HARRAP'S NEW SHORTER
FRENCH AND ENGLISH
DICTIONARY

by

J. E. MANSION, M.A.

Revised by

M. FERLIN, *Agrégé de l'Université*, O.✳
and P. FORBES, B.A.(Oxon)

Edited by

D. M. LEDÉSERT, M.A. ❶ and
R. P. L. LEDÉSERT, *Licencié-ès-Lettres, Licencié en Droit* ❶

PART TWO

ENGLISH–FRENCH

HARRAP **&** BORDAS
LONDON   CANADA

First published in Great Britain 1940
by GEORGE G. HARRAP & CO. LTD
182–184 High Holborn, London WC1V 7AX

Reprinted: 1944; 1945; 1946; 1950; 1952 (*twice*);
1953; 1954; 1955; 1957; 1958; 1960; 1961; 1963;
1964; 1965 (*twice*); 1966

Completely revised, enlarged and reset edition 1967
Reprinted and updated: 1968; 1969; 1970; 1971
Reprinted: 1971; 1972
Reprinted and updated: 1972; 1973; 1974
Reprinted: 1975; 1976 (*twice*); 1977

ISBN 0 245 59062 5

Printed in Great Britain by offset lithography by
Billing & Sons Ltd, Guildford, London and Worcester

PREFACE

This work is a completely revised edition of *Harrap's Shorter French and English Dictionary*, reprinted in 1972 with numerous corrections to help American readers. It incorporates words and phrases that have become established in the French or English language in recent years. Obsolete terms, particularly dated colloquialisms, have been deleted. Numerous French-Canadianisms and specifically American idioms have been added. It is about one quarter longer than the original work.

British spellings of English words are used throughout. Common alternative spellings are given in the English-French part, though it should be noted that for words with the alternative suffixes -ise or -ize and -isation or -ization, -ize and -ization have been adopted throughout. American users will notice the following spelling differences:

(*a*) the English use of -our in words that in American usage are spelled with -or (e.g. *Eng:* colour, *U.S:* color).

(*b*) the use of the final -re in words where American usage favors -er (e.g. *Eng:* theatre, *U.S:* theater).

(*c*) the doubling of the l before an ending beginning with a vowel, irrespective of accentuation (e.g. *Eng:* woollen, *U.S:* woolen; *Eng:* travelling, *U.S.:* traveling).

(*d*) the single l before a final syllable beginning with a consonant, where the American usage is ll (e.g. *Eng:* skilful, *U.S:* skillful; *Eng:* enrolment, *U.S:* enrollment).

(*e*) the use of a c in certain words where American usage favors an s (e.g. *Eng:* defence, *U.S:* defense).

(*f*) the use of ae in certain words where American usage favors e (e.g. *Eng:* aesthete, *U.S:* esthete).

The pronunciation of both French and English words is indicated with the symbols of the International Phonetic Association.

To keep the work within a manageable number of pages, several space-saving devices are used. When the headword itself is repeated within the entry in exactly the same form it is represented by the initial letter, though plural nouns or verb conjugations in which the form differs from the infinitive are written in full.

> e.g. **gentleman,** *s.* . . . **Young g.,** jeune homme . . . **Gentlemen's hairdresser,** coiffeur pour hommes.
> **gain,** *v. tr.* . . . **To g. strength,** (re)prendre des forces . . . **You will g. nothing by it,** vous n'y gagnerez rien . . . **He is gaining in weight,** il prend du poids.

Similarly, compound words appearing in examples are represented by the two initial letters:

> e.g. **gate-legged,** *a.* **G.-l. table,** table à abattants.

This method of abbreviation also applies to the English compound verbs when the two component parts are not separated; when they are separated, however, it has generally been considered clearer to write them in full.

> e.g. **get through,** *v.* . . . **To g.t. an examination,** être reçu à un examen . . . **To get sth. through the customs,** (faire) passer qch. à la douane.

In the French–English part a certain number of adverbs and simple derivatives follow a headword when no difficulty in meaning is involved:

arros/er . . ., to water . . . *a.* **-able.** *s.m.* **-age.** *s.m.* **-ement.**
abrupt, *a.* Abrupt . . . *adv.* **-ement.**
aud/ible, *a.* Audible. *s. f.* **-ibilité.**

In the English–French part, adverbs in **-ly** normally follow the adjectives:

new, *a.* Nouveau, -el, -elle . . . **-ly,** *adv.* Récemment, nouvellement.

noisy, *a.* Bruyant . . . **-ily,** *adv.* Bruyamment . . .

Hyphenated words are normally entered under the headword forming their first element:

night, *s.* . . . **night-bird,** *s.* . . . **night-blindness,** *s.* . . . *etc.*

This system has, however, caused considerable difficulties, as North American usage appears to have rejected to a great extent the use of the hyphen, while in England many words which only a few years ago would have been written with a hyphen now appear either as a single word or as two separate words. Where the usage is not yet fully established the hyphen has been placed in brackets; but, as there are no definable rules for the use of the hyphen, the user should bear in mind that he may find a compound word listed either under the headword which forms its first element, or in its strict alphabetical place.

For English verbs with compound forms, the simple form is treated first, and then follow under the same headword (i) the compound forms, each with any participial adjective or gerund; (ii) participial forms of the simple verb; and (iii) any hyphenated compounds of the headword.

e.g. **to break; . . . to break down, break-down,** *s.,* **broken-down,** *a.* . . . **to break up, break-up,** *s.,* **breaking up; broken,** *a.,* **-ly,** *adv.,* **broken-backed,** etc.; **breaking,** *s.,* **breaking-point; break-neck.**

The following conventions have also been observed:

GENDER, FEMININES, PLURALS. Common nouns have been described as 'substantives', being listed as *s.m.* or *s. f.* in the French–English part. In the English–French part the gender is given after the French word, except where the English word is given its gender (e.g. **man,** *s.m.*). Irregular plurals are given, as are the feminine forms of French adjectives which do not form their feminine by the simple addition of an **-e.**

VERBS. The principal parts of irregular verbs are given after the infinitive.

The French pronominal verbs are dealt with in a separate article following the simple verb whenever the verb in the pronominal form assumes new meanings or constructions. Thus the verb **battre** is followed by a special entry for the verb **se battre,** to fight. But if the pronominal form is merely a reflexive use of the simple verb, implying no change of meaning, it is not treated as a separate entity.

PUNCTUATION. Within the sub-headings (1, 2, (*a*), (*b*) etc.) indicating different meanings of a word, a comma is deemed to imply a virtual synonym, while a semi-colon indicates a different shade of meaning. An example shown in brackets after a meaning does not necessarily imply that the construction can be used for no other example (e.g. **susciter,** *v.tr.* . . . To (a)rouse (envy); envy suggests only one of the feelings which might be aroused).

Owing to the different systems of administration, etc. in different countries, it is not always possible to give true translations for different functions or offices. In such cases the sign = has been used to indicate the nearest equivalent.

We should like to thank Mr C. B. Johnson, B.A., Miss M. Holland Smith, Mrs P. Brading, M.A., and Mrs E. A. H. Strick, M.A., for their help in the revision work; Mrs F. Collin, M.A. (Montréal), for providing a list of French Canadianisms; Mr J. D. O'Connor, B.A., for his help in the revision of the English phonetics; Miss V. Brown, B.A., Mr P. H. Collin, M.A., and Mr F. G. S. Parker, M.A., for reading the proofs and bringing to our notice many omissions and imperfections which had escaped us.

Revisers:

M. Ferlin, *Agrégé de l'Université, O.*✳

Patricia Forbes, B.A.

Editors:

R. P. L. Ledésert, *Licencié en Droit, Licencié-ès-Lettres,* ◖

Margaret Ledésert, M.A. ◖

PREFACE

Cet ouvrage est l'édition entièrement révisée du Harrap's Shorter French and English Dictionary, augmentée du supplément paru en 1961, des mots et locutions qui ont acquis droit de cité en français ou en anglais au cours de ces dernières années, et allégée des termes tombés en désuétude, en particulier des tournures familières vieillies. Cette nouvelle édition présente une particularité par rapport à l'ancienne: l'adjonction de canadianismes français et de nombreux américanismes supplémentaires. Elle est plus longue que l'édition originale d'à peu près un quart.

L'orthographe des mots anglais respecte l'usage britannique. Les variantes usuelles figurent dans la partie anglais–français; il faut cependant signaler que pour les deux formes des suffixes -ise ou -ize, et -isation ou -ization l'orthographe -ize et -ization a été adoptée dans les deux parties du dictionnaire.

Nous attirons l'attention du lecteur américain sur quelques différences particulièrement frappantes:

(a) l'emploi anglais de -our dans des mots pour lesquels l'américain emploierait l'orthographe -or (ex. *angl:* colour, *U.S:* color).

(b) l'emploi de la finale -re dans des mots pour lesquels l'usage américain donne la préférence à la forme -er (ex. *angl:* theatre, *U.S:* theater).

(c) le redoublement de la lettre l devant une voyelle (ex. *angl:* woollen, *U.S:* woolen; *angl:* travelling, *U.S:* traveling).

(d) l'emploi de l'l simple devant une syllabe finale commençant par une consonne, alors que l'usage américain est ll (ex. *angl:* skilful, *U.S:* skillful; *angl:* enrolment, *U.S:* enrollment).

(e) l'emploi d'un c dans certains mots pour lesquels l'américain donne la préférence à l's (ex. *angl:* defence, *U.S:* defense).

Pour la transcription phonétique des mots français et anglais, nous employons les signes de l'Association phonétique internationale.

Afin d'éviter d'accroître démesurément le volume du présent ouvrage, un certain nombre de règles typographiques de l'édition originale du Harrap's Shorter French and English Dictionary ont été conservées. Quand, dans un exemple, un mot principal est repété sans changement, il est représenté par sa première lettre, alors que les noms au pluriel, ou les formes des verbes pour lesquels l'orthographe change (ce qui n'est pas toujours le cas en anglais), sont écrits en toutes lettres.

> ex. **gentleman,** *s.* . . . **Young g.,** jeune homme . . . **Gentlemen's hairdresser,** coiffeur pour hommes.
> **gain,** *v. tr.* . . . **To g. strength,** (re)prendre des forces . . . **You will g. nothing by it,** vous n'y gagnerez rien . . . **He is gaining in weight,** il prend du poids.

De même, les mots composés qui figurent dans les exemples sont représentés par la première lettre de chacun des composants.

> ex. **gate-legged,** *a.* **G.-l. table,** table à abattants.

Cette méthode d'abréviation s'applique aussi aux verbes composés anglais lorsque les deux composants du verbe ne sont pas séparés, mais lorsqu'un complément les sépare nous avons cru préférable de les écrire en toutes lettres, afin d'en rendre la lecture plus aisée.

> ex. **get through,** *v.* . . . **To g.t. an examination,** être reçu à un examen . . . **To get sth. through the customs,** (faire) passer qch. à la douane.

Dans la partie français-anglais, un certain nombre d'adverbes et de dérivés simples sont insérés à la suite du mot principal, à condition que ceci n'entraîne aucune difficulté de compréhension:

> **arros/er** . . . , to water . . . *a.* **-able.** *s.m.* **-age.** *s.m.* **-ement.**
> **abrupt,** *a.* Abrupt . . . adv. **-ement.**
> **aud/ible,** *a.* Audible. *s.f.* **-ibilité.**

Dans la partie anglais-français, les adverbes en **-ly** suivent normalement les adjectifs:

> **new,** *a.* Nouveau, -el, -elle . . . **-ly,** *adv.* Récemment, nouvellement.
> **noisy,** *a.* Bruyant . . . **-ily,** *adv.* Bruyamment . . .

Les mots composés à trait d'union figurent normalement sous leur premier composant:

> **night,** *s.* . . . . **night-bird,** *s.* . . . . **night-blindness,** *s.* . . . . *etc.*

Ce procédé présente toutefois des difficultés considérables. En effet, l'usage américain semble avoir rejeté dans une très large mesure l'emploi du trait d'union, et en Angleterre de nombreux mots qui, il y a seulement quelques années, eussent été écrits avec un trait d'union, s'écrivent maintenant soit en un seul mot, soit en deux mots séparés. Quant aux mots dont l'orthographe n'est pas encore définitivement établie, le trait d'union est entre parenthèses; mais comme il n'y a pas de règles bien définies, l'usager du dictionnaire doit toujours avoir présent à l'esprit qu'il peut éventuellement trouver un mot composé soit sous le mot principal formant son premier élément, soit à sa place strictement alphabétique.

En ce qui concerne les verbes anglais avec postposition, on trouvera d'abord le verbe simple, puis, sous le même article, (a) les verbes à postposition, avec pour chacun, les adjectifs participiaux ou les gérondifs; (b) les formes participiales du verbe simple et (c) tous les composés à trait d'union du verbe simple.

> ex. **to break;** . . . **to break down,** *s.,* **broken-down,** *a.* . . . . **to break up, break-up,** *s.,* **breaking up; broken,** *a.* **-ly,** *adv.,* **broken-backed,** etc.; **breaking,** *s.,* **breaking-point; break-neck.**

Les conventions suivantes ont été respectées:

GENRES, FÉMININS, PLURIELS. Les noms communs ont été classés comme substantifs et catalogués *s.m.* ou *s.f.* dans la partie français–anglais. Dans la partie anglais–français le genre est indiqué après le mot français, sauf dans les cas où le genre est donné pour le mot anglais (ex. **man**, *s.m.*). Les pluriels irréguliers sont indiqués, ainsi que le féminin des adjectifs français, lorsque celui-ci n'est pas formé par la simple adjonction d'un **-e**.

VERBES. Les temps principaux des verbes irréguliers sont indiqués à la suite de l'infinitif.

Les verbes pronominaux français sont traités dans un paragraphe séparé à la suite du verbe simple chaque fois que le verbe sous sa forme pronominale implique un sens nouveau ou une construction nouvelle. Ainsi, le verbe **battre** est suivi d'un article spécial pour le verbe **se battre**, to fight. Mais quand la forme pronominale n'est qu'un emploi réfléchi du verbe simple, et n'implique aucun changement de sens, celui-ci n'est pas traité dans un article séparé.

PONCTUATION. Les différents sens d'un mot sont donnés sous les sous-titres (1, 2, (*a*), (*b*), etc.); une virgule indique en quelque sorte un synonyme, tandis qu'un point-virgule marque une légère différence de sens. Lorsque, après une signification donnée, un exemple est indiqué entre parenthèses, cela n'implique pas nécessairement que cette construction ne soit admise que pour ce seul exemple (ex. **susciter**, *v.tr.* To (a)rouse (envy); l'envie ne suggère que l'un des sentiments qui peuvent être suscités).

Etant donné les différences dans les structures administratives et autres des pays, il n'est pas toujours possible de traduire exactement les diverses charges, fonctions etc. Dans de tels cas, le signe = a été utilisé pour indiquer l'équivalent le plus proche.

Nous tenons à remercier Mr C. B. Johnson, B.A., Miss M. Holland Smith, Mrs. P. Brading, M.A., et Mrs E. A. H. Strick, M.A., qui nous ont aidés au travail de révision; Mrs F. Collin, M.A. (Montréal), qui nous a fourni une liste de canadianismes français; Mr J. D. O'Connor, B.A., qui a contribué à la révision de la phonétique anglaise; et Miss V. Brown, B.A., Mr P. H. Collin, M.A., et Mr F. G. S. Parker, M.A., qui ont lu les épreuves et ont attiré notre attention sur de nombreuses omissions et imperfections qui nous avaient échappé.

Réviseurs:

M. Ferlin, *Agrégé de l'Université*, O.✲

Patricia Forbes, B.A.

Rédacteurs:

R. P. L. Ledésert, *Licencié en Droit, Licencié-ès-Lettres*, ◖.

Margaret Ledésert, M.A. ◖

ABBREVIATIONS USED IN THE DICTIONARY

a., adj.	*Adjective*	Adjectif	*Cav:*	*Cavalry*	Cavalerie
A:	*Archaism; ancient; in former use*	Sens vieilli; désuet	*Cer:*	*Ceramics*	Céramique
			Cf.	*Refer to*	Conferatur
Abs.	*Absolutely, absolute use*	Emploi absolu	*Ch:*	*Chemistry*	Chimie
			Chr:	*Chronology*	Chronologie
Ac:	*Acoustics*	Acoustique	*Cin:*	*Cinematography*	Cinématographie
acc.	*Accusative*	Accusatif	*Civ:*	*Civilisation*	Civilisation
Adm:	*Administration*	Administration	*Civ.E:*	*Civil Engineering*	Génie civil
adv.	*Adverb, adverbial*	Adverbe, adverbial	*Cl:*	*Classical*	Classique; antiquité grecque ou romaine
Adv.phr.	*Adverbial phrase*	Locution adverbiale			
Aer:	*Aeronautics*	Aéronautique	*Clockm:*	*Clock and watch making*	Horlogerie
Agr:	*Agriculture*	Agriculture			
A.Hist:	*Ancient history*	Histoire ancienne	*Coel:*	*Coelenterata*	Cœlentérés
Alg:	*Algebra*	Algèbre	*cogn.acc.*	*Cognate accusative*	Accusatif de d'objet interne
	Algae	Algues			
Amph:	*Amphibia*	Amphibiens			
Anat:	*Anatomy*	Anatomie	*Coll:*	*Collective*	Collectif
Ann:	*Annelida*	Annelés	*Com:*	*Commerce*	Commerce
Ant:	*Antiquity, -ies*	Antiquité	*comb.fm*	*Combining form*	Forme de combinaison
Anthr:	*Anthropology*	Anthropologie			
Ap:	*Apiculture*	Apiculture	*Comest:*	*Comestibles*	Comestibles
approx.	*Approximately*	Sens approché	*comp.*	*Comparative*	Comparatif
Ar:	*Arithmetic*	Arithmétique	*Conc:*	*Concrete*	Concret
Arach:	*Arachnida*	Arachnides	*Conch:*	*Conchology*	Conchyliologie
Arb:	*Arboriculture*	Arboriculture; sylviculture	*condit.*	*Conditional*	Conditionnel
			conj.	*Conjunction*	Conjonction
Arch:	*Architecture*	Architecture	*Conj. like*	*Conjugated like*	Conjugué de même que
Archeol:	*Archaeology*	Archéologie			
Arm:	*Armour*	Armures	*Const:*	*Construction*	Bâtiment
	Arms	Armes	*Coop:*	*Cooperage*	Tonnellerie
	Art	Beaux-arts	*Corr:*	*Correspondence*	Correspondance
Artil:	*Artillery*	Artillerie	*Cost:*	*Costume, clothing*	Costume
Astr:	*Astronomy*	Astronomie	*Cp.*	*Compare*	Comparer
Astrol:	*Astrology*	Astrologie	*Cr:*	*Cricket*	Cricket
Atom.Ph:	*Atomic physics*	Sciences atomiques	*Crust:*	*Crustacea*	Crustacés
attrib.	*Attributive*	Attributif	*Cryst:*	*Crystallography*	Cristallographie
Austr:	*Australia; Australian*	Australie; australien	*Cu:*	*Culinary; cuisine*	Cuisine
			Cust:	*Customs*	Douanes
Aut:	*Automobilism*	Automobilisme	*Cy:*	*Cycles: cycling*	Cycles; cyclisme
aux.	*Auxiliary*	Auxiliaire			
Av:	*Aviation*	Aviation	*Danc:*	*Dancing*	Danse
			dat.	*Dative*	Datif
B:	*Biblical; Bible*	Biblique; Bible	*def.*	*Definite*	Défini
Bac:	*Bacteriology*	Bactériologie	*def.*	*Defective*	Défectif
Bak:	*Baking*	Boulangerie	*dem.*	*Demonstrative*	Démonstratif
Ball:	*Ballistics*	Balistique	*Dent:*	*Dentistry*	Art dentaire
Bank:	*Banking*	Opérations de banque	*Dial:*	*Dialect*	Dialectal
			Dim:	*Diminutive*	Diminutif
B.Hist:	*Bible History*	Histoire sainte	*Dipl:*	*Diplomacy*	Diplomatie
Bib:	*Bibliography*	Bibliographie	*Dist:*	*Distilling*	Distillation
Bill:	*Billiards*	Jeu de billard	*Dom.Ec:*	*Domestic Economy*	Économie domestique
Bio-Ch:	*Biochemistry*	Biochimie			
Biol:	*Biology*	Biologie			
Bookb:	*Bookbinding*	Reliure	*Draw:*	*Drawing*	Dessin
Book-k:	*Book-keeping*	Tenue des livres	*Dressm:*	*Dressmaking*	Couture et modes
Bootm:	*Bootmaking*	Cordonnerie	*Dy:*	*Dyeing*	Teinture
Bot:	*Botany*	Botanique			
Box:	*Boxing*	Boxe	*E.*	*East*	Est
Breed:	*Breeding*	Élevage	*E:*	*Engineering*	Art de l'ingénieur; industries mécaniques
Brew:	*Brewing*	Brasserie			
Brickm:	*Brickmaking*	Briqueterie			
			Ecc:	*Ecclesiastical*	Église et clergé
card.a.	*Cardinal adjective*	Adjectif cardinal	*Echin:*	*Echinodermata*	Échinodermes
	Cards	Jeux de cartes	*e.g.*	*For example*	Par exemple
Carp:	*Carpentry*	Charpenterie; menuiserie du bâtiment	*El:*	*Electricity; electrical*	Électricité; électrique
			El.-Ch:	*Electro-Chemistry*	Électro-chimie

El.E:	Electrical engineering	Électrotechnique	*inf.*	Infinitive	Infinitif
			Ins:	Insurance	Assurances
Eng.	English; England	Anglais; Angleterre	*int.*	Interjection	Interjection
Engr:	Engraving	Gravure	*interr.*	Interrogative	Interrogatif
Ent:	Entomology	Entomologie	*inv.*	Invariable	Invariable
epith.	Epithet (adjective)	(Adjectif) qualificatif	*Iron:*	Ironical(ly)	Ironique(ment)
Equit:	Equitation	Équitation			
esp.	Especially	Surtout	*Jew.*	Jewish	Juif; juive
etc.	Et cetera	Et cætera	*Join:*	Joinery	Menuiserie
Eth:	Ethics	Morale	*Journ:*	Journalism	Journalisme
Ethn:	Ethnology	Ethnologie	*Jur:*	Jurisprudence: law	Droit; terme de palais
excl.	Exclamation; exclamative	Exclamation; exclamatif			
				Knitting	Tricot
Exp:	Explosives	Explosifs			
			Lap:	Lapidary Arts	Arts lapidaires; taillerie
f.	Feminine	Féminin			
F:	Colloquial	Familier; style de la conversation	*Laund:*	Laundering	Blanchissage
			Leath:	Leatherwork	Travail du cuir
Farr:	Farriery	Maréchalerie	*Ling:*	Linguistics	Linguistique
Fb:	Football	Football	*Lit:*	Literary use; literature; literary	Forme littéraire; littérature; littéraire
Fenc:	Fencing	Escrime			
	Ferns	Fougères			
Fin:	Finance	Finances	*Lith:*	Lithography	Lithographie
Fish:	Fishing	Pêche	*Locksm:*	Locksmithery	Serrurerie
For:	Forestry	Forêts	*Log:*	Logic	Logique
Fort:	Fortification	Fortification	*Lt.*	Latin	Latin
Fr.	French; France	Français; France			
Fr.C:	French Canadian	Canadien français	*m.*	Masculine	Masculin
fu.	Future	Futur	*Magn:*	Magnetism	Magnétisme
	Fuel	Combustibles	*Mapm:*	Mapmaking	Cartographie
Fung:	Fungi	Champignons	*Mch:*	Machines	Machines; machines à vapeur
Furn:	Furniture	Mobilier			
			Meas:	Weights and Measures	Poids et mesures
	Games	Jeux			
Gasm:	Gasmaking	Industries du gaz	*Mec:*	Mechanics	Mécanique
Geog:	Geography	Géographie	*Mec.E:*	Mechanical Engineering	Industries mécaniques
Geol:	Geology	Géologie			
Geom:	Geometry	Géométrie	*Med:*	Medicine	Médecine
ger.	Gerund	Gérondif	*Mediev:*	Medieval	Du moyen âge
Glassm:	Glassmaking	Verrerie	*Metall:*	Metallurgy	Métallurgie
Gr.	Greek	Grec	*Metalw:*	Metalworking	Travail des métaux
Gr.Alph:	Greek Alphabet	Alphabet grec	*Metaph:*	Metaphysics	Métaphysique
Gr.Ant:	Greek Antiquity	Antiquité grecque	*Meteor:*	Meteorology	Météorologie
Gr.Civ:	Greek Civilization	Civilisation grecque	*Mil:*	Military	Militaire; art militaire
Gram:	Grammar	Grammaire			
	Gramophones	Phonographes	*Mill:*	Milling	Meunerie
Gym:	Gymnastics	Gymnastique	*Min:*	Mining and quarrying	Exploitation des mines et carrières
Hairdr:	Hairdressing	Coiffure	*Miner:*	Mineralogy	Minéralogie
Harn:	Harness	Sellerie; harnais	*M.Ins:*	Maritime Insurance	Assurance maritime
Her:	Heraldry	Blason			
Hist:	History; historical	Histoire; historique	*Moham:*	Mohammedan	Musulman
			Moll:	Molluscs	Mollusques
Hor:	Horology	Horométrie	*Moss:*	Mosses and lichens	Muscinées
Hort:	Horticulture	Horticulture	*Mount:*	Mountaineering	Alpinisme
Hum:	Humorous	Par facétie	*Mth:*	Mathematics	Mathématiques
Husb:	Husbandry	Économie rurale	*Mus:*	Music	Musique
Hyd:	Hydraulics; hydrostatics	Hydraulique; hydrostatique	*Myr:*	Myriapods	Myriapodes
Hyg:	Hygiene	Hygiène	*Myth:*	Myth and legend, mythology	Mythes et légendes; mythologie
i.	Intransitive	Intransitif			
I.C.E:	Internal Combustion Engines	Moteurs à combustion interne	*n.*		Nous
			N.	North	Nord
Ich:	Ichthyology	Ichtyologie	*N.Arch:*	Naval Architecture	Architecture navale
imp.	Imperative	Impératif	*Nat.Hist:*	Natural History	Histoire naturelle
impers.	Impersonal	Impersonnel	*Nau:*	Nautical	Terme de marine
ind.	Indicative	Indicatif	*Nav:*	Navigation	Navigation
Ind:	Industry	Industrie; arts industriels		Navy	Marine militaire
			Needlew:	Needlework	Travaux à l'aiguille; couture
indef.	Indefinite	Indéfini			
ind.tr.	Indirectly transitive	Transitif avec régime indirect	*neg.*	Negative	Négatif
			neut.	Neuter	Neutre

nom.	*Nominative*	Nominatif	*qch.*	*Something*	Quelque chose
Num:	*Numismatics*	Numismatique	*qn*	*Someone*	Quelqu'un
num.a.	*Numeral adjective*	Adjectif numéral	*q.v.*	*See this word*	Se reporter à ce mot
O:	*Obsolescent*	Vieilli	*Rac:*	*Racing*	Courses
Obst:	*Obstetrics*	Obstétrique	*Rad.-A:*	*Radio-activity*	Radio-activité
Oc:	*Oceanography*	Océanographie	*Rail:*	*Railways*	Chemins de fer
occ.	*Occasionally*	Parfois; par occasion	*R.C.Ch:*	*Roman Catholic Church*	Église catholique
Onomat:	*Onomatopoeia*	Onomatopée			
Opt:	*Optics*	Optique	*rel.*	*Relative*	Relatif
Orn:	*Ornithology*	Ornithologie	*Rel:*	*Religion(s)*	Religion(s)
Ost:	*Ostreiculture*	Ostréiculture	*Rel.H:*	*Religious History*	Histoire des religion
			Rept:	*Reptiles*	Reptiles
p.	(i) *Participle;* (ii) *past*	(i) Participe; (ii) passé	*Rh:*	*Rhetoric*	Rhétorique
				Rockets	Fusées
P:	*Uneducated expression; slang*	Expression populaire; argot	*Rom.*	*Roman*	Romain, romaine
			Ropem:	*Ropemaking*	Corderie
Paint:	*Painting trade*	Peinture en bâtiment	*Row:*	*Rowing*	Aviron
			R.t.m.	*Registered trade mark*	Marque déposee
Pal:	*Paleography*	Paléographie			
Paleont:	*Paleontology*	Paléontologie	*S.*	*South*	Sud
Paperm:	*Papermaking*	Fabrication du papier	*s., sb.*	*Substantive, noun*	Substantif, nom
			S.a., S.a.	*See also*	Voir
Parl:	*Parliament*	Parlement	*Sch:*	*Schools and universities*	Université; écoles
Path:	*Pathology*	Pathologie			
p.d.	*Past descriptive; imperfect tense*	Passé descriptif; imparfait (de l'indicatif)	*Scot:*	*Scottish*	Écossais
				Scouting	Scoutisme
Pej:	*Pejorative*	Sens péjoratif	*Sculp:*	*Sculpture*	Sculpture
Perf.	*Perfect*	Parfait	*Ser:*	*Sericulture*	Sériciculture
pers.	*Person; personal*	Personne; personnel	*sg.*	*Singular*	Singulier
p.h.	*Past historic; past definite*	Passé historique; passé défini	*Sm.a:*	*Small arms*	Armes portatives
			s.o.	*Someone*	Quelqu'un
Ph:	*Physics*	Physique	*Soapm:*	*Soapmaking*	Savonnerie
Pharm:	*Pharmacy*	Pharmacie	*Sp:*	*Sport*	Sport
Ph.Geog:	*Physical geography*	Géographie physique	*Spong:*	*Sponges*	Spongiaires
			St.Exch:	*Stock Exchange*	Terme de Bourse
Phil:	*Philosophy*	Philosophie	*sth.*	*Something*	Quelque chose
Phot:	*Photography*	Photographie	*Stonew:*	*Stoneworking*	Taille de la pierre
Phot.Engr:	*Photo-engraving; process work*	Procédés photomécaniques; photogravure	*sub.*	*Subjunctive*	Subjonctif
			suff.	*Suffix*	Suffixe
			Sug.-R:	*Sugar-Refining*	Raffinerie du sucre
phr.	*Phrase*	Locution	*sup.*	*Superlative*	Superlatif
Physiol:	*Physiology*	Physiologie	*Surg:*	*Surgery*	Chirurgie
Pisc:	*Pisciculture*	Pisciculture	*Surv:*	*Surveying*	Géodésie et levé de plans
pl.	*Plural*	Pluriel			
Plumb:	*Plumbing*	Plomberie	*Swim:*	*Swimming*	Natation
P.N:	*Public notices*	Affichage; avis au public			
			Tail:	*Tailoring*	Vêtements d'hommes
Poet:	*Poetical*	Style poétique	*Tan:*	*Tanning*	Tannage des cuirs
Pol:	*Politics*	Politique	*Tchn:*	*Technical*	Terme(s) technique(s); terme(s) de métier
Pol.Ec.	*Political Economy*	Économie politique			
poss.	*Possessive*	Possessif			
Post:	*Postal Service*	Postes et télégraphes	*Ten:*	*Tennis*	Tennis
p.p.	*Past participle*	Participe passé	*Tex:*	*Textiles*	Industries textiles
pr.	*Present*	Présent	*Tg:*	*Telegraphy*	Télégraphie
pred.	*Predicate; predicative*	Attribut; attributif	*Th:*	*Theatre*	Théâtre
			Theol:	*Theology*	Théologie
pref.	*Prefix*	Préfixe	*thg*	*Thing*	Chose; objet
Prehist:	*Prehistory*	Préhistoire	*Tls:*	*Tools*	Outils
prep.	*Preposition*	Préposition	*Toil:*	*Toilet; make-up*	Toilette; maquillage
Prep.phr.	*Prepositional phrase*	Locution prépositive	*Town P:*	*Town Planning*	Urbanisme
			Tp:	*Telephony*	Téléphonie
Pr.n.	*Proper name*	Nom propre	*tr.*	*Transitive*	Transitif
pron.	*Pronoun*	Pronom	*Trans:*	*Transport*	Transports
Pros:	*Prosody*	Prosodie; métrique	*Trig:*	*Trigonometry*	Trigonométrie
Prot:	*Protozoa*	Protozoaires		*Turf*	Turf
Prov:	*Proverb*	Proverbe	*T.V:*	*Television*	Télévision
pr.p.	*Present participle*	Participe présent	*Typ:*	*Typography*	Typographie
Psy:	*Psychology*	Psychologie	*Typewr:*	*Typewriting*	Dactylographie
Publ:	*Publishing*	Édition			
Pyr:	*Pyrotechnics*	Pyrotechnie	*U.S:*	*United States*	États-Unis

usu.	*Usually*	D'ordinaire	*W.*	*West*	Ouest	
			Wine-m:	*Wine-making*	Vinification	
v.	*Verb*	Verbe	*Wr:*	*Wrestling*	Lutte	
v.		Vous	*W.Tel:*	*Wireless Tele-*	Téléphonie et	
V:	*Vulgar; not in*	Trivial; bas		*phony and*	télégraphie sans fil;	
	polite use			*Telegraphy*	T.S.F.	
Veh:	*Vehicles*	Véhicules	*W.Tg:*	*Wireless Tele-*	Télégraphie sans fil	
Ven:	*Venery*	Chasse		*graphy*		
Vet:	*Veterinary science*	Art vétérinaire	*W.Tp:*	*Wireless Tele-*	Téléphonie sans fil	
v.i.	*Intransitive verb*	Verbe intransitif		*phony*		
v.ind.tr.	*Verb indirectly*	Verbe transitif				
	transitive	indirect		*X Rays*	Rayons X	
Vit:	*Viticulture*	Viticulture				
Voc:	*Vocative*	Vocatif	*Y:*	*Yachting*	Yachting	
v.pr.	*Pronominal verb*	Verbe pronominal				
v.tr.	*Transitive verb*	Verbe transitif	*Z:*	*Zoology*	Zoologie	

HARRAP'S NEW SHORTER

FRENCH AND ENGLISH
DICTIONARY

Completely revised edition

PART TWO

ENGLISH-FRENCH

PRONUNCIATION

A table of the phonetic symbols—those of the International Phonetic Association—used to represent the English words is given below; the following points, however, call for special attention:

(i) Symbols appearing between round brackets, e.g. *nation* [neiʃ(ə)n]; *postcard* [pous(t)kɑːd] show that there are alternative and equally acceptable pronunciations with or without the corresponding sound.

(ii) Words such as *which, why, what* have been consistently shown with the [h]-symbol in parentheses, i.e. [(h)witʃ], [(h)wai], [(h)wɔt], as the [h] is frequently dropped especially in quick speech.

(iii) Word-stress is indicated by an accent preceding the stressed syllable, e.g. *abbot* [ˈæbət]; *abide* [əˈbaid]. Certain words have the possibility of two stresses, *e.g. examination* [igˌzæmiˈneiʃ(ə)n]; *qualification* [ˌkwɔlifiˈkeiʃ(ə)n]. The lowered accent-mark implies optional stress on the following syllable; where a second stress *must* be present, for example in many compounds, the high accent-mark is used, *e.g. electro-magnet* [iˈlektrouˈmægnit]; *post-war* [ˈpoustˈwɔːr].

(iv) The sound [r] does not usually occur before consonants or before a pause; the italicised symbol [*r*] is used at the ends of words such as *better, four, here* to show that the [r]- sound may occur there if, and only if, the following word in the phrase begins with a vowel and there is no intervening pause, as in *here and now*.

(v) In compounds entered under the head-word which forms their first element the pronunciation is not shown unless there is any room for doubt, but the fall of the stress is indicated.

For further information on this system of phonetic notation the reader is referred to Professor Daniel Jones' *English Pronouncing Dictionary* (Dent, 1960) and *Outline of English Phonetics* (Heffer, 1960).

PRONONCIATION

Un tableau des signes phonétiques employés pour les mots anglais—ceux de l'Association phonétique internationale—est donné ci-dessous; nous attirons toutefois l'attention du lecteur sur les points suivants:

(i) Les caractères mis entre parenthèses, p.ex. *nation* [neiʃ(ə)n]; *postcard* [pous(t)kɑːd] signifient que le mot peut se prononcer aussi bien avec que sans le son correspondant à cette lettre.

(ii) Les mots tels que *which, why, what* ont été uniformément transcrits avec l'[h] entre parenthèses, à savoir [(h)witʃ], [(h)wai], [(h)wɔt]; on peut néanmoins prononcer ces mots sans [h], surtout en parlant vite.

(iii) L'accent tonique est indiqué par un accent précédant la syllabe accentuée, p.ex. *abbot* ['æbɔt]; *abide* [ə'baid]. Certains mots peuvent avoir deux accents toniques, p.ex. *examination* [ig‚zæmi'neiʃ(ə)n]; *qualification* [‚kwɔlifi'keiʃ(ə)n]; l'accent du bas implique un accent facultatif sur la syllabe qui suit; lorsqu'un second accent est obligatoire, p.ex. dans de nombreux composés, on emploie l'accent du haut pour les deux, p.ex. *electro-magnet* [i'lektrou'mægnit]; *post-war* ['poust'wɔːr].

(iv) Le son [r] ne s'entend généralement pas devant une consonne ou devant une pause; on emploie le caractère en italique [*r*] à la fin des mots tels que *better, four, here*, pour indiquer que le son [r] peut se faire entendre dans ces mots dans le cas, et uniquement dans le cas, où le mot suivant dans la phrase commence par une voyelle sans qu'il ait de pause, p.ex. *here and now.*

(v) Pour les composés enregistrés à la suite de l'article qui en forme le premier élément, on n'a donné la prononciation que s'il y a un doute possible, mais on a indiqué l'accent tonique.

Pour plus de détails sur ce système de notation phonétique, nous renvoyons le lecteur aux ouvrages de M. le Professeur Daniel Jones: *English Pronouncing Dictionary* (Dent, 1960), et *Outline of English Phonetics* (Heffer, 1960).

TABLE OF PHONETIC SYMBOLS

VOWELS

[i:]	bee, fever, sea, police		[ɔi]	boil, toy, oyster, loyal
[iə]	beer, appear, real		[ou]	low, soap, rope
[i]	bit, added, physic		[o]	obey, coherent, plutocrat
[e]	bet, menace, leopard, said, bury		[u]	put, wool, would, full
[ei]	date, day, nail		[u:]	shoe, prove, too, frugal
[ɛə]	bear, bare, there, heir, airy		[uə]	poor, sure, tour, boorish
[æ]	bat, add		[ʌ]	cut, sun, son, some, cover, rough
[ai]	aisle, height, life, fly, type		[ə:]	burn, learn, herb, whirl, myrrh
[ɑ:]	art, car, ask		[ə]	rodent, guttural, treacherous
[au]	fowl, house, bough		[y]	
[ɔ]	lot, was, what		[ø]	In foreign words as in Part I
[ɔ:]	all, haul, short, saw		[œ]	

CONSONANTS

[p]	pat, tap		[tʃ]	chat, search, chisel, thatch, rich
[b]	bat, tab		[ʒ]	pleasure, azure, vision
[m]	mat, ram, prism		[dʒ]	rage, edge, verger, pigeon, jet, digit, spinach
[f]	fat, laugh, ruff, rough, elephant		[k]	cat, ache, pique, kitten
[v]	vat, avail, rave		[ks]	except, exercise, expect
[t]	tap, pat, patter, trap		[kʃ]	action, eviction
[d]	dab, bad, build		[g]	go, ghost, guard, again, egg
[n]	nab, ban, banner, pancake		[gz]	exist, exact
[nj]	pinion, onion		[h]	hat, cohere
[s]	sat, scene, mouse, psychology		[χ]	loch, pibroch
[θ]	thatch, ether, faith, breath		[ŋ]	bang, sing, link, anchor
[z]	zinc, buzz, houses		[ŋg]	anger, finger, English
[dz]	adze, adds		[r]	rat, arise, barring
[ð]	that, the, mother, breathe		[r]	sailor, martyr, finger, here; (sounded only when final and carried onto the next word, as in) here and now
[l]	lad, all, table, chisel			
[lj]	bullion, pillion			
[ʃ]	sham, dish, pressure, ocean, nation, machine			

SEMI-CONSONANTS

[j]	yam, yet, beauty, pure, duration		[w]	wall, well, await
			[hj]	hew, hue, huge

NOTE: The attention of the reader is directed to the Preface and the List of Abbreviations used in the dictionary, which are printed at the beginning of PART ONE.

A, a¹ [ei], *s.* **1.** (La lettre) A, a *m*. **It is spelt with two a's,** cela s'écrit avec deux a. *Tp:* A for Andrew, A comme Anatole. A1 [ei'wʌn], *U.S:* A No. 1, (i) *Nau:* A1 (*at Lloyd's*), de première cote (au Lloyd); (ii) de première qualité; de premier ordre. (*In house numbering*) Number 51a, numéro 51 bis. **2.** *Mus:* La *m.* **In A flat,** en la bémol. **3. A-bomb,** Bombe *f* A.

a², *before word beginning with vowel usu.* an [*stressed* ei, æn; *unstressed* ə, ən], *indef. art.* **1.** Un, une. **A man,** un homme. **A history,** une histoire. **A unit,** une unité. **An apple,** une pomme. **An M.P.** [an'em'pi:], = un député. **A man and (a) woman,** un homme et une femme. **A wife and mother,** une épouse et mère. **2.** (*Def. art. in Fr.*) (*a*) **To have a big mouth,** avoir la bouche grande. (*b*) **To have a taste for sth.,** avoir le goût de qch. **A fine excuse indeed!** la belle excuse! (*c*) (*Generalizing use*) **A woman takes life too seriously,** les femmes prennent la vie trop au sérieux. **3.** (*Distributive use*) (*a*) **Apples at fivepence a pound,** pommes à cinq pence la livre. **Five francs a head,** cinq francs par tête. (*b*) (*Time*) **Three times a week, a month, a year,** trois fois par semaine, par mois, par an, *occ.* trois fois l'an. **4.** (*Partitive in Fr.*) **It has given me an appetite,** cela m'a donné de l'appétit. **5.** (*a*) (= *A certain, a particular*) **I know a Doctor Smith,** je connais un certain docteur Smith. **In a sense,** dans un certain sens. (*b*) (= *The same; with 'at', 'of'*) **To eat two at a time,** en manger deux à la fois. **To come in two at a time,** entrer deux par deux. **To be of a size,** être de la même grandeur, de (la) même taille. (*c*) (= *A single*) **I haven't understood a word,** je n'ai pas compris un seul mot. **6.** (*Omitted in Fr.*) (*a*) (*Before unqualified pred. nouns*) **He is an Englishman,** a father, il est Anglais; il est père. **He was a barrister,** il était avocat. (*But* C'est un Anglais de passage.) (*b*) (*Before nouns in apposition*) **Caen, a large town in Normandy,** Caen, grande ville de Normandie. (*c*) (*In many verb-phrases*) **To put an end to sth.,** mettre fin à qch. **To make a fortune,** faire fortune. (*d*) **What a man!** quel homme! **What a pity!** quel dommage! (*e*) **To live like a prince,** vivre en prince. **To sell sth. at a loss,** vendre qch. à perte. **Within a short time,** à bref délai.

Aachen [ɑːxən]. *Pr. n. Geog:* Aix-la-Chapelle.

aardvark ['ɑːdvɑːk], *s. Z:* Oryctérope *m*.

aardwolf ['ɑːdwulf], *s. Z:* Protèle *m*.

aback [ə'bæk], *adv.* (*a*) *Nau:* (Voile) masquée, coiffée. (*Of ship*) **To be a.,** avoir le vent dessus. **To be caught a., taken a.,** être pris devant, vent dessus; être masqué. (*b*) **To be taken a.,** être, rester, déconcerté, interdit, interloqué; se déconcerter.

abacus, *pl.* **-ci, -cuses,** ['æbəkəs, -sai, -kəsiz], *s.* **1.** *Mth:* Boulier compteur *m*, abaque *m*. **2.** *Arch:* Abaque, tailloir *m*.

abaft [ə'bɑːft]. *Nau:* **1.** *adv.* Sur l'arrière; vers l'arrière. **2.** *prep.* A. the mast, sur l'arrière, en arrière, du mât.

abandon¹ [ə'bændən, abɑ'dɔ̃], *s.* (*a*) Abandon *m*; laisser-aller *m*. (*b*) Entrain *m*; désinvolture *f*.

abandon² [ə'bændən], *v.tr.* Abandonner; délaisser (sa famille, etc.); renoncer à (un plan, des poursuites). *Nau:* **To a. ship,** abandonner, évacuer, le bâtiment. **To a. oneself to despair,** s'abandonner, se livrer, laisser aller, au désespoir. **abandoned,** *a.* Dévergondé; dépravé. **abandoning,** *s.* = ABANDONMENT.

abandonment [ə'bændənmənt], *s.* Abandon(nement) *m* (de qn, de qch.); délaissement *m*.

abase [ə'beis], *v.tr.* Abaisser, humilier, ravaler (qn). **To a. oneself,** s'abaisser, s'humilier.

abasement [ə'beismənt], *s.* Abaissement *m*. **1.** Ravalement *m*; humiliation *f*, abjection *f*. **2.** Humilité *f*.

abash [ə'bæʃ], *v.tr.* Confondre, interloquer, décontenancer, déconcerter, interdire. **To be abashed at sth.,** être confus, tout interdit, de qch. **Nothing can a. him,** rien ne le démonte.

abashment [ə'bæʃmənt], *s.* Confusion *f*, embarras *m* (de qn).

abate [ə'beit]. **1.** *v.tr.* Diminuer (l'orgueil, le zèle, etc.); affaiblir (le courage); relâcher, ralentir (son activité); diminuer, faire cesser (la douleur, le bruit, etc.). **2.** *v.i.* (*Of storm, courage*) Diminuer, faiblir, s'affaiblir; (*of storm, fear, pain*) se calmer, s'apaiser; se modérer; (*of flood*) baisser, diminuer. **The wind abated,** le vent tomba.

abatement [ə'beitmənt], *s.* **1.** Diminution *f*, affaiblissement *m*; apaisement *m* (de la tempête); relâchement *m* (du temps); baisse *f* (des eaux). **2.** *Com:* Rabais *m*, remise *f* (sur le prix).

abattoir ['æbətwɑːr], *s.* Abattoir *m*.

abbacy ['æbəsi], *s.* **1.** Dignité *f* abbatiale. **2.** Abbaye *f*, bénéfice *m*.

abbess ['æbes, -is], *s.f.* Abbesse; supérieure (de couvent); mère abbesse.

abbey ['æbi], *s.* **1.** Abbaye *f*. **2.** A. (**church**), église abbatiale, abbatiale *f*.

abbot ['æbət], *s.m.* Abbé (d'un monastère); (père) supérieur.

abbreviate [æ'briːvieit], *v.tr.* Abréger.

abbreviation [əbriːvi'eiʃ(ə)n], *s.* Abréviation *f*.

ABC, abc [eibiː'siː]. **1.** ABC, abc *m. S.a.* SIMPLE 1. **2.** *s. Sch:* Abécédaire *m*.

abdicate ['æbdikeit], *v.tr.* **1.** Abdiquer (un trône); se démettre (d'une charge); renoncer à (un droit). **2.** *Abs.* Abdiquer; résigner le pouvoir. **Abdicating,** *a.* Abdicataire.

abdication [æbdi'keiʃ(ə)n], *s.* Abdication *f* (d'un trône); renonciation *f* (à un droit); démission *f* (d'une charge).

abdicator [æbdikeitər], *s.* Abdicataire *mf*.

abdomen ['æbdomen], *s.* Abdomen *m*.

abdominal [æb'dominl], *a.* Abdominal, -aux.

abduct [æb'dʌkt], *v.tr. Jur:* Enlever (qn).

abduction [æb'dʌkʃ(ə)n], *s. Jur:* Enlèvement *m* (de qn). **A. by force,** rapt *m*.

abductor [æb'dʌktər]. **1.** *s. Jur:* Ravisseur *m*; auteur *m* de l'enlèvement. **2.** *a. & s. Anat:* **A.** (**muscle**), muscle abducteur.

abeam [ə'biːm], *adv. Nau:* Par le travers; en belle.

abed [ə'bed], *adv. Au lit;* couché.

aberrance [æ'berəns], *s.* Déviation *f*, erreur *f*.

aberrant [æ'berənt], *a.* **1.** Aberrant; égaré (du droit chemin); dévoyé. **2.** *Biol:* Aberrant; anormal, -aux.

aberration [æbə'reiʃ(ə)n], *s.* **1.** Aberration *f*, déviation *f*. **2.** (*a*) Égarement *m* (des passions, etc.). **Mental a.,** égarement d'esprit; aberration; *Jur:* démence *f*. (*b*) Écart *m* (de conduite). **3.** *Astr: Mth: Opt:* Aberration. **4.** *Biol:* Structure anormale; anomalie *f*.

abet [ə'bet], *v.tr.* (abetted) **1. To a. s.o. in a crime,** encourager qn à un crime. *Jur:* **To aid and a. s.o.,** être le complice de qn. **2.** Encourager (un vice, le crime). **abetting,** *s.* (**Aiding and**) a., complicité *f*.

abettor [ə'betər], *s.* **A. of a crime,** complice *mf*, fauteur, -trice, d'un crime.

abeyance [ə'be(i)əns], *s.* Suspension *f* (d'une loi); vacation *f* (de droits); vacance *f* (d'un poste). **The matter is still in a.,** la question est toujours pendante, en suspens. **Law in a.,** loi inappliquée. **To fall into a.,** tomber en désuétude. *Jur:* **Estate in a.,** succession vacante.

abhor [əb'hɔːr], *v.tr.* (abhorred) Abhorrer; avoir horreur de; avoir (qn, qch.) en horreur.

abhorrence [əb'hɔrəns], *s.* Horreur *f* (of, de); extrême aversion *f* (of, pour, de).

abhorrent [əb'hɔrənt], *a.* **1.** (*Of pers., thg*) **To be a. to s.o.,** être répugnant, en horreur, à qn. **2.** (*Of thg*) **A. to, from, sth.,** contraire à qch.; incompatible avec qch.

abide [ə'baid], *v.* (*p.t.* abided, abode [ə'boud]; *p.p.* abided, abode) **1.** *v.i.* (*a*) *A. & Lit:* Rester, séjourner, demeurer. (*b*) **To a. by a promise,** rester fidèle à, tenir, une promesse. **To a. by a decision,** maintenir une décision. **I a. by what I said,** je maintiens mon dire. (c) (Of thg) Durer, subsister, demeurer. **2.** v.tr. (a) To a. the test, subir l'épreuve. (b) Attendre. (c) (Neg. and interr.) F: I can't a. him, je ne peux pas le sentir. **abiding,** a. Permanent, durable.

ability [ə'biliti], s. (a) Capacité f, pouvoir m (to do sth., de faire qch.). (b) Jur: Habilité f (à succéder; etc.); capacité légale. **2.** Habileté, capacité, intelligence f: To do sth. to the best of one's a., faire qch. dans la mesure de ses moyens; faire qch. de son mieux.

abject ['æbdʒekt], a. **1.** Abject, misérable. To live **in a. poverty,** F: ramper dans la misère. **2.** (a) Bas, vil. (b) Servile. **-ly,** adv. Abjectement. **1.** Misérablement. **2.** Bassement.

abjection [æb'dʒekʃ(ə)n], s. Abjection f; misère f.

abjectness ['æbdʒektnis], s. Abjection f; misère f.

abjuration [æbdʒuə'reiʃ(ə)n], s. Abjuration f.

abjure [əb'dʒuər], v.tr. Abjurer (sa foi, ses erreurs); renier (sa religion); renoncer (sous serment) à (ses droits).

abjurer [əb'dʒurər], s. Renieur m (of, de).

ablation [æb'leiʃən], s. Geol: Surg: Ablation f.

ablative ['æblətiv], a. & s. Gram: Ablatif (m). In the a., à l'ablatif. A. absolute, ablatif absolu.

ablaut ['æblaut], s. Ling: Apophonie f.

ablaze [ə'bleiz], adv. & pred.a. En feu, en flammes; enflammé, embrasé. To be a., flamber. A. with light, resplendissant de lumière. A. with anger, enflammé de colère.

able ['eibl], a. **1.** (a) Capable, compétent, habile. A very a. man, un homme de haute capacité. Jur: A. **in body and mind,** sain de corps et d'esprit. S.a. SEAMAN 1. (b) To be a. to do sth., (i) savoir, être capable de, faire qch.; (ii) (as infinitive to the vb. CAN) pouvoir, être à même de, être en état de, faire qch. **I shall not be a. to come,** je ne pourrai pas venir. **Better a. to do sth.,** plus capable, mieux à même, de faire qch. A. to pay, en mesure de payer. (c) Jur: A. to devise property, to inherit, apte, habile, à léguer, à succéder. **2.** A. **piece of work,** œuvre de talent; travail bien fait. **'ably,** adv. Habilement; avec maîtrise. **'able-'bodied,** a. Fort, robuste, vigoureux. Mil: (i) Valide; (ii) bon pour le service. S.a. SEAMAN 1. **'able-'minded,** a. Intelligent; de haute capacité intellectuelle.

ablution [əb'lu:ʃ(ə)n], s. Ablution f.

abnegate ['æbnigeit], v.tr. Renoncer à (une croyance, un privilège). To a. one's religion, renoncer (à) sa foi.

abnegation [æbni'geiʃ(ə)n], s. **1.** Abnégation f; renoncement m, renonciation f. **2.** Désaveu m, reniement m (d'une doctrine, etc.).

abnormal [əb'nɔ:məl], a. Anormal, -aux. **-ally,** adv. Anormalement.

abnormality [æbnɔ:'mæliti], s. **1.** Caractère anormal (de qch.); anomalie f. **2.** (a) Difformité f. (b) Bizarrerie f.

abnormity [æb'nɔ:miti], s. **1.** = ABNORMALITY. **2.** (a) Monstruosité f. (b) Monstre m.

aboard [ə'bɔ:d]. **1.** adv. A bord. To go a., aller, monter, à bord; s'embarquer. All a.! embarquez! **2.** prep. A. (a) ship, à bord d'un navire.

abode[1] [ə'boud], s. **1.** Lit: Demeure f, habitation f, résidence f. **2.** (Lieu m de) séjour m. Jur: Place of a., domicile m. Of, with, no fixed a., sans domicile fixe.

abode[2]. See ABIDE.

abolish [ə'bɔliʃ], v.tr. Abolir, supprimer.

abolition [æbə'liʃ(ə)n], s. Abolissement m, abolition f; suppression f.

abolitionism [æbə'liʃənizm], s. Hist: Abolitionnisme m.

abolitionist [æbə'liʃənist], s. & a. Hist: Abolitionniste mf, antiesclavagiste mf.

abominable [ə'bɔminəbl], a. Abominable; odieux. **-ably,** adv. Abominablement.

abominate [ə'bɔmineit], v.tr. Abominer; avoir (qch.) en abomination, en horreur. To a. doing sth., détester faire qch.

abomination [ə,bɔmi'neiʃ(ə)n], s. Abomination f.

aboriginal [æbə'ridʒən(ə)l]. **1.** a. (a) Primitif. (b) Indigène, aborigène. **2.** s. Aborigène m, indigène m.

aborigine [æbə'ridʒini:], s. Aborigène m, indigène m.

abort [ə'bɔ:t], v.i. Biol: Obst: Avorter.

abortion [ə'bɔ:ʃ(ə)n], s. **1.** (Miscarriage) Avortement m, esp. avortement provoqué. **2.** F: (a) (Dwarfed creature) Avorton m. (b) Œuvre mal venue.

abortionist [ə'bɔ:ʃ(ə)nist], s. Médecin avorteur; avorteuse f, F: faiseuse d'anges.

abortive [ə'bɔ:tiv]. **1.** a. & s. Abortif (m). **2.** a. (Of plan, etc.) Avorté, mort-né, manqué. (Of plan) To prove a., ne pas aboutir; n'aboutir à rien; échouer, avorter. **-ly,** adv. **1.** (Naître) avant terme. **2.** F: Sans succès; sans aboutir.

abortiveness [ə'bɔ:tivnis], s. Insuccès m, non-réussite f (d'un projet).

abound [ə'baund], v.i. Abonder (in, with, en); foisonner. **abounding,** a. Abondant.

about [ə'baut], adv. & prep. **1.** (a) Autour (de). The hills (round) a. the town, les collines autour de la ville. The people a. us, les gens auprès de nous, qui nous entourent. He went a long way a., il fit un long détour. (b) De côté et d'autre. To stroll a., se promener de ci, de là. Don't leave those papers lying a., ne laissez pas traîner ces papiers. A. here, par ici, dans ces parages. To walk a. the streets, marcher dans, par, les rues. He is a. again, il est de nouveau sur pied. (c) There is something uncommon a. him, il y a dans sa personne quelque chose de pas ordinaire. There's something a. a horse that . . ., il y a chez le cheval un je ne sais quoi qui. . . . (d) To do sth. turn (and turn) a., faire qch. à tour de rôle, tour à tour. S.a. DAY 1, TURN[1] 4. **2.** To turn sth. a., retourner qch. To turn a., faire demi-tour; se retourner. Mil: A. turn! a. face! demi-tour! S.a. RIGHT-ABOUT. Nau: Ready a.! paré à virer! S.a. GO ABOUT 1, PUT ABOUT 3, TACK[2] 2. **3.** Environ, presque. There are a. thirty, il y en a environ trente; il y en a une trentaine. A. as big, à peu près aussi grand. That's a. right, c'est à peu près cela. **Haven't we had a. enough of this?** Ça va durer longtemps cette plaisanterie? It is a. time, (i) il est presque temps; (ii) Iron: il est grand temps! He came a. three o'clock, il est venu vers trois heures, sur les trois heures. A. midday, a. one o'clock, sur les midi, sur les une heure. **4.** Au sujet de. To quarrel a. nothing, se quereller à propos de rien. Much ado a. nothing, beaucoup de bruit pour rien. A. that, là-dessus, à ce sujet, à cet égard. A. what? what a.? à quel sujet? à quel propos? What is it all a.? de quoi s'agit-il? He told me all a. it, il m'a mis au courant, il m'a dit ce qu'il en était. The doubts I entertained a. his intelligence, les doutes que j'ai éprouvés quant à son intelligence. To speak a. sth., parler de qch. To be uneasy a. s.o., être inquiet à l'égard, sur le compte, de qn. F: What a. my bath? et mon bain? How a. a game of bridge? si on faisait un bridge? **5.** (a) To be a. to do sth., être sur le point de, près de, faire qch. What were you a. to say? qu'est-ce que vous alliez dire? (b) To go a. one's task, faire sa besogne. This is how I go a. it, voici comment je m'y prends. To know what one is a., savoir, connaître, son affaire. What are you a.? qu'est-ce que vous faites là? Mind what you are a.! faites attention! You haven't been long a. it, il ne vous a pas fallu longtemps (pour le faire). While you are a. it, pendant que vous y êtes. To send s.o. a. his business, envoyer promener qn.

above [ə'bʌv], adv. & prep. **1.** Au-dessus (de). (a) The water reached a. their knees, l'eau leur montait jusqu'au-dessus des genoux. (b) To hover a. the town, planer au-dessus de la ville. The tenants of the flat a., les locataires du dessus. A voice from a., une voix d'en haut. The Powers a., les puissances célestes. A mountain rises a. the lake, une montagne s'élève au-dessus du lac, domine le lac. His voice was heard a. the din, on entendit sa voix par-dessus le tumulte. The Seine valley a. Paris, la vallée de la Seine en amont de Paris. (d) He is a. me in rank, il est mon supérieur hiérarchique. You must show yourself a. prejudice, il faut vous montrer supérieur aux préjugés. To live a. one's means, vivre au-delà de ses moyens. A. criticism, hors de l'atteinte de la critique. S.a. LAW 2. A. all . . ., surtout . . ., sur toutes choses . . . (surtout et) avant tout . . . par-dessus tout. . . . **2.** (In book) Ci-dessus. See the paragraph a., voir le paragraphe ci-dessus. As a., comme ci-dessus. **3.** (*Of pers.*) **To be a.** (all) **suspicion,** être au-dessus de tout soupçon. **I am a. doing that,** je me respecte trop pour faire cela; je dédaigne de faire cela. **He is a. telling a lie,** il ne saurait s'abaisser, jusqu'à mentir. **4. A. twenty,** plus de vingt. **a'bove-board. 1.** *adv.* **To play fair and a.-b.,** jouer cartes sur table; agir ouvertement, loyalement. **2.** *Pred.a.* Loyal; franc, franche. **His conduct was a.-b.,** sa conduite a été franche et ouverte. *S.a.* GROUND 5. **a'bove-'mentioned, a'bove-'named,** *a.* Susmentionné, susnommé, susdit; mentionné ci-dessus.

abracadabra [ˌæbrəkə'dæbrə], *s.* (*a*) (*Magic formula*) Abracadabra *m.* (*b*) Jargon *m.*

abrade [ə'breid], *v.tr.* Abraser, user (qch.) par le frottement, par abrasion; écorcher (la peau, etc.).

abrasion [ə'breiʒ(ə)n], *s.* **1.** Abrasion *f*; (usure par le) frottement *m.* **2.** *Med:* Écorchure *f*, éraflure *f.*

abrasive [ə'breisiv], *a. & s.,* Abrasif (*m*).

abreast [ə'brest], *adv.* (*a*) De front; sur la même ligne. *Navy:* **Line a.,** en ligne de front. **To come a. of a car,** arriver à la hauteur d'une voiture. (*b*) (*Of people*) **To walk a.,** marcher côte à côte. **To march two a.,** marcher par deux. **To be, keep, a. with, of, the times,** être de son temps, suivre son temps; *F:* être à la page.

abridge [ə'bridʒ], *v.tr.* **1.** Abréger. **Abridged edition,** édition réduite. **2.** Diminuer, restreindre, retrancher (l'autorité, les droits, de qn).

abridg(e)ment [ə'bridʒmənt], *s.* **1.** (*a*) Raccourcissement *m.* (*b*) Diminution *f*; restriction *f.* **2.** Abrégé *m*, précis *m*, résumé *m.*

abroad [ə'brɔːd], *adv.* **1.** (*a*) A l'étranger; en voyage. **To live a.,** vivre à l'étranger. **He is just back from a.,** il revient de l'étranger. **Our colleagues from a.,** nos collègues d'outre-mer. *S.a.* HOME I. 2. (*b*) *O:* (*Of pers.*) Sorti; (au) dehors. **2.** Au loin. **Scattered a.,** éparpillé de tous côtés. **The news got a.,** la nouvelle se répandit. **There is a rumour a. that . . .,** le bruit court que. . . . *S.a.* NOISE², TRUMPET² 2.

abrogate ['æbrogeit], *v.tr.* Abroger (une loi).

abrogation [ˌæbro'geiʃ(ə)n], *s.* Abrogation *f.*

abrupt [ə'brʌpt], *a.* (Départ, personne) brusque; (départ) brusqué, précipité; (ton) cassant; (style) heurté, saccadé, abrupt. **-ly,** *adv.* **1.** Brusquement; sans transition. **2.** Abruptement, à pic.

abruptness [ə'brʌptnis], *s.* **1.** (*a*) Brusquerie *f.* (*b*) Précipitation *f.* (*c*) Allure saccadée (du style). **2.** Raideur *f* (d'un sentier).

abscess ['æbses], *s.* Abcès *m*; foyer purulent. **To lance, drain, an a.,** ouvrir, percer, vider, un abcès. **To turn into an a.,** abcéder.

abscissa, *pl.* **-ae, -as** [æb'sisə, -iː, -əz], *s.* *Mth:* Abscisse *f.*

abscission [æb'siʒən], *s.* *Surg:* Abscission *f*, excision *f.*

abscond [əb'skɔnd], *v.i.* (*a*) Se soustraire à la justice; s'enfuir, s'évader (from, de). (*b*) *F:* Décamper, filer; mettre la clef sous le paillasson. **absconding**¹, *a.* En fuite. **absconding**², *s.* Fuite *f*, évasion *f.*

absconder [əb'skɔndər], *s.* **1.** Fugitif; évadé. **2.** *Jur:* Contumace *m*; défaillant *m.*

abseiling [æb'seiliŋ], *s.* *Mount:* Rappel *m.*

absence ['æbs(ə)ns], *s.* **1.** Absence *f*, éloignement *m* (from, de). **To be conspicuous by one's a.,** briller par son absence. *Jur:* **Sentenced in his, her, a.,** condamné(e) par contumace. **2. In the a. of definite information,** faute de, à défaut de, renseignements précis. **3. A. of mind,** distraction *f*, préoccupation *f.*

absent¹ ['æbs(ə)nt], *a.* **1.** (*a*) Absent (from, de). *Mil: etc:* **A. without leave,** en (position d') absence illégale, porté manquant. (*b*) Manquant. **2.** *Occ.* = ABSENT-MINDED. **-ly,** *adv.* Distraitement; d'un air distrait; d'un ton préoccupé. **absent-'minded,** *a.* Distrait. **-ly,** *adv.* Distraitement; d'un air distrait; d'une oreille distraite. **absent-'mindedness,** *s.* Distraction *f.*

absent² [æb'sent], *v.pr.* **To a. oneself,** s'absenter (from, de).

absentee [ˌæbs(ə)n'tiː]. **1.** *s.* (*a*) Absent *m.* (*b*) Manquant *m* (à l'appel). **2.** *a. & s. Hist:* **A.** (landlord), absentéiste *m.*

absenteeism [ˌæbsən'tiːizm], *s.* Absentéisme *m.*

absinth(e) ['æbsinθ], *s.* Absinthe *f.*

absolute ['æbsəl(j)uːt]. **1.** *a.* (*a*) Absolu. **A. power,** pouvoir absolu, illimité. **A. alcohol,** alcool absolu. **Case of a. necessity,** cas *m* de force majeure. *Jur:* **Decree a.,** décret irrévocable. *Gram:* **Ablative a.,** ablatif absolu. (*b*) Autoritaire; (ton) absolu. (*c*) *F:* **It's an a. scandal,** c'est un véritable scandale. **He's an a. idiot,** c'est un parfait imbécile. **2.** *s. Phil:* **The a.,** l'absolu *m.* **-ly,** *adv.* Absolument. **It is a. forbidden to . . .,** il est formellement interdit de. . . . **Verb used a.,** verbe employé dans un sens absolu.

absoluteness ['æbsəl(j)uːtnis], *s.* **1.** Pouvoir absolu. **2.** Caractère absolu (de qch.); réalité *f.*

absolution [ˌæbsə'l(j)uːʃ(ə)n], *s. Ecc:* Absolution *f.*

absolutism ['æbsə'l(j)uːtizm], *s.* Absolutisme *m.*

absolutist [ˌæbsə'l(j)uːtist], *s.* Absolutiste *mf.*

absolve [əb'zɔlv], *v.tr.* **1.** (*a*) Absoudre (s.o. of a sin, qn d'un péché). (*b*) Remettre (un péché). **He was absolved from all blame,** il fut reconnu qu'il n'était aucunement responsable. **2. To a. s.o. from a vow,** affranchir, délier, dispenser, qn d'un vœu. **absolving,** *s.* Dispensation *f* (from, de).

absorb [əb'sɔːb], *v.tr.* **1.** (*a*) Absorber (un liquide, la chaleur), (*b*) **To a. a shock, a sound,** amortir un choc, un son. **2.** (*a*) **His business absorbs him,** ses affaires l'absorbent. (*b*) **To become absorbed in sth.,** s'absorber dans qch. **absorbing,** *a.* Absorbant.

absorbedly [əb'sɔːbidli], *adv.* D'un air absorbé.

absorbent [əb'sɔːbənt], *a. & s.* Absorbant (*m*). *Med:* **A. cotton-wool,** coton hydrophile.

absorber [əb'sɔːbər], *s. Ch: Ph:* Absorbeur *m.* **2.** Amortisseur *m* (de son, d'oscillations). *S.a.* SHOCK³.

absorption [əb'sɔːpʃ(ə)n], *s.* **1.** Absorption *f* (de chaleur, etc.). **2.** Absorbement *m* (de l'esprit).

absorptive [əb'sɔːptiv], *a.* Absorptif; absorbant. **A. power,** force *f* d'absorption.

abstain [əbs'tein], *v.i.* **1.** S'abstenir (from sth., from doing sth., de qch., de faire qch.). *R.C.Ch:* **To a. from meat,** faire maigre. **2.** *Abs.* S'abstenir de boissons alcooliques. **abstaining,** *s.* = ABSTINENCE.

abstainer [əbs'teinər], *s.* Abstème *mf*; abstinent, -ente, buveur d'eau. **To be a total a. (from alcohol),** ne pas boire d'alcool; ne boire que de l'eau.

abstemious [əbs'tiːmiəs], *a.* (*a*) Sobre, tempérant, abstinent, abstème. (*b*) **An a. meal,** un repas frugal. **-ly,** *adv.* Sobrement; frugalement.

abstemiousness [əbs'tiːmiəsnis], *s.* Sobriété *f*, tempérance *f*; abstinence *f.*

abstention [əbs'tenʃ(ə)n], *s.* **1.** Abstention *f*, abstinence *f* (from, de). **2.** *Pol:* Abstention; abstentionnisme *m.*

abstentionist [əbs'tenʃ(ə)nist], *s. Pol:* Abstentionniste *m.*

abstinence ['æbstinəns], *s.* (*a*) Abstinence *f* (from, de). (*b*) **Total a.,** abstinence complète de boissons alcooliques.

abstinency ['æbstinənsi], *s.* Habitudes *fpl* de tempérance, de frugalité.

abstinent ['æbstinənt], *a.* Abstinent, tempérant, sobre.

abstract¹ ['æbstrækt]. **1.** *a.* Abstrait. (*a*) **A. number,** nombre abstrait. *Gram:* **A. noun,** nom abstrait. **A. art,** art abstrait. (*b*) **Abstrus.** **2.** *s.* **The a.,** l'abstrait *m.* **To know sth. in the a.,** avoir une connaissance abstraite, théorique, de qch.

abstract² ['æbstrækt], *s.* Résumé *m*, abrégé *m.*

abstract³ [æbs'trækt], *v.tr.* **1.** (*a*) Soustraire, dérober, voler (sth. from s.o., qch. à qn). (*b*) Détourner (l'attention de qn). **2.** (*a*) **To a. a quality, a conception,** faire abstraction d'une qualité, d'une conception. (*b*) *Ch: Ind:* Extraire (par distillation). **3.** Résumer, abréger (un livre); relever (un compte). **abstracted,** *a.* Distrait; rêveur. **-ly,** *adv.* = ABSENT-MINDEDLY.

abstractedness [æbs'træktidnis], *s.* Absence *f* (d'esprit); préoccupation *f.*

abstraction [æbs'trækʃ(ə)n], *s.* **1.** Soustraction *f* (d'argent, de papiers, etc.); détournement *m*, vol *m.* **2.** (*a*) *Phil:* Abstraction *f.* (*b*) Idée abstraite. **3. A. of mind,** distraction *f*, préoccupation *f.* **A fit of a.,** un moment d'absence.

abstractive [æbs'træktiv], *a.* Abstractif, -ive.

abstruse [æbs'truːs], *a.* Abstrus. **-ly,** *adv.* D'une manière compliquée.

abstruseness [æbs'tru:snis], *s.* Caractère abstrus (de qch.); complexité *f*; obscurité *f*; hermétisme *m* (d'un texte, etc.).

absurd [əb'sə:d], *a.* Absurde; déraisonnable; *F:* impossible. It's a.! *F:* c'est idiot! **-ly,** *adv.* Absurdement.

absurdity [əb'sə:diti], **absurdness** [əb'sə:dnis], *s.* Absurdité *f.*

abundance [ə'bʌndəns], *s.* 1. Abondance *f*, affluence *f.* In a., en abondance, *F:* à foison. To live in a., vivre dans l'abondance. 2. (*At solo whist*) Demande *f* de neuf levées.

abundant [ə'bʌndənt], *a.* Abondant (in, en); fertile (en blé, etc.); copieux. **-ly,** *adv.* Abondamment; copieusement.

abuse¹ [ə'bju:s], *s.* 1. (*a*) Abus *m* (of, de). A. of administrative authority, abus d'autorité, de pouvoir. A. of trust, prévarication *f.* (*b*) To remedy an a., redresser un abus. (*c*) Emploi abusif (d'un terme). (*d*) Dommage (infligé). A. of the highway, dommage, dégradations *fpl*, à la route. 2. Insultes *fpl*, injures *fpl.*

abuse² [ə'bju:z], *v.tr.* ·1. Abuser de (son autorité, etc.); mésuser de (son pouvoir); faire abus de (qch.). A much-abused word un mot trop, mal, employé. 2. Maltraiter, houspiller (qn). 3. (*a*) Médire, dire du mâl, de (qn); dénigrer (qn). (*b*) Injurier; dire des injures, des sottises, à (qn).

abuser [ə'bju:zər], *s.* Détracteur, -trice.

abusive [ə'bju:siv], *a.* 1. (Emploi) abusif (d'un mot). 2. (Propos) injurieux; (homme) grossier. **-ly,** *adv.* 1. (Employer un mot) abusivement. 2. (Parler) injurieusement.

abusiveness [ə'bju:sivnis], *s.* Grossièreté *f.*

abut [ə'bʌt], *v.i. & tr.* (abutted) 1. To a. sth. ; to a. on, against, sth., aboutir, confiner, à un endroit. 2. *Const:* To a. on, against (a wall, etc.), s'appuyer, buter, contre (une paroi). 3. *Carp:* (*a*) *v.i.* (S') abouter. (*b*) *v.tr.* Abouter (deux pièces). **abutting,** *a.* 1. Aboutissant, attenant (on, à). 2. A. joint, assemblage en about. A. surface, surface de contact.

abutment [ə'bʌtmənt], *s.* 1. *Carp:* Aboutement *m.* 2. (*a*) Arc-boutant *m* (d'une muraille); contrefort *m.* (*b*) Butée *f*, culée *f* (d'un pont); pied-droit *m* (d'une voûte).

abysmal [ə'bizm(ə)l], *a.* Sans fond; insondable; (ignorance) profonde. **-ally,** *adv.* A. ignorant, d'une ignorance profonde.

abyss [ə'bis], *s.* Abîme *m*, gouffre *m.*

abyssal [ə'bis(ə)l], *a. Oc: Geol:* Abyssal, -aux.

Abyssinia [ˌæbi'sinjə]. *Pr.n. Geog:* L'Éthiopie *f*; l'Abyssinie *f.*

Abyssinian [ˌæbi'sinjən], *a. & s.* Éthiopien, -ienne, abyssinien, -ienne.

acacia [ə'keiʃə], *s. Bot:* Acacia *m.*

academic [ˌækə'demik], *a.* Académique. (*a*) *Phil:* Qui se rapporte à l'école platonicienne. (*b*) A. discussion, débat académique; discussion abstraite. (*c*) *Pej:* (Style) compassé, guindé. (*d*) (Carrière, etc.) universitaire. (*e*) *Art:* (Peinture, etc.) académique.

academical [ˌækə'demik(ə)l]. 1. *a.* Universitaire. 2. *s.pl.* Academicals, costume *m* académique. **-ally,** *adv.* Académiquement.

academician [əˌkædə'miʃ(ə)n], *s.* Académicien *m. Esp.* Royal A., R.A., membre de la '*Royal Academy*' (des Beaux-Arts).

academism [ə'kædəmizm], *s. Art:* Académisme *m.*

academist [ə'kædəmist], *s.* 1. *Phil:* Platonicien *m.* 2. Académicien *m*; membre d'une Académie.

academy [ə'kædəmi], *s.* 1. *Gr.Phil:* L'Académie *f* (de Platon). 2. (*a*) Académie. The Royal A. (of Arts), (i) l'Académie royale des Beaux-Arts; (ii) le Salon (de Londres). Fencing a., salle *f* d'escrime. (*b*) Military A., École *f* militaire. A. of music, conservatoire *m.* 3. (*a*) *A:* École (privée); pension *f*, pensionnat *m.* (*b*) (*In Scot.*) = lycée *m.*

acanthus [ə'kænθəs], *s.* 1. *Bot:* Acanthe *f.* 2. *Arch:* (Feuille *f* d')acanthe.

acarpous [ə'kɑ:pəs], *a. Bot:* Acarpe.

accede [æk'si:d], *v.i.* 1. To a. to an office, entrer en possession d'une charge. To a. to the throne, monter sur le trône, accéder au trône. 2. To a. to a treaty, adhérer à un traité. To a. to a request, accueillir une demande.

accelerate [æk'seləreit]. 1. *v.tr.* (*a*) Accélérer (la marche, un travail); précipiter (les événements); activer (un travail). *Abs. Aut:* Accélérer. (*b*) Hâter, précipiter. To a. proceedings, hâter une procédure. 2. *v.i.* (*Of motion, etc.*) S'accélérer. **accelerated,** *a.* (Mouvement) accéléré. *Cin:* Accelerated motion, accéléré *m.* **accelerating,** *a.* Accélérateur, -trice.

acceleration [ækˌselə'reiʃ(ə)n], *s.* Accélération *f.* Negative a., accélération retardatrice, négative; retardation *f.* Constant a., accélération uniforme. Uniform a., vitesse uniformément accélérée. Gravitational a., accélération de la pesanteur.

accelerator [æk'seləreitər]. 1. *a. & s.* Accélérateur, -trice. 2. *s. Aut: Clockm: Phot: Atom.Ph:* Accélérateur *m. Aut:* A. pedal, pédale d'accélération, *F:* champignon *m.*

accelerograph [æk'selərəgræf], *s.* Accélérographe *m.*

accelerometer [ækselə'rəmetər], *s. Mec:* Accéléromètre *m.*

accent¹ ['æks(ə)nt], *s.* Accent *m.* 1. (*a*) To have a German a., avoir l'accent allemand. (*b*) In broken accents, d'une voix brisée, entrecoupée. 2. (*a*) *Pros:* Temps marqué. (*b*) *Mus:* (i) Temps fort; (ii) accent (mélodique). 3. Grammatical accents, accents grammaticaux. Acute a., grave a., accent aigu, accent grave.

accent² [æk'sent], *v.tr.* Accentuer (une syllabe, une voyelle, etc.); appuyer sur (une syllabe).

accentuate [æk'sentjueit], *v.tr.* Accentuer, souligner, appuyer sur, faire ressortir, rehausser (un détail, etc.). **accentuated,** *a.* Fortement marqué; accentué.

accentuation [ækˌsentju'eiʃ(ə)n], *s.* Accentuation *f.*

accept [ək'sept], *v.tr. & ind.tr.* Accepter (un cadeau, une offre); agréer (les prières de qn); admettre (les raisons, les excuses, de qn); se soumettre (à son destin); donner son adhésion à (un traité). To be accepted, être accepté; passer. The accepted custom, l'usage (admis). *Com:* To a. a bill, accepter un effet.

acceptability [əkˌseptə'biliti], *s.* **acceptableness** [ək'septəb(ə)lnis], *s.* Acceptabilité *f.*

acceptable [ək'septəbl], *a.* (*a*) Acceptable, agréable (to, à). Your cheque was most a., votre chèque est arrivé fort à propos. (*b*) Possible. She considered him as an a. husband, elle le considérait comme un mari possible. **-ably,** *adv.* Acceptablement; assez bien.

acceptance [ək'septəns], *s.* (*a*) Acceptation *f*; consentement *m* à recevoir (qch.); accueil *m* favorable (de qch.). A. of a proposal, agrément donné à une proposition. To secure a. of sth., faire accepter qch. This proposal met with general a., cette proposition a rallié tous les suffrages. To find a. (*of story, etc.*), trouver créance. *Com:* To present a bill for a., présenter une traite à l'acceptation. (*b*) *Th:* Réception *f* (d'une pièce par le comité de lecture). (*c*) *Com: Ind:* Réception (d'un article commandé). A. test, trial, essai de réception, de recette. (*d*) *Jur:* A. of persons, partialité *f.* Without a. of persons, sans faire acception de personne.

acceptant [ək'septənt], *a. & s. Com:* Acceptant, -ante.

acceptation [ˌæksep'teiʃ(ə)n], *s.* Acception *f*, signification *f* (d'un mot).

acceptor [ək'septər], *s. Com:* Tiré *m*; accepteur *m* (d'une lettre de change).

access ['ækses], *s.* 1. Accès *m*, abord *m.* Difficult of a., d'un accès difficile, d'un abord difficile; difficile à approcher. Easy of a., abordable, accostable. Door that gives a. to a room, porte qui donne accès à, qui commande, une pièce. A. to the door is by a flight of steps, on accède à la porte par un escalier. To find, obtain, a. to s.o., trouver accès auprès de qn. To have a. to s.o., avoir accès chez, auprès de qn; avoir son entrée, ses entrées, chez qn. 2. A. of fever, of rage, accès de fièvre, de rage. A. of joy, saisissement *m* de joie.

accessibility [ækˌsesi'biliti], *s.* Accessibilité *f*; commodité *f*, facilité *f*, d'accès.

accessible [æk'sesəbl], *a.* 1. (Endroit, personne, etc.) accessible, abordable, approchable. Knowledge a. to everyone, connaissances à la portée de tout le monde, accessibles à tous. 2. (*Of pers.*) (*a*) Accueillant. (*b*) He was a. to bribery, il n'était pas incorruptible.

accession [æk'seʃ(ə)n], s. 1. A. of light, of air, admission f de lumière, d'air. A. of funds from abroad, arrivage m de fonds de l'étranger. 2. (a) Accroissement m (par addition). List of accessions to a library, registre m des additions à une bibliothèque. A. to one's income, augmentation f de revenus. (b) Adhésion f (à un parti). 3. (a) A. to manhood, arrivée f à l'âge d'homme. (b) A. to power, accession f au pouvoir. A. to the throne, avènement m au trône. A. to an estate, entrée en possession, en jouissance, d'un patrimoine.

accessory [æk'sesəri]. 1. a. Accessoire, subsidiaire (to, à). 2. s. (a) Accessoire m (d'une machine, etc.); article m d'équipement. Toilet accessories, objets m, ustensiles m, de toilette. (b) pl. Th: Accessoires mpl (d'une pièce). 3. s. & pred. a. A. to a crime, complice m, fauteur m, d'un crime. Jur: A. before the fact, complice par instigation. A. after the fact, complice après coup.

accidence ['æksid(ə)ns], s. Gram: Morphologie f.

accident ['æksid(ə)nt]. 1. a. (a) Accidentel, fortuit; de hasard. (b) Accessoire, subsidiaire. 2. s. Mus: Accident m; signe accidentel. -ally, adv. Accidentellement. (a) Par hasard, fortuitement. (b) Par mégarde.

acclaim [ə'kleim], v.tr. Acclamer; accueillir (qn) par des acclamations. Charlemagne was acclaimed emperor, Charlemagne fut acclamé, proclamé, empereur.

acclamation [æklə'meiʃ(ə)n], s. Acclamation f. Carried by a., adopté par acclamation.

acclamatory [æk'læmətəri], a. Acclamatif, -ive.

acclimatization [ə,klaimətai'zeiʃ(ə)n], s. Acclimatation f, accoutumance f (to, à); naturalisation f.

acclimatize [ə'klaimətaiz], v.tr. Acclimater; naturaliser. To get, become, acclimatized, s'acclimater.

acclivity [ə'kliviti], s. Montée f, côte f; rampe f.

accolade [æko'leid], s. (a) Accolade f (i) coup du plat de l'épée; (ii) Mus: trait de plume; (b) Arch: Arc m en accolade.

accommodate [ə'kɔmədeit], v.tr. 1. (a) Accommoder, conformer (ses goûts à ceux d'un autre). To a. oneself to circumstances, s'accommoder, s'adapter, s'harmoniser, aux circonstances. (b) Ajuster, adapter (qch. à qch.). (c) Arranger (une querelle); concilier (des opinions). 2. To a. s.o., accommoder, servir, obliger, rendre service à, qn. To a. s.o. with sth., donner, fournir, qch. à qn; fournir qn de qch. To a. s.o. with a loan, faire un prêt à qn. 3. Loger, recevoir (tant de personnes). accommodating, a. (a) Complaisant, obligeant, serviable, accommodant; peu difficile (with regard to, sur). (b) Pej: (Of morals, religion, etc.) Accommodant, commode, facile. -ly, adv. Complaisamment.

accommodation [ə,kɔmə'deiʃ(ə)n], s. 1. (a) Ajustement m, adaptation f (to, à). (b) Accommodement m, arrangement m, ajustement (d'une dispute). To come to an a., arriver à un compromis; s'arranger à l'amiable. 2. (a) Commodité f, facilités fpl. For your a., pour votre commodité. Com: A. bill, billet de complaisance. Nau: A. ladder, échelle de poupe, de coupée; échelle de commandement. Rail: U.S: A. (train), (train) omnibus. (b) Logement m; installation matérielle. We have no sleeping a., nous n'avons pas de chambres. A: A. for man and beast, (ici) on loge à pied et à cheval. (c) Avance f, prêt m (d'argent).

accommo'dation-'unit, s. Adm: Bloc-logement m.

accompaniment [ə'kʌmp(ə)nimənt], s. (a) Accompagnement m; accessoires mpl. (b) Mus: Accompagnement (on the piano, au piano).

accompanist [ə'kʌmp(ə)nist], s. Mus: Accompagnateur, -trice.

accompany [ə'kʌmp(ə)ni], v.tr. Accompagner. 1. To be accompanied by s.o., être accompagné de (occ. par) qn. 2. (a) He accompanied these words with a smile, il accompagna ces mots d'un sourire. (b) Fever accompanied by, with, delirium, fièvre accompagnée de délire. 3. Mus: To a. s.o. on the piano, accompagner qn au piano. accompanying, a. (Symptôme, etc.) concomitant.

accomplice [ə'kɔmplis], s. Complice mf. To be an a. in a crime, tremper dans un crime, être complice d'un crime.

accomplish [ə'kɔmpliʃ], v.tr. Accomplir, exécuter, achever, venir à bout de (qch.); mener à bonne fin (une tâche); réaliser (une prédiction). To a. one's object, atteindre son but. accomplished, a. (a) (Musicien, etc.) accompli, achevé. A. fact, fait accompli. (b) Qui possède de nombreux talents.

accomplishment [ə'kɔmpliʃmənt], s. 1. (a) Accomplissement m, achèvement m, exécution f, consommation f (d'une tâche); réalisation f (d'un projet). Difficult of a., difficile à réaliser. (b) Chose accomplie, réalisée. 2. Usu.pl. Art(s) m d'agrément, talent(s) m (d'agrément).

accord[1] [ə'kɔːd], s. 1. Accord m, consentement m. With one a., d'un commun accord. 2. To do sth. of one's own a., faire qch. de son plein gré, de son propre gré, de sa propre volonté.

accord[2]. 1. v.i. S'accorder, être d'accord, concorder (with, avec). 2. v.tr. Accorder, concéder, octroyer (to, à). according, adv. Used only in: 1. Conj.phr. A. as, selon que, suivant que, + ind. We see things differently a. as we are rich or poor, on voit les choses différemment selon qu'on est riche ou pauvre. 2. Prep.phr. (a) A. to the orders, selon, suivant, d'après, les ordres; conformément aux ordres. A. to age, to height, par rang d'âge, de taille. (b) A. to him, d'après lui; à l'en croire; à ce qu'il dit. A. to that, d'après cela. The Gospel a. to St. Luke, l'Évangile selon saint Luc. -ly, adv. 1. (a) To act a., agir en conséquence, à l'avenant. (b) A. as = according as. 2. (Therefore) A. I wrote to him, je lui ai donc écrit; en conséquence je lui ai écrit.

accordance [ə'kɔːd(ə)ns], s. Accord m, conformité f. In a. with your instructions, en conformité avec, conformément à, vos ordres; suivant vos ordres. Statement in a. with the truth, affirmation conforme à, d'accord avec, la vérité.

accordant [ə'kɔːd(ə)nt], a. 1. Concordant; d'accord. 2. D'accord (to, with, avec); conforme (to, with, à); en harmonie (avec).

accordion [ə'kɔːdiən], s. Accordéon m. Dressm: A.-pleated, (plié) en accordéon; en plis d'accordéon, plissé soleil. accordion-player, s. = ACCORDIONIST.

accordionist [ə'kɔːdiənist], s. Accordéoniste mf.

accost [ə'kɔst], v.tr. (a) Accoster, aborder. (b) Racoler. accosting, s. Jur: Raccrochage m; racolage m.

accouchement [ə'kuːʃmɑ̃ː(ŋ)], s. Obst: Accouchement m.

account[1] [ə'kaunt], s. 1. (Calculation) To cast an a., faire un calcul. 2. (a) Com: Fin: Compte m, note f. Detailed a., compte spécifié. Book-k: Accounts payable, dettes passives. Accounts receivable, dettes actives. Current a., compte courant. My bank a., mon compte en banque. To settle an a., régler une note, un compte. The accounts (of a firm), la comptabilité. To keep the accounts, tenir les livres, les écritures, les comptes. In a. with s.o., en compte avec qn. To pay a sum on a., payer une somme en acompte, à compte, à valoir; payer un acompte. To give ten pounds on a., donner un acompte de dix livres. On, for, a. of s.o., pour le compte de qn, à valoir sur qn. (b) Exposé m, état m, note. A. of expenses, état, note, de dépenses. (c) To find one's a. in . . ., trouver son compte à. . . . To turn, put, sth. to a., tirer parti, avantage, de qch.; faire valoir qch.; utiliser qch. To turn sth. to the best a., tirer tout le profit, parti, possible de qch. He can turn everything to a., il fait profit de tout; il fait flèche de tout bois. (d) To call s.o. to a. (for sth., for doing sth.), demander une explication à qn; demander compte à qn (de qch.); prendre qn à partie (d'avoir fait qch.). To bring s.o. to a., faire payer ses méfaits à qn. He has gone to his a., il est mort; il a payé sa dette à la nature. To give

a. of sth., rendre raison de qch. He gave quite a good a. of himself, il s'est bien acquitté; il s'en est bien tiré. 3. (a) (*Person, thing*) of some a., of high a., of small a., (personne, chose) qui compte, qui compte pour beaucoup, qui ne compte guère. Competitors of little a., des concurrents peu dangereux, peu sérieux. To make much, little, a. of sth., faire grand cas, peu de cas, de qch. To be held in a., to be of some a., être (tenu) en grande estime. To take sth. into a., to take a. of sth., tenir compte de qch., faire état de qch. To leave sth. out of a., to take no a. of sth., ne pas tenir compte de qch.; négliger (une circonstance). (b) On a. of s.o., à cause de, par égard pour, qn. I was nervous on his a., j'avais peur pour lui. On a. of sth., à cause de, en considération de, qch. On every a., sous tous les rapports. On no a., not on any a., dans aucun cas, pour rien au monde. (c) To act on one's ówn a., agir de sa propre initiative, de soi-même. 4. Récit m, relation (d'un fait). To give an a. of sth., faire le récit, la relation, de qch. To give an a. of the position of affairs, faire un exposé de la situation. To give an a. of oneself, (i) rendre compte de ses faits et gestes; (ii) décliner ses titres et qualités. By his own a. . . ., (i) d'après son propre dire . . ., selon son dire . . ., à ce qu'il dit . . ; (ii) à l'en croire. . . . By all accounts, au dire de tout le monde. ac'count-book, s. Livre de comptes m. ac'count-day, s. St.Exch: (Jour de) règlement m.

account², *v.tr. & ind.tr.* 1. *Pred.* To a. (to be) wise, guilty, tenir qn pour sage, coupable; regarder, considérer, qn comme sage, coupable. To a. oneself lucky, s'estimer heureux. 2. (a) Comptabiliser. To a. for (sth.), rendre raison de, justifier (de) (sa conduite); expliquer (une circonstance). To a. for a sum of money, for an expenditure, rendre compte d'une somme; justifier une dépense. Submarines accounted for 60% of the enemy's losses, les sous-marins ont été responsables de 60% des pertes de l'ennemi. (b) I can't a. for it, je n'y comprends rien, je ne me l'explique pas. There is no accounting for tastes, des goûts et des couleurs, on ne discute pas; chacun son goût. (c) F: To a. for (= *kill*) s.o., faire son affaire à qn. **accounting,¹** a. Com: etc: A. machine, machine f comptable. **accounting,²** s. = ACCOUNTANCY. The a. department, la comptabilité.

accountability [ə,kauntə'biliti], s. Responsabilité f.

accountable [ə'kauntəbl], a. To be a. to s.o. for sth., être responsable de qch. envers qn. To be a. for a sum of money, être redevable d'une somme d'argent. He is not a. for his actions, il est irresponsable.

accountableness [ə'kauntəblnis], s. = ACCOUNTABILITY.

accountancy [ə'kauntənsi], s. 1. Comptabilité f; profession f de comptable. 2. Tenue f des livres.

accountant [ə'kauntənt], s. (a) Agent m comptable; comptable m; teneur m de livres. Chief a., chef m de (la) comptabilité; chef comptable. The accountant's department, la comptabilité. (b) Chartered a., C.A., = expert m comptable; conseiller m fiscal.

accountantship [ə'kauntəntʃip], s. 1. Place f de comptable. 2. Poste m de chef de (la) comptabilité.

accoutrement(s) [ə'ku:trəmənt(s)], s.(pl.) (a) Harnachement m; caparaçon m (d'un destrier). (b) Équipement m, fourniment m (du soldat).

accredit [ə'kredit], v.tr. 1. Accréditer (qn, qch.); mettre (qn, qch.) en crédit, en réputation. 2. To a. an ambassador to a government, accréditer un ambassadeur auprès d'un gouvernement. **accredited**, a. 1. (Of pers.) Accrédité, autorisé. 2. A. opinions, opinions reçues, orthodoxes.

accretion [ə'kri:ʃ(ə)n], s. (a) Accroissement m organique. (b) Accroissement par alluvion, par addition; addition f (to, à).

accrue [ə'kru:], v.i. 1. (a) Provenir, dériver (from, de). (b) (Of moneys, land, etc.) To a. to s.o., revenir à qn. 2. (Of interest) Courir, s'accumuler. **accruing,** a. Fin: (a) Portion a. to each heir, portion afférente à chaque héritier. (b) Intérêts à échoir.

accumulate [ə'kju:mjuleit], 1. v.tr. Accumuler, amasser (une fortune, etc.); amonceler; emmagasiner (de l'électricité, de la chaleur). 2. v.i. S'accumuler, s'amonceler.

accumulation [ə,kju:mju'leiʃ(ə)n], s. 1. Accumulation f, amoncellement m, emmagasinage m, de la chaleur, de l'électricité. A. of capital, accroissement m du capital (auquel viennent s'ajouter les intérêts). Improper accumulations, réserves abusives. 2. Amas m, monceau m, accumulation.

accumulator [ə'kju:mjuleitər], s. 1. (Pers.) Accumulateur, -trice. 2. (a) Mec.E: Civ.E: Accumulateur m (d'énergie). (b) El: (Storage battery) Accumulateur, F: accu m. A. capacity indicator, accumètre m.

accuracy ['ækjurəsi], s. (a) Exactitude f; (degré m de) justesse f; précision f. (b) Fidélité f (de mémoire, d'une traduction).

accurate ['ækjurit], a. (a) Exact, juste, précis. To be (strictly) a. . . ., pour être tout à fait exact. . . . To take a. aim, viser juste. (b) (Mémoire, traduction) fidèle; (dessin) correct, fidèle. -ly, adv. Exactement, avec précision.

accursed [ə'kə:sid], a. 1. Lit: Maudit. 2. F: Maudit, exécrable, détestable.

accusation [,ækju'zeiʃ(ə)n], s. Accusation f; Jur: incrimination f.

accusative [ə'kju:zətiv], a. & s. Gram: (Cas) accusatif m; régime direct.

accuse [ə'kju:z], v.tr. Accuser (s.o. of sth., of doing sth., qn de qch., de faire qch.); Jur: incriminer (qn). **accused,** s. Jur: The a., l'inculpé(e) (in all cases); l'accusé(e) (d'un crime); l'incriminé(e) le, la prévenu(e). **accusing,** a. Accusateur, -trice. -ly, adv. D'une manière accusatrice.

accuser [ə'kju:zər], s. Accusateur, -trice.

accustom [ə'kʌstəm], v.tr. Accoutumer, habituer (s.o. to sth., to doing sth., qn à qch., à faire qch.); aguerrir (qn à, contre, la fatigue, etc.). To a. oneself to discipline, se faire à la discipline. **accustomed,** a. 1. Accoutumé, habitué (to, à). To be a. to . . ., (i) avoir coutume de . . ., (ii) être accoutumé à . . . . To get a. to sth., s'accoutumer à qch.; se faire à qch. That is not what I am a. to, (i) ce n'est pas dans mes habitudes; (ii) ce n'est pas ce à quoi je suis accoutumé. 2. Habituel, familier, ordinaire; d'usage.

ace [eis], s. 1. (Of dice, dominoes, cards) As m. 2. Av: (Of pers.) As. attrib. F: An a. reporter, journaliste mf de premier ordre. 3. F: Within an a. of sth., à deux doigts de qch. I was within an a. of + ger., j'ai bien failli, bien manqué + inf.

acephalous [ə'sefələs], a. Biol: Acéphale.

acerbity [ə'sə:biti], s. Acerbité f; aigreur f, âpreté f (de ton).

acetate ['æsiteit], s. Ch: Acétate m. Cellulose a., acétocellulose f. Gramophones: F: Disque m souple.

acetic [ə'setik, ə'si:tik], a. Ch: Acétique. Glacial a. acid, acide acétique concentré.

acetify [ə'setifai], 1. v.tr. Acétifier. 2. v.i. S'acétifier; tourner au vinaigre.

acetone ['æsitoun], s. Ch: Acétone f.

acetous ['æsetəs], a. Acéteux, -euse.

acetylene [ə'setili:n], s. Ch: Acétylène m. A. lamp, lampe, lanterne, à acétylène. A. blow-lamp, chalumeau m à acétylène.

ache¹ [eik], s. Mal m, douleur f. All aches and pains, tout courbaturé, tout moulu. S.a. HEADACHE, TOOTHACHE.

ache², v.i. My head aches, la tête me fait mal; j'ai mal à la tête. It makes my head a., cela me donne le, un, mal de tête. The exercise has made my legs a., l'exercise m'a fatigué, courbaturé, les jambes. It makes my heart a., cela me serre le cœur. F: He was aching to join in the fight, il brûlait de prendre part au combat. **aching,** a. Douloureux, endolori. A. tooth, une dent malade. A. heart, cœur dolent. S.a. VOID II.

achene [ə'ki:n], s. Bot: Akène m.

achieve [ə'tʃi:v], v.tr. 1. Accomplir (un exploit); exécuter, réaliser (une entreprise). 2. Acquérir (de l'honneur); parvenir (aux honneurs); se faire (une réputation). 3. Atteindre (à), arriver à (un but). To a. one's purpose, one's end, parvenir à ses fins. To a. victory, remporter la victoire. He has achieved the impossible, il est venu à bout d'une tâche qui semblait impossible. He will never a. anything, il n'arrivera jamais à rien. **achieving,** s. 1. Accomplissement m, exécution f. 2. Obtention f (d'un résultat).

achievement [ə'tʃiːvmənt], s. 1. Accomplissement m, réalisation f, exécution f (d'un projet, etc.). 2. (a) Exploit m, (haut) fait. (b) When we consider his a., lorsque nous considérons (i) son œuvre, (ii) l'effort qu'il a accompli.

Achilles [ə'kiliːz]. Pr.n.m. Achille. A. tendon, tendon m d'Achille.

acid ['æsid]. 1. a. (a) Acide. A. drops, bonbons acidulés. (b) Revêche, aigre. To make (stomach, etc.) a., aciduler. S.a. TEST[1] 1 (b). 2. s. Acide m. -ly, adv. Aigrement; avec acerbité. 'acid-proof, 'acid-resisting, a. Qui résiste aux acides.

acidify [ə'sidifai]. 1. v.tr. Acidifier. Pharm: Aiguiser (un médicament). 2. v.i. S'acidifier.

acidimeter [æsi'dimitər], s. Acidimètre m; acido-mètre m, pèse-acide m, pl. pèse-acides.

acidity [ə'siditi], s. 1. Acidité f; verdeur f (des fruits, du vin). 2. Aigreur f (d'une réponse).

acidosis [æsi'dousis], s. Med: Acidose f.

acidulate [ə'sidjuleit], v.tr. Aciduler (une boisson, etc.).

acidulous [ə'sidjuləs], a. Acidulé.

ack-ack ['æk'æk], s. Mil: Défense f contre-avions (D.C.A.), défense antiaérienne.

acknowledge [ək'nɔlidʒ], v.tr. 1. (a) Reconnaître, avouer (qch.); reconnaître (qn). He acknowledged having organized the plot, il reconnut avoir organisé le complot. He was acknowledged as king, il fut reconnu pour roi. To a. oneself beaten, s'avouer, se reconnaître, vaincu. Fenc: To a. a hit, accuser un coup. 1. Reconnaître (un service). 2. Répondre à (une courtoisie, un salut, etc.). To a. (receipt of) a letter, accuser réception d'une lettre. acknowledged, a. 1. (Fait) reconnu, avéré, notoire. 2. Qui fait autorité.

acknowledg(e)ment [ək'nɔlidʒmənt], s. 1. (a) Constatation f; reconnaissance f (d'un bienfait). Com: Reçu m, quittance f (d'un paiement). A. of receipt, accusé m de réception (d'une lettre, d'un colis). To make an a. of sth., reconnaître qch. Jur: A. of indebtedness (in writing), reconnaissance de dette. (b) Aveu m (d'une faute). 2. Acknowledgements, remerciements mpl.

acme ['ækmi], s. Plus haut point; comble m (de la perfection, du bonheur); sommet m, faîte m (de la gloire, des honneurs); apogée m (de la puissance); plus haut période (de la gloire, de l'éloquence).

acne ['ækni], s. Med: Acné f. A. rosacea, couperose f.

acolyte ['ækəlait], s. Ecc: etc: Acolyte m.

aconite ['ækənait], s. Bot: Aconit m.

aconitin(e) [ə'kɔniti(:)n, -tain], s. Ch: Aconitine f.

acorn ['eikɔːn], s. Bot: Gland m (du chêne). 'acorn-cup, s. Bot: Cupule f.

acotyledon [ækɔti'liːd(ə)n], s. Bot: Acotylédone f, acotylédonée f.

acoustic(al) [ə'kuːstik(əl)], a. Acoustique.

acoustician [əkuːs'tiʃ(ə)n], s. Acousticien m.

acoustics [ə'kuːstiks], s.pl. (With sg. or pl. const.) Acoustique f. A. is the science of sound, l'acoustique est la science des sons. The a. of this hall are excellent, cette salle a une bonne acoustique.

acquaint [ə'kweint], v.tr. 1. To a. s.o. with sth., of a fact, informer, avertir, qn de qch.; faire savoir qch. à qn. To a. s.o. with the facts (of the case), mettre qn au courant (des faits); mettre qn au fait (de la situation). 2. (a) To be acquainted with s.o., sth., connaître qn; connaître, savoir, qch. (b) To become, make oneself, acquainted with s.o., faire, lier, connaissance avec qn. They became acquainted in 1966, ils se sont connus en 1966. To become, make oneself, acquainted with sth., prendre connaissance (des faits); apprendre, s'initier à, étudier (une langue, une science).

acquaintance [ə'kweintəns], s. 1. Connaissance f (with, de). (a) His a. with the classical tongues, sa connaissance des langues classiques. (b) Long a. with s.o., relations f de longue date avec qn. To make s.o.'s a., faire la connaissance de qn. He improves upon a., il gagne à être connu. 2. (Pers.) Personne f de connaissance; connaissance. To have a wide circle of acquaintances, a wide a., avoir des relations très étendues.

acquaintanceship [ə'kweintənsʃip], s. 1. Relations fpl, rapports mpl. 2. Coll. Cercle m de connaissances, relations. Wide a., relations étendues.

acquiesce [ækwi'es]. 1. v.i. Acquiescer (in a request, à une demande); donner son assentiment (in, à). 2. Se soumettre, se plier (to, à) (une doctrine, des exigences).

acquiescence [ækwi'esns], s. 1. Acquiescement m (in, à); assentiment m. 2. Soumission f (in, à).

acquiescent [ækwi'esnt], a. Disposé à acquiescer; consentant; conciliant; soumis.

acquire [ə'kwaiər], v.tr. Acquérir (qch.); se rendre propriétaire de (qch.). To a. a habit, prendre, contracter, une habitude. To a. a taste for sth., prendre goût à qch. Whisky is an acquired taste, le goût du whisky ne s'acquiert qu'avec l'habitude. To a. knowledge, apprendre; élargir ses connaissances. He has acquired a certain knowledge of the language, il possède une certaine connaissance de la langue.

acquirement [ə'kwaiəmənt], s. 1. Acquisition f (of, de). 2. (a) Talent (acquis). (b) pl. Connaissances fpl.

acquirer [ə'kwaiərər], s. Acquéreur m.

acquisition [ækwi'ziʃ(ə)n], s. Acquisition f ((i) action d'acquérir, (ii) chose acquise); acquêt m.

acquisitive [ə'kwizitiv], a. 1. Thésauriseur. 2. Apre au gain.

acquit [ə'kwit], v.tr. (acquitted) 1. To a. a debt, s'acquitter d'une dette, acquitter une dette. 2. Acquitter (un accusé). To a. s.o. of sth., absoudre qn de qch. 3. (a) To a. oneself of a duty, of a task, s'acquitter d'un devoir, d'une tâche. (b) To a. oneself well, ill, se bien, mal, acquitter.

acquittal [ə'kwitl], s. 1. Jur: Acquittement m (d'un accusé, d'un débiteur). 2. Exécution f, accomplissement m (d'un devoir).

acquittance [ə'kwitəns], s. Com: Jur: Acquit m, acquittement m (d'une dette).

acre ['eikər], s. 1. A: Champ m, pré m. (Still so used in) God's a., le champ de repos, le cimetière. 2. Meas: Acre f (0.4 hectare); (approx. =) arpent m, demi-hectare m.

acreage ['eikəridʒ], s. Superficie f (en mesures agraires).

acrid ['ækrid], a. 1. (Goût, fumée) âcre. 2. (Style) mordant; (critique) acerbe. -ly, adv. Avec âcreté; avec acerbité.

acridity [æ'kriditi], s. **acridness** ['ækridnis], s. Acreté f.

acrimonious [ækri'mounjəs], a. Acrimonieux, atrabilaire; (of woman) acariâtre. -ly, adv. Avec acrimonie; acrimonieusement.

acrimony ['ækriməni], **acrimoniousness** [ækri'mounjəsnis], s. Acrimonie f; aigreur f.

acrobat ['ækrəbæt], s. Acrobate m/f.

acrobatic [ækro'bætik]. 1. a. Acrobatique. A. feat, tour d'acrobatie. 2. s.pl. Acrobatics, acrobatie f.

acrobatism ['ækrəbætizm], s. Acrobatisme m, acrobatie f.

acropolis [ə'krɔpəlis], s. Acropole f.

across [ə'krɔs], adv. & prep. En croix; en travers (de). 1. With arms, Nau: with yards, a., les bras, les vergues, en croix. With arms folded a. his breast, les bras croisés sur la poitrine. 2. (a) To walk a. (a street), traverser (une rue). To go a. a bridge, passer (sur) un pont; franchir un pont. We shall soon be a., (i) nous serons bientôt de l'autre côté; (ii) la traversée sera bientôt faite. F: He didn't manage to put it a., il n'a pas pu faire adopter son idée. (b) To lay sth. a. (sth.), mettre qch. en travers (de qch.). To throw a bridge a. a river, jeter un pont sur une rivière. (c) F: To come, drop, a. s.o., sth., rencontrer qn, trouver qch. (par hasard). 3. (a) The distance a., (i) la distance en largeur; (ii) la longueur de la traversée. The river is a mile a., le fleuve a un mille de large. (b) He lives a. the street, il demeure de l'autre côté de la rue.

acrostic [ə'krɔstik], a. & s. Acrostiche (m).

acrylic [ə'krilik], a. Ch: Acrylique.

act[1] [ækt], s. 1. Acte m. (a) A. of justice, of kindness, acte de justice, de bonté. (b) A. of Parliament, loi f, décret m. (c) (Instrument in writing) The Acts of the Apostles, les Actes des Apôtres. I deliver this as my a. and deed, signé de ma main; fait de ma main. 2. Action f. The a. of walking, l'action de marcher. An a. of folly, une folie. To catch, take, s.o. in the (very) a., prendre qn sur le fait, en flagrant délit. Jur: Ins: A. of God, (i) (cas m de) force majeure; (ii) cas fortuit; cause naturelle. 3. Th: Acte (d'une pièce).

act². 1. *v.tr.* (*a*) To a. a play, a character, jouer, représenter, une pièce, un personnage. To a. a part, remplir un rôle. To a. Hamlet, jouer, faire, Hamlet. To a. the fool, faire l'imbécile. (*b*) To a. a part, feindre; faire, jouer, la comédie. To a. fear, simuler la crainte. He was only acting, il faisait semblant. (*c*) To a. the part of an honest man, se conduire, agir, en honnête homme. 2. *v.i.* Agir; prendre des mesures. (*a*) It is time to a., il est temps d'agir. He did not know how to a., il ne savait quel parti prendre. To a. like a friend, agir en ami, se conduire en ami. I acted for the best, j'ai fait pour le mieux. To a. for s.o., agir au nom de qn; représenter qn. To a. as secretary, faire office, exercer les fonctions, de secrétaire. His daughter acts as his secretary, sa fille lui sert de secrétaire. To a. upon a letter, donner suite à une lettre. To a. upon advice, suivre un avis. To a. up to one's principles, agir conformément à ses principes; mettre ses principes en pratique. (*b*) The pump is not acting well, la pompe ne fonctionne, ne marche, pas bien. The engine acts as a brake, le moteur fait fonction de frein. (*c*) To a. (up)on the brain, the bowels, agir, exercer une action, sur le cerveau, sur l'intestin. (*d*) *Th: Cin:* Jouer. To a. for the films, faire du cinéma. To a. in a film, tourner dans un film. **acting¹**, *a.* Remplissant les fonctions de . . .; (i) suppléant; (ii) intérimaire. **A. manager**, (i) directeur gérant; (ii) directeur intérimaire; gérant provisoire. *Adm:* **A. allowance**, indemnité *f* de fonction. **Lieutenant a. captain**, lieutenant faisant fonction de capitaine. **acting²**, *s.* 1. Action *f.* 2. (*a*) *Th:* Jeu *m* (d'un acteur); exécution *f*, production *f* (d'une pièce de théâtre). (*b*) To go in for a., faire du théâtre. (*c*) It is mere a., c'est de la comédie.

actinic [æk'tinik], *a.* *Ph:* Actinique. **A. spectrum**, spectre *m* chimique.

actinism ['æktinizm], *s.* *Ph:* Actinisme *m.*

actinium [æk'tiniəm], *s.* *Ch:* Actinium *m.* **The a. series**, les actinides *mpl.*

actinometer [ækti'nɔmitər], *s.* *Ph: Phot:* Actinomètre *m*; photomètre *m* de tirage, de pose.

action ['ækʃ(ə)n], *s.* 1. Action *f* (d'une personne, d'un remède, etc.). To take a., agir; prendre des mesures. Man of a., homme de main, d'action. To suit the a. to the word, joindre le geste à la parole. To put, set, sth. in a.; to bring, call, sth. into a., mettre qch. en action, en œuvre, en jeu, en train, en mouvement; faire agir, faire marcher, faire jouer, faire fonctionner, qch. To come into a., entrer en action, en jeu. To bring the law into a., faire intervenir la loi. Out of a., hors de service. To put (sth.) out of a., (i) débrayer, dégager (une machine, etc.); (ii) *I.C.E:* arrêter, couper (l'allumage, etc.); (iii) détraquer, mettre en panne (une machine, etc.). 2. (*Deed*) Action, acte *m*, fait *m.* Splendid a., action d'éclat; haut fait. 3. *Th:* Action (d'une pièce). The scene of a. is . . ., la scène se passe à . . . 4. (*a*) Action, gestes *mpl* (d'un joueur); train *m*, allure *f*, action (d'un cheval). (*b*) Mécanisme *m* (d'une montre, etc.); jeu *m* (d'une pompe, d'une serrure); mécanique *f* (d'un piano, d'un orgue). 5. *Jur:* **A. at law**, action en justice; procès *m* (civil ou criminel). **To bring an a. against s.o.**, intenter une action, un procès, à, contre, qn; exercer des poursuites contre qn. 6. *Mil: Navy:* Action, combat *m*, engagement *m.* **Naval a.**, combat naval. To go into a., engager le combat; donner. **Killed in a.**, tué au feu, à l'ennemi. **Out of a.**, hors de combat.

actionable ['ækʃənəbl], *a.* *Jur:* Actionnable; poursuivable; (mot, action) qui expose à des poursuites judiciaires.

actionless ['ækʃ(ə)nlis], *a.* *Ch: etc:* Inerte.

activate ['æktiveit], *v.tr.* Activer; accélérer, presser. *Atom.Ph:* Rendre (un corps) radio-actif.

activator ['æktiveitər], *s.* *Ch:* Activeur *m.*

active ['æktiv], *a.* 1. Actif; agile, alerte. **To be still a.**, être encore allant, alerte, ingambe. **A. volcano**, volcan en activité. **There is an a. demand for wool**, les laines sont très recherchées. **A. brain**, cerveau éveillé. **A. imagination**, imagination vive. 2. *Gram:* **Verb in the a. voice**, verbe à l'actif, à la voix active. 3. **To take an a. part in sth.**, prendre une part active, effective, à qch. *Jur: Adm: etc:* **A. consideration**,

examen approfondi. 4. **A. list**, *Mil: Navy:* cadre d'activité, *Mil:* rôles de l'armée active. (*Of official*) **To be in a. employment**, *Mil:* to be on the a. list, être en activité (de service). *Mil:* **A. service**, (i) service actif; (ii) (= *field service*) service en campagne. **On a. service**, en campagne. 5. *Med:* **A. immunity**, immunité par (les) anticorps. **A. poison**, poison rapide. *El:* **A. cell**, élément (d'accu) chargé. *Atom. Ph:* = RADIOACTIVE. **-ly**, *adv.* Activement. **'active-'minded**, *a.* A l'esprit actif.

activism ['æktivizm], *s.* *Pol:* Activisme *m.*

activist ['æktivist], *s.* *Pol:* Activiste *mf.*

activistic [ækti'vistik], *a.* *Pol:* Activiste.

activity [æk'tiviti], *s.* 1. Activité *f.* **Man of a.**, homme actif. **The a. of a large town**, le mouvement d'une grande ville. 2. **That does not come within my activities**, cela ne rentre pas dans mes fonctions; c'est en dehors de ma sphère d'action, *Pol:* **Subversive activities**, menées subversives. 3. *pl.* **Activities**, activités, occupations.

actor ['æktər], *s.* (*a*) Acteur *m*; comédien *m.* **Tragic a.**, tragédien *m.* **Film a.**, acteur de cinéma. (*b*) **The chief a. in this event**, le principal acteur dans cet événement.

actress ['æktris], *s.f.* Actrice; comédienne. **Tragic a.**, tragédienne *f.* **Film a.**, actrice de cinéma. **She is a film a.**, elle fait du cinéma.

actual ['æktju(ə)l], *a.* 1. Réel, véritable. **It's an a. fact**, c'est un fait positif. **To take an a. case**, pour prendre un cas concret. **To give the a. figures**, donner les chiffres mêmes. **A. possession**, possession de fait. **In a. fact . . .**, en fait. . . . 2. (*Present*) Actuel, présent. **The a. position of affairs**, l'état de choses actuel. **-ally**, *adv.* 1. (*a*) Réellement, véritablement, effectivement, positivement; de, en, fait. (*b*) **I a. found the door open**, à mon grand étonnement je trouvai la porte ouverte. **He a. swore**, il alla (même) jusqu'à lâcher un juron. 2. Actuellement, à présent; à l'heure actuelle.

actuality [æktju'æliti], *s.* (*a*) Réalité *f.* (*b*) Le temps présent.

actuary ['æktjuəri], *s.* *Ins:* Actuaire *m.* **Actuaries' tables**, tables *f* de mortalité.

actuate ['æktjueit], *v.tr.* 1. Mettre en action, mettre en mouvement, mener, actionner (une machine). 2. Animer, pousser, faire agir (qn). **Actuated by jealousy**, poussé, mû, inspiré, par la jalousie. **actuating**, *a.* 1. (Mécanisme) de commande, de manœuvre. 2. (Motif) qui fait agir.

acuity [ə'kju:iti] *s.* Acuité *f.*

acumen ['ækju:men], *s.* Pénétration *f*, finesse *f* (d'esprit); clairvoyance *f*, perspicacité *f.*

acupunctor ['ækjupʌnktər], *s.* *Surg:* Acuponcteur *m.*

acupuncture ['ækjupʌnkt(ə)r], *s.* *Surg:* Acuponcture *f.*

acute [ə'kju:t], *a.* 1. (*a*) (Angle) aigu; (pointe) aiguë. (*b*) *Gram:* **A. accent**, accent aigu. 2. (*a*) (Son) aigu; (douleur) aiguë, intense; vif. **A. remorse**, remords cruels, poignants. (*b*) **A. stage of disease**, période aiguë d'une maladie. 3. (*a*) **A. ear**, oreille fine, ouïe fine. **A. sight**, vue perçante. (*b*) (Esprit) fin, pénétrant. **-ly**, *adv.* 1. Vivement; intensément. 2. Avec finesse; finement. **acute-angled**, *a.* (Triangle *m*) acutangle.

acuteness [ə'kju:tnis], *s.* 1. Aiguïté *f* (d'un angle). 2. (*a*) Acuité *f* (d'une douleur, d'un son); intensité *f* (d'une douleur, d'un remords). (*b*) Caractère aigu (d'une maladie). 3. (*a*) Finesse *f* (d'ouïe), acuité (de la vision); vivacité *f* (d'un sentiment). (*b*) Pénétration *f*, perspicacité *f* (de l'esprit).

ad [æd], *s.* *F:* (*In newspaper*) Annonce *f.* **To put an ad in the paper**, mettre une annonce dans le journal.

ad-man, *s.* *F:* Annoncier *m*, agent *m* de publicité.

adage ['ædidʒ], *s.* Adage *m*; maxime *f.*

adagio [ə'dɑ:dʒiou], *adv. & s.* Adagio (*m*).

Adam ['ædəm]. *Pr.n.m.* Adam. **Adam's apple**, pomme *f* d'Adam. *F:* **Adam's ale**, château *m* la Pompe. *F:* **Not to know s.o. from A.**, ne connaître qn ni d'Ève ni d'Adam. *S.a.* OLD 3.

adamant ['ædəmənt], *a.* Dur; inflexible, intransigeant.

adamantine [ædə'mæntain], *a.* *Miner:* **A. spar**, spath adamantin. **A. courage**, courage indomptable.

adapt [ə'dæpt], *v.tr.* Adapter, ajuster, approprier (sth. to sth., qch. à qch.). **To a. oneself to circumstances**, s'adapter, s'ajuster, s'accommoder, aux circonstances.

To a. one's language to the circumstances, approprier son langage aux circonstances. adapted, a. 1. A. to sth., approprié à, fait pour, qch. Well a. for a purpose, bien adapté à un but; qui se prête à un but. 2. Play a. from the French, pièce adaptée du français.

adaptability [ə,dæptə'biliti], s. Faculté f d'adaptation; souplesse f.

adaptable [ə'dæptəbl], a. 1. (a) Adaptable, ajustable, qui peut s'adapter (to, à). (b) Susceptible d'être utilisé (for, pour; to an end, dans un but). 2. A. person, personne qui s'accommode à toutes les circonstances. A. mind, esprit souple.

adaptation [,ædæp'teiʃ(ə)n], s. 1. Adaptation f, appropriation f (of sth. to sth., de qch. à qch.). 2. Adaptation (littéraire).

adapter, adaptor [ə'dæptər], s. 1. Auteur m d'une adaptation; remanieur m, adaptateur m. 2. Intermédiaire m de raccord. El: Raccord m (de lampe). Phot: Lens a., bague f porte-objectif. Gramophones: Centreur m.

add [æd], v.tr. 1. (a) Ajouter, joindre (to, à). To a. s.o. to a committee, adjoindre qn à un comité. To a. the interest to the capital, ajouter l'intérêt au capital. This news adds to our joy, cette nouvelle augmente, accroît, notre joie. To a. to one's house, agrandir sa maison. Added to which . . ., en outre de quoi. . . . To a. to my work . . ., par surcroît de besogne. . . . To a. to my distress . . ., pour mettre le comble à mon chagrin. To a. sth. in, ajouter, inclure, qch.; faire entrer qch. en ligne de compte. (b) (Say besides) Ajouter. He added that . . ., il ajouta que. . . . 2. Ar: To a. (up, together) ten numbers, additionner dix nombres. To a. up a column of figures, totaliser une colonne de chiffres. (Passive use) The assets a. up to two millions, l'actif se totalise par deux millions. 'adding-machine, s. Machine f à calculer; calculatrice f.

addendum, pl. -a [ə'dendəm, -ə], s. (a) Addenda m inv. (b) Addition f (à un livre, etc.); supplément m.

adder ['ædər], s. Vipère f, péliade f. Young a., vipereau m. adder's-tongue, s. Bot: Ophioglosse m vulgaire, langue f de serpent.

addict[1] ['ædikt], s. Personne adonnée à (l'opium, etc.); -mane m. Morphia a., morphinomane mf. Med: Intoxiqué, -ée; F: Sp: Danc: etc: fanatique mf.

addict[2] [ə'dikt], v.tr. To a. oneself to study, drink, s'adonner, se livrer, à l'étude, à la boisson.

addiction [ə'dikʃ(ə)n], s. (a) A. to study, science, good, evil, attachement m à l'étude, inclination f pour les sciences, penchant m au bien, au mal. (b) Med: Manie f pathologique; intoxication f. A. to morphia, morphinomanie f.

addition [ə'diʃ(ə)n], s. 1. (a) Addition f. A welcome a. to my salary, un heureux surcroît d'appointements. Additions to the staff, adjonction f de personnel. In a., en outre, en sus, de plus, par surcroît. In a. to sth., en plus, en sus, de qch. (b) Publ: (To M.S., proof, contract) Ajout m, ajouté m. 2. Mth: Addition. I'm doing an a., j'additionne.

additional [ə'diʃn(ə)l], a. Additionnel, supplémentaire. A. postage, surtaxe f. Com: A. payment, supplément m. A. reason, nouvelle raison, raison de plus. -ally, adv. En outre (to, de); en sus.

additive ['æditiv]. 1. a. Additif, -ive. 2. s. I.C.E: Anti-carbon a., carburant additionnel décalaminant.

addle[1] ['ædl], a. 1. (Œuf) pourri, gâté, couvi. 2. F: (Cerveau) (i) vide, creux, (ii) trouble, brouillé. A.-headed, s. a.-brain, -pate, (homme) écervelé.

addle[2]. 1. v.tr. (a) Pourrir, gâter (un œuf). (b) F: Troubler, brouiller (le cerveau, la tête). 2. v.i. (Of egg) Se pourrir, se gâter. 'addled, a. = ADDLE[1].

address[1] [ə'dres], s. 1. Adresse f, habileté f. 2. Adresse (d'une personne, d'une lettre). What is your a.? où demeurez-vous? Of no a., sans domicile connu. Home a., adresse privée, personnelle. 3. (a) Abord m. (b) O: To pay one's addresses to a lady, faire la cour à une femme. 4. Discours m, allocution f. 5. Form of a., titre m (à donner en s'adressant à qn). ad'dressbook, s. Carnet m d'adresses, (carnet-)répertoire m.

address[2], v.tr. 1. (a) To a. a letter to s.o., adresser une lettre à qn. (b) To a. a letter, mettre, écrire, l'adresse sur une lettre. 2. (a) To a. one's prayers to God, adresser ses prières à Dieu. (b) To a. s.o., (i) aborder,

accoster, qn; (ii) adresser la parole à qn. To a. oneself to s.o., s'adresser à qn. (c) To a. the crowd, haranguer la foule. Pol: When he addresses the House, quand il parle à la Chambre, (in Fr.) quand il monte à la tribune. 3. Golf: Viser (la balle). 4. To a. oneself to a task, se mettre à une tâche.

addressee [ædre'si:], s. Destinataire mf.

addressograph [ə'dresogræf, -gra:f], s. R.t.m: Machine f à imprimer les adresses.

adduce [ə'dju:s], v.tr. Alléguer, apporter (des raisons, des preuves); produire (un témoin); invoquer, citer (une autorité).

Adelaide ['ædəleid]. Pr.n. Geog: etc: Adélaïde.

adenoids['ædinoidz], s.pl. Med: Végétations f adénoïdes.

adenoma [,ædi'noumə], s. Med: Adénome m.

adept. 1. a. [æ'dept]. To be a. in sth., at doing sth., être expert, habile, à qch., à faire qch. 2. s. ['ædept]. Adepte mf; initié(e); expert m (in, en).

adequacy ['ædikwəsi], s. Suffisance f (d'une récompense, etc.); justesse f; adéquation f.

adequate ['ædikwit], a. 1. (a) Suffisant (to, à). A. reward, juste récompense; récompense adéquate, suffisante. A. help, aide efficace. (b) Proportionné (to, à). 2. I can find no one a. to the task, je ne trouve personne qui soit à la hauteur de la tâche. -ly, adv. Suffisamment, congrûment, convenablement, en juste proportion.

adequateness ['ædikwitnis], s. = ADEQUACY.

adhere [əd'hiər], v.i. 1. (Of thg) Adhérer, se coller. (Of clay, cigarette) To a. to the tongue, to the lips, happer à la langue, aux lèvres. 2. (Of pers.) (a) To a. to a proposal, to a party, adhérer, donner, son adhésion, à une proposition, à un parti. (b) To a. to one's decision, persister dans sa décision. I a. to my statement, je maintiens mon dire.

adherence [əd'hiərəns], s. 1. (Of thg) Adhérence f, (to, à). 2. (Of pers.) (a) Attachement m (à un parti). (b) Accession f, adhésion (à un parti).

adherent [əd'hiərənt]. 1. a. Adhérent (to, à); collé, attaché (to, à). 2. s. Adhérent m; partisan m.

adhesion [əd'hi:ʒ(ə)n], s. 1. Adhésion f (to, à); accession f (à un parti); approbation f (d'un projet). 2. Mec: Med: Surg: Adhérence f.

adhesive [əd'hi:siv], a. 1. Adhésif, collant; agglutinant. 2. Adhérent. Mec: A. capacity, pouvoir adhérent. S.a. PLASTER[1] 1. 3. s. Adhésif m.

adhesiveness [əd'hi:sivnis], s. Force f d'adhésion; tendance f à se coller.

ad hoc ['æd'hɔk]. Lt.adv.phr: Ad hoc. Ad h. committee, comité spécial, ad hoc.

adiabatic [,ædiə'bætik], a. Ph: A. chart, diagramme adiabatique. A. lapse rate, vitesse f de refroidissement m, d'échauffement m, adiabatique.

adieu [ə'dju:]. int. & s. Adieu (m).

ad infinitum [æd,infi'naitəm]. Lt.adv.phr: A l'infini; F: à n'en plus finir.

ad interim [æd'intərim]. Lt.adv.phr: Jur: Par intérim; provisoire.

adipose ['ædipous]. 1. a. Adipeux, -euse. 2. s. Graisse animale.

adiposity [,ædi'pɔsiti], s. Adiposité f.

adjacency [ə'dʒeisə)nsi], s. Contiguïté f (to a place, à un lieu); proximité f, adjacence f.

adjacent [ə'dʒeis(ə)nt], a. (Angle, terrain) adjacent; contigu, -guë, attenant(to, à); (pays) limitrophe (to, de).

adjectival ['ædʒik'taiv(ə)l], a. Gram: Adjectif, -ive. -ally, adv. Adjectivement.

adjective ['ædʒiktiv], s. Adjectif m.

adjoin [ə'dʒɔin]. 1. v.tr. Avoisiner (un lieu); être contigu à (qch.); toucher à, attenir à (qch.). 2. v.i. The two houses a., les deux maisons sont contiguës, se touchent. adjoining, a. (a) Contigu, -uë; avoisinant. Garden a. mine, jardin attenant au mien. (b) The a. room, la pièce voisine.

adjourn [ə'dʒə:n]. 1. v.tr. To a. sth. to, till, the next day, for a week, ajourner, différer, remettre, renvoyer, qch. au lendemain, à huitaine. 2. v.i. (a) (Of meeting, etc.) (i) S'ajourner (until, à); (ii) lever la séance; clore les débats. (b) O: (Of persons) To a. to the drawing-room, passer au salon.

adjournment [ə'dʒə:nmənt], s. (a) Ajournement m, suspension f (d'une séance, etc.). (b) Renvoi m, remise f (d'une affaire, etc.).

adjudge [ə'dʒʌdʒ], v.tr. **1.** Prononcer sur, juger, décider judiciairement (une querelle, etć.). **2.** Pred. To a. s.o. (to be) guilty, déclarer qn coupable. **3.** To a. a prize to s.o., adjuger, décerner, une récompense à qn.

adjudicate [ə'dʒu:dikeit], v.tr. & i. Juger, décider (une affaire); prononcer sur (une affaire); adjuger, discerner(un prix).To a.a claim, juger une réclamation.

adjudication [ə,dʒu:di'keiʃ(ə)n], s. Jugement m, décision f, arrêt m. A. of bankruptcy, jugement déclaratif de faillite.

adjudicator [ə'dʒu:dikeitər], s. (a) Arbitre m; juge m. (b) (In competitions, etc.) Membre m du jury.

adjunct ['ædʒʌŋkt], s. **1.** (a) (Pers.) Adjoint (to, de); auxiliaire mf. (b) (Thg) Accessoire m (of, de). **2.** Gram: Complément m (du verbe, etc.).

adjuration [,ædʒuə'reiʃ(ə)n], s. Adjuration f.

adjure [ə'dʒuər], v.tr. To a. s.o. to do sth., adjurer, conjurer, supplier, qn de faire qch.

adjust [ə'dʒʌst], v.tr. **1.** Arranger (une affaire, une querelle); concilier, régler (un différend). **2.** (a) Ajuster (qch. à qch.). To a. oneself to new conditions, s'adapter aux conditions nouvelles. (b) Régler, ajuster (une balance, une montre, etc.); monter (un appareil); étalonner (un instrument); mettre (un microscope, un moteur) au point; égaliser (la pression, etc.). Nau: To a. the compasses, compenser, corriger, les compas. Chess: To a. a piece, adouber une pièce. (c) Ajuster, arranger (son chapeau, ses vêtements). **adjusting,** s. Mise f au point; réglage m. A. screw, vis de réglage.

adjustable [ə'dʒʌstəbl], a. (a) (Différend) susceptible d'accommodement. (b) Mec.E: etc: Ajustable, réglable.

adjuster [ə'dʒʌstər], s. **1.** (Pers.) Ajusteur m; régleur m; metteur m au point. M.Ins: Average a., dispacheur m. **2.** Appareil m de réglage.

adjustment [ə'dʒʌstmənt], s. **1.** Ajustement m (d'un differend, etc.); adaptation f; arrangement m (d'une affaire). Social a., adaptation au milieu social. M.Ins: Average a., dispache f. **2.** Ajustement (d'une balance); rectification f (d'un outil, d'un instrument); réglage m (d'un mécanisme). Nau: Compensation f, correction f (des compas). Final a., mise f au point.

adjutancy ['ædʒutənsi], s. Mil: Fonctions fpl de capitaine adjudant-major, de capitaine adjoint.

adjutant ['ædʒutənt], s. Mil: (Garrison duty) O: capitaine m adjudant-major; F: le major; (Battalion, regimental) capitaine adjoint. A. general, approx. = Chef m du 1er Bureau de l'État-Major de l'Armée, (E.M.A.). 'adjutant(-bird, -crane, -stork), s. Orn: Adjudant m, marabout m (des Indes).

ad libitum, ad lib. [æd'libitəm, æd'lib], Lt.adv.phr. A volonté; (of food) à discrétion.

administer [əd'ministər], v. (a) Administrer, régir (un pays); gérer (des affaires, des biens); appliquer (les lois). To a. justice, dispenser, rendre, la justice. (b) To a. the last sacraments to s.o., administrer (les derniers sacrements) à qn. To a. an oath, the oath, to s.o., faire prêter serment à qn; assermenter qn.

administrate [əd'ministreit], v.tr. U.S: = ADMINISTER.

administration [əd,minis'treiʃ(ə)n], s. **1.** (a) Administration f, gestion f (d'une fortune, etc.); régie f (d'une succession, etc.). (b) Jur: Curatelle f (des biens d'un mineur). (c) Administration (de la justice, des sacrements, d'un remède). **2.** Coll. L'administration, le gouvernement, les pouvoirs publics.

administrative [əd'ministrətiv], a. Administratif, -ive. A. details, détails d'ordre administratif.

administrator [əd'ministreitər], s. **1.** Administrateur m; gestionnaire m. **2.** Jur: Curateur m.

administratorship [əd'ministreitəʃip], s. Gestion f, gérance f. Jur: Curatelle f.

administratrix, -trices [əd'ministrətriks, -trisi:z], s.f. **1.** Administratrice; gestionnaire f. **2.** Jur: Curatrice.

admirable ['ædm(ə)rəbl], a. Admirable. **-ably,** adv. Admirablement. He succeeded a.,il a réussi à merveille.

admiral ['ædm(ə)rəl], s. **1.** (a) Amiral m, pl. -aux. A. of the Fleet = amiral commandant en chef. A. Nelson, l'amiral Nelson. (b) Commandant m en chef (d'une flotte marchande). **2.** Ent: Red A., vulcain m. White A., petit sylvain.

admiralship ['ædm(ə)rəlʃip], s. Dignité f, rang m, d'amiral; amiralat m.

admiralty [ædm(ə)rəlti], s. The A., l'Amirauté f; (in France) le Ministère de la Marine, F: la Marine. First Lord of the A. = Ministre de la Marine. Court of A., Tribunal m maritime. Geog: The A. Islands, les îles de l'Amirauté. A. Island (British Columbia), Ile de l'Amirauté.

admiration [,ædmə'reiʃ(ə)n], s. (a) Admiration f (of, for, pour). To be struck with a., être saisi d'admiration. (b) To be the a. of everyone, faire l'admiration de tous.

admire [əd'maiər], v.tr. **1.** Admirer. To a. oneself in a glass, se mirer dans une glace. **2.** Exprimer son admiration de (qch.); s'extasier (devant qch.). **3.** U.S: P: I'd a. to see . . ., je voudrais bien voir . . . **admiring,** a. (Regard, ton, etc.) admiratif.

admirer [əd'maiərər], s. (a) Admirateur, -trice. (b) Adorateur, -trice; soupirant m (d'une femme).

admissibility [əd,misi'biliti], s. Admissibilité f.

admissible [əd'misibl], a. (Idée, projet) admissible. Jur: (Pourvoi) recevable.

admission [əd'miʃ(ə)n], s. **1.** Admission f, accès m (à une école, à un emploi). A. free, entrée libre. **2.** (a) Admission, acceptation f (d'un argument, d'une preuve). (b) Jur: Reconnaissance f (d'un fait allégué); confession f (d'un crime, etc.); aveu m. To make full admission (of guilt), faire des aveux complets. **3.** Mch: I.C.E: Admission, aspiration f (de la vapeur, des gaz, etc.); injection f (de l'eau). A. pipe, tuyau, conduite, d'amenée.

admit [əd'mit], v. (admitted) **1.** v.tr. (a) Admettre (qn à qch., dans un endroit); laisser entrer (qn); livrer passage à (qn). 'A. bearer,' "laissez passer." To a. s.o. to one's friendship, admettre qn dans son intimité. (b) The windows do not a. enough air, les fenêtres ne laissent pas entrer assez d'air. (c) Harbour that admits large ships, port qui reçoit de grands navires. (d) Admettre (une vérité, des excuses); reconnaître (un principe, sa faute); concéder (qu'on a tort). It must be admitted that . . ., il faut reconnaître que + ind. To a. one's guilt, s'avouer coupable; faire des aveux; avouer. I was wrong, I a., j'ai eu tort, j'en conviens. Let it be admitted! avouons-le! (e) To a. a claim, faire droit à, accueillir, une réclamation. **2.** v.ind.tr. It admits of no doubt, cela ne permet, ne souffre, aucun doute. **admitted,** a. **1.** A. custom, usage admis. **2.** A. truth, vérité reconnue, avouée. An a. thief, un voleur avéré, reconnu pour tel. **-ly,** adv. No a., entrée interdite. The country is a. ill-governed, le pays, de l'aveu général, est mal gouverné. He's a bad lad a., but how charming! C'est un mauvais garçon, il est vrai, mais si charmant!

admittance [əd'mit(ə)ns], s. **1.** Permission f d'entrer; entrée f (to, dans); accès m (à un endroit, auprès de qn). To give s.o. a., laisser entrer qn; admettre qn. He was denied, refused, a., on ne voulut pas le laisser entrer. No a., entrée interdite. **2.** El: Admittance f.

admix [əd'miks]. **1.** v.tr. Mélanger qch. avec qch. **2.** v.i. (Of substances) Se mélanger.

admixture [əd'mikstʃər], s. **1.** Mélange m. **2.** Pharm: (Ad)mixtion f. Water with an a. of alcohol, eau additionnée d'alcool.

admonish [əd'məniʃ], v.tr. **1.** (a) Admonester, reprendre (qn). (b) To a. s.o. to do sth., exhorter qn à faire qch. **2.** A: To a. s.o. of a danger, avertir, prévenir, qn d'un danger.

admonishment [əd'məniʃmənt], **admonition** [,ædmə'niʃ(ə)n], s. Remontrance f, admonestation f. Ecc: Admonition f, exhortation f.

admonitory [əd'mənit(ə)ri], a. Admonitif, -ive (lettre, etc.) de remontrances.

ad nauseam [æd'nɔ:ziəm], Lt.adv.phr: A satiété; jusqu'à la nausée.

ado [ə'du:], s. **1.** Agitation f, activité f; bruit m, affairement m. Without (any) more a., without further a., sans plus de façons, de cérémonie, d'embarras, F: d'histoires. To make much a. about nothing, faire beaucoup de bruit pour rien. **2.** Difficulté f, peine f.

adobe [ə'doubi, ə'doub], s. Adobe m (brique ou maison).

adolescence [,ædo'les(ə)ns], s. Adolescence f.

adolescent [ˌædoˈles(ə)nt], *a. & s.* Adolescent.

adonis [əˈdounis], *s. Bot: Ent:* Adonis *m.*

adopt [əˈdɔpt], *v.tr.* 1. Adopter (un enfant). *Pred.* To a. s.o. as son, adopter qn pour fils. 2. Adopter (une ligne de conduite); choisir, embrasser (une carrière). The course to a., la marche à suivre. **adopted,** *a.* (Enfant, mot) adopté. **A. son,** fils adoptif. **My a. country,** mon pays d'adoption.

adoptable [əˈdɔptabl], *a.* Adoptable.

adoptee [ədɔptˈiː], *s. Jur:* Adopté, -ée.

adopter [əˈdɔptər], *s. Jur:* Adoptant, -ante (d'un enfant).

adoption [əˈdɔpʃ(ə)n], *s.* Adoption *f* (d'un enfant, d'une coutume, d'un pays); choix *m* (d'une carrière).

adoptive [əˈdɔptiv], *a.* (Enfant, père) adoptif; (parent) adoptant; (enfant) adopté.

adorable [əˈdɔːrabl], *a.* Adorable. **-ably,** *adv.* Adorablement; à ravir.

adoration [ˌædoˈreif(ə)n], *s.* Adoration *f.* **His a. for my cousin,** l'amour, le culte, qu'il portait à ma cousine.

adore [əˈdɔːr], *v.tr.* Adorer (qn, qch.); aimer (qn) à l'adoration.

adorer [əˈdɔːrər], *s.* Adorateur, -trice. **Her adorers,** ses adorateurs; ses soupirants.

adorn [əˈdɔːn], *v.tr.* Orner, parer, embellir (**with,** de). **To a. oneself,** se parer (**with,** de); se faire beau, belle.

adornment [əˈdɔːnmənt], *s.* 1. Ornementation *f.* 2. Ornement *m,* parure *f.* **In all her adornments,** dans tous ses atours.

adrenal [əˈdriːn(ə)l]. 1. *a.* Surrénal. 2. *s.pl.* **Adrenals,** capsules surrénales.

adrenalin(e) [əˈdrenəlin], *s. Med:* Adrénaline *f.*

Adriatic [ˌeidriˈætik], *a. & s. Geog:* (La mer) Adriatique.

adrift [əˈdrift], *adv. Nau:* A la dérive. (*Of ship*) **To run, go, a.,** aller à la dérive; dériver. **To break a.,** partir en dérive. **To be a.,** être en dérive, à l'abandon. **You are all a.,** vous divaguez! **To turn s.o. a.,** abandonner qn; mettre qn sur le pavé. **He was turned a. in the world,** il fut abandonné à ses propres ressources. **To cut a boat a.,** couper l'amarre. **To cut (oneself) a. from s.o.,** rompre avec qn.

adroit [əˈdrɔit], *a.* Adroit; habile. **-ly,** *adv.* Adroitement.

adroitness [əˈdrɔitnis], *s.* Adresse *f,* dextérité *f.*

adulate [ˈædjuleit], *v.tr.* Aduler, flatter, flagorner.

adulation [ˌædjuˈleiʃ(ə)n], *s.* Adulation *f,* flatterie *f.*

adulator [ˈædjuleitər], *s.* Adulateur, -trice.

adulatory [ˈædjuleitəri], *a.* Adulateur, -trice.

adult [əˈdʌlt], *a. & s.* Adulte (*mf*).

adulterant [əˈdʌltərənt], *s.* Adultérant *m.*

adulterate [əˈdʌltəreit], *v.tr.* Adultérer (une substance); altérer, falsifier (les monnaies); frelater (du vin, du lait).

adulteration [əˌdʌltəˈreiʃ(ə)n], *s.* Adultération *f;* altération *f,* falsification *f* (des monnaies); frelatage *m* (des boissons).

adulterator [əˈdʌltəreitər], *s.* Falsificateur, -trice; sophistiqueur *m;* adultérateur *m;* frelateur *m* (d'aliments).

adulterer, f. -eress [əˈdʌltərər, -əris], *s.* Adultère *mf* (violateur, -trice, de la foi conjugale).

adulterous [əˈdʌlt(ə)rəs], *a.* Adultère. **-ly,** *adv.* 1. Par adultère. 2. (Vivre) en état d'adultère.

adultery [əˈdʌltəri], *s.* Adultère *m.*

adumbrate [ˈædʌmbreit], *v.tr.* 1. Ébaucher, esquisser (un plan). 2. Faire pressentir, laisser pressentir (de nouvelles démarches).

adumbration [ˌædʌmˈbreiʃ(ə)n], *s.* 1. Ébauche *f,* esquisse *f.* 2. (*a*) Signes précurseurs. (*b*) Pressentiment *m.*

ad valorem [ˈædvəˈlɔːrem]. *Lt.phr. Com: Ind:* **Ad v. duty,** droit ad valorem; droit proportionnel.

advance¹ [ədˈvɑːns], *s.* 1. (*a*) Marche *f* en avant; mouvement *m* en avant. **To make an a.,** avancer. **A. towards sth.,** acheminement *m* à, vers, qch. *Adm:* **A. in seniority,** majoration *f* d'ancienneté. *Mil:* **A. guard,** avant-garde *f.* **A. party,** pointe *f* d'avant-garde. (*b*) **In a.,** (i) en avant; (ii) en avance; (iii) avant la lettre. **To arrive in a.,** arriver en avance. **To arrive in a. of the others,** arriver avant les autres. **To pay in a.,** payer d'avance, par avance. *Th: etc:* **To book in a.,** louer à l'avance. **A. payment,** paiement par anticipation. (*c*) *I.C.E:* **A. of the ignition,** avance *f*

à l'allumage. 2. Avancement *m,* progrès *m,* développement *m* (des sciences, etc.). **The a. of thought,** le cheminement, le progrès, de la pensée. 3. **To make an a., advances, to s.o.,** faire une avance, des avances, à, auprès de, qn; faire les premières démarches. **To respond to s.o.'s advances,** répondre aux invites de qn. *F:* (*Of woman*) **To make advances to a man,** provoquer, *F:* aguicher, un homme. 4. *Com: Fin:* (*a*) Avance (de fonds); à valoir, *m.inv.* **Advances on securities,** prêts *m* sur titres. (*b*) Augmentation *f* (de prix); renchérissement *m;* hausse *f.* (*At an auction sale*) **Any a.?** Qui dit mieux?

advance². I. *v.tr.* 1. (*a*) Avancer (le pied, *Chess:* un pion). (*b*) Avancer (l'heure d'un paiement). *I.C.E:* **To a. the ignition,** mettre de l'avance à l'allumage. (*c*) Avancer, présenter, mettre en avant (une opinion). 2. (*a*) Faire progresser, faire avancer (les sciences, etc.); faire avancer (des troupes); reculer (une frontière). (*b*) Élever, faire avancer (qn à un grade supérieur). (*c*) Accélérer (la croissance, le développement, etc.). 3. Augmenter, hausser (le prix de qch.). 4. **To a. s.o. money,** avancer de l'argent à qn. II. **advance,** *v.i.* 1. S'avancer (**towards,** vers); (*of troops*) se porter en avant. **He advanced on me (threateningly),** il vint sur moi. 2. (*a*) Avancer en âge, dans ses études. **The work is advancing,** le travail avance, fait des progrès. *S.a.* YEAR. (*b*) (*Of officers, etc.*) Recevoir de l'avancement; monter (en grade). 3. Augmenter de prix; hausser. **advanced,** *a.* 1. (*a*) (Poste) avancé; (études, opinions) avancées; (peuple) évolué. **To be very a., to hold very a. ideas,** avoir des idées très avancées. **An a. book,** un livre d'avant-garde. (*b*) **A. mathematics,** mathématiques supérieures. 2. **The night is a.,** il est tard dans la nuit. **The season is a.,** c'est la fin de saison. 3. **The a. cost of living,** l'augmentation du coût de la vie.

advancement [ədˈvɑːnsmənt], *s.* Avancement *m* (d'une personne, des sciences); progrès *m.*

advantage¹ [ədˈvɑːntidʒ], *s.* 1. Avantage *m.* **To have the a. of, over, s.o.;** **to gain the a. over s.o.,** avoir, remporter, l'avantage sur qn; l'emporter sur qn; avoir le dessus. **To take s.o. at a.,** prendre qn au dépourvu. **To have the a. of, in, numbers,** avoir l'avantage du nombre. **I gained little a. from it,** j'en ai eu, j'en ai remporté, peu de profit. **You might with a. apply to . . .,** vous pourriez utilement vous adresser à. . . . **To take a. of sth.,** profiter de qch.; tirer avantage, profit, de qch. **To take a. of s.o.,** abuser de la crédulité, de la bonne volonté, de qn; exploiter qn. **To turn sth. to a.,** tirer parti de qch.; mettre qch. à profit; faire tourner qch. à son avantage. (*Of event*) **To turn out to s.o.'s a.,** tourner à l'avantage de qn; profiter à qn. **To show off sth. to a.,** faire valoir qch. **To show to (great) a.,** faire (très) bonne figure. **To execute an order to the best a.,** exécuter un ordre au mieux. *Ten:* **A. in, a. server,** avantage dedans, au servant. **A. out, a. striker,** avantage dehors, au relanceur. *Mec:* Multiplication *f* (d'un levier).

advantage², *v.tr.* Avantager, favoriser (qn, qch.).

advantageous [ˌædvənˈteidʒəs], *a.* Avantageux (**to,** pour); profitable, utile. **-ly,** *adv.* Avantageusement; utilement.

advantageousness [ˌædvənˈteidʒəsnis], *s.* Avantage *m;* utilité *f.*

advent [ˈædvənt], *s.* 1. *Ecc:* (*a*) Avent *m.* **A. Sunday,** le premier dimanche de l'Avent. (*b*) **The second A.,** le second Avènement. 2. Arrivée *f;* venue *f.* **The a. of the motor car,** l'avènement *m* de l'automobile.

Adventist [ˈædvəntist], *s. Rel.H:* Adventiste *mf.* **Seventh-Day A.,** Adventiste du septième jour.

adventitious [ˌædvenˈtiʃəs], *a.* Advantice. (*a*) (Fait) accessoire. (*b*) Accidentel, fortuit. **-ly,** *adv.* D'une manière adventice. (*a*) Accessoirement. (*b*) Accidentellement, fortuitement.

adventure¹ [ədˈventʃər], *s.* 1. Aventure *f.* **a.** Entreprise hasardeuse. **Life of a.,** vie d'aventure, vie aventureuse. (*b*) Événement *m* (qui arrive à qn). **He told us all his adventures,** il nous a raconté toutes ses aventures. 2. *Com:* Spéculation hasardée.

adventure². *O:* 1. *v.tr.* Aventurer, hasarder, risquer (sa fortune, sa vie, etc.). 2. *v.i. & pr.* **To a. (oneself) (up)on an undertaking,** s'aventurer, se hasarder, dans une entreprise.

adventurer [əd'ventʃərər], s. (*In all senses*) Aventurier m; homme m d'aventures. *Pej:* Chevalier m d'industrie.

adventuresome [əd'ventʃərsəm], a. Aventureux; téméraire.

adventuress [əd'ventʃəris], s.f. *Pej:* Aventurière; intrigante.

adventurous [əd'ventʃərəs], a. Aventureux, -euse. -ly, adv. Aventureusement, d'une façon aventureuse.

adventurousness [əd'ventʃərəsnis], s. Hardiesse f; audace f; esprit m d'aventure.

adverb ['ædvə:b], s. *Gram:* Adverbe m.

adverbial [əd'və:biəl], a. *Gram:* Adverbial, -aux. A. phrase, locution adverbiale. -ally, adv. Adverbialement.

adversary ['ædvəs(ə)ri], s. Adversaire mf.

adverse ['ædvə:s], a. 1. Adverse. (a) Contraire, opposé (to, à). A. wind, vent contraire. (b) Ennemi (to, de); hostile (to, à, envers). A. fortune, fortune adverse. (c) Défavorable. 2. Opposé; en face. -ly, adv. (a) To act a. to s.o., agir (tout) au contraire de qn; prendre le contre-pied de ce que fait qn. (b) To influence s.o. a., exercer une influence défavorable sur qn.

adversity [əd'və:siti], s. Adversité f, infortune f.

advert[1] [əd'və:t], v.i. To a. to sth., faire allusion à qch.; parler de qch.; citer qch.

advert[2] ['ædvə:t], s. F: = ADVERTISEMENT.

advertise ['ædvətaiz], v.tr. & i. 1. A: Avertir (s.o. of sth., qn de qch.). 2. (a) (i) (Faire) annoncer, faire savoir, faire connaître (un événement dans les journaux); (ii) afficher (une vente, etc.). To a. in a paper, (faire) insérer une annonce dans un journal. (b) Faire de la réclame, de la publicité, de la propagande, pour (un produit). *Abs.* Faire de la réclame, de la publicité. *F:* You needn't a. the fact, vous n'avez pas besoin de le crier sur les toits. advertising, s. Publicité f, réclame f; annonces fpl. A. medium, agency, agent, organe, bureau, entrepreneur, agent, de publicité. A. manager, chef de la publicité.

advertisement [əd'və:tismənt], s. 1. Publicité f. 2. (a) (*In newspaper*) Annonce f. Classified advertisements, petites annonces. A. manager, annoncier m. (b) (*On a wall*) Affiche f.

advertiser ['ædvətaizər], s. (a) Auteur m de l'annonce. (b) Faiseur m de réclame.

advice [əd'vais], s. (*The pl. is rare, except in* 3) 1. Conseil(s) m(pl), avis m. Piece of a., conseil. To ask for a., demander (des) conseil(s). To ask, seek, s.o.'s a., prendre conseil de qn; prendre l'avis de qn. To take s.o.'s a., suivre le conseil de qn; se conformer à l'avis de qn. To act on s.o.'s a., agir selon, sur, le conseil de qn. To take medical a., consulter un médecin. At, by, on, under, s.o.'s a., sur l'avis de qn; suivant les conseils de qn. 2. Avis. *Com:* A.-note, letter of a., lettre, note, d'avis. 3. *pl. O:* Nouvelles f, avis. We have advices from abroad, nous avons reçu des informations, des avis, de l'étranger.

ad'vice-boat, s. A: *Navy:* Aviso m, mouche f (d'escadre).

advisability [əd,vaizə'biliti], s. = ADVISABLENESS.

advisable [əd'vaizəbl], a. 1. (Démarche) recommandable, conseillable, judicieuse. It would be a. to lock up these papers, il serait prudent d'enfermer ces papiers. 2. Opportun, à propos; convenable (for, pour). It might be a. to . . ., peut-être conviendrait-il de. . . . As shall be deemed a., ainsi qu'on le jugera utile; ainsi qu'il appartiendra. If you deem it a., si bon vous semble.

advisableness [əd'vaizəblnis], s. Opportunité f, convenance f.

advise [əd'vaiz]. I. v.tr. 1. (a) To a. s.o., conseiller qn. To a. s.o. to do sth., conseiller à qn de faire qch. I strongly a. you to . . ., je vous recommande (instamment) de. . . . What do you a. me to do? que me conseillez-vous? (b) To a. sth., recommander qch. (à qn). (c) To a. s.o. against sth., against doing sth., déconseiller qch. à qn; déconseiller à qn de faire qch. 2. To a. s.o. on a question, renseigner qn sur une question. To a. on a question, servir de conseil pour une question. 3. To a. s.o. of sth., avertir, prévenir, instruire, qn de qch. To a. s.o. that . . ., avertir,

prévenir, qn que. . . . II. advise, v.i. O: To a. with s.o., (i) consulter qn; (ii) se consulter avec qn. advised, a. 1. (Acte) réfléchi, délibéré. 2. *See* ILL-ADVISED, WELL-ADVISED.

advisedly [əd'vaizidli], adv. 1. De propos délibéré; à dessein. 2. En connaissance de cause; après mûre considération.

adviser [əd'vaizər], s. Conseiller m. Legal a., conseiller juridique. Spiritual a., directeur m de conscience.

advisory [əd'vaizəri], a. Consultatif, -ive. A. services, services de documentation. In an a. capacity, dans des fonctions consultatives, comme conseiller.

advocacy ['ædvəkəsi], s. 1. Profession f, fonction f, d'avocat. 2. A. of a cause, plaidoyer m en faveur d'une cause; appui donné à une cause.

advocate[1] ['ædvəkit], s. 1. *Jur:* (*In Scot.*) Avocat m. The Lord A. = le Procureur général (en Écosse). 2. Avocat; défenseur m (d'une doctrine, etc.). The advocates of free trade, les partisans du libre-échange.

advocate[2] ['ædvəkeit], v.tr. Plaider en faveur de (qch.); préconiser (un remède).

advowson [əd'vauz(ə)n], s. *Ecc:* Droit m de présentation (à un bénéfice).

adze [ædz], s. *Tls:* (H)erminette f; doloire f.

aedile ['i:dail], s. *Rom.Ant:* Édile m.

Aegean [i(:)'dʒi:ən], a. & s. *Geog:* (La mer) Égée.

Aegeus ['i:dʒju:s]. *Pr.n.m. Gr.Myth:* Égée.

aegis ['i:dʒis], s. *Gr.Myth:* Égide f. Under the a. of . . ., sous l'égide de. . . .

Aeneas [i(:)'ni:æs]. *Pr.n.m. Lt.Lit:* Énée.

Aeneid ['i:niid], s. The A., l'Énéide f.

Aeolian [i(:)'oulian], a. *A.Geog:* Éolien. A. harp, harpe éolienne. *Geog:* A. erosion, érosion éolienne.

aeon ['i:ən], s. Durée f (de l'univers); éon m.

aerate ['εəreit], v.tr. 1. (a) Aérer. (b) *Physiol:* Artérialiser, oxygéner (le sang). 2. Gazéifier (l'eau). aerated, a. (a) (Pain) aéré. (b) (Eau) gazeuse.

aeration [εə'reiʃ(ə)n], s. 1. Aération f; aérage m (de l'eau, etc.). 2. *Med:* Oxygénation f, artérialisation f (du sang). 3. Gazéification f (des eaux minérales).

aerial ['εəriəl]. 1. a. Aérien. A. railway, voie ferrée aérienne. 2. s. *W.Tel:* Antenne f. Sending, transmitting a., antenne de transmission. A. wire, brin, fil, d'antenne. Television aerial, antenne de télévision. *Radar:* Aérien m.

aerialist ['εəriəlist], s. *U.S:* Acrobate (aérien).

aerobatics [εəro'bætiks], s.pl. *Av: F:* Acrobaties (aériennes), vol m acrobatique.

aerobe ['εəroub], s. *Biol:* Aérobie f.

aerodrome ['εərodroum], s. Aérodrome m.

aerodynamic [εərodai'næmik, -di-], a. Aérodynamique. A. axis, axe de poussée. A. centre, centre de poussée.

aerodynamics ['εərodai'næmiks, -di-], s.pl. (*Usu. with sg. const.*) Aérodynamique f.

aerodyne ['εərodain], s. *Av:* Aérodyne m.

aero-engine ['εəro'endʒin], s. Moteur m d'avion.

aerofoil ['εərofoil], s. *Av:* Plan m à profil d'aile; voilure f; surface portante.

aerogram(me) ['εərogræm], s. Aérogramme m.

aerolite ['εərolait], aerolith ['εəroliθ], s. Aérolithe m.

aerology [εə'rələdʒi], s. Aérologie f.

aerometer [εə'rɔmitər], s. Aéromètre m.

aerometry [εə'rɔmətri], s. Aérométrie f.

aeromodelling ['εəro'mɔdliŋ], s. Aéromodélisme m.

aeronaut ['εəronɔ:t], s. Aéronaute m.

aeronautic(al) [εəro'nɔ:tik(l)], a. Aéronautique.

aeronautics [εəro'nɔ:tiks], s.pl. (*Usu. with sg. const.*) Aéronautique f.

aerophagia [εəro'feidʒiə], s. *Med:* Aérophagie f.

aeroplane ['εəroplein], s. Avion m.

aeropulse ['εəropʌls], s. aero-resonator ['εəro'rezonatər], s. Avion m à réaction; pulsoréacteur m.

aerosol ['εərosɔl], s. Aérosol m.

aerostat ['εərostæt], s. *Av:* Aérostat m.

aerostatics ['εəro'stætiks], s.pl. (*Usu. with sg. const.*) Aérostatique f.

aerotechnics ['εəroteknics], s. *Av:* Aérotechnique f.

aerotherapeutics ['εəro,θerə'pju:tiks], s. Aérothérapie f.

Aeschylus ['i:skiləs]. *Pr.n.m.* Eschyle.

Aesop ['i:sɔp]. *Pr.n.m. Gr.Lit:* Ésope.

aesthete ['i:sθi:t], s. Esthète mf.
aesthetic(al) [i:s'θetik(l)], a. **1.** Esthétique. **2.** De bon goût. **-ally,** adv. Esthétiquement.
aesthetics [i:s'θetiks], s.pl. (Usu. with sg. const.) Esthétique f.
aestivation [i:sti'vaiʃən], s. **1.** Bot: Estivation f, préfloraison f. **2.** Z: Estivation.
afar [ə'fɑ:r], adv. Chiefly Lit: From a., de loin. **A. off,** au loin; éloigné.
affability [æfə'biliti], s. Affabilité f (towards, envers, avec); aménité f, courtoisie f.
affable ['æfəbl], a. Affable, courtois (to, with, envers, avec). **-ably,** adv. Avec courtoisie, avec affabilité.
affableness ['æfəb(ə)lnis], s. = AFFABILITY.
affair [ə'fɛər], s. Affaire f. **That is my a.,** ça, c'est mon affaire. **(Love-)a.,** affaire de cœur. **Unhappy love a.,** déception sentimentale. **A. of honour,** affaire d'honneur; duel m. **The affairs of this world,** les choses f de ce monde. F: **What a ghastly a.!** En voilà du propre!
affect¹ [ə'fekt], v.tr. **1.** (a) Affecter (une forme). (b) Affecter (une manière, une vertu, etc.). **He affects generosity,** il fait parade de (la) générosité. (c) Simuler (la piété, etc.). **To a. stupidity,** faire la bête. **2.** (Of animals) Fréquenter, hanter (une région). **affected¹,** a. (Of pers., manners) (a) Affecté, maniéré, mignard, affété; (of pers.) minaudier, grimacier. (b) Simulé. **-ly,** adv. Avec affectation.
affect², v.tr. **1.** (a) Atteindre, attaquer, toucher (qn); affecter (un organe, etc.); influer sur (qch.). **To be affected by a fall in prices,** être atteint par une baisse de prix. **The climate has affected his health,** le climat a altéré sa santé. **It affects me personally,** cela me touche, m'intéresse, personnellement. (b) Med: Intéresser. **Bowel complaint that also affects the liver,** maladie intestinale qui intéresse le foie. **2.** Affecter, affliger, toucher (qn). **To be affected at the sight of sth.,** se laisser attendrir au spectacle de qch. **3.** Toucher, concerner (qn, qch.). **That does not a. the matter,** cela ne fait rien à l'affaire. **To a. events,** influer sur les événements. **affected²,** a. (a) To be well, ill, a. towards s.o., être bien, mal, disposé pour qn. (b) To be a. with a disease, être atteint d'une maladie. **The lung is a.,** le poumon est atteint, attaqué, touché. (c) Ému, touché. **To be much a. by sth.,** ressentir vivement qch. **affecting,** a. Touchant, attendrissant.
affectation [æfek'teiʃ(ə)n], s. **1.** A. of interest, affectation f, simulation f, d'intérêt. **2.** Affectation, affèteterie f; apprêt m (de langage); mignardise f, mièvrerie f; simagrées fpl.
affectedness [ə'fektidnis], s. Affectation f.
affection [ə'fekʃ(ə)n], s. **1.** Affection f, tendresse f; amitié f, attachement m. **To have an a. for s.o., to feel a. towards s.o.,** avoir, ressentir, de l'affection pour qn; affectionner qn. **To gain, win, s.o.'s a.,** se faire aimer de qn. **2.** Med: Affection (de poitrine, etc.).
affectionate [ə'fekʃənit], a. Affectueux, aimant. **Your a. son,** votre fils affectionné. **-ly,** adv. Affectueusement. **affectionnément. Yours a.,** bien affectueusement.
affiance [ə'faiəns], v.tr. Lit: Fiancer (s.o. to s.o., qn avec qn).
affidavit [æfi'deivit], s. Jur: Déclaration par écrit et sous serment, enregistrée sur acte timbré; affirmation f. **Evidence taken on a.,** dépositions recueillies sous serment. **A. made by process server,** constat d'huissier.
affiliate [ə'filieit], v.tr. **1.** (Of a society) To a. members, s'affilier des membres. **2.** To a. a member to, with, a society, affilier un membre à une société. **To a. (oneself) to, with, a society,** s'affilier à une société. **Affiliated firm, filiale f.**
affiliation [ə,fili'eiʃ(ə)n], s. (a) Affiliation f (à une société). (b) U.S: Political affiliations, attaches f politiques. (c) Jur: Procédure f en recherche de paternité.
affinity [ə'finiti], s. (a) Affinité f (with, to, avec; between, entre). **Spiritual a.,** affinité spirituelle. (b) Conformité f de caractère. (c) Ch: A. for a body, affinité pour un corps. (d) Parenté f par alliance; affinité.
affirm [ə'fə:m], v.tr. **1.** Affirmer, soutenir (that, que). **To a. sth. to s.o.,** affirmer, assurer, qch. à qn. **2.** Jur: Confirmer, homologuer (un jugement).

affirmation [æfə:'meiʃ(ə)n], s. **1.** (a) Affirmation f, assertion f. (b) Jur: Déclaration solennelle (tenant lieu de serment) (p. ex. lorsque le témoin n'a pas de foi religieuse). **2.** Jur: Confirmation f, homologation f (d'un jugement).
affirmative [ə'fə:mətiv]. **1.** a. Affirmatif. **To make an a. sign,** faire signe que oui. **2.** s. If he replies in the a., s'il répond affirmativement. • The answer is in the a., la réponse est oui. **-ly,** adv. Affirmativement.
affirmatory [ə'fə:mət(ə)ri], a. Affirmatif.
affix [ə'fiks], v.tr. Attacher (sth. to sth., qch. à qch.). **To a. a seal, a stamp, to a document,** apposer un sceau, un timbre, à, sur, un document.
afflict [ə'flikt], v.tr. Affliger, tourmenter; désoler. s. **The afflicted,** les affligés.
affliction [ə'flikʃ(ə)n], s. **1.** Affliction f. **These forms are my a.,** ces formules font mon désespoir. **2.** Calamité f, revers m. **3.** The afflictions of old age, les infirmités f de la vieillesse.
affluence ['æfluəns], s. **1.** Affluence f; grand concours (de gens, etc.). **2.** Abondance f, richesse f.
affluent¹ ['æfluənt], a. **1.** Abondant, riche (in, en). **2.** Opulent, riche. **In a. circumstance,** dans l'aisance.
affluent², s. Geog: Affluent m (d'une rivière).
afflux ['æflʌks], s. **1.** Afflux m, affluence f (du sang, etc.). **2.** Concours m (de gens).
afford [ə'fɔ:d], v.tr. **1.** (Usu. with 'can') (a) Avoir les moyens (pécuniaires) (de faire qch.); être en mesure (de faire qch.). **I cannot a. to be idle,** je ne suis pas à même de ne rien faire. **I can't a. it,** mes moyens ne le permettent pas; c'est trop cher pour moi. **He can well a. to build,** il a largement les moyens de bâtir. (b) **I can a. to wait,** je peux attendre. **Can you a. the time?** disposez-vous du temps (nécessaire)? **2.** (Give, provide) Fournir, offrir. **These trees afforded us little shelter,** ces arbres ne nous fournissaient qu'un piètre abri.
afforest [ə'forest], v.tr. Boiser (une terre, une région); soumettre (une région) au régime forestier.
afforestation [ə,foris'teiʃ(ə)n], s. Boisement m, afforestation f.
affranchise [ə'fræn(t)ʃaiz], v.tr. Affranchir.
affranchisement [ə'fræntʃizmənt], s. Affranchissement m (d'un serf, d'un esclave).
affray [ə'frei], s. **1.** Bagarre f, échauffourée f. **2.** (Between two men) Rixe f.
affront¹ [ə'frʌnt], s. Affront m, offense f. **To suffer an a. (at the hands of s.o.),** essuyer une avanie (de la part de qn). **To pocket an a.,** avaler un affront.
affront², v.tr. (a) Insulter, offenser; faire (un) affront à (qn). (b) Faire rougir, faire honte à (qn).
Afghanistan [æf,gænis'tɑ:n], Pr.n. Geog: Afghanistan m.
afield [ə'fi:ld], adv. (a) Lit: To be a., (of labourer) être aux champs; (of warrior) être en campagne. (b) **To go far a., farther a.,** aller très loin, plus loin.
afire [ə'faiər], adv. & pred.a. A. & Lit: En feu; embrasé. **To be (all) a. with the desire to...,** brûler du désir de....
aflame [ə'fleim], adv. & pred. a. Lit: En flammes; embrasé. **To be a. with colour,** briller de vives couleurs; rutiler. **To be a. with curiosity,** brûler de curiosité.
afloat [ə'flout], adv. & pred. a. **1.** (a) A flot; sur l'eau; à la mer. (Of ship, F: of pers.) To be a., être à flot. **To set a ship a.,** lancer, mettre à la mer, mettre à l'eau, un navire. **To keep a ship a.,** maintenir un navire à flot. **What had remained a. from the wreck,** ce qui avait surnagé du naufrage. (Of pers.) **To keep a.,** se maintenir à flot; surnager. (b) **The deck was a.,** le pont était submergé. **2.** (Of rumour, etc.) **To be a.,** courir, circuler.
afoot [ə'fut], adv. **1.** A: To be, to go, to come a., être, aller, venir, à pied. **2.** O: To be a., être sur pied, en mouvement. **3.** A plan is a. to..., on envisage, on a formé, un projet pour...; on a formé le projet de.... **There's something a.,** il se prépare, il se trame, quelque chose. **There is some mischief a.,** il se prépare un mauvais coup.
afore [ə'fɔ:r], adv. & prep. **1.** Nau: A. the mast, sur l'avant (du mât). **2.** A. & Dial: = BEFORE. **3.** a. Jur: A.-cited, -mentioned, -named, aforesaid, précité, susmentionné, susdit; (pers.) prénommé.

aforethought [ə'fɔ:θɔ:t], *a. Jur:* **With, of, malice a.** avec préméditation.

afraid [ə'freid], *pred. a.* Pris de peur. **To be a. (of s.o., of sth.),** avoir peur (de qn, de qch.); craindre (qn, qch.). **Don't be a.,** n'ayez pas peur; ne craignez rien, **To make s.o. a.,** faire peur à qn; effrayer qn. **To be a. to do, of doing, sth.,** ne pas oser faire qch.; avoir peur, craindre, de faire qch. **I am a. he will die,** je crains qu'il ne meure. **I am a. that he will not come, of his not coming,** j'ai peur qu'il ne vienne pas. **I'm a. it is so!** j'en ai (bien) peur! **I'm a. I can't tell you,** je ne saurais guère vous le dire. **I am a. he is out,** je crois bien qu'il est sorti. **I'm a. that it is too true,** je crains bien que ce ne soit que trop vrai.

afresh [ə'freʃ], *adv.* De nouveau, à nouveau. **To start sth. a.,** recommencer qch.

Africa ['æfrikə]. *Pr.n. Geog:* L'Afrique *f*.

African ['æfrikən], *a. & s. Geog:* Africain, -aine.

Africanist ['æfrikənist], *a. & s.* Africaniste *mf*.

Afrikaans [æfri'ka:ns], *s. Ling·* Afrika(a)ns *m*.

Afrikander [ˌæfri'kændər], *s. & a. Geog:* Afrikander *mf*.

Africanization [ˌæfrikənai'zeiʃən], *s.* Africanisation *f*.

Afro-Asian [ˌæfro'eiʃn, -'eizn], *a. & s.* Afro-asiatique *mf*.

aft [ɑːft], *adv. Nau:* Sur, à, vers, l'arrière. **To berth a.,** coucher à l'arrière. **A. of the mast,** sur l'arrière du mât. *S.a.* FORE-AND-AFT. **'aft-gate,** *s.* Porte *f* (d')aval (d'une écluse).

after ['ɑːftər]. I. *adv.* Après. 1. (*Place, order*) **To come a.,** venir après, venir à la suite. **You speak first, I shall speak a.,** parlez d'abord, je parlerai ensuite. 2. (*Time*) **I never spoke to him a.,** je ne lui ai jamais parlé après. **I heard of it a.,** je l'ai appris plus tard. **He was ill for months a.,** il en est resté malade pendant des mois. **Soon, long, a.,** bientôt, longtemps, après. **The night, the week, a.,** la nuit, la semaine, d'après. *S.a.* EVER 1, MORNING 1. II. *after, prep.* Après. 1. (*Place*) (*a*) **To walk a. s.o.,** marcher après qn. **He closed the door a. him,** il referma la porte sur lui. (*b*) **To run, shout, a. s.o.,** courir, crier, après qn. *F:* **To be a. s.o., sth.,** être après qn, qch.; être en quête de qn, de qch. **The police are a. you,** la police est à vos trousses. **The boys are a. your fruit,** les gamins en veulent à vos fruits. **What is he a.?** (i) qu'est-ce qu'il a en tête? (ii) qu'est-ce qu'il cherche? **I see what you're a.,** je vois où vous voulez en venir. 2. (*Time*) **To reign a. s.o.,** régner après qn. **A. this date . . .,** passé cette date. . . . **On and a. the 15th,** à partir du quinze. **A. hours,** (i) après le travail; (ii) après les heures de service; (iii) après l'heure de fermeture. **A. all** (said and done), au bout du compte; à la fin des fins; après tout; enfin. **The day a. tomorrow,** après-demain. **It is a. five (o'clock),** il est plus de cinq heures; il est cinq heures passées. *U.S:* **It is half a. four,** il est quatre heures et demie. **They entered one a. the other,** ils entrèrent à la file, les uns après les autres. **He read page a. page,** il lut page sur page. **Time a. time,** maintes (et maintes) fois. **Charge a. charge,** des assauts répétés. **Day a. day,** jour après jour. 3. (*Order*) (*a*) **'A. you, sir,'** "après vous, monsieur." (*b*) **I put Milton a.** Dante, je mets Milton au-dessous de Dante. 4. (*Manner*) **A. a pattern,** d'après, suivant, selon, un modèle. **He's a man a. my own heart,** c'est un homme qui a les mêmes idées que moi. **Landscape a.** Turner, paysage d'après Turner, à la manière de Turner. III. *after, conj.* Après que + *ind.* **I come a. he goes,** je viens après qu'il est parti. IV. **after-,** *a.* 1. Après. 2. A venir. 3. Arrière. *S.a.* GUN¹ 1. **'after-cabin,** *s. Nau:* Chambre *f* de l'arrière. **'after-care,** *s.* Surveillance *f* (de convalescents, de jeunes criminels). **'after-damp,** *s. Min:* Gaz *m* délétères (provenant d'une explosion de grisou); mofette *f*. **'after-days,** *s.pl.* La suite des temps. **In a.-days,** (i) dans les jours à venir; (ii) dans les jours qui suivirent; dans la suite. **'after-deck,** *s. Nau:* Arrière-pont *m*, pont arrière. **'after-effect(s),** *s.(pl.)* Suites *fpl*, contre-coup *m*, répercussion *f* (d'un événement); séquelles *fpl* (d'une maladie). **'after-hold,** *s. Nau:* Cale *f* arrière. **'after-life,** *s.* 1. La vie future. 2. Suite *f* de la vie. **In a.-l.,** plus tard dans la vie. **'after-pains,** *s.pl. Obst:* Tranchées utérines. **'after-sensation,** *s. Phil:* Image consécutive. **'after-shave,** *a.* **A.-s. lotion,**

lotion *f* après rasage. **'after-taste,** *s.* Arrière-goût *m*; (*of wine*) déboire *m*. **'after-treatment,** *s.* Soins ultérieurs (à un convalescent); traitement ultérieur (d'un produit). **'after-wit,** *s.* Esprit *m* de l'escalier. **'after-world,** *s.* La vie future, l'au-delà *m*.

afterbirth ['ɑːftəbə:θ], *s.* 1. *Obst:* Arrière-faix *m*, délivre *m*, secondines *fpl*. 2. *Jur:* Naissance posthume ou postérieure au testament.

afterclap ['ɑːftəklæp], *s.* Contre-coup *m* (d'un événement, etc.).

aftercrop ['ɑːftəkrɔp], *s.* Regain *m*; seconde récolte.

afterglow ['ɑːftəglou], *s.* Dernières lueurs, derniers reflets, du soleil couchant.

aftermath ['ɑːftəmæθ], *s.* 1. *Agr:* Regain *m*. 2. Suites *fpl* (d'un événement).

aftermost ['ɑːftəmoust], *a. Nau:* The a. part, la partie la plus en arrière, la plus à l'arrière.

afternoon [ɑːftə'nuːn], *s.* Après-midi *m or f. inv.* **I shall see him this a.,** je le verrai cet après-midi. **At half past two in the a.,** à deux heures et demie de l'après-midi; *Jur: etc:* à deux heures et demie du soir. **Every a.,** tous les après-midi. **I saw him on Tuesday a.,** je l'ai vu mardi après-midi. **Good a.!** bonjour! *S.a.* TEA 1.

afters ['ɑːftəz], *s.pl. Cu: F:* Dessert *m* ou fromage *m*.

after-shave [ɑːftə'ʃeiv], *a.* **a.-s. lotion,** lotion *f* après rasage.

afterthought ['ɑːftəθɔːt], *s.* Réflexion *f* après coup.

afterwards ['ɑːftəwədz], *adv.* Après, plus tard, ensuite; dans la suite, par la suite. **I only heard of it a.,** je ne l'ai su qu'après coup.

again [ə'gen], *adv. With a vb. often rendered by the pref.* re-: **to begin a.,** recommencer; **to bring a.,** ramener, rapporter; **to do a.,** refaire; **to come down, up, a.,** redescendre, remonter. 1. (*a*) De nouveau, encore; *Lit:* derechef. **Once a.,** encore une fois, une fois de plus. **Here we are a.!** *F:* nous revoilà! **Don't do it a.!** ne recommencez pas! **Never a.,** (ne . . .) jamais plus; plus jamais (. . . ne). **A'. and a.,** time **and a.,** maintes et maintes fois; à plusieurs reprises. **Now and a.,** de temps en temps; de temps à autre. **As much a.,** deux fois autant. **As large a.,** deux fois aussi grand. **Half as much a.,** (de) moitié plus. (*b*) (*Back*) **To send, give, sth. back a.,** renvoyer, rendre, qch. **To come a.,** revenir. (*c*) *F:* **What's his name a.?** comment s'appelle-t-il déjà? (*d*) (*Intensive*) **The blow made his ears ring a.,** ce fut un coup à lui faire tinter les oreilles. **The loaded table groaned a.,** la table chargée gémissait sous le poids. 2. (*a*) De plus, d'ailleurs, en outre. (*b*) (**Then**) **a.;** (**and**) **a.,** d'autre part; d'un autre côté.

against [ə'genst], *prep.* Contre. 1. (*a*) **To fight a. s.o.,** se battre contre qn. **To march a. the enemy,** marcher à l'ennemi. **I have nothing to say a. it,** je n'ai rien à dire là-contre. **To be a. sth. being done,** être opposé à ce que quelque chose se fasse. **They fought man a. man,** ils se battirent homme à homme. **I did it a. my will,** je l'ai fait malgré moi, à contre-cœur. **Action that is a. the rules,** action contraire aux règlements. **Conditions are a. us,** les conditions (nous) sont défavorables. **There is no law a. it,** il n'y a pas de loi qui s'y oppose. **To brush a hat a. the nap,** brosser un chapeau à rebrousse-poil. (*b*) **Warned a. s.o., sth.,** mis en garde contre qn, qch. (*c*) **To run, dash, a. the wall,** courir, donner, contre le mur. *F:* **To run up a. s.o.,** rencontrer qn par hasard. *S.a.* COME UP, UP¹ I. 5. (*d*) **Leaning a. the wall,** appuyé contre le mur. (*e*) A l'encontre de. **Never go a.** Nature, il ne faut jamais aller à l'encontre de la Nature. 2. **My rights (as) a. the Government,** mes droits vis-à-vis du Gouvernement. 3. **To show up a. a background,** se détacher sur un fond. 4. **To make preparation a. his return,** faire des préparatifs pour son retour. **To buy preserves a. the winter,** acheter des conserves en prévision de l'hiver. 5. **Three deaths this year as a. thirty in 1964,** trois morts cette année contre trente, comparées à trente, en 1964.

agape [ə'geip], *adv. & pred. a.* Bouche bée.

agar-agar ['eiga:r'eiga:], *s.* Agar-agar *m*.

agaric ['ægərik, ə'gærik], *s. Fung:* Agaric *m*. **Fly-a.,** (amanite *f*) tue-mouches *m*, fausse oronge. **Royal a.,** oronge.

agate ['ægət], *s.* Agate *f*.

agave ['ægeiv], *s. Bot:* Agave *m*.

age¹ [eidȝ], *s.* **1.** Age *m.* (*a*) Middle a., âge mûr. To be past middle a., être sur le retour; être sur le déclin de la vie. Of uncertain a., entre deux âges. To be twenty years of a., être âgé de vingt ans. What a. are you? quel âge avez-vous? He has a daughter your a., il a une fille de votre âge. At his a., à son âge, à l'âge qu'il a. To be under a., être mineur. Full a., âge légal; (état *m* de) majorité *f.* To be of (full) a., être majeur. To come of a., atteindre sa majorité. On, at, his coming of a., à sa majorité. To be over a. to do sth., être trop âgé pour faire qch. To be of an a. to marry, être en âge de se marier. He does not look his a., il ne porte pas son âge. She might be any a., elle n'a pas d'âge. They are of an a., ils sont du même âge. (*b*) (Old) a., vieillesse *f. S.a.* OLD 1. **2.** (*a*) Age, époque *f*, siècle *m.* From a. to a., d'âge en âge. The a. we live in, le siècle où nous vivons; notre siècle. In our a., à notre époque. The present a., la génération actuelle. *Prehist:* The stone a., l'âge de pierre. The ice a., l'âge des glaciers. The iron a., l'âge du fer. *Hist:* The Middle Ages, le moyen âge. The atomic a., l'ère *f* atomique. *Myth:* The golden a., l'âge d'or. The iron a., l'âge de fer. (*b*) *F:* It is an a., it is ages, since I saw him, I haven't seen him for ages, il y a une éternité que je ne l'ai vu. 'age-group, *s. Mil: etc:* Classe *f.*

age², *v.* (aged [eidȝd], ag(e)ing ['eidȝiŋ]) **1.** *v.i.* Vieillir; prendre de l'âge. **2.** *v.tr.* Vieillir; rendre (qn) vieux. **aged,** *a.* **1.** ['eidȝid] Âgé, vieux. An a. man, un vieillard. *s.* The a., les vieillards, les vieux. **2.** [eidȝd] (*a*) A. twenty years, âgé de vingt ans. (*b*) I found him greatly a., je le trouvai bien vieilli. **ageing¹,** *a.* Vieillissant. **ageing²,** *s.* Vieillissement *m.*

ageless ['eidȝlis], *a.* **1.** Toujours jeune. **2.** Éternel.

agency ['eidȝənsi], *s.* **1.** (*a*) Action, opération *f.* Through the a. of water, par l'action de l'eau. (*b*) Agent *m.* Natural agencies, agents naturels. (*c*) Entremise *f.* Through s.o.'s a., par l'entremise, par l'intermédiaire *m*, de qn. **2.** *Com:* Agence *f*, bureau *m.* A. office, bureau d'affaires. Travel a., agence de voyages.

agenda [ə'dȝendə], *s.pl.* (*Usu. with sing. concord*) Ordre *m* du jour (d'une réunion). **Agenda(-book),** agenda *m.*

agent ['eidȝənt], *s.* **1.** (*a*) Agent *m.* To be a free a., avoir son libre arbitre. (*b*) Homme *m* d'affaires; régisseur *m* (d'une propriété). *Com:* Agent, représentant *m.* A. on the spot, agent à demeure. To be sole a. for . . ., avoir la représentation exclusive de. . . . Forwarding a., entrepreneur *m* de transports. Mercantile a., commissionnaire *m.* Bank a., directeur *m* d'une succursale de banque. *Pol:* Electioneering a., agent électoral. (*c*) Mandataire *mf*; fondé(e) de pouvoir. *S.a.* PRINCIPAL II. 1. **2.** Chemical a., agent chimique.

agglomerate¹ [ə'glɔmərit, -eit]. **1.** *a.* Aggloméré. **2.** *s. Geol: Min:* Agglomérat.

agglomerate² [ə'glɔməreit]. **1.** *v.tr.* Agglomérer. **2.** *v.i.* S'agglomérer.

agglomeration [ə,glɔmə'reiʃ(ə)n], *s.* Agglomération *f.*

agglutinate [ə'glu:tineit]. **1.** *v.tr.* Agglutiner. **2.** *v.i.* S'agglutiner.

agglutination [ə,glu:ti'neiʃ(ə)n], *s.* Agglutination *f.*

agglutinative [ə'glu:tinətiv], *a. Ling:* Agglutinant.

aggrandizement [ə'grændizmənt], *s.* Agrandissement *m.*

aggravate ['ægrəveit], *v.tr.* **1.** (*a*) Aggraver (une faute, une difficulté); empirer (un mal); envenimer (une querelle). *Jur:* Aggravated larceny, vol qualifié. (*b*) Augmenter (l'indignation, la douleur). **2.** *F:* Agacer, exaspérer (qn). **aggravating,** *a.* **1.** A. circumstance, circonstance aggravante. **2.** *F:* Exaspérant, assommant.

aggravation [,ægrə'veiʃ(ə)n], *s.* **1.** (*a*) Aggravation *f* (d'un crime, d'une maladie); envenimement *m* (d'une querelle). (*b*) *F:* Agacement *m*, exaspération *f.* **2.** Circonstance aggravante.

aggregate¹ ['ægrigit]. **1.** *a.* Collectif. *Ind:* A. output, rendement global, total, d'ensemble. (*b*) *Bot: Geol: Z:* Agrégé. **2.** *s.* (*a*) Ensemble *m*, total *m.* (*b*) Masse *f*, assemblage *m*, agrégation *f. Miner:* Agrégat *m.* In the a., en somme, dans l'ensemble.

aggregate² ['ægrigeit]. **1.** *v.tr.* (*a*) *Ph:* Agréger. (*b*) To a. s.o. to a society, agréger qn à une compagnie. **2.** *v.i.* (*a*) These armies aggregated 300,000 men, ces armées s'élevaient à un total de 300,000 hommes. (*b*) *Ph:* S'agréger.

aggregation [,ægri'geiʃ(ə)n], *s.* **1.** (*a*) *Ph:* Agrégation *f*, agglomération *f.* (*b*) A. of people, assemblage *m* de personnes. **2.** Agrégat *m.*

aggression [ə'greʃ(ə)n], *s.* Agression *f.*

aggressive [ə'gresiv], *a.* Agressif. A. policy, politique militante. **-ly,** *adv.* D'une manière agressive; d'un ton agressif.

aggressiveness [ə'gresivnis], *s.* Agressivité *f*, caractère agressif.

aggressor [ə'gresər], *s.* Agresseur *m.*

aggrieve [ə'gri:v], *v.tr.* (*Usu. passive*) Chagriner, blesser.

aghast [ə'gɑ:st], *pred. a.* Consterné. To stand a. (at sth.), être stupéfait, consterné, médusé, ébahi (de qch.); *F:* être sidéré.

agile ['ædȝail], *a.* Agile, leste. **-ly,** *adv.* Agilement.

agility [ə'dȝiliti], *s.* Agilité *f.*

Agincourt ['ædȝinkɔ:t]. *Pr.n. Geog: Hist:* Azincourt *m.*

agio ['ædȝiou], *s. Fin:* **1.** Agio *m*; prix *m* du change. **2.** Commerce *m* du change.

agiotage ['ædȝətidȝ], *s. Fin:* Agiotage *m.*

agitate ['ædȝiteit], *v.tr.* **1.** Agiter, remuer (qch.). **2.** Agiter, émouvoir, troubler (qn, l'esprit de qn). **3.** (*a*) Agiter (une question). (*b*) *Abs.* To a. for sth., against sth., faire de l'agitation en faveur de qch., contre qch. **agitated,** *a.* Agité; ému; troublé. **agitating,** *a.* Émouvant; troublant.

agitation [,ædȝi'teiʃ(ə)n], *s.* **1.** Agitation *f* (de la mer); mouvement *m.* **2.** (*a*) Agitation, émotion *f*, trouble *m.* (*b*) Agitation (ouvrière, etc.); troubles. **3.** Discussion *f* (d'une question).

agitator ['ædȝiteitər], *s.* **1.** Agitateur *m.* Political a., fauteur *m* de troubles; meneur *m.* **2.** *Ind:* (Appareil) brasseur *m*; agitateur.

aglow [ə'glou], *adv. & pred. a.* **1.** (*Of thg*) Enflammé, embrasé. To be a. with colour, briller de vives couleurs. **2.** (*Of pers.*) I was all a., (l'exercice, etc.) m'avait fouetté le sang. Face a. with health, visage resplendissant de santé.

agnail ['ægneil], *s.* Envie *f* (filet de peau qui s'est détaché de l'ongle).

agnostic [æg'nɔstik], *a. & s.* Agnostique (*mf*); libre penseur *m.*

agnosticism [æg'nɔstisizm], *s.* Agnosticisme *m*; libre pensée *f.*

ago [ə'gou]. **1.** *a.* Ten years a., il y a dix ans; cela date de dix ans. He arrived an hour a., il est arrivé il y a déjà une heure; il est là depuis une heure. A little while a., tout à l'heure; tantôt. **2.** *adv.* Long a., il y a longtemps. Not long a., il n'y a pas longtemps; naguère. How long a. is it since . . .? combien de temps y a-t-il que. . . .? As long a., as 1840, déjà en 1840; dès 1840. No longer a. than last week, pas plus tard que la semaine dernière.

agog [ə'gɔg], *adv. & pred. a.* To be a. for sth., être dans l'attente, dans l'expectative, de qch. To be (all) a. (with excitement) about sth., être en l'air, en émoi, à cause de qch. To be (all) a. to do sth., être impatient de faire qch.; griller d'envie de faire qch. The whole town was a., toute la ville était en émoi. To set s.o. (all) a., mettre qn en train, en émoi; *F:* aguicher qn. To set the town a., mettre la ville en rumeur.

agonize ['ægənaiz], *v.* **1.** *v.tr.* Torturer; mettre (qn) au supplice, au martyre, à la torture. **2.** *v.i. Lit:* Être au supplice, au martyre. **agonized,** *a.* **1.** (Cri) d'angoisse, d'angoisse. **2.** I was a. at the thought, idea, that . . ., j'étais au supplice, angoissé, à l'idée que. . . . **agonizing,** *a.* (*Of pain*) Atroce; (*of spectacle*) navrant, poignant, angoissant. A. cry, cri déchirant. *Pol:* A. reappraisal, réévaluation déchirante. **-ly,** *adv.* Avec angoisse.

agony ['ægəni], *s.* **1.** Angoisse *f.* To suffer agonies, to be in agonies, être au supplice, au martyre. To be in an a. of terror, être au comble de l'épouvante. *Journ: F:* A. column, annonces personnelles. **2.** To be in the death a., être à l'agonie.

agoraphobia [,ægərə'foubiə], *s. Psy:* Agoraphobie *f.*

agouti, agouty [ə'gu:ti], *s. Z:* Agouti *m.*

agraffe [ə'græf], *s. Surg: etc:* Agrafe *f.*

agraphia [ə'græfjə], *s. Med:* Agraphie *f.*

agrarian [ə'greəriən]. **1.** *a.* (Loi, mesure) agraire. **2.** *a. & s. Pol:* Agrarien (*m*).

agrarianism [ə'grɛəriənizm], s. Pol: Agrarianisme m.
agree [ə'griː]. I. v.i. & tr. 1. Consentir, donner son adhésion (to, à); faire droit (à une requête). To a. formally to sth., approuver qch. officiellement. To a. to do sth., accepter, convenir, de faire qch.; consentir à faire qch. I a. that he was mistaken, je vous accorde, j'admets, qu'il s'est trompé. To a. upon, as to, certain conditions, convenir de, accepter, tomber d'accord sur, certaines conditions. They have agreed about the prices, ils sont convenus des prix. To a. to sth. being done, accepter que qch. se fasse. Unless otherwise agreed, sauf arrangement contraire. 2. (Of pers.) (a) S'accorder; être d'accord; tomber d'accord. (b) To a. with s.o., entrer dans les idées de qn; donner raison à qn; penser comme qn. To a. with s.o. on, in, a matter, être du même avis que qn sur une question; s'accorder, être d'accord, avec qn sur une question; accepter (un point de vue). I quite a. with you on that point, je suis tout à fait de votre avis là-dessus. I don't a. with this theory, je n'accepte pas cette théorie. (c) "That is so," he agreed, "c'est vrai," acquiesça-t-il. 3. (Of thgs) (a) S'accorder, concorder (ensemble); (of ideas, opinions) se rencontrer. (b) Gram: S'accorder. (c) Convenir, réussir (with, à). The climate, wine, does not a. with him, le climat ne lui convient pas; le vin lui est contraire. F: Lobster does not a. with me, le homard ne me réussit pas. II. agree, v.tr. Book-k: To a. the books, faire accorder les livres. **agreed**, a. 1. (Of pers.) To be a. (with s.o.), être, demeurer, d'accord (avec qn) (on, about, sth., sur qch.). We are a. about the prices, nous sommes convenus des prix. 2. (Of thgs) A. upon, convenu. (That is) a.! c'est convenu! c'est entendu! soit! d'accord! A. unanimously, adopté à l'unanimité.
agreeable [ə'griəbl], a. 1. Agréable (to, à); (of pers.) aimable (to, envers). If that is a. to you, si cela vous convient. 2. Pred. (Of pers.) Consentant. To be a. to sth., to do sth., consentir à qch., à faire qch.; accepter de faire qch. I am (quite) a., je veux bien. -ably, adv. 1. Agréablement. 2. Conformément (to, with, à). 3. De bon gré; volontiers.
agreeableness [ə'griəblnis], s. (a) (Of pers.) Amabilité f. (b) (Of place, etc.) Agrément m. (c) Consentement.
agreement [ə'griːmənt], s. 1. Convention f, acte m, contrat m, traité m, arrangement m. Jur: Real a., bail m. Written a., convention par écrit. To enter into, conclude, an a., with s.o., passer un traité, un contrat, avec qn. Collective a., contrat collectif. 2. (a) Accord m. To be in a. with s.o., être d'accord avec qn. To be in a. with a decision, se rallier à, approuver, une décision. To come to an a., tomber d'accord. By mutual a., de gré à gré; à l'amiable. Com: As per a., comme convenu. (b) A. between powers, concert m des puissances. Ind: A. between producers, entente f entre producteurs. 3. (a) Conformité f, concordance f. (b) Gram: Accord (with, avec); concordance.
agricultural [ˌægri'kʌltʃər(ə)l], a. (Nation, produit) agricole; (peuple) agriculteur. A. engineer, ingénieur agronome. A. college, école (nationale) d'agriculture. A. show, comice f agricole.
agriculture ['ægrikʌltʃər], s. Agriculture f.
agricultur(al)ist [ˌægri'kʌltʃər(ə)list], s. Agriculteur m; agronome m.
agrimony ['ægriməni], s. Bot: 1. Common a., aigremoine f. 2. Hemp a., chanvre m d'eau.
agronomic(al) [ˌægro'nomik(l)], a. Agronomique.
agronomist [ə'grɒnəmist], s. Agronome m.
agronomy [ə'grɒnəmi], s. Agronomie f.
aground [ə'graund], adv. Nau: Échoué; au sec. To run a ship a. (faire) échouer un navire; mettre un navire à la côte. (Of ship) To run a., échouer (à la côte); s'échouer.
ague ['eigjuː], s. Med: A: Fièvre (paludéenne) intermittente. Fit of a., accès m de fièvre.
ah [ɑː], int. Ah! ha! heu!
aha [ɑː'hɑː], int. Haha!
ahead [ə'hed], adv. 1. Nau: (a) To be a., être sur l'avant, en avant (du navire). The ship was right a., le navire était droit devant. To draw a. of s.o., a ship, dépasser qn, un navire; gagner l'avant d'un navire. To go a., aller de l'avant; avancer; faire

route. Full speed a.! en avant à toute vitesse! en avant toute! (b) Wind a., vent debout. 2. (Of pers., car, etc.) (a) To get a., prendre de l'avance. To go on a., prendre les devants. Go on a.! filez devant! A. of s.o., en avant de qn. To be two hours a. of s.o., avoir deux heures d'avance sur qn. He is going a., il fait des progrès, il va de l'avant. To look a., penser à l'avenir. (b) Go a.! (i) allez! marchez! (ii) continuez!
ahem [m'mm], int. Hum!
ahoy [ə'hɔi], int. Nau: Boat a.! ohé, du canot!
ai ['ɑːi], s. Z: Aï m, paresseux m.
aid[1] [eid], s. 1. (a) Aide f, assistance f, secours m, appui m. With, by, the a. of s.o., sth., avec l'aide de qn; à l'aide de qch. To go to s.o.'s a., aller, se porter, au secours de qn. In a. of, au profit de. Collection in a., of . . ., quête f en faveur de. . . . Mutual a., entr'aide f; secours mutuels. Medical a., soins médicaux. S.a. FIRST-AID. (b) Deaf a., hearing a., aide auditif, aide-ouie m inv. Audio-visual aids, aides audiovisuelles. 2. Usu.pl. Aids to health, conseils m pour se bien porter. 3. (Pers.) Aide mf; auxiliaire mf.
aid[2], v.tr. 1. Aider, assister, secourir (qn); venir en aide à, venir à l'aide de (qn). To a. s.o. to do sth., aider (à) qn à faire qch. To a. one another, s'aider les uns les autres; s'entr'aider. S.a. ABET 1. 2. Soutenir, venir en aide à (une entreprise). **aiding**, s. Aide f. S.a. ABETTING.
aide-de-camp ['eid(d)əkɒŋ], s. (pl. aides-de-camp ['eid(d)əkɒŋ]) Mil: Officier m d'ordonnance.
aigrette ['eigret], s. Aigrette f.
aiguille ['eigwiː], s. Geog: Mount: Aiguille f, piton m (d'une montagne).
ail [eil], v.tr. (With indef. subject, esp. in interrog.) Faire souffrir (qn). O: What ails you? de quoi souffrez-vous? qu'est-ce que vous avez? **ailing**, a. Souffrant, malade, mal portant. She has been a. for a long time, elle souffre depuis longtemps. He is always a., il a une petite santé.
aileron ['eilərən], s. Av: Aileron m. A. roll, tonneau lent. A. turn, tonneau en descendant.
ailment ['eilmənt], s. Mal m; maladie (légère).
aim[1] [eim], s. 1. (a) Action f de viser. To miss one's a., (i) (with fire-arm) manquer le but, manquer son coup; (ii) frapper à faux. To take a. at s.o., viser, ajuster, qn; coucher qn en joue. Abs. To take a., mettre en joue. (b) But m. Missiles that fall short of their a., projectiles qui n'atteignent pas le but. 2. But, objet m, dessein m; visées fpl. He has one a. and object in life, sa vie n'a qu'un (seul) but. With the a. of doing sth., dans le dessein de faire qch.
aim[2]. 1. v.tr. (a) To a. a stone, a blow, at s.o., lancer une pierre, porter, allonger, un coup, à qn. (b) Viser. Artil: Pointer. To a. a gun, a pistol, at s.o., ajuster, viser, qn. Well-aimed fire, feu bien ajusté. He aimed his telescope at . . ., il braqua sa lunette sur. . . . (c) To a. one's remarks at s.o., parler à l'adresse de qn. Measures aimed against our trade, mesures dirigées contre notre commerce. 2. v.ind.tr. (a) To a. at s.o. (with a gun), ajuster, viser, qn; mettre, coucher, qn en joue. (b) To aim at becoming sth., aspirer, viser, à devenir qch. What are you aiming at? quel but poursuivez-vous? Decree that aims at altering . . ., arrêt qui vise à changer. . . . **aiming**, s. Visée f. Artil: Pointage m.
aimer ['eimə], s. Viseur, -euse. Av: Bomb-a., viseur de bombardement, de tir aérien.
aimless ['eimlis], a. Sans but, sans objet. An a. sort of life, une vie désœuvrée, qui ne mène à rien. -ly, adv. Sans but.
aimlessness ['eimlisnis], s. Manque m d'ambition. The a. of his remarks, l'inanité f de ses observations.
ain't [eint]. A. & P: = am not, is not, are not.
air[1] [ɛər], s. I. Air m. (a) Breath of a., souffle m (d'air). Fresh a., air frais. Foul a., air vicié. S.a. OPEN[1]. OPEN-AIR. The fowls of the a., les oiseaux des cieux. F: I can't live on a., je ne peux pas vivre de l'air du temps. To carry goods by a., transporter des marchandises par avion. Journey by a., voyage aérien, en avion. To throw sth. into the a., jeter qch. en l'air. F: To walk on a., ne pas se sentir de joie. There is something in the a., il se prépare, il se trame quelque

chose. **The idea was in the a.,** l'idée était dans l'air. **It's all in the a.** as yet, ce ne sont encore que de vagues projets, des projets en l'air. *Mil:* **Their left flank was in the a.,** le flanc gauche était en l'air, exposé. **All that money has vanished into thin a.,** tout cet argent a passé au bleu. (*b*) *Attrib.* **A. raid,** attaque aérienne. **A. representative,** représentant aérien. *Av:* **The Fleet A. Arm** = l'Aéronavale. **The Royal A. Force,** *U.S:* **the United States A. Force** = l'Armée *f.* de l'air, l'Aviation *f.* (*c*) *W. Tel: F:* **To be on a.,** parler à la radio. **His speech will be on the a.,** son discours sera radiodiffusé. II. **air.** *Mus:* Air. III. **air.** Air, mine *f,* apparence *f.* **There is an a.** of comfort everywhere, il y a partout une apparence, un air, de confort. *F:* **He has an a.** about him, il a beaucoup de cachet, de chic; il a du panache. **To carry it off with an a.,** y mettre du panache. **To give oneself airs, to put on airs,** se donner des airs; prendre de grands airs; faire des embarras; faire l'important, *F:* enfler le jabot. **To put on airs with s.o.,** traiter qn de haut. **'air-balloon,** *s.* (*Toy*) Ballon *m* à air. *Aer: etc:* Aérostat. **'air-base,** *s.* Base *f* d'aviation. **'air-bladder,** *s.* **1.** *Ich:* Vésicule aérienne; vessie *f* natatoire. **2.** *Algae:* Vésicule, aérocyste *f.* **'air-brake,** *s.* Frein *m* à air comprimé. **'air-bridge,** *s.* *Av:* Pont aérien; liaison aérienne. **'air-brush,** *s.* *Paint:* Aérographe *m;* pinceau *m* à air; pistolet *m* (vaporisateur). **'air-cell,** *s.* Vésicule (aérienne, pulmonaire). **'air-chamber,** *s.* **1.** Chambre *f* à air; (*of torpedo, etc.*) réservoir *m* d'air comprimé. **2.** Cloche *f* d'air (d'une pompe). **'air-channel,** *s.* Conduit *m* d'air; conduit à vent; *Min:* buse *f* d'aérage. **'Air-Chief-'Marshal,** *s.* *Av:* Général d'Armée aérienne. **Air-Commodore,** *s.* *Av:* Général de brigade aérienne. **'air-condition,** *v.tr.* Climatiser, conditionner. **'air-conditioned,** *a.* Climatisé, conditionné. **'air-conditioning,** *s.* Climatisation *f,* conditionnement *m* (de l'air). **'air-conditioner,** *s.* Conditionneur *m* d'air. **'air-conveyance,** *s.* Transport par air, par avion. **'air-cooled,** *a.* Refroidi par l'air; (moteur) à refroidissement par air. **'air-cooler,** *s.* Refroidisseur *m* d'air. **'air-cooling,** *s.* Refroidissement *m* par air. *Av:* **'air-cover,** *s.* Force de protection aérienne. **'air-cushion,** *s.* Coussin *m* à air, pneumatique. **'air-display,** *s.* Fête *f* aéronautique. **'air-drill,** *s.* *Tls:* Perforatrice *f* à air comprimé. **'air-duct,** *s.* **1.** Canal aérien (des poissons, etc.). **2.** *Ind: etc:* Porte-vent *m inv.* **'air-ferry,** *s.* Avion transbordeur. **'air-gun,** *s.* Carabine *f,* fusil *m,* à air comprimé. **'air-hole,** *s.* **1.** (*Ventilator*) Aspirail *m,* soupirail *m;* trou *m* d'évent; prise *f* d'air. **Air-holes of bellows,** venteaux *m* d'un soufflet. **2.** (*In metal*) Soufflure *f;* bulle *f* d'air; globule *m.* **'air-hostess,** *s.* *Av:* Hôtesse *f* de l'air. **'air-inlet, -intake,** *s.* Prise *f* d'air. **'air-letter,** *s.* Aérogramme *m.* **'air-lift,** *s.* Pont *m* aérien. **'air(-)line,** *s.* Service *m* de transports aériens, de transport par avion. **'air(-)liner,** *s.* Avion *m* de ligne. **'air-lock,** *s.* **1.** (*a*) *Civ.E:* Écluse *f,* sas *m* pneumatique, à air, clapet *m* à air (d'un caisson). (*b*) *Nau:* Sas (de la chaufferie). **2.** *Mch:* Poche *f* d'air, retenue d'air. **'air-mail,** *s.* Courrier *m* par avion; service postal aérien. **By air-mail,** par avion. *attrib.* **A.-m. letter,** aérogramme *f.* **'air-mail,** *v.tr.* Envoyer par avion. **Air-Marshal,** *s.* Général *m* de corps d'armée aérien. **'air-mattress,** *s.* matelas *m* pneumatique. **'air-mechanic,** *s.* Mécanicien d'avion. **'air-minded,** *a.* **To be a.-m.,** avoir le sens de l'air. **'air-passages,** *s.pl.* *Anat:* Voies *f* aérifères. **'air-pilot,** *s.m.* Pilote aviateur. **'air-pocket,** *s.* **1.** *Av:* Trou *m* d'air. **2.** *Hyd.E:* Poche *f* d'air (dans une canalisation). **'air-port,** *s.* *Nau:* Sabord *m* d'aérage; hublot *m.* **'air-pressure,** *s.* Pression *f* atmosphérique. **'air-pump,** *s.* Pompe *f* à air. *Ph:* Machine *f* pneumatique. **air-raid,** *s.* *Av:* attaque aérienne, bombardement *m.* **A.-r. precautions,** défense antiaérienne, défense passive. **'air-scoop,** *s.* *Aer:* Prise *f* d'air. **'air-screw,** *s.* *Av:* Hélice *f.* **'air-sea,** *a.* **A.-s. rescue,** sauvetage *m* aéro(-)maritime. **'air-shaft,** *s.* *Min:* Puits *m,* buse *f,* d'aérage. *Nau:* Manche *f* (à vent, à air). **air-show,** *s.* *Av:* (i) Meeting *m* d'aviation, (ii)

= AIR-DISPLAY. **'air-sock,** *s.* *Av:* Manche *f* à air. **'air-sickness,** *s.* Mal *m* de l'air, d'avion. **'air-speed,** *s.* Vitesse relative. **A.-s. indicator,** badin *m.* **'air-terminal,** *s.* *Av:* Aérogare *f.* **'air-tight,** *a.* (Récipient) à clôture hermétique, étanche (à l'air); (vêtement) imperméable à l'air. *Com:* **A.-t. container,** étouffoir *m.* **air-to-air,** *a.* Air-air. **A.-to-a. missile,** engin *m* air-air. **'air-to-'ground,** *a.* Air-sol. **A.-to-g. missile,** engin *m* air-sol. **'air-tube,** *s.* **1.** Tuyau *m* à air. **2.** Chambre *f* à air (d'un pneu). **'air-valve,** *s.* Soupape *f* à air; reniflard *m.* **'Air Vice-Marshal,** *s.* Général de division aérienne.

air², *v.tr.* **1.** (*a*) **To a. a room,** aérer, rafraîchir, une pièce; renouveler l'air d'une pièce. **To a. clothes (out of doors),** mettre des effets à l'air, au vent. **To a. linen, a bed,** chauffer, aérer, le linge; bassiner un lit; (*before the fire*) donner un coup de feu au linge. (*b*) **The question needs to be aired,** la question demande à être discutée. **To a. personal grievances,** exposer des griefs personnels. **2. To a. one's opinions, one's knowledge,** faire parade de ses opinions, de son savoir. **airing,** *s.* **1.** (*a*) Ventilation *f,* renouvellement *m* de l'air (d'une salle, etc.); aérage *m,* aération *f.* (*b*) Éventage *m* (de vêtements); exposition *f* à l'air. **A.-cupboard,** chauffe-linge *m.* **2.** (Petite) promenade. **To take an a.,** prendre l'air; faire un petit tour.

airborne ['ɛəbɔːn], *a.* Aéroporté. **A. troops,** troupes aéroportées. **A. radar,** radar d'avion.

aircraft ['ɛəkrɑːft], *s.* **1.** (*No pl.*) Navigation aérienne (en tant que science). **2.** (*inv. in pl.*) Avion *m.* **Carrier-borne a.,** aviation embarquée. **Rocket-propelled a.,** avion (à) fusée. **Nuclear a.,** avion à propulseur atomique. **Torpedo-carrying a.,** avion torpilleur. **Vertical take-off a.,** avion à décollage et atterrissage verticaux. **A. manufacturer,** avionneur *m.*

aircraftman, -men ['ɛəkrɑːftmən], *s.* *Av:* Soldat *m* (de l'Armée de l'air). **A. first-class,** soldat de première classe. **Leading a.,** caporal *m.*

aircraftwoman, -women ['ɛəkrɑːftˌwumən, -ˌwimen], *s.* Femme soldat de la W.R.A.F. **Leading a.,** femme caporal de la W.R.A.F.

aircrew ['ɛəkruː], *s.* *Av:* Équipage *m* d'avion.

airdrome ['ɛədroum], *s.* *U.S:* = AERODROME.

airfield ['ɛəfiːld], *s.* Champ *m,* terrain *m,* d'aviation.

airflow ['ɛəflou], *s.* *U.S: Aut:* **A. body,** carrosserie *f* aérodynamique.

airframe ['ɛəfreim], *s.* Cellule *f* d'avion.

airgraph ['ɛəgræf], *s.* *R.t.m:* Lettre *f* microphotographique.

airiness ['ɛərinis], *s.* **1.** (*a*) Situation aérée. (*b*) Bonne ventilation. **2.** Légèreté *f* (d'esprit); désinvolture *f.*

airless ['ɛəlis], *a.* **1.** Privé d'air; renfermé. **2.** (Temps) calme, tranquille, sans vent.

airman, -men ['ɛəmən], *s.m.* Aviateur.

airplane ['ɛəplein], *s.* *U.S:* = AEROPLANE.

airport ['ɛəpɔːt], *s.* *Av:* Aéroport *m.*

airship ['ɛəʃip], *s.* (Ballon) dirigeable *m.*

airstrip ['ɛəstrip], *s.* *Av:* **1.** Terrain *m* d'atterrissage. **Emergency a.,** terrain *m* de secours. **2.** Secteur *m* de reconnaissances aériennes, d'observation aérienne.

airway ['ɛəwei], *s.* *Av:* (*a*) Aéroroute *f.* (*b*) Radio-alignement *m.* **Airways navigation, flying airways,** radiobalisage *m.* **To fly airways,** radiobaliser.

airwoman, -women ['ɛəwumən, -wimen], *s.f.* Aviatrice.

airworthiness ['ɛəˌwɔːðinis], *s.* Tenue *f* en l'air, navigabilité *f* (d'un avion.).

airworthy ['ɛəˌwɔːði], *a.* *Aer:* Muni d'un certificat de navigabilité.

airy ['ɛəri], *a.* **1.** Bien aéré; ouvert à l'air. **2.** *Poet:* Élevé, aérien. **3.** (*Of material, etc.*) Léger, ténu. **4.** (*a*) (*Of conduct, etc.*) Léger, insouciant, désinvolte, dégagé. (*b*) **A. promises,** promesses vaines; promesses en l'air. **-ily,** *adv.* Légèrement; avec désinvolture. **'airy-'fairy,** *a.* Impraticable, infaisable.

aisle [ail], *s.* **1.** *Ecc. Arch:* Nef latérale; bas-côté *m.* **The bride walked up the a.,** la mariée remonta l'allée centrale. **2.** Passage *m* (entre bancs).

aitch [eitʃ], *s.* (La lettre) h *m.* **To drop one's aitches, ne pas aspirer les h,** ou les aspirer mal à propos (indice d'un niveau social peu élevé).

aitchbone ['eitʃboun], *s.* Culotte *f* (de bœuf).

ajar [ə'dʒɑːr], *adv. & pred. a.* (*Of door*) Entrebâillé, entrouvert.

akimbo [ə'kimbou], *adv.* With arms a., les (deux) poings sur les hanches.
akin [ə'kin], *adv. & pred. a.* 1. A. to s.o., parent de qn; apparenté à, avec, qn. 2. To be a. to sth., ressembler à qch.; avoir des rapports avec qch. Passion a. to love, passion qui tient de l'amour. Trades closely a., métiers connexes.
alabaster [ælə'bɑːstər], *s.* Albâtre *m.*
alacrity [ə'lækriti], *s.* Empressement *m*, alacrité *f.*
alarm¹ [ə'lɑːm], *s.* 1. Alarme *f*, alerte *f.* To raise the a., donner l'éveil. To give the a. to s.o., donner l'alarme, l'alerte, à qn; alerter qn. To sound the a., sonner le tocsin, l'alarme, l'appel aux armes. **Alarms and excursions**, (i) *Th:* A: alertes et échauffourées *fpl*; (ii) alertes; remue-ménage *m.* To take (the) a., prendre l'alarme; s'alarmer. False a., fausse alerte. 2. (*a*) Avertisseur *m*, signal *m.* *Mch:* Low-water a., sifflet-avertisseur *m* de bas niveau. (*b*) = ALARM-CLOCK. **a'larm-bell**, *s.* (*a*) Tocsin *m*; cloche *f* d'alarme. (*b*) Timbre avertisseur; sonnerie *f* d'alarme. **a'larm-clock**, *s.* Réveille-matin *m inv.*; réveil *m.* **a'larm-gun**, *s.* Canon *m* d'alarme. **a'larm-signal**, *s.* Signal *m* d'alarme. **a'larm-thermometer**, *s.* Thermo-avertisseur *m.*
alarm², *v.tr.* 1. (*a*) Alarmer, donner l'alarme à (qn). (*b*) Alerter (des troupes). 2. (*Frighten*) Alarmer, effrayer. To be alarmed at sth., s'alarmer, s'émouvoir, de qch. **alarming**, *a.* Alarmant; angoissant. **-ly**, *adv.* D'une manière alarmante.
alarmist [ə'lɑːmist], *s.* Alarmiste *mf*, *F:* paniquard *m.*
alarum [ə'lɛərəm, ə'lærəm], *s.* 1. A: = ALARM¹ 1. *Esp. Th:* A: Alerte *f.* 2. O: Réveille-matin *m inv.*
alas [ə'lɑːs], *int.* Hélas!
alb [ælb], *s.* *Ecc.Cost:* Aube *f.*
Albania [æl'beinjə]. *Pr.n. Geog:* L'Albanie *f.*
Albanian [æl'beinjən], *a. & s.* Albanais, -aise.
albatross [ˈælbətrɔs], *s.* Albatros *m.*
albeit [ɔːl'biːit], *conj. Lit:* Quoique, bien que, + *sub.*
Albert [ˈælbət]. 1. *Pr.n.m.* Albert. 2. *s.* *A.Cost:* A. (chain), chaîne (de montre) giletière à gros maillons.
Albigenses [ælbi'dʒensiːz], *s.pl.* *Hist:* Albigeois *m.*
albinism [ˈælbinizm], *s.* *Med:* Albinisme *m.*
albino, *pl.* -os [æl'biːnou, -ouz]. 1. *s.* Albinos *mf.* 2. *a.* A. negro, nègre blanc. A. rabbit, lapin *m* russe.
album [ˈælbəm], *s.* Album *m.* Loose-leaf a., album à feuilles mobiles.
albumen [ˈælbjumin], *s.* 1. Albumen *m*; blanc d'œuf. 2. Albumine *f* (du sang). 3. *Bot:* Albumen (de l'embryon).
albumin [ˈælbjumin, æl'bjuːmin], *s.* *Biol: Ch:* Albumine *f.*
alchemist [ˈælkimist], *s.m.* Alchimiste *m.*
alchemy [ˈælkimi], *s.* Alchimie *f.*
alcohol [ˈælkəhɔl], *s.* Alcool *m.* Pure a., alcool absolu. Denatured a., alcool dénaturé. Ethyl a., alcool éthylique.
alcoholic [ælkə'hɔlik]. 1. *a.* Alcoolique. 2. *s.* (*Pers.*) Alcoolique *mf.*
alcoholism [ˈælkəhɔlizm], *s.* *Med:* Alcoolisme *m.*
alcoholization [ælkəhɔlai'zeiʃ(ə)n], *s.* Alcoolisation *f.*
alcoholize [ˈælkəhɔ'laiz], *v.tr.* Alcooliser.
alcoholometer [ˈælkəhɔ'lɔmitər], *s.* Alcoolomètre *m*, alcoomètre *m*; pèse-liqueur *m*; *pl.* pèse-liqueurs.
Alcoran [ælkə'rɑːn], *s.* = KORAN.
alcove [ˈælkouv], *s.* 1. Alcôve *f* (de chambre). 2. Niche *f*, enfoncement *m* (dans un mur).
aldehyde [ˈældihaid], *s.* *Ch:* Aldéhyde *f.*
alder [ˈɔːldər], *s.* *Bot:* 1. Au(l)ne *m.* 2. Black a., a. buckthorn, bourdaine *f*, frangule *f.*
alderman, **-men** [ˈɔːldəmən], *s.m.* Conseiller(municipal).
Alderney [ˈɔːldəni]. *Pr.n. Geog:* Aurigny *m.*
ale [eil], *s.* 1. Bière anglaise (légère); ale *f.* Pale a., bière blonde; pale-ale *m.* *S.a.* ADAM. 2. *See* GINGER-ALE. **'ale-house**, *s.* A: Cabaret *m.* **ale-wife**, *s.f.* A: Cabaretière.
aleatory [ˈeiliət(ə)ri], *a.* (Contrat, etc.) aléatoire.
Alec(k) [ˈælik]. *Pr.n.m.* Alexandre. *F:* A smart A., un finaud; *F:* un combinard.
alee [ə'liː], *adv. Nau:* Sous le vent. To put the helm a., mettre la barre dessous.
alembic [ə'lembik], *s.* Alambic *m.*
Aleppo [ə'lepou]. *Pr.n. Geog:* Alep *Med:* A. boil, ulcer, bouton *m* d'Alep, ulcère *m* d'Orient.

alert¹ [ə'ləːt]. 1. *a.* (*a*) Alerte, vigilant, éveillé. (*b*) Actif, vif, preste. 2. *s.* Alerte *f.* To be on the a., être sur le qui-vive, être en alerte. To keep s.o. on the a., tenir qn en éveil. **-ly**, *adv.* D'une manière alerte; prestement.
alert², *v.tr.* Alerter.
alertness [ə'ləːtnis], *s.* 1. (*a*) Vigilance *f.* (*b*) Promptitude *f.* 2. Vivacité *f*, prestesse *f.*
Alexander [ælig'zɑːndər]. *Pr.n.m.* Alexandre.
Alexandria [ælig'zɑːndriə]. *Pr.n. Geog:* Alexandrie.
Alexandrian [ælig'zɑːndriən], *a.* Alexandrin.
Alexandrine [ælig'zɑːndrain], *a. & s.* *Pros:* Alexandrin (*m*).
alfa(-grass) [ˈælfə(grɑːs)], *s.* *Bot:* Alfa *m.*
alfalfa [æl'fælfə], *s.* *Bot:* Luzerne *f.*
alfresco [æl'freskou], *a. & adv.* En plein air.
alga, *pl.* -ae [ˈælgə, ˈældʒiː], *s.* *Bot:* Algue *f.*
algebra [ˈældʒibrə], *s.* Algèbre *f.*
algebraic(al) [ældʒi'breiik(l)], *a.* Algébrique. **-ally**, *adv.* Algébriquement.
algebr(a)ist [ˈældʒibr(ei)ist], *s.* Algébriste *m.*
Algeria [æl'dʒiəriə]. *Pr.n. Geog:* L'Algérie *f.*
Algerian [æl'dʒiəriən], *a. & s.* 1. (*Of Algeria*) Algérien, -ienne. 2. (*Of Algiers*) Algérois.
Algiers [æl'dʒiəz]. *Pr.n. Geog:* Alger.
alias [ˈeiliæs]. 1. *adv.* Autrement dit, autrement nommé, alias. 2. *s.* (*pl.* **aliases** [ˈeiliəsiz]) Nom d'emprunt, faux nom.
alibi [ˈælibai], *s.* Alibi *m.* To plead an a., plaider l'alibi. To produce an a., fournir un alibi. To establish an a., prouver son alibi.
alien [ˈeiliən]. 1. *a. & s.* Étranger (non naturalisé). 2. *a.* A. from sth., étranger à qch., éloigné de qch. A. to sth., contraire, opposé, à qch.; qui répugne à qch.
alienability [eiliənə'biliti], *s.* *Jur:* Aliénabilité *f*, mutabilité *f* (d'une terre, etc.).
alienable [ˈeiliənəbl], *a.* *Jur:* (Bien) aliénable, mutable.
alienate [ˈeiliəneit], *v.tr.* 1. *Jur:* Aliéner (des biens, etc.). 2. Détacher, éloigner, (s')aliéner (qn).
alienation [eiliə'neiʃ(ə)n], *s.* 1. *Jur:* Aliénation *f* (de biens). 2. Aliénation (de cœurs); désaffection *f.* 3. Mental a., aliénation (mentale); égarement *m* d'esprit.
alienator [ˈeiliəneitər], *s.* *Jur:* Aliénateur, -trice.
alienee [ˈeiliə'niː], *s.* *Jur:* Aliénataire *mf.*
alienism [ˈeiliənizm], *s.* 1. Qualité *f* d'étranger. *Med:* Aliénisme *m.*
alienist [ˈeiliənist], *s.* (Médecin) aliéniste *m.*
alight¹ [ə'lait], *v.i.* Descendre. 1. To a. from horseback, descendre de cheval; mettre pied à terre. 2. (*a*) (*Of birds*) S'abattre, se poser. (*b*) *Av:* Atterrir; (*on sea*) amerrir, amérir. **alighting**, *s.* *Av:* Atterrissage *m*; amerrissage *m*, amérissage *m.*
alight², *pred. a.* Allumé; en feu. To catch a., s'allumer; prendre feu. To set sth. a., mettre le feu à qch.
align [ə'lain]. 1. *v.tr.* Aligner (des soldats, etc.); mettre (des objets) en ligne. 2. *v.i.* S'aligner; se mettre en ligne.
alignment [ə'lainmənt], *s.* Alignement *m.* Out of a., désaligné; *Typ:* (ligne) sortante.
alike [ə'laik]. 1. *pred. a.* Semblable, pareil, ressemblant. You are all a.! vous vous ressemblez tous! vous êtes tous pareils! All things are a. to him, tout lui est égal, indifférent. 2. *adv.* Pareillement; de même; de la même manière; également. Dressed a., habillés de même. Summer and winter a., été comme hiver.
aliment¹ [ˈælimənt], *s.* Aliment *m.*
aliment² [ˈæliment], *v.tr.* Alimenter; nourrir.
alimentary [æli'mentəri], *a.* Alimentaire. *Anat:* A. canal, tube digestif.
alimentation [ælimen'teiʃ(ə)n], *s.* Alimentation *f.*
alimony [ˈæliməni], *s.* *Jur:* Pension *f* alimentaire.
aliquot [ˈælikwɔt], *a. & s.* *Mth:* A. (part), (partie *f*) aliquote (*f*).
alive [ə'laiv], *a.* (*Always pred. unless modified by an adv. Cf.* DEAD-ALIVE) 1. (*a*) (*Of pers.*) To be (still) a., être (encore) vivant, en vie; vivre (encore). If he is still a., s'il est encore de ce monde. To keep s.o. a., maintenir qn en vie. To be burnt, buried, a., être brûlé, enterré, vif. It's good to be a.! il fait bon vivre! Dead or a., mort ou vif. Misjudged while a., méconnu de son vivant. The best man a., le meilleur homme du monde. He will do it better than any man a., il le fera mieux que personne. *O: F:* Man a.,

par exemple! (b) (Of thg) To keep a memory a., garder, entretenir un souvenir. To keep the conversation a., entretenir la conversation. 2. To be a. to an impression, ressentir une impression. To be fully a. to the danger, avoir pleinement conscience du danger. To be a. to the importance of . . ., se rendre compte de l'importance de. . . . I am a. to the fact that . ., je n'ignore pas que. . . . 3. He is very much a., (i) il est très remuant; (ii) il a l'esprit très éveillé. Look a.! remuez-vous (donc)! dépêchez-vous! 4. The cheese was a. with worms, le fromage grouillait de vers. The heath is a. with game, la lande foisonne de gibier. The street was a. with people, la rue fourmillait de monde. 5. El.E: (Fil, etc.) sous tension.

alkalescence [ælkə′lesəns], s. Ch: Alcalescence f.

alkalescent [ælkə′lesənt], a. Ch: Alcalescent.

alkali [′ælkəlai], s. Ch: Alcali m.

alkaline [′ælkəlain], a. Ch: Alcalin.

alkaloid [′ælkələid], a. & s. Alcaloïde (m). Ch: To test for alkaloids, faire la réaction des alcaloïdes.

all [ɔ:l]. I. a., pron., & adv. 1. Tout, tous. (a) (With noun or pronoun expressed) A. France, toute la France. A. day, (pendant) toute la journée. A. men, tous les hommes. A. the others, tous les autres. Try to be a. things to a. men, tâchez d'être tout à tous. A. his life, toute sa vie. A. the way, tout le long du chemin. Is that a. the luggage you are taking? c'est tout ce que vous emportez de bagages? For a. his wealth . . ., en dépit de, malgré, sa fortune. . . . With a. speed, au plus vite, à toute vitesse. At a. hours, à toute heure. You are not as ill as a. that, vous n'êtes pas malade à ce point-là; vous n'êtes pas (aus)si malade que ça. (b) Almost a., presque tous. A. of us, nous tous; tous tant que nous sommes. A. together, tous, toutes, à la fois, ensemble. A. whom I saw, tous ceux, toutes celles, que j'ai vu(e)s. (c) We a. love him, nous l'aimons tous. I know it a., (i) je sais tout cela; (ii) (of poem, etc.) je le sais par entier. Take it a., prenez le tout. Games: We're five a., nous sommes cinq à cinq. Ten: Four a., quatre jeux partout. Fifteen a., quinze a, quinze A. (d) neut. Almost a., presque tout. A. is lost, tout est perdu. A. (that) I did, tout ce que j'ai fait. For a. he may say, en dépit de ses dires; quoi qu'il en dise. That's a., c'est tout, voilà tout. Is that a.? (i) est-ce tout? (ii) Iron: n'est-ce que cela? la belle affaire! If that is a. (the difficulty), s'il ne tient qu'à cela. All's well, tout va bien. S.a. WELL³ II. 2. When a. is said and done, somme toute; quand tout est dit. 2. (a) Once for a., une fois pour toutes. For a. I know, autant que je sache. For a. I care, pour (tout) ce que cela me fait. S.a. FOR¹ I. 9. Thirty men in a., trente hommes en tout. (b) Most of a., surtout; le plus. (The) best of a. would be to . . ., le mieux serait de. . . . S.a. FIRST III. 1. (c) At a. (i) Did you speak at a.? avez-vous dit quoi que ce soit? Do you know him at a.? le connaissez-vous aucunement? Not at a., pas du tout; F: du tout! Nothing at a., rien du tout. I don't know at a., je n'en sais rien (du tout). (ii) If he comes at a., si tant est qu'il vienne. If you hesitate at a. . . ., pour peu que vous hésitiez. . . . If you are at a. anxious, si vous êtes tant soit peu inquiet. If there is any wind at a., s'il y a le moindre vent. (d) A. but, A. but impossible, presque impossible. I a. but fell, j'ai failli tomber. He a. but embraced me, c'est tout juste s'il ne m'embrassa pas. (e) A. in a. Taking it, take it, a. in a., à tout prendre. They were a. in a. to each other, ils étaient dévoués l'un à l'autre. He imagines that he is a. in a. to the business, il s'imagine qu'il est indispensable. (f) F: And a., et (tout) le reste. (g) P: Damn a., que dalle. I've done damn a. today, je n'ai fichu que dalle aujourd'hui. 3. adv. Tout. He is, she is, a. alone, il est tout seul, elle est toute seule. To be (dressed) a. in black, être habillé tout en noir, tout de noir. His hands were a. tar, ses mains étaient couvertes de goudron. She is a. ears, a. impatience, elle est tout oreilles, tout impatience. He is not a. bad, il n'est pas entièrement mauvais. A. the better, a. the worse (for me), tant mieux, tant pis (pour moi). You will be a. the better for it, vous vous en trouverez (d'autant) mieux. The hour came a. too soon, l'heure n'arriva que trop tôt. A. at once, (i) (suddenly) tout à coup, subitement; (ii)

(at one time) tout d'un coup, tous à la fois. F: He's not a. there, il est un peu simple d'esprit. II. all, s. Tout m, totalité f. My a., mon tout; tout mon avoir. We must stake our a., il faut risquer le tout pour le tout. To lose one's a., perdre son pécule, tout son petit avoir. 'all-'clear, s. (Signal m de) fin f d'alerte. 'All 'Fools' Day, s. Le premier avril. 'All 'Hallows' (Day), s. (Le jour de) la Toussaint. all-im′portant, a. De la plus haute importance; de toute importance. 'all-in, a. 1. El: A.-i. agreement, police mixte (force et lumière). Ins: A.-i. policy, police tous risques. Com: A.-i. price, prix inclusif, exempt de tout supplément, prix tout compris. 2. Sp: A.-i. wrestling, catch m. 'all-'mains, a. El: W.Tel: etc: Tous courants. 'all-'night, a. (Veillée, etc.) de la nuit entière. A.-n. service, permanence de nuit. Mil: etc: A.-n. pass, permission de la nuit. 'all-'out, a. A.-o. effort, effort m maximum, à outrance. 'all-'powerful, a. Tout-puissant, toute-puissante. 'all-'purpose, a. Répondant à tous les besoins; universel; à tout faire. 'all-'round, a. F: (Athlète, etc.) complet. An a.-r. man, un homme universel. A.-r. improvement, amélioration totale, sur toute la ligne. all-'rounder, s. F: Homme universel. 'All 'Saints' Day, s. (Le jour de) la Toussaint. 'All 'Souls' Day, s. Le jour, la fête, des Morts. 'all-'star, a. Th: A.-s. performance, (pièce) jouée exclusivement par des vedettes. 'all-time a. Sans précédent, inouï, jamais atteint auparavant. A.-t. low, record m de médiocrité. A.-t. high, record le plus élevé. 'all-up, a. Av: A.-u. weight, poids m global en vol. 'all-weather, a. De toute saison.

allay [ə′lei], v.tr. (a) Apaiser, calmer (une tempête, une colère); tempérer, modérer (l'ardeur). (b) Apaiser (une querelle); calmer (la frayeur); endormir, dissiper (les soupçons). (c) Alléger, soulager, calmer, amortir, assoupir (la douleur); apaiser (la soif, la faim). **allaying**, s. Apaisement m, soulagement m.

allegation [ˌæli′geif(ə)n], s. Allégation f.

allege [ə′ledʒ], v.tr. 1. Alléguer, prétendre (that, que + ind.). To a. an urgent appointment, prétexter un rendez-vous urgent. He was alleged to be dead, on le prétendait mort, on le disait mort. To allege sth. against s.o., objecter qch. à qn. 2. Plaider, citer (un exemple). **alleged**, a. A. reason, raison alléguée. The a. thief, le voleur présumé.

allegiance [ə′li:dʒ(ə)ns], s. 1. Fidélité f, obéissance f (to, à). Profession of a., soumission f. To own a. to a party, être inféodé à un parti. To cast off one's a. to a party, se détacher d'un parti. 2. To take the oath of a., prêter serment d'allégeance.

allegoric(al) [ˌæli′gɔrik(ə)l], a. Allégorique. -ally, adv. Allégoriquement; par allégorie.

allegorist [′æligərist], s. Allégoriste m.

allegorize [′ælegəraiz], v.tr. & i. Allégoriser.

allegory [′æligəri], s. Allégorie f.

allergen [′ælədʒin], s. Med: Allergène m.

allergic [ə′lə:dʒik], a. Med: Allergique. F: I am a. to fish, je suis allergique au poisson, le poisson ne me convient pas, ne me réussit pas. Med: A. infection, allergide f.

allergy [′ælədʒi], s. Med: Allergie f.

alleviate [ə′li:vieit], v.tr. Alléger, soulager (la douleur); adoucir (le chagrin); apaiser (la soif). **alleviative**, a. & s. Adoucissant (m), calmant (m); Med: anodin (m).

alleviation [əˌli:vi′eif(ə)n], s. Allègement m (de la douleur); soulagement m, adoucissement m.

alley [′æli], s. (a) (In garden) Allée f; (in town) ruelle f, passage m. S.a. BLIND¹ 3. (b) See BOWLING-ALLEY, SKITTLE 2. **'alley-way**, s. 1. Ruelle f. 2. N.Arch: Coursive f.

alliance [ə′laiəns], s. 1. Alliance f. To enter into an a., s'allier (with, avec). 2. A. by marriage, alliance; apparentage m.

allied [′ælaid], a. 1. Allié (to, with, à, avec). The A. Powers, les puissances alliées. The a. nations, les nations coalisées. 2. Biol: Med: De la même famille, du même ordre; de la même nature. Closely a. industries, industries connexes.

alligator [′æligeitər], s. 1. Rept: Caïman; alligator m. 2. Bot: A. pear, (poire f d') avocat m.

alliterate [ə′litəreit], v.i. Allitérer.

alliteration [ə,litə'reiʃ(ə)n], s. Allitération f.

alliterative [ə'litəreitiv], a. Allitératif.

allocate ['ælokeit], v.tr. (a) Allouer, assigner (qch. à qn, à qch.). (b) To a. a sum amongst several people, répartir une somme entre plusieurs personnes. To a. duties, attribuer des fonctions (to, à).

allocatee [ələkə'ti:], s. Adm: Allocataire mf.

allocation [,ælo'keiʃ(ə)n], s. 1. Allocation f, affectation f (d'une somme). (b) Répartition f (de dépenses); attribution f (de fonctions). (c) A. of contract, adjudication f. 2. Part ou somme assignée.

allocution [,ælo'kju:ʃ(ə)n], s. Allocution f.

allopath ['ælopæθ], s. Med: Allopathe mf.

allopathic [,ælo'pæθik], a. Med: Allopathique.

allopathy [ə'lɔpəθi], s. Med: Allopathie f.

allot [ə'lɔt], v.tr. (allotted) 1. To a. sth. to s.o., attribuer, assigner, qch. à qn. To a. sth. to, for, an object, affecter, destiner, qch. à un but. Mil: To a. a portion of one's pay to a relative, faire une délégation de solde à un parent. 2. Répartir, distribuer (des fonctions, des sièges, Fin: des actions).

allotment [ə'lɔtmənt], s. 1. (a) Attribution f (de qch. à qn); affectation f (d'une somme à un but). Mil: Navy: A. of pay (to wife, etc.), délégation f de solde (à une épouse, etc.). (b) Partage m, répartition f; distribution f; lotissement m. A. of time, emploi m du temps. 2. (a) Portion f, part f, lot m. (b) Lopin m de terre. Allotments, jardins ouvriers.

allotropy [ə'lɔtrəpi], s. Ch: Allotropie f.

allottee [,ælɔ'ti:], s. Fin: Attributaire mf.

allow [ə'lau], v.tr. 1. (a) Admettre. To a. sth. to be true, admettre, reconnaître, qch. pour vrai. (b) To a. a request, a claim, faire droit à une demande, à une réclamation; admettre une requête. 2. (a) (Permit) Permettre, souffrir, tolérer, admettre (qch.). To a. s.o. sth., permettre qch. à qn. To a. s.o. to do sth., permettre à qn de faire qch. A. me to tell you the truth, souffrez que je vous dise la vérité. Circumstances will not a. it, les circonstances s'y opposent. A. me! permettez(-moi)! The law allows you twenty days' grace, la loi vous impartit, vous accorde, un délai de vingt jours. To a. an item of expenditure, allouer une dépense. (b) To a. sth. to be lost, laisser perdre qch. To a. oneself to be led, to be deceived, se laisser mener, se laisser tromper. (c) ind.tr. (Of thg) Tone which allowed of no reply, ton qui n'admettait pas de réplique. The matter allows of no delay, l'affaire ne souffre pas de retard. His condition would not a. him to go out, son état ne lui permettait pas de sortir. 3. (a) To a. s.o. £100 a year, faire, accorder, allouer, à qn une rente de £100. To a. a debtor time to pay, accorder un délai à un débiteur. (b) Com: Fin: To a. s.o. a discount, consentir, accorder, faire, une remise à qn. (c) ind.tr. To a. for sth., tenir compte de qch.; faire la part de qch.; avoir égard à qch. After allowing for . . ., déduction faite de. . . . To a. for readjustments, prévoir des rectifications. To a. so much for carriage, (i) ajouter tant pour le port; (ii) déduire tant pour le port. Allowing for the circumstances . . ., eu égard aux circonstances. . . .

allowable [ə'lauəbl], a. Admissible, admis, légitime.

allowance [ə'lauəns], s. 1. (a) Tolérance f (d'un abus, etc.). (b) Jur: A. of items in an account, allocation f des articles dans un compte. 2. (a) Pension f alimentaire; rente f; argent m de poche (pour un enfant). (b) Adm: Jur: Allocation; prestation f; dégrèvement m (pour charges de famille, etc.). (c) Mil: Navy: etc: Field-a., indemnité f de campagne. Mess a., indemnité de table. Acting a., indemnité de fonctions. Marriage a., indemnité d'homme marié. Adm: Office a., frais mpl de bureau. Travelling a., frais de route, de voyage; indemnité de déplacement. Adm: Family allowances, allocations familiales. (d) (Of food, etc.) Ration f. To put s.o. on (short) a., mettre qn à la ration; rationner qn. 3. Com: Remise f, rabais m, déduction f, concession f. 4. (a) Mec.E: etc: Tolérance f. Num: Tolérance; faiblage m. (b) To make allowance(s) for sth., tenir compte de, faire la part de, avoir égard à, qch.

allowedly [ə'lauidli], adv. De l'aveu de tous; de l'aveu général.

alloy¹ ['æloi], s. Alliage m. Lit: [ə'lɔi] Happiness without a., bonheur sans mélange.

alloy² [ə'lɔi], v.tr. Allier (l'or avec l'argent, etc.). Nothing happened to a. our happiness, rien ne vint altérer, diminuer, notre bonheur.

allspice ['ɔ:lspais], s. Bot: Cu: Poivre m de Jamaïque; toute-épice f.

allude [ə'l(j)u:d], v.ind.tr. To a. to sth., to s.o., (of pers.) faire allusion à qch., à qn; (of phrase) avoir trait à, se rapporter à, qch., qn.

allure [ə'l(j)uər], v.tr. 1. O: To a. s.o. to(wards) oneself, (in)to a party, attirer qn à, vers, soi; à, dans, un parti. 2. Attirer, allécher, séduire. alluring, a. Attrayant, alléchant, séduisant. -ly, adv. D'une manière attrayante, séduisante.

allurement [ə'l(j)uəmənt], s. Attrait m; appât m, amorce f; allèchement m, séduction f.

allusion [ə'l(j)u:ʒ(ə)n], s. Allusion f.

allusive [ə'l(j)u:siv], a. (Style, etc.) allusif, plein d'allusions. -ly, adv. Par (voie d')allusion(s).

alluvial [ə'l(j)u:viəl], a. Geol: (Terrain) alluvial, d'alluvion; (gîte) alluvien, alluvionnaire.

alluvion [ə'l(j)u:vian], s. Alluvion f.

alluvium, pl. -ia [ə'l(j)u:viəm, -iə], s. Geol: (a) Alluvion f. (b) pl. Terrains alluviaux, terres f d'alluvion.

ally¹ [æ'lai], s. Allié, -e, coallié, -e. To become allies, s'allier (ensemble); se coaliser.

ally² [ə'lai]. 1. v.tr. Allier (qn, qch.) (to, with, à, avec). To a. by marriage, apparenter (deux familles, etc.). 2. v.i. S'allier (to, with, à, avec).

Alma Mater ['ælmə'meitər], s. L'université f, le collège, où l'on a fait ses études; alma mater f.

almanac ['ɔ:lmənæk], s. 1. Almanach m. 2. Annuaire m.

almightiness [ɔ:l'maitinis], s. Toute-puissance f, omnipotence f.

almighty [ɔ:l'maiti], a. & s. 1. Tout-puissant, omnipotent. The A., le Tout-Puissant, le Très-Haut. 2. F: They're making an a. row, ils font un bruit de tous les diables.

almond ['a:mənd], s. 1. Amande f. Sweet a., amande douce. Burnt almonds, amandes grillées; pralines f. Shelled almonds, amandes décortiquées. Ground almonds, amandes pilées. A.(-shaped) eyes, yeux (taillés) en amande. S.a. SUGAR-ALMOND. 2. A. (-tree), amandier m. 'almond-'eyed, a. Aux yeux en amande. 'almond-'oil, s. Huile f d'amande. Sweet-a. oil, huile d'amandes douces. 'almond-'paste, s. Cu: Pâte f d'amandes.

almoner ['a:mənər], s. Aumônier m. A: Assistante sociale.

almonry ['a:mənri], s. Aumônerie f.

almost ['ɔ:lmoust], adv. Presque; à peu près; quasi. A. always, presque toujours. It is a. noon, il est près de midi, bientôt midi. He a. fell, peu s'en fallut qu'il ne tombât; il faillit tomber. He is a. the master here, il est quasi, quasiment, le maître ici.

alms [a:mz], s.sg. or pl. Aumône f. To give a. to s.o., donner, faire, l'aumône à qn; faire la charité à qn. 'alms-box, s. Tronc m pour les pauvres. 'alms-giving, s. L'aumône f. 'alms-house, s. Maison f de retraite pour les vieillards.

aloe ['ælou], s. 1. Bot: Aloès m. 2. pl. (Usu. with sg. constr.) Pharm: Aloes ['ælouz], aloès. Bitter aloes, amer m d'aloès.

aloft [ə'lɔft], adv. Nau: En haut (dans la mâture). A. there! ohé de la hune! Away a.! en haut les gabiers!

alone [ə'loun], pred. a. 1. Seul. He lives (all) a., il demeure (tout) seul. An expert a. could advise us, seul un expert pourrait nous conseiller. I did it a., je l'ai fait à moi seul. London a. has a population equal to . . ., Londres à lui seul a une population égale à. . . . To believe s.o. on his word a., croire qn sur (sa) simple parole. I want to speak to you a., je voudrais vous parler seul à seul. His silence a. is sufficient proof against him, rien que son silence le condamne. With that charm which is his a., avec ce charme qui lui est propre, qui n'appartient qu'à lui. 2. (a) To let, leave, s.o., sth., a., (i) laisser qn tranquille, en paix; (ii) laisser qn faire; (iii) ne pas se mêler de qch. Your work is all right, leave it a., votre travail est bien, n'y retouchez pas. Prov: Let well a., le mieux est (souvent) l'ennemi du bien. (b) Let a. . . ., sans parler de . . ., sans compter. . . .

along [ə'lɔŋ]. **1.** *prep.* Le long de. (*a*) **To walk a. the shore**, longer la plage, se promener (tout) le long de la plage. **To go a. a street**, suivre une rue; passer par une rue. **To sail a. the land, the coast**, serrer la terre; longer, suivre, la côte. **To creep a. the wall**, se faufiler le long du mur. (*b*) **Trees a. the river**, arbres qui bordent la rivière, sur le bord de la rivière. **2.** *adv.* (*Often expletive, with a general implication of progress*) (*a*) **To move a.**, avancer. **To walk, stride, a.**, avancer à grandes enjambées; *F:* arpenter le terrain. **Come a. with me**, venez(-vous-en) avec moi. **Come a.!** arrivez donc! venez donc! *P:* **Get a. with you!** allez, ouste! (ii) (= je n'en crois rien) allons donc! (*b*) **I knew that all a.**, je le savais dès, depuis, le commencement. (*c*) *F:* **A. with**, avec.

alongshore [ə'lɔŋ'ʃɔ:r], *adv.* Le long de la côte. **To sail a.**, longer la terre.

alongside [ə'lɔŋsaid], *adv. & prep. Nau:* Accosté (le long de . . .). **To make a boat fast (close) a. a ship**, amarrer (un canot) le long du bord. **To come a.** (a ship), **a. of a ship**, accoster, aborder (un navire). **Come a.!** accostez! **A. the quay**, le long du quai, bord à quai. **To come a. (the quay)**, aborder à quai. **The car drew up a. the kerb**, la voiture s'est arrêtée le long du trottoir.

aloof [ə'lu:f], *adv. & pred. a.* **1.** *Nau:* Au large et au vent. **Keep a.!** passez au large! **2. To keep, hold, a. (from sth.)**, se tenir (visiblement) à l'écart, à distance, éloigné (de qch.); s'abstraire (de qch.). **To stand a. from a cause**, se tenir en dehors d'une cause. **To hold, stand, a.**, s'abstenir (lorsqu'il s'agit de faire qch.). **He kept very much a.**, il s'est montré très distant.

aloofness [ə'lu:fnis], *s.* Attitude distante; désintéressement *m*, réserve *f* (from, à l'égard de).

alopecia [ælo'pi:ʃə], *s. Med:* Alopécie *f*.

aloud [ə'laud], *adv.* A haute voix; (tout) haut. **Half a.**, entre haut et bas.

alp [ælp], *s.* Alpe *f*; pâturage *m* de montagne. *Geog:* **The Alps**, les Alpes.

alpaca [æl'pækə], *s.* **1.** *Z:* Alpaca *m*. **2.** *Tex:* Alpaga *m*.

alpenstock ['ælpinstɔk], *s.* Alpenstock *m*; bâton ferré.

alpha ['ælfə], *s. Gr.Alph:* Alpha *m*. *Ph:* **A. particle**, particule *f* alpha. **A. rays**, rayons *m* alpha.

alphabet ['ælfəbit], *s.* Alphabet *m*, abc *m inv.*

alphabetical [ælfə'betik(ə)l], *a.* Alphabétique. **-ally**, *adv.* Alphabétiquement; par ordre alphabétique.

alpine ['ælpain], *a.* (Club, chasseur) alpin; (site, paysage, climat) alpestre. *Geog:* **A. range**, chaîne de montagnes alpines. **A. pasture**, alpage *m.* **A. climbing**, alpinisme *m. Bot:* **A. plants**, plantes alpines, alpicoles.

alpinist ['ælpinist], *s.* Alpiniste *mf.*

already [ɔ:l'redi], *adv.* Déjà; dès à présent. **Ten o'clock a.!** déjà dix heures!

Alsace [æl'zæs, 'ælsæs]. *Pr.n. Geog:* Alsace *f.*

Alsatian [æl'seiʃ(ə)n], *a. & s. Geog:* Alsacien, -ienne. **A. (wolf-hound)**, berger allemand; chien-loup *m.*

also ['ɔ:lsou], *adv.* Aussi. **I a. discovered that . . .**, (i) moi aussi j'ai trouvé que . . ., (ii) j'ai encore trouvé que. . . . **He saw it a.**, il l'a vu également. **Not only . . . but a. . . .**, non seulement . . . mais encore . . ., mais aussi. . . . *Turf:* **A. ran . . .**, non-classés. . . .

altar ['ɔ:ltər], *s.* Autel *m.* **High a.**, maître(-)autel *m.* **Table a.**, autel improvisé. **Side a.**, autel latéral. **To set up an a.**, dresser un autel. **To lay one's ambitions on the a.**, sacrifier ses ambitions; faire le sacrifice de ses ambitions. **To lead to the a.**, épouser. **'altar-cloth**, *s.* Nappe *f* d'autel. **'altar-boy**, *s.* Enfant *m* de chœur (faisant fonction de répondant). **'altar-piece**, *s.* Tableau *m* d'autel; retable *m.* **'altar-rail**, *s.* Balustrade *f*, grille *f*, (du sanctuaire) de l'autel. **'altar-screen**, *s.* Retable *m.* **'altar-stone, -table**, *s.* Pierre *f* d'autel.

alter ['ɔ:ltər]. **1.** *v.tr.* (*a*) Remanier (une comédie); retoucher (un dessin); modifier (ses plans); changer de (plans). **To a. the place of sth.**, changer qch. de place. **To a. one's mind**, changer d'avis. **That alters the case**, voilà qui change les choses; *F:* ça, c'est une autre paire de manches. **To a. sth. for the better**, améliorer qch. **To a. sth. for the worse**, altérer qch. **To a. one's course**, changer de route. *Nau:* **To a. (the)**

course, changer, modifier, la route. (*b*) Fausser (les faits); altérer (un texte). **2.** *v.i.* **He has greatly altered**, il a bien changé. **To a. for the better**, s'améliorer; s'amender; (*of pers.*) changer en mieux. **To a. for the worse**, s'altérer, perdre.

alterability [ɔltərə'biliti], *s.* Variabilité *f.*

alterable ['ɔltərəbl], *a.* Variable; modifiable.

alteration [ɔltə'reiʃ(ə)n], *s.* (*a*) Remaniement *m*, retouche *f*, modification *f*; changement *m.* **To make an a. to a dress**, faire une modification, une retouche, à une robe. (*b*) **Marginal a.**, renvoi *m* en marge.

altercation [ɔltə'keiʃ(ə)n], *s.* Altercation *f*, dispute *f*, querelle *f.*

alternate¹ [ɔ:l'tə:nit], *a.* **1.** Alternatif, alterné, alternant. **The a. action of sun and rain**, l'action alternative, alternée, du soleil et de la pluie. **To come on a. days**, venir de deux jours l'un, tous les deux jours. **Trees planted in a. rows**, arbres en quinconce. **Professors lecturing on a. days**, professeurs alternants. **2.** *Geom: Bot:* (Angles, feuilles) alternes. **3.** *Pros:* (Rimes) croisées. **-ly**, *adv.* Alternativement; tour à tour.

alternate² ['ɔ:ltəneit]. **1.** *v.tr.* Faire alterner; employer tour à tour, alternativement. **2.** *v.i.* Alterner (**with**, avec); se succéder (tour à tour). **alternating**, *a.* **1.** Alternant, alterné. **2.** (*a*) *El.E:* (Courant) alternatif. (*b*) *Mec.E:* (Mouvement) alternatif, de va-et-vient.

alternation [ɔ:ltə'neiʃ(ə)n], *s.* **1.** Alternation *f* (d'un mouvement). **2.** Alternance *f* (du jour et de la nuit, etc.). **3. Alternations of rain and sun**, alternatives *f* de pluie et de soleil.

alternative [ɔ:l'tə:nətiv]. **1.** *a.* (*a*) Alternatif. **An a. proposal**, une contre-proposition. (*b*) **An a. route**, un second, un autre, itinéraire. **2.** *s.* Alternative *f.* **There is no a.**, il n'y a pas d'alternative. **To have no a.**, n'avoir pas le choix. **-ly**, *adv.* Avec l'alternative de. . .

alternator ['ɔ:ltəneitər], *s. El.E:* Alternateur *m.*

although [ɔ:l'ðou], *conj.* = THOUGH I. 1.

altimeter ['æltimətər], *s. Av: etc:* Altimètre *m.*

altitude ['æltitju:d], *s.* **1.** (*a*) Altitude *f*, élévation *f* (au-dessus du niveau de la mer). (*b*) Hauteur *f* (d'un astre, d'un triangle). **2.** *Usu.pl.* Hauteur(s).

alto ['æltou], *s. Mus:* **1.** Alto *m.* **2.** (*a*) (*Male*) Haute-contre *f.* (*b*) (*Female*) Contralto *m.*

altogether [ɔ:ltə'geðər], *adv.* (*a*) (*Wholly*) Entièrement, tout à fait. **You are a. right**, vous avez entièrement, grandement, raison. (*b*) (*On the whole*) Somme toute. . . . **Taking things a.; taken a.**, à tout prendre. (*c*) **How much a.?** combien en tout? combien tout compris? (*d*) *s. F:* **The a.**, la nudité absolue.

alto-relievo ['æltouri'li:vou], *s.* Haut-relief *m.*

altruism ['æltruizm], *s.* Altruisme *m.*

altruist ['æltruist], *s.* Altruiste *mf.*

altruistic [æltru'istik], *a.* Altruiste.

alum ['æləm], *s.* Alun *m. Phot:* **A. bath**, bain aluné.

alumina [ə'lju:minə], *s. Miner:* Alumine *f.*

aluminium [ælju'miniəm], *s.* Aluminium *m.*

aluminum [ə'lu:minəm], *s. U.S:* = ALUMINIUM.

alumnus, *pl.* **alumna**, *pl.* **-i, -ae** [ə'lʌmnəs, -ə, -ai, -i], *s.m. U.S:* (*a*) Ancien(-ne) élève (d'un college). (*b*) Ancien, -ne étudiant(e) (à une université); diplômé(e) (d'une université).

alunite ['æljunait], *s. Miner:* Alunite *f.*

alveolar [ælvi'oulər], *a.* Alvéolaire.

alveolate ['ælviouleit], *a.* Alvéolé.

alveole ['ælvioul], **alveolus**, *pl.* **-i** ['ælvi'ouləs], *s.* Alvéole *m.*

always ['ɔ:lwəz], *adv.* Toujours. **He is nearly a. here**, il est presque toujours ici. **Office a. open**, permanence *f.*

alyssum ['ælis(ə)m], *s. Bot:* Alysson *m*, alysse *m.*

am. *See* BE.

amalgam [ə'mælgəm], *s.* Amalgame *m.*

amalgamate [ə'mælgəmeit]. **1.** *v.tr.* (*a*) Amalgamer (l'or, etc.). (*b*) Amalgamer (des idées); fusionner, fondre (des sociétés); unifier (les industries). **2.** *v.i.* (*a*) (*Of metals*) S'amalgamer. (*b*) (*Of ideas*) S'amalgamer; (*of companies*) fusionner; (*of races*) se mélanger.

amalgamation [əmælgə'meiʃ(ə)n], *s.* **1.** Amalgamation *f* (des métaux). **2.** Fusion *f*, fusionnement *m* (de deux sociétés); mélange *m* (de races, etc.).

amanita [æmə'nitə], s. Fung: Amanite f. **A. phalloides**, amanite phalloïde.

amanuensis, pl. -es [ə,mænju'ensis, -iːz], s. A: Secrétaire mf.

amarant(h) ['æmərænt, -ænθ], s. Amarante f. a.inv. Amarante.

amateur [æmə'təːr, 'æmətəːr], s. Amateur m. (a) Amateur. **He is an a. of painting**, c'est un amateur de belles peintures; il s'intéresse à la peinture. (b) Amateur, dilettante m. **He paints as an a.**, il peint en amateur, la peinture c'est son violon d'Ingres. Pej: **He is an a. at painting**, il peint en amateur, c'est un barbouilleur. (c) Sp: Amateur. (d) attrib: **A. painter**, peintre m amateur. **A. work**, travail m d'amateur, de dilettante.

amateurish [,æmə'təːriʃ], a. Pej: (Travail, etc.) d'amateur; (travail) maladroit. **-ly**, adv. En amateur; maladroitement.

amateurishness [,æmə'təːriʃnis], s. Inexpérience f, manque m de maitrise; maladresse f.

amateurism ['æmətəːrizm], 1. Dilettantisme m. 2. Sp: Amateurisme m.

amatory ['æmətəri], a. (Sentiment) amoureux; (lettre) d'amour; (poète, poème) érotique.

amaze [ə'meiz], v.tr. Confondre, stupéfier, frapper de stupeur. **His courage amazed me**, j'ai été stupéfait de son courage. Iron: **You a. me!** vraiment? **amazed**, a. Confondu, stupéfait; ébahi; F: renversé. **I'm a. at it**, j'en reste confondu(e). **amazing**, a. Stupéfiant; F: renversant. **It's a.**, je n'en reviens pas. Com: **A. offer!** offre exceptionnelle! **-ly**, adv. Étonnamment. **He's doing a. well**, il réussit à merveille.

amazement [ə'meizmənt], s. Stupéfaction f; stupeur f; ébahissement m.

Amazon ['æməz(ə)n]. 1. s.f. Myth: etc: Amazone, guerrière f. 2. Pr.n. Geog: **The river A.**, l'Amazone f.

Amazonia [æmə'zouniə]. Pr.n. Geog: Amazonie f.

ambassador [æm'bæsədər], s. Ambassadeur m. **Woman a.**, ambassadrice f.

ambassadorial [,æmbæsə'dɔːriəl], a. Ambassadorial, -aux; d'ambassadeur.

ambassadorship [æm'bæsədəʃip], s. Ambassade f.

ambassadress [æm'bæsədris], s.f. Ambassadrice.

amber ['æmbər], s. Ambre m. Yellow a., ambre jaune; succin m. **A. colour**, nuance ambrée. Adm: **A. light**, feu jaune. **'amber-coloured**, a. Ambré.

ambergris ['æmbəgriːs], s. Ambre gris.

ambidexter ['æmbi'dekstər], s. Ambidextre mf.

ambidexterity ['æmbideks'teriti], s. Ambidextérité f.

ambidextrous ['æmbi'dekstrəs], a. Ambidextre.

ambience ['æmbiəns], s. Ambiance f, atmosphère f.

ambient ['æmbiənt], a. Ambiant.

ambiguity [æmbi'gjuiti], s. 1. Ambiguïté f. 2. Équivoque f.

ambiguous [æm'bigjuəs], a. 1. Ambigu, f. -uë; équivoque. 2. Incertain. 3. Obscur; (style) confus. **-ly**, adv. Avec ambiguïté; d'une manière équivoque.

ambiguousness [æm'bigjuəsnis], s. = AMBIGUITY 1.

ambition [æm'biʃ(ə)n], s. Ambition f. **The a. to shine**, l'ambition de briller. **To make it one's a. to do sth.**, mettre son ambition à faire qch.

ambitious [æm'biʃəs], a. Ambitieux. **-ly**, adv. Ambitieusement.

ambitiousness [æm'biʃəsnis], s. 1. Ambition f. 2. Caractère ambitieux.

ambivalence [æmbi'veiləns], s. Ambivalence f.

ambivalent [æmbi'veilənt], a. Ambivalent.

amble¹ ['æmbl], s. 1. Equit: (a) Amble m, entrepas m. (b) (Of horse) Traquenard m. 2. (Of pers.) Pas m tranquille; allure f tranquille.

amble², v.i. 1. Equit: (a) Aller (à) l'amble. (b) (Of horse) Aller le traquenard. 2. F: (Of pers.) **To a. along**, aller, marcher, d'un pas tranquille.

ambler ['æmblər], s. 1. Cheval ambleur. 2. Promeneur m sans but; flâneur m.

ambrosia [æm'brouziə], s. Ambroisie f.

ambrosial [æm'brouziəl], a. Ambrosiaque; au parfum d'ambroisie.

ambulance ['æmbjuləns], s. Ambulance f. Mil: **Field a.**, ambulance divisionnaire. **A. train**, train m sanitaire. **A. ship**, navire m hôpital. **Flying a.**, avion sanitaire. attrib. **A. man**, ambulancier (-brancardier) m; infirmier m.

ambulatory¹ ['æmbjulətəri], a. Ambulant, mobile.

ambulatory², s. Promenoir m, préau m. Ecc. Arch: Déambulatoire m.

ambush¹ ['æmbuʃ], s. Embuscade f; guet-apens m, pl. guets-apens. **To lay an a.**, dresser une embuscade. **To fall into an a.**, donner, tomber, dans une embuscade. **To be, lie, in a.**, être, se tenir, en embuscade; être à l'affût. **Troops in a.**, troupes embusquées.

ambush². 1. v.tr. **To a. the enemy**, attirer l'ennemi dans un piège. **To be ambushed**, tomber dans une embuscade. 2. v.i. S'embusquer.

ameliorate [ə'miːliəreit]. 1. v.tr. Améliorer. 2. v.i. S'améliorer, s'amender.

amelioration [ə,miːliə'reiʃ(ə)n], s. Amélioration f.

ameliorative [ə'miːliəreitiv], a. Améliorateur, -trice, amélioratif, -ive.

amen ['ɑː men, 'ei'men], int. Amen; ainsi soit-il.

amenability [ə,miːnə biliti], s. = AMENABLENESS.

amenable [ə'miːnəbl], a. 1. Jur: Justiciable, ressortissant, relevant (to a court, d'un tribunal); responsable (to s.o., envers qn). **A. to a fine**, passible d'une amende. 2. (a) Soumis (à la loi, à la discipline); docile (aux conseils); sensible (à la bonté). **A. to reason**, raisonnable. (b) (Enfant) soumis, docile. **-ably**, adv. D'une façon soumise.

amenableness [ə'miːnəblnis], s. 1. Jur: Justiciabilité f (to, de); responsabilité f (to, envers). 2. Soumission f, docilité f.

amend [ə'mend]. 1. v.tr. (a) Amender, modifier (un projet de loi); rectifier (un compte); corriger (un texte). (b) Réformer (sa vie). **To a. one's ways**, s'amender. 2. v.i. S'amender, se corriger. **amending**, a. Correctif.

amendment [ə'mendmənt], s. (a) Modification f; rectification f; redressement m (d'une erreur). (b) Parl: etc: Amendement m.

amends [ə'mendz], s.pl. Réparation f, dédommagement m, compensation f. Used esp. in **To make a. for (an injury)**, réparer (un tort).

amenity [ə'miːniti], s. 1. Aménité f, agrément m, charme m (d'un lieu). 2. Aménité, amabilité f, affabilité f. 3. pl. **Amenities**. (a) Aménités, civilités fpl. (b) **The amenities of life**, les agréments m de l'existence. **Educational amenities**, ressources intellectuelles et artistiques. Jur: **Compensation for loss of amenities**, dommages-intérêts mpl pour atteinte portée à l'agrément (d'une propriété).

amenorrhoea [ə,menə'riə], s. Med: Aménorrhée f.

America [ə'merikə]. Pr.n. L'Amérique f. **North, South, A.**, l'Amérique du Nord, du Sud. **Latin A.**, l'Amérique latine.

American [ə'merikən], a. & s. 1. Américain, -aine. **A. Indian**, Amérindien, -ienne. 2. Des États-Unis. S.a. CLOTH 1.

Americanism [ə'merikənizm], s. Ling: etc: Américanisme m.

Americanist [ə'merikənist], s. Américaniste mf.

Americanize [ə'merikənaiz]. 1. v.tr. Américaniser. 2. v.i. S'américaniser.

Amerind ['æmər'ind], s. Ethn: Amérindien, -ienne.

Amerindian [,æmər'indiən, -diən], a. Amérindien, -ienne.

amethyst ['æmiθist], s. Améthyste f.

amiability [,eimjə'biliti], s. Amabilité f (to, envers).

amiable ['eimjəbl], a. Aimable (to, envers). **To make oneself a. to s.o.**, faire l'aimable auprès de qn. **-ably**, adv. Aimablement.

amiableness ['eimjəb(ə)lnis], s. = AMIABILITY.

amiantosis [,æmiæn'tousis], s. Med: Fr.C: Amiantose f.

amicability [,æmikə'biliti], s. 1. Nature, disposition, amicale. 2. Concorde f.

amicable ['æmikəbl], a. 1. (Of manner, etc.) Amical; (of pers.) bien disposé. 2. Jur: **A. settlement**, arrangement à l'amiable. **-ably**, adv. (i) Amicalement; (ii) à l'amiable.

amicableness ['æmikəb(ə)lnis], s. = AMICABILITY.

amid(st) [ə'mid(st)], prep. Au milieu de; parmi.

amidships [ə'midʃips], adv. Nau: 1. Au milieu du navire; par le travers. **The boat parted a.**, le navire s'ouvrit par le milieu. 2. **To put the helm a.**, mettre la barre droite. **Helm a.!** zéro (la barre)!

amino-plastic ['æminou'plæstik], s. Ch: Aminoplaste m.

amir ['æmiːr], s. Émir m.

amiss [ə'mis], *adv. & pred. a.* **1.** (*Wrongly*) Mal; **de travers.** To judge a., mal juger. To take sth. a., prendre qch. de travers, en mal, en mauvaise part. **2.** (*Out of order*) Mal à propos. **That would not come a.**, cela n'arriverait pas mal (à propos). **Something is a.**, il y a quelque chose qui cloche.

amity ['æmiti], *s.* Amitié *f*, concorde *f*, bonne intelligence, bons rapports, bonnes relations.

ammeter ['æmitər], *s.* El: Ampèremètre *m*.

ammo ['æmou], *s. Mil: F:* = AMMUNITION.

ammonia [ə'mounjə], *s. Ch:* Ammoniaque *f*; gaz ammoniac. **A. hydrate, a. solution**, *F:* a., (solution aqueuse d')ammoniaque.

ammoniac [ə'mounjæk], *a.* Ammoniac, -aque. *Esp.* **Sal a.**, sel ammoniac.

ammoniated [ə'mounieitid], *a. Pharm: etc:* Ammoniacé, ammoniaqué.

ammonite ['æmounait], *s. Paleont:* Ammonite *f*.

ammonium [ə'mounjəm], *s. Ch:* Ammonium *m*. **A. carbonate**, carbonate *m* d'ammonium.

ammunition [æmju'niʃ(ə)n], *s. Mil:* **1.** Munitions *fpl* de guerre. *S.a.* ROUND[1] II. 6. **2.** *Attrib.* D'ordonnance. **ammu'nition-pouch**, *s.* Cartouchière *f*, giberne *f*.

amnesia [æm'ni:ziə], *s. Med:* Amnésie *f*.

amnesic [æm'ni:zik], *a.* Amnésique.

amnesty¹ ['æmnisti], *s.* Amnistie *f*.

amnesty², *v.tr.* Amnistier.

amoeba, *pl.* **-as, -ae** [ə'mi:bə, -əz, -i:], *s.* Amibe *f*.

amoebic [ə'mi:bik], *a.* Amibien, -ienne.

amoeboid [ə'mi:bɔid], *a.* Amiboïde.

amok [ə'mʌk]. **1.** *a.* Amok. **2.** *adv.* (a) **To run a.**, tomber dans la folie furieuse de l'amok. (b) *F:* (i) Devenir fou furieux. (ii) Perdre son sang-froid; voir rouge. **3.** *s.* Amok *m*.

among(st) [ə'mʌŋ(st)], *prep.* Parmi, entre. (a) **Sitting a. her children**, assise au milieu de ses enfants. **To wander a. the ruins**, errer dans les ruines. (b) **We are a. friends**, nous sommes entre amis. (c) **To count s.o. a. one's friends**, compter qn au nombre de ses amis. **He is a. those who . . .**, il est du nombre de ceux qui. . . . **A. them are several . . .**, parmi eux il y en a plusieurs. . . . **Not one a. them**, pas un d'entre eux. **He is one a. many**, il n'est pas seul. (d) **Nations divided a. themselves**, nations divisées entre elles. **You've made a hash of it a. you**, à vous tous vous avez fait un beau gâchis.

amoral [ei'mɔrəl], *a.* Amoral, -aux.

amorality [eimɔr'æliti], *s.* Amoralité *f*.

amorous ['æmərəs], *a.* Amoureux (of s.o., de qn); porté vers l'amour. **A. verse**, poésie érotique. **-ly**, *adv.* Amoureusement.

amorousness ['æmərəsnis], *s.* Tempérament amoureux.

amorphia [ə'mɔ:fiə], **amorphism** [ə'mɔ:fizm], *s.* Amorphie *f*, amorphisme *m*.

amorphous [ə'mɔ:fəs], *a.* **1.** *Biol: etc:* Amorphe. **2.** (Opinions) sans forme; (projet) vague, amorphe.

amorphousness [ə'mɔ:fəsnis], *s.* État *m* amorphe; *Biol:* Amorphie *f*.

amortization [əmɔ:ti'zeiʃ(ə)n], *s.* Amortissement *m* (d'une dette, etc.).

amortize [ə'mɔ:taiz], *v.tr.* **1.** Amortir (une dette). **2.** *Jur:* Aliéner (une terre) en mainmorte.

amortizement [ə'mɔ:tizmənt], *s.* **1.** = AMORTIZATION. **2.** *Arch:* Amortissement *m*.

amount¹ [ə'maunt], *s.* **1.** *Com:* Somme *f*, montant *m*, total *m* (d'une facture, etc.). **Have you the right a.?** avez-vous votre compte? **What is the a. of their business?** quel est leur chiffre d'affaires? (Up) to the a. of . . ., jusqu'à concurrence de. . . . **2.** (a) Quantité *f*. **In small amounts**, par petites quantités. *F:* **To spend any a. of money**, dépenser énormément d'argent. **He has any a. of money**, il a de l'argent tant et plus. **Any a. of people saw it**, nombre de gens l'ont vu. (b) (*Percentage*) Teneur *f*. **A. of grease in a leather**, teneur en graisse d'un cuir. **3.** Valeur *f*, importance *f* (d'une affirmation, etc.).

amount², *v.i.* **1.** (*Of money, etc.*) S'élever, (se) monter (to, à). *Com:* **The stocks a. to so much**, les stocks s'élèvent à tant, atteignent tant. **I don't know what my debts a. to**, j'ignore le montant de mes dettes. **2.** (*Be equivalent*) Équivaloir, revenir; se résumer, se borner, se ramener (to, à). **It amounts to the same**

thing, cela revient au même; *F:* c'est tout comme. **3.** *F:* **He will never a. to much**, il ne sera, ne fera, jamais grand-chose.

amour [ə'muər], *s.* Intrigue galante.

amp [æmp], *s. F:* = AMPERE.

amperage ['æmpəridʒ], *s. El:* Ampérage *m*.

ampere ['æmpeər], *s. El.Meas:* Ampère *m*. **'ampere-hour**, *s.* Ampère-heure *m*, *pl.* ampères-heures.

ampersand ['æmpəsænd], *s. Typ:* Et *m* commercial.

amphibia [æm'fibiə], *s.pl. Z:* Amphibiens *mpl*.

amphibian [æm'fibiən], *a. & s.* **1.** *Z:* Amphibie (*m*). **2.** *Mil: Av: etc:* (Véhicule, char, etc.) amphibie (*m*); (avion) amphibie (*m*).

amphibious [æm'fibiəs], *a. Z: Mil: etc:* Amphibie. (a) **The frog is a.**, la grenouille est un amphibie. (b) **An a. military operation**, une opération militaire amphibie.

amphitheatre ['æmfi,θiətər], *s.* Amphithéâtre *m*.

amphora, *pl.* **-ae** ['æmfərə, -i:], *s.* Amphore *f*.

ample [æmpl], *a.* Ample. **1. An a. garment**, un ample, large, vêtement. **A. resources**, d'abondantes ressources. **2.** (*Enough*) **You have a. time**, vous avez amplement, grandement, largement, le temps. **To make a. apologies**, faire d'amples excuses. **-ply**, *adv.* Amplement, grandement.

ampleness ['æmplnis], *s.* Ampleur *f*; abondance *f* (de ressources).

amplification ['æmplifi'keiʃ(ə)n], *s.* Amplification *f*.

amplifier ['æmplifaiər], *s.* **1.** *Phot:* (Lentille) amplificatrice. **2.** *W.Tel:* Amplificateur *m*, haut-parleur *m*, *pl.* haut-parleurs.

amplify ['æmplifai], *v.tr.* Amplifier (une idée, *El:* le courant). **To a. a story** développer une histoire. **amplifying**, *a* Amplificateur, -trice; amplifiant.

amplitude ['æmplitju:d], *s.* **1.** Amplitude *f*. *Ph:* **A. of swing**, amplitude des oscillations (d'un pendule). **2.** Abondance *f*, ampleur *f* (de style).

ampoule ['æmpu:l], *s. Med:* Ampoule *f*.

ampulla, *pl.* **-ae** [æm'pula, -i:], *s.* Ampoule *f*.

amputate ['æmpjuteit], *v.tr.* Amputer, faire l'amputation de (la jambe, etc.). **His right leg was amputated**, il fut amputé de la jambe droite.

amputation [æmpju'teiʃ(ə)n], *s.* Amputation *f*.

amuck [ə'mʌk] = AMOK.

amulet ['æmjulit], *s.* Amulette *f*.

amuse [ə'mju:z], *v.tr.* Amuser, divertir, égayer, faire rire (qn). **To amuse oneself by, with, doing sth.**, s'amuser, se récréer, à faire qch., en faisant qch. **To a. oneself with sth.**, s'amuser avec qch. **To be amused at, by, sth.**, être amusé de qch.; s'amuser de qch. **amusing**, *a.* Amusant, divertissant. **Highly a.**, désopilant. **The a. thing about it is that . . .**, le plaisant de l'affaire c'est que. . . . **-ly**, *adv.* D'une manière amusante, divertissante.

amusement [ə'mju:zmənt], *s.* **1.** Amusement *m*; divertissement *m*. **We have few amusements here**, nous avons ici peu de distractions. **A. park**, parc *m* d'attractions. **2. Money for one's amusements**, argent pour menus plaisirs.

Amy ['eimi]. *Pr.n.f.* Aimée.

amyl ['æmil], *s. Ch:* Amyle *m*.

an. *See* A².

Anabaptist ['ænə'bæptist], *a. & s. Rel:* Anabaptiste (*mf*).

anacard ['ænəkɑ:d], *s. Bot:* Anacarde *m*.

anachronism [ə'nækrənizm], *s.* Anachronisme *m*.

anachronistic [ə,nækrə'nistik], *a.* Anachronique.

anaconda [ænə'kɔndə], *s.* Anaconda *m*, eunecte *m*.

anaemia [ə'ni:miə], *s.* Anémie *f*. **Pernicious anaemia**, anémie pernicieuse progressive.

anaemic [ə'ni:mik], *a.* Anémique. **To become a.**, s'anémier.

anaerobe, *pl.* **anaerobia** [æ'neəroub, -iə], *s. Bac:* Anaérobie *m*.

anaerobic [,æneə'roubik], *a. Bac:* Anaérobe.

anaesthesia [ænes'θi:ziə], *s.* Anesthésie *f*.

anaesthesiologist [ænəsθi:zi'ɔlədʒist], *s.* Anesthésiologiste *mf*.

anaesthesiology [ænəsθi:zi'ɔlədʒi], *s.* Anesthésiologie *f*.

anaesthetic [ænəs'θetik], *a. & s.* Anesthésique (*m*). **Under the a.**, sous l'effet *m* de l'anesthésique.

anaesthetist [ə'ni:sθətist], *s.* Anesthésiste *m*.

anaesthetization [ə,ni:sθətai'zeiʃ(ə)n], *s.* Administration *f* d'un anesthésique; insensibilisation *f*.

anaesthetize [ə'niːsθətaiz], *v.tr. Med:* Anesthésier; *F:* endormir.

anagram ['ænəgram], *s.* Anagramme *f.*

anagrammatic(al) [ænəgrəm'ætik(l)], *a.* Anagrammatique. **-ally,** *adv.* Anagrammatiquement.

anal ['ein(ə)l], *a. Anat:* Anal, -aux.

analgesia [ænæl'dʒiːziə], *s. Med:* Analgésie *f;* analgie *f.*

analgesic [ænæl'dʒiːsik], **analgetic** [ænæl'dʒetik], *a. & s. Med:* Analgésique (*m*); anodin (*m*).

analogical [ænə'lɒdʒik(ə)l], *a.* Analogique. **-ally,** *adv.* Analogiquement; par analogie.

analogist [ə'nælədʒist], *s.* Analogiste *mf.*

analogous [ə'næləgəs], *a.* Analogue (to, with, à).

analogue ['ænəlɒg], *s.* Analogue *m.*

analogy [ə'nælədʒi], *s.* Analogie *f* (to, with, avec; between, entre). To argue from a., raisonner par analogie. On the a. of . . ., par analogie avec. . . .

analysable ['ænəlaizəbl], *a.* Analysable.

analyse ['ænəlaiz], *v.tr.* Analyser; faire l'analyse de (qch.). *Gram:* To a. a sentence, faire l'analyse logique d'une phrase.

analysis, *pl.* **-es** [ə'næləsis, -iːz], *s.* Analyse *f. Ch:* Quantitative a., dosage *m.* Wet a., analyse par voie humide. Dry a., analyse par voie sèche. *Gram:* A. of a sentence, analyse logique d'une phrase.

analyst ['ænəlist], *s. Ch:* Analyste *m.*

analytic(al) [ænə'litik(əl)], *a.* Analytique. **-ally,** *adv.* Analytiquement; par l'analyse.

anapaest ['ænəpiːst], *s. Pros:* Anapeste *m.*

anarchic(al) [ə'nɑːkik(əl)], *a.* Anarchique. **-ally,** *adv.* Anarchiquement.

anarchism ['ænəkizm], *s.* Anarchisme *m.*

anarchist ['ænəkist], *s.* Anarchiste *mf.*

anarchy ['ænəki], *s.* Anarchie *f.*

anastigmat [ænæ'stigmæt], *s. Opt: Phot:* Objectif *m* anastigmatique; anastigmat *m.*

anastigmatic [ə,næstig'mætic], *a. Opt:* Anastigmat, anastigmatique.

anastomosis [ænəstə'mousis], *s. Bot: Anat: Surg:* Anastomose *f.*

anathema [ə'næθəmə], *s.* Anathème *m* ((i) malédiction *f;* (ii) personne frappée de malédiction). *F:* It's, he's, a. to me, c'est ma bête noire.

anathematize [ə'næθəmətaiːz], *v.tr.* (a) Anathématiser (qn); frapper (qn) d'anathème. (b) Maudire (qn).

Anatolia [ænə'touljə]. *Pr.n. Geog:* Anatolie *f.*

anatomical [ænə'tɒmik(ə)l], *a.* Anatomique. A. specimen, pièce d'anatomie. **-ally,** *adv.* Anatomiquement.

anatomist [ə'nætəmist], *s.* Anatomiste *m.*

anatomize [ən'ætəmaiz], *v.tr.* Anatomiser; disséquer.

anatomy [ə'nætəmi], *s.* Anatomie *f.*

ancestor ['ænsistər], *s.* Ancêtre *m;* aïeul *m, pl.* aïeux.

ancestral [æn'sestrəl], *a.* (a) Héréditaire; de famille. His a. castle, le château de ses ancêtres. (b) *Biol:* Ancestral, -aux.

ancestress ['ænsistris], *s.f.* Ancêtre, aïeule.

ancestry ['ænsistri], *s.* **1.** Race *f;* lignée *f,* lignage *m;* longue suite d'ancêtres; ascendance *f.* **2.** *Coll.* Ancêtres *mpl;* ascendants *mpl;* aïeux *mpl.*

anchor¹ ['æŋkər], *s.* Ancre *f. Nau:* Grappling a., grappin *m. S.a.* BOWER², KEDGE¹, SHEET-ANCHOR. Stand by the a.! paré à mouiller! To let go, drop, the a., jeter, mouiller, l'ancre. Let go the a.! mouillez! To come to a., s'ancrer, mouiller. (*Of pers.*) To cast a., to come to a., s'ancrer (quelque part). To lie, ride, at a., être à l'ancre; être mouillé, au mouillage. Foul a., ancre surjalée, engagée. **'anchor-plate,** *s. Civ.E:* Plaque *f* d'ancrage; contre-plaque *f.* **'anchor-ring,** *s.* Organeau *m,* cigale *f.* **'anchor-tie,** *s. Const: etc:* Tige *f* d'ancrage. **'anchor-watch,** *s. Nau:* Quart *m* au mouillage; quart de rade.

anchor², **1.** *v.tr.* (a) Ancrer (un navire); mettre (un navire) à l'ancre, au mouillage. (b) *Const:* Affermir (qch.) par des ancres. (c) (*Of aerial, etc.*) Haubanner. (d) *Nau: etc:* Hauban(n)er. **2.** *v.i.* (a) Jeter l'ancre; mouiller. To a. by the stern, mouiller par l'arrière. (b) S'ancrer (dans un lieu). **anchored,** *a.* (a) Ancré, mouillé; à l'ancre. *Fish:* A. net, rets sédentaire. (b) Firmly a. faith, foi solidement ancrée. **anchoring,** *s.* Ancrage *m,* mouillage *m.* A.-gear, apparaux *mpl* de mouillage. A.-ground, -place, -berth, ancrage, mouillage.

anchorage ['æŋkəridʒ], *s. Nau:* (a) Ancrage *m,* mouillage *m.* To leave the a., dérader. (b) Droits *mpl* d'ancrage, de stationnement.

anchorite ['æŋkərait], *s.* Anachorète *m.*

anchovy ['æntʃəvi, æn'tʃouvi], *s.* Anchois *m.* A. paste, beurre *m,* pâte *f,* d'anchois. A. toast, toast *m* aux anchois, au beurre d'anchois.

anchylose ['æŋkilouz]. **1.** *v.tr.* Ankyloser. **2.** *v.i.* S'ankyloser. (*Of bones*) To become anchylosed, s'ankyloser, se souder.

anchylosis [æŋki'lousis], *s. Med:* Ankylose *f.*

ancient ['einʃ(ə)nt], *a.* Ancien. (a) De vieille date. Family of a. descent, famille ancienne, de longue lignée. A. oak, chêne centenaire. *s. B:* The A. of Days, l'Ancien des jours; l'Éternel. *S.a.* LIGHT¹ 4. (b) A. Rome, la Rome antique. The a. world, le monde antique. *s.* The ancients, les anciens. *S.a.* HISTORY 1.

ancillary [æn'siləri], *a.* Subordonné, ancillaire.

and [ænd, ənd], *conj.* Et. **1.** (a) A knife a. fork, un couteau et une fourchette. The president a./or secretary, le président ou le secrétaire, ou tous les deux. (b) (*With numerals*) (i) A. & Lit: Five a. twenty (= twenty-five), vingt-cinq. (ii) Two hundred a. two, deux cent deux. Four a. a half, quatre et demi. Four a. three quarters, quatre trois quarts. An hour a. twenty minutes, une heure vingt minutes. (c) Ham a. eggs, des œufs au jambon. Carriage a. pair, voiture à deux chevaux. To walk two a. two, marcher deux à deux, deux par deux. Now a. then, de temps en temps. (d) (*After 'without'*) Ni. He had come without pens a. without pencils, il était venu sans plumes ni crayons. (e) (*Intensive repetition*) For miles a. miles, pendant des milles et des milles. Better a. better, de mieux en mieux. Worse a. worse, de pis en pis. Smaller a. smaller, de plus en plus petit. I knocked a. knocked, but . . ., je frappai tant et plus, mais . . . **2.** (*Connecting clauses*) (a) He sang a. danced, il chantait et dansait. (b) Go a. look for it, allez le chercher. Come a. see me, venez me voir. Wait a. see, attendez voir. Try a. help me, tâchez de m'aider.

Andalusia [ændə'luːziə]. *Pr.n. Geog:* L'Andalousie *f.*

Andalusian [ændə'luːziən], *a. & s.* Andalou, -ouse.

Andes ['ændiːz]. *Pr.n. Geog:* The A., les Andes *f.*

andiron ['ændaiən], *s.* (a) Landier *m.* (b) Chenet *m.*

Andorra [æn'dɒrə]. *Pr.n. Geog:* (La République d') Andorre.

Andrew ['ændruː]. *Pr.n.m.* André.

androgen ['ændrodʒin], *s. Biol:* Androgène *m.*

androgenic [ændro'dʒenik], *a. Biol:* Androgène.

androgynous [æn'drɒdʒinəs], *a. Biol:* Androgyne.

anecdotal ['ænikdout(ə)l], *a.* Anecdotique.

anecdote ['ænikdout], *s.* Anecdote *f.*

anecdotist ['ænikdoutist], *s.* Anecdotier, -ière.

anemograph [ə'neməgræf], *s. Meteor:* Anémographe *m.*

anemometer [æni'mɒmitər], *s.* Anémomètre *m.*

anemometry [æni'mɒmitri], *s. Meteor:* Anémométrie *f.*

anemone [ə'nemoni], *s. Bot:* Anémone *f. S.a.* SEA-ANEMONE.

aneroid ['ænəroid], *a. & s.* A. (barometer), (baromètre *m*) anéroïde (*m*).

anesthesia [ænəs'θiːziə], *s. Med:* = ANAESTHESIA.

aneurism, **aneurysm** ['ænjurizm], *s. Med:* Anévrisme *m.*

anew [ə'njuː], *adv.* **1.** (*Once more*) De nouveau. To begin a., recommencer. **2.** (*In a new way*) A nouveau. To create sth. a., créer qch. sous une forme nouvelle, à nouveau.

anfractuosity [ænfræktju'ɒsiti], *s.* (a) *Lit:* Anfractuosité *f.* (b) *pl.* Sinuosités *f;* détours *m. Anat:* The anfractuosities of the brain, les anfractuosités du cerveau.

angel ['eindʒəl], *s.* **1.** Ange *m.* Little a., angelet *m.* Guardian a., ange gardien; *F:* You're an a.! tu es chic! tu es un amour! *F:* An a. passes, un ange passe. *Prov:* Talk of angels and you will hear the flutter of their wings, quand on parle du loup on en voit la queue. **2.** *Cu:* Angels on horseback, friture *f* d'huîtres au bacon. A.(-food) cake, (variété de) gâteau *m* de Savoie. **3.** *U.S: F:* (Associé *m*) commanditaire. **'angel-fish,** *s. Ich:* Ange *m* de mer.

angelic, angelical [æn'dʒelik, -(ə)l], *a.* Angélique. **An a. smile,** un sourire d'ange.

angelica [æn'dʒelikə], *s. Bot: Cu:* Angélique *f.*

angelus ['ændʒələs], *s. Ecc:* Angélus *m.*

anger[1] ['æŋɡər], *s.* Colère *f;* emportement *m; Lit:* courroux *m.* **Fit of a.,** accès *m* de colère. **To act in a.,** agir sous le coup de la colère. **In great a.,** courroucé. **In a. against s.o.,** en colère contre qn.

anger[2], *v.tr.* Irriter. *Lit:* courroucer (qn); mettre (qn) ·en colère. **He is easily angered,** il se met facilement en colère; il est irascible.

Angevin(e) ['ændʒəvin], *a.* Angevin; d'Anjou.

angina [æn'dʒainə], *s. Med:* 1. Angine *f.* 2. **A. pectoris** ['pektəris], angine de poitrine.

angiology [,ændʒi'ɔlədʒi], *s. Med:* Angiologie *f.*

angle[1] [æŋɡl], *s.* (a) Angle *m.* **Acute a.,** angle aigu. **Obtuse a.,** angle obtus. **Sharp a.,** angle vif. **Straight a.,** angle plat. **At an a. of . . .,** sous un angle de. . . . **At an a.,** en biais. **The house stands at an a. to the street,** la maison fait angle sur la rue. **A. of elevation,** angle de mire. **The problem has been discussed from every a.,** la question a été étudiée sur toutes ses faces, sous tous les angles. *Aer:* **Leading a.,** angle d'attaque. *S.a.* RIGHT[1] I. 1. (b) (*Corner, nook*) Coin *n.* 'angle-bar, *s.* Cornière *f* (en fer). 'angle-brace, *s. Tls:* Foret *m* à angle. 'angle-iron, *s.* Cornière *f;* fer *m* d'angle.

angle[2], *v.i.* Pêcher à la ligne. **To a. for trout,** pêcher la truite. *F:* **To a. for compliments,** quêter des compliments. **To a. for a husband,** essayer de pêcher un mari. **angling,** *s.* Pêche *f* à la ligne. **A. for trout,** la pêche de la truite.

angledozer ['æŋɡl,douzər], *s. Constr: R.t.m:* Angle-dozer *m.*

angler ['æŋɡlər], *s.* Pêcheur *m* à la ligne.

Anglican ['æŋɡlikən], *a. & s. Ecc:* Anglican, -ane. **The A. Church,** l'Église anglicane.

Anglicanism ['æŋɡlikənizm], *s. Ecc:* Anglicanisme *m.*

anglice ['æŋɡlisi], *Lt.adv.* En anglais.

anglicism ['æŋɡlisizm], *s.* (*In speaking or writing a foreign language*) Anglicisme *m.*

anglicize ['æŋɡlisaiz], *v.tr.* Angliciser.

Anglo-Catholic ['æŋɡlou'kæθ(ə)lik], *a. & s. Rel.H:* Anglo-catholique (*mf*).

Anglo-Indian ['æŋɡlou'indjən], *a. & s.* Anglo-Indien, -ienne. 1. *Adm:* Métis, -isse (issu(e) du croisement entre Anglais(e) et Hindou(e)). 2. *F: A:* (Anglais) (i) né dans l'Inde, aux Indes, (ii) servant ou ayant servi dans l'Inde.

anglomania ['æŋɡlou'meiniə], *s.* Anglomanie *f.*

anglomaniac [æŋɡlo'meiniæk], *s.* Anglomane *mf.*

Anglo-Norman ['æŋɡlou'nɔ:mən], *a. & s.* Anglo-Normand, -ande.

Anglophil(e) ['æŋɡlofail], *s.* Anglophile *mf.*

anglophilia [æŋɡlo'filiə], *s.* Anglophilie *f.*

anglophobe ['æŋɡlofoub], *s.* Anglophobe *mf.*

anglophobia [æŋɡlo'foubiə], *s.* Anglophobie *f.*

Anglo-Saxon ['æŋɡlou'sæks(ə)n]. 1. *a. & s.* Anglo-Saxon, -onne. 2. *s. Ling:* L'anglo-saxon *m.*

angora [æŋ'ɡɔ:rə], *s.* 1. Angora *inv.* **A. cat, goat, rabbit,** chat *m,* chèvre *f,* lapin *m,* angora; angora *m. s. Tex:* (Tissu *m*) angora (*m*).

angostura [æŋɡə'stjuərə], *s.* Angusture *f.*

angry ['æŋɡri], *a.* Fâché, irrité, courroucé (**with s.o. about sth.,** contre qn de qch.). **He was a. at being kept waiting,** il était irrité qu'on le fît attendre. **He sent me an a. letter,** il m'a envoyé une lettre courroucée. **To get a.,** se mettre en colère; se fâcher, s'irriter. **To get a. with s.o.,** se fâcher contre qn. **To make s.o. a.,** fâcher, exaspérer, qn; mettre qn en colère. **A. voices,** voix irritées. **The a. sea,** la mer courroucée, en courroux. **A. sky,** ciel à l'orage. *Med:* **A. sore,** plaie irritée, enflammée. **-ily,** *adv.* En colère, avec colère.

angström ['æŋstrɔ:m], *s. Ph.Meas:* **A. (unit),** unité d'Angström, angström *m.*

anguish ['æŋɡwiʃ], *s.* Angoisse *f;* douleur *f;* bourrèlement *m.* **To be in a.,** être au supplice; être angoissé.

angularity [æŋɡju'læriti], *s.* Angularité *f.*

angular ['æŋɡulər], *a.* 1. (Vitesse, etc.) angulaire. 2. (Rocher, visage) anguleux. *F:* (*Of pers.*) Maigre, décharné.

anhydride [æn'haidraid], *s. Ch:* Anhydride *m.*

anhydrous [æn'haidrəs], *a. Ch:* Anhydre.

anil ['ænil], *s.* 1. (a) *Bot:* Anil *m,* indigotier *m.* (b) *Dy:* Indigo *m.* 2. *Ch:* Anil.

aniline ['ænili:n], *s. Ch: Dy:* Aniline *f.* **A. dyes,** colorants azoïques.

animadversion [,ænimæd'və:ʃ(ə)n], *s.* Animadversion *f,* censure *f,* blâme *m.*

animadvert ['ænimæd'və:t], *v.i.* **To a. on s.o.'s action,** critiquer, blâmer, censurer, l'action de qn.

animal ['ænim(ə)l]. 1. *s.* Animal *m.* **A. painter,** animalier *m.* **A. house,** animalerie *f.* 2. *a.* **A. life,** vie animale. **The a. kingdom,** le règne animal. **A. nature,** animalité *f.*

animalcule, *pl.* **-cules, -cula, -culae** [æni'mælkju:l, -kju:lz, -kjulə, -kjuli:], *s.* Animalcule *m.*

animalism ['æniməlizm], *s.* Animalisme *m.*

animalist ['ænimɔlist], *s. Art:* Animalier *m.*

animality [æni'mæliti], *s.* 1. Animalité *f.* 2. Bestialité *f.*

animalize ['ænimɔlaiz], *v.tr.* 1. *Physiol:* Animaliser (les aliments). 2. Sensualiser (une passion, etc.).

animate[1] ['ænimət], *a.* Animé; doué de vie.·

animate[2] ['ænimeit], *v.tr.* Animer. **To be animated by the best intentions,** être animé des meilleures intentions. (b) Encourager, stimuler. **animated,** *a.* Animé. *Cin:* **A. cartoons,** dessins animés. **To become a.,** s'animer. **-ly,** *adv.* D'un ton, regard, animé; avec entrain.

animation ['æni'meiʃ(ə)n], *s.* 1. Animation *f;* vivacité *f;* chaleur *f* (du style); feu *m,* entrain *m,* verve *f* (d'un orateur). 2. Stimulation *f,* encouragement *m.*

animism ['ænimizm], *s. Phil: Rel:* Animisme *m.*

animist ['ænimist], *s. Phil: Rel:* Animiste.

animosity [æni'mɔsiti], *s.* Animosité *f.*

anion ['ænaiən], *s. Ph:* Anion *m.*

anise ['ænis], *s. Bot:* Anis *m.*

aniseed ['ænisi:d], *s.* (Graine *f* d')anis *m.* **To flavour with a.,** anisé.

ankle ['æŋkl], *s.* Cheville *f* (du pied). **A.-deep,** jusqu'à la cheville. **A.-ring,** anneau de cheville. 'ankle-bone, *s.* Astragale *m.* 'ankle-joint, *s.* Cheville *f;* attache *f* du pied. 'ankle-strap, *s.* Barrette *f* (de soulier). 'ankle-sock, *s.* Socquette *f,* (*R.t.m.*)

anklet ['æŋklit], *s.* Anneau attaché autour de la cheville. (a) Manille *f* (de forçat). (b) Bracelet *m* de jambe, de cheville.

ankylosis [,æŋki'lousis], *s. Med:* = ANCHYLOSIS.

annalist ['ænəlist], *s.* Annaliste *m.*

annals ['æn(ə)lz], *s.pl.* Annales *f.*

Annamese [ænə'mi:z], **Annamite** ['ænəmait], *a. & s. Geog:* Annamite.

Anne [æn]. *Pr.n.f.* Anne. *F:* **Queen A.'s dead,** c'est de l'histoire ancienne.

anneal [ə'ni:l], *v.tr. Metall:* Recuire, adoucir (un métal, le verre). **annealing,** *s.* Recuit *m,* recuite *f.*

annelid, *pl.* **-ida** ['ænəlid, ə'nelidə], *s.* Annélide *m.*

annex [ə'neks], *v.tr.* 1. Annexer (**sth. to sth.,** qch. à qch.); ajouter, joindre (une pièce à un mémoire). 2. **To a. a province,** annexer une province.

annex(e) ['æneks], *s.* Annexe *f* (d'un hôtel, etc.).

annexation [ænek'seiʃ(ə)n], *s.* Annexion *f* (**of,.** de); mainmise *f* (**of,** sur).

annihilate [ə'naiəleit], *v.tr.* Anéantir (une flotte, etc.); annihiler, supprimer.

annihilation [ə,naiə'leiʃ(ə)n], *s.* Anéantissement *m;* annihilation *f.*

annihilator [ə'naiəleitər], *s.* (*Pers.*) Annihilateur, -trice; destructeur *m.*

anniversary [æni'və:s(ə)ri], *s.* Anniversaire *m.*

Anno Domini ['ænou'dɔminai]. *Lt.phr:* 1. (*Abbr:* A.D.) En l'an du Seigneur, de grâce. **In 1066 A.D.,** en 1066 après J.-C. (Jésus-Christ). 2. *F:* Les ans, la vieillesse qui vient.

annotate ['ænoteit], *v.tr.* Annoter (un livre, etc.); commenter (un texte).

annotation [æno'teiʃ(ə)n], *s.* Annotation *f.* 1. Commentaire *m.* 2. Note *f.*

announce [ə'nauns], *v.tr.* Annoncer (qn, qch.). **He announced his intentions to me,** il me fit part de ses intentions.

announcement [ə'naunsmənt], *s.* Annonce *f,* avis *m;* (*of birth, marriage, etc.*) faire-part *m.*

announcer [ə'naunsər], *s.* 1. Annonceur *m.* 2. *W.Tel: T.V:* Speaker *m,* speakerine *f.*

annoy [ə'nɔi], *v.tr.* **1.** (*Vex*) Contrarier, tracasser; impatienter. **2.** (*a*) (*Inconvenience*) Gêner, incommoder, ennuyer, importuner, *F*: embêter. (*b*) (*Molest*) Molester (qn); harceler (l'ennemi). *Fr.C*: *P*: Bâdrer. **annoyed,** *a.* Contrarié, ennuyé. To get **a. at, about, sth.,** se vexer, se fâcher, de qch. **annoying,** *a.* Contrariant, ennuyeux, ennuyant.

annoyance [ə'nɔiəns], *s.* **1.** Contrariété *f*, chagrin *m*. Look of a., air contrarié, fâché. **2.** Désagrément *m*, ennui *m*. *Fr.C*: *P*: Bâdrage *m*.

annual ['ænju(ə)l]. **1.** *a.* Annuel. **2.** *s.* (*a*) *Bot*: Plante annuelle. *S.a.* HARDY 2. (*b*) (*Book, etc.*) Annuaire *m*; publication annuelle. **-ally,** *adv.* Annuellement; tous les ans.

annuitant [ə'njuit(ə)nt], *s.* **1.** Pensionnaire *mf*. **2.** Rentier, -ière (en viager).

annuity [ə'njuiti], *s.* **1.** A. **in redemption of debt,** annuité *f*. **2.** Rente (annuelle). **Government a.,** rente sur l'État. **Life a.,** rente viagère, pension viagère. To pay s.o. **an a.,** servir, faire, une rente à qn.

annul [ə'nʌl], *v.tr.* (**annulled**) Annuler, résilier (un acte); dissoudre (un mariage); abroger (une loi). *Jur*: Annihiler. **annulling,** *a.* Qui annule. *Jur*: **A. clause,** clause *f* abrogatoire. *Nau*: **A. signal,** annulement *m*.

annular ['ænjulə], *a.* (Éclipse, doigt, espace) annulaire.

annulate ['ænjuleit], **annulated** ['ænjuleitid], *a.* *Bot*: *Z*: Annelé.

annulment [ə'nʌlmənt], *s.* Annulation *f*, résiliation *f*; dissolution *f* (d'un mariage); abrogation *f* (d'une loi), abolition *f* (d'un décret). *Jur*: A. of judgment, arrêt *m* d'annulement.

annunciate [ə'nʌnʃieit], *v.tr.* Annoncer, proclamer (une nouvelle, la venue du Messie).

annunciation [ə,nʌnsi'eiʃ(ə)n], *s.* *Ecc*: **The A.,** l'Annonciation *f*.

anode ['ænoud], *s.* *El*: Anode *f*. **A. voltage,** tension *f* de plaque.

anodal [ə'noud(ə)l], **anodic** [ə'nɔdik], *a.* *El*: Anodique.

anodyne ['ænodain], *a. & s.* *Med*: Anodin (*m*); calmant (*m*); antalgique (*m*).

anoint [ə'nɔint], *v.tr.* Oindre. To **a. s.o. with oil,** oindre qn d'huile. *Pred*: To **a. s.o. king,** sacrer qn roi. **The Lord's Anointed,** l'Oint du Seigneur. **anointing,** *s.* **1.** Onction *f*. **2.** Sacre *m* (d'un roi, d'un évêque).

anomalous [ə'nɔmələs], *a.* **1.** Anomal, -aux. **2.** Irrégulier, -ière, exceptionnel, -elle; anormal, -aux. **-ly,** *adv.* Irrégulièrement.

anomaly [ə'nɔməli], *s.* Anomalie *f*.

anon¹ [ə'nɔn], *adv.* *A*: & *F*: Tout à l'heure, bientôt; à l'instant.

anon², *a.* = ANONYMOUS.

anonymity ['ænə'nimiti], *s.* Anonyme *m*, anonymat *m*.

anonymous [ə'nɔniməs], *a.* Anonyme. **A. writer,** anonyme *m*. To **remain a.,** garder l'anonyme, l'anonymat. **-ly,** *adv.* Anonymement.

anopheles [ə'nɔfiliːz], *s.* *Ent*: Anophèle *m*.

anorak ['ænəræk], *s.* *Cost*: Anorak *m*.

anorexia [ano'reksiə], *s.* *Med*: Anorexie *f*.

another [ə'nʌðər], *a. & pron.* **1.** (*An additional*) Encore (un). **A. cup of tea,** encore une tasse de thé. **In a. ten years,** dans dix ans d'ici. I **have received a. three hundred francs,** j'ai reçu trois cents autres francs. **Without a. word . . .,** sans plus . . .; sans un mot de plus. . . . **2.** (*A similar*) (Un(e) autre, un(e) second(e). Such a., un autre du même genre, du même modèle. **3.** (*a*) (*A different*) Un(e) autre. **A. was there before me,** un autre m'avait devancé. **That is (quite) a. matter,** c'est tout autre chose; *F*: c'est une autre paire de manches. **A. time,** une autre fois. *F*: Tell me **a.!** allez, va, conter ça ailleurs. (*b*) She now has **a. husband,** elle a maintenant un nouvel époux. **One . . . a.** (*a*) **Science is one thing, art is a.,** la science est une chose, l'art en est une autre. (*b*) (Taking) **one year with a.,** bon an mal an. **Taking one (thing) with a.,** we just manage, l'un dans l'autre, l'un portant l'autre, on arrive à joindre les deux bouts. *S.a.* THING 3. (*c*) (*Reciprocal pron.*) **One a.,** l'un l'autre, les uns les autres. **Love one a.,** aimez-vous les uns les autres. **Near one a.,** l'un près de l'autre; près l'un de l'autre. **To help one a.,** s'entr'aider.

anoxemia ['ænɔk'siːmiə], *s.* *Med*: Anoxémie *f*.

answer¹ ['ɑːnsər], *s.* **1.** Réponse *f* (à une question, à une lettre); réplique *f* (à une observation, à une critique). **To give an a. to s.o. about sth.,** répondre, faire une réponse, à qn sur qch., au sujet de qch. **He has an a. to everything,** il a réponse à tout. *F*: He **knows all the answers,** c'est un finaud, un combinard. I **could find no a.,** je n'ai rien trouvé à répondre. **A. to a charge,** réponse à une accusation. **Her only a. was to break into sobs,** pour toute réponse, elle éclata en sanglots. *Com*: **In a. to your letter . . .,** en réponse à votre lettre. . . . *F*: **It's the a. to a maiden's prayer,** c'est exactement ce qu'il nous fallait, ce qu'il nous faut, c'est ce que nous cherchions, attendions, voulions. **2.** Solution *f* (d'un problème).

answer², *v.tr. & i.* **1.** Répondre. (*a*) To **a. s.o.,** répondre à qn. **Not to a. a syllable,** ne pas répondre un mot. **He answered that he knew nothing about it,** il répondit qu'il n'en savait rien; il répondit n'en rien savoir. **To a. back,** répliquer. **Don't a. back!** Pas de répliques! (*Of dog*) To **a. to the name of Rover,** répondre au nom de Rover. (*b*) To **a. a question,** a letter, répondre, faire réponse, à une question, à une lettre. **The question was not answered,** la question resta sans réponse. **To a. for** (= *instead of*) s.o., répondre pour qn. (*Cp.* 3) (*c*) To **a. the roll,** to a. one's name, répondre à l'appel. **To a. the bell,** répondre à un coup de sonnette. **To a. the door,** aller ouvrir; venir ouvrir. (*d*) (*Of ship*) To **a. the helm,** obéir à la barre. (*e*) To **a. a charge,** répondre à, réfuter, une accusation. (*f*) To **a. (to) a description** répondre à un signalement. (*g*) To **a. (to) a prayer,** exaucer une prière. **2.** To **a. the requirements of . . .,** répondre aux besoins de. . . . **To a. the purpose,** remplir le but. **That will a. my purpose,** cela fera mon affaire. **3.** To **a.** (= *vouch*) for s.o., for s.o.'s honesty, répondre de qn; se porter, se rendre, garant de qn, de l'intégrité de qn. (*Cp.* 1 (*b*).) I will **a. for it that . . .,** je vous suis caution que. . . . He **has a lot to a. for,** il est responsable de bien des choses. **answering,** *a.* **1.** An a. cry, un cri jeté en réponse. **2.** Qui répond, correspond, est équivalent (to, à).

answerable ['ɑːnsərəbl], *a.* **1.** (*a*) Garant, responsable, comptable (to s.o. for sth., envers qn de qch.). (*b*) **To be a. to an authority,** relever d'une autorité. **2.** **The question is not a.,** c'est une question (i) à laquelle on ne peut pas répondre, (ii) que l'on ne peut pas résoudre.

ant [ænt], *s.* Fourmi *f*. **Wood a.,** red a., fourmi rouge, fauve. **White a.,** fourmi blanche; termite *m*. **'ant-bear,** *s.* *Z*: Tamanoir *m*. **'ant-eater,** *s.* *Z*: Fourmilier *m*. **'ant-hill,** *s.* Fourmilière *f*.

antagonism [æn'tægənizm], *s.* Antagonisme *m*, opposition *f*.

antagonist [æn'tægənist], *s.* Antagoniste *mf*, adversaire *mf*.

antagonistic [æn,tægə'nistik], *a.* Opposé, contraire (to, à). **A. environment,** milieu antagonique. **-ally,** *adv.* D'une façon, manière, antagonique, hostile.

antagonize [æn'tægənaiz], *v.tr.* **1.** (*Of a force*) S'opposer à (une autre force); contrarier (une force). **2.** Éveiller l'antagonisme, l'hostilité, de (qn).

antarctic [ænt'ɑːktik]. **1.** *a.* Antarctique. **2.** *s.* **The A.,** l'Antarctique *m*.

Antarctica [ænt'ɑːktikə]. *Pr.n.* *Geog*: L'Antarctique *f*.

antecedence [ænti'siːd(ə)ns], *s.* **1.** (*a*) Antériorité *f*. (*b*) Priorité *f*. **2.** *Astr*: Antécédence *f*.

antecedent [ænti'siːd(ə)nt]. **1.** *a.* Antécédent; antérieur (to, à). **2.** *s.* (*a*) *Gram*: *etc*: Antécédent *m*. (*b*) *Mus*: Thème *m* (d'une fugue). (*c*) *pl.* His antecedents, ses antécédents.

antechamber ['æntitʃeimbər], *s.* Antichambre *f*.

ante-chapel ['æntitʃæpl], *s.* *Arch*: Avant-corps *m* de la chapelle.

antedate ['ænti'deit], *v.tr.* **1.** Antidater (un document). **2.** Précéder, venir avant (un événement).

antediluvian [æntidi'ljuːviən], *a. & s.* Antédiluvien, -ienne.

antelope ['æntiloup], *s.* *Z*: Antilope *f*.

ante meridiem [æntimə'ridiem], *Lt.phr.* (*Abbr.* a.m. ['eiem]) Avant midi. **Five a.m.,** cinq heures du matin.

ante-natal ['ænti'neit(ə)l], *a.* Prénatal, -als.
antenna, *pl.* **-ae** [æn'tenə, -iː], *s.* **1.** *Ent: Crust:* Antenne *f. Moll:* Tentacule *m;* corne *f* (de limaçon). **2.** *W.Tel: T.V:* Antenne.
antenuptial ['ænti'nʌpʃ(ə)l], *a.* Anténuptial, -aux; prénuptial, -aux.
antepenult ['æntipi'nʌlt], **antepenultimate** ['æntipi-'nʌltimit], *a. & s.* Antépénultième (*f*).
anterior [æn'tiəriər], *a.* Antérieur, -e (**to**, à).
ante(-)room ['æntirum], *s.* Antichambre *f.*
anthelion, *pl.* **-ia** [æn'θiːliən, -iə], *s. Meteor:* Anthélie *f.*
anthem ['ænθəm], *s.* **1.** *Ecc.Mus:* Motet *m.* **2.** National a., hymne national.
anther ['ænθər], *s. Bot:* Anthère *f.*
anthology [æn'θɔlədʒi], *s.* Anthologie *f,* florilège *m.*
Anthony ['æntəni]. *Pr.n.m.* Antoine. (**St.**) **Anthony's fire**, érysipèle *m.*
Anthozoa ['ænθə'zouə], *s.pl. Z:* Anthozoaires *mpl.*
anthracite ['ænθrəsait], *s. Min:* Anthracite *m.*
anthrax ['ænθræks], *s.* (*a*) *Vet: Med:* Charbon *m.* (*b*) *Med:* Pustule charbonneuse. (*c*) *Ent:* Anthrax *m.*
anthropocentric [,ænθropo'sentrik], *a. Phil:* Anthropocentrique.
anthropography [,ænθro'pɔgrəfi], *s.* Anthropographie *f.*
anthropoid ['ænθropɔid], *a. & s.* (*a*) Anthropoïde (*m*). (*b*) *Z:* (Singe *m*) anthropomorphe; anthropoïde (*m*).
anthropological [,ænθropo'lɔdʒik(ə)l], *a.* Anthropologique.
anthropologist [,ænθro'pɔlədʒist], *s.* Anthropologiste *mf,* anthropologue *mf.*
anthropology [,ænθro'pɔlədʒi], *s.* Anthropologie *f.*
anthropometric(al) [,ænθropo'metrikl], *a.* Anthropométrique.
anthropometry [,ænθro'pɔmitri], *s.* Anthropométrie *f,* bertillonage *m.* **Criminal a. department**, service anthropométrique.
anthropomorphism [,ænθropo'mɔːfizm], *s. Rel.H:* Anthropomorphisme *m.*
anthropophagi [,ænθro'pɔfədʒai], *s.pl.* Anthropophages *mf.*
anthropophagous [,ænθro'pɔfəgəs], *a.* Anthropophage.
anthropophagy [,ænθro'pɔfədʒi], *s.* Anthropophagie *f.*
anti-aircraft ['ænti'ɛəkrɑːft], *a.* **A.-a. gun**, canon anti-aérien, contre-avion(s).
anti-alcohol(ic) ['æntiælko'hɔl(ik)], *a.* Antialcoolique.
anti-atomic ['æntiə'tɔmik], *a.* Antiatomique.
antibiotic ['æntibai'ɔtik], *s.* Antibiotique *m.*
antibody ['æntibɔdi], *s. Physiol:* Anticorps *m.*
antic ['æntik], *s.* (*Usu. pl.*) (*a*) Bouffonnerie *f,* singerie *f,* cocasserie *f.* **To perform antics**, faire le bouffon, faire des singeries, des farces. (*b*) *pl.* Gambades *f,* cabrioles *f.*
anticathode ['ænti'kæθoud], *s. El:* Anticathode *f.*
antichrist ['æntikraist], *s.* Antéchrist *m.*
antichristian ['ænti'kristjən], *a.* Antichrétien, -ienne.
anticipate [æn'tisipeit], *v.tr.* **1.** (*a*) **To a. events**, one's income, anticiper sur les événements, sur son revenu. **To a. a pleasure**, savourer un plaisir d'avance. (*b*) Escompter (un résultat, un vote). **2. To a. s.o.**, prévenir, devancer, qn. **To a. s.o.'s orders**, s.o.'s desires, prévenir les ordres de qn; aller au-devant des désirs de qn. **3.** Anticiper, avancer (un paiement, l'heure de son arrivée). **4.** Prévoir, envisager, s'attendre à (une difficulté, etc.); se promettre (un plaisir).
anticipation [æn,tisi'peiʃ(ə)n], *s.* Anticipation *f.* **1.** Action *f* d'escompter (un résultat, etc.). *Com:* 'Thanking you in a.,' "avec mes remerciements anticipés." **2.** Prévision *f.* **3.** Attente *f,* expectative *f.*
anticipatory [æn'tisipeitəri], *a.* Anticipé, anticipatif; par anticipation.
anticlerical ['ænti'klerikl], *a. & s.* Anti-clérical, -aux.
anticlericalism ['ænti'kleriklizm], *s.* Anticléricalisme *m.*
anticlimax ['ænti'klaimæks], *s.* **1.** *Rh:* Anti-climax *m;* gradation *f* inverse. **2. The fifth act forms an a.**, avec le cinquième acte nous retombons dans l'ordinaire. **The arrival of the mayor was an a.**, l'arrivée du maire nous a fait revenir au terre à terre.
anticline ['æntiklain], *s. Geol:* Anticlinal, -aux *m.*

anti-clockwise ['ænti'klɔkwaiz], *adv. & pred. a.* Dans le sens inverse des aiguilles d'une montre.
anticoagulant ['æntikou'ægjulənt]. **1.** *a.* Anticoagulant. **2.** *s.* Anticoagulant *m.*
anticolonialism [æntikə'lounjəlizm], *s. Pol:* Anticolonialisme *m.*
anticonstitutional ['ænti'kɔnsti'tjuːʃn(ə)l], *a.* Anticonstitutionnel, -elle. **-ally**, *adv.* Anticonstitutionnellement.
anticyclone ['ænti'saikloun], *s.* Anticyclone *m.*
anti-dazzle ['ænti'dazl], *a.* Anti-aveuglant. *Aut:* **Anti-d. shield**, pare-lumière *m.* **Anti-d. head-lights**, phares-code *m.*
anti-dazzling ['ænti'dæzliŋ], *a.* Anti-aveuglant, anti-éblouissant.
antidotal ['æntidoutl], *a.* Antivénéneux, -euse.
antidote ['æntidout], *s.* Antidote *m,* contre-poison *m;* antivénéneux *m.*
antifading ['ænti'feidiŋ], *a. W.Tel: T.V:* Antifading.
anti-flu ['ænti'fluː], *a.* Antigrippal.
anti-freeze ['ænti'friːz], *s. Aut:* Anti-gel *m inv.*
anti-French ['ænti'fren(t)ʃ], *a.* (Démonstration, etc.) gallophobe, anti-française.
anti-friction ['ænti'frikʃn], *a. Mec.E:* (Garniture, etc.) anti-friction.
anti-G. suit, *F:* **anti-G.** ['ænti'dʒiːsjuːt], *s. Av:* Vêtement anti-g.
antigen ['æntidʒen], *s. Med:* Antigène *m.*
anti-glare ['ænti'glɛə], *a. Aut:* = ANTI-DAZZLE.
antihistamine ['ænt:'histəmin], *s. Med: Pharm:* Antihistaminique *m.*
anti-icer ['ænti'aisər], *s. Av:* Antigivreur *m,* antigivrant *m.*
anti-icing ['ænti'aisiŋ], *s.* Antigivrage *m.*
anti-Jewish ['ænti'dʒuːiʃ], *a.* Antisémitique, antisémite.
anti-knock ['ænti'nɔk], *a. I.C.E: Aut:* (Produit) antidétonant.
Antilles (the) [ðiæn'tiliːz]. *Pr.n.pl. Geog:* Les Antilles *f.*
antilog ['æntilɔg], *s. F:* = ANTILOGARITHM.
antilogarithm ['ænti'lɔgəriθm], *s. Mth:* Antilogarithme *m.*
antimacassar ['æntimə'kæsər], *s.* Têtière *f* (de fauteuil).
antimagnetic ['æntimæg'netik], *a. El: Phy:* Antimagnétique.
antimilitarism ['ænti'militarizm], *s.* Antimilitarisme *m.*
antimilitarist ['ænti'militərist], *s.* Antimilitariste *mf.*
anti-mist ['ænti'mist], *a.* **A.** (**device**), (dispositif) antibuée.
antimony ['æntiməni], *s.* Antimoine *m.* **Grey a.**, stibine *f.*
antinazi ['ænti'nɑːtsi], *a. & s.* Antinazi, -ie.
antineuralgic ['æntinju'rældʒik], *a. & s. Pharm:* Antinévralgique (*m*).
antinode ['æntinoud], *s. Ph:* Antinœud *m,* ventre *m* (d'onde).
antinomy [æn'tinəmi], *s. Phil: Jur:* Antinomie *f.*
antinuclear [,ænti'njuːkliər], *a.* Antiatomique, anti-nucléaire.
Antioch ['æntiɔk]. *Pr.n. A.Geog:* Antioche *f.*
antioxygen ['ænti'ɔksidʒən], *s. Ch:* Antioxygène *m.*
antiparliamentary ['ænti'pɑːlə'ment(ə)ri], *a.* Antiparlementaire.
antipathetic(al) ['æntipə'θetik(əl)], *a.* Antipathique (**to**, à).
antipathy [æn'tipəθi], *s.* Antipathie *f* (**to**, **against**, pour, contre).
anti-personnel ['æntipə:sə'nel], *a.* **A.-p. bomb**, bombe *f* antipersonnel.
antiphon ['æntifən], *s. Ecc.Mus:* Antienne *f.*
antiphonal [æn'tifənl]. **1.** *a.* (*a*) (En forme) d'antienne. (*b*) En contre-chant. **2.** *s.* = ANTIPHONARY.
antiphonary [æn'tifənəri], *s.* Antiphonaire *m.*
antiphony [æn'tifəni], *s.* = ANTIPHON.
antipodal [æn'tipədl], *a. Geog:* Antipodal, -aux.
antipodes [æn'tipədiːz], *s.pl. Geog:* **The a.**, les antipodes *m.*
antipoison ['æntipɔizn], *s.* Contre-poison *m.*
antipope ['æntipoup], *s. Ecc.Hist:* Antipape *m.*
antiproton ['ænti'proutən], *s. Atom.Ph:* Antiproton *m.*
antipyretic ['æntipai'retik], *a. & s. Med:* Fébrifuge (*m*); antipyrétique (*m*).

antiquarian [ˌæntiˈkwɛəriən]. **1.** a. Ancien, -ienne. **A. bookseller**, libraire m qui vend des vieilles éditions; bouquiniste m. **A. collection**, collection d'antiquités. **2.** s. (a) = ANTIQUARY. (b) Com: Antiquaire m.

antiquarianism [ˌæntiˈkwɛəriənizm], s. Goût m des antiquités.

antiquary [ˈæntikwəri], s. Étudiant m ou amateur m d'antiquités.

antiquated [ˈæntikweitid], a. Vieilli; désuet, -ète. **A. dress**, habit démodé, suranné. **A. person**, personne vieux jeu.

antique [ænˈtiːk]. **1.** a. Antique. (a) A: Des anciens. (b) Lit: & Hum: Ancien, vénérable. (c) Suranné. (d) **A. books, prints**, livres anciens, gravures anciennes. (Genuine) a. furniture, meubles d'époque. **2.** s. (a) Art: The a., l'antique m. (b) Objet m antique. **A. shop**, magasin d'antiquités. **A. dealer**, antiquaire m.

antiquity [ænˈtikwiti], s. **1.** (a) Ancienneté f (d'un usage, etc.). (b) L'antiquité (grecque, romaine). **2.** pl. Antiquités.

anti-rabic [ˈæntiˈræbik], a. Med: Vet: Antirabique.

anti-rachitic [ˈæntirəˈkitik], a. Med: (Vitamine f, etc.) antirachitique.

anti-radar [ˈæntiˈreidɑr], a. Mil: Navy: Av: (Mesure de défense) antiradar.

antireligious [ˌæntiriˈlidʒəs], a. Antireligieux, -euse.

antirepublican [ˌæntiriˈpʌblikən], a. & s. Pol: Antirépublicain, -aine.

antirevolutionary [ˈæntiˌrevəˈluːʃən(ə)ri], a. & s. Antirévolutionnaire (mf).

antirrhinum [æntiˈrainəm], s. Bot: Muflier m, F: gueule-de-loup f.

anti-Semite [ˈæntiˈsiːmait], s. Antisémite.

anti-Semitic [ˈæntisiˈmitik], a. Antisémitique, antisémite.

anti-Semitism [ˈæntiˈsemitizm], s. Antisémitisme m.

antisepsis [ˈæntiˈsepsis], s. Med: Antisepsie f.

antiseptic [ˈæntiˈseptik], a. & s. Med: Antiseptique (m).

antisepticize [ˌæntiˈseptisaiz], v.tr. Antiseptiser.

antiserum [ˈæntiˈsiərəm], s. Med: Antisérum m.

anti-skidding [ˈæntiˈskidiŋ], a. Aut: etc: **A.-s. device**, antipatinant (m), antidérapant (m).

antislavery [ˈæntiˈsleivəri], s. Antiesclavagisme m.

antisocial [ˈæntiˈsouʃ(ə)l] a. Antisocial, -aux.

antispark [ˈæntiˈspɑːk], a. Anti-étincelles inv.

antispasmodic [ˈæntispæzˈmɔdik], a. & s. Med: Pharm: Antispasmodique (m).

anti-splash [ˈæntiˈsplæʃ], a. **A.-s. tap-nozzle**, brise-jet m.inv.

anti-striker [ˈæntiˈstraikər], s. Antigréviste mf.

anti-submarine [ˈæntiˈsʌbməˈriːn], a. Navy: **A.-s. warfare**, guerre anti-sous-marine.

antistrophe [ænˈtistrəfi], s. Antistrophe f.

anti-tank [ˈæntiˈtæŋk], a. Mil: Anti-chars, anti-tank.

antitetanic [ˈæntiteˈtænik], a. & s. Med: Pharm: Antitétanique (m).

anti-theft [ˈæntiˈθeft], a. Antivol inv.

antithesis, pl. -es [ænˈtiθisis, -iːz], s. **1.** Antithèse (between, entre; to, of, de). **2.** Opposé m, contraire m (de).

antithetic(al) [ˈæntiˈθetik(əl)], a. Antithétique. **-ally**, adv. Par antithèse.

antitoxic [ˈæntiˈtɔksik], a. Med: Antitoxique; antivénéneux, -euse.

antitoxin [ˈæntiˈtɔksin], s. Med: Antitoxine f.

anti-tubercular [ˈæntitjuˈbəːkjulər], a. Med: Antituberculeux, -euse.

antivirus [ˈæntiˈvaiərəs], s. Bac: Med: Antivirus m.

antivivisectionist [ˈæntivivisekˈʃnist], s. Anti-vivisection(n)iste mf.

antler [ˈæntlər], s. Andouiller m (d'un cerf, etc.). **The antlers**, le bois, les bois.

Antony [ˈæntəni]. Pr.n.m. Antoine. **Mark A.**, Marc Antoine.

antonym [ˈæntənim], s. Antonyme m.

Antwerp [ˈæntwəːp]. Pr.n. Geog: Anvers m. 🏴

anuclear [eiˈnjuːkliər], a. Atom.Ph: Anucléaire.

anus [ˈeinəs], s. Anat: Anus m.

antrum [ˈæntrəm], s. Anat: Antre m, sinus m.

anvil [ˈænvil], s. **1.** Metalw: Enclume f. **Two-horned a.**, bigorne f. **2.** Anat: Enclume (de l'oreille). **'anvil-bed, -block**, s. Billot m d'enclume; semelle f, souche f, d'enclume.

anxiety [æŋˈzaiəti], s. (a) Inquiétude f. **Deep a.**, anxiété f, angoisse f. (b) **A. for s.o.'s safety**, sollicitude f pour la sûreté de qn. (c) **A. for knowledge**, désir m de savoir.

anxious [ˈæŋ(k)ʃəs], a. **1.** (a) Inquiet, ennuyé, soucieux (about, sur, de, au sujet de). **Very a., extremely a.**, tourmenté, angoissé. **To be a. for s.o.'s safety**, (i) être plein de sollicitude pour la sûreté de qn; (ii) craindre pour qn. (b) Inquiétant. **An a. moment**, un moment d'anxiété. **2.** Désireux. **To be a. for sth.**, désirer vivement qch. **To be a. to do sth.**, désirer faire qch.; tenir à faire qch.; être désireux, soucieux, impatient, de faire qch. **Not very a. to meet her**, peu soucieux de se rencontrer avec elle. **I am very a. that he should come**, je tiens beaucoup à ce qu'il vienne. **-ly**, adv. **1.** (a) Avec inquiétude; soucieusement. (b) Anxieusement. **2.** Avec sollicitude. **3.** Avec impatience.

any [ˈeni]. **I.** a. & pron. **1.** (Some(one); in interr. and hypothetical sentences) **Is there a. Englishman who . . .?** y a-t-il un Anglais qui . . .? **Have you a. milk?** avez-vous du lait? **Have you a.?** en avez-vous? **If a. of them should see him**, si aucun d'entre eux le voyait. **If it's in a. way inconvenient**, pour peu que cela vous dérange. . . . **In a. village of a. importance**, dans tout village tant soit peu considérable. **There is little, are few, if a.**, il y en a peu ou pas, si tant est qu'il y en ait. **He knows English if a. man does**, il sait l'anglais comme pas un. **2.** (a) **Not a.**, ne . . . aucun, nul. **He hasn't a. reason to complain**, il n'a aucune raison de se plaindre. **I don't owe a. man a penny**, je ne dois un centime à qui que ce soit. **I can't find a.**, je n'en trouve pas. **I don't think a. of them have arrived**, je ne pense pas qu'aucun d'eux soit arrivé. (b) (With implied negation) **The impossibility of giving him a. education**, l'impossibilité de lui donner aucune éducation. **3.** (a) (No matter which) N'importe (le)quel. **Come a. day (you like)**, venez n'importe quel jour. **Not under a. pretext**, sous aucun prétexte. **A. but he would have refused**, tout autre que lui aurait refusé. **That may happen a. day**, cela peut arriver d'un jour à l'autre. **Draw a. two cards**, tirez deux cartes quelconques. (b) (A. and every) **A. pupil who forgets his books . . .**, tout élève qui oubliera ses livres. . . . **At a. hour of the day**, à toute heure de la journée. **II.** any, adv. (Not translated) **I cannot go a. further**, je ne peux aller plus loin. **Will you have a. more tea?** voulez-vous encore du thé?

anybody [ˈenibɔdi], **anyone** [ˈeniwʌn], s. & pron. **1.** (= 'Someone' in hypothetical and interr. sentences) Quelqu'un; (with implied negation) personne. **Do you see a. over there?** voyez-vous quelqu'un là-bas? **Does a. dare to say so?** y a-t-il personne qui ose le dire? **You may bring along a. you like**, vous amènerez qui vous voudrez. F: **Is he a.?** est-il quelqu'un? **2.** (In neg. sentences) **Not a., not anyone**, ne . . . personne. **There was hardly a.**, il n'y avait presque personne. **3.** (No matter who) N'importe qui; tout le monde. **A. will tell you so**, le premier venu vous le dira. **A. would think him mad**, on le croirait fou. **A. who had seen him at that time . . .**, quiconque l'aurait vu alors. . . . **A. but he**, tout autre que lui. S.a. ELSE 2.

anyhow [ˈenihau]. **1.** adv. **To do sth. a.**, faire qch. (i) d'une manière quelconque, (ii) n'importe comment, tant bien que mal. **Things are (going) all a.**, tout est en désordre, en pagaille. F: **You look all a.**, vous paraissez tout chose. **2.** conj. (At any rate) En tout cas, de toute façon; toujours est-il que. **A. you can try**, vous pouvez toujours essayer.

anything [ˈeniθiŋ], pron. & s. **1.** (= Something, in interr. and hypothetical sentences) Quelque chose; (with implied negation) rien. **Can I do a. for you?** puis-je vous être utile à quelque chose? **Is there a. more pleasant than . . .?** est-il rien de plus agréable que . . .? **If a. should happen to him . . .**, s'il lui arrivait quelque malheur. . . . **He must be earning a. from £40 to £50 a week**, il doit gagner au moins dans les 40 à 50 Livres par semaine. **2.** (In neg. sentences) **Not a.**, ne . . . rien. **He doesn't do a.**, il ne fait rien. **Without doing a.**, sans rien faire. **Hardly a.**, presque rien. **3.** (No matter what) N'importe quoi;

tout. He eats a., il mange de tout. A. you like, tout ce que vous voudrez. He is a. but mad, il n'est rien moins que fou. *S.a.* BUT 3, ELSE 2, IF 1. **4.** *Adv.phr.* (*Intensive*) F: Like a. To work like a., travailler avec acharnement. To run like a., courir à toutes jambes. It is raining like a., il pleut tant qu'il peut.

anyway ['eniwei], *adv. & conj.* = ANYHOW 2.

anywhere ['eniwɛər], *adv.* **1.** N'importe où; dans quelque endroit que ce soit. Can you see it a.? peux-tu le voir quelque part? A. else, partout ailleurs. Are you going a.? allez-vous quelque part? faites-vous quelque chose? **2.** Not . . . a., nulle part; en aucun endroit, en aucun lieu.

anywise ['einiwaiz], *adv.* (*also in a.*). A: **1.** D'une manière quelconque. **2.** En aucune façon; d'aucune façon. If he has in a. offended you, s'il vous a offensé en aucune façon.

Anzac ['ænzæk], *s.m. Hist:* Membre de l'Australian and New Zealand Army Corps (1914-1918).

aorta [ei'ɔːtə], *s. Anat:* Aorte *f. Med:* Inflammation of the a., aortite *f.*

aortal [ei'ɔːtl], **aortic** [ei'ɔːtik], *a. Anat:* Aortique. *Med:* A. insufficiency, insuffisance *f* aortique.

apace [ə'peis], *adv. Lit:* A grands pas; vite, rapidement. Winter is coming on a., voici déjà l'hiver.

Apache [ə'pætʃi], *s.* **1.** *Ethn:* Apache *m.* **2.** F: [ə'pæʃ] (*Hooligan*) Apache.

apanage ['æpənidʒ], *s.* Apanage *m.*

apart [ə'pɑːt], *adv.* A part. **1.** (*Aside*) De côté. To live a. from the world, vivre éloigné du monde. A class a., un genre à part. **2.** (*Asunder, separate*) To get two things a., séparer deux choses. The boys and girls were kept a., on tenait séparés les garçons et les filles. To move a., se séparer. To come a., se détacher, se défaire, se désunir. To take a machine a., démonter, désassembler, une machine. It is difficult to tell them a., il est difficile de les distinguer l'un de l'autre. To stand with one's feet wide a., se tenir les jambes écartées. **3.** (*a*) (*Distant*) They are a mile a., ils sont à un mille l'un de l'autre. Lines ten centimetres a., lignes espacées de dix centimètres. (*b*) A. from the fact that . . ., hormis que . . ., outre que. . . . A. from these reasons . . ., en dehors de ces raisons . . ., ces raisons mises à part. . . . Jesting, joking, a., plaisanterie à part; F: sans blague.

apartheid [ə'pɑːteit, -eid], *s.* (*In South Africa*) Ségrégation *f.*

apartment [ə'pɑːtmənt], *s.* (*a*) Salle *f*, chambre *f*; pièce *f.* (*b*) (*Usu. pl.*) Logement *m*; appartement *m.* To take apartments, retenir, prendre, un appartement. To let furnished apartments, louer en meublé. *Pej:* en garni. (*c*) *U.S:* (*Flat*) Appartement *m.* A. house, Maison *f* de rapport; immeuble *m* d'habitation, de logement.

apathetic [æpə'θetik], *a.* Apathique, indifférent. **-ally,** *adv.* Apathiquement; nonchalamment.

apathy ['æpəθi], *s.* Apathie *f*, nonchalance *f.*

ape¹ [eip], *s. Z:* (Grand) singe (sans queue).

ape², *v.tr.* Singer; imiter; mimer; contrefaire.

apeak [ə'piːk], *adv. & pred. a. Nau:* **1.** (Ancre) à pic, dérapée. **2.** Yard-arms a., vergues en pantenne, apiquées. Oars a., avirons mâtés.

Apennines (the) [ði:'æpinainz]. *Pr.n.pl. Geog:* Les Apennins *m.pl.*

apepsia [ə'pepsiə], **apepsy** [ə'pepsi], *s. Med:* Apepsie *f.*

aperient [ə'piəriənt], *a. & s. Med:* Laxatif (*m*).

aperiodic [ˌei,piəri'ɔdik], *a. Mec:* Apériodique.

apéritif [ə'peritif], *s.* Apéritif *m.*

aperitive [ə'peritiv]. **1.** *a.* Laxatif, -ive. **2.** *s.* = APÉRITIF.

aperture ['æpətjuər], *s.* (*a*) Ouverture *f*, orifice *m.* (*b*) *Phot:* Ouverture (d'un objectif, du diaphragme). A. ratio, relative a., ouverture relative.

apex, *pl.* **apexes, apices** ['eipeks, -iz, 'eipisiːz], *s.* Sommet *m*, apex *m* (d'un triangle, d'une montagne). Point culminant, apogée *m* (d'une carrière).

aphasia [ə'feiziə], *s. Med:* Aphasie *f.*

aphasi(a)c [ə'feizi(æ)k], *a. & s. Med:* Aphasique (*mf*).

aphelion [æ'fiːliən], *s. Astr:* Aphélie *f.*

aphis, *pl.* **-ides** ['eifis, 'æfis, -idiːz], *s. Ent:* Aphis *m*; puceron *m.*

aphonia [æ'founjə], *s. Med:* Aphonie *f.*

aphonic [æ'fɔnik], *a.* **1.** *Med: etc:* Aphone. **2.** *Ling:* (Phonème) sourd.

aphorism ['æfərizm], *s.* Aphorisme *m.*

aphoristic [ˌæfə'ristik], *a.* Aphoristique. **-ally,** *adv.* Par aphorisme.

aphrodisiac [ˌæfro'diziæk], *a. & s.* Aphrodisiaque (*m*).

Aphrodite [ˌæfro'daiti]. *Pr.n.f. Gr.Myth:* Aphrodite.

aphtha, *pl.* **-ae** ['æfθə, -iː], *s. Med: Vet:* (*a*) Pustule aphteuse. (*b*) *pl.* Aphtes *m.*

apiarian [eipi'ɛəriən], *a.* (Société) abeillère; (appareil) apicole.

apiarist ['eipiərist], *s.* Apiculteur *m.*

apiary ['eipiəri], *s.* Rucher *m.*

apices. *See* APEX.

apiculture ['eipikʌltʃər], *s.* Apiculture *f.*

apiculturist [ˌeipi'kʌltʃərist], *s.* Apiculteur, -trice.

apiece [ə'piːs], *adv.* Chacun. To cost a penny a., coûter un penny (la) pièce. He gave them five francs a., il leur donna cinq francs chacun.

apish ['eipiʃ], *a.* **1.** Simiesque. A. trick, singerie *f.* **2.** Imitateur, -trice. **-ly,** *adv.* En singe.

apishness ['eipiʃnis], *s.* Singeries *fpl*; sotte imitation.

aplomb [ə'plɔm], *s.* Sang-froid *m*; confiance *f* en soi.

apocalypse [ə'pokəlips], *s.* Apocalypse *f.*

apocalyptic(al) [ə,pokə'liptik(əl)], *a.* Apocalyptique. **-ally,** *adv.* D'une manière apocalyptique.

apocope [ə'pokəpi], *s. Ling:* Apocope *f.*

Apocrypha (the) [ði:ə'pokrifə], *s.pl. B. Lit:* Les Apocryphes *m.*

apocryphal [ə'pokrifəl], *a.* Apocryphe.

apod(e), *pl.* **-es, -a, -s** ['æpɔd, -oud, *pl.* 'æpodiːz, 'æpodə, 'æpodz], *a. & s. Z:* Apode *m.*

apodosis, *pl.* **-es** [ə'podəsis, -iːz], *s. Gram:* Apodose *f.*

apogee ['æpodʒiː], *s.* Apogée *m.* The moon is at a., la lune est à son apogée.

Apollo [ə'polou]. *Pr.n.m. Myth:* Apollon.

Apollyon [ə'poljən]. *Pr.n.m.* L'Ange de l'abîme; Satan.

apologetic(al) [ə,polə'dʒetik(əl)], *a.* **1.** (Ton, etc.) d'excuse. He was quite a. about it, il s'en excusa vivement. **2.** (Livre, etc.) apologétique. **-ally,** *adv.* **1.** En manière d'excuse; pour s'excuser; en s'excusant. **2.** Sous forme d'apologie.

apologetics [ə,polə'dʒetiks], *s.pl.* (*usu. with sing. concord.*) Apologétique *f.*

apologia [ˌæpə'loudʒ(i)ə], *s.* Justification *f* (de sa vie, etc.).

apologist [ə'polədʒist], *s.* Apologiste *m.*

apologize [ə'polədʒaiz], *v.i.* To a. to s.o. for sth., s'excuser de qch. auprès de qn. To a. for doing sth., s'excuser de faire qch. To a. for one's attire, s'excuser sur sa tenue.

apologue ['æpolog], *s.* Apologue *m.*

apology [ə'polədʒi], *s.* **1.** (*a*) Excuses *fpl.* Letter of a., lettre d'excuses. To make, offer, an a., faire, présenter, des excuses. To demand an a., exiger des excuses. To be profuse in one's apologies, se répandre, se confondre, en excuses. (*b*) F: An a. for a dinner, un semblant de dîner, un piètre dîner. **2.** Apologie *f* (for, de); justification *f.*

apophony [ə'pofəni], *s. Ling:* Alternance *f* (de voyelles); ablaut *m*; apophonie *f.*

apoplectic [ˌæpə'plektik], *a.* (Personne) apoplectique; (attaque) d'apoplexie.

apoplexy ['æpəpleksi], *s. Med:* Apoplexie *f*; congestion (cérébrale). Heat a., coup *m* de chaleur; coup de soleil.

apostasy [ə'postəsi], *s.* Apostasie *f.*

apostate [ə'postit], *a. & s.* Apostat (*m*).

apostatize [ə'postətaiz], *v.i.* Apostasier. To a. from one's faith, apostasier sa foi.

apostle [ə'posl], *s.* Apôtre *m.* The Apostles' Creed, le Symbole des Apôtres. A. spoon, cuillère *f* avec figurine d'apôtre.

apostleship [ə'poslʃip], **apostolate** [ə'postəlit], *s.* Apostolat *m.*

apostolic(al) [ˌæpə'stolik(əl)], *a.* Apostolique. **-ally,** *adv.* Apostoliquement.

apostrophe [ə'postrəfi], *s.* Apostrophe *f.*

apostrophize [ə'postrəfaiz], *v.tr.* Apostropher.

apothecary [ə'poθikəri], *s.* A: Apothicaire *m*, pharmacien *m.* Apothecary's shop, pharmacie *f.*

apotheosis, *pl.* -oses [ə‚pɒθi'ousis, -'ousi:z], *s.* Apothéose *f.*
apotheosize [ə'pɒθiosaiz], *v.tr.* Apothéoser.
appal [ə'pɔːl], *v.tr.* (**appalled**) Consterner; épouvanter. **appalling**, *a.* Épouvantable, effroyable. *F:* You're making an a. row, vous faites un bruit de tous les diables. **-ly**, *adv.* Épouvantablement, effroyablement.
Appalachian [‚æpə'leitʃiən, -'lætʃ], *a. Geog:* Appalachien, -ienne. The Appalachians, A. Mountains, les (monts) Appalaches *mpl.*
apparatus, *pl.* -us, -uses [‚æpə'reitəs, -əsiz], *s.* (*Pl. more usu.* pieces of a.) (*a*) Appareil *m,* dispositif *m.* (*b*) Fishing a., attirail *m* de pêche.
apparel [ə'pær(ə)l], *s.* (*No pl.*) *A:* Vêtement(s) *m,* habillement *m,* habits *mpl.*
apparent [ə'pær(ə)nt, ə'peər(ə)nt], *a.* (Qui est ou qui semble être) apparent, manifeste, évident. The truth became a. to him, la vérité lui apparut. In spite of his a. indifference, malgré son air d'indifférence. *S.a.* HEIR. **-ly**, *adv.* 1. Évidemment, manifestement. 2. Apparemment. This is a. true, il paraît que c'est vrai.
apparition [‚æpə'riʃ(ə)n], *s.* 1. Apparition *f.* 2. Fantôme *m,* revenant *m.*
apparitor [ə'pæritər], *s.m.* Appariteur.
appeal¹ [ə'piːl], *s.* 1. Appel *m,* recours *m.* A. to arms, recours aux armes. *Jur:* A. at law, appel. A. from a sentence, appel d'une condamnation. Court of A., cour d'appel. To hear an a. from a decision, juger en appel d'une décision. Without a., sans appel; en dernier ressort. Notice of a., intimation *f* (d'appel). To lodge an a., interjeter appel, se pourvoir en appel. To lodge an a. with the Supreme Court, se pourvoir en cassation. The condemned men have been informed of the rejection of their a., les condamnés ont été informés du rejet de leur recours *m* en grâce. 2. (*a*) To make an a. to s.o.'s generosity, faire appel à la générosité de qn. (*b*) The a. of the sea, l'attrait *m* de la mer. 3. Prière *f,* supplication *f.*
appeal², *v.i.* 1. *Jur: etc:* (*a*) To a. to the law, invoquer l'aide de la justice, de la loi. To a. from a judgment, appeler d'un jugement. To a. to the Supreme Court, se pourvoir en cassation. To a. to the sword, to the country, en appeler à l'épée, au pays. To a. to s.o.'s indulgence, faire appel à l'indulgence de qn. (*b*) *Abs.* Interjeter appel. 2. To a. to s.o. for help, demander des secours à qn; avoir recours à qn; faire appel à qn. To a. for a cause, adresser, lancer, un appel en faveur d'une cause. 3. To a. to s.o.'s imagination, s'adresser à l'imagination de qn; (*of thg*) attirer, séduire, charmer, l'imagination. If it appeals to you, si le cœur vous en dit, vous en chante. The plan appeals to me, le projet me sourit. That doesn't a. to me, cela ne me dit rien. **appealing**, *a.* 1. (Regard, etc.) suppliant. 2. (Ton) émouvant. 3. (Personnalité) sympathique. **-ly**, *adv.* D'un ton, d'un regard, suppliant.
appear [ə'piər], *v.i.* 1. (*Become visible*) Paraître, apparaître; devenir visible; se montrer. When Christ shall a., quand le Christ paraîtra. A ghost appeared to him, un spectre lui apparut. 2. (*Present oneself publicly*) (*a*) Se présenter. *Jur:* To a. before a court, comparaître devant un tribunal. To a. for s.o., représenter qn; (*of counsel*) plaider pour qn. (*b*) (*Of actor*) To a. on the stage, entrer en scène; paraître sur la scène. (*c*) (*Of book*) Paraître. 3. (*a*) (*Seem*) To a. sad, paraître, sembler, triste. He appeared to hesitate, il paraissait hésiter. So it appears, so it would a., il paraît que oui. It appears not, il paraît que non. The boat, it appears, did not call at . . ., le navire, à ce qu'il paraît, n'a pas fait escale à. . . . (*b*) (*Be manifest*) As will presently a., comme on le verra bientôt.
appearance [ə'piərəns], *s.* 1. (*a*) Apparition *f;* entrée *f.* To make an a., one's a., paraître, faire son apparition, se montrer, se présenter, arriver. To put in an a., faire acte de présence. *Th:* First a. of Miss X, début *m* de Mlle X. To make one's first a., débuter; faire ses débuts. 2. *Jur:* Comparution *f* (devant un tribunal). (*c*) *Publ:* Parution *f* (d'un livre). 2. (*a*) (*Look, aspect*) Apparence *f,* aspect *m,* air *m,* figure *f,* mine *f,* dehors *m.* A pleasing a., un extérieur aimable; des dehors agréables. To have a good a., faire bonne

figure. The a. of the streets, l'aspect des rues. At first a., à première vue; au premier abord. One should not judge by appearances, il ne faut pas juger sur l'apparence, sur les dehors. (*b*) (*Semblance*) Apparence. To, by, all appearance(s), selon toute apparence; apparemment. For the sake of appearances, pour sauver les apparences; pour la forme.
appease [ə'piːz], *v.tr.* (*a*) Apaiser, tranquilliser (qn). (*b*) Apaiser, assouvir (la faim).
appeasement [ə'piːzmənt], *s.* (*a*) Apaisement *m.* (*b*) Assouvissement *m.* (*c*) A. policy, politique *f* d'apaisement, de conciliation *f.*
appeaser [ə'piːzər], *s.* Conciliateur, -trice.
appellant [ə'pelənt], *a. & s. Jur:* Appelant *m.*
appellate [ə'pelit], *a. Jur:* A. jurisdiction, juridiction *f* d'appel.
appellation [æpe'leiʃ(ə)n], *s.* Appellation *f,* nom *m,* titre *m,* désignation *f.*
appellative [ə'pelətiv]. 1. *Gram:* (*a*) *a.* Appellatif; (nom) commun. (*b*) *s.* Nom commun; nom générique. 2. *s.* Appellation *f.*
append [ə'pend], *v.tr.* (*a*) Attacher, joindre (qch. à qch.). *Esp.* (*b*) To a. a signature to a document, apposer une signature sur un document. To a. a document to a dossier, annexer un document à un dossier. To a. notes, ajouter des notes.
appendage [ə'pendidʒ], *s.* 1. Accessoire *m,* apanage *m* (to, de). The house and its appendages, la maison et ses dépendances *f,* et ses annexes *f.* 2. *Anat: Nat.Hist:* Appendice *m.*
append(ic)ectomy [ə‚pend(is)'ektəmi], *s. Surg:* Appendicectomie *f.*
appendicitis [ə‚pendi'saitis], *s.* Appendicite *f.*
appendix, *pl.* -ixes, -ices [ə'pendiks, -iksiz -isi:z], *s.* Appendice *m.* 1. *Anat:* Vermiform a., appendice vermiforme. 2. Annexe *f* (d'un rapport, etc.); appendice (d'un livre).
appertain [æpə'tein], *v.i. Adm. & Lit:* 1. Appartenir (to, à). 2. As appertains to my office, comme il appartient à mes fonctions. 3. Se rapporter (to, à).
appetite ['æpitait], *s.* (*a*) Appétit *m.* To have a good a., avoir bon appétit. To spoil, take away, s.o.'s a., gâter, couper, l'appétit à qn. To eat with (an) a., manger de bon appétit. I have quite lost my a., j'en ai perdu le boire et le manger. (*b*) A. for revenge, soif *f* de vengeance.
appetizer ['æpitaizər], *s.* (*a*) Apéritif *m.* (*b*) Amuse-gueule *m, pl.* amuse-gueule(s). (*c*) A walk is a good a., une promenade vous ouvre l'appétit.
appetizing ['æpitaiziŋ], *a.* Appétissant, alléchant.
applaud [ə'plɔːd], *v.tr.* 1. Applaudir (qn.) 2. To a. s.o.'s efforts, applaudir aux efforts de qn.
applause [ə'plɔːz], *s.* 1. Applaudissements *mpl.* To meet, be greeted, with a., être applaudi. To win a., se faire applaudir (from, par, de). 2. Approbation *f.*
apple ['æpl], *s.* 1. Pomme *f.* Eating a., dessert a., pomme au couteau. Stewed apples, compote *f* de pommes; pommes en compote. Baked a., pomme cuite au four. *S.a.* ADAM, DUMPLING, TURN-OVER 3. 2. A. of the eye, prunelle *f* de l'œil. apple-'brandy, *s.* Calvados *m.* 'apple-cart, *s.* Voiture *f* à bras (de marchand des quatre saisons). *F:* To upset s.o.'s a.-c., bouleverser, chambarder, les plans de qn. 'apple-cheeked, *a.* Aux joues pleines et vermeilles; à figure de pomme d'api. 'apple-core, *s.* Trognon *m* de pomme. apple-'green, *a. & s.* Vert pomme *m inv.* 'apple-jack, *s.* = APPLE-BRANDY. 'apple-orchard, *s.* Pommeraie *f.* apple-'pie, *s.* Tourte *f* aux pommes. *F:* In 'a.-p. order, en ordre parfait. 'A.-p. bed, lit *m* en portefeuille. 'apple-polisher, *s. U.S:* Flagorneur, -euse; lécheur, -euse (de bottes). apple-'sauce, *s.* Compote *f* de pommes. apple-'tart, *s.* Tourte *f,* tarte *f,* aux pommes. 'apple-tree, *s.* Pommier *m.*
appliance [ə'plaiəns], *s.* (*a*) Appareil *m,* instrument *m,* dispositif *m;* engin *m.* (*b*) *pl.* Accessoires *m* (d'une machine, etc.); attirail *m.*
applicability [ə‚plikə'biliti], *s.* Applicabilité *f.*
applicable ['æplikəbl], *a.* 1. Applicable (to, à). 2. Approprié (to, à).
applicant ['æplikənt], *s.* 1. A. for a post, candidat *m* à un emploi. 2. *Jur:* Demandeur, -deresse; requérant, -ante.

application [ˌæpliˈkeiʃ(ə)n], s. **1.** (a) Application f, applicage m (of sth. to sth., de qch. à, sur, qch.). *Pharm:* 'For external a.' "pour l'usage externe." (b) (*Thing applied*) Application; enduit m. (c) Industrial applications of a discovery, applications industrielles d'une découverte. Practical applications of a process, réalisations f d'un procédé. **2.** Assiduité f, application (à l'étude, etc.). **3.** Demande f, sollicitation f, requête f. A. for a job, for help, for a patent, demande d'emploi, de secours, de brevet. To make a. to s.o. for sth., s'adresser à qn pour avoir qch. Samples are sent on a., on envoie des échantillons sur demande.

applicator [æplikeitər], s. *Pharm: Com:* Applicateur m.

appliqué [æˈpliːkei], s. *Dressm:* Aplat m, appliqué m. *Needlew:* Broderie-application f. A. lace, dentelle f princesse.

apply [əˈplai], v.tr. & i. **1.** (a) Appliquer (sth. to sth., qch. sur qch.); faire l'application de (qch. à qch.). To a. a poultice, appliquer un cataplasme. *Aut:* To a. the brake, freiner, serrer le frein. (b) To a. a system, appliquer un système; mettre un système en pratique. This applies to my case, ceci s'applique à mon propre cas. (c) To a. one's mind to sth., appliquer son esprit à qch.; s'appliquer à qch. To a. oneself to one's work, travailler avec application; s'attacher à son travail. **2.** To a. to s.o. for sth., s'adresser, recourir, avoir recours, à qn pour obtenir qch. To a. for a post, poser sa candidature à un emploi; solliciter, postuler, un emploi. **applied**, a. The a. sciences, les sciences appliquées. A. arts, arts industriels.

appoggiatura [əˌpɔdʒəˈtuərə], s. *Mus:* Appog(g)iature f.

appoint [əˈpoint], v.tr. **1.** Nommer. (a) *Pred.* To a. s.o. (to be) mayor, nommer qn maire. (b) To a. s.o. to sth., to do sth., nommer qn à qch.; désigner qn pour faire qch. To a. s.o. to a post, to a ship, désigner qn à, pour, un poste, un bateau. He was appointed headmaster of Eton (College), il fut choisi comme directeur du Collège d'Eton. **2.** (a) Fixer, désigner, assigner (l'heure, l'endroit); arrêter (un jour). (b) To a. that sth. shall be done, décider que qch. se fera; prescrire que qch. se fasse. **appointed**, a. **1.** Désigné. (a) At the a. time, à l'heure dite, convenue, indiquée. (b) A. agent, agent attitré. **2.** Équipé, monté. Well-a. house, maison bien installée.

appointment [əˈpointmənt], s. **1.** Rendez-vous m; (*for business*) entrevue f; *Adm:* convocation f. To make, accept, an a. for three o'clock, prendre rendez-vous pour trois heures. To break an a., manquer au rendez-vous. **2.** (a) A. of s.o. to a post, to a ship, nomination f de qn à un emploi; *Adm:* désignation f de qn pour un emploi, un navire. Purveyor by special a. to His, Her, Majesty, fournisseur breveté, attitré, de sa Majesté. (b) Place f, charge f, emploi m. *Journ:* 'Appointments Vacant,' "Situations vacantes." **3.** pl. Aménagement m, installation f (d'une maison); équipement m (d'une auto, etc.).

apportion [əˈpɔːʃ(ə)n], v.tr. *Fin:* Répartir (les frais); lotir (une propriété). *Book-k:* Ventiler. To a. sth. to s.o., assigner qch. à qn.

apportionment [əˈpɔːʃ(ə)nmənt], s. Partage m, répartition f; allocation f; lotissement m. *Book-k:* Ventilation f.

appose [æˈpouz], v.tr. To a. one's signature to a document, revêtir un document de sa signature.

apposite [ˈæpozit], a. Juste; approprié (to, à); (fait) à propos. **-ly**, adv. A propos; convenablement.

appositeness [ˈæpozitnis], s. Justesse f, à-propos m; opportunité f (d'une action).

apposition [æpoˈziʃ(ə)n], s. *Gram: etc:* Apposition f. Words in a., mots appositifs.

appraisal [əˈpreiz(ə)l], **appraisement** [əˈpreizmənt], s. Évaluation f, estimation f, appréciation f. Official appraisement, expertise f.

appraise [əˈpreiz], v.tr. Priser, estimer, évaluer (qch.) (at so much, à tant); faire l'expertise (des dégâts).

appraiser [əˈpreizər], s. Estimateur m, priseur m, évaluateur m. Official a., (of property, etc.), commissaire-priseur m; expert m.

appreciable [əˈpriːʃəbl], a. Appréciable; sensible. **-ably**, adv. Sensiblement.

appreciate [əˈpriːʃieit]. **1.** v.tr. (a) Évaluer (des marchandises); estimer la valeur de (qch.). (b) Apprécier; faire cas de (qch.). Songs greatly appreciated, chansons très goûtées. I fully a. the fact that . . ., je me rends clairement compte que. . . . I fully a. all you have done, je ne méconnais pas vos services. **2.** *Fin:* (a) v.tr. Hausser la valeur de (qch.). To a. the coinage, rehausser les monnaies. (b) v.i. (*Of goods*) Augmenter de valeur; hausser de prix; monter.

appreciation [əˌpriːʃiˈeiʃ(ə)n], s. **1.** (a) Appréciation f (i) du prix, de la valeur, de qch.; (ii) d'un service, de la situation, etc.); estimation f (de la valeur de qch.); évaluation f. To show a. (of s.o.'s kindness), apprécier la bonté de qn, remercier qn. (b) To give, write, an a. of a new play, faire la critique d'une nouvelle pièce. *Sch:* (Literary) a. of a text, explication f de texte. **2.** Accroissement m, hausse f, de valeur.

appreciative [əˈpriːʃiətiv], **appreciatory** [əˈpriːʃiət(ə)ri], a. **1.** (Jugement, etc.) élogieux. **2.** To be appreciative of music, être sensible à la musique; apprécier la musique. **-ively**, adv. (a) Favorablement. (b) Avec satisfaction. (c) Avec gratitude.

apprehend [æpriˈhend], v.tr. **1.** *Jur:* Arrêter (qn); appréhender (qn) (au corps); saisir (qn) au corps. **2.** *Lit:* (a) Percevoir. (b) Comprendre, saisir (le sens d'une phrase). **3.** *Lit:* Appréhender, redouter.

apprehensible [æpriˈhensibl], a. Appréhensible (to, by, the senses, par les sens); perceptible.

apprehension [æpriˈhen(ʃ)(ə)n], s. **1.** *Jur:* Arrestation f; prise f de corps. **2.** *Lit:* (a) Perception f; compréhension f. (b) *Psy:* Entendement m. **3.** Appréhension f, crainte f.

apprehensive [æpriˈhensiv], a. **1.** The a. faculty, la faculté de comprendre, de percevoir. The a. faculties, les facultés perceptives. **2.** Timide, craintif. To be a. of danger, redouter le danger. To be a. of failure, craindre d'échouer. **-ly**, adv. Avec appréhension, avec crainte.

apprehensiveness [æpriˈhensivnis], s. **1.** *Lit:* Faculté f de comprendre, de percevoir. **2.** Appréhension f; timidité f.

apprentice¹ [əˈprentis], s. (a) Apprenti, -ie. (b) *Nau:* Apprenti marin; novice m. *Av:* A.-pilot, aspirant m pilote. (c) Élève (d'un architecte).

apprentice², v.tr. To a. s.o. to s.o., placer, mettre, qn (i) en apprentissage chez qn, (ii) comme élève chez un architecte. **apprenticed**, a. En apprentissage (to, chez).

apprenticeship [əˈprentisʃip], s. Apprentissage m.

apprise [əˈpraiz], v.tr. *Lit:* To a. s.o. of sth., apprendre qch. à qn; prévenir qn de qch. To be apprised of a fact, avoir connaissance d'un fait.

appro [ˈæprou], s. *F: Com:* On a., à condition, à l'examen, à l'essai.

approach¹ [əˈproutʃ], s. Approche f. **1.** (a) The a. of death, l'approche, les approches, de la mort. (b) Abord m. His a. to the problem, sa méthode d'attaque du problème, la façon dont il aborde le problème. Freshness of a., fraîcheur f d'imagination. I don't like his a., il n'aime pas sa façon de s'y prendre. (c) To make approaches to s.o., faire des avances à qn. **2.** Voie f d'accès. The a. to a town, les abords, approches, d'une ville. **3.** Rapprochement m. It is an a. to perfection, cela approche de la perfection. **4.** *Golf:* A. shot, coup m d'approche.

approach². **1.** v.i. Approcher, s'approcher. *Golf:* Jouer le coup d'approche. To a. to perfection, approcher de la perfection. **2.** v.tr. (a) We are approaching London, nous approchons de Londres. (b) S'approcher de (qn); aborder, approcher (qn); entrer en communication avec (qn). To a. s.o. on the subject of . . ., faire une démarche auprès de qn au sujet de. . . . To be easy, difficult, to a., avoir l'abord facile, difficile. (c) To a. a question, aborder, s'attaquer à, une question. **approaching**, a. Approchant. (a) His a. death, sa mort prochaine. (b) The a. car, la voiture qui venait en sens inverse. (c) Avoisinant. It was with sth. a. a feeling of relief that . . ., ce fut avec un sentiment presque de soulagement que. . . .

approachability [ə‚proutʃə'biliti], s. Accessibilité f.
approachable [ə'proutʃəbl], a. Accessible, approchable; (personne, côte)' abordable.
approbate ['æprobeit], v.tr. U.S: = APPROVE.
approbation [‚æpro'beiʃ(ə)n], s. Approbation f. 1. Agrément m, consentement m. 2. Jugement m favorable. **To show one's a.**, manifester son approbation. **Smile of a.**, sourire approbateur.
appropriate¹ [ə'proupriit], a. 1. Approprié. **Style a. to the subject**, style qui' convient au sujet; style approprié au sujet. 2. Propre, convenable (to, for, à). **The remark is a.**, l'observation est juste, à propos. **-ly**, adv. Convenablement, proprement; à propos; comme il convient.
appropriate² [ə'prouprieit], v.tr. 1. S'approprier (qch.); s'emparer de (qch.). 2. Approprier, affecter, consacrer (sth. to, for, a purpose, qch. à une destination).
appropriateness [ə'prouprⅰitnis], s. Convenance f, justesse f, à-propos m, applicabilité f.
appropriation [ə‚proupri'eiʃ(ə)n], s. 1. Appropriation f, prise f de possession (of, de). 2. (a) Appropriation, affectation f (de qch. à un usage). (b) Affectation de fonds. 3. Crédit m (budgétaire); budget m.
appropriator [ə'proupri‚eitər], s. Usurpateur, -trice (of, de). **To be an a. of sth.**, s'approprier qch.
approvable [ə'pru:vəbl], a. Digne d'approbation f; qui mérite l'approbation.
approval [ə'pru:v(ə)l], s. 1. Approbation f, agrément m. **I hope it will meet with your a.**, j'espère que vous en serez satisfait. **Gesture, sign, of a.**, geste, signe, approbateur. **To nod a.**, approuver de la tête. 2. Adm: Ratification f, homologation f. 3. Com: **On a.**, à condition, à l'examen, à l'essai.
approve [ə'pru:v]. 1. v.tr. (a) A: **To a. oneself**, faire ses preuves. **The old approved methods**, les méthodes classiques. (b) Approuver, sanctionner (une action); ratifier, homologuer (une décision); agréer (un contrat). **Read and approved**, lu et approuvé. Adm: **Approved society**, compagnie d'assurances agréée par l'État. **Approved school** = maison de redressement; maison d'éducation surveillée. 2. v.ind.tr. **To a. of sth.**, approuver qch. **To a. of a suitor**, agréer un prétendant. **I don't a. of your friends**, vos amis ne me plaisent pəs. **To a. of s.o.'s doing sth.**, approuver, trouver bon, que qn fasse qch. **approving**, a. Approbateur, -trice; approbatif. **-ly**, adv. D'un air, d'un ton, approbateur.
approver [ə'pru:vər], s. 1. Approbateur, -trice. 2. Jur: Complice m dénonciateur de ses camarades.
approximate¹ [ə'prɔks(i)mit], a. 1. Biol: Ph: Rapproché, proche, voisin. 2. (Calcul, etc.) approximatif, approché. **-ly**, adv. Approximativement.
approximate² [ə'prɔksimeit]. 1. v.tr. Rapprocher (deux cas, etc.). 2. v.i. **To a. to the truth**, approcher, se rapprocher, de la vérité.
approximation [ə‚prɔksi'meiʃ(ə)n], s. 1. Rapprochement m. 2. Approximation f. **A. to the truth**, approximation de la vérité. **To be satisfied with an a.**, se contenter d'un à-peu-près.
approximative [ə'prɔksimətiv], a. Approximatif. **-ly**, adv. Par approximation.
appurtenance [ə'pə:tinəns], s. 1. Jur: (a) Appartenance f. (b) Droit m accessoire, servitude f (d'un immeuble). 2. pl. Accessoires m, attirail m.
appurtenant [ə'pə:tinənt], a. Jur: (a) **A. to sth.**, appartenant à qch.; dépendant de qch. (b) Propre, particulier (to, à).
après-ski [apreski], a. **A.-s. outfit**, tenue f d'après-ski.
apricot ['eiprikət], s. 1. Abricot m. 2. **A.(-tree)**, abricotier m.
April ['eipril], s. Avril m. **In A.**, au mois d'avril, en avril. **(On) the first, the seventh, of A.**, le premier, le sept, avril. **A. Fools' Day**, le premier avril. **To make an A.-fool of s.o.**, donner, faire, un poisson d'avril à qn.
a priori [‚eiprai'ɔ:rai], adv. A priori. **A p. reasoning**, apriorisme m.
apriorism [‚eiprai'ɔrizm], s. Apriorisme m.
apron ['eiprən], s. 1. Cost: Tablier m. 2. (a) Veh: Aut: Tablier m. (b) Th: **A.(-stage)**, avant-scène f. (c) Av: Aire f de manœuvre et de stationnement. '**apron-strings**, s.pl. Cordons m de tablier. F: **To be tied to one's mother's a.-s.**, être pendu aux jupes, aux jupons, de sa mère.

apropos ['æprə'pou]. 1. s. A-propos m; opportunité f (d'une observation, etc.). 2. a. **A very a. remark**, une observation très à propos. 3. Prep.phr. **It was mentioned a. of the holidays**, il en a été parlé à propos des vacances.
apse [æps], s. Ecc.Arch: Abside f, apside f.
apsidal ['æpsidl], a. Absidal, -aux.
apsidiole [æp'sidioul], s. Ecc.Arch: Absidiole f.
apt [æpt], a. 1. (Mot) juste; (expression) heureuse, qui convient. 2. **A. to do sth.** (a) (Of pers.) Enclin, porté, à faire qch. **He is a. to forget**, il oublie facilement. **We are a. to believe that . . .**, on croit volontiers que. . . . (b) (Of thg) Sujet à, susceptible de, faire qch. **Toys a. to go wrong**, jouets sujets à se détraquer. **Iron is a. to rust**, le fer se rouille facilement. 3. (Élève, etc.) intelligent. **To be a. at sth.**, at doing sth., être habile à qch., à faire qch. **-ly**, adv. 1. Avec justesse; convenablement; avec à-propos. 2. Adroitement, habilement.
aptera ['æptərə], s.pl. Ent: Aptères m.
apterous ['æptərəs], a. Ent: Aptère.
aptitude ['æptitju:d], s. **A. for sth.**, aptitude f à, pour qch.; disposition(s) f pour qch.
aptness ['æptnis], s. 1. Justesse f, à-propos m. 2. Penchant m, tendance f (to do sth., à faire qch.). 3. = APTITUDE.
aqua ['ækwə], s. (Used to form compounds in) Ch: Pharm: **A. fortis**, eau-forte f. **A. regia** ['ri:dʒiə], eau régale. **A. vitae** ['vaiti], eau-de-vie f.
aquafortist [ækwə'fɔ:tist], s. Engr: Aquafortiste mf.
aqualung ['ækwəlʌŋ], s. Scaphandre m autonome.
aquamarine ['ækwəmə'ri:n], s. Aigue-marine f.
aquaplane¹ ['ækwəplein], s. Sp: Aquaplane m.
aquaplane², v.i. Faire de l'aquaplane m.
aquarelle [ækwə'rel], s. Art: Aquarelle f.
aquarium [ə'kwɛəriəm], s. Aquarium m.
Aquarius [ə'kwɛəriəs]. Pr.n. Astr: Le Verseau.
aquatic [ə'kwætik], a. 1. (Plante, etc.) aquatique. 2. **A. sports**, s.pl. **aquatics**, sports nautiques.
aquatint ['ækwətint], s. Engr: Aquatinte f.
aqueduct ['ækwidʌkt], s. Aqueduc m.
aqueous ['eikwiəs], a. Aqueux. **A. solution**, soluté m.
aquiline ['ækwilain], a. Aquilin. **A. nose**, nez aquilin, busqué, en bec d'aigle.
Arab ['ærəb], a. & s. 1. Ethn: Arabe (mf). S.a. STREET-ARAB. 2. (Cheval) arabe (m).
arabesque [ærə'besk], s. Arabesque f.
Arabia [ə'reibiə]. Pr.n. L'Arabie f. **Saudi A.**, L'Arabie Séoudite. A.Geog: **A. Petraea**, L'Arabie Pétrée.
Arabian [ə'reibiən]. 1. a. Arabe, d'Arabie. Arch: Arabesque. **The A. Gulf**, le golfe Arabique. 2. s. Arabe mf.
Arabic ['ærəbik]. 1. a. (Gomme) arabique; (langue) arabe. **A. numeral**, chiffre m arabe. 2. s. Ling: L'arabe m. **A. scholar**, arabisant m.
Arabist ['ærəbist], s. Arabisant m.
arable ['ærəbl], a. (Terre) arable, labourable.
arachnid, pl. **-ida** [ə'ræknid, -idə], s. Z: Arachnide m; acarien m.
Aramaean [ærə'mi(:)ən], a. & s. B.Hist: Araméen, -enne.
Aramaic [ærə'meiik], a. Ling: Araméen, -enne.
araucaria [ærɔ:'kɛəriə], Bot: Araucaria m.
arbiter ['ɑ:bitər], s. Arbitre m.
arbitral ['ɑ:bitr(ə)l], a. Arbitral, -aux.
arbitrary ['ɑ:bitrəri], a. Arbitraire. **-ily**, adv. Arbitrairement.
arbitrate ['ɑ:bitreit]. 1. v.tr. Arbitrer, juger, trancher (un différend). 2. v.i. Décider en qualité d'arbitre; arbitrer.
arbitration [ɑ:bi'treiʃ(ə)n], s. Arbitrage m. **Procedure by a.**, procédure arbitrale. **A. court**, tribunal arbitral.
arbitrator ['ɑ:bitreitər], s. Jur: Arbitre m; arbitre-juge m.
arbor ['ɑ:bər], s. Mec.E: (a) Arbre m (de roue); arbre, axe m (de meule). (b) Mandrin m (de tour).
arboreal [ɑ:'bo:riəl], a. 1. D'arbre(s). 2. (Animal) arboricole; (existence) sur les arbres.
arborescence [ɑ:bə'resns], s. Arborescence f.
arborescent [ɑ:bə'resnt], a. Arborescent. **A. shrub**, arbuste m.
arboriculture [ɑ:bəri'kʌltʃər], s. Arboriculture f.

arboriculturist [ˌɑːbəri'kʌltʃərist], s. Arboriculteur m, pépiniériste m.

arbour ['ɑːbər], s. Berceau m de verdure; tonnelle f, charmille f. Vine a., treille f.

arbutus [ɑː'bjuːtus], s. Bot: Arbousier m. A. berry, arbouse f.

arc [ɑːk], s. 1. Arc m. A. of a circle, arc de cercle. 2. Electric a., voltaic a., arc électrique, voltaïque. 'arc-brazing, s. Soudo-brasage m à l'arc. 'arc-lamp, s. Lampe f à arc. 'arc-weld, v.tr. Metalw: Souder à l'arc (électrique).

arcade [ɑː'keid], s. (a) Arcade(s) f (en bord de rue); galeries fpl. (b) Passage m (à magasins).

arcature ['ɑːkətʃər], s. Arch: Arcature f.

arch[1] [ɑːtʃ], s. 1. Voûte f, arc m; cintre m. Row of arches, arcade f. Centre a., voûte maîtresse. A. of a vault, arceau m. Semicircular a., round a., arc (en) plein cintre. Pointed a., arc brisé. 2. (a) Civ.E: Arche f (d'un pont, d'un viaduc). (b) A. of a furnace, voûte d'un fourneau. 3. A. of a saddle, arcade f d'une selle. Anat: A. of the eybrows, arc des sourcils. The orbital arches, les arcades orbitaires. A. of the instep, cambrure f du pied. 'arch-stone, s. Arch: Voussoir m, claveau m.

arch[2]. 1. v.tr. (a) Voûter (une porte, un passage). (b) Arquer, cintrer; cambrer. The cat arches its back, le chat bombe, arque, le dos, fait le gros dos. 2. v.i. Se voûter, former voûte, bomber. arched, a. (a) A arc, en voûte; voûté; voussé. A. window, fenêtre (i) cintrée, (ii) en arc brisé. (b) Arqué, cintré; cambré. A. nose, nez busqué.

arch[3], a. (Usu. attrib. and only of women and children) Espiègle; malin, f. -igne; malicieux, -euse. An a. glance, un coup d'œil espiègle et moqueur. -ly, adv. D'un air espiègle, malin; malicieusement.

arch-, a. & pref. Archi-, grand, insigne. A.-traitor, traître insigne; architraître. A.-deceiver, maître en fourberie. A.-liar, menteur fieffé.

archaeological [ˌɑːkiə'lɔdʒikəl], a. Archéologique.

archaeologist [ˌɑːki'ɔlədʒist], s. Archéologue mf.

archaeology [ˌɑːki'ɔlədʒi], s. Archéologie f.

archaic [ɑː'keiik], a. Archaïque.

archaism ['ɑːkeiizm], s. Archaïsme m.

archangel ['ɑːkˌeindʒ(ə)l], s. Archange m.

archangelic(al) [ˌɑːkən'dʒelik(l)], a. Archangélique.

archbishop ['ɑːtʃ'biʃəp], s.m. Archevêque.

archbishopric [ɑːtʃ'biʃəprik], s. 1. Archevêché m. 2. Archiépiscopat m.

archdeacon ['ɑːtʃ'diːk(ə)n], s.m. Archidiacre.

archdiocese ['ɑːtʃ'daiəsis], s. = ARCHBISHOPRIC 1.

archducal [ɑːtʃ'djuːk(ə)l], a. Archiducal, -aux.

archduchess [ɑːtʃ'dʌtʃis], s.f. Archiduchesse.

archduchy ['ɑːtʃ'dʌtʃi], s. Archiduché m.

archduke ['ɑːtʃ'djuːk], s.m. Archiduc.

archer ['ɑːtʃər], s. 1. Archer m. 2. Astr: The A., le Sagittaire.

archery ['ɑːtʃəri], s. Tir m à l'arc.

archetype ['ɑːkitaip], s. Archétype m.

arch-fiend [ɑːtʃ'fiːnd], s. The a., Satan m.

archidiaconal [ˌɑːkidai'ækənl], a. D'archidiacre.

archiepiscopacy [ˌɑːkiiˈpiskəpəsi], s. Archiépiscopat m.

archiepiscopal [ˌɑːkiiˈpiskəp(ə)l], a. Archiépiscopal, -aux.

archiepiscopate [ˌɑːkiiˈpiskəpit], s. Archiépiscopat m.

Archimedean [ˌɑːkiˈmiːdiən], a. D'Archimède.

Archimedes [ˌɑːkiˈmiːdiːz]. Pr.n.m. Gr.Hist: Archimède.

archipelago, pl. -oes [ˌɑːkiˈpeləgou, -ouz], s. Archipel m.

architect ['ɑːkitekt], s. 1. Architecte m. 2. Naval a., ingénieur m des constructions navales, du génie maritime.

architectural [ˌɑːkiˈtektjur(ə)l], a. Architectural, -aux.

architecture ['ɑːkitektʃər], s. Architecture f.

architrave ['ɑːkitreiv], s. 1. Arch: Architrave f. 2. Const: Encadrement m (de porte, de fenêtre).

archives ['ɑːkaivz], s.pl. Archives f.

archivist ['ɑːkivist], s. Archiviste mf.

archness ['ɑːtʃnis], s. (Of women and children) Malice f, espièglerie f (du regard, du sourire).

archpriest ['ɑːtʃ'priːst], s.m. Archiprêtre.

archway ['ɑːtʃwei], s. Passage voûté; porte cintrée, voûte f d'entrée; arcade f, portail m.

arctic ['ɑːktik], a. Arctique.

ardent ['ɑːdnt], a. Ardent. -ly, adv. Ardemment; avec ardeur.

ardour ['ɑːdər], s. Ardeur f.

arduous ['ɑːdjuəs], a. (Sentier, travail) ardu; (chemin) escarpé; (travail) rude. -ly, adv. Péniblement, malaisément.

arduousness ['ɑːdjuəsnis], s. Arduité, f, difficulté f.

are. See BE.

area ['ɛəriə], s. 1. (a) Terrain vide, inoccupé. (b) Parterre m (de salle de concert, de cinéma). 2. Cour f d'entrée en sous-sol (sur la rue). 3. (a) Aire f, superficie f, contenance f (d'un cercle, d'un champ, etc.). (b) Surface f. Wall a., surface de paroi. 4. Étendue f (de pays); territoire m, région f. Disturbed a., zone troublée. Postal a., zone postale. The whole London a., l'agglomération londonienne. Av: Servicing a., aire d'entretien. Pol.Ec: Sterling a., zone sterling. Town P: Clearance a., tache f insalubre (à démolir).

areca [æ'riːkə], s. Bot: Arec m. A. palm(-tree), aréquier m. A.-nut, (noix f. d')arec.

arena, pl. -as [ə'riːnə, -əz], s. (a) Arène f. (b) Champ m (d'une activité, etc.). The a. of the war, le théâtre de la guerre.

arenaceous [ˌæri'neiʃəs], a. Geol: Arénacé.

aren't [ɑːnt] = Are not.

areola, pl. -ae [æ'riːoulə, -iː], s. Aréole f. Anat: Halo m, aréole (du mamelon). Med: Zone f rouge (de vaccination).

areometer [ˌæri'ɔmitər, ɛəri-], s. Ph: Aréomètre m.

arête [æ'ret], s. Geog: Arête f (d'une montagne).

argent ['ɑːdʒ(ə)nt]. Her: & Poet: 1. s. Argent m. 2. a. Argenté; Her: d'argent, argent inv.

Argentina [ˌɑːdʒ(ə)n'tiːnə]. Pr.n. Geog: L'Argentine f; la République Argentine.

argentine[1] ['ɑːdʒ(ə)ntain], a. Argentin.

Argentine[2], a. Geog: The A. (Republic), la République Argentine.

argillaceous [ˌɑːdʒi'leifəs], a. Argileux, -euse.

argle-bargle ['ɑːgl'bɑːgl], v.i. F: Discutailler; discuter le coup.

argol ['ɑːgɔl], s. Tartre brut.

argon ['ɑːgɔn], s. Ch: Argon m.

Argonaut ['ɑːgənɔːt], s. 1. Gr.Myth: Argonaute m. 2. Moll: Voilier m, argonaute.

arguable ['ɑːgjuəbl], a. Discutable, soutenable.

argue ['ɑːgjuː]. (arguing; argued) 1. v.tr. (a) (Indicate) Prouver, indiquer, démontrer. His action argues him (to be) a coward, son action prouve, accuse, décèle, sa lâcheté. (b) Discuter, débattre; raisonner sur (une question, une affaire, etc.). To a. that sth. is impossible, soutenir, prétendre, que qch. est impossible. 2. v.i. (a) Argumenter (against s.o., contre qn; about sth., sur qch.). To a. from sth., tirer argument de qch. (b) Discuter, (se) disputer, raisonner (with s.o. about sth., avec qn sur qch.); plaider (for, against, sth., pour, contre, qch.).

arguer ['ɑːgjuər], s. Argumentateur, -trice; discuteur, -euse.

argufy ['ɑːgjufai], v.i. P: (a) Argumenter, raisonner; faire le raisonneur. (b) Disputailler.

argument ['ɑːgjumənt], s. 1. Argument m (for, against, en faveur de, contre). To follow s.o.'s (line of) a., suivre le raisonnement de qn. His a. is that gold should be done away with, sa thèse est qu'il faudrait abolir l'or. For the sake of a., (i) pour le plaisir de discuter; (ii) à titre d'exemple. 2. Discussion f, dispute f, débat m. 3. (a) A: Argument, thèse f (d'un discours, d'une pièce de théâtre). (b) (Synopsis) Argument, sommaire m.

argumentation [ˌɑːgjumen'teiʃ(ə)n], s. Argumentation f.

argumentative [ˌɑːgju'mentətiv], a. 1. (Ouvrage) raisonné, critique. 2. (Of pers.) Raisonneur; disposé à argumenter, à disputailler.

argumentativeness [ˌɑːgju'mentətivnis], s. Disposition f à argumenter; esprit raisonneur.

Argus ['ɑːgəs]. Pr.n.m. Myth: Argus. A.-eyed, aux yeux d'Argus.

aria ['ɑːriə], s. Mus: Aria f.

Ariadne [ˌæri'ædni]. Pr.n.f. Gr.Myth: Ariane.

Arian ['ɛəriən], a. & s. Rel.H: Arien, -ienne.

Arianism ['ɛəriənizm], s. *Rel.Hist:* Arianisme *m*.
arid ['ærid], *a*. (Terre, sujet) aride.
aridity [æ'riditi], **aridness** ['æridnis], *s*. Aridité *f*.
Aries ['ɛərii:z]. *Pr.n. Astr:* Le Bélier.
arietta [ˌæri'etə], *s. Mus:* Ariette *f*.
aright [ə'rait], *adv*. Bien, juste, correctement.
Ariosto ['æri'ostou]. *Pr.n.m. Lit.Hist:* L'Arioste.
arise [ə'raiz], *v.i.* (arose [ə'rouz]; arisen [ə'rizn]) 1. S'élever. (*a*) (*Of pers.*) A prophet arose, un prophète surgit, se révéla. (*b*) *B:* To a. from the dead, ressusciter (des morts). 2. (*Of thg*) (*a*) S'élever, surgir, survenir, s'offrir, se présenter, se produire. A storm arose, il survint une tempête. Another difficulty then arose, alors survint, surgit, se présenta, une nouvelle difficulté. Should the occasion a. . . ., le cas échéant. . . . (*b*) Émaner, provenir, résulter (from, de). Obligations that a. from a clause, obligations qui émanent d'une clause. Arising from (this proposal, etc.), comme suite à (cette proposition, etc.).
aristocracy [ˌæris'tɔkrəsi], *s*. Aristocratie *f*.
aristocrat ['æristəkræt, ə'ris-], *s*. Aristocrate *mf*.
aristocratic [ˌæristə'krætik], *a*. Aristocratique. **-ally**, *adv*. Aristocratiquement.
Aristophanes [ˌæris'tɔfəni:z]. *Pr.n.m.* Aristophane.
Aristotelian [ˌæristə'ti:ljən], *a. & s*. Aristotélicien, -ienne; (doctrine) aristotélique.
Aristotle ['æristɔtl]. *Pr.n.m.* Aristote.
arithmetic [ə'riθmətik], *s*. Arithmétique *f*, calcul *m*.
arithmetical [ˌæriθ'metik(ə)l], *a*. Arithmétique. *S.a.* PROGRESSION 2. **-ally**, *adv*. Arithmétiquement.
arithmetician [ˌæriθme'tiʃ(ə)n], *s*. Arithméticien, -ienne; calculateur, -trice.
ark [ɑːk], *s*. Arche *f*. 1. Noah's a., l'arche de Noé. *F:* It looks as if it had come out of the a., ça a l'air de remonter au déluge. 2. The A. of the Covenant, l'Arche d'alliance, l'Arche sainte.
arm¹ [ɑːm], *s*. 1. Bras *m* (de personne; *Farr:* de cheval). Upper a., haut *m* du bras, arrière-bras *m*. *S.a.* FOREARM. To carry a child in one's arms, porter un enfant au bras, dans ses bras. To give one's a. to s.o., donner le bras à qn. A.-in-a., bras dessus bras dessous. She took my a., elle me prit le bras; elle passa sa main dans mon bras. To put one's a. round s.o., prendre qn par la taille. To carry sth. at arm's length, porter qch. à bras tendu, à bout de bras. *F:* To keep s.o. at arm's length, tenir qn à distance. To welcome s.o. with open arms, recevoir qn à bras ouverts, faire à qn un accueil cordial. (*Traffic signal*) To put one's a. out, étendre le bras. 2. Bras (de mer, d'un fleuve, de fauteuil, de levier, de manivelle); fléau *m* (de balance); accoudoir *m* (de fauteuil). 'arm-band, *s*. Brassard *m*; *esp*. brassard de deuil. 'arm(-)chair, *s*. Fauteuil *m. attrib. F:* A. general, général *m* en chambre. A strategist, politician, tacticien *m*, politicien *m*, du Café du Commerce. 'arm-rest, *s. Veh:* Accoudoir *m*, accotoir *m*; appui(e)-bras *m*.
arm², *s. Usu. pl.* 1. Arme *f*. (*a*) Small arms, armes portatives. Side-arms, armes blanches. To take up arms, to rise up in arms, prendre les armes (against, contre). To arms! aux armes! To bear, carry, arms, porter les armes. To lay down one's arms, mettre bas les armes; rendre les armes. Nation in arms, under arms, nation sous les armes. Arms factory, fabrique d'armes. *F:* To be up in arms, se gendarmer (against, contre). Arms race, course *f* aux armements. (*b*) *Mil:* (*Branch of service*) Arme. 2. *pl. Her:* Armoiries *f*, armes. *S.a.* COAT¹ 1.
arm³, *v.tr.* (*a*) Armer. To a. oneself with an umbrella, s'armer, se nantir, d'un parapluie. (*b*) *Tchn:* Armer (une poutre, un aimant, etc.); renforcer (une poutre, etc.). 2. *v.i.* S'armer; prendre les armes. armed¹, *a.* Armé (with, de). A. ship, (i) navire armé en guerre; (ii) vaisseau cuirassé. The a. forces, les forces armées. A. to the teeth, armé jusqu'aux dents. arming, *s*. 1. A. of a fuse, armement *m* d'une amorce. 2. *Nau:* Suif *m* (de la grande sonde).
armada [ɑː'mɑːdə], *s*. (*a*) *Hist:* The Invincible A., l'Invincible Armada. (*b*) Grande flotte de guerre.
armadillo [ɑːmə'dilou], *s*. 1. *Z:* Tatou *m*. 2. *Crust:* (*Wood-louse*) Armadille *m* or *f*.
Armageddon [ɑːmə'gedn], *s*. (*a*) *B.Lit:* Armageddon *m*. (*b*) La lutte suprême.

armament ['ɑːməmənt], *s*. 1. Armement *m*. Naval armaments, armements navals. A. factory, usine de matériel de guerre. 2. Forces *fpl*; armée *f*, flotte navale.
armature ['ɑːmətjuər], *s*. 1. *Biol: etc:* Armure *f*. 2. *El:* Induit *m* (de condensateur, dynamo); armature *f* (de magnéto). A. winding, enroulement *m* d'induit.
-armed² ['ɑːmd], *a*. Long-a., au(x) bras long(s).
Armenia [ɑː'miːnjə]. *Pr.n. Geog:* L'Arménie *f*.
Armenian [ɑː'miːnjən], *a. & s. Geog:* Arménien, -ienne.
armful ['ɑːmful], *s*. Brassée *f*. In armfuls, by the a., à pleins bras, plein les bras.
armhole ['ɑːmhoul], *s*. Emmanchure *f*, entournure *f*.
armistice ['ɑːmistis], *s*. Armistice *m*. A. day, l'anniversaire de l'Armistice (de 1918).
armless ['ɑːmlis], *a*. Sans bras.
armlet ['ɑːmlit], *s*. 1. Bracelet (porté au-dessus du coude). 2. Bra²sard *m*. 3. Petit bras de mer.
armorial [ɑː'mɔːriəl]. 1.*a*. Armorial, -aux; héraldique. A. bearings, armoiries *fpl*. 2. *s*. Armorial *m*.
armorist ['ɑːmərist], *s*. Armoriste *m*; héraldiste *m*.
armory ['ɑːməri], *s*. L'art *m* héraldique.
armour¹ ['ɑːmər], *s*. 1. Armure *f* (de chevalier, etc.). Suit of a., armure complète. In full a., armé de pied en cap. 2. (*a*) Blindage *m* (de véhicule blindé). (*b*) *N.Arch:* Cuirasse *f*, blindage. (*c*) Unités blindées, blindés *mpl*., chars *mpl*. 'armour-bearer, *s. A:* Écuyer *m*. 'armour-belt, *s. N.Arch:* Cuirasse *f* de ceinture; ceinture blindée, cuirassée. 'armour-clad, *a*. Blindé, cuirassé. 'armour-piercing, *a*. (Obus) perforant, de rupture. 'armour-plate, *s. N.Arch: etc:* Plaque *f* de cuirasse, de blindage. 'armour-plated, *a*. Cuirassé; blindé.
armour², *v.tr.* Cuirasser (un navire); blinder (un train, etc.); *El.E:* armer (un câble). armoured, *a*. Cuirassé, blindé. A. cruiser, croiseur *m* cuirassé, *s*. cuirassé *m*. A. car, automobile blindée; *U.S:* fourgon *m* bancaire. Light a. car, auto-mitrailleuse *f*, *pl*. auto-mitrailleuses.
armourer ['ɑːmərər], *s*. Armurier *m*.
armoury ['ɑːməri], *s*. 1. Magasin *m* d'armes. 2. (*In barracks*) Armurerie *f*.
armpit ['ɑːmpit], *s*. Aisselle *f*.
army ['ɑːmi], *s*. 1. (*a*) Armée *f*. To be in the a., être dans l'armée; être soldat, militaire. To go into the a., to join the army, s'engager, s'enrôler, se faire soldat; entrer au service. Standing a., regular a., armée permanente, active. A. corps, corps *m* d'armée. A. list = L'Annuaire *m* militaire. (*b*) The Salvation A., l'Armée du Salut. 2. Foule *f*, multitude *f* (d'hommes, etc.).
arnica ['ɑːnikə], *s*. Arnica *f*.
aroma [ə'roumə], *s*. Arome *m*; bouquet *m* (d'un vin, d'un cigare).
aromatic [ˌærə'mætik]. 1. *a*. Aromatique; (parfum) balsamique. 2. *s*. Aromate *m*.
aromatize [ə'roumətaiz], *v.tr.* Aromatiser.
around [ə'raund]. 1. *adv*. Autour, à l'entour. All a., tout autour. The woods (all) a., les bois d'alentour. 2. *prep*. Autour de. The country a. the town, les environs de la ville. A. London, à la périphérie de Londres.
arouse [ə'rauz], *v.tr.* 1. (*a*) Réveiller, éveiller (qn). To a. s.o. from his sleep, tirer qn de son sommeil. (*b*) Secouer (qn) (de sa paresse); stimuler (qn). 2. Exciter, éveiller, susciter (un sentiment); soulever (des passions).
arpeggio [ɑː'pedʒiou], *s. Mus:* Arpège *m*.
arrack ['æræk], *s. Dist:* Arack *m*, arac *m*.
arraign [ə'rein], *v.tr.* (*a*) *Jur:* Mettre (qn) en accusation; accuser, inculper (qn) (for, de); traduire (qn) devant un tribunal. (*b*) Attaquer (qn, une opinion); s'en prendre à (qn).
arraignment [ə'reinmənt], *s*. 1. *Jur:* (*a*) Mise *f* en accusation. (*b*) Acte *m* d'accusation. 2. Censure *f*, critique *f* hostile.
arrange [ə'rein(d)ʒ], *v.tr.* Arranger, aménager. 1. (*a*) (*Set in order*) Disposer, ranger (les meubles, etc.); ordonner (un cortège). To a. one's affairs, régler ses affaires. (*b*) Piece arranged for the piano, morceau adapté, arrangé, pour piano. 2. (*Plan beforehand*) To a. a marriage, arranger un mariage. To a. to do sth.,

(i) s'arranger, prendre ses dispositions, pour faire qch.; (ii) s'arranger avec qn pour faire qch.; convenir de faire qch. **To a. a time for sth.**, fixer une heure pour qch. **It was arranged that . . .**, il fut convenu que. . . . 3. (*Settle*) Accommoder, ajuster, arranger (un différend). **arranging,** *s.* Arrangement *m*, aménagement *m*, ajustement *m*, règlement *m*.

arrangement [ə'rein(d)ʒmənt], *s.* 1. Arrangement *m*, disposition *f*, aménagement *m*, mise *f* en ordre. **To make arrangements to do sth., for sth. to be done**, prendre des dispositions, des mesures, faire des préparatifs, pour faire qch., pour que qch. se fasse. *Mus:* **A. for piano**, ar:angement, adaptation *f*, réduction *f*, pour piano. 2. Accommodement *m* (d'un différend); accord *m*, entente *f*. *Jur:* Transaction *f*. *Com:* **To come to an a.**, **with** s.o., entrer en arrangement, passer un compromis, avec qn. **Price by a.**, prix à débattre. 3. Dispositif *m* (de mise en marche, etc.).

arrant ['ær(ə)nt], *a.* *Pej:* Insigne, achevé. **A. rogue**, coquin fieffé; franc coquin.

arras ['ærəs], *s.* *A:* Tenture(s) *f*; tapisserie(s) *f*.

array¹ [ə'rei], *s.* 1. (*a*) Rangs *mpl.* **In close a.**, en rangs serrés. **In battle a.**, en ordre de bataille. (*b*) Étalage *m.* **An imposing a. of tools**, un imposant déploiement d'outils. 2. *Poet:* *A:* Parure *f*, atours *mpl.*

array², *v.tr.* 1. Ranger, mettre en ordre; disposer, déployer (des troupes) (en ordre de bataille). 2. *Poet:* *A:* Revêtir, orner, parer (s.o. in sth., qn de qch.).

arrear(s) [ər'iər(z)], *s.* Arriéré *m*, arrérages *mpl.* **Arrears of rent**, arriéré de loyer. **Arrears of wages**, arrérages de salaires. **Rent in a.**, loyer arriéré, en retard. **To get, fall, into arrears**, (*of pers.*) se mettre en retard; s'arriérer. **Arrears of interest**, intérêts moratoires; arrérages.

arrest¹ [ə'rest], *s.* 1. (*a*) Arrestation *f*. *Jur:* Prise *f* de corps. **Under a.**, en état d'arrestation. *S.a.* WARRANT¹ 3. (*b*) *Mil: Navy:* Arrêts *mpl.* **Under a.**, aux arrêts. **House a.**, arrêts à la chambre. 2. Arrêt *m*, suspension *f* (d'un mouvement, du progrès).

arrest², *v.tr.* 1. Arrêter (un mouvement, le progrès). 2. Arrêter (un malfaiteur); appréhender (qn) (au corps). 3. Arrêter, fixer, retenir (l'attention, les regards). 4. *Jur:* **To a. judgment**, suspendre l'exécution d'un jugement. **arresting**, *a.* Attachant, frappant; qui arrête l'attention.

arrester, (also *pers.*) **arrestor**, [ə'restər], *s.* 1. Celui qui arrête (un malfaiteur). 2. *Jur:* Saisissant *m* (de biens mobiliers). 3. **Lightning-a.**, paratonnerre. *Navy:* *Av:* **A.-gear**, brin *m* d'arrêt (á l'appontage). **A.-hook**, crosse *f* d'arrêt à l'appontage.

arris ['æris], *s.* Arête vive (d'un prisme, d'une cannelure).

arrival [ə'raiv(ə)l], *s.* 1. (*a*) Arrivée *f*. **On a.**, à l'arrivée. (*b*) *Com:* Arrivage *m* (de marchandises). (*c*) *Nau:* Entrée *f* (d'un vaisseau). *S.a.* PLATFORM 2. 2. (*Of pers.*) **A new a.**, un nouveau venu, un nouvel arrivant.

arrive [ə'raiv], *v.i.* 1. (*a*) Arriver (at, in, à, dans). **We arrived at three o'clock**, nous sommes arrivés à trois heures. **As soon as he arrived in London**, dès son arrivée à Londres. **To a. on the scene, to a. unexpectedly**, survenir. (*b*) *O:* **To a. at the age of sixty**, atteindre, parvenir à, l'âge de soixante ans. 2. **To a. at a conclusion**, arriver, aboutir, à une conclusion. **To a. at a price**, fixer un prix.

arrogance ['ærəgəns], *s.* Arrogance *f*; morgue *f*.

arrogant ['ærəgənt], *a.* Arrogant. **A. tone**, ton *m* rogue. **-ly**, *adv.* Avec arrogance.

arrogate ['ærəgeit], *v.tr.* 1. **To a. sth. to oneself**, s'arroger qch., s'attribuer qch. 2. **To a. sth. to s.o.**, attribuer injustement qch. à qn.

arrogation [ærə'geif(ə)n], *s.* Prétention mal fondée. **A. of sth.**, usurpation *f* de qch.

arrow¹ ['ærou], *s.* Flèche *f*. **To shoot, let fly, an a.**, lancer, décocher, une flèche. *F:* **The arrows of calumny**, les traits *m* de la calomnie. *Adm:* *A:* **Broad a.** = marque *f* de l'État. **'arrow-head,** *s.* Tête *f*, fer *m*, pointe *f*, de flèche.

arrow², *v.tr.* Indiquer au moyen d'une flèche. (*Road direction*) Flécher (une route, une direction). **arrowing,** *s.* Fléchage *m*.

arrowroot ['ærɔruːt], *s.* 1. *Bot:* Marante *f*. 2. *Cu:* Arrow-root *m*, fécule extraite du rhizome de la marante.

arse [ɑːs], *s.* *V:* Cul *m*, derrière *m*. **A. over tip**, à la renverse. **'arse a'bout,** *v.i.* *V:* Don't you go arsing about in there, va pas faire le con là-dedans. **'arse-crawler, 'arse-licker,** *s.* *V:* Lèche-cul *m.inv.*

arsenal ['ɑːsinl], *s.* Arsenal *m*, -aux.

arsenate ['ɑːsəneit], *s.* *Ch:* Arséniate *m*.

arsenic¹ ['ɑːsnik], *s.* Arsenic *m*. **White a., flowers of a.**, acide arsénieux.

arsenic² [ɑː'senik], *a.* *Ch:* (Acide) arsénique.

arsenical [ɑː'senik(ə)l], *a.* Arsenical, -aux. **A. poisoning**, arsenicisme *m*.

arsenide ['ɑːsənaid], *s.* *Ch:* Arséniure *m*.

arson ['ɑːsn], *s.* Incendie *m* volontaire, par malveillance. *Jur:* Crime *m* d'incendie.

art¹. *See* BE.

art² [ɑːt], *s.* 1. Art *m*. (*a*) **The (fine) arts**, les beaux-arts. **Work of a., œuvre** *f* d'art. *S.a.* GALLERY 2. (*b*) **The liberal arts**, les arts libéraux. *Sch:* **Faculty of arts**, faculté *f* des lettres. *S.a.* BACHELOR 3, MASTER¹ 1. **Arts and crafts**, production artistique des métiers artisanaux, y compris dessin décoratif. (*c*) **The a. of war**, l'art militaire. **The black a.**, la magie noire. 2. (*a*) (*Dexterity, cunning*) Adresse *f*, habileté *f*, artifice *m*, art. **To use every a. in order to . . .**, user de tous les artifices pour. . . . (*b*) *Jur:* **To have a. and part in sth.**, être fauteur et complice de qch. **I had no a. or part in it**, je n'y suis pour rien. **'art-critic,** *s.* Critique *m* d'art. **'art(-)exhibition,(-)show,** *s.* Exposition *f* des beaux-arts. **'art-school,** *s.* École *f* des beaux-arts; *esp.* école, académie *f*, de dessin.

artefact ['ɑːtifækt], *s.* 1. *Prehist:* Objet façonné. 2. *Biol:* Artefact *m*.

arterial [ɑː'tiəriəl], *a.* 1. *Anat:* Artériel. 2. **A. road**, grande voie de communication.

arteriosclerosis [ɑː'tiəriousgliə'rousis], *s.* *Med:* Artériosclérose *f*.

arteritis [ɑːti'raitis], *s.* *Med:* Artérite *f*.

artery ['ɑːtəri], *s.* 1. *Anat:* Artère *f*. 2. (= *route*). Artère (de circulation).

artesian [ɑː'tiːzjən, -'tiːʒən], *a.* Artésien, -ienne; de l'Artois. **A. well**, puits artésien.

artful ['ɑːtf(u)l], *a.* (*a*) Adroit, habile, ingénieux, -euse. (*b*) Rusé, artificieux, -euse, astucieux, -euse. *F:* malin, *f.* -igne. **He's as a. as a monkey**, il est malin comme un singe. **-fully**, *adv.* 1. Adroitement. 2. Artificieusement.

artfulness ['ɑːtf(u)lnis], *s.* 1. Art *m*, adresse *f*, habileté *f*, ingéniosité *f*. 2. Astuce *f*.

arthralgia [ɑː'θrældʒə], *s.* *Med:* Arthralgie *f*.

arthritic [ɑː'θritik], *a.* *Med:* Arthritique.

arthritis [ɑː'θraitis], *s.* *Med:* Arthrite *f*. **Rheumatoid a.**, poly-arthrite chronique évolutive.

arthritism ['ɑːθritizm], *s.* *Med:* Arthritisme *m*.

arthropod, *pl.* **-s, -oda** ['ɑːθropɔd, -z, ɑː'θrɔ,podə], *s.* *Z:* Arthropode *m*.

arthrosis [ɑː'θrousis], *s.* *Med:* Arthrose *f*.

Arthurian [ɑː'θjuəriən], *a.* *Lit.Hist:* (Cycle *m*, etc.) d'Arthur; (roman) arthurien.

artichoke ['ɑːtitʃouk], *s.* 1. Artichaut *m*. 2. **Jerusalem a.**, topinambour *m*. 3. **Chinese, Japanese a.**, crosne *m*.

article¹ ['ɑːtikl], *s.* 1. *Bot:* *Ent:* Article *m*; point *m* d'articulation. 2. (*a*) *Com:* *Jur:* Article, clause *f* (d'un contrat, d'un traité). **Articles of apprenticeship, of a partnership**, contrat *m* d'apprentissage, de société; acte *m* de société. **Articles of war,** *Mil:* code *m* (de justice) militaire; *Navy:* code de justice maritime. (*b*) *Theol:* **A. of faith**, article de foi. **The Articles of Religion, the Thirty-nine Articles**, les Articles de religion (de l'Église anglicane). (*c*) *Jur:* Chef *m* d'accusation. 3. Article (de journal, de revue). *Journ:* *F:* Papier *m*. *S.a.* LEADING² 2. 4. (*a*) Article, objet *m*. (*b*) **A. of clothing**, article d'habillement. 5. *Gram:* **Definite, indefinite, a.**, article défini, indéfini.

article², *v.tr.* **To a. s.o. to an architect**, etc., placer qn (comme élève) chez un architecte, etc. **Articled clerk**, clerc d'avoué, de notaire, lié par un contrat d'apprentissage.

articular [ɑː'tikjulər], *a.* *Nat. Hist:* *Med:* Articulaire.

articulate¹ [ɑː'tikjulit]. 1. *a.* & *s.* *Z:* Articulé (*m*). 2. *a.* (*a*) **A. speech**, langage articulé. (*b*) (*Of utterance*) Net, distinct. **-ly**, *adv.* (Parler) distinctement.

articulate² [ɑːˈtikjuleit], v.tr. & i. 1. Anat: Articuler (un squelette, etc.). 2. Articuler, énoncer (un mot, etc.). He doesn't a. clearly, son énonciation est mauvaise.

articulation [ɑːˌtikjuˈleiʃ(ə)n], s. Articulation f.

artifact [ˈɑːtifækt], s. = ARTEFACT.

artifice [ˈɑːtifis], s. 1. Artifice m, ruse f; combinaison f. 2. Art m, habileté f, adresse f.

artificer [ɑːˈtifisər], s. Artisan m, ouvrier m. Mil: Artificier m. Navy: Engine-room a., mécanicien m.

artificial [ɑːtiˈfiʃ(ə)l] a. 1. Artificiel; simili-. A. stone, similipierre f. A. limb, prothèse f orthopédique. A. beauty, beauté empruntée. A. hair, teeth, cheveux postiches, fausses dents. Med: A. respiration, respiration artificielle. Agr: A. manure, engrais chimiques. S.a. SILK 1. 2. Factice, simulé. A. tears, larmes factices, feintes. -ally, adv. Artificiellement.

artificiality [ɑːtifiʃiˈæliti], s. Nature artificielle (d'un produit); caractère artificiel, manque m de naturel.

artillery [ɑːˈtiləri], s. (Ordnance, gunnery, or one of the arms of the service) Artillerie f. Heavy a., artillerie lourde. Naval a., artillerie de bord.

artilleryman, pl. -men [ɑːˈtilərimən], s.m. Artilleur.

Artiodactyla [ɑːtioˈdæktilə], s.pl. Z: Les artiodactyles.

artisan [ɑːtiˈzæn], s. Artisan m, ouvrier m.

artist [ˈɑːtist], s. (a) Artiste mf. Esp. (b) Artiste-peintre mf. He is an a., il est peintre.

artiste [ɑːˈtiːst], s. Th: Artiste mf.

artistic(al) [ɑːˈtistik(əl)], a. (Arrangement) artistique; (style, tempérament) artiste. -ally, adv. Artistement, avec art; artistiquement.

artistry [ˈɑːtistri], s. Art m (avec lequel qch. a été ordonné, truqué, etc.).

artless [ˈɑːtlis], a. 1. Sans art. 2. Naturel; sans artifice. 3. Naïf, ingénu, candide. -ly, adv. 1. Sans art. 2. Naturellement, simplement. 3. Naïvement, ingénument.

artlessness [ˈɑːtlisnis], s. 1. Naturel m, simplicité f. 2. Naïveté f, ingénuité f, candeur f.

arty [ˈɑːti], a. F: Qui affiche des goûts artistiques; prétentieux. 'arty-'crafty, a. F: Bohème, artiste (genre St Germain-des-Prés).

arum [ˈɛərəm], s. Bot: Arum m; F: gouet m. A. lily, arum; richardie f.

Aryan [ˈɛəriən], a. & s. Ling: Aryen, -enne. Nazi Pol: Aryen, -enne (non-Juif).

as [æz, əz]. I. adv. 1. (In principal clause) Aussi, si. I am as tall as you, je suis aussi grand que vous. Is it as high as that? est-ce si haut que ça? 2. I shall help you as far as I can, je vous aiderai autant que je pourrai. I worked as hard as I could, j'ai travaillé tant que j'ai pu. S.a. SOON 1. 3. As regards that, as for that, as to that, quant à cela. S.a. FOR¹ I. 9. To question s.o. as to his motives, interroger qn sur ses motifs. As to, for, you, quant à vous; pour ce qui est de vous. II. as, conj. & rel. adv. (In subordinate clause) 1. (Degree) (a) Que. You are as tall as he, vous êtes aussi grand que lui. You are not so tall as he, vous n'êtes pas si, aussi, grand que lui. He is as generous as he is wealthy, il est libéral autant que riche. By day as well as by night, le jour comme la nuit; de jour comme de nuit. S.a. WELL² I. 4. (b) (In intensifying similes) Comme. As pale as death, pâle comme un mort. As white as a sheet, blanc comme un linge. 2. (Concessive) Delightful as London is . . ., si agréable que soit Londres. . . . Ignorant as he is . . ., tout ignorant qu'il est. . . . S.a. MUCH 4. Be that as it may, quoi qu'il en soit. 3. (Manner) (a) Comme. Do as you like, faites comme vous voudrez. Pronounce the a as in "father," prononcez l'a comme dans father. As often happens. . . ., comme il arrive souvent . . .; ainsi qu'il arrive souvent. . . . A is to B as C is to D, A est à B comme C est à D. Leave it as it is, laissez-le tel quel, tel qu'il est. As it is, we must . . ., les choses étant ainsi, il nous faut. . . . S.a. BE 6 (c), GO² 2, 3, IF 1 (e), so I. 1, THOUGH I. 3. (b) As . . ., so . . . (Just) as we must know how to command, so must we know how to obey, de même qu'il faut savoir commander, (de même) il faut savoir obéir. As the parents act so will the children, tel font les parents, tel feront les enfants. (c) O: He will keep silent, as I am an honest man, il se taira, (sur ma) foi d'honnête homme. As I live, I

saw him strike the blow! aussi vrai que je suis en vie, je l'ai vu frapper le coup! (d) To consider s.o. as a friend, considérer qn comme un ami. To treat s.o. as a stranger, traiter qn en étranger. I had him as a master, je l'ai eu pour maître. He was often ill as a child, enfant il fut souvent malade; il fut souvent malade dans son enfance. To act as secretary, (i) servir de secrétaire; (ii) agir en qualité de secrétaire. A study of Dumas as a writer and as a man, une étude de Dumas en tant qu'écrivain et en tant qu'homme. To act as a father, agir en père. To be dressed as a page, être habillé en page. (e) They rose as one man, ils se sont levés comme un seul homme. 4. (Time) (a) He went out (just) as I came in, il sortit comme, au moment (même) où, j'entrais. One day as I was sitting . . ., un jour que j'étais assis. . . . They were murdered as they lay asleep, ils furent assassinés pendant qu'ils dormaient, pendant leur sommeil. S.a. JUST II. 1. (b) He grew more charitable as he grew older, il devenait plus charitable à mesure qu'il vieillissait, en vieillissant. 5. (Reason) As you are not ready, we cannot go, comme, puisque, vous n'êtes pas prêt, nous ne pouvons pas partir. 6. (Result) He so arranged matters as to please everyone, il arrangea les choses de manière, de façon, à contenter tout le monde. Be so good as to come, soyez assez bon pour venir. He is not so foolish as to believe it, il n'est pas assez stupide pour le croire. S.a. so I. 4. III. as, rel.pron. I had the same trouble as you, j'ai eu les mêmes difficultés que vous. Beasts of prey, (such) as the lion or tiger, les bêtes fauves, telles que, comme, le lion ou le tigre.

asafoetida [æsəˈfetidə, -ˈfiː-], s. 1. Bot: Férule f persique. 2. Pharm: etc: Assafœtida f.

asbestos [æzˈbestəs], s. Asbeste m, amiante m. A. sheet, carton m d'amiante. A. cement, fibro(-)ciment m.

ascaris, pl. -ides [ˈæskəris, æsˈkæridiːz], s. Ann: Ascaride m, ascaris m, lombric (intestinal).

ascend [əˈsend]. 1. v.i. (a) Monter, s'élever. (b) (Of genealogical line) Remonter. 2. v.tr. (a) To a. the throne, monter sur le trône. (b) To a. a mountain, a hill, faire l'ascension d'une montagne; gravir une colline. (c) To a. a river, remonter un fleuve.

ascending, a. 1. Astr: Mth: etc: Ascendant. Mus: A. scale, gamme ascendante. 2. (Sentier) montant, remontant.

ascendancy, -ency [əˈsendənsi], s. 1. Ascendant m, pouvoir m, influence f (over s.o., sur qn). 2. (Of nation, etc.) To rise to a., arriver à la suprématie.

ascendant, -ent [əˈsendənt]. 1. a. Ascendant. 2. s. (a) Astrol: Ascendant m. To be in the a., (i) (of point of the ecliptic) être à l'ascendant; (ii) Lit: avoir le dessus; s'affirmer; prédominer. (b) Jur: (Father, grandfather, etc.) Ascendant.

ascension [əˈsenʃ(ə)n], s. 1. Ascension f. Esp. Ecc: A.-day, jour, fête, de l'Ascension. 2. Pr.n. Geog: A. Island, (Île de) l'Ascension.

Ascensiontide [əˈsenʃəntaid], s. Le temps de l'Ascension.

ascent [əˈsent], s. 1. Ascension f (d'une montagne); montée f (d'une tour, etc.). Mount: First a., première f. 2. Montée, pente f, rampe f. 3. Jur: Line of a., ascendance f.

ascertain [æsəˈtein], v.tr. Constater (un fait); s'assurer, s'informer, de (la vérité de qch.). It is difficult to a. whether . . ., il est difficile de savoir si. . . .

ascertainable [æsəˈteinəbl], a. (Fait) que l'on peut constater; (fait) vérifiable.

ascertainment [æsəˈteinmənt], s. Constatation f (d'un fait).

ascetic [əˈsetik]. 1. a. Ascétique. 2. s. Ascète mf, ascétique mf.

asceticism [əˈsetisizm], s. Ascétisme m.

ascribe [əˈskraib], v.tr. Attribuer, imputer (to, à).

ascription [əˈskripʃ(ə)n], s. Attribution f, imputation f (of sth. to sth., de qch. à qch.).

asdic [ˈæzdik], s. Nav: (From Anti-submarine detection investigation committee) Asdic m.

asepsis [eiˈsepsis], s. Med: Asepsie f.

aseptic [eiˈseptik], a. & s. Med: Aseptique (m).

asexual [eiˈseksjuəl], a. Biol: Asexué, asexuel, -elle.

ash¹ [æʃ], s. Bot: Frêne m. S.a. MOUNTAIN ASH. 'ash-grove, s. Frênaie f. 'ash-key, s. Bot: Samare f de frêne.

ash², s. (Usu. in pl.) **1.** (a) Cendre(s) f(pl). Cigar a., cendre de cigare. To reduce, burn, sth. to ashes, réduire qch. en cendres. S.a. SACKCLOTH. (b) pl. Mch: Escarbilles f. **2.** (a) Cendres (des morts); dépouille mortelle. S.a. DUST¹ **2.** (b) Cr: The Ashes, trophée m (que se disputent les équipes anglaises et australiennes). 'ash-bin, s. Boîte f à ordures. 'ash-blond, a. Blond cendré inv. 'ash-box, s. Cendrier m (de locomotive). 'ash-can, s. U.S: = ASH-BIN. 'ash-cloud, s. Nuée f de cendres (au-dessus d'un volcan). 'ash-coloured, ash-'grey, a. Cendré; gris cendré inv. 'ash-heap, s. Metall: Crassier m. 'ash-hole, -pit, s. **1.** Trou m à cendres; fosse f aux cendres. **2.** Cendrier m, fosse à escarbilles (de foyer de machine). 'ash-pan, s. Cendrier m (de poêle); garde-cendres m inv. 'ash-tray, s. Cendrier m (de fumeur). Ash 'Wednesday, s. Le mercredi des Cendres.

ashamed [ə'ʃeimd], a. **1.** Honteux, confus. To be a. of s.o., of sth., avoir honte de qn, de qch. I am a. of you, vous me faites honte. To be, feel, a. to do sth., of doing sth., avoir honte. être honteux. de faire qch.; avoir honte à faire qch. You make me feel a., (i) vous me rendez confus; (ii) vous me faites honte. You ought to be a. of yourself, vous devriez avoir honte. **2.** He was a. to beg, il était trop fier pour mendier.

ashen¹ [æʃn], a. De frêne, en frêne.

ashen², a. Cendré; couleur de cendres; (of face) blême, pâle comme la mort.

ashlar [ˈæʃlər], s. (a) Pierre f de taille; moellon m d'appareil. A. work, appareil en moellons. (b) Parements mpl. revêtement m (des murs d'un édifice).

ashore [ə'ʃɔːr], adv. Nau: **1.** A terre. To go a., aller, descendre, à terre; débarquer. To set, put, (passengers) a., débarquer (des passagers). **2.** Échoué. (Of ship) To run a., s'échouer; faire côte.

ashy [ˈæʃi], a. **1.** Cendreux; couvert de cendres. **2.** = ASHEN².

Asia [ˈeiʃə]. Pr.n. Geog: L'Asie f. A. Minor, l'Asie Mineure.

Asian [ˈeiʃn, ˈeiʒn]. **1.** a. Geog: Asiatique. A. 'flu, grippe f asiatique. **2.** s. Asiate.

Asiatic [ˌeiʃi'ætik], a. & s. Asiatique (mf).

aside [ə'said]. **1.** adv. De côté; à l'écart; à part. To draw (a curtain) a., écarter (un rideau). To lay, put, sth. a., mettre qch. de côté. S.a. LAY ASIDE. To stand a., (i) se tenir à l'écart, à part; (ii) se ranger. To step a., s'écarter, se ranger. To turn a., se détourner (from, de). Putting that a . . . , à part cela . . . , laissant cela de côté. . . . I took, drew, him a., je le pris à part, à l'écart. Th: (Words spoken) a., (paroles dites) en aparté. S.a. SET ASIDE. **2.** U.S: En plus de; excepté. A. from, à part. A. from my own interest, I think . . ., mon propre intérêt à part, je pense que. . . . **3.** s. Remarque faite à l'écart; à-côté m. Th: Aparté m. In an a., en aparté.

asinine [ˈasinain], a. (a) (Race) asine. (b) F: Stupide, sot; digne d'un âne.

ask [ɑːsk], v.tr. & i. (asked [ɑːs(k)t]) Demander. **1.** (Inquire) To a. s.o. sth., demander qch. à qn. A. (him) his name, demandez(-lui) son nom. To a. the time, demander l'heure. To a. s.o. a question, poser, faire, adresser, une question à qn. A. a policeman, adressez-vous à un agent de police. F: A. me another! je n'ai pas la moindre idée. If you a. me . . ., à mon avis. . . . **2.** (Beg for, request to be given) (a) To a. a favour of s.o., to a. s.o. a favour, demander une faveur à qn. (b) (Of price) How much are you asking for it? combien en voulez-vous? To a. six francs for sth., demander six francs pour qch., de qch. **3.** (Request) (a) To a. to do sth., demander à faire qch.; demander la permission, l'autorisation, de faire qch. He asked to be admitted, il demanda à être admis. (b) To a. s.o. to do sth., demander à qn, prier qn, de faire qch. **4.** (a) To a. about sth., se renseigner sur qch. To a. s.o. about sth., interroger qn sur qch.; se renseigner sur qch. auprès de qn. He asked me about him, il m'a demandé de ses nouvelles. (b) To a. after s.o., after s.o.'s health, demander des nouvelles

de (la santé de) qn; s'informer de la santé de qn. **5.** (a) To a. for s.o., demander à voir qn. I asked for the manager, je demandai à parler au gérant. (b) To a. for sth., demander qch.; solliciter qch. To a. s.o. for sth., demander qch. à qn. To a. for something to eat, demander à manger. To a. for something to read, demander qch. à lire. To be asking for trouble, F: for it, aller au devant des ennuis. F: He's been asking for it, il l'a bien cherché. **6.** Ecc: (a) A: To a. the bans, publier les bans. (b) 'This is the first time of asking', "C'est ici la première publication." **7.** Inviter. To a. s.o. to lunch, inviter qn à déjeuner. To a. s.o. in, out, up, demander à qn, prier qn, d'entrer, de sortir, de monter. **ask back**, v.tr. **1.** To a. for sth. back, redemander (un objet prêté, son argent, etc.). **2.** To a. s.o. back, inviter qn pour lui rendre la politesse. **asking**, s. You may have it for the a., il ne vous en coûtera que la peine de le demander; il n'y a qu'à le demander.

askance [ə'skæns], adv. De côté, du coin de l'œil, obliquement. Esp. To look a. at s.o., at sth., regarder qn, qch., de travers, avec méfiance, d'un œil malveillant.

askew [ə'skjuː], adv. De biais, de côté.

aslant [ə'slɑːnt], adv. Obliquement, de travers, de biais.

asleep [ə'sliːp], adv. & pred. a. Endormi. **1.** To be a., dormir, sommeiller. To be fast, sound, a., être profondément endormi, plongé dans le sommeil; dormir profondément. He lay a., il dormait. To fall, drop, a., s'endormir. **2.** My foot is a., j'ai le pied engourdi, endormi.

asp [æsp], s. (Vipère f) aspic m.

asparagus [əs'pærəgəs], s. Coll. Asperges fpl. A stick of a., une asperge. A. tips, pointes d'asperges. Bundle of a., botte d'asperges. **as'paragus-fern**, s. Bot: Asparagus m.

aspect [ˈæspekt], s. **1.** Exposition f, vue f; orientation f. To have a northern a., être exposé au nord; avoir une exposition nord. **2.** Aspect m, air m. All the aspects of a subject, tous les aspects d'un sujet. To see sth. in its true a., voir qch. sous son vrai jour. **'aspect-ratio**, s. Av: (Of wings) allongement m.

aspen [ˈæspən], s. Bot: (Peuplier m) tremble m. A. leaf, feuille de tremble.

asperges [æs'pɜːdʒiːz], s. Ecc: Aspergès m.

aspergillum [ˌæspə'dʒiləm], s. Ecc: Goupillon m.

asperity [æs'periti], s. **1.** (a) Âpreté f. (b) Rigueur f, sévérité f (du climat). (c) Rudesse f (de caractère); âpérité f (de style). **2.** (Rough excrescence) Aspérité.

aspersion [ə'spɜːʃ(ə)n], s. **1.** (Sprinkling) Aspersion f. **2.** Calomnie f. To cast aspersions upon s.o., répandre des calomnies sur qn; dénigrer qn.

asphalt¹ [ˈæsfælt], s. Asphalte m; (often loosely) bitume m; goudron minéral.

asphalt², v.tr. Asphalter, bitumer.

asphodel [ˈæsfədel], s. Bot: Asphodèle m.

asphyxia [æs'fiksiə], s. Asphyxie f.

asphyxiate [æs'fiksieit], v.tr. Asphyxier.

asphyxiation [æsˌfiksi'eiʃ(ə)n], s. Asphyxie f.

aspic¹ [ˈæspik], s. = ASP.

aspic², s. Cu: Aspic m.

aspidistra [ˌæspi'distrə], s. Bot: Aspidistra m.

aspirant [ə'spaiər(ə)nt], s. Aspirant, -ante (to, after, à); candidat m.

aspirate¹ [ˈæsp(ə)rit]. Ling: **1.** a. Aspiré. **2.** s. (a) (Lettre) aspirée f. (b) (La lettre) h.

aspirate² [ˈæspəreit], v.tr. Aspirer (une voyelle, un liquide). **Aspirating filter**, filtre à vide.

aspiration [ˌæspə'reiʃ(ə)n], s. **1.** Aspiration f ((i) de l'air, d'un fluide; (ii) de l'h). **2.** A. for, after, fame, aspiration à la gloire.

aspirator [ˈæspəreitər], s. **1.** Ph: Med: Aspirateur m. **2.** (Filter-pump) Trompe f.

aspiratory [ˈæspər'eit(ə)ri], a. Aspirateur, -trice; aspiratoire.

aspire [ə'spaiər], v.i. Aspirer. To a. to, after, sth., aspirer, prétendre, viser, à qch.; ambitionner qch. To a. to do sth., aspirer à faire qch. **aspiring**, a. Ambitieux.

aspirin [ˈæspərin], s. Pharm: Aspirine f. Take an a. prenez un comprimé d'aspirine.

ass [æs, ɑ:s], *s.* 1. Ane, *f.* ânesse. Ass's foal, ass's colt, ânon *m.* Ass's milk, lait d'ânesse. 2. *F:* Sot, *f.* sotte; âne; idiot, -te. He is a perfect a., c'est un âne bâté; il est bête à manger du foin. *S.a.* SILLY 1. **To make an a. of oneself,** (i) agir d'une manière stupide, idiote; faire des âneries; (ii) se donner en spectacle; se faire moquer de soi.

assail [ə'seil], *v.tr.* Assaillir, attaquer (l'ennemi, une place forte).

assailant [ə'seilənt], *s.* Assaillant *m.*

assassin [ə'sæsin], *s.* Assassin *m.*

assassinate [ə'sæsineit], *v.tr.* Assassiner.

assassination [ə,sæsi'neiʃ(ə)n], *s.* Assassinat *m.*

assault¹ [ə'sɔ:lt], *s.* 1. (*a*) Assaut *m.* To take, carry, a town by a., prendre une ville|d'assaut. *Fenc:* A. of, at, arms, assaut d'armes. (*b*) Attaque (brusquée). 2. *Jur:* Tentative *f* de voie de fait. Unprovoked a., agression *f.* A. and battery, (menaces *fpl* et) voies de fait; coups *mpl* et blessures *fpl.* Criminal a., tentative *f* de viol. Indecent a., attentat *m* à la pudeur; outrage *m* aux mœurs. To commit an a., se porter, se livrer, à des voies de fait (on, sur).

assault², *v.tr.* 1. Attaquer, assaillir (une position); donner l'assaut à (une ville, etc.). 2. Attaquer, violenter (qn). To be assaulted, être victime d'une agression.

assaulter [ə'sɔ:ltər], *s.* Assaillant *m*, agresseur *m.*

assay¹ [ə'sei], *s. Metall:* Essai *m* (d'un métal précieux, d'un minerai).

assay², *v.tr. Metall:* Essayer, titrer (un métal précieux, un minerai). assaying, *s.* Essai *m*, titrage *m.*

assegai ['æsigai], *s.* Zagaie *f*, sagaie *f.*

assemblage [ə'semblidʒ], *s.* 1. Assemblage *m* (de pièces de menuiserie, etc.). 2. (*a*) Réunion *f*, concours *m* (de personnes). (*b*) Collection *f* (d'objets).

assemble [ə'sembl]. 1. *v.tr.* (*a*) Assembler (des personnes); convoquer (un parlement). *Mil:* Rassembler (des troupes). (*b*) Assembler (des pièces de menuiserie, etc.); ajuster, monter (une machine). 2. *v.i.* S'assembler; se rassembler. assembling, *s.* Assemblage *m*; rassemblement *m*; convocation *f.*

assembler [ə'semblər], *s. Ind:* Monteur, -euse; ajusteur, -euse.

assembly [ə'sembli], *s.* 1. (*a*) Assemblée *f.* In open a., en séance publique. (*b*) *Mil:* (Sonnerie *f* du) rassemblement *m.* (*c*) *Jur:* Unlawful a., attroupement *m.* ¡2. Assemblement *m*, réunion *f.* Place of a., lieu de réunion. A. rooms, salle *f* des fêtes. 3. Assemblage *m*, montage *m* (d'une machine). A. line, banc *m*, chaîne *f* de montage. A. shop, atelier *m* d'assemblage. A. mark, repère *m* de montage, d'ajustage.

assent¹ [ə'sent], *s.* Assentiment *m*, consentement *m*, acquiescement *m. Jur:* Agrément *m.* The royal a., le consentement, la sanction, du souverain. *S.a.* NOD².

assent², *v.i.* 1. (*a*) Accéder, acquiescer, donner son assentiment (to, à). (*b*) (*Of sovereign, etc.*) Sanctionner (une loi, etc.). 2. To a. to the truth of sth., reconnaître la vérité de qch. To a. to a theory, admettre une théorie.

assert [ə'sə:t], *v.tr.* 1. (*a*) To a. one's rights, revendiquer, faire valoir, ses droits. (*b*) To a. oneself, soutenir ses droits; s'affirmer; s'imposer. 2. Affirmer. To a. that . . ., affirmer, prétendre, soutenir, que. . . . To a. one's innocence, protester de son innocence.

assertion [ə'sə:ʃ(ə)n], *s.* 1. A. of one's rights, revendication *f* de ses droits. 2. Affirmation *f*; assertion *f. S.a.* SELF-ASSERTION.

assertive [ə'sə:tiv], *a.* (*a*) = SELF-ASSERTIVE. (*b*) (Ton, etc.) péremptoire, cassant. -ly, *adv.* Avec assurance; d'un ton cassant.

assertiveness [ə'sə:tivnis], *s.* Assurance *f*; ton *m*, manière *f* autoritaire.

assess [ə'ses], *v.tr.* 1. (*a*) Répartir, établir (un impôt). (*b*) Estimer, inventorier, évaluer. *Jur:* To a. the damages, fixer les dommages-intérêts. 2. To a. a loan, an estate, etc., upon s.o., imposer un prêt, etc., à qn. 3. *Adm:* To a. s.o. in, at, so much, coter, imposer, taxer, qn à tant. 4. To a. a property (for taxation), évaluer une propriété. Assessed taxes, impôts directs.

assessable [ə'sesəbl], *a.* 1. (Dommage) évaluable. 2. (Propriété) imposable.

assessment [ə'sesmənt], *s.* 1. (*a*) Répartition *f*, assiette *f* (d'un impôt). (*b*) Évaluation *f* (de dégâts, *Nau:* d'avarie). *Jur:* A. of damages, fixation *f* de dommages-intérêts. (*c*) Imposition *f* (d'une commune, d'un immeuble). (*d*) Cotisation *f* (du contribuable). 2. (*Amount*) Cote *f*; taxe officielle. A. on landed property, cote foncière. A. on income, impôt *m* sur le revenu. Notice of a., feuille *f* d'impôt.

assessor [ə'sesər], *s.* 1. *Jur:* Assesseur (adjoint à un juge). 2. Répartiteur *m.* A. of taxes, contrôleur *m* des contributions (directes).

asset ['æset], *s.* I. Chose *f* dont on peut tirer avantage; possession *f*; avoir *m.* He is one of our assets, c'est une de nos valeurs. II. assets, *s.pl.* 1. *Jur:* Masse *f* d'une succession, d'une société. Personal a., biens *m* meubles. Real a., biens immobiliers. *S.a.* LIQUID 1. 2. *Com: Fin:* Actif *m*; avoir *m*; avoirs *mpl.*

asseverate [ə'sevəreit], *v.tr.* Affirmer (solennellement) (that, que + *ind*).

asseveration [ə,sevə'reiʃ(ə)n], *s.* Affirmation (solennelle); protestation *f* (d'innocence).

assiduity ['æsi'djuiti], *s.* Assiduité *f*, diligence *f* (in doing sth., à faire qch.).

assiduous [ə'sidjuəs], *a.* 1. (*Of pers.*) Assidu; diligent. 2. (Travail) assidu. -ly, *adv.* Assidûment.

assiduousness [ə'sidjuəsnis], *s.* = ASSIDUITY.

assign¹ [ə'sain], *s. Jur:* Ayant cause *m*, ayant droit *m* (*pl.* ayants cause, ayants droit); délégué, -ée; mandataire *mf*; attributaire *mf.*

assign², *v.tr.* 1. Assigner (to, à). Donner (qch.) en partage (à qn). (*b*) To a. a reason for sth., donner la raison de qch. Object assigned to a certain use, objet affecté, consacré, à un certain usage. To a. a salary to an office, attribuer un traitement à un emploi. (*c*) To a. an hour, a place, fixer une heure, un lieu. (*d*) To a. a task to s.o., assigner, attribuer, une tâche à qn. 2. *Jur:* To a. a property to s.o., céder, transférer, une propriété à qn.

assignable [ə'sainəbl], *a.* 1. (*a*) Assignable, attribuable (to, à). (*b*) (Date, etc.) que l'on peut fixer, que l'on peut déterminer. 2. *Jur:* (Bien) cessible, transférable.

assignation [,æsig'neiʃ(ə)n], *s.* 1. Distribution *f*, répartition *f*, attribution *f* (de biens). 2. *Jur:* Cession *f*, transfert *m* (de biens, de dettes). (*In bankruptcy*) Deed of a., acte de transfert; acte attributif. 3. (*a*) Fixation *f* (d'une heure, etc.). (*b*) Rendez-vous galant.

assignee [,æsai'ni:], *s. Jur:* 1. (*a*) = ASSIGN¹. (*b*) (Administrateur-)séquestre *m*; syndic *m.* 2. Cessionnaire *mf* (d'une créance, etc.).

assignment [ə'sainmənt], *s.* 1. (*a*) = ASSIGNATION 1, 2. (*b*) (*Allocation*) Affectation *f*, allocation *f*, attribution *f* (de qch. à qch., à qn). (*c*) Citation *f*, production *f* (de raisons); attribution (de cause) (to, à). 2. *Sch: U.S:* Tâche assignée.

assimilable [ə'similəbl], *a.* 1. (Aliment) assimilable. 2. Comparable, assimilable (to, à).

assimilate [ə'simileit], *v.tr.* 1. (*a*) Assimiler, comparer (to, à). (*b*) *v.i.* (*Of consonants*) S'assimiler. 2. To a. food, assimiler des aliments. assimilating, assimilative, assimilatory, *a.* Assimilateur, -trice.

assimilation [ə,simi'leiʃ(ə)n], *s.* 1. (*a*) Assimilation *f* (to, with, à). (*b*) (*Comparison*) Assimilation (to, à); comparaison *f* (to, avec). 2. Assimilation (des aliments).

assist [ə'sist], 1. *v.tr.* (*a*) Aider (qn); prêter son concours, prêter assistance, à (qn). To a. one another, s'entr'aider. To a. s.o. in doing sth., aider qn à faire qch. (*b*) To a. s.o. in misfortune, secourir, assister, qn dans le malheur. 2. *v.i.* To a. at a ceremony, (i) prendre part à une cérémonie; (ii) (*be present*) assister à une cérémonie.

assistance [ə'sistəns], *s.* Aide *f*, secours *m*, assistance *f.* To come to s.o.'s a., venir à l'aide de, en aide à, au secours de, qn. With the a. of sth., of s.o., à l'aide de qch., avec l'aide de qn. To be of a. to s.o., aider qn, être utile à qn. *Adm:* National A., l'Assistance publique.

assistant [ə'sistənt]. 1. *a.* Qui aide; auxiliaire; adjoint; sous-. A. manager, sous-directeur *m*; sous-gérant *m. Sch:* A. master, mistress, professeur *m* (de lycée). *Th:* A. director, régisseur *m.* 2. *s.* Aide *mf*; adjoint, -ointe; auxiliaire *mf. Com:* Commis *m* (de magasin); vendeur, -euse; employé, -ée. *S.a.* SHOP-ASSISTANT.

assize [ə'saiz], *s.* (*Usu. in pl.*) *Jur:* (Court of) assizes, a.-court, (cour *f* d')assises *fpl*.

associate¹ [ə'souʃiit]. 1. *a.* Associé. A. judge, juge-assesseur *m*. 2. *s.* (*a*) Associé *m*, adjoint *m*; membre correspondant (d'une académie). Associates in crime, in intrigue, consorts *m*. (*b*) Compagnon *m*, camarade *mf*.

associate² [ə'souʃieit]. 1. *v.tr.* Associer (with, avec qn, à qch.). To a. oneself with s.o. in an undertaking, s'associer avec qn pour une entreprise. Associated territories, territoires associés. To be associated with a plot, tremper dans un complot. *Phil:* To a. ideas, associer des idées. 2. *v.i.* (*a*) To a. with s.o. in doing sth., s'associer avec qn pour faire qch. (*b*) To a. with s.o., fréquenter qn; frayer avec qn.

association [ə,sousi'eiʃ(ə)n], *s.* 1. (*a*) Association *f* (d'idées, etc.). Land full of historic associations, pays fertile en souvenirs historiques. (*b*) Fréquentation *f* (with s.o., de qn). To form associations, se faire des relations. (*c*) A. football, football *m* association. 2. Association, société *f*, amicale *f* (de professeurs, etc.). Young Men's Christian A., Union chrétienne de jeunes gens. To form an a., constituer une société.

associationism [ə,sousi'eiʃ(ə)nizm], *s.* *Phil:* Associationisme *m*.

assonance ['æsənəns], *s.* *Pros:* Assonance *f*.

assonant ['æsənənt], *a.* *Pros: Ling:* Assonant.

assort [ə'sɔːt]. 1. *v.tr.* (*a*) Assortir (with, à). To a. colours, assortir des couleurs; marier des couleurs. (*b*) Classer, ranger (with, parmi). 2. *v.i.* To a. well, ill, with sth., (s')assortir bien, mal, avec qch. To a. well, ill, aller ensemble, ne pas aller ensemble.

assortment [ə'sɔːtmənt], *s.* 1. Assortiment *m*; jeu *m* (d'outils). 2. Classement *m*, classification *f* (par sortes).

assuage [ə'sweidʒ], *v.tr.* Apaiser, adoucir, soulager, calmer (les souffrances); apaiser, satisfaire (un appétit).

assuagement [ə'sweidʒmənt], *s.* Apaisement *m*, adoucissement *m*, soulagement *m* (de la douleur).

assume [ə'sjuːm], *v.tr.* 1. Prendre, se donner (un air, une mine); affecter, revêtir (une forme, un caractère). 2. (*a*) Prendre sur soi, prendre à son compte, assumer (une charge, une responsabilité); se charger (d'un devoir). *Com:* To a. all risks, assumer tous les risques. (*b*) To a. power, authority, prendre possession du pouvoir. 3. S'attribuer, s'arroger, s'approprier (un droit, un titre). To a. a name, adopter un nom. *Jur:* To a. ownership, faire acte de propriétaire. 4. Simuler, affecter (une vertu). 5. Présumer, supposer (qch.); tenir (qch.) comme établi. *Geom:* Admettre (qch.) en postulat. I a. that he will come, je présume qu'il viendra. He was assumed to be wealthy, on le supposait riche. Let us a. that such is the case, mettons qu'il en soit ainsi. To a. the existence of . . ., présumer l'existence de . . . Assuming the truth of the story . . ., en supposant que l'histoire soit vraie . . . assumed, *a.* Supposé, feint, faux *f*, fausse. With a. nonchalance, avec une affectation d'indifférence. A. piety, fausse dévotion. A. name, pseudonyme *m*; nom de guerre. assuming, *a.* Présomptueux, -euse, prétentieux, -euse.

assumption [ə'sʌm(p)ʃ(ə)n], *s.* 1. *Ecc:* Assomption *f* (de la Vierge). 2. (*a*) Action *f* de prendre (une forme, un caractère). (*b*) A. of office, entrée *f* en fonctions. 3. (*a*) Affectation *f* (de vertu, etc.). (*b*) Arrogance *f*, prétention(s) *f*, présomption *f*. 4. Supposition *f*, hypothèse *f*. *Phil:* Postulat *m*.

assurable [ə'ʃuərəbl], *a.* Assurable.

assurance [ə'ʃuər(ə)ns], *s.* 1. (*a*) (*Certainty*) Assurance *f*. To make a. double sure, pour plus de sûreté; pour surcroît de sûreté. (*b*) Promesse (formelle). (*c*) Affirmation *f*. 2. *Ins:* Life-a., assurance sur la vie. 3. (*a*) Assurance, fermeté *f*; *F:* aplomb *m*. S.a. SELF-ASSURANCE. (*b*) Hardiesse *f*, présomption *f*; *F:* toupet *m*.

assure [ə'ʃuər], *v.tr.* (*a*) (*Make safe*) To a. s.o. against sth., assurer qn contre qch. To a. s.o.'s life, assurer la vie de qn. To a. one's life, s'assurer (sur la vie). (*b*) (*Make certain*) To a. the peace, the happiness, of s.o., assurer la paix, le bonheur, de qn. (*c*) (*Affirm*) To a.

s.o. of sth., assurer qn de qch.; assurer qch. à qn. He will do it, I can a. you! il le fera, je vous en réponds! You may rest assured that . . ., vous pouvez tenir pour certain que. . . .

assuredly [ə'ʃuəridli], *adv.* Assurément; à coup sûr. A. not, non certes.

assuredness [ə'ʃuəridnis], *s.* 1. Certitude. 2. = ASSURANCE 3.

assurer, assuror [ə'ʃuərər], *s.* *Ins:* Assureur *m*.

Assyria [ə'siriə]. *Pr.n. A.Geog:* L'Assyrie *f*.

Assyrian [ə'siriən], *a. & s.* *A.Hist:* Assyrien, -ienne.

aster ['æstər], *s.* *Bot:* Aster *m*. China a., aster de Chine; reine-marguerite *f*.

asterisk ['æst(ə)risk], *s.* Astérisque *m*.

astern [ə'stəːn]. 1. *adv.* (*a*) (*Position on ship*) A l'arrière, sur l'arrière. (*b*) (*Backwards*) To go, come, a., culer; aller de l'arrière; marcher en arrière. Full speed a.! toute vitesse en arrière! (*c*) (*Behind*) To make a boat fast a., amarrer un canot derrière. To have the wind a., avoir le vent en arrière. 2. A. of a ship, derrière un bateau; sur l'arrière d'un bateau.

asteroid ['æstərɔid]. 1. *a.* En forme d'étoile. 2. *s.* Astéroïde *m*.

asthenia [æs'θiːniə], *s.* *Med:* Asthénie *f*.

asthma ['æsmə], *s.* Asthme *m*. To suffer from a., être asthmatique.

asthmatic [æs'mætik], *a. & s.* Asthmatique (*mf*).

astigmatic [æstig'mætik], *a.* Astigmate.

astigmatism [æ'stigmətizm], *s.* Astigmatisme *m*.

astir [ə'stəːr], *adv. & pred.a.* 1. Actif; en mouvement; animé. To set sth. a., mettre qch. en mouvement, en branle. 2. Debout, levé. 3. En émoi; agité.

astonish [ə'stɔniʃ], *v.tr.* Étonner, surprendre. You a. me, vous m'étonnez. To be astonished at seeing sth., to see sth., être étonné, s'étonner, de voir qch. I am astonished that . . ., cela m'étonne que + *sub.* astonishing, *a.* Étonnant, surprenant. -ly, *adv.* Étonnamment.

astonishment [ə'stɔniʃmənt], *s.* Étonnement *m*, surprise *f*. My a. at seeing him, mon étonnement, l'étonnement où j'étais, de le voir. A look of blank a., un air ébahi.

astound [ə'staund], *v.tr.* Confondre, abasourdir; stupéfier; ébahir. I'm astounded! je n'en reviens pas! astounding, *a.* (*a*) Abasourdissant. (*b*) (*Désastre*) épouvantable; (*nouvelle*) atterrante.

astragal ['æstrəg(ə)l], *s.* Astragale *m*, chapelet *m* (d'une colonne).

Astrak(h)an [æstrə'kæn]. 1. *Pr.n. Geog:* Astrak(h)an. 2. *s.* (*Fur*) Astrakan *m*.

astral ['æstr(ə)l], *a.* Astral, -aux.

astray [ə'strei], *adv. & pred.a.* (i) Égaré; (ii) *Pej:* dévoyé. To go a., (i) s'égarer; s'écarter de la route, faire fausse route; (ii) *Pej:* se dévoyer. To lead s.o. a., (i) égarer qn; induire qn en erreur; (ii) débaucher, dévoyer, qn.

astride [ə'straid], *adv., pred.a., & prep.* A califourchon; jambe deçà, jambe delà (sur qch.). To sit a. sth., être à cheval, chevaucher, être à califourchon, sur qch.

astringency [ə'strin(d)ʒənsi], *s.* Astringence *f*.

astringent [ə'strin(d)ʒ(ə)nt], *a. & s.* Astringent (*m*); styptique (*m*), constipant (*m*).

astrionics [æstri'ɔniks], *s.* Électronique appliquée à l'astronautique.

astrobiology ['æstrobai'ɔlədʒi], *s.* *Ph:* Astrobiologie *f*.

astrodome ['æstrodoum], *s.* *Av:* Coupole vitrée avant; astrodôme *m*.

astrolabe ['æstroleib], *s.* *Astr:* Astrolabe *m*.

astrologer [ə'strɔlədʒər], *s.* Astrologue *m*.

astrological [æstrə'lɔdʒik(ə)l], *a.* Astrologique. -ally, *adv.* Astrologiquement.

astrology [ə'strɔlədʒi], *s.* Astrologie *f*.

astronaut ['æstrɔnɔːt], *s.* Astronaute *m*.

astronautics [æstro'nɔːtiks], *s.pl.* Astronautique *f*.

astronomer [ə'strɔnəmər], *s.* Astronome *m*.

astronomic(al) [æstrə'nɔmik(əl)], *a.* Astronomique. *F:* The sales reach astronomical figures, la vente atteint des chiffres astronomiques. -ally, *adv.* Astronomiquement.

astronomy [ə'strɔnəmi], *s.* Astronomie *f*.

astrophysical ['æstro'fizik(ə)l], *a.* Astrophysique.

astrophysics ['æstrou'fiziks], *s.pl.* Astrophysique *f*.

Asturias [æs'tjuəriæs, æst'juəriəs]. *Pr.n. Geog:* Les Asturies *fpl.*

astute [əs'tju:t], *a.* 1. Fin, avisé, pénétrant. 2. *Pej:* Astucieux, matois, rusé. -ly, *adv.* 1. Avec finesse. 2. Astucieusement.

astuteness [əs'tju:tnis], *s.* 1. Finesse , sagacité *f;* pénétration *f.* 2. *Pej:* Astuce *f.*

Asuncion [ə‚sunsi'oun]. *Pr.n. Geog:* Assomption (capitale du Paraguay).

asunder [ə'sʌndər], *adv.* 1. Éloignés, écartés (l'un de l'autre). 2. To tear sth. a., déchirer qch. en deux. (*Of parts*) To come a., se désunir, se disjoindre.

asylum [ə'sailəm], *s.* 1. (*a*) *Hist:* Asile *m* (inviolable). (*b*) Asile, (lieu *m* de) refuge *m.* To afford a. to s.o., donner asile, offrir un asile, à qn. 2. *A:* (*a*) Hospice *m.* (*b*) *O:* (Lunatic) a., maison *f*, hospice, asile, d'aliénés.

asymmetrical [‚æsi'metrik(ə)l], *a.* Asymétrique, dissymétrique.

asymmetry [æ'simitri], *s.* Asymétrie *f;* dissymétrie *f.*

at [æt], *prep.* A. 1. (*Position*) (*a*) At the centre, at the top, au centre, au sommet. At table, at church, at school, à table, à l'église, à l'école. The dog was at his heels, le chien marchait sur ses talons. At hand, sous la main. At sea, at war, en mer, en guerre. (*b*) At home, à la maison, chez soi. At the tailor's, chez le tailleur. (*c*) To sit at the window, se tenir (au-)près de la fenêtre. He came in at the window, il entra par la fenêtre. 2. (*Time*) At six o'clock, à six heures. At present, à présent. Two at a time, deux par deux; deux à la fois. *S.a.* TIME¹ 5. At night, la nuit, le soir. 3. (*Price*) At two francs a pound, à deux francs la livre. 4. At my request, sur ma demande. At all events, en tout cas. 5. Swift at repartee, prompt à la repartie. Good at games, sportif, -ive. 6. (*a*) To look at sth., regarder qch. To be surprised at sth., être étonné de qch. To catch at sth., s'accrocher à qch. (*b*) To laugh at s.o., se moquer de qn. To swear at s.o., jurer contre qn. (*c*) To be at work, être au travail, travailler. To be at sth., être occupé à faire qch. *F:* She's at it again (i.e. crying, etc.), voilà qu'elle recommence! While we are at it, why not . . ., pendant que nous y sommes, pourquoi ne pas. . . . (*d*) *F:* To be at s.o., être acharné contre qn; rudoyer qn. They are at me again, voilà encore qu'on s'en prend à moi. *Mil:* At them! chargez! en avant! (*To dog*) At him! pille! pille!

atavism ['ætəvizm], *s.* Atavisme *m.*

atavistic [ætə'vistik], *a.* Atavique.

ataxic [ə'tæksik], *a. Med:* Ataxique.

ataxy [ə'tæksi], *s. Med:* Ataxie *f.* Locomotor a., ataxie locomotrice (progressive).

ate. *See* EAT.

Athanasian [æθə'neiʃ(ə)n], *a.* Athanasien. The A. Creed, le Symbole de St. Athanase.

atheism ['eiθiizm], *s.* Athéisme *m.*

atheist ['eiθiist], *s.* Athée *mf.*

atheistic(al) [‚eiθi'istik(ə)l], *a.* 1. (Doctrine) athéistique. 2. (Personne) athée. -ally, *adv.* En athée; avec impiété.

athenaeum [‚æθi'ni(:)əm], *s.* Athénée *m.*

Athenian [ə'θi:niən], *a. & s.* Athénien, -ienne; d'Athènes; attique.

Athens ['æθinz]. *Pr.n.* Athènes *f.*

atheroma [æθə'roumə], *s. Med:* Athérome *m.*

athirst [ə'θə:st], *pred. a. Lit:* Altéré, assoiffé (for, de).

athlete ['æθli:t], *s.* 1. Athlète *m.* 2. Sportif, -ive. *Med:* Athlete's foot, pied *m* de l'athlète.

athletic [æθ'letik], *a.* 1. Athlétique. A. meeting, réunion sportive. *Med: F:* A. heart, *F:* cœur claqué. 2. He looks a., il a l'air vigoureux, solide, bien taillé, sportif. -ically, *adv.* Athlétiquement.

athleticism [æθ'letisizm], *s.* Athlétisme *m.*

athletics [æθ'letiks], *s.pl.* (*Usu. with sg. const.*) Sports *m* (athlétiques).

at-home [ət'houm], *s.* Réception *f;* soirée *f.*

athwart [ə'θwɔ:t]. 1. *adv.* En travers; *Nau:* par le travers. 2. *prep.* En travers de.

Atlantic [ət'læntik], *a. & s.* The A. (Ocean), l'(océan) Atlantique *m.*

Atlantis [ət'læntis]. *Pr.n. Myth:* L'Atlantide *f.*

Atlas ['ætləs]. 1. *Pr.n.m. Gr.Myth:* Atlas. *Geog:* The A. Mountains, l'Atlas *m.* 2. *s.* (*pl.* atlases ['ætləsiz]) Atlas *m.*

atmosphere ['ætməsfiər], *s.* 1. Atmosphère *f.* I don't like the a., l'ambiance *f* ne me plaît pas. *Ph:* Sensible a., atmosphère permettant la sustentation aérodynamique. 2. *Ph:* (*Pressure of 15 lb. per sq. inch*) Atmosphère.

atmospheric(al) [‚ætməs'ferik(ə)l]. 1. *a.* Atmosphérique. 2. *s.pl. W.Tel:* Atmospherics, perturbations *fpl*, parasites *mpl.*

atoll ['ætɔl], *s.* Atoll *m.*

atom ['ætəm], *s. Ch: Ph:* Atome *m. Mil:* A. bomb, bombe *f* atomique. Not an a. of truth, pas un grain de vérité. Smashed to atoms, réduit en miettes, en poussière. 'atom-free, *a.* A.-f. zone, zone dénucléarisée.

atomic [ə'tɔmik], *a.* Atomique. A. age, âge *m*, ère *m*, atomique. A. energy, énergie *f* atomique. A. pile, pile *f* atomique. A. physicist, scientist, atomiste *m. Ph:* A. number, numéro *m* atomique. A. weight, poids *m* atomique. *Mil:* A. warfare, guerre *f* atomique. A. missile, projectile *m* atomique. The a. theory, (i) *Phil:* atomisme *m;* (ii) *Atom.Ph:* atomistique *f*, théorie *f* atomistique. *s.* Atomics, sciences *fpl.* atomiques.

atomicity [‚ætə'misiti], *s. Ch: Ph:* Atomicité *f*, valence *f.*

atomism ['ætəmizm], *s. Phil: Atom.Ph:* Atomisme *m.*

atomist ['ætəmist], *s. Phil:* Atomiste *m.*

atomistic [‚ætə'mistik], *a. Phil: Atom.Ph:* Atomistique.

atomize ['ætəmaiz], *v.tr.* Pulvériser (un liquide); vaporiser; atomiser.

atomizer ['ætəmaizər], *s.* 1. Pulvérisateur *m*, atomiseur *m.* 2. *I.C.E:* Gicleur-pulvérisateur *m.*

atonable [ə'tounəbl], *a.* Expiable; (faute *f*) réparable.

atonal [æ'tounl, ə't-], *a. Mus:* Atonal, -aux.

atonality [‚ætou'næliti], *s. Mus:* Atonalité *f.*

atone [ə'toun], *v.tr. or ind.tr.* To a. (for) a fault (by doing sth.), expier, racheter, réparer, une faute (en faisant qch.).

atonement [ə'tounmənt], *s.* Expiation *f*, réparation *f* (for, de). *Theol:* Rachat *m.* Offering of a., sacrifice *m* expiatoire. To make a. for a fault, réparer une faute. *Jew.Rel:* Day of A., fête *f* du Grand Pardon.

atonic [ə'tɔnik]. 1. *a. Med:* (*Of muscle, etc.*) Atonique. 2. *a. & s.* (Syllabe) atone (*f*).

atrocious [ə'trouʃəs], *a.* 1. (Crime) atroce. 2. *F:* (Jeu de mots) exécrable; (chapeau) affreux. -ly, *adv.* 1. Atrocement. 2. *F:* Exécrablement.

atrociousness [ə'trouʃəsnis], *s.* Atrocité *f* (d'un supplice).

atrocity [ə'trɔsiti], *s.* Atrocité *f* (d'un crime). To witness atrocities, assister à des atrocités.

atrophy¹ ['ætrəfi], *s.* Atrophie *f.*

atrophy². 1. *v.tr.* Atrophier. 2. *v.i.* S'atrophier.

atropine ['ætropi(:)n], *s. Ch: Pharm:* Atropine *f.*

attach [ə'tætʃ]. 1. *v.tr.* (*a*) Attacher, lier, fixer (sth. to sth., qch. à qch.); annexer (un document). (*b*) *Jur:* Arrêter (qn); contraindre (qn) par corps; saisir, mettre une saisie-arrêt sur (des biens mobiliers). (*c*) To a. credence to sth., ajouter foi à qch. *S.a.* IMPORTANCE. 2. *v.i.* S'attacher. The blame which attaches to a crime, la honte qui s'attache à un crime.

attached, *a.* (*a*) Attaché (to, à); adjoint (à un personnel). Official temporarily a. to another department, fonctionnaire détaché à un autre service. (*Of ship*) To be a. to a squadron, faire partie d'une escadre. Salary a. to a post, traitement afférent à un emploi. (*b*) To be deeply a. to s.o., être fortement attaché à qn. (*c*) *Cost:* Shirt with collar a., chemise col tenant.

attachable [ə'tætʃəbl], *a.* 1. Qui peut être attaché (to, à); facile à attacher, à fixer. 2. *Jur:* (*Of property*) Saisissable.

attaché [ə'tæʃei], *s. Dipl: etc:* Attaché *m.* at'taché-case, *s. O:* Mallette *f* (pour documents).

attachment [ə'tætʃmənt], *s.* 1. (*a*) Action *f* d'attacher (qch. à qch.); attachement *m. Techn:* A. flange, collerette *f* de fixation. (*b*) Attache *f*, lien *m.* 2. Accessoire *m* (d'une machine à coudre, etc.). 3. (*Affection*) Attachement (of s.o. for s.o., de qn pour qn); affection *f* (for, pour). 4. *Jur:* (*a*) Saisie-arrêt *f*, opposition *f.* (*b*) Contrainte *f* par corps.

attack¹ [ə'tæk], s. **1.** Attaque f, assaut m. **To make an a. upon s.o., sth.,** attaquer qn, qch.; s'attaquer à (un problème, un travail). *Mil:* **Surprise a.,** coup m de main. **To rush to the a.,** se précipiter à l'assaut. **To return to the a.,** revenir à la charge. **2.** (a) Attaque, crise f (de goutte, etc.). **A. of fever, of giddiness,** accès m de fièvre, de vertige. **A. of nerves,** crise de nerfs. *F:* **To have an a.,** piquer une crise. (b) **A. on s.o.'s life,** attentat m à la vie de qn.

attack², v.tr. (a) *Mil:* Attaquer (l'ennemi). **The attacking forces,** les troupes engagées dans l'attaque. **To be attacked,** subir une attaque; être attaqué. (b) **To a. s.o., s.o.'s rights,** attaquer qn, les droits de qn; s'en prendre à qn; s'attaquer à qn. (c) **To a. a task,** s'attaquer à un travail.

attacker [ə'tækər], s. Attaquant m; agresseur m.

attain [ə'tein]. **1.** v.tr. Atteindre, arriver à (un endroit); atteindre, parvenir à, arriver à (un grand âge). **To a. knowledge,** acquérir des connaissances. **2.** v.ind.tr. **To a. to perfection,** atteindre à la perfection.

attainability [ə'teinə'biliti], s. Accessibilité f (d'un but, etc.).

attainable [ə'teinəbl], a. Accessible; que l'on peut atteindre; à la portée (by, de).

attainableness [ə'teinəb(ə)lnis], s. = ATTAINABILITY.

attainder [ə'teindər], s. *Jur: A:* Act, bill, of a., décret m de confiscation de biens et de mort civile.

attainment [ə'teinmənt], s. **1.** (*No pl.*) Arrivée f (à ses fins); obtention f, réalisation f. **For the a. of his purpose,** pour atteindre, arriver, à ses fins. **End easy, difficult, of a.,** but facile, difficile, à atteindre. **2.** (*Often in pl.*) Connaissance(s) f; savoir m.

attar ['ætər], s. **A. of roses,** essence f de roses.

attempt¹ [ə'tem(p)t], s. **1.** Tentative f, essai m, effort m. **A. at theft,** tentative de vol. **To make an a. at sth., at doing sth., to do sth.,** essayer, tâcher, de faire qch.; s'essayer à faire qch. **You made a good a. at it,** (i) vous vous êtes acquitté de façon très méritoire; (ii) vous êtes arrivé fort près du but. **No a. will be made to . . .,** on n'essaiera pas de. . . . **First a., coup m d'essai;** première tentative. **To be successful at the first a.,** réussir du premier coup; emporter une affaire d'emblée. **I will do it or perish in the a.,** je le ferai ou j'y perdrai la vie. **To give up the a.,** y renoncer. **2. A. on s.o.'s life,** attentat m contre la vie de qn.

attempt², v.tr. (a) **To a. to do sth.,** essayer, tenter, s'efforcer, tâcher, de faire qch. **He attempted to rise,** il voulut se lever. (b) **To a. resistance,** essayer de résister. **He attempted a smile,** il s'efforça de sourire. **To a. the impossible,** tenter l'impossible. **Attempted murder, theft,** tentative f d'assassinat, de vol.

attend [ə'tend]. **1.** v.ind.tr. (*Give heed*) (a) **To a. to sth.,** prêter attention à qch. (b) **To a. to s.o.,** écouter qn. **I shall a. to you in a minute,** je serai à vous dans une minute. (c) **To a. to sth.,** s'occuper, se charger, se préoccuper de qch. **To a. to one's studies,** s'appliquer à ses études. **To a. to one's business,** vaquer à ses affaires. (d) **To a. to a customer,** servir un client. **2.** v.tr. (*Of doctor*) Soigner, donner des soins à (un malade). **3.** v.tr. & ind.tr. (a) **To a. s.o.; to a. on, upon, s.o.,** (i) servir qn, être au service de qn, être de service auprès de qn; (ii) se rendre auprès de qn, se rendre aux ordres de qn. **To a. (upon) a prince,** suivre, accompagner, un prince. (b) **Measure attended by unexpected consequences,** mesure suivie, accompagnée, de conséquences inattendues. **Method attended by great difficulties,** méthode qui comporte de grandes difficultés. **4.** v.tr. **To a. church, school,** aller à l'église, à l'école. **To a. a lecture, a meeting,** assister à une conférence, à une réunion. **To a. (a course of) lectures,** suivre un cours.

attendance [ə'tendəns], s. **1.** (a) (*In hotel, shop*) Service m. (b) (*Of doctor*) **A. on s.o.,** soins mpl pour qn; visites fpl à qn. (c) **To be in a. (up)on the king,** être de service auprès du roi. **To dance a. on s.o.,** faire antichambre chez qn. **2.** (a) **At a meeting,** présence f à une réunion. **School a.,** scolarisation f, fréquentation f scolaire. **Regular a.,** assiduité f; régularité f de présence. **3. There was a good a. at the meeting,** il y avait une nombreuse assistance à la réunion.

attendant [ə'tendənt]. **1.** a. (a) **A. on s.o.,** qui escorte, qui suit, qui accompagne, qui sert, qn. (b) The a.

crowd, la foule qui y assistait. **2.** s. (a) Serviteur m, domestique mf; surveillant, -ante; *Adm:* préposé, -ée; (*in museum, etc.*) gardien, -ienne; (*in theatre*) ouvreuse f; (*in laboratory*) appariteur m. *Med:* **Medical a.,** médecin traitant. (b) (*Usu.pl.*) Suivants m, gens m (d'un roi, etc.); personnel m (d'un magasin, etc.); personnel de service. **The prince and his attendants,** le prince et sa suite, et son cortège.

attention [ə'tenʃ(ə)n], s. **1.** (a) Attention f (**to,** à) **To give one's a. to sth.,** se préoccuper de qch. **To turn one's a. to sth.,** diriger son attention vers qch.; porter son attention sur qch. **We will now turn our a. to . . .,** nous allons maintenant nous occuper de. . . . *Com:* **For the a. of Mr X.,** à l'attention de M. X. **To pay a. to sth.,** faire attention à qch.; tenir compte de qch. **To pay particular a. to sth.,** s'attacher (surtout) à qch. **To pay a. to s.o., to give one's a. to s.o.,** prêter (son) attention à qn. **Pay a.!** faites attention! **To call, attract, draw, s.o.'s a. to sth.,** appeler, attirer, porter, l'attention (de qn) sur qch. **To catch s.o.'s a.,** attirer, fixer, l'attention de qn. **To attract a.,** se faire remarquer. (b) Soins mpl, entretien m. **The batteries require daily a.,** les accus exigent un entretien journalier. **2.** (*Often in pl.*) Attention(s), soins, prévenance(s) f. **To require a great deal of a.,** demander beaucoup de soins. **3.** *Mil:* **A.!** *F:* **'shun!** garde à vous! **To come to a.,** se mettre au garde-à-vous. **To stand at a.,** prendre l'attitude militaire; être, se tenir, au garde-à-vous.

attentive [ə'tentiv], a. **1.** Attentif (**to,** à), soigneux, soucieux (**to,** de). **2. A. to s.o.,** assidu, empressé, auprès de qn; prévenant pour qn; plein d'égards, d'attentions, pour qn. **To be very a. to s.o.,** être aux petits soins pour qn; être très attentionné pour qn. **-ly,** adv. Attentivement; avec attention.

attentiveness [ə'tentivnis], s. **1.** Attention f. **2.** Prévenances fpl (**to** s.o., pour qn).

attenuate [ə'tenjueit]. **1.** v.tr. Atténuer. (a) Amincir. **His attenuated body,** son corps amaigri. (b) Raréfier (un gaz, etc.). (c) **To a. a statement,** atténuer une affirmation. **2.** v.i. S'atténuer; (*of gas*) se raréfier.

attest [ə'test]. **1.** v.tr. (a) Attester, certifier (un fait). **To a. that . . .,** attester, certifier que + ind. *Vet:* **Attested herds,** troupeaux tuberculinés. (b) Affirmer sous serment. **Attested copy,** copie certifiée, conforme. **To a. a signature,** légaliser une signature. (c) v.ind.tr. **To a. to sth.,** (i) témoigner de qch.; (ii) attester qch.; se porter garant, témoin, de qch. **2.** (a) *Jur:* Assermenter. (b) *Mil:* Faire prêter serment à (des volontaires). (c) v.i. *Mil:* Prêter serment.

attestation [ætes'teiʃ(ə)n], s. **1.** *Jur:* (a) Déposition f; témoignage m. (b) Attestation f; légalisation f. **2.** (a) Assermentation f (d'une recrue). (b) Prestation f de serment.

Attic¹ ['ætik], a. Attique.

attic², s. (a) Mansarde f. **To live in the attics,** loger sous les toits. (b) Grenier m.

Attica ['ætikə]. *Pr.n. A.Geog:* L'Attique f.

atticism ['ætisizm], s. Atticisme m.

attire¹ [ə'taiər], s. (a) Vêtement(s) m; costume m. (b) *Poet:* Parure f, atours mpl (de femme). (c) *Her: Ven:* Ramure f (d'un cerf).

attire², v.tr. *Lit:* (*Usu. passive or reflexive*) Vêtir; parer.

attitude ['ætitjuːd], s. (a) Attitude f, pose f; port m (de la tête). (b) **A. of mind,** manière f de penser, de voir; disposition f d'esprit. **To maintain a firm a.,** (i) rester ferme; (ii) garder bonne contenance. *S.a.* STRIKE² I. 10. (c) *Av:* **A. of a machine,** position f d'un avion en vol. **Landing a.,** position d'atterrissage. **Steep a.,** vol cabré.

attitudinize [æti'tjuːdinaiz], v.i. Poser; faire des grâces; *F:* la faire à la pose.

attitudinizer [æti'tjuːdinaizər], s. Poseur, euse.

attorney¹ [ə'təːni], s. **1.** *Jur:* **1. A:** A.-at-law = SOLICITOR. *S.a.* PETTIFOG. **2.** *U.S:* Avoué m. **3. A.-general,** Avocat m du Gouvernement (avec fonctions ministérielles, et toujours membre du Parlement) et chef du barreau. **4.** Mandataire m; fondé m de pouvoir(s).

attorney², s. **Letter, power, warrant, of a.,** procuration f, mandat m, pouvoirs mpl.

attorneyship [ə'tə:niʃip], s. *Jur:* **1.** Procuration f, mandat m. **2.** Charge f de procureur, A: d'avoué.

attract [ə'trækt], v.tr. **1.** Attirer (to, à, vers). A magnet attracts iron, l'aimant attire le fer. *S.a.* ATTENTION 1. *Jur:* To a. a penalty (*of crime, etc.*) entraîner une peine. **2.** Séduire, attirer; exercer une attraction sur (qn); avoir de l'attrait pour (qn).

attractability [ə,træktə'biliti], s. *Ph: etc.* Pouvoir m d'attraction; propriété f d'être attiré.

attractable [ə'træktəbl], a. *Ph: etc:* Attirable.

attractile [ə'træktail], a. *Ph:* Attracteur, -trice.

attraction [ə'trækʃ(ə)n], s. **1.** Attraction f (to, towards, vers). The a. of gravity, l'attraction. *S.a.* CENTRE[1] 1. **2.** (*Usu. in pl.*) Séduction f; attractions, attraits mpl. **3.** The chief a. (at a party, etc.), le clou (de la fête, etc.).

attractive [ə'træktiv], a. **1.** (*Of magnet, etc.*) Attractif, attirant. **2.** (*Of pers., offer, manner*) Attrayant, attirant, séduisant; alléchant. A. flat, appartement coquet. **-ly,** adv. D'une manière attrayante.

attractiveness [ə'træktivnis], s. Attrait m, charme m, agrément m, attraction f.

attractivity [æ,træk'tiviti], s. *Ph:* Attractivité f.

attribute[1] ['ætribju:t], s. **1.** Attribut m, qualité f, apanage m. Speech is an a. of man, la parole est un attribut de l'homme. **2.** Symbole m, attribut. The sword, as an a. of justice, le glaive, en tant qu'attribut de la justice. **3.** *Gram:* Épithète f.

attribute[2] [ə'tribju(:)t], v.tr. Attribuer, imputer (to, à). You a. to him qualities that he does not possess, vous lui prêtez des qualités qu'il n'a pas.

attribution [,ætri'bju:ʃ(ə)n], s. **1.** Attribution f, imputation f (to, à). **2.** That lies outside my attributions, cela sort de mes attributions.

attributive [ə'tribjutiv], a. *Gram:* A. adjective, épithète f; adjectif o' alificatif.

attrition [ə'triʃ(ə)n], ,. Attrition f; usure f par le frottement. War of a., guerre d'usure.

attune [ə'tju:n], v.tr. *Lit:* Accorder, harmoniser (to, avec). Tastes attuned to mine, goûts à l'unisson des miens.

aubergine ['oubə:dʒi:n], s. *Bot: Cu:* Aubergine f.

auburn ['ɔ:bən], a. A. hair, cheveux châtain roux, auburn.

auction[1] ['ɔ:kʃ(ə)n], s. (Sale by) a., a.-sale, vente f à l'enchère, aux enchères; vente à l'encan; (vente à la) criée f. To put sth. up to, for, a., mettre qch. aux enchères. *S.a.* BRIDGE[2]. **'auction-room,** s. Salle f des ventes.

auction[2], v.tr. Vendre (qch.) aux enchères, à l'encan; mettre (qch.) aux enchères; vendre (des denrées) à la criée.

auctioneer[1] [,ɔ:kʃə'niər], s. **1.** (*Auctioneer and valuer*) Commissaire-priseur m. **2.** Directeur m de la vente; crieur m.

auctioneer[2], v.tr. *F:* = AUCTION[2].

audacious [ɔ:'deiʃəs], a. **1.** Audacieux, -euse, hardi, intrépide. **2.** *Pej:* Effronté, hardi, cynique. **-ly,** adv. **1.** Audacieusement; avec audace; hardiment. **2.** *Pej:* Effrontément; avec cynisme.

audaciousness [ɔ:'deiʃəsnis], **audacity** [ɔ:'dæsiti], s. Audace f. **1.** Intrépidité f, hardiesse f. **2.** *Pej:* Effronterie f, hardiesse, cynisme m.

audibility [,ɔ:di'biliti], **audibleness** ['ɔ:diblnis], s. Perceptibilité f (d'un son), audibilité f.

audible ['ɔ:dibl], a. Perceptible (à l'oreille); audible; (*of speech, voice*) distinct, intelligible; qu'on peut entendre. He was scarcely a., on l'entendait à peine. Above the a. range, ultra-sonore. **-ibly,** adv. Distinctement, intelligiblement.

audience ['ɔ:djəns], s. **1.** Audience f. To grant s.o. an a., accorder audience à qn. *Attrib.* A. chamber, salle f d'audience. **2.** (*At meeting, etc.*) Assistance f, assistants mpl; (*at theatre*) spectateurs mpl, auditoire m, public m; (*at concert*) auditeurs mpl.

audio-frequency ['ɔ:dio'fri:kwənsi], s. *W.Tel:* Fréquence téléphonique.

audiometer [ɔ:di'ɔmitər], s. Audiomètre m.

audio-lingual ['ɔ:dio'liŋgwəl], a. Audio-oral.

audio-visual ['ɔ:dio'vizju(ə)l], a. Audiovisuel, -elle.

audit[1] ['ɔ:dit], s. Vérification f, apurement m (de comptes); vérification(s) comptable(s). *Adm:* Audit Office, Cour des comptes.

audit[2], v.tr. Vérifier, apurer (des comptes). **auditing,** s. Apurement m.

audition[1] [ɔ:'diʃ(ə)n], s. **1.** Ouïe f. **2.** Séance f d'essai (d'un chanteur, etc.); audition f.

audition[2], v.tr. *F:* Auditionner.

auditive ['ɔ:ditiv], a. Auditif.

auditor ['ɔ:ditər], s. **1.** Auditeur m (d'une conférence, etc.). **2.** (*a*) *Adm:* Commissaire m aux comptes; vérificateur m des comptes. (*b*) Expert m comptable; vérificateur comptable.

auditorium [,ɔ:di'tɔ:riəm], s. **1.** *Th:* Salle f. **2.** *Ecc:* Parloir m (d'un couvent).

auditory ['ɔ:dit(ə)ri], a. = AUDITIVE.

auger[1] ['ɔ:gər], s. *Tls:* **1.** Perçoir m, foret m; amorçoir m; tarière f. **2.** *Min:* Sonde; tarière (de sondage). **'auger-shell,** s. *Conch:* Térèbre f.

auger[2], v.tr. Percer; forer; sonder. *U.S: Av: F:* To a. in, mal atterrir; casser du bois; s'écraser (au sol).

aught [ɔ:t], s. *Lit:* Quelque chose m; quoi que ce soit. If you have a. to say, si vous avez quelque chose à dire. For aught I know, (pour) autant que je sache.

augment [ɔ:g'ment]. **1.** v.tr. Augmenter, accroître (with, by, de). **2.** v.i. Augmenter, s'accroître.

augmentation [,ɔ:gmen'teiʃ(ə)n], s. Augmentation f, accroissement m (de fortune, etc.).

augur[1] ['ɔ:gər], s. *Rom.Ant:* (*Pers.*) Augure m.

augur[2], v.tr. & i. Augurer, présager, prédire. It augurs no good, cela ne présage, n'annonce, rien de bon. It augurs well, ill, cela est de bon, de mauvais, augure.

augury ['ɔ:gjuri], s. **1.** Augure m; présage m. The priests took the auguries, les prêtres prirent les augures. **2.** Science f des augures.

august[1] [ɔ:'gʌst], a. Auguste; imposant, majestueux. **-ly,** adv. Majestueusement, augustement.

August[2] ['ɔ:gəst], s. Août m. In A., au mois d'août. On the fifth of A., le cinq août.

Augustan [ɔ:'gʌstən], a. The A. age, (i) *Lt.Lit:* le siècle d'Auguste; (ii) *Engl.Lit:* l'époque de la reine Anne.

Augustinian [,ɔgəs'tiniən], a. & s. *Ecc.Hist:* **1.** De l'ordre de St. Augustin. **2.** The A. Friars, les Augustins. The A. Canons, les chanoines réguliers de St. Augustin.

Augustus [ɔ:'gʌstəs]. *Pr.n.m.* Auguste.

auk [ɔ:k], s. *Orn:* **1.** Pingouin m. Great a., grand pingouin. **2.** Little a. = RAZORBILL.

auld [ɔ:ld], a. *Scot:* = OLD. A. lang syne, le temps jadis; le bon vieux temps. 'A. Reekie,' la vieille Enfumée (Édimbourg).

aunt [ɑ:nt], s.f. **1.** Tante. A.-in-law, tante par alliance. **2.** *F:* A. Sally (i) = jeu m de massacre; (ii) objet m de dérision.

auntie, aunty ['ɑ:nti], s.f. *F:* Ma tante, tantine.

aura ['ɔ:rə], s. *Psy: etc:* Aura f.

aural ['ɔ:rəl], a. De l'oreille. A. surgeon, auriste m. **-ally,** adv. Avec l'oreille; (perçu) par l'oreille.

Aurelius [ɔ:'ri:ljəs]. *Pr.n.m. Hist:* Marcus A., Marc Aurèle.

aureola [ɔ:'ri:ələ], **aureole** ['ɔ:rioul], s. *Art:* Auréole f, gloire f (d'un saint).

aureomycin ['ɔ:riou'maisin], s. *Pharm:* Auréomycine f.

auricle ['ɔ:rikl], s. (*a*) Auricule f; pavillon m (de l'oreille). (*b*) Oreillette f (du cœur).

auricula, pl. -ae [ə'rikjulə, -i:], s. **1.** *Bot:* Auricule f. **2.** *Moll:* Auricule.

auricular [ɔ:'rikjulər]. **1.** a. Auriculaire. (*a*) De l'oreille; des oreillettes du cœur. (*b*) A. confession, confession auriculaire. A. witness, témoin auriculaire. **2.** s. (*Little finger*) Auriculaire m.

auriferous [ɔ:'rifərəs], a. Aurifère.

aurist ['ɔ:rist], s. *Med:* (*Ear specialist*) Auriste m, otologiste m.

aurochs ['ɔ:rɔks], s. Aurochs m; bœuf m urus.

Aurora [ɔ:'rɔ:rə]. **1.** *Pr.n.f. Myth:* Aurore. **2.** s. Aurore f. A. borealis, aurore boréale.

auscultate ['ɔ:skəlteit], v.tr. *Med:* Ausculter.

auscultation [,ɔsk(ə)l'teiʃ(ə)n], s. Auscultation f.

auspices ['ɔ:spisiz], s.pl. Auspices m. Under favourable a., sous d'heureux auspices.

auspicious [ɔːsˈpiʃəs], a. 1. (a) (Vent, etc.) propice, favorable. (b) (Signe) de bon augure. 2. (Age) heureux, prospère, de prospérité. -ly, adv. (a) Sous d'heureux auspices. (b) Favorablement.

auspiciousness [ɔːsˈpiʃəsnis], s. Aspect m favorable, propice (d'une entreprise, etc.).

Aussie ['ɔsi], s.m. F: = AUSTRALIAN.

austere [ɔːsˈtiər], a. Austère; (appartement) sans luxe, d'un goût sévère. -ly, adv. Austèrement; avec austérité.

austereness [ɔːsˈtiːənis], **austerity** [ɔsˈteriti], s. Austérité f; absence f de luxe; sévérité f de goût. The days of austerity, le temps des restrictions.

Austin ['ɔːstin]. Pr.n. Ecc: The A. friars, les Augustins.

austral ['ɔːstrəl], a. Austral, -als, -aux.

Australasia ['ɔːstrəˈleisjə], Pr.n. Geog: Australasie f.

Australasian ['ɔːstrəˈleisj(ə)n], a. Australasien, -ienne.

Australia [ɔːsˈtreiliə] Pr.n. L'Australie f. South A. l'Australie méridionale. Western A., l'Australie occidentale.

Australian [ɔːsˈtreiliən], a. & s. Australien, -ienne. Great A. Bight, Grande Baie australienne.

Austria ['ɔːstriə]. Pr.n. L'Autriche f.

Austrian ['ɔːstriən], a. & s. Autrichien, -ienne.

autarchic(al) [ɔːˈtɑːkik(l)], a. Autarchique.

autarchy ['ɔːtɑːki], s. Autarchie f.

autarky ['ɔːtɑːki], s. Autarcie f.

authentic [ɔːˈθentik], a. Authentique; digne de foi. -ally, adv. Authentiquement.

authenticate [ɔːˈθentikeit], v.tr. 1. Certifier, homologuer, légaliser, valider, viser (un acte, etc.). 2. Établir l'authenticité de (qch.); vérifier. **authenticated**, a. 1. Authentique. 2. D'une authenticité établie.

authentication [ɔːˌθentiˈkeiʃ(ə)n], s. Certification f (d'une signature, etc.); homologation f, légalisation f, validation f.

authenticity [ɔːθenˈtisiti], s. Authenticité f.

author ['ɔːθər], s. Auteur m.

authoress ['ɔːθəris], s.f. Femme auteur; femme écrivain.

authoritarian [ɔːˌθɔriˈtɛəriən], a. & s. Autoritaire (m); partisan m de l'autorité.

authoritarianism [ɔːˌθɔriˈtɛəriənizm], s. Autoritarisme m.

authoritative [ɔːˈθɔritətiv], a. 1. (Caractère) autoritaire; (ton) péremptoire, d'autorité. 2. Revêtu d'autorité. (a) (Document) qui fait foi, qui fait autorité. (b) (Renseignement) de bonne source. -ly, adv. 1. Autoritairement; péremptoirement. 2. Avec autorité.

authoritativeness [ɔːˈθɔriˈteitivnis], s. 1. Air m d'autorité; ton m péremptoire. 2. Autorité f (d'un document, etc.).

authority [ɔːˈθɔriti], s. Autorité f. 1. To have, exercise, a. over s.o., (i) avoir, exercer, une autorité sur qn; (ii) avoir de l'ascendant sur qn. Who is in a. here? qui est-ce qui commande ici? To be under s.o.'s a., être sous les ordres de qn. 2. Autorisation f, mandat m. To have a. to act, avoir qualité f pour agir. To give s.o. a. to do sth., autoriser qn à faire qch. To act on s.o.'s a., agir sur l'autorité de qn. To do sth. without a., faire qch. sans autorisation, sans mandat. 3. (a) To be an a. on sth., faire autorité en matière de qch. (b) To have sth. on good a., tenir, savoir, qch. de bonne part, de source autorisée. 4. Adm: Public a., administrative a., corps constitué; service administratif. The authorities, l'administration f; les autorités.

authorization [ɔːθ(ə)raiˈzeiʃ(ə)n], s. Autorisation f (to do sth., de faire qch.); pouvoir m; mandat m.

authorize ['ɔːθəraiz], v.tr. Autoriser (qch.). To a. s.o. to do sth., autoriser qn à faire qch. **Authorized by** custom, sanctionné par l'usage. **authorized**, a. Autorisé. To apply to an a. person, s'adresser à qui de droit. The A. Version (of the Bible), la traduction anglaise de la Bible de 1611. A. charges, prix homologués.

authorship ['ɔːθəʃip], s. 1. Profession f ou qualité f d'auteur. 2. To establish the a. of a book, identifier l'auteur d'un livre.

autism ['ɔːtizm], s. Psy: Autisme m; introversion f.

auto¹ ['ɔːtou], s. F: A. & U.S: Automobile f, auto f; F: voiture f. 'auto-cycle, s. Cyclomoteur m. A.-c. rider, cyclomotoriste mf.

auto². Pref: Auto-. **auto-intoxication**, s. Med: Auto-intoxication f. **auto-suggestion**, s. Med: Psy: Auto-suggestion f. **auto-vaccine**, s. Med: Auto-vaccin m.

autobiographer [ɔːtobaiˈɔgrəfər], s. Autobiographe m.

autobiographic(al) ['ɔːtobaioˈgræfik(əl)], a. Autobiographique.

autobiography [ɔːtobaiˈɔgrəfi], s. Autobiographie f.

autobus ['ɔːtobʌs], s. U.S: Autobus m.

autochthonous [ɔːˈtɔkθənəs], a. Autochtone.

autoclave ['ɔːtoklɑːv], a. & s. Ch: Ind: Marmite f autoclave; autoclave m.

autocracy [ɔːˈtɔkrəsi], s. Autocratie f.

autocrat ['ɔːtokræt], s. Autocrate m.

autocratic(al) [ɔːtəˈkrætik(əl)], a. Autocratique; (of pers.) autocrate; (caractère) absolu. -ally, adv. Autocratiquement.

auto-da-fé, pl. **autos-da-fé** ['ɔːtodɑːˈfei, 'ɔːtozdɑːˈfei], s. Autodafé m.

autodidact [ɔtoˈdaidækt], s. Autodidacte mf.

autogiro ['ɔːtouˈdʒairou], s. Av: = AUTOGYRO.

autograft ['ɔːtogrɑːft], s. Surg: Autogreffe f.

autograph¹ ['ɔːtogrɑːf, -græf]. 1. s. (a) Autographe m. A. album, cahier m, album m d'autographes; cahier de souvenirs. (b) Reproduction autographiée. 2. a. A. letter of Byron, lettre autographe de Byron.

autograph², v.tr. 1. Écrire (une lettre, etc.) de sa propre main. 2. Écrire son autographe dans (un livre); signer, dédicacer (un exemplaire). 3. Lith: Autographier.

autographic(al) [ɔːtəˈgræfik(əl)], a. 1. (Lettre) autographe. 2. Lith: (Encre, papier) autographique.

autogyro ['ɔːtouˈdʒairou], s. Av: Autogyre m.

auto-ignition ['ɔːtoigˈniʃ(ə)n], s. I.C.E: Auto-allumage m.

autokinetic ['ɔːtokaiˈnetik], a. Automobile.

autolithography ['ɔːtoliˈθɔgrəfi], s. Autographie f.

automat ['ɔːtomæt], s. 1. U.S: Restaurant m à distributeurs automatiques. 2. Phot: Obturateur toujours armé.

automatic [ɔːtəˈmætik], a. (a) Automatique. A. machine (delivering sweets, etc.), distributeur m. Sm.a: A. (pistol), automatique m. Tp: A. telephone, F: the a., automatique m. Aut: A. clutch, auto-débrayage m. A. working, automaticité f. (b) A. motion, mouvement inconscient, machinal. -ally, adv. 1. Automatiquement. 2. Machinalement.

automatics [ɔːtəˈmætiks], s. Tchn: Automatique f.

automation [ɔːtəˈmeiʃ(ə)n], s. Automation f, automatisation f, automatique f.

automatism [ɔːˈtɔmətizm], s. Automatisme m.

automatize [ɔːˈtɔmətaiz], v.tr. Automatiser.

automatization [ɔːˌtɔmətaiˈzeiʃ(ə)n], s. Automatisation f.

automaton, pl. **-ons**, **-a** [ɔːˈtɔmət(ə)n, -(ə)nz, -ə], s. Automate m.

automobile ['ɔːtəmɔbiːl], s. U.S: Automobile f; F: auto f, voiture f.

automotive [ɔːtoˈmoutiv], a. Automoteur, -trice. U.S: A. industry, industrie f automobile.

autonomist [ɔːˈtɔnəmist], s. Autonomiste m.

autonomous [ɔːˈtɔnəməs], a. Autonome.

autonomy [ɔːˈtɔnəmi], s. Autonomie f.

autoplasty ['ɔːtoplæsti], s. Surg: Autoplastie f.

autopsy ['ɔːtəpsi], s. Autopsie f.

autumn ['ɔːtəm], s. L'automne m; l'arrière-saison f. In a., en automne.

autumnal [ɔːˈtʌmnəl], a. Automnal; d'automne.

auxiliary [ɔːgˈziljəri], a. & s. Auxiliaire (mf); subsidiaire (to, à). Gram: A. verb, verbe auxiliaire.

avail¹ [əˈveil], s. Lit: Avantage m, utilité f. Of no a., sans effet. To be of use to s.o., être peu utile à qn. It is of no a., cela ne sert à rien. Without a., sans effet; inutile(ment).

avail², v.tr. & i. 1. Lit: Servir, être utile, à (qn); être efficace. 2. To a. oneself of sth., se servir, s'aider, de qch.; user de qch.; profiter de qch. To a. oneself of the opportunity to do sth., saisir l'occasion de faire qch.

availability [əˌveiləˈbiliti], s. 1. Disponibilité f (de matériaux, d'hommes). 2. Rail: etc: (Durée et rayon de) validité f (d'un billet).

available [ə'veiləbl], *a.* **1.** (*a*) Disponible; *Bank:* réalisable. To try every a. means, essayer de tous les moyens dont on dispose. A. funds, fonds liquides, disponibles. Capital that can be made a., capitaux mobilisables. (*b*) Accessible. Train a. for passengers covering a distance of . . ., train accessible aux voyageurs effectuant un parcours de. . . . **2.** (*Of ticket, etc.*) Valable, bon, valide (pour deux mois, etc.).

avalanche ['ævəlɑ:nʃ], *s.* Avalanche *f.*

avarice ['ævəris], *s.* Avarice *f.*

avaricious [ævə'riʃəs], *a.* Avare, avaricieux. -ly, *adv.* Avaricieusement.

avariciousness [ævə'riʃəsnis], *s.* Avarice *f.*

avast [ə'vɑ:st], *int. Nau:* Tiens bon! tenez bon! baste! A. heaving! tenez bon virer!

avatar [ævə'tɑ:r], *s.* **1.** *Hindu Rel:* Avatar *m.* **2.** Manifestation *f*, phase *f.*

ave ['ɑvei, 'ɑ:vi]. **1.** *Lt.int. Ecc. & Lit:* (*a*) Salut! (*b*) Adieu! **2.** *s.* Avé (Maria) *m.*

aven ['ævən], *s. Geol:* Aven *m.*

avenge [ə'ven(d)ʒ], *v.tr.* Venger (qn, une injure). To a. oneself, be avenged, on one's enemies, se venger de, sur, ses ennemis; prendre, tirer, vengeance de ses ennemis. avenging, *a.* Vengeur, *f.* -eresse.

avenger [ə'ven(d)ʒər], *s.* Vengeur, -eresse.

avens ['ævənz], *s. Bot:* Wood a., benoîte commune *f.* Water a., benoîte des ruisseaux.

avenue ['ævinju:], *s.* (*a*) Avenue *f.* (*b*) *Esp. U.S:* (Belle) rue; boulevard *m.* (*c*) Chemin *m* d'accès. (*d*) Promenade plantée d'arbres.

aver [ə'və:r], *v.tr.* (averred) **1.** Avérer, déclarer, affirmer (que). **2.** *Jur:* Prouver (son dire).

average[1] ['ævəridʒ], *s.* **1.** Moyenne *f.* On an a., en moyenne. To take an a. of results, faire la moyenne des résultats. **2.** *M.Ins:* Avarie(s) *f.* Particular a., avarie particulière. General a., avaries communes. A. adjustment, dispache *f. S.a.* ADJUSTER.

average[2], *a.* Moyen. The a. Englishman, l'Anglais moyen, l'Anglais en général. Man of a. abilities, homme ordinaire. A. specimen, échantillon normal.

average[3], *v.tr. & i.* **1.** Prendre, établir, faire, la moyenne (des résultats, etc.). **2.** (*a*) To a. (up to) so much, donner, atteindre, rendre, une moyenne de tant. (*b*) He averages eight hours' work a day, il travaille en moyenne huit heures par jour.

averment [ə'və:mənt], *s.* **1.** Affirmation *f. Jur:* Allégation *f.* **2.** *Jur:* Preuve *f* (d'une allégation).

averse [ə'və:s], *a.* Opposé. To be a. to, from, sth., répugner à qch.; être opposé à qch. I am a. to acknowledging that . . ., il me répugne d'admettre que. . . . He is not a. to a glass of beer, il prend volontiers un verre de bière.

aversion [ə'və:ʃ(ə)n], *s.* **1.** Aversion *f*, répugnance *f.* To feel an a. to, for, s.o., se sentir de l'aversion pour, envers, qn. To feel a. to doing sth., répugner à faire qch. To have an a. to s.o., avoir qn en aversion. To take, conceive, an a. to s.o., prendre qn en aversion, en grippe. **2.** *F:* Objet *m* d'aversion. My pet a., ma bête noire.

avert [ə'və:t], *v.tr.* **1.** Détourner (les yeux, etc.) (from, de). **2.** Écarter, éloigner, prévenir (des soupçons, un danger); détourner (un coup).

aviary ['eiviəri], *s.* Volière *f.*

aviation [eivi'eiʃ(ə)n], *s.* Aviation *f.* Naval A., Aéronavale *f.*

aviator ['eivieitər], *s.* Aviateur, -trice.

avid ['ævid], *a.* Avide (of, for, de). -ly, *adv.* Avidement; avec avidité.

avidity [ə'viditi], *s.* Avidité *f* (for, de, pour).

avionics ['eivi'ɔniks], *s.pl. Av:* Avionique *f.*

avocado [ævə'kɑ:dou], *s. Bot:* **1.** Avocatier *m.* **2.** A. (-pear), (poire *f* d')avocat *m.*

avocet ['ævoset], *s. Orn:* Avocette *f.*

avoid [ə'void], *v.tr.* **1.** Éviter. To a. doing sth., éviter de faire qch. To a. s.o., se cacher à qn. **2.** (*Evade*) Se soustraire (au châtiment); esquiver (un coup, une difficulté). To a. notice, se dérober aux regards. **3.** *Jur:* Résoudre, résilier, annuler (un contrat, etc.).

avoidable [ə'voidəbl], *a.* Évitable.

avoidance [ə'voidəns], *s.* **1.** Action *f* d'éviter. **2.** *Jur:* A. of an agreement (owing to breach, etc.), résolution *f*, annulation *f*, résiliation *f*, d'un contrat.

avoirdupois [ævədə'pɔiz], *s.* Poids *m* du commerce. Ounce a., once *f* avoirdupois, du commerce.

avow [ə'vau], *v.tr.* (*a*) Avouer; reconnaître. (*b*) Déclarer, affirmer. avowed, *a.* (Ennemi, etc.) avéré. He is an avowed atheist, il est franchement athée.

avowal [ə'vauəl], *s.* Aveu *m.* To make an a., faire un aveu.

avowedly [ə'vauidli], *adv.* Ouvertement, franchement.

avuncular [ə'vʌŋkjulər], *a.* Avunculaire.

await [ə'weit], *v.tr.* **1.** (*a*) (*Of pers.*) Attendre (qch., occ. qn). *Com:* Awaiting your orders, dans l'attente de vos ordres. (*b*) Parcels awaiting delivery, colis *m* en souffrance. (*c*) The fate that awaits him, le sort qui l'attend, qui lui est réservé.

awake[1] [ə'weik], *v.* (*p.t.* awoke [ə'wouk]; *p.p.* awoke, awaked [ə'weikt]) **1.** *v.i.* (*a*) S'éveiller, se réveiller. (*b*) To a. to the danger, se rendre compte, prendre conscience, du danger. **2.** *v.tr.* (*a*) Éveiller, réveiller (qn, les remords); éveiller (la curiosité, les soupçons). (*b*) = AWAKEN 1.

awake[2], *pred.a.* **1.** Éveillé. To lie a., to keep a., rester éveillé. I was a., je ne dormais pas. To keep s.o. a., tenir qn éveillé. Wide a., (i) bien éveillé, tout éveillé; (ii) *F:* averti, malin, avisé. He's wide a.! il a l'œil ouvert! **2.** To be a. to a danger, avoir conscience d'un danger, se rendre compte d'un danger.

awaken [ə'weik(ə)n], *v.tr. & i.* **1.** To a. s.o. to a sense of his position, ouvrir les yeux à qn sur sa position. **2.** = AWAKE[1]. awakening, *a.* (Passion, etc.) qui s'éveille. awakening[2], *s.* (*a*) Réveil *m.* (*b*) A rude a., une amère désillusion.

award[1] [ə'wɔ:d], *s.* **1.** *Jur:* Arbitrage *m*; sentence arbitrale; décision (arbitrale); adjudication *f.* To make an a., rendre un jugement (arbitral). **2.** (*a*) *Jur:* Dommages-intérêts *mpl.* (*b*) *Sch: etc:* Récompense *f.* To make an a., décerner un prix, une récompense.

award[2], *v.tr.* Adjuger, décerner (sth. to s.o., qch. à qn); adjuger (un marché); conférer (un bénéfice, une dignité). awarding, *s.* Décernement *m* (d'un prix, etc.); adjudication *f* (d'un marché); attribution *f* (d'une récompense, etc.).

aware [ə'wɛər], *a.* Avisé, informé, instruit (of sth., de qch.). To be a. of sth., avoir connaissance, avoir conscience, de qch.; savoir, ne pas ignorer, qch. Fully a. of the gravity of . . ., conscient de la gravité de. . . . Not that I am a. of, pas que je sache. To become a. of sth., apprendre qch.; prendre connaissance (d'un fait). I became a. of a smell of burning, j'ai senti une odeur de brûlé.

awareness [ə'wɛənis], *s.* Conscience *f* (de qch.); perception *f* (de qch.).

awash [ə'wɔʃ], *adv.* **1.** (*Of submarine, etc.*) A fleur d'eau. Reef a., écueil ras. **2.** Flottant sur l'eau; surnageant. **3.** The deck was a., le pont était inondé.

away [ə'wei], *adv.* Loin; au loin. **1.** (*With verbs expressing sense of removal*) (*a*) To go a., partir, s'en aller. To walk, drive, ride, a., partir à pied, en voiture, à cheval. To gallop a., partir, s'éloigner, au galop. The ball rolled a., la balle roula plus loin. *S.a.* MAKE AWAY. (*b*) (*Sense shown by a prefix on-, em-*) To run, fly, a., s'enfuir, s'envoler. To take s.o., sth., a., emmener qn, emporter qch. To carry a., emporter. (Uses (*a*) and (*b*) above are dealt with under the respective verbs; *see* GET, GIVE, PUT, SEND, THROW, *etc.*). **2.** (*Elliptical uses*) A. with you! allez-vous-en! *F:* fichez le camp! A. with it! take it a.! emportez-le! I ordered him a., je lui ai ordonné de s'en aller. A: I must a.! il me faut partir! **3.** (*Continuousness*) (*a*) To work a., travailler toujours; continuer à travailler. (*b*) To do sth. right a., faire qch. tout de suite, sur-le-champ. *S.a.* FIRE[2] 2, RIGHT[1] III. 1. **4.** (*Distant*) Loin. (*a*) Far a., dans le lointain; au loin. A. back in the distance, tout au loin. We are five miles a. from the station, nous sommes à huit kilomètres de la gare. Five paces a. stood . . ., à cinq pas de là se tenait. . . . This is far and a. the best, c'est de beaucoup le meilleur. That is far and a. better, cela vaut infiniment mieux. (*b*) To hold sth. a. from sth., tenir qch. éloigné, loin, de qch. To turn (one's face) a. from sth., détourner la tête de qch. *S.a.* LOOK AWAY. (*c*) A. from home, absent (de chez lui, de chez moi). When he is a., lorsqu'il n'est pas là.

When I have to be a., lorsque je dois m'absenter. My occupation keeps me a. from town, mon occupation me tient éloigné de la ville. To stay a., rester absent, ne pas venir. To keep a., se tenir à l'écart. *Sp:* A. ground, terrain *m* adverse. A. match, match *m* à l'extérieur. To play a., jouer à l'extérieur. 5. *(Time)* I knew him a. back in 1900, je l'ai connu dès 1900.

awe[1] [ɔː], *s.* Crainte *f*, terreur *f*; *occ.* respect *m*. To strike s.o. with a., (i) *(of pers.)* imposer à qn un respect mêlé de crainte; (ii) *(of phenomenon)* frapper qn d'une terreur mystérieuse. To hold, keep, s.o. in a., (en) imposer à qn; tenir qn en respect. To stand in a. of s.o., (i) craindre, redouter, qn; (ii) avoir une crainte respectueuse de qn. 'awe-inspiring, *a.* Terrifiant, imposant, impressionnant. A.-i. sight, spectacle grandiose. 'awe-stricken, 'awe-struck, *a.* 1. Frappé d'une terreur profonde, mystérieuse, etc. 2. Intimidé.

awe[2], *v.tr.* = To strike with a., *q.v. above.*

awesome ['ɔːsəm], *a.* = AWE-INSPIRING.

awful ['ɔːful], *a.* 1. Terrible, redoutable, effroyable. To die an a. death, mourir d'une mort terrible. 2. *(a)* Terrifiant. *(b)* Imposant, solennel. 3. *(Intensive) F:* An a. hat, un chapeau affreux. You were an a. fool! vous avez été rudement bête! What a. weather! quel chien de temps! An a. row, un bruit de tous les diables. -fully, *adv.* 1. Terriblement, effroyablement. 2. Solennellement. 3. *F: (Intensive)* I am a. sorry, je regrette infiniment. A. funny, drôle comme tout. *O:* Thanks a.! merci mille fois!

awfulness ['ɔːfulnis], *s.* Caractère imposant; solennité *f*; caractère terrible (de la situation).

awhile [ə'wail], *adv.* Pendant quelque temps; un moment. Wait a., attendez un peu.

awkward ['ɔːkwəd], *a.* 1. *(Clumsy)* Gauche, maladroit, disgracieux. To be a., avoir l'air emprunté. The a. age, l'âge ingrat. A. fellow, *F:* empoté *m*. *Mil: F:* The a. squad, le peloton des arriérés; les bleus. To be a. with one's hands, avoir la main maladroite. A. sentence, phrase gauche. 2. *(Ill at ease)* Embarrassé, gêné. 3. Fâcheux, malencontreux, embarrassant, gênant. An a. situation, un mauvais pas. 4. Incommode, peu commode. A. tool, outil peu maniable. A. corner, virage difficile, assez dangereux. *F:* He's an a. customer, c'est un homme difficile; il n'est pas commode. -ly, *adv.* 1. *(a)* Gauchement, maladroitement. *(b)* Mal à propos. 2. D'une manière embarrassée, d'un ton embarrassé, gêné. 3. D'une façon gênante, embarrassante. To be a. situated, se trouver dans une situation embarrassante.

awkwardness ['ɔːkwədnis], *s.* 1. *(a)* Gaucherie *f*; maladresse *f*. *(b)* Manque *m* de grâce; balourdise *f*. 2. Embarras *m*, gêne *f*. 3. *(Of situation)* Inconvénient *m*, incommodité *f*.

awl [ɔːl], *s. Tls:* Alêne *f*, poinçon *m*, perçoir *m*.

awn [ɔːn], *s. Bot:* Barbe *f*, barbelure *f* (d'avoine, etc.); arête *f*.

awning ['ɔːniŋ], *s.* 1. *(a)* Tente *f*, vélum *m*; banne *f* (de boutique); bâche *f* (de charrette). *(b) Nau:* Tente, tendelet *m*. 2. Marquise *f* (de gare, d'hôtel, etc.) 'awning-deck, *s.* Pont-abri *m. pl.* ponts-abris.

awoke. *See* AWAKE[1].

awry [ə'rai], *adv. & pred.a.* De travers; de guingois. *(Of plans, etc.)* To go all a., aller tout de travers; avorter.

ax, axe[1], *pl.* axes [æks, 'æksiz], *s.* 1. Hache *f*. Woodman's a., felling a., hache d'abattage; cognée *f* de bûcheron. Broad a., doloire *f*. *F:* To have an a. to grind, avoir un intérêt personnel à servir; agir dans un but intéressé. *S.a.* BATTLE-AXE, ICE-AXE, POLE-AXE[1]. 2. *F:* The a., coupe *f* sombre dans les prévisions budgétaires; réductions *fpl* sur les traitements; diminutions *fpl* de personnel. axe'head, *s.* Fer *m* de hache.

axe[2], *v.tr. Adm: F:* 1. To a. expenditure, réduire les dépenses, porter la hache dans les dépenses. 2. To a. a number of officials, of officers, mettre à pied un certain nombre de fonctionnaires, d'officiers.

axial ['æksiəl], *a.* Axial, -aux.

axil ['æksil], **axilla** [æk'silə], *s. Bot:* Aisselle *f* (d'une feuille).

axillary [æk'siləri], *a.* Axillaire.

axiom ['æksiəm], *s.* Axiome *m*.

axiomatic(al) [æksiə'mætik(l)], *a.* *(a)* Axiomatique. *(b)* Évident.

axis, *pl.* -es ['æksis, 'æksiːz], *s.* Axe *m*. Major a. of an ellipse, grand axe d'une ellipse. *Opt:* A. of vision, axe visuel. *Radar:* Scan a., axe radioélectrique. *Hist:* Rome-Berlin A., l'Axe Rome-Berlin.

axle ['æksl], *s.* 1. A.(-tree), essieu *m*. Live a., essieu tournant. Dead a., essieu fixe. Driving-a., essieu moteur; *(of electric locomotive)* pont *m. Aut:* Rear a., pont (arrière); essieu arrière. 2. Tourillon *m*, arbre *m*, axe *m* (d'une roue, etc.). 'axle-arm, *s.* Fusée *f* (de l'essieu). 'axle-box, *s.* Boîte *f* de l'essieu; boîte à graisse. 'axle-cap, *s. Veh:* Chapeau *m*, capot *m*, de moyeu. 'axle-pin, *s.* Clavette *f* d'essieu. 'axle-shaft, *s. Aut:* Demi-essieu *m* (du pont arrière).

ay(e)[1] [ai]. 1. *adv. & int. (a) (Esp. in Scot.)* Oui; mais oui. *(b) Nau:* A., a., sir! (i) oui commandant! bien, capitaine! (ii) paré! 2. *s. (In voting)* Ayes and noes, voix *f* pour et contre. The ayes have it, le vote est pour. Thirty ayes and twenty noes, trente oui et vingt non.

ay(e)[2] [ei], *adv. Lit:* Toujours. For (ever and) a., pour toujours; à tout jamais.

azalea [ə'zeiljə], *s. Bot:* Azalée *f*.

azimuth ['æzimθ], *s.* Azimut *m*. A. compass, compas de relèvement, compas azimutal.

azimuthal [æzi'mjuːθ(ə)l], *a. Astr: Surv:* Azimutal, -aux.

azoic [ə'zouik], *a. Geol:* (Terrain *m*) azoïque, azootique.

Azores (the) [ðiə'zɔːz]. *Pr.n.pl.* Les Açores *f*.

Aztec ['æztek], *a. & s. Ethn: Hist:* Aztèque *(mf)*.

azure ['æʒər, eiʒər]. 1. *s.* Azur *m*. 2. *Attrib.* An a. sky, un ciel d'azur.

B, b [biː]. **1.** (La lettre) B, b *m. Tp:* **B for Bertie,** B comme Berthe. **2.** *Mus:* Si *m.* **B flat,** si bémol.

baa¹ [baː], *s.* Bêlement *m.* **Baa!** bê! **B.-lamb,** petit agneau.

baa², *v.i.* (baaed, baa'd [baːd]) Bêler.

Baal, *pl.* **Baalim** ['beiəl, 'beiəlim], *s. Rel.H:* (*a*) Baal *m.* (*b*) Faux dieu.

babbitt-metal, *F:* **babbitt** ['bæbit(met(ə)l)], *s.* Métal *m* antifriction; régule *m.*

babble¹ ['bæbl], *s.* **1.** Babil *m*, babillage *m*, babillement *m. Ven:* (*Of hound*) Clabaudage *m.* **2.** Jaserie *f,* bavardage *m.* **3.** Murmure *m* (d'un ruisseau).

babble². **1.** *v.i.* (*a*) Babiller. (*b*) Bavarder, jaser. (*c*) (*Of stream*) Murmurer, babiller. (*d*) *Ven:* Clabauder. **2.** *v.tr.* **To b.** (**out**) **a secret,** laisser échapper un secret. **babbling,** *a.* Babillard, bavard, jaseur, -euse; (*of stream*) murmurant.

babbler ['bæblər], *s.* **1.** Babillard, -arde; bavard, -arde. *Ven:* Clabaudeur *m.* **2.** Jaseur, -euse (qui laisse échapper les secrets).

babe [beib], *s.* Enfant *m* (en bas âge); petit enfant, *F:* bambin *m.*

Babel ['beib(ə)l]. **1.** *Pr.n.* **The Tower of B.,** la Tour de Babel. **2.** *s.* **B. of talk,** brouhaha *m* de conversation. **It was an absolute b.,** c'était un vacarme à ne pas s'entendre.

baboon [bə'buːn], *s. Z:* Babouin *m.* **Dog-faced b.,** cynocéphale *m.*

baboosh, babouche [bə'buːʃ], *s.* Babouche *f.*

baby ['beibi], *s.* **1.** (*m., f., or neut.*) Bébé *m*; poupon *m*, poupard *m.* **I have known him from a b.,** je l'ai vu naître. **The b. of the family,** le benjamin. *S.a.* CRY-BABY. *F:* **To hold, carry, the b.,** avoir l'affaire sur les bras. *F:* **That's your b.,** c'est votre affaire; tire-toi d'affaire tout seul; débrouille-toi. **2.** *Attrib.* (*a*) D'enfant, de bébé. **B. talk,** babil enfantin. *F:* **B. face,** visage poupard. (*b*) *F:* De petites dimensions. *Esp.* **B. grand,** piano *m* (à) demi-queue; crapaud *m.* (*c*) (*Used for the young of animals*) **B. gazelle,** bébé gazelle. **'baby-carriage,** *s. U.S:* Voiture *f* d'enfant; poussette *f.* **'baby-carrier,** *s.* Moïse *m* de toile. **'baby-farm,** *s.* Pouponnière *f*, garderie *f* d'enfants. **'baby-farmer,** *s.* Gardeuse *f* d'enfants. **'baby-linen,** *s.* Layette *f.* **'baby-sit,** *v.i.* Garder les bébés. **'baby-sitter,** *s.* Gardien, -ienne, d'enfants, garde-bébé *mf, pl.* gardes-bébés. **'baby-sitting,** *s.* Garde *f* des bébés; *F:* Service *m* biberon. **'baby-snatching,** *s.* (*a*) Enlèvement *m*, rapt *m*, d'enfant, kidnapping *m.* (*b*) *F:* Détournement *m* de mineur. **'baby-(weighing-) scales,** *s.pl.* Pèse-bébé *m, pl.* pèse-bébés.

babyhood ['beibihud], *s.* Première enfance; bas âge.

babyish ['beibiiʃ], *a.* De bébé; puéril.

Babylon ['bæbilən]. *Pr.n.* Babylone *f.*

Babylonia [ˌbæbi'lounjə]. *Pr.n. A.Geog:* Babylonie *f.*

Babylonian [ˌbæbi'lounjən]. **1.** *a. & s.* Babylonien, -ienne. **The B. Captivity,** la Captivité de Babylone. **2.** *a. F:* Immense.

baccarat ['bækəraː], *s. Cards:* Baccara *m.*

bacchanal ['bækənəl], *s.* (*a*) (*Reveller*) Tapageur, -euse; noceur, -euse. (*b*) (*Revelry*) Bacchanal *m.* (*c*) (*Dance*) Bacchanale *f.*

bacchante [bə'kænti], *s.f.* Bacchante, ménade.

baccy ['bæki], *s. O: P:* = TOBACCO.

bach [bætʃ], *v.i. U.S: F:* Vivre en célibataire.

bachelor ['bætʃələr], *s.m.* **1.** *Hist:* Bachelier (aspirant à la chevalerie). **2.** Célibataire, garçon. Old b., vieux garçon. **B. girl,** jeune fille indépendante. **3.** *Sch:* **B. of Arts, of Science,** *approx.* = licencié ès lettres, ès sciences.

bachelorhood ['bætʃələhud], *s.* Célibat *m.*

bacillary [bə'siləri], *a. Biol:* Bacillaire.

bacillus, *pl.* -i [bə'siləs, -ai], *s. Biol:* Bacille *m.*

back¹ [bæk]. **I.** *s.* **1.** (*a*) Dos *m.* **To fall on one's b.,** tomber à la renverse. *F:* **I have no clothes, I haven't a rag, to my b.,** je n'ai rien à me mettre sur le dos. She wears her hair down her b., elle porte les cheveux dans le dos. **To carry, sling, sth. across one's b.,** porter, mettre, qch. en bandoulière. **To be at the b. of s.o.,** (i) être derrière qn; (ii) soutenir qn. **The Government has a broad b.,** le gouvernement a bon dos. **To do sth. behind s.o.'s back,** faire qch. à l'insu de qn. **To turn one's b. on s.o.,** (i) tourner le dos à qn; (ii) abandonner qn. **To stand, sit, with one's b. to s.o.,** tourner le dos à qn. **To be glad to see the b. of s.o.,** être content de voir partir qn, d'être débarrassé de qn. **To be on one's b.,** (i) être étendu sur le dos; (ii) (*to be ill*) être alité. **The cat sets up its b.,** le chat fait le gros dos, arque le dos. *F:* **To put, set, get, s.o.'s b. up,** mettre qn en colère; fâcher qn; faire rebiffer qn. **To make a b.** (*at leap-frog*), faire le mouton. **To make a b. for s.o.,** to lend a b. to s.o., faire la courte échelle à qn. **B. to b.,** dos à dos; adossés. **B. to front,** sens devant derrière. **With one's b. to the wall,** (i) adossé au mur; (ii) poussé au pied du mur; acculé; aux abois. *F:* **To put one's b. into sth.,** s'appliquer à qch.; s'y mettre, travailler, énergiquement. **S.a.** PAT². (*b*) **Les reins** *m; F:* l'échine *f. S.a.* SMALL II 1. **To break one's b.,** se casser les reins, l'échine. **To break the b. of the work,** faire le plus dur, le plus fort, du travail. (*c*) (*Of ship*) **To break her b.,** se briser en deux; se casser. **2.** (*a*) Dos (d'un couteau, d'un livre); envers *m* (d'une étoffe); verso *m* (d'une page, d'une carte postale); dos, verso (d'un chèque). *Fin:* **Bills as per b.,** effets comme au verso. **The vocabulary is at the b. of the book,** le vocabulaire est à la fin du livre. (*b*) Dossier *m* (d'une chaise). (*c*) Revers *m* (d'une colline, d'une médaille). **The b. of the hand,** le revers de la main. **He knows London like the b. of his hand,** il connaît Londres comme (le fond de) sa poche. (*d*) Derrière *m* (de la tête, d'une maison); arrière *m* (d'une maison, d'une voiture). **The dress fastens at the b.,** la robe s'agrafe dans le dos. *F:* **The third floor b.,** le troisième sur la cour, sur le derrière. **Idea at the b. of one's mind,** idée de derrière la tête; arrière-pensée *f.* **There is something at the b. of it,** il y a une raison secrète derrière tout cela. **To get to the b. of a policy,** voir le dessous des cartes. **3.** *Arch:* Extrados *m* (d'une voûte). **4.** Fond *m* (d'une armoire, d'une salle). *Th:* **The b. of the stage,** le fond de la scène; l'arrière-scène *f.* **At the very b. of . . .,** au fin fond de. . . . *S.a.* BEYOND 3. **5.** *Fb:* Arrière *m*, **The backs,** l'arrière-défense *f. S.a.* HALF-BACK. **II. back,** *a.* (Place, etc.) arrière, de derrière. **B. room,** pièce sur le derrière. **The b. streets of a town,** les bas quartiers d'une ville. *Mil:* **The b. area,** l'arrière *m.* **B. wheel,** roue arrière. *Aut:* **B. axle,** pont arrière. **III. back,** *adv.* **1.** (*Of place*) (*a*) En arrière. **Stand b.!** arrière! rangez-vous! **To step b. a pace,** faire un pas en arrière. **Far b.,** loin derrière (les autres, etc.). **House standing b. from the road,** maison écartée du chemin; maison en retrait. (*b*) Dans le sens contraire. **To hit, strike, b.,** rendre coup pour coup. **If anyone hits me, I hit b.,** si on me frappe, je rends la pareille. *F:* **It was a bit of his own b.,** c'était une revanche. (*With a v. often rendered by the pref.* re-) **To call s.o. b.,** rappeler qn. **To come b., revenir. **To go, drive, ride, sail, walk, b.,** (i) retourner (to, à); (ii) rebrousser chemin. **To drive, chase, s.o. b.,** faire rebrousser chemin à qn. **To make one's way b.,** s'en retourner. **Ship chartered to Lisbon and b. to London,** navire affrété pour voyage à Lisbonne avec retour sur Londres. **To hasten b.,** retourner en toute hâte. (*c*) **To arrive, come, b.,** rentrer. **When will he be b.?** quand sera-t-il de retour? **As soon as I get b.,** dès mon retour. *S.a.* THERE I. 1. *Attrib.* **B. action,** mouvement inverse. **B. current,** contre-courant *m.* **2.** (*Of time*) **Some few years b.,** il y a (déjà) quelques années. **Far b. in the Middle Ages,** à une période reculée du moyen âge. **As far b. as 1914,** déjà en 1914; dès 1914. **back-'answer,** *s. F:* Réplique impertinente. **'back-'bench,** *s. Eng. Parl:* Banc pour les membres qui n'ont pas de portefeuille. **back-'bencher,** *s. Parl:* Membre *m* sans portefeuille.

'back-breaking, a. (Travail, etc.) éreintant. 'back-chat, s. F: Impertinence f. 'back-cloth, -curtain, s. Th: Toile f de fond; arrière-scène f. 'back-current, s. El.É: etc: Courant m de retour; contre-courant m, pl. contre-courants. 'back-date, v.tr. Antidater. back-'door, s. Porte f de derrière, de service. F: To get into a profession through the b.-d., entrer dans une profession par la petite porte. 'back-drop, s. (a) Th: Toile f de fond. (b) arrière-plan m. 'back-end, s. 1. Arrière m (d'une voiture, etc.). 2. Arrière-automne m, arrière-saison f. back-'fire¹, s. I.C.E: (a) Allumage prématuré; contre-allumage m. B.-fire kick, retour m de manivelle. (b) Retour de flamme (au carburateur). back-'fire², v.i. I.C.E: 1. S'allumer prématurément; pétarader; avoir des retours. 2. Donner des retours de flamme. back-'firing, s. Retours mpl de flamme; pétarades fpl. back-'garden, s. Jardin m de derrière. back-'hair, s. Chignon m. 'back-hand, s. 1. B.-h. blow, stroke, coup m de revers. 2. Écriture renversée, penchée à gauche. 3. B.-h. welding, soudure f à droite (en arrière). 'back-handed, a. 1. B.-h. blow, coup inattendu, déloyal. B.-h. compliment, compliment équivoque, à rebours. 2. B.-h. writing, écriture renversée, penchée à gauche. 'back-hander, s. F: 1. Coup m du revers de la main. 2. Riposte inattendue; attaque indirecte, déloyale. 'back-iron, s. Tls: Contre-fer m (de rabot). back-'kitchen, s. Arrière-cuisine f. 'back-lash, s. 1. Mec.E: Jeu m (nuisible); secousse f, battement m, saccade f. 2. Contre-coup m, répercussion f (d'une explosion). 'back-marker, s. Sp: Scratch m, champion, -ionne. back'number, s. (a) Vieux numéro (d'un journal). (b) F: Objet démodé. (Of pers.) P: croulant. To be a b.-n., être vieux jeu. back-'pay, s. Mil: Navy: Arriéré m de solde; rappel m de solde. back-'pedal, v.i. Contre-pédaler, F: faire machine arrière. 'back-pedalling, s. Contre-pédalage m. B.-p brake, frein m par contre-pédalage, dans le moyeu. 'back-premises, s. Arrière-corps m (d'un bâtiment). 'back-pressure, s. 1. Contre-pression f. B.-p. valve, clapet de retenue. 2. El: Contre-tension f. 'back-room, s. Pièce f de derrière. F: B.-r. boy, savant m (qui travaille à l'arrière-plan). 'back-scratcher, s. 1. Gratte-dos m. inv. 2. P: Flagorneur m. 'back-scratching, s. P: 1. Flagornerie f. 2. = LOG-ROLLING 2. back 'seat, s. Siège m de derrière; siège arrière. To take a b. s., (i) s'asseoir sur un banc de derrière; (ii) F: passer au second plan; se trouver relégué au deuxième rang; céder le pas à d'autres. 'back-set, s. Contre-courant m. back-'shop, s. Arrière-boutique f, pl. -boutiques. back-'sight, s. Sm.a: Hausse f. (Sighting notch of) b.-s., cran m de mire. 'back-slapper, s. Personne f d'une exubérance intolérable. 'back-spacer, s. Typewr: Rappel m de chariot. 'back-stitch, s. Needlew: Point m arrière, arrière-point m, point de piqûre. 'back-street, s. 1. Petite rue écartée. 2. Pej: Rue pauvre, mal fréquentée. 'back-stroke, s. 1. (a) Coup m de revers. (b) Contre-coup m. 2. Course f de retour (d'un piston, etc.). 3. Swim: Nage f sur le dos. 'back-talk, s. U.S: F: = BACK-ANSWER, BACK-CHAT. back-'tooth, s. Dent f du fond; molaire f. back-'yard, s. Arrière-cour f.

back², I. v.tr. 1. (a) Renforcer (un mur, une carte); endosser (un livre); maroufler (une toile). (b) Sp: To b. a horse, parier, miser, sur un cheval; jouer un cheval. To b. the wrong horse, mettre sur le mauvais cheval. To b. (a horse) each way, U.S: win, place or show, across the board, jouer (un cheval) gagnant et placé. Well-backed horse, cheval très coté. Com: etc: To b. s.o., financer qn. To b. a bill, endosser un effet. 2. (a) Reculer (une charrette); faire (re)culer (un cheval). Mch: Mettre en marche arrière; refouler (un train). (b) Nau: To b. the oars, to b. water, (i) ramer à rebours, nager à culer; (ii) (to stop way) scier, dénager. (c) Nau: Masquer, coiffer (une voile). 3. Servir de fond à (qch.). The hills that b. the town, les collines qui s'élèvent derrière la ville. II. back, v.i. 1. (a) Aller en arrière; marcher à reculons; (of horse) reculer; Aut: etc: faire marche arrière. Aut: To b. into the garage, entrer dans le garage en marche arrière. (b) Nau: (Of wind)

(Re)descendre, ravaler. 2. The house backs on the road, la maison donne par derrière sur la route. back down, v.i. 1. (a) Descendre (une échelle, etc.) à reculons. (b) The engine is backing down, la machine revient sur le train. 2. (a) Avouer qu'on est dans son tort; rabattre ses prétentions; en rabattre. (b) P: Caner; caler; filer doux. back out, v.i. 1. (Of pers., etc.) Sortir à reculons; (of car) sortir en marche arrière. 2. F: Retirer sa promesse; se dédire, se dérober. To b. out of an argument, se soustraire à une discussion. back up, v.tr. Soutenir, appuyer, qn, qch.; prêter son appui à qn. backed, a. 1. B. on to sth., adossé à qch. 2. (a) Red-b., à dossier. B. saw, scie à dosseret. (b) Broad-b., à large dos, qui a le dos large. S.a. HUMPBACKED. backing s. 1. (a) Renforcement m (d'un mur, d'une carte). Bookb: Endossage m (d'un livre). 2. Sp: B. of a horse, paris mpl sur un cheval. 2. Renfort m, support m, soutien m (d'un mur). 3. (a) Recul m, reculement m (d'un cheval); acculement m (d'un cheval); refoulement m (d'un train); marche arrière (d'une voiture). (b) Nage f à culer (d'un canot). (c) Renversement m (du vent).

backache ['bækeik], s. (a) Douleurs fpl de reins. (b) Courbature f.

backbite ['bækbait], v.tr. Médire de (qn). backbiting, s. Médisance f.

backbiter ['bæk'baitər], s. Médisant, -ante; mauvaise langue.

backbone ['bækboun], s. (i) Épine dorsale, colonne vertébrale; échine f; (ii) grande arête (de poisson). English to the b., anglais jusqu'à la moelle des os. He has got b., il a du caractère. He has no b., il manque de fermeté, d'énergie, de caractère; c'est un emplâtre. He is the b. of the movement, c'est lui qui mène le mouvement.

backer ['bækər], s. 1. Sp: esp. Rac: Parieur, -euse. 2. Com: (a) B. of a bill, donneur m d'aval. (b) Commanditaire m. 3. Partisan, -e.

backgammon [bæk'gæmən], s. (Jeu m de) trictrac m; (jeu de) jacquet m.

background ['bækgraund], s. Fond m, arrière-plan m. In the b., dans le fond, à l'arrière-plan. Against a dark b., sur (un) fond sombre. To keep (oneself) in the b., s'effacer; se tenir dans l'ombre.

backless ['bæklis], a. (Robe, etc.) sans dos; (banc, etc.) sans dossier.

backlog ['bæklog], s. F: Arriéré m (de travail).

backmost ['bækmoust], a. Dernier; le plus éloigné, le plus reculé.

backsheesh ['bækʃi:ʃ], s. = BAKSHEESH.

backside ['bæksaid], s. Anat: F: Derrière m; Fr.C: califourchon m.

backslide ['bækslaid], v.i. (backslid) Retomber dans l'erreur, dans le vice; récidiver. 'back-sliding, s. Rechute f dans le péché, dans le vice; récidive f.

backslider ['bæk'slaidər], s. Relaps, f. relapse.

backstair(s) [,bæk'steər, -eəz], s. (i) Escalier m de service; (ii) escalier dérobé. F: B. influence, (i) protections en haut lieu; (ii) menées sourdes, secrètes. B. gossip, propos d'antichambre.

backward ['bækwəd]. 1. a. (a) B. motion, mouvement rétrograde, en arrière. B. glance, regard en arrière. (b) B. harvest, moisson en retard. B. child, enfant attardé, arriéré. (c) To be b. in doing sth., être lent, peu empressé, à faire qch. 2. adv. = BACKWARDS.

backwardness ['bækwədnis], s. 1. Retard m, arriération f (d'un enfant, de la moisson); lenteur f d'intelligence. 2. B. in doing sth., hésitation f, lenteur, à faire qch.

backwards ['bækwədz], adv. En arrière. To jump, lean, b., sauter, se pencher, en arrière. F: To lean over b. to do sth. for s.o., se mettre en quatre pour faire qch. pour qn. To go, walk, b., aller, marcher, à reculons. To fall b., tomber à la renverse. (Of water) To flow b., couler à contre-courant; refouler. To reckon b. to a date, remonter jusqu'à une date. To stroke the cat b., caresser le chat à rebrousse-poil. B. and forwards, d'avant en arrière et d'arrière en avant. To walk b. and forwards, aller et venir; se promener de long en large; faire les cent pas.

backwash ['bækwɔʃ], s. Remous m.
backwater¹ ['bækwɔ:tər], s. **1.** Eau arrêtée (par un bief, etc.). **2.** Bras m de décharge (d'une rivière). **3.** Remous m (d'une roue à aubes).
backwater², v.i. = back water, q.v. under BACK² I. 2.
backwoods ['bækwudz], s.pl. Forêts f vierges (de l'Amérique du Nord).
backwoodsman, pl. -men [,bæk'wudzmən], s.m. Colon des forêts (de l'Amérique du Nord); défricheur m de forêts; A: coureur des bois.
bacon ['beik(ə)n], s. Lard m; porc salé et fumé; bacon m. F: To save one's b., sauver sa peau.
bacterial [bæk'tiəriəl], a. Bactérien, -ienne.
bactericidal [bæktiəri'saidl], a. Biol: Bactéricide.
bactericide [bæk'tiərisaid], s. Biol: Bactéricide.
bacteriological [bæktiəriə'lɔdʒikl], a. Bactériologique.
bacteriologist [bæk,tiəri'ɔlədʒist], s. Bactériologiste mf; bactériologue mf.
bacteriology [bæk,tiəri'ɔlədʒi], s. Bactériologie f.
bacteriophage [bæk'tiəriofeidʒ], s. Biol: Bactériophage m.
bacteriostatic [bæk,tiəriɔ'stætik], a. Bactériostatique.
bacterium, pl. -ia [bæk'tiəriəm, -iə], s. Bactérie f.
bad [bæd]. I. a. (worse [wə:s], worst [wə:st]) Mauvais. **1.** (a) (Inferior) B. food, mauvaise nourriture; nourriture de mauvaise qualité. B. air, air vicié. B. meat, viande gâtée, avariée. B. coin, pièce fausse. B. debt, mauvaise créance; créance douteuse, véreuse, irrécouvrable. Very b. work, travail détestable. Nau: In holding-ground, fond sans tenue. (Of food, etc.) To go b., se gâter, s'avarier. (b) (Incorrect) B. translation, mauvaise traduction, traduction incorrecte. He speaks b. French, il parle mal le français; son français est mauvais. B. shot, coup mal visé; coup qui manque le but. To be b. at (lying, etc.), s'entendre mal à (mentir, etc.). F: It's not b., not so b., P: it isn't half b., ce n'est pas si mal; ce n'est pas mal du tout; c'est très passable. (c) (Unfortunate) It's a b. business! F: it's a b. job! c'est une mauvaise affaire! c'est une triste affaire! To be in a b. way, être en mauvais, piteux, état; être dans de beaux draps; (health) filer un mauvais coton. He will come to a b. end, il finira mal. He has a b. name, il a (une) mauvaise réputation. It would not be a b. thing, a b. plan, to . . ., on ne ferait pas mal de. . . . Things are going from b. to worse, les choses vont de mal en pis. (d) Jur: B. claim, réclamation mal fondée. B. voting paper, bulletin de vote nul. This is b. law, b. history, c'est fausser la loi, l'histoire. (e) Word taken in a b. sense, mot avec un sens péjoratif. **2.** (a) (Wicked) B. man, méchant homme. B. book, mauvais livre. B. life, mauvaise vie; vie déréglée. Don't call people b. names, n'injuriez pas les gens. S.a. LANGUAGE 2. He's a b. lot, F: a b. egg, a b. hat, c'est un vilain oiseau, un vilain coco, un vaurien, une fripouille. He isn't as b. as he looks, il n'est pas si diable qu'il est noir. (b) (Unpleasant) B. news, mauvaise nouvelle. B. smell, mauvaise odeur. To have a b. cold, a b. headache, avoir un gros rhume, un violent mal de tête. To be on b. terms with s.o., être mal, en mauvais termes, avec qn. It is very b. of you to . . ., c'est très mal à vous, de votre part, de. . . . It is (really) too b.! that's too b.! c'est (par) trop fort! par trop violent! ça c'est raide! It's too b. of him! ce n'est vraiment pas bien de sa part! (c) B. accident, grave accident. B. mistake, faute grave; lourde méprise. To be b. for s.o., for sth., ne rien valoir à qn, pour qch. It is b. for the health, cela ne vaut rien pour la santé. (d) F: (Ill, diseased) She is very b. to-day, elle est très mal aujourd'hui. I feel b., je ne me sens pas bien. She has a b. finger, elle a mal au doigt. B. tooth, dent cariée. My b. leg, ma jambe malade. F: I'm not so b., je ne vais pas trop mal. How's business?—Not so b., comment vont les affaires?—Pas si mal. P: She took b., was taken b., elle s'est sentie indisposée, a été prise d'un malaise. **-ly**, adv. (worse, worst) **1.** Mal. B. dressed, mal habillé. To do, come off, b., mal réussir. I came off b. in that affair, cette affaire a tourné à mon désavantage. To be doing b., faire de mauvaises affaires. Things are going, turning out, b., les choses vont mal, tournent mal. He took it very b., il a très mal pris la

chose. (Of machine, etc.) To work b., mal fonctionner. **2.** B. wounded, gravement, grièvement, blessé. The badly disabled, les grands infirmes, les grands mutilés. B. beaten, battu à plate couture. **3.** To want sth. b., (i) avoir grand besoin de qch; (ii) avoir grande envie de qch. II. bad, s. Ce qui est mal ou mauvais. (a) To take the b. with the good, accepter la mauvaise fortune aussi bien que la bonne. (b) (Of pers.) To go to the b., mal tourner. (c) I am 500 francs to the b., je perds 500 francs. **bad-'looking**, a. F: He is not b.-l., il n'est pas mal (de sa personne); F: il n'est pas mal fichu. **bad-'tempered**, a. Grincheux. She is b.-t. to-day, elle est de mauvaise humeur aujourd'hui.
bade. See BID².
badge [bædʒ], s. **1.** (a) Insigne m (d'un membre d'une société); insigne de casquette; plaque f (de cocher); médaille f (de porteur, etc.); Mil: attribut m (d'un régiment, etc.); écusson m (d'un régiment). B. of rank, insigne de grade. (b) (Of boy-scout) Brevet m; badge m. **2.** Symbole m, marque f; signe distinctif.
badger¹ ['bædʒər], s. **1.** Z: Blaireau m. **2.** (Brush) Blaireau.
badger², v.tr. Harceler, tourmenter, tracasser, importuner (qn). To b. s.o. for sth., harceler qn pour obtenir qch. **badgering**¹, a. Importun. **badgering**², s. Harcèlement m.
ba`lands ['bædlændz], s. Geog: Bad-lands fpl.
badminton ['bædmintən], s. Games: Badminton m, volant m au filet.
badness ['bædnis], s. **1.** (a) Mauvaise qualité; mauvais état. (b) The b. of the weather, le mauvais temps. **2.** (Of pers.) Méchanceté f.
Baffin ['bæfin]. Pr.n. Geog: B. Island, la Terre de Baffin.
baffle¹ ['bæfl], s. Déflecteur m; chicane f; contre-porte f.
baffle², v.tr. **1.** (a) Confondre, déconcerter, dérouter (qn); dépister (la police); dérouter (les soupçons). (b) Déjouer, faire échouer (un projet); frustrer, décevoir (un espoir); tromper, éluder (la vigilance). To b. definition, échapper à toute définition. **2.** Établir des chicanes dans (un conduit, etc.). **baffling**, a. (a) Déconcertant. (b) Nau: B. winds, brises folles.
bag¹ [bæg], s. **1.** Sac m. Money-bag, (i) bourse f; (ii) (of bus conductors, etc.) sacoche f, (iii) (for church collections) bourse. Travelling bag, sac de voyage. Paper bag, sac de, en, papier. Diplomatic b., F: the b., valise f diplomatique, F: la valise. S.a. GAME-BAG, GAS-BAG, ICE-BAG, KIT-BAG, MAIL-BAG, NOSE-BAG, SLEEPING-BAG, TOOL-BAG, STRING-BAG, WORK-BAG. F: To pack up b. and baggage, plier bagage; prendre ses cliques et ses claques; faire son baluchon. P: There are bags of it, il y en a des tas, il y en a à gogo. **2.** (a) Nat.Hist: Sac, poche f. Tear b., sac lacrymal. Poison b., glande f, vésicule f, à venin. (b) Husb: Pis m, mamelle f (de vache). (c) F: Bags under the eyes, poches sous les yeux. Bags at the knees, poches aux genoux (d'un pantalon). **3.** (a) Ven: The b., le tableau (de chasse). To secure a good bag, faire bonne chasse. (b) F: In the b., (i) sûr et certain, dans le sac; (ii) Mil.Av: (of enemy aircraft) au tableau. **4.** pl. F: Pantalon m. **bag-sleeve**, s. Dressm: Manche bouffante.
bag², v. (bagged) **1.** v.tr. (a) To bag (up) sth., mettre qch. en sac; ensacher (du minerai, etc.). (b) Ven: Abattre, tuer (du gibier). (c) F: Empocher; s'emparer de (qch.); mettre la main sur (qch.). Bags (that)! à moi ça! (d) P: Voler, chiper. **2.** v.i. (Se) gonfler, s'enfler; (of garment, etc.) bouffer, avoir trop d'ampleur; (of sail, etc.) faire sac. **bagging**, s. **1.** Mise f en sac. **2.** Toile f à sac.
bagatelle [,bægə'tel], s. **1.** Bagatelle f. **2.** Billard anglais.
bagful ['bægful], s. Sac plein; plein sac; sachée f.
baggage ['bægidʒ], s. **1.** (a) Mil: Bagage m. (b) O: F: A saucy b., une jeune effrontée. **2.** U.S: = LUGGAGE. B. car, Rail: fourgon m à bagages. **'baggage-check**, s. U.S: Bulletin m de bagages. **'baggage-room**, s. U.S: Soute f aux bagages.

baggy ['bægi], *a.* (Vêtement) trop ample, trop lâche, mal coupé; (pantalon) flottant, bouffant. **B. cheeks,** joues pendantes; bajoues *f.*

bagman, *pl.* -men ['bægmən], *s.m. A: F:* Commis voyageur.

bagpipe(s) ['bægpaip(s)], *s.* Cornemuse *f.*

bagpiper ['bæg,paipər], *s.* Joueur *m* de cornemuse.

Bahama [bə'hɑːmə]. *Pr.n.* **The B. Islands, the Bahamas,** les Lucayes *f,* les Bahamas *f.*

bail¹ [beil], *s. Jur:* (*a*) Cautionnement *m.* (*b*) (*Pers.*) Caution *f,* garant *m,* répondant *m.* (*c*) Somme fournie à titre de cautionnement. **To grant b.,** admettre une caution. **To go b. for s.o.,** se porter, se rendre, garant de qn; fournir caution pour qn (pour sa libération provisoire). **To find b.,** fournir caution. '**bail-bond,** *s. Jur:* Engagement signé par la caution.

bail², *v.tr.* To b. s.o. (out), se porter caution pour obtenir l'élargissement provisoire de qn.

bail³, *s.* 1. *O:* (Swinging) b. (*in stable*), bat-flanc(s) *m inv.* 2. *pl. Cr:* Barrettes *f,* bâtonnets *m* (qui couronnent le guichet).

bail⁴, *v.tr.* **To b. a boat (out), to b. (out) the water,** écoper, vider, un canot; vider, écoper, l'eau d'une embarcation.

bailer ['beilər], *s.* Écope *f;* épuisette *f.*

bailey¹ ['beili], *s. F:* **The Old B.** (= the Central Criminal Court), la Cour d'Assises (à Londres).

Bailey², *pr.n. Mil: Constr:* **B. bridge,** pont Bailey (du nom de l'inventeur).

bailiff ['beilif], *s.* 1. **Sheriff's b.,** agent *m* de poursuites; huissier *m;* porteur *m* de contraintes. 2. Régisseur *m,* intendant *m* (d'un domaine). *S.a.* WATER-BAILIFF. 3. *Hist:* Bailli *m.*

bain-marie [,bæ(n)mə'riː], *s.* Bain-marie *m, pl.* bains-marie.

bairn [bɛərn], *s. Dial:* (*In Scot.*) Enfant *mf.*

bait¹ [beit], *s.* (*a*) *Fish:* Amorce *f,* appât *m,* achée *f.* (*b*) Appât, leurre *m.* **To take, nibble at, rise to, swallow, the b.,** mordre à l'hameçon, à l'appât; gober l'appât; *F:* gober le morceau.

bait². 1. *v.tr.* Harceler (un animal). **To b. a bull with dogs,** lancer, faire combattre, des chiens contre un taureau. *F:* **To b. s.o.,** harceler, tourmenter, qn. 2. *v.tr.* Faire manger (un cheval pendant une halte). 3. *v.tr.* Amorcer, appâter, garnir (un hameçon, etc.). **baiting,** *s.* 1. Harcèlement *m.* 2. Amorçage *m* (d'un hameçon).

baize [beiz], *s.* Feutrine *f,* gros tissu (d'ameublement). Green b., tapis vert. (Green-)b. door, porte rembourrée, matelassée.

bake [beik]. 1. *v.tr.* (*a*) Cuire, faire cuire (qch.) (au four). *Abs.* **Do you know how to b.?** savez-vous boulanger? *S.a.* HALF-BAKED. (*b*) Cuire (des briques). **Earth baked by the sun,** sol durci, desséché, par le soleil. 2. *v.i.* (*Of bread, etc.*) Cuire (au four). *F:* **We are baking in the heat,** nous brûlons par cette chaleur. **baking,** *s.* 1. (*a*) Cuisson *f* (du pain, etc.). *Attrib.* **B. apples, pears, pommes** *f,* poires *f,* à cuire (au four). *Mil:* **The b. section,** la boulangerie. (*b*) Cuisson, cuite *f* (des briques, de la porcelaine). 2. (*Batch*) (*a*) Fournée *f* (de pain). (*b*) Cuite (de briques, etc.). **baking-dish,** *s. Cu:* Plat *m* à rôtir, plat allant au four. '**baking-powder,** *s. Cu:* Poudre *f* à lever; levure artificielle, minérale, chimique; *R.t.m:* Levure Alsacienne.

bakehouse ['beikhaus], *s.* Fournil *m,* boulangerie *f.*

bakelite ['beikəlait], *s.* Bakélite *f.*

baker ['beikər], *s.* Boulanger *m.* **The b.'s wife,** la boulangère. **B.'s man,** garçon boulanger, *F:* mitron. **B.'s shop,** boulangerie *f. S.a.* DOZEN 2.

bakery ['beikəri], *s.* Boulangerie *f.*

baksheesh ['bækʃiːʃ], *s.* Bakhchich *m;* pot-de-vin *m.*

Balaclava [,bælə'klɑːvə]. *Pr.n. Geog:* Balaklava. **B. helmet,** passe-montagne *m.*

balaenoptera [,bælein'ɔptərə], *s.pl. Z:* Balénoptères *m.*

balalaïka [,bælə'laikə], *s. Mus:* Balalaïka *f.*

balance¹ ['bæləns], *s.* 1. Balance *f.* **Roman b.,** balance romaine. **Spring b.,** peson *m.* **Analytical, chemical, precision, b.,** balance de précision; (*if small*) trébuchet *m.* **To turn the b.,** faire pencher la balance.

To be, hang, in the b., être, rester, en balance. 2. Équilibre *m,* aplomb *m.* **To keep, lose, recover, one's b.,** se tenir en équilibre; perdre l'équilibre; retrouver, reprendre, son équilibre. **To throw s.o. off his b.,** (i) faire perdre l'équilibre à qn; (ii) interloquer qn. **Mind off its b.,** esprit désaxé, déséquilibré. *Hist:* **The b. of power,** l'équilibre des puissances; la balance politique, la balance des pouvoirs. 3. *Com: Fin:* (*a*) Solde *m,* reliquat *m* (d'un compte). **B. in hand,** solde créditeur. **B. carried forward,** report *m* à nouveau, solde à nouveau. **B. due,** (i) solde débiteur; (ii) solde de compte. **B. of payments,** balance des paiements. (*b*) Bilan *m.* **To strike a b.,** dresser, établir, le bilan. **On b. . . .,** à tout prendre. '**balance-beam,** *s.* Fléau *m* de balance. '**balance-sheet,** *s. Com:* Bilan *m* (d'inventaire); tableau *m* par doit et avoir. '**balance-weight,** *s.* Contrepoids *m.* '**balance-wheel,** *s. Clockm: etc:* Balancier *m* (de montre); roue *f* de balance (d'une horloge).

balance². 1. *v.tr.* (*a*) Balancer, peser (les conséquences, etc.). (*b*) Mettre, maintenir, (un objet) en équilibre; équilibrer, stabiliser, compenser (des forces); faire contrepoids à (qch.). **To b. oneself on one foot,** s'équilibrer sur un seul pied. (*c*) **One thing balances another,** une chose balance, compense, l'autre. (*d*) *Com: Fin:* Balancer, solder (un compte). *Book-k:* **To b. the books,** régler les livres. **To b. the budget,** équilibrer le budget. 2. *v.i.* (*a*) Se faire contrepoids. (*Of scales*) Se faire équilibre. (*Of accounts*) Se balancer, s'équilibrer, se solder. (*b*) Osciller, balancer. (*Of pers.*) Hésiter; balancer, (entre deux partis). **balanced,** *a.* 1. Équilibré, compensé. *Biol:* Stabilisé. *Med:* **B. diet,** régime équilibré. **To have a well-, ill-b. mind,** avoir l'esprit bien, mal, équilibré. 2. En nombre égal; de force ou de valeur égale. **balancing¹,** *a.* 1. (*a*) (Mouvement) de bascule. (*b*) (Caractère) hésitant. 2. (*a*) (*Of power*) Pondérateur, -trice. (*b*) (*Of spring, etc.*) Compensateur, -trice. **balancing²,** *s.* 1. Balancement *m,* hésitation *f* (entre deux choses). 2. (*a*) Mise *f* en équilibre; équilibrage *m;* stabilisation *f.* (*b*) **B. of accounts,** règlement *m,* solde *m,* alignement *m,* des comptes. 3. Ajustement *m* (de deux choses); compensation *f. W.Tel:* **B. aerial,** antenne de compensation. '**balancing-pole,** *s.* Contrepoids *m,* balancier *m* (de danseur de corde).

balancer ['bælənsər], *s.* 1. Balancier *m.* 2. *Ent:* Balancier, aileron *m* (des diptères).

balcony ['bælkəni], *s.* 1. Balcon *m.* 2. *Th:* Balcon. *U.S:* Fauteuils *mpl,* stalles *fpl,* de deuxième galerie.

bald [bɔːld], *a.* 1. Chauve. *F:* déplumé. **B. patch,** région chauve; (*on head*) petite tonsure. **To be b. at the temples,** avoir les tempes dégarnies. 2. (*Of style, etc.*) Décharné; plat; sec, *f.* sèche. 3. (*Marked with white*) **B. horse,** cheval belle-face. **-ly,** *adv.* Nûment, platement, sèchement. '**bald-head,** *s.* Tête *f* chauve; *F:* caillou déplumé. *F:* **An old b.-h.,** un vieux déplumé. '**bald-headed,** *a.* (A la tête) chauve. *F:* **To go at it b.-'h.,** y aller tête baissée. '**bald-pate,** *s.* = BALD-HEAD.

baldachin ['bɔːldəkin], *s.* Baldaquin *m.*

balderdash ['bɔːldədæʃ], *s.* Bêtises *fpl,* balivernes *fpl,* fadaises *fpl.*

balding ['bɔːldiŋ], *a. F:* Devenant chauve. **He is a b. thirty,** à trente ans, il se déplume.

baldness ['bɔːldnis], *s.* 1. (*a*) Calvitie *f;* alopécie *f.* (*b*) Nudité *f* (d'une montagne, etc.). 2. Platitude *f,* pauvreté *f,* sécheresse *f* (du style, etc.).

baldric ['bɔːldrik], *s. A:* Baudrier *m.*

bale¹ [beil], *s. Com:* Balle *f,* ballot *m* (de marchandises).

bale², *v.tr.* Emballotter, paqueter, empaqueter. **baling,** *s.* Mise *f* en balles; paquetage *m.*

bale³, *v.tr.* = BAIL⁴. **bale out,** *v.i. Av:* Sauter (en parachute).

Balearic [bæli'ærik], *a. Geog:* **The B. Islands, les Iles Baléares.**

baleful ['beilful], *a. Lit:* Sinistre, funeste. **-fully,** *adv.* Sinistrement.

balk¹ [bɔːk], *s.* 1. *Agr:* (*a*) Bande *f* de délimitation entre deux champs. (*b*) Billon *m.* 2. (*a*) (i) Pierre *f* d'achoppement; obstacle *m;* contretemps *m;* (ii) déception f. (b) Bill: Espace m derrière la ligne de départ. 3. Const: (Grosse) poutre, solive f, billon.

balk². 1. v.tr. Contrarier. (a) To b. s.o.'s plans, déjouer, contrecarrer, les desseins de qn. To b. s.o. of his prey, frustrer qn de sa proie. (b) Se mettre en travers de (qn qui va sauter, etc.); entraver (qn). (c) Éviter (un sujet); se soustraire à (une obligation); laisser passer (une occasion). 2. v.i. (Of horse) Refuser; se dérober. To b. at sth., s'arrêter, reculer, hésiter, devant qch.; regimber contre qch.

Balkan ['bɔːlkən], a. Geog: The B. mountains, the Balkans, les (monts) Balkans m. The B. States, the Balkans, les États balkaniques. The B. Peninsula, la péninsule des Balkans.

ball¹ [bɔːl], s. 1. (a) Boule f (de croquet, de neige); balle f (de cricket, de tennis, de hockey, etc.); ballon m (d'enfant, de football); bille f (de billard); balle (de fusil); boulet m (de canon); pompon (d'une frange); pelote f, peloton m (de laine, de ficelle). To wind wool into a b., (em)peloter, pelotonner, de la laine; mettre (de la laine) en pelote. The three (golden) balls, P: the three brass balls, les trois boules (enseigne du prêteur sur gages). Meteor: B. of fire, b. lightning, globe m de feu; éclair m en boule. S.a. FIRE-BALL. Sm.a: To load with b., charger à balle. Cr: No b., fausse balle. Ten: etc: To knock the balls about, peloter; Bill: caramboler les billes. F: To keep the b. rolling, continuer, soutenir, la conversation; ne pas laisser languir la conversation, le jeu. To start the b. rolling, to set the b. a-rolling, déclencher la conversation; mener le branle. To have the b. at one's feet, avoir la balle belle, avoir la partie belle; n'avoir qu'à saisir l'occasion. F: To play b., coopérer avec qn, être en cheville avec qn. S.a. RACE³ 4. (c) B.-(and-socket) joint, (i) Anat: emboîtement m réciproque; énarthrose f; (ii) Mec.E: joint m à rotule, à boulet, à genou; joint sphérique. (d) pl. V: 'Balls,' les couilles f, c'est de la couille, quelle connerie! quelle couillonnade! 2. (a) Lentille f (de pendule). (b) Éminence métatarsienne (du pied); éminence thénar (du pouce). To walk on the b. of the foot, marcher sur la demi-pointe des pieds. (c) Globe m (de l'œil). 3. Cu: Meat-b., boulette f. 4. U.S: Ball (game) = BASEBALL. 'ball-bearing(s), s.(pl.) Mec.E: Roulement m à billes. 'ball-cartridge, s. Cartouche à balle. 'ball-cock, s. Robinet m, soupape f, à flotteur. 'ball-pen, s. Stylo m à bille. 'ball-planting, s. For: Plantation en mottes. 'ball-point, s. Pointe-bille f. B.-p. pen, stylo m à bille, crayon à bille. 'ball-shaped, a. Spherique. 'ball-valve, s. 1. Soupape f à boulet; clapet m sphérique. 2. = BALL-COCK.

ball². 1. v.tr. (a) Agglomérer. Metall: Baller (le fer). (b) Tex: Mettre (la laine) en pelote. F: (Of speaker) To be balled up, être embrouillé. To get balled up, s'embrouiller. 2. v.i. S'agglomérer; (of snow) botter.

ball³, s. Danc: Bal m, pl. bals. S.a. FANCY¹ II, MASK¹ 1. To open the b., (i) ouvrir le bal; mettre le bal en train; (ii) mettre les choses en branle; ouvrir le bal. 'ball-room, s. Salle f de bal.

ballad ['bæləd], s. 1. Mus: Romance f; ballade f. 2. Lit: Ballade f.

ballade [bæ'lɑːd], s. Lit: Ballade f.

ballast¹ ['bæləst], s. 1. Nau: Aer: Lest m. Ship in b.(-trim), navire sur lest. To take in b., faire son lest. To discharge, throw out, b., se délester; jeter du lest. F: (Of pers.) To have b., avoir l'esprit rassis. To lack b., ne pas avoir de plomb dans la cervelle. 2. (a) Civ.E: Pierraille f, caillloutage m. (b) Rail: Ballast m, empierrement m.

ballast², v.tr. 1. Nau: Aer: Lester. 2. Civ.E: (a) Empierrer, caillouter. (b) Rail: etc: Ballaster. **ballasting,** s. 1. Nau: Aer: Lestage m. 2. Civ.E: Empierrement m, ensablement m, caillloutage m. Rail: Ballastage m.

ballerina [ˌbælə'riːnə], s.f. 1. Ballerine. Prima b., première danseuse, danseuse f étoile. 2. Bootm: Ballerine f.

ballet ['bælei], s. 1. Ballet m. 2. Corps m de ballet. 'ballet-dancer, s. Danseur, -euse, d'opéra; ballerine

f. 'ballet-girl, s.f. Figurante. 'ballet-master, -mistress, s. Directeur, -trice des ballets. 'ballet-shoe, s. Chausson m. 'ballet-skirt, s. Tutu m.

balletomane ['bælito,mein], s. Balletomane mf; fanatique mf de ballet.

ballistic [bə'listik], a. Balistique.

ballistics [bə'listiks], s.pl. (Usu. with sg. const.) Balistique f.

ballon(n)et ['bælənet], s. Aer: Ballonnet compensateur.

balloon¹ [bə'luːn], s. 1. (a) Aer: Ballon m, aérostat m. To go up in a b., monter en ballon. Mil: Met: Sounding b., ballon sonde. Com: Advertising b., ballon réclame; (in comic strip) banderole f. S.a. DIRIGIBLE, BARRAGE. (b) Air-b., toy-b., ballon à air. 2. Ch: B.(-flask), ballon. B. glass, verre m à dégustation. bal'loon-tyre, s. Pneu m. ballon, pneu confort.

balloon², v.i. 1. Bouffer; se ballonner. 2. F: Monter en ballon.

ballot¹ ['bælət], s. 1. B.(-ball), boule f de scrutin. 2. (a) Tour m de scrutin. To vote by b., voter au scrutin. (b) Scrutin m, vote m. To take a b., procéder à un scrutin, à un vote. 3. Parl: Tirage m au sort (pour la priorité du droit de soumettre des résolutions, etc.). To hold a b., procéder à un tirage au sort. 'ballot-box, s. Urne f de scrutin. 'ballot-paper, s. Bulletin m de vote.

ballot², v.i. (a) Voter au scrutin (secret). To b. against s.o., voter contre qn; F: blackbouler qn. (b) Tirer au sort. To b. for a place, tirer une place au sort. **balloting,** s. 1. Élection f au scrutin. 2. Tirage m au sort.

ballyhoo [ˌbæli'huː], s. U.S: P: 1. Grosse réclame; F: battage m. 2. Bourrage m de crâne.

ballyrag ['bæliræg], v.tr. **ballyragging** ['bæliræɡiŋ], s. O: = RAG².

balm [bɑːm], s. 1. Baume m. 2. Bot: Mélisse officinale; citronnelle f. 'balm-cricket, s. Ent: Cigale f.

balmy ['bɑːmi], a. 1. Balsamique. 2. (a) (Air, temps) embaumé, parfumé; d'une douceur délicieuse. (b) Lit: Calmant, adoucissant. 3. P: Toqué, loufoque.

balneology [ˌbælni'ɔlədʒi], s. Thermalisme m.

balneotherapy [ˌbælniəˈθerəpi], s. Balnéothérapie f.

baloney [bə'louni], s. P: Blague f. foutaise f.

balsa ['bɔːlsə], s. B. wood, balsa m.

balsam ['bɔːlsəm], s. 1. Baume m. Copalba b., baume de Copahu. B. of Peru, baume du Pérou. 2. Bot: Garden, yellow, b., balsamine f. 3. B. fir, sapin baumier.

balsamic [bɔːl'sæmik], a. Balsamique.

balsamine ['bɔːlsəmiːn], s. Bot: Balsamine f.

Baltic ['bɔːltik], a. & s. Geog: 1. The B. (Sea), la (mer) Baltique. 2. B. port, port baltique.

baluster ['bæləstər], s. 1. Balustre m. 2. pl. = BANISTERS.

balustrade [ˌbæləs'treid], s. (a) Balustrade f. (b) Accoudoir m, allège f, appui m (de fenêtre, etc.).

bamboo [bæm'buː], s. Bambou m.

bamboozle [bæm'buːzl], v.tr. F: Mystifier, enjôler, embobeliner (qn). To b. s.o. out of sth., (i) frauder qn de qch.; (ii) soutirer qch. à qn.

bamboozlement [bæm'buːzlmənt], s. F: Enjôlement m, duperie f, tromperie f.

ban¹ [bæn], s. (a) (Sentence of banishment, of outlawry) Ban m, bannissement m, proscription f. (b) Ecc: Interdit m. To place s.o. under the b. of public opinion, mettre qn au ban de l'opinion.

ban², v.tr. (banned) Interdire (qn, qch.); mettre (un livre) à l'index. To be banned by public opinion, être au ban de l'opinion (publique).

banal [bə'nɑːl, 'beinl], a. Banal -aux; ordinaire.

banality [bə'næliti], s. Banalité f.

banana [bə'nɑːnə], s. Banane f. B.-tree, bananier m. Nau: B. boat, bananier m. El.E: B. plug, fiche f banane. ba'nana-plan'tation, s. Bananeraie f, bananerie f.

band¹ [bænd], s. 1. (a) Lien m (de fer); frette f; cercle m (d'un tonneau); bandage m (d'une roue); ruban m (d'un chapeau). Bookb: Nerf m, nervure f. Narrow b., bandelette f. Crape b. (round arm), brassard m de deuil. Elastic b., anneau m en caoutchouc; F: élastique m. S.a. NECK-BAND, WAISTBAND.

Mil: Cap-b., bandeau *m.* *Nau:* (*In Merchant Service*) Bands, galons *mpl.* (*b*) Bande *f* (de gazon, de toile). Paper b., bande de papier; (*round cigar*) bague *f.* (*c*) *Opt:* Bands of the spectrum, bandes du spectre. (*d*) *W.Tel:* Frequency b., bande de fréquence. (*e*) *Gramophones:* Plage *f* (d'un disque). 2. *Mec.E:* Bande, courroie *f* (de transmission). *Ind:* Endless b. (*in mass production*), b.-conveyor, tapis roulant; transporteur *m* à toile sans fin. Moving-b. production, travail à la chaîne. 3. *pl. Ecc.Cost: etc:* Bands, rabat *m.* 'band-brake, *s.* Frein *m* à collier, à bande. 'band-clutch, *s.* Embrayage *m* à ruban. 'band-pulley, *s.* Poulie *f* à courroie. 'band-saw, *s.* Scie *f* à ruban; scie sans fin. 'band-wheel, *s. Mec.E:* Roue *f* de transmission.

band², *v.tr.* Bander (un ballot); fretter (un four, etc.); mettre (un journal) sous bande; baguer (un pigeon).

band³, *s.* 1. (*a*) Bande *f*, troupe *f.* (*b*) Compagnie *f*; *Pej:* clique *f.* 2. *Mus:* (*a*) Orchestre *m.* (*b*) *Mil: etc:* Musique *f.* The regimental b., la musique du régiment. Brass b., fanfare *f.* Brass and reed b., harmonie *f.* *Mil:* The drum and bugle b., la batterie. The members of the b., les musiciens. 'band-waggon, *s. U.S:* Char *m* des musiciens (en tête de la cavalcade). *Esp. U.S: F:* To jump on the b.-w., se mettre dans le mouvement; se ranger du bon côté.

band⁴, *v.i.* To b. (together), (i) se réunir en bande; (ii) s'ameuter.

bandage¹ ['bændidʒ], *s.* (*a*) *Esp. Med:* Bandage *m*, bande *f*; (*for blindfolding*) bandeau *m.* Crêpe b., bande Velpeau. (*b*) *Surg:* Bande de pansement; pansement *m.* Head swathed in bandages, tête enveloppée de linges. To remove a b. from a wound, débander une plaie.

bandage², *v.tr.* Bander (une plaie); poser un appareil, mettre un pansement, sur (une plaie).

bandan(n)a [bæn'dænə], *s.* 1. Foulard *m.* 2. *F:* Mouchoir *m.*

bandbox ['bændbɔks], *s.* Carton *m* à chapeau(x); carton de modiste. To look as if one had just stepped out of a b., être tiré à quatre épingles.

banderilla [ˌbændə'riljə], *s. Bull-fighting:* Banderille *f.*

banderol(e) ['bændərɔl], *s.* (*a*) Banderole *f.* (*b*) Oriflamme *f.*

bandit ['bændit], *s.* Bandit *m*, brigand *m.*

banditry ['bænditri], *s.* Brigandage *m.*

bandmaster ['bændmɑːstər], *s.* (*a*) Chef *m* d'orchestre. (*b*) *Mil: etc:* Chef de musique, de fanfare.

bandoleer, bandolier [ˌbændə'liər], *s.* 1. Bandoulière *f.* 2. Cartouchière (portée en écharpe).

bandsman, *pl.* -men ['bændzmən], *s.m.* Musicien (d'un orchestre, d'une fanfare).

bandstand ['bændstænd], *s.* Kiosque *m* à musique.

bandy¹ ['bændi], *v.tr.* (Se) renvoyer (une balle, des paroles); échanger (des plaisanteries, des coups). To b. words, se chamailler.

bandy², *a.* 1. B. legs, jambes arquées, bancales. *Furn:* B. leg, pied-de-biche *m.* 2. (*Of pers.*) = BANDY-LEGGED. 'bandy-legged, *a.* (*Of pers.*) Bancal, -als.

bane [bein], *s.* 1. Fléau *m*, peste *f.* 2. *A:* Poison *m.*

baneful ['beinful], *a.* Funeste, fatal, -als; pernicieux. -fully, *adv.* Pernicieusement.

bang¹ [bæŋ], *s.* Coup (violent); détonation *f*; fracas *m*; claquement *m* (de porte). (*Of firework, etc.*) To go off with a b., détoner. *Av:* Double b., double bang *m.*

bang². 1. *v.i.* (*a*) To b. at, on, the door, frapper à la porte avec bruit; heurter à la porte. To b. on the table with one's fist, frapper la table du poing. (*b*) (*Of door*) To b., claquer, battre. 2. *v.tr.* (*a*) Frapper (violemment). I banged his head on a stone, je lui ai cogné la tête sur une pierre. (*b*) To b. the door, (faire) claquer la porte, fermer la porte avec fracas, frapper la porte. To b. down the lid, abattre violemment le couvercle. banging, *s.* (*a*) Coups violents; claquement *m.* (*b*) Détonations *fpl.*

bang³. 1. *int.* Pan! v'lan! boum! 2. *adv. F:* To go b., éclater. He crashed b. into the tree, il est rentré pile dans l'arbre. *Adv.phr:* B. off, sur-le-champ. *P:* B. on. It's b. on, c'est drôlement nickel. B. on! au poil!

bang⁴, *s.* Coiffure *f* à la chien; coiffure en frange.

bang-tail, *s.* Cheval *m* (à la queue) écourté(e).

banger ['bæŋər], *s. P:* 1. Mensonge *m* énorme. 2. *P:* Saucisse *f.*

bangle ['bæŋgl], *s.* Bracelet *m.*

banian ['bæniən], *s. Bot:* B.-(tree), arbre *m* des banians; banian *m*; figuier *m* de l'Inde.

banish ['bæniʃ], *v.tr.* 1. Bannir, exiler; proscrire (qn). 2. To b. fear, care, bannir, chasser, la crainte, les soucis.

banishment ['bæniʃmənt], *s.* Bannissement *m*, proscription *f*, exil *m.*

banister ['bænistər], *s.* (*Usu. in pl.*) 1. Balustre *m* (d'escalier). 2. Rampe *f* (d'escalier).

banjo, *pl.* -os, -oes ['bændʒou, -z], *s. Mus:* Banjo *m.*

banjoist ['bændʒouist], *s.* Joueur, -euse, de banjo.

bank¹ [bæŋk], *s.* 1. (*a*) Talus *m*; terrasse *f. Civ.E:* Banquette *f*, remblai *m. Rail:* Rampe *f.* B. of flowers, tertre *m* de fleurs. (*b*) (*In river, sea*) Banc *m* (de sable, de roches). *S.a.* SANDBANK. *Geog:* The Banks of Newfoundland, le Banc de Terre-Neuve. (*c*) Digue *f.* 2. (*a*) (*Steep side*) Berge *f* (d'une rivière, etc.). (*b*) (*Side*) Bord *m*, rive *f* (d'une rivière, d'un lac). 3. *Av:* Virage incliné.

bank². 1. *v.tr.* (*a*) To b. a river, endiguer une rivière. (*b*) To b. up, remblayer, terrasser, amonceler (de la terre, de la neige). *Civ.E:* To b. a road (at a corner), surhausser, relever, un virage. Banked edge (of road, etc.), berge *f.* (*c*) *Mch:* To b. (up) fires, couvrir, coucher, les feux. 2. *v.i.* (*Of snow, clouds, etc.*) S'entasser, s'accumuler, s'amonceler. 3. *v.i. Av:* Pencher l'avion; virer (sur l'aile). banking¹, *s.* 1. (*a*) Remblayage *m*; surhaussement *m*, relèvement *m* (d'un virage). (*b*) B. up a river, haussement *m* du niveau d'une rivière. 2. Remblai *m.* 3. *Av:* Virage incliné.

bank³, *s.* 1. (*a*) Banque *f.* The B. of England, la Banque d'Angleterre. It's as safe as the B. of England, *F:* c'est de l'or en barre. Merchant b., banque d'affaires. B. account, compte en banque. B. clerk, commis, employé, de banque. (*b*) (Bureau *m* de) banque. Branch b., succursale *f*, agence *f. S.a.* BLOOD-BANK. 2. *Gaming:* Banque. To break the b., faire sauter la banque. 'bank-bill, *s.* Effet (tiré par une banque sur une autre). 'bank-book, *s.* Livret *m* de banque. bank-'holiday, *s.* Jour férié. bank-'messenger, *s.* Garçon *m* de recette. 'bank-note, *s.* Billet *m* de banque. bank-rate, *s. Fin:* Taux *m* d'escompte.

bank⁴, *v.tr. & i.* 1. Mettre, déposer, (de l'argent) en banque. 2. *Gaming:* Tenir la banque. 3. *F:* To b. on sth., compter sur qch.; caver, miser, sur (un événement). banking², *s.* 1. Affaires *fpl*, opérations *fpl*, de banque *f.* B. house, maison *d* de banque. B. account, compte en banque. 2. Profession *f* de banquier; la banque.

bank⁵, *s.* 1. *Nau: A:* (*a*) Banc *m* (de rameurs). Rang *m* (de rames, d'avirons). 2. *Mus:* Clavier *m* (d'un orgue). Organ with three banks, orgue à trois claviers. *Typewr:* Rang *m.* A three-b. machine, une machine à trois rangs de touches. 3. *Ind:* Groupe *f*, batterie *f* (de chaudières, de cornues, de lampes électriques, etc.). *Cin:* B. of projectors, rampe *f* de projecteurs.

bankable ['bæŋkəbl], *a. Fin:* (Effet *m*) bancable, banquable, négociable en banque.

banker¹ ['bæŋkər], *s.* 1. Banquier *m.* Banker's draft, chèque *m* bancaire. 2. *Gaming:* Banquier, tailleur *m.*

banker², *s.* Banquier *m*, banquais *m* (qui pêche la morue); morutier *m*, terre-neuvas *m*, terre-neuvien *m.*

bankrupt¹ ['bæŋkrʌpt], *a. & s.* 1. (*a*) (Commerçant) failli (*m*). To go b., (i) faire faillite; (ii) (*of business*) *F:* sauter. To be b., être en faillite. Bankrupt's certificate, concordat *m. S.a.* UNDISCHARGED 1. (*b*) Fraudulent or negligent b., banqueroutier *m.* (*c*) *O:* B. of intelligence, dépourvu d'intelligence. 2. *F:* (Homme) criblé de dettes, sans ressources.

bankrupt², *v.tr.* Mettre (qn) en faillite.

bankruptcy ['bæŋkrəp(t)si], *s.* 1. (*a*) Faillite *f.* (*b*) Fraudulent b., banqueroute *f.* 2. *F:* Ruine *f.*

banksman, *pl.* **-men** ['bæŋksmən], *s.m. Min:* Receveur *m*; porion *m* de surface.

banner ['bænər], *s.* (*a*) Bannière *f*, étendard *m.* (*b*) *Ecc:* Bannière. (*c*) *U.S: Journ:* B. **headlines**, des titres flamboyants.

banneret ['bænəret], *s. Hist:* **1.** Banneret *m.* **2.** Knight b., chevalier banneret.

bannock ['bænək], *s.* (*In Scot.*) Pain plat et rond cuit sans levain.

banns [bænz], *s.pl.* Bans *m* (de mariage). **To put up, publish, the b.**, (faire) publier les bans. **To forbid the b.**, faire, mettre, opposition à un mariage.

banquet¹ ['bæŋkwit], *s.* Banquet *m*; dîner *m* de gala, d'apparat.

banquet². **1.** *v.tr.* Offrir un banquet, un dîner de gala, à (qn). **2.** *v.i. F:* Banqueter; faire festin.

banshee ['bæn'ʃi:], *s.* (*In Ireland and Scot.*) Dame blanche (dont les cris présagent la mort).

bant [bænt], *v.i. F:* Suivre un régime amaigrissant.

banting, *s.* Régime amaigrissant; cure *f* d'amaigrissement.

bantam ['bæntəm], *s.* Bantam *m*, coq *m*, poule *f*, (de) Bantam; coq nain. **'bantam-weight**, *s. Box:* Poids *m* coq.

banter¹ ['bæntər], *s.* (*a*) Badinage *m.* (*b*) Ironie *f*, raillerie *f*, persiflage *m.*

banter², *v.tr. & i.* (*a*) Badiner. (*b*) Gouailler, railler; (*ill-naturedly*) persifler. **bantering**, *a.* Railleur, -euse; goguenard. **-ly**, *adv.* Railleusement, d'un ton goguenard, gouailleur.

banterer ['bæntərər], *s.* Railleur, -euse, gouailleur, -euse; (*ill-natured*) persifleur, -euse.

Bantu ['bæn'tu:], *a. & s. Ethn:* Bantou, -oue.

banyan(-tree) ['bæniən], *s. Bot:* = BANIAN.

baobab(-tree) ['beiobæb], *s. Bot:* Baobab *m.*

baptism ['bæptizm], *s.* Baptême *m.* **To receive b.**, recevoir le baptême. **Certificate of b.**, extrait de baptême; extrait baptistaire.

baptismal [bæp'tizm(ə)l], *a.* (Registre) baptistaire; (nom) de baptême.

baptist ['bæptist], *s.* **1.** John the B., saint Jean-Baptiste. **2.** *Ecc:* Anabaptiste *mf.*

baptist(e)ry ['bæptistri], *s.* Baptistère *m.*

baptize [bæp'taiz], *v.tr.* **1.** Baptiser. **To be baptized**, recevoir le baptême. **2.** Baptiser, bénir (une cloche, un navire).

bar¹ [bɑ:r], *s.* **1.** (*a*) Barre *f* (de fer, de bois, de chocolat); barre, brique *f* (de savon); lingot *m* (d'or). B. **of a medal**, barrette *f* d'une médaille. B. **of a door**, bâcle *f* d'une porte; barre de porte. *Gym:* **Parallel bars**, barres parallèles. **Horizontal b.**, barre fixe. (*b*) *pl.* Barreaux *m* (d'une fenêtre, d'une grille, d'une cage). **The bars of the grate**, la grille du foyer. **To be behind the prison bars**, être sous les verrous. (*c*) *pl.* Barrettes (de souliers de dames). (*d*) *pl.* Barres (de la bouche d'un cheval). (*e*) (*In river, harbour*) Barre (de sable); traverse *f.* **To cross the b.**, passer, franchir, la barre. *S.a.* SAND-BAR. **2.** (*a*) Empêchement *m*, obstacle *m.* **To be a b. to sth.**, être un empêchement, faire obstacle, à qch. **The colour b.**, racisme *m*; ségrégation raciale. (*b*) *Jur:* Exception *f*; fin de non-recevoir. *S.a.* PLEA 1. **3.** *Jur:* (*a*) Barre (des accusés). **The prisoner at the b.**, l'accusé. **To appear at the b.**, paraître à la barre. (*b*) Barreau (des avocats). **To read for the b.**, faire son droit. **To be called, to come, go, to the b.**, être reçu, se faire inscrire, au barreau; être reçu avocat. **4.** (*a*) Bar *m*; (*in N. of Fr.*) estaminet *m. Rail: Th:* Buvette *f. S.a.* SNACK. (*b*) (*In public house*) Comptoir *m*, bar. **5.** (*a*) Barre, ligne *f*, trait *m.* (*b*) *Mus:* B.(-line), barre. **Double b.**, double barre; division *f.* (*c*) *Mus:* Mesure *f.* **6.** *Meteor: Meas:* Bar. **'bar-iron**, *s. Com:* Fer *m* en barres. **'bar-keeper**, *s.* **1.** Cabaretier *m.* **2.** (Toll)b.-k., péagier *m.* **bar-'lounge**, *s.* Salon *m* du bar. **'bar-soap**, *s.* Savon *m* en barres.

bar², *v.tr.* (**barred**) **1.** Barrer; bâcler (une porte); griller (une fenêtre). **To b. oneself in**, se barricader. **2.** (*a*) (*Obstruct*) Barrer (un chemin). **To b. s.o.'s way**, barrer la route à qn. (*b*) = DEBAR. **3.** (*a*) Défendre, prohiber, interdire (une action); exclure (un sujet de conversation). **To b. a motion**, s'opposer à une motion. (*b*) *F:* Ne pas supporter, ne pas

approuver (une personne, une habitude). (*c*) *Jur:* Opposer une fin de non-recevoir à (une action). **4.** Rayer (de lignes); barrer. **barred**, *a.* **1.** (*a*) Barré; muni d'une grille, de barreaux. B. **window**, fenêtre grillée. (*b*) *Mus:* **Barred C**, C barré. **2.** (Drap, etc.) rayé. **3.** (Port) obstrué par une barre de sable.

bar³, **barring**, *prep. F:* Excepté, sauf; à l'exception de. **Barring accidents**, sauf accident, à moins d'accident(s). B. **none**, sans exception.

bar⁴, *s. Ich:* Maigre *m.*

barb¹, [bɑ:b], *s.* **1.** (*a*) Barbillon *m* (d'un hameçon); barbelure *f* (d'une flèche). (*b*) *Engr: Metalw:* Barbe *f*, bavure *f* (de métal). **2.** *pl.* (*a*) *Ich: Vet:* Barbillons. *Bot:* Arêtes *f.* (*b*) Barbes (d'une plume).

barb², *v.tr.* Garnir de barbelures, de barbillons. **barbed**, *a.* **1.** *Bot:* Aristé; hameçonné. **2.** Barbelé. B. **wire**, (fil de fer) barbelé (*m*). *Mil:* B.**-wire entanglements**, les barbelés *m.*

barb³, *s.* Cheval *m* barbe; barbe *m.*

Barbados [bɑ:'beidouz, -os]. *Pr.n. Geog:* La Barbade.

Barbaresque ['bɑ:bə'resk], *a. Ethn:* Barbaresque; berbère.

barbarian [bɑ:'bɛəriən], *a. & s.* Barbare (*mf*).

barbaric [bɑ:'bærik], *a.* Barbare.

barbarism ['bɑ:bərizm], *s.* **1.** *Gram: Ling:* Barbarisme *m.* **2.** Barbarie *f.*

barbarity [bɑ:'bæriti], *s.* Barbarie *f*, cruauté *f.*

barbarize ['bɑ:bəraiz]. **1.** *v.tr.* Barbariser (un peuple, une langue). **2.** *v.i.* (*a*) Commettre des barbarismes (de langue). (*b*) Devenir barbare.

barbarous ['bɑ:bərəs], *a.* **1.** Barbare. **2.** Cruel, barbare, inhumain. **-ly**, *adv.* Cruellement.

barbarousness ['bɑ:bərəsnis], *s.* = BARBARITY.

Barbary ['bɑ:bəri]. *Pr.n. Geog:* La Barbarie; les États *m* barbaresques.

barbate ['bɑ:beit], *a.* **1.** *Bot:* Barbé, aristé. **2.** *Z:* Barbu.

barbecue¹ ['bɑ:bikju:], *s.* Barbecue *m.*

barbecue², *v.tr. Cu:* **1.** Rôtir un animal tout entier. **2.** Rôtir, griller de la viande en barbecue.

barbel ['bɑ:b(ə)l], *s.* **1.** *Ich:* Barbeau *m.* **2.** *pl.* Barbillons *m*, palpes *f*, cirres *m* (d'un poisson).

barber ['bɑ:bər], *s.* Barbier *m*, coiffeur *m.* **Barber's pole**, enseigne de barbier.

barbershop ['bɑ:bə'ʃop], *s. U.S:* Salon *m* de coiffure pour hommes.

barberry ['bɑ:beri], *s. Bot:* Épine-vinette *f.*

barbican ['bɑ:bikən], *s. Fort:* Barbacane *f.*

barbitone ['bɑ:bitoun], *s. Med:* Véronal *m.*

barbiturate [bɑ:'bitjureit], *s. Ch:* Barbiturate *m*, barbiturique *m.*

barbituric [bɑ:'bitjurik], *a. Ch:* B. **acid**, acide *m* barbiturique.

barcarol(l)e ['bɑ:kəroul], *s. Mus:* Barcarolle *f.*

Barcelona ['bɑ:si'lounə], *Pr.n. Geog:* Barcelone.

bard¹ [bɑ:d], *s.* **1.** (*a*) (*Celtic, esp. of Wales*) Barde *m.* (*b*) (*Of ancient Greece*) Aède *m.* **2.** *Lit:* Poète *m.*

bard², *s.* **1.** *Arm:* Barde *f* (de cheval d'armes). **2.** *Cu:* Barde (de lard).

bard³, *v.tr.* **1.** *Arm:* Barder (un cheval). **2.** *Cu:* Barder (une volaille).

bardic ['bɑ:dik], *a.* Concernant la poésie celtique ou les concours de poésie au Pays de Galles.

bare¹ ['bɛər], *a.* **1.** Nu; dénudé. B. **legs**, jambes nues. *F:* B. **as the back of my hand**, nu comme la main. B. **countryside**, pays nu, dénudé, pelé. **The trees are already bare**, les arbres sont déjà dépouillés. B. **cupboard, cupboard b. of food**, placard vide; buffet dégarni. **To lie, sleep, on the b. ground, on the b. boards**, coucher sur la dure. **To lay b.**, mettre à nu, exposer (une surface, son cœur); dévoiler (un secret, une fraude). B. **chest**, poitrine découverte. *El:* B. **wire**, fil dénudé. *Nau:* **To run, scud, under b. poles**, filer, courir, fuir, à sec (de toiles). *Cards:* **Ace b., king b.**, as sec, roi sec. **2.** **To earn a b. living**, gagner tout juste, à peine, de quoi vivre; gagner sa vie et rien de plus. *S.a.* NECESSITY 2. B. **majority**, faible majorité. **The b. thought frightens me**, cette seule pensée m'effraie. **His success is a b. possibility**, son succès est tout juste possible, est possible, sans plus. **A b. thank you**, un merci tout sec. **-ly**, *adv.* **1.** Room b. **furnished**, (i) pièce dont le mobilier se réduit à l'essentiel; (ii) pièce pauvrement meublée. 2. A peine, tout juste. I b. **know** him, c'est à peine si je le connais. He is b. **thirty,** c'est tout juste s'il a trente ans. **'bare-backed.** 1. *a.* A dos nu, le dos nu. **B.-b. horse,** cheval nu, à poil. 2. *adv.* = BAREBACK. **'bare-headed,** *a. & adv.* Nu-tête, (la) tête nue; découvert. **'bare-legged,** *a. & adv.* Nu-jambes, (les) jambes nues; aux jambes nues.

bare², *v.tr.* Mettre (qch.) à nu; découvrir (une plaie, etc.); se découvrir (la tête); déchausser (une dent, des racines, etc.).

bare³. *See* BEAR².

bareback ['bɛəbæk], *adv.* To ride b., monter (un cheval) à nu, à cru, à poil.

bareboned ['bɛə'bound], *a.* F: Maigre, décharné, squelettique.

barefaced ['bɛəfeist], *a.* 1. A visage imberbe. 2. (*a*) Sans masque. (*b*) F: (Mensonge, etc.) éhonté, cynique. -ly, *adv.* Effrontément.

barefacedness [bɛə'feisidnis], *s.* Effronterie *f*; cynisme *m*.

barefoot ['bɛəfut]. 1. *adv.* Nu-pieds; (à) pieds nus. 2. *a.* = BAREFOOTED.

barefooted ['bɛə'futid], *a.* Aux pieds nus; les pieds nus. *Ecc:* B. Carmelites, carmes déchaussés.

barege [bæ'reiʒ], *s. Tex:* Barège *m*.

bareness ['bɛənis], *s.* 1. Nudité *f*, dénuement *m.* 2. Pauvreté *f*, sécheresse *f* (de style).

barfly ['bɑ:flai], *s. U.S:* F: Pilier *m* de cabaret.

bargain¹ ['bɑ:gin], *s.* 1. Marché *m*, affaire *f.* To make a good b., faire une bonne affaire, un bon marché. To get the best of the b., avoir l'avantage (dans un marché). To **strike, drive,** a b. with s.o., conclure un marché avec qn. *S.a.* BEST¹ 1. A real b., une véritable occasion. Into the b., par-dessus le marché; par surcroît; en plus. It's a b.! c'est entendu! c'est convenu! 2. (*a*) B. sale, vente de soldes. B. **prices,** prix de solde. (*b*) (*Of article*) To be a b., être (à un prix) intéressant. **'bargain-counter,** *s. Com:* Rayon *m* des soldes.

bargain², *v.i.* (*a*) Entrer en négociations, négocier (with s.o., avec qn). To b. with s.o. for sth., traiter, faire marché, de qch. avec qn. F: I didn't b. for that, je ne m'attendais pas à cela. *F:* He got more than he **bargained** for, il a eu du fil à retordre. (*b*) (*Haggle*) To b. with s.o., marchander qn. To b. **over an article,** marchander un article. **bargaining,** *s.* Marchandage *m.* Collective b. = convention collective.

bargainer ['bɑ:ginər], *s.* Marchandeur, -euse.

barge¹ [bɑ:dʒ], *s.* (*a*) Chaland *m*, péniche *f*, barge *f.* Canal b., bélandre *f.* Motor b., chaland à moteur. (*b*) (*With sails*) Gabare *f.* (*c*) *Navy:* Canot *m.* Admiral's b., canot de l'amiral. (*d*) State b., barque *f* de cérémonie. **'barge-pole,** *s.* Gaffe *f.* F: I wouldn't touch it with a b.-p., je n'en veux à aucun prix. I wouldn't touch him with a b.-p., (i) il me dégoûte; (ii) je ne veux rien avoir à faire avec lui.

barge². 1. *v.tr. U.S:* Transporter (qch.) en péniche. 2. *v.i.* F: To b. **into, against,** s.o., venir se heurter contre qn; bousculer qn. To b. **in,** intervenir mal à propos.

bargee [bɑ:'dʒi:], *s.* (*a*) Chalandier *m.* (*b*) Gabarier *m.* (*c*) *F:* Batelier *m*, marinier *m.*

bargemaster ['bɑ:dʒmɑ:stər], *s.* Patron *m* de chaland ou de gabare.

baritone ['bæritoun], *s. Mus:* Baryton *m.*

barium ['bɛəriəm], *s. Ch:* Baryum *m. Med:* B. **meal,** bouillie barytée.

bark¹ [bɑ:k], *s.* 1. Écorce *f* (d'arbre). Inner b., liber *m.* To strip the b. off a tree, écorcer un arbre. **Peruvian b.,** quinquina *m.* 2. Tanner's b., tan *m.* **'bark pit,** *s. Tan:* Fosse *f* de tanneur; fosse à tan.

bark². *v.tr.* (*a*) Écorcer, décortiquer (un arbre). (*b*) *F:* To b. one's shins, s'écorcher, s'érafler, les tibias.

bark³, *s.* (*a*) Aboiement *m*, aboi *m.* To give a b., pousser un aboiement. His b. **is worse than his bite,** il aboie plus qu'il ne mord; il fait plus de bruit que de mal. (*b*) (*Of fox*) Glapissement *m.*

bark⁴, *v.i.* 1. (*a*) Aboyer (at, après, contre). To b. **up the wrong tree,** suivre une fausse piste; accuser qn à

tort. (*b*) (*Of fox*) Glapir. 2. Dire (qch.) d'un ton sec, cassant. 3. *F:* Tousser. **barking¹,** *a.* (Chien) aboyeur. **barking²,** *s.* (*a*) Aboiement *m.* (*b*) (*Of fox*) Glapissement *m.*

bark⁵, *s.* 1. *Nau:* Trois-mâts barque *m.* 2. *Poet:* Barque *f.*

barker ['bɑ:kər], *s.* 1. Aboyeur, -euse; bonimenteur *m.* 2. *P:* Pistolet *m* ou revolver *m.*

barley ['bɑ:li], *s.* Orge *f; but m. in:* hulled b., orge mondé, *and* pearl b., orge perlé. **'barley-sugar,** *s.* Sucre *m* d'orge. **'barley-water,** *s.* Tisane *f* d'orge.

barleycorn ['bɑ:likɔ:n], *s.* Grain *m* d'orge. *F:* **John B.,** le whisky.

barm [bɑ:m], *s.* Levure *f* (de bière).

barmaid ['bɑ:meid], *s.f.* Barmaid *f*, serveuse *f.*

barman, -men ['bɑ:mən], *s.m.* Garçon de comptoir (d'un débit de boisson); barman *m*, *pl.* barmen.

barmy ['bɑ:mi], *a.* 1. Écumeux, -euse. 2. *F:* = BALMY 3.

barn [bɑ:n], *s.* (*a*) Grange *f.* (*b*) *U.S:* Étable *f*, écurie *f.* **barn-'door,** *s.* Porte *f* de grange. **'B.-d. fowls,** volaille de basse-cour. *F:* He couldn't hit a b.-d., il manquerait un éléphant dans un tunnel. **barn-'floor,** *s.* Aire *f* (de grange). **'barn-owl,** *s. Orn:* Effraie *f.* **'barn-stormer,** *s. F:* Cabotin *m.* **'barn-yard,** *s.* Basse-cour *f.*

Barnabite ['bɑ:nəbait], *s. Ecc:* Barnabite *m.*

barnacle ['bɑ:nəkl], *s.* 1. *Orn:* B. (goose), bernacle *f*, bernache *f*; oie marine. 2. (*a*) *Crust:* Stalked b., ship b., bernache, bernacle; anatife *m*, balane *m.* (*b*) *F:* (*pers.*) Crampon *m.*

barogram ['bærogræm], *s.* Barogramme *m.*

barograph ['bærogræf], *s.* Barographe *m.*

barometer [bə'rɒmitər], *s.* Baromètre *m.* **Recording b.,** baromètre enregistreur. The b. **points to rain, to set fair,** le baromètre est à la pluie, au beau fixe. *S.a.* ANEROID.

barometric(al) ['bærə'metrik(əl)], *a.* Barométrique.

baron ['bærən], *s.* 1. (*a*) Baron *m.* (*b*) *U.S:* F: Grand manitou (industriel). 2. B. **of beef,** double aloyau *m*; selle *f* de bœuf.

baronage ['bærənidʒ], *s.* 1. Baronnage *m.* 2. Annuaire *m* de la noblesse.

baroness ['bærənis], *s.f.* Baronne.

baronet ['bærənit], *s.m.* Baronnet.

baronetage ['bærənitidʒ], *s.* 1. Les baronnets *m.* 2. Annuaire *m* des baronnets.

baronetcy ['bærənitsi], *s.* Dignité *f* de baronnet. To be given a b., être élevé au rang de baronnet.

baronial [bə'rouniəl], *a.* Baronnial. B. **hall,** demeure seigneuriale.

barony ['bærəni], *s.* 1. Baronnie *f.* 2. (*In Scot.*) Grande propriété terrienne.

baroque [bə'rɒk], *a. & s. Art:* Baroque (*m*).

baroscope ['bærəskoup], *s. Ph:* Baroscope *m.*

barque [bɑ:k], *s. Nau:* = BARK⁵ 1.

barrack¹ ['bærək], *s.* 1. (*a*) *Mil:* (*Usu. in pl.*) Caserne *f*; (*of cavalry*) quartier *m.* To **live in barracks,** (i) (*of officers*) loger, vivre, à la caserne, au quartier; (ii) (*of the soldiers*) être casernés. **Life in barracks,** la vie de caserne. **Confinement to barracks,** *F:* C.B., consigne au quartier. To **be confined to barracks,** être consigné. (*b*) **Naval barracks,** dépôt *m* des équipages de la flotte. 2. *Pej: F:* Grand bâtiment qui ressemble à une caserne; *F:* caserne. **'barrack room,** *s.* Chambrée *f.* **B.-r. language,** expressions de caserne, de chambrée. **B.-r. joke,** plaisanterie *f* de corps-de-garde. **barrack 'square,** *s.* Cour *f* du quartier.

barrack², *v.tr.* 1. *Mil:* Caserner (des troupes). 2. *P:* Conspuer, huer (une équipe de joueurs). *Abs.* Faire du chahut; chahuter.

barracuda [ˌbærə'kju:də], *s. Ich:* Barracuda *m.*

barrage ['bæra:ʒ], *s.* 1. *Hyd.E:* Barrage *m* (d'un fleuve). 2. *Mil:* (*a*) (*also* [bə'rɑ:ʒ]) Tir *m* de barrage; tir sur zone. (*b*) B. **balloon,** ballon *m* de protection.

barratry ['bærətri], *s. Nau:* Baraterie *f.*

barrel¹ ['bærəl], *s.* 1. (*a*) Tonneau *m*, barrique *f*, futaille *f*, fût *m* (de vin, etc.); caque *f*, baril *m* (de) harengs. (*b*) Biscuit b., seau *m* à biscuits. 2. (*a*) Cylindre *m*; partie *f* cylindrique; fût; caisse *f* (d'un tambour); tuyau *m* (de plume d'oiseau); canon *m*

((i) de fusil, (ii) de seringue, (iii) de serrure, de clef); corps m, barillet m (de pompe); cylindre, barillet (de serrure); fusée f, mèche f, tambour m, cloche f (de cabestan, de treuil). *Clockm:* Barillet, boîte f à ressort (de montre). *Mus:* Cylindre noté (d'un orgue mécanique). *S.a.* LOCK² 3. (*b*) *Anat:* B. of the ear, caisse du tympan. **barrel-'bellied**, *a.* Ventru, pansu. **barrel-'head**, *s.* Fond m de tonneau. **'barrel-organ**, *s. Mus:* (*a*) Orgue m mécanique. (*b*) (*Of street-player*) (i) Orgue de Barbarie; (ii) piano m mécanique (à cylindre). **'barrel-roll**, *s. Av:* Tonneau, m. **'barrel-roof**, *s.* Toit cintré. **'barrel-stand**, *s.* Porte-fût(s) m inv; chantier m. **'barrel-vault**, *s.* Voûte f en berceau.
barrel², *v.tr.* (**barrelled**) Mettre (qch.) en fût; entonner, enfutailler (du vin); (en)caquer, embariller (des harengs). **barrelled**, *a.* 1. (Vin m) en tonneau(x), en fûts; (harengs m) en caque. 2. En forme de tonneau; bombé. **barrelling**, *s.* Enfûtage m; entonnage m; encaquement m.
barren ['bærən], *a.* 1. *a.* (*a*) Stérile, improductif; (d'un animal) bréhaigne; (terrain) aride; infertile. (*b*) **B. subject**, sujet maigre, ingrat, aride. **Mind b. of ideas**, esprit peu fertile en idées. 2. *s.* Lande f; pays nus. **-ly**, *adv.* Stérilement; sans résultats.
barrenness ['bærənnis], *s.* Stérilité f.
barricade¹ ['bærikeid], *s.* Barricade f.
barricade², *v.tr.* Barricader.
barrier ['bæriər], *s.* Barrière f. *Rail:* **Ticket b.**, barrière. **B. to progress**, obstacle m au progrès. *Geog:* **The Great B. Reef**, la Grande Barrière. *S.a.* SOUND¹ (*a*).
barring ['bɑːriŋ], *prep. See* BAR².
barrister ['bæristər], *s. Jur:* **B.-at-law**, avocat m. **Consulting b.**, avocat consultant, avocat conseil.
barrow¹ ['bærou], *s.* 1. (Wheel-)b., brouette f. 2. = HAND-BARROW. 3. (*a*) (*With two wheels*) **Hawker's b.**, baladeuse f; voiture f à bras. (*b*) *Rail:* **Luggage-b.**, diable m. **'barrow-boy**, *s.* Marchand m des quatre-saisons.
barrow², *s. Archeol:* Tumulus m; tertre m (funéraire); tombeau m. **Long b.**, tombeau de forme allongée. **Round b.**, tombeau de forme arrondie.
barrowful ['bærouful], *s.* Brouettée f.
bartender ['bɑːtendər], *s. U.S:* = BARMAN.
barter¹ ['bɑːtər], *s.* Échange m; troc m.
barter², *v.tr.* **To b. sth. for sth.**, échanger, troquer, qch. contre qch. **barter away**, *v.tr. Pej:* Vendre, faire traffic de (son honneur, etc.).
barterer ['bɑːtərər], *s.* Troqueur, -euse.
Bartholomew [bɑː'θɔləmjuː]. *Pr.n.m.* Barthélemy. *Hist:* **The Massacre of St B.**, le Massacre de la Saint-Barthélemy.
barye ['bɛəri], *s. Ph.Meas:* Barye f.
baryta [bə'raitə], *s. Ch:* Baryte f; oxyde m de baryum.
barytes [bə'raitiːz], *s. Miner:* Barytine f.
barytone ['bæritoun]. *Mus:* (*a*) *s.* Baryton m. (*b*) *a.* **B. voice**, voix de baryton.
basal ['beisl], *a.* Fondamental, -a   *Cryst:* (Clivage) basique.
basalt ['bæsɔlt], *s.* Basalte m.
basaltic [bə'sɔːltik], *a.* Basaltique.
bascule ['bæskjuːl], *s. Civ.E:* Bascule f. *Esp.* **B.-bridge**, pont m à bascule.
base¹ [beis], *s.* 1. (*a*) Base f (de triangle, etc.). **Aviation b.**, base d'aviation. **Submarine b.**, nid m de sous-marins. *S.a.* NAVAL, PRISONER 3, ROCKET². (*b*) *Mth:* Base (logarithmique, d'un système de numération). (*v*) *Ch:* Base (d'un sel). 2. (*a*) Partie inférieure; fondement m; base; *Arch: Const:* soubassement m; (*of apparatus*) socle m, pied m, embase f. *El:* **Insulating b.**, socle isolant. *Phot: Cin:* **B. of the film**, support m du film, de l'émulsion. (*b*) *Her:* Pied (de l'écu). 3. (Metal) b. (*of sporting cartridge, electric lamp*), culot m. *S.a.* WHEELBASE. **'base-line**, *s.* 1. (*a*) *Surv:* Base f. (*b*) *Mch:* Ligne f zéro (du diagramme). (*c*) *Ten:* Ligne de fond. 2. *Art:* Ligne de fuite.
base², *v.tr.* Baser, fonder (on, sur). **To b. oneself on sth.**, se fonder, se baser, sur qch. **To b. taxation on income**, asseoir l'impôt sur le revenu. *Av:* **A British-based U.S. aircraft**, un avion américain basé en Grande-Bretagne.

base³, *a.* (*a*) Bas, vil. **B. motive**, motif bas, indigne. **B. action**, action ignoble, lâche. (*b*) (*Of little value*) **B. metals**, métaux vils, basses étoffes f. (*c*) **B. coin(age)**, (i) monnaie de mauvais aloi; (ii) fausse monnaie. **-ly**, *adv.* Bassement, vilement. **'base-born**, *a.* 1. De basse extraction, de basse naissance. 2. Bâtard.
baseball ['beisbɔl], *s. U.S: Sp:* Base-ball m.
Basel ['bɑːzl]. *Pr.n. Geog:* Bâle.
baseless ['beislis], *a.* Sans base, sans fondement; (critique) qui manque de fondement. **B. charge**, accusation f sans fond.
basement ['beismənt], *s.* 1. Soubassement m (d'une construction); allège f (d'une fenêtre). 2. Sous-sol m. **B. flat**, sous-sol.
baseness ['beisnis], *s.* Bassesse f, abjection f. **B. of birth**, (i) bassesse de naissance; (ii) illégitimité f.
bash¹ [bæʃ], *s. F:* (*a*) Coup m, enfoncement m. **The tea-pot has had a b.**, la théière est bosselée. *F:* **To have a b. at sth.**, s'attaquer à, s'essayer à, qch., *F:* tenter le coup. (*b*) Coup (sur la figure); coup de poing violent; *P:* gnon m.
bash², *v.tr. F:* **To b. one's head**, se cogner la tête. **To b. (in) a hat**, aplatir, cabosser, un chapeau (d'un coup de poing). **To b. in a box**, défoncer une boîte. **To b. s.o. about**, houspiller, maltraiter qn. **He bashed him on the head**, il l'assomma. **bashing**, *s. F: Mil: etc:* **To take, get, a b.**, prendre quelque chose.
Bashan ['beiʃæn]. *Pr.n. B:* Basan.
basher ['bæʃər], *s. F:* Cogneur m, pugiliste m.
bashful ['bæʃf(u)l], *a.* (*a*) Timide. **B. lover**, amoureux transi. (*b*) Modeste, pudique. **-fully**, *adv.* (*a*) Timidement. (*b*) Pudiquement.
bashfulness ['bæʃf(u)lnis], *s.* Timidité f; fausse honte.
basic ['beisik], *a.* 1. (Principe, etc.) fondamental. **B. pay**, salaire m de base. *Pol. Ec:* **B. commodity**, denrée f témoin. *Ling:* **B. vocabulary**, vocabulaire m de base. **B. English**, l'anglais de base. 2. (*a*) *Ch: Geol:* Basique. **B. slag**, scorie f basique. (*b*) *Ch:* Sous-. **B. salt**, sous-sel m. **B. nitrate**, sous-nitrate m. **-ally**, *adv.* Fondamentalement; à la base.
basicity [bei'sisiti], *s. Ch: Metall:* Basicité f.
basil¹ ['bæzl], *s. Bot:* Basilic m.
basil², *s. Leath:* Basane f.
basilica [bə'silikə], *s.* Basilique f.
basilicon [bə'zilikən], *s.* Basilicon f, basilicum f.
basilisk ['bæzilisk], *s. Myth: Rept:* Basilic m.
basin ['beisn], *s.* 1. (*a*) Bassin m; (*for soup, etc.*) écuelle f, bol m; (*for milk*) jatte f. **B. of a fountain**, vasque f, coupe f, d'une fontaine. *S.a.* SUGAR-BASIN. (*b*) (Wash-hand-)b., (i) cuvette f; (ii) *Plumbing:* lavabo m. 2. *Geog:* Bassin (d'un fleuve). 3. (*a*) *Geog:* Port naturel; rade fermée. (*b*) *Nau:* Bassin. (*c*) (*In canal, river*) Garage m.
basinful ['beisnful], *s.* 1. Plein bol, écuellée f (de soupe, etc.). 2. Pleine cuvette (d'eau). 3. *P:* **To have a b.**, en avoir marre; en avoir tout son saoul.
basis, *pl.* **bases** ['beisis, -iːz], *s.* Base f (de négociations, etc.); fondement m (d'une opinion, etc.). **B. of a tax**, assiette f d'un impôt.
bask [bɑːsk], *v.i.* **To b. in the sun**, se chauffer (au soleil); prendre le soleil, *F:* faire le lézard.
basket ['bɑːskit], *s.* 1. (*Without a handle*) Corbeille f; (*with a handle*) panier m; (*carried in front*) éventaire m; (*carried on the back*) hotte f; (*for coal, etc.*) banne f, manne f; (*small*) banneau m, bannette f. **Laundry b.**, corbeille à linge. **Linen-b.**, panier à linge. *S.a.* WORK-BASKET. **B. handle**, anse f de panier. *Cu:* **Frying b.**, panier m à friture. 2. *Ent:* Pollen b. (*of bee*), corbeille. **'basket-ball**, *s. Games:* Basket-ball m, *F:* basket m. **B.-b. player**, basketeur, -euse. **'basket-chair**, *s.* Chaise f en osier. **'basket-furniture**, *s. Coll:* Meubles m en rotin. **'basket-maker**, *s.* Vannier m. **'basket-work**, *s.* Vannerie f.
basketful ['bɑːskitful], *s.* Plein panier; panerée f; hottée f.
Basle [bɑːl]. *Pr.n. Geog:* Bâle f.
Basque [bæsk]. 1. *a. & s. Ethn: etc:* Basque (mf). *a.* Basquais. *s.f.* Basquaise. 2. *s. Cost:* Basque f.
bas-relief ['bæsriliːf, 'bɑːri-], *s.* Bas-relief m.
bass¹ [bæs], *s. Ich:* 1. Perche commune. 2. Bar(s) m.

bass² [bæs], *s.* 1. (*a*) *Bot:* Liber *m.* (*b*) Tille *f*, teille *f*, filasse *f.* 2. (*a*) B.(-mat), paillasson *m* en fibre, en tille, etc. (*b*) (*Basket*) (Workman's) b., cabas *m.* ʹbass-wood, *s. Bot: Com:* Tilleul *m* d'Amérique.

bass³ [beis], *a. & s. Mus:* Basse *f.* 1. (*a*) B. voice, voix de basse. Deep b., basse profonde. *S.a.* CLEF. (*b*) (*In brass bands*) E-flat b., B-flat b., contrebasse *f* en mi bémol, en si bémol. *S.a.* DOUBLE-BASS, DRUM¹ 1, VIOL. 2. Figured b., basse chiffrée.

basset [ʹbæsit], *s.* 1. (Chien) basset *m.* 2. B. horn, cor de basset.

bassinet(te) [ʹbæsiʹnet], *s.* 1. Berceau *m*; bercelonnette *f* ou moïse *m.* 2. Voiture *f* d'enfant.

bassobn [bəʹsuːn], *s.* Basson *m.* Double b., contrebasson *m.*

bassoonist [bəʹsuːnist], *s. Mus:* Bassoniste *m.*

bast [bæst], *s.* = BASS² 1.

bastard [ʹbæstəd, ʹbɑː-], 1. *s.* (*a*) Bâtard, -arde; *Jur:* enfant naturel. (*b*) *P:* Salaud *m. V:* That's a b., ça c'est couille. 2. *a.* Faux, *f* fausse; (*of paper, book*) bâtard.

bastardize [ʹbæstədaiz, ʹbɑː-], *v.tr.* 1. Déclarer (un enfant) bâtard. 2. Abâtardir.

bastardy [ʹbæstədi, ʹbɑː-], *s.* Bâtardise *f. Jur:* B. case, action en désaveu de paternité.

baste¹ [beist], *v.tr. Needlew:* Bâtir, faufiler, baguer (un corsage, etc.). **basting¹,** *s.* Bâti *m*, faufilure *f.* B. thread, bâti *m*, faufil *m.*

baste², *v.tr.* 1. *Cu:* Arroser (de sa graisse) (un rôti, une volaille). 2. *F:* Bâtonner (qn). **basting²,** *s.* 1. Arrosement *m*, arrosage *m* (d'un rôti). 2. *F:* Bastonnade *f*; rossée *f.*

bastion [ʹbæstiən], *s. Fort:* Bastion *m.*

bat¹ [bæt], *s. Z:* Chauve-souris *f*, *pl.* chauves-souris. Long-eared b., oreillard *m. S.a.* BLIND¹ 1. *F:* To have bats in the belfry, to be bats, avoir une araignée au plafond; être toqué.

bat², *s.* 1. Batte *f* (de cricket, de base-ball). *Cr:* To carry one's b., rester au guichet jusqu'à la fin de la partie. *F:* To do sth. off one's own b., faire qch. de sa propre initiative, de son (propre) chef. 2. Palette *f*, raquette *f* (de ping-pong); battoir *m* (de blanchisseuse). 3. (Harlequin's) b., batte.

bat³, *v.i.* (**batted**) Manier la batte (au cricket, au base-ball). *Cr:* Être au guichet.

bat⁴, *s.* 1. *F:* Pas *m*, allure *f.* He went off at the hell of a b., il est parti à toute allure. 2. *P:* Noce, *f* bombe *f.* He's on the b., il fait la noce.

bat⁵, *v.tr. F:* He never batted an eyelid, il n'a pas sourcillé, bronché.

batata [bəʹtɑːtə], *s. Hort:* Patate *f.*

batch¹ [bætʃ], *s.* 1. Fournée *f* (de pain). B. of prisoners, fournée de prisonniers. A whole b. of letters, tout un paquet de lettres. 2. Lot *m* (de marchandises). 3. Gâchée *f* (de ciment, de béton).

batch², *v.tr. Civ.E:* Mesurer, doser (les agrégats du béton).

bate [beit], *v.tr. A:* Réduire, diminuer, retrancher. (*Still used in*) To speak with bated breath, parler en baissant la voix, dans un souffle.

bath¹, *pl.* **baths** [bɑːθ, bɑːðz], *s.* 1. Bain *m.* To take, have, a b., prendre un bain. To give a child a b., baigner un enfant. *U.S:* Bain (de mer), baignade *f* (= *Eng.* bathe). Public baths, (i) établissement *m* de bains; (ii) (*swimming*) piscine *f.* Turkish baths, hammam *m.* The Order of the B., l'Ordre du Bain. *S.a.* FOOT-BATH, SHOWER-BATH, SWIMMING-BATH. 2. (*a*) Baignoire *f.* (*b*) *Phot: etc:* Cuvette *f.* 3. (*Liquid*) Acid, alkaline, b., bain acide, alcalin. *Phot:* Alum b., hardening b., bain aluné. ʹbath attendant, *s.* Baigneur, -euse. ʹbath-heater, *s.* Chauffe-bain *m.* ʹbath-mat, *s.* Descente *f* de bain. ʹbath-room, *s.* Salle *f* de bain(s). ʹbath salts, *spl.* Sels *m* pour le bain. ʹbath-sheet, *s.* Drap *m* de bain. ʹbath-towel, *s.* Serviette *f* de bain. ʹbath-tub, *s.* Baignoire *f.* ʹbath-wrap, *s.* Peignoir *m* de bain.

bath², 1. *v.tr.* Baigner, donner un bain à (qn). 2. *v.i. & pr.* Prendre un bain; se baigner.

Bath³, *Pr.n. Geog:* Bath. ʹBath bun, *s.* 'Bun' (*q.v.*) saupoudré de sucre. ʹBath-ʹchair, *s.* Voiture *f* de malade; fauteuil roulant.

bathe¹ [beiθ], *s.* Bain *m* (de rivière, en mer); baignade *f.*

bathe². 1. *v.tr.* (*a*) Baigner. To b. one's face, se baigner la figure. Face bathed in tears, visage baigné, arrosé, de larmes. (*b*) Laver, lotionner (une plaie). (*c*) The seas that b. England, les mers qui baignent l'Angleterre. 2. *v.i.* Se baigner. **bathing** [ʹbeiðiŋ], *s.* 1. Bains *mpl* (de mer, de rivière); baignades *fpl.* Sea b., bains de mer. *S.a.* SUN-BATHING. 2. Bassinage *m*, lotion *f* (d'une plaie, etc.). ʹbathing-cap, *s.* Bonnet *m* de bain. ʹbathing-costume, -dress, *s.* Costume *m* de bain(s); maillot *m* (de bain). ʹbathing-hut, *s.* Cabine *f* de bains (de plage). ʹbathing-place, *s.* Baignade *f*; endroit *m* où l'on peut se baigner. ʹbathing-resort, *s.* Station *f* balnéaire; *F:* plage *f.* ʹbathing-trunks, *s.* Caleçon *m* de bain. ʹbathing-wrap, *s.* Peignoir *m* de bain.

bather [ʹbeiðər], *s.* Baigneur, -euse.

bathometer [bəʹθɔmitər], *s. Oc:* Bathomètre, *m*, bathymètre *m.*

bathos [ʹbeiθɔs], *s.* L'ampoulé *m* (du style); enflure *f*; affectation *f* ridicule du sublime.

bathrobe [bɑːθroub], *s.* (i) = BATH-WRAP. (ii) *U.S:* Robe *f* de chambre.

Bathsheba [ʹbæθʃibə, bæθʹʃiːbə], *Pr.n.f. B.Hist:* Bethsabée.

bathymeter [bæʹθimiːtər], *s. Oc:* = BATHOMETER.

bathymetry [bəʹθimitri] *s. Oc:* Bathymétrie *f.*

bathyscaph [ʹbæθiskæf], *s.* Bathyscaphe *m.*

bathysphere [ʹbæθisfiər], *s.* Bathysphère *f.*

batiste [bæʹtiːst], *s. Tex:* Batiste *f.*

batman, *pl.* **-men** [ʹbætmən], *s. Mil: O:* Ordonnance *f* or *m.*

baton [ʹbæt(ə)n], *s.* 1. Bâton *m.* Conductor's b., bâton de chef d'orchestre. Field-marshal's b., bâton de maréchal. 2. = TRUNCHEON.

batrachian [bəʹtreikiən], *a. & s.* Batracien (*m*).

batsman, *pl.* **-men** [ʹbætsmən], *s.m. Cr:* Batteur.

battalion [bəʹtæljən], *s. Mil:* Bataillon *m.*

batten¹ [ʹbætn], *s.* 1. (*a*) (i) (*Bead or moulding*) Couvrejoint *m*; baguette *f*; (ii) latte *f*; liteau *m.* (*b*) *Nau:* Barre *f*, latte, tringle *f.* 2. *Th:* The battens, les herses *f* (d'éclairage). 3. Planche *f* (de parquet).

batten², *v.tr.* (*a*) *Carp:* Latter, voliger. (*b*) *Nau:* To b. down the hatches, (i) mettre les panneaux en place; (ii) condamner les panneaux, les descentes; assujettir, coincer, les panneaux. (*c*) *Const:* Planchéier (un parquet).

batten³, *v.i. Lit:* S'engraisser, se bourrer, se repaître (on, de). To b. on others, s'enrichir aux dépens des autres.

batter¹ [ʹbætər], *s.* 1. *Cu:* Pâte *f* lisse; pâte à frire. 2. *Typ:* (*a*) Écrasement *m* (des caractères). (*b*) Caractère écrasé.

batter². 1. *v.tr.* (*a*) Battre. *Artil:* Battre en brèche, canonner (une ville). (*b*) Bossuer (de la vaisselle d'argent, etc.). 2. *v.i.* To b. at the door, frapper avec violence à la porte. **batter about,** *v.tr.* Maltraiter (qn); rouer (qn) de coups. **batter down,** *v.tr.* Abattre, démolir. **batter in,** *v.tr.* Enfoncer (une porte, etc.); défoncer (le crâne à qn). **battered,** *a.* Délabré, bossué. Old b. hat, vieux chapeau cabossé. B. face, visage meurtri. **battering,** *s.* Action *f* de battre en brèche, de démolir. ʹbattering-ram, *s. Mil: A:* Bélier *m.*

batter³, *s. Civ.E:* (*a*) Fruit *m* (d'un mur, etc.). (*b*) B. of an embankment, talus *m* d'un remblai.

batter⁴. 1. *v.tr. Civ.E:* Donner du fruit à (une muraille); taluter (un remblai). 2. *v.i.* (*Of wall*) Avoir du fruit; (*of revetment, etc.*) aller en talus.

battery [ʹbætəri], *s.* 1. *Jur:* (*a*) Rixe *f.* (*b*) Voie *f* de fait. *S.a.* ASSAULT¹ 2. 2. *Artil:* Batterie *f.* Horse b., batterie à cheval, batterie volante. *A:* B. fire, tir par salves. 3. (*a*) Batterie (de fours à coke, de chaudières, etc.). (*b*) *Phot:* B. of lenses, trousse *f* d'objectifs. (*c*) *El:* Pile *f*, batterie. *El.E:* Booster b., batterie de renfort. (*d*) *El:* (Storage-)b., accumulateur *m*, *F:* accu *m.* (*e*) *Husb:* Éleveuse *f* (à poulets), batterie.

battle¹ [ʹbætl], *s.* Bataille *f*, combat *m.* Pitched b., bataille rangée. Army drawn up in b. array, in b. order, armée rangée en bataille, en ordre de bataille. *S.a.* ORDER¹ 3. To fight a b., livrer une bataille, un combat. To give, offer, b., donner, livrer, bataille; engager le combat. To win a b., gagner une bataille;

remporter une victoire. **Killed in b.**, tué à l'ennemi. *Lit:* To do b. for, against, s.o., livrer bataille pour qn; livrer bataille à, contre, qn. To join b. with s.o., entrer en lutte avec qn. That's half the b., c'est bataille à moitié gagnée. To fight s.o.'s battles, prendre le parti de qn; livrer bataille pour qn. **B. royal**, bataille en règle; mêlée générale. **'battle-axe**, *s.* Hache *f* d'armes. *F:* What a b.-a.! Quelle virago! **'battle-cruiser**, *s. Nau: O:* Croiseur *m* de combat, de bataille. **'battle-cry**, *s.* Cri *m* de guerre. **'battle-dress**, *s. Mil:* Tenue *f* de campagne. **'battle-field**, *s.* Champ *m* de bataille.

battle², *v.i.* Se battre, lutter, rivaliser *(with s.o. for sth.*, avec qn pour qch.). To b. with, against, public opinion, combattre l'opinion. To b. against the wind, lutter contre le vent.

battledore ['bætldɔːr], *s.* **1.** (*a*) *Laund: A:* Battoir *m*. (*b*) *Bak:* Pelle *f* à enfourner. **2.** *Sp:* Raquette *f* (de jeu de volant). To play at b. and shuttlecock, jouer au volant.

battlemented ['bætlməntid], *a.* Crénelé.

battlements ['bætlmənts], *s.pl.* (*a*) Créneaux *m.* (*b*) Parapet *m*, rempart *m*.

battleship ['bætlʃip], *s. O:* Cuirassé *m* (de ligne).

battlewagon ['bætlwægən], *s. Mil: etc: F:* Char *m* ou véhicule blindé.

battleworthy ['bætlwəːði], *a.* Militairement fort.

battue [bæ'tuː], *s.* **1.** *Ven:* Battue *f.* **2.** *F:* Massacre *m* en masse.

batty ['bæti], *a. P:* Toqué; dingo *inv*; cinglé.

bauble [bɔːbl], *s.* **1.** Jester's b., marotte *f.* **2.** (*Worthless thing*) Babiole *f.*

baulk¹,² [bɔːk], *s. & v.* = BALK¹,².

bauxite ['bɔːksait], *s. Miner:* Bauxite *f.*

Bavaria [bə'vɛəriə], *Pr.n. Geog:* La Bavière.

Bavarian [bə'vɛəriən], *a. & s. Geog:* Bavarois, -oise. *Cu:* **B. cream**, bavaroise *f.*

bawd [bɔːd], *s.f. A:* (*a*) Procureuse, proxénète, entremetteuse. (*b*) Propriétaire *f* d'une maison close; *P:* maquerelle *f.* (*c*) Poissarde *f.*

bawdiness ['bɔːdinis], *s.* Obscénité *f.*

bawdy ['bɔːdi], *a.* Obscène, impudique. **B. talk**, propos orduriers.

bawl [bɔːl], *v.tr. & i.* (*a*) Brailler; crier à tue-tête; *F:* beugler (**at s.o.**, contre qn). To b. out abuse, brailler, hurler, des injures. (*b*) To b. for help, crier au secours.

bay¹ [bei], *s. Bot:* Sweet b., b. laurel, laurier commun. *Cu:* **B. leaf**, feuille *f* de laurier. **B.-tree**, laurier. **B. wreath**, bays, couronne *f* de laurier(s)

bay², *s. Geog:* Baie *f*; (*if small*) anse *f.* **Hudson B.**, la Baie d'Hudson. **The B. of Biscay**, le Golfe de Gascogne.

bay³, *s.* **1.** (*Of bridge, roof, etc.*) Travée *f.* **2.** (*a*) Enfoncement *m.* (*Space for door, etc.*) Baie *f. S.a.* SICK-BAY. (*b*) *Ind:* Hall *m* (d'usine). (*c*) **Parking b.**, place *f* de stationnement (à un parcomètre). **Loading b.**, quai *m* de chargement. **bay-'window**, *s.* Fenêtre *f* en baie, en saillie; baie *f.*

bay⁴, *s.* Aboi *m*, aboiement *m* (d'un chien de chasse). To bring a stag to b., mettre un cerf aux abois; acculer un cerf. To be at b., être aux abois.

bay⁵, *v.i.* (*a*) (*Of hound*) Aboyer; donner de la voix. (*b*) To b. (**at**) the moon, hurler, aboyer, à la lune. **baying**, *s.* Aboiement *m.*

bay⁶, *a. & s.* (Cheval) bai (*m*). **Light b.**, bai châtain; (cheval) isabelle (*m*).

bayonet¹ ['beiənit], *s. Mil:* Baïonnette *f.* To fix bayonets, mettre (la) baïonnette au canon. **B. charge**, charge à la baïonnette. **'bayonet-frog**, *s.* Portebaïonnette *m inv.* **'bayonet-joint**, *s.* joint *m* en baïonnette. **B.-j. base, socket**, culot, douille, à baïonnette (de lampe électrique).

bayonet², *v.tr.* (bayoneted) Percer (qn) d'un coup de baïonnette, *F:* passer (qn) à la baïonnette.

bay-salt ['beisɔːlt], *s.* Sel gris, sel marin; gros sel.

bazaar [bə'zɑːr], *s.* **1.** (*a*) Bazar *m* (oriental). (*b*) Bazar; magasin *m* à bon marché. **2.** Vente *f* de charité.

bazooka [bə'zuːkə], *s. Artil:* Bazooka *m.*

be [stressed biː: unstressed bi(ː)], *v.i.* (*pr. ind.* am, art, is, *pl.* are; *past ind.* was, wast, was, *pl.* were; *pr.sub.* be; *past sub.* were, wert; *pr. p.* being, *p.p.*

been; *imp.* be) Être. **1.** (*a*) Mary is pretty, Marie est jolie. The weather was fine, le temps était beau. Seeing is believing, voir c'est croire. Yours, his, is a fine house, c'est une belle maison que la vôtre, que la sienne. Isn't he lucky? n'est-ce pas qu'il a de la chance? *P:* He's one of them, il en est. (*b*) His father is a doctor, son père est médecin. He is an Englishman, il est Anglais, c'est un Anglais. If I were you, à votre place; si j'étais (que) de vous. (*c*) Unity is strength, l'union fait la force. Three and two are five, trois et deux font cinq. You would be as well to . . ., vous feriez (aussi) bien de. . . . **2.** (*a*) The books are on the table, les livres sont, se trouvent, sur la table. He was a long time reaching the shore, il mit longtemps à gagner le rivage. Don't be long, ne tardez pas (à revenir). To be in danger, se trouver en danger. I was at the meeting, j'ai été, j'ai assisté, à la réunion. I don't know where I am, (i) je ne sais pas où je suis; (ii) *F:* je suis tout désorienté; je ne sais pas où j'en suis. Here I am, me voici. So you are back again, vous voilà donc de retour. (*b*) (*Of health*) How are you? comment allez-vous? comment vous portez-vous? I am better, je vais mieux, je me trouve mieux; je me sens mieux. (*c*) How much is that? combien cela coûte-t-il? How much is that in all? combien cela fait-il? How far is it to London? combien y a-t-il d'ici à Londres? It is a mile from here, c'est à un mille (d'ici). (*d*) (*Time*) When is the concert? quand le concert aura-t-il lieu? Christmas is on a Sunday this year, Noël tombe un dimanche cette année. To-morrow is Friday, c'est demain vendredi. **3.** (*a*) To be (= *feel*) cold, afraid, etc., avoir froid, peur, etc. *S.a.* AFRAID, ASHAMED, COLD, *etc.* My hands are cold, j'ai froid aux mains. How cold your hands are! comme vous avez les mains froides! (*b*) To be twenty (years old), avoir vingt ans, être âgé de vingt ans. The wall is six foot high, le mur a six pieds de haut, est haut de six pieds. **4.** (*Exist, occur, remain*) (*a*) To be or not to be, être, ou ne pas être. The time of steel ships was not yet, on n'en était pas encore au temps des navires d'acier. The greatest genius that ever was, le plus grand génie qui ait jamais existé, qui fut jamais. That may be, cela se peut. So be it! ainsi soit-il! Well, so be it! eh bien, soit! Everything must remain just as it is, tout doit rester tel quel. However that may be, quoi qu'il en soit. How is it that . . .? comment se fait-il que + *sub.*, d'où vient(-il) que . . .? (*b*) *Impers:* There is, there are. (i) Il y a. There is a man in the garden, il y a un homme dans le jardin. What is there to see? qu'est-ce qu'il y a à voir? There will be dancing, on dansera. There were a dozen of us, nous étions une douzaine. (ii) (*In a wide, permanent sense*) *Lit:* Il est. There are men on whom Fortune always smiles, il est des hommes à qui tout sourit. (iii) There was once a princess, il était une fois une princesse. **5.** (*Go or come*) Are you for Bristol? allez-vous à Bristol? I have been to see Jones, j'ai été voir Jones. He had been and inspected the land, il était allé inspecter le terrain. I have been into every room, j'ai visité toutes les pièces. He was into the room like a flash, il entra dans la pièce en coup de foudre. Where have you been? d'où venez-vous? Has anyone been? est-il venu quelqu'un? **6.** *Impers:* (*a*) It is six o'clock, il est six heures. It is late, il est tard. It is a fortnight since I saw him, il y a quinze jours, voilà quinze jours, que je ne l'ai vu. (*b*) It is fine, cold, *etc.*, il fait beau (temps), il fait froid, etc. (*c*) It is easy to do so, il est facile de le faire. It is right that . . ., il est juste que + *sub.* It is said that . . ., on dit que. . . . It is you I am speaking to, c'est à vous que je parle. It is for you to decide, c'est à vous à décider. What is it? (i) que voulez-vous? (ii) de quoi s'agit-il? qu'est-ce qu'il y a? As it were, pour ainsi dire; en quelque sorte. Were it only to please me, ne fût-ce que pour me plaire. Were it not for my rheumatism, si ce n'était mon rhumatisme. Had it not been for the rain . . ., n'eût été la pluie. . . . Had it not been for him . . ., sans lui . . ., n'eût été lui. . . . *F:* Well, well, if it isn't George! Georges! En voilà une surprise! **7.** (*Auxiliary uses*) (*a*) I am, was, doing sth., je fais, je faisais, qch.; je suis, j'étais, en train de faire qch. They are always laughing, ils sont toujours à rire. **The house is building, is being built,** on est en train de bâtir la maison. **I have (just) been writing,** je viens d'écrire. **I have been waiting for a long time,** il y a longtemps que j'attends; j'attends depuis longtemps. (*Emphatic*) **Why are you not working?—I *am* working!** pourquoi ne travaillez-vous pas?—Mais si je travaille! mais je travaille, voyons! (*b*) **The sun is set,** le soleil est couché. **The guests were all gone,** les invités étaient tous partis. (*c*) (*Forming passive voice*) (i) **He was killed,** il fut tué. **He is respected by all,** il est respecté de tous. **The loft was reached by means of a ladder,** on accédait au grenier au moyen d'une échelle. **He is allowed to smoke,** on lui permet de fumer. **He was laughed at,** on s'est moqué de lui. (ii) **He is to be pitied,** il est à plaindre, on doit le plaindre. **The house is to be let,** la maison est à louer. **How is it to be done?** comment le faire? **What is to be done?** que faire? (*d*) (*Denoting futurity*) **I am to see him to-morrow,** je dois le voir demain. **He was never to see them again,** il ne devait plus les revoir. **I was to have come, but . . .,** je devais venir, mais. . . . (*e*) (*Necessity, duty*) **Am I to do it or not?** faut-il que je le fasse ou non? **You are to be at school to-morrow,** il faut que vous soyez à l'école demain. **8.** (*a*) **The bride to be,** la future, la fiancée. *S.a.* HAS-BEEN. (*b*) **To be for s.o., sth.,** tenir pour qn, qch. **I am for reform,** je suis pour, je suis partisan de, la réforme. (*c*) (*Belong*) **The battle is to the strong,** la victoire est aux forts. **3.** (*Elliptical*) **Is your book published?—It is,** est-ce que votre livre est publié?—Oui, il l'est. **Are you happy?—I am,** êtes-vous heureux?—Oui, *or* je le suis, *or* oui, je le suis, *or* mais oui! **You are angry.—No, I'm not.—Oh, but you are!** vous voilà fâché.—Pas du tout.—Oh, mais si! **He's back.—Is he?** il est de retour.—Vraiment? **So you are back, are you?** alors vous voilà de retour?

being¹, *a.* **For the time b.,** pour le moment, pour le quart d'heure, pour l'heure. **being²,** *s.* **1.** Existence *f*, être *m*. (*a*) **Those to whom you owe your b.,** ceux qui vous ont donné le jour. (*b*) **To come into b.,** prendre forme, prendre naissance. **The coming into b. of a new industry,** la naissance d'une nouvelle industrie. **To bring a plan into b.,** réaliser un projet. **2.** Être. (*a*) **All my b. revolts at the idea,** tout mon être se révolte à cette idée. (*b*) **A human b.,** un être humain. **Human beings,** le genre humain, les humains. **The Supreme B.,** l'Être Suprême.

beach¹ [biːtʃ], *s.* Plage *f*, grève *f*, rivage *m*. *S.a.* PEBBLE¹ 1. 'beach-comber, *s.* **1.** Vague déferlante. **2.** *F:* (*Of pers.*) Batteur *m* de grève. 'beach-guard, *s.* Brigade *f*, équipe *f*, de sauvetage (sur une plage). 'beach-head, *s.* *Mil:* Tête *f* de pont. 'beach-hut, *s.* Cabine *f*.

beach², *v.tr.* **1.** Échouer, mettre à l'échouage (un navire). **2.** Tirer (une embarcation) à sec.

beachwear ['biːtʃwɛər], *s.* Vêtements *mpl* de plage.

beacon¹ ['biːk(ə)n], *s.* **1.** (*a*) *A:* Feu *m* d'alarme. (*b*) Tour *f* ou colline *f* du feu d'alarme. **2.** Feu de joie. **3.** *Nau:* *Av:* B.(-light), fanal *m*, phare *m*. **Airway b.,** phare de ligne. **4.** *Nau:* Balise *f*. **5.** *Adm:* *Aut:* **Belisha b.,** sphère orange, indiquant un passage clouté.

beacon², *v.tr.* *Nau:* *Av:* Baliser, éclairer (un chenal, une piste d'envol).

beaconage ['biːk(ə)nidz], *s.* **1.** Balisage *m*. **2.** Droits *mpl* de balisage.

bead¹ [biːd], *s.* **1.** (*For prayers*) Grain *m*. (**String of**) **beads,** chapelet *m*. **To tell one's beads,** égrener, dire, son chapelet; dire le rosaire. **2.** (*a*) (*For ornament*) Perle *f* (de verroterie, d'émail). (**String of**) **beads,** collier *m*. **To thread beads,** enfiler des perles. (*b*) (*Drop*) Goutte *f*, perle. **Beads of dew,** perles de rosée. (*c*) Bulle *f* (sur le vin, l'eau-de-vie). (*d*) *Arch: Join:* Perle, baguette *f*, arête *f* (de moulure). **3.** (*Of tyre*) Talon *m*, bourrelet *m*. **Clincher b.,** talon à crochet. **4.** *Sm.a:* Guidon *m*, mire *f* (de fusil); grain-d'orge *m*. *F:* **To draw a b. on s.o.,** ajuster, viser, qn.

bead². **1.** *v.tr.* (*a*) Couvrir, orner (qch.) de perles. (*b*) *Join:* Appliquer une baguette sur (qch.). **2.** *v.i.* (*Of liquids*) Perler, faire la perle. **beaded,** *a.* **1.** *Tex:* (*Of*

material) Perlé. **2.** **B. edge,** talon *m* (de pneu). **B. tyre,** pneu à talons, à bourrelets. **B. rim,** jante à rebord. **3.** **Brow b. with perspiration,** front emperlé de sueur. **beading,** *s.* **1.** Garniture *f* de perles. **2.** (*a*) *Join:* Baguette *f*. (*b*) (*Of tyre*) Talon *m*, bourrelet *m*.

beadle ['biːdl], *s.m.* Bedeau; massier.

beady ['biːdi], *a.* **1.** (Yeux) en trou de vrille. **2.** (Liquide) qui perle. 'beady-'eyed, *a.* Aux yeux en vrille.

beagle ['biːgl], *s.* (Chien *m*) bigle *m*; briquet *m*.

beak¹ [biːk], *s.* Bec *m* (d'oiseau, de tortue, d'enclume); *F:* nez crochu.

beak², *s.m.* (*a*) *P:* Magistrat (du commissariat de police). (*b*) *Sch:* *F:* Professeur *m*, *F:* pion *m*.

beaked [biːkt], *a.* **1.** (Animal) à bec. **2.** (Nez) crochu.

beaker ['biːkər], *s.* Gobelet *m*; coupe *f*.

beakful ['biːkful], *s.* Pleine becquée.

beam¹ [biːm], *s.* **1.** (*a*) Poutre *f* (en bois); solive *f*, madrier *m*; (*small*) poutrelle *f*. **Main b.,** maîtresse poutre. **Longitudinal b.,** longeron *m*, longrine *f*. *S.a.* CROSS-BEAM 1, TIE-BEAM. (*b*) Fléau *m*, verge *f* (d'une balance). (*c*) Age *m*, timon *m*, flèche *f* (d'une charrue). (*d*) Balancier *m* (d'une machine). **2.** *N. Arch:* Bau *m*. **Deck-b.,** barrot *m* de pont. **The beams,** les barrots. **On the starboard b.,** par le travers tribord. **On the weather b.,** par le travers au vent. (**Breadth of**) **b.** (*of a ship*), largeur *f* (d'un navire). **Broad in the b.,** (i) (vaisseau) à larges baux; (ii) *F:* (personne) aux larges hanches. **3.** (*a*) **Rayon** *m* (de lumière, de soleil). **Stray b. of sunshine,** coulée *f* de soleil. **B. of delight,** large sourire *m*. (*b*) **B. of rays,** faisceau lumineux. **B. of a lighthouse, head-light,** faisceau d'un phare. *W.Tg:* **B. system,** émission aux ondes dirigées. *F:* **We're not on the same b.,** on n'est pas sur la même longueur d'onde. **B. navigation,** navigation *f* radiogoniométrique. *El:* **Wireless b.,** faisceau hertzien. *T.V:* **Electron b.,** faisceau *m* électronique. **Scanning electron b.,** faisceau cathodique explorateur. *F:* **To be off b.,** dérailler, *F:* être à la côte. 'beam-compass, *s.* Compas *m* à trusquin, à verge (de dessinateur). beam-'ends, *s.pl.* (*Of ship*) **To be on her b.-e.,** être engagé. **To throw a ship on her b.-e.,** coucher un navire. *F:* (*Of pers.*) **To be on one's b.-e.,** être, se trouver, à bout de ressources. 'beam-tree, *s.* *Bot:* (White) **b.-t.,** Alisier blanc.

beam². **1.** *v.tr.* (*Of the sun*) **To b. (forth) rays,** envoyer, lancer, darder, des rayons. **2.** *v.i.* (*Of the sun*) Rayonner. (*b*) (*Of pers.*) **To b. (with satisfaction),** rayonner (de satisfaction). (*c*) *W.Tel:* Émettre. (**To be**) **beamed in (on),** être dirigé vers.... **beaming,** *a.* Rayonnant; (soleil, visage) radieux.

beamy ['biːmi], *a.* (*a*) Massif. (*b*) (*Of ship*) A larges baux.

bean [biːn], *s.* **1.** **Broad b.** (grosse) fève. **Kidney b., haricot b.,** haricot *m*, soissons *m*. **French beans,** haricots verts. **Dried beans,** haricots secs. *S.a.* BUTTER-BEAN, RUNNER 3, SOYA-BEAN. *F:* **To be full of beans,** (i) être gaillard; se porter à merveille; (ii) être plein d'entrain. **To give s.o. beans,** attraper qn; donner un savon, laver la tête, à qn. **He knows how many beans make five,** c'est un malin. **He hasn't a b.,** il n'a pas le sou, *P:* pas un radis. **To spill the beans,** (i) mettre les pieds dans le plat; gaffer; (ii) vendre la mèche. **2.** **Grain** *m* (de café). 'bean-feast, *s.* *F:* **1.** *A:* Petite fête (annuelle) offerte aux ouvriers par le patron. **2.** Partie *f* de plaisir; noce *f*, régal *m*. 'bean-king, *s.* Roi *m* (on Twelfth Night). 'bean-pole, *s.* *F:* *U.S:* (*Woman*) (Grande) perche, asperge *f*.

beano ['biːnou], *s.* *F:* = BEAN-FEAST 2.

bear¹ ['bɛər], *s.* **1.** (*a*) Ours *m*. **She-b.,** ourse *f*. **Young b., bear's cub,** ourson *m*. **Polar b.,** ours blanc. *S.a.* GRIZZLY 2. *F:* **He's like a b. with a sore head,** il n'est pas à prendre avec des pincettes. **What a b.!** quel maussade! quel ours! (*b*) *Astr:* **The Great, Little, B.,** la Grande, la Petite, Ourse. **2.** *St.Exch:* Baissier *m*; joueur *m* à la baisse. 'bear-baiting, *s.* *A:* *Sp:* Combats *mpl* d'ours et de chiens. 'bear-fight, *s.* *F:* Scène *f* de désordre; bousculade *f*. 'bear-garden, *s.* **1.** Fosse *f* aux ours. **2.** *F:* Pétaudière *f*. **To turn the place into a b.-g.,** mettre le désordre partout. 'bear-leader, *s.* Montreur *m* d'ours; meneur *m* d'ours.

bear², *v.tr.* (beared) *St.Exch:* To b. the market, chercher à faire baisser les cours. *Abs.* To b., spéculer à la baisse.

bear³, *v.tr. & i.* (*p.t.* bore ['bɔːr], A. & B: bare ['bɛər]; *p.p.* borne [bɔːn]) (a) Porter (un fardeau, des armes, un nom, une date). The document bears your signature, le document porte votre signature. To b. a good character, jouir d'une bonne réputation. To b. oneself well, se bien comporter. The love she bore him, l'affection qu'elle lui portait. (b) Supporter, soutenir (un poids); supporter, endurer (la souffrance); supporter (les frais, les conséquences); souffrir (la douleur, la fatigue, une perte). To b. the penalty of one's misdeeds, porter la peine de ses méfaits. To b. a part in sth., jouer un rôle dans qch. The charge will not b. examination, cette accusation ne supporte pas l'examen. He could b. it no longer, il ne pouvait plus y tenir. *S.a.* GRIN². I cannot b. him, b. the sight of him, je ne peux pas le souffrir, le sentir. I cannot b. to see it, je ne peux pas en supporter la vue. To b. with s.o., être, se montrer, indulgent pour qn. (c) (*Press*) We were borne backwards (by the crowd, etc.), nous fûmes refoulés (par la foule, etc.). It was gradually borne in upon him that . . ., peu à peu il se laissa persuader que.... To b. (to the) right, prendre à droite; appuyer à droite. To b. hard, heavily, on s.o., (i) (*of pers.*) être dur pour qn; (ii) (*of thg*) peser lourdement sur qn. Law that bears unjustly on s.o., loi qui défavorise qn. Question that bears on the welfare of the country, question qui intéresse le bien-être du pays. That does not b. on the question, cela n'a aucun trait à la question. (*Of pers.*) To b. on a lever, peser sur un levier. (d) Bring to b. To bring all one's strength to b. on a lever, peser (de toutes ses forces) sur un levier. To bring one's mind to b. on sth., porter son attention sur qch. *S.a.* PRESSURE 2. To bring a telescope to b. on sth., braquer une lunette sur qch. To bring a gun to b. on a mark, pointer un canon sur un but. (e) *Nau:* The cape bears north-north-west, on relève le cap au nord-nord-ouest. How does the land b.? comment relève-t-on la terre? (*f*) (*Produce*) To b. a child, donner naissance à un enfant, mettre au jour un enfant. She has borne him three sons, elle lui a donné trois fils. *S.a.* BORN. Capital that bears interest, capital qui porte intérêt. *S.a.* FRUIT 1. **bear away**, *v.tr.* Emporter, enlever (qch.). To b. away the prize, remporter le prix. **bear down**. 1. *v.tr.* To b. down all resistance, briser, vaincre, venir à bout de, toute résistance. 2. *v.i. Nau:* To b. down (up)on sth., courir sur qch. To b. down on the enemy, foncer sur l'ennemi. **bear off**. 1. *v.tr.* = BEAR AWAY. 2. *v.i. Nau:* To b. off from the land, s'éloigner, s'écarter, de la terre. **bear out**, *v.tr.* 1. To b. o. a body, etc., emporter un cadavre, etc. 2. To b. o. a statement, confirmer, justifier, une assertion. To b. s.o. out, corroborer le dire de qn. **bear up**. 1. *v.tr.* Soutenir (qn, qch.). 2. *v.i.* To b. up against pain, résister à la douleur. To b. up against, under, misfortune, faire face, tenir tête, au malheur. B. up! tenez bon! du courage! **bearing¹**, *a.* 1. Porteur, -euse. B. axle, essieu porteur. B. surface, surface d'appui; surface portante. 2. (a) (Sol) productif. (b) Interest-b. capital, capital producteur d'intérêts; capital qui rapporte. (c) (*In scientific compounds often*) -fère. Lead-b., plombifère. Silver-b., argentifère. **bearing²**, *s.* 1. (a) Port *m* (d'armes, de nouvelles). (b) (*Of pers.*) Port, maintien *m*, conduite *f*. Majestic b., port majestueux. Modest b., maintien modeste. Soldierly b., allure martiale. (c) *pl. Her:* (Armorial) bearings, armoiries *f*, blason *m*. 2. (a) Capacité *f* de supporter (des maux, des souffrances). Beyond (all) b., insupportable. (b) (Appareil *m* d'appui *m* (d'un pont métallique); surface *f* d'appui (d'une poutre), portée *f* (de poutres); chape *f* (d'une balance). (*Of beam, etc.*) To take its b. on sth., prendre appui sur qch. (c) *Mec.E:* (i) Palier *m*; roulement *m*; (ii) coussinet *m*. Thrust b., palier de butée. Big end b., coussinet de tête de bielle. B.-brasses, coussinet antifriction. *S.a.* BALL-BEARING(s). (d) *Nau:* Relèvement *m. Surv:* Orientation *f*. To take the bearings of a coast, relever une côte. To take the ship's bearings, faire le point. Radio b. station, poste radiogoniométrique. *F:* To take one's

bearings, s'orienter, se repérer. To lose one's bearings, perdre le nord; se trouver désorienté. To find, get, one's bearings, se retrouver, se reconnaître. (e) Portée *f* (d'une question, d'un argument). B. on a question, rapport *m* avec une question. I had not understood the b. of his words, je n'avais pas saisi la portée de ses paroles. To examine a question in all its bearings, examiner une question sous tous ses aspects. 3. (a) (*Of tree, etc.*) To be in full b., être en plein rapport. (b) B. of a child, mise *f* au monde d'un enfant.

bearable ['bɛərəbl], *a.* Supportable.

beard¹ ['biəd], *s.* (a) Barbe *f*. To have a b., avoir de la barbe; porter la barbe. Man with a b., (homme) barbu. (b) Barbiche *f* (de chèvre). (c) *Bot:* Arête *f* (d'épi). (d) Barbelure *f* (d'une flèche, d'un hameçon).

beard², *v.tr.* Braver, défier, narguer (qn). To b. the lion in his den, aller défier qn chez lui.

bearded ['biədid], *a.* (Homme, blé, poisson) barbu; (blé) aristé. **Black-b. man**, homme à barbe noire.

beardless ['biədlis], *a.* Imberbe; sans barbe.

bearer ['bɛərər], *s.* 1. (*Pers.*) (a) Porteur, -euse. B. of good news, porteur de bonnes nouvelles. B. of evil tidings, messager *m* de malheur. *S.a.* STANDARD-BEARER, STRETCHER-BEARER. (b) B. of a cheque, of a passport, porteur d'un chèque, titulaire *mf* d'un passeport. *Fin:* B. bond, cheque, titre, chèque, au porteur. (c) (*At funeral*) The bearers, les porteurs. 2. (*Of tree*) To be a good b., être de bon rapport. 3. Support *m*. Bearers of a rolling-mill, colonnes *f* d'un laminoir.

bearish ['bɛəriʃ], *a.* (a) (Manières) d'ours. (b) (*Of pers.*) Bourru.

bearskin ['bɛəskin], *s.* 1. Peau *f* d'ours. 2. *Mil.Cost:* Bonnet *m* à poil; bonnet d'oursin.

beast [biːst], *s.* 1. Bête *f; esp.* quadrupède *m*. Wild b., (i) bête sauvage; (ii) bête féroce. The brute beasts, les brutes *f*. The king of (the) beasts, le roi des animaux. 2. (a) Bête de somme ou de trait. (b) *pl. Husb:* Bétail *m*, bestiaux *mpl*; cheptel *m*. Herd of forty beast(s), troupeau de quarante têtes de bétail. 3. *F:* To make a b. of oneself, s'abrutir. What a b.! quel animal! Quel abruti! That b. of a foreman, cette vache, ce chameau, de contremaître!

beastliness ['biːstlinis], *s.* 1. Bestialité *f*, brutalité *f*. 2. Saleté *f* (d'esprit).

beastly ['biːstli]. 1. *a.* (a) Bestial, brutal, -aux. (b) *F:* Sale, dégoûtant, infect. What b. weather! quel sale temps! 2. *adv. F:* (*Intensive*) Terriblement, bigrement. It's b. cold, il fait bigrement froid.

beat¹ [biːt], *s.* 1. (a) Battement *m* (du cœur, etc.); pulsation *f* (du cœur); batterie *f* (de tambour); son *m* (du tambour). (b) *Mus:* Mesure *f*, temps ·*m*. Strong b., temps fort. 2. *Ph:* Battement (d'ondes sonores). 3. Secteur *m* de surveillance (d'une sentinelle, etc.); ronde *f* (d'un agent de police). *F:* It's off my b. altogether, ça n'est pas de ma compétence; ce n'est pas mon rayon. 4. *Ven:* (Terrain de) battue *f*. 5. *U.S: F:* (a) = DEAD-BEAT² 2. (b) Beatnik *m*.

beat², *v.tr. & i.* (beat; beaten) Battre (qn, qch.). 1. (a) To b. s.o. with a stick, donner des coups de bâton à qn. To b. s.o. black and blue, meurtrir, rouer, qn de coups; mettre qn en capilotade. To b. one's breast, se frapper la poitrine. To b. on the door, frapper, cogner, à la porte. To b. a drum, battre du tambour. To b. to arms, battre le rappel. To b. the retreat (on drum), battre la retraite. To b. a retreat. (i) *Mil:* battre en retraite; (ii) se retirer, se dérober. To b. time (to music), battre la mesure. His heart beats with joy, son cœur bat de joie. To b. a wood (for game), battre un bois. *F:* To b. about the bush, tourner autour du pot; accumuler les mais, les si et les car. Not to b. about the bush, (i) aller droit au but, droit au fait; (ii) répondre sans ambages, carrément. *Nau:* To b. to windward, against the wind, louvoyer; tirer des bordées; gagner au vent. *P:* To b. it, tirer au large. Now then, b. it! allons, file! décampe! fiche le camp! (b) (*Of bird*) To b. its wings, battre des ailes. 2. (*Conquer, surpass*) (a) To b. the enemy, battre l'ennemi. To b. s.o. at chess, battre qn aux échecs. *S.a*

HOLLOW¹ II 2. *F*: **That beats me!** cela me passe! ça me dépasse! **That beats everything!** ça c'est fort! ça c'est le comble! c'est le bouquet! il ne manquait plus que ça! **Can you b. it?** y a-t-il plus fort que ça? (*b*) **To b. the record,** battre le record. **beat back,** *v.tr.* Repousser, refouler (qn). **To b. back the flames,** rabattre les flammes. **beat down.** 1. *v.tr.* (*a*) **To b. sth. down,** (r)abattre qch. **The rain has beaten down the corn,** la pluie a couché les blés. (*b*) **To b. down the price of sth.,** marchander sur le prix de qch. **To b. s.o. down,** marchander (avec) qn. 2. *v.i.* **The sun beats down upon our heads,** le soleil donne (à plomb) sur nos têtes. **beat in,** *v.tr.* Enfoncer, défoncer (une porte). **beat off,** *v.tr.* **To b. off an attack,** repousser un assaut. **beat out,** *v.tr.* 1. (*a*) **To b. out a path,** frayer un chemin. (*b*) **To b. out iron,** battre, aplatir, le fer. 2. **To b. s.o.'s brains out,** assommer qn. **beat up.** 1. *v.tr.* (*a*) **To b. up eggs, cream,** battre, fouetter, les œufs, la crème. (*b*) **To b. up game,** *F*: **customers,** rabattre, traquer, le gibier, des clients. (*c*) *F*: **To b. up s.o.,** rosser, *P*: tabasser, qn. **To b. it up,** faire la bringue, la noce. *U.S*: He beats it up a lot, il mène une vie de patachon, il fait la nouba, la fête, la bombe. 2. *v.i. Nau*: **To b. up,** louvoyer vers la terre; gagner vers la terre. **To b. up to windward,** remonter le vent. **beat³,** *a. P*: = BEATEN. **You have me b.,** j'y renonce. **beaten,** *a.* 1. **The b. track,** le chemin battu; les vieux sentiers rebattus. **House off the b. track,** maison écartée. 2. (Or, fer) battu, martelé. *S.a.* WEATHER-BEATEN. **beating,** *s.* 1. (*a*) Battement *m* (d'ailes, du cœur, etc.). (*b*) *Tchn*: Battage *m*. 2. (*a*) Coups *mpl*; raclée *f*, rossée *f*. (*b*) Défaite *f*.

beater ['bi:tər], *s.* 1. (*Pers.*) (*a*) Batteur, -euse. (*b*) *Ven*: Rabatteur *m*, traqueur *m*. 2. Batte *f*; battoir *m* (de laveuse); fouloir *m* (de foulon).

beatific [bi(:)ə'tifik], *a.* Béatifique.

beatification [bi(:),ætifi'keiʃ(ə)n], *s. Ecc*: Béatification *f*.

beatify [bi(:)'ætifai], *v.tr. Ecc*: Béatifier.

beatitude [bi(:)'ætitju:d], *s.* Béatitude *f*.

beatnik ['bi:tnik], *s.* Beatnik *m*.

beau, *pl.* **beaus, beaux** 'bou, bouz], *s.m.* 1. *O*: Élégant, dandy; petit-maître, *pl.* petits-maîtres. **An old b.,** un vieux beau. 2. *U.S*: Prétendant (d'une jeune fille); galant.

Beaufort ['boufə:t]. *Pr.n. Meteor*: **B. scale,** échelle *f* de Beaufort.

beau-ideal [,bouai'diəl], *s.* Idéal *m*. **The b.-i. of a perfect knight,** le type achevé du chevalier.

beauteous ['bju:tiəs], *a. Poet*: = BEAUTIFUL.

beautician [bju'tiʃiən], *s. U.S*: Esthéticienne *f*.; Visagiste *mf. R.t.m.*

beautiful ['bju:tif(u)l], *a.* 1. (Très) beau, (très) belle. **A b. face,** un très beau visage. **At twenty she was b.,** à vingt ans c'était une beauté. 2. Magnifique; admirable. 3. *s.* **The b.,** le beau. **-fully,** *adv.* Admirablement; on ne peut mieux; parfaitement.

beautify ['bju:tifai], *v.tr.* Embellir, enjoliver.

beauty ['bju:ti], *s.* Beauté *f*. 1. **To be in the flower of one's b.,** être dans toute sa beauté. **B. cream,** crème *f* de beauté. **B. treatment,** soins *mpl* de beauté. **specialist** = BEAUTICIAN. *Prov*: **B. is in the eye of the beholder,** il n'y a point de laides amours. **The b. of it is that . . .,** le beau côté, le joli, de l'affaire, c'est que. . . . **That's the b. of it!** (i) voilà ce qui en fait le charme! (ii) c'est là le plus beau de l'affaire! 2. **She was a b. in her day,** elle a été une beauté dans le temps. *F*: **She's a b.!** c'est un rêve! *F*: **Well, you're a b.!** eh bien, tu es encore un drôle de type, toi! *P*: **I'm going to spoil his b. for him,** je vais lui abîmer le portrait. **The Sleeping B.,** la Belle au bois dormant. **'beauty-parlour,** *s.* Institut *m* de beauté. **'beauty-sleep,** *s.* Sommeil *m* avant minuit. **'beauty-spot,** *s.* 1. (*Applied on face*) Mouche *f*. 2. Site *m*, coin *m*, pittoresque.

beaver ['bi:vər], *s. Z*: Castor *m*. *F*: **Eager b.,** fayot *m*.

becalm [bi'ka:m], *v.tr.* Abriter, déventer (un navire). (*Of ship*) **To be becalmed,** être accalminé.

became. *See* BECOME.

because [bi'kɔ(:)z]. 1. *conj.* Parce que. **I eat b. I'm hungry,** je mange parce que j'ai faim. **If I said so it was b. it had to be said,** si je l'ai dit c'est qu'il fallait le dire. **B. he dashed off a sonnet he thinks himself a poet,** pour avoir bâclé un sonnet il se croit poète. 2. *Prep.phr.* **B. of sth.,** à cause de, en raison de qch.

Béchamel ['beʃəmel]. *Pr.n. Cu*: **B. sauce,** béchamelle *f*, sauce à la Béchamel.

bêche-de-mer ['beʃdə'mɛər], *s.* (*a*) Trépang *m*; bêche-de-mer *f*, *pl.* bêches-de-mer. (*b*) **B.-de-m. English,** bichlamar *m*, sabir polynésien.

beck¹ [bek], *s.* Ruisseau *m* (de montagne).

beck², *s.* Signe *m* (de tête, de la main). **To have s.o. at one's b. and call,** avoir qn à ses ordres. **To be at s.o.'s b. and call,** être à qn au doigt et à l'œil.

beckon ['bek(ə)n], *v.tr. & i.* Faire signe (to s.o., à qn); appeler (qn) de la main, d'un geste. **To b. s.o. in,** faire signe à qn d'entrer.

become [bi'kʌm], *v.* (**became** [bi'keim]; **become**) 1. *v.i.* Devenir; se faire. (*a*) **To b. great, king, etc.,** devenir grand, roi, etc. **To b. old, thin,** vieillir, maigrir. **They have b. more amiable,** ils se sont faits plus aimables. **To b. a priest, a doctor,** se faire prêtre, médecin. **To b. accustomed, interested,** s'accoutumer, s'intéresser. (*Of pers.*) **To b. known,** commencer à être connu; se faire connaître. (*b*) **What has b. of X?** qu'est devenu X? qu'est-il advenu de X? 2. *v.tr.* (*a*) **To b. s.o.,** aller (bien) à. **Hat that does not b. him,** chapeau qui ne lui sied pas, qui ne lui va pas. *S.a.* ILL III. 2. **becoming,** *a.* 1. (*a*) Convenable, bienséant. (*b*) **B. to the occasion,** digne de l'occasion. 2. (*Of dress, etc.*) Seyant (to, à); qui sied (à); qui va bien (à). **B. dress,** robe avantageuse. **-ly,** *adv.* Convenablement; comme il convient.

bed¹ [bed], *s.* Lit *m*; *Lit*: couche *f*. 1. (*a*) **Single b.,** lit à une place, pour une personne. **Double b.,** lit à deux places, pour deux personnes. **Twin beds,** lits jumeaux. **Spare b.,** lit de la chambre d'ami. *S.a.* CAMP-BED, FEATHER-BED, TRUCKLE-BED, WATER-BED. **To give b. and board to s.o.,** donner à qn le logement et la nourriture, le vivre et le couvert. **The marriage b.,** le lit conjugal. *Jur*: **Separation from b. and board,** séparation de corps (et de biens). **To sleep in separate beds,** faire lit à part. **To be brought to b. of a boy,** accoucher d'un petit garçon. **To be in b.,** (i) être couché; (ii) (*through illness*) être alité, garder le lit. **To go to b.,** se coucher. **To take to one's b.,** s'aliter. **To keep to one's b.,** garder le lit. **B. of sickness,** lit de douleur. *S.a.* SICK-BED. **Three days in b.,** trois jours d'alitement. **To get into b.,** se mettre au lit. **To get out of b.,** se lever. **To put a child to b.,** coucher un enfant. **To make the beds,** faire les lits. *Prov*: **As you make your b. so you must lie on it,** comme on fait son lit on se couche. *S.a.* DEATH-BED, ROSE¹ 1. (*b*) = BEDSTEAD. (*c*) Spring-b., sommier *m* (à ressorts). 2. (*a*) Lit (d'une rivière); banc *m* (d'huîtres). *Hort*: **(Rectangular) b.,** planche *f*, carré *m* (de légumes, etc.). **(Flower-)b.,** parterre *m*, plate-bande *f*, *pl.* plates-bandes. *S.a.* OYSTER-BED, SEED-BED. (*b*) *Geol*: Assise *f*; couche *f. Miner*: Gisement *m. S.a.* COAL-BED, *Const*: *etc*: **B. of concrete,** assise de béton. (*c*) **(Engine-)b.,** support *m*, bâti *m*, de moteur. (*d*) *Typ*: Marbre *m*. **The paper has gone to b.,** le journal est tombé. **'bed-bug,** *s.* Punaise *f* des lits. **'bed-cover,** *s.* Dessus *m* de lit. **'bed-frame,** *s.* Bois *m* de lit. **'bed-hangings,** *s.* *See* HANGING² 2. **'bed-head,** *s.* Chevet *m*; tête *f* (du lit). **'bed-jacket,** *s.* Liseuse *f*. **'bed-linen,** *s.* Draps *mpl* de lit et taies *fpl* d'oreillers. **'bed-pan,** *s. Hyg*: Bassin *m*. **Slipper b.-p.,** pantoufle *f*. **'bed-plate,** *s. Mch*: Bâti *m*, sole *f*, semelle *f*, socle *m*; plaque *f* de fondation (d'une machine). *Metall*: Sole *f* (du fourneau). *Rail*: Plaque *f* d'aiguille. **'bed-rest,** *s.* Dossier *m* de malade. **'bed-rock,** *s.* (*a*) *Geol*: Roche *f* de fond. (*b*) Fondement *m* (de sa croyance, etc.). **To get down to the b.-r.,** descendre au fond des choses. **B.-r. price,** dernier prix; prix le plus bas. **'bed-'settee,** *s.* Canapé-lit *m. pl.* canapés-lits. **'bed-'sitting-room,** *s. F*: **'bed-'sitter, 'bed-'sit,** *s.* (Appartement-)studio *m*; pièce *f* unique (d'étudiant, etc.) avec divan; chambre meublée. **'bed-sore,** *s.* Escarre *f*, eschare *f. Med*: **'bed-table,** *s.* Table *f* de malade. **'bed-warmer,** *s.* 1. Chauffe-lit *m*, couverture chauffante. 2. Bouillotte *f*. **'bed-wetting,** *s. Med*: *Psy*: 1. *a.* Incontinent. 2. *s.* Incontinence *f* nocturne.

bed². **1.** *v.tr.* (bedded) (*a*) To b. (up, down) the horses, faire la litière aux chevaux. (*b*) To b. (out) plants, dépoter des plantes. To b. (in) seedlings, repiquer des plants. (*c*) *Const:* Sceller (une poutre dans un mur, etc.); asseoir (une pierre, les fondations). **2.** *v.i.* (*a*) (*Of animal*) Se gîter. (*b*) (*Of foundations, etc.*) To b. (down), prendre son assiette; se tasser. **bedding**, *s.* **1.** (*a*) Parcage *m* (des huîtres). (*b*) *Civ.E:* Enrochement *m* (d'un bâtardeau, etc.). (*c*) Scellement *m* (d'une poutre dans un mur, etc.); assiette *f* (d'une pierre). (*d*) *Hort:* B.-out, dépotage *m*, dépotement *m* (de plantes). **2.** (*a*) Literie *f*; fournitures *fpl* (d'un lit). (*b*) *Mil: Navy:* (Matériel *m* de) couchage *m*. **3.** (*a*) *Husb:* Litière *f*. (*b*) *Civ.E:* Matériau *m* d'enrochement, d'assise. **4.** Lit (d'une chaudière).

bedaub [bi'dɔːb], *v.tr.* Barbouiller (de peinture).

bedchamber ['bedt∫eimbər], *s.* *A:* Chambre *f* à coucher. (*At court*) The Gentleman of the B., les gentilshommes de la chambre.

bedclothes ['bedklou(ð)z], *s.pl.* Couvertures *f* et draps *m* de lit.

bedeck [bi'dek], *v.tr.* *Lit:* Parer, orner (s.o. with sth., qn de qch.). *Pej: A:* To b. oneself, s'attifer.

bedevil [bi'devl], *v.tr.* **1.** Ensorceler (qn). **2.** Taquiner, tourmenter, lutiner (qn).

bedevilment [bi'devlmənt], *s.* **1.** Ensorcellement *m.* **2.** Taquinerie *f.*

bedew [bi'djuː], *v.tr.* *Pej: Lit:* Humecter de rosée.

bedfellow ['bedfelou], *s.* Camarade *mf* de lit. He is an unpleasant b., il est mauvais coucheur.

bedizen [bi'daizn], *v.tr.* *Pej:* Attifer, chamarrer.

Bedlam ['bedləm]. **1.** *Pr.n.* (*Corrupt. of Bethlehem*) *A:* Hôpital *m* (d'aliénés) de Ste-Marie-Bethléem. **2.** *s.* *F:* (*a*) Maison *f* de fous, d'aliénés. (*b*) Charivari *m*, tohu-bohu *m*, chahut *m* à tout casser.

Bedouin ['beduin, -iːn], *a. & s. inv.* Bédouin, -ine.

bedpost ['bedpoust], *s.* Colonne *f* de lit; quenouille *f* (de lit à colonnes).

bedraggled [bi'dragld], *a.* (*a*) Crotté. (*b*) Dépenaillé.

bedridden ['bed'ridn], *a.* Cloué au lit.

bedroom ['bedrum], *s.* Chambre *f* (à coucher). Spare b., chambre d'ami.

bedroomed ['bedrumd], *a.* A three-b. house, une maison avec trois chambres à coucher.

bedside ['bedsaid], *s.* Chevet *m*; bord *m* du lit. At s.o.'s b., au chevet de qn. B. carpet, rug, descente *f* de lit. B. lamp, lampe de chevet. B. table, table de nuit, de chevet. B. books, livres de chevet. (*Of doctor*) To have a good b. manner, avoir un comportement agréable auprès d'un malade.

bedsock ['bedsɔk], *s.* Chausson *m* de nuit.

bedspread ['bedspred], *s.* Courtepointe *f*; dessus *m* de lit, couvre-lit *m.*

bedstead ['bedsted], *s.* Châlit *m*; bois *m* de lit. Folding b., lit-cage *m.*

bedtick(ing) ['bed'tik(iŋ)], *s.* Toile *f* à matelas.

bedtime ['bedtaim], *s.* Heure *f* du coucher. It is b., il est l'heure d'aller se coucher.

bee [biː], *s.* **1.** Abeille *f.* Hive-b., abeille domestique. Worker b., (abeille) ouvrière. To keep bees, élever des abeilles. *F:* To have a b. in one's bonnet, (i) être timbré; avoir une araignée au plafond; (ii) avoir une idée fixe. *S.a.* BUMBLE-BEE, HONEY-BEE, QUEEN-BEE. **2.** *U.S:* (*a*) Réunion *f* (pour travaux en commun). (*b*) Concours *m.* *S.a.* SPELLING-BEE. 'bee-bread, *s.* Nourriture *f* (miel, pollen, eau) du couvain. 'bee-eater, *s.* *Orn:* Guépier *m.* 'bee-keeper, *s.* Apiculteur *m.* 'bee-keeping, *s.* Apiculture *f.* 'bee-line, *s.* Ligne *f*, droite. In a b.-l., à vol d'oiseau. *F:* To make a b.-l. for sth., aller droit vers qch, s'avancer en droite ligne vers qch.

beech [biːt∫], *s.* Hêtre *m.* Copper b., hêtre rouge. B. wood furniture, meubles en hêtre. 'beech-grove, *s.* Hêtraie *f.* 'beech-mast, *s.* Faînes *fpl.* 'beech-nut, *s.* Faine *f.*

beef [biːf], *s.* (*No pl.*) *Cu:* Bœuf *m.* Roast b., rôti *m* de bœuf; rosbif *m.* Salt b., bœuf salé, mariné. Corned b., corned-beef *m, F: Mil:* singe *m.* *F:* To have plenty of b., avoir du muscle; *F:* être costaud. 'beef(-)tea, *s.* Bouillon *m.*

beefeater ['biːfiːtər], *s.* **1.** Hallebardier *m* ((i) de la garde du corps, (ii) à la Tour de Londres). **2.** *Orn:* Pique-bœuf *m.*

beefsteak [biːf'steik], *s.* *Cu:* Biftock *m.*

beefy ['biːfi], *a.* *F:* Musculeux, -euse, musclé; *F:* costaud.

beehive ['biːhaiv], *s.* *Ap:* Ruche *f.*

Beelzebub [bi'elzibʌb]. *Pr.n.m.* **1.** *B.Lit:* Belzébuth. **2.** *F:* Le Diable.

been. *See* BE.

beer ['biər], *s.* Bière *f.* *U.S:* Bière d'Alsace, bière blonde (allemande). Bottled b., bière en can(n)ette. Small b., petite bière. *F:* To think no small b. of oneself, ne pas se prendre pour de la petite bière; se croire le premier moutardier du pape; *P:* se gober. Fortune made in b., fortune faite dans la brasserie. *F:* Life is not all b. and skittles, tout n'est pas rose(s) dans ce (bas) monde. 'beer-barrel, *s.* Tonneau *m* à bière. 'beer-engine, *s.* Pompe *f* à bière (sous pression). 'beer-garden, *s.* Café *m* en plein air; guinguette *f.* 'beer-glass, *s.* Bock *m*; chope *f.* 'beer-house, *s.* Cabaret *m*; brasserie *f.* 'beer-mat, *s.* Sous-bock *m.*

beery ['biəri], *a.* **1.** (Atmosphère) qui sent la bière. **2.** Un peu gris. B. voice = voix avinée.

beeswax ['biːzwæks], *s.* (*a*) Cire *f* d'abeilles. (*b*) Cire à parquet.

beeswing ['biːzwiŋ], *s.* **1.** Pellicules *fpl* (du vin de Porto). **2.** Vieux porto.

beet [biːt], *s.* Betterave *f.* White b., (i) (bette) poirée *f*; (ii) betterave à sucre. *S.a.* SUGAR-BEET. B. sugar, sucre de betterave. B.-worker, betteravier *m.* (Sugar-)b. industry, industrie betteravière.

beetle¹ ['biːtl], *s.* Mailloche *f*, masse *f* (en bois); maillet *m; (for paving)* hie *f*, demoiselle *f*; dame *f.* *Laund:* Battoir *m.*

beetle², *s.* *Ent:* Coléoptère *m*; hister *m*, escarbot *m*, scarabée *m.* *S.a.* BLACK-BEETLE, STAG-BEETLE, etc. 'beetle-crushers, *s.pl.* *F:* **1.** Pieds *m; P:* arpions *m.* **2.** *P:* Godillots *m*; godasses *f*; bateaux *m*; croquenots *m.*

beetle³, *a.* B. brows, (i) Sourcils touffus; (ii) front sourcilleux. 'beetle-browed, *a.* Sourcilleux; aux sourcils épais, touffus.

beetle⁴, *v.i.* Surplomber. **beetling**, *a.* **1.** (*Of rock*) Surplombant, menaçant. B. height, précipice *m.* **2.** = BEETLE³.

beetroot ['biːtruːt], *s.* Betterave (potagère).

befall [bi'fɔːl], *v.tr. & i.* (*Conj. like* FALL; *used only in 3rd pers.*) Arriver, survenir (à qn). It so befell that . . ., il arriva que. . . .

befit [bi'fit], *v.tr.* (befitted) (*Used only in 3rd pers.*) *A:* Convenir, seoir (à qn, à qch.).

before [bi'fɔːr]. **1.** *adv.* (*a*) (*In space*) En avant; devant. To go on b., marcher en avant, prendre les devants; (*take precedence*) passer le premier. There were trees b. and behind, il y avait des arbres devant et derrière. This page and the one b., cette page et la précédente. (*b*) (*In time*) Auparavant, avant. Two days b., deux jours auparavant; l'avant-veille *f.* The day b., le jour précédent; la veille. The evening b., la veille au soir. The year b., l'année d'auparavant. A moment b., un moment auparavant. I have seen him b., je l'ai déjà vu. I have never seen him b., je le vois pour la première fois. **2.** *prep.* (*a*) (*Place*) Devant. To stand b. s.o., se tenir devant qn. B. my (very) eyes, sous mes (propres) yeux. He said so b. me, il l'a dit en ma présence. *S.a.* WIND¹ 1. (*b*) (*Time*) Avant. B. Christ, B.C., avant Jésus-Christ, av. J.-C. B. long, avant longtemps. He will leave us b. long, il nous quittera sous peu. It ought to have been done b. now, ce devrait être déjà fait. To arrive an hour b. the time, arriver (avec) une heure d'avance. We are b. our time, nous sommes en avance. The day b. the battle, la veille de la bataille. Two days b. Christmas, l'avant-veille de Noël. B. answering, avant de répondre. *Fin:* Redemption b. due date, remboursement anticipé. (*c*) (*Preference, order*) B. everything else . . ., avant tout. . . . Ladies b. gentlemen, les dames avant les messieurs. **3.** *conj.* Avant que (ne) + *sub.* (*a*) Come and see me b. you leave, venez me voir avant que vous (ne) partiez, avant de partir, avant votre départ. It will be long b. we see him again, on ne le reverra pas d'ici longtemps. It was long b. he came, il fut longtemps à venir. (*b*)

I will die b. I yield, je préfère mourir plutôt que de céder. (c) B. I forget, they expect you this evening, pendant que j'y pense, ils vous attendent ce soir.

beforehand [biˈfɔːhænd], *adv* Préalablement, au préalable; d'avance; auparavant. **You ought to have told me b.**, vous auriez dû me prévenir. **To be b. with the rent,** (i) payer son loyer avant le terme; (ii) avoir en main l'argent du terme.

befriend [biˈfrend], *v.tr.* Venir en aide à, à l'aide de (qn); secourir (qn); se montrer l'ami de (qn).

beg [beg], *v.tr. & i.* (begged) 1. Mendier; tendre la main. **To b.** (for) one's bread, mendier son pain. *(To dog)* B.! fais le beau! **These jobs go begging,** ce sont des emplois qui trouvent peu d'amateurs. 2. **To b. a favour of s.o.,** solliciter une faveur de qn. **To b.** (of) s.o. to do sth., prier, supplier, qn de faire qch. *Com:* I b. to inform you that . . ., j'ai l'honneur de vous faire savoir que . . . *Com:* We b. to hand you a cheque for . . ., nous avons l'avantage de vous remettre un chèque de. . . . I b. (of) you! de grâce! je vous en prie! **To b. the question,** supposer vrai ce qui est en question; faire une pétition de principe. *S.a.* PARDON[1] 1. **begging**[1], *a.* (Frère, ordre) mendiant. **begging**[2], *s.* 1. Mendicité *f*; quémanderie *f*. 2. B. the question, pétition *f* de principe.

began. *See* BEGIN.

beget [biˈget], *v.tr.* (begot [biˈgɔt], B: begat [biˈgæt]; begotten [biˈgɔtn]) 1. Engendrer, procréer. **Abraham begat Isaac,** Abraham engendra Isaac. 2. *O:* Causer, susciter; faire naître (des difficultés, etc.).

begetter ˈbiˈgetər], *s.* 1. Père *m*; géniteur *m*; auteur *m* (of, de). 2. Cause *f* (of, de).

beggar[1] [ˈbegər], *s.* 1. B.(-man, -woman), mendiant, -e, gueux, -euse, pauvre, -esse. *A:* Sturdy b., truand *m*. *Prov:* Beggars cannot be choosers, ne choisit pas qui emprunte. *S.a.* HORSEBACK. 2. Individu *m*. Funny little b., drôle *m* de petit bonhomme. Poor b.! pauvre diable! Lucky b.! veinard!

beggar[2], *v.tr.* (beggared (beggared) 1. **To b. s.o.,** réduire qn à la mendicité; mettre qn sur la paille. 2. *O:* To b. description, défier toute description. **Beggar-my-neighbour,** *s. Cards:* Bataille *f*.

beggarly [ˈbegəli], *a.* Chétif, minable, misérable, mesquin. B. wage, salaire dérisoire.

beggary [ˈbegəri], *s.* Mendicité *f*, misère *f*. **To be reduced to b.,** être réduit à la mendicité; être dans la misère.

begin [biˈgin], *v.tr. & i.* (began [biˈgæn]; begun [biˈgʌn]) Commencer (un discours, une tâche); entamer, amorcer (une conversation). **To b. at the beginning,** commencer par le commencement. **He began life as a grocer,** il débuta dans la vie comme épicier. **Before winter begins,** avant le début de l'hiver. **The day began well, badly,** la journée s'annonça bien, mal. **To b. to do sth., to b. doing sth.,** commencer à, de, faire qch. **To b. to laugh, to cry; to b. laughing, crying,** se mettre à rire, à pleurer; se prendre à pleurer. **To b. by doing sth.,** débuter, commencer, par faire qch. **To b. with,** tout d'abord; pour commencer. **To b. again,** recommencer. *Prov:* Well begun is half done, à moitié fait qui commence bien. **beginning,** *s.* Commencement *m*; début *m* (d'une carrière, etc.); origine *f*, naissance *f* (du monde, etc.). **In the b.,** au commencement, au début. **From the b.,** dès le commencement. **From b. to end,** depuis le commencement jusqu'à la fin; de bout en bout. **To make a b.,** commencer, débuter. **To start again from the very b.,** reprendre le travail à pied d'œuvre. *Aut:* B. of a skid, amorce *f* de dérapage.

beginner [biˈginər], *s.* 1. Premier *m* à agir; auteur *m* (d'une querelle, etc.). 2. Commençant, -ante, débutant, -ante; novice *mf*.

begonia [biˈgounjə], *s. Bot:* Bégonia *m*.

begot(ten). *See* BEGET.

begrime [biˈgraim], *v.tr.* Noircir, salir, barbouiller. **Begrimed with smoke,** noirci de fumée.

begrudge [biˈgrʌdʒ], *v.tr.* Donner (qch.) à contre-cœur. **To b. s.o. sth.,** (i) mesurer, (ii) envier, qch. à qn.

begrudgingly [biˈgrʌdʒiŋli], *adv.* 1. A contre-cœur. 2. Envieusement. 3. Chichement.

beguile [biˈgail], *v.tr. Lit:* 1. Enjôler, séduire, tromper (qn). *B:* The serpent beguiled me, le serpent m'a séduite. **To b. s.o. with promises,** bercer qn de promesses. 2. Distraire, charmer, amuser.

begum [ˈbiːgəm], *s.f.* Bégum.

begun. *See* BEGIN.

behalf [biˈhɑːf], *s.* 1. On b. of s.o., au nom de qn; *Com:* au compte, au profit, de qn. I come on b. of Mr X, je viens de la part de M. X. 2. To plead in, on, s.o.'s b., plaider en faveur de qn. 3. Don't be uneasy on my b., ne vous inquiétez pas à mon sujet.

behave [biˈheiv], *v.i.* (Usu. with adv.) **To b. well, badly, prudently,** se conduire, se comporter, bien, mal, prudemment. **To b. well to, towards, s.o.,** bien agir envers qn; se bien conduire à l'égard de, envers, qn. **To know how to b.,** savoir vivre. *(To child)* B. yourself! sois sage! tiens-toi bien! **behaved,** *a.* (With adv. prefixed, e.g.) Well-b., sage; poli; qui se conduit bien. Ill-b., badly b., qui se conduit mal; sans tenue.

behaviour [biˈheivjər], *s.* 1. Façon *f* de se comporter, d'agir; tenue *f*, maintien *m*; conduite *f*; comportement *m* (to, towards, s.o., avec, envers, qn). Good b., bonne conduite. **To be on one's best b.,** se surveiller; se conduire de son mieux. 2. Allure *f*, fonctionnement *m* (d'une machine); comportement *m*; tenue (d'une auto).

behaviourism [biˈheivjərizm], *s. Psy:* Behaviorisme *m*, psychologie *f* du comportement.

behead [biˈhed], *v.tr.* Décapiter; faire tomber la tête de (qn). **beheading,** *s.* Décapitation *f*.

beheld. *See* BEHOLD.

behest [biˈhest], *s. Lit:* Commandement *m*, ordre *m*. **At s.o.'s b.,** sur l'ordre de qn.

behind [biˈhaind]. 1. *adv.* Derrière; par derrière. (a) Hair cropped close b., cheveux coupés ras par derrière. **To attack s.o. from b.,** attaquer qn par derrière. **To come b.,** venir derrière; suivre. **To ride b.,** (i) suivre à cheval; (ii) monter en croupe. **To fall, lag, b.,** s'attarder; traîner en arrière; se laisser distancer. **To stay, remain, b.,** rester, demeurer, en arrière. (b) **To be b. with one's studies, with one's work,** être en retard pour ses études, dans son travail. 2. *prep.* (a) Derrière. **He hid b. it,** il se cacha derrière. **Look b. you,** regardez derrière vous. **To walk, follow, close b. s.o.,** marcher sur les talons de qn. **What is b. all this?** qu'y a-t-il derrière tout cela? **To be b.** (= to support) s.o., soutenir qn. **To put a thought b. one,** rejeter une pensée. (b) En arrière de, en retard sur (qn, qch.). **Country (far) b. its neighbours,** pays (très) en arrière de ses voisins. **Here we are far b. Paris,** ici nous sommes très en retard sur Paris (en matière de modes, etc.). *S.a.* TIME[1] 4, 6. 3. *s. F:* Derrière *m*, *P:* cul *m*. **To kick s.o.'s b.,** botter le derrière de, à, qn. **To sit on one's b.,** ne rien faire.

behindhand [biˈhaindhænd], *adv. & pred. a.* En arrière; en retard; attardé. **To be b. with the rent,** être en retard pour, avec, le loyer. **He is not b. in generosity,** il n'est pas en reste de générosité.

behold [biˈhould], *v.tr.* (beheld [biˈheld]; beheld) *Lit:* 1. Voir; apercevoir. 2. *imp.* B.! voyez!

beholden [biˈhouldn], *a.* **To be b. to s.o.,** être redevable à qn (for, de).

beholder [biˈhouldər], *s.* Spectateur, -trice; assistant, -ante; témoin *m*.

behoof [biˈhuːf], *s. A:* To, for, on, s.o.'s b., à l'avantage, au profit, de qn. **For one's own b.,** dans son propre intérêt.

behove [biˈhouv], *v.tr. impers.* 1. Incomber (à). It behoves him to . . ., il lui appartient de. . . . 2. It does not b. him to boast, mal lui sied de se vanter.

beige [beiʒ]. 1. *s. Tex:* Beige. 2. *a.* (Couleur *f*) beige.

being, *s. See* BE.

bejewelled [biˈdʒuː(ː)ild], *a.* Paré(e) de bijoux. **She was very much b.,** elle était parée comme une châsse.

bel [bel], *s. Ph: Ac:* Bel *m*.

belabour [biˈleibər], *v.tr. O:* T. b. s.o. (soundly), battre qn à coups redoublés; rouer qn de coups.

belated [biˈleitid], *a.* 1. (Voyageur, etc.) attardé; surpris par la nuit. 2. (Repentir, renseignement) tardif; (invité) en retard. **-ly,** *adv.* Un peu tard, tardivement, sur le tard, trop tard.

belaud [bi'lɔːd], *v.tr. A:* Combler (qn) de louanges.

belay¹ [bi'lei], *s. Mount:* Point *m* d'assurance.

belay², *v.tr. Nau:* Tourner, amarrer (une manœuvre). **B.!** amarrez! *Mount:* Assurer. **be'laying-pin, -cleat,** *s.* Cabillot *m*, taquet *m*.

belch¹ [bel(t)ʃ], *s.* **1.** Éructation *f;* (*not in polite use*) rot *m.* **2.** Vomissement *m* (de flammes, etc.).

belch². **1.** *v.i.* Éructer; (*not in polite use*) roter. **2.** *v.tr.* To b. (forth, out) **flames, smoke,** vomir des flammes, de la fumée.

beldam(e) ['beldəm], *s.f. A:* Vieille sorcière; mégère.

beleaguer [bi'liːgər], *v.tr.* Assiéger. **Beleaguered city,** ville investie.

belemnite ['beləmnait], *s.* Bélemnite *f.*

belfry ['belfri], *s.* Beffroi *m*, clocher *m. S.a.* BAT¹.

Belgian ['beldʒən], *a. & s.* Belge (*mf*); de Belgique. **B. turn of phrase,** belgicisme *m.*

Belgium ['beldʒəm]. *Pr.n.* La Belgique.

belie [bi'lai], *v.tr.* (*pr.p.* **belying** [bi'laiiŋ]) Donner un démenti à (des paroles); démentir (une promesse, des espérances); faire mentir (un proverbe).

belief [bi'liːf], *s.* **1.** Croyance *f*, conviction *f.* **B. in ghosts,** croyance aux revenants. **B. in God,** croyance en Dieu. **To the best of my b.,** à ce que je crois; autant que je sache. **2. B. in s.o., in sth.,** foi *f*, confiance *f*, en qn, en qch.

believable [bi'liːvəbl], *a.* Croyable.

believe [bi'liːv]. **1.** *v.tr.* (*a*) Croire (une nouvelle, etc.); ajouter foi à (une rumeur); accorder créance à (une affirmation). **I b. (that) I am right,** je crois avoir raison. **The house was believed to be haunted,** la maison passait pour être hantée. **He is believed to have a chance,** on lui croit des chances (de réussir). **I b. not,** je crois que non; je ne le crois pas. **I b. so,** je crois que oui; je le crois. **Seeing is believing,** voir c'est croire. **To make s.o. b. that . . . ,** faire accroire à qn que. . . . *F:* **Don't you b. it!** N'en croyez rien! **I can well b. it,** je suis prêt à le croire. **B. it or not, I'm in love with her (him),** je l'aime, figure-toi. (*b*) **To b. s.o.,** croire qn; accorder créance au dire de qn. **If he is to be believed . . . ,** à l'en croire . . . ; s'il faut l'en croire. . . . **2.** *v.i.* (*a*) **To b. in God,** croire en Dieu. **To b. in one God,** croire à un seul Dieu. (*b*) **To b. in s.o.'s word,** croire à la parole de qn. **I don't b. in doctors,** je n'ai pas confiance dans les médecins. **He believes in change,** il en est pour les changements. **3. To make b. to do sth.,** feindre, faire semblant, de faire qch. *S.a.* MAKE-BELIEVE.

believer [bi'liːvər], *s.* **1.** Croyant, -ante. **2. To be a b. in sth.,** (i) croire à qch.; (ii) être partisan de qch.

belittle [bi'litl], *v.tr.* Rabaisser, déprécier, amoindrir (qn, le mérite de qn); décrier (qn). **To b. oneself,** se déprécier.

Belisha [bi'liːʃə]. *Pr.n. See* BEACON¹ 5.

bell¹ [bel], *s.* **1.** (*a*) (Clapper-)b. (*in church, etc.*), cloche *f*; (*smaller*) clochette *f*; (*in house*) sonnette *f*; (*fixed bell*) timbre *m*; (*for cattle, sheep*) clochette, clarine *f*, sonnaille *f.* **Globular b., sleigh-b.,** grelot *m.* **Electric b.,** sonnerie *f* (électrique). *Med: etc:* **Night-b.,** sonnette de nuit. **Set of bells** (*of church, etc.*), sonnerie. **Great b.** (*of church*), bourdon *m.* **Chime of bells, carillon** *m.* **There's a ring at the b., there's the b.,** on sonne. **To ring the b.,** (i) sonner; (ii) (*handbell*) agiter la sonnette; (iii) (*at a fair*) faire sonner le timbre de la tête de Turc. *F:* **This rings a b.,** cela me rappelle, dit, quelque chose. *S.a.* CANTERBURY, SOUND⁸ I. 1. (*b*) **The dinner-b.,** la cloche du dîner. *S.a.* PASSING-BELL. (*c*) *Nau:* **To strike the bells,** piquer l'heure. **Six bells,** six coups (de cloche). **To strike eight bells,** piquer midi. **2.** Calice *m*, clochette (d'une fleur); pavillon *m* (d'une trompette, etc.); cloche (de gazomètre). **'bell-boy,** *s.m. U.S:* Groom (d'hôtel); chasseur. **'bell-buoy,** *s.* Bouée *f* à cloche. **'bell-crank,** *attrib. B.-c.* lever, levier coudé, à renvoi. **'bell-flower,** *s.* Campanule *f.* **'bell-founder,** *s.* Fondeur *m* de cloches. **'bell-foundry,** *s.* Fonderie *f* de cloches. **'bell-handle,** *s.* **1.** Tirant *m* (de cloche, de sonnette). **2.** Poignée *f* (de sonnette à main). **'bell-hop,** *s.m. U.S: F:* = BELL-BOY. **'bell-metal,** *s.* Métal *m*, bronze *m*, de cloche(s). **'bell-mouth,** *s.* Évasement *m*, égueulement *m.* **'bell-mouthed,** *a.*

Évasé; (entrée *f*) en entonnoir. **'bell-pull,** *s.* Cordon *m* de sonnette. **'bell-push,** *s.* Bouton *m* (de sonnerie électrique); bouton (à) poussoir. **'bell-ringer,** *s.* (*a*) Sonneur *m.* (*b*) Carillonneur *m.* **'bell-ringing,** *s.* **1.** Carillonnement *m.* **2.** Art *m* campanaire. **'bell-rope,** *s.* Corde *f* de cloche; cordon *m* de sonnette. **'bell-shaped,** *a.* En forme de cloche. **'bell-tower,** *s.* Clocher *m*; campanile *m.* **'bell-wether,** *s.m.* **1.** *Husb:* Sonnailler; bélier meneur du troupeau. **2.** *Pej:* Chef de bande; meneur.

bell². **1.** *v.tr. F:* **To b. the cat,** attacher le grelot. **2.** *v.i.* (*Of skirt, etc.*) Faire cloche; ballonner.

bell³, *s.* Bramement *m* (du cerf).

bell⁴, *v.i.* (*Of deer*) Bramer, raire.

belladonna [ˌbelə'dɔnə], *s.* Belladone *f.*

belle [bel], *s.f. (Pers.)* Beauté *f.* **The b. of the ball,** la reine, la beauté, du bal.

belles-lettres ['bel'letr], *s.pl. Lit:* Belles-lettres *fpl.*

bellicose ['belikous], *a.* Belliqueux, -euse.

bellicosity [ˌbeli'kɔsiti], *s.* Humeur belliqueuse; caractère belliqueux.

-bellied ['belid], *a.* (*With adj. prefixed*) Big-b., ventru, pansu. *S.a.* POT-BELLIED.

belligerency [bi'lidʒər(ə)nsi], *s.* Belligérance *f.*

belligerent [be'lidʒər(ə)nt], *a. & s.* Belligérant (*m*).

bellow¹ ['belou], *s.* (*a*) Beuglement *m*, mugissement *m.* (*b*) Hurlement *m* (de douleur, etc.).

bellow². **1.** *v.i.* (*Of bull*) Beugler, mugir; (*of pers., ocean*) mugir, hurler. **2.** *v.tr. F:* **To b. (out) a song,** *F:* beugler une chanson.

bellows ['belouz], *s.pl.* **1.** Soufflet *m* (pour le feu). **A pair of b.,** un soufflet; *F:* **My b.,** mes poumons *m.* **2.** Soufflerie *f* (d'un orgue, d'une forge).

belly¹ ['beli], *s.* **1.** Ventre *m*; *P:* panse *f*, bedaine *f.* **2.** (*a*) Ventre, panse (d'une cruche). (*b*) *Mus:* Table *f* d'harmonie (d'un violon, d'un piano). **3.** *Nau:* Creux *m*, fond *m* (d'une voile). **'belly-ache¹,** *s. F:* Mal *m* de ventre; colique *f.* **'belly-ache²,** *v.i. P:* Ronchonner, rouspéter, bougonner, se plaindre. **'belly-button,** *s. F:* Nombril *m.* **'belly-flop,** *s. Swim: F:* **To do a b.-f.,** faire un plat ventre *inv.* **'belly-land,** *v.tr. & i. Av:* Atterrir sur le ventre. **'belly-landing,** *s. Av:* Atterrissage *m* sur le ventre.

belly². *Nau:* **1.** *v.tr. (Of wind)* To b. (out) **the sails,** enfler, gonfler, les voiles. **2.** *v.i. (Of sail)* Faire (le) sac.

bellyful ['beliful], *s.* Plein ventre; *F:* ventrée *f. F:* **To have a b.,** en avoir une gavée; en avoir tout son soûl; *P:* en avoir marre; en avoir plein le dos.

belong [bi'lɔŋ], *v.i.* **1.** Appartenir, être **(to, à).** **That book belongs to me,** ce livre m'appartient, est à moi. **It belongs to me to decide,** il m'appartient de décider. **That belongs to my duties,** cela relève de mes attributions. *(Of land)* **To b. to the Crown,** dépendre de la Couronne. **2.** *(Be appropriate)* Être propre (à qch.). **Such amusements do not b. to his age,** de tels amusements ne sont pas de son âge. *U.S:* **To b. with,** aller avec. **Cheese belongs with salad,** le fromage va avec la salade. **3.** *(Be connected)* **To b. to a society,** faire partie, être membre, d'une société. **To b. to a place,** (i) être (natif, originaire) d'un endroit; (ii) résider à un endroit. **I b. here,** je suis d'ici. **Put it back where it belongs,** remets-le à sa place.

belongings [bi'lɔŋiŋz], *s.pl.* Affaires *f*, effets *m* (appartenant à qn). **Personal b.,** objets personnels. **With all one's b.,** avec armes et bagages.

beloved. **1.** *p.p. & pred. a.* [bi'lʌvd] Aimé. **B. by all,** aimé de tous. **B. of the gods,** aimé, chéri, des dieux. **2.** *a. & s.* [bi'lʌvid] Bien-aimé(e), chéri(e). **My b.,** mon, ma, bien-aimé(e).

below [bi'lou]. **1.** *adv.* (*a*) En bas, (au-)dessous. **The tenants of the flat b.,** les locataires du dessous. **Here b. (on earth),** ici-bas. *Nau:* **All hands b.!** tout le monde en bas! *S.a.* DOWN⁸ I. 2. (*b*) *Jur:* **The court b.,** le tribunal inférieur. (*c*) **The passage quoted b.,** le passage cité (i) ci-dessous, (ii) plus loin, ci-après. **2.** *prep.* Au-dessous de. (*a*) **B. the knee,** au-dessous du genou. **On the table and b. it,** sur la table et (au-)dessous. *S.a.* BELT¹ 1. (*b*) **B. the average,** au-dessous de la moyenne. **Temperature b. normal,** température inférieure à la normale. (*c*) **B. the surface,** sous la surface. *Th:* **B.-stage,** les dessous *m.* (*d*) **B. the**

bridge, en aval du pont. (*e*) To be b. s.o. in rank, occuper un rang inférieur à qn.

belt[1] [belt], *s.* **1.** (Waist-)b., ceinture *f*, *Mil:* ceinturon *m.* (**Shoulder-**)b., baudrier *m*, banderole *f*. **Suspender**, *U.S:* garter, b., gaine *f*, porte-jarretelles *m. inv. S.a.* HALF-BELT, LIFE-BELT. *Box:* **Blow below the b.**, donner à qn un coup en traître; frapper qn déloyalement. *Av: Aut:* **Seat b.**, ceinture de sécurité. **2.** *Mec.E.:* Courroie *f* (de transmission). *Mil:* **Loading b.** (**of machine gun**), bande-chargeur *f*, *pl.* bandes-chargeur (**machine gun**), bande-chargeur *f*, *pl.* bandes-chargeurs. **3.** B. of hills, ceinture de collines. **B. of land**, bande *f* de terre. **Coal b.**, zone houillère. **The belts of Jupiter**, les zones, les bandes, de Jupiter. **Tradewind b.**, zone des (vents) alizés. **Standard-time b.**, fuseau *m* horaire. *Adm:* **Green b.**, zone verte, zone de verdure. **'belt-driven**, *a.* Mû, actionné, par courroie.

belt[2], *v.tr.* **1.** Ceinturer, ceindre (qn, qch.). **2.** (*Surround*) Entourer (qch.) d'une ceinture. **3.** *F:* To b. along, aller à toute allure. **belted**, *a.* Ceinture; à ceinture.

belting, *s.* **1.** (*a*) Ceinture(s) *f(pl)*. (*b*) Matière *f* à courroies. **2.** *Mec.E:* Transmission *f*. **3.** *F:* To give a child a good b., administrer une correction à un enfant (avec une courroie).

belvedere ['belvidiər], *s.* *Arch:* Belvédère *m*; mirador *m.*

bemire [bi'maiər], *v.tr.* *O:* Crotter; embourber (qn).

bemoan [bi'moun], *v.tr.* Pleurer, déplorer (qch.).

bemuse [bi'mju:z], *v.tr.* Stupéfier.

Ben[1] [ben]. *Pr.n.m.* Benjamin. *S.a.* BIG BEN.

ben[2], *s. Geog:* (*Scot.*) Sommet *m*. B. Nevis, le mont Nevis.

ben[3], *s. Bot:* Ben *m*. Oil of b., huile de ben. **'ben-nut**, *s.* Noix de ben.

bench[1] [ben(t)ʃ], *s.* **1.** (*a*) Banc *m*; banquette *f*; gradin *m* (d'amphithéâtre). *Parl:* The Treasury B., le banc ministériel. *Jur:* The judge's b., le siège du juge. (*b*) *Jur:* The B., (i) la magistrature, (ii) (*the judges*), la Cour. Queen's B., *Fr.C:* Cour du Banc de la Reine. **2.** (*a*) Établi *m* (de menuisier). (*b*) *Mec.E:* Testing-b., banc d'essai, d'épreuve. **3.** *Civ.E:* Accotement *m*, berme *f* (d'un chemin). **'bench-mark**, *s. Surv:* Repère *m*. **'bench-stop**, *s. Carp:* Griffe *f* d'établi. **'bench-test**, *s. Mec.E:* Essai *m* au banc.

bench[2], *v.tr.* **1.** To b. a dog, exhiber un chien (à une exposition canine). **2.** *Const:* To b. out the ground, préparer le sol (pour des fondations). **3.** *Sp:* *U.S:* To b. a player, retirer un joueur (du jeu).

bencher ['ben(t)ʃər], *s.* Avocat appartenant au corps des doyens des '*Inns of Court*,' *q.v. under* INN 2.

bend[1] [bend], *s. Nau:* Nœud *m*, ajut *m*. Fisherman's b., nœud de grappin; nœud anglais.

bend[2], *s. Her:* Bande *f*. B. sinister, barre *f*.

bend[3], *s.* **1.** Courbure *f*; courbe *f*; (*of road, pipe*) coude *m*; (*of road*) tournant *m*, virage *m*; (*of river*) méandre *m*, boucle *f*. To take a b., prendre un virage. *S.a.* HAIRPIN. *P.N:* Bends for 3 miles, virages sur 5 kilomètres. *Cy:* B. of the handle-bar, cintre *m* du guidon. *Mec.E:* Expansion b., arc compensateur. U-b., (i) courbe de retour; (ii) tube *m* en U, coude en U. *P:* To be round the b., être fou, cinglé, dingo. *P:* To go on the b., faire la bombe. **2.** *Med:* *F:* The bends, mal *m* des caissons.

bend[4], *v.tr. & i.* (**bent**) *p.p.* **bent**, *Lit: occ.* **bended**), **1.** Courber (un osier, le corps); plier (le bras, etc.); ployer, fléchir (le genou); baisser (la tête); arquer (le dos); cambrer, cintrer (un tuyau, un rail). To b. one's head over a book, pencher la tête sur un livre. To b. to s.o.'s will, se plier à, fléchir devant, la volonté de qn. Better b. than break, mieux vaut plier que rompre. The road, river, bends to the right, la route, la rivière, tourne, s'infléchit, fait un coude, vers la droite. To b. beneath a burden, plier, fléchir, se courber, sous un fardeau. *S.a.* KNEE 1. *F:* To catch s.o. bending, surprendre qn en mauvaise posture. To b. the elbow, lever le coude. **2.** (*a*) *v.tr.* To b. a rod, a key, out of shape, forcer, fausser, une barre de fer, une clef. (*b*) *v.i.* To b. under a strain, (*of wood, iron*) b. idiot, ce sacré imbécile. **3.** (*Make tense*) Tendre, bander (un arc, un ressort). **4.** (*Direct*) (*a*) To b. one's steps towards a place, diriger, porter, ses pas, se diriger, vers un endroit. (*b*) *Lit:* To b. one's

gaze on sth., fixer ses regards sur qch. **5.** *Nau:* (*a*) Étalinguer (un câble); frapper (une manœuvre); enverguer (une voile). (*b*) Abouter (deux cordages).

bend back, **1.** *v.tr.* Reployer en arrière; replier; recourber (une lame, etc.); réfléchir (la lumière). **2.** *v.i.* (*a*) Se recourber; se réfléchir. (*b*) (*Of pers.*) Se pencher en arrière. **bend down. 1.** *v.tr.* Courber, ployer (une branche). **2.** *v.i.* Se courber, se baisser.

bend forward, *v.i.* Se pencher en avant. **bent**, *a.* **1.** (*a*) Courbé, plié, arqué. **B. back**, dos voûté. (*b*) Faussé, fléchi, gauchi. To become b., (i) s'arquer, se courber; (*with age*) se voûter; (ii) (*of rod, spring, etc.*) fléchir, gauchir. **2.** (*Determined*) Déterminé, résolu, décidé (*on doing sth.*, à faire qch.). He is b. on ruining you, il est acharné à votre perte. He is b. on seeing me, il veut absolument me voir. To be b. on gain, être âpre au gain. **3.** To be homeward b., diriger ses pas, s'acheminer, vers la maison. **bending**, *s.* (*a*) Ployage *m*, cintrage *m*. (*b*) *Mec.E: etc:* Arcure *f*. (*c*) *Mec:* B. strength, résistance à la flexion. **B. moment**, moment de flexion.

bender [bendər], *s.* **1.** (*Pers.*) *Metalw:* Cintreur *m*. **2.** *Mec.E:* Cintreuse *f*. **3.** *U.S:* *P:* To go on a b., faire la noce, la bombe.

beneath [bi'ni:θ]. **1.** *adv.* Dessous, au-dessous, en bas. From b., de dessous. **2.** *prep.* (*a*) (*Lower than*) Audessous de; sous. It is b. him to complain, il est indigne de lui de se plaindre; il dédaigne de se plaindre. *S.a.* MARRY[1] 2. (*b*) (*Under*) The plank gave way b. me, la planche céda sous mon poids. To bend b. a burden, plier sous un fardeau.

Benedict ['benidikt]. *Pr.n.m.* Benoît, Benoist.

benedictine ['beni'diktin]. **1.** *Ecc: a. & s.* Bénédictin, -ine. **2.** *s.* (*also* [-ti:n]) (*Liqueur*) Bénédictine *f*.

benediction ['beni'dik[(ə)n], *s.* **1.** Bénédiction *f*. **2.** (*At meals*) Bénédicité *m*.

benedictory ['beni'diktəri], *a.* De bénédiction. **B. prayer**, bénédiction *f*.

benefaction [,beni'fæk[(ə)n], *s.* **1.** Bienfait *m*. **2.** (*a*) Œuvre *f* de bienfaisance. (*b*) Donation *f*.

benefactor, -tress ['benifæktər, -tris], *s.* **1.** Bienfaiteur, -trice. **2.** Donateur, -trice.

benefice ['benifis], *s. Ecc:* Bénéfice *m*.

beneficed ['benifist], *a. Ecc:* Pourvu d'un bénéfice. **B. clergyman**, bénéficier *m*.

beneficence [bi'nefisəns], *s.* **1.** Bienfaisance *f*. **2.** Œuvre *f* de bienfaisance.

beneficent [bi'nefisənt], *a.* **1.** Bienfaisant. **2.** Salutaire. **-ly**, *adv.* **1.** Avec bienfaisance. **2.** Salutairement.

beneficial [,beni'fi[(ə)l], *a.* **1.** Salutaire, profitable, utile, avantageux. **2.** *Jur:* B. owner, occupant, usufruitier, -ière. **-ally**, *adv.* Avantageusement.

beneficiary [,beni'fi[əri], *a. & s. Ecc: Jur:* Bénéficier, -ière ; bénéficiaire (*m*); ayant-droit *m*.

benefit[1] ['benifit], *s.* **1.** Avantage *m*, profit *m*. To derive, reap, b. from sth., profiter de qch. *Jur:* B. of the doubt, bénéfice *m* du doute. **B. club, b. society**, société de secours mutuels. *Th: Sp:* B. (performance, match), représentation, match, au bénéfice de qn. **2.** *Adm:* Indemnité *f*, allocation *f*. Unemployment b., indemnité de chômage; prestation *f*. Medical b., secours médical. **Maternity b.**, allocation de maternité.

benefit[2]. **1.** *v.tr.* Faire du bien, être avantageux, profiter, à (qn, qch.). **2.** *v.i.* To b. by, from, sth., profiter de qch.; gagner à qch.; se trouver bien de qch.

Benelux ['beniLʌks]. *Pr.n.Geog:* (Le) Bénélux.

benevolence [bi'nevələns], *s.* **1.** Bienveillance *f*, bonté *f*. **2.** Bienfait *m*; don *m* charitable.

benevolent [bi'nevələnt], *a.* **1.** Bienveillant (to, envers). **2.** Bienfaisant, charitable (to, envers). **B. society**, association de bienfaisance; société de secours mutuels. **-ly**, *adv.* Avec bienveillance.

Bengal [ben'gɔ:l]. *Pr.n.Geog:* Le Bengale. **B. light**, feu *m* de Bengale.

Bengali [ben'gɔ:li], *a. & s. Ethn: Ling:* Bengali *mf*.

benighted [bi'naitid], *a.* **1.** Anuité; surpris par la nuit. **2.** Plongé dans les ténèbres de l'ignorance. *F:* That b. idiot, ce sacré imbécile.

benign [bi'nain], *a.* Bénin, *f.* bénigne; doux, *f.* douce; favorable. (*b*) *Med:* Bénin. **-ly**, *adv.* Bénignement.

benignant [bi'nignənt], *a.* Bénin, *f.* bénigne; bon, bienveillant. **-ly,** *adv.* Avec bienveillance.

benignity [bi'nigniti], *s.* **1.** Bienveillance *f,* bonté *f.* **2.** Bénignité *f* (du climat, d'une fièvre).

Benjamin¹ ['ben(d)ʒ(ə)min]. *Pr.n.m.* Benjamin. The B., le Benjamin (de la famille); le favori, le gâté.

benjamin², *s. Bot:* Benjoin *m.*

bent¹ [bent], *s.* Penchant *m,* inclination *f,* disposition *f* (**for,** pour). **To have a b. towards sth.,** avoir du goût pour qch., un penchant à qch., des dispositions naturelles pour qch. **To follow one's b.,** suivre son penchant.

bent². *See* BEND⁴.

benumb [bi'nʌm], *v.tr.* (*a*) Engourdir, transir. (*b*) Paralyser, engourdir (l'esprit).

Benzedrine ['benzidri:n], *s. R.t.m.:* Benzédrine *f.*

benzene, benzine ['benzi:n, ben'zi:n], *s.* Benzine *f.*

benzoate ['benzoeit], *s. Ch:* Benzoate *m.*

benzoic [ben'zouik], *a. Ch:* (Acide m) benzoïque.

benzoin ['benzoin], *s.* (Gum) b., benjoin *m.*

benzol ['benzɔl], *s. Ch: Com:* Benzol *m.*

benzoline ['benzoli:n], *s. Ch:* Essence minérale.

beplaster [bi'pla:stər], *v.tr.* Barbouiller, enduire grossièrement; plâtrer; torcher.

bequeath [bi'kwi:ð], *v.tr.* Léguer (**to,** à).

bequest [bi'kwest], *s.* Legs *m.* (*In museum*) Fonds *m.*

berate [bi'reit], *v.tr.* Gronder, réprimander, morigéner.

Berber ['bə:bər]. **1.** *a. & s. Ethn:* Berbère *mf.* **2.** *s. Ling:* Le berbère.

berceuse [beə'sə:z], *s. Mus:* Berceuse *f.*

bereave [bi'ri:v], *v.tr.* (*p.t. & p.p.* **bereft** [bi'reft], **bereaved;** *usu.* **bereft** *in* 1 *and* **bereaved** *in* 2) Priver déposséder (s.o. of sth., qn de qch.). **1.** Indignation had bereft him of speech, l'indignation l'avait privé de la parole. **2. An accident bereaved him of his father, of his parents,** un accident lui a ravi son père, l'a rendu orphelin. *s.pl.* **The bereaved,** la famille du mort; les affligés.

bereavement [bi'ri:vmənt], *s.* Perte *f* (d'un parent); deuil *m.*

bereft. *See* BEREAVE.

beret ['berei, 'beret], *s. Cost:* Béret *m.*

bergamot¹ ['bə:gəmɔt], *s.* (*Orange or lemon*) Bergamote *f.* **B. tree,** bergamotier *m.*

bergamot², *s.* (*Pear*) Bergamote *f,* crassane *f.*

bergschrund ['beəgʃrund], *s. Geol: Mount:* Rimaye *f.*

Bergsonism ['bə:gsənizm], *s. Phil:* Bergsonisme *m.*

beriberi ['beri'beri], *s. Med:* Béribéri *m.*

berkelium ['bə:kliəm], *s. Ch:* Berkélium *m.*

Berlin [bə:'lin]. *Pr.n. Geog:* Berlin. **B. wool,** laine *f* à tricoter, à broder.

berm [bə:m], *s. Civ.E:* Berme *f,* banquette *f;* risberme *f* (d'un barrage).

Bermudas (the) [ðəbə(:)'mju:dəz]. *Pr.n. Geog:* Les Bermudes *f.*

Bernardine ['bə:nədin], *a. & s. Ecc.Hist:* Bernardin, -ine.

Bern(e) ['bə:n]. *Pr.n. Geog:* Berne.

berry¹ ['beri], *s.* **1.** *Bot:* Baie *f.* **2.** (*a*) Frai *m* (de poisson). (*b*) Œufs *mpl* (de crustacé). **Lobster in b.,** homard œuvé.

berry², *v.i.* (*Of shrub*) Se garnir de baies. **berried,** *a.* **1.** *Bot:* A baies; couvert de baies. **2.** (Crustacé) œuvé.

berserk [bə:'sə:k], *s.* Berserk *m.* **To go b.,** devenir fou furieux.

berth¹ [bə:θ], *s.* **1.** *Nau:* (*a*) Évitée *f,* évitage *m.* **To give a ship a wide b.,** éviter, parer, un navire; passer au large d'un navire. **To give s.o. a wide b.,** éviter qn. (*b*) (*Anchoring*) Poste *m* de mouillage, d'amarrage. (*c*) Poste à quai; emplacement *m.* **2.** (*a*) *Nau: Rail:* Couchette *f* (de voyageur). (*b*) *Nau:* Cadre *m* (d'officier, d'homme d'équipage). **3.** (*a*) Emplacement (de qch.). (*b*) *F:* Place, emploi *m.* *F:* **To find a b.,** arriver à se caser. *F:* **To find a soft b.,** trouver un emploi pépère.

berth². **1.** *v.tr.* (*a*) Donner, assigner, un poste à (un navire). (*b*) Accoster (un navire) le long du quai. **2.** *v.i.* (*a*) (*Of ship*) (i) Mouiller. (ii) Aborder à quai. (*b*) **To b. forward,** aft, coucher à l'avant, à l'arrière.

beryl ['beril], *s. Miner:* Béryl *m.*

berylline ['berəli:n], *a.* Qui ressemble au béryl; de béryl.

beryllium [be'riliəm], *s. Ch:* Béryllium, *m,* glucinium *m.*

beseech [bi'si:tʃ], *v.tr.* (**besought** [bi'sɔ:t]) *Lit:* **1.** Supplier, adjurer, conjurer (s.o. to do sth., qn de faire qch.). **2. To b. s.o.'s pardon,** implorer le pardon de qn. **beseeching,** *a.* (Air, ton) suppliant. **-ly,** *adv.* D'un air, d'un ton, suppliant.

beseem [bi'si:m], *v.tr.* (*Impers.*) *Lit:* **It would ill b. me to . . .,** je serais mal venu à . . . **beseeming,** *a.* Convenable, seyant.

beset [bi'set], *v.tr.* (*p.t.* **beset;** *p.p.* **beset; besetting**) *Lit:* **1.** Cerner (des troupes); assaillir, obséder (qn); serrer (qn) de près. **B. with dangers, with difficulties,** environné, entouré, de dangers, de difficultés. **2.** (*Of misfortunes, etc.*) Assaillir (qn). **besetting,** *a.* **B. sin,** péché d'habitude; péché mignon.

beside [bi'said], *prep.* **1.** A côté, auprès, de (qn, qch.). **Seated b. me,** assis à côté de moi. **There is no one to set b. him,** il n'y a personne qui lui soit comparable. **2.** (*a*) **B. the question, b. the point,** à côté de la question; en dehors du sujet. (*b*) **To be b. oneself,** être hors de soi; (*with joy*) être transporté de joie.

besides [bi'saidz]. **1.** *adv.* (*a*) En outre, en plus; bien plus. **Many more b.,** encore bien d'autres. **Nothing b.,** rien de plus. (*b*) **It is too late; b., I am tired,** il est trop tard; d'ailleurs, du reste, je suis fatigué. **2.** *prep.* **Others b. him,** d'autres que lui. **We were four b. John,** nous étions quatre sans compter Jean. **Who b. him?** Qui hormis lui, à part lui?

besiege [bi'si:dʒ], *v.tr.* Assiéger; mettre le siège devant (une ville); faire le siège (d'une ville). **besieged.** **1.** *a.* **The b. town,** la ville assiégée, investie. **2.** *s.* **The b.,** les assiégés.

besieger [bi'si:dʒər], *s.* Assiégeant *m.*

beslobber [bi'slɔbər], *v.tr. F: O:* **1.** Baver sur (qch.). **2.** Prodiguer des baisers (baveux) à (qn).

besmear [bi'smiər], *v.tr.* Barbouiller, souiller.

besmirch [bi'smə:tʃ], *v.tr. O:* Salir, tacher, souiller (qch.); salir, ternir (la mémoire de qn, etc.).

besom ['bi:zəm], *s.* Balai *m* (de jonc, de bruyère).

besot [bi'sɔt], *v.tr.* (**besotted**) Abrutir (**with,** de). **besotted,** *a.* Abruti (par la boisson, etc.).

besought. *See* BESEECH.

bespatter [bi'spætər], *v.tr.* Eclabousser. **Bespattered with mud,** tout couvert de boue.

bespeak [bi'spi:k], *v.tr.* (*Conj. like* SPEAK) **1.** Commander (des souliers, etc.); retenir, arrêter (une place, une chambre à l'hôtel). **2.** Accuser, annoncer. **His conversation bespeaks a man of wit,** sa conversation annonce un homme d'esprit. **bespoke,** *a.* (*a*) **B. garment,** vêtement (fait) sur commande, sur mesure. (*b*) **B. shoemaker,** cordonnier à façon.

bespeckle [bi'spekl], *v.tr.* Tacheter, moucheter.

bespectacled [bi'spektəkld], *a.* Qui porte des lunettes; portant lunettes; à lunettes.

besprinkle [bi'spriŋkl], *v.tr. Lit:* (*a*) Arroser, asperger (**with,** de). (*b*) Saupoudrer (**with,** de). (*c*) Parsemer (**with,** de).

Bess [bes]. *Pr.n.f. F:* (*Dim. of Elizabeth*) Lisette. *A:* **Brown B.,** fusil *m* à pierre; mousquet *m. Hist: F:* **Good Queen B.,** la bonne reine Élisabeth (1533-1603).

Bessarabia [,besə'reibjə]. *Pr.m. Geog:* (La) Bessarabie.

best¹ [best]. **1.** *a. & s.* (*a*) (Le) meilleur, (la) meilleure; (*neuter*) le mieux. **B. man** (*at a wedding*), garçon d'honneur. **We drank of the b., of his b.,** nous avons bu du meilleur, de son meilleur. (*Dressed*) **in one's b.** (*clothes*), endimanché; (*of woman*) dans ses plus beaux atours; *F:* sur son trente et un. **He can sing with the b.,** il chante comme pas un. **The b. of the matter, the b. of it, is that . . .,** le plus beau de l'affaire c'est que. . . . **The b. part of the way, of the year,** la plus grande partie du chemin, de l'année. **To know what is b. for s.o.,** savoir ce qui convient le mieux à qn. **It would be b. to . . .,** le b. plan would be to . . ., le mieux serait de. . . . **To do one's b., the b. one can,** faire de son mieux, faire tout son possible. **I did my b. to comfort her,** je la consolai de mon mieux. **He did his b. to smile,** il s'efforça de sourire. **To look one's**

b., être, paraître, à son avantage; (*of woman*) être en beauté. **To be at one's b.**, être en train, en forme. **She was at her b. at thirty**, c'est à trente ans qu'elle a été le plus belle. **To get, have, the b. of it, of the bargain**; **to come off b.**, l'emporter; avoir l'avantage; avoir le dessus. **To make the b. of sth.**, s'accommoder de qch. **To make the b. of a bad job, of a bad bargain**, faire bonne mine à mauvais jeu; faire contre mauvaise fortune bon cœur. *S.a.* FOOT¹ 1, NEXT I. 2, SECOND-BEST. (*b*) *Adv.phr.* **At (the) b.** **To sell at b.**, vendre au mieux. **At (the) b. it is a poor piece of work**, pour dire le mieux c'est un piètre travail. **To act for the b.**, agir pour le mieux. **To do sth. to the b. of one's ability**, faire qch. de son mieux. **To the b. of my belief, knowledge, recollection**, à ce que je crois; autant que je sache; (pour) autant que je puisse m'en souvenir. **2.** *adv.* (*a*) **He does it (the) b.**, c'est lui qui le fait le mieux. **I comforted her as b. I could**, je la consolai de mon mieux. **You know b.**, c'est vous (qui êtes) le mieux placé pour en juger. **Do as you think b.**, faites comme bon vous semble(ra). (*b*) **The b. dressed man**, l'homme le mieux habillé. **The b. known book**, le livre le mieux, le plus, connu. **best-'seller**, *s.* F: **1.** Best-seller, livre *m* à succès, à fort tirage, à forte vente. **2.** Auteur *m* à gros tirages. **3.** Article *m* de grosse vente.

best², *v.tr.* F: L'emporter sur (qn).

bestial ['bestjəl], *a.* Bestial, -aux. **-ally**, *adv.* Bestialement.

bestiality [ˌbesti'æliti], *s.* Bestialité *f.*

bestialize ['bestiəlaiz], *v.tr.* Bestialiser, abrutir.

bestir [bi'stəːr], *v.pr.* (*Conj. like* STIR) **To b. oneself**, se remuer. s'actionner. s'activer.

bestow [bi'stou], *v.tr.* Lit: Accorder, octroyer, donner (sth. upon s.o., qch. à qn). **To b. a title on s.o.**, conférer un titre à qn. **To b. one's affection on s.o.**, placer son affection sur qn. *O:* **To b. one's hand on s.o.**, donner sa main à qn.

bestowal [bi'stouəl], *s.* Don *m*, octroi *m* (de qch.).

bestrew [bi'struː], *v.tr.* (*p.t.* bestrewed; *p.p.* bestrewed *or* bestrewn [bi'struːn]) Lit: Parsemer, joncher (with, de).

bestride [bi'straid], *v.tr.* (bestrode [bi'stroud], bestridden [bi'stridn]) **1.** (*a*) Être à cheval, à califourchon, sur (qch.). (*b*) Se tenir les jambes écartées au-dessus de (qch.). **2.** (*a*) Enjamber (un fossé). (*b*) Enfourcher (un cheval).

bet¹ [bet], *s.* Pari *m*, gageure *f.* **To make, lay, a b.**, parier; faire un pari. **To take (up) a b.**, tenir, accepter, un pari. *S.a.* EVEN² 3.

bet², *v.tr.* (*p.t.* bet; *p.p.* bet; betting) Parier (une somme). **To b. ten to one that . . .**, parier à dix contre un que. . . . **To b. two to one**, parier le double contre le simple. **To b. against s.o.**, parier contre qn. **To b. that one will do sth.**, parier de faire qch. **To b. on sth.**, parier sur qch. F: **You b.!** pour sûr! *P:* **tu parles!** **I b. you don't!** *P:* Chiche (que tu ne le feras pas)! **B. you I will!** Chiche (que je le fais)! **I'll b. you anything you like**, j'en mettrais ma tête à couper. **betting**, *s.* Les paris *m.* **The b. ran high**, on a parié gros. **B. shop** = bureau du pari mutuel.

beta ['biːtə], *s.* (*a*) Gr.Alph: Bêta *m.* (*b*) Ph: **B. particle**, particule *f* bêta.

betake [bi'teik], *v.pr.* (*Conj. like* TAKE). A: **To b. oneself to a place**, (s'en) aller, se rendre, dans, à, un endroit.

betatron ['biːtətron], *s.* Atom.Ph: Bêtatron *m.*

betel ['biːt(ə)l], *s.* Bétel *m.* **B.-nut**, (noix *f* d')arec *m.*

Bethany ['beθəni]. *Pr.n.* B.Hist: Béthanie *f.*

Bethel ['beθəl]. **1.** *Pr.n.* B.Hist: Béthel *m.* **2.** *s.* Temple *m* (d'une secte dissidente).

bethink [bi'θiŋk], *v.pr.* (*Conj. like* THINK). A: **1.** **To b. oneself**, réfléchir, considérer. **To b. oneself of sth., to do sth.**, s'aviser de qch., de faire qch. **2.** Se rappeler (that, que).

Bethlehem ['beθlihem]. *Pr.n.* B.Hist: Bethléem *m.*

bethought. See BETHINK.

betide [bi'taid], *v.* (*Used only in 3rd sing. pres. sub.* A. & *Lit:* **1.** *v.i.* Whate'er b., quoi qu'il arrive; advienne que pourra. **2.** *v.tr.* Woe b. him if ever . . ., malheur à lui si jamais. . . .

betimes [bi'taimz], *adv.* Lit: De bonne heure.

betoken [bi'touk(ə)n], *v.tr.* Lit: **1.** Être signe de (qch.); accuser, dénoter, révéler. **2.** Présager, annoncer (le beau temps, etc.).

betony ['betəni], *s.* Bot: Bétoine *f.*

betook. See BETAKE.

betray [bi'trei], *v.tr.* **1.** Trahir (qn, sa patrie, sa foi); vendre (qn). **To b. s.o. into s.o.'s hands**, livrer qn aux mains de qn (par trahison). **2.** **To b. s.o. into error**, entraîner qn dans l'erreur. **3.** Révéler, montrer, laisser voir, laisser deviner, trahir (son ignorance, son émotion); livrer, révéler (un secret).

betrayal [bi'treiəl], *s.* **1.** Action *f* de trahir; trahison *f.* **2.** Révélation *f* (de son ignorance, etc.).

betrayer [bi'treiər], *s.* (*a*) Traître, -esse. **B. of his country**, traître envers sa patrie. (*b*) Révélateur, -trice (d'un secret).

betroth [bi'trouð], *v.tr.* A: Lit: Promettre (sa fille) en mariage (to, à); fiancer (to, à, avec).

betrothal [bi'trouðəl], *s.* Fiançailles *fpl* (to, avec).

better¹ ['betər]. **1.** *a. & s.* Meilleur. **B. days**, des jours meilleurs. **They have seen b. days**, ils ont eu des malheurs. *S.a.* DAY 3. **You will find no b. hotel**, vous ne trouverez pas mieux comme hôtel. **He's a b. man than you**, il est votre supérieur; il vaut plus que vous. (*At games, etc.*) **You are b. than I**, vous êtes plus fort que moi. **He is no b. than his brother**, il ne vaut pas mieux que son frère. **The respect due to your betters**, le respect dû à vos supérieurs. **A street of b.-class houses**, une rue de maisons de bonne apparence. **I had hoped for b. things**, j'avais espéré mieux. **For the b. part of the day**, pendant la plus grande partie du jour. *S.a.* HALF 1, WORLD 1. **2.** (*Neuter*) Mieux. (*a*) **That's b.**, voilà qui est mieux. **That's b.!** à la bonne heure! **Nothing could be b., it couldn't be b.**, c'est on ne peut mieux. **So much the b.**, tant mieux. **To do sth. for b. or worse**, faire qch. vaille que vaille. **To take s.o. for b. or worse**, prendre qn pour le meilleur et pour le pire. **To get b.**, (i) (*of thgs*) s'améliorer, s'amender; (ii) (*of pers.*) guérir, se remettre, se rétablir. **The weather is b.**, il fait meilleur. **To be b. (in health)**, aller, se porter, mieux. **Change for the b.**, amélioration *f.* **There is a change for the b.**, il y a un mieux. **To get the b. of s.o.**, (i) l'emporter sur qn; (ii) (*cheat*) refaire qn; mettre qn dedans; rouler qn. **To be (all) the b. for doing sth.**, se trouver bien d'avoir fait qch. *S.a.* ALL I. 3. **To go one b. than s.o.**, (r)enchérir, surenchérir sur qn; F: damer le pion à qn. (*b*) **It is b. that it should be so**; b. so, il vaut mieux qu'il en soit ainsi. **It is b. to go away than stay**, il vaut mieux, mieux vaut, partir que de rester. **It is b. to suffer than to lie**, plutôt souffrir que mentir. **It would be b. to see him again**, il serait préférable de le revoir. **3.** *adv.* (*a*) Mieux. **B. and b.**, de mieux en mieux. **I know that b. than you**, je sais cela mieux que vous. **I can understand it all the b. because . . .**, je le conçois d'autant mieux que. . . . **You had b. stay**, il vaut mieux que vous restiez; vous ferez, feriez, bien de rester. **To think b. of it**, changer d'opinion; se raviser. **B. still . . .**, (i) mieux encore . . ., (ii) qui mieux est. . . . *S.a.* LATE II. 1. (*b*) **B. dressed**, mieux habillé. **B. known**, plus connu.

better². **1.** *v.tr.* (*a*) Améliorer; rendre meilleur. **To b. oneself**, améliorer sa position, sa condition. (*b*) Surpasser (un exploit). **2.** *v.i.* (*Of thg*) S'améliorer.

better³, bettor ['betər], *s.* Parieur *m.*

betterment ['betəmənt], *s.* **1.** Amélioration *f.* **2.** Plus-value *f.*

between [bi'twiːn]. **1.** *prep.* Entre. (*a*) **B. the two hedges**, entre les deux haies. **No one can come b. us**, personne ne peut nous séparer. *S.a.* DEVIL¹ 1, FIRE¹ 4, STOOL¹ 1. (*b*) **B. eight and nine o'clock**, entre huit et neuf heures. **B. now and Monday**, d'ici (à) lundi. **B. twenty and thirty**, de vingt à trente. **B. trains**, entre deux trains. (*c*) **You must choose b. them**, il faut choisir entre les deux. (*d*) **We bought it b. us**, nous l'avons acheté à nous deux, à nous trois, etc. (*e*) **They shared the loot b. them**, ils se sont partagé le butin. **B. ourselves**, entre nous; de vous à moi. **2.** *adv.* **He separated them by rushing b.**, il les a séparés en se jetant entre eux. *S.a.* FAR-BETWEEN,

GO-BETWEEN. **be'tween-decks.** *Nau:* 1. *adv.* Dans l'entre-pont; sous barrots. 2. *s.* L'entrepont *m.* **be'tween-season,** *s.* Demi-saison *f, pl.* demi-saisons. *Attrib.* **B.-s. prices,** prix (réduits) de demi-saison. **be'tween-time(s), -while(s),** *adv.* 1. Dans l'intervalle; entre-temps. 2. De temps en temps.

betwixt [bi'twikst]. 1. *prep.* Entre. 2. *adv.* F: **B. and between,** entre les deux.

bevatron ['bevətrən], *s. Atom.Ph:* Bévatron *m.*

bevel ['bev(ə)l], *s.* 1. Angle *m* oblique. (*a*) Biseau *m,* biais *m.* **B.-edge,** bord biseauté, en chanfrein. (*b*) Conicité *f* (d'un engrenage, etc.). **B.-gear,** engrenage conique. **B.-wheel,** roue dentée conique; pignon conique. 2. *Tls:* **B.-rule, -square,** fausse équerre.

bevel², *v.* (bevelled) 1. *v.tr.* Biseauter, chanfreiner; tailler (qch.) en biseau, en sifflet. 2. *v.i.* (*Of thg*) Biaiser; aller de biais; aller en biseau. **bevelled,** *a.* (Bord) biseauté, en biseau. **bevelling,** *s.* Biseautage *m,* équerrage *m,* chanfreinage *m.* **B. machine,** biseauteuse *f;* biseautoir *m* mécanique.

beveller ['bev(ə)lər], *s. Glassm:* Biseauteur, -euse.

beverage ['bevəridʒ], *s.* Breuvage *m,* boisson *f.*

bevy ['bevi], *s.* 1. Bande *f,* troupe *f. Esp.* B. of girls, bande, essaim *m,* de jeunes filles. 2. *Ven:* (*Of larks, quails*) Volée *f;* (*of roes*) harde *f,* troupe.

bewail [bi'weil], *v.tr. Lit:* Pleurer (qch.). To b. one's lot, se lamenter sur son sort. **bewailing,** *s.* Lamentation *f* (of, sur).

beware [bi'weər], *v.ind.tr. & Poet: v.tr.* (Only in inf. and imp.) To b. of s.o., se méfier, se défier, de qn. To b. of sth., se garder de qch.; prendre garde à qch. B.! prenez garde! *P.N:* **'B. of pickpockets,'** "se méfier des pickpockets." **'B. of the trains!'** "attention aux trains!" To b. of doing sth., se garder de faire qch.

bewilder [bi'wildər], *v.tr.* Désorienter, égarer (qn); F: ahurir (qn). **bewildered,** *a.* (*a*) Désorienté; F: ahuri. **B. air,** air hébété. I am b., j'y perds la tête. (*b*) Abasourdi, confondu. **bewildering,** *a.* Déroutant; F: ahurissant.

bewilderment [bi'wildəmənt], *s.* (*a*) Désorientation *f;* trouble *m;* F: ahurissement *m.* (*b*) Abasourdissement *m.*

bewitch [bi'witʃ], *v.tr.* Ensorceler. (*a*) Jeter un sort sur (qn). (*b*) Charmer, enchanter (qn). **bewitching,** *a.* Ensorcelant, ravissant; enchanteur, -eresse. **-ly,** *adv.* A ravir. She smiled at him b., elle lui adressa un sourire ensorcelant. **bewitchment,** *s.* Ensorcellement *m;* charme *m.*

beyond [bi'jɔnd]. 1. *adv.* Au-delà, par-delà, plus loin. 2. *prep.* Au-delà de, par-delà. (*a*) The house is b. the church, la maison est au-delà de, plus loin que, l'église. The countries b. the Rhine, b. the seas, les pays d'outre-Rhin, d'outre-mer. To be b. the pale, être au ban de la société. *S.a.* REACH¹ 2. (*b*) To stay b. one's time, rester trop longtemps. B. a certain date, passé une certaine date. (*c*) (*Surpassing*) B. all praise, au-dessus de tout éloge. To succeed b. one's hopes, réussir au-delà de ses espérances. To go b. one's authority, outrepasser ses pouvoirs. This work is b. me, ce travail dépasse mes forces, mes moyens. It is b. me, cela me dépasse; je n'y comprends rien. *S.a.* CONTROL¹ 1, POWER 1. B. doubt, hors de doute. B. belief, incroyable(ment). *S.a.* MEASURE¹ 3, QUESTION¹ 2. That is (going) b. a joke, cela dépasse les bornes de la plaisanterie. (*d*) (*Except*) He has nothing b. his wages, il n'a rien que ses gages. 3. *s.* The b., l'au-delà. F: At the back of b., tout au bout du monde. He lives at the back of b., il habite un trou perdu, au diable (vau)vert, en plein bled.

bezel ['bezl], *s.* 1. *Lap:* Biseau *m* (d'une pierre taillée). 2. Chaton *m,* portée *f* (de bague). 3. Drageoir *m,* biseau (du boîtier de montre).

bezique [bi'zi:k], *s. Cards:* Bésigue *m.*

bezoar ['bezouər], *s.* Bézoard *m.*

biannual, [bai'ænjuəl]. 1. *a.* Biennal, -aux; bisannuel, semestriel. 2. *s. Bot:* = BIENNIAL 2.

bias¹ ['baiəs], *s.* 1. *Needlew:* Biais *m.* **Material cut on the b.,** étoffe coupée en biais, de biais. 2. *Bowls:* (*a*) Décentrement *m,* fort *m* (de la boule). (*b*) Déviation *f.* 3. (*a*) Prévention *f* (towards, en faveur de; against, contre); parti pris. (*b*) Penchant *m* (pour qch.),

tendance *f* (à qch.). **Vocational b.,** déformation professionnelle. 4. *W.Tel:* **Grid b.,** polarisation *f* de la grille.

bias², *v.tr.* **(bias(s)ed)** 1. *Bowls:* Décentrer (la boule). 2. Rendre (qn) partial; prédisposer, prévenir (qn) (towards, en faveur de; against, contre). **biased,** *a.* Partial, -aux. To be b. against s.o., avoir une prévention contre qn.

bib [bib], *s.* 1. Bavette *f,* bavoir *m* (d'enfant). 2. Bavette *f* (de tablier).

bibasic [bai'beisik], *a. Ch:* Bibasique.

Bible ['baibl], *s.* Bible *f.* **B.-oath,** serment prêté sur la Bible. **B. class,** (i) classe d'histoire sainte; (ii) (classe du) catéchisme. **B. paper,** papier *m* bible. F: **This book is my b.,** je ne puis rien faire sans ce livre, ce livre est mon Évangile.

biblical ['biblik(ə)l], *a.* Biblique.

bibliographer [,bibli'ɔgrəfər], *s.* Bibliographe *m.*

bibliographic(al) [,biblio'græfik(ə)l], *a.* Bibliographique.

bibliography [,bibli'ɔgrəfi], *s.* Bibliographie *f.*

bibliomania [,biblio'meinjə], *s.* Bibliomanie *f.*

bibliomaniac [,biblio'meiniæk], *s.* Bibliomane *m.*

bibliophile ['bibliofail], *s.* Bibliophile *m.*

bibulous ['bibjuləs], *a.* Adonné à la boisson; buveur. F: **B. nose,** nez d'ivrogne.

bicamera, 'bai'kæmər(ə)l], *a.* Bicaméral. *Pol:* **B. system,** bicamérisme *m.*

bicarbide [bai'kɑ:baid], *s. Ch:* Bicarbure *m.*

bicarbonate [bai'kɑ:bənit], *s.* Bicarbonate *m.*

bicarburetted ['bai'kɑ:b(j)əretid], *a. Ch:* Bicarboné.

bice [bais], *s. Ind:* Bleu *m* de cobalt. **Green b.,** vert de cobalt.

bicentenary ['baisen'ti:nəri], *a. & s.* Bicentenaire (*m*).

bicephalous [bai'sefələs], *a.* Bicéphale.

biceps ['baiseps], *s. Anat:* Biceps *m.* **B. muscles,** muscles bijumeaux.

bichloride ['bai'klɔ:raid], *s. Ch:* Bichlorure *m.*

bichromate ['bai'kroumit], *s.* Bichromate *m.*

bicker ['bikər], *v.i.* 1. Se quereller, se chamailler. 2. (*Of stream*) Murmurer. **bickerer,** *s.* Querelleur, -euse, chamailleur, -euse. **bickering¹,** *a.* 1. Querelleur. 2. (*Of stream*) Murmurant. **bickering²,** *s.* Querelles *fpl;* chamailleries *fpl.*

bicolour(ed) ['baikʌlər,(-kʌləd)], *a. Bot: etc:* Bicolore.

biconcave [bai'kɔnkeiv], *a.* Biconcave.

biconvex [bai'kɔnveks], *a.* Biconvexe.

bicycle¹ ['baisikl], *s.* Bicyclette *f,* F: vélo *m;* bécane *f.* **Motor-assisted b.,** bicyclette à moteur auxiliaire. **Water b.,** pédalo *m.* **B. track,** piste cyclable. **bicycle-rickshaw,** vélo-pousse *m;* vélotaxi *m.*

bicycle², *v.i.* 1. Faire de la bicyclette, du vélo. 2. To b. to Bristol, aller à bicyclette à Bristol.

bid¹ [bid], *s.* (*a*) Enchère *f,* offre *f,* mise *f.* **To make a b. for a property,** (i) faire une offre pour, (ii) mettre (une) enchère sur, un immeuble. Further b., higher b., surenchère *f;* offre supérieure. The last b., la dernière mise. To make a b. for power, (i) viser au pouvoir; (ii) tenter un coup d'État. (*b*) *Cards:* Appel *m;* demande *f.* (*At bridge*) **To raise the b.,** relancer. No b.! Parole!

bid², *v.tr. & i.* (*p.t.* bade [bæd, beid], bid; *p.p.* bidden [bidn], bid; bidding) 1. *O:* Commander, ordonner (s.o. (to) do sth., à qn de faire qch.). B. him come in, dites-lui d'entrer. Do as you are b., faites ce qu'on vous dit. 2. *O:* (*a*) To b. s.o. to dinner, inviter qn à dîner. (*b*) To b. s.o. welcome, good-day, souhaiter la bienvenue, donner le bonjour, à qn. *S.a.* DEFIANCE, FAREWELL. (*c*) The weather bids fair to be fine, le temps s'annonce beau. 3. (*p.t. & p.p.* bid) (*a*) (*At auction sale*) **To b. for sth.,** (i) faire une offre pour qch.; (ii) mettre une enchère sur qch. **To b. ten pounds,** faire une offre de dix livres. **To start to b. for a picture at £5,000,** mettre un tableau à prix £5,000. (*b*) *Cards:* **To b. three diamonds,** demander, appeler, trois carreaux. **bidding,** *s.* 1. (*a*) Commandement *m,* ordre *m.* To be at s.o.'s b., être aux ordres de qn. (*b*) *O:* Invitation *f.* 2. (*a*) Enchères *fpl,* mises *fpl.* (*b*) *Cards: etc:* The b. is closed, l'enchère est faite.

biddable ['bidəbl], *a.* Obéissant, docile.

bidder ['bidər], s. (At sale) Enchérisseur m. The highest b., le plus offrant; le dernier enchérisseur.
bide [baid], v.tr. & i. (bided) A: = ABIDE. (Still used in) To b. one's time, attendre l'heure, attendre le bon moment; se réserver.
bidet ['bi:dei], s. Hyg: Bidet m (de toilette).
bi-dentate [bai'denteit], a. Nat.Hist: Bidenté; (animal) à deux dents.
biennale [bi:e'nɑ:lei], s. (Exhibition) Biennale f.
biennial [bai'enjəl]. 1. a. Biennal, -aux. 2. a. & s. Bot: B. (plant), plante bisannuelle. -ally, adv. Tous les deux ans.
bier ['biər], s. (a) Civière f (pour porter un mort). (b) (Hearse) Corbillard m.
bif(f)¹ [bif], s. P: Gnon m, beigne f, torgnole f.
bif(f)², v.tr. P: Flanquer un gnon à qn. To b. s.o. on the nose, bouffer le blair à qn.
bifocal ['bai'fouk(ə)l]. Opt: (a) a. Bifocal, -aux; à double foyer. (b) s.pl. Bifocals, verres mpl à double foyer.
bifoliate [bai'fouliit], a. Bot: Bifolié.
biform ['baifɔːm], a. Biforme.
bifurcate ['baifə'keit]. 1. v.tr. Bifurquer. 2. v.i. (Se) bifurquer.
bifurcation ['baifə:'keiʃ(ə)n], s. Bifurcation f, embranchement m.
big [big]. (bigger ['bigər]; biggest) 1. a. (a) (Large) Grand; (bulky) gros. B. hotel, grand hôtel. B. man, (i) homme de grande taille, (ii) gros homme, (iii) homme marquant. B. girl, grande jeune fille. B. enough to defend oneself, de taille à se défendre. B. fortune, grosse fortune. F: He earns b. money, il gagne gros. B. drop in prices, forte baisse de prix. F: B. pot, b. noise, gros bonnet. F: He has b. ideas, il voit grand. The b. scene (of the play), la grande scène. To grow big(ger), (i) grandir; (ii) grossir. B. drum, grosse caisse. Ven: B. game, (i) gros gibier; (ii) les grands fauves. S.a. END¹ 1, STICK¹ 1. (b) B. with child, grosse, enceinte. B. with consequences, gros, lourd, de conséquences. 2. adv. F: To talk big, faire l'important; fanfaronner. 'big-'bellied, a. Ventru, pansu. 'Big 'Ben, s. La grosse cloche du Palais du Parlement. 'big-'boned, a. Ossu; fortement charpenté. 'big-'headed, a. F: Vaniteux, -euse, prétentieux, -euse, suffisant.
bigamist ['bigəmist], s. Bigame mf.
bigamous ['bigəməs], a. Bigame.
bigamy ['bigəmi], s. Bigamie f.
bigger, biggest. See BIG.
biggish ['bigiʃ], a. 1. Assez grand. 2. Assez gros.
bight [bait], s. 1. Double m, bal(l)ant m, anse f (d'un cordage). 2. Geog: The Great Australian B., la Grande Baie Australienne. B. of Benin, le Golfe de Bénin.
bigness ['bignis], s. 1. Grandeur f. 2. Grosseur f.
bigot ['bigət], s. Fanatique mf (en politique, etc.); sectaire mf.
bigoted ['bigətid], a. Fanatique; au zèle ou à l'esprit étroit.
bigotry ['bigətri], s. Bigotisme m, bigoterie f; fanatisme m; étroitesse f d'esprit.
bigwig ['bigwig], s. F: Personnage important; gros bonnet; P: grosse légume.
bijou ['bi:ʒu], s. Bijou m; objet m d'art de facture délicate. Attrib. B. flat to let, petit appartement coquet à louer.
bike [baik], s. F: = BICYCLE¹.
bikini [bi'ki:ni], s. Cost: Bikini m (costume de bain).
bilabial [bai'leibiəl], a. & s. Ling: (Consonne) bilabiale (f).
bilateral [bai'læt(ə)r(ə)l], a. Bilatéral, -aux.
bilberry ['bilbəri], s. Bot: Airelle f, myrtille f.
bile [bail], s. Physiol: Bile f. F: To stir s.o.'s b., échauffer la bile à qn. 'bile-stones, s.pl. Med: Calculs m biliaires.
bilge [bildʒ], s. Nau: (a) Fond m de cale. The bilges, les mailles f. (b) B.(-water), eau f de cale. F: Get rid of all that b., débarrassez-vous de tout ce fatras. P: To talk b., dire des bêtises. 'bilge-keel, s. Quille f de bouchain; quille de roulis. 'bilge-pump, s. Pompe f de cale.
biliary ['biljəri], a. Physiol: Biliaire.

bilinear [bai'liniər], a. Mth: Bilinéaire.
bilingual [bai'liŋgw(ə)l], a. Bilingue.
bilingualism [bai'liŋgwəlizm], s. Bilinguisme m.
bilinguist [bai'liŋgwist], s. Personne f bilingue.
bilious ['biljəs], a. Bilieux; (tempérament) cholérique. B. attack, accès m de bile.
biliousness ['biljəsnis], s. Attaque f de bile; crise f hépatique; bile f.
bilk [bilk], v.tr. F: 1. Tromper, escroquer (qn); payer (qn) en monnaie de singe. 2. Fausser compagnie à (qn); filouter (un conducteur de taxi).
bill¹ [bil], s. Arm: Hallebarde f. 'bill-hook, s. Tls: Serpe f; vouge m.
bill², s. 1. Bec m (d'oiseau, d'ancre). S.a. CRANE'S-BILL, RAZOR-BILL, SCISSOR-BILL. 2. Geog: Bec, promontoire m. Portland B., le Bec de Portland.
bill³, v.i. (Of birds) Se becqueter. F: (Of pers.) To b. and coo, faire les tourtereaux.
bill⁴, s. 1. Com: Note f, facture f, mémoire m; (in restaurant) addition f. To make out a b., faire, rédiger, une facture. To draw up a stiff b., F: saler la note. Jur: B. of costs, état m de frais. 2. (a) Effet m (de commerce); billet m. Long(-dated) bills, papier, effets, à longue échéance. B. of exchange, lettre f de change; traite f. (b) U.S: Billet de banque. 3. Affiche f, placard m, écriteau m. To stick bills on a wall, placarder un mur. P.N: Stick no bills! défense d'afficher. Th: (Play-)b., affiche; programme m du spectacle. F: It tops the b., c'est le comble. S.a. FLY-BILL, HANDBILL. 4. (a) B. of fare, carte f du jour; menu m. (b) Nau: B. of lading, connaissement m; police f de chargement. (Clean, foul) b. of health, patente f de santé (nette, suspecte, brute). (c) B. of sale, acte m, contrat m, de vente; facture. 5. Projet m de loi. S.a. ATTAINDER. 6. Jur: Résumé des chefs d'accusation (présenté au jury). (Of Grand Jury) To find a true b. against s.o., déclarer fondés ses chefs d'accusation. 'bill(-)board, s. Panneau m (d'affichage); panneau-réclame. 'bill-book, s. Carnet m d'échéances; F: échéancier m. 'bill-broker, s. Courtier m de change; agent m de change. 'bill-fold, s. U.S: Portefeuille m. 'bill-head, s. En-tête m de facture, pl. en-têtes. 'bill-poster, -sticker, s. Afficheur m, colleur m d'affiches. 'bill-posting, -sticking, s. Affichage m.
bill⁵, v.tr. 1. Facturer (des marchandises). 2. Afficher; Th: mettre (une pièce) à l'affiche.
Bill⁶. Pr.n.m. (Dim. of William) Guillaume.
billet¹ ['bilit], s. Mil: 1. Billet m de logement. (b) Logement m (chez l'habitant). O: Every bullet has its b., toute balle a sa destination; on ne lutte pas contre le sort. 2. F: Place f, emploi m.
billet², v. (billeted) 1. v.tr. Mil: To b. troops on s.o., on, in, a town, loger des troupes chez qn; cantonner des troupes dans une ville. 2. v.i. Mil: Loger (with, chez). **billeting**, s. Cantonnement m. 'billeting-officer, s. Chef m de campement m, cantonnement. 'billeting-party, s. Détachement m de campement, cantonnement.
billet³, s. 1. Bûche f; rondin m; bille f, billette f (de bois de chauffage, etc.). 2. Metall: Billette (d'acier); lopin m.
billiards ['biljədz], s.pl. (Jeu m de) billard m. To play b., jouer au billard. To have a game of b., faire une partie de billard. (The sg. is used as a comb.fm.) Billiard ball, bille f de billard. Billiard cloth, tapis m de billard. B. cue, queue f de billard. Billiard marker, garçon m de billard. 'billiard-table, s. Billard m.
Billingsgate ['biliŋzgit]. 1. Pr.n. Marché m au poisson (à Londres). 2. s. F: Langage m des halles, des poissardes.
billion ['biljən], s. Billion m; U.S: milliard m.
billow¹ ['bilou], s. Grande vague; lame f (de mer).
billow², v.i. (Of the sea) Se soulever en vagues; (of clouds, flames) ondoyer.
billowy ['bilǝui], a. (Flot) houleux; (mer) houleuse.
Billy ['bili]. 1. Pr.n.m. Guillaume. 2. s. (In Austr.) B.(-can), gamelle f; bouilloire f (à thé).
billygoat ['biligout], s. Bouc m.
bilobate [bai'loubit], bilobed [bai'loubd], a. Bilobé.
bimanous ['baimənəs], a. Z: Bimane.

bimetallic ['baimi'tælik], *a.* Bimétallique.
bimetallism [bai'metəlizm], *s. Pol.Ec:* Bimétallisme *m.*
bimetallist ['bai'metəlist], *s.* Bimétalliste *m.*
bimillenary ['baimi'lenəri], *s.* Bimillénaire *m.*
bi-monthly ['bai'mΛnθli]. **1.** *a.* (*a*) Bimensuel, semi-mensuel. (*b*) Bimestriel, -elle. **2.** *adv.* (*a*) Bimensuelle-ment. (*b*) Tous les deux mois.
bin [bin], *s.* (*a*) Coffre *m*, huche *f*, bac *m.* Corn b. (*in stable*), coffre à avoine. *S.a.* DUSTBIN. (*b*) Wine b., casier à bouteilles. *Constr:* Cement b., silo *m* à ciment.
binary ['bainəri], *a. Mth: etc:* Binaire.
bind¹ [baind], *s.* **1.** *Mus:* Ligature *f*, liaison *f.* **2.** (*a*) Coincement *m*, grippage *m.* (*b*) Gommage *m.* **3.** *F:* (*of thg*) Scie *f*; (*of pers*) crampon *m*, cassepieds *m.inv.* It's a(n awful) b.! c'est cassepieds!
bind², *v.tr.* (bound [baund]; bound) Attacher, lier. **1.** (*Tie fast*) (*a*) To b. a prisoner, s.o.'s hands, lier, attacher, ligoter, un prisonnier; lier les mains à qn. Bound hand and foot, pieds et poings liés. Bound by a spell, retenu par un charme. *S.a.* SPELL-BOUND. To be bound to s.o. by gratitude, être attaché à qn par la reconnaissance. (*b*) To b. sth. (down) to, on, sth., attacher, fixer, qch. à qch.; serrer (une pièce sur l'établi). *Sp:* To b. on one's skis, fixer ses skis. (*c*) To b. a bargain, ratifier, confirmer, un marché. (*d*) Food that binds the bowels, nourriture constipante. **2.** (*a*) To b. (up) a wound, bandər, panser, une blessure. To b. an artery, ligaturer une artère. (*b*) To b. a wreath about s.o.'s head, ceindre d'une couronne la tête de qn. (*c*) Border (un manteau, un chapeau); bordurer (une étoffe). **3.** (*Tie together*) (*a*) To b. (up) a sheaf, lier une gerbe. (*b*) Relier (un livre). Bound in paper, paper-bound, broché. Bound in boards, cartonné. Full-bound in morocco, relié en plein maroquin. (*c*) (i) Lier, agglutiner (du sable, etc.). (ii) *v.i.* (*Of gravel, etc.*) Se lier, s'agglomérer; s'agré-ger; (*of cement*) durcir, prendre. (*d*) *v.i.* (*Of machine parts, etc.*) (Se) coincer; (*of bearings*) gripper; (*of cylinders, etc.*) coller, gommer. **4.** Lier, engager (qn). To b. s.o. to obedience, astreindre qn à l'obéissance. To b. s.o. apprentice, mettre qn en apprentissage (with s.o., chez qn). To b. oneself to do sth., s'engager à faire qch. **5.** *v.i.* F: Ronchonner. **bind down,** *v.tr.* To b. s.o. down to do sth., astreindre, contraindre, qn à faire qch. **bind over,** *v.tr. Jur:* To b. s.o. over to keep the peace, exiger de qn sous caution qu'il ne se livrera à aucune voie de fait. **bound,** *a.* **1.** (*a*) Lié. They are very much b. up in each other, ils sont très attachés l'un à l'autre. The present is b. up with the past, le présent se relie au passé, est lié au passé. (*b*) (*With s. prefixed, e.g.*) Tide-b., retenu par la marée. *S.a.* HIDE-BOUND, ICE-BOUND, SNOW-BOUND, WEATHER-BOUND, WIND-BOUND. **2.** (*a*) To be b. to do sth., être obligé, tenu, de faire qch. You are in duty b. to do it, votre devoir vous y oblige. To be in honour b. to do sth., être engagé d'honneur à faire qch.; mettre son honneur à faire qch. To be b. by strict rules, être soumis à des règles strictes. (*b*) He's b. to come, il ne peut pas manquer de venir. It's b. to happen, c'est fatal. We are b. to be successful, nous réussirons à coup sûr. (*c*) *F:* He'll come, I'll be b., il viendra, j'en suis sûr! je vous le promets! **binding¹,** *a.* **1.** (Agent) agglomérant, agglutinant. **2.** Obli-gatoire (upon s.o., pour qn). Agreement b. (up)on s.o., contrat qui lie qn. **3.** *Med:* Astringent, constipant, échauffant. **binding²,** *s.* **1.** (*a*) Agglutination *f*, agrégation *f.* (*b*) Fixation *f*; serrage *m*; cerclage *m* (d'une roue). *Sp:* Ski b., Fixation, attache *f.* B. screw, (i) vis de pression; (ii) El: serre-fil *m.* (*c*) = BIND¹ 2. **2.** (*a*) Lien *m*, ligature *f*; bandage *m* (d'une poutre, etc.); frette *f.* *El.E:* Armature b., frette d'induit. (*b*) Reliure *f* (d'un livre). Quarter-b., demi-reliure *f.* Library b., reliure amateur. Spring b. (*for holding papers*) reliure électrique; auto-relieur *m.* *S.a.* LIMP³. (*c*) Bordure *f*, liséré *m* (d'une robe, etc.).
binder ['baindər], *s.* **1.** (Pers.) (*a*) Husb: etc: Lieur, -euse. (*b*) = BOOKBINDER. **2.** (Thg) (*a*) Husb: Lieuse *f* (de gerbes); botteleur *m*, botteleuse *f*; lien *m*, hart *f*, (de fagot, etc.). (*b*) Bande *f*, ceinture *f* (de flanelle); bandage *m* de corps. (*e*) (Spring-back) b.,

auto-relieur *m.* (*f*) *Civ.E:* Liant *m*, agglomérant *m*; matériau *m* d'agrégation (d'une route).
bindery ['baindəri], *s.* Atelier *m* de reliure.
bindweed ['baindwi:d], *s. Bot:* Liseron *m.*
bine [bain], *s. Bot:* Sarment *m*; tige *f* (de houblon, etc.). *S.a.* WOODBINE.
binge [bin(d)ʒ], *s. P:* Ribote *f*, bombe *f*, ribouldingue *f.*
binnacle ['binəkl], *s. Nau:* Habitacle *m.*
binocular [bi'nɔkjulər, bai-]. *Opt:* **1.** *a.* Binoculaire. **2.** *s.pl.* Binoculars, jumelle(s) *f.*
binomial [bai'noumiəl]. *Mth:* **1.** *a.* Binôme. The b. theorem, le théorème de Newton. **2.** *s.* Binôme *m.*
biochemic(al) ['baio'kemik(əl], *a.* Biochimique.
biochemistry ['baio'kemistri], *s.* Biochimie *f.*
biodynamics ['baiodɔi'næmiks], *s.* Biodynamique *f.*
biogenesis ['baio'dʒenisis], *s. Biol:* Biogenèse *f.*
biogenetic ['baiodʒi'netik], *a.* Biogénétique.
biographer [bai'ɔgrəfər], *s.* Biographe *m.*
biographic(al) [baio'græfik(əl], *a.* Biographique. Biographical novel, biographie romancée.
biography [bai'ɔgrəfi], *s.* Biographie *f.*
biokinetics ['baioki'netiks], *s.* Biomécanique *f.*
biologic(al) ['baio'lɔdʒik(əl)], *a.* Biologique.
biologist [bai'ɔlədʒist], *s.* Biologiste *m.*
biology [bai'ɔlədʒi], *s.* Biologie *f.*
biometry ['bai'ɔmitri], *s.* Biométrie *f.*
biophysics ['baiou'fiziks], *s.* Biophysique *f.*
biopsy ['baiɔpsi], *s. Surg:* Biopsie *f.*
biosatellite ['baiou'sætəlait], *s.* Satellite habité.
biosphere ['baiosfiər], *s.* Biosphère *f.*
biotherapy ['baiou'θerəpi], *s. Med:* Biothérapie *f.*
bipartite [bai'pɑ:tait], *a.* **1.** *Nat.Hist:* Biparti, -ite. **2.** (Document) rédigé en double.
biped ['baiped], *a. & s.* Bipède (*m*).
biphase ['baifeiz], *a. El.E:* Biphasé, diphasé.
biplane ['baiplein], *s.* Avion biplan; biplan *m.*
bipod ['baipɔd], *s. Mil:* Bipied *m* (d'un fusil-mitrail-leur).
bipolar [bai'poulər], *a. El:* Bipolaire.
biquadratic ['baikwə'drætik], *a. Mth:* Bicarré.
birch¹ [bə:tʃ], *s.* **1.** *Bot:* Bouleau *m.* Lady b., silver b., white b., bouleau blanc. B. plantation, boulaie *f.* **2.** B.(-rod), verge *f*, poignée *f* de verges (pour fouetter).
birch², *v.tr.* Donner les verges, le fouet, à (qn); fouetter qn.
bird [bə:d], *s.* **1.** (*a*) Oiseau *m.* Hen b., oiseau femelle. Song-b., oiseau chanteur. Little b., oiselet *m*, oisillon *m.* *F:* A little b. toid me so, mon petit doigt me l'a dit. To give s.o. the b., (i) envoyer promener qn; (ii) *Th: etc:* huer, siffler, qn. *Prov:* The early b. catches the worm, à qui se lève matin Dieu aide et prête la main. A b. in the hand is worth two in the bush, un 'tiens' vaut mieux que deux 'tu l'auras.' *S.a.* KILL¹ 1. (*b*) *Cu:* Volaille *f.* (*c*) The birds are shy this year, le gibier est timide cette année. **2.** *P:* Type *m*, individu *m.* Who's that old b.? qu'est-ce que c'est que ce vieux type-là? He's a rare b., c'est un mouton à cinq pattes. **3.** (*a*) *P:* Femme *f* (volage); poule *f.* (*b*) *P:* Pépée *f.* '**bird-cage,** *s.* Cage *f* d'oiseau. '**bird-call,** *s.* Appeau *m*, pipeau *m.* '**bird-catcher,** *s.* Oiseleur *m.* '**bird-fancier,** *s.* (*a*) Oiselier *m*; aviculteur *m.* (*b*) Connaisseur *m* en oiseaux. '**bird-lime,** *s.* Glu *f.* '**bird's-eye,** *s.* **1.** *Bot:* Véronique *f.* **2.** B.'s-e. view, perspective, vue, perspective, à vol d'oiseau. **3.** B.'s-e. mahogany, acajou moucheté. B.'s-e. maple, érable à broussin, érable madré. **4.** Tabac cordé et haché. '**bird('s)-nest,¹** *s.* **1.** Nid *m* d'oiseaux. **2.** *Cu:* Nid d'hirondelle. **bird('s)-'nest²,** *v.i.* Dénicher des oiseaux. '**bird('s)-nester,** *s.* Dénicheur, -euse, de nids.
biretta [bi'retə], *s. Ecc.Cost:* Barrette *f.*
birth [bə:θ], *s.* **1.** Naissance *f.* Premature b., accouche-ment *m* avant terme. To give b. to a child, donner naissance, donner le jour, à un enfant. To give b. to a poem, enfanter un poème. Irish by b., Irlandais de naissance. Of high b., de haute naissance. By right of b., par droit de naissance. The b. of an idea, genèse d'une idée. **2.** Mise *f* bas (d'un animal). (*Of animal*) To give b. to . . ., mettre bas. . . . '**birth-cer'tificate,** *s.* Acte *m*, extrait *m*, de naissance.

'birth-control, s. Limitation f des naissances, conception dirigée; contrôle m des naissances. 'birth-mark, s. Envie f; tache f de naissance. 'birth-place, s. (a) Lieu m de naissance; (i) pays natal; (ii) maison natale. (b) Berceau m (d'une religion, etc.). 'birth-rate, s. Natalité f. The trend of the b.-r., le mouvement des natalités. Fall in the b.-r., dénatalité f.

birthday ['bəːθdei], s. Anniversaire m (de naissance); B. present, cadeau d'anniversaire. B. party, réunion d'anniversaire. F: To be in one's b. suit, être à poil.

birthright ['bəːθrait], s. 1. Droit m d'aînesse. 2. Droit de naissance. droit du sang.

Biscay ['biskei]. Pr.n. Geog: La Biscaye (en Espagne). The Bay of B., le golfe de Gascogne.

biscuit ['biskit], s. 1. (a) Biscuit m. U.S: = SCONE. Fancy biscuits, gâteaux secs; petits fours. P: He takes the b.! à lui le pompon! That takes the b.! ça, c'est fort! B. factory, biscuiterie f. B. trade, biscuiterie. (b) a. & s. (Colour) Biscuit inv; isabelle inv. 2. Cer: B. ware, biscuit.

bisect [bai'sekt]. 1. v.tr. Couper, diviser, (une ligne, un angle) en deux parties égales. 2. v.i. (Of road, etc.) Bifurquer.

bisection [bai'sekʃ(ə)n], s. Bissection f.

bisector [bai'sektər], s. Bissectrice f.

bisexual [bai'seksjuəl], a. Bot: etc: Bis(s)exué, bis(s)exuel.

bishop ['biʃəp], s. 1. Ecc: Évêque m. Bishop's palace, palais épiscopal; évêché m. 2. Chess: Fou m. 3. (Mulled wine) Bi(s)chof m.

bishopric ['biʃəprik], s. Évêché m.

bismuth ['bizməθ], s. Miner: Bismuth m.

bison ['baisn], s. Bison m.

bisque¹ [bisk], s. Ten: Bisque f.

bisque², s. Cer: (a) Biscuit m. (b) Porcelaine blanche sans couverte.

bisque³, s. Cu: (Shell-fish soup) Bisque f (d'écrevisses, etc.).

bissextile [bi'sekstail]. 1. a. Bissextil. 2. s. Année bissextile.

bistoury ['bisturi], s. Surg: Bistouri m.

bistre ['bistər], s. & a. Bistre (m).

bisulphate [bai'sʌlfeit], s. Ch: Bisulfate m.

bisulphite [bai'sʌlfait], s. Ch: Bisulfite m.

bit¹ [bit], s. 1. Harn: Mors m (d'une bride). To champ the b., (of horse) mâcher son mors; (of pers.) ronger son frein. (Of horse, pers.) To take the b. between its, one's, teeth, prendre le mors aux dents; s'emballer. S.a. BRIDLE-BIT, CURB-BIT. 2. Tls: (a) Mèche f (de vilebrequin). S.a. CENTRE-BIT, SPOON-BIT, TWIST-BIT. (b) Copper-b., soldering-b., fer m à souder.

bit², s. 1. (a) Morceau m (de pain, de fromage, etc.). F: To have a b. of something, manger un morceau. (b) Bout m, brin m. B. of paper, of string, bout m de papier, de ficelle. B. of straw, brin m de paille. A (little) b. of hope, un peu, un petit brin, d'espoir. O: I did my b., j'ai servi pendant la guerre. (c) F: (Coin) Pièce f. Threepenny b., pièce de trois pence. 2. (a) A b. (of), un peu (de). A tiny little b., un tout petit peu. He is a b. jealous, il est quelque peu jaloux. He is a b. of a liar, il est tant soit peu menteur. Wait a b.! attendez un peu, un instant! F: A good b. older, sensiblement plus âgé. B. by b., peu à peu; petit à petit; brin à brin. Not a b. (of it)! pas le moins du monde! n'en croyez rien! It's not a b. of use, cela ne sert absolument à rien. S.a. EVERY. (b) F: A b. of news, une nouvelle. A b. of advice, un conseil. A b. of luck, une chance; une aubaine. (c) F: After the accident he was picked up in bits, après l'accident on l'a ramassé en pièces détachées.

bit³. See BITE².

bitch¹ [bitʃ], s. 1. (a) Chienne f. (b) Terrier b., terrier m femelle. (c) Femelle f (du renard, du loup). 2. P: (Of woman) Garce f.

bitch², v.tr. P: Gâcher, saboter (l'ouvrage). She bitched up the whole business for us, elle nous a gâché toute l'affaire.

bite¹ [bait], s. 1. (a) Coup m de dent. S.a. BARK³, CHERRY 1. (b) Fish: Touche f. F: Got a b.? ça mord? 2. (a) (Wound) Morsure f. S.a. FROST-BITE. (b) Piqûre f, morsure f (d'un insecte). S.a. FLEA-BITE.

3. F: Bouchée f, morceau m. I haven't had a b. all day, je n'ai rien mangé de la journée. Without b. or sup, sans boire ni manger. 4. (a) Tchn: Mordant m (d'une lime, etc.). (b) Piquant m (d'une sauce).

bite², v.tr. (p.t. bit; p.p. bitten, A: bit, see BITER) Mordre. 1. Donner un coup de dent à (qn, qch.); (of insect) piquer. To b. one's lips, one's nails, se mordre les lèvres, se ronger les ongles. To b. the dust, mordre la poussière. The fish bites, le poisson mord (à l'hameçon). Prov: Once bitten, twice shy, chat échaudé craint l'eau froide. To get bitten, se faire mordre; se faire piquer. To be bitten with a desire to do sth., brûler de faire qch. F: I've been badly bitten, on m'a mis dedans. 2. The wind bites the face, le vent coupe le visage. Frost bites the leaves, la gelée brûle les feuilles. Pepper bites the tongue, le poivre pique la langue. bite off, v.tr. Enlever, détacher, (qch.) avec les dents, d'un coup de dent(s). F: To b. s.o.'s head off, rembarrer qn. To b. off more than one can chew, entreprendre une trop forte tâche; tenter qch. au-dessus de ses forces. biting, a. Mordant; (of cold) cuisant, âpre, perçant; (of wind) cinglant, piquant; (of style, wit, epigram) mordant, caustique. -ly, adv. D'un ton mordant.

biter ['baitər], s. Animal m qui mord.

bitten. See BITE².

bitter ['bitər]. 1. a. (Goût) amer; (vin) acerbe; (vent) aigre, piquant; (ennemi) implacable; (conflit) aigu; (temps) rigoureux; (ton) aigre, âpre. B. cold, wind, froid, vent, glacial, cinglant. B. beer, bière forte-ment houblonnée. B. enemies, ennemis à mort. B. hatred, haine acharnée. B. remorse, remords cuisants. B. experience, amère déception; expérience cruelle. S.a. PILL. To be b. against a project, critiquer un projet avec âpreté. 2. s. (a) = bitter beer. (b) pl. Bitters, bitter(s) m, amer(s) m. -ly, adv. Amèrement, avec amertume, avec aigreur. It was b. cold, il faisait un froid de loup. To feel sth. b., ressentir beaucoup d'amertume de qch. 'bitter-'sweet. 1. a. Aigre-doux, -douce. 2. s. Bot: Douce-amère f.

bitter-end ['bitər'end], s. Nau: Étalingure f du puits. To the b.-e., à outrance; jusqu'au bout.

bittern ['bitə(:)n], s. Orn: Butor m.

bitterness ['bitənis], s. 1. (a) Amertume f. (b) Rigueur f, âpreté f (du temps); aigreur f, acrimonie f (de paroles, d'une querelle). 2. Rancune f, rancœur f.

bitts [bits], s.pl. Nau: Bittes f (d'amarrage).

bitumen ['bitjumin], s. Bitume m; goudron minéral; asphalte minéral.

bituminize [bi'tju:minaiz], v.tr. Bituminer, bitumer.

bituminous [bi'tju:minəs], a. Bitumineux, -euse. B. coal, houille grasse, collante.

bivalence ['bai'veiləns], s. Ch: Bivalence f.

bivalent ['bai'veilənt], a. Ch: Bivalent, divalent.

bivalve ['baivælv], a. & s. Moll: Bivalve (m).

bivalved ['baivælvd], bivalvular [bai'vælvjulər], a. Bivalulaire; bivalve.

bivouac¹ ['bivuæk], s. Mil: Bivouac m.

bivouac², v.i. (bivouacked) Bivouaquer.

bivvy ['bivi], s. (a) = BIVOUAC. (b) P: Tente indi-viduelle (de campeur).

bi-weekly ['baiwi:kli]. 1. (a) a. De tous les quinze jours. (b) adv. Tous les quinze jours. 2. (a) a. Bi-hebdomadaire. (b) adv. Deux fois par semaine.

bizarre [bi'zɑːr], a. Bizarre.

blab¹ [blæb], blabber ['blæbər], s. F: Jaseur, -euse; indiscret, -ète; bavard, -arde.

blab², v. (blabbed) F: 1. v.i. Jaser, bavarder; causer (indiscrètement). 2. v.tr. To b. out a secret, laisser échapper un secret.

black¹ [blæk]. I. a. Noir. 1. (a) B. coat, habit noir. B. spot (on furniture, etc.), noircissure f. The night was as b. as pitch, il faisait noir comme dans un four. As b. as ebony, d'un noir d'ébène. S.a. PITCH-BLACK. To be b. in the face, avoir le visage tout conges-tionné. To look b., faire une vilaine figure, une vilaine moue. To look as b. as thunder, avoir l'air furieux. To beat s.o. b. and blue, meurtrir, rosser, qn de coups. To be b. and blue (all over), être tout meurtri (de coups); être couvert de bleus, d'ecchymoses. B. eye, œil poché; F: œil au beurre noir. S.a. EYE¹ 1. B. market, marché noir. Hist: The B. Death, la

Peste Noire. *S.a.* LIST². *Geog:* The B. Sea, la Mer Noire. *S.a.* COAL-BLACK, CURRANT 1, JACK III. 3, JET-BLACK, MARIA, RUST¹ 2, SHEEP. (*b*) The b. races, les races noires. B. woman, noire *f*. B. servant, domestique nègre. (*c*) His hands were b., il avait les mains sales, les mains toutes noires. The B. Country, la région sidérurgique (du Staffordshire et du Warwickshire); le "Pays Noir" de l'Angleterre. 2. B. despair, sombre désespoir. B. tidings, triste(s) nouvelle(s). B. ingratitude, noire ingratitude. *S.a.* ART² 1. II. black, *s.* Noir *m*. 1. Ivory b., noir d'ivoire. Bone b., noir animal. Lamp b., noir de fumée. Carbon b., noir *m* de fumée, de pétrole. Brunswick b., laque *f* à l'asphalte. 2. (*a*) She always wears b., elle est toujours en noir. (*b*) To work in b. and white, faire du dessin à l'encre, au crayon noir. B.-and-white artist, dessinateur à l'encre. B.-and-white postcard, carte en noir. To set sth. down in b. and white, coucher qch. par écrit. 3. (*pers.*) Noir, noire. 4. *F:* He put up a b., il a fait une gaffe. 'black-beetle, *s.* (i) Blatte *f*, cafard *m*; (ii) escarbot *m*. 'black-coated, *a.* Vêtu de noir; à jaquette noire. The b.-c. workers, les employés de bureau (par opposition à l'artisanat). 'black(-)cock, *s. Orn:* Tétras *m* lyre; petit coq de bruyère. black(-)'hole, *s.* Cachot *m*. black-'lead, *s.* 1. Mine *f* de plomb; plombagine *f*. 2. Crayon *m* de mine de plomb. 'black letter, *s. Typ:* Caractères *m* gothiques, 'black-list, *v.tr.* 1. Inscrire, mettre, (qn) sur la liste des punitions, des suspects. *Cf.* black list, under LIST². 2. Mettre (un livre, un atelier) à l'index. Black-listed, à l'index. 'black-marke'teer, *s.* Profiteur *m* du marché noir. black-'pudding, *s. Cu:* Boudin *m*.
black², *v.tr.* 1. Noircir (qch.). To b. boots, cirer des bottes, des bottines. *F:* To b. s.o.'s eye, pocher l'œil à qn. 2. To b. sth. out, effacer, rayer, qch. (d'un gros trait noir). *Th:* To b. out, éteindre la rampe, couper la lumière; *Cin:* fermer en fondu. 'blacking-brush, *s.* Brosse *f* à cirer. 'black-out, *s.* 1. *Civil Defence:* Black-out *m*; extinction *f* des lumières. 2. Panne *f* d'électricité. 3. *Physiol: Av: F:* Voile noir. To have a black-out, (i) tomber faible, (ii) tomber en syncope. black out, *v.* 1. *v.i.* Éteindre les lumières; faire le black-out. 2. *v.tr.* To b.o. a house, faire le black-out dans une maison.
blackamoor ['blækəmuər], *s. Pej:* Noir, -e; nègre, *f.* négresse; moricaud, -e.
blackball ['blækbɔ:l], *v.tr.* Blackbouler (qn).
blackberry ['blækb(ə)ri], *s.* Mûre *f* (de ronce). B. bush, ronce *f*, mûrier *m* des haies.
blackbird ['blækbə:d], *s. Orn:* Merle *m*.
blackboard ['blækbɔ:d], *s.* Tableau noir.
blackcap ['blækkæp], *s.* Fauvette *f* à tête noire.
blacken ['blæk(ə)n]. 1. *v.tr.* Noircir (un mur, la réputation de qn); obscurcir (le ciel); (*with smoke*) enfumer. To b. s.o.'s character, calomnier qn. 2. *v.i.* (Se) noircir; devenir noir; s'assombrir. blackening, *s.* Noircissement *m*.
blackguard¹ ['blæga:d], *s.* Ignoble personnage *m*; canaille *f*, gouape *f*, vaurien *m*.
blackguard², *v.tr.* Lancer des injures à (qn); agonir (qn) d'injures.
blackguardly ['blæga:dli], *a.* Ignoble, canaille.
blackhead ['blækhed], *s.* Comédon *m*; tanne *f*; point noir (sur le visage).
blackish ['blækiʃ], *a.* Noirâtre; tirant sur le noir.
blackleg¹ ['blækleg], *s. Ind: F:* Renard *m*; jaune *m*; traître *m*.
blackleg², *v.tr.* (blacklegged) *Ind:* Prendre la place (des grévistes, etc.). *Abs.* Trahir ses camarades.
blackmail¹ ['blækmeil], *s.* Chantage *m*.
blackmail², *v.tr.* Soumettre (qn) à un chantage; *F:* faire chanter (qn).
blackmailer ['blækmeilər], *s.* Maître chanteur *m*.
blackness ['blæknis], *s.* Noirceur *f*; (*of the night*) obscurité *f*.
Blackshirt ['blækʃə:t], *s.* Fasciste *m*; chemise noire.
blacksmith ['blæksmiθ], *s.* Forgeron *m*; maréchal-ferrant. B. welding, soudage *m* à la forge.
blackthorn ['blækθɔ:n], *s.* 1. *Bot:* Épine noire. 2. B. (cudgel), gourdin *m* (d'épine).

bladder ['blædər], *s.* (*a*) *Anat:* Vessie *f.* (*b*) *Anat: Bot:* Vésicule *f. S.a.* AIR-BLADDER, GALL-BLADDER. (*c*) Outre remplie d'air. *Fb:* Vessie (de ballon). 'bladder-wort, *s. Bot:* Utriculaire *f.* 'bladder-wrack, *s. Algae:* Raisin *m* de mer.
blade [bleid], *s.* 1. Brin *m* (d'herbe); pampe *f* (de blé). Corn in the b., blé en herbe. 2. (*a*) Lame *f* (de couteau, d'épée, de rasoir, *Bot:* de feuille); feuille *f*, lame (d'une scie). (*b*) *F:* Sabre *m* ou épée *f. F: A:* He's a (regular) b., c'est un gaillard, un luron. 3. Pelle *f*, plat *m*, pale *f* (d'aviron); aile *f*, pale *f* (d'hélice); ailette *f*, vanne *f* (de ventilateur); ailette, aube *f* (de turbine); fer *m* (de bêche). 4. B. of the tongue, plat de la langue. *S.a.* SHOULDER-BLADE. 'blade-bone, *s.* 1. *Anat:* Omoplate *f.* 2. *Cu:* Paleron *m*.
bladed ['bleidid], *a.* A lame(s), à aile(s), à pales, à ailettes. Three-b. propeller, hélice à trois ailes, à trois pales.
blah ['blɑː], *s. F:* Bla-bla-bla *m*, baratin *m*.
blamable ['bleiməbl], *a.* = BLAMEWORTHY.
blame¹ [bleim], *s.* 1. Reproches *mpl*; condamnation *f.* To deserve b., mériter des reproches. 2. Responsabilité *f*; faute *f.* The b. is mine, la faute en est à moi. To lay, put, cast, the b. (for sth.) upon s.o., rejeter, faire retomber, le blâme ou la faute (de qch.) sur qn; incriminer qn. To bear the b., supporter le blâme; endosser la faute.
blame², *v.tr.* 1. Blâmer, condamner (qn). To b. s.o. for sth., blâmer qn de qch.; reprocher qch. à qn; attribuer (un malheur, etc.) à qn. To b. s.o. for doing sth., reprocher à qn de faire, d'avoir fait, qch. They b. each other, ils s'en prennent l'un à l'autre. I am not blaming you, ce n'est pas à vous que j'en ai. To have only oneself to b., n'avoir à s'en prendre qu'à soi-même. You have only yourself to b.! Vous l'avez voulu! He is to b., il y a de sa faute. To b. sth. for an accident, etc., attribuer un accident, etc., à qch.
blameless ['bleimlis], *a.* Innocent, irréprochable; sans tache. -ly, *adv.* Irréprochablement.
blamelessness ['bleimlisnis], *s.* Innocence *f*, irréprochabilité *f.*
blameworthy ['bleimwə:ði], *a.* 1. Blâmable; digne de reproches. 2. (*Of conduct*) Répréhensible; déméritoire.
blanch [blɑːn(t)ʃ]. 1. *v.tr.* (*a*) Blanchir (des légumes, un métal). To b. almonds, monder, dérober, des amandes. (*b*) *Poet:* (*Of illness, etc.*) Pâlir, rendre pâle (qn, le teint de qn); (*of fear, etc.*) blêmir (le visage). 2. *v.i.* (*a*) (*Of hair, etc.*) Blanchir. (*b*) (*Of pers.*) Blêmir, pâlir.
blancmange [blə'rɔ:nʒ], *s.* Blanc-manger *m*.
bland [blænd], *a.* 1. (*Of pers., speech*) (*a*) Doux, *f.* douce; aimable; affable; débonnaire. *Iron:* Doucereux. (*b*) (Sourire) narquois. 2. (*Of air, food, drink*) Doux, suave. -ly, *adv.* (*a*) Avec affabilité; *Iron:* mielleusement. (*b*) D'un air un peu narquois.
blandish ['blændiʃ], *v.tr.* Cajoler, flatter.
blandishment ['blændiʃmənt], *s.* Flatterie *f. Usu. pl.* Cajoleries *fpl.* câlineries *fpl.*
blandness ['blændnis], *s.* 1. *a*) Douceur *f*, suavité *f*, affabilité *f.* (*b*) Affabilité un peu narquoise. 2. Douceur (du climat, etc.).
blank [blæŋk]. I. *a.* 1. (*a*) B. paper, papier blanc. B. page, page vierge, blanche. (*b*) B. cheque, credit, chèque, crédit, en blanc. (*c*) B. space, espace en blanc; blanc *m*. B. map, carte muette. (*d*) B. verse, vers blancs, non rimés. *S.a.* CARTRIDGE 1. 2. (*a*) B. existence, existence vide. B. look, regard sans expression. (*b*) To look b., avoir l'air confondu, déconcerté. *S.a.* ASTONISHMENT. (*c*) B. despair, profond découragement. B. impossibility, impossibilité absolue. -ly, *adv.* 1. To look b. at s.o., regarder qn (i) d'un air confondu, déconcerté, (ii) sans expression. 2. To deny sth. b., nier qch. absolument, carrément. II. blank, *s.* 1. (*a*) *U.S:* Formulaire *m*, formule *f*, Telegraph b., formule de télégramme; imprimé *m* à télégramme. To fill out a b., remplir, compléter, une formule, une feuille, un imprimé. (*In document, etc.*) Blanc *m*, vide *m*; (*in one's memory*) trou *m*, lacune *f*, vide. Paper signed in b., blanc-seing *m*, *pl.* blancs-seings. To leave blanks, laisser des blancs. His

death leaves a b., sa mort laisse un vide. **His mind is a b.,** (i) sa mémoire est une table rase; (ii) il a, il se sent, la tête vide. (b) **To fire off b.** (shot), tirer à blanc. (c) Blanc (d'une cible). *S.a.* POINT-BLANK. (d) *Dominoes:* Double b., double blanc *m*. 2. (*In lottery*) Billet blanc, billet perdant. *S.a.* DRAW² 3. 3. (a) *Mint:* Flan *m* (de métal). (b) *Metalw:* Flan; masselotte *f*.

lanket¹ ['blæŋkit], *s*. 1. (a) Couverture *f* (de lit, de cheval). **Electric b.,** couverture chauffante (électrique). **To toss s.o. in a b.,** berner qn, *F:* passer qn à la couverte. *F:* **To be born on the wrong side of the b.,** être de naissance illégitime. *S.a.* WET BLANKET. (b) Couverture ou pagne *m* (d'indigène). 2. *Type:* (Press-)b., blanchet *m*. 3. *Attrib.* Général; applicable à tous les cas. **B. order,** ordre d'une portée générale.

lanket², *v.tr.* 1. Mettre une couverture à (qch.), fournir (un lit) de couvertures. 2. (a) *Nau:* Déventer, abriter (un navire, un yacht); manger le vent à (un autre navire). (b) *Navy:* Se mettre en travers du feu de (ses propres vaisseaux). **blanketed,** *a*. Couvert, recouvert. **Streets b. with snow,** rues feutrées de neige. **blanketing,** *s*. 1. *Coll:* Couvertures *fpl*. 2. *Tex: Com:* Lainages *mpl* pour couvertures.

blankness ['blæŋknis], *s*. 1. Air confus, décontenancé. 2. Vide *m*, néant *m* (de la pensée, etc.).

blanquette ['blɔŋket], *s*. *Cu:* **B. (of veal),** blanquette *f* (de veau).

blare¹ ['blɛər], *s*. Sonnerie *f*, accents cuivrés (de la trompette).

blare². 1. *v.i.* (*Of trumpet*) Sonner. *Mus:* Cuivrer le son. **The radio is blaring away,** la radio fonctionne à casser les oreilles. 2. *v.tr.* **The band blared (out) a quickstep,** la fanfare fit retentir une marche.

blarney¹ ['blɑːni], *s*. *F:* Eau bénite de cour; patelinage *m*; boniments *mpl* à la graisse d'oie.

blarney², *v.tr.* *F:* Cajoler, enjôler (qn).

blasé ['blɑːzei], *a*. Blasé.

blaspheme [blæs'fiːm], *v.i. & tr.* Blasphémer.

blasphemer [blæs'fiːmər], *s*. Blasphémateur, -trice.

blasphemous ['blæsfiməs], *a*. (*Of pers.*) Blasphémateur, -trice; (*of words*) blasphématoire, impie. **-ly,** *adv.* Avec impiété. **To speak b.,** blasphémer; outrager Dieu.

blasphemy ['blæsfimi], *s*. Blasphème *m*.

blast¹ [blɑːst], *s*. 1. (a) Bouffée *f* de vent, coup *m* de vent; rafale *f*. **B. of steam,** jet *m* de vapeur. (b) Souffle *m* (du vent). 2. **B. on the whistle, on the siren,** coup de sifflet, de sirène. **B. on the trumpet,** sonnerie *f* de trompette. *Nau:* **To sound a b.,** faire entendre un coup de sirène. 3. *Metall:* Air *m*, vent *m* (de la soufflerie); soufflerie *f*, soufflage *m* (d'un haut-fourneau). (*Of furnace*) **To be in b.,** être allumé, en marche. **To be in full b.,** être en pleine activité. *S.a.* SAND-BLAST. 4. (a) *Ball:* Souffle. (b) *Min:* (i) Coup de mine. (ii) Charge *f* d'explosif. 'blast-effect, *s*. *Mil:* Effet *m* du souffle. 'blast-engine, *s*. *Ind:* (Machine) soufflante (*f*), soufflerie *f*. 'blast-furnace, *s*. Haut-fourneau *m*. 'blast-off, *s*. *Aer:* Mise à feu (d'un engin, d'une fusée). 'blast-pipe, *s*. *Metall: Av: Aer:* Tuyère *f* (de fusée, de moteur à réaction). 'blast screen, *s*. *Av:* Déflecteur *m* de souffle.

blast². *v.tr.* (a) *Min:* Faire sauter (à la dynamite, etc.); pétarder (des roches). (b) Brûler, flétrir (une plante); ruiner, briser (l'avenir de qn); détruire, anéantir (des espérances). **Blasted heath,** lande désolée. (c) (*Of lightning*) Foudroyer (un arbre, etc.). (d) *int. P:* **Blast (it, you)!** Zut! **blasted,** *a. P:* = DAMNED 2. **blasting,** *s*. 1. (a) Travail *m* aux explosifs; exploitation *f* à la mine; abattage *m* à la poudre. *S.a.* GELATINE. (b) Anéantissement *m* (d'un espoir, etc.); ruine *f* (d'une carrière). (c) Foudroiement *m* (d'un arbre). 2. *W.Tel:* Poussées *fpl* d'intensité (dans le haut-parleur); réception hurlante. 'blasting-powder, *s*. Poudre *f* de mine, de démolition.

blastema [blæs'tiːmə], *s*. *Biol:* Blastème *m*.

blastoderm ['blæstodɔːm], *s*. *Biol:* Blastoderme *m*.

blastodermic [,blæsto'dɔːmik], *a*. *Biol:* Blastodermique.

blastogenesis ['blæsto'genisis], *s*. *Biol:* Blastogenèse *f*.

blatancy ['bleit(ə)nsi], *s*. Vulgarité criarde.

blatant ['bleit(ə)nt], *a*. 1. (*Of pers., manners*) D'une vulgarité criarde. 2. (Injustice) criante; (mensonge) flagrant. **-ly,** *adv.* Avec une vulgarité criarde.

blather ['blæðər], *v. & s.* = BLETHER¹,².

blaze¹ [bleiz], *s*. 1. (a) Flamme(s) *f*, feu *m*, conflagration *f*, flambée *f*. **In a b.,** en feu, en flammes. **To set sth. in a b.,** enflammer, embraser, qch. **The whole of Europe was in a b.,** toute l'Europe était en feu. **To burst (out) into a b.,** se mettre à flamber; s'enflammer. **In the b. of day,** en plein midi. (b) **B. of anger,** éclat *m* de colère. 2. Flamboiement *m* (du soleil); éclat (des couleurs, des diamants, etc.). **To end in a b. of glory,** finir en beauté *f*. 3. *pl. F:* (= HELL) (a) **Go to blazes!** allez au diable! (b) (*Intensive*) **What the blazes . . .,** que diable (me veut-il, etc.).

blaze², *v.i.* (a) (*Of fire, etc.*) Flamber; (*of sun, colours*) flamboyer; (*of jewels, metals*) étinceler. **Uniforms blazing with gold lace,** uniformes resplendissants de galons d'or. (b) (*Of pers.*) **To b. with anger,** être enflammé de colère; être furieux. **blaze away,** *v.i.* 1. (*Of fire*) Continuer à flamber. 2. **To b. away at the enemy,** maintenir un feu nourri contre l'ennemi. **blaze down,** *v.i.* (*Of sun*) Darder, déverser, ses rayons (on, sur). **blaze out,** *v.i.* 1. (a) (*Of fire*) Se mettre à flamber. (b) (*Of the sun*) Apparaître tout à coup (parmi les nuages). 2. Éclater en reproches, en injures, etc. **To b. out at s.o.,** s'en prendre violemment à qn. **blaze up,** *v.i.* 1. S'embraser, s'enflamer. 2. (*Of pers.*). S'emporter; se fâcher tout rouge. **To b. up at a proposal,** s'insurger contre une proposition. **blazing,** *a*. (a) En feu; enflammé; embrasé. (b) (Feu, soleil) flambant, ardent. (c) *Ven:* **B. scent,** fumet tout récent; piste toute fraîche.

blaze³, *s*. 1. (*On face of horse, ox*) Étoile *f*. 2. (*On tree*) B.(-mark), blanchis *m*, griffe *f*.

blaze⁴, *v.tr.* Griffer, blanchir, marquer, layer (un arbre). **To b. a trail,** tracer un chemin, frayer le chemin; (*through forest*) layer une forêt; poser des jalons (dans une science, etc.).

blaze⁵, *v.tr.* **To b. a rumour abroad,** répandre un bruit partout.

blazer ['bleizər], *s*. *Cost: Sp:* Blazer *m*.

blazon¹ [bleizn], *s*. *Her:* (a) Blason *m*. (b) Armoiries *fpl*. (c) Étendard armorié.

blazon², *v.tr.* 1. *Her:* Blasonner; marquer (qch.) aux armoiries de qn. 2. Embellir, orner (de dessins héraldiques). 3. Célébrer, exalter (les vertus de qn). 4. **To b. forth, out,** publier, proclamer, qch.

blazoning ['bleizəniŋ], *s*. *Her:* Blasonnement *m*.

bleach¹ [bliːtʃ], *s*. Agent *m* de blanchiment; décolorant *m*. *Hairdr:* Oxygénée *f*.

bleach², *v.tr. & i.* Blanchir; *Ch: etc:* (se) décolorer. **To b. the hair,** blondir, oxygéner, les cheveux. *Tex:* **Half-bleached,** demi-blanc. **bleaching,** *s*. Blanchiment *m*; *Ch:* décoloration *f*. 'bleaching-powder, *s*. Poudre *f* à blanchir; chlorure *m* de chaux.

bleak¹ [bliːk], *s*. *Ich:* Ablette *f*.

bleak², *a*. 1. (Terrain) désert, sans abri, exposé au vent. 2. (Temps) triste; (vent) froid. 3. **B. prospects,** avenir morne. **B. smile,** sourire pâle. **-ly,** *adv.* Froidement, tristement; d'un air morne.

bleakness ['bliːknis], *s*. Tristesse *f*, froidure *f*; aspect *m* morne.

blear¹ ['bliər], **bleary** ['bliəri], *a*. 1. (*Of eyes*) Troubles larmoyants, chassieux. 2. (*Of outline*) Vague, indécis, imprécis. 'blear-eyed, 'bleary-eyed, *a*. Aux yeux troubles, larmoyants, chassieux.

blear², *v.tr.* 1. Rendre (les yeux) troubles. 2. Obscurcir, embrumer, estomper (des contours).

bleat¹ [bliːt], *s*. Bêlement *m*.

bleat², *v.i.* Bêler; (*d'une chèvre*) bégueter; (*d'une chèvre, d'un vieillard*) chevroter. *F:* **What's he bleating about?** de quoi se plaint-il? **bleating,** *s*. Bêlement *m*.

bleb [bleb], *s*. 1. Bouillon *m*, bulle *f*, cloche *f* (dans le verre, etc.). 2. Bouton *m*, petite ampoule (sur la peau).

bleed [bliːd], *v*. (bled; bled) 1. *v.tr.* Saigner. **To b. s.o. in the arm,** saigner qn au bras. **To b. s.o.** (for money), saigner, gruger, qn; extorquer de l'argent à qn; *P:* faire casquer, faire cracher, qn. **To b. oneself**

white to pay, se saigner aux quatre veines pour payer.
2. *v.i.* (*a*) Saigner; perdre du sang. He is bleeding at
the nose, his nose is bleeding, il saigne du nez. (*b*) (*Of
tree, etc.*) Pleurer, perdre sa sève. (*c*) *Civ.E: etc:*
(*Of riveted joints; of water, gas, etc.*) Fuir. *Typ:*
Bled-off illustrations, illustrations à marges perdues.
bleeding[1], *a.* 1. Saignant; (i) en train de saigner;
(ii) ensanglanté. With a b. heart, le cœur navré de
douleur. 2.*P: Euphemism for* BLOODY 2. **bleeding**[2],
s. 1. (*a*) Écoulement *m* de sang, de sève; (*of vine,
etc.*) pleurs *mpl.* B. at the nose, saignement *m* de nez.
(*b*) *Surg:* Saignée *f.* 2. Fuite *f* (de gaz, etc.).
blemish[1] ['blemiʃ], *s.* 1. Défaut *m*; défectuosité *f*,
imperfection *f.* 2. Souillure *f*, tache *f*, tare *f.*
blemish[2], *v.tr.* 1. Tacher, entacher, souiller (une
réputation, etc.). 2. Abîmer, gâter (un travail).
blench [blenʃ], *v.i.* (*a*) Sourciller, broncher. (*b*) Pâlir,
blêmir.
blend[1] [blend], *s.* Mélange *m* (de thés, etc.).
blend[2], *v.* (*p.t. & p.p.* blended, *Lit:* blent) 1. *v.tr.* (*a*)
To b. sth. with sth., mêler qch. à, avec, qch.; joindre,
unir, qch. à qch. To b. one colour with another, (i)
mélanger une couleur avec une autre; (ii) fondre
deux couleurs; (iii) allier, marier, deux couleurs. (*b*)
(Re)couper (des vins, des whiskys). (*c*) Mélanger
(des thés, des cafés; des races). 2. *v.i.* Se mêler, se
mélanger, se confondre (into, en); (*of voices, etc.*) se
marier harmonieusement; (*of colours*) s'allier, se
marier; (*of parties, etc.*) fusionner. **blending**, *s.*
Mélange *m* (de thés, de tabacs, etc.); alliance *f* (de
deux qualités).
blende [blend], *s. Min:* Blende *f.*
blennorrhagia [ˌblenəˈreidʒiə], *s. Med:* Blennorr(h)a-
gie *f.*
blennorrhoea [ˌblenəˈriə], *s. Med:* Blennorrhée
f.
blepharitis [ˌblefəˈraitis], *s. Med:* Blépharite *f.*
Ciliary, marginal, b., blépharite ciliaire.
bless [bles], *v.tr.* (*p.t. & p.p.* blessed [blest], *A. & Poet:*
blest) Bénir. 1. To b. God, bénir, adorer, Dieu. 2.
(*Of the priest*) To b. the people, bénir le peuple. To
b. a bell, consacrer, baptiser, une cloche. God b.
you! que Dieu vous bénisse! à vos souhaits! 3.
God blessed them with children, Dieu leur accorda le
bonheur d'avoir des enfants. To be blessed, blest,
with sth., jouir de qch.; avoir le bonheur de posséder
qch. I blessed my stars that . . ., je me félicitai de ce
que . . .; je bénis mon étoile de ce que. . . . God
b. me! miséricorde! mon Dieu! B. my soul! tiens,
tiens, tiens! Well, I'm blest! par exemple! *F:* (I'll be)
blest if I know, que le diable m'emporte si je le sais.
blessed ['blesid], *a.* (*a*) The B. Virgin, la Sainte Vierge.
B. be Thy name, que votre nom soit sanctifié. (*b*)
R.C.Ch: The B. Martyrs, les bienheureux martyrs.
B. are the poor in spirit, bienheureux sont les pauvres
en esprit. (*c*) *P:* (*Intensive*) What a b. nuisance! quel
fichu contretemps! The whole b. day, toute la sainte
journée. That b. boy! ce sacré gamin! **blessing**,
s. Bénédiction *f.* To give, pronounce, the b., donner
la bénédiction. To ask a b. (at a meal), dire le
bénédicité. With the b. of God, par la grâce de Dieu.
The blessings of civilization, etc., les avantages *m*,
bienfaits *m*, de la civilisation, etc. Blessings upon
you! Dieu vous bénisse! To count one's blessings,
s'estimer heureux avec ce qu'on a.
blessedness ['blesidnis], *s.* Béatitude *f*; félicité *f.*
blest [blest]. 1. *a.* Bienheureux. 2. *s. Coll:* Les
Bienheureux, les saints au Paradis.
blether[1] ['bleðər], *s. Scot:* Paroles *fpl* en l'air;
sottises *fpl*, bêtises *fpl.*
blether[2], *v.i. Scot:* Parler à tort et à travers; dire des
inepties, des bêtises.
blew. *See* BLOW[2],[4].
blight[1] [blait], *s.* 1. (*a*) Rouille *f*, brûlure *f*; charbon
m, nielle *f* (des céréales); brunissure *f* (des pommes
de terre); cloque *f* (des pêchers, etc.). (*b*) (*By the sun*)
Brouissure *f.* 2. *Ent:* (*Plant-louse*) Puceron *m.* 3.
Influence *f* néfaste; fléau *m.*
blight[2], *v.tr.* Rouiller, nieller (le blé); (*of the sun*)
brouir; (*of the wind*) flétrir. To b. s.o.'s hopes,
flétrir les espérances de qn. **blighting**, *s.* Niellure *f*
(du blé); flétrissure *f.*

blighter ['blaitər], *s. P:* 1. Bon à rien. You b.! espec
d'animal! 2. Individu *m*, *F:* type *m*; *P:* zèbre *m*
A poor b., un pauvre hère. You lucky b.!
veinard!
blighty ['blaiti], *s. Mil: F: A:* 1. L'Angleterre *f*
(le) retour dans les foyers. 2. A b., la bonne blessure
blimey ['blaimi], *int. P:* Zut alors!
blimp [blimp], *s.* 1. *Aer:* Dirigeable *m* de reconnaissance; vedette aérienne. 2. *Cin: U.S:* Blindage
m insonore (de la caméra). 3. He's a true Colonel
B., c'est une vraie culotte de peau, un scrongneugneu
blind[1] [blaind], *a.* 1. Aveugle. (*a*) B. in one eye,
borgne. A b. man, woman, un, une, aveugle. The b.,
les aveugles. B. from birth, aveugle-né(e). To be
struck b., être frappé de cécité *f.* It is a case of the b.
leading the b., c'est un aveugle qui en conduit un
autre. He is as b. as a bat, a mole, il n'y voit pas plus
clair qu'une taupe. *F:* To turn a b. eye to sth.,
refuser de voir qch. (In) b. man's holiday, entre chien
et loup. *Av:* B. flying, vol *m* sans visibilité, vol en
P.S.V. (pilotage sans visibilité). B. with anger,
aveuglé par la colère. *S.a.* COLOUR-BLIND, DAY-
BLIND, STONE-BLIND, *etc.* (*b*) To be b. to one's own
interests, to s.o.'s faults, ne pas voir ses propres
intérêts, les défauts de qn. (*c*) *adv. F:* To go at a
thing b., se lancer à l'aveugle dans une entreprise.
Av: To fly b., être dans le cirage. *S.a.* DRUNK 1. 2.
(*Hidden*) B. ditch, saut *m* de loup. *Needlew:* B. hem-
ming, point d'ourlet invisible. *S.a.* CORNER[1] 3. 3. B.
path, chemin sans issue. B. alley, cul-de-sac *m*, impasse *f.* B.-alley occupation, situation sans avenir.
Arch: B. door, window, fausse porte; fenêtre feinte,
aveugle. **-ly,** *adv.* Aveuglément; en aveugle; à
l'aveuglette. **'blind-man's-'buff,** *s.* Colin-maillard
m. **'blind-stor(e)y,** *s. Arch:* Triforium *m.* **'blind-
worm,** *s. Rept:* Orvet *m.*
blind[2], *v.tr.* 1. Aveugler. (*a*) Rendre (qn) aveugle;
frapper (qn) de cécité; crever les yeux à (qn). Blinded
ex-service men, aveugles de guerre. (*b*) Éblouir. 2.
(*a*) Ensabler (une chaussée, une voie ferrée). (*b*) *Min:*
Blinder (une galerie). **blinding**[1], *a.* 1. Aveuglant.
2. Éblouissant. **blinding**[2], *s.* 1. B. by headlights, etc.
éblouissement *m* par les phares, etc. 2. *Civ.E:*
Ensablement *m.* *Mil: Min:* Blindage *m.*
blind[3], *s.* 1. (Awning-)b., (outside sun-)b., store *m* (à
l'italienne); abat-jour *m inv.* Roller b., store sur
rouleau. Venetian b., jalousie *f* (à lames mobiles).
2. His piety is only a b., sa piété n'est qu'un masque,
qu'une feinte.
blindfold[1] ['blain(d)fould], *a. & adv.* 1. Les yeux
bandés. 2. (*Recklessly*) Aveuglément.
blindfold[2], *v.tr.* Bander les yeux à, de, (qn).
blindness ['blaindnis], *s.* 1. Cécité *f. S.a.* COLOUR-
BLINDNESS, DAY-BLINDNESS,, *etc.* 2. (*Ignorance, folly*)
Aveuglement *m.* B. to the facts, refus *m* d'envisager
les faits.
blink[1] [bliŋk], *s.* 1. Battement *m*, clignotement *m*, de
paupières. 2. (*Gleam*) Lueur (momentanée); (*glimpse*)
vision momentanée.
blink[2]. 1. *v.i.* (*a*) Battre des paupières; cligner des
paupières; clignoter. (*b*) (*Of light*) Papilloter. 2.
Fermer les yeux à demi. (*a*) *v.tr.* To b. the facts,
fermer les yeux sur la vérité. There is no blinking the
fact that . . ., il n'y a pas à dissimuler que. . . . (*b*)
v.i. To b. at a fault, fermer les yeux sur un défaut.
blinking[1], *a.* 1. (*a*) Clignotant. (*b*) (Feu) papillotant.
2. *P: Euphemism for* BLOODY 2. **blinking**[2], *s.* 1.
Clignotement *m*; papillotement *m*; papillotage *m.*
2. B. of a fact, refus *m* d'envisager un fait.
blinker ['bliŋkər], *s.* Phare *m* à éclats (sur les aéro-
dromes).
blinkers ['bliŋkəz], *s.pl. Harn:* Œillères *f. F:* (*Of
pers.*) He goes about in b., il a, porte, des œillères.
bliss [blis], *s.* Béatitude *f*, félicité *f.*
blissful ['blisful], *a.* (Bien)heureux. B. days, jours
sereins. **-fully,** *adv.* Heureusement.
blister[1] ['blistər], *s.* (*a*) (*On skin*) Ampoule *f*, bulle *f.*
Water b., cloque *f.* (*b*) Cloque, boursouflure *f* (de la
peinture). *Glassm:* Bulle, cloche *f. Metall:*
Soufflure *f*, paille *f.* (*c*) *Med:* Vésicatoire *m.*
blister[2]. 1. *v.tr.* (*a*) Couvrir d'ampoules; faire venir
les ampoules à (la main, etc.). (*b*) *Med:* Appliquer
un vésicatoire à. 2. *v.i.* Se couvrir d'ampoules; (*of

paint) (se) cloquer; gondoler. ˈblistering, *s.* **1.** *Med:* Vésication *f.* **2.** Formation *f* d'ampoules. **3.** Cloquage *m*, gondolage *m*.

blithe(some) [ˈblaiθ(səm)], *a.* Joyeux, folâtre.

blithely [ˈblaiθli], *adv.* Joyeusement.

blithering [ˈbliðəriŋ], *a. F:* B. idiot, (type absolument) idiot.

blitz¹ [blits], *s. F:* Bombardement aérien, *F:* arrosage *m*.

blitz², *v.tr.* The house was blitzed, la maison a été endommagée, détruite, par un bombardement.

blitzkrieg [ˈblitskriːg], *s.* Guerre *f* éclair.

blizzard [ˈblizəd], *s.* Tempête *f* de neige; blizzard *m*.

bloat [blout], *s.* (a) Boursoufler; gonfler; bouffir. bloated, *a.* (a) Boursouflé, gonflé, bouffi. (b) B. face, visage congestionné.

bloater [ˈbloutər], *s.* Hareng bouffi; craquelot *m*.

blob¹ [blɔb], *s.* (a) Tache *f* (de couleur); pâté *m* (d'encre). (b) Goutte *f* d'eau (sur la table, etc.).

blob², *v.i.* My fountain-pen is blobbing, mon stylo coule, bave; mon stylo fait des pâtés.

bloc [blɔk], *s. Pol:* Bloc *m*. **The Western b.,** le bloc occidental.

block¹ [blɔk], *s.* **1.** (a) Bloc *m* (de marbre, de fer); bille *f*, tronçon *m* (de bois); quartier *m* (de roche); tête *f* à perruque (de coiffeur); poupée *f* (de modiste). *I.C.E:* Four-cylinder b., bloc de quatre cylindres. *Aut: Av:* Engine b., bloc *m* moteur. *Toys:* Building blocks, cubes *mpl*; jeu *m* de constructions. *S.a.* CALENDAR 1, CHIP¹ 1, HAT-BLOCK, *etc.* (b) (Chopping-, anvil-)b., billot *m*. *Hist:* To perish on the b., périr sur le billot. (c) (Mounting-)b., horse-b., montoir *m*. (d) (Chock) Tin *m*, hausse *f*, cale *f*. (e) Sabot *m* (de frein). (f) *P:* Tête *f*; *P:* caboche *f*. **2.** (a) Pâté *m*, îlot *m*, de maisons (entre quatre rues); ensemble *m* de bâtiments. **B. of flats,** immeuble *m*. (Large modern) b. (of flats, etc.), building *m*. *U.S:* He lives two blocks from us, il habite à deux rues de nous. *Sch:* School b., groupe *m* scolaire. (b) (*In Australia*) Lot *m* (de terrains). (c) *Fin:* B of shares, tranche *f* d'actions. **3.** (a) Traffic b., encombrement *m*, embarras *m* (de voitures); embouteillage *m*. (b) *Cr:* Point en avant du guichet où le batteur appuie sa batte. **4.** *Rail:* Tronçon *m* (de ligne); canton *m*. B. system, cantonnement *m*; block-système *m*. **5.** *Engr:* Planche *f*; bois *m*; (*metal*) cliché *m*. **6.** Poulie *f*; moufle *m*. **Differential b.,** moufle différentielle *f*. ˈblock-ˈbuster, *s. Mil:* Bombe *f* de très gros calibre. ˈblock ˈcapitals, *s.pl.* Majuscules *f* d'imprimerie. ˈblock-chain, *s. Mec.E:* Chaîne *f* d'articulation; chaîne à maillons pleins, à galets. *F:* Chaîne de bicyclette *f*. ˈblock-ˈletter, *s.* (a) *Typ:* Lettre moulée; caractère gras. (b) *pl.* = BLOCK-CAPITALS. ˈblock-maker, *s.* (a) Photograveur *m*. (b) *Typ:* Clicheur *m*. ˈblock-signal, *s. Rail:* Disque *m* de fermeture (de la voie). ˈblock-train, *s. Rail:* Rame indépendante.

block², *v.tr.* **1.** Bloquer, obstruer. **To b. the traffic,** entraver, gêner, la circulation. **To b. s.o.'s way,** barrer le passage à qn. *P.N:* 'Road blocked.' "rue barrée." **To b. progress,** arrêter le progrès. **To b. a wheel,** bloquer, enrayer, une roue. *Rail:* **To b. the line,** fermer la voie. **2.** *Games:* (a) *Cr:* **To b. the ball,** arrêter la balle sans la relancer; bloquer la balle. (b) *Dominoes:* **To b. the game,** fermer le jeu. (c) *Fb:* Gêner (un adversaire). **3.** *Bookb:* Gaufrer, frapper (la couverture d'un livre). **block out,** *v.tr.* **1.** (*Of censor*) Caviarder (un passage d'un journal). **2.** Ébaucher (une statue, etc.). **block up,** *v.tr.* (a) Boucher, bloquer, (un trou); condamner, murer (une porte, une fenêtre); *Nau:* bâcler (un port). (b) Obstruer (un tuyau, etc.). blocking, *s.* **1.** Encombrement *m*. **2.** *Bookb:* Gaufrage *m*, frappe *f*.

blockade¹ [blɔˈkeid], *s.* Blocus *m*. **To run the b.,** forcer le blocus. **To raise the b.,** lever le blocus. blocˈkade-runner, *s.* Forceur *m* de blocus. blocˈkade-running, *s.* Forcement *m* du blocus.

blockade², *v.tr.* Bloquer (une ville, un port); faire le blocus (d'une place forte).

blockage [ˈblɔkidʒ], *s.* Obstruction *f*.

blockhead [ˈblɔkhed], *s. F:* Lourdaud *m*; sot *m*. He's a b., c'est une tête de bois.

blockheaded [ˈblɔkˈhedid], *a.* Sot, -te; idiot; (esprit) épais.

blockhouse [ˈblɔkhaus], *s. Mil:* Blockhaus *m*.

bloke [blouk], *s. P:* Individu *m*, type *m*, zèbre *m*.

blond, *f.* blonde [blɔnd], *a. & s.* **1.** Blond, -e. **2.** *F:* Blondin, -ine. **3.** B. (lace), blonde *f*.

blondness [ˈblɔndnis], *s.* Blondeur *f*.

blood¹ [blʌd], *s.* **1.** Sang *m*. (a) To shed, spill, b., répandre, verser, le sang. Without shedding of b., sans effusion de sang. To draw b., faire saigner qn. To flog s.o. till one draws b., fouetter qn jusqu'au sang. To fight until b. is drawn (and no longer), se battre au premier sang. To spit b., cracher du sang; cracher rouge. *F:* He's out for b., il va se montrer intraitable, féroce. *Prov:* One can't get b. out of a stone, on ne saurait tirer de l'huile d'un mur. The b. stream, le cours du sang. It makes my b. boil, cela me fait bouillir le sang; cela m'indigne. His b. boiled, his b. was up, le sang lui bouillait dans les veines; il était monté. *F:* To spit b., voir rouge. His b. ran cold, son sang se glaça, se figea (dans ses veines). To commit a crime in cold b., commettre un crime de sang-froid. His b. is on his own head, son sang est sur lui. There is bad b., ill b., between them, il y a de vieilles rancunes entre eux. To infuse new b. into an undertaking, vivifier une entreprise. The committee needs new b., le comité a besoin d'être rajeuni. *Med:* To have high b. pressure, faire de l'hypertension *f*. B. culture, hémoculture *f*. *S.a.* FLESH 2, PRESSURE 1. (b) (*Kindred*) They are near in b., ils sont proches parents. It runs in the b., cela tient de famille; c'est dans le sang. The call of the b., la voix du sang. (c) (*Birth, race*) Prince of the b., prince du sang. Blue b., sang royal, aristocratique. *Prov:* B. will tell, bon sang ne peut mentir. B. horse, cheval de race; (cheval) pur-sang *m*. **2.** (a) *A:* Petit-maître *m*, dandy *m*. (b) *F:* Young b., un des jeunes du parti (politique, etc.). ˈblood-and-ˈthunder, *attrib.* B.-and-t. play, pièce *f* à gros effets; mélo *m*. B.-and t. novel, roman à sensation. ˈblood-bank, *s. Med:* Banque *f* du sang. ˈblood-blister, *s. Med: F:* Pinçon *m*. ˈblood-cell, *s. Med:* Globule *m*. ˈblood-coloured, *a.* Couleur *f* de sang. ˈblood-count, *s. Med:* Numération *f* globulaire. ˈblood-curdling, *a.* A vous tourner les sangs; qui (vous) fige le sang. ˈblood-donor, *s. Med:* Donneur, -euse, de sang. ˈblood-group, *s.* Groupe sanguin. ˈblood-ˈgrouping, *s. Med:* Recherche *f* du groupe sanguin. ˈblood-heat, *s.* Température *f* du sang. ˈblood-letting, *s. Med: A:* Saignée *f*. ˈblood-money, *s.* Prix *m* du sang. ˈblood-orange, *s.* (Orange) sanguine *f*. ˈblood-poisoning, *s. Med:* Empoisonnement *m* du sang; septicémie *f*, toxémie *f*. ˈblood-pressure, *s. Med:* Tension artérielle. To suffer from high b.-p., avoir, faire, de la tension, de l'hypertension. ˈblood-red, *a.* Rouge sang. blood-relation, *s.* Parent(e) par le sang. ˈblood ˈsausage, *s. U.S:* Boudin *m*. ˈblood-sports, *s.* La chasse. ˈblood-stain, *s.* Tache *f* de sang. ˈblood-stained, *a.* Taché de sang; souillé de sang. ˈblood-sucker, *s.* **1.** *Ann:* Sangsue *f*. **2.** *F:* Sangsue, vampire *m*. blood-sugar, *s. Physiol:* Glucose *m* or *f* sanguin(e). ˈblood-tax, *s.* L'impôt *m* du sang. ˈblood-test, *s. Med: Bac:* Examen *m* du sang. *F:* Prise *f* de sang. ˈblood-typing, *s. Med: Bac:* = BLOOD-GROUPING. ˈblood-vessel, *s.* Vaisseau sanguin. *F:* He nearly burst a b.-v., il a failli crever d'un coup de sang.

blood², *v.tr.* (a) *Ven:* Acharner (les chiens), leur donner le goût du sang. (b) *Mil:* To b. the troops, donner aux troupes le baptême du feu.

-blooded [ˈblʌdid], *a.* Warm-, cold-b. animals, animaux à sang chaud, à sang froid.

bloodhound [ˈblʌdhaund], *s.* **1.** Chien *m* de Saint-Hubert; limier *m*. **2.** *F:* (*Of pers.*) Limier.

bloodiness [ˈblʌdinis], *s.* (a) Taché sanglant. (b) Disposition *f* sanguinaire.

bloodless [ˈblʌdlis], *a.* **1.** Exsangue, anémié. **2.** B. victory, victoire sans effusion de sang. -ly, *adv.* Sans effusion de sang.

bloodshed [ˈblʌdʃed], *s.* **1.** Effusion *f* de sang. **2.** Carnage *m*.

bloodshot [ˈblʌdʃɔt], *a.* B. eye, œil injecté de sang. (*Of eye*) To become b., s'injecter.

bloodstock [ˈblʌdstɔk], s. Bêtes de race pure, pur-sang m.inv.

bloodstone [ˈblʌdstoun], s. Lap: Sanguine f.

bloodthirstiness [ˈblʌdθəːstinis], s. Soif f de sang.

bloodthirsty [ˈblʌdθəːsti], a. Sanguinaire; altéré de sang, assoiffé de sang.

bloody¹ [ˈblʌdi], a. 1. Sanglant, ensanglanté, taché de sang; (combat) sanglant, sanguinaire; (tyran) sanguinaire, cruel. 2. P: (a) a. (Intensive) Sacré. A b. liar, un sacré menteur. You b. fool! bougre d'idiot! Stop that b. row! assez de chahut! (b) adv. It's b. hot, il fait bigrement chaud. Not b. likely! pas de danger. ˈbloody-ˈminded, a. P: Pas commode. A b.-m. fellow, un mauvais coucheur. ˈbloodyˈmindedness, s. P: Disposition f peu commode. I'm sick of you and your b.-m.! j'en ai marre de vous et de votre sale caractère!

bloody², v.tr. (bloodied) Ensanglanter; souiller (ses mains, etc.) de sang.

bloom¹ [bluːm], s. 1. (i) Fleur f; (ii) floraison f, épanouissement m. To burst into b., fleurir. Flower in b., fleur éclose. In full b., épanoui; en pleine fleur. F: In the b. of youth, à, dans, la fleur de l'âge; en pleine jeunesse. Beauty that has lost its b., beauté défraîchie. 2. Velouté m, duvet m (du raisin).

bloom², v.i. Fleurir; être en fleur. To b. into sth., devenir qch. (de beau). blooming¹, a. 1. (a) Fleurissant; en fleur. (b) (Flourishing) Florissant. 2. P: O: You b. idiot! sacré imbécile! blooming², s. Floraison f, fleuraison f.

bloom³, s. Metall: Masse f de fer cinglé; loupe f. bloom m, lopin m, masseau m.

bloomer [ˈbluːmer], s. P: blooper [ˈbluːpər], s.F: Bévue f, gaffe f.

bloomers [ˈbluːməz], s.pl. A: Cost: Culotte bouffante (de femme).

blossom¹ [ˈblɔsəm], s. Fleur f (des arbres). Tree in b., arbre en fleur(s). Orange b., fleur d'oranger.

blossom², v.i. (Of tree) Fleurir. To b. (out) into sth., devenir qch. (de beau). blossom out, v.i. S'épanouir. blossoming, s. Fleuraison f, floraison f.

blot¹ [blɔt], s. (a) Tache f; (of ink) pâté m. (b) A b. on s.o.'s honour, une tache, une souillure, à l'honneur de qn.

blot², v.tr. (blotted) 1. (a) Tacher, souiller. (b) (Of ink) Faire des pâtés sur (qch.). 2. Sécher l'encre (d'une lettre, etc.), F: buvarder. To b. (up) the ink, passer le buvard sur l'encre. 3. Abs. (Of blotting-paper) Boire l'encre. blot out, v.tr. 1. Effacer. 2. (Of fog, etc.) Cacher, masquer (l'horizon, etc.). 3. Lit: Exterminer (une race). blotting, s. 1. Séchage m (au papier buvard). 2. Maculage m (du papier). ˈblotting-pad, s. (Bloc) buvard m; sous-main m. ˈblotting-paper, s. Papier buvard, papier brouillard.

blotch¹ [blɔtʃ], s. 1. Tache f, éclaboussure f (d'encre, de couleur). 2. (a) Tache rouge (sur la peau). (b) Pustule f.

blotch², v.tr. Couvrir (la peau) de taches, de rougeurs. The cold blotches the skin, le froid marbre la peau.

blotchiness [ˈblɔtʃinis], s. Couperose f.

blotchy [ˈblɔtʃi], a. 1. (Teint) brouillé, couperosé; (peau) couverte de rougeurs. 2. Tacheté.

blotter [ˈblɔtər], s. Buvard m; bloc m buvard. Hand b., tampon m buvard.

blotto [ˈblɔtou], a. P: Complètement ivre; P: rétamé.

blouse [blauz], s. 1. Corsage m; occ. blouse f. 2. Mil: U.S: Vareuse f.

blow¹ [blou], s. 1. Coup m de vent. To go for a b., sortir prendre l'air. 2. Souffle m. Every morning he has a b. at his trombone, tous les matins il souffle dans son trombone. 3. = FLY-BLOW.

blow², v. (blew) [bluː]; blown [bloun], P: blowed [bloud] I. v.i. Souffler. 1. (a) (Of wind) It is blowing, il fait du vent, il vente. It is blowing hard, le vent souffle fort; il fait grand vent. It is blowing a gale, le vent souffle en tempête, the vent fait rage. It is blowing up for rain, le vent annonce de la pluie. S.a. WIND¹ 1. B. high, b. low . . ., quoi qu'il advienne. . . . S.a. FRESH¹ 1, HOT¹ 1. (b) Pred. The door blew open, la porte s'ouvrit sous la poussée du vent. 2. (a) (Of pers.) To b. on one's fingers, souffler dans ses

doigts. (b) (Of whale) Rejeter l'eau par les évents F: (Of pers.) To b. like a grampus, souffler comme une baleine, comme un phoque, comme un bœuf. 3. (Of electric lamp) Claquer, griller; (of fuse) fondre, sauter. II. blow, v.tr. 1. The wind blows the rain against the windows, le vent chasse la pluie contre les vitres. (Of wind) To b. a ship ashore, pousser un navire à la côte. 2. (a) (Of pers.) To b. the dust off a book, souffler sur un livre (pour enlever la poussière). F: To b. s.o. a kiss, envoyer un baiser à qn. (b) To b. (up) the fire, ranimer le feu. To b. the organ, souffler l'orgue. (c) To b. one's nose, se moucher. To b. a trumpet, souffler dans une trompette. To b. the horn, sonner du cor. F: To b. one's own trumpet, chanter ses propres louanges. (d) To b. air into sth., insuffler de l'air dans qch. Mch: To b. a boiler, évacuer une chaudière. Nau: To b. the tanks (of a submarine), chasser aux ballasts. To b. bubbles, faire des bulles (de savon). To b. glass, souffler le verre. 3. Essouffler (un cheval, etc.). 4. El: To b. a fuse, faire fondre un fusible; faire sauter les plombs. 5. (Of fly) Pondre des œufs (dans la viande, etc.). (S.a. FLY-BLOWN.) 6. P: B. the expense! expense be blowed! je me moque de la dépense! You be blowed! zut pour vous! I'll be blowed if . . ., que le diable m'emporte si. . . . blow about. 1. v.i. (Of leaves, etc.) Voler çà et là; s'envoler. 2. v.tr. Faire voler (qch.) çà et là; disperser (des feuilles, etc.). blow away, v.tr. Emporter. 1. To b. away the dust, souffler sur la poussière (pour l'enlever). 2. The sails were blown away, les voiles furent emportées par le vent. blow down, v.tr. (Of wind) Abattre, renverser (un arbre); verser (les blés). blow in. 1. v.tr. (Of wind, etc.) Enfoncer (une vitre, une porte). 2. v.i. (a) The wind blows in at the window, le vent entre par la fenêtre. (b) F: (Of pers.) Entrer en passant; s'amener. blow off. 1. v.tr. (a) The wind has blown his hat off, le vent a emporté son chapeau. To b. the dust off, souffler la poussière. (b) Mch: To b. off steam, purger, laisser échapper, lâcher, de la vapeur. S.a. STEAM¹. 2. v.i. (Of hat) S'envoler. ˈblow-off, a. & s. 1. Hyg: B.-o. (pipe), ventilateur m, tuyau m d'évent. 2. Mch: B.-o. (gear, cock), robinet m, bouchon m, de vidange; purgeur m de vapeur. B.-o. valve, clapet m de décharge. blow out. 1. v.tr. (a) Souffler, éteindre (une bougie). (b) To b. out one's cheeks, gonfler, enfler, les joues. (c) To b. the air out (from gas-pipes, etc.), chasser, expulser, l'air. To b. out a boiler, évacuer l'eau d'une chaudière. S.a. BRAIN¹ 2. 2. v.i. (a) (Of candle, etc.) S'éteindre. (b) Aut: (Of tyre) Éclater; faire hernie. (c) El: (Of fuse) Sauter. (d) My paper blew out of the window, mon journal s'est envolé par la fenêtre. ˈblow-out, s. P: Gueuleton m. blow over. 1. v.tr. = BLOW DOWN. 2. v.i. (a) The storm has blown over, la tempête s'est calmée, est passée. The scandal soon blew over, le scandale fut bientôt oublié. (b) (Of crops) Verser. blow up. 1. v.i. (a) (Of mine, etc.) Éclater, sauter; (of boiler) crever, exploser. (b) Nau: It is blowing up for a gale, il vente grand frais. 2. v.tr. (a) Faire sauter (une mine, un pont, etc.); faire exploser (une mine). (b) Gonfler (un pneu). F: Blown up with pride, bouffi d'orgueil. (c) F: Semoncer, tancer. blowing up, s. 1. Explosion f. 2. Gonflement m (d'un pneu). 3. Semonce f. 4. Phot: F: Agrandissement m d'une photographie. blown, a. 1. Essoufflé; hors d'haleine; à bout de souffle. 2. (Of food) Gâté. blowing, s. 1. Soufflement m (du vent). 2. Soufflage m (d'un fourneau, etc.). ˈblow-cock, s. Mch: Robinet m de vidange. ˈblow gun, s. Sarbacane f.

blow³, s. (In the phr.) In full b., en pleine fleuraison, en plein épanouissement.

blow⁴, v.i. (blew; blown) (Of flower) S'épanouir, fleurir.

blow⁵, s. 1. Coup m; (with fist) coup de poing; (with stick) coup de bâton. At the first b., du premier coup. At a (single) b., d'un (seul) coup. To strike a b., porter, asséner, donner, un coup. Without striking a b., sans coup férir. To deal s.o. a b., porter un coup à qn. S.a. FETCH¹ 5. To come to blows, en venir aux mains; Jur: en arriver aux voies de fait. Blows fell thick and fast, il pleuvait des coups. Knock-out b., (i) coup d'assommoir; (ii) Box: knock-out m. F:

K.-O., *m. Prov:* The first b. is half the battle, le premier coup en vaut deux. B. to s.o.'s credit, atteinte *f* au crédit de qn. To aim a b. at s.o.'s authority, porter atteinte à l'autorité de qn. 2. Coup, (du sort). It came as a crushing b. to us, ce fut un coup d'assommoir pour nous.

blowball ['bloubɔːl], *s. Bot: F:* Chandelle *f* (de pissenlit).

blower ['blouər], *s.* 1. (a) Soufleur, -euse (de verre, etc.). (b) Horn b., sonneur *m* de cor. (c) *F:* Téléphone *m; P:* ronfleur *m*, tube *m*. 2. (a) Tablier *m*, rideau *m* (de cheminée). (b) *Ind: etc:* Ventilateur soufflant; machine *f* à vent; souffleur *m*. (c) Insufflateur *m*, soufflet *m* (à poudre insecticide).

blowfly, *pl.* -flies [blouflai, -flaiz], *s.* Mouche *f* à viande.

blowhole ['blouhoul], *s.* 1. Évent *m* (d'une baleine). 2. Ventilateur *m* (d'un tunnel).

blowlamp, -torch ['bloulæmp, -tɔːtʃ], *s.* 1. Lampe *f* à souder, à braser; chalumeau *m*. 2. Brûloir *m* (de peintre en bâtiments).

blowpipe ['bloupaip], *s.* 1. Sarbacane *f*. 2. (a) *Ch: Metall:* Chalumeau *m*. (b) *Glassm:* Canne *f* (de souffleur).

blowy ['bloui], *a.* Venteux; tempétueux.

blowzy ['blauzi], *a.* (*Of woman*) (a) Rougeaude. (b) Ébouriffée; mal peignée. The maid was a b., frowzy girl, la bonne était une grosse souillon.

blubber[1] ['blʌbər], *s.* Graisse *f*, lard *m*, de baleine.

blubber[2], *attrib.a.* B. lip, lippe *f*. B.-lipped, lippu.

blubber[3]. *F:* 1. *v.i.* (a) Pleurer bruyamment, *F:* pleurer comme un veau (over, sur). (b) Pleurnicher. 2. *v.tr.* (a) To b. out sth., dire qch. en pleurant. (b) Checks blubbered with tears, joues barbouillées de larmes, bouffies par les larmes.

blubberer ['blʌbərər], *s.* **blubbering,** *a.* Pleurard, -arde; pleurnicheur, -euse.

bludgeon[1] ['blʌdʒən], *s.* Gourdin *m*, matraque *f*.

bludgeon[2], *v.tr.* Matraquer, asséner un coup de gourdin, de matraque, à (qn).

blue[1] [bluː]. I. *a.* (a) Bleu, azuré. B. spectacles, lunettes bleutées. B. ribbon, (i) ruban bleu (de l'Ordre de la jarretière, des buveurs d'eau, de la traversée de l'Atlantique); (ii) prix principal (d'une réunion de course, etc.). *F:* B. water, the b. sea, la haute mer; le large. *Med:* B. pill, pilule *f* au mercure. *S.a.* BLOOD[1] 1, BOOK[1] 1, MOON[1], PETER[1] 2, *etc.* (b) (*Of pers.*) To go b., prendre une teinte violacée. You may talk till you are b. in the face, till all's b., vous avez beau parler. *S.a.* BLACK[1] I. 1. (c) *F:* To look b., avoir l'air (i) triste, sombre; (ii) déconcerté. To feel b., avoir le cafard. II. blue, *s.* 1. Bleu *m*, azur *m*. A light b. dress, une robe bleu clair. Dark b. socks, des chaussettes bleu foncé. Sky-b., bleu ciel; azur *m inv.* Cambridge b., bleu clair. Oxford b., bleu foncé. Steely b., bleu acier. Navy b., bleu marine *inv.* The b. (sky), le firmament. Out of the b., soudainement. *S.a.* BOLT[1] 2. 2. *Pol:* A true b., un patriote, partisan *m* de la droite; *F:* un vrai de vrai. To win, get, one's b., être choisi pour représenter son université dans un match universitaire. 3. (Washing-)b., indigo *m*; bleu (d'empois). 4. *s.pl.* The blues, humeur noire, papillons noirs. To have (a fit of) the blues, avoir des idées noires; avoir le cafard. 'blue 'baby, *s. Med:* Enfant bleu. 'blue bag, *s. Laund:* Sachet *m* à bleu. 'blue-'black, *a.* Bleu-noir. blue-'eyed, *a.* 1. Aux yeux bleus. 2. *F:* Innocent, candide. Mother's b.-e. boy, le chouchou de maman. blue-'grass, *s. Bot:* Pâturin *m* des prés. 'blue-grey, *a.* & *s.* Gris bleuté. 'blue jeans, *s. Cost:* Bleus *mpl* (de travail); bluejean *m.* blue-'pencil, *v.tr.* Marquer au crayon bleu; censurer. 'blue-print, *s.* Dessin négatif, photocalque *m; F:* bleu *m;* plan *m*, projet *m.* 'blue(-)stocking, *s.* (*Of woman*) Bas-bleu *m.*

blue[2], *v.tr.* 1. (a) Bleuir; teindre (qch.) en bleu. *Laund:* Azurer (le linge); mettre, passer, (le linge) au bleu. (b) Blued spectacles, lunettes bleutées. 2. *F:* To b. one's money, gaspiller, manger, son argent.

Bluebeard ['bluːbiəd], *Pr.n.m.* Barbe-bleue *m*.

bluebell ['bluːbel], *s.* 1. Jacinthe *f* des prés, des bois. 2. *Scot:* Campanule *f*.

blueberry ['bluːbəri], *s. Bot: U.S:* Airelle *f; Fr.C:* bleuet *m.*

bluebottle ['bluːbɔtl], *s.* 1. Bleuet *m*, bleuet *m*. 2. Mouche *f* à viande.

bluejacket ['bluːdʒækit], *s.* Marin *m*, matelot *m*, de l'État; col-bleu *m.*

blueness ['bluːnis], *s.* Couleur bleue, coloration bleue.

Bluenose ['bluːnouz], *s. U.S:* 1. Puritain, -aine. 2. *Geog: F:* Habitant, -ante, de la Nouvelle-Écosse.

bluff[1] [blʌf]. I. *a.* (a) (*Of cliff, coast*) Accore, escarpé, à pic. *Nau:* B.(-bowed), (navire) renflé de l'avant. (b) (*Of pers.*) Brusque; un peu bourru. A straightforward, b. man, un homme tout rond. II. bluff, *s. Geog:* Cap *m* à pic; à-pic *m*; falaise *f*.

bluff[2], *s.* (a) *Cards:* (*At poker*) Bluff *m*. (b) *F:* Bluff, battage *m.* (c) Menaces exagérées. To call s.o.'s b., (i) (*at poker*) inviter l'adversaire à mettre cartes sur table; (ii) relever un défi.

bluff[3], *v.tr. Cards & F:* Bluffer (qn). *Abs.* Faire du bluff, *F:* de l'épate.

bluffer ['blʌfər], *s.* Épateur *m*; bluffeur, -euse.

bluffness ['blʌfnis], *s.* Brusquerie (amicale); franc-parler *m.*

bluish ['bluːiʃ], *a.* Bleuâtre; bleuté. B.-green, bleuvert, glauque. B.-grey, gris-bleu, ardoisé.

blunder[1] ['blʌndər], *s.* Bévue *f*, maladresse *f*, erreur *f.* Social b., solécisme *m* de conduite; *F:* gaffe *f*, impair *m.*

blunder[2], *v.i. & tr.* 1. Faire une bévue, une gaffe, une maladresse, un faux pas; *F:* gaffer. 2. To b. against, into, s.o., se heurter contre qn; heurter qn. To b. one's way along, avancer à l'aveuglette. To b. upon the truth, découvrir la vérité par hasard. He managed to b. through, il s'en est tiré tant bien que mal. **blundering,** *a.* Brouillon, maladroit. **-ly,** *adv.* A l'aveuglette; au petit bonheur.

blunderbuss ['blʌndəbʌs], *s.* Tromblon, *m*, espingole *f.*

blunderer ['blʌndərər], *s.* Brouillon, -onne; maladroit, -e; gaffeur, -euse.

blunderhead ['blʌndəhed], *s.* = DUNDERHEAD.

blunt[1] [blʌnt], *a.* 1. (*Not sharpened*) Mousse; (*having lost its edge*) émoussé; (*having lost its point*) épointé, (instrument) contondant; (angle) obtus. 2. (*Of pers.*) Brusque, carré. The b. fact, le fait brutal. **-ly,** *adv.* Brusquement, carrément. To announce news b., annoncer une nouvelle sans ménagements.

blunt[2], *v.tr.* Émousser (un couteau); épointer (un crayon). To b. the feelings, émousser les sentiments. To b. the palate, blaser le palais.

bluntness ['blʌntnis], *s.* 1. État émoussé, épointé; manque *m* de tranchant. 2. Brusquerie *f*, franchise *f.* B. of speech, franc-parler *m.*

blur[1] [bləːr], *s.* 1. Tache *f*, macule *f*, barbouillage *m*, bavochure *m* (d'encre, etc.). 2. (a) Apparence confuse; brouillard *m.* (b) Buée *f* (sur un miroir, etc.). 3. Ternissure *f.*

blur[2], *v.tr.* (blurred) 1. Barbouiller (d'encre, etc.). *Typ:* Maculer. 2. Brouiller, troubler. Eyes blurred with tears, yeux voilés de larmes. **blur out,** *v.tr.* Effacer, cacher (l'horizon).

blurb [bləːb], *s. Publ: F:* (a) Annonce avantageuse d'un livre sur le point de paraître; prière d'insérer; *F:* jus *m.* (b) Annonce sur le couvre-livre, sur la bande de nouveauté.

blurt [bləːt], *v.tr.* To b. out a secret, laisser échapper, trahir maladroitement, un secret.

blush[1] [blʌʃ], *s.* 1. Aspect *m.* At the first b., au premier abord, au premier aspect. In the first b. of youth, aux prémices de la jeunesse. 2. (a) Rougeur *f* (de modestie, de honte). (b) Incarnat *m* (des roses). The first b. of dawn, les premières rougeurs de l'aube.

blush[2], *v.i.* 1. (*Of pers*) Rougir. To b. for shame, rougir de honte. To make s.o. b., (i) faire rougir qn; (ii) faire honte à qn. I b. for you, vous me faites rougir. To b. to the roots of one's hair, rougir jusqu'au blanc des yeux, jusqu'aux oreilles. 2. (*Of flower, dawn*) Rougir. **blushing,** *a.* 1. Rougissant; timide. 2. (*Of flower, etc.*) Rouge, rougissant. **-ly,** *adv.* En rougissant; timidement; pudiquement.

bluster[1] ['blʌstər], *s.* (a) Fureur *f*, fracas *m* (de l'orage). (b) Air bravache, rodomontades *fpl.*

bluster², *v.i.* (a) (*Of wind*) Souffler en rafales. (b) (*Of pers.*) Faire du fracas; parler haut; faire le rodomont. *v.tr.* To b. out threats, se répandre en menaces; déblatérer des menaces. **blustering,** *a.* (a) (Vent) violent. (b) Bravache, tonitruant. -ly, *adv.* D'un air bravache.

blusterer ['blʌstərər], *s.* Bravache *m*, fanfaron *m*.

boa ['bouə], *s.* 1. *Z:* Boa *m*. B. **constrictor,** boa constricteur. 2. *Cost:* Feather b., boa.

boar ['bɔːr], *s.* Verrat *m*. Wild b., sanglier *m*. Young wild b., marcassin *m*. Old b., solitaire *m*. *S.a.* HEAD¹ 1. **'boar-hunting,** *s.* Chasse *f* au sanglier.

board¹ [bɔːd], *s.* 1. (a) Planche *f*, ais *m*; (thick) madrier *m*. Bread b., planche à (couper le) pain. Ironing b., planche à repasser. *S.a.* DIVING-BOARD, KNIFE-BOARD, *etc.* (b) (Notice-)b., tableau *m* de publicité, d'annonces, d'affichage. *Sch:* Tableau noir. *Sp:* Telegraph b., tableau d'affichage. *Aut:* (Fascia-)b., (instrument-)b., tableau de bord. *S.a.* DASH-BOARD, SIGNBOARD, *etc.* (c) *pl. Th:* The **boards,** la scène, le théâtre, *F:* les planches. To go **on the boards,** aborder la scène; monter sur les planches, sur les tréteaux. *S.a.* DIVING-BOARD, *m. Bookb:* (i) (Binding in) paper boards, cartonnage *m*, emboîtage *m*. In paper boards, cartonné. (Binding in) cloth boards, emboîtage pleine toile. (ii) *pl.* The **boards,** les plats *m* (d'un livre). 2. (a) Table *f*. The festive b., la table du festin. (b) Table, nourriture *f*, pension *f*. **B. and lodging,** b. (and) residence, pension et chambre(s). Partial b., demi-pension *f*. With b. **and lodging,** nourri et logé. (c) (Gaming) b., table de jeu. To clean the b., faire tapis net. (d) *Chess:* Tablier *m* (de l'échiquier). 3. (a) B. of enquiry commission *f* d'enquête. B. of examiners, jury *m*, commission, d'examen. (b) The B. of Trade, le Ministère du Commerce. *U.S:* B. of Trade, chambre *f* de commerce. (c) *Com:* B. of Directors, of Managers, (conseil *m* d')administration *f*; bureau *m* (d'une société). B. meeting, réunion du conseil. 4. *Nau:* (a) Bord *m*. On b. (ship), à bord (d'un navire). On b. my ship, à mon bord. To take **goods on b.,** embarquer des marchandises. To go on b., monter à bord; s'embarquer. To go by the b., s'en aller par-dessus bord; tomber à la mer. *F:* To let sth. go by the b., négliger, abandonner qch. (b) Bordée *f*, bord. To make a b., courir une bordée; courir un bord. **'board-room,** *s.* Salle *f*, chambre *f*, du conseil. **'board-school,** *s.* A: = École primaire communale. **board-'wages,** *s.pl.* (of domestic employee) Indemnité *f* de logement, de nourriture. To be on b.-w., toucher pour sa nourriture. **'board-walk,** *s.* U.S: trottoir *m* en planches.

board². 1. *v.tr.* (a) Planchéier (le sol d'un appartement). (b) *Bookb:* Cartonner (un livre). 2. (a) *v.i.* Être en pension. To b. with the family, prendre pension dans la famille. To b. at the school, être pensionnaire à l'école. (b) *v.tr.* Nourrir (des élèves, etc.). 3. *v.tr. Nau:* (a) Aborder, accoster, *Adm:* arraisonner (un navire). (b) *Adm:* Aller, monter, à bord (d'un navire). To b. a train, monter dans un train. (c) *Navy:* Aborder (un navire). **board out,** *v.tr.* Mettre (des enfants) en pension; placer (des enfants) dans une famille. **board up,** *v.tr.* Boucher (une fenêtre); condamner (une porte). **boarding,** *s.* 1. (a) *Const:* Planchéiage *m*. (b) Cartonnage *m* (d'un livre). 2. (a) *Nau:* Accostage *m*; arraisonnement *m*. (b) *Navy:* Abordage *m*. 3. *Coll.* Planches *fpl.* **'boarding-house,** *s.* 1. Pension *f* de famille. Small b.-h., maison *f* de famille. 2. *Sch:* Maison *f* où logent les internes. **'boarding-school,** *s.* Pension *f*, pensionnat *m*, internat *m*. To send a child to a b.-s., mettre un enfant en pension.

boarder ['bɔːdər], *s.* Pensionnaire *mf*; (in schools) interne *mf*. Weekly b., pensionnaire à la semaine.

boast¹ [boust], *s.* Vanterie *f*. To make a b. of sth., se faire gloire, se vanter, de qch.

boast². 1. *v.i.* Se vanter; fanfaronner; *F:* hâbler. To b. that one can do, has done, sth., se vanter de pouvoir faire, d'avoir fait, qch. To b. of, about, sth., se vanter, se faire gloire, de qch. That's nothing to b. of, il n'y a pas là de quoi être fier. Without wishing to b. . . ., sans vanité . . .; sans forfanterie . . .

2. *v.tr.* (Se glorifier de) posséder (qch.). The school boasts a fine library, l'école possède une belle bibliothèque. **boasting,** *s.* Vantardise *f*; gloriole *f*; jactance *f*, fanfaronnade *f*. -ly, *adv.* D'un air fanfaron, avec vantardise *f*.

boaster ['boustər], *s.* Vantard *m*, fanfaron *m*.

boastful ['boustful], *a.* Vantard. **-fully,** *adv.* Avec vanterie, avec jactance.

boastfulness ['boustfulnis], *s.* Vantardise *f*, jactance *f*. fanfaronnade *f*.

boat¹ [bout], *s.* Bateau *m*; (i) canot *m*; barque *f* (de pêcheur); embarcation *f*; (ii) navire (marchand). Ship's b., embarcation de bord. Canal-b., péniche *f*. *S.a.* FERRY-BOAT, FISHING-BOAT, MAIL-BOAT, *etc.* We **took (the) b. at** . . ., nous nous sommes embarqués à . . ., nous avons pris le bateau à . . . . To go by b., prendre le bateau. To lower the boats, mettre les embarcations à la mer. *F:* To be all in the same b., être tous logés à la même enseigne; être tous dans le même cas, dans le même panier. To burn one's **boats,** brûler ses vaisseaux. To miss the b., manquer le coche. **'boat-builder,** *s.* Constructeur *m* de canots, de bateaux. **'boat-deck,** *s. Nau:* Pont *m* des embarcations. **'boat-hook,** *s. Nau:* Gaffe *f*; croc *m* de marinier. **'boat(-)house,(-)shed,** *s.* Hangar *m* à bateaux, pour canots; garage *m* (pour canots). **'boat-keeper,** *s.* Loueur *m* d'embarcations. **'boat-race,** *s.* Course *f* de bateaux; *esp.* match *m* d'aviron; régate(s) *f* (pl). **'boat-train,** *s. Rail:* Train *m* du bateau; train-paquebot *m*. **'boat-yard,** *s.* Chantier *m* pour bateaux de plaisance; chantier pour canots.

boat². 1. *v.i.* Aller, se promener, en bateau; canoter; faire du canotage. 2. *v.tr.* To b. oars, rentrer les avirons. **boating,** *s.* Canotage *m*. B.-club, cercle de canotage, d'aviron.

boater ['boutər], *s.* (Hat) Canotier *m*.

boatful ['boutful], *s.*, **boatload** ['boutloud], *s.* 1. Barquée *f*; batelée *f* (de bois, etc.). 2. Plein bateau (de personnes).

boatman, *pl.* -men ['boutmən], *s.m.* 1. Batelier. 2. Loueur de canots. 3. Good b., bon canotier.

boatswain [bousn], *s. Nau:* (F: bos'n, bosun) Maître *m* d'équipage. Boatswain's mate, second maître d'équipage. Bosun's chair, cradle, chaise de gabier, de riveur, de calfat.

Boaz ['bouæz]. *Pr.n.m. B.Hist:* Booz.

bob¹ [bɔb], *s.* 1. *Mec: etc:* (a) Lentille *f* (d'un pendule); plomb *m* (d'un fil à plomb); queue *f* (d'un cerf-volant). (b) *Fish:* Bouchon *m* (de ligne). 2. (a) B. of hair, chignon *m*. (b) Coiffure *f* à la Ninon, à la Jeanne d'Arc. (c) Queue écourtée (d'un cheval). 3. *U.S:* (a) Patin *m* (de traîneau). (b) = BOB-SLEIGH. **'bob-sled, -sleigh,** *s.* Bob-sleigh *m*; bob *m*.

bob², *v.tr.* (bobbed) 1. (Of woman) To b. one's hair, faire couper les cheveux à la nuque; porter les cheveux à la Ninon. 2. To b. a horse's tail, écourter la queue d'un cheval.

bob³, *v.i.* Se mouvoir de haut en bas et de bas en haut; s'agiter. 1. Something was bobbing on the water, quelque chose s'agitait sur l'eau. To b. up and down in the water, danser sur l'eau. 2. To b. to s.o., to b. a curtsey, faire une petite révérence (à qn). 3. To b. for apples, chercher à saisir avec les dents des pommes flottant dans un baquet. **'bob-cherry,** *s.* Cerises jumelles; grappe *f* de deux ou trois cerises; *F:* "boucle *f* d'oreille." **bob down,** *v.i.* Baisser brusquement la tête. **bob under,** *v.i.* (Of fisherman's float) Plonger. **bob up,** *v.i.* Surgir brusquement. To b. up again, revenir à la surface; revenir sur l'eau.

bob⁴, *s.* 1. Petite secousse; petit coup. 2. (Curtsey) Petite révérence. 2. *Bellringing:* (a) Carillon *m*. (b) Chacune des variations du carillon.

Bob⁵. 1. *Pr.n.m.* Robert, Bob. 2. *s.m. F:* (At Eton) Dry b., joueur *m* de cricket. Wet b., canotier *m*.

bob⁶, *s.inv. F:* Shilling *m*.

bobbin ['bɔbin], *s.* 1. (a) Bobine *f*. (b) Lace b., bloquet *m*, fuseau *m*, de dentellière, brodoir *m*. 2. *El:* Corps *m* de bobine. **'bobbin-frame,** *s. Tex:* Bobinoir *m*.

Bobby ['bɔbi]. 1. *Pr.n.m.* Dim. of ROBERT. 2. *s. F:* = POLICEMAN. **'bobby-pin,** *s.* U.S: Pince *f* à cheveux. **'bobby-sock,** *s. F:* R.t.m. Socquette *f*. **'bobby-soxer,** *s.f. P:* Jeune fille à l'âge ingrat.

bobstay ['bɔbstei], *s. Nau:* Sous-barbe *f inv.*

bobtail ['bɔbteil], *a. & s.*, '**bobtailed**, *a.* (Cheval, chien) à queue écourtée. *S.a.* RAG-TAG.

bocage ['bɔkɑːʒ], *s. Geog:* Bocage *m.*

Boccaccio [bɔ'kætʃiou]. *Pr.n.m.* Boccace.

bode [boud], *v.tr. & i. Lit:* Présager. It **bodes no good**, cela ne présage, n'annonce, rien de bon. To b. **well, ill**, être de bon, de mauvais, augure. b ding, *s.* (a) Présage *m*, augure *m.* (b) Pressentiment *m.*

bodega [bɔ'deigə], *s. U.S:* Épicerie *f* (avec patente de débit de boissons).

bodice ['bɔdis], *s.* Corsage *m*; corselet *m.*

-bodied ['bɔdid], *a.* Strong-b., fort, robuste, Able-b., valide. **Full-b. wine, tobacco**, vin, tabac, qui a du corps.

bodiless ['bɔdilis], *a.* Sans corps.

bodily ['bɔdili]. 1. *a.* Corporel, physique. To **supply one's b. wants**, pourvoir à ses besoins matériels. **B. pain**, douleur physique. To **go about in b. fear**, craindre pour sa sûreté personnelle. 2. *adv.* (a) Corporellement. (b) They resigned b., ils ont donné leur démission en corps.

bodkin ['bɔdkin], *s.* (a) Passe-lacet *m*, passe-cordon *m.* (b) *Needlew:* Poinçon *m.* (c) (Grande) épingle.

body ['bɔdi], *s.* Corps *m.* 1. (a) **Human b.**, corps humain. To **belong to s.o. b. and soul**, appartenir, être, à qn corps et âme. To **keep b. and soul together**, vivre tout juste; vivoter. **B. linen**, linge de corps. *S.a.* SOUND[1] I. 1. (b) (Dead) b., corps (mort); cadavre *m.* **Over my dead b.!** à mon corps défendant! **The resurrection of the b.**, la résurrection de la chair. (c) Sève *f*, générosité *f* (d'un vin). To **give b. to wine**, corser le vin. (Of wine) To **acquire b.**, s'enforcir. (d) Consistance *f.* **Paper without enough b.**, papier qui manque de consistance, de corps. 2. (a) **Legislative b.**, corps législatif. **Public b.**, corporation *f.* **Examining b.**, jury *m* d'examen. **Electoral b.**, collège électoral. (b) **Large b. of people**, nombreuse société; foule nombreuse. **Little b. of disciples**, petite bande de disciples. To **come in a b.**, venir en masse, en corps. (c) *Jur:* **Strong b. of evidence**, forte accumulation de preuves. **B. of laws**, recueil *m* de lois. 3. *F:* (Person) (a) A **very decent old b.**, une vieille personne très respectable. (b) **A queer b.**, un drôle de type. 4. (Main part) (a) Corps (de document, de bâtiment); nef *f*, vaisseau *m* (d'église); fuselage *m* (d'avion). **The b. of a speech**, le fond, la substance, d'un discours. (b) *Veh:* Bâti *m*, corps, caisse *f*; carrosserie *f*; nacelle *f* (de voiture *f* d'enfant). *Av: Aut:* **Stream-lined b.**, carène *f. Aut:* **Integral all-steel welded b.**, carrosserie (mono)coque, coque auto-porteuse. 5. *Astr: Ch:* Corps. **Heavenly b.**, astre *m*; corps céleste. '**body-builder**, *s. Veh: Aut:* Carrossier *m.* '**body-colour**, *s.* Couleur *f* opaque. *Art:* Gouache *f.* To **paint in b.-c.**, peindre à la gouache. '**body-guard**, *s.* 1. (a) Garde *f* du corps; sauvegarde *f.* (b) Cortège *m* (à la suite de qn). 2. Garde *m* du corps. '**body-snatcher**, *s.* Déterreur *m* (de cadavres); résurrectionniste *m.*

Boer ['buər, 'bouər], *s. & a.* Boer (*mf*).

boffin ['bɔfin], *s. F:* Savant *m.*

bog[1] [bɔg], *s.* 1. Fondrière *f*; marécage *m.* 2. *F:* **What an awful b.!** quelle gaffe!

bog[2], *v.* (bogged) 1. *v.tr.* Embourber, enliser. To **get bogged**, s'embourber, s'enliser. 2. *v.i.* (Of horse, etc.) To **b. down**, s'enfoncer dans une fondrière.

bog[3], *s. P:* Latrines *fpl*; cabinets *mpl*; *P:* goguenots *mpl*, chiottes *fpl.*

bogey ['bougi], *s.* 1. (a) Épouvantail *m.* (b) Fantôme *m*, spectre *m.* 2. *Golf:* To **play against b.**, jouer contre la normale. '**bogey-man**, *s.* The b.-m., croquemitaine *m*; le Père Fouettard (des enfants).

boggle ['bɔgl], *v.i.* (a) Reculer, rechigner (at, over, sth., devant qch.; at, about, doing sth., à faire qch.). (b) (Bungle) To **b. over an exercise**, over the adverbs, patauger dans un devoir, parmi les adverbes.

boggy ['bɔgi], *a.* Marécageux, tourbeux.

bogie ['bougi], *s. Rail:* Bog(g)ie *m.* **B. carriage**, voiture à bog(g)ie.

bogle ['bougl], *s. Scot:* 1. = BOGEY 1. 2. Spectre *m*, revenant *m.*

bogus ['bougəs], *a.* Faux, *f.* fausse; feint, simulé. *Com:* **B. company**, (i) société qui n'existe pas; société fantôme; (ii) société véreuse.

bogy ['bougi], *s.* = BOGEY 1.

Bohemia [bo'hi:miə]. *Pr.r.* 1. *Geog:* La Bohème. 2. (Unconventional life) Bohème *f.*

Bohemian [bo'hi:miən]. 1. *a. & s. Geog:* Bohémien, -ienne. 2. *s.* (a) (Gipsy) Bohémien, -ienne. (b) Bohème *mf*, *a.* **B. life**, vie de bohème.

bohemianism [bo'hi:miənizm], *s.* Mœurs *fpl* de bohème, vie *f* de bohème; bohémianisme *m.*

boil[1] [bɔil], *s. Med:* Furoncle *m*, *F:* clou *m.*

boil[2], *s.* 1. (Of water, etc.) To **come to the b.**, commencer à bouillir. **The kettle is on the b.**, l'eau bout. To **go off the b.**, cesser de bouillir. 2. Tourbillon *m* (dans un cours d'eau); remous *m.*

boil[3]. 1. *v.i.* Bouillir; (violently) bouillonner. To **begin to b.**, entrer en ébullition. To **b. fast**, gently, bouillir à gros, à petits, bouillons. *Cu:* **Allow to b. gently, slowly**, faites mijoter. To **keep the pot boiling**, (i) faire bouillir la marmite; (ii) *F:* pourvoir aux besoins du ménage; (iii) *F:* maintenir l'entrain (dans une réunion). *S.a.* BLOOD[1] 1. 2. *v.tr.* (a) Faire bouillir (de l'eau, etc.); cuire (du sucre). *Cu:* Cuire, faire cuire, (des pois, etc.) à l'eau. **Boiled egg**, œuf à la coque. (b) *Laund:* Lessiver (le linge). *S.a.* SHIRT. **boil away**, *v.i.* (Of sauce, etc.) (Se) réduire. **boil down**. 1. *v.tr.* Réduire (une solution); (faire) réduire (un sirop, etc.). *F:* To **b. down a newspaper article**, résumer, condenser, un article de journal. 2. *v.i.* Se réduire, *F:* se ramener, se borner, se résumer, revenir (to, à). *F:* **This is what his argument boils down to**, voici à quoi se ramène, se résume, se borne, revient, son raisonnement. **boil over**, *v.i.* (Of liquid in pan) Verser, se sauver. *F:* To **b. over with rage**, bouillir de colère. **boil up**, *v.i.* (Of milk, etc.) Monter, partir. **boiling**[1], *a.* Bouillant, bouillonnant. *adv.* **B. hot**, tout bouillant. **boiling**[2], *s.* 1. Bouillonnement *m*, ébullition *f.* 2. *P:* **The whole b.**, toute la bande; tout le bazar; toute la boutique. '**boiling-point**, *s.* Point *m* d'ébullition.

boiler ['bɔilər], *s.* 1. Fabricant *m*, raffineur *m* (de sucre, etc.). 2. Chaudière *f.* **Direct-tube b.**, chaudière à flamme directe. **French b.**, chaudière à bouilleurs. **Oil-fuel b.**, chaudière au mazout. *Dom.Ec:* **Range b.**, chaudière de cuisine. **Double b.**, bain-marie *m.* 3. *Cu: F:* Poule *f* (à bouillir). '**boiler-deck**, *s. Nau:* Pont inférieur (d'un vapeur). '**boiler-house**, *s. Ind:* Salle *f*, bâtiment *m*, des chaudières. '**boiler-maker**, *s.* Chaudronnier *m.* '**boiler-making**, *s.* Chaudronnerie *f.* '**boiler-man**, *s.* Chauffeur *m.* '**boiler-plate**, *s.* Tôle *f* à chaudières. '**boiler-room**, *s.* 1. = BOILER-HOUSE. 2. *Nau:* Chambre *f* de chauffe. **The boiler-rooms**, la chaufferie. '**boiler-suit**, *s. Ind:* Bleus *mpl*; bleu *m* de chauffe; combinaison *f.* '**boiler-tube**, *s.* 1. (Fire-tube) Tube *m* de chaudière, de fumée. 2. (Water-tube) Bouilleur *m*; tube d'eau.

boisterous ['bɔist(ə)rəs], *a.* (Of pers.) Bruyant, turbulent; tapageur; (of wind) violent; (of sea), rude, houleux, tumultueux, (of weather) tempétueux. **B. spirits**, gaieté débordante, bruyante. **-ly**, *adv.* (a) Bruyamment; avec une gaieté bruyante. (b) Tempétueusement.

boisterousness ['bɔist(ə)rəsnis], *s.* Turbulence *f*; violence *f* (du vent); agitation *f* (de la mer).

bold [bould], *a.* 1. Hardi; (i) peu timide; (ii) audacieux, téméraire; (ton, regard) assuré, confiant. **B. stroke** (i) coup hardi; (ii) coup d'audace. **B. to act**, hardi à agir. To **make b. with s.o.**, prendre des libertés avec qn. To **make (so) b. (as) to do sth.**, s'enhardir jusqu'à faire qch.; oser faire qch.; se permettre de faire qch. To **put a b. face on the matter**, payer d'audace. 2. Impudent, effronté. **As b. as brass**, effronté comme un page. To **answer as b. as brass**, répondre sans sourciller. 3. (Prominent) (a) **B. headland**, promontoire à pic, accore. **B. cliff**, falaise escarpée. *S.a.* TYPE[2] 1. (b) *Art:* **B. style**, style hardi. **In b. relief**, en puissant relief. **-ly**, *adv.* 1. Hardiment; audacieusement; avec audace. To **assert sth. b.**, affirmer qch. carrément, avec confiance. 2. Effrontément. **bold-faced**, *a.* 1. Effronté. 2. *Typ:* **B.-f. type**, caractères gras.

boldness ['bouldnis], *s.* **1.** Hardiesse *f* (de conduite, etc.); audace *f*, intrépidité *f*. **2.** Effronterie *f*. **3.** Escarpement *m* (d'une falaise).

bole [boul], *s.* Fût *m*, tronc *m*, tige *f* (d'un arbre).

bolero [bə'lɛrou, 'bɔlərou], *s. Danc: Cost:* Boléro *m*.

boletus [bə'li:təs], *s. Fung:* Bolet *m*; cèpe *m*.

bolivar ['bɔliva:r], *s. Num:* Bolivar *m*.

Bolivia [bə'liviə]. *Pr.n. Geog:* (La) Bolivie.

Bolivian [bə'liviən], *a. & s.* Bolivien, -ienne.

boll [boul, bɔl], *s.* Capsule *f* (du cotonnier, du lin). **'boll-weevil**, *s. Ent:* Anthonome *m* des cultures de cotonnier.

bollard ['bɔləd], *s. Nau:* (a) (*On wharf*) Pieu *m*, canon *m*, borne *f*, d'amarrage. (b) (*On ship*) Bitte *f* (de tournage).

Bologna [bə'lounjə]. *Pr.n. Geog:* Bologne *f*. **B. sausage**, mortadelle *f*.

bolometer [bə'lɔmitər], *s. Ph:* Bolomètre *m*.

boloney [bə'louni], *s. F:* It's all b., c'est des histoires! *P:* c'est de la foutaise, des conneries!

Bolshevik ['bɔlʃəvik], **Bolshevist** ['bɔlʃəvist], *a. & s.* Bolchevik (*mf*), bolcheviste (*mf*).

Bolshevism ['bɔlʃəvizm], *s.* Bolchevisme *m*.

bolshevization [ˌbɔlʃəvaizeiʃ(ə)n], *s.* Bolchevisation *f*.

bolshevize ['bɔlʃəvaiz], *v.tr.* Bolcheviser.

Bolshie, Bolshy ['bɔlʃi], *a. & s. F:* Moscoutaire (*mf*). He's feeling a bit b. today, il n'est pas à prendre avec des pincettes aujourd'hui.

bolster[1] ['boulstər], *s.* **1.** Traversin *m*; coussin *m* (de canapé). *Rail: Veh:* Sommier *m*. **2.** Épaulement *m* (de couteau, etc.). **3.** (a) *Mec.E:* Coussinet *m*. (b) *Metalw:* Matrice *f*; étampe inférieure *f*. **4.** *Const:* Racinal, -aux *m*; sous-poutre *f*.

bolster[2], *v.tr.* To b. s.o. up, (i) soutenir, relever, la tête de qn avec des oreillers; (ii) *F:* appuyer, soutenir, qn (qui a tort).

bolt[1] [boult], *s.* **1.** Carreau *m* (d'arbalète). *F:* He has shot his last b., il a vidé son carquois. **2.** Éclair *m*; coup *m* de foudre. *F:* B. from the blue, événement imprévu. **3.** (a) (**Sliding**) **b.**, verrou *m* (de porte); pêne *m* (de serrure). **To shoot the bolts**, pousser, mettre, les verrous. (b) *Sm.a:* Rifle-b., culasse *f* mobile; fermeture *f* de culasse. **4.** *Mec.E:* Boulon *m*; cheville *f*. **Main bolt**, cheville ouvrière. **Nuts and bolts**, boulonnerie *f*. *S.a.* EYE-BOLT, KING-BOLT, RING-BOLT, SCREW-BOLT, etc. **5.** (a) Pièce *f* (de toile). (b) Botte *f* (d'osier). **'bolt-head**, *s.* **1.** Tête *f* de boulon. **2.** Tête mobile (de fusil). **'bolt-lever**, *s.* Levier *m* (de fusil). **'bolt-rope**, *s. Nau:* Ralingue *f*.

bolt[2]. **1.** *v.i.* (a) (*Of pers.*) *F:* (i) Décamper, déguerpir. (*Of game*) To b. from cover, débouler. (ii) To b. out of the room, sortir précipitamment, brusquement, de la salle. (b) (*Of horse*) S'emballer, s'emporter. **2.** *v.tr.* Gober; avaler à grosses bouchées, sans mâcher. To b. one's dinner, expédier, *F:* bouffer, son dîner. **3.** *v.tr.* (a) Verrouiller; fermer (une porte) au verrou; bâcler (une porte). To b. the door, mettre les verrous. (b) Boulonner, cheviller. **bolt in**, *v.tr.* Enfermer (qn) au verrou. **bolt out**, *v.tr.* Mettre les verrous contre (qn). **bolting**[1], *s.* **1.** Verrouillage *m*. **2.** Boulonnage *m*, chevillage *m*.

bolt[3], *adv.* B. upright, tout droit; droit comme un piquet.

bolt[4], *s. F:* Élan soudain; fuite *f*. To make a b. for sth., s'élancer sur, vers, qch. To make a b. for it, décamper, déguerpir, filer. **'bolt-hole**, *s.* **1.** Trou *m*, terrier *m* de refuge (d'un animal). *Mil:* Abri *m* (de bombardement). **2.** Échappée *f*. *F:* To arrange oneself a b.-h., se ménager une (porte de) sortie.

bolt[5], *v.tr. Mill:* Bluter, tamiser, sasser (la farine). **bolting**[2], *s.* Blutage *m*, tamisage *m*.

bolter ['boultər], *s.* Cheval porté à s'emballer.

bomb[1] [bɔm], *s.* (a) Bombe *f*. **Cobalt b.**, bombe au cobalt. **Depth b.**, bombe sous-marine. **Delayed-action b.**, bombe à retardement. **Flying b.**, bombe volante. **Glide(r) b.**, bombe planante. **H-b.**, bombe à (l')hydrogène. **Incendiary b.**, bombe incendiaire. **Plastic b.**, (bombe au) plastic, plastique *m*. **Smoke b.**,

bombe fumigène. **Tear-gas b.**, bombe lacrymogène. **Uranium b.**, bombe à l'uranium. **Mills b.**, grenade *f* de Mills. **To release a b.**, lâcher une bombe. **B. clearance, disposal**, (i) désobusage *m*; (ii) déminage *m*. **B. disposal squad**, équipe *f* de déminage. *S.a.* ATOM, NAPALM. (b) *Geol:* Volcanic b., bombe volcanique. (c) *Med:* Cobalt b., bombe au cobalt. **'bomb-aimer**, *s. Av:* Bombardier *m*. **'bomb-bay**, *s. Av:* Soute *f* à bombes. **'bomb-carrier**, *s. Av:* Dispositif *m* porte-bombes. **'bomb-crater**, *s. Mil:* Entonnoir *m*, cratère *m*. **'bomb-load**, *s.* Charge *f* de bombes. **'bomb-proof**, *a.* A l'épreuve des bombes; blindé. **'bomb-rack**, *s.* Casier *m*, ratelier *m*, à bombes. **'bomb-release**, *s. Av:* Commande *f* de lance-bombes. **'bomb-sight**, *s. Av:* Viseur *m*. **'bomb-thrower**, *s.* **1.** (*Pers.*) Lanceur *m* de bombes. **2.** (*Appareil m*) lance-bombes *m inv*.

bomb[2], *v.tr. Esp. Av:* Bombarder, lancer des bombes sur (une ville). **bombed out**, *a.* Sinistré. **bomb up**, *v.i. Av:* Prendre sa charge de bombes. **bombing**. **1.** *Av:* Bombardement *m*. **Dive b.**, bombardement en piqué. **Pin-point b.**, (i) bombardement sur objectif ponctuel; (ii) bombardement de précision. **B. raid**, raid *m* de bombardement. **2.** Attaque *f* à la grenade.

bombard [bɔm'ba:d], *v.tr. Mil: Navy:* Bombarder (une ville, un port).

bombardier [bɔmbə'diər], *s.* **1.** *A:* Bombardier *m*. **2.** *Artil:* (*In Brit. army*) Brigadier *m*. **3.** *U.S: Mil: Av:* Bombardier. **4.** *Ent:* B. beetle, brachyne tirailleur, bombardier.

bombardment [bɔm'ba:dmənt], *s.* Bombardement *m*. *Ph:* B. of the electrons, bombardement électronique.

bombasine, bombazine [bɔmbə'zi:n], *s. Tex:* Bombasin *m*.

bombast ['bɔmbæst], *s.* Emphase *f*, enflure *f*, boursouflure *f* (de style); grandiloquence *f*.

bombastic [bɔm'bæstik], *a.* (Style) ampoulé, enflé, emphatique. **-ally**, *adv.* D'un style ampoulé, enflé; emphatiquement; avec emphase.

bomber ['bɔmər], *s.* **1.** (*Pers.*) (a) *Mil:* Grenadier *m*. (b) *Av:* Bombardier *m*. **2.** *Av:* (*aircraft*) Bombardier *m*, avion *m* de bombardement. **B. command**, l'aviation *f* de bombardement.

bombshell ['bɔmʃel], *s.* (a) *A:* (= SHELL[1] 4) Obus *m*. (b) This was a b. to us all, cette nouvelle nous consterna. This letter came like a b., cette lettre nous tomba des nues.

bona fide ['bounə'faidi], *a. & adv.* De bonne foi. **B. f. offer**, offre sérieuse.

bonanza [bə'nænzə]. **1.** *s. U.S:* Bonanza *f*; filon riche. **To strike a b.**, rencontrer un filon riche. **2.** *a. F:* Prospère. **B. year**, année *f* de prospérité, d'abondance.

Bonapartist ['bounəpɑ:tist], *s. Hist:* Bonapartiste *m*.

bond[1] [bɔnd], *s.* Lien *m*; attache *f*. **1.** *pl. A:* Fers *m*, liens, chaînes *f*. **To burst one's bonds, to break from one's bonds**, rompre, briser, ses liens. **2.** (a) Lien (d'osier, pour fagots, etc.). **Bonds of friendship**, liens d'amitié. (b) *Const:* (System of) b., appareil *m* (en liaison). **Old English b.**, appareil anglais. (c) Assemblage *m* ou joint *m*. **Thermit(e) b.**, joint à la thermite. **3.** (a) Engagement *m*, contrat *m*; obligation *f*. **Mortgage b.**, titre *m* hypothécaire. (b) *Fin:* Bon *m*. **Treasury bonds**, bons du Trésor. **Bearer b.**, bon au porteur. **Registered b.**, bon nominatif. **Government bonds**, (i) rentes *f* sur l'État; (ii) titres de rente. **Premium bonds**, bons à lots. (c) *Jur:* Caution *f*. **4.** *Com:* Dépôt *m*, entreposage *m*. (*Of goods*) To be in b., être à l'entrepôt, être entreposé. **To take goods out of b.**, dédouaner des marchandises. **'bond-note**, *s. Cust:* Acquit-à-caution *m*, *pl.* acquits-à-caution. **'bond-stone**, *s. Const:* Parpaing *m*, boutisse *f*. **'bond-store**, *s. Cust:* Entrepôt *m*.

bond[2], *v.tr.* **1.** *Const:* (a) Liaisonner (des pierres). (b) Appareiller (un mur). **2.** *Com:* Entreposer, mettre en dépôt, à l'entrepôt (des marchandises). *S.a.* WAREHOUSE[1] 1.

bondage ['bɔndidʒ], *s.* **1.** Esclavage *m*, servitude *f*, asservissement *m*. **To be in b. to s.o.**, être sous la coupe, sous la férule, de qn. **2.** *Hist:* Servage *m*. **3.** *Poet:* Captivité *f*.

bondholder ['bɔndhouldər], s. Fin: Obligataire m; porteur m de bons, d'obligations.

bondman, pl. -men ['bɔndmən], s.m. (a) Hist: Serf. (b) Esclave.

bondsman, pl. -men ['bɔndsmən], s.m. 1. = BONDMAN. 2. To be b. for s.o., être le garant de qn; s'être porté caution pour qn:

bone[1] [boun], s. 1. Os m. Fish-b., arête f. S.a. ANKLE-BONE, BACKBONE, CHEEK-BONE, WHALEBONE, etc. Horse with plenty of b., cheval fortement membré. Hard words break no bones, une parole rude ne casse rien. F: He is (nothing but) a bag of bones, il n'a que la peau et les os. He won't make old bones, il ne fera pas de vieux os. I feel it in my bones, j'en ai le pressentiment. To make no bones about doing sth., ne pas se gêner, ne pas faire de manières, pour faire qch.; ne pas hésiter à faire qch. attrib: B. china, demi-porcelaine f, porcelaine tendre anglaise. S.a. BREED[2] I., CHILL[3] 1, CONTENTION 1, PICK[3] 3. 2. pl. (a) (Of the dead) Ossements m. (b) F: (i) Dés m à jouer. (ii) Dominos m. (c) (i) Mus: Cliquettes f. (ii) Le joueur de cliquettes (dans une troupe nègre). 'bone-black, s. Noir m animal. 'bone-dry, a. Absolument sec, archisec. 'bone-'idle, a. = BONE-LAZY. 'bone-lace, s. Dentelle f au fuseau. 'bone-'lazy, a. Paresseux, -euse, comme une couleuvre. 'bone-'meal, s. Engrais m d'os (broyés). 'bone-setter, s. Rebouteur m. 'bone-shaker, s. 1. A: F: Vélocipède m à bandages de fer. 2. (Of car, bicycle) F: Vieux clou; vieille guimbarde.

bone[2], v.tr. 1. Désosser (la viande); ôter les arêtes (du poisson). 2. Garnir (un corset) de baleines. 3. P: Chiper, escamoter, voler (qch.). 4. v.tr. & i. U.S: P: To b. (up on) a subject, potasser un sujet. Abs. Potasser.

bonehead ['bounhed], s. P: Tête de bois.

boneless ['bounlis], a. 1. Désossé; sans os; sans arêtes. 2. F: Mou; sans énergie.

boner ['bounə], s. Sch: U.S: P: Bourde f.

Boney ['bouni]. Pr.n.m. F: A: Bonaparte.

bonfire ['bɔnfaiər], s. Feu m de joie; feu de jardin.

bonhomie ['bɔnɔmi], s. Bonhomie f.

bonnet ['bɔnit], s. 1. Cost: (Men) Bonnet (a)(écossais); béret (écossais). S.a. BEE 1. (b) (Women) Chapeau m à brides; capote f, bonnet; béguin m (d'enfant). 2. Aut: Av: Capot m. Aut: B. to tail, pare-chocs à pare-chocs m. 3. Nau: Bonnette maillée, basse (de voile).

bonny ['bɔni], a. Scot: Joli; gentil, f. gentille. A b. baby, un bébé magnifique.

bonus, pl. -uses ['bounəs, -əsiz], s. Surpaye f, boni m; prime f; part f de bénéfice; gratification f. Cost-of-living b., indemnité f de vie chère. B. on shares, bonification f sur les actions. Ins: No-claim b., bonification pour non-sinistre.

bony ['bouni], a. 1. Osseux. 2. (a) (Personne) à gros os; (corps) anguleux. (b) (Doigt, visage) décharné. 3. (Of meat) Plein d'os; (of fish) plein d'arêtes.

bonza ['bɔnzə]. a. F: Austr: Épatant.

bonze ['bɔnz], s. Rel: Bonze m. B. monastery, bonzerie f.

boo[1] [bu:]. 1. int. Hou! (d'aversion ou de mépris). F: He can't say b. to a goose, c'est un timide; un nigaud. 2. s. Huée f.

boo[2], v.tr. & i. To b. (at) s.o., huer, conspuer, qn. To be booed off the stage, quitter la scène au milieu des huées. booing, s. Huées fpl.

boob[1] [bu:b], s. P: (a) U.S: = BOOBY 1 (a). (b) Gaffe f, boulette f.

boob[2], v.i. P: Faire une gaffe, une boulette.

booby ['bu:bi], s. 1. (a) Nigaud m, benêt m, grand dadais. (b) Le dernier (dans un concours, etc.). 2. Orn: F: Fou m. 'booby-trap, s. A: Attrape-nigaud m. (b) Mil: Piège m; mine-piège f.

boodle ['bu:dl], s. P: Argent m, P: pèze m, fric m.

boohoo[1] [bu:'hu:]. 1. int. Heu, heu, heu! 2. s. F: Pleurnichement m.

boohoo[2], v.i. F: Pleurer bruyamment; pleurnicher.

book[1] [buk], s. 1. (a) Livre m; F: bouquin m. To talk like a b., parler comme un livre. To speak by the b., citer ses autorités. B. knowledge, connaissances livresques. School b., text b., livre classique, de classe. (b) Livret m (d'un opéra). (c) (Bible) To swear on the B., prêter serment sur la Bible. (d) Blue b., (i) Adm: = livre jaune; (ii) U.S: registre m (des employés de l'État, etc.); (iii) U.S: = Bottin mondain; (iv) U.S: Sch: cahier bleu dans lequel les candidats écrivent leurs copies d'examen. F: To do a blue b., passer un examen. 2. Registre. (a) Account b., livre de comptes. Book-k: To put on the books, faire passer aux écritures. Bank-b., livret, carnet m, de banque. S.a. DAY-BOOK, NOTE-BOOK, PASS-BOOK, etc. To keep the books of a firm, tenir les livres d'une maison. F: To be in s.o.'s good books, être dans les petits papiers de qn. To be in s.o.'s bad books, être mal vu de qn. To bring s.o. to b. for sth., forcer qn à rendre compte de qch. (b) Nau: Ship's books, livres de bord. (c) Exercise-b., cahier m. S.a. 1, (d). (d) Turf: Betting-b., livre de paris. To make a b., faire un livre. F: That just suits my b., ça fait mon beurre. (e) Savings-bank b., livret de caisse d'épargne. B. of tickets, carnet de billets. (f) The telephone b., l'annuaire m du téléphone. 3. B. of matches, pochette f d'allumettes. 'book-club, s. Club m du livre. 'book-ends, s.pl. Serre-livres m inv. 'book-hunter, s. Bibliophile m, bouquineur m. 'book-hunting, s. Bouquinerie f. 'book-jacket, s. Protège-livre m, pl. protège-livres; jaquette f. 'book(-)keeper, s. Teneur m de livres; comptable m. 'book(-)keeping, s. Tenue f des livres; comptabilité f. Double-entry book-keeping, digraphie f; tenue des livres en partie double. 'book-learning, s. Savoir acquis dans les livres; connaissances f livresques; érudition f. 'bookmark(er), s. Signet m. 'book-muslin, s. Tex: Organdi m. 'book-plate, s. Ex-libris m. 'book-post, s. Service postal des imprimés (journaux exceptés). 'book-rest, s. Appui-livre(s) m inv.; liseuse f. 'book-trade, s. Industrie f du livre; (commerce m de) librairie f.

book[2], v.tr. 1. Inscrire, enregistrer (une commande, etc.). Com: Shall I b. it for you, madam? dois-je l'inscrire à votre compte, madame? 2. Retenir, réserver (une chambre, une place); louer (une place) d'avance. 3. Rail: Délivrer un billet à (un voyageur). Abs. (Of passenger) To b., prendre son billet. 4. Aut: F: I was booked for speeding = j'ai eu une contravention (pour excès) de vitesse. booking, s. (a) Enregistrement m, inscription f. Th: B. of tickets, location f de billets. Rail: B. of seats, réservation f des places. (b) Th: (Of artist) Engagement m. 'booking-clerk, s. Rail: Préposé m à la distribution des billets; employé m du guichet. 'booking-office, s. Rail: Guichet m.

bookable ['bukəbl], a. Qui peut être loué, retenu, réservé.

bookbinder ['bukbaindər], s. Relieur m.

bookbinding ['bukbaindiŋ], s.f. Reliure f. B. machine, relieuse f.

bookcase ['bukkeis], s. Bibliothèque f.

bookie ['buki], s. F: = BOOKMAKER 2.

bookish ['bukiʃ], a. 1. Adonné à la lecture; studieux. 2. Pédantesque, livresque.

booklet ['buklit], s. Livret m; opuscule m.

booklover ['buklʌvər], s. Bibliophile m.

bookmaker ['bukmeikər], s. 1. Faiseur m de livres. 2. Turf: Bookmaker m, F: book m.

bookmobile ['bukmobi:l], s. U.S: Bibliobus m.

bookseller ['bukselər], s. Libraire mf. Second-hand b., bouquiniste m.

bookshelf, pl. -ves ['bukʃelf, -elvz], s. Rayon m.

bookshop ['bukʃɔp], s. Librairie f.

bookstall ['bukstɔ:l], **bookstand** ['bukstænd], s. 1. Étalage m de livres. Second-hand b., étalage de bouquiniste. 2. Rail: Bibliothèque f (de gare).

bookworm ['bukwə:m], s. 1. Ent: Anobium m. 2. F: (Of pers.) Dévoreur de livres, liseur acharné; bouquineur m.

boom[1] [bu:m], s. 1. (At harbour mouth) (Pannes fpl de) barrage m; chaîne f (de fermeture); barre f. 2. Nau: (a) Bout-dehors m (de foc); gui m. Spinnaker b., tangon m, bout-dehors, de spinnaker. S.a. JIB-BOOM. (b) Swinging b., tangon. (c) Derrick-b., mât m de charge. (d) Flèche f (d'une grue). 3. Av: Longeron m.

boom², s. Grondement m, retentissement m, bruit m (du canon, du tonnerre); mugissement m (du vent); tons m sonores (de la voix); ronflement m (de l'orgue); bourdonnement m.

boom³, v.i. (Of wind. etc.) Retentir, gronder, mugir (sourdement); (of guns) gronder, tonner; (of organ) ronfler; (of insects) bourdonner.

boom⁴, s. Com: 1. Hausse f rapide; boom m. 2. (a) Vague f de prospérité. (b) (Période de) vogue f.

boom⁵. 1. v.tr. Faire une grosse publicité en faveur de (qch.); faire du battage autour de (qn, qch.). 2. v.i. Être en hausse. **Trade is booming,** le commerce va très fort.

boomerang ['buːməræŋ], s. Boumerang m, boomerang m.

boon¹ [buːn], s. 1. A: Don m, faveur f. **To grant a b.,** accorder une faveur. 2. Bienfait m, avantage m.

boon², a. B. **companion,** gai compagnon; bon vivant; vive-la-joie m inv.

boor ['buər], s. Rustre m, rustaud m; goujat m. **What a b.!** quel ours!

boorish ['buəriʃ], a. Rustre, rustaud, grossier; malappris. **-ly,** adv. Grossièrement; en rustre.

boorishness ['buəriʃnis], s. Grossièreté f; manque m de savoir-vivre.

boost¹ [buːst], s. 1. (a) **To give s.o. a b.,** (i) soulever qn par derrière; (ii) faire de la réclame pour qn. (b) Relance f. 2. B. **pressure,** pression f d'admission, de suralimentation (d'un moteur).

boost², v.tr. 1. (a) Soulever (qn) par derrière. (b) F: Faire de la réclame, du battage, pour, en faveur de (qn, qch.); vanter, faire valoir (sa marchandise). 2. El.E: Survolter. **boosting,** s. 1. F: Battage m, réclame f. 2. El.E: Survoltage m. '**boost-'glide,** a. B.-g. **vehicle,** véhicule mi-balistique mi-planeur m.

booster ['buːstər], s. 1. Prôneur m, réclamiste m. 2. El.E: Survolteur m. 3. Bac: B. **dose,** dose f de rappel m. B. **injection,** injection f de rappel. '**booster(-rocket),** s. Aer: Fusée f de lancement, fusée porteuse.

boot¹ [buːt], s. 1. Chaussure f, bottine f; (high b.) botte f; (strong, laced b.) brodequin m. **Ankle b.,** bottillon m. **Riding-boots,** bottes à l'écuyère. B. **and shoe manufacturer,** fabricant de chaussures. **To put on one's boots,** (i) se chausser; (ii) (riding-boots) se botter. **To take off one's boots,,** se déchausser. S.a. JACK-BOOTS, TOP-BOOTS, etc. F: **The b. is on the other foot,** (i) c'est tout (juste) le contraire; (ii) les rôles sont renversés. P: **To give s.o. the (order of the) b.,** mettre, flanquer, qn à la porte. **To get the b.,** être congédié. **To die with one's boots on,** mourir à la tâche. **To lick s.o.'s boots,** lécher les bottes à qn. Geog: **The b. of Italy,** la botte de l'Italie. S.a. HEART¹ 1, PUSS¹, SEVEN-LEAGUE. 2. Veh: Coffre m, malle f. '**boot-jack,** s. Arrache-chaussures m inv, tire-botte m (pour se débotter). '**boot-maker,** s. Bottier m, cordonnier m. '**boot-polish,** s. Crème f à chaussures. '**boot-tree,** s. 1. Embauchoir m (pour botte). 2. Tendeur m (pour chaussures).

boot², v.tr. 1. Chausser (qn). 2. F: Flanquer des coups de pied à (qn). **To b. s.o. out,** flanquer qn à la porte. **To b. s.o. upstairs,** donner de l'avancement à qn, avancer, promouvoir qn (pour s'en débarrasser).

boot³, s. (In the phrase) **To b.,** par surcroît, en sus, de plus.

boot⁴, v.tr.impers. A. & Lit: **What boots it to . . .?** à quoi sert-il de . . .? **It boots not to . . .,** rien ne sert de. . . .

bootblack ['buːtblæk], s. Décrotteur m, cireur m (de chaussures).

bootee [buː'tiː], s. (a) Bottine f d'intérieur (pour dame). (b) Bottine d'enfant; bottillon m; chausson tricoté de bébé.

booth [buːð], s. Baraque f, tente f (de marché, de forains); loge f (de foire). Cin: **Projection b.,** cabine f de projection. Tp: **Telephone b.,** cabine téléphonique. S.a. POLLING-BOOTH.

bootlace ['buːtleis], s. Lacet m (de chaussure).

bootleg ['buːtleg], v.i. U.S: F: (a) Trafiquer en boissons alcooliques. (b) Faire la contrebande des boissons alcooliques. **bootlegging,** s. (a) Trafic m en alcool. (b) Contrebande f de l'alcool.

bootlegger ['buːtlegər], s. U.S: F: (a) Trafiquant m en boissons alcooliques, F: bootlegger m. (b) Contrebandier m de boissons alcooliques.

bootless¹ ['buːtlis], a. Sans chaussures.

bootless², a. A. & Lit: Inutile, vain.

bootlick ['buːtlik], v.tr. F: Lécher les bottes à (qn).

bootlicker ['buːtlikər], s. F: Louangeur m; lécheur m (de bottes), lèche-bottes m.

boots [buːts], s. Garçon m d'étage (dans un hôtel); cireur m de chaussures (dans un pensionnat, etc.).

booty ['buːti], s. Butin m.

booze¹ [buːz], v.i. P: Faire (la) ribote.

booze², s. P: 1. Boisson f (alcoolique). 2. **To be on the b.,** être en ribote.

boozer ['buːzər], s. P: 1. Ivrogne m, poivrot m. 2. Bistrot m.

boozy ['buːzi], a. P: 1. Riboteur, ivrogne. 2. Un peu gris, pompette.

boracic [bə'ræsik], a. Ch: Borique. B. **ointment,** pommade à l'acide borique. B. **powder,** poudre boriquée.

borage ['bɔridʒ], s. Bot: Pharm: Bourrache f.

borate ['bɔːreit], s. Ch: Borate m.

borated ['bɔːreitid], a. Ch: Boraté.

borax ['bɔːræks], s. Borax m.

border¹ ['bɔːdər], s. 1. Bord m (d'un lac); lisière f, bordure f (d'un bois); marge f (d'un chemin); frontière f, confins mpl (d'un pays). **The B.,** (i) la frontière écossaise (et les comtés limitrophes). (ii) U.S: la frontière entre les États-Unis et le Mexique. B. **town,** ville frontière. 2. (a) (Edging) Galon m, bordé m (d'un habit); bordure (d'un tableau, d'un tapis, etc.); encadrement m (d'un panneau). (b) Grass b., turf b., cordon m de gazon. '**border-line,** s. 1. Ligne f de séparation (entre deux catégories, etc.); pl. limites fpl, bornes fpl (d'une catégorie, etc.); frontière f (entre deux états). 2. B.-l. **case,** (i) cas limite; (ii) cas indéterminé.

border². 1. v.tr. (a) Border (un habit, un chemin); lisérer (un mouchoir); encadrer. (b) Border; confiner à (un pays, etc.). 2. v.i. **To b. on (sth.).** (a) (Of territory) Toucher, confiner, à (un autre pays); être limitrophe (d'un autre pays). (b) **To b. on insanity,** approcher, être voisin, de la folie; friser la folie. **bordering,** a. (a) Contigu, -uë; touchant, aboutissant (on, à); voisin (on, de); limitrophe (on, de). (b) Colour b. **on red,** couleur qui tire sur le rouge. **Statement b. on truth, on falsehood,** déclaration qui côtoie la vérité, qui frise le mensonge.

borderer ['bɔːdərər], s. Habitant m, -ante, (i) de la frontière, esp (ii) de la frontière d'Écosse; frontalier m.

borderland ['bɔːdələænd], s. Pays m frontière, limitrophe; marche f.

bore¹ ['bɔːr], s. 1. (a) Calibre m, alésage m (d'un tuyau, etc.); calibre (d'une arme à feu). (b) Ame f (d'une arme à feu). 2. Min: Trou m de sonde. '**bore-hole,** s. Min: 1. Trou m de sonde. 2. Trou de mine. 3. Bure f.

bore², v.tr. & i. 1. **To b. (out),** creuser; (i) forer, (ii) foncer (un puits); forer, percer (un trou); aléser (un cylindre). **To b. through sth.,** percer, perforer, qch. Min: **To b. for water, minerals,** faire un sondage, sonder, pour trouver de l'eau, des minéraux. 2. (Of horse) Bourrer, encenser. 3. (a) Turf: Abs. Couper un concurrent, couper la ligne. (b) (Of pers.) **To b. (one's way) through the crowd,** se frayer (brutalement) un chemin à travers la foule. **boring¹,** s. Percement m. Mec.E: Forage m, perçage m; (of cylinder) alésage m. Min: Sondage m. '**boring-machine,** s. Foreuse f, perceuse f; (for cylinders) alésoir m, aléseuse f.

bore³, s. F: (a) (Of pers.) Fâcheux, -euse; importun m; raseur, -euse. (b) (Of thg) Ennui m, scie f, corvée f.

bore⁴, v.tr. F: Ennuyer; F: raser, assommer, enquiquiner (qn); scier le dos à (qn). **To b. s.o. to death;** to b. s.o. stiff, ennuyer qn à mourir; empoisonner qn. **To be bored to death, bored stiff,** s'ennuyer à mourir; se morfondre; F: s'empoisonner; avoir le cafard. **To be bored with doing sth.,** s'ennuyer à faire qch. **boring²,** a. Ennuyeux, ennuyant, F: assommant, rasant, sciant, barbant, enquiquinant.

bore³, s. (In tidal wave) Mascaret m.
bore⁴. See BEAR².
boreal ['bɔːriəl], a. Boréal, -aux.
boredom ['bɔːdəm], s. Ennui m.
borer ['bɔːrər], s. 1. Foreur m, perceur m; sondeur m (de puits). 2. Appareil m ou outil m de perforation. (a) Foret m, tarière f; perçoir m, vrille f. (b) Alésoir m. (c) Civ.E: Perforatrice f. 3. Cheval m qui se braque. 4. Ent: (Insecte m) térébrant (m).
boric ['bɔrik], a. Ch: Borique.
boride ['bɔraid], s. Ch: Borure m.
born [bɔːn]. 1. p.p. To be b., naître; venir au monde. To be b. again, renaître. To have been b., être né. London b., natif de Londres. French b., Français de naissance. He was b. in 1870, il naquit, il est né, en 1870. In this town a hundred children are b. every month, il naît dans cette ville cent enfants par mois. F: Do you think I was b. yesterday? croyez-vous que je suis né d'hier? S.a. BLANKET¹ 1, CAUL 1, LUCKY¹, PURPLE II. High-b., de haute naissance. S.a. BASE-BORN, NEW-BORN, etc. Confidence is b. of knowledge, la confiance vient du savoir. 2. a. He is a b. poet, a poet b., il est né poète, poète-né. A gentleman b., un gentilhomme de naissance. A Londoner b. and bred, un vrai Londonien de Londres. F: B. fool, parfait idiot. 3. s. Her latest b., son dernier né, sa dernière née.
borne. See BEAR².
boron ['bɔːrɔn], s. Ch: Bore m.
borough ['bʌrə], s. (a) Ville f (avec municipalité). County b., grande commune (dont le système administratif est semblable à celui d'un comté). (b) Circonscription électorale (urbaine). Hist: Rotten b., bourg pourri.
Borromean [bɔrə'miː(ə)n], a. Geog: The B. Islands, les îles Borromées.
borrow ['bɔrou], v.tr. Emprunter (from, of, à). To b. at interest, emprunter à intérêt. Borrowed feathers, plumes, plumes d'emprunt. borrowing, s. Emprunts mpl. To live by b., vivre d'emprunts. This word is a b. from Latin, ce mot est un emprunt au latin.
borrower ['bɔrouər], s. Emprunteur, -euse.
Borstal ['bɔːst(ə)l]. Pr.n. Geog: Borstal (ville du comté de Kent). Adm: B. Institution, école de réforme, maison de redressement pour jeunes gens âgés de plus de 16 ans.
bort [bɔːt], s. Lap: Égrisée f; bort m.
borzoi ['bɔːzɔi], s. Lévrier m russe; borzoï m.
bosh [bɔʃ], s. & int. F: Bêtises fpl, blague f; propos idiots. That's all b., tout ça c'est de la blague.
bos'n [bousn]. See BOATSWAIN.
bosom ['buzəm], s. (a) Sein m; poitrine f. Ample b., poitrine opulente. (b) In the b. of one's family, of the Church, au sein de sa famille; dans le giron de l'Église. S.a. FRIEND 1.
Bosphorus ['bɔsfərəs], **Bosporus** ['bɔspərəs]. Pr.n. Geog: The B., le Bosphore.
boss¹ [bɔs], s. Protubérance f, renflement m; bossage m. Arch: osci. Arm: Bosse f. I.C.E: (Gudgeon-pin) bosses of the piston, bossages du piston. Av: Nau: B. of the propeller, moyeu m de l'hélice.
boss². 1. s. F: (a) The b., le patron, le chef. She's the b., c'est elle qui porte la culotte. (b) Ind: Contre-maître m. 2. a. U.S: F: Épatant.
boss³, v.tr. F: Mener, diriger (qn, qch.). He bosses everybody, il régente tout le monde. Here, it is Mr. X who bosses the show, ici, c'est M. X qui fait la loi.
boss⁴, a. & s. P: To make a b. of sth., louper qch. To make a b. shot, rater, manquer, son coup. 'boss-eyed, a. P: Qui louche.
bossiness ['bɔsinis], s. F: Autoritarisme m; façons f autoritaires.
bossy ['bɔsi], a. F: Autoritaire.
bosun [bousn], s. See BOATSWAIN.
bot(t) [bɔt], s. Ann: Larve f d'œstre. 'bot-fly, s. Œstre m; mouche f des chevaux.
botanic(al) [bə'tænik(ə)l], a. Botanique.
botanist ['bɔtənist], s. Botaniste mf.
botanize ['bɔtənaiz], v.i. Herboriser, botaniser. botanizing, s. Herborisation f.

botany ['bɔtəni], s. Botanique f.
botch¹ [bɔtʃ], s. 1. Pustule f (sur la peau). 2. F: Travail mal fait; F: travail bousillé. To make a b. of sth., saboter un travail.
botch², v.tr. F: 1. Bousiller, saboter (un travail, etc.). 2. To b. up, réparer grossièrement, rafistoler (des souliers, un appareil, etc.).
botcher ['bɔtʃər], s. F: Bousilleur m; ravaudeur m; loupeur, -euse.
botchy ['bɔtʃi], a. 1. Pustuleux, -euse. 2. (Travail) bousillé, saboté.
both [bouθ]. 1. a. & pron. Tous (les) deux, toutes (les) deux; l'un(e) et l'autre. B. (of them) are dead, ils sont morts tous (les) deux. B. of these possibilities must be taken into account, il faut tenir compte de l'une et l'autre de ces possibilités. To hold sth. in b. hands, tenir qch. à deux mains. On b. sides, des deux côtés. S.a. SIDE¹ 3, 4. B. alike, l'un comme l'autre. B. of us saw it, nous l'avons vu tous (les) deux. You can't have it b. ways, on ne peut pas avoir le drap et l'argent. 2. adv. B. you and I, (et) vous et moi. B. John and I came, John and I b. came, Jean et moi sommes venus tous les deux. She b. attracts and repels me, elle m'attire et me repousse à la fois. I am fond of music b. ancient and modern, j'aime la musique tant ancienne que moderne.
bother¹ ['bɔðər], s. Ennui m, F: embêtement m, tracas m, aria m. B.! zut!
bother². 1. v.tr. Gêner, ennuyer, tracasser, tourmenter (qn); F: embêter (qn). To b. s.o. about sth., importuner qn au sujet de qch. Don't b. me! laissez-moi tranquille! Don't b. (your head) about me! ne vous inquiétez pas de moi! F: I can't be bothered, ça m'embête. B. it! b. the thing! zut! I can't be bothered to do it, j'ai la flemme de le faire. F: Don't b. to bring a mac, ce n'est pas la peine de prendre votre imper. 2. v.i. He doesn't b. about anything, il ne s'inquiète de rien. bothered, a. Inquiet; embarrassé. S.a. HOT¹ 1.
bothersome ['bɔðəsəm], a. Importun, gênant.
bottle¹ ['bɔtl], s. 1. (a) Bouteille f; (small) flacon m; fiole f; (wide-mouthed) bocal m. Wine b., bouteille à vin. B. of wine, bouteille de vin. Half-b. (of wine), demi-bouteille. Cider in a stone b., du cidre dans un cruchon. F: To take to the b., se livrer à la boisson. To hit the b., caresser la bouteille. (b) Flacon m (de parfum etc). 2. Feeding b., baby's b., biberon m. Baby brought up on the b., enfant élevé au biberon. 3. Hot-water b., bouillotte f (de lit). 'bottle-brush, s. Goupillon m; hérisson m. 'bottle-corking machine, s. Bouche-bouteilles m inv. 'bottle-drainer, s. Égouttoir m à bouteilles; hérisson m. 'bottle-fed, a. Nourri au biberon. 'bottle-feeding, s. Allaitement artificiel. 'bottle-glass, s. Verre m à bouteilles; verre vert. 'bottle-'green, a. & s. Vert bouteille (m) inv. 'bottle-holder, s. Box: Soigneur m, second m. 'bottle-neck, s. 1. Goulot m (de bouteille). 2. Embouteillage m (dans une rue); goulet m (d'un port). 'bottle-nosed, a. 1. A gros nez. 2. Z: B.-n. whale, hyperoodon m. 'bottle-opener, s. Ouvre-bouteille(s) m, pl. ouvre-bouteilles; décapsuleur m; débouchoir m. 'bottle-party, s. Réunion intime, à laquelle chacun apporte à boire. 'bottle-rack, s. Porte-bouteilles m inv; casier m, à bouteilles. 'bottle-washer, s. 1. Laveur, -euse de bouteilles; plongeur m. F: Head cook and b.-w., (i) factotum m; (ii) homme qui mène toute l'affaire. 2. (Machine) Rince-bouteilles m inv.
bottle², v.tr. Mettre (du vin) en bouteilles; mettre (des fruits) en bocal. bottled, a. (i) En bouteille. (ii) F: Ivre. bottle up, v.tr. 1. Embouteiller (une flotte, la circulation). 2. F: To b. up one's feelings, one's anger, étouffer ses sentiments; comprimer, ravaler, sa colère. bottling, s. Mise f en bouteille(s), en bocal.
bottle³, s. Botte f (de foin, etc.)
bottler ['bɔtlər], s. Metteur m en bouteilles, embouteilleur m.
bottom¹ ['bɔtəm], s. 1. (a) Bas m (d'une colline, d'un escalier, d'une robe, d'une page). S.a. TOP¹ I. 1. (b) Fond m (d'un puits, d'une boîte, de la mer); ballast m, assiette f (d'une chaussée, etc.). At the b. of the garden,

au fond du jardin. At the b. of the table, of the class, au (bas) bout de la table, à la queue de la classe. To send a ship to the b., envoyer un bâtiment au fond, par le fond. (*Of ship*) To go to the b., couler à fond. Prices have touched b., les prix sont au plus bas. *S.a.* ROCK-BOTTOM. (*Of swimmer*) To find b. again, reprendre fond; reprendre pied. To sift sth. to the b., examiner qch. à fond. At b. he's not a bad fellow, au fond ce n'est pas un mauvais garçon. From the very b. of the heart, du fond du cœur. To be at the b. of sth., (*of pers.*) être l'instigateur de qch. To get to the b. of sth., découvrir la cause de qch. *Nau:* Gravel, rocky, sandy, muddy, b., fond de gravier, de roche, de sable, de vase. (*c*) Résistance *f*, fond. 2. Bas-fond *m* (de terrain); creux *m*; vallée *f*. *U.S:* B. lands, plaine alluviale. 3. (*a*) (i) Fond, (ii) dessous *m* (d'assiette, de verre, etc.); siège *m* (d'une chaise). To set sth. b. up(wards), mettre qch. sens dessus dessous. *F:* Bottoms up! Videz vos verres! *F:* To knock the b. out of an argument, démolir un argument. The b. has fallen out of the market, le marché s'est effondré. (*b*) *Bill:* To put b. on a ball, faire de l'effet rétrograde; faire un rétro. 4. *F:* Derrière *m*, postérieur *m*; fondement *m*; *Fr.C:* califourchon *m*. (d'une personne). To kick s.o.'s b., *F:* botter le derrière à qn. 5. *Nau:* (*a*) Carène *f*, fond (d'un navire). Double b., double fond. (*b*) Navire *m*. In British bottoms, sous pavillon anglais. 6. *attrib.* B. half (*of a box, etc.*), partie inférieure. B. boy of the class, dernier élève de la classe. *U.S:* *F:* My b. dollar, mon dernier sou. *S.a.* GEAR[1] 3.

bottom[2]. 1. *v.tr.* Mettre ou remettre un fond à (une boîte), un siège à (une chaise). 2. *v.i.* (*Of ship*) Toucher le fond. -bottomed, *a.* Leather-b. easy chair, fauteuil à siège de cuir. Flat-b. boat, bateau à fond plat.

bottomless ['bɔtəmlis], *a.* Sans fond. 1. (Chaise) sans siège. 2. Insondable. B: The b. pit, l'abîme *m*.

bottomry ['bɔtəmri], *s. Nau:* Emprunt *m* à la grosse aventure.

boudoir ['bu:dwɑ:r], *s.* Boudoir *m*.

bougainvillea [,bugən'viliə], *s. Bot:* Bougainvillée *f*.

bough [bau], *s.* Branche *f*, rameau *m* (d'arbre).

bought. See BUY.

bouillabaisse ['bu:jəbes], *s. Cu:* Bouillabaisse *f*.

bouillon ['bu:jɔn], *s. Cu:* Bouillon *m*, consommé *m*.

boulder ['bouldər], *s.* (Gros) bloc de pierre roulé; gros galet. 'boulder-clay, *s.* Argile *f* à blocaux.

boulevard ['bu:ləvɑ:r], *s.* 1. Boulevard *m*. 2. *U.S:* Grande voie de communication.

bounce[1] [bauns], *s.* 1. (*Of ball*) Rebond *m*, rebondissement *m*; bond *m*. To take, catch, the ball on the b., prendre la balle au bond. 2. *F:* (*Of pers.*) Jactance *f*, vantardise *f*, épate *f*.

bounce[2]. 1. *v.i.* (*a*) (*Of ball*) Rebondir. (*b*) (*Of pers.*) To b. in, out, entrer, sortir, en coup de vent, à l'improviste. (*c*) *F:* (*Of pers.*) Faire l'important; faire de l'esbrouffe, de l'épate. (*d*) I hope this cheque won't b., j'espère que ce n'est pas un chèque sans provision. 2. *v.tr.* (*a*) Faire rebondir (une balle). (*b*) *F:* Ne pas laisser à (qn) le temps de réfléchir. To b. s.o. into doing sth., arriver à force d'esbrouffe à faire faire qch. à qn. (*c*) *U.S:* *F:* Donner son congé à (qn); flanquer (qn) à la porte (du cabaret, etc.). **bouncing**, *a.* 1. Rebondissant. 2. *F:* B. baby, enfant *mf* plein(e) de vie et de santé.

bouncer ['baunsər], *s.* 1. Épateur *m*, vantard *m*, hâbleur *m*. 2. *U.S:* = CHUCKER-OUT. 3. *F:* Chèque *m* sans provision.

bound[1] [baund], *s.* (*Usu. pl.*) Limite(s) *f*, bornes *fpl*. *Sch:* The village is out of bounds, l'accès du village est défendu aux élèves. *Golf:* *Fb:* *etc:* Out of bounds, hors des limites, hors (du) jeu. To set bounds to one's ambition, mettre des bornes, fixer une limite, à son ambition; borner son ambition. To go beyond all bounds, to pass all bounds, to know no bounds, dépasser toutes les bornes, n'avoir pas de bornes. To keep within bounds, rester dans la juste mesure; user de modération. Within the bounds of probability, dans les limites du probable. *S.a.* BREAK[2] I. 4.

bound[2], *v.tr.* Borner, limiter.

bound[3], *s.* Bond *m*, saut *m*. At a b., d'un (seul) bond, d'un saut.

bound[4], *v.i.* Bondir, sauter; (*of ball, etc.*) rebondir; (*of horse*) soubresauter. To b. away, (*of pers.*) s'en aller en bondissant; (*of ball*) (re)bondir au loin. His heart bounded with joy, son cœur tressaillit, sursauta, de joie.

bound[5], *a. Nau:* Ship b. for a country, navire en partance pour, en route pour, allant à, un pays. The ship was b. for Japan, le navire (i) partait pour, (ii) faisait route vers, le Japon.

bound[6]. See BIND[2].

boundary ['baundri], *s.* Limite *f*, bornes *fpl*, frontière *f*; bornage *m* (d'une concession, etc.). B. (line), ligne frontière, ligne de démarcation; *Sp:* limites du jeu. B. post, stone, poteau *m*, pierre *f*, de bornage; borne. *Av:* B. layer, couche *f* limite.

bounden ['baundən], *a. O:* (Devoir) impérieux, obligatoire.

bounder ['baundər], *s. F:* Épateur *m*, plastronneur *m*; bluffeur *m*; arriviste *m*; homme prétentieux et mal élevé.

boundless ['baundlis], *a.* Sans bornes; illimité, infini. -ly, *adv.* Infiniment.

boundlessness ['baundlisnis], *s.* Infinité *f*, infinitude *f*.

bounteous ['bauntiəs], *a.* 1. *O:* (*Of pers.*) Libéral, -aux; généreux. 2. B. harvest, moisson abondante. -ly, *adv.* Libéralement, généreusement.

bounteousness ['bauntiəsnis], *s.* 1. Libéralité *f*, générosité *f*. 2. (*Of crops, etc.*) Abondance *f*.

bountiful ['bauntiful], *a.* 1. Bienfaisant. B. rains, pluies fécondes. 2. Généreux; libéral, -aux.

bountifulness ['bauntifulnis], *s.* = BOUNTEOUSNESS.

bounty ['baunti], *s.* 1. *Lit:* Générosité *f*, munificence *f*. 2. (*a*) Don *m*, gratification *f* (à un employé, etc.). (*b*) *Adm:* *Ind:* Indemnité *f*; prime *f* (d'exportation, etc.); subvention *f*. (*c*) *Mil:* *Nau:* Prime d'engagement.

bouquet [bu'kei, 'bukei], *s.* 1. Bouquet *m* (de fleurs, de feu d'artifice). 2. ['bukei] Bouquet *m* (du vin).

Bourbon ['buəbən]. 1. *Pr.n. Hist:* Bourbon. 2. *s. Pol:* *U.S:* A b., un réactionnaire. 3. *s. U.S:* Whisky *m* de maïs.

bourdon[1] ['buəd(ə)n], *s. Mus:* 1. (*Organ stop*) Bourdon *m*. 2. (*Of bagpipe*) Bourdon.

bourdon[2], *s.* Bourdon *m*, bâton *m* de pèlerin.

bourgeois ['buəʒwɑ:], *a. & s. Pej:* Bourgeois, -oise.

bourn(e) [buən], *s. Poet:* 1. Borne *f*, terme *m*, but *m*. 2. Frontière *f*. The b. from which no traveller returns, l'au-delà *m*.

bout[1] [baut], *s.* 1. (*At games*) Tour *m*, reprise *f*. Fencing b., passe *f* d'armes. Wrestling b., assaut *m* de lutte. 2. Accès *m* (de fièvre); attaque *f* (de goutte, de grippe); crise *f* (de rhumatisme). *S.a.* DRINKING-BOUT.

'bout[2], *adv.* (= ABOUT) *Nau:* 'B. ship! envoyez!

boutique [bu'ti:k], *s.* (*a*) Petit magasin de modes. (*b*) (*In department store*) Rayon *m* de frivolités, boutique *f*; Teen-age b., le coin des jeunes.

Bovidae ['bɔvidi:], *s.pl. Z:* Bovidés *mpl.*

bovine ['bouvain]. 1. *a.* (*a*) Bovin. (*b*) (Esprit) lourd. 2. *s.pl.* Bovines, bovinés *m*, bovins *m*.

bow[1] [bou], *s.* 1. Arc *m*. To draw a b., bander, tendre un arc. To draw the b., tirer de l'arc. To have two strings to one's b., avoir deux cordes à son arc. I have still one string to my b., il me reste encore une ressource. 2. *Mus:* (*a*) Archet *m* (de violon, etc.). (*b*) Coup *m* d'archet. 3. Nœud *m* (de ruban). Butterfly b., nœud (de) papillon. 4. *Harn:* (Saddle-)b., arçon *m*, pontet *m*. 'bow-compass, *s.* (*Also* pair of bow-compasses) Compas *m* à balustre. 'bow-drill, *s. Tls:* Foret *m* à archet; touret *m*. 'bow-fronted, *a. Furn:* A devant bombé. 'bow-legged, *a.* Bancal, -als. 'bow-legs, *s.pl.* Jambes bancales, arquées. 'bow-saw, *s. Tls:* Scie *f* à chantourner. 'bow-spring, *s. Mec.E:* Ressort *m* à arc. 'bow-tie, *s. Cost:* Nœud papillon. bow-'window, *s.* Fenêtre *f* en saillie (courbe); bow-window *m*.

bow[2] [bou], *v.tr.* 1. Courber (qch.). *Nau:* To b. a mast, arquer un mât. 2. *Mus:* To b. a passage, gouverner l'archet dans un passage. **bowing**, *s.* 1. Courbage *m*. 2. *Mus:* Manière *f* de gouverner l'archet; coup *m* d'archet.

bow³ [bau], s. Salut m; (i) révérence f; (ii) inclination f de tête. O: To make one's b. to the company, se présenter; débuter; O: To make one's b. to the company (and depart), tirer sa révérence à la compagnie. With a b., en saluant, en s'inclinant. To make a deep, low, b. to s.o., saluer qn profondément.

bow⁴ [bau]. 1. v.i. (a) (i) S'incliner; baisser la tête; (ii) faire une génuflexion. To b. to s.o., adresser un salut à qn; saluer qn. To b. low to s.o., faire un grand salut à qn. To b. and scrape to s.o., faire force révérences à qn; faire des courbettes à qn. To b. (down) to, before, s.o., (i) se prosterner devant qn; (ii) faire des courbettes devant qn. (b) With cogn. acc. To b. one's assent, signifier son consentement d'une inclination de tête. (c) To b. to s.o., s'incliner devant qn. To b. to the inevitable, s'incliner devant les faits. 2. v.tr. (a) Incliner, baisser (la tête); fléchir (le genou). (b) Courber, voûter (le dos, les épaules, de qn). To become bowed, se voûter. bow down, v.i. Se baisser. bow in, v.tr. To b. s.o. in, faire entrer qn (avec force saluts). bow out, v.tr. To b. s.o. out, (i) prendre congé de qn (à la porte) avec force saluts; (ii) congédier qn avec un salut.

bow⁵ [bau], s. 1. Nau: (Often in pl.) Avant m, étrave f; A. & Lit: proue f. On the b., par l'avant, par le bossoir. On the port b., par bâbord devant. To cross the bows of a ship, couper la route d'un navire. 2. Av: Proue de la coque; nez m. 3. Row: Nageur m de tête; le brigadier. 'bow-chaser, s. Navy: Canon m de chasse. 'bow-side, s. Row: Tribord m.

bowdlerize ['baudləraiz], v.tr. Expurger (une œuvre littéraire).

bowel ['bauəl], s. Anat: etc: (a) Intestin m. (b) pl. Intestins, entrailles f, F: boyaux m. B. complaint, affection intestinale. To have one's bowels open, free, avoir le ventre libre. The bowels of the earth, les entrailles, le sein, de la terre. (c) A: Bowels of compassion, sentiment m de compassion; F: entrailles.

bower¹ ['bauər], s. 1. Berceau m de verdure; charmille f, tonnelle f. 2. Poet: A: (a) Demeure f. (b) Appartement m (d'une dame); boudoir m.

bower², s. Nau: B.(-anchor), ancre f de bossoir.

bowie(-knife, pl. -ves) ['bəui(naif, -naivz)], s. U.S: Couteau-poignard m; couteau m de chasse.

bowl¹ [boul], s. 1. (a) Bol m, jatte f; (small wooden) sébile f (de mendiant); coupe f (de cristal, etc.). Mil: Gamelle f. (b) (Basin) Cuvette f, bassin m. (c) Contenu m d'un bol, etc. A b. of milk, un bol de lait. 2. Fourneau m (de pipe à tabac); cuilleron m (de cuiller); culot m (de lampe). Nau: Cuvette f (du compas). El: (Electric) b. fire, radiateur m parabolique. 3. U.S: (a) Geog: Cuvette, bassin. (b) Amphithéâtre m.

bowl², s. Boule f. (Game of) bowls, (i) (jeu m de) boules, pétanque f; (ii) U.S: (jeu de) quilles f.

bowl³, v.tr. (a) Rouler, faire courir (un cerceau). (b) Bowls: Lancer, rouler (la boule). (c) Cr: Bôler, servir (la balle). bowl along, v.i. (Of carriage) A: Rouler rapidement; (of ship) voguer rapidement. bowl (out), v.tr. To b. s.o. out, (i) Cr: renverser le guichet de qn; mettre qn hors jeu; F: réduire (qn) à quia. bowl over, v.tr. (a) Renverser (les quilles avec la boule). (b) F: Déconcerter, renverser (qn). You can't b. him over, il ne se laisse pas démonter; rien ne l'épate. bowling, s. 1. (a) Jeu m de boules. B. match, match de boules. (b) U.S: Jeu de quilles. 2. Cr: Lancement m de la balle. 'bowling-alley, s. Boulodrome m, bowling m. 'bowling-green, s. (Terrain m pour) jeu m de boules.

bowler¹ ['boulər], s. 1. Joueur m de boules; boulomane m. 2. Cr: Bôleur m, serveur m, lanceur m.

bowler², s. B. (hat), chapeau rond, (chapeau) melon m. Mil: P: Battle b., casque m. Mil: Av: F: To give s.o. his b. hat, v.tr. to b.-h. s.o., renvoyer qn à la vie civile, limoger qn.

bowlful ['boulful], s. Plein bol, bolée f (de qch.); jattée f (de lait).

bowline ['boulin], s. Nau: Bouline f. B.-knot, -hitch, nœud m de chaise, nœud de bouline. To sail on a b., courir près du vent.

bowman¹, pl. -men ['boumən], s.m. Archer.

bowman², pl. -men ['baumən], s.m. Row: Brigadier (d'un canot).

bowshot ['bouʃɔt], s. Portée f de trait. Within b., à portée d'arc, de trait.

bowsprit ['bousprit], s. Nau: Beaupré m.

bowstring ['boustriŋ], s. 1. Corde f d'arc. 2. (As mode of execution) Lacet m, cordon m.

bow-wow ['bau'wau]. 1. int. Ouâ-ouâ! 2. s. F: (Child's language) Toutou m.

box¹ [bɔks], s. Bot: Buis m.

box², s. 1. (a) Boîte f; (small) coffret m; (large wooden) caisse f, coffre m; (for packing) caisse, layette f; (for shrubs) bac m; (for travelling) malle f; (of cardboard) carton m (à chapeaux, etc.); (for dicing) cornet m. B. of chocolates, boîte de chocolats. Tool-b., coffre à outils. Jewel-b., coffret à bijoux. El: Accumulator b., bac. Posting-b., boîte aux lettres. Post: B. number, boîte, case, postale No. S.a. CHRISTMAS-BOX, LETTER-BOX, SNUFF-BOX, etc. (b) Ecc: (For alms) Tronc m. 2. Veh: A: Siège m (du cocher). 3. (a) Th: Loge f. (b) (In stable) Stalle f, box m, pl. boxes. (c) Jur: Witness-b. = barre f des témoins. To be in the b., paraître à la barre. (d) Mil: Sentry-b., guérite f. Rail: Signal-b., cabine f (de signaleur); poste m d'aiguillage. (e) (Fishing-, shooting-)b., pavillon m (de pêche, de chasse). (f) Rail: (Horse-)b., wagon m à chevaux, wagon-box(e) m. 4. Tchn: Boîte (d'essieu, de frein); moyeu m (de roue); palastre m (d'une serrure). Aut: (Of gear) Carter m. Mec.E: Coupling b., manchon m d'accouplement, d'assemblage. S.a. FIRE-BOX, SOUND-BOX, etc. 'box-attendant, s. Th: Ouvreuse f. 'box-bed, s. Lit clos; lit en armoire. 'box-camera, s. Phot: Appareil m rigide. 'box-car, s. Rail: U.S: Fourgon m. 'box-kite, s. Cerf-volant m cellulaire. 'box-office, s. Th: Bureau m de location; caisse f, guichet m. 'box-pleat, s. Dressm: Pli creux. 'box-room, s. Chambre f de débarras. 'box-spanner, s. Tls: Clef f à douille. 'box-tricycle, s. Triporteur m. 'box-wrench, s. Tls: = BOX-SPANNER.

box³, v.tr. (a) Emboîter, encaisser, encartonner (qch.); mettre (qch.) en boîte. To b. a horse, mettre un cheval dans une stalle à part, dans un box. (b) To b. the compass, (i) Nau: réciter, dire, la rose des vents; répéter le compas; (ii) F: revenir à son point de départ (dans ses opinions). To b. off a room, cloisonner, compartimenter, une pièce. boxed, a. Com: Ind: En boîte ou en étui. B. in, encaissé; sans issue. To feel b. up, se sentir à l'étroit. boxing¹, s. Emboîtage m; encaissement m (d'un oranger).

box⁴, s. B. on the ear, gifle f, claque f.

box⁵. 1. v.tr. To b. s.o.'s ears, gifler qn; flanquer une claque à qn. 2. v.i. Sp: Boxer; faire de la boxe. boxing², s. La boxe, le pugilat. 'boxing-gloves, s.pl. Gants bourrés; gants de boxe m. 'boxing-match, s. Match m de boxe.

box-calf ['bɔks'kɑːf], s. Leath: Veau chromé; box-calf m, pl. box-calfs.

boxer¹ ['bɔksər], s. Boxeur m, pugiliste m.

boxer², s. Boxer m (chien).

boxful ['bɔksful], s. Pleine boîte, pleine caisse.

Boxing-day ['bɔksiŋdei], s. Le lendemain de Noël.

boxwood ['bɔkswud], s. Buis m.

boy [bɔi], s.m. (a) Garçon; (on the street) gamin m. Little b., garçonnet m. An English b., un jeune Anglais. Blind b., jeune aveugle. S.a. SCOUT¹ 1. When I was a b., quand j'étais petit; quand j'étais enfant. I have known him from a b., je le connais (i) depuis ma jeunesse, (ii) depuis sa jeunesse. Boys will be boys, il faut que jeunesse se passe. She ought to have been a b., c'est un garçon manqué. F: O: My dear b.! mon cher (ami)! mon bon! Old b.! mon vieux! The old b., (i) le paternel; (ii) le patron. (b) Sch: Élève m. An old b., un ancien élève. (c) F: One of the boys, un joyeux vivant, un gai luron. (d) P: Her b. (friend), son flirt, son amoureux. (e) F: This is my b., voici mon fils, mon garçon. (f) F: Barrow boy = marchand m des quatre saisons. 2. (a) (In Africa, etc.) Domestique m ou ouvrier m indigène; boy. (b) The grocer's boy, le garçon épicier. S.a. STABLE-BOY, TELEGRAPH BOY.

boycott¹ ['bɔikət], *s.* Mise *f* en interdit; boycottage *m.*
boycott², *v.tr.* Boycotter (qn). **boycotting,** *s.* Boycottage *m.*
boycotter ['bɔikətər], *s.* Boycotteur *m.*
boyhood ['bɔihud], *s.* Enfance *f,* première jeunesse, ou adolescence *f* (d'un garçon).
boyish ['bɔiiʃ], *a.* **1.** Puéril, enfantin, d'enfant. **2.** (Nature) jeune. **3.** (Manières) de garçon. **-ly,** *adv.* (*a*) En petit garçon. (*b*) Comme un petit garçon.
boyishness ['bɔiiʃnis], *s.* Manières, air, de petit garçon.
Boyle [bɔil]. *Pr.n.* *Ph:* Boyle's law, la loi de Mariotte.
boylike ['bɔilaik]. **1.** *a.* De gamin. **2.** *adv.* En vrai enfant; en vrai(s) garçon(s).
bra [brɑː], *s.* *F:* = BRASSIÈRE.
Brabant [brə'bænt, 'brɑːbænt], *Pr.n.* *Geog:* Brabant *m.*
brace¹ [breis], *s.* **1.** *Const: etc:* (*In tension*) Attache *f,* lien *m,* entretoise *f,* étrésillon *f;* croisillon *m;* (*in compression*) contrefiche *f,* moise *f;* jambe *f* de force. (Anchor-)b., ancre *f,* ancrure *f.* Cross-b., diagonal b., écharpe *f;* moise en écharpe. *Surg:* Surgical b., armature *f* orthopédique. *Dent:* Dental b., rectificateur *m* dentaire. **2.** (*a*) *pl.* *Cost:* Bretelles *f.* (*b*) Tirant *m,* corde *f* (de tambour). **3.** *inv.* Couple *f* (de perdrix); paire *f* (de pistolets, etc.). *S.a.* SHAKE¹ 1. **4.** *Tls:* B. (and bit), vilebrequin *m* (à main). B.-chuck, porte-outil(s) *m inv.* **5.** *Nau:* Bras *m* (de vergue). **6.** *Mus: Typ:* Accolade *f.*
brace², *v.tr.* **1.** *Const: etc:* Ancrer, amarrer (une construction); armer (une poutre); entretoiser, étrésillonner (une charpente); moiser (des étais); hauban(n)er (un mât). **2.** Fortifier (le corps); tonifier (les nerfs). To b. s.o. up, retremper qn; (re)donner de la vigueur à qn; *F:* remonter, ravigoter, qn. To b. oneself (up) to do sth., raidir ses forces, se raidir, pour faire qch. **3.** Bander (un tambour). To b. the knees, tendre les jarrets. **4.** *Typ:* Accolader, accoler (des mots). *Mus:* Accolader (les portées). **5.** *Nau:* Brasser (les vergues). **bracing¹,** *a.* (Air, etc.) fortifiant, tonifiant. **bracing²,** *s.* **1.** Ancrage *m,* entretoisement *m;* armement *m* (d'une poutre); consolidation *f,* renforcement *m* (d'un mur). **2.** Retrempe *f* (du corps); tonification *f* (des nerfs). **3.** *Nau:* Brassage *m* (des vergues).
bracelet ['breislit], *s.* **1.** Bracelet *m.* **2.** *pl.* *P:* = HANDCUFFS.
bracer ['breisər], *s.* *F:* Petit verre (de spiritueux); cordial *m.*
brachial [bræ'kiəl], *a.* *Anat:* Brachial (artère, etc.).
brachiopod ['bræikiəpɔd], *s.* *Moll:* Brachiopode *m.*
brachycephalic [,brækise'fælik], *a.* Brachycéphale.
bracken ['bræk(ə)n], *s.* Fougère *f* (arborescente).
bracket¹ ['brækit], *s.* **1.** Support *m.* (*a*) Console *f;* potence *f.* *Arch:* Corbeau *m.* (*b*) Tasseau *m;* taquet *m* de soutien. (*c*) **(Gas-)b., (electric-)b.,** applique *f* (à gaz, électrique). *Cy:* Lamp-b., support *m* de phare. **2.** (*a*) *Typ: etc:* Square b., crochet *m.* Round b., parenthèse *f.* (*b*) (*Brace*) Accolade *f.* (*c*) *Artil:* (*In ranging*) Fourchette *f.* **3.** *Adm:* The middle-income b., la tranche des salariés moyens.
bracket², *v.tr.* (**bracketed**) **1.** Mettre (des mots) entre crochets, entre parenthèses. **2.** Réunir (des mots) par une accolade; accoupler (les noms de deux personnes); associer (deux idées). **3.** *Artil:* Encadrer (le but); prendre (le but) en fourchette.
brackish ['brækiʃ], *a.* Saumâtre.
brackishness ['brækiʃnis], *s.* Nature saumâtre (d'une eau stagnante).
bract [brækt], *s.* *Bot:* Bractée *f.*
brad [bræd], *s.* Pointe *f;* clou *m* à tête perdue.
bradawl ['brædɔːl], *s.* *Tls:* Alêne plate; poinçon *m.*
brae [brei], *s.* *Scot:* Pente *f,* côte *f,* colline *f.*
brag¹ [bræg], *s.* **1.** (*Piece of*) b., vanterie *f,* vantardise *f,* hâblerie *f,* fanfaronnade *f.* **2.** (*Pers.*) Fanfaron *m;* vantard *m.*
brag², *v.i.* (**bragged** [brægd]) Hâbler, se vanter; fanfaronner. To b. of, about, sth., se vanter de qch. **bragging¹,** *a.* Vantard. **bragging²,** *s.* Vantardise *f.*
Braganza [brə'gænzə]. *Pr.n.* *Geog:* Bragance *f.*
braggadocio ['brægə'doutʃiou], *s.* **1.** (*Pers.*) Bravache *m,* fanfaron *m.* **2.** Fanfaronnade *f.*

braggart ['brægət], *a. & s.* Fanfaron (*m*), vantard (*m*).
brahman, brahmin ['brɑːmən, -min], *s.m.* **1.** Brahmane, brame. **2.** *U.S:* *F:* Brahmin, intellectuel *m.*
Brahmanic(al) [brɑː'mænik(əl)], **Brahminic(al)** [brɑː'minik(əl)], *a.* Brahmanique.
Brahmanism ['brɑːmənizm], **Brahminism** ['brɑːminizm], *s.* Brahmanisme *m.*
braid¹ [breid], *s.* **1.** (*a*) Tresse *f* (de cheveux). (*b*) *Poet:* Bandeau *m* (pour les cheveux). **2.** (*a*) Galon *m,* ganse *f,* tresse. Gold b. (*of officers*), galon. (*b*) *El.E:* Guipage *m* (de fils conducteurs).
braid², *v.tr.* **1.** (*a*) Tresser, natter (ses cheveux, de la paille). (*b*) *Poet:* Mettre un bandeau sur (ses cheveux). **2.** Galonner, soutacher; passementer. **3.** *El.E:* Tresser, guiper (un câble). **braided,** *a.* Tressé; (*d'un cours d'eau*) anastomosé. **braiding,** *s.* **1.** Tressage *m.* **2.** (Garniture *f* de) galon *m;* soutache *f.*
brail¹ [breil], *s.* *Nau:* Cargue *f.*
brail², *v.tr.* *Nau:* To b. (up), carguer (une voile).
braille [breil], *s.* Braille *m.* B. type, caractères *mpl* Braille.
brain¹ [brein], *s.* **1.** Cerveau *m.* Electronic b., cerveau électronique. B. diseases, maladies cérébrales. *F:* To turn s.o.'s b., tourner la tête à qn. To have an idea on the b., être monomane; avoir l'obsession d'une idée. To get sth. on the b., être hanté par l'image, par la pensée, de qch, *F:* avoir qch. dans le ciboulot. **2.** *pl.* **Brains,** cervelle *f.* (*a*) Matière cérébrale. *Cu:* Calves' brains, cervelle de veau. To blow s.o.'s brains out, brûler, faire sauter, la cervelle à qn. (*b*) *F:* The brains, personnes qui font partie d'un brain-trust. (*c*) To rack, cudgel, one's brains, se creuser la cervelle, *F:* les méninges *fpl.* Man of brains, homme de tête. He has brains, il est intelligent. **'brain-child,** *s.* *F:* Idée, conception originale. *F:* That's my b.-c., ça c'est mon idée à moi. **'brain-drain,** *s.* Fuite *f* des cerveaux. **'brain-pan,** *s.* Crâne *m;* boîte crânienne; calotte *f* du crâne. **'brain-storm,** *s.* Transport *m* au cerveau. **'brains trust,** *s.* Brain-trust *m,* *pl.* brain-trusts. **'brain-wave,** *s.* **1.** *Psychics:* Onde *f* télépathique. **2.** *F:* Inspiration *f,* trouvaille *f,* idée lumineuse. **'brain-work,** *s.* Travail cérébral; travail de tête.
brain², *v.tr.* Défoncer le crâne à (qn); casser la tête à (qn); assommer (qn).
braininess ['breininis], *s.* *F:* Intelligence *f.*
brainless ['breinlis], *a.* *F:* Sans cervelle; stupide.
brainwash ['breinwɔʃ], *v.tr.* *F:* Désintoxiquer et endoctriner (qn), faire un lavage de crâne, de cerveau (à qn).
brainwashing ['breinwɔʃiŋ], *s.* *F:* Lavage *m* de crâne, de cerveau.
brainy ['breini], *a.* *F:* Intelligent, débrouillard.
braise [breiz], *v.tr.* *Cu:* Braiser; cuire (qch.) à l'étouffée. Braised beef, bœuf en daube.
brake¹ [breik], *s.* Fourré *m,* hallier *m;* *Ven:* breuil *m.*
brake², *s.* *Veh: etc:* Frein *m.* To put a b. on s.o.'s activities, freiner qn. *Aut:* Four-wheel brakes, freins sur quatre roues; freinage intégral. Band-b., frein à ruban, à bande. Hand-b., frein à main; frein de stationnement. Air b., frein à air (comprimé). Disk b., frein à disque. Drum b., frein à tambour. B. gear, timonerie *f.* *Cy:* Rim b., frein sur jante. To put on, apply, the b., serrer le frein. To release the b., lâcher le frein. B. pedal, pédale *f* de frein. **brake-band,** *s.* *Aut: etc:* Bandage *m,* collier *m,* ruban *m,* de frein. **'brake-block,** *s.* Sabot *m* de frein; patin *m.* **'brake-drum,** *s.* *Aut:* Tambour *m* de frein. **'brake fluid,** *s.* *Aut:* Liquide *m* pour freins (hydrauliques). **'brake-lining,** *s.* *Tchn:* Fourrure *f,* garniture *f,* de frein. **'brake-shoes,** *s.* *Aut:* Mâchoires *f,* sabots *m,* segments *m,* de frein. **'brake-van,** *s.* *Rail:* Wagon-frein; fourgon *m.*
brake³, *v.tr.* Appliquer le frein sur (les roues). *Abs.* Serrer le frein; freiner; enrayer. **braking,** *s.* Freinage *m;* serrage *m* des freins. B. distance, distance *f* d'arrêt, de freinage.
brake⁴. 1. = BREAK³. **2.** *Aut:* Shooting b., break *m* de chasse, canadienne *f.*
brakesman, *pl.* -men, *U.S:* **brakeman,** *pl.* -men ['breik(s)mən], *s.m.* *Rail:* Serre-frein(s).

bramble ['bræmbl], s. **1.** Ronce sauvage, commune; mûrier m des haies. **2.** Brambles, ronces. 'bramble-berry, s. Mûre f sauvage. 'bramble-bush, s. Roncier m, roncière f. 'bramble-rose, s. **1.** (*Flower*) Églantine f. **2.** (*Bush*) Églantier m.

bran [bræn], s. *Mill:* Son m; remoulage m; bran m. 'bran-mash, s. *Husb:* Son mouillé; eau blanche; mash m. bran-'pie, 'bran-tub, s. Baquet rempli de son où l'on plonge la main pour en retirer une surprise (à une vente de charité, à une soirée enfantine).

branch[1] [brɑːn(t)ʃ], s. **1.** Branche f, rameau m (d'un arbre). **2.** (*a*) Ramification f; rameau (d'une chaîne de montagnes); branche, bras m (d'un fleuve); embranchement m (d'une route, d'un chemin de fer). *U.S:* affluent m (d'un fleuve). (*b*) Branche (d'une famille, etc.). (*c*) Succursale f, filiale f (d'une société, d'une maison de commerce). Main b. (*of a business*), établissement principal. *attrib.* B. office, (i) agence f; (ii) bureau m de quartier. B. depot, dépôt m auxiliaire. (*d*) *Mil:* Arme f; service m. 'branch-line, s. *Rail:* Embranchement m; ligne f d'intérêt local.

branch[2]. **1.** *v.i.* (*Of plants*) To b. (forth), pousser des branches. To b. (out), se ramifier; (*of an organization, etc.*) étendre au loin ses ramifications. **2.** *v.i.* (*Of road(s), etc.*) To b. (off, away), (se) bifurquer, s'embrancher (from, sur). **3.** *v.tr. El:* Brancher (un circuit); dériver (le courant). branching[1], a. **1.** (*Of tree*) Branchu, rameux. **2.** (*Of road, etc.*) D'embranchement. branching[2] (off), s. Bifurcation f. branchement m, dérivation f.

branchia ['bræŋkiə], s.pl. branchiae ['bræŋkiiː], s.pl. Branchies f; ouïes f.

Branchiopoda [ˌbræŋki'ɔpədə], s.pl. *Crust:* Branchiopodes m.

branchless ['brɑːn(t)ʃlis], a. Sans branches; dépourvu de branches.

brand[1] [brænd], s. **1.** Brandon m, tison m. F: A b. from the burning, un tison arraché au feu; un nouveau converti. *Poet:* Flambeau m. **3.** (*a*) Fer chaud. (*b*) Marque (faite avec un fer chaud); flétrissure f. **4.** *Com:* (*a*) Marque (de fabrique). (*b*) F: Sorte f, qualité f (d'une marchandise). **5.** *Poet:* Glaive m, épée f. **6.** *Agr:* Brûlure f; rouille f (des plantes). 'brand-'new, a. Tout (battant) neuf, tout flambant neuf.

brand[2], *v.tr.* **1.** To b. with a hot iron, marquer au fer chaud; flétrir (qn). **2.** To b. sth. on s.o.'s memory, graver qch. dans la mémoire de qn. **3.** To b. s.o. with infamy, flétrir, stigmatiser, qn; noter qn d'infamie. branded, a. (*a*) Marqué à chaud. (*b*) B. goods, des produits de marque. B. petrol, supercarburant m. branding, s. Impression f au fer chaud. 'branding-iron, s. Fer m à marquer.

brandish ['brændiʃ], *v.tr.* Brandir (une arme, etc.). brandishing, s. Brandissement m.

brandling ['brændliŋ], s. *Fish:* Ver m rouge.

brandy ['brændi], s. Eau-de-vie f, cognac m. **Liqueur b.,** fine champagne. B. and soda, fine f à l'eau.

bran-new ['bræn'njuː], a. = BRAND-NEW.

brash [bræʃ], a. Fougueux, impétueux; effronté, présomptueux, indiscret.

brass [brɑːs], s. **1.** Cuivre m jaune; laiton m; *Lit:* airain m. *Bookb:* Fer m. B. foundry, fonderie f de cuivre; robinetterie f. B. plate, plaque f de cuivre. F: B.-hat, officier d'état-major. P: Top b., les grosses légumes, les gros bonnets. **2.** (*a*) Les cuivres, robinets, etc. (du ménage, à bord). To do the brass(es), faire les cuivres. (*b*) *Usu. pl. Mec.E:* Coussinet m de bielle, de palier; coquille f (de coussinets). (*c*) *Mus:* The b. (*in band, orchestra*), les cuivres. (*d*) (*In church*) Brasses, plaques f mortuaires en cuivre. **3.** P: Argent m, pépettes fpl, galette f. **4.** P: (*Cheek*) Toupet m, culot m. 'brass 'rags, s.pl. **1.** Chiffons m à astiquer les cuivres. **2.** P: To part b. r., se brouiller, rompre. 'brass 'tacks, s.pl. Let's get down to b. t., venons-en aux faits, aux réalités essentielles. 'brass-ware, s. Dinanderie f. 'brass-work, s. **1.** Les cuivres m. **2.** *Ind:* Cuivrerie f.

brassie ['brɑːsi], s. *Golf:* Brassie f.

brassière [bræˈsiɛər], s. Soutien-gorge m inv. **Strapless b.,** bustier m. **Half-cup b.,** balconet m. **Uplift b.,** soutien-gorge pigeonnant.

brassiness ['brɑːsinis], s. **1.** Apparence cuivreuse d'un bijou, etc. en toc. **2.** Sons cuivrés (d'une musique).

brass off ['brɑːs'ɔːf], *v.tr.* P: I'm brassed off, j'ai le cafard.

brassy[1] ['brɑːsi], s. *Golf:* = BRASSIE.

brassy[2], a. **1.** (*a*) (*Of colour, etc.*) Qui ressemble au cuivre; tapageur. (*b*) (Son) cuivré, claironnant. **2.** P: (*Of pers.*) Effronté.

brat [bræt], s. *Usu. Pej:* Marmot m, mioche mf, moutard m.

bravado [brəˈvɑːdou], s. Bravade f. Out of b., par bravade.

brave[1] [breiv]. **1.** a. (*a*) Courageux, brave. (*b*) A. & F: (i) Beau, élégant; (ii) excellent, fameux. **2.** s. Brave m (guerrier Peau-rouge). -ly, adv. Courageusement.

brave[2], *v.tr.* Braver, défier (qn); affronter (un danger, etc.). To b. it out, ne pas se laisser démonter.

bravery ['breivəri], s. **1.** Bravoure f, vaillance f. **2.** A. & F: Beaux habits.

bravo[1], pl. -os, -oes ['brɑːvou, -ouz], s. Bravo m, pl. bravi; spadassin m.

bravo[2], int. Bravo!

brawl[1] [brɔːl], s. **1.** Rixe f, bagarre f. Drunken b., querelle f d'ivrognes. **2.** = BRAWLING[2] **2.**

brawl[2], *v.i.* **1.** (*Of pers.*) Brailler; se chamailler. **2.** (*Of streams*) Murmurer, bruire. brawling[1], a. **1.** (*Of pers.*) Braillard, tapageur. **2.** (*Of stream*) Murmurant, bruissant. brawling[2], s. **1.** Braillement m, clabauderie f. **2.** Murmure m, bruissement m (d'un ruisseau, etc.).

brawler ['brɔːlər], s. Braillard, -arde; tapageur, -euse; querelleur, -euse.

brawn [brɔːn], s. **1.** Muscles mpl; partie charnue (des membres). **2.** *Cu:* Fromage m de tête.

brawniness ['brɔːninis], s. Carrure musclée, forte carrure; force f (de corps); musculature f.

brawny ['brɔːni], a. (*Of pers.*) Musclé; bien bâti.

bray[1] [brei], s. **1.** Braiment m (d'un âne). **2.** Son éclatant (d'une trompette).

bray[2], *v.i.* **1.** (*Of ass*) Braire. **2.** (*Of trumpet, etc.*) Émettre un son strident, éclatant. braying, s. Braicment m.

bray[3], *v.tr.* Broyer, piler, concasser.

braze [breiz], *v.tr.* Braser; souder (qch.) au laiton. brazing, s. Brasage m; brasement m; soudure f (au laiton); soudure forte.

brazen[1] ['breizn], a. **1.** D'airain. **2.** F: B.(-faced), au front d'airain; effronté, impudent, cynique. To tell a b. lie, mentir impudemment, cyniquement. -ly, adv. Effrontément, cyniquement.

brazen[2], *v.tr.* To b. it out, payer d'effronterie, de toupet; crâner.

brazenness ['breiznnis], s. Cynisme m.

brazier ['breizjər], s. Brasero m.

Brazil [brəˈzil]. *Pr.n. Geog:* Le Brésil. Bra'zil-'nut, s. Noix f du Brésil.

Brazilian [brəˈziljən], a. & s. Brésilien, -ienne.

breach[1] [briːtʃ], s. **1.** Infraction f. B. of rules, infraction aux règles. B. of the law, violation f de la loi. B. of duty, manquement m au devoir. B. of faith, violation de foi; manque m de parole. B. of trust, abus m de confiance. B. of privilege, atteinte portée aux privilèges. B. of police regulations, contravention f. B. of the peace, attentat m, délit m, contre l'ordre public. B. of promise, (i) manque m de parole; (ii) violation de promesse de mariage. *S.a.* CONTRACT[1] **2.** **2.** Brouille f, rupture f (entre deux amis, etc.). **3.** Brèche f (dans un mur, etc.). *Mil:* To make a b. in the enemy's lines, trouer, percer, les lignes de l'ennemi.

breach[2]. **1.** *v.tr.* Ouvrir une brèche dans (une digue, un mur). **2.** *v.i.* (*a*) (*Of embankment, etc.*) Se rompre. (*b*) (*Of whale*) Sauter, émerger.

bread[1] [bred], s. Pain m. Brown b., pain bis, pain de son. New, fresh, b., pain frais. Wholemeal b., pain complet. French b., flûte f; baguette f. *S.a.* RYE. Ship's b., biscuit m (de mer). A loaf of b., un pain, une miche. B. and butter, (i) pain beurré; (ii) F: moyens de subsistance. Slice of b. and butter, tartine de beurre, tartine beurrée. Poetry doesn't earn one's

b. and butter, la poésie ne nourrit pas son homme. *F:* **B.-and-butter letter,** lettre de remerciements *m* (après avoir séjourné chez qn), lettre de digestion, de château. *F:* **To earn one's b. and butter, one's daily b.,** gagner sa croûte. *F:* **To quarrel with one's b. and butter,** casser la marmite. **He knows on which side his b. is buttered,** il sait où est son avantage, son intérêt. **To live on b. and cheese,** vivre chichement, frugalement. **B. and milk,** panade *f* au lait; soupe *f* au lait. **To be on b. and water,** être au pain (sec) et à l'eau. *Ecc:* **The b. and wine,** les espèces *f*. **To take the b. out of s.o.'s mouth,** ôter le pain à qn. 'bread-basket, *s.* 1. Corbeille *f* à pain. 2. *P:* Estomac *m*, bedaine *f*. 'bread-bin, *s.* Boîte *f* à pain; maie *f*. 'bread(-)crumb¹, *s.* (*a*) Mie *f* (du pain); mie de pain. (*b*) Miette *f* (de pain). *Cu:* **B.(-)crumbs,** chapelure *f*; (*when cooked*) gratin *m*. 'bread(-)crumb², *v.tr. Cu:* Paner (des côtelettes); gratiner (une sole). 'bread-cutter, *s.* Tranche-pain *m inv*. 'bread-fruit, *s. Bot:* Fruit *m* à pain. **B.-fruit tree,** arbre *m* à pain; jaquier *m*. 'bread-making, *s.* Boulange *f*. 'bread-'poul-tice, *s.* Cataplasme *m* à la mie de pain. 'bread-'sauce, *s.* Sauce *f* à la mie de pain. 'bread-stuffs, *s.pl.* 1. Farines *f*. 2. Céréales *f* panifiables. 'bread-winner, *s.* Gagne-pain *m inv*; (i) soutien *m* de famille, chef *m* de famille; (ii) instrument *m* de travail.

bread², *v.tr. U.S: Cu:* Paner.

breadth [bredθ], *s.* 1. Largeur *f*. **Finger's b.,** travers *m* de doigt. **B. of wings** (*of bird, aircraft*), envergure *f*. **The table is three feet in b.,** la table a trois pieds de large. 2. Largeur (de pensée, de vues); facture *f* large (d'un tableau); ampleur *f* (de style). *S.a.* LENGTH 1.

break¹ [breik], *s.* 1. Rupture *f*. (*a*) Brisure *f*, cassure *f*, fracture *f*; trouée *f*, percée *f*, brèche *f*, ouverture *f* (dans une haie); éclaircie *f* (à travers les nuages); lacune *f* (dans une succession). **B. in the voice,** (i) altération *f* de la voix (par l'émotion); (ii) mue *f* (à la puberté). **B. of continuity,** solution *f* de continuité. **B. in a journey,** arrêt *m*. **To work without a b.,** travailler sans interruption, sans désemparer. *El.E:* **B. in the circuit,** rupture *f* du circuit. *W.Tel: T.V:* **B. in transmission,** incident *m* technique. (*b*) **B. in the weather,** changement *m* de temps. (*c*) **B. between two friends,** rupture, brouille *f*, entre deux amis. (*d*) Brisure (d'une ligne). (*e*) Déviation *f. Games:* Effet *m* (de la balle). (*f*) *F:* **To make a bad b.,** faire une bourde, une gaffe. 2. (*a*) (Moment *m* de) repos *m*, répit *m*. **With an hour's b. for lunch,** avec une heure de battement pour déjeuner. **The coffee b.,** la pause du café, la pause-café. (*b*) *Sch:* Intervalle *m* entre les classes; récréation *f*. 3. **B. of day,** point *m* du jour; aube *f*, aurore *f*. 4. *Bill:* Série *f*, suite *f*, (de carambolages, etc.).

break², *v.* (broke [brouk], *A:* brake [breik]; *p.p.* broken]broukn], *F:* broke) I. *v.tr.* 1. (*a*) Casser, briser (un verre); casser, rompre (un bâton); briser, rompre (ses chaînes); rompre (les rangs). **To b. one's arm, one's neck,** se casser le bras, se rompre le cou. **To b. sth. in(to) pieces,** mettre, briser, qch. en morceaux. **To b. the sound barrier,** franchir le mur du son. **To b. bread with s.o.,** rompre le pain avec qn. **To b. the enemy's lines,** enfoncer, rompre, les lignes ennemies, **To b. the skin,** entamer la peau. **To b. (new) ground,** (i) défricher une terre; donner les premiers coups de pioche; (ii) faire œuvre de pionnier. (*b*) *Com:* Décompléter, dépareiller (un service d'argen-terie). (*c*) *El:* Interrompre (le courant); rompre, couper, ouvrir (le circuit). (*d*) **To b. step,** rompre le pas. **To b. a charm, (the) silence, one's fast,** rompre un charme, le silence, le jeûne. **To b. one's journey at . . . ,** interrompre son voyage à . . . ; faire étape à . . . ; *Nau:* faire escale à . . . . *Abs:* **To b. even,** joindre les deux bouts. 2. **To b. a branch from a tree,** détacher une branche d'un arbre. 3. **To b. s.o. of a bad habit,** faire perdre à qn une mauvaise habitude. 4. (*a*) **To b. a way,** se frayer, s'ouvrir, un chemin. (*b*) **To b. gaol,** forcer sa prison; s'évader de prison. *Mil: etc:* **To b. bounds,** violer la consigne. 5. **To b. s.o.'s heart,** briser, crever, le cœur à qn. *S.a.* HEART¹ 1. **To b. s.o.'s spirit,** briser le courage de qn. **To b. (down) s.o.'s resistance,** briser la résistance de qn. **To b. s.o.**

into a type of work, rompre qn à un travail. *Equit:* **To b. a horse,** rompre, dresser, un cheval. *S.a.* BREAK IN 1. 6. (*a*) **To b. a fall, a blow,** amortir une chute, un coup. (*b*) **To b. the news gently to s.o.,** apprendre une (mauvaise) nouvelle doucement à qn. 7. (*a*) **To b. s.o.,** (i) (*of losses, etc.*) ruiner qn; (ii) (*of grief*) briser qn; (iii) (*of age, illness*) casser qn. **To b. the bank,** faire sauter la banque. (*b*) *Mil:* Casser (un officier). 8. (*a*) Violer, enfreindre, ne pas observer (la loi); rompre, enfreindre, violer (une trêve). **To b. the peace,** troubler, violer, l'ordre public. **To b. one's word, one's promise,** manquer de parole (à qn); fausser parole (à qn); violer sa promesse. **To b. an appointment,** manquer à un rendez-vous. (*b*) Résilier (un contrat). 9. *Nau:* **To b. a flag,** déferler un signal. II. **break,** *v.i.* 1. (*a*) Se casser, se rompre, se briser; (*of limb, etc.*) se fracturer; (*of wave*) déferler; (*of bubble, abscess*) crever. **The clouds are breaking,** les nuages se dissipent, se dispersent. (*b*) (*Of troops*) Se débander. 2. (*a*) (*Of heart*) Se briser; se fendre, crever; (*of health*) s'altérer, se détraquer; (*of weather*) changer, (i) s'améliorer, (ii) se gâter; (*of heat-wave*) passer. **The frost has broken,** le temps est, se met, au dégel. (*b*) **Their spirit did not b.,** ils ne se laissèrent pas abattre. **His voice is beginning to b.,** sa voix commence à muer. **His voice broke (with emotion),** sa voix s'altéra, se troubla. 3. (*Of business*) Faire faillite; (*of bank*) sauter. 4. **To b. with s.o.,** rompre, briser, avec qn, avec la vie traditionnelle. 5. (*a*) **To b. into a house,** entrer de force, pénétrer, dans une maison; (*of burglar*) cambrioler une maison. (*b*) **To b. (out), into a laugh, into sobs,** éclater de rire, en sanglots. **Her face broke into a smile,** son visage s'épanouit en un sourire. **To b. into a trot,** prendre le trot. 6. (*a*) **To b. out of prison,** s'échapper, s'évader, de prison. (*b*) **A cry broke from his lips,** un cri s'échappa de ses lèvres. (*c*) (*Of ideas, etc.*) **To b. in upon s.o.,** se présenter, s'offrir, à (l'esprit de) qn. (*d*) **Day was beginning to b.,** le jour commençait à poindre, à se lever. (*e*) **The storm broke,** la tempête éclata. 7. *Sp:* **The ball breaks,** la balle fait faux bond. **break away.** 1. *v.tr.* Détacher (qch.) (from, de). 2. *v.i.* (*a*) (*Of thg*) Se détacher (from, de); (*of pers.*) se dégager, se détacher (from, de); (*of prisoner*) s'échapper, s'évader. *Box:* **To make fighters b. away,** briser un corps-à-corps. **B. (away)!** séparez! (*b*) *Mil:* (*Of troops*) Rompre les rangs. 'break-away, *s.* 1. Sécession *f*, désertion *f* (from, de). 2. *Box:* Séparation *f*. 3. *Rail:* Dérive *f* (de wagons). **break down.** 1. *v.tr.* (*a*) Abattre, (un mur, etc.); rompre (un pont); analyser (des statistiques). **To b. down all opposition,** vaincre, avoir raison de, toute opposition. (*b*) **To b. down a sub-stance,** (i) concasser, broyer, (ii) *Ch:* décomposer, une substance. 2. *v.i.* (*a*) (*Of health*) S'altérer, se détra-quer; (*of the mind*) s'ébranler, sombrer; (*of plan*) échouer, s'effondrer; (*of bridge*) s'effondrer. (*b*) (*Of pers.*) (i) S'arrêter tout court, demeurer court (dans un discours); (ii) éclater en sanglots, fondre en larmes; (iii) tomber malade (de fatigue). (*c*) (*Of motor car, train*) Rester, être, en panne, avoir une panne. 'breakdown, *s.* 1. (*a*) Insuccès *m* (d'une tentative); rupture *f* (de négociations); écroulement *m* (d'un système); arrêt complet (dans un service). (*b*) Ré-partition *f* (de la population par classes, âge, *etc.*). 2. **B. in health,** débâcle *f*, écroulement, de la santé. **Ner-vous B.,** dépression nerveuse. 3. (*a*) *Aut: Nau: etc:* Avarie *f* de route; panne *f*; *Mch:* arrêt inopiné. **B. gang,** (i) *Aut:* équipe de dépannage; (ii) *Rail:* corvée de secours. **B. lorry,** dépanneuse *f*. **B.-van,** *s.* Camion-grue *m*, *pl.* camions-grues. (*b*) *Ind: Rail: etc:* Perturbation *f* dans le service. **broken down,** *a.* (*Of pers.*) Cassé; brisé (par la douleur); (*of horse*) usé, fourbu; (*of health, furniture*) délabré; (*of motor car, etc.*) (i) en panne; (ii) en mauvais état; (*of any mechanism*) détraqué. **break in.** 1. *v.tr.* (*a*) Enfoncer (une porte); défoncer (un tonneau). (*b*) Rompre, mater, dresser (un cheval); culotter (une pipe); briser des souliers neufs; *U.S:* roder (une voiture). **To b. oneself in to sth.,** se rompre à qch. 2. *v.i.* (*Of roof, etc.*) Se défoncer, s'effondrer. 3. *v.i.* (*a*) **To b. in on s.o.,** a conversation, interrompre qn, conversation. To b. in on a gathering, faire irruption dans une réunion. *Abs.* To b. in, intervenir, s'interposer. (b) (*Of burglars, etc.*) S'introduire par effraction. breaking in, *s.* 1. (a) Enfoncement *m* (d'une porte); défonçage *m*, défoncement *m* (d'un tonneau). (b) Effraction *f*. 2. Dressage *m* (d'un cheval); adaptation *f*, formation *f*; culottage *m* (d'une pipe). 3. Irruption *f* (dans une réunion); interruption *f* (d'une conversation). break loose, *v.i.* 1. Se dégager de ses liens; s'évader, s'échapper, s'affranchir (from, de). (*Of dog*) Casser sa chaîne. 2. His fury broke loose, sa fureur se déchaîna. 3. (*Of ship*) Partir à la dérive. break off. 1. *v.tr.* (a) Casser, rompre (qch.); détacher (qch.) (from, de). (b) Interrompre, abandonner (son travail, une discussion); cesser (des relations d'affaires, etc.); rompre (des négociations). The engagement is broken off, le mariage est rompu. 2. *v.i.* (a) Se détacher, se dégager (from sth., de qch.); se détacher (net); casser (net). (b) Discontinuer. *Abs.* To b. o. for ten minutes, prendre dix minutes de repos. To b. o. talking, s'interrompre de parler. (c) To b. o. with s.o., rompre avec qn. breaking off, *s.* Rupture *f* (d'un mariage, des négociations); interruption *f* (d'un travail). break open, *v.tr.* To b. open a door, a safe, a case, enfoncer, forcer, une porte; forcer une serrure, un coffre-fort; défoncer une caisse. break out, *v.i.* 1. (a) (*Of war, fire, disease*) Éclater; se déclarer. (b) (*Of the face, etc.*) To b. out into pimples, se couvrir de boutons. To b. out into a sweat, se mettre à transpirer; entrer en moiteur. 2. (a) S'échapper, s'évader (de prison, etc.). (b) Faire une fugue. To b. out into excesses, se livrer à des excès. 3. S'écrier. break through¹, *v.tr.* To b. through a barrier, *abs.* to b. through, enfoncer une barrière; se frayer un passage. *Av:* To b. t. the sound barrier, franchir le mur du son. To b. through a wall, faire une brèche dans, à, un mur. The sun breaks through (the clouds), le soleil perce les nuages. *Mil:* To b. through (the enemy lines), faire une percée. 'break-through², *s.* (a) *Mil:* Percée *f* (des lignes de l'ennemi). (b) Poussée *f*, hausse soudaine (des prix). (c) Solution soudaine (à un problème scientifique); découverte sensationnelle. break up. 1. *v.tr.* Mettre (qch.) en morceaux; démolir (un bâtiment, etc.); défoncer, ameublir (un terrain); *Ch:* résoudre (un composé); morceler (une propriété); démembrer, fragmenter (un empire); disperser (la foule); dissoudre (une assemblée); rompre, interrompre (une conférence); rompre (une coalition). The country was broken up into factions, le pays était divisé en factions. To b. up a fight, séparer des combattants. *F:* B. it up! la paix! *P:* That's right, b. up the happy home! faites chauffer la colle! *Ten:* To b. up an opponent's game, casser la cadence d'un adversaire. 2. *v.i.* (*Of empire, ship, etc.*) Se démembrer. (*of crowd, etc.*) se disperser; (*of road surface, etc.*) se désagréger; (*of ice*) débâcler. Ship breaking up, navire en perdition. *F:* She is beginning to b. up, il commence à se casser, à décliner. (b) (*Of company, meeting*) Se séparer; (*of groups*) se disjoindre. (c) *Sch:* Entrer en vacances. We b. up on the fourth, nos vacances commencent le quatre. (d) (*Of weather*) Se gâter, se brouiller. 'break-up, *s.* 1. Dissolution *f*, fin *f* (d'un empire, d'une assemblée); affaissement *m* (des forces physiques); bris *m* (d'un navire). 2. *Sch:* Entrée *f* en vacances. 3. Changement *m* (du temps); débâcle *f* (des glaces). breaking up, *s.* 1. Démolition *f*; défoncement *m* (d'un terrain); décomposition *f* (d'une substance); dissolution *f* (d'une assemblée); dispersion *f* (d'une foule); morcellement *m* (d'une propriété); démembrement *m*, déchirage *m* (d'un navire). 2. (a) Séparation *f*. On the b. up of the meeting, au sortir, à l'issue, de la réunion. (b) *Sch:* Entrée *f* en vacances. (c) Débâcle *f* (des glaces). broken, *a.* (a) Cassé, brisé, rompu. B. ribs, côtes enfoncées. He is b. in health, sa santé est délabrée, détraquée. His spirit is b., il est abattu, découragé. A b. man, (i) un homme ruiné; (ii) un homme au cœur brisé. (b) (*Terrain*) accidenté; (chemin) raboteux, défoncé; (sommeil) interrompu; (temps) incertain, variable. B. outline, contour anfractueux. In a b. voice, d'une voix

entrecoupée, altérée. In b. French, en mauvais français. -ly, *adv.* Sans suite; par à-coups; (parler) à mots entrecoupés. broken-'backed, *a.* (a) Aux reins cassés, brisés. (b) *Nau:* (Navire) arqué, cassé. 'broken-'down, *a.* *Mec.E:* *Aut:* etc: En panne; détraqué. broken-'hearted, *a.* Au cœur brisé. To die b.-h., mourir de chagrin. breaking, *s.* 1. (a) Rupture *f*; brisement *m* (d'une statue); concassage *m* (du minerai). *Jur:* (i) Bris *m* (d'une vitre, de scellés); (ii) levée *f* (de scellés). *El.E:* B. of the circuit, rupture du circuit. (b) B. into a house, entrée *f* par effraction dans une maison. (c) B. of the law, violation *f* de la loi, infraction *f* à la loi. B. of one's word, manque *m* de parole. (d) Amortissement *m* (d'une chute). (e) Brisement *m* (des vagues). 2. B. of the voice, (at manhood) mue *f*; (ii) (with emotion) altération *f* de la voix. 3. B. of new ground, (i) Défrichage *m*, (ii) œuvre *f* de pionnier. 'breaking ('down)-point, *s.* *Mec.E:* Limite *f* critique (de résistance); point *m* de rupture. 'break-neck, *a.* It was a b.-n. path, le sentier était un véritable casse-cou. To go at a b.-n. speed, filer à une allure folle; galoper, marcher, à tombeau ouvert, à fond de train.

break³, *s.* 1. *Veh:* Break *m*. 2. Voiture *f* de dressage (des chevaux).

breakable ['breikəbl]. 1. *a.* Cassant, fragile. 2. *s.pl.* Breakables, objets *m* fragiles.

breakage ['breikidʒ], *s.* 1. Rupture *f*; bris *m*, fracture *f* (du verre, etc.). 2. Casse *f*. To pay for breakages, payer la casse.

breaker ['breikər], *s.* 1. (*Pers.*) (a) Casseur, briseur. (b) Dresseur, entraîneur (de chevaux). (c) Violateur, -trice (d'une loi). 2. Brisoir *m*, concasseur *m*. 3. *Nau:* Brisant *m*; vague déferlante. Breakers ahead! des brisants devant!

breakfast¹ ['brekfəst], *s.* (Petit) déjeuner *m*. Continental b., café complet. Wedding b., repas *m* de noces. To have b., to eat one's b., déjeuner. (Large) b. cup and saucer, déjeuner.

breakfast², *v.i.* Déjeuner (le matin).

breakwater ['breikwɔːtər], *s.* 1. Brise-lames *m*; môle *m*; jetée *f*. 2. Éperon *m* (d'un pont).

bream [briːm], *s.* *Ich:* Brème *f*.

breast¹ [brest], *s.* 1. Sein *m*, mamelle *f*. To give a child the b., donner le sein à un enfant. Child at the b., enfant à la mamelle. 2. Poitrine *f*; poitrail *m* (de cheval). *Cu:* Blanc *m* (de volaille); avant-cœur *m* (de bœuf). B. of a coat, of a shirt, devant *m* d'un habit, d'une chemise. *S.a.* DOUBLE-BREASTED, SINGLE-BREASTED. To press s.o. to one's b., serrer qn sur son cœur. *F:* To make a clean b. of it, tout avouer; faire des aveux complets. 3. *Min:* Front *m* de taille, d'abattage. 'breast-'deep, *adv.* Jusqu'à la poitrine. 'breast-drill, *s.* *Tls:* Vilebrequin *m* à engrenages; chignole, *f*; porte-foret *m* (à conscience). 'breast-'feeding, *s.* Allaitement naturel. 'breastharness, *s.* Bricole *f*. 'breast-'high, *adv.* 1. A hauteur de poitrine. 2. A hauteur d'appui. 'breast-'pocket, *s.* Poche *f* de poitrine. Inside b.-p., poche intérieure. 'breast-stroke, *s.* *Swim:* Brasse *f*. 'breast-wall, *s.* *Civ.E:* Mur *m* de soutènement.

breast², *v.tr.* Affronter, faire front à, lutter contre (une tempête, un danger). To b. a hill, affronter, gravir, une colline.

breast(-)bone ['brestboun], *s.* *Anat:* Sternum *m*; bréchet *m* (d'un oiseau).

breastplate ['brestpleit], *s.* 1. (a) Plastron *m*; cuirasse *f*. (b) *Rel:* Pectoral *m*. 2. *Tls:* Conscience *f* (de vilebrequin).

breastwork ['brestwəːk], *s.* Parapet *m*, garde-corps *m inv.* *Nau:* Rambarde *f*.

breath [breθ], *s.* Haleine *f*, souffle *m*, respiration *f*. To draw b., respirer. To draw a deep, long b., respirer profondément. To draw one's last b., exhaler son dernier souffle; rendre le dernier soupir. To have sweet b., avoir l'haleine douce. To have bad b., avoir mauvaise haleine. It is the very b. of life to me, cela m'est aussi précieux que la vie même. All in the same b., tout d'une haleine. In one b., d'une seule émission de voix. To hold one's b., retenir son souffle. To gasp for b., haleter. He caught his b., il eut un sursaut; la respiration lui manqua. To lose one's

b., perdre haleine. **To waste one's b.**, perdre son temps en discours inutiles; perdre ses paroles. **To be short of b.**, (i) avoir l'haleine courte; (ii) être essoufflé. **Out of b.**, hors d'haleine; à bout de souffle; essoufflé. **To get out of b.**, perdre haleine. **To take s.o.'s b. away**, couper la respiration, le souffle, à qn; suffoquer, interloquer, qn. **To take b.**; **to get, recover, one's b.**, souffler; reprendre haleine. **To speak below, under, one's b.**, parler à (de)mi-voix, à voix basse. **To swear under one's b.**, jurer en sourdine. **The first b. of spring**, les premiers effluves du printemps. **To go out for a b. of air**, sortir prendre l'air _m_. **There is not a b. of wind**, il n'y a pas un souffle de vent. **B. of stale tobacco**, relent _m_ de tabac. _S.a._ AIR[1] I. BATB. **'breath-taking**, _a._ _F:_ Ahurissant. **It's b.-t.**, c'est à vous couper le souffle.
breathalyser ['breθəlaizər], _s._ B. (test), alcotest _m_.
breathe [bri:ð]. I. _v.i._ Respirer, souffler. **To b. hard**, (i) haleter; respirer avec peine; (ii) souffler fort, à pleins poumons. **To b. heavily**, (i) respirer bruyamment; (ii) respirer péniblement. **To b. again, freely**, respirer de nouveau, librement. II. **breathe**, _v.tr._ 1. Respirer (l'air). **To b. the air, in, out**, aspirer, exhaler, l'air. **To b. air into sth.**, insuffler de l'air dans qch. 2. **To b. new life into s.o.**, animer qn. 3. (_a_) **To b. a sigh**, exhaler, laisser échapper, un soupir. **To b. a prayer**, murmurer une prière. **To b. one's last**, rendre le dernier soupir. **Don't b. a word of it!** n'en soufflez pas un mot! (_b_) **To b. forth, b. out, threats**, s'exhaler en menaces; proférer des menaces. (_Of a flower_) **To b. forth perfume**, exhaler un parfum. (_c_) _Ling:_ Aspirer (un son). 4. Laisser souffler (un cheval). **breathing**[1], _a._ (_Of picture, statue_) Vivant; qui respire. **breathing**[2], _s._ 1. Respiration _f_; souffle _m_. **Heavy b.**, (i) respiration bruyante; (ii) respiration pénible; oppression _f_. **B. apparatus**, appareil _m_ respiratoire. 2. _Ling:_ (_a_) Aspiration _f_ (d'un son). (_b_) _Gr.Gram:_ Rough, smooth, b., esprit rude, doux. **'breathing-space**, _s._ Le temps de souffler, de respirer; répit _m_.
breather ['bri:ðər], _s._ _F:_ Moment _m_ de repos. **To give a horse a b.**, laisser souffler un cheval. **To go out for a b.**, sortir prendre l'air.
breathless ['breθlis], _a._ 1. Hors d'haleine; essoufflé, haletant. **B. with running**, essoufflé d'avoir couru. 2. **B. suspense**, attente fiévreuse. **-ly**, _adv._ 1. En haletant. 2. (Attendre, écouter) en retenant son haleine.
breathlessness ['breθlisnis], _s._ Essoufflement _m_; (_of patient_) manque _m_ de souffle; oppression _f_.
bred. _See_ BREED[2].
breech [bri:tʃ], _s._ 1. _A:_ _Anat:_ Le derrière. 2. (_a_) (Pair of) breeches ['britʃiz], culotte _f_. _A:_ **To put a child into breeches**, mettre un enfant en culotte. (_b_) _F:_ Pantalon _m_, _F:_ culotte. (_Of wife_) **To wear the breeches**, porter la culotte. 3. _Artil:_ _Sm.a:_ Culasse _f_. **B. action**, mécanisme de culasse. **'breech-block**, _s._ _Artil:_ Bloc _m_ de culasse. **'breech-birth**, _s._ _Obst:_ Accouchement _m_ par le siège. **'breeches-buoy**, _s._ _Nau:_ Bouée-culotte _f_. **'breech-delivery**, _s._ _Obst:_ = BREECH-BIRTH. **'breech-loader**, _s._ Fusil _m_, pièce _f_, se chargeant par la culasse. **'breech-loading**, _s._ Chargement _m_ par la culasse.
breed[1] [bri:d], _s._ Race _f_ (d'hommes, d'animaux); lignée _f_. _S.a._ CROSS-BREED[1], HALF-BREED.
breed[2], _v._ (bred; bred) I. _v.tr._ 1. Produire, engendrer; faire naître, donner naissance à (des vices, etc.). _S.a._ FAMILIARITY 1. 2. (_a_) Élever (du bétail, etc.). _Abs._ Faire de l'élevage. _Prov:_ **What's bred in the bone will come out in the flesh**, (i) bon chien chasse de race; (ii) chassez le naturel, il revient au galop. (_b_) **He was bred to the law**, il fut destiné au barreau. **He had been bred a sailor**, il avait été élevé pour faire un marin. **Country-bred**, élevé à la campagne. _S.a._ BORN 2, HALF-BRED, ILL-BRED, PURE-BRED. II. **breed**, _v.i._ (_a_) (_Of animals, people_) Multiplier; se reproduire. (_b_) (_Of opinions, etc._) Se propager.
breeding, _s._ 1. (_a_) Reproduction _f_. (_b_) Élevage _m_ (d'animaux domestiques, etc.). **He goes in for b.**, il fait de l'élevage. **Silkworm b.**, éducation _f_ des vers à soie. 2. (_a_) Éducation _f_ (d'un enfant, etc.). (_b_) (**Good**) **b.**, bonnes manières; savoir-vivre _m_. _S.a._

ILL-BREEDING. **'breeding-season**, _s._ (_Of birds_) Couvaison _f_; (_of domestic animals_) monte _f_.
breeder ['bri:dər], _s._ 1. Reproducteur, -trice. **Good b.** (jument) bonne poulinière. 2. Éleveur _m_ (d'animaux). _S.a._ SILKWORM. 3. _Atom.Ph:_ _attrib._ **B. reactor**, réacteur (expérimental) (auto-)régénérateur.
breeks [bri:ks], _s.pl._ _F:_ (_In Scot._) = breeches, _q.v._ _under_ BREECH 2.
breeze[1] [bri:z], _s._ 1. Vent assez fort; brise _f_. **Land b.**, brise de terre. **Sea b.**, brise de mer, du large. _Nau:_ **Strong b., stiff b.**, vent frais, grosse brise. 2. _F:_ Scène _f_, querelle _f_. _P:_ **There was a bit of a b. when he came home**, il y a eu du grabuge quand il est rentré.
breeze[2], _v.i._ 1. _Nau:_ (_Of wind_) **To b. up**, fraîchir. 2. _P:_ _U.S:_ S'échapper de prison. 3. _F:_ **To b. in, out**, entrer, sortir, en coup de vent.
breeze[3], _s._ (_Cinders_) Braise _f_ de houille; fraisil _m_. **'breeze-block**, _s._ Parpaing _m_.
breezily ['bri:zili], _adv._ _F:_ Avec jovialité.
breeziness ['bri:zinis], _s._ _F:_ Cordialité bruyante; jovialité _f_; verve _f_ (d'un discours).
breezy ['bri:zi], _a._ 1. Venteux. 2. _F:_ (_Of pers., manners_) Jovial; désinvolte; (_of speech_) plein de verve. **B. welcome**, accueil cordial (et bruyant).
Bremen ['breimən]. _Pr.n._ _Geog:_ Brême.
Bren-gun ['brengʌn], _s._ _Mil:_ = Fusil mitrailleur.
brent-goose ['brentgu:s], _s._ _Orn:_ Bernache _f_, barnache _f_; cravant _m_.
brethren ['breðrin], _s.pl._ _See_ BROTHER.
Breton ['bret(ə)n]. 1. _a. & s._ Breton, -onne. 2. _s._ _Ling:_ Le breton.
breve ['bri:v], _s._ 1. _Hist:_ Bref _m_ (du pape). 2. _Pros:_ Brève _f_.
brevet ['brevit], _s._ _Mil:_ Brevet _m_. **B. officer**, officier breveté. **B. rank**, grade honoraire.
breviary ['bri:viəri], _s._ _Ecc:_ Bréviaire _m_.
brevity ['breviti], _s._ Brièveté _f_. 1. Concision _f_. 2. Courte durée (de la vie, etc.).
brew[1] [bru:], _s._ 1. (_a_) Brassage _m_ (de la bière). (_b_) Brassin _m_, cuvée _f_. 2. Infusion _f_ (de thé); tisane _f_ (de plantes).
brew[2]. 1. _v.tr._ (_a_) Brasser (la bière). (_b_) _Abs._ Brasser; faire de la bière. (_c_) **To b. tea**, faire infuser le thé. 2. _v.i._ (_a_) (_Of tea, etc._) S'infuser. (_b_) **There is a storm brewing**, il y a un orage qui couve. _F:_ **There is something brewing**, il se trame quelque chose. **brewing**, _s._ = BREW[1] 1. **brew up**, _v.tr._ _F:_ _Mil:_ Faire infuser le thé, = "faire le jus."
brewer ['bru(:)ər], _s._ Brasseur _m_.
brewery ['bru(:)əri], _s._ Brasserie _f_.
briar ['braiər], _s._ (_a_) **Wild b.**, églantier commun; rosier _m_ sauvage. **Sweet b.**, églantier odorant. (_b_) **Briars**, ronces _f_. (_c_) = BRIER. **'briar-rose**, _s._ Églantine _f_.
bribe[1] [braib], _s._ Payement _m_ illicite; _F:_ pot-de-vin _m_. **To take a b.**, bribes, se laisser corrompre.
bribe[2], _v.tr._ Corrompre, acheter, soudoyer; _F:_ graisser la patte à (qn). **To b. a witness**, suborner un témoin. **bribing**, _s._ Corruption _f_; subornation _f_ (de témoins).
briber ['braibər], _s._ Corrupteur, -trice; suborneur _m_.
bribery ['braibəri], _s._ Corruption _f_. **Open to b.**, corruptible.
bric-à-brac ['brikəbræk], _s._ Bric-à-brac _m_.
brick[1] [brik], _s._ 1. (_a_) Brique _f_. **Glazed b.**, brique vernissée. **B. house**, maison en briques. _F:_ **To drop a b.**, faire une boulette, une bourde, une gaffe. **I can't make bricks without straw**, je ne peux pas faire un miracle. _F:_ **He came down on me like a ton of bricks**, il m'est tombé dessus. _S.a._ WALL[1] 1. (_b_) (_Toy_) **Box of bricks**, boîte de constructions. 2. _F:_ **He's a b.!** c'est un chic type. **Be a b.!** soyez chic! **'brick-clay**, _s._ Argile _f_, terre _f_, à briques. **'brickfield**, _s._ Briqueterie _f_. **'brick-kiln**, _s._ Four _m_ à briques; briqueterie _f_. **'brick-'red**, _a._ Rouge brique _inv._
brick[2], _v.tr._ Briqueter; garnir (qch.) en briques. **To b. up a window**, murer une fenêtre.
brickbat [brikbæt], _s._ Fragment _m_ de brique; briquaillon _m_.

bricklayer ['brikleiǝr], *s.* Maçon *m*; briqueteur *m*.

brickmaker ['brikmeikǝr], *s.* Briquetier *m*.

brickmaking ['brikmeikiṅ], *s.* Briqueterie *f*.

brickwork ['brikwǝ:k], *s.* Briquetage *m*; maçonnerie *f* de brique. *pl.* **Brickworks**, briqueterie *f*.

brickyard ['brikjɑ:d], *s.* Briqueterie *f*.

bridal ['braid(ǝ)l]. **1.** *s. Poet:* Noce(s) *f*. **2.** *a.* Nuptial, -aux, de noce(s). **B.** veil, voile *m* de mariée.

bride [braid], *s.f.* **1.** Future, fiancée (sur le point de se marier). **2.** Épousée; (nouvelle) mariée. **The b. and bridegroom,** (i) les futurs conjoints; (ii) les nouveaux mariés.

bridegroom ['braidgrum], *s.m.* **1.** Futur, prétendu (sur le point de se marier). **2.** (Nouveau) marié.

bridesmaid ['braidzmeid], *s.f.* Demoiselle d'honneur (de la mariée).

bridge¹ [bridʒ], *s.* **1.** Pont *m*. **To throw a b. across a river,** jeter un pont sur un fleuve. **Swing-b.,** pont tournant. **Suspension b.,** pont suspendu. *F:* **We'll cross that b. when we get to it,** chaque chose en son temps. **2.** *Nau:* (*a*) Passerelle *f* (de commandement). (*b*) (*From ship to shore*) **Ladder b.,** passerelle à taquets. **3.** *El:* (*a*) **Measuring-b.,** pont de mesure. **Induction b.,** balance *f* d'induction. (*b*) **B.-piece,** pont polaire (d'accus). **4.** Dos *m*, arête *f* (du nez); chevalet *m* (d'un violon); arcade *f* (d'une paire de lunettes). *Dent:* Bridge *m*. **5.** *Mil:* Charnière *f*. **Bailey b.,** pont Bailey, pont provisoire. **'bridge-building,** *s.* Pontage *m*; construction *f* de ponts. **'bridge-crane,** *s.* Pont-grue *m*. **'bridge-head,** *s. Mil:* Tête *f* de pont. **'bridge-house,** *s. Nau:* Rouf central. **'bridge-keeper,** *s.* Pontier *m*. **'bridge-train,** *s. Mil:* (i) Train *m* de pontons; (ii) corps *m* des pontonniers.

bridge², *v.tr.* **To b. a river,** jeter, construire, un pont sur un fleuve. **To b. a gap,** relier les bords d'une brèche; combler une lacune. *Pol.Ec:* **To b. the gap,** faire la soudure.

bridge³, *s. Cards:* Bridge *m*. **Auction b.,** bridge aux enchères. **Contract b.,** bridge contrat. **B. player,** bridgeur, -euse. **B.-marker,** carnet-bloc *m* (de bridge). **B.-party,** (i) soirée, (ii) réunion, de bridge. **To play b.,** bridger.

bridle¹ [braidl], *s.* **1.** (*a*) *Harn:* Bride *f*. **To give a horse the b.,** lâcher, rendre, la bride à un cheval. (*b*) **Frein** *m*. **To put a b. on one's passions,** mettre un frein à ses passions. **2.** *Nau:* Branche *f*. **3.** Frein, filet *m* (de la langue). **'bridle-bit,** *s. Harn:* Mors *m* de bride. **'bridle-path, -way,** *s.* Sentier *m* pour cavaliers; piste cavalière; chemin muletier.

bridle². **1.** *v.tr.* (*a*) Brider, rêner, (un cheval). (*b*) Maîtriser, brider, mettre un frein à, refréner (ses passions). **2.** *v.i.* **To b. (up),** (i) redresser la tête; se rengorger; (ii) se rebiffer; prendre la mouche.

brief¹ [bri:f], *a.* Bref, *f.* brève; court. **B. stay, visit,** séjour passager, de peu de durée. **In b.,** en raccourci, en résumé, bref, en deux mots. **-ly,** *adv.* Brièvement; en peu de mots.

brief², *s.* **1.** *Ecc:* Bref *m*. **Apostolic b.,** bref apostolique, bref du pape. **2.** Abrégé *m*, résumé *m*, exposé *m*. *Jur:* Dossier *m* (d'une procédure). **To hold a b.,** être chargé d'une cause. **To hold a b. for s.o.,** représenter qn en justice. *F:* **I don't hold much b. for him,** je n'ai guère confiance en lui. **3.** *Cost:* Briefs, slip *m*. **'brief-case,** *s.* Serviette *f* (en cuir).

brief³, *v.tr.* **1.** **To b. a case,** rédiger, établir, le dossier d'une affaire. **2.** **To b. a barrister,** confier une cause à un avocat; constituer un avoué. **3.** Donner une mission à, munir d'instructions, fournir des directives à, *Av: F:* briefer. **briefing,** *s.* **1.** **B. of a case,** constitution *f* du dossier d'une affaire. **2.** **B. of a lawyer,** constitution d'avoué. **3.** Instructions *f,* directives *f. Av:* Briefing *m, F:* amphi *m*.

briefless ['bri:flis], *a.* (Avocat) sans cause.

briefness ['bri:fnis], *s.* Brièveté *f*; concision *f*.

brier ['braiǝr], *s.* **1.** Bruyère (arborescente). **2.** **B. (pipe),** pipe *f* en bruyère. **'brier-root,** *s.* Racine *f* de bruyère.

brig [brig], *s. Nau:* Brick *m*.

brigade¹ [bri'geid], *s.* **1.** Brigade *f* (de cavalerie, d'artillerie). *F:* **One of the old b.,** un vieux de la vieille; (*of woman*) une vieille garde. **2.** Corps organisé (pour un service public, etc.). *See esp.* FIRE-BRIGADE.

brigade², *v.tr. Mil:* Embrigader.

brigadier [ˌbrigǝ'diǝr], *s. Mil:* Général *m* de brigade.

brigand ['brigǝnd], *s.* Brigand *m*, bandit *m*.

brigandage ['brigǝndidʒ], **brigandism** ['brigǝndizm], *s.* Brigandage *m*.

brigantine ['brigǝnti:n], *s. Nau:* Brigantin *m*.

bright [brait], *a.* **1.** Lumineux. (*a*) (*Of star, gem, etc.*) Brillant; (*of sun*) éclatant. **B. fire,** feu clair, vif. **B. light,** lumière vive. **B. eyes,** yeux brillants, lumineux. **B. steel,** acier poli. *F:* **As b. as a button,** brillant comme un sou neuf. (*b*) (*Of day, weather*) Clair. **To become brighter,** s'éclaircir. (*c*) (*Of colour*) Vif, éclatant. **B. red,** rouge vif. (*d*) **Brighter days,** des jours plus heureux. **To look on the b. side of things,** prendre les choses par le bon côté. **2.** (*a*) (*Vivacious*) Vif, animé, sémillant. (*b*) *F:* **B. lad,** garçon éveillé, intelligent. **He's not very b.,** il n'est pas très intelligent. **A b. idea,** une idée lumineuse. **-ly,** *adv.* **1.** Brillamment; avec éclat. **2.** **To reply b.,** répondre (i) gaiement, (ii) avec intelligence.

Bright². *Pr.n. Med:* **Bright's disease,** maladie *f* de Bright, néphrite *f* chronique.

brighten ['brait(ǝ)n]. **1.** *v.tr.* **To b. sth. (up),** faire briller, faire reluire, qch.; fourbir (le métal); aviver (une couleur); égayer (la conversation). (*Of joy, etc.*) **To b. s.o.'s face,** dérider, faire épanouir, le visage de qn. **2.** *v.i.* **To b. (up),** (*of face*) s'épanouir, s'éclaircir, se dérider; (*of weather*) s'éclaircir. **His eyes brightened,** ses yeux s'allumèrent. **He began to b. up,** il commença à s'animer.

brightness ['braitnis], *s.* Éclat *m* (du soleil, du teint); intensité *f* d'éclairage; brillant *m* (de l'acier); clarté *f* (du jour); vivacité *f* (de l'intelligence, d'une couleur); intelligence *f* (d'un enfant). *Mus:* Brio *m. f.*

brill [bril], *s. Ich:* Barbue *f*.

brilliance ['briljǝns], **brilliancy** ['briljǝnsi], *s.* Éclat *m*, brillant *m*, lustre *m*; *Opt:* brillance *f*.

brilliant¹ ['briljǝnt], *a.* (*a*) (Fait d'armes, éclairage) brillant, éclatant. (*b*) (*Of pers.*) Très intelligent, très doué, brillant. **B. idea,** idée lumineuse. **-ly,** *adv.* Brillamment; avec éclat.

brilliant², *s. Lap:* Brillant *m*.

brilliantine [ˌbriljǝn'ti:n], *s. Toil:* Brillantine *f*. **Solid b.,** *F:* gomina *f*.

brim¹ [brim], *s.* Bord *m* (de verre, de chapeau, etc.) **To fill s.o.'s glass to the b.,** verser du vin à qn à ras bord. **'brim-'full,** *a.* Plein jusqu'au bord; débordant.

brim², *v.* (brimmed) **1.** *v.tr.* **To b. the bowl,** remplir la coupe jusqu'au bord. **2.** *v.i.* **To b. over (with sth.),** déborder, regorger (de qch.). **Brimming (over),** débordant (with, de). **Eyes brimming (over) with tears,** yeux noyés de larmes.

brimful ['brimful], *a.* **B. of health, of life,** débordant de santé, de vie.

brimstone ['brimstǝn], *s.* Soufre (brut). *Ent:* **B. (butterfly),** citron *m*.

brindle(d) ['brindl(d)], *a.* (Chat) tacheté, tavelé; (taureau) bringé.

brine [brain], *s.* Eau salée; saumure *f*.

bring [briṅ], *v.tr.* (*p.t.* **brought** [brɔ:t]; *p.p.* **brought**) (*a*) Amener (qn, un animal, une voiture); apporter (qch., une réponse, des nouvelles). **He was brought before the judge,** on l'amena, on le fit comparaître, devant le juge. **To be brought before the assizes,** être traduit en cour d'assises. *S.a.* WORD¹ 3. (*b*) **To b. tears (in)to s.o.'s eyes,** faire venir, faire monter, les larmes aux yeux de qn. **To b. s.o. luck, bad luck,** porter bonheur, malheur, à qn. **To b. misfortune on s.o.,** attirer un malheur sur qn. **You have brought it on yourself,** vous vous l'êtes attiré vous-même. (*c*) **To b. an action against s.o.,** intenter un procès à qn. *S.a.* CHARGE¹ 6. (*d*) **To b. s.o. into difficulties, into danger,** mettre qn dans l'embarras, dans le danger. **To b. sth. into action, into play,** mettre qch. en œuvre. *S.a.* FASHION¹ 3. (*e*) **To b. s.o. to beggary,** réduire qn

à la mendicité. **To b. sth. to perfection,** porter qch.
à la perfection. **To b. sth. to a successful issue,** faire
aboutir qch. *S.a.* END[1] 3, HOME II. 2, JUSTICE 1,
LIGHT[1] 1, LOW[1] I. 2, MIND[1] 1, NOTICE[1] 3, TRIAL 1. (*f*)
To b. sth. to pass, amener, faire arriver, qch. *S.a.*
BEAR[3] (*d*). (*g*) **To b. s.o. to do sth.,** amener qn à faire
qch. **To b. oneself to do sth.,** se résoudre, se décider, à
faire qch. **bring about,** *v.tr.* **1.** (*a*) (*Cause*) Amener,
causer, déterminer, occasionner (qch.). **To b. about**
s.o.'s ruin, entraîner la ruine de qn. **To b. about an**
accident, a reform, provoquer un accident, une réforme. (*b*) Effectuer, accomplir, opérer (qch.).
To b. about a change, opérer un changement. **2.** *Nau:*
Retourner, faire virer (un navire). **bring along,** *v.tr.*
Amener (qn); apporter (qch.). **bring away,** *v.tr.*
Emmener (qn); emporter (qch.) **bring back,** *v.tr.*
Rapporter (qch.); ramener (qn). **This brings back**
to me my childhood, cela me rappelle mon enfance.
bring down, *v.tr.* **1.** (*a*) Abattre, descendre (un arbre,
du gibier); faire tomber (le fruit d'un arbre);
faire crouler, faire effondrer (une maison); terrasser
(un adversaire). *Th: F:* To b. down the house, faire
crouler la salle (sous les applaudissements). (*b*)
Ar: **To b. down a figure,** abaisser un chiffre. **2.** (*a*)
Faire descendre (qn). (*b*) Descendre (un objet du
grenier, etc.). **3.** (*a*) Abaisser (l'orgueil de qn). (*b*)
Abaisser, faire baisser (le prix). **4.** (*a*) **To b. down a**
sword on s.o.'s head, abattre un sabre sur la tête de
qn. (*b*) **To b. down s.o.'s wrath on s.o.,** attirer la
colère de qn sur qn. **5.** To b. down a swelling, réduire
une enflure. **6. To b. down a history to modern times,**
amener une histoire jusqu'aux temps modernes.
bring forth, *v.tr.* **1.** Mettre au monde (des enfants);
(*of animal*) mettre bas (des petits); (*of plant*) produire (des fruits). **What the future will b. forth,** ce
que l'avenir produira, apportera. **2. To b. forth**
protests, provoquer des protestations. **bring for-**
ward, *v.tr.* (*a*) Avancer (une chaise, etc.); faire
avancer, faire approcher (qn); produire (un témoin);
avancer (un argument). (*b*) Avancer (une réunion,
etc.). (*c*) *Com:* Reporter (une somme). **Brought**
forward, à reporter; report *m.* **bring in,** *v.tr.* **1.** (*a*)
Introduire, faire entrer (qn); apporter, rentrer
(qch.). **B. him in,** faites-le entrer. **Dinner was brought**
in, on servit le dîner. *S.a.* MONEY 1. (*b*) Introduire
(une coutume); lancer (une mode). (*c*) Faire intervenir (qn). **2.** (*Of capital, investment*) To b. in interest,
rapporter; porter intérêt. **3.** (*a*) Déposer, présenter
(un projet de loi). (*b*) (*Of jury*) To b. in a verdict,
rendre un verdict. **To b. s.o. in guilty,** déclarer qn
coupable. (*c*) (Faire) intervenir qn. **bring off,** *v.tr.*
1. (*a*) Ramener (qn) à bord ou à terre. (*b*) Renflouer
(un navire). **2.** Réussir, boucler, conduire à bien
(une affaire). *F:* **To b. it off,** réussir le coup. **bring**
on, *v.tr.* **1.** Produire, occasionner (une maladie, etc.).
2. The sun is bringing on the plants, le soleil fait
pousser les plantes. **3.** *Th:* Amener ou apporter sur
la scène. **bring out,** *v.tr.* **1.** Apporter (qch.) dehors;
faire sortir (qn); conduire (qn) dehors. **To b. sth.**
out (*of a box, etc.*), sortir qch. **2.** Faire ressortir,
mettre en relief, mettre en évidence (le sens de qch.);
faire valoir (une couleur); mettre en lumière (un
défaut, etc.). **3.** (*a*) Introduire, faire débuter, (une
jeune fille) dans le monde; lancer (une actrice). (*b*)
The sun brings out the roses, le soleil fait épanouir
les roses. (*c*) Publier, faire paraître (un livre).
bringing out, *s.* Publication *f* (d'un livre); lancement
m (d'une actrice); présentation *f* (d'une jeune fille)
dans le monde. **bring over,** *v.tr.* **1.** Transporter,
amener (**from,** de). **2. To b. s.o. over to a cause,**
convertir, gagner, qn à une cause. **bring round,** *v.tr.*
1. Apporter (qch.); amener, faire venir (qn). **2.**
(*a*) Rappeler, ramener, (qn) à la vie; faire reprendre
connaissance à (qn). (*b*) Remettre (qn) de bonne
humeur. **3.** (*a*) Rallier (qn à un parti). (*b*) To b. the
conversation round to a subject, (r)amener la conversation sur un sujet. **bring through,** *v.tr.* **1.** Faire
passer, faire traverser (qn, qch.). **2. To b. a patient**
through, sauver un malade. **bring to,** *v.tr.* **1.** *Nau:*
Mettre (un navire) en panne; couper l'erre à (un
navire). *v.i.* (*Of ship*) Mettre en panne, prendre la
panne. **2.** *F:* **To b. s.o. to,** faire reprendre connaissance à qn. **bring together,** *v.tr.* Réunir; mettre

(des personnes) en contact; affronter (des plaques
de métal). **To b. persons together again,** réconcilier
des personnes. I brought them together, je leur fis
faire connaissance. **Chance brought us together,** le
hasard m'a fait le, la, rencontrer. **bring under,** *v.tr.*
1. Soumettre, subjuguer, assujettir (qn). **2.** (*Prep.*
use) **To b. s.o. under discipline,** plier qn à la discipline.
bring up, *v.tr.* **1.** (*a*) Monter (du vin de la cave);
faire monter (qn). (*b*) **To b. up one's food,** vomir;
rendre ce qu'on a mangé. **2.** Apporter, approcher,
avancer (qch.); amener, faire approcher (qn). **B.**
up your chair to the fire, approchez votre chaise du
feu. **3.** Élever (des enfants). **4. To b. s.o. up before**
the court, citer qn en justice. **5.** (*Bring to a standstill*)
(*a*) **To be brought up short by sth.,** buter contre qch.
(*b*) *Nau:* Mouiller ou arrêter (un navire). *v.i.* (*Of*
ship) Mouiller; casser son erre; accoster (**along,** le
long de). *S.a.* STANDING[1] 4. **6. To b. up a subject,**
mettre une question sur le tapis, en avant. **To b. up a**
subject again, revenir sur un sujet. **To b. sth. up**
against s.o., objecter qch. à qn. **bringing up,** *s.* **1.**
Apport *m* (de munitions, etc.). **2.** Éducation *f* (des
enfants).
brink [briŋk], *s.* Bord *m* (d'un précipice, d'un fleuve).
To be on the b. of ruin, être à deux doigts, à la veille,
de la ruine; être sur le bord de l'abîme. **To be on the**
b. of tears, avoir peine à retenir ses larmes; être
près d'éclater en sanglots.
brinkmanship ['briŋkmənʃip], *s.* Diplomatie *f* du bord
du gouffre, politique *f* du bord de l'abîme.
briny ['braini]. **1.** *a.* Saumâtre, salé. **2.** *s.* *F:* The
b., la mer, la grande tasse.
brio ['bri(:)ou], *s.* *Mus:* Brio *m.*
briony ['braiəni], *s.* = BRYONY.
briquette [bri'ket], *s.* Briquette *f.*
brisk[1] [brisk], *a.* **1.** Vif, actif, alerte, animé; plein
d'entrain. **B. old man,** vieillard ingambe, guilleret.
At a b. pace, à vive allure. **B. trade,** commerce actif.
B. market, marché animé. (i) feu vif; (ii)
Mil: feu nourri. **2.** (Air) vivifiant. **-ly,** *adv.* Vivement, activement; avec entrain.
brisk[2]. **1.** *v.tr.* **To b. s.o. up,** animer, activer, émoustiller, qn. **2.** *v.i.* **To b. up,** s'animer.
brisket ['briskit], *s.* *Cu:* Poitrine *f* (de bœuf).
briskness ['brisknis], *s.* (*a*) Vivacité *f,* animation *f,*
entrain *m.* (*b*) Activité *f* (des affaires). **2.** Fraîcheur
f (de l'air).
brisling ['brisliŋ], *s.* *Ich:* Sprat *m,* anchois *m* de
Norvège.
bristle[1] ['brisl], *s.* **1.** Soie *f* (de porc, de brosse); poil
m raide (de la barbe). **2.** *Bot:* Soie, poil.
bristle[2]. **1.** *v.tr.* (*Of animal*) Hérisser (ses poils, ses
soies). **2.** *v.i.* (*a*) (*Of animal, hair, etc.*) To b. (up),
se hérisser; *F:* (*of pers.*) se rebiffer, se hérisser. (*b*)
F: **To b. with bayonets, with difficulties,** être hérissé
de baïonnettes, de difficultés. **bristling,** *a.* Hérissé
(**with,** de). **A b. moustache,** une moustache en
bataille.
bristly ['brisli], *a.* Couvert ou garni de soies, de poils
raides; poilu. **B. moustache,** moustache hérissée,
raide.
Britain ['brit(ə)n]. *Pr.n.* **1.** *Hist:* La Bretagne (plus
tard l'Angleterre). **2.** *Geog:* (Great) **B.,** la Grande-
Bretagne.
Britannia [bri'tænjə]. *Pr.n.* (Nom symbolique de) la
Grande-Bretagne. *Com:* B. metal, *F:* b., métal
(blanc) anglais.
Britannic [bri'tænik], *a.* His, Her, B. Majesty, Sa
Majesté Britannique.
Briticism ['britisizm], *s.* *U.S:* Anglicisme *m;* tour-
nure (de phrase) anglaise.
British ['britiʃ], *a.* **1.** Britannique; de la Grande-
Bretagne; (*in Fr. usu.*) anglais, d'Angleterre. The
B. Isles, les Iles Britanniques. *s.pl.* The B. les
Anglais *m.* **2.** *Hist:* Breton (de la Grande-Bretagne).
Britisher ['britiʃər], *s.* *U.S: Austr:* Anglais, -aise.
Briton ['brit(ə)n], *s.* **1.** *Hist:* Breton, -onne (de la
Grande-Bretagne). **2.** *F:* Anglais, -aise.
Brittany ['britəni]. *Pr.n.* La Bretagne.
brittle [britl], *a.* Fragile, cassant. *Metalw:* Aigre.
brittleness ['britlnis], *s.* Fragilité *f.*

broach[1] [broutʃ], s. **1.** Cu: Broche f (à rôtir). **2.** Arch: Flèche f, aiguille f (d'église). **3.** Tls: (a) Équarrissoir m; alésoir m. (b) Coop: Perçoir m.

broach[2], v.tr. **1.** Cu: Embrocher. **2.** (a) Metalw: Aléser (un trou, un tube); équarrir. (b) Coop: Percer, entamer (un fût); mettre (un fût, du vin) en perce. **3.** Entamer, aborder (une question, etc.). **broaching**, s. **1.** Alésage m; mandrinage m. **2.** Mise f en perce (d'un fût).

broach[3], v. Nau: **1.** v.i. (Of ship) To b. (to), venir en travers; faire chapelle. **2.** v.tr. To b. a ship to, lancer un vaisseau dans le vent.

broad [brɔːd]. **1.** a. (a) Large. The road is forty foot b., la route est large de quarante pieds, a quarante pieds de large, de largeur. To have a b. back, (i) avoir une forte carrure; (ii) F: avoir bon dos. B. grin, sourire épanoui. In b. daylight, en plein jour; au grand jour. F: It is as b. as it is long, cela revient au même; c'est bonnet blanc et blanc bonnet. S.a. ARROW, OUTLINE[1] 2, BEAN, GAUGE[1] 1. (b) The b. facts, les faits tout simples. B. rule, règle de principe. (c) B. accent, speech, accent, langage, rustique. To speak b. Scotch, parler l'anglais avec un accent écossais. S.a. HINT[1]. (d) B. story, histoire hardie, risquée, F: salée, corsée. B. humour, grosse gaieté. To be b. in one's conversation, être libre, leste, dans ses discours. (e) B. Church, Église libérale. B. views, idées larges. **2.** s. (a) The b. of the back, toute la largeur du dos; le milieu du dos. (b) pl. Geog: The (Norfolk) Broads, la région de lacs et de marécages du Norfolk. (c) U.S: P: Femme f de mœurs faciles; poule f. **3.** adv. B. awake, tout éveillé. **-ly**, adv. Largement. **B. speaking**, généralement parlant. **'broad-'brimmed**, a. A larges bords. **broad-'minded**, a. To be b.-m., avoir l'esprit large, les idées larges; être tolérant. **broad-'mindedness**, s. Largeur f, ouverture f, d'esprit; tolérance f. **broad-'shouldered**, a. Large d'épaules, trapu.

broadcast[1] ['brɔːdkɑːst]. **1.** adv. Agr: To sow b., semer à tout vent, à la volée. To scatter money b., semer l'argent à pleines mains. **2.** a. (a) Agr: Semé à la volée. (b) W.Tel: T.V: Radiodiffusé. B. announcement, annonce f par radio. B. account of a sports event, radio-reportage m d'une réunion sportive.

broadcast[2]. **I.** v.tr. (broadcast; broadcast) **1.** (a) Agr: Semer (le grain) à la volée. (b) Faire savoir (qch.) partout, de tous côtés; diffuser, répandre (une nouvelle). **2.** W.Tel: T.V: (broadcasted) broad-cast(ed)) Radiodiffuser. **broadcasting**, s. **1.** Agr: Semaille f à la volée. **2.** W.Tel: T.V: Radio-émission f, radiodiffusion f, radiophonie f. B. station, station de radiodiffusion; poste émetteur. A good broadcasting voice, une voix radiogénique. **II. broadcast**, s. W.Tel: T.V: Émission f (d'informations); radio-émission; audition (musicale, etc.). Live b., (i) W.Tel: transmission directe; (ii) T.V: prise f de vue directe. W.Tel: Recorded b., transmission différée, en différé.

broadcaster ['brɔːdkɑːstər], s. W.Tel: T.V: **1.** (Appareil) émetteur m, diffuseur m. **2.** (Pers.) Chroniqueur, -euse, speaker, -ine.

broadcloth ['brɔːdklɔθ], s. Tex: Drap noir fin, de première qualité; U.S: popeline f.

broaden ['brɔːd(ə)n]. **1.** v.tr. Élargir. **2.** v.i. S'élargir, s'évaser.

broadness ['brɔːdnis], s. **1.** Largeur f. **2.** (a) Grossièreté f, vulgarité f (d'une plaisanterie, etc.). (b) Accent prononcé.

broadsheet ['brɔːdʃiːt], s. **1.** Typ: In-plano m inv. **2.** Lit.Hist: Canard m; feuille imprimée (relatant ou satirisant un fait du jour).

broadside ['brɔːdsaid], s. **1.** Nau: (a) Flanc m, travers m (du navire). On the b., par le travers. (Of ship) To be b. on to sth., présenter le côté, le travers, à qch. Collision b. on, abordage par le travers. (b) To fire a b., tirer une bordée. **2.** = BROADSHEET.

broadsword ['brɔːdsɔːd], s. Sabre m; latte f.

brocade[1] [bro'keid], s. Tex: Brocart m. Gold b., brocart, drap m d'or.

brocade[2], v.tr. Tex: Brocher. **brocaded**, a. Tex: Broché. B. dress, robe f de brocart. B. in gold, broché d'or.

broc(c)oli ['brɔkəli], s. Hort: Brocoli m.

brochure [bro'ʃuər], s. Brochure f, dépliant m; prospectus m publicitaire.

broderie Anglaise ['brɔdri ɑːŋ'gleiz], s. Needlew: Broderie ajourée anglaise.

brogue[1] [broug], s. **1.** A: Chaussure f en cuir cru. **2.** Soulier m de golf. **3.** Fishing brogues, brodequins m de pêche.

brogue[2], s. (a) Accent m de terroir. (b) Accent irlandais.

broil[1] [brɔil], s. Querelle f; bagarre f; rixe f.

broil[2], s. U.S: Viande grillée; grillade f.

broil[3], v.tr. & i. Griller; (faire) cuire sur le gril. **broiling**, a. F: (Of the sun) Ardent, brûlant. B. weather, chaleur torride. adv. It's b. hot in this room, on cuit dans cette salle.

broiler ['brɔilər], s. (a) Rôtissoire f électrique, gril m. (b) F: Poulet m (à rôtir) élevé en batterie. B. house, élevage m en batteries pour la chair.

broke [brouk]. **1.** See BREAK[2]. **2.** a. P: (=broken) Fauché. To be (stony) b., dead b., U.S: flat b., être sans le sou, dans la purée; être décavé, à sec, fauché (comme les blés).

broken, -ly. See BREAK[2].

broker ['broukər], s. **1.** (a) Courtier m (de commerce). Bill-b., courtier de change. Cotton-b., courtier en coton. S.a. PAWNBROKER, SHIP-BROKER. (b) (Stock-) b., agent m de change. S.a. EXCHANGE[1] 2. **2.** (Second-hand) Brocanteur, -euse.

brokerage ['broukəridʒ], s. **1.** (Profession) Courtage m. **2.** (Commission) (Frais mpl de) courtage.

brolly ['brɔli], s. F: Parapluie m; F: pépin m.

bromal ['broum(ə)l], s. Pharm: Bromal m.

bromate ['broumeit], s. Ch: Bromate m.

bromic ['broumik], a. Ch: Bromique.

bromide ['broumaid], s. **1.** Ch: Bromure m. Phot: B. paper, papier au gélatinobromure; papier au bromure (d'argent). **2.** U.S: F: (a) Homme ennuyeux; raseur m. (b) Banalité f; lieu commun.

bromine ['broumi(:)n, -ain], s. Ch: Brome m.

bronchia ['brɔŋkiə], s.pl. Anat: Bronches f.

bronchial ['brɔŋkiəl], a. Anat: Bronchial, -aux; des bronches.

bronchiole ['brɔŋkioul], s. Anat: Bronchiole f.

bronchitic [brɔŋ'kitik], a. Med: Bronchitique.

bronchitis [brɔŋ'kaitis], s. Med: Bronchite f.

broncho-pneumonia ['brɔŋkounju(:)'mounjə], s. Med: Broncho-pneumonie f.

bronchoscopy [brɔŋ'kɔskəpi], s. Med: Bronchoscopie f.

bronco ['brɔŋkou], s. Cheval sauvage de l'Amérique. U.S: F: Cheval non dressé.

brontosaurus ['brɔntə'sɔːrəs], s. Paleont: Brontosaure m.

bronze[1] [brɔnz]. **1.** s. (a) Bronze m. (b) Art: (Objet m en) bronze. (c) pl. Bronzes (in general), bronzerie f. Maker of bronzes, bronzier m. **2.** Attrib. (a) B. statue, statue de, en, bronze. (b) (Cuir) bronzé, mordoré.

bronze[2]. **1.** v.tr. (a) Bronzer (le fer, etc.). Bronzed skin, peau bronzée, basanée. (b) Mordorer (le cuir). **2.** v.i. Se bronzer. **bronzing**, s. Bronzage m.

brooch [broutʃ], s. Cost: Broche f, épingle f. B. pin, queue de broche.

brood[1] [bruːd], s. **1.** Couvée f (de poussins); nichée f (de canetons); volée f (de pigeons); naissain m (d'huîtres). **2.** F: (a) Enfants mpl; F: marmaille f. (b) Pej: B. of scoundrels, engeance f de scélérats. **'brood-hen**, s.f. Couveuse. **'brood-mare**, s.f. (Jument) poulinière.

brood[2], v.i. **1.** (Of hen) Couver. **2.** (a) Broyer du noir; rêver noir. To b. on, over, sth., rêver à qch.; songer sombrement à qch.; ruminer (une idée); couver (un projet). To b. over the fire, couver le feu. (b) The storm brooding over us, l'orage qui plane, qui couve sur nos têtes.

brooder ['bruːdər], s. (a) (Poule) couveuse f. (b) Husb: Couveuse (artificielle).

broody ['bruːdi], a. (a) B. hen, poule couveuse, qui demande à couver. (b) F: (Of pers.) Distrait, rêveur, -euse.

brook[1] [bruk], s. Ruisseau m. **'brook-trout**, s. Ich: Saumon m de fontaine.

brook², *v.tr.* (*In neg. sentences*) (Ne pas) souffrir; (ne pas) endurer. **The matter brooks no delay**, l'affaire ne souffre pas de retard.

brooklet ['bruklit], *s.* Ruisselet *m*; petit ruisseau.

brookweed ['brukwi:d], *s.* Pimprenelle *f* aquatique; mouron *m* d'eau.

broom [bru:m, brum], *s.* **1.** *Bot:* Genêt *m* (à balai). **2.** Balai *m*. **Small b.**, balayette *f*. **Wall-b.**, tête-de-loup *f*. *Prov:* **A new b. sweeps clean**, il n'est ferveur que de novice; tout nouveau, tout beau.

broomstick ['bru(:)mstik], *s.* **1.** Manche *m* à balai. **2.** *pl. F:* Jambes *f* comme des allumettes.

broth [brɔθ], *s.* (*a*) Bouillon *m*, potage *m*. (*b*) Scotch **b.**, soupe *f* (de tête de mouton) avec orge et légumes.

brothel ['brɔθ(ə)l], *s.* Bordel *m*.

brother, *pl.* **-ers**; (*in sense* 2) *pl.* brethren ['brʌðər, -əːz, 'breðrin], *s.* **1.** Frère *m*. **Older b.**, frère aîné. **Younger b.**, (frère) cadet *m*. *Com:* **Smith Brothers, Bros.**, (Maison *f*) Smith Frères. **2.** (*a*) (*Fellow-member of a society*) Frère. *Ecc:* **Dearly beloved brethren**, mes très chers frères. (*b*) Confrère *m* (d'un corps de métier). **3.** *Ecc:* (*pl. Brothers*) Frère (d'une communauté). **4.** *Attrib.* **B.-'writer, -'teacher, -'doctor, -'officer**, etc., confrère *m*, collègue *m*. **'brother-in-'arms**, *s.m.* (*pl.* brothers-in-arms) Compagnon d'armes; frère d'armes. **'brother-in-law**, *s.m.* Beau-frère, *pl.* beaux-frères.

brotherhood ['brʌðəhud], *s.* **1.** Fraternité *f*. **2.** (*a*) Confraternité *f*, société *f*; (*religious*) confrérie *f*. (*b*) *U.S:* Syndicat ouvrier.

brotherlike ['brʌðəlaik], **brotherly** ['brʌðəli]. **1.** *a.* De frère; fraternel. **2.** *adv.* En frère; fraternellement.

brotherliness ['brʌðəlinis], *s.* **1.** Amour fraternel. **2.** Confraternité *f*.

brougham ['bru:əm, bru:m], *s.* *A: Veh:* Brougham *m*.

brought. *See* BRING.

brow [brau], *s.* **1.** (*Usu. pl.*) (*a*) Arcade(s) sourcilière(s). (*b*) Sourcil(s) *m*. **To pucker one's brows**, froncer les sourcils. *S.a.* KNIT² 2. **2.** (*Forehead*) Front *m*. *S.a.* HIGHBROW, LOWBROW. **3.** Front, croupe *f* (de colline); bord *m* (de précipice).

browbeat ['braubi:t], *v.tr.* Intimider, brusquer, rudoyer (qn).

brown¹ [braun]. **I.** *a.* (*a*) Brun, marron. **B. hair**, cheveux bruns, châtains. **Light-b. hair**, cheveux châtain clair. *Tex:* **B. holland**, toile écrue. *Cu:* **B. butter**, beurre roux, beurre noisette. *S.a.* BREAD, OWL, PAPER, STUDY 2, SUGAR. (*b*) Bruni (par le soleil); bronzé. **II.** *s.* Brun *m*; marron *m*. **'brown-stone**, *s.* *U.S: Constr:* Grès *m* (de construction).

brown². **1.** *v.tr.* (*a*) Brunir. **Face browned by the sun**, teint bruni au soleil. (*b*) *Cu:* Rissoler (la viande); faire dorer (le poisson); faire roussir (une sauce). *Metall:* Bronzer, brunir. **2.** *v.i.* (*a*) (Se) brunir. (*b*) *Cu:* Prendre couleur; roussir. **'brown 'off**, *v.tr. F:* Décourager (qn). **To be browned off**, avoir le cafard, être découragé. **browning¹**, *s.* **1.** Brunissement *m*; bronzage *m*. **2.** *Cu:* Caramel *m*.

Brownian ['braunian], *a.* *Ph:* (mouvement) Brownien.

brownie ['brauni], *s.* **1.** *Scot:* Farfadet *m*. **2.** *Scouting:* Jeannette *f*.

Browning² ['braunin], *s.* *Sm.a:* Browning *m*; pistolet *m* automatique.

brownish ['brauniʃ], *a.* Brunâtre.

browse [brauz], *v.tr. & i.* (*a*) **To b.** (on) **leaves**, brouter des feuilles. (*b*) (= GRAZE) Brouter (l'herbe); paître. **To b. among books**, butiner dans les livres.

Bruin ['bru(:)in]. *Pr.n. Lit:* Brun *m*; l'Ours *m*, *F:* (l'ours) Martin.

bruise¹ [bru:z], *s.* Meurtrissure *f*; contusion *f*; bleu *m*; (*on fruit*) talure *f*; (*on metal*) bosse *f*. *Surg:* Coup *m* orbe.

bruise², *v.tr.* **1.** (*a*) Meurtrir, contusionner, froisser (une partie du corps); écraser (un fruit, un doigt); taler (un fruit). **To b. one's arm**, se meurtrir le bras. (*b*) (*With passive force*) (*Of fruit*) Se meurtrir, se tacher. **2.** Bosseler, bossuer. **3.** Broyer. **bruising**, *s.* **1.** Écrasement *m* (des chairs); contusion *f*, froissement *m*. **2.** Broyage *m*.

bruiser ['bru:zər], *s.* *Box: F:* Boxeur (brutal); cogneur *m*.

brunch [brʌnʃ], *s.* *F:* Repas *m* mixte de mi-matin (tenant lieu de "*breakfast*" et de "*lunch*").

brunette [bru(:)'net], *a. & s.* (*Of woman*) Brune (*f*).

brunt [brʌnt], *s.* Choc *m*. **To bear the b. of the attack** soutenir le plus fort, le choc, de l'attaque. **The b. o the battle**, le plus fort de la bataille. **To bear the b** (*of work or fight*), payer de sa personne. **To bear the b. of the expense**, faire la plupart des frais.

brush¹ [brʌʃ], *s.* **1.** (*a*) = BRUSHWOOD. (*b*) *U.S: etc.* Brousse *f*. **2.** (*a*) Brosse *f*; (*for bottles*) goupillon *m*. **Long-handled (Turk's head) b.**, tête-de-loup *f*. **Hearth-, banister-b.**, balayette *f*, époussette *f*. **Shoe b.** (*hard*), brosse à décrotter. (*b*) (Paint-)b., pinceau *m*. **Flat b.**, queue-de-morue *f*. **Paste-b.**, pinceau à colle. **Whitewash b.**, badigeon *m*. **Air-b.**, pinceau vaporisateur. (*c*) *Ven:* Queue *f* (de renard). (*d*) *El.E:* Balai (de commutateur); frottoir *m* (de dynamo). **3.** Faisceau *m* de rayons électriques. **4.** Coup *m* de brosse (à des vêtements, etc.). **5.** Rencontre *f*, échauffourée *f* (avec l'ennemi). **At the first b.**, au premier abord. **'brush-factory, -trade**, *s.* Brosserie *f*. **'brush-holder**, *s.* *El.E:* Porte-balais *m inv* (de dynamo). **'brush-maker**, *s.* Brossier *m*; fabricant *m* de brosses. **'brush-proof**, *s.* *Typ:* Épreuve *f* à la brosse; morasse *f*. **'brush-ware**, *s.* Brosserie *f*. **'brush-work**, *s.* **1.** Travail *m* au pinceau. **2.** *Art:* Touche *f* (du peintre); facture *f*.

brush². **1.** *v.tr.* (*a*) Brosser (un habit, les cheveux); balayer (un tapis). (*b*) Effleurer, raser, frôler (une surface). (*c*) Gratter (la laine). (*d*) **To b. the dust off sth.**, enlever la poussière de qch. (à la brosse). *U.S:* **To b. off one's hat**, brosser son chapeau. **To b. sth. clean**, nettoyer qch. avec une brosse, à la brosse. **2.** *v.i.* **To b. against, by, past, s.o.**, frôler, qn en passant. **brush aside**, *v.tr.* Écarter (qn, une pensée, une difficulté). **brush away**, *v.tr.* Enlever (la boue, etc.) d'un coup de brosse ou de balai; écarter (une difficulté). **brush down**, *v.tr.* Donner un coup de brosse à (qn); brosser, panser (un cheval). **'brush-off**, *s.* *F:* Affront *m*, rebuffade *f*; *F:* soufflet *m*. **To get the b.-o.**, essuyer une mortification, un affront (de la part de qn). **To give s.o. the b.-o.**, *F:* Snober (qn). **brush over**, *v.tr.* Enduire (une surface) à la brosse; badigeonner (une surface) (with, de). **brush up**, *v.tr.* (*a*) Donner un coup de brosse à (un chapeau, etc.). *F:* **To b. up a subject**, se remettre à un sujet; repasser, rafraîchir un sujet. **To b. up one's French**, dérouiller son français. (*b*) **To b. up wool**, gratter la laine. (*c*) **To b. up the crumbs**, ramasser les miettes (avec la brosse). **brush-'up**, *s.* **1.** Coup *m* de brosse. **2.** **To give one's French a b.-up**, dérouiller son français. **brushing**, *s.* Coup *m* de brosse; brossage *m*, balayage *m*.

brushwood ['brʌʃwud], *s.* (*a*) Broussailles *fpl*; bois taillis; fourré *m*. (*b*) Mort-bois *m*; menu bois. **'brushwood-killer**, *s.* Débroussaillant *m*.

brushy ['brʌʃi], *a.* **1.** En brosse; hérissé. **2. B. tail**, queue bien fournie.

brusque [bru(:)sk], *a.* Brusque; (ton) rude, bourru. **-ly**, *adv.* Avec rudesse, avec brusquerie.

brusqueness ['bru(:)sknis], *s.* Brusquerie *f*, rudesse *f*.

Brussels ['brʌslz]. *Pr.n. Geog:* Bruxelles. *S.a.* CARPET¹, SPROUT¹ 2.

brutal ['bru:tl], *a.* Brutal, -aux; (instinct) animal, de brute. **-ally**, *adv.* Brutalement.

brutality [bru:'tæliti], *s.* **1.** Brutalité *f* (to, envers). **2.** *Jur:* Sévices *mpl* (envers).

brutalization [ˌbru:təlai'zeiʃ(ə)n], *s.* Abrutissement *m*.

brutalize ['bru:təlaiz], *v.tr.* Abrutir.

brute [bru:t]. **1.** *s.* (*a*) Brute *f*; bête *f* brute. **Alcohol turns men into brutes**, l'alcool abrutit les hommes. (*b*) *F:* (*Of pers.*) Brute; brutal, -aux *m*. **You b.!** espèce d'animal! (*c*) *F:* **It was a b. of a job**, c'était un métier, un travail, de chien. **2.** *a.* (*a*) **B. beast**, bête brute. (*b*) **B. force**, la force brutale. **By b. force**, de vive force. (*c*) **B. matter**, matière brute.

brutish ['bru:tiʃ], *a.* **1.** De brute; bestial, -aux. **2.** Abruti. **-ly**, *adv.* Brutalement; en brute; comme une brute.

brutishness ['bru:tiʃnis], *s.* **1.** Bestialité *f*. **2.** Abrutissement *m*.

bryony ['braiəni], s. *Bot:* 1. White b., bryone *f*, couleuvrée *f*. 2. Black b., tami(ni)er *m*.

bubble¹ [bʌbl], s. 1. (a) Bulle *f* (d'air, de savon); (*in boiling liquid*) bouillon *m*. (b) *Glassm: Metall:* Soufflure *f*; *Cer:* cloche *f*. 2. Projet *m* chimérique; chimère *f*, illusion *f*; tromperie *f*. *Hist:* The South Sea B., l'affaire des Mers du Sud (1720). B. scheme, entreprise véreuse; duperie *f*. 3. Bouillonnement *m*. **'bubble-and-'squeak,** s. *Cu:* Réchauffé *m* en friture de pommes de terre et de choux.

bubble², v.i. (a) Bouillonner; dégager des bulles; (*of wine*) pétiller; (*of gas through liquid*) barboter. (b) (*Of liquid poured*) Faire glouglou; glouglouter. **bubble over,** v.i. Déborder. F: To b. over with vitality, with high spirits, déborder de vie, de gaieté. **bubble up,** v.i. (*Of spring*) Sortir à gros bouillons. **bubbling,** a. Bouillonnant; (of wine) pétillant.

bubbly ['bʌbli]. 1. a. Plein de bulles; pétillant. 2. s. P: (Vin de) champagne (*m*).

bubo, pl. -oes ['bju:bou, -ouz], s. *Med:* Bubon *m*.

bubonic [bju(:)'bɔnik], a. *Med:* Bubonique. B. plague, peste *f* bubonique.

bubs [bʌbz], s.pl. V: Les nichons *m*.

buccal ['bʌk(ə)l], a. *Anat:* Buccal, -aux.

buccaneer [ˌbʌkə'niər], s. (a) *Hist:* Flibustier *m*. (b) Boucanier *m*, flibustier *m*; pirate *m*.

Bucharest ['bju:kərest, 'bu:-]. Pr.n. *Geog:* Bucarest.

buck¹ [bʌk], s. 1. (a) Daim *m* ou chevreuil *m* (mâle). (b) Mâle *m* (du renne, du chamois, du lapin, du lièvre). (c) U.S: Indien mâle; jeune nègre. 2. F: A. & Hist: Dandy *m*, élégant *m*. Old b., vieux marcheur. 3. *Equit:* = BUCK-JUMP¹. 4. U.S: P: = DOLLAR. **'buck-fever,** s. U.S: F: Fièvre de la chasse. **'buck-jump¹,** s. (Of horse) Saut *m* de mouton. **'buck-jump²,** v.i. (Of horse) Faire le saut de mouton; faire un haut-le-corps. **'buck-shot,** s. *Ven:* Chevrotine *f*; gros plomb. **'buck-teeth,** s.pl. F: Dents saillantes.

buck². 1. v.i. = BUCK-JUMP². 2. v.tr. (Of horse) To b. s.o. off, désarçonner qn.

buck³, F: 1. v.tr. To b. s.o. up, remonter le courage de qn; stimuler, ragaillardir, qn. I was tremendously bucked to hear the news, j'ai été enchanté d'apprendre la nouvelle. 2. v.i. To b. up, (i) reprendre courage, se ressaisir; (ii) se hâter; se remuer. B. up! (i) courage! dépêche-toi! P: grouille-toi!

buck⁴, s. U.S: *Cards:* Couteau *m* etc., que l'on place devant un joueur pour marquer que c'est à lui de donner. To pass the b., F: (i) passer la décision à qn; (ii) se débrouiller sur le voisin.

bucket ['bʌkit], s. 1. (a) Seau *m*. Canvas b., wooden b., seau en toile, en bois. *S.a.* DROP¹ 1, KICK² 2. (b) *Ind:* Baquet *m*. *Nau:* Tar b., baille *f* à goudron. 2. Piston *m* (à clapet) (d'une pompe); chopine *f*. 3. *Hyd.E:* (a) Auget *m* (d'une roue hydraulique). (b) Chain of buckets, (pompe à) chapelet *m*. 4. Godet *m*, benne *f* (d'une drague). 5. *Mil:* Botte *f* (pour carabine); godet (pour hampe de lance, etc.). **'bucket-seat,** s. *Aut:* (Siège *m* en) baquet *m*. **'bucket-shop,** s. *Fin:* Bureau *m* d'un courtier marron.

bucketful ['bʌkitful], s. Plein seau. F: It is raining (in) bucketfuls, il pleut à seaux.

buckle¹ ['bʌkl], s. 1. Boucle *f*, agrafe *f*. 2. *Tchn:* Flambement *m*, gauchissement *m* (d'une tige, d'une surface); voile *m* (d'une roue); flambage *m*.

buckle². 1. v.tr. (a) Boucler (une valise, un soulier, etc.); agrafer, serrer, attacher (une ceinture, etc.). (b) *Tchn:* Déjeter; gauchir; voiler (une roue); faire flamber (une tige de métal, etc.). 2. v.i. (a) (Of shoe, belt) Se boucler. (b) F: (Of pers.) To b. to a task, s'appliquer, s'atteler, à un travail. To b. to, s'y atteler; s'y mettre. 3. v.i. To b. (up), (of metal, etc.) se déformer, se déjeter, (se) gondoler, gauchir, flamber, arquer; (of wheel) se voiler. **buckling¹,** s. 1. Agrafage *m*. 2. (Of metal) Déformation *f*, flambage *m*, gauchissement *m*, déjettement *m*, voilure *f*; gondolage *m* (d'une tôle, de plaques d'accu). 3. F: B. to, (i) application assidue au travail; (ii) commencement *m* du travail.

buckler ['bʌklər], s. 1. *Arm:* Écu *m*, bouclier *m*. 2. *Nau:* Tampon *m*, tape *f* (d'écubier).

buckling², ['bʌkliŋ], s. Hareng cuit et fumé.

buckram ['bʌkrəm], s. *Tex:* Bougran *m*.

bucksaw ['bʌksɔ:], s. *Tls:* Scie *f* à bûches.

buckshee ['bʌk'ʃi:], a. & adv. P: Gratis; à l'œil.

buckskin ['bʌkskin], s. Peau *f* de daim. B. breeches, s.pl. buckskins, culotte *f* de peau.

buckthorn ['bʌkθɔ:n], s. *Bot:* Nerprun *m*.

buckwheat ['bʌkwi:t], s. Sarrasin *m*; blé noir.

bucolic [bju(:)'kɔlik], a. & s. Bucolique (*f*).

bud¹ [bʌd], s. 1. *Hort:* Bourgeon *m*; œil *m* (d'une plante); écusson *m*. (Of tree) To be in b., bourgeonner. Sedition in the b., sédition en germe. *S.a.* NIP² 2. 2. *Bot:* Bouton *m* (de fleur). 3. s.m. U.S: F: Copain *m*. 4. *Anat:* Taste b., papille gustative.

bud², v. (budded) 1. v.i. (a) (Of tree, plant) Bourgeonner; se couvrir de bourgeons. (b) (Of flower) Boutonner; commencer à éclore. (c) F: (Of talent, etc.) Commencer à éclore, à se révéler. 2. v.tr. Greffer (un arbre fruitier) par œil détaché; écussonner (un arbre). **budding¹,** a. (a) Qui bourgeonne ou qui boutonne. A b. rose, un bouton de rose; une rose en bouton. (b) B. **artist,** artiste en herbe. **budding²,** s. 1. (a) Bourgeonnement *m*. (b) Poussée *f* des boutons. 2. *Hort:* Greffe *f* par œil détaché; écussonnage *m*. **'budding-knife,** s. Écussonnoir *m*.

Buddha ['budə], s. (Le) Bouddha.

Buddhism ['budizm], s. Bouddhisme *m*.

Buddhist ['budist]. 1. s. Bouddhiste *mf*. 2. a. Bouddhique.

buddy ['bʌdi], s. U.S: F: Ami *m*, copain *m*.

budge [bʌdʒ]. 1. v.i. (a) Bouger, céder; reculer. I won't b. **an inch,** je ne reculerai pas d'un centimètre. (b) Bouger, remuer. 2. v.tr. I **couldn't b. him,** il est resté inébranlable.

budgerigar ['bʌdʒəri'ga:r], s. Perruche *f* inséparable.

budget¹ ['bʌdʒit], s. Budget *m*. To **introduce, open, the b.,** présenter le budget. To pass the b., voter le budget. Household b., budget du ménage. *S.a.* BALANCE² 1.

budget², v.i. Budgétiser. To b. **for a certain expenditure,** porter, inscrire, certaines dépenses au budget.

budgetary ['bʌdʒit(ə)ri], a. Budgétaire.

buff¹ [bʌf], s. 1. (a) Peau *f* de buffle; cuir épais. B.-leather, buffle *m*. 2. Couleur *f* chamois; jaune clair *inv*. 3. F: In the b., tout nu. To strip to the b., se mettre dans le costume d'Adam; P: se mettre à poil. **'buff-stick,** s. *Metalw:* Buffle *m*, polissoir *m*.

buff², v.tr. Polir, émeuler (un métal, etc.) (au buffle). **buffing,** s. Polissage *m*, émeulage *m*, **'buffing-wheel,** s. Meule *f* à polir.

buffalo¹, pl. -oes ['bʌfəlou, -ouz], s. Z: (a) Buffle *m*. Cow b., bufflesse *f*. Young b., bufflon, -onne. (b) U.S: F: Bison *m*.

buffalo², v.tr. U.S: F: 1. Blouser (qn). 2. Intimider, terroriser (qn).

buffer¹ ['bʌfər], s. Appareil *m* de choc; amortisseur *m*. 1. (a) *Rail:* Tampon *m* (de choc). *El.E:* Accumulator forming b., accumulateur en tampon. (b) = BUFFER-STOP. 2. *Artil:* Recoil-b., frein *m* (de tir). **'buffer(-)state,** s. *Pol:* État *m* tampon. **'buffer-stocks,** s.pl. Stocks régulateurs. **'buffer-stop,** s. *Rail:* Butoir *m*, heurtoir *m*; tampon *m* d'arrêt.

buffer², s. F: Old b., (i) vieux copain; (ii) vieux bonze.

buffet¹ ['bʌfit], s. Coup *m* (de poing).

buffet², v.tr. & i. (a) Flanquer une torgn(i)ole à (qn); bourrer (qn) de coups. (b) To b. with the waves, lutter contre les vagues. (Of ship) Buffeted by the waves, by the wind, battu, ballotté, par les vagues; secoué par le vent. **buffeting,** s. Succession *f* de coups, de chocs. We got a b. **in the Bay of Biscay,** nous avons été fortement secoués dans le golfe de Gascogne.

buffet³, s. 1. ['bʌfei or 'bufei] (Sideboard) Buffet *m*. 2. ['bʌfei] (a) Buffet. There will be a b. (meal), il y aura un buffet. (b) (On menu) Cold b., viandes froides; assiette anglaise. **'buffet car,** s. *Rail:* Voiture-bar *f*, voiture-buffet *f*.

buffoon [bʌ'fu:n], s. Bouffon *m*, paillasse *m*. F: To play the b., bouffonner, faire le bouffon.

buffoonery [bʌ'fuːnəri], s. Bouffonneries *fpl*, F: baladinage *m*.

bug[1] [bʌg], s. 1. (a) Punaise *f*. (b) U.S: Insecte m. (c) F: Microbe m. (d) F: Microphone clandestin. 2. F: (*Of pers.*) Big b., gros bonnet. **The big bugs**, les huiles f. **'bug-eyed**, a. U.S: F: Aux yeux exorbités; qui ouvre de grands yeux (d'étonnement). **'bug(-)house**, s. U.S: F: (a) (*Place*) F: Maison de fous; cabanon m. (b) (*Pers.*) He's b.-h., il est fou, F: cinglé, louftingue, piqué, toqué, P: dingo. **'bug-hunter**, s. F: Entomologiste m; naturaliste m.

bug[2], v.tr. F: Camoufler un microphone clandestin (dans une pièce).

bugaboo ['bʌgəbuː], s. U.S: (a) Objet m d'épouvante (pour les enfants): F: croquemitaine m, loup-garou m. (b) F: Sujet m de grosse inquiétude; cauchemar m.

bugbear ['bʌgbɛər], s. (a) = BUGABOO. (b) F: That man's my b., cet homme-là, je ne peux pas le sentir.

bugger ['bʌgər], s. 1. Jur: Pédéraste m. 2. P: Bougre m.

buggy ['bʌgi], s. Veh: Buggy m.

bugle[1] [bjuːgl], s. Clairon m. **Key(ed) b.**, bugle m. **B. band**, fanfare *f*. S.a. CALL[1] 2.

bugle[2], v.i. Sonner du clairon.

bugle[3], s. Bot: Bugle *f*.

bugler ['bjuːglər], s. Clairon m; sonneur m de clairon.

bugloss ['bjuːglɔs], s. Bot: 1. Corn, field, b., buglosse *f*. 2. Viper's b., vipérine *f*; herbe *f* aux vipères. 3. Dyer's b., orcanette *f*.

bugs [bʌgz], a. U.S: F: = BUG-HOUSE (b).

buhl [buːl], s. (Marqueterie *f* de) Boul(l)e m. **B. cabinet**, cabinet de boulle.

build[1] [bild], s. 1. Construction *f*; façons *fpl* (d'un navire, etc.); style m (d'un édifice). 2. Carrure *f*, taille *f*, conformation *f* (d'une personne). **Man of powerful b.**, homme à forte membrure. **Man of slight b.**, homme fluet.

build[2], v.tr. (built [bilt]; built) 1. (Faire) bâtir (une maison, etc.); construire (un vaisseau, un pont, une route, une machine); édifier (un temple); faire, bâtir (un nid). **To b. over, upon, a piece of land**, bâtir un terrain. **The stables are built on to the house**, les écuries tiennent à la maison. **To b. upon sand**, bâtir sur le sable. F: **I'm built that way**, je suis comme ça. **I'm not built that way**, cela ne s'accorde pas avec mes principes; ce n'est pas mon genre. 2. **To b. vain hopes on sth.**, fonder de vaines espérances sur qch. **build in**, v.tr. 1. Murer, boucher, bloquer (une fenêtre, etc.). 2. **Built-in beam**, poutre encastrée. **Built-in cupboard**, placard m. **build up**[1]. 1. v.tr. (a) Affermir (la santé). (b) Bâtir, échafauder (une théorie, etc.). **To b. up a connection**, se créer une clientèle. (c) (*Of magnetic field*) **To b. up**, s'amorcer. (d) Built-up area, agglomération (urbaine). 2. v.i. **Pressure is building up**, la pression s'accumule. **'build-up**[2], s. 1. = BUILDING-UP. 2. **The N.A.T.O. military b.-u.**, l'organisation *f* militaire de l'O.T.A.N. 3. Publicité *f*. **building up**, s. 1. Affermissement m, consolidation *f* (de la santé, etc.); échafaudage (de projets). 2. El.E: Amorçage m (du champ, d'une dynamo). **built**, a. British b., de construction anglaise. **Well-b. man**, homme bien bâti, solidement charpenté. **building**, s. 1. Construction *f*. attrib. **B. ground, b. land**, terrain à bâtir. **B. estate**, lotissement m. **B. plot**, lot m. **B. contractor**, entrepreneur de bâtiment. **B. maniac**, bâtisseur m. **The b.-trade**, le bâtiment, l'industrie *f* du bâtiment. **B. materials**, matériaux *mpl* de construction. 2. Bâtiment m; immeuble m; maison *f*; local m, -aux; (*large b.*) édifice m. **Public b.**, édifice public; monument m. **'building-slip**, s. N.Arch: Cale *f* de construction. **'building(-)society**, s. Société immobilière.

builder ['bildər], s. Entrepreneur m (en bâtiments); constructeur m (de navires).

built. See BUILD[2].

bulb [bʌlb], s. 1. Bot: Bulbe m, oignon m (de tulipe, etc.). 2. Anat: **Hair-b.**, bulbe pileux. 3. El: Ampoule *f*; lampe *f*. 4. Ph: Boule *f*, ampoule (de thermomètre). 5. Poire *f* (en caoutchouc).

bulbous ['bʌlbəs], a. Bulbeux. **B. nose**, gros nez, F: piton m.

Bulgaria [bʌl'gɛəriə]. Pr.n. La Bulgarie.

Bulgarian [bʌl'gɛəriən], a. & s. Bulgare (*mf*).

bulge[1] [bʌldʒ], s. Bombement m, ventre m, renflement m; (*of tase, etc.*) panse *f*. Pol.Ec: 'The b.' le "ventre" (de la courbe), la poussée.

bulge[2], v.tr. & i. **To b. (out)**, bomber, ballonner; faire ventre; faire saillie. **Sack bulging with potatoes**, sac bourré de pommes de terre. **bulging**, a. (Front, etc.) bombé; (ventre) ballonnant; (bouteille, etc.) pansu. **B. eyes**, yeux protubérants; F: yeux en boules de loto.

bulimia ['bjuːlimiə], **bulimy** ['bjuːlimi], s. Med: Boulimie *f*.

bulk[1] [bʌlk], s. 1. Nau: Charge *f*; chargement arrimé. **To break b.**, désarrimer; rompre charge; entrer en déchargement. **To load (a ship) in b.**, charger un navire en volume, en vrac. Com: **In b.**, en bloc, globalement; en gros, en quantité. **B. buying**, achat massif, en gros. 2. Grandeur *f*, grosseur *f*, masse *f*, volume m (d'un colis). 3. **The b. of mankind**, la masse, la plupart, des hommes. **To lose the b. of one's goods**, perdre le plus gros de ses biens.

bulk[2], v.i. **To b. large**, occuper une place importante, faire figure importante (*in s.o.'s eyes*, aux yeux de qn). **To b. up**, s'amasser. **To b. up to . . .**, s'élever au total de . . . **bulking**[1], a. Publ: **B. paper**, papier bouffant. **bulking**[2], s. Com: Groupage m, (de colis). **bulk up**, v.tr. Publ: Imprimer un livre sur papier bouffant.

bulkhead ['bʌlkhed], s. N.Arch: Cloison *f*. **Fire-proof b.**, cloison coupe-feu.

bulkiness ['bʌlkinis], s. 1. Volume excessif; encombrement m. 2. Grosseur *f*.

bulky ['bʌlki], a. 1. Volumineux, encombrant, peu portatif. **B. book**, livre épais. 2. Gros, *f* grosse.

bull[1] [bul], s. 1. (a) Taureau m. F: **To take the b. by the horns**, prendre le taureau par les cornes. **He is like a b. in a china shop**, il est comme un taureau en rupture d'étable. F: **cou de brise-fer**. (b) B. elephant, whale, éléphant m mâle, baleine *f* mâle. (c) U.S: F: Agent m de police, *f* flic m. (d) Astr: **The B.**, le Taureau. 2. St.Exch: Spéculateur m à la hausse; haussier m. F: = BULL'S-EYE 4. **'bull-baiting**, s. Combat m de chiens contre un taureau. **'bull-calf**, s. 1. Jeune taureau m; taurillon m. 2. F: Niais m, innocent m. **'bull-headed**, a. 1. Au front de taureau. 2. D'une impétuosité de taureau. **'bull-pen**, s. Toril m. **'bull-pup**, s. Jeune bouledogue. **'bull's-eye**, s. 1. Glassm: Boudine *f*. 2. Nau: (Verre m de) hublot m; lentille *f*. 3. B.-e. window, œil-de-bœuf m, pl. œils-de-bœuf. 4. Noir m, blanc m, mouche *f* (d'une cible). **To make a b.-e.**, faire mouche, faire un rigodon. 5. F: Gros bonbon (en boule) à la menthe. **bull-'terrier**, s. (Chien) bull-terrier m.

bull[2], v.tr. (a) **To b. the market**, chercher à faire hausser les cours. (b) Abs. Spéculer à la hausse.

bull[3], s. Ecc: Bulle *f*. **Benefice conferred by a b.**, bénéfice bullé.

bull[4], s. 1. **Irish b.**, inconséquence *f*; coq-à-l'âne m. 2. Bévue *f* (comique); gaffe *f*.

bulldog ['buldɔg], s. 1. Bouledogue m. 2. F: (i) Personne d'un courage obstiné; (ii) appariteur m du censeur (aux universités d'Oxford et de Cambridge). F: **One of the b. breed**, un homme qui a du cran.

bulldoze ['buldouz]. 1. Metalw: Civ.E: Passer au bulldozer. 2. U.S: P: Menacer, intimider, brutaliser (qn) (pour lui faire faire qch.).

bulldozer ['buldouzər], s. 1. Metalw: Machine *f* à refouler, à cintrer. 2. Civ.E: Bulldozer m, bélier m mécanique.

bullet ['bulit], s. Balle *f* (de fusil, de revolver). **'bullet-headed**, a. A tête ronde. **'bullet-proof**, a. A l'épreuve des balles.

bulletin ['bulitin], s. Bulletin m, communiqué m. U.S: **B. board**, tableau m d'annonces; porte-affiches m inv. **News b.**, bulletin d'actualités; W.Tel: T.V: Cin: journal parlé, télévisé, filmé; informations *fpl*, actualités *fpl*.

bullfight ['bulfait], s. Corrida *f*; course *f* de taureaux.

bullfighter ['bulfaitər], s. Toréador m.

bullfighting ['bulfaitiŋ], s. Courses *fpl* de taureaux; tauromachie *f*.

bullfinch ['bulfin(t)ʃ], s. **1.** Orn: Bouvreuil m. **2.** Equit: Haie f avec fossé, bullfinch m.

bullfrog ['bulfrɔg], s. Grenouille f taureau, Fr.C: ouaouaron m.

bullhead ['bulhed], s. Ich: Chabot m de rivière; meunier m.

bullion¹ ['buljən], s. Or m en barres; or, argent m, en lingot(s); valeurs fpl en espèces. **B. reserve,** réserve métallique. **B. van,** fourgon m bancaire.

bullion², s. Tex: (a) Cannetille f. (b) Mil: Torsades fpl; franges fpl.

bullock ['bulək], s. Husb: Bœuf m. **Young b.,** bouvillon m. **'bullock-cart,** s. Char m à bœufs.

bullring ['bulriŋ], s. Arène f (pour les courses de taureaux).

bully¹ ['buli], s. **1.** (a) A: Bravache m. **To play the b.,** faire le fendant. (b) F: Brute f, tyran m. Sch: Brimeur m. (c) Homme de main (d'un aventurier politique, etc.). **2.** (Pimp) Souteneur m.

bully², v.tr. Intimider, malmener, brutaliser. **To b. s.o. into doing sth.,** faire faire qch. à qn à force de menaces. **bullying¹,** a. Brutal, -aux; bravache. **bullying²,** s. **1.** Intimidation f, brutalité f. **2.** Sch: Brimades fpl.

bully³, a. & int. U.S: P: Fameux, épatant, bœuf.

bully⁴, s. Hockey: Engagement m (du jeu).

bully⁵, v.i. Hockey: **To b. (off),** engager (le jeu); mettre la balle en jeu.

bully⁶, s. F: **B. (beef),** bœuf m de conserve; corned-beef m; Mil: F: singe m.

bullyrag ['bulirӕg], v. = RAG³.

bulrush ['bulrʌʃ], s. Bot: **1.** Jonc m des marais. **2.** Massette f, quenouille f.

bulwark ['bulwək], s. **1.** A.Fort: Rempart m, boulevard m. **2.** pl. Nau: Pavois m, bastingage m.

bum¹ [bʌm], s. F: Derrière m; P: cul m. **'bum-freezer,** s. Cost: P: Pet-en-l'air m inv., veston m rase-pet. **'bum-sucker,** s. V: Lèche-cul m inv.

bum². U.S: P: **1.** a. Sans valeur; misérable, P: moche. **B. steer,** faux renseignement, tuyau crevé. **2.** s. Fainéant m; clochard m.

bum³, v.i. (bummed) U.S: P: **1.** Flâner, fainéanter. **2.** Être, vivre aux crochets de qn. **3.** v.tr. (a) Emprunter (qch.). (b) **To b. a dinner off s.o.,** se faire payer à dîner par qn.

bumble-bee ['bʌmblbi:], s. Ent: Bourdon m.

bum-boat ['bʌmbout], s. Nau: Bateau m à provisions.

bumf [bʌmf], s. P: **1.** Papier m hygiénique; P: papier torchecul. **2.** Paperasserie f.

bummaree ['bʌməri], s. (a) Courtier m en poisson (au marché de Billingsgate). (b) Courtier en viande (au marché de Smithfield).

bump¹ [bʌmp], s. **1.** Choc (sourd); secousse f, heurt m, coup m; cahot m (d'une voiture). **2.** Bosse f; (in phrenology) protubérance f, bosse f. **Bumps in a road,** inégalités f, cahots, d'un chemin. **To have the b. of invention,** avoir la bosse de l'invention. **3.** Av: Trou m d'air.

bump². **1.** v.tr. Cogner, frapper. **To b. one's head on, against, sth.,** se cogner la tête contre qch. **2.** v.i. (a) Se cogner, se heurter, buter (into, against, sth., contre qch.); entrer en collision (avec qch.). F: **I bumped into him in the Tube,** je l'ai rencontré par hasard, je suis tombé sur lui, dans le Métro. **To b. along** (in cart, etc.), avancer avec force cahots. (b) Nau: (Of ship) Talonner; toucher (le fond). **bump off,** v.tr. P: Assassiner, supprimer (qn). **bumping,** s. Heurtement m, cahotement m.

bump³, adv. & int. Pan! boum!

bumper ['bʌmpər], s. **1.** Rasade f (de champagne, etc.). F: **B. crop,** récolte magnifique. Th: **B. house,** salle comble. **2.** (a) Rail: U.S: Tampon m. (b) Aut: Pare-choc(s) m inv.

bumpkin ['bʌm(p)kin], s. Rustre m, lourdaud m.

bumptious ['bʌm(p)ʃəs], a. Présomptueux, suffisant, outrecuidant. **-ly,** adv. D'un air suffisant; avec suffisance.

bumptiousness ['bʌm(p)ʃəsnis], s. Suffisance f, outrecuidance f.

bumpy ['bʌmpi], a. **1.** (Chemin, etc.) cahoteux, défoncé. Av: **B. flight,** vol chahuté. **2.** Couvert de bosses.

bun [bʌn], s. **1.** Cu: Petit pain au lait (avec ou sans raisins). **2.** (Cheveux enroulés en) chignon m. **3.** Fung: F: **Penny b.,** cèpe m.

Buna ['bu:nə], s. R.t.m: Caoutchouc m synthétique.

bunch¹ [bʌn(t)ʃ], s. (a) Botte f (de radis); bouquet m (de fleurs); grappe f (de raisins); houppe f (de plumes); trousseau m (de clefs); flot m (de rubans); régime m (de bananes); poignée f (de brindilles, etc.). (b) F: Groupe m (de personnes). **He's the best of the b.,** c'est lui le meilleur (de la bande). **What a b.!** quelle engeance!

bunch². **1.** v.tr. Grouper; botteler (des radis, etc.); lier (des fleurs) en bouquet. **To b. up one's skirt,** retrousser sa jupe. **2.** v.i. **To b. (together),** se presser en foule; se serrer; se pelotonner.

bundle¹ ['bʌndl], s. Paquet m (de linge, etc.); ballot m (de marchandises); F: baluchon m (d'effets); botte f (d'asperges, etc.); faisceau m (de cannes, de fils); liasse f (de papiers); fagot m (de bois).

bundle². **1.** v.tr. (a) **To b. (up),** empaqueter; mettre, lier, (qch.) en paquet; mettre (des documents) en liasse. F: **To b. everything up,** tout ramasser en pagaïe. **He bundled all the papers into the drawer,** il fourra pêle-mêle tous les papiers dans le tiroir. (b) F: **To b. s.o. out of the house,** jeter, flanquer, qn à la porte. **To b. sth. into a corner,** fourrer qch. dans un coin. **2.** v.i. **To b. in, out,** s'introduire, sortir, à la hâte. **To b. off,** s'en aller (sans cérémonie).

bung¹ [bʌŋ], s. Bondon m (de fût); tampon m de liège. **'bung-drawer,** s. Tire-bonde m, pl. tire-bondes. **'bung-hole,** s. Bonde f.

bung², v.tr. **To b. (up),** bondonner (un fût); boucher (un orifice). F: **Eyes bunged up,** yeux pochés.

bung³, v.tr. P: Lancer, jeter (des pierres, etc.).

bungaloid ['bʌŋgəlɔid], a. F: Pej: **A horrid b. growth,** une éruption de petits bungalows affreux (et mal bâtis).

bungalow ['bʌŋgəlou], s. **1.** (In India) Bungalow m; villa f à véranda. **2.** Bungalow, maison f sans étage.

bungle¹ ['bʌŋgl], s. Gâchis m, maladresse f, bousillage m. **To make a b. of sth.,** bousiller, gâcher, qch.

bungle², v.tr. Bousiller, gâcher, saboter; F: ravauder; P: louper (un travail); rater (une affaire). **bungling¹,** a. Maladroit. **B. attempt,** tentative gauche. **bungling²,** s. **1.** Bousillage m, gâchis m, F: ravaudage m. **2.** Maladresse f.

bungler ['bʌŋglər], s. (a) Bousilleur, -euse (de travail); gâcheur, -euse. (b) Maladroit, -e.

bunion ['bʌnjən], s. Med: F: Oignon m.

bunk¹ [bʌŋk], s. (a) Lit-placard m. (b) Nau: Rail: Couchette f.

bunk², v.i. & s. F: **To b. (off), to do a b.,** déguerpir, filer, décamper.

bunk³, s. P: = BUNKUM.

bunker¹ ['bʌŋkər], s. **1.** Nau: Soute f (à charbon, etc.). **2.** (a) Golf: Bunker m. (b) Mil: Blockhaus m; abri bétonné.

bunker², v.tr. **1.** Nau: Mettre (du charbon) en soute. **2. To be bunkered,** (i) Golf: se trouver derrière un bunker; (ii) F: se trouver dans une impasse.

bunkum ['bʌŋkəm], s. F: Blague f, bêtises fpl. **That's all b.!** tout ça c'est des histoires, des balivernes!

bunny ['bʌni], s. F: Jeannot lapin m.

bunting¹ ['bʌntiŋ], s. Orn: Bruant m. **Corn b., common b.,** bruant proyer.

bunting², s. **1.** Tex: Étamine f (à pavillon); burat m. **2.** Coll. Drapeaux m, pavillons m. **To put out b.,** pavoiser.

buoy¹ [bɔi], s. Nau: Bouée f; balise flottante. **Mooring-b.,** (bouée de) corps-mort m. **To put down a b.,** mouiller une bouée. S.a. BELL-BUOY, BREECHES-BUOY, LIFE-BUOY. **'buoy-rope,** s. Orin m.

buoy², v.tr. Nau: **1. To b. up an object,** faire flotter un objet; soutenir un objet sur l'eau. F: **To b. s.o. up,** soutenir, appuyer, qn. **2.** Baliser (un chenal).

buoyancy ['bɔiənsi], s. **1.** (a) Flottabilité f (d'un objet); légèreté f sur l'eau. (b) Poussée f (d'un liquide). **Centre of b.,** centre de poussée. **2.** Entrain m; élasticité f de caractère; ressort m.

buoyant ['bɔiənt], a. **1.** (a) Flottable; léger. (b) **Salt water is more b. than fresh,** l'eau salée porte mieux que l'eau douce. **2.** (Of pers.) Plein d'entrain; qui a du ressort. **B. step,** pas élastique. Com.: **B market,** marché soutenu. **-ly,** adv. Avec entrain; avec optimisme.

bur [bəːr], s. Bot: (a) Capsule épineuse. (Of burdock) Bouton m de pompier; teigne f (de bardane). Chestnut-b., bogue f. Teasel-b., carde f. (b) = BURDOCK. (c) F: (Of pers.) Crampon m.

Burberry ['bəːberi], s. R.t.m: Imperméable m.

burble[1] [bəːbl], s. Murmure m (de paroles); sons inarticulés.

burble[2], v.i. (a) Murmurer (des sons inarticulés). (b) F: Débiter des inepties.

burbot ['bəːbɔt], s. Ich: Lotte f, barbot m.

burden[1] [bəːdn], s. 1. (a) Fardeau m, charge f. The b. of years, of taxation, le poids des années, des impôts. Jur: B. of proof, charge de la preuve. To be a b. to s.o., être à charge à qn. To become a b. on s.o., tomber à la charge de qn. To make s.o.'s life a b., rendre la vie dure à qn. Beast of b., bête de somme, de charge. (b) Nau: Charge, contenance f, d'un navire. Ship of five thousand tons b., navire qui jauge cinq mille tonneaux. 2. O: (a) Refrain m (d'une chanson). (b) Substance f, fond m (d'un discours, d'une plainte).

burden[2], v.tr. (a) Charger, alourdir (s.o. with sth., qn de qch.). To b. the people with taxes, accabler le peuple d'impôts. Burdened estate, domaine grevé d'hypothèques. (b) Être un fardeau pour (qn).

burdensome ['bəːdnsəm], a. Onéreux (to, à); fâcheux, ennuyeux.

burdock ['bəːdɔk], s. Bardane f, glouteron m.

bureau, pl. -eaux ['bjuərou, -ouz], s. 1. Furn: Bureau m; secrétaire m. U.S: Commode f. 2. (a) (Office) Bureau. Information b., bureau de renseignements. (b) U.S: Bureau; service m (du gouvernement).

bureaucracy [bjuə'rɔkrəsi], s. Bureaucratie f.

bureaucrat ['bjuərəkræt], s. Bureaucrate m; F: rond-de-cuir m, pl. ronds-de-cuir.

bureaucratic [,bjuərə'krætik], a. Bureaucratique.

burette [bjuə'ret], s. 1. Ecc: Burette f. 2. Ch: Éprouvette graduée.

burg [bəːg], s. U.S: Pej: F: Ville f, bourg m.

burgeon ['bəːdʒ(ə)n], s. & v.i. Lit: = BUD[1],[2].

burgess ['bəːdʒis], s. 1. Adm: Électeur m (dans une ville). 2. (a) Hist: Député représentant une ville ou une université. (b) U.S: Conseiller municipal.

burgh ['bʌrə], s. Scot: Ville f, municipalité f.

burgher ['bəːgər], s. Hist: Bourgeois m, citoyen m. The Burghers of Calais, les Bourgeois de Calais.

burglar ['bəːglər], s. Cambrioleur m; dévaliseur m de maisons. S.a. CAT-BURGLAR. 'burglar-proof, a. (Coffre-fort) incrochetable, inviolable.

burglarize [bəːgləraiz], v.tr. U.S: Cambrioler, dévaliser (une maison).

burglary ['bəːgləri], s. (a) Jur: Vol m de nuit avec effraction. (b) F: Vol avec effraction; cambriolage m.

burgle [bəːgl], v.tr. F: Cambrioler, dévaliser (une maison). **burgling**, s. Cambriolage m.

burgomaster ['bəːgəmɑːstər], s. Bourgmestre m.

Burgrave ['bəːgreiv], s Hist: Burgrave m.

Burgundian [bəː'gʌndiən], a. & s. Geog: Bourguignon, -onne.

Burgundy ['bəːgəndi]. 1. Pr.n. La Bourgogne. 2. s. (Vin m de) bourgogne m.

burial ['beriəl], s. Enterrement m, inhumation f. Christian b., sépulture f en terre sainte. 'burial-ground, s. Cimetière m. 'burial-place, s. Lieu m de sépulture. 'burial-service, s. Office m des morts.

burke [bəːk], v.tr. Étouffer, étrangler (un scandale). To b. the question, escamoter la vraie question.

burlap ['bəːlæp], s. Toile f d'emballage.

burlesque[1] ['bəːlesk]. 1. a. Burlesque. 2. s. (a) Burlesque m. (b) Parodie f.

burlesque[2], v.tr. Travestir, parodier.

burliness ['bəːlinis], s. Corpulence f; forte carrure.

burly ['bəːli], a. Solidement bâti. A big b. fellow, un grand gaillard de forte carrure.

Burma ['bəːmə]. Pr.n. La Birmanie.

Burmese [,bəː'miːz], a. & s. Birman, -ane. B. cat, chat, chatte, de Birmanie.

burn[1] [bəːn], s. Brûlure f.

burn[2], v. (burnt; burnt; occ. burned; burned) 1. v.tr. (a) Brûler. To b. sth. to ashes, réduire qch. en cendres. To b. one's fingers, se brûler les doigts. F: He burnt his fingers over it, il lui en a cuit. To be

burnt alive, être brûlé vif. To be burnt to death, être brûlé vif; (in house fire, etc.) être carbonisé. F: Money burns his fingers, burns a hole in his pocket, l'argent lui fond dans les mains. To have money to b., avoir de l'argent à n'en savoir que faire. S.a. BOAT[1], CANDLE 1. (b) Ind: Cuire (des briques). (c) Surg: Cautériser (une plaie). 2. v.i. (a) Brûler. To b. like matchwood, flamber comme une allumette. To b. like tinder, brûler comme de l'amadou; brûler sec. My head burns, la tête me brûle. My wound was burning, ma blessure cuisait. To b. with desire, brûler de désir. To b. to do sth., brûler de faire qch. To b. with impatience, griller d'impatience. Pred: Magnesium burns white, le magnésium brûle avec une flamme blanche. (b) I.C.E: (Of mixture) Exploser. **burn away**. 1. v.tr. Brûler, consumer (qch.). 2. v.i. Se consumer. **burn down**, v.tr. Brûler, incendier (une ville, etc.); burn in, v.tr. Graver (qch.) par le feu. **burn into**, v.i. Acid that burns into a metal, acide m qui ronge un métal. **burn off**, v.tr. Brûler, décaper (la peinture). **burn out**. 1. v.tr. (a) To b. s.o.'s eyes out, brûler les yeux à qn. (b) They were burnt out of house and home, leur maison fut réduite en cendres. (c) The candle has burnt itself out, la chandelle est brûlée jusqu'au bout. (d) El: Brûler, court-circuiter (une bobine); griller (une lampe). (e) Aut: To burn out the brake lining, brûler la garniture des freins, brûler ses freins. 2. v.i. Se consumer; brûler; (of electric lamp) griller. **burn up**. 1. v.tr. Brûler (entièrement); consumer. 2. v.i. (Of fire) Se ranimer, flamber. '**burn-up**, s. Atom.Ph: etc: Volatilisation f. **burnt**, a. 1. (a) Brûlé, carbonisé. A b. child dreads the fire, expérience passe science. (b) Face b. by the sun, figure bronzée par le soleil. 2. B. taste, goût de brûlé. **burning**[1], a. 1. Brûlant, ardent. B. question, question brûlante. 2. B. coals, du charbon embrasé, allumé. B. town, ville incendiée, en feu. 3. B. bush. (i) B: Buisson ardent; (ii) Bot: F: fraxinelle f. '**burning-'hot**, a. Brûlant. **burning**[2], s. 1. Brûlage m; incendie m (d'une maison). B. sensation, (i) sensation de chaleur; (ii) douleur cuisante. There is a smell of b., ça sent le brûlé. 2. (a) Cuite f, cuisson f (de briques, de tuiles). (b) Fournée f.

burn[3], s. Scot: Ruisseau m.

burner ['bəːnər], s. 1. (Pers.) Brûleur, -euse. 2. (a) (Of gas-cooker, etc.) Brûleur. (b) Bec m (de gaz). Bunsen b., bec Bunsen.

burnet ['bəːnit], s. Bot: Grande pimprenelle.

burnish[1] ['bəːniʃ], s. Bruni m, brunissure f.

burnish[2]. 1. v.tr. (a) Brunir; polir, lisser (un métal). (b) Phot: Satiner (une épreuve). 2. v.i. Se polir; prendre de l'éclat. **burnishing**, s. (a) Brunissage m, lissage m. (b) Satinage m.

burnisher ['bəːniʃər], s. 1. (Pers.) (a) Brunisseur m. (b) Satineur m. 2. Tls: Brunissoir m.

burnous(e) [bəː'nuːs], s. Arab Cost: Burnous m.

burp[1] [bəːp], s. U.S: Éructation f, rot m.

burp[2], v.i. U.S: Éructer, roter.

burr[1] [bəːr], s. = BUR.

burr[2], s. 1. Engr: Metalw: Barbe f, bavure f. 2. Ling: Grasseyement m. To speak with a b., grasseyer.

burr[3], v.tr. 1. To b. one's r's, grasseyer. 2. Mater (l'extrémité d'un boulon, etc.); rabattre (un clou).

burrow[1] ['bʌrou], s. Terrier m (de renard, de lapin).

burrow[2]. 1. v.i. (Of rabbits, etc.) (i) Fouir la terre; (ii) (se) terrer. To b. into the archives, fouiller dans les archives. 2. v.tr. To b. one's way underground, creuser un chemin sous terre.

burrower ['bʌrouər], s. (Animal) fouisseur m.

bursar ['bəːsər], s. 1. Sch: Économe m; intendant, -ante. 2. (Esp. in Scot.) Boursier, -ière.

bursary ['bəːsəri], s. 1. Économat m, intendance f. 2. Bourse f (d'études).

burst[1] [bəːst], s. 1. Éclatement m, explosion f (d'une bombe, etc.). (Aerobatics) Bomb b., éclatement m d'une formation. 2. Jaillissement m, jet m (de flamme); coup m (de tonnerre); éclat m (de rire); salve f (d'applaudissements). B. of activity, emballement m; poussée f d'activité. B. of gun-fire, rafale f. B. (of a machine-gun), F: giclée f. Sp: B. of speed, emballage m. Final b., finish m.

burst[2], *v.* (burst; burst) **1.** *v.i.* (*a*) (*Of boiler, bomb, etc.*) Éclater, exploser, faire explosion; (*of boiler*) sauter; (*of abscess*) crever, percer; (*of bubble, tyre*) crever; (*of bud*) éclore. **To b. in pieces,** voler en éclats. (*b*) **The sacks were bursting,** les sacs étaient pleins à crever; les sacs regorgeaient. **To be bursting with laughter,** crever de rire. **To be bursting with health,** déborder, regorger, de santé. **Bursting with impatience,** bouillant d'impatience. **I was bursting to tell him so,** je mourais d'envie de le lui dire. (*c*) **A cry b. from his lips,** un cri s'échappa de ses lèvres. (*d*) (*Of flower*) **To b. into bloom,** fleurir, s'épanouir. **The horses b. into a gallop,** les chevaux prirent le galop. **To b. into tears,** fondre en larmes. *S.a.* FLAME[1] 1, SONG 1. (*e*) **To b. into a room,** entrer dans une pièce en coup de vent. (*Of sun*) **To b. through a cloud,** percer un nuage. (*f*) **To b. upon s.o.'s sight,** se présenter, se découvrir, aux yeux de qn. **The truth b. (in) upon me,** soudain la vérité m'apparut. **2.** *v.tr.* Faire éclater (qch.); crever, éclater (un ballon); faire sauter (une chaudière); rompre (ses liens). **To b. a door open,** enfoncer, briser, une porte. *F:* **He nearly b. a blood-vessel,** il a failli crever d'un coup de sang. *Bac:* **Bursting factor,** facteur déchainant. **burst asunder.** *Lit:* **1.** *v.tr.* Rompre (ses liens). **2.** *v.i.* Se rompre. **burst forth,** *v.i.* (*Of sun*) Se montrer tout à coup; (*of tears*) jaillir. **To b. forth into explanations,** se répandre en explications. **burst in. 1.** *v.tr.* Enfoncer (une porte). **2.** *v.i.* Faire irruption; (*of pers.*) entrer en coup de vent. **burst open. 1.** *v.tr.* Enfoncer (une porte); faire sauter (le couvercle). **2.** *v.i.* (*Of door*) S'ouvrir tout d'un coup. **burst out,** *v.i.* (*Of pers.*) S'écrier, s'exclamer; (*of liquid*) jaillir. **To b. out laughing,** éclater, pouffer, de rire. **bursting,** *s.* Éclatement *m*, explosion *f* (d'une chaudière); crevaison *f* (de pneu); rupture *f* (de liens).

Burton ['bə:tn]. **1.** *Pr.n. Geog:* Burton (sur le Trent). **2.** *s.* B.(ale), bière *f* de Burton. *P:* **He's gone for a B.,** il est mort, manquant; *Av: F:* il a fait un trou dans l'eau.

bury ['beri], *v.tr.* (*p.p. & p.t.* buried) Enterrer, inhumer, ensevelir (un mort); enfouir (une bête). **To b. at sea,** immerger. **Buried in the ruins,** enseveli sous les décombres. **To b. one's face in one's hands,** se couvrir la figure de ses mains. **To b. oneself in one's studies,** s'enfermer dans ses études. *F:* **To b. oneself,** se reléguer (à la campagne, etc.). **I found it buried under my papers,** je l'ai trouvé enfoui sous mes papiers. **burying**[1], *s.* **burying beetle,** *s. Ent:* Nécrophore *m.* **burying**[2], *s.* **1.** Enterrement *m*; ensevelissement *m.* **2.** Enfouissement *m.*

bus[1], *pl.* buses [bʌs, 'bʌsiz], *s.* (Country-) b., car *m.* **Double decker b.,** autobus à impériale. **We went there by b.,** nous y sommes allés en autobus. **To miss the b.,** (i) manquer, rater, l'autobus (ii) *F:* laisser échapper l'occasion, manquer le coche. *P.N:* **All buses stop here,** arrêt obligatoire (de l'autobus). **School b. service,** service *m* de ramassage des écoliers. *Aut: F:* **My old b.,** ma vieille bagnole. *Av: P:* Coucou *m.* *S.a.* STATION[1] 3, CONDUCTOR 1, DRIVER 1.

bus[2], *v.i.* (bussed) Aller en autobus. **2.** *v.tr. U.S: F:* **To b. the dishes,** desservir la table (dans un restaurant).

busboy ['bʌsbɔi], *s. U.S:* Aide-serveur *m* (dans un restaurant).

busby ['bʌzbi], *s.* Bonnet *m* de hussard; colback *m.*

bush[1] [buʃ], *s.* **1.** (*a*) Buisson *m*; (*of lilac, etc.*) arbrisseau *m.* Rose-b., rosier *m.* **Raspberry-b.,** framboisier *m.* (*b*) Fourré *m*, taillis *m. S.a.* BEAT[2] 1. **To grow into a b.,** buissonner. **2.** *A:* (*Vintner's*) Bouchon *m. S.a.* WINE[1]. **3.** (*Africa, Austr.*) The b., la brousse. 'bush baby, *s. Z:* Galago *m.* 'bush-fighter, *s.* Guérillero *m.* 'bush-fighting, *s.* Guerre *f* de buissons, d'embuscades. 'bush-ranger, *s.* **1.** *U.S:* Trappeur *m.* **2.** (*In Austr.*) Brigand *m* (réfugié dans la brousse). 'bush-shirt, *s.* = Saharienne *f.* 'bush 'telegraph, *s. F:* Téléphone *m* arabe.

bush[2], *s. Mec.E:* Fourrure *f* métallique; bague *f*; coussinet *m* (de palier).

bush[3], *v.tr. Mec.E:* Baguer, manchonner; mettre coussinet à (un palier). **bushing,** *s.* **1.** Manchonnage, *m.* **2.** Manchon *m*; coussinet *m* métallique; douille *f*, bague *f.*

bushed [buʃt], *a.* (*In Austr.*) (*a*) Perdu, égaré, dans la brousse. (*b*) *F:* Désorienté, interdit.

bushel ['buʃl], *s.* Boisseau *m* (= *approx.* 36 litres).

bushman, *pl.* -men ['buʃmən], *s.* **1.** *Ethn:* (*In S. Africa*) Boschiman *m.* **2.** Colon *m* (de la brousse australienne).

bushy ['buʃi], *a.* Touffu; épais, -aisse; buissonneux, -euse, broussailleux, -euse. **B. beard,** barbe fournie.

busily [bizili], *adv.* **1.** Activement, avec empressement, d'un air affairé. **2.** Avec trop de zèle.

business ['biznis], *s.* **1.** (*a*) Affaire *f*, besogne *f*, occupation *f*, devoir *m.* **To make it one's b. to do sth.,** se faire un devoir, se mettre en devoir, de faire qch. **To have b. with s.o.,** avoir affaire avec qn. **That's the manager's b.,** ça c'est l'affaire du gérant. **It is my b. to . . . ,** c'est à moi de. . . . **It's none of your b.,** ce n'est pas votre affaire; cela ne vous regarde pas. **What b. had you to tell him so?** était-ce à vous de le lui dire? *F:* **To send s.o. about his b.,** envoyer promener qn. *S.a.* MIND[2] 2. **It's a bad, a sorry, b.,** c'est une malheureuse affaire. (*b*) **B. meeting,** séance de travail (d'une société). **The b. before the meeting,** l'agenda *m*; l'ordre *m* du jour. **2.** (*a*) **Les affaires *f.* B. is b.,** les affaires sont les affaires. **To set up in b. as a grocer,** s'établir épicier. **To go into b.,** entrer dans les affaires. **To follow a b.,** exercer un métier. **To do b. with s.o.,** faire des affaires avec qn. **To give up b.,** se retirer des affaires. He is in b. for himself, il travaille à son compte. **Piece of b.,** affaire; opération (commerciale). **To mean b.,** avoir des intentions sérieuses; ne pas plaisanter. *Attrib.* **B. hours,** heures d'ouverture, d'affaires, des affaires. **B. house,** maison de commerce. **B. man,** homme d'affaires. **Big b. man,** brasseur *m* d'affaires. *F:* **The b. end of a chisel,** le tranchant *m* d'un ciseau. (*b*) **Fonds *m* de commerce. Manager of two different businesses,** directeur de deux établissements différents. **3.** *Th:* Jeux *mpl* de scène. **4.** Métier *m.* **To make a b. of one's religion,** faire métier de sa religion. 'business girl, *s.f.* (Jeune) employée de bureau, de magasin, etc. 'business-like, *a.* **1.** (*Of pers.*) Capable; pratique; (*of transaction*) régulier, sérieux. **2.** (*Of style*) Net, précis; (*of manner*) sérieux, carré. 'business suit, *s. U.S: Cost:* Complet veston *m* (de ville).

busman, *pl.* -men ['bʌsmən], *s.m.* (i) Conducteur (d'autobus); (ii) (= *conductor*) receveur. *F:* **To take a busman's holiday,** faire du métier en guise de congé ou de loisirs.

bust[1] [bʌst], *s.* **1.** *Sculp:* Buste *m.* **2.** Buste, gorge *f*, poitrine *f* (de femme).

bust[2], *P:* **1.** *a.* **To be completely b.,** être sans le sou. **To go b.,** faire faillite. **2.** *s.* **To go on the b.,** faire la bombe. **3.** *v.tr. Mil:* **To b. (a sergeant),** rétrograder (un sergent). 'bust-up, *s. P:* Rupture *f.* **They've had a b.-up,** ils ont rompu.

bustard ['bʌstəd], *s. Orn:* Outarde *f.*

buster ['bʌstər], *s. U.S:* **1.** *P:* Chose *f* énorme. (*b*) Mensonge *m* énorme. **2.** (Bronco-) buster, dresseur *m* de chevaux.

bustle[1] ['bʌsl], *s.* Remue-ménage *m.*

bustle[2]. **1.** *v.i.* **To b. (about),** se remuer, s'activer, s'affairer; faire l'empressé. **They b. in and out,** ils entrent et sortent d'un air affairé. **2.** *v.tr.* Faire dépêcher (qn). **To b. s.o. out of the house,** pousser qn dehors. **bustling,** *a.* Affairé; agissant, allant; empressé.

bustle[3], *s. Cost: A:* Tournure *f* (de derrière de jupe).

busy[1] ['bizi]. **1.** *a.* (busier, busiest) Affairé, occupé; actif, allant; empêché. **B. day,** jour chargé. **B. street,** rue mouvementée, passante. **To be b. with, over, sth.,** être occupé à, de, qch. **To be b. doing sth.,** être occupé à faire qch.; être en train de faire qch. **To keep oneself b.,** s'activer. *F:* **To get b.,** se mettre à la tâche; s'y mettre. **To look b.,** faire l'empêché. *F:* **Get b.!** Grouille-toi! **2.** *s. P:* Agent *m*, ou inspecteur *m* de la Sûreté; détective *m.*

busy[2], *v.tr. & pr.* **To b. oneself, one's hands, with sth.,** s'occuper à, se mêler de, qch. **To b. oneself (with) doing sth.,** s'occuper à, de, faire qch.

busybody ['bizibɔdi], *s.* Officieux, -euse; important *m*, la mouche du coche.

but [bʌt]. **1.** *conj.* (a) Mais. **A rich b. honest family,** une famille riche mais honnête. **B. I tell you I saw it!** (mais) puisque je vous dis que je l'ai vu! **B. yet . . .,** néanmoins . . ., toutefois. . . . (b) (*Subordinating*) O: **I never pass there b. I think of you,** je ne passe jamais par-là sans penser à vous. **Never a year passes b. he writes to us,** il ne se passe jamais une année qu'il ne nous écrive. **Who knows b. that he may come?** qui sait s'il ne viendra pas? **I cannot b. believe that . . .,** il m'est impossible de ne pas croire que. . . . (c) (*Intensive*) **Not only once, b. twice,** par deux fois. **2.** *adv.* Ne . . . que; seulement. **She is b. a child,** ce n'est qu'une enfant. **He talks b. little,** il parle assez peu. **One can b. try,** on peut toujours essayer. **B. a moment ago,** il n'y a qu'un instant. **B. yesterday,** pas plus tard qu'hier. **Had I b. known! si j'avais su! If I could b. see him!** si je pouvais seulement le voir! *S.a.* ALL 2. **3.** *conj. or prep.* (*Except*). (a) **Who will do it b. me?** qui le fera si ce n'est moi, sinon moi? **All b. he, b. him,** tous excepté lui; tous sauf lui. **None b. he,** personne d'autre que lui. **Anyone b. me,** tout autre que moi. **Anything b. that,** tout plutôt que cela. **He is anything b. a hero,** il n'est rien moins qu'un héros. **There is nothing for it b. to obey,** il n'y a qu'à obéir. **What could I do b. invite him?** que pouvais-je faire d'autre que de l'inviter? **2.** (b) **B. for,** sans. **B. for you I was done for,** sans vous j'étais perdu. **B. for that, à part cela;** excepté cela. **4.** *s.* **There is a b.,** il y a un mais. **There are no buts about it,** il n'y a pas d'objections; pas d'objection!

butane ['bjuːtein], *s. Ch:* Butane *m.*

butcher[1] ['butʃər], *s.* **1.** (a) Boucher *m.* **The b.'s wife,** la bouchère. **B.'s boy,** garçon boucher. **B.'s shop, trade,** boucherie *f.* (b) *F:* Boucher, massacreur *m.* (c) *F:* Chirurgien incompétent; *P:* charcutier *m.* **2.** *U.S: Th: Rail:* Vendeur *m* (de fruits, cigarettes, etc.).

butcher[2], *v.tr.* **1.** *U.S:* Abattre (des bêtes de boucherie). **2.** Égorger, massacrer. **3.** *F:* Massacrer, saboter (un travail, une symphonie). (*Of surgeon*) **To b. a patient,** charcuter un patient. **butchering,** *s.* Tuerie *f*, massacre *m* (of, de).

butchery ['butʃəri], *s.* **1.** (*Trade*) Boucherie *f.* **2.** *F:* Tuerie *f*, boucherie, massacre *m.*

butler ['bʌtlər], *s.* Maître *m* d'hôtel (d'une maison privée).

butt[1] [bʌt], *s.* (a) Barrique *f*, futaille *f*; gros tonneau. (b) Tonneau *m* (pour l'eau de pluie).

butt[2], *s.* **1.** Bout *m*; souche *f* (d'arbre, de chèque); bout, *P:* mégot *m* (de cigare, cigarette). *Join: etc:* **B. and b.,** bout à bout. **2.** Gros bout, talon *m* (d'une canne à pêche). **3.** *Bill:* Masse *f*, talon (de la queue). **4.** *Sm.a:* Crosse *f* (de fusil). **5.** Poisson plat. **'butt-end,** *s.* Extrémité inférieure; pied *m*; gros bout. **'butt-joint,** *s. Carp: Mec.E: etc:* Assemblage *m* bout à bout; joint *m* en about.

butt[3], *s.* **1.** *Mil:* (*Stop-butt*) Butte *f.* **The butts,** le champ de tir. **2.** (*Thing aimed at*) But *m*, cible *f. Esp.* (*Of pers.*) Souffre-douleur *m inv.* **To be a b. for s.o.'s jokes,** servir de plastron à qn, être la tête de turc de qn.

butt[4], *s.* Coup *m* de (la) tête; coup de corne (d'un bélier, etc.).

butt[5], *v.i. & tr.* **To b. (into, against) sth.,** donner du front, buter, contre qch. (*Of ram, etc.*) **To b. (at) s.o.,** donner un coup de corne à qn. *F:* **To b. into the conversation, to b. in,** intervenir sans façon (dans la conversation).

butter[1] ['bʌtər], *s.* Beurre *m.* **B. factory,** beurrerie *f.* **Whiting with melted b.,** merlan sauce au beurre. **With brown b. sauce,** au beurre noir. *F:* **B. wouldn't melt in her mouth,** elle fait la sainte nitouche, la sucrée. **'butter-bean,** *s. Hort:* Haricot *m* beurre. **'butter-cloth, -muslin,** *s.* Étamine *f.* **'butter-cooler,** *s.* Beurrier rafraîchissant. **'butter-dish,** *s.* Beurrier *m.* **'butter-fingered,** *a. F:* Maladroit, empoté. **'butter-fingers,** *s. F:* Maladroit, -e; empoté, -ée; *F:* brise-tout *m inv.* **'butter-knife,** *s.* Couteau *m* à beurre. **'butter-paper,** *s.* Papier sulfurisé; papier beurre. **'butter-pat,** *s. Dom.Ec:* **1.** Palette *f*, spatule *f*, à beurre. **2.** Médaillon *m* de beurre. **'butter(-)scotch,** *s.* Caramel *m* au beurre.

butter[2], *v.tr.* Beurrer (du pain). *S.a.* BREAD. *F:* **To b. s.o. up,** flatter, pateliner qn.

buttercup ['bʌtəkʌp], *s. Bot:* Renoncule *f* des champs; *F:* bouton m d'or.

butterfat ['bʌtəfæt], *s.* Matière grasse. **The b. content of milk,** la teneur du lait en matière grasse.

butterfly ['bʌtəflai], *s.* **1.** *Ent:* Papillon *m. Swim:* **B. (stroke), (nage *f*)** papillon. *S.a.* BOW[1] 3. **2.** *F:* Personne *f* frivole; papillon.

buttermilk ['bʌtəmilk], *s.* Babeurre *m*, petit-lait *m.*

buttery ['bʌtəri], *s. Sch:* Dépense *f*, office *f.*

buttock ['bʌtək], *s.* **1.** (a) Fesse *f.* (b) *pl.* **The buttocks,** le derrière, le postérieur, les fesses. (c) *Cu:* Culotte *f* (de bœuf). **2.** *pl.* Croupe *f* (de cheval, de bœuf).

button[1] ['bʌtn], *s.* **1.** Bouton *m* (pour attacher). **Bachelor's buttons,** boutons automatiques (pour vêtements). *F:* **Buttons,** chasseur *m* (d'hôtel, de club); groom *m.* **2.** (a) Bouton(-poussoir) *m* (de sonnerie électrique, etc.). *F:* **You've only to press the b.,** ça se fait tout seul; c'est automatique. (b) Bouton, mouche *f* (de fleuret). (c) **B. mushroom,** champignon *m* encore en bouton.

button[2], *v.tr.* **1.** (a) **To b. (up) sth.,** boutonner qch. *F:* **Buttoned up mouth,** bouche cousue. (b) (*With passive force*) **Dress that buttons behind,** robe qui se boutonne par derrière. **2.** *Fenc:* Moucheter (une épée).

buttonhole[1] ['bʌtnhoul], *s.* **1.** Boutonnière *f.* **To wear a b.,** porter une fleur à sa boutonnière. **B. stitch,** point de feston, de boutonnière. **2.** *Surg:* Boutonnière; petite incision.

buttonhole[2], *v.tr. F:* **To b. s.o.,** retenir, cramponner, accrocher, qn (au passage).

buttress[1] ['bʌtris], *s. Const:* Contrefort *m*, contreboutant *m. S.a.* FLYING-BUTTRESS.

buttress[2], *v.tr. Const:* Arc-bouter, étayer.

buxom ['bʌksəm], *a.* (Femme) fraîche et rondelette; grassouillette.

buxomness ['bʌksəmnis], *s.* Ampleur *f* de formes; fraîcheur *f* robuste (d'une femme).

buy [bai]. **1.** *v.tr.* (**bought; bought**) Acheter (*sth. from, of, s.o.,* qch. à qn); prendre (un billet de chemin de fer, etc.). **I bought this horse cheap,** j'ai eu ce cheval à bon marché. **Money cannot b. it,** cela ne se paie pas. **A dearly bought advantage,** un avantage chèrement payé. **To b. s.o. sth.,** acheter qch. à, pour, qn. *F:* **I'll b. it!** je donne ma langue au chat! *P:* **He has bought it,** il est foutu. *S.a.* PIG. **2.** *s. F:* Achat *m*, affaire *f.* **It's a good b.,** c'est un bon placement, une bonne affaire. **buy back,** *v.tr.* Racheter. **buying back,** *s.* Rachat *m.* **buy in,** *v.tr.* **1.** (*At auction sales*) Racheter (pour le compte du vendeur). **2.** S'approvisionner de (denrées, etc.). **buy off,** *v.tr.* Se débarrasser de (qn) en lui payant une somme d'argent; *F:* acheter (qn). **buy out,** *v.tr.* Désintéresser (un associé). **buy over,** *v.tr.* Corrompre, acheter (qn). **buy up,** *v.tr.* Rafler, accaparer (des denrées, etc.). **buying up,** *s.* Accaparement *m.*

buyer ['baiər], *s.* **1.** Acheteur, -euse; acquéreur *m.* **2.** *Com:* Chef *m* de rayon.

buzz[1] [bʌz], *s.* Bourdonnement *m*, vrombissement *m* (d'un insecte); brouhaha *m* (de conversations). *W.Tel:* Ronflement *m*; (bruits *mpl* de) friture *f. Tp:* **I'll give you a b.,** je vous passerai un coup de téléphone. **'buzz-saw,** *s. U.S:* Scie *f* circulaire.

buzz[2]. **1.** *v.i.* Bourdonner, vrombir. **My ears were buzzing,** les oreilles me tintaient. **2.** *v.tr.* (a) *F:* Lancer (une pierre, etc.). (b) *Av:* Harceler (un avion). (c) *F: U.S:* Téléphoner à qn. (d) *P:* **Let's b. the bottle,** vidons la bouteille. **buzz about, around,** *v.i. F:* S'activer; faire l'empressé. **buzz off,** *v.i. P:* Décamper, filer, se tailler. **buzzing,** *s.* = BUZZ[1]. **B. in the ears,** tintement *m* des oreilles; *Med:* bourdonnement *m.*

buzzard ['bʌzəd], *s. Orn:* Buse *f*, busard *m.*

buzzer ['bʌzər], *s.* (a) *Nau: Ind:* Sirène *f.* (b) *El: Tp:* Vibreur *m*, vibrateur *m.* **B. call,** appel vibré.

by [bai]. **I.** *prep.* **1.** (*Near*) (a) (Au)près de, à côté de. **Sitting by the fire,** assis près du feu. **By the sea,** au bord de la mer. **By oneself,** seul; à l'écart. **He kept by himself,** il se tenait à l'écart. **I have no**

money by me, (i) je n'ai pas d'argent sous la main; (ii) je n'ai pas d'argent disponible. (b) North by East, Nord quart nord-est. **2.** (*Along, via*) Par. By land and sea, par terre et par mer. **3.** (*Agency, means*) (a) Par, de. To be punished by s.o., être puni par qn. To die by one's own hand, mourir de ses propres mains. Made by hand, by machine, fait à la main, à la machine. Known by the name of X, connu sous le nom d'X. By force, de force. By (an) error, par suite d'une erreur. By chance, par hasard. To do sth. (all) by oneself, faire qch. (tout) seul. Three feet by two, trois pieds sur deux. To travel by rail, voyager par le, *F:* en, chemin de fer. By tram, by car, by motor cycle, by mule, en tramway, en auto, à motocyclette, à dos de mulet. (b) (*With gerund*) By doing that you will offend him, en faisant cela vous l'offenserez. What do you gain by doing that? que gagnez-vous à faire cela? We shall lose nothing by waiting, nous ne perdrons rien pour attendre. **4.** By rote, par routine. By right, de droit. By rights, de toute justice. By the clock it is three, d'après l'horloge il est trois heures. To judge by appearances, juger sur l'apparence. By (the terms of) article 5 . . ., aux termes, selon les termes, de l'article 5. . . . To sell sth. by the pound, vendre qch. à la livre. **5.** By degrees, par degrés. By turn(s), tour à tour. One by one, un à un. By twos and threes, par deux ou trois. **6.** By day, de jour, le jour. **7.** (*Of point in time*) He will be here by three o'clock, il sera ici avant, pour, trois heures. By Monday, d'ici lundi. He ought to be here by now, by this time, il devrait être déjà ici. **8.** Longer by two feet, plus long de deux pieds. By far, de beaucoup. **9.** I know him by name, by sight, je le connais de nom, de vue. He is a grocer by trade, il est épicier de son métier. To do one's duty by s.o., faire son devoir envers qn. *F:* Is that all right by you? Cela vous va-t-il? **10.** (*In oaths*) By God, au nom de Dieu. To swear by all one holds sacred, jurer par tout ce qu'on a de plus sacré. **II. by,** *adv.* **1.** Près. Close by, hard by, tout près, ici près, tout à côté. *Nau:* By and large! près et plein! *F:* Taking it by and large . . ., à tout prendre. . . . **2.** (*Aside*) To lay, set, put, sth. by, mettre qch. de côté. **3.** (*Past*) To go, pass, by, passer. The time is gone by when . . ., le temps est passé où. . . . **4.** *Adv.phr.* By and by, tout à l'heure, bientôt, tantôt. By the by(e) . . ., à propos. . . .

III. by(e¹), *a.* By(e) effect, effet secondaire, indirect; contre-coup *m.* '**by-election,** *s. Pol:* Élection partielle. '**by(-)pass¹,** *s.* **1.** *Mch: etc:* Conduit *m* de dérivation. B.-p. **engine,** turboréacteur *m* double flux. **2.** (*Of gas burner*) Veilleuse *f.* **3.** *Aut: etc:* B.-p. (road), route *f* d'évitement, de contournement, déviation *f. Civ.E: Mil:* Rocade *f.* **4.** *W.Tel:* Filtre *m* B.-p. **condenser,** condensateur shunté. '**by(-)pass²,** *v.tr.* **1.** (a) *Mch:* Amener (la vapeur, etc.) en dérivation. (b) *W.Tel:* Filtrer (un poste émetteur). **2.** (a) (*Of road or pers.*) Contourner, éviter (une ville, etc.). (b) To b-p. the traffic, dévier la circulation. '**by(-)path,** *s.* Sentier écarté, détourné. '**by-product,** *s. Ind:* Sous-produit *m;* produit secondaire; dérivé *m.* '**by-road,** *s.* (a) Chemin détourné. (b) Chemin vicinal. '**by(-)street,** *s.* Rue écartée; ruelle *f.* '**by(-)way,** *s.* Chemin détourné, voie indirecte. B.-ways of history, à-côtés *m* de l'histoire.

bye² [bai], *s.* **1.** *Cr:* Balle passée. **2.** *Sp:* (*Of player*) To have a b., être exempt (d'une épreuve dans un tournoi).

bye-bye ['bai'bai]. **1.** *int. F:* Adieu! au revoir! **2.** *s. F:* To go to bye-byes, aller faire dodo.

by(e)-law ['bailɔː], *s.* (a) Statut *m* émanant d'une autorité locale; arrêté municipal. (b) *U.S:* Règlement (d'une Société).

Byelorussia [bi:'elou'rʌʃə]. *Pr.n. Geog:* Biélorussie *f,* Russie Blanche.

bygone ['baigɔn]. **1.** *a.* Passé, écoulé, ancien, d'autrefois. In b. days, dans l'ancien temps. **2.** *s.pl.* Let bygones be bygones, oublions le passé; passons l'éponge (là-dessus).

by-play ['baiplei], *s. Th:* Jeu *m* accessoire; aparté mimé.

byre ['baiər], *s.* Vacherie *f;* étable *f* à vaches.

Byronic [bai'rɔnik], *a.* Byronien.

bystander ['baistændər], *s.* Assistant *m;* spectateur, -trice.

byword [baiwəːd], *s.* **1.** Proverbe *m,* dicton *m.* **2.** To be the b. of the village, être la fable, la risée, du village.

Byzantine [bi'zæntain, bai'zæntain], *a. & s.* Byzantin, -ine.

Byzantium [bi'zænʃiəm, bai'zæntiəm]. *Pr.n. Geog:* Byzance *f.*

C, c [si:]. **1.** (La lettre) C, c m. *Tp:* C for Charlie, C comme Célestin. C.-spring, ressort m en C. **2.** *Mus:* Ut m, do m. **In C sharp,** en ut dièse. **3.** *Mil:* F: **C.B.,** *see* BARRACK[1] 1. **4.** A C3 man, homme classé dans la dernière catégorie par le conseil de révision. F: C3 nation, nation aveulie.

cab [kæb], s. **1.** Voiture f de place. (a) A: Fiacre m. (b) A: Hansom c., cab m. (c) Taxi m. **To call a c.,** héler un taxi; faire avancer un taxi. **2.** Guérite f, cabine f (de conducteur de camion, etc.); abri m, poste m de conduite (de locomotive). 'cab-driver, s. = CABMAN. 'cab-rank, s. Station f de, pour, taxis.

cabal[1] [kə'bæl], s. **1.** Cabale f, brigue f. **2.** Coterie f.

cabal[2], v.i. (caballed) Cabaler, comploter.

cabaret ['kæbərei], s. **1.** Cabaret m (genre montmartrois). **2.** C. (show), concert m genre music-hall (donné dans un restaurant, etc.); attractions fpl.

cabbage ['kæbidʒ], s. **1.** Chou m, pl. choux. Garden c., chou pommé, chou cabus. 'cabbage(-)lettuce, s. Laitue pommée. 'cabbage-patch, s. Carré m, plant m, de choux. 'cabbage-stump, s. Trognon m de chou. 'cabbage 'white (butterfly), s. Ent: Piéride f du chou; papillon blanc du chou.

cab(b)ala ['kæbələ], s. Jew.Rel.H: Cabale f.

cab(b)alist ['kæbəlist], s. Cabaliste mf.

cab(b)alistic [,kæbə'listik], a. Cabalistique.

cabby ['kæbi], s. F: **1.** A: Cocher m (de fiacre). **2.** O: Chauffeur de taxi.

caber ['keibər], s. Sp: Tronc m de mélèze, de pin, ou de sapin. **Tossing the c.,** sport écossais qui consiste à lancer le tronc (tenu verticalement par le petit bout) de manière à le faire retomber aussi loin que possible sur le gros bout.

cabin[1] ['kæbin], s. **1.** (a) Cabane f, case f. (b) Rail: Guérite f, cabine f (de signaux); vigie f. (c) El.Rail: Driver's c., loge f; poste m de conduite. **2.** (a) Nau: Cabine. (b) Av: Carlingue f. Pressurized c., cabine pressurisée. 'cabin-boy, s.m. Nau: Mousse. 'cabin-class, s. Nau: Classe f cabine. 'cabin-trunk, s. Malle f (de) cabine; malle (de) paquebot.

cabinet ['kæbinit], s. **1.** (a) Meuble m à tiroirs. Music-c., casier m à musique. (b) Wireless c., coffret m, ébénisterie f, de poste de radio. (c) Glass c., vitrine f. **2.** (a) A: Petite chambre; cabinet m. (b) Pol: Cabinet, ministère m. **C. minister,** ministre d'État. **C. crisis,** crise ministérielle. **3.** Phot: C. size, format album. 'cabinet-maker, s. Ébéniste m. 'cabinet-work, s. Ébénisterie f.

cable[1] [keibl], s. **1.** Nau: etc: Câble m. C.('s)-length (one-tenth of a nautical mile, = 185.2 m.), encâblure f. **2.** Nau: Chaîne f (d'ancre). **3.** El.E: Câble. **To lay a c.,** poser un câble. **4.** = CABLEGRAM. 'cable-laying, s. Pose f de câbles sous-marins. 'cable(-)railway, s. Funiculaire m. 'cable(-)re'lease, s. Phot: Déclencheur m. 'cable(-)ship, s. Câblier m. 'cable(-)stitch, s. Knitting: Point natté m.

cable[2], v.tr. Câbler (un message). Abs. To c. (to) s.o., câbler à qn; aviser qn par câble.

cablegram ['keiblgræm], s. Câblogramme m.

cableway ['keiblwei], s. Blondin m.

cabman, pl. -men ['kæbmən], s.m. **1.** A: Cocher de fiacre. **2.** O: Chauffeur de taxi.

cabochon [kə'bouʃon], s. Lap: Cabochon m.

caboodle [kə'bu:dl], s. P: The whole c., tout le bazar; tout le tremblement.

caboose [kə'bu:s], s. **1.** Nau: Cambuse f. **2.** Rail: U.S: Wagon-frein m, pl. wagons-freins; fourgon m. **3.** Cabane f, hutte f.

cabstand ['kæbstænd], s. U.S: = CAB-RANK.

ca'canny ['ka:'kæni]. **1.** int. Scot: Allez-y doucement! **2.** v.i. F: To c., travailler sans se (la) fouler; Ind: faire la grève perlée.

cacao [kə'ka:ou, kə'keiou], s. **1.** C.(-bean), cacao m. **2.** Cacaotier m.

cachalot ['kæʃələt], s. Z: Cachalot m.

cache [kæʃ], s. Cache f, cachette f (d'explorateur).

cachectic [kə'kektik], a. Med: Cachectique.

cachet ['kæʃei], s. **1.** (Of a work, etc.) To have a certain c., avoir un certain cachet. **2.** (i) Cachet (d'aspirine); (ii) capsule f (d'huile de foie de morue).

cachexy [kə'keksi], s. Med: Cachexie f.

cachou [kə'ʃu:], s. Cachou m.

cack [kæk], s. P: Caca m.

cackle[1] ['kækl], s. **1.** (Of hen, F: of pers.) Caquet m. P: **Cut your c.!** en voilà assez! **2.** Ricanement m; rire saccadé.

cackle[2], v.i. **1.** (Of hen) Caqueter. **2.** Ricaner; faire entendre un petit rire sec. **cackling. 1.** a. C. (laughter), (rire) saccadé. **2.** s. Caquetage m; ricanement m.

cackler ['kæklər], s. **1.** Poule f qui caquette. **2.** F: (Pers.) (a) Caqueteur, -euse. (b) Ricaneur, -euse.

cacophony [kæ'kɔfəni], s. Cacophonie f.

cactus ['kæktəs], s. Bot: Cactus m, cactier m.

cad [kæd], s.m. **1.** Goujat, pleutre, cuistre. **2.** Canaille f; P: fripouille f, arsouille m.

cadastral [kə'dæstrəl], a. Cadastral, -aux. C. survey, cadastre m.

cadaveric [kə'dæverik], a. (Rigidité) cadavérique.

cadaverous [kə'dævərəs], a. Cadavéreux, -euse.

caddie[1] ['kædi], s. Golf: Cadet m, caddie m.

caddie[2], v.i. Golf: Servir de cadet (for s.o., à qn).

caddis ['kædis], s. C.(-fly), phrygane f. C.(-worm), Fish: c.-bait, larve f de phrygane.

caddish ['kædiʃ], a. F: Voyou, arsouille.

caddishness ['kædiʃnis], s. Goujaterie f.

caddy ['kædi], s. (Tea-)c., boîte f à thé.

cadence ['keid(ə)ns], s. **1.** Cadence f, rythme m, battement m. **2.** Mus: Cadence. **3.** C. of the voice, (i) chute f de la voix; (ii) intonation f.

cadet [kə'det], s.m. **1.** A: (Younger son) Cadet. **2.** (a) Élève d'une école militaire; cadet. (b) Sch: Élève de la préparation militaire. C. corps, préparation f militaire.

cadge [kædʒ], v.tr. & i. **1.** A: Colporter. **2.** (a) Mendier. (b) Écornifler, chiner (qch.). F: To c. sth. from s.o., taper qn de qch.

cadger ['kædʒər], s.m. **1.** A: Marchand ambulant; colporteur m. **2.** (a) Mendiant. (b) Écornifleur; chineur.

Cadiz [kə'diz]. Pr.n. Geog: Cadix.

cadmium ['kædmiəm], s. Ch: Cadmium m.

cadre ['ka:dr, kædr], s. **1.** Plan m (d'un ouvrage). **2.** Mil: Cadre m.

caecal ['si:k(ə)l], a. Anat: Cæcal, -aux.

caecum, pl. -a, ['si:kəm, -ə], s. Anat: Cæcum m.

Caesar ['si:zər]. Pr.n.m. Julius C., Jules César.

Caesarean, Caesarian [si(:)'zɛəriən], a. & s. **1.** Hist: Pol: Césarien, -ienne. **2.** Obst: C. operation, section, (opération) césarienne (f).

caesium ['si:ziəm], s. Ch: Césium m.

caesura [si'zjuərə], s. Pros: Césure f.

café ['kæfei], s. Café(-restaurant) m. 'café au lait, attrib.a. (As a colour) Café au lait inv. 'café-'owner, s. Cafetier, -ière.

cafeteria [,kæfi'tiəriə], s. Cafeteria f, F: (Café) libre-service m, pl. libres-services.

caffeine ['kæfi:n], s. Ch: etc: Caféine f. 'caffeine-free, a. Décaféiné.

cage[1] [keidʒ], s. **1.** Cage f. **2.** (a) Cabine f (d'ascenseur). (b) Min: Shaft-c., cage de puits. 'cage-bird, s. Oiseau m de volière, d'appartement.

cage[2], v.tr. Encager; mettre (un oiseau) en cage.

cagey ['keidʒi], a. F: Prudent, circonspect, défiant; cauteleux, précautionneux. My father was c. about his age, mon père cachait astucieusement son âge.

cahoot [kə'hu:t], s. U.S: F: To be in c.(s) with s.o., être d'intelligence avec qn, F: être de mèche avec qn. F: To go cahoot(s) with s.o., partager avec qn.

caiman ['keimən], s. Rept: = CAYMAN.

Cain [kein]. Pr.n.m. B: Caïn. F: To raise C., (i) faire un bruit infernal; (ii) faire une scène (à propos de qch.).

cairn ['kɛən], s. Cairn (commémoratif); mont-joie m, pl. monts-joie; tumulus m de pierres.

Cairo ['kaiərou]. Pr.n. Geog: Le Caire.

caisson ['keis(ə)n], s. Hyd.E: Caisson m, bâtardeau m.

caitiff ['keitif], s. A: Misérable m; lâche m.

cajole [kə'dʒoul], v.tr. Cajoler; enjôler. To c. s.o. into doing sth., persuader à qn de faire qch. To c. sth. out of s.o., obtenir qch. de qn à force de cajoleries; soutirer (de l'argent) à qn. **cajoling**, a. Cajoleur, -euse.

cajoler [kə'dʒoulər], s. Cajoleur, -euse.

cajolery [kə'dʒouləri], s. Cajolerie(s) f(pl); enjôlement m.

cake[1] [keik], s. 1. (a) Gâteau m. S.a. CHEESE-CAKE, FRUIT-CAKE, SPONGE-CAKE. F: To take the c., remporter la palme. That takes the c.! c'est la fin des haricots! He takes the c.! à lui le pompon! They're going, selling, like hot cakes, ça se vend comme des petits pains. F: It's a piece of c., c'est en or, c'est du gâteau, c'est donné. (b) (Small) cakes, pâtisserie légère; gâteaux, pâtisseries. (c) Oat-c., galette f d'avoine. (d) Rissole f. S.a. FISH-CAKE. 2. (a) Pain m (de savon, etc.); tablette f (de chocolat). (b) Oil-, linseed-c., tourteau m de lin. Husb: Cattle c., cow c., tourteau. 3. Masse f, croûte f (de sang coagulé); motte f (de terre, etc.); agglutination f (de houille, etc.). 'cake-shop, s. Pâtisserie f.

cake[2], v.i. (a) Former une croûte; faire croûte. (b) (Of coal, etc.) (Se) coller; (se) prendre; s'agglutiner; (of blood, etc.) se cailler. Caked with mud, with blood, plaqué de boue, de sang. **caking**, s. Agglomération f, agglutination f (de la houille); coagulation f (du sang).

calabar ['kæləbɑːr], s. Furs: Petit-gris m.

calabash ['kæləbæʃ], s. Calebasse f, gourde f. C. tree, calebassier m.

Calabria [kə'læbriə]. Pr.n. Geog: La Calabre.

calamar(y) ['kæləmɑː(ri)], s. Moll: Calmar m; encornet m.

calamine ['kæləmain], s. Miner: Calamine f.

calamitous [kə'læmitəs], a. Calamiteux, -euse, désastreux, -euse.

calamity [kə'læmiti], s. 1. Calamité f, infortune f, malheur m. 2. Désastre m; sinistre m.

calamus ['kæləməs], s. Bot: 1. Calamus m, rotin m. 2. Sweet c., jonc odorant.

calcareous [kæl'kɛəriəs], a. Geol: etc: Calcaire.

calceolaria [kælsiə'lɛəriə], s. Bot: Calcéolaire f.

calcification [kælsifi'keiʃ(ə)n], s. Calcification f.

calcify ['kælsifai]. 1. v.tr. Calcifier. (a) Convertir en carbonate de chaux. (b) Pétrifier (le bois). 2. v.i. Se calcifier.

calcination [kælsi'neiʃ(ə)n], s. Ch: Ind: Calcination f; cuisson f; grillage m.

calcine ['kælsain]. 1. v.tr. Calciner; cuire (le gypse, etc.). Metall: Griller (le minerai). 2. v.i. Se calciner.

calcite ['kælsait], s. Miner: Calcite f.

calcium ['kælsiəm], s. Ch: Calcium m. C. carbide, carbure m de calcium.

calculable ['kælkjuləbl], a. Calculable, chiffrable.

calculate ['kælkjuleit], v.tr. & i. 1. (a) Calculer, évaluer; estimer (une distance); calculer, mesurer (ses paroles); faire le compte de (sa fortune). Abs. Faire un calcul; compter. (b) To c. upon sth., on doing sth., compter sur qch.; compter faire qch. 2. U.S: F: Croire, supposer (that, que). **calculated**, a. (a) C. insolence, insolence délibérée, calculée. (b) News c. to astonish him, nouvelle faite pour l'étonner, Words c. to reassure us, paroles propres à nous rassurer. **calculating**[1], a. (Of pers.) Calculateur, -trice; réfléchi. **calculating**[2], s. Calcul m, estimation f. C. machine, machine à calculer.

calculation [kælkju'leiʃ(ə)n], s. Calcul m. To be out in one's calculations, être loin de son compte.

calculator ['kælkjuleitər], s. 1. (Pers.) Calculateur, -trice. 2. Machine f à calculer. 3. Barème m.

calculous ['kælkjuləs], a. Med: Calculeux, -euse.

calculus ['kælkjuləs], s. 1. Med: (pl. calculi ['kælkjulai]) Calcul (vésical, etc.). 2. Mth: Calcul infinitésimal.

Caledonia [kæli'dounjə]. Pr.n. A: La Calédonie, l'Écosse f.

Caledonian [kæli'dounjən], a. & s. Calédonien, -ienne. The C. canal, le Canal calédonien.

calendar ['kælindər], s. 1. Calendrier m. Tear-off c., block-c., calendrier bloc; calendrier éphéméride, à effeuiller. 2. Jur: Liste f des accusés, des causes au criminel; rôle m des assises. U.S: Ordre m du jour (du Congrès).

calender[1] ['kælindər], s. Calandre f.

calender[2], v.tr. Calandrer, cylindrer (des étoffes, etc.). **calendering**, s. Calandrage m.

calends ['kælindz], s.pl. Rom.Ant: Calendes f. On the Greek c., aux calendes grecques.

calf[1], pl. **calves** [kɑːf, kɑːvz], s. 1. (a) Veau m. Cow in, with, c., vache pleine. attrib. C. love, amours enfantines; les premières amours. (b) Leath: Veau; vachette f. S.a. BOX-CALF. 2. (a) Petit m de certains animaux. Whale-c., baleineau m. Elephant-c., éléphanteau m. (b) Glaçon (détaché d'un iceberg); veau. 'calf's-foot jelly, 'calves-foot jelly, s. Cu: Gelée f de pied de veau.

calf[2], pl. **calves**, s. Mollet m (de la jambe).

calfskin ['kɑːfskin], s. (Cuir m de) veau m.

calibrate ['kælibreit], v.tr. Étalonner (un compteur); calibrer (un tube); graduer (un thermomètre); tarer (un ressort).

calibration [kæli'breiʃ(ə)n], s. Étalonnage m; calibrage m (d'un tube); tarage m (d'un ressort).

calibre ['kælibər], s. (a) Calibre m, alésage m (d'un canon, d'un tube). (b) A man of his c., un homme de son calibre, de son envergure.

-calibred ['kælibəd], a. Small[1]-, large-c., de petit, gros, calibre.

calico ['kælikou], s. 1. Tex: (a) Calicot m. Printed c., indienne f. (b) Dressm: Percaline f (pour doublures). 2. a. U.S: Varié, bigarré.

California [kæli'fɔːnjə]. Pr.n. La Californie.

Californian ['kæli'fɔːnjən], a. & s. Californien, -ienne.

californium [kæli'fɔːnjəm], s. Ch: Californium m.

caliper ['kælipər], s. = CALLIPER.

caliph ['keilif], s. Calife m.

caliphate ['kælifeit], s. Califat m.

calk[1] [kɔːk], s. Crampon m (de fer à cheval). Bootm: Crampon à glace.

calk[2], v.tr. Ferrer (un cheval) à glace. **calking**, s. Ferrage m à glace.

call[1] [kɔːl], s. 1. (a) (Shout) Appel m, cri m; cri d'appel. (b) Cri (d'un oiseau). 2. (Summons). (a) Appel. To come at, to answer, s.o.'s c., venir, répondre, à l'appel de qn. To be within c., être à portée de voix. To give s.o. a c., appeler qn. To answer the c. of duty, se rendre à son devoir. You have no c. to do so, vous n'avez aucune raison de le faire. F: To have a close c., l'échapper belle. S.a. BECK[2], BLOOD[1] 1. (b) Mil: Bugle-c., trumpet-c., sonnerie f, coup m, appel, de clairon, de trompette. (c) (Roll-)c., c.-over, appel nominal. (d) He felt a c. (to the ministry), il se sentait la vocation. (e) Tp: Telephone c., appel téléphonique; coup de téléphone. Local c., communication locale, urbaine. Personal, U.S: person-to-person, c., appel m avec préavis. I'll give you a c., je vous téléphonerai. To put a c. through, donner la communication. To pay for twenty calls, payer vingt conversations f. (f) Cards: (At bridge) Appel; (at solo whist) demande f. C. for trumps, invite f d'atout. A c. of three diamonds, une annonce de trois carreaux. (g) Th: Rappel m (d'un acteur). When she took her c., lorsqu'elle parut devant le rideau. 3. Visite f. To pay, make, a c. on s.o., faire (une) visite à qn. To pay calls, faire des visites. Com: Passage m (d'un représentant). F: To pay a c., aller faire pipi, aller faire une petite commission. Nau: Port of c., port d'escale, de relâche. 4. Demande (d'argent). Fin: Appel de fonds, de versement. Payable at c., remboursable sur demande, à présentation, à vue. 'call-box, s. Tp: Cabine f (téléphonique). 'call-boy, s. 1. Th: Avertisseur m. 2.(In hotel) U.S: Chasseur m. 'call-girl, s.f. Prostituée (sur rendez-vous téléphonique), call-girl. 'call-money, s. Com: Fin: Emprunt(s) remboursable(s) sur demande. 'call-number, s. U.S: Fiche f de référence (d'un livre dans une bibliothèque). 'call-sign, s. W.Tel: Av: etc: Indicatif m (d'appel).

call². I. *v.tr.* **1.** (*a*) Appeler (qn); crier (qch.). *Abs.* Who is calling? qui est-ce qui appelle? To c. (out) 'fire,' crier au feu. To c. the banns, publier les bans. To c. a halt, (i) crier halte; (ii) faire halte. To c. the roll, faire l'appel. *Nau:* To c. the soundings, chanter le fond. (*b*) To c. to s.o. to do sth., crier à qn de faire qch. **2.** (*a*) (*Summon*) Appeler (qn); héler (un taxi); convoquer (une assemblée); *U.S:* téléphoner à (qn). *Th:* Rappeler (un acteur). To c. (in) the doctor, faire venir, appeler, le médecin. *Mil:* To c. to arms, battre la générale. To c. into play all one's powers, faire appel à toutes ses facultés. *S.a.* ACCOUNT¹ 2, BAR¹ 3, MIND¹ 1. (*b*) C. me at six o'clock, réveillez-moi à six heures. **3.** He is called John, il s'appelle Jean. To c. s.o. after s.o., donner le nom de qn à qn. To c. oneself a colonel, se qualifier de colonel. To c. s.o. names, injurier, invectiver, qn. To c. s.o. a liar, traiter qn de menteur. *F:* We'll c. it three francs, (i) mettons trois francs; (ii) va pour trois francs. **4.** *Cards:* Appeler, déclarer (deux carreaux, etc.). **5.** To c. a strike, décréter, ordonner, une grève. II. **call**, *v.i.* (*a*) To c. at s.o.'s house, (i) faire une visite chez qn; (ii) passer, se rendre, se présenter, chez qn. Has anyone called? est-il venu quelqu'un? I must c. at the grocer's, il faut que je passe chez l'épicier. To c. again, repasser (on, chez). (*b*) The train calls at every station, le train s'arrête à toutes les gares. *Nau:* (*Of ship*) To c. at a port, faire escale, relâcher, toucher, à un port. **call aside**, *v.tr.* Prendre, tirer, (qn) à part. **call away**, *v.tr.* I am called away on business, je suis obligé de m'absenter pour affaires. **call back. 1.** *v.tr.* Rappeler (qn). **2.** *v.tr.* I called back 'don't forget,' je me suis retourné pour crier "n'oubliez pas." **3.** *v.i.* I shall c. back for it, je repasserai le prendre. **call down**, *v.tr.* (*a*) Faire descendre (qn). (*b*) To c. down curses on s.o.'s head, appeler des malédictions sur la tête de qn. (*c*) *U.S:* Reprendre (qn). **call for**, *v.ind.tr.* (*a*) Appeler, faire venir (qn); faire apporter (qch.); commander (une consommation, etc.). To c. for help, appeler, crier, au secours. (*b*) Venir prendre, venir chercher (qn, qch.). 'To be (left till) called for,' "à laisser jusqu'à ce qu'on vienne le chercher"; *Post:* "poste restante"; *Rail:* "en gare." (*c*) To c. for an explanation, for an apology, demander, exiger, une explication, des excuses. (*d*) Demander, comporter, réclamer, exiger (l'attention, des réformes). **call forth**, *v.tr.* (*a*) Produire, faire naître (des protestations); évoquer (un souvenir); exciter (l'admiration). (*b*) Faire appel à (tout son courage). (*c*) Évoquer (un esprit). **call in**, *v.tr.* **1.** Faire entrer (qn); faire rentrer (les enfants). **2.** Retirer (une monnaie) de la circulation. **3.** To c. in a specialist, faire appel, avoir recours, à un spécialiste. **call off. 1.** *v.tr.* (*a*) Rappeler (un chien). (*b*) To c. off a strike, décommander une grève. To c. off a deal, rompre, annuler, un marché. **2.** *v.i.* Se dédire; revenir sur sa parole. **call on**, *v.i.* **1.** Faire visite chez (qn); passer chez (qn); aller voir (qn). To c. on s.o. again, repasser chez qn. **2.** = CALL UPON. **call out. 1.** *v.tr* (*a*) Faire sortir (qn); appeler (les pompiers). To c. out the military, faire intervenir la force armée. To c. out workers, faire mettre en grève, donner l'ordre de grève à, des ouvriers. (*b*) Provoquer (qn) en duel. **2.** *v.i.* (*a*) Appeler; appeler au secours. (*b*) To c. out for sth., demander qch. à grands cris. **call over**, *v.tr.* (*a*) To c. over (the names), faire l'appel. (*b*) I called him over, je lui fis signe de venir nous retrouver. 'call-over, *s. Sch: etc:* L'appel *m*. **call together**, *v.tr.* Convoquer, réunir (une assemblée); assembler (des gens). **call up**, *v.tr.* **1.** Faire monter (qn). **2.** Évoquer (un esprit, un souvenir). **3.** Appeler (qn) au téléphone. **4.** *Mil:* Mobiliser (un réserviste); appeler (qn) sous les armes. 'call-up, *s. Mil:* Appel *m* sous les drapeaux. C.-up papers, ordre d'appel *m*. **call upon**, *v.i.* (*a*) Invoquer (le nom de Dieu). (*b*) To c. upon s.o. for sth., demander qch. à qn; réclamer qch. à qn. (*c*) To c. upon s.o. to do sth., sommer qn de faire qch. To c. upon s.o.'s help, faire appel à qn, à l'aide de qn. To c. upon s.o. to apologize, exiger de qn qu'il fasse des excuses. I feel called upon to warn you that . . ., je me sens dans l'obligation de vous avertir que. . . . I now c. upon Mr S., la parole est à M. S. **calling**, *s.* **1.** (*a*) Appel *m*, cri *m*. (*b*) Con-

vocation *f* (d'une assemblée, etc.). **2.** Visite *f* (on, à). **3.** Vocation *f*, état *m*, métier *m*.

caller ['kɔ:lər], *s.* **1.** Personne *f* qui appelle. **2.** Visiteur -euse. **3.** (*a*) C.(-up), éveilleur, -euse. (*b*) *Tp:* Demandeur, -euse.

calligraphy [kə'ligrəfi], *s.* Calligraphie *f*.

cal(l)iper¹ ['kælipər], *s.* (*Sg. only in compounds*) C. compasses, (pair of) callipers, compas *m* à calibrer. In and out callipers, maître-à-danser *m*. Figure-of-eight c., huit-de-chiffre(s) *m*. C. square, pied *m* à coulisse. *Surg:* C.(-splint), étrier *m* de réduction, de traction; attelle-étrier *f*, *pl.* attelles-étriers.

cal(l)iper², *v.tr.* Calibrer (un tube); mesurer (qch.) (au compas à coulisse).

callisthenics [,kælis'θeniks], *s.pl.* (*Usu. with sg. const.*) Callisthénie *f*.

callosity [kæ'lositi], *s.* Callosité *f*, durillon *m*.

callous ['kæləs], *a.* **1.** (*Of skin*) Calleux, -euse. **2.** (Homme, cœur) insensible, endurci; (homme) dur, sans cœur. **-ly**, *adv.* Sans pitié, sans cœur.

callousness ['kæləsnis], *s.* Insensibilité *f* (to, à); dureté *f*; manque *m* de cœur, de pitié.

callow ['kælou], *a.* (*Of fledgling*) Sans plumes. C. youth, la verte jeunesse. A c. youth, un blanc-bec.

callus ['kæləs], *s.* **1.** Callosité *f*. **2.** *Surg:* Cal *m*, *pl.* cals.

calm¹ [kɑ:m], *s.* Calme *m*; tranquillité *f*, sérénité *f* (d'esprit); *Nau:* bonace *f* (avant une tempête). Dead c., calme plat.

calm², *a.* Calme, tranquille. The sea was as c. as a mill-pond, nous avions une mer d'huile. To remain c. and collected, rester serein; ne pas perdre la tête. To keep c., rester calme; se modérer. **-ly**, *adv.* Avec calme; tranquillement; sans s'émouvoir.

calm³. 1. *v.tr.* Calmer, apaiser (la tempête); tranquilliser (l'esprit); atténuer, adoucir (la douleur). C. yourself, remettez-vous! To c. s.o. down, pacifier qn. **2.** *v.i.* (*Of storm, grief*) To c. down, se calmer, s'apaiser. **calming** (down), *s.* Apaisement *m*; adoucissement *m*.

calmative ['ka:mətiv], *a. & s. Med:* Calmant (*m*).

calmness ['kɑ:mnis], *s.* Tranquillité *f*, calme *m*.

calomel ['kæləmel], *s. Pharm:* Calomel *m*.

caloric [kə'lɔrik], *s. Ph:* Calorique *m*. C. energy, énergie thermique.

caloricity [,kælə'risiti], *s. Physiol:* Caloricité *f*.

calorie ['kæləri], *s. Ph:* Calorie *f*.

calorific [,kælə'rifik], *a. Ph:* Calorifique *f*.

calorimeter [,kælə'rimitər], *s.* Calorimètre *m*.

calorimetric(al) [kə,lɔri'metrik(əl)], *a. Ph:* Calorimétrique *f*.

calorimetry [kælə'rimitri], *s. Ph:* Calorimétrie *f*.

calorization [,kælərai'zeiʃ(ə)n], *s. Metalw:* Calorisation *f*.

calorize ['kæləraiz], *v.tr. Metalw:* Caloriser.

calotte [kə'lɔt], *s. R.C.Ch: Geol:* Calotte *f*.

calumet ['kæljumet], *s.* Calumet *m*.

calumniate [kə'lʌmnieit], *v.tr.* Calomnier.

calumniation [kə,lʌmni'eiʃ(ə)n], *s.* Calomnie *f*.

calumniator [kə'lʌmnieitər], *s.* Calomniateur, -trice.

calumny ['kæləmni], *s.* Calomnie *f*.

Calvary ['kælvəri]. **1.** *Pr.n.* (Mount) C., le Calvaire. **2.** *s.* Calvaire *m*.

calve [kɑ:v], *v.i.* (*Of cow, iceberg*) Vêler. **calving**, *s.* Vêlage *m*, vêlement *m*.

calves¹,². *See* CALF¹,².

Calvinism ['kælvinizm], *s.* Calvinisme *m*.

Calvinist ['kælvinist], *s. Rel.H:* Calviniste *mf*.

Calvinistic [,kælvi'nistik], *a.* Calviniste.

calypso [kə'lipsou], *s. Poet: Mus: Danc:* (*In West Indies*) Calypso *m*.

calyx, *pl.* -yxes, -yces ['keiliks, -iksiz, -isi:z], *s. Bot:* Calice *m*; vase *m* (de tulipe).

cam [kæm], *s. Mec.E:* Came *f*; excentrique *m*. 'camshaft, *s. Mec.E:* Arbre *m* à cames. *I.C.E:* Arbre de distribution.

camber¹ ['kæmbər], *s.* Cambrure *f* (d'une poutre); courbure *f*; bombement *m* (d'une chaussée). **Rise of c.**, flèche *f* (d'une poutre).

camber². 1. *v.tr.* Bomber (une chaussée); cambrer (une poutre). **2.** *v.i.* (*a*) Se bomber, se cambrer. (*b*) Avoir de la cambrure, bomber. **cambered**, *a.* Arqué, courbé, cambré. **cambering**, *s.* Bombement *m*, cambrage *m*; cintrement *m*.

Cambodia [kæm'boudiə]. *Pr.n. Geog:* Le Cambodge.
Cambrian ['kæmbriən], *a. & s.* **1.** *Geog:* Gallois, -oise. **2.** *Geol:* Cambrien, -ienne.
cambric ['keimbrik], *s. Tex:* Batiste *f* (de lin).
came. *See* COME.
camel ['kæm(ə)l], *s.* **1.** Chameau *m.* She-c., chamelle *f.* Racing c., méhari *m. Mil:* C. Corps, (compagnies *f*) méharistes. Camel's hair, poil de chameau. C.-hair brush, pinceau en petit-gris (pour l'aquarelle). **2.** *Nau:* Chameau (de renflouage). 'camel-driver, *s.* Chamelier *m.*
camellia [kə'mi:ljə], *s. Bot:* Camélia *m.*
cameo ['kæmiou], *s.* Camée *m.*
camera ['kæm(ə)rə], *s.* **1.** (*a*) *Phot:* Appareil *m.* Plate c., appareil à plaques. Folding c., appareil pliant. Miniature c., appareil de petit format. *Cin:* Cine c., caméra *f.* Motor(-driven) c., motocaméra *f, T.V:* Caméra. (*b*) *Opt:* C. obscura, chambre noire. **2.** *Jur:* Cabinet *m* du Président; chambre du Conseil. In c., à huis clos. 'camera-gun, *s.* Cinémitrailleuse *f.* 'camera-man, *pl.* -men, *s.m.* **1.** Photographe de la presse. **2.** *Cin:* (*a*) Opérateur *m.* (*b*) Cinéaste *m,* cameraman *m, pl.* les cameramen.
Cameroons (the) [ðə,kæmə'ru:nz]. *Pr.n.pl. Geog:* Le Cameroun.
cami-knickers ['kæmi'nikəz], *s.pl. Cost:* Chemise-culotte *f.*
camisole ['kæmisoul], *s. Cost: O:* Cache-corset *m inv.*
camomile ['kæməmail], *s. Bot:* **1.** Camomille *f.* **2.** Stinking c., camomille puante; maroute *f.* 'camo-mile-'tea, *s.* (Tisane *f* de) camomille *f.*
camouflage[1] ['kæmuflɑ:ʒ], *s.* Camouflage *m.*
camouflage[2], *v.tr.* Camoufler. *Mil:* Camouflaged combat clothing, tenue *f* léopard.
camp[1] [kæmp], *s.* Camp *m;* campement *m.* To pitch a c., asseoir, établir, un camp. To strike, break (up), c., lever le camp. Holiday c., camp de vacances; camping *m; (for children),* colonie *f* de vacances. Work c., agricultural c., chantier *m* (de travail). 'camp-bed, *s.* Lit *m* de camp. 'camp-chair, *s.* Chaise pliante. 'camp-'craft, *s. Sp:* Art *m* du camping. 'camp(-)e'quipment, *s. Sp:* Matériel *m* de campement, de camping. 'camp 'fire, *s.* Feu *m* de camp. camp-'followers, *s.pl. A:* Non-combattants à la suite de l'armée. camp-'meeting, *s. U.S:* Assemblée religieuse en plein air. 'camp-stool, *s.* Pliant *m.*
camp[2]. **1.** *v.i.* To c. (out), camper. **2.** *v.tr.* Camper (une armée). camping, *s.* **1.** *Mil: etc:* Campement *m.* **2.** Camping *m.* To go c., faire du camping. 'camping-ground, *s.* (*a*) Campement *m* (de bohémiens, etc.). (*b*) Terrain *m* de camping, camping *m.*
campaign[1] [kæm'pein], *s.* Campagne *f* (militaire). Electoral c., campagne électorale. To lead, conduct, a c. against s.o., mener (une) campagne contre qn. Sales c., campagne de vente.
campaign[2], *v.i.* Faire (une) campagne; faire des campagnes. campaigning, *s.* Vie *f* de soldat; campagnes *fpl.*
campaigner [kæm'peinər], *s.* **1.** Soldat *m* en campagne. **2.** Old c., vieux soldat; vieux routier; vétéran *m.*
campanile [,kæmpə'ni:li], *s. Arch:* Campanile *m.*
campanology [,kæmpə'nɔlədʒi], *s.* **1.** Science *f* de la fonte des cloches. **2.** Art *m* campanaire.
campanula [kəm'pænjulə], *s. Bot:* Campanule *f.*
camper ['kæmpər], *s.* Campeur, -euse.
camphor ['kæmfər], *s.* Camphre *m.* 'camphor-tree, *s.* Camphrier *m.*
camphorated ['kæmfəreitid], *a.* C. oil, huile camphrée.
campion ['kæmpjən], *s. Bot:* Lychnis *m.* White c., compagnon blanc. Bladder c., silène enflé.
campus ['kæmpəs], *s. U.S:* (University) c., campus *m* (universitaire).
can[1] [kæn], *s.* **1.** (*a*) Bidon *m,* broc *m,* pot *m* (pour liquides). *S.a.* WATER-CAN. *F:* To carry the c. (back), payer les pots cassés. (*b*) Milk-c., boîte *f* à lait. (*c*) *Ind:* Burette *f* (à huile, etc.). **2.** (*a*) Boîte (de conserves). (*b*) *U.S: P:* (i) Taule *f*; (ii) lieux *m pl* d'aisance. 'can-opener, *s. U.S:* Ouvre-boîte(s) *m.*
can[2], *v.tr. Esp. U.S:* Mettre, conserver (de la viande, etc.) en boîte. canned, *a.* **1.** (*Of meat*) Conservé en boîtes (de fer blanc). *U.S: F:* C. music, musique enregistrée. **2.** *P:* Soûl. canning, *s.* C. industry,

industrie des conserves alimentaires. C. factory, conserverie *f.*
can[3], *modal aux. v.* (*pr.* can, canst, can, *pl.* can ; *neg.* cannot ['kænɔt], canst not ; *p.t.* could [kud], could(e)st ; *inf., pr.p. & p.p.* wanting: *defective parts are supplied from 'to be able to.'* 'Cannot' *and* 'could not' *are often contracted into* can't (kɑ:nt], couldn't ['kudnt]) **1.** Pouvoir. I c. do it, je peux, je puis le faire. I cannot allow that, je ne saurais permettre cela. As soon as I c., aussitôt que je pourrai. As often as I possibly c., aussi souvent que possible. I took every step that I possibly could, j'ai fait toutes les démarches possibles. He will do what he c., il fera ce qu'il pourra; il fera son possible. I will help you all I c., je vous aiderai de mon mieux. (*b*) (*Possibility*) It cannot be done, cela ne peut pas se faire; c'est impossible (à faire). That cannot be, cela ne se peut pas. What c. it be? qu'est-ce que cela peut bien être? C. it be that . . .? se peut-il, est-il possible, que + *sub.*? (*c*) (*Emphatic*) I never could understand music, je n'ai jamais été capable de comprendre la musique. Mr X? what 'c. he want? M. X? qu'est-ce qu'il peut bien me vouloir? How 'could you? vous! faire ça! dire ça! à quoi pensez-vous? She is as pleased as c. 'be, elle est on ne peut plus contente. As soon as c. 'be, aussi tôt que possible. **2.** Savoir. I c. swim, je sais nager. **3.** (*a*) You don't know how silly a girl c. be, vous ne savez pas à quel point les jeunes filles sont parfois sottes. (*b*) (*Permission,* = 'may') When c. I move in? quand pourrai-je emménager? You c. go, vous pouvez vous retirer. You c. go if you like, vous pouvez y aller si vous le voulez. **4.** (*Not translated*) I c. understand your doing it, je comprends que vous le fassiez. I c. see nothing, je ne vois rien. How c. you tell? comment le savez-vous? **5.** (*a*) He could have done it if he had wanted to, il aurait pu le faire s'il avait voulu. (*b*) I could have wished it otherwise, j'aurais préféré qu'il en fût autrement. (*c*) I could have wept, je me sentais près de pleurer; j'en aurais pleuré! **6.** You cannot but succeed, vous ne pouvez pas ne pas réussir. You c. but try, vous pouvez toujours essayer.
Canaan ['keinən]. *Pr.n. B.Hist:* The land of C., la terre, le pays, de Chanaan.
Canada ['kænədə]. *Pr.n. Geog:* Le Canada. In C., au Canada.
Canadian [kə'neidjən], *a. & s,* Canadien, -ienne.
canal [kə'næl], *s.* **1.** Canal, -aux *m.* The Suez C., le Canal de Suez. Branch c., canal de dérivation. **2.** *Anat:* The alimentary c., le canal alimentaire. Auditory c., conduit auditif.
canalization [,kænəlai'zeiʃ(ə)n], *s.* Canalisation *f.* (*For water supply*) Adduction *f.*
canalize ['kænəlaiz]. **1.** *v.tr.* Canaliser. **2.** *v.i.* (*Of opinion, etc.*) Se canaliser.
canapé ['kænəpe], *s. Cu:* Canapé *m.*
canard ['kænɑ:d], *s.* Canard *m,* fausse nouvelle.
Canary [kə'nɛəri]. **1.** *Pr.n. Geog:* The C. Islands, the Canaries, les îles Canaries. **2.** *s. Orn:* Serin *m.* C. yellow, jaune serin *inv.* ca'nary-seed, *s.* (Grains *mpl* de) millet *m.*
canasta [kə'næstə], *s. Cards:* Canasta *f.*
cancan ['kænkæn], *s. Danc:* French c., cancan *m.*
cancel[1] ['kæns(ə)l], *s.* **1.** *Typ:* C.(-page), onglet *m.* **2.** Oblitérateur *m,* poinçon *m.*
cancel[2], *v.tr.* (cancelled) **1.** Annuler (une commande); résilier, résoudre, *Jur:* rescinder (un contrat); révoquer (un acte); rappeler (un message); contremander (un ordre); rapporter (une décision); supprimer (un train); décommander (une réunion); infirmer (une lettre); oblitérer (un timbre); biffer (un mot). *Mil:* Lever (une consigne). Cancelling stamp, mark, biffe *f.* To c. one's booking, décommander sa place. **2.** *Mth:* To c. x, y, éliminer x, y. cancel out, *v.i.* S'éliminer.
cancellation [,kænsə'leiʃ(ə)n], *s.* Annulation *f*; résiliation *f* (d'une commande); résolution *f* (d'une vente); défection *f.* C. of an order, contre-ordre *m.*
cancer ['kænsər], *s.* **1.** *Med:* Cancer *m.* C. serum, sérum anticancéreux. C. patient, cancéreux, -euse. C. hospital, centre *m* anticancéreux. C. specialist, cancérologue *m.* **2.** *Astr:* Le Cancer.
cancerigenic [,kænsəri'dʒenik], *a.* Cancérigène.

cancerous ['kæns(ə)rəs], *a. Med:* Cancéreux, -euse.

cancroid ['kæŋkrɔid]. **1.** *a. Crust: Med:* Cancroïde; cancériforme. **2.** *s. Med:* Cancroïde *m*.

candelabra, *pl.* **-as** [ˌkændi'lɑːbrə, -əz], **candelabrum,** *pl.* **-a** [ˌkændi'lɑːbrəm, -ə], *s.* Candélabre *m*.

candescent [kæn'des(ə)nt], *a.* D'une blancheur éblouissante; (métal, etc.) chauffé à blanc.

candid ['kændid], *a.* **1.** Franc, *f.* franche; sincère. **2.** Impartial, -aux. **-ly,** *adv.* **1.** Franchement, sincèrement, de bonne foi. **2.** Impartialement.

candidacy ['kændidəsi], *s. U.S:* = CANDIDATURE.

candidate ['kændidit], *s.* Candidat *m*, aspirant *m*, prétendant *m* (for sth., à qch.). To be a c., être sur les rangs.

candidature ['kændidətʃər], *s.* Candidature *f*.

candidness ['kændidnis], *s.* = CANDOUR.

candle ['kændl], *s.* **1.** Wax c., bougie *f*. Tallow c., chandelle *f*. Church c., cierge *f*. To burn the c. at both ends, brûler la chandelle par les deux bouts. The game is not worth the c., le jeu n'en vaut pas la chandelle. He cannot hold a c. to you, il vous est très inférieur. **2.** *Pyr:* Roman c., chandelle romaine. 'candle'end, *s.* Bout *m* de chandelle; lumignon *m*. 'candle-grease, *s.* Suif *m*.

candle², *v.tr. Husb: Com:* Mirer (des œufs). **candling,** *s.* Mirage *m* (des œufs).

candlelight ['kændllait], *s.* Lumière *f* de chandelle, de bougie. By c., à la chandelle, à la bougie.

Candlemas ['kændlməs], *s. Ecc:* La Chandeleur.

candlestick ['kændlstik], *s.* Chandelier *m*. Flat c. bougeoir *m*.

candlewick ['kændlwik], *s. Tex:* Candlewick *m*, chenille *f* de coton.

candour ['kændər], *s.* **1.** Franchise *f*, bonne foi, sincérité *f*. **2.** Impartialité *f*.

candy¹ ['kændi], *s.* **1.** (Sugar-)candy, sucre candi. **2.** *U.S:* Bonbon *m*. Box of candies, boîte *f* de bonbons. C. store, confiserie *f*. 'candy-floss, *s. Comest:* Barbe *f* à papa. 'candy-striped, *a.* Pékiné.

candy², *v.tr.* **1.** (*a*) Faire candir (le sucre). (*b*) Glacer (des fruits). **2.** *v.i.* (*Of sugar*) Se cristalliser; se candir. **candied,** *a.* Candi; confit (au sucre). *S.a.* PEEL¹.

candytuft ['kænditʌft], *s. Bot:* Ibéride *f*.

cane¹ [kein], *s.* (*a*) Canne *f*, jonc *m*; rotin *m*. Raspberry c., (tige *f* de) framboisier (*m*). (*b*) (*Walking-stick*) Canne. Malacca c., (canne de) jonc. (*c*) (*Switch*) Badine *f*. (*d*) (*For chastisement*) Canne. To get the c., être fouetté. 'cane(-bottomed) chair, *s.* Chaise cannée. 'cane-juice, *s. Sug-R:* Vesou *m*. 'cane-plantation, *s.* Cannaie *f*. 'cane-sugar, *s.* Sucre *m* de canne.

cane², *v.tr.* **1.** Battre, frapper (qn) à coups de canne. **2.** Canner (une chaise). **caning,** *s.* **1.** *Sch:* Correction *f*. **2.** Cannage *m* (de chaises).

canful ['kænful], *s.* Plein bidon, plein broc.

canicular [kə'nikjulər], *a.* Caniculaire.

canine ['kænain, 'kænin]. **1.** *a.* Canin; de chien. **2.** *s.* C. (tooth), canine *f*; (dent) œillère *f*.

canister ['kænistər], *s.* **1.** Boîte *f* (en fer blanc). Ammonia c., cartouche *f* d'ammoniaque. **2.** *A. Mil:* Mitraille *f*. **3.** *Ecc:* Boîte à hosties.

canker¹ ['kæŋkər], *s.* **1.** *Hort: Med: Vet:* Chancre *m*. **2.** Influence corruptrice; plaie *f*, fléau *m*. **3.** *Vet:* Crapaud *m* (au sabot).

canker², *v.tr.* (*a*) Ronger (un arbre); nécroser (le bois). (*b*) Corrompre (une âme). **cankered,** *a.* Atteint par le chancre; rongé.

cankerous ['kæŋkərəs], *a.* Chancreux, -euse.

cankerworm ['kæŋkəwəːm], *s.* Ver rongeur.

canna ['kænə], *s. Bot:* Balisier *m*; canna *m*. 'canna-seed, *s.* Balise *f*.

cannery ['kænəri], *s.* Conserverie *f*.

cannibal ['kænibəl], *s. & a.* Cannibale (*mf*); anthropophage (*mf*).

cannibalism ['kænibəlizm], *s.* Cannibalisme *m*, anthropophagie *f*.

cannibalistic [ˌkænibə'listik], *a.* Cannibale.

cannibalize ['kænibəlaiz], *v.tr. F:* Cannibaliser, démonter (pour utiliser les pièces détachées). To c. an engine, démonter un moteur.

cannily ['kænili], *adv. Scot:* Prudemment. To go c., jouer serré.

cannon¹ ['kænən], *s.* **1.** *Artil:* (*pl. usu.* cannon) Cano *m*; pièce *f* d'artillerie. **2.** *Harn:* C.(-bit), canon (d mors). **3.** *Bill:* Carambolage *m.* **4.** Canon (de clef) 'cannon-ball, *s.* Boulet *m* (de canon). *Tennis* C.-b. service, service canon. 'cannon-bone s Canon *m* (de la jambe du cheval). 'cannon-fodder *s. F:* Chair *f* à canon. 'cannon-shot, *s.* (*a*) Cou *m* de canon. (*b*) Within c.-shot, à portée de canon

cannon², *v.i.* (**cannoned**) **1.** *Bill:* Caramboler. To c off the red, caramboler par le rouge. **2.** To c. int s.o., heurter violemment qn.

cannonade [ˌkænə'neid], *s.* Canonnade *f*.

cannot. *See* CAN³.

canny ['kæni], *a.* Prudent, finaud. C. answer, répons de Normand. *S.a.* CA'CANNY.

canoe¹ [kə'nuː], *s.* **1.** *Sp:* (Canadian) c., canoë *m* *Fr.C:* canot *m*. Rob-Roy c., périssoire *f.* **2.** (*I tropics*) Pirogue *f. S.a.* PADDLE².

canoe², *v.i.* Faire du canoë, de la périssoire. *Fr.C.* Canoter. **canoeing,** *s.* Canoéisme *m*; (le) canoë.

canoeist [kə'nu(ː)ist], *s.* Canoéiste *mf; Fr.C:* canoteu *m*.

canon¹ ['kænən], *s.* **1.** (*a*) Canon *m* (de la messe). C law, droit canon. (*b*) Règle *f*, critère *m.* **2.** *Mus.* Canon.

canon², *s. Ecc:* Chanoine *m*.

cañon ['kænjən], *s.* = CANYON.

canoness ['kænənis], *s.f. Ecc:* Chanoinesse.

canonical [kə'nɔnik(ə)l], *a.* **1.** (Devoir) canonial, -aux (droit) canonique. **2.** C. dress, *s.pl.* canonicals, vêtements sacerdotaux.

canonization [ˌkænənai'zeiʃ(ə)n], *s.* Canonisation *f*.

canonize ['kænənaiz], *v.tr. Ecc:* **1.** Canoniser (qn). **2.** Sanctionner (un usage).

canonry ['kænənri], *s.* Canonicat *m*.

canoodle [kə'nuːdl], *v. P:* **1.** *v.tr.* Faire des mamours à (qn). **2.** *v.i.* Se faire des mamours.

canopy¹ ['kænəpi], *s.* **1.** Dais *m* (d'un trône); baldaquin *m* (de lit); ciel *m* (d'autel); (*over doorway*) auvent *m*, marquise *f. Lit:* The c. of heaven, la voûte du ciel. **2.** *Arch:* Gable *m* (de fenêtre). **3.** *Av:* Verrière *f*.

canopy², *v.tr.* Couvrir d'un dais, d'un baldaquin.

cant¹ [kænt], *s.* **1.** *Arch: Carp:* Pan coupé. *Mec.E.* Arête *f* (de boulon). **2.** (*a*) (*Slope*) Inclinaison *f* dévers *m*. (*b*) To have a c., pencher. 'cant-hook, *s.* Croc *m* à levier.

cant². **1.** *v.tr.* (*a*) *Carp:* To c. off an angle, délarder une arête. (*b*) To c. a beam, incliner une poutre. *Rail:* To c. the outer rail, surhausser le rail extérieur. (*c*) Renverser. *Nau:* To c. a boat for repairs, cabaner un canot pour le réparer. **2.** *v.i.* (*a*) S'incliner. (*b*) Pencher. (*c*) (*Of ship*) Éviter.

cant³. **1.** *s.* (*a*) Jargon *m*, argot *m*. (*b*) Langage *m* hypocrite. **2.** *a.* C. phrase, cliché *m*.

can't. *F.* = cannot, *q.v. under* CAN³.

cantaloup(e) ['kæntəluːp], *s. Hort:* Cantaloup *m*.

cantankerous [kæn'tæŋk(ə)rəs], *a.* Revêche, acariâtre; d'humeur hargneuse; tracassier, -ière. To be c., avoir mauvais caractère. **-ly,** *adv.* D'une manière acariâtre.

cantankerousness [kæn'tæŋk(ə)rəsnis], *s.* Humeur *f* revêche, acariâtre.

cantata [kæn'tɑːtə], *s. Mus:* Cantate *f*.

cantatrice ['kæntətriːs], *s.f. Mus:* Cantatrice *f*.

canteen [kæn'tiːn], *s.* **1.** *Mil: Ind:* Cantine *f. Nau:* Cambuse *f.,* C.-keeper, cantinier; cambusier. **2.** *Mil:* (*a*) Bidon *m*. (*b*) Gamelle *f.* **3.** C. of cutlery, service *m* de table en coffre; ménagère *f*.

canter¹ ['kæntər], *s. Equit:* Petit galop. *Rac:* To win in a c., arriver bon premier; *F:* arriver dans un fauteuil. Trial c. (before a race), canter *m*.

canter². **1.** *v.i.* Aller au petit galop. **2.** *v.tr.* Faire aller, mener (un cheval) au petit galop.

Canterbury ['kæntəb(ə)ri]. *Pr.n.* Cantorbéry *m*. C. bell, campanule *f* à grosses fleurs.

cantharis, *pl.* **cantharides** ['kænθəris, kæn'θæridiːz], *s.* Cantharide *f*.

canticle ['kæntikl], *s.* Cantique *m*.

cantilena [kænti'liːnə], *s. Lit: Mus:* Cantilène *f*.

cantilever ['kæntiliːvər], *s.* (*a*) *Arch:* Encorbellement *m*. (*b*) *Civ.E:* Cantilever *m*. C. bridge, pont *m* en encorbellement, à consoles; cantilever *m*.

anting ['kæntiŋ], a. 1. Hypocrite. 2. Her: C. arms, armes parlantes.

anto ['kæntou], s. Chant m (d'un poème).

anton [kæn'tɔn, 'kæntən], s. Canton m.

antonese ['kæntən'iːz], a. & s. Cantonais, -aise.

antonment [ˌkən'tɔːnmənt], s. Mil: Cantonnement m.

antor ['kæntər], s. Ecc: Chantre m.

anvas ['kænvəs], s. 1. Tex: (a) (Grosse) toile; toile à voiles, toile de tente. Aut: C. of a tyre, toiles d'un pneu. Tailor's c., toile tailleur. Under c., (i) Mil: sous la tente; (ii) Nau: sous voile. S.a. STRETCHER 1. (b) Needlew: C. work, tapisserie au, sur, canevas. 2. Art: A fine c., une belle toile. 'canvas-back, s. Orn: Canard m d'Amérique.

anvass[1] ['kænvəs], s. Pol: Com: Sollicitation f de suffrages, de commandes; tournée électorale.

anvass[2], v.tr. 1. Discuter (une affaire); éplucher (une réputation). 2. Solliciter (des suffrages, des commandes). Abs. To c., faire une tournée électorale. Com: To c. from door to door, faire la place. **canvassing**, s. 1. Discussion f; épluchage m (de réputations). 2. Sollicitation f (de suffrages); prospection f. 3. Com: Démarchage m.

anvasser ['kænvəsər], s. Solliciteur, -euse. Com: Placier m (de marchandises), démarcheur, -euse. Pol: Agent électoral.

anyon ['kænjən], s. Geog: Cañon m.

ap[1] [kæp], s. 1. (a) (Brimless) Bonnet m; (with peak) casquette f; toque f (de jockey, universitaire); képi m (de militaire); béret m (de marin); barrette f (de cardinal). Skull c., calotte f. Huntsman's, horseman's c., bombe f. Sp: Football c., cape f. To win one's c., gagner sa cape. C. and bells, marotte f (de bouffon). Sch: In c. and gown, en toque et en toge; en costume académique. To come c. in hand, se présenter le bonnet à la main. F: (Of woman) To set one's c. at a man, entreprendre la conquête d'un homme. If the c. fits, wear it! qui se sent morveux se mouche! à bon entendeur salut! S.a. THINKING[2]. (b) Orn: Capuchon m, chapeau m (d'un oiseau). 2. (a) Chapeau (de champignon). (b) Tchn: Chapeau (de protection); capuchon (de stylo). Mec.E: Lubricator c., chapeau graisseur. 3. Exp: Amorce f, capsule f. 'cap-lamp, s. Min: etc: Photophore m, lampe frontale. 'cap-screw, s. Vis f à tête cubique. 'cap-stone, s. 1. Const: Chaperon m (d'un toit). 2. Prehist: Table f (couronnant un dolmen).

ap[2], v.tr. (capped [kæpt]) 1. (a) Coiffer (qn). (b) Sch: (In Scot.) To c. a candidate, conférer un grade à un candidat. (c) Sp: Donner (à qn) sa cape. 2. Coiffer, couronner (sth. with sth., qch. de qch.); capsuler (une bouteille); armer (un aimant); amorcer (un obus). 3. F: (Outdo) Surpasser. To c. it all . . ., pour comble. . . That caps all! ça c'est le bouquet! **capped**, a. Coiffé. Snow-c. mountain, montagne coiffée, couronnée, couverte, de neige. Screw-c. bottle, flacon m à couvercle vissé. **capping**, s. 1. (a) Capsulage m (d'un flacon). (b) Amorçage m (d'un obus). (c) Nau: Capelage m (de câbles). 2. Chapeau m, chape f (d'une charpente).

ap[3], s. Typ: F: = CAPITAL[2] II. 2.

apability [ˌkeipə'biliti], s. 1. Capacité f (of doing sth., pour faire qch.); faculté f (to do sth., de faire qch.). 2. The boy has capabilities, c'est un enfant bien doué.

apable ['keipəbl], a. 1. (a) Capable (of sth., de qch.). (b) Very c. doctor, médecin très compétent. C. woman, maîtresse femme. 2. Susceptible (d'amélioration). **-ably**, adv. Avec compétence.

apacious [kə'peiʃəs], a. Vaste, spacieux, -se; ample.

apaciousness [kə'peiʃəsnis], s. Amples proportions fpl (d'une salle, etc.).

apacitance [kə'pæsitəns], s. El: Résistance f de capacité, capacité f électrostatique.

apacitate [kə'pæsiteit], v.tr. 1. Rendre (qn) capable (for sth., de qch.). 2. Jur: Donner qualité à (qn) (to act, pour agir).

apacitor [kə'pæsitər], s. El: Condensateur m.

apacity [kə'pæsiti], s. 1. (a) Capacité f (d'un cylindre, El: d'un accumulateur); contenance f (d'un tonneau). Nau: C. of the bunkers, volume m des soutes. (b) Rendement m (d'une locomotive). Carrying c., charge f utile; capacité f de transport.

S.a. LIFTING. Seating c., nombre m de places assises (dans une voiture, etc.). Th: To play to c., jouer à bureaux fermés. House filled to c., salle comble. 2. Capacité (for, pour). C. for doing sth., aptitude f à faire qch. To show one's c., donner sa mesure. 3. To have c. to act, avoir qualité pour agir. To act in one's official c., agir dans l'exercice de ses fonctions.

cap-a-pie [ˌkæpə'piː], adv. (Armé) de pied en cap.

cape[1] [keip], s. 1. Cost: (a) Pèlerine f, cape f; (small) collet m. (b) Ecc: Camail m, pl. -ails. 2. Orn: Collier m.

cape[2], s. Cap m, promontoire m. Geog: The C. (of Good Hope), le Cap (de Bonne Espérance). Hist: C. Colony, la colonie du Cap. The C. to Cairo railway, le transafricain. 'cape'coloured, a. & s. Métis, -isse (de l'Afrique du sud). C. pigeon, pétrel damier, pigeon m du Cap.

capella[1] [kə'pelə], s. Ecc: C. ardente, chapelle ardente.

capella[2], s. Astr: La Chèvre.

caper[1] ['keipər], s. Bot: 1. Câpre f. Cu: C. sauce, sauce f aux câpres. 2. C.(-bush, -plant), câprier m.

caper[2], s. Entrechat m, cabriole f, gambade f. To cut capers, (i) faire des entrechats; (ii) F: faire des siennes.

caper[3], v.i. To c. (about), faire des entrechats, des cabrioles; gambader.

capercaillie [ˌkæpə'keilji], **capercailzie** [ˌkæpə'kelzi], s. Coq m de bruyère (d'Écosse); grand tétras.

Capernaum [kæ'pɔːniəm]. Pr.n. B.Hist: Capharnaüm.

capful ['kæpful], s. Pleine casquette. Nau: A c. of wind, une bouffée de vent.

capillarity [ˌkæpi'læriti], s. Ph: Capillarité f.

capillary [kə'piləri], a. Capillaire.

capital[1] ['kæpitl], s. Arch: Chapiteau m.

capital[2]. I. a. 1. Capital, -aux. C. letter, s. c., (lettre) capitale, (lettre) majuscule (f). C. city, s. c., (ville) capitale. (f). 2. Jur: C. punishment, peine capitale. 3. It is of c. importance, c'est de la plus haute importance. S.a. SHIP[1]. 4. A c. fellow, un excellent garçon. C.! fameux! -ally, adv. Admirablement (bien). II. capital, s. 1. Fin: Capital m, capitaux mpl. fonds mpl. Paid-up c., capital versé. Working c., fonds de roulement. Funded c., capitaux investis. F: To make c. of sth., profiter de qch.; exploiter qch. C. levy, prélèvement m sur le capital. 2. Typ: Large capitals, grandes capitales; majuscules f.

capitalism ['kæpitəlizm], s. Capitalisme m.

capitalist ['kæpitəlist], s. Capitaliste mf.

capitalistic [ˌkæpitə'listik], a. Capitaliste.

capitalization [ˌkæpitəlai'zeiʃ(ə)n], s. 1. Capitalisation f (des intérêts). 2. Emploi m des majuscules.

capitalize ['kæpitəlaiz], v.tr. 1. Capitaliser. 2. Écrire (un mot) avec une majuscule.

capitate ['kæpiteit], **capitated** ['kæpiteitid], a. Bot: En capitule; capité.

capitation [ˌkæpi'teiʃ(ə)n], s. Adm: Capitation f. C. grant, allocation f (de tant) par tête.

Capitol (the) [ðə'kæpitəl], s. Le Capitole (A: de Rome; U.S: de Washington).

capitular [kə'pitjulər], a. 1. Jur: Ecc: Capitulaire. 2. Bot: Capitulé.

capitulary [kə'pitjuləri], s. Hist: Capitulaire m.

capitulate [kə'pitjuleit], v.i. Capituler.

capitulation [kəˌpitju'leiʃ(ə)n], s. 1. Énumération f des chapitres, des articles (d'un traité). 2. Capitulation f, reddition f (d'une place forte).

capon ['keipən], s. Cu: Chapon m, poulet m.

caponize ['keipənaiz], v.tr. Husb: Chaponner, châtrer (un poulet).

capot ['kæpɔt], s. Cards: (Piquet) Capot m.

capper ['kæpər], s. Capsuleur, -euse (de bouteilles).

caprice [kə'priːs], s. 1. Caprice m, lubie f. 2. Mus: Caprice.

capricious [kə'priʃəs], a. Capricieux, -euse. -ly, adv. Capricieusement.

capriciousness [kə'priʃəsnis], s. Humeur capricieuse, inégale. C. of temper, inégalité f d'humeur.

Capricorn ['kæprikɔːn], s. Astr: Le Capricorne. The Tropic of C., le tropique du Capricorne.

caprine ['kæprain], a. Z: Caprin.

capriole[1] ['kæprioul], s. Equit: Cabriole f.

capriole², *v.i.* (*Of horse*) Cabrioler.
capsicum ['kæpsikəm], *s.* 1. *Bot:* Piment *m.* 2. *Cu:* Piment, poivron *m.*
capsize [kæp'saiz]. 1. *v.i.* (*Of boat*) Chavirer. (*Of car*) Capoter. 2. *v.tr.* Faire chavirer. **capsizing,** *s.* Chavirement *m;* capotage *m.*
capstan ['kæpstən], *s.* 1. Cabestan *m.* To man the c., armer le cabestan. 2. *Mec.E:* Revolver *m* (de tour). *S.a.* LATHE 1.
capsular ['kæpsjulər], *a.* (Fruit) capsulaire.
capsule ['kæpsju:l], *s.* Capsule *f* (de fleur, de bouteille, pharmaceutique, etc.). *Astronautics:* Capsule *f.*
captain¹ ['kæptin], *s.* 1. (*a*) Chef *m,* capitaine *m.* **Captains of industry,** les capitaines de l'industrie. (*b*) *Sp:* Chef d'équipe. *A. Artil:* C. of the gun, chef de pièce. 2. *Mil: Nau:* (*Rank*) Capitaine. (*W.R.A.C.*) Première classe. *Mil.Av:* Group c., colonel *m.* *Civil Av:* (Pilote) commandant de bord; (*as title*) Commandant. 3. *Ich:* Grondin gris.
captain², *v.tr.* 1. Commander (une compagnie). 2. Conduire (une expédition). *Sp:* To c. a team, mener, diriger, une équipe.
captaincy ['kæptinsi], *s.* 1. Grade *m* de capitaine. To obtain one's c., passer capitaine. 2. Conduite *f,* commandement *m.*
caption ['kæpʃ(ə)n], *s.* 1. (*In book*) En-tête *m.* (*Of illustration*) Légende *f.* *Cin:* Sous-titre *m.* *Journ:* Rubrique *f.* *Jur:* Arrestation *f.* 3. *Jur:* Indication *f* d'origine.
captious ['kæpʃəs], *a.* 1. (Raisonnement) captieux, insidieux. 2. (*Of pers.*) Pointilleux, -euse, chicaneur, -euse, vétilleux, -euse. **-ly,** *adv.* Pointilleusement.
captiousness ['kæpʃəsnis], *s.* 1. Caractère *m* sophistique (d'un argument). 2. Pointillerie *f,* chicanerie *f;* esprit *m* de chicane.
captivate ['kæptiveit], *v.tr.* Charmer, captiver; séduire.
captivation [kæpti'veiʃ(ə)n], *s.* Séduction *f;* charme fascinateur.
captive ['kæptiv]. 1. *a.* (*a*) Captif, -ive. (*b*) C. state, état *m* de captivité. 2. *s.* Captif, -ive, prisonnier, -ière.
captivity [kæp'tiviti], *s.* Captivité *f.*
captor ['kæptər], *s.* 1. Celui qui s'est emparé de qn; ravisseur *m.* 2. *Navy:* Capteur *m.*
capture¹ ['kæptʃər], *s.* 1. (*Action*) Capture *f,* prise *f.* 2. (*Thg. or pers. taken*) Prise.
capture², *v.tr.* 1. Capturer (un navire); prendre (une ville) (from, à). *Com:* To c. the market, accaparer la vente. 2. *W.Tel:* To c. Hertzian waves, capter des ondes hertziennes. **capturing,** *s.* 1. Capture *f* (d'un navire); prise *f* (d'une ville). 2. *W.Tel:* Captage *m.*
Capuchin ['kæpjuʃin], *s.* 1. *Ecc:* Capucin. 2. *A: Cost:* Capeline *f.* 3. (*Monkey*) Saï *m.*
capybara [kæpi'bɑ:rə], *s.* *Z:* Cabiai *m.*
car [kɑ:r], *s.* 1. *Lit:* (*Chariot*) Char *m.* 2. (Motor) c., auto(mobile) *f,* voiture *f.* **Radio c.,** voiture radio. **Private c.,** voiture de tourisme. *S.a.* STREETCAR. 3. *Rail:* (*a*) *U.S:* Voiture; wagon *m.* (*b*) **Dining-c.,** wagon-restaurant *m.* *S.a.* SLEEPING-CAR. 4. (*a*) Nacelle *f* (d'un pont transbordeur, d'un ballon). (*b*) *U.S:* Cabine *f* (d'un ascenseur). **'car(-)fare,** *s.* Prix *m* du trajet (par tramway, autobus). **'car-ferry,** *s.* Bac *m* à voitures; ferry-boat *m,* F: car-ferry. **'car-licence,** *s.* Permis *m* de circulation (= carte grise). **'car-'park,** *s.* Stationnement autorisé (pour voitures), parc *m* (à voitures), F: parking *m.* **'car-'sickness,** *s.* Mal *m* de voiture. **'car-'sleeper,** *s.* *Rail:* Train *m* auto-couchette(s).
carabineer [kærəbi'niər], *s.* *Mil:* Carabinier *m.*
caracal ['kærəkæl], *s.* *Z:* Caracal *m, pl.* -als.
caracole¹ ['kærəkoul], *s.* *Equit:* Caracole *f.*
caracole², *v.i.* *Equit:* Caracoler.
caracul ['kærəkʌl], *s.* *Z:* Caracul *m.* *Com:* (Fourrure *f* de) caracul.
carafe [kə'rɑ:f], *s.* Carafe *f.*
caramel ['kærəməl], *s.* 1. Caramel *m.* *Cu:* **Crème caramel,** crème *f* caramel. 2. Bonbon *m* au caramel.
caramelize ['kærəməlaiz], *v.tr.* Caraméliser.
carapace ['kærəpeis], *s.* *Crust:* Carapace *f;* bouclier *m.*

carat ['kærət], *s.* *Meas:* Carat *m.* Eighteen-c. gol[d] or au titre 750.
Caravaggio [kærə'vædʒiou]. *Pr.n.m.* Le Caravage.
caravan¹ ['kærəvæn], *s.* 1. Caravane *f* (de l'Orient[). 2. *Veh:* (*a*) Roulotte *f* (de forains). (*b*) *Aut:* Cara[vane. (Touring) c., remorque *f* camping, *F:* campin[g *m;* remorque roulotte.
caravan², *v.i.* Faire du caravan(n)ing. **caravan(n)ing,** *s.* Caravan(n)ing *m.*
caravaneer [kærəvə'ni:ər], *s.* Caravanier *m* (d[e l'Orient).
caravan(n)er [kærə'vænər], *s.* Caravanier *m,* amateu[r *m* de caravan(n)ing.
caravanserai [kærə'vænsərai], *s.* Caravansérail *m.*
caravel ['kærəvel], *s.* *Nau: A:* Caravelle *f.*
caraway ['kærəwei], *s.* *Bot:* Carvi *m.* **'caraway seeds,** *s.pl.* Graines *f* de carvi.
carbide ['kɑ:baid], *s.* *Ch: Ind:* Carbure *m.*
carbine ['kɑ:bain], *s.* Carabine *f.*
carbo-hydrate ['kɑ:bou'haidreit], *s.* *Ch:* Hydrate *n[* de carbone.
carbolated ['kɑ:boleitid], *a.* Phéniqué.
carbolic [kɑ:'bɔlik], *a.* *Ch:* Phénique. *Com:* **C. acid[,** phénol *m.*
carbolize ['kɑ:bolaiz], *v.tr.* *Med:* Phéniquer.
carbon ['kɑ:bən], *s.* 1. *Ch:* Carbone *m.* **C. monoxide[,** oxyde *m* de carbone. **C. dioxide,** anhydride *m[* acide *m,* carbonique. **C. dioxide snow,** neige *f* car[bo]bonique. 2. (*a*) **Gas c.,** charbon *m* de cornue. (*b[* *Phot:* C. print, épreuve au charbon. (*c*) *I.C.E:* etc[**C. deposit,** calamine *f.* 3. *Typwr:* (*a*) Papier *n[* carbone. (*b*) = CARBON-COPY. 4. *Lap:* Carbonad[e *m.* **'carbon-copy,** *s.* *Typewr:* Copie *f,* double *m[* au (papier) carbone. **'carbon-holder,** *s.* *El.E[:* Porte-charbon *m inv.* **'carbon paper,** *s.* 1. *Phot[:* Papier *m* au charbon. 2. *Typewr:* Papier carbone.
carbonaceous [kɑ:bə'neiʃəs], *a.* *Ch:* Carboné. 2[*Geol:* Charbonneux, -euse.
carbonate ['kɑ:bənit], *s.* *Ch:* Carbonate *m.*
carbonic [kɑ:'bɔnik], *a.* *Ch:* Carbonique. **C. acid gas[,** anhydride *m* carbonique.
carboniferous [kɑ:bə'nifərəs], *a.* Carbonifère.
carbonization [kɑ:bənai'zeiʃ(ə)n], *s.* 1. Carbonisatio[n *f.* 2. *I.C.E:* Calaminage *m.*
carbonize ['kɑ:bənaiz], *v.tr.* Carboniser; *I.C.E[:* carburer. **carbonizing,** *s.* = CARBONIZATION.
carbonyl ['kɑ:bonil], *s.* *Ch:* Carbonyle *m.*
carborundum [kɑ:bə'rʌndəm], *s.* Carborundum *m[* **C. wheel,** meule en carborundum.
carboy ['kɑ:bɔi], *s.* Tourie *f;* bonbonne *f.*
carbuncle ['kɑ:bʌŋkl], *s.* 1. *Lap:* Escarboucle *f.* 2[*Med:* Anthrax *m;* bourgeon *m* (sur le nez).
carbuncular [kɑ:'bʌŋkjulər], *a.* *Med:* Charbonneux[-euse; rouge et enflammé. **C. tumour,** tumeu[r charbonneuse.
carburant ['kɑ:bjurənt], *s.* *I.C.E:* Carburant *m.*
carburate ['kɑ:bjureit], *v.tr.* Carburer.
carburation [kɑ:bju'reiʃ(ə)n], *s.* Carburation *f.*
carburetted ['kɑ:bjuretid], *a.* Carburé. **C. hydrogen[,** hydrogène carburé.
carburetter, -or [kɑ:bju'retər], *s.* *I.C.E:* Carburateu[r *m.*
carburetting ['kɑ:bjuretiŋ], *s.* Carburation *f.*
carburize ['kɑ:bjuraiz], *v.tr.* 1. Carburer (un gaz). 2[*Metall:* Carburer (l'acier).
carcajou ['kɑ:kəʒu], *s.* *Z: Fr.C:* Carcajou *m.*
carcase, carcass ['kɑ:kəs], *s.* 1. *F:* (i) Cadavre[(humain); (ii) corps *m.* To save one's c., sauver s[a peau. 2. Cadavre, carcasse *f* (d'un animal). 3. Car[casse, charpente *f* (d'une maison).
carcinoma [kɑ:si'noumə], *a.* *Med:* Carcinome *m.*
carcinomatous [kɑ:si'noumətəs], *a.* *Med:* Carcino[mateux, -euse.
card¹ [kɑ:d], *s.* 1. (Playing-)c., carte *f* (à jouer). Gam[e of cards,** partie de cartes. **Pack,** *U.S:* **deck, o[r cards,** jeu de cartes. **To play one's cards well, bie[n jouer son jeu. **To lay one's cards on the table,** mettr[e cartes sur table. **To have a c. up one's sleeve,** avoi[r encore une ressource. **It is (quite) on the cards tha[t . . .,** il est bien possible que. . . . *S.a.* THROW IN 4[*O:* **He's a queer c.,** c'est un drôle de type. *P:* He'[s a c.,** c'est un original. 2. (*a*) (Visiting-)c., *U.S[:* **calling c.,** carte (de visite). **Business c.,** carte d[e

adresse, d'affaires. (b) **Admission c.,** carte, billet *m*, d'entrée. *Adm:* **Passport control c.,** fiche de voyageur. **Identity c.,** carte d'identité. (c) **Carte postale. Correspondence c.,** carte correspondance. *S.a.* CHRISTMAS CARD, POSTCARD. (d) *Com:* **(Index-)c.,** (carte-) fiche *f.* (e) *Golf:* Carte du parcours. *Rac:* Programme *m* des courses. (f) *Mec.E:* **Indicator c.,** diagramme *m* d'indicateur. (g) *O:* **Dance c.,** carnet *m* de bal. 3. *Dominoes:* Dé *m.* '**card-case,** *s.* Porte-cartes *m inv.* '**card index**[1], *s.* 1. Fichier *m*; classeur *m.* 2. Catalogue *m* sur fiches. **card-'index**[2], *v.tr.* Mettre sur fiches; encarter. '**card-'indexing,** *s.* Mise *f* sur fiches. '**card-player,** *s.* Joueur, -euse, de cartes. '**card-playing,** *s.* Jeu *m.* '**card-sharper,** *s.* Tricheur *m*; bonneteur *m*, escroc *m.* '**card-table,** *s.* Table *f* de jeu.

card[2], *v.tr.* Mettre (des notes) sur fiche.

card[3], *s. Tex:* Carde *f*, peigne *m.*

card[4], *v.tr. Tex:* Carder, peigner (la laine, etc.). **carding,** *s.* 1. Cardage *m*, peignage *m*, écharpage *m* (de laine). 2. *pl.* Peignons *m.*

cardamom ['kɑ:dəməm], *s. Bot:* Cardamome *m.*

cardan ['kɑ:d(ə)n], *s. Mec.E:* **C. joint,** joint *m* de Cardan, joint universel.

cardboard ['kɑ:dbɔ:d], *s.* Carton *m.* **C. trade,** cartonnerie *f.*

carder ['kɑ:dər], *s. Tex:* (a) (*Pers.*) Cardeur, -euse. (b) (*Machine*) Cardeuse *f.*

cardiac ['kɑ:diæk], *a. Med:* Cardiaque.

cardialgia [kɑ:di'ældʒə], *s. Med:* Cardialgie *f.*

cardigan ['kɑ:digən], *s.* Gilet *m* de tricot, cardigan *m.*

cardinal ['kɑ:dinl]. I. *a.* 1. Cardinal, -aux. **The c. numbers, points,** les nombres, points, cardinaux. **The c. virtues,** les vertus cardinales. 2. (*Colour*) Pourpre; cardinal *inv.* **-ally,** *adv.* Fondamentalement. II. **cardinal,** *s.* 1. *Ecc:* Cardinal *m.* 2. *Orn:* **C.(-bird),** cardinal. '**cardinal-flower,** *s. Bot:* Cardinale *f.*

cardiogram ['kɑ:diougræm], *s. Med:* Cardiogramme *m.*

cardiograph ['kɑ:diougræf], *s. Med:* Cardiographe *m.*

cardiographer [kɑ:di'ogrəfər], *s. Med:* Cardiographe *m.*

cardiologist [kɑ:di'ɔlədʒist], *s. Med:* Cardiologue *m.*

cardiology [kɑ:di'ɔlədʒi], *s. Med:* Cardiologie *f.*

cardiotonic [kɑ:diou'tonik], *a. & s. Med:* Cardiotonique (*m*), tonicardiaque (*m*).

cardoon [kɑ:'du:n], *s. Hort:* Cardon *m.*

care[1] [keər], *s.* 1. Souci *m*, inquiétude *f.* **My greatest c.,** ma plus grande préoccupation. **Gnawing c.,** soucis rongeurs. 2. Soin(s) *m(pl)*, attention *f*, ménagement *m.* **Constant c.,** soins assidus. **C. for details,** attention aux détails. **To take c. in doing sth.,** apporter du soin à faire qch. **To take c. not to do sth.,** se garder, prendre garde, de faire qch. **Take c.!** *O:* **have a c.!** (i) faites attention! prenez garde! (ii) ne vous y frottez pas! **To take c. of one's health,** ménager sa santé. **To take c. that sth. shall be done,** veiller à ce que qch. se fasse. **That matter will take c. of itself,** cela s'arrangera tout seul. '(Glass) with c.,' "fragile." 3. Soin(s), charge *f*, tenue *f.* **C. of the aged, of old people,** soins des personnes âgées. **C. and treatment of animals,** soins et traitement des animaux. **Write to me c. of Mrs X,** écrivez-moi aux bons soins de Mme X. **C. and maintenance of a car,** entretien *m* d'une voiture. **Want of c.,** incurie *f*, négligence *f.* 4. **Cares of State,** responsabilités *f* d'État. **That shall be my c.,** je m'en charge. '**care(-)free,** *a.* Libre de soucis; insouciant; sans souci. '**care(-)worn,** *a.* Rongé par le chagrin, les soucis.

care[2], *v.i.* 1. Se soucier, s'inquiéter, se préoccuper (for, about, de). **That's all he cares about,** il n'y a que cela qui l'intéresse. **I don't c. what he says,** peu m'importe ce qu'il dit. **What do I c.?** qu'est-ce que cela me fait? **I don't c. much for it,** je n'y tiens pas. *F:* **I couldn't c. less,** je m'en fiche éperdument, c'est le moindre de mes soucis. **To c. for nothing,** se désintéresser de tout; ne se soucier de rien. **Not that I c.,** non pas que ça me fasse quelque chose. **For all I c.,** pour (tout) ce que ça me fait. **I don't c.! as if I cared!** ça m'est égal! **I don't c. either way,** cela m'est indifférent. *F:* **I don't c. a damn, two hoots,** je m'en

moque pas mal; ça m'est absolument égal; *F:* je m'en fiche. **He doesn't c. for anybody or anything,** il se moque du tiers comme du quart. 2. **To c. for invalids,** soigner les malades. **Well cared-for appearance,** apparence soignée. 3. '**To c. for s.o.,** aimer qn. **He doesn't c. for her,** elle ne lui plaît pas. **I don't c. for this music,** cette musique ne me dit rien. *F:* **I don't c. if I do,** je veux bien; je ne dis pas non. **If you c. to join us,** si vous voulez vous joindre à nous. **If you c. to,** si le cœur vous en dit.

careen [kə'ri:n]. 1. *v.tr.* (a) Abattre, mettre, (un navire) en carène. (b) Caréner (un navire); nettoyer la carène (d'un navire). 2. *v.i.* (*Of ship*) Donner de la bande; plier sous le vent. **careening,** *s.* 1. Carénage *m*; abattage *m* en carène. **C. basin,** bassin de carénage. 2. *Nau:* Bande dangereuse.

careenage [kə'ri:nidʒ], *s. Nau:* 1. = CAREENING 1. 2. Frais *mpl* de carénage. 3. Chantier *m* de carénage.

career[1] [kə'riər], *s.* 1. Course (précipitée). **To stop in mid c.,** rester, demeurer, en (beau) chemin. 2. Carrière *f.* **To take up a c.,** embrasser une carrière. *Sch:* **Careers master, mistress,** orienteur, -euse, professionnel(le).

career[2], *v.i.* Courir rapidement, follement. **To c. along,** aller à toute vitesse.

careerist [kə'riːrist], *s.* Arriviste *mf.*

careful ['keəful], *a.* 1. Soigneux, -euse (of, de); attentif, -ive (of, à). **Be c. of it!** ayez-en soin! **Be c. what you are doing,** faites attention à ce que vous faites. **Be c.!** prenez garde! faites attention! 2. Prudent, circonspect. **C. housewife,** ménagère très regardante. **A c. answer,** une réponse bien pesée. **-fully,** *adv.* 1. Soigneusement, avec soin; attentivement. 2. Prudemment; avec circonspection. **To live c.,** (i) soigner sa santé; (ii) vivre avec économie.

carefulness ['keəf(u)lnis], *s.* 1. Soin *m*, attention *f.* 2. Prudence *f.*

careless ['keəlis], *a.* 1. (a) Insouciant (of, about, de); nonchalant. (b) **A c. remark,** une observation à la légère. **C. mistake,** faute d'inattention. 2. Négligent; sans soin. **-ly,** *adv.* Avec insouciance; négligemment; sans soin.

carelessness ['keəlisnis], *s.* 1. (a) Insouciance *f.* (b) Inattention *f.* **Piece of c.,** étourderie *f.* 2. Manque *m* de soin; négligence *f.*

caress[1] [kə'res], *s.* Caresse *f.*

caress[2], *v.tr.* Caresser. **caressing,** *a.* Caressant. **C. tones,** tons câlins.

caret ['kærət], *s. Typ:* Signe *m* d'omission.

caretake [keə'teik], *v.tr.* Servir de concierge pour (un immeuble); avoir la charge de qch. **caretaking,** *s.* Gardiennage *m.*

caretaker ['keə:teikər], *s.* 1. Concierge *mf* (de maison); gardien *m* (d'un immeuble, d'un musée). 2. *Sch:* Dépensier, -ière. *Pol: Attrib. use:* **C. cabinet,** cabinet *m* intérimaire.

carful ['kɑ:ful], *s.* Pleine voiture, pleine auto (de touristes, etc.); *F:* voiturée *f.*

cargo, *pl.* **-oes** ['kɑ:gou, -ouz], *s. Nau:* Cargaison *f*, chargement *m.* **To take in c.,** charger des marchandises. '**cargo-boat,** *s.* Cargo *m.*

Carib ['kærib], *a. & s. Ethn:* Caraïbe (*mf*).

Caribbean [kæri'bi(:)ən], *a. C.* **Sea, Islands,** mer des Antilles, des Caraïbes; les Antilles.

caribou ['kæribu:], *s. Z:* Caribou *m, pl.* -ous.

caricature[1] ['kærikətjuər], *s.* Caricature *f*, charge *f.*

caricature[2] [kærikə'tjuər], *v.tr.* Caricaturer. *Th:* **To c. a part,** charger un rôle.

caricaturist [kærikə'tjuərist], *s.* Caricaturiste *m.*

caries ['keərii:z], *s. Med: Dent:* Carie *f.*

carillon [kə'riljən], *s. Mus:* Carillon *m.*

carious ['keəriəs], *a. Med:* (Os) carié.

carking ['kɑ:kiŋ], *a. Lit:* **C. care,** soucis rongeurs.

carline ['kɑ:lin], *s. Bot:* **C. thistle,** carline *f* vulgaire.

carload ['kɑ:loud], *s.* = CARFUL.

carman, *pl.* **-men** ['kɑ:mən], *s.m.* (a) Camionneur. (b) *Com:* Livreur.

Carmelite ['kɑ:məlait], *s. Rel.H:* Carme *m.* **C. nun,** carmélite *f.* **The C. order,** l'ordre du Carmel.

carmine ['kɑ:main, -min]. 1. *s.* Carmin *m.* 2. *a.* Carminé; carmin *inv.*

carnage ['kɑ:nidʒ], *s.* Carnage *m.*

carnal ['kɑːnl], a. Charnel; (i) sensuel; (ii) sexuel. C. sins, péchés de la chair. -ally, adv. Charnellement, sensuellement. 'carnal-'minded, a. 1. Charnel, sensuel. 2. Mondain. 'carnal-'mindedness, s. 1. Sensualité f. 2. Mondanité f.

carnality [kɑː'næliti], s. Sensualité f.

carnation[1] [kɑː'neif(ə)n]. (a) s. Incarnat m. (b) a. (Teint) incarnat, incarnadin.

carnation,[2] s. Bot: Œillet m.

carnival ['kɑːniv(ə)l], s. Carnaval m, pl. -als. U.S: = FUN FAIR.

Carnivora [kɑː'nivərə], s.pl. Z: Carnassiers m.

carnivore ['kɑːnivɔːr], s. 1. Z: Carnassier m. 2. Bot: Plante f carnivore.

carnivorous [kɑː'niv(ə)rəs], a. 1. (Of animal) Carnassier. 2. (Of pers., plant) Carnivore.

carob ['kærəb], s. 1. C.(-bean), caroube f, carouge f. 2. C.(-tree), caroubier m.

carol[1] ['kær(ə)l], s. (a) Chant m, chanson f. Christmas c., (chant de) noël m. (b) Tire-lire m (de l'alouette).

carol[2], v.i. & tr. (carolled) (a) Chanter (joyeusement). (b) (Of lark) Tire-lirer.

Carolina [kærə'lainə]. Pr.n. Geog: North, South, C., la Caroline du Nord, du Sud.

Caroline ['kærəlain, -lin]. 1. Pr.n.f. Caroline. 2. a. (a) = CAROLINGIAN (b) Eng.Hist: Qui appartient aux rois Charles; du temps des rois Charles. (c) Geog: The C. Islands, l'archipel m des Carolines.

Carolingian [kærə'lindʒiən], a. & s. Hist: Carolingien, -ienne.

carom[1] ['kærəm], s. Bill: U.S: Carambolage m.

carom[2], v.i. Bill: U.S: Caramboler; faire un carambolage.

carotene ['kærətiːn], s. Ch: Carotène m.

carotid [kə'rɔtid], a. & s. Anat: Carotide (f).

carousal [kə'rauz(ə)l], **carouse**[1] [kə'rɑːuz], s. O: B(e)uverie f; F: bombe f; bamboche f.

carouse[2], v.i. O: Faire la fête, F: la bombe.

carouser [kə'rauzər], s. O: Fêtard m, noceur m.

carp[1] [kɑːp], s. (Usu. inv. in pl.) Ich: Carpe f. Young c., carpeau m.

carp[2], v.i. Épiloguer, gloser (at, sur). To c. at sth., trouver à redire à qch. **carping**[1], a. Chicanier, -ière. C. criticism, critique pointilleuse. -ly, adv. Pointilleusement. **carping**[2], s. Critique (malveillante).

carpal ['kɑːp(ə)l]. Anat: 1. a. Carpien; du carpe. 2. s. Os carpien.

Carpathian [kɑː'peiθiən], a. Geog: The C. Mountains, s. the Carpathians, les (Monts) Karpates, Carpates.

carpel ['kɑːpəl], s. Bot: Carpelle m.

carpenter[1] ['kɑːpintər], s. Charpentier m; menuisier m en bâtiments. Nau: Ship's c., matelot m charpentier. C. shop, atelier de menuiserie.

carpenter[2], v.i. Faire de la charpenterie, de la menuiserie.

carpentry ['kɑːpintri], s. 1. Charpenterie f; grosse menuiserie. 2. Charpente f.

carper ['kɑːpər], s. (a) Critique malveillant. (b) F: Ronchonneur.

carpet[1] ['kɑːpit], s. Tapis m. (a) Brussels c., moquette f de Bruxelles. Thick-pile c., tapis de haute laine. Short-pile c., tapis de laine rase. To lay a c., poser un tapis. F: To be on the c., (of pers.) être sur la sellette; (of question) être sur le tapis. (b) Tapis (de verdure, etc.). **carpet(-)'bagger**, s. F: U.S: Aventurier m politique. **carpet-beater,** s. Tapette f. **'carpet-'slippers,** s.pl. Pantoufles f. **'carpet-sweeper,** s. Balai m mécanique.

carpet[2], v.tr. Recouvrir d'un tapis. **carpeted,** a. Couvert d'un tapis. Slope c. with flowers, pente tapissée de fleurs. **carpeting,** s. (a) Pose f de tapis. (b) Coll. Tapis mpl en pièce.

carport ['kɑːpɔːt], s. Abri-garage m.pl. Des abris-garages.

carpus ['kɑːpəs], s. Anat: Z: Carpe m.

Carrara [kə'rɑːrə]. Pr.n. Geog: Carrare f.

carriage ['kæridʒ], s. 1. Port m, transport m. Com: C. free, franc de port; franco. C. paid, port payé; franc de port. C. forward, (en) port dû. 2. Port, maintien m. Free, easy, c., allure dégagée. 3. (a) Veh: Voiture f; équipage m, attelage m. C. and pair, voiture à deux chevaux. Baby c., voiture d'enfant. (b) Rail: Voiture, wagon m. 4. (a) Artil: (Gun-)c., affût m. (b) Veh: Train m (de la voiture). (c) Mec.E: Chariot m (d'un tour, d'une machine à écrire).

'carriage-builder, s. Carrossier m. **'carriage-building,** s. Carrosserie f. **'carriage clock,** s. Pendule(tte) f (de voiture). **'carriage-drive,** s. Avenue f pour voitures.

carriageway ['kæridʒwei], s. Dual c., route jumelée, à double voie.

carrier ['kæriər], s. 1. (Pers.) (a) Porteur, -euse. Med: (Germ) c., porteur, -euse de bacilles. (b) Com: Camionneur m, messagiste m. Jur: Common c., (i) voiturier public; (ii) entrepreneur m de messageries maritimes. (c) Mil: (Of ammunition) Ravitailleur m. 2. (a) Support m. (b) Mec.E: Toc m, doguin m (de tour); (heart-shaped) cœur m de tour. Sm.a: Cartridge c., chargeur m. (c) Ind: Overhead c., transporteur aérien. 3. Navy: Aircraft c., (navire m) porte-avions m inv. Mil: Bren-gun c. = chenillette f. C. platoon, section f de véhicules porte-mitrailleuses. C. rocket, fusée porteuse. 4. C.-pigeon, pigeon voyageur. 5. W.Tel: C. wave, onde porteuse. **'carrier-bag,** s. (Grand) sac (en papier gris). **'carrier-'borne,** a. Av: Nau: Embarqué. C.-b. aircraft, l'aviation embarquée.

carrion ['kæriən], s. Charogne f. S.a. CROW[1] 1.

carrot ['kærət], s. Hort: Carotte f. F: **Carrots,** (i) cheveux m rouges; (ii) (pers.) rouquin, -ine.

carroty ['kærəti], a. F: Roux, f. rousse.

carry[1] ['kæri], s. 1. Mil: Sword at the c., sabre en main. 2. (a) Portée f (d'un fusil). (b) Golf: Trajet m (d'une balle).

carry[2], v.tr. (carried) 1. Porter (un fardeau); transporter (des marchandises); rentrer (la moisson). To c. one's life in one's hands, risquer sa vie. S.a. CAN[1], FETCH[2] 1, LEG[1] 1. 2. (Of wires) Conduire (le son); (of pipes) amener (l'eau). 3. To c. pipes under a street, faire passer des tuyaux par-dessous une rue. To c. sth. in one's head, retenir qch. dans sa tête. Liberty carried to the point of effrontery, licence poussée jusqu'au cynisme. To c. sth. into effect, mettre qch. à exécution. 4. Enlever (une forteresse); emporter (une position) d'assaut. To c. all before one, (i) remporter tous les prix; (ii) vaincre toutes les résistances. To c. one's hearers with one, entraîner son auditoire. To c. one's point, imposer sa manière de voir. S.a. DAY 1 (b), FOOT[1] 1. 5. (i) Adopter, (ii) faire adopter (une proposition). (Of a bill) To be carried, être voté. 6. (a) Porter (une montre, etc.) sur soi. To c. authority, avoir du poids, de l'autorité. (Of money) To c. interest, porter intérêt. (b) (Of shop) Avoir (des marchandises) en magasin, en dépôt. 7. Mil: To c. swords, mettre le sabre en main. 8. To c. one's head high, porter la tête haute. To c. one's liquor well, bien supporter la boisson. 9. Porter, supporter (une poutre, une voûte). 10. Ar: To c. a figure, retenir un chiffre. C. two and seven are nine, deux de retenue et sept font neuf. 11. Abs. (Of gun) Porter. His voice carries well, il a une voix qui porte bien. 12. St.Exch: Accorder un crédit à (un client). **carry across,** v.tr. Transporter (qch.) de l'autre côté. **carry along,** v.tr. Emporter, entraîner (qn, qch.). The mud carried along by the stream, la vase charriée par le ruisseau. **carry away,** v.tr. 1. = CARRY OFF 1. 2. Transporter (qn de joie). Carried away by his feelings, entraîné par ses émotions. **carry back,** v.tr. 1. Rapporter (qch.); ramener (qn). 2. (a) Reporter (qch.); remmener (qn). (b) That carries me back to my youth, cela me rappelle ma jeunesse. **carry down,** v.tr. Descendre (qch.). **carry forward,** v.tr. 1. Avancer (qch.). 2. Book-k: To c. an item forward, reporter un article. Carried forward, report m; à reporter. **carry-'forward,** s. Book-k: Report m. **carry off,** v.tr. 1. Emporter (qch.); emmener, enlever (qn). 2. To c. off the prize, remporter le prix. 3. F: To c. it off, (i) faire passer la chose; (ii) réussir le coup. S.a. AIR[1] III. **carry on.** 1. v.tr. Poursuivre; continuer (une tradition); exercer (un commerce); entretenir (une correspondence); soutenir (une conversation). 2. v.i. (a) To c. on during s.o.'s absence, (i) continuer le travail, (ii) diriger les affaires, pendant l'absence de qn; Adm: assurer l'intérim. C. on! continuez! (b) Persévérer, persister. I shall c. on to the end, j'irai jusqu'au bout. (c) F: Se comporter. I don't like the way she carries on, je n'aime pas ses façons. (d)

P: **She carried on dreadfully,** elle nous a fait une scène terrible. **Don't c. on like that!** ne vous emballez pas comme ça! (*e*) F: **To c. on with s.o.,** faire des coquetteries à qn. **carrying on,** *s.* **1.** Continuation *f* (d'un travail, de la guerre). **2.** F: **Such carryings on!** quelle manière de se conduire! **carry out,** *v.tr.* **1.** Porter (qch.) dehors. **2.** Mettre à exécution, réaliser (un projet); remplir (les instructions de qn); exécuter (un programme); exercer (un mandat); se décharger (d'une commission); s'acquitter (d'une fonction). **To c. out the law,** appliquer la loi. *Mil:* **Movement smartly carried out,** mouvement bien enlevé. **carry over,** *v.tr.* **1.** Transporter de l'autre côté. **2.** *Book-k:* Reporter (une somme). **To c. over a balance,** transporter un solde. **3.** *St. Exch:* **To c. over stock,** reporter des titres. **'carry-over,** *s. St.Exch: Typ:* Report *m.* **carrying over,** *s.* **1.** Transport *m.* **2.** *St.Exch:* Report *m.* **carry through,** *v.tr.* **1.** Transporter (qch.). **2.** Mener (une entreprise) à bonne fin. **3.** **His strong constitution carried him through (his illness),** sa forte santé l'aida à surmonter cette maladie. **carry up,** *v.tr.* Monter (qch.). **carrying,** *s.* **1.** (*a*) Port *m,* transport *m.* **C. business,** entreprise de transports. **C. capacity,** (capacité de) charge *f* utile. (*b*) **C. of arms,** port d'armes. **2.** Enlèvement *m* (d'une forteresse). **3.** Adoption *f,* vote *m* (d'un projet de loi). **'carry-cot,** *s.* Moïse *m* de toile; porte-bébé *m inv.*

cart¹ [kɑːt], *s.* Charrette *f. Mil:* Fourgon *m.* **Bullock, ox, c.,** char *m* à bœufs. **Hay c.,** charrette à foin. **Tip-c.,** tombereau *m. F:* **To put the c. before the horse,** mettre la charrue devant les bœufs. *F:* **To be in the c.,** être dans le pétrin, dans de beaux draps. **'cart-horse,** *s.* Cheval *m* de (gros) trait. **'cart-load,** *s.* Charretée *f,* voiturée *f* (of, de). **C.-l. of coal,** tombereau *m* de charbon. *F:* **A c.-l. of trouble,** toute une accumulation de malheurs. **'cart-track,** *s.* Chemin *m* de charroi; route charretière, chemin charretier. **'cart-wheel,** *s.* **1.** Roue *f* de charrette. **2.** *Gym:* **To turn c.-wheels,** faire la roue (sur les pieds et les mains).

cart², *v.tr.* Charrier, charroyer. **cart about,** *v.tr. F:* Trimbaler (qn, qch.). **carting,** *s.* = CARTAGE.

cartage ['kɑːtidʒ], *s.* Charroi *m,* charriage *m.*

carte (à la) [ˌæləˈkɑːt]. *Fr.a.phr. & adv.phr.* **A la c. dinner,** dîner à la carte.

carte blanche ['kɑːtˈblɑ̃(n)ʃ], *s.* **To give (s.o.) c.b.,** donner carte blanche (à qn).

cartel [kɑːˈtel], *s.* Cartel *m.*

carter ['kɑːtər], *s.* Charretier *m.*

Cartesian [kɑːˈtiːziən], *a. & s. Phil: Mth:* Cartésien, -enne. *Ph:* **C. diver, imp, ludion** *m.*

cartful ['kɑːtful], *s.* Charretée *f.*

Carthaginian [kɑːθəˈdʒiniən], *a.&s.* Carthaginois, -oise.

Carthusian [kɑːˈθjuːziən], *a. & s.* **1.** Chartreux, -euse; des chartreux. **The C. friars,** les chartreux. **2.** (Élève ou ancien élève) de l'école de Charterhouse.

cartilage ['kɑːtilidʒ], *s.* Cartilage *m.*

cartilaginous [ˌkɑːtiˈlædʒinəs], *a.* Cartilagineux, -euse.

cartographer [kɑːˈtogrəfər], *s.* Cartographe *m.*

cartographical [ˌkɑːtoˈgræfik(ə)l], *a.* Cartographique.

cartography [kɑːˈtogrəfi], *s.* Cartographie *f.*

cartomancy ['kɑːtomænsi], *s.* Cartomancie *f.*

carton ['kɑːtən], *s.* (*a*) Carton *m.* (*b*) (Petite boîte en) carton. (*c*) **C.** Cartouche *f* (de cigarettes).

cartoon¹ [kɑːˈtuːn], *s.* **1.** *Art:* Carton *m* (dessin ou peinture sur carton). **2.** *Journ:* (*a*) Caricature *f* (sur les événements du jour). (*b*) Portrait caricaturé. (*c*) *Cin:* Dessin animé, cartoon *m.*

cartoon², *v.tr.* Faire la caricature (de qn).

cartoonist [kɑːˈtuːnist], *s.* **1.** Caricaturiste *m;* dessinateur *m* humoristique ou satirique. **2.** *Cin:* Dessinateur de dessins animés.

cartouche [kɑːˈtuːʃ], *s. Arch: etc:* Cartouche *m.*

cartridge ['kɑːtridʒ], *s.* **1.** (*a*) Cartouche *f.* **To fire blank c.,** tirer à blanc. (*b*) Gargousse *f* (de grosse pièce). **2.** *Ind:* Filter c., cartouche filtrante; cartouche à filtre. **'cartridge-belt,** *s.* **1.** Ceinture-cartouchière *f.* **2.** Bande-chargeur *f* (de mitrailleuse). **'cartridge-case,** *s.* **1.** Étui *m,* douille *f.* **2.** *Artil:* Gargoussier *m.* **'cartridge-clip,** *s. Sm.a:* Chargeur *m.* **'cartridge-factory,** *s.* Cartoucherie *f.* **'cartridge-paper,** *s.* Papier fort. **'cartridge-pouch,** *s.* Cartouchière *f.*

cartwright ['kɑːtrait], *s.* Charron *m.*

caruncle ['kærəŋkl, kəˈrʌŋkl], *s. Biol:* Caroncule *f.*

carve [kɑːv], *v.tr.* **1.** Sculpter, graver, ciseler. **To c. one's way,** se tailler un chemin. **2.** Découper (la viande); dépecer (un poulet). **carving,** *s.* **1.** *Art:* Sculpture *f,* gravure *f,* ciselure *f.* **2.** Découpage *m* de la viande. *S.a.* KNIFE¹ **1.**

carvel ['kɑːvil], *s. A:* = CARAVEL. **'carvel-built,** *a.* Bordé à franc-bord.

carver ['kɑːvər], *s.* **1.** (*a*) Ciseleur *m.* (*b*) (*At table*) Découpeur; (*hotel*) serveur. **2.** Couteau *m* à découper. *pl.* Serv.:e *m* à découper.

caryatid [ˌkæriˈætid], *s. Arch:* Caryatide *f.*

caryopsis [ˌkæriˈopsis], *s. Bot:* Caryopse *m.*

cascade¹ [kæsˈkeid], *s.* Chute *f* d'eau; cascade *f.*

cascade², *v.i.* Tomber en cascade; cascader.

case¹ [keis], *s.* **1.** Cas *m.* **The c. in point,** le cas dont il s'agit. *Jur:* **A c. in point,** un cas d'espèce. **To quote a c. in point,** citer un exemple topique. **In this particular c.,** en l'espèce. **In every c.,** en toute hypothèse. **Should the c. occur,** le cas échéant. **This is not the c.,** ce n'est pas le cas; il n'en est rien. **If that is the c.,** s'il en est ainsi. **That is often the c.,** cela arrive souvent. **That alters the c.,** c'est une autre affaire. **It is a hard c.,** c'est dur pour lui. **It is a c. for the doctor,** c'est affaire au médecin. **In any c.,** en tout cas; dans tous les cas; de toute façon. **As in the c. of . . .,** comme pour. . . . **Do it, just in c.,** faites-le tout hasard. **Such being the c. . . .,** cela étant. . . . **In most cases,** en général. **2.** *Med:* (*a*) Cas (de choléra). (*b*) *F:* **Malade** *mf;* blessé. *Mil:* **The serious cases,** les grands blessés. **3.** *Jur:* (*a*) Cause *f,* affaire. **Famous cases,** causes célèbres. **To state the c.,** faire l'exposé des faits. (*b*) **The c. for the Crown,** l'accusation *f.* **There is no c. against you,** vous êtes hors de cause. **You have no c.,** vous serez débouté (de votre demande). **To make out a c.,** établir une réclamation. **The c. for,** arguments en faveur de. . . . **To put up a strong c. for (s.o.),** (i) prendre le parti de (qn), défendre (qn); (ii) recommander (qn) très chaudement. **4.** *Gram:* Cas. **The c. endings,** les flexions casuelles. **'case-book,** *s.* Recueil *m* de jurisprudence. **'case 'history,** *s. Med:* Dossier *m* (médical). **'case-law,** *s.* Jurisprudence *f.*

case², *s.* **1. C. of goods,** caisse *f* de marchandises; colis *m. A. Mil:* **Uniform c.,** cantine *f* (d'officier). **2.** (*a*) Mallette *f;* étui *m;* écrin *m* (pour bijoux); étui (à lunettes); trousse *f* (d'instruments); boîte *f* (de violon). (*b*) (**Display**) **c.,** vitrine *f.* **3.** (*a*) Coffre *m,* caisse (de piano); buffet *m* (d'orgue). (*b*) Boîtier *m* (de montre). **4.** = CASING **2.** **Wheel c.,** bâche *f* (of a turbine). *Ball:* **Bomb c.,** corps *m* de bombe. **5.** *Bookb:* Couverture *f.* **6.** *Dom.Ec:* **Pillow-c.,** taie *f* d'oreiller. **7.** *Typ:* Casse *f.* **Upper c.,** haut *m* de casse. **Lower-c. letters,** lettres (de) bas de casse; minuscules *f.* **'case-binding,** *s. Bookb:* Emboîtage *m;* reliure *f* Bradel. **'case-harden,** *v.tr.* Cémenter, aciérer (le fer). **'case-hardened,** *a.* **1.** Cémenté, aciéré. **2.** *F:* (*Of pers.*) Endurci. **'case-opener,** *s.* Ciseau *m* à déballer.

case³, *v.tr.* **1. To c. goods (up),** encaisser des marchandises. **2.** (*a*) Envelopper (with, de). **To c. a boiler,** chemiser une chaudière. **To c. a turbine,** bâcher une turbine. (*b*) *Bookb:* Cartonner (un livre). **3. To c. a well,** tuber, cuveler, un puits. **casing,** *s.* **1.** (*a*) Encaissage *m* (de marchandises); clissage *m* (d'une bouteille). *Bookb:* **C. (in),** cartonnage *m.* (*b*) Coffrage *m* (d'un puits de mine). **2.** Enveloppe *f* (d'une pompe); chemise *f* (d'un cylindre); bâche *f* (d'une turbine); revêtement *m* (d'une maçonnerie); chambranle *m* (d'une porte). *Min:* Boisage *m* (d'une galerie). *N.Arch:* Cadre *m* (d'une hélice). *El.E:* **Armature c.,** enveloppe d'induit. *Aut:* **Differential c.,** carter *m* du différentiel. **Tyre c.,** enveloppe (extérieure) de pneu.

casein ['keisiin], *s. Ch: Ind:* Caséine *f.*

casemate¹ ['keismeit], *s. Fort:* Casemate *f,* coffre *m. N.Arch:* **Gun c.,** réduit *m.*

casemate², *v.tr. Fort:* Casemater.

casement ['keismənt], *s.* Châssis *m* de fenêtre à deux battants. **'casement(-)cloth,** *s.* Toile *f* pour rideaux. **'casement-window,** *s.* Croisée *f.*

cash[1] [kæʃ], s. *No pl.* Espèces *fpl*; argent comptant; valeurs *fpl* en espèces. **To be out of, short of, c.,** (i) ne pas avoir d'argent comptant (sur soi); (ii) ne pas être en fonds; *F:* être à sec. **Hard c.,** espèces sonnantes. **C. down,** argent (au) comptant. **To pay c. down,** payer comptant, *F:* payer cash. **Terms c.,** payable au comptant. **C. less discount,** comptant avec escompte. **C. price,** prix au comptant. **C. on delivery parcel,** colis expédié contre remboursement. **C. with order,** payable à la commande. *Jur:* **C. offer,** offre réelle. *Book-k:* **C. in hand,** espèces en caisse. **To balance the c.,** faire la caisse. **'cash-account,** s. Compte *m* de caisse. **'cash and 'carry,** s. Paiement comptant, marchandises à transporter par l'acheteur. **'cash-'balance,** s. Solde *m* de caisse. **'cash-book,** s. Livre *m* de caisse; sommier *m.* **'cash-box,** s. Caisse *f*; cassette *f.* **cash-desk,** s. Caisse *f.* **'cash-'discount,** s. *Com:* Escompte *m* au comptant. **'cash(-)register,** s. Caisse enregistreuse; caisse *f* automatique. **'cash-sale,** s. Transaction *f* au comptant.

cash[2], *v.tr.* Toucher (un chèque); encaisser (un coupon). **cash in,** *v.tr.* **1.** Déposer (de l'argent) en banque. **2.** (*a*) *Abs.* Verser sa recette à la caisse; régler ses comptes. (*b*) *U.S: P:* **To c. in one's chips,** mourir; lâcher la rampe. **3.** *F:* **To c. in on one's influence,** monnayer son influence.

cash[3], s. *Num:* Sapèque *f.*

cashew [kæ'ʃuː], s. *Bot:* Acajou *m* à pommes; anacardier *m.* **C. nut,** noix *f* d'acajou.

cashier[1] [kə'ʃiər], s. Caissier, -ière. **C.'s desk, office, caisse** *f*; comptoir *m* de recette.

cashier[2], *v.tr.* Casser (un officier).

Cashmere [kæʃ'miər]. **1.** *Pr.n.* Le Cachemire. **2.** s. *Tex:* Cachemire *m.* **C. shawl,** cachemire de l'Inde.

casino [kə'siːnou], s. Casino *m.*

cask [kɑːsk], s. (*a*) Barrique *f*, fût *m*, tonneau *m.* (*b*) (*For dry goods*) Boucaut *m.*

casket ['kɑːskit], s. **1.** Coffret *m*, cassette *f.* **2.** *U.S:* (*Coffin*) Cercueil *m* rectangulaire; cercueil de luxe.

Caspian ['kæspiən], *a.* **The C. Sea,** la mer Caspienne.

cassation [kə'seiʃən], s. *Jur:* Cassation *f.*

cassava [kə'sɑːvə], s. Cassave *f*, manioc *m.*

casserole ['kæsəroul], s. *Cu:* **1.** Cocotte *f* (en terre). **2.** Ragoût *m* en cocotte.

cassette [kæ set], s. *Phot:* Chargeur *m.*

cassia ['kæsiə], s. **1.** *Bot:* (*a*) Casse *f*, canéfice *f.* (*b*) **C.(-tree),** cassier *m.* **2.** *Pharm:* Casse.

Cassino [kæ'siːnou]. *Pr.n. Geog:* **Monte C.,** le Mont Cassin.

cassock ['kæsək], s. *Ecc:* Soutane *f.*

cassowary ['kæsəwɛəri], s. *Orn:* Casoar *m.*

cast[1] [kɑːst], s. **1.** (*a*) Jet *m* (d'une pierre); coup *m* (de dés); lancer *m* (du filet). *Nau:* **C. of the lead,** coup de sonde. (*b*) *Fish:* Bas *m* de ligne. **2.** (*a*) *Earthworm* casts, déjections *f* de lombric. (*b*) *Husb:* Agneaux *pl* mis bas. **3.** *Ap:* Jet (d'abeilles); rejet *m* (d'essaim). **4.** (*a*) *Metall:* Coulée *f.* (*b*) Pièce moulée. **Plaster c.,** moulage *m* au plâtre. **To take a c. of sth.,** mouler qch. **5.** (*a*) **A man of his c.,** un homme de sa trempe. **C. of mind,** tournure *f* d'esprit. **C. of features,** physionomie *f.* (*b*) (*Arrangement*) **C. of a sentence,** ordonnance *f*, allure *f*, d'une phrase. **6.** **To have a c. in one's eye,** avoir une tendance à loucher. **7.** Addition *f* (de chiffres). **8.** *Th:* Distribution *f* (des rôles); la troupe. **With the following c. . . . ,** avec le concours de. . . .

cast[2], *v.tr.* (*p.t.* **cast**; *p.p.* **cast**) **1.** (*a*) Jeter, lancer (une pierre); projeter (une ombre). **The die is c.,** le dé, le sort, en est jeté. **You needn't c. it in his teeth,** ce n'est pas la peine de revenir là-dessus. **To c. a glance at s.o.,** jeter un coup d'œil, un regard, sur qn. *Nau:* **To c. the lead,** donner un coup de sonde. *S.a.* ASPERSION 2. (*b*) (*Of reptile*) **To c. its slough,** jeter sa dépouille. (*Of bird*) **To c. its feathers,** muer. (*Of pers.*) *O:* **To c. a garment,** se dévêtir de qch.; ôter un vêtement. *S.a.* SHOE[1] 2. (*c*) *Husb:* (*Of dam*) **To c. her young,** mettre bas (un petit) avant terme. **2.** *Fish:* **To c. the line,** lancer la ligne. **3.** Donner (un suffrage). **Number of votes c.,** nombre de voix, de suffrages. **4.** *Astrol:* **To c. a horoscope,** dresser un horoscope. *S.a.* LOT 1. **5.** **To c. (up) figures,** additionner des chiffres. *S.a.* ACCOUNT[1] 1. **6.** **To c. a horse,** jeter un cheval par terre. **7.** *Jur:*

To be c. in damages, être condamné à des dommages-intérêts. **8.** *Metall:* Fondre (du métal); mouler (un cylindre). **To c. a statue,** couler une statue. **Cast in one piece,** coulé en bloc. *Typ:* **To c. a page,** clicher une page. *S.a.* MOULD[2] 2. **9.** *Th:* **To c. a play,** distribuer les rôles d'une pièce. **To c. s.o. for a part,** assigner un rôle à qn. **cast about. 1.** *v.tr.* **To c. one's eyes about,** promener ses regards de tous côtés. **2.** *v.i.* (*a*) **To c. about for an excuse,** chercher une excuse. (*b*) *Nau:* Virer. **cast aside,** *v.tr.* Se défaire de (qch.); mettre (qch.) de côté. **cast away,** *v.tr.* (*a*) Jeter au loin; rejeter. (*b*) *Nau:* **To be c. away,** faire naufrage. **cast back.** (*a*) *v.tr.* Renvoyer (une pierre, etc.). (*b*) Ramener, reporter, (ses pensées) en arrière. **cast down,** *v.tr.* (*a*) Jeter bas. (*b*) Baisser (les yeux). (*c*) **To be c. down,** être abattu, déprimé. **cast loose,** *v.tr. Nau:* Larguer (une amarre). *Abs.* **To c. loose,** larguer. **cast off. 1.** *v.tr.* (*a*) Rejeter. **He was c. off by his family,** il a été renié par sa famille. (*b*) Se dévêtir de (ses vêtements). **C.-o. clothing, c.-offs,** vêtements *mpl* de rebut; défroque *f.* (*c*) **To c. off all sense of shame,** abjurer toute pudeur. (*d*) *Nau:* **To c. off the hawsers,** larguer les amarres. (*e*) *Knitting:* **To c. off five stitches,** fermer cinq mailles. *Abs.* **To c. off,** rabattre, arrêter, rejeter, les mailles. (*f*) *Typ:* **To c. off a manuscript,** évaluer le nombre de pages imprimées auquel se montera un manuscrit. **2.** *v.i.* (*Of ship*) Abattre sous le vent. **cast on,** *v.tr. Knitting:* **To c. on twenty stitches,** monter vingt mailles. *Abs.* **To c. on,** monter les mailles. **casting on,** s. *Knitting:* Montage *m* (des mailles). **cast out,** *v.tr.* Mettre (qn) dehors; exorciser (des démons). **cast up,** *v.tr.* **1.** Lever (les yeux) au ciel. **2.** Flotsam c. up on the shore, épaves rejetées sur le rivage. **cast**[3], *a.* **1.** *Art:* **C. shadow,** ombre portée. **2.** *Metall:* Coulé. **C. iron,** fonte *f* (de fer). **'C.-iron excuse,** alibi, excuse *f*, alibi *m* irréfutable. **casting**[1], *a.* **The chairman has the c. vote,** la voix du président est prépondérante. **To give the c. vote,** départager les voix. **casting**[2], s. **1.** (*a*) Jet *m* (d'une pierre); *Fish:* pêche *f* au lancer. (*b*) *Metall:* Moulage *m*, fonte *f.* (*c*) *Th:* Distribution *f* des rôles. (*d*) **C. (up) of figures,** addition *f* de chiffres. **2.** *Metall:* Pièce coulée, pièce de fonte. **Heavy castings,** grosses pièces. **'cast(ing)-net,** s. *Fish:* Épervier *m.*

castanets [,kæstə'nets], *s.pl.* Castagnettes *f.*

castaway ['kɑːstəwei], s. (*a*) Naufragé, -ée. (*b*) = OUTCAST.

caste [kɑːst], s. Caste *f.* **To lose c.,** déroger (à son rang).

castellated ['kæstileitid], *a.* Crénelé.

castigate ['kæstigeit], *v.tr.* Châtier, corriger (qn).

castigation [,kæsti'geiʃ(ə)n], s. Châtiment *m*, correction *f.*

castigator ['kæstigeitər], s. Châtieur *m*; critique *m* sévère.

Castile [kæs'tiːl]. *Pr.n. Geog:* La Castille. *Com:* **C. soap,** savon blanc.

Castilian [kæs'tilian], *a. & s.* Castillan, -ane.

castle[1] ['kɑːsl], s. **1.** Château (fort). **To build castles in the air,** bâtir des châteaux en Espagne. *Prov:* **An Englishman's home is his c.,** charbonnier est maître chez lui. **2.** *Chess:* Tour *f.* **'castle-nut,** s. Écrou crénelé à entailles.

castle[2], *v.tr. Chess:* **To c. the king,** *abs.* to c., roquer. **castling,** s. *Chess:* Roque *m.*

castor[1] ['kɑːstər], s. **1.** Saupoudroir *m.* *S.a.* SUGAR[1] 1. **2.** Roulette *f* (de fauteuil).

castor[2], s. Châtaigne *f* (de jambe de cheval).

castor oil ['kɑːstər'ɔil], s. Huile *f* de ricin.

castrate [kæs'treit], *v.tr.* Châtrer.

castration [kæs'treiʃ(ə)n], s. Castration *f.*

castrato [kæs'trɑːtou], *s.m. Mus:* Castrat *m.*

casual ['kæʒju(ə)l]. **1.** *a.* (*a*) Fortuit, accidentel, -elle. **To engage in c. conversation,** parler de choses et d'autres. **C. labour,** main-d'œuvre temporaire. **C. profit,** produit casuel. (*b*) Insouciant. **To give a c. answer,** répondre d'un air désinvolte. *Cost:* **C. clothes, clothes for c. wear,** costume *m* sport. **2.** s. (*a*) *A:* Indigent *m* de passage. **C. ward,** asile *m* de nuit (d'un hospice). (*b*) *Bootm:* *pl.* Casuals, mocassins *mpl.* **-ally,** *adv.* (*a*) Fortuitement, par hasard, en passant. (*b*) Négligemment; avec désinvolture.

casualness ['kæʒjuəlnis], s. Indifférence *f*; insouciance *f*; manque *f* de méthode.

casualty ['kæʒju(ə)lti], s. **1.** (*a*) Accident *m* (de personne). **C. ward**, salle des accidentés. (*b*) pl. Mil: Pertes *f*. **2.** Mort *m*; blessé, -ée.

casuist ['kæzjuist], s. Casuiste *m*.

casuistic(al) [kæzju'istik(ə)l], *a*. De casuiste.

casuistry ['kæzjuistri], s. Casuistique *f*.

cat¹ [kæt], s. **1.** (*a*) Chat, *f*. chatte. **Tom c.**, matou *m*. **Persian cat**, (chat) angora. (*Ordinary*) **domestic**, *F*: **alley, c.**, chat de gouttière. **Tabby c.**, chat tigré. **Siamese c.**, chat siamois. **C. door**, chatière *f*. *F*: **To be like a c. on hot bricks**, être sur des épines. **To see which way the c. jumps**, prendre l'aire du vent. **There's not room to swing a c.** in his study, son cabinet est grand comme un mouchoir de poche. **To let the c. out of the bag**, éventer la mèche. **The c. is out of the bag**, le grand mot est lâché. **They quarrel like c. and dog**, ils s'accordent comme chien et chat. *S.a.* RAIN². **It would make a c. laugh**, c'est à mourir de rire. *Prov:* **A c. may look at a king**, un chien regarde bien un évêque. **When the cat's away the mice will play**, le chat parti les souris dansent. *S.a.* CARE¹ 1, GRIN². (*b*) *F*: (*Of pers.*) **An old c.**, une vieille chipie. **2.** *Z*: **Wild c.**, chat sauvage. **The (great) cats**, les grands félins. **3.** = CAT-O'-NINE-TAILS. 'cat(-)burglar, s. *F*: Monte-en-l'air *m inv.* 'cat(-)fish, s. Loup marin; chat marin; poisson-chat *m*. 'cat-footed, *a*. Qui marche à pas feutrés. 'cat-ice, s. Nau: Glace pourrie. 'cat-lap, s. *F*: Lavasse *f*, thé *m*, trop faible. 'cat(-)nap, s. Sieste *f*, somme *m*. cat-o'-'nine-tails, s. Nau: Chat *m* à neuf queues. 'cat's-'cradle, s. (Jeu *m* de la) scie; (jeu du) berceau. 'cat's-eye, s. Lap: Œil-de-chat *m*. Opt: Catadioptre *m*, R.t.m: Cataphote *m*. 'cat-lick, s. *F*: **To have a c.-l.**, se laver le bout du nez. **Cat's meat**, c. Viande *f* pour chats. *F*: **To make c. m. of s.o.**, abîmer le portrait à, de, qn. 'cat's-paw, s. **1.** Petite bouffée de vent. **2.** *F*: **To be made a c.-p. of**, tirer les marrons du feu (pour qn). 'cat's-tail, s. Bot: Massette *f*. 'cat-walk, s. Nau: Cin: etc: Passerelle *f* de visite.

cat². **1.** *v.tr.* Nau: Caponner (l'ancre). **2.** *v.i.* *P*: Dégobiller.

cataclysm ['kætəklizm], s. Cataclysme *m*.

catacombs ['kætəkoumz], s.pl. Catacombes *f*.

catafalque ['kætəfælk], s. Catafalque *m*.

Catalan [kætə'læn], *a*. & *s*. Geog: Catalan, -ane.

catalepsy ['kætələpsi], s. Med: Catalepsie *f*.

cataleptic [kætə'leptik], *a*. & *s*. Med: Cataleptique (*mf*).

catalogue¹ ['kætələg], s. **1.** Catalogue *m*, liste *f*. **Subject c.**, catalogue raisonné. **2.** Com: Catalogue, prix-courant *m*.

catalogue², *v.tr.* Cataloguer.

Catalonia [kætə'lounjə]. Pr.n. Geog: La Catalogne.

catalpa [kæt'ælpə], s. Bot: Catalpa *m*.

catalyse ['kætəlaiz], *v.tr.* Ch: Catalyser.

catalyser ['kætəlaizər], catalyst ['kætəlist], s. Ch: Catalyseur *m*.

catalysis [kə'tælisis], s. Ch: Catalyse *f*.

catalytic [kætə'litik], *a*. Ch: Catalytique.

cataplasm ['kætəplæzm], s. Med: Cataplasme *m*.

catapult¹ ['kætəpʌlt], s. **1.** Lance-pierre *m*. **2.** Av: Catapulte *f* (de lancement).

catapult², *v.tr.* Av: Lancer, catapulter (un avion). **catapulting**, s. Av: Lancement *m*, catapultage *m*. *attrib.* **C. hook**, crochet de catapultage.

cataract ['kætərækt], s. **1.** Cataracte *f* (d'un fleuve, de l'œil). Med: **To couch a c.**, faire une kératotomie, *F*: enlever une cataracte.

catarrh [kə'tɑːr], s. Med: Catarrhe *m*.

catarrhal [kə'tɑːr(ə)l], *a*. Med: Catarrhal, -aux.

catastrophe [kə'tæstrəfi], s. **1.** Catastrophe *f*; désastre *m*. **The victims of the c.**, les sinistrés. **2.** Gr.Drama: Catastrophe, dénouement *m*.

catastrophic [kætə'strɔfik], *a*. Désastreux, -euse; catastrophique.

catbird ['kætbəːd], s. Orn: Oiseau-chat *m*.

catcall¹ ['kætkɔːl], s. Th: (Coup *m* de) sifflet *m*.

catcall², *v.i.* Siffler (un acteur); chahuter.

catch¹ [kætʃ], s. **1.** Prise *f*. (*a*) Cr: Prise au vol de la balle. (*b*) **C. of the breath**, soubresaut *m*. **2.** (*a*) Fish: Prise, pêche *f*. **To have a good c.**, faire (une) bonne

pêche. (*b*) *F*: Bon parti (à épouser). (*c*) *F*: **It's no great c.**, ce n'est pas le Pérou. **3.** Fragment *m*, bribe *f* (de conversation). **4.** (*On door*) Loquet *m*, loqueteau *m*; (*of buckle*) ardillon *m*; (*on garment*) agrafe *f*. Mec.E: Déclic *m*; cliquet *m*. **5.** (*Deception*) Attrape *f*. **There's a c. in it**, c'est une attrape. Sch: etc: **C. question**, colle *f*. **6.** Mus: Chant *m* à reprises; canon *m*.

catch², *v.* (*p.t.* **caught** [kɔːt]; *p.p.* **caught**) I. *v.tr.* **1.** (*a*) Attraper, prendre (un poisson); attraper, saisir (une balle, une allusion); ne pas manquer (le train). Fish: Ven: **To c. nothing**, revenir bredouille. Nau: (*Of sail, etc.*) **To c. the wind**, prendre le vent. *S.a.* BREATH, HARE¹. (*b*) = CATCH UP 3. (*c*) **To c. s.o. doing sth.**, surprendre qn à faire qch. **If I c. them at it!** si je les y prends! *F*: **C. me** (doing such a thing)! il n'y a pas de danger! **You won't c. me doing that again!** on ne m'y reprendra plus! (*d*) **We were caught in the storm**, l'orage nous a surpris. **2.** (*a*) Saisir (des sons); rencontrer (le regard de qn). **A sound caught my ear**, un son me frappa l'oreille. **The artist has caught the likeness**, l'artiste a bien saisi la ressemblance. (*b*) **I did not c. what you said**, je n'ai pas bien entendu ce que vous disiez. **I didn't quite c. that**, pardon? plaît-il? (*c*) Accrocher, happer. **A nail caught my dress**, un clou a accroché ma robe. **To c. one's foot** (in sth.), se prendre le pied (dans qch.). **3.** Attraper (une maladie); contracter (une habitude). **4.** *F*: (*a*) **To c. s.o. a blow**, flanquer un coup à qn. (*b*) **You'll c. it!** vous allez être grondé! votre affaire est bonne! *F*: (*Entrap*) Attraper. **You don't c. me!** ça ne prend pas (avec moi)! II. **catch**, *v.i.* **1.** **To c. at sth.**, s'accrocher à qch. **2.** (*a*) (*Of cog-wheel*) Mordre; (*of door-bolt*) s'engager. *b*) (*Of fire*) Prendre. **3.** Cu: **To c. s.o. up** (in a speech), relever les paroles de qn. **3.** (*Overtake*) **To c. s.o. up**, *v.i.* to **c. up with s.o.**, rattraper qn. **He caught us up at the village**, il nous a rejoints au village. **catching¹**, *a*. (*Of disease*) Contagieux, -euse, infectieux, -euse; (*of laughter*) communicatif, -ive; (*of melody*) (i) entraînant, (ii) facile à retenir. **catching²**, *s*. Prise *f*. (*a*) Capture *f*. (*b*) Accrochage *m*. 'catch-as-catch 'can, *s*. Wr: Lutte *f* libre; catch *m*. 'catch-phrase, *s*. *F*: Rengaine *f*; scie *f*; slogan *m*. 'catch-points, s.pl. Rail: Aiguille prise en pointe.

catchall ['kætʃɔːl], s. *U.S:* Débarras *m*; fourre-tout *m*.

catcher ['kætʃər], s. Attrapeur, -euse; preneur, -euse. *Baseball:* Receveur *m*, attrapeur *m*.

catchment ['kætʃmənt], s. Hyd.E: (*a*) (Water-)c., captage *m* (d'eaux). (*b*) **C. basin**, surface *f* de captation des eaux; bassin *m* de réception.

catchpenny ['kætʃpeni], s. (*Of thg*) Attrape-sou *m*; camelote *f* de réclame.

catchword ['kætʃwəːd], s. **1.** (*a*) Pol: Mot *m* de ralliement. (*b*) Scie *f*, rengaine *f*. **2.** Typ: Mot-souche *m*. **3.** Th: Réplique *f*.

catchy ['kætʃi], *a*. *F*: **1.** (*Of tune, etc.*) (i) Entraînant; (ii) facile à retenir, accrochant. **2.** **C. question**, question insidieuse.

catechism ['kætəkizm], s. Catéchisme *m*.

catechist ['kætəkist], s. Catéchiste *m*.

catechize ['kætəkaiz], *v.tr.* **1.** Catéchiser. **2.** *F*: Poser une série de questions à (qn).

catechizer ['kætəkaizər], s. **1.** Catéchiste *m*. **2.** Interrogateur, -trice.

catechumen [kætə'kjuːmən], s. Ecc: Catéchumène *m*.

categoric(al) [kætə'gɔrik(ə)l], *a*. Catégorique. **-ally**, *adv.* Catégoriquement.

category ['kætəgəri], s. Catégorie *f*.

catenary [kæ'tiːnəri], catenarian [kæti'neəriən], *a*. & *s*. Caténaire (*f*); (ligne *f* de) chaînette *f*. **C. curve**, funiculaire *f*.

cater ['keitər], *v.i.* **To c. for s.o.**, (i) approvisionner qn; (ii) pourvoir aux plaisirs de qn. **To c. for all tastes**, pourvoir à tous les goûts. **catering**, *s*. Approvisionnement *m*.

caterer ['keitərər], s. 1. Approvisionneur m; pourvoyeur m. 2. (Supplying banquet, etc.) Traiteur m.

caterpillar ['kætəpilər], s. 1. Chenille f. 2. (a) R.t.m. C. (-tractor), autochenille f. (b) C. wheel, roue à chenille.

caterwaul ['kætəwɔːl], v.i. 1. Miauler. 2. F: Crier (comme les chats la nuit); faire un vrai sabbat. **caterwauling**, s. 1. Miaulements mpl. 2. F: Sabbat m de chats; charivari m.

catgut ['kætgʌt], s. Corde f de boyau (pour cordes (i) de violon, (ii) de raquette). Surg: Catgut m.

cathedral [kə'θiːdrəl]. 1. a. Cathédral, -aux. C. church, église cathédrale. 2. s. Cathédrale f. C. city, ville épiscopale, évêché m.

Catherine ['kæθ(ə)rin]. 1. Pr.n.f. Catherine. 2. Pyr: C. wheel, soleil m; roue f à feu.

catheter ['kæθitər], s. Surg: Cathéter m.

cathode ['kæθoud], a. El: T.V: Cathode f. C. rays, rayons cathodiques. C.-ray tube, oscillographe m cathodique, tube m cathodique.

cathodic [kə'θɒdik], a. El: T.V: Cathodique. C. beam, faisceau m cathodique.

catholic ['kæθ(ə)lik]. 1. a. (a) Universel, -elle. (b) Tolérant. C. mind, esprit large. C. taste, goûts éclectiques. 2. a. & s. Ecc: (a) Orthodoxe (mf), catholique (mf). The C. Church, toute la chrétienté. (b) (Roman Catholic) Catholique. I believe in one holy, Catholic and apostolic Church, je crois en l'Église, une, sainte, catholique et apostolique.

catholicism [kə'θɒlisizm], s. Catholicisme m.

catholicity [ˌkæθə'lisiti], s. 1. (a) Universalité f. (b) Largeur f (d'esprit); tolérance f; éclectisme m. 2. Theol: Orthodoxie f, catholicité f.

cathouse ['kæthaus], s. P: U.S: Bordel m.

cation ['kætaiən], s. El: Cation m.

catkin ['kætkin], s. Bot: Chaton m.

catlike ['kætlaik], a. Comme un chat; félin. To walk with c. tread, marcher à pas de loup.

catmint ['kætmint], U.S: catnip ['kætnip], s. Bot: Cataire f; herbe f aux chats.

catoptrics [kə'tɒptriks], s. Ph: Catoptrique f.

cattery ['kætəri], s. F; Pension f pour chats.

cattiness ['kætinis], s. = CATTISHNESS.

cattish ['kætiʃ], a. F: (Esp. of woman) Méchant(e), rosse. C. answer, réponse aigre-douce. -ly, adv. Méchamment.

cattishness ['kætiʃnis], s. F: Méchanceté f, rosserie f.

cattle ['kætl], s. Coll. inv. 1. Bétail m; bestiaux mpl. Horned c., bêtes fpl à cornes. C. breeding, élevage m du bétail. P.N: 'C. crossing,' "passage m de troupeaux." 2. A: Chevaux mpl. 'cattle-'drover, s. Bouvier m; toucheur m de bœufs. 'cattle-pen, s. Parc m à bestiaux. 'cattle-plague, s. Peste bovine. 'cattle-rustling, s. U.S: Vol m de bétail. 'cattle-show, s. Comice m agricole. 'cattle-truck, s. Fourgon m à bestiaux.

catty ['kæti], a. F: = CATTISH. C. remark, rosserie f.

Caucasian [kɔː'keizjən], a. & s. Caucasien, -ienne.

Caucasus (the) [ðə'kɔːkəsəs]. Pr.n. Geog: Le Caucase.

caucus ['kɔːkəs], s. Comité électoral; clique f politique.

caudal ['kɔːdl], a. Z: Caudal, -aux.

caught. See CATCH².

caul [kɔːl], s. 1. Coiffe f (de nouveau-né). Born with a c., né coiffé. 2. Cu: Crépine f.

cauldron ['kɔːldrən], s. 1. (a) Chaudron m. (b) Ind: Chaudière f. 2. Oc: Gouffre m.

cauliflower ['kɒliflauər], s. Chou-fleur m. Box: C. ear, oreille en chou-fleur.

caulk [kɔːk], v.tr. 1. (a) Calfater (un navire). (b) Calfeutrer (une fenêtre). 2. Mater (un rivet). **caulking**, s. 1. (a) Calfatage m (d'un navire). (b) Calfeutrage m, calfeutrement m. 2. Matage m (de tôles). 'caulking-iron, s. 1. Calfait m; ciseau m de calfat. 2. Metalw: Matoir m.

caulker ['kɔːkər], s. Calfat m.

causal ['kɔːz(ə)l], a. Causal (no mpl). Gram: C. conjunction, conjonction causative.

causality [kɔː'zæliti], s. Phil: Causalité f.

causation [kɔː'zeiʃən], s. 1. Causation f. 2. = CAUSA-LITY.

causative ['kɔːzətiv], a. Esp. Gram: Factitif, -ive (verbe, etc.); causatif, -ive (voix, etc.).

cause¹ [kɔːz], s. 1. Cause f. Prime c., cause première. To be the c. of an accident, être (la) cause d'un accident. 2. Raison f, motif m, sujet m. C. for litigation, matière f à procès. I have c. to be thankful, j'ai lieu d'être reconnaissant. To have good c. for doing sth., faire qch. à bon droit. And with good c., et pour cause. To show c., exposer ses raisons. To give serious c. for complaint, donner de grands sujets de plainte. 3. (a) Jur: Cause; procès m. To plead s.o.'s c., plaider la cause de qn. (b) To take up s.o.'s c., épouser la querelle de qn. To work in a good c., travailler pour une bonne cause. W.Tel: T.V: The week's good c., appel m à la radio pour une œuvre charitable. 'cause-list, s. Jur: Rôle m d'audience.

cause², v.tr. 1. Causer, occasionner (un malheur). To c. a fire, provoquer un incendie. 2. To c. s.o. to do sth., faire faire qch. à qn. To c. s.o. to be punished, faire punir qn.

causeway ['kɔːzwei], s. (a) Chaussée f. (b) Levée f, digue f.

caustic ['kɔːstik]. 1. a. Caustique. C. wit, esprit mordant. C. humour, causticité f. 2. s. Pharm: Caustique m. 3. Opt: Caustique f. -ally, adv. D'un ton mordant.

causticity [kɔːs'tisiti], s. Ch: Causticité f.

cauterization [kɔːtərai'zeiʃ(ə)n], s. Cautérisation f.

cauterize ['kɔːtəraiz], v.tr. Cautériser.

cautery ['kɔːtəri], s. Cautère m.

caution¹ ['kɔːʃ(ə)n], s. 1. Précaution f, prévoyance f, prudence f, circonspection f. To do sth. with great c., faire qch. avec de grands ménagements. 2. (a) Avis m, avertissement m. C.! attention! (b) Mil: Commandement m préparatoire. (c) Réprimande f. He was let off with a c., il s'en est tiré avec une réprimande. To inflict a punishment as a c. to others, infliger une punition pour l'exemple. 3. P: A c., un drôle de numéro; une drôle de femme; un vrai type. She's a c., elle est formidable.

caution², v.tr. 1. Avertir (qn); mettre (qn) sur ses gardes. To c. s.o. against sth., mettre qn en garde contre qch. 2. Menacer (qn) de poursuites à la prochaine occasion.

cautionary ['kɔːʃənəri], a. D'avertissement. C. signal, signal m d'avertissement. C. tales, contes moraux.

cautious ['kɔːʃəs], a. Circonspect, prudent. C. judgment, jugement retenu. To be c. in doing sth., faire qch. avec circonspection. To play a c. game, jouer serré. -ly, adv. Avec circonspection; prudemment; avec ménagement(s).

cautiousness ['kɔːʃəsnis], s. Prudence f.

cavalcade [ˌkæv(ə)l'keid], s. Cavalcade f.

cavalier [ˌkævə'liər]. 1. s.m. (a) Cavalier; gentilhomme. Eng.Hist: Royaliste. The Cavaliers and the Roundheads, les Cavaliers et les Têtes rondes. (b) A: Galant; chevalier servant (d'une dame). 2. a. Cavalier, -ière, désinvolte.

cavalry ['kæv(ə)lri], s. Cavalerie f. Heavy c., grosse cavalerie, les dragons mpl. Light c., cavalerie légère, Hist: les chevau-légers mpl.

cavalryman, pl. -men ['kævəlrimən], s.m. Mil: Cavalier; soldat de cavalerie.

cave¹ [keiv], s. 1. Caverne f, antre m, souterrain m, grotte f. Art: (attrib. use) C. art, art m rupestre. C. hunting, spéléologie f. Paleont: C. bear, ours des cavernes. 'cave-dweller, s. Troglodyte mf. 'cave-man, pl. -men, s.m. 1. Prehist: Homme m des cavernes. 2. F: Homme à la manière forte (avec les femmes).

cave², v.i. To c. in. 1. S'effondrer, s'ébouler. 2. F: (Of pers.) Céder, se rendre.

cave³ ['keivi], int. F: Vingt-deux! To keep c., faire le guet.

caveat ['kæviæt], s. Jur: (a) Opposition f (to, à). To enter a c., mettre opposition (against, à). (b) Avis m d'opposition.

cavern ['kæv(ə)n], s. Caverne f; souterrain m.

cavernous ['kævənəs], a. Caverneux, -euse.

caviar(e) ['kæviɑːr], s. Caviar m.

cavil ['kæv(i)l], v.i. (cavilled) Chicaner, ergoter. He is always cavilling, il trouve à redire sur tout. To c. at sth., pointiller sur qch. **cavilling**, a. Argutieux, -euse; chicaneur, -euse.

caviller ['kævilər], s. Chicaneur, -euse; chicanier, -ière; ergoteur, -euse.

cavity ['kæviti], s. Cavité f; creux m; alvéole m; trou m, pl. trous. *Metall:* Grumelure f (dans la fonte). *Anat:* The nasal c., les fosses nasales.

cavort [kə'vɔːt], v.i. *F:* Cabrioler; faire des galopades, des galipettes.

cavy ['keivi], s. 1. Cobaye m; cochon m d'Inde. 2. Water c., cabiai m.

caw[1] [kɔː], s. Croassement m.

caw[2], v.i. (Of crow) Croasser. **cawing,** s. Croassement m.

Cayenne [kei'en]. 1. *Pr.n. Geog:* Cayenne f. 2. s. C. (pepper), poivre m de Cayenne, cayenne m.

cayman ['keimən], s. *Rept:* Caïman m.

cease[1] [siːs], s. Without c., sans cesse.

cease[2], v.tr. & i. 1. Cesser ((from) doing sth., de faire qch.). He has ceased to see anybody, il ne voit plus personne. 2. Cesser (ses efforts, etc.). To c. from work, cesser son travail. To c. work, cesser le travail; arrêter les travaux. The noise ceased, le bruit cessa. The noise ceased for a moment, le bruit s'interrompit quelques instants. 'cease-'fire, s. *Mil:* Cessez-le-feu m. **ceasing,** s. Cessation f. Without ceasing, sans arrêt.

ceaseless ['siːslis], a. Incessant; sans arrêt; sans fin. **-ly,** adv. Sans cesse, sans arrêt.

cedar ['siːdər], s. *Bot:* C.(-tree, -wood), cèdre m.

cede [siːd], v.tr. Céder (un bien immobilier).

cedilla [si'dilə], s. Cédille f.

ceiling ['siːliŋ], s. 1. Plafond m. C. beam, doubleau m. C. light, lamp, plafonnier m. *F:* To hit the c., entrer dans une colère bleue. 2. *Av:* (Valeur f de) plafond (d'un avion), *Com:* Plafond. *F:* He's hit the c., il plafonne. 3. *Nau:* Vaigres fpl, vaigrage m.

-ceilinged ['siːliŋd], a. High-, low-c., haut, bas, de plafond.

celandine ['seləndain], s. *Bot:* Éclaire f.

celebrant ['selibrənt], s. *Ecc:* Célébrant m.

celebrate ['selibreit], v.tr. 1. *Ecc:* Célébrer (la messe). 2. Célébrer, glorifier (la mémoire de qn); commémorer (un événement). 3. *F:* Fêter (un événement).

celebrated, a. Célèbre (for, par); renommé (for, pour).

celebration [seli'breiʃ(ə)n], s. 1. *Ecc:* Célébration f (de la messe). 2. Célébration, commémoration f (d'un événement, etc.). 3. *F:* This calls for a c., il faut fêter, arroser, ça.

celebrator ['selibreitər], s. Célébrateur m.

celebrity [si'lebriti], s. 1. Célébrité f, renommée f. 2. (Pers.) Célébrité f.

celeriac [se'leriæk], s. *Hort:* Céleri-rave m.

celerity [si'leriti], s. Célérité f.

celery ['seləri], s. *Hort:* Céleri m. Head of c., pied m de céleri. *Bot:* Wild c., ache f.

celestial [si'lestiəl]. a. Céleste. *Aer:* C. navigation, navigation f par visée astronomique.

celibacy ['selibəsi], s. Célibat m.

celibate ['selibit]. 1. a. (Personne) célibataire; (vie) de célibataire. 2. s. Célibataire mf.

cell [sel], s. 1. Compartiment m. (a) (In monastery) Cellule f; (in prison) cellule, cachot m. Cells (of police station), les locaux m disciplinaires (d'un poste de police). *Mil:* The cells, la prison, *P:* le bloc. (b) *Ap:* Cellule, alvéole m. (c) The brain cells, les territoires cérébraux. 2. *El:* Élément m (de pile); couple m. Dry c., pile sèche. 3. (a) *Biol:* Cellule. White blood-cells, globules blancs, leucocytes m. Red blood-cells, globules rouges, hématies f. C.-wall, paroi f cellulaire. (b) *Bot:* Loge f. 4. (a) *Mil:* Groupe m de combat. (b) Communist c., cellule communiste; noyau m communiste.

cellar[1] ['selər], s. Cave f; (small) caveau m. To keep a good c., avoir une bonne cave.

cellar[2], v.tr. Encaver (du vin); mettre (du vin) en cave, en chai.

cellarage ['seləridʒ], s. 1. Emmagasinage m (en cave). 2. *Coll.* Caves fpl.

cellarer ['selərər], s.m. *Ecc:* (Frère-) cellérier m.

cellarman, pl. -men ['seləmən], s.m. Caviste; sommelier m.

cellad [seld], a. 1. *Biol:* Cellulé. 2. *Biol: etc:* One-c., two-c., à une cellule, à deux cellules.

cellist ['tʃelist], s. = VIOLONCELLIST.

cello ['tʃelo], s. = VIOLONCELLO.

cellophane ['seləfein], s. *R.t.m:* Cellophane f.

cellular ['seljulər], a. 1. *Biol:* Cellulaire, celluleux, -euse. 2. Cellulaire, alvéolaire. C. girder, poutre cellulaire. *I.C.E:* C. radiator, radiateur cellulaire, à nid d'abeilles. *Dom.Ec:* C. blanket, couverture f (de lit) en maille aérée.

cellule ['selju:l], s. *Nat.Hist:* Cellule f.

cellulitis [selju'laitis], s. *Med:* Cellulite f.

celluloid ['seljulɔid], s. Celluloïd(e) m.

cellulose ['seljulous]. 1.a. Celluleux, -euse. 2. s. Cellulose f. C. varnish, vernis cellulosique.

Celt [kelt], s. *Ethn:* Celte mf.

Celtic ['keltik]. 1. a. Celtique; celte. 2. s. *Ling:* Le celtique.

cement[1] [si'ment], s. 1. *Const:* Ciment m. Hydraulic c., mortier m hydraulique. Asbestos c., fibro-ciment m (R.t.m.). C. bin, silo m à ciment. 2. *Cer: Dent: etc:* Mastic m, lut m. 3. *Anat:* Cément m (d'une dent). 4. *Metall:* Cément. ce'ment-mixer, s. Bétonnière f.

cement[2], v.tr. 1. Cimenter (des pierres); cimenter, consolider (une amitié). 2. Lier au ciment; coller. Cemented lens, objectif à lentilles collées. 3. *Metall:* Cémenter (le fer).

cementation [siːmen'teiʃ(ə)n], s. 1. Cimentage m, cimentation f; collage m. 2. *Metall:* Cémentation f.

cemetery ['semətri], s. Cimetière m.

cenotaph ['senətæf], s. Cénotaphe m.

cense [sens], v.tr. *Ecc:* Encenser.

censer ['sensər], s. *Ecc:* Encensoir m, 'censer-bearer, s. Encenseur m, thuriféraire m.

censor[1] ['sensər], s. *Adm:* Censeur m. The Board of Censors, la censure. Banned by the C., interdit par la censure.

censor[2], v.tr. 1. Interdire (une pièce de théâtre, etc.). 2. To be censored, (i) (of play, etc.) passer par la censure; (of letter) passer par le contrôle; (ii) être interdit, supprimé, par la censure; (iii) être expurgé. **censoring,** s. Censure f (des journaux, etc.).

censorial [sen'sɔːriəl], a. Censorial, -aux.

censorious [sen'sɔːriəs], a. Porté à censurer; sévère (of, upon, pour).

censorship ['sensəʃip], s. *Adm:* (a) The C., la censure. (b) Postal c., contrôle postal.

censurable ['senʃərəbl], a. Censurable, blâmable.

censure[1] ['senʃər], s. Censure f, blâme m; réprobation f. *Jur:* Réprimande f. Deserving of c., réprimandable. To pass c. on the Government, blâmer le Gouvernement. Vote of c., motion f de censure.

censure[2], v.tr. Censurer; (i) blâmer, condamner; (ii) critiquer.

census ['sensəs], s. Recensement m. *Adm:* To take a c. of the population, faire le recensement de la population; dénombrer la population.

cent [sent], s. 1. *Num:* (a) *U.S: etc:* Cent m. (b) *F:* (Small coin) Sou m, liard m. I haven't got a red c., je n'ai pas le sou. 2. Per c., pour cent.

centaur ['sentɔːr], s.m. *Myth:* Centaure.

centaury ['sentɔːri], s. *Bot:* Centaurée f.

centenarian [senti'nɛəriən], a. & s. Centenaire (mf).

centenary [sen'tiːnəri, -'ten-], a. & s. (Anniversaire) centenaire (m).

centennial [sen'teniəl]. 1. a. Centennal, -aux; séculaire. 2. s. *U.S:* = CENTENARY.

centesimal [sen'tesim(ə)l], a. Centésimal, -aux.

centigrade ['sentigreid], a. Centigrade.

centigramme ['sentigræm], s. Centigramme m.

centilitre ['sentiliːtər], s. Centilitre m.

centimetre ['sentimiːtər], s. Centimètre m.

centipede ['sentipiːd], s. *Myr:* Centipède m; *F:* mille-pattes m inv.

central ['sentr(ə)l]. 1. a. Central, -aux. 2. s. *U.S: Tp:* (a) Central m téléphonique. (b) Standardiste mf. **-ally,** adv. Centralement.

centralization [sentrəlai'zeiʃ(ə)n], s. Centralisation f.

centralize ['sentrəlaiz]. 1. v.tr. Centraliser. 2. v.i. Se centraliser. **centralizing,** a. Centralisateur, -trice.

centre[1] ['sentər], s. 1. Centre m (d'un cercle, etc.); milieu m (d'une table); foyer m (d'érudition, d'infection). In the c., au centre. Infant welfare c., consultation f de nourrissons. Maternity and child welfare c., centre de protection maternelle et infantile.

(Rural) health c., centre médical, d'hygiène (rural). Rest c., centre d'accueil. *Ph:* C. of gravity, centre de gravité. C. of attraction, (i) *Ph:* centre d'attraction, de gravitation; (ii) clou *m* (d'une fête, etc.). Out of c., décentré. *S.a.* DEAD-CENTRE. 2. *Mec.E:* Pointe *f* (d'un tour). 3. *attrib.* Central, -aux. The c. arch, l'arche centrale, du centre. *Pol:* The C. party, les membres du Centre; les centristes. 'centre-bit, *s. Tls:* Mèche anglaise. 'centre-board, *s. Nau:* (Quille *f* de) dérive *f*. centre-'forward, *s. Fb:* (*Pers.*) Avant-centre *m.* centre-'half, *s. Fb:* (*Pers.*) Demi-centre *m.* 'centre-line, *s.* Ligne médiane. 'centre-piece, *s.* Pièce *f* de milieu, surtout *m.* 'centre-pin, *s.* Cheville ouvrière. 'centre-punch, *s. Tls:* Pointeau *m.* 'centre-'rail, *s.* Crémaillère *f* (de chemin de fer de montagne). 'centre-second(s), *s. Clockm:* Grande aiguille trotteuse.

centre². 1. *v.tr.* (a) Placer (qch.) au centre. To c. one's affections on s.o., concentrer, rassembler, toute son affection sur qn. (b) Centrer (une pièce sur le tour). *Mch:* Axer. (c) *Fb:* Centrer (le ballon); *abs.* centrer. 2. *v.i.* To c. in, on, round, s.o., sth., se concentrer dans, sur,·autour de, qn, qch. -centred, *a.* Two-c. arch, arc à deux centres. *S.a.* SELF-CENTRED. centring, *s.* 1. Centrage *m* (d'une pièce sur le tour, etc.). 2. *Const:* (a) Cintrage *m* (d'une voûte). (b) Cintre *m.* 3. *Cin:* Cadrage *m* (du film).

centric(al) ['sentrik(əl)], *a.* Du centre; central, -aux. centrifugal [sen'trifjug(ə)l], *a.* Centrifuge. C. machine, centrifugeur *m*, centrifugeuse *f*. centrifuge¹ ['sentrifjudʒ], *v.tr. Ind:* Centrifuger (un liquide). centrifuge², *s.* Centrifugeur *m*, centrifugeuse *f*. centripetal [sen'tripətl], *a.* Centripète. centuple¹ ['sentju:pl], *a. & s.* Centuple (*m*). centuple², centuplicate [sen'tju:plikeit], *v.tr.* Centupler. centurion [sen'tju:rən], *s. Rom.Ant:* Centurion *m.* century ['sentʃəri], *s.* 1. (a) Siècle *m.* In the nineteenth c., au dix-neuvième siècle. (b) *Rom.Ant:* Centurie *f.* 2. *Cr:* Centaine *f.* cep(e) [sep], *s. Fung:* Cèpe *m.* cephalic [si'fælik], *a.* Céphalique. cephalopod ['sefələpɔd], *s. Moll:* Céphalopode *m.* ceramic [sə'ræmik], *a.* Céramique. ceramics [sə'ræmiks], *s.pl.* (*Usu. with sg. const.*) La céramique. ceramist ['serəmist], *s.* Céramiste *m.* Cerberus ['sɔ:bərəs]. *Pr.n.m. Myth:* Cerbère. *S.a.* SOP¹ 2. cere [siər], *s. Orn:* Cire *f* (du bec d'un oiseau). cereal ['siəriəl]. 1. *a.* Céréale; céréalier, -ière. 2. *s. usu.pl.* (a) To grow cereals, cultiver des céréales *fpl.* (b) (Breakfast) cereals, céréales en flocons. cerebellum [,seri'beləm], *s. Anat:* Cervelet *m.* cerebral ['seribrəl], *a.* Cérébral, -aux. cerebrate ['seri'breit], *v.i. U.S:* Penser, cogiter. cerebration [,seri'breiʃ(ə)n], *s. Physiol:* Cérébration *f.* cerebro-spinal ['seribrou'spain(ə)l], *a. Anat: Med:* Cérébro-spinal, -aux. cerebrum ['serəbrəm], *s. Anat:* Cerveau *m.* cerement(s) ['siːəmənt(s)], *s.* (*Usu. pl.*) 1. Toile(s) *f* d'embaumement. 2. *Lit:* Linceul *m*, suaire *m.* ceremonial [,seri'mounjəl]. 1. *a.* De cérémonie. 2. *s.* Cérémonial *m.* -ally, *adv.* En grande cérémonie. ceremonious [,seri'mounjəs], *a.* Cérémonieux, -euse. -ly, *adv.* Cérémonieusement. ceremoniousness [,seri'mounjəsnis], *s.* Manières cérémonieuses. ceremony ['seriməni], *s.* Cérémonie *f.* With c., solennellement. Without c., sans cérémonie, sans façon. To stand (up)on c., faire des façons. Master of ceremonies, ordonnateur *m.* To attend a c., assister à une cérémonie. Ceres ['siːəriz]. *Pr.n.f. Myth:* Cérès. cerise [sə'riːs], *a. & s.* (*Colour*) Cerise (*m*) *inv.* cerium ['siːrjəm], *s. Ch:* Cérium *m.* cert [sɔ:t], *s. F:* = CERTAINTY. A dead c., une certitude (absolue); une affaire sûre. It's a c., c'est couru. certain ['sɔ:t(ə)n], *a.* Certain. 1. (*Assured*) (a) This much is c. that . . ., ce qu'il y a de sûr, de certain, c'est que. . . . He is c. to come, il viendra sûrement; il est certain qu'il viendra. (b) (*Of pers.*) To be c. of

sth., être certain, sûr, de qch. I am almost c. of it, j'en ai la presque certitude. I am not c. that he will come, je ne suis pas certain qu'il vienne. (c) To know sth. for c., être bien sûr de qch.; savoir qch. à n'en pouvoir douter. (d) To make c. of sth., (i) s'assurer de qch.; (ii) s'assurer qch. To make c. of a seat, s'assurer une place. 2. (a) (*Undetermined*) There are c. things that . . ., il y a a certaines choses que. . . . With women of a c. age . . ., chez les femmes d'un certain âge. *Pej:* A c. person, (une) certaine personne. C. people, (de) certaines gens; certains *mpl.* A c. Mr Smith, un certain M. Smith. (b) He used to write on a c. day, il m'écrivait à jour fixe. -ly, *adv.* (a) Certainement; certes; assurément; à coup sûr. (b) (*Assent*) Assurément; parfaitement. May I?—C.! vous permettez?—Je vous en prie. C. not! non certes! non, par exemple!

certainty ['sɔ:tnti], *s.* (a) Certitude *f*; chose certaine, fait certain. For a c., of a c., à coup sûr; certainement. It's a dead c., c'est une certitude absolue. To bet on a c., parier à coup sûr. (b) Certitude (morale); conviction *f.* certifiable [sɔ:ti'faiəbl], *a.* Que l'on peut certifier. C. lunatic, personne dont un médecin se jugera autorisé à attester l'aliénation mentale. *F:* He's c., il est fou à lier. certificate¹ [sɔ'tifikit], *s.* 1. (a) Certificat *m*, attestation *f. Fin:* Titre *m* (d'actions). (b) *Jur:* (Acte *m* de) concordat *m* (entre un failli et ses créanciers). 2. C. (of competency), certificat (d'aptitude); diplôme *m*, brevet *m. Nau:* Master's c., brevet de capitaine. *Sch:* General C. of Education, Ordinary Level = certificat *m* de fin d'études secondaires. General C. of Education, Advanced Level = Baccalauréat-ès-lettres, -ès-sciences. 3. Acte. Birth c., acte de naissance. Death c., (i) acte de décès; (ii) extrait mortuaire. *Aer:* C. of airworthiness, certificat de navigabilité. *S.a.* REGISTRY 1. certificate² [sɔ'tifikeit], *v.tr.* Diplômer, breveter (qn.) certificated, *a.* 1. Diplômé, titré. 2. *Jur:* C. bankrupt, concordataire *mf.* certification [sɔtifi'keiʃ(ə)n], *s.* (a) Certification *f.* (b) C. of aircraft, délivrance *f* du certificat de navigabilité. certifier ['sɔ:tifaiər], *s.* Certificateur *m.* certify ['sɔ:tifai], *v.tr.* 1. (a) Certifier, déclarer, attester. To c. a death, constater un décès. *Jur:* Certified lunatic, aliéné interdit. (b) Authentiquer, homologuer, légaliser (un document). *Com:* U.S: Certified cheque, chèque visé. *S.a.* COPY¹ 2. (c) Diplômer, breveter (qn). Certified broker, courtier attitré. 2. *v.ind.tr.* To c. to sth., attester qch. certifying¹, *a.* (Document) certificatif. certifying², *s.* 1. Attestation *f.* 2. Approbation *f* (d'un document); homologation *f.* 3. Interdiction *f* (d'un aliéné). certitude ['sɔ:titju:d], *s.* Certitude *f.* cerulean [si'ru:liən], *a. Lit:* Bleu céleste *inv*; cérulé, céruléen, azuré. cerumen [sə'ru:mən], *s. Physiol:* Cérumen *m.* cervical [sɔ:'vik(ə)l], *a. Anat:* Cervical, -aux. cervix, *pl.* -vices [sɔ:'viks, -visiz], *s. Anat:* Col *m* (du fémur, etc.). cessation [se'seiʃ(ə)n], *s.* Cessation *f*, arrêt *m. Mil:* C. of hostilities, armistice *m.* cession ['seʃ(ə)n], *s.* Cession *f*; abandon *m* (de marchandises, de droits, etc.). cessionary ['seʃənəri], *s.* 1. *a.* Cessionnaire. 2. *s. Jur:* Ayant cause *m, pl.* ayants cause. cesspit ['sespit], *s.* 1. Fosse *f* à fumier et à purin. 2. = CESSPOOL. cesspool ['sespu:l], *s.* Fosse *f* d'aisances. A c. of iniquity, un cloaque de vice. Cetacea [si'teisiə, -ʃiə], *s.pl. Z:* Les cétacés *m.* cetacean [si'teisiən, -ʃən], *a. & s.* Cétacé (*m*). cetaceous [si'teisiəs, -ʃəs], *a.* Cétacé. Ceylon [si'lɔn]. *Pr.n. Geog:* Ceylan *m.* chad [tʃæd], *s. Ich:* 1. Dorade (bilunée). 2. = SHAD. chafe¹ [tʃeif], *s.* 1. = CHAFING. 2. Écorchure *f.* chafe². 1. *v.tr.* (a) Frictionner, dégourdir (les membres). (b) User, échauffer, (qch.) par le frottement; écorcher (la peau); érailler (un cordage). (c) Irriter, énerver (qn). 2. *v.i.* (a) S'user par le frottement; (of rope) s'érailler, raguer. (b) (Of caged animal) To

c. against the bars, s'user en vains efforts contre les barreaux. (*Of pers.*) To c. at, under, sth., s'énerver de qch. To c. under restraint, ronger son frein.

chafing, *s.* **1.** Friction *f.* **2.** (*a*) Écorchement *m* (de la peau). (*b*) Usure *f*, frottement *m*, échauffement *m* (d'une corde). **3.** (*Of pers.*) Irritation *f*, énervement *m.* **'chafing-dish,** *s. Cu:* Réchaud *m* (de table); chauffe-plat *m, pl.* chauffe-plats.

chafer ['tʃeifər], *s. Ent:* = COCKCHAFER.

chaff[1] [tʃæf, tʃɑːf], *s.* **1.** (*a*) Balle(s) *f* (du grain). (*b*) *Husb:* (i) Menue paille, paille d'avoine; (ii) paille hachée. (*c*) *F:* Choses *fpl* sans importance; vétilles *fpl.* **2.** *F:* Raillerie *f*; persiflage *m.* **'chaff-cutter,** *s. Husb:* Hache-paille *m.inv.*

chaff[2], *v.tr.* Railler, taquiner (qn); persifler (qn).

chaffer[1] ['tʃæfər], *s. F:* Railleur *m*; persifleur *m.*

chaffer[2], *v.i. A:* Marchander, barguigner. To c. with s.o., marchander qn. To c. over the price, débattre le prix.

chaffinch ['tʃæfin(t)ʃ], *s. Orn:* Pinson *m.*

chaffingly ['tʃæfiŋli], *adv.* En taquinant, en badinant, en riant.

chagrin[1] ['ʃæ'griːn], *s.* Chagrin *m*, dépit *m*; vive contrariété; déplaisir *m.*

chagrin[2], *v.tr.* Chagriner, dépiter (qn). To be chagrined at sth., être mortifié de qch.

chain[1] [tʃein], *s.* **1.** (*a*) Chaîne *f*; (*small*) chaînette *f.* To put a dog on the c., mettre un chien à l'attache, à la chaîne. Prisoner in chains, prisonnier enchaîné. To burst one's chains, rompre ses chaînes; briser ses fers. Watch-c., chaîne de montre. *Aut:* (Wheel) chains, chaînes (à neige). *Mec.E:* Driving c., chaîne de transmission. *Hyg:* To pull the c., tirer la chasse d'eau. (*b*) Chaîne (de montagnes); enchaînement *m* (d'idées); suite *f*, série *f* (d'événements); cordon *m* (de sentinelles). C. reaction, réaction *f* en chaîne. **2.** *Surv.Meas:* Longueur *f* de 20 m, 116; double décamètre. **'chain-adjuster,** *s.* Tendeur *m* de chaîne; patte *f* de tension. **'chain(-)armour,** *s. Arm:* (*a*) Mailles *fpl.* (*b*) Cotte *f* de mailles. **'chain(-)bridge,** *s.* Pont *m* suspendu. **'chain-case,** *s. Cy:* Carter *m.* **'chain-gang,** *s. A. & U.S:* Chaîne *f*, cadène *f* (de forçats). **'chain-lock,** *s. Cy: etc:* Chaîne *f* anti-vol. **'chain 'measuring,** *s. Surv:* Chaînage *m.* **'chain-pulley,** *s. Mec.E:* Barbotin *m.* **'chain-saw,** *s. Tls:* Scie *f* à chaîne. **'chain-smoker,** *s.* Fumeur, -euse, de cigarettes à la file. **'chain-stitch,** *s. Needlew:* Point *m* de chaînette. **'chain(-)store,** *s.* (*a*) Magasin *m* à succursales multiples. (*b*) Succursale *f* de grand magasin. **chain-work,** *s.* Travail *m* à la chaîne.

chain[2], *v.tr.* **1.** To c. sth. to sth., attacher qch. à qch. par une chaîne, par des chaînes. **2.** To c. sth. down, retenir qch. par une chaîne, par des chaînes. To c. s.o. (down), enchaîner qn. Chained to one's desk, cloué à son bureau. To c. up a dog, mettre un chien à la chaîne, à l'attache. Chained up, chained together, à la chaîne. **3.** Fermer (un port, etc.) avec des chaînes. **4.** *Surv:* Chaîner (un champ).

chair[1] [tʃɛər], *s.* **1.** (*a*) Chaise *f*, siège *m.* Folding c., chaise pliante; pliant *m.* High c., chaise haute (pour enfants). Grandfather c., bergère *f* à oreilles. Club c., fauteuil *m* club. Self-propelling c., fauteuil roulant. *Jur: U.S:* Electric c., chaise, fauteuil, électrique. To take a c., s'asseoir. Musical chairs, le jeu, la polka, des chaises. *S.a.* ARM(-)CHAIR, BATH-CHAIR, DECK-CHAIR, BOATSWAIN, EASY-CHAIR, IN-VALID[3], ROCKING-CHAIR. (*b*) *Sch:* Chaire *f* (de professeur de faculté). (*c*) Siège (de juge); fauteuil *m* (de président). To be in the c., to occupy, fill, the c., occuper le fauteuil présidentiel; présider. To take the c., prendre la présidence. To leave, vacate, the c., lever la séance. C.! C.! à l'ordre! à l'ordre! **2.** *Rail:* Coussinet *m*, chaise (de rail). **'chair-attendant,** *s.* Chaisier, -ière; loueur, -euse, de chaises (dans un parc, etc.) ou de fauteuils roulants (pour malades). **'chair-back,** *s.* Dossier *m* de chaise. **'chair-bed,** *s.* Fauteuil-lit *m.* **'chair-car,** *s. Rail: U.S:* Voiture *f* salon. **'chair-lift,** *s.* Télésiège *m.* **'chair-maker,** *s.* Chaisier; fabricant *m* de chaises. **'chair-mender,** *s.* Rempailleur de chaises. **'chair-rail,** *s.* **1.** Barreau *m*, bâton *m* (de chaise). **2.** Antibois *m* (d'une salle).

chair[2], *v.tr.* Porter (qn) en triomphe.

chairman, *pl.* -men ['tʃɛəmən, -mən], *s.* **1.** Président, -ente. Mr C., Madam C., Monsieur le Président, Madame la Présidente. **2.** Chaisier *m*; loueur *m* de chaises. **3.** *A:* Porteur *m* (de chaise à porteurs).

chairmanship ['tʃɛəmənʃip], *s.* Présidence *f.*

chaise [ʃeiz], *s. Veh: A:* Chaise *f*, cabriolet *m.* **'chaise 'longue,** *s. Furn:* Chaise longue.

chalcedony [kæl'sedəni], *s. Lap:* Calcédoine *f.*

Chaldea [kæl'di(ː)ə]. *Pr.n. A.Geog:* La Chaldée.

Chaldean [kæl'di(ː)ən], **Chaldee** [kæl'diː], *a. & s. A.Geog:* Chaldéen, -enne.

chalet ['ʃælei], *s.* Chalet *m* (suisse); petite villa.

chalice ['tʃælis], *s. Ecc:* Calice *m.*

chalk[1] [tʃɔːk], *s.* **1.** Craie *f*; (*coloured c. for drawing*) pastel *m. Bill:* Blanc *m.* French c., talc *m*, stéatite *f. S.a.* RED 1. *F:* He doesn't know c. from cheese, il ne sait rien de rien, il ne sait ni A ni B. **2.** *A:* Compte *m* des consommations (à l'ardoise). *F:* Not by a long c., tant s'en faut. **'chalk-pit,** *s.* (i) Carrière *f* de craie; crayère *f*; (ii) plâtrière *f.* **'chalk-stone,** *s. Med:* Concrétion *f* calcaire.

chalk[2], *v.tr.* **1.** (*a*) Marquer (qch.) à la craie. (*b*) Blanchir (qch.) avec de la craie. (*c*) Talquer; saupoudrer de talc. **2.** To c. (up) sth. on sth., écrire qch. à la craie sur qch. *F:* C. it up, mettez-le à mon compte.

chalkiness ['tʃɔːkinis], *s.* **1.** Nature crayeuse (du sol). **2.** Extrême pâleur (du teint).

chalky ['tʃɔːki], *a.* **1.** Crayeux, -euse, crétacé. *S.a.* DEPOSIT[1] 3. **2.** (Teint) pâle, terreux.

challenge[1] ['tʃælən(d)ʒ], *s.* **1.** (*a*) Défi *m*; provocation *f* (en duel, etc.). This work is a c. to me, ce travail est une vraie gageure pour moi. *Sp:* To issue a c., lancer un challenge. (*b*) *Mil:* Qui-vive *m inv.* **2.** *Jur:* Récusation *f* (du jury). **'challenge-cup,** *s. Sp:* Coupe challenge *f.* **'challenge-match,** *s. Sp:* Challenge *m.*

challenge[2], *v.tr.* **1.** (*a*) To c. s.o., (i) provoquer qn (au combat), jeter le gant à qn; (ii) challenger qn. To c. s.o. to do sth., défier qn de faire qch. (*b*) *Mil:* (*Of sentry*) To c. s.o., interpeller qn. **2.** (*a*) Disputer, relever (une affirmation); mettre en question, en doute (la parole de qn). (*b*) Récuser (un juré). **3.** Provoquer (l'admiration, etc.). **challenging,** *a.* (*Of look, remark*) Provocateur, -trice; (air) de défi.

challenger ['tʃælən(d)ʒər], *s.* **1.** (*a*) Provocateur, -trice. (*b*) *Sp:* Lanceur *m* d'un challenge, challenger *m.* **2.** *Jur:* Récusant.

chalybeate [kə'libiit], *a. Ch:* Ferrugineux, -euse.

chamber ['tʃeimbər], *s.* **1.** (*a*) *A. & Lit:* (*Room*) Chambre *f*, pièce *f*, salle *f.* (*Still so used in*) Audience c., salle d'audience. *S.a.* COUNCIL-CHAMBER, LETHAL. (*b*) *Lit:* (Bed-)c., chambre (à coucher). Gentleman of the Privy C., gentilhomme de la Chambre du Roi. (*c*) C.(-pot), pot *m* de chambre, vase *m* de nuit. **2.** C. of Commerce, of Trade, chambre de commerce, de métiers. *Pol:* The double c. system, le système bicaméral. **3.** *pl.* Chambers. (*a*) Appartement *m* de garçon. (*b*) Cabinet *m* de consultation (d'un avocat); étude *f* (d'un avoué). (*c*) *Jur:* To hear a case in chambers, juger une cause en référé. *S.a.* COUNSEL[1] 4. **4.** *Tchn:* (*a*) Cavité *f* alvéolaire; alvéole *m.* (*b*) Chambre, tonnerre *m* (d'une arme à feu). *I.C.E:* Chambre d'explosion; culasse *f. Conch:* Loge *f.* **'chamber-'concert,** *s.* Concert *m* de musique de chambre. **'chamber-counsel,** *s. Jur:* Avocat consultant; avocat conseil. **'chamber-music,** *s.* Musique *f* de chambre.

chambered ['tʃeimbəd], *a.* Évidé, chambré. Six-c. revolver, revolver à six coups.

chamberlain ['tʃeimbəlin], *s.* Chambellan *m.*

chambermaid ['tʃeimbəmeid], *s.f.* Fille, femme, de chambre (d'hôtel).

chameleon [kə'miːljən], *s. Rept:* Caméléon *m.* **chameleon-like,** *a.* Versicolore.

chamfer[1] ['tʃæmfər], *s.* Biseau *m*, chanfrein *m.*

chamfer[2], *v.tr.* **1.** *Carp: etc:* Biseauter, chanfreiner; abattre (une arête). **2.** Canneler (une colonne).

chamfering, *s.* Biseautage *m.*

chamois ['ʃæmwɑː], *s.* Chamois *m.* **chamois-leather,** ['ʃæmi'leðər], *s.* (Peau *f* de) chamois *m.*

champ [tʃæmp], *v.tr.* (*Of horse, etc.*) Mâcher bruyamment (le fourrage); ronger, mâcher, mâchonner (le mors). *F:* (*Of pers.*) He was champing at the bit, il rongeait son frein. **champing,** *s.* Mâchonnement *m.*

Champagne [ʃæmˈpein]. **1.** *Pr.n. Geog:* La Champagne. Wet, Dry, C., Champagne humide, pouilleuse. **2.** *s.* Vin *m* de Champagne; champagne *m*. C. cider, cidre champagnisé, mousseux.

champaign [ˈtʃæmpein], *s. A. & Lit:* Plaine *f*; campagne ouverte.

champion¹ [ˈtʃæmpjən], *s.* **1.** (*a*) Champion *m*. (*b*) *Sp:* Recordman *m*; champion, -ionne. **2.** (*a*) *attrib.* C. driver, champion de vitesse. (*b*) *a. Dial:* (*N. of Engl.*) That's c.! à la bonne heure! bravo!

champion², *v.tr.* Soutenir, défendre (une cause); prendre fait et cause pour (qn).

championship [ˈtʃæmpjənʃip], *s.* **1.** *Sp: etc:* Championnat *m. Aut: etc:* C. race, Grand Prix. **2.** Défense *f* (d'une cause).

chance¹ [tʃɑːns], *s.* **1.** (*a*) Chance *f*, hasard *m*, sort *m*. Game of c., jeu de hasard. By (mere) c., par hasard. Shall we see you there by any c.? est-ce que par hasard on vous y verra? C. so ordained it that . . ., le hasard voulut, le hasard fit, que + *ind. or sub.* To leave everything to c., s'en remettre au hasard. The chances are against me, les chances sont contre moi. The chances are that . . ., il y a fort à parier que. . . . Off c., chance moyenne. To do sth. on the off c., faire qch. à tout hasard. (*b*) **To submit to the c. of war,** se soumettre au sort, à la fortune, de la guerre. To keep an eye on the main c., ne pas perdre de vue son propre intérêt; s'attacher au solide. **2.** Occasion *f*. Now's your c.! vous avez beau jeu! To have a good c. of doing sth., avoir beau jeu, une belle occasion, de faire qch. To stand a c., avoir des chances de succès. He hasn't the ghost of a c. of succeeding, il n'a pas la moindre chance, l'ombre d'une chance, de réussir. To have even chances, avoir des chances égales. To give s.o. a c., (i) mettre qn à l'essai; (ii) entendre qn jusqu'au bout; agir loyalement avec qn. To take one's c., risquer les chances. **3.** Risque *m*. To take a c., encourir un risque. To take a long c., risquer beaucoup. **4.** *attrib.* Fortuit, accidentel, -elle. A c. acquaintance, une connaissance fortuite, de rencontre. C. meeting, rencontre occasionnelle.

chance². **1.** *v.i.* (*a*) To c. to do sth., faire qch. par hasard. If I c. to find it, si je viens à le trouver. (*b*) To c. upon s.o., upon sth., trouver, rencontrer, qn, qch., par hasard. **2.** *v.tr.* To c. it, risquer le coup. To c. one's luck, tenter la fortune. *F:* To c. one's arm, tenter sa chance.

chancel [ˈtʃɑːnsəl], *s. Ecc.Arch:* Chœur *m* (et sanctuaire *m*).

chancellery, -ory [ˈtʃɑːnsəlri], *s.* Chancellerie *f*.

chancellor [ˈtʃɑːnsələr], *s.* Chancelier *m*. C. of the Exchequer = Ministre *m* des Finances.

chancellorship [ˈtʃɑːnsələʃip], *s.* Cancellariat *m*.

chancery [ˈtʃɑːnsəri], *s.* **1.** *Jur:* (Court of) c., cour *f* de la chancellerie. *S.a.* WARD¹ **1. 2.** *Wr:* Hold in c., cravate *f*.

chancre [ˈʃæŋkə], *s. Med:* Chancre vénérien.

chancrous [ˈʃæŋkrəs], *a. Med:* Chancreux.

chancy [ˈtʃɑːnsi], *a. F:* Chanceux, -euse, incertain; risqué.

chandelier [ˌʃændiˈliər], *s.* Lustre *m* (d'éclairage).

chandler [ˈtʃɑːndlər], *s. O:* (*a*) Épicier-droguiste *m*. (*b*) Fournisseur *m. S.a.* CORN-CHANDLER, SHIP-CHANDLER.

chandlery [ˈtʃɑːndləri], *s.* **1.** *O:* Épicerie-droguerie *f*. **2.** Ship's c., fournitures *fpl* pour la marine.

change¹ [tʃein(d)ʒ], *s.* **1.** Changement *m*; retour *m* (de la marée); revirement *m* (d'opinion, de fortune). C. of domicile, changement de domicile; déplacement *m*. C. for the better, worse, changement en mieux, en mal. Barometer at 'c.', baromètre à "variable." To make a c., effectuer un changement (in, à). This journey will be (a bit of) a c. for you, ce voyage vous changera un peu. For a c., comme distraction; pour changer. *Physiol:* C. of life, retour *m* d'âge. *Aut:* Gear c., changement de vitesse. *El:* C. of connection, commutation *f*. C. of front, (i) *Mil:* mouvement *m* de conversion; (ii) volte-face *f inv.* (politique). **2.** (*a*) C. of clothes, vêtements de rechange. (*b*) *A:* C. of horses, relais *m*. **3.** (*Exchange*) Change *m*. **4.** (*a*) Monnaie *f*. Small c., petite monnaie. To give c. for £5, donner, rendre, la monnaie de cinq livres. 'No c. given,' "on ne rend pas de monnaie"; "le public est tenu de faire l'appoint."

F: He won't get much c. out of me, il perdra ses peines avec moi. (*b*) = EXCHANGE¹ **3. 5.** (*Campanology*) To ring the changes, carillonner avec permutations. **To ring the changes on a subject,** ressasser, rabâcher, un sujet. 'change 'ringing, *s.* (*Campanology*) Sonnerie *f* à permutations.

change². **1.** *v.tr.* Changer. (*a*) Modifier (ses plans). To c. one thing (in)to another, changer, transformer, une chose en une autre. To c. one's note, one's tune, changer de ton. To c. the subject, changer de sujet; passer à autre chose. *S.a.* MIND¹ **2.** (*b*) To c. one's clothes, *abs.* to c., changer de vêtements; se changer. *S.a.* GEAR¹ **3.** (*c*) To c. one's seat, changer de place. *Rail:* To c. trains, *abs.* to change changer de train. All c.! tout le monde descend! To c. colour, changer de couleur, de visage. To c. front, (i) *Mil:* changer de front; (ii) faire volte-face. To c. the guard, relever la garde. *S.a.* HAND¹ **1,** PLACE¹ **2,** SIDE¹ **5.** (*d*) To c. one thing for another, échanger, troquer, une chose contre une autre. (*e*) To c. a (bank)note, (i) changer un billet (de banque); (ii) donner la monnaie d'un billet (de banque). **2.** *v.i.* (Se) changer (into, en); se modifier; varier. To c. for the better, changer en mieux; (*of weather*) tourner au beau. I could not wish it changed, je ne voudrais pas qu'il en fût autrement. *P:* He hasn't half changed! il a drôlement décollé! *S.a.* CHOP¹ **1,** MANNER **3. change down,** *v.i. Aut:* Passer à une vitesse inférieure. **change over,** *v.i.* **1.** Passer (d'un système à un autre). **2.** (*Of sentries*) Se relever. **3.** *El:* Permuter, commuter. 'change-over, *s.* **1.** Changement *m* (d'un système à un autre). **2.** Renversement *m* (politique, etc.). **3.** Relève *f* (de factionnaires). **4.** *El:* Commutation *f*. **change up,** *v.i. Aut:* Passer à une vitesse supérieure; monter les vitesses. **changing¹**, *a.* Changeant; (expression) mobile. **changing²**, *s.* Changement *m*; relève *f* (de la garde). 'changing-room, *s.* Vestiaire *m*.

changeability [ˌtʃein(d)ʒəˈbiliti], **changeableness** [ˈtʃein(d)ʒəblnis], *s.* Variabilité *f* (du temps); mobilité *f* (de caractère); versatilité *f*.

changeable [ˈtʃein(d)ʒəbl], *a.* **1.** (*Of pers., colour, etc.*) Changeant; (*of weather*) variable, inconstant; (*of character*) mobile. **2.** C. at will, modifiable à discrétion.

changeful [ˈtʃein(d)ʒful], *a. Lit:* Capricieux, -euse, inconstant.

changeless [ˈtʃein(d)ʒlis], *a.* Immuable.

changeling [ˈtʃein(d)ʒliŋ], *s.* Enfant changé en nourrice, ou par les fées.

changer [ˈtʃein(d)ʒər], *s.* **1.** See MONEY-CHANGER. **2.** *W.Tel:* Frequency c., changeur *m* de fréquence. **3.** *Gramophones:* (Automatic) record c., changeur de disques (automatique).

channel¹ [tʃænl], *s.* **1.** Lit *m* (d'une rivière). **2.** (*a*) Passe *f*, chenal *m* (d'un port). (*b*) *Geog:* Détroit *m*, canal *m*. The (English) C., la Manche. The C. Islands, les îles Anglo-Normandes, de la Manche. **3.** Canal, conduit *m*; goulotte *f*. Oil-c., rainure *f* de graissage; *pl.* pattes *f* d'araignée. **4.** Cannelure *f*, rainure (d'une colonne); gorge *f*, goujure *f* (d'une poulie). **5.** Rigole *f* (d'irrigation, de rue). **6.** Voie *f. Adm:* To go through official channels, suivre la filière, suivre la voie hiérarchique. Through the ordinary channels of diplomacy, par voie diplomatique. Channels of communication (of a country), artères *f* (d'un pays). **7.** New channels for trade, nouveaux débouchés pour le commerce. **8.** *T.V:* Canal *m*.

channel², *v.tr.* (channelled) **1.** Creuser des rigoles dans (un terrain). **2.** (*a*) Canneler, rainurer. To c. out a groove, tailler une rainure. (*b*) Évider (une lame de sabre, etc.).

chant¹ [tʃɑːnt], *s. Mus:* Chant *m* (monotone), mélopée *f*; (*in church*) (i) plain-chant *m*, (ii) psalmodie *f*. Gregorian c., chant grégorien.

chant², *v.tr.* (*a*) *A:* Chanter (*Still used in*) To c. s.o.'s praises, chanter les louanges de qn. (*b*) *Ecc:* Psalmodier.

chanter [ˈtʃɑːntər], *s.* **1.** *Ecc:* Chantre *m*. **2.** *Mus:* Chalumeau *m* (de la cornemuse).

chanterelle [ˌtʃɑːntəˈrel], *s. Fung:* Chanterelle *f*, girolle *f*.

chanticleer [,tʃænti'kliər], s. Lit: Chantecler m (le coq).
chantry ['tʃɑːntri], s. Ecc: 1. Fondation f de messes (pour le repos de l'âme du fondateur). 2. Chant(r)erie f.
chaos ['keios], s. Chaos m.
chaotic [kei'ɔtik], a. Chaotique, désorganisé. **-ally**, adv. Sans ordre.
chap¹ [tʃæp], s. Gerçure f, crevasse f.
chap², v.tr. (chapped) Gercer, crevasser (la peau). (Of hands) To get chapped, v.i. to c., se gercer, se crevasser.
chap³, s. (Usu. pl.) Bajoue(s) f (d'un cochon). Cu: Bath c., joue de porc fumée.
chap⁴, s. 1. A: = CHAPMAN. 2. F: Garçon m, type m, individu m. Old c., mon vieux. A queer c., un drôle de bonhomme.
chapel [tʃæpl], s. (a) Chapelle f; oratoire (particulier). Mortuary c., chapelle ardente. Sch: A: To keep a c., faire acte de présence à un office. C. of ease, (chapelle de) secours m. (b) Temple (dissident). (c) Typ: Atelier (syndiqué).
chaperon¹ ['ʃæpəroun], s. Chaperon m. To act as c., jouer le rôle de chaperon.
chaperon², v.tr. (chaperoned) Chaperonner (une jeune fille).
chaplain ['tʃæplin], s. Ecc: Aumônier m; chapelain m.
chaplaincy ['tʃæplinsi], **chaplainship** ['tʃæplinʃip], s. Aumônerie f.
chaplet ['tʃæplit], s. 1. Ecc: Chapelet m (d'un tiers du rosaire). 2. Arch: Moulure f en perles.
chapman, pl. -men ['tʃæpmən], s.m. A: Colporteur.
chaps ['ʃæps], s.pl. Pantalon m de cuir (de cowboy).
chapter ['tʃæptər], s. 1. Chapitre m. To give c. and verse, citer ses autorités, fournir des documents. A c. of accidents, une suite de malheurs. 2. Ecc: Chapitre (de chanoines). 'chapter-house, s. Salle f du chapitre.
char¹ [tʃɑːr], s. Ich: Omble-chevalier m.
char², s.f. F: = CHARWOMAN.
char³, v.i. F: To go out charring, travailler à la journée; aller en journée; faire des ménages.
char⁴. 1. v.tr. (charred) Carboniser. 2. v.i. Se carboniser. **charring**, s. Carbonisation f.
char⁵, s. P: Thé m. A cup of c., une tasse de thé.
char(-)à(-)banc ['ʃærəbæŋ], s. A: Autocar m.
character ['kæriktər], s. 1. Typ: Caractère m, lettre f. 2. (a) Caractère; marque distinctive. Books of that c., les livres de ce genre. To be in c. with sth., être à l'unisson de qch.; s'harmoniser avec qch. It is out of c. with . . ., cela ne s'accorde guère avec. . . . In his c. of . . ., en (sa) qualité de. . . . (b) Work that lacks c., œuvre qui manque de caractère, de cachet. To assume, take on, c., se caractériser. 3. Man of (strong) c., homme de caractère, de volonté. He lacks (strength of) c., il n'a pas de (force de) caractère. 4. (a) Of bad c., de mauvaise réputation; mal famé. (b) F: Certificat m (de moralité). F: To give s.o. a good c., dire du bien de qn. 5. (a) Personnage m (de roman, etc.). (Of acting) In c., dans le ton, la note. Out of c., pas dans son rôle. C. actor, acteur de genre. Th: Characters (in order of appearance), personnages f (par ordre d'entrée en scène). W.Tel: Characters (in order of speaking), distribution f (par ordre d'entrée en ondes). Cin: Rôle de composition. (b) A public c., une personnalité. A bad c., un mauvais sujet. F: He's a c., c'est un type, un original, F: un numéro.
characterial [kærək'tiəriəl], a. Caractériel, -elle.
characteristic [,kæriktə'ristik]. 1. a. Caractéristique. Adm: C. signs, signalement m. Med: C. symptoms, symptômes m diacritiques. 2. s. (a) Trait m, signe m, caractéristique, particularité f. (b) Mth: Caractéristique f (d'un logarithme). **-ally**, adv. D'une manière caractéristique.
characterization ['kæriktərai'zeiʃ(ə)n], s. Caractérisation f.
characterize ['kæriktəraiz], v.tr. Caractériser; être caractéristique de (qn).
characterless ['kæriktəlis], a. 1. Dépourvu de caractère. 2. Dépourvu de certificat (de bonne conduite).
charade [ʃə'rɑːd], s. Charade f. Dumb c., charade mimée.

charcoal ['tʃɑːkoul], s. 1. (a) Charbon m (de bois). (b) Animal c., noir animal, charbon animal. 2. Art: Fusain m. C. drawing, (dessin m au) fusain. 'charcoal-burner, s. Charbonnier m. 'charcoal 'grey, a. Gris foncé, gris charbon.
chard [tʃɑːd], s. Cu: Carde f. Swiss c., bette poirée.
charge¹ [tʃɑːdʒ], s. 1. (a) Charge f (d'une cartouche). Blank c., charge de salut. S.a. DEPTH-CHARGE. (b) (Of kiln, etc.) Fournée f. (c) El: Charge. 2. (a) Frais mpl, prix m; Adm: droits mpl. List of charges, tarif m. C. for admission, prix m d'entrée. No c. for admission, entrée gratuite. To make a c. for sth., compter qch. Free of c., (i) Com: Bank: exempt de frais, sans frais; (ii) gratis, franco; (iii) à titre gratuit, à titre gracieux. At a c. of . . ., moyennant. . . . S.a. EXTRA 1. Overnight c., hébergement m. Bank: Capital c., intérêt m, service m, des capitaux (investis). (b) Jur: Privilège m, droit m. Subject to the c., grevé du privilège. Right of c., droit de constitution de privilège. Charges on an estate, charges d'une succession. To be a c. on s.o., être à la charge de qn. 3. (a) Commission f, devoir m. (b) Charge; emploi m; fonction f; (of clergy) cure f. 4. (a) Garde f, soin m. To take c. of s.o., (i) se charger, avoir soin, de qn; (ii) (provide for) prendre qn à sa charge. Nurse in c. of a child, bonne commise à la garde d'un enfant. Child in c. of a nurse, enfant sous la garde d'une bonne. To give s.o. c. of, over, sth., confier qch. à (la garde de) qn. (Of official) To have c., be in c., of sth., être préposé à la garde de qch. Person in c., préposé (of, à). Jur: To take s.o. in c., arrêter qn. To give s.o. in c., faire arrêter qn. C. sheet, cahier m des délits. Mil: To take sth. on c., porter qch. sur les contrôles. (b) Personne, chose, confiée à la garde de qn. 5. Recommandation f; exhortation f; résumé m (du juge après cause entendue). 6. Jur: Charge; chef m d'accusation. To bring, lay, a c. against s.o., porter une accusation, porter plainte, contre qn. To lay sth. to s.o.'s c., charger, accuser, qn de qch. On a c. of . . ., sous l'inculpation de. . . . 7. (a) Mil: Charge, attaque f. To return to the c., revenir à la charge. (b) Fb: Choc m, charge. 'charge-hand, s. Chef m d'équipe.
charge², v.tr. 1. Charger (un fusil, un accumulateur) (with, de). El: Charged conductor, conducteur chargé, sous tension. 2. (a) To c. s.o. with a commission, charger qn d'une commission. (b) Jur: (Of judge) To c. the jury, faire le résumé des débats. 3. To c. s.o. with a crime, imputer un crime à qn. To c. s.o. with having done sth., accuser qn, reprocher à qn, d'avoir fait qch. 4. (a) Com: Charger, imputer. To c. the postage to the customer, débiter les frais de poste au client. To c. an expense on, to, an account, imputer, passer, mettre, une dépense à un compte. C. it on the bill, portez-le sur la note. (b) To c. a fee, percevoir un droit. To c. s.o. a price for sth., prendre, compter, demander, un prix à qn pour qch. To c. five francs a yard (for sth.), demander cinq francs du mètre. How much will you c. for the lot? combien me faites-vous le tout? 5. v.tr. & i. Charger (l'ennemi). F: To c. into sth., donner (de la tête) contre qch. To c. down upon s.o., foncer sur qn. **charging**, s. Chargement m; remplissage m. El.E: Battery c., (re)charge f des accus.
chargeable ['tʃɑːdʒəbl], a. 1. (Of pers.) Accusable, inculpable (with, de). 2. (Of pers., thg) A la charge (to, de). 3. Imputable (to a cause, à une cause). 4. (Of land) Affectable; grevé (d'un impôt).
chargé d'affaires ['ʃaːʒeidæ'feər], s. Dipl: Chargé m d'affaires.
charger¹ ['tʃɑːdʒər], s. 1. Cheval m de bataille. 2. Chargeur m (d'accumulateur); chargeuse f mécanique. S.a. TRICKLE-CHARGER.
charger², s. A: Grand plat.
charily ['tʃɛərili], adv. 1. Avec précaution; avec circonspection. 2. Avec parcimonie, parcimonieusement.
chariness ['tʃɛərinis], s. 1. Circonspection f, prudence f (of doing sth., à faire qch.). 2. Parcimonie f (de paroles, de louanges).
chariot ['tʃæriət], s. Char m.
charioteer [,tʃæriə'tiər], s. Conducteur m de char.

charitable ['tʃæritəbl], *a.* **1.** (Personne) charitable. **2.** (Œuvre) de bienfaisance, de charité. **C. work,** bonnes œuvres. **-ably,** *adv.* Charitablement.

charity ['tʃæriti], *s.* **1.** Charité *f.* Out of c., for charity's sake, par charité. *Ecc:* To be in c. with one's neighbour, vouloir du bien à son prochain. *Prov:* C. begins at home, charité bien ordonnée commence par soi(-même). **2.** *(a)* Acte *m* de charité. *(b)* Charité, aumônes *fpl,* bienfaisance *f.* To live on c., vivre d'aumônes, être à la charité. **C. ball,** bal de bienfaisance. **C. bazaar,** vente *f* de charité. **3.** Œuvre *f* de bienfaisance, de charité; fondation pieuse. *pl.* **Charities,** bonnes œuvres, œuvres charitables.

charivari ['ʃɑːri'vɑːri], *s.* Charivari *m.*

charlady ['tʃɑːleidi], *s.f.* *F:* = CHARWOMAN.

charlatan ['ʃɑːlət(ə)n], *s.* Charlatan *m.*

charlatanism ['ʃɑːlət(ə)nizm], *s.* Charlatanisme *m.*

charlatanry ['ʃɑːlətənri], *s.* Charlatanerie *f.*

Charles ['tʃɑːlz], *Pr.n.m.* Charles. *Fr.Hist:* **C. the Bold,** Charles le Téméraire. *S.a.* WAIN 2.

Charley, Charlie ['tʃɑːli]. *Pr.n.m.* Charlot. *Cin:* **C. Chaplin,** Charlot.

charlock ['tʃɑːlək], *s.* *Bot:* Sanve *f.*

Charlotte ['tʃɑːlət]. **1.** *Pr.n.f.* Charlotte. **2.** *s.* *Cu:* **Apple c.,** charlotte *f* aux pommes. **C. russe,** charlotte russe.

charm¹ [tʃɑːm], *s.* **1.** Charme *m* (**against,** contre); sortilège *m,* sort *m.* To be under the c., se trouver sous le charme. **2.** *(a)* Amulette *f,* fétiche *m.* *(b)* Breloque *f;* porte-bonheur *m inv.* **3.** Charme, agrément *m.* To be devoid of c., manquer de charme.

charm², *v.tr.* Charmer, enchanter. To c. away s.o.'s cares, charmer les ennuis de qn. He bears a charmed life, sa vie est sous un charme; *F:* il est verni. **charming,** *a.* Charmant, ravissant. **-ly,** *adv.* *(a)* D'une façon charmante. *(b)* D'une façon ravissante; à ravir.

charmer ['tʃɑːmər], *s.* Charmeur, -euse.

charmless ['tʃɑːmlis], *a.* Sans charme.

charnel-house ['tʃɑːnlhaus], *s.* Charnier *m,* ossuaire *m.*

chart¹ [tʃɑːt], *s.* **1.** *Nau:* Carte *f* (marine). **Wind c.,** carte des vents. **2.** *(a)* *(Of statistics, etc.)* Graphique *m,* diagramme *m.* *(b)* Tableau *m* (de graissage, etc.). *(c)* *Computers:* **Operating c.,** organigramme *m.* **'chart-house, -room,** *s.* *Nau:* Cabine *f,* chambre *f,* des cartes; kiosque *m* de navigation.

chart², *v.tr.* **1.** *Nau:* *(a)* Porter (un rocher, etc.) sur une carte. *(b)* Dresser la carte (d'une côte, etc.); faire l'hydrographie (d'une mer, etc.). **2.** Établir le graphique (d'une série de relèvements). **charting,** *s.* Reconnaissance *f* (du littoral); relèvement *m* (d'un récif, etc.).

charter¹ ['tʃɑːtər], *s.* **1.** Charte *f* (d'une ville); statuts *m* (d'une société). **Bank c.,** privilège *m* de la Banque. *Pol:* **The Atlantic C.,** la Charte de l'Atlantique. *U.S:* **C. member,** membre *m* fondateur (d'une société, etc.). **2.** *Nau:* Affrètement *m.* **Trip c., time c.,** affrètement au voyage, à temps. *Av:* **C. plane,** avion-taxi *m.* **On c.,** (i) affrété, (ii) loué, (iii) sous contrat. **'charter-party,** *s.* *Nau:* Charte-partie *f,* *pl.* chartes-parties.

charter², *v.tr.* **1.** Instituer (une compagnie) par charte. **2.** *Nau:* Affréter, fréter. *Av:* To c. an aircraft, affréter un avion. **chartered,** *a.* (Compagnie) à charte. **C. bank,** banque privilégiée. *S.a.* ACCOUNTANT. **chartering,** *s.* (Af)frètement *m,* nolisement *m.*

charterer ['tʃɑːtərər], *s.* *Nau:* (Af)fréteur *m,* nolis(at)eur *m.*

Charterhouse ['tʃɑːtəhaus]. **1.** *s.* *A:* Couvent *m* de chartreux. **2.** *Pr.n.* Une des grandes écoles d'enseignement secondaire d'Angleterre.

chartless ['tʃɑːtlis], *a.* *(a)* (Littoral, etc.) non hydrographié. *(b)* (Navire) sans cartes marines.

charwoman, *pl.* **-women** ['tʃɑːwumən, -wimin], *s.f.* Femme de journée, femme de ménage.

chary ['tʃɛəri], *a.* **1.** Prudent, circonspect. To be c. of, in, doing sth., hésiter à faire qch. **2.** C. of praise, avare de louanges. **C. of one's words,** économe, chiche, de paroles.

chase¹ [tʃeis], *s.* **1.** *(a)* Chasse *f,* poursuite *f.* To give c. to s.o., donner la chasse à qn. *F:* **Wild goose c.,** poursuite vaine. To go on a wild goose c., courir après la lune. *(b)* *Ven:* Chasse (à courre). **2.** (Terrain non enclos réservé à la) chasse.

chase², *v.tr.* **1.** Chasser, pourchasser (le cerf). Poursuivre; donner la chasse à (un voleur, etc.). To c. away a dog, chasser un chien. **3.** *v.i.* *F:* To c. off after sth., partir à la poursuite de qch.

chase³, *v.tr.* **1.** *(a)* Ciseler, bretteler (l'or). *(b)* Relever (le métal) en bosse; repousser (le métal). **2.** Enchâsser, sertir (un diamant). **chasing,** *s.* *(a)* Ciselage *m,* ciselure *f,* brettelure *f.* *(b)* Repoussage *m.*

chase⁴, *s.* *Typ:* Châssis *m* (de mise en pages).

chaser¹ ['tʃeisər], *s.* **1.** *A:* Chasseur *m* (du cerf). **2.** *Navy:* *(a)* (Navire) chasseur. **Submarine-c.,** chasseur de sous-marins. *(b)* Pièce *f* de canon. *S.a.* BOW-CHASER, STERN-CHASER. **3.** *F:* *(a)* Pousse-café *m inv.* *(b)* Verre de bière pris après un verre de whisky, etc.

chaser², *s.* *Metalw:* **1.** (Pers.) Ciseleur *m.* **2.** Peigne *m* à fileter (pour vis).

chasm ['kæz(ə)m], *s.* **1.** Gouffre béant. **2.** Abîme *m* (entre deux personnes). **3.** Vide *m* énorme.

chassé ['ʃæsei], *s.* *Danc:* Chassé *m.*

chassis ['ʃæsi], *s.* *inv.* *Aut: etc:* Châssis *m.* **Stripped c.,** châssis nu.

chaste [tʃeist], *a.* **1.** *(Of pers.)* Chaste, pudique. **2.** *(Of style)* Pur, châtié. **-ly,** *adv.* Chastement, pudiquement; purement.

chasten ['tʃeisn], *v.tr.* *(a)* Châtier, éprouver (qn). *(b)* Châtier (ses passions, son style). *(c)* Rabattre l'orgueil de (qn); assagir (qn). **chastened,** *a.* Assagi (par un déboire); désillusionné; radouci.

chasteness ['tʃeistnis], *s.* = CHASTITY.

chastise [tʃæs'taiz], *v.tr.* Châtier; infliger une correction à (qn); corriger (un enfant).

chastisement ['tʃæstizmənt, tʃæs'taizmənt], *s.* Châtiment *m.*

chastity ['tʃæstiti], *s.* **1.** Chasteté *f.* **2.** *Art: etc:* Pureté *f,* simplicité *f* (de style).

chasuble ['tʃæzjubl], *s.* *Ecc:* Chasuble *f.*

chat¹ [tʃæt], *s.* Causerie *f,* causette *f.* He was glad of a c., il était content de pouvoir bavarder.

chat², *v.i.* (chatted) Causer, bavarder.

chat³, *s.* *Orn:* Tarier *m.*

chattel [tʃætl], *s.* *Jur:* *(a)* Bien *m* meuble, bien mobilier. *(b)* *pl.* Objets mobiliers; meubles *m.* **Goods and chattels,** biens et effets *m.*

chatter¹ ['tʃætər], *s.* **1.** Caquet(age) *m,* jacasserie *f* (d'oiseaux, de commères); bavardage *m.* **2.** Claquement *m* (d'une machine).

chatter², *v.i.* **1.** *(Of birds)* Caqueter, jacasser, jaser; *(of pers.)* bavarder, caqueter. To c. like a magpie, jaser comme une pie (borgne). **2.** *(a)* *(Of teeth)* Claquer. *(b)* *(Of machinery, etc.)* Faire du bruit; cogner. **chattering,** *s.* **1.** = CHATTER¹. **2.** Claquement *m* (des dents).

chatterer ['tʃætərər], *F:* **chatterbox** ['tʃætəbɔks], *s.* Babillard, -arde; grand(e) bavard(e). *F:* To be a great c., avoir la langue bien pendue.

chatty ['tʃæti], *a.* *(Of pers.)* Causeur, -euse; (dîner) très causant. **C. article on . . .,** article sur le ton de la conversation sur. . . .

chauffeur ['ʃoufər], *f.* **chauffeuse** ['ʃoufəːz], *s.* Chauffeur, -euse (salarié(e)) d'automobile.

chauvinism [ʃouvinizm], *s.* Chauvinisme *m.*

chaw¹ [tʃɔː], *s.* Chique *f* (de tabac).

chaw², *v.tr.* *F:* *(a)* Mâcher. *(b)* Chiquer (du tabac).

cheap [tʃiːp]. **1.** *a.* *(a)* À bon marché. *Pol.Ec:* **C. money policy,** politique *f* de facilités d'escompte, de l'argent à bon marché. To buy sth. c., acheter qch. (à) bon marché, à bon compte, pour pas cher. **Cheaper,** (à) meilleur marché, moins cher. It comes cheaper to take a whole bottle, on a avantage à prendre la bouteille entière. **Dirt c.,** à vil prix; pour rien. It's c. and nasty, c'est camelote. **C. seats** (theatre, etc.), places populaires, petites places. To do sth. on the c., faire qch. (i) à peu de frais, (ii) chichement, au rabais. *(b)* De peu de valeur. *F:* To feel c., (i) être honteux; (ii) ne pas être dans son assiette; *F:* être mal fichu. To make oneself c., déroger; se déprécier. To hold sth. c., faire bon marché, peu de cas, de qch. *S.a.* JACK¹ II 1. **2.** *adv.* *F:* = CHEAPLY. **-ly,** *adv.* À bon marché; à bas prix; à peu de frais. *F:* He got off cheap(ly), il en est quitte à bon compte.

cheapen ['tʃiːp(ə)n]. **1.** *v.tr.* (Ra)baisser le prix de (qch.); diminuer la valeur de (qch.). **2.** *v.i.* Diminuer de prix.

cheapness ['tʃiːpnis], s. **1.** Bon marché; bas prix (de qch.). **2.** Médiocrité f (de qch.).

cheat¹ [tʃiːt], s. **1.** (a) Trompeur m; escroc m. (b) (At games) Tricheur m. **2.** A: Tromperie f, fourberie f, escroquerie f.

cheat², v.tr. **1.** Tromper; frauder (qn); voler (qn). To c. the gallows, échapper à la potence. To c. s.o. out of sth., frustrer qn de qch. **2.** (At games) Tricher (qn); abs. tricher. **cheating¹**, a. **1.** Trompeur, -euse. **2.** Tricheur, -euse. **cheating²**, s. **1.** Tromperie f; fourberie f. **2.** Cards: Tricherie f.

check¹ [tʃek], s. **1.** (a) Chess: Échec m. To give c. to the king, faire échec au roi. 'C.!' "échec au roi!" (b) Revers m, échec. (c) Ven: (Of pack) To come to a c., venir à bout de voie; perdre la voie. **2.** Arrêt m, pause f, anicroche f, à-coup m. **3.** (Restraint) Frein m. To keep, to hold, the enemy in c., tenir l'ennemi en échec; faire échec à l'ennemi. **4.** Butée f, arrêt. Aut: etc: Door-c., arrêt de porte. **5.** Contrôle m. (a) Com: Vérification f (d'un compte, etc.). C. sample, échantillon témoin. (Cross-)checks (on information), (moyens m de) recoupement m. To keep a c. on sth., contrôler qch. (b) Billet m; (at cloakroom, etc.) ticket m. Luggage c., bulletin m de bagages. (c) U.S: (P: in Engl.) Addition f, note f (dans un restaurant). (d) U.S: Jeton m de présence (à une séance). P: To hand in one's checks, mourir, P: poser sa chique. (e) U.S: To put a c. against a name, pointer un nom, faire une coche après un nom. **6.** U.S: = CHEQUE. **check-a'nalysis**, s. Contre-analyse f. **'check-inspection**, s. Med: visite f de contrôle; contre-visite f. **'check-list**, s. Liste de contrôle. **'check-nut**, s. Contre-écrou m. **'check-point**, s. Sp: Aut: Rac: Contrôle m. **'check(-)room**, s. Rail: U.S: Consigne f, salle f des bagages. **'check-screw**, s. Contre-vis f inv. **'check-valve**, s. Mch: Hyd.E: Soupape f de retenue.

check². **1.** v.tr. (a) Chess: Mettre (le roi) en échec; faire échec (au roi). (b) Faire échec à (qn, qch.); contenir (l'ennemi); enrayer (une crise); arrêter (une attaque). Nau: Stopper (un câble). (c) Refouler, comprimer, retenir (ses larmes, sa colère); modérer (sa violence); réprimer, refréner (une passion); freiner (la production). (d) Réprimander, reprendre (un enfant, etc.). (e) Vérifier, apurer (un compte); vérifier (la pression, etc.); collationner, compulser (un document). Typ: (i) Réviser, (ii) conférer (des épreuves). To c. (off), pointer (des noms sur une liste). To c. (up) information, U.S: to c. up on information, contrôler des renseignements. Checked, double-checked and cross-checked, vérifié et revérifié. (f) Contrôler (une expérience, etc.; Rail: les billets). (g) (Faire) enregistrer (ses bagages). **2.** v.i. Hésiter, s'arrêter (at, devant); (of horse) refuser. **check in**, v.i. **1.** U.S: S'inscrire (à l'hôtel, etc.). **2.** Ind: Signer à l'arrivée. **check out**, v.tr. Retirer. U.S: To c.o. baggage, retirer des bagages. **2.** v.i. F: Quitter, partir. **check over**, v.tr. Vérifier. **'check(-)up**, s. Med: Examen médical complet; vérification, inspection médicale. To have a c.-up, passer une visite médicale. **checking**, s. **1.** Répression f; enrayage m. (a) Contrôle m; vérification f; apurement m; pointage m. (b) Enregistrement m (de bagages).

check³, s. Tex: Carreau m; (tissu) à carreaux, en damier. Broken c., pied-de-poule m.

checked [tʃekt], a. A carreaux; quadrillé.

checker¹ ['tʃekər], s. Contrôleur m, pointeur m.

checker², s. & v.tr. = CHEQUER¹,².

checkers ['tʃekəz], s.pl. U.S: Jeu m de dames. **'checker-board**, s. U.S: Damier m.

checkmate¹ ['tʃekmeit], s. Chess: Échec et mat m.

checkmate², v.tr. **1.** Chess: A: =¦MATE². **2.** Faire échec et mat à (qn). **3.** Contrecarrer, déjouer (les projets de qn).

cheddar ['tʃedər], s. (Fromage m de) Cheddar m.

cheek¹ [tʃiːk], s. **1.** Joue f. C. by jowl with s.o., côte à côte avec qn. S.a. TONGUE¹ 1. **2.** F: (a) Toupet m, effronterie f, impudence f. To have the c. to do, say, sth., avoir l'aplomb de faire, de dire, qch. It's a piece of damned c.! F: c'est se ficher du monde! What c.! quel toupet! He has plenty of c., P: il a un culot monstre! (b) Impertinences fpl. **3.** Joue

(de poulie, de coussinet); flasque m, bras m (de manivelle); mâchoire f (d'étau). **'cheek-bone**, s.

cheek², v.tr. F: Faire l'insolent avec (qn); F: se payer la tête de (qn).

-cheeked ['tʃiːkt], a. Rosy-c., aux joues vermeilles. S.a. APPLE-CHEEKED.

cheekiness ['tʃiːkinis], s. F: Effronterie f.

cheeky ['tʃiːki], a. F: Effronté. **-ily**, adv. F: D'un air ou d'un ton effronté.

cheep¹ [tʃiːp], s. Piaulement m.

cheep², v.i. (Of young birds) Piauler.

cheer¹ [tʃiər], s. **1.** Bonne disposition (d'esprit). (So used esp. in) Words of c., paroles consolatrices, d'encouragement. A: (& P: when usu. written wotcher?) What c.? comment ça va? A: (Food) Bonne chère. **3.** Hourra m; pl. acclamations f, bravos m, vivats m. 'Loud cheers,' "vifs applaudissements." To give three cheers = accorder un ban à qn. Three cheers for X! vive X! (When having a drink) Cheers! A la vôtre!

cheer². **1.** v.tr. (a) To c. s.o. (up), égayer, ragaillardir, dérider, qn; relever le moral de qn. To c. s.o. on (to do sth.), encourager qn (à faire qch.). (b) Acclamer, applaudir (qn). **2.** v.i. (a) To c. up, reprendre sa gaieté; se ragaillardir. C. up! courage! (b) Pousser des hourras, des vivats; applaudir. **cheering¹**, a. Encourageant, réjouissant. **cheering²**, s. Acclamation f; applaudissements mpl.

cheerful ['tʃiəf(u)l], a. (Of pers.) Gai; de bonne humeur; allègre; (of room) d'aspect agréable, riant; (of fire, news) réconfortant; (of conversation, music) égayant. **-fully**, adv. **1.** Gaiement, allégrement. **2.** De bon cœur; volontiers.

cheerfulness ['tʃiəf(u)lnis], s. (a) (Of pers.) Gaieté f, belle humeur; contentement m. His c. in misfortune, sa sérénité dans le malheur. (b) Aspect riant (du paysage); air m agréable (d'un intérieur).

cheeriness ['tʃiərinis], s. Joyeux caractère; gaieté communicative; sérénité f.

cheerio ['tʃiəri'ou], int. P: **1.** A bientôt! bon courage! adieu! **2.** (When having a drink) A la vôtre! à la tienne!

cheerless ['tʃiəlis], a. Morne, triste, sombre. **-ly**, adv. Tristement.

cheery ['tʃiəri], a. **1.** (Of pers.) Joyeux, -euse, gai, guilleret. **2.** = CHEERING¹. **-ily**, adv. Gaiement.

cheese¹ [tʃiːz], s. **1.** Fromage m. To believe the moon is made of green c., prendre des vessies pour des lanternes. S.a. CHALK¹. **2.** (With pl. cheeses) A c., un fromage (entier). Cheshire c., chester m. Cream c., fromage blanc; petit suisse. Goat's-milk c., fromage de chèvre. Dutch c., (i) fromage de Hollande, (ii) F: Tête f de maure, de mort. Blue c., (fromage) bleu. Processed c., fromage fondu, fromage industriel, crème f (de gruyère, etc.). **3.** Gelée f (de prunes de Damas, etc.). S.a. LEMON-CHEESE. Ciderm: Marc m de pommes. U.S: P: Big c., grosse légume. **'cheese-'biscuit**, s. Biscuit non sucré. **'cheese-cake**, s. (a) Cu: Tarte f au fromage blanc parfumée au citron. (b) F: Pin up f, **'cheese-cloth**, s. Gaze f; étamine f. **'cheese-cover**, s. Cloche f à fromage. **'cheese-'finger**, s. Cu: Biscuit fourré au fromage. **'cheese-maker**, s. Fromager, -ère. **'cheese-paring**, s. **1.** Croûte f de fromage. **2.** Parcimonie f, lésine f. a. C.-p. economy, économies de bouts de chandelle. **'cheese-'straws**, s. Cu: Allumettes f au fromage, pailles f au parmesan.

cheese², v. P: (Used in the phr.) C. it! en voilà assez! la ferme! fiche le camp! **cheese off**, v.tr. P: Décourager (qn). To be cheesed off, avoir le cafard, être découragé.

cheesemonger ['tʃiːzmʌŋgər], s. Marchand m de fromage.

cheesy ['tʃiːzi], a. **1.** Caséeux, -euse, caséiforme. **2.** (Odeur) de fromage. **3.** U.S: P: Miteux, minable.

cheetah ['tʃiːtə], s. Z: Guépard m.

chef [ʃef], s.m. Chef m de cuisine.

chemical ['kemik(ə)l]. **1.** a. Chimique. C. balance, balance de laboratoire. C. warfare, guerre f chimique. C. engineering, chimie industrielle. **2.** s.pl. Chemicals, produits m chimiques. Com: Ind: Drogues f. **-ally**, adv. Chimiquement.

chemise [ʃə'miːz], s. Chemise f (de femme).

chemist ['kemist], s. 1. Pharmacien m. Chemist's shop, pharmacie f. 2. Chimiste m. Analytical c., chimiste (analyste).

chemistry ['kemistri], s. Chimie f. Inorganic c., chimie minérale. Organic c., chimie organique. Applied c., chimie appliquée. C. of metals, métallochimie f.

chemotherapy ['kemou'θerəpi], s. Med: Chimio-thérapie f.

cheque [tʃek], s. Com: Chèque m. Crossed c., chèque barré. Open, uncrossed, c., chèque ouvert, non barré. Com: Dud c., c. without cover, worthless c., chèque m sans provision, sans contre-partie. S.a. BLANK I. 1, TRAVELLER 1. 'cheque-book, s. Carnet m de chèques; (esp. of large counting-houses) Chéquier m.

chequer[1] ['tʃekər], s. Usu. pl. Quadrillage m.

chequer[2], v.tr. 1. Quadriller (une étoffe, etc.). 2. Diaprer, bigarrer. 3. F: Diversifier, varier. chequered, a. 1. Quadrillé, à carreaux, en damier, en échiquier. 2. Diapré, bigarré. 3. C. career, vie accidentée, mouvementée. chequering, s. Quadrillage m (d'une étoffe); guillochage m (d'une montre).

cherish ['tʃeriʃ], v.tr. 1. Chérir; soigner tendrement (un enfant). 2. Bercer, caresser (un espoir); nourrir, entretenir (une idée, une haine, des illusions). His most cherished hopes, ses espérances les plus chères.

cheroot [ʃə'ruːt], s. Manille m (à bouts coupés).

cherry ['tʃeri]. 1. s. Cerise f. Black-heart c., guigne noire. White-heart c., bigarreau m. Wild c., merise f. Not to make two bites at a c., ne pas s'y prendre à deux fois; y aller sans hésiter. 2. s. C.(-tree, -wood), cerisier m. Wild c.(-tree), merisier m. Heart-c.(-tree), guignier m. 3. a. C.(-red), cerise inv; (of lips) vermeil. cherry-'bay, -'laurel, s. Bot: Laurier-cerise m. 'cherry 'brandy, s. Cherry-brandy m, F: cherry m. 'cherry-orchard, s. Cerisaie f. cherry-'pie, s. 1. Tourte f aux cerises. 2. Bot: Héliotrope m (du Pérou). 'cherry-stone, s. 1. Noyau m de cerise. 2. U.S: Moll: Palourde f. 'cherry-wood, s. (Bois m de) cerisier m. C.-w. pipe, pipe en merisier.

cherub, pl. **cherubs** B: **cherubim** ['tʃerəb, -z, -əbim], s. Chérubin m.

cherubic [tʃi'ruːbik], a. Chérubique; de chérubin.

chervil ['tʃəːvil], s. Bot: Cerfeuil m.

Cheshire ['tʃeʃiːr], Pr.n. Geog: Le (comté de) Cheshire, de Chester. Com: C. cheese, fromage m de Chester; chester m.

chess [tʃes], s. Jeu m d'échecs. 'chess-board, s. Échiquier m. 'chess-men, s.pl. Pièces f (du jeu d'échecs).

chest [tʃest], s. 1. Coffre m, caisse f, boîte f. Furn: C. of drawers, commode f. Sea c., coffre de marin. S.a. ICE-CHEST, MEDICINE-CHEST, TEA-CHEST, TOOL-CHEST. 2. Anat: Poitrine f. C. specialist, pneumologue mf. Cold on the c., c. cold, rhume de poitrine. To have a weak c., avoir les bronches délicates. To throw out one's c., bomber la poitrine, le torse. F: To get it off one's c., dire ce qu'on a sur le cœur, F: se déboutonner. 'chest-protector, s. Plastron m hygiénique. 'chest-voice, s. Voix f de poitrine.

-chested ['tʃestid], a. Broad-c., à large poitrine.

chesterfield ['tʃestəfiːld], s. Furn: Canapé rembourré et capitonné (à deux accoudoirs).

chestnut ['tʃes(t)nʌt]. 1. s. (a) (Sweet, Spanish) c., (i) châtaigne f (comestible); (ii) (if very large) marron m. S.a. HORSE-CHESTNUT. (b) (Sweet) c.(-tree), châtaignier commun; marronnier m. (c) F: Plaisanterie usée; vieille histoire. 2. Attrib. (a) (Wood) De châtaignier. (b) (Colour) Châtain; (cheval) bai-châtain, alezan. 'chestnut-grove, s. Châtaigneraie f.

chesty ['tʃesti], a. 1. U.S: P: Vaniteux, -euse. 2. F: Délicat des bronches.

cheval-glass [ʃe'vælglɑːs], s. Furn: Psyché f.

chevet ['ʃevei], s. Arch: Chevet m (d'une église).

cheviot ['tʃeviət, 'tʃiː-]. 1. Pr.n. Geog: The Cheviots, les Cheviots m. 2. s. (a) Husb: (Mouton) cheviot (m). (b) Tex: Cheviot (cloth), cheviot(t)e f.

chevron ['ʃevrən], s. Her: Mil: Chevron m.

chew[1] [tʃuː], s. 1. To have a c. at sth., mâchonner qch. 2. Chique f (de tabac).

chew[2], v.tr. Mâcher, mastiquer (des aliments, etc.); chiquer (du tabac); mâchonner (un cigare). F: To c. over sth., méditer sur qch.; ruminer (une idée). To c. sth. up, abîmer qch.; mettre qch. en morceaux. P: To c. the rag, the fat, (i) ronchonner; (ii) parler. chewing, s. Mastication f, mâchonnement m. 'chewing-gum, s. Chewing-gum m. Pharm: Masticatoire m.

chewer ['tʃuːər], s. Chiqueur m (de tabac).

chiaroscuro [ki,ɑːros'kuərou], s. Art: Clair-obscur m.

chic [ʃiːk]. 1. a. (Robe, manteau) chic. 2. s. F: She has some c. about her, elle a du chic, elle est toujours à la mode.

chicane[1] [ʃi'kein], s. Chicane f; avocasserie f.

chicane[2]. 1. v.i. Chicaner. 2. v.tr. Chicaner (qn).

chicanery [ʃi'keinəri], s. 1. Chicanerie f, chicane f, tracasserie f. 2. Arguties fpl; subtilités fpl.

chichi, chi-chi [ʃiʃi, ʃiːʃiː], a. Recherché, prétentieux, -euse, précieux, -euse.

chick [tʃik], s. (i) (Unfledged) Poussin m; (ii) poulet m; (iii) U.S: P: pépée f. To have neither c. nor child, être sans enfant.

chickabiddy ['tʃikəbidi], s. F: Cocot(t)e f (poule ou enfant).

chicken[1] ['tʃikin], s. 1. (a) (Recently hatched) Poussin m. (b) (Fledged) Poulet m. Don't count your chickens before they are hatched, il ne faut pas vendre la peau de l'ours avant de l'avoir tué. F: She is no c., elle n'est plus dans sa première jeunesse. Orn: F: Mother Car(e)y's c., pétrel m de tempête. 2. Cu: Poulet. Spring c., poussin. 3. Coll: Volaille f. 'chicken-'breasted, a. Med: Rachitique. 'chicken-feed, s. (a) Husb: Nourriture f pour les volailles. (b) F: It's just c.-f., c'est de la gnognote. 'chicken-farm, s. Élevage m avicole, de volaille. 'chicken-hearted, -livered, a. F: Poltron; F: capon, froussard. To be c.-h., être une poule mouillée. 'chicken-pox, s. Med: Varicelle f. 'chicken-run, s. Enclos grillagé d'un poulailler.

chicken[2], a. U.S: F: 1. = CHICKEN-HEARTED. 2. Tatillon, -onne.

chicken[3], v.i. U.S: P: To c. out, P: caner.

chickling ['tʃiklin], s. Bot: Gesse f.

chick-pea [,tʃik-'piː], s. Bot: Pois m chiche.

chickweed ['tʃikwiːd], s. Bot: Mouron m des oiseaux.

chicory ['tʃikəri], s. 1. Bot: Chicorée f. Broad-leaved c., endive f. Wild c., (i) Bot: chicorée sauvage; (ii) Hort: barbe-de-capucin f. 2. Com: (Ground) c., (poudre f de) chicorée. Coffee with c., café m à la chicorée.

chide [tʃaid], v.tr. & i. (p.t. chid, occ. chided; p.p. chidden or chid, occ. chided) A. & Lit: Réprimander, gronder (qn). To c. s.o. for sth., for doing sth., reprocher à qn d'avoir fait qch.

chief [tʃiːf]. I. s. (a) (Pers.) Chef m (de tribu). F: The c., le patron. (b) In c., en chef. Commander-in-c., commandant en chef. II. chief, a. Principal, -aux; premier, -ière; (en) chef. C. engineer, ingénieur en chef. C. stoker, chef de chauffe. C. guest, hôte m d'honneur. C. object, but principal. To play a c. part in . . ., jouer un rôle capital dans. . . . -ly, adv. 1. Surtout, avant tout. 2. Principalement.

chieftain ['tʃiːftən], s.m. Chef (de clan).

chieftainship ['tʃiːftənʃip], s. Dignité f, rang m, de chef (de clan).

chiffon ['ʃifon], s. Tex: Mousseline f de soie.

chiffonier [,ʃifə'niər], s. Furn: Chiffonnier m (à tiroirs).

chignon ['ʃiːnjɔ̃ːŋ], s. Chignon m.

chilblain ['tʃilblein], s. Engelure f.

child, pl. **children** [tʃaild, 'tʃildrən], s. (a) Enfant mf. A: To be with c., être enceinte. Be a good c.! sois sage! I'm taking the c. with me, j'emmène le petit, la petite. From a c. . . ., dès son enfance, depuis son plus jeune âge. . . . Problem c., difficult c., enfant difficile. Adj. use, C. psychiatry, psychiatrie infantile. C. welfare, protection f de l'enfance. C. welfare centre, centre m de protection infantile. (b) Lit: B: Descendant; enfant. Our children's children, nos arrière-neveux m. 'child-bearing, s. 1. = CHILD-BIRTH. 2. Gestation f, grossesse f. 'child-bed, s. Couches fpl. 'child-birth, s. Enfantement m; couches fpl; accouchement m. 'child's play, s. Jeu m d'enfant. To make c.-p. of sth., faire qch. en se jouant. That's only c.-p., ce n'est que l'enfance de l'art.

childhood ['tʃaildhud], s. (a) Enfance f. (b) Med: Later c., deuxième, seconde enfance. **In one's second c.**, retombé en enfance.

childish ['tʃaildiʃ], a. 1. Enfantin, d'enfant, d'enfance. 2. Pej: (Of grown-up pers.) Enfant, puéril, F: bébête. **Don't be so c.**, ne faites pas l'enfant. 3. (Of aged pers.) **To grow c.**, retomber en enfance. **-ly**, adv. Comme un enfant; puérilement.

childishness ['tʃaildiʃnis], s. Pej: Enfantillage m, puérilité f.

childless ['tʃaildlis], a. Sans enfant(s).

childlike ['tʃaildlaik], a. Enfantin; naïf, -ïve.

Chile ['tʃili]. Pr.n. Geog: Le Chili.

Chilean ['tʃiliən], a. & s. Geog: Chilien, -ienne.

chill¹ [tʃil], s. 1. (a) Med: Coup m de froid. **To catch a c.**, prendre froid; F: attraper un chaud et froid. (b) **C. of fear**, frisson m de crainte. 2. (a) Froideur f (de l'eau, etc.). **To take the c. off (sth.)**, (faire) dégourdir, (faire) tiédir (l'eau); chambrer (le vin). (b) **To cast a c. over the company**, jeter un froid sur l'assemblée. 3. Metall: C.(-mould), moule m en fonte; coquille f.

chill², a. Froid, glacé. **The wind blows c.**, il souffle un vent glacial. (Of blood) **To run c.**, se glacer.

chill³. 1. v.tr. (a) Refroidir, glacer; faire frissonner (qn); donner le frisson à (qn). **Chilled to the bone**, morfondu; transi de froid. (b) Réfrigérer (la viande, etc.). **Chilled meat**, viande frigorifiée. (c) Metall: **To c. (-harden)**, tremper, couler, (le fer) en coquille. 2. v.i. Se refroidir, se glacer. **chilling¹**, a. (Vent, accueil) glacial, -als. **chilling²**, s. 1. Réfrigeration f (des aliments). 2. Metall: Trempe f en coquille.

chilli ['tʃili], s. Cu: Piment m. **Red c.**, piment rouge.

chilliness ['tʃilinis], s. (a) Froid m, froideur f, fraîcheur f. (b) Froideur (d'un accueil).

chilly ['tʃili], a. 1. (Of pers.) (a) Frileux, -euse. (b) **To feel c.**, avoir froid. 2. (Of weather, etc.) Frais, f. fraîche; (un peu) froid. **It is getting c.**, il commence à faire frisquet. 3. (Of pers., manner) Froid. **C. politeness**, politesse glaciale.

chime¹ [tʃaim], s. C., chimes (of bells), carillon m. **The full chimes**, la grosse sonnerie.

chime². 1. v.i. Carillonner. **To c. together**, s'accorder, être d'accord. **To c. in with s.o.'s ideas**, s'harmoniser, tomber d'accord, avec les idées de qn. F: **To c. in**, placer son mot, intervenir (dans la conversation). **To c. in with the laughter**, s'associer aux rires. 2. v.tr. (Of clock) **To c. the hour**, carillonner l'heure. **chiming¹**, a. Carillonnant. **C. clock**, pendule à carillon. **chiming²**, s. Carillonnement m, carillon m, sonnerie f.

chime³, s. Jable m (d'un tonneau).

chimera, -æra, [ki'miərə], s. 1. Myth: Chimère f. 2. Ich: Chimère.

chimerical [kai'merik(ə)l], a. Chimérique. **-ally**, adv. Chimériquement.

chimney ['tʃimni], s. 1. Cheminée f (de maison). **C. on fire**, feu m de cheminée. A: **C. boy**, petit ramoneur. 2. (Funnel) Cheminée (de bateau à vapeur). **Lamp c.**, verre m de lampe. 3. Mountaineering: Cheminée, varappe f. **To climb a c.**, ramoner. **'chimney-corner**, s. Coin m de cheminée; coin du feu. **'chimney-flue**, s. Const: Conduit m de fumée; tuyau m de tirage. **'chimney-jack**, s. Mitre f (de cheminée) à tête mobile; gueule-de-loup f. **'chimney-piece**, s. Chambranle m de cheminée; la cheminée. **'chimney-pot**, s. Mitre f; pot m de cheminée. **'chimney-stack, -stalk**, s. 1. (Corps de) cheminée f; souche f. 2. Cheminée d'usine. **'chimney-sweep**, s. (Pers.) Ramoneur m. **'chimney-sweeper**, s. 1. (Brush) Ramoneuse f; hérisson m. 2. = CHIMNEY-SWEEP. **'chimney-sweeping**, s. Ramonage m.

chimpanzee [ˌtʃimpæn'ziː], s. Chimpanzé m.

chin [tʃin], s. Menton m. **Double c.**, double menton. **Chins up!** (i) Mil: levez la tête! (ii) F: courage! **'chin-rest**, s. Mentonnière f (de violon). **'chin-strap**, s. Mil: Jugulaire f, (sous-)mentonnière f (de casque, etc.). **'chin-wag**, s. F: O: Conversation f, causette f.

China ['tʃainə]. 1. Pr.n. Geog: La Chine. **Communist C.** = CHINESE PEOPLE'S REPUBLIC. 2. s. (No pl.) (i) Porcelaine f; faïence fine; (ii) vaisselle f de porce-

laine. S.a. ASTER. **'china-clay**, s. Kaolin m. **'china-closet**, s. 1. Armoire f à porcelaine. 2. Vitrine f à porcelaine. **'china-paper**, s. Paperm: Papier m de Chine. **'china(-)ware**, s. (Vaisselle f de) porcelaine.

Chinaman, pl. -men ['tʃainəmən], s.m. Pej: Chinois.

Chinatown ['tʃainətaun]. Pr.n. Quartier chinois (d'une ville).

chinchilla [tʃin'tʃilə], s. (Rat, rabbit) Chinchilla m.

chin-chin ['tʃin'tʃin], int. & s. P: O: 1. (a) Salut m, bonjour m. (b) Adieu m; au revoir m. 2. A la vôtre!

chine¹ [tʃain], s. Geol: Ravinée f, ravin m.

chine², s. 1. Anat: Échine f. 2. Arête f, crête f (d'une montagne).

Chinee [tʃai'niː], s. A: P: Chinois m.

Chinese [ˌtʃai'niːz]. 1. a. & s. inv. Chinois, -oise. **C. People's Republic**, République f populaire de Chine. **C. Nationalist Government**, Gouvernement m de la Chine nationaliste. **C. white**, blanc de Chine. 2. s. Ling: Le chinois.

chink¹ [tʃiŋk], s. Fente f, crevasse f, lézarde f (dans un mur); entrebâillement m (de la porte).

chink², s. Tintement m (du métal, du verre). **I heard a c. of money**, j'entends sonner des pièces de monnaie.

chink³. 1. v.tr. Faire sonner (son argent); faire tinter (des verres, etc.). 2. v.i. Sonner (sec).

Chink⁴, s. P: Pej: Chinois m.

chinless ['tʃinlis], a. Au menton fuyant. **-chinned** [tʃind], a. Double-c., à double menton.

chinook [tʃi'nuk], s. Meteor: Chinook m.

chintz [tʃints], s. Tex: Perse f, indienne f, chintz m.

chip¹ [tʃip], s. 1. Éclat m, copeau m (de bois); écaille f, éclat (de marbre). **To have a c. on one's shoulder**, chercher noise à tout le monde. **He is a c. of the old block**, c'est bien le fils de son père. 2. (Fracture) Brisure f, écornure f (d'assiette). 3. Cu: **Chips** (pommes de terre) frites(f). **Game chips**, croustilles f. 4. Cards: etc: Jeton m. P: **He's had his chips**, il est cuit, fichu.

chip², v.tr. (chipped) 1. Tailler par éclats; hacher ou doler (le bois). 2. (a) Ébrécher (une tasse, un couteau); écorner (un meuble). **To c. a piece off sth.**, enlever un morceau à qch. (b) Piquer (les incrustations d'une chaudière). (c) F: **To c. (at) s.o.**, persifler qn; se moquer de qn. **chip in**, v.i. 1. Cards: Miser. 2. F: Intervenir; placer son mot. **chip off**, 1. v.i. (Of paint, etc.) S'écailler. 2. v.tr. **To c. off the scale of a boiler**, piquer une chaudière. **chipped**, a. 1. Ébréché, écaillé. 2. **Chipped potatoes**, pommes de terre frites, frites fpl. **chipping**, s. 1. (a) Taille f par éclats; écaillement m; clivage m (de pierre); burinage m (de métal); piquage m au marteau (d'une chaudière). (b) F: Persiflage m, taquinerie f. 2. pl. **Chippings**, éclats m, copeaux m. P.N: **Loose chippings**, gravillons mpl.

chipmunk ['tʃipmʌŋk], s. Z: Chipmunk m, tamia rayé, Fr.C: suisse rayé.

chipper ['tʃipər], a. U.S: F: Gai, vif, f. vive, bien en train.

chippy ['tʃipi], a. 1. F: (Esp. of food) Sec, f. sèche; sans saveur. 2. P: **To feel c.**, avoir la gueule de bois.

chiromancer ['kaiərəmænsər], s. Chiromancien, -ienne.

chiromancy ['kaiərəmænsi], s. Chiromancie f.

chiropodist [ki'rɔpədist], s. Pédicure mf.

chiropody [ki'rɔpədi], s. Chirurgie f pédicure.

chiropractic ['kaiərəpræktik], s. Chiropractie f.

chiropractor ['kaiərəpræktər], s. Chiropracteur m.

Chiroptera [kai'rɔptərə], s.pl. Z: Ché(i)roptères mpl.

chirp¹ [tʃəːp], s. Pépiement m, gazouillement m, gazouillis m, piaulement m (d'oiseaux); grésillement m (du grillon).

chirp², v.i. (Of bird) Pépier, gazouiller, ramager; (of grasshopper) grésiller. **chirp up**, v.i. F: (a) Faire entendre sa petite voix. (b) Se ragaillardir.

chirpiness ['tʃəːpinis], s. F: Humeur gaie, gaillarde.

chirpy ['tʃəːpi], a. F: D'humeur gaie; bien en train.

chirr¹ [tʃəːr], s. Grésillement m (du grillon).

chirr², v.i. (Of cricket) Grésiller, chanter.

chirrup ['tʃirəp], s. & v.i. = CHIRP¹,².

chisel ['tʃizl], s. 1. Ciseau m. **Mortise c.**, bédane m. S.a. COLD-CHISEL. 2. Engr: Burin m. 3. Anvil c., tranche f. 4. P: Filouterie f; sale coup m.

chisel², *v.tr.* **1.** Ciseler; buriner (le métal). **To c. sth. off**, enlever, détacher, qch. au ciseau, au burin. **Chiselled features**, traits finement ciselés. **2.** *P:* Duper, filouter, rouler, carotter (qn). **chiselling**, *s.* **1.** Ciselure *f*; burinage *m.* **2.** *P: O:* Escroquerie *f.*

chiseller ['tʃizlər], *s.* **1.** Ciseleur *m*, burineur *m.* **2.** *P: O:* Escroc *m*, carotteur *m.*

chit¹ [tʃit], *s.* *F: Usu. Pej:* Mioche *mf*, gosse *mf*; bambin *m.*

chit², *s.* *F:* **1.** Lettre *f*, billet *m.* **2.** Billet, reconnaissance *f* de dette.

chit-chat ['tʃitʃæt], *s.* *F:* Bavardages *mpl*, commérages *mpl.*

chitterlings ['tʃitəliŋz], *s.pl.* *Cu:* = Andouille *f.*

chivalrous ['ʃivəlrəs], *a.* Chevaleresque; courtois. -ly, *adv.* Chevaleresquement.

chivalrousness ['ʃivəlrəsnis, 'tʃ-], *s.* = CHIVALRY 2.

chivalry ['ʃivəlri], *s.* **1.** Chevalerie *f.* **2.** Conduite *f* chevaleresque; courtoisie *f.*

chives [tʃaivz], *s.pl.* Ciboulette *f*, civette *f.*

chivy, chivvy ['tʃivi], *v.tr.* Poursuivre, chasser. **To c. s.o. about**, ne laisser aucun repos à qn.

chloral ['klɔ:rəl], *s.* *Ch:* Chloral *m.*

chlorate ['klɔ:reit], *s.* *Ch:* Chlorate *m.*

chloric ['klɔ:rik], *a.* *Ch:* Chlorique.

chloride ['klɔ:raid], *s.* *Ch:* Chlorure *m.*

chlorinate ['klɔrineit], *v.tr.* **1.** Chlorurer. **2.** *Hyg:* Javelliser, chlorer (l'eau).

chlorination [,klɔri'neiʃ(ə)n], *s.* **1.** Chloruration *f.* **2.** *Hyg:* Javellisation *f.*

chlorine ['klɔ:ri:n], *s.* *Ch:* Chlore *m.*

chloroform¹ ['klɔrəfɔ:m], *s.* *Med:* Chloroforme *m.*

chloroform², *v.tr.* Chloroformer, chloroformiser.

chloromycetin [,klɔrəmai'si:tin], *s.* *R.t.m:* *Pharm:* Tifomycine *f.* *Med:* Chloromycétine *f.*

chlorophyll(l) ['klɔrəfil], *s.* Chlorophylle *f.*

chlorosis [klɔ:'rousis], *s.* *Med: Bot:* Chlorose *f.*

choc-ice ['tʃɔkais], *s.* *F:* Esquimau *m*, chocolat glacé.

chock¹ [tʃɔk], *s.* Cale *f*; tin *m*, coin *m.* *Av: etc:* **To withdraw the chocks**, enlever les cales. **Chocks away!** Enlevez les cales!

chock², *v.tr.* **To c. (up)**, caler (un meuble), coincer (des rails). **chocking**, *s.* **1.** Calage *m.* **2.** Coinçage *m.*

chock-a-block ['tʃɔkə'blɔk], *a.* **1.** (Poulie) à bloc. **2.** *F:* = CHOCK-FULL.

chock-full ['tʃɔk'ful], *a.* *F:* Plein comme un œuf. *Th:* **The house was c.-f.**, la salle était comble.

chocolate ['tʃɔklit]. **1.** *s.* Chocolat *m.* **Slab of c.**, tablette *f* de chocolat. **Cooking c.**, chocolat à cuire. **Eating c.**, chocolat à croquer. **A cup of c.**, une tasse de chocolat. **A box of chocolates**, une boîte de chocolats. **A c.**, une crotte de chocolat. **C. factory, trade**, chocolaterie *f.* **C. manufacturer**, chocolatier, -ière. **C. pot**, chocolatière *f.* **2.** *a.* (De couleur) chocolat *inv.*

choice¹ [tʃɔis], *s.* **1.** Choix *m.* (a) Préférence *f.* **For c.**, de préférence. **The country of my c.**, mon pays d'élection. (b) Alternative *f.* **You have no c. in the matter**, vous n'avez pas le choix. **2.** (*Variety*) Assortiment *m*, choix. **To have a wide c.**, trouver grandement de quoi choisir.

choice², *a.* **1.** Bien choisi. **2.** *Com:* **C. article**, article de choix; article surfin.

choiceness ['tʃɔisnis], *s.* Excellence *f.*

choir ['kwaiər], *s.* **1.** *Arch:* Chœur *m* (d'église). **2.** (a) Chœur (de chanteurs) (d'anges). **Male-voice c.**, orphéon *m.* (b) *Ecc:* Maîtrise *f.* **'choir-boy**, *s.m.* *Ecc:* Jeune choriste. **'choir-master**, *s.m.* Maître de chapelle. **'choir-school**, *s.* Maîtrise *f*; manécanterie *f.*

choirman, *pl.* -men ['kwaiəmən], *s.m.* *Ecc:* Chantre.

choke¹ [tʃouk], *s.* **1.** (a) Étranglement *m* (de canon de fusil). (b) *I.C.E:* Starter *m.* **To pull out the c.**, tirer sur le starter. **2.** Étranglement (de la voix). **3.** *Bot:* Foin *m* (d'un artichaut).

choke². **I.** *v.* **1.** *v.tr.* (a) Étouffer, suffoquer, étrangler (qn). **Voice choked with sobs**, voix suffoquée par les sanglots. (b) Étrangler (une cartouche). (c) **To c. (up) a pipe**, obstruer, engorger, boucher, un tuyau (with, de). *I.C.E:* **Choked jet (of carburettor)**, gicleur bouché. **Harbour choked (up) with sand**, port ensablé. **2.** *v.i.* (a) Étouffer, étrangler (with, de). **To**

c. with laughter, suffoquer de rire. (b) S'engorger s'obstruer, se boucher (with, de); (of filter, etc.) se colmater. **choke back**, *v.tr.* Refouler (ses larmes).

choke down, *v.tr.* Étouffer, ravaler (un sanglot).

choke off, *v.tr.* *F:* (a) **To c. s.o. off from doing sth.** dissuader qn de faire qch. (b) Se débarrasser de (qn); écarter (un importun). **choking**, *s.* **1.** Étouffement *m*, suffocation *f*, étranglement *m.* **2.** Engorgement *m*, obstruction *f*; ensablement *m.* **II.** choke-, *comb.fm.* **'choke-bore**, *s.* *Sm.a:* **1.** Étranglement *m* (du canon). **2.** Fusil *m* de chasse à choke-bore. **'choke-damp**, *s.* *Min:* Moffette *f.*

choker ['tʃoukər], *s.* *F:* **1.** (a) Foulard *m* (d'ouvrier). (b) (**Ladies fur**) c., cravate *f* de fourrure; tour *m* de cou. **Bead c.**, collier *m* (de perles) court. (c) = DOG-COLLAR 2. **2.** = CHOKE¹ 1 (b).

choky ['tʃouki], *a.* *F:* **To feel c.**, étouffer d'émotion. **C. atmosphere**, atmosphère suffocante.

cholera ['kɔlərə], *s.* Choléra *m.* **A c. patient**, un, une, cholérique.

choleraic [kɔlə'reiik], *a.* *Med:* Cholérique.

choleric ['kɔlərik], *a.* Colérique, irascible.

cholesterol [kɔ'lestərɔl], *s.* *Med:* Cholestérol *m.*

choose [tʃu:z], *v.tr.* (chose [tʃouz]; chosen [tʃouzn]) **1.** (a) Choisir; faire choix de (qch.). **To c. a method**, adopter une méthode. *Pred.* **To c. s.o. (for a) king**, choisir qn comme roi. (b) **He cannot c. but obey**, il ne peut faire autrement qu'obéir. (c) **To c. from, between, several persons**, choisir, opter, entre plusieurs personnes. **To c. an apple from the basket**, choisir une pomme dans le panier. **War or peace? they chose war**, la guerre ou la paix; ils optèrent pour la guerre. **There is nothing to c. between them**, l'un vaut l'autre; ils se valent. **2.** **I do not c. to do so**, il ne me plaît pas de le faire. **When I c.**, quand je voudrai. **I do as I c.**, je fais comme il me plaît, comme je l'entends. **To do sth. when one chooses**, faire qch. à son bon plaisir. **chosen**, *a.* Choisi. **To address a c. few**, s'adresser à quelques auditeurs choisis. **C. candidate**, candidat élu. *s.* **The c.**, les élus. **choosing**, *s.* Choix *m.* **The difficulty of c.**, l'embarras du choix.

chooser ['tʃu:zər], *s.* Personne *f* qui choisit. *S.a.* BEGGAR¹ 1.

choosy ['tʃu:zi], *s.* *F:* Difficile. **A c. customer**, un client, une personne, difficile.

chop¹ [tʃɔp], *s.* **1.** Coup *m* de hache, de couperet. **2.** *Cu:* Côtelette *f* (de mouton, de porc). **3.** Clapotage *m*, clapotis *m* (de la mer). **4.** *Ten:* **C.(-stroke)**, volée coupée, arrêtée. **'chop-house**, *s.* Restaurant *m* (où on sert surtout des côtelettes et des steaks).

chop², *v.* (chopped) **1.** *v.tr.* (a) Couper, fendre (du bois), hacher (les légumes). **Chopped wood**, menu bois. **To c. sth. to pieces**, hacher qch. (b) *Ten:* **To c. the ball**, couper, choper, la balle. **2.** *v.i.* (Of sea) Clapoter. **chop away**, *v.tr.* Détacher (qch. à coups de cognée); trancher (qch.). **chop down**, *v.tr.* Abattre (un arbre). **chop off**, *v.tr.* Trancher, couper, abattre. **chop up**, *v.tr.* Couper (qch.) en morceaux. **chopping¹**, *s.* **1.** Coupe *f* (du bois); hachage *m* (des légumes, etc.). **2.** Clapotage *m*, clapotis *m* (de la mer). **'chopping-block**, *s.* Hachoir *m*, billot *m.* **'chopping-knife**, *s.* Couperet *m*, hachoir *m.*

chop³, *s.* = CHAP³. **To lick one's chops**, se (pour)lécher les babines. **The chops of the Channel**, l'entrée *f* de la Manche.

chop⁴, *s.* **C. of the wind**, saute *f* de vent.

chop⁵. *v.i.* (a) **To c. and change**, manquer de suite; girouetter. **He's always chopping and changing**, c'est une vraie girouette. (b) *Nau:* **The wind keeps chopping about**, le vent varie à chaque instant. **chopping²**, *s.* *F:* **C. and changing**, girouetteries *fpl.*

chop⁶, *s.* (*In Africa*) Manger *m*, déjeuner *m.*

chopper ['tʃɔpər], *s.* Couperet *m*, hachoir *m.*

choppiness ['tʃɔpinis], *s.* Agitation *f* (de la mer).

choppy¹ ['tʃɔpi], *a.* *Nau:* Clapoteux, -euse. **C. sea**, mer hachée, heurtée; lame courte.

choppy², *a.* (Vent) changeant, variable.

chopsticks ['tʃɔpstiks], *s.pl.* Bâtonnets *m*, baguettes *f.*

chop suey [tʃɔp'su:i], *s.* (Sorte de) ragoût chinois.

choral ['kɔ:r(ə)l], *a.* *Mus:* **1.** Choral, *pl.* -aux, -ales. **C. society**, Société chorale; chorale *f*; (of male voices) orphéon *m.* **2.** Chanté en chœur.

choral(e) [kə'rɑːl], *s. Mus:* Choral *m, pl.* -als; cantique *m.*

chord¹ [kɔːd], *s.* **1.** *Poet:* Corde *f* (d'une harpe). **To touch the right c.,** faire vibrer la corde sensible. **2.** = CORD¹ (*d*). **3.** *Geom:* Corde (d'un arc).

chord², *s. Mus:* Accord *m.* **Common c.,** accord parfait. **Broken c.,** spread c., arpège *m.*

chore [tʃɔːr], *s.* Corvée *f.* **The daily chores,** le travail quotidien, la corvée quotidienne. **To do the chores,** faire le ménage.

chorea [kɔ'riə], *s. Med:* Chorée *f;* danse *f* de Saint-Guy.

choreographer [ˌkɔri'ɔgrəfər], *s.* Choréographe *mf.*

choreographic [ˌkɔriou'græfik], *a.* Chorégraphique.

choreography [ˌkɔri'ɔgrəfi], *s.* Chorégraphie *f.*

chorister ['kɔristər], *s.m.* Choriste; *esp. Ecc:* chantre.

chortle¹ [tʃɔːtl], *s. F:* Gloussement *m* (de gaieté).

chortle², *v.i. F:* Glousser de joie.

chorus¹, *pl.* -uses ['kɔːrəs, -əsiz], *s.* **1.** Chœur *m.* (*a*) C. of praise, concert *m* de louanges. (*b*) She belongs to the c., elle fait partie du chœur. **2.** Refrain *m* (d'une chanson). **To join in the c.,** faire chœur. **'chorus-girl,** *s.f.* Girl (of music-hall). **'chorus-singer,** *s.* (*In opera*) Choriste *mf.*

chorus², *v.* (chorused) **1.** *v.i.* Faire chorus; reprendre en chœur. **2.** *v.tr.* **To c. sth.,** répéter qch. en chœur.

chose, chosen. *See* CHOOSE.

chou [ʃuː], *s. Cu:* Chou *m.* **C. pastry,** pâte à choux.

chough [tʃʌf], *s. Orn:* Crave *m.*

chow¹ [tʃau], *s.* (Chien) chow-chow (*m*).

chow², *s. Mil: P:* Mangeaille *f.* **C. time,** l'heure du repas.

chow-chow ['tʃautʃau], *s.* **1.** *Cu:* (*a*) Fruits exotiques conservés dans un sirop. (*b*) Conserve chinoise de légumes à la moutarde. **2.** = CHOW¹.

chowder ['tʃaudər], *s. Cu:* (Recette américaine de) soupe *f* aux poissons ou aux coquillages.

chrestomathy [kres'tɔməθi], *s.* Chrestomathie *f.*

chrism ['kriz(ə)m], *s. Ecc:* (Saint) chrême.

Ch-ist [kraist]. *Pr.n.m.* Le Christ; Jésus-Christ.

christen ['krisn], *v.tr.* **1.** Baptiser (qn, un bateau). **To c. a child after s.o.,** donner à un enfant le nom de qn. **2. To c. a new dress,** étrenner une nouvelle robe. **christening,** *s.* Baptême *m.*

Christendom ['krisndəm], *s.* La chrétienté.

Christian ['kristjən], *a. & s.* Chrétien,-ienne. **The C. era,** l'ère chrétienne. *S.a.* BURIAL, NAME¹ 1.

christiania [ˌkristi'ɑːniə], *s. Skiing:* Christiania *m.*

Christianity [ˌkristi'æniti], *s.* Christianisme *m.*

Christlike ['kraistlaik], *a.* Ressemblant au Christ. **C. patience,** patience *f* évangélique.

Christmas ['krisməs], *s.* Noël *m.* **At C.,** à Noël, à la Noël. **A merry C.!** joyeux Noël! **Father C.,** le Père Noël. **C. comes but once a year,** ce n'est pas tous les jours fête. **C. party,** réunion de Noël. **C. present,** cadeau *m* de Noël. **'Christmas box,** *s.* = Étrennes *fpl;* gratification *f.* **'Christmas card,** *s.* Carte *f* de Noël. **Christmas 'carol,** *s.* Chant *m* de Noël; noël *m.* **Christmas 'Day,** *s.* Le jour de Noël. **Christmas 'Eve,** *s.* La veille de Noël. **'Christmas(-)'rose,** *s. Bot:* Rose *f* de Noël, ellébore noir. **'Christmas 'stocking,** *s.* = Sabot *m* de Noël. **'Christmas tree,** *s.* Arbre *m* de Noël.

chromate ['kroumit], *s. Ch:* Chromate *m.*

chromatic [kro'mætik], *a.* Chromatique. **1.** (Impression) polychrome. **2.** *Mus:* **C. scale,** gamme chromatique.

chromatics [kro'mætiks], *s. Opt: Art:* Chromatique *f.*

chrome [kroum], *s.* (*a*) **C. leather,** cuir chromé. **C. tanning,** tannage aux sels de chrome. (*b*) **C. steel,** acier chromé. (*c*) **C. yellow,** jaune de chrome.

chromic ['kroumik], *a.* **C.** Chromique.

chromium ['kroumiəm], *s. Ch:* Chrome *m.* **C. steel,** acier chromé, au chrome. **'chromium-plating,** *s.* Chromage *m.*

chromolithograph ['kroumou'liθəgrɑːf, -græf], *s.* (*Colour-print*) Chromolithographie *f.*

chromolithography ['kroumouli'θɔgrəfi], *s.* (*Process*) Chromolithographie *f.*

chromosome ['kroumə'sɔum], *s. Biol:* Chromosome *m.*

chronic ['krɔnik], *a.* **1.** (*a*) *Med:* Chronique. **C. ill-health,** invalidité *f.* (*b*) *F:* Constant, continuel. **2.** *P:* Insupportable. **A c. headache,** un mal de tête fou. **-ally,** *adv.* Chroniquement.

chronicle¹ ['krɔnikl], *s.* Chronique *f.*

chronicle², *v.tr.* **To c. events,** faire la chronique des événements; enregistrer, raconter, les faits.

chronicler ['krɔniklər], *s.* Chroniqueur *m.*

chronologer [krə'nɔlədʒər], *s.* Chronologiste *m.*

chronological [ˌkrɔnə'lɔdʒik(ə)l], *a.* Chronologique. **In c. order,** par ordre de dates. **-ally,** *adv.* Chronologiquement.

chronologist [krə'nɔlədʒist], *s.* = CHRONOLOGER.

chronology [krə'nɔlədʒi], *s.* Chronologie *f.*

chronometer [krə'nɔmitər], *s.* Chronomètre *m.*

chrysalis, *pl.* **chrysalides, chrysalises** ['krisəlis, kri'sælidiːz, 'krisəlisiz], *s.* Chrysalide *f.*

chrysanthemum [kri'zænθ(ə)məm], *s.* Chrysanthème *m.*

chub ['tʃʌbi], *s. Ich:* Chevesne *m.*

chubby ['tʃʌbi], *a.* Boulot, -otte; (*of face*) joufflu. **'chubby-cheeked,** *a.* Joufflu.

chuck¹. **1.** *s.* Gloussement *m* (de la volaille). **2.** (*Call to fowls*) **C.! c.!** petit! petit!

chuck², *v.i.* (*a*) (*Of fowls*) Glousser. (*b*) *F:* (*Of pers.*) Clapper (de la langue).

chuck³, *s. U.S: F:* (*a*) Mangeaille *f.* (*b*) Repas *m..*

chuck⁴, *s.* **1.** Petite tape (sous le menton). **2.** Action de lancer qch. *O:* **To give s.o. the c.,** (i) *O:* plaquer qn; (ii) congédier (un employé). **To get the c.,** recevoir son congé.

chuck⁵, *v.tr.* **1. To c. s.o. under the chin,** relever le menton à qn. **2.** (*a*) *F:* Jeter, lancer (une pierre). (*b*) *P:* Lâcher, plaquer (qn). (*c*) *P:* **C. it!** en voilà assez! **chuck about,** *v.tr. F:* Gaspiller (son argent). **To c. one's weight about,** faire l'important. **chuck away,** *v.tr. F:* Jeter (qch.) (pour s'en défaire); gaspiller (son argent). **chuck out,** *v.tr. F:* Flanquer (qn) à la porte. **chuck up,** *v.tr. F:* (*a*) Abandonner (un travail). **To c. it up,** y renoncer; quitter la partie. (*b*) **To c. up one's job,** lâcher son emploi; démissionner.

chuck⁶, *s.* **1.** Mandrin *m,* plateau *m* (d'un tour). **2.** *Cu:* Paleron *m* de bœuf.

chucker-out ['tʃʌkər'aut], *s. F:* Expulseur *m,* videur *m.*

chuckle¹ ['tʃʌkl], *s.* Rire étouffé; petit rire.

chuckle², *v.i.* Rire tout bas, en soi-même, sous cape (at, over, sth., de qch).

chuckle-head ['tʃʌklhed], *s. F:* Nigaud *m,* benêt *m.*

chuckle-headed ['tʃʌklhedid], *a. F:* Sans cervelle.

chug [tʃʌg], *v.i.* **1.** *Rail:* Souffler (en parlant d'une locomotive). **2.** *Aut:* **To c. along,** rouler doucement, en père de famille.

chum¹ [tʃʌm], *s. F: O:* Camarade *mf;* copain *m,* copine *f.*

chum², *v.i.* (chummed) *F: O:* **To c. (up) with s.o.,** se lier d'amitié avec qn.

chump [tʃʌmp], *s.* **1.** (*a*) Tronçon *m* (de bois). (*b*) **C.-chop,** côtelette *f* de gigot. **2.** *P:* (*a*) **Off one's c.,** timbré, loufoque, ballot. (*b*) **A (silly) c.,** un nigaud, une cruche.

chunk [tʃʌŋk], *s.* Gros morceau (de bois, etc.); quignon *m* (de pain).

church [tʃəːtʃ], *s.* **1.** Église *f;* (*protestant*) temple *m, Fr.C:* mitaine *f.* **C. hall,** salle paroissiale, salle d'œuvres. **2.** (*a*) **The Established C.,** l'Église établie. **The C. of England,** l'Église anglicane. **To go into the C.,** entrer dans les ordres. **To be received into the C.,** (i) prendre le voile; (ii) faire sa première communion; (iii) devenir chrétien par le baptême. (*b*) **C. service,** office *m;* service (divin). **To go to c.,** aller à l'office, (in R.C.Ch.) à la messe. **I shall see you after c.,** je vous verrai après l'office; après la messe. **To be a c.-goer,** être pratiquant, -ante. **'church-worker,** *s.* Personne *f* qui prend une part active aux œuvres de l'église.

church², *v.tr.* (*Of woman after childbirth*) **To be churched,** faire ses relevailles. **churching,** *s.* Relevailles *fpl.*

churchman, *pl.* **-men** ['tʃəːtʃmən], *s.* **1.** Homme *m* d'église; ecclésiastique *m.* **2. He's a good c.,** il est pratiquant; (in Eng. often =) c'est un bon anglican.

churchwarden ['tʃəːtʃwɔːdən], *s.* **1.** Marguillier *m,* fabricien *m.* **2.** Longue pipe (en terre); pipe hollandaise.

churchwoman, *pl.* **women** ['tʃəːtʃwumən, -wimin], *s.f.* **She's a good c.,** elle est pratiquante; (in Eng. often =) c'est une bonne anglicane.

churchy ['tʃɔːtʃi], *a. Pej:* Bigot. **C. person,** calotin *m*; bondieusard, -arde. **C. old women,** *P:* vieilles punaises de sacristie.

churchyard ['tʃɔːtʃjɑːd], *s.* Cimetière *m. F:* **C. cough,** toux qui sent le sapin.

churl [tʃəːl], *s.* (*a*) *Hist:* Manant *m.* (*b*) *F:* Rustre *m.* (*c*) *F:* Grincheux *m.*

churlish ['tʃəːliʃ], *a.* (*a*) Mal élevé; grossier, -ière. (*b*) Hargneux, -euse, grincheux, -euse. **-ly,** *adv.* Avec mauvaise grâce.

churlishness ['tʃəːliʃnis], *s.* (*a*) Grossièreté *f.* (*b*) Tempérament hargneux.

churn[1] [tʃəːn], *s.* 1. Baratte *f.* 2. Bidon *m* à lait.

churn[2]. 1. *v.tr.* (*a*) Baratter (la crème); battre (le beurre). (*b*) **To c. up the foam,** brasser l'écume. 2. *v.i.* (*Of sea*) Bouillonner.

chute [ʃuːt], *s.* (*a*) Chute *f* d'eau. (*b*) *Sp:* Piste *f*, glissière *f* (pour toboggans); (*in swimming bath*) toboggan *m.*

chutney ['tʃʌtni], *s. Cu:* Chutney *m* (condiment épicé).

chyle [kail], *s. Physiol:* Chyle *m.*

chyme [kaim], *s. Physiol:* Chyme *m.*

ciborium [si'bɔːriəm], *s.* 1. *Ecc.Arch:* Ciborium *m.* 2. *Ecc:* Ciboire *m.*

cicada [si'kɑːdə], *s. Ent:* Cigale *f.*

cicatrice, cicatrix, *pl.* -ices ['sikətris, -triks, -isiz], *s.* Cicatrice *f.*

cicatrization [ˌsikətraiˈzeiʃ(ə)n], *s.* Cicatrisation *f.*

cicatrize ['sikətraiz]. 1. *v.tr.* Cicatriser. 2. *v.i.* Se cicatriser.

Cicero ['sisərou]. *Pr.n.m.* Cicéron.

cicerone [ˌtʃitʃəˈrouni], *s.* Cicerone *m.*

cider ['saidər], *s.* Cidre *m.* **'cider-cup,** *s.* Boisson glacée au cidre. **'cider-press,** *s.* Pressoir *m* (à pommes).

cigar [si'gɑːr], *s.* Cigare *m.* **ci'gar-case,** *s.* Étui *m* à cigares. **ci'gar-cutter,** *s.* Coupe-cigares *m inv.* **ci'gar-holder,** *s.* Fume-cigare *m*, porte-cigare *m.* **ci'gar store,** *s. U.S:* Bureau *m* de tabac.

cigarette [ˌsigəˈret], *s.* Cigarette *f.* **C. paper,** papier *m* à cigarettes. **C. card,** vignette *f* (réclame). **ciga'rette-case,** *s.* Étui *m* à cigarettes. **ciga'rette-holder** *s.* Porte-cigarette *m.*

cilia ['siliə], *s.pl. Biol:* Cils *m* vibratiles.

ciliary ['siliəri], *a. Nat. Hist:* Ciliaire.

cilice ['silis], *s. Ecc:* Cilice *m.*

cinch [sin(t)ʃ], *s. U.S:* 1. *Harn:* Sangle *f*; sous-ventrière *f.* 2.*P:* Certitude *f.* **It's a c.,** (i) c'est certain; (ii) *P:* c'est du tout cuit.

cinchona [siŋˈkounə], *s.* Quinquina *m.*

cinder ['sindər], *s.* 1. Cendre *f.* **To cook a joint to a c.,** calciner un rôti. **To rake out the cinders,** racler les cendres (du foyer). 2. *pl.* (*a*) (*Partly burnt coal*) Escarbilles *fpl.* (*b*) *Metall:* Scorie(s) *f(pl).* **'cinder-path, -track,** *s.* Piste (en) cendrée. **'cinder-sifter,** *s.* Crible *m* à escarbilles.

Cinderella [ˌsindəˈrelə]. *Pr.n.f.* Cendrillon.

cine camera ['sinikæmərə], *s.* Caméra *f.*

cine club ['siniklʌb], *s.* Ciné-club *m*, *pl.* ciné-clubs.

cinema ['sinimə], *s.* (*a*) Le cinéma. (*b*) (Salle *f* de) cinéma.

cinemascope ['sinəməskoup], *s.* Cinémascope *m.*

cinematic [siniˈmætik], *a.* Cinématographique; relatif au cinéma.

cinematics [siniˈmætiks], *s.pl. Mth:* Cinématique *f.*

cinematograph [siniˈmætəgræf], *s.* Cinématographe *m.*

cinematography [ˌsinəˈtɔgrəfi], *s.* Cinématographie *f.*

cine-projector [siniprəˈdʒektər], *s.* Projecteur *m.*

cinerama [ˌsinəˈrɑːmə], *s. R.t.m:* Cinérama *m.*

cineraria [ˌsinəˈreəriə], *s. Bot:* Cinéraire *f.*

cinerarium [ˌsinəˈreəriəm], *s.* Cinéraire *m.*

cinerary ['sinərəri], *a.* Cinéraire.

Cingalese [ˌsiŋɡəˈliːz]. 1. *a. & s. Geog:* Cingalais, -aise. 2. *s. Ling:* Le Cingalais.

cinnabar ['sinəbɑːr], *s.* (*a*) *Miner:* Cinabre *m*; vermillon naturel. (*b*) *Ind:* Vermillon.

cinnamon ['sinəmən], *s.* 1. **C.(-bark),** cannelle *f.* 2. **C. (-tree),** cannelier *m.*

cinquecento [ˌtʃiŋkwiˈtʃentou], *s.* L'art italien du XVIᵉ siècle.

cinquefoil ['siŋkfɔil], *s.* 1. *Bot:* Potentille rampante, quintefeuille *f.* 2. *Arch:* Quintefeuille *m.*

cipher[1] ['saifər], *s.* 1. *Mth:* Zéro *m.* **He's a mere c.,** c'est une nullité, un homme qui ne compte pas. 2. (*a*) (*Secret writing*) Chiffre *m.* **To send a message in c.,** transmettre une dépêche en chiffre. **C. department** (*in service ministry, etc.*), service *m* du chiffre. **C. officer,** officier *m* du chiffre. (*b*) Message chiffré. (*c*) Clef *f* (d'un chiffre). 3. (*Monogram*) Chiffre. 4. *Mus:* Cornement *m* (d'un tuyau d'orgue).

cipher[2]. 1. *v.tr.* Chiffrer (une dépêche). 2. *v.i.* (*a*) Chiffrer, calculer. (*b*) *Mus:* (*Of organ pipe*) Corner.

circle[1] ['səːkl], *s.* 1. (*a*) Cercle *m.* **To stand in a c.,** faire cercle. *Geog:* **Polar c.,** cercle polaire. **Arctic c.,** cercle arctique. *Nav:* **Great c.,** grand cercle. **To have circles round the eyes,** avoir les yeux cernés. *Aut:* **Turning c.,** rayon *m* de braquage. (*b*) *Log:* **Vicious c.,** cercle vicieux. (*c*) *Adm:* **U.S:** **Traffic c.,** rond-point *m*, *pl.* ronds-points. 2. Révolution *f*, orbite *f* (d'une planète). **To come full c.,** compléter son orbite. 3. *Th:* **Dress c.,** (premier) balcon. **Upper c.** seconde galerie. 4. Milieu *m*, coterie *f.* **The family c.,** le sein de la famille. **In certain circles,** dans certains milieux. **In theatrical circles,** dans le monde des théâtres. **The inner c.,** le cercle intime (d'amis); le groupe dirigeant (d'un parti politique, etc.).

circle[2]. 1. *v.tr.* (*a*) Ceindre, entourer (with, de). (*b*) (*Go round*) Faire le tour de (qch.). 2. *v.i.* **To c. round, about, sth.,** tournoyer autour de qch. **The plane was circling over the airport,** l'avion décrivait des cercles au-dessus de l'aéroport.

circs [səːks], *s.pl. P:* = CIRCUMSTANCES. **Under the c.,** dans ces circonstances.

circuit ['səːkit], *s.* 1. (*a*) Pourtour *m* (d'une ville); enceinte *f* (de murailles). (*b*) *Sp:* Circuit *m*, parcours *m.* 2. (*a*) Révolution *f* (du soleil). (*b*) Tournée *f*, circuit. (*Of judge*) **To go on c.,** aller en tournée. (*c*) Circonscription *f* (de tournée). 3. Détour *m.* **To make a wide c.,** faire un grand détour. 4. *El:* Circuit. **Branch c.,** branchement *m.* **To close, make, the c.,** fermer le circuit. **To break the c.,** rompre le circuit. **Short c.,** court-circuit *m.* **Closed-c.** television, télévision à circuit fermé. **'circuit-breaker,** *s. El.E:* Coupe-circuit *m inv.*, interrupteur *m*, disjoncteur *m.* **'circuit-closer,** *s. El.E:* Conjoncteur *m*, ferme-circuit, *m inv.*

circuitous [səːˈkjuːitəs], *a.* (Chemin) détourné. **To take a c. road,** faire un détour. **By c. means,** par des moyens détournés. **-ly,** *adv.* Par des moyens indirects.

circular ['səːkjulər]. 1. *a.* Circulaire. (*a*) **C. arc,** arc de cercle. (*b*) **C. letter,** lettre circulaire; circulaire *f.* **C. tour,** tour circulaire. 2. *s.* (*a*) = **circular letter.** (*b*) Prospectus *m.* (*c*) **The Court c.,** la chronique mondaine. **-ly,** *adv.* Circulairement; en rond.

circularize ['səːkjuləraiz], *v.tr.* Circulariser, toucher (ses clients, etc.) au moyen de circulaires. **circularizing,** *s.* Envoi *m* de circulaires, de prospectus.

circulate ['səːkjuleit]. 1. *v.i.* Circuler. 2. *v.tr.* (*a*) Faire circuler (l'air, le vin, etc.). (*b*) Distribuer, communiquer, faire communiquer; mettre en circulation (de l'argent, des nouvelles); faire circuler (un bruit). **circulating,** *s.* Circulation *f.*

circulation [ˌsəːkjuˈleiʃ(ə)n], *s.* Circulation *f* (du sang, de l'argent); tirage *m* (d'un journal). **C. of capital,** roulement *m* de fonds. *Publ:* **For private c.,** hors commerce. **Newspaper with a wide c.,** journal à grand tirage. **To restore the c. in one's legs,** se dégourdir les jambes. **To put forged notes into c.,** écouler de faux billets. **Notes in c.,** billets circulants. *I.C.E:* **Gravity c.,** circulation (de l'eau) par gravité. **Forced-feed c.,** circulation sous pression (de l'eau, de l'huile).

circulatory ['səːkjulət(ə)ri], *a. Anat:* Circulatoire.

circumcise ['səːkəmsaiz], *v.tr.* Circoncire. **circumcised,** *a.* Circoncis.

circumcision [ˌsəːkəmˈsiʒ(ə)n], *s.* Circoncision *f.*

circumference [səˈkʌmfərəns], *s.* Circonférence *f*; périphérie *f*; pourtour *m* (d'un piston). **On the c.,** à la circonférence.

circumflex ['səːkəmfleks], *a. & s.* **C. (accent),** accent *m* circonflexe.

circumlocution [ˌsəːkəmləˈkjuːʃ(ə)n], *s.* Circonlocution *f.*

circumnavigate [ˌsəːkəmˈnævigeit], *v.tr.* Circumnaviguer.

circumnavigation ['sə:kəmnævi'geiʃ(ə)n], s. Circumnavigation f.
circumscribe ['sɔ:kəmskraib], v.tr. 1. Circonscrire. 2. Limiter (des pouvoirs). **circumscribed**, a. 1. Geom: Circonscrit. 2. Restreint, limité. C. **intellect**, esprit borné.
circumscription [‚sɔ:kəm'skripʃ(ə)n], s. 1. Geom: Circonscription f. 2. Restriction f. 3. Région f, circonscription (administrative).
circumspect ['sɔ:kəmspekt], a. Circonspect; avisé. **-ly**, adv. Prudemment; avec circonspection.
circumspection [‚sɔ:kəm'spekʃ(ə)n], s. Circonspection f.
circumstance ['sɔ:kəmstəns], s. 1. pl. (a) Circonstances f. In, under, **the circumstances**, dans ces circonstances; puisqu'il en est ainsi. **Under any circumstances**, en tout état de cause. **In, under, no circumstances**, en aucun cas; sous aucun prétexte; d'aucune manière. **Under similar circumstances**, en pareille occasion. **That depends on circumstances**, c'est selon. **We must take the circumstances into account**, il faut faire la part des circonstances. **Circumstances alter cases**, les cas changent avec les circonstances. Jur: Aggravating, extenuating, **circumstances** (of crime), circonstances aggravantes, atténuantes. (b) **If his circumstances allow**, si ses moyens le permettent. **In easy circumstances**, dans l'aisance. 2. sing. Circonstance, détail, fait. **Without omitting a single c.**, sans omettre aucun détail. **Were it not for the c. that . . .**, n'était le fait que.... 3. sing. Pompe f. **To receive s.o. with pomp and c.**, recevoir qn en grande cérémonie.
circumstantial [‚sɔ:kəm'stænʃ(ə)l], a. 1. Circonstanciel, -ielle. C. **evidence**, preuves indirectes. 2. Accessoire, accidentel, -elle. 3. (Récit) circonstancié, détaillé. **-ally**, adv. 1. Accessoirement. 2. En détail.
circumvent [‚sɔ:kəm'vent], v.tr. Circonvenir.
circumvention [‚sɔ:kəm'venʃ(ə)n], s. Circonvention f (de la loi, etc.).
circus, pl. **-uses** ['sɔ:kəs, -əsiz], s. 1. Rom. Ant: Cirque m. 2. Cirque. **Travelling c.**, cirque forain.
cirque [siək, sɔ:k], s. Geol: Cirque m.
cirrhosis [si'rousis], s. Med: Cirrhose f.
cirro-cumulus ['sirou'kju:mjuləs], s. Meteor: Cirro-cumulus m inv.
cirro-stratus ['sirou'strɑ:təs], s. Meteor: Cirro-stratus m inv.
cirrus, pl. **-ri** ['sirəs, -rai], s. 1. Meteor: Cirrus m; 2. Bot: Cirre m.
Cisalpine [sis'ælpain], a. Hist: Cisalpin.
cissy ['sisi], s. = SISSY.
cist [sist], s. Sépulture f préhistorique en dalles de pierre.
Cistercian [sis'tɔ:ʃ(ə)n], a. & s. Cistercien, -ienne. **The C. Order**, l'ordre de Cîteaux.
cistern ['sistən], s. (a) Réservoir m à eau (sous les combles). (b) (Underground) Citerne f. (c) (In W.C.) Réservoir de chasse f d'eau.
citadel ['sitədel], s. (a) Citadelle f. (b) Lieu m de refuge.
citation [sai'teiʃ(ə)n], s. 1. Jur: = SUMMONS. 2. Citation f d'un auteur, d'une autorité. Mil: esp. U.S: Citation (pour une action méritoire, une décoration).
cite [sait], v.tr. 1. Jur: (a) Citer (qn devant un tribunal). (b) Assigner (un témoin). (c) (Patents) Citer. 2. (a) Citer (un auteur). (b) Alléguer (un auteur). 3. Mil: U.S: Citer (un militaire pour son courage).
citizen ['sitiz(ə)n], s. (a) Citoyen, -enne; bourgeois, -oise; citadin m. **My fellow-citizens**, mes concitoyens. (b) (Adjectival) Civique. U.S: C. **rights**, droits m civiques.
citizenry ['sitiz(ə)nri], s. U.S: Masse f des citoyens.
citizenship ['sitiz(ə)nʃip], s. 1. Droit m de cité, de bourgeoisie. 2. Good c., civisme m. 3. Nationalité f.
citrate ['sitreit], s. Ch: Citrate m.
citric ['sitrik], a. Ch: Citrique. **'citron-wood**, s. Bois m de thuya m.
citron ['sitrən], s. Cédrat m.
citronella [sitrə'nelə], s. Bot: Pharm: Citronelle f.
citrus ['sitrəs], s. Bot: Citron m. C. **fruit**, agrumes mpl.

city ['siti], s. 1. (a) Grande ville; U.S: ville; (in Engl.) ville épiscopale; Poet: cité f. **The c. dwellers**, la population urbaine. (b) Cité, agglomération f. **Garden-c.**, (i) cité-jardin f; (ii) cité ouvrière. 2. **The C.**, la Cité de Londres. F: **He's in the C.**, il est dans les affaires. **'city-bred**, a. Élevé en ville. A c.-b. **child**, un(e) enfant de la ville. **'City 'Hall**, s. Hôtel m de ville. **'city 'state**, s. Hist: État-cité m, pl. états-cités.
civet ['sivit], s. C.(-cat), civette f.
civic ['sivik], a. Civique. **The c. authorities**, les autorités municipales. Town P: C. **centre**, centre civique, social.
civics ['siviks], s.pl. (Usu. with sg. const.) Sch: Instruction f civique.
civil ['siv(ə)l], a. 1. Civil. C. **rights**, droits civiques. C. **war**, guerre civile. **In c. life**, dans le civil. Adm: **The C. List**, la liste civile. C. **List pension**, pension sur les fonds de la Couronne. C. **servant**, fonctionnaire mf. **Established c. servants**, fonctionnaires titularisés. 2. Poli, honnête, courtois. **-illy**, adv. Civilement, poliment.
civilian [si'viljən]. 1. s. Civil m. Hist: **Indian c.**, fonctionnaire m de l'administration des Indes. 2. a. Civil. **In c. life**, dans le civil.
civility [si'viliti], s. Civilité f; politesse f.
civilization [‚sivilai'zeiʃ(ə)n], s. Civilisation f.
civilize ['sivilaiz], v.tr. Civiliser. **To become civilized**, se civiliser. **civilizing**, a. Civilisant; civilisateur, -trice.
civvies ['siviz], s. pl. F: Vêtements civils. **In c.**, en civil.
civvy ['sivi], Mil: F: 1. = CIVILIAN 1. 2. C. **Street**, la vie civile.
clack[1] [klæk], s. 1. Bruit sec; claquement m. C.-c., clic-clac m. 2. (a) C.(-valve), (soupape f à) clapet m. (b) (Mill-)c., traquet m. 3. F: = CHATTER[1] 1. **Stop your c.**, P: la ferme! ferme ça!
clack[2], v.i. 1. (Of ring) Claquer. 2. F: (Of pers.) Caqueter, bavarder, jacasser.
clad. See CLOTHE.
claim[1] [kleim], s. 1. Demande f (de secours, etc.); revendication f, réclamation f. Adm: **Fares c.**, demande de remboursement de voyage. 2. Droit m, titre m, prétention f (to sth., à qch.). **To lay c. to sth.**, (i) prétendre à qch.; (ii) s'attribuer qch. **Legal c. to sth.**, titre juridique à qch. **To put in a c.**, faire valoir ses droits. **To set up a c.**, émettre une revendication. **To renounce one's claims**, renoncer à ses prétentions. 3. (Debt) Créance f. 4. (a) Jur: Réclamation. **To set up a c.**, faire une réclamation. **To make, put in, a c. for damages**, réclamer des dommages-intérêts. Ins: **To put in a c.**, réclamer l'indemnité (d'assurance). Adm: **Disputed claims office**, le contentieux. (b) **I have some claims on his friendship**, j'ai des titres à son amitié. **I have many claims on my time**, mon temps est entièrement pris. 5. (In U.S. and Austr.) Concession (minière).
claim[2], v.tr. (a) Réclamer (un droit); revendiquer (un honneur); demander (de l'attention). **To c. sth. from s.o.**, réclamer qch. à qn. **To c. a privilege**, prétendre à un privilège. **To c. the right to do sth.**, revendiquer le droit de faire qch. **To claim one's due**, faire valoir ses droits. **The sea claims many victims**, la mer fait de nombreuses victimes. (b) **To c. that . . .**, prétendre, avancer, affirmer, soutenir, que.... **To c. a virtue**, s'attribuer une vertu. **To c. kinship with s.o.**, se prétendre parent de qn. **Family that claims descent from . . .**, famille qui rapporte son origine à....
claimant ['kleimənt], **claimer** ['kleimər], s. Prétendant, -ante; revendicateur m; Jur: réclamant, -ante; demandeur, -eresse. **Rightful c.**, ayant droit m. **Estate without a c.**, succession vacante.
clairvoyance [kleə'voiəns], s. 1. Lucidité f (somnambulique). 2. (Penetration of mind) Clairvoyance f.
clairvoyant [kleə'voiənt]. 1. a. (a) Doué de seconde vue. (b) (Shrewd) Clairvoyant. 2. s. (f. occ. clairvoyante) Voyant, -ante; somnambule mf lucide.
clam[1] [klæm], s. (a) Moll: Palourde f; praire f (venus verrucosa). F: **To shut up like a c.**, refuser de parler. (b) U.S: F: (Homme) taciturne. **'clam 'chowder**, s. U.S: Cu: Soupe f aux palourdes. **'clam-shell**, s. 1. Moll: Coquille f de peigne. 2. Civ.E: C.-s. **bucket**, benne preneuse.

clam², *v.i. U.S: F:* To c. up, se taire.
clambake ['klæmbeik], *s. U.S:* 1. Pique-nique *m* au bord de la mer. 2. *esp.Pol: F:* Réunion tapageuse. 3. *F: T.V: W.Tel:* Four *m*, fiasco *m*.
clamber¹ ['klæmbər], *s.* Escalade *f*.
clamber², *v.i.* Grimper (des pieds et des mains). To c. up, over, a wall, escalader un mur.
clamminess ['klæminis], *s.* Moiteur froide.
clammy ['klæmi], *a.* 1. (*Of skin*) (Froid et) moite; (*of atmosphere*) (froid et) humide. 2. Gluant, collant.
clamorous ['klæmərəs], *a.* Bruyant, braillard. A c. crowd, une foule vociférante.
clamour¹ ['klæmər], *s.* Clameur *f*; cris *mpl*.
clamour², *v.i.* Vociférer; pousser des clameurs. To c. for sth., réclamer qch. à grands cris.
clamp¹ [klæmp], *s.* (*a*) Crampon *m*, presse *f*; main *f* de fer. (*b*) *Const:* Agrafe *f*, happe *f*. (*c*) Bride *f* de serrage; patte *f* d'attache. (*d*) *Carp:* Serre-joint *m*, valet *m*. (*e*) Mordache *f* (d'étau). (*f*) *El.E:* Attache-fil(s) *m inv*; borne *f*. (*g*) *Surg:* Clamp *m*.
clamp². 1. *v.tr.* (*a*) Agrafer (deux pierres); brider (un tuyau). (*b*) Bloquer; caler (un télescope). 2. *v.i. F:* To c. down on s.o., visser (qn). To c. down on an abuse, mettre le holà à un abus.
clamp³, *s. Agr:* Silo *m* (temporaire) (de pommes de terre, etc.).
clan¹ [klæn], *s.* 1. Clan *m*. The head of the c., le chef de clan. 2. (*a*) Tribu *f*. (*b*) *F:* Coterie *f*.
clan², *v.i.* (**clanned**) *F:* To c. together, se soutenir mutuellement.
clandestine [klæn'destin], *a.* Clandestin, subreptice. **-ly**, *adv.* Clandestinement; à la dérobée.
clang¹ [klæŋ], *s.* Son *m* métallique; bruit strident, retentissant; résonnement *m* (de cloches).
clang², *v.i.* Retentir, résonner. **clanging**, *s.* = CLANG¹.
clanger ['klæŋər], *s. F:* To drop a c., faire une boulette.
clangour ['klæŋgər], *s. Lit:* = CLANG¹.
clank¹ [klæŋk], *s.* Bruit sec (de fers); cliquetis *m*.
clank². 1. *v.i.* Rendre un bruit métallique (sans résonance). 2. *v.tr.* The prisoners c. their chains, les prisonniers font sonner leurs fers. **clanking**, *s.* = CLANK¹.
clannish ['klæniʃ], *a.* Dévoué aux intérêts de son clan, de sa coterie.
clannishness ['klæniʃnis], *s.* Esprit *m* de corps (des membres d'un clan, d'une famille, d'une coterie).
clansman, *pl.* -**men** ['klænzmən], *s.* Membre *m*. d'un clan, d'une tribu.
clap¹ [klæp], *s.* 1. (*a*) Battement *m* (de mains); applaudissements *mpl*. To give s.o. a c., applaudir qn. (*b*) Coup *m*, tape *f* (de la main). 2. (Thunder-)c., coup de tonnerre.
clap². 1.*v.tr.* (**clapped**) (*a*) To c. one's hands, battre, claquer, des mains. To c. s.o. on the back, donner à qn une tape dans le dos. To c. a performer, applaudir un artiste. (*b*) (*Of bird*) To c. its wings, battre des ailes. (*c*) To c. s.o. in prison, fourrer qn en prison. To c. a pistol to s.o.'s head, appuyer brusquement un pistolet sur la tempe de qn. To c. on one's hat, camper son chapeau sur sa tête. To c. on more sail, augmenter de toile. *F:* To c. eyes on s.o., voir qn (tout à coup). 2. *v.i.* Applaudir; frapper des, dans les, dans ses, mains. **clap to**, *v.i.* Se refermer (avec un bruit sec). **clapping**, *s.* Battements *m* des mains; applaudissements *mpl*.
clap³, *s. V:* Blennorragie *f*; gonorrhée *f*; chaude-pisse.
clapboard ['klæpbɔːd], *s. Constr: U.S:* Planche *f* à recouvrement.
clapper ['klæpər], *s.* 1. Battant *m* (de cloche); claquet *m*, traquet *m*. (de moulin). 2. *Ecc:* Claquette *f*. 3. (*Pers.*) Applaudisseur *m*; (*hired*) claqueur *m*. The (hired) clappers, la claque.
claptrap ['klæptræp], *s.* Boniment *m*; phrases *f* vides. To talk c., parler pour la galerie; parler pour ne rien dire.
clarendon ['klær(ə)ndən], *s. Typ:* Caractère gras; égyptienne *f*; "en noir."
claret ['klærət], *s.* Vin *m* de Bordeaux (rouge); bordeaux *m*. 'claret-cup, *s.* Boisson sucrée au vin rouge.
clarification [ˌklærifiˈkeiʃ(ə)n], *s.* 1. Clarification *f*. 2. *Pharm: Sug.-R:* Défécation *f*.

clarify ['klærifai]. 1. *v.tr.* Clarifier (le beurre, le sirop); éclaircir (l'esprit). *Sug.R:* Déféquer. To c. a question, matter, débroussailler une question. 2. *v.i.* Se clarifier, s'éclaircir. **clarifying**, *s.* Clarification *f* (d'un liquide).
clarinet [ˌklæriˈnet], *s.* Clarinette *f*.
clarion ['klæriən], *s. Poet:* Clairon *m*.
clarity ['klæriti], *s.* Clarté *f*.
clash¹ [klæʃ], *s.* Choc violent et sonore. 1. Fracas *m*; résonnement *m* (de cloches); choc (de verres); cliquetis *m* (d'épées). 2. (*a*) Conflit *m*, choc (d'opinions); (*between mobs*) échauffourée *f*. (*b*) Disparate *f* (de couleurs).
clash². 1. *v.i.* (*a*) (*Of bells*) Résonner (bruyamment); (*of arms*) s'entrechoquer. (*b*) (*Of colours*) Jurer; faire disparate; (*of opinions, etc.*) s'opposer; (*of interests*) se heurter. The two dates c., les deux réunions, etc., tombent le même jour. 2. *v.tr.* Faire résonner (des cymbales).
clasp¹ [klɑːsp], *s.* 1. Agrafe *f* (de broche); fermeture *f* (de collier); fermoir *m* (de porte-monnaie). Staple-c. (*for padlocking*), moraillon *m*. 2. Hand-c., serrement *m* de mains. 'clasp-knife, *s.* Couteau pliant; (*with lock-back*) couteau à cran d'arrêt.
clasp², *v.tr.* Agrafer (un bracelet). *v.i.* This bracelet won't c., ce bracelet ne veut pas s'agrafer. 2. (*a*) Serrer, étreindre (qn). To c. s.o. to one's breast, serrer qn contre sa poitrine. To be clasped in each other's arms, se tenir étroitement embrassés. (*b*) To c. s.o.'s hand, serrer la main à qn. To c. one's hands, joindre les mains.
class¹ [klɑːs], *s.* Classe *f*. 1. The upper c., les gens du monde. The governing c., les classes dirigeantes. C. consciousness, (i) esprit de caste; (ii) conscience de classe; (iii) *Pol:* esprit *m* de (la) solidarité de classe. C. war, lutte des classes. The lower classes, le prolétariat. The middle c., la bourgeoisie; les classes moyennes. 2. *Sch:* Classe; *U.S:* promotion *f*. The French c., la classe de français. Evening classes, cours *m* du soir, Dancing c., cours de danse. In c., en classe *f*. To hold classes for discussion, organiser des séances de discussion. 3. (*a*) Catégorie *f*, sorte *f*, genre *m*. Arrangement in classes, classification *f*. This article stands in a c. by itself, cet article est unique. C. of ships, type *m* de navires. (*b*) *Ins:* C. of a ship, cote *f* d'un navire (au Lloyd). (*c*) *Sch:* (*At university*) Mention obtenue.
class², *v.tr.* (*a*) Classer; ranger (des candidats) par classes. Classed first, classé premier. Not classed, (i) non classé; (ii) (*at exhibitions*) hors concours. To c. as, assimiler à. (*b*) *Ins:* Coter (un navire).
classic ['klæsik]. 1. *a.* Classique. *Turf:* C. (race), course *f* classique. 2. *s.* (*a*) Classique *m* (grec, français, etc.). Author who has now become a c., auteur *m* qui est maintenant un classique. (*b*) *Sch:* Humaniste *m*. (*c*) *pl.* (*Usu. with sg. const.*) Études *f* classiques; humanités *f*. To study classics, étudier les classiques, faire ses humanités.
classical ['klæsik(ə)l], *a.* Classique. C. scholar, humaniste *m*.
classicism ['klæsisizm], *s.* Classicisme *m*.
classicist ['klæsisist], *s.* 1. *Lit.Hist:* Classique *m*. 2. *Sch:* Humaniste *mf*. 3. Partisan *m* des études classiques.
classification [ˌklæsifiˈkeiʃ(ə)n], *s.* Classification *f* (des plantes); classement *m* (de papiers); cote *f* (d'un navire); codification *f* (des lois).
classifier ['klæsifaiər], *s.* 1. (*Pers.*) Classificateur *m*. 2. Classeur *m*.
classify ['klæsifai], *v.tr.* Classifier, classer. *Adm:* Classified documents, documents classifiés. Classified results, résultats *m* et classements *m*. *Sch:* Classified vocabulary, vocabulaire *m* arrangé par centres d'intérêt. *Journ: F:* Classified Ads, petites annonces.
classmate ['klɑːsmeit], *s. U.S:* (*a*) Camarade *mf* de classe. (*b*) Camarade de promotion.
classroom ['klɑːsruːm], *s.* (Salle *f* de) classe *f*.
classy ['klɑːsi], *a. F:* Bon genre; chic.
clatter¹ ['klætər], *s.* 1. Bruit *m*, vacarme *m*; ferraillement *m*. 2. Brouhaha *m* (de conversation).
clatter². 1. *v.i.* Faire du bruit; se choquer avec fracas. To c. downstairs, descendre bruyamment l'escalier. To come clattering down, dégringoler. 2. *v.tr.* Faire résonner.

clause [klɔːz], s. 1. Clause f, article m (d'un traité). C. of a will, disposition f testamentaire. **Customary c., clause d'usage. 2.** Gram: Membre m de phrase. Head c., main c., proposition principale.

claustral ['klɔːstr(ə)l], a. Claustral, -aux.

claustrophobia [ˌklɔːstrə'foubiə], s. Med: Claustrophobie f.

clavicle ['klævikl], s. Anat: Clavicule f.

claw¹ [klɔː], s. 1. Griffe f (de félin); serre f (d'oiseau de proie); pince f (d'une écrevisse). (Of cat) To sharpen its claws, faire ses griffes. To draw in its claws, faire patte de velours. F: To cut s.o.'s claws, rogner les ongles à qn. 2. Coup m de griffe, d'ongle, de patte. 3. (a) (Of bench) Valet m; (of vice) mordache f. (b) C. of a grapnel, patte f d'un grappin. (c) (Of hammer) Panne fendue. 'claw-hammer, s. Marteau m à panne fendue, marteau fendu.

claw². 1. v.tr. Griffer, égratigner; déchirer (qch.) avec ses griffes. 2. v.i. To c. at sth., s'accrocher à qch.; agripper qch.

clay [klei], s. 1. Argile f; (terre-)glaise f. Pottery c., argile figuline. C. soil, sol argileux, glaiseux. Sp: C. pigeon, pigeon artificiel. 2. C.(-pipe), pipe f en terre. 'clay-pit, s. Argilière f, glaisière f.

clayey ['kleii], a. Argileux, -euse, glaiseux, -euse.

clean¹ [kliːn]. I. a. 1. Propre, net. As c. as a new pin, propre comme un sou neuf. To make sth. c., nettoyer qch. To keep sth. c., tenir qch. propre. Keep the conversation c., pas de grossièretés f. C. plate, assiette nette. C. land, terrain sans herbes. Nau: C. anchorage, mouillage sain. C. jump, saut franc. C. break, cassure nette, franche. Nau: C. bill of health, patente nette. The doctor gave me a clean bill of health, le docteur m'a trouvé en pleine forme. C. hands, (i) mains propres; (ii) (clean from crime) mains nettes. Jur: C. sheet, casier m judiciaire vierge. To make a c. breast of sth., vider son sac. 2. C. (out)lines, contours nets. Car with c. lines, auto qui a de la ligne. Nau: C. ship, navire fin. Farr: C. hocks (of horse), jarrets vides. II. clean, adv. 1. F: Tout à fait. I c. forgot, j'ai absolument oublié. They got c. away, ils ont décampé sans laisser de traces. 2. To cut c. through sth., couper, traverser, qch. de part en part. To break off c., casser net. 'clean-'cut, a. Net, clair. clean-'handed, a. Aux mains nettes. clean-'shaven, a. Sans barbe ni moustache; (visage) glabre, entièrement rasé.

clean², s. Nettoyage m. To give sth. a c. (up), nettoyer qch.

clean³, v.tr. Nettoyer (qch.); récurer (les casseroles); balayer (les rues); faire (une chambre); vider (le poisson); sarcler, désherber, nettoyer (un champ); défricher (un terrain). Nau: To c. the brasswork, faire le fourbissage. To c. one's teeth, one's nails, se brosser les dents; se curer les ongles. F: To c. oneself (up), se débarbouiller. clean out, v.tr. 1. Ranger (une armoire); curer, décrasser (un fourneau); vidanger (une fosse). I.C.E: To c. out the jet, déboucher le gicleur. 2. F: To c. s.o. out, mettre qn à sec. Cleaned out, décavé, lessivé. clean up, v.tr. 1. Nettoyer (un champ). 2. Abs. Faire le nettoyage. 'clean-up, s. Nettoyage m. cleaning, s. Nettoyage m, nettoiement m. (Household) c. materials, produits mpl d'entretien. U.S: C. woman, femme f de ménage. 'cleaning-rod, s. Baguette f (de fusil).

cleaner ['kliːnər], s. 1. (Pers.) Nettoyeur, -euse; décrotteur m; femme f de ménage. French, dry, c., nettoyeur à sec. Window c., laveur m de vitres. 2. (Device) Nettoyeuse f; (device, preparation) dégraisseur m. S.a. VACUUM-CLEANER.

cleanliness ['klenlinis], s. Propreté f; netteté f.

cleanly¹ ['klenli], a. Propre (par habitude).

cleanly² ['kliːnli], adv. Proprement, nettement.

cleanness ['kliːnnis], s. 1. Propreté f. 2. Netteté f (de contours).

cleanse [klenz], v.tr. 1. Assainir, curer (un égout). 2. Purifier, dépurer (le sang). cleansing¹, a. Assainissant, purifiant. cleansing², s. 1. Assainissement m, curage m (d'un égout). 2. Purification f (du sang, de l'âme); dépuration f (du sang). Toil: C. cream, crème f de démaquillage, démaquillant m.

cleanser ['klenzər], s. Toil: Face c., cleaner m.

clear¹ [kliər]. I. a. 1. (a) Clair, limpide; net. On a c. day, par temps clair. As c. as day, as crystal, clair comme le jour, comme de l'eau de roche. As c. as mud, pas clair du tout. (b) C. conscience, conscience nette. (c) C. voice, voix claire, nette. 2. (Manifest) C. indication, signe certain, évident. C. case of bribery, cas de corruption manifeste. To make one's meaning, oneself, c., se faire comprendre. I wish to make it c. that . . ., je tiens à préciser que. . . . To make c., expliciter. C. thinker, esprit lucide. s. To send a message in c., transmettre une dépêche en clair. 4. To be c. about sth., être convaincu, certain, de qch. 5. (a) C. profit, bénéfice clair et net. C. loss, perte sèche. C. majority, majorité absolue. (b) Jur: Three c. days, trois jours francs. 6. Libre, dégagé (of, de). C. estate, bien franc d'hypothèque. C. space, espace libre. C. road, chemin libre; route bien dégagée. (Of pers.) To be c. of sth., être débarrassé de qch. The train was c. of the station, le train était sorti de la gare. Horizon c. of haze, horizon dégagé de brume. The town was c. of the enemy, la ville avait été évacuée par l'ennemi. The roads are c., les routes sont débloquées. Rail: C. road, 'road c.', "voie libre." 'All c.!' Mil: "fin d'alerte"; Nau: "paré!" C. coast, côte saine. F: The coast is c., le champ est libre. II. clear, a. or adv. To steer c. of a rock, passer au large d'un écueil. To stand c., s'écarter, se garer (pour éviter un danger). To pull s.o. c. (of sth.), dégager qn (de qch.). To keep, steer, c. of sth., éviter qch.; se garer de qch. Stand c. of the doorway! dégagez la porte! I keep c. of him as far as possible, je l'évite le plus possible. To get c. of debt, se débarrasser de ses dettes. To get c., se tirer d'affaire. -ly, adv. 1. Clairement, nettement. To see, speak, c., voir, parler, clair. It was too dark to see c., il faisait trop noir pour bien distinguer. You must c. understand that . . ., il vous faut bien comprendre que. . . . 2. Évidemment. (a) He is c. wrong, il est clair qu'il a tort. (b) I was wrong?—C., j'ai eu tort?—Évidemment. 'clear-cut, a. C.c. features, traits nettement dessinés. C.c. division, division nette. 'clear-'eyed, a. 1. Aux yeux clairs. 2. = CLEAR-SIGHTED. 'clear-'headed, a. 1. Perspicace. 2. I was quite c.-h., j'avais toute ma tête, toute ma lucidité d'esprit. 'clear-'headedness, s. Perspicacité f. 'clear-'sighted, a. Clairvoyant; qui voit juste. 'clear-'toned, a. Au timbre clair, pur.

clear², v. I. v.tr. 1. (a) Éclaircir. To c. the air, (i) (of thunderstorm) rafraîchir l'air; (ii) (of discussion) mettre les choses au point. (b) Clarifier (un liquide); dépurer (le sang). 2. To c. s.o. of a charge, innocenter qn d'une accusation. To c. oneself, se disculper. 3. Dégager (une route); désencombrer (une salle); défricher (un terrain); (from rubbish) déblayer (un terrain). Mil: Dégager (la frontière). To c. (of mines), déminer. To c. of sand, désensabler. Jur: To c. the court, faire évacuer la salle. To c. one's conscience, décharger sa conscience. C. the way! faites place! To c. a way for oneself, se frayer (un) passage. To c. the ground for negotiations, déblayer le terrain. To c. the table, débarrasser la table, enlever le couvert. Navy: To c. (the decks) for action, faire le branle-bas de combat. A cup of coffee clears the head, une tasse de café dégage le cerveau. Com: To c. goods, solder des marchandises. 'To c.,' "en solde," "solde." 'Must be cleared,' "vente à tout prix." Nau: To c. a cable, an anchor, parer un câble, une ancre. Rail: To c. the line, dégager la voie; (after an accident) déblayer la voie. To c. a choked pipe, désobstruer un tuyau. To c. a filter, décolmater un filtre. Town P: To c. slums, supprimer les taudis. F: C. all this out of here, débarrassez-moi de tout cela. 4. To c. one's plate, faire assiette nette. To c. a barrier (by five centimetres), franchir une barrière (avec cinq centimètres de reste). To jack up a wheel until it clears the ground, soulever une roue jusqu'à ce qu'elle ne touche plus le sol. (b) Nau: To c. the harbour, sortir du port; quitter le port. To c. the land, parer la terre. Vessel cleared, navire sorti. 6. (a) Acquitter (une dette); affranchir (une propriété); solder, liquider (un compte); arrêter (un compte, le solde de dépôt). (b) *Nau:* (*Of ship*) To c. its quaran-tine, purger la quarantaine. To c. goods, dédouaner des marchandises. 7. To c. ten per cent, faire un bénéfice net de dix pour cent. Not to c. one's expenses, ne pas faire ses frais. 8. *Fin:* Compenser, virer (un chèque). II. clear, *v.i.* 1. (a) (*Of the weather*) To c. (up), s'éclaircir; se mettre au beau. (*Of mist*) To c. (away), se dissiper. The sky is clearing, le ciel se dégage. His brow cleared, son front se rasséréna. (b) (*Of liquid*) Se clarifier. 2. (*Of ship*) Prendre la mer. **clear away,** *v.tr.* Enlever, ôter (qch.); écarter (un obstacle). *Abs.* Débarrasser la table. **clear off.** 1. *v.tr.* S'acquitter de (ses dettes). *Com:* Solder (des marchandises). To c. off one's debts, a mortgage, payer ses dettes, purger une hypothèque. To c. off arrears of work, rattraper l'arriéré de besogne. 2. *v.i.* (*Of intruders*) S'enfuir, filer, décamper. **clear out,** 1. *v.tr.* Nettoyer (une chambre); vider (une armoire); balayer (tout le personnel); liquider (le stock). 2. *v.i.* Filer, déguerpir. C. out! filez! hors d'ici! 'clear-out, s. Nettoyage *m.* **clear up,** *v.tr.* (a) Éclaircir, élucider (un mystère). To c. up a matter, tirer une affaire au clair. (b) (Re)mettre (une pièce) en ordre. *S.a.* CLEAR² II 1. (a). **clearing,** *s.* 1. C. of s.o. (from a charge), désinculpation *f* de qn. 2. Dégagement *m,* déblaiement *m* (d'une voie); enlèvement *m* (de débris); défrichement *m* (d'un terrain). 3. Franchissement *m* (d'une barrière). 4. (a) *Cust:* Dédouanement *m.* (b) Acquittement *m* (de dettes). (c) *Fin:* Compensation *f* (de chèques). Under the c. procedure, par voie *f* de compensation. C. agreement, accord *m* de compensation. 5. (*In forest*) Éclaircie *f,* clairière *f*; (*for cultivation*) défriche *f,* défriché *m.* 'clearing-bank, *s.* Bank: Banque *f* de virement. 'clearing-house, *s.* 1. *Fin:* Chambre *f* de compensation. 2. *Rail:* Bureau central. **clearance** ['kliərəns], *s.* 1. C. sale, (vente *f* de) soldes *f,* réalisation *f* du stock. *Town Cp:* C. area, tache, quartier (insalubre), à démolir. *Mil:* Bomb, shell c., désobusage *m.* Mine c., déminage *m.* 2. (a) *Cust:* Dédouanage *m,* dédouanement *m.* C. certificate, lettre *f* de mer. C. inwards, permis *m* d'entrée. (b) *Nau:* Départ *m* (du port). 3. *Bank:* Compensation *f* (de chèques), présentation *f* à l'encaissement (d'un chèque). 4. *Tchn:* Espace *m* libre; jeu *m*; voie *f* (d'une scie). Permissible c., jeu tolérable. There is not enough c. for the barges under the bridge, le pont manque de hauteur pour laisser passer les péniches. **clearness** ['kliənis], *s.* 1. Clarté *f* (de l'atmosphère). 2. Netteté *f* (d'une image, des idées). **clearway** ['kliə'wei], *s.* Route *f* à stationnement interdit. **cleat** [kli:t], *s.* Tasseau *m,* taquet *m.* **cleavable** ['kli:vəbl], *a.* Fissile. *Miner:* clivable. **cleavage** ['kli:vidʒ], *s.* 1. Fendage *m.* *Miner:* Clivage *m.* 2. Scission *f* (dans un parti). 3. *F:* Échancrure provocante du corsage. **cleave¹** [kli:v], *v.* (*p.t.* cleaved, cleft [kleft], *Lit:* clove [klouv]; *p.p.* cleaved, cleft, *Lit:* cloven [klouvn]) 1. *v.tr.* (a) Fendre (le bois, le fer). Cleft stick, piquet fourchu. To be in a cleft stick, se trouver dans une impasse. Cleft palate, palais fendu. Cloven hoof, pied fendu, fourchu. To show, display, the cloven hoof, montrer le pied fourchu; laisser passer le bout de l'oreille. (b) *Miner:* Cliver (un cristal). (c) (*Of bird, ship*) Fendre (l'air, les eaux). 2. *v.i.* (a) To c. (asunder), se fendre. (b) (*Of crystals*) Se cliver. **cleave²,** *v.i.* (*p.t.* cleaved [kli:vd], cleft; *p.p.* cleaved) *O:* Adhérer, s'attacher, être fidèle (à un parti). **cleaver** ['kli:vər], *s.* Fendoir *m*; (*for meat*) couperet *m.* **cleavers** ['kli:vəz], *s. Bot:* Grat(t)eron *m.* **clef** [klef], *s. Mus:* Clef *f.* The bass c., la clef de fa. The treble c., la clef de sol. The C c., la clef d'ut. **cleft¹** [kleft], *s.* Fente *f,* fissure *f,* crevasse *f.* **cleft².** See CLEAVE¹. **clem** [klem], *v.tr. & i.* (*N. of Eng.*) *F:* I'm fair clemmed, je crève de faim. I'm clemmed with cold, je suis transi de froid. **clematis** ['klemətis, kli'meitis], *s. Bot:* Clématite *f.* **clemency** ['klemənsi], *s.* 1. Clémence *f* (to, envers, pour). 2. Douceur *f* (du temps). **clement** ['klemənt], *a.* 1. Clément, indulgent (to, envers, pour). 2. (*Of weather*) Doux, *f.* douce. **clementine** ['klemɔntain], *s. Hort:* Clémentine *f.*

clench [klen(t)ʃ], *v.tr.* 1. ═ CLINCH² I. 2. Serrer (les dents, le poing). With clenched hands, les mains crispées. 3. *v.i.* Se serrer; se crisper. **Cleopatra** [ˌkli:o'pætrə]. *Pr.n.f. A.Hist:* Cléopâtre. **clepsydra** ['klepsidrə], *s. Archeol:* Clepsydre *f.* **clerestory** ['kli:əsto:ri], *s. Ecc.Arch:* Fenêtres hautes. **clergy** ['klə:dʒi], *s.* (*No pl.*) 1. *Coll.* Clergé *m.* 2. (*With pl. const.*) Membres *m* du clergé. **clergyman,** *pl.* -men ['klə:dʒimən], *s.m.* Ecclésiastique; ministre (du culte); pasteur (protestant). **cleric** ['klerik], *s.* ═ CLERGYMAN. **clerical** ['klerik(ə)l], *a.* 1. Clérical, -aux; du clergé. 2. (a) C. error, faute de copiste; *Book-k:* erreur d'écritures. (b) C. work, travail de bureau. **clericalism** ['klerik(ə)lizm], *s.* Cléricalisme *m.* **clerk¹** [klɑ:k, *U.S:* klɔ:k], *s.* 1. (a) Employé, -ée, de bureau; commis *m*; buraliste *mf*; clerc *m* (d'avoué). Counter c., guichetier *m* (dans une banque). Filing c., documentaliste *mf.* Chief c., chef *m* de bureau. Junior c., petit employé. (b) *Jur:* C. of the Court, greffier *m.* C. of the court's office, greffe *m.* 2. *Ecc:* C. (in holy orders), clerc; ecclésiastique *m.* 3. (a) C. of the works, conducteur *m,* surveillant *m,* des travaux. (b) *F:* The C. of the weather, la providence qui régit la pluie et le beau temps. (c) *Rac:* C. of the course, commissaire *m* de la piste. 4. *U.S:* Vendeur, -euse (de magasin). **clerk²,** *v.i. U.S:* 1. Être commis *m* (for s.o., chez qn). 2. To c. in a store, travailler comme vendeur, -euse, dans un magasin. **clerkly** ['klɑ:kli], *a.* 1. De bureau. C. hand, écriture moulée. 2. *A:* Docte, savant, lettré. **clerkship** ['klɑ:kʃip], *s.* Emploi *m* ou place *f* de commis, d'employé, *Jur:* de clerc. **clever** ['klevər], *a.* 1. Habile, adroit. He is c. with his hands, il est adroit de ses mains. C. at doing sth., habile, ingénieux, à faire qch. To be c. with one's pencil, se servir adroitement de son crayon. *P:* That's not very c., c'est pas malin. 2. (a) To be c., être intelligent. A c. child, un enfant à l'intelligence éveillée. *Sch:* C. at mathematics, fort en mathématiques. (b) *F:* (*Smart*) He was too c. for us, il nous a roulés. (c) A c. parody, une parodie pleine de finesse. (d) C. device, dispositif ingénieux. -ly, *adv.* Habilement, adroitement; avec intelligence. **cleverness** ['klevənis], *s.* 1. Habileté *f,* adresse *f,* dextérité *f.* C. at doing sth., habileté à faire qch. 2. Intelligence *f.* 3. Ingéniosité *f.* **clew¹** [klu:], *s.* 1. Pelote *f* (de fil). 2. *Nau:* (a) Araignée *f* (de hamac). (b) Point *m* d'écoute (de voile). 'clew-garnet, -line, *s. Nau:* Cargue-point *m.* **clew²,** *v.tr.* To c. (up) the sails, carguer les voiles. **cliché** ['kli:ʃei], *s.* Cliché *m.* **click¹** [klik], *s.* 1. Bruit sec; clic *m*; cliquetis *m* (d'épées). 2. *Ling:* C. (of the tongue), clappement *m* (de la langue). 3. *Tchn:* Cliquet *m*; déclic *m.* 'click-beetle, *s.* Élatère *m*; *F:* taupin *m.* 'click-clack, *s.* Tic-tac *m* (d'un moulin). 'click-wheel, *s.* Roue *f* à cliquet, à rochet. **click²,** *v.tr. & i.* Cliqueter; faire tic-tac. To c. one's heels, (faire) claquer les talons (en saluant). **clicking,** *s.* ═ CLICK¹ 1, 2. **click³,** *v.i. F:* (a) (*Of two pers.*) Se plaire du premier coup. (b) (*Of things*) Aller ensemble. (c) That clicks! ça me rappelle quelque chose. **client** ['klaiənt], *s.* 1. *Rom.Ant:* Client *m.* 2. (a) Client, ·ente (dans les professions libérales). (b) *Com:* ═ CUSTOMER 1. **clientele** [klaiən'tel, kliɑ̃'tɛl], *s.* Clientèle *f.* **cliff** [klif], *s.* Falaise *f*; (*inland*) escarpement *m.* 'cliff-dweller, *s.* (a) *Prehist:* Troglodyte *mf.* (b) *U.S:* *F:* Locataire *mf* d'un gratte-ciel. 'cliff-hanger, *s. Cin: T.V:* Drame-feuilleton *m.* **climate** ['klaimit], *s.* Climat *m.* **climatic** [klai'mætik], *a.* (a) Climat(ér)ique. (b) *Biol:* C. variation, variation climatologique. **climatological** [ˌklaimə'tɔlədʒikl], *a.* Climatologique. **climatology** [ˌklaimə'tɔlədʒi], *s.* Climatologie *f.* **climax** ['klaimæks], *s.* 1. *Rh:* Gradation (ascendante). 2. Comble *m,* apogée *m*; plus haut point. This brought matters to a c., ce fut le comble. *Th: etc:* To work up to a c., corser l'action; amener la grande scène. 3. *Nat.Hist:* Climax *m.*

climb¹ [klaim], s. **1.** Ascension f. *Aut: Sp:* Hill c., course f de côte. *Av:* Rate of c., vitesse ascensionnelle. **C. indicator,** variomètre m; indicateur m de vitesse ascensionnelle. **2.** Côte f, montée f. **Steep c.,** grimpette f. **Stiff c.,** grimpée f.

climb², *v.tr. & i.* **1.** (a) Monter, gravir (l'escalier); grimper à (un arbre); monter à (l'échelle); escalader (une falaise) To c. a mountain, faire l'ascension d'une montagne. **To (rock-)c.,** varapper. **To c. over the wall,** franchir le mur. **To c. down the cliff,** descendre la falaise. **To c. out of a hole,** sortir en grimpant d'un trou; se tirer d'un trou. *F:* **To c. up the wall,** être à bout de forces, *P:* être cinglé, dingo. (b) **The road climbs,** la route va en montant. **2. To c. to power,** s'élever au pouvoir. **3.** *Av:* Prendre de l'altitude, monter. **climb down,** *v.i.* **1.** Descendre. **2.** *F:* En rabattre; baisser pavillon; *P:* se dégonfler. **'climb-down,** s. **1.** Descente f. **2.** *F:* Défaite f. **A miserable c.-d.,** une honteuse reculade. **climbing¹,** a. **C. plant,** plante grimpante. **climbing²,** s. Escalade f; montée f. **Mountain c.,** alpinisme m. *Aut:* **C. ability,** tenue en côte. **C. speed,** vitesse en montée. *Aer:* **C. speed,** vitesse ascensionnelle. **'climbing-irons,** s.pl. (a) *Mount:* Crampons m. (b) Grimpettes fpl, grappins mpl.

climber ['klaimər], s. **1.** Ascensionniste mf (de montagne; alpiniste m; grimpeur m (à un arbre). **2.** *F:* Arriviste mf. **3.** (a) *Bot:* Plante grimpante. (b) *Orn:* Grimpeur.

clime [klaim], s. *Poet:* Climat m; pays m.

clinch¹ [klin(t)ʃ], s. **1.** (a) Rivet m, crampon m (b) *Nau:* Étalingure f. **2.** *Box:* Corps-à-corps m; clinch m.

clinch². **1.** *v.tr.* (a) River. (b) *Nau:* Étalinguer (une chaîne). (c) Conclure (un marché). **That clinches it,** voilà qui tranche la question. **2.** *v.i.* *Box:* Se prendre corps-à-corps. **'clinch-nail,** s. Clou rivé à river.

clincher ['klinʃər], s. **1.** *F:* Argument m sans réplique. **That was a c. for him!** ça lui a rivé son clou! **2.** *Aut: Cy:* (Of wheel-rim) Gouttière f. **C. tyre,** pneu à talon.

cling [kliŋ], *v.i.* (clung [klʌŋ]; clung) (a) (Of pers.) S'attacher, s'accrocher, se cramponner (to, à); (of burr) s'attraper (to, à). **She clung to me,** elle se prit à moi. **To c. close to s.o.,** se serrer, se coller, contre qn. **To c. together,** to one another, (i) rester attachés l'un à l'autre; rester étroitement unis; (ii) se tenir étroitement enlacés. (b) **To c. to an opinion,** rester attaché à une opinion. (c) Adhérer (to, à). (O garment) **To c. to the figure,** coller au corps. **The ivy is clinging to the tree,** le lierre s'attache, se noue, à l'arbre. **clinging,** a. Qui s'attache; qui colle; qui s'accroche. **C. material,** tissu qui moule le corps. **C. nature,** naturel affectueux. **C. perfume,** parfum m tenace.

clinger ['kliŋər], s. *F:* Crampon m; *P:* pot m de colle.

clingstone ['kliŋstoun], s. **C.** (peach, etc.), (pêche, etc.) à noyau adhérent.

clinic ['klinik], s. *Med:* Clinique f.

clinical ['klinik(ə)l], a. (Leçon, etc.) clinique. **C. thermometer,** thermomètre médical.

clink¹ [kliŋk], s. Tintement m, choc m (de verres); cliquetis m (d'épées).

clink². **1.** *v.i.* (Of glasses) Tinter. **2.** *v.tr.* Faire tinter, faire résonner. **To c. glasses,** trinquer.

clink³, s. *P:* Prison f; *Mil: P:* bloc m, taule f. **To go to c.,** être fourré au bloc.

clinker ['kliŋkər], s. **1.** Brique vitrifiée. **2.** Mâchefer m; scories vitreuses; escarbilles fpl.

clinometer [klai'nomitər], s. *Surv: Nau:* Clinomètre m.

clip¹ [klip], s. **1.** Pince f, attache f; griffe f, collier m, étrier m de serrage. **Paper-c.,** agrafe f (pour papiers); happeur m; attache-papiers m inv; (wire) (attache) trombone m. **Fountain-pen c., bague-agrafe f,** clip m. *Surg:* **Artery-c.,** pince hémostatique. *Cy:* **Trouser clips,** pince-pantalons f. **2.** *El:* Cosse f (de fil). **3.** *Mil:* (Loading-)c., chargeur m (pour cartouches).

clip², *v.tr.* (clipped [klipt]) Pincer, serrer. **To c. papers together,** agrafer des papiers.

clip³, s. **1.** (a) Tonte f (de moutons). (b) Tonte de la saison. **2.** *F:* Taloche f. *Box:* **C. on the jaw,** coup sec à la mâchoire. **3.** *U.S: F:* To go at a good c., marcher à grande vitesse.

clip⁴, *v.tr.* **1.** Tondre (un mouton); tailler une haie); rogner, cisailler (la monnaie). **To c. the wings of a bird,** rogner les ailes à une volaille. *F:* **To c. one's words,** écourter ses mots. **2.** Poinçonner (un billet). **3.** *P:* **To c. s.o.'s ear,** flanquer une taloche à qn.

clipping, s. **1.** (a) Tondage m (de chevaux); tonte f (de moutons). (b) Poinçonnage m (de billets). **2.** (a) *U.S:* Coupure (prise dans un journal). (b) pl. Rognures f.

clipper ['klipər], s. **1.** (Pers.) Tondeur, -euse. **2.** pl. *Tls:* Tondeuse f. **3.** *Nau:* Fin voilier. **C.-built,** à formes élancées. *Av: O:* Long courrier.

clippie ['klipi], s.f. *F:* Receveuse (d'autobus).

clique [kli:k], s. Coterie f; petite chapelle.

cliquishness ['kli:kiʃnis], s. Esprit m de coterie.

cloaca, pl. -ae [klo'eikə, -i:], s. Cloaque m.

cloak¹ [klouk], s. Manteau m. **Evening c.,** sortie f de bal, de théâtre. **Under the c. of night,** sous le voile de la nuit. **Under the c. of religion,** sous le manteau de la religion. **C.-and-dagger story,** roman de cape et d'épée. *Adm: Mil: F:* **The c.-and-dagger boys,** le contre-espionnage m. **'cloak-room,** s. **1.** *Th:* Vestiaire m. **'Ladies' c.-room,'** "Dames." **2.** *Rail:* Consigne f.

cloak², *v.tr.* (a) Couvrir, revêtir, (qn) d'un manteau. (b) Masquer (ses projets).

clobber ['klobər], s. *F:* Frusques fpl; hardes fpl, affaires fpl.

cloche [kloʃ], s. **1.** *Hort:* Cloche f (à melons, etc.). **Continuous c.,** cloche tunnel. **2.** *Cost:* **C. hat,** cloche.

clock¹ [klok], s. (a) (Large) Horloge f; (smaller) pendule f. *Nau:* Montre f. *Aut:* **Dashboard c.,** montre de bord. **Town c.,** horloge de ville. **Grandfather c.,** horloge de parquet, comtoise, normande. **Wall c.,** cartel m. *Tp:* **The speaking c.,** l'horloge parlante. **It is one, two, o'clock,** il est une heure, deux heures. **It took him ten minutes by the c.,** cela lui a pris dix minutes montre en main. *F:* **To sleep the c. round,** faire le tour du cadran. *Ind:* **To work round the c.,** faire trois équipes f (dans les 24 heures). **We are working round the c. to finish this dictionary,** nous travaillons d'arrache-pied pour finir ce dictionnaire. (b) **C. of taxi-cab,** compteur m (horo-)kilométrique. **'clock 'golf,** s. Jeu m de clock-golf. **'clock-maker,** s. Horloger m.

clock², **1.** *v.tr.* *F:* Chronométrer. **2.** *v.i.* *Ind:* **To c. on, off, in, out,** pointer à l'arrivée, au départ.

clock³, s. (On sock) Baguette f; grisotte f.

clocklike ['kloklaik], a. (D'une régularité) d'horloge; (d'une régularité) monotone.

clockwise ['klokwaiz], a. & adv. Dans le sens des aiguilles d'une montre; à droite; dextrorsum.

clockwork ['klokwə:k], s. Rouage m d'horloge; mouvement m d'horlogerie. **C. train,** chemin de fer mécanique. **F: Everything is going like c.,** tout va comme sur des roulettes. *S.a.* REGULAR I 1.

clod [klod], s. **1.** (a) Motte f (de terre). *Agr:* **To break (up) the clods,** émotter la terre. (b) **The c.,** la terre (des champs). **2.** = CLODHOPPER.

clodhopper ['klodhopər], s. Rustre m, lourdaud m.

clog¹ [klog], s. **1.** (a) Entrave f; billot m (pour vache). (b) *F:* Empêchement m. **2.** (a) *A:* (Overshoe) Socque f, galoche f. (b) Sabot m.

clog², *v.tr.* (clogged) **1.** *v.tr.* (a) Entraver (une bête). (b) Boucher, obstruer (un tuyau); colmater (un filtre); empâter (une lime). **To c. the wheels of the administration,** entraver la marche des services. **2.** *v.i.* Se boucher, s'obstruer.

cloisonné [klwæ'zonei], a. & s. *Ind: Art:* **C.** (enamel), cloisonné m.

cloister¹ ['kloistər], s. Usu.pl. Cloître m.

cloister², *v.tr.* Cloîtrer. **To lead a cloistered life,** mener une vie monacale.

cloistral ['kloistrəl], a. Claustral, -aux.

close¹ [klous]. **I.** a. **1.** (a) Bien fermé; clos. *Ling:* **C. vowel,** voyelle fermée, entravée. (b) **C. air,** air renfermé. **The room smells c.,** ça sent le renfermé ici. **C. weather,** temps lourd. (c) **C. secret,** secret impénétrable. (d) **C. corporation,** société exclusive. (e) *Ven:* **C. time, season,** chasse fermée. **2. C. carpeting,** tapis ajusté. *Typ:* **C. matter,** composition compacte. **C. grain,** grain fin, dense. **In c. order,** *Navy:* à distance serrée; *Mil:* en rangs serrés. **3. When I saw him at c. quarters,** quand je le vis de près. **C. connexion between two facts,** rapport étroit entre deux faits. **C. friend,** ami(e) intime. **C. resemblance,** ressemblance exacte. **C. translation,** traduction fidèle. **C. attention,** attention soutenue. **To keep c. watch on s.o.,** surveiller qn de près. **C. prisoner,** prisonnier étroitement gardé. **To cut hair c.,** couper les cheveux ras. *Rac:* **C. finish,** arrivée serrée. **C. election,** élection vivement contestée. **4.** Peu communicatif. **To be c. about sth.,** être réservé à l'égard de qch. **To play a c. game,** jouer serré. **5.** Avare, regardant. **-ly,** *adv.* **1.** = CLOSE¹ II. 1. **2.** *(a)* **C. guarded,** étroitement gardé. *(b)* **C. cut,** tondu ras. **C. contested,** vivement contesté. *(c)* (Surveiller qn) de près; (interroger qn) à fond; (écouter) attentivement. **3. C. packed in a box,** serrés dans une boîte. II. **close,** *adv.* **1. C. shut,** étroitement, hermétiquement, fermé, bouché. **2.** Près, de près, auprès. **To follow c. behind s.o.,** suivre qn de près. **To keep c. to the door,** se tenir tout près de la porte. *(Of garment)* **To fit c.,** bien prendre la taille. **To stand c. together,** se tenir serrés. **3. To lie c.,** se tenir tapi. **4.** *(a)* **C. at hand, c. by,** tout près, tout proche; à peu de distance. *(b)* **Nau: To stand c. in** (to the land), serrer la terre. *(c)* **C. on nine o'clock,** tout près de neuf heures. **To be c. on fifty,** friser la cinquantaine. *(d)* **C. to, c. by** (sth.), tout près, à proximité, de (qch.). **C. to the door,** tout contre la porte. **C. to the ground,** à fleur de terre. **close-'cropped, -'cut,** *a.* *(Of hair)* Coupé ras; *(of grass)* tondu de près. **close-'fisted,** *a.* Ladre; peu donnant, *F:* pingre, dur à la détente. **'close-fitting,** *a.* (Vêtement) ajusté, collant. **close-'grained,** *a.* *(Of wood)* Serré; à grain(s) fin(s). **close-'hauled,** *a.* Nau: Au plus près serré. **close-'meshed,** *a.* A petites mailles. **close-'mouthed, -'tongued,** *a.* Économe de paroles; peu communicatif; cadenassé; taciturne. **close-'reefed,** *a.* Nau: Au bas ris. **close-'set,** *a.* *(Of eyes, etc.)* Rapprochés. **close'shaven,** *a.* Rasé de près. **close-'up,** *s.* Cin: (Vue *f* de) premier plan. **C.-up (detail),** détail *m* (vu de près). **'close-'woven,** *a.* (Toile *f*) d'un tissu serré.

close² [klous], *s.* **1.** *Jur:* Clôture *f.* **2.** *(a)* Clos *m*, enclos *m.* *(b)* Enceinte *f* (de cathédrale). **3.** *(In Scot.)* Passage *m.*

close³ [klouz], *s.* **1.** Fin *f*, conclusion *f*; bout *m* (de l'année); clôture *f* (d'une séance). **The evening drew to a c.,** la soirée prit fin. **C. of the season,** fermeture *f* de la pêche, de la chasse. **2.** *(Of wrestlers)* **To come to a c.,** en venir au corps-à-corps.

close⁴ [klouz]. I. *v.tr.* **1.** Fermer; replier (un parapluie); barrer (une rue); Nau: bâcler (un port). **Road closed to traffic,** route interdite à la circulation. **Cold closes the pores,** le froid resserre les pores. **Book-k: To c. the books,** régler les livres; balancer les comptes. **2.** Conclure, terminer; clore, fermer (un débat); arrêter (un compte). **To declare the discussion closed,** prononcer la clôture des débats. **3. To c. the ranks,** serrer les rangs. **Navy: To c. the columns,** resserrer les colonnes. II. **close,** *v.i.* **1.** (Se) fermer; se refermer. **The theatres c. on Good Friday,** les théâtres font relâche le vendredi saint. *El.E:* **The cut-out has closed,** le conjoncteur est collé. **2.** Finir; se terminer. **The day is closing,** le jour tire à sa fin. **3. To c. about, round** (s.o.), cerner, encercler (qn). **4. To c. with s.o.,** (i) conclure le marché avec qn; *F:* toper; (ii) se prendre corps à corps avec qn. **close down. 1.** *v.tr.* Fermer (une usine). **2.** *v.i.* *(a)* *(Of factory)* Fermer; chômer. *(b)* W.Tel: Terminer l'émission. **close in,** *v.i.* *(a)* **The night closes in,** la nuit tombe. **The days are closing in,** les jours (se) raccourcissent. *(b)* **To c. in on s.o.,** cerner qn de près. **close up. 1.** *v.tr.* *(a)* Boucher; barrer. *(b)* Typ: Rapprocher (les caractères). **2.** *v.i.* *(a)* *(Of aperture)* S'obturer; *(of wound, etc.)* se refermer. *(b)* Se serrer, se tasser. *Mil:* **C. up!** serrez les rangs! **closed,** *a.* **1.** Fermé; *(of pipe)* obturé, bouché. **With c. eyes,** les yeux clos. **'Road c.,'** "rue barrée." *Th:* **'C.,'** "relâche." **'C. for the season,'** "clôture." **2. C. shop,** entreprise industrielle fermée aux travailleurs non-syndiqués. **In c. session,** en séance *f* à huis clos.

closing¹, *a.* *(a)* Qui (se) ferme. *(b)* Dernier; final, -als. **The c. bid,** la dernière enchère. **C. session,** séance de clôture. **C. prices,** derniers cours. **closing²,** *s.* **1.** Fermeture *f.* **C.(-down) of a factory,** fermeture d'une usine. **Com: Sunday c.,** repos *m* hebdomadaire. **C.-time,** heure *f* de fermeture (d'un magasin). **'C. time!' "on ferme!"** **2.** Clôture *f* (d'un compte, d'une séance).

closeness ['klousnis], *s.* **1.** *(a)* Rapprochement *m*, proximité *f.* **The c. of their friendship,** leur grande intimité. *(b)* Contexture serrée (d'un tissu, etc.). **2.** Exactitude *f.* **The c. of the resemblance,** la ressemblance frappante. **3.** *(a)* Manque *m* d'air. *(b)* Lourdeur *f* (du temps). **4.** Réserve *f*, caractère peu communicatif (de qn). **5.** Ladrerie *f*; *F:* pingrerie *f.*

closet¹ ['klɔzit], *s.* **1.** *(a)* Cabinet *m.* *(b)* A: Boudoir *m*; cabinet de travail. *(c)* A: = WATER-CLOSET. **2.** Armoire *f*, placard *m*; *(under staircase)* soupente *f* (d'escalier).

closet², *v.tr.* (closeted) To be closeted with s.o., être enfermé avec qn (pour conférer).

closure¹ ['klouʒər], *s.* **1.** *(a)* Clôture *f*, fermeture *f* (d'une séance). *(b)* Parl: To move the c., voter la clôture. **2.** Fermeture, occlusion *f* (d'une soupape, etc.).

closure², *v.tr.* Clôturer (un débat).

clot¹ [klɔt], *s.* **1.** Caillot *m* (de sang); bourbillon *m* (d'encre). **C. on the brain,** embolie cérébrale. **2.** *F:* Idiot *m*, imbécile *m*, *V:* con *m.*

clot², *v.* (clotted) **1.** *v.i.* *(Of milk)* Se cailler; *(of blood)* se figer, se coaguler. **2.** *v.tr.* Caillebotter, cailler (le lait); figer (le sang). **Clotted cream,** crème caillebottée (par échaudage). **clotting,** *s.* Caillement *m*, figement *m.*

cloth, *pl.* **cloths** [klɔθ, klɔθs], *s.* **1.** *Tex:* *(a)* Tissu *m f* de laine; drap *m.* *(b)* *(Linen, cotton)* Toile *f.* **Map mounted on c.,** carte entoilée. *Pub:* **C. binding,** reliure *f* toile. *(c)* **American c.,** *(also oil-c.)* toile cirée; molesquine *f.* **2.** *(a)* Linge *m*; *(for cleaning)* torchon *m.* *(b)* (Table)-c., nappe *f.* **To lay the c.,** (i) mettre la nappe; (ii) mettre, dresser, le couvert. *(c)* Tapis (de billard). *(d)* Th: Toile (de décor). *S.a.* FLOOR-CLOTH, TEA-CLOTH, TRAY-CLOTH. **3.** *F:* **The c.,** (i) l'habit *m* ecclésiastique; (ii) le clergé. **'cloth-hall,** *s.* A: Halle *f* aux draps. **'cloth-maker,** *s.* Fabricant *m* de drap; drapier *m.*

clothe [klouð], *v.tr.* *(p.t. & p.p.* clad [klad] *or* clothed [klouðd]) Vêtir, revêtir, habiller (in, with, de). **Warmly clad,** chaudement vêtu. **Wall clad with ivy,** mur revêtu, tapissé, de lierre. *S.a.* IRONCLAD. **clothing,** *s.* **1.** Action *f* de vêtir ou de se vêtir. **The c. trade,** l'industrie *f* du vêtement, l'industrie vestimentaire. **2.** Coll. Habillement *m*; vêtements *mpl.*

clothes [klouðz], *s.pl.* **1.** Vêtements *m*, habits *m*, effets *m.* **Suit of c.,** complet *m.* **In one's best c.,** dans ses habits de cérémonie, *(of women)* en toilette *f*; *F:* endimanché. **To put on, take off, one's c.,** s'habiller, se vêtir; se déshabiller, se dévêtir. *S.a.* LONG-CLOTHES, MOTH 1, READY-MADE, SUNDAY, SWADDLING-CLOTHES. **2.** Linge *m.* **Soiled c.,** linge sale. **3.** = BED-CLOTHES. **'clothes-basket,** *s.* Panier *m* au linge (sale). **'clothes-brush,** *s.* Brosse *f* à habits. **'clothes-horse,** *s.* Séchoir *m.* **'clothes-line,** *s.* Corde *f* à (étendre le) linge; étendoir *m.* **'clothes-peg,** U.S: -pin, *s.* Pince *f* à linge. **'clothes-press,** *s.* Armoire *f* à linge. **'clothes-prop,** *s.* Perche *f* d'étendoir. **'clothes-rack,** *s.* Porte-habit(s) *m.inv.*

clothier ['klouðiər], *s.* *(a)* Drapier *m.* *(b)* Marchand *m* de confections.

cloud¹ [klaud], *s.* **1.** Nuage *m*; *Poet:* nuée *f*, nue *f.* **To be in the clouds,** être dans les nuages. *(Of stranger, etc.)* **To drop from the clouds,** tomber des nues. *Prov:* **Every c. has a silver lining,** après la pluie le beau temps. **To be under a c.,** être en défaveur; être l'objet de soupçons. **2.** Nuage, voile *m* (de fumée, de poussière). **Under the c. of night,** sous le voile de la nuit. **3.** *(In liquid)* Nuage, turbidité *f*; *(on glass)* buée *f.* **4.** Nuée (de sauterelles, de flèches). **5.** *Ph:* **C. chamber,** chambre d'ionisation *f.* **'cloudburst,** *s.* Trombe *f*; rafale *f* de pluie. **'cloud-cover,** *s.* Nébulosité *f.* **'cloud-'cuckoo-land,** *s.* Pays *m* de cocagne.

cloud². **1.** *v.tr.* Couvrir, voiler, obscurcir (le ciel); troubler (un liquide); couvrir (une vitre) de buée; ternir (un miroir). **To c. s.o.'s mind,** troubler, obscurcir, la raison de qn. **To c. the issue,** embrouiller la question. **2.** *v.i.* *(Of sky)* **To c.** (up, over), se couvrir, se voiler, de nuages, s'ennuager. **His brow clouded (over),** son front s'assombrit. **clouded,** *a.* (Ciel) couvert (de nuages); (verre) embué, couvert de buée; (liquide) trouble.

cloudiness ['klaudinis], *s.* **1.** Aspect nuageux (du ciel). **2.** Turbidité *f* (d'un liquide).

cloudless ['klaudlis], *a.* (Ciel) sans nuages.

cloudy ['klaudi], *a.* **1.** (Temps) couvert; (ciel) nuageux, assombri. **2.** (Liquide) trouble. **C. ideas,** idées fumeuses, nébuleuses. **3.** *Lap:* Jardineux, -euse. **Ravin.**

clough [klʌf], *s.* Ravin *m*, gorge *f.*

clout¹ [klaut], *s.* **1.** *A: & Dial:* (a) Chiffon *m,* linge *m,* torchon *m.* (b) Vêtement *m.* *Prov:* Ne'er cast a c. **till May be out** = en avril ne quitte pas un fil. **3.** *F:* Beigne *f,* claque *f,* taloche *f* (sur la tête).

clout², *v.tr.* **1.** *A. & Dial:* Rapiécer, rapetasser (un viel habit). **2.** *F:* **To c. s.o. on the head,** flanquer une taloche, *P:* une beigne, à qn.

clove¹ [klouv]. *See* CLEAVE¹.

clove², *s.* **C. of garlic,** gousse *f* d'ail.

clove³, *s.* **1.** Clou *m* de girofle. **C.-tree,** giroflier *m.* **2.** *Bot:* **C.-pink,** œillet *m* des fleuristes.

clove-hitch ['klouv'hitʃ], *s.* *Nau:* Demi-clefs *fpl* à capeler.

cloven [klouv(ə)n]. *See* CLEAVE¹. **cloven-'footed, -'hoofed,** *a.* *Z:* Fissipède; au pied fourchu.

clover ['klouvər], *s.* *Bot:* Trèfle *m;* *F:* lupinelle *f.* **Four-leaved c.,** trèfle à quatre feuilles. *F:* **To be, to live (like pigs) in c.,** être, vivre, comme un coq en pâte. **'clover-leaf,** *s.* Feuille *f* de trèfle. *Civ.E:* **C.-l. intersection,** croisement *m* en trèfle.

clown¹ [klaun], *s.* **1.** *A:* Paysan *m.* **2.** Rustre *m,* manant *m.* **3.** *Th:* (a) Bouffon *m,* paillasse *m,* pitre *m.* (b) Clown *m* (de cirque).

clown², *v.i.* Faire le clown, le pitre.

clownery ['klaunəri], *s.* Bouffonnerie *f.*

clownish ['klauniʃ], *a.* **1.** *A:* Campagnard, agreste. **2.** (a) Gauche, empoté. (b) Grossier; mal élevé. **3.** Clownesque. **-ly,** *adv.* **1.** Gauchement; d'un air empoté. **2.** Grossièrement.

cloy [klɔi], *v.tr.* *(Of food)* Rassasier; écœurer. **cloying,** *a.* Rassasiant, affadissant.

club¹ [klʌb], *s.* **1.** (a) Massue *f,* gourdin *m,* assommoir *m.* *Gym:* **Indian c.,** mil *m.* (b) *Golf:* Crosse *f,* club *m.* **2.** *Cards:* Trèfle *m.* **3.** (a) Club *m* (politique, littéraire, etc.). **C. chair,** fauteuil *m* club. (b) **Literary c.,** cercle *m,* cénacle *m,* littéraire. (c) **Association f,** société *f,* club. **Youth c.,** foyer *m* des jeunes. **Tennis c.,** club de tennis. **'club-foot,** *s.* Pied bot *m.* **'club-footed,** *a.* (Qui a le) pied bot. **'club-house,** *s.* *Sp:* Pavillon *m.* **'club-root,** *s.* *Hort:* Hernie *f* (d'un chou, etc.).

club², *v.* (clubbed) **1.** *v.tr.* Frapper (qn) avec une massue, avec un gourdin; matraquer (qn). **To c. s.o. to death,** assommer qn à coups de gourdin. **2.** *v.tr.* **To c. one's resources (together),** mettre ses ressources en commun; faire bourse commune. **3.** *v.i.* (a) Se réunir, s'associer (avec d'autres pour faire qch.). (b) **To c. together,** se cotiser; mettre son argent en commun.

cluck¹ [klʌk], *s.* *(Of hen)* Gloussement *m.*

cluck², *v.i.* (a) *(Of hen)* Glousser. (b) *F:* Claquer la langue. **clucking,** *s.* Gloussement *m.*

clue [klu:], *s.* **1.** = CLEW¹ 1, 2. **2.** Indication *f,* indice *m.* **To get, find, the c. to sth.,** trouver, découvrir, la clef de qch., le fin mot. **To give s.o. a c.,** mettre qn sur la voie, sur la piste. **The clues of a cross-word puzzle,** les définitions *f. F:* **I haven't a c.,** je n'en sais rien. *F:* **He hasn't a c.,** il ne sait rien de rien, il ne sait jamais rien, il n'en a pas la moindre idée.

clueless ['klu:lis], *a.* *F:* **He's quite c.,** il ne sait jamais rien.

clump¹ [klʌmp], *s.* **1.** (a) Bloc *m,* masse *f* (de bois, d'argile). (b) Groupe *m,* bouquet *m* (d'arbres); massif *m* (de fleurs). **2.** Pas lourd.

clump², *v.i.* **1.** Se grouper en masse compacte. **2.** **To c. (about),** marcher lourdement.

clumsiness ['klʌmzinis], *s.* Maladresse *f,* gaucherie *f.*

---

clumsy ['klʌmzi], *a.* **1.** Maladroit, malhabile, gauche. **2.** *(Of shape)* Lourd, informe. **-ily,** *adv.* Maladroitement, gauchement.

clung. *See* CLING.

cluster¹ ['klʌstər], *s.* Bouquet *m* (de fleurs); massif *m,* groupe *m* (d'arbres); grappe *f* (de raisins); nœud *m* (de diamants); amas *m* (d'étoiles); agglomération *f* (d'îles).

cluster². **1.** *v.tr.* Grouper; rassembler en groupes. **2.** *v.i.* **To c. round s.o., sth.,** se grouper, se rassembler, autour de qn, de qch. *(Of particles, etc.)* **To c. together,** s'agglomérer. **clustered,** *a.* **Heavy-c. branch,** branche grappue, lourdement chargée. *Arch:* **C. columns,** colonnes en faisceau.

clutch¹ [klʌtʃ], *s.* **1.** (a) Griffe *f* (d'un animal); serre *f* (d'un oiseau de proie). **To be in s.o.'s clutches,** dans les griffes de qn. **To fall into s.o.'s clutches,** tomber sous la patte de qn. **To escape from s.o.'s clutches,** se tirer des pattes de qn. (b) **To make a c. at sth.,** tâcher de saisir qch. **2.** *Mec.E:* (Manchon *m* d')embrayage *m.* *Aut:* **Single-plate c.,** embrayage à plateau, par disque unique. **Multiple-disc c.,** embrayage à disques. **Automatic c.,** autodébrayage *m.* **To let in the c.,** embrayer. **To disengage, put out, the c.,** débrayer. **'clutch-disc, -plate,** *s.* Disque *m* d'embrayage. **'clutch-housing,** *s.* Carter *m* d'embrayage.

clutch², *v.tr. & ind.tr.* Saisir, empoigner, étreindre. **To c. sth. with both hands,** saisir qch. à deux mains. **To c. at sth., to c. hold of sth.,** se raccrocher, s'agripper, à qch. **To c. at every straw,** se raccrocher à tout. **To c. at shadows,** essayer de saisir des ombres.

clutch³, *s.* Couvée *f* (d'œufs).

clutter¹ ['klʌtər], *s.* Encombrement *m,* mélimélo *m,* confusion *f;* (em)brouillamini *m.*

clutter². **1.** *v.i.* = CLATTER². **2.** *v.tr.* **To c. up a room,** encombrer une pièce (with, de). **Everything is cluttered up,** tout est en pagaille.

coach¹ [koutʃ], *s.* **1.** (a) *A:* Carrosse *m* ou coche *m.* **C. and six,** carrosse à six chevaux. (b) *(Auto)* car *m.* **C. station,** gare routière. **2.** *Rail:* Voiture *f,* wagon *m.* **3.** (a) *Sch:* Professeur *m* qui donne des leçons particulières (pour préparer à un examen); répétiteur *m.* (b) *Sp:* Entraîneur *m.* **'coach-builder,** *s.* Carrossier *m.* **'coach-building,** *s.* Carrosserie *f.* **'coach-horse,** *s.* **1.** Cheval *m* de carrosse. **2.** *Ent:* **Devil's c.-h.,** staphylin *m.* **'coach-house,** *s.* Remise *f.* **'coach-work,** *s.* Carrosserie *f.*

coach², *v.tr.* (a) *Sch:* Donner des leçons particulières à (qn); *F:* chauffer (qn). *Th:* **To c. s.o. in a part,** faire répéter son rôle à qn. (b) *Sp:* Entraîner (une équipe). **coaching,** *s.* **1. The old c. days,** le temps où l'on voyageait en diligence. **2.** (a) *Sch:* Répétitions *fpl.* **To give private c.,** donner des répétitions. (b) *Sp:* Entraînement *m* (de l'équipe).

coachman, *pl.* **-men** ['koutʃmən], *s.m.* Cocher.

coadjutor [kou'ædʒuːtər], *s.* Aide *m,* collègue *m.* *Ecc:* Coadjuteur *m.*

co-administrator, -trix [ˌkouəd'ministreitər, -triks], *s.* *Com: etc:* Cogérant, -ante.

coagulable [kou'ægjuləbl], *a.* Coagulable.

coagulant [kou'ægjulənt], *s.* Coagulant *m.*

coagulate [kou'ægjuleit]. **1.** *v.tr.* Coaguler, figer; cailler (le lait). **2.** *v.i.* Se coaguler, se figer; *(of milk)* se cailler.

coagulation [kouˌægjuˈleiʃ(ə)n], *s.* Coagulation *f,* figement *m.*

coal¹ [koul], *s.* (a) Charbon *m* (de terre); houille *f.* **Bituminous c.,** houille grasse. **Brown c.,** lignite *m.* **C. industry,** industrie houillère. (b) Morceau *m* de charbon. **Live coals,** braise *f;* charbons ardents. **To carry coals to Newcastle,** porter de l'eau à la rivière, à la mer. **To heap coals of fire on s.o.'s head,** faire repentir qn de son ingratitude, sa méchanceté. *F:* **To haul s.o. over the coals,** réprimander, semoncer, qn. **'coal-barge,** *s.* Chaland *m* à charbon. **'coal-bearing,** *a.* Carbonifère; houiller, -ère. **'coal-black,** *a.* Noir comme du charbon. **'coal bunker,** *s.* *Dom.Ec:* Coffre *m* à charbon. **'coal-cellar,** *s.* Cave *f* à charbon. **'coal-face,** *s.* Taille *f.* **'coal(-)field,** *s.* *Min:* Bassin houiller. **'coal-gas,** *s.* Gaz *m* de houille. **'coal-heaver,** *s.* Porteur *m,* coltineur *m,* de charbon; *(from ship)* déchargeur *m.* **'coal-**

hole, s. Cave f, réduit m, à charbon. **'coal-merchant,** s. 1. Négociant m en charbon. 2. Marchand m de charbon; charbonnier m. **'coal-mine,** s. Mine f de houille; houillère f. **'coal-miner,** s. (Ouvrier) mineur m, houilleur. **'coal-mining,** s. Exploitation f de la houille; charbonnage m. **'coal-oil,** s. U.S: Ch: etc: 1. Huile minérale. 2. Pétrole m (lampant). **'coal-pit,** s. (Puits m de) mine f de houille. **'coal-scuttle,** s. Seau m à charbon. **'coal-seam,** s. Couche f de houille. **'coal-shovel, 'coal-scoop,** s. Pelle f à charbon. **'coal-'tar,** s. Goudron m (de houille). **'coal-tit,** s. Orn: Mésange charbonnière.

coal², v.tr. O: Approvisionner (un navire) de charbon. To c. **ship,** abs. to c., faire le charbon. **coaling,** s. Nau: Charbonnage m.

coalesce [ˌkouə'les], v.i. 1. (a) S'unir; se fondre (ensemble). (b) Ch: Se combiner. 2. (Of parties, etc.) Fusionner. **coalescing,** s. 1. Union f, coalescence f. 2. Fusion f, fusionnement m (de partis).

coalescence [ˌkouə'lesəns], s. (a) Coalescence f, fusion f. (b) Ch: Combinaison f.

coalfish ['koulfiʃ], F: **coalie** ['kouli], s. Ich: Colin m.

coalite ['koulait], s. R.t.m: Semi-coke m; coalite f.

coalition [ˌkouə'liʃ(ə)n], s. Coalition f. Pol: The left wing c., le cartel, le bloc, des Gauches.

coalman, pl. -men ['koulmən], s.m. Marchand m. de charbon.

coarse [kɔːs], a. 1. Grossier, -ière, vulgaire. C. **laugh,** rire brutal; gros rire. C. **voice,** voix commune. C. **words,** mots grossiers; grossièretés f. 2. (a) (Of material) Gros, f grosse, grossier, rude. To have a c. **skin,** avoir la peau rude. (b) (Of food) Grossier. **-ly,** adv. Grossièrement. **'coarse-'cut,** a. (Tabac) haché gros. **'coarse-'featured,** a. Aux traits grossiers, épais. **'coarse-fibred, -grained,** a. A gros grain(s); à grain grossier; (of wood) à gros grain. **'coarse-'minded,** a. A l'esprit grossier.

coarsen ['kɔːsn]. 1. v.tr. Rendre plus grossier, plus rude. 2. v.i. Devenir plus grossier; (of features) s'épaissir.

coarseness ['kɔːsnis], s. 1. Grossièreté f, brutalité f (des manières, etc.). 2. Rudesse f (de la peau); grosseur f de fil (d'une étoffe); gros grain (de la pierre, du bois).

coast¹ [koust], s. 1. Côte f, rivage m; littoral m. From c. to c., d'une mer à l'autre. 2. Descente f (en toboggan); Cy: descente en roue libre. **'coast(-)guard,** s. 1. Garde-côte m, pl. gardes -côte. 2. C.-g. **path,** sentier douanier.

coast², v.i. & tr. 1. Nau: (a) To c. **(along),** suivre la côte; côtoyer le rivage. (b) Nau: Caboter. 2. To c. (down a hill), descendre en toboggan; Cy: descendre en roue libre; Aut: descendre (une côte) le moteur débrayé. **coasting,** s. 1. (a) Navigation côtière. (b) Cabotage m. C. **vessel,** caboteur m. 2. (a) Cy: Aut: Descente f de côte en roue libre. (b) Aut: Marche f au débrayé.

coastal ['koust(ə)l], a. Côtier, -ière; littoral. C. **navigation,** navigation côtière; cabotage m. C. **defence,** défense côtière. C. **defence ship,** navire m garde-côte.

coaster ['koustər], s. 1. (Of pers. or ship) Caboteur m. 2. Dessous m de bouteille, de carafe.

coastline ['koustlain], s. Littoral m.

coastwise ['koustwaiz]. 1. adv. Le long de la côte. 2. a. Côtier. C. **trade,** commerce caboteur.

coat¹ [kout], s. 1. (a) (For men) Veste f; veston m. To **take off one's c.,** F: tomber la veste. **Dress c.,** habit (à queue); frac m. **Morning c., jacquette** f. **(Over)c., (top-)c.,** pardessus m. Arm: **C. of mail,** cotte f de mailles. To cut one's c. **according to one's cloth,** subordonner ses dépenses à son revenu. (b) (For women) (short) Jaquette f. (long) manteau m. **House c.,** robe f d'intérieur, déshabillé m. (c) Her: **C. armour,** cotte d'armes. **C. of arms,** armes fpl, armoiries fpl; écusson m. 2. Robe f (d'un chien, d'un cheval); pelage m (d'un renard, d'un cerf, d'un fauve). 3. (a) Couche f, application f (de peinture). **First c.,** couche de teinte, de finition. (b) Anat: Paroi f (de l'estomac, du crâne). **'coat-hanger,** s. Cintre m; porte-vêtements m inv. **'coat-hook, -peg,** s. Patère f. **'coat-rack,** s. Portemanteau m.

coat², v.tr. Enduire (sth. with paint, tar, etc., qch. de peinture, de goudron, etc.). El.E: To c. **a cable,** revêtir, couvrir, armer, un câble (with, de). Pharm: To c. **a pill,** dragéifier une pilule. Cu: To c. **sth. with chocolate, with yolk of egg,** enrober qch. de chocolat, dorer qch. au jaune d'œuf. **coated,** a. Enduit, couvert, recouvert, enrobé (with, de). C. **tongue,** langue chargée, pâteuse. C. **paper,** papier couché. **coating,** s. 1. Enduisage m. 2. Enduit m, revêtement m, couche f (de peinture, etc.). Anat: Paroi f (de l'estomac). Const: **Rough c.** (of plaster), crépi m. 3. Com: Tissu m pour pardessus.

coatee ['koutiː], s. Jaquette courte.

co-author ['kou'ɔːθər], s. Coauteur m.

coax [kouks], v.tr. Cajoler, enjôler, câliner. To c. **s.o. into doing sth.,** faire faire qch. à qn à force de cajoleries. To c. **sth. out of s.o.,** obtenir qch. de qn en le cajolant. **coaxing¹,** a. Câlin, cajoleur, -euse. **-ly,** adv. D'un ton cajoleur. **coaxing²,** s. Cajolerie f, enjôlement m.

coaxer ['kouksər], s. Cajoleur, -euse; enjôleur, -euse; câlin, -e.

cob¹ [kɔb], s. 1. (Horse) Cob m, bidet m. 2. C. (**-swan**), cygne m mâle. 3. C.(**-nut**), grosse noisette. 4. (Corn-)c., épi m de maïs. 5. C.(**-coal**), cobs, gaillette f, gailletin m.

cob², s. Const: Pisé m, torchis m.

cobalt ['koubɔːlt], s. Ch: Cobalt m. C. **blue,** cobalt d'outremer; bleu de cobalt. Mil: C. **bomb,** bombe f au cobalt.

cobber ['kɔbər], s. F: Austr: Camarade m, copain m.

cobble¹ ['kɔbl], s. 1. C.(**-stone**), galet m, caillou m (de chaussée). 2. pl. (Charbon m en) gaillette(s) f(pl).

cobble², v.tr. Paver en cailloutis.

cobble³, v.tr. Rapetasser (des vêtements, des souliers, etc.).

cobbler ['kɔblər], s. Cordonnier m (qui fait les raccommodages). **'cobbler's 'wax,** s. Poix f de cordonnier.

cobra ['koubrə], s. Rept: Cobra m; serpent m à lunettes.

cobweb ['kɔbweb], s. 1. Toile f d'araignée. To blow away the cobwebs, prendre l'air; se rafraîchir les idées. 2. Fil m d'araignée.

coca ['koukə], s. Bot: Coca m or f.

cocaine [ko'kein], s. Pharm: Cocaïne f. C.-**addict,** cocaïnomane mf.

coccyx ['kɔksiks], s. Anat: Coccyx m.

Cochin-China [kɔtʃin'tʃainə]. Pr.n. Geog: La Cochinchine.

cochineal ['kɔtʃiniːl], s. Dy: Ent: Cochenille f. Bot: C.-**fig, -cactus,** cochenillier m, nopal m.

cock¹ [kɔk], s. 1. (a) Coq m. As **bold as a c. on his own dunghill,** hardi comme un coq sur son fumier. The c. **of the walk,** of **the roost,** le coq du village, de la paroisse. P: **Old c.!** mon vieux! F: C.-**and-bull story,** histoire à dormir debout. (b) C.-**bird,** oiseau m mâle. C. **lobster,** homard m mâle. 2. (a) Robinet m. Nau: **Sea-c.,** robinet de prise d'eau à la mer. (b) Sm.a: Chien m (de fusil). At **full c.,** au cran d'armé. S.a. HALF-COCK. **'cock-a-doodle-'doo!** Cocorico! **'cock-a-'hoop,** a. & adv. (En) jubilant; triomphant, exultant. **'cock-crow,** s. At c.-crow, au (premier) chant du coq; à l'aube. **'cock-fight,** s. Combat m de coqs. **'cock-loft,** s. Grenier m. **'cock-shy,** s. 1. Coup visé. To have a c.-s. at sth., lancer une pierre, etc., à, contre, qch. 2. Jeu m de massacre. **cock-'sure,** a. Sûr de soi; outrecuidant. To be c.-s. **of, about, sth.,** n'avoir aucun doute sur qch. **cock-'sureness,** s. Outrecuidance f.

cock², v.tr. 1. (a) To c. **one's eye at s.o.,** lancer une œillade à qn; regarder qn de côté. (b) To c. **its, one's ears,** (of animal) dresser les oreilles; F: (of pers.) dresser l'oreille. To c. **one's little finger,** dresser le petit doigt. 2. To c. **one's hat,** (i) mettre son chapeau de travers, sur l'oreille; (ii) relever, retrousser, son chapeau. **Cocked hat,** (i) chapeau à cornes; (two-pointed) bicorne m; (three-pointed) tricorne m. F: To **knock s.o. into a cocked hat,** (i) battre qn à plates coutures; (ii) abasourdir qn. 3. To c. **a gun,** armer un fusil.

cock³, s. Agr: Meulon m, meule f (de foin).

cockade [kə'keid], s. Cocarde f.

cockatoo [ˌkɔkə'tuː], *s. Orn:* Cacatoès *m*, cacatois *m*.

cockatrice ['kɔkətrais], *s. Myth:* Basilic *m*.

cockchafer ['kɔktʃeifər], *s. Ent:* Hanneton *m*.

cocker ['kɔkər], *s.* **C. (spaniel)**, (épagneul) cocker *m*.

cockerel ['kɔk(ə)r(ə)l], *s.* Jeune coq.

cock-eyed ['kɔkaid], *a. F:* 1. Qui louche. 2. De biais, de travers. **Cock-eyed story**, histoire *f* à dormir debout.

cockiness ['kɔkinis], *s. F:* Toupet *m*, suffisance *f*.

cockle¹ ['kɔkl], *s.* 1. *Bot:* (Corn-)c., nielle *f* des champs, des blés. 2. *Agr:* (*Disease*) Nielle.

cockle², *s.* (*a*) *Moll:* Coque *f*, clovisse *f*. (*b*) *Hist:* Coquille *f* de pèlerin. (*c*) *A:* **Cockles of the heart**, le cœur. *S.a.* WARM³ 1. '**cockle-shell**, *s.* 1. Bucarde *f*, coque *f*. 2. *F:* (*Boat*) Coquille *f* de noix.

cockle³. 1. *v.tr.* (Re)coquiller (une feuille de papier); faire goder (une étoffe). 2. *v.i.* Se recroqueviller; (*of paper*) (se) gondoler; se crisper; (*of tissue*) goder, coquiller. **cockling¹**, *s.* Gondolement *m*, gondolage *m*.

cockling² ['kɔkliŋ], *s.* La pêche aux coquillages.

cockney ['kɔkni], *a. & s.* Londonien, -ienne (des quartiers populaires de l'est de Londres). **C. accent**, accent *m* populaire (de Londres).

cockneyism ['kɔkniizm], *s.* Locution *f*, ou particularité *f* de prononciation populaire propre aux Londoniens.

cockpit ['kɔkpit], *s.* 1. Arène *f*, parc *m*, de combats de coqs. 2. *Navy: A:* Poste *m* des blessés. 3. *Av:* Carlingue *f*; poste du pilote; cockpit *m*.

cockroach ['kɔkroutʃ], *s. Ent:* Blatte *f*; *F:* cafard *m*.

cockscomb ['kɔkskoum], *s.* 1. Crête *f* de coq. 2. *Bot:* Célosie *f* à crête(s); crête-de-coq *f*. 3. = COXCOMB.

cockspur ['kɔkspəːr], *s.* Ergot *m* de coq.

cocktail ['kɔkteil], *s.* (*Drink*) Cocktail *m*. **C. party**, cocktail *m*. **C. snack**, amuse-gueule *m*, *pl.* amuse-gueules.

cocky ['kɔki], *a. F:* Suffisant, outrecuidant. **-ily**, *adv.* Effrontément; avec suffisance.

cocoa ['koukou], *s.* 1. Cacao *m*. 2. **C.-tree**, cacaotier *m*, cacaoyer *m*. '**cocoa-bean**, *s.* Graine *f*, fève *f*, de cacao. '**cocoa-nib**, *s.* Graine *f* de cacao décortiquée.

coconut ['koukənʌt], *s.* 1. (Noix *f* de) coco *m*. **C. milk**, eau *f*, lait *m*, de coco. *Cu:* **Desiccated c.**, noix de coco déshydratée. **C. fibre**, fibre *f* de coco; coir *m*. **C. oil**, huile *f* de coprah. **C. matting**, (i) tapis végétal; (ii) (*doormat*) tapis-brosse *m*, *pl.* tapis-brosses. **C. shy**, jeu *m* de massacre. 2. **C. palm**, cocotier *m*. **C. plantation**, cocoteraie *f*.

cocoon¹ [kə'kuːn], *s.* Cocon *m* (de ver à soie, etc.).

cocoon², *v.i.* (*Of caterpillar*) Coconner; filer son cocon.

cod¹ [kɔd], *s.* **C.(-fish)**, morue *f*. **Fresh c.**, cabillaud, *m*. **Dried c.**, morue sèche. '**cod-bank**, *s. Fish:* Banc *m* de morues. '**cod-fisher**, *s.* Morutier *m*. '**cod-fishing**, *s.* Pêche *f* de la morue. '**cod-liver-oil**, *s. Pharm:* Huile *f* de foie de morue.

cod², *v.tr. & i.* (**codded**) *A: P:* Tromper, mettre (qn) dedans.

coddle ['kɔdl], *v.tr.* Gâter, choyer; élever (qn) dans le coton, dans la ouate. **To c. oneself**, s'écouter; se dorloter; se mijoter.

code¹ [koud], *s.* 1. Code *m*. **The highway c.**, le code de la route. 2. (*a*) *Tg: etc:* Telegraphic c., code télégraphique. **C. word**, mot convenu. **C. letter**, indicatif littéral. (*b*) (*Secret*) Chiffre *m*. **To write a dispatch in c.**, chiffrer une dépêche. **C. book**, dictionnaire chiffré.

code², *v.tr.* 1. Coder (une dépêche). 2. Mettre en chiffre, chiffrer (une dépêche).

codeine ['koudiːn], *s. Pharm:* Codéine *f*.

codex, *pl.* **-ices** ['koudeks, -isiːz], *s.* 1. Manuscrit (ancien). 2. *Pharm:* Codex *m*.

codger ['kɔdʒər], *s. F:* Type *m*. **Old c.**, vieux bonhomme. **Funny old c.**, drôle de type, drôle de coco *m*.

codicil ['kɔdisil], *s.* Codicille *m* (d'un testament); avenant *m* (d'un traité).

codification [ˌkoudifi'keiʃ(ə)n], *s.* Codification *f*.

codify ['koudifai], *v.tr.* Codifier.

co-director [ˌkoudi'rektər], *s.* Codirecteur *m*; co-administrateur *m*.

codlin(g) ['kɔdlin, -iŋ], *s.* Pomme *f* à cuire.

codling ['kɔdliŋ], *s. Ich:* Jeune morue *f*.

co-education ['kou,edju'keiʃ(ə)n], *s.* Coéducation *f*.

co-educational ['koued ju'keiʃ(ə)nl], *a.* Coéducationnel, -elle. **Co-educational school**, école mixte.

coefficient [ˌkoui'ifiʃənt], *s.* Coefficient *m*. *Mec.E:* **C. of safety**, facteur *m* de sûreté, de sécurité.

cœlacanth ['siːləkænθ], *s. Ich:* Cœlacanthe *m*.

Cœlenterata [siːˌlentə'reitə], *s.pl. Z:* Cœlentérés *m*.

cœnobite, ['siːnəbait], *s.* Cénobite *m*.

coerce [kou'əːs], *v.tr.* Forcer, contraindre (**s.o. into doing sth.**, qn à faire qch.).

coercible [kou'əːsibl], *a.* 1. (*Of pers.*) Contraignable. 2. (*Of gas*) Coercible.

coercion [kou'əːʃ(ə)n], *s.* Coercition *f*, contrainte *f*. **To act under c.**, agir par contrainte; agir à son corps défendant.

coercive [kou'əːsiv], *a.* Coercitif, -ive; *Jur:* coactif, -ive. **-ly**, *adv.* Par la force, par contrainte.

coeternal [kou'iːtəːnl], *a.* Coéternel.

coeval [kou'iːv(ə)l]. 1. *a.* **C. with sth.**, contemporain de qch.; de l'âge de qch. 2. *s.* Contemporain, -aine.

co-executor, -trix ['kouig'zekjutər, -triks], *s. Jur:* Coexécuteur, -trice (testamentaire).

coexist ['kouig'zist], *v.i.* Coexister (**with**, avec).

coexistence ['kouig'zistəns], *s.* Coexistence *f*. *Pol:* **Peaceful c.**, coexistence pacifique.

coexistent ['kouig'zistənt], *a.* Coexistant (avec).

coextensive ['kouiks'tensiv], *a.* (i) De même étendue, (ii) de même durée, (**with**, que).

coffee ['kɔfi], *s.* Café *m*. **Black c.**, café noir; (*in Switzerland*) café nature. **White c.**, café au lait, café crème. **Ground c.**, café moulu. **Instant c.**, café soluble. '**coffee-bean**, *s.* Grain *m* de café. '**coffee-break**, *s.* Pause-café *f*, pause *f* du café. '**coffee-burner, -roaster**, *s.* Brûloir *m*. '**coffee-coloured**, *a.* (Couleur) café au lait *inv.* '**coffee-cup**, *s.* Tasse *f* à café. '**coffee-house**, *s. A:* Café *m*. '**coffee-mill**, *s.* Moulin *m* à café. '**coffee-percolator**, *s.* Percolateur *m*; cafetière *f* automatique, cafetière russe. '**coffee-pot**, *s.* Cafetière *f*. '**coffee-room**, *s.* Salle *f* des voyageurs, salle à manger (d'hôtel). **coffee(-)shrub**, *s.* Caféier *m*. '**coffee(-)spoon**, *s.* Cuillère *f* à moka. '**coffee-stall**, *s.* Bar *m*, cantine *f*, de coin de rue (sur roulettes). '**coffee-table**, table *f* de salon.

coffer¹ ['kɔfər], *s.* 1. Coffre *m*. **The coffers of State**, les fonds publics. 2. *Arch:* Caisson *m* (de plafond).

coffer², *v.tr.* 1. *Min:* Coffrer (un puits). 2. Diviser (un plafond) en caissons.

cofferdam ['kɔfədæm], *s. Hyd.E:* Bâtardeau *m*; caisson *m* hydraulique.

coffin ['kɔfin], *s.* 1. Cercueil *m*, bière *f*. 2. *Farr:* Cavité *f* du sabot (d'un cheval).

cog¹ [kɔg], *s. Mec.E:* Dent *f* (d'une roue dentée). **I am only a c. in the machinery**, je ne suis qu'un rouage de la machine. **To slip a c.**, (i) (*of pawl*) glisser sur une dent; (ii) (*of the mind*) avoir un moment d'absence. '**cog-rail**, *s. Rail:* Crémaillère *f*. '**cog-wheel**, *s. Mec.E:* Roue dentée.

cog², *v.* (**cogged**) 1. *v.tr.* Denter, endenter (une roue). 2. *v.i.* (*Of wheels*) S'engrener; encliqueter.

cog³, *v.tr.* Piper (des dés). **Cogged dice**, dés pipés.

cogency ['koudʒənsi], *s.* Force *f*, puissance *f* (d'un argument).

cogent ['koudʒənt], *a.* (Argument) irrésistible; (motif) puissant; (raison) valable. **-ly**, *adv.* Avec force; fortement.

cogitate ['kɔdʒiteit]. 1. *v.i.* Méditer, réfléchir (**upon, over**, sur). 2. *v.tr.* **To c. mischief**, méditer un mauvais coup.

cogitation [ˌkɔdʒi'teiʃ(ə)n], *s.* Réflexion *f*, délibération *f* (**upon, over**, sur).

cognac ['kɔnjæk], *s. Vit: Dist:* Cognac *m*.

cognate ['kɔgneit]. 1. *s. Jur:* Cognat *m*; parent *m*. 2. *a.* **C. (with sth.)**, qui a du rapport (avec qch.); analogue (à qch.). **C. words**, mots congénères, apparentés. **C. accusative**, accusatif de qualification.

cognizance ['kɔgnizəns, *Jur:* 'kɔnizəns], *s.* 1. Connaissance *f. Jur:* **To take c. of sth.**, prendre connaissance de qch. **The child acted without c.**, l'enfant a agi sans discernement. 2. *Jur:* Compétence *f*. **Within the c. of a court**, du ressort d'une cour.

cognizant ['kɔgnizənt, *Jur:* 'kɔnizənt], *a.* **To be c. of a fact**, être instruit d'un fait.

cognomen [kɔg'noumen], s. 1. *Rom.Hist:* Cognomen *m.* 2. (a) Surnom *m,* sobriquet *m.* (b) Nom *m* de famille.

cohabit [kou'hæbit], v.i. (cohabited) Cohabiter.

cohabitation ['kouhæbi'teiʃ(ə)n], s. Cohabitation *f.*

coheir, *f.* -ess ['kou'ɛər, -is], s. Cohéritier, -ière.

cohere [kou'hiər], v.i. (a) (Of whole, of parts) Se tenir ensemble; adhérer. (b) S'agglomérer. (c) (Of argument) Être conséquent; se tenir.

coherer [kou'hiərər], s. *Ph: W.Tel: etc:* Cohéreur *m,* radioconducteur *m.*

coherence, -ency [kou'hiərəns, -ənsi], s. 1. = COHESION. 2. (Of argument, style) Suite *f* (logique); cohérence *f.*

coherent [kou'hiər(ə)nt], a. 1. (Of whole, of parts) Cohérent(s); lié(s) ensemble. 2. (Of argument, etc.) Conséquent, cohérent; (of thinker) qui a de la suite dans ses idées. **-ly,** adv. (Parler) avec cohérence.

cohesion [kou'hi:ʒ(ə)n], s. (a) Cohésion *f;* adhérence *f.* (b) **Attack that lacks c.,** attaque qui manque d'ensemble.

cohesive [kou'hi:siv], a. Cohésif, -ive.

cohesiveness [kou'hi:sivnis], s. Cohésion *f.*

cohort ['kouhɔ:t], s. Cohorte *f.*

coif [kɔif], s. (a) A: Coiffe *f,* béguin *m.* (b) Cornette *f* (de nonne).

coil¹ [kɔil], s. 1. (a) Rouleau *m* (de corde); Nau: glène *f* (de câble). (b) (Coiled tube) Serpentin *m.* 2. (a) Pli *m,* repli *m* (d'un cordage); repli, anneau *m* (d'un serpent). (b) **Coils of smoke,** tourbillons *m* de fumée. (c) El: Enroulement *m,* bobine *f.* **C. winding,** solénoïde *m.*

coil². 1. v.tr. (En)rouler, gléner (un cordage). El: Bobiner (des fils). To **c.** (itself) up, (of snake) s'enrouler, se lover; (of cat) se mettre en rond. **Coiled spring,** ressort en spirale; ressort à boudin. 2. v.i. Serpenter. **coiling,** s. Enroulement *m;* bobinage *m.*

coin¹ [kɔin], s. 1. Pièce *f* de monnaie. 2. *Coll.* Monnaie(s) *f,* numéraire *m,* espèces *fpl.* **Small c.,** monnaie divisionnaire. To **pay in c.** of the realm, payer en espèces. *S.a.* PAY BACK 2.

coin², v.tr. 1. To **c. money,** (i) frapper de la monnaie, battre monnaie; (ii) faire des affaires d'or. 2. Inventer, forger (un mot nouveau).

coinage ['kɔinidʒ], s. 1. (a) Monnayage *m;* frappe *f* (de la monnaie). (b) Invention *f* (d'un mot). 2. (a) Système *m* monétaire (d'un pays). (b) Monnaie(s) *f;* numéraire *m.*

coincide [,kouin'said], v.i. 1. Coïncider (**with,** avec). 2. S'accorder, être d'accord (**with,** avec).

coincidence [kou'insidəns], s. 1. (In space, time) Coïncidence *f.* 2. Coïncidence, rencontre *f,* concours *m* (d'événements).

coincident [kou'insidənt], a. Coïncident; d'accord (**with,** avec).

coincidental [,kouinsi'dent(ə)l], a. (Effet *m*) de coïncidence.

coiner ['kɔinər], s. 1. Monnayeur *m.* 2. Faux monnayeur. 3. Fabricateur *m,* inventeur *m* (d'un mensonge, etc.).

coir ['kɔiər], s. Coir *m;* fibre *f* de coco; bastin *m.* **C. mat,** paillasson *m;* tapis-brosse *m, pl.* tapis-brosses.

coition [kou'iʃən], **coitus** [kou'itəs], s. Coït *m.*

coke¹ [kouk], s. Coke *m.* **C. oven,** four *m* à coke.

coke², v.tr. Cokéfier. **'coking-plant,** s. Ind: Cokerie *f.*

coke³, s. P: (= cocaine) Coco *f.*

coke⁴, s. P: R.t.m: Coca-Cola.

cokernut ['koukənʌt], s. F: = COCONUT.

col [kɔl], s. Geog: Col *m;* (in Pyrences) port *m.*

colander ['kʌləndər], s. Cu: Passoire *f.*

colchicum ['kɔltʃikəm], s. Bot: Colchique *m.*

cold¹ [kould], a. Froid. 1. (a) It is **c.,** il fait froid. Meteor: **C. front,** front froid. To **get, grow, c.,** se refroidir. **C. steel,** l'arme blanche. **Soluble when c.,** soluble à froid. Com: **C. storage,** conservation par le froid. **C. room** (for storage), chambre frigorifique. **C. store,** entrepôt frigorifique. To **give s.o. the c. shoulder,** battre froid à qn. Pol: **The c. war,** la guerre froide. (b) (Of pers.) **To be c., to feel c.,** avoir froid. **My feet are as cold as ice,** j'ai les pieds glacés. F: **To have c. feet,** P: avoir la frousse. 2. **A c. reception,** un accueil froid. **To be c. with s.o., se montrer froid avec qn.** F: **That leaves me c.,** cela ne me fait ni chaud ni froid. F: **To knock s.o. c.,** (i) étendre qn raide (d'un coup); (ii) rendre qn ahuri, stupéfait. 3. Metalw: C.-pressed, pressé à froid. **C. riveting,** rivure à froid. **-ly,** adv. Froidement. **'cold-blooded,** a. 1. (Animal) à sang froid. 2. (Of pers.) Froid, insensible; (of action) prémédité, délibéré. **'cold-'chisel,** s. Ciseau *m* à froid. **'cold(-)'cream,** s. Pharm: Cold-cream *m.* **'cold-drawn,** a. Metalw: Étiré à froid. **'cold-hammer,** v.tr. Écrouir (le fer); battre, marteler, (le fer) à froid. **cold-'hearted,** a. Au cœur froid, sec. **cold-'press,** v.tr. Tex: etc: Catir (le drap), satiner (le drap, le papier) à froid. Metalw: Presser (la tôle, etc.) à froid. **cold-'shoulder,** v.tr. Battre froid à (qn); tourner le dos à (qn); F: snober (qn).

cold², s. 1. Froid *m.* **C. wave,** vague de froid. **C. snap,** courte offensive du froid. F: **To leave s.o. out in the c.,** laisser qn à l'écart. 2. Med: Rhume *m.* **To have a c.,** être enrhumé; avoir un rhume. **C. in the head,** rhume de cerveau. **C. on the chest, chest c.,** rhume de poitrine. **To catch (a) c.,** attraper un rhume; s'enrhumer; prendre froid; P: choper un rhume. F: **You will catch your death of c.,** vous allez attraper la mort par ce froid. **C. in the eye,** coup *m* d'air dans l'œil.

coldish ['kouldiʃ], a. F: Un peu froid; frais, F: frisquet. **It is c.,** il fait frisquet. **C. reception,** accueil plutôt froid.

coldness ['kouldnis], s. 1. Froideur *f;* froidure *f* (du climat). 2. **There is a c. between them,** il y a de la froideur, du froid, entre eux.

Coleoptera [,kɔli'optərə], s.pl. Z: (L'ordre *m* des) coléoptères *m.*

coleslaw ['koulslɔ:], s. U.S: Cu: Salade *f* de chou cru.

colic ['kɔlik], s. Med: Colique *f,* épreintes *fpl.*

Coliseum (the) [ðə'kɔli'siəm], s. Rom.Ant: Le Colisée.

colitis [kə'laitis], s. Med: Côlite *f.*

collaborate [kə'læbəreit], v.i. Collaborer (**with,** avec).

collaboration [kə,læbə'reiʃ(ə)n], s. Collaboration *f;* Pej: collaborationnisme *m.*

collaborationist [kə,læbə'reiʃənist], s. Pol: Hist: Pej: Collaborationniste *mf.*

collaborator [kə'læbəreitər], s. Collaborateur, -trice.

collage [kə'lɑ:ʒ], s. Art: Collage *m.*

collapse¹ [kə'læps], s. 1. (a) Écroulement *m,* effondrement *m;* dégonflement *m* (d'un ballon); débâcle *f* (d'un pays). (b) Mec.E: etc: Gauchissement *m,* flexion *f* (d'une plaque, etc.). (c) Com: Chute *f* (de prix); effondrement (du marché); dégringolade *f* (du franc). 2. Med: Affaissement subit; prostration *f;* collapsus *m.* **C. therapy,** collapsothérapie *f.*

collapse², v.i. 1. (a) S'affaisser, s'écrouler, s'effondrer; (of balloon) se dégonfler; (of pers.) s'effondrer; tomber comme une masse. (b) Mec.E: etc: (Of support, etc.) Gauchir, fléchir. (c) (Of car hood) Se rabattre. (d) (Of prices) S'effondrer. 2. Med: (Of pers.) S'affaisser (subitement). To **c. a lung,** collaber un poumon. **collapsing,** s. Med: Collapsus *m* (du poumon).

collapsible [kə'læpsəbl], a. Pliant, repliable, démontable; escamotable; rabattable.

collar¹ ['kɔlər], s. 1. (a) Col *m* (de robe); collet *m* (de manteau); tour *m* de cou (en fourrure, etc.); collier *m* (d'un ordre, etc.). Lace c., collerette *f.* **Non-detachable** shirt c., col de chemise. **To seize s.o. by the c.,** prendre, saisir, qn au collet. (b) (Detachable) c., faux col. **Soft c.,** col mou, souple. **Stiff c.,** col raide, empesé. **Size in collars,** encolure *f.* 2. Collier (de chien, de cheval). 3. Mec.E: Anneau *m,* collier, collet. **Set c.,** bague *f* d'arrêt, de butée. **'collar-beam,** s. Arch: Const: Entrait retroussé; (between rafters) traversière *f.* **'collar-bone,** s. Clavicule *f.* **'collar-stud,** s. Bouton *m* de col.

collar², v.tr. 1. (a) Colleter (qn); saisir, prendre (qn) au collet. (b) Fb: Arrêter (l'adversaire). **To c. s.o. low,** ceinturer qn. (c) F: Saisir, pincer, mettre la main sur (qn, qch.). 2. Cu: Rouler (de la viande, pour la ficeler); mettre (du poisson, etc.) en roulades.

collate [kə'leit], v.tr. Collationner, conférer (un texte) (**with,** avec).

collateral [kɔ'læt(ə)r(ə)l], a. 1. Collatéral, -aux. 2. (Of knowledge) Concomitant, additionnel. Com: Jur: C. security, garantie additionnelle, accessoire; nantissement m subsidiaire. -ally, adv. 1. Parallèlement (with, à). 2. Indirectement, subsidiairement.

collation [kɔ'leiʃ(ə)n], s. 1. Collation f, confrontation f (de textes). 2. Collation, goûter m. Cold c., repas froid. 3. Ecc: Collation (d'un bénéfice).

collator [kɔ'leitər], s. 1. (a) The c. of two texts, celui qui collationne deux textes. (b) Bookb: Collateur m (de feuillets). 2. Ecc: Collateur (d'un bénéfice).

colleague ['kɔliːg], s. Collègue mf; confrère m.

collect¹ ['kɔlekt], s. Ecc: (Prayer) Collecte f.

collect² [kɔ'lekt]. 1. v.tr. (a) Rassembler (la foule); assembler (des matériaux); relever (les blessés); amasser (une fortune); recueillir (des données). Civ.E: To c. the water, capter, réunir, les eaux. (b) Collectionner (des timbres, etc.). (c) Percevoir, lever (les impôts); toucher (une traite). To c. a debt, faire rentrer une créance; faire un recouvrement. Abs. To c. for charity, quêter, faire la quête, pour une œuvre de bienfaisance. Collecting-box, tronc m (d'église, de quêteur). (d) Aller chercher (sa valise, etc.). (e) Recueillir, rassembler (ses idées); ramasser (ses forces). To c. oneself, se reprendre. To c. one's thoughts, se recueillir. 2. v.i. (Of pers.) S'assembler, se rassembler; (of thgs) s'amasser. collected, a. (a) Recueilli. (b) (Plein) de sang-froid. -ly, adv. (a) Avec recueillement. (b) Avec calme; avec sang-froid.

collectedness [kɔ'lektidnis], s. 1. Recueillement m. 2. Sang-froid m.

collection [kɔ'lekʃ(ə)n], s. 1. Rassemblement m; relèvement m (des blessés); recouvrement m (d'une somme); perception f (des impôts); encaissement m (d'un billet); levée f (des lettres); enlèvement m, prise f à domicile (de colis); captage m (d'eau, de courant électrique, etc.); collectionnement m (de tableaux, de livres). 2. Ecc: etc: Quête f, collecte f. To take (up) a c., faire la quête. 3. Amas, m assemblage m. 4. Collection f (de papillons, de timbres); recueil m (de proverbes).

collective [kɔ'lektiv], a. Collectif, -ive. Pol.Ec: C. farm, ferme collective. Ind: C. agreement, contrat collectif. C. bargaining = convention collective. -ly, adv. Collectivement; en commun.

collectivism [kɔ'lektivizm], s. Pol.Ec: Collectivisme m.

collectivist [kɔ'lektivist], s. Pol.Ec: Collectiviste m.

collectivity [ˌkɔlek'tiviti], s. Collectivité f.

collectivization [kɔˌlektivai'zeiʃ(ə)n], s. Collectivisation f.

collectivize [kɔ'lektivaiz], v.tr. Collectiviser.

collector [kɔ'lektər], s. 1. (a) Encaisseur m (d'un chèque, d'un billet); quêteur, -euse (d'aumônes); collecteur, -trice (de cotisations). Rail: Ticket-c., contrôleur m. (b) Encaisseur (de la Compagnie du gaz, etc.). Adm: Percepteur m (des contributions directes); receveur m (des contributions indirectes). (c) Collectionneur, -euse. S.a. STAMP-COLLECTOR. 2. (Device) Collecteur (d'huile, etc.). El.E: Current c., prise f de courant.

college ['kɔlidʒ], s. 1. Collège m. Ecc: The Sacred C., le Sacré Collège. Her: The C. of Arms, le collège des hérauts. 2. Sch: (a) = L'université. F: When I was at c., quand j'étais à la faculté. (b) Military, naval, c., école f militaire, navale. (c) College of education = école normale. Agricultural c. = institut m agronomique. (d) = Lycée m. Technical c. = lycée technique. (As Pr.n.) Eton C., le collège d'Eton.

collegiate [kɔ'liːdʒiit], a. Collégial, -aux. C. church, collégiale f.

collet ['kɔlit], s. 1. Douille f (de serrage). 2. Chaton m (de bague); sertissure f.

collide [kɔ'laid], v.i. (Of vehicles, etc.) Se rencontrer, se heurter; entrer en collision; F: s'emboutir. To c. with sth., heurter qch.; Nau: Aborder (un navire).

collie ['kɔli], s. Chien de berger écossais, colley m.

collier ['kɔliər], s. 1. (Pers.) Houilleur m; mineur m (de charbon). 2. Nau: (Navire m) charbonnier m.

colliery ['kɔljəri], s. Houillère f; mine f de houille.

collimator ['kɔlimeitər], s. Opt: Collimateur m.

collision [kɔ'liʒ(ə)n], s. Collision f, rencontre f; tamponnement m (de trains); abordage m (de navires); collision, choc m, conflit m (d'intérêts). Head-on c., collision de plein fouet. To come into c. with . . ., entrer en collision avec (un train, etc.); se heurter à, contre (qn). Atom.Ph: Nuclear c., collision nucléaire.

collodion [kɔ'loudiən], s. Collodion m.

colloid ['kɔlɔid], a. & s. Ch: Colloïde (m).

colloidal [kɔ'lɔidl], a. Ch: Colloïdal, -aux.

collop ['kɔlɔp], s. Tranche f de viande. Scot: Minced collops, hachis m.

colloquial [kɔ'loukwiəl], a. Familier; de (la) conversation; parlé. C. English, l'anglais parlé. -ally, adv. Familièrement.

colloquialism [kɔ'loukwiəlizm], s. Expression familière.

colloquy ['kɔləkwi], s. Colloque m, entretien m.

collotype ['kɔlotaip], s. 1. Phototype m. 2. (Process) Phototypie f; collotypie f.

collusion [kɔ'ljuːʒ(ə)n], s. Collusion f. To act in c. with s.o., agir de complicité, de connivence, avec qn.

collusive [kɔ'ljusiv], a. Collusoire. -ly, adv. Collusoirement.

collywobbles ['kɔliwɔblz], s.pl. F: To have the c., (i) avoir des borborygmes m; (ii) avoir mal au ventre; (iii) avoir la colique.

Colombia [kɔ'lʌmbiə]. Pr.n.Geog: La Colombie.

colon¹ ['koulən], s. Anat: Côlon m.

colon², s. Deux-points m.

colonel ['kəːnl], s. Colonel m. C.'s wife, F: la colonelle. Queen Elizabeth, c.-in-chief of the London Scottish, la reine Elisabeth, colonelle d'honneur des London Scottish.

colonelcy ['kəːnlsi], **colonelship** ['kəːnlʃip], s. Grade m de colonel.

colonial [kɔ'lounjəl], a. & s. Colonial, -aux.

colonialism [kɔ'lounjəlizm], s. Pol: Colonialisme m.

colonialist [kɔ'lounjəlist], a. & s. Pol: Colonialiste (mf); qui soutient le colonialisme.

colonist ['kɔlənist], s. Colon m.

colonization [ˌkɔlənai'zeiʃ(ə)n], s. Colonisation f.

colonize ['kɔlənaiz], v.tr. Coloniser.

colonizer ['kɔlənaizər], s. Colonisateur m.

colonnade [ˌkɔlə'neid], s. Colonnade f.

colony ['kɔləni], s. Colonie f.

colophon ['kɔlɔfən], s. Typ: Chiffre m (de l'éditeur); marque f typographique, colophon m.

Colorado [ˌkɔlə'rɑːdou]. 1. Pr.n. Geog: Le Colorado. 2. Ent: C. beetle, doryphore m.

coloration [ˌkʌlə'reiʃ(ə)n], s. Coloration f; coloris m.

colossal [kɔ'lɔs(ə)l], a. Colossal, -aux; démesuré. -ally, adv, Colossalement, démesurément.

colossus, pl. -i, -uses [kɔ'lɔsəs, -ai, -əsiz], s. Colosse m.

colour¹ ['kʌlər], s. 1. (a) Couleur f. What c. is it? de quelle couleur est-ce? To take the c. out of sth., décolorer qch. The c. problem, le problème du racisme; le racisme. To see things in their true colours, voir les choses comme elles sont. F: I've still to see the c. of his money, je n'ai pas encore vu la couleur de son argent. (b) Art: etc: Coloris m. Primary colours, couleurs primaires, génératrices; Dy: couleurs matrices. Secondary colours, couleurs binaires, composites. 2. (Material) Matière colorante; pigment m. Water c., (i) couleur pour l'aquarelle f; (ii) Art: aquarelle. Oil c., couleur à l'huile. 3. Teint m, couleurs. To lose c., perdre ses couleurs; devenir pâle. To get back one's c., retrouver ses couleurs. To change c., changer de visage. High c., vivacité f de teint. F: To be off c., être pâle; ne pas être dans son assiette. 4. Usu. pl. (a) Couleurs (d'un parti). Nau: Pavillon m. To show, display, one's colours, montrer son pavillon; montrer les couleurs. Hoisting the colours, lever m des couleurs. (Regimental) colours, drapeau m. C. party, garde f du drapeau. Nav: Mus: 'Colours,' (salut) au drapeau. S.a. TROOP² 2. To call s.o. to the colours, appeler qn sous les drapeaux. With colours flying (à) enseignes déployées. F: To pass (an examination) with flying colours, passer haut la main. To sail under false colours, (i) naviguer sous un faux pavillon; (ii) F: se faire passer pour quelqu'un d'autre. F: To stick to one's colours, rester fidèle à ses principes. To show oneself in one's true colours, jeter le masque.

To nail one's colours to the mast, clouer son pavillon. (b) *Turf:* Couleurs (d'un jockey). *Sp: Sch:* **To be awarded one's colours,** recevoir une haute distinction sportive. **5.** (a) **To give, lend, c. to a story,** rendre une histoire vraisemblable; colorer un récit. (b) Prétexte *m*, couleur, fausse apparence. **Under c.** of law, of reason, sous l'apparence de la légalité, du bon sens. **'colour-bar,** s. Ségrégation raciale. **'colour-bearer,** s. *Mil:* Porte-drapeau *m inv.* **'colour-blind,** a. Daltonien, -ienne. **'colour-blindness,** s. Daltonisme *m.* **'colour-line,** s. *U.S:* = COLOUR-BAR. **'colour-pho'tography,** s. Photographie *f* en couleurs. **'colour-print,** s. Reproduction *f* en couleurs. **'colour-sergeant,** s. *Mil:* = Sergent-chef *m* (de la garde du drapeau), *pl.* sergents-chefs.

colour². **1.** v.tr. (a) Colorer; colorier (une carte); enluminer (une gravure). To c. sth. blue, colorer qch. en bleu. (b) Donner de l'éclat à (une description); imager (son style). (c) Présenter (un fait) sous un faux jour; déguiser (un mensonge). **2.** v.i. (a) (*Of thg*) Se colorer. (b) (*Of pers.*) Rougir. **coloured,** a. **1.** Coloré; (*of drawing*) colorié. **C. shirt,** chemise de couleur. **C. person,** personne de couleur. **C. sketch,** croquis en couleurs. **2. Highly c. narrative,** récit coloré. **3.** s. *Dom.Ec: F:* (*Clothes*) **Coloureds,** couleurs *fpl.* **colouring,** s. **1.** Coloration *f*, coloriage *m* (de cartes, etc.). **2.** (a) *Art:* Coloris *m.* (b) Colorant *m.* (c) Teint *m.* **People with high c.,** gens hauts en couleur. **3.** Apparence *f.* To give a false c. to the facts, dénaturer, travestir, les faits.

colourable ['kʌlərəbl], a. **1.** Plausible; (argument) spécieux. **2.** Trompeur, -euse.

colourful ['kʌləful], a. (Ciel, style) coloré; (style) pittoresque. **C. portrait, landscape,** portrait vif, brillant, paysage éclatant. *F:* **What a c. character!** Quel type original, pittoresque!

colourist ['kʌlərist], s. *Lit: Art:* Coloriste *m.*

colourless ['kʌləlis], a. **1.** Sans couleur; incolore. **2.** (a) Terne; (visage) décoloré; (lumière) pâle, falote. (b) **C. style,** style insipide.

colt¹ [koult], s. **1.** Poulain *m.* **2.** *F:* Débutant *m*, novice *m.*

Colt². *Pr.n. Sm.a:* *U.S:* **C. revolver,** (revolver) Colt *m.* **C. pistol,** pistolet automatique.

coltish ['koultiʃ], a. **1.** Sans expérience. **2.** Folâtre.

coltsfoot ['koultsfut], s. *Bot:* Tussilage *m*; *F:* pas-d'âne *m.*

Columbia [kə'lʌmbiə]. *Pr.n. Geog:* **1. British C.,** la Colombie britannique. **2. (District of) C.,** (le District fédéral de) Columbia.

columbine¹ ['kɔləmbain], s. *Bot:* Ancolie *f.*

Columbine². *Pr.n f. Th:* Colombine.

Columbus [kə'lʌmbəs]. *Pr.n.m.* **Christopher C.,** Christophe Colomb.

column ['kɔləm], s. **1.** Colonne *f.* *Anat:* **Spinal c.,** colonne vertébrale. **2.** *Av:* **Control c.,** levier *m* de commande. *Aut:* **Steering c.,** colonne de direction. **3.** *Mil:* **C. of fours,** colonne par quatre. *Pol:* **Fifth c.,** cinquième colonne *f.* **4. Page of two columns,** page de deux colonnes. *Journ:* **The theatrical c.,** le courrier, la rubrique, des théâtres.

columnist ['kɔləmist], s. *Journ:* Journaliste *m*; collaborateur régulier, attitré, d'un journal.

colza ['kɔlzə]. s. *Bot:* Colza *m.*

coma ['koumə], s. *Med:* Coma *m.*

comatose ['koumətous], a. *Med:* (État) comateux; (sommeil) soporeux.

comb¹ [koum], s. **1.** Peigne *m.* **Dressing c.,** démêloir *m.* (Fine) **tooth c.,** peigne fin. To go over sth. with a fine tooth c., passer qch. au peigne fin. **2.** (a) *Tex:* Peigne, carde *f.* (b) *El:* Collecteur *m.* **3.** (a) Crête *f* (de coq). (b) Crête (de vague, etc.). **4.** = HONEY-COMB¹.

comb², s. *F:* To give one's hair a c., donner un coup de peigne à ses cheveux.

comb³. **1.** v.tr. (a) Peigner (les cheveux). To c. one's hair, se peigner. To c. down a horse, étriller un cheval. (b) *Tex:* Peigner, carder (la laine). **2.** v.i. (*Of wave*) Se briser en écumant, déferler. **comb out,** v.tr. **1.** Démêler (les cheveux). **2.** *F:* (a) To c. out a department, (i) éliminer les incapables d'un service; (ii) (*in wartime*) éplucher, ratisser, élaguer, le personnel d'un service (pour trouver des combattants). (b)

(*Of police*) To c. out a district, faire une rafle (de suspects), ratisser un quartier. **'comb(ing) out,** s. *F:* (a) *Mil:* Ratissage (d'une zone). (b) (*Police, etc.*) Rafle *f.* **combing,** s. **1.** (a) Coup *m* de peigne. (b) *Tex:* Peignage *m*, cardage *m.* **2.** *pl.* **Combings,** peignures *f*, démêlures *f.*

combat¹ ['kɔmbæt, 'kɔmbət], s. Combat *m.* *U.S:* **C. fatigue,** psychose *f* traumatique.

combat². **1.** v.i. (**combated**) Combattre (**with, against,** contre). **2.** v.tr. Lutter contre, combattre (une maladie).

combatant ['kɔmbətənt, 'kʌm-], a. & s. Combattant (*m*).

combative ['kɔmbətiv, 'kʌm-], a. Combatif, -ive; agressif, -ive.

comber ['koumər], s. **1.** (a) (*Pers.*) Peigneur, -euse; cardeur, -euse (de laine). (b) (*Machine*) Peigneuse *f.* **2.** Longue lame déferlante.

combination [,kɔmbi'neiʃ(ə)n], s. **1.** Combinaison *f.* (a) **To enter into c. with . . .,** se combiner avec . . . (b) *Ch:* Combiné *m*, mélange *m.* **2.** Association *f* (de personnes); *Pej:* coalition *f.* **3.** *pl.* *Cost:* (A pair of) **combinations,** une combinaison-culotte (en laine). **4.** Chiffre *m* (de la serrure d'un coffre-fort). **5.** (Motorcycle) **c.,** motocyclette *f* à side-car.

combine¹ ['kɔmbain], s. Combinaison financière; entente industrielle; cartel *m*; trust *m*; (*in U.S.S.R.*) combinat *m.* **'combine-'harvester,** s. Moissonneuse-batteuse *f.*

combine² [kəm'bain]. **1.** v.tr. Combiner; allier (des qualités, des mots, etc.) (**with,** à). To c. forces, one's efforts, joindre ses forces, ses efforts. To c. business with pleasure, joindre l'utile à l'agréable. **2.** v.i. (a) (*Of pers.*) S'unir, s'associer (**against,** contre); (*of workers*) se syndiquer. (b) (*Of parties*) Fusionner. (c) *Ch:* (*Of elements*) Se combiner. **combined,** a. **C. efforts,** efforts réunis, conjugués. **C. work,** travail fait en collaboration. *Mec.E:* **C. strength,** résistance composée. **C. operation** (i) *Mil:* opération *f* interarmes; (ii) *Mil: Navy: Av:* opération *f* amphibie. **C. operations school,** école *f* interarmes.

combustibility [kəm,bʌsti'biliti], s. Combustibilité *f.*

combustible [kəm'bʌstibl]. **1.** a. (a) Combustible. (b) *F:* (*Of a crowd, etc.*) Inflammable. **2.** s. (a) Matière *f* inflammable. (b) (*Fuel*) Combustible *m.*

combustion [kəm'bʌstʃ(ə)n], s. Combustion *f.* **Spontaneous c.,** inflammation spontanée; autoallumage *m.* **Internal c. engine,** moteur à explosion, à combustion interne. **Slow-c. stove,** poêle à combustion continue.

come [kʌm], v.i. (*p.t.* **came** [keim]; *p.p.* **come**) **1.** Venir, arriver. To c. to a place, venir, arriver, à un endroit. **He has just c. from Paris,** il arrive de Paris. *F:* **Let 'em all c.!** qu'ils viennent tous! ils seront tous les bienvenus. **He comes this way every week,** il passe par ici tous les huit jours. **Here he comes!** le voilà qui arrive! **Coming!** voilà! on y va! j'y vais! He came to see me yesterday, il est venu me voir hier. **C. to, and, see me tomorrow,** venez me voir, me trouver, demain. To c. for s.o., for sth., venir chercher qn, qch. To c. to s.o., venir trouver qn. **You have c. to the wrong person,** vous vous adressez mal. To c. to the throne, monter sur le trône. To c. to years of discretion, arriver à l'âge de raison. *F:* **What are things coming to?** où allons-nous? To c. and go, aller et venir. To c. to the surface again, remonter sur l'eau. *int.* **C. now!** allons! voyons! **C., c.!** a little silence! allons, allons! un peu de silence! *Prov:* **Easy c. easy go,** l'argent ne lui coûte guère. *F:* **He had it coming to him,** ça lui pendait au nez. (b) **To c. to (oneself),** (i) reprendre connaissance; (ii) recouvrer sa raison; (iii) revenir de ses erreurs; se ressaisir. (c) *F:* **A week c. Tuesday,** il y aura mardi huit jours. **He will be ten c. January,** il aura dix ans au mois de janvier. **2.** (*Occur, happen*) (a) **That comes on the next page,** cela se trouve à la page suivante. **C. what may,** advienne que pourra. (b) **How does the door c. to be open?** comment se fait-il que la porte soit ouverte? **Now that I c. to think of it,** maintenant que j'y songe. **3.** (a) **What will c. of it?** qu'en adviendra-t-il? qu'en résultera-t-il? **That's what comes of doing . . .,** voilà ce qu'il en est sorti de faire. . . . (b) **To c. of a good family,** être, sortir, d'une bonne famille. **4.** (*a*) **The total comes to ten shillings,** la somme s'élève à dix shillings. **How much does it c. to?** combien cela fait-il? **It comes to this, that . . .,** cela revient à ceci, que. . . . *S.a.* NOTHING II. **2.** (*b*) **If it comes to that . . .,** à ce compte-là. . . . **It must c. to that,** il faudra bien en arriver là. **What he knows does not c. to much,** ce qu'il sait ce n'est pas grand-chose. **He will never c.to much,**il ne sera,ne fera, jamais grand-chose. **That is what his argument comes to,** voici à quoi se ramène, se résume, se réduit,revient, son raisonnement. **C. to that, what are you doing here?** mais à propos, qu'est-ce que vous faites ici? (*c*) **That doesn't c. within my duties,** cela ne rentre pas dans mes fonctions. **5.** (*a*) **That comes easy, natural, to him,**cela lui est facile,naturel. **To c. expensive,cheap,** coûter cher, revenir cher; coûter peu. (*Of seam, etc.*) **To c. unstitched,** se découdre. (*b*) **You c. first,** vous venez en premier; c'est vous le premier. **You c. third,** vous êtes le troisième. **6. I have c. to believe that . . .,** j'en suis venu, j'en suis arrivé, à croire que. . . . **I came to like him,** il me devint sympathique. **When she came to know him,** quand elle vint à le connaître. **7. The time to c.,** le temps à venir; l'avenir *m.* **The life to c.,** la vie future. **For three months to c.,** pendant trois mois encore. **8.** *P:* **To c. it strong,** exagérer; y aller fort. **To c. it over s.o.,** faire la loi à qn. **To c. the old soldier over s.o.,** la faire au vieux sergent; chercher à en imposer à qn; rudoyer qn. **come about,** *v.i.* **1.** Arriver, se passer, se produire, avoir lieu. **2.** (*a*) *Nau:* Virer de bord. (*b*) (*Of the wind*) Tourner. **come across,** *v.i.* (*a*) Traverser (la mer, les champs). (*b*) Trouver, rencontrer, (qn, qch.) sur son chemin; tomber sur (qn). **come after,** *v.i.* **1.** (*Prep. use*) (*a*) Suivre (qn, qch.). (*b*) Succéder à (qn). **2.** (*Adv. use*) Suivre; venir plus tard. **come again,** *v.i.* Revenir. *F:* **C. again!** Répétez, s'il vous plaît. *S.a.* CUT² **1. come against,** *v.i.* (*Prep. use*) Heurter, frapper (qch.). **come along,** *v.i.* **1.** Arriver, venir. **C. along!** (i) amène-toi! arrive! (ii) allons-y! allons-nous-en! **2.** (*Happen*) *F:* Survenir. **come apart, asunder,** *v.i.* (*a*) Se séparer, se défaire. (*b*) Se décoller. **come at,** *v.i.* *F:* Attaquer, se jeter sur (qn). **come-at-able,** *a.* *F:* Accessible. **come away,** *v.i.* **1.** Partir, s'en aller (d'un lieu); quitter (un lieu). **2.** Se détacher; se décoller. **come back,** *v.i.* **1.** Revenir. **It's all coming back to me,** cela me revient à la mémoire. **To c. back to what I was saying . . .,** pour en revenir à ce que je disais. . . . **2.** (*Of fashion, etc.*) Revenir en vogue. *F:* **C. back all I said,** oublie tout ce que je viens de dire. **'come-back,** *s.* **1.** Retour *m* (en vogue); retour au pouvoir (d'un homme politique, etc.). **2.** *U.S:* Réplique *f.* **No come-backs!** pas de complications! pas de reproches! **come before,** *v.i.* **1.** *Jur:* **The case comes before the court to-morrow,** le procès aura lieu demain. **2.** Précéder (qn, qch.). **3.** (*Of thg*) Primer (qch.en importance); (*of pers.*)prendre le pas sur (qn). **come between,** *v.i.* Intervenir, s'entremettre, s'interposer, entre (deux personnes). **come by,** *v.i.* **1.** (*a*) **To c. by the house,** passer par la maison. (*b*) **To c. by money,** obtenir de l'argent. **Horestly c. by,** honnêtement acquis. **2.** *adv. use* **I heard him c. by,** je l'ai entendu passer. **come clean,** *v.i.* *F:* Avouer; *P:* vider son sac (devant le juge, etc.). **come down,** *v.i.* **1.** Descendre (l'échelle, l'escalier); faire la descente de (la montagne, etc.). **2.** (*a*) **To c. down to breakfast,** descendre déjeuner. **To c. down to s.o.'s level,** s'abaisser jusqu'au niveau (d'esprit) de qn. *F:* **To c. down (in the world),** déchoir. **Prices are coming down,** les prix baissent, sont en baisse. *F:* **To c. down a peg,** (i) en rabattre; déchanter; (ii) descendre d'un cran. (*b*) *F:* **To c. down upon s.o.,** (i) semoncer vertement qn; (ii) blâmer sévèrement qn. (*c*) *F:* **To c. down handsomely,** se montrer généreux; *F:* se fendre. (*d*) (*Of rain, etc.*) Tomber. (*e*) **Her hair came down to her knees,** ses cheveux lui descendaient jusqu'aux genoux. (*f*) Venir (de nos aïeux). **All the tales that have come down to us,** tous les contes qui nous ont été transmis par la tradition. (*g*) (*Of pers., horse*) S'abattre; (*of structure*) s'écrouler. (*h*) (*Of problem, etc.*) Se résumer. **The expenses c. down to board and lodging,** les dépenses se réduisent aux frais de pension. **'come-down,** *s.* *F:* Humiliation *f*;

déchéance *f.* **come forth,** *v.i.* Sortir, s'avancer. **come forward,** *v.i.* **1.** S'avancer. *Iron:* **He's not backward in coming forward,** il ne se gêne pas. **2. To c. forward as a candidate,** se présenter comme candidat; se porter candidat. **come-'hither,** *a.* *F:* (Regard) aguichant. **come in,** *v.i.* **1.** Entrer. **That's just where the mistake comes in,** voilà justement où est l'erreur. **2.** (*Of tide*) Monter; (*of ship*) arriver; (*of year*) commencer; (*of fashion*) entrer en vogue. **As soon as oysters come in,** dès que les huîtres sont de saison. **3.** (*Of funds*) Rentrer. **4.** (*a*) **To c. in useful to s.o., for sth.,** servir à qn, à qch. (*b*) *Sp:* **To c. in first, second,** arriver premier, second. **5.** *F:* **To c. in for sth.,** recevoir (une part des bénéfices, une semonce, etc.). **To c. in for a fortune,** succéder à une fortune. **And where do I c. in?** et moi, qu'est-ce que j'y gagne? **come into,** *v.i.* **1.** Entrer dans (une chambre). (*Of idea*) **To c. into s.o.'s mind,** se présenter à l'esprit de qn. **2. To c. into a property,** entrer en possession d'un domaine. **come off,** *v.i.* **1.** (*Prep. use*) (*a*) Descendre de (la table, etc.). **To c. off one's horse,** tomber de (son) cheval. *F:* **C. off it!** en voilà assez! allons donc! allez raconter ça ailleurs! (*b*) **To c. off the gold standard,** abandonner l'étalon or. **2.** (*Adv. use*) (*a*) (*Of button, etc.*) Se détacher, sauter; (*of smell, etc.*) se dégager; (*of stain, etc.*) s'enlever, s'en aller. **The colour came off on my dress,** la couleur a déteint sur ma robe. (*b*) (*Of ship aground*) Se déséchouer; partir. (*c*) (*Of event*) Avoir lieu; (*of attempt, etc.*) réussir, aboutir. *F:* **The marriage didn't c. off,** le mariage ne s'est pas fait. (*d*) **To c. off badly,** s'en mal tirer. **He came off victorious,** il en sortit vainqueur. **come on,** *v.i.* (*a*) S'avancer. (*Of boys!*) (i) allons-y, les gars! (ii) arrivez, mes enfants! **C. on, let's have a game!** allons! faisons une partie! **C. on!** (i) en avant! (ii) arrivez! (iii) *F:* (*as a challenge*) viens-y donc! (*b*) (*Of plants, children, etc.*) (Bien) venir; se développer; faire des progrès. (*c*) (*Of illness, etc.*) Survenir; (*of winter etc.*) venir, arriver; (*of night*) tomber. **It came on to rain,** il s'est mis à pleuvoir. (*d*) (*Of question*) **To c. on** (*for discussion*), venir en discussion. (*Of lawsuit*) **The case comes on tomorrow,** la cause sera entendue demain. (*e*) *Th:* (*of actor*) Entrer en scène. **I see the *Tempest*'s coming on again,** je vois qu'on redonne la Tempête. **come out,** *v.i.* **1.** (*Prep. use*) **To c. out of a place, of a room,** sortir d'un lieu, quitter une salle. **2.** (*Adv. use*) (*a*) Sortir. *Ind:* **To c. out (on strike),** se mettre en grève. (*b*) **Do c. out to Australia,** venez donc nous retrouver en Australie. (*c*) *Sch:* **To c. out first, second,** être reçu premier, second. (*d*) (*Of stars*) Paraître; (*of buds*) éclore; *Phot:* (*of image*) se développer, se révéler; (*of rash, pimples*) sortir, se montrer; (*of the truth*) se découvrir. (*Of pers.*) **To c. out in a rash,** (i) avoir une poussée de boutons; (ii) avoir une poussée d'urticaire. (*e*) (i) *Art: etc:* (*Of details*) Ressortir; se détacher (sur le fond). (ii) *Phot:* (*Of detail in negative*) Apparaître. (iii) *Phot:* **You have come out well,** vous êtes très réussi. (*f*) (*Of stain*) S'enlever, s'effacer. (*g*) (*Of book*) Paraître. (*h*) (*Of problem*) Se résoudre. (*Of average, etc.*) **To c. out at . . .,** être de . . ., être de l'ordre de . . ., se monter à. . . . (*i*) (*Of pers.*) Débuter (au théâtre); débuter, faire son entrée dans le monde. (*j*) **To c. out with a remark,** lâcher, laisser échapper, une observation. **coming out,** *s.* Début *m* (dans le monde). **come over,** *v.i.* **1.** (*Prep. use*) (*a*) Traverser (la mer). (*b*) Envahir, gagner, saisir (qn). **What has c. over you?** qu'est-ce qui vous prend? **2.** (*Adv. use*) (*a*) **To c. over from a place,** arriver, venir, d'un lieu. (*b*) **To c. over to s.o.'s side,** passer du côté de qn. (*c*) *P:* **To c. over funny, queer,** se sentir mal; *F:* se sentir tout chose. **come round,** *v.i.* **1.** (*Prep. use*) (*a*) Entourer (qn). (*b*) Faire le tour de (qch.); contourner (qch.). **2.** (*Adv. use*) (*a*) Faire le tour, un détour. **Conversation that comes round to the same subjects again,** conversation qui retombe sur les mêmes sujets. (*b*) **C. round and see me one day,** venez me voir un de ces jours. (*c*) **When my turn came round again,** quand ce fut de nouveau mon tour. (*d*) Reprendre connaissance; revenir à soi. (*e*) **To c. round to s.o.'s way of thinking,** se ranger à l'avis de qn. **come through,** *v.i.* **1.** (*Prep. use*) (*a*) Passer par, à travers (le bois). **The rain has c. through his clothes,** la pluie a traversé, percé, ses vêtements. (*b*) **To c. through trials,** passer par des épreuves. **To c. through an illness,** surmonter une maladie. **2.** (*Adv. use*) (*a*) **The water, the rain, is coming through,** l'eau, la pluie, pénètre. (*b*) **He came through without a scratch,** il s'en est tiré indemne. **come to,** *v.i.* F: = COME ROUND 2 (*d*). **come together,** *v.i.* S'assembler, se réunir. **come under,** *v.i.* **1. To c. under s.o.'s influence,** être soumis à, tomber sous, subir, l'influence de qn. F: (*In an office, etc.*) **He comes under Mr Martin,** c'est M. Martin qui est son chef. **2. To c. under a heading,** être compris sous un article. **come up,** *v.i.* **1.** (*Prep. use*) Monter (l'échelle, etc.). **2.** (*Adv. use*) (*a*) **Come up to my rooms,** montez chez moi. **To c. up out of the abyss,** surgir de l'abîme. **To c. up to the surface again,** remonter sur l'eau. (*b*) **To c. up to town,** venir en ville. **To c. up (to the university),** commencer ses études universitaires. (*c*) **To c. up to s.o.,** s'approcher de qn. *Ten:* **To c. up to the net,** monter au filet. *Jur:* **To c. up before the Court,** comparaître (devant le tribunal). (*d*) (*Of plants*) Sortir de terre; pousser. (*e*) **To c. up (for discussion),** venir en discussion; venir sur le tapis. **The case comes up for hearing tomorrow,** la cause sera entendue demain. *Sch:* **This question has never c. up yet,** cette question n'est jamais encore sortie (à l'examen). (*f*) **To c. up to sth.,** atteindre, s'élever, jusqu'à, qch. **He does not c. up to my waist,** il ne me vient pas à la ceinture. **To c. up to s.o.'s expectations,** répondre à l'attente de qn. (*g*) **As a violinist he doesn't c. up to X,** comme violoniste il n'égale pas X, il ne vaut pas X. (*h*) **To c. up against sth.,** se heurter, se cogner, à, contre, qch. **To c. up against s.o.,** entrer en conflit avec qn. (*i*) **To c. up with s.o.,** rattraper, rejoindre, qn. (*j*) F: **The table comes up well when you polish it,** la table revient bien à l'astiquage. **come upon,** *v.i.* (*a*) Tomber, fondre, sur (qn). (*b*) **To c. upon s.o. for a sum of money,** réclamer une somme à qn. (*c*) **To c. upon s.o.,** rencontrer qn par hasard. **come within,** *v.i.* Rentrer dans (les fonctions de qn); être couvert par (une définition). **coming**[1], *a.* **The c. year,** l'année qui vient, l'année prochaine. **The c. storm,** l'orage qui approche. **The c. generations,** les générations futures, à venir. **A c. man,** un homme d'avenir. **coming**[2], *s.* Venue *f*, arrivée *f*; approche *f* (de la nuit, etc.); avènement *m* (du Messie). **There was a great deal of c. and going,** il y avait beaucoup de va-et-vient. **Comings and goings,** allées et venues. **comedian** [kə'miːdiən], *s.* **1.** (*a*) Comédien, -ienne. (*b*) Comique *m* (de music hall, etc.). **2.** *A:* Auteur de comédies. **comedienne** [kɔmiːdi'en], *s.f.* Comédienne *f*. **comedy** ['kɔmədi], *s.* **1.** La comédie; le genre comique. **2.** (*Play*) Comédie. **Musical c.,** opérette *f*. **comeliness** ['kʌmlinis], *s.* Charme *m*; grâce *f*; mine fraîche et avenante. **comely** ['kʌmli], *a.* (*Of pers.*) Avenant; (femme) fraîche et avenante. **comer** ['kʌmər], *s.* **1.** Arrivant, -ante; venant, -ante. **Open to all comers,** ouvert à tout le monde. **2. First c.,** premier venu; premier arrivé. *S.a.* LATE-COMER, NEW-COMER. **comet** ['kɔmit], *s.* Comète *f*. **The C. year,** l'année de la comète (1811). **comfit** ['kʌmfit], *s.* *O:* Bonbon *m*; dragée *f*. **C.-box,** bonbonnière *f*. **comfort**[1] ['kʌmfət], *s.* **1.** Consolation *f*; motif *m* de consolation; soulagement *m*. *A:* **Be of good c.!** prenez courage! **To take c.,** se consoler. **That is cold c.,** c'est une piètre consolation. **To be a great c. to s.o.,** être un grand sujet de consolation à qn. **2.** Bien-être *m*. **I like c.,** j'aime mes aises. **3.** (*a*) Confort *m*; confortable *m*; aisance *f*. (*At hotel, etc.*) **Every modern c.,** tout le confort moderne. **To live in c.,** vivre dans l'aisance, à l'aise. (*b*) *U.S:* **C. station, c. room,** toilettes publiques. **4.** *pl.* **The comforts of life,** les commodités *f*, les agréments *m*, les douceurs *f*, de la vie. **comfort**[2], *v.tr.* **1.** Consoler, soulager. **2.** (*a*) (*Of beverage*) Réconforter. (*b*) Redonner du courage à (qn). **comforting,** *a.* Réconfortant. **C. words,** paroles de consolation, de réconfort.

comfortable ['kʌmf(ə)təbl], *a.* **1.** (*a*) (*Of bed, etc.*) Confortable; (*of dress*) commode, aisé; (*of warmth*) agréable. **These shoes are c.,** on est à l'aise dans ces chaussures. **To make oneself c.,** se mettre à son aise. **To feel c.,** se trouver bien; se sentir à l'aise. **It is so c. here,** on est si bien ici; il fait si bon ici. (*b*) (*Of patient*) **To be c.,** ne pas souffrir. **2. C. income,** revenu suffisant. **To make s.o. c. for the rest of his days,** assurer la vie de qn pour le restant de ses jours. **3.** Sans inquiétude; tranquille, rassuré. **-ably,** *adv.* Confortablement, commodément, agréablement. **To be c. off,** avoir de quoi (vivre); être à l'aise. **To live c.,** vivre à l'aise, à son aise. **comforter** ['kʌmfətər], *s.* **1.** Consolateur, -trice. **2.** Cache-nez *m inv* (de laine). **3.** (*Baby's*) Tétine *f* (sur anneau); sucette *f*. **4.** *U.S:* Couvre-pieds *inv.* piqué. **comfortless** ['kʌmfətlis], *a.* **1.** Incommode; sans confort *m*, dépourvu de confort; peu confortable. **2.** (*Of pers.*) Abandonné; inconsolé, sans consolation *f*. **comfrey** ['kʌmfri], *s.* *Bot:* Consoude *f*. **comfy** ['kʌmfi], *a.* F: = COMFORTABLE 1. **comic** ['kɔmik]. **1.** *a.* Comique. **C. opera,** opéra bouffe. **The c. side of a situation,** le côté ridicule d'une situation. **2.** *s.* (*a*) Comédien, -ienne (de music-hall); comique *m*. (*b*) *Journ:* Journal de bandes illustrées. **3.** *s.pl.* *Journ:* **Comics,** comics *mpl*; bande illustrée. **comical** ['kɔmik(ə)l], *a.* Comique, risible; qui prête à rire. **What a c. idea!** quelle drôle d'idée! **-ally,** *adv.* Comiquement; drôlement. **Cominform** ['kɔminfɔːm], *s.* *Hist:* Kominform *m*. **Comintern** ['kɔmintəːn], *s.* *Hist:* Komintern. **comity** ['kɔmiti], *s.* Courtoisie *f*, politesse *f*. **The c. of nations,** le bon accord entre les nations. **comma** ['kɔmə], *s.* (*a*) Virgule *f*. (*b*) **Inverted commas,** guillemets *m*. **Between inverted commas,** entre guillemets. **To put (word, etc.) in inverted commas,** guillemeter (un mot). **command**[1] [kə'mɑːnd], *s.* **1.** Ordre *m*, commandement *m*. **Done by, s.o.'s c.,** fait d'après les ordres de qn. **To be at s.o.'s c.,** être aux ordres de qn. **Word of c.,** commandement. **By royal c.,** sur l'invitation du Souverain. *Th:* **C. Performance,** représentation commandée par le souverain. **2.** Commandement (of, de; over, sur); gouvernement *m* (d'une place forte). **Second in c.,** commandant *m* en second. **Under (the) c. of . . .,** sous le commandement de. . . . *Mil:* **The Higher C.,** le commandement supérieur. *Mil:* *Av:* **Coastal Defence C.,** zone fortifiée de défense côtière. **C. post,** poste *m* de commandement. **3.** (*a*) **To be in c. of a pass,** commander, dominer, un défilé. (*b*) **Connaissance** *f*, maîtrise *f* (d'une langue). **To have several languages at one's c.,** to have a c. of several languages, posséder plusieurs langues. (*c*) **C. over oneself,** maîtrise *f* de soi. (*d*) **C. of the seas,** maîtrise des mers. (*e*) **The money at my c.,** les fonds à ma disposition. **command**[2], *v.tr.* **1.** Ordonner, commander (s.o. to do sth., à qn de faire qch.). **2.** (*a*) Commander (un régiment). *Abs.* **To c. in chief,** commander en chef. (*b*) **To c. oneself,** rester maître de soi. **To c. one's temper,** se contenir. **With money one commands the world,** avec de l'argent on est maître du monde. **3.** Avoir (qch.) à sa disposition. O: **You may c. me,** vous pouvez disposer de moi. **4.** (*a*) **To c. respect, admiration,** commander, inspirer, le respect, l'admiration. **To c. attention,** forcer l'attention. (*b*) **To c. a high price,** se vendre à un haut prix. **5.** (*Of fort, etc.*) Commander, dominer (une ville, etc.). **commanding,** *a.* **1.** **C. officer,** officier commandant; *Mil:* chef *m* de corps. **2.** (Ton) d'autorité, de commandement. **3.** **C. presence,** air, port, imposant. **4.** (Lieu) éminent. **commandant** [ˌkɔmən'dænt], *s.* Commandant *m*. **commandeer** [ˌkɔmən'diːər], *v.tr.* Réquisitionner. **commander** [kə'mɑːndər], *s.* **1.** (*a*) *Mil:* Commandant *m*. **C.-in-chief,** commandant en chef; généralissime *m*. (*b*) *Navy:* Capitaine *m* de frégate. **2.** (*Of knights*) Commandeur *m*. **commandership** [kə'mɑːndəʃip], *s.* Commandement *m*; poste *m* de commandant ou de capitaine de frégate.

commandment [kə'mɑ:ndmənt], s. Commandement (divin).

commando [kə'mɑ:ndou], s. *Mil:* (a) Commando m, corps franc. (b) Soldat m membre d'un commando.

commemorate [kə'meməreit], v.tr. Commémorer (qn, le souvenir de qn); solenniser, célébrer, le souvenir de (qn, qch.).

commemoration [kə,memə'reiʃ(ə)n], s. Commémoration f. In c. of s.o., en mémoire de qn.

commemorative [kə'meməreitiv], a. Commémoratif, -ive (of, de).

commence [kə'mens], v.tr. & i. Commencer (sth., qch.). To c. to do sth., to c. doing sth., commencer à, de, faire qch. *Mil:* To c. operations, entamer les opérations.

commencement [kə'mensmənt], s. 1. Commencement m, début m. 2. *Sch: U.S:* Collation f des grades universitaires.

commend [kə'mend], v.tr. 1. Recommander, confier (qch. à qn, aux soins de qn). 2. (a) Louer. To c. s.o. for his bravery, louer qn de sa bravoure. To c. s.o. for doing sth., approuver qn d'avoir fait qch. (b) A course of action that did not c. itself to me, une ligne de conduite qui n'était pas à mon goût.

commendable [kə'mendəbl], a. Louable. -ably, adv. Louablement, d'une manière louable.

commendation ['komen'deiʃ(ə)n], s. Éloge m, louange f, approbation f.

commendatory [kə'mendətəri], a. 1. Élogieux, -euse. 2. *Ecc:* (Abbé, abbaye) commendataire.

commensal [kə'mensl]. 1. s. *Esp. Biol:* Commensal m, -aux. 2. a. (a) Qui mange à la même table. (b) *Biol:* Commensal.

commensurable [kə'menʃərəbl], a. 1. Commensurable (with, to, avec). 2. = COMMENSURATE 2.

commensurate [kə'menʃərit], a. 1. Coétendu (with, à). 2. Proportionné (to, with, à). -ly, adv. Proportionnellement (to, with, à).

comment[1] ['koment], s. Commentaire m. Comments on a work, appréciation f d'un ouvrage. No comments, please! pas d'observations, s'il vous plaît! To call for c., provoquer des critiques.

comment[2] ['koment], v.i. 1. To c. on a text, commenter un texte. 2. To c. on s.o.'s behaviour, critiquer la conduite de qn. Several people commented on his absence, plusieurs firent des observations sur son absence.

commentary ['komənt(ə)ri], s. 1. Commentaire m, glose f. 2. *W.Tel:* (Running) c., radio-reportage m; reportage m en direct.

commentate ['komənteit], v.i. Faire un commentaire (on, sur).

commentator ['komənteitər], s. 1. Commentateur, -trice. 2. *W.Tel: T.V:* Radio-reporter m.

commerce ['komə:s], s. Le commerce; les affaires f.

commercial [kə'mə:ʃ(ə)l]. 1. a. (a) Commercial, -aux. C. bank, banque commerciale, de commerce. C. vehicle, voiture f de livraison. C. efficiency (of machine), rendement économique. The c. world, le commerce. (b) (Esprit) mercantile. 2. s. *F:* (a) Commis voyageur. C. room, salle rseérvée aux voyageurs de commerce. (b) *T.V: F:* Émission f publicitaire. -ally, adv. Commercialement.

commercialese [kə,mə:ʃə'li:z], s. *F:* Style commercial. He writes in c., il écrit dans le style du commerce.

commercialism [kə'mə:ʃ(ə)lizm], s. Esprit commerçant, mercantilisme m; esprit commercial.

commercialization [kə,mə:ʃ(ə)lai'zeiʃən], s. 1. *Fin:* Commercialisation f. 2. The c. of sport is deplorable, la commercialisation du sport est à déplorer.

commercialize [kə'mə:ʃ(ə)laiz], v.tr. Commercialiser.

commination [,komi'neiʃ(ə)n], s. 1. *Ecc:* Commination f. 2. Dénonciation f; menaces fpl.

comminatory ['kominət(ə)ri], a. Comminatoire.

commingle [ko'miŋgl]. 1. v.tr. Mêler ensemble; mélanger. 2. v.i. Se mêler (with, avec).

comminute ['kominju:t], v.tr. 1. Pulvériser; réduire en fragments. *Surg:* Comminuted fracture, fracture esquilleuse. 2. Morceler (une propriété).

comminution [,komi'nju:ʃ(ə)n], s. 1. Comminution f; pulvérisation f. 2. Morcellement m.

commiserate [kə'mizəreit], v.tr. & i. To c. (with) s.o., s'apitoyer sur le sort de qn.

commiseration [kə,mizə'reiʃ(ə)n], s. Commisération f, compassion f (with, pour).

commiserative [kə'mizərətiv], a. Compatissant.

commissar [komi'sɑ:r], s. *Russ.Adm:* Commissaire m (du peuple).

commissariat [,komi'sɛəriət], s. 1. *Mil:* Intendance f. 2. *Russ.Adm:* Service m; ministère m.

commissary ['komisəri], s. 1. Commissaire m, délégué m. 2. *Mil:* C. general, intendant général d'armée. 3. *Ecc:* Vicaire général (délégué par l'évêque).

commission[1] [kə'miʃ(ə)n], s. Commission f. 1. Délégation f (d'autorité). 2. Brevet m. C. of the peace, charge f de juge de tribunal d'instance. *Mil:* To get a, one's, c., être nommé officier, passer officier, gagner l'épaulette. To resign one's c., démissionner. 3. Ordre m, mandat m. To carry out a c., s'acquitter d'une commission. 4. Royal C., commission d'enquête ordonnée par décret parlementaire, *Fr.C:* commission royale. Fact-finding c., commission d'enquête. 5. *Nau:* Armement m (d'un navire). To put a ship into c., armer un navire. To put a ship out of c., désarmer un navire; mettre un navire en réserve. Aircraft in c., avion en service. *F:* My car is out of c., ma voiture est en réparation. 6. *Com:* Commission; pourcentage m. Illicit c., remise f illicite; *F:* pot m de vin. 7. Perpétration f (d'un crime). com'mission agency, s. Maison f de commission. com'mission agent, s. Commissionnaire m en marchandises. com'mission-day, s. *Jur:* Jour m de l'ouverture des assises.

commission[2], v.tr. 1. (a) Commissionner (qn). (b) Préposer, déléguer, (qn) à une fonction; nommer (un officier) à un commandement. (c) Commander (un livre, un tableau). 2. *Nau:* (a) Armer (un navire). (b) v.i. (Of ship) Armer. commissioned, a. 1. Muni de pouvoirs; commissionné. 2. C. officer, officier m.

commissionaire [kə,miʃə'nɛər], s. Commissionnaire m. 1. (a) Chasseur m (d'hôtel). (b) Concierge m, portier m. 2. Messager patenté (sociétaire du *Corps of Commissionnaires*).

commissioner [kə'miʃ(ə)nər], s. Commissaire m. (a) Membre m d'une commission. (b) Délégué m d'une commission. C. of police = préfet m de police. C. for oaths, avoué m ayant qualité pour recevoir les déclarations sous serment. (In Canada) School c., *Fr.C:* commissaire m d'école.

commissure ['komiʃuər], s. *Anat:* Commissure f (des lèvres, etc.).

commit [kə'mit], v.tr. (committed) 1. Commettre, confier (sth. to s.o.'s care, qch. aux soins, à la garde, de qn). To c. sth. to writing, coucher qch. par écrit. 2. To c. s.o. to prison, abs. to c. s.o., envoyer qn en prison. To c. s.o. for trial, renvoyer (un prévenu) aux assises. 3. (a) Engager (sa parole, etc.). (b) To c. oneself, se compromettre. I am too deeply committed to draw back, je suis trop engagé pour reculer. Without committing myself, sous toutes réserves. Committed literature, littérature engagée. 4. Commettre (un crime, une erreur). *S.a.* SUICIDE[2].

commitment [kə'mitmənt], s. 1. = COMMITTAL. 2. Engagement financier. My commitments do not allow me to . . ., mes engagements ne me permettent pas de. . . .

committal [kə'mitl]. s. 1. Délégation f (d'une tâche, etc.) (to, à). 2. (a) C. of a body to the earth, mise f en terre d'un cadavre. (b) *Jur:* Mise en prison. C. order, mandat de dépôt. 3. Perpétration f (d'un délit). 4. Engagement m (de sa parole).

committee [kə'miti], s. 1. Comité m, commission f, conseil m. To be on a c., faire partie d'un comité. C. of management, conseil d'administration. Organizing c., comité d'organisation. Joint Production C., comité d'entreprise. C. of ways and means, = commission du budget. To send a bill to a c., renvoyer un projet de loi à une commission. C. rooms (of parliamentary candidate), permanence électorale. *Jur:* [komi'ti:] Tuteur, -trice, curateur, -trice (d'un faible d'esprit).

commode [kə'moud], s. *Furn:* 1. Commode f. 2. (Night) c., chaise percée.

commodious [kə'moudiəs], a. (a) Spacieux. (b) (Appartement m) commode, confortable, convenable.

commodiousness [kə'moudiəsnis], s. Amples dimensions f, confort m (d'une maison, d'une pièce).

commodity [kə'mɔditi], s. Marchandise f, denrée f, article m. **Primary, basic, c.**, produit m de b̈ase; (*of food*) denrée f témoin.

commodore ['kɔmədɔːr], s. (*a*) *Navy:* Chef m de division (par intérim); commodore m. Chef d'escadre. (*b*) Le capitaine (d'un corps de pilotes, d'un yacht-club). (*c*) *Av:* **Air-c.**, général m de brigade (aérienne).

common¹ ['kɔmən], a. 1. Commun (to, à). **C. wall**, mur mitoyen. **C. report**, rumeur publique; *Jur:* commune renommée. **C. property**, choses communes. **The c. opinion**, l'opinion courante. *S.a.* SENSE¹ 4. *Gram:* **C. noun**, nom commun. *Mth:* **C. divisor**, commun diviseur. *Ecc:* The Book of C. Prayer, liturgie anglicane. 2. (*a*) Ordinaire. **C. name (of a plant)**, nom m vulgaire (d'une plante). **C. occurrence**, chose fréquente. **C. honesty**, la probité la plus élémentaire. **In c. use**, d'usage courant. **In c. parlance**, en langage ordinaire. (*Of news, etc.*) **To be c. talk**, courir les rues. **The c. soldiery**, les simples soldats m. **They are as c. as blackberries**, les rues en sont pavées. (*b*) De peu de valeur. **C. material**, étoffe ordinaire. **The c. people**, les gens du peuple; le menu peuple. 3. Vulgaire; trivial, -als. **C. manners**, manières vulgaires, communes. **-ly**, *adv.* 1. Communément, ordinairement; d'habitude. 2. Vulgairement. **common-'lawyer**, s. Civiliste m. **'common-room**, s. *Sch:* Salle commune. (*At university*) **Junior c.-r.**, salle des étudiants. **Senior c.-r.**, Salle des professeurs.

common², s. 1. (*a*) Pâtis m, friche f. (*b*) Terrain, pré, communal. *Jur:* Vaine pâture. 2. **To have sth. in c. with s.o.**, avoir qch. en commun avec qn. **They have nothing in c.**, ils n'ont rien de commun. **It is out of the c.**, cela sort de l'ordinaire. **Nothing out of the c.**, rien d'extraordinaire.

commonage ['kɔmənidʒ], s. *Hist: Jur:* Droit m de vaine pâture; droit de parcours.

commonalty ['kɔmənəlti], s. 1. Le commun des hommes. 2. La bourgeoisie.

commoner ['kɔmənər], s. 1. Homme m du peuple; bourgeois m. 2. *Sch:* Étudiant m ordinaire.

commonness ['kɔmənnis], s. 1. Fréquence f (d'un événement). 2. Banalité f; vulgarité f.

commonplace ['kɔmənpleis]. 1. s. (*a*) Lieu commun. (*b*) Banalité f. **C.-book**, mémorandum m. 2. a. Banal, -als.

commons ['kɔmənz], s. 1. Le peuple; le tiers état. The House of C., la Chambre des Communes. 2. *Sch:* Ordinaire m (de la table). **To be on short c.**, faire maigre chère.

commonweal (the) [ðə'kɔmənwiːl], s. Le bien public; la chose publique.

commonwealth ['kɔmənwelθ], s. (*a*) État m; république f. (*b*) The C., la chose publique. *Hist:* The C. of England, la République d'Angleterre (1649-60). (*c*) The British Commonwealth of Nations, le Commonwealth britannique.

commotion [kə'mouʃ(ə)n], s. 1. Confusion f, agitation f, ommotion f, ébranlement m. **In a state of c.**, en émoi. **The c. in the streets**, le brouhaha de la rue. 2. Troubles mpl.

communal [kə'muːn(ə)l], a. Communal, -aux; communautaire. *Jur:* **C. estate**, communauté (conjugale).

commune [kə'mjuːn], v.i. 1. *Lit:* Converser, s'entretenir (with s.o., avec qn). **To c. with oneself**, se recueillir. 2. *U.S: Ecc:* Communier.

communicable [kə'mjuːnikəbl], a. Communicable. *Med:* Contagieux, -euse, transmissible.

communicant [kə'mjuːnikənt], s. 1. Informateur, -trice. 2. *Ecc:* Communiant, -ante. **To be a regular c.**, fréquenter les sacrements.

communicate [kə'mjuːnikeit]. 1. v.tr. **To c. (sth.) to sth., to s.o.**, communiquer (la chaleur, etc.) à qch.; communiquer, faire connaître (une nouvelle) à qn. 2. v.i. (*a*) **To c. with s.o.**, communiquer avec qn. **To c. by letter**, communiquer par lettre. (*b*) **Rooms that c. with one another**, chambres qui communiquent entre elles, qui se commandent. 3. *Ecc:* (*a*) v.tr. Communier (qn), donner la communion (à qn). (*b*) v.i. Communier; recevoir la communion.

communication [kə,mjuːni'keiʃ(ə)n], s. 1. (*a*) C. of a piece of news to s.o., communication f d'une nouvelle à qn. (*b*) **To read a c.**, lire une communication. 2. **To get into c. with s.o.**, communiquer avec qn. **To be in close c. with one another**, être en relations suivies. 3. **Line of c.**, voie d'intercommunication. **Means of c.**, moyens (i) de communication, (ii) de transport. *Rail:* **C. cord**, corde f de signal d'alarme; sonnette f d'alarme.

communicative [kə'mjuːnikətiv], a. Communicatif, -ive; expansif, -ive.

communicativeness [kə'mjuːnikətivnis], s. Caractère expansif; humeur bavarde.

communicator [kə'mjuːnikeitər], s. Communicateur m (de mouvement, etc.); transmetteur m.

communion [kə'mjuːnjən], s. 1. Relations fpl, rapports mpl (with s.o., avec qn). **Self-c.**, recueillement m. 2. **The c. of saints**, la communion des saints. 3. *Ecc:* **The (Holy) C.**, la communion, la (Sainte) Cène. **The C. table**, la Sainte Table. **To administer Holy C. (to s.o.)**, communier (qn).

communiqué [kə'mjuːnikei], s. Communiqué m.

communism ['kɔmjunizm], s. Communisme m.

communist ['kɔmjunist], s. Communiste mf.

communistic [kɔmju'nistik], a. Communiste; communisant. **A trade union with c. tendencies**, un syndicat ouvrier à tendances communisantes. **-ally**, adv. A la façon communiste. **C. inclined**, à tendances f communistes.

community [kə'mjuːniti], s. 1. Communauté f (de biens); solidarité f (d'intérêts). 2. *Ecc:* Communauté (religieuse). 3. (*a*) The c., l'État m; le public. **All classes of the c.**, toutes les classes de la société. (*b*) **C. singing**, chansons populaires reprises en chœur par l'assistance. (*c*) **C. centre**, centre m, salle f, de loisirs, de récréation (d'une ville, etc.). *U.S:* **C. chest**, fonds m de secours, fonds communs.

commutability [kə,mjutə'biliti], s. 1. Permutabilité f. 2. *Jur:* Commuabilité f (d'une peine).

commutable [kə'mjuːtəbl], a. 1. Permutable; interchangeable. 2. (Peine) commuable.

commutate ['kɔmjuteit], v.tr. *El.E:* Commuter, permuter.

commutation [,kɔmju'teiʃ(ə)n], s. 1.(*a*) C. of sentence, commutation f de peine. (*b*) C. of an easement, rachat m d'une servitude. 2. *U.S: Rail:* C. ticket, carte f d'abonnement.

commutative [kə'mjuːtətiv, 'kɔmjəteitiv], a. Commutatif.

commutator ['kɔmju:teitər], s. El: Commutateur m. **C. ring**, bague f de collecteur.

commute [kə'mjuːt], v.tr. 1. Permuter, interchanger. 2. (*a*) Échanger (for, into, pour, contre); racheter (une servitude). *Jur:* Commuer (une peine). (*b*) *Abs.* Faire un long trajet journalier entre la résidence et le lieu de travail. 3. *El.E:* = COMMUTATE. **commuting**, s. (Action de faire un) long trajet journalier entre la résidence et le lieu de travail.

commuter [kə'mjuːtər], s. *Rail: etc:* Abonné, -ée; personne qui fait un long trajet journalier entre la résidence et le lieu de travail, banlieusard, -e.

compact¹ ['kɔmpækt], s. Convention f, accord m, pacte m.

compact² [kəm'pækt], a. 1. Compact; serré, tassé; (style) concis. 2. Formé, composé (of, de). **-ly**, adv. D'une manière compacte.

compact³ ['kɔmpækt], s. 1. *Toil:* Poudrier m (de sac à main). 2. *U.S: Aut:* Petite voiture.

compact⁴ [kəm'pækt], v.tr. 1. Rendre (qch.) compact; tasser. 2. **To be compacted of . . .**, être composé de. . . .

compactness [kəm'pæktnis], s. Compacité f; concision f (de style).

companion¹ [kəm'pænjən], s. 1. (*a*) Compagnon, f. compagne. **Companions in distress**, compagnons d'infortune. (*b*) **(Lady-)c.**, dame f de compagnie. (*c*) Compagnon (d'un ordre). 2. Manuel m; vademecum m. 3. Pendant m (à un tableau, etc.).

companion², s. *Nau:* 1. **C.(-hatch)**, capot m (de descente). 2. **C.(-ladder)**, échelle f d'honneur, de commandement. **C.(-way)**, escalier m des cabines.

companionable [kəm'pænjənəbl], a. D'une société agréable. **-ably**, adv. Sociablement.

companionship [kəm'pænjənʃip], s. (a) Compagnie f. (b) Camaraderie f.

company ['kʌmpəni], s. 1. Compagnie f. To keep s.o. c., tenir compagnie à qn. To part c. (with s.o.), (i) se séparer (de qn); (ii) n'être plus d'accord (avec qn). Prov: Two's c., three's none, deux s'amusent, trois s'embêtent. 2. (a) Assemblée f, compagnie; bande f. Select c., assemblée choisie. Present c. excepted, les présents exceptés. (b) O: (Guests) Monde m. To put on one's c. manners, soigner sa tenue, son langage. 3. (Associates) Compagnie, société f. To keep good c., fréquenter la bonne compagnie. Avoid bad c., prenez garde aux mauvaises fréquentations. A man is known by the c. he keeps, dis-moi qui tu hantes, je te dirai qui tu es. He is very good c., il est fort amusant. 4. Com: Ind: (a) (i) Compagnie; (ii) société (financière, commerciale, industrielle). Joint stock c., société par actions. (In England) Limited (liability) c., société = à responsabilité limitée. Smith and C. (usu. and Co.), Smith et Compagnie; Smith et Cie. Fin: Holding c., holding m. (b) Corporation f de marchands. 5. (a) Th: Troupe f. Touring c., troupe ambulante. (b) Nau: The ship's c., l'équipage m. 6. Mil: Compagnie. Half-c., peloton m. F: (In British Army) To get one's c., être promu commandant; recevoir le commandement d'une compagnie.

comparable ['kɔmpərəbl], a. Comparable (with, to, avec, à). **-ably**, adv. Comparablement.

comparative [kəm'pærətiv], a. 1. (a) Comparatif, -ive. Gram: C. adverb, adverbe comparatif. C. degree, le comparatif. (b) C. philology, philologie comparée. 2. Relatif, -ive. He's a c. stranger to me, je ne le connais guère. **-ly**, adv. 1. Comparativement, par comparaison (to, à). 2. Relativement.

compare¹ [kəm'peər], s. Beyond c., hors de comparaison; (beauté) sans pareille.

compare². 1. v.tr. (a) Comparer (to, with, à, avec). C. the two things! faites la comparaison! They are not to be compared, on ne saurait les comparer. (As) compared with, to . . ., en comparaison de . . ., auprès de.... To c. a copy with the original, confronter une copie avec l'original. To c. notes, échanger ses impressions avec qn. (b) To c. an adjective, former les degrés de comparaison d'un adjectif. 2. v.i. He can't c. with you, il ne vous est pas comparable. To c. favourably with sth., ne le céder en rien à qch. **comparing,** s. Comparaison f.

comparison [kəm'pæris(ə)n], s. Comparaison f. In c. with . . ., en comparaison de . . .; auprès de . . ., Gram: Degrees of c., degrés de comparaison.

compartment [kəm'pa:tmənt], s. 1. Compartiment m. To divide (sth.) into compartments, compartimenter (qch.). N.Arch: Watertight c., compartiment étanche. Rail: First-class c., compartiment de première classe. Smoking c., compartiment (pour) fumeurs. Luggage c., soute f à (aux) bagages. 2. Case f (d'un tiroir).

compartmentalize [ˌkɔmpɑt'məntəlaiz], v.tr. Compartimenter.

compartmentation [kəm,pɑ:tmən'teiʃ(ə)n], s. 1. N. Arch: Compartimentage m (d'un sous-marin, d'un porte-avions). Constr: Cloisonnement m (d'une maison, d'un immeuble). 2. Administrative c. inevitably results in mutual misunderstanding, le compartimentage administratif mène inévitablement au manque réciproque de compréhension.

compass¹ ['kʌmpəs], s. 1. (A pair of) compasses, un compas. Proportional compasses, compas à, de, réduction. 2. (a) Limite(s) f(pl) (d'un endroit). (b) Pourtour m (d'un bâtiment). 3. (a) Étendue f. Knowledge within my c., connaissances à la portée de mon esprit. In small c., sous un volume restreint. (b) Mus: Étendue, registre m (de la voix); clavier m (de la clarinette). 4. (With moving needle) Boussole f; (with moving card) compas. Pocket c., boussole de poche. Mariner's c., compas (de mer). Gyroscopic c., compas m gyroscopique. The points of the c., les aires f de vent. Nau: To take a c. bearing, prendre un relèvement au compas. **'compass-card,** s. Nau: Rose f des vents. **'compass-saw,** s. Scie f à chantourner.

compass², v.tr. 1. Faire le tour de (qch.). 2. O: Compassed about by, with, enemies, entouré d'ennemis. 3. Comprendre; saisir. 4. Jur: Comploter (la mort, la ruine, de qn).

compassion [kəm'pæʃ(ə)n], s. Compassion f. To have c. on s.o., avoir compassion de qn. To arouse c., faire pitié.

compassionate [kəm'pæʃənit], a. Compatissant (to, towards, à, pour). Mil: etc: C. leave, permission exceptionnelle (pour raisons familiales). **-ly,** adv. Avec compassion.

compatibility [kəm,pætə'biliti], s. Compatibilité f.

compatible [kəm'pætəbl], a. Compatible (with, avec). **-ibly,** adv. D'une manière compatible (with, avec).

compatriot [kəm'pætriət], s. Compatriote mf.

compel [kəm'pel], v.tr. (compelled) To c. s.o. to do sth., contraindre, forcer, obliger, qn à, occ. de, faire qch. To be compelled to do sth., se voir forcé de faire qch. He compels respect, il impose le respect. **compelling,** a. C. force, force compulsive. C. curiosity, curiosité irrésistible.

compendious [kəm'pendiəs], a. Abrégé, succinct. **-ly,** adv. En abrégé; succinctement.

compendium, pl. -ums [kəm'pendiəm(z)], s. 1. Abrégé m, compendium m inv. (d'une science, etc.). C. of laws, recueil m des lois. 2. Com: Pochette f (de papeterie).

compensate ['kɔmpənseit]. 1. v.tr. (a) To c. s.o. for sth., dédommager qn de qch. (b) Rémunérer (qn). (c) Mec: Compenser (un pendule, etc.). These errors c. one another, ces erreurs se compensent. 2. v.i. To c. for sth., (i) remplacer, racheter, qch.; (ii) compenser qch. Mec.E: To c. for wear, compenser l'usure. **compensating,** a. 1. C. errors, erreurs qui se compensent. 2. Compensateur, -trice. C. magnet, aimant correcteur. C. arm, bras m de rappel.

compensation [kɔmpən'seiʃ(ə)n], s. 1. Compensation f; dédommagement m; indemnité f; indemnisation f. War damage c., dommages mpl de guerre. Workmen's C. Act, loi f sur les accidents du travail. In c., en revanche. Ph: C. for temperature, compensation en température. 2. U.S: Salaire m.

compensative [kəm'pensətiv], a. Compensateur, -trice; compensatif, -ive.

compensator ['kɔmpənseitər], s. El: Ph: Compensateur m. Aut: Palonnier m (du frein).

compensatory [kəm'pensətri], a. Compensatoire; compensateur, -trice; compensatif, -ive.

compère¹ ['kɔmpeər], s. Th: etc: Compère m.

compère², v.tr. W.Tel: T.V: etc: Être le compère (d'un programme).

compete [kəm'pi:t], v.i. 1. To c. with s.o., faire concurrence à qn. 2. To c. for a prize, concourir pour un prix. To c. with s.o. for a prize, disputer un prix à qn. 3. To c. with s.o. in talent, ardour, le disputer en talent avec qn; rivaliser d'ardeur avec qn.

competence ['kɔmpitəns], s. 1. Compétence f; capacité f. Competence in a subject, compétence en un sujet. 2. Attributions fpl (d'un fonctionnaire); Jur: compétence. It lies beyond my c., cela dépasse ma compétence. 3. A modest c., une modeste indépendance.

competency ['kɔmpitənsi], s. 1. Suffisance f de moyens d'existence. To have a bare c., avoir tout juste de quoi vivre. 2. Capacité f, compétence f.

competent ['kɔmpitənt], a. 1. Capable. 2. Compétent (in a matter, en une matière). 3. (Tribunal) compétent. Jur: Fit and c. to make a will, apte et idoine à tester. 4. C. knowledge of English, connaissance suffisante de l'anglais. **-ly,** adv. 1. Avec compétence. 2. D'une manière suffisante.

competition [ˌkɔmpə'tiʃ(ə)n], s. 1. Rivalité f, concurrence f; compétition f. There was keen c. for it, il y avait un grand nombre de concurrents. 2. Concours m. Chess c., tournoi m d'échecs. The place will be filled by open c., le poste sera mis au concours. 3. Com: Concurrence. Unfair c., concurrence déloyale.

competitive [kəm'petitiv], a. C. spirit, esprit de concurrence. C. design, dessin de concours. C. prices, prix concurrentiels.

competitor [kəm'petitər], s. Concurrent, -ente; compétiteur, -trice. To be a c., être sur les rangs.

compilation [ˌkɔmpaiˈleiʃ(ə)n, ˌkɔmpiˈleiʃ(ə)n], s. Compilation f.

compile [kəmˈpail], v.tr. Compiler. To c. a catalogue, dresser un catalogue.

compiler [kəmˈpailər], s. Compilateur, -trice.

complacence [kəmˈpleis(ə)ns], **complacency** [kəmˈpleis(ə)nsi], s. 1. Satisfaction f. 2. Contentement m de soi-même; suffisance f.

complacent [kəmˈpleis(ə)nt], a. Content de soi-même. C. air, air suffisant. C. optimism, optimisme béat. -ly, adv. Avec satisfaction; avec suffisance.

complain [kəmˈplein], v.i. 1. Se plaindre (of, de). To c. that . . ., se plaindre que + sub. or ind., de ce que + ind. He complains of the heat, il se plaint de la chaleur. I have nothing to c. of, je n'ai pas à me plaindre; je n'ai à me plaindre de rien. 2. Porter plainte (against s.o., contre qn). What do you c. of? sur quoi porte votre plainte? 3. Poet: Se lamenter.

complainant [kəmˈpleinənt], s. Jur: Plaignant, -e.

complainer [kəmˈpleinər], s. Réclamant, -ante; mécontent, -ente.

complaint [kəmˈpleint], s. 1. Lit: (a) Plainte f, doléances fpl. (b) Lit.Hist: Complainte f. 2. (a) Grief m. I have no cause of c., je n'ai aucun sujet de plainte. Let us hear your complaints, exposez vos griefs. That is the general c., tout le monde s'en plaint. (b) To lodge a c. against s.o., porter plainte contre qn. 3. Maladie f, mal m. What is your c.? de quoi souffrez-vous?

complaisance [kəmˈpleiz(ə)ns], s. Complaisance f. obligeance f.

complaisant [kəmˈpleiz(ə)nt], a. Complaisant, obligeant. -ly, adv. Avec complaisance.

complement[1] [ˈkɔmplimənt], s. 1. (a) Plein m (de combustibles, etc.). (b) Navy: etc. Effectif m. Full c., effectif complet. 2. Complément m (d'un verbe, d'un angle, d'un logarithme). Gram: Attribut m.

complement[2] [ˈkɔmpliˈment], v.tr. Compléter.

complementary [ˌkɔmpliˈment(ə)ri], a. (Angle, etc.) complémentaire. The two books are c. to each other, les deux livres se complètent (l'un l'autre).

complete[1] [kəmˈpliːt], a. 1. (a) Complet, -ète; entier, -ière, total. My happiness is c., rien ne manque à mon bonheur. The staff is c., le personnel est au complet. To have c. charge of the business, avoir l'entière direction de la maison. (b) Terminé. My report is not yet c., mon rapport n'est pas encore achevé. 2. Parfait, achevé, accompli. F: A c. idiot, un parfait idiot. -ly, adv. Complètement, totalement.

complete[2], v.tr. 1. Compléter, achever, accomplir. He has completed his twentieth year, il a vingt ans accomplis, révolus. To c. the misfortune . . ., pour comble de malheur. . . . 2. To c. a form, remplir une formule.

completeness [kəmˈpliːtnis], s. État complet; plénitude f (d'une victoire).

completion [kəmˈpliːʃ(ə)n], s. 1. Achèvement m, complètement m. In process of c., en (cours d')achèvement; en voie d'achèvement. Near c., près d'être achevé. (Of house property) Possession on c., prise f de possession dès la signature du contrat. 2. Accomplissement m (d'un vœu); pleine réalisation.

complex [ˈkɔmpleks]. 1. a. Complexe. 2. s. (a) Tout (formé de parties). The industrial c. at Lacq, le complexe industriel de Lacq. (b) Psy: Complexe m. Inferiority c., complexe d'infériorité.

complexion [kəmˈplekʃ(ə)n], s. 1. Teint m. To have a fine c., avoir un joli teint. 2. Aspect m. The affair has assumed a serious c., l'affaire a revêtu un caractère grave.

-complexioned [kəmˈplekʃ(ə)nd], a. To be fair-, dark-c., être blond, brun. Fresh-c., au teint frais.

complexity [kəmˈpleksiti], s. Complexité f.

compliance [kəmˈplaiəns], s. 1. Acquiescement m (with, à). In c. with your wishes, conformément à vos désirs. To refuse c. with an order, refuser d'obéir à un ordre. Pej: (Base) c., soumission (abjecte). Questionable c., complaisance f d'une moralité douteuse.

compliant [kəmˈplaiənt], a. 1. Obligeant, accommodant. 2. D'une complaisance servile; souple.

complicate [ˈkɔmplikeit], v.tr. Compliquer (with, de).

complicated, a. Compliqué; (affaire) embrouillée.

complication [ˌkɔmpliˈkeiʃ(ə)n], s. Complication f.

complicity [kəmˈplisiti], s. Complicité f (in, à).

compliment[1] [ˈkɔmplimənt], s. Compliment m. To pay a c. to s.o., faire, adresser, un compliment à qn. Mil: Navy: To pay compliments, rendre les honneurs m. (At end of letter) To send one's compliments to s.o., se rappeler au bon souvenir de qn. Compliments of the season, meilleurs souhaits de nouvel an. With the publisher's compliments, hommage de l'éditeur.

compliment[2] [ˈkɔmpliˈment], v.tr. Complimenter, féliciter (qn) (on, de).

complimentary [ˌkɔmpliˈment(ə)ri], a. 1. Flatteur, -euse. 2. Gracieux, -euse. C. copy, exemplaire envoyé à titre gracieux.

complin(e) [ˈkɔmplin], s. Ecc: Complies fpl.

comply [kəmˈplai], v.i. To c. with (sth.), se conformer à (une formalité); se soumettre à (la loi); observer (une règle); accéder à (une demande); obéir à (un ordre). He complied gracefully, il s'exécuta avec grâce. Your wishes have been complied with, vos désirs ont reçu satisfaction.

component [kəmˈpounənt]. 1. a. C. parts, parties constituantes. Mec: C. forces, forces composantes. 2. s. (a) Composant m; partie composante. (b) Organe m (d'une machine). (c) Opt: Four-c. lens, objectif à quatre lentilles.

comport [kəmˈpɔːt]. 1. v.i. S'accorder, convenir (with, à). 2. v.pr. To c. oneself, se comporter.

comportment [kəmˈpɔːtmənt], s. Conduite f, maintien m.

compose [kəmˈpouz], v.tr. 1. Composer. Typ: To c. a line, composer une ligne. An engine is composed of many parts, un moteur se compose, est composé, de nombreux organes. 2. Art: To c. the figures in a picture, arranger les personnages d'un tableau. 3. Arranger, accommoder (un différend). 4. (a) To c. one's features, se composer le visage. To c. oneself to sleep, se disposer au sommeil. (b) C. yourself! calmez-vous! **composed**, a. Calme, tranquille. **composing**, s. Composition f. Typ: C.-stick, composteur m.

composedly [kəmˈpouzidli], adv. Tranquillement; avec calme.

composer [kəmˈpouzər], s. Compositeur, -trice (de musique).

Compositae [kəmˈpɔziti:], s.pl. Bot: Composacées fpl.

composite [ˈkɔmpɔzit]. 1. a. (a) (Fleur) composée. Arch: (Chapiteau) composite. (b) (Train) mixte. (c) Cin: C. shot, impression combinée. 2. s. Composé m. Bot: Composée f.

composition [ˌkɔmpəˈziʃ(ə)n], s. 1. (a) Action f de composer; composition f (de qch.). Mec: C. of forces, la composition des forces. (b) Composition, constitution f (de l'air, etc.). Art: Composition. 2. Mélange m, composé m. 3. (a) A musical c., une composition musicale. (b) Sch: Dissertation f, rédaction f; narration f. (c) Sch: Thème m. To do a paper in French c., faire un thème français. 4. (a) Accommodement m, entente f. To enter into a c. with s.o. over sth., composer avec qn sur qch. (b) Transaction f. C. for stamp duty, (taxe f d')abonnement m au timbre. (c) Accommodement (avec des créanciers); concordat m.

compositor [kəmˈpɔzitər], s. Typ: Compositeur m, typographe m.

compos mentis [ˈkɔmpɔsˈmentis], a. Jur: Sain d'esprit. Non c. (m.), aliéné.

compost[1] [ˈkɔmpɔst], s. Hort: Compost m; terreau m.

compost[2], v.tr. Composter; terreauter.

composure [kəmˈpouʒər], s. Calme m, sang-froid m. To retain one's c., garder son sang-froid.

compound[1] [ˈkɔmpaund]. 1. a. (a) Composé. Gram: C. word, mot composé. C. interest, intérêts composés. S.a. FRACTURE[1] 1. (b) Complexe. C. addition, addition de nombres complexes. (c) El.E: C. steel, acier compound inv. El.E: C. wound, à enroulement compoundé. II. compound, s. 1. (Corps m) composé m. 2. Tchn: Composition f, mastic m. 3. Gram: Mot composé.

compound² [kəm'paund]. 1. v.tr. (a) Composer, mélanger (une boisson, etc.); combiner (des éléments). (b) Accommoder, arranger (un différend); régler (un différend) à l'amiable. (c) To c. a felony, pactiser avec un crime. (d) El.E: Compounder (une dynamo). 2. v.i. S'arranger, composer (with s.o., avec qn); transiger (avec sa conscience). compounding, s. 1. Composition f; confection f (de drogues). 2. El.E: Compoundage m.

compoundable [kəm'paundəbl], a. (Dette f, etc.) qui peut s'arranger à l'amiable, sur laquelle on peut venir à composition.

comprehend [‚kɔmpri'hend], v.tr. Comprendre. 1. Se rendre compte de (qch.). 2. Englober. comprehending, a. Qui comprend; plein de compréhension; compréhensif, -ive.

comprehensibility [‚kɔmpri,hensi'biliti], s. Compréhensibilité f; intelligibilité f.

comprehensible [‚kɔmpri'hensəbl], a. Compréhensible, intelligible. -ibly, adv. D'une manière compréhensible, intelligible.

comprehension [‚kɔmpri'henʃ(ə)n], s. Compréhension f. 1. Entendement m. 2. Portée f, étendue f.

comprehensive [‚kɔmpri'hensiv], a. Compréhensif, -ive. 1. Phil: The c. faculty, l'entendement m. 2. C. study, étude d'ensemble. C. knowledge, connaissances étendues; vaste érudition. -ly, adv. Dans un sens très étendu; largement.

comprehensiveness [‚kɔmpri'hensivnis], s. Étendue f, portée f (d'un mot, d'une offre).

compress¹ ['kɔmpres], s. Surg: Compresse f.

compress² [kəm'pres], v.tr. (a) Comprimer (un gaz); bander (un ressort); (of compressor) refouler (l'air). (b) (With passive force) (Of gas, etc.) Se comprimer; (of spring) fléchir. 2. Condenser (un discours); concentrer (son style). compressed, a. Comprimé. C. air, air comprimé. compressing, a. Comprimant; compresseur, -euse.

compressibility [kəm,presi'biliti], s. Compressibilité f.

compressible [kəm'presəbl], a. Compressible, comprimable.

compression [kəm'preʃ(ə)n], s. 1. Compression f. I.C.E: C. tap, robinet de décompression. 2. Concentration f (du style).

compressive [kəm'presiv], a. Compressif, -ive. C. stress, effort de compression.

compressor [kəm'presər], s. Compresseur m (de gaz, d'air, etc.). Dom.Ec: C.-type refrigerator, réfrigérateur m à compresseur. Constr: C.-unit, compresseur mobile (à moteur) Diesel.

comprise [kəm'praiz], v.tr. Comprendre, comporter, renfermer.

compromise¹ ['kɔmprəmaiz], s. Compromis m. To agree to a c., accepter une transaction; transiger. Policy of c., politique d'accommodements. Policy of no c., politique intransigeante.

compromise². 1. v.tr. (a) Compromettre (son honneur, etc.). To c. oneself with s.o., se compromettre avec qn. (b) Arranger (un différend). 2. v.i. Compromettre, transiger. If he agrees to c., s'il accepte un compromis. compromising,¹ a. Compromettant. compromising², s. 1. Compromission f (de son honneur). 2. Composition f (d'un différend).

comptometer [kɔmp'tɔmitər]. s. R.t.m: Machine f à calculer.

comptroller [kən'troulər], s. 1. Administrateur m (d'une maison royale, etc.). 2. Contrôleur m; vérificateur m (de comptes).

compulsion [kəm'pʌlʃ(ə)n], s. 1. Contrainte f, compulsion f. Under c., par contrainte. To obey only under c., n'obéir qu'à son corps défendant. 2. Psy: Impulsion f.

compulsive [kəm'pʌlsiv], a. 1. = COMPULSORY 2. 2. Psy: Impulsif, -ive. A c. act, action commise sous une impulsion (psychologique). -ly, adv. 1. Par force, par contrainte. 2. Psy: Impulsivement; par impulsion (psychologique).

compulsory [kəm'pʌls(ə)ri], a. 1. Obligatoire. C. loan, emprunt forcé. 2. C. powers, pouvoirs coercitifs. -ily, adv. Obligatoirement.

compunction [kəm'pʌŋ(k)ʃ(ə)n], s. Componction f; remords m. Without c., sans scrupule.

computable [kəm'pju:təbl], a. Calculable.

computation [‚kɔmpju(:)'teiʃ(ə)n], s. Calcul m, estimation f. Ecc: Comput m (du calendrier). To make a c. of sth., calculer qch. Beyond c., incalculable.

compute [kəm'pju:t], v.tr. Computer, calculer, estimer. Computed horse-power, chevaux-vapeur estimés.

computer [kəm'pju:tər], s. 1. (Pers.) Calculateur m. 2. Machine f mécanographique, ordinateur m; F: machine à calculer. Electronic c., calculateur m, calculatrice f, électronique.

comrade ['kɔmreid], s. (a) Camarade m, compagnon m. Comrades in arms, compagnons d'armes. (b) (As term of address between Communists) Camarade mf.

comradeship ['kɔmreidʃip], s. Camaraderie f.

con¹ [kɔn], v.tr. (conned) O: Étudier (un rôle).

con², v.tr. Nau: Gouverner (un navire). To c. the ship, diriger, commander, la manœuvre. 'conning-tower, s. Navy: Tourelle f de commandement; kiosque m (de sous-marin).

con³, a. U.S: F: attrib. = CONFIDENCE 4. C.-man, escroc m.

con⁴, v.tr. U.S: F: Escroquer (qn).

con⁵, prep. & s. See PRO.

concatenation [kɔn,kæti'neiʃ(ə)n], s. Enchaînement m (d'idées); concours m (de circonstances).

concave ['kɔnkeiv], a. Concave.

concavity [kɔn'kæviti], s. Concavité f.

conceal [kən'si:l], v.tr. (a) Cacher; celer, dissimuler (la vérité, son chagrin, etc.); masquer (ses projets, une fenêtre); voiler (ses pensées); tenir secret (un projet). I do not c. the fact that it is so, je ne dissimule pas qu'il en est ainsi, qu'il n'en soit ainsi. To c. sth. from s.o., cacher qch. à qn; taire qch. à qn. To c. one's movements from the enemy, dérober sa marche à l'ennemi. (b) Jur: Receler (un malfaiteur, un objet volé). concealed, a. Caché, dissimulé, invisible, masqué. C. lighting, éclairage indirect.

concealment [kən'si:lmənt], s. 1. Dissimulation f. 2. Jur: (a) Cel m, recel m. C. of birth, recel d'enfant; non-présentation f d'enfant. (b) Réticence f. 3. Action f de cacher ou de se cacher. To find a place of c., trouver une cachette, une retraite.

concede [kən'si:d], v.tr. 1. Concéder. I will c. nothing, je ne ferai aucune concession. 2. To c. that one is wrong, concéder, admettre, qu'on a tort.

conceit [kən'si:t], s. 1. Vanité f, suffisance f. Eaten up with c., pétri d'amour-propre. 2. He has a very good c. of himself, il est très satisfait de sa petite personne. 3. A: Trait m d'esprit. pl. Conceits, concetti m.

conceited [kən'si:tid], a. Suffisant, vaniteux, -euse. A c. young idiot, un jeune prétentieux. A c. little minx, une petite mijaurée. -ly, adv. Avec suffisance.

conceivable [kən'si:vəbl], a. Concevable, imaginable. -ably, adv. He may c. have reached the summit, il est concevable qu'il ait pu atteindre jusqu'au sommet.

conceive [kən'si:v], v.tr. 1. Concevoir (un enfant). Who was conceived by the Holy Ghost, qui a été conçu du Saint-Esprit. 2. (a) Concevoir (un projet). To c. a dislike for s.o., prendre qn en aversion. (b) I cannot c. why you should allow it, je ne conçois pas pourquoi vous le permettriez. 3. v.i. To c. of sth., (s')imaginer, comprendre, qch. That is not the case, as you may well c., vous pouvez bien vous imaginer qu'il n'en est pas ainsi.

concentrate¹ ['kɔnsəntreit], s. Concentré m. Tomato c., concentré de tomate.

concentrate². 1. v.tr. Concentrer (des troupes, son attention). Mil: To c. the fire of a battery, faire converger les feux d'une batterie. 2. v.i. (a) Se concentrer. (b) To c. on sth., concentrer son attention sur qch. concentrated, a. Concentré. C. orange juice, jus m d'orange concentré. Mil: C. fire, tir convergent. Art: C. composition, composition ramassée.

concentration [‚kɔnsen'treiʃ(ə)n], s. 1. (a) Concentration f (d'une solution, etc.); Mil: convergence f (des feux). Pol: C. camp, camp m de concentration. Prisoner in c. camp, concentrationnaire mf. (b) Ch: (Degree of) c., titre m (d'un acide). 2. Power of c., faculté f de concentration, d'application. 3. Hostile c., rassemblement ennemi.

concentre [kɔn'sentər], v. Opt: Phys: etc: **1.** v.tr. Réunir (des rayons, etc.) en un centre commun; concentrer (des éléments). **2.** v.i. Se concentrer; se réunir.

concentric [kɔn'sentrik], a. Concentrique. **-ally,** adv. Concentriquement.

concentricity [ˌkɔnsen'trisiti], s. Arrangement m concentrique; concentricité f. Techn: Centrage m.

concept ['kɔnsept], s. Concept m; idée générale.

conception [kɔn'sepʃ(ə)n], s. Conception f (d'un enfant, d'une idée). **To have a clear c. of sth.,** se représenter clairement qch. par la pensée. F: **I haven't the remotest c.,** je n'en ai pas la moindre idée.

concern[1] [kɔn'sə:n], s. **1.** (a) Rapport m. (b) Intérêt m (in, dans). **It's no c. of mine,** cela ne me regarde pas; ce n'est pas mon affaire. **2.** Souci m, anxiété f, inquiétude f (about, à l'égard de). **He enquired with c. . . .,** il demanda avec sollicitude f. . . . **He showed deep c. at the news,** il s'est montré très affecté de cette nouvelle. **3.** (a) Com: Ind: Entreprise f; maison f de commerce, fonds m de commerce. **The whole c. is for sale,** toute l'entreprise est mise en vente. F: **I'm sick of the whole c.,** j'en ai marre de tout le bataclan. (b) F: Appareil m, machin m, truc m. **He smashed the whole c.,** il a démoli tout l'appareil.

concern[2], v.tr. **1.** (a) Concerner, regarder, intéresser (qn, qch.); se rapporter à (qn, qch.). **That does not c. me,** cela ne me regarde pas. **You are the most closely concerned,** c'est vous le premier intéressé. **It concerns him to know . . .,** il lui importe de savoir. . . . **To whom it may c.,** à toutes fins utiles. **Treaty concerning a country,** traité relatif à un pays. **As concerns . . .,** quant à . . ., pour ce qui est de. . . . (b) **To c. oneself with, about, in, sth.,** s'intéresser à, s'occuper de, se mêler de, qch. **2.** (a) **To be concerned in, with, sth.,** s'intéresser à, s'occuper de, qch.; être en cause. **His honour is concerned,** il s'agit de son honneur. **The parties, persons, concerned,** les intéressés. **As far as I am concerned,** en ce qui me concerne; quant à moi. **This book is concerned with . . .,** ce livre traite de . . ., il s'agit dans ce livre de . . . **To pass on to the department concerned,** transmettre au service compétent. (b) **To be concerned about sth.,** s'inquiéter, être inquiet, de qch. **I am concerned for his health,** sa santé me donne des inquiétudes. **He looked very much concerned,** il avait l'air très soucieux. **concerning,** prep. Concernant, touchant, en ce qui concerne, au sujet de (qn, qch.).

concernedly [kɔn'sə:nidli], adv. Avec inquiétude; d'un air soucieux.

concert[1] ['kɔnsət], s. **1.** Concert m, accord m. **To sing in c.,** chanter à l'unisson. **To act in c. (with s.o.),** agir de concert, d'accord (avec qn). **2.** Mus: Concert; séance musicale. **C. performer,** concertiste mf. **'concert-'grand,** s. Mus: Piano m à grande queue. **'concert-hall,** s. Salle f de concert. **'concert-pitch,** s. Diapason m de concert (anglais). (Of pers.) **To keep up to c.-p.,** se maintenir en forme.

concert[2] [kɔn'sə:t], v. **1.** v.tr. Concerter (des mesures). **2.** v.i. Se concerter, tenir conseil (with, avec). **concerted,** a. Concerté. **To act with no c. plan,** agir sans plan concerté. **C. action,** action f d'ensemble. Mus: **C. piece,** morceau concertant.

concertina [ˌkɔnsə'ti:nə], s. **1.** Mus: Accordéon hexagonal. **2.** Rail: **C. vestibule** (joining coaches), soufflet m.

concerto [kə'ntʃeətou], s. Mus: Concerto m.

concession [kɔn'seʃ(ə)n], s. Concession f (de terrain, d'opinion). **Mining c.,** concession minière. Com: Réduction f.

concession(n)aire [kɔnˌseʃə'nɛər], s. Concessionnaire m.

concessionary [kɔn'seʃənri]. **1.** a. (a) (Compagnie f, etc.) concessionnaire. (b) (Subside, etc.) concédé. **2.** s. = CONCESSION(N)AIRE.

concessive [kɔn'sesiv], a. Concessif, -ive.

conch [kɔŋk, kɔn(t)ʃ], s. Conque f.

concha ['kɔŋkə], s. **1.** Conque f (de l'oreille); oreille f externe. **2.** Voûte f d'abside.

conchie ['kɔnʃi], s. P: = CONCHY.

conchoidal [kɔŋ'kɔid(ə)l], a. Geom: etc: Conchoïdal, -aux.

conchology [kɔŋ'kɔlədʒi], s. Nat.Hist: Conchyliologie f.

conchy ['kɔnʃi], s. P: = conscientious objector, q.v. under CONSCIENTIOUS.

conciliate [kɔn'silieit], v.tr. **1.** Concilier, réconcilier (des intérêts opposés). **2. To c. s.o.'s favour,** se concilier la faveur de qn.

conciliation [kɔnˌsili'eiʃ(ə)n], s. Conciliation f. Ind: **C. board,** conseil m d'arbitrage.

conciliator [kɔn'silieitər], s. Conciliateur, -trice.

conciliatory [kɔn'siliət(ə)ri], a. Conciliant; conciliatoire.

concise [kɔn'sais], a. Concis. **-ly,** adv. Avec concision.

conciseness [kɔn'saisnis], s. Concision f.

concision [kɔn'siʒ(ə)n], s. Concision f.

conclave ['kɔnkleiv], s. **1.** R.C.Ch: Conclave m. **2.** (a) Assemblée f, réunion f. (b) Conseil (tenu à huis clos).

conclavist ['kɔnkleivist], s. Ecc: Conclaviste m.

conclude [kɔn'klu:d], v.tr. & i. **1.** Conclure (un traité, etc.); arranger, régler (une affaire). **2.** (a) Terminer, conclure, achever. **To c. by saying,** dire en terminant. **To be concluded in our next issue,** la fin au prochain numéro. (b) v.i. **The report concludes as follows,** le rapport se termine comme (il) suit. **3.** **From this I c. that . . .,** de ceci je conclus, j'estime, que. . . . **4. To c. in favour of a course of action,** conclure à une ligne de conduite. **concluding,** a. Final, -als.

conclusion [kɔn'klu:ʒ(ə)n], s. **1.** Conclusion f (d'un traité). **2.** Fin f, conclusion (d'une lettre); clôture f (d'une session). **In c.,** pour conclure. **3.** (a) Log: Conclusion (d'un syllogisme). (b) **Conclusions arrived at,** décisions prises. **To come to the c. that . . .,** conclure que. . . . **It was a foregone c.,** c'était prévu. **It's up to you to draw your own conclusions,** à vous d'en juger. F: **To try conclusions with s.o.,** se mesurer avec, contre, qn. S.a. JUMP[2] I 1.

conclusive [kɔn'klu:siv], a. **1.** (Of argument) Concluant, décisif, -ive. (Of test) Probant. **-ly,** adv. D'une manière concluante, probante.

concoct [kɔn'kɔkt], v.tr. **1.** Composer (un cocktail); confectionner (un plat). **2.** Imaginer, combiner (un plan); tramer (un complot).

concoction [kɔn'kɔkʃ(ə)n], s. **1.** (a) Confectionnement m (d'un plat, etc.). (b) Boisson f, potion f. **2.** (a) Conception f; machination f (d'un complot). (b) **C. of lies,** tissu m de mensonges.

concomitant [kɔn'kɔmit(ə)nt]. **1.** a. Concomitant (with, de). **2.** s. Accessoire m, accompagnement m.

concord ['kɔnkɔ:d], s. **1.** Concorde f, harmonie f, paix f, entente f. **To live in c.,** vivre en bon accord (with, avec). **2.** Gram: Concordance f. **The concords, les règles f d'accord. **3.** Mus: Accord.

concordance [kɔn'kɔ:d(ə)ns], s. **1.** Concordance f, accord m (with, avec); harmonie f. **2.** Index m, concordance (de la Bible, des œuvres d'un auteur).

concordant [kɔn'kɔ:d(ə)nt], a. **1.** Qui s'accorde, concordant (with, avec). **2.** Mus: Consonant.

concordat [kɔn'kɔ:dæt], s. Concordat m.

concours ['kɔnkuə], s. Aut: **C. d'élégance,** concours d'élégance. **Hors c.,** hors concours.

concourse ['kɔnkɔ:s], s. **1.** (a) Foule f, rassemblement m, concours m (de personnes). (b) Carrefour m. **2.** **Unforeseen c. of circumstances,** concours inattendu de circonstances.

concrescence [kɔn'kresns], s. Biol: Concrétion f.

concrete[1] ['kɔnkri:t]. **1.** a. Concret, -ète. Jur: **C. case,** cas d'espèce. **C. suggestion, proposal, application** f, proposition f, pratique, concrète. **2.** s. Béton m (de ciment). **Reinforced c.,** béton armé. **C. work,** bétonnage m. **-ly,** adv. D'une manière concrète. **'concrete-mixer,** s. Bétonneuse f.

concrete[2] ['kɔnkri:t, kɔn'kri:t]. **1.** v.tr. Const: Bétonner. **2.** v.i. Se solidifier; se prendre en masse. **concreting,** s. Bétonnage m.

concretion [kɔn'kri:ʃ(ə)n], s. Concrétion f.

concubinage [kɔn'kju:binidʒ], s. Concubinage m.

concubinary [kɔn'kju:binri]. **1.** a. Concubin. **2.** s. Concubinaire m.

concubine ['kɔŋkjubain], s.f. Concubine.

concupiscence [kɔn'kju:pisns], s. Concupiscence f.

concupiscent [kɔn'kju:pisənt], a. Libidineux, -euse.

concur [kən'kəːr], v.i. (concurred) 1. (a) (Of events) Concourir, coïncider. (b) To c. to produce a result, contribuer à produire un résultat. 2. (Of pers.) Être d'accord (with s.o., avec qn); partager l'opinion (de qn). All c. in the belief that . . ., tous s'accordent à croire que. . . .

concurrence [kən'kʌr(ə)ns], s. 1. (a) Concours m (de circonstances); coopération f (de personnes). Geom: Point of c., point de concours. (b) Simultanéité f. 2. (Of pers.) (a) Accord m. (b) Assentiment m, approbation f. 3. Jur: Conflit m, concurrence f (de droits).

concurrent [kən'kʌr(ə)nt], a. 1. (a) Geom: C. lines, lignes concourantes. (b) Simultané; coexistant. (c) C. cause, cause contribuante. 2. Unanime, concordant. -ly, adv. Concurremment (with, avec). Jur: The two sentences to run c., avec confusion des deux peines.

concuss [kən'kʌs], v.tr. (a) Ébranler, secouer (qch.). (b) Med: F: Commotionner (le cerveau).

concussion [kən'kʌʃ(ə)n], s. Secousse f, ébranlement m. Med: Commotion (cérébrale). Artil: C. fuse, fusée percutante.

condemn [kən'dem], v.tr. Condamner. 1. To c. s.o. to death, condamner qn à (la) mort. **Condemned cell,** cellule des condamnés. **The condemned man (on the scaffold),** le patient. **Condemned to lead a hopeless existence,** condamné à vivre sans espoir. 2. To c. stores, condamner, réformer, du matériel. 3. Déclarer coupable. His looks c. him, sa mine le condamne. 4. Censurer, blâmer.

condemnation [ˌkɔndem'neiʃ(ə)n], s. 1. (a) Condamnation f. (b) Censure f, blâme m. 2. Mil: Réforme f (du matériel).

condemnatory [kən'demnətri], a. (Silence m, etc.) condamnatoire.

condensable [kən'densəbl], a. Condensable.

condensation [ˌkɔnden'seiʃ(ə)n], s. 1. Condensation f (de la vapeur, d'un gaz). 2. Liquide condensé.

condense [kən'dens]. 1. v.tr. Condenser (un gaz, une pensée); serrer (son style); concentrer (un produit). 2. v.i. Se condenser. **condensed,** a. Condensé. C. milk, lait concentré, condensé.

condenser [kən'densər], s. 1. (a) Mch: Gasm: Condenseur m. (b) Nau: Fresh-water c., distillateur m. 2. El: Opt: Condensateur m.

condescend [ˌkɔndi'send], v.i. 1. Condescendre (to do sth., à faire qch.); s'abaisser (à, jusqu'à, faire qch.). 2. Se montrer condescendant (to s.o., envers qn). **condescending,** a. Condescendant (to, envers). -ly, adv. Avec condescendance. To treat s.o. c., traiter qn de haut en bas.

condescension [ˌkɔndi'senʃ(ə)n], s. 1. Condescendance f (to, envers, pour). 2. Complaisance f.

condign [kən'dain], a. (Châtiment) mérité, exemplaire; juste (punition).

condiment ['kɔndimənt], s. Condiment m; assaisonnement m.

condition¹ [kən'diʃ(ə)n], s. Condition f. 1. To impose conditions on s.o., poser des conditions à qn. **Conditions laid down in an agreement,** stipulations f d'un contrat. On c. that . . ., à (la) condition que. . . . 2. (a) État m, situation f. In (a) good, bad, c., en bon, mauvais, état. F: She's in an interesting c., elle est dans une situation intéressante, elle est enceinte. To be in a (fit) c. to do sth., être à même, en état, de faire qch. Not in a c. to do sth., hors d'état de faire qch. To keep oneself in c., se maintenir en forme. Ind: Working conditions in the factory, les conditions de travail à l'usine. The c. of the workers, la situation des ouvriers. Com: Conditions of sale, conditions de vente. (b) État civil. To change one's c., changer d'état; se marier. (c) O: People of humble c., gens de simple condition. 3. pl. Weather conditions, conditions atmosphériques.

condition², v.tr. 1. Conditionner; soumettre (qch.) à une condition. **The receipts are conditioned by the capacity of the hall,** les recettes dépendent de la capacité de la salle. **Everything that conditions laws,** tout ce qui conditionne les lois. 2. Ind: Conditionner (la soie, l'air d'un cinéma, etc.). **conditioned,** a. (Of proposition) Conditionné. Med: C. reflex, réflexe conditionné. S.a. AIR-CONDITIONED.

conditional [kən'diʃnəl]. 1. a. Conditionnel, -elle. (a) My promise was c., ma promesse était soumise à certaines réserves. (b) C. on sth., dépendant de qch. (c) Gram: C. mood, mode conditionnel. 2. s. Gram: Verb in the c., verbe au conditionnel. -ally, adv. Conditionnellement; sous certaines conditions. C. on . . ., à la condition que. . . .

condolatory [kən'doulət(ə)ri], a. (Lettre, etc.) de condoléance.

condole [kən'doul], v.i. To c. with s.o., exprimer ses condoléances à qn.

condolence [kən'douləns], s. Condoléance f.

condominium [ˌkɔndə'miniəm], s. Condominium m.

condonation [ˌkɔndo'neiʃ(ə)n], s. Pardon m; indulgence f (of, pour).

condone [kən'doun], v.tr. 1. Pardonner. 2. (Of action) Racheter (une offense).

condor ['kɔndəːr], s. Orn: Condor m.

conduce [kən'djuːs], v.i. Contribuer, tendre (to, à). Virtues that c. to success, vertus qui favorisent le succès.

conducive [kən'djuːsiv], a. Qui contribue (à qch.); favorable (à qch.).

conduct¹ ['kɔndʌkt], s. Conduite f. 1. C. of affairs, conduite, gestion f, maniement m, des affaires. Unprofessional c., manquement m aux devoirs de la profession. S.a. SAFE-CONDUCT. 2. Allure f; manière f de se conduire. C. towards s.o., conduite à l'égard de, envers qn.

conduct² [kən'dʌkt], v.tr. 1. Conduire, (a)mener (qn). Conducted tours, excursions accompagnées; vacances fpl en groupe. 2. (a) Mener, gérer (des affaires); diriger (des opérations). Who will c. the negotiations? qui va mener les négociations? Jur: To c. one's own case, plaider soi-même sa cause. (b) Mus: Diriger (un orchestre). 3. To c. oneself, se comporter, se conduire (bien, mal). 4. Ph: Être conducteur de. . . . Substance that conducts heat, substance conductrice de la chaleur. **conducting¹,** a. Conducteur, -trice. **conducting²,** s. 1. Conduite f (de touristes, etc.). 2. Exécution f (d'un essai); conduite f (d'une entreprise, etc.). 3. L'art de diriger (un orchestre).

conductance [kən'dʌktəns], s. El: Conductance f.

conductibility [kənˌdʌkti'biliti], s. Ph: Conductibilité f.

conductible [kən'dʌktəbl], a. Ph: Conductible.

conduction [kən'dʌkʃ(ə)n], s. Ph: Conduction f, transmission f (de la chaleur).

conductive [kən'dʌktiv], a. Conducteur, -trice.

conductivity [ˌkɔndʌk'tiviti], s. Ph: Conductivité f, conductibilité f.

conductor [kən'dʌktər], s. 1. (a) Conducteur m (de personnes). (b) Receveur m (d'un autobus). Rail: U.S: Chef m de train. (c) Mus: Chef d'orchestre. 2. Conducteur m (de la chaleur, de l'électricité). S.a. LIGHTNING-CONDUCTOR.

conductress [kən'dʌktris], s.f. Receveuse f (d'un autobus).

conduit ['kɔndjuit, 'kɔnd(w)it], s. (a) Hyd.E: C.(-pipe), conduit m; tuyau conducteur. (b) El.E: Cable-c., tube m guide-fils; manchon m pour câbles.

cone¹ [koun], s. 1. (a) Cône m. Truncated c., tronc m de cône. Ball: C. of fire, of dispersion, gerbe f (de dispersion), cône d'éclatement. Mil: Nose c. (of rocket), ogive f. (b) Ice-(cream) c., cornet m de glace, de crème glacée. 2. Blast-furnace c., cloche f, trémie f, de haut-fourneau. S.a. STORM-CONE. 3. Bot: Pomme f, cône (de pin, de houblon). 4. Cône (d'un volcan). **'cone-bearing,** a. Bot: Conifère. **'cone-clutch,** s. Mec.E: Embrayage m à cône. **'cone-pulley,** s. Poulie étagée. **'cone-shaped,** a. En forme de cône; côné, conique. **'cone-wheel,** s. Mec.E: Roue f conique (à friction).

cone², v.tr. Av: Prendre (un avion) dans un cône de projecteurs.

coney ['kouni], s. 1. (a) F: Lapin m. (b) Com: Peau f de lapin. 2. Daman m.

confab¹ ['kɔnfæb], s. F: = CONFABULATION. There's a family c. going on, toute la famille est en train de conférer.

confab², v.i. F: = CONFABULATE.

confabulate [kən'fæbjuleit], v.i. Tenir un colloque; causer; conférer.

confabulation [kənfæbju'leiʃ(ə)n], s. Causerie f intime; entretien familier; colloque m; conciliabule m.

confect [kən'fekt], v.tr. U.S: 1. Mélanger, combiner, fabriquer (un plat, des médicaments). 2. Iron: Composer, élucubrer (un poème, un roman). 3. Dressm: Confectionner (une robe).

confection [kən'fekʃ(ə)n], s. Confection f.

confectioner [kən'fekʃənər], s. Confiseur m. Baker and c., boulanger-pâtissier m.

confectionery [kən'fekʃən(ə)ri], s. Confiserie f; pâtisserie f.

confederacy [kən'fed(ə)rəsi], s. 1. Confédération f (d'États). 2. Conspiration f.

confederate[1] [kən'fed(ə)rit]. 1. a. Confédéré (with, avec). 2. s. (a) Confédéré m. (b) Jur: Complice m (with, de). (c) Conjuror's c., comparse m.

confederate[2] [kən'fedəreit]. 1. v.tr. Confédérer (des États). 2. v.i. (a) Se confédérer (with, avec). (b) Conspirer (against, contre).

confederation [kən,fedə'reiʃ(ə)n], s. Confédération f. Hist: The Fathers of the C., les pères de la Confédération.

confer [kən'fə:r], v. (conferred) 1. v.tr. Conférer (a title on s.o., un titre à qn). To c. a favour on s.o., accorder une faveur· à qn. 2. v.i. Conférer, entrer en consultation (with s.o. on sth., about sth., avec qn sur qch.). **conferring**, s. 1. = CONFERMENT. 2. Consultation f.

conference ['kɔnf(ə)r(ə)ns], s. 1. Conférence f, entretien m, consultation f. Press c., conférence f de presse. 2. International c., congrès international.

conferment [kən'fə:mənt], s. 1. Collation f (d'un titre). 2. Octroi m (d'une faveur).

confess [kən'fes], v.tr. 1. (a) Confesser, avouer (une faute). To c. oneself (to be) guilty, s'avouer coupable. I was wrong, I c., j'ai eu tort, je l'avoue, j'en conviens. (b) Abs. (Of criminal) Faire des aveux. (c) v.ind.tr. To c. to having done sth., se confesser de qch. To c. to a crime, avouer un crime. To c. to a liking for . . ., avouer avoir un penchant, un faible, pour. . . . 2. Ecc: (a) To c. one's sins, confesser ses péchés. To c. (oneself), faire sa confession, se confesser (to s.o., à qn, auprès de qn). (b) (Of priest) Confesser (un pénitent). 3. To c. the faith, confesser sa foi. **confessed**, a. Confessé, avoué. The c. murderer of . . ., le meurtrier avoué de. . . . To stand confessed as . . ., se révéler, s'accuser, comme. . . .

confessedly [kən'fesidli], adv. 1. De l'aveu général. 2. Ouvertement.

confession [kən'feʃ(ə)n], s. 1. Confession f, aveu (de qch.). To make a full c., faire des aveux complets. By general c., de l'aveu de tout le monde. 2. Ecc: (Auricular) c., confession (auriculaire, privée). The seal of c., le secret du confessional. To go to c., aller à confesse. To hear s.o.'s c., confesser qn. To make one's c., faire sa confession. 3. C. of faith, confession de foi. People of all confessions, des gens de toutes les confessions.

confessional [kən'feʃənl]. 1. a. Confessionnel, -elle. 2. s. Ecc: Confessionnal m.

confessor [kən'fesər], s. 1. Personne f qui avoue (un crime). 2. (Priest) Confesseur m. 3. Confesseur (de sa foi).

confetti [kən'feti(:)], s.pl. Confetti m.

confidant, f. **confidante** [ˌkɔnfi'dænt], s. Confident, -ente.

confide [kən'faid]. 1. v.tr. Confier. (a) He confided to me that . . ., il m'avoua en confidence que. . . . (b) To c. sth. to s.o.'s care, confier qch. à la garde de qn. 2. v.i. To c. in s.o., (i) se fier à qn; (ii) se confier à qn. **confiding**, a. Confiant; sans soupçons. To be of a c. nature, être peu soupçonneux, -euse. -ly, adv. Avec confiance; d'un air confiant.

confidence ['kɔnfidəns], s. 1. (a) Confiance f (in, en). To put one's c. in s.o., mettre sa confiance en qn. To have every c. in s.o., faire toute confiance à qn. To lose the c. of the public, perdre toute créance. Parl: To ask for a vote of c., poser la question de confiance. Motion of no c., motion de défiance f. (b) Assurance f, confiance, hardiesse f. I have every c. that he will succeed, j'ai l'assurance qu'il réussira. 2. Confidence f. To tell s.o. sth. in c., dire qch. à qn en confidence. In strict c., à titre essentiellement confidentiel. 3.

To make a c. to s.o., faire une confidence à qn. 4. C. trick, U.S: c. game, vol m à l'américaine. C. man, c. trickster, escroc m, chevalier m d'industrie.

confident ['kɔnfidənt]. 1. a. (a) Assuré, sûr (of, de); confiant. C. of success, sûr de réussir. (b) Pej: Plein de hardiesse; effronté. 2. s. Confident, -ente. -ly, 1. adv. Avec, de, confiance. 2. Avec assurance.

confidential [ˌkɔnfi'denʃ(ə)l], a. 1. (Avis, etc.) confidentiel. 2. To be c. with s.o., faire des confidences à qn. 3. C. clerk, homme de confiance. C. secretary, secrétaire particulier, particulière. -ally, adv. Confidentiellement; à titre confidentiel.

configuration [kən,figju'reiʃ(ə)n], s. Configuration f.

confine [kən'fain], v.tr. (a) (R)enfermer (qn dans une prison, etc.); emprisonner (qn). To be confined to bed, être obligé de garder le lit; être alité. (b) To c. oneself to doing sth., se borner, se limiter, à faire qch. All their knowledge is confined to this, toute leur science se borne à cela. To c. oneself to facts, s'en tenir aux faits. (c) Resserrer (une rivière dans son lit). To be confined (for space), être à l'étroit. Confined space, espace resserré, restreint. (d) (Of woman) To be confined, faire ses couches.

confinement [kən'fainmənt], s. 1. Emprisonnement m, réclusion f. In close c., in solitary c., au secret; dans une réclusion rigoureuse. 2. (a) C. to one's bed, alitement m. (b) Couches fpl, accouchement m. 3. Limitation f, restriction f (to, à).

confines ['kɔnfainz], s.pl. (a) Confins m (d'un lieu, etc.). The utmost c. of the earth, of space, les derniers confins, les dernières limites, de la terre, de l'espace. The c. of science, les confins de la science. (b) Eaux f (d'un port).

confirm [kən'fə:m], v.tr. 1. (R)affermir (son pouvoir); fortifier (une résolution); confirmer (qn dans une opinion). 2. Confirmer (un traité); Jur: entériner (une décision); homologuer (un arrêt). 3. Confirmer, corroborer (une nouvelle). Confirming my letter, en confirmation de ma lettre. 4. Ecc: Confirmer. To be confirmed, recevoir la confirmation. **confirmed**, a. (Habitude) invétérée; (ivrogne) incorrigible; (célibataire) endurci.

confirmand [kən'fɑ:mənd], s. Ecc: Confirmand, -e.

confirmation [ˌkɔnfə'meiʃ(ə)n], s. 1. (R)affermissement m (de l'autorité de qn); confirmation f (d'un traité, d'une nouvelle). In c. of . . ., pour confirmer. . . . 2. Ecc: Confirmation.

confirmative [kən'fə:mətiv], a. Confirmatif, -ive (of, de).

confirmatory [kən'fə:mətri], a. Corroboratif, -ive.

confiscate ['kɔnfiskeit], v.tr. Confisquer.

confiscation [ˌkɔnfis'keiʃ(ə)n], s. Confiscation f.

conflagration [ˌkɔnflə'greiʃ(ə)n], s. (a) Conflagration f, embrasement m. (b) Incendie m.

conflict[1] ['kɔnflikt], s. Conflit m, lutte f; antagonisme m (d'intérêts). To come into c. with s.o., entrer en conflit avec qn.

conflict[2] [kən'flikt], v.i. 1. A: Lutter (with, contre). 2. Être en conflit, en contradiction, en désaccord (with, avec). When interests c., lorsque les intérêts se heurtent. **conflicting**, a. Opposé (with, à); incompatible (with, avec). C. evidence, témoignages discordants.

confluence ['kɔnfluəns], s. 1. Confluent m (de cours d'eau). 2. A: Affluence f, concours m (de monde).

confluent ['kɔnfluənt]. 1. a. (Of streams) Qui confluent; (of marks, spots) qui se confondent. 2. s. Affluent m (d'un fleuve).

conform [kən'fɔ:m]. 1. v.tr. Conformer (sth. to sth., qch. à qch.). 2. v.i. Se conformer (to, with, à). (a) To c. to fashion, suivre la mode. To c. to the law, obéir aux lois. (b) (Of a part) To c. (in shape) to another part, s'adapter à une autre pièce. (c) Rel.H: Faire acte de conformité.

conformability [kən,fɔ:mə'biliti], s. Geol: etc: Conformité f.

conformable [kən'fɔ:məbl], a. 1. Conforme (to, à). 2. (Of pers.) (a) Accommodant. (b) Docile, soumis (to, à). 3. Geol: C. strata, couches conformes, concordantes. -ably, adv. C. to . . ., conformément à (vos désirs, etc.).

conformation [ˌkɔnfɔ'meiʃ(ə)n], s. Conformation f, structure f.

conformist [kən'fɔːmist], s. Conformiste m.
conformity [kən'fɔːmiti], s. 1. Conformité f (to, with, à). In c. with your instructions, conformément à vos ordres. 2. Rel.H: Conformisme m; conformité; orthodoxie f.
confound [kən'faund], v.tr. 1. Confondre, déconcerter (les plans de qn). 2. Bouleverser, confondre (qn). 3. Lit: (a) Mêler, brouiller. (b) To c. sth. with sth., confondre qch. avec qch. 4. C. him! que le diable l'emporte! C. it! zut! confounded, a. F: Maudit, satané, sacré. -ly, adv. F: It was c. cold, il faisait bigrement froid.
confraternity [,kɔnfrə'təːniti], s. 1. Confrérie f. Treaty of c., traité de confraternité.
confront [kən'frʌnt], v.tr. 1. To c. s.o., être en face, se trouver en présence, de qn. 2. To c. the enemy, a danger, affronter, faire face à, l'ennemi, un danger. 3. To c. s.o. with witnesses, confronter qn avec des témoins.
confrontation [,kɔnfrʌn'teiʃ(ə)n], s. Confrontation f (de témoins, etc.).
Confucianism [kən'fjuːʃjənizm], s. Confucianisme m.
confuse [kən'fjuːz], v.tr. 1. Mêler, brouiller. To c. accounts, embrouiller des comptes. 2. To c. sth. with sth., confondre qch. avec qch. 3. (a) Embrouiller (qn). To get confused, s'embrouiller. (b) Bouleverser, troubler (qn). To get confused, se troubler; devenir confus. confused, a. 1. (a) Embrouillé. C. mind, esprit trouble. (b) Bouleversé, F: ahuri. (c) Confus, interdit. 2. C. speech, discours confus. confusing, a. Embrouillant; déroutant. It is very c., on s'y perd.
confusedly [kən'fjuːzidli], adv. 1. Confusément. 2. (Regarder qn) d'un air confus, interdit.
confusion [kən'fjuːʒ(ə)n], s. 1. Confusion f. To put s.o. to c., couvrir qn de confusion, de honte. 2. Désordre m, remue-ménage m. Everything was in c., tout était sens dessus dessous. To retire in c., se retirer à la débandade. To fall into c., se désorganiser. 3. C. of sth. with sth., confusion de qch. avec qch.
confutation [,kɔnfju'teiʃ(ə)n], s. Réfutation f.
confute [kən'fjuːt], v.tr. 1. Convaincre (qn) d'erreur. 2. Réfuter (un argument).
congeal [kən'dʒiːl]. 1. v.tr. (a) Congeler, geler. (b) Coaguler; cailler (le sang); figer (l'huile, le sang). 2. v.i. (a) Se congeler; geler. (b) (Of oil, blood) Se figer.
congealment [kən'dʒiːlmənt], congelation [,kɔndʒi-'leiʃ(ə)n], s. Congélation f.
congener ['kɔndʒinər]. 1. s. Congénère m (of, de). a. Congénère (to, de).
congeneric [,kɔndʒi'nerik], a. Congénère.
congenial [kən'dʒiːniəl], a. 1. (a) C. with sth., du même caractère, de la même nature, que qch. We have c. tastes, nous avons des goûts en commun. (b) C. spirit, esprit sympathique, aimable. C. employment, travail agréable. 2. Propre, convenable, qui convient (to, à). If I could find some c. employment, si je pouvais trouver un emploi qui me convienne. -ally, adv. Agréablement; d'un ton aimable.
congeniality [kən,dʒiːni'æliti], s. Accord m de sentiments, d'humeur; communauté f (de goûts).
congenital [kən'dʒenitl], a. Congénital, -aux. C. idiot, (i) idiot de naissance; (ii) F: parfait idiot. -ally, adv. De naissance.
conger ['kɔŋgər], s. Ich: C.(-eel), congre m; anguille f de mer.
congest [kən'dʒest]. 1. v.tr. (a) Med: Congestionner; engorger. (b) Encombrer, embouteiller (la circulation, les rues, etc.). 2. v.i. (a) Med: Se congestionner. (b) (Of traffic, etc.) S'embouteiller. congested, a. 1. Med: Congestionné. 2. Bot: Congestif, -ive. 3. (Of traffic) Encombré, embouteillé. The streets are very congested, les rues sont très congestionnées. C. area, région surpeuplée.
congestion [kən'dʒestʃ(ə)n], s. 1. Med: Congestion f; engorgement m. C. of the brain, of the lungs, congestion cérébrale, pulmonaire. 2. (a) Encombrement m de rue, de circulation; presse f. (b) Surpeuplement m.
congestive [kən'dʒestiv], a. Med: Congestif, -ive.
conglomerate¹ [kən'glɔmərət]. 1. a. Congloméré. 2. s. Geol: Conglomérat m, aggloméré.

conglomerate² [kən'glɔməreit]. 1. v.tr. Conglomérer. 2. v.i. Se conglomérer. Geol: S'agglomérer.
conglomeration [kən,glɔmə'reiʃ(ə)n], s. Conglomération f; agrégation f (de roches, etc.).
Congo ['kɔŋgou]. Pr.n. 1. (The River) C., le Congo. 2. Republic of the C., la République du Congo.
Congolese [kɔŋgou'liːz], a. & s. Geog: Congolais, -aise. The C. Republic, la République fédérale du Congo.
congratulate [kən'grætjuleit], v.tr. To c. s.o. on sth., féliciter qn de qch. I c. you, (je vous en fais) mes compliments, félicitations!
congratulation [kən,grætju'leiʃ(ə)n], s. Félicitation f. Congratulations! je vous en félicite! félicitations!
congratulatory [kən,grætju'leitəri], a. (Lettre) de félicitations.
congregate ['kɔŋgrigeit]. 1. v.tr. Rassembler, réunir. 2. v.i. Se rassembler, s'assembler.
congregation [,kɔŋgri'geiʃ(ə)n], s. 1. Rassemblement m. 2. (a) A: Assemblée f. (b) (In church) L'assistance f, les paroissiens m. To preach to a large c., prêcher devant une nombreuse assistance.
congregational [,kɔŋgri'geiʃnl], a. En assemblée. Rel.H: The C. Church, l'Église congrégationaliste.
Congregationalism [,kɔŋgri'geiʃ(ə)nəlizm], s. Rel.H: Congrégationalisme m.
Congregationalist [,kɔŋgri'geiʃ(ə)nəlist], s. Rel.H: Congrégationaliste mf.
congress ['kɔŋgres], s. 1. Réunion f (d'atomes, de personnes). 2. (a) Congrès m. (d'une église, d'hommes d'état, etc.). (b) U.S: Session f du Congrès. (c) Pol: Trade Union C. = Confédération Générale du Travail.
congressman, pl. -men ['kɔŋgresmən], s.m. congresswoman, pl. -women ['kɔŋgres,wumən, -wimin], s.f. U.S: (a) Membre du Congrès. (b) Congressiste mf.
congressional [kən'greʃənl], a. (Réunion f, etc.) du congrès; congressionnel, -elle.
congruence ['kɔŋgruəns], congruency ['kɔŋgruənsi], s. 1. Conformité f (with, avec). 2. Mth: Congruence f.
congruent ['kɔŋgruənt], a. 1. Conforme (with, à). 2. Mth: Congruent (with, à).
congruity [kɔŋ'gruːiti], s. = CONGRUENCE.
congruous ['kɔŋgruəs], a. = CONGRUENT 1. -ly, adv. Congrûment, convenablement (to, with, à).
conic(al) ['kɔnik(əl)], a. Geom: Conique. Conic sections, sections coniques.
conics ['kɔniks], s.pl. Mth: Sections f coniques.
conifer ['kounifər], s. Bot: Conifère m.
coniferous [kə'nifərəs], a. Bot: Conifère.
conjectural [k(ə)n'dʒekt(ə)r(ə)l], a. Conjectural, -aux. -ally, adv. Conjecturalement; par conjecture.
conjecture¹ [kən'dʒektʃər], s. Conjecture f.
conjecture², v.tr. Conjecturer.
conjoin [kən'dʒɔin]. 1. v.tr. Conjoindre. 2. v.i. S'unir; se joindre ensemble; s'associer. conjoined, a. Conjoint; (planètes) en conjonction.
conjoint [kən'dʒɔint], a. Conjoint, associé. -ly, adv. Conjointement, ensemble.
conjugal ['kɔndʒug(ə)l], a. Conjugal, -aux. -ally, adv. Conjugalement.
conjugate¹ ['kɔndʒugət], a. Conjugué.
conjugate² ['kɔndʒugeit]. 1. v.tr. Conjuguer (un verbe). 2. v.i. Biol: (Of cells) Se conjuguer.
conjugation [,kɔndʒu'geiʃ(ə)n], s. Conjugaison f.
conjunct [kən'dʒʌŋ(k)t], a. Conjoint, associé. -ly, adv. Conjointement.
conjunction [kən'dʒʌŋ(k)ʃ(ə)n], s. Conjonction f. In c. with s.o., de concert avec qn. In c. with sth., concurremment avec qch.
conjunctiva [,kɔn(d)ʒʌŋ(k)'taivə], s. Conjonctive f (de l'œil).
conjunctive [kən'dʒʌŋ(k)tiv]. 1. a. (Tissu) conjonctif. 2. a. & s. Gram: (Mode) conjonctif (m). -ly, adv. 1. Conjointement. 2. Gram: Words used c., locution conjonctive.
conjunctivitis [kən,(d)ʒʌŋ(k)ti'vaitis], s. Med: Conjonctivite f.
conjuncture [kən'dʒʌŋ(k)tʃər], s. Conjoncture f, circonstance f, occasion f.
conjuration [,kɔndʒu(ə)'reiʃ(ə)n], s. Conjuration f. 1. Évocation f (des démons). 2. Incantation f.

conjure, v. 1. [kən'dʒuər], v.tr. Conjurer (s.o. to do sth., qn de faire qch.). 2. ['kʌndʒər] (a) v.tr. Conjurer (un démon). To c. up, évoquer (un esprit). To c. up memories, évoquer des souvenirs. A name to c. with, un nom tout-puissant. (b) v.i. Faire des tours de passe-passe. **conjuring**, s. 1. Conjuration f (des esprits). C. up, évocation f. 2. Prestidigitation f; tours mpl de passe-passe.

conjurer, conjuror ['kʌn(d)ʒ(ə)rər], s. Prestidigitateur m.

conk[1] [kɔŋk], s. P: 1. Nez m; P: blair m, pif m. 2. Tête f; F: caboche f. 3. Coup m; P: gnon m.

conk[2]. 1. v.tr. P: To c. s.o., P: flanquer un gnon à (qn). 2. v.i. F: (Of machinery, etc.) To c. out, tomber en panne; claquer; caler.

conker ['kɔŋkər], s. F: Marron m d'Inde.

connate ['kɔneit], a. (a) C. ideas, idées innées. (b) C. with . . ., né en même temps que. . . . Path: Congénital, -aux.

connect [kə'nekt]. 1. v.tr. (a) (Re)lier, (ré)unir; rattacher, joindre (with, to, à). Connected by telephone, relié par téléphone. Tp: To c. two subscribers, mettre deux abonnés en communication. El: To c. to earth, relier à la terre. Connected to the mains, branché sur le secteur. (Of power stations) Connected up, interconnectés. (b) Associer (with, avec, à); relier (des idées). (c) (Of pers.) To be connected with a family, être allié à, avec, une famille. 2. v.i. Se lier, se relier, se joindre, se réunir. Rail: etc: To c. with a train, faire correspondance avec un train. **connected**, a. 1. (a) C. speech, discours suivi. (b) Two closely c. trades, deux métiers connexes. 2. (O, pers.) To be well c., être bien apparenté. 3. Bot: Jur: Connexe. **-ly**, adv. To think c., avoir de la suite dans les idées. **connecting**, a. C. wire, fil de connexion. C. gear, embrayage m. C. rod, bielle motrice.

connection [kə'nekʃ(ə)n], s. 1. Rapport m, liaison f (des choses); connexion f, suite f (des idées). This question has no c. with . . ., cette question n'a rien à voir avec. . . . In c. with . . ., à propos de . . ., relatif à. . . . In this c., à ce propos; à cet égard. In another c., d'autre part. 2. To form a c. with s.o. établir des rapports, des relations, avec qn. To break off a c., rompre des relations. 3. (a) Parenté f; liens mpl de famille. (b) He, she, is a c. of mine, c'est un(e) de mes parent(e)s. 4. Com: Wide c., belle clientèle; achalandage m considérable. Commercial traveller with a wide c., F: commis voyageur bien relationné. 5. Rail: Correspondance f; train correspondant. 6. Mec.E: Connexion f; assemblage m; embrayage m. Tp: Wrong c., fausse communication. 7. (a) Raccord m (entre deux tuyaux). (b) El.E: Contact m; prise f de courant.

connective [kə'nektiv], a. Connectif. Anat: C. tissue, tissu cellulaire, connectif, conjonctif.

connexion [kə'nekʃ(ə)n], s. = CONNECTION.

connivance [kə'naivəns], s. Connivence f; complicité f (at, in, dans). This was done with his c., cela s'est fait d'intelligence avec lui.

connive [kə'naiv], v.i. To c. at an abuse, tolérer, fermer les yeux sur, un abus.

connoisseur [kɔnə'səːr], s. Connaisseur m.

connotation [kɔnə'teiʃ(ə)n], s. 1. Signification f (d'un mot). 2. Phil: Compréhension f (d'un nom générique).

connote [kə'nout], v.tr. Log: Connoter. 2. Comporter (une signification secondaire, etc.). 3. Signifier; impliquer.

connubial [kə'njuːbiəl], a. Conjugal, -aux.

conquer ['kɔŋkər], v.tr. 1. Conquérir. To c. all hearts, subjuguer tous les cœurs. 2. Vaincre. **conquering**, a. 1. Conquérant. 2. Victorieux. The c. hero, le héros triomphant.

conqueror ['kɔŋk(ə)rər], s. 1. Conquérant m (d'un pays). Hist: (William) the C., Guillaume le Conquérant. 2. Vainqueur m.

conquest ['kɔŋkwest], s. Conquête f.

consanguin [kɔn'sæŋgwin], **consanguineous** [kɔnsæŋ-'gwiniəs], a. Consanguin.

consanguinity [kɔnsæŋ'gwiniti], s. Consanguinité f.

conscience ['kɔnʃəns], s. Conscience f. To have a clear, an easy, c., avoir la conscience nette, tranquille.

With a clear c., en (toute) sûreté de conscience. Accommodating c., conscience large. To have no c., être sans conscience. I did it for c. sake, je l'ai fait par acquit de conscience. In (all) c., en vérité, assurément, certes. It would go against my c. to do it, cela irait contre ma conscience de le faire. '**conscience money,** s. Somme restituée par remords de conscience. '**conscience-stricken,** a. Pris de remords.

conscienceless ['kɔnʃənslis], a. Sans scrupule; sans conscience.

conscientious [kɔnʃi'enʃəs], a. 1. Consciencieux, -euse. 2. C. scruple, scrupule de conscience. C. objector, réfractaire m; objecteur m de conscience. **-ly,** adv. Consciencieusement.

conscientiousness [kɔnʃi'enʃəsnis], s. Conscience f; droiture f.

conscious ['kɔnʃəs], a. 1. (a) To be c. of sth., avoir conscience de qch. I was not c. of having moved, je n'avais pas conscience d'avoir bougé. To become c. of sth., s'apercevoir de qch. I was c. that he was looking at me, je sentais qu'il me regardait. (b) C. movement, mouvement conscient. (c) (= SELF-CONSCIOUS) Phil: Man as a c. being, l'homme en tant qu'être conscient. (d) Fashion c., qui suit de près la mode. Food c., qui se préoccupe beaucoup de sa nourriture. 2. To be c., avoir sa connaissance. To become c., reprendre connaissance; revenir de son évanouissement. **-ly,** adv. Consciemment.

consciousness ['kɔnʃəsnis], s. 1. (a) Conscience f, sentiment m (of, de). The c. of being watched, le sentiment qu'on vous regarde. (b) Sentiment intime, persuasion f intime. C. that all is not well, pressentiment m de malheur. 2. Phil: (a) Conscience (de l'être conscient). (b) Moral c., conscience morale. 3. To lose c., perdre connaissance; s'évanouir. To regain c., revenir à soi.

conscript[1] ['kɔnskript], a. & s. Conscrit (m).

conscript[2] [kən'skript], v.tr. Enrôler, engager (des troupes) par la conscription.

conscription [kən'skripʃ(ə)n], s. Conscription f.

consecrate[1] ['kɔnsikr(e)it], a. Consacré (to, à).

consecrate[2] ['kɔnsikreit], v.tr. 1. (a) Ecc: Consacrer (une église); bénir (le pain); sacrer (un évêque). (b) Custom consecrated by time, coutume consacrée par le temps. 2. To c. one's life to a work, consacrer, vouer, sa vie à un travail; se vouer à un travail. **consecrated,** a. (Of church, phrase) Consacré; (of bread) bénit. In c. ground, en terre sainte, en terre bénite.

consecration [kɔnsi'kreiʃ(ə)n], s. 1. Consécration f; sacre m (d'un roi). 2. The c. of a whole life to a single object, le dévouement d'une vie entière à un seul but.

consecutive [kən'sekjutiv], a. Consécutif, -ive. 1. On three c. days, trois jours de suite. Mus: C. fifths, quintes consécutives. 2. Gram: C. clause, proposition consécutive. **-ly,** adv. Consécutivement; de suite.

consensus [kən'sensəs], s. Consensus m, unanimité f (d'opinions, de témoignages).

consent[1] [kən'sent], s. Consentement m, assentiment m. Age of c., âge m nubile. C. to a request, agrément donné à une requête. By common c., d'une commune voix; de l'aveu de tout le monde. With one c., d'un commun accord. By mutual c., de gré à gré.

consent[2], v.i. To c. to sth., consentir à qch. I c., j'y consens; je veux bien.

consequence ['kɔns(i)kwəns], s. 1. Conséquence f; suites fpl. In c., par conséquent. In c. of . . ., par suite de. . . . To take the consequences, to put up with the consequences, subir, accepter, les conséquences. (Game of) consequences, (jeu des) petits papiers. 2. Importance f; conséquence f. It is of no c., cela ne tire pas à conséquence; cela ne fait rien. He is of no c., il ne compte pas. People of c. in the town, les personnalités f de la ville.

consequent[1] ['kɔns(i)kwənt], s. Mth: Conséquent m. 2. Log: Conclusion f.

consequent[2], a. 1. Résultant. Infirmity c. on a wound, infirmité consécutive à une blessure. 2. Log: Conséquent (from, de). 3. (Consistent) Conséquent, logique. **-ly,** 1. adv. & conj. Par conséquent; conséquemment. 2. adv. Logiquement.

consequential [ˌkɔnsiˈkwenʃ(ə)l], a. 1. Conséquent, consécutif, -ive (to, à). 2. (Of pers.) Suffisant; plein d'importance. -ally, adv. 1. Indirectement, secondairement. 2. D'un air important.

consequentiality [ˌkɔnsikwenʃiˈæliti], s. 1. Log: Conséquence f, suite f (dans les idées). 2. (Of pers.) Importance f, suffisance f.

conservancy [kənˈsəːv(ə)nsi], s. 1. Commission f de conservation. The Thames C., la Commission fluviale (de la Tamise). 2. Conservation f, protection f (des forêts, etc.).

conservation [ˌkɔnsəˈ(ː)veiʃ(ə)n], s. Conservation f, protection f.

conservatism [kənˈsəːvətizm], s. Pol: Conservatisme m.

conservative [kənˈsəːv(ə)tiv]. 1. a. (a) Préservateur, -trice; conservateur, -trice. (b) At a c. estimate, au bas mot. On c. lines, selon la méthode consacrée par l'usage. 2. a. & s. Pol: Conservateur, -trice. -ly, adv. It was c. estimated . . ., selon des estimations modérées. . . .

conservatory [kənˈsəːvətri], s. (a) Hort: Serre f. (b) U.S: Conservatoire m (de musique, etc.).

conserve [kənˈsəːv], v.tr. Conserver, préserver.

conserves [kənˈsəːvz], s.pl. Cu: O: Confiture(s) f, conserves f (de fruits).

conshie, conshy [kɔnʃi], s. P: = conscientious objector, q.v. under CONSCIENTIOUS.

consider [kənˈsidər], v.tr. 1. (a) Considérer (une question); envisager (une possibilité). I will c. it, j'y réfléchirai; j'y songerai. Considered opinion, opinion motivée, réfléchie. All things considered, tout bien considéré; (toute) réflexion faite. (b) Prendre (une offre) en considération; étudier, examiner (une proposition). 2. (a) To c. s.o., s.o.'s feelings, avoir égard à la sensibilité de qn; ménager qn. To c. the expense, regarder à la dépense. (b) When one considers that . . ., quand on pense que. . . . 3. (a) Pred. I c. him (to be) crazy, je le considère, regarde, comme fou; je le tiens pour fou. C. it (as) done, tenez cela pour fait. He is considered rich, on le dit riche. To c. oneself happy, s'estimer heureux. (b) We c. that he ought to do it, à notre avis il doit le faire. considering, prep. Eu égard à (qch.). C. his age, étant donné son âge. C. the circumstances, vu les circonstances. C. that . . ., vu, attendu, que. . . . F: It is not so bad c., somme toute, ce n'est pas si mal.

considerable [kənˈsid(ə)rəbl], a. Considérable. A c. number of . . ., un nombre considérable de. . . . To a c. extent, dans une forte mesure. -ably, adv. Considérablement.

considerate [kənˈsid(ə)rit], a. Prévenant, attentionné, plein d'égards (towards, pour, envers). It is very c. of you, c'est très aimable de votre part. If you had been more c., si vous aviez tenu compte de son état, etc., si vous aviez montré plus de discrétion, plus de délicatesse. -ly, adv. Avec égards, avec prévenance. He acted very c., il a agi avec une grande délicatesse.

considerateness [kənˈsid(ə)ritnis], s. Attentions fpl, égards mpl (to, for, envers, pour).

consideration [kənˌsidəˈreiʃn], s. 1. Considération f. (a) To take sth. into c., prendre qch. en considération; tenir compte de qch. Taking all things into c., tout bien considéré. Fact that has been left out of c., fait auquel on n'a pas pris garde. In c. of . . ., en considération de . . ., eu égard à. . . . Question under c., question en délibération, à l'examen, à l'étude. After due c., après mûre réflexion; tout bien considéré. A list for your c., une liste que nous vous prions de bien vouloir examiner. (b) Money is always the first c., la question d'argent vient toujours en premier. Material considerations, préoccupations matérielles. On no c. . . ., à aucun prix . . ., pour rien au monde. . . . 2. Compensation f, rémunération f. For a c., contre espèces; F: moyennant finance. 3. Out of c. for s.o., par égard, par considération, pour qn. To treat s.o. with c., to show s.o. c., ménager qn. 4. Of great, of no, c., de grande importance; d'aucune importance. Money is no c., l'argent n'entre pas en ligne de compte.

consign [kənˈsain], v.tr. 1. Consigner, expédier (des marchandises) (to s.o., à qn, à l'adresse de qn); envoyer (des marchandises) en consignation (à qn). 2. Confier, livrer (sth. to s.o.'s care, qch. à qn, entre les mains de qn). To c. sth. to oblivion, ensevelir qch. dans l'oubli.

consignee [ˌkɔnsaiˈniː], s. Consignataire m.

consignment [kənˈsainmənt], s. 1. (a) Envoi m, expédition f (de marchandises). For c. abroad, à destination de l'étranger. C. note, (i) lettre f de voiture; (ii) Rail: récépissé m. (b) Com: On c., en consignation, en dépôt (permanent). 2. Envoi, arrivage m (de marchandises).

consignor [kənˈsainər], s. Com: Consignateur m, expéditeur m.

consist [kənˈsist], v.i. (a) To c. of sth., consister en, dans, se composer de, qch. (b) True happiness consists in desiring little, le vrai bonheur consiste à modérer ses désirs.

consistence [kənˈsist(ə)ns], s. Consistance f (d'un sirop, etc.); compacité f (du sol, etc.).

consistency [kənˈsist(ə)nsi], s. 1. = CONSISTENCE. 2 Uniformité f (de conduite). Your actions lack c., vos actions manquent de suite f, de logique f.

consistent [kənˈsist(ə)nt], a. 1. (Of pers.) Conséquent; logique. Ideas that are not c., idées qui ne se tiennent pas. 2. Compatible, d'accord (with, avec). -ly, adv. 1. Conséquemment; avec conséquence, avec logique. 2. Conformément (with, à).

consistorial [ˌkɔnsisˈtɔːriəl], a. Ecc: Consistorial, -aux.

consistory [kənˈsistəri], s. Ecc: Consistoire m.

consolable [kənˈsoulabl], a. Consolable.

consolation [ˌkɔnsəˈleiʃ(ə)n], s. Consolation f. C. prize, prix de consolation.

consolatory [kənˈsɔlətri], a. Consolateur, -trice.

console¹ [ˈkɔnsoul], s. 1. Arch: Console f. 2. Console (d'orgue).

console² [kənˈsoul], v.tr. Consoler (s.o. for a loss, qn d'une perte). consoling, a. Consolant; consolateur, -trice.

consoler [kənˈsoulər], s. Consolateur, -trice.

consolidate [kənˈsɔlideit], 1. v.tr. (a) Consolider, (r)affermir. (b) Consolider, (ré)unir (deux propriétés); unifier (une dette). The consolidated annuities, les fonds consolidés. 2. v.i. Se consolider; (of road) se tasser.

consolidation [kənˌsɔliˈdeiʃ(ə)n], s. 1. Consolidation f, (r)affermissement m; tassement m (de terres). 2. Unification f (des lois, etc.). 3. Rural Ec: (a) Remembrement m, réorganisation foncière. (b) Remaniement m, regroupement m parcellaire.

consols [kənˈsɔlz], s.pl. Fin: Fonds consolidés.

consommé [kənˈsɔmei], s. Cu: Consommé m; bouillon m.

consonance [ˈkɔnsənəns], s. 1. Consonance f; Mus: accord m. 2. Accord, communion f (d'idées).

consonant¹ [ˈkɔnsənənt], a. 1. Consonant. 2. C. with duty, qui s'accorde avec le devoir.

consonant², s. Ling: Consonne f.

consort¹ [ˈkɔnsɔːt], s. 1. Époux, -ouse, conjoint, -e. Prince c., prince consort. 2. To act in c. with s.o., agir de concert avec qn. Nau: To sail in c., naviguer de conserve.

consort² [kənˈsɔːt], v.i. 1. To c. with s.o., frayer avec qn; fréquenter qn. 2. (Of thg.) To c. with sth., s'accorder avec qch.

consortium [kənˈsɔːtjəm], s. Pol.Ec: Consortium m.

conspectus [kənˈspektəs], s. Aperçu général.

conspicuous [kənˈspikjuəs], a. 1. Qui donne dans la vue; (repère) voyant. In a c. position, bien en évidence. To be c., attirer les regards. F: To be c. by one's absence, briller par son absence. 2. Frappant, marquant. To make oneself c., se faire remarquer; se singulariser; se particulariser; se signaler (by, through, par). C. gallantry, bravoure insigne. -ly, adv. Manifestement; bien en évidence.

conspicuousness [kənˈspikjuəsnis], s. 1. Évidence f, visibilité f (de qch.); éclat m, voyant m (d'un uniforme etc.). 2. Caractère m insigne (d'une action); éminence f.

conspiracy [kənˈspirəsi], s. 1. Conspiration f, conjuration f. 2. Jur: Entente délictueuse.

conspirator [kənˈspirətər], s. Conspirateur, -trice; conjuré, -ée.

conspiratorial [kənspirəˈtɔːriəl], a. Conspirateur, -trice

conspire [kən'spaiər], *v.i.* (*a*) Conspirer (against, contre); agir de concert (avec qn). To c. to do sth., comploter de faire qch.; s'entendre pour faire qch. (*b*) (*Of events*) Concourir, conspirer (to, à).

constable ['kʌnstəbl], *s.* 1. (*a*) *Hist:* Connétable *m.* (*b*) Gouverneur *m* (d'un château). 2. (Police) c., agent *m* de police; gendarme *m.* **Chief c.** = commissaire *m* de police. **Special c.**, citoyen assermenté faisant fonction d'agent de police.

constabulary [kən'stæbjuləri], *s.* *Coll:* La police. **The County C.** = la gendarmerie départementale.

constancy ['kɔnst(ə)nsi], *s.* 1. Constance *f*, fermeté *f* (de caractère); fidélité *f* (d'un ami). 2. Constance (de la température); régularité *f* (du vent).

constant ['kɔnst(ə)nt]. 1. *a.* (*a*) Constant; (équilibre) stable; (pression) invariable; *El:* (courant) continu. (*b*) Incessant, continuel, -elle; (travail) assidu, soutenu. **Through c. repetition**, à force de répéter. (*c*) (Ami) loyal, -aux; (au cœur) fidèle. 2. *s.* *Mth: Ph:* Constante *f.* **-ly**, *adv.* Constamment, continuellement.

constellation [ˌkɔnstə'leiʃ(ə)n], *s.* Constellation *f.*

consternated ['kɔnstəneitid], *a.* Consterné, atterré, accablé (by . . ., par . . .).

consternation [ˌkɔnstə(:)'neiʃ(ə)n], *s.* Consternation *f*; atterrement *m.* **They looked at each other in c.**, ils se regardaient atterrés, consternés.

constipate ['kɔnstipeit], *v.tr.* *Med:* Constiper. **To be constipated**, être constipé. **constipating**, *a.* Constipant; échauffant.

constipation [ˌkɔnsti'peiʃ(ə)n], *s.* Constipation *f.*

constituency [kən'stitjuənsi], *s.* 1. Collège (électoral); électeurs *mpl.* 2. Circonscription électorale.

constituent [kən'stitjuənt]. 1. *a.* Constituant, constitutif, -ive. 2. *s.* Élément constitutif; composant *m.* 3. *s.pl.* Mandants *m* (d'un député); électeurs *m.*

constitute ['kɔnstitjuːt], *v.tr.* Constituer. 1. **Constituted authority**, les autorités constituées. **To c. s.o. arbitrator**, constituer, nommer, qn arbitre. 2. Constituer, faire (le bonheur de qn). 3. **So constituted that . . .**, ainsi fait que. . .

constitution [ˌkɔnsti'tjuːʃ(ə)n], *s.* 1. Constitution *f*, composition *f* (de qch.). 2. Complexion *f*, constitution (du corps). **Iron c.**, santé *f* de fer. 3. *Pol:* Constitution (d'un État). 4. *pl. Hist:* Constitutions, arrêts *m.*

constitutional [ˌkɔnsti'tjuːʃnl]. 1. *a.* (*a*) (Monarque) constitutionnel. (*b*) *Med:* (Affection) diathésique. 2. *s.* **To take, go for, one's c.**, faire sa promenade quotidienne. **-ally**, *adv.* 1. Constitutionnellement; conformément à la constitution (de l'État). 2. Par tempérament.

constitutionalist [ˌkɔnsti'tjuːʃənəlist], *s.* 1. Spécialiste *m*, historien *m*, des constitutions politiques. 2. *Pol:* Constitutionnel *m.*

constitutive ['kɔnstitjutiv], *a.* Constitutif, -ive.

constrain [kən'strein], *v.tr.* 1. **To c. s.o. to do sth.**, contraindre, forcer, qn à, de, faire qch. **To feel constrained to do sth.**, se voir dans la nécessité de faire qch. 2. Retenir (qn) de force; tenir (qn) en contrainte. **constrained**, *a.* (Sourire) forcé; (air) gêné.

constraint [kən'streint], *s.* 1. Contrainte *f.* **To put s.o. under c.**, retenir qn de force; enfermer, interner (un aliéné). 2. (*a*) (*Of manner*) Gêne *f*, contrainte. (*b*) Retenue *f.* **To speak without c.**, parler à cœur ouvert.

constrict [kən'strikt], *v.tr.* 1. Resserrer, étrangler, rétrécir (une ouverture). 2. Brider, serrer, gêner.

constriction [kən'strikʃ(ə)n], *s.* Resserrement *m*, étranglement *m*; *Med:* strangulation *f* (des artères); *Physiol:* constriction *f* (des muscles, etc.).

constrictor [kən'striktər], *s.* 1. (Muscle) constricteur (*m*). 2. = *boa-constrictor, q.v. under* BOA.

construct [kən'strʌkt], *v.tr.* Construire; bâtir (un édifice); établir (un chemin de fer); confectionner, charpenter (un drame).

construction [kən'strʌkʃ(ə)n], *s.* 1. (*a*) Construction *f*, établissement *m* (d'une machine, d'un édifice). **Under c., in course of c.**, en construction. (*b*) Construction, édifice *m*, bâtiment *m.* 2. (*a*) *Gram:* Construction (de la phrase). (*b*) **To put a good, bad, c. on s.o.'s words**, interpréter en bien, en mal, les paroles de qn. **To put a wrong c. on sth.**, mal interpréter qch.; entendre qch. de travers.

constructional [kən'strʌkʃənl], *a.* De construction. **C. engineering**, construction *f* mécanique. **C. toy**, jeu *m* de construction.

constructive [kən'strʌktiv], *a.* 1. Constructif, -ive; (esprit) créateur. *Jur:* Par déduction. *S.a.* LOSS 2. **-ly**, *adv.* Par interprétation, par induction.

constructor [kən'strʌktər], *s.* Constructeur *m*; ingénieur *m* (des constructions navales).

construe ['kɔnstruː, kən'struː], *v.tr.* 1. (*a*) *Sch:* O: Faire le mot à mot (d'un passage); analyser, décomposer (une phrase). (*b*) *Gram:* **Preposition construed with the dative**, préposition qui gouverne le datif. 2. Interpréter (les paroles de qn); expliquer (la conduite de qn).

consubstantiate [ˌkɔnsəb'stænʃieit], *v. Theol:* 1. *v.tr.* Unir (qch.) dans une seule et même substance (with, avec). 2. *v.i.* S'unir dans une seule et même substance.

consubstantiation [ˌkɔnsəbstænʃi'eiʃən], *s. Theol:* Consubstantiation *f.*

consul ['kɔns(ə)l], *s.* Consul *m.*

consular ['kɔnsjulər], *a.* Consulaire.

consulate ['kɔnsjulit], *s.* Consulat *m.*

consult [kən'sʌlt]. 1. *v.tr.* (*a*) Consulter (s.o. on, about, sth., qn sur qch.). (*b*) **To c. one's own interests, one's own safety**, consulter ses intérêts; pourvoir à son propre salut. **To c. s.o.'s feelings**, avoir égard à la sensibilité de qn. 2. *v.i.* Consulter (avec qn). **To c. together**, délibérer; se consulter. **consulting**, *a.* **C. physician**, médecin consultant. **C. engineer**, ingénieur conseil. **con'sulting-hours**, *s.pl.* Heures *f* de consultation. **con'sulting-room**, *s.* Cabinet *m* de consultation.

consultant [kən'sʌltənt], *s.* (*a*) Médecin ou chirurgien consultant. (*b*) *Ind:* Expert *m* conseil.

consultation [ˌkɔns(ə)l'teiʃ(ə)n], *s.* 1. Consultation *f* (d'un dictionnaire, etc.). 2. Consultation, délibération *f* (entre médecins, etc.). **To hold a c.**, consulter, délibérer, conférer.

consultative [kən'sʌltətiv], *a.* Consultatif, -ive.

consumable [kən'sjuːməbl], *a.* 1. Consumable (par le feu). 2. (*a*) (Aliment *m*) consommable. (*b*) *s.pl.* **Consumables**, aliments *m*, comestibles *m*, denrées *f.*

consume [kən'sjuːm], *v.tr.* 1. (*a*) (*Of fire*) Consumer, dévorer. **The town was consumed by fire**, la ville fut la proie des flammes. (*b*) Consommer (des vivres). (*c*) **Engine that consumes a lot of fuel**, machine qui consomme, qui brûle, beaucoup de combustible. (*d*) **To be consumed with thirst**, être consumé par la soif. **To be consumed with desire, jealousy**, brûler de désir; être dévoré, rongé, de jalousie. **To be consumed with boredom**, sécher d'ennui. (*e*) Épuiser (ses vivres, etc.).

consumer [kən'sjuːmər], *s.* Consommateur, -trice (d'une denrée). **Consumers of gas**, abonnés au gaz. *Pol.Ec:* **C. goods**, biens *m* de consommation.

consummate¹ [kən'sʌmit], *a.* (*a*) (Art, artiste) consommé, achevé. **To be a c. master of one's craft**, être passé maître dans son métier. (*b*) *F:* **C. liar**, menteur achevé. **-ly**, *adv.* Parfaitement, complètement.

consummate² ['kɔnsəmeit], *v.tr.* Consommer (un mariage, un sacrifice).

consummation [ˌkɔnsə'meiʃ(ə)n], *s.* 1. Consommation *f* (d'un mariage, d'un crime). 2. Perfection *f* (d'un art, etc.). 3. Fin *f*; but *m*; comble *m* (des désirs). **The c. of a splendid life**, le couronnement d'une belle vie.

consumption [kən'sʌm(p)ʃ(ə)n], *s.* 1. (*a*) Consommation *f* (de denrées). (*b*) Consommation, dépense *f* (de chaleur, de charbon). 2. *Med: F:* Phtisie *f*; consomption *f* pulmonaire. *S.a.* GALLOPING 2.

consumptive [kən'sʌm(p)tiv], *a. & s. Med: F:* Poitrinaire (*mf*), phtisique (*mf*), tuberculeux, -euse. **C. cough**, toux de poitrinaire.

contact¹ ['kɔntækt], *s.* Contact *m.* 1. (*a*) **Point of c.**, point de contact, de tangence, d'attouchement (de deux courbes, etc.). *Opt:* **C. lens**, verre *m*, lentille *f*, de contact. (*b*) **To be in c. with s.o.**, être en contact, en rapport, avec qn. **Preliminary contacts**, prise *f* de contact. *Com:* **C. man**, agent *m* de liaison. 2. *El:* (*a*) **C. to earth**, contact avec la terre; mise *f* à terre. **To make c.**, établir le contact. **To break c.**, rompre le contact; couper le circuit. (*b*) **C.**

(-piece), contact, touche *f*; (*button*) goutte-de-suif *f*; (*stud*) plot *m*. Floor c., pédale *f* de parquet. Bulb c., plot de lampe. *S.a.* SLIDING¹. 3. *Med:* Personne *f* ayant approché un malade contagieux. 4. *Av:* C. flying, vol *m* au contact. 'contact-breaker, *s. El.E:* Dispositif *m* de rupture; (inter)rupteur *m*; trembleur *m*. 'contact-pin, *s. El.E:* Cheville *f* de contact.

contact², *v.tr.* Contacter (qn); s'aboucher, prendre contact, se mettre en relation (avec qn).

contagion [kən'teidʒ(ə)n], *s.* Contagion *f*.

contagious [kən'teidʒəs], *a.* (*Of disease, laughter*) Contagieux, -euse; (*of laughter*) communicatif, -ive. -ly, *adv.* (*a*) Par contagion. (*b*) D'une façon contagieuse.

contagiousness [kən'teidʒəsnis], *s.* Contagiosité *f*.

contain [kən'tein], *v.tr.* 1. (*a*) Contenir. (*b*) (*Comprise, include*) Contenir, renfermer; comprendre, comporter. Machine that contains all the latest improvements, machine qui comporte tous les derniers perfectionnements. Substance that contains arsenic, substance où il entre de l'arsenic. 2. (*Restrain*) Contenir, maîtriser (son indignation); retenir, refouler (ses sentiments). 3. *Mil:* Contenir, maintenir (l'ennemi).

container [kən'teinər], *s.* (*a*) Récipient *m*; réservoir *m*. *El:* Bac *m* (d'accumulateur); vase *m*. *Com:* Boîte *f*. *Av:* (Supply) c., gaine *f* à matériel (pour parachutages), bombe *f* de ravitaillement, container *m*, conteneur *m*. *Rail:* (Freight) c., cadre *m* de déménagement, container, conteneur.

contaminate [kən'tæmineit], *v.tr.* Contaminer; corrompre; souiller. Contaminated air, air vicié. contaminating, *a.* Viciateur, -trice.

contamination [kən,tæmi'nei∫(ə)n], *s.* Contamination *f*, souillure *f*.

contango, *pl.* -oes [kən'tæŋgou, -ouz], *s. St.Exch:* (Intérêt *m* de) report *m*. Payer of c., reporté *m*.

contemplate ['kəntempleit], *v.tr.* 1. (*a*) Contempler, considérer. (*b*) *v.i.* Se recueillir; méditer. 2. (*a*) Prévoir, envisager (qch.). (*b*) To c. sth., doing sth., projeter, se proposer, qch., de faire qch. To c. suicide, songer au suicide.

contemplation [,kəntem'plei∫(ə)n], *s.* 1. (*a*) Contemplation *f*. (*b*) Recueillement *m*, méditation *f*. 2. (*a*) It is as yet only in c., ce n'est encore qu'à l'état de projet. (*b*) In c. of an attack, en prévision d'une attaque.

contemplative ['kəntempleitiv, kən'templətiv], *a.* Contemplatif, -ive, recueilli.

contemplator ['kəntempleitər], *s.* Contemplateur,-trice.

contemporaneous [kən,tempə'reinjəs], *a.* Contemporain (with, de). -ly, *adv.* C. with . . ., à la même époque que. . .

contemporary [kən'temp(ə)rəri]. 1. *a.* Contemporain (with, de). C. events, événements actuels. 2. *s.* Our contemporaries, nos contemporains *m*.

contempt [kən'tempt], *s.* 1. Mépris *m*; dédain *m*. To hold s.o. in c., mépriser qn; tenir qn en mépris. To bring s.o. into c., faire tomber qn dans le mépris; faire mépriser qn. In c. of . . ., au, en, mépris de. . . . Beneath c., tout ce qu'il y a de plus méprisable. 2. *Jur:* C. of court, (i) outrage *m* ou offense *f* au tribunal; désobéissance *f*; (ii) refus *m* de comparaître; contumace *f*.

contemptibility [kən,temptə'biliti], *s.* Caractère *m* méprisable; platitude *f*, bassesse *f* (d'une action).

contemptible [kən'temptəbl], *a.* Méprisable; (conduite) indigne. *Hist:* The Old Contemptibles, les survivants *m* de l'armée britannique de 1914. -ibly, *adv.* D'une manière méprisable.

contemptuous [kən'temptjuəs], *a.* 1. Dédaigneux, -euse (of, de). 2. (Air) méprisant; (geste) de mépris. -ly, *adv.* Avec mépris; d'un air, d'un ton, méprisant.

contemptuousness [kən'temptjuəsnis], *s.* Mépris *m*; caractère méprisant.

contend [kən'tend]. 1. *v.i.* Combattre, lutter (with, against, contre); disputer; discuter (avec qn sur qch.). To have a powerful enemy to c. with, avoir affaire à forte partie. To c. with s.o. for sth., disputer, contester, qch. à qn. 2. *v.tr.* To c. that . . ., prétendre, soutenir, que + *ind.* contending, *a.* C. parties, contestants *m*; partis *m* en lutte. C. armies, armées opposées.

content¹ ['kəntent], *s.* 1. (*a*) Contenu *m*, volume *m* (d'un solide); contenance *f* (d'un vase). (*b*) *pl.* Contents, contenu *m* (d'une bouteille, d'une lettre, etc.). (*Of book*) (Table of) contents, table des matières. 2. *Ch: Miner:* Teneur *f*, titre *m*. Gold c., teneur en or. (Food) with a high protein c., (aliment *m*) riche en protéine *f*.

content² [kən'tent], *s.* 1. Contentement *m*, satisfaction *f*. *S.a.* HEART' 2. 2. (*In House of Lords*) (*a*) Vote affirmatif. (*b*) Membre *m* qui a voté pour la motion.

content³ [kən'tent], *a.* 1. Satisfait (with, de). To be c. to do sth., s'accommoder de qch. I am c. to live at home, je n'en demande pas davantage que de vivre à la maison. To be c. with sth., se contenter de qch. 2. (*In House of Lords*) C., pour. Not c., contre.

content⁴ [kən'tent], *v.tr.* 1. Contenter, satisfaire (qn). 2. To c. oneself with (doing) sth., se contenter de (faire) qch.; se borner à faire qch. contented, *a.* Satisfait, content (with, de). -ly, *adv.* Sans se plaindre; (vivre) content.

contentedness [kən'tentidnis], *s.* Contentement *m*.

contention [kən'ten∫(ə)n], *s.* 1. Dispute *f*, démêlé *m*, débat *m*. To be a bone of c., être un sujet de dispute, une pomme de discorde; donner lieu à des contestations. 2. Affirmation *f*, prétention *f*. My c. is that . . ., je soutiens que + *ind.*

contentious [kən'ten∫əs], *a.* 1. Disputeur, -euse; chicaneur, -euse; disputailleur, -euse. 2. (*Of issue*) Contentieux, -euse.

contentment [kən'tentmənt], *s.* Contentement *m* de son sort.

contest¹ ['kəntest], *s.* (*a*) Combat *m*, lutte *f* (with, avec, contre; between, entre). (*b*) Concours *m* (de musique, etc.). *Sp:* Épreuve *f*, match *m*, partie *f*. C. of eloquence, joute *f* oratoire. *W.Tel: T.V:* Talent c., crochet *m* (radiophonique).

contest² [kən'test]. 1. *v.tr.* (*a*) Contester, débattre (une question). (*b*) To c. s.o.'s right to do sth., contester à qn le droit de faire qch. *Sp:* It was a well-contested match, la lutte a été chaude. To c. a seat in Parliament, disputer un siège au Parlement. (*c*) *Jur:* Attaquer (un testament); contester (une dette). 2. *v.i.* (*a*) Se disputer (with, against, avec). (*b*) To c. for a prize, disputer un prix.

contestable [kən'testəbl], *a.* Contestable; (question) débattable; (testament) attaquable.

contestant [kən'testənt], *s.* 1. Contestant, -ante. 2. Compétiteur, -trice; concurrent *m*.

contestation [,kəntes'tei∫(ə)n], *s.* Contestation *f* (d'un droit). Matters in c., matières en contestation, en litige.

context ['kəntekst], *s.* Contexte *m*.

contiguity [,kənti'gju:iti], *s.* Contiguïté *f*. In c., contigu, -uë (with, à).

contiguous [kən'tigju:)əs], *a.* C. to sth., contigu, -uë, à qch., avec qch.; attenant à qch. To be c., se toucher. -ly, *adv.* En contiguïté (to, avec).

continence ['kəntinəns], *s.* Continence *f*, chasteté *f*.

continent¹ ['kəntinənt], *a.* Continent, chaste.

continent², *s. Geog:* (*a*) Continent *m*. The five continents, les cinq parties *f* du monde. (*b*) *F:* The C., l'Europe (continentale).

continental [,kənti'nentl]. 1. *a.* Continental, -aux. 2. *s.* Continental, -e; habitant, -e, de l'Europe (continentale, -e.

contingency [kən'tindʒənsi], *s.* (*a*) Éventualité *f*; cas imprévu. Should a c. arise, in case of a c., en cas d'imprévu. (*b*) *Com:* Contingencies, faux frais divers. To provide for contingencies, parer à l'imprévu.

contingent [kən'tindʒənt]. 1. *a.* (*a*) *Phil:* Contingent. (*b*) Éventuel, -elle, fortuit, accidentel, -elle; (profit) aléatoire. C. expenses, dépenses imprévues. (*c*) C. on sth., sous (la) réserve de qch. (*Of event*) To be c. upon sth., dépendre de qch. 2. *s. Mil:* Contingent *m*.

continual [kən'tinju(:)əl], *a.* Continuel, -elle. -ally, *adv.* Continuellement; sans cesse, sans arrêt.

continuance [kən'tinju(:)əns], *s.* Continuation *f*. 1. Perpétuation *f*. 2. Persistance *f*, durée *f*.

continuation [kən,tinju(:)'ei∫(ə)n], *s.* 1. Continuation *f*. 2. Prolongement *m* (d'un mur); suite *f* (d'un roman). 3. *St.Exch:* Report *m*.

continue [kən'tinju:]. **1.** *v.tr.* (*a*) Continuer; prolonger (une droite); poursuivre (un travail); reprendre (une conversation). *Journ:* 'To be continued,' "à suivre." (*b*) Perpétuer (la race, une tradition); maintenir (qn dans un emploi). (*c*) To c. (on) one's **way,** continuer son chemin; se remettre en marche. (*d*) To c. to do sth., continuer à, de, faire qch. **2.** *v.i.* (*a*) (Se) continuer, se soutenir; (*of line*) se prolonger. (*b*) To c. **impenitent,** rester impénitent. To c. **in office,** garder sa charge. **continued,** *a.* **C. existence of a race,** permanence *f* d'une race. **C. interest,** intérêt soutenu. *Mth:* **C. fraction, line,** fraction, ligne, continue.

continuity [ˌkɔnti'nju(:)iti], *s.* **1.** Continuité *f.* *El:* Uniformité *f* (du courant). **To break the c. of s.o.'s ideas,** couper le fil des idées de qn. **2.** *Cin:* Scénario *m.* **C. man,** découpeur *m.* **c. girl,** script-girl *f*, *pl.* script-girls.

continuous [kən'tinju(:)əs], *a.* Continu. **C. studies,** études suivies. *El:* **C. waves,** ondes entretenues. *Cin:* **C. performance,** spectacle permanent. -**ly,** *adv.* Continûment; sans interruption.

contort [kən'tɔːt], *v.tr.* Tordre, contourner (les traits, etc.); dévier (un organe). **Face contorted by pain,** visage tordu, crispé, par la douleur. **contorted,** *a.* Contorsionné, contourné; (visage *m*) tourmenté, crispé.

contortion [kən'tɔːʃ(ə)n], *s.* Contorsion *f.*

contortionist [kən'tɔːʃənist], *s.* Contorsionniste *mf.*

contour¹ ['kɔntuər], *s.* Contour *m*; profil *m* (du terrain); tracé *m* (d'un plan). *attrib. Mapm:* **C. (line),** courbe *f* de niveau. **C. intervals,** équidistances *fpl.* **C. map,** carte *f* en courbes de niveau. *attrib. Agr:* **C. farming,** culture *f* en courbes de niveau.

contour², *v.tr.* **1.** *Surv:* Lever les courbes de niveau de (la région). **2.** *Civ.E:* Construire (une route) en corniche.

contra ['kɔntrə], *s.* *Book-k:* **Per c.,** par contre. **As per c.,** en contre-partie, porté ci-contre. **C. entry,** écriture *f* inverse; contre-écriture *f.*

contraband ['kɔntrəbænd], *s.* Contrebande *f.* **C. goods,** marchandises de contrebande.

contrabass ['kɔntrə'beis], *s.* *Mus:* Basse-contre *f* (voix ou instrument).

contraception [kɔntrə'sepʃən], *s.* *Med:* Contraception *f*; méthodes anticonceptionnelles.

contraceptive [kɔntrə'septiv], *a.* Anticonceptionnel, -elle. *Hyg:* **C. sheath,** préservatif *m*, condom *m.*

contract¹ ['kɔntrækt], *s.* **1.** (*a*) Pacte *m*; contrat *m* (de mariage). (*b*) Acte *m* de vente; contrat translatif de propriété. **By private c.,** à l'amiable; de gré à gré. *S.a.* SIMPLE 1. **2.** Entreprise *f*; soumission *f*, adjudication *f*; convention *f* forfaitaire. **To make a c. for a supply of coal,** passer marché pour une fourniture de charbon. **C. for a bridge,** entreprise d'un pont. **C. work,** travail à l'entreprise, à forfait. **To enter into a c.,** passer (un) contrat (**with,** avec). **To put work up to c.,** mettre un travail en adjudication. **To put work out to c.,** mettre un travail à l'entreprise. **To place the c. for an undertaking,** concéder, adjuger l'exécution d'une entreprise. **To get, secure, a c. for sth.,** être déclaré adjudicataire de qch. **Breach of c.,** rupture de contrat. *Cards:* (*Bridge*) Déclaration *f*; contrat. **To make one's c.,** réaliser son contrat.

contract² [kən'trækt], *v.* **I. 1.** *v.tr.* (*Make smaller*) (*a*) Contracter; crisper (les traits); rétrécir, resserrer (les tissus). (*b*) *Ling:* To c. **'shall not'** into **'shan't,'** contracter "shall not" en "shan't." **2.** *v.i.* Se contracter, se resserrer, se rétrécir. **II. contract. 1.** *v.tr.* (*a*) (*Incur*) Contracter (une obligation, une dette, une maladie); prendre, contracter (une habitude). **To c. a liking for sth.,** prendre goût à qch. (*b*) *Com:* To c. to do sth., s'engager par traité à faire qch. **2.** *v.i.* *Com:* To c. **for a supply of sth.,** entreprendre une fourniture. **To c. for work,** entreprendre des travaux à forfait. **To c. out,** renoncer par contrat. **contracted,** *a.* **1.** (*Of features, etc.*) Contracté; (*of outlook*) rétréci. **2.** *Gram:* **C. article,** article contracté. **contracting**¹, *a.* (*a*) **High c. parties,** hautes parties contractantes. (*b*) *Com:* **C. party,** contractant *m*; *esp.* partie *f* adjudicataire. **contracting**², *s.* (*a*) Affermage *m.* (*b*) *Ind:* Recours *m* à l'entreprise.

contractible [kən'træktibl], **contractile** [kən'træktail], *a.* Contractile.

contraction [kən'trækʃ(ə)n], *s.* **1.** (*a*) Contraction *f*; rétrécissement *m*; retrait *m* (des métaux). (*b*) *Com:* Amoindrissement *m* (de crédit). **2.** (*a*) Contraction (de deux mots en un seul). (*b*) Mot contracté; contraction. **3.** Prise *f* (d'une habitude). **C. of debts,** endettement *m.*

contractor [kən'træktər], *s.* Entrepreneur *m*, pourvoyeur *m*; (*of public works*) adjudicataire *m.* **Army c.,** fournisseur *m* de l'armée.

contractual [kən'træktjuəl], *a.* Contractuel, -elle.

contradict [ˌkɔntrə'dikt], *v.tr.* Contredire (qn); démentir (qn, un bruit). **To c. a statement,** opposer un démenti à une déclaration.

contradiction [ˌkɔntrə'dikʃ(ə)n], *s.* Contradiction *f.* **1.** Démenti *m.* **To give a flat c. to a statement,** démentir formellement une assertion. **2. In c. with . . .,** en contradiction avec. . . . **C. in terms,** contradiction dans les termes.

contradictor [ˌkɔntrə'diktər], *s.* Contradicteur *m.*

contradictory [ˌkɔntrə'dikt(ə)ri], *a.* Contradictoire; opposé (**to,** à).

contradistinction [ˌkɔntrədis'tiŋ(k)ʃ(ə)n], *s.* **In c. to . . .,** par opposition à. . . .

contra-indicate [ˌkɔntrə'indikeit], *v.tr.* *Med:* Contre-indiquer (un régime, etc.).

contra-indication [ˌkɔntrəindi'keiʃən], *s.* *Med:* Contre-indication *f.*

contralto [kən'træltou], *s.* *Mus:* Contralto *m.*

contraption [kən'træpʃ(ə)n], *s.* *F:* Dispositif *m*, machin *m*; truc *m.*

contrapuntal [ˌkɔntrə'pʌntl], *a.* *Mus:* (Morceau, accompagnement) en contrepoint.

contrariety [ˌkɔntrə'raiəti], *s.* Contrariété *f* (d'intérêts, d'opinions).

contrariness [kən'trɛərinis], *s.* *F:* Esprit de contra-diction, de contrariété.

contrariwise ['kɔntrəriwaiz], *adv.* **1.** Au contraire; d'autre part. **2.** En sens opposé. **3.** *F:* [kən'trɛəri-waiz] Par esprit de contrariété.

contrary ['kɔntrəri]. **1.** *a.* (*a*) Contraire (**to,** à); (*of interests, etc.*) opposé, en opposition (avec). **In a c. direction,** en sens opposé, inverse. **C. to nature,** contre nature. **C. winds,** vents contraires. (*b*) [kən'trɛəri] Indocile; qui prend plaisir à contrarier. **2.** *s.* Contraire *m.* **Quite the c.,** tout au contraire; c'est tout l'opposé. **On the c.,** au contraire. **Unless you hear to the c.,** à moins d'avis contraire; sauf contre-avis. **I have nothing to say to the c.,** je n'ai rien à objecter; je n'ai rien à dire contre. **3.** *adv.* Contrairement (**to,** à); en opposition (**to,** à, **with,** avec); à, au, rebours (**to, de**). **C. to accepted opinions,** à l'encontre des idées reçues. **C. to his usual custom,** contrairement à son habitude.

contrast¹ ['kɔntrɑːst], *s.* Contraste *m* (**between,** entre). **In c. with sth.,** par contraste avec qch. **Colours in c.,** couleurs en opposition. **To form a c. to . . .,** faire contraste avec. . . . **To stand out in sharp c. to sth.,** se détacher nettement sur, contre, qch.

contrast² [kən'trɑːst]. **1.** *v.tr.* Faire contraster, mettre en contraste (**with,** avec); opposer (le vice à la vertu). **2.** *v.i.* Contraster, faire contraste (**with,** avec). **To c. strongly,** trancher (**with,** sur). **Contrasting colours,** tons opposés.

contravene [ˌkɔntrə'viːn], *v.tr.* **1.** Transgresser, enfreindre (la loi, etc.). **To c. the regulations,** contrevenir aux règlements. **2.** Aller à l'encontre de (qch.); opposer un démenti à (une affirmation).

contravener [ˌkɔntrə'viːnər], *s.* Transgresseur *m* (d'une loi, etc.).

contravention [ˌkɔntrə'venʃ(ə)n], *s.* **C. of a law,** contravention *f*, infraction *f*, à la loi. **To act in c. of a rule,** agir en violation d'une règle.

contretemps ['kɔntrətɑ̃(ŋ)], *s.* Contretemps *m.*

contribute [kən'tribju:]t], *v.tr. & i.* **To c. one's share,** payer sa (quote-)part. **To c. a sum of money,** contribuer, cotiser, pour une somme. **To c. to a charity,** contribuer à, souscrire pour, une bonne œuvre. **To c. to a newspaper,** collaborer à un journal. **To c. to the success,** aider au succès.

contribution [ˌkɔntri'bju:ʃ(ə)n], s. **1.** (a) Contribution f (à une œuvre de bienfaisance, etc.); cotisation f. Fin: C. of capital, apport m de capitaux. (b) Mil: etc: Contribution; réquisition f. **The whole country has been laid under c.,** on a fait contribuer tout le pays. **2.** C. to a newspaper, article écrit pour un journal.

contributive [kən'tribjutiv], a. Contributif, -ive.

contributor [kən'tribjutər], s. **1.** Fin: Apporteur m (de capitaux). **2.** Collaborateur, -trice (**to a paper,** d'un journal).

contributory [kən'tribjut(ə)ri], a. Contribuant, contributif, -ive. C. causes, causes contribuantes. Jur: Ins: C. negligence, manque m de précautions, imprudence f, de la part de l'accidenté.

contrite ['kɔntrait], a. Contrit, pénitent, repentant. **-ly,** adv. D'un air pénitent; avec contrition.

contrition [kən'triʃ(ə)n], s. Contrition f, pénitence f.

contrivance [kən'traiv(ə)ns], s. **1.** Invention f (d'un appareil); combinaison f, adaptation f (d'un moyen). **2.** (a) Invention; artifice m. (b) Pej: Machination f; manigance f. **3.** Appareil m, dispositif m; engin m, F: truc m.

contrive [kən'traiv], v.tr. (a) Inventer, imaginer, combiner. (b) Pratiquer, ménager. **To c. to do sth.,** trouver moyen de, venir à bout de, faire qch. (c) Pej: Machiner (un complot, etc.). **contrived,** a. (Pièce, histoire) artificielle, qui sonne faux.

contriver [kən'traivər], s. Inventeur, -trice; combinateur, -trice; agenceur, -euse. **He is a good c.,** il est débrouillard. **She is a good c.,** elle est bonne ménagère.

control¹ [kən'troul], s. **1.** (a) Autorité f. **To have c. of an undertaking,** être à la tête d'une entreprise. **She has no c. over her children,** elle ne sait pas tenir ses enfants. (b) Maîtrise f, contrainte f. **Circumstances beyond our c.,** circonstances en dehors de notre action, de notre volonté. (Of pers.) **To get out of c.,** s'affranchir de toute autorité. **To have one's horse under c.,** avoir son cheval bien en main. **Everything is under c.,** tout est fin prêt. **To bring a disease under c.,** enrayer une maladie. **To have absolute c. over s.o.,** avoir un empire absolu sur qn. **To lose c. of oneself,** ne plus se maîtriser, se dominer. Av: C. tower, tour f de contrôle. (c) Gouverne f, manœuvre f (d'un train, d'un navire). **The driver had lost c. of the train,** le mécanicien n'était plus maître du train. **Ship out of c.,** navire qui n'est plus maître de sa manœuvre. Av: Out of c., désemparé. Mec.E: C. lever, levier m, manette f, de commande, d'asservissement. Av: C. column, levier de commande. (d) Surveillance f. **Under government c.,** assujetti au contrôle du gouvernement. Fin: **Exchange c.,** contrôle des changes. **2.** Tchn: (Organe m de) commande f. I.C.E: Ignition c., commande d'allumage. W.Tel: Volume c., contrôle m de volume; modérateur m de son. Remote c., commande à distance. **3.** Sp: (In reliability run, etc.) C. point, contrôle m. Med: C. case, cas témoin.

control², v.tr. (controlled) **1.** Diriger (des affaires, la production); régler (la dépense). **To c. men, one's fate,** commander aux hommes, au destin. **He cannot c. his pupils,** il ne sait pas tenir ses élèves. Adm: **To c. the traffic,** réglementer la circulation. **2.** Maîtriser, gouverner (un cheval); réprimer (un soulèvement); gouverner, dompter (ses passions). **To c. oneself,** se maîtriser, se dominer. **C. yourself!** modérez-vous! retenez-vous! **controlled,** a. (a) Dirigé. (b) Sold at the c. price, vendu à la taxe. **To fix a c. price for a food-product,** taxer une denrée.

controllable [kən'trouləbl], a. **1.** Qui peut être gouverné; (machine, vaisseau) maniable, manœuvrable. **2.** (Passion, cheval) maîtrisable.

controller [kən'troulər], s. **1.** (Pers.) Contrôleur, -euse. **2.** (Appareil) contrôleur m; commande f.

controversial [ˌkɔntrə'və:ʃ(ə)l], a. **1.** Controversable. **2.** (Of pers.) Enclin à la controverse; disputailleur, -euse. **-ally,** adv. C. inclined, enclin à la polémique; chicaneur, -euse.

controversialist [ˌkɔntrə'və:ʃəlist], s. Controversiste m, polémiste m.

controversy ['kɔntrəvə:si], s. Polémique f; controverse f. **To hold, carry on, a c. (with, against, s.o.) on sth.,** soutenir une polémique, une controverse, (contre qn) au sujet de qch. **Beyond c.,** hors de controverse. **Question which has given rise to much c.,** question fort controversée.

controvert ['kɔntrəvə:t], v.tr. **1.** Controverser (une question). **2.** Disputer; mettre en doute (la vérité de qch.).

controvertible [ˌkɔntrə'və:təbl], a. Controversable.

contumacious [ˌkɔntju'meiʃəs], a. Rebelle, récalcitrant. Jur: Contumace.

contumacy ['kɔntjuməsi], s. Entêtement m, obstination f. Jur: Contumace f.

contumelious [ˌkɔntju'mi:ljəs], a. **1.** (Of words, actions) Outrageant. **2.** (Of pers.) Insolent.

contumely [kən'tjumili], s. **1.** Insolence f; souverain mépris. **2.** Honte f.

contuse [kən'tju:z], v.tr. Contusionner. **Contused wound,** plaie contuse.

contusion [kən'tju:ʒ(ə)n], s. Contusion f; meurtrissure f.

contusive [kən'tju:ziv], a. (Coup, instrument) contondant.

conundrum [kə'nʌndrəm], s. **1.** Devinette f. **2.** Énigme f.

conurbation [ˌkɔnə:'beiʃ(ə)n], s. Conurbation f.

convalesce [ˌkɔnvə'les], v.i. Relever de maladie. **He is convalescing at Brighton,** il est en convalescence à Brighton.

convalescence [ˌkɔnvə'les(ə)ns], s. Convalescence f.

convalescent [ˌkɔnvə'les(ə)nt], a. & s. **1.** Convalescent, -ente. **2.** C. home, maison de convalescence.

convection [kən'vekʃ(ə)n], s. Ph: Convection f.

convector [kən'vektər], s. Appareil m de chauffage par convection.

convene [kən'vi:n]. **1.** v.tr. Convoquer, réunir (une assemblée). **2.** v.i. S'assembler, se réunir.

convener [kən'vi:nər], s. Convocateur m (d'une assemblée, etc.).

convenience [kən'vi:njəns], s. **1.** Commodité f, convenance f. **Marriage of convenience,** mariage de convenance, de raison. **At your c.,** à votre convenance, à votre bon plaisir. **At your earliest c.,** le plus tôt (qu'il vous sera) possible. **It is a great c. to be able to . . .,** c'est bien commode, pratique, de pouvoir. . . . **To make a c. of s.o.,** abuser de la bonté de qn. **2.** (Public) c., W.C. public. **3.** pl. Commodités, agréments m. **All modern conveniences,** tout le confort moderne.

convenient [kən'vi:njənt], a. Commode. **If it is c. to you,** si cela ne vous dérange pas; si vous n'y voyez pas d'inconvénient. **To make it c. to do sth.,** s'arranger de manière à faire qch. F: **That's a c. little gadget!** voilà un petit truc bien pratique! **-ly,** adv. Commodément; sans inconvénient.

convent ['kɔnvənt], s. Couvent m (de femmes). **She goes to the c.** (school), elle fait ses études au couvent, F: chez les bonnes sœurs.

convention [kən'venʃ(ə)n], s. **1.** (a) Convention f. **The Hague Conventions,** les Conventions, les actes, m de la Haye. (b) Accord m, contrat m. **2.** Usu. pl. Convenances fpl, bienséances fpl. **Social conventions,** les conventions sociales. **3.** Hist: Assemblée f, convention.

conventional [kən'venʃən(ə)l], a. **1.** Conventionnel, -elle; de convention. Art: C. design, dessin stylisé. **2.** (a) Courant; normal, -aux. **The c. type of car,** la voiture ordinaire, classique. Mil: C. weapons, armes classiques. (b) Sans originalité. **-ally,** adv. **1.** Conventionnellement. **2.** Normalement. **3.** Sans originalité.

conventionality [kənvenʃə'næliti], s. **1.** (a) Convention f; usage m. (b) Les conventions (sociales); les bienséances f. **2.** Caractère conventionnel, ordinaire, banal (d'un salon, d'un tableau, d'un livre).

conventionalize [kən'venʃ(ə)nəlaiz], v.tr. Rendre conventionnel; styliser; banaliser.

conventual [kən'ventjuəl], a. Conventuel, -elle.

converge [kən'və:dʒ]. **1.** v.i. Converger (on, sur). **2.** v.tr. Faire converger (des rayons lumineux, etc.). **converging,** a. Convergent, concourant. C. point, point de concours.

convergence [kən'və:dʒəns], s. Convergence f.

convergent [kən'və:dʒənt], a. Convergent.

conversant [kən'vɜːs(ə)nt], *a.* Familier, intime (avec qn). **C. with** sth., versé dans, au courant de, qch.; compétent en matière de (finance).

conversation [ˌkɒnvəˈseiʃ(ə)n], *s.* **1.** Conversation *f*, entretien *m.* **To hold a c. with** s.o., s'entretenir avec qn. **To enter, fall, into c.** (with s.o.), entrer en conversation (avec qn). **Preliminary c.,** prise *f* de contact. **To be the subject of c.,** défrayer la conversation; faire les frais de la conversation. *Art:* **C. piece,** scène *f* d'intérieur; tableau *m* de genre.

conversational [ˌkɒnvəˈseiʃ(ə)l], *a.* **1.** De (la) conversation. **In a c. tone,** sur le ton de la conversation. **2.** (*Of pers.*) Qui aime à causer. **-ally,** *adv.* He writes c., il écrit sur le ton de la conversation, comme s'il vous parlait.

conversation(al)ist [ˌkɒnvəˈseiʃən(əl)ist], *s.* Causeur, -euse.

converse[1] [kənˈvɜːs], *v.i.* Causer. **To c. with** s.o. **on, about, sth.,** converser avec qn sur qch.; s'entretenir avec qn de qch.

converse[2] ['kɒnvɜːs], *a. & s.* **1.** *Log:* (Proposition) converse (*f*). **2.** *Mth:* (Proposition) réciproque (*f*)

conversely [kənˈvɜːsli], *adv.* Réciproquement.

conversion [kənˈvɜːʃ(ə)n], *s.* **1.** Conversion *f* (de qn). **2.** (*a*) **C. of water into steam,** conversion de l'eau en vapeur. **Improper c. of funds,** détournement *m* de fonds. *St.Exch:* **Fraudulent c. of stocks,** lavage *m* des titres. (*b*) **C. of a room to office use,** transformation *f* d'une pièce en bureau.

convert[1] ['kɒnvɜːt], *s.* Converti, -ie. **To become a c. to** sth., se convertir à qch.

convert[2] [kənˈvɜːt], *v.tr.* **1.** Convertir (qn (à une religion). **To preach to the converted,** prêcher un converti. **2.** Transformer, changer, convertir (**sth. into** sth., qch. en qch.). (*a*) *Rugby Fb:* **Converted goal,** but de transformation. *S.a.* TRY[1] 2. (*b*) **To c. a room to office use,** transformer, aménager, une pièce en bureau. **3.** **To c. funds to one's own use,** détourner des fonds. **To c. (property) fraudulently,** carambouiller.

converter [kənˈvɜːtər], *s.* (Appareil) convertisseur *m.* *W.Tel:* Adapteur *m.* *El.E:* **Static c.,** convertisseur, transformateur *m.* **Rotary c.,** commutatrice *f.*

convertibility [kənˌvɜːtiˈbiliti], *s.* Convertibilité *f.*

convertible [kənˈvɜːtəbl], *a.* Convertible, convertissable (**into,** en). **C. (car),** (voiture *f*) décapotable (*f*). *Ling:* **C. terms,** termes *m* synonymes, interchangeables.

convex ['kɒnveks], *a.* Convexe. **Double c.,** biconvexe.

convexity [kɒnˈveksiti], *s.* Convexité *f.*

convey [kənˈvei], *v.tr.* **1.** Transporter, porter, conduire; (a)mener (qn). **2.** (*Of air, etc.*) Transmettre (le son, une odeur). **3.** Transmettre (un ordre, des remerciements); communiquer (une nouvelle) (**to,** à). **To c. one's meaning,** communiquer, rendre, sa pensée. **To c. to** s.o. **that . . .,** faire comprendre à qn que. . . . **The name conveys nothing to me,** ce nom ne me dit rien. **4.** *Jur:* Faire cession (d'un bien); transmettre, céder (un bien) (**to,** à).

conveyance [kənˈveiəns], *s.* **1.** Transport *m*; moyens *m* de transport; transmission *f.* **Public means of c.,** les transports en commun. **2.** *Jur:* Transmission, translation *f*, transfert *m* (de biens). **3.** *Jur:* Acte translatif de propriété. **4.** Véhicule *m* (de transport); voiture *f.* *Adm:* **Public c.,** véhicule de transport(s) en commun; voiture publique.

conveyancing [kənˈveiənsiŋ], *s.* *Jur:* Rédaction *f* des actes translatifs de propriété.

conveyor, -er [kənˈveiər], *s.* *Ind:* (Appareil) transporteur *m*; transporteuse *f.* **C. belt,** bande transporteuse; courroie *f* de transport. **Portable c.,** transporteur *m* à courroies mobile, sauterelle *f.* **Spiral c.,** vis transporteuse; transporteur à vis (sans fin). *Mec.E:* **Assembly c.,** chaîne *f* de montage; tapis roulant. **Work on the c. belt,** travail *m* à la chaîne.

convict[1] ['kɒnvikt], *s.* Détenu *m*; forçat *m*; bagnard *m*; réclusionnaire *m.*

convict[2] [kənˈvikt], *v.tr.* (*a*) **To c.** s.o. **of a crime,** convaincre qn d'un crime. **He was convicted,** il fut déclaré, reconnu, coupable. (*b*) **To c.** s.o. **of error,** convaincre qn d'erreur. (*c*) **You stand convicted by your own words,** vos propres paroles vous condamnent.

conviction [kənˈvikʃ(ə)n], *s.* **1.** Condamnation *f.* *Jur:* **Previous convictions,** dossier *m* du prévenu. **2.** **To be open to c.,** être accessible à la persuasion; ne demander qu'à être convaincu. **3.** (*Belief*) Conviction *f.* (*Of evidence, etc.*) **To carry c.,** emporter conviction. **It is my c. that . . .,** je suis persuadé que. . . . *S.a.* COURAGE.

convince [kənˈvins], *v.tr.* Convaincre, persuader (s.o. **of** sth., qn de qch.). **I am convinced that he is still alive,** j'ai la conviction, je suis persuadé, qu'il est encore vivant. **convincing,** *a.* (Argument) convaincant; (langage) persuasif. **-ly,** *adv.* D'un ton, d'un air, qui emporte conviction.

convivial [kənˈviviəl], *a.* **1.** **C. evening,** dîner entre camarades; soirée passée à table ou à boire. **2.** (*Of pers.*) Jovial (à table); bon convive; bon vivant (entre convives).

conviviality [kənˌviviˈæliti], *s.* Gaieté *f* (dans un repas, une noce).

convocation [ˌkɒnvəˈkeiʃ(ə)n], *s.* **1.** Convocation *f* (d'une assemblée). **2.** *Ecc:* Assemblée *f*, synode *m.*

convoke [kənˈvouk], *v.tr.* Convoquer (une assemblée).

convolute ['kɒnvəluːt], **1.** *a.* *Bot:* Convoluté, contourné. *Conch:* Contourné. **2.** *s.* *Nat.Hist: etc:* Enroulement *m.*

convolution [ˌkɒnvəˈljuːʃ(ə)n], *s.* Circonvolution *f* (du cerveau, etc.).

convolvulus, -uses [kənˈvɒlvjuləs, -əsiz], *s.* *Bot:* Volubilis *m*, liseron *m*; belle-de-jour *f*, *pl.* belles-de-jour.

convoy[1] ['kɒnvɔi], *s.* *Mil: Nau:* Convoi *m.* **C.-ship,** convoyeur *m*; (bâtiment d') escorte *f.* **To sail under c.,** naviguer de conserve, en convoi.

convoy[2], *v.tr.* *Mil: Nau:* Convoyer, escorter.

convulse [kənˈvʌls], *v.tr.* **1.** Bouleverser (qn, la vie de qn); ébranler (la terre). **2.** *Med:* Convulsionner; convulser (un muscle); donner des convulsions à (qn). **To be convulsed with laughter,** se tordre de rire. **Face convulsed with terror,** visage décomposé par la terreur.

convulsion [kənˈvʌlʃ(ə)n], *s.* **1.** *Med:* (*Usu. pl.*) Convulsions *fpl.* **2.** **To be seized with convulsions of laughter,** se tordre de rire. **3.** Agitation violente (de la mer); bouleversement *m*, commotion *f* (de la terre).

convulsive [kənˈvʌlsiv], *a.* Convulsif, -ive. **C. movements** (*of the limbs*), soubresauts *m.*

cony ['kouni], *s.* = CONEY.

coo[1] [kuː], *s.* Roucoulement *m.*

coo[2], *v.i.* Roucouler; (*of baby*) gazouiller. *S.a.* BILL[8]. **cooing,** *s.* Roucoulement *m.*

coo[3], *int.* *P:* Tiens! mazette!

cook[1] [kuk], *s.* (*a*) Cuisinier, -ière. **She's a first-rate c.,** c'est un cordon-bleu. **C.-general,** cuisinière et bonne à tout faire. (*b*) *Nau:* Cuisinier; maître-coq *m.* *Mil: F:* Cuistot *m.* **'cook-house,** *s.* *Mil: Nau:* Cuisine *f.* *Mil:* **To be on c.-h. fatigue, to be c.-h. orderly,** être (de corvée) de soupe.

cook[2]. **1.** *v.tr.* (*a*) (Faire) cuire (de la viande, etc.). *Abs.* Faire la cuisine; cuisiner. *S.a.* READY-COOKED. *F:* **To c.** s.o.**'s goose,** (i) contrecarrer qn; (ii) faire son affaire à qn. **His goose is cooked,** il a son compte; il est flambé. (*b*) *F:* **To c. accounts,** fricoter; tripoter, truquer, les comptes. **2.** *v.i.* (*Of food*) Cuire. *F:* **What's cooking?** qu'est-ce qui se passe? **cook up,** *v.tr.* *F:* Inventer, imaginer (une excuse, etc.); forger (un mensonge); mijoter (une revanche).

cooking, *s.* **1.** Cuisson *f* (de la viande, etc.). **C. apple,** pomme *f* à cuire. **2.** Cuisine *f.* **(Good) home c.,** cuisine bourgeoise. **To do the c.,** faire la cuisine. **C. utensils,** batterie *f* de cuisine. **3.** *F:* **C. of accounts,** trucage *m* des comptes; tripotages *mpl* de caisse. **'cooking-stove,** *s.* Fourneau *m* de cuisine; cuisinière *f.*

cookbook ['kukbuk], *s.* *U.S:* Livre *m* de cuisine.

cooker ['kukər], *s.* **1.** (*Kitchen stove*) Cuisinière *f.* **Electric c.,** cuisinière, fourneau *m*, électrique. **Gas-c.,** cuisinière à gaz. *S.a.* PRESSURE-COOKER. **2.** Pomme *f* à cuire.

cookery ['kukəri], *s.* (L'art de la) cuisine. **C.-book,** livre de cuisine.

cookstove ['kukstouv], *s.* *U.S:* = COOKING-STOVE.

cookie ['kuki], *s.* *U.S: Cu:* Biscuit *m*; petit gâteau.

cool¹ [ku:l]. **1.** *a.* (*a*) Frais, *f.* fraîche. **C. drink,** boisson rafraîchissante. **It is c.,** il fait frais. **It is turning c.,** le temps se rafraîchit. **'To be kept in a c. place,' "**craint la chaleur"; "tenir au frais." (*b*) **To keep c.** (**calm and collected**), garder son sang-froid. *F:* **As c. as a cucumber,** avec un sang-froid imperturbable. **Keep c.!** du calme! *F:* ne vous emballez pas! (*c*) **To be c. towards s.o.,** être froid, tiède, envers qn. **To give s.o. a c. reception,** faire un accueil froid à qn. (*d*) *F:* **He is a c. customer,** il ne se laisse pas démonter; il en prend à son aise. **I lost a c. thousand,** j'ai perdu mille livres bien comptées. **2.** *s.* **In the c.,** au frais. **In the c. of the evening,** dans la fraîcheur du soir: à la fraîche. **To enjoy the c. of the evening,** prendre le frais. **-ily,** *adv.* **1.** Fraîchement. **2.** (Agir) de sang-froid, de sens rassis. **3.** (Recevoir qn) avec froideur, froidement. **4.** Effrontément; sans gêne. **cool-'headed,** *a.* A l'esprit calme; que rien ne démonte.

cool². **1.** *v.tr.* Rafraîchir, refroidir (l'eau, l'air); rafraîchir (le sang). *S.a.* AIR-COOLED. **2.** *v.i.* (*Of liquid*) Se rafraîchir, (se) refroidir; (*of anger, etc.*) se refroidir. **cool down,** *v.i.* (*After exertion*) Se rafraîchir; (*after anger*) s'apaiser, se calmer. **cool off.** **1.** *v.i. F:* (*Of affection, enthusiasm*) Se refroidir, tiédir. **2.** *v.tr. F:* **The government's mistakes have cooled off his enthusiasm for the Socialist party,** les fautes du gouvernement ont refroidi son enthousiasme pour le parti socialiste. **cooling¹,** *a.* (*a*) Rafraîchissant. (*b*) *Ind: etc:* Réfrigérant. **C. agent,** agent *m* de refroidissement. **cooling²,** *s.* (*a*) Rafraîchissement *m*, refroidissement *m*. (*b*) *Ind:* Réfrigération *f. I.C.E: etc:* **Air c.,** refroidissement par courant d'air. *Ind:* **C. tower,** tour *f* de réfrigération; refroidisseur *m.*

coolant ['ku:lənt], *s.* Agent *m* de refroidissement.

cooler ['ku:lər], *s.* **1.** (*a*) (Appareil) rafraîchisseur *m. S.a.* WINE-COOLER. (*b*) *Ind:* Réfrigérant *m*, refroidisseur *m.* **2.** *F:* (*Drink*) Boisson rafraîchissante. **3.** *P:* Taule *f*, tôle *f*, prison *f.*

coolie ['ku:li], *s.* (*In India, China*) Coolie *m.*

coolish ['ku:liʃ], *a.* **1.** Un peu frais, *f* fraîche. **2.** A c. reception, un accueil plutôt froid.

coolness ['ku:lnis], *s.* **1.** Fraîcheur *f* (de l'air, du soir). **2.** (*a*) Sang-froid *m*, flegme *m.* (*b*) *F:* Aplomb *m*; culot *m*, toupet *m.* **3.** Froideur *f* (de qn, d'un accueil). **There's a certain c. between them,** ils sont en froid.

coon [ku:n], *s. U.S: F:* **1.** *Z:* = RAC(C)OON. **2.** *O:* **He's a gone c.,** il est fichu. **3.** *O: Pej:* Nègre *m.* **C. songs,** chansons nègres.

coop¹ [ku:p], *s.* (*a*) Cage *f* à poules; mue *f.* **Fattening c.,** épinette *f*, cageot *m* d'engraissement. (*b*) Poussinière *f.*

coop², *v.tr.* Enfermer (des poules) dans une mue. *F:* **To c. s.o. up,** tenir qn enfermé; claquemurer, cloîtrer, qn. **To feel cooped up,** se sentir à l'étroit.

co-op [kou'ɔp], *s. F:* = *co-operative stores, q.v. under* CO-OPERATIVE.

cooper ['ku:pər], *s.* **1.** (Wet) c., fabricant *m* de tonneaux, de barils, tonnelier *m.* **Dry c.,** boisselier *m.* **2.** = WINE-COOPER.

cooperage ['ku:pəridʒ], *s.* Tonnellerie *f*; tonnelage *m.*

co-operate [kou'ɔpəreit], *v.i.* **1.** Coopérer (**with s.o. in sth.,** avec qn à qch.); agir en commun. **2.** (*Of thgs*) Concourir, contribuer (in, à).

co-operation [kou'ɔpə'reiʃ(ə)n], *s.* Coopération *f*, concours *m* (in, à).

co-operative [kou'ɔp(ə)rətiv]. **1.** *a.* (*a*) Coopératif, -ive. **C.** (**supply**) **stores,** société coopérative de consommation. (*b*) **He isn't c.,** on ne peut pas travailler avec lui. **2.** *s.* (**Wine-making**) **c.,** coopérative *f* (vinicole).

co-operator [kou'ɔpəreitər], *s.* Coopérateur, -trice.

co-opt [kou'ɔpt], *v.tr.* Coopter.

co-option [kou'ɔpʃ(ə)n], *s.* Cooptation *f.*

co-ordinate¹ [kou'ɔ:dinit]. **1.** *a. Gram:* (*Of clause*) Coordonné. **2.** *s.pl.* **Coordinates,** *Mth:* Coordonnées *f. Cost: Com:* Coordonnées *f.*

co-ordinate² [kou'ɔ:dineit], *v.tr.* Coordonner (with, à).

co-ordinating, *a.* **1.** Coordonnateur, -trice. **2.** *Gram:* Coordonnant.

co-ordination [kou'ɔ:di'neiʃ(ə)n], *s.* Coordination *f.*

coot [ku:t], *s. Orn:* (Bald-)c., foulque noire. *F:* **Bald as a c.,** chauve comme un œuf.

cop¹ [kɔp], *s. F:* (= *policeman*) Flic *m. S.a.* SPEED(-)COP, COURTESY.

cop², *v.tr. P:* Attraper, pincer (qn). **To get copped,** se faire pincer. **To c. it,** (i) écoper; (ii) recevoir un savon.

copal ['koupəl], *s.* (Gum) c., copal *m.*

copartner [kou'pɑ:tnər], *s. Com:* Coassocié *m.*

copartnership [kou'pɑ:tnəʃip], *s.* Coassociation *f*; société *f* en nom collectif.

cope¹ [koup], *s. Ecc:* Chape *f.*

cope², *v.i.* **To c. with s.o.** (**difficult**), tenir tête à qn. **She manages to c. with all those children,** elle sait se débattre avec tous ces enfants. **To c. with a situation,** faire face à une situation. **To c. with a difficulty,** venir à bout d'une difficulté. **To be able to c. with one's job,** être à la hauteur de sa tâche. **I just can't c.,** c'est au-dessus de mes forces. **I'll c.,** je me débrouillerai (tout(e) seul(e)). **I'll c. (with it, him),** je m'en occuperai.

Copenhagen [,koupən'heigən]. *Pr.n.* Copenhague *f.*

copier ['kɔpiər], *s.* **1.** Copiste *mf.* **2.** Imitateur, -trice. **3.** Duplicateur *m.*

co-pilot ['kou'pailət], *s. Av:* Pilote *m* de relève; copilote *m.*

coping ['koupiŋ], *s. Const: etc:* Couronnement *m*, toit *m* (d'un mur); margelle *f* (d'un puits). **'coping-stone,** *s. Const:* Tablette *f* (de couronnement).

copious ['koupjəs], *a.* Copieux, -euse, abondant, ample. **-ly,** *adv.* Copieusement.

copper¹ ['kɔpər], *s.* **1.** Cuivre *m* (rouge). **2.** (*a*) *Dom.Ec:* Cuve *f* à lessive; lessiveuse *f*; chaudron *m.* (*b*) *F:* (*Coin*) = Sou *m. pl.* Petite monnaie. **3.** *attrib.* (*a*) De cuivre, en cuivre. **C. wire,** fil de cuivre. (*b*) (**C.-coloured**) Cuivré. **C. complexion,** teint cuivré, bronzé. *S.a.* BEECH. **'copper-ware,** *s.* Dinanderie *f.*

copper², *v.tr.* *Metalw:* **1.** Cuivrer. **2.** Doubler, recouvrir (qch.) de cuivre.

copper³, *s.* = COP¹.

copperhead ['kɔpəhed], *s. Rept: F:* Mocassin *m.*

copperplate¹ ['kɔpəpleit], *s.* **1.** Plaque *f* de cuivre. **2. C. engraving,** (gravure *f* en) taille-douce *f*; gravure sur cuivre. **C. writing,** écriture moulée, calligraphiée.

copperplate², *v.tr.* Cuivrer (un métal).

coppersmith ['kɔpə:smiθ], *s.* Chaudronnier *m* en cuivre.

coppice ['kɔpis], *s.* Taillis *m*, hallier *m.*

copra ['kɔprə], *s. Com:* Copra *m.*

co-property ['kou'prɔpəti], *s. Jur:* Copropriété *f.*

co-proprietor ['koupra'praiətər], *s. Jur:* Copropriétaire *m.*

copse [kɔps], *s.* = COPPICE.

copulate ['kɔpjuleit], *v.i.* S'accoupler.

copulation [kɔpju'leiʃ(ə)n], *s. Physiol:* Copulation *f*; coït *m*; accouplement *m* (des animaux).

copy¹ ['kɔpi], *s.* **1.** Copie *f*, reproduction *f.* **2.** (*a*) Copie, transcription *f* (d'une lettre, etc.); *Typ:* double *m.* **Top c.,** original *m.* **Rough c.,** brouillon *m.* **Fair c.,** copie (au net). **To take a c. of a letter,** prendre copie d'une lettre. (*b*) *Jur:* Expédition *f* (d'un acte). **Certified c.,** copie authentique; ampliation *f.* **'Certified true c.,' "**pour copie conforme." **True c.,** copie conforme. **3.** Modèle *m*, exemple *m* (d'écriture). **4.** Exemplaire *m* (d'un livre); numéro *m* (d'un journal). **5.** (*a*) Manuscrit (destiné à l'impression); copie. (*b*) *Journ:* Matière *f* à reportage; sujet *m* d'article. **'copy-book,** *s.* Cahier *m* d'écriture. *F:* **To blot one's c.-b.,** ternir sa réputation. **'copy-reader,** *s. U.S: Journ:* = SUB-EDITOR. **'copy typist,** *s.* Dactylo *f.*

copy², *v.tr.* Copier. **1.** (*a*) Imiter, reproduire (une œuvre d'art, etc.). **Copied from the original,** copié sur l'original. (*b*) **To c. s.o.,** se modeler sur qn. *Art: Lit:* **To c. s.o.'s style,** copier, pasticher, le style de qn. (*c*) *Journ:* "**Australian papers please c.,**" "prière d'insérer dans les journaux australiens." (*d*) *Abs: Sch:* Copier (sur un autre élève). **2. To c. (out) a letter,** copier, transcrire, une lettre. **Copying clerk,** expéditionnaire *m.* **copying,** *s.* Transcription *f*, imitation *f. S.a.* INK¹¹.

copyist ['kɔpiist], *s.* Copiste *mf*; scribe *m.*

copyright¹ ['kɔpirait], *s.* Copyright *m.* **Out of c.,** (tombé) dans le domaine public. **C. reserved,** tous droits réservés.

copyright², *v.tr. Publ:* Déposer (un livre).
copyright³, *a.* (Livre) qui est protégé par des droits d'auteur; (article) dont le droit de reproduction est réservé.
coquetry ['kɔkitri], *s.* Coquetterie *f*, chatteries *fpl*.
coquette [kə'ket], *s.* Coquette *f*.
coquettish [kə'ketiʃ], *a.* (Sourire) provocant, *F:* aguichant. **-ly**, *adv.* D'un air provocant.
cor¹ [kɔːr], *s. Mus:* C. anglais, cor *m* anglais.
cor² [kɔː], *int. P:* Ça alors! C.! she's a smasher! *V:* merde! ce qu'elle est belle!
coral ['kɔrəl], *s.* Corail *m*, -aux. C. fisher, corailleur *m*. C. fishery, la pêche du corail. C. island, île corallienne, de corail. C. necklace, collier de corail. *Bot:* C. tree, flamboyant *m. Rept:* C. snake, serpent corail.
coralline ['kɔrəlain], *a.* (*a*) Corallien, -ienne. (*b*) (*Pinkish-red*) Corallin.
corbel¹ ['kɔːbl], *s. Arch:* Corbeau *m*, console *f*.
corbel², *v.tr.* Encorbeller. **To be corbelled out**, porter en saillie. **corbelled**, *a. Arch:* En encorbellement. **corbelling**, *s.* Encorbellement *m*.
cord¹ [kɔːd], *s.* (*a*) Corde *f* (mince); cordon *m*; ficelle *f*. Stranded, twisted, c., cordon câblé. (*b*) *El.E:* Conducteur *m* souple; cordon. (*c*) Bandereau *m* (de trompette). *Dressm: Tail:* Ganse *f. Bookb:* Nerf *m* (de dos de livre). (*d*) *Anat:* The vocal cords, les cordes vocales. The spinal c., le cordon médullaire. The umbilical c., le cordon ombilical. (*e*) *Min:* Cordeau *m*; mèche *f*.
cord², *v.tr.* Corder; attacher, lier, avec une corde; ligoter (un fagot, etc.). **corded**, *a.* (*a*) *Tex:* Côtelé; à côtes. (*b*) *Needlew:* C. cotton, coton perlé.
cordage ['kɔːdidʒ], *s. Coll.* Cordages *m pl*, filin *m*.
cordate ['kɔːdeit], *a.* Cordé, cordiforme; en forme de cœur.
cordial ['kɔːdjəl]. **1.** *a.* Cordial, -aux; chaleureux, -euse. **2.** *s.* Cordial *m*. **-ally**, *adv.* Cordialement, chaleureusement.
cordiality ['kɔːdi'æliti], *s.* Cordialité *f*.
cordillera [kɔːdi'ljeərə], *s. Geog:* Cordillère *f*.
cordite ['kɔːdait], *s. Exp:* Cordite *f*.
Cordoba ['kɔdəbə]. *Pr.n. Geog:* **1.** Cordoba (Argentine). **2.** Cordoue (Espagne).
cordon¹ ['kɔːdən], *s.* **1.** (*a*) Cordon *m*, tresse *f*. (*b*) [kɔr'dɔ̃] Cordon (d'un ordre de chevalerie). **2.** Cordon (de police, de troupes). *Hyg:* Sanitary c., cordon sanitaire.
cordon², *v.tr.* To c. (a district, etc.) off, isoler (un quartier, un secteur) par un cordon (de police, de troupes).
Cordova ['kɔːdəvə]. *Pr.n. Geog:* Cordoue *f*.
corduroy¹ ['kɔːdərɔi], *s. & a. Tex:* Velours (de coton) côtelé, à côtes. C. road, chemin de rondins; route fascinée.
corduroy², *v.tr.* Construire (un chemin) de rondins; fasciner un chemin.
core¹ ['kɔːr], *s.* **1.** Cœur *m* (du bois, etc.); trognon *m* (d'une pomme, etc.). Selfish to the c., d'un égoïsme foncier. *S.a.* ROTTEN 1. **2.** Bourbillon *m* (d'un abcès); cornillon *m* (d'une corne). **3.** (*a*) *Geol: Metall:* Noyau *m*. (*b*) *El:* Noyau (d'un aimant). (*c*) Mèche *f*, âme *f* (d'un câble). (*d*) *Civ.E:* Watertight c., noyau d'étanchéité. **'core-drill**, *s. Min:* Carottage *m*. **'core-sample**, *s. Min:* Carotte *f*, témoin *m*.
core², *v.tr.* **1.** To c. an apple, enlever le cœur d'une pomme; vider une pomme. **2.** To c. (out) a mould, noyauter, évider, un moule.
co-religionist ['kouri'lidʒənist], *s.* Coreligionnaire *m*.
co-respondent ['kouris'pɔndənt], *s. Jur:* Co-défendeur *m* (en adultère).
Corfu [kɔː'fuː]. *Pr.n. Geog:* Corfou *m*.
corgi ['kɔːgi], *s. Z:* (Chien) corgi *m*.
coriaceous [kɔri'eiʃər], *a.* Coriace. *Nat.Hist:* Coriacé.
coriander [kɔri'ændər], *s. Bot:* Coriandre *f*.
Corinth ['kɔrinθ]. *Pr.n. A.Geog:* Corinthe *f*.
Corinthian [kə'rinθiən], *a. & s.* Corinthien, -ienne.
cork¹ [kɔːk], *s.* **1.** Liège *m*. C. sole, semelle de, en, liège. **2.** Bouchon *m* (de liège). **To draw the c. of a bottle**, déboucher une bouteille. **'cork-oak**, *s. Bot:* Chêne-liège *m*, *pl.* chênes-lièges. **'cork-tipped**, *a.* (Cigarette) à bout de liège.

cork², *v.tr.* **1.** (*a*) To c. (up) a bottle, boucher une bouteille. (*b*) Garnir (un filet, etc.) de bouchons. **2.** Se noircir (le visage) au bouchon. **corked**, *a.* (Of wine) Qui sent le bouchon. **corking**, *a. P:* Épatant, fameux, -euse, bath.
corker ['kɔːkər], *s. P:* (*a*) Mensonge un peu fort. (*b*) Réponse *f* qui vous en bouche un coin.
corkscrew¹ ['kɔːkskruː], *s.* Tire-bouchon *m. Hairdr: A:* C. curl, tire-bouchon; boudin *m. Av:* C. spin, descente *f* en tire-bouchon.
corkscrew², *v.i.* (*Of wire, etc.*) Vriller; tire-bouchonner; tourner en colimaçon.
corkwood ['kɔːkwud], *s.* (*a*) Bois *m* de liège. (*b*) Balsa *m*.
corm ['kɔːm], *s. Bot: Hort:* Bulbe *m*.
cormorant ['kɔːmərənt], *s.* **1.** *Orn:* Cormoran *m*. **2.** Homme *m* d'une rapacité de cormoran.
corn¹ [kɔːn], *s.* **1.** Grain *m* (de blé, etc.). **2.** (*a*) (*Coll. sg.*) Grains, blé(s) *m*, céréales *f*. (*b*) *U.S:* (Indian) c., maïs *m*. (*c*) *esp. Scot:* Avoine *f. corn bread, s. U.S:* Pain de maïs. **'corn chandler**, *s. Com:* Marchand *m* de grains, grainetier *m.* **'corn-cob**, *s.* Épi *m* de maïs. **'corn-coloured**, *a.* Paille *inv.* **'corn(-)field**, *s.* Champ de blé, *U.S:* de maïs. **'corn 'pone**, *s. U.S:* (*a*) Galette *f* de maïs. (*b*) Pain *m* de maïs. **'corn 'salad**, *s. Bot:* Mâche *f.* **'corn-stalk**, *s.* **1.** Tige *f* de maïs. **2.** *U.S: F:* (*Pers.*) Grande perche.
corn², *s.* **1.** Cor *m* (à l'orteil); oignon *m* (au pied); durillon *m* (sous le pied). Soft c., œil-de-perdrix, *pl.* œils-de-perdrix. *F:* To tread on s.o.'s corns, toucher qn à l'endroit sensible; froisser qn. *Vet:* Bleime *f*.
corncrake ['kɔːnkreik], *s. Orn:* Râle *m* des genêts.
cornea ['kɔːniə], *Anat:* Cornée *f* (de l'œil).
corneal ['kɔːniəl], *a.* Cornéal, -aux; cornéen. *Med:* C. grafting, greffe *f* de la cornée.
corned [kɔːnd], *a.* C. beef, bœuf de conserve; corned-beef *m*.
cornelian [kɔː'niːljən], *s. Lap:* Cornaline *f*.
corner¹ ['kɔːnər], *s.* **1.** Coin *m*, angle *m. F:* To rub the corners off s.o., dégourdir, dégrossir, qn. **2.** Coin; encoignure *f* (d'une salle, etc.); commissure *f* (des lèvres). To put a child in the c., mettre un enfant en pénitence. To drive s.o. into a c., (i) acculer qn; (ii) *F:* mettre qn au pied du mur. C. seat, place de coin. Chimney c., coin du feu. Nooks and corners, coins et recoins. *S.a.* FOUR. *Fb:* C.(-kick), corner *m*. **3.** (*a*) Coin, angle (de rue). C. house, maison qui fait le coin, l'angle, de la rue. C. shop, boutique d'angle. You will find the grocer's round the c., vous trouverez l'épicerie en tournant le coin. To turn the c., passer le moment critique. (*b*) Tournant *m; Aut: Sp:* virage *m*. He disappeared round the c., il a disparu au tournant. To cut off a c., (i) prendre le plus court; (ii) éviter un détour. *Aut:* Blind c., virage masqué, sans visibilité. To take a corner, virer; prendre un virage. *U.S: F:* To cut corners, (i) rogner les dépenses; (ii) bâcler un travail. *Mount:* Open c., dièdre *m*. **4.** *Com:* Monopole *m*. To make a corner in wheat, accaparer le blé. **'corner-cupboard**, *s.* Encoignure *f.* **'corner-flag**, *s. Fb:* Piquet *m* de coin. **'corner-plate**, *s.* Équerre *f* en fer, en tôle. **'corner-stone**, *s. Const:* Pierre *f* angulaire; pierre de refend. **'corner-tile**, *s. Const:* Tuile cornière.
corner², *v.tr.* **1.** (*a*) Acculer (qn); mettre (un animal) à l'accul. (*b*) *F:* Mettre (qn) au pied du mur, à quia. **2.** Accaparer (une denrée, le marché). **3.** *Abs.Aut:* Prendre un virage; virer. To c. sharply, virer court. **-cornered**, *a.* Sharp-c., à angles saillants. Three-c., à trois coins; triangulaire; (*of hat*) tricorne.
cornet¹ ['kɔːnit], *s.* **1.** *Mus:* Cornet *m* à pistons; piston *m*. C. (player), cornettiste *m*. **2.** Cornet (en papier). Ice-cream c., cornet *m* de crème glacée, de glace.
cornet², *s.* **1.** Cornette *f* (de religieuse). **2.** *Mil: A:* (*a*) Étendard *m* (de cavalerie). (*b*) (*Pers.*) Cornette *m*.
cornflakes ['kɔːnfleiks], *s.pl.* = Paillettes *f* de maïs.
cornflour ['kɔːnflauər], *s.* Farine *f* de maïs.
cornflower ['kɔːnflauər], *s. Bot:* Bleuet *m*, bluet *m*, barbeau *m*. C. blue, bleu barbeau *inv.*
cornice ['kɔːnis], *s.* Corniche *f*.

Cornish ['kɔːniʃ], a. Cornouaillais.
cornstarch ['kɔːnstɑːtʃ], s. U.S: = CORNFLOUR.
cornucopia, pl. -as [ˌkɔːnjuˈkoupiə, -əz], s. Corne d'abondance.
Cornwall ['kɔːnw(ə)l]. Pr.n. (Le comté de) Cornouailles.
corny ['kɔːni], a. F: Usé, vieux, vieille. A c. joke, une plaisanterie usée.
corolla [kəˈrɔlə], s. Bot: Corolle f.
corollary [kəˈrɔləri], s. Log: Mth: Corollaire m.
corona, pl. -ae [kəˈrounə, -iː], s. Couronne f (solaire, d'une dent, etc.).
coronary ['kɔrənəri], a. Anat: Coronaire. Med: C. thrombosis, infarctus m du myocarde.
coronation [ˌkɔrəˈneiʃ(ə)n], s. Couronnement m; sacre m.
coroner ['kɔrənər], s. Jur: Coroner m (officier civil chargé d'instruire en cas de mort suspecte). S.a. INQUEST.
coronet ['kɔrənit], s. (a) (Petite) couronne (ducale, etc.); cercle m; tortil m (de baron). (b) (Lady's) Diadème m ou bandeau m.
corporal[1] ['kɔːp(ə)r(ə)l], a. Corporel, -elle. S.a. PUNISHMENT.
corporal[2], s. (a) Mil: (Of infantry) Caporal m, -aux; (of cavalry, artillery) brigadier m. Mil: Mess c., caporal d'ordinaire. Mil.Av: Caporal-chef m. (Women's Services) Sixième catégorie f.
corporate ['kɔːp(ə)rit], a. 1. Jur: Body c., c. body, corps constitué; personne morale, civile, juridique. 2. C. feeling, esprit m de corps.
corporation [kɔːpəˈreiʃ(ə)n], s. 1. (a) Corporation f; corps constitué. (b) Hist: Corps de métier. 2. Com: Société enregistrée. 3. Jur: Personne morale, civile. 4. (Municipal) c., conseil municipal. 5. F: Bedaine f, bedon m. To develop a c., prendre du ventre.
corporeal [kɔːˈpɔːriəl], a. Corporel, -elle, matériel, -elle.
corps [kɔːr, pl. kɔːz], s. inv. Corps m. Army c., corps d'armée. The diplomatic c., le corps diplomatique.
corpse [kɔːps], s. Cadavre m; corps (mort).
corpulence ['kɔːpjuləns], s. Corpulence f.
corpulent ['kɔːpjulənt], a. Corpulent.
corpus ['kɔːpəs], s. 1. (a) Corpus m, recueil m (d'inscriptions, etc.). (b) Jur: C. delicti [diˈlikti], le corps du délit. 2. C. Christi ['kristi], la Fête-Dieu, la Fête du Saint-Sacrement.
corpuscle ['kɔːpʌsl], s. Corpuscule m. Blood corpuscles, globules sanguins.
corpuscular [kɔːˈpʌskjulər], a. Corpusculaire.
corral[1] [kəˈrɑːl], s. Corral m, pl. -als.
corral[2], v.tr. Renfermer (des chevaux etc.) dans un corral.
correct[1] [kəˈrekt], v.tr. 1. Relever les fautes (d'un thème, etc.); corriger (une épreuve, une mauvaise habitude). 2. Rectifier (une erreur). Ph: Volume corrected for temperature and pressure, volume ramené aux conditions normales de température et de pression. 3. (a) Reprendre, faire la leçon à (un enfant). To stand corrected, reconnaître son erreur. To c. oneself, se reprendre. (b) Punir (qn), infliger une correction à (qn). 4. Neutraliser, contrebalancer (une influence).
correct[2], a. 1. Correct, exact; (réponse) juste. His prediction proved c., sa prédiction s'est vérifiée. 2. Bienséant; conforme à l'usage. It's the c. thing, c'est l'usage. -ly, adv. Correctement, exactement, justement.
correction [kəˈrekʃ(ə)n], s. 1. Correction f (d'une épreuve, d'un devoir, etc.); rectification f (d'une erreur). Under c., sauf erreur, sauf correction. 2. Correction, châtiment m, punition f.
corrective [kəˈrektiv], a. Correctif, -ive.
correctness [kəˈrektnis], s. Correction f, convenance f (de tenue, etc.); exactitude f, justesse f; pureté f (de style).
corrector [kəˈrektər], s. Correcteur, -trice.
correlate ['kɔrileit]. 1. v.i. Correspondre, être corrélatif (with, to, à). 2. v.tr. Mettre (qch.) en corrélation (with, avec).
correlation [kɔriˈleiʃ(ə)n], s. Corrélation f.
correlative [kɔˈrelətiv], a. & s. Corrélatif (m).

correspond ['kɔrisˈpɔnd], v.i. 1. (a) Correspondre, être conforme (with, to, à). (b) Correspondre (to, avec). The two windows do not c., les deux fenêtres ne correspondent pas, ne se répondent pas. 2. (Communicate) Correspondre (with s.o., avec qn). They correspond, ils s'écrivent. **corresponding**, a. Correspondant. C. to the original, conforme à l'original. Book-k: C. entry, écriture conforme. -ly, adv. Également; à l'avenant.
correspondence ['kɔrisˈpɔndəns], s. 1. Correspondance f (with, to, avec). 2. (a) To be in c. with s.o., être en relations, en correspondance, avec qn. (b) Correspondance, courrier m. Com: C. clerk, correspondancier, -ière. Sch: C. course, cours m par correspondance. C. school, école d'enseignement par correspondance.
correspondent ['kɔrisˈpɔndənt], s. Correspondant m. Journ: Answers to correspondents, la petite poste. From our special c., de notre envoyé spécial.
corridor ['kɔridɔːr], s. Couloir m, corridor m. Rail: C. carriage, wagon m à couloir, wagon-couloir m. Hist: The Polish C., le Couloir de Dantzig.
corrie ['kɔri], s. Geog: Cirque m.
corrigendum, pl. -da [kɔriˈdʒendəm, -də], s. Typ: Erratum m, pl. errata m.
corroborate [kəˈrɔbəreit], v.tr. Corroborer, confirmer (une déclaration). The facts c. his statements, les faits viennent à l'appui de ce qu'il dit.
corroboration [kəˈrɔbəˈreiʃ(ə)n], s. Corroboration f, confirmation f. In c. of . . ., à l'appui de. . . .
corroborative [kəˈrɔbərətiv]. **corroboratory** [kərɔbə-rɔtri], a. Corroboratif, -ive.
corroborator [kəˈrɔbəreitər], s. Témoin m à l'appui.
corrode [kəˈroud]. 1. v.tr. Corroder, attaquer (le métal); ronger (le métal). 2. v.i. Se corroder.
corrodent [kəˈroud(ə)nt], s. Corrodant m.
corrosion [kəˈrouʒ(ə)n], s. Corrosion f.
corrosive [kəˈrousiv], a. & s. Corrosif (m), corrodant (m).
corrosiveness [kəˈrouzivnis], s. Corrosivité f; action corrosive; mordant m (d'un acide).
corrugate ['kɔrugeit], v.tr. Strier de nervures; strier (le verre); onduler (la tôle); gaufrer (le papier). **corrugated**, a. Ridé, plissé, rugueux; (verre) strié, cannelé; (papier) gaufré; (carton) ondulé. C. iron, tôle ondulée.
corrugation ['kɔruˈgeiʃ(ə)n], s. Plissement m, ondulation f, cannelure f.
corrupt[1] [kəˈrʌpt], a. Corrompu. (a) C. practices, (i) tractations f malhonnêtes; (ii) trafic m d'influence. C. press, presse vénale. (b) (Texte) corrompu, altéré. -ly, adv. D'une manière corrompue; par corruption; vénalement.
corrupt[2]. 1. v.tr. Corrompre, altérer (un texte, le caractère); suborner (un témoin); dépraver, dévoyer (la jeunesse). 2. v.i. Se corrompre.
corrupter [kəˈrʌptər], s. Corrupteur, -trice, démoralisateur, -trice.
corruptibility [kəˈrʌptiˈbiliti], s. Corruptibilité f; vénalité f.
corruptible [kəˈrʌptibl], a. Corruptible; vénal, -aux.
corruption [kəˈrʌpʃ(ə)n], s. 1. (a) Corruption f, putréfaction f. (b) Dépravation f. 2. Jur: Subornation f (de témoins). Bribery and c., corruption, subornation.
corruptness [kəˈrʌptnis], s. Corruption f; vénalité f.
corsage [kɔːˈsɑːʒ], s. 1. Cost: Corsage m. 2. U.S: Bouquet m (porté au corsage).
corsair ['kɔːsɛər], s. 1. Corsaire m (vaisseau ou marin). 2. Flibustier m, pirate m.
corselet ['kɔːslit], s. Cost: Gaine-combinaison f, combiné m.
corset ['kɔːsit], s. (Often pl.) Cost: Corset m; gaine f. **'corset-maker**, s. Corsetier, -ière.
Corsica ['kɔːsikə]. Pr.n. Geog: La Corse.
Corsican ['kɔːsikən], a. & s. Corse (mf).
cortège [kɔːˈteiʒ], s. Cortège m (funéraire).
cortex, pl. -ices ['kɔːteks, -isiːz], s. Bot: Anat: Cortex m.
cortisone ['kɔːtizoun], s. Med: Cortisone f.
corundum [kəˈrʌndəm], s. Miner: Corindon m. Ind: C. wheel, meule en corindon.
corvette [kɔːˈvet], s. Navy: Corvette f.

coryza [kə'raizə], *s. Med:* Coryza *m*.
cos[1] [kɔs], *s Hort:* **C.** (lettuce), (laitue) romaine *f*.
cos[2] [kɔz], *s. F:* = COSINE.
cosec ['kousek], *s. F:* = COSECANT.
cosecant ['kou'sekənt], *s. Mth:* Cosécante *f*.
cosh[1] [kɔʃ], *s. P:* Matraque *f*; assommoir *m*.
cosh[2], *v.tr. P:* Matraquer (qn), assommer (qn).
co-signatory ['kou'signətri], *s.* Cosignataire *m*.
cosily ['kouzili], *adv.* Confortablement, douillette-ment; à l'aise.
cosine ['kousain], *s. Trig:* Cosinus *m*. **C.** curve, cosinusoïde *f*.
cosiness ['kouzinis], *s.* Confortable *m* (d'un fauteuil); chaleur *f* agréable (du coin du feu, etc.).
cosmetic [kɔz'metik], *a. & s.* Cosmétique (*m*).
cosmic ['kɔzmik], *a.* Cosmique. **C. radiation,** rayonne-ment *m* cosmique. **C. rays,** rayons *m* cosmiques.
cosmographer [kɔz'mɔgrəfər], *s.* Cosmographe *m*.
cosmographic(al) [kɔzmə'græfik(l)],*a.*Cosmographique.
cosmography [kɔz'mɔgrəfi], *s.* Cosmographie *f*.
cosmological [kɔzmə'lɔdʒikl], *a.* Cosmologique.
cosmology [kɔz'mɔlədʒi], *s.* Cosmologie *f*.
cosmonaut ['kɔzmonɔːt], *s.* Cosmonaute *m*.
cosmopolitan ['kɔzmə'pɔlit(ə)n], *a. & s.* Cosmopolite (*mf*).
cosmopolitanism [kɔzmə'pɔlit(ə)nizm], *s.* Cosmopoli-tisme *m*.
cosmos ['kɔzmɔs], *s.* Cosmos *m*. **The c.,** l'univers *m*.
Cossack ['kɔsæk], *a. & s.* Cosaque (*mf*).
cosset ['kɔsit], *v.tr. F:* Dorloter, choyer, gâter, câliner, chouchouter (qn).
cost[1] [kɔst], *s.* **1.** Coût *m*, frais *mpl*. **C. of living,** coût *m* de la vie. **C. of living bonus,** indemnité *f* de cherté de vie, allocation *f* de vie chère. **To bear the c. of an undertaking,** faire les frais d'une entreprise; défrayer une entreprise. **At the c. of one's life,** au prix de sa vie. **At little c.,** à peu de frais. **At great c.,** à grands frais. **At any c., at all costs,** à tout prix; à toute force; coûte que coûte. **I learnt it to my c.,** je l'ai appris à mes dépens. **Com:** Prime c., net c., prix de revient, prix coûtant. **C.-plus contract,** contrat en régie *f*. *S.a.* PRICE[1]. **2.** *pl. Jur:* Frais d'instance; dépens *mpl*. **To allow costs,** accorder les frais et dépens. **They were ordered to pay costs,** ils furent condamnés aux frais. **'cost-book,** *s.* Livre de(s) charges.
cost[2]. **1.** *v.i.* (cost; cost) Coûter. **His house has c. him 50,000 francs,** sa maison lui revient à 50,000 francs. **That will c. him a lot of trouble,** cela lui coûtera beau-coup de peine. **The attempt c. him his life,** cette tentative lui coûta la vie. **C. what it may,** coûte que coûte. **It costs me a little civility,** j'en suis quitte pour une petite politesse. **2.** *v.tr.* (costed ; cost) *Com: Ind:* **To c. an article,** établir le prix de revient d'un article. **To c. a job,** évaluer le coût d'un travail. **costing,** *s.* Établissement *m* du prix de revient.
coster(monger) ['kɔstərmʌŋgər], *s.* Marchand ambulant; marchand des quatre saisons.
costive ['kɔstiv], *a.* Constipé.
costliness ['kɔstlinis], *s.* **1.** Somptuosité *f* (de l'ameuble-ment, etc.). **2.** Haut prix; prix élevé.
costly ['kɔstli], *a.* **1.** (*a*) Précieux, -euse; de grand prix. (*b*) (Ameublement, etc.) riche, somptueux, -euse; de luxe. **2.** Coûteux, -euse, dispendieux, -euse.
costmary ['kɔstmɛəri], *s. Bot:* Balsamite *f*.
costume ['kɔstjuːm], *s.* Costume *m*. **1.** *Th:* **C. play,** pièce historique. **2. (Lady's tailor-made) c.,** (cos-tume) tailleur (*m*). **C. jewellery,** bijoux *m* en toc. **Bathing c.,** maillot *m* de bain.
costumier [kɔs'tjuːmiər], *s.* Costumier *m*.
cosy ['kouzi]. **1.** *a.* Chaud, confortable. (*of pers.*) **It is c. here,** il fait bon ici. *F:* **C. little house,** petite maison sympathique. **2.** *s.* = EGG-COSY, TEA-COSY.
cot[1] [kɔt], *s.* **1.** *Poet:* (Cottage) Chaumière *f*, chaumine *f*. **2.** Abri *m*.
cot[2], *s.* Lit *m* d'enfant; couchette *f*. *S.a.* CARRY-COT.
cot[3], *s. F:* = COTANGENT.
cotangent [kou'tæn(d)ʒ(ə)nt], *s. Trig:* Cotangente *f*.
cote [kɔt, kout], *s.* **Dove-c.,** colombier *m*, pigeonnier *m*.
co-tenant [kou'tenənt], *s.* Colocataire *mf*; copreneur, -euse.

coterie ['koutəri], *s.* Coterie *f*; cénacle *m* (littéraire etc.).
cotill(i)on [kə'tiljən], *s. Danc:* Cotillon *m*.
cottage ['kɔtidʒ], *s.* **1.** Chaumière *f*. **2.** Villa *f*; petite maison de campagne. (Country) c., cottage *m*. **C. hospital,** hôpital de petite ville. **Summer c.,** *Fr.C:* camp *m* d'été. *S.a.* LOAF[1].
cottager ['kɔtidʒər], *s. O:* Paysan, -anne; villageois, -oise.
cottar, cotter[1], ['kɔtər], *s. Mec.E: etc:* (*Also* **cotter-pin**) Clavette *f*, goupille *f*.
cotter[2], *v.tr. Mec.E:* Claveter; goupiller; caler (une pièce).
cotton[1] ['kɔtn], *s.* **1.** (*a*) *Bot:* Cotonnier *m*. (*b*) Coton *m*. **Raw c.,** coton en laine. **C. industry,** industrie cotonnière. *Pharm:* (Absorbent) c. wool, *U.S:* **absorbent cotton,** ouate *f*, coton, hydrophile. *F:* **bring up a child in c. wool,** élever un enfant dans du coton. **2.** *Tex:* (*a*) **C. yarn,** fil *m* de coton. (*b*) **C. goods, cottons,** cotonnades *f*. **C.(-cloth),** (toile *f* de) coton; cotonnade, percale *f*. **Printed c.,** indienne *f*. **3.** (Sewing-)c., fil à coudre; fil de coton. **Embroidery c.,** coton à broder. **'cotton-cake,** *s. Husb:* Tour-teau *m*. **'cotton-gin,** *s. Tex:* Machine *f* à égrener le coton. **'cotton-mill,** *s.* Filature *f* de coton; cotonnerie *f*. **'cotton-plantation,** *s.* Cotonnerie *f*. **'cotton-seed,** *s.* Graine *f* de coton. **C.-s. oil,** huile *f*. de coton. **'cotton-spinner,** *s.* **1.** (*Owner*) Filateur *m* de coton. **2.** (*Worker*) Fileur, -euse, de coton.
cotton[2], *v.i.* **1.** (*Of material*) (Se) cotonner. **2.** *F:* **To c. (with s.o.),** s'accorder, faire bon ménage (avec qn). **3. To c. up to s.o.,** faire des avances à qn. **4.** (*a*) **To c. (on) to s.o.,** se sentir attiré par qn; prendre qn en amitié. (*b*) **To c. (on) to (sth.),** mordre à (l'algèbre, etc.).
cottontail ['kɔt(ə)nteil], *s. F: U.S:* Lapin *m*.
cottonwood ['kɔtnwud], *s. U.S:* (Variété *f* de) peuplier *m*.
cottony ['kɔtni], *a.* Cotonneux, -euse.
cotyledon [kɔti'liːd(ə)n], *s. Bot:* Cotylédon *m*.
cotyledonous [kɔti'liːdənəs], *a.* Cotylédoné.
couch[1] [kautʃ], *s.* **1.** *Lit:* Lit *m*, couche *f*. **2.** *Furn:* Canapé *m*, divan *m*. **Studio c.,** banquette-lit *f*, *pl.* banquettes-lits. **3.** *Brew:* Couche, lit (de grains).
couch[2]. **1.** *v.tr.* (*a*) *Lit:* **To be couched on the ground,** être couché par terre. (*b*) Mettre (sa lance) en arrêt. (*c*) *A. & Adm:* **To c. a request in writing,** coucher une demande par écrit. **Letter couched in these terms,** lettre ainsi conçue. **2.** *v.i.* (*Of animal*) **Se coucher, être couché** (dans sa tanière); se terrer; gîter. (*b*) (*Of dog, pers.*) Se tapir (devant qn); s'aplatir. (*c*) Se tenir embusqué. **3.** *v.tr. Surg:* Enlever (une cataracte).
couch[3](-grass) ['kautʃ(grɑːs), 'kuːtʃ-], *s. Bot:* Chien-dent *m*.
couchant ['kautʃənt], *a. Her:* Couché.
couchette [kuː'ʃet], *s. Rail:* Couchette *f*.
cougar ['kuːgər], *s. Z:* Couguar *m*, puma *m*.
cough[1] [kɔf], *s.* Toux *f*. **To have a c.,** tousser. **He gave a c. to warn me,** il toussa pour m'avertir. **'cough-drop, -lozenge,** *s.* Pastille pectorale.
cough[2]. **1.** *v.i.* Tousser. **2.** *v.tr.* **To c. up sth.,** cracher qch. (en toussant). *P:* **To c. up money,** *abs.* **to c. up,** payer, *P:* cracher. **coughing,** *s.* Toux *f*. **Fit of c.,** accès *m*, quinte *f*, de toux.
could. *See* CAN[2]. **couldn't-care-'less,** *a. F:* **C.-c.-l. attitude,** je m'en-fichisme *m*, je m'en-foutisme *m*.
coulomb [kuː'lɔm], *s. El.Meas:* Coulomb *m*; ampère-seconde *m*, *pl.* ampères-secondes.
council ['kaunsl], *s.* **1.** Conseil *m*. **C. of State,** Conseil d'État. **The Army C., the Air C.,** Conseil supérieur de la guerre, de l'armée de l'air. **Security C.,** Conseil de Sécurité (de l'O.N.U.). **Town c., city c.,** conseil municipal. **County c.** = conseil général, conseil départemental. **To hold c. ; to be, meet, in c.,** tenir conseil. **C. house, flat** = habitation *f* à loyer modéré (H.L.M.). *S.a.* ORDER[1] 11, PRIVY I, 2. **2.** *Ecc:* Concile *m*. **'council-chamber,** *s.* Salle *f* du conseil. **'council-school,** *s. A:* = École com-munale.
councillor ['kaunsilər], *s.* Conseiller *m*; membre *m* du conseil. **County c.** = conseiller général.

counsel¹ ['kauns(ə)l], s. 1. Délibération *f*; consultation *f*. **To take c. with s.o.,** (i) prendre conseil de qn; (ii) délibérer, consulter, avec qn. **To take c. together,** se consulter, se concerter. 2. Conseil *m*, avis *m*. **C. of perfection,** idéal *m* difficile à atteindre. 3. Dessein *m*, intention *f*. **To keep one's (own) c.,** garder ses projets pour soi; observer le silence. 4. *Jur:* (*a*) Avocat *m*; conseil *m*. **To be represented by c.,** comparaître par avoué. **C. in chambers,** avocat consultant. (*b*) **King's, Queen's c.,** conseiller du Roi, de la Reine (titre conféré à des membres éminents du barreau de Londres).

counsel², *v.tr.* (**counselled**) *Lit:* Recommander (une ligne de conduite). **To c. s.o. to do sth.,** conseiller, recommander, à qn de faire qch.

counsellor ['kauns(ə)lər], s. Conseiller *m*. *Dipl:* Conseiller d'ambassade.

count¹ [kaunt], s. 1. (*a*) Compte *m*, calcul *m*; (*of votes*) dépouillement *m*; (*of people*) dénombrement *m*. **To keep c. of . . .,** compter . . .; tenir le compte de. . . . **To lose c.,** perdre le compte. **To ask for a c.,** demander le scrutin. *Med:* **Blood c.,** numération *f* globulaire. **Blood-c. cell,** hématimètre *m*. *Techn:* **C. down,** compte à rebours. (*b*) Total *m*. 2. *Jur:* Chef *m* (d'accusation). 3. *Tex:* Numéro *m* (du fil). 4. *Box:* Compte (de dix secondes). **To take the c.** (**out**), rester sur le plancher pour le compte; être mis knock-out.

count². 1. *v.tr.* (*a*) Compter; dénombrer (ses troupeaux, etc.). **To c. the cost,** compter, calculer, la dépense. **To c. up sth.,** compter, faire le compte de, qch. *S.a.* CHICKEN 1. **To c. the votes** (*at election*), dépouiller le scrutin. **Counting from to-morrow . . .,** à compter de demain. (*b*) **To c. s.o. among one's friends,** compter qn parmi ses amis. (*c*) *Pred:* **To c. s.o. as dead,** tenir, compter, qn pour mort. 2. *v.i.* (*a*) *A:* Faire des projets. **To c. on, upon, s.o.,** compter sur qn. **To c. on doing sth.,** compter faire qch. 3. *v.i.* (*a*) **He counts among my best friends,** il compte parmi, au nombre de, mes meilleurs amis. *Cards:* **Card that counts,** (carte) marquante. **This person counts as two,** cette personne compte pour deux. **He doesn't c. for much,** il ne compte guère. (*b*) Avoir de l'importance. **Every minute counts,** il n'y a pas une minute à perdre. **Every penny counts,** il faut regarder à chaque sou. **count in,** *v.tr.* Faire entrer en ligne de compte. **Don't c. me in,** ne me mettez pas du nombre. **count off,** *v.tr. & i.* Dénombrer; séparer en comptant. **count out,** *v.tr.* 1. Compter (de l'argent, etc.) pièce par pièce. 2. *Box:* **To be counted out,** rester sur le plancher pour le compte. 3. *F:* **You can c. me out of that show,** ne comptez pas sur moi dans cette affaire. **countable,** *a.* Nombrable. **counting,** *s.* Compte *m*, calcul *m*; dépouillement *m* (du scrutin); dénombrement *m* (de personnes). **'counting-frame,** *s.* Boulier compteur. **'counting-house,** *s.* (Bureau *m* de) la comptabilité.

count³, *s.m.* (*Title*) Comte.

countenance¹ ['kauntinəns], s. 1. Expression *f* du visage; visage, figure *f*, mine *f*. **To keep one's c.,** (i) ne pas se laisser décontenancer; (ii) se donner, se faire, une contenance. **To put s.o. out of c.,** décontenancer qn. **To lose c., se décontenancer;** perdre contenance. **To stare s.o. out of c.,** dévisager qn. 2. **To give, lend, c. to s.o., to sth.,** appuyer, favoriser, encourager, qn, qch.; accréditer (une nouvelle, etc.).

countenance², *v.tr.* 1. Autoriser, approuver, sanctionner (une action). 2. Encourager, appuyer, soutenir (qn) (in, dans).

counter¹ ['kauntər], s. 1. (*Pers.*) Compteur, -euse. 2. *Mec.E:* Compteur *m*. 3. *Games:* (i) (*Square*) Fiche *f* (en os, etc.). (ii) (*Round*) Jeton *m*. 4. (*a*) (*In bank, etc.*) Guichets *mpl*; caisse *f*. (*b*) (*In shop*) Comptoir *m*. *F:* **To sell under the c.,** vendre en cachette. **'counter-hand,** *s. Com:* Vendeur, -euse.

counter², *s.* 1. *N.Arch:* Voûte *f* d'arcasse. 2. Creux *m* (d'un poinçon, etc.).

counter³, *s. Bootm:* Contrefort *m*.

counter⁴. 1. *s.* (*a*) *Fenc:* Contre *m*. (*b*) *Box:* Coup *m* d'arrêt; contre. 2. *a.* (*a*) Contraire, opposé (to, à). (*b*) *In compounds often translated by* contre-. 3. *adv.* En sens inverse; à contresens. **To run c. to**

one's orders, agir contrairement à ses instructions; aller à l'encontre de ses instructions. **'counter-ad'vice,** *s.* Contre-avis *m.* **'counter-at'tack¹,** *s.* Contre-attaque *f.* **'counter-at'tack²,** *v.tr. & i.* Contre-attaquer. **'counter-at'traction²,** *s.* 1. Attraction opposée. 2. Attraction destinée à faire concurrence au clou de la fête. **'counter-brace¹,** *s. Civ.E:* Entretoise *f.* **'counter-brace²,** *v.tr.* Entretoiser. **'counter-charge,** *s.* Contre-accusation *f.* **'counter-check,** *s.* 1. *Mec:* Force opposée; force antagoniste. 2. Recoupement *m*; recoupage *m*; vérification *f.* **'counter-check²,** *v.tr.* Recouper; vérifier. **'counter-claim¹,** *s. Jur:* Demande reconventionnelle; défense *f* au contraire. **'counter-claim²,** *v.tr. Jur:* Faire, opposer, une demande reconventionnelle (en dommages-intérêts, etc.). **'counter-'clockwise,** *adv.* En sens inverse des aiguilles d'une montre; sinistrorsum. **'counter-'current,** *s.* Contre-courant *m.* **'counter-decla'ration,** *s.* Contre-déclaration *f.* **'counter-demon'stration,** *s.* Contre-manifestation *f.* **'counter-'effort,** *s.* Contre-effort *m.* **'counter-en'quiry,** *s. Jur:* Contre-enquête *f.* **'counter-espionage,** *s.* Contre-espionnage *m.* **'counter-intelligence,** *s. Mil:* Contre-espionnage *m.* **'counter-'irritant,** *a. & s. Med:* (Médicament) révulsif (*m*), dérivatif (*m*). **'counter-irritation,** *s. Med:* Révulsion *f*, dérivation *f.* **'counter-o'ffensive,** *s. Mil:* Contre-offensive *f.* **'counter-'order,** *s.* Contrordre *m.* **'counter-preparation,** *s. Mil:* Contre-préparation *f.* **'counter-'pressure,** *s.* Contre-pression *f.* **'counter-propa'ganda,** *s.* Contre-propagande *f.* **'counter-punch,** *s. Tls:* Contre-poinçon *m.* **'counter-re'connaissance,** *s. Mil:* Contre-reconnaissance *f.* **'counter-reform'ation,** *s. Rel.H:* Contre-réforme *f*, contre-réformation *f.* **'counter-revo'lution,** *s.* Contre-révolution *f.* **'counter-revo'lutionary,** *a.* Contre-révolutionnaire. **'counter-seal¹,** *s.* Contre-sceau *m.* **'counter-'seal²,** *v.tr.* Contre-sceller. **'counter-'signature,** *s.* 1. Contreseing *m.* 2. Approuvé *m.* **'counter-'spy,** *s.* Contre-espion *m.* **'counter-stroke,** *s. Mil:* Retour offensif. **'counter-'tenor,** *s. Mus:* (Voix) haute-contre *f.* **'counter-'trade,** *s. Meteor:* Contre-alizé *m.* **'counter-valu'ation,** *s.* Contre-expertise *f.*

counter⁵, *v.tr.* Aller à l'encontre de, contrarier (qn, qch.); contrecarrer (les desseins de qn). *Box:* **To c.** (*a blow*), parer, bloquer (un coup) et riposter en même temps.

counteract [kauntə'rækt], *v.tr.* Neutraliser (une influence); parer à (un résultat).

counteraction ['kauntə'rækʃ(ə)n], *s.* 1. Action *f* contraire; mouvement opposé; opposition *f.* 2. Neutralisation *f* (d'une influence, etc.).

counterbalance¹ ['kauntəbæləns], *s.* Contre-poids *m.*

counterbalance² ['kauntə'bæləns], *v.tr.* Contre-balancer; faire contrepoids à (qch.); compenser (une force, etc.).

countercharge ['kauntətʃɑːdʒ], *s. Jur:* Contre-accusation *f.*

counterfeit¹ ['kauntəfiːt], s. 1. *a.* Contrefait; faux, fausse. **C. coin,** fausse monnaie. 2. *s.* Contrefaçon *f.*

counterfeit², *v.tr.* 1. Contrefaire (la monnaie, etc.). 2. Simuler, feindre (une passion, etc.). **counte̶-feiting,** *s.* 1. (*a*) Contrefaction *f.* (*b*) Contrefaçon *f.* 2. Simulation *f.*

counterfeiter ['kauntəfiːtər], s. 1. Contrefacteur *m*; faux monnayeur. 2. Simulateur, -trice.

counterfoil ['kauntəfoil], s. Souche *f*, talon *m* (de chèque, etc.).

countermand ['kauntə'mɑːnd], *v.tr.* Contremander; décommander (une grève); révoquer, rappeler (un ordre). **Unless countermanded,** sauf contre-ordre, sauf contre-avis.

countermarch ['kauntəmɑːtʃ], s. Contremarche *f.*

countermeasure ['kauntəmeʒər], s. Contre-mesure *f.*

countermine [kauntə'main], *v.tr. & i.* Contre-miner.

counterpane ['kauntəpein], s. Courtepointe *f*; couvre-lit *m*, couvre-pied(s) *m.*

counterpart ['kauntəpɑːt], s. Contrepartie *f*; pendant *m* (d'un tableau, etc.).

counterplot ['kauntəplɔt], s. Contre-ruse *f*, contre-trame *f.*

counterpoint ['kauntəpoint], s. *Mus:* Contrepoint *m.*

counterpoise¹ ['kauntəpɔːiz], *s.* **1.** Contrepoids *m.* **2.** Équilibre *m.* **In c.,** en équilibre.

counterpoise², *v.tr.* Contrebalancer; faire contrepoids à (qch.).

counterscarp ['kauntəskɑːp], *s. Fort:* Contrescarpe *f.*

countershaft ['kauntəʃɑːft], *s. Mec.E:* Arbre *m* intermédiaire, de renvoi. *Aut:* Contre-arbre *m.*

countersign¹ ['kauntəsain], *s.* **1.** Contreseing *m.* **2.** Mot d'ordre; mot de ralliement.

countersign² ['kauntə'sain], *v.tr.* Contresigner, signer en second, viser.

countersink¹ ['kauntəsiŋk], *s.* **1.** *Tls:* Fraise *f.* **2.** C. (hole), fraisure *f* (d'un trou); noyure *f* (pour tête de vis).

countersink², *v.tr.* (*Conj. like* SINK) **1.** Fraiser (un trou). **2.** Encastrer (la tête d'un rivet); noyer (la tête d'une vis).

counterweight¹ ['kauntəweit], *s.* Contrepoids *m.*

counterweight², *v.tr.* Contrebalancer; équilibrer.

countess ['kauntis], *s.f.* Comtesse.

countless ['kauntlis], *a.* Innombrable.

countrified ['kʌntrifaid], *a.* Aux allures campagnardes; provincial; agreste. **To become c.,** se provincialiser. **They are very c.,** *F:* ils sont très province.

country ['kʌntri], *s.* **1.** (*a*) Pays *m,* contrée *f,* région *f.* **To go up c.,** remonter vers l'intérieur du pays. **Open c.,** rase campagne. **Broken c.,** pays accidenté. *Pol:* **To appeal, go, to the c.,** en appeler au pays; consulter le corps électoral. (*b*) (*Native country*) Patrie *f.* **To die for King and c.,** mourir pour la patrie. **Mother c.,** mère patrie *f.* **2.** (*a*) (*Opposed to capital*) Province *f.* **In the c.,** en province. (*b*) (*Opposed to town*) Campagne *f.* **In the c.,** à la campagne. **Surrounding c.,** pays d'alentour. **C. life,** vie de, à la, campagne; vie de province. **She's a real c. girl,** elle n'aime que la vie de campagne. **country 'dance,** *s.* Danse *f* folklorique. **country 'house,** *s.* **1.** Maison *f* de campagne. **2.** Château *m;* gentilhommière *f;* manoir *m.* **country-seat,** *s.* = COUNTRY-HOUSE 2.

countryman, *pl.* **-men** ['kʌntrimən, -mən], *s.m.* **1.** Compatriote. **2.** Paysan, campagnard.

countryside (the) [ðə'kʌntrisaid], *s.* La région, le pays.

countrywoman, *pl.* **-women** ['kʌntriwumən, -wimin], *s f.* **1.** Compatriote. **2.** Paysanne, campagnarde.

county ['kaunti], *s.* Comté *m.* **C. town,** *U.S:* **c. seat,** chef-lieu *m* de comté, *pl.* chefs-lieux. **A c. family,** une des familles terriennes du comté. *S.a.* COUNCIL 1, COUNCILLOR, COURT¹ 1.

coup [kuː], *s.* (*a*) Coup (audacieux). **To bring off a c.,** faire réussir un coup. (*b*) (*Empruntés au français*): **c. d'état; c. de grâce;** *Prehist:* **c. de poing; c. de théâtre.**

coupé ['kuːpei], *s. Veh:* Coupé *m.*

couple¹ ['kʌpl], *s.* **1.** Couple *f* (d'attache, pour chiens de chasse). **2.** Couple *f* (de pigeons, d'œufs, etc.). **To work in couples,** se mettre à deux pour travailler. *F:* **I'll come in a c. of minutes,** je viens dans un instant. **3.** (*a*) Couple *m* (de chiens de chasse). *O:* **To hunt in couples,** être toujours ensemble. (*b*) Couple *m* (d'époux, de danseurs). **The newly married c.,** les nouveaux mariés; le nouveau ménage. **The young c.,** les deux jeunes époux. **4.** *Mec:* Couple *m* (de torsion); couple moteur.

couple², *v.tr.* (*a*) Coupler, accoupler (des bœufs, deux idées); accoupler, apparier (le mâle et la femelle); associer, accoler (des noms, etc.). *Organ:* **To c. two manuals,** accoupler deux claviers. (*b*) *Mec.E:* etc: Engrener, embrayer (une machine); raccorder (des tuyaux). **Coupled direct to the motor,** en prise directe avec le moteur. (*c*) *El:* Associer, grouper, accoupler (des piles). (*d*) *Rail:* **To c. up, c. on, a carriage,** accrocher un wagon. **coupling,** *s.* **1.** Accouplement *m* (de deux choses); appariement *m* (des animaux); association *f* (d'idées, etc.); accolement *m* (de deux noms). **2.** *Tchn:* (*a*) Accouplement, assemblage *m,* couplage *m* (de deux roues, etc.); emmanchement *m* (de deux tuyaux). **C.-box, c.-sleeve,** manchon *m* d'accouplement. (*b*) *Rail:* Accrochage *m* (des wagons). (*c*) *El:* Couplage, association *f,* groupement *m* (d'éléments de pile, etc.). **3.** (*Coupling device*) Accouplement, raccord *m;* (*for transmitting motion*) embrayage *m.* *Rail:* Attelage *m.* **coupling-rod,** *s. Mech:* (*a*) Allonge *f.* (*b*) Bielle *f* d'accouplement.

coupler ['kʌplər], *s. Organ:* (i) Tirant *m* à accoupler; (ii) pédale *f* d'accouplement.

couplet ['kʌplit], *s. Pros:* Distique *m.*

coupon ['kuːpɔn], *s.* Coupon *m. Post:* **International reply c.,** coupon-réponse international. *Hist: Adm:* **Petrol c.,** bon *m* d'essence. **Clothing coupons,** points *m* textiles; *F:* des points. **Bread c.,** ticket *m* de pain. *Com:* **Free-gift c.,** bon-prime *m, pl.* bons-primes.

courage ['kʌridʒ], *s.* Courage *m.* **To have the c. of one's convictions,** avoir le courage de ses opinions. **To take, pluck up, muster up, c.,** prendre son courage à deux mains; faire appel à tout son courage. *S.a.* DUTCH 1.

courageous [kə'reidʒəs], *a.* Courageux, -euse. **-ly,** *adv.* Courageusement.

courier ['kuriər], *s.* (*a*) Courrier *m,* messager *m.* (*b*) (*Of tourist party*) Guide *m.*

course¹ [kɔːs], *s.* **1.** (*a*) Cours *m* (d'un fleuve, du temps); courant *m* (des affaires, etc.); cours, marche *f* (des événements); cours, trajet *m* (d'une balle, etc.). **In the c. of the sitting,** au cours de la séance. **In (the) c. of time,** avec le temps; à la longue. **In the ordinary c. of things,** normalement. **To do sth. in due c.,** faire qch. en temps voulu, en temps utile. **This will probably happen in the c. of three or four months,** ceci se produira probablement d'ici trois ou quatre mois. **In c. of construction,** en cours de construction. **The fever must run its c.,** il faut que la fièvre suive son cours. **To let nature take her c.,** donner libre cours à la nature. **Let things take their c.,** laissez faire. (*b*) **Of c.,** bien entendu; naturellement. **Of course not!** bien sûr que non! (*c*) **That is a matter of c.,** cela va sans dire; cela va de soi. **As a matter of c.,** comme de juste, comme de raison. **2.** (*a*) *Sch:* Cours. **To give a c. of lectures,** professer un cours. **To go through a c., to take a c.,** suivre un cours (de physique, etc.). **To publish a French c.,** publier une méthode de français. (*b*) *Med:* Traitement *m,* régime *m.* **3.** (*a*) Route *f,* direction *f.* **To hold (on) one's c.,** suivre tout droit son chemin; *Nau:* maintenir son cap. **To be on (the) c.,** suivre le cap fixé. **To change one's c.,** changer de direction; *Nau:* changer le cap. **To veer off one's c.,** dévier du cap fixé. *Nau:* **To set the c. (on the chart),** tracer la route (sur la carte). **To steer a c.,** suivre une route. (*b*) **To take a c. of action,** adopter une ligne de conduite. **To take one's own c.,** agir à sa guise. **There was no c. open to me but flight,** je n'avais d'autre ressource que la fuite. **To hesitate between two courses,** hésiter entre deux partis. **The best c., the right c.,** le parti le plus sûr; la bonne voie. *S.a.* MIDDLE 1. (*c*) *Mch:* Upward c. of a piston, course ascendante, ascensionnelle, d'un piston. **4.** (*Of meal*) Service *m,* plat *m.* **5.** *Sp:* (*a*) Champ *m,* terrain *m* (de courses). (*b*) Piste *f.* **Closed c.,** circuit *m* (sur piste). **6.** *Const:* Assise *f* (de briques, de charpente). *S.a.* DAMP-COURSE.

course². **1.** *v.tr.* (*a*) *Ven:* Courir (un lièvre). (*b*) Faire courir (un chien, un cheval). **2.** *v.i. Lit:* (*Of liquids*) Courir, couler. **The blood courses through the veins,** le sang circule dans les veines. **coursing,** *s.* Chasse *f* à courre au lièvre.

court¹ [kɔːt], *s.* **1.** (*a*) = COURTYARD. (*b*) (*Off street*) Ruelle *f;* impasse *f.* **2.** (*a*) Cour (royale). **The C. of St James's,** la cour de la Reine d'Angleterre. (*b*) **To pay c. to s.o.,** faire la cour à qn. **3.** *Jur:* (*a*) Cour *f,* tribunal *m.* **C.-room,** salle *f* d'audience. **The Law Courts,** le palais de justice. **County c.** = tribunal de grande instance. **Juvenile c.,** tribunal d'enfants; tribunal pour enfants et adolescents. **Magistrates', police, c.** = tribunal d'instance. **In open c.,** en plein tribunal, en pleine audience; à huis ouvert. **To arrange, settle, a case out of c.,** arranger une affaire à l'amiable. **To be ruled, put, out of c.,** être mis hors de cour; être débouté de sa demande. (*b*) *Mil: Navy:* **C. of inquiry,** commission *f* d'enquête. **4.** (*a*) (i) Jeu *m* de paume. (ii) Terrain *m* (de jeu de paume). (*b*) (i) Tennis *m.* **Porous cement tennis c.,** quick *m.* (ii) Court *m* (de tennis). (iii) **Service-c.,** rectangle *m* de service. **'court-card,** *s. Cards:* Figure *f;* carte peinte. **'court-day,** *s. Jur:* Jour *m* d'audience. **'court-dress,** *s.* (*a*) Habit *m* de cour. (*b*) (*Of lady*) Robe *f* de cour. **'court-house,** *s.*

Palais *m* de justice; tribunal *m*. **court-'martial**[1], *s*. (*pl*. **courts-martial**) *Mil*: Conseil *m* de guerre. **To be tried by c.-m.,** passer en conseil de guerre. **court-martial**[2], *v.tr*. (**court-martialled**) Faire passer (qn) en conseil de guerre.

court[2], *v.tr*. 1. Courtiser; faire la cour à (une femme). 2. Briguer, rechercher (une alliance, etc.); (re)chercher, solliciter (les applaudissements, etc.). **To c. danger,** aller au-devant du danger.

courteous ['kɔːtjes], *a*. Courtois, poli, gracieux, -euse (**to, towards,** envers). **-ly,** *adv*. Courtoisement.

courteousness ['kɔːtjesnis], *s*. Courtoisie *f*, politesse *f*.

courtesan ['kɔːti'zæn], *s*. Courtisane *f*.

courtesy ['kɔːtesi], *s*. Courtoisie *f*, politesse *f*. **By c., as a matter of c.,** à titre gracieux. **By c. of . . .,** avec la gracieuse permission de . . ., avec l'aimable concours de . . .. **Road c.,** politesse *f* de la route (entre automobilistes, etc.). *F*: **C. cop,** motard *m*. **Exchange of courtesies,** échange de bons procédés. **C. title,** titre de courtoisie. **'courtesy-light,** *s*. *Aut*: Éclairage *m* intérieur automatique.

courtier ['kɔːtiər], *s*. Courtisan *m*.

courtliness ['kɔːtlinis], *s*. 1. Courtoisie *f*. 2. Élégance *f*; grand air.

courtly ['kɔːtli], *a*. 1. Courtois. 2. Élégant; à l'air digne et aristocratique.

courtship ['kɔːtʃip], *s*. Cour (faite à une femme).

courtyard ['kɔːtjɑːd], *s*. Cour *f* (de maison).

couscous ['kuskus], *s*. *Cu*: Couscous *m*.

cousin ['kʌzn], *s*. Cousin, -ine. **First c.,** cousin(e) germain(e). **Second c.,** cousin(e) issu(e) de germains.

couture [kuː'tjuər], *s*. **Haute c.,** haute couture.

couturier [kuː'tjuriei], *s*. Couturier *m*.

cove[1] [kouv], *s*. *Ph.Geog*: Anse *f*; petite baie.

cove[2], *s*. *P*: *O*: Type *m*, individu *m*.

covenant[1] ['kʌvenənt], *s*. 1. *Jur*: Convention *f*, contrat *m*. **Deed of c.,** contrat. 2. *Pol*: Pacte *m*, traité *m*. 3. *B*: Alliance *f* (entre Dieu et les Israélites).

covenant[2]. 1. *v.tr*. (*a*) Promettre, accorder (qch.) par contrat. (*b*) Stipuler (une somme). (*c*) **To c. to do sth.,** convenir de, s'engager à, faire qch. 2. *v.i*. **To c. with s.o. for sth.,** convenir (par contrat) de qch. avec qn. **covenanted,** *a*. Stipulé par contrat; contractuel.

covenanter ['kʌvenəntər], *s*. 1. Partie contractante. 2. *Eng.Rel.H*: [kʌve'nantər] Covenantaire *m*.

Coventry ['kʌventri, 'kɔ-]. *Pr.n*. *Geog*: Coventry. *F*: **To send s.o. to C.,** mettre qn en quarantaine; frapper qn d'ostracisme.

cover[1] ['kʌvər], *s*. 1. Couverture *f*; tapis *m* (de table); dessus *m* (de buffet); fourreau *m* (de parapluie); bâche *f* (d'automobile). **Loose c.** (*of chair*), housse *f*. **Outer c. of tyre,** enveloppe *f* de pneu. **C.** Couvercle *m* (de marmite, etc.); cloche *f* (pour plat); plaque *f* (d'égout). **Chain c.,** carter *m* de chaîne. 3. **Couverture** (d'un livre); *Bookb*: les plats *m*. **To read a book from c. to c.,** lire un livre d'un bout à l'autre. 4. *Post*: Enveloppe *f*. **Under separate c.,** sous pli séparé. 5. (*a*) Abri *m*. **To give s.o. c.,** abriter qn. **To seek, take, c.,** se mettre à l'abri; s'abriter. **To be under c.,** être à couvert, à l'abri. (*b*) *Ven*: *etc*: (i) Abri, couvert *m*, fourré *m*; (ii) gîte *m*, retraite *f*. **To break c.,** sortir de son terrier, d'un fourré; débucher. *Mil*: **To take c. from the enemy's fire,** se défiler du feu de l'ennemi. (*c*) **To place troops under c.,** embusquer des troupes. **To take c.,** s'embusquer. 6. Voile *m*, masque *m*. **Under the c. of darkness, of night,** sous le couvert de la nuit. **Under (the) c. of friendship,** sous le masque de l'amitié. 7. *Com*: *Ins*: Couverture, provision *f*, marge *f*. **To operate without c.,** opérer à découvert. *Fin*: **Call for additional c.,** appel *m* de marge. *Ins*: **Full c.,** garantie totale. **'cover-charge,** *s*. (*At restaurant*) Couvert *m*. **'cover-girl,** *s.f*, Cover-girl. **'cover-glass, -slip,** *s*. (Lamelle *f*) couvre-objet *m* (d'une préparation microscopique). **'cover-plate,** *s*. Plaque *f* de couverture; plaque-couvercle *f*, *pl*. plaques-couvercles.

cover[2], *v.tr*. 1. (*a*) Couvrir (qn, qch.) (**with,** de). **To c. one's head,** se couvrir (la tête); se coiffer. **To be well covered,** (i) être bien couvert, chaudement vêtu; (ii) *F*: être bien en chair. **To c. oneself up,** se vêtir chaudement. (*b*) **To c. s.o. with ridicule,** couvrir qn de ridicule. 2. **The cavalry covered the retreat,** la

cavalerie couvrait la retraite. 3. Couvrir, recouvrir, gainer, envelopper, revêtir. **To c. a book,** couvrir un livre (de papier gris). *El.E*: *etc*: **To c. a wire,** guiper un fil conducteur. 4. **To c. a distance,** couvrir, franchir, parcourir, une distance. 5. Couvrir, dissimuler (son inquiétude, etc.). 6. **To c. s.o. with a revolver,** braquer un revolver sur qn. 7. Comprendre, englober. **This explanation does not c. all the facts,** cette explication n'embrasse pas tous les faits. **In order to c. all eventualities . . .,** pour parer à toute éventualité. . . . 8. (*a*) Couvrir (un risque). **To c. a bill,** faire la provision d'une lettre de change. (*b*) **To c. (one's) expenses,** faire ses frais; couvrir ses dépenses. **To c. a deficit,** combler un déficit. *Journ*: *F*: Couvrir (une réunion, un incident politique). 9. *Breed*: Couvrir, saillir (la femelle); monter (une jument). **cover in, cover over,** *v.tr*. Recouvrir (une canalisation sous terre, etc.); remplir (la tranchée). **cover up,** *v.tr*. Couvrir entièrement; recouvrir; dissimuler (la vérité). **covering**[1], *a*. **C. letter,** lettre confirmative (d'une autre); lettre d'introduction. *Com*: **C. note,** garantie *f*. **covering**[2], *s*. 1. Recouvrement *m* (de qch.). 2. Couverture *f*, enveloppe *f*, revêtement *m*, recouvrement, gainage *m*. *El.E*: Guipage *m* (d'un câble, etc.).

coverage ['kʌv(ə)ridʒ], *s*. Champ *m* d'application. *Journ*: News *c.*, l'ensemble des informations *fpl*.

coverlet ['kʌvəlit], *s*. Couvre-lit *m*; dessus *m* de lit; couvre-pied(s) *m inv*.

covert[1] ['kʌvət], *a*. (*Of threat, etc*.) Caché, voilé; (*of attack*) indirect; (*of enemy*) couvert, secret. **-ly,** *adv*. Secrètement; en secret.

covert[2], *s*. *Ven*: = COVER[1] 5 (*b*) 2. *Orn*: Tail-coverts, wing-coverts, (plumes) tectrices (*f*) de la queue, des ailes.

covet ['kʌvit], *v.tr*. (*a*) Convoiter. (*b*) Ambitionner (qch.); aspirer à (qch.).

coveter ['kʌvitər], *s*. Convoiteur, -euse.

covetous ['kʌvitəs], *a*. 1. Avide (**of gain,** de gain). 2. **To be c. of sth.,** convoiter qch. **To cast c. eyes on sth.,** convoiter qch. des yeux; regarder qch. d'un œil de convoitise. **-ly,** *adv*. Avec convoitise; avidement.

covetousness ['kʌvitəsnis], *s*. 1. Cupidité *f*, avidité *f*. 2. Convoitise *f*.

covey ['kʌvi], *s*. Compagnie *f*, vol *m* (de perdrix).

cow[1] [kau], *s*. (*pl*. **cows,** *A*: **kine** [kain]). 1. Vache *f*. **Milch, milking, c.,** vache laitière. **C. in calf,** vache pleine. *F*: **Wait till the cows come home,** attendez jusqu'à la semaine des quatre jeudis. 2. (*Of elephant, seal, etc*.) Femelle *f*. 3. *a*. *Austr*: *P*: **It's, he's, a fair c.,** que c'est, qu'il est, moche. **'cow-bell,** *s*. Clochette *f*, sonnette *f*, sonnaille *f*, clarine *f*. **'cow-catcher,** *s*. *U.S*: Chasse-bestiaux *m inv*, chasse-corps *m inv*. (de locomotive); *F*: ramasse-piétons *m inv*. (de camion). **'cow(-)girl,** *s.f*. Vachère. **'cow-hand,** *s.m*. Vacher, bouvier. **'cow-heel,** *s*. *Cu*: Pied *m* de vache en gelée. **'cow-hide,** *s*. *Leath*: (Peau *f* de) vache *f*. **'cow-parsley,** *s*. Cerfeuil *m* sauvage. **'cow-pat(ch),** *s*. Bouse *f* (de vache). **'cow-pox,** *s*. *Med*: *Vet*: Cow-pox *m*; vaccine *f*. **'cow-puncher,** *s*. *U.S*: *F*: = COWBOY.

cow[2], *v.tr*. 1. Intimider, dompter (qn). **Cowed look,** air de chien battu. 2. Accouardir (un chien).

coward ['kauəd], *s*. & *a*. 1. Lâche (*mf*). 2. **I'm a terrible c. in the dark,** je suis très poltron quand il fait nuit.

cowardice ['kauədis], **cowardliness** ['kauədlinis], *s*. Lâcheté *f*, poltronnerie *f*.

cowardly ['kauədli]. 1. *a*. Lâche, poltron. 2. *adv*. Lâchement; en lâche, en poltron.

cowboy ['kauboi], *s.m*. Cowboy.

cower ['kauər], *v.i*. Se blottir, se tapir (à terre). **To c. before s.o.,** trembler, se faire tout petit, devant qn.

cowherd ['kauhɜːd], *s.m*. Vacher; bouvier.

cowl [kaul], *s*. 1. (*a*) Capuchon *m* (de moine). Penitent's c., cagoule *f*. (*b*) Têtière *f* (d'un capuchon). 2. (*a*) Capuchon, mitre *f*, abat-vent *m inv* (de cheminée). (*b*) *Av*: *Nau*: Capot *m* (de moteur, de cheminée).

cowled [kauld], *a*. Capuchonné; encapuchonné.

cowlick ['kaulik], *s*. Épi *m* (de cheveux).

cowling ['kauliŋ], s. 1. Capuchonnement m (de cheminée). 2. Capot m, capotage m (de moteur).
cowman, pl. -men ['kaumən], s.m. Vacher.
cowrie ['kauəri], s. 1. Conch: Moll: Porcelaine f. 2. (Money) Cauris m.
cowshed ['kauʃed], s. Étable f.
cowslip ['kauslip], s. Bot: Primevère f, (fleur f de) coucou m.
cox¹ [kɔks], s. F: = COXSWAIN.
cox², v.tr. Diriger, gouverner, barrer (un canot).
coxal ['kɔksəl], a. Anat: Coxal, -aux.
coxalgia [kɔks'ældʒiə], s. Med: Coxalgie f.
coxcomb ['kɔkskoum], s. Petit-maître m, pl. petits-maîtres; fat m.
coxswain ['kɔksn], s. 1. Nau: Patron m (d'une chaloupe). 2. Row: Barreur m.
coy [kɔi], a. (Of girl) Timide, modeste, farouche; qui fait la Sainte-Nitouche. -ly, adv. Modestement, timidement.
coyness ['kɔinis], s. Timidité f, réserve f.
coyote ['kɔiout, kɔi'out(i)], s. Z: Coyote m.
coypu [kɔipu:], s. Z: Coypou m, myopotame m.
cozen ['kʌzn], v.tr. A: Tromper, duper (qn). To c. s.o. out of sth., filouter qch. à qn.
crab¹ [kræb], s. 1. Crust: Crabe m, cancre m. Shore c., green c., crabe commun. F: (Rowing) To catch a c., (i) engager un aviron; (ii) attaquer en sifflet, faire fausse rame. 2. Astr: Le Cancer. 3. Ind: etc: Treuil (roulant, portatif); chèvre f. Ceiling c.. chariot (transporteur) à poutre de plafond. 'crab-pot, s. Nasse f, casier m (à crabes).
crab², s. C.(-apple), pomme f sauvage. C.-tree, pommier m sauvage.
crab³, v.tr. (crabbed). 1. Fish: Pêcher des crabes. 2. F: (a) Décrier, dénigrer (qn, qch.); débiner (qn). (b) Mettre des bâtons dans les roues à (qn). 3. v.i. Nau: Av: Dériver; marcher en diagonale, en crabe.
crabbed ['kræb(i)d], a. 1. (Of pers.) Maussade, grognon, grincheux, -euse, revêche. 2. C. style, style pénible, rébarbatif. C. writing, écriture illisible, en pattes de mouche.
crabwise ['kræbwaiz], adv. Comme un crabe; (marcher) de biais.
crack¹ [kræk]. I. s. 1. (n) Craquement m (de branches, etc.); claquement m, clic-clac m (de fouet); détonation f, coup sec (de fusil). (b) C. on the head, coup violent sur la tête. 2. (a) Fente f, fissure f; (in skin) gerçure f, crevasse f; (in wall, ground) crevasse, lézarde f; (in pottery, bell, etc.) fêlure f. (b) Entre-bâillement m (d'une porte). 3. (a) Scot: Causerie f, causette f. (b) A c. at the socialists, une plaisanterie aux dépens des socialistes. II. crack, a. F: Fameux; d'élite; de première force. C. player, etc., as m, crack m. 'crack-'brained, a. Au cerveau timbré, fêlé.
crack², int. Clac! crac! pan!
crack³. I. v.tr. 1. Faire claquer (un fouet); faire craquer (ses doigts, etc.). 2. (a) Fêler (une cloche, un verre); gercer, crevasser (la peau); lézarder, crevasser (un mur); fendre, fendiller (une pierre, etc.); fracturer (un os). (b) Casser (une noisette). To c. one's skull, se casser la tête. F: To c. a bottle (with s.o.), vider, boire, une bouteille (avec qn). P: To c. a crib, cambrioler une maison. S.a. NUT 1. (c) Ind: Fractionner (une huile lourde); opérer le cracking, le craquage, (du pétrole etc.). 3. To c. a joke, faire, lâcher, lancer, une plaisanterie. II. crack, v.i. 1. Craquer; (of whip) claquer. A rifle cracked, un coup de fusil partit. 2. Se fêler; se fissurer; se crevasser; (of wall) se lézarder; (of skin) se gercer; se fendre, se fendiller. 3. (Of voice) Se casser, se fausser; (at puberty) muer. 4. Scot: Causer, faire la causette (avec qn). 5. F: To get cracking, s'y mettre. Get cracking! Grouille-toi! crack along, v.i. Sp: Aut: F: etc. Faire de la vitesse. crack down, v.i. F: To c. d. on s.o., F: laver la tête à qn; P: engueuler qn. crack up. 1. v.tr. F: Vanter, prôner (qn, qch.). 2. v.i. F: Craquer (of empire) se démembrer; (of firm) faire faillite; (of pers.) flancher, s'effondrer. cracked, a. 1. Fêlé, fendu; (of wall) lézardé; (of tree, timber) gerçuré. C. voice, voix cassée. To sound c., sonner le fêlé. 2. F: Timbré, toqué; loufoque. cracking,

s. 1. Claquement m, craquement m. 2. Fendillement m; craquelure f (de la peinture). 3. Cracking m, craquage m (du pétrole). C. plant (installation de) cracking m. 'crack-jaw, a. (Nom, etc.) impossible à prononcer.
cracker ['krækər], s. 1. (Pers.) C. of jokes, faiseur, -euse, de plaisanteries. 2. F: Mensonge m, craque f. 3. (a) Pétard m. Jumping c., crapaud m. (b) (Christmas-)c., diablotin m; papillote f à pétard. 4. (Nut-)crackers, casse-noisette(s) m inv, casse-noix m inv. 5. U.S: Biscuit (sec); craquelin m.
crackerjack ['krækədʒæk]. U.S: F: 1. s. Grosse légume. 2. a. Chouette, chic.
crackers ['krækəz], a. F: He's c., il est cinglé.
crackle¹ ['krækl], s. 1. Craquement m, crépitement m. W.Tel: Crachements mpl, friture f. 2. Fendillement m. 'crackle-ware, s. Cer: Porcelaine f, faïence f, craquelée; craquelé m.
crackle². 1. v.i. (a) Craqueter; (of salt on fire, etc.) crépiter; (of sth. frying) grésiller; (of fire) pétiller. (b) Se fendiller. 2. v.tr. Fendiller. crackling, s. 1. = CRACKLE¹. 2. Peau croquante (du porc rôti); couenne f.
cracknel ['kræknəl], s. (Biscuit) Craquelin m, croquignole f.
crackpot ['krækpɔt], F: 1. a. C. ideas, des idées extravagantes, fantaisistes, un peu folles. 2. s. He's a c., il est dingo, cinglé, toqué.
cracksman, pl. -men ['kræksmən], s.m. F: Cambrioleur.
Cracow ['krækau]. Pr.n. Geog: Cracovie f.
cradle¹ ['kreidl], s. 1. (a) Berceau m (d'un enfant). Wicker c., moïse m. (b) Lit: Berceau (d'une science, etc.) Greece, the cradle of European philosophy, la Grèce, berceau de la philosophie européenne. 2. (a) Ind: Berceau (d'une machine); cadre m. (b) N.Arch: Ber m (de lancement). (c) Tp: Fourche interruptrice. 3. Const: Échafaud(age) volant; pont volant. 4. (a) Med: (Over bed) Arceau m. (b) Surg: Gouttière f. cradle-song, s. Berceuse f.
cradle², v.tr. Mettre, coucher (un enfant) dans un berceau. Cradled in luxury, bercé dans le luxe.
craft [krɑːft], s. 1. (a) A: Habileté f, adresse f. (b) Ruse f, artifice m; fourberie f. 2. (i) Métier manuel; (ii) profession f. 3. Corps m de métier. 4. Nau: (pl. craft) Bateau m, embarcation f. craft union, s. U.S: Syndicat artisanal.
craftiness ['krɑːftinis], s. Ruse f, astuce f.
craftsman, pl. -men ['krɑːftsmən], s.m. 1. Artisan, ouvrier qualifié; homme de métier. Coll: pl. Craftsmen, artisanat m. 2. Artiste dans son métier.
craftsmanship ['krɑːftsmənʃip], s. 1. Dextérité manuelle. 2. (In writer, etc.) Connaissance f du métier.
crafty ['krɑːfti], a. Artificieux, -euse, astucieux, -euse, rusé, cauteleux, -euse. -ily, adv. Artificieusement, astucieusement, cauteleusement.
crag [kræg], s. Flanc de montagne escarpé; rocher à pic.
cragginess ['kræginis], s. Aspect anfractueux, rocailleux (d'une montagne).
craggy ['krægi], a. Rocailleux, -euse, anfractueux, -euse.
cram [kræm], v. (crammed) 1. v.tr. (a) Fourrer (sth. into sth., qch. dans qch.). (b) To c. one's hat down over one ear, enfoncer son chapeau sur l'oreille. Room crammed to suffocation, salle bondée où l'on s'étouffe. Cupboards crammed with linen, armoires bourrées de linge. (b) To c. s.o. with sth., bourrer qn de qch. (c) Husb: Empâter, gaver, embecquer, gorger (une volaille). (d) Sch: Chauffer (un candidat pour un examen). To c. a pupil with Greek, bourrer, gaver, un élève de grec. 2. v.i. F: (a) S'entasser (into, dans). (b) Se gorger de nourriture; s'empiffrer, se gaver (with, de). (c) To c. for an examination, F: bachoter, potasser un examen. cramming, s. 1. Entassement m. 2. Gavage m. 3. Sch: Chauffage m, F: bachotage m (pour un examen).
crambo ['kræmbou], s. Bouts-rimés; corbillon m. Dumb c., charade mimée.
crammer ['kræmər], s. Sch: F: (a) Répétiteur m, F: bachoteur m. (b) (also crammer's). Boîte f à bachot.
cram-full ['kræm'fu:l], a. F: Tout plein; bondé. Book c.-f. of quotations, livre bourré de citations, qui regorge de citations.

cramp¹ [kræmp], *s. Med:* Crampe *f.*
cramp², *s.* (*a*) *Const: etc:* Happe *f,* agrafe *f,* crampon *m.* (*b*) *Tls:* Serre-joint *m.* (*c*) *Typ:* Cornière *f.* 'cramp-iron, *s.* = CRAMP² (*a*).
cramp³, *v.tr.* 1. Donner des crampes à (qn). Limbs cramped by the cold, membres engourdis par le froid. 2. Gêner (les mouvements, etc.). *F:* To c. s.o.'s style, priver qn de ses moyens. 3. (*a*) *Const:* Cramponner, agrafer (des pierres, etc.). (*b*) Presser, serrer (à l'étau, au serre-joint). **cramped,** *a.* A l'étroit; gêné. To be, feel, c. for room, être, se sentir, à l'étroit. C. handwriting, écriture gênée. C. style, style contraint.
crampon ['kræmpən], *s. Mount:* Crampon *m* à glace.
cranberry ['krænbəri], *s. Bot:* Canneberge *f; Fr.C:* atoca *m.*
crane¹ [krein], *s.* 1. *Orn:* Grue *f.* 2. *Mec.E:* Grue. Overhead travelling c., pont-grue *m;* pont roulant; (chariot *m*) transporteur *m.* Floating c., ponton-grue *m.* 'crane-fly, *s. Ent:* Tipule *f.* 'crane's-bill, *s. Bot:* Bec-de-grue *m;* géranium *m.* 'crane-tower, *s.* Sapine *f.*
crane². 1. *v.tr.* To c. one's neck, tendre, allonger, le cou. 2. *v.i.* To c. forward, allonger le cou, la tête, en avant.
cranial ['kreiniəl], *a.* Crânien, -ienne.
cranium, *pl.* -ia ['kreiniəm, -iə], *s.* Crâne *m.*
crank¹ [kræŋk], *s.* 1. *Mec.E:* Manivelle *f.* 'crank-arm, *s.* Bras *m,* corps *m,* de manivelle. 'crank-axle, *s.* 1. Essieu coudé. 2. *Cy:* Axe pédalier. 'crank-case, *s. I.C.E:* Carter *m* (du moteur). 'crank-pin, *s.* Tourillon *m,* maneton *m,* de manivelle. 'crank-shaft, *s.* Vilebrequin *m;* arbre-manivelle *m,* arbre coudé.
crank², *v.tr.* 1. Couder (un essieu). 2. To c. up a car, faire démarrer une voiture à la manivelle.
crank³, *s. F:* 1. Marotte *f,* manie *f.* 2. (*Pers.*) Maniaque *mf,* excentrique *mf,* original, -e.
crank⁴, *a.* (*Of machinery*) Détraqué; délabré.
crank⁵, *a.* (*Navire*) instable, mal équilibré.
crankiness ['kræŋkinis], *s.* 1. Humeur *f* difficile. 2. (*a*) État délabré. (*b*) Chavirabilité *f,* instabilité *f* (d'un navire).
cranky ['kræŋki], *a.* 1. D'humeur difficile; capricieux. 2. (*a*) = CRANK⁴. (*b*) = CRANK⁵.
cranny ['kræni], *s.* (*a*) Fente *f,* crevasse *f.* (*b*) Enfoncement *m,* niche *f.*
crap¹ ['kræp], *s. V:* 1. Merde *f.* 2. Foutaise *f.*
crap², *v.i. V:* 1. Chier. 2. Don't c. about like that, fais pas le con!
crape¹ [kreip], *s. Tex:* Crêpe noir.
crape², *v.tr.* Draper de crêpe (en signe de deuil).
crapehanger ['kreiphæŋər], *s. U.S: P:* Rabat-joie *m inv.*
craps [kræps], *s. pl. U.S:* To shoot c., jouer aux dés.
crapulous ['kræpjuləs], *a.* Crapuleux, -euse.
crash¹ [kræʃ], *s.* 1. Fracas *m.* A c. of thunder, un coup de tonnerre. 2. Catastrophe *f,* débâcle *f. Fin:* Krach *m.* 3. Écrasement *m;* chute *f. Av:* Atterrissage brutal. Air, plane, c., accident *m* d'avion. *Aut:* Collision *f,* accident *m.* 4. *int.* Patatras! He went, drove, c. into the wall, il alla s'emboutir contre, percuter, le mur. 'crash-dive, *s.* Plongée *f* raide (d'un sous-marin). 'crash-helmet, *s.* Serre-tête *m inv;* casque protecteur. 'crash-'land, *v.i. Av:* Atterrir brutalement, *F:* casser du bois, faire un crash. 'crash-'landing, *s. Av:* Atterrissage brutal, crash *m.* 'crash-proof, *a.* Résistant au choc, antichoc.
crash². 1. *v.i.* (*a*) Retentir; éclater avec fracas. (*b*) To c. (down), tomber avec fracas; s'abattre. The roof crashed in, le toit s'effondra. To c. into a shop-window, enfoncer une vitrine. *Aut:* To c. into a tree, s'emboutir sur, tamponner, un arbre. (*c*) *Av:* (i) (*Of plane*) S'écraser sur le sol. (ii) (*Of pilot*) Atterrir brutalement; *F:* casser du bois. 2. *v.tr.* Briser, fracasser. *Av:* Écraser (son avion) sur le sol.
crash³, *s. Tex:* Toile *f* à serviettes (de toilette).
crass [kræs], *a.* C. stupidity, stupidité grossière. C. ignorance, ignorance crasse.
crate¹ [kreit], *s.* 1. Caisse *f* à claire-voie; cageot *m,* cageotte *f;* (*for glass, bicycle, etc.*) harasse *f.* 2. (i) *Av: P:* (*Plane*) Coucou *m,* zinc *m.* (ii) *Aut: P:* (*Car*) Bagnole *f.*

crate², *v.tr.* Emballer (des marchandises) dans une caisse à claire-voie, etc.
crater ['kreitər], *s.* 1. Cratère *m* (de volcan). 2. (*Shell-hole*) Entonnoir *m.* 3. Cratère (de l'arc électrique). 4. *Gr.Ant:* Cratère.
cravat [krə'væt], *s.* 1. *A:* Cravate *f.* 2. Foulard *m.*
crave [kreiv], *v.tr & i.* 1. *O:* To c. sth. from s.o., of s.o., implorer avec instance qch. de qn. To c. s.o.'s pardon, demander pardon à qn. To c. the attention of the audience, solliciter l'attention du public. 2. To c. for, after, sth., désirer ardemment qch.
craving, *s.* Désir ardent, obsédant; appétit *m* insatiable (for, de). To have a c. for praise, être assoiffé de louanges; avoir soif de louanges.
craven ['kreivn], *a. & s. A:* Poltron (*m*), lâche (*m*).
cravenness ['kreivnnis], *s. A:* Lâcheté *f,* couardise .
crawfish ['krɔːfiʃ], *s.* = CRAYFISH.
crawl¹ [krɔːl], *s.* (*a*) *Pisc:* Vivier *m;* bordigue *f.* (*b*) Parc *m* à tortues, à homards.
crawl², *s.* 1. Rampement *m* (d'un serpent). 2. Mouvement traînant (d'une personne). *S.a.* PUB-CRAWL¹. 3. *Swim:* Crawl *m.*
crawl³, *v.i.* 1. Ramper. To c. in, out, entrer, sortir, en rampant. *F:* To c. before s.o., ramper, s'aplatir, devant qn. 2. (*a*) (*Of pers.*) To c. (along), se traîner. To c. on one's hands and knees, aller à quatre pattes. (*b*) Avancer lentement. (*Of taxi*) Marauder. *F: Aut:* Faire du surplace. 3. To be crawling with vermin, grouiller de vermine. 4. *Swim:* Crawler, faire du crawl. **crawling,** *a.* 1. Rampant. 2. C. taxi, taxi en maraude. 3. Grouillant (with, de).
crawler ['krɔːlər], *s.* 1. (*a*) Qn, qch., qui rampe; traînard *m.* (*b*) *Swim:* Crawleur *m.* (*c*) *F:* Lécheur *m* de bottes. 2. *pl. Cost:* Crawlers, tablier-combinaison *m;* barboteuse *f* (pour enfants).
crayfish ['kreifiʃ], *s.* 1. *Crust:* 1. (Fresh-water) c., écrevisse *f.* 2. *F:* (= spiny lobster) Langouste *f.*
crayon ['kreiən], *s.* Craie *f* à dessiner; crayon *m* de pastel.
craze¹ [kreiz], *s.* Manie *f, F:* toquade *f* (for sth., de qch.). Camping is the latest c., le camping c'est la dernière rage, le camping fait fureur.
craze², *v.tr.* (*a*) Rendre (qn) fou; déranger (l'esprit). (*b*) *Cer:* Fendiller, craqueler (la porcelaine).
craziness ['kreizinis], *s.* (*Of pers.*) Folie *f,* démence *f.*
crazy ['kreizi], *a.* 1. (*Of pers.*) Fou, *f.* folle (à lier); *F:* toqué. C. with fear, affolé (de terreur). To drive, send, s.o. c., rendre qn fou; affoler qn. *F:* faire tourner qn en bourrique. To be c. over, about, s.o., être fou de qn. To be c. to do sth., brûler de faire qch. It's like sth. out of a c. show, on dirait une histoire de fous. 2. (*Of building*) Délabré; qui menace ruine. C. furniture, meubles branlants. 3. Composé de morceaux rapportés; irrégulier. C. paving, dallage irrégulier. -ily, *adv.* Follement.
creak¹ [kriːk], *s.* Cri *m,* grincement *m* (de gonds, etc.); craquement *m.*
creak², *v.i.* (*Of hinge, etc.*) Crier, grincer; (*of timber, shoes*) craquer.
cream¹ [kriːm], *s.* 1. (*a*) Crème *f* (du lait). Clotted c., Devonshire cream, crème caillée (par échaudage). C. bun, chou *m* à la crème. To take the c. off the milk, écrémer le lait. C. cheese, fromage *m* à la crème; petit suisse; fromage blanc. (*b*) (Le) meilleur; *F:* (le) dessus du panier. The c. of society, la crème de la société. The c. of the joke, le plus beau, le plus drôle, le piquant, de l'histoire. 2. (*a*) Chocolate c., chocolat fourré à la crème. C. of tomato soup, crème de tomates. C. of tartar, crème de tartre. (*c*) Crème (à chaussures, de beauté, etc.). *Toil:* Cleansing c., crème de démaquillage, démaquillant *m.* Cold c., cold-cream *m.* 3. *attrib.* C.(-coloured), crème *inv;* (cheval) isabelle *inv.* 'cream-jug, *s.* Pot *m* à crème. 'cream-'laid, *a.* (Papier) vergé blanc. 'cream-'wove, *a.* (Papier *m*) vélin blanc.
cream². 1. *v.tr.* (*a*) Écrémer. (*b*) *Cu:* Battre (du beurre et du sucre) en crème. 2. *v.i.* (*Of milk*) Se couvrir de crème; crémer.
creamer ['kriːmər], *s.* 1. (*Pan*) Crémeuse *f.* 2. Écrémeuse *f* centrifuge.
creamery ['kriːməri], *s.* 1. Crémerie *f.* 2. Laiterie (industrielle); coopérative laitière. C. butter, beurre laitier.

creamy ['kri:mi], *a.* Crémeux, -euse. C. complexion, teint velouté.

crease[1] [kri:s], *s.* (Faux) pli *m*; (*in paper*) fronce *f.* 'crease-resisting, *a. Tex:* C.-r. material, tissu *m* infroissable.

crease[2]. 1. *v.tr.* (a) Plisser, faire des (faux) plis à qch.). Well-creased trousers, pantalon avec un pli impeccable. (b) Chiffonner, froisser (une robe, etc.). 2. *v.i.* Se plisser; prendre un faux pli. creasing, *s.* 1. Plissement *m*; froncement *m.* 2. Pli *m.*

create [kri'eit], *v.tr.* 1. Créer. To c. s.o. a knight, créer qn chevalier. 2. (a) Créer, faire naître, susciter (une difficulté); faire, produire (une impression). To c. a scandal, (i) causer un scandale; (ii) faire de l'esclandre. (b) *Abs. P:* To c., rouspéter; faire une scène (about, à propos de). (c) *Com:* To c. a fashion, créer, lancer, une mode.

creation [kri'eiʃ(ə)n], *s.* Création *f.* The latest creations, les dernières modes, créations.

creative [kri'eitiv], *a.* Créateur, -trice; créatif, -ive.

creativeness [kri'eitivnəs], *s.* Esprit *m* de création.

creator [kri'eitər], *s.* Créateur, -trice.

creature ['kri:tʃər], *s.* 1. Créature *f*, être *m*; *esp.* être vivant. 2. Animal *m*, bête *f.* Dumb creatures, les bêtes, les animaux. 3. Poor c.! le pauvre homme! la pauvre femme! le, la, pauvre enfant! Not a c. was to be seen, on ne voyait âme qui vive. 4. La créature, l'âme damnée (d'un homme puissant). 5. Man is the c. of circumstances, l'homme dépend des circonstances. 6. *attrib.* C. comforts, l'aisance matérielle.

crèche [kreiʃ], *s.* (a) Crèche *f*; pouponnière *f.* (b) *U.S:* Orphelinat *m.* (c) *U.S: Ecc:* Crèche *f.*

credence ['kri:d(ə)ns], *s.* 1. Créance *f*, croyance *f*, foi *f.* To give, attach, c. to sth., ajouter foi à qch. 2. *Ecc:* C.(-table), crédence *f.*

credentials [kri'denʃ(ə)lz], *s.pl.* 1. Lettres *fpl* de créance. To show one's c., (i) montrer ses pouvoirs; (ii) faire preuve de ses titres. 2. Pièces justificatives, d'identité.

credibility [,kredi'biliti], *s.* Crédibilité *f.*

credible ['kredibl], *a.* Croyable; digne de foi. -ibly, *adv.* D'une façon qui inspire la confiance. To be c. informed of sth., tenir qch. de bonne source.

credit[1] ['kredit], *s.* 1. Croyance *f*, créance *f*, foi *f.* Rumour that is gaining c., bruit qui prend de la consistance. To give c. to . . ., ajouter foi à . . . (*Of report*) To gain c., s'accréditer. 2. Crédit *m*, influence *f*, réputation *f* (with, auprès de). He has c. at court, il est bien en cour. 3. Mérite *m*, honneur *m.* To take c. for an action, s'attribuer le mérite d'une action. He came out of it with c., il en est sorti à son honneur. *Sch:* To pass an examination with c., être reçu avec mention assez bien. I gave him c. for more sense, je lui croyais, lui supposais, plus de jugement. It must be said to his c. that . . ., on doit dire à son honneur que. . . . It does him c., cela lui fait honneur. *Cin:* C. titles, générique *m.* 4. (a) *Com:* Crédit. To give s.o. c., faire crédit à qn. To sell on credit, vendre à crédit, à terme. C. slip, bulletin de versement. *Bank:* Letter of c., lettre de crédit; accréditif *m*; lettre accréditive. To enter, put, a sum to s.o.'s c., porter une somme au crédit, à l'actif, de qn. C. balance, solde créditeur. C. card, carte *f* de crédit. (b) *Book-k:* C. side, avoir *m.* 5. *Com:* Réputation de solvabilité; crédit. 6. *Parl:* = Douzième *m* provisoire.

credit[2], *v.tr.* 1. Ajouter foi à, donner, accorder, créance à (un bruit); croire (qn). 2. (a) (*Attribute*) Attribuer, prêter (s.o. with a quality, une qualité à qn). I credited you with more sense, je vous croyais plus de jugement. To be credited with having done sth., passer pour avoir fait qch. He hasn't as much money as people c. him with, il n'a pas la grosse fortune qu'on lui prête. (b) (*Recognise*) To c. s.o. with a quality, reconnaître une qualité à qn. 3. *Com:* To c. a sum to s.o., to c. s.o. with a sum, créditer qn d'une somme; porter une somme au crédit de qn.

creditable ['kreditəbl], *a.* (Action) estimable, honorable. -ably, *adv.* Honorablement; avec honneur.

creditor ['kreditər], *s.* Créancier, -ière.

credulity [kri'dju:liti], *s.* Crédulité *f.*

credulous ['kredjuləs], *a.* Crédule. -ly, *adv.* Avec crédulité.

credulousness ['kredjuləsnis], *s.* Crédulité *f.*

creed [kri:d], *s.* 1. *Theol:* Credo *m.* The (Apostles') C., le symbole des Apôtres. 2. Croyance *f*; foi (confessionnelle). 3. Profession *f* de foi; credo (politique).

creek [kri:k], *s.* 1. Crique *f*, anse *f.* 2. *U.S:* (a) Ruisseau *m*, affluent *m.* (b) Petite vallée.

creel [kri:l], *s.* (a) Panier *m* de pêche. (b) Casier *m* à homards.

creep[1] [kri:p], *s.* 1. *pl. F:* Chair *f* de poule. He, it, gives me the creeps, ça me met les nerfs en pelote. 2. Glissement *m*, cheminement *m* (d'un pneu sur la jante, etc.). 3. *U.S: P:* Personnage déplaisant; flagorneur, -euse, *V:* lèche-cul *m inv*; chapardeur, -euse. 4. *Geog:* Solifluction *f.*

creep[2], *v.i.* (crept [krept]; crept) 1. Ramper; (*of pers.*) se traîner, se glisser; *F:* ramper (devant les grands). To c. into bed, se glisser dans son lit. To c. into the room, entrer tout doucement, à pas de loup, dans la pièce. To c. into a hole, se couler dans un trou. A feeling of uneasiness creeps over me, une inquiétude commence à me gagner. *S.a.* FLESH 1. 2. (*Of rails, etc.*) Cheminer; (*of transmission belt*) glisser, ramper; (*of tyre*) glisser, cheminer, sur la jante. 3. (*Of plant, etc.*) Grimper. creep along, *v.i.* S'avancer en rampant, furtivement. To c. along the wall, se faufiler le long du mur. creep away, *v.i.* S'éloigner (i) en rampant, (ii) à pas de loup. creep on, *v.i.* Avancer lentement. Old age is creeping on, la vieillesse s'approche à pas lents. creep up, *v.i.* 1. Avancer furtivement, à pas de loup. 2. *Aut: etc:* The speedometer crept up to 100, l'aiguille avança lentement jusqu' à 100. creeping, *s.* 1. Rampement *m.* 2. Grimpement *m*, ascension *f* capillaire (de l'acide *f* un accu). 3. (*Of skin*) Chair *f* de poule.

creeper ['kri:pər], *s.* 1. *Bot:* Plante rampante, grimpante. *S.a.* VIRGINIA 1. 2. Vis *f* de transport.

creepy ['kri:pi], *a. F:* 1. Rampant. 2. To feel c., avoir la chair de poule. C. story, récit qui donne la chair de poule. 'creepy-'crawly. *F:* 1. a. C.-c. feeling, (i) fourmillement *m*; (ii) chair *f* de poule. 2. a. (*Of pers.*) Rampant, servile. 3. *s. F:* Insecte, etc., rampant.

cremate [kri'meit], *v.tr.* Incinérer (un mort).

cremation [kri'meiʃ(ə)n], *s.* Incinération *f*; crémation *f.*

crematorium [,kremə'tɔ:riəm], *s.* Crématorium *m*; (four *m*) crématoire *m.*

crenel(l)ate ['krenəleit], *v.tr.* Créneler.

crenel(l)ation [,krenə'leiʃ(ə)n], *s.* Crénelure *f*, crénelage *m.*

creole ['kri:oul], *a. & s.* Créole (*mf*).

creosote[1] ['kri:əsout], *s. Ch:* Créosote *f.*

creosote[2], *v.tr.* Créosoter; injecter (le bois) à la créosote.

crêpe [kreip], *s.* 1. *Tex:* Crêpe *m.* C. de chine, crêpe de chine. Satin c., crêpe satin. 2. C.(-rubber) soles, semelles *f* (de) crêpe. 3. *Med:* C. bandage, bande *f* Velpeau. 4. C. paper, papier *m* crêpe.

crepitate ['krepiteit], *v.i.* Crépiter.

crepitation [,krepi'teiʃ(ə)n], *s.* Crépitation *f.*

crept. See CREEP[2].

crepuscular [kre'pʌskjulər], *a.* Crépusculaire.

crescendo [kri'ʃendou]. *Mus:* 1. *adv.* Crescendo; en augmentant. 2. *s.* Crescendo *m.*

crescent ['kres(ə)nt]. 1. *s.* (a) Le premier quartier de la lune. (b) Croissant *m* (de la lune qui croît ou décroît). (c) *Her: etc:* Croissant. (d) Rue *f* ou côté *m* de rue en arc de cercle. 2. *a.* The c. moon, le croissant de la lune.

cress [kres], *s. Bot:* Cresson *m.* 'cress-bed, *s.* Cressonnière *f.*

crest[1] [krest], *s.* 1. Crête *f* (de coq); huppe *f* (d'alouette); aigrette *f* (de paon). 2. Cimier *m*, crête (de casque). 3. Crête, sommet *m*, arête *f* (de colline); crête (d'une vague). 4. *Arch:* Crête, faîte *m*, faîtage *m.* 5. *Her:* Cimier; (*on helmet*) timbre *m.* 6. (*On seal*) Armoiries *fpl*; écusson *m.*

crest[2], *v.tr.* (a) Gravir (une colline) jusqu'à la crête. (b) Franchir la crête (d'une vague). crested, *a.* 1. *Orn: etc:* A crête; huppé, houppé. 2. (a) (*Of helmet*) Orné d'un cimier. (b) Armorié.

crestfallen ['krestfɔ:l(ə)n], *a.* (*Of pers.*) Abattu, découragé; (*of look*) déconfit, penaud.
cretaceous [kri'teiʃəs], *a.* Crétacé. *s.* The C., le Crétacé.
Cretan ['kri:t(ə)n], *a. & s.* Crétois, -oise.
Crete [kri:t]. *Pr.n. Geog:* Crète *f.*
cretin ['kretin], *s.* Crétin *m.*
cretinism ['kretinizm], *s.* Crétinisme *m.*
cretinous ['kretinəs], *a.* Crétineux, -euse.
cretonne ['kretən], *s. Tex:* Cretonne *f.*
crevasse [kri'væs], *s.* Crevasse *f* (glaciaire).
crevice ['krevis], *s.* Fente *f*; crevasse *f*, lézarde *f* (de mur); fissure *f* (de rocher).
crew[1] [kru:], *s.* **1.** *Nau:* Équipage *m*; (*of rowing boat*) équipe *f.* **2.** (*a*) (*Gang*) Équipe. *Artil:* Gun c., servants *mpl* d'une pièce. (*b*) *Aut: Mil:* The c. of a lorry, l'équipage *m* d'un camion. **3.** *Pej:* Bande *f*, troupe *f.* 'crew cut, *s. Hairdr:* Coupe *f* (de cheveux) en brosse.
crew[2]. *See* CROW[3].
crewel ['kru:əl], *s.* Laine *f* à broder, à tapisserie. 'crewel-needle, *s.* Aiguille *f* à tapisserie. 'crewel-work, *s.* Tapisserie *f* (sur canevas).
crib[1] [krib], *s.* **1.** Mangeoire *f*, râtelier *m.* **2.** Lit *m* d'enfant. *Ecc:* Crèche *f.* **3.** *F:* Plagiat *m.* (*b*) *Sch:* Traduction *f* (d'auteur), corrigé *m* (de thèmes, etc.) (employés subrepticement). **4.** *O:* Hutte *f*, cabane *f. P:* To crack a c., cambrioler une maison.
crib[2], *v.tr.* (cribbed) **1.** *A:* Claquemurer, enfermer. *Lit:* To be cribbed, cabined and confined, être à l'étroit. **2.** *F:* (*a*) Voler, plagier (qn). (*b*) To c. from an author, plagier un auteur. (*c*) *Sch:* To c. an exercise from another boy, *abs.* to crib, copier un devoir sur un camarade. **cribbing,** *s. Sch:* Emploi déloyal de traductions.
crick[1] [krik], *s.* **1.** Crampe *f.* **C. in the neck,** torticolis *m.* **2.** Effort *m*, foulure *f.* **C. in the back,** tour *m* de reins.
crick[2], *v.tr.* **1.** To c. one's neck, se donner le torticolis. **2.** To c. one's back, se donner un tour de reins.
cricket[1] ['krikit], *s. Ent:* Grillon *m*; cricri *m.*
cricket[2], *s. Games:* Cricket *m.* *F:* That's not c., cela n'est pas loyal; cela ne se fait pas. 'cricket-field, -ground, *s.* Terrain *m* de cricket, de jeu.
cricketer ['krikitər], *s.* Joueur *m* de cricket.
crier ['kraiər], *s.* (*a*) Crieur *m* (à une vente, etc.). (*b*) Public c., town-c., crieur public. (*c*) Court c., audiencier *m* (du tribunal).
crikey ['kraiki], *int. P:* Mince alors! Fichtre!
crime [kraim], *s.* (*a*) Crime *m.* (*b*) Délit *m.* (*c*) *Mil:* Manquement *m* à la discipline; infraction *f*, faute *f.* C. sheet, feuille *f* de punitions.
Crimea [krai'miə]. *Pr.n. Geog:* La Crimée.
Crimean [krai'miən], *a.* The C. War, la guerre de Crimée.
criminal ['krimin(ə)l]. **1.** *a.* Criminel, -elle. To take c. proceedings against s.o., poursuivre qn criminellement, au criminel. The Criminal Investigation Department, *F:* the C.I.D. = la Police Judiciaire, *F:* la P.J. C. lawyer, avocat d'assises. **2.** *s.* (*a*) Criminel *m.* Habitual c., repris *m* de justice; récidiviste *mf.* (*b*) *F:* Le coupable. -ally, *adv.* Criminellement.
criminality [krimi'næliti], *s.* Criminalité *f.*
criminate ['krimineit], *v.tr.* **1.** Incriminer, accuser (qn). **2.** Convaincre (qn) d'un crime.
criminologist [krimi'nɔlədʒist], *s.* Criminaliste *m*; criminologiste *m.*
criminology [krimi'nɔlədʒi], *s.* Criminologie *f.*
crimp[1] [krimp], *s. A:* Racoleur *m* (de marins, etc.).
crimp[2], *v.tr. A:* Racoler (des marins, etc.). **crimping**[1], *s.* Racolage *m.*
crimp[3], *s.* Gaufrage *m*; pli *m* (d'un drap); frisure *f*, crêpage *m* (des cheveux).
crimp[4], *v.tr.* (*a*) Gaufrer (à la paille), plisser, crêper, friser (l'étoffe, etc.). (*b*) Friser, frisotter, crêper (les cheveux). **crimping**[2], *s.* Plissement *m*, gaufrage *m*, crêpage *m.*
crimson ['krimz(ə)n], *a. & s.* Cramoisi (*m*); pourpre (*m*). C. with rage, rouge de colère.
cringe[1] [krindʒ], *s.* **1.** Mouvement craintif. **2.** Courbette *f* servile.
cringe[2], *v.i.* **1.** Se faire tout petit; se dérober (par crainte d'un coup). **2.** S'humilier, ramper, se mettre

à plat ventre (to, before, s.o., devant qn). **cringing,** *a.* **1.** (Geste) craintif. **2.** Servile, obséquieux, -euse. -ly, *adv.* **1.** Craintivement. **2.** Servilement, obséquieusement.
crinkle[1] ['kriŋkl], *s.* Pli *m*, ride *f*; fronce *f* (dans le papier).
crinkle[2]. **1.** *v.tr.* Froisser, chiffonner (le papier). Crinkled paper, papier ondulé, gaufré; papier crêpe. **2.** *v.i.* Se froisser, se chiffonner.
crinkly ['kriŋkli], *a.* Froissé, chiffonné, gaufré, froncé.
crinoline ['krinəlin], *s. A. Cost:* Crinoline *f.*
cripple[1] ['kripl], *s.* Estropié, -ée; boiteux, -euse; infirme *m.*
cripple[2], *v.tr.* (*a*) Estropier (qn). **Crippled with rheumatism,** perclus de rhumatismes. (*b*) Disloquer (une machine); paralyser (l'industrie, la volonté); désemparer (un navire).
crisis, *pl.* **crises** ['kraisis, -i:z], *s.* Crise *f.*
crisp [krisp]. **1.** *a.* (*a*) (Cheveux) crêpés, crépus, frisés. (*b*) (Biscuit) croquant, croustillant, cassant. (*c*) (Style) nerveux; (ton) tranchant. (*d*) The c. air of an autumn morning, l'air vif d'une matinée d'automne. **2.** *s.* Potato crisps, pommes *f* chip, chips *mpl.* -ly, *adv.* (Parler) d'un ton tranchant.
crispness ['krispnis], *s.* **1.** Qualité croustillante (d'un gâteau, etc.). **2.** Netteté *f* (de style, *Mus:* d'exécution). **3.** Froid vif (de l'air).
criss-cross[1] ['kriskrɔs]. **1.** *a.* (*a*) Entrecroisé, treillissé. (*b*) (Humeur, personne) revêche. **2.** *adv.* De travers. **3.** *s.* Entrecroisement *m.* C.-c. of wires, enchevêtrement *m* de fils de fer. C.-c. of footpaths, réseau *m* de sentiers.
criss-cross[2]. **1.** *v.tr.* Entrecroiser. **2.** *v.i.* S'entrecroiser.
criterion, *pl.* **-ia** [krai'tiəriən, -iə], *s.* Critérium *m*, critère *m.*
critic ['kritik], *s.* (*a*) Critique *m* (littéraire, etc.). Dramatic c., critique dramatique. Armchair c., critique en chambre. (*b*) Censeur *m* (de la conduite d'autrui, etc.); critiqueur *m.*
critical ['kritik(ə)l], *a.* Critique. **1.** To look on sth. with a c. eye, regarder qch. d'un œil sévère. **2.** C. situation, situation critique, dangereuse. *Med:* In a c. state, dans un état critique. **3.** *Ph:* C. temperature, température critique; point de transformation. *Opt:* C. angle, angle limite. -ally, *adv.* **1.** To look at sth. c., considérer qch. en critique. **2.** C. ill, dangereusement malade.
criticism ['kritisizm], *s.* Critique *f.*
criticize ['kritisaiz], *v.tr.* **1.** Critiquer, faire la critique de (qch.). **2.** Censurer, blâmer.
criticizer ['kritisaizər], *s.* Critiqueur, -euse; censeur *m.*
critique [kri'ti:k], *s.* **1.** Critique *f* (littéraire, artistique). **2.** L'art *m* de la critique.
croak[1] [krouk], *s.* Coassement *m* (de grenouille); croassement *m* (de corbeau).
croak[2], *v.i.* **1.** (*Of frog*) Coasser; (*of raven*) croasser. **2.** *F:* (a) Grogner, ronchonner. **3.** (*a*) *P:* Mourir. (*b*) *v.tr. P: U.S:* Tuer, descendre (qn). **croaking,** *s.* Coassement *m*; croassement *m.*
croaker ['kroukər], *s.* **1.** Ronchonneur *m*; grognon *mf.* **2.** Prophète *m* de malheur; prêche-malheur *mf inv.*
croaky ['krouki], *a.* (Voix) enrouée, rauque.
crochet[1] ['krouʃei], *s.* (Travail *m* au) crochet *m.* 'crochet-hook, *s.* Crochet *m.* 'crochet-work, *s.* (Travail *m*, ouvrage *m*, au) crochet *m.*
crochet[2], *v.tr.* (*p.p. & p.t.* crocheted ['krouʃeid]). Faire (qch.) au crochet. *Abs.* Faire du crochet.
crock[1] [krɔk], *s.* (*a*) Cruche *f.* (*b*) Pot *m* de terre.
crock[2], *s. F:* **1.** Cheval claqué; vieille rosse. **2.** *Aut:* Vieux clou; tacot *m*, vieille guimbarde; (*of pers.*) bonhomme fini, claqué.
crock[3]. **1.** *v.i. F:* To c. (up), tomber malade; flancher. **2.** *v.tr.* Mettre (un athlète) hors de combat; claquer, abîmer (un cheval).
crockery ['krɔkəri], *s.* Faïence *f*, poterie *f.*
crocky ['krɔki], *a. F:* His illness left him with a c. heart, sa maladie lui laissa le cœur affaibli.
crocodile ['krɔkədail], *s.* (*a*) Crocodile *m.* C. tears, larmes de crocodile. (*b*) *F:* Élèves marchant deux à deux, en rang(s) d'oignons. 'crocodile-bird, *s. Orn:* Pluvian *m.*

crocus, *pl.* **-uses** ['kroukəs, -əsiz], *s. Bot:* Crocus *m.* Autumn c., safran cultivé.

croft [krɔft], *s.* 1. Petit clos. 2. Petite ferme.

crofter ['krɔftər], *s.* Petit fermier.

cromlech ['krɔmlek], *s. Prehist:* Cromlech *m.*

crone [kroun], *s.* Vieille (femme); commère *f.*

crony ['krouni], *s.* Compère *m*, commère *f.* **An old c.,** *F:* un vieux copain.

crook¹ [kruk], *s.* 1. (*a*) Croc *m*, crochet *m.* (*b*) Houlette *f* (de berger); crosse *f* (d'évêque). (*c*) *Mus:* Ton *m* de rechange (d'un cor d'harmonie). 2. Angle *m*, courbure *f*; détour *m*, coude *m.* 3. *F:* Escroc *m*; chevalier *m* d'industrie. 4. *a. F: Austr:* Malade; souffrant. **'crook-back,** *s.* Bossu, -ue. **'crook-backed,** *a.* Bossu.

crook², *v.tr.* Courber, recourber. **crooked** ['krukid], *a.* 1. (*a*) Courbé (en crosse); crochu; tordu, recourbé; (*of path*) tortueux; (*of limb, tree*) contourné, déjeté. **Your tie's crooked,** votre cravate est de travers. (*b*) Malhonnête, déshonnête. 2. [krukt] (Canne, etc.) à béquille. **-ly** ['krukidli], *adv.* 1. Tortueusement, 2. De travers.

crookedness ['krukidnis], *s.* 1. Sinuosité *f* (d'un sentier, etc.). 2. (*a*) Perversité *f.* (*b*) Manque *m* de franchise, de droiture.

croon¹ [kru:n], *s.* (*a*) Chanson *f* à demi-voix; fredonnement *m.* (*b*) Plainte *f*; gémissement plaintif.

croon², *v.tr.* Chantonner; fredonner (une chanson).

crooner ['kru:nər], *s.* Chanteur, -euse, de charme.

crop¹ [krɔp], *s.* 1. Jabot *m* (d'un oiseau). 2. Manche *m* (d'un fouet). **Hunting-c.,** stick *m* de chasse. 3. Récolte *f*, moisson *f*; (*of fruit*) cueillette *f.* **Second c. (of hay),** regain *m.* *U.S:* **Cover c.,** culture *f* intercalaire. **The crops,** la récolte. **Companion crops,** cultures associées. 4. Coupe *f* (des cheveux). **To give s.o. a close c.,** tondre les cheveux de qn. *O:* **Eton c.,** cheveux *mpl* à la garçonne. **'crop-eared,** *a.* 1. (Chien) courtaud, essorillé. 2. *Hist:* (Têtes-rondes) aux cheveux coupés ras.

crop², *v.* (**cropped**) 1. *v.tr.* (*a*) Tondre, tailler, couper (une haie, etc.); écourter, couper (les oreilles, la queue); essoriller (un chien). *Tex:* Tondre, raser (une étoffe). **Hair cropped close,** cheveux coupés ras. (*b*) (*Of cattle*) Brouter, paître (l'herbe). 2. (*a*) *v.i.* (*Of land*) Donner une récolte. (*b*) *v.tr.* Cultiver. **crop up,** *v.i. F:* Surgir. **cropping,** *s.* 1. Tondage *m.* *Tex:* Affinage *m* (des étoffes). 2. *Agr:* Mise *f* en culture, défrichage *m*, emblavage *m* (d'une terre). **Share-c.,** métayage *m.*

cropper ['krɔpər], *s.* 1. (*Pers.*) Tondeur *m* (de drap). 2. *F:* **To come a c.,** (i) faire une chute (de cheval, de bicyclette); faire la culbute; (ii) faire faillite; (iii) se heurter à un obstacle imprévu. **I came a c. in history,** j'ai été collé en histoire. 3. *Agr:* **Share c.,** métayer *m.*

croquet ['kroukei, -ki], *s.* (Jeu *m* de) croquet *m.*

croquette [krou'ket], *s. Cu:* Croquette *f.*

crosier ['krouʒiər], *s.* Crosse *f* (d'évêque).

cross¹ [krɔs], *s.* 1. Croix *f.* **To make the sign of the c.,** tracer, faire, le signe de croix; se signer. **The Stations of the C.,** le chemin de Croix. **Market c.,** croix de la place du marché. **Wayside c.,** calvaire *m.* (*Of crusader*) **To take the c.,** prendre la croix; se croiser. **C. of Lorraine,** croix de Lorraine. **Maltese c.,** croix de Malte. *Med:* **The Red C.,** la Croix rouge. 2. Contrariété *f*, ennui *m.* 3. *Husb:* (*a*) Croisement *m* (de races). (*b*) Métis, -isse. **To be a c. between sth. and sth.,** être un mélange de qch. et de qch. 4. (*Of cloth*) Biais *m.* **On the c.,** en biais. **'cross-bearer,** *s.* Porte-croix *m inv.* **'cross-stitch,** *s. Needlew:* Point croisé.

cross². 1. *v.tr.* (*a*) Croiser (deux bâtons, etc.). (*b*) *Ecc:* **To c. oneself,** faire le signe de la croix; se signer. *F:* **C. my heart,** croix de bois croix de fer; boule de feu boule de fer. (*c*) Barrer (un chèque). **To cross one's t's,** mettre les points sur les i. (*d*) Passer (la mer); traverser (la rue, la mer); franchir (le seuil). **To c. a bridge,** passer (sur) un pont. (*Of thought*) **To c. s.o.'s mind,** passer par, traverser, l'esprit de qn. **To c.** Croiser (qn dans la rue). **To c. s.o.,** s.o.'s path, se trouver sur le chemin de qn. **To c. s.o.,** s.o.'s plans, contrecarrer qn, les desseins de qn. **Crossed in love,** contrarié dans ses amours. (*f*) **To c. breeds,** croiser,

métisser, des races. 2. *v.i.* (*a*) (*Of roads, breeds*) Se croiser. (*b*) Passer (d'un lieu à un autre). **To c. from Dover to Calais,** faire la traversée de Douvres à Calais. **cross out,** *v.tr.* Biffer, barrer, rayer (un mot). **cross over,** *v.i.* Passer de l'autre côté (de la rue, etc.). **'cross-over,** *s.* Croisement *m.* *Rail:* Voie *f* de croisement, de passage. **crossing,** *s.* 1. Barrement *m* (d'un chèque). 2. (*a*) Traversée *f* (de la mer); passage *m* (d'un fleuve, des Alpes). (*b*) (Street-)c., passage (d'un trottoir à l'autre). **Pedestrian c.,** passage pour piétons. 3. Croisement *m* (de lignes, de fils, etc.); intersection *f* (de voies). *Rail:* **Level c.,** passage à niveau. 4. *Breed:* Croisement, mélange *m* (de deux espèces). **'crossing-sweeper,** *s. A:* Balayeur *m* (entre trottoirs).

cross³. 1. *a. & comb.fm.* (*a*) Transversal, -aux; oblique; mis en travers. (*b*) (*Intersecting*) (Entre-)croisé. (*c*) (*Opposed*) Contraire, opposé (to, à). 2. *a. F:* (*Of pers.*) Maussade, de mauvaise humeur, fâché. **To be as c. as two sticks, as a bear,** être d'une humeur massacrante; être comme un crin; *F:* être inabordable. **Don't be c. with me,** il ne faut pas m'en vouloir. **-ly,** *adv.* Avec (mauvaise) humeur. **'cross-bar,** *s.* (*a*) (Barre *f* de) traverse *f*; entretoise *f*; (*of window*) croisillon *m.* (*b*) *Fb:* Barre (de but). **'cross-beam,** *s. Const:* Sommier *m*, traverse *f.* **'cross-'bearings,** *s.pl. Nau:* Relèvements croisés, simultanés. **'cross-bones,** *s.pl.* Os *m* en croix. *S.a.* SKULL. **'cross-bow,** *s.* Arbalète *f.* **'cross-brace¹,** *s.* Entretoise *f*; croisillon *m.* **cross-'brace²,** *v.tr.* Entretoiser; croisillonner. **'cross-'bred,** *a.* Métis, -isse. **'cross-'breed¹,** *s.* 1. *Husb:* Race croisée. 2. *F:* Métis, -isse. **cross-'breed²,** *v.tr.* (*p.t. & p.p.* cross-bred) Croiser, métisser (des races). **'cross-'breeding,** *s.* Croisement *m* de races; métissage *m.* **'cross-'check,** *s. Surv: etc:* Recoupement *m.* **cross-'check,** *v.tr.* Recouper. **'cross-'country** *attrib. a.* (Chemin, promenade, etc.) à travers champs. *Sp:* **C.-c. running,** cross (-country) *m.* **C.-c. runner,** crossman *m, pl.* crossmen. **'cross-cut,** *s.* 1. (*a*) Coupe *f* en travers. (*b*) Contre-taille *f.* 2. Raccourci *m*; (chemin *m* de) traverse *f.* **cross-exami'nation,** *s. Jur:* Contre-interrogatoire *m, pl.* contre-interrogatoires. **cross-ex'amine,** *v.tr Jur:* Contre-interroger. **cross-ex'aminer,** *s.* Interrogateur, -trice. **'cross-eye,** *s. Med:* Strabisme *m.* **'cross-eyed,** *a.* Louche; qui louche; strabique. **'cross-fertili'sation,** *s. Bot:* Allogamie *f.* **'cross-fire,** *s.* Feu croisé. **Exposed to c.-f.,** pris entre deux feux. **'cross-grain,** *s. Carp:* 1. Fibre torse. 2. Coupe transversale. **'cross-grained,** *a.* 1. (*Of wood*) Aux fibres irrégulières. 2. *F:* (*Of pers.*) (a) Revêche, grincheux, -euse. (*b*) Bourru, ronchonneur, -euse. **'cross-hairs,** *s.pl. Opt:* Fils *m* en croix, fils d'araignée; réticule *m.* **'cross-hatch** *v.tr. Engr:* Contrehacher, contre-tailler. **'cross-hatching,** *s.* Contrehachure *f.* **'cross-'head,** *s.* 1. *Mch:* Pied *m* de bielle; crosse *f*, tête *f* (de piston). 2. (Barre *f* de) traverse *f.* **'cross-'keys,** *s.pl. Her: etc:* Clefs *f* en sautoir. **'cross-'legged,** *a.* Les jambes croisées. **'cross-patch,** *s. F:* Grincheux, euse; grognon *mf.* **'cross-piece,** *s.* (Barre *f* de) traverse *f*; entretoise *f*; moise *f.* **'cross-'purposes,** *s.pl.* Malentendu *m*, quiproquo *m.* **We are at c.-p.,** (i) il y a malentendu; (ii) nous nous contrecarrons. **cross-'question,** *v.tr.* = CROSS-EXAMINE. **'cross-'reference¹,** *s.* Renvoi *m* (dans un livre). **'cross-'reference²,** *v.tr.* **To c.-r. a book,** établir les renvois d'un livre. **'cross-road,** *s.* 1. Chemin de traverse. 2. Cross-roads, carrefour *m*; croisée *f* de chemins. **We are now at the cross-roads,** c'est l'heure des décisions irrévocables. **'cross-'section,** *s.* Coupe *f* en travers; coupe, section transversale. **A c.-s. of life,** une tranche de vie. **'cross-'talk,** *s.* Répliques *fpl.* **cross-wind** ['krɔs'wind], *s.* Vent *m* de travers.

crossbill ['krɔsbil], *s. Orn:* Bec-croisé *m.*

crossbowman, *pl.* **-men** ['krɔsboumən], *s.m. A.Mil:* Arbalétrier.

crossness ['krɔsnis], *s.* Mauvaise humeur; maussaderie *f.*

crossways ['krɔsweiz], **crosswise** ['krɔswaiz], *adv.* En croix, en travers; en sautoir.

crossword ['krɔswə:d], *s.* **C.** (**puzzle**) mots croisés.

crotch [krɔtʃ], s. Fourche f, enfourchure f (d'un arbre, des jambes d'un pantalon), entrejambes m.

crotchet ['krɔtʃit], s. 1. Mus: Noire f. 2. F: (a) Lubie f, caprice m, toquade f. (b) Idée f fixe; manie f. (c) pl. Préjugés m.

crotchetiness ['krɔtʃitinis], s. Caractère capricieux; inégalité f d'humeur.

crotchety ['krɔtʃiti], a. Sujet à des lubies; capricieux, -euse, fantasque; à l'humeur difficile.

crouch[1] [krautʃ], s. Accroupissement m.

crouch[2], v.i. Se blottir, se tapir, s'accroupir. **crouching,** s. Accroupissement m.

croup[1] [kru:p], s. Croupe f (de cheval).

croup[2], s. Med: Croup m; laryngite diphtérique.

croupier ['kru:piər], s. Croupier m.

crow[1] [krou], s. 1. (a) Orn: Corneille f. The crows (as a class), les corbeaux m. Carrion c., corbeau, corneille m. As the c. flies, à vol d'oiseau. U.S: To eat c., avaler des couleuvres. 2. Tls: C.(-bar), pince f (à levier); aspect m. 'crow's-foot, pl. -feet, s. Patte f d'oie (au coin de l'œil). 'crow's-nest, s. Nau: Nid m de pie.

crow[2], s. Chant m du coq; F: coquerico m, cocorico m.

crow[3], v.i. (p.t. crowed [kroud], Lit: crew [kru:]; p.p. crowed). 1. (Of cock) Chanter. F: To c. over s.o., chanter victoire sur qn. 2. (Of infant) Gazouiller; pousser de petits cris de joie. **crowing,** s. 1. Chant m (du coq). 2. Gazouillement m (de bébé).

crowd[1] [kraud], s. 1. Foule f, affluence f, rassemblement m. To force one's way through the c., fendre la presse. F: It might pass in a c., ce n'est pas bon mais cela passerait. 2. F: (a) Bande f (de personnes). Pej: I don't belong to that c., je ne suis pas de ce monde-là. (b) Th: Cin: The c., les figurants m. 3. Nau: Under a c. of sail, toutes voiles dehors.

crowd[2]. 1. v.tr. (a) Serrer, (en)tasser. We are too crowded here, on est gêné ici. (b) Remplir, bourrer. Room crowded with furniture, pièce encombrée de meubles. The hall was crowded with people, la salle était bondée. The streets were crowded, il y avait foule dans les rues. Th: Crowded house, salle comble. Crowded profession, profession encombrée. Streets crowded with traffic, rues à circulation intense. (c) Sp: To c. a competitor, entraver la marche d'un concurrent. To be crowded off the pavement, être forcé de quitter le trottoir. U.S: Fin: To c. a debtor, importuner, relancer, un débiteur. (d) Nau: To c. (on) sail, faire force de voiles. 2. v.i. (a) To c. (together), se presser en foule; s'attrouper. (b) Nau: Se hâter, se presser; (of sailing ship) courir à toutes voiles. **crowd in,** v.i. Entrer en foule. **crowd into,** v.i. S'empiler (dans); arriver en foule. **crowd out.** 1. v.i. Sortir en foule. 2. v.tr. (a) Ne pas laisser de place à (qn, qch.). Journ: Matter crowded out, matière restée sur le marbre. (b) U.S: Évincer (qn).

crowfoot ['kroufut], s. Bot: Renoncule f.

crown[1] [kraun], s. 1. (a) Couronne f (de fleurs, d'or). (b) attrib: C. Colony, colonie f de la Couronne. C. jewels, joyaux mpl de la Couronne. C. lands, terres relevant de la Couronne. C. lawyer, avocat du Gouvernement. C. witness, témoin à charge. C. prince, prince héritier. C. princess, (i) princesse royale; (ii) femme du prince héritier. 2. Num: Couronne (de cinq shillings). Half a c., une demi-couronne. 3. Sommet m, haut m (de la tête). 4. C. of a hat, calotte f, forme f, d'un chapeau. 5. Couronne (de dent); sommet, clef f (de voûte); bombement m (d'un pont); cime f (d'un arbre). Aut: To drive on the c. of the road, conduire sur l'axe m de la chaussée. 6. Paperm: C.(size), (papier m) couronne. 'crown 'cap, s. U.S: = CROWN(-)CORK. 'crown(-)'cork, s. capsule f (métallique) de bouteille. C.(-)c. opener, décapsul(at)eur m. 'crown-glass, s. Opt: Glassm: Crown-glass m. 'crown-wheel, s. Mec.E: Roue dentée sur une surface latérale; roue de champ.

crown[2], v.tr. 1. Couronner. To c. s.o. king, couronner, sacrer, qn roi. Crowned with roses, couronné de roses. 2. (a) Couronner, récompenser (les efforts de qn). (b) F: To c. all, pour y mettre le comble. That crowns all! il ne manquait plus que cela! 3. (At draughts) Damer (un pion). 4. Couronner (une dent).

5. F: Flanquer un coup à la tête de qn. **crowning**[1], a. Final, -als; suprême. That would be the c. mistake, il ne manquerait plus que cela! **crowning**[2], s. 1. Couronnement m (d'un prince, etc.). 2. Bombement m (d'une route).

-crowned [kraund], a. High-, low-c. hat, chapeau haut, bas, de forme.

crozier ['krouʒiər], s. = CROSIER.

crucial ['kru:ʃiəl, 'kru:ʃ(ə)l], a. 1. Crucial, -aux; en forme de croix. 2. (Point) décisif, crucial, critique. The c. test, l'épreuve décisive.

crucible ['kru:sibl], s. Ch: Ind: Creuset m.

crucifer ['kru:sifər], s. Bot: Crucifère f.

cruciferous [kru:'sifərəs], a. Bot: Crucifère.

crucifix ['kru:sifiks], s. Crucifix m, christ m. Roadside c., calvaire m.

crucifixion [,kru:si'fikʃ(ə)n], s. Crucifixion f, crucifiement m; mise f en croix.

cruciform ['kru:sifɔ:m], a. Cruciforme.

crucify ['kru:sifai], v.tr. Crucifier (qn, la chair, etc.); mettre (qn) en croix.

crude [kru:d], a. 1. (a) (A l'état) brut. (b) (Of fruit) Vert; (of colour) cru. C. expression, expression crue. (c) (Of method, style) Informe, grossier. C. manners, manières frustes. C. statement of the facts, exposition brutale des faits. (d) (Of literary work) Indigeste. 2. Physiol: (Aliment) non assimilé. -ly, adv. 1. Crûment, grossièrement. 2. D'une manière fruste.

crudeness ['kru:dnis], **crudity** ['kru:diti], s. Crudité f (de l'eau, d'expression, Art: de tons); verdeur f (d'expression); grossièreté f (de manières, etc.).

cruel ['kruəl], a. Cruel, -elle. (a) C. disposition, naturel brutal. (b) A c. death, une mort cruelle. -lly, adv. Cruellement.

cruelty ['kruəlti], s. (a) Cruauté f (to, towards, envers). Society for the prevention of c. to animals, société protectrice des animaux. (b) Jur: Sévices mpl (to one's wife, envers sa femme).

cruet ['kruit], s. Huilier m. Ecc: (Altar) c., burette f.

cruise[1] [kru:z], s. Croisière f.

cruise[2], v.i. Nau: Croiser. Navy: To be cruising, tenir croisière. Aut: Av: Nau: Cruising speed vitesse f économique, vitesse de croisière. 2. (O taxi) Cruising, a. 1. En croisière. C. fleet, croisière f. 2. (Of taxi) En maraude.

cruiser ['kru:zər], s. Navy: Croiseur m. Armed merchant c., croiseur auxiliaire. 'cruiser-weight, s. Box: Poids mi-lourd.

crumb[1] [krʌm], s. 1. Miette f (de pain). He didn't leave a c., il n'en a pas laissé une miette. O: C. of comfort, brin m de consolation. 2. (Opposed to crust) Mie f.

crumb[2], v.tr. Cu: Paner (des côtelettes, etc.).

crumble ['krʌmbl]. 1. v.tr. Émietter (du pain); effriter (les pierres). To c. glass, gruger le verre. To c. sth. up, réduire qch. en miettes. 2. v.i. (Of bread) S'émietter; (of stone) s'effriter; brésiller; (of masonry) s'écrouler; (of earth) s'ébouler; (of empire) crouler. **crumbling,** s. 1. Émiettement m, effritement m, désagrégation f. 2. Éboulement m; écroulement m.

crumbly ['krʌmbli], a. Friable.

crummy ['krʌmi], a. P: Moche.

crump [krʌmp], s. 1. Coup violent. 2. F: Obus m qui éclate.

crumpet ['krʌmpit], s. 1. Sorte de crêpe peu sucrée (servie rôtie et beurrée). 2. P: O: Tête f, caboche f. Off one's c., maboul, loufoque.

crumple ['krʌmpl]. 1. v.tr. Friper, froisser. Aut: Crumpled (up) bumper, pare-chocs en accordéon. 2. v.i. To c. (up). (a) Se friper, se froisser; (of leaves, parchment) se recroqueviller. (b) (Of opposition; Sp: of pers., horse) S'effondrer. (c) (Of car) Se mettre en accordéon.

crunch[1] [krʌn(t)ʃ], s. 1. Coup m de dents. 2. Bruit m de broiement. 3. F: Le moment critique.

crunch[2]. 1. v.tr. Croquer, broyer (qch. avec les dents). 2. v.i. (of snow, etc.) Crisser, craquer, s'écraser (sous les pieds).

crupper ['krʌpər], s. 1. Harn: Croupière f, culière f. 2. Croupe f (de cheval).

crusade[1] [kru:'seid], s. Croisade f.

crusade², *v.i.* 1. Aller en croisade. 2. Mener une croisade, une campagne (for, pour, against, contre).
crusader [kru:'seidər], *s.* Croisé *m*.
cruse [kru:z], *s. B:* Pot *m*, jarre *f*.
crush¹ [krʌʃ], *s.* 1. Écrasement *m*. 2. Presse *f*, foule *f* bousculade *f. F:* An awful c., un monde fou. 3. *F:* To have a c. on s.o., avoir un béguin pour qn. 'crush-barrier, *s.* Barrière *f* pour contenir la foule. 'crush-'hat, *s.* (Chapeau) claque *m*; gibus *m*.
crush². 1. *v.tr. (a)* Écraser; aplatir (un chapeau); pressurer (des fruits). To c. one's leg in falling, se broyer la jambe en tombant. To c. sth. into a box, fourrer qch. dans une boîte. We were nearly crushed to death, la presse était à mourir. *(b)* Crushed with grief, accablé de douleur. *(c)* Froisser (une robe). *(d) Min: etc:* Broyer, concasser. 2. *v.i.* Se presser en foule. To c. one's way through the crowd, se frayer un chemin à travers la foule. **crushing¹**, *a.* 1. *(Of roller)* Concasseur. 2. *(Of news, defeat)* Écrasant; terrassant. *(b)* A c. reply, une réponse écrasante, humiliante. **-ly**, *adv.* (Répondre, parler) d'un ton écrasant. **crushing²**, *s.* Aplatissage *m*, écrasement *m*; broyage *m* (du minerai).
crusher ['krʌʃər], *s. Min: etc:* Broyeur *m*, écraseur *m*; concasseur *m*. Ore-c., pileur *m* de minerai.
crust¹ [krʌst], *s.* 1. Croûte *f* (de pain, de pâté). Not a c. to eat, pas une croûte à manger. 2. Écorce *f*, croûte (terrestre); carapace *f* (de homard); paroi *f* (de sabot de cheval); couche *f* (de rouille). *F: O:* The upper c., la fine fleur de la société, *F:* le gratin. 3. Dépôt *m* (de vin en bouteille). 4. Croûte (d'une plaie). 5. *P:* Du toupet.
crust². 1. *v.tr.* Encroûter; couvrir d'une croûte (de rouille). 2. *v.i.* Se couvrir d'une croûte. **crusted**, *a.* 1. C. over, couvert d'une croûte. C. snow, tôlée *f*, neige tôlée. 2. (Vin) qui a du dépôt. Old .c. port, vieux porto de derrière les fagots.
crustacea [krʌs'teiʃiə], *s.pl. Z:* Crustacés *m*.
crustacean [krʌs'teiʃiən], *s.* Crustacé *m*.
crustiness ['krʌstinis], *s.* 1. Dureté *f* de croûte (du pain). 2. Humeur bourrue.
crusty ['krʌsti], *a.* 1. *Cu: (a)* (Pain) qui a une forte croûte. *(b)* (Pâté, biscuit) croustillant. 2. *F: (Of pers.) (a)* Bourru. *(b)* Hargneux, -euse, irritable. He's a c. fellow, c'est un ours. **-ily**, *adv. (a)* D'un ton bourru. *(b)* Avec humeur.
crutch [krʌtʃ], *s.* 1. Béquille *f*. 2. *(a) Ind: Const:* Support *m*; béquille; étançon *m*. *(b) Row:* Tolet *m* à fourche. *(c)* Support arrière (de motocyclette). 3. *Tail:* Fourche *f*, fourchet *m*, entrejambes *m* (du pantalon).
crux [krʌks], *s.* Nœud *m* (d'une difficulté, de la question).
cry¹ [krai], *s.* 1. Cri *m. Within c.*, à portée de voix. It is a far c. from here to . . ., il y a loin d'ici à. . . . War-c., cri de guerre. The pack is in full c., toute la meute aboie. The thief fled with the street in full c. after him, le voleur détala, avec toute la rue à ses trousses. 2. Cri (de douleur); plainte *f*. 3. Action *f* de pleurer; pleurs *mpl*. To have a good c., pleurer libre cours à ses larmes. To have one's c. out, pleurer tout son content.
cry², *v.tr. & i.* (cried [kraid]; cried). 1. *(a)* Crier; pousser un cri, des cris. To c. aloud, pousser de grands cris. To c. for help, crier au secours. Evil that cries (out) for a remedy, mal qui réclame un remède. *(b)* To c. fish (for sale), crier son poisson (dans la rue). *O:* To c. stinking fish, dénigrer sa propre marchandise, dire du mal des siens. *(c) Ven: (Of hounds)* Donner de la voix; aboyer. 2. S'écrier. "It's not true!" he cried, "c'est faux!" s'écria-t-il. 3. Pleurer; verser des larmes. To c. for sth., demander qch. en pleurant. To c. one's eyes out, pleurer toutes les larmes de ses yeux. **cry down**, *v.tr.* Décrier, déprécier (qn, qch.). **cry off.** 1. *v.i.* Se dédire, se récuser. 2. *v.tr.* To c. off a deal, annuler une affaire. **cry out.** 1. *v.tr.* To c. out a name, crier un nom. 2. *v.i. (a)* Pousser des cris; s'écrier. *(b)* To c. out against s.o., se récrier contre qn. **cry up**, *v.tr.* Prôner, vanter (qn, qch.). **crying¹**, *a.* 1. C. injustice, injustice criante. C. evil, abus scandaleux. 2. Pleurant; qui pleure. **crying²**, *s.* 1. Cri(s) *m(pl)*; clameur *f*. 2. Pleurs *mpl*, larmes *fpl*. Fit of c., crise *f* de larmes. 'cry-baby, *s.* Pleurard, -arde; pleurnicheur, -euse.

crypt [kript], *s.* Crypte *f*.
cryptic ['kriptik], *a.* Secret, occulte. To maintain a c. silence, se renfermer dans un silence énigmatique. **-ally**, *adv.* (Parler) à mots couverts.
crypto-communist ['kripto'kɔmjunist], *s. Pol:* Crypto-communiste *mf*.
cryptogam ['kriptogæm], *s. Bot:* Cryptogame *f*.
cryptogamic [kripto'gæmik], **cryptogamous** [krip'tɔgæməs], *a. Bot:* Cryptogamique.
cryptogram [kriptogræm], *s.* Cryptogramme *m*.
cryptographer [krip'tɔgrəfər], *s.* Cryptographe *mf*.
cryptography [krip'tɔgrəfi], *s.* Cryptographie *f*.
crystal ['kristl], *s.* 1. Cristal *m*, -aux. Twin(ned) c., macle *f*. C. clear, clair comme le jour. 2. *(a)* C. (-glass), cristal. *(b) a.* The c. waters of the fountain, les eaux cristallines, limpides, de la source. 3. *U.S:* Verre *m* de montre. 4. *Psychics:* Boule *f* de cristal. 'crystal-gazer, *s.* Voyant, -ante, qui pratique la divination par la boule de cristal.
crystalline ['kristəlain], *a.* Cristallin.
crystallization [kristəlai'zeiʃ(ə)n], *s.* Cristallisation *f*.
crystallize ['kristəlaiz]. 1. *v.tr. (a)* Cristalliser. *(b)* Crystallized fruits, fruits confits. 2. *v.i.* (Se) cristalliser.
crystallography [kristə'lɔgrəfi], *s.* Cristallographie *f*.
cub¹ [kʌb], *s.* Petit *m* (d'un animal); *(of fox)* renardeau *m*; *(of bear)* ourson *m*; *(of lion)* lionceau *m*; *(of wolf)* louveteau *m. Scouting:* Louveteau. *F:* Unlicked, young c., ours mal léché. 'cub-hunting, *s.* Chasse *f* au renardeau.
cub², *v.i.* (cubbed; cubbing). Mettre bas (des petits); faire des petits. **cubbing**, *s.* 1. Mise *f* bas. 2. Chasse *f* au renardeau.
Cuba ['kju:bə]. *Pr.n. Geog:* (L'île *f* de) Cuba. In C., à Cuba.
Cuban ['kju:b(ə)n], *a. & s. Geog:* Cubain, -aine.
cubby-hole ['kʌbihoul], *s.* 1. Cachette *f*. 2. Placard *m. Aut:* Vide-poche(s) *m. inv.*
cube¹ [kju:b], *s.* 1. Cube *m.* C. root, racine cubique. 2. Tablette *f* (de soupe); dé *m* (de pain).
cube², *v.tr. Mth:* Cuber.
cubic ['kju:bik], *a.* 1. *(Cube-shaped)* Cubique. 2. *Meas:* C. foot, pied cube. C. capacity, volume *m; Mch:* cylindrée *f*. 3. C. equation, équation du troisième degré.
cubicle ['kju:bikl], *s.* 1. Alcôve *f* (d'un dortoir). *Tail: etc:* Cabine d'essayage. 2. Cabine *f* (d'une piscine, etc.).
cubism ['kju:bizm], *s. Art:* Cubisme *m*.
cubist ['kju:bist], *s. Art:* Cubiste *m*.
cubit ['kju:bit], *s. A.Meas:* Coudée *f*.
cubitus ['kju:bitəs], *s. Anat:* Cubitus *m*; avant-bras *m*.
cubmaster ['kʌbmastər], *s. Scouting:* (Woman) c., cheftaine *f* (de louveteaux).
cuckold¹ ['kʌkəld, -ould], *s.m.* Cocu *m, P:* cornard *m*.
cuckold², *v.tr.* Cocufier.
cuckoo¹ ['kuku:], *s.* 1. *(a) Orn:* Coucou *m. (b) int.* Coucou! 2. *F:* Niais, -se, benêt *m*. He's c., il est cinglé, loufoque. 'cuckoo-clock, *s.* (Pendule *f* à) coucou *m*. 'cuckoo-flower, *s. Bot:* Cardamine *f* des prés; cresson élégant, cresson des prés. 'cuckoo-pint, *s. Bot:* Arum maculé; gouet *m*.
cuckoo², *v.i.* Coucouer, coucouler.
cucumber ['kju:kʌmbər], *s.* Concombre *m*.
cud [kʌd], *s.* Bol *m* alimentaire (d'un ruminant). To chew the c., ruminer.
cuddle¹ ['kʌdl], *s.* Étreinte *f*, embrassade *f*.
cuddle². 1. *v.tr.* Serrer (qn) doucement dans ses bras. 2. *v.i. (a)* Se peloter (l'un l'autre). *(b)* To c. up to s.o., se pelotonner contre qn. **cuddling**, *s.* Pelotage *m*.
cuddly ['kʌdli], *a.* (Enfant, chiot, poupée) qui invite aux caresses.
cudgel¹ ['kʌdʒəl], *s.* Gourdin *m*, trique *f*. To take up the cudgels for s.o., prendre fait et cause pour qn.
cudgel², *v.tr.* (cudgelled) Bâtonner. To c. s.o. to death, assommer qn à coups de gourdin. **cudgelling**, *s.* (Volée *f* de) coups *mpl* de bâton.
cue¹ [kju:], *s. (a) Th:* Fin *f* de tirade; réplique *f*. To take (up) one's c., donner la réplique. *(b)* Avis *m*, mot *m*, indication *f*. To give s.o. the c., donner le mot à qn. To take one's c. from s.o., s'ajuster sur qn. *Pol:* Hungary takes her c. from Russia, la Hongrie s'aligne sur la Russie. *(c) Mus:* Indication *f* de rentrée (d'un instrument).

cue², s. Queue f (de billard). '**cue-rack**, s. *Bill:* Porte-queues m inv. '**cue-tip**, s. *Bill:* Procédé m.

cuff¹ [kʌf], s. 1. Poignet m (de chemise); manchette f. 2. (*Of coat sleeve*) Parement m; revers m. 3. *U.S:* (*Trouser*) cuffs, revers de pantalon. 4. *F:* **Off the c.**, (discours) impromptu. '**cuff-links**, s. Boutons m pl de manchettes (jumelés).

cuff², s. Taloche f, calotte f.

cuff², v.tr. Talocher, calotter (qn); flanquer une taloche à (qn).

cuirass [kwiˈræs], s. Cuirasse f.

cuirassier [ˌkwirəˈsiər], s. *Mil:* Cuirassier m.

cul-de-sac [ˈkʌldəsæk], s. Impasse f; cul-de-sac m, pl. culs-de-sac.

culinary [ˈkʌlinəri], a. Culinaire.

cull [kʌl], v.tr. *Lit:* 1. Choisir, recueillir (**from**, dans). 2. Cueillir (des fleurs, des fruits).

culm [kʌlm], s. *Bot:* Chaume m, stipe m, tige f.

culminant [ˈkʌlminənt], a. 1. (Astre) culminant, au méridien. 2. (Point) culminant.

culminate [ˈkʌlmineit], v.i. 1. (*Of star*) Culminer; passer au méridien. 2. **To c. in sth.**, aboutir à, se terminer en, qch. **Culminating point**, point culminant.

culmination [ˌkʌlmiˈneiʃ(ə)n], s. 1. *Astr:* Culmination f. 2. Aboutissement m; point culminant; apogée m.

culpability [ˌkʌlpəˈbiliti], s. Culpabilité f.

culpable [ˈkʌlpəbl], a. Coupable. **To hold s.o. c.**, tenir qn pour coupable. **-ably**, adv. Coupablement.

culprit [ˈkʌlprit], s. 1. *Jur:* Accusé, -ée; prévenu, -ue. 2. Coupable mf.

cult [kʌlt], s. Culte m (of, de).

cultivate [ˈkʌltiveit], v.tr. 1. (a) Cultiver, exploiter (la terre, un champ). (b) Cultiver (des légumes). 2. **To c.s.o.'s friendship**, cultiver l'amitié de qn. **cultivated**, a. (Voix) qui accuse une bonne éducation; (esprit) cultivé.

cultivation [ˌkʌltiˈveiʃ(ə)n], s. Culture f. **Fields under c.**, cultures fpl. **To bring land into c.**, mettre des terres ṛ valeur; défricher des terrains.

cultivato. [ˈkʌltiveitər], s. 1. (*Pers.*) Cultivateur, -trice. 2. (*Implement*) Cultivateur; motoculteur m.

cultural [ˈkʌltʃər(ə)l], a. Culturel, -elle.

culture [ˈkʌltʃər], s. 1. Culture f (des champs). 2. *Bac:* Culture. **C. tube**, tube à culture. 3. **He lacks c.**, il n'a aucune culture.

cultured [ˈkʌltʃəd], a. Cultivé, lettré.

culvert [ˈkʌlvət], s. 1. *Civ.E:* (a) Ponceau m. (b) Open c., rigole f, cassis m. **Closed c.**, canal couvert. 2. *El.E:* Conduit souterrain.

cumber [ˈkʌmbər], v.tr. Embarrasser, encombrer (**with**, de).

cumbersome [ˈkʌmbəsəm], **cumbrous** [ˈkʌmbrəs], a. Encombrant, gênant, incommode.

cumulative [ˈkjuːmjulətiv], a. Cumulatif, -ive. **-ly**, adv. Cumulativement.

cumulo-nimbus [ˈkjuːmjuloˈnimbəs], s. *Meteor:* Cumulo-nimbus m inv.

cumulo-stratus [ˈkjuːmjuloˈstrɑːtəs], s. *Meteor:* Cumulo-stratus m inv.

cumulus, pl. **-li** [ˈkjuːmjuləs, -lai], s. *Meteor:* Cumulus m.

cuneiform [ˈkjuːni(i)fɔːm], a. Cunéiforme.

cunning¹ [ˈkʌniŋ], s. 1. (a) Ruse f, finesse f. (b) *Pej:* Fourberie f, astuce f. **Man of low c.**, homme plein d'astuce. 2. Adresse f, habileté f.

cunning², a. 1. Rusé; malin, f. maligne; madré, astucieux, -euse. 2. (a) *A:* Adroit. (b) **C. device**, dispositif ingénieux. (c) *U.S:* gentil, -ly, adv. 1. (a) *F:* Avec ruse; astucieusement. 2. *A:* Habilement.

cup¹ [kʌp], s. 1. Tasse f. **Tea-c.**, tasse à thé. **C. of tea**, tasse de thé. *F:* **That's just my c. of tea**, c'est tout à fait dans mes cordes. *F:* **That's, it's, not my c. of tea**, je ne mange pas de ce pain-là, *P:* c'est pas mes oignons. *F:* **That's another c. of tea**, ça, c'est autre chose, c'est une autre affaire, c'est une autre paire de manches. *F:* **That might not be everyone's c. of tea**, il se pourrait que ce ne soit pas du goût de tout le monde. 2. (*Metal*) Gobelet m, timbale f. 3. (a) *Lit:* Coupe f. *Ecc:* Calice m (du Saint Sacrement). **Stirrup c.**, le coup de l'étrier. **To drain the c.** (of sorrow) **to the dregs**, boire le calice jusqu'à la lie. *Prov:* **There's many a slip 'twixt the c. and the lip**, il y a loin de la coupe aux lèvres. *F:* **To be in one's cups**,

être pris de boisson. **To be quarrelsome in one's cups**, avoir le vin mauvais. (b) *Sp:* **To win a c.**, remporter une coupe. **The Davis C.**, la coupe Davis. 4. *Cu:* Champagne, wine, c., marquise f. 5. (a) *Bot:* Calice (d'une fleur). (b) *Anat:* Emboîture f (d'un os). (c) **C.-and-ball**, (jeu m de) bilboquet m. *Mec.E:* **C.-and-ball joint**, joint à rotule. (d) *Mec.E:* Lubricating c., godet graisseur. (e) *Med:* **Dry c.**, ventouse sèche. **Wet c.**, ventouse scarifiée. (f) (*Of brassière*) Bonnet m. '**cup-bearer**, s. Échanson m. '**cup-final**, s. *Fb:* Finale f du championnat. '**cup-tie**, s. *Fb:* Match m éliminatoire. '**cup-valve**, s. Soupape f à cloche.

cup², v.tr. (cupped) 1. *Surg:* Ventouser (qn). 2. **With her chin cupped in her hand**, le menton dans le creux de la main. **To c. one's hand around one's mouth**, mettre la main en porte-voix. **cupping**, s. Application f de ventouses. **C. glass**, ventouse f.

cupboard [ˈkʌbəd], s. Armoire f; (*in wall*) placard m. *F:* **C. love**, amour intéressé.

cupel¹ [ˈkjuːpəl], s. *Metall:* Coupelle f.

cupel², v.tr. (cupelled [ˈkjuːpəld]), *Metall:* Coupeller (l'or, l'argent).

cupful [ˈkʌpful], s. Pleine tasse, tassée f. **Add two cupfuls of milk**, ajouter deux tasses de lait.

Cupid [ˈkjuːpid]. 1. *Pr.n.m.* Cupidon. 2. s. **Chubby little Cupids**, Amours joufflus.

cupidity [kjuːˈpiditi], s. Cupidité f.

cupola [ˈkjuːpələ], s. *Arch:* Coupole f.

cuppa [ˈkʌpə], s. *P:* **Let's have a c.**, prenons une tasse de thé.

cupreous [ˈkjuːpriəs], a. Cuivreux, -euse.

cupric [ˈkjuːprik], a. *Ch:* (Acide) cuprique.

cupriferous [kjuːˈprifərəs], a. Cuprifère.

cuprous [ˈkjuːprəs], a. *Ch:* (Sel) cuivreux.

cur [kəːr], s. 1. Roquet m; chien m sans race, corniaud m. 2. *F:* Homme m méprisable; malotru m.

curable [ˈkjuərəbl], a. Guérissable; curable.

curaçao, curaçoa [kjuərəˈsou], s. Curaçao m.

curacy [ˈkjuərəsi], s. *Ecc:* Vicariat m, vicairie f.

curare [kjuˈrɑːri], s. *Med: etc:* Curare m.

curate [ˈkjuərit], s. Vicaire m. **C. in charge**, desservant m.

curative [ˈkjuərətiv], a. & s. Curatif (m).

curator [kjuəˈreitər], s. Conservateur m (de musée).

curb¹ [kəːb], s. 1. *Harn:* Gourmette f. **To put a c. on one's passions**, mettre un frein à ses passions. 2. **C.(-stone)**, bordure f (de trottoir); margelle f (de puits). *Aut:* **To hit the c.**, heurter le trottoir. '**curb-bit**, s. *Harn:* Mors m de bride. '**curb-roof**, s. *Arch:* Comble brisé; toit m en mansarde.

curb², v.tr. 1. Gourmer (un cheval). 2. Réprimer, refréner, contenir (sa colère); brider (ses passions).

curd [kəːd], s. (Lait) caillé m; caillebotte f. **Curds and whey**, lait caillé sucré.

curdle [ˈkəːdl]. 1. v.tr. Cailler (le lait); glacer, figer (le sang). 2. v.i. (*Of milk*) Se cailler; (*of blood*) se figer.

cure¹ [ˈkjuər], s. 1. Guérison f. **To effect cures**, opérer des guérisons. 2. (a) Cure f. **Milk c.**, cure de lait. **To take a c.**, suivre un traitement. (b) Remède m. **There is a c. for everything but death**, il y a remède à tout sauf à la mort. 3. *Ecc:* **C. of souls**, charge f d'âmes.

cure², v.tr. 1. **To c. s.o. of an illness**, guérir qn d'une maladie. *Prov:* **What can't be cured must be endured**, où il n'y a pas de remède il faut se résigner. 2. (a) Saler, fumer (la viande); saurer (des harengs). (b) *Leath:* Saler (les peaux). **curing**, s. 1. Guérison f. 2. Salaison f. '**cure-all**, s. Panacée f.

curfew [ˈkəːfjuː], s. Couvre-feu m inv.

curie [ˈkjuəri], s. *Atom Ph: Meas:* Curie f.

curio [ˈkjuəriou], s. Curiosité f; bibelot m. **C. hunter**, bibeloteur m.

curiosity [ˌkjuəriˈɔsiti], s. 1. Curiosité f. **I was burning with c.**, je brûlais d'en savoir plus long; j'étais fort intrigué. 2. **I referred to it as a matter of c.**, j'en ai fait mention à titre de curiosité. 3. Objet curieux; rareté f.

curious [ˈkjuəriəs], a. 1. (a) Curieux, -euse. **I felt c. to know**, la curiosité me prit de savoir. (b) *Pej:* Curieux; indiscret, -ète. 2. Curieux, singulier, -ière. **The c. part about it**, le curieux de l'affaire. **-ly**, adv. 1. Curieusement. 2. Singulièrement. **C. enough . . .**, chose assez singulière. . . .

curium ['kjuəriəm], *s. Atom Ph:* Curium *m.*

curl¹ [kɔːl], *s.* **1.** (*a*) Boucle *f* (de cheveux); frisure *f.* Loose curls, boucles éparses. (*b*) Spirale *f* (de fumée); volute *f.* **2.** (*a*) Action *f* de se recourber. C. of the lips, moue *f* de dédain. (*b*) (*Of hair*) In c., bouclé, frisé. My hair is out of c., je suis toute défrisée. **'curl-paper**, *s. A:* Papillote *f.*

curl². **1.** *v.tr.* (*a*) Boucler, onduler, friser (les cheveux). (*b*) To c. one's lip, faire la moue. (*c*) To c. sth. round sth., enrouler qch. autour de qch. **2.** *v.i.* (*a*) (*Of hair*) Boucler, friser; (*of paper*) se recroqueviller. (*b*) (*Of smoke*) S'élever en spirales; tire-bouchonner; (*of waves*) onduler ou déferler; (*of lip*) s'abaisser avec dédain. **curl up. 1.** *v.tr.* (*a*) To c. up one's lip, retrousser la lèvre. (*b*) To c. (oneself) up, se rouler en boule, se pelotonner. **2.** *v.i.* (*a*) (*Of paper*) S'enrouler; (*of nail, point*) se rebrousser. (*b*) (*Of hedgehog*) Se mettre en boule. **curling**, *s.* Frisure *f*, ondulation *f* (des cheveux); ondulation *f*, déferlement *m* (des vagues). *Sp:* Curling *m.* **'curling-tongs**, *s.pl.* Fer *m* à friser; frisoir *m.*

curler ['kɔːlər], *s. Haird:* Bigoudi *m.*

curlew ['kɔːljuː], *s. Orn:* Courlis *m*, courlieu *m.*

curlicue ['kɔːlikjuː], *s.* **1.** (*With the pen*) Trait *m* de plume en paraphe; enjolivure *f.* **2.** (*In skating*) Figure compliquée.

curly ['kɔːli], *a.* Bouclé, frisé; en spirale. **C. lettuce** (laitue) frisée. **'curly-headed**, *a.* A la tête bouclée; (*of negro*) crépu.

curmudgeon [kɔːˈmʌdʒən], *s.* Bourru *m.*

currant ['kʌrənt], *s.* **1.** Groseille *f* (à grappes). Red c., groseille (rouge); *Fr.C:* gadelle *f.* Black c., cassis *m.* **2.** Raisin *m* de Corinthe. **currant-bush**, *s.* Groseillier *m.*

currency ['kʌrənsi], *s.* **1.** Circulation *f*, cours *m.* To give c. to a rumour, mettre un bruit en circulation. **2.** Unité *f* monétaire (d'un pays); monnaie *f.* Paper c., monnaie fiduciaire. Export of c., exportation *f* de capitaux. Foreign c., (i) monnaie étrangère, (ii) devise (étrangère). Payable in c., payable en espèces. *Pol.Ec:* Hard c., devise forte. Countries with hard currencies, pays à change élevé, à devises fortes.

current¹ ['kʌrənt], *a.* Courant; en cours. **C. number** (of a periodical), dernier numéro (d'une publication); numéro du jour. **C. reports**, bruits qui courent. To be c., être accepté; ϵvoir cours. **In c. use**, d'usage courant; très usité. **C. events**, actualités *f. Fin: etc:* **C. loan**, prêt en cours, non remboursé, consenti. **-ly**, *adv.* Couramment. It is c. reported that . . ., le bruit court que. . . .

current², *s.* **1.** (*a*) Courant *m*; fil *m* de l'eau. *Nau:* Back c., revolin *m.* To drift with the c., se laisser aller au fil de l'eau. *Meteor:* Air, atmospheric, c., courant (d'air). (*b*) The c. of events, le cours des événements. **2.** Electric c., courant électrique. Direct c., courant continu. Alternating c., courant alternatif.

curriculum [kəˈrikjuləm], *s. Sch:* Programme *m* d'études; plan *m* d'études.

currier ['kʌriər], *s. Leath:* Corroyeur *m.*

curry¹ ['kʌri], *s. Cu:* Curry *m.*

curry², *v.tr. Cu:* Apprêter (qch.) au curry.

curry³, *v.tr.* **1.** Étriller (un cheval). **2.** Corroyer (le cuir). **3.** To c. favour with s.o., s'insinuer dans les bonnes grâces de qn. **'curry-comb**, *s.* Étrille *f.*

curse¹ [kɔːs], *s.* **1.** (*a*) Malédiction *f*, anathème *m.* A c. on the day when . . .! maudit soit le jour où . . .! To lie under a c., être sous le coup d'une malédiction. (*b*) Imprécation *f*; juron *m*; gros mot. **2.** (*a*) Fléau *m*, calamité *f.* Here the rabbits are a c., ici les lapins sont un fléau. (*b*) *F:* The c., règles *fpl*, menstrue *f.*

curse². **1.** *v.tr.* Maudire, anathématiser. He is cursed with a violent temper, il est affligé d'un mauvais caractère. **C. it!** malédiction! **2.** *v.i.* Blasphémer; sacrer, jurer. **cursed** ['kɔːsid, kɔːst], *a.* **1.** Maudit. **2.** *F:* What c. weather! quel fichu temps! **cursing**, *s.* **1.** Malédiction(s) *f* (*pl*). **2.** Jurons *mpl*; gros mots *pl.*

cursive ['kɔːsiv], *a.* Cursif, -ive. **C. handwriting**, *s.* c., cursive *f.*

cursoriness ['kɔːsərinis], *s.* Rapidité *f*, caractère superficiel (d'un examen, d'un coup d'œil).

cursory ['kɔːsəri], *a.* (Coup d'œil) rapide, superficiel. **-ily**, *adv.* Rapidement; à la hâte.

curt [kɔːt], *a.* Brusque; sec, *f.* sèche. **C. answer** réponse sèche, brève. He might have been a little less c., il aurait pu le prendre sur un ton moins cassant. **-ly**, *adv.* Brusquement, sèchement.

curtail [kɔːˈteil], *v.tr.* **1.** Raccourcir; écourter; tronquer (un ouvrage). **2.** Diminuer (l'autorité de qn); restreindre (ses dépenses). **3.** To c. s.o. of his privileges, enlever ses privilèges à qn.

curtailment [kɔːˈteilmənt], *s.* Raccourcissement *m*; restriction *f*, diminution *f* (d'autorité).

curtain¹ [ˈkɔːtn], *s.* **1.** Rideau *m.* Door-c., portière *f. Mil:* Fire-c., rideau *m* de feu. *Pol: Hist:* Iron c., rideau de fer. **2.** *Th:* Rideau. To ring down the c., sonner pour le baisser du rideau. The c. rises at eight sharp, rideau à huit heures précises. Fire-proof c., safety c., rideau métallique. *U.S: P:* It'll be curtains for you if . . ., vous y laisserez votre peau si . . . **3.** *Fort:* Courtine *f.* **'curtain-call**, *s. Th:* Rappel *m* (d'un acteur) devant le rideau. To take three c.-calls, être rappelé trois fois. **'curtain-lecture**, *s.* Semonce conjugale; sermon *m* d'alcôve. **'curtain-raiser**, *s.* (*Short play*) Lever *m* de rideau. **'curtain-rod**, *s.* Tringle *f* (de rideau).

curtain², *v.tr.* Garnir de rideaux. To c. off part of a room, séparer une partie de la salle par des rideaux.

curtness ['kɔːtnis], *s.* Brusquerie *f.*

curts(e)y¹ ['kɔːtsi], *s.* Révérence *f* (que fait une femme en pliant le genou).

curts(e)y², *v.i.* (*Of woman*) Faire une révérence (to s.o., à qn).

curvature ['kɔːvətʃər], *s.* Courbure *f. Med:* C. of the spine, déviation *f* de la colonne vertébrale. *Ph:* C. of space, courbure de l'espace. *Opt:* C. of field, courbure de champ.

curve¹ [kɔːv], *s.* (*a*) Courbe *f.* Flat c., courbe ouverte. Taking of curves (by train), inscription *f* des courbes. C. of an arch, voussure *f* d'une voûte. (*b*) C. in the road, tournant *m*; *Aut:* virage *m.* (*c*) C. of the back, ensellure *f.*

curve². **1.** *v.tr.* Courber, cintrer. **2.** *v.i.* Se courber; décrire une courbe. **curved**, *a.* Courbé, courbe.

curvet¹ [kɔːˈvet], *s. Equit:* Courbette *f.*

curvet², *v.i.* (curvet(t)ed) *Equit:* Faire des courbettes.

curvilinear ['kɔːviˈliniər], *a.* Curviligne.

cusec ['kjusek], *s. Meas:* Pied *m* cubique par seconde.

cushion¹ ['kuʃ(ə)n], *s.* **1.** Coussin *m.* Leather c., (i) coussin de cuir, (ii) (*on office-chair*) rond *m* de cuir. Upholstered c., coussin capitonné. **2.** *Bill:* Bande *f.* Off the c., par la bande. To play off the c., bricoler. **3.** *Mch:* Steam c., matelas *m* de vapeur. **4.** (*Pad*) Bourrelet *m.* **5.** Fourchette *f* (de sabot de cheval). **'cushion-tyre**, *s. Aut:* Pneu *m* à basse pression.

cushion², *v.tr.* **1.** (*a*) Garnir (un siège) de coussins. (*b*) Rembourrer (un siège). **2.** Amortir (un coup). *Mch:* Matelasser (le piston).

cushy ['kuʃi], *a. F:* (Emploi) facile et grassement rétribué. **C. job**, *F:* prébende *f.* To have a c. time, se chouchouter. **A c. life**, *F:* une vie pépère.

cusp [kʌsp], *s.* **1.** Pointe *f.* C. of the moon, corne *f* de la lune. **2.** *Geom:* Point *m* de rebroussement (d'une courbe). **3.** *Bot:* Cuspide *f.*

cuspidate ['kʌspideit], *a. Bot:* Cuspidé.

cuspidor ['kʌspidɔr], *s. U.S:* Crachoir *m.*

cuss [kʌs], *s. F:* (= *curse*) **1.** Juron *m.* It's not worth a (tinker's) c., ça ne vaut pas un pet de lapin. **2.** (*Of pers.*) Individu *m*, type *m.*

cussed ['kʌsid], *a. F:* = CURSED **2.** **-ly**, *adv. F:* (*intensive*) Diablement, bigrement.

cussedness ['kʌsidnis], *s. F:* (= *cursedness*) Perversité *f.* Out of pure, sheer, c., rien que pour embêter le monde. The c. of things, l'ironie *m* des choses.

custard ['kʌstəd], *s. Cu:* Crème *f* (au lait); œuf(s) *m* au lait. Baked c., flan *m.* Caramel c., crème brûlée, renversée, au caramel. **'custard-apple**, *s. Bot:* Corossol *m.*

custodian [kʌsˈtoudiən], *s.* Gardien, -ienne; (*of museum*) conservateur *m.*

custody ['kʌstədi], *s.* **1.** Garde *f* (d'enfants, etc.). In safe c., sous bonne garde, en lieu sûr. **2.** Emprisonnement *m*; détention *f.* To take s.o. into c., arrêter qn; constituer qn prisonnier. To be in c., être en détention préventive.

custom ['kʌstəm], *s.* **1.** Coutume *f*, usage *m*, habitude *f*. **The manners and customs** (*of a country*), les us *m* et coutumes. **2.** *Jur:* Droit coutumier, coutume (d'un pays). **3.** *pl. Adm:* Douane *f*. **Customs officer**, douanier *m*. **Customs station**, poste de douane. **Custom(s) house**, (bureau *m* de la) douane. **Custom(s) duties**, droits de douane. **The customs examination**, la visite douanière. **To clear one's luggage through the customs**, dédouaner ses bagages. **4.** *Com:* (*a*) (*Of shop, business*) Clientèle *f*. **The shop is losing c.**, le magasin perd des clients, de la clientèle. (*b*) Patronage *m* (du client). (*c*) *U.S:* **C.-made, -built**, fait sur commande; *Ind:* hors série. *Aut:* **C.(-built) body**, carrosserie spéciales. *Tail.* **C.-made clothes**, vêtements (faits) sur meaure. **C. tailor**, tailleur *m* à façon. **'customs 'union**, *s. Pol:* Union douanière (entre États).

customary ['kʌstəməri], *a.* (*a*) Accoutumé, habituel, d'usage. **It is c. to . . .**, il est de coutume, d'usage, de. . . . (*b*) *Jur:* **C. clause**, clause d'usage. **-ily**, *adv.* Ordinairement, habituellement.

customer ['kʌstəmər], *s.* **1.** (*Of shop, business*) Client, -ente. **2.** *F:* **A queer c.**, un drôle de type. **Rough, ugly, c.**, vilain bonhomme; **sale type. Sly, shifty, c.**, faux bonhomme.

customize ['kʌstəmaiz], *v.tr. U.S:* Modifier, remanier (une voiture etc.) selon les demandes d'un acheteur particulier.

cut[1] [kʌt], *s.* **1.** (*a*) Coupe *f*. **To make a clean c.**, trancher nettement. **Crew c.**, cheveux taillés en brosse. (*b*) Coupure *f* (dans une pièce de théâtre). (*c*) **Wage cuts**, réductions *f* de salaires, sur le traitement. (**Electricity**) **c.**, coupure *f* du courant. (*d*) *Cards:* Coupe. **C. for partners**, tirage *m* pour les places. (*e*) *Cr: Ten:* Coup tranchant. **2.** (*a*) Coup *m* (d'épée); taillade *f*. *Pol:* **The c. and thrust of parliamentary debate**, le jeu d'attaques et de ripostes des débats parlementaires. (*b*) **C. with a whip**, coup de fouet; cinglon *m*. **The unkindest c. of all**, le coup de pied de l'âne. **3.** *Metalw: etc:* (*a*) Taille *f*, entaille *f* (d'une lime). (*b*) Passe *f* (de machine-outil). (*c*) **Saw c.**, trait *m* de scie. **4.** (*a*) (*Wound, gash*) Coupure; balafre *f*; entaille. (*b*) *Hort:* Enture *f*. (*c*) *Civ.E:* Tranchée *f*. *Mec.E:* Saignée *f* (pour graissage). **5.** (*a*) Illustration *f*, gravure *f*; (*woodcut*) gravure sur bois. (*b*) Diagramme *m*. **6.** Coupe (d'un vêtement); taille (d'une pierre précieuse). **7.** *F:* **To be a c. above s.o.**, être supérieur à qn. **That's a c. above me**, ça me dépasse. **8.** *Cu:* **C. off the joint**, tranche *f*, morceau *m*, de rôti. **Prime c.**, morceau de (premier) choix. **Cheap cuts**, bas morceaux. *U.S:* **Cold cuts**, assiette anglaise. **9. Short c.**, raccourci *m*; chemin *m* de traverse.

cut[2], *v.tr & i.* (*p.t.* cut; *p.p.* cut; *pr.p.* cutting) **1.** Couper, tailler; (*in slices*) trancher; hacher (le tabac); brillanter (un diamant). **To c. one's finger**, se couper au doigt. **To have one's hair c.**, se faire tailler les cheveux. **This remark c. him to the quick**, cette parole le piqua au vif. **That cuts both ways**, c'est un argument à deux tranchants. *F:* **To c. and come again**, revenir au plat. **To c. into a loaf**, entamer un pain. *Bill:* **To c. the cloth**, faire un accroc au tapis. *Com:* **To c. prices**, faire des prix de concurrence. *Aut: etc:* **To c. a corner (close)**, prendre un virage à la corde. *Nau:* **To c. one's moorings**, couper ses amarres. **To c. and run**, (i) *Nau:* filer le câble; (ii) *F:* filer (en vitesse); prendre ses jambes à son cou. **2.** (*a*) **To c. sth. to ribbons**, déchiqueter qch. (*b*) **To c. an actor's lines**, faire des coupures dans le rôle d'un acteur. **To c. sth. short**, couper court à qch. **To c. a speech short**, raccourcir un discours. **To c. s.o. short**, couper la parole à qn. **To c. a long story short** she left him, tant (il) y a qu'elle l'a quitté. *F:* **C. it short!** abrégez! **3. To c. an opening in a wall**, pratiquer une ouverture dans un mur. **To c. a channel**, creuser, percer, un canal. *Mount:* **To c. steps**, tailler. **4.** (*a*) **To c. one's way through the wood**, se frayer un chemin à travers le bois. **To c. across country**, couper à travers champs. (*b*) **To c. into the conversation**, intervenir dans la conversation. **5.** *Cards:* Couper (les cartes). **To c. for deal**, tirer pour la donne. **6.** *Cr: Ten:* Trancher, couper (la balle). **7. To c. s.o. (dead)**, faire

semblant de ne pas voir qn. **He c. me dead**, il m'a passé raide (sans me saluer). **8.** *F:* (*a*) Manquer exprès à (un rendez-vous). *Sch:* Sécher (un cours, une classe). (*b*) **To c. the whole concern**, abandonner l'affaire; renoncer à l'affaire. **cut away**[1], *v.tr.* (*a*) Retrancher, élaguer. (*b*) Évider. **'cut-a'way**[2], *a.* Entaillé, évidé. **C.-a. illustration**, vue en coupe. **cut back. 1.** *v.tr.* Élaguer. **2.** *v.i. F:* Rebrousser chemin. **cut down**, *v.tr.* **1.** (*a*) Abattre (un arbre). (*b*) Sabrer (un adversaire); faucher (les troupes ennemies). **2.** Rogner (des dépenses). *Ind:* Restreindre (la production). **3. She cuts down her dresses for her child**, elle taille dans ses robes pour habiller la petite. **cut in**, *v.i.* **1.** *Cards:* (R)entrer dans le jeu. **2.** Se mêler à la conversation. *Danc:* Enlever la danseuse de qn. **3.** *Rac:* Couper un concurrent. *Aut:* Couper la route à qn (après avoir doublé) **4.** *v.tr.El:* **To c. in a resistance**, intercaler une résistance. **'cut-in**, *s.* **1.** *Cin:* (*a*) Sous-titre *m*. (*b*) Scène *f* raccord. **2.** *El.E:* Conjoncteur *m*. **cut off. 1.** *v.tr.* (*a*) Couper, détacher. **To c. off s.o.'s head**, trancher, abattre, la tête à qn. **To be c. off in one's prime**, être fauché à la fleur de l'âge. (*b*) **To c. off s.o.'s retreat**, couper la retraite à qn. (*c*) *Tp:* **Don't c. me off**, ne coupez pas. (*d*) *El:* **To c. off the current**, interrompre le courant. *Av:* **To land with the engine c. off**, atterrir hélice calée. **To c. off s.o.'s supplies**, couper les vivres à qn. (*e*) **To c. s.o. off with a shilling**, déshériter qn. **2.** *v.i. F:* Décamper. **I told him to c. off**, je lui ai dit de filer. **'cut-off**, *attrib.a. Cin:* **C.-off period**, phase *f* d'escamotage. **cut out**, *v.tr.* **1.** (*a*) Couper, enlever; exciser. (*b*) *F:* **To c. s.o. out**, supplanter qn. **2.** Découper (des images). **To c. out a garment**, tailler un vêtement. *F:* **To be c. out for sth.**, être fait, taillé, pour qch.; avoir des dispositions pour qch. **To be cut out for a teacher**, avoir la vocation du professorat. **3.** Supprimer, retrancher (un organe). **To c. out superfluous details**, élaguer des détails superflus. **4.** *v.i. Cards:* Couper à qui se retirera du jeu. **cut-'out**, *s. El.E:* Coupe-circuit *m inv.* **Time-lag c.-out**, coupe-circuit à action différée. **cut up**, *v.tr.* **1.** Couper, débiter (le bois); découper, dépecer (une volaille); *F:* critiquer sévèrement (un livre). **To c. up the bread**, tailler le pain par morceaux. **Road c. up by the rains**, route ravinée par les pluies. **2.** *F:* (*a*) **Don't be so c. up about it**, ne vous affligez pas ainsi. (*b*) *v.i.* **To c. up rough**, se fâcher; se mettre en colère. **He c. up very rough (about it)**, il a très mal pris la chose. **cut**[8], *a.* **1. C. glass**, cristal taillé. **Well-c. suit**, complet de bonne coupe. **Low-c. dress**, robe décolletée. **C. and dried opinions**, opinions toutes faites. **2. C. prices**, prix réduits. **cutting**[1], *a.* **1. C. edge**, tranchant *m* (d'un outil). **2. C. wind**, vent cinglant. **3. C. remark**, réponse mordante. **-ly**, *adv.* Caustiquement; d'un ton mordant. **cutting**[2], *s.* **1.** (*a*) Coupe *f*, coupage *m*. (*b*) Taille *f* (d'un diamant). (*c*) Découpage *m* (de la tôle, d'un film). (*d*) **C. of prices**, réduction *f* des prix. **2.** (*Piece cut off*) (*a*) Coupon *m*, bout *m* (d'étoffe, etc.). **C. from a newspaper**, coupure prise dans un journal. (*b*) *Hort:* Bouture *f*. **3.** *Civ.E: etc:* Tranchée *f*; voie *f* en tranchée. **Road running through a c.**, route encaissée. *Mount:* **Step c.**, taille *f*.

cutaneous [kju'teiniəs], *a.* Cutané.

cute [kju:t], *a. F:* **1.** (*a*) (*Of pers*) Malin, -igne; rusé. (*b*) **C. idea**, idée originale. **2.** *U.S:* Gentil, -ille; coquet, -ette. **-ly**, *adv. F:* Avec ruse; ingénieusement.

cuteness ['kju:tnis], *s. F:* Intelligence *f*, finesse *f*.

cuticle ['kju:tikl], *s.* **1.** Épiderme *m*. **2.** *Bot: Biol:* Cuticule *f*.

cutie ['kju:ti], *s.f. U.S: P:* Petite rusée; petite délurée.

cutis ['kju:tis], *s. Anat:* Derme *m*.

cutlass ['kʌtləs], *s.* **1.** *Nau:* Sabre *m* d'abordage. **2.** *U.S:* Couteau *m* de chasse.

cutler ['kʌtlər], *s.* Coutelier *m*.

cutlery ['kʌtləri], *s.* Coutellerie *f*.

cutlet ['kʌtlit], *s.* (*a*) Côtelette *f* (de mouton); côte *f* (de veau). (*b*) *Cu:* Croquette *f* de viande.

cutter ['kʌtər], *s.* **1.** (*Pers.*) Coupeur *m*; tailleur *m* (de pierre). **2.** *Tls:* Coupoir *m*, lame *f*. **Rotary c.**, roue *f* à couteaux. **3.** *Nau:* Canot *m* (d'un bâtiment de guerre).

cut(-)throat ['kʌtθrout], s. 1. Coupe-jarret m; escarpe m. C. den, coupe-gorge m inv. 2. (a) C. competition, concurrence acharnée. (b) Cards: C. (bridge), bridge m à trois.
cuttlebone ['kʌtlboun], s. Os m de seiche.
cuttlefish ['kʌtlfiʃ], s. Moll: Seiche f.
cutwater ['kʌtwɔːtər], s. 1. N.Arch: (Taquet m de) taille-mer m; éperon m; guibre f. 2. Civ.E: Bec m (d'une pile de pont).
cwm [kuːm], s. Geol: Cirque m.
cyanamide [sai'ænəmaid], s. Ch: Cyanamide f.
cyanide ['saiənaid], s. Ch: Cyanure m. C. process, procédé de cyanuration.
cyanogen [sai'ænədʒin], s. Ch: Cyanogène m.
cyanosis [ˌsaiə'nousis], s. Med: Cyanose f.
cybernetics ['saibə'netiks], s. Cybernétique f.
cyclamen ['sikləmən], s. Bot: Cyclamen m.
cycle¹ ['saikl], s. 1. Cycle m (de mouvements, de poèmes); Geol: période f. Ph: Carnot's c., le cycle de Carnot. I.C.E: Four-stroke c., cycle à quatre temps. 2. = BICYCLE¹. Pedal c., bicyclette f (sans moteur). C. track, piste f cyclable. C.-racing track, vélodrome m. 'cycle-car, s. Cyclecar m.
cycle², v.i. Faire de la bicyclette; aller à bicyclette. cycling¹, a. Cycliste. cycling², s. Cyclisme m.
cyclic ['siklik], a. Cyclique. C. novel, roman-fleuve, roman-cycle.
cyclist ['saiklist], s. Cycliste mf. Racing c., coureur cycliste.
cycloid ['saiklɔid], s. Geom: Cycloïde f.
cycloidal [sai'klɔid(ə)l], a. Cycloïdal, -aux.
cyclometer [sai'klɔmitər], s. Compteur m kilométrique (pour bicyclettes).
cyclone ['saikloun], s. Meteor: Cyclone m.
cyclonic [sai'klɔnik], a. Meteor: Cyclonique.
cyclopaedia [ˌsaiklə'piːdiə], s. = ENCYCLOPAEDIA.
Cyclopean [ˌsaiklə'piən], a. Cyclopéen; gigantesque.
Cyclops ['saiklɔps], s. Myth: Cyclope m.
cyclorama [saiklə'rɑːmə], s. Cin: Cyclorama m.
cyclostyle ['saiklostail], s. Appareil m à polycopier par stencils.
cyclotron ['saiklotron], s. Atom. Ph: Cyclotron m.
cygnet ['signit], s. Orn: Geom: Jeune cygne m.

cylinder ['silindər], s. 1. Geom: Cylindre m. 2. Cylindre (de machine à vapeur); barillet m (de revolver). Typewr: Rouleau m porte-papier. C. of compressed gas, bouteille f, cylindre, de gaz comprimé. A six-c. car, F: une six-cylindres. 'cylinder-head, s. I.C.E: Culasse f.
cylindrical [si'lindrik(ə)l], a. Cylindrique.
cyma, pl. -mas ['saimə(z)], s. 1. Arch: Cimaise f (de corniche). 2. Bot: = CYME.
cymbal ['simb(ə)l], s. Cymbale f.
cymbalist ['simbəlist], s. Cymbalier m.
cyme [saim], s. Bot: Cyme f.
Cymric ['kimrik, 'kʌm-], a. Kymrique; gallois.
cynegetic [ˌsaini'dʒetik], a. Cynégétique.
cynegetics [ˌsaini'dʒetiks], s.pl. (With sg. const.) Cynégétique f.
cynic ['sinik]. 1. a. & s. Hist. of Phil: Cynique (m). 2. s. Censeur m caustique; railleur m; sceptique m.
cynical ['sinik(ə)l], a. 1. Hist. of Phil: Cynique. 2. Sarcastique; sceptique; désabusé. -ally, adv. D'un ton sceptique; caustiquement.
cynicism ['sinisizm], s. 1. Hist. of Phil: Cynisme m. 2. Scepticisme railleur; désillusionnement m. 3. Mot m caustique.
cynocephalus [ˌsaino'sefələs], s. Z: Cynocéphale m.
cynosure ['sainəsjuər], s. Lit: The c. of every eye, le point de mire de tous les yeux.
cypher ['saifər], s. = CIPHER.
cypress ['saipris], s. Bot: Cyprès m.
Cypriot ['sipriət], a. & s. Geog: Cypriote (mf).
Cyprus ['saiprəs]. Pr.n. L'île de Chypre.
cyrillic [si'rilik], a. (L'alphabet) cyrillien, cyrillique.
cyst [sist], s. 1. (a) Biol: Anat: Sac m; vésicule f. (b) Bot: Kyste m. 2. Med: Kyste m.
cystitis [sis'taitis], s. Med: Cystite f.
cystotomy [sis'tɔtəmi], s. Surg: Cystotomie f.
cytoblast ['saitoblɑːst], s. Biol: Cytoblaste m.
czar [zɑːr], s. Tsar m.
czarevitch [zɑː'rivitʃ], s. Tsarévitch m.
czarina [zɑː'riːnə], s.f. Tsarine.
Czech [tʃek], a. & s. Tchèque (mf).
Czechoslovakia ['tʃekouslə'vækiə]. Pr.n. La Tchécoslovaquie.

D, d [diː], s. 1. (La lettre) D, d m. Tp: D for David, D comme Désiré. 2. Mus: Ré m. 3. (Abbr. for Lt. 'denarius') Penny m, pence mpl. 4. Mil: D-day, le jour J.

dab¹ [dæb], s. 1. Coup léger; tape f. 2. (a) Tache f (d'encre, de peinture). F: pl. Empreintes digitales. A d. of butter, un petit morceau de beurre. (b) Petit coup de tampon.

dab², v.tr. (dabbed) 1. Donner une tape à (qn). 2. Tapoter; (with pad) tamponner. To d. one's eyes with a handkerchief, se tamponner les yeux.

dab³, s. Ich: Limande f.

dab⁴, s. F: To be a d. hand at sth., s'entendre à qch. He's a d. hand at algebra, il est calé, c'est un as, en algèbre.

dabber [dæbər], s. Tampon m.

dabble [dæbl]. 1. v.tr. Humecter, mouiller. 2. v.i. (a) Barboter (dans l'eau). (b) F: To d. in, at, law, s'occuper un peu de droit. To d. in politics, politicailler, se mêler de politique.

dabbler [dæblər], s. To be a d. in sth., se mêler un peu de qch.; faire qch. en amateur.

dabster [dæbstər], s. F: 1. Expert m. 2. Art: Barbouilleur.

dace [deis], s. Ich: Vandoise f; dard m.

dachshund [dækshund], s. Basset allemand, teckel m.

dacoit [dæ'kɔit], s. Dacoït m (brigand de l'Inde).

dacron [dækrɔn], s. Tex: R.t.m: Dacron m.

dactyl [dæktil], s. Pros: Dactyle m.

dactylology [dækti'lɔlədʒi], s. Dactylologie f.

dactyloscopy [dækti'lɔskəpi], s. Dactyloscopie f; étude f des empreintes digitales.

dad [dæd], s. F: Papa m; petit père.

dadaism [dɑː'dəizm], s. Art: Dadaïsme m.

dadaist [dɑː'dəist], s. Art: Dadaïste mf.

daddy [dædi], s. ≐ DAD. **daddy-'long-legs**, s. Ent: F: Tipule f.

dado [deidou], s. 1. Arch: (a) Dé m (de piédestal). (b) Cimaise f. 2. Lambris m (d'appui).

Daedalus [diː'dələs]. Pr.n.m. Gr.Myth: Dédale.

daffodil [dæfədil], s. Bot: 1. Hort: Jonquille f. 2. Narcisse m sauvage, des bois.

daft [dɑːft], a. 1. Écervelé. 2. Toqué, braque. To go d. over sth., s'enticher de qch.

daftness [dɑːftnis], s. F: Loufoquerie f.

dagger [dægər], s. 1. Poignard m, dague f. F: To be at daggers drawn, être à couteaux tirés (with, avec). To look daggers at s.o., lancer un regard furibond à qn. 2. Typ: Croix f.

dago [deigou], s. P: Pej: Sud-américain m (de race latine); métèque m.

daguerreotype [də'gerotaip], s. Daguerréotype m.

dahlia [deiljə], s. Bot: Dahlia m.

daily [deili]. 1. a. Journalier, quotidien. D. help, F: s. daily, femme f de ménage. 2. adv. Journellement, quotidiennement, tous les jours. 3. s. Journ: Quotidien m. Our leading dailies, nos grands quotidiens.

daintiness [deintinis], s. Délicatesse f, raffinement m (de goût); mignonnesse f (de taille).

dainty¹ [deinti], s. Friandise f.

dainty², a. 1. (Of food) Friand, délicat. 2. (Of pers.) Délicat, exquis. She's a d. little thing, elle est mignonne. 3. To be d., être délicat sur la nourriture. -ily, adv. Délicatement; d'une manière raffinée.

dairy [dɛəri], s. 1. Laiterie f. 2. (Shop) Laiterie; crémerie f. **'dairy-butter**, s. Beurre fermier, laitier. **'dairy cattle**, s. Vaches laitières. **'dairy-farm**, s. Ferme laitière. **'dairy-farming**, s. L'industrie laitière. **'dairy-produce**, s. Produits laitiers; laitages mpl.

dairymaid [dɛərimeid], s.f. Fille de laiterie; laitière.

dairyman, pl. -men [dɛərimən], s.m. 1. Husb: Nourrisseur. 2. Com: Laitier; crémier.

dais [deiis], s. (a) Estrade f (d'honneur); dais m. (b) Dais (recouvrant l'estrade).

daisy [deizi], s. 1. Bot: Marguerite f. Common d., pâquerette f. D.-chain guirlande f de pâquerettes. P: To be pushing up the daisies, être mort et enterré; P: manger les pissenlits par les racines. 2. P: She's a d., c'est une perle.

dale [deil], s. Vallée f, vallon m.

dalesman, pl. -men [deilzmən, -mən], s.m. Habitant des vallées (du nord de l'Angleterre).

dalliance [dæliəns], s. Lit: Échange m de tendresses; badinage m.

dally [dæli], v.i. Lit: 1. (a) To d. with an idea, caresser une idée. (b) Badiner, flirter, (with, avec). 2. Tarder, baguenauder.

dalmatic [dæl'mætik], s. Ecc.Cost: Dalmatique f.

daltonian [dɔːl'touniən], a. & s. Med: Daltonien, -ienne.

daltonism [dɔːlt(ə)nizm], s. Med: Daltonisme m.

dam¹ [dæm], s. Hyd.E: (a) Barrage m (de retenue d'un grand réservoir). Earth d., barrage en terre. Gravity d., barrage poids. Arch d., barrage voûte. Arch-gravity d., barrage voûte-poids. Rock-filled, barrage en enrochements. (b) F: Eau retenue (par un barrage); retenue f. **'dam-buster**, s. Av: Hist: 1. Torpille aérienne lourde. 2. Pilote m d'avion chargé de détruire un barrage.

dam², v.tr. (dammed) To d. (up), contenir, endiguer (un cours d'eau, un lac).

dam³, s. Mère f (en parlant des animaux).

damage¹ [dæmidʒ], s. 1. Dommage(s) m(pl), dégâts mpl; (to engine, ship, etc.) avarie(s) f(pl). Jur: Sinistre m. D. in transit, avarie(s) en cours de route. F: There's no great d. done, il n'y a pas grand mal. 2. Préjudice m, tort m. To cause s.o. d., porter préjudice à qn. 3. pl. Jur: Dommages-intérêts m, indemnité f. To sue s.o. for damages, poursuivre qn en dommages-intérêts. D. to property, dommages matériels. War d., dommages de guerre. 4. F: What's the d.? à combien se monte la note? c'est combien?

damage², v.tr. 1. Endommager; avarier (une marchandise, une machine); abîmer (qch.); F: amocher, esquinter (qch.). 2. Faire tort, nuire, à (qn). **damaged**, a. Avarié, endommagé; F: (of car, etc.) accidenté. **damaging**, a. Préjudiciable, nuisible.

damascene [dæmə'siːn], v.tr. Metalw: Damasquiner.

Damascus [də'mæskəs]. Pr.n. Geog: Damas m.

damask [dæmask], a. & s. 1. Tex: D. (silk, linen), damas m; soie damassée, linge damassé. 2. D. steel, acier damassé. 3. (a) D. rose, rose de Damas. (b) D. (colour), incarnat m. Her d. cheeks, ses joues vermeilles.

dame [deim], s. 1. A: = LADY. F: An old d., une vieille dame. U.S: P: Femme f, gonzesse f. 2. Titre accordé aux femmes titulaires de certaines décorations. **'dame-school**, s. A: École enfantine (tenue par une femme).

damfool [dæmfuːl]. P: 1. a. Stupide, idiot. 2. s. Sacré idiot! imbécile mf, crétin m.

dammit [dæmit], int. Sacristi! sacrebleu! It was as near as d., il était moins une.

damn¹ [dæm], s. (Occ. written d——) Juron m; gros mot. Not to be worth a (tuppenny) d., ne pas valoir chipette. P: Not to give a d. (for), se moquer de, se soucier de, qch. comme de sa première culotte.

damn², v.tr. 1. (a) Condamner, critiquer défavorablement (un livre). (b) Perdre, ruiner (qn, un projet). 2. (a) Theol: Damner; (of God) réprouver. (b) F: Well, I'm damned [dæmd]! ça c'est fort! I'll see him damned first! qu'il aille au diable! 3. (a) D. your impudence! que le diable vous emporte! (b) int. Sacristi! sacrebleu! D. it! zut! **damned**, a. 1. Damné, réprouvé. The d., les damnés. 2. F: (Occ. written d——d) (a) Sacré, satané. F: What a d. nuisance! Quel empoisonnement! He's a d. nuisance! Comme il est enquiquineur! (b) adv. Diablement, bigrement, F: vachement. It's d. hard, c'est vachement difficile. (c) s. To do one's damnedest [dæmdist], faire tout son possible. **damning¹**

['dæmiŋ], *a.* Portant condamnation. **D. evidence,** preuves accablantes. *F:* **D. praise,** éreintement *m* avec des fleurs. **damning²** ['dæmiŋ], *s.* 1. Condamnation *f.* 2. Damnation *f.*

damn³, *a.* 1. *P:* = DAMNED 2. 2. *F:* **He's doing d. all,** il ne fiche rien.

damnable ['dæmnəbl], *a.* 1. Damnable. 2. *F:* Maudit, odieux. **-ably,** *adv.* Odieusement; diablement, *F:* bigrement (mauvais, etc.).

damnation [dæm'neiʃ(ə)n], *s.* 1. Damnation *f. Theol:* Eternal d., peine *f* du dam. 2. Éreintement *m* (d'une pièce de théâtre, etc.). 3. *int. F:* Sacrebleu!

Damocles ['dæməkliːz]. *Pr.n.m.* **The sword of D.,** l'épée de Damoclès.

damp¹ [dæmp], *s.* 1. (*a*) Humidité *f.* (*b*) *O:* **To cast a d. over the company,** jeter un froid sur la compagnie. 2. *Min:* (**Black**) **d.** = CHOKE-DAMP. *S.a.* FIRE-DAMP. **'damp-course,** *s. Const:* Couche isolante, hydrofuge. **'damp-proof,** *a.* Hydrofuge; imperméable.

damp², *v.tr.* 1. Mouiller; humecter (le linge); amoitir (la peau). 2. Étouffer (le feu); assourdir (un son). **To d. down a furnace,** boucher un haut fourneau. 3. *Ph:* (*a*) **Damped waves,** ondes amorties. (*b*) *v.i.* **The oscillations d. down,** les vibrations s'amortissent. 4. Refroidir (l'ardeur, le courage). **To d. s.o.'s spirits,** décourager qn. **damping,** *s.* 1. (*a*) Humectation *f.* (*b*) **A general d. of spirits,** un froid général jeté sur la compagnie. 2. Amortissement *m. Aer:* **Aerodynamic d.,** résistance *f* aux forces aérodynamiques. **'damping-cloth,** *s. Dom.Ec:* Pattemouille *f.*

damp³, *a.* Humide; (*of skin*) moite. **D. heat,** chaleur humide, moite.

dampen ['dæmpən]. 1. *v.tr. U.S:* = DAMP² 1, 4. 2. *v.i.* (*a*) Devenir humide. (*b*) (*Of ardour*) Se refroidir.

damper ['dæmpər], *s.* 1. *F:* (*a*) (*Pers.*) Rabat-joie *m inv.* (*b*) Événement déprimant. **To put a d. on the company,** jeter un froid sur la compagnie. 2. (*In Austr.*) Pain *m* en galette, sans levain. 3. (*Of piano, sound*) Étouffoir *m.* 4. Registre *m* (de foyer). 5. *Mec.E: El.E: Aut:* Amortisseur m.

dampish ['dæmpiʃ], *a.* Un peu humide; à peine humide.

dampness ['dæmpnis], *s.* Humidité *f;* moiteur *f* (de la peau).

damsel ['dæmz(ə)l], *s.f. A. & Lit:* Demoiselle; jeune fille.

damson ['dæmz(ə)n]. 1. *s.* (*a*) Prune *f* de Damas. (*b*) Prunier *m* de Damas. 2. *a.* (*Colour*) Prune *inv.*

dance¹ [dɑːns], *s.* 1. (*a*) Danse *f.* **D. music,** musique *f* de danse. *F:* **To lead s.o. a d.,** (i) donner du fil à retordre à qn; (ii) faire voir bien du chemin à qn. **The D. of Death,** la danse macabre. (*b*) (Air *m* de) danse. 2. Bal *m, pl.* bals; soirée dansante. **'dance-band,** orchestre *m* de musique de danse. **'dance-dress,** *s.* Robe *f* de bal. **'dance-hall,** *s.* Bal public; dancing *m.* **'dance-hostess,** *s.f.* Entraîneuse *f.* **'dance-programme,** *s.* Carnet *m* de bal. **'dance-shoes,** *s.pl.* Souliers *m* de bal; (*for men*) escarpins *m.*

dance². 1. *v.i.* (*a*) Danser. **To d. with s.o.,** faire danser qn. *F:* **I'll make him d. to a different tune!** je vais le faire chanter sur un autre ton. **To d. to every fiddle,** tourner à tous les vents. (*b*) **To d. for joy,** danser de joie. **To d. with rage,** trépigner de colère. 2. *v.tr.* (*a*) Danser (une valse, etc.). (*b*) **To d. attendance on s.o.,** faire l'empressé auprès de qn; faire les trente-six volontés de qn. **dancing¹,** *a.* Dansant. **D. dervish,** derviche tourneur. **'dancing-girl,** *s.f.* Bayadère. **dancing²,** *s.* Danse *f.* **'dancing-master,** *s.* Maître *m* de danse. **'dancing-partner,** *s.* Cavalier *m,* dame *f;* partenaire *mf;* danseur, -euse.

dancer ['dɑːnsər], *s.* Danseur, -euse.

dandelion ['dændilaiən], *s. Bot:* Pissenlit *m.*

dander ['dændər], *s. F:* **To get s.o.'s d. up,** mettre qn en colère; échauffer la bile à qn. **He got his d. up,** la moutarde lui a monté au nez.

dandified ['dændifaid], *a.* Vêtu en dandy. **D. young man,** (i) jeune gommeux; (ii) jeune fat.

dandle ['dændl], *v.tr.* 1. (*a*) Faire sauter (un enfant sur ses genoux). (*b*) Dodeliner (un enfant). 2. Câliner (qn).

dandruff ['dændrəf], *s.* Pellicules *fpl* (du cuir chevelu).

dandy ['dændi]. 1. *s.* Dandy *m,* gommeux *m.* 2. *a. U.S:* Épatant, chic, chouette.

Dane [dein], *s.* 1. Danois, -oise. 2. (*Dog*) (**Great**) **D.,** (grand) danois.

danger ['deindʒər], *s.* Danger *m,* péril *m.* **To be in d.,** courir un danger. **Out of d.,** hors de danger; *F:* hors d'affaire. **To run into d.,** s'exposer au danger. **To be in d. of falling,** courir le risque de tomber. **To ward off a d.,** écarter un danger. **Rock that is a d. to navigation,** écueil dangereux pour la navigation. *P.N:* **'D., road up,'** "attention aux travaux." *Rail:* **Signal at d.,** signal à l'arrêt. **'danger-signal,** *s. Rail:* Arrêt *m.* **'danger-zone,** *s. Mil: etc:* Zone dangereuse.

dangerous ['dein(d)ʒrəs], *a.* (*a*) Dangereux, périlleux. **D. illness,** maladie grave. *F:* **You are on d. ground,** vous êtes sur un terrain brûlant. **D. situation,** mauvais pas. (*b*) **D. example,** exemple pernicieux. **-ly,** *adv.* Dangereusement.

dangle [dæŋgl]. 1. *v.i.* Pendiller, pendre. **With one's legs dangling,** les jambes ballantes. *F: O:* **To d. after a woman,** être pendu aux jupes d'une femme. 2. *v.tr.* Faire pendiller. *F:* **To d. a prospect before s.o.'s eyes,** faire miroiter une perspective aux yeux de qn.

Danish ['deiniʃ]. 1. *a.* Danois. 2. *s. Ling:* Le danois.

dank [dæŋk], *a.* (Cachot) humide (et froid).

danseuse [dɑːn'səːz], *s.f.* Ballerine *f.*

Danube (**The**) [ðə'dænjuːb]. *Pr.n. Geog:* Le Danube.

Danzig ['dæntzig]. *Pr.n.m. Geog:* Dantzig.

Danziger ['dæntzigər], *a. & s. Geog:* Dantzikois, -oise.

Daphne ['dæfni]. 1. *Pr.n.f. Myth:* Daphné. 2. *s. Bot:* Daphné *m,* lauréole *f.*

dapper ['dæpər], *a.* Pimpant. **A d. little man,** un petit homme tiré à quatre épingles.

dapple [dæpl]. 1. *v.tr.* Tacheter, pommeler. 2. *v.i.* Se tacheter; (*of sky*) se pommeler. **dappled,** *a.* Tacheté, (cheval bai) miroité, à miroir.

dapple-grey ['dæpl'grei], *a. & s.* (Cheval) gris pommelé.

darbies ['dɑːbiz], *s.pl. P:* Menottes *f.*

Darby ['dɑːbi]. *Pr.n. F:* **D. and Joan** = Philémon et Baucis. **D. and Joan club,** club *m* des vieux.

dare¹ ['deər], *s.* (*a*) Coup *m* d'audace. (*b*) Défi *m.*

dare², *v.* 1. *Modal aux.* (*3rd sg.pr.* **he dare;** *O:* **durst** [dəːrst], **dared, dare;** *no p.p.*) Oser. **He dared not contradict me,** il n'osa (pas) me contredire. **Don't you d. touch him!** n'ayez pas l'audace de le toucher! **How d. you!** vous osez! **I d. say,** sans doute; peut-être bien; je (le) crois bien. 2. *v.tr.* (*3rd sg.pr.* **he dares;** *p.t.* **dared;** *p.p.* **dared**) (*a*) **To d. to do sth.,** oser faire qch. **To d. all things,** tout oser. (*b*) Braver, affronter (la mort). (*c*) **To d. s.o. to do sth.,** défier qn de faire qch. **daring¹,** *a.* (i) Audacieux, hardi; (ii) téméraire. **Greatly d.,** fort osé. **-ly,** *adv.* Audacieusement, témérairement. **daring²,** *s.* (i) Audace *f,* hardiesse *f;* (ii) témérité *f.* **'dare-devil.** 1. *s.* Casse-cou *m inv;* cervelle brûlée. 2. *a.* Qui ne craint ni Dieu ni diable.

dark¹ [dɑːk], *a.* 1. Sombre, obscur, noir. **It is d.,** il fait nuit, il fait noir. **It is getting d.,** il commence à faire sombre. **The sky grew d.,** le ciel s'assombrit. 2. (*Of colour*) Foncé, sombre. **D. blue (dresses),** (des robes *f*) bleu foncé. 3. (*Of pers.*) Brun; basané. 4. **The d. race,** la race nègre. 5. (*a*) Sombre, triste. **D. future,** sombre avenir. **To look on the d. side of things,** voir tout en noir. (*b*) Ténébreux, mauvais. **To utter d. threats,** proférer de sourdes menaces. 6. **D. saying,** mot mystérieux. **To keep sth. d.,** tenir qch. secret. **Keep it d.!** gardez le secret! Motus! **D. horse,** (i) cheval, homme dont on ne sait rien; (ii) *F:* concurrent que l'on ne croyait pas dangereux. **He's a d. horse,** c'est une quantité inconnue. 7. **The D. Ages,** l'âge des ténèbres. **-ly,** *adv.* (*a*) Obscurément. (*b*) **To look d. at s.o.,** regarder qn d'un air sombre. **'dark-'eyed,** *a.* Aux yeux noirs. **'dark-'lantern,** *s.* Lanterne sourde. **'dark-room,** *s. Phot:* Cabinet noir. **'dark-'skinned,** *a.* 1. A peau brune. 2. (Race) nègre. **'dark-slide,** *s. Phot:* Châssis *m* photographique.

dark², *s.* 1. Ténèbres *fpl,* obscurité *f.* **After d.,** à (la) nuit close. **The d. of the moon,** la nouvelle lune. 2. **To be (kept) in the d.,** être (laissé) dans l'ignorance. **We are in the d. as to his plans,** nous ignorons ses projets. *S.a.* LEAP¹ 1.

darken ['dɑ:k(ə)n]. **1.** *v.tr.* Obscurcir; assombrir (le ciel); brunir (le teint); foncer (une couleur); attrister (la vie de qn). A cloud darkened the sun, un nuage voila la face du soleil. **Never d. my doors again!** ne remettez plus les pieds chez moi! **2.** *v.i.* S'obscurcir; (*of sky, brow*) s'assombrir. **darkening,** s. Assombrissement *m*.

darkish ['dɑ:kiʃ], *a.* Un peu sombre; (*of hair*) plutôt brun.

darkness ['dɑ:knis], *s.* **1.** Obscurité *f*, ténèbres *fpl*. The room was in complete d., il faisait tout à fait noir dans la salle. **2.** Teinte foncée. **D. of complexion,** teint bronzé. **3.** Ignorance *f* (as to, de).

darkie, darky ['dɑ:ki], *s.* F: Pej: Nègre *m*.

darling ['dɑ:liŋ], *s. & a.* Favori, -ite; bien-aimé, -ée. **My d.!** mon chéri! ma chérie! **She's a little d.,** c'est un petit amour. **A mother's d.,** un enfant gâté. **The d. of the people,** l'idole *f* du peuple.

darn¹ [dɑ:n], *s.* Reprise *f*.

darn², *v.tr.* Raccommoder, ravauder; repriser, passefiler (des bas). **darning,** s. Reprise *f*, ravaudage *m*. **'darning-egg,** s. Œuf *m* à repriser. **'darning-needle,** s. Aiguille *f* à repriser.

darn³, darned [dɑ:nd], *a.* F: Sacré.

darnel ['dɑ:nl], *s. Bot:* Ivraie (enivrante).

darner ['dɑ:nər], s. **1.** (*Pers.*) Repriseur, -euse, ravaudeur, -euse. **2.** (*a*) = DARNING-NEEDLE. (*b*) = DARNING-EGG.

dart¹ [dɑ:t], s. **1.** (*a*) Dard *m*, trait *m*, javelot *m*. (*b*) *Games:* Fléchette *f*. (*c*) *Dressm:* Pince *f*. **2.** Mouvement soudain en avant. **To make a sudden d. on sth.,** foncer, se précipiter sur qch.

dart². **1.** *v.tr.* Darder (des rayons); lancer (un harpon, un regard). **2.** *v.i.* Se précipiter, s'élancer, foncer (at, upon, sur). **To d. in, out, away,** entrer, sortir, partir, comme un trait.

Dartmoor ['dɑ:tmuər]. *Pr.n.* (*a*) *Geog:* Massif *m* de Dartmoor. (*b*) Prison *f* pour forçats.

dartre ['dɑ:tər], *s. Med:* Dartre *f*.

dartrous ['dɑ:trəs], *a.* Dartreux; herpétique.

dash¹ [dæʃ], s. **1.** Coup *m*, heurt *m*, choc *m*. **2.** Soupçon *m*, goutte *f* (de cognac, etc.); pointe *f* (de vanille, etc.); filet *m* (de vinaigre). **3.** D. of colour, tache *f* de couleur (dans le paysage, etc.); touche *f* de couleur (dans un tableau). **4.** Trait *m* (de plume, de l'alphabet Morse). *Typ:* (i) Tiret *m*; (ii) moins *m*. *Mth:* A d. (A′), a prime. **5.** (i) Attaque soudaine; (ii) course *f* à toute vitesse; élan *m*; ruée *f*. **To make a d. forward,** s'élancer en avant. **To make a d. at sth.,** se précipiter, se ruer, sur qch. **D. across the desert,** raid *m* à travers le désert. **6.** Élan, impétuosité *f*, fougue *f*, entrain *m*, allant *m*. *Mus:* **To play with d.,** jouer avec brio. **7.** F: **To cut a d.,** faire (brillante) figure; faire de l'effet; faire de l'épate.

dash². **1.** *v.tr.* (*a*) Lancer violemment (qch. contre qch.); jeter; flanquer (qch. par terre). **To d. sth. to pieces,** fracasser qch.; briser qch. en morceaux. **To d. one's head against sth.,** se casser la tête contre qch. (*b*) **To d. water over sth.,** jeter, flaquer, de l'eau sur qch. (*c*) **To d. sth. with mud,** éclabousser qch. de boue. **Dashed with colour,** rehaussé de touches de couleur. (*d*) Déconcerter, confondre (qn); anéantir, détruire (les espérances). **To d. s.o.'s spirits,** abattre le courage, l'entrain, de qn. (*e*) *int. F: Euphemism for* DAMN² (*b*). **2.** *v.i.* (*a*) **To d. against sth.,** se heurter, se jeter, contre qch. (*b*) **To d. at s.o., at sth.,** se précipiter, s'élancer, sur qn, qch. **To d. down the street,** descendre la rue à toute vitesse. **dash along,** *v.i.* Avancer, filer, à fond de train. **dash away.** **1.** *v.tr.* Écarter violemment (qch.). **2.** *v.i.* S'éloigner en coup de vent. **dash in,** *v.i.* Entrer en trombe, précipitamment. **dash off.** **1.** *v.tr.* Dessiner (un croquis) en un tour de main; bâcler, enlever (une lettre, etc.). **2.** *v.i.* = DASH AWAY 2. **dash out.** **1.** *v.tr.* **To d. out one's brains,** se fracasser la cervelle. **2.** *v.i.* S'élancer dehors. **dashed,** *a. Euphemism for* DAMNED 2. **dashing,** *a.* (*Of pers.*) Impétueux; plein d'élan; (*of horse*) fougueux. **D. young man,** beau cavalier. **-ly,** *adv.* (*a*) (S'habiller) avec une élégance tapageuse. (*b*) (Se conduire) avec fougue, avec brio.

dashboard ['dæʃbɔ:d], s. **1.** *Veh: A:* Garde-boue *m inv*, pare-boue *m inv*. **2.** *Aut:* Tablier *m*; tableau *m*. de bord.

dastard ['dæstəd], *s. Lit:* Lâche *m*.

dastardliness ['dæstədlinis], s. **1.** Lâcheté *f*. **2.** Infamie *f* (d'une action).

dastardly ['dæstədli], *a.* **1.** Lâche. **2.** (Crime, etc.) infâme.

data ['deitə], *s.pl. See* DATUM.

datable ['deitəbl], *a.* Datable, qu'on peut dater (from, à partir de).

date¹ [deit], s. *Bot:* **1.** Datte *f*. **2.** D.(-palm), dattier *m*.

date², s. Date *f*; (*on coins, books*) millésime *m*; (*of month*) quantième *m*. Under the d. of June 4th, en date du 4 juin. **To be up to d.,** être au niveau des derniers progrès; être dans le train; *F:* être à la page. **To be up to d. with one's work,** être à jour dans son travail. **To bring up to d.,** remettre au point (une question, etc.). **To bring, keep, one's diary up to d.,** mettre, tenir, son journal à jour. **Out of d.,** (i) (*of pers.*) de la vieille école; (ii) (*of thg*) démodé. *Com:* **Interest to d.,** intérêts à ce jour. **D. of a bill,** terme *m*, échéance *f*, d'un billet. **Three months after d.,** at three months' d., à trois mois de date. *F:* **To have a d. with s.o.,** avoir rendez-vous avec qn. **'date-cancel,** *v.tr.* Oblitérer (un timbre mobile) avec le timbre dateur. **'date line,** s. **1.** *Geog:* Ligne *f* de changement de date; **2.** *F:* Your latest d.l. is . . ., votre dernière limite est. . . . **'date-marker, -stamp,** s. Dateur *m*; timbre *m* à date.

date³. **1.** *v.tr.* (*a*) Dater (une lettre, etc.); composter (un billet de chemin de fer, etc.); (*Vintage wine bottles*) millésimer. *S.a.* LONG-DATED, SHORT-DATED. (*b*) Assigner une date à (une œuvre). (*c*) **To d. back,** antidater. (*d*) *U.S: F:* Prendre rendez-vous avec (qn). **2.** *v.i.* (*a*) **Church dating from, dating back to, the XIIIth century,** église qui remonte au XIIIe siècle, qui date du XIIIe siècle. (*b*) **His style has dated, is beginning to d.,** son style commence à dater. **dating,** s. Datation *f*.

dateless ['deitlis], *a.* Sans date.

dative ['deitiv], *a. & s. Gram:* Datif (*m*). **In the d.,** au datif.

datum, *pl.* **data** ['deitəm, 'deitə], s. **1.** Donnée *f*. **2.** (*a*) *Surv:* D.-line, ligne *f* de repère; ligne, plan *m*, de niveau. D.-plan, plan de comparaison. (*b*) *Mec.E: etc:* (Point *m* de) repère *m*. *S.a.* PROCESSING, REDUCTION 1.

daub¹ [dɔ:b], s. **1.** (*a*) Enduit *m*, barbouillage *m*. (*b*) *Const:* Torchis *m*, gobetage *m*. **2.** (*Picture*) Croûte *f*.

daub², *v.tr.* **1.** Barbouiller, enduire (with, de). **Wall daubed with clay,** mur enduit de torchis. **2.** *Art: F:* Peintur(lur)er (une toile).

dauber ['dɔ:bər], **daubster** ['dɔ:bstər], s. *Art: F:* Barbouilleur, -euse.

daughter ['dɔ:tər], *s.f.* Fille (par rapport au père et à la mère). **'daughter-in-law,** *s.f.* Belle-fille, *pl.* belles-filles; bru.

daughterly ['dɔ:təli], *a.* Filial, -als, -aux.

daunt [dɔ:nt], *v.tr.* Intimider, décourager. **Nothing daunted,** aucunement intimidé; sans se laisser abattre.

dauntless ['dɔ:ntlis], *a.* Intrépide. **-ly,** *adv.* Intrépidement.

dauntlessness ['dɔ:ntlisnis], s. Intrépidité *f*.

Dauphin, Dauphiness ['dɔ:fin, -inis], s. *Fr.Hist:* Dauphin, -ine.

davenport ['dævnpɔ:t], s. **1.** Petit bureau-pupitre secrétaire *m* de salon. **2.** *U.S:* Canapé-lit *m*, divan *m*.

davit ['dævit], s. *Nau:* Bossoir *m*, davier *m* (d'embarcation).

Davy Jones ['deivi'dʒounz]. *Pr.n. Nau: F:* **D. J.'s locker,** le port des navires perdus.

dawdle ['dɔ:dl]. **1.** *v.i.* Flâner, musarder, lambiner. **2.** *v.tr.* **To d. away one's time,** passer son temps à flâner; gaspiller le temps. **dawdling¹,** *a.* Flâneur, musard, lambin. **dawdling²,** s. Flânerie *f*, musardise *f*; traînerie *f*.

dawdler ['dɔ:dlər], s. Flâneur, -euse; lambin, -ine; traînard *m*.

dawn¹ [dɔ:n], s. **1.** Aube *f*, aurore *f*. **At d.,** au point du jour. **2.** Aube de la vie, de l'histoire; commencement *m* (de la civilisation); naissance *f* (d'une idée).

dawn², *v.i.* (*Of day*) Poindre; (commencer à) paraître; naître. **Day is dawning,** le jour se lève. **At length it dawned on me that . . .,** enfin il me vint à l'esprit que. . . . **The truth dawned on him,** la vérité se fit jour dans son esprit. **dawning,** *a.* (Jour, espoir) naissant.

day [dei], s. 1. (a) Jour m; (whole day in regard to work, etc.) journée f. It's a fine d., il fait beau aujourd'hui. To work d. and night, travailler nuit et jour. All d. (long), all the d., toute la journée. To work by the d., travailler à la journée. F: It's all in the day's work, ça fait partie de ma routine; j'en vois bien d'autres! Twice a d., deux fois par jour. Thiʳ d., ce jour-ci, aujourd'hui. This d. week, (d')aujourd'hui en huit. The d. before sth., la veille de qch. Two days before sth., l'avant-veille f de qch. The d. after (sth.), le lendemain (de qch.). Two days after, later, deux jours après; le surlendemain. Every other d., O: d. about, tous les deux jours. D. in d. out, d. after d., à longueur f de journée. D. after d., year after year, au fil des jours et des ans. D. by d., jour par jour; de jour en jour. From d. to d., de jour en jour. (b) To carry, win, the d., gagner la journée; remporter la victoire. F: Let's call it a d., we'd better call it a d., tenons-nous-en là. 2. (a) Before d., avant le jour. At break of d., au point du jour. (b) (Daylight) To travel by d., in the d., voyager le jour, de jour. It was broad d., il faisait grand jour. 3. (a) D. of the month, quantième m du mois. What is the d. of the month? c'est le combien aujourd'hui? One summer d., par un jour d'été. One d., some d., one of these (fine) days, un de ces (beaux) jours. I saw him the other d., je l'ai vu l'autre jour. He may arrive any d., il peut arriver d'un jour à l'autre. It is many a long d. since you did that, il y a beau jour que vous n'avez fait cela. Thursday is my (at-home) d., mon jour (de réception) est le jeudi. D. off, jour de congé (d'un employé). F: To name the d., fixer le jour du mariage. Prov: The better the d. the better the deed, bon jour bonne œuvre. S.a. TIME[1] 6. (b) Fête f. All Saints' D., (la fête de) la Toussaint. Easter D., le jour de Pâques. 4. The good old days, le bon vieux temps. In the days of . . ., au temps de . . ., du temps de. . . . In the days of old, autrefois; au temps jadis. In these days, in our days, de nos jours; de notre temps. I was a student in those days, j'étais étudiant à ce moment-là, à cette époque. Those were happy days, those were the days, c'était la bonne vie (alors). At, to, this (very) d., encore aujourd'hui. In days to come, dans un temps futur. Of other, former, days, d'autrefois. The man of the d., l'homme du jour. (Of theory, etc.) To have had its d., avoir fait son temps. **'day-blind**, a. Nyctalope. **'day-blindness**, s. Nyctalopie f. **'day-boarder**, s. Sch: Demi-pensionnaire mf. **'day-book**, s. Com: Journal m, -aux; main courante; brouillard m. **'day-boy, -girl**, s. Sch: Externe mf. **'day-dream[1]**, s. Rêverie f, rêvasserie f. **'day-dream[2]**, v.i. Rêver creux; rêvasser. **'day-dreaming**, s. Rêverie f, songerie f. **'day-dreamer**, s. Rêveur, -euse; songecreux m inv. **'day-labour**, s. Travail m à la journée. **'day-'labourer**, s. Journalier m; ouvrier m à la journée. **'day-nursery**, s. 1. Salle f des enfants. 2. Adm: Pouponnière f; garderie f (d'enfants). **'day-pupil**, s. Sch: Externe mf. **'day-shift**, s. Ind: Équipe f du jour. **'day-scholar**, s. O: Externe mf. **'day-school**, s. Externat m. **'day-temperature**, s. Meteor: Température diurne. **'day-time**, s. Le jour, la journée. In the d.-t., pendant la journée.

daybreak ['deibreik], s. Point m du jour; lever m du jour; aube f. At d., au jour levant.

daylight ['deilait], s. 1. Jour m; lumière f du jour. By d., de jour, le jour. In broad d., en plein jour; au grand jour. It is broad d., il fait grand jour. O: D.-saving time, l'heure f d'été. Before d., avant le jour. Attrib. De jour. D. bombing, bombardement m de jour. 2. Espace m libre; ouverture f; jour, intervalle m. F: To (begin to) see d. through a piece of work, (i) apercevoir la fin du travail; approcher du but; (ii) (commencer à) voir clair dans une affaire.

daylong ['deiloŋ]. 1. a. Qui dure toute la journée. 2. adv. Toute la journée, tout le long du jour.

daze[1] [deiz], s. Étourdissement m, stupéfaction f. To be in a d., être hébété, stupéfait.

daze[2], v.tr. 1. (a) (Of drug, etc.) Stupéfier, hébéter. (b) (Of blow) Étourdir. (c) F: Abasourdir, ahurir (qn). 2. = DAZZLE[2]. dazed, a. (a) Stupéfié (par un narcotique); hébété. (b) Tout étourdi (par un coup). (c) F: Abasourdi, ahuri, sidéré.

dazzle[1] ['dæzl], s. 1. Éblouissement m; aveuglement m. 2. Navy: Camouflage m.

dazzle[2], v.tr. Éblouir, aveugler. dazzling, a. Éblouissant, aveuglant. -ly, adv. D'une manière éblouissante. D. beautiful, d'une beauté éblouissante.

deacon ['di:kən], s. Ecc: 1. Diacre m. 2. (Presbyterian Ch.) Membre m du conseil de fabrique.

deaconess ['di:kənis], s.f. Diaconesse.

dead [ded]. I. a. 1. Mort. (a) He is d., il est mort, décédé. The d. man, woman, le mort, la morte. S.a. SHOE[1] 1. Prov: D. men tell no tales, morte la bête mort le venin. S.a. FLOG. To strike, kill, s.o. (stone) d., tuer qn raide. To drop down d., tomber mort. F: D. as a door-nail, as mutton, mort et bien mort. D. and gone, d. and buried, mort et enterré. D. to the world, mort pour le monde. F: D. and done for, flambé, fichu, fini. (Of regulation) To become a d. letter, tomber en désuétude. Post: D. letters, lettres tombées au rebut. D. language, langue morte. (Doigt) mort, engourdi par le froid. (Of limb) To go d., s'engourdir. 2. D. to reason, sourd à la raison. 3. D. coal, charbon éteint. D. colour, couleur terne. D. white, blanc mat. D. sound, son mat. D. well, puits perdu. El.E: D. wire, fil (i) hors courant, (ii) sans tension, sans courant. El: D. cell, pile épuisée, à plat. Typ: D. matter, matière à distribuer. 4. D. season, morte-saison f. D. period, période f d'inactivité. The d. hours, (i) la nuit; (ii) Ind: etc: les heures creuses. D. spring, ressort qui a perdu son élasticité. D. axle, essieu fixe. D. air-screw, hélice calée. Fb: D. ball, ballon mort. Ph: D. beat, oscillation amortie. 5. D. stop, arrêt brusque, halte subite. To come to a d. stop, s'arrêter net. Nau: D. calm, calme plat. D. silence, silence de mort. D. secret, profond secret. D. level, niveau parfait. To be d. on time, être à la minute. D. loss, perte sèche. F: A dead loss, un propre à rien, un crétin. To be in d. earnest, être tout à fait sérieux. He's a d. shot, il ne manque, ne rate, jamais son coup. Golf: (Of ball) To lie d., être au bord du trou. S.a. CERT, SPIT[1] 1. II. dead, s. 1. pl. The d., les morts m; les trépassés m. To rise from the d., ressusciter d'entre les morts. 2. At d. of night, au milieu de la nuit. In the d. of winter, au (plus) fort de l'hiver. III. dead, adv. (a) Absolument. D. drunk, ivre mort. D. tired, mort de fatigue; éreinté. D. sure, absolument certain. F: D. broke, fauché. To go d. slow, aller au grand ralenti. To stop d., s'arrêter net, F: s'arrêter pile. (c) (Of pers.) To be d. against sth., être absolument opposé à qch. D. smooth surface, surface parfaitement plane. D. on time, à l'heure tapante, à l'heure pile. **'dead(-and)-a'live**, a. (Endroit) mort, triste, sans animation. **'dead-'beat[1]**, attrib. a. El: (Instrument) apériodique. **'dead-'beat[2]**. 1. a. F: Épuisé, éreinté, fourbu. 2. s. U.S: P: (a) Clochard m. (b) Chevalier m d'industrie; filou m. **'dead-'centre**, s. 1. Mch: Point mort (du piston). 2. (Of lathe) Pointe f de la poupée mobile. **dead-'end**, s. Cul-de-sac m. **'dead-fall**, s. (Piège m) assommoir m; traquenard m. **dead(-)line**, s. Délimitation f; ligne f. de repère Tomorrow is our d.(-)l., demain c'est notre date f limite, notre dernière limite. **'dead(-)lock**, s. 1. Serrure f à pêne dormant. 2. Impasse f; situation f inextricable. **'dead 'march**, s. Mus: Marche f funèbre. **'dead(-)pan[1]**, esp. U.S: F: 1. (a) a. (Visage) figé. (b) s. (i) Pince-sans-rire m. Master of d. p., roi m du pince-sans-rire. (ii) Un visage figé. **'dead(-)pan[2]**, v.i. esp. U.S: Être pince-sans-rire. **'dead-'reckoning**, s. Nau: Av: Estime f (du point); route f à l'estime. Latitude by d.-r., latitude estimée. **'dead-'weight**, s. 1. Poids mort, poids accablant (de dettes, etc.). 2. Nau: Port m en lourd. **'dead-wood**, s. Bois mort. To cut out the d.-w. from the staff, élaguer le personnel.

deaden ['dedn], v.tr. Amortir (un coup); assourdir, étouffer (un son); émousser, assoupir, aveulir (les sens). To d. one's footsteps, ouater, feutrer, ses pas. deadening, s. Amortissement m; assourdissement m (du bruit, d'un son).

deadliness ['dedlinis], s. Nature mortelle (d'un poison, etc.).

deadly ['dedli]. **1.** *a.* (*a*) (*Of poison, blow, etc.*) Mortel. **D. hatred,** haine mortelle, implacable. **D. insult,** insulte mortelle. **The seven d. sins,** les sept péchés capitaux. (*b*) = DEATHLIKE. (*c*) **Her life was d.,** elle s'ennuyait à mourir. **To be in d. earnest,** être tout à fait sérieux. **2.** *adv.* Mortellement. **D. pale,** d'une pâleur mortelle. **It was d. cold,** il faisait un froid de loup. *S.a.* DULL¹ 5.

deadness ['dednis], *s.* Torpeur *f*; engourdissement *m* (des membres); stagnation *f* (des affaires).

deaf [def], *a.* Sourd. **D. and dumb,** sourd-muet. **D. as a door-post,** sourd comme un pot. **To turn a d. ear to s.o.,** faire la sourde oreille à ce que dit qn; refuser d'écouter qn. **-ly,** *adv.* Comme un sourd. **'deaf-'mute,** *s.* Sourd-muet, *f.* sourde-muette.

deafen ['defn], *v.tr.* Assourdir (qn); rendre (qn) sourd. **deafening,** *a.* Assourdissant.

deafness ['defnis], *s.* Surdité *f.*

deal¹ [di:l], *s.* (*Usu.* **a great d., a good d.**) (Grande) quantité; beaucoup. **A good d. to do,** bien des choses à faire. **That's saying a good d.,** ce n'est pas peu dire. *adv.* **He is a good d. better,** il va beaucoup mieux. **He is a great d. wiser than you,** il est de beaucoup plus sage que vous.

deal², *s.* **1.** *Cards:* La donne; la main. **Whose d. is it?** à qui de faire, de donner? **2.** *Com:* **F:** Affaire *f*, marché *m.* **To do a d. with s.o.,** conclure un marché avec qn. **Hole and corner d.,** affaire conclue sous (la) main. **F: To give s.o. a square d.,** agir loyalement envers qn. **F: To give s.o. a raw d.,** en faire voir de dures à qn; **it's a raw d.,** c'est dur à avaler. *Pej:* **D. between parties,** tractation *f* entre partis.

deal³, *v.* (**dealt** [delt]; **dealt**) I. *v.tr.* **1.** **To d. out gifts,** distribuer, répartir, partager, des dons (**to, among, entre**). **2.** **To d. a blow,** donner, porter, allonger, asséner, un coup (**at, à**). **3.** Donner, distribuer (les cartes). II. **deal,** *v.i.* **1.** (*a*) **To (have to) d. with s.o.,** avoir affaire à, avec, qn. **Man easy to d. with,** homme commode, accommodant. (*b*) **To d. with a subject,** traiter, s'occuper, d'un sujet. **2.** (*a*) **To d. with a piece of business,** conclure, terminer, une affaire. **To d. with a difficulty,** venir à bout d'une difficulté. (*b*) **To d. with a culprit,** disposer d'un coupable; faire justice à un coupable. **I know how to d. with him,** je sais comment il faut le traiter. **To d. well, badly, by s.o.,** en user bien, mal, avec qn. **3.** *Com:* **To d. with s.o.,** traiter, négocier, avec qn. **To d. in leather,** faire le commerce des cuirs. **To d. in politics,** se mêler de politique. **4.** *Cards:* La donne; donner; *F:* faire. **dealing,** *s.* **1.** **D.** (**out**), distribution *f* (de dons, etc.); distribution, donne *f* (de cartes). **2.** *pl.* (*a*) **To have dealings with s.o.,** avoir des relations, des rapports, entretenir des relations, avec qn. (*b*) *Pej:* Accointances *f*, tractations *f* (**with,** avec); tripotage *m.* **Underhand dealings,** menées sourdes, sournoises. **3.** Conduite *f*, procédé *m.* **Fair, square, dealing(s),** loyauté *f*, honnêteté *f* (en affaires). *S.a.* DOUBLE-DEALING.

deal⁴, *s.* **1.** (*a*) Madrier *m.* (*b*) Planche *f* (à planchéier). **2.** Bois *m* de pin ou de sapin; *esp.* **white d.,** sapin blanc, bois blanc.

dealer ['di:lər], *s.* **1.** *Cards:* Donneur *m.* **2.** *Com:* (*a*) Négociant *m* (**in,** en); distributeur *m* (**in,** de). (*b*) Marchand, -ande, fournisseur *m* (**in,** de). **Record d.,** disquaire *m.* (*c*) *St.Exch:* = JOBBER 3.

dean [di:n], *s.* *Ecc: Sch:* Doyen *m.*

deanery ['di:nəri], *s.* *Ecc:* **1.** Doyenné *m.* **2.** Résidence *f* du doyen.

deanship ['di:nʃip], *s.* *Ecc:* Décanat *m*, doyenné *m.* *Sch:* (*Of a faculty*) Doyennat *m.*

dear ['diər]. I. *a.* (*a*) Cher (**to, à**). **To hold s.o. d.,** chérir, aimer, qn. *F:* **My d. fellow,** mon cher; mon ami. **D. Madam,** Madame, Mademoiselle. **D. Sir, D. Mr Smith,** Cher Monsieur. **To run for d. life,** courir de toutes ses forces. (*b*) Cher, coûteux. (*Of food, etc.*) **To get d.,** devenir plus cher, enchérir, renchérir. **-ly,** *adv.* **1.** Cher, chèrement. **You shall pay d. for this,** cela vous coûtera cher. **2. D. loved,** tendrement aimé(e), bien aimé(e). **He d. loves his house,** il est fort attaché à sa maison. II. **dear,** *s.* Cher *f* chère. **My d.,** cher ami, mon ami(e). **Be a d., and . . . ,** sois gentil(le) et . . . III. **dear,** *adv.* **1.** (Vendre, payer) cher. **2. He sold his life d.,** il vendit chèrement sa vie.

IV. dear, *int.* **D. d! d. me!** mon Dieu, mon Dieu! **Oh d.!** (i) diable! (ii) hélas!

dearie ['diəri], *s.* *P:* (Mon petit) chéri, (ma petite) chérie.

dearness ['diənis], *s.* **1.** Cherté *f* (des vivres, etc.). **2.** (*a*) Tendresse *f.* (*b*) Degré *m* d'affection.

dearth [də:θ], *s.* Disette *f*, pénurie *f* (de vivres, de livres, etc.); dénuement *m*, stérilité *f* (d'idées). **D. of man-power,** manque *m* de main-d'œuvre.

death [deθ], *s.* **1.** Mort *f*; *Lit:* trépas *m.* **To die a violent d.,** mourir de mort violente. *Hist:* **The Black D.,** la peste noire. **Till d.,** pour la vie. **Faithful unto d.,** fidèle jusqu'au tombeau. *F:* **You will catch your d. if you go out in this weather,** vous allez attraper la mort si vous sortez par ce temps. *F:* **He'll be the d. of me,** (i) il me fera mourir; (ii) il me fait mourir de rire. *F:* **To be d. on sth.,** ne pas souffrir qch. **To put s.o. to d.,** mettre qn à mort; exécuter qn. **To do s.o. to d.,** faire souffrir une mort cruelle à qn; *F:* égorger qn. *F:* **Meat done to d.,** viande carbonisée. **Fashion that has been done to d.,** mode qui a été copiée jusqu'à la nausée. **Wounded to the d.,** blessé à mort. **To be sick (un)to d.,** être malade à mourir. *F:* **To be sick to d. of sth.,** en avoir plein le dos. **To drink oneself to d.,** se tuer à force de boire. **To be in at the d.,** (i) *Ven:* être à la curée, à l'hallali; (ii) *F:* être présent au bon moment, pour le bouquet. **2.** *Jur:* Décès *m.* **To notify a d.,** notifier un décès. **D. notices** (*in newspaper*), avis *m* mortuaires. *Journ:* **Deaths,** Nécrologie *f.* **3.** La mort. **To be at death's door,** être à toute extrémité; être à l'article de la mort, être voisin(e) de la mort. **'death-bed,** *s.* Lit *m* de mort. **D.-b. confession,** aveu fait au lit de mort. **'death-bell,** *s.* Glas *m.* **'death-blow,** *s.* Coup mortel, fatal. **'death-chamber,** *s.* (*a*) Chambre *f* mortuaire. (*b*) *U.S:* Salle *f* d'exécution (dans une prison). **'death-duty,** *s.* *Adm:* Droit *m* de mutation par décès; droit de succession. **'death-mask,** *s.* Masque *m* mortuaire. **'death-rate,** *s.* (Taux *m* de la) mortalité. **Infant d.-r.,** mortalité infantile. **'death-rattle,** *s.* Râle *m* (de la mort). **'death-roll,** *s.* Liste *f* des morts; nécrologe *m.* **'death's-head,** *s.* Tête *f* de mort. **'death-trance,** *s.* *Med:* Léthargie *f.* **'death-trap,** *s.* Endroit dangereux pour la vie; casse-cou *m inv.* *Aut:* Croisement dangereux. **'death-warrant,** *s.* *Jur:* Ordre *m* d'exécution; arrêt *m* de mort. **'death-watch (-beetle),** *s.* *Ent:* Horloge *f* de la mort; vrillette *f.* **'death-wound,** *s.* Blessure mortelle.

deathless ['deθlis], *a.* Impérissable, immortel. **-ly,** *adv.* Immortellement.

deathlessness ['deθlisnis], *s.* Immortalité *f.*

deathlike ['deθlaik], *a.* De mort; (teint) cadavéreux.

deathly ['deθli]. *Lit:* **1.** *a.* (*a*) = DEADLY 1 (*a*). (*b*) = DEATHLIKE. **2.** *adv.* **D. pale,** d'une pâleur mortelle.

de-atomization ['di:ˌætəmai'zeiʃn], *s.* Désatomisation *f.*

de-atomize ['di:ˈætəmaiz], *v.tr.* Désatomiser.

debacle [dei'ba:kl], *s.* Débâcle *f.*

debar [di'ba:r], *v.tr.* (**debarred**) **1.** **To d. s.o. from sth.,** exclure, priver, qn de qch. **To d. s.o. from doing sth.,** défendre, interdire, à qn de faire qch. **2. To d. s.o. a right,** refuser un droit à qn; priver qn d'un droit.

debase [di'beis], *v.tr.* **1.** Avilir, ravilir, ravaler, dégrader (qn); rabaisser, trivialiser (son style). **2.** (*a*) Altérer (la monnaie). (*b*) Déprécier (la monnaie). **debasing,** *a.* Avilissant.

debasement [di'beismənt], *s.* **1.** Avilissement *m*, dégradation *f.* **2.** Altération *f* (des monnaies).

debatable [di'beitəbl], *a.* Contestable, discutable; (frontière, etc.) en litige.

debate¹ [di'beit], *s.* Débat *m*, discussion *f*; conférence *f* contradictoire. **The question in d., under d.,** la question en discussion.

debate². 1. *v.tr.* Débattre contradictoirement, discuter, agiter (une question, etc.). **A much debated question,** une question fort controversée. **I was debating in my mind whether . . . ,** je délibérais si . . . . **2.** *v.i.* Discuter, disputer (**with s.o. on sth.,** avec qn sur qch.). **debating,** *attrib.a.* **D. society,** société *f* d'exercices oratoires, *F:* parlot(t)e *f.* **D. point,** matière *f* à controverse.

debater [di'beitər], *s.* Orateur *m* (qui brille dans les débats).

debauch[1] [di'bɔːtʃ], s. La débauche.

debauch[2], v.tr. Débaucher, corrompre (qn); vicier (le goût). **debauched**, a. Débauché, corrompu.

debauchee [,dibɔː'tʃiː], s. Débauché m.

debaucher [di'bɔːtʃər], s. Débaucheur, -euse; corrupteur, -trice (des gens, des mœurs); séducteur m (de femmes).

debauchery [di'bɔːtʃəri], s. Débauche f; dérèglement m de mœurs.

debenture [di'ben(t)ʃər], s. Fin: Obligation f. Mortgage d., obligation hypothécaire. **de'benture-'holder**, s. Fin: Porteur, -euse, d'obligations; obligataire m.

debilitate [di'biliteit], v.tr. Débiliter.

debility [di'biliti], s. Med: Débilité f; affaiblissement m.

debit[1] ['debit], s. Book-k: Débit m, doit m. To enter sth. to the d.(-side) of an account, porter qch. au débit, au doit, d'un compte. D. balance, solde débiteur. Account showing a d. balance, compte déficitaire.

debit[2], v.tr. Book-k: 1. Débiter (un compte). 2. To d. s.o. with a sum, inscrire, porter, une somme au débit de qn.

debonair [,debə'nɛər], a. Lit: Jovial, -aux.

debouch [di'bautʃ], v.i. Déboucher (into, dans).

debouchment [di'bautʃmənt], s. 1. Débouchement m (de troupes, d'un fleuve). 2. Débouché m, sortie f (d'un défilé, etc.).

Debrett [də'bret]. Pr.n. Debrett's (Peerage), almanach m nobiliaire.

debris ['debriː], s. (a) Débris mpl; détritus mpl (géologiques). (b) (Of buildings, etc.) Décombres mpl.

debt [det], s. Dette f; créance f. Bad debts, mauvaises créances, créances véreuses. To be in d., être endetté; avoir des dettes. To be head over ears, up to the eyes, in d., être criblé de dettes; avoir des dettes par-dessus la tête. How much am I in your d.? Combien vous dois-je? I shall always be in your d., je serai toujours votre obligé; je vous serai toujours redevable. To be twenty francs in d., avoir vingt francs de dettes. To be out of d., être quitte de dettes; n'avoir plus de dettes. Funded d., consolidated d., fonds consolidés. Floating d., dette courante. National D., Dette publique. To pay the d. of, to, nature, payer sa dette, le tribut, à l'humanité, à la nature. **'debt-collector**, s. Com: Agent m de recouvrements.

debtor ['detər], s. 1. Débiteur, -trice. I am your d. for £100, je vous suis redevable de £100. 2. Book-k: D. side, débit m, doit m. D. account, compte débiteur. D. and creditor account, compte par doit et avoir.

debunk [di'bʌŋk], v.tr. P: Découronner, détrôner (un grand nom); déboulonner (qn).

debut ['deibjuː; 'deˈbyː], s. Début m; (in society) entrée f dans le monde.

debutante ['deibjuː'tɑ̃ː(n)t, deby'tãt], s.f. Débutante.

decade ['dekəd, di'keid], s. 1. Période f de dix ans, décade f; décennie f. 2. Ecc: Dizain m de chapelet.

decadence ['dekəd(ə)ns], s. Décadence f.

decadent ['dekəd(ə)nt], a. En décadence; décadent.

decaffeinate [di'kæfiːineit], **decaffeinize** [diˈkæfiːinaiz], v.tr. Décaféiner.

decagon ['dekəgən], s. Geom: Décagone m.

decagram(me) ['dekəgræm], s. Meas: Décagramme m.

decalcification ['diːˌkælsifiˈkeiʃən], s. Med: Décalcification f.

decalcify [di'kælsifai], v.tr. Med: Décalcifier.

decalitre ['dekəˌliːtər], s. Meas: Décalitre m.

Decalogue (The) [ðəˈdekələg], s. Ecc: Décalogue m.

decametre ['dekəˌmiːtər], s. Meas: Décamètre m.

decamp [di'kæmp], v.i. 1. Mil: Lever le camp. 2. F: Décamper, filer.

decant [di'kænt], v.tr. Décanter, transvaser (un liquide); tirer (un liquide) au clair.

decantation [,diːkæn'teiʃ(ə)n], s. Décantation f, décantage m; transvasement m.

decanter [di'kæntər], s. (a) Carafe f (à liqueur, à vin). (b) Transvaseur m (personne ou appareil).

decapitate [di'kæpiteit], v.tr. Décapiter; couper la tête à (qn).

decapitation [di,kæpi'teiʃ(ə)n], s. Décapitation f; décollation f.

Decapoda [dekə'poudə], s.pl. Crust: Décapodes m.

decarbonization [diːˌkɑːbənaiˈzeiʃ(ə)n], s. I.C.E: Décarbonisation f, décalaminage m, décrassage m.

decarbonize [diːˈkɑːbənaiz], v.tr. 1. Metall: Ind: Décarburer (la fonte, etc.). 2. I.C.E: Décarboniser, décalaminer (un cylindre). **decarbonizing**, s. Décalaminage m.

decarburize [diːˈkɑːbju(ə)raiz], v.tr. Ind: = DECARBONIZE 1.

decasyllable ['dekəsiləbl], s. Pros: Décasyllabe m.

decay[1] [di'kei], s. 1. Décadence f (d'une famille, d'un pays); déclin m (de la beauté, d'une fortune); délabrement m (d'un bâtiment). Senile d., affaiblissement m sénile. To fall into d., (of house) tomber en ruine, se délabrer; (of state) tomber en décadence; (of custom) tomber en désuétude. To be in a state of d., être en ruine, en décadence. 2. (a) Pourriture f, corruption f; putréfaction f; altération f (du caoutchouc, etc.). (b) Carie f (des dents).

decay[2]. 1. v.i. (a) Tomber en décadence; (of building) tomber en ruine; se délabrer; (of race, plant) dépérir; (of empire) décliner; (of custom) se perdre. (b) (Of meat, fruit) Se gâter, s'altérer, s'avarier, pourrir; (of teeth) se carier. 2. v.tr. Pourrir (le bois, etc.); carier (les dents). **decayed**, a. 1. (Famille) déchue, ruinée; (fleur, beauté) passée, flétrie; (maison, fortune) délabrée. D. gentlewoman, dame (bien née) tombée dans la gêne. 2. (Bois) pourri; (fruit) gâté. D. tooth, dent gâtée, cariée.

Deccan ['dekən]. Pr.n. Geog: Deccan, Dekkan m.

decease[1] [di'siːs], s. Jur: Adm: Décès m.

decease[2], v.i. Jur: Adm: Décéder. **deceased**. 1. a. (a) Décédé. John Smith, d., (le) feu John Smith. Mary Smith, d., feu Mary Smith. (b) D'un décédé. D. estate, succession f. 2. s. Le défunt, la défunte. The house of the d., la maison mortuaire.

decedent [də'siːdənt], a. & s. U.S: = DECEASED.

deceit [di'siːt], s. Tromperie f, duperie f, fourberie f. A piece of d., une supercherie.

deceitful [di'siːtf(u)l], a. Trompeur, -euse; fourbe; faux, f. fausse; (regard) mensonger. -**fully**, adv. 1. Frauduleusement; par supercherie. 2. Faussement; avec duplicité.

deceitfulness [di'siːtf(u)lnis], s. Nature trompeuse; fausseté f.

deceive [di'siːv], v.tr. Tromper, abuser (qn); en imposer à (qn). To d. oneself, se tromper, s'abuser. To d. oneself with a fond hope, se leurrer d'un espoir. I thought my eyes were deceiving me, F: j'ai cru avoir la berlue. **deceiving**, a. Trompeur, -euse; décevant. -**ly**, adv. Trompeusement.

decelerate [,diː'seləreit], v.i. Aut: etc: Ralentir; modérer son allure; freiner.

deceleration ['diːˌseləˈreiʃən], s. 1. Ralentissement m (des trains, etc.). 2. Mec: Aut: etc: Décélération f; freinage m.

December [di'sembər], s. Décembre m. In D., au mois de décembre, en décembre. (On) the first, the seventh, of D., le premier, le sept, décembre.

decency ['diːsnsi], s. 1. Décence f, bienséance f (de costume, etc.). 2. Bienséance, convenance(s) f(pl), décence, honnêteté f. The decencies, common d., les convenances (sociales); le respect humain. 3. (Sense of) d., pudeur f.

decennial [di'senjəl], a. Décennal, -aux. -**ally**, adv. Tous les dix ans.

decent ['diːsnt], a. 1. (a) Bienséant, convenable. (b) Décent, honnête, modeste, pudique. F: Are you d.? Es-tu habillé (convenablement)? 2. Passable; assez bon. To have a d. competence, avoir une honnête aisance. F: The food is d. enough, la nourriture est convenable. 3. F: A very d. (sort of) fellow, un très bon garçon; un brave garçon. Quite d. people, des gens comme il faut. F: D.-sized house, maison d'une grandeur raisonnable. -**ly**, adv. 1. Décemment, convenablement. 2. Passablement; assez bien.

decentralization [diːˌsentrəlaiˈzeiʃ(ə)n], s. Décentralisation (administrative, etc.).

decentralize [diː'sentrəlaiz], v.tr. Décentraliser. **decentralizing**, a. Décentralisateur, -trice.

decentre [diː'sentər], v.tr. Opt: Ph: etc: Décentrer. **decentring**, s. Décentrage m, décentration f; décentrement m.

deception [di'sepʃ(ə)n], s. **1.** Tromperie f, duperie f; fraude f. **2.** (Piece of) d., supercherie f.

deceptive [di'septiv], a. (Of thg, appearance) Trompeur, -euse; décevant, mensonger. **-ly,** adv. Trompeusement, mensongèrement.

deceptiveness [di'septivnis], s. Caractère mensonger, trompeur (d'un mirage, etc.).

dechristianize [di:'kristjənaiz], v.tr. Déchristianiser (qn).

decibel ['desibel], s. Ph: Décibel m.

decide [di'said]. **1.** v.tr. (a) Décider (une question, une querelle); trancher (une question); juger (un différend); statuer sur (une affaire). (b) Décider de (qch.). To d. s.o.'s fate, décider du sort de qn. Nothing has been decided yet, il n'y a encore rien de décidé. (c) To d. s.o. to do sth., décider qn à faire qch. (d) To d. to do sth., se décider, se résoudre, à faire qch.; décider, résoudre, de faire qch. It was decided to await his reply, on décida d'attendre sa réponse. I have decided what I shall do, mon parti est pris. **2.** v.i. To d. (up)on sth., se décider à qch. To d. on doing sth., se décider à, décider de, faire qch. To d. upon a day, fixer un jour. To d. for, in favour of, s.o., se décider pour, en faveur de, qn. **decided,** a. **1.** (a) They are quite d. about it, ils sont tout à fait décidés (là-dessus). (b) (Of opinion) Arrêté; (of manner) décidé. In a d. tone, d'un ton net, résolu, tranchant. A d. refusal, un refus catégorique. **2.** (Of improvement, etc.) Incontestable. A d. difference, une différence marquée. **-ly,** adv. **1.** (Agir, répondre) résolument, avec décision. **2.** Incontestablement, décidément. **deciding,** a. Décisif.

decidedness [di'saididnis], s. Esprit m de décision.

deciduous [di'sidjuəs], a. Caduc, f. caduque.

decigram(me) ['desigræm], s. Meas: Décigramme m.

decilitre ['desi,li:tər], s. Meas: Décilitre m.

decimal ['desim(ə)l]. **1.** a. Décimal, -aux. Mth: D. point = virgule f. **2.** s. Décimale f. Recurring d., fraction f périodique. Correct to five places of decimals, exact jusqu'à la cinquième décimale.

decimalization [desiməli'zeiʃ(ə)n], s. Décimalisation f.

decimate ['desimeit], v.tr. Décimer (des mutinés, etc.).

decimation [,desi'meiʃ(ə)n], s. Décimation f.

decimetre ['desimi:tər], s. Meas: Décimètre m.

decipher [di'saifər], v.tr. Déchiffrer; transcrire en clair (une dépêche chiffrée). **deciphering,** s. Déchiffrement m; transcription f en clair.

decipherable [di'saif(ə)rəbl], a. Déchiffrable.

decision [di'siʒ(ə)n], s. **1.** (a) Décision f (d'une question); délibération f (d'une assemblée). (b) Décision, jugement m, arrêt m. **2.** Décision, résolution f. To come to, reach, a d., arriver à, prendre une décision; prendre un parti. To abide by one's d., s'en tenir à sa décision. **3.** Résolution (de caractère); fermeté f, décision.

decisive [di'saisiv], a. **1.** Décisif; (of experiment) concluant. **2.** (a) (Ton) tranchant, net. (b) = DECIDED 2. **-ly,** adv. Décisivement.

deck¹ [dek], s. **1.** (a) Nau: Pont m. (On aircraft carrier) Flight d., pont d'envol. Aft(er)-d., pont arrière. Lower d., pont inférieur; premier pont. Upper d., pont supérieur. Forecastle d., (pont de) gaillard m avant. Orlop d., faux-pont m. (On train-ferry) Train d., pont des voies. To come, go, on d., monter sur le pont. Navy: To clear the decks (for action), faire le branle-bas (de combat). The lower-d. ratings, F: the lower d., le personnel non officier. Upper-d. ratings, hommes du pont. (b) Top d. (of bus, etc.) impériale f. **2.** Civ.E: Tablier m; plancher m (d'un pont). **3.** U.S: D. of cards, jeu m de cartes. 'deck-cargo, s. Pontée f. 'deck-chair, s. Transatlantique m; F: transa(t) m. 'deck-hand, s. Homme m de pont, matelot m de pont. 'deck-house, s. Navy: Rouf m, roufle m. 'deck-land, v.i. Navy: Av: Apponter. 'deck-landing, s. Navy: Appontage m. 'deck-light, s. Nau: Claire-voie f (dans le pont). 'deck-load, s. Pontée f.

deck², v.tr. **1.** Parer, orner, agrémenter (with, de). To d. oneself out, s'endimancher; se mettre sur son trente et un. S.a. FLAG¹ 1. **2.** N.Arch: To d. a ship, ponter un navire. **-decked,** a. Nau: Two-, three-d., à deux, à trois, ponts. **decking,** s. **1.** D. (out), décoration f. **2.** Pontage m (d'un navire). **3.** Coll: (Les) ponts m (d'un navire).

-decker ['dekər], s. Nau: A three-d., un vaisseau à trois ponts; un trois-ponts. S.a. DOUBLE-DECKER.

deckle-edged ['dekl'edʒd], a. (Papier) à bords non ébarbés, à bords déchiquetés.

declaim [di'kleim]. **1.** v.i. Déclamer (against, contre). **2.** v.tr. Déclamer.

declamation ['deklə'meiʃ(ə)n], s. Déclamation f.

declamatory [di'klæmət(ə)ri], a. (Style) déclamatoire.

declaration [,deklə'reiʃ(ə)n], s. (a) Déclaration f. Customs d., déclaration de, en, douane. (b) Cards: Annonce f.

declare [di'kleər]. **1.** v.tr. (a) Déclarer (sth. to s.o., qch. à qn). He declared he had seen nothing, il déclara, affirma, n'avoir rien vu. To d. war, déclarer la guerre (on, against, à). (At the customs) Have you anything to d.? avez-vous quelque chose à déclarer? S.a. POLL¹ 2. (b) Pred. To d. s.o. guilty, déclarer qn coupable. To d. s.o. king, déclarer qn roi. To d. the bargain off, rompre le marché. (c) Cards: To d. trumps, appeler l'atout. Abs. To d., annoncer son jeu. To d. one's hand, avouer ses intentions. (d) To d. oneself, (i) prendre parti; (ii) (of suitor) faire sa déclaration. (Of disease) To d. itself, se déclarer, éclater. **2.** v.i. To d. for, against, sth., se déclarer, se prononcer, pour, contre, qch. **declared,** a. Ouvert, avoué, déclaré.

declaredly [di'kleərədli], adv. Ouvertement.

declarer [di'kleərər], s. **1.** Déclarateur, -trice. **2.** Cards: Demandeur, -euse.

déclassé [dei'klæsei], a. Déclassé, déchu (de sa classe sociale).

declension [di'klenʃ(ə)n], s. Gram: Déclinaison f.

declinable [di'klainəbl], a. Gram: Déclinable.

declination [,dekli'neiʃ(ə)n], s. **1.** Déclination f. Astr: Déclinaison f. **2.** U.S: Refus m (courtois, mais formel).

decline¹ [di'klain], s. **1.** Déclin m (du jour, d'un empire); baisse f (de prix). To be on the d., être sur le déclin; décliner; (of pers.) être sur le retour (d'âge); (of prices) être en baisse. **2.** A: Maladie f de langueur; consomption f, phtisie f. To go into a d., entrer en consomption.

decline² [di'klain]. **I.** v.tr. **1.** (a) Refuser courtoisement (une invitation); décliner (un honneur). Abs. S'excuser. (b) Refuser; repousser (l'intervention de qn). To d. to do sth., refuser de faire qch. **2.** Gram: Décliner (un nom, etc.). **II.** decline, v.i. **1.** (Of ground, etc.) S'incliner; être en pente. **2.** (a) (Of sun, etc.) Décliner; (of day) tirer à sa fin. (b) (Of health, etc.) Décliner, baisser; (of empire) tomber en décadence; (of prices) baisser; être en baisse. **declining,** a. Sur son déclin. D. sun, soleil couchant. In one's d. years, au déclin de la vie.

declivitous [di'klivitəs], a. Déclive; escarpé.

declivity [di'kliviti], s. Déclivité f, pente f.

declutch [di:'klʌtʃ], v.i. Aut: Débrayer.

decoction [di'kɔkʃən], s. **1.** (Process) Décoction f. **2.** (Resultant liquid) Décoction. Pharm: Décocté m.

decode ['di:'koud], v.tr. Déchiffrer, transcrire en clair (une dépêche). **decoding,** s. Déchiffrement m; transcription f en clair.

decoder ['di:'koudə], s. **1.** Mil: (Officier) déchiffreur. **2.** Décrypteur.

decoke [di:'kouk], v.tr. F: = DECARBONIZE 2.

décolletage [dei'kɔltə:ʒ], s. Dressm: Décolleté m.

décolleté [dei'kɔltei]. **1.** a. (Vêtement) décolleté. **2.** s. Décolletage.

decolonization [di:,kɔlənai'zeiʃən], s. Décolonisation f.

decolo(u)rization [di:,kʌlərai'zeiʃən], s. Décoloration f.

decolo(u)rize [di:'kʌləraiz], v.tr. Décolorer. **decolo(u)rizing,** a. Décolorant.

decomposable ['di:kəm'pouzəbl], a. (a) Décomposable (into, en). (b) Ch: (Of double salts) Dédoublable.

decompose ['di:kəm'pouz]. **1.** v.tr. (a) Décomposer, analyser (la lumière, etc.). (b) Décomposer, corrompre (la matière). **2.** v.i. (a) Se décomposer. (b) Entrer en décomposition; pourrir.

decomposite [di:'kɔmpəzit], a. Bot: Décomposé (feuilles, etc.).

decomposition ['di:,kɔmpə'ziʃ(ə)n], s. Décomposition f. **1.** Resolution f en parties simples. **2.** Désintégration f; putréfaction f.

decompress [di:kəm'pres], *v.tr.* Décomprimer (un gaz, etc.).

decompression [ˌdi:kəm'preʃ(ə)n], *s. Mch: etc:* Décompression *f Av:* Décompensation *f.*

decompressor [ˌdi:kəm'presər], *s. I.C.E:* Décompresseur *m.*

deconsecrate [di:'kɔnsikreit], *v.tr.* Séculariser, désaffecter (une église).

deconsecration ['di:ˌkɔnsi'kreiʃ(ə)n], *s.* Sécularisation *f*, désaffectation *f.*

decontaminate ['di:kən'tæmineit], *v.tr.* 1. Désinfecter. 2. Décontaminer.

decontamination ['di:kənˌtæmi'neiʃən], *s.* 1. Désinfection *f.* 2. Décontamination *f.*

decontrol [ˌdi:kən'troul], *v.tr.* (a) Libérer (le commerce, etc.) des contraintes du gouvernement. (b) *Adm:* To d. the price of meat, détaxer la viande. (c) *Adm:* Decontrolled road, route sur laquelle on a supprimé la limite de vitesse.

décor ['deikɔ:], *s. Th: etc:* Décor *m.*

decorate ['dekəreit], *v.tr.* 1. (a) Décorer, orner, agrémenter (with, de); pavoiser (une rue). (b) Peindre (et tapisser), décorer (un appartement). *Arch:* Decorated style = style flamboyant. 2. Médailler, décorer (un soldat, etc.).

decoration [ˌdekə'reiʃ(ə)n], *s.* 1. (a) Décoration *f*; parement *m* (d'une façade); pavoisement *m* (des rues). (b) Remise *f* d'une décoration (à qn). 2. (a) *Usu. pl.* (Les) décorations (d'une ville en fête, etc.); décor *m* (d'un appartement, etc.). (b) Décoration, médaille *f.*

decorative ['dek(ə)rətiv], *a.* Décoratif, -ive.

decorator ['dekəreitər], *s.* Décorateur *m.* (House) d., peintre décorateur (d'appartements); tapissier *m.*

decorous ['dekərəs], *a.* Bienséant, convenable; comme il faut.

decorticate [di'kɔ:tikeit], *v.tr.* Décortiquer.

decorum [di'kɔ:rəm], *s.* Décorum *m*, bienséance *f.*

decoy¹ [di'kɔi], *s.* Appât *m*, piège *m*, leurre *m*, amorce *f.* **D.-bird**, (oiseau *m* de) leurre; moquette *f*; *F:* chanterelle *f.*

decoy², *v.tr.* 1. Piper, leurrer (des oiseaux). 2. Leurrer, amorcer (qn). To d. s.o. into a trap, entraîner, attirer, qn dans un piège. To d. s.o. into doing sth., entraîner qn à faire qch.

decrease¹ ['di:kri:s], *s.* Diminution *f*, décroissance *f*, amoindrissement *m.* D. in speed, ralentissement *m.* Imports are on the d., les importations sont en décroissance.

decrease² [di'kri:s]. 1. *v.tr.* (a) Diminuer, faire décroître, amoindrir. (b) *Abs.* (Knitting) Fermer des mailles; diminuer. 2. *v.i.* Diminuer; décroître; s'amoindrir. **decreasing**, *a.* Décroissant, diminuant; (tarif) dégressif, (taxe) dégressive. -ly, *adv.* De moins en moins, en diminuant, en décroissant; dégressivement.

decree¹ [di'kri:], *s.* 1. *Adm:* Décret *m*, édit *m*, arrêté *m*; ordonnance (royale). To issue a d., promulguer un décret. 2. *Jur:* Décision *f*, arrêt *m*, jugement *m.* D. nisi ['naisai], jugement provisoire (en matière de divorce).

decree², *v.tr.* Décréter, ordonner.

decrement ['dekrimənt], *s.* 1. Décroissement *m*, décroissance *f.* 2. *Mth: Ch: El.E: etc:* Perte *f*, diminution *f*; décrément *m.* Atténuation *f*, amortissement *m* (des sons).

decrepit [di'krepit], *a.* 1. (Of pers.) Décrépit; caduc, -uque 2. (Of thg) Vermoulu; qui tombe en ruine.

decrepitude [di'krepitju:d], *s.* 1. Décrépitude *f*; caducité *f.* 2. Vermoulure *f.*

decrescendo [ˌdi:kri'ʃendou], *adv. & s. Mus:* Decrescendo (m).

decrescent [di'kres(ə)nt], *a.* Décroissant; en décroissance.

decry [di'krai], *v.tr.* Décrier, dénigrer.

decuple¹ ['dekjupl], *a. & s.* Décuple (m).

decuple². 1. *v.tr.* Décupler. 2. *v.i.* Se décupler.

dedicate ['dedikeit], *v.tr.* 1. Dédier, consacrer (une église). To d. oneself, one's life, to sth., se vouer à qch. 2. Dédier (un livre, etc.) (to, à).

dedication [ˌdedi'keiʃ(ə)n], *s.* 1. Dédicace *f*, consécration *f* (d'une église). 2. Dédicace (d'un livre).

dedicatory ['dedi'keitəri], *a.* Dédicatoire.

deduce [di'dju:s], *v.tr.* Déduire, inférer, conclure (from, de).

deducible [di'dju:səbl], *a.* D. proofs, preuves que l'on peut inférer (de certains faits connus).

deduct [di'dʌkt], *v.tr.* Déduire, retrancher (from, de). To d. sth. from the price, rabattre qch. sur le prix.

deductible [di'dʌktəbl], *a.* Déductible.

deduction [di'dʌkʃ(ə)n], *s.* 1. Déduction *f* (from a quantity, sur une quantité); (of pay) retenue *f.* 2. (a) Raisonnement déductif; déduction. (b) Déduction, conclusion *f* (from, tirée de).

deductive [di'dʌktiv], *a.* Déductif. -ly, *adv.* Par déduction.

deed¹ [di:d], *s.* 1. (a) Action *f*, acte *m.* Man of deeds, homme d'action, d'exécution. (b) D. of valour, haut fait; exploit *m.* (c) Foul d., forfait *m.* (d) Fait. He was ruler in d., though not in name, il était chef en fait, sinon en titre. 2. *Jur:* Acte notarié, sur papier timbré, et signé par les parties. To draw up a d., rédiger un acte. **'deed-box**, *s.* Coffret *m* à documents. **'deed(-), poll**, *s. Jur:* Acte unilatéral.

deed², *v.tr. U.S:* Transférer (qch.) par un acte.

deem [di:m], *v.tr. Lit:* Juger, estimer, croire. I do not d. it necessary to . . ., je ne juge pas, ne crois pas, nécessaire de. . . . To d. highly of s.o., avoir une haute opinion de qn. *S.a.* ADVISABLE 2.

deemster ['di:mstər], *s.* Juge *m* (dans l'île de Man).

deep [di:p]. I. *a.* 1. (a) Profond. To be ten feet d., avoir dix pieds de profondeur; être profond de dix pieds. D. end, bout le plus profond (de la piscine). *P:* To go (in) off the d. end, (i) se mettre en colère; (ii) prendre les choses au tragique. D. in debt, in study, criblé de dettes; absorbé, plongé, dans l'étude. *S.a.* ANKLE, KNEE-DEEP, WAIST-DEEP. (b) D. shelves, rayons larges. Man d. in the chest, homme à forte poitrine. *Mil:* Two, three, d., sur deux, trois rangs. The crowd on the pavement was twelve d., sur le trottoir la foule formait une haie d'une douzaine de rangs. (c) D. sigh, profond soupir. D. thinker, penseur profond. 2. (a) (Of colour) Foncé, sombre. (b) (Of sound) Profond, grave. In a d. voice, d'une voix profonde. 3. D. sorrow, despair, chagrin profond, profond désespoir. D. concern, vive préoccupation. *S.a.* MOURNING 2. 4. (Of conduct) Difficile à pénétrer; (of pers.) rusé, malin, astucieux. D. scheme, projet ténébreux. -ly, *adv.* Profondément. To go d. into sth., pénétrer, entrer, fort avant dans qch. To be d. read in a subject, être versé, érudit, instruit, dans une matière. II. deep, *adv.* 1. Profondément. D.-lying causes, causes profondes. *Prov:* Still waters run d., il n'y a pire eau que l'eau qui dort. 2. The harpoon sank d. into the flesh, le harpon pénétra très avant dans les chairs. D. into the night, très avant dans la nuit. 3. To play d., jouer gros. To drink d., boire à longs traits. To breathe d., respirer à pleins poumons. III. deep, *s.* 1. The d. (a) Les profondeurs *f*, l'abîme *m*, le gouffre. (b) L'océan *m.* The ocean deeps, l'abysse *m*; la région abyssale. To commit a body to the d., immerger un mort. 2. In the d. of winter, au plus profond de l'hiver. **'deep-'chested**, *a.* (Homme) à forte poitrine. **'deep-'drawn**, *a.* (Soupir) profond. **'deep-'dyed**, *a.* = DOUBLE-DYED. **'Deep-'freeze**, *s. R.t:m:* Quick-freezing *m.* **'deep-'freeze**, *v.tr.* Surgeler. **'deep-'fry**, *v.tr. & i. Cu:* (Faire) cuire en friteuse. **'deep-'laid**, *a.* (Complot) ténébreux. **'deep-'rooted**, *a.* Profondément enraciné. **'deep-'sea**, *attrib. a.* D.-s. fishery, (i) pêche hauturière; (ii) grande pêche (de Terre-Neuve, etc.). *S.a.* PILOT¹ 1. **'deep-'seated**, *a.* Profond, enraciné. **'deep-'set**, *a.* (Yeux) enfoncés, creux.

deepen ['di:p(ə)n]. 1. *v.tr.* (a) Approfondir, creuser (un puits, etc.). (b) Rendre (un sentiment) plus intense. (c) Foncer (une couleur); rendre (un son) plus grave, plus sonore. 2. *v.i.* (a) Devenir plus profond; s'approfondir. The river deepens below London, le fleuve prend de la profondeur en aval de Londres. (b) (Of colour) Devenir plus foncé; (of sound) devenir plus grave. **deepening**, *s.* 1. Approfondissement *m.* 2. Augmentation *f* de profondeur, d'intensité. 3. *Meteor:* D. of a depression, creusement *m* d'une dépression.

deepness ['di:pnis], s. 1. Profondeur f (de la voix, etc.). *Mus:* Gravité f (d'un son). 2. Astuce f (d'une personne).

deer ['diər], s.inv. (Red) d., (i) cerf commun; (ii) *Coll.* cervidés *mpl.* **Fallow d.,** daim m. **'deer-hound,** s. Limier m; lévrier m d'Écosse. **'deer(-)stalker,** s. 1. Chasseur m (de cerf) à l'approche. 2. Chapeau m de chasse. **'deer(-)stalking,** s. Chasse f (du cerf) à l'approche.

deerskin ['diəskin], s. Peau f de daim.

deface [di'feis], v.tr. Défigurer; mutiler (une statue); dégrader (une porte); lacérer (une affiche); oblitérer (un timbre).

defacement [di'feismənt], s. Défiguration f, mutilation f (d'une statue, etc.); lacération f (d'une affiche); oblitération f.

de facto [di:'fæktou], *Lat. phr. Jur:* De facto. De f. **and de jure,** de droit et de fait.

defalcate ['di(:)fælkeit], v.i. Détourner des fonds.

defalcation ['di:fæl'keiʃ(ə)n], s. 1. Détournement m de fonds. 2. Fonds manquants; déficit m (de caisse).

defamation [,defə'meiʃ(ə)n], s. Diffamation f.

defamatory [di'fæmət(ə)ri], a. Diffamatoire, diffamant.

defame [di'feim], v.tr. Diffamer (qn); salir le nom de (qn).

defamer [di'feimər], s. Diffamateur, -trice.

default[1] [di'fɔ:lt], s. 1. (a) Manquement m (à un engagement). (b) *St.Exch:* Déconfiture f. 2. *Jur:* Défaut m; non-comparution f; (criminal law) contumace f. **Judgment by d.,** jugement par défaut, par contumace. *Sp:* Match won by d., match gagné par forfait. 3. Carence f. (a) *Com:* D. in paying, défaut de paiement. (b) *Jur:* D. of heirs, déshérence f. (c) *Prep.phr.* In d. of . . ., à, au, défaut de . . .; faute de. . . .

default[2], v.i. (a) *Jur:* Faire défaut; être en état de contumace. (b) *St.Exch:* Manquer à ses engagements; tomber en déconfiture.

defaulter [di'fɔ:ltər], s. 1. (a) Délinquant, -ante. (b) *Jur:* Contumace mf. 2. *Mil: Navy:* (a) Retardataire m, réfractaire m. (b) (Undergoing punishment) Consigné m. 3. Auteur m de détournements de fonds; (of public money) concussionnaire m. 4. *St.Exch:* Défaillant m.

defeat[1] [di'fi:t], s. 1. Défaite f. **To suffer, sustain, a d.,** essuyer une défaite. 2. Renversement m (d'un projet); insuccès m (d'une entreprise).

defeat[2], v.tr. 1. Battre, défaire, vaincre (une armée). 2. Renverser, faire échouer (un projet). *Pol:* **The government was defeated in Parliament,** le Gouvernement a été mis en minorité au Parlement. **To d. the ends of justice,** contrarier la justice. **To d. one's own object,** aller à l'encontre de ses propres intentions.

defeated, a. (Armée) vaincue, en déroute, défaite; (espoir) frustré; (projet) échoué, renversé, détruit; (justice) contrariée.

defeatism [di'fi:tizm], s. Défaitisme m.

defeatist [di'fi:tist], s. Défaitiste mf.

defecate ['defikeit], v.i. Déféquer.

defecation [defi'keiʃ(ə)n], s. Défécation f.

defect[1] ['di:fekt], s. 1. Défaut m, insuffisance f, manque m (of, de). 2. Défaut, imperfection f; défectuosité f, vice m (de construction); tare f. **Physical d.,** défaut; vice m de conformation.

defect[2] [di'fekt], v.i. Déserter.

defection [di'fekʃ(ə)n], s. Défection f.

defective [di'fektiv], a. 1. a. (a) Défectueux, imparfait; (of formation) vicieux. **D. child,** enfant anormal. *S.a.* MENTALLY. **D. brakes,** freins mauvais. (b) *Gram:* (Verbe, etc.) défectif. 2. ,s. Mental m, see MENTAL. **-ly,** adv. Défectueusement.

defectiveness [di'fektivnis], s. 1. État défectueux; défectuosité f, imperfection f. 2. *Gram:* Défectivité f.

defence [di'fens], s. 1. Défense f, protection f. *S.a.* SELF-DEFENCE. 2. *Mil:* **Defences,** défenses. **Civil d.,** protection civile. **Anti-aircraft d.,** défense contre avions, D.C.A. **Coastal d.,** défense côtière. 3. (a) Défense, justification f, apologie f. (b) *Jur:* Défense. **Counsel for the d.,** défenseur m; (in civil law) avocat m de la défense. **Witness for the d.,** témoin m à décharge. **To set up a d.,** établir, présenter, une défense. **In his d. it may be said that . . .,** l'on pourrait dire à sa décharge que. . . .

defenceless [di'fenslis], a. Sans défense. 1. (a) Sans protection. (b) Incapable de se défendre. 2. Désarmé; sans moyen de défense.

defend [di'fend], v.tr. 1. Défendre, protéger (from, against, contre). 2. (a) Faire l'apologie de (qn). (b) Défendre, justifier (une opinion). 3. *Jur:* Défendre (un accusé).

defendant [di'fendənt], a. & s. *Jur:* (a) Défendeur, -eresse. (b) (In criminal case) Accusé, -ée.

defender [di'fendər], s. Défenseur m.

defensible [di'fensəbl], a. 1. (Frontière, cause) défendable. 2. (Opinion) soutenable. **-ibly,** adv. D'une manière justifiable.

defensive [di'fensiv]. 1. a. Défensif. 2. s. Défensive f. **To be, stand, on the d.,** se tenir, rester, sur la défensive. **-ly,** adv. Défensivement.

defer[1] [di'fə:r], v.tr. (deferred) Différer, ajourner, renvoyer, retarder (une affaire); reculer, arriérer (un payement); suspendre (un jugement). **To d. doing sth.,** différer à, de, faire qch. **deferred,** a. (Of share, telegram, etc.) Différé. **D. payment,** paiement par versements échelonnés, paiement différé.

defer[2], v.i. Déférer. **To d. to s.o.'s opinion,** déférer, se rendre, à l'avis de qn. *Mil:* Mettre en sursis (d'appel). **To d. s.o. on medical grounds,** ajourner qn. **Deferred conscript,** sursitaire m.

deference ['def(ə)r(ə)ns], s. Déférence f. **To pay, show, d. to s.o.,** témoigner de la déférence à, envers, qn. **In, out of, d. to . . .,** par déférence pour. . . . **With all due d. to you,** sauf votre respect. **With all due d. to your father,** n'en déplaise à monsieur votre père.

deferential [,defə'renʃ(ə)l], a. Déférent; (air, ton) de déférence. **-ally,** adv. Avec déférence.

deferment [di'fə:mənt], s. Ajournement m, remise f (d'une affaire). *Mil:* Ajournement (pour raison de santé). **To be on d.** (of call-up), être en sursis. **To apply for d.** (of call-up), faire une demande de sursis (d'appel).

defiance [di'faiəns], s. Défi m. **To bid d. to s.o.,** lancer, porter, jeter, un défi à qn. **To set s.o. at d.,** défier qn. **In d. of the law,** au mépris de la loi.

defiant [di'faiənt], a. (a) Provocant; (regard, parole) de défi. (b) Qui repousse les avances; intraitable. **-ly,** adv. D'un air de défi.

deficiency [di'fiʃənsi], s. 1. Manque m, insuffisance f, défaut m (of, de). *S.a.* MENTAL. 2. Défaut, faiblesse f, imperfection f. 3. Déficit m. 4. *Med:* Carence f (in, of, de); déficience f. **D. diseases,** maladies f par, de, carence, maladies carentielles.

deficient [di'fiʃənt], a. (a) Défectueux, insuffisant, incomplet. **To be d. in sth.,** manquer, être dépourvu, de qch. (b) (Personne) à petite mentalité. *S.a.* MENTAL, MENTALLY.

deficit ['defisit, 'di:fisit], s. *Fin: Com:* Déficit m. **Budget that shows a d.,** budget en déficit, déficitaire.

defile[1] ['di:fail], s. Défilé m; détroit m (entre montagnes).

defile[2] [di'fail], v.i. (Of troops) Défiler. **defiling,** s. Défilé m.

defile[3] [di'fail], v.tr. Souiller, salir (ses mains); polluer (un lieu saint).

defilement [di'failmənt], s. Souillure f; pollution f. **Free from d.,** sans tache, sans souillure.

definable [di'fainəbl], a. Définissable.

define [di'fain], v.tr. 1. Définir. **To d. one's position,** préciser son attitude (politique, etc.). 2. Déterminer (l'étendue de qch.); formuler (des pensées); délimiter (un territoire). 3. **Well-defined outlines,** contours nettement dessinés.

definite ['definit], a. 1. Défini; bien déterminé. **D. answer,** réponse catégorique. **D. intentions,** intentions bien arrêtées. *Com:* **D. order,** commande ferme. 2. *Gram:* **D. article,** article défini. **Past d.,** passé défini. **-ly,** adv. D'une manière précise, bien déterminée. **He is d. better,** il va décidément mieux. **D. superior,** nettement supérieur.

definiteness ['definitnis], s. Précision f, exactitude f, netteté f.

definition [,defi'niʃ(ə)n], s. 1. Définition f. 2. *Opt: W.Tel: T.V:* Netteté f (du son, de l'image).

definitive [di'finitiv], a. (Jugement, résultat) définitif. **-ly,** adv. Définitivement; en définitive.

deflagrate ['deflagreit]. *Ch:* 1. *v.tr.* Faire déflagrer (du salpêtre, etc.). 2. *v.i.* Déflagrer, fuser.

deflagration [,defla'greiʃ(ə)n], *s. Ch:* Déflagration *f.*

deflate [di:'fleit], *v.tr.* (*a*) Dégonfler. Deflated tyre, pneu aplati, à plat. (*b*) To d. the currency, *abs.* to d., amener la déflation de la monnaie.

deflation [di:'fleiʃ(ə)n], *s.* 1. Dégonflement *m* (d'un ballon). 2. *Fin:* Déflation *f.*

deflationary [di'fleiʃənri], *a. Pol.Ec:* (Politique, etc.) déflationniste, de déflation.

deflationist [di'fleiʃənist], *a. & s.* Déflationniste *mf.*

deflect [di'flekt]. 1. *v.tr.* Dévier; détourner; défléchir. *Aut:* To d. the front wheels, braquer les roues avant. *El:* Deflecting field, champ *m* de déviation. 2. *v.i.* (*a*) (Se) dévier, se détourner; défléchir. (*b*) S'incurver; faire flèche.

deflection, deflexion [di'flekʃ(ə)n], *s.* 1. Déflexion *f* (de la lumière); déviation *f* (de l'aiguille du compas). 2. Déjettement *m*, déformation *f.* (*Sag*) Flèche *f*, flexion *f.* D. under load, flexion, affaissement *m*, sous charge. 3. *Aut:* Braquage *m* (des roues avant).

deflector [di'flektər], *s. Mch: etc:* Déflecteur *m.*

defoliant [di'fouliənt], *s.* Défoliant *m.*

defoliate [di:'foulieit], *v.tr.* Défeuiller (un arbuste, etc.).

defoliation [,di:fouli'eiʃən], *s.* Défeuillaison *f*, défoliation *f.*

deforest [di:'forist], *v.tr.* 1. Déboiser. 2. Défricher.

deforestation [,di:foris'teiʃ(ə)n], *s.* 1. Déboisement *m.* 2. Défrichement *m.*

deform [di'fo:m], *v.tr.* Déformer. deformed, *a.* 1. (*Of pers.*) Contrefait, difforme. 2. *Ph:* D. wave, onde faussée, déformée.

deformation [,di:fo:'meiʃ(ə)n], *s.* Déformation *f.*

deformity [di'fo:miti], *s.* Difformité *f.*

defraud [di'fro:d], *v.tr.* 1. Frauder (le fisc, etc.). 2. To d. s.o. of sth., frustrer qn de qch.; escroquer qch. à qn. defrauding, *s.* 1. Fraude *f.* 2. Frustration *f* (de ses créanciers, etc.).

defrauder [di'fro:dər], *s.* Fraudeur *m* (du fisc).

defray [di'frei], *v.tr.* To d. s.o.'s expenses, défrayer qn. To d. the cost of sth., couvrir les frais de qch.

defrayable [di'freiəbl], *a.* A la charge (by, de). Expenses d. out of taxes, frais *m* imputables aux impôts.

defrayment [di'freimənt], *s.* Payement *m*, paiement *m*, remboursement *m* (des frais).

de-freeze [di:'fri:z], *v.tr.* Décongeler. defreezing, *s.* Décongélation *f.*

defrost [di:'frost], *v.tr.* 1. Dégivrer (un réfrigérateur). 2. Décongeler (la viande frigorifiée).

defroster [di:'frostər], *s.* Dégivreur *m.*

deft [deft], *a.* Adroit, habile. D. hand, main exercée; main preste. -ly, *adv.* Adroitement, prestement.

deftness ['deftnis], *s.* Adresse *f*, habileté *f*, dextérité *f*, prestesse *f.*

defunct [di'fʌŋkt], *a.* Défunt, -e; décédé, -ée.

defuse [,di:'fju:z], *v.tr.* Désamorcer.

defy [di'fai], *v.tr.* Défier (qn); mettre (qn) au défi. I d. you to do so, je vous mets au défi, je vous défie, de le faire. To d. description, défier toute description.

degauss [di'gaus], *v.tr. Nau:* Dégausser, démagnétiser. degaussing, *s.* Démagnétisation *f.*

degeneracy [di'dʒen(ə)rəsi], *s.* Dégénération *f.*

degenerate[1] [di'dʒen(ə)rit], *a. & s.* Dégénéré, -ée; *a.* abâtardi.

degenerate[2] [di'dʒenəreit], *v.i.* Dégénérer (from, de; into, en); s'abâtardir. degenerating, *a. Med:* Dégénérescent.

degeneration [di,dʒenə'reiʃ(ə)n], *s.* Dégénérescence *f*, dégénération *f*; abâtardissement *m.*

degradation [,degrə'deiʃ(ə)n], *s.* 1. Dégradation *f*; cassation *f* (d'un officier, etc.). 2. Avilissement *m*, dégradation, abrutissement *m.*

degrade [di'greid], *v.tr.* (*a*) Dégrader, casser (un officier, etc.). (*b*) Avilir, ravilir, dégrader (qn). degrading, *a.* Avilissant, dégradant.

degree [di'gri:], *s.* 1. *A:* Degré *m*, marche *f* (d'autel). 2. (*a*) To some d., à un certain degré; (jusqu')à un certain point. In the highest d., au plus haut degré, au suprême degré. In some d., dans une certaine mesure. To a d., au plus haut degré; éminemment. By degrees, par degrés; petit à petit. By slow degrees, graduellement, lentement. *Gram:* D. of comparison,

degré de comparaison. D. of humidity, titre *m* d'eau; teneur *f* en eau. *F:* Third d., passage *m* à tabac; cuisinage *m.* To put a prisoner through the third d., cuisiner un prisonnier. (*b*) *Mth: Ph: etc:* Degré (d'un cercle, de température). Angle of 30 degrees, angle de 30 degrés. Twenty degrees west of Greenwich, sous le méridien de vingt degrés à l'ouest de Greenwich. 3. *Mus:* Échelon *m* (de la gamme); degré (de la portée). 4. *A. & Lit:* Rang *m*, condition *f.* Of high d., de haut rang, de haut lignage. Of low d., *F:* de bas étage. 5. *Sch:* Grade *m* (universitaire). To take one's d., passer sa licence. He has his d., il a ses diplômes. Honorary d., diplôme *m* honoris causa.

degression [di'greʃən], *s.* Diminution progressive; dégression *f.*

degressive [di'gresiv], *a.* D. tariff, taxation, tarif dégressif, impôts dégressifs.

dehiscence [di'his(ə)ns], *s. Bot:* Déhiscence *f.*

dehumidify ['di:'hju(:)'midifai], *v.tr.* Déshydrater (l'air etc.); sécher, dessécher.

dehydrate [di:'haidreit], *v.tr.* Déshydrater. Dehydrated eggs, œufs en poudre. Dehydrated vegetables, légumes déshydratés.

dehydration [,di:hai'dreiʃ(ə)n], *s. Ch: Ind:* Déshydratation *f.*

de-ice ['di:'ais], *v.tr. Av: Aut:* Dégivrer. de-icing, *s. Av: Aut:* Dégivrage *m.*

de-icer ['di'aisər], *s. Av: Aut:* Dégivreur *m.*

deification [,di:ifi'keiʃ(ə)n], *s.* Déification *f*; divinisation *f.*

deify ['di:ifai], *v.tr.* Déifier, diviniser (qn).

deign [dein], *v.tr.* 1. To d. to do sth., daigner faire qch.; condescendre à faire qch. 2. *Usu. neg.* He did not d. to answer, il ne daigna pas répondre.

deism ['di:izm], *s.* Déisme *m.*

deist ['di:ist], *s.* Déiste *m.*

deistic [di:'istik], *a.* Déiste.

deity ['di:iti], *s.* 1. Divinité *f* (de Jésus-Christ, etc.). 2. Dieu *m*, déesse *f*; déité *f*, divinité.

deject [di'dʒekt], *v.tr.* Abattre, décourager, déprimer (qn). dejected, *a.* Triste, abattu, déprimé. -ly, *adv.* D'un air découragé; tristement.

dejection [di'dʒekʃ(ə)n], *s.* 1. Découragement *m*, tristesse *f*, abattement *m.* 2. *Med:* Déjection *f.*

dekko ['dekou], *s. P:* Let's have a d., fais-moi voir.

delay[1] [di'lei], *s.* 1. Sursis *m*, remise *f*; délai *m*, retard *m*; traînerie *f.* Without d., sans délai; tout de suite. Without further d., sans plus tarder. To make no d., ne pas traîner, ne pas tarder (in doing sth., à faire qch.). The law's delays, les lenteurs *f* de la loi. 2. Retardement *m*, arrêt *m*, entrave *f* (du progrès).

delay[2]. 1. *v.tr.* (*a*) Différer, retarder, remettre (une affaire); arriérer (un paiement). (*b*) Retenir, arrêter, retarder (qn); entraver, retarder (le progrès). 2. *v.i.* (*a*) Tarder, différer (in doing sth., à faire qch.). (*b*) S'attarder. delayed, *a.* Retardé. *Phot:* D. action shutter, obturateur *m* à action différée. *Mil: etc:* D. action fuse, bomb, mine, etc. Fusée *f*, bombe *f*, mine *f*, engin *m*, à retardement. delaying, *a.* D. action, action *f* dilatoire, de retardement.

delectable [di'lektəbl], *a. Lit:* Délectable, délicieux. -ably, *adv.* Délectablement.

delectation [,di:lek'teiʃ(ə)n], *s.* Délectation *f.*

delegate[1] ['deligit], *s.* Délégué *m.*

delegate[2] ['deligeit], *v.tr.* Déléguer.

delegation [,deli'geiʃ(ə)n], *s.* (*a*) Délégation *f*; subrogation *f* (de droits, etc.). (*b*) Délégation (de qn). (*c*) A delegation, une délégation.

delegator [,deli'geitər], *s. Jur:* Délégateur, -trice.

delete [di'li:t], *v.tr.* Effacer, rayer (un mot, etc.). *Typ:* 'D.,' "à supprimer."

deleterious [,deli'tiəriəs], *a.* 1. Nuisible à la santé. 2. (Gaz, etc.) délétère.

deletion [di'li:ʃ(ə)n], *s.* 1. Rature *f*, suppression *f* (d'un passage). 2. Passage supprimé.

delf(t) [delf(t)], *s. Cer:* Faïence *f* de Delft. D. blue, bleu *m* de faïence.

deliberate[1] [di'lib(ə)rit], *a.* 1. Délibéré, prémédité, intentionnel, voulu. D. insolence, insolence calculée. 2. (*Of pers.*) (*a*) Réfléchi, circonspect, avisé. (*b*) Lent; sans hâte. D. tread, pas mesuré. -ly, *adv.* 1. De propos délibéré; à dessein; exprès; à bon escient. 2. (Agir) posément, sans hâte, délibérément.

deliberate[2] [di'libəreit], *v.tr. & i.* Délibérer (on, de, sur). To d. over,'on, a question, délibérer d'une question.

deliberateness [di'lib(ə)ritnis], *s.* 1. Intention marquée (d'une insulte). 2. Sage lenteur *f*, mesure *f* (dans les actions).

deliberation [di'libə'reiʃ(ə)n], *s.* 1. (*a*) Délibération *f*. After due d., après mûre délibération; après mûre réflexion. (*b*) The deliberations of an assembly, les débats *m* d'une assemblée. 2. (*a*) To act with d., agir avec circonspection, après réflexion. (*b*) Sage lenteur *f*. With d., posément; sans hâte.

delicacy ['delikəsi], *s.* Délicatesse *f*. 1. (*a*) Finesse *f* (d'un dessin); sensibilité *f* (d'un instrument de précision). (*b*) Délicatesse, faiblesse *f* (de santé). (*c*) To outrage s.o.'s d., faire outrage à la pudeur de qn. To feel a d. about doing sth., se faire scrupule de faire qch. Negotiations of the utmost d., négociations très délicates. 2. Table delicacies, délicatesses, friandises *f*, de table.

delicate ['delikit], *a.* Délicat. 1. (*a*) To have a d. touch, avoir de la légèreté de touche, de doigté. To have a d. wit, avoir l'esprit fin. (*b*) D. feelings, sentiments délicats, raffinés. 2. D. situation, situation délicate, difficile. D. question, question épineuse. To tread on d. ground, toucher à des questions délicates. 3. D. health, santé délicate, faible. -ly, *adv.* Délicatement; avec délicatesse.

delicateness ['delikətnis], *s.* = DELICACY 1.

delicatessen ['delikə'tes(ə)n], *s.* Plats cuisinés; charcuterie *f*. D. shop, charcuterie.

delicious [di'liʃəs], *a.* Délicieux, exquis. -ly, *adv.* Délicieusement.

delight[1] [di'lait], *s.* 1. Délices *fpl*, délice *m*, délectation *f*. It is such a d. to . . ., c'est si bon de. . . . *S.a.* TURKISH DELIGHT. 2. Joie *f*. Much to the d. of . . ., to the great d. of . . ., à la grande joie de. . . . 3. To take d. in sth. = to delight in sth.

delight[2]. 1. *v.tr.* Enchanter, ravir, réjouir (qn); faire les délices de (qn). 2. *v.i.* To d. in sth., se délecter à (l'étude), dans (le péché); faire ses délices de qch. To d. in doing sth., se complaire à faire qch. **delighted**, *a.* Enchanté, ravi (with, at, de). To be d. to do sth., être enchanté de faire qch. I shall be d., je ne demande pas mieux.

delightful [di'laitful], *a.* Délicieux, ravissant; enchanteur, -eresse; charmant. -fully, *adv.* Délicieusement; (chanter, etc.) à ravir.

delightfulness [di'laitfulnis], *s.* Charme *m*, plaisir *m*, enchantement *m*.

delimit [di:'limit], *v.tr.* Délimiter (un terrain, des pouvoirs).

delimitation [di,limi'teiʃ(ə)n], *s.* Délimitation *f*.

delineate [di'linieit], *v.tr.* 1. Tracer, décrire (un triangle, etc.). 2. Dessiner (un paysage); délinéer (un profil).

delineation [di,lini'eiʃ(ə)n], *s.* 1. Délinéation *f*. 2. Tracé *m*, dessin *m*.

delinquency [di'liŋkwənsi], *s.* 1. Culpabilité *f*; délinquance *f*. Juvenile d., criminalité *f*, délinquance, juvénile. 2. Délit *m*, faute *f*; écart *m* de conduite.

delinquent [di'liŋkwənt], *a. & s.* 1. Délinquant, -ante; coupable (*mf*). 2. *U.S:* D. taxes, impôts non payés.

deliquesce [,deli'kwes], *v.i.* Tomber en déliquescence.

deliquescence [,deli'kwesns], *s.* Déliquescence *f*.

deliquescent [,deli'kwes(ə)nt], *a.* Déliquescent.

delirious [di'liriəs], *a.* (Malade) en délire, délirant; (divagations) du délire. To be d., avoir le délire; délirer. *F:* D. with joy, fou, délirant, de joie.

delirium [di'liriəm], *s.* Délire *m*. D. tremens, delirium *m* tremens.

deliver [di'livər], *v.tr.* 1. Délivrer, sauver (s.o. from sth., qn de qch.). To d. s.o. from captivity, (re)tirer qn de (la) captivité. 2. (*a*) To d. a woman (of a child), (faire) accoucher une femme. (*b*) To be delivered of a child, accoucher d'un enfant. 3. To d. s.o., sth., (up, over) to s.o., livrer, délivrer, qn, qch., à qn. *S.a.* STAND[2] I. 3. To d. up, restituer, rendre (to, à). To d. over, céder, transférer, transmettre (un bien, etc.) (to, à). 4. (*a*) Remettre, livrer (un paquet, etc.); distribuer (des lettres); livrer (des marchandises). To d. sth. into s.o.'s charge, confier qch. à qn, à la garde de qn. To d. a message, faire une commission. *Com:* Delivered free, rendu à domicile; livraison franco. (*b*) (Of dynamo, etc.) Débiter, fournir (du courant); (of pump) refouler (l'eau). 5. Porter, donner (un coup); faire, lancer (une attaque); livrer (un assaut). 6. Faire, prononcer (un discours); faire (une conférence). *Jur:* Prononcer, rendre (un jugement).

deliverable [di'liv(ə)rəbl], *a. Com: Fin:* Livrable.

deliverance [di'liv(ə)r(ə)ns], *s.* Délivrance *f*, libération *f* (from, de).

deliverer [di'liv(ə)rər], *s. Lit:* Libérateur, -trice; sauveur *m*.

delivery [di'liv(ə)ri], *s.* 1. *Obst:* Accouchement *m*. 2. *Mil:* Reddition *f* (d'une ville, d'un prisonnier). 3. (*a*) D. of a message, exécution *f* d'une commission. (*b*) Livraison *f*, remise *f* (d'un paquet, etc.); remise (d'une lettre); distribution *f* (des lettres). *Jur:* D. of a writ, signification *f* d'un acte. *Com:* D. price, prix rendu. D. note, bulletin *m* de livraison. Free d., livraison franco. D.-man, livreur. To pay on d., payer sur livraison. Payment on d., livraison contre remboursement. Cash on d., payable à livraison. *Ind:* To accept d. of sth., prendre qch. en recette. *Post:* Free d. area (*for telegrams. etc.*) circonscription *f* de remise gratuite. *U.S:* General d., = poste restante. 4. (*a*) D. of a speech, prononciation *f* d'un discours. (*b*) Débit *m*, diction *f* (d'un orateur). 5. (*a*) Distribution (de courant électrique, etc.). (*b*) Débit (de courant, etc.); refoulement *m* (d'une pompe). D. pipe, tuyau *m*, conduite *f*, d'amenée.

dell [del], *s.* Vallon *m*, combe *f*.

delouse ['di:'laus], *v.tr.* Épouiller (qn). **delousing**, *s.* Épouillage *m*.

Delphi ['delfi]. *Pr.n Geog:* Delphes *f*.

Delphic ['delfik], *a.* The D. Oracle, l'Oracle *m* de Delphes.

delphinium [del'finiəm], *s. Bot:* Delphinium *m*.

delta ['deltə], *s.* 1. *Gr.Alph: Geog:* Delta *m*. 2. *Metall:* D. metal, (métal *m*) delta. *Ph:* D. rays, rayons *m* delta. *Aer:* D. wing aircraft, avion *m* aux ailes en delta.

deltoid ['deltoid], *a. & s. Anat:* (Muscle *m*) deltoïde *m*.

delude [di'lju:d], *v.tr.* 1. Abuser, tromper (qn); induire (qn) en erreur. To d. oneself, s'abuser; se faire illusion. To d. oneself with false hopes, se bercer, se leurrer, de vaines espérances. 2. Duper (qn); en faire accroire à (qn).

deluge[1] ['delju:dʒ], *s.* Déluge *m*.

deluge[2], *v.tr.* Inonder (with, de). To be deluged with letters, être inondé de lettres.

delusion [di'lju:ʒ(ə)n], *s.* Illusion *f*, hallucination *f*, erreur *f*. To be under a d., se faire illusion; s'abuser; s'illusionner. To suffer from delusions, être sujet aux hallucinations.

delusive [di'lju:siv], *a.* Illusoire; trompeur, -euse. -ly, *adv.* Illusoirement; trompeusement.

delusiveness [di'lju:sivnis], *s.* Caractère illusoire, trompeur (d'une apparence, d'une promesse).

de luxe [də'luks], *a. Com:* De luxe *m*, (marchandise *f*) de qualité supérieure.

delve [delv], *v.i.* (*a*) *A. & Lit:* Fouiller le sol. (*b*) To d. into the past, fouiller, remonter, dans le passé.

demagnetization [di:,mægnətai'zeiʃ(ə)n], *s.* Désaimantation *f*; démagnétisation *f*.

demagnetize [di:'mægnətaiz], *v.tr.* Démagnétiser; désaimanter.

demagogue ['deməgɔg], *s.* Démagogue *m*.

demagogy ['deməgɔgi, -dʒi], *s.* Démagogie *f*.

demand[1] [di'mɑːnd], *s.* 1. Demande *f*, réclamation *f*, revendication *f*. Payable on d., payable sur demande, à vue. *attrib. Bank: U.S:* D. deposit = current account. 2. *Pol.Ec:* Supply and d., l'offre et la demande. To be in (great, little) d., être (très, peu) demandé, recherché. *Com:* Goods in firm d., marchandises constamment demandées. 3. *pl.* To make great demands upon s.o.'s energy, exiger de qn beaucoup d'énergie. I have many demands upon my time, je suis très pris. Excessive demands, prétentions excessives.

demand[2], *v.tr.* 1. To d. sth. of, from, s.o., demander (formellement), réclamer, qch. à qn; exiger qch. de qn. To d. to know whether . ., insister pour savoir si. . . . To d. that . . ., demander, exiger, que + *sub*. 2. The matter demands great care, l'affaire demande, exige, réclame, beaucoup de soin. **demanding**, *a.* Revendicatif, -ive; exigeant.

demarcate ['di:mɑ:keit], *v.tr.* Délimiter (un terrain). **demarcating,** *a.* Démarcatif, -ive.

demarcation [,di:mɑ:'keiʃ(ə)n], *s.* Démarcation *f*; délimitation *f.*

démarche ['deimɑ:ʃ], *s. Pol: Journ:* Démarche *f* politique ou diplomatique.

demean [di'mi:n], *v.pr.* To d. oneself, s'abaisser, se dégrader.

demeanour [di'mi:nər], *s.* Air *m*, tenue *f*, maintien *m.*

demented [di'mentid], *a.* Fou, *f.* folle; en démence.

dementia [di'menʃiə], *s. Med:* Démence *f.*

Demerara [,demə'rɛərə]. *Pr.n. Geog:* Demerara. **D. sugar,** cassonade *f*, sucre roux.

demerit [di:'merit], *s.* Démérite *m.* **The merits and demerits of the case,** le pour et le contre.

demesne [di'mein], *s.* 1. *Jur:* Possession *f.* 2. Domaine *m.*

demigod ['demigɔd], *s.* Demi-dieu *m.*

demijohn ['demidʒɔn], *s. Ind: etc:* Dame-jeanne *f*, bonbonne *f*, tourie *f.*

demilitarization ['di:,milit(ə)rai'zeiʃ(ə)n], *s.* Démilitarisation *f.*

demilitarize [di:'militəraiz], *v.tr.* Démilitariser.

demi-mondaine ['demi'mɔndein], *s.* Demi-mondaine *f*, *pl.* demi-mondaines.

demi-monde ['demi'mɔ:nd], *s.* Demi-monde *m.*

demise¹ [di'maiz], *s.* 1. *Jur:* Cession *f*, transmission *f* (par testament, etc.); transfert *m* (d'un titre, etc.). 2. Décès *m*, mort *f* (de qn).

demise², *v.tr. Jur:* Céder, transmettre (un bien).

demisemiquaver ['demi'semi'kweivər], *s. Mus:* Triple croche *f.*

demist [di:'mist], *v.tr. Aut: etc:* Enlever la buée (d'une glace, d'un pare-brise, etc.).

demister [,di:'mistər], *s. Aut:* (Dispositif) antibuée *m.*

demi-tasse ['demi-'tæs], *s. U.S:* (a) (Une tasse de) café noir. (b) Petite tasse à café.

demob¹ ['di:'mɔb], *s. F:* = DEMOBILIZATION.

demob², *v.tr.* (**demobbed**) *F:* = DEMOBILIZE.

demobilization ['di:,moubilai'zeiʃ(ə)n], *s.* Démobilisation *f.*

demobilize [di:'moubilaiz], *v.tr. Mil:* Démobiliser.

democracy [di'mɔkrəsi], *s.* Démocratie *f.* **People's d.,** démocratie populaire. **To tend towards d.,** se démocratiser.

democrat ['deməkræt], *s.* Démocrate *mf.*

democratic [,demə'krætik], *a.* Démocratique. **-ally,** *adv.* Démocratiquement.

democratize [di'mɔkrətaiz], *v.tr.* Démocratiser.

demograph ['deməgrɑ:f], *s.* Démographe *m.*

demographer [di'mɔgrəfə], *s.* Démographe *m.*

demographic [demə'græfik]. *a.* Démographique.

demography [di:'mɔgrəfi], *s.* Démographie *f.*

demolish [di'mɔliʃ], *v.tr.* Démolir.

demolition [,demo'liʃ(ə)n], *s.* Démolition *f.*

demon ['di:mən], *s.* 1. (a) *Gr.Myth:* Démon *m*, esprit *m.* (b) *Myth:* Démon, génie *m.* 2. Démon, diable *m.*

demonetization [di:,mʌnitai'zeiʃ(ə)n], *s.* Démonétisation *f.*

demonetize [di:'mʌnitaiz], *v.tr.* Démonétiser (une monnaie).

demoniac [di'mouniæk], *a. & s.* Démoniaque (*mf*).

demoniacal [,di:mə'naiək(ə)l], *a.* Démoniaque, diabolique.

demonology [,di:mən'ɔlədʒi], *s.* Démonologie *f.*

demonstrable ['demənstrəbl], *a.* Démontrable. **-ably,** *adv.* **Statement d. false,** affirmation dont la fausseté peut être prouvée.

demonstrate ['demənstreit]. 1. *v.tr.* (a) Démontrer (une vérité). (b) Décrire, expliquer (un système). *Com:* To d. a car, etc.), faire la démonstration (d'une voiture, etc.). 2. *v.i. Pol:* Manifester; prendre part à une manifestation.

demonstration [,demən'streiʃ(ə)n], *s.* 1. (a) Démonstration *f* (d'une vérité). (b) Démonstration (d'un appareil). *attrib. Com:* **D. model,** appareil *m* de démonstration. 2. **Demonstrations of love,** témoignages *m*, démonstrations, de tendresse. 3. Manifestation *f* (politique). **To make a d.,** manifester.

demonstrative [di'mɔnstrətiv], *a.* Démonstratif, -ive. **-ly,** *adv.* (Accueillir qn) avec effusion.

demonstrator ['demənstreitər], *s.* 1. (a) Démonstrateur *m.* (b) *Sch:* Préparateur *m* (d'un professeur de sciences, etc.); démonstrateur (en anatomie). 2. Manifestant *m* (politique).

demoralization [di'mɔrəlai'zeiʃ(ə)n], *s.* Démoralisation *f.*

demoralize [di'mɔrəlaiz], *v.tr.* 1. Dépraver, corrompre. 2. Démoraliser (les troupes, etc.). **demoralizing,** *a.* Démoralisateur, -trice; corrupteur, -trice.

demote [di'mout], *v.tr. Mil: etc:* Réduire à un grade inférieur, à une classe inférieure.

demount ['di:'maunt], *v.tr. U.S: Mech.E: etc:* Démonter (une roue, un moteur).

demur¹ [di'mə:r], *s.* Hésitation *f.* **To make no d.,** ne faire aucune difficulté, aucune objection.

demur², *v.i.* (**demurred**) Faire des difficultés; soulever des objections (**at, to,** contre).

demure [di'mjuər], *a.* (*Used chiefly of young women*) 1. Posé(e), grave; réservé(e). 2. D'une modestie affectée. **D. look,** petit air de Sainte-Nitouche. **-ly,** *adv.* 1. D'un air posé, modeste. 2. Avec une modestie affectée; d'un air de Sainte-Nitouche.

demureness [di'mjuənis], *s.* 1. Gravité *f* de maintien. 2. Modestie affectée; air *m* de Sainte-Nitouche.

demurrage [di'mʌridʒ], *s.* 1. *Nau:* Surestarie(s) *f*(*pl*). 2. *Rail:* Magasinage *m.*

den [den], *s.* 1. Tanière *f*, antre *m*, repaire *m* (de bêtes féroces). **Bear's d.,** *Fr.C:* ouache *f.* *B:* **D. of lions,** fosse *f* aux lions. *S.a.* BEARD². **D. of thieves,** retraite *f* de voleurs. 2. *F:* Cabinet *m* de travail ou fumoir *m*; *P:* turne *f.* 3. *F:* Bouge *m.* *S.a.* GAMBLING.

denationalization [di:,næʃənəlai'zeiʃ(ə)n], *s.* Dénationalisation *f.*

denationalize [di:'næʃnəlaiz], *v.tr.* Dénationaliser (qn, une industrie, etc.).

denaturalization [di:,nætʃərəlai'zeiʃ(ə)n], *s.* Dénaturalisation *f.*

denaturalize [di:'nætʃərəlaiz], *v.tr.* 1. Dénaturer (qch.). 2. To d. oneself, se dénaturaliser, se dénationaliser.

denature [di:'neitʃər], **denaturize** [di:'neitʃəraiz], *v.tr.* Dénaturer (un produit).

denazification [di:,nɑ:tsifi'keiʃ(ə)n], *s.* Dénazification *f.*

denazify [di:'nɑ:tsifai], *v.tr.* Dénazifier.

dendrite ['dendrait], *s. Miner: Cryst:* Arborisation *f*, dendrite *f.*

deniable [di'naiəbl], *a.* Niable.

denial [di'naiəl], *s.* 1. (*Refusal*) Déni *m*, refus *m.* I will take no d., il faut absolument que vous veniez, que vous le fassiez, etc. 2. Dénégation *f*, démenti *m* (de la vérité de qch.). 3. *B:* (Le) reniement (de saint Pierre).

denicotinize ['di:'nikəti:naiz], *v.tr.* Dénicotiniser (le tabac).

denier ['deniei], *s. Hosiery:* Denier *m.* **A 15 denier stocking,** un bas 15 deniers.

denigrate ['denigreit], *v.tr. Lit:* (a) Noircir (la réputation de qn); diffamer (qn). (b) Dénigrer (qn, un projet).

denigration [,deni'greiʃ(ə)n], *s. Lit:* (a) Diffamation *f.* (b) Dénigrement *m.*

denigrator ['denigreitər], *s. Lit:* (a) Diffamateur *m.* (b) Dénigreur *m.*

denim ['denim], *s. Tex:* 1. Serge *f* de coton. 2. *Mil:* *pl.* Denims, treillis *mpl.*

denizen ['denizn], *s.* 1. *Poet:* Habitant, -ante. Denizens of the forest, hôtes *m*, habitants, des bois. 2. *Nat. Hist:* Animal acclimaté; plante acclimatée.

Denmark ['denmɑ:k]. *Pr.n.* Le Danemark.

denominate [di'nɔmineit], *v.tr.* Dénommer.

denomination [di,nɔmi'neiʃ(ə)n], *s.* 1. Dénomination *f.* 2. *Ecc:* Culte *m*, secte *f*, confession *f.* 3. Catégorie *f.* **Coins of all denominations,** pièces de toutes valeurs.

denominational [di,nɔmi'neiʃnl], *a. Ecc:* Confessionnel, sectaire. **D. school,** école confessionnelle.

denominator [di'nɔmineitər], *s. Mth:* Dénominateur *m.* **Common d.,** dénominateur commun.

denotation [,di:nou'teiʃ(ə)n], *s.* 1. Désignation *f*, indication *f* (**of** sth. **by** sth., de qch. par qch.). 2. Signification *f* (d'un mot).

denote [di'nout], *v.tr.* 1. Dénoter, indiquer. **Face that denotes energy,** visage qui dénote l'énergie. **Here everything denotes peace,** ici tout respire la paix. 2. Signifier.

dénouement [dei'nuːmãː(ŋ)], s. *Lit:* Dénouement *m*.

denounce [di'nauns], v.tr. 1. (a) Dénoncer. To d. s.o. to the authorities, déférer qn à la justice. (b) Démasquer (un imposteur). (c) *Pred.* To d. s.o. as an imposter, taxer qn d'imposture. 2. S'élever contre (un abus). 3. To d. a treaty, dénoncer un traité.

de novo [diː'nouvou]. *Lt.adv.phr.* A nouveau.

dense [dens], a. 1. *Ph:* Dense. 2. (*Of smoke*) Épais, -aisse. D. darkness, obscurité profonde. D. crowd, foule compacte. 3. *F:* Stupide, bête; (esprit) lourd, obtus. 4. *Phot:* D. negative, cliché opaque. -ly, adv. D. wooded country, pays couvert de forêts épaisses. D. populated region, région très peuplée.

denseness ['densnis], s. 1. Épaisseur *m* (du brouillard, etc.). 2. *F:* Stupidité *f*.

density ['densiti], s. 1. *Ph:* Densité *f*. 2. Compacité (du sol); densité (de la population). 3. *F:* Stupidité *f*. 4. *Phot:* Opacité *f* (d'un cliché).

dent¹ [dent], s. (a) Marque *f* de coup; bosselure *f*; renfoncement *m*. (b) Brèche *f* (dans une lame).

dent², v.tr. (a) Bosseler, bossuer. (b) Ébrécher (une lame).

dental ['dentl], a. 1. Dentaire. D. surgeon, chirurgien dentiste. 2. *Ling:* Dental, -aux. s. (Consonne) dentale *f*.

dentate ['denteit], a. Denté.

dentation [den'teiʃ(ə)n], s. Denteture *f*.

dentifrice ['dentifris], s. Dentifrice *m*.

dentist ['dentist], s. Dentiste *m*.

dentistry ['dentistri], s. Art *m* dentaire.

dentition [den'tiʃ(ə)n], s. Dentition *f*.

denture ['den(t)ʃər], s. 1. *Z:* Denture *f*. 2. (*Of artificial teeth*) Dentier *m*; *F:* râtelier *m*.

denudation [ˌdiːnjuː(ː)'deiʃ(ə)n], s. Dénudation *f*.

denude [di'njuːd], v.tr. Dénuder (qch.). Tree denuded of leaves, arbre dégarni de feuilles.

denunciation [diˌnʌnsi'eiʃ(ə)n], s. 1. Dénonciation *f*. 2. (a) Condamnation *f* (d'un abus). (b) Accusation publique (de qn). 3. Dénonciation (d'un traité).

denunciative [di'nʌnsieitiv], **denunciatory** [di'nʌnsi-eitəri], a. Dénonciateur, -trice.

deny [di'nai], v.tr. 1. Nier (un fait); démentir (une nouvelle). *Jur:* Dénier (un crime); repousser (une accusation). I don't d. it, je n'en disconviens pas. I do not d. that we have common interests, je ne nie pas que nous avons, que nous ayons, des intérêts communs. There is no denying the fact, c'est un fait indéniable. I do not d. the fact that . . ., j'apprécie le fait que. . . There's no denying that . . ., on ne saurait nier que. . . . 2. Renier (qn, sa foi). To d. God, nier Dieu. 3. To d. s.o. sth., refuser qch. à qn. To d. the door to s.o., fermer sa porte à qn. To be denied a right, se voir frustré d'un droit. He is not to be denied, il n'acceptera pas de refus. 4. (a) To d. oneself sth., se refuser qch.; se priver de qch. (b) To d. oneself, faire abnégation de soi-même.

deodar ['dioudɑːr], s. Cèdre *m* de l'Himalaya.

deodorant [diː'oudərənt], s. Désodorisant *m*.

deodorize [diː'oudəraiz], v.tr. Désodoriser.

deodorizer [diː'oudəraizər], s. Désodorisant *m*.

deoxidization [diːˌɔksidai'zeiʃən], s. *Ch: Ind:* Désoxydation *f*.

deoxidize [diː'ɔksidaiz], v.tr. *Ch: Ind:* Désoxyder.

deoxidizer [diː'ɔksidaizər], s. *Ch: Ind:* Désoxydant *m*.

deoxygenate [diː'ɔksidʒineit], v.tr. *Ch: Ind:* Désoxygéner.

deoxygenation [diːˌɔksidʒi'neiʃən], v.tr. *Ch: Ind:* Désoxygénation *f*.

depart [di'pɑːt], v.i. 1. (a) S'en aller, partir; (*of train*) partir. (b) To d. (from) this life, mourir; quitter ce monde. 2. To d. from a rule, s'écarter d'une règle.

departed, a. 1. (*Of glory, etc.*) Passé, évanoui. 2. Mort, défunt. s. The d., (i) le défunt; (ii) *pl.* les morts.

department [di'pɑːtmənt], s. 1. (a) *Adm:* Département *m*, service *m*. The different departments, les différents bureaux. Heads of departments, chefs *m* de service. (b) (*In shop*) Rayon *m*, comptoir *m*. D. store, grand magasin. 2. *U.S:* Ministère *m*. State D. = Ministère des Affaires Étrangères.

departmental [ˌdiːpɑːt'mentl], a. Départemental, -aux; qui se rapporte à un service.

departure [di'pɑːtʃər], s. 1. Départ *m*. To take one's d., s'en aller; partir. 2. D. from a principle, déviation *f* d'un principe. A d. from his usual habits, procédé *m* contraire à ses habitudes. 3. A new d., (i) une nouvelle tendance; (ii) un nouvel usage.

depend [di'pend], v.i. 1. *A:* Pendre (from, à). 2. Dépendre (on, de). That depends entirely on you, cela ne tient qu'à vous. That depends, it all depends, cela dépend; *F:* c'est selon. It depends whether he's married, ça dépend s'il est marié. 3. (a) To d. on s.o., se trouver à la charge de qn; recevoir une pension de qn. (b) To d. on foreign supplies, être tributaire de l'étranger. To d. on oneself, *F:* voler de ses propres ailes. 4. (*Rely*) To d. upon s.o., compter sur, faire fond sur, qn. I can d. on him, je suis sûr de lui. You may d. upon it that what I say is true, vous pouvez être sûr que ce que je vous dis est la vérité. (You may) d. upon it, comptez là-dessus.

dependable [di'pendəbl], a. (*Of pers.*) Digne de confiance; (*of information*) sûr, bien fondé.

dependant [di'pendənt], s. Protégé, -ée. *pl.* Dependants, (i) domesticité *f*; (ii) charges *f* de famille.

dependence [di'pendəns], s. 1. (a) D. on s.o., dépendance *f* de qn. (b) D. on s.o., le fait d'être à la charge de qn. 2. Confiance *f* (on, en). To place d. on s.o., se fier à qn.

dependency [di'pendənsi], s. Dépendance *f*. *Esp. pl.* Dependencies of an estate, dépendances d'une terre.

dependent [di'pendənt]. 1. a. (a) Dépendant (on, de). To be d. on alms, subsister d'aumônes. (b) *Gram:* D. clause, proposition subordonnée. (c) To be d. on s.o., être à la charge de qn. Two d. children, deux enfants à charge. (d) *Surg:* D. drainage, drainage *m* au point déclive. 2. s. = DEPENDANT.

depersonalize [diː'pəːsnəlaiz], v.tr. *Med: Psy:* Dépersonnaliser (qn).

depict [di'pikt], v.tr. Peindre, dépeindre, décrire, représenter.

depiction [di'pikʃən], s. Peinture *f*, description *f*.

depilate ['depileit], v.tr. Dépiler. *Toil:* Épiler. *Leath:* Peler (des peaux).

depilation ['depi'leiʃ(ə)n], s. *Toil:* Épilation *f*. *Leath:* Dépilage *m*, épilage *m*.

depilatory [di'pilətəri], a. & s. Dépilatoire (*m*).

deplete [di'pliːt], v.tr. Épuiser (des provisions, etc.).

depletion [di'pliːʃ(ə)n], s. Épuisement *m* (des ressources).

deplorable [di'plɔːrəbl], a. Déplorable, lamentable. -ably, adv. Lamentablement.

deplore [di'plɔːr], v.i. Déplorer; regretter vivement. To d. one's fate, se lamenter sur son sort.

deploy [di'plɔi]. *Mil: Navy:* 1. v.tr. Déployer (une armée). 2. v.i. se déployer.

deployment [di'plɔimənt], s. *Mil: Navy:* Déploiement *m*.

depolarization [diː'poulərai'zeiʃ(ə)n], s. *Ph: El:* Dépolarisation *f*.

depolarize [diː'poulraiz], v.tr. *Ph: El:* Dépolariser.

depolarizer [diː'pouləraizər], s. *Ph: El:* Dépolarisant *m*.

deponent [di'pounənt], a. & s. 1. *Gram:* (Verbe) déponent (*m*). 2. *Jur:* (Témoin) déposant *m*.

depopulate [diː'pɔpjuleit], v.tr. Dépeupler.

depopulation ['diːˌpɔpju'leiʃ(ə)n], s. Dépopulation *f* (d'un pays); dépeuplement *m* (d'une forêt). Rural d., exode rural, désertion *f* des campagnes.

deport [di'pɔːt]. 1. v.tr. (a) Expulser (un étranger). (b) Déporter (de force, les habitants d'un pays). 2. v.pr. To d. oneself, se comporter (bien, mal).

deportation ['diːpɔː'teiʃ(ə)n], s. Expulsion *f* (d'un étranger). D. order, arrêté *m* d'expulsion. (b) Déportation (forcée, d'un peuple).

deportee ['diːpɔː'tiː], s. Déporté, -ée.

deportment [di'pɔːtmənt], s. (a) Tenue *f*, maintien *m*. (b) Conduite *f*; manière *f* d'agir.

depose [di'pouz], v.tr. 1. (a) *A:* Poser (qch.). (b) Déposer (un roi). 2. *Jur:* (a) Déposer, témoigner (that, que + *ind.*). (b) v.i. To d. to a fact, témoigner d'un fait.

deposit¹ [di'pɔzit], s. 1. Bank d., dépôt *m* en banque. D. account, compte *m* de dépôts. 2. To pay a d., verser une somme à titre de provision; donner des arrhes *fpl*. 3. Dépôt(s) *m(pl)*; sédiment *m*. *Geol:* Gisement *m*, couche *f*. To form a d., se déposer. *Med:* Chalky d., encroûtement *m* calcique. *I.C.E:* Carbon d., encrassement charbonneux; calamine *f*.

deposit², *v.tr.* **1.** Déposer (sth. on sth., qch. sur qch.). **2.** (*a*) **To d. money with s.o.**, consigner de l'argent chez qn. (*b*) *Com:* **To d. £100**, laisser, payer, cent livres comme provision. *Cust:* **To d. the duty (repayable)**, cautionner les droits. **3.** (*Of liquid*) Déposer.
depositary [di'pozit(ə)ri], *s.* Dépositaire *m.*
deposition [ˌdiːpə'ziʃ(ə)n], *s.* **1.** Déposition *f* (d'un roi). **2.** *Jur:* Déposition, témoignage *m.* **3.** Dépôt *m* (d'un sédiment). *Geog:* Remblaiement *m.*
depositor [di'pozitər], *s. Bank:* Déposant *m.*
depository [di'pozit(ə)ri], *s.* Dépôt *m*, entrepôt *m.* **Furniture d.**, garde-meubles *m inv.*
depot ['depou], *s.* **1.** *Mil: Navy:* Dépôt *m. Navy:* **D. ship**, (transport) ravitailleur *m.* **2.** (*a*) *Com:* Dépôt, entrepôt *m.* (*b*) **Bus d.**, garage *m* d'autobus. *Rail:* **Goods d.**, dépôt de marchandises. (*c*) *U.S:* ['diːpou] Gare *f* (de chemin de fer).
depravation [ˌdeprə'veiʃ(ə)n], *s.* Dépravation *f.*
deprave [di'preiv], *v.tr.* Dépraver.
depravity [di'præviti], *s.* Dépravation *f*; perversité *f.*
deprecate ['deprikeit], *v.tr.* Désapprouver, déconseiller (une action). **deprecating**, *a.* Désapprobateur, -trice. **-ly**, *adv.* D'un air, d'un ton désapprobateur.
deprecation ['depri'keiʃ(ə)n], *s.* Désapprobation *f.*
deprecatory ['deprikeitəri], *a.* (Rire, *etc.*) qui va au-devant des reproches, de la critique.
depreciable [di'priːʃiabl], *a.* Dépréciable.
depreciate [di'priːʃieit]. **1.** *v.tr.* (*a*) Déprécier; avilir (les marchandises). (*b*) Déprécier, dénigrer (qn). **2.** *v.i.* Se déprécier; diminuer de valeur; (*of shares, etc.*) baisser.
depreciation [di'priːʃi'eiʃ(ə)n], *s.* **1.** (*a*) Dépréciation *f*, rabais *m* (de l'argent); moins-value *f.* (*b*) *Ind:* **Annual d.**, amortissement annuel. **2.** Dépréciation, dénigrement *m.*
depreciative [di'priːʃiətiv], **depreciatory** [di'priːʃi'eitəri], *a.* Dépréciateur, -trice; péjoratif, -ive.
depreciator [di'priːʃi'eitər], *s.* Dépréciateur, -trice; dénigreur, -euse.
depredation [ˌdepri'deiʃ(ə)n], *s.* Déprédation *f.*
depredator ['deprideitər], *s.* Déprédateur, -trice.
depress [di'pres], *v.tr.* **1.** Abaisser; baisser (qch.); appuyer sur (la pédale). **2.** (*a*) Abattre (les forces); faire languir (le commerce). (*b*) Attrister, décourager. **depressed**, *a.* **1.** *Arch:* (Arc) surbaissé. **2.** *Com:* (Marché) languissant. **D. area**, région touchée par la crise. **3.** Triste, abattu. **He is easily d.**, un rien l'abat. **To feel d.**, *F:* avoir le cafard. **depressing**, *a.* Attristant; dépressif, -ive; déprimant. **D. landscape**, paysage triste, maussade.
depression [di'preʃ(ə)n], *s.* **1.** (*a*) Abaissement *m* (de qch.). (*b*) *Astr:* Dépression *f* (d'un astre). **2.** *Meteor:* Dépression, cyclone *m.* **3.** Dépression, creux *m* (de terrain). **4.** *Pol.Ec:* **Economic d.**, dépression économique, crise *f. Com:* Affaissement *m*, marasme *m* (des affaires). **5.** Découragement *m*, abattement *m.*
depressor [di'presər], *s.* **1.** *Anat:* (Muscle) abaisseur *m.* **2.** *Surg:* Dépressoir *m.* **3.** *Ch:* Dépresseur *m.*
deprival [di'praivəl], *s.* Privation *f* (**of**, de).
deprivation [ˌdepri'veiʃ(ə)n], *s.* **1.** Privation *f*, perte *f* (de droits). **2.** Dépossession *f.*
deprive [di'praiv], *v.tr.* **1. To d. s.o. of sth.**, priver qn de qch. **To d. oneself**, s'infliger des privations. **2.** Déposséder (qn) d'une charge; destituer (un prêtre).
depth [depθ], *s.* **1.** Profondeur *f.* **At a d. of 50 fathoms**, par 50 brasses de fond. **2.** Fond *m*, hauteur *f* (de l'eau). **To get out of one's d.**, (i) perdre pied; (ii) sortir de sa compétence. **3.** Hauteur (d'un faux col); épaisseur *f* (d'une couche). **4.** (*a*) Gravité *f* (d'un son). (*b*) Portée *f* (de l'intelligence). (*c*) Intensité *f* (de coloris). **5.** Fond (d'une forêt, d'une caverne); milieu *m* (de la nuit). **In the d. of winter**, au plus fort de l'hiver. **6.** *pl.* **The depths.** (*a*) *Lit:* L'abîme *m*, le gouffre. (*b*) Profondeurs (de l'océan); ténèbres *f* (de l'ignorance). **In the depths of despair**, dans le plus profond désespoir. **'depth-charge**, *s. Navy:* Grenade sous-marine. **'depth-finder, -gauge**, *s. Oc: Nau:* Sondeur *m.* **Sonic d.-f.**, sondeur sonore.
deputation [ˌdepju(ː)'teiʃ(ə)n], *s.* Députation *f*, délégation *f.*

depute [di'pjuːt], *v.tr.* **1.** Déléguer (powers to s.o., des pouvoirs à qn). **2. To d. s.o. to do sth.**, députer, déléguer, qn pour faire qch.
deputize ['depjutaiz], *v.i.* **To d. for s.o.**, faire l'intérim de qn; remplacer qn.
deputy ['depjuti], *s.* Fondé *m* de pouvoir. **1.** Substitut *m* (d'un juge); délégué *m* (d'un fonctionnaire). **To act as d. for s.o.**, suppléer qn. **D.-chairman**, vice-président *m.* **D.-governor**, sous-gouverneur *m.* **D.-judge**, juge *m* suppléant. **D.-mayor**, maire *m* adjoint. **2.** Délégué; *occ.* député *m.*
derail [di'reil], *v.tr.* Faire dérailler (un train).
derailment [di'reilmənt], *s.* Déraillement *m.*
derange [di'rein(d)ʒ], *v.tr.* Déranger.
derangement [di'rein(d)ʒmənt], *s.* Dérèglement *m.* **D. of mind**, dérangement d'esprit.
derat [diː'ræt], *v.tr. U.S:* Dératiser.
derate [diː'reit], *v.tr.* Dégrever (une industrie, etc.). **derating**, *s.* Dégrèvement *m.*
deration [diː'ræʃ(ə)n], *v.tr.* Mettre en vente libre. **derationing**, *s.* Mise *f* en vente libre.
Derby ['daːbi]. **1.** *Pr.n. Geog:* Derby. **2.** *Sp:* **The D.**, la course classique du Derby; le Derby. **3.** *Cost:* (*a*) *U.S:* [dəːbi], Chapeau *m* melon. (*b*) (*Shoe*) Derby *m.*
derelict ['derilikt]. **1.** *a.* Abandonné, délaissé, à l'abandon. **2.** *s.* (*a*) Objet abandonné. *Esp. Nau:* Navire abandonné (en mer); épave *f.* (*b*) Épave humaine.
dereliction [ˌderi'likʃ(ə)n], *s.* **1.** Abandon *m*, délaissement *m.* **2. D. of duty**, manquement *m* au devoir.
derequisition [ˌdiːrekwi'ziʃ(ə)n], *v.tr.* Déréquisitionner.
derestrict [ˌdiːri'strikt], *v.tr. Adm: Aut:* **To d. a road**, libérer une route de toute restriction de vitesse.
deride [di'raid], *v.tr.* Tourner en dérision; bafouer, railler, se moquer de (qn).
derision [di'riʒ(ə)n], *s.* **1.** Dérision *f.* **Object of d.**, objet de risée. **To hold s.o. in d.**, se moquer de qn. **2.** Objet *m* de dérision.
derisive [di'raisiv], *a.* **1.** Moqueur, -euse. **2. D. offer**, offre dérisoire. **-ly**, *adv.* D'un air moqueur.
derisory [di'raisəri], *a.* = DERISIVE.
derivation [ˌderi'veiʃ(ə)n], *s.* Dérivation *f.*
derivative [di'rivətiv]. **1.** *a.* & *s. Gram:* (Mot) dérivé (*m*), dérivatif *m.* **2.** *s.* (*a*) *Ch: Ind:* Dérivé *m.* (*b*) *Mth:* Dérivée *f.* (*c*) *Mus:* Accord dérivé. **-ly**, *adv.* Par dérivation.
derive [di'raiv], *v.tr.* & *i.* **1.** (*a*) **To d. sth. from sth.**, tirer (son origine) de qch.; devoir (son bonheur) à qch.; trouver (du plaisir) à qch. **Income derived from an investment**, revenu provenant d'un placement. (*b*) *Ling:* **Word derived from Latin**, mot qui vient du latin. **2. To be derived**, *v.i.* **to d.**, dériver, (pro)venir (**from**, de).
derm(a) [dəːm(ə)], *s. Anat:* Derme *m.*
dermal ['dəːm(ə)l], **dermic** ['dəːmik], *a.* Cutané.
dermatitis [ˌdəːmə'taitis], *s. Med:* Dermite *f*, dermatite *f.*
dermatological [ˌdəːmətə'lədʒikl], *a.* Dermatologique.
dermatologist [ˌdəːmə'tolədʒist], *s.* Dermatologiste *m.*
dermatology [ˌdəːmə'tolədʒi], *s.* Dermatologie *f.*
dermatosis [ˌdəːmə'tousis], *s.* Dermatose *f.*
derogate ['derogeit], *v.i.* **1.** *A:* **To d. from a right**, porter atteinte à un droit. **To d. from s.o.'s authority**, diminuer l'autorité de qn. **2. To d.** (**from one's dignity**), déroger (à sa dignité).
derogation [ˌdero'geiʃ(ə)n], *s.* **1. D. of a law**, dérogation *f* à une loi. **2. D. from a right**, atteinte portée à un droit. **3. Without d.**, sans déroger (**from dignity**, à la dignité).
derogatory [di'rogət(ə)ri], *a.* **1.** (*a*) Dérogatoire (**from**, à). (*b*) **D. to a right**, attentatoire à un droit. **2.** Dérogeant, qui déroge (**to**, à). **To do sth. d. to one's position**, se manquer à soi-même.
derrick ['derik], *s.* (*a*) Chevalement *m*; potence *f*, chèvre *f.* (*b*) *Nau:* Mât *m* de charge. (*c*) *Oil ind:* Derrick *m.*
derv [dəːv], *s.* (*Initials of Diesel-engined road vehicle*). Gas-oil *m*, gaz-oil *m.*
dervish ['dəːviʃ], *s.* Derviche *m.*
desalting [ˌdi'səltiŋ], *s.* Dessalage *m*, dessalaison *f.*, dessalement *m* (du poisson, de la viande).
descant ['deskænt], *s. Mus:* (*Esp. Ecc:*) Déchant *m.*

descend [di'send]. **1.** *v.i.* (a) Descendre; (of rain) tomber. (b) To d. on s.o., s'abattre, tomber, sur qn. (c) To d. to s.o.'s level, s'abaisser au niveau de qn. To d. to lying, descendre jusqu'au mensonge. (d) To d., be descended, from s.o., descendre de qn; tirer son origine (d'une maison royale, etc.). (e) (Of property) To d. from s.o. to s.o., passer de qn à qn. **2.** *v.tr.* Descendre, dévaler (une colline, un escalier).

descendant, -ent [di'sendənt], *s.* Descendant, -ante. *pl.* **Descendants,** descendance *f*, postérité *f*.

descent [di'sent], *s.* **1.** Descente *f*. **2.** (Attack) Descente, irruption *f* (on, dans, à, sur). **3.** Chute *f* (de température). **4.** (Lineage) Descendance *f*. **Person of noble d.,** personne de haut parage. **5.** *Jur:* Transmission *f* (d'un bien) par héritage.

describe [dis'kraib], *v.tr.* **1.** (a) Décrire, dépeindre. (b) *Pred.* To d. s.o. as . . ., qualifier qn de . . ., représenter qn comme. . . . (c) Donner le signalement (d'un homme recherché par la police). **2.** Décrire (une courbe).

description [dis'kripʃ(ə)n], *s.* **1.** (a) Description *f*. **Beyond d.,** indescriptible. (b) (Formally) (i) (For Police purposes) (in a card index) fiche *f* signalétique; (ii) (On passport, etc.), profession *f*, qualité *f*. **To answer to the d.,** répondre au signalement *m*. (c) *Com:* Désignation *f* (de marchandises). **2.** Sorte *f*, espèce *f*, genre *m*. **People of this d.,** les gens de cette espèce, de cette sorte.

descriptive [dis'kriptiv], *a.* Descriptif, -ive.

descry [dis'krai], *v.tr. Lit:* Apercevoir, aviser (dans le lointain).

desecrate ['desikreit], *v.tr.* Profaner (un lieu saint).

desecration ['desi'kreiʃ(ə)n], *s.* Profanation *f*.

desecrator ['desikreitər], *s.* Profanateur, -trice.

desensitize [di:'sensitaiz], *v.tr. Phot:* Désensibiliser (une plaque).

desensitizer [di:'sensitaizər], *s.Phot:* Désensibilisateur *m*.

desert¹ [di'zə:t], *s.* Mérite *m. Usu. pl.* Mérites; ce qu'on mérite; dû *m*. **To everyone according to his deserts,** à chacun son dû. **To get one's deserts,** avoir ce que l'on mérite.

desert² ['dezət]. **1.** *a.* (Of region, etc.) Désert; désertique. **2.** *s.* Désert *m*.

desert³ [di'zə:t], *v.tr.* (a) Déserter (son poste); quitter (un lieu). *Abs. Mil:* Déserter. (b) Abandonner, délaisser (qn). *Pol:* To d. one's party, faire défection.

deserted, *a.* (Of pers.) Abandonné; (of place) désert.

deserter [di'zə:tər], *s.* Déserteur *m*.

desertion [di'zə:ʃ(ə)n], *s.* **1.** Abandon *m*, délaissement *m* (de qn). **2.** *Mil:* Désertion *f. Pol:* **D. of one's party,** défection *f*.

deserve [di'zə:v], *v.tr.* Mériter (qch.). **To d. praise,** être digne d'éloges. **He (richly) deserves it!** *F:* il ne l'a pas volé! **deserving,** *a.* (Of pers.) Méritant; (of action) méritoire. **D. case,** cas digne d'intérêt.

deservedly [di'zə:vidli], *adv.* A juste titre; à bon droit.

desiccate ['desikeit], *v.tr.* Dessécher; déshydrater.

desiccation [,desi'keiʃ(ə)n], *s.* Dessiccation *f*; dessèchement *m*; déshydratation *f*.

desideratum, *pl.* -a [di,zidə'ra:təm, -ə], *s.* Desideratum *m, pl.* desiderata.

design¹ [di'zain], *s.* **1.** (a) Dessein *m*, intention *f*, projet *m*. **By d.,** à dessein. *F:* **To have designs on s.o.,** avoir des desseins sur qn, *esp.* avoir des vues matrimoniales sur qn. **To have designs on sth.,** jeter son dévolu sur qch. (b) **With this d . . . .,** dans ce but. . . . **2.** (Decorative) d., dessin d'ornement. **3.** *Ind:* Étude *f*, avant-projet *m* (d'une machine, etc.). **4.** Dessin, type *m*, forme *f*, modèle *m* (d'une machine, etc.). **Machine of faulty d.,** machine mal étudiée, de construction fautive. **Car of the latest d.,** voiture dernier modèle. **D. is as important as construction,** la présentation a autant d'importance que la fabrication.

design², *v.tr.* **1.** *O:* Destiner (for, à). **To d. s.o. for the church,** destiner qn à la prêtrise. **2. Machine designed for a special purpose,** machine construite, étudiée, dans un but spécial. **3.** (a) Préparer (un projet); combiner (un coup). (b) Créer (une robe); établir le plan (d'un avion), étudier, calculer. **Well-designed piece of furniture,** meuble *m* aux lignes étudiées. **designing¹,** *a.* Artificieux, -euse, intrigant. **designing²,** *s.* Dessin *m*, création *f* (d'une machine, etc.).

designate¹ ['dezigneit], *a.* (Bishop) d., (évêque) désigné.

designate², *v.tr. Usu. Adm: or Jur:* **1.** (a) Désigner, nommer (s.o. to an office, qn à une fonction). (b) **To d. s.o. as, for, one's successor,** désigner qn pour, comme, son successeur. **2. Designated by the name of . . .,** désigné sous le nom de. . . . **Rulings designated as arbitrary,** décisions qualifiées d'arbitraires. **3.** (Of things) Indiquer (qch.).

designation [,dezig'neiʃ(ə)n], *s. Usu. Adm: or Jur:* **1.** Désignation *f* (d'une personne). **2. D. to a post,** nomination *f* à un emploi. **3.** Désignation, nom *m*.

designedly [di'zainidli], *adv.* A dessein; avec préméditation; avec intention.

designer [di'zainər], *s.* **1.** *Ind: Com:* Dessinateur, -trice. *Th:* **Stage d.,** décorateur *m* de théâtre. **2.** Intrigant, -ante.

desirability [di,zaiərə'biliti], **desirableness** [di'zaiərəblnis], *s.* Caractère *m* désirable; avantage *m*; attrait *m* (d'une femme).

desirable [di'zaiərəbl], *a.* Désirable. (a) A désirer; souhaitable; avantageux. *Com:* **D. property for sale,** belle maison à vendre. (b) (Of pers., esp. of woman) Attrayant.

desire¹ [di'zaiər], *s.* **1.** (a) Désir *m*, souhait *m*. **I feel no d. to . . .,** je n'éprouve aucune envie de . . . (b) Désir, appétit charnel. **2. At, by, s.o.'s d.,** à, sur, la demande de qn.

desire², *v.tr.* **1.** Désirer (qch.); avoir envie de (qch.). **To d. to do sth.,** désirer faire qch. **Since you d. it,** puisque vous y tenez. **It leaves much to be desired,** cela laisse beaucoup à désirer. **2.** (a) **To d. sth. of s.o.,** demander qch. à qn. (b) **To d. s.o. to do sth.,** prier qn de faire qch.

desirous [di'zaiərəs], *a.* Désireux (of, de).

desist [di'zist], *v.i. Lit:* **1.** Cesser (from doing sth., de faire qch.). **2. To d. from sth.,** renoncer à qch.; se désister de qch.

desk [desk], *s.* **1.** (a) (Scholar's) Pupitre *m*; (in office) bureau *m*; (schoolmaster's) chaire *f*. (b) *Journ: U.S:* **The d.,** le secrétariat de la rédaction. **2.** Caisse *f*. **Pay at the d.!** payez à la caisse! **'desk-pad,** *s.* Sousmain *m.inv.*; bloc-notes *m, pl.* blocs-notes.

desolate¹ ['desəlit], *a.* **1.** (Lieu) désert. **2.** Affligé. **-ly,** *adv.* (Vivre) dans la solitude; d'un air désolé; avec désolation.

desolate² ['desəleit], *v.tr.* Désoler. **1.** Ravager (un pays). **2.** Affliger (qn).

desolation [,desə'leiʃ(ə)n], *s.* Désolation *f*.

despair¹ [dis'pɛər], *s.* (a) Désespoir *m*; désespérance *f*. **To be in d.,** être au désespoir. **A dumb d.,** un accablement muet. **To give up (the attempt) in d.,** y renoncer en désespoir de cause. **To drive s.o. to d.,** pousser qn au désespoir. **To give way to d.,** s'abandonner au désespoir. (b) **Child who is the d. of his parents,** enfant qui fait le désespoir des siens.

despair², *v.i.* (a) Désespérer (of, de). **To d. of doing sth.,** désespérer de faire qch. **His life is despaired of,** on désespère de sa vie, on n'a plus d'espoir. (b) *Abs.* Perdre espoir; (se) désespérer. **despairing,** *a.* Désespéré. **In a d. tone,** d'un ton de désespoir. **-ly,** *adv.* En désespéré.

despatch [dis'pætʃ], *s. & v.* = DISPATCH¹,².

desperado [,despə'ra:dou], *s.m.* Homme capable de tout; cerveau brûlé; risque-tout *inv.*

desperate ['despə(ə)rit], *a.* **1.** (a) (Of condition, malady) Désespéré. (b) **D. remedy,** remède héroïque. **D. cases require d. remedies,** aux grands maux les grands remèdes. **2.** (a) A d. man, un désespéré. (b) **D. energy,** l'énergie du désespoir. **D. conflict,** combat acharné. **To do something d.,** faire un malheur. **-ly,** *adv.* **1.** (Lutter) désespérément, avec acharnement. **2. D. ill,** gravement malade; près de la mort. **3.** *F:* **D. in love,** éperdument amoureux (with, de).

desperation [,despə'reiʃ(ə)n], *s.* (Outrance *f* du) désespoir *m*. **To drive s.o. to d.,** pousser qn à bout. **In d.,** en désespoir de cause. **I was in d.,** j'étais au désespoir, *F:* j'étais aux cent coups.

despicable ['despikəbl, dis'pik-], *a.* Méprisable. **-ably,** *adv.* Bassement.

despise [dis'paiz], *v.tr.* (a) Mépriser (qn); faire mépris de (qch.). (b) Dédaigner (qch.).

despite [dis'pait]. **1.** *s. Lit:* Dépit *m*. **2.** *prep. & prep.phr.* **D., in d. of,** (sth.), en dépit de (qch.).

despoil [dis'pɔil], *v.tr.* Dépouiller, spolier (qn) (of, de).
despoiler [dis'pɔilər], *s.* Spoliateur, -trice.
despond[1] [dis'pɔnd], *s. Lit:* The slough of d., le bourbier du découragement.
despond[2], *v.i.* Perdre courage.
despondency [dis'pɔndənsi], *s.* Découragement *m*, abattement *m*.
despondent [dis'pɔndənt], *a.* Découragé, abattu. To feel d., se sentir déprimé. **-ly,** *adv.* D'un air découragé.
despot ['despɔt], *s.* Despote *m*; tyran *m*.
despotic [dis'pɔtik], *a.* 1. (Pouvoir) despotique. 2. (Of pers.) Arbitraire, despote. **-ally,** *adv.* Despotiquement, arbitrairement.
despotism ['despɔtizm], *s.* Despotisme *m*.
desquamate ['deskwəmeit], *v.i.* Se desquamer; s'exfolier.
dessert [di'zə:t], *s.* (a) Dessert *m*. (b) Entremets sucré. *attrib.* D. **apple,** pomme *f* au couteau. D. **grapes,** raisins *mpl.* de table. D. **wine,** vin *m* de liqueur. **des'sert-plate,** *s.* Assiette *f* à dessert. **des'sert-service,** *s.* Service *m* à dessert. **des'sert-spoon,** *s.* Cuiller *f* à dessert.
destination [,desti'neiʃ(ə)n], *s.* Destination *f*.
destine ['destin], *v.tr.* 1. Destiner. He was destined for the church, il fut destiné à l'église. I was destined to be unhappy, j'étais destiné à être malheureux. He was destined never to see her again, il ne devait plus la revoir. 2. *Lit:* The ship was destined for the Cape, le vaisseau était en partance pour le Cap.
destiny ['destini], *s.* Destin *m*, destinée *f*; le sort.
destitute ['destitju:t], *a.* Dépourvu, dénué (of, de). 2. Indigent; sans ressources; *F:* sans le sou. To be utterly d., manquer de tout.
destitution [,desti'tju:ʃ(ə)n], *s.* Dénuement *m*, indigence *f*; la misère.
destroy [dis'trɔi], *v.tr.* 1. Détruire; anéantir (des espérances). 2. Tuer, abattre (une bête). To d. oneself, se suicider. **destroying,** *a.* Destructeur, -trice.
destroyer [dis'trɔiər], *s.* 1. Destructeur, -trice. 2. *Navy:* Destroyer *m*. 3. *Mil:* Tank d., chasseur *m* de chars.
destructibility [dis,trʌkti'biliti], *s.* Destructibilité *f*.
destructible [dis'trʌktibl], *a.* Destructible.
destruction [dis'trʌkʃ(ə)n], *s.* Destruction *f*. He is rushing to his own d., il court à sa perte. The d. caused by the fire, les ravages *m* du feu. Gambling was his d., le jeu a causé sa perte.
destructive [dis'trʌktiv], *a.* Destructeur, -trice; destructif, -ive. D. **criticism,** critique destructive. A d. **child,** *F:* un brise-tout *inv.*
destructiveness [dis'trʌktivnis], *s.* Destructivité *f*. 1. Effet destructeur, pouvoir destructeur (d'un explosif). 2. (Of child) Penchant *m* à détruire.
destructor [dis'trʌktər], *s.* 1. Destructeur, -trice. 2. Refuse d., incinérateur *m*.
desuetude [di'sjuitju:d], *s.* Désuétude *f*. Law fallen into d., loi caduque, désuète.
desulphurization ['di:,sʌlfərai'zeiʃən], *s. Ch: Ind:* Désulfuration *f*.
desulphurize ['di:'sʌlfəraiz], *v.tr. Ch: Ind:* Désulfurer.
desultoriness ['desəltərinis], *s.* Manque *m* de suite, de méthode.
desultory ['desəlt(ə)ri], *a.* Décousu; sans suite. D. **conversation,** conversation à bâtons rompus. D. **reading,** lectures décousues. **-ily,** *adv.* D'une manière décousue; sans suite, sans méthode, à bâtons rompus.
detach [di'tætʃ], *v.tr.* 1. Détacher, séparer (from, de); dételer (des wagons). 2. *Mil:* Détacher (des troupes). **detached,** *a.* Détaché. 1. Séparé (from, de); à part. D. **house,** maison séparée. *S.a.* SEMI-DETACHED. *Mil:* D. **post,** poste isolé. 2. (a) (Of pers.) Désintéressé. (b) D. **manner,** manière désinvolte.
detachable [di'tætʃəbl], *a.* Détachable; amovible.
detachment [di'tætʃmənt], *s.* 1. (a) Séparation *f* (from, de). (b) Action de se détacher; décollement *m*. *Med:* D. of the retina, décollement de la rétine. 2. (a) Détachement *m* (de l'esprit) (from, de). (b) Indifférence *f* (from, envers). 3. *Mil:* Détachement. On d., détaché.

detail[1] ['di:teil], *s.* 1. Détail *m*, particularité *f*. To go, enter, into all the details, donner, entrer dans, tous les détails. In every d., de point en point. 2. Organe *m*, pièce composante (d'une machine). 3. *Mil:* Détachement *m* (de corvée). *U.S:* Détachement *m* (de policiers); groupe *f* (de journalistes).
detail[2] [di'teil], *v.tr.* 1. Détailler; raconter en détail. To d. the facts, énumérer les faits. 2. *Mil:* To d. s.o. for a duty, affecter qn à un service. **detailed,** *a.* Détaillé; (récit) circonstancié, détaillé. *Surv:* D. **survey,** levé *m* de détail.
detain [di'tein], *v.tr.* 1. Détenir (qn en prison). 2. (a) Retenir (qn); empêcher (qn) de partir. (b) Consigner (un élève).
detainee [,di:tei'ni:], *s. Jur: etc:* Détenu *m*.
detainer [di'teinər], *s. Jur:* 1. Détention *f* (d'un objet). 2. (Writ of) **detainer,** mandat *m* de dépôt.
detect [di'tekt], *v.tr.* 1. Découvrir (le coupable). To d. s.o. in the act, prendre qn en flagrant délit. 2. Apercevoir; détecter; discerner. 3. (a) Localiser (une fuite de gaz, etc.). (b) *W.Tel:* Détecter. **detecting,** *a.* Détecteur, -trice. *W.Tel:* D. **valve,** lampe détectrice.
detectaphone [di'tektəfoun], *s.* Espion *m*, microphone caché.
detection [di'tekʃ(ə)n], *s.* 1. Découverte *f*. To escape d., (i) se dérober aux recherches; (ii) (of mistake) passer inaperçu. 2. *W.Tel:* Détection *f*. 3. *Mil: Av:* Sound d., détection par le son. *Mil:* Mine d., détection (des mines).
detective [di'tektiv]. 1. *a.* Révélateur, -trice. 2. *s.* Agent *m* de la Police Judiciaire, de la Sûreté. Private d., détective *m*. D. **story,** roman policier.
detector [di'tektər], *s.* 1. (Pers.) Découvreur, -euse (d'erreurs, etc.). 2. *Tchn:* (a) Détecteur *m* (de grisou); indicateur *m* (de gaz). (b) Signal *m* d'alarme (d'incendie); avertisseur *m*. (c) *Mil:* Mine d., détecteur de mines. *Mil: Av:* Sound d., appareil *m* de repérage par le son. (d) Lie d., détecteur de mensonges.
détente [,dei'tɑ:nt], *s.* Détente *f* (diplomatique).
detention [di'tenʃ(ə)n], *s.* 1. (a) Détention *f* (en prison). (b) *Sch:* Consigne *f*, retenue *f*. 2. (a) Retard *m* (inévitable); arrêt *m*. (b) *Nau:* Arrêt (d'un navire).
deter [di'tə:r], *v.tr.* (deterred) Détourner, décourager (s.o. from doing sth., qn de faire qch.). Nothing will d. him, rien ne le fera hésiter.
detergent [di'tə:dʒənt], *a. & s.* Détersif (*m*), détergent (*m*); lessive *f*.
deteriorate [di'tiəriəreit]. 1. *v.tr.* Détériorer. 2. *v.i.* (a) (Se) détériorer. (b) Diminuer de valeur. (c) (Of race) Dégénérer.
deterioration [di,tiəriə'reiʃ(ə)n], *s.* (a) Détérioration *f*. (b) Diminution *f* de valeur. (c) Dégénération *f* (d'une race).
determinable [di'tə:minəbl], *a.* 1. (Quantité) déterminable. 2. *Jur:* (Contrat) résoluble.
determinant [di'tə:minənt]. 1. *a.* Déterminant. D. of sth., qui détermine qch. 2. *s.* (a) Cause déterminante (de qch.). (b) *Mth: Biol:* Déterminant *m*.
determinate [di'tə:minit], *a.* (a) Déterminé; précis; bien défini. (b) Définitif.
determination [di,tə:mi'neiʃ(ə)n], *s.* 1. (a) Détermination *f* (d'une date). (b) Délimitation *f* (d'une frontière). 2. (Of pers.) Détermination, résolution *f*. Air of d., air résolu. 3. *Jur:* (a) Décision *f* (d'une affaire). (b) Arrêt *m*, décision. 4. (a) *Jur:* Résolution (d'un contrat, etc.). (b) Expiration *f* (d'un contrat).
determinative [di'tə:minətiv]. 1. *a.* Déterminant. 2. *a. & s. Gram:* Déterminatif (*m*).
determine [di'tə:min], *v.tr. & i.* (a) Déterminer (une date). Conditions to be determined, conditions à fixer. (b) Délimiter (une frontière). (c) Constater (la nature de qch.). 2. Décider (une question). 3. To d. to do sth., décider de faire qch. To d. that . . ., décider, résoudre, que . . . 4. *Jur:* (a) *v.tr.* Résoudre (un contrat). (b) *v.i.* (Of lease) Prendre fin.
determined, *a.* 1. (Prix) déterminé. 2. (Of pers.) Déterminé, résolu. D. **chin,** menton volontaire. To be d. to do sth., être résolu à, vouloir absolument, faire qch. **-ly,** *adv.* Résolument.
deterrent [di'terənt], *s. Mil: Pol:* Arme *f* de dissuasion. To act as a d., exercer un effet préventif.

detersive [di'tə:siv], *a. & s. Med: Dom.Ec:* Détersif (*m*).
detest [di'test], *v.tr.* Détester; abhorrer.
detestable [di'testəbl], *a.* Détestable. **-ably,** *adv.* Détestablement.
detestation [,di:tes'teiʃ(ə)n], *s.* 1. Détestation *f* (of, de). 2. Chose *f* détestable; abomination *f.*
dethrone [di'θroun], *v.tr.* Détrôner.
dethronement [di'θrounmənt], *s.* Détrônement *m.*
detonate ['detəneit]. 1. *v.tr.* Faire détoner (un explosif); faire sauter (une mine). 2. *v.i.* Détoner. **detonating,** *a.* Détonant, explosif.
detonation [,detə'neiʃ(ə)n], *s.* Détonation *f*, explosion *f.*
detonative ['detənətiv], *a.* Détonant, explosif. **D. power,** force explosive.
detonator ['detəneitər], *s.* 1. Détonateur *m*; amorce *f.* 2. *Rail:* Pétard *m.*
detour ['deituər], *s.* (*a*) Détour *m.* (*b*) *U.S:* Déviation *f* (de la circulation, d'itinéraire, etc.).
detoxicate [di:'tɔksikeit], *v.tr. Med:* Désintoxiquer, détoxiquer.
detoxication [di:,tɔksi'keiʃ(ə)n], *s.* Désintoxication *f,* détoxication *f.*
detract [di'trækt]. 1. *v.i.* To d. from s.o.'s merit, rabaisser le mérite de qn. 2. *v.tr. O:* To d. something from s.o.'s pleasure, diminuer un peu le plaisir de qn.
detraction [di'trækʃ(ə)n], *s.* (*a*) Dénigrement *m.* (*b*) This is no d. from his merits, ceci n'enlève rien à son mérite.
detractor [di'træktər], *s.* Détracteur, -trice.
detriment ['detrimənt], *s.* Détriment *m,* dommage *m.* To the d. of . . ., au détriment, au préjudice, de. . . .
detrimental [,detri'mentl], *a.* Nuisible (to, à). It would be d. to my interests, cela desservirait mes intérêts. **-ally,** *adv.* Nuisiblement.
detritus [di'traitəs], *s. Geol:* Détritus *m(pl).*
deuce[1] [dju:s], *s.* 1. (*Of dice, dominoes, cards*) Deux *m.* 2. *Ten:* A deux; égalité *f* (à quarante).
deuce[2], *s. F: O:* Diantre *m*, diable *m.* Go to the d.! allez vous promener! va-t-en au diable! To play the d. with sth., ruiner, gâcher, qch. He's the d. of a liar, c'est un satané menteur. A d. of a mess, un joli gâchis.
deuced ['dju:sid]. *F: O:* 1. *a.* A d. lot of trouble, une peine du diable. 2. *adv.* What d. bad luck! quelle fichue guigne! **-ly,** *adv. F: O:* Diablement, diantrement.
deuterium [dju(:)'tiəriəm], *s. Atom.Ph:* Deutérium *m.*
Deuteronomy [,dju:tə'rɔnəmi], *s. B:* Deutéronome *m.*
devaluate [di:'væljueit], *v.tr.* = DEVALUE.
devaluation [di:,vælju'eiʃ(ə)n], *s. Pol.Ec:* Dévaluation *f.* **The d. rate,** le taux dévaluateur.
devalue [di:'vælju], *v.tr. Pol.Ec:* Dévaluer, dévaloriser (une monnaie).
devastate ['devəsteit], *v.tr.* Dévaster, ravager. **devastating,** *a.* 1. (*Of storm*) Dévastateur, -trice. 2. (Argument) accablant; *F:* (charme) fatal. **-ly,** *adv. F:* **D.** funny, d'un comique à se tordre. *F:* **She's d. beautiful,** elle est belle à vous rendre fou.
devastation [,devə'steiʃ(ə)n], *s.* Dévastation *f.*
devastator ['devəsteitər], *s.* Dévastateur, -trice.
develop [di'veləp], *v.* (developed [di'veləpt]) I. *v.tr.* 1. *Mth:* Développer (une surface, une fonction). 2. (*a*) Développer (les facultés). (*b*) Développer, amplifier (une pensée). (*c*) *Mil:* To d. an attack, développer une attaque. 3. To d. a district, exploiter, mettre en valeur, une région. *Town P:* Lotir. 4. To d. heat, engendrer de la chaleur. 5. Contracter (une maladie, une mauvaise habitude); manifester (une tendance à . . .). 6. *Phot:* Révéler, développer (une pellicule). II. develop, *v.i.* 1. (*a*) (*Of the body*) Se développer. We must let things d., il faut laisser les choses suivre leur cours. *Bot:* (*Of plant*) To d. imperfectly, avorter. (*b*) London developed into the general mart of Europe, Londres devint peu à peu le grand marché de l'Europe. 2. Se manifester. (*a*) An abscess developed, il s'était formé un abcès. (*b*) *U.S:* They waited to see what would d. next, ils attendaient voir ce qui se passerait ensuite. 3. *U.S:* It developed today that . . ., il advint aujourd'hui que . . . **developing,** *s.* 1. Développement *m*; mise *f* en valeur (d'une région). **D. countries,** pays en voie de développement. 2. *Phot:* Développement. **D. of prints,** tirage *m* par développement. **D. bath,** (bain) révélateur *m.*

developer [di'veləpər], *s.* 1. *Town P:* Lotisseur *m.* 2. *Phot:* (*a*) (*Pers.*) Développeur *m.* (*b*) (*Agent*) Révélateur *m.*
development [di'veləpmənt], *s.* 1. *Mth:* Développement *m* (d'une surface, d'une fonction). 2. (*a*) Développement (des facultés). **Retarded d.,** infantilisme *m.* (*b*) Développement, amplification *f* (d'un sujet). 3. *Town P: etc:* Exploitation *f,* aménagement *m,* mise *f* en valeur (d'une région). **D. area,** région *f* à mettre en valeur. **D. of building land,** lotissement *m* d'un terrain à bâtir. **D. companies,** sociétés *f* d'exploitation. 4. *Phot:* Développement. 5. Développement; déroulement *m* (des événements). 6. Fait nouveau. **To await further developments,** attendre la suite des événements.
deviate ['di:vieit], *v.i.* Dévier, s'écarter (from, de). *Ph:* (*Of beam*) S'infléchir. (*Of projectile*) Dériver.
deviation [,di:vi'eiʃ(ə)n], *s.* Déviation *f* (from, de); écart *m.* **D. from one's instructions,** dérogation *f* à ses instructions.
deviationism ['di:vi'eiʃənizm], *s. Pol:* Déviationnisme *m.*
deviationist [,di:vi'eiʃənist], *a. & s.* Déviationniste (*mf*).
device [di'vais], *s.* 1. (*a*) Expédient *m,* moyen *m.* **To leave s.o. to his own devices,** abandonner qn à ses propres moyens; livrer qn à lui-même. (*b*) Stratagème *m,* ruse *f.* 2. Dispositif *m,* appareil *m*; *F:* truc *m.* **A new d.,** un nouveau système. 3. Emblème *m,* devise *f.*
devil[1] ['devl], *s.* 1. (*a*) Diable *m.* **To be between the d. and the deep sea,** être entre l'enclume et le marteau; être entre Charybde et Scylla. **Talk of the d. and he's sure to appear,** quand on parle du loup, on en voit la queue. **To paint the d. blacker than he is,** faire le diable plus noir qu'il n'est. **The d. rebuking sin,** le diable qui s'est fait ermite. **D. take it!** que le diable l'emporte! **To go to the d.,** se ruiner. **Go to the d.!** allez au diable! **To play the d. with sth.,** mettre la confusion dans qch. **That child is a little d.,** cet enfant est un petit monstre. (*b*) *F:* **What the d. are you doing?** que diable faites-vous là? **How the d. . . .?** comment diable . . .? **To work like the d.,** travailler avec acharnement. *F:* **There'll be the d. to pay,** ça nous, vous, coûtera cher. (*Of a task, etc.*) **It's the d.,** c'est le diable. **He has the d. of a temper,** il est mauvais coucheur. 2. Démon *m.* **D. worship,** démonolâtrie *f.* **To raise the d. in s.o.,** évoquer les pires passions chez qn. **Poor d.!** pauvre diable! 3. (*a*) Nègre *m* (d'un avocat). (*b*) *Typ:* Printer's d., apprenti imprimeur. 4. *Geog:* (Dust-)d., tourbillon *m* de poussière. 'devil-fish, *s.* Pieuvre *f,* poulpe *m.* 'devil-may-'care, *a. & s.* Cerveau brûlé; tête brûlée. **D.-m.-c. spirit,** esprit (i) téméraire, (ii) insouciant.
devil[2], *v.* (devilled). 1. *v.i.* To d. (for a barrister), servir de nègre (à un avocat). 2. *v.tr.* Griller de la viande fortement épicée.
devilish ['deviliʃ]. 1. *a.* Diabolique. (*b*) Maudit, satané. 2. *adv. F: O:* **It's d. hot!** il fait diablement chaud! **-ly,** *adv.* 1. Diaboliquement. 2. *F:* Diantrement, bigrement.
devilishness ['deviliʃnis], *s.* 1. Nature *f* diabolique (d'une invention, etc.). 2. Diablerie *f.*
devilment ['devlmənt], **devilry** ['devlri], *s.* 1. Méchanceté *f.* **There's some d. afoot,** il se trame quelque chose. 2. **To be full of d.,** avoir le diable au corps.
devious ['di:viəs], *a.* Détourné, tortueux. **To achieve one's end by d. ways,** prendre les voies détournées pour arriver à son but.
deviousness ['di:viəsnis], *s.* Détours *mpl,* tortuosité *f.*
devisable [di'vaizəbl], *a.* 1. Imaginable. 2. *Jur:* (Bien immobilier) disponible (par testament).
devise[1] [di'vaiz], *s.* 1. Dispositions *f* testamentaires de biens immobiliers. 2. Legs (immobilier).
devise[2], *v.tr.* 1. Combiner (un projet); inventer, imaginer (un appareil); tramer (un complot). **To d. a good plan,** s'aviser d'un bon expédient. 2. *Jur:* Disposer par testament de (biens immobiliers).
devisee [divai'zi:], *s. Jur:* Légataire *mf.*
deviser [di'vaizər], *s.* Inventeur (d'un appareil, etc.).
devisor [di'vaizər], *s. Jur:* Testateur, -trice.
devoid [di'vɔid], *a.* Dénué, dépourvu (of, de).

devolution [,di:vəˈlju:ʃ(ə)n], s. 1. *Biol:* Dégénération *f* (d'une espèce). 2. *Jur:* Dévolution *f*; transmission *f*. 3. *Pol:* (a) Délégation *f* (de pouvoir). (b) Décentralisation administrative.
devolve [diˈvɔlv]. 1. *v.tr.* Déléguer, transmettre (des fonctions). 2. *v.i.* (a) Incomber (on, upon, à). The duty devolved upon me to . . ., le devoir m'échut de. . . . (b) *Jur:* (Of property) To d. to, upon, s.o., être dévolu à qn. The estate devolved upon him, c'est lui qui a hérité.
Devonian [deˈvouniən], a. 1. *Geol:* Dévonien, -ienne. 2. (Habitant *m*, natif *m*) du Devon.
devote [diˈvout], *v.tr.* Vouer, consacrer; accorder (du temps à qch.). To d. oneself to sth., se vouer à (une occupation); s'adonner à (l'étude). **devoted,** a. Dévoué, attaché (to, à). D. to work, assidu au travail. **-ly,** adv. Avec dévouement.
devotedness [diˈvoutidnis], s. = DEVOTION 3.
devotee [,devouˈti:], s. Fervent *m* (of sport, du sport). Surrounded by his devotees, entouré de thuriféraires *m*.
devotion [diˈvouʃ(ə)n], s. 1. Dévotion *f* (à Dieu). 2. To be at one's devotions, faire ses dévotions, ses prières. 3. Dévouement *m* (to s.o., à, pour, qn). D. to work, assiduité *f* au travail.
devotional [diˈvouʃnl], a. (Livre) de dévotion. D. attitude, attitude de prière.
devour [diˈvauər], *v.tr.* Dévorer. **devouring,** a. Dévorateur, -trice.
devout [diˈvaut], a. 1. Dévot, pieux. 2. (Of wish) Fervent, sincère. **-ly,** adv. 1. Dévotement, avec dévotion. 2. Sincèrement. It is d. to be hoped that . . ., on ne saurait trop espérer que. . . .
devoutness [diˈvautnis], s. Dévotion *f*, piété *f*.
dew[1] [dju:], s. Rosée *f*. Evening dew, serein *m*; rosée du soir. Dew is falling, il tombe de la rosée. ˈdew(-)claw, s. Z: Ergot *m* (des chiens, etc.). ˈdew(-)fall, s. Serein *m*. ˈdew-point, s. Ph: Meteor: Point *m* de rosée.
dew[2], *v.tr.* Humecter (l'herbe) de rosée.
dewberry [ˈdju:beri], s. Bot: (a) Mûre *f* des haies. (b) (The shrub) Ronce bleue.
dewdrop [ˈdju:drɔp], s. (a) Goutte *f* de rosée. (b) F: Goutte au bout du nez; roupie *f*.
dewlap [ˈdju:læp], s. 1. Fanon *m* (de la vache). 2. F: Double menton *m*.
dewpond [ˈdju:pɔnd], s. Mare artificielle.
dewy [ˈdju:i], a. Humecté de rosée.
dexterity [deksˈteriti], s. Dextérité *f*; habileté *f*.
dext(e)rous [ˈdekst(ə)rəs], a. Adroit, habile (in doing sth., à faire qch.). **-ly,** adv. Avec dextérité; habilement.
dextrin [ˈdekstrin, -i:n], s. Ch: Ind: Dextrine *f*.
dextrose [ˈdekstrous], s. Dextrose *m*.
dhoti [ˈdouti], s. (In India) Pagne *m*.
diabetes [,daiəˈbi:ti:z], s. Med: Diabète *m*.
diabetic [,daiəˈbetik], a. & s. Diabétique (*mf*).
diabolical [,daiəˈbɔlik(ə)l], a. (Cruauté) diabolique; (complot) infernal, -aux. D. grin, ricanement satanique. **-ally,** adv. Diaboliquement.
diabolism [daiˈæbəlizəm], s. 1. Diablerie *f*, magie noire; sorcellerie *f*. 2. Satanisme *m*.
diaconal [daiˈækənl], a. Ecc: Diaconal, -aux.
diaconate [daiˈækənit], s. Ecc: Diaconat *m*.
diacritical [,daiəˈkritik(ə)l], a. 1. Gram: (Signe) diacritique. 2. D. mind, esprit fin.
diadem [ˈdaiədəm], s. Diadème *m*; bandeau royal.
diaeresis, pl. **-eses** [daiˈiərəsis, -əsi:z], s. 1. Gram: Tréma *m*; diérèse *f*. 2. Surg: Diérèse *f*.
diagnose [ˈdaiəgˈnouz], *v.tr.* Diagnostiquer.
diagnosis, pl. **-oses** [,daiəgˈnousis, -ousi:z], s. Med: Diagnostic *m* (d'une maladie); diagnose *f*.
diagonal [daiˈægənl]. 1. a. Diagonal, -aux. 2. s. Diagonale *f*. **-ally,** adv. Diagonalement; en diagonale.
diagram [ˈdaiəgræm], s. 1. Diagramme *m*, tracé *m*, schéma *m*. Geometrical d., figure *f* géométrique. 2. Graphique *m* (de température, de pression, etc.). Mch: Indicator d., diagramme d'indicateur.
diagrammatic [,daiəgrəˈmætik], a. Schématique. **-ally,** adv. Schématiquement.
dial[1] [ˈdaiəl], s. 1. (a) Cadran *m*. S.a. SUN-DIAL. (b) Nau: Compass d., rose *f* des vents. 2. P: Visage *m*, P: museau *m*.

dial[2], (dialled). Tp: (a) v.tr. Appeler (qn) à l'automatique. To d. 999, téléphoner à la police, appeler Police Secours. (b) abs. Composer, faire, chiffrer, un numéro. **dialling,** s. Tp: Composition *f* du numéro. D. tone, signal *m* de manœuvre, tonalité continue.
dialect [ˈdaiəlekt], s. Dialecte *m*. Provincial d., patois *m*.
dialectal [,daiəˈlektl], a. Dialectal, -aux.
dialectic(s) [,daiəˈlektik(s)], s.(pl.) Dialectique *f*.
dialectician [,daiəlekˈtiʃ(ə)n], s. Dialecticien, -ienne.
dialogist [daiˈælədʒist], s. Cin: Dialoguiste *mf*.
dialogue [ˈdaiəlɔg], s. Dialogue *m*.
diameter [daiˈæmitər], s. Diamètre *m*. Wheel 60 inches in d., roue qui a 60 pouces de diamètre. Opt: Magnification of eight diameters, grossissement *m* de huit fois.
diametrical [,daiəˈmetrik(ə)l], a. Diamétral, -aux. **-ally,** adv. Diamétralement. That is d. opposed to the truth, c'est le rebours de la vérité.
diamond [ˈdaiəmənd], s. 1. Diamant *m*. D. of the first water, diamant de première eau. Rough d., diamant brut. He's a rough d., c'est un diamant dans sa gangue. To set (sth.), make (sth.), sparkle, with diamonds, diamanter (qch.). D. cutter, merchant, diamantaire *m*. Ind: D. dust, égrisée *f*. Tls: Cutting d., diamant de vitrier. S.a. WEDDING. 2. (a) Losange *m*. D. panes, vitres en forme de losange. (b) Cards: Carreau *m*. (c) Sp: U.S: Terrain *m* de baseball. 3. Typ: Corps quatre. ˈdiamond-bearing, a. Geol: Diamantifère. ˈdiamond-shaped, a. En losange.
Diana [daiˈænə]. Pr.n.f. Diane.
diapason [,daiəˈpeisən], s. 1. (a) A. & Lit: Crescendo harmonieux. (b) Diapason *m*, étendue *f* (d'un instrument). 2. Diapason, (hauteur *f* du) ton *m* (d'un instrument). 3. Principaux jeux de fond (d'un orgue). D.(-stop), prestant *m*.
diaper [ˈdaiəpər], s. 1. Tex: Linge ouvré, damassé *m*; toile gaufrée. 2. (a) Serviette (ouvrée). (b) (For babies) Couche *f*. 3. Arch: Motif *m* (d'ornementation) en simples formes géométriques.
diaphanous [daiˈæfənəs], a. Diaphane.
diaphragm [ˈdaiəfræm], s. 1. Anat: Diaphragme *m*. 2. (a) Diaphragme, membrane *f*. Porous d., membrane poreuse. Tp: etc: Carbon d., membrane de charbon. (b) Phot: Iris d., diaphragme iris.
diarist [ˈdaiərist], s. Auteur *m* d'un journal (particulier).
diarrhoea [,daiəˈriːə], s. Med: Diarrhée *f*. F: Verbal d., verbomanie *f*.
diary [ˈdaiəri], s. 1. Journal *m* (intime). 2. Calendrier *m*. Desk d., bloc *m* calendrier. 3. Journ: etc: D. (of social events), carnet mondain.
diascopy [daiˈæskəpi], s. Opt: Diascopie *f*.
diastole [daiˈæstəli], s. Physiol: Diastole *f*.
diathermic [,daiəˈθə:mik], a. Ph: Med: Diathermique.
diathermy [ˈdaiəθə:mi], s. Med: Diathermie *f*.
diathesis, pl. **-eses** [daiˈæθisis, -isiːz], s. Med: Diathèse *f*; prédisposition *f* (à l'arthrite, etc.).
diatom [ˈdaiətɔm], s. Algae: Diatomée *f*.
diatomic [,daiəˈtɔmik], a. Diatomique, biatomique.
diatonic [,daiəˈtɔnik], a. Mus: (Gamme) diatonique.
diatribe [ˈdaiətraib], s. Diatribe *f*.
dibasic [daiˈbeisik], a. Ch: Bibasique, dibasique.
dibber [ˈdibər], **dibble** [ˈdibl], s. Tls: Plantoir *m*.
dibbling [ˈdiblin], s. Semis *m* en poquets.
dibs [dibz], s.pl. 1. (Game) Osselets *mpl*. 2. F: Argent *m*; P: pognon *m*, pépette *f*. He's got the d., c'est un richard.
dice[1] [dais], s.pl. See DIE[1] I. ˈdice-box, s. Cornet *m* à dés.
dice[2]. 1. v.i. Jouer aux dés. 2. v.tr. (a) To d. away a fortune, perdre une fortune au jeu. (b) Cu: Couper (des légumes) en cubes.
dicey [ˈdaisi], a. P: Hasardeux, -euse.
dichotomy [daiˈkɔtəmi], s. Astr: Bot: Log: Dichotomie *f*.
dichromatic [,daikrouˈmætik], a. Dichromatique.
Dick [ˈdik]. 1. Pr.n.m. (Dim. of Richard) Richard. 2. s.m. P: Policier *m*, détective *m*. P: poulet *m*, bourre *m*.
dickens [ˈdikinz], s. F: Euphemism for DEVIL, DEUCE, (q.v.) in such phrases as What the d. . . .?
dicker [ˈdikər], v.tr. & i. U.S: Marchander.
dicky[1], **dickey** [ˈdiki], s. F: 1. Dial: Bourricot *m*, âne *m*. 2. F: (Baby-talk) D.(-bird), petit oiseau. 3. Faux plastron (de chemise). 4. Aut: O: Spider *m*.
dicky[2], a. F: (a) Défectueux; peu solide. (b) Malade, indisposé.

dicotyledon ['dai‚kɔti'liːd(ə)n], s. Bot: Dicotylédone f, dicotylédonée f.
dicotyledonous ['dai‚kɔti'liːdənəs], a. Bot: Dicotylédone, dicotylédoné.
dictaphone ['diktəfoun], s. R.t.m: Dictaphone m.
dictate¹ ['dikteit], s. Commandement m. The dictates of conscience, la voix de la conscience. The dictates of fashion, les exigences f de la mode.
dictate² [dik'teit]. 1. v.tr. Dicter (une lettre, des conditions de paix). Abs: Faire la loi. 2. v.i. F: I won't be dictated to, je n'ai pas d'ordres à recevoir; on ne me régente pas.
dictation [dik'teif(ə)n], s. 1. Dictée f. Passage taken down from d., passage dicté. Sch: To do d., faire la dictée. 2. Étalage m d'autorité. These people won't submit to d., on ne fait pas la loi à ces gens-là.
dictator [dik'teitər], s. (a) Pol: Dictateur m. (b) Dictators of fashion, les dictateurs de la mode.
dictatorial [‚diktə'tɔːriəl], a. 1. (Pouvoir) dictatorial, -aux. 2. (Ton) impérieux. To be d., avoir le verbe haut. -ally, adv. Impérieusement; autoritairement.
dictatorship [dik'teitəfip], s. Dictature f.
diction ['dikf(ə)n], s. 1. Style m (d'un orateur). 2. Diction f.
dictionary ['dikf(ə)nri], s. Dictionnaire m. 'dictionary maker, s. Lexicographe mf. 'dictionary-making, s. Lexicographie f.
dictum, pl. -ums, -a ['diktəm, -əmz, -ə], s. 1. Affirmation f. 2. Maxime f, dicton m. 3. Opinion prononcée par un juge.
did. See DO¹.
didactic [di'dæktik], a. Didactique. -ally, adv. Didactiquement.
didactics [di'dæktiks], s.pl. La didactique.
diddle ['didl], v.tr. 1. P: Duper, rouler, carotter (qn). 2. (Esp. U.S:) To d. (away) (one's time, etc.), flâner.
diddler ['didlə], s. P: Carotteur, -euse.
dido ['daidou], s. U.S: Frasque f.
die¹ [dai], s. I. pl. dice [dais]. 1. Dé m (à jouer); (with twelve faces) cochonnet m. The cast of the d., le coup de dés. The d. is cast, le sort en est jeté. 2. pl. To play dice, jouer aux dés. To cast the dice, jeter les dés. II. die, pl. dies [da:iz]. 1. Arch: Dé f. 2. Minting: Coin m. 3. Metalw: Matrice f. D. forging, forgeage m par matriçage. Stamping d., étampe f. 'die-cast, a. Coulé sous pression; matricé. D.-c. moulding, moulage matricé. 'die-casting, s. Moulage m mécanique, en coquille. 'die-sinker, s. (Pers.) Graveur m d'étampes, médailleur m.
die², v.i. (died [daid]; dying ['daiiŋ]) 1. Mourir; (prematurely) périr; (of animals) crever. To be dying, être à l'agonie, se mourir. He died yesterday, il est mort hier. It is five years since he died, il y a cinq ans qu'il est mort. To d. a natural death, mourir de sa belle mort. To d. before one's time, mourir avant l'âge. To d. a martyr to the cause, mourir martyr pour une cause. They died like heroes, ils se firent tuer en braves. To d. by one's own hand, périr de sa propre main. To d. by inches, mourir à petit feu. To d. hard, (of pers.) vendre chèrement sa vie; (of an abuse, etc.) être dur à tuer. This superstition will d. hard, cette superstition aura la vie dure. Never say d.! il ne faut jamais désespérer. 2. To d. of laughing, mourir de rire. I am dying of thirst, je meurs de soif. To be dying to do sth., brûler, mourir d'envie, de faire qch. 3. His fortune dies with him, sa fortune s'éteindra avec lui. His secret died with him, il emporta son secret dans le tombeau. Day is dying, le jour s'en va. **die away**, v.i. Se mourir; (of sound) s'affaiblir; (of voice) s'éteindre; Mth: (of curve, etc.) décroître. The sound died away in the distance, le son alla se perdre au loin. **die down**, v.i. (of fire) Baisser; (of wind) s'apaiser; (of sound) s'éteindre; (of excitement) se calmer; (of plant) perdre ses feuilles. **die off**, v.i. Mourir les uns après les autres. **die out**, v.i. Se mourir; (of fire) s'éteindre; (of custom) disparaître; (of race) s'éteindre. **dying¹**, a. Mourant, agonisant. In a d. voice, d'une voix éteinte. **dying²**, s. 1. Agonie f, mort f. 2. Coll: The d., les mourants, les moribonds. Prayers for the d., prières des agonisants. 'die(-)hard, s. Conservateur m à outrance; réactionnaire endurci; jusqu'auboutiste m. The die(-)hards, les irréductibles m.

diesel ['diːz(ə)l], a. I.C.E: D. engine, diesel m. D. oil, gas-oil m, gaz-oil m. s. A d., (i) une locomotive diesel; (ii) un moteur diesel.
dies non ['daiiːz'nɔn], s. Jur: 1. Jour férié. 2. Jour dont il n'est pas tenu compte.
diet¹ ['daiət], s. 1. Nourriture f, alimentation f. 2. To be on a d., être au régime. Milk d., régime lacté, diète lactée. Starvation d., diète absolue.
diet², v.tr. Mettre (qn) au régime. To d. (oneself), se mettre au régime.
diet³, s. Pol: Diète f.
dietary ['daiət(ə)ri]. 1. s. Régime m (alimentaire) (d'un malade, d'une prison). 2. a. Diététique. D. survey, enquête f alimentaire.
dietetic [‚daiə'tetik], a. Diététique.
dietetics [‚daiə'tetiks], s.pl. (Usu. with sing. constr.) Diététique f.
dietician, dietitian ['daiə'tif(ə)n], s. Diététicien, -ienne.
differ ['difər], v.i. 1. Différer (from, de); être différent (de). 2. To d. in opinion, différer d'opinion. To d. about sth., ne pas s'accorder sur qch. I beg to d., permettez-moi d'être d'un autre avis. To agree to d., garder chacun son opinion.
difference ['difr(ə)ns], s. 1. Différence f, écart m (between, entre). I don't quite see the d., je ne saisis pas la nuance. To tell the d., faire la différence (entre deux choses). What a d. from . . ., quelle différence avec. . . . D. in age, différence d'âge. D. in temperature, écart de température. With a slight d., à peu de chose près. With this d. that . . ., à la différence que. . . . F: With a d., pas comme le reste, les autres. It makes no d. (to me), cela ne (me) fait rien; cela m'est parfaitement égal. It will make no d., F: cela ne fera ni chaud ni froid. That makes all the d., voilà qui change les choses du tout au tout. 2. Différence (entre deux nombres). Com: To split the d., partager le différend. Rail: To pay the d., payer le supplément. 3. Dispute f, différend m. Differences arose, des démêlés m survinrent. Settle your differences, mettez-vous d'accord.
different ['difr(ə)nt], a. 1. Différent (from, to, de). I feel a d. man, je me sens tout autre. To do sth. quite d., faire tout autre chose. To do sth. out of a desire to be d. from other people, faire qch. par esprit de singularité. That's quite a d. matter, ça, c'est une autre affaire. He wears a d. suit every day, il met tous les jours un nouveau costume. 2. Divers, différent. D. people saw him, différentes personnes l'ont vu. At d. times, à diverses reprises. -ly, adv. 1. Différemment. He speaks d. from you, il parle autrement que vous. 2. Diversement.
differential [‚difə'renf(ə)l]. 1. a. (a) Différentiel. Mth: D. calculus, calcul différentiel. (b) Distinctif. 2. s. (a) Mth: Différentielle f. (b) Aut: Différentiel m.
differentiate [‚difə'renfieit], v.tr. (a) Différencier (sth. from sth., qch. de qch.). Abs. To d. between two things, faire la différence entre deux choses. (b) Mth: Différentier (une fonction).
differentiation [‚difərenfi'eif(ə)n], s. Différenciation f.
difficult ['difikəlt], a. (a) Difficile, malaisé, laborieux, -euse, pénible, ardu. There's nothing d. in that, cela ne présente aucune difficulté. Only the beginning is d., il n'y a que le premier pas qui coûte. Person d. of approach, personne d'accès difficile. It is d. to deny that . . ., on ne saurait nier que. . . . It is d. to believe that . . ., on a peine à croire que + sub. (b) (Of pers., character) Difficile; peu commode. Person d. to get on with, personne difficile à vivre.
difficulty ['difikəlti], s. Difficulté f. 1. Work of some d., travail assez difficile. There will be no d. about that, cela ne fera pas de difficulté. The d. is to . . ., le difficile, c'est de. . . . The d. of choice, l'embarras m du choix. With great d., à grand-peine. 2. Obstacle m. I see no d. about it, je n'y vois pas d'inconvénient. To raise, make, difficulties, soulever des objections f; faire des difficultés. To look for difficulties where there are none, F: chercher midi à quatorze heures. 3. Embarras m, ennui m. To be in a d., être dans l'embarras. Ship in difficulties, navire en détresse. Pecuniary difficulties, soucis mpl d'argent; la gêne. To get out of one's difficulties, se tirer d'affaire. He knows how to get out of a d., il sait se débrouiller.

diffidence ['difidəns], s. Manque m d'assurance; modestie excessive.
diffident [difidənt], a. Qui manque d'assurance. To be d., se défier de soi-même. I was d. about speaking to him, j'hésitais à lui parler. -ly, adv. Timidement; en hésitant.
diffract [di'frækt], v.tr. Opt: Diffracter.
diffraction [di'frækʃ(ə)n], s. Opt: Diffraction f.
diffractive [di'fræktiv], a. Opt: Diffractif, -ive, diffringent.
diffuse[1] [di'fju:s], a. (Of light) Diffus; (of style) diffus, prolixe. -ly, adv. Avec prolixité.
diffuse[2] [di'fju:z]. 1. v.tr. Répandre; diffuser. Diffused lighting, éclairage diffusé. 2. v.i. Se répandre; (of light) se diffuser.
diffusion [di'fju:ʒ(ə)n], s. Diffusion f; rayonnement m (des idées, d'un art). Ph: Dispersion f (des rayons). attrib. Phot: D. screen, écran diffuseur.
diffusive [di'fju:siv], a. Diffusif, -ive.
dig[1] [dig], s. F: 1. I've been having a d. in, at, the garden, je viens de donner un coup de bêche au jardin. 2. (a) To give s.o. a d. in the ribs, pousser (qn) du coude. (b) To have a d. at s.o., donner un coup de patte, de bec, à qn; lancer un sarcasme à qn. That's a d. at you, c'est une pierre dans votre jardin. 3. Archeol: We're working on a d. in Egypt, nous explorons une fouille (d'intérêt archéologique) en Égypte.
dig[2], v. (dug [dʌg]; dug; digging) 1. v.tr. (a) Bêcher, retourner (la terre). (b) To d. (up) potatoes, arracher des pommes de terre. (c) Creuser (un trou). To d. a grave, creuser une fosse. (d) Abs. Travailler la terre; fouir. To d. into, through, sth., creuser, percer, qch. 2. v.tr. Enfoncer (sth. into sth., qch. dans qch.). To d. one's spurs into one's horse, éperonner son cheval. To d. s.o. in the ribs, pousser qn du coude. 3. v.i. F: Loger en garni. 4. v.i. F: Archaeol: Faire des fouilles. **dig in**, v.tr. (a) Enterrer (le fumier). Mil: To d. oneself in, se retrancher. F: To d. oneself in (to a place), s'incruster, s'ancrer, s'accrocher (à). (b) To d. one's toes in, (i) s'assurer, se tenir de pied ferme. (ii) F: Se buter, s'entêter. **dig out**, v.tr. (a) Extraire, déterrer (qch.). (b) F: Déterrer (un secret). Documents dug out of the archives, documents exhumés des archives. **dig up**, v.tr. Déraciner (une plante); mettre à jour (un trésor); piocher (la rue); déterrer, exhumer (un corps). **digging**, s. 1. (a) Bêchage m (de la terre); excavation f. (b) Fouilles fpl. 2. pl. **Diggings**. (a) Min: Placer m. (b) F: O: = DIGS.
digest[1] ['daidʒest], s. 1. Sommaire m, abrégé m, résumé m (d'une science). 2. Journ: Condensé m, F: digest m.
digest[2] [di'dʒest, dai-], v.tr. 1. (a) Mettre en ordre (des faits). (b) Résumer (un compte rendu). 2. Digérer, élaborer (un projet). 3. (a) Digérer (les aliments). (b) To d. what one reads, digérer, s'assimiler, ce qu'on lit.
digestibility [di,dʒestə'biliti], s. Digestibilité f.
digestible [di'dʒestəbl], a. Digestible.
digestion [di'dʒestʃ(ə)n], s. (a) Digestion f. (b) Sluggish d., digestion laborieuse. To spoil one's d., s'abîmer l'estomac.
digestive [di'dʒestiv], a. Digestif, -ive.
digger ['digər], s. 1. Bêcheur m; piqueur m (de la houille); terrassier m (de fossés); fouilleur m (de monuments). Austr: P: Australien m. 2. Tls: Plantoir m. Agr: Défonceuse f, arrachoir m; (potato-)d., arracheuse f.
digit ['didʒit], s. 1. (a) Doigt m. (b) Doigt de pied; orteil m. 2. Meas: A: (Grandeur f d'un travers de) doigt. 3. Mth: Chiffre m (arabe). The ten digits, les neuf chiffres et le zéro.
digital ['didʒitl]. 1. a. Digital, -aux. D. computer, calculateur m, calculatrice f, numérique, arithmétique. 2. s. Mus: Touche f (du piano).
digitalin [didʒi'teilin], s. Pharm: Digitaline f.
digitalis [,didʒi'teilis], s. 1. Bot: Digitale f. 2. Pharm: Digitaline f.
dignify ['dignifai], v.tr. Donner de la dignité à (qch.); revêtir (qch.) d'un air de majesté. **dignified**, a. Plein de dignité; (air) digne.
dignitary ['dignit(ə)ri], s. Dignitaire m.

dignity ['digniti], s. 1. Dignité f. To preserve one's d., soutenir sa dignité. To be, stand, on one's d. (with (s.o.), se tenir sur son quant-à-soi; le prendre de haut (avec qn). It is beneath your d. to accept, vous ne pouvez pas vous abaisser (jusqu')à accepter. 2. Dignité; haut rang. To maintain the d. of one's (official) position, représenter dignement (son rang).
digraph ['daigra:f], s. Gram: Typ: Digramme m.
digress [dai'gres], v.i. Faire une digression (from, de); s'écarter (du sujet).
digression [dai'greʃ(ə)n], s. Digression f, écart m. This by way of d., ceci soit dit en passant.
digressive [dai'gresiv], a. Digressif, -ive; (of pers.) enclin aux digressions.
digs [digz], s.pl. F: Logement m, garni m. To live in d., loger en garni. I called at his d., je suis passé chez lui.
dihedral [dai'hi:drəl]. 1. a. Dièdre. 2. s. Angle m dièdre.
dihedron [dai'hi:drən], s. Dièdre m.
dike[1] [daik], s. See DYKE[1].
dike[2], v.tr. See DYKE[2].
dilapidate [di'læpideit], v.tr. Délabrer, dégrader (un édifice). **dilapidated**, a. Délabré, décrépit; F: calamiteux. D.-looking car, auto décrépite. D. hat, chapeau dépenaillé.
dilapidation [di,læpi'deiʃ(ə)n], s. (a) Délabrement m, dégradation f (d'un mur). (b) pl. Jur: Dilapidations, détériorations f, dégradations.
dilatability [dai,leitə'biliti], s. Ph: Dilatabilité f.
dilatable [dai'leitəbl], a. Dilatable.
dilatation [,dailei'teiʃ(ə)n], **dilation** [dai'leiʃ(ə)n], s. Dilatation f. Med: Élargissement m (du cœur, etc.).
dilate [dai'leit]. 1. v.tr. Dilater. 2. v.i. (a) (Of eyes) Se dilater. (b) To d. (up)on a topic, s'étendre sur un sujet. **dilating**, a. Dilatateur, -trice, dilatant.
dilator [dai'leitər], s. Surg: Dilatateur m, dilatant m.
dilatoriness ['dilət(ə)rinis], s. Lenteur f (à agir).
dilatory ['dilət(ə)ri], a. (Of pers.) Lent (à agir); (of action) tardif, -ive; Jur: etc: dilatoire.
dilemma [dai'lemə], s. 1. Log: Dilemme m. 2. Embarras m. To be in a d., être fort embarrassé.
dilettante, pl. -ti [,dili'tænti, -ti]. 1. a. En amateur, en dilettante. To work in a d. fashion, travailler en dilettante. 2. s. Dilettante m.
dilettantism [,dili'tæntizm], s. Dilettantisme m.
diligence ['dilidʒ(ə)ns], s. Assiduité f, application f, diligence f.
diligent ['dilidʒ(ə)nt], a. Assidu, appliqué, diligent. -ly, adv. Avec assiduité, avec application; diligemment.
dill [dil], s. Bot: Aneth odorant.
dilly-dally ['dilidæli], v.i. F: Lanterner, traînasser; barguigner; baguenauder.
dilute[1] [dai'lju:t, di-], a. 1. (Of acid) Dilué. 2. Atténué; (socialisme) à l'eau de rose.
dilute[2], v.tr. 1. Diluer; mouiller, arroser, couper, (le vin, le lait). 2. Atténuer, édulcorer (une doctrine). 3. Délaver, délayer (une couleur).
diluter [dai'lju:tə], s. Diluant m.
dilution [dai'lju:ʃ(ə)n, di-], s. 1. Dilution f; mouillage m (du vin); dédoublage m (de l'alcool). 2. D. of labour, adjonction f de main-d'œuvre non professionnelle.
diluvial [di'lju:viəl], **diluvian** [di'lju:viən], a. Geol: Diluvien, -ienne; diluvial, -aux.
dim[1] [dim], a. (dimmer) (Of light) Faible, pâle; (of colour) effacé; (of sight) faible; (of memory) incertain, vague. Eyes d. with tears, yeux voilés de larmes. D. forebodings, d'obscurs pressentiments. To grow d., (of light) baisser; (of recollection) s'effacer; (of understanding) s'affaiblir; (of sight) se troubler; (of colour) pâlir. F: To take a d. view of (s.o., sth.), avoir une piètre opinion de (qn, qch.). He's a d. sort of chap, F: C'est un mou; il est moche. -ly, adv. Faiblement, sans éclat; vaguement; obscurément; confusément. **'dim-'sighted**, a. Qui a la vue trouble ou faible. **'dim(-)wit**, s. F: Espèce f d'idiot. **'dim-'witted**, a. F: Stupide.
dim[2], s. U.S: (a) Feu m de position. (b) Phare-code m.

dim³, *v.* (dimmed) 1. *v.tr.* (*a*) Obscurcir; ternir (un miroir). Eyes dimmed with weeping, yeux ternis de pleurs, embués de larmes. (*b*) Réduire (la lumière); mettre (l'électricité) en veilleuse. *Aut: U.S:* To d. the headlights, mettre les phares en code. 2. *v.i.* (*Of light*) Baisser; (*of eyes*) s'obscurcir; (*of outlines*) s'effacer. **'dim(-)out**, *s. U.S: F:* Camouflage partiel des lumières; blackout partiel.

dime [daim], *s. U.S: Num:* Dîme *f* (= ¹⁄₁₀ de dollar). *F:* D. novel, roman *m* populaire, roman à sensation. D. store, magasin *m* à prix unique.

dimension [dai'menʃ(ə)n, di-], *s.* Dimension *f; Ind:* cote *f.* D. figures of a machine, cotes d'une machine.

dimensional [dai'menʃənəl, di-], *a.* Two-, three-d. space, espace à deux, à trois, dimensions. *Cin:* 3D(imensional) film, film à réfraction *f.*

diminish [di'miniʃ]. 1. *v.tr.* Diminuer, réduire, amoindrir. 2. *v.i.* Diminuer, décroître; aller en diminuant. **diminished**, *a.* Diminué, amoindri. *Mus:* D. interval, intervalle diminué. **diminishing**, *a.* Qui diminue, qui va en diminuant. (*of value, etc.*) baissant. *Pol.Ec:* Law of d. returns, loi *f* du rendement non-proportionnel.

diminuendo [di,minju'endou], *adv. & s. Mus:* Diminuendo (*m*).

diminution [,dimi'nju:ʃ(ə)n], *s.* Diminution *f;* réduction *f;* amoindrissement *m.*

diminutive [di'minjutiv]. 1. *a. & s. Gram:* Diminutif (*m*). 2. *a.* Tout petit; minuscule.

dimity ['dimiti], *s. Tex:* Basin *m,* brillanté *m.*

dimmer ['dimər], *s.* Réducteur *m* d'éclairage.

dimness ['dimnis], *s.* 1. Faiblesse *f* (d'éclairage, de la vue); obscurité *f* (d'une salle). 2. Imprécision *f* (d'un contour). 3. *F:* Stupidité *f.*

dimorphism [dai'mɔrfizm], *s. Cryst: Biol: etc:* Dimorphisme *m.*

dimple ['dimpl], *s.* (*On cheek, chin*) Fossette *f.*

dimpled ['dimpld], *a.* A fossette(s).

din¹ [din], *s.* Tapage *m,* fracas *m,* vacarme *m. F:* To kick up a d., faire un charivari de tous les diables. What a d.! quel vacarme!

din², *v.* (dinned) 1. *v.tr.* To d. sth. into s.o.'s ears, corner qch. aux oreilles à qn. 2. *v.i.* (*Of voice*) To d. in s.o.'s ears, retentir dans l'oreille de qn.

dine [dain], *v.i.* Dîner. To d. on, off, sth., dîner de qch. To d. out, dîner (i) en ville, dans un restaurant; (ii) chez des amis. **'dining-car**, *s.* Wagon-restaurant *m.* **'dining-room**, *s.* Salle *f* à manger.

diner ['dainər], *s.* 1. Dîneur, -euse. 2. *Rail:* = DINING-CAR.

dinette [di'net], *s.* Coin-repas *m* (dans un studio, une caravane).

ding-dong ['diŋ'dɔŋ]. 1. *adv.* Digue-din-don. 2. *s.* Tintement *m* (des cloches). 3. *a. Sp:* D.-d. match, partie durement disputée.

dinghy ['diŋ(g)i], *s. Nau:* Canot *m,* youyou *m.* Collapsible d., berthon *m.* Rubber d., canot pneumatique.

dinginess ['dindʒinis], *s.* Aspect enfumé, manque *m* de fraîcheur (du mobilier); propreté douteuse (d'une maison, du mobilier).

dingle ['diŋl], *s.* Vallon (boisé).

dingo ['diŋgou], *s.* Dingo *m;* chien *m* sauvage (de l'Australie).

dingy ['dindʒi], *a.* Qui manque d'éclat, de fraîcheur; (*of furniture*) défraîchi; (*of colour*) terne; (*of linen*) crasseux. D. white, d'un blanc sale.

dinkum ['diŋkəm], *a. Austr: F:* (*Of pers.*) Franc, franche, sincère; (*of goods*) authentique.

dinky ['diŋki], *a. F:* Coquet, mignon.

dinner ['dinər], *s.* Dîner *m.* I have s.o. in to d., j'ai quelqu'un à dîner. To be at d., être à table. We were having d., nous étions en train de dîner. To go out to d., dîner (i) en ville, (ii) chez des amis. Public d., banquet *m. Rail:* Second d., deuxième service *m.* To do d. duty (in schools) (i) surveiller, faire le service de la cantine; (ii) surveiller au réfectoire. **'dinner-dance**, *s.* Dîner-dansant *m.* **'dinner-hour**, *s.* L'heure *f* du dîner. **'dinner-jacket**, *s.* (Veston *m*) smoking *m.* **'dinner-lift**, *s.* Monte-plats *m inv.* **'dinner-mat**, *s.* Dessous de plat, d'assiette. **'dinner-party**, *s.* Dîner prié. To give a d.-p., avoir du monde à dîner. **'dinner-service**, *s.* Service *m* de table. **'dinner-time**, *s.* L'heure *f* du dîner. **'dinner(-)trolley**, **'dinner(-)wagon**, *s. Furn:* Table (desserte) roulante, à roulettes.

dinosaur ['dainəsɔ:r], *s.* Dinosaure *m.*

dint¹ [dint], *s.* 1. = DENT¹. 2. By d. of . . ., à force de. . . .

dint², *v.tr.* = DENT².

diocesan [dai'ɔsisən], *a. & s. Ecc:* Diocésain (*m*).

diocese ['daiəsis], *s.* Diocèse *m.*

diode ['daioud], *s. W.Tel:* (Lampe *f*) diode *f.* Cross-connected d., diode en montage croisé.

diopter [dai'ɔptər], *s. Opt.Meas:* Dioptrie *f.*

dioptric [dai'ɔptrik], *a. Ph:* Dioptrique.

dioptrics [dai'ɔptriks], *s.pl.* (*Usu. sing. const.*) Dioptrique *f.*

diorama ['daiə'rɑ:mə], *s.* Diorama *m.*

dioxide [dai'ɔksaid], *s. Ch:* Bioxyde *m.*

dip¹ [dip], *s.* 1. Plongement *m,* immersion *f* (de qch. dans un liquide). 2. (*a*) Inclinaison *f* (de l'aiguille aimantée). (*b*) Plongée *f* (du terrain); déclivité *f.* (*c*) Caniveau *m* (dans une route). 3. *Nau:* Salut *m* (avec le pavillon). Flag at the d., pavillon à mi-drisse. 4. *F:* Baignade *f.* I'm going for a d., je vais me baigner. 5. Sheep-d., bain parasiticide (pour moutons). **'dip-needle**, *s.* Boussole *f* d'inclinaison. **'dip-pipe**, **-trap**, *s. Plumb:* Siphon *m.* **'dip-stick**, *s. Aut:* jauge *f* d'huile, pige *f* de niveau d'huile.

dip², *v.* (dipped) I. *v.tr.* 1. Plonger, tremper (les mains dans l'eau). *F:* I am always dipping my hand into my pocket, je suis toujours à débourser. 2. Immerger, décaper, dérocher (un métal). *Husb:* To d. the sheep, baigner les moutons (dans un bain parasiticide). 3. Baisser (qch.) subitement. *Aut:* To d. the head-lights, baisser les phares; se mettre en code. *Nau:* To d. one's flag, *abs.* to d., to a ship, saluer un navire avec son pavillon; *abs.* saluer. *Av:* To d. (one's wings), saluer. 4. He dipped his spoon into the pot, il puisa dans la marmite avec sa cuiller. II. dip, *v.i.* 1. Plonger (dans l'eau). 2. (*Of sun*) Baisser. The sun dipped below the sea, le soleil s'enfonça dans la mer. 3. (*Of compass-needle*) Incliner; (*of scale*) pencher. The road dips sharply, la route plonge brusquement. 4. To d. into a book, feuilleter un livre. To d. into one's purse, puiser dans sa bourse. To d. deep into the past, sonder le passé. 5. *Av:* (*Of machine*) Piquer. **dipping**, *s.* Plongée *f,* immersion *f; Metalw:* dérochage *m,* décapage *m.*

diphase ['dai'feiz], **diphasic** [dai'feizik], *a. El.E:* (Circuit, etc.) diphasé.

diphtheria [dif'θiəriə], *s. Med:* Diphtérie *f.*

diphthong ['difθɔŋ], *s. Ling:* Diphtongue *f.*

diplegia [dai'pli:dʒiə], *s. Med:* Diplégie *f.*

diplodocus [dai'plɔdəkəs], *s. Paleont:* Diplodocus *m.*

diploma [di'ploumə], *s.* Diplôme *m.*

diplomacy [di'plouməsi], *s.* Diplomatie *f.*

diplomat ['diploumæt], *s.* Diplomate *m.*

diplomatic [,diplə'mætik], *a.* 1. Diplomatique. To enter the d. service, entrer dans la diplomatie. He's in the d. service, il est dans la diplomatie, *F:* il est de la carrière. 2. Adroit, prudent. D. answer, réponse *f* politique. **-ally**, *adv.* 1. Diplomatiquement. 2. Avec tact.

diplomatist [di'ploumətist], *s.* Diplomate *m.*

dipper ['dipər], *s.* 1. *Ind:* (*Pers.*) Plongeur, -euse. 2. *Orn:* Merle *m* d'eau. 3. (*a*) *U.S:* Cuiller *f* à pot, louche *f.* (*b*) *Astr: U.S:* The (Great) D., la Grande Ourse. 4. (*a*) *I.C.E:* Oil d., plongeur *m* (de tête de bielle). (*b*) *Aut:* = DIP-STICK.

dippy ['dipi], *a. P:* Maboul, loufoque, timbré.

dipsomania [,dipso'meiniə], *s.* Dipsomanie *f.*

dipsomaniac [,dipso'meiniæk], *a. & s.* Dipsomane (*mf*).

diptera ['diptərə], *s.pl. Ent:* Diptères *m.*

dipterous ['diptərəs], *a. Ent:* Diptère.

diptych ['diptik], *s.* Diptyque *m.*

dire ['daiər], *a.* 1. Désastreux, néfaste, affreux. D. necessity, nécessité implacable. D. poverty, misère noire. D. forebodings, pressentiments lugubres. To be in d. distress, se trouver dans la dernière misère.

direct¹ [dai'rekt, di-], *v.tr.* 1. Adresser (une lettre) (to s.o., à qn). Letter directed to s.o., lettre à l'adresse de qn. 2. Gouverner (sa conduite); gérer, régir (une entreprise). 3. (*a*) To d. s.o.'s attention to sth., attirer l'attention de qn sur qch. (*b*) To d. one's efforts to(wards) an end, orienter ses efforts vers un but. 4. Could you d. me to the station? pourriez-vous m'indiquer le chemin de la gare? 5. (a) To d. s.o. to do sth., ordonner à qn, charger qn, de faire qch. As directed, selon les instructions. I was directed to . . ., je reçus l'ordre de. . . . (b) (Of judge) To d. the jury, instruire le jury.

direct². 1. a. (a) Direct. D. cause, cause immédiate. D. taxation, contributions directes. To be a d. descendant of s.o., descendre de qn en ligne directe. The d. opposite of sth., juste l'opposé de qch. Gram: D. object, complément direct. (b) (Of pers.) Franc, f. franche. (c) Absolu, formel. D. answer, réponse catégorique. (d) El: D. current, courant continu. W.Tel: D. coupled aerial, antenne montée en direct. 2. adv. (Aller) directement, tout droit. -ly. 1. adv. (a) (Aller) directement, tout droit. To go d. to the point, aller droit au fait. I am not d. concerned, cela ne m'intéresse pas personnellement. (b) Absolument. D. opposite views, des points de vue diamétralement opposés. He lives d. opposite the church, il demeure juste en face de l'église. (c) Tout de suite, tout à l'heure. The doctor came d., le médecin vint aussitôt. 2. conj. F: Aussitôt que, dès que. I will come d. I've finished, je viendrai dès que j'aurai fini.

direction [dai'rekʃ(ə)n, di-], s. 1. Direction f, administration f (d'une société). Under the d. of . . ., sous la conduite de. . . . 2. Adresse f (d'une lettre). 3. (a) Direction, sens m. In every d., en tous sens. In the opposite d., en sens inverse. To lose one's sense of d., perdre le sens de l'orientation f. Mth: Positive d., sens direct. Negative d., sens rétrograde. (b) Improvements in many directions, améliorations sous bien des rapports m. 4. (Usu. pl.) Instruction(s) f(pl). D. (of play, film), mise f en scène. Com: Directions (for use), notice f; mode f d'emploi. Sailing directions, instructions nautiques. Stage d., indication f scénique. di'rection-finder, s. W.Tel: Electronics: (Radio)goniomètre m, F: gonio m. direction-finding¹, a. Radiogoniométrique. di'rection-'finding,² s. (Radio)goniométrie f, F: gonio f. D.-f. station, station f radiogoniométrique, de radiogoniométrie. di'rection-indicator, s. Aut: Semaphore-type d.-i., flèche f de direction. Winking-light, flashing-light, d.-i., clignotant m.

directional [dai'rekʃən(ə)l, di-], a. W.Tel: Electronics: Directionnel, -elle; dirigé. D. radio transmission, liaison radio dirigée. D. relay, relai directionnel.

directive¹ [dai'rektiv, di-], a. Directif. D. function, fonction directrice.

directive², s. Mil: etc: Directive f.

directness [dai'rektnis, di-], s. Franchise f (d'une réponse).

director [dai'rektər, di-], s. 1. (Pers.) (a) Administrateur m, directeur m (d'une société); gérant m (d'une entreprise). Board of Directors, conseil m d'administration. Th: Cin: Metteur m en scène; réalisateur m. Assistant d., régisseur m. (b) R.C.Ch: Directeur de conscience. 2. (a) Navy: D. top, hune f de télépointage. (b) Appareil m de visée (de torpille). (e) Mec.E: etc: Guide m (d'un mouvement).

directorate [dai'rektərit, di-], s. (Conseil m d')administration f.

directorial [,dairek'tɔːriəl], a. Directorial, -aux.

directorship [dai'rektəʃip, di-], s. Directorat m. 1. Poste m, fonctions fpl de directeur, d'administrateur. 2. During my d., au cours de mon administration.

directory [dai'rektəri, di-], s. 1. Répertoire m d'adresses; annuaire m (des téléphones). 2. U.S: Le conseil d'administration (d'une compagnie, etc.).

directress [dai'rektris, di-], s.f. Directrice.

direful [ˈdaiəful], a. Poet: = DIRE. -fully, adv. Désastreusement, affreusement.

dirge [dəːdʒ], s. Hymne m, chant m funèbre.

dirigible [ˈdiridʒibl], a. & s. D. (balloon), (ballon) dirigeable (m).

dirk [dəːk], s. Poignard m.

dirt [dəːt], s. Saleté f. 1. (a) Boue f, crotte f, ordure f; (body dirt) crasse f. Hands ingrained with d., mains encrassées. F: To throw d. at s.o., éclabousser la réputation de qn. To treat s.o. like d., traiter qn comme de la saleté. F: To eat d., être forcé de faire des excuses; F: avaler des couleuvres. To talk d., parler grossièrement, P: raconter des cochonneries f. F: It's d. cheap, c'est pour trois fois rien. (b) I.C.E:

D. in the carburettor, encrassement m du carburateur. (c) Min: Terre f aurifère. 2. Malpropreté f. 3. Attrib: U.S: D. floor, sol m en terre battue. D. roof, toiture f en tourbe. D. road, chemin non macadamisé. D. wagon, = DUST-CART. 'dirt farmer, s. U.S: Exploitant m agricole. 'dirt farming, s. U.S: Exploitation f agricole. 'dirt-proof, a. Insalissable. 'dirt-track, s. Sp: Piste f en cendrée.

dirtiness [ˈdəːtinis], s. 1. Saleté f, malpropreté f. 2. F: (Of speech) Saleté f, grossièreté f; P: cochonnerie; (of action) bassesse f.

dirty¹ [ˈdəːti], a. 1. Sale, malpropre, crasseux; crotté; encrassé. D. hands, mains sales. D. face, visage barbouillé. D. shoes, souliers crottés. D. streets, rues fangeuses. Don't get your gloves d., ne salissez pas vos gants. 2. D. weather, mauvais temps; Nau: gros temps. 3. D. mind, esprit tourné vers l'obscénité. P: He has a d. mind, il a l'esprit cochon. How d. minded she is! Comme elle est cochonne (,cette fille)! 4. To play s.o. a d. trick, jouer un vilain tour à qn. It's a d. business, c'est une sale affaire. F: To do the d. on s.o., faire une crasse à qn; jouer un sale coup à qn. -ily, adv. Salement. 1. Malproprement. 2. Bassement.

dirty². 1. v.tr. Salir, crotter, encrasser. To d. one's hands, se salir les mains. 2. v.i. (Of material) To d. easily, se salir facilement.

disability [,disə'biliti], s. 1. (a) Incapacité f. (b) Physical d., infirmité f. (c) Adm: Invalidité f. D. pension, pension f d'invalidité. 2. Jur: Inhabilité f (à faire qch.).

disable [dis'eibl], v.tr. Mettre (qn) hors de combat; estropier (qn); désemparer (un navire). Disabled by rheumatism, rendu impotent par les rhumatismes, perclus de rhumatismes. Disabled soldier, invalide m. Disabled ex-service-men, mutilés m de guerre. The badly disabled, (i) les grands infirmes; (ii) les grands mutilés. (Of ship) To be disabled, avoir des avaries; être en panne.

disablement [dis'eiblmənt], s. 1. Mise f hors de combat. 2. Invalidité f; incapacité f de travail. Adm: Degree of d., coefficient m d'invalidité. Permanent d., incapacité permanente.

disabuse [,disə'bjuːz], v.tr. Désabuser (of, de); désaveugler (qn).

disadvantage [,disəd'vaːntidʒ], s. Désavantage m, inconvénient m. To take s.o. at a d., prendre qn au dépourvu; surprendre (qn) dans un moment embarrassant. To show oneself to d., se montrer sous un jour désavantageux, se montrer handicapé.

disadvantageous [,disədvaːn'teidʒəs], a. Désavantageux, défavorable (to, à).

disaffection [disə'fekʃ(ə)n], s. Désaffection f.

disagree [,disə'griː], v.i. 1. (a) Être en désaccord, n'être pas d'accord (with, avec). (b) To d. with s.o., donner tort à qn. I d., je ne suis pas de cet avis. 2. (a) (Quarrel) Se brouiller (with, avec). (b) They had always disagreed, ils avaient toujours vécu en mésintelligence. 3. The climate disagrees with him, le climat ne lui convient pas. Wine disagrees with him, le vin lui est contraire.

disagreeable [,disə'griː(ː)əbl], a. (a) Désagréable (to, à); déplaisant (to, à). (b) A d. incident, un incident fâcheux. (c) (Of pers.) Désagréable, maussade. -ably, adv. Désagréablement; fâcheusement; d'un ton désobligeant.

disagreeableness [,disə'griː(ː)əblnis], s. 1. Désagrément m. 2. (a) Mauvaise humeur. (b) Désobligeance f (to, envers).

disagreement [,disə'griːmənt], s. 1. Différence f (between, entre); discordance f. 2. Désaccord m (with s.o. on, about, sth., avec qn sur qch.). 3. (a) Différend m, querelle f, brouille f. (b) Mésintelligence f, mésentente f (between, entre).

disallow [,disə'lau], v.tr. 1. Ne pas admettre (une réclamation). Jur: Rebuter, rejeter (un témoignage). 2. Ne pas permettre; interdire.

disappear [,disə'piər], v.i. Disparaître (from a place, d'un endroit), (of difficulties) s'aplanir. He disappeared from our sight, il disparut à nos yeux. Since he disappeared, depuis sa disparition. disappearing, a. (Cible, etc.) à éclipse; escamotable.

disappearance [,disə'piərəns], s. Disparition f.

disappoint [ˌdisəˈpɔint], v.tr. (a) Désappointer (qn). (after promising) manquer de parole à (qn). (b) Décevoir, chagriner (qn). Are you disappointed? c'est une déception? He was greatly disappointed, il a eu un grave mécompte. To be disappointed in love, avoir des chagrins d'amour. (c) Décevoir (les espérances de qn); tromper (l'attente de qn). I was very, most, disappointed with it, cela n'a répondait aucunement à mon attente. **disappointing**, a. 1. Décevant. 2. How d.! quel contretemps!

disappointment [ˌdisəˈpɔintmənt], s. Déception f, désappointement m; mécompte m; déboire m.

disapprobation [ˌdisæprəˈbeiʃ(ə)n], s. Désapprobation f (of, de).

disappropriate [ˌdisəˈprouprieit], v.tr. Jur: Désapproprier.

disapproval [ˌdisəˈpruːv(ə)l], s. Désapprobation f (of, de); improbation f. Look of d., regard désapprobateur.

disapprove [ˌdisəˈpruːv]. 1. v.tr. Désapprouver (qn); réprouver. 2. v.i. To d. of sth., désapprouver qch. To d. of sth. being done, désapprouver, trouver mauvais, que l'on fasse qch.

disapprovingly [ˌdisəˈpruːviŋli], adv. D'un air ou d'un ton désapprobateur.

disarm [disˈɑːm]. 1. v.tr. Désarmer (un prisonnier, etc.). 2. v.i. Désarmer. **disarming**[1], a. (Franchise, etc.) qui vous désarme. -ly, adv. He was d. frank, il montrait une franchise qui vous désarmait. **disarming**[2], s. Désarmement m.

disarmament [disˈɑːməmənt], s. Désarmement m.

disarrange [ˌdisəˈreindʒ], v.tr. Déranger; désagencer (une machine); mettre (qch.) en désordre. **Disarranged hair**, cheveux défaits.

disarrangement [ˌdisəˈreindʒmənt], s. Dérangement m, désajustement m désagencement m (d'une machine); désordre m.

disarray[1] [ˌdisəˈrei], s. Désarroi m; désordre m.

disarray[2], v.tr. (a) Mettre (des troupes) en désarroi, en déroute. (b) Mettre en désordre.

disaster [diˈzɑːstər], s. Désastre m; (by shipwreck, fire, flood) sinistre m. Public d., calamité publique. Railway d., catastrophe f de chemin de fer. He is heading for d., il court à sa perte.

disastrous [diˈzɑːstrəs], a. Désastreux; funeste. -ly, adv. Désastreusement.

disavow [ˌdisəˈvau], v.tr. Désavouer; renier (sa foi, une action).

disavowal [ˌdisəˈvauəl], s. Désaveu m; reniement m (de sa foi).

disband [disˈbænd]. 1. v.tr. Licencier, congédier (des troupes). 2. v.i. (Of troops) (a) Se débander. (b) Être licencié. **disbanding**, s. Licenciement m.

disbandment [disˈbæn(d)mənt], s. Licenciement m.

disbar [disˈbɑːr], v.tr. (disbarred) Rayer (un avocat) du tableau de l'ordre.

disbelief [ˌdisbiˈliːf], s. 1. D. in sth., incrédulité f à l'égard de qch.; refus m de croire à qch. 2. Theol: Incrédulité.

disbelieve [ˌdisbiˈliːv]. 1. v.tr. Ne pas croire (qch.); refuser créance à (qn). 2. v.i. To d. in sth., ne pas croire à qch.

disbeliever [ˌdisbiˈliːvər], s. Incrédule mf.

disbud [disˈbʌd], v.tr. (disbudded) Hort: For: Ébourgeonner, épincer (un arbre fruitier).

disburse [disˈbəːs], v.tr. Débourser (de l'argent).

disbursement [disˈbəːsmənt], s. 1. Déboursement m. 2. pl. Disbursements, débours mpl.

disc [disk], s. (a) Disque m (de la lune). (b) Disque, rondelle f. Gramophones: Disque. Mil: etc: Identity d., plaque d'identité. Rail: D. signal, disque. Aut: Wheel d., enjoliveur m. (c) Anat: (Intervertebral) d., disque intervertébral. Med: Slipped d., hernie discale. '**disc-brake**, s. Aut: Frein m à disque. '**disc-clutch**, s. Aut: Embrayage m à disques. '**disc-harrow**, s. Agr: Pulvériseur m. '**disc-jockey**, s. W. Tel: T.V: Présentateur m (de disques).

discard[1] [disˈkɑːd], s. 1. (a) (At cribbage) Écart m (action ou carte). (b) (At bridge) Défausse f. 2. Ind: Com: Pièce f de rebut, déchet m.

discard[2], v.tr. 1. (a) (At cribbage) Écarter (une carte). (b) (At bridge) To d. a suit, se défausser d'une couleur. Abs. To d., se défausser. 2. Mettre (qch.) de côté; se défaire de (qch.); abandonner (un projet); quitter (une habitude); renoncer à (une croyance). To d. one's winter clothing, laisser de côté ses vêtements d'hiver. 3. Ball: To d. (the larger part of a rocket) in flight, larguer, lâcher. **discarding**, s. 1. Cards: (a) Écart m. (b) (At bridge) Défausse f. 2. Mise f de côté (de qch.); mise au rancart (d'une théorie).

discern [diˈsəːn], v.tr. (a) Distinguer, discerner, apercevoir. (b) To d. good from bad, discerner le bien d'avec le mal. **discerning**, a. (Of pers.) Judicieux; (of intelligence) pénétrant; (of taste) sûr.

discernible [diˈsəːnibl], a. Perceptible.

discernment [diˈsəːnmənt], s. Discernement m.

discharge[1] ['distʃɑːdʒ], s. 1. Déchargement m (d'un navire). 2. Décharge f (d'artillerie). 3. (a) Décharge, déversement m; dégagement m (de gaz); débit m (d'une pompe). D. pipe, tuyau m d'évacuation, de vidange. El: Décharge. (c) Med: (i) Écoulement m; (ii) suppuration f. 4. (a) Renvoi m (d'un employé). (b) Libération f (d'un militaire); (after active service) démobilisation f. To take one's d., prendre son congé. (c) Mil: Navy: etc: (For unfitness) Réforme f. 5. Jur: (a) Mise f en liberté, élargissement m (d'un prisonnier). (b) Acquittement m (d'un accusé). (c) D. in bankruptcy, réhabilitation f (d'un failli). 6. Accomplissement m (d'un devoir). In the d. of his duties, dans l'exercice m de ses fonctions. 7. (a) Paiement m (d'une dette). (b) Quittance f. In full d., pour acquit.

discharge[2] [disˈtʃɑːdʒ]. I. v.tr. 1. Décharger (un navire). 2. (a) Décharger (une arme à feu). (b) El: Décharger (une pile, etc.). 3. (a) Décharger, débarder (une cargaison). (b) (Of vehicle) To d. passengers, déposer des voyageurs. 4. (a) Congédier (un employé); débaucher (un ouvrier); destituer (un fonctionnaire). (b) Libérer (un homme) du service militaire. Navy: Débarquer (un équipage). Mil: Navy: etc: (For unfitness) Réformer. (c) To d. a patient (from hospital), renvoyer un malade guéri. 5. Jur: (a) Libérer (un prisonnier). (b) Acquitter (un accusé). 6. Discharged bankrupt, (failli) réhabilité. 7. (a) Lancer (un projectile). (b) (Of abscess) To d. pus, jeter du pus. Abs. To d. (of abscess) se dégorger; (of wound) suppurer. (c) (Of chemical reaction) Dégager, émettre (un gaz). (d) River that discharges into a lake, rivière qui se déverse dans un lac. 8. (a) S'acquitter de (son devoir). (b) Acquitter, régler, solder (une dette). II. discharge, v.i. 1. (Of ship) Être en déchargement, se décharger. 2. (Of gun) Partir. **discharging**, s. Décharge f, déchargement m.

discharger [disˈtʃɑːdʒə], s. El: Ph: Excitateur m.

disciple [diˈsaipl], s. Disciple m.

disciplinarian [ˌdisipliˈneəriən], s. Disciplinaire m. He is a good d., il a de la discipline. He's no d., il n'a pas de discipline.

disciplinary [disiˈplinəri], a. (Punition) disciplinaire; (établissement) de discipline. Mil: D. company, compagnie f disciplinaire, section spéciale.

discipline[1] ['disiplin], s. Discipline f. Iron d., discipline de fer. To enforce d., maintenir la discipline.

discipline[2], v.tr. (a) Discipliner (des élèves). (b) Former (le caractère). (c) Punir.

disclaim [disˈkleim], v.tr. 1. Renoncer à (un droit). 2. Désavouer (qch.). To d. all responsibility, dénier toute responsabilité. 3. Renier (l'autorité de qn).

disclaimer [disˈkleimər], s. (a) Jur: D. of a right, renonciation f à un droit. (b) D. of responsibility, déni m de responsabilité.

disclose [disˈklouz], v.tr. Découvrir, révéler (qch.); divulguer (un secret).

disclosure [disˈklouʒər], s. Mise f à découvert (d'un trésor); révélation f (de sa pensée); divulgation f (d'un secret).

discoid(al) ['diskɔid, ˌdisˈkɔid(ə)l], a. Discoïde, discoïdal, -aux.

discolour [disˈkʌlər], v.tr. (a) Décolorer. (b) Ternir, délaver (un tissu).

discolo(u)ration [ˌdisˌkʌləˈreiʃ(ə)n], s. Décoloration f.

discomfiture [dis'kʌmfitʃər], s. 1. Lit: Déconfiture f (d'une armée). 2. Déconvenue f (de qn).

discomfort [dis'kʌmfət], s. (a) Inconfort m, manque m de confort. (b) Malaise m, gêne f. (c) Med: Malaise.

discommode [ˌdiskə'moud], v.tr. Incommoder (qn).

discompose [ˌdiskəm'pouz], v.tr. Troubler, agiter (qn). Discomposed countenance, visage défait.

discomposure [ˌdiskəm'pouʒər], s. Trouble m, agitation f; perturbation f (d'esprit).

disconcert [ˌdiskən'səːt], v.tr. Déconcerter, interloquer; déconfire (qn). **disconcerting**, a. Déconcertant, troublant.

disconnect [ˌdiskə'nekt], v.tr. 1. Désunir, séparer, détacher, disjoindre (sth. with, from, sth., qch. de qch.); décrocher (des wagons); débrayer (une machine). 2. El: Débrancher (une prise, un circuit, un secteur). To d. a telephone line, (i) débrancher, couper la ligne; (ii) couper la communication. **disconnected**, a. 1. (a) Détaché, isolé. (b) Mec.E: Débrayé. 2. (Of speech) Décousu. **-ly**, adv. (Parler, penser) sans suite, à bâtons rompus. **disconnecting**, s. 1. Désunion f (des parties d'une machine); désassemblage m; décrochage m (d'un wagon); Mec.E: débrayage m (d'une machine). 2. El: Débranchage m (d'un circuit, etc.), mise f hors circuit. D. plug, switch, disjoncteur m.

disconnectedness [ˌdiskə'nektidnis], s. Incohérence f, manque m de suite (des idées).

disconsolate [dis'kɔnsəlit], a. Tout triste; inconsolable; désolé. **-ly**, adv. Tristement; d'un air, d'un ton, désolé.

discontent [ˌdiskən'tent], s. (a) Mécontentement m. (b) Sujet m de mécontentement; grief m.

discontented [ˌdiskən'tentid], a. Mécontent (with, de); peu satisfait (de son sort). **-ly**, adv. Avec mécontentement.

discontentedness [ˌdiskən'tentidnis], s. Mécontentement m (de son sort).

discontinuance [ˌdiskən'tinju(:)əns], s. Discontinuation f, cessation f (de fabrication).

discontinue [ˌdiskən'tinju:]. 1. v.tr. Discontinuer (qch.). To d. one's visits, cesser ses visites. 2. v.i. Cesser.

discontinuity [ˌdiskɔnti'nju(:)iti], s. 1. Discontinuité f. 2. Med: Ch: Ph: Solution f de continuité; intervalle m.

discontinuous [ˌdiskən'tinju(:)əs], a. Discontinu. Mth: D. quantity, quantité discrète. **-ly**, adv. Sans continuité; d'une façon intermittente.

discord ['diskɔːd], s. 1. Discorde f, désunion f. To sow d., semer la discorde, la zizanie. Civil d., dissensions civiles. 2. Mus: (i) Dissonance f; (ii) accord dissonant.

discordance [dis'kɔːd(ə)ns], s. 1. Discordance f, inharmonie f (des sons). 2. D. of opinions, désaccord m d'opinions.

discordant [dis'kɔːd(ə)nt], a. 1. (a) (Of sound) Discordant; peu harmonieux. (b) Mus: Dissonant. 2. D. opinions, opinions opposées.

discount[1] ['diskaunt], s. 1. Com: Remise f, ristourne f, rabais m. To sell sth. at a d., vendre qch. au rabais. D. for quantities, réductions fpl sur la quantité. D. for cash, escompte m au comptant. 2. Fin: Escompte. (Of shares) To stand at a d., accuser une perte. Politeness is at a d., on fait peu de cas de la politesse. 'discount price, s. Com: Prix m faible.

discount[2] [dis'kaunt, 'diskaunt], v.tr. 1. Fin: Escompter; faire l'escompte (d'un effet). 2. (a) Ne pas tenir compte de (qn, qch.). (b) Faire peu de cas de (l'avis de qn). You must d. half of what he says, il faut rabattre la moitié de ce qu'il dit.

discountenance [dis'kauntinəns], v.tr. 1. Décontenancer; déconcerter (qn). 2. Décourager (un projet); désapprouver.

discourage [dis'kʌridʒ], v.tr. Décourager, abattre (qn). To become discouraged, se décourager. **discouraging**, a. Décourageant. **-ly**, adv. D'une manière décourageante.

discouragement [dis'kʌridʒmənt], s. 1. Découragement m. To meet with d., essuyer des déboires m. 2. Désapprobation f (d'un projet).

discourse[1] ['diskɔːs], s. Lit: Discours m; dissertation f (on, sur).

discourse[2] [dis'kɔːs], v.i. Lit: (a) Discourir (on, of, sur). (b) Causer, s'entretenir (de).

discourteous [dis'kɔːtiəs], a. Discourtois, impoli. **-ly** adv. To behave d. to s.o., faire une impolitesse à qn.

discourtesy [dis'kɔːtəsi], s. Impolitesse f; discourtoisie f.

discover [dis'kʌvər], v.tr. 1. Découvrir, trouver. (a) To d. a new gas, découvrir un gaz nouveau. (b) I discovered too late that . . ., je m'aperçus trop tard que. . . . 2. (a) A. & Lit: Révéler, laisser voir (qch.); divulguer (un secret). (b) Th: To be discovered as the curtain rises, être en scène au lever du rideau.

discoverer [dis'kʌvərər], s. Découvreur, -euse.

discovery [dis'kʌvəri], s. 1. Découverte f. Voyage of d., voyage m d'exploration. A great d., (i) une grande découverte; (ii) F: (of a find) une trouvaille. 2. A. & Lit: Révélation f (d'un secret); divulgation f.

discredit[1] [dis'kredit], s. 1. Doute m. To throw d. upon a statement, mettre en doute une affirmation. 2. Discrédit m (de qn, de qch.); déconsidération f (de qn). To reflect d. on . . ., jeter du discrédit sur. . . .

discredit[2], v.tr. 1. Ne pas croire (un bruit); mettre en doute (un bruit). 2. Discréditer (une opinion); déconsidérer (qn).

discreditable [dis'kreditəbl], a. 1. Peu digne. D. acquaintances, connaissances interlopes. 2. D. examination paper, composition qui ne fait pas honneur au candidat. **-ably**, adv. De façon indigne, déshonorante.

discreet [dis'kriːt], a. 1. Avisé, sage. A d. smile, un petit sourire contenu. 2. Discret, -ète. **-ly**, adv. 1. Avec réserve. 2. Discrètement.

discrepancy [dis'krepənsi], s. Désaccord m; divergence f (de témoignages). There is a d. between the two stories, les deux récits ne cadrent pas.

discrepant [dis'krepənt], a. Différent (from, de). D. accounts, récits contradictoires.

discrete [dis'kriːt], a. Mth: Discret, -ète; discontinu.

discretion [dis'kreʃ(ə)n], s. 1. Discrétion f. I shall use my own d., je ferai comme bon me semblera. To leave sth. to s.o.'s d., laisser qch. à la discrétion de qn. 2. Sagesse f, jugement m, prudence f. To use d., agir avec discrétion. To come to years of d., atteindre l'âge de raison. He thought d. the better part of valour, il abandonna le champ à de plus dignes. 3. Discrétion; silence judicieux.

discretionary [dis'kreʃən(ə)ri], a. (Pouvoir) discrétionnaire.

discriminant [dis'kriminənt], s. Mth: Discriminant m.

discriminate [dis'krimineit]. 1. v.tr. Distinguer (from, de, d'avec). 2. v.i. (a) Distinguer, discriminer, établir une distinction (between, entre). (b) To d. in favour of s.o., faire des distinctions en faveur de qn. **discriminating**, a. 1. (Of pers.) Plein de discernement. D. purchaser, acheteur avisé. D. ear, oreille fine. 2. Adm: D. tariff, tarif différentiel. **-ly**, adv. Avec discernement.

discrimination [disˌkrimi'neiʃ(ə)n], s. 1. Discernement m. 2. Jugement m; discrimination f. Man of d., homme judicieux. 3. Distinction f, préférence f; mesures f discriminatoires. Racial d., discrimination raciale.

discriminatory [dis'kriminətəri], a. Discriminatoire.

discursive [dis'kəːsiv], a. 1. (Style) décousu, sans suite. He is too d., il ne s'attache pas assez à son sujet. 2. Log: Discursif, déductif. **-ly**, adv. 1. D'une manière décousue. 2. Log: Par déduction.

discus ['diskəs], s. Gr.Ant: Sp: Disque m. D. thrower, discobole m; lanceur m de disque.

discuss [dis'kʌs], v.tr. 1. Discuter, débattre (un problème); délibérer (d'une question); agiter (une question). D. the matter with him, concertez-vous avec lui là-dessus. 2. To d. a bottle of wine, déguster une bouteille de vin.

discussion [dis'kʌʃ(ə)n], s. Discussion f; agitation f (d'une question). Oral d., débat m. A subject for d., un sujet de discussion. Question under d., question en discussion. To start a d., entamer une discussion.

disdain[1] [dis'dein], s. Dédain m (of, de).

disdain[2], v.tr. Dédaigner.

disdainful [dis'deinful], a. Dédaigneux (of, de). **-fully**, adv. Dédaigneusement.

disease [di'ziːz], s. Maladie f; mal m, affection f.
diseased [di'ziːzd], a. 1. Malade. 2. Morbide.
disembark [ˌdisem'baːk], v.tr. & i. Débarquer.
disembarkation [ˌdisembaː'keiʃ(ə)n], s. Débarquement m.
disembarrass [ˌdisim'bærəs], v.tr. Débarrasser (of, de); dégager (from, de).
disembody [ˌdisim'bɔdi], v.tr. Désincorporer. Disembodied spirit, esprit désincarné.
disembowel [ˌdisim'bauəl], v.tr. Éventrer; éviscérer.
disenchant ['disin'tʃaːnt], v.tr. 1. Désenchanter, désensorceler (qn). 2. Désillusionner (qn).
disenchantment [ˌdisin'tʃaːntmənt], s. Désenchantement m, désensorcellement m; désillusion f.
disencumber [ˌdisin'kʌmbər], v.tr. (a) Débarrasser (of, de); désencombrer (qn). (b) Purger l'hypothèque sur (une terre).
disengage [ˌdisin'geidʒ], 1. v.tr. (a) Dégager (sth. from sth., qch. de qch.). (b) Mec.E: Déclencher; désengrener; débrayer. (c) Ch: To d. oxygen, dégager de l'oxygène. (d) Abs. Fenc: Dégager (le fer). 2. v.i. (a) Se dégager. (b) Se déclencher. **disengaged**, a. 1. (Of pers.) Libre, inoccupé, visible. 2. (Of seat) Libre; pas occupé.
disentail [ˌdisin'teil], v.tr. Jur: Libérer (une propriété substituée).
disentangle [ˌdisin'tæŋgl], v.tr. (a) Dégager, F: dépêtrer (from, de). (b) Démêler, désentortiller (une ficelle); débrouiller (une situation).
disentanglement [ˌdisin'tæŋglmənt], s. Débrouillement m, dégagement m; démêlage m (d'un écheveau).
disestablish [ˌdisis'tæbliʃ], v.tr. Séparer (l'Église) de l'État.
disestablishment [ˌdisis'tæbliʃmənt], s. Séparation f de l'Église et de l'État.
disfavour [dis'feivər], s. Défaveur f. To fall into d., tomber en disgrâce. At the risk of incurring s.o.'s d., au risque de déplaire à qn.
disfiguration [disˌfigə'reiʃ(ə)n], s. = DISFIGUREMENT.
disfigure [dis'figər], v.tr. Défigurer; enlaidir. Factory chimneys that d. the view, cheminées d'usine qui gâtent le paysage. **disfigured**, a. Défiguré; au visage ravagé (par une blessure, etc.); F: au visage abîmé.
disfigurement [dis'figəmənt], s. Défiguration f; enlaidissement m.
disfranchise [dis'frænfaiz], v.tr. Priver (qn) du droit électoral; priver (un bourg pourri, etc.) de ses droits de représentation.
disfranchisement [dis'frænfizmənt], s. Privation f du droit de vote, des droits civiques.
disgorge [dis'gɔːdʒ], v.tr. (a) Dégorger, rendre (la nourriture). To make a bird d. its prey, faire dégorger un oiseau. (b) River that disgorges its waters into . . . rivière qui décharge ses eaux dans. . . . (c) Dégorger (ce qu'on a volé, etc.). Abs. To make s.o. d., faire dégorger qn.
disgrace¹ [dis'greis], s. 1. Disgrâce f. To be in d., être en disgrâce; (of child) être en pénitence f. 2. Honte f, déshonneur m. To bring d. on one's family, déshonorer sa famille. To be a d. to one's family, être la honte de sa famille. These slums are a d. to the town, ces taudis m sont la honte de la ville.
disgrace², v.tr. 1. Disgracier (un courtisan, etc.). 2. Déshonorer.
disgraceful [dis'greisful], a. Honteux, déshonorant, scandaleux. **-fully**, adv. Honteusement; d'une manière scandaleuse. He acted d., sa conduite a été indigne.
disgracefulness [dis'greisfulnis], s. Honte f, ignominie f, infamie f.
disgruntled [dis'grʌntld], a. Contrarié, mécontent (at, de); maussade.
disguise¹ [dis'gaiz], s. 1. Déguisement m; travestissement m. In d., déguisé. 2. Feinte f; fausse apparence. To throw off all d., laisser tomber le masque.
disguise², v.tr. 1. Déguiser, travestir (qn). 2. (a) Déguiser (sa pensée); masquer (une odeur). (b) There is no disguising the fact that . . ., il faut avouer que. . . . (c) To d. one's feelings, dissimuler ses sentiments.
disgust¹ [dis'gʌst], s. 1. Dégoût (profond) (at, for, towards, pour). 2. Profond mécontentement. He resigned in d., écœuré, il donna sa démission.

disgust², v.tr. Dégoûter; écœurer. To be disgusted at, with, by, sth., être profondément mécontent de qch.
disgusting, a. Dégoûtant. 1. Qui répugne au goût, à la vue. 2. Écœurant. It's d.! F: C'est du propre! **-ly**, adv. He is d. mean, il est d'une ladrerie dégoûtante.
dish¹ [diʃ], s. 1. Plat m. Earthenware d., terrine f. Vegetable d., légumier m. To wash (up) the dishes, laver la vaisselle. 2. Cu: Plat (de viande, etc.); mets m. Dainty d., mets délicat. 3. Récipient m. Ch: Capsule f. Phot: Cuvette f. 4. U.S: P: Jolie fille. 'dish-cloth, s. 1. Torchon m. 2. Lavette f. 'dish-cover, s. 1. Couvercle m (de plat). 2. Cloche f. 'dish-mop, s. Lavette f. 'dish-warmer, s. Chauffe-plat, pl. chauffe-plats. 'dish-washer, s. (a) (Pers., in a restaurant, etc.) Plongeur m. (b) Machine f à laver la vaisselle. 'dish-water, s. 1. Eau f de vaisselle; eau grasse. 2. P: (a) (Thin soup, etc.) Lavasse f. (b) Thé m, café m, sans goût.
dish², v.tr. 1. To d. (up) meat, servir, dresser, la viande. F: To d. up well-known facts in a new form, donner un réchauffé de faits bien connus. 2. F: To d. one's opponents, rouler, enfoncer, ses adversaires. To d. oneself, s'enferrer. He's dished! il est flambé, fini, fichu! 3. Donner une forme concave ou convexe à (une surface). Veh: Dished wheel, roue désaxée. Metalw: Dished plate, tôle emboutie; tôle bombée.
dishearten [dis'haːtn], v.tr. Décourager, abattre, démoraliser, rebuter. Don't get disheartened, ne perdez pas courage. **disheartening**, a. Décourageant; (travail) ingrat.
dishevel [di'ʃev(ə)l], v.tr. Ébouriffer (qn, les cheveux). **dishevelled**, a. 1. Échevelé, dépeigné; ébouriffé. 2. Aux vêtements chiffonnés.
dishful ['diʃful], s. Platée f; plein un plat (of, de).
dishonest [dis'ɔnist], a. Malhonnête; déloyal, -aux. **-ly**, adv. Malhonnêtement.
dishonesty [dis'ɔnisti], s. Improbité f, malhonnêteté f. Piece of d., malhonnêteté.
dishonour¹ [dis'ɔnər], s. 1. Déshonneur m. To bring d. on one's family, déshonorer sa famille. 2. Chose déshonorante.
dishonour², v.tr. 1. Déshonorer. 2. (a) To d. one's word, manquer à sa parole. (b) Com: To d. a bill, ne pas honorer un effet. Dishonoured cheque, chèque impayé.
dishonourable [dis'ɔnərəbl], a. 1. (Of pers.) Sans honneur. 2. (Of action) Déshonorant, honteux, indigne. **-ably**, adv. D'une façon peu honorable.
dishpan ['diʃpæn], s. U.S: Bassine f à vaisselle.
disillusion¹ [ˌdisi'ljuːʒ(ə)n], s. Désillusion f, désabusement m, désenchantement m.
disillusion², disillusionize [ˌdisi'ljuːʒənaiz], v.tr. Désillusionner, désabuser, désenchanter.
disillusionment [ˌdisi'ljuːʒənmənt], s. Désillusionnement m, désenchantement m.
disincarnate [disin'kaːnit], a. Psychics: Désincarné.
disinclination [ˌdisinkli'neiʃ(ə)n], s. Répugnance f, aversion f (for, to, pour). To show a d. to do sth., montrer peu d'empressement à faire qch.
disinclined [ˌdisin'klaind], a. Peu disposé (for, to, sth., à qch.).
disincrustant [disin'krʌstənt], s. Désincrustant m (de chaudière).
disinfect [ˌdisin'fekt], v.tr. Désinfecter.
disinfectant [ˌdisin'fektənt], a. & s. Désinfectant (m).
disinfection [ˌdisin'fekʃ(ə)n], s. Désinfection f.
disinfestation [ˌdisinfes'teiʃ(ə)n], s. (Of lice) Épouillage m; (of fleas) épuçage m. Rat d., dératisation f.
disingenuous [ˌdisin'dʒenjuəs], a. Sans franchise; faux, f. fausse. **-ly**, adv. Sans franchise.
disingenuousness [ˌdisin'dʒenjuəsnis], s. Manque m de franchise; mauvaise foi.
disinherit [ˌdisin'herit], v.tr. Déshériter.
disintegrate [dis'intigreit], 1. v.tr. Désagréger; effriter (la pierre). 2. v.i. Se désagréger; s'effriter.
disintegration [disˌinti'greiʃ(ə)n], s. (a) Désagrégation f, effritement m, détrition f (de la pierre). (b) Désagrégation f (de la société, etc.). (c) Nuclear d., désintégration f.
disinter [ˌdisin'təːr], v.tr. (disinterred) Déterrer, exhumer.

disinterested [dis'intərestid], a. **1.** Désintéressé. **His action is not entirely d.,** F: ce qu'il en fait ce n'est pas pour vos beaux yeux. **2.** Non intéressé (**in,** dans), indifférent (**to,** à). **-ly,** adv. Avec désintéressement.

disinterestedness [dis'intrəstidnis], s. Désintéressement m.

disinterment [,disin'tə:mənt], s. Déterrement m; exhumation f.

disjoint [dis'dʒɔint], v.tr. Disjoindre, démembrer (une volaille). Surg: Désarticuler (l'épaule). **disjointed,** a. Disjoint, disloqué; (discours) sans suite; (style) décousu.

disjunction [dis'dʒʌŋ(k)ʃ(ə)n], s. Disjonction f.

disjunctive [dis'dʒʌŋ(k)tiv], a. Disjonctif, -ive.

disk [disk], s. = DISC.

dislike¹ [dis'laik], s. Aversion f, répugnance f (**to, of, for, pour**). **To take a d. to s.o.,** prendre qn en grippe.

dislike², v.tr. Ne pas aimer; détester. **He dislikes you,** vous lui êtes antipathique. **I don't d. him,** il ne me déplaît pas. **I d. his coming so often,** je n'aime pas qu'il vienne si souvent. **To be disliked by all,** être mal vu de tous.

dislocate ['disləkeit], v.tr. (a) Disloquer (une machine); désorganiser (les affaires). (b) Luxer, déboîter (un membre). **To d. one's jaw,** se décrocher la mâchoire. (Of horse) **To d. its hip,** se déhancher.

dislocation [,dislə'keiʃ(ə)n], s. (a) Dislocation f (d'une machine); désorganisation f (des affaires). (b) Luxation f, déboîtement m (d'un membre). Med: Vet: **D. of the hip,** déhanchement m.

dislodge [dis'lodʒ], v.tr. **1.** Déloger (un renard, etc.); débucher (un cerf). **2.** Détacher. **Several bricks had become dislodged,** plusieurs briques s'étaient détachées.

dislodg(e)ment [dis'lodʒmənt], s. **1.** Délogement m, débusquement m (de l'ennemi, etc.). Ven: Débucher m. **2.** Déplacement m (d'une pierre, etc.).

disloyal [dis'lɔiəl], a. Infidèle (à l'amitié); déloyal, -aux. **A d. act,** une déloyauté. **-ally,** adv. Infidèlement, déloyalement, perfidement.

disloyalty [dis'lɔiəlti], s. Infidélité f, déloyauté f, perfidie f.

dismal ['dizməl], a. Sombre, triste; lugubre; (paysage) morne. **A d. Jemmy,** un broyeur de noir. **-ally,** adv. Lugubrement, tristement.

dismantle [dis'mæntl], v.tr. **1.** Dégarnir (**of,** de). **2.** (a) Démanteler (une forteresse). (b) Démonter (une machine).

dismast [dis'mɑ:st], v.tr. Démâter.

dismay¹ [dis'mei], s. Consternation f; épouvante f. **In (blank) d.,** consterné.

dismay², v.tr. Consterner, épouvanter. **We were dismayed at the news,** la nouvelle nous jeta dans la consternation.

dismember [dis'membər], v.tr. Démembrer (un poulet). **His body was dismembered,** son corps fut écartelé.

dismemberment [dis'membəmənt], s. Démembrement m.

dismiss [dis'mis], v.tr. **1.** Congédier (qn); donner congé a (qn); chasser (un domestique); révoquer, destituer (un fonctionnaire). **2.** (a) Congédier (aimablement) (qn). (b) Congédier, éconduire (un importun, etc.). (c) Dissoudre (une assemblée). (d) **To d. troops (after service),** renvoyer des troupes dans leurs foyers. **3. To d. sth. from one's thoughts,** bannir, chasser, qch. de ses pensées. **4. Let us d. the subject,** n'en parlons plus; brisons là. **The subject is not to be dismissed lightly,** l'on ne saurait écarter cette question aussi légèrement. **5.** (a) Écarter (une proposition). Jur: Rejeter (une demande). **To d. a charge,** rendre une ordonnance de non-lieu. (b) **To d. the accused,** acquitter l'inculpé. **6.** Mil: **D.!** rompez (les rangs)!

dismissal [dis'misəl], s. **1.** Congédiement m, renvoi m (d'un employé); révocation f, destitution f (d'un fonctionnaire). **He threatened him with d.,** il menaça de le renvoyer. **2.** Jur: (a) Fin f de non-recevoir; rejet m (d'un appel). (b) Acquittement m (de l'inculpé).

dismount [dis'maunt]. **1.** v.i. **To d. (from a horse),** descendre (de cheval); mettre pied à terre. **2.** v.tr. (a) Démonter, désarçonner (un cavalier). (b) Mil: Mettre à pied (des troupes montées). **3.** v.tr. Démonter (un canon, une machine).

disobedience [,disə'bi:djəns], s. Désobéissance f (**to s.o.,** à qn; **to a rule,** à une règle).

disobedient [,disə'bi:djənt], a. Désobéissant. **To be d. to s.o.,** désobéir à qn.

disobey [,disə'bei], v.tr. Désobéir à (qn). **My orders were disobeyed,** mes ordres ont été désobéis.

disobliging [,disə'blaidʒiŋ], a. Désobligeant, peu complaisant.

disobligingness [,disə'blaidʒiŋnis], s. Désobligeance f; manque m de complaisance (**to,** envers).

disorder¹ [dis'ɔ:dər], s. **1.** Désordre m, confusion f. **In d.,** en désordre. **To throw the ranks into d.,** mettre le désordre dans les rangs. **They fled in d.,** ils s'enfuirent à la débandade. **2.** (Civil disorder) Désordre, tumulte m. **3.** Med: Désordre; affection f. **Disorders of the mind,** dérangement m d'esprit.

disorder², v.tr. **1.** Déranger; mettre le désordre, la confusion, dans (les rangs, etc.). **2.** O: Déranger (l'estomac); F: détraquer (la santé). **disordered,** a. **1.** Désordonné; en désordre. **2.** (Foie, esprit) malade.

disorderliness [dis'ɔ:dəlinis], s. **1.** Désordre m; manque m d'ordre. **2.** Conduite f contraire aux bonnes mœurs. **3.** Turbulence f.

disorderly [dis'ɔ:dəli], a. **1.** Qui manque d'ordre; désordonné; en désordre. **2.** (Of mob) Turbulent. **3.** (Of pers.) Désordonné, déréglé. **D. conduct,** conduite f contraire aux bonnes mœurs. **To lead a d. life,** vivre dans le dérèglement. **4.** Jur: **D. house,** (i) maison f de débauche. (ii) Maison de jeu.

disorganization [dis'ɔ:gənai'zeiʃ(ə)n], s. Désorganisation f; désagencement m.

disorganize [dis'ɔ:gənaiz], v.tr. Désorganiser; désagencer. **disorganizing,** a. Désorganisateur, -trice.

disorientate [dis'ɔ:rienteit], v.tr. Désorienter.

disown [dis'oun], v.tr. Désavouer (qch., qn); renier (l'autorité de qn, sa signature).

disparage [dis'pæridʒ], v.tr. **1.** Déprécier, dénigrer; battre (qn) en brèche. **2.** Déshonorer, discréditer. **disparaging,** a. **1.** (Terme) de dénigrement; dépréciateur, -trice. **2.** Peu flatteur, -euse; déshonorant. **-ly,** adv. **To speak d. of s.o.,** parler de qn en termes peu flatteurs.

disparagement [dis'pæridʒmənt], s. Dénigrement m, dépréciation f.

disparager [dis'pæridʒər], s. Dénigreur, -euse; détracteur, -trice.

disparity [dis'pæriti], s. Inégalité f (**of, de**). **D. of age,** différence f, disparité f, d'âge.

dispassionate [dis'pæʃənit], a. **1.** Sans passion; calme. **2.** Impartial, -aux. **-ly,** adv. **1.** Sans passion; avec calme. **2.** Sans parti pris.

dispatch¹ [dis'pætʃ], s. **1.** Expédition f; envoi m (de qn, de qch.). Com: **D. office,** service m des expéditions. **D. note,** bulletin m, bordereau m d'expédition. Post: Office of d., bureau m d'origine. **2.** Mise f à mort. **3.** (a) Expédition (d'une affaire.) (b) Promptitude f, diligence f. **With d.,** promptement. **With all possible d.,** with the utmost d., en toute diligence; au plus vite. **4.** Dépêche f. Mil: **To be mentioned in dispatches,** être cité (à l'ordre du jour). **5.** Nau: **D.(-boat, -vessel),** aviso m. **dis'patch-box,** s. Boîte f à documents. **dis'patch-case,** s. Serviette f (en cuir). **dis'patch-rider,** s. Mil: Estafette f.

dispatch², v.tr. **1.** Dépêcher (un courrier); expédier (des marchandises); envoyer (qn); faire partir (des troupes). **2.** (a) **To d. a wounded animal,** achever un animal. (b) **The executioner soon dispatched the prisoners,** le bourreau eut vite fait d'expédier les prisonniers. **3. To d. current business,** expédier les affaires courantes. **4.** F: Expédier (un repas).

dispatcher [dis'pætʃər], s. **1.** Expéditeur, -trice. **2.** Rail: (Train) d., dispatcher m, régulateur m.

dispel [dis'pel], v.tr. (**dispelled**) Chasser, dissiper (des illusions, les craintes).

dispensable [dis'pensəbl], a. **1.** Dont on peut se passer. **2.** Ecc: (Vœu m, etc.) dispensable.

dispensary [dis'pensəri], s. **1.** (a) Dispensaire m; policlinique f. (b) (In a hospital) Dépense f. **2.** (a) Officine f (d'une pharmacie). (b) Pharmacie f.

dispensation [,dispen'seiʃ(ə)n], s. **1.** Dispensation f, distribution f (des aumônes). **2.** Décret m, arrêt m (de la Providence). **3.** Ecc: **D. from fasting,** dispense f du jeûne. **4. D. from sth.,** fait m d'être dispensé de qch.

dispense [dis'pens]. 1. *v.tr.* (*a*) Dispenser, distribuer (des aumônes). (*b*) Administrer (la justice). (*c*) *Pharm:* Préparer (des médicaments). **To d. a prescription**, exécuter, préparer, une ordonnance. 2. *v.tr.* **To d. s.o. from sth.**, dispenser qn de qch. 3. *v.i.* **To d. with sth.**, se passer de qch. **dispensing**, *s.* 1. Dispensation *f*, distribution *f* (des aumônes). 2. *Pharm:* Préparation *f* (des ordonnances). **D. chemist**, pharmacien diplômé. (*In large stores*) **D. counter**, rayon *m* d'ordonnances médicales.

dispenser [dis'pensər], *s.* 1. (*a*) Dispensateur, -trice (d'aumônes). (*b*) (*In hospital*) Dépensier, -ière. (*c*) Pharmacien *m*. (*d*) (*Razor-blade*) d., distributeur *m* (de lames de rasoir). 2. Administrateur *m* (des lois).

dispersal [dis'pə:s(ə)l], *s.* Dispersion *f*. *Av:* **D. area**, *F:* dispersal *m*.

disperse [dis'pə:s]. 1. *v.tr.* (*a*) Disperser; dissiper (les nuages). (*b*) Répandre, disséminer (des nouvelles). (*c*) *Med:* Résoudre (une tumeur). (*d*) *Opt:* (*Of prism, etc.*) Disperser (la lumière). 2. *v.i.* Se disperser.

dispersion [dis'pə:ʃ(ə)n], *s.* Dispersion *f*; diffusion *f* (de la chaleur, etc.). **D. of a diamond**, feux *mpl* (d'un diamant).

dispirit [di'spirit], *v.tr.* Décourager, abattre (qn). **dispirited**, *a.* Découragé, abattu. **-ly**, *adv.* D'un air, d'un ton, découragé, abattu.

displace [dis'pleis], *v.tr.* 1. Déplacer (qch.). *El.E:* **To d. the brushes**, décaler les balais. 2. (*a*) Déplacer, destituer (un fonctionnaire). (*b*) Remplacer (by, par). (*c*) Évincer (qn). **To d. s.o. in s.o.'s affections**, supplanter qn. (*d*) *Pol:* **Displaced persons**, personnes déplacées.

displacement [dis'pleismənt], *s.* (*a*) Déplacement *m* (de qch.); changement *m* de place. *El.E:* Décalage *m* (des balais). (*b*) *N.Arch:* Déplacement (d'un navire). **Light d.**, déplacement lège. **Load d.**, déplacement en charge.

display[1] [dis'plei], *s.* 1. Étalage *m*, déploiement *m* (de marchandises); manifestation *f* (de colère). **D. of courage**, déploiement de courage. **Air d.**, fête *f* aéronautique. *Com:* **D. case**, coffret *m* d'étalage. **D. unit**, présentoir *m*. **D. window**, vitrine *f*. *Electronics:* Affichage *m*. 2. Étalage (de luxe); parade *f*, apparat *m*; affichage *m* (d'opinions). **To make a great d. of sorrow**, faire montre de douleur, afficher sa douleur. 3. *Typ:* Lignes *fpl*, matières *fpl*, en vedette.

display[2], *v.tr.* 1. Exhiber, étaler, exposer (des marchandises). **To d. a notice**, afficher un avis. 2. Montrer, manifester (du courage); faire preuve de (courage). **To d. a taste for . . .**, témoigner d'un goût pour. . . . 3. Étaler, afficher (son luxe). 4. Découvrir, révéler (son ignorance). 5. *Typ:* Mettre (une ligne, etc.) en vedette.

displease [dis'pli:z], *v.tr.* Déplaire à (qn); contrarier, mécontenter (qn). *Abs.* Déplaire. **To be displeased at sth., with s.o.**, être mécontent de qch., de qn. **displeasing**, *a.* Déplaisant, désagréable (to, à).

displeasure [dis'pleʒər], *s.* Déplaisir *m*, mécontentement *m*. **To incur s.o.'s d.**, s'attirer le courroux de qn.

disport [dis'pɔ:t], *v.pr. & i.* **To d. (oneself)**, (i) se divertir, s'amuser; (ii) s'ébattre; folâtrer.

disposable [dis'pouzəbl], *a.* 1. (*Money, possessions, etc.*) Disponible. 2. *Com:* **D. handkerchiefs**, mouchoirs *m* en tissu cellulose, *F:* mouchoirs en papier. **D. wrapping**, emballage perdu.

disposal [dis'pouzəl], *s.* 1. (*a*) Action *f* de disposer (de qch.). **The d. of one's money**, ce qu'il faut faire de son argent. **D. of a piece of business**, expédition *f* d'une affaire. **D. of a question**, résolution *f* d'une question. **D. of household refuse**, destruction *f* des ordures ménagères. **D. unit**, broyeur *m* d'ordures. *Mil:* **Bomb d. squad**, équipe *f* de désobusage. (*b*) **At s.o.'s d.**, à la disposition de qn. **It is entirely at your d.**, c'est tout à votre service. **The means at my d.**, les moyens dont je dispose. 2. Disposition *f*, cession *f* (de biens). **For d.**, à vendre. 3. Disposition (des troupes sur le terrain).

dispose [dis'pouz], *v.tr. & i.* 1. (*a*) Disposer, arranger (des objets); ordonner (une maison). **Man proposes, God disposes**, l'homme propose et Dieu dispose. (*b*) **To d. of s.o.'s fate**, décider du sort de qn. 2. **To d. of sth., s.o.**, se défaire de qch., de qn; *F:* faire un sort à qch., à qn; tuer qn. **To d. of an opponent**, vaincre un adversaire. **To d. of a matter**, régler une affaire. *F:* **To d. of a meal**, expédier un repas. 3. *Com:* (*Sell*) **To d. of goods, of an article**, écouler des marchandises; vendre, placer, un article. **To d. of one's business**, céder son fonds. **To be disposed of**, à vendre, à céder. 4. Disposer, incliner, porter (s.o. to do sth., qn à faire qch.). 5. **To d. oneself to sleep**, se disposer à dormir. **disposed**, *a.* 1. Intentionné, disposé. **To be well disposed (towards s.o.)**, être bien intentionné (envers qn). **If you feel so d.**, si le cœur vous en dit. 2. (*a*) **D. to sth.**, enclin, porté, à qch. **To be d. to pity**, incliner à la pitié. (*b*) **I am d. to help you**, je suis (tout) disposé à vous aider.

disposition [ˌdispə'ziʃ(ə)n], *s.* 1. (*a*) Disposition *f*, agencement *m*. (*b*) *Jur:* Disposition (testamentaire). 2. = DISPOSAL 1 (*b*). 3. Caractère *m*, naturel *m*, humeur *f*. **He is of a kindly d.**, c'est une bonne nature. 4. (*a*) **D. to do sth.**, désir *m* de faire qch. **There was a general d. to remain**, tous étaient disposés à rester. (*b*) Penchant *m*, tendance *f* (to, à).

dispossess [ˌdispə'zes], *v.tr.* (*a*) Déposséder (qn) (of, de). (*b*) Exproprier (qn).

dispossession [ˌdispə'zeʃ(ə)n], *s.* (*a*) Dépossession *f*. (*b*) Expropriation *f*.

disproof [dis'pru:f], *s.* Réfutation *f*.

disproportion [ˌdisprə'pɔ:ʃ(ə)n], *s.* Disproportion *f*; défaut *m* de proportion.

disproportional [ˌdisprə'pɔ:ʃ(ə)nl], *a.* Disproportionnel, -elle.

disproportionate [ˌdisprə'pɔ:ʃənit], *a.* Disproportionné (to, à). **-ly**, *adv.* D'une façon disproportionnée.

disprove [dis'pru:v], *v.tr.* Réfuter (un dire); démontrer la fausseté (d'un dire).

disputable [dis'pju:təbl], *a.* Contestable. **-ably**, *adv.* Contestablement.

disputant [dis'pju:tənt], *a. & s.* Discuteur, -euse; controversiste (*mf*).

disputation [ˌdispju'teiʃ(ə)n], *s.* Débat *m*.

disputatious [ˌdispju(:)'teiʃəs], *a.* Disputeur, -euse; chicanier, -ière; *F:* disputailleur, -euse.

dispute[1] [dis'pju:t, 'dispju:t], *s.* 1. Contestation *f*, débat *m*. **The matter in d.**, l'affaire dont il s'agit. **Beyond d.**, incontestable. **Without d.**, sans contredit. *Jur:* **Case under d.**, cas en litige. 2. Querelle *f*, dispute *f* (as to, relative à). **Trade d.**, conflit *m* du travail. **Industrial disputes**, conflits ouvriers.

dispute[2] [dis'pju:t]. 1. *v.i.* (*a*) **To d. with s.o. about sth.**, débattre qch. avec qn. (*b*) Se disputer. 2. *v.tr.* (*a*) Débattre (une question); contester (une affirmation). (*b*) **To d. (the possession of) sth. with s.o.**, disputer qch. à qn.

disqualification [disˌkwɔlifi'keiʃ(ə)n], *s.* 1. Incapacité *f*; *Jur:* inhabilité *f* (to act, à agir). 2. Cause *f* d'incapacité (for, à). 3. (*a*) Mise *f* en état d'incapacité. (*b*) *Sp:* Disqualification *f*.

disqualify [dis'kwɔlifai], *v.tr.* 1. Rendre incapable (for sth., de faire qch.). 2. (*a*) *Jur:* **Disqualified from making a will**, inhabile à tester. (*b*) **To d. s.o. from driving**, retirer le permis de conduire à qn. 3. *Sp:* Disqualifier (un joueur).

disquiet[1] [dis'kwaiət], *s.* Inquiétude *f*; agitation *f*.

disquiet[2], **disquieten** [dis'kwaiət(n)], *v.tr.* Inquiéter; troubler. **disquieting**, *a.* Inquiétant; peu rassurant.

disquietude [dis'kwaiətju:d], *s.* 1. Inquiétude *f*, anxiété *f*. 2. Manque *m* de calme; agitation *f*.

disquisition [ˌdiskwi'ziʃ(ə)n], *s.* Dissertation *f* (on, sur).

disrate [dis'reit], *v.tr.* *Navy:* Déclasser (un homme).

disregard[1] [ˌdisri'gɑ:d], *s.* Indifférence *f*, insouciance *f* (of, for, à l'égard de); irrespect *m*. **D. of a rule**, désobéissance *f* à une règle. **D. of the law**, inobservation *f* de la loi.

disregard[2], *v.tr.* Ne tenir aucun compte de (qn, qch.); méconnaître (un devoir).

disremember [disri'membər], *v.tr.* *U.S:* *F:* Oublier.

disrepair [ˌdisri'pɛər], *s.* Délabrement *m* (d'une maison). **To fall into d.**, tomber en ruines; se délabrer, se dégrader. **In a state of d.**, délabré.

disreputable [dis'repjutəbl], a. **1.** (*Of action*) Déshonorant; honteux. **2.** (*Of pers.*) De mauvaise réputation; taré, perdu d'honneur. **D. house,** maison mal famée, louche. **3.** (*Of garments*) Minable. **D. old hat,** vieux chapeau digne d'un chiffonnier. **-ably,** *adv.* Honteusement; d'une façon peu honorable. **dis'reputable-looking,** a. De mauvaise mine; d'aspect louche.

disrepute [disri'pju:t], s. **To bring sth. into d.,** discréditer qch.; faire tomber qch. dans le discrédit. **To fall into d.,** tomber dans le mépris.

disrespect [,disris'pekt], s. Manque m d'égards, de respect (**for,** envers); irrespect m, irrévérence f. **To treat s.o. with d.,** manquer de respect à qn.

disrespectful [,disris'pektful], a. Irrespectueux, irrévérencieux. **To be d. to s.o.,** manquer de respect à qn. **-fully,** *adv.* **To speak d. of s.o.,** parler de qn avec irrévérence.

disrobe [dis'roub]. **1.** *v.tr.* Aider (un magistrat, etc.) à se dévêtir de sa robe. **2.** *v.i.* (*Of judge*) Se dévêtir de sa robe.

disrupt [dis'rʌpt], *v.tr.* **1.** Rompre, briser, disloquer. **The train services are often disrupted on British Railways,** les relations ferroviaires sont souvent interrompues dans les chemins de fer britanniques. **2.** Démembrer (un empire); faire crouler (une administration); rompre (une coalition). **To d. our plans,** ruiner nos plans, nos projets.

disruptive [dis'rʌptiv], a. Disruptif, -ive.

disruption [dis'rʌpʃ(ə)n], s. **1.** Dislocation (violente). **2.** Démembrement m (d'un empire).

dissatisfaction [di,sætis'fækʃ(ə)n], s. Dissatisfaction f; mécontentement m (**with, at,** de).

dissatisfy [di'sætisfai], *v.tr.* Mécontenter; dissatisfaire; ne pas satisfaire. **dissatisfied,** a. Mécontent (**with, at,** de).

dissect [di'sekt], *v.tr.* Disséquer.

dissection [di'sekʃ(ə)n], s. **1.** Dissection f. **2.** Découpage m. **3.** *T.V:* **Vertical d.,** exploration f par lignes verticales.

dissemble [di'sembl], *v.tr.* Dissimuler (ses sentiments); passer (un fait) sous silence. *Abs.* User de dissimulation; déguiser sa pensée. **dissembling,** s. Dissimulation f.

dissembler [di'semblər], s. Dissimulateur, -trice; hypocrite mf.

disseminate [di'semineit], *v.tr.* Disséminer, semer (le grain); propager, répandre (les idées).

dissemination [di,semi'neiʃ(ə)n], s. Dissémination f, propagation f. **D. (of technical knowledge),** diffusion f (des connaissances techniques).

disseminator [di'semineitər], s. Disséminateur, -trice; propagateur, -trice (d'idées, etc.).

dissension [di'senʃ(ə)n], s. Dissension f.

dissent¹ [di'sent], s. **1.** Dissentiment m; avis m contraire. **2.** *Ecc:* Dissidence f.

dissent², *v.i.* **1.** Différer (**from s.o. about sth.,** de qn sur qch.). **2.** *Ecc:* Être dissident. **dissenting,** a. Dissident.

dissenter [di'sentər], s. Dissident, -e.

dissentient [di'senʃjənt], a. & s. Dissident, -e. **With one d. vote,** à l'unanimité moins une voix.

dissertation [,disə'teiʃ(ə)n], s. Dissertation f.

disservice [di'sə:vis], s. Mauvais service rendu. **To do s.o. a d.,** desservir qn.

dissidence ['disid(ə)ns], s. Dissidence f.

dissident ['disid(ə)nt], a. & s. (a) Dissident (m). (b) Membre dissident (d'un parti).

dissimilar [di'similər], a. Dissemblable (**to,** à, de); différent (**to,** de); dissemblant.

dissimilarity [di,simi'læriti], a. Dissemblance f, dissimilitude f (**to,** de); dissimilarité f.

dissimulate [di'simjuleit], *v.tr.* (a) Dissimuler; cacher (un fait). (b) *Abs.* Feindre.

dissimulation [di,simju'leiʃ(ə)n], s. Dissimulation f.

dissimulator [di'simjuleitər], s. Dissimulateur, -trice.

dissipate ['disipeit]. **1.** *v.tr.* Dissiper (une fortune). **To d. one's efforts,** disperser ses efforts. **2.** *v.i.* Se dissiper. **dissipated,** a. Dissipé. **D. man, woman,** noceur, noceuse.

dissipation [,disi'peiʃ(ə)n], s. **1.** Dissipation f (du brouillard); gaspillage m (d'une fortune). **2.** Divertissement m. **3.** Dissipation; vie désordonnée; le plaisir.

dissociable [di'souʃjəbl], a. *Ch:* Dissociable (**from, de**).

dissociate [di'souʃieit], *v.tr.* (a) Désassocier (des personnes) (**from, de**). **To d. oneself from a question,** se désintéresser d'une affaire. (b) *Ch:* Dissocier (un composé).

dissociation [di,sousi'eiʃ(ə)n], s. *Ch:* Dissociation f.

dissolubility [di,sɔlju'biliti], s. *Ch:* Dissolubilité f.

dissoluble [di'sɔljubl], a. **1.** *Ph: etc:* Dissoluble (**in, dans**). **2.** *Jur:* Dissoluble.

dissolute ['disɔlju:t], a. Dissolu, débauché. **To lead a d. life,** vivre dans la débauche. **-ly,** *adv.* Dissolument.

dissoluteness ['disɔlju:tnis], s. Dérèglement m.

dissolution [,disɔ'lju:ʃ(ə)n], s. **1.** Dissolution f, fonte f, liquéfaction f. **2.** Dissolution (d'une assemblée, d'un mariage).

dissolvable [di'zɔlvəbl], a. (Assemblée f etc.) dissoluble; (association commerciale) terminable.

dissolve¹ [di'zɔlv], s. *Cin:* Fondu m. **D.-in, -out,** ouverture f, fermeture f, en fondu.

dissolve². **1.** *v.tr.* (a) Dissoudre, faire dissoudre (un sel, etc.). (b) Dissoudre (une assemblée, un mariage). **2.** *v.i.* (a) Se dissoudre; fondre. **To d. into thin air,** partir, s'en aller, en fumée. (b) (*Of Parliament*) se dissoudre. (c) *Cin:* **Dissolving views,** fondus m.

dissolvent [di'zɔlvənt], s. *Ph: etc:* Dissolvant m.

dissonance ['disənəns], s. **1.** *Mus:* Dissonance f. **2.** Désaccord m (**between,** entre).

dissonant ['disənənt], a. **1.** *Mus:* Dissonant. **2.** En désaccord (**from, to,** avec).

dissuade [di'sweid], *v.tr.* **To d. s.o. from doing sth.,** dissuader, détourner, qn de faire qch.

dissuasion [di'sweiʒ(ə)n], s. Dissuasion f.

dissuasive [di'sweisiv], a. Dissuasif.

distaff ['dista:f], s. Quenouille f. **The d. side (of a family),** le côté maternel.

distance ['distəns], s. **1.** (a) Distance f, éloignement m. **Within speaking d.,** à portée de voix. **It is no d. (away),** *F:* ce n'est qu'une promenade. **Seen from a d.,** vu de loin. **D. lends enchantment to the view,** tout paraît beau vu de loin. **Customers who come from a d.,** clients venus du dehors. (b) Lointain m. **Away in the d.,** dans le lointain. **The countryside with its vast distances,** la campagne aux vastes horizons. *Art:* **Middle-d.,** second plan. (c) (*Time*) **At this d. of time,** après cet intervalle (de temps). **A d. of three centuries,** un intervalle de trois siècles. **2. To go part of the d. on foot,** faire une partie du trajet à pied. **3.** Distance, intervalle m. **To keep s.o. at a d.,** tenir qn à distance. *Rail:* **D. between rails,** écartement m de voie. **4. D. of manner,** air distant; réserve f.

distant ['distənt], a. **1.** *O:* **Three miles d.,** à trois milles de distance. **Not far d. from . . .,** à peu de distance de. . . . **2.** (a) (Endroit) éloigné; (pays) lointain. **To have a d. view of sth.,** voir qch. de loin. *Rail:* **D. signal,** signal à distance; signal avancé. **D. look,** regard perdu dans le vague. (b) (*In time*) Éloigné, reculé. **D. recollection,** souvenir lointain. **In the d. future,** dans un avenir lointain. **3.** (*Of pers.*) Réservé, froid, distant. **-ly,** *adv.* **1.** De loin. **D. related,** d'une parenté éloignée. **2.** Avec réserve; froidement.

distaste [dis'teist], s. Dégoût m (**for, de**); aversion f, répugnance f (**for,** pour).

distasteful [dis'teistful], a. **1.** Désagréable au goût. **2.** Désagréable, déplaisant, antipathique (**to, à**). **To be d. to s.o.,** répugner à qn.

distemper¹ [dis'tempər], s. (a) *A:* Maladie f. (b) *Vet:* Maladie du jeune âge.

distemper², *v.tr.* *A:* Rendre (qn) malade. **Distempered mind,** esprit dérangé, troublé.

distemper³, s. **1.** *Art:* Détrempe f. **2.** (*For housedecoration*) Détrempe, badigeon m.

distemper⁴, *v.tr.* **1.** *Art:* Peindre (un tableau) en détrempe. **2.** Badigeonner (un mur). **distempering,** s. **1.** Peinture f en détrempe. **2.** Badigeonnage m.

distend [dis'tend]. **1.** *v.tr.* (a) Dilater, gonfler (un ballon). (b) Distendre, dilater, ballonner (l'estomac); *Vet:* météoriser (l'estomac). **2.** *v.i.* (a) Se dilater, enfler. (b) Se distendre.

distension, (*mainly U.S.*) **distention** [dis'tenʃ(ə)n], s. Dilatation f, distension f, gonflement m.

distich ['distik], s. *Pros:* Distique m.

distil [dis'til], v. (distilled) 1. v.tr. (a) Distiller (l'eau, le vin, etc.); brûler (le vin); raffiner (le pétrole). They d. their own brandy, ils brûlent leur vin. (b) Laisser tomber goutte à goutte. To d. poison into s.o.'s mind, faire couler du poison dans l'âme de qn. 2. v.i. (a) To d. (over), se distiller. (b) Distiller, couler doucement.

distillation [‚disti'leiʃ(ə)n], s. Distillation f.

distiller [dis'tilər], s. 1. (Pers.) Ind: Distillateur m. 2. (Apparatus) Ind: etc: Distillateur; bouilleur m (pour eau-de-vie, etc.).

distillery [dis'tiləri], s. Ind: Distillerie f.

distinct [dis'tiŋ(k)t], a. 1. Distinct, différent (from, de). To keep two things d., distinguer entre deux choses. 2. (Clear) Distinct, net. D. memory, souvenir clair. D. promise, promesse formelle. 3. Caractérisé, marqué. D. preference, préférence marquée. -ly, adv. 1. (a) (Parler) distinctement, clairement. (b) I told him d., je le lui ai dit expressément. 2. Indéniablement, décidément. (Of health) He is d. better, il y a un mieux sensible.

distinction [dis'tiŋ(k)ʃ(ə)n], s. 1. Distinction f (between, entre). 2. Academic distinctions, distinctions académiques. 3. (Excellence) Distinction. To gain d., se distinguer. Man of d., homme distingué, homme de marque.

distinctive [dis'tiŋ(k)tiv], a. Distinctif, -ive.

distinctiveness [dis'tiŋ(k)tivnis], s. Caractère particulier, distinctif (of, de).

distinctness [dis'tiŋ(k)tnis], s. 1. Clarté f, netteté f. 2. D. of sth. from sth., caractère nettement différent de deux choses.

distinguish [dis'tiŋgwiʃ]. 1. v.tr. (a) Distinguer, discerner. (b) Distinguer, différencier (from, de). This tinguishing mark, signe distinctif. (c) To d. oneself by . . ., se signaler, se faire remarquer, par. . . . 2. v.i. Faire une distinction (between, entre). To d. between two things, distinguer entre, faire une distinction entre, deux choses. To d. between people, faire la distinction de personnes. distinguished, a. 1. Distingué. D. writer, écrivain de distinction. D. people, personnages de marque. He is d. for his strength, il est remarquable par sa force. 2. To look d., avoir l'air distingué.

distinguishable [dis'tiŋgwiʃəbl], a. 1. Que l'on peut distinguer (from, de). 2. Perceptible, reconnaissable.

distort [dis'tɔːt], v.tr. Tordre, distordre, contourner (qch.); décomposer, déformer. Techn: Déformer (le champ électrique, visuel, la réception (à la radio, à la T.V., etc.)). (b) Défigurer (la vérité); fausser, dénaturer (les faits). distorted, a. Tordu, contourné, tourmenté. Face d. by rage, visage convulsé par la fureur. D. ideas, idées biscornues. Phot: T.V: D. image, image déformée. Ac: W.Tel: Tp: D. sound, son déformé. distorting, a. Déformant.

distortion [dis'tɔːʃ(ə)n], s. 1. (a) Distorsion f; décomposition f (des traits). (b) Déformation f (des faits). 2. (a) Opt: Déformation, distortion. (b) W.Tel: Déformation (de la réception). T.V: Déformation (de l'image).

distract [dis'trækt], v.tr. 1. (a) Distraire, détourner (the attention from, l'attention de). (b) Brouiller (l'esprit). 2. Affoler (qn). distracted, a. 1. Distrait, inattentif. 2. Affolé, éperdu. I shall go d., je deviendrai fou. Like one d., comme un affolé. -ly, adv. 1. Comme un affolé. 2. (Aimer qn) éperdument. distracting, a. 1. Qui distrait (l'attention). The radio is a little d. to my work, la radio me distrait pas mal quand je travaille. 2. Affolant. -ly, adv. A rendre fou. She is d. beautiful, elle est belle à vous rendre fou.

distraction [dis'trækʃ(ə)n], s. 1. Distraction f. (a) Divertissement m. (b) Interruption f. 2. Confusion f, désordre m. 3. Affolement m. To drive s.o. to d., mettre qn hors de soi. To love s.o. to d., aimer qn éperdument.

distrain [dis'trein], v.i. Jur: To d. upon s.o.'s belongings, saisir les meubles de qn. To d. upon a debtor, exécuter un débiteur.

distrainable [dis'treinəbl], a. Jur: Saisissable.

distraint [dis'treint], s. Jur: Saisie f.

distraught [dis'trɔːt], a. Lit: = DISTRACTED.

distress¹ [dis'tres], s. 1. Détresse f, angoisse f. 2. Misère (profonde); gêne f. 3. Détresse, embarras m. Companions in d., compagnons d'infortune. Nau: D. signal, signal de détresse. 4. Jur: = DISTRAINT. dis'tress-warrant, s. Jur: Mandat m de saisie.

distress², v.tr. 1. Affliger, angoisser, chagriner. 2. Épuiser, excéder. distressed [dis'trest], a. 1. Affligé, désolé. 2. Économiquement faible. D. area, zone f de dépression économique. 3. Épuisé, essoufflé. distressing, a. Affligeant, angoissant; fâcheux, -euse. -ly, adv. Péniblement, douloureusement, fâcheusement.

distribute [dis'tribju(ː)t], v.tr. Distribuer, répartir. Com: Être concessionnaire de, vendre (un produit). To d. a dividend, répartir un dividende. Load evenly distributed, charge uniformément répartie. Typ: To d. the type, distribuer la composition.

distribution [‚distri'bju:ʃ(ə)n], s. 1. (Mise f en) distribution f; répartition f. Pol.Ec: D. of wealth, répartition des richesses. 2. Typ: Mise en casse.

distributive [dis'tribjutiv], a. Gram: Distributif, -ive.

distributor [dis'tribjutər], s. 1. (a) Distributeur, -trice. (b) Concessionnaire m (d'une marque d'automobiles). 2. El.E: Distributeur de courant. 3. Aut: Distributeur de l'allumage, F: Delco (R.t.m.). D. arm, rotor m du Delco.

district ['distrikt], s. 1. Région f, contrée f, territoire m, district m. Mining d., région minière. 2. Adm: (a) District, secteur m. Electoral d., circonscription électorale. U.S: D. attorney = Procureur m de la République. D. Court, = Tribunal m d'Instance. Com: D. manager, directeur régional. (b) Quartier m (d'une ville). district-'nurse, s.f. (Infirmière) visiteuse.

distrust¹ [dis'trʌst], s. Méfiance f, défiance f.

distrust², v.tr. Se méfier, se défier, de (qn). To d. one's own eyes, n'en pas croire ses propres yeux.

distrustful [dis'trʌstful], a. 1. Défiant, méfiant (of, de); soupçonneux. 2. Timide. He was d. of his own capabilities, il manquait de foi en ses propres capacités. -fully, adv. Avec méfiance, avec défiance.

disturb [dis'təːb], v.tr. 1. Déranger; troubler (le repos); agiter, remuer (une surface). Please don't d. yourself, ne vous dérangez pas. 2. Ph: Ébranler (l'éther); amener la perturbation dans (le champ magnétique). 3. Inquiéter, troubler (qn). To d. s.o.'s mind, jeter le trouble dans l'esprit de qn. disturbing, a. Perturbateur, -trice. D. news, nouvelle fâcheuse.

disturbance [dis'təːbəns], s. 1. Trouble m; dérangement m. Atmospheric d., perturbation f atmosphérique. Tp: W.Tel: T.V: Perturbation; (bruit) parasite m, friture f. 2. Bruit m, tapage m, émeute f. To make a d., troubler l'ordre public. Nocturnal d., tapage nocturne. 3. Agitation f, trouble (d'esprit).

disturber [dis'təːbər], s. 1. Dérangeur, -euse 2. Perturbateur, -trice (de l'ordre).

disulphide [dai'sʌlfaid], s. Ch: Bisulfure m.

disunion [dis'juːnjən], s. Désunion f.

disunite [‚disju(ː)'nait], v.tr. Désunir.

disuse [dis'juːs], s. Désuétude f. To fall into d., (i) tomber en désuétude; (ii) être mis au rancart. Customs that are falling into d., usages m qui se perdent.

disused [dis'juːzd], a. Hors d'usage; (of public building) désaffecté; (of door, etc.) condamné; (of word) désuet, vieilli.

disyllabic [‚disi'læbik, -dai], a. (Mot) dissyllabe; (vers) dissyllabique.

disyllable [di'siləbl], s. Dissyllabe m.

ditch¹ [ditʃ], s. Fossé m; rigole f; caniveau m; (between fields) douve f. To die in a d., mourir sur le bord de la route. 'ditch-water, s. Eaux stagnantes (d'un fossé). F: It's as clear as d.-w., c'est la bouteille à l'encre.

ditch². 1. v.tr. (a) Entourer (un champ) de fossés; creuser des fossés. (b) Aut: To d. one's car, verser son auto dans le fossé. F: To be ditched, (i) échouer; (ii) être dans le pétrin. U.S: To d. sth., jeter qch. 2. v.i. Av: Faire un amerrissage forcé. ditching, s. 1. Hedging and d., entretien m des haies et fossés. 2. Av: Amerrissage forcé.

dither ['diðər], v.i. F: 1. Trembloter. 2. S'agiter sans but.

dithery ['diðəri], *a. F:* Agité, nerveux, -se. **To feel d.,** *F:* se sentir tout chose.

dithionate [ˌdai'θaiəneit], *s. Ch:* Hyposulfite *m.*

dittany ['ditəni], *s. Bot:* Dictame *m.*

ditto ['ditou], *a. & s. (Abbr. do)* Idem; de même. **To say d.,** être du même avis, opiner du bonnet.

ditty ['diti], *s.* Chanson *f.* **Old ditties,** vieux refrains, vieilles chansons.

ditty-bag, -box ['ditibag, -bɔks], *s. Nau:* Nécessaire *m* de marin.

diuresis [ˌdaijuə'riːsis], *s. Med:* Diurèse *f.*

diuretic [ˌdaijuə'retik], *a.* Diurétique.

diurnal [dai'əːn(ə)l], *a.* Diurne.

diva ['diːvə], *s.f. Th:* Diva, cantatrice.

divagate ['daivəgeit], *v.i.* Divaguer. **1.** Errer çà et là. **2.** S'écarter de son sujet.

divagation [ˌdaivə'geiʃ(ə)n], *s.* Divagation *f.*

divalent [ˌdai'veilənt], *a. Ch:* Divalent, bivalent.

divan [di'væn], *s.* Divan *m.* **divan-bed,** *s.* Lit-divan *m,* divan-lit *m.*

dive[1] [daiv], *s.* **1.** (*a*) Plongeon *m.* **High d.,** plongeon de haut vol. **Swallow d.,** saut *m* de l'ange. *S.a.* SKIN-DIVE.[1] (*b*) Plongée *f* (d'un sous-marin). (*c*) *Av:* Vol piqué; piqué *m.* **Spinning d.,** descente *f* en vrille. **2.** *P:* (*a*) Cabaret *m* borgne. (*b*) Gargote *f.* 'dive-bomb, *v.tr. Av:* Bombarder, attaquer en piqué. 'dive-bomber, *s. Av:* Bombardier *m* en piqué. 'dive-bombing, *s. Av:* Bombardement *m,* attaque *f* en piqué.

dive[2], *v.i.* **1.** (*a*) Plonger (**into,** dans); (*head first*) piquer une tête. *S.a.* SKIN-DIVE.[2] **To d. for pearls,** pêcher des perles. *Nau: F: (Of ship)* **To d. into it,** piquer du nez. (*b*) *Av:* **To (nose-)d.,** piquer (du nez). (*c*) *(Of submarine)* Plonger; effectuer une plongée. **2.** *F:* **To d. into a shop,** s'engouffrer dans un magasin. **diving,** *s.* Action *f* de plonger. **I'm not good at d.,** je ne suis pas fort pour plonger. *S.a.* SKIN-DIVING. 'diving-bell, *s.* Cloche *f* à, de, plongeur(s). 'diving-board, *s.* Plongeoir *m,* tremplin *m.* 'diving-dress, -suit, *s.* Scaphandre *m.*

diver ['daivər], *s.* **1.** (*a*) Plongeur *m.* (*b*) *(In diver's dress)* Scaphandrier *m. S.a.* SKIN-DIVER. **2.** *Orn:* Plongeon *m.*

diverge [dai'vəːdʒ], *v.i. (Of roads, lines)* Diverger, s'écarter. **To d. from the beaten track,** s'écarter du chemin battu. **diverging,** *a.* Divergent.

divergence [dai'vəːdʒəns], *s.* Divergence *f.*

divergent [dai'vəːdʒənt], *a.* Divergent.

divers ['daivəz], *a.pl. A: Lit:* Divers, plusieurs. **On d. occasions,** en diverses occasions; à diverses reprises.

diverse [dai'vəːs, di-], *a.* **1.** Divers, différent. **2.** Divers, varié. **-ly,** *adv.* Diversement.

diversification [dai,vəːsifi'keiʃən], *s.* Diversité *f* (de goûts, des opinions); variété *f*; variation *f.*

diversify [dai'vəːsifai, di-], *v.tr.* Diversifier.

diversion [dai'vəːʃ(ə)n, di-], *s.* **1.** Détournement *m,* déroutement *m,* déviation *f* (d'une route, de la circulation); dérivation *f* (d'un cours d'eau). **2.** *Mil:* Diversion *f.* **3.** (*a*) Diversion (de l'esprit). **To create a d.,** faire diversion. (*b*) Divertissement *m,* distraction *f,* jeu *m.*

diversionary [dai'vəːʃənəri], *a.* **D. (demonstrations),** (des démonstrations) destinées à faire diversion. *Mil:* **D. landing,** débarquement *m* de diversion.

diversity [dai'vəːsiti, di-], *s.* Diversité *f.*

divert [dai'vəːt, di-], *v.tr.* **1.** Détourner, dériver (un cours d'eau); écarter (un coup); détourner, dévier (la circulation) (**from,** de). *Nau: or Rail:* Dérouter. **To d. s.o.'s attention,** distraire l'attention de qn. **2.** Divertir, amuser. **diverting,** *a.* Divertissant, amusant.

Dives ['daiviːz], *s. B:* Le mauvais riche.

divest [dai'vest], *v.tr.* **1.** **To d. s.o. of his clothes,** dévêtir qn. **2.** Dépouiller, priver (qn de qch.). **To d. oneself of a right,** renoncer à un droit.

divide[1] [di'vaid], *s. Geol: esp. U.S:* Ligne *f* de partage des eaux.

divide[2]. **1.** *v.tr.* (*a*) Diviser (un héritage). **To d. into parts,** diviser en parties; sectionner, fractionner. **Divided between hatred and pity,** partagé entre la haine et la pitié. *Parl:* **To d. the House,** aller aux voix. (*b*) *(Share out)* Partager, répartir (**among,** entre). **We d. the work among us,** nous nous partageons le travail. (*c*) *Mth:* Diviser. **Twelve divides by three,** douze est divisible par trois. (*d*) Séparer (**from,** de). (*e*) Désunir (une famille). **House divided against itself,** maison désunie. **A policy of d. and rule,** une politique de diviser pour régner. (*f*) **Opinions are divided,** les avis sont partagés. **A divided mind,** esprit indécis. **2.** *v.i.* (*a*) Se diviser, se partager (**into, en**); *(of road)* fourcher, (se) bifurquer. *Parl:* Aller aux voix. **divide up,** *v.tr.* Démembrer (un royaume); détailler (de la viande, etc.). **dividing,** *a.* (Ligne) de démarcation, divisoire. **D. wall,** mur mitoyen.

dividend ['dividend], *s. Mth: Fin:* Dividende *m.* **D. on shares,** dividende d'actions. **Interim d.,** dividende provisoire. **Final d.,** solde *m* de dividende.

dividers [di'vaidəz], *s.pl.* Compas *m* à pointes sèches.

divination [ˌdivi'neiʃ(ə)n], *s.* Divination *f.*

divine[1] [di'vain]. **1.** *a.* (*a*) Divin. (*b*) *F:* Divin, admirable. **2.** *s.* (*a*) Théologien *m.* (*b*) *A:* Ecclésiastique *m.* **-ly,** *adv.* Divinement; adorablement.

divine[2], *v.tr.* Deviner (l'avenir). **di'vining-rod,** *s.* Baguette *f* divinatoire; baguette de sourcier.

diviner [di'vainər], *s.* Devin *m,* devineresse *f.* **Water d.** = DOWSER.

divinity [di'viniti], *s.* **1.** (*a*) *(Divine nature)* Divinité *f.* (*b*) Divinité, dieu *m.* **2.** (*a*) Théologie *f.* **Doctor of D.,** docteur en théologie. (*b*) *Sch:* Enseignement religieux.

divisibility [di,vizi'biliti], *s.* Divisibilité *f.*

divisible [di'vizibl], *a.* Divisible (**by,** par). *Fin:* **D. profits,** profits répartissables.

division [di'viʒ(ə)n], *s.* **1.** Division *f,* partage *m* (**into, en**); scission *f* (d'un parti). **2.** Répartition *f,* partage (des bénéfices). **3.** Division, désunion *f.* **4.** *Mth:* Division. *Ar:* Simple d., division à un chiffre. **5.** *Parl:* Vote *m.* **There will be a d.,** on ira aux voix. **To challenge a d.,** provoquer un vote. **6.** (*a*) Division (d'un livre). (*b*) *Biol:* Groupe *m,* classe *f.* (*c*) *Mil:* Division. (*d*) **Parliamentary d.,** circonscription électorale. **7.** Cloison *f.*

divisional [di'viʒən(ə)l], *a.* Divisionnaire. *Jur:* **D. Court,** cour *f* d'Appel.

divisor [di'vaizər], *s. Mth:* Diviseur *m.*

divisory [di'vaizəri], *a. Jur:* (Procès, etc.) divisoire.

divorce[1] [di'vɔːs], *s.* Divorce *m.*

divorce[2], *v.tr. Jur:* (*a*) *(Of judge)* Prononcer le divorce (entre deux époux). (*b*) *(Of husband or wife)* **To d. s.o.,** divorcer d'avec qn. (*c*) Séparer (**from,** de). **To d. Church from State,** séparer l'Église et l'État.

divorcee [di'vɔːsiː], *s.* Divorcé, -ée.

divot ['divət], *s. Golf:* Motte *f* (de gazon).

divulgation [ˌdivʌl'geiʃ(ə)n, ˌdai-], **divulgement** [di'vʌldʒmənt, dai-], **divulgence** [dai'vʌldʒəns], *s.* Divulgation *f.*

divulge [di'vʌldʒ, dai-], *v.tr.* Divulguer.

dixie, dixy ['diksi], *s. Mil: F:* Gamelle *f*; marmite *f* (de campement); bouteillon *m.*

dizziness ['dizinis], *s.* Étourdissement *m,* vertige(s) *m(pl).* **Fit of d.,** éblouissement *m.*

dizzy ['dizi], *a.* **1.** Pris d'étourdissement; pris de vertige. **To feel d.,** avoir le vertige. **To make s.o. d.,** étourdir qn. **My head is d.,** la tête me tourne. **2.** *F: (Of height, speed)* Vertigineux. **-ily,** *adv.* Vertigineusement.

Djibuti [dʒi'buːti]. *Pr.n.Geog:* Djibouti *m.*

do[1] [duː]. **I.** *v.tr.* (*pr. ind. sg.* 1st *pers.* do; 2nd *pers.* **doest** ['duest], *as aux.* dost [dʌst]; 3rd *pers.* **does** [dʌz], *A:* **doth** [dʌθ], **doeth** ['dueθ]; *pl.* do; *past ind.* did, didst; *pr. sub. sg. & pl.* do; *p.p.* done [dʌn]) **1.** (*a*) *(Perform)* Faire (une bonne action, son devoir). **What do you do (for a living)?** quel est votre métier, votre profession? **What are you doing?** (i) qu'est-ce que vous faites? qu'est-ce que vous êtes en train de faire? (ii) que devenez-vous? (iii) mais qu'est-ce que tu es en train de faire? où as-tu la tête? **To do good,** faire le bien. **To do right,** bien faire. **He did brilliantly in his examination,** il a réussi brillamment (son examen). **You would do well to . . .,** vous feriez bien de. . . . **To do one's military service,** faire son service militaire. *Sch:* **Are you doing German?**

faites-vous de l'allemand? *F:* We're doing *Hamlet* this term, on étudie *Hamlet* ce trimestre-ci. To do three miles on foot, faire trois milles à pied. The car was doing sixty, l'auto faisait du soixante, filait à soixante. *F:* To do ten years (in prison), faire dix ans de prison. Are you doing anything to-morrow? avez-vous quelque chose en vue pour demain? *F:* It isn't done, cela ne se fait pas. It's as good as done, c'est une affaire faite ou autant vaut. *Prov:* What is done cannot be undone, à chose faite point de remède. I shall do nothing of the sort, no such thing, je n'en ferai rien. What is to be done? What can, could, I, he, we, do? que faire? I don't know what to do, je ne sais que faire. It cannot be done, c'est (chose) impossible. She did nothing but cry, elle ne faisait que pleurer. What can I do for you? en quoi puis-je vous aider, vous être utile, vous servir? Que puis-je faire pour vous, pour toi? What do you do for water? comment faites-vous pour vous procurer de l'eau? What are you going to do about it? que vous proposez-vous de faire? Do what we would . . ., malgré tous nos efforts. . . . Well done! très bien! bravo! à la bonne heure! *F:* That's done it!, ça c'est le bouquet, c'est la fin de tout, c'est la fin des haricots! (*b*) *F:* He came to see what was doing, il est venu voir ce qui se faisait. *Com:* There is nothing doing, le marché est mort, est nul. *F:* Nothing doing! rien à faire! ça ne prend pas! 2. (*a*) Faire (la correspondance, une chambre, les cheveux à qn). He does repairs, il se charge des réparations. (*b*) Cuire, faire cuire (la viande). Done to a turn, cuit à point. (*c*) To do a sum, a problem, faire un calcul; résoudre un problème. (*d*) (*Act a play*) Faire (*Hamlet*, etc.). (*e*) *F:* Visiter, *F:* faire (une ville, un musée, etc.). (*f*) *F:* (*Cheat*) Refaire, faire, enfoncer (qn); mettre (qn) dedans. To do s.o. out of sth., soutirer, filouter, qch. à qn. To do s.o. out of a job, supplanter qn. (*g*) *F:* They do you very well at this hotel, on mange très bien à cet hôtel. To do oneself well, faire bonne chère. (*h*) *Com:* *F:* We can do you this article at . . ., nous pouvons vous faire cet article à. . . . 3. (*In perfect tenses and past participle*) (*a*) Done, have done, avoir fini. It's done, c'est fini, c'est fait, *F:* ça y est. *O:* *Lit:* Be done! have done! finissez donc! (*b*) *F:* (*Of pers.*) To be done (to the wide), être éreinté, exténué; n'en pouvoir plus. (*c*) (*After a bargain made*) Done! tope là! c'est marché fait! tenu! 4. How do you do? (i) comment vous portez-vous? comment allez-vous? (ii) (*on being introduced to s.o.*) enchanté (de faire votre connaissance)! To be doing well, être en bonne voie, faire de bonnes affaires; (*of invalid*) être en voie de guérison; (*of business*) bien aller, réussir. He's a young man who will do well, c'est un garçon qui réussira. 5. (*To serve, suffice*) That will do, (i) c'est bien (comme cela); cela va; (ii) cela suffira; en voilà assez! This room will do for the office, cette pièce ira bien pour le bureau. That won't do, cela ne fera pas l'affaire. That won't do here, cela ne passe pas ici. It would hardly have done to . . ., il n'aurait pas été convenable de. . . . I will make it do, je m'en arrangerai. You must make do with what you have, il faut vous arranger avec ce que vous avez. *F:* To have just enough to do on, avoir tout juste de quoi vivre. *F:* That will do me, cela fera mon affaire. Nothing would do but for me to go home with him, il a fallu absolument que je rentre avec lui. II. do, *verb substitute.* 1. I replied as the others had done, j'ai répondu comme avaient fait les autres. Why act as you do? pourquoi agir comme vous le faites? He writes better than I do, il écrit mieux que moi. He envies me as much as I do him, il me porte autant d'envie que je lui en porte. 2. (*Elliptical auxiliary*) May I open these letters?—Please do, puis-je ouvrir ces lettres?—Faites donc! Je vous en prie! Did you see him?—I did, l'avez-vous vu?—Oui (, je l'ai vu). Do you like her?—I don't, l'aimez-vous?—Non (, je ne l'aime pas). I like coffee; do 'you? j'aime le café; et vous? You like him, don't you? vous l'aimez, n'est-ce pas? You like him, do you? vous l'aimez, alors? He said so, did he? il a dit cela, ah vraiment? Don't! ne faites pas cela! finissez! 3. I wanted to see

him and I did (so), j'ai voulu le voir, et je l'ai vu. You like Paris? so do I, vous aimez Paris? moi aussi. III. do, *v.aux.* 1. (*For emphasis*) He 'did go, il y est bien allé. He threatened to go, and he 'did go, and go he 'did, il menaça de partir, et il partit en effet. Do you remember him?—'Do I remember him! vous souvenez-vous de lui?—Si je m'en souviens! Why don't you work?—I 'do work! pourquoi ne travaillez-vous pas?—Mais si, je travaille! 'Did he indeed? non vraiment? 'Do sit down, veuillez (donc) vous asseoir; asseyez-vous donc! Do shut up! voulez-vous bien vous taire! 2. (*Inversion*) Never did I spend such a night, jamais je n'ai passé une nuit pareille. 3. (*Usual form in questions and negative statements*) Do you see him? le voyez-vous? We do not know, nous ne le savons pas. Don't do it! n'en faites rien! *F:* D'you mind? ça ne vous fait rien? IV. do, *with certain prepositions.* 1. To do well, badly, by s.o., bien, mal, agir envers qn. He has been hard done by, il a été traité durement. 2. *F:* Do for. (*a*) To do for s.o., faire, tenir, le ménage de qn. He can do for himself, il peut se subvenir à lui-même. (*b*) Tuer (qn); faire son affaire à (qn). I'm done for, j'ai mon compte; je suis perdu. (*c*) Détruire, ruiner, couler (qn). 3. (*a*) To have to do with s.o., avoir affaire à qn. To have to do with sth., (*of pers.*) être mêlé à qch.; avoir à voir à qch.; (*of thg*) avoir rapport à qch. To have nothing to do with the business, (*of pers.*) n'être pour rien dans l'affaire. Jealousy has a lot to do with it, la jalousie y est pour beaucoup. (*b*) What have I done with my umbrella, où ai-je mis mon parapluie? (*c*) I cannot do with any noise, je ne peux pas supporter le bruit. He does with very little food, il s'accommode de très peu de nourriture. (*d*) How many can you do with? combien en désirez-vous? combien vous en faut-il? *F:* I could do with a cup of tea, je prendrais bien une tasse de thé. (*e*) It's all over and done with, c'est fini, tout ça. 4. Do without, se passer de (qch.). V. do, *s.* 1. (*a*) The do's and don'ts (of society), ce qui se fait et ce qui ne se fait pas. A diet with numerous do's and don'ts, un régime comportant de nombreuses prescriptions et proscriptions. (*b*) *F:* Manière *f* de traiter qn. It's a poor do! c'est plutôt minable! 2. *F:* *O:* Attrape *f*, fourberie *f*, escroquerie *f.* 3. *F:* (*a*) Réception *f*; soirée *f*; réunion *f.* (*b*) Exposition *f.* *Mil:* *etc:* Défilé *m.* do again, *v.tr.* 1. Refaire (qch.). 2. I won't do it again, je ne le ferai plus, je ne recommencerai plus. do away, *v.i.* To do away with, abolir (un usage); supprimer (des frais, etc.); détruire, faire disparaître (un édifice); tuer, *F:* supprimer (qn); se défaire de (qn). do in, *v.tr.* (*a*) *P:* Tuer, assassiner (qn). (*b*) *F:* I'm feeling absolutely done in, je me sens absolument fourbu, éreinté, je n'en peux plus. do out, *v.tr.* Faire, nettoyer (une chambre, une salle). do up, *v.tr.* 1. (*a*) Réparer (qch.); remettre (qch.) à neuf; décorer (une maison, etc.). *F:* To do oneself up, faire toilette. Done up to kill, sur son grand tralala. (*b*) Blanchir (le linge). 2. *Cu:* Accommoder (un plat, des restes). 3. Faire, envelopper, ficeler (un paquet); emballer, empaqueter (des marchandises); mettre (un journal) sous bande; boutonner, agrafer (un vêtement). 4. *F:* To be done up, être éreinté, fourbu; n'en pouvoir plus. doing, *s.* 1. (*a*) Action *f* de faire. There is a great difference between d. and saying, il y a loin du faire au dire. *F:* That takes some d., ce n'est pas facile. (*b*) All this is your d., c'est vous qui êtes la cause de tout cela. It was none of my d., ce n'est pas à moi qu'il faut s'en prendre. 2. (*Usu. in pl.*) Ce qu'on fait; événements *mpl*; faits *mpl.* 3. *F:* The doings, le machin, le truc.

do² [dou], *s.* *Mus:* 1. (*Fixed do*) Do *m*, ut *m.* 2. (*Movable do*) La tonique.

do³ ['ditou] = DITTO.

doc [dɔk], *s.* *U.S:* *F:* = DOCTOR.

docile ['dousail], *a.* Docile. -ely, *adv.* Docilement.

docility [do'siliti], *s.* Docilité *f.*

dock¹ [dɔk], *s.* *Bot:* Patience *f.*

dock², *v.tr.* 1. *A:* To d. a horse, a horse's tail, couper la queue à, écourter, un cheval. 2. (*a*) Diminuer, rogner, ou supprimer (le traitement de qn). (*b*) To d. s.o. of his ration, retrancher sa ration à qn.

dock³, *s. Nau:* (*a*) Bassin *m* (d'un port). **Outer d.,** avant-bassin *m.* **Inner d.,** arrière-bassin *m.* **Flooding d.,** bassin à flot. **To go into d.,** entrer au bassin. **The docks,** les docks *m.* (*b*) **Dry d., graving d.,** cale sèche; bassin de radoub. **Ship in dry d.,** navire en radoub. *F:* **To be in d.,** être en réparation (avion, automobile). (*c*) **Floating d.,** dock flottant. **Floating (dry) d.,** cale sèche flottante. (*d*) *pl.* **Naval docks** = DOCKYARD.

dock⁴. 1. *v.tr.* Faire entrer (un navire) au bassin. **2.** *v.i.* (*Of ship*) Entrer au bassin. **docking,** *s.* (*a*) Entrée *f* au bassin. (*b*) Arrimage *m* (d'engins spatiaux).

dock⁵, *s. Jur:* Banc *m,* box *m,* des accusés, des prévenus. **To be in the d.,** être au banc des prévenus; être dans le box des accusés.

dockage ['dɔkidʒ], *s. Nau:* Droits *mpl* de bassin.

docker ['dɔkər], *s.* Déchargeur *m,* débardeur *m,* docker *m.*

docket¹ ['dɔkit], *s.* Étiquette *f,* fiche *f* (d'un document). **Wages d.,** bordereau *m* de paye.

docket², *v.tr.* Étiqueter, classer (des papiers).

dockyard ['dɔkjɑːd], *s.* Chantier *m* de construction de navires. **Naval d.,** arsenal *m* maritime.

doctor¹ ['dɔktər], *s.* **1.** *A:* (*Learned man*) Docteur *m.* **2.** *Sch:* **D. of Divinity,** docteur en theologie. **D. of Science,** docteur ès sciences. *S.a.* LAW 3. **3.** Docteur, médecin *m.* **Woman d.,** femme docteur, doctoresse *f.* **D.** (*abbr.* **Dr.**) **Smith,** (Monsieur) le docteur Smith. **To call in a d.,** appeler un médecin. **Come in, D.,** entrez, docteur.

doctor², *v.tr.* **1.** (*a*) Soigner (un malade). (*b*) *Turf:* Droguer, doper (un cheval). (*c*) *F:* Châtrer (un chat). **2.** *F:* Réparer, raccommoder (un objet). **3.** *F:* Falsifier, fausser, truquer (des comptes); frelater (du vin, etc.). **doctoring,** *s.* **1.** Soins (donnés à qn). **2.** *F:* Profession *f* de médecin. **3.** *F:* Falsification *f* (des comptes).

doctoral ['dɔktərəl], *a.* Doctoral, -aux.

doctorate ['dɔktərit], *s. Sch:* Doctorat *m.*

doctrinal [dɔk'train(ə)l], *a.* Doctrinal, -aux.

doctrinaire ['dɔktri'nɛər], **doctrinarian** ['dɔktri'nɛəriən], *s.* Doctrinaire *m;* théoricien *m,* idéologue *m.*

doctrine ['dɔktrin], *s.* Doctrine *f.*

document¹ ['dɔkjumənt], *s.* Document *m,* pièce *f,* titre *m;* *F:* papier *m.* **Legal d.,** acte *m* authentique. *Jur:* **Documents pertaining to the case,** dossier *m* (de l'affaire); pièces en instance. **'document-case,** *s.* Porte-documents *m. inv.*

document² ['dɔkjument], *v.tr.* Documenter.

documentary [,dɔkju'ment(ə)ri]. **1.** *a.* Documentaire. *S.a.* EVIDENCE 3. **2.** *a. & s. Cin:* Documentaire *m.*

documentation [,dɔkjumen'teiʃ(ə)n], *s.* Documentation *f.*

dodder¹ ['dɔdər], *s. Bot:* Cuscute *f.*

dodder², *v.i.* (*Of aged pers.*) Trembloter. **To d. along,** marcher en branlant bras et jambes. **doddering,** *a.* **1. D. gait, head,** démarche, tête, branlante. **2.** (*Of pers.*) Gaga *inv.*

dodderer ['dɔdərər], *s. F:* Vieux gaga, gâteux *m.*

doddery ['dɔdəri], *a. F:* Tremblant, tremblotant.

dodecagon [dou'dekəgən], *s. Geom: Cryst:* Dodécagone *m.*

dodecahedron [,doudekə'hiːdrən], *s.* Dodécaèdre *m.*

dodecaphonic ['doudikə'fɔnik], *s. Mus:* Dodécaphonique.

dodge¹ [dɔdʒ], *s.* **1.** Mouvement *m* de côté. *Box: Fb:* Esquive *f.* **2.** (*a*) Ruse *f,* artifice *m.* (*b*) Truc *m,* ficelle *f;* tour *m* de main. **Trade dodges,** recettes *f* de métier. **To be up to all the dodges,** connaître tous les trucs. **An old d.,** un coup classique.

dodge². 1. *v.i.* (*a*) Se jeter de côté. (*b*) *Box: Fb:* Esquiver, éviter. *Fb:* **To d. a player,** dépister un joueur. (*c*) Biaiser; user d'artifices. **2.** *v.tr.* Se jeter de côté pour éviter (un coup); esquiver (un coup); éviter (qn); esquiver, tourner (une difficulté). *F:* **To d. the column,** tirer au flanc. **To d. a question,** éluder une question.

dodgem ['dɔdʒəm], *a. & s.* **Dodgem cars,** *s.* **dodgems,** autos tamponneuses.

dodger ['dɔdʒər], *s.* **1.** *F:* (*a*) Malin *m,* roublard *m.* (*b*) *Mil:* Embusqué *m.* **2.** *U.S:* Prospectus *m.*

dodgy ['dɔdʒi], *a. F:* **D. situation,** situation délicate.

dodo, *pl.* **-o(e)s** ['doudou, -ouz], *s. Orn:* Dodo *m. F:* **As dead as the d.,** vieux comme Hérode.

doe [dou], *s. Z:* **1.** Daine *f.* **2.** (*Of rabbit*) Lapine *f;* (*of wild rabbit and hare*) hase *f.*

doer ['duər], *s.* **1.** Faiseur, -euse; auteur *m* (d'une action). *P:* **She's no end of a d.,** c'est une femme très agissante. **2.** (*Of domestic animal*) **He's a good d.,** il profite bien (de sa nourriture).

does, doest. *See* DO¹.

doeskin ['douskin], *s.* (*a*) Peau *f* de daim. (*b*) *Tex:* Simili-daim *m.*

doff [dɔf], *v.tr. O: Lit:* Enlever, ôter (un vêtement).

dog¹ [dɔg], *s.* **1.** Chien *m,* chienne *f.* **House-d.,** chien de garde, d'attache. **Sporting d.,** chien de chasse. **Gun d.,** chien d'arrêt. **D. racing,** *F:* **the dogs,** courses de lévriers. *F:* **To go to the dogs,** (i) aller aux courses de lévriers; (ii) gâcher sa vie, se dégrader, se débaucher; marcher à la ruine; (*of business*) aller à vau-l'eau. **To lead a dog's life,** mener une vie de chien. **To help a lame d. over a stile,** tirer qn d'un mauvais pas. *F:* **To take a hair of the d. that bit you,** reprendre du poil de la bête. *U.S: F:* **To put on the d.,** *P:* faire de l'épate. *Prov:* **Every ⊂. has his day,** à chacun son heure de gloire. **Give a d. a bad name, and hang him,** qui veut noyer son chien l'accuse de la rage. **D. does not eat d.,** les loups ne se mangent pas entre eux. *F:* **To see a man about a d.,** aller faire pipi. *Cu:* **Hot d.,** (petit pain fourré d'une) saucisse de Francfort chaude. **2. Mâle** *m* (de certains animaux). **D. fox,** renard *m* mâle. **D. hyena,** hyène *f* mâle. **3.** *F:* **Lucky d.!** (le) veinard! **Gay d.,** (i) *Pej:* viveur *m,* noceur *m;* (ii) joyeux gaillard. *P:* **Dirty d.,** sale type *m.* **To be a dead d.,** être inutile. **4.** (*a*) (*Pawl*) Chien, cliquet *m,* détente *f.* (*b*) (*Of lathe*) Toc *m* (d'entraînement). (*c*) *Mec.E:* Crabot *m,* dent *f.* **5. Fire-d.,** chenet *m.* **6.** *pl. P:* Les pieds. **'dog-biscuit,** *s.* Biscuit *m* de chien. **'dog-cart,** *s. Veh:* Charrette anglaise. **'dog-clutch,** *s. Mec.E:* Clabotage *m.* **'dog-collar,** *s.* **1.** Collier *m* de chien. **2.** *F:* Faux col d'ecclésiastique. **'dog-days,** *s.pl.* (La) canicule. **'dog-faced,** *a. Z:* Cynocéphale. **'dog-fight,** *s.* **1.** Combat de chiens. **2.** *F:* Mêlée générale. **3.** *Av: F:* Duel aérien. **'dog-fish,** *s. Ich:* Chien *m* de mer; roussette *f.* **'dog-food,** *s.* Pâtée *f* (pour chiens). **'dog-headed,** *a.* Cynocéphale. **'dog('-)house,** *s.* **1.** *U.S:* = KENNEL 1. **2.** *F:* **To be in the d.(-)h.,** être en défaveur (auprès de qn). **'dog-in-the-manger,** *s.* Chien *m* du jardinier; égoïste outré. **'dog-'Latin,** *s.* Latin *m* de cuisine. **'dog-paddle,** *v.i.* Nager à la chien. **'dog-rose,** *s. Bot:* **1.** Églantine *f.* **2.** (*Bush*) Rosier *m* sauvage; églantier *m.* **'dog('s)-ear¹,** *s.* Corne (faite à la page d'un livre); (*not cut*) larron *m.* **'dog('s)-ear²,** *v.tr.* Corner (la page d'un livre). **'dog-show,** *s.* Exposition canine. **'dog-spike,** *s.* **1.** Clou *m* à large tête. **2.** *Rail:* Crampon *m.* **'Dog-star (the),** *s. Astr:* La Canicule. Sirius *m.* **'dog-'tired,** *a. F:* Éreinté, vanné, fourbu. **'dog-watch,** *s. Nau:* Petit quart; quart de deux heures.

dog², *v.tr.* (**dogged** [dɔgd]) Suivre (qn) à la piste; filer (qn). **To dog s.o.'s footsteps,** s'attacher aux pas de qn; talonner (qn); marcher sur les pas de qn. **Dogged by ill fortune,** poursuivi par la guigne.

dogberry ['dɔgbəri], *s. Bot:* Cornouille *f.*

doge [doudʒ], *s. Hist:* Doge *m.*

dogged ['dɔgid], *a.* Obstiné, résolu, tenace. **-ly,** *adv.* Avec ténacité; opiniâtrement.

doggedness ['dɔgidnis], *s.* Courage *m* tenace; persévérance *f.*

doggerel ['dɔgərəl], *a. & s.* (i) (Poésie *f*) burlesque; (ii) (vers *mpl*) de mirliton.

doggie ['dɔgi], *s. F:* Toutou *m.*

doggo ['dɔgou], *adv. F:* **To lie d.,** se tenir coi; faire le mort.

doggish ['dɔgiʃ], *a.* **1.** *F:* Qui ressemble à un chien; qui a un air de chien. **2.** *U.S: F:* Faraud; crâneur, -euse; plastronneur, -euse.

doggy ['dɔgi], *a.* **1.** (*a*) Canin; de chien. (*b*) *F: O:* Chic. (*c*) **With a d. air,** avec un petit air crâne. **2.** *s. F:* = DOGGIE.

dogie, dogey, dogy ['dougi], *s. U.S:* Veau *m,* génisse *f* (dont la mère est morte).

dogma, *pl.* **-as** ['dɔgmə, -əz], *s.* Dogme *m.*

dogmatic [dɔg'mætik], *a.* **1.** Dogmatique. **2.** *F:* Autoritaire, tranchant. **-ally,** *adv.* D'un ton autoritaire, tranchant.

dogmatism ['dɔgmətizm], s. Dogmatisme m.
dogmatist ['dɔgmətist], s. Dogmatiste m.
dogmatize ['dɔgmətaiz], v.i. Dogmatiser.
dogsbody ['dɔgzbɔdi], s. F: Sous-verge m. inv.
dogwood ['dɔgwud], s. Bot: Cornouiller m.
doh [dou], s. = DO² 2.
doily ['dɔili], s. 1. Petit napperon. 2. Dessus m d'assiette.
doldrums ['dɔldrəmz], s.pl. The d., (i) le cafard; (ii) Nau: la zone des calmes; le pot au noir. To be in the d., (i) (of pers.) avoir le cafard; (ii) Nau: être dans les calmes équatoriaux; (iii) F: (of business) être dans le marasme.
dole¹ [doul], s. 1. A: Portion échue en partage. 2. (a) Aumône f. (b) Adm: F: Unemployment d., secours m, allocation f, indemnité f de chômage. To go on the d., s'inscrire au chômage.
dole², v.tr. To d. out sth., distribuer (parcimonieusement) qch.
doleful ['doulful], a. (Mine) lugubre; (cri) dolent, douloureux; (of pers.) triste, larmoyant. -fully, adv. Tristement, douloureusement.
dolichocephalic ['dɔlikousi'fælik], a. Anthr: Dolichocéphale.
doll¹ [dɔl], s. 1. Poupée f. Doll's house, maison de poupée. F: (Of woman) Pretty little d., jolie poupée. 2. U.S: Jeune fille.
doll², v.tr. To d. up a child, a woman, pouponner un enfant, une femme. To d. oneself up, se bichonner, se pomponner.
dollar ['dɔlər], s. Num: U.S: etc: Dollar m. D. diplomacy, diplomatie f du dollar. D. area, zone f dollar.
dollop ['dɔləp], s. P: Morceau m (informe); motte f (de qch. de mou). A good d. of jam, une bonne cuillerée de confiture.
dolly ['dɔli], s. 1. F: (a) Poupée f. (b) (Bandaged finger) Poupée. 2. Agitateur m (pour le linge). D.-tub, baquet m à lessive. 3. Metalw: (a) Tas m à river. (b) Bouterolle f (de riveur). 4. Cin: Travelling m. D. shot, travelling en poursuite. 5. Rail: Av: etc: U.S: Chariot m.
dolman ['dɔlmən], s. Cost: Dolman m.
dolmen ['dɔlmen], s. Prehist: Dolmen m.
dolomite ['dɔləmait]. 1. s. Miner: Dolomi(t)e f. 2. Pr.n.Geog: The Dolomites, les Dolomites f.
dolomitic [dɔlə'mitik], a. Geol: Dolomitique.
dolorous ['dɔlərəs], a. A. & Poet: 1. Douloureux. 2. Triste, plaintif. -ly, adv. Tristement, plaintivement.
dolphin ['dɔlfin], s. 1. Z: Her: Dauphin m. (b) Ich: Dorade f. 2. Nau: (a) Baderne f; bourrelet m de défense (de mât). (b) Bouée f de corps-mort.
dolt [doult], s. Sot m, benêt m; lourdaud m; P: cruche f, gourde f.
doltish ['doultiʃ], a. Sot, lourdaud.
Dom [dɔm], s. Ecc: Dom m.
domain [də'mein], s. Domaine m; terres fpl; propriété f. O: It does not come within my d., cela n'est pas de mon domaine.
dome [doum], s. 1. Arch: Dôme m. 2. Dôme, calotte f (des cieux, de verdure); calotte (du crâne).
domed [doumd], a. (a) (Édifice) à dôme. (b) En forme de dôme.
domestic [də'mestik], a. 1. (Vertu) domestique; (charbon) de ménage. D. quarrels, scènes de ménage. D. life, la vie de famille. D. (servant), domestique mf, bonne f. D. economy, l'économie f domestique. D. science, (i) les arts ménagers; (ii) enseignement ménager. Com: U.S: (In store) "Domestics," pl. articles ménagers. 2. (a) (Commerce) intérieur. Post: U.S: D. mail, correspondance f à destination de l'intérieur. D. postal rates, tarif m d'affranchissement m en régime intérieur. (b) Domestic animal, animal domestique. 3. (Of pers.) Casanier; (femme) d'intérieur. -ally, adv. Domestiquement.
domesticate [də'mestikeit], v.tr. 1. Domestiquer, apprivoiser (un animal). 2. Domesticated woman, femme d'intérieur.
domestication [də,mesti'keiʃ(ə)n], s. 1. Domestication f (d'un animal). 2. Acclimatation f.
domesticity [doumes'tisiti], s. (a) Attachement m au foyer; goûts m domestiques. (b) Vie f de famille.
domicile¹ ['dɔmisail], s. Domicile m. To elect d. at a place, élire domicile dans un endroit.

domicile², v.tr. Com: Domicilier (un effet). **domiciled**, a. Domicilié, demeurant (at, à).
domiciliary [,dɔmi'siljəri], a. (Visite) domiciliaire.
dominance ['dɔminəns], s. Dominance f (d'une maladie); prédominance f (d'une race).
dominant ['dɔminənt]. 1. a. Dominant. 2. s. Mus: Dominante f. D. seventh, septième f de dominante.
dominate ['dɔmineit], v.tr. & i. To d. (over) s.o., a people, dominer (sur) qn, un peuple. The fortress dominates the town, la forteresse commande la ville. **dominating**, a. Dominant.
domination [,dɔmi'neiʃ(ə)n], s. Domination f.
domineer [,dɔmi'niər], v.i. 1. Se montrer autoritaire. 2. To d. over s.o., tyranniser qn; régenter qn. **domineering**, a. Autoritaire. A d. person, petit tyran, tyranneau m.
dominical [də'minik(ə)l], a. Ecc: Dominical, -aux.
Dominican [də'minikən], a. & s. Dominicain, -aine. The D. Republic, la République Dominicaine.
dominion [də'minjən], s. 1. Domination f, maîtrise f, autorité f. To hold dominion over . . ., exercer son empire sur. . . . 2. Dominion m. The D. of Canada, le Dominion du Canada.
domino, pl. -oes ['dɔminou, -ouz], s. 1. Domino m (de bal masqué). 2. Games: Domino. To play (at) dominoes, jouer aux dominos.
don¹ [dɔn], s.m. 1. (Spanish title) Don. 2. Sch: F: Professeur (d'université).
don², v.tr. (donned) Lit: Revêtir, endosser (un uniforme, etc.); mettre, coiffer (un chapeau).
donate [də'neit], v.tr. 1. Faire un don de (qch.). Med: To d. blood, donner du sang. 2. U.S: Donner (to, à).
donation [də'neiʃ(ə)n], s. Donation f, don m. Jur: D. inter vivos, donation entre vifs.
done. See DO¹.
donkey ['dɔŋki], s. 1. Ane, f. ânesse f; baudet m. To ride a d., aller à âne. D. ride, promenade à âne. She would talk the hind-leg off a d., elle jase comme une pie borgne. F: D. work, travail de routine. I haven't seen him for d.'s years, il y a une éternité que je ne l'ai vu. F: Imbécile mf, âne m. 'donkey-boiler, s. Nau: Chaudière f auxiliaire; petite chaudière. 'donkey-cart, s. Charrette f à âne. 'donkey-driver, s. Anier, -ière. 'donkey-engine, s. 1. Mch: Petit cheval. 2. Treuil m à vapeur. 'donkey-load, s. Anée f. 'donkey-man, pl. -men, s.m. Anier.
donnish ['dɔniʃ], a. F: Pédant. He has rather a d. manner, il a un petit air professoral.
donor ['dounər], s. 1. Jur: Donateur, -trice. 2. Surg: Blood d., donneur, -euse, de sang.
don't [dount]. = do not.
doodah ['du:dɑ:], U.S: **doodad** ['du:dæd], s. F: Truc m, machin m.
doodle¹ ['du:dl], s. F: Griffonnage m, gribouillage m.
doodle², v.i. F: Griffonner, faire des petits dessins, en pensant à autre chose.
doodle-bug ['du:dlbʌg], s. F: A: Mil: Bombe volante.
doom¹ [du:m], s. 1. Destin m (funeste); sort (malheureux). He met his d. at . . ., il trouva la mort à. . . . 2. Perte f, ruine f. His d. is sealed, c'en est fait de lui. 3. The Day of d., le jugement dernier. Until the crack of d., jusqu'au jugement dernier.
doom², v.tr. Condamner (to, à). Doomed man, homme perdu. To be doomed to failure, être voué à l'échec.
doomsday ['du:mzdei], s. Le (jour du) jugement dernier. Till d., (i) jusqu'à la fin du monde; (ii) F: indéfiniment.
door ['dɔ:r], s. 1. Porte f. Entrance-d., usu. street-d., front-d., porte d'entrée, porte de (la) rue. Side-d., porte latérale. S.a. BACK-DOOR. Carriage-d., porte cochère. Double d., folding d., porte brisée, à deux battants. Sliding d., porte à coulisse, à glissières. Revolving d., tambour m. Two doors away, deux portes plus loin. To show s.o. the d., éconduire qn. To show s.o. to the d., conduire qn jusqu'à la porte; reconduire qn. To turn s.o. out of doors, mettre qn à la porte. To play out of doors, jouer dehors, en plein air. To be denied the d., trouver porte close. To open the d. to abuses, prêter aux abus. To open the d. to a settlement, rendre possible un arrangement. To close the d. to, against, s.o., fermer sa porte à qn. To close the d. upon any discussion, empêcher, rendre impossible,

aucune discussion. **To lay a charge at s.o.'s d.**, imputer qch. à qn. **The fault lies at my d.**, la faute en est à moi. *Com:* **D. to d. transport, canvassing, selling**, porte à porte *m*. **D. to d. salesman**, placier *m*. **From d. to d.**, de domicile à domicile. **2.** Portière *f* (de wagon, d'auto, etc.). **'door-bell**, *s*. **1.** (*Swinging*) Sonnette *f*. **2.** (*Fixed*) Timbre *m*. **'door-'curtain**, *s*. Portière *f*. **'door-frame**, *s*. Chambranle *m*, châssis *m* de porte. **'door-handle**, *s*. Poignée *f* de porte, de portière. **'door-hinge**, *s*. Gond *m*. **'door-keeper**, *s*. Portier *m*; concierge *mf*. **'door-knob**, *s*. Poignée (ronde) de porte; bouton *m*. **'door-mat**, *s*. Paillasson *m*; essuie-pieds *m inv*. **'door-nail**, *s*. Clou *m* de porte. *S.a.* DEAD I. 1. **'door-plate**, *s*. Plaque *f* de porte. **'door-post**, *s*. Montant *m* de porte. **'door-scraper**, *s*. Décrottoir *m*; gratte-pieds *m inv*. **'door-spring**, *s*. Ferme-porte *m inv*. (automatique) **'door-step**, *s*. **1.** Seuil *m*, pas *m* (de la porte). **2.** *F:* Grosse tartine (de pain beurré). **'door-stop**, *s*. Butoir *m*.

doorman, *pl.* **-men** ['dɔrmən], *s.m.* Portier.

doorway ['dɔːwei], *s*. (Encadrement *m* de la) porte. **In the d.**, sous la porte; dans l'encadrement de la porte.

dooryard ['dɔrjɑːd], *s. U.S:* Arrière-cour *f*; jardin *m* de derrière.

dope¹ [doup], *s*. **1.** *Av:* Enduit *m*. *Aut:* Laque *f* (de carrosserie). **2.** *F:* Stupéfiant *m*, narcotique *m*. *Turf:* Doping (administré à un cheval). **3.** *I.C.E:* Doping (du combustible). **4.** *F:* (*a*) Renseignement *m*, tuyau *m*. (*b*) Faux renseignements; bourrage *m* de crâne. **5.** *P:* **What a d. the chap is!** Quel crétin, quelle nouille, que ce garçon! **'dope-fiend**, *s*. *F:* Morphinomane *mf*, toxicomane *mf*. **'dope-habit**, *s*. *F:* Toxicomanie *f*. **'dope-peddler**, *s*. (*esp.*) *U.S: F:* Trafiquant *m* en stupéfiants.

dope², *v.tr.* **1.** *Av:* Enduire (les ailes). **2.** Administrer un narcotique à (qn). *Turf:* Doper (un cheval). *F:* **To d.** (**oneself**), prendre des stupéfiants. **3.** *Aut: Av:* Doper (le combustible). **4.** Mêler un narcotique à (un verre de vin); narcotiser (une cigarette). **doping**, *s. Turf:* Doping *m*.

dop(e)y ['doupi], *a*. (*a*) Stupéfié, hébété (par un narcotique). (*b*) Abruti (de fatigue).

dorado [dəˈrɑːdou], *s. Ich:* Dorade *f*.

Doric ['dɔrik], *a. & s. Arch:* Dorique (*m*).

dorm [dɔːm], *s. Sch: F:* = DORMITORY.

dormant ['dɔːmənt], *a*. (*a*) (*Of passion*) Assoupi, endormi. **To lie d.**, sommeiller, dormir. (*b*) (Volcan) en repos, assoupi.

dormer(-window) ['dɔːmə(windou)], *s*. Lucarne *f*; (fenêtre f en) mansarde *f*.

dormitory ['dɔːmətri], *s*. Dortoir *m*. *U.S: Sch:* Foyer *m* d'étudiants. **D. town**, ville *f* dortoir.

dormouse, *pl.* **-mice** ['dɔːmaus, -mais], *s. Z:* Loir *m*, muscardin *m*. **Garden d.**, lérot *m*.

dorsal ['dɔːs(ə)l], *a. Anat: Nat.Hist:* Dorsal, -aux. **D. fin**, (*of fish*), nageoire dorsale.

dory ['dɔːri], *s. Ich:* (**John**) **D.**, zée *m* forgeron, (poisson) Saint-Pierre.

dosage ['dousidʒ], *s*. Posologie *f*, dosage *m* (d'un médicament).

dose¹ [dous], *s. Med: Pharm:* Dose *f* (de médicament).

dose², *v.tr.* **1.** Doser (un médicament). **2.** Médicamenter, droguer (qn). **She was heavily dosed with sedatives**, on lui administrait de fortes doses de sédatifs.

doss¹ [dɔs], *s. P:* Lit *m* (dans un asile de nuit). **'doss-house**, *s. P:* Asile *m* de nuit.

doss², *v.i. P:* **1.** Coucher à l'asile de nuit. **2. To d. down**, se coucher.

dossier ['dosiei], *s. Adm:* Dossier *m*.

dost. *See* DO¹.

dot¹ [dɔt], *s*. Point *m*. *Tg:* **Dots and dashes**, points et traits *m*; brèves *f* et longues *f*. *F:* **He arrived on the d.**, il est arrivé à l'heure tapante.

dot², *v.tr.* (**dotted**) **1.** Mettre un point sur (un i). *S.a.* I¹. **2.** Marquer (une surface) avec des points; pointiller. **Dotted line**, ligne en pointillé. **Hillside dotted with chalets**, coteau parsemé de chalets. **3.** *Mus:* Pointer (une note). **4. To d. and carry one,** (i) *Ar: A:* reporter un chiffre; (ii) *F:* boiter (en marchant); clopiner. **5.** *P:* **To d. him one,** lui flanquer un gnon.

dotage ['doutidʒ], *s*. Radotage *m*; seconde enfance; gâtisme *m*.

dotal ['dout(ə)l], *a*. Dotal, -aux.

dotard ['doutəd], *s*. Vieillard) radoteur; *F:* gâteux *m*.

dote¹ [dout], *s*. Pourriture *f* du bois.

dote², *v.i.* **1.** Radoter; tomber dans la sénilité. **2. To d.** (**up**)**on s.o.**, aimer qn à la folie. **doting**, *a*. **1.** Radoteur, -euse; sénile. **2.** Qui montre une tendresse ou une indulgence ridicule.

doth. *See* DO¹.

dott(e)rel ['dɔt(ə)rəl], *s. Orn:* (Pluvier *m*) guignard *m*.

dottle ['dɔtl], *s. F:* Culot *m* (de pipe).

dotty ['dɔti], *a*. **1.** Marqué de points; moucheté. **2.** *F:* Toqué, piqué, maboul. **To go d.**, perdre la boule.

double¹ ['dʌbl]. **I.** *a*. **1.** (*a*) Double. **With a d. meaning**, à deux sens, à double sens. **To give a d. knock**, frapper d'un coup redoublé. **D. bed**, lit *m* à deux places, grand lit. **D. bedroom**, chambre à deux personnes. 'All' is spelt 'a, d. l,' "all" s'écrit "a, deux l." **To play a d. game**, jouer double jeu; ménager la chèvre et le chou. **To lead a d. life**, (i) mener une vie double; (ii) avoir deux ménages. **D. saucepan**, *U.S:* **d. boiler**, bain-marie *m*. (*b*) De grandeur ou de force double. **D. whisky**, double (consommation *f* de) whisky. **2. To fold a sheet d.**, plier une feuille en deux (*Of pers.*) **Bent d.**, courbé en deux. **3. D. the number**, le double; deux fois autant. **I am d. your age**, je suis deux fois plus âgé que vous. **D. the length of . . .**, deux fois plus long que. . . . **4. D. time**, pas redoublé. **II. double**, *adv.* **To see d.**, voir double. **III. double**, *s*. **1.** Double *m*; deux fois autant. **To toss d. or quits**, jouer (à) quitte ou double. **2.** (*Of pers.*) Double; *F:* sosie *m*. **3.** *Mil:* **At the d.**, au pas de course; au pas gymnastique. **4.** *Ten:* **Men's doubles**, double *m* messieurs. **'double-'acting**, *a. Mec.E:* (Cylindre) à double effet. **'double-'barrelled**, *a*. (*a*) (Fusil) à deux coups. (*b*) *F:* **D.-b. name**, nom à charnière, à rallonge. **'double-bass** [beis], *s. Mus:* Contrebasse *f* (à cordes). **'double-'breasted**, *a*. (Gilet, pardessus) croisé. **'double-'bottomed**, *a*. À fond double. **'double-'cross**, *v.tr. F:* Duper, tromper. **'double-'crosser**, *s. F:* Faux frère; faux jeton. **'double-dealing**, *s*. Duplicité *f*, fourberie *f*. **'double-'decker**, *s*. (*a*) *Av:* Deux-ponts *m inv*. *Aut:* Autobus *m* à impériale. (*b*) *Cu:* **D.-d.** (**sandwich**), sandwich *m* double. **'double-de'clutch**, *v.i. Aut:* Faire un double débrayage. **'double 'Dutch**, *s. F:* **To talk d. D.**, baragouiner; parler un langage inintelligible. **'double-dyed**, *a*. **1.** *Tex:* (Étoffe) bon teint *inv*. **2.** *F:* **D.-d. villain**, gredin fieffé. **'double-edged**, *a*. (Épée, argument) à deux tranchants. **double-entendre** ['duːblɑ̃ˈtɑ̃ːdr], *s*. Double entente *f*. **'double-faced**, *a*. **1.** *Tex:* (Étoffe) sans envers, à double envers. **2.** (Homme) à deux visages, hypocrite. **'double-headed**, *a*. A deux têtes; bicéphale. **'double-'jointed**, *a*. (*Of pers., limb*) Désarticulé. **double-'lock**, *v.tr.* Fermer (une porte) à double tour. **double-'park**, *v.tr. Aut:* Stationner (une voiture) en double file. **'double-'parking**, *s. Aut:* Stationnement *m* en double file. **'double-quick**, *a. & adv.* **In d.-q. time**, **d.-q.**, (i) au pas gymnastique; (ii) *F:* en mois de rien. **'double-'scull¹**, *s. Row:* Aviron *m* à couple. **double-'scull²**, *v.i. Row:* Nager à, en couple. **'double-'width**, *a*. **D.-w. cloth**, tissu *m* grande largeur.

double². **I.** *v.tr.* **1.** Doubler (un nombre, etc.). *Mus:* **To d. a note**, doubler, redoubler, une note (à l'octave). *Th:* **To d. parts**, jouer deux rôles. **2.** *Nau:* **To d. a cape**, doubler un cap. **3.** *Cards:* (*At bridge*) Contrer. **II. double**, *v.i.* **1.** (*Of population, etc.*) Doubler, se doubler. **2.** Prendre le pas gymnastique, le pas de course. **3.** (*Of pers., hunted animal*) **To d.** (**back**), faire un brusque crochet; doubler ses voies. **double back**, *v.tr.* Replier, rabattre (une couverture, etc.). **double up**. **1.** *v.i.* (*a*) Se plier (en deux); se replier. **To d. up with laughter**, se tordre de rire. (*b*) Accourir au pas gymnastique. (*c*) *F:* **To d. up with s.o.**, partager une chambre etc. avec qn. **2.** *v.tr.* (*a*) Replier (qch.). (*b*) (*Of blow, etc.*) Faire plier (qn) en deux.

doublet ['dʌblit], *s*. **1.** *A.Cost:* Pourpoint *m*, doublet *m*. **2.** *Ling:* Doublet.

doubly ['dʌbli], *adv.* Doublement.
doubt[1] [daut], *s.* Doute *m.* To be in d., être en doute, dans le doute. To cast doubts on sth., mettre qch. en doute. To have one's doubts about, as to, sth., avoir des doutes sur, au sujet de, qch. I have my doubts whether he will come, je doute qu'il vienne. There is no room for d., le doute n'est pas permis. Beyond (a) d., sans le moindre doute; à n'en pas douter. No d. he will come, sans doute qu'il viendra. There seems to be no d. that . . ., il ne semble faire aucun doute que (ne) + *sub., more usu.* que + *ind.* Without (a) d., sans aucun doute. There is no d. about it, cela ne fait point de doute.
doubt[2]. 1. *v.tr.* Douter. To d. s.o., s.o.'s word, douter de qn, de la parole de qn. I d. whether he will come, je doute qu'il vienne, je me demande s'il viendra. I do not d. that he will come, je ne doute pas qu'il ne vienne. 2. *v.i.* He doubted no longer, il n'hésita plus. **doubting,** *a.* Douteur, -euse.
doubter ['dautər], *s.* Douteur, -euse; incrédule *mf.*
doubtful ['dautful], *a.* 1. (*Of thg*) Douteux. *Com:* D. debt, dette véreuse. 2. (*Of pers.*) (*a*) Indécis, incertain. I was still d. about speaking to him, j'hésitais encore à lui parler. (*b*) To be d. of, as to, sth., douter de qch. 3. (Caractère) équivoque, suspect; (question) discutable. D. society, compagnie louche. In d. taste, d'un goût douteux. **-fully,** *adv.* 1. D'un air de doute. 2. En hésitant. 3. Vaguement.
doubtfulness ['dautfulnis], *s.* 1. Ambiguïté *f.* 2. Incertitude *f* (du temps, de l'avenir). 3. Irrésolution *f,* indécision *f.*
doubtless ['dautlis], *adv.* Sans doute; très probablement.
douche[1] [duːʃ], *s. Esp. Med:* Douche *f.*
douche[2]. 1. *v.tr.* Doucher. 2. *v.i.* Se doucher.
dough [dou], *s.* 1. Pâte *f* (à pain). 2. *F:* Argent *m; P:* galette *f;* fric *m.* 'dough(-)boy, *s.* 1. *Cu: A:* = DUMPLING. 2. *U.S: F: O:* Soldat (américain).
doughnut ['dounʌt], *s. Cu:* Beigne *m* (*Fr.C.*).
doughty ['dauti], *a. A:* Vaillant, preux. D. deeds, hauts faits.
doughy ['doui], *a.* 1. (Pain) pâteux. 2. *F:* (Visage) terreux.
dour ['duər], *a. Scot:* 1. Austère, froid, sévère. 2. Obstiné; buté. **-ly,** *adv.* 1. Avec une austérité froide. 2. Avec obstination.
douse[1] [daus], *v.tr. F:* 1. Plonger, tremper, (qch.) dans l'eau. 2. Arroser, asperger (qn); administrer unedouche à (qn). **dousing,** *s.* (*a*) Plongeon *m.* (*b*) Douche *f.*
douse[2], *v.tr. Nau:* 1. (*a*) Amener rondement (une voile). (*b*) Fermer (un sabord). 2. *A:* Éteindre (la lumière).
dove[1] [dʌv]. 1. *s.* Colombe *f.* 2. *a.* D. (-coloured, -grey), colombin; gorge-de-pigeon *inv.*
dove[2] [douv], *U.S: p.h. of* DIVE[1], *v.i., q.v.*
dovecot(e) ['dʌvkɔt], *s.* Colombier *m,* pigeonnier *m.*
Dover ['douvər]. *Pr.n. Geog:* Douvres *m.* The Straits of D., le Pas de Calais.
dovetail[1] ['dʌvteil], *s. Carp:* Queue-d'aronde *f.*
dovetail[2], *v.tr.* 1. Assembler à queue-d'aronde. Dovetailed joint, assemblage endenté, à queue-d'aronde. 2. (*a*) To d. two schemes (into each other), opérer le raccord entre deux entreprises. (*b*) *v.i.* (*Of schemes, etc.*) Se rejoindre, se raccorder.
dowager ['dauədʒər], *s.f.* Douairière.
dowdiness ['daudinis], *s.* Manque *m* d'élégance (dans la toilette).
dowdy ['daudi], *a.* (Femme ou toilette) peu élégante, sans élégance. **-ily,** *adv.* (Vêtue) sans élégance.
dowel[1] ['dauəl], *s. Carp:* Goujon *m* (d'assemblage); cheville *f* (en bois).
dowel[2], *v.tr.* (dowelled) Goujonner.
dower[1] ['dauər], *s.* 1. (*Widow's*) Douaire *m.* 2. *A. & Lit:* = DOWRY.
dower[2], *v.tr.* 1. Assigner un douaire à (une veuve). 2. Doter (une jeune fille).
dowerless ['dauəlis], *a.* Sans dot.
down[1] [daun], *s. Geog:* 1. Dune *f.* 2. *usu.pl.* Collines crayeuses. The (North, South) Downs, les Downs *m.* 3. The D., la rade au large de Deal.
down[2], *s.* 1. (*On birds*) Duvet *m.* D. mattress, duvet. D. pillow, oreiller de plume. 2. (*On pers.*) Duvet; poil follet. 3. (*On plants, fruit*) Duvet.

down[3]. I. *adv.* 1. (*Motion*) Vers le bas; (de haut) en bas; à terre; par terre. To go d., aller en bas; descendre. To lay d. one's arms, mettre bas les armes. To fall d., tomber (i) à terre, (ii) par terre. Cash d., argent (au) comptant, sur table. D. with the traitors! à bas les traîtres! *F:* D. with so-and-so! un tel au poteau! (*To a dog*) D.! à bas! couché! à bas les pattes! 2. (*Position*) D. below, en bas, en contre-bas. D. there, là-bas (en contre-bas). D. in the country, (au loin) à la campagne, en province. D. here, ici; dans ces parages. *F:* D. under, aux antipodes. The blinds were d., les stores étaient baissés. The curtains are d., on a enlevé les rideaux. Face d., face en dessous. Head d., la tête en bas. To be d., (i) être tombé (par terre); (ii) (*of student*) être rentré chez soi (à la fin du trimestre); (iii) n'être plus à l'université. He is not d. (from his bedroom) yet, il n'est pas encore descendu. To hit a man when he is d., frapper un homme à terre. He is (put) d. for £20, il est inscrit pour (une cotisation de) 20 livres. He is £20 d., il a un déficit de 20 livres. D. with fever, alité, frappé, par la fièvre. D. with 'flu, il est grippé. The sun is d., le soleil est couché. The wind is d., le vent est tombé. The tide is d., la mer est basse. Bread is d., le pain a baissé. His nerves are d., ses cheveux sont dénoués, défaits. *Aut: etc:* Your tyres are d., vos pneus sont dégonflés, à plat. *Games:* To be ten points d., avoir dix points de moins. *Cards:* To be two d., avoir deux de chute. Ship d. by the head, navire enfoncé par l'avant. 3. *From prince d. to pedlar,* du prince jusqu'au colporteur. D. to recent times, jusqu'au temps présent; jusqu'à présent. D. to here, (en descendant) jusqu'ici. 4. *F:* To be d. on s.o., en vouloir à qn; être toujours sur le dos de qn. To be d. in the mouth, être découragé, abattu. To be d. and out, être ruiné, décavé, à bout de ressources. II. **down,** *prep.* To lower s.o. d. a precipice, descendre qn le long d'un précipice. Her hair is hanging d. her back, les cheveux lui pendent dans le dos. To go d. the street, d. a hill, descendre la rue, une colline. D. (the) river, en aval. To fall d. the stairs, tomber en bas de l'escalier. Water is running d. the wall, l'eau *f* coule, dégouline, le long du mur. D. town, en ville. *S.a.* UP[1] II. 2. III. **down,** *a.* 1. *Rail:* D. train, d. platform, train montant, quai montant. 2. *Mus:* D. beat, temps fort. 3. *Com:* D. payment, acompte *m. F:* = DOWN-HEARTED. IV. **down,** *s.* 1. *In the phr.* Ups and downs, *q.v. under* UP[1] IV. 2. *F:* To have a d. on s.o., en vouloir à qn; avoir une dent contre qn. 'down-and-'out(er), *s.* Clochard *m;* (homme) ruiné, fichu, fini. down-at-'heel, *a.* (Soulier) éculé; (*of pers.*) râpé. *F:* décheux. 'down-draught, *s.* Courant d'air descendant. *I.C.E:* D.-d. carburettor, carburateur inversé. down(-)'hearted, *a.* Découragé; déprimé, abattu. 'down-lead, *s. W.Tel: etc:* Descente d'antenne. 'down-side. *s. Tg:* Aval *m.* 'down-'stage, *adv. & a. Th:* Sur le devant (de la scène). 'down-stroke, *s.* 1. (*In writing*) Jambage *m,* plein *m.* 2. *Mch:* Course descendante (du piston). 'down-wash, *s. Av:* Déplacement m d'air.
down[4], *v.tr.* 1. *F:* Terrasser, abattre. 2. *Ind:* To d. tools, (i) cesser le travail; (ii) se mettre en grève. 3. *F:* Avaler, s'enfoncer (une boisson).
downcast ['daunkɑːst], *a.* 1. (*Of pers.*) Abattu déprimé. 2. (*Of look*) Baissé (vers la terre).
downfall ['daunfɔːl], *s.* Chute *f;* ruine *f;* écroulement *m,* effondrement *m* (d'un empire, etc.).
downgrade[1] ['daungreid], *s.* 1. *Rail:* Rampe descendante; descente *f.* 2. Décadence *f.* To be on the d., être sur le déclin, *F:* sur le retour.
downgrade[2], *v.tr.* Réduire à un niveau inférieur.
downhill. 1. ['daun'hil], *a.* En pente; incliné. 2. [daun'hil], *adv.* To go d., (*of road*) aller en descendant; (*of car, etc.*) descendre (la côte); *F:* (*of pers.*) être sur le déclin.
downpour ['daunpɔːr], *s.* Forte pluie; grosse averse; pluie battante, diluvienne.
downright ['daunrait]. 1. *adv.* (*a*) Tout à fait; complètement. (*b*) (Refuser) nettement, catégoriquement, carrément. 2. *a.* (*a*) (*Of pers., language*) Direct; franc, *f.* franche; carré. (*b*) Absolu, véritable. D. lie, mensonge éclatant. (*b*) swindle, véritable escroquerie. A d. no, un non catégorique.

downstairs. **1.** *adv.* [daun'stɛəz]. En bas (de l'escalier). **To come, go, d.,** descendre (l'escalier). *(b)* En bas, au rez-de-chaussée. **Our neighbours d.,** nos voisins, (i) de l'étage-au-dessous; (ii) du rez-de-chaussée. **2.** *a.* ['daunstɛəz] The d. **rooms,** les pièces d'en bas, du rez-de-chaussée.

downstream ['daun'striːm]. **1.** *adv.* En aval. **2.** *a.* D'aval.

downtown ['daun'taun]. *U.S:* **1.** *a. & s.* D. (sector), centre, quartier, commercial (d'une ville). **The d. church,** l'église au centre (de la ville). **2.** *adv.* **I'm going d.,** je vais en ville.

downtrodden ['daun͵trɔdn], *a.* Foulé aux pieds; (peuple) opprimé, tyrannisé.

downward ['daunwəd]. **1.** *a.* (Mouvement) descendant, de haut en bas; (regard) dirigé en bas. *Lit:* **The d. path,** la pente fatale. **2.** *adv.* = DOWNWARDS.

downwards ['daunwədz], *adv.* *(a)* De haut en bas; en descendant; *(on river)* en aval. **Face d.,** face à terre; en dessous. *(b)* **From the twelfth century d.,** à partir du douzième siècle.

downy ['dauni], *a.* **1.** *(a)* Duveteux; couvert de duvet. *Bot:* Lanugineux, pubescent. *(b)* *(Of fruit)* Velouté. *(c)* (Lit)douillet, moelleux. **2.** *F: O:* **A d. bird, cove,** un malin, un rusé.

dowry ['dauəri], *s.* Dot *f*; biens dotaux.

dowse ['dauz], *v.i.* Faire de l'hydroscopie, de la radiesthésie. **dowsing,** *s.* Hydroscopie *f*, radiesthésie *f*. **'dowsing-rod,** *s.* Baguette *f* divinatoire, de sourcier.

dowser ['aauzər], *s.* Sourcier *m*; hydroscope *m*, radiesthésiste *mf*.

doxology [dɔk'sɔlədʒi], *s.* Doxologie *f*.

doyen ['dɔiən], *s.* Doyen *m* *(esp.* du corps diplomatique).

doze[1] [douz], *s.* Petit somme. **To have a d.,** faire un petit somme.

doze[2], *v.i.* Sommeiller; être assoupi. **To d. off,** s'assoupir.

dozen ['dʌzn], *s.* Douzaine *f*. **1.** *(Inv. in pl.)* **Half a d.,** une demi-douzaine. **Six d. bottles,** six douzaines de bouteilles. *F:* **Daily d.,** gymnastique *f* du matin. **2.** *(pl.* dozens*)* **To sell articles in (sets of) dozens, by the d.,** vendre des articles à la douzaine. **Dozens and dozens of times,** maintes et maintes fois. **A long d.,** a **baker's d.,** treize douze; treize à la douzaine, une treizaine. *F:* **To talk nineteen to the d.,** jaser comme une pie borgne, avoir la langue bien pendue.

drab[1] [dræb], *s.f.* *(a)* Souillon. *(b)* Prostituée.

drab[2], *a. & s.* *(a)* Gris-brun *(m)*; beige. *(b)* D. existence, existence terne, décolorée.

drachm [dræm], *s.* *Pharm.Meas:* Drachme *f*.

drachma, *pl.* -mas, -mae ['drækmə, -əz, -i], *s.* *Num:* Drachme *f*.

Draconian [dræ'kounian], *a.* Draconien, -ienne; sévère.

draft[1] [drɑːft], *s.* I. **1.** *Mil:* *(a)* Détachement *m* (de troupes); contingent *m* (de recrues). *(b)* Membre *m* d'un détachement, d'un contingent. *(c)* *U.S:* Conscription *f*. **2.** *Com:* *(a)* Tirage *m* (d'un effet). *(b)* Traite *f*; lettre *f* de change; effet *m*. **D. at sight,** effet à vue. **3.** Dessin *m* schématique; plan *m*, tracé *m*; ébauche *f*. **4.** Projet *m* (de contrat); brouillon *m* (de lettre). **First d. of a novel,** premier jet d'un roman. II. **draft,** *s.* = DRAUGHT[1] I.

draft[2], *v.tr.* **1.** *Mil:* *(a)* Détacher, envoyer en détachement (des troupes). *(b)* *U.S:* Appeler (des soldats) sous les drapeaux. **2.** **To d. s.o. to a post,** désigner, affecter, qn pour, à, un poste. **3,** Rédiger (un acte); faire le brouillon (d'une lettre).

draftee [drɑː'fːti:], *s.* *Mil:* *U.S:* Conscrit *m*; recrue *f*.

drafter ['drɑːftər], *s.* **1.** Rédacteur *m* (d'un acte). **2.** *U.S:* Cheval *m* de trait.

draftsman, *pl.* -men ['drɑːftsmən], *s.* = DRAUGHTS-MAN 1.

drag[1] [dræg], *s.* **1.** *Veh:* Drag *m*, mail-coach *m* (à quatre chevaux). *Agr:* Herse *f*. **2.** *(a)* *(Dredging)* Drague*f*.*(b)**(For retrieving lost object)* Araignée *f*; *Nau:* grappin *m* à main. *(c)* *Fish:* = DRAG-NET. **3.** *(a)* Sabot *m*, patin *m* (d'enrayage). **To put a d. on a wheel,** enrayer une roue. *(b)* Entrave *f*. **To be a d. on s.o.,** entraver qn; être un boulet au pied de qn. **He is a d. on me,**

je le traîne comme un boulet. *(c)* *Nau:* = DRAG-ANCHOR. **4.** *(a)* Tirage *m*, résistance *f* (à l'avancement); frottement excessif. *(b)* *Av:* Effort *m* de traînée. *(c)* **To walk with a d.,** marcher en traînant la jambe. **'drag-anchor,** *s.* *Nau:* Ancre flottante, ancre de cape. **'drag-net,** *s.* *Fish:* Drague *f*, drège *f*, chalut *m*, seine *f*; filet *m* à la trôle. *Ven:* Traîneau *m*, traînasse *f*, tirasse *f*.

drag[2], *v.* (dragged [drægd]) **1.** *v.tr.* *(a)* Traîner, tirer; entraîner (qn) (contre sa volonté). **To d. one's feet,** (i) traîner les pieds; (ii) *F:* Montrer peu d'empressement à faire qch. *F:* **We had to d. him here,** il n'est venu qu'à son corps défendant. *(b)* *Nau:* *(Of ship)* **To d. her anchor,** chasser sur ses ancres; déraper. *(c)* Draguer (un étang). **2.** *v.i.* *(a)* *(Of pers.)* Traîner, rester en arrière; *(of thg)* traîner (à terre); *(of lawsuit, etc.)* traîner en longueur; *(of conversation)* languir, s'éterniser. *(b)* Offrir de la résistance; *(of brakes)* frotter (sur les roues). *(c)* *Nau:* *(Of anchor)* Raguer le fond, labourer le fond. *(d)* Draguer (for sth., à la recherche de qch.). *Fish:* Pêcher à la drague. **drag about,** *v.tr.* Traîner, *F:* trimbaler (qn, qch.). **drag along,** *v.tr.* Traîner, entraîner (qn, qch.). **drag away,** *v.tr.* *(a)* Entraîner, emmener (qn) de force; traîner (qch.) dehors, etc. *(b)* Arracher (qn, qch.) **(from,** à, de). **drag down,** *v.tr.* Tirer, entraîner (qn, qch.) en bas. **He has dragged me down with him,** il m'a entraîné dans sa chute. **drag in,** *v.tr.* Faire entrer de force (qn, qch.). **drag on,** *v.i.* *(Of affair, etc.)* Traîner en longueur; s'éterniser. **drag out,** *v.tr.* **1.** **To d. s.o. out of bed,** tirer qn de son lit. **To d. the truth out of s.o.,** arracher la vérité à qn. **2.** Faire traîner (une affaire). **3.** **To d. out a wretched existence,** poursuivre, traîner, jusqu'à sa fin une existence misérable. **drag up,** *v.tr.* **1.** Entraîner, tirer (qn, qch.) jusqu'en haut. **2.** Repêcher (un cadavre, etc.) à la drague. *F:* **Why do you d. up that old story?** pourquoi ressortir cette vieille histoire? **3.** *F:* *(Of child)* Dragged up, élevé à la va-comme-je-te-pousse, tant bien que mal. **dragging,** *s.* **1.** Traînage *m*, traînement *m* (d'un fardeau). *Nau:* **D. of the anchor,** dérapage *m*. **2.** *(a)* Dragage *m* (d'un étang, etc.). *(b)* *Fish:* Pêche *f* à la trôle.

dragée ['drædʒei], *s.* *Comest:* *Pharm:* Dragée *f*.

draggle [drægl]. **1.** *v.tr.* Traîner (sa jupe, etc.) dans la boue; crotter (ses vêtements). **2.** *v.i.* Traîner; rester en arrière.

dragon ['drægən], *s.* Dragon *m*. **'dragon-fly,** *s.* *Ent:* Libellule *f*.

dragoon[1] [drə'guːn], *s.* *Mil:* Dragon *m*.

dragoon[2], *v.tr.* **1.** *Hist:* Dragonner (le peuple). **2.** Tyranniser (qn). **To d. s.o. into doing sth.,** contraindre qn à faire qch.

drain[1] [drein], *s.* **1.** Canal *m*, -aux (de décharge); tranchée *f*, caniveau *m*, rigole *f*. **Open d.,** tranchée à ciel ouvert. **2.** *(a)* Égout *m*. *F:* **To throw money down the d.,** jeter son argent par la fenêtre. *(b)* **The drains of a house,** la canalisation sanitaire d'une maison. **3.** *(a)* Tuyau *m* d'écoulement, de vidange. *(b)* *Surg:* Drain *m*. **4.** Perte *f*, fuite *f* (d'énergie, etc.). **Constant d. on the resources,** saignée continuelle. **'drain-cock,** *s.* Robinet *m* de purge, de vidange. **'drain-pipe,** *s.* **1.** Tuyau *m* d'écoulement, d'échappement; gouttière *f*. **2.** *Cost:* *F:* D.-p. **trousers,** pantalons *m* fuseaux.

drain[2], *v.tr.* *(a)* **To d. water (away, off),** (i) évacuer, faire écouler, des eaux; (ii) faire égoutter l'eau. **The Paris Basin is drained by the Seine and its tributaries,** la Seine et ses affluents arrosent le Bassin parisien. *(b)* Boire (un liquide) jusqu'à la dernière goutte; vider (un fût, un verre). *(c)* Assécher (un terrain); mettre à sec, vider (un étang); assécher, drainer, épuiser (une mine); (faire) égoutter (des bouteilles, des légumes*)*. *I.C.E:* **To d. the sump,** vidanger le carter. *(d)* Épuiser, saigner (qn, la bourse). **To d. a country of money,** épuiser l'argent d'un pays. *F:* **To d. s.o. dry,** saigner qn à blanc. **2.** *v.i.* *(a)* *(Of water, etc.)* **To d. (away),** s'écouler. *(b)* *(Of thg)* **(S')**égoutter. **draining,** *s.* Écoulement *m* (des eaux); assèchement *m* (d'un marais); drainage *m* (d'un terrain); égouttage *m* (des bouteilles). **'draining-board,** *s.* Égouttoir *m* (d'évier). **'draining-rack,** *s.* Égouttoir *m* (à assiettes, etc.).

drainage ['dreinidʒ], s. 1. = DRAINING 1. 2. (i) Système m d'écoulement des eaux; (ii) système d'égouts. Main d., tout à l'égout. Geog: D. area, surface f 'captation des eaux, bassin m hydrographique. 'drainage-tube, s. Surg: Drain m.

drainer ['dreinər], s. Égouttoir m.

drake [dreik], s. Canard m mâle.

dram [dræm], s. 1. = DRACHM. 2. F: Goutte f (à boire); petit verre.

drama ['drɑːmə], s. 1. Drame m. 2. (The) d., l'art m dramatique; le théâtre.

dramatic [drə'mætik], a. Dramatique. A d. effect, un effet théâtral. The d. works of Corneille, le théâtre de Corneille. -ally, adv. Dramatiquement.

dramatics [drə'mætiks], s.pl. Le théâtre.

dramatis personae ['drɑːmətispɑː'sounai], s. Th: Personnages mpl.

dramatist ['dræmətist], s. Auteur m dramatique; dramaturge m.

dramatize ['dræmətaiz], v.tr. Dramatiser; adapter (un roman) à la scène.

drank. See DRINK².

drape¹ [dreip], s. U.S: Rideau m.

drape², v.tr. (a) Draper, tendre (with, in, de). (b) Art: Draper (une étoffe).

draper ['dreipər], s. Marchand m de tissus, de nouveautés, drapier m. Draper's shop, magasin de nouveautés; mercerie f. S.a. LINEN-DRAPER.

drapery ['dreipəri], s. Draperie f. 1. (a) Commerce m des tissus. (b) Magasin m de nouveautés; mercerie f. 2. Tentures fpl; vêtements drapés.

drastic ['dræstik], a. 1. Med: Drastique. 2. To take d. measures, prendre des mesures énergiques, rigoureuses; trancher dans le vif. -ally, adv. Énergiquement, rigoureusement.

drat [dræt], v.tr. F: (Used only in third pers. sub.) D. the child! au diable cet enfant! quel sacré mioche! D. (it)! nom de nom! **dratted,** a. F: Maudit (mioche, etc.).

draught¹ ['drɑːft], s. I. 1. Traction f, tirage m. D. animal, bête de trait. 2. Fish: Coup m de filet; pêche f. 3. (Drinking) Trait m, coup m, gorgée f. At a d., d'un seul trait, d'un seul coup. 4. Med: Potion f, breuvage m. 5. Nau: Tirant m d'eau (d'un vaisseau). Load d., tirant d'eau en charge. Light d., tirant d'eau en lège. 6. pl. Draughts, (jeu m de) dames fpl. D.-board, damier m. 7. (a) (In room) Courant m d'air. (b) (Induced) d. (of chimney), tirage; appel m d'air. 8. Beer on d., d. beer, bière f à la pompe, à la pression; bière au tonneau, détaillée du fût. II. draught, s. = DRAFT¹ I. 'draught-excluder, s. Bourrelet m (de porte); brise-bise m inv. 'draught-harness, s. Harnais m d'attelage. 'draught-regulator, s. Mch: etc: Registre (régulateur) de tirage.

draught², v.tr. = DRAFT².

draughtsman, pl. -men ['drɑːftsmən], s. 1. Ind: Dessinateur m, traceur m (d'épures, etc.). 2. Games: Pion m (du jeu de dames).

draughtsmanship ['drɑːftsmənʃip], s. 1. L'art m du dessin industriel; Ind: le dessin. 2. Talent m de dessinateur.

draughty ['drɑːfti], a. 1. Plein de courants d'air. 2. (Coin de rue, etc.) exposé à tous les vents.

draw¹ [drɔː], s. 1. (a) Tirage m. (b) F: This was meant as a d., but he did not rise to it, on a dit ça pour l'attirer sur ce sujet, mais il n'a pas mordu. (c) F: To be quick on the d., (i) avoir la gâchette facile; (ii) avoir la repartie facile. 2. (a) Tirage au sort. (b) Loterie f; tombola f. 3. F: Attraction f; clou m (de la fête, etc.). (Of play, etc.) To be a d., faire recette. 4. Sp: Partie nulle; résultat nul.

draw², v. (drew [druː]; drawn [drɔːn]) I. v.tr. 1. (a) Tirer (un verrou, un rideau); lever (un pont-levis). To d. the curtains, (i) fermer les rideaux; (ii) ouvrir les rideaux. To d. the blinds, baisser les stores. To d. one's hand across one's forehead, passer la main sur son front. To d. a bow, bander, tendre, un arc. (b) Tirer, traîner (une voiture). Drawn by a locomotive, remorqué par une locomotive. 2. (a) (Take in) Tirer, aspirer (l'air dans ses poumons). (b) (Attract)

Attirer. To d. a crowd, crowds, attirer une foule; provoquer un rassemblement. Abs. To d., attirer la foule, le public. To d. s.o. into the conversation, faire entrer qn dans la conversation. To d. s.o. into a conspiracy, engager, entraîner, qn dans une conspiration. To d. s.o. into doing sth., amener qn à faire qch. To feel drawn to s.o., se sentir attiré vers qn. I feel drawn to him, il m'est sympathique. The Government has refused to be drawn, le Gouvernement a refusé de se commettre. 3. (a) Tirer, retirer, ôter (sth. from, out of, sth., qch. de qch.). To d. (one's sword), tirer l'épée; dégainer. To d. (lots) for sth., tirer qch. au sort. The number drawn, le numéro sortant. To d. a blank, (i) tirer un numéro blanc; (ii) F: éprouver une déception; faire chou blanc. Cp. 4 (b). To d. straws, tirer à la courte paille. (b) Arracher (un clou, une dent, etc.). To d. tears from s.o., tirer, arracher, des larmes à qn. F: To d. s.o.'s teeth, mettre qn hors d'état de nuire. (c) To d. water from the river, puiser, tirer, de l'eau à la rivière. To have a bath drawn for one, se faire préparer un bain. To d. wine (from a barrel), tirer du vin (d'un tonneau). To d. a conclusion from sth., tirer une conclusion de qch. (d) Toucher (de l'argent, un salaire). Abs. To d. upon one's savings, prendre sur ses économies. To d. upon one's memory, faire appel à sa mémoire. (e) Tchn: To d. the fire(s), mettre bas les feux. (f) Ven: To d. a fox, lancer, mettre sur pied, un renard. Mil: To d. the enemy's fire, attirer sur soi le feu de l'ennemi. To d. s.o.'s fire, provoquer une attaque sur soi-même. F: To try to d. s.o., essayer de faire parler qn. 4. (a) Vider (une volaille). To be hanged, drawn and quartered, être pendu, éviscéré et écartelé. (b) Ven: To d. a covert, battre un taillis. To d. a blank, (i) faire buisson creux; (ii) F: revenir bredouille. Cp. 3 (a). 5. To d. the tea, faire infuser le thé. 6. Metall: Étirer, tirer (des tubes, etc.); tréfiler (un métal). 7. (a) (Trace) Tracer (un plan); tirer, mener (une ligne). (b) To d. a map, (i) (of surveyor) dresser une carte; (ii) (of schoolboy) faire, dessiner, une carte. (c) Dessiner (un paysage). To d. a picture of s.o., faire le portrait de qn. (d) Faire, établir (une distinction, des comparaisons). 8. To d. a cheque on a bank, tirer un chèque sur une banque. To d. a bill, abs. to d., (up)on s.o. for £ . . ., tirer sur qn pour £. . . 9. Nau: To d. twenty feet of water, tirer, jauger, vingt pieds d'eau. 10. To d. (a game) with s.o., faire partie nulle, match nul, avec qn. The battle was drawn, la bataille resta indécise. II. draw, v.i. 1. (a) To d. near to s.o., se rapprocher de qn; s'approcher de qn. The crowd drew to one side, la foule se rangea (de côté). The train drew into the station, le train entra en gare. To d. round the table, s'assembler autour de la table. (b) (Of the day, etc.) To d. to an end, tirer, toucher, à sa fin. 2. (Of chimney) Tirer; (of pump) aspirer. To let the tea d., laisser infuser le thé. **draw along,** v.tr. Traîner, entraîner (qn, qch.). **draw apart.** 1. v.tr. Séparer, écarter. 2. v.i. Se séparer, s'écarter. **draw aside.** 1. v.tr. (a) Détourner, écarter (qch.); tirer (les rideaux). (b) Prendre (qn) à l'écart. 2. v.i. S'écarter; se ranger. **draw away.** 1. v.tr. (a) Entraîner (qn). (b) Détourner (s.o. from sth., qn de qch.). 2. v.i. S'éloigner. **draw back.** 1. v.tr. (a) Tirer en arrière; retirer (sa main). (b) Tirer, ouvrir (les rideaux). 2. v.i. (Se) reculer; se retirer en arrière. **draw down,** v.tr. Faire descendre (qch.); baisser (les stores). **draw in.** 1. v.tr. (a) Faire entrer (qch.) (en tirant); (of cat) rentrer, rétracter (ses griffes). (b) Aspirer (l'air) (à pleins poumons). (c) Abs. Réduire sa dépense; faire des économies. 2. v.i. The day is drawing in, le jour baisse. The days are drawing in, les jours diminuent. 3. v.i. The car drew in to the curb, la voiture se rapprocha à frôler le (bord du) trottoir. **draw off,** v.tr. (a) Retirer, ôter (ses gants). (b) Détourner (l'attention). (c) Soutirer (un liquide). Med: To d. off blood, prendre du sang. Mch: D.-o. plug, bouchon m de vidange. **draw on.** 1. v.tr. (a) O: Mettre (ses gants); passer, enfiler (un vêtement). (b) To d. s.o. on to do sth., entraîner qn à faire qch. 2. v.i. (a) S'avancer. (b) Evening was drawing on, la nuit approchait. **draw out,** v.tr. 1. Sortir, retirer (qch. de qch.); arracher (un clou, une dent). 2. F: Encourager (qn) à sortir de sa réserve;

faire parler (qn). 3. (a) Allonger (un cordage); étirer (le fer). (b) Prolonger (un repas); tirer (une affaire) en longueur; (faire) traîner (une affaire). (e) The days are drawing out, les journées se prolongent. **draw to,** v.tr. Tirer, fermer (les rideaux). **draw together,** v.tr. (a) Rassembler, réunir, rapprocher (des personnes, des choses). (b) = DRAW TO. **draw up. 1.** v.tr. (a) Tirer (qch.) en haut; faire (re)monter (qch.); lever (un store); relever (ses manches); aspirer (de l'eau). **To d. oneself up (to one's full height),** se (re)dresser (de toute sa hauteur). (b) **To d. up a chair (to the table),** approcher une chaise (de la table). (c) Ranger, aligner (des troupes). (d) Dresser, rédiger, libeller (un document); établir (un compte); arrêter (un programme); élaborer (un projet). **2.** v.i. **To d. up to the table,** s'approcher de la table. **To d. up with s.o.,** arriver à la hauteur de qn. (b) (Of car) S'arrêter, stopper. (c) (Of troops) Se ranger, s'aligner. **drawn,** a. **1. With d. curtains,** les rideaux tirés. **2. With d. swords,** sabre au clair. **3.** (a) Metalw: **D. tube,** tube étiré. (b) **D. features,** traits tirés, contractés, décomposés. **4. D. battle,** bataille indécise. **D. match,** partie égale, nulle. **'drawn-'thread-work,** s. Needlew: Ouvrage m à jour(s). **To do d.-t.-w.,** F: faire des jours. **drawing,** s. **1.** (a) Tirage m; (of water) puisage m, puisement m; (of teeth, nails) extraction f. (b) Attraction f (towards, vers). **D. power,** pouvoir attractif. (c) Metalw: Étirage m. **2.** (a) Dessin m. **To learn d.,** apprendre le dessin. **Freehand d.,** dessin à main levée. **Out of d.,** mal dessiné. **Mechanical drawing,** dessin industriel. (b) **Pencil d.,** dessin au crayon, **Rough d.,** ébauche f, croquis m. **Sectional d.,** (vue f en) coupe f. (c) Ind: Épure f. **Wash d.,** épure au lavis. **'drawing-account,** s. U.S: = current account, q.v. under ACCOUNT¹ 1. **'drawing-board,** s. Planche f à dessin. **'drawing-book,** s. Cahier m de dessin. **'drawing-knife,** s. Tls: Plane f, plaine f (de charron). **'drawing-master,** s.m. Professeur de dessin. **'drawing-mill,** s. Metalw: Tréfilerie f. **'drawing-paper,** s. Papier m à dessin. **'drawing-pen,** s. Tire-ligne m, pl. tire-lignes. **'drawing-pin,** s. Punaise f (pour papier à dessin).

draw³-, comb.fm. **'draw-bar,** s. Barre f d'attelage, de tirage. **'draw-bench,** s. Metalw: Banc m à étirer, à tréfiler. **'draw-hole,** s. Metall: Trou m de coulée (de haut-fourneau). **'draw-hook,** s. Crochet m d'attelage. **'draw-knife,** s. Tls: = DRAWING-KNIFE. **'draw-net,** s. Ven: Tirasse f. **drav-sheet,** s. Alaise f, alèse f. **'draw-slide, -tube,** s. Opt: Tube m à tirage (d'un microscope).

drawback ['drɔːbæk], s. **1.** Inconvénient m, désavantage m. **2.** Cust: Remboursement m (à la sortie) des droits d'importation; drawback m.

drawbridge ['drɔːbridʒ], s. **1.** Pont-levis m. **2.** Civ.E: Pont basculant.

drawee ['drɔː'iː], s. Tiré m, accepteur m (d'une lettre de change).

drawer ['drɔːər], s. **1.** (Pers.) (a) Tireur, -euse; (of water) puiseur, -euse; (of teeth) arracheur, -euse. (b) Tireur de vin, de bière. (c) Tireur, souscripteur m (d'une lettre de change). (d) Dessinateur m, traceur m. (e) **D. (up),** rédacteur m (d'un document). **2.** (Device) Extracteur m. **3.** (a) Tiroir m. **Chest of drawers,** commode f. **Nest of drawers,** classeur m à tiroirs. **Sth. for one's bottom d.,** quelque chose pour son trousseau. (b) **Cash-d.,** tiroir-caisse m. **4.** pl. O: (a) (Underwear) (**Pair of) drawers,** (for men) caleçon m; (for women) culotte f; slip m. (b) **Running drawers,** culotte f (de coureur); short m.

drawing-room ['drɔːiŋrum], s. **1.** (a) Salon m. (b) Rail: U.S: = Voiture-lit f, wagon-lit m. **2.** (At court) Réception f.

drawl¹ [drɔːl], s. Voix traînante; débit traînant.

drawl². 1. v.i. Parler d'une voix traînante. **2.** v.tr. **To d. out sth.,** dire qch. avec une nonchalance affectée.

dray [drei], s. Veh: (a) Camion m (de brasseur). (b) Fardier m. **'dray-horse,** s. Cheval m de camion, de charrette; cheval de gros trait.

drayman, pl. **-men** ['dreimən, -mən], s.m. Livreur de brasserie; camionneur.

dread¹ [dred], s. Crainte f, terreur f, épouvante f; effroi m; F: phobie f. **In d. of doing sth.,** de crainte de faire qch. **To be, stand, in d. of s.o.,** craindre, redouter, qn.

dread², v.tr. Redouter, craindre. **To d. that . . .,** redouter que (ne) + sub.

dreadful ['dredf(u)l], a. **1.** Terrible, redoutable. **2.** Atroce, épouvantable. **It is something d.,** c'est quelque chose d'affreux. F: **It's a d. bore!** c'est assommant! **I've been hearing d. things about you,** on m'a raconté des horreurs sur votre compte. **-fully,** adv. **1.** Terriblement, affreusement, atrocement. **2.** (Intensive) F: **D. ugly,** affreusement laid. **I am d. sorry,** je regrette infiniment.

dreadnought ['drednɔːt], s. Navy: A: (Cuirassé m du type) Dreadnought m.

dream¹ [driːm], s. Rêve m. (a) Songe m. **To have a d.,** faire un rêve, un songe. **Sweet dreams!** faites de beaux rêves! **To see sth. in a d.,** voir qch. en songe. (b) **Waking d., day-d.,** rêverie f, rêvasserie f, songerie f. **To be in a d.,** être dans un rêve. attrib. **D. house,** maison de rêve. F: **It's a d. of a hat!** c'est un chapeau rêvé, un amour de chapeau!

dream², v.tr. & i. (p.t. & p.p. dreamt or dreamed [dremt]). **1.** (During sleep) **To d. of, about, sth.,** rêver de qch. **2.** Laisser vaguer ses pensées; rêvasser. **To d. empty dreams,** rêver creux. **3. I shouldn't d. of doing it,** jamais je ne m'aviserais de faire cela. **Little did I d. that . . .,** je ne songeais guère que. **dream away,** v.tr. Passer, perdre (son temps) à rêver. **dream up,** v.tr. F: Inventer, imaginer. **dreaming,** s. Rêves mpl, songes mpl.

dreamer ['driːmər], s. **1.** Rêveur, -euse. **2.** F: Rêveur; (esprit) songeur m. **3.** Pej: Cerveau creux; songe-creux m inv.

dreaminess ['driːminis], s. (État m de) rêverie f.

dreamland ['driːmlænd], s. Le pays des rêves.

dreamless ['driːmlis], a. (Sommeil m) sans rêves.

dreamy ['driːmi], a. Rêveur; songeur; langoureux. **-ily,** adv. D'un air, d'un ton, rêveur; rêveusement.

dreariness ['driərinis], s. Tristesse f, aspect m morne (d'un paysage, etc.).

dreary ['driəri], a. (Paysage) triste, morne; (discours) morne, ennuyeux. **-ily,** adv. Tristement; lugubrement.

dredge¹ [dredʒ], s. Fish: Drague f. **'dredge-boat,** s. (On canal) Revoyeur m.

dredge², v.tr. & i. Draguer, curer, dévaser (un chenal, un canal). **To d. for sth.,** draguer à la recherche de qch. **dredging¹,** s. Dragage m.

dredge³, v.tr. Cu: Saupoudrer. **dredging²,** s. Saupoudrage m.

dredger¹ ['dredʒər], s. **1.** (Pers.) (Ouvrier) dragueur m. **2.** (Machine) Drague f; cure-môle m.

dredger², s. Saupoudroir m (à sucre, etc.).

dreg [dreg], s. (Usu. pl.) **To drink the cup to the dregs,** boire la coupe jusqu'à la lie. **The dregs of the population,** la lie du peuple.

drench¹ [dren(t)ʃ], s. Vet: Breuvage m, purge f.

drench², v.tr. **1.** Tremper, mouiller (with, de). **To get drenched,** F: se faire saucer. **Drenched to the skin,** trempé jusqu'aux os; trempé comme une soupe. **2.** Vet: Administrer un médicament à (une bête). **drenching,** a. **D. rain,** pluie battante, diluvienne.

drencher [dren(t)ʃər], s. **1.** Grosse averse, F: saucée f. **2.** Vet: Appareil m pour administrer un breuvage (à une bête).

Dresden ['drezdən]. Pr.n. Geog: Dresde f. **D. china,** porcelaine f de Saxe.

dress¹ [dres], s. **1.** Habillement m; habits mpl; vêtements mpl. **In full d.,** en grande toilette; en grand costume; en grande tenue. **Morning d.,** (i) (of women) négligé m; (ii) costume de cérémonie. **Evening d.,** tenue de soirée. **Faultless d.,** mise f irréprochable. **To talk d.,** causer chiffons. **D. materials,** tissus pour robes, pour costumes. **2.** Robe f, costume, toilette. **Ball d.,** robe de bal. **Bathing d.** = BATHING-COSTUME. Com: **Ladies' dresses,** modes f. **'dress-'circle,** s. Th: (Premier) balcon. **'dress-preserver, -shield,** s. Cost: Sous-bras m inv. **'dress-re'hearsal,** s. Th: (Répétition) générale. **'dress-stand,** s. Mannequin m (de vitrine, etc.). **'dress-'suit,** s. Habit m (de soirée).

dress², *v.tr.* (dressed [drest]) 1. (*a*) Habiller, vêtir (qn). Well dressed, bien habillé, bien mis; élégant. To be plainly dressed, avoir une mise simple. Badly dressed, mal habillé; mal mis. *Th:* To d. a play, costumer une pièce. (*b*) *v.pr. & i.* To d. (oneself), s'habiller; faire sa toilette. To d. with taste, se mettre avec goût. To d. (for dinner), (i) (*of man*) se mettre en habit; (ii) se mettre en toilette du soir. 2. Orner, parer (with, de). *Com:* To d. the window, faire la vitrine; faire l'étalage. *Nau:* To d. a ship, pavoiser un navire. 3. *Mil:* Aligner (des troupes). *v.i.* (*Of troops*) S'aligner. Right d.! à droite alignement! 4. *Med:* Panser (une blessure). 5. (*a*) *Tchn:* Apprêter (une surface); dresser, tailler, parer (des pierres). To d. timber roughly, dégrossir le bois. To d. cloth, (i) apprêter, (ii) lainer, un tissu. (*b*) To d. s.o.'s hair, coiffer qn. (*c*) *Cu:* Apprêter, accommoder (un mets); assaisonner, garnir (une salade). (*d*) *Agr:* Donner une façon à (un champ). dress down, *v.tr. F:* Chapitrer (qn); laver la tête à (qn). dressing down, *s. F:* Verte semonce. dress up, *v.tr.* Habiller, parer, *F:* attifer (qn). To d. oneself up, *v.i.* to d. up, as a soldier, s'habiller, se costumer, en soldat. *P:* To be dressed up to the nines, être tiré à quatre épingles; être sur son trente et un. *S.a.* KILL³ 1. dressing, *s.* 1. (*a*) Habillement *m*, toilette *f*. (*b*) Arrangement *m* (des cheveux). (*c*) *Agr: Hort:* Façon *f*. *Vit:* First d., sombrage *m*. *Arb:* Traitement *m*. (*d*) *Cu:* Accommodage *m*, apprêt *m*, assaisonnement *m* (des mets). (*e*) Pansement *m* (d'une blessure). (*f*) Alignement *m* (des troupes). (*g*) Pavoisement *m*. (*h*) *Tchn:* Apprêt *m*, apprêtage *m* (des étoffes); dressage *m*, taille *f* (des pierres). 2. (*a*) *Cu:* (Salad-)d., assaisonnement *m* (pour la salade) genre sauce mayonnaise. French d., vinaigrette *f*. (*b*) Produit *m* d'entretien; enduit *m* (pour cuirs, etc.); graisse *f* (pour courroies). *Agr:* Fumages *mpl.* A heavy d. of manure, un gros apport de fumier. Light d., engrais légers. Surface d., top d., couche *f* d'engrais. (*c*) *Med:* Pansement *m*. (*d*) *Tex:* Apprêt, empois *m*. 'dressing-case, *s.* Nécessaire *m*, sac *m* (de toilette, de voyage). (Fitted) d.-c., mallette garnie. 'dressing-gown, *s.* Robe *f* de chambre; (*for women*) peignoir *m*. 'dressing-room, *s.* 1. Cabinet *m* de toilette. 1. *Th:* Loge *f* (d'acteur, d'actrice). 'dressing-station, *s. Mil: Med:* Poste *m* de secours. Field dressing-station, antenne *f* chirurgicale. 'dressing-table, *s.* (Table *f* de) toilette *f*; coiffeuse *f*.

dressage [dre'sɑː3], *s. Equit:* Dressage *m*.

dresser¹ ['dresər], *s. Furn:* 1. Buffet *m* de cuisine; dressoir *m*; vaisselier *m*. 2. *U.S:* = DRESSING-TABLE.

dresser², *s.* 1. *Ind:* Apprêteur, -euse. *S.a.* WINDOW-DRESSER. 2. *Th:* Habilleur, -euse. 3. Externe *m* (des hôpitaux); panseur, -euse.

dressiness ['dresinis], *s. Often Pej:* Recherche *f* dans sa mise, dans sa toilette.

dressmaker ['dresmeikər], *s.* (*a*) Couturière *f*. (*b*) Couturier *m*. (*c*) Visiting d., ouvrière *f* maison, couturière à la journée.

dressmaking ['dresmeikiŋ], *s.* 1. Couture *f*. 2. Confections *fpl* pour dames; confection de robes. To be in the d. trade, (i) être dans la (haute) couture; (ii) être dans la confection.

dressy ['dresi], *a. Often Pej:* 1. (*Of pers.*) Mis avec recherche; (*of woman*) qui aime la toilette; coquette. 2. (*Of clothes, etc.*) Chic, élégant.

drew. *See* DRAW².

dribble¹ ['dribl], *s.* 1. (*a*) Dégouttement *m*, égouttage *m*. (*b*) (*Of child*) Bave *f*. 2, *Fb:* Dribbling *m*, dribble *m*.

dribble². 1. *v.i.* (*a*) Dégoutter; tomber goutte à goutte. *F:* The men came dribbling back, les ouvriers revenaient par deux ou trois, par petits groupes. (*b*) (*Of child, idiot*) Baver. 2. *v.tr. Fb:* Dribbler (le ballon). dribbling, *s.* 1. Dégouttement *m*, égouttage *m* (d'un liquide). 2. *Fb:* Dribbling *m*.

dribbler ['driblər], *s.* 1. Baveux, -euse. 2, *Fb:* Dribbleur *m*.

drib(b)let ['driblit], *s.* Petite quantité. In, by, driblets, par petits paquets. To pay in driblets, payer sou par sou, petit à petit.

dried. *See* DRY².

drier, driest, *a. See* DRY¹.

drift¹ [drift], *s.* 1. (*a*) Mouvement *m*. *Ph:* Ether d., mouvement relatif de la terrre et de l'éther. (*b*) (i) Direction *f*, sens *m* (d'un courant); (ii) vitesse *f* (d'un courant). (*c*) Cours *m*, marche *f* (des événements). 2. (*a*) *Artil:* Dérivation *f* (d'un projectile). (*b*) *Av: Nau:* Dérive *f*. *Av:* D. indicator, dérivomètre *m*. D. angle, angle *m* de dérive. *Pol: etc:* Laisser-faire *m*. 3. But *m*, tendance *f*, sens général, portée *f*. What is the d. of these questions? où tendent ces questions? 4. (*a*) Amoncellement *m* (de neige, de sable). (*b*) *Geol:* Apport(s) *m(pl)*. Glacial d., moraine *f*; argile *f* à blocaux. 5. *Tls:* (*a*) D. (punch), chasse-clef *m*, chasse-clavette *m*; poinçon *m*. (*b*) (*For virent-holes*) Broche *f* d'assemblage; mandrin *m*. 'drift-ice, *s.* Glaces flottantes; glaçons *mpl* en dérive. 'drift-net, *s.* Filet traînant; traîne *f*. 'drift-sand, *s.* Sable mouvant. 'drift-wood, *s.* Bois flottant, bois flotté.

drift². 1. *v.i.* (*a*) Flotter; être charrié, entraîné. *Nau:* Dériver, aller en dérive; *Av:* déporter. *Nau:* To d. to leeward, être dépalé, drossé. To d. on shore, abattre à la côte. To d. with the current, se laisser aller au fil de l'eau. (*b*) To d. into vice, se laisser aller au vice. To let oneself d., to let things d., se laisser aller; laisser aller les choses. *F:* (*Of pers.*) To d. along, flâner. To d. in, entrer en passant; s'amener (chez qn). (*c*) (*Of snow*) S'amonceler, s'amasser. (*d*) (*Of questions, events*) Tendre (vers un but). 2. *v.tr* (*a*) Flotter (du bois); (*of current*) charrier, entraîner (qch.). (*b*) (*Of wind*) Amonceler, entasser (la neige, le sable). (*c*) Brocher, mandriner (un trou de rivet).

drifter ['driftər], *s.* 1. *Nau:* (*a*) Pêcheur *m* au filet traînant; chalutier *m*. (*b*) (*Boat*) Chalutier *m*. 2. *F:* Personne qui se laisse aller.

drill¹ [dril], *s.* 1. (*a*) *Tls:* Foret *m*, pointe *f* à forer, mèche *f*; perforateur *m*. *Min:* Fleuret *m*. Pneumatic d., marteau *m* pneumatique. Wall-d. (for plugging), tamponnoir *m*. (*b*) *Tls:* Vilebrequin *m*. Hand-d., drille *f*, perceuse *f* à main. *Med:* (Dentist's) d., fraise *f*. 2. *Mil:* Exercice(s) *m(pl)*, manœuvre(s) *f(pl)*. Company d., école *f* de compagnie. Company at d., compagnie à l'exercice. To do punishment d., faire la pelote. *F:* What's the d.? Quel est le programme? Qu'est-ce qu'on fait? *S.a.* GROUND³ 5, PACK-DRILL, RECRUIT¹. 'drill-book, *s. Mil:* Théorie *f* (du soldat). 'drill-ground, *s. Mil:* Terrain *m* d'exercice, de manœuvres. 'drill-hall, *s. Mil:* Salle *f* d'exercice. 'drill-sergeant, *s. Mil:* Sergent instructeur.

drill². 1. *v.tr.* Forer, driller (un puits); perforer (une plaque); percer (un trou). *Dent:* To d. a tooth, fraiser une dent. 2. *v.tr.* Faire faire l'exercice à (des hommes); instruire, faire manœuvrer (des soldats). 3. *v.i.* Faire l'exercice; manœuvrer. drilling, *s.* 1. *Metalw: Min: etc:* Forage *m*, perçage *m*; perforation *f* (des roches, etc.); sondage *m* (d'un puits). *Dent:* Fraisage *m*. 2. *Mil:* Exercices *mpl*; manœuvres *fpl.*

drill³, *s. Agr: Hort:* 1. Ligne *f*, rayon *m*, sillon *m*. To sow in drills, semer par sillons. 2. Semeuse *f* (à cuillers); semoir *m* en lignes. 'drill-plough, *s. Agr:* Sillonneur *m*.

drill⁴, *v.tr. Agr:* Semer en lignes, par sillons.

drill⁵, *s. Tex:* Coutil *m*, treillis *m*.

drily ['draili], *adv.* = DRYLY.

drink¹ [driŋk], *s.* 1. (*Liquid drunk*) (*a*) Boire *m*. Food and d., (i) le boire et le manger; (ii) à boire et à manger. (*b*) To give s.o. a d., donner à boire à qn; faire boire qn. To have a d., se désaltérer. To have a long d., boire un bon coup. Give me a d. of water, donnez-moi un peu d'eau à boire. (*c*) Consommation *f*. To have a d., prendre quelque chose; *F:* boire un coup. (Will you) have a d.? voulez-vous boire quelque chose? qu'est-ce que vous allez prendre? (*d*) *Nau: P:* The d., la mer, la grande tasse. 2. (*Beverage*) Boisson *f*, breuvage *m*. Strong d., liqueurs fortes; spiritueux *mpl.* Soft d., boisson sans alcool; sirop *m*, limonade *f*, etc.; *Fr.C:* liqueur douce. Long d., grand verre de bière, de cidre, etc.; gin *m*, whisky *m*, à l'eau. Short d., apéritif *m*, verre de vin, d'alcool, etc. 3. Boisson; ivrognerie *f*. To take to d., s'adonner à la boisson. The d. question, la question de l'alcoolisme. To be in d., the worse for d., under the influence of d., avoir trop bu; être ivre, soûl; *Jur:* être en état d'ébriété. To smell of d., puer l'alcool.

drink², *v.tr.* (*p.t.* **drank**; *p.p.* **drunk**) Boire. **1. To d.** water, wine, boire de l'eau, du vin. **To d. the waters,** prendre les eaux. **D. your soup,** mange ta soupe. **Will you have something to d.?** voulez-vous boire quelque chose? **Fit to d.,** bon à boire; buvable, potable. **To d. from the bottle,** boire à (même) la bouteille. **To d. (a toast) to s.o.,** boire à qn, porter un toast à qn. **To d. success to s.o., to s.o.'s success,** boire au succès de qn. **To d. oneself drunk,** se soûler. **To d. s.o. under the table,** mettre qn sous la table. *S.a.* DEATH, HEALTH. **2.** *Abs.* Être adonné à la boisson. **To d. hard, heavily,** (i) boire sec, raide; (ii) s'alcooliser. **To d. like a fish,** boire comme une éponge. **drink away,** *v.tr.* Boire (sa fortune); noyer (ses soucis, etc.). **drink down,** *v.tr.* Boire, avaler (un breuvage). **drink in,** *v.tr.* **1.** Absorber, boire (l'eau); s'imbiber (d'eau). **2.** *F:* Boire (les paroles de qn). **3.** *F:* **He drank it all in,** il a avalé ça doux comme lait. **drink off,** *v.tr.* Boire (un verre) d'un coup, d'un trait. **drink up,** *v.tr.* **1.** Achever de boire; vider (un verre). **2.** (*Of plants, etc.*) = DRINK IN 1. **drunk. 1.** *Pred. a.* (*a*) Ivre, gris; soûl (with, de). **To be d.,** être pris de boisson. **To get d.,** s'enivrer, se griser, se soûler. **Dead d.,** ivre-mort, *pl.* ivres-morts. **Blind d.,** soûl perdu. **As d. as a fiddler, as a lord,** soûl comme une grive. **D. as an owl,** soûl comme une bourrique. *Jur:* **D. and disorderly,** en état d'ivresse manifeste. (*b*) Enivré, grisé (**with success,** par le succès). **D. with carnage,** ivre de carnage. **2.** *s. F:* Homme pris de boisson; ivrogne *m.* **3.** *s. F:* Ribote *f.* **drinking,** *s.* **1.** After d., après boire. **2.** Ivrognerie *f*, alcoolisme *m.* 'drinking-bout, *s.* Beuverie *f*, *P:* soûlerie *f*, ribote *f.* 'drinking-fountain, *s.* Borne-fontaine *f*, *pl.* bornes-fontaines; fontaine publique. 'drinking-song, *s.* Chanson *f* à boire; chanson bachique. 'drinking-trough, *s.* Abreuvoir *m*, auge *f.* 'drinking-water, *s.* Eau *f* potable.

drinkable ['driŋkəbl]. **1.** *a.* (*a*) Buvable. (*b*) (Eau) potable. **2.** *s.pl. F:* **We've forgotten the drinkables,** nous avons oublié la boisson.

drinker ['driŋkər], *s.* Buveur, -euse. **Hard d.,** grand buveur; alcoolique *mf.*

drip¹ [drip], *s.* **1.** Dégouttement *m*; égouttement *m* (d'un robinet). *Mch:* **D. receiver,** godet *m.* **2.** Goutte *f*; *pl.* égoutture *f.* **3.** *Arch:* Larmier *m* (de corniche). **4.** *F:* **He's, she's, a d.,** c'est une nouille. 'drip-cock, *s. Mch:* (Robinet) purgeur *m.* 'drip-feed, *s. Mch:* Distributeur *m* compte-gouttes (d'huile). 'drip-stone, *s. Arch:* Capucine *f*; larmier *m.*

drip², *v.* (**dripped**) **1.** *v.i.* Dégoutter, s'égoutter, goutter; tomber goutte à goutte. **Wall that drips,** mur qui suinte. **2.** *v.tr.* Laisser tomber (du liquide) goutte à goutte. **dripping¹,** *a.* Ruisselant; (robinet) qui pleure. **To be d. wet,** être trempé (comme une soupe). **dripping²,** *s.* **1.** Dégouttement *m*, égouttement *m.* **2.** *pl.* Égoutture *fpl* (des arbres); dégouttures *fpl* (du toit). **3.** *Cu:* Graisse *f* de rôti. **Bread and d.,** tartine *f* à la graisse. 'dripping-pan, *s. Cu:* Lèche-frite *f.* 'dripping-tube, *s.* Pipette *f* compte-gouttes.

drip-dry ['dripdrai], *a.* Ne nécessitant aucun repassage.

drive¹ [draiv], *s.* **1.** Promenade *f* en voiture; course *f.* **To go for a d.,** faire une promenade en voiture. **2.** *Ven:* Battue *f* (du gibier). **3.** *Mec.E:* (Mouvement *m* de) propulsion *f*; (i) attaque *f* (d'un organe); (ii) commande *f* (par un organe); transmission *f*, actionnement *m.* **Belt d.,** entraînement *m* par courroie. *Aut:* Conduite *f.* **Left-hand d.,** conduite à gauche. **Direct d.,** prise directe, attaque directe. **Front-wheel d.,** traction *f* avant. **Rear d.,** pont *m* arrière. **4.** *Sp:* *Golf:* Coup *m* de départ. (*b*) *Ten:* Drive *m.* **Forearm d.,** drive de coup droit. **5.** (*a*) **D. of business,** urgence *f* des affaires. (*b*) (*Of pers.*) **To have plenty of d.,** avoir de l'énergie, du dynamisme; être très entreprenant. *F:* **He's got a lot of d.,** il est très dynamique. (*c*) Campagne *f.* **Output d.,** campagne en faveur de, pour, la production. **6.** (*a*) Avenue *f* (dans une forêt). (*b*) = CARRIAGE-DRIVE. **7. Bridge, whist, d.,** tournoi *m* de bridge, de whist.

drive², *v.* (*p.t.* **drove** [drouv]; *p.p.* **driven** ['drivn]) **I.** *v.tr.* **1.** (*a*) Chasser pousser, faire aller (devant soi). **To d. cattle to the fields,** conduire, mener, le bétail aux champs. **To d. s.o. from, out of, the house,** chasser qn de la maison. *F:* **To d. sth. out of s.o.'s**

head, faire oublier qch. à qn. **To be driven out of one's course,** être entraîné hors de sa route. **To be driven ashore,** être drossé, poussé, à la côte. (*b*) *Ven:* **To d. the game,** rabattre le gibier. **2.** (*a*) Faire marcher (une machine); conduire (un cheval, une auto, une locomotive). *Abs.* **Can you d.?** savez-vous conduire? *Jur:* **He was driving to the public danger,** il conduisait au mépris de la sécurité publique. (*b*) **To d. s.o. to the station,** conduire qn à la gare. **3.** (*a*) Pousser (qn à une action); contraindre (qn à faire qch.). **He was driven to it,** on lui a forcé la main. *S.a.* NEEDS. (*b*) **To d. s.o. out of his senses,** rendre qn fou. **4.** Surcharger (qn) de travail; exploiter (qn); surmener (ses employés). **5.** Enfoncer (un clou); foncer, battre, ficher (un pieu). **6.** Percer, forer, avancer (un tunnel). **7. To d. a bargain,** faire, conclure, passer, un marché. **8.** *Sp:* **To d. the ball,** *abs.* **to d.,** *Ten:* jouer un drive; *Golf:* jouer une crossée. **9.** (*a*) Actionner, faire marcher, commander (une machine). (*b*) (*Of part*) **To d. another part,** actionner, entraîner, attaquer, un organe. (*b*) *A: F:* (*Of pers.*) **To d. a pen,** a quill, écrire; manier la plume; gratter le papier. **II. drive,** *v.i.* **1.** (*a*) (*Of clouds, etc.*) **To d. before the wind,** chasser, être charrié, devant le vent. **To let d. at s.o.,** décocher un coup à qn. (*b*) (*Of snow*) S'amonceler. (*c*) *Nau:* (*Of ship*) Dériver. **Driving ashore,** dérivant à la côte. **2. To d. (along the road),** rouler (sur la route). **To d. to a place,** se rendre en voiture à un endroit. **I don't like to d. at night,** je n'aime pas conduire, voyager, la nuit. **To d. on the right (of the road),** circuler à droite; tenir la droite. **drive along. 1.** *v.tr.* Chasser, pousser (qn, qch.). **2.** *v.i.* Cheminer (en voiture); rouler. **drive at,** *v.i.* **1.** Travailler (à qch.) sans relâche; *F:* bûcher (qch.). **2.** *F:* **What are you driving at?** à quoi voulez-vous en venir? où tendent ces questions? **I see what you're driving at,** je vous vois venir. **drive away. 1.** (*a*) *v.tr.* Chasser, éloigner, repousser. (*b*) *v.i.* Partir, s'en aller, en voiture; *Aut:* démarrer. **2.** *v.i.* **To d. a. at one's work,** travailler d'arrache-pied. **drive back. 1.** *v.tr.* (*a*) Repousser, refouler, faire reculer. (*b*) Reconduire, ramener, (qn) en voiture. **2.** *v.i.* Rentrer, revenir, retourner, en voiture. **drive down.** **1.** *v.tr.* **To d. s.o. down to, into, the country,** conduire qn (en voiture) à la campagne. **2.** *v.i.* Se rendre en voiture (de la ville à la campagne, de Londres en province). **drive in. 1.** *v.tr.* (*a*) Enfoncer (un clou); visser (une vis). (*b*) (*Of chauffeur, etc.*) Faire entrer (qn). **2.** *v.i.* Entrer (en voiture). 'drive-in, *s.* (*a*) *Aut:* Piste *f* de ravitaillement. (*b*) *U.S:* Cinéma en plein air, auquel on assiste en auto. (*c*) *U.S:* Restaurant *m* en bordure de route, restoroute *m.* **D.-in Bank,** banque *f* en bordure de route (où on peut régler ses affaires de sa voiture). **drive-off,** *v.tr. & i.* = DRIVE AWAY 1. **drive on. 1.** *v.tr.* Pousser, entraîner (qn). **2.** *v.i.* Continuer sa route. **drive out. 1.** *v.tr.* Chasser (qn, qch.); faire sortir (qn). **2.** *v.i.* Sortir (en voiture). **drive over,** *v.i.* Venir, se rendre, (à un endroit) en voiture. **drive through. 1.** *v.tr.* **To d. one's sword through s.o.'s body,** passer son sabre à travers le corps à qn. **2.** *v.i.* Traverser, passer par, (une ville) en voiture. **driven,** *a.* **1. Tempest-d. ship,** vaisseau battu par les tempêtes. *S.a.* SNOW¹ 1. **2.** *Mec.E:* **D. shaft,** arbre commandé. **Electrically d.,** actionné par l'électricité; à commande électrique. **Belt-d.,** à entraînement par courroie. **driving¹,** *a.* **1.** *Mec.E:* (*Of wheel, etc.*) Moteur, -trice. *S.a.* AXLE 1, SHAFT¹ 5. **D. force,** force motrice. **2. D. rain,** pluie battante. **driving²,** *s.* Conduite *f* (d'une voiture, etc.). 'driving-band, -belt, *s.* Courroie *f* de commande, d'entraînement, de transmission. 'driving-chain, *s. Mec.E:* Chaîne *f* de transmission. 'driving-gear, *s. Mec.E:* (Engrenage(s) *m(pl)* de) transmission *f*; commande *f.* 'driving-iron, *s. Golf.* Driver *m.* 'driving-pulley, *s.* Poulie conductrice, de commande. 'driving-school, *s. Aut:* Auto-école *f.* 'driving-test, *s. Aut:* Examen *m* pour permis de conduire. 'driving-wheel, *s.* **1.** Roue motrice (de locomotive, etc.). **2.** Roue de transmission. **3.** *Aut:* Volant *m.*

drivel¹ ['drivl], *s.* **1.** Bave *f.* **2.** *F:* Radotage *m* balivernes *fpl.* **To talk d.,** radoter.

drivel², *v.i.* (**drivelled**) **1.** Baver. **2.** *F:* Radoter.

driveller ['drivlər], s. 1. Baveur, -euse. 2. F: Radoteur, -euse.

driver ['draivər], s. 1. (a) Mécanicien m (de locomotive); conducteur m (d'autobus); conducteur, -trice, chauffeur, -euse (d'automobile); cocher m (de voiture); voiturier m (de charrette). He is a good d., il conduit bien. Aut: Racing car d., coureur m (automobile). Rac: (In trotting races) Driver m. (b) Conducteur (de bestiaux). (c) Surveillant m (d'esclaves). 2. Tls: (a) Poinçon m. (b) Chasse-clavette m. 3. (a) = DRIVING-WHEEL 1. (b) = DRIVING-PULLEY. 4. Golf: Driver m.

drizzle[1] ['drizl], s. Bruine f, crachin m, brouillasse f; pluie fine et pénétrante.

drizzle[2], v.i. Bruiner, crachiner; F: pleuvasser, pleuvoter; pleuvoir à petites gouttes.

drizzly ['drizli], a. A d. sort of day, un jour bruineux, de bruine.

droll [droul]. 1. s. A: Bouffon m. 2. a. Drôle, drolatique, bouffon, plaisant. O: A d. fellow, (i) un drôle de corps; (ii) un farceur.

drollery ['drouləri], s. Drôlerie f, plaisanterie f, bouffonnerie f.

drollness ['droulnis], s. Caractère m drôle (de qch.).

dromedary ['drʌməd(ə)ri, 'drɔm-], s. Dromadaire m.

drone[1] [droun], s. 1. (a) Ent: Abeille f mâle; faux-bourdon. (b) F: Fainéant m, parasite m. The drones, les inutiles m. 2. (a) Bourdonnement m (des abeilles). F: The parson's endless d., le débit monotone du pasteur. Av: D. of the engine, ronronnement m, vrombissement m, du moteur. (b) Mus: Bourdon m (de cornemuse). 3. Av: Mil: Avion-cible m, pl. avions-cibles.

drone[2]. 1. v.i. (a) (Of bee, etc.) Bourdonner. (b) Fainéanter. 2. v.tr. To d. (out) sth., débiter (une prière, etc.) d'un ton monotone.

drool [dru:l], s. & v.i. = DRIVEL[1,2].

droop[1] [dru:p], s. 1. (a) Attitude penchée (de la tête). (b) Abaissement m (des paupières). 2. Langueur f, abattement m, affaissement m.

droop[2]. 1. v.i. (a) (Of head, etc.) (Se) pencher; (of eyelids) s'abaisser; (of feathers) pendre, retomber. (b) (Of flower) Pencher, languir. (c) (Of pers.) Languir, s'affaiblir, s'affaisser. To revive s.o.'s drooping spirits, remonter le courage à qn. 2. v.tr. Baisser, pencher (la tête); abaisser (les paupières); (of bird) laisser pendre (les ailes).

drop[1] [drɔp], s. 1. (a) Goutte f. Water falling d. by d., eau qui tombe goutte à goutte. F: It's only a d. in the bucket, in the ocean, ce n'est qu'une goutte d'eau dans la mer. A d. of wine, une goutte, un doigt, de vin. Cu: A few drops of vinegar, un filet de vinaigre. F: To take a d., boire la goutte. He has had a d. too much, il a bu un coup de trop. (b) pl. Pharm: Gouttes. (c) (Of necklace, chandelier, etc.) Pendant m, pendeloque f. (d) Peppermint, chocolate, d., pastille f de menthe, de chocolat. S.a. ACID 1. 2. Chute f. Surv: D. in the ground, dénivellation f du terrain. D. in prices, chute, baisse f, de prix. El.E: D. in voltage, perte f de charge, chute f de tension. Av: Mil: Parachutage m; droppage m. Av: Ouverture f. Delayed d., ouverture retardée (d'un parachute). 3. (a) (Of lock) Cache-entrée m inv. (b) Th: = DROP-CURTAIN. (c) (In gallows) Bascule f, trappe f. (d) (Crane) Drop m. Pw: 4. F: (To do sth.) at the d. of a hat, (faire qch.) (i) sans hésiter, (ii) au signal donné. 'drop-curtain, s. Th: Rideau m d'entr'acte. 'drop-forge, v.tr. Metalw: Étamper, estamper; emboutir; forger à la presse. 'drop-forging, s. 1. Estampage m; matriçage m. 2. Pièce emboutie, étampée; pièce matricée. 'drop-hammer, s. Marteau-pilon m à friction, pl. marteaux-pilons; mouton m. 'drop-head, s. Aut: Capote f rabattable. 'drop-kick, s. Fb: Coup tombé. 'drop-leaf, s. Furn: Battant m, volet m (de table). 'drop-scene, s. Th: (a) Toile f de fond. (b) = DROP-CURTAIN. 'drop-shutter, s. Phot: Obturateur m à guillotine. 'drop-valve, s. I.C.E: Soupape renversée.

drop[2], v. (dropped [drɔpt]) I. v.i. 1. Tomber goutte à goutte, dégoutter (from, de); s'égoutter. 2. Tomber; (of pers.) se laisser tomber; (of ground) s'abaisser. To d. into a chair, s'écrouler sur une chaise; s'affaler dans un fauteuil. F: He almost dropped (with sur-

prise), il pensa tomber de son haut. I am ready to d., je tombe de fatigue (ou de sommeil). S.a. PIN[1] 1. 3. (Of prices, temperature) Baisser; (of wind) tomber, se calmer. 4. There the matter dropped, l'affaire en resta là. 5. (a) To d. to the rear, rester en arrière; se laisser dépasser. (Of pers., car) To d. into place, prendre sa place (dans la file); prendre la file. (b) To d. into the habit, the way of . . ., prendre l'habitude de. . . . 6. (a) To d. into one's club, entrer en passant à son cercle. (b) To d. upon, across, s.o., rencontrer qn par hasard. To d. on to a secret, surprendre un secret. 7. F: To d. (up)on s.o. (like a ton of bricks), attraper qn; rembarrer qn. II. drop, v.tr. 1. Verser (une larme). To d. oil into sth., verser de l'huile goutte à goutte dans qch. 2. (a) Laisser tomber; lâcher (qch.); baisser (un rideau); lancer, larguer (une bombe); (in knitting) sauter, laisser échapper (une maille). To d. a remark, laisser échapper une remarque. Rugby: To d. a goal, marquer un but sur coup tombé. Dropped goal, drop m, drop-goal m. Nau: To d. the pilot, débarquer le pilote. Geom: To d. a perpendicular to, on, a line, abaisser une perpendiculaire à une ligne. S.a. ANCHOR[1], BRICK[1] 1. (b) (Of sheep, etc.) Mettre bas (des petits). (c) Laisser échapper (une observation). To d. a word in s.o.'s ear, couler, glisser, un mot à l'oreille de qn. S.a. HINT[1]. (d) To d. a letter into the pillar-box, jeter une lettre à la poste. F: To d. s.o. a line, a card, envoyer, écrire, un mot, une carte, à qn. 3. Perdre (de l'argent) (over sth., sur qch.). 4. (Cause to drop) Abattre (qn, une pièce de gibier, un avion) (d'un coup de feu). 5. (Set down) I shall d. you at your door, je vous déposerai chez vous en passant. Will you d. this parcel at Mrs Smith's, voulez-vous avoir l'obligeance de remettre ce paquet chez madame Smith. 6. (a) Omettre, supprimer (une lettre, une syllabe). (b) Ne pas prononcer (les h, etc.). S.a. AITCH. 7. Baisser (les yeux); baisser, laisser tomber (la voix). 8. (a) Abandonner, délaisser (un travail); cesser, lâcher (une poursuite); se départir (d'une habitude). To d. the idea of doing sth., renoncer à (l'idée de) faire qch. Let us d. the subject, laissons ce sujet, qu'il n'en soit plus question. F: D. it! finissez! en voilà assez! (b) F: To d. s.o., cesser de voir qn; cesser ses relations avec qn. (c) Av: To d. a wing, piquer de l'aile. To d. a parachutist, lâcher un parachutiste. drop away, v.i. 1. The members of the family have dropped away, la famille s'est égrenée; les membres de la famille ont disparu un à un. 2. (Of members, receipts) Diminuer. drop behind, v.i. Rester en arrière; se laisser dépasser; se laisser distancer. drop in. 1. v.tr. Ajouter (qch.) goutte à goutte; glisser, laisser tomber, (qch.) dedans. 2. v.i. Entrer en passant. To d. in on s.o., faire une petite visite, un bout de visite, à qn. drop off, v.i. 1. (Of leaves, etc.) Tomber, se détacher. 2. F: To d. off (to sleep), s'assoupir, s'endormir. 3. = DROP AWAY 2. drop out. 1. v.tr. Omettre, supprimer. 2. v.i. (a) Tomber dehors. To d. out of a contest, se retirer. Two of the runners dropped out, deux des coureurs ont renoncé. Mil: (Of man unable to keep up with his troop) Sortir des rangs; rester en arrière. dropped, a. Aut: etc: D. axle, etc., essieu, etc., surbaissé. dropping, s. 1. (a) Dégouttement m (d'un liquide). (b) Descente f, chute f (d'un objet); abaissement m, baisse f, chute (des prix); suppression f (d'un mot); abandon m (d'un projet). (c) Ball: D. angle, angle m de visée f. Mil: Av: D. zone, zone f de droppage. 2. pl. Droppings, (a) Gouttes fpl; égouttures f. (b) (Of animals) Fiente f; (of sheep) crottes fpl.

droplet ['drɔplit], s. Gouttelette f.

dropper ['drɔpər], s. 1. Compte-gouttes m inv. 2. Fish: Bout m de ligne.

dropsical ['drɔpsik(ə)l], a. Med: Vet: Hydropique; ascitique.

dropsy ['drɔpsi], s. Med: Hydropisie f; ascite f.

drosera ['drɔs(ə)rə], s. Bot: Drosère m, rossolis m.

dross [drɔs], s. 1. Metall: Scories fpl, crasse f, laitier m. 2. (a) Impuretés fpl (de toutes sortes); déchet m. (b) F: Rebut m.

drought [draut], s. (Période f de) sécheresse f; disette f d'eau.

drove[1] [drouv], s. (a) Troupeau m (de bœufs) en marche. (b) F: Multitude f, foule f (de personnes en marche).

drove[2]. See DRIVE[2].

drover ['drouvər], s. Conducteur m de bestiaux; toucheur m.

drown [draun], v.tr. 1. Noyer. To d. oneself, se noyer; se jeter à l'eau. To be drowned, v.i. to d. (by accident), se noyer; être noyé. A drowning man, un homme qui se noie. Drowned at sea, noyé en mer. F: To d. one's sorrow in drink, noyer son chagrin dans la boisson. 2. (a) Inonder, submerger (une prairie). (b) To be drowned out, être chassé (de sa demeure, etc.) par l'inondation. Étouffer, couvrir (un son). drowned, a. 1. Noyé. A d. man, un noyé. 2. D. lands, terrains noyés, inondés. drowning, s. 1. Death by d., asphyxie f par submersion. 2. Inondation f (des champs).

drowse [drauz]. 1. v.i. Somnoler, s'assoupir. To d. away, off, s'assoupir. 2. v.tr. To d. the time away, passer le temps à dormir, à somnoler.

drowsiness ['drauzinis], s. Somnolence f.

drowsy ['drauzi], a. Assoupi, somnolent. To grow d., s'assoupir. To be, feel d., avoir envie de dormir; avoir sommeil. To make s.o. d., assoupir qn. D. afternoon, après-midi lourd. -ily, adv. D'un air, d'un ton somnolent; à demi endormi.

drub [drʌb], v.tr. (drubbed) Battre, rosser (qn, l'ennemi); F: flanquer une raclée, une tripotée, à (qn). drubbing, s. (a) Volée f de coups (de bâton, de poing); F: tripotée f. (b) Défaite f.

drudge[1] [drʌdʒ], s. Femme f, homme m, de peine. The d. of the household, le souffre-douleur inv de la maison; la cendrillon.

drudge[2], v.i. Trimer, peiner. To d. and slave, mener une vie de forçat, de galérien.

drudgery ['drʌdʒ(ə)ri], s. Travail pénible, ingrat; besognes fastidieuses; métier m d'esclave.

drug[1] [drʌg], s. 1. Produit m pharmaceutique; drogue f. 2. Narcotique m, stupéfiant m. To take drugs, faire usage de stupéfiants; s'adonner aux stupéfiants. F: Truth d., sérum m de vérité. D. traffic, trafic m des stupéfiants. 3. (Of goods) To be a d. in the market, être invendable. 'drug-addict, F: 'drug-fiend, s. Morphinomane mf ou cocaïnomane mf; toxicomane mf. 'drug-habit, s. Toxicomanie f.

drug[2], v.tr. (drugged) 1. Donner, administrer, un narcotique, des stupéfiants, à (qn); F: endormir (qn). To d. oneself, faire usage de stupéfiants; s'adonner aux stupéfiants. 2. They had drugged his wine, on avait mis, mêlé, un narcotique à son vin.

drugget ['drʌgit], s. Tex: Droguet m.

druggist ['drʌgist], s. Pharmacien m.

drugstore ['drʌgstɔ:r], s. U.S: Magasin m où l'on vend des produits pharmaceutiques, des articles de toilette, de la confiserie, de la papeterie, des journaux et où l'on sert des repas rapides.

Druid ['dru(:)id], s.m. Druide.

Druidess ['dru(:)ides], s.f. Druidesse.

Druidical [dru'idikl], a. Druidique.

Druidism ['dru(:)idizm], s. Druidisme m.

drum[1] [drʌm], s. 1. Mus: Tambour m, caisse f. Big d., bass d., grosse caisse. Long d., tenor d., caisse roulante. Mil: The drums, la batterie. To play the d., battre du tambour. To beat the d., battre le tambour. With drums beating, tambour(s) battant(s). 2. Tambourinage m. 3. Anat: (Caisse f, membrane f, du) tympan m. 4. Tonneau m en fer; tonnelet m; gonne f (à goudron); bidon m, tambour, estagnon m (à huile). 5. (a) Arch: Tambour (d'une colonne); vase m (d'un chapiteau). (b) Tambour, touret m (de treuil). Capstan d., tambour, cloche f, de cabestan. Cable d., tambour, bobine f, dévidoir m (de câble électrique). Mch: D. of the pressure gauge, barillet m de l'indicateur de pression. Concrete mixing d., bétonnière f. 'drum-brake, s. Aut: Frein m à tambour. drum-'major, s. Tambour-major m.

drum[2], v. (drummed) 1. v.i. (a) Tambouriner; battre du tambour. (Of pers., rain) To d. on the window-panes, tambouriner sur les vitres. (b) (Of insects) Bourdonner. (c) (Of car, etc.) Ferrailler, tambouriner. 2. v.tr. To d. a tune on sth., tambouriner un air sur qch. F: To d. sth. into s.o.'s head, enfoncer, fourrer, qch. dans la tête de qn. drum out, v.tr. Mil: To d.

s.o. out, expulser qn au son du tambour; dégrader qn. drum up, v.tr. Racoler (des partisans). To d. up recruits, faire du recrutement. F: To d. up one's friends, battre le rappel de ses amis. drumming, s. (a) Tambourinage m; bruit m de tambour. (b) Bourdonnement m (d'un insecte, des oreilles). (c) F: (Of car) Ferraillement m.

drummer ['drʌmər], s. 1. Tambour m (qui joue du tambour). Big d., joueur m de grosse caisse; F: grosse caisse. 2. U.S: Commis voyageur. 'drummer-boy, s.m. Petit tambour.

drumhead ['drʌmhed], s. 1. Peau f de tambour. Mil: D. service, office divin en plein air. 2. Tête f, chapeau m (de cabestan).

drumstick ['drʌmstik], s. 1. Baguette f de tambour. Bass-d., tampon m, mailloche f. Kettle-d., baguette de timbale. 2. Cu: Pilon m (d'une volaille).

drunk. See DRINK[2].

drunkard ['drʌŋkəd], s. Ivrogne, f. ivrognesse; F: pochard m.

drunken ['drʌŋk(ə)n], a. 1. Ivrogne. 2. D. state, état d'ivresse, d'ébriété. -ly, adv. (a) En ivrogne; comme un ivrogne. (b) Hors d'aplomb.

drunkenness ['drʌŋk(ə)nnis], s. 1. Ivresse f. 2. Ivrognerie f.

drupe [dru:p], s. Bot: Drupe m.

dry[1] [drai], a. (drier, driest) Sec, f. sèche. 1. (a) (Of well, etc.) Tari, à sec; (of country) aride. D. land, terre ferme. S.a. DOCK[2]. To pump a well d., épuiser l'eau d'un puits; assécher un puits. To wring linen d., essorer le linge. To run d., to go d., (of channel) se dessécher, (s')assécher; (of spring, well) s'épuiser, (se) tarir. (Of speaker, writer) He soon runs d., il a l'haleine courte. D. weather, temps sec. It has been d. (weather) for a week, il fait sec depuis huit jours. S.a. HIGH I. 7. (b) Ind: etc: D. process, procédé par voie sèche. D. crushing, broyage à sec. D. masonry, maçonnerie à sec. S.a. WALL[1], ICE[1]. (c) To put on d. clothing, mettre des vêtements secs. D. bread, pain sec. (Of goods, etc.) 'To be kept dry,' "craint l'humidité." (d) (Of pers.) To be, feel, d., avoir le gosier sec; avoir soif. D. work, travail qui donne soif. (e) (Of wine) Sec, brut. Medium d., demi-sec. 2. F: D. country, pays "sec" (où les boissons alcooliques sont prohibées). These States are d., ces États ont le régime sec. 3. Aride; sans intérêt. A d. subject, un sujet aride. 4. (a) D. smile, sourire teinté d'ironie. D. humour, esprit caustique, mordant. A man of d. humour, un pince-sans-rire. (b) D. reception, accueil peu cordial. 5. U.S: D. goods, articles m de nouveauté; étoffes f, tissus m; mercerie f. -ly, adv. 1. D'un ton sec; sèchement. 2. Avec une pointe d'ironie contenue. 'dry-bulb, attrib. a. D.-bulb thermometer (of hygrometer), thermomètre à boule sèche; thermomètre sec. 'dry-'clean, v.tr. Nettoyer à sec; dégraisser (des vêtements). 'dry-'cleaning, s. Nettoyage m à sec; dégraissage m; F: pressing m. 'dry-'cleaner's, s. F: Pressing m. 'dry-'dock. 1. v.tr. Mettre (un navire) en cale sèche. 2. v.i. (Of ship) Entrer, passer, en cale sèche. 'dry-'eyed, a. To look on d.-e., regarder d'un œil sec. 'dry farming, s. Dry-farming m, culture f à sec. 'dry-foot(ed), a. & adv. A pied sec. 'dry-nurse[2], v.tr. 1. Élever (un enfant) au biberon. 2. F: Servir de mentor à (qn). 'dry-point, s. Engr: 1. Tls: Pointe sèche. 2. (Process or etched engraving) Gravure f à la pointe sèche; pointe-sèche f. 'dry-'rot, s. (a) Carie sèche, pourriture sèche (du bois). (b) F: Political d.-r., désintégration f. 'dry-'shod, a. & adv. A pied sec. 'dry(-)'wash, s. Dom.Ec: Blanchissage non-calandré, non-repassé.

dry[2], v. (dried [draid]; drying) 1. v.tr. Sécher (qch.); faire sécher (le linge). To d. sth. with a cloth, essuyer qch. avec un torchon. To d. (up) the dishes, essuyer la vaisselle, les plats. To d. one's eyes, s'essuyer les yeux. To d. one's tears, sécher ses larmes. Wind that dries (up) the skin, vent qui dessèche, ratatine, la peau. 2. v.i. (a) Sécher, se dessécher. To put sth. out to d., mettre qch. à sécher dehors. 2. Husb: (Of cow) Tarir; se sécher. dry off, dry out. 1. v.tr. Faire évaporer (l'eau, etc.); faire sécher (qch.). 2. v.i. (Of moisture) S'évaporer, se dessécher. dry up, v.i. 1. (Of well, pool) Se dessécher, (s')assécher, tarir. Little

dried-up man, petit homme sec. **2.** *F:* Cesser de parler. *P:* **D. up!** la ferme! **3.** *v.tr. Abs.* Essuyer la vaisselle. **dried**, *a.* Séché, desséché. **D. fruits**, fruits secs. **D. apples, pears**, pommes, poires, tapées. **D. eggs**, œufs *m* en poudre. **drying**, *s.* **1.** Séchage *m*; assèchement *m*, dessèchement *m*. (*With a cloth*) Essuyage *m. Ind:* Dessiccation *f.* **Spin.**, essorage *m. Ind:* **D. cupboard**, d. closet, étuve *f*; chambre chaude. **2. D. quality** (of a varnish), siccativité *f.*

dryad ['draiəd], *s.f. Myth:* Dryade.

dryer ['draiər], *s. Ind:* Séchoir *m*; dessiccateur *m.* **Centrifugal d.**, essoreuse *f* centrifuge. *Dom.Ec:* **Spin d.**, essoreuse. **2.** *Paint:* Siccatif *m.*

dryness ['drainis], *s.* **1.** Sécheresse *f*; aridité *f* (du sol). **2.** Sécheresse, sévérité *f* (de ton); aridité (d'un discours); causticité *f* (de l'esprit).

drysalter ['drai'sɔːltər], *s.* (*a*) Marchand *m* de conserves. (*b*) Marchand de couleurs; droguiste *m.*

D.T.'s ['diː'tiːz], *s.pl. F:* Delirium tremens.

dual ['djuː(ə)l], *s.* **1.** *a.* Double. *I.C.E:* **D. ignition**, double allumage. **D. tyres**, pneus jumelés. *Aut:* **D. carriage-way**, route *f* à double chaussée. *W.Tel:* **D. loud-speakers**, haut-parleurs accouplés. *Psy:* **D. personality**, dédoublement *m* de la personnalité. **2.** *a. & s. Gram:* **D.** (number), duel (*m*).

dub¹ [dʌb], *v.tr.* (**dubbed**) **1.** (*a*) **To d. s.o.** (a) **knight**, armer, adouber, qn chevalier; donner l'accolade à qn. (*b*) **To d. s.o. a quack**, qualifier qn de charlatan. **2.** *Leath:* Préparer (le cuir) avec le dégras.

dub², *v.tr. Cin:* Doubler (un film) en langue étrangère.

dubbing, *s. Cin:* Doublage *m*, transposition *f* (en langue étrangère).

dubbin ['dʌbin], *s. Leath:* Dégras *m.*

dubiety [djuː(ː)'baiəti], *s.* (Sentiment *m* de) doute *m*; incertitude *f* (**regarding**, à l'égard de).

dubious ['djuːbiəs], *a.* **1.** Douteux. (*a*) Incertain, vague. **D. result**, résultat incertain. (*b*) Équivoque, louche. **D. company**, compagnie douteuse, louche. **2.** Hésitant; qui doute. **D. expression**, air de doute. **-ly**, *adv.* D'un air ou d'un ton de doute.

dubiousness ['djuːbiəsnis], *s.* **1.** Incertitude *f* (du résultat, etc.). **2.** Caractère douteux, équivoque *f* (d'un compliment, etc.). **3.** = DUBIETY.

ducal ['djuːk(ə)l], *a.* Ducal, -aux; de duc.

duchess ['dʌtʃis], *s.f.* Duchesse.

duchy ['dʌtʃi], *s.* **1.** Duché *m.* **2. The Duchies**, les duchés de Cornouailles et de Lancastre.

duck¹ [dʌk], *s.* **1.** *Orn:* (*a*) (*Female of drake*) Cane *f.* (*b*) (*Generic*) Canard *m.* **Wild d.**, canard sauvage. **Mandarin d.**, canard mandarin. *Cu:* **D. and green peas**, canard aux petits pois. **To take to Latin like a d. to water**, mordre au latin. **To play at ducks and drakes**, faire des ricochets (sur l'eau). **To play ducks and drakes with one's money, with one's life**, jeter son argent par les fenêtres; gâcher sa vie. *F:* **That's like pouring water on a duck's back**, c'est comme si on chantait. **To behave like a dying d.** (in a thunderstorm), faire la carpe pâmée, faire des yeux de merlan frit. **2.** (*a*) *F:* **A lame d.**, (i) un malheureux; une malheureuse; (ii) un pauvre type. (*b*) *P:* **Duck(s)**, mon cher, ma chère. (*c*) *Cr:* Zero *m.* **To make a d.**, faire chou blanc. **3.** *Mil:* Véhicule *m* amphibie. **'duck-bill**, *s. Z:* Ornithor(h)ynque *m.* **'duck-boards**, *s.pl. Mil:* Caillebotis *m.* **'duck-gun**, *s. Sm.a:* Canardière *f.* **'duck(-)pond**, *s.* Canardière *f*, mare *f* aux canards, barbotière *f.* **'duck-shooting**, *s.* Chasse *f* aux canards (sauvages). **'duck-shot**, *s.* Plomb *m* à canard.

duck², *s. Tex:* Coutil *m*; toile fine (pour voiles). **D. trousers**, *pl.* **D: ducks**, pantalon blanc; pantalon de coutil, de toile. **The crew were in ducks**, l'équipage était en blanc.

duck³, *s.* **1.** Plongeon *m*, bain (inattendu ou involontaire). **2.** Mouvement instinctif de la tête (pour se dérober). *Box:* Esquive *f.*

duck⁴. **1.** *v.i.* (*a*) Plonger dans l'eau; faire le plongeon. (*Of water-fowl*) Replonger. (*b*) Baisser la tête, se baisser (subitement, instinctivement). *Box:* Esquiver de la tête. **2.** *v.tr.* (*a*) Plonger (qn) dans l'eau; faire faire le plongeon à (qn). (*b*) Baisser subitement (la tête). **ducking**, *s.* Plongeon *m* (involontaire); bain forcé. **To give s.o. a d.**, *F:* faire boire une tasse à qn.

duckling ['dʌkliŋ], *s. Orn:* Canardeau *m*; (*drake*) caneton *m*; (*duck*) canette *f.*

duckweed ['dʌkwiːd], *s. Bot:* Lentille *f* d'eau; lenticule *f.*

ducky ['dʌki]. **1.** *s. P:* (My) **d.**, mon petit chat, ma petite chatte; ma poupoule, ma cocotte; mon chou. **2.** *a. F:* Mignon, -onne: coquet, -ette.

duct [dʌkt], *s.* **1.** Conduit *m*, conduite *f*; caniveau *m*; *El.E:* canalisation *f* (pour câbles, etc.). **2.** *Anat:* Canal *m*, -aux; vaisseau *m*, voie *f.* **Auditory d.**, conduit auditif. **3.** *Bot:* Trachée *f*, canal.

ductile ['dʌktail], *a.* (*a*) Ductile; malléable. (*b*) **D. character**, caractère docile, malléable, souple.

ductility [dʌk'tiliti], *s.* (*a*) Ductilité *f*; malléabilité *f.* (*b*) Docilité *f*, souplesse *f* (de caractère).

ductless ['dʌktlis], *a. Anat:* **D. glands**, glandes closes, endocrines.

dud [dʌd]. *F:* **1.** *s.pl. O:* **Duds**, frusques *fpl*; nippes *fpl.* **2.** *s. & a.* (*a*) Incapable. **He's a d.**, (i) c'est un type nul; c'est un zéro. (ii) c'est un raté. (b) Mauvais; *P:* moche. *Artil:* **D.** (shell), obus qui a raté. **D. cheque**, chèque sans provision. **The note was a d.**, le billet était faux.

dude [djuːd], *s. U.S:* *F:* **1.** Gommeux *m*, poseur, -euse. **2.** Touriste venu des États de l'est (aux États Unis). **D. ranch**, ranch-hôtel *m* pour touristes.

dudgeon ['dʌdʒən], *s.* Colère *f*, ressentiment *m.* **In high d.**, fort en colère.

due¹ [djuː]. **1.** *a.* (*a*) (*Of debt*) Exigible; (*of bill*) échéant, échu. **Bill due on 1st May**, effet payable le premier mai. **The balance due to us**, le solde qui nous revient. **Balance d. to us** (from Mr Smith), redoit M. Smith. **Debts d. to us**, to the firm, dettes actives; créances *f.* **Debts d. by us**, by the firm, dettes passives. (*Of bill, etc.*) **To fall d.**, échoir; venir à (l')échéance. **When d.**, à l'échéance. *F:* **I'm a d. for a shampoo**, je suis bon pour un shampooing. (*b*) Dû, *f* due; juste, mérité. **It is d. to him to say . . .**, il n'est que juste envers lui de dire. . . . **With d. care**, avec tout le soin requis. **In d. form**, dans les formes voulues; en bonne forme; en règle; dans les règles. **After d. consideration**, après mûre réflexion; tout bien considéré. *S.a.* COURSE¹ 1, DEFERENCE, RESPECT¹ 3, TIME¹ 5. (*c*) (*In consequence of*) **D. to . . .**, dû à . . . ; occasionné, causé, par . . . ; attribuable à . . . **It is d. to him, to his negligence**, c'est lui, c'est sa négligence, qui en est (la) cause. **What is it d. to?** à quoi cela tient-il? *prep.phr. U.S: & F:* **D. to . . .**, par suite de . . ., à cause de. . . . (*d*) (*Expected*) **The train is d.** (to arrive), is d. in, at two o'clock, le train arrive à deux heures. **2.** *adv.* **D. north, east**, plein nord, plein est, droit vers le nord, vers l'est.

due², *s.* **1.** Dû *m.* **To give s.o. his d.**, donner à qn ce qui lui est dû, ce qui lui revient; rendre justice à qn. **To pay one's dues**, payer ce qu'on doit. **2.** *pl.* (*a*) Droits *mpl*, frais *mpl.* **Taxes and dues**, impôts *m* et taxes. *Nau:* **Port dues**, droits de port. (*b*) *U.S:* = SUBSCRIPTION 3.

duel¹ ['djuː(ː)əl], *s.* **1.** Duel *m*; affaire *f* d'honneur; rencontre *f.* **To fight a d.**, se battre en duel; aller sur le terrain. **2.** Lutte *f*, contestation *f.*

duel², *v.i.* (**duelled**) Se battre en duel. **duelling**, *s.* Le duel. *S.a.* PISTOL.

duellist ['djuː(ː)əlist], *s.* Duelliste *m.*

duenna [djuː(ː)'enə], *s.f.* Duègne.

duet [djuː(ː)'et], *s.* Duo *m.* (*for piano*) morceau *m* à quatre mains.

duettist [djuː(ː)'etist], *s.* Duettiste *mf.*

duffel, duffle ['dʌfl], *s.* **1.** Drap molletonné; molleton *m.* **2.** *U.S:* (*usu.* **duffle**) = KIT¹ 1. **'duffle-bag**, *s. Mil: etc:* = KIT-BAG 2. **'duffle-coat**, *s.* Duffel-coat *m*, duffle-coat *m.*

duffer ['dʌfər], *s. F: Sch: O:* Cancre *m*, croûte *f. Sp:* Maladroit, -oite; mazette *f.*

dug¹ [dʌg], *s.* (*a*) Mamelle *f* (d'un animal); pis *m* (de vache). (*b*) Trayon *m*, tétin *m.*

dug². See DIG².

dugong ['duːgɔŋ], *s. Z:* Dugong *m*, vache marine.

dug-out ['dʌgaut], *s.* **1.** Canot creusé dans un tronc d'arbre; pirogue *f.* **2.** *Mil:* Abri (blindé). **Deep d.-o.**, abri-caverne *m.*

duke [djuːk], *s.* Duc *m.*

dukedom ['dju:kdəm], *s.* **1.** Duché *m.* **2.** Dignité *f* de duc.

dulcet ['dʌlsit], *a. Lit:* (Son) doux, suave, agréable.

dulcify ['dʌlsifai], *v.tr.* Dulcifier; adoucir.

dulcimer ['dʌlsimər], *s. Mus:* Tympanon *m.*

dulcitone ['dʌlsitoun], *s. Mus:* Typophone *m.*

dull[1] [dʌl], *a.* **1.** (*Of pers.*) Lent, lourd; à l'esprit obtus, épais. **D.** sense of touch, d. hearing, toucher *m*, ouïe *f*, peu sensible. **To be d.** of sight, of hearing, avoir la vue faible; avoir l'oreille dure. *Sch:* The d. boys, les élèves peu brillants; *F:* les cancres *m.* **2.** (*a*) A **d. ache**, une douleur sourde. (*b*) (Bruit) sourd, étouffé, mat. **3.** *Com:* (Marché) calme, inactif, lourd, inanimé. **The d. season**, la morte-saison. **4.** (*Depressed*) Triste, morne, déprimé. **I feel d.**, je m'ennuie; j'ai le cafard. **In a d. mood**, maussade. **5.** Triste, ennuyeux, peu intéressant. **As d. as ditch-water**, ennuyeux comme un jour de pluie. **A deadly d. task**, une besogne abrutissante, assommante. **A thoroughly d. evening**, une soirée tout à fait assommante. **6.** (*Blunt*) Émoussé. (*Of tool, etc.*) To become **d.**, s'émousser. **7.** (*Of colour, surface*) Terne, mat. **D. eyes**, yeux morts, sans éclat. **A d. fire**, un feu triste; un pauvre feu. **8.** (*Of weather*) Lourd, triste, sombre. **-ly,** *adv.* **1.** Lourdement; ennuyeusement; tristement. **2.** Sourdement, faiblement; sans éclat. **'dull-'eyed,** *a.* Au regard terne. **'dull-'witted,** *a.* A l'esprit lourd, obtus, épais.

dull[2]. **I.** *v.tr.* **1.** (*a*) Hébéter (qn). (*b*) Alourdir, appesantir (l'esprit); émousser (les sens). **2.** Émousser (un outil). **3.** (*a*) Amortir, assourdir (le son); ternir (les couleurs, un miroir); dépolir (une surface); mater (un métal). (*b*) Amortir (une douleur); rendre moins vif (le plaisir). **II. dull,** *v.i.* **1.** (*Of senses, etc.*) S'engourdir, s'alourdir. **2.** (*Of colour*) Se ternir; (*of metal, etc.*) se dépolir.

dullard ['dʌləd], *s.* Lourdaud *m. Sch:* Cancre *m*, crétin *m.*

dul(l)ness ['dʌlnis], *s.* **1.** Lenteur *f*, pesanteur *f*, butorderie *f*, de l'esprit; épaisseur *f* de l'intelligence; abêtissement *m*; émoussement *m* (des sens). **D.** of hearing, dureté *f* d'oreille. **2.** Matité *f* (d'un son). **3.** Ennui *m*, tristesse *f*; monotonie *f.* **4.** *Com:* Stagnation *f*, marasme *m* (des affaires); peu *m* d'activité (du marché). **5.** Manque *m* de tranchant, de fil (d'une lame); émoussement *m* (d'une pointe, d'un tranchant). **6.** Manque d'éclat; faiblesse *f* (d'un son, d'une lumière); bruit sourd (d'un coup).

duly ['dju:li], *adv.* **1.** Dûment, justement; comme de juste; convenablement. **2.** En temps voulu; en temps utile.

dumb [dʌm], *a.* **1.** Muet, *f.* muette. **Deaf and d.**, sourd-muet, *f.* sourde-muette. **Born d.**, muet de naissance. *F:* **D. as a fish,** as an **oyster**, muet comme un poisson, comme une carpe. **D. animals**, les bêtes, les animaux. **To strike s.o. d.**, (i) frapper qn de mutisme; (ii) *F:* rendre qn muet; abasourdir, *F:* sidérer, qn. **In d. show**, pantomime *f*; jeu muet. **To act a scene in d. show**, mimer une scène. **2.** (*Wanting some essential detail*) **D. piano**, piano *m* sans cordes; clavier *m* (pour l'étude du doigté, etc.). *Nau:* **D.** craft, bateaux *mpl* sans voiles; chalands *mpl.* **3.** *F:* Sot, *f.* sotte. **D. blonde**, blonde évaporée. **-ly,** *adv.* Sans rien dire, sans mot dire; en silence. **'dumb(-)bell,** *s.* Haltère *m.* **D.-b. wielder**, haltérophile *m.* **D.-b. wielding**, haltérophilie *f.* **2.** *U.S: F:* Sot *m*, imbécile *m.* **'dumb-'waiter,** *s. Furn:* Servante *f*, desserte *f.* **2.** *U.S:* Monte-plats *m inv.*

dumbfound [dʌm'faund], *v.tr.* Abasourdir, stupéfier, ahurir, confondre, ébahir. **dumbfounded,** *a.* Abasourdi, ahuri. **I am d.**, je n'en reviens pas.

dumbness ['dʌmnis], *s.* **1.** Mutisme *m.* **2.** *F:* Silence *m.* **3.** *F:* Sottise *f*; bêtise *f*; niaiserie *f.*

dummy ['dʌmi], *s.* **1.** Homme *m* de paille; prête-nom *m inv.* **2.** (*a*) *Dressm: Tail:* Mannequin *m. Fb:* To give, sell, the **d.**, faire une feinte de passe. (*b*) *Com:* (*for window display*) Factice *m. Publ:* Maquette *f* (d'un livre). (*c*) (*Baby's*) **d.**, sucette *f*; tétine *f* sur anneau. **3.** *Cards:* Mort *m.* To be, play, **d.**, faire le mort. **D. bridge**, bridge à trois (personnes). **4.** *Attrib.* Postiche; faux, *f.* fausse. **D. cartridge**, fausse cartouche.

dump[1] [dʌmp], *s.* **1.** Coup sourd (d'une masse qui tombe). **2.** Tas *m*, amas *m* (de déchets, de déblais, de minerai, etc.). *Min:* Halde *f.* **3.** Chantier *m* de dépôt; dépôt *m* des déblais; (lieu *m* de) décharge *f. U.S:* **D. truck**, camion *m* à bascule, à benne basculante. (**Town**) **Council Rubbish D.**, décharge publique. **4.** Dépôt (de vivres, de munitions). *Mil:* **Ammunition d.**, parc *m* à munitions. **5.** *F:* **What a d.!** (i) (*of place*) quel trou! quel bled! (ii) (*of hotel, etc.*) etc.) quelle boîte!

dump[2], *v.tr.* **1.** (*a*) Décharger, déverser (une charretée de sable, de matériau). (*b*) **To d. (down)**, déposer, jeter, culbuter (qch.) (avec un bruit sourd); laisser tomber lourdement (un ballot, etc.). (*c*) Se défaire de (qch.). **2.** Faire un dépôt de (vivres, etc.). **3.** *Com:* **To d. goods on a foreign market**, faire du dumping.

dumping, *s.* **1.** (*a*) Déversement *m*, versage *m* (du contenu d'un chariot). (*b*) Dépôt *m.* **D.-ground**, (lieu *m* de) décharge *f*; déversement; (*for refuse*) dépotoir *m.* **2.** *Com:* Dumping *m.*

dumpling ['dʌmpliŋ], *s. Cu:* (*a*) Boulette (de pâte) (servie avec le bœuf bouilli, etc.). (*b*) **Apple d.**, pomme enrobée (cuite au four). *F:* **Little d.**, petit boulot (d'enfant).

dumps [dʌmps], *s.pl. F:* Cafard *m*; idées noires. **To be (down) in the d.**, to have the **d.**, broyer du noir; avoir le cafard.

dumpty ['dʌmpti], *s. Furn: F:* Pouf *m.*

dumpy ['dʌmpi]. **1.** *a.* Trapu; boulot, -otte; replet, -ète. **A d. little man**, un petit homme replet; un courtaud. **2.** *s.* (*a*) (*Umbrella*) Tom-pouce *m.* (*b*) *Furn: F:* Pouf *m.*

dun[1] [dʌn]. **1.** *a.* (*a*) Brun grisâtre. (*b*) *Poet:* Sombre, obscur. **2.** *a. & s.* (Cheval) gris louvet. **Yellow-d.**, bai doré; louvet.

dun[2], *s.* **1.** (*a*) Créancier importun. (*b*) Agent *m* de recouvrement (de dettes). **2.** Demande pressante (de payement).

dun[3], *v.tr.* (**dunned**) Importuner, harceler, relancer (un débiteur). **To be dunned on all sides**, être accablé de dettes criardes.

dunce [dʌns], *s.* Ignorant, -ante; *F:* crétin, -ine; âne *m. Sch: F:* Cancre *m*, crétin. **D.'s cap**, bonnet *m* d'âne.

dunderhead ['dʌndəhed], *s. F:* (*a*) Lourdaud, -aude. (*b*) Imbécile *mf.*

dune [dju:n], *s.* (Sand-)d., dune *f.*

dung[1] [dʌŋ], *s.* **1.** Fiente *f*, crotte *f*; bouse *f* (de vache); crottin *m* (de cheval). **2.** *Agr:* Fumier *m*, engrais *m.* **'dung-beetle,** *s. Ent:* Bousier *m.*

dung[2]. **1.** *v.tr. Agr:* Fumer (un champ). **2.** *v.i.* (*Of animal*) Bouser.

dungaree ['dʌŋgə'ri:], *s.* **1.** Tissu de coton grossier (de l'Inde); cotonnade *f*, treillis *m.* **2.** *pl. Ind:* **Dungarees**, combinaison *f*, *F:* salopette *f*; bleus *mpl* (de mécanicien). *Mil:* (Jeu *m* de) treillis.

dungeon ['dʌn(d)ʒ(ə)n], *s.* Cachot *m* (d'un château du moyen âge).

dunghill ['dʌŋhil], *s.* Tas *m* de fumier; fumier *m. S.a.* COCK[1] 1.

dunk [dʌŋk], *v.tr. esp. U.S: F:* To d. (a doughnut, etc.), tremper (= une brioche, etc.). *Abs. F:* Faire la trempette.

Dunkirk [dʌn'kə:k]. *Pr.n. Geog:* Dunkerque.

dunlin ['dʌnlin], *s. Orn:* Bécasseau *m* variable; alouette *f* de mer.

duo [dju:ou], *s. Mus:* = DUET.

duodecimal [dju(:)o'desim(ə)l], *a.* Duodécimal, -aux.

duodecimo [dju(:)o'desimou], *s. Typ:* In-douze *m inv.*

duodenal [dju(:)o'di:n(ə)l], *a.* Duodénal, -aux. **D. ulcer**, ulcère au duodénum.

duodenitis [dju:odn'aitis], *s. Med:* Duodénite *f.*

duodenum [dju(:)o'di:nəm], *s.* Duodénum *m.*

duopoly [dju'ɔpəli], *s. Pol:* Duopole *m.*

dupe[1] [dju:p], *s.* Dupe *f.*

dupe[2], *v.tr.* Duper, tromper.

dupery ['dju:pəri], *s.* Duperie *f.*

duple ['dju:pl], *a. Mus:* **D. time**, mesure *f* à deux temps; mesure binaire.

duplex[1] ['dju:pleks], *a.* Double. **D. pump**, pompe duplex *inv.* jumelle. **D. telegraphy**, télégraphie duplex. *U.S:* **D. (house)**, pavillon *m*, maison *f*, pour deux familles. **D. apartment**, appartement *m* à deux étages.

duplex², *v.tr.* **1.** Doubler. **2.** *W.Tel: etc:* Duplexer, dupliquer.
duplicate¹ ['djuplikit]. **1.** *a.* Double. D. **parts**, pièces de rechange. **2.** *s.* (*a*) *Tel:* receipt, reçu en duplicata. **2.** *s.* (*a*) Double *m*, répétition *f* (d'une œuvre d'art, etc.). (*b*) Duplicata *m* (d'un chèque égaré, etc.); double, contre-partie *f* (d'un écrit); ampliation *f* (d'un acte). **In d.**, en, par, duplicata; en double exemplaire, en double expédition. (*c*) Reconnaissance *f* (de prêteur sur gages).
duplicate² ['djuplikeit], *v.tr.* (*a*) Faire le double de (qch.); reproduire (un document) en double exemplaire. (*b*) Tirer un certain nombre de copies (d'un document) au duplicateur. **duplicating**, *s.* **1.** Duplication *f*. **2.** Reproduction *f* au duplicateur. '**duplicating-book**, *s.* Manifold *m*. '**duplicating-machine**, *s.* Duplicateur *m*.
duplication [,dju:pli'keiʃ(ə)n], *s.* **1.** Duplication *f*, reproduction *f*. **2.** *Opt:* Dédoublement *m*.
duplicator ['dju:plikeitər], *s.* *Typewr: etc:* Duplicateur *m*.
duplicity [dju'plisiti], *s.* Duplicité *f*; mauvaise foi.
durability [,djuərə'biliti], **durableness** ['djuərəblnis], *s.* Durabilité *f*; durée *f* (d'une étoffe); stabilité *f* (d'une administration).
durable ['djuərəbl], *a.* Durable; résistant.
duralumin [djuə'ræljumin], **duraluminium** [djuə,ræl-ju'minjəm], *s.* *R.t.m:* *Metall:* Duralumin *m*.
duramen [djuə'reimən], *s.* Duramen *m*; cœur *m* du bois.
duration [dju'reiʃ(ə)n], *s.* Durée *f*; étendue *f* (de la vie).
duress [djuə'res], *s.* **1.** Emprisonnement *m*. **2.** *Jur:* Contrainte *f*, violence *f*. **To act under d.**, agir à son corps défendant; céder à la force.
during ['djuəriŋ], *prep.* Pendant, durant. **D. his life**, pendant (toute) sa vie; sa vie durant. **D. the winter**, au cours de l'hiver. **D. that time**, (i) pendant ce temps; (ii) sur ces entrefaites.
durst. *See* DARE.
dusk [dʌsk]. **1.** *a.* It is growing d., la nuit tombe. **2.** *s.* (*a*) Obscurité *f*, ténèbres *fpl*. (*b*) Crépuscule *m*; *Fr.C:* brunante *f*. **At d.**, à la brune, à la nuit tombante; entre chien et loup.
duskiness ['dʌskinis], *s.* **1.** Obscurité *f*. **2.** (*Of complexion*) Teint brun, bistré. (*b*) Teint noiraud.
dusky ['dʌski], *a.* **1.** Sombre, obscur. **2.** (*a*) (*Of complexion*) Brun foncé *inv*; bistré. (*b*) Noirâtre; (*of pers.*) noiraud, moricaud.
dust¹ [dʌst], *s.* **1.** Poussière *f*. **To raise the d.**, faire de la poussière. **To cover with d.**, empoussiérer. **To reduce sth. to d.**, mettre, réduire, qch. en poussière. *Lit:* **To bite the d.**, mordre la poussière. *F:* **To throw d. in s.o.'s eyes**, jeter de la poudre aux yeux de qn. *F:* **To kick up a d.**, **to raise a d.**, faire une scène; *P:* faire du barouf. **Marble d.**, sciure *f* de marbre. **2.** Cendres *fpl* (d'un mort). **Ashes to ashes, d. to d.**, cendres aux cendres, poudre à la poudre. '**dust-bath**, *s.* (*Of bird*) To take a dust-bath, faire la poudrette. '**dust(-)bowl**, *s.* *Geog:* Région dénudée, zone *f* semi-aride, semi-désertique. '**dust-cart**, *s.* Tombereau *m* aux ordures; voiture *f* de boueur. '**dust-coloured**, *a.* Cendré. '**dust-cover**, '**dust-jacket**, '**dust-wrapper**, *s.* Bookb: protège-livre *m*; liseuse *f*; jaquette *f*. **To put a d.-c. on a book**, enchemiser, recouvrir, un livre. '**dust-destructor**, *s.* Incinérateur *m* d'ordures. '**dust(-)devil**, *s.* Tourbillon *m* de poussière. '**dust-proof**, *a.* Étanche, imperméable (à la poussière). '**dust-sheet**, *s.* Toile *f* de protection contre la poussière; housse *f*. '**dust-shoot**, *s.* Lieu *m* de décharge; dépotoir *m*. '**dust-shot**, *s.* *Sm.a.:* Cendrée *f*; petit plomb. '**dust-trap**, *s.* Nid *m* à poussière.
dust², *v.tr.* **1.** (*a*) Saupoudrer (un gâteau, etc.) (**with**, de). (*b*) *Metall:* Tamponner (un moule, etc.). **2.** Épousseter (une pièce, un meuble). *v.i.* (*Of bird*) S'ébrouer dans la poussière, faire la poudrette. **dusting**, *s.* **1.** (*a*) Saupoudrage *m*; *Phot:* poudrage *m*. (*b*) *Metall:* Tamponnement *m*. **2.** (*a*) Époussetage *m*. (*b*) *F:* Frottée *f*, raclée *f*, tripotée *f*. **3.** *Nau:* *F:* Gros temps; *F:* coup *m* de tabac. '**dust-up**, *s.* **1.** Querelle *f*; *F:* prise *f* de bec. **2.** *Sp:* Pointe *f* de vitesse.

dustbin ['dʌs(t)bin], *s.* **1.** Poubelle *f*, boîte *f* ou bac *m* à ordures (ménagères). **2.** *Av:* *F:* Tourelle de mitrailleuse intérieure, *F:* baignoire *f*.
dust cloth ['dʌstklɔθ], *s.* *U.S:* **1.** = DUSTER. **2.** = DUST-SHEET.
duster ['dʌstər], *s.* Chiffon *m* (à épousseter); torchon *m*. **Feather d.**, plumeau *m*, époussette *f*. *Sch:* Board d., torchon *m*.
dustman, *pl.* **-men** ['dʌs(t)mən, -mən], *s.m.* Boueur, boueux.
dustpan ['dʌstpæn], *s.* Pelle *f* à main; ramasse-poussière *m inv*.
dusty ['dʌsti], *a.* **1.** Poussiéreux, poudreux; empoussiéré: recouvert de poussière. **2.** Aride; dépourvu d'intérêt. **3.** *F:* *O:* It's not so d., ce n'est pas si mauvais; *F:* c'est pas si moche; *F:* c'est pas mal du tout. **4.** To get a d. answer, éprouver une désillusion. '**dusty-'miller**, *s.* *Bot:* Auricule *f*.
Dutch [dʌtʃ]. **1.** *a.* Hollandais; de Hollande. The D. Government, le Gouvernement néerlandais. D. cheese, fromage de Hollande; tête-de-Maure, -More, -mort. *F:* D. courage, bravoure après boire; courage puisé dans la bouteille. D. treat, partie *f* de plaisir, régal *m*, où chacun paye son écot. *adv.* To go d., payer chacun son écot. *S.a.* UNCLE. **2.** *s.* (*a*) The D. (people), les Hollandais. (*b*) *Ling:* Le hollandais.
Dutchman, *pl.* **-men** ['dʌtʃmən, -mən], *s.* **1.** Hollandais *m*. **2.** (*a*) *U.S:* Américain de souche allemande. (*b*) *Nau:* Matelot étranger.
dutiable ['dju:tiəbl], *a.* (*Of goods*) Soumis aux droits de douane; taxable.
dutiful ['dju:tif(u)l], *a.* (*Of child, etc.*) Respectueux, soumis. A. d. husband, un mari plein d'égards pour sa femme. **-fully**, *adv.* Avec soumission; suivant son devoir.
dutifulness ['dju:tif(u)lnis], *s.* Obéissance *f*, soumission *f*.
duty ['dju:ti], *s.* **1.** Obéissance *f*, respect *m*. **To pay one's d. to s.o.**, présenter ses respects, ses hommages, à qn. **2.** Devoir *m* (to, envers). **To do one's d.**, s'acquitter de son devoir; faire son devoir. **Do your d. come what may**, fais ce que dois, advienne que pourra. **I shall make it my d.**, a point of d., to help him, je prendrai à tâche de l'aider. **As in d. bound**, comme il est de mon devoir. *S.a.* BOUND⁶ 2. **From a sense of d.**, par devoir. **To pay a d call¹**, faire une visite obligée, une visite de politesse. (*Of mutineer, etc.*) **To return to d.**, rentrer dans le devoir. *F:* **Have you done your d.?** as-tu fait caca? **3.** Fonction(s) *f(pl)*, tâche *f*. **Public duties**, fonctions publiques. **Duties of various officials**, attributions *fpl* de divers fonctionnaires. **To enter upon, take up, one's duties**, entrer en fonctions, en charge. **To do d. for s.o.**, remplacer qn. **4.** *Mil: etc:* Service *m*. **To be on d.**, être de service, de garde *f*; *Nau:* être de quart *m*. **To be on sentry d.**, être en faction *f*. *Navy:* D. men, hommes de corvée. *Sch:* **To be on d. for the day**, être de jour. **To do dinner d.**, surveiller le réfectoire. **5.** Droit *m*. (*a*) Customs d., droit(s) de douane. **Liable to d.**, passible de droits; soumis aux droits. **D. paid**, franc de douane. (*b*) Stamp duties, droit de timbre. **6.** *Mec.E:* Heavy-d. engine, machine de grande puissance. '**duty-'free**, *a.* *Cust:* Exempt de droits; (importé) en franchise; non tarifé.
duvetyn ['dju:və'ti:n], *s.* *Tex:* *R.t.m:* Duvetine *f*.
dwarf¹ [dwɔ:f], *s. & a.* Nain, -e; nabot, -cte; (*of plant*) (i) nain; (ii) rabougri.
dwarf², *v.tr.* **1.** Empêcher de croître; rabougrir ou naniser (une plante). **2.** Rapetisser (par contraste).
dwarfish ['dwɔ:fiʃ], *a.* (De) nain; chétif, (*of pers.*) nabot, -ote.
dwell [dwel], *v.i.* (**dwelt**; **dwelt**) **1.** *Lit:* To d. **in a place**, habiter (dans) un lieu; demeurer, résider, dans un lieu. **2.** Rester; se fixer; être fixé. Her memory dwells with me, son souvenir reste présent à ma mémoire. **3.** **To d. on sth.**, s'étendre sur, s'appesantir sur (un sujet); appuyer sur (une syllabe). **We will not d. on that**, glissons là-dessus. *Mus:* **To d. on a note**, appuyer (sur) une note. **dwelling**, *s.* **1.** (*a*) Séjour *m*, résidence *f* (dans un endroit). (*b*) Insistance *f* (sur un fait). **2.** Lieu *m* de séjour; logis *m*, demeure *f*. '**dwelling-house**, *s.* Maison *f* d'habitation. '**dwelling-place**, *s.* Demeure *f*, résidence *f*.

dweller ['dwelər], s. Habitant, -ante (in, on, de).
dwindle ['dwindl], v.i. To d. (away), diminuer, dépérir, s'affaiblir. dwindling, s. Diminution f, dépérissement m, affaiblissement m.
dye¹ [dai], s. 1. (a) Dy: Teinture f, teint m. Fast d., bon teint, grand teint. (b) Teinte f. Lit: O: Villain of the deepest d., coquin fieffé; triple coquin. 2. Matière colorante; teinture, colorant m. 'dyeworks, s. Teinturerie f.
dye², v.tr. (a) Teindre. To d. sth. black, teindre qch. en noir. To have a dress dyed, faire teindre une robe. (b) Teinter (un film, etc.). (c) v.i. Material that dyes well, tissu qui prend bien la teinture. S.a. wool 1. dyeing, s. 1. (a) Teinture f (d'étoffes, des cheveux). (b) Teintage m. 2. D.(-trade), la teinturerie.
dyer ['daiər], s. Teinturier m. Bot: D.'s moss, orseille f. D.'s (green)weed, (réséda m) gaude (f).
dying. See DIE².
dyke¹ [daik], s. 1. (a) Digue f, levée f. (b) Chaussée surélevée. 2. Fossé m. 3. Geol: Dyke m, filon m d'injection. 4. Esp.Scot: Dry(-stone)d., muraillon m.
dyke², v.tr. 1. Endiguer (un terrain, un fleuve). 2. Drainer (un terrain en faisant des fossés).
dynamic [dai'næmik], a. Dynamique. D. personality, caractère énergique.
dynamics [dai'næmiks], s.pl. Dynamique f.

dynamism ['dainəmizm], s. Dynamisme m.
dynamist ['dainəmist], s. Dynamiste m.
dynamite¹]'dainəmait], s. Dynamite f. D. factory, dynamiterie f.
dynamite², v.tr. Faire sauter (des roches, etc.) à la dynamite; dynamiter (un édifice).
dynamiter ['dainəmaitər], s. Dynamiteur m.
dynamo, pl. -os ['dainəmou, -ouz], s. Dynamo f; génératrice f, générateur m (de courant). 'dynamo-e'lectric, a. Dynamo-électrique.
dynamograph ['dainəmogræf], s. Dynamographe m.
dynamometer [,dainə'momitər], s. Dynamomètre m. Recording d., dynamographe m.
dynast ['dinəst], s. Dynaste m.
dynastic [di'næstik], a. Dynastique.
dynasty ['dinəsti], s. Dynastie f.
dyne [dain], s. Ph.Meas: Dyne f. A million dynes, mégadyne f.
dysenteric [,disn'terik], a. Med: Dysentérique.
dysentery ['disntri], s. Dysenterie f.
dysmenorrhœa [,dismenə'riə], s. Med: Dysménorrhée f.
dyspepsia [dis'pepsiə], s. Med: Dyspepsie f, apepsie f.
dyspeptic [dis'peptik], a. & s. Dyspepsique (mf). dyspeptique (mf).
dyspnoea [dis'pni(:)ə], s. Med: Dyspnée f.

E, e [i:], s. **1.** (La lettre) E, e m. Tp: E for Edward, E comme Eugène. **2.** Mus: Mi m. Key of E flat, clef de mi bémol.

each [i:tʃ]. **1.** a. Chaque. **E. man,** chaque homme. E. **day,** chaque jour; tous les jours. E. **one of us,** chacun, chacune, de nous, d'entre nous. **2.** pron. (a) Chacun, -une. E. **of us,** chacun de nous; chacun d'entre nous. (b) **We e. earn one pound, we earn one pound e.,** nous gagnons une livre chacun. **Peaches that cost a shilling e.,** pêches qui coûtent un shilling chacune, un shilling pièce. **Three groups of ten men e.,** trois groupes de chacun dix hommes. (c) **E. other,** l'un à l'autre, les uns les autres. **For e. other,** l'un pour l'autre. **Separated from e. other,** séparés l'un de l'autre. **To strike against e. other,** s'entrechoquer.

eager ['i:gər], a. (a) Ardent, passionné. **E. for gain,** âpre au gain. **E. for, after, fame,** avide, assoiffé, de gloire. **E. in pursuit of the enemy,** ardent à poursuivre l'ennemi. **To be e. to do sth.,** être impatient de faire qch.; désirer ardemment faire qch.; F: brûler de faire qch. **To be e. for sth.,** ambitionner qch.; désirer ardemment qch. (b) **E. glance,** œillade avide. **E. pursuit,** âpre poursuite. **E. desire,** vif désir. **-ly,** adv. Ardemment, passionnément, avidement.

eagerness ['i:gənis], s. Ardeur f; impatience f; empressement m; vif désir. **E. for praise,** soif f d'éloges.

eagle [i:gl], s. **1.** Orn: Aigle mf. **Golden e.,** aigle royal. **2.** Her: Aigle f. **3.** Ecc: (Lectern) Aigle m. **4.** (a) **The Roman Eagles,** les aigles romaines. (b) Fr.Hist: **The Imperial E.,** le drapeau impérial; l'aigle impériale. **5.** U.S: (= 10 dollars) Aigle m. **'eagle-eyed,** a. Aux yeux d'aigle; au regard d'aigle.

eaglet ['i:glit], s. **1.** Aiglon m. **2.** Her: Aiglette f.

eagre ['eigər, 'i:gər], s. = BORE³.

ear¹ [iər], s. **1.** Oreille f. Med: **E. specialist,** auriste m. **To wear rings in one's ears,** porter des anneaux aux oreilles. **Your ears must have burned, must have been tingling,** les oreilles ont dû vous corner, vous tinter. **Up to the ears,** jusqu'au cou. F: **To be up to the ears, over head and ears, in work,** être accablé, débordé, de travail; avoir du travail par-dessus la tête. S.a. DEBT, LOVE¹ 1. **To set people by the ears,** brouiller les gens; mettre des personnes aux prises. F: **To send s.o. away with a flea in his e.,** (i) renvoyer qn avec un refus net et catégorique; (ii) éconduire qn avec une verte semonce; lui dire ses quatre vérités. **He went off with a flea in his e.,** il est parti l'oreille basse, tout penaud. P: **To give s.o. a thick e.,** flanquer une gifle à qn. S.a. BOX¹ 1. Prov: **Walls have ears,** les murs ont des oreilles. **To have sharp ears,** avoir l'oreille, l'ouïe, fine. F: **To be all ears,** être tout ouïe, tout oreilles. **To have an e., a fine e., for music;** to have a good e., avoir l'oreille musicienne, juste; avoir de l'oreille. **To play by e.,** jouer d'instinct. **To keep one's ears open,** être, se tenir, aux écoutes. **To have s.o.'s e.,** avoir, posséder, l'oreille de qn. **To gain s.o.'s e.,** s'assurer l'attention bienveillante de qn. **To give ear, lend an e., lend one's e., to s.o.,** prêter l'oreille à qn. **To close one's ears to the truth,** fermer l'oreille à la vérité. **If it should come to the ears of . . .,** si cela parvient aux oreilles de. . . . S.a. DEAF. **2.** Tchn: Anse f, oreille (de vase); anse (de cloche); orillon m (d'une écuelle, etc.). **'ear(-)ache,** s. Mal m, maux mpl, d'oreille(s); Med: otalgie f. **To have e.-a.,** avoir mal à l'oreille, aux oreilles. **'ear-drop,** s. Pendant m d'oreille; pendeloque f. **'ear-drum,** s. (Caisse f du) tympan m. **'ear-flap,** s. **1.** Lobe m de l'oreille. **2.** Oreillette f (de casquette). **'ear-mark¹,** s. **1.** Husb: Marque à l'oreille (à laquelle on reconnaît les moutons). **2.** Marque particulière, distinctive. **'ear-mark²,** v.tr. **1.** Husb: Marquer (les moutons, etc.) à l'oreille. **2.** **To e.-m. funds,** spécialiser des fonds. **To e.-m. funds for a purpose,** assigner, affecter, des fonds à un projet. **'ear-pendant,** s. Pendant m d'oreille. **'ear-phone,** s. W.Tel: = HEAD-PHONE. **'ear-piece,**

s. Tp: Écouteur m, pavillon m (de récepteur). **'ear-plug,** s. Protège-tympan m. inv. **'ear-ring,** s. Boucle f d'oreille. **Stud e.-r.,** dormeuse f. **'ear-shields,** s. pl. Fb: Pare-oreilles m. **'ear-shot,** s. **Within e.-s.,** à portée de voix, de l'ouïe. **Out of e.-s.,** hors de portée de la voix. **'ear-splitting,** a. (Cri) qui vous fend les oreilles. **E.-s. noise,** bruit à briser le tympan, à fendre la tête. **'ear-trumpet,** s. Cornet m acoustique. **'ear-wax,** s. Physiol: Cérumen m.

ear², s. Épi m (de blé, de maïs). **Wheat in the e.,** blé en épi.

ear³, v.i. (Of corn) Monter en épi; épier. **eared,** a. À épis. **E. corn, wheat,** blé en épi; blé épié. **Full-eared,** à épis pleins.

earl [ə:l], s. (f. countess, q.v.) Comte m.

earldom ['ə:ldəm], s. Comté m; titre m de comte.

earliness ['ə:linis], s. **1.** (a) Heure peu avancée (du jour). (b) Heure prématurée (de la mort de qn). **2.** Précocité f (d'un fruit).

early ['ə:li]. I. a. (earlier, earliest) **1.** Qui appartient au commencement (du jour, de l'année, de la vie). (a) **The e. cock,** le coq matinal. **In the e. morning,** de bon matin; de grand matin. **In the e. afternoon,** au commencement de l'après-midi. **To have an e. dinner,** dîner de bonne heure. **To be an e. riser,** F: **an e. bird,** être (un) matineux; être toujours matinal; se lever (de bon) matin. S.a. BIRD 1. **To keep e. hours,** se coucher tôt (et se lever tôt). **A cold morning in e. spring,** une froide matinée du début du printemps. **During the earlier months of the year,** pendant les premiers mois de l'année. Com: **E. closing day,** jour où les magasins sont fermés l'après-midi. **It is e. days yet to make up one's mind,** il est encore trop tôt pour se décider. (b) **The earliest times,** les temps les plus reculés. **The e. Church,** l'Église primitive. **In the e. nineteenth century,** au début du dix-neuvième siècle. **In e. days,** (i) dans l'ancien temps; (ii) de bonne heure (dans le passé). **At an e. date,** de bonne heure (dans le passé). (Cp. 3.) Hist. of Art: **The e. masters,** les primitifs. (c) **E. youth,** première jeunesse. **In his earliest youth,** dans sa prime jeunesse. **E. age,** âge tendre, bas âge, premier âge. **At an e. age,** tout jeune; dès l'enfance. **My earliest recollections,** mes souvenirs les plus lointains. **2.** Précoce, hâtif. **E. death,** mort prématurée. **E. beans,** (i) haricots précoces, hâtifs; (ii) haricots de primeur. **E. vegetables, e. fruit, e. produce,** primeurs fpl. **3.** Prochain, rapproché. **At an e. date,** prochainement; sous peu; bientôt. Cp. 1 (b). **At an earlier date,** (i) à une date antérieure; (ii) à une date plus rapprochée. **At the earliest possible moment,** dans le plus bref délai possible; au plus tôt. S.a. CONVENIENCE 1. II. **early,** adv. **1.** (a) De bonne heure; tôt. **Earlier, de meilleure heure; plus tôt. Earlier than . . .,** avant. . . . **Too e.,** trop tôt; de trop bonne heure. **I am half an hour e.,** je suis en avance d'une demi-heure. **Too e. in the morning,** trop matin. **E. in the morning,** le matin de bonne heure; de grand matin. **It was e. in the afternoon,** c'était au commencement de l'après-midi. **E. in the evening,** très tôt dans la soirée. **To rise e.,** se lever de bonne heure; être matineux. **E. enough,** à temps. **E. in the winter,** dans, dès, les premiers jours de l'hiver; à l'entrée de l'hiver. **E. in the year,** au commencement, au début, de l'année. **E. in (his) life,** dans ses jeunes années; dans sa jeunesse. **E. in his career,** au début de sa carrière. **As e. as the tenth century,** dès le dixième siècle. **As e. as possible,** le plus tôt possible. (b) **To die e.,** (i) mourir jeune; (ii) mourir prématurément. **2.** **E. in the list,** tout au commencement de la liste.

earn [ə:n], v.tr. **1.** Gagner (de l'argent). **To e. one's living by writing,** gagner sa vie à écrire, en écrivant. **2.** Mériter, gagner (des éloges, l'affection de qn).

earnest¹ ['ə:nist]. **1.** a. (a) (Of pers.) Sérieux. **E. worker,** ouvrier consciencieux. (b) **An e. Christian,** un chrétien sincère et convaincu. (c) **E. request, E. prayer,** prière fervente. **E.**

effort, sérieux effort; effort soutenu. 2. *s.* In e., sérieusement; pour de bon. To be in e., être sérieux; ne pas plaisanter. It is raining in real e., il pleut pour (tout) de bon. He is very much in e., (i) il est terriblement convaincu; (ii) il prend son rôle à cœur. *S.a.* DEAD I. 5. -ly, *adv.* (Parler) sérieusement, d'un ton convaincu, d'un ton sérieux; (travailler) de bon cœur, avec ardeur, avec zèle. To entreat s.o. e., prier qn instamment.

earnest², *s.* 1. *Com: etc:* Arrhes *fpl.* E. money, dépôt *m* de garantie; arrhes. 2. Gage *m*, garantie *f*.

earnestness ['əːnistnis], *s.* Gravité *f*, sérieux *m* (de ton); ardeur *f*, ferveur *f* (d'une prière).

earnings ['əːniŋz], *s.pl.* 1. Fruit *m* du travail; salaire *m*, gages *mpl.* 2. Profits *mpl*, bénéfices *mpl* (d'une entreprise).

earth¹ [əːθ], *s.* 1. Terre *f.* (*a*) Le monde; le globe terrestre. He is just back from the ends of the e., il revient du bout du monde. On e., sur terre. *F:* Where on e. have you been? où diable étiez-vous? Why on e. . . . .? pourquoi diable . . .? (*b*) Le sol. *F:* To come back to e., retomber des nues; sortir de sa rêverie. Down to e., terre à terre; réaliste, *F:* qui a les pieds sur terre. *Mil:* Scorched e. policy, tactique de la terre brûlée. 2. (*a*) To till the e., cultiver la terre. Heavy e., terre(s) grasse(s); terroir gras. (*b*) Alkaline earths, terres alcalines. 3. *El.E:* Terre. E. cable, câble de terre; prise de terre; (*in engine, car, etc.*) fil de masse. E. leakage, perte à la terre. E. to frame (*of a car, etc.*), contact *m* à la masse. 4. Terrier *m*, tanière *f* (de renard). (*Of fox*) To go to e., se terrer. To run to e., (i) chasser (un renard) jusqu'à son terrier; dépister (le gibier); (ii) découvrir la source, l'origine (d'une citation, d'une erreur de calcul, etc.); dépister, dénicher (qn); découvrir la retraite de (qn). '**earth-bound**, *a.* (*a*) Terre à terre *inv.* (*b*) (Fantôme) qui ne peut pas quitter le monde des vivants. (*c*) qui se dirige vers la terre. '**earth-closet**, *s.* *Hyg:* Cabinets *mpl.* '**earth-nut**, *s.* *Bot:* Arachide *f.*

earth². 1. *v.tr.* (*a*) *Hort:* To e. (up), butter, terrer (une plante). (*b*) *El:* Mettre à la terre; (*in car*) mettre à la masse. 2. *v.i.* *Ven:* (*Of fox*) Se terrer.

earthen ['əːθ(ə)n], *a.* De terre, en argile cuite.

earthenware ['əːθ(ə)nwɛər], *s.* Poterie *f* (de terre); argile cuite. Glazed e., (i) faïence *f*; (ii) grès flambé.

earthliness ['əːθlinis], *s.* 1. Caractère *m* terrestre. 2. Attachement *m* aux choses de ce monde.

earthly ['əːθli], *a.* 1. Terrestre. 2. *F:* There is no e. reason for . . ., il n'y a pas la moindre raison (du monde) pour. . . . For no e. reason, à propos de rien; à propos de bottes. He hasn't an e. chance, *P:* an e., il n'a pas la moindre chance, pas l'ombre d'une chance (de réussir). 3. E.-minded, attaché aux choses de ce monde; terre à terre *inv.*

earthquake ['əːθkweik], *s.* 1. Tremblement *m* de terre; séisme *m.* 2. Convulsion *f*, bouleversement *m* (politique, etc.).

earthward ['əːθwəd], *adv.* Vers la terre.

earthwork ['əːθwəːk], *s.* 1. (Travaux *mpl* de) terrassement *m.* 2. *pl.* *Civ.E:* Earthworks, travaux en terre.

earthworm ['əːθwəːm], *s.* *Ann:* Lombric *m*; ver *m* de terre.

earthy ['əːθi], *a.* 1. Terreux. E. taste, goût de terre. 2. (*Of pers.*) Matériel, grossier; terre à terre *inv.*

earwig ['iəwig], *s.* *Ent:* Forficule *f*, perce-oreille *m.*

ease¹ [iːz], *s.* 1. (*a*) Tranquillité *f* (d'esprit); repos *m*, bien-être *m*, aise *f* (du corps). To be at e., avoir l'esprit tranquille. *S.a.* ILL III. 3. To be at one's e., (i) être à son aise; (ii) être tranquille. To set s.o. at e., (i) mettre qn à son aise; (ii) tranquilliser qn. To set s.o.'s mind at e., tirer qn de son inquiétude. To take one's e., prendre ses aises. *Mil:* To stand at e., se mettre, se tenir, au repos. Stand at ease! repos! (*b*) E. from pain, adoucissement *m* de douleur; soulagement *m.* *S.a.* CHAPEL. 2. (*a*) Loisir *m.* (*b*) Oisiveté *f.* To live a life of e., vivre dans l'oisiveté, vivre une vie de loisirs. 3. (*a*) Aisance *f* (de manières, etc.); moelleux *m* (des mouvements). (*b*) Simplicité *f* (de réglage); douceur *f*, facilité *f* (de manœuvre). With e., facilement; aisément; avec aisance.

ease², *v.tr.* (*a*) Adoucir, calmer, alléger, atténuer (la souffrance); soulager (un malade). *v.i.* The pain has

eased, la douleur s'est atténuée. (*b*) Calmer, tranquilliser (l'esprit). 2. Débarrasser, délivrer (s.o. of, from, sth., qn de qch.). To e. oneself of a burden, se soulager d'un fardeau. *F:* To e. s.o. of his purse, soulager qn de son porte-monnaie. 3. (*a*) Détendre, relâcher, soulager (un cordage, un ressort); desserrer (une vis); *Nau:* mollir (une manœuvre); *Mch:* modérer, soulager (la pression); ralentir (la vitesse). To e. (the strain on) a girder, alléger, soulager, une poutre. *Nau:* E. the engines! lentement la machine! To e. the helm (down), mettre moins de barre; *Row:* E. all! stop(pe)! (*b*) *Dressm:* Donner plus d'ampleur à (une robe, etc.). ease off. 1. *v.tr.* (*a*) *Nau:* Filer, choquer (un cordage). (*b*) Dégager (une surface). 2. *v.i.* (*a*) = EASE UP 2 (*a*). (*b*) *Nau:* S'éloigner un peu du rivage. ease up. 1. *v.tr.* *Nau:* Soulager (un palan). 2. *v.i.* (*a*) *F:* Se relâcher; moins travailler; se détendre. (*b*) Diminuer la vitesse; ralentir.

easing ['iːziŋ], *s.* 1. Soulagement *m* (de la souffrance); allègement *m* (d'une poutre). 2. E. of the tension in diplomatic circles, détente *f* dans les milieux diplomatiques.

easel ['iːzl], *s.* Chevalet *m* (de peintre).

easement ['iːzmənt], *s.* *Jur:* Servitude *f*; service foncier; droit *m* d'usage.

easiness ['iːzinis], *s.* 1. Bien-être *m*, commodité *f.* 2. Aisance *f*, grâce *f* (des manières, du style). 3. Indifférence *f*, insouciance *f.* 4. Facilité *f* (du travail). 5. (*a*) Complaisance *f*; humeur *f* facile. (*b*) Jeu *m* facile (d'une machine); douceur *f* (de roulement).

east [iːst]. 1. *s.* (*a*) Est *m*, orient *m*, levant *m.* House facing (the) e., maison exposée à l'est. On the e., to the e., à l'est (of, de). (*b*) The E., l'Orient, le Levant. In the E., en Orient. The Far E., l'Extrême-Orient. The Middle E., le Moyen-Orient. The Near E., Proche-Orient. *U.S:* The E., les États de l'Est. 2. *adv.* A l'est, à l'orient. To travel e., voyager vers l'est. *Prov:* Too far e. is west, les extrêmes se touchent. 3. *adj.* (Vent) d'est; (pays) de l'est, oriental; (fenêtre) qui fait face à l'est. The E. Indies, les Indes orientales. '**East-'End** (the), *s.* Quartiers populeux de la partie est de Londres.

Easter ['iːstər], *s.* Pâques *m.* E. (Sun)day, le jour de Pâques. E. Monday, le lundi de Pâques. E. egg, œuf de Pâques. To do one's E. duties, faire ses pâques. E. communion, communion pascale. *Geog:* E. Island, l'Ile *f* de Pâques.

easterly ['iːstəli]. 1. *a.* E. wind, vent (d')est. E. current, courant qui se dirige vers l'est. 2. *adv.* Vers l'est.

eastern ['iːstən], *a.* Est, de l'est; oriental, -aux. The E. Church, l'Église d'Orient.

Eastertide ['iːstətaid], *s.* Pâques *m.*

eastward ['iːstwəd]. 1. *s.* To the e., vers l'est. 2. *a.* (*a*) A l'est; dans l'est. (*b*) Du côté de l'est.

eastwards ['iːstwədz], *adv.* A l'est; vers l'est; vers l'orient.

easy ['iːzi] (easier, easiest) I. *a.* 1. (*a*) A l'aise. To feel easier, se sentir plus à son aise; se sentir mieux. (*b*) Tranquille; sans inquiétude. To make one's mind e. about sth., se tranquilliser, se rassurer, sur qch. E. life, vie sans souci, sans tracas. *S.a.* CIRCUMSTANCE 1. 2. (*a*) (*Of manners, etc.*) Aisé, libre, dégagé. E. style, style facile, coulant. (*b*) Coat of an e. fit, veston ample, dans lequel on est à l'aise. (*c*) E. movement, mouvement moelleux. *Nau:* E. rolling, roulis doux. *Mec.E:* E. fit, ajustage lâche. 3. E. task, travail facile, aisé. That is e. to see, cela se voit; il y paraît. It is e. for him to . . ., il lui est facile de. . . . It is e. to say . . ., on a vite fait de dire. . . . House within e. distance, within e. reach, of . . ., maison à distance commode de. . . . *F:* As e. as anything, simple comme bonjour. *P:* Esp. *U.S:* (*Of pers.*) E. mark, jobard *m.* (*b*) (*Of pers.*) Facile, accommodant, complaisant; débonnaire. E. person to get on with, personne d'un commerce facile. *S.a.* FREE¹ 5. (*c*) To travel by e. stages, voyager à petites étapes. At an e. trot, au petit trot. *Com:* By e. payments, on e. terms, avec facilités de payement. *Sp: etc:* To come in an e. first, arriver bon premier. *F:* To make e. money, gagner de l'argent facilement. 4. *Com:* E. market, marché tranquille, calme. Cotton was easier, le coton a accusé une détente. 5. *Cards:*

Honours e., honneurs partagés. -ily, adv. 1. Tranquillement, à son aise, paisiblement. **To take things, life, e.,** prendre le temps comme il vient; se laisser vivre; F: se la couler douce. 2. (a) Doucement; sans secousse. **The door shuts e.,** la porte se ferme sans effort. (b) Avec confort. **The car holds six people e.,** on tient à l'aise six dans cette voiture. 3. Facilement, sans difficulté, avec aisance. **To speak e.,** parler avec facilité. **He came in e. first,** il est arrivé bon premier. **He is e. forty,** il a bien quarante ans. II. **easy** adv. F: 1. (a) **To take things e.,** prendre les choses en douceur. **To take it e.,** en prendre tout à son aise, F: se la couler douce. **Take it e.!** ne vous faites pas de bile! F: ne vous en faites pas! **To take life e.,** se laisser vivre. **To go e. with, on, sth.,** ménager qch. (b) Nau: Row: **E. (ahead)!** (en avant) doucement! **E. all!** stop(pe)! (c) Mil: **Stand e.!** repos! 2. P: Facilement. F: **Easier said than done,** c'est plus facile à dire qu'à faire; c'est bon à dire. **'easy-'chair,** s. Fauteuil m; bergère f. **'easy-going,** a. (Of pers.) (a) Qui prend les choses tranquillement; insouciant; qui ne se fait pas de bile. (b) Accommodant; peu exigeant; peu tracassier. (c) D'humeur facile. **An e.-g. man,** un homme facile à vivre; un bon garçon.

eat [iːt], v.tr. (p.t. **ate** [et]; p.p. **eaten** [iːtn]) (a) Manger. **To e. one's breakfast, dinner, supper,** déjeuner, dîner, souper. **To ask for something to e.,** demander à manger. **Fit to e.,** bon à manger; mangeable. **To e. like a wolf, a horse,** manger comme un ogre; dévorer. S.a. FILL¹ 1. **To e. one's heart out,** se ronger le cœur. F: **He eats out of my hand,** il m'obéit comme un chien. F: **I thought he was going to e. me,** j'ai cru qu'il allait m'avaler. **To e. one's words,** (i) se rétracter; (ii) bafouiller; manger ses mots. (Of insect, worm) **To e. into wood,** ronger, mouliner, le bois. Sch: Jur: **To e. one's dinners,** faire ses études d'avocat. (b) Prendre ses repas; dîner. **We e. at seven,** nous dînons à sept heures. 2. F: **What's eating you?** quelle mouche vous pique? Qu'est-ce qui vous prend? **eat away,** v.tr. (a) Ronger, éroder (une falaise); saper (des fondations). (b) (Of acid) Mordre, dissoudre, attaquer (un métal). **eat off,** v.tr. **To e. its head off,** (of horse, etc.) s'engraisser à ne rien faire; (of factory) marcher à vide. **eat up,** v.tr. 1. Manger jusqu'à la dernière miette (un gâteau, etc.); achever de manger (qch.). **E. up your bread!** finis ton pain! (Of car, etc.) **To e. up the miles,** dévorer la route. 2. Consumer (qch.) sans profit. **Stove that eats up the coal,** poêle qui mange beaucoup de charbon. 3. F: **To be eaten up (with sth.),** être dévoré (d'orgueil), etc.; consumé (par l'ambition); perclus (de rhumatismes). **eating,** s. Manger m. **Pheasants make good e.,** les faisans sont bons à manger. attrib. **E. chocolate,** chocolat à croquer. **E. apple,** pomme f de dessert, à couteau. **'eating-house,** s. Restaurant m. Pej: gargotte f.

eatable ['iːtəbl]. 1. a. Mangeable; bon à manger. 2. s.pl. **Eatables,** provisions f de bouche; comestibles m.

eater ['iːtər], s. 1. Mangeur, -euse. **He's not a big e.,** il ne mange pas beaucoup. 2. Fruit m à couteau. **These apples are good eaters,** ces pommes se laissent manger.

eaves [iːvz], s.pl. Const: Avancée f (du toit); avanttoit m.

eavesdrop ['iːvzdrɒp], v.i. (**eavesdropped**) Écouter aux portes, à la porte. **être aux écoutes.**

eavesdropper ['iːvzdrɒpər], s. Écouteur, -euse, aux portes; indiscret, -ète.

ebb¹ [eb], s. 1. Reflux m, jusant m; baisse f (de la marée). **The e. and flow,** le flux et le reflux. **Set of the e.,** direction f du jusant. **Slack of the e.,** étale m du jusant. 2. Déclin m (de la fortune, de la vie). **The patient is at a low e.,** le malade est très bas. **'ebb-'tide,** s. Marée descendante; marée de jusant; reflux m.

ebb², v.i. 1. (Of tide) Baisser, refluer. **To e. and flow,** monter et baisser. **The tide is ebbing,** la marée baisse. 2. (Of life, etc.) Décliner; être sur le déclin; décroître, baisser. **To e. away,** s'écouler. **Ebbing strength,** forces qui s'en vont.

ebonite ['ebənait], s. Ébonite f; vulcanite f.

ebony ['ebəni], s. (a) Ébène f; bois m d'ébène. (b) (Plaqueminier) ébénier.

Ebro ['iːbrou]. Pr.n. Geog: L'Èbre m.

ebullience [i'bʌliəns], **ebulliency** [i'bʌliənsi], s. Bouillonnement m, effervescence f (de la colère, de la jeunesse).

ebullient [i'bʌliənt], a. 1. Bouillonnant. 2. (Sentiment) débordant, exubérant; (homme) plein de vie.

ebullition [ebʌ'liʃ(ə)n], s. 1. Ébullition f, bouillonnement m. 2. **E. of feeling,** transport m, exubérance f.

eccentric [ik'sentrik], a. & s. (a) Excentrique (m); désaxé. **E. load,** charge décentrée. (b) (Of pers.) Excentrique (mf); original, -ale, -aux.

eccentricity ['eksen'trisiti], s. (a) Excentricité f, désaxage m, décentrement m. (b) Excentricité (de caractère); bizarrerie f, originalité f.

ecclesiastic [i'kliːzi'æstik], a. & s. Ecclésiastique (m).

ecclesiastical [i'kliːzi'æstikl], a. Ecclésiastique. **The e. body,** le sacerdoce. Adm: **E. matters,** les Cultes m.

echelon¹ ['eʃələn], s. Mil: Échelon m.

echelon², v.tr. Mil: Échelonner (des troupes). **echeloned,** a. Mil: En échelon.

echo¹ ['ekou], s. (pl. echoes) Écho m.

echo². 1. v.tr. Répéter (en écho). **To e. s.o.'s opinions,** se faire l'écho des opinions de qn. **To e. back a shout,** faire écho à un cri. 2. v.i. (a) Faire écho. (b) Retentir. **His voice echoed through the room,** sa voix retentit, résonna, dans la salle.

echoless ['ekouliss], a. Sans écho. Cin: **E. studio,** studio complètement sourd.

eclair [ei'klɛər], s. Cu: Éclair m (à la crème, etc.).

éclat [ei'klɑː], s. Éclat m, gloire f.

eclectic [i'klektik], a. & s. Éclectique (m). -ally, adv. Éclectiquement.

eclecticism [i'klektisizm], s. Éclectisme m.

eclipse¹ [i'klips], s. Éclipse f (de soleil, de lune; d'un phare). **To be under an e.,** être éclipsé; se trouver relégué dans l'ombre.

eclipse², v.tr. Éclipser.

ecliptic [i'kliptik], a. & s. Astr: Écliptique (f).

eclogue ['eklɔg], s. Lit: Églogue f.

ecology [iː'kɔlədʒi], s. Écologie f.

economic [iːkə'nɔmik], a. Qui se rapporte à l'économie (politique); (problème) économique. **An e. rent,** un loyer rentable, qui rapporte.

economical [iːkə'nɔmikl], a. (a) (Of pers.) Économe. (b) (Of method, apparatus, etc.) Économique. -ally, adv. Économiquement. **To use sth e.,** ménager qch.

economics [iːkə'nɔmiks], s.pl. 1. Les sciences f économiques, l'économie f politique. 2. Rentabilité f. **The e. of town planning,** les aspects financiers de l'urbanisme.

economist [iː(ː)'kɔnəmist], s. (Political) e., économiste m. **Agricultural e.,** agronome m.

economize [iː(ː)'kɔnəmaiz], v.tr. Économiser, ménager (le temps, l'argent, etc.). Abs. Faire des économies.

economy [iː(ː)'kɔnəmi], s. 1. Économie f. **To practise e.,** économiser. **E. run,** concours m de consommation. 2. Political e., économie politique. **Planned e.,** économie planifiée. **Controlled e.,** économie dirigée. S.a. DOMESTIC 1.

ecstasy ['ekstəsi], s. 1. Transport m (de joie); ravissement m. **To be in an e. of joy,** se pâmer de joie. **To go into ecstasies over sth.,** s'extasier devant qch. 2. Extase (religieuse, etc.).

ecstatic [ik'stætik], a. Extatique. -ally, adv. **E. happy,** heureux jusqu'au ravissement. **To gaze e. at s.o.,** tomber en extase devant qn.

ectoderm ['ektədəːm], s. Anat: Ectoderme m.

ectoplasm ['ektəplæzm], s. Biol: Ectoplasme m.

Ecuador ['ekwədɔːr]. Pr.n. Geog: (La République de) l'Équateur m.

ecumenical [iːkjuː'menik(ə)l], a. Ecc: Œcuménique.

eczema ['eksimə], s. Med: Eczéma m.

eczematous [ek'semətəs], a. Eczémateux.

eddy¹ ['edi], s. 1. Remous m; tourbillon m; tournoiement m. Nau: revolin m. El: **E. currents,** courants m de Foucault. **'eddy-chamber,** s. Chambre f, boîte f, aérodynamique (pour étude des remous). **'eddy-wind,** s. Nau: Revolin m.

eddy², v.i. (Of water) Faire des remous; (of wind) tourbillonner, tournoyer.

edelweiss ['eidlvais], *s. Bot:* Édelweiss *m.*

Eden [i:dn]. *Pr.n.* **(The Garden of)** E., l'Éden *m.*

edentate [i'denteit], *a. & s. Z:* Édenté (*m*).

edge¹ [edʒ], *s.* **1.** Fil *m*, tranchant *m* (d'une lame). *F:* The thin e. of the wedge, le premier pas (qui mène à une mauvaise habitude, etc.). **Knife with a keen e. on it,** couteau à tranchant aigu, acéré. **To put an e. on a blade,** (re)donner du fil à, aiguiser, affiler, une lame. **To take the e. off sth.,** émousser (un couteau, l'appétit, le plaisir). **Not to put too fine an e. upon it,** pour ne pas mâcher les mots. **2.** (*a*) Arête *f*, angle *m* (d'une pierre, etc.). **Sharp e.,** arête vive. (*b*) *Carp: Tls:* **Straight e.,** limande *f.* **3.** Bord *m*, rebord *m* (de table); tranche *f*, chant *m* (d'une planche); ourlet *m* (d'un cratère); tranche (d'une pièce de monnaie, d'un livre). *Bookb:* **Gilt edges,** tranches dorées. **With gilt edges,** doré sur tranches. **On e.,** (i) (*of brick*) de chant; (ii) (*of pers.*) énervé, nerveux. **It sets my teeth on e.,** cela me crispe; cela me fait mal aux dents. **My nerves are all on e.,** j'ai les nerfs à fleur de peau, en pelote. **She is on e. to-day,** elle est nerveuse aujourd'hui. **4.** Lisière *f*, bordure *f*, orée *f* (d'un bois); bord, rive *f* (d'une rivière); liséré *m*, bord (d'une étoffe, etc.). **At the e. of a precipice,** au bord d'un précipice. **'edge-'tool,** *s.* Outil tranchant, coupant.

edge², *v.tr. & i.* **1.** Affiler, aiguiser (un couteau); affûter (un outil). **2.** Border (une étoffe, la route) **(with,** de); lisérer (une jupe). **3. To e.** (one's way) **into a room; to e. in,** se faufiler, se glisser, dans une pièce. **To e. in a word,** placer son mot; glisser un mot. **To e. to(wards) the right,** obliquer vers la droite. **edge away,** *v.i.* S'éloigner, se reculer, s'écarter, tout doucement **(from,** de). **edged,** *a.* **1.** (*Of tool, etc.*) Tranchant, acéré. **To play with e. tools,** jouer avec le feu; jouer un jeu dangereux. **2.** (*a*) A tranchant. **edging,** *s. Dressm: etc:* Liséré *m*, cordonnet *m*, passement *m*, ganse *f. Hort:* Bordure *f* (de parterre, etc.). **'edging-shears,** *s.pl. Hort:* Cisaille *f* à bordures.

edgeways ['edʒweiz], **edgewise** ['edʒwaiz], *adv.* **1.** (Vu) latéralement, de côté. **2.** (Placé) de chant, sur chant. *F:* **I can't get a word in e.,** impossible de placer un mot (dans la conversation).

edginess ['edʒinis], *s. F:* Nervosité *f.*

edgy ['edʒi], *a.* **1.** (*Of rock, etc.*) Aux arêtes vives; (*of picture*) aux lignes dures. **2.** *F:* (*Of person*) Au caractère anguleux. (*b*) Énervé.

edible ['edibl], *a.* **1.** *a.* Comestible; bon à manger. **2.** *s.pl.* Edibles, comestibles *m.*

edict ['i:dikt], *s. Hist:* Édit *m.*

edification [ˌedifi'keiʃ(ə)n], *s.* Édification *f*, instruction *f.*

edifice ['edifis], *s.* Édifice *m.*

edify ['edifai], *v.tr.* Édifier (qn).

Edinburgh ['ed(i)nbrə]. *Pr.n.* Édimbourg.

edit ['edit], *v.tr.* (*a*) Annoter, éditer (le texte d'un auteur); diriger (une série de textes, etc.). (*b*) Rédiger, (un journal). **Edited by . . .,** (série, journal, etc.) sous la direction de. . . . **editing,** *s.* **1.** Préparation *f*, annotation *f* (d'un texte). **2.** Rédaction *f*, direction *f* (d'un journal). **3.** *Cin:* Montage *m.*

edition [i'diʃ(ə)n], *s. Publ:* Édition *f.* **School e.,** édition classique. **Limited e.,** édition à tirage limité. **Pirated e.,** édition frauduleuse. **Book in its fourth e.,** livre à sa quatrième édition.

editor ['editər], *s.* **1.** Annotateur *m*, éditeur *m* (d'un texte); auteur *m* (d'une édition critique). **2.** (*a*) Surveillant *m* de la publication; directeur *m* (d'une série, d'un dictionnaire). (*b*) Rédacteur *m* en chef, directeur (d'un journal). **Managing e.,** rédacteur gérant. **News e.,** rédacteur aux informations. **Publicity e.,** annoncier *m.* (*c*) *W.Tel:* Programme e., éditorialiste *mf.*

editorial [ˌedi'tɔ:riəl]. **1.** *a.* Éditorial, -aux. **The e. staff,** la rédaction. **2.** *s. Journ:* Article *m* de fond, de tête; éditorial *m.*

editorship ['editəʃip], *s.* **1.** Rôle *m* d'annotateur (d'un texte). **2.** **Series published under the e. of . . .,** série publiée sous la direction de. . . . **3.** Direction *f*, rédaction *f* (d'un journal).

educate ['edjukeit], *v.tr.* **1.** (*a*) Donner de l'instruction à, instruire (qn). **He was educated in France,** il a fait ses études en France. (*b*) (i) Faire faire ses études à (un enfant); (ii) pourvoir à l'instruction de (son enfant). **To e. one's son for the bar,** diriger son fils vers le barreau. **2.** Former (qn, le goût de qn). **Educated man,** homme instruit; esprit cultivé. **3.** Dresser (des animaux).

education [ˌedju'keiʃ(ə)n], *s.* **1.** Éducation *f.* **2.** Enseignement *m*, instruction *f.* **Ministry of E.,** Ministère *m* de l'Éducation nationale. **He has had a classical e.,** il a fait ses études classiques. **He has had a good e.,** il a fait de fortes études. **Adult e.,** enseignement post-scolaire, enseignement des adultes. **Further e.,** les œuvres post-scolaires. **General e.,** l'éducation de base. **Progressive e.,** l'éducation nouvelle. **University e.,** enseignement supérieur. **3.** Dressage *m* (des animaux).

educational [ˌedju'keiʃən(ə)l], *a.* (Maison, ouvrage) d'éducation, d'enseignement; (procédé) éducatif, pédagogique. **E. film,** film éducatif.

educative ['edjukətiv], *a.* Éducatif.

educator ['edjukeitər], *s.* Éducateur, -trice.

Edward ['edwəd]. *Pr.n.m.* Édouard.

eel [i:l], *s.* **1.** Anguille *f.* **2. Electric e.,** gymnote *m.* **'eel-basket, -buck,** *s.* Nasse *f* à anguilles. **'eel-pond,** *s.* Anguillère *f.* **'eel-pout,** *s. Ich:* Lotte (commune); barbot *m.* **'eel-prong, -spear,** *s.* Foène *f.*

e'en [i:n], *adv. Poet:* = EVEN³.

e'er ['ɛər], *adv. Poet:* = EVER.

eerie, eery ['iəri], *a.* Étrange, mystérieux; qui donne le frisson. **-ily,** *adv.* Étrangement; d'une façon à donner le frisson.

efface [i'feis], *v.tr.* (*a*) Effacer; oblitérer. (*b*) **To e. oneself,** s'effacer.

effacement [i'feismənt], *s.* Effacement *m.*

effect¹ [i'fekt], *s.* **1.** (*a*) Effet *m*, action *f*, influence *f*; résultat *m*, conséquence *f.* **The e. of heat upon metals,** l'action de la chaleur sur les métaux. **To feel the effects of an illness,** ressentir les effets d'une maladie. **To have an e. on s.o.,** produire de l'effet sur qn; affecter qn. **To be of no e.; to have, produce, no e.,** ne produire aucun effet; rester sans action. **Nothing has any e. on it,** rien n'y fait. **It has little e.,** cela ne fait pas grand-chose. **To take e.,** (i) faire (son) effet; (ii) (*of regulation*) entrer en vigueur; (iii) (*of drugs*) agir, opérer; (*of vaccination*) prendre; (iv) (*of shot*) porter. **Of no e.,** (i) sans effet, inutile, inefficace; (ii) *Jur:* non avenu. **To no e.,** en vain; sans résultat. **To give e. to sth.,** exécuter (un décret); donner suite à (une décision). **To carry into e.,** mettre (qch.) à exécution. (*b*) Sens *m*, teneur *f* (d'un document). **I received a telegram to the same e.,** j'ai reçu une dépêche dans le même sens. **That is what he said, or words to that e.,** voilà ce qu'il a dit, ou quelque chose d'approchant. **2.** (*a*) *Th:* **Stage effects,** effets scéniques, jeux *m* scéniques. (*b*) **Words meant for e.,** phrases à effet. **To do sth. for e.,** faire qch. pour se faire remarquer. **3. In e.,** en fait, en réalité. **4.** *pl.* (Personal) **effects,** effets, biens (personnels). *Bank:* 'No effects,' "défaut de provision."

effect², *v.tr.* Effectuer, accomplir, réaliser (qch.). **To e. an entrance,** forcer la porte, la fenêtre. **To e. a payment,** effectuer un payement.

effective [i'fektiv]. **1.** *a.* (*a*) Efficace. **The medicine was e.,** le médicament a produit son effet. (*b*) (*Actual*) Effectif. *Mec.E:* **E. power,** rendement *m*; puissance effective; effet *m* utile. (*c*) **E. contrast,** contraste frappant, saisissant. **E. picture,** tableau qui fait de l'effet. (*d*) *Mil:* **E. troops,** troupes valides. (*e*) (*Of decree, etc.*) **To become e.,** entrer en vigueur. **2.** *s.pl. Mil:* **Effectives,** effectifs *m.* **-ly,** *adv.* **1.** Avec effet, efficacement, utilement. **2.** Effectivement; en réalité. **3.** D'une façon frappante.

effectiveness [i'fektivnis], *s.* **1.** Efficacité *f.* **2.** L'effet heureux (produit par un tableau, etc.).

effectual [i'fektjuəl], *a.* **1.** Efficace. **2.** (Contrat) valide; (règlement) en vigueur. **-ally,** *adv.* Efficacement.

effeminacy [i'feminəsi], *s.* Caractère efféminé; mollesse *f.*

effeminate [i'feminit], *a. & s.* Efféminé (*m*). **To grow e.,** s'efféminer, s'amollir.

effervesce [ˌefə'ves], v.i. Être, entrer en effervescence; (of drinks) mousser.

effervescence [ˌefə'ves(ə)ns], s. Effervescence f (d'un liquide).

effervescent [ˌefə'ves(ə)nt], a. Effervescent.

effete [i'fiːt], a. (Of method, etc.) Caduc, -uque, qui a fait son temps.

efficacious [ˌefi'keiʃəs], a. Efficace. **-ly**, adv. Efficacement; avec efficacité.

efficaciousness [ˌefi'keiʃəsnis], **efficacy** ['efikəsi], s. Efficacité f.

efficiency [i'fiʃ(ə)nsi], s. 1. Efficacité f (d'un remède, etc.). 2. (a) Mec.E: Rendement (industriel); coefficient m de rendement, d'effet utile. **High e. engine**, moteur à grand, bon, rendement. (b) Bon fonctionnement (d'une administration, etc.). 3. (Of pers.) Capacité f; compétence f; valeur f; efficience f. Mil: E. pay, prime payée aux hommes qui ont fait leurs classes.

efficient [i'fiʃ(ə)nt], a. (a) Phil: E. cause, cause efficiente. (b) (Of method, work) Effectif, efficace. (c) E. machine, (i) machine à bon rendement; (ii) machine d'un fonctionnement sûr. (d) (Of pers.) Capable, compétent, efficient. **-ly**, adv. 1. Efficacement. 2. Work e. done, travail exécuté avec compétence.

effigy ['efidʒi], s. Effigie f. **To burn, hang, s.o. in e.**, brûler, pendre, qn en effigie.

efflorescence [ˌeflɔ'res(ə)ns], s. Efflorescence f.

efflorescent [ˌeflɔ'res(ə)nt], a. Efflorescent.

effluence ['efluəns], s. Émanation f.

effluvium, pl. -ia [i'fluːviəm, -iə], s. (a) Effluve m, émanation f. (b) Pej: Émanation désagréable; exhalaison. f.

efflux ['eflʌks], s. Flux m, écoulement m (de liquide).

effort ['efət], s. 1. (a) Effort m. **To make an e. to do sth.**, faire (un) effort pour faire qch.; s'efforcer de faire qch. **Make an e.!** secouez-vous! **He spares no e.**, il ne s'épargne pas; rien ne lui coûte. **Supported by voluntary e.**, subventionné par l'initiative privée. (b) **You've seen his latest e.?** vous avez vu son dernier ouvrage, sa dernière œuvre? 2. Mec: Effort (de traction, etc.); poussée f, travail m.

effortless ['efətlis], a. (a) Sans effort. (b) Facile.

effrontery [i'frʌntəri], s. Effronterie f.

effulgence [i'fʌldʒəns], s. Éclat m, splendeur f.

effulgent [i'fʌldʒənt], a. Resplendissant, éclatant.

effusion [i'fjuːʒ(ə)n], s. 1. Effusion f, épanchement m (de sang, etc.). 2. Effusion (de tendresse, etc.); épanchement de cœur. F: **Have you ever read such an e.?** avez-vous jamais lu une tartine pareille?

effusive [i'fjuːsiv], a. Démonstratif, expansif. **To be e. in one's compliments**, se répandre en compliments. **To be e. in one's thanks**, se confondre en remerciements. **-ly**, adv. Avec effusion, avec expansion. **To thank s.o. e.**, se confondre en remerciements auprès de qn.

effusiveness [i'fjuːsivnis], s. Effusion f; volubilité f.

eft [eft], s. = NEWT.

egad [i'gæd], int. A: Parbleu! morbleu!

egalitarian [igæli'teəriən], a. Égalitaire.

egg¹ [eg], s. 1. (a) Œuf m. (Farm-)fresh e., œuf du jour. New-laid e., œuf frais. Dehydrated, dried, e., œuf en poudre. Boiled e., œuf à la coque. Hard-boiled e., œuf dur. Soft-boiled e., œuf mollet. Fried e., œuf sur le plat. Poached e., œuf poché. Scrambled eggs, œufs brouillés. The goose with the golden eggs, la poule aux œufs d'or. A bad e., (i) un œuf pourri; (ii) F: un bon à rien, un vaurien. (b) Œuf (d'insecte); lente f (de pou). Silkworm's eggs, F: graines f de vers à soie. Needlew: Darning e., œuf à repriser. **'egg-cosy**, s. Cosy m (pour œufs à la coque). **'egg-cup**, s. Coquetier m. **'egg-flip**, s. Boisson chaude composée d'un œuf battu dans de la bière, de l'alcool; (non-alcoholic) lait m de poule. **'egg-man**, pl. -men, **'egg-merchant**, s.m. Coquetier; marchand d'œufs. **'egg-nog**, s. = EGG-FLIP. **'egg-plant**, s. Bot: Hort: Aubergine f. **egg-powder**, s. Cu: Œufs mpl en poudre. **'egg-shaped**, a. Ovoïde. **'egg-shell**, s. Coquille f d'œuf. **E.-s. china**, coquille d'œuf. **'egg-spoon**, s. Cuiller f à œufs. **'egg-stand**, s. Œufrier m. **'egg-timer**, s. Cu: Sablier m. **'egg-whisk**, s. Batteur m., fouet m, à œufs.

egg², v.tr. **To e. s.o. on (to do sth.)**, pousser, inciter, encourager, qn (à faire qch.).

egghead ['eghed], s. F: Intellectuel m.

eglantine ['eglantain], s. Bot: 1. Églantine f. 2. (Bush) Églantier m.

ego ['egou, 'iːgou], s. Phil: The e., le moi.

egocentric [ˌego'sentrik], a. Psy: Égocentrique.

egoism ['egoizm], s. 1. Égoïsme m; égocentrisme m. 2. = EGOTISM.

egoist ['egoist], s. = EGOTIST.

egoistic(al) [ˌegou'istik(l)], a. 1. Égoïste. 2. F: Entiché de sa personne; rempli de sa propre importance.

egotism ['egotizm], s. Égotisme m; culte du moi.

egotist ['egotist], s. Égotiste mf.

egress ['iːgres], s. (a) Sortie f, issue f. (b) Mch: etc: Échappement m.

egret ['iːgrit], s. 1. Orn: Aigrette f; héron argenté. 2. Bot: Aigrette (de chardon).

Egypt ['iːdʒipt]. Pr.n. Geog: L'Égypte f.

Egyptian [i'dʒipʃ(ə)n], a. & s. Égyptien, -ienne.

Egyptologist [ˌiːdʒiptə'lədʒist], s. Égyptologue mf.

Egyptology [ˌiːdʒiptə'lədʒi], s. Égyptologie f.

eh [ei], int. Eh! hé! hein?

eider(-duck) ['aidər, 'aidədʌk], s. Orn: Eider m. **eider-down**, s. 1. Duvet m d'eider. 2. Édredon m.

eight [eit]. 1. num. a. & s. Huit (m). **Twenty e.**, vingt-huit. **E. and six (pence)**, huit shillings six pence. **To be e. (years old)**, avoir huit ans. **There were e. of us**, nous étions huit. **Page e.**, page huit. **It's e. o'clock**, il est huit heures. **E. day clock**, huitaine f. P: **He's had one over the e.**, il a bu un coup de trop. 2. s. Sp: (i) Équipe f de huit rameurs; (ii) canot m à huit rameurs; huit de pointe.

eighteen [ˌei'tiːn], num. a. & s. Dix-huit (m).

eighteenth [ˌei'tiːnθ], num. a. & s. (a) Dix-huitième. (b) (On) the e. (of May), le dix-huit (mai). **Louis the E.**, Louis dix-huit.

eightfold ['eitfould]. 1. a. Octuple. 2. adv. Huit fois autant.

eighth [eitθ]. 1. num. a. & s. (a) Huitième. **In the e. place**, huitièmement. (b) (On) the e. (of April), le huit (avril). **Henry the E.**, Henri Huit. 2. s. (Fractional) Huitième m.

eightieth ['eitiiθ], num. a. & s. Quatre-vingtième (m).

eighty ['eiti], num. a & s. Quatre-vingts (m); octante (Suisse), huitante (en Suisse, en Belgique). **E.-one**, quatre-vingt-un. **E.-first**, quatre-vingt-unième. **Page e.**, page quatre-vingt.

eikon ['aikən], s. Icone f.

eikonogen [ai'konədʒin], s. Phot: Iconogène m.

Eire ['ɛərə]. Pr.n. Geog: Eire f, la République d' Irlande.

either ['aiðər]. 1. a. & pron. (a) L'un(e) et l'autre, chaque, chacun(e). **On e. side**, de chaque côté; des deux côtés. (b) L'un(e) ou l'autre. **E. of them**, soit l'un(e), soit l'autre. **I don't believe e. of you**, je ne vous crois ni l'un ni l'autre. **You can do it e. way**, vous pouvez le faire d'une manière ou de l'autre, des deux façons l'une. **Do you want this one or that one?—E.**, voulez-vous celui-ci ou celui-là?—L'un ou l'autre; n'importe lequel. 2. conj. & adv. (a) **E. . . . or . . .**, ou . . ., ou . . .; soit . . ., soit . . . **E. come in or go out**, entrez ou sortez. (b) **Not . . . e.**, ne . . . non plus. **Nor I e.!** ni moi non plus.

ejaculate [i'dʒækjuleit], v.tr. (a) Physiol: Éjaculer. (b) Pousser (un cri); lancer (un juron, etc.).

ejaculation [i'dʒækju'leiʃ(ə)n], s. (a) Éjaculation f. (b) Cri m, exclamation f.

eject [i'dʒekt], v.tr. 1. Jeter, émettre (des flammes, etc.); expulser, évacuer (de la bile). 2. (a) Expulser, F: éjecter, sortir (un agitateur d'une réunion). (b) Jur: Expulser (un locataire).

ejection [i'dʒekʃ(ə)n], s. (a) Jet m (de flammes); éjection f (de la vapeur, d'une cartouche); expulsion f (de qn); évacuation f (de la bile). (b) Éviction f, expulsion f (d'un locataire).

ejector [i'dʒektər], s. 1. Sm.a: Mch: Éjecteur m. 2. Av: E. seat, siège éjectable.

eke [iːk], v.tr. **To e. out**, suppléer à l'insuffisance de, augmenter (ses revenus); ménager, faire durer (les vivres). **To e. out the soup, the sauce** (with water), allonger la soupe, la sauce. **To e. out one's income by writing**, gagner un petit surplus en écrivant.

elaborate[1] [i'læb(ə)rit], *a.* (*Of mechanism*) Compliqué; (*of work*) soigné, fini; (*of style*) travaillé; (*of inspection*) minutieux, -euse. E. **dress**, toilette recherchée, étudiée. **-ly**, *adv.* Avec soin; soigneusement; minutieusement.

elaborate[2] [i'læbəreit], *v.tr.* (*a*) Élaborer (une théorie); fouiller, pousser (une œuvre d'art). (*b*) *Physiol:* Élaborer (un suc, etc.).

elaborateness [i'læb(ə)ritnis], *s.* Complication *f* (d'un mécanisme); fini *m* (d'un travail); minutie *f* (de recherches).

elaboration [i,læbə'reiʃ(ə)n], *s. Physiol: etc:* Élaboration *f.*

elapse [i'læps], *v.i.* (*Of time*) S'écouler; (se) passer.

elastic [i'læstik]. **1.** *a.* (*a*) Élastique; (bois, etc.) flexible. To be e., (i) faire ressort; (ii) *F:* (*of pers.*) avoir du ressort. (*b*) *F:* (Règlement, etc.) élastique. **2.** *s.* Élastique *m.*

elasticity [ɪːlæs'tisiti, el-], *s.* Élasticité *f*; ressort *m* (de caractère); souplesse *f* (de corps).

elate [i'leit], *v.tr.* Exalter, transporter. To be **elated with joy, with success**, être transporté de joie, enivré de succès.

elater ['elətər], *s. Ent:* Élater *m*; *F:* taupin *m.*

elation [i'leiʃ(ə)n], *s.* **1.** Exaltation *f*; ivresse *f* (du succès). **2.** Joie *f*, gaieté *f.*

Elba ['elbə]. *Pr.n.Geog:* (L'île d')Elbe *f.*

Elbe ['elb]. *Pr.n.Geog:* (The River) E., l'Elbe *m.*

elbow[1] ['elbou], *s.* **1.** Coude *m* (du bras). To rest one's e. on sth., s'accouder sur qch. To be out at elbow(s), (i) (*of coat*) être troué, percé, aux coudes; (ii) *F:* (*of pers.*) être loqueteux, déguenillé. *F:* To lift one's e., lever le coude; être adonné à la boisson. To rub elbows with s.o., coudoyer qn. To be at s.o.'s e., se tenir aux côtés de qn. **2.** (*a*) Coude, genou *m*, jarret *m* (d'un tuyau). **'elbow-grease**, *s. F:* Huile *f* de bras, de coude. Put a bit of e.-g. into it, mettez-y un peu de nerf. **'elbow-'high**, *adv.* **1.** Jusqu'au coude. **2.** *Const:* A hauteur d'appui. **'elbow-joint**, *s.* **1.** *Anat:* Articulation *f* du coude. **2.** *Mec.E: etc:* Joint articulé; (joint à) genou *m.* **'elbow-rest**, *s.* Accoudoir *m*, accotoir *m.* **'elbow-room**, *s.* To have e.-r., avoir ses coudées franches; être au large.

elbow[2], *v.tr. & i.* (*a*) Coudoyer (qn); pousser (qn) du coude, des coudes. To e. s.o. aside, écarter qn d'un coup de coude. (*b*) To e. (one's way) through the crowd, se frayer un passage à travers la foule; jouer des coudes. **elbowing**, *s.* Coudoiement *m.*

elder[1] ['eldər]. **1.** *a.* Aîné, plus âgé (de deux personnes). Pliny the E., Pline l'Ancien. The elder girls (of the school), les grandes. The E. Statesmen, les vétérans de la politique. **2.** *s.* (*a*) Aîné, -ée; plus âgé, -ée. (*b*) *pl.* Obey your elders! obéissez à vos aînés! (*c*) *Ecc:* Ancien *m.*

elder[2], *s. Bot:* Elder(-tree), sureau *m.* Ground e., sureau hièble, petit sureau. **'elder-berry**, *s.* Baie *f* de sureau.

elderly ['eldəli], *a.* D'un certain âge. *s.* The e., les personnes âgées.

eldest ['eldist], *a.* Aîné.

eldritch ['eldritʃ], *a. Scot:* Surnaturel, -elle.

elect[1] [i'lekt], *a.* Élu. The Lord Mayor e., le futur Lord Maire. *s. Theol:* The e., les élus *m.*

elect[2], *v.tr.* **1.** To e. to do sth., choisir de faire qch.; se décider à faire qch. **2.** Élire. (*a*) To e. s.o. (a) member, s.o. to be a member, élire qn député. (*b*) *Jur:* To e. domicile, élire domicile.

election [i'lekʃ(ə)n], *s.* Élection *f.* **Parliamentary elections**, élections législatives.

electioneering [ilekʃə'niːəriŋ], *s.* Propagande électorale; tournée électorale.

elective [i'lektiv], *a.* **1.** Électif. **2.** *Sch: U.S:* Facultatif.

elector [i'lektər], *s.* **1.** Électeur *m*, votant *m.* **2.** *Hist:* Électeur (de Brandebourg, de Saxe).

electoral [i'lektərəl], *a.* Électoral, -aux. *U.S:* The E. College, le Collège électoral (qui élit le Président).

electorate [i'lektərit], *s.* **1.** *Hist:* Électorat *m.* **2.** *Pol:* Corps électoral; les votants *mpl.*

electric [i'lektrik], *a.* Électrique. E. **shock treatment**, traitement *m* par électrochocs. *S.a.* CHAIR.

electrical [i'lektrik(ə)l], *a.* **1.** Électrique. E. **engineering industry**, industrie *f* de l'équipement électrique. **2.** E. **fitter**, monteur-électricien *m.* *S.a.* ENGINEER[1] 1, **-ally**, *adv.* Électriquement. E. **driven**, actionné par électromoteur.

electrician [ilek'triʃ(ə)n], *s. Ind:* (Monteur-)électricien *m.*

electricity [ilek'trisiti], *s.* Électricité *f.*

electrification [i,lektrifi'keiʃ(ə)n], *s.* **1.** Électrisation *f* (d'un corps). **2.** Électrification *f* (d'un chemin de fer).

electrify [i'lektrifai], *v.tr.* **1.** Électriser (un corps, son auditoire). **2.** Électrifier (un chemin de fer). **electrifying**[1], *a.* Électrisant. **electrifying**[2], *s.* **1.** Électrisation *f.* **2.** Électrification *f.*

electro [i'lektrou], *s. & v.tr.* F: **1.** = ELECTRO-PLATE[1,2]. **2.** = ELECTROTYPE[1,2].

electro-, *comb. fm:* e**'lectro-'cardiogram**, *s.* Électro-cardiogramme *m.* e**'lectro-'chemistry**, *s.* Électro-chimie *f.* e**'lectro-de'posit**, *s.* Dépôt *m* galvanoplastique; dépôt électrolytique. e**'lectro-'magnet**, *s.* Électro-aimant *m.* e**'lectro-plate**[1], *s.* (*a*) Articles plaqués. (*b*) Articles argentés; couverts *mpl* en ruolz. e**'lectro-plate**[2], *v.tr.* (*a*) Plaquer (un métal). (*b*) Argenter. e**'lectro-'plating**, *s.* (*a*) Plaqué *m.* (*b*) Argenture *f* (galvanique). e**'lectro-'technology**, *s.* Électrotechnique *f.* e**'lectro-'therapy**, *s. Med:* Électrothérapie *f.* e**'lectro-'thermic, -thermi'onic**, *a.* Électrothermique.

electrocute [i'lektrəkju:t], *v.tr.* Électrocuter.

electrocution [i,lektrə'kju:ʃ(ə)n], *s.* Électrocution *f.*

electrode [i'lektroud], *s.* Électrode *f.* *W.Tel:* Three-e. valve, lampe à trois électrodes.

electrodynamics [i,lektroudai'næmiks], *s.pl.* Électrodynamique *f.*

electroencephalogram [i'lektrouin'sefələgræm], *s. Med:* Électroencéphalogramme *m.*

electroencephalography [i'lektrouin,sefə'lɔgrəfi], *s. Med:* Électroencéphalographie *f.*

electrolyse [i'lektrəlaiz], *v.tr.* Électrolyser.

electrolysis [ilek'trɔlisis], *s.* Électrolyse *f.*

electrolyte [i'lektrəlait], *s. El:* Électrolyte *m*; liquide excitateur.

electromotive [i,lektrou'moutiv], *a.* E. **force**, force électromotrice.

electromotor [i,lektrou'moutər], *s.* Électromoteur *m.*

electron [i'lektrɔn], *s.* Électron *m.* *T.V:* E. **gun**, canon *m* à électrons. E. **lens**, lentille *f* électronique.

electronic [ilek'trɔnik]. **1.** *a.* Électronique. **2.** *s.pl.* **Electronics**, électronique *f.* E. **specialist**, électronicien, -ienne.

electropathy [ilek'trɔpəθi], *s. Med:* Électrothérapie *f.*

electroscope [i'lektrəskoup], *s.* Électroscope *m.*

electrostatic [i'lektrou'stætik], *a.* Électrostatique.

electrotechnology [i'lektroutek'nɔlədʒi], *s.* Électrotechnique *f.*

electrotype[1] [i'lektrətaip], *s.* **1.** Électrotype *m*; cliché *m* galvano, galvanotype *m*; *F:* galvano *m.* **2.** = ELECTROTYPING.

electrotype[2], *v.tr.* Clicher (par électrotypie). **electrotyping**, *s.* Électrotypie *f*, galvanoplastie *f*; clichage *m.*

elegance ['elɪgəns], *s.* Élégance *f.*

elegant ['elɪgənt], *a.* **1.** Élégant. **2.** *U.S: F:* Excellent; de premier ordre. **-ly**, *adv.* Élégamment.

elegiac [ˌelɪ'dʒaiək]. **1.** *a.* Élégiaque. **2.** *s.pl.* **Elegiacs**, vers *m* élégiaques.

elegist ['elɪdʒist], *s.* Poète *m* élégiaque.

elegy ['elɪdʒi], *s.* Élégie *f.*

element ['elɪmənt], *s.* Élément *m.* **1.** To brave the elements, braver les éléments. To be in one's e., être dans son élément, *F:* être à son affaire. To be out of one's e., être hors de son élément; être dépaysé. **2.** (*a*) The personal e., le facteur humain. (*b*) *Ph:* (d'un tout). Battery of fifty elements, batterie de cinquante éléments. **3.** *Ch:* Corps *m* simple. *Biol:* Trace e., oligo-élément *m.* **4.** *pl.* Éléments, rudiments *m* (d'une science).

elemental [ˌelə'ment(ə)l], *a.* **1.** (Culte, etc.) des éléments, des esprits élémentaires. **2.** (*Of substance*) Élémentaire. **3.** E. truths, vérités premières.

elementary [,elə'ment(ə)ri], a. Élémentaire. A: E. school, école primaire. Sch: E. algebra, rudiments mpl d'algèbre. E. prudence demands that . . ., la simple prudence veut que. . . .
elephant ['eləfənt], s. (Bull) e., éléphant m (mâle). Cow e., éléphant femelle. Young e., éléphanteau m. White e., (i) éléphant blanc; (ii) F: objet m, cadeau m, d'une certaine valeur mais inutile et encombrant. 'elephant-driver, s. Cornac m. 'elephant's ear, s. Bot: Bégonia m.
elephantine [,elə'fæntain], a. 1. Éléphantin. E. wit, esprit lourd. 2. (Of proportions, etc.) Éléphantesque.
elevate ['eləveit], v.tr. Élever (l'hostie, etc.); relever (son style); hausser, élever (la voix). elevated, a. 1. Élevé. E. position, position élevée. F: To be slightly e., être un peu gris, un peu parti. 2. (Overhead) Surélevé. U.S: E. railroad, chemin de fer aérien.
elevating, a. 1. (Of discourse, etc.) Qui élève l'esprit. 2. Élévatoire; élévateur; (organe) de relevage. E. screw (of gun), vis f de pointage en hauteur. Av: E. power, force ascensionnelle.
elevation [,elə'veiʃ(ə)n], s. 1. Élévation f (de qn à un rang supérieur, de l'hostie). 2. (a) E. above sea-level, altitude f, hauteur f, au-dessus du niveau de la mer. (b) Élévation (d'un astre). (c) Artil: Élévation; hausse f; pointage m en hauteur. 3. (Hill) Élévation, éminence f. 4. Geom.Draw: Arch: Élévation (d'un édifice, etc.) Sectional e., coupe verticale. Front e., façade f. 5. Élévation, noblesse f, grandeur f.
elevator ['eləveitər], s. 1. (a) Élévateur m; U.S: monte-charge(s) m inv. (b) U.S: Ascenseur m. (c) Grain e., aspirateur m à céréales. 2. Av: Gouvernail m de profondeur, d'altitude.
eleven [i'levn]. 1. num. a. & s. Onze (m). They are only e., ils ne sont que onze, F: qu'onze. Sch: E. plus examination = examen m d'entrée en sixième. (For other phrases see EIGHT.) 2. s. Sp: Cr: Équipe f de onze joueurs, le onze. 3. s.pl. Elevenses, casse-croûte m (pris à onze heures du matin).
eleventh [i'levnθ], num. a. & s. Onzième. At the e. hour, (i) B: à la onzième heure; (ii) au dernier moment; à la dernière heure. (For other phrases see EIGHTH.)
elevon ['eləvən], s. Av: Élevon m.
elf, pl. **elves** [elf, elvz], s. Elfe m, lutin m lutine f.
elfin ['elfin], a. D'elfe, de lutin, de fée.
elfish ['elfiʃ], a. (a) Des elfes, de lutin. (b) (Of child) Espiègle.
Elias [i'laiəs]. Pr.n.m. B.Hist: Élie.
elicit [i'lisit], v.tr. Faire jaillir (qch. de caché); découvrir (la vérité); déduire, mettre au jour (des vérités d'après des données). To e. the facts, tirer les faits au clair. To e. a reply from s.o., tirer, obtenir, une réponse de qn.
elide [i'laid], v.tr. Élider (une voyelle, etc.).
eligibility [elidʒi'biliti], s. Éligibilité f.
eligible ['elidʒibl], a. 1. Éligible (en droit) (to, à). To be e., avoir droit (for, à). 2. E. for an occupation, admissible à un emploi. E. young man, jeune homme acceptable; bon parti; parti avantageux, F: sortable.
Elijah [i'laidʒə]. Pr.n.m. B.Hist: Élie.
eliminable [i'liminəbl], a. Éliminable.
eliminate [i'limineit], v.tr. Éliminer (des matières toxiques, Mth: une inconnue); supprimer, écarter (une éventualité). eliminating, a. Éliminateur, -trice. Sp: E. heats, épreuves éliminatoires.
elimination [i'limi'neiʃ(ə)n], s. Élimination f.
eliminative [i'liminətiv], a. Éliminateur, -trice.
eliminator [i'limineitər], s. 1. Éliminateur m. 2. W.Tel: Dispositif m de filtrage du courant du secteur.
Elisha [i'laiʃə]. Pr.n.m. B.Hist: Élisée.
elision [i'liʒ(ə)n], s. Élision f.
elite [ei'li:t], s. Élite f.
elixir [i'liksər], s. Élixir m.
Elizabethan [i,lizə'bi:θ(ə)n], a. & s. Élisabéthain; du règne de la reine Élisabeth.
elk [elk], s. Z: Scandinavian e., Élan m. Canadian e., orignal m. American e., wapiti m.
ell [el], s. A.Meas: (a) Aune f. (b) Aunée f (de drap, etc.).

ellipse [i'lips], s. Geom: Ellipse f.
ellipsis, pl. **-ses** [i'lipsis, -si:z], s. Gram: Ellipse f.
elliptic(al) [i'liptik(əl)], a. Gram: Geom: Elliptique.
elm [elm], s. Orme m. Young e., ormeau m. Wych e., Scotch e., orme blanc, orme de(s) montagne(s). E. grove, ormaie f.
elocution [,elə'kju:ʃ(ə)n], s. Élocution f, diction f.
elocutionist [,elə'kju:ʃ(ə)nist], s. (a) Diseur, -euse. (b) Professeur m de diction.
elongate ['i:lɔŋgeit]. 1. v.tr. Allonger, étendre. 2. v.i. S'allonger, s'étendre.
elongation [,i:lɔŋ'geiʃ(ə)n], s. (a) Allongement m. (b) Allonge f; prolongement m (d'une ligne). (c) Astr: Path: Élongation f.
elope [i'loup], v.i. (Of daughter, wife) S'enfuir avec un amant; se faire enlever. They eloped, ils ont pris la fuite.
elopement [i'loupmənt], s. Fuite f (de la maison paternelle, du domicile conjugal); enlèvement (consenti).
eloquence ['eləkwəns], s. Éloquence f.
eloquent ['eləkwənt], a. Éloquent. E. look, regard qui en dit long. -ly, adv. Éloquemment.
else [els]. 1. adv. Autrement; ou bien. Come in or e. go out, entrez ou bien sortez. Give me back my book, or e. . . .! Rendez-moi mon livre, sinon . . .! 2. (a) a. or adv. Anyone e., anybody e., (i) toute autre personne; tout autre, n'importe qui d'autre. (ii) (Interrog.) Can I speak to anyone e.? y a-t-il quelqu'un d'autre à qui je puisse parler? Did you see anybody e.? avez-vous vu encore quelqu'un? Anything e., (i) n'importe quoi d'autre. (ii) (Interrog.) (In shop) Anything e., madam? et avec cela, madame? Someone e., somebody e., quelqu'un d'autre, un autre. Something e., quelque autre chose m. No one e., nobody e., personne m d'autre, aucun autre, nul autre. Nothing e., rien m d'autre. Nothing e., thank you, plus rien, merci. Who e.? qui d'autre? qui encore? What e.? quoi encore? quoi de plus? What e. can I do? que puis-je faire d'autre, de mieux? Everything e., tout le reste. S.a. EVERYONE. Little e., pas grand-chose d'autre. Much e., encore beaucoup. (b) Where e.? (i) où encore? (ii) en quel autre lieu? Everywhere e., partout ailleurs. Somewhere e., U.S: some place e., autre part; ailleurs. Nowhere e., nulle part ailleurs; en aucun autre lieu. Anywhere e., (i) n'importe où (ailleurs); partout ailleurs. (ii) (Interrog.) Can I find some anywhere e.? puis-je en trouver ailleurs? How e., de quelle autre manière?
elsewhere [els(')wɛər], adv. Ailleurs; autre part.
elucidate [i'lju:sideit], v.tr. Élucider, éclaircir; porter la lumière dans (une question).
elucidation [i,lju:si'deiʃ(ə)n], s. Élucidation f; éclaircissement m.
elude [i'lju:d], v.tr. Éluder (une question); tourner (la loi); esquiver, éviter (un coup); échapper à (la poursuite); se soustraire à (la justice). To e. s.o.'s grasp, échapper aux mains de qn.
elusive [i'lju:siv], a. Insaisissable, intangible. E. reply, réponse évasive. -ly, adv. Évasivement.
elusory [i'lju:səri], a. Évasif.
elver ['elvə], s. Ich: Civelle.
elves [elvz]. See ELF.
Elysian [i'liziən], a. Myth: Élyséen. The E. fields, les Champs m Élysées.
Elysium [i'liziəm]. Pr.n. Myth: L'Élysée m.
elytron, pl. **-tra** ['elitrɔn, -trə], s. Ent: Élytre m.
em [em], s. (La lettre) m m. S.a. QUADRAT.
emaciate [i'meiʃieit], v.tr. Amaigrir; faire maigrir; émacier, dessécher (le corps); appauvrir (le sol).
emaciated [i'meiʃieitid], a. Émacié, amaigri, décharné, hâve, étique. To become e., s'étioler, s'atrophier.
emaciation [i,meisi'eiʃ(ə)n], s. Amaigrissement m, émaciation f.
emanate ['eməneit], v.i. Émaner (from, de).
emanation [,emə'neiʃ(ə)n], s. Émanation f.
emancipate [i'mænsipeit], v.tr. Émanciper (un mineur, les femmes); affranchir (un esclave).
emancipation [i,mænsi'peiʃ(ə)n], s. Émancipation f (d'un mineur); affranchissement m (d'un esclave).
emancipator [i'mænsipeitər], s. Émancipateur, -trice; affranchisseur m.

emasculate [i'mæskjuleit], v.tr. Émasculer, châtrer.

emasculation [i,mæskju'leiʃ(ə)n], s. Émasculation f. castration f (d'un animal).

embalm [im'bɑːm], v.tr. 1. Embaumer (un cadavre). 2. Embaumer, parfumer (l'air). **embalming**, s. Embaumement m.

embank [im'bæŋk], v.tr. Encaisser, endiguer (un fleuve); remblayer (une route). **embanking**, s. Endiguement m; remblayage m, remblaiement m.

embankment [im'bæŋkmənt], s. 1. = EMBANKING. 2. (a) Digue f; levée f de terre. (b) Talus m; remblai m, banquette f (d'une route). River e., berge f, quai m, d'un fleuve.

embargo, pl. -oes [im'bɑːgou, -ouz], s. Embargo m, séquestre m. To lay an e. on a ship, mettre l'embargo, l'arrêt, sur un navire. To raise, take off, the e., lever l'embargo. (Of ship, goods) To be under an e., être séquestré. To put an e. on the import of horses, mettre un embargo sur, défendre, l'importation des chevaux.

embark [im'bɑːk]. 1. v.tr. Embarquer (des troupes, etc.). 2. v.i. S'embarquer (à bord d'un navire, dans une affaire).

embarkation [,embɑː'keiʃ(ə)n], s. Embarquement m. E. card, carte f d'accès à bord.

embarrass [im'bærəs], v.tr. Embarrasser, gêner (qn, les mouvements de qn); déconcerter (qn). **embarrassed**, a. Embarrassé; dans l'embarras; gêné. To be e., être confus; se sentir gêné. **embarrassing**, a. Embarrassant, gênant.

embarrassment [im'bærəsmənt], s. Embarras m, gêne f.

embassy ['embəsi], s. Ambassade f. The French E., l'Ambassade de France.

embattle [im'bætl], v.tr. 1. Ranger en bataille. 2. Fortifier; garnir de créneaux. **embattled**, a. Arch: Her: Crénelé.

embed [im'bed], v.tr. (embedded) Enfoncer, noyer (un clou dans un mur); encastrer, enchâsser, enrober, sceller (une plaque dans un mur).

embellish [im'beliʃ], v.tr. Embellir, orner, agrémenter (qch.); enjoliver (un récit).

embellishment [im'beliʃmənt], s. Embellissement m, ornement m, agrément m.

ember¹ ['embər], s. (Usu. pl.) Braise f; charbon (ardent); pl. cendres ardentes.

Ember², attrib. Ecc: E. days, les Quatre-Temps m. E. eve, vigile f des Quatre-Temps.

embezzle [im'bezl], v.tr. Détourner, distraire, s'approprier (des fonds).

embezzlement [im'bezlmənt], s. Détournement m de fonds.

embezzler [im'bezlər], s. Auteur d'un détournement; déprédateur, -trice.

embitter [im'bitər], v.tr. Remplir d'amertume, enfieller (qn); aigrir (le caractère); envenimer, aggraver (une querelle, etc.). **embittered**, a. Aigri (by, par); (cœur) ulcéré. **embittering**, s. Aigrissement m (de qn); envenimement m, aggravation f (d'une querelle).

emblazon [im'bleiz(ə)n], v.tr. Blasonner.

emblem ['emblim], s. Emblème m, symbole m; insigne (sportif); Her: devise f.

emblematic(al) [,embli'mætik(əl)], a. Emblématique.

embodiment [im'bodimənt], s. Incorporation f; incarnation f; personnification f.

embody [im'bodi], v.tr. (embodied; embodying) 1. Incarner. 2. Réaliser (une conception); mettre en application (un principe); concrétiser (une idée); personnifier (une qualité). 3. Incorporer (un article dans une loi); renfermer, contenir. 4. Réunir, rassembler, organiser (des troupes).

embolden [im'bould(ə)n], v.tr. Enhardir (s.o. to do sth., qn à faire qch.).

embolism ['embəlizm], s. Med: Embolie f.

emboss [im'bos], v.tr. Graver en relief; travailler en relief, en bosse; repousser, estamper (le métal); frapper, gaufrer (le cuir). **embossing**, s. Bosselage m (du métal); estampage m, repoussage m (du métal, du cuir); gaufrage m (du cuir). E. punch, repoussoir m.

embower [im'bauər], v.tr. Lit: Abriter (dans un berceau de verdure).

embrace¹ [im'breis], v.tr. Étreinte f. embrassement m.

embrace², v.tr. 1. Embrasser, étreindre. 2. Embrasser (une carrière); adopter (une cause); profiter de, saisir (une occasion). 3. (Include) Embrasser (in, dans); contenir, renfermer (in, dans); comporter, comprendre (des sujets).

embrasure [im'breizər], s. Embrasure f.

embrocation [embrə'keiʃ(ə)n], s. Med: Embrocation f.

embroider [im'broidər], v.tr. 1. Needlew: Broder. 2. Broder, enjoliver (un récit). To e. the story, broder l'histoire; broder sur le canevas.

embroiderer [im'broidərər], s. Brodeur, -euse.

embroidery [im'broidəri], s. 1. Needlew: Broderie f. E. scissors, ciseaux à broder. 2. F: Broderie, enjolivure f (d'un récit).

embroil [im'broil], v.tr. (a) Brouiller, embrouiller (une affaire). Motorist embroiled with the law, automobiliste aux prises avec la loi.

embroilment [im'broilmənt], s. 1. Brouillement m, embrouillement m, complication f (d'une affaire). 2. Brouille f (entre deux personnes).

embryo, pl. -os ['embriou, -ouz], s. Biol: Embryon m. In e., (i) (à l'état) embryonnaire; (ii) Plans in e., projets m embryonnaires, en germe.

embryonic [embri'ɔnik], a. 1. Biol: Embryonnaire. 2. En germe.

emend [i'mend], v.tr. Corriger (un texte).

emendation [iːmen'deiʃ(ə)n], s. Émendation f.

emerald ['emərəld], s. Émeraude f. The E. Isle, la verte Irlande. 'emerald-'green, a. & s. Vert (m) d'émeraude.

emerge [i'məːdʒ], v.i. 1. Émerger (from, de); surgir, s'élever (de l'eau, etc.). 2. Déboucher (from, de); sortir (d'un trou, de l'enfance). 3. (a) (Of difficulty) Se dresser; surgir. (b) From these facts it emerges that . . ., de ces faits il apparaît, il ressort, que . . .

emergence [i'məːdʒəns], s. Émergence f (d'un rayon lumineux); émersion f (d'un rocher).

emergency [i'məːdʒənsi], s. Circonstance f critique; cas urgent, cas imprévu. Med: An e., une urgence. E. ward, salle f d'urgence. E. operation, opération à chaud. To provide for emergencies, parer aux éventualités, à l'imprévu. To rise to the e., être, se montrer, à la hauteur de la situation, des circonstances. In this e., en cette conjoncture; en cette occurrence. In case of e., au besoin; en cas d'urgence. State of e., état m d'urgence. E. legislation, mesures d'exception. E. repairs, réparations d'urgence. E. brake, frein de secours. E. exit, sortie de secours.

emeritus [i'meritəs], a. (Professeur) honoraire.

emery ['eməri], s. Émeri m. E. paper, papier émerisé; papier d'émeri. E.-cloth, toile f (d')émeri. E.-wheel, meule f en émeri.

emetic [i'metik], a. & s. Émétique (m).

emigrant ['emigrənt], a. & s. Émigrant, -ante.

emigrate ['emigreit], v.i. Émigrer.

emigration [,emi'greiʃ(ə)n], s. Émigration f.

émigré ['emigrei], s. Émigré, ée.

eminence ['eminəns], s. Éminence f. 1. (a) Élévation f (de terrain); monticule m. (b) Anat: Saillie f. 2. Grandeur f, distinction f. 3. Ecc: (Title of cardinal) Your E., votre Éminence.

eminent ['eminənt], a. Éminent. Most e., éminentissime (cardinal, etc.). -ly, adv. Éminemment; par excellence. An e. respectable family, une famille des plus honorables.

emir ['emiər], s. Émir m.

emissary ['emisəri], s. Émissaire m.

emission [i'miʃ(ə)n], s. Émission f, dégagement m (de chaleur, etc.).

emit [i'mit], v.tr. 1. Dégager, émettre (de la chaleur); exhaler, répandre (une odeur); lancer (des étincelles); rendre (un son). 2. Émettre (du papier-monnaie, un avis).

emollient [i'moliənt], a. & s. Émollient (m).

emolument [i'moljumənt], s. (Usu. pl.) Émolument mpl, appointements mpl, traitement m.

emotion [i'mouʃ(ə)n], s. Émotion f; trouble m, attendrissement m. To appeal to the emotions, faire appel aux sentiments. Voice touched with e., voix émue.

emotional [i'mouʃn(ə)l], a. Émotionnable; émotif, -ive. To be e., s'attendrir facilement.

empanel [im'pæn(ə)l], v.tr. (empanelled) Jur: To empanel a jury, dresser la liste du jury; constituer le jury.

empennage [im'penidʒ], s. Av: Empennage m.

emperor ['empərər], s. Empereur m. Ent: Purple e., grand mars. E. moth, saturnie f, paon m de nuit.

emphasis ['emfəsis], s. 1. Force f; (énergie f d')accentuation f. 2. To ask with e., demander avec insistance. To lay e. on a fact, souligner, faire ressortir, insister sur, appuyer sur, un fait. 3. Ling: Accent m d'insistance.

emphasize ['emfəsaiz], v.tr. Accentuer, appuyer sur, souligner (un fait); faire ressortir, mettre en relief (une qualité).

emphatic [im'fætik], a. (Manière) énergique (de s'exprimer); (dénégation) absolue, énergique; (ton) autoritaire; (refus) positif, net, absolu. -ally, adv. 1. Énergiquement, positivement; (refuser) carrément, catégoriquement. 2. En termes pressants.

empire ['empaiər], s. Empire m. Hist: The Roman E., l'Empire romain. The Holy Roman E., le Saint Empire Romain. The British E., l'Empire britannique. Fr.Hist: The (First) E., l'Empire. The Second E., le second Empire. Art: E. style, style empire. U.S: The Empire City, State, la ville, l'État, de New York.

empiric(al) [im'pirik(əl)], a. Empirique. -ally, adv. Empiriquement.

empiricism [im'pirisizm], s. Empirisme m.

emplacement [im'pleismənt], s. Mil: Emplacement m (d'un canon).

employ¹ [im'pləi], s. Emploi m.

employ², v.tr. 1. Employer (qn, son temps, etc.); faire usage de (la force, etc.). To e. twenty workmen, employer vingt ouvriers. 2. To e. oneself (in doing sth.), s'occuper (à faire qch.). To be employed in doing sth., être occupé à faire qch. To keep s.o. well employed, donner de quoi faire à qn.

employable [im'pləiəbl], a. Employable.

employee [im'pləii:], s. Employé, -ée. Coll: The employees of Messrs. Martin & Co., le personnel de la maison Martin.

employer [im'pləiər], s. Ind: Patron, patronne; maître, maîtresse. The big employers of labour, les grands employeurs de main-d'œuvre. Employers' union, syndicat patronal.

employment [im'pləimənt], s. 1. Emploi m (de l'argent, etc.). 2. Emploi, travail m; place f, situation f; occupation f. To find e. for s.o., placer, caser, qn. E. agency, bureau m de placement; (for workmen) service m d'embauche. Pol.Ec: Full e., plein emploi. Full time e., emploi à temps complet. Part-time e., emploi à temps incomplet.

emporium [im'po:riəm], s. 1. Entrepôt m; marché m; centre commercial. 2. O: (Pompous style) Grand(s) magasin(s).

empower [im'pauər], v.tr. 1. Jur: Donner pouvoir, donner procuration, à (qn). 2. To e. s.o. to do sth., autoriser, habiliter, qn à faire qch.; donner, conférer, plein(s) pouvoir(s) à qn pour faire qch.

empress ['empris], s.f. Impératrice.

emptiness ['em(p)tinis], s. 1. Vide m (d'une chambre, etc.). 2. Néant m, vanité f (des plaisirs).

empty¹ ['em(p)ti]. 1. a. Vide (of, de). (a) Building standing e., immeuble inoccupé. E. stomach, estomac creux. 'To be taken on an e. stomach,' "à prendre à jeun." (b) E. head, mind, tête vide; esprit creux, nul. (c) E. words, vaines paroles. E. threats, menaces en l'air. 2. s.pl. Com: Empties, caisses f vides; bouteilles f vides. empty-'handed, a. Les mains vides. To return empty-handed, F: revenir bredouille. empty-'headed, a. Sans cervelle.

empty². 1. v.tr. Vider; décharger (un wagon); débourrer (une pipe); vidanger (une fosse d'aisance, un carter). 2. v.i. (a) (Of river, etc.) Se décharger, se déverser (into, dans). (b) (Of hall) Se dégarnir, se vider.

empyrean [ˌempi'riən, em'piriən], a. & s. Empyrée (m).

emu ['i:mju:], s. Orn: Émeu m.

emulate ['emjuleit], v.tr. Être l'émule de (qn); rivaliser avec, imiter (qn, qch.).

emulation [ˌemju'leiʃ(ə)n], s. Émulation f.

emulative ['emjulətiv], a. Plein d'émulation.

emulator ['emjuleitər], s. Émule mf (of, de).

emulous ['emjuləs], a. Émulateur, -trice (of, de); rival; ambitieux (de).

emulsifier [i'mʌlsifaiər], s. Émulseur m.

emulsify [i'mʌlsifai], v.tr. Émulsionner.

emulsion [i'mʌlʃ(ə)n], s. Émulsion f.

en [en], s. (La lettre) n m. S.a. QUADRAT.

enable [i'neibl], v.tr. To e. s.o. to do sth., (i) rendre qn capable, mettre qn à même, permettre à qn, de faire qch.; (ii) Jur: habiliter qn à faire qch.; donner pouvoir à qn de faire qch.

enact [i'nækt], v.tr. 1. Jur: Rendre (un arrêt); promulguer (une loi); ordonner, arrêter, décréter (une mesure). 2. Lit: Jouer, représenter (une tragédie); procéder à, accomplir (une cérémonie); jouer (un rôle).

enactment [i'næktmənt], s. 1. Promulgation f (d'une loi). 2. Loi, ordonnance f; décret m.

enamel¹ [i'næm(ə)l], s. 1. Émail m, pl. émaux. (a) Niello enamels, émaux de niellure. (b) The e. of the teeth, l'émail des dents. 2. Vernis m; émail, pl. émails; laque f. E. paint, peinture f au vernis. U.S: Nail e., vernis à ongles. e'namel-ware, s. Ustensiles mpl en fer émaillé. e'namel-work, s. 1. Émaillure f. 2. Peinture f sur émail.

enamel², v.tr. (enamelled) 1. Émailler (la porcelaine, etc.). 2. Peindre au Ripolin (R.t.m.); ripoliner; vernir, vernisser (le fer, le cuir); glacer (le papier); Phot: émailler, satiner (une épreuve). Enamelled saucepan, casserole en fer émaillé. Enamelled tile, carreau vernissé. enamelling, s. (a) Émaillage m. (b) (Art of enamelling) Émaillure f. (c) Vernissage m (du fer, du cuir, etc.); glaçage m (du papier, etc.).

enameller [i'næmələr], s. Émailleur, -euse.

enamour [i'næmər], v.tr. Enamourer (qn); rendre (qn) amoureux. To be enamoured of, with, s.o., être amoureux, épris, de qn. To be enamoured of, with, sth., être passionné pour qch., être féru de qch.

en bloc ['ɑ̃(n)'blɔk], adv. En bloc.

encage [in'keidʒ], v.tr. Mettre en cage.

encamp [in'kæmp]. 1. v.tr. (Faire) camper (une armée). 2. v.i. Camper.

encampment [in'kæmpmənt], s. Campement m.

encase [in'keis], v.tr. 1. Encaisser, enfermer (in, dans). 2. (a) Munir (qch.) d'une enveloppe; blinder (un mécanisme). (b) F: Revêtir, recouvrir (s.o. in sth., qn de qch.).

encasement [in'keismənt], s. 1. Revêtement m; enveloppe f. 2. Anat: Emboîtement m (de deux os).

encash [in'kæʃ], v.tr. Encaisser (un chèque).

encashment [in'kæʃmənt], s. 1. Encaissement m. 2. Recette f, rentrée f.

encaustic [en'kɔ:stik], a. & s. Art: Encaustique (f). E. tile, carreau m céramique.

enceinte¹ [ɑ̃:n'sɛ̃nt, ɔn'sænt], a.f. Obst: Enceinte.

enceinte², s. Fort: Enceinte f.

encephalic [ˌense'fælik], a. Encéphalique.

encephalitis [ˌensefə'laitis], s. Med: Encéphalite f.

encephalogram [en'sefəˌgræm], s. Med: (Électro-) encéphalogramme m.

encephalography [enˌsefə'lɔgrəfi], s. Med: (Électro-) encéphalographie f.

encephalon [en'sefələn], s. Encéphale m.

enchain [in'tʃein], v.tr. Lit: Enchaîner.

enchant [in'tʃɑ:nt], v.tr. 1. Enchanter, ensorceler. 2. Enchanter, charmer, ravir. enchanting, a. Enchanteur, -eresse; ravissant, charmant. -ly, adv. A ravir; d'une manière ravissante.

enchanter [in'tʃɑ:ntər], s. Enchanteur m.

enchantment [in'tʃɑ:ntmənt], s. 1. Enchantement m. 1. Ensorcellement m. 2. Ravissement m.

enchantress [in'tʃɑ:ntris], s.f. Enchanteresse.

encircle [in'sə:kl], v.tr. Ceindre, encercler; envelopper, cerner (une armée); entourer (une armée, la taille).

encircling, s. Encerclement m.

enclave¹ [en'kleiv], s. Enclave f.

enclave², v.tr. Enclaver.

enclitic [en'klitik], a. & s. Gram: Enclitique (f).

enclose [in'klouz], *v.tr.* **1.** (*a*) Enclore, clôturer, enceindre (un champ) (**with**, de); entourer (l'ennemi, une ville). (*b*) Blinder; enfermer (un mécanisme) dans un carter. **2.** *Ecc:* Cloîtrer (une femme). **3.** Inclure, joindre. **Enclosed** (**herewith**) **please find . . .**, veuillez trouver ci-inclus, ci-joint, sous ce pli. . . . **Enclosed sea**, mer fermée.

enclosure [in'klouʒər], *s.* **1.** Clôture *f*. *Ecc:* Clôture, claustration *f* (de religieuses). **2.** (*a*) Enclos *m*, clos *m*. (*b*) *Turf:* Le pesage. **The public enclosures**, la pelouse. **The royal e.**, l'enceinte réservée pour la famille royale. **3.** *Com:* Pièce annexée; pièce jointe, document *m* ci-joint.

encomium, *pl.* -**ums** [in'koumiəm(z)], *s.* Panégyrique *m*, éloge *m*, louange *f*.

encompass [in'kʌmpəs], *v.tr.* **1.** Entourer, environner, ceindre (**with**, de). **2.** Envelopper, renfermer (**with**, **within**, dans).

encore[1] [ɔŋ'kɔːr], *s. & int.* Bis *m*, rappel *m*.

encore[2], *v.tr.* Bisser (un passage, un acteur). *Abs:* Crier bis.

encounter[1] [in'kauntər], *s.* **1.** Rencontre *f*. **2.** (*a*) Rencontre (hostile); combat *m*. (*b*) Duel *m*. (*c*) **E. of wits**, assaut *m* d'esprit.

encounter[2], *v.tr.* Rencontrer (un obstacle); éprouver, essuyer (des difficultés); affronter, aborder (l'ennemi).

encourage [in'kʌridʒ], *v.tr.* **1.** Encourager, enhardir (qn). **2.** Encourager, inciter (qn à faire qch.). **3.** Favoriser (les arts); encourager (une croyance). **encouraging**, *a.* Encourageant. -**ly**, *adv.* D'une manière encourageante.

encouragement [in'kʌridʒmənt], *s.* Encouragement *m*.

encroach [in'krout∫], *v.i.* **To e. (up)on sth.**, empiéter sur (une terre, etc.); entamer (son capital). **The sea is encroaching upon the land**, la mer gagne du terrain. **To e. upon s.o.'s time**, abuser du temps de qn.

encroachment [in'krout∫mənt], *s.* Empiètement *m* (**on**, sur). **E. upon s.o.'s rights**, usurpation *f* des droits de qn.

encrust [in'krʌst], *v.tr.* (*a*) Incruster. (*b*) Couvrir d'une croûte; encroûter (**with**, de).

encumber [in'kʌmbər], *v.tr.* **1.** Encombrer (**with**, de); embarrasser, gêner (qn, le mouvement), empêtrer. **2.** **Encumbered estate**, propriété grevée de dettes, d'hypothèques.

encumbrance [in'kʌmbrəns], *s.* **1.** Embarras *m*, charge *f*. **To be an e. to s.o.**, être à charge à qn. **Without** (**family**) **encumbrances**, sans charges de famille. **2.** *Jur:* (*a*) Charges (d'une succession). **To free an estate from encumbrances**, dégrever une propriété. (*b*) Servitude *f*.

encyclic(al) [in'siklik(əl)], *a.&s. R.C.Ch:* Encyclique(*f*).

encyclopaedia [in,saiklə'piːdiə], *s.* Encyclopédie *f*.

encyclopaedic [in,saiklə'piːdik], *a.* Encyclopédique.

encyclopaedist [in,saiklə'piːdist], *s.* Encyclopédiste *m*.

end[1] [end], *s.* **1.** (*a*) Bout *m*, extrémité *f*; fin *f* (d'un livre); queue *f* (d'une procession). **The upper e. of the table**, le haut bout de la table. *Swim:* **Deep, shallow e.**, grand, petit, fond (d'une piscine). *Fb:* **To change ends**, changer de camp. **The e. house of the street**, la dernière maison de la rue. *F:* **To have the right e. of the stick**, tenir le bon bout. **To get, have, hold of the wrong e. of the stick**, comprendre à travers, à rebours. **To begin, start, at the wrong e.**, brider l'âne par la queue. **To keep one's e. up**, (i) *Cr:* maintenir son guichet intact; (ii) *F:* ne pas se laisser démonter; tenir bon. *Adv.phrs.* **E. to e.**, bout à bout. **From e. to e.**, d'un bout à l'autre; de bout en bout. **On e.** (i) (*Of barrel, etc.*) Debout; sur bout. *S.a.* HAIR 1. (ii) **Two hours on e.**, (pendant) deux heures de suite, d'affilée. **Straight on e.**, **right on e.**, de suite; consécutivement. **E. on**, bout à bout. *Nau:* (*Of ships*) **To meet e. on**, se rencontrer nez à nez. *S.a.* DEAD-END, DEEP I. 1, LOOSE[1] 1. (*b*) *I.C.E:* **Big e.**, tête *f* de bielle. **Small e.**, pied *m* de bielle. (*c*) Tronçon *m* (de mât, etc.); tronche *f* (de câble). **Candle e.**, bout de chandelle. **2.** Limite *f*, borne *f*. **To the ends of the earth**, jusqu'au bout du monde. **3.** Bout, fin (du mois); issue *f* (d'une réunion); terme *m* (d'un procès, etc.). **The lease is at an e.**, le bail est expiré. **We shall never hear the e. of the matter**, cela va être des commérages sans fin. **And there's an e. of it!** et voilà tout! **There's no e. to it**, cela n'en finit pas. **To make an e. of sth.** ; **to put an e. to sth.** ; **to**

bring sth. to an e., en finir avec qch.; achever qch.; mettre fin à (un abus, etc.). **To draw to an e.**, tirer, toucher, à sa fin. **To come to an e.**, prendre fin; arriver à son terme. **To be at an e.**, (i) (*of resources*) être épuisé; (ii) (*of time*) être accompli; (iii) (*of action*) être terminé, fini, achevé. **To be at the e. of one's resources**, être au bout de ses ressources. **At the e. of (the) winter**, au sortir de l'hiver. **At the e. of the six months allowed**, au bout des six mois. **In the e.**, (i) à la longue, avec le temps; (ii) à la fin; enfin; en fin de compte. *F:* **No e.**, à n'en plus finir. *P:* **No e. of . . .**, une infinité de . . ., force. . . . **It'll do you no e. of good**, ça vous fera énormément de bien. *P:* **No e. of money**, un argent fou. *P:* **He thinks no e. of himself**, il se gobe. **To come to a bad e.**, mal finir. **To meet one's e.**, trouver la mort. **To be near one's e.**, n'en avoir plus pour longtemps. **To come to an untimely e.**, mourir avant l'âge. **4.** Fin, but *m*, dessein *m*. **Private ends**, intérêt(s) personnel(s). **To gain, attain, one's ends**, en venir, parvenir, à ses fins. **With this e. in view**, dans ce but; à cet effet. **For, to, this e.**, à cet effet; dans ce dessein. **To the e. that . . .**, afin que + *sub.* '**end-paper**, *s. Bookb:* (Feuille de) garde *f*. '**end-play**, *s. Mec.E:* '**end-thrust**, *s. Mec.E:* Poussée axiale. '**end-ways**, '**end-wise**, *adv.* **1.** (*a*) De chant, debout. (*b*) **Endways on**, avec le bout en avant. **2.** (*End to end*) Bout à bout. **3.** Longitudinalement.

end[2]. **1.** *v.tr.* Finir, achever, terminer (un ouvrage); conclure, clore (un discours). **To e. war**, mettre un terme aux guerres. **To e. off, up, a speech with a quotation**, conclure un discours avec une citation. **In order to e. the matter**, pour en finir. **It is ended and done with**, (i) c'est fini et bien fini; (ii) il n'y a plus à revenir là-dessus. **2.** *v.i.* Finir, se terminer. **All stories e. (up) like that**, toutes les histoires finissent de cette manière. **He ended by insulting me**, il finit par m'injurier. **To e. in a point**, aboutir, se terminer, en pointe. *F:* **To e. in smoke**, n'aboutir à rien; s'en aller en fumée. **ending**, *s.* **1.** Terminaison *f*, achèvement *m*. **2.** Fin *f*, conclusion *f*, (d'un ouvrage). **Happy e.**, dénouement heureux. **3.** *Gram:* Désinence *f*, terminaison.

endanger [in'deindʒər], *v.tr.* Mettre en danger; exposer, hasarder, risquer (sa vie, etc.); compromettre (des intérêts).

endear [in'diər], *v.tr.* Rendre cher (**to**, à). **endearing** *a.* **1.** Qui inspire l'affection. **2.** (Mot) tendre, affectueux. -**ly**, *adv.* Tendrement, affectueusement.

endearments [in'diəmənts], *s.pl.* Caresses *f*; mots tendres.

endeavour[1] [in'devər], *s.* Effort *m*, tentative *f*. **To use, make, every e. to . . .**, faire tous ses efforts, tout son possible, pour. . . .

endeavour[2], *v.i.* **To e. to do sth.**, s'efforcer, essayer, tâcher, de faire qch.; chercher à faire qch.

endemic [en'demik]. **1.** *a.* Endémique. **2.** *s.* Endémie *f*; maladie *f* endémique.

endive ['endiv], *s.* Chicorée *f* endive. **Curled e.**, chicorée frisée. **Broad-leaved e.**, endive *f*, (e)scarole *f. U.S:* (French) endive, endive *f*.

endless ['endlis], *a.* **1.** (*a*) (Vis, voyage) sans fin. (*b*) Sans bornes; infini. **E. speculation**, raisonnement *m* à perte de vue. **2.** (*In time*) (*a*) Sans fin; éternel. **It is an e. task**, c'est à n'en plus finir. (*b*) (*Of pain, etc.*) Continuel, incessant; (*of chatter, etc.*) intarissable. -**ly**, *adv.* Sans fin; sans cesse, éternellement, perpétuellement, intarissablement.

endocarditis ['endouka:'daitis], *s. Med:* Endocardite *f*.

endocardium ['endo'ka:diəm], *s.* Endocarde *m*.

endocarp ['endoka:p], *s. Bot:* Endocarpe *m*.

endocrine ['endokrain], *a. & s.* (Glande *f*) endocrine; à sécrétion interne.

endogamy [en'dogəmi], *s. Anthr:* Endogamie *f*.

endorse [in'dɔːs], *v.tr.* **1.** Endosser (un document, un chèque); viser (un passeport). *Adm:* **To e. a driving licence**, inscrire les détails d'un délit au verso du permis de conduire. **To e. sth. on a document**, to **a document with sth.**, mentionner qch. au verso d'un document. *Com:* **To e. a bill**, avaliser un effet. **To e. back a bill to drawer**, contre-passer un effet au tireur. **2.** Appuyer, venir à l'appui de (l'opinion de qn); souscrire à (une décision).

endorsee [endɔ:'si:], s. *Fin:* Endossataire *mf*.
endorsement [in'dɔ:smənt], s. 1. Endossement *m*, endos *m* (d'une lettre de change, d'un chèque); (*on passport, etc.*) mention spéciale. 2. Approbation *f* (d'une action); adhésion *f* (à une opinion).
endorser [in'dɔ:sər], s. *Fin:* Endosseur *m*.
endosperm ['endɔspə:m], s. *Bot:* Endosperme *m*.
endow [in'dau], v.tr. Doter (qn, une église) (with, de); assurer un revenu à (sa fille, sa femme). **To e. a bed in a hospital,** fonder un lit dans un hôpital. **Endowed with great talents,** doué de grands talents.
endowment [in'daumənt], s. 1. (a) Dotation *f*. (b) Fondation (léguée à une œuvre, etc.). (c) E. **assurance,** assurance *f* en cas de vie; assurance à terme fixe, à dotation. 2. Don (naturel).
endue [in'dju:], v.tr. *Lit:* Revêtir (qn d'une dignité, etc.) **To be endued with a quality,** être doué d'une qualité.
endurable [in'djuərəbl], a. Supportable, endurable.
endurance [in'djuərəns], s. 1. (a) Endurance *f*, résistance *f*. **To have great powers of e.,** être dur à la fatigue, au mal. **Beyond e.,** insupportable, intolérable. (b) E. **test,** (i) *Mec.E:* essai *m* de durée; (ii) *Sp:* épreuve *f* d'endurance. 2. Patience *f*, longanimité *f*.
endure [in'djuər]. 1. v.tr. Supporter, endurer (des insultes, etc.). **I can't e. being disturbed,** je ne peux pas souffrir qu'on vienne me déranger. 2. v.i. Durer, rester. **enduring,** a. 1. Durable, permanent. E. **evil,** mal qui persiste. E. **remorse,** remords vivace. 2. Patient, endurant. **-ly,** adv. D'une manière durable.
enema ['enimə], s. *Med:* 1. Lavement *m*. 2. Appareil *m* à lavements; irrigateur *m*.
enemy ['enəmi, -ni-]. 1. s. (a) Ennemi, -e. **To be one's own (worst) e.,** se desservir soi-même. E.**-occupied territory,** territoire occupé (par l'ennemi). *S.a.* PUBLIC 1. (b) *Coll:* **The e.,** l'ennemi, l'adversaire *m*. 2. a. **The e. fleet,** la flotte ennemie.
energetic [enə'dʒetik]. 1. a. Énergique. 2. s.pl. Energetics, énergétique *f*. **-ally,** adv. Énergiquement.
energize ['enədʒaiz], v.tr. (a) Donner de l'énergie à (qn); stimuler (qn). (b) *El:* Aimanter (l'âme d'une bobine, etc.); amorcer (une dynamo). **energizing,** a. 1. Stimulant, activant; (nourriture) énergétique. 2. *El:* E. **circuit,** circuit d'aimantation; circuit d'amorçage.
energumen [enə'gjumən], s. Énergumène *m*.
energy ['enədʒi], s. 1. Énergie *f*, force *f*, vigueur *f*. 2. *Mec:* Énergie, travail *m*. **Atomic e.,** énergie *f* atomique. **Kinetic e.,** énergie cinétique.
enervate ['enəveit], v.tr. Affaiblir, amollir, énerver (le corps, la volonté).
enervation [enə'veiʃ(ə)n], s. 1. Affaiblissement *m*, aveulissement *m*; énervation *f*. 2. Mollesse *f*.
enfant terrible [ɑ̃fɑ̃te'ri:bl], s. (a) Enfant *mf* impossible. (b) **The e.t. of the Romantic movement,** l'enfant terrible du Romantisme.
enfeeble [in'fi:bl], v.tr. Affaiblir (qn).
enfold [in'fould], v.tr. Envelopper (**in, with,** dans). **To e. s.o. in one's arms,** étreindre, embrasser qn.
enforce [in'fɔ:s], v.tr. 1. Faire valoir (un argument); appuyer (une demande). 2. Mettre en vigueur. **To e. one's rights,** faire valoir ses droits. **To e. the law,** appliquer la loi. **To e. the blockade,** rendre le blocus effectif. 3. **To e. a rule,** faire observer un règlement. **To e. obedience,** se faire obéir. **To e. one's will on s.o.,** imposer sa volonté à qn.
enforceable [in'fɔ:səbl], a. (Contrat) exécutoire.
enforcement [in'fɔ:smənt], s. *Jur:* Exécution *f*, mise *f* en vigueur, application *f* (d'une loi).
enfranchise [in'frænʃaiz], v.tr. 1. Affranchir (un esclave). 2. *Pol:* (a) Accorder le droit de vote à (qn). (b) Conférer la franchise, les droits municipaux à (une ville).
enfranchisement [in'frænʃizmənt], s. 1. Affranchissement *m* (d'un esclave). 2. *Pol:* Admission *f* (d'un citoyen) au suffrage; concession *f* de droits municipaux (à une ville).
engage [in'geidʒ], v.tr. & i. 1. Engager (sa parole, son honneur). **To e. (oneself) to do sth.,** s'engager, s'obliger, à faire qch. 2. (a) Engager, prendre (un domestique); embaucher (des ouvriers). (b) Retenir, réserver (une chambre, etc.); louer (un taxi). 3. Occuper (qn); fixer (l'attention); attirer, gagner (l'affection). **To e. s.o. in conversation,** lier conversa-

tion, entrer en conversation, avec qn. 4. **To e. the enemy,** en venir aux prises avec, attaquer, l'ennemi; donner. 5. (a) Mettre en prise (un engrenage). (b) v.i. (*Of cog-wheel*) (S')engrener, se mettre en prise (with, avec). **engage in,** v.i. **To e. in battle,** engager le combat. **To e. in conversation with s.o.,** entrer en conversation avec qn. **To e. in politics,** s'embarquer, se lancer, dans la politique. **engaged,** a. 1. E. (**to be married**), fiancé. **To become e.,** se fiancer. 2. Occupé, pris. **Are you e.?** êtes-vous occupé? (*to taxi-driver*) êtes-vous libre? 3. **This seat is e.,** cette place est retenue, prise. *Tp:* 'Line e.,' "ligne occupée." 4. *Mec.E:* (*Of gear-wheels, etc.*) En prise. **engaging,** a. Engageant, attrayant, séduisant.
engagement [in'geidʒmənt], s. 1. Engagement *m*, promesse *f*, obligation *f*. **To enter into an e.,** prendre, contracter, un engagement. *Com:* **To meet one's engagements,** faire face à ses engagements. **Owing to a previous e.,** à cause d'une promesse antérieure. **Social engagements,** invitations *fpl* dans le monde. **To have an e.,** être pris. E. **book,** agenda *m*. 2. (a) Engagement (de domestiques). (b) Poste *m*, situation *f* (de domestique, de secrétaire). 3. Fiançailles *fpl*. E. **ring,** anneau, bague, de fiançailles. 4. *Mil: Navy:* Combat *m*, action *f*, engagement. 5. *Mec.E:* Mise *f* en prise; embrayage *m*.
engender [in'dʒendər], v.tr. Faire naître, produire (un effet); engendrer (une maladie).
engine ['endʒin], s. 1. Machine *f*, appareil *m*. **Pumping e.,** pompe *f* d'épuisement. *S.a.* FIRE-ENGINE. 2. (a) (Steam) e., machine à vapeur. **Auxiliary e.,** (machine) auxiliaire (*f*). *S.a.* DONKEY-ENGINE, TRACTION-ENGINE. (b) *Rail:* Locomotive *f*. **Electric e.,** (i) locomotive électrique; (ii) locomotrice *f*. **To sit facing the e.,** s'asseoir dans le sens (de la marche) du train. 3. **Moteur** *m*. **Internal combustion e.,** moteur à combustion interne. **Two-stroke e.,** moteur à deux temps. **Side-valve e.,** moteur à soupapes latérales. **Overhead-valve e.,** moteur à soupapes en tête. **Rotary e.,** moteur rotatif. 'engine-driver, *s.* Mécanicien *m*. 'engine-oil, *s.* (a) Huile *f* pour moteurs. (b) Huile à graisser. 'engine-room, *s.* 1. Salle *f* des machines, hall *m* aux machines. 2. Chambre *f* de la machine, du moteur. *Nau:* Chambre des machines. 'engine-shed, *s.* Garage *m*, dépôt *m*, de machines, de locomotives.
engineer[1] [endʒi'niər], s. 1. Ingénieur *m*. **Consulting e.,** ingénieur conseil. **Civil e.,** ingénieur civil. **Electrical e.,** ingénieur électricien. **Mechanical e.,** ingénieur mécanicien. **Mining e.,** ingénieur des mines. **Naval e.,** ingénieur maritime. *Cin:* **Sound e.,** ingénieur du son. 2. *Nau:* Mécanicien *m*. 3. *Mil:* Soldat *m* du génie. **The Engineers,** le génie.
engineer[2], v.tr. 1. Construire (en qualité d'ingénieur). 2. Machiner (un coup); manigancer (une affaire).
engineering [endʒi'niəriŋ], s. 1. Technique *f* de l'ingénieur. **Civil e.,** le génie civil. **Chemical e.,** chimie *f* industrielle. **Electrical e.,** électrotechnique *f*. **Electrical e. industry,** industrie *f* de l'équipement électrique. **Industrial e.,** organisation industrielle. (**Mechanical**) **e.,** l'industrie mécanique, constructions *f* mécaniques. **Nuclear e.,** génie atomique. **Production e.,** technique de la production. **Human e.,** psychanalyse (industrielle). 2. *Usu. Pej:* Manœuvres *fpl*, machinations *fpl*.
England ['iŋglənd]. *Pr.n.* Angleterre *f*. **In E.,** en Angleterre. *S.a.* NEW ENGLAND.
English ['iŋgliʃ]. 1. a. & s. Anglais, -aise. *Arch:* **Early E. (style),** gothique *m* du XIIIe. siècle. *S.a.* CHANNEL[1] 2. 2. s. *Ling:* L'anglais, la langue anglaise. **To speak E.,** parler anglais. **What is the E. for . . .?** comment dit-on en anglais . . .? **The King's, Queen's, E.,** l'anglais correct. 'English-'born, *a.* D'origine, de naissance, anglaise. 'English-'speaking, *a.* Anglophone, de langue anglaise.
Englishman, *pl.* -men ['iŋgliʃmən], s.m. Anglais.
Englishwoman, *pl.* -women ['iŋgliʃwumən, -wimin], s.f. Anglaise.
engrave [in'greiv], v.tr. Graver (des caractères). **Engraved on the memory,** gravé dans la mémoire. **engraving,** s. (*Process or print*) Gravure *f*; (*print*) estampe *f*. **Wood e.,** gravure sur bois. **Half-tone e.,** similigravure *f*.

engraver [in'greivər], s. Graveur m.

engross [in'grous], v.tr. **1.** Jur: (a) Écrire(un document) en grosse; grossoyer (un document). (b) Rédiger (un document). **2.** Absorber, occuper (qn, l'attention). To be engrossed in one's work, être tout entier à son travail. To become engrossed in sth., s'absorber dans qch.

engrossment [in'grousmənt], s. **1.** Jur: Grosse f. **2.** Accaparement m, absorption f (de l'attention) (in, dans).

engulf [in'gʌlf], v.tr. Engloutir, engouffrer.

enhance [in'hɑːns], v.tr. Rehausser (le mérite de qch.); augmenter, accroître (le plaisir); mettre en valeur, relever (la beauté de qn).

enharmonic [ˌenhɑː'mɔnik], a. Mus: (Note f) enharmonique. E. change, enharmonie f.

enigma [i'nigmə], s. (a) Énigme f. To solve the enigma, trouver le mot de l'énigme. (b) Personne énigmatique, mystérieuse.

enigmatic(al) [ˌenigˈmætik(ə)l], a. Énigmatique.

enjoin [in'dʒɔin], v.tr. Enjoindre, prescrire, imposer (sth. on s.o., qch. à qn).

enjoy [in'dʒɔi], v.tr. **1.** Aimer, goûter; prendre plaisir à (qch.). To e. one's dinner, trouver le dîner bon. To e. a pipe, savourer une pipe. Have you enjoyed your holidays? avez-vous passé de bonnes vacances? To e. oneself, s'amuser, se divertir. He enjoys life, il sait jouir de la vie. To e. doing sth., prendre plaisir, trouver (du) plaisir, à faire qch. **2.** Jouir de, posséder (une fortune, la confiance de qn). To e. good health, jouir d'une bonne santé.

enjoyable [in'dʒɔiəbl], a. (Séjour, etc.) agréable; (mets) savoureux. We had a most e. evening, nous avons passé une excellente soirée. -ably, adv. Agréablement; avec plaisir.

enjoyment [in'dʒɔimənt], s. **1.** Jur: Jouissance f (d'un droit, etc.). **2.** Plaisir m.

enlarge [in'lɑːdʒ]. **1.** v.tr. (a) Agrandir; accroître, augmenter (sa fortune); élargir (un trou). Phot: Agrandir (un cliché). Med: Enlarged heart, hypertrophie f du cœur. (b) Développer, élargir (l'intelligence, etc.); amplifier (une idée). **2.** v.i. (a) S'agrandir, s'étendre, s'élargir. (b) To e. upon . . ., s'étendre sur, discourir longuement sur (un sujet).

enlargement [in'lɑːdʒmənt], s. Agrandissement m; accroissement m (d'une fortune); élargissement m (d'un trou); augmentation f. Phot: Agrandissement. Med: Hypertrophie f (du cœur).

enlarger [in'lɑːdʒər], s. Phot: Agrandisseur m.

enlighten [in'laitn], v.tr. To e. s.o. on a subject, éclairer qn sur un sujet. **enlightened**, a. (Of pers., mind) Éclairé. Often Iron: In these e. days, en ce siècle de lumières.

enlightenment [in'laitnmənt], s. **1.** Éclaircissements mpl (on, sur). **2.** Age of e., siècle m de lumières.

enlist [in'list]. **1.** v.tr. (a) Mil: Enrôler (un soldat). (b) Enrôler, recruter (des partisans). To e. the services of s.o., s'assurer le concours de qn. **2.** v.i. (Of soldier) S'engager, s'enrôler. **enlisted**, a. Mil: U.S: E. man, simple soldat, marin; gradé.

enlistment [in'listmənt], s. Mil: Engagement m, enrôlement m.

enliven [in'laiv(ə)n], v.tr. (a) Animer (qn, une discussion); stimuler (les affaires). (b) Égayer (un tableau, une fête).

en masse [ɑn'mæs], adv.phr. En masse, tous ensemble.

enmity ['enmiti], s. Inimitié f, hostilité f. At e. with s.o., en guerre ouverte avec qn.

ennoble [i'noubl], v.tr. **1.** Anoblir (un roturier). **2.** Ennoblir (qn, le caractère).

enormity [i'nɔːmiti], s. Énormité f (d'un crime).

enormous [i'nɔːməs], a. Énorme; colossal, -aux; (succès) fou. -ly, adv. Énormément.

enough [i'nʌf]. **1.** a. & s. Assez. E. money, assez d'argent. F: I've had e. of it, j'en ai assez. That's e., (i) cela suffit; (ii) en voilà assez! More than e., plus qu'il n'en faut. Have you e. to pay the bill? avez-vous de quoi payer? He has e. to live on, il a de quoi vivre. E. said! assez parlé! brisons là! One word was e. to prove that . . ., il a suffi d'un mot pour prouver que . . . It was e. to drive one crazy, c'était à vous rendre fou. S.a. SPARE² 2. **2.** adv. (a) Good e., assez bon. It's a good e. reason, c'est une raison

comme une autre. (b) (Intensive) You know well e. what I mean, vous savez très bien ce que je veux dire. Curiously e. . . ., chose curieuse. . . . S.a. SURE 2. (c) (Disparaging) She sings well e., elle ne chante pas mal. It is good e. in its way, but . . ., ce n'est pas si mal en son genre, mais. . . .

en passant [ɑː'pɑsɑ̃], adv.phr. En passant, incidemment.

enquire [in'kwaiər], v. = INQUIRE.

enquiry [in'kwaiəri], s. = INQUIRY.

enrage [in'reidʒ], v.tr. Rendre (qn) furieux; faire enrager (qn).

enrapture [in'ræptʃər], v.tr. Ravir, enchanter, transporter (un auditoire).

enrich [in'ritʃ], v.tr. Enrichir; meubler (l'esprit); fertiliser, amender (la terre). Enriched with gold, rehaussé d'or. I.C.E: To e. the mixture, enrichir le mélange.

enrichment [in'ritʃmənt], s. Enrichissement m.

enrockment [in'rɔkmənt], s. Civ.E: Hyd.E: Enrochement m.

enrol [in'roul], v.tr. (enrolled) Enrôler, encadrer (des recrues); embaucher (des ouvriers); immatriculer (des étudiants). To e. (oneself) in the army, s'enrôler, s'engager, dans l'armée. To e. for a course of lectures, se faire inscrire pour un cours.

enrolment [in'roulmənt], s. Enrôlement m (de soldats); engagement m, embauche f (d'ouvriers).

ensconce [in'skɔns], v.tr. To e. oneself in a corner, in an armchair, se nicher dans un coin, se rencogner dans un angle; se camper dans un fauteuil.

ensemble [ɔn'sɔmbl], s. Cost: Mus: etc: Ensemble m.

enshrine [in'ʃrain], v.tr. Enchâsser (une relique, une image) (in, dans).

enshroud [in'ʃraud], v.tr. Ensevelir (comme dans un linceul); recouvrir.

ensign ['ensain, 'ens(ə)n], s. **1.** Étendard m, drapeau m. Nau: Pavillon national. White e., pavillon de la Marine anglaise. Red e. = pavillon marchand. **2.** (a) Mil: A: Porte-drapeau m inv, enseigne m. (b) U.S: Navy: Enseigne m (de vaisseau).

ensilage ['insilidʒ], s. Husb: Ensilage m (de blé, etc.).

enslave [in'sleiv], v.tr. Réduire en esclavage; asservir. To e. hearts, captiver, enjôler, les cœurs.

enslavement [in'sleivmənt], s. Asservissement m.

ensnare [in'snɛər], v.tr. Prendre (qn) au piège.

ensue [in'sjuː], v.i. S'ensuivre. A long silence ensued, il se fit un long silence. **ensuing**, a. (An, jour) suivant; (événement) subséquent.

ensure [in'ʃuər], v.tr. **1.** Assurer (against, from, contre); garantir (de). **2.** (a) Assurer (le succès); réaliser (une guérison). (b) To e. s.o. enough to live on, assurer à qn de quoi vivre.

entablature [in'tæblətʃər], s. Arch: Entablement m.

entail¹ [in'teil], s. Jur: Substitution f (d'héritiers). **2.** Bien substitué, indisponible; majorat m.

entail², v.tr. **1.** Jur: To e. an estate (on s.o.), substituer un bien (au profit de qn). **2.** (Of actions) Amener, entraîner (des conséquences); occasionner (des dépenses); comporter (des difficultés).

entangle [in'tæŋgl], v.tr. **1.** Empêtrer. To get entangled in the seaweed, s'empêtrer dans les algues. To get entangled in a shady business, se trouver entraîné dans une affaire louche. **2.** Emmêler (les cheveux, du fil); enchevêtrer; embrouiller.

entanglement [in'tæŋglmənt], s. **1.** Embrouillement m, enchevêtrement m. S.a. WIRE¹ 1. **2.** Implication f.

entente [ɑːn'tɑːnt, ɔ̃:n'tɔ̃:nt], s. Entente f; esp. Dipl: entente cordiale.

enter ['entər], v. (entered) **I.** v.i. Entrer (into, through, dans, par). Th: E. Hamlet, Hamlet entre. **II.** enter, v.tr. **1.** (a) Entrer, pénétrer, dans (une maison); monter dans (une voiture); s'engager (dans un défilé, sur une route). S.a. HEAD¹ 2. (b) Faire entrer. **2.** To e. the Army, the Navy, entrer au service; se faire soldat, se faire marin. **3.** (a) To e. a name on a list, inscrire, porter, un nom sur une liste. To e. a horse for a race, engager un cheval dans une course. Abs. To e. for a race, se faire inscrire, s'engager, pour une course. S.a. EXAMINATION 2. (b) Com: To e. (up) an item in the ledger, porter un article au grand livre. E. that to me, mettez cela à mon compte. (c) To e. an action against s.o., intenter un procès à qn. **To e. a protest,** protester formellement. **enter into,** v.i. **1.** (a) **To e. into relations with s.o.,** entrer en relations, entamer des relations, avec qn. **To e. into a bargain, a contract,** conclure un marché; passer un contrat. **To e. into explanations,** fournir des explications; s'expliquer. (b) Prendre part à (un complot, etc.). **2. To e. into s.o.'s feelings,** partager les sentiments de qn. **To e. into the spirit of the game,** entrer dans le jeu. **enter on, upon,** v.i. Entrer en (fonctions, etc.); entreprendre (une tâche); débuter dans(une carrière); entamer (des négociations).

enteric [en'terik], a. Med: Entérique.

enteritis [entə'raitis], s. Med: Entérite f.

enterprise ['entəpraiz], s. **1.** Entreprise f. Pol.Ec: Private e., secteur privé. State e., secteur public. **2.** Esprit m d'entreprise; hardiesse f.

enterprising ['entəpraiziŋ], a. Entreprenant. **-ly,** adv. Hardiment, résolument.

entertain [entə'tein], v.tr. **1.** (a) Amuser, divertir (qn). **To e. s.o. with a story,** raconter une histoire à qn pour le distraire. (b) Faire la conversation à (qn). **2.** Régaler, fêter (qn). **To e. s.o. to dinner,** offrir un dîner à qn. Abs. Donner une réception. **They e. a great deal,** ils reçoivent beaucoup. **3.** Admettre, accueillir (une proposition); faire bon accueil à (une demande). **4.** Concevoir (une idée, des doutes); éprouver (des craintes); nourrir, caresser (un espoir); chérir (une illusion). **entertaining,** a. Amusant, divertissant.

entertainer [entə'teinər], s. **1.** Hôte m, hôtesse f. **2.** Amuseur; diseur, -euse (de monologues, etc.); comique m.

entertainment [entə'teinmənt], s. **1.** (a) Divertissement m. **Much to the e. of the crowd,** au grand amusement de la foule. (b) Th: Spectacle m. **E. tax,** taxe sur les spectacles. **2.** Hospitalité f. Adm: **E. allowance,** frais de représentation.

enthral(l) [in'θrɔ:l], v.tr. **(enthralled)** Captiver, charmer, ensorceler.

enthrone [in'θroun], v.tr. (a) Introniser (un évêque). (b) Mettre (un roi) sur le trône.

enthuse [in'θju:z], v.i., v.tr. F: S'enthousiasmer, se passionner **(over, about, sth.,** de, pour, qch.).

enthusiasm [in'θju:ziæzm], s. Enthousiasme m (for, about, pour). **Book that arouses e.,** livre qui passionne.

enthusiast [in'θju:ziæst], s. Enthousiaste mf (for, de). **Golf e.,** fervent(e) du golf; F: enragé(e) de golf.

enthusiastic [in,θju:zi'æstik], a. Enthousiaste. **E. fisherman,** pêcheur passionné, enragé. **To become, wax, e. over sth.,** s'enthousiasmer pour qch. **-ally,** adv. Avec enthousiasme.

entice [in'tais], v.tr. Attirer, séduire, allécher. **To e. s.o. to do sth.,** entraîner qn à faire qch. **To e. s.o. away,** entraîner qn à sa suite. **To e. s.o. into a place,** attirer qn dans un endroit. **enticing,** a. (Of offer) Séduisant, attrayant, alléchant; (of dish) affriandant, alléchant.

enticement [in'taismənt], s. **1.** Séduction f. **2.** Attrait m, charme m. **3.** Appât m.

entire [in'taiər], a. (a) Entier, tout. **The e. population,** la population (tout) entière. (b) Entier, complet. **An e. delusion,** une illusion complète. **An e. success,** un véritable succès. **-ly,** adv. Entièrement, tout à fait. **To agree e. with s.o.,** être entièrement d'accord avec qn; être tout à fait du même avis que qn. **E. unnecessary,** absolument inutile. **You are e. mistaken,** vous vous trompez du tout au tout.

entirety [in'taiərəti], s. Intégralité f. **In its e.,** en entier; totalement. **To fulfil an order in its e.,** exécuter intégralement une commande.

entitle [in'taitl], v.tr. **1.** Intituler (un livre). **2.** Donner à (qn) le titre de (duc, etc.). **3.** **To e. s.o. to do sth.,** donner à qn le droit de faire qch. **entitled,** a. **To be e. to sth.,** avoir droit à qch. **To be e. to do sth.,** avoir qualité pour faire qch.; être en droit, avoir le droit, de faire qch. **To be e. to say that . . .,** pouvoir dire à juste titre que. . . . Jur: **To be e. to inherit,** avoir habilité à hériter.

entity ['entiti], s. Phil: Entité f.

entomb [in'tu:m], v.tr. **1.** Mettre au tombeau; enterrer, ensevelir (un mort). **2.** Servir de tombeau à (un mort).

entomological [entəmə'lɔdʒikl], a. Entomologique.

entomology [entə'mɔlədʒi], s. Entomologie f.

entourage [ontu'ra:ʒ], s. Entourage m.

entr'acte ['ɑ̃ntrækt, 'ɔn-], s. Th: Entracte m.

entrails ['entreilz], s.pl. Entrailles f.

entrain [in'trein]. **1.** v.tr. (Faire) embarquer (des troupes, etc.) en chemin de fer. **2.** v.i. S'embarquer (en chemin de fer).

entrance¹ ['entrəns], s. **1.** Entrée f. (a) **To make one's e.,** faire son entrée. Actor's e. (on the stage), entrée en scène d'un acteur. **E. gate,** barrière f; grille f d'entrée. (b) Admission f, accès m. **To give e. to a room,** donner accès à une pièce. **2.** (Way in) **Main e.,** entrée principale. **Side e.,** entrée latérale; porte f de service. S.a. HALL 3. **'entrance-fee,** s. (a) Prix m d'entrée. (b) Droit m d'inscription; cotisation f d'admission (à un club, etc.).

entrance² [in'trɑ:ns], v.tr. Extasier, ravir, transporter (qn). **To be entranced,** tomber en extase. **To be entranced by . . .,** s'extasier sur. . . . **entrancing,** a. Enchanteur, -eresse; ravissant; (conte) passionnant; (paysage) d'une beauté féerique.

entrant ['entrənt], s. (a) Débutant, -ante (dans une profession, etc.). (b) Inscrit, -ite (pour une course).

entrap [in'træp], v.tr. **(entrapped)** Prendre (qn) au piège. **To e. s.o. into doing sth.,** user d'artifices pour faire faire qch. à qn.

entreat [in'tri:t], v.tr. **To e. s.o. to do sth.,** prier, supplier, qn de faire qch.; demander instamment à qn de faire qch. **I e. your indulgence,** je réclame votre indulgence. **entreating,** a. (Ton, regard) suppliant. **-ly,** adv. D'un air, d'un ton, suppliant.

entreaty [in'tri:ti], s. Prière f, supplication f, adjuration f. **At the urgent e. of s.o.,** sur les vives instances de qn. **Look of e.,** regard suppliant.

entrechat ['ontrəʃa:], s. Danc: Entrechat m.

entrée ['ontrei, 'ɑ̃:tre], s. **1.** Entrée f (to, into, dans). **2.** Cu: Entrée.

entrench [in'trenʃ], v.tr. Mil: Retrancher (un camp). **To e. oneself,** se retrancher, se terrer. **Entrenching tool,** pelle-bêche f.

entrenchment [in'trenʃmənt], s. Mil: Retranchement m.

entrepôt ['ontrəpou], s. Entrepôt m. **E. port,** port m franc.

entrust [in'trʌst], v.tr. **To e. s.o. with sth.,** charger qn (d'une tâche, etc.); investir qn (d'une mission). **To e. sth. to s.o.,** confier (un secret, un enfant) à qn. **To e. s.o. with the care of sth.,** s'en remettre à qn du soin de qch. **To e. a sum to s.o.,** remettre (en confiance) une somme à qn.

entry ['entri], s. **1.** (a) Entrée f. P.N: **No e.,** passage interdit au public; défense d'entrer; (one-way street) sens interdit. (b) **To make one's e.,** faire son entrée; Th: entrer en scène. (c) Mus: Entrée. (d) Début m (dans la politique, etc.). **2.** (a) Enregistrement m (d'un acte, etc.); inscription f (d'un nom sur une liste). (b) Book-k: (i) Passation f d'écriture. **Single, double, e.,** comptabilité f en partie simple, en partie double. (ii) (Item) Article m, rubrique f, écriture f. Nau: **E. in the log,** élément m du journal. **3.** Sp: Engagement m, inscription (d'un concurrent). **E. form,** feuille f d'inscription.

entwine [in'twain]. **1.** v.tr. (a) Entrelacer. (b) Enlacer (with, de). **The ivy entwines the elms,** le lierre enlace, embrasse, les ormes. **2.** v.i. S'entrelacer.

enucleate [i'nju:klieit], v.tr. **1.** Surg: Énucléer (un œil, une tumeur). **2.** Expliquer, élucider.

enucleation [i,nju:kli'ei(ə)n], s. Énucléation f.

enumerate [i'nju:məreit], v.tr. Énumérer, détailler, dénombrer.

enumeration [i,nju:mə'reiʃ(ə)n], s. Énumération f, dénombrement m.

enunciate [i'nʌnsieit], v.tr. **1.** Énoncer, exprimer (une opinion, etc.). **2.** Prononcer, articuler. **To e. clearly,** articuler distinctement.

enunciation [i,nʌnsi'eiʃ(ə)n], s. **1.** Énonciation f (d'une opinion). **2.** Articulation f, énonciation.

envelop [in'veləp], v.tr. **(enveloped)** Envelopper (in, dans, de). Mil: **Enveloping movement,** manœuvre m d'enveloppement.

envelope ['envəloup, 'ɔn-], s. **1.** (Covering) Enveloppe f. Biol: Tunique f (d'un organe). **2.** Enveloppe (d'une lettre). **Window e., e. with transparent window,** enveloppe vitrifiée, à panneau transparent. **To put a letter in an e.,** mettre une lettre sous enveloppe. **In a sealed e.,** sous pli cacheté.

envelopment [in'veləpmənt], s. Enveloppement m.
envenom [in'venəm], v.tr. Envenimer, aigrir (une discussion).
enviable ['enviəbl], a. Enviable; digne d'envie.
envious ['enviəs], a. Envieux. E. looks, regards d'envie. To be e. of s.o., porter envie à qn. To make s.o. e. of sth., faire envier qch. à qn. (Of thg) To make s.o. e., faire envie à qn. -ly, adv. Avec envie; (regarder qch.) d'un œil d'envie.
environment [in'vaiərənmənt], s. Milieu m, entourage m; ambiance f, environnement m.
environs [in'vaiərənz], s.pl. Environs m, alentours m.
envisage [in'vizidʒ], v.tr. 1. Envisager (une difficulté, un danger). 2. Faire face à (un danger, etc.).
envoy ['envoi], s. Envoyé, -e (diplomatique); ambassadeur m.
envy[1] ['envi], s. 1. Envie f. F: He'd have been green with e., il en aurait fait une jaunisse. 2. Objet m d'envie. To be the e. of s.o., être l'objet d'envie de qn; faire envie à qn.
envy[2], v.tr. Envier, porter envie à (qn). To e. s.o. sth., envier qch. à qn. To be envied by s.o., s'attirer l'envie de qn.
enzyme ['enza(:)im], s, Ch: Enzyme f; diastase f.
eocene ['i:(ə)si:n], a. & s. Geol: Éocène (m).
eon ['i:ən], s = AEON.
epaulet(te) ['epəlet], s. Épaulette f.
ephedrin(e) ['efidrin, i'fedrin], s. Pharm: Éphédrine f.
ephemeral [i'femərəl], a. Éphémère. E. passion, passion fugitive. Their beauty is e., leur beauté n'est que d'un jour.
ephemeridae [,efi'meridi:], s.pl. Ent: Éphéméridés m.
ephemeris, pl. **ephemerides** [i'feməris, ,efi'meridi:z], s. Astr: Éphéméride f.
epic ['epik]. 1. a. Épique; (combat) légendaire. 2. s. Poème m épique; épopée f.
epicarp ['epikɑ:p], s. Bot: Épicarpe m.
epicentre ['episentər], s. Geol: Épicentre m (d'un séisme).
epicure ['epikjuər], s. Gourmet m, gastronome m.
epicurean [,epikjuə'riən], a. & s. Épicurien, -ienne.
epicureanism [,epikjuə'riənizm], **epicurism** ['epikjuə-rizm], s. Épicurisme m.
epicycle ['episaikl], s. Astr: Épicycle m.
epicyclic [,epi'saiklik], a. Mec.E: Épicycloïdal, -aux.
epicycloid [,epi'saikləid], s. Geom: Épicycloïde f.
epidemic [,epi'demik]. 1. a. Épidémique. 2. s. Épidémie f.
epidemical [,epi'demik(ə)l], a. Épidémique.
epidermis [,epi'də:mis], s. Anat: Épiderme m.
epigastrium [,epi'gæstriəm], s. Anat: Épigastre m.
epiglottis [,epi'glɔtis], s. Épiglotte f.
epigram ['epigræm], s. Épigramme f.
epigrammatic [,epigrə'mætik], a. Épigrammatique. -ally, adv. Épigrammatiquement.
epigraph ['epigrɑ:f, -græf], s. Épigraphe f.
epigraphy [i'pigrəfi], s. Épigraphie f.
epilepsy ['epilepsi], s. Épilepsie f.
epileptic [,epi'leptik], a. & s. Épileptique (mf). Epileptic fit, crise f d'épilepsie.
epilogue ['epilɔg], s. Épilogue m.
Epiphany [i'pifəni], s. Ecc: L'Épiphanie f; F: le jour, la fête, des Rois.
episcopal [i'piskəp(ə)l], a. Épiscopal, -aux. E. ring, anneau pastoral. (In U.S. & Scot.) The E. Church, l'Église épiscopale.
episcopalian [i,piskə'peiliən], a. & s. (U.S. & Scot.) Épiscopalien, -ienne; (membre m) de l'Église épiscopale.
episcopate [i'piskəpeit], s. Épiscopat m.
episode ['episoud], s. Épisode m.
episodic(al) [,epi'sɔdik(əl)], a. Épisodique.
epistle [i'pisl], s. Épître f.
epistolary [i'pistələri], a. Épistolaire.
epistyle ['epistail], s. Arch: Épistyle m.
epitaph ['epitɑ:f, -tæf], s. Épitaphe f.
epithet ['epiθet], s. Épithète f.
epithetic(al) [,epi'θetik(əl)], a. Épithétique.
epitome [i'pitəmi], s. Épitomé m, abrégé m, résumé m (d'un livre); raccourci m; quintessence f (de l'élégance).

epitomize [i'pitəmaiz], v.tr. Faire un abrégé, résumer (un discours, etc.); incarner (qch.).
epizootic [,epizou'ɔtik], a. Vet: (Maladie) épizootique.
epoch ['i:pɔk], s. Époque f, âge m. To make, mark, an e., faire époque, faire date. 'epoch-,making, 'epoch-,marking, a. Qui fait époque; historique, mémorable, inoubliable.
Epsom ['epsəm]. Pr.n. E. salts, sulfate m de magnésie; sels m d'Epsom, sels anglais.
equability [,i:kwə'biliti, ,ek-], s. Uniformité f (de climat); égalité f, régularité f (d'humeur).
equable ['ekwəbl], a. Uniforme, régulier; égal, -aux. E. temperament, humeur égale.
equal[1] ['i:kwəl]. 1. a. (a) Égal, -aux (to, with, à). To fight on e. terms, combattre à armes égales. To be on e. terms with s.o., être sur un pied d'égalité avec qn. All things being e., toutes choses égales (d'ailleurs). F: To get e. with s.o., se venger de qn; prendre sa revanche. (b) To be e. to the occasion, to a task, être à la hauteur de la situation, d'une tâche. To be e. to doing sth., être de force à, de taille à, à même de, faire qch. I don't feel e. to (doing) it, je ne m'en sens pas le courage, la force. 2. s. Égal, -ale; pair m. Your equals, vos pareils, vos égaux. You will not find his e., vous ne trouverez pas son pareil. To treat s.o. as an e., traiter qn d'égal à égal. -ally, adv. Également, pareillement. E. exhausted, tout aussi éreintés. E. with s.o., à l'égal de qn.
equal[2], v.tr. (equalled) Égaler (in, en). Not to be equalled, sans égal; qui n'a pas son égal.
equality [i'kwɔliti], s. Égalité f. On a footing of e., on an e., sur un pied d'égalité, d'égal à égal (with, avec).
equalization [,i:kwəlai'zeiʃ(ə)n], s. 1. Égalisation f. 2. Compensation f; péréquation f; équilibrage m (de forces, etc.).
equalize ['i:kwəlaiz]. 1. v.tr. (a) Égaliser. Fb: To e. (the score), marquer égalité de points; égaliser (la marque). (b) Compenser, équilibrer (des forces, etc.). 2. v.i. (a) S'égaliser. (b) Se compenser, s'équilibrer.
equanimity [,ekwə'nimiti], s. Égalité f d'âme, de caractère; tranquillité f d'esprit; équanimité f. To recover one's e., se ressaisir; se rasséréner.
equate [i'kweit], v.tr. (a) Égaler (to, with, à). Mth: Mettre (deux expressions, etc.) en équation. (b) Assimiler (with, à).
equation [i'kweiʃ(ə)n], s. 1. (a) Astr: E. of time, équation f du temps. (b) Psy: Personal e., équation personnelle. 2. Mth: Simple, quadratic, e., équation du premier, du deuxième, degré.
equator [i'kweitər], s. Équateur m. At the e., sous l'équateur.
equatorial [,ekwə'tɔ:riəl, ,i:k-], a. Équatorial, -aux.
equerry ['ekwəri], s.m. 1. Écuyer. 2. Officier de la maison du souverain.
equestrian [i'kwestriən]. 1. a. (Statue, etc.) équestre. 2. s. (f. occ. equestrienne) (a) Cavalier, -ière. (b) Écuyer, -ère (de cirque).
equidae ['i:kwidi:], s.pl. Z: Équidés mpl.
equidistant [,i:kwi'distənt], a. Geom: Équidistant.
equilateral [,i:kwi'læt(ə)rəl], a. Geom: Équilatéral, -aux.
equilibrate [i:'kwilibreit]. 1. v.tr. Équilibrer; mettre en équilibre. 2. v.i. S'équilibrer; être en équilibre.
equilibration [i:,kwili'breiʃ(ə)n], s. Équilibration f; mise f en équilibre.
equilibrist [i:'kwilibrist], s. Équilibriste mf; funambule mf.
equilibrium [,i:kwi'libriəm], s. Équilibre m, aplomb m.
equine ['i:kwain, 'ekwain], a. Équin; de cheval. E. race, race chevaline.
equinoctial [,i:kwi'nɔkʃ(ə)l, ,ekwi-], a. (a) Équinoxial, -aux. (b) E. tides, grandes marées.
equinox ['i:kwinɔks, 'ekwi-], s. Équinoxe m.
equip [i'kwip], v.tr. (equipped) 1. Équiper, armer (un navire, un soldat). 2. Meubler, monter (une maison); installer, doter (une ferme, etc.); outiller, monter (une usine). To e. s.o. with sth., munir, pourvoir, qn de qch. Well equipped, bien équipé; (laboratoire) bien installé, bien agencé; (ménage) bien monté.

equipment [i'kwipmənt], s. **1.** Équipement m (d'une expédition); armement m (d'un navire); outillage m (d'une usine); installation f (d'un laboratoire). **2.** (Objets mpl d')équipement; équipage m. **Electrical e. of a motor car**, appareillage m électrique d'une auto. **Camping e.**, matériel m de camping. **A soldier's e.**, les effets m, le fourniment, d'un soldat. **Works with modern e.**, usine avec outillage moderne. **School e.**, matériel scolaire.

equipoise ['ekwipɔiz], s. (a) Équilibre m. **To preserve the e. of sth.**, maintenir qch. en équilibre. (b) Contrepoids m.

equitable ['ekwitəbl], a. Équitable, juste. **-ably**, adv. Équitablement; avec justice.

equitation [ˌekwi'teiʃ(ə)n], s. Équitation f.

equity ['ekwiti], s. **1.** Équité f, justice f. **2.** Th: Le syndicat des artistes de la scène. **3.** Fin: **E. securities, equities**, actions f ordinaires.

equivalence [i'kwivələns], s. Équivalence f. Fin: **E. of exchange**, parité f de change.

equivalent [i'kwivələnt]. **1.** a. Équivalent. **To be e. to sth.**, être équivalent, équivaloir, à qch. **2.** s. Équivalent m.

equivocal [i'kwivɔk(ə)l], a. Équivoque. (a) Ambigu, -uë; (mot) à double entente. **To give an e. answer**, répondre d'une façon équivoque. (b) Incertain, douteux. (c) Suspect, douteux; louche. **-ally**, adv. D'une manière équivoque.

equivocate [i'kwivɔkeit], v.i. User d'équivoque, jouer sur les mots; équivoquer, tergiverser.

equivocation [iˌkwivɔ'keiʃ(ə)n], s. Equivocation f. tergiversation f.

era ['iərə], s. Ère f. **To mark an e.**, faire époque.

eradicate [i'rædikeit], v.tr. (a) Déraciner (une plante). (b) Extirper, déraciner (des préjugés).

eradication [iˌrædi'keiʃ(ə)n], s. Déracinement m (d'un arbre). Extirpation f (d'un préjugé).

erase [i'reiz], v.tr. Effacer; raturer ou gommer (un mot).

eraser [i'reizər], s. (a) Grattoir m. (b) Gomme f (à effacer). **Ink e.**, gomme à encre.

erasure [i'reiʒər], s. Rature f; grattage m.

ere ['eər]. A. & Poet: **1.** prep. Avant. S.a. LONG¹ II. **2.** 2. conj. Avant que + sub.

erect¹ [i'rekt], a. (Of pers.) Droit, debout. **With tail e.**, la queue levée, dressée. **With head e.**, la tête haute, le front haut. **To stand e.**, se tenir droit; se redresser.

erect², v.tr. **1.** Dresser; arborer (un mât, etc.). **2.** Ériger, construire (un édifice); élever, ériger (une statue); dresser (un échafaudage); monter, installer (une machine); imaginer, édifier (un système). **3.** Opt: Redresser (une image renversée). **erecting**, s. **1.** = ERECTION 1. **2.** Redressement m (d'une image). **E. prism**, prisme redresseur.

erection [i'rekʃ(ə)n], s. **1.** (a) Dressage m (d'un mât, etc.). (b) Construction f (d'un édifice); érection f (d'une statue); montage m, installation f (d'une machine). **2.** Bâtisse f, construction, édifice m.

erg¹ [əːg], s. Ph.Meas: Erg m.

erg², s. Geog: Erg m.

ergot ['ɔːgot], s. Agr: Pharm: Ergot m.

Erie ['iəri]. Pr.n. Geog: **Lake E.**, le Lac Érié.

Erin ['iərin]. Pr.n. A. & Poet: L'Irlande f.

ermine ['əːmin], s. **1.** Z: Hermine f. **2.** (Fur) Hermine. Com: roselet m.

erode [i'roud], v.tr. Éroder; ronger; (of acid) corroder (le fer, etc.).

erosion [i'rouʒ(ə)n], s. Érosion f; usure f (d'une chaudière). Dent: Érosion dentaire. Geog: Érosion, dénudation f. **Cycle of e.**, cycle m d'érosion.

erosive [i'rousiv], a. Érosif, -ive.

erotic [i'rɔtik], a. Érotique.

eroticism [e'rɔtisizm], s. Érotisme m.

err [əːr], v.i. (a) S'égarer, s'écarter (from, de). (b) Pécher. **He does not e. on the side of modesty**, il ne pèche pas par la modestie. **To e. out of ignorance**, pécher par ignorance. (c) Errer; être dans l'erreur; faire erreur; se tromper. **erring**, a. Dévoyé, égaré; tombé dans l'erreur.

errand ['er(ə)nd], s. Commission f, course f. **To go, run, errands**, faire les commissions, des courses. **'errand-boy**, s.m. Garçon de courses; petit commissionnaire.

erratic [i'rætik], a. **1.** Med: (Douleur) erratique. **2.** Irrégulier. Aut: **E. driving**, conduite mal assurée. **3.** (Of pers.) Excentrique, fantasque, velléitaire. **E. life**, vie désordonnée. **4.** s. Geol: Bloc m erratique. **-ally**, adv. Sans méthode, sans règle; (travailler) à bâtons rompus, par boutades.

erratum, pl. **-ta** [i'rɑːtəm, -tə], s. Erratum m, pl. errata.

erroneous [i'rounjəs], a. Erroné; faux, f. fausse. **-ly**, adv. A tort; par erreur.

error ['erər], s. **1.** Erreur f, faute méprise f. **E. of, in, judgment**, erreur de jugement Printer's e., faute d'impression; F: coquille f. **Typing e.**, erreur, faute, de frappe. **Clerical e.**, erreur d'écriture, de transcription. Com: **Errors and omissions excepted**, sauf erreur ou omission. Mil: **E. in range**, écart m en portée. **To make, commit, an e.**, faire, commettre, une erreur; se tromper. **It is an e. to suppose that . . .**, on aurait tort de croire que. . . . **2.** (a) **To be in e.**, être dans l'erreur; avoir tort. **Goods sent in e.**, marchandises envoyées par erreur. (b) **He has seen the e. of his ways**, il est revenu de ses égarements. **3.** Écart (de conduite).

Erse [əːs], a. & s. Ling: (a) Erse (m), gaélique (m). (b) F: (not used in Eire) Irlandais (m).

erstwhile ['əːstwail], adv. A. & Poet: Autrefois, jadis.

eructation [ˌiːrʌk'teiʃ(ə)n], s. Éructation f.

erudite ['eru(ː)dait], a. Érudit, savant.

erudition [ˌeru(ː)'diʃ(ə)n], s. Érudition f.

erupt [i'rʌpt], v.i. **1.** (Of teeth) Percer. **2.** (Of volcano) Entrer en éruption; faire éruption.

eruption [i'rʌpʃ(ə)n], s. **1.** (a) Éruption f. (b) Éclat m, accès m (de colère, etc.). **2.** Éruption, poussée f (de boutons); éruption (des dents).

erysipelas [ˌeri'sipiləs], Med: Érysipèle m, érésipèle m.

escalade¹ [ˌeskə'leid], s. Escalade f.

escalade², v.tr. Escalader.

escalate ['eskəleit], v.i. Pol: Mil: transformer un conflit localisé en une guerre plus étendue.

escalation [ˌeskə'leiʃ(ə)n], s. **1.** Pol.Ec: Ajustement m (des prix). **2.** Escalade f, transformation f d'un conflit localisé en une guerre plus étendue.

escalator ['eskəleitər], s. Escalier roulant, escalator m.

escapade [ˌeskə'peid], s. Escapade f; frasque f, F: fredaine f.

escape¹ [is'keip], s. **1.** (a) Fuite f, évasion f, dérobade f. **To make one's e.**, s'échapper, se sauver. **To make good one's e.**, réussir, parvenir, à s'échapper. **To have a narrow e.**, l'échapper belle. **He had a narrow e. from falling**, il a failli tomber. **There's no e. from it**, il n'y a pas moyen d'y échapper, il faut en passer par là. **Way of e.**, issue f. attrib. **E. clause**, clause échappatoire. (b) Échappement m, fuite, dégagement m (de gaz, d'eau, etc.). (c) **E. from the earth's gravitational pull**, libération f de l'attraction terrestre. **2.** (Fire-)e., échelle f de sauvetage; escalier m de secours. **es'cape-valve**, s. Soupape f d'échappement, de décharge.

escape². **1.** v.i. (a) (S')échapper (from, out of, de); prendre la fuite; (d'un liquide) déborder. **To e. from prison**, s'évader. **To e. to the mountains**, gagner les montagnes. **Escaped prisoner**, évadé m. (b) **To e. by the skin of one's teeth**, échapper, s'en tirer, tout juste. **He escaped with a fright**, il en a été quitte pour la peur. (c) (Of gases, fluids) Se dégager; s'échapper, fuir. **2.** v.tr. (a) (Of pers.) Échapper à (un danger). **To e. pursuit**, se dérober aux poursuites. **He narrowly escaped death**, il a échappé tout juste à la mort. **He just escaped being killed**, il a manqué (de) se faire tuer. (b) (Of thgs) **To e. notice**, échapper à l'attention; passer inaperçu. **That fact escaped me**, ce fait m'avait échappé. (c) **An oath escaped him**, il laissa échapper un juron. **Not a word escaped his lips**, pas un mot n'échappa de ses lèvres.

escapee [eskei'piː], s. Évadé, -ée.

escapement [is'keipmənt], s. (a) Issue f, débouché m. (b) Clockm: etc: Échappement m.

escapism [is'keipizm], s. Évasion f (de la réalité).

escapist [is'keipist], a. **E. literature**, littérature f d'évasion.

escarpment [is'kɑːpmənt], s. Escarpement m.

eschew [is'tʃuː], v.tr. O: Éviter (qch.); renoncer à (qch.); s'abstenir de (qch.).

escort¹ ['eskɔːt], s. (a) Mil: etc: Escorte f. **Under the e. of . . .,** sous l'escorte de. . . . **Under e.,** sous escorte. (b) Cavalier m (qui accompagne une dame).

escort² [es'kɔːrt], v.tr. Escorter, faire escorte à (un général, un convoi); servir de cavalier à (une dame). **May I e. you home?** puis-je vous reconduire?

escritoire [ˌeskriː'twɑːr], s. Furn: Secrétaire m.

escutcheon [is'kʌtʃ(ə)n], s. 1. (a) Her: Écu m, écusson m. (b) N.Arch: Tableau m. 2. Tchn: Écusson, entrée f (de serrure).

Eskimo, pl. -o(e)s ['eskimou, -ouz], a. & s. (pl. also **Eskimo**) Esquimau (m), -aux. **E. woman,** esquimaude.

esoteric [ˌesoˈterik], a. Ésotérique; secret.

espalier [is'pæljər], s. Espalier m ((i) treillage, (ii) arbre). **Fan-shaped e.,** palmette f.

esparto(-grass) [es'pɑːtou(grɑːs)], s. Spart(e) m; alfa m. **E. products,** sparterie f.

especial [is'peʃ(ə)l], a. Spécial, -aux; particulier. **-ally,** adv. Surtout, particulièrement.

espionage [ˌespiəˈnɑːʒ], s. Espionnage m.

esplanade [ˌesplə'neid], s. Esplanade f.

espouse [is'pauz], v.tr. 1. Lit: Épouser (une femme). 2. Épouser, embrasser (une cause).

espresso [es'presou], a. & s. 1. **E. (coffee),** (café m) expresso, F: café express. 2. **E. (machine),** cafetière f à pression, expresso (m).

esprit de corps ['espriːdə'kɔːr], s. Esprit m de corps.

espy [is'pai], v.tr. Apercevoir, aviser, entrevoir (au loin), découvrir.

esquire [is'kwaiər], s. Titre m honorifique d'un "gentleman." **John Smith, Esq.** = Monsieur John Smith.

essay¹ ['esei], s. 1. Essai m, effort m; tentative f (at, de). 2. (a) Lit: Essai. (b) Sch: Dissertation f; composition f (littéraire); narration f.

essay² [e'sei], v.tr. Lit: 1. Mettre à l'épreuve. 2. Essayer (sth., to do sth., qch., de faire qch.).

essayist ['eseiist], s. Lit: Essayiste mf.

essence ['esns], s. Essence f. **The e. of the matter,** le fond de l'affaire. **The e. of a book,** le suc, la moelle, d'un livre. **Meat e.,** extrait m de viande.

essential [i'senʃ(ə)l]. 1. a. (a) Essentiel, indispensable; capital, -aux. **E. foodstuffs,** denrées de première nécessité. **E. tool,** outil de première utilité. **It is e. that . . .,** il est indispensable que + sub. **Prudence is e.,** la prudence s'impose. (b) See OIL¹ 3. 2. s. Usu. pl. L'essentiel. **Reduced to its essentials,** dépouillé. **-ally,** adv. Essentiellement; au premier chef.

establish [is'tæbliʃ], v.tr. 1. (a) Affermir (sa foi); asseoir (des fondements, son crédit). (b) Jur: **To e. one's right,** faire apparoir son bon droit. 2. Établir (un gouvernement); édifier (un système); fonder (une maison de commerce); créer, instituer (une agence). **To e. a reputation for scholarship,** se faire une réputation de savant. **To e. s.o., oneself (in business, etc.),** établir qn, s'établir. **To e. oneself in the country,** s'installer à la campagne. 3. Établir, constater (un fait); démontrer (l'identité de qn).

established, a. Établi (réputation) solide; (fait) avéré, acquis. **Well-e. business, fortune,** maison solide; fortune bien assise. S.a. CHURCH¹ 1.

establishment [is'tæbliʃmənt], s. 1. (a) Constatation f (d'un fait, etc.). (b) Établissement m (d'un gouvernement, d'une industrie); création f (d'un système); fondation f (d'une maison de commerce). 2. Établissement, maison f. **Business e.,** maison de commerce. **To keep up an e.,** avoir un grand train de maison. 3. (a) Personnel m (d'une maison). **To be on the e.,** faire partie du personnel. (b) Mil: Navy: Effectif m (d'une unité, etc.). **Peace e.,** effectifs (en temps) de paix. **On a war e.,** sur le pied de guerre. 4. **The E.** (a) L'Église officielle; (in Eng.) anglicane. (b) Les classes régnantes, l'ordre établi.

estate [is'teit], s. 1. État m, condition f. **Man's e.,** l'âge d'homme. Ecc: **The holy e. of matrimony,** le saint état de mariage. 2. Rang m, condition. 3. Hist: **The Third E.,** le Tiers État; la bourgeoisie. 4. Jur: (a) Bien m, domaine m, immeuble m. **Personal e.,** biens mobiliers, biens meubles. **Life e.,** biens en viager. S.a. REAL 2. (b) Succession f (d'un défunt).

E. duty, droits de succession. (c) Actif m (d'un failli). 5. (a) Terre f, propriété f. (b) **Housing e.,** cité f; lotissement m. **es'tate-agency,** s. Agence f de location; agence immobilière. **es'tate-agent,** s. Agent m de location; agent immobilier. **es'tate-car,** s. Aut: Familiale f; commerciale f; break m.

esteem¹ [is'tiːm], s. Estime f, considération f. **To hold s.o. in high e.,** avoir qn en haute estime. **Held in low e.,** peu estimé, mal vu. **To rise, fall, in s.o.'s e.,** monter, baisser, dans l'estime de qn.

esteem², v.tr. 1. Estimer (qn); priser (qch.). **Man highly esteemed,** homme fort estimé. 2. Estimer, considérer (as, comme). **To e. oneself happy,** s'estimer heureux.

estimable ['estiməbl], a. Estimable.

estimate¹ ['estimit], s. 1. Appréciation f, évaluation f, calcul m (des pertes, du contenu de qch.). **To form a correct e. of sth.,** se faire une idée exacte de qch. **These figures are only a rough e.,** ces chiffres sont très approximatifs. **On, at, a rough e.,** par aperçu, F: à vue de nez. **At the lowest e.,** au bas mot. 2. Com: Devis (estimatif). **Building e.,** devis de construction. **To make an e.,** établir un devis. **To put in an e.,** soumissionner. **E. of expenditure,** chiffre prévu pour les dépenses. Pol: **The Estimates,** les prévisions f budgétaires; les crédits m. **Navy estimates,** budget m de la marine.

estimate² ['estimeit], v.tr. Estimer, évaluer (les frais); apprécier (une distance, etc.). **His fortune is estimated at . . .,** on évalue sa fortune à. . . . **Estimated cost,** coût estimatif.

estimation [ˌestiˈmeiʃ(ə)n], s. (a) Jugement m. **In my e.,** à mon avis. (b) Estime f, considération f. **To hold s.o. in e.,** tenir qn en grande estime.

Estonia [es'tounjə, -iə]. Pr.n. Geog: L'Estonie f.

estrange [es'treindʒ], v.tr. (a) **To e. s.o.,** s'aliéner l'estime, l'affection, de qn. **To become estranged from s.o.,** se détacher de qn. **Estranged friends,** amis brouillés. (b) **To e. s.o. from s.o.,** indisposer qn contre qn.

estrangement [es'trein(d)ʒmənt], s. Aliénation f (de qn); désaffection f; éloignement m; brouille f (between, entre).

estuary ['estjuəri], s. Estuaire m.

etcetera [et'set(ə)rə], Lt.phr. (abbr. etc.) Et cætera. 2. s. (pl. etceteras) Et cætera m.inv; extras mpl.

etch [etʃ], v.tr. 1. Graver à l'eau-forte. **To e. away the metal,** enlever le métal à l'eau-forte. 2. Abs. Faire de la gravure à l'eau-forte. **etching,** s. 1. Gravure f à l'eau-forte. **Etching-needle,** pointe sèche (à graver). 2. (Print) Gravure à l'eau-forte; eau-forte f.

etcher ['etʃər], s. Graveur m à l'eau-forte; aquafortiste mf.

eternal [i(ː)'təːnl]. 1. a. (a) Éternel. (b) F: Continuel; sans fin; sempiternel. 2. s. **The E.,** l'Éternel m. **-ally,** adv. Éternellement.

eternity [i(ː)'təːniti], s. (a) Éternité f. (b) pl. **The eternities,** les vérités éternelles.

eternize [iː'təːnaiz], v.tr. Éterniser.

Etesian [i'tiːʒiən], a. Meteor: (Vent) étésien.

ethane ['eθein], s. Ch: Éthane m.

ether ['iːθər], s. Ph: Ch: Med: Éther m. **E. addict,** éthéromane.

ethereal [i(ː)'θiəriəl], a. 1. (Of regions, love) Éthéré; (of form, vision) impalpable; qui n'est pas de ce monde. 2. Ch: (Of liquid) Éthéré, volatil.

etherize ['iːθəraiz], v.tr. Éthériser.

ethic(al) ['eθik(əl)], a. 1. Moral, -aux. 2. Gram: **Ethic dative,** datif m éthique.

ethics ['eθiks], s.pl. Éthique f, morale f.

Ethiopia [ˌiːθi'oupjə]. Pr.n. L'Éthiopie f.

Ethiopian [ˌiːθi'oupjən], a. & s. Éthiopien, -ienne.

ethnic(al) ['eθnik(əl)], a. Ethnique, ethnologique.

ethnographer [eθ'nɔgrəfər], s. Ethnographe mf.

ethnography [eθ'nɔgrəfi], s. Ethnographie f.

ethnologist [eθ'nɔlədʒist], s. Ethnologue mf.

ethnology [eθ'nɔlədʒi], s. Ethnologie f.

ethyl ['eθil], s. Ch: Éthyle m.

ethylene ['eθiliːn], s. Ch: Éthylène m.

etiquette ['etiket], s. (a) Étiquette f; (les) convenances f; Dipl: le protocole. **Court e.,** le cérémonial de cour. (b) **The e. of the Bar,** les règles f du Barreau.

Eton ['iːtn]. *Pr.n.* Eton College, l'école d'Eton (une des grandes *"public schools"*). 'Eton 'blue, *a.* Bleu clair *inv.* 'Eton 'jacket, *s.* Veste noire courte.

Etruria [iˈtruəriə]. *Pr.n. A.Geog:* L'Étrurie *f.*

Etruscan [iˈtraskən], *a. & s.* Étrusque (*mf*).

etymological [ˌetiməˈlɔdʒik(ə)l], *a.* Étymologique. **-ally,** *adv.* Étymologiquement.

etymologist [ˌetiˈmɔlədʒist], *s.* Étymologiste *mf.*

etymology [ˌetiˈmɔlədʒi], *s.* Étymologie *f.*

eucalyptus [juːkəˈliptəs], *s.* Eucalyptus *m.* E. oil, essence *f* d'eucalyptus.

eucharist (the) [ðəˈjuːkərist], *s. Ecc:* L'eucharistie *f.*

Euclid ['juːklid]. *Pr.n.m.* Euclide.

eugenics [juˈdʒeniks], *s.pl.* (*Usu. with sg. const.*) Eugénisme *m,* eugénique *f.*

eulogist ['juːlədʒist], *s.* Panégyriste *m.*

eulogistic(al) [ˌjuːləˈdʒistik(əl)], *a.* Élogieux.

eulogize ['juːlədʒaiz], *v.tr.* (*a*) Faire l'éloge, le panégyrique de (qn, qch.). (*b*) Adresser des éloges à (qn).

eulogy ['juːlədʒi], *s.* Panégyrique *m.*

eunuch ['juːnək], *s.* Eunuque *m.*

euphemism ['juːfimizm], *s.* Euphémisme *m.*

euphemistic [ˌjuːfiˈmistik], *a.* Euphémique. **-ally,** *adv.* Euphémiquement; par euphémisme.

euphonic [juˈfɔnik], *a.* Euphonique.

euphonium [juˈfouniəm], *s. Mus:* Saxhorn *m* basse; basse *f* (des cuivres). E. player, bassiste *m.*

euphony ['juːfəni], *s.* Euphonie *f.*

euphorbia [juˈfɔːbiə], *s. Bot:* Euphorbe *f.*

euphoria [juˈfɔːriə], *s.* Euphorie *f.*

euphuism ['juːfjuːizm], *s.* **1.** *Lit.Hist:* Euphuisme *m.* **2.** = Préciosité *f;* affectation *f* (de langage).

euphuistic [ˌjuːfjuːˈistik], *a.* Euphuistique, euphuiste (parler) précieux, affecté.

Eurasia [juˈreiʒə]. *Pr.n. Geog:* Eurasie *f.*

Euratom [juəˈrætəm]. *Pr.n.* Euratom *f.*

eurhythmic [juˈriθmik]. **1.** *a.* Eurythmique. **2.** *s.pl.* Eurhythmics, gymnastique *f* rythmique.

Europa [juˈroupə]. *Pr.n.f. Gr.Myth:* Europe *f.*

Europe ['juərəp]. *Pr.n.* L'Europe *f.*

European [ˌjuərəˈpi(ː)ən], *a. & s.* Européen, -enne.

Eurovision [juərəˈviʒ(ə)n]. *Pr.n.* Eurovision *f.*

Eustachian [juːsˈteiʃən], *a. Anat:* The E. tube, trompe d'Eustache.

euthanasia [ˌjuːθəˈneiziə], *s.* Euthanasie *f.*

evacuate [iˈvækjueit], *v.tr.* **1.** (*a*) Évacuer (une forteresse, etc.). (*b*) Évacuer, décharger (le ventre). **2.** Évacuer (les blessés, etc.). **3.** Expulser, refouler (les gaz brûlés d'un moteur, etc.).

evacuation [iˌvækjuˈeif(ə)n], *s.* **1.** Évacuation *f* (d'une ville, etc.). **2.** (*a*) Évacuation, décharge *f* (du ventre). (*b*) *Usu. pl.* Déjections *f,* selles *f.* **3.** Évacuation (des blessés, etc.).

evacuee [iˌvækjuˈiː], *s.* Évacué, -ée.

evade [iˈveid], *v.tr.* **1.** Éviter (un coup, un danger); esquiver (un coup); se soustraire à (un châtiment); éluder, tourner (une question, la loi); déjouer (la vigilance de qn). **2.** (*Of thgs*) Échapper à (l'intelligence).

evaluate [iˈvæljueit], *v.tr.* Évaluer; estimer le montant (des dommages).

evaluation [iˌvæljuˈeif(ə)n], *s.* Évaluation *f.*

evanescent [ˌiːvəˈnesənt], *a.* Évanescent; (gloire, etc.) éphémère.

evangelic [ˌiːvænˈdʒelik], *a. Ecc:* Évangélique; conforme à l'Évangile.

evangelical [ˌiːvænˈdʒelik(ə)l]. **1.** *a.* = EVANGELIC. **2.** (*a*) *a.* Qui appartient à la religion réformée. (*b*) *s.* Protestant *m* évangélique.

evangelist [iˈvæn(d)ʒilist], *s.* Évangéliste *m.*

evangelize [iˈvæn(d)ʒilaiz], *v.tr.* Évangéliser; prêcher l'Évangile à (qn).

evaporate [iˈvæpəreit]. **1.** *v.tr.* Faire évaporer (un liquide). E. down, réduire par évaporation. **2.** *v.i.* (*Of liquid*) S'évaporer, se vaporiser; (*of acid*) se volatiliser.

evaporation [iˌvæpəˈreif(ə)n], *s.* Évaporation *f;* volatilisation *f* (d'un acide).

evaporator [iˈvæpəreitər], *s. Ind:* Évaporateur *m,* vaporisateur *m;* bouilleur *m.*

evasion [iˈveiʒ(ə)n], *s.* **1.** Évitement *m;* moyen *m* d'éluder (une question); dérobade *f.* **2.** Échappatoire *f,* faux-fuyant *m.* To resort to evasions, to use evasions, user de détours; biaiser. Without e., sans détours.

evasive [iˈveisiv], *a.* Évasif. **-ly,** *adv.* (Répondre) évasivement.

Eve[1] [iːv]. *Pr.n.f.* Ève.

eve[2], *s.* (*a*) *Ecc:* Vigile *f* (de fête). (*b*) Veille *f.* Christmas E., la veille de Noël. On the eve of . . ., (à) la veille de. . . .

even[1] ['iːv(ə)n], *s. Poet:* Soir *m.*

even[2], *a.* **1.** (*a*) (*Of surface*) Uni; plan; égal, -aux; uniforme. (*b*) To be e. with sth., être à fleur de, à ras de, qch.; affleurer qch. (*c*) (*Of spacing, weights, etc.*) Égal, -aux. To make e., aplanir (une surface); affleurer (deux planches, etc.); *Typ:* espacer (la composition). **2.** (Souffle, pouls) égal, régulier, uniforme. E. pace, allure uniforme. E. temper, humeur égale. **3.** (*a*) E. bet, pari avec enjeu égal. To lay e. odds, *F:* to lay evens, parier à égalité. (*b*) *Games:* To be e., être manche à manche. *F:* To get e. with s.o., rendre la pareille à qn, se venger de qn. I'll be e. with him yet, je le lui revaudrai; *F:* il ne l'emportera pas en paradis. (*c*) E. bargain, marché équitable, juste. **4.** (*a*) (Nombre) pair. Odd or e., pair ou impair. (*b*) E. money, compte rond. To make up the e. money, faire l'appoint. **5.** *Com:* Of e. date, de même date. **-ly,** *adv.* **1.** Uniment. **2.** (*a*) Régulièrement; (diviser) également. (*b*) E. matched, de force égale. 'even-'handed, *a.* Équitable; impartial, -aux.

even[3], *adv.* Même; (*with comparative*) encore; (*with negative*) seulement, même. E. the cleverest, même les plus habiles. E. the children knew, les enfants mêmes le savaient. To love e. one's enemies, aimer même ses ennemis. To jest e. on the scaffold, plaisanter jusque sur l'échafaud. I never e. saw it, je ne l'ai même pas vu. That would be e. worse, ce serait encore pis. E. sadder than usual, encore plus triste que de coutume. Without e. speaking, sans seulement parler. E. if, e. though, he failed, même s'il échouait; alors même qu'il échouerait; quand même il échouerait. If e. one could speak to him, si encore on pouvait lui parler. E. so, mais cependant, quand même. *B:* E. so must the Son of Man be lifted up, ainsi il faut que le Fils de l'Homme soit élevé. E. now, à l'instant même. E. then, dès cette époque; déjà.

even[4], *v.tr.* **1.** Aplanir, niveler, égaliser (une surface); affleurer (deux planches). **2.** Rendre égal. *Typ:* To e. (out) the spacing, égaliser l'espacement. *F:* That will e. things up, cela rétablira l'équilibre.

evening ['iːvniŋ], *s.* **1.** Soir *m;* (*duration of e.*) soirée *f.* To-morrow e., demain (au) soir. In the e., le soir, au soir. At nine o'clock in the e., à neuf heures du soir. (On) that e., ce soir-là. (On) the previous e., la veille au soir. On the e. of the first of May, le premier mai au soir. On the e. of the next day, le lendemain soir. One, on a, fine summer e., (par) un beau soir d'été. Every e., tous les soirs. Every Monday e., tous les lundis soir. All the e., toute la soirée. Long winter evenings, longues veillées d'hiver. E. paper, journal du soir. *Th:* E. performance, (représentation de) soirée. **2.** Musical e., soirée musicale. 'evening-'dress, *s.* **1.** (*Man*) Tenue *f* de soirée. In e.-d., en tenue de soirée. (*Woman*) Robe *f* du soir. In e.-d., en toilette de soirée. In full e.-d., en grand décolleté.

evenness ['iːv(ə)nnis], *s.* **1.** Égalité *f;* régularité *f* (de mouvement). **2.** Sérénité *f,* calme *m* (d'esprit); égalité (d'humeur).

evensong ['iːv(ə)nsɔŋ], *s. Ecc:* Vêpres *fpl* et salut *m;* office *m* du soir.

event [iˈvent], *s.* **1.** Cas *m.* In the e. of his refusing, au cas, dans le cas, où il refuserait. **2.** Événement *m.* (*a*) In the course of events . . ., au cours des événements . . ., par la suite. . . . (*b*) Issue *f,* résultat *m.* In either e. you will lose nothing, dans l'un ou l'autre cas vous ne perdrez rien. Wise after the e., sage après coup. At all events, dans tous les cas; en tout cas; quoi qu'il arrive. **3.** *Sp:* (*a*) Réunion sportive. (*b*) (*Athletics*) Field events, concours *m,* épreuves *fpl,* sur terrain. Track events, courses *fpl* sur piste.

eventful [i'ventful], a. (Of story, life) Plein d'événements; mouvementé; (jour) mémorable, qui fait époque; (semaine) fertile en événements.

eventide ['i:vəntaid], s. Poet: Soir m; Poet: la chute du jour. O: E. home, hospice m pour vieillards.

eventration [i:ven'treiʃ(ə)n], s. Surg: Éventration f.

eventual [i'ventjuəl], a. 1. (Profit, etc.) éventuel. 2. Définitif; final, -aux. His prodigality and his e. ruin, sa prodigalité et sa ruine finale. -ally, adv. Finalement, en fin de compte, par la suite. He will do it e., il finira bien par le faire.

eventuality [i,ventju'æliti], s. Éventualité f.

ever ['evər], adv. 1. Jamais. (a) I read seldom if e., je ne lis jamais, ou rarement. Now if e. is the time to . . ., c'est maintenant ou jamais le moment de. . . . If e. I catch him, si jamais je l'attrape. Nothing e. happens, il n'arrive jamais rien. He hardly e., scarcely e., smokes, il ne fume presque jamais. Do you e. miss the train? vous arrive-t-il (jamais) de manquer le train? He is a liar if e. there was one, c'est un menteur, s'il en fut (jamais). It started to rain faster than e., il se mit à pleuvoir de plus belle. It is as warm as e., il fait toujours aussi chaud. S.a. WORSE 3. (b) They lived happy e. after, depuis lors, à partir de ce jour, ils vécurent toujours heureux. (c) E. since (then), dès lors, depuis (lors). 2. (a) Toujours. E.-increasing influence, influence toujours plus étendue. Corr: Yours e., bien cordialement à vous; tout(e) à vous. (b) For e., pour toujours; à jamais; à perpétuité. Gone for e., parti sans retour. For e. and e., à tout jamais jusqu'à la fin des siècles. Scotland for e.! vive l'Écosse! To live for e., vivre éternellement. He is for e. grumbling, il grogne sans cesse. To be for e. chopping and changing, changer (d'opinion) à tout bout de champ. 3. (Intensive) (a) As quick as e. you can, du plus vite que vous pourrez. As soon as e. he comes home, aussitôt qu'il rentrera. Worst e., best e., sans précédent. F: E. so difficult, difficile au possible; tout ce qu'il y a de plus difficile. F: E. so much easier, infiniment plus simple. E. so long ago, il y a bien, bien longtemps. E. so many times, je ne sais combien de fois. P: Thank you e. so much, merci mille fois; merci infiniment. (b) How e. did you manage? comment diable avez-vous fait? What e. shall we do? qu'est-ce que nous allons bien faire? What e.'s the matter with you? mais qu'est-ce que vous avez donc? What e. can it be? qu'est-ce que ça peut bien être? When e. will he come? quand donc viendra-t-il? Where e. can he be? où peut-il bien être? Who e. told you that? qui est-ce qui a bien pu vous dire cela? Why e. not? mais pourquoi pas?

everglade ['evəgleid], s. U.S: Terrain marécageux (du sud de la Floride).

evergreen ['evəgri:n]. 1. a. Toujours vert; Bot: à feuilles persistantes. E. topic, question toujours d'actualité. 2. s. Arbre (toujours) vert. Evergreens, plantes vertes.

everlasting [evə'la:stiŋ]. 1. a. (a) Éternel. (b) E. flower, immortelle f. E. pea, pois vivace. (c) (Of object, etc.) Inusable, solide, durable. (d) F: Perpétuel, sempiternel. E. complaints, plaintes sans fin. 2. s. Éternité f. The E., Dieu. -ly, adv. 1. Éternellement. 2. F: Sempiternellement.

evermore [evə'mɔ:r], adv. Toujours. For e., à jamais, pour toujours. Their name liveth for e., leur nom vivra éternellement.

eversion [i'və:ʃ(ə)n], s. (a) Surg: Éversion f, retournement m (d'un organe). (b) E. of the eyelid, ectropion m; éraillement m de la paupière.

every ['evri], a. (a) Chaque; tout; tous les. . . . E. day, chaque jour, tous les jours. In e. Frenchman there is an idealist, chez tout Français il y a un idéaliste. His desire to meet your e. wish, son désir d'aller au-devant de chacun de vos désirs. E. other day, e. second day, tous les deux jours; un jour sur deux. E. other Sunday, un dimanche sur deux. E. three days, tous les trois jours; un jour sur trois. E. third man was chosen, on choisissait un homme sur trois. To do sth. e. quarter of an hour, faire qch. tous les quarts d'heure. S.a. NOW I. 1. E. few minutes, F: toutes les cinq minutes. I expect him e. minute, je l'attends d'un instant à l'autre. (b) (Intensive) He was e. inch a republican, il était républicain jusqu'au

bout des ongles, des doigts. I have e. reason to believe that . . ., j'ai toute raison, tout lieu, de croire que. . . . E. bit as good as . . ., tout aussi bon que. . . . I shall give you e. assistance, je vous aiderai de tout mon pouvoir. (c) E. 'one, chacun, chacune; tout le monde. E. one of us, tous tant que nous sommes. Cf. EVERYONE. E. man for himself, (i) chacun pour soi; (ii) (in danger) sauve qui peut! F: E. man Jack of them, tous sans exception.

everybody ['evribədi, -bɔdi], indef.pron. = EVERYONE.

everyday ['evri'dei], a. Journalier, quotidien. E. occurrence, (i) fait journalier; (ii) fait banal. E. life, la vie quotidienne. My e. clothes, mes vêtements de tous les jours. E. English, l'anglais usuel. Words in e. use, mots d'usage courant; mots très usités. E. knowledge, connaissances usuelles.

everyone ['evriwʌn], indef.pron. Chacun; tout le monde; tous. As e. knows, comme chacun (le) sait. E. knows that, le premier venu, n'importe qui, sait cela. E. else knows it, tous les autres le savent. E. we know, tout notre cercle de connaissances.

everything ['evriθiŋ], indef.pron. (a) Tout. E. in its place, chaque chose f à sa place. We must show him e., il faut tout lui montrer. E. good, tout ce qu'il y a de bon. They sell e., on y vend de tout. Com: E. for cyclists, tout pour le cyclisme. (b) (As predicate) De première importance. Money is e., l'argent fait tout. She is very pretty.—Beauty isn't e., elle est très jolie.—Il n'y a pas que la beauté (qui compte).

everywhere ['evriwɛər], adv. Partout; en tout lieu; en tous lieux. To look e. for s.o., chercher qn partout, de tous côtés. E. you go, partout où vous allez.

evict [i'vikt], v.tr. Évincer, expulser (un locataire) (from, de); F: faire déguerpir (un locataire).

eviction [i'vikʃ(ə)n], s. Éviction f, expulsion f (d'un locataire), dépossession f.

evidence ['evid(ə)ns], s. 1. Évidence f. (a) To fly in the face of e., se refuser à l'évidence. (b) To be in e., être en évidence. A man much in e., un homme très en vue. 2. Signe m, marque f. To bear evidence(s) of, give e. of, sth., porter la marque, les marques, de qch. To give e. of intelligence, (i) (of action) marquer l'intelligence; (ii) (of pers.) faire preuve d'intelligence. 3. (a) Preuve f. Internal e., preuves intrinsèques. (b) Jur: Preuve testimoniale; témoignage m. Documentary e., in writing, document probant; preuve littérale. To give e., témoigner; déposer (en justice); porter témoignage. The e. was strongly against him, les témoignages pesaient contre lui. The e. of the senses, le témoignage des sens. S.a. CIRCUMSTANTIAL 1. 4. Jur: (Pers.) Témoin(s) m(pl). The e. for the prosecution, for the defence, les témoins à charge, à décharge. To turn King's, Queen's, U.S: State's, e., témoigner contre ses complices (sous promesse de pardon); dénoncer ses complices.

evident ['evid(ə)nt], a. Évident. E. truth, vérité patente. He had drunk too much, as was e. from his gait, il avait trop bu, et il y paraissait à sa démarche. -ly, adv. Évidemment, manifestement. He was e. afraid, il était manifeste qu'il avait peur.

evil ['i:v(i)l]. 1. a. Mauvais. (a) House of e. repute, lieu mal famé. E. tidings, fâcheuses nouvelles. E. omen, présage de malheur. Of e. omen, de mauvais présage. An e. day, un jour malheureux. To fall on e. days, tomber dans l'infortune. (b) Méchant. E. spirit, esprit malfaisant, malin. The E. One, l'Esprit malin, le Malin. E. influence, influence néfaste. E. eye, mauvais œil; (in Italy) jettature f. E. tongue, mauvaise langue. 2. s. Mal m, pl. maux. (a) A social e., une plaie sociale. To speak e. of s.o., dire du mal de qn. (b) A: The King's e., les écrouelles f, la scrofule. **evil-'doer**, s. Malfaiteur, -trice. **'evil-looking**, a. De mauvaise mine; qui ne dit rien de bon. **evil-'minded**, a. Porté au mal; malintentionné, malveillant. **evil-'smelling**, a. Nauséabond. **evil-'speaking, -'tongued**, a. Médisant. An e.-t. person, une mauvaise langue, une langue de vipère.

evince [i'vins], v.tr. Montrer, témoigner, faire preuve de (qch.). To e. curiosity, manifester de la curiosité. To e. intelligence, faire paraître de l'intelligence. To e. a taste for . . ., témoigner d'un goût pour. . . .

eviscerate [i'visəreit], v.tr. Éviscérer, éventrer.

evocation [evə'keiʃ(ə)n], s. Évocation f.

evocative [i'vɔkətiv], a. Évocateur, -trice.

evocatory [i'vɔkət(ə)ri], a. Évocatoire.

evoke [i'vouk], v.tr. Évoquer. **This remark evoked a smile,** cette observation provoqua, suscita, un sourire.

evolution [ˌiːvə'ljuːʃ(ə)n], s. 1. (a) Biol: Évolution f, développement m. (b) **The e. of events,** le déroulement des événements. 2. Évolution (d'un acrobate, d'une flotte). 3. Geom: Déroulement m (d'une courbe). 4. Dégagement m (de chaleur).

evolutionary [ˌiːvə'ljuʃən(ə)ri], a. Biol: Évolutionnaire.

evolutionism [ˌiːvə'ljuːʃənizm], s. Biol: Évolutionnisme m.

evolutionist [ˌiːvə'ljuːʃənist, ev-], s. Biol: Évolutionniste mf.

evolve [i'vɔlv]. 1. v.tr. (a) Dérouler, développer (des projets); élaborer (une méthode); développer, déduire (une théorie) (**from,** de). (b) Ch: Dégager (de la chaleur). 2. v.i. (a) (Of events) Se dérouler. (b) (Of race) Se développer, évoluer.

ewe [juː], s. Brebis f. S.a. LAMB[1].

ewer ['juər], s. O: Pot m à eau; aiguière f.

ex[1] [eks], prep. 1. (Out of) Com: **Ex ship,** transbordé. **Ex store,** en magasin. 2. Fin: **Shares quoted ex dividend,** actions cotées coupon détaché.

ex-[2], pref. Ancien; ex-. **Ex-Minister,** ex-ministre. **Ex-schoolmistress,** ancien professeur (femme); ancienne institutrice. **Ex-husband,** -wife, ex-mari, ex-femme.

exacerbate [eks'æsə(ː)beit], v.tr. Irriter, exaspérer (qn); exacerber, aggraver (une douleur).

exact[1] [ig'zækt], a. Exact. 1. (a) Précis. **To give e. details,** donner des précisions; préciser. **To be more e. . .,** pour mieux dire. . . . **E. copy of a document,** copie textuelle d'un document. (b) **The e. word,** le mot juste. **The public must tender the e. amount,** le public est tenu de faire l'appoint. 2. **To be e. in carrying out one's duties,** être exact à s'acquitter de ses devoirs. **E. in business,** strict en affaires. **-ly,** adv. Exactement; tout juste, justement. **I don't know e. what happened,** je ne sais pas au juste ce qui est arrivé. **Exactly!** précisément! parfaitement! **Three months e.,** trois mois jour pour jour. **He is not e. a scholar,** ce n'est pas à proprement parler un savant.

exact[2], v.tr. 1. (a) Exiger (un impôt) (**from, of,** de). (b) Extorquer (une rançon à qn). 2. Exiger, réclamer (beaucoup de soins). **exacting,** a. (Of pers.) Exigeant; (of work) astreignant. **To be too e. with s.o.,** en demander trop à qn.

exaction [ig'zækʃ(ə)n], s. (a) Exaction f d'impôts. (b) Exaction, demande exorbitante (d'argent).

exactitude [ig'zæktitjuːd], s. Exactitude f.

exactness [ig'zæktnis], s. Exactitude f, précision f; justesse f (d'un calcul).

exaggerate [ig'zædʒəreit], v.tr. Exagérer; grandir (un incident); outrer (une mode, des éloges). Abs. Exagérer; forcer la note. **exaggerated,** a. Exagéré. **To attach e. importance to sth.,** prêter une importance excessive à qch.

exaggeration [igzædʒə'reiʃ(ə)n], s. Exagération f.

exalt [ig'zɔlt], v.tr. 1. Élever (qn en rang, etc.). 2. Exalter, louer (les vertus de qn). **To e. s.o. to the skies,** porter, élever, qn aux nues. 3. Exciter, exalter (l'imagination). **exalted,** a. 1. (Rang) élevé. **E. personage,** personnage haut placé. 2. **To speak in an e. strain,** parler d'un ton élevé.

exaltation [ˌegzɔl'teiʃ(ə)n], s. 1. Élévation f (**to a dignity,** à une dignité). 2. Exaltation f.

exam [ig'zæm], s. F: = EXAMINATION 2.

examination [igˌzæmi'neiʃ(ə)n], s. Examen m. 1. Inspection f, visite f (des machines); vérification f (de comptes). **Under e.,** à l'examen. **To undergo a medical e.,** passer une visite médicale. 2. Sch: Entrance e., examen d'entrée. **Competitive e.,** concours m. **To go up, sit, enter, for an e.,** se présenter à un examen; passer un examen. 3. Jur: Interrogatoire m (d'un accusé); audition f (de témoins).

examine [ig'zæmin], v.tr. Examiner. 1. Inspecter (une machine); Cust: visiter (les bagages); vérifier (des comptes); contrôler (un passeport); compulser (des dossiers). **To e. a question thoroughly,** approfondir une question. Nau: **To stop and e. a ship,** arraisonner un navire. 2. Jur: Interroger (un témoin). Sch: Faire passer un examen (à qn). Sch: Abs. Corriger des copies d'examen.

examinee [igˌzæmi'niː], s. Sch: Candidat m.

examiner [ig'zæminər], s. 1. Inspecteur, -trice, vérificateur m (de machines, de bagages). 2. Sch: Examinateur, -trice. **The examiners,** le jury (d'examen).

example [ig'zɑːmpl], s. Exemple m. 1. **To quote sth. as an e.,** citer qch. en exemple. **Practical e.,** cas concret. **For e., by way of e.,** par exemple. 2. Précédent m. **Beyond, without, e.,** sans exemple, sans précédent. 3. **To set an e.,** donner l'exemple. **To take s.o. as an e.,** prendre exemple sur qn. **Following the e. of . . .,** à l'exemple de. . . . **To make an e. of s.o.,** faire un exemple de qn; infliger à qn un châtiment exemplaire.

exasperate [ig'zɑːspəreit], v.tr. 1. Exaspérer, aggraver (la haine, une douleur). 2. Exaspérer, irriter (qn). **Exasperated at, by, his insolence,** exaspéré de son insolence. **exasperating,** a. (Ton) exaspérant, irritant.

exasperation [igˌzɑːspə'reiʃ(ə)n], s. 1. Exaspération f, aggravation f (d'une douleur). 2. (Of pers.) Exaspération, irritation f. **To drive s.o. to e.,** pousser qn à bout.

excavate ['ekskəveit], v.tr. Excaver, creuser (un tunnel); fouiller (la terre). Abs. Faire des fouilles (dans un endroit).

excavation [ˌekskə'veiʃ(ə)n], s. Excavation f. 1. Fouillement m (de la terre). 2. Terrain excavé; fouille f. **The excavations at Pompeii,** les fouilles de Pompéi.

excavator ['ekskəveitər], s. 1. Civ.E: Excavateur m; excavatrice f. 2. (Pers.) Fouilleur m.

exceed [ik'siːd]. 1. v.tr. (a) Excéder, dépasser, outrepasser (ses droits). **Not exceeding ten pounds,** ne dépassant pas dix livres. **To e. one's instructions,** aller au-delà de ses instructions. **To e. one's powers,** sortir de sa compétence. Aut: **To e. the speed limit,** dépasser la vitesse légale. (b) Surpasser (**in,** en). **It exceeded my expectations,** cela a été au-dessus de mon attente. 2. v.i. Manger, boire, à l'excès. **exceedingly,** adv. Très, extrêmement, excessivement.

excel [ik'sel], v. (**excelled**) 1. v.i. Exceller (**in, at, sth.,** à qch.). **To e. in an art,** être éminent dans un art. **To e. at a game,** exceller à un jeu. 2. v.tr. Surpasser (qn). **To e. oneself,** se surpasser. **To e. all one's rivals,** l'emporter sur tous ses rivaux.

excellence ['eksələns], s. Excellence f. 1. Perfection f (d'un ouvrage). 2. Mérite m, qualité f (de qn, de qch.).

excellency ['eksələnsi], s. **Your E.,** votre Excellence f. **It is I, your E., who . . .,** c'est moi, Excellence, qui. . . .

excellent ['eksələnt], a. Excellent, parfait. **E. business,** affaire d'or. **-ly,** adv. Excellemment.

except[1] [ik'sept], v.tr. Excepter, exclure (**from,** de). **Present company excepted,** les présents exceptés.

except[2]. 1. prep. (a) Excepté; à l'exception de; sauf. **He does nothing e. eat and drink,** il ne fait rien sinon manger et boire. **Nobody heard it e. myself,** il n'y a que moi qui l'aie entendu. **E. by agreement between the parties . . .,** sauf accord entre les parties. . . . (b) **E. for . . .,** à part . . .; si ce n'est. . . . **The dress is ready, e. for the buttons,** la robe est prête, à l'exception des boutons. 2. (a) conj. A: & Lit: A moins que. (b) Conj.phr. **E. that,** excepté que, sauf que.

exception [ik'sepʃ(ə)n], s. 1. Exception f. **To be an e. to a rule,** faire exception à une règle. **With that e., we are agreed,** à cela près nous sommes d'accord. **Without e.,** sans exception. **With the e. of . . .,** à l'exception de . . ., exception faite de. . . . **With certain exceptions,** sauf exceptions. 2. Objection f. **To take e. to sth.,** (i) trouver à redire à qch.; (ii) se froisser de qch. **E. was taken to his youth,** on lui objecta sa jeunesse. Jur: **To take e. to a witness,** récuser un témoin. **To take e. to s.o.'s doing sth.,** trouver mauvais que qn fasse qch.

exceptionable [ik'sepʃənəbl], a. Blâmable, répréhensible.

exceptional [ik'sepʃən(ə)l], a. Exceptionnel. **-ally,** adv. Exceptionnellement. 1. Par exception. 2. **E. cheap,** d'un bon marché exceptionnel.

excerpt ['eksəːpt], s. Extrait m, citation f.

excess [ik'ses], s. 1. (a) Excès m (de lumière, etc.). E. of precaution, luxe m de précautions. In e., to e., (jusqu')à l'excès. Indulgence carried to e., indulgence poussée trop loin. (b) To commit excesses, commettre des excès. 2. Excédent m (de poids, etc.), surplus m. Rail: etc: E. fare, supplément m. E. luggage, excédent de bagages.

excessive [ik'sesiv], a. Excessif; (of zeal) immodéré; (of thirst) extrême. -ly, adv. Excessivement; (manger) à l'excès. To be e. generous, être par trop généreux.

exchange[1] [iks'tʃeindʒ], s. 1. Échange m. E. and barter, troc m. In e. (for sth.), en échange (de qch.). Car, etc., taken in part e., reprise f. Adm: E. of posts, permutation f (de deux fonctionnaires). 2. Fin: (a) Foreign e., change (extérieur). Operations in foreign e., opérations de change. (Rate of) e., taux m du change. At the current rate of e., au change du jour. (Foreign) e. broker, cambiste m, agent m de change. (b) Bill of e., effet m, traite f; lettre f de change. 3. (a) Bourse f (des valeurs). Corn e., halle f aux blés. (b) Telephone e., central m (téléphonique).

exchange[2], v.tr. To e. sth. for sth., échanger, troquer, qch. pour, contre, qch. To e. glances, échanger un regard. They had exchanged hats, ils avaient fait un échange de chapeaux. Adm: To e. (posts) with s.o., permuter avec qn.

exchangeable [iks'tʃeindʒəbl], a. Échangeable (for, pour, contre).

exchequer [iks'tʃekər], s. 1. The E., (i) la Trésorerie, le fisc; (ii) le Trésor public; (iii) = le Ministère des Finances. The Chancellor of the E. = le Ministre des Finances. E. bill, bon m du Trésor. 2. F: Finances fpl (d'un particulier). My e. is empty, je ne suis pas en fonds.

excise[1] ['eksaiz], s. Contributions indirectes. The E. Office, la Régie. E. officer, employé de la régie. 'excise-bond, s. Cust: Acquit-à-caution m.

excise[2] [ek'saiz], v.tr. Surg: Exciser, retrancher (un organe).

excision [ek'siʒ(ə)n], s. Excision f.

excitability [ik'saitə'biliti], s. 1. Émotivité f. 2. El: Physiol: Excitabilité f.

excitable [ik'saitəbl], a. 1. (Of pers.) Émotionnable, surexcitable. 2. El: Physiol: Excitable.

excitant [ik'saitənt], a. & s. Med: Excitant (m), stimulant (m).

excitation [eksi'teiʃ(ə)n], s. (a) Physiol: Excitation f. (b) El: Amorçage m (d'une dynamo).

excite [ik'sait], v.tr. 1. (a) Provoquer, exciter (un sentiment); susciter (de l'intérêt). To e. s.o.'s curiosity, piquer la curiosité de qn. (b) Physiol: Exciter, stimuler (un nerf). (c) El: Exciter, amorcer (une dynamo). 2. (a) Exciter, enflammer (une passion). (b) Agiter, émouvoir, surexciter (qn). To e. the mob, passionner la foule. Easily excited, surexcitable, émotionnable. **excited**, a. 1. El: Physiol: Excité. 2. (Of pers.) Agité, surexcité. Don't get e.! ne vous énervez pas! F: ne vous frappez pas! He gets e. over nothing, F: il s'emballe pour un rien. -ly, adv. D'une manière agitée; avec fièvre. **exciting**, a. 1. Passionnant, émouvant, captivant. An e. novel, un roman palpitant d'intérêt. An e. game, une partie mouvementée. 2. El: E. dynamo, excitatrice f. E. battery, batterie f d'excitation.

excitement [ik'saitmənt], s. 1. Surexcitation f (d'un organe). 2. Agitation f, surexcitation; fièvre f. The thirst for e., la soif des sensations fortes. The e. of departure, l'émoi m du départ. To cause great e., faire sensation. F: What's all the e. about? qu'est-ce qui se passe donc?

exclaim [eks'kleim]. 1. v.i. S'écrier, s'exclamer. To e. at, against, an injustice, se récrier contre une injustice. 2. v.tr. He exclaimed that he would rather die, il s'écria qu'il aimerait mieux mourir.

exclamation [ekskla'meiʃ(ə)n], s. Exclamation f. E. mark, U.S: point, point m d'exclamation.

exclamatory [eks'klæmət(ə)ri], a. Exclamatif.

exclude [iks'kluːd], v.tr. (a) Exclure (from, de). To e the sun, empêcher le soleil d'entrer. Aliens are excluded from these posts, les étrangers ne sont pas

admis à ces emplois. Ecc: To e. s.o. from the sacraments, refuser les sacrements à qn. Excluding . . ., à l'exclusion de. . . . (b) Écarter (le doute). This excludes all possibility of doubt, le doute n'est plus permis.

exclusion [iks'kluːʒ(ə)n], s. 1. Exclusion f (from, de). To the e. of . . ., à l'exclusion de. 2. Refus m d'admission (from, à).

exclusive [iks'kluːsiv], a. 1. Exclusif. Two qualities that are mutually e., deux qualités qui s'excluent. 2. (a) (Droit) exclusif. To have e. rights in a production, avoir l'exclusivité f d'une production. Cin: E. film, film en exclusivité. (b) Seul, unique. The e. work of . . ., exclusivement l'œuvre de. . . . (c) U.S: Choisi; de choix. (d) E. profession, profession très fermée. Very e. club, cercle très fermé. 3. adv. Sans compter les extras. Rent (of flat, etc.) £300 a year e., loyer m (d'un appartement, etc.) £300 par an, contributions et charges en plus. Price of the dinner e. of wine, prix du dîner, vin non compris. -ly, adv. Exclusivement.

exclusiveness [iks'kluːsivnis], s. Caractère exclusif (de qch.). E. of mind, esprit m de caste.

excogitate [eks'kɔdʒiteit], v.tr. Imaginer, combiner (un projet, etc.).

excommunicate [,eksə'mjuːnikeit], v.tr. Excommunier.

excommunication ['eksə,mjuːni'keiʃ(ə)n], s. Excommunication f.

excoriate [eks'kɔːrieit], v.tr. Excorier.

excoriation [eks,kɔri'eiʃ(ə)n], s. Excoriation f.

excrement ['ekskrimənt], s. Excrément m.

excrescence [iks'kresns], s. Excroissance f. Bot: (On tree trunk) Bourrelet m, loupe f.

excreta [eks'kriːtə], s.pl. Excréta m, excrétions f.

excrete [eks'kriːt], v.tr. Excréter; (of plant) sécréter (un suc).

excretion [eks'kriːʃ(ə)n], s. Excrétion f.

excruciate [iks'kruːʃieit], v.tr. Lit: A: Mettre au supplice; torturer. **excruciating**, a. (Of pain) Atroce, affreux. An e. joke, une plaisanterie atroce. -ly, adv. Atrocement, affreusement. F: It's e. funny, c'est à se tordre, à mourir de rire.

exculpate ['ekskʌlpeit], v.tr. Disculper (from, de).

exculpation [,ekskʌl'peiʃ(ə)n], s. Disculpation f.

excursion [iks'kəːʃ(ə)n], s. 1. Excursion f; voyage m d'agrément; partie f de plaisir; sortie f. Aut: Cy: Randonnée f. Rail: E. ticket, billet d'excursion. 2. Excursion, digression f (dans un discours).

excursionist [iks'kəːʃnist], s. Excursionniste mf.

excusable [iks'kjuːzəbl], a. Excusable, pardonnable. -ably, adv. Excusablement.

excuse[1] [iks'kjuːs], s. 1. Excuse f. His conduct admits of no e., sa conduite est inexcusable. Ignorance of the law is no e., nul n'est censé ignorer la loi. 2. Excuse, prétexte m. By way of e. he alleged that . . ., en guise d'excuse il allégua que. . . . To offer a reasonable e., donner, fournir, une excuse valable.

excuse[2] [eks'kjuːz], v.tr. (a) Excuser, pardonner. E. my being late, excusez-moi d'être en retard. He may be excused for laughing, il est excusable d'avoir ri. If you will e. the expression, si vous voulez me passer l'expression. E. me! (i) excusez-moi! (ii) pardon! Sch: May I be excused? est-ce que je peux sortir? (b) To e. s.o. from doing sth., excuser, dispenser, qn de faire qch. To e. s.o. from attendance, excuser qn. F: E. me getting up, pardonnez-moi si je ne me lève pas. Mil: Navy: To be excused a fatigue, être exempté d'une corvée. On the excused list, exempt de service.

exeat ['eksiæt], s. Ecc: Sch: Exeat m.

execrable ['eksikrəbl], a. Exécrable, détestable. -ably, adv. Détestablement.

execrate ['eksikreit], v.tr. 1. Exécrer, détester. 2. Abs. Proférer des imprécations.

execration [,eksi'kreiʃ(ə)n], s. Exécration f.

executant [ig'zekjutənt], s. Mus: Exécutant, -ante.

execute ['eksikjuːt], v.tr. 1. (a) Exécuter (un travail); s'acquitter (d'une tâche). Fin: Effectuer (un transfert). To e. a deed, souscrire un acte. (b) Exécuter, jouer (un morceau de musique). 2. Exécuter (un criminel).

execution [ˌeksi'kjuːʃ(ə)n], s. **1.** (a) Exécution f (d'un projet). **In the e. of one's duty,** dans l'exercice de ses fonctions. (b) *Jur:* Souscription f (d'un acte). (c) (i) Exécution (d'un morceau de musique); (ii) jeu m (d'un musicien). **2.** *Jur:* Saisie-exécution f. **Writ of e.,** exécutoire m. **3.** Exécution (d'un criminel); exécution capitale.

executioner [ˌeksi'kjuːʃnər], s. Bourreau m.

executive [ig'zekjutiv]. **1.** a. Exécutif. *Adm: Mil:* **E. duties,** service m de détail. *Adm:* **E. (officer)** = rédacteur m (de ministère). **2.** s. (a) Pouvoir exécutif, exécutif m (d'un gouvernement). (b) Bureau m (d'une association). (c) Administrateur m. **Sales e.,** directeur commercial.

executor, s. **1.** ['eksikjuːtər] Exécuteur, -trice (d'un ordre). **2.** [ig'sekjutər] *Jur:* Exécuteur testamentaire (d'un testateur).

executory [ig'zekjut(ə)ri], a. *Jur:* (a) (Jugement) exécutoire. (b) = EXECUTIVE 1.

executrix [ig'zekjutriks], s.f. *Jur:* Exécutrice testamentaire.

exegesis [ˌeksi'dʒiːsis], s. *Theol:* Exégèse f.

exemplary [ig'zempləri], a. Exemplaire. **An e. husband,** un époux modèle. **E. punishment,** punition f exemplaire.

exemplification [ig,zemplifi'keiʃ(ə)n], s. **1.** Démonstration f au moyen d'exemples. **2.** Exemple m. **3.** *Jur:* Ampliation f.

exemplify [ig'zemplifai], v.tr. **1.** Démontrer par des exemples. **To e. a rule,** donner un exemple d'une règle. **2.** Servir d'exemple à (une règle). **3.** *Jur:* Faire une ampliation (d'un acte).

exempt¹ [ig'zem(p)t], a. Exempt, dispensé. **E. from taxation,** franc, f. franche, d'impôts.

exempt², v.tr. **e. s.o. (from sth.),** exempter, exonérer, dispenser, qn (de qch.).

exemption [ig'zem(p)ʃ(ə)n], s. **E. from sth.,** exemption f, exonération f, dispense f, de qch.

exercise¹ ['eksəsaiz], s. **1.** Exercice m (d'une faculté). **In the e. of one's duties,** dans l'exercice de ses fonctions. **2.** (a) Mental e., exercice de l'esprit. **Outdoor e.,** exercice au grand air. **To take e.,** prendre de l'exercice. (b) *Mil:* **Tactical exercises,** évolutions f tactiques. (c) **School e.,** exercice scolaire. **Written e.,** exercice écrit; devoir m. (d) **Religious exercises,** exercices spirituels, pratiques religieuses. **'exercise-book,** s. Cahier m.

exercise², v.tr. **1.** Exercer (un droit, une influence, etc.); pratiquer (un métier). **2.** (a) Exercer (le corps, l'esprit). **To e. oneself,** prendre de l'exercice. **To e. troops,** faire faire l'exercice à des troupes. **To e. a horse,** promener un cheval. **To e. one's wits in order to do sth.,** s'ingénier à faire qch. (b) v.i. S'entraîner; *Mil:* faire l'exercice. **3.** Tourmenter, tracasser. **To e. s.o.'s patience,** mettre à l'épreuve la patience de qn. **The problem that is exercising our minds,** le problème qui nous préoccupe.

exergue [eg'zəːg], s. *Num:* Exergue m.

exert [ig'zəːt], v.tr. **1.** Employer (la force); mettre en œuvre (la force, son talent); déployer (son talent); exercer (une influence). **2. To e. oneself,** s'employer; se donner du mal. **To e. oneself to do sth.,** s'efforcer de faire qch.

exertion [ig'zəːʃ(ə)n], s. **1.** Usage m, emploi m (de la force). **2.** Effort m, efforts. **Being now unequal to the e. of travelling,** n'étant plus à même de soutenir la fatigue d'un voyage.

exeunt ['eksiʌnt], *Lt.v.i. Th:* (Un tel et un tel) sortent. **E. omnes,** tous sortent.

exfoliate [eks'foulieit], v.i. (*Of bone, etc.*) S'exfolier (*of rock*) s'effeuiller, se déliter.

exfoliation [eks,fouli'eiʃ(ə)n], s. **1.** Exfoliation f. *Geol:* Exfoliation, desquamation f. **2.** Squame f.

ex gratia [eks'grɑːʃiə]. **1.** a. **Ex g. payment,** paiement m à titre de faveur. **2.** adv. **He was not eligible for a pension but the firm gave him a lump sum ex g.,** il n'avait pas droit à une retraite, mais la maison lui a donné un capital à titre de faveur.

exhalation [eks(h)ə'leiʃ(ə)n], s. **1.** (a) Exhalation f (de vapeurs). (b) Expiration f (du souffle). **2.** Effluve m, exhalaison f.

exhale [eks'heil]. **1.** v.tr. Exhaler. **2.** v.i. (*Of vapour, etc.*) S'exhaler.

exhaust¹ [ig'zɔːst], s. **1.** *Mch: I.C.E:* (a) Échappement m (de la vapeur, des gaz). *I.C.E:* **E. stroke,** échappement, évacuation f. (b) Gaz m d'échappement. **2.** (a) Production f du vide (dans un cylindre). **E. fan,** ventilateur aspirant; aspirateur m. (b) = EXHAUST-PIPE. **ex'haust-pipe,** s. *I.C.E:* Tuyau m d'échappement.

exhaust², v.tr. (a) Aspirer (l'air). (b) Épuiser, tarir (une source, ses ressources). **To e. a bulb (of air),** faire le vide dans une ampoule. (c) Épuiser, éreinter, exténuer (qn). **exhausted,** a. **1.** (*Of bulb*) Vide d'air. **2.** (a) Épuisé. **E. land,** terre usée. (b) (*Of pers., animal*) Épuisé, exténué. **I am e.,** je n'en peux plus. **exhausting,** a. (Effort) épuisant.

exhaustion [ig'zɔːstʃ(ə)n], s. **1.** *Ph:* Aspiration f, exhaustion f (d'un gaz). **2.** Épuisement m (du sol). **3.** Épuisement; affalement m. **To be in a state of e.,** être à bout de forces.

exhaustive [ig'zɔːstiv], a. Qui épuise toutes les hypothèses. **E. enquiry,** enquête approfondie. **-ly,** adv. **To treat a subject e.,** traiter un sujet à fond.

exhibit¹ [ig'zibit], s. **1.** *Jur:* Pièce f à conviction (en procédure criminelle); pièce ou document m à l'appui. **2.** Objet exposé (à une exposition). **There are several interesting exhibits,** il y a plusieurs envois intéressants.

exhibit², v.tr. **1.** Exhiber, montrer (un objet); faire preuve de (courage). **2.** Offrir, présenter (qch. à la vue). **3. To e. goods in shop windows,** exposer des marchandises à l'étalage. **4.** *Jur:* Exhiber, produire (des pièces à l'appui).

exhibition [ˌeksi'biʃ(ə)n], s. **1.** (a) Exposition f, étalage m (de marchandises). **To make an e. of oneself,** se donner en spectacle. (b) Démonstration f (d'un procédé). (c) *Jur:* **E. of documents,** production f des pièces. **2.** (a) Exposition. (b) *Com:* **E. room,** salon d'exposition (d'automobiles). (c) *Cin:* Présentation f (d'un film). **3.** *Sch:* Bourse f.

exhibitioner [ˌeksi'biʃnər], s. *Sch:* Boursier, -ière (à une université, un collège).

exhibitionism ['eksi'biʃ(ə)nizəm], s. Exhibitionnisme m.

exhibitionist ['eksi'biʃ(ə)nist], s. Exhibitionniste mf.

exhibitor [ig'zibitər], s. **1.** (*At exhibition*) Exposant, -ante. **2.** *Cin:* Exploitant m d'une salle.

exhilarate [ig'ziləreit], v.tr. Vivifier; mettre à (qn) la joie au cœur; *F:* émoustiller. **exhilarated,** a. Ragaillardi, émoustillé. **exhilarating,** a. Vivifiant, émoustillant. **E. wine,** vin capiteux.

exhilaration [ig,zilə'reiʃ(ə)n], s. Gaieté f; joie f de vivre.

exhort [ig'zɔːt], v.tr. (a) Exhorter, encourager (**s.o. to (do) sth.,** qn à (faire) qch.). (b) Préconiser (une réforme, etc.).

exhortation [ˌegzɔː'teiʃ(ə)n], s. Exhortation f.

exhumation [ˌeks(h)juː'meiʃ(ə)n], s. Exhumation f.

exhume [eks'hjuːm], v.tr. Exhumer.

exigence ['eksidʒəns], **exigency** [ek'sidʒənsi], s. **1.** Exigence f, nécessité f. **2.** Situation f critique; cas pressant. **In this e.,** dans cette extrémité.

exigent ['eksidʒənt], a. **1.** Urgent. **2.** Exigeant.

exigible ['eksidʒəbl], a. Exigible.

exiguity [eksi'gjuiti], s. Exiguïté f (d'un logement); modicité f (d'un revenu).

exiguous [eg'zigjuəs], a. Exigu, -uë.

exile¹ ['eksail], s. Exil m; bannissement m.

exile², s. Exilé, -ée; banni, -ie.

exile³, v.tr. Exiler, bannir (**from,** de). **To e. oneself,** se dépayser.

exist [ig'zist], v.i. Exister. **I think, therefore I e.,** je pense, donc je suis. **To continue to e.,** subsister. **Wherever these conditions e.,** partout où règnent ces conditions. **How do you manage to e. here?** comment parvenez-vous à vivre ici? **existing,** a. Existant, actuel, présent. **In e. circumstances,** dans les circonstances actuelles.

existence [ig'zist(ə)ns], s. **1.** Existence f. **The firm has been in e. for fifty years,** la maison existe depuis cinquante ans. **To come into e.,** naître. **2.** Existence, vie f.

existent [ig'zist(ə)nt], a. Existant.

existential [ˌegzis'tenʃəl], a. *Phil:* Existentiel, -elle.

existentialism [egzis'tenʃəlizm], s. *Phil:* Existentialisme m.
existentialist [egzis'tenʃəlist], a. & s. *Phil:* Existentialiste (mf).
exit[1] ['eksit], s. 1. Sortie f. *Th:* **Sham e.,** fausse sortie. **To make one's e.,** quitter la scène. 2. Sortie; (porte f de) dégagement m (d'un théâtre). **To provide for exits,** ménager des issues f. **Emergency e.,** sortie de secours. **E. only,** (porte exclusivement affectée à la) sortie.
exit[2], v.i. 1. *Th:* E. **Macbeth,** Macbeth sort. 2. Sortir; faire sa sortie.
exodus ['eksədəs], s. (a) Exode m (des Hébreux, etc.). **(The Book of) E.,** l'Exode. (b) Départ m, sortie f (d'un groupe de gens). **After the chairman's speech there was a general e.,** après le discours du président il y eut une sortie générale.
ex(-)officio ['eksə'fiʃiou], adv.phr: **Ex(-)officio member,** membre de droit, de par ses fonctions.
exonerate [ig'zɔnəreit], v.tr. 1. Exonérer, dispenser (from, de). 2. **To e. s.o.** (from blame), disculper qn. **Evidence that exonerates you,** témoignage à votre décharge.
exoneration [ig,zɔnə'reiʃ(ə)n], s. 1. Exonération f, décharge f, dispense f (from, de). 2. **E. from blame,** disculpation f.
exorbitance [ig'zɔ:bit(ə)ns], s. Exorbitance f, énormité f, extravagance f (des prix).
exorbitant [ig'zɔ:bit(ə)nt], a. Exorbitant, extravagant. **E. price,** prix exorbitant.
exorcism ['eksɔ:sizm], s. Exorcisme m; conjuration f.
exorcist ['eksɔ:sist], s. Exorciste m.
exorcise ['eksɔ:saiz], v.tr. Exorciser (un démon); conjurer (un esprit). **exorcising,** s. Exorcisation f, exorcisme m.
exordium [ek'sɔ:diəm[, s. Exorde m.
exosmosis [,eksɔs'mousis], s. *Ph:* Exosmose f.
exoteric [,eksɔ'terik], a. (a) (*Doctrine, etc.*) exotérique. (b) Populaire; facile à comprendre.
exotic [eg'zɔtik], a. Exotique.
expand [iks'pænd]. 1. v.tr. (a) Dilater (un gaz); développer (un abrégé); élargir (l'esprit). *Mch:* Détendre (la vapeur). (b) Déployer (les ailes). 2. v.i. (a) (*Of solid, air*) Se dilater; (*of steam*) se détendre; (*of chest*) se développer. **His mind is expanding,** son intelligence se développe. (b) (*Of pers.*) Devenir expansif. **expanding,** a. 1. **The e. universe,** l'univers en expansion. 2. **E. bracelet,** bracelet extensible.
expander [iks'pændər], s. *Gym:* (**Chest**) **e.,** extenseur m, sandow m.
expanse [iks'pæns], s. Étendue f (de pays).
expansibility [iks'pænsə'biliti], s. Expansibilité f. *Ph:* Dilatabilité f.
expansible [iks'pænsəbl], a. Expansible. *Ph:* Dilatable.
expansion [iks'pænʃ(ə)n], s. Dilatation f (d'un gaz, d'un métal); développement m (d'un abrégé, de la poitrine). *Mch:* Détente f (de la vapeur).
expansionist [iks'pænʃ(ə)nist], s. Expansionniste mf.
expansive [iks'pænsiv], a. 1. (*Of force*) Expansif. 2. (*of pers.*) Expansif, démonstratif. 3. Vaste, étendu.
expansiveness [iks'pænsivnis],s. Expansibilité f, expansivité f.
ex parte ['eks'pɑ:ti], *Lt.adv.* & *a.phr. Jur:* (Déclaration) émanant d'une seule partie; unilatéral, -aux.
expatiate [eks'peiʃieit], v.i. Discourir (longuement), s'étendre (on, upon, sur). **To be for ever expatiating on . . . ,** ne pas tarir sur. . . .
expatiation [eks,peiʃi'eiʃ(ə)n], s. Dissertation f; long discours.
expatriate[1] [eks'pætrieit], a. & s. Expatrié, -iée.
expatriate[2], v.tr. Expatrier (qn).
expatriation [eks,pætri'eiʃ(ə)n], s. Expatriation f.
expect [iks'pekt], v.tr. 1. Attendre (qn); s'attendre à (un événement); compter sur (l'arrivée de qn). **I expected as much,** je m'y attendais. **I knew what to e.,** je savais à quoi m'attendre. **As one might e.,** comme on doit s'y attendre. *F:* **I wouldn't have expected that of him,** je n'aurais pas cru ça de lui. **To e. that s.o. will do sth.,** s'attendre à ce que qn fasse qch. **It is to be expected that . . . ,** il est vraisemblable que + ind. **It is hardly to be expected that . . . ,** il y a peu

de chances (pour) que + sub. **To e. to do sth.,** compter faire qch. **Don't e. me till you see me,** ne m'attendez pas à l'heure. *Abs. F:* **She's expecting,** elle attend un bébé. 2. **To e. sth. from s.o.,** attendre, exiger, qch. de qn. **I e. you to be punctual,** je vous demanderai d'arriver à l'heure. **What do you e. me to do?** qu'attendez-vous de moi? **How do you e. me to do it?** comment voulez-vous que je le fasse? **It is not expected of you,** vous n'êtes pas tenu de le faire. 3. **I e. so,** je pense que oui. **expected,** a. Attendu, espéré.
expectancy [iks'pekt(ə)nsi], s. Attente f; expectative f.
expectant [iks'pekt(ə)nt], a. (a) Qui attend; d'attente; expectant. (b) **E. mother,** femme enceinte. *Jur:* **E. heir,** héritier en expectative. **-ly,** adv. **To gaze at s.o. e.,** regarder qn avec un air d'attendre qch.
expectation [,ekspek'teiʃ(ə)n], s. 1. Attente f, espérance f, prévision f. **To come up to, fall short of, s.o.'s expectations,** répondre à, tromper, l'attente de qn. **Contrary to all expectations,** contre toute attente. 2. (a) *Jur:* Expectative f d'héritage. (b) pl. **Expectations,** espérances. 3. Probabilité f. *Ins:* **E. of life,** espérance de vie. **E. of life tables,** tables de survie.
expectative [eks'pektətiv], a. Expectatif.
expectorate [eks'pektəreit], v.tr. Expectorer. *Abs.* Cracher.
expectoration [eks,pektə'reiʃ(ə)n], s. Expectoration f; (i) crachement m; (ii) crachat m.
expediency [iks'pi:diənsi], s. (a) Convenance f, opportunité f (d'une mesure). (b) Opportunisme m.
expedient [iks'pi:diənt]. 1. a. Expédient, convenable, opportun. **Do what you think e.,** faites ce que vous jugerez à propos. 2. s. Expédient m, moyen m. **-ly,** adv. Convenablement.
expedite ['ekspidait], v.tr. 1. Activer (une mesure); accélérer (un processus). 2. Expédier, dépêcher (une affaire).
expedition [,ekspi'diʃ(ə)n], s. 1. (a) *Mil: etc:* Expédition f. **To be on an e.,** être en expédition. **E. to the South Pole,** expédition au Pôle Sud. (b) Excursion f. 2. Célérité f, promptitude f.
expeditionary [,ekspi'diʃnəri], a. (Corps, armée) expéditionnaire.
expeditious [,ekspi'diʃəs], a. (Procédé) expéditif; (trajet) rapide; (réponse) prompte. **-ly,** adv. Avec célérité; promptement.
expel [iks'pel], v.tr. (expelled) Expulser (un locataire); chasser (l'ennemi). **To e. s.o. from a society,** bannir qn d'une société. **To e. a boy from school,** renvoyer un élève (de l'école).
expend [iks'pend], v.tr. 1. (a) Dépenser (de l'argent, etc.). (b) **To e. care, time, in doing sth.,** employer du soin, du temps, à faire qch. 2. (a) **Having expended all their cartridges . . . ,** ayant épuisé leurs cartouches. . . . (b) **To e. too much ammunition,** consommer trop de munitions. **expendable,** a. Non-récupérable; sacrifiable. **expendables,** s.pl. esp. *Mil:* Troupes; munitions, etc., sacrifiables.
expenditure [iks'penditʃər], s. 1. Dépense f (d'argent); consommation f (de munitions). 2. Dépense(s). **The national e.,** les dépenses de l'État.
expense [iks'pens], s. 1. (a) Dépense f, frais mpl. **Regardless of e.,** sans regarder à la dépense. **Free of e.,** sans frais; franco. **To go to great e.,** faire de grands, *F:* gros, frais, *F:* se mettre en frais. **To put s.o. to e.,** occasionner des frais à qn. (b) **E. account,** indemnité f pour frais professionnels. pl. **Expenses,** dépenses, frais; *Com:* sorties f. **Travelling expenses,** frais de déplacement. (*Of a car*) **Running expenses,** dépenses d'utilisation. **Petty expenses,** menus frais. **Incidental expenses,** faux frais. **Household expenses,** dépenses du ménage. **To have all expenses paid,** être défrayé de tout. 2. Dépens m. **A laugh at my e.,** un éclat de rire à mes dépens. 3. **To be a great e. to s.o.,** être une grande charge pour qn.
expensive [iks'pensiv], a. (Objet) coûteux, cher; (procédé) dispendieux. **E. car,** voiture de luxe. **To be e.,** coûter cher inv. **Little places that are not too e.,** petits trous pas chers. **-ly,** adv. (S'habiller) coûteusement; (construire, etc.) à grands frais. **To live e.,** mener la vie large; dépenser beaucoup d'argent.
expensiveness [iks'pensivnis], s. Cherté f (d'une denrée); prix élevé (de qch.).

experience[1] [iks'piəriəns], *s.* Expérience *f.* 1. Épreuve personnelle. To go through painful experiences, passer par de rudes épreuves. It was a new e. for them, ce fut une nouveauté pour eux. 2. We profit by e., l'expérience nous rend habiles. Practical e., la pratique. E. in driving, expérience de la route; habitude *f* de conduire. He still lacks e., il manque encore de pratique. Facts within my e., faits à ma connaissance. Have you had any previous e.? avez-vous déjà travaillé dans ce métier?

experience[2], *v.tr.* 1. Éprouver; faire l'expérience de (qch.). To e. difficult times, passer par des temps difficiles. 2. Apprendre (par expérience) (that, que). 3. *U.S:* To e. religion, se convertir. **experienced**, *a.* Qui a de l'expérience, du métier; expérimenté; (observateur) averti; (œil) exercé (in, à). E. in business, rompu aux affaires.

experiment[1] [iks'periment], *s.* Expérience *f*; essai *m.* To carry out an e., procéder à une expérience. As an e., by way of e., à titre d'essai.

experiment[2], *v.i.* Expérimenter, faire une expérience, des expériences (on, with, sur, avec). **experimenting**, *s.* Expérimentation *f.*

experimental [eks,peri'mentl], *a.* 1. (Savoir) expérimental, -aux. 2. *Ind:* The e. department, le service des essais. -ally, *adv.* Expérimentalement.

experimentation [eks,perimen'teiʃ(ə)n], *s.* Expérimentation *f.*

experimenter [iks'perimentər], *s.* Expérimentateur, -trice.

expert[1] ['ekspə:t], *a.* Habile, expert. E. advice, avis autorisé. -ly, *adv.* Habilement, expertement.

expert[2] ['ekspə:t], *s.* Expert *m*; spécialiste *m.* The experts, les gens *m* du métier, les techniciens *m.* With the eye of an e., d'un regard connaisseur. Expert's report, expertise *f.*

expertise [ekspə:'ti:z], *s.* 1. Expertise *f.* 2. Compétence *f*; connaissances *f* techniques.

expertness ['ekspə:tnis], *s.* Habileté *f*, compétence *f.*

expiate ['ekspieit], *v.tr.* Expier.

expiation [ekspi'eiʃ(ə)n], *s.* Expiation *f.*

expiatory ['ekspieitəri], *a.* Expiatoire.

expiration [ekspai(ə)'reiʃ(ə)n], *s.* Expiration *f.* 1. E. of air from the lungs, expiration de l'air des poumons. 2. Cessation *f*, terme *m* (d'une concession); échéance *f* (d'un marché à prime).

expire [iks'paiər], 1. *v.tr.* Expirer, exhaler (l'air des poumons). 2. *v.i.* (a) Expirer, mourir; (of hope) s'évanouir. (b) Expirer, cesser, prendre fin. *Com:* Expired bill, effet périmé. *Ins:* Expired policy, police déchue.

expiry [iks'paiəri], *s.* Expiration *f*, terminaison *f*; terme *m.*

explain [iks'plein], *v.tr.* Expliquer, éclaircir. That explains matters, voilà qui explique tout. That is easily explained, cela s'explique facilement. To e. oneself, (i) s'expliquer; (ii) se justifier. **explain away**, *v.tr.* Donner une explication satisfaisante de (propos offensants).

explainable [iks'pleinəbl], *a.* Explicable; (conduite) justifiable.

explanation [ekspla'neiʃ(ə)n], *s.* Explication *f*; éclaircissement *m.* To give an e. of one's conduct, rendre raison de sa conduite.

explanatory [iks'plænət(ə)ri], *a.* Explicatif.

expletive [eks'pli:tiv]. 1. *a.* Explétif. 2. *s.* (a) *Gram:* Explétif *m.* (b) Juron *m.*

explicable [eks'plikəbl], *a.* Explicable.

explicit [iks'plisit], *a.* Explicite; formel, catégorique. To be more e. in one's statements, préciser ses affirmations. -ly, *adv.* Explicitement; catégoriquement.

explode [iks'ploud]. 1. *v.tr.* (a) Démontrer la fausseté de (qch.); discréditer (une théorie). (b) Faire éclater (un obus); faire sauter (une mine). 2. *v.i.* Faire explosion. (a) (Of shell) Éclater; (of mine) sauter. (b) (Of gunpowder) Exploser, détoner. (c) To e. with laughter, éclater de rire. **exploded**, *a.* 1. E. theory, théorie discréditée. 2. (Obus) éclaté; (mine) qui a sauté.

exploit[1] ['eksploit], *s.* Exploit *m*; haut fait.

exploit[2] [iks'ploit], *v.tr.* (a) Exploiter (une mine). (b) Exploiter (qn).

exploitable [iks'ploitəbl], *a.* Exploitable.

exploitation [eksploi'teiʃ(ə)n], *s.* Exploitation *f.*

exploration [eksplo'reiʃ(ə)n], *s.* Exploration *f.* Voyage of e., voyage *m* de découverte.

exploratory [eks'plo:rətəri], *a.* Exploratif; explorateur, -trice.

explore [iks'plə:r], *v.tr.* (a) Explorer (une région). (b) *Med:* Explorer, sonder (une plaie).

explorer [iks'plo:rər], *s.* Explorateur, -trice.

explosion [iks'plouʒ(ə)n], *s.* 1. Explosion *f.* *Min:* Fire-damp e., coup *m* de grisou. To cause an e., provoquer une explosion. *I.C.E:* E. stroke, détente *f.* 2. Détonation *f.* 3. *F:* Débordement *m* (de fureur); explosion (de rires).

explosive [iks'plousiv]. 1. *a.* (Matière) explosible; (mélange) explosif. *I.C.E:* E. mixture, mélange détonant. 2. *s.* (a) Explosif *m*, détonant *m*; *F:* (generic term) poudre *f.* High e., explosif puissant, brisant. (b) *Ling:* (Consonne) explosive (*f*).

exponent [eks'pounənt], *s.* 1. Interprète *mf* (d'un système, etc.). *Mus:* Interprète, exécutant, -ante. 2. *Mth:* Exposant *m* (d'une quantité).

exponential [ekspo'nenʃ(ə)l], *a.* *Mth:* Exponentiel.

export[1] ['ekspo:t], *s.* 1. *pl.* Exports, (i) articles m d'exportation; (ii) exportations *f.* 2. *Attrib.* E. trade, commerce d'exportation. E. duty, droit(s) de sortie, d'exportation.

export[2] [eks'po:t], *v.tr.* Exporter.

exportation [ekspo:'teiʃ(ə)n], *s.* Exportation *f.*

exporter [eks'po:tər], *s.* Exportateur, -trice.

expose [iks'pouz], *v.tr.* Exposer. 1. (a) Laisser sans abri. 'Not to be exposed to the air,' "ne pas laisser à l'air." (b) To e. oneself to danger, s'exposer au danger. (c) *Phot:* Exposer (un film). 2. (a) Mettre (qch.) à découvert, à nu, à jour, en évidence. To e. one's ignorance, afficher son ignorance. (b) To e. goods for sale, exposer, étaler, des marchandises pour la vente. 3. Éventer (un secret); démasquer (un hypocrite); dévoiler (un crime). **exposed**, *a.* (a) Exposé (à la vue). E. goods, marchandises étalées, en montre. *Mil:* E. position, endroit exposé. (Of troops) To be e., être en l'air. (b) (Laid bare) A nu; (of root) déchaussé.

exposition [ekspo'ziʃ(ə)n], *s.* 1. Exposition *f*; interprétation *f* (d'une œuvre littéraire). 2. *U.S:* = EXHIBITION 2.

expostulate [iks'postjuleit], *v.i.* Faire des remontrances (with s.o., à qn).

expostulation [iks,postju'leiʃ(ə)n], *s.* (a) Remontrances *fpl.* (b) Remontrance. E. proved useless, j'ai eu beau le raisonner.

exposure [iks'pouʒər], *s.* 1. (a) Exposition *f* (à l'air). To die of e., mourir de froid. (b) *Phot:* (Temps *m* de) pose *f.* Time e., pose. Double e., surimpression *f*, superposition *f.* E. meter, posemètre *m.* 2. (a) Exposition, étalage *m* (de marchandises) pour la vente. (b) Dévoilement *m* (d'un crime). The fear of e., la crainte d'un éclat, d'un scandale. 3. Exposition, orientation *f* (d'un lieu). Southerly e., exposition au midi.

expound [iks'paund], *v.tr.* 1. Exposer (une doctrine). 2. Expliquer, interpréter.

express[1] [iks'pres]. 1. *a.* (a) E. image, image exacte, fidèle (of, de). (b) (Of order) Exprès, formel. For this e. purpose, pour cela même. (c) *Post:* By e. messenger, par exprès. (d) *U.S:* E. company, compagnie *f* de messageries. (e) *U.S:* E. (high)way, autoroute *f.* 2. *adv.* (a) To go e., aller en toute hâte. (b) Sans arrêt. 3. *s.* (a) (Messager) exprès *m.* (b) *Rail:* E. (train), express *m*; rapide *m.*

express[2], *v.tr.* 1. Exprimer (le jus, l'huile) (out of, from, de). 2. Énoncer (un principe); exprimer (ses sentiments, une pensée). To e. a wish, formuler un souhait. To e. one's appreciation, témoigner son appréciation. To e. one's thoughts on paper, traduire ses pensées sur le papier. 3. To e. oneself in French, s'exprimer en français.

express[3], *v.tr.* (a) Envoyer (une lettre) par exprès. (b) *U.S:* Envoyer (qch.) par les messageries.

expression [iks'preʃ(ə)n], *s.* 1. Expression *f* (du jus d'une orange). 2. Expression (d'une pensée). Beyond, past, e., inexprimable. To give e. to one's gratitude, témoigner sa reconnaissance. 3. (a)

Expression, locution *f.* **Unguarded e.**, mot malheureux. (*b*) **Algebraical e.**, expression, formule *f*, algébrique. **4.** (*a*) Expression (du visage). (*b*) *Mus:* **To sing with e.**, chanter avec expression.

expressionism [iks'preʃnizm], *s.* Expressionnisme *m.*

expressionist [iks'preʃnist], *s.* Expressionniste *mf.*

expressionless [iks'preʃ(ə)nlis], *a.* Sans expression; (visage) inexpressif, impassible.

expressive [iks'presiv], *a.* Expressif; plein d'expression. **-ly**, *adv.* Avec expression.

expressiveness [iks'presivnis], *s.* Caractère expressif, force *f* d'expression (d'une langue, d'un mot).

expressly [iks'presli], *adv.* **1.** Expressément, formellement (défendu). **2. I did it e.** to please you, je l'ai fait à seule fin de vous plaire.

expressman [iks'presmən], *s. U.S:* Employé *m* d'une compagnie de messageries.

expropriate [iks'prouprieit], *v.tr.* Exproprier.

expropriation [eks,proupri'eiʃ(ə)n], *s.* Expropriation *f.*

expulsion [iks'pʌlʃ(ə)n], *s.* Expulsion *f*; renvoi *m* (d'un élève).

expulsive [iks'pʌlsiv], *a.* Expulsif.

expunge [eks'pʌndʒ], *v.tr.* Effacer, rayer (un nom d'une liste).

expurgate ['ekspə:geit], *v.tr.* Expurger, épurer (un livre).

expurgation [,ekspə:'geiʃ(ə)n], *s.* Expurgation *f.*

exquisite ['ekskwizit]. **1.** *a.* (*a*) (*Of workmanship*) Exquis. (*b*) (*Of pleasure*) Vif. (*c*) (*Of s.o.'s taste*) Très sensible, délicat. **-ly**, *adv.* D'une manière exquise; excessivement.

ex-serviceman, *pl.* **-men** ['eks'sə:vismən], *s.m.* Ancien combattant; ancien mobilisé.

extant [ek'stænt], *a.* Existant; qui existe; subsistant.

extemporaneous [eks,tempə'reinjəs], *a.* Improvisé; impromptu *inv.* **-ly**, *adv.* = EXTEMPORE 1.

extempore [eks'tempəri]. **1.** *adv.* **To speak e.**, parler d'abondance, impromptu. **2.** *a.* Improvisé, impromptu *inv.* **To make an e. speech**, improviser un discours.

extemporize [iks'tempəraiz]. **1.** *v.tr.* Improviser (un discours). **2.** *v.i.* (*a*) Improviser; parler d'abondance. (*b*) *Mus:* Improviser.

extend [iks'tend]. **I.** *v.tr.* **1.** (*a*) Étendre, allonger (le corps); prolonger (une ligne). (*b*) *Book-k.:* Reporter. (*c*) Étendre, déployer (des troupes). (*d*) **To e. a horse**, pousser un cheval. **2.** Prolonger (une période de temps); *Com:* proroger (l'échéance d'un billet). **3.** Étendre, porter plus loin (les limites); accroître (un commerce); agrandir (son pouvoir). **4.** (*a*) Tendre (la main). (*b*) **To e. a welcome to s.o.**, souhaiter la bienvenue à qn. **5.** *Jur:* Évaluer; saisir (des biens). **II. extend**, *v.i.* **1.** S'étendre, s'allonger. **Estate that extends to the sea**, propriété qui s'étend jusqu'à la mer. **To e. beyond the wall**, saillir, faire saillie, au delà du mur. **2.** (*Of period of time*) Se prolonger, continuer. **extended**, *a. Gramophones:* **An e. play record**, un super 45 tours, un disque à durée prolongée.

extensibility [iks,tensə'biliti], *s.* Extensibilité *f.*

extensible [iks'tensəbl], *a.* Extensible.

extension [iks'tenʃ(ə)n], *s.* **1.** (*a*) Extension *f* (du bras); prolongement *m* (d'un canal); agrandissement *m* (d'une usine). **E. ladder**, échelle *f* à coulisse. (*b*) *Phot:* Tirage *m* (du soufflet). (*c*) *U.S:* **E. services**, services *m* de vulgarisation *f.* **2.** Extension, accroissement *m* (des affaires). **3.** (*a*) (R)allonge *f* (de table). *Rail:* **Line with extensions to . . .**, ligne avec prolongements jusqu'à. . . . *Tp:* **E. 35**, poste *m*, *Fr.C:* local *m*, 35. (*b*) *U.S:* Annexe *f* (d'un bâtiment). (*c*) *Gram:* Complément *m* (du sujet). **4.** Prolongation *f* (de congé). **To get an e. of time**, obtenir un délai. **5.** *Phil:* Étendue *f*, extension (de la matière).

extensive [iks'tensiv], *a.* **1.** Étendu, vaste, ample. **E. knowledge**, connaissances étendues. **E. researches**, travaux approfondis. **2. E. agriculture**, l'agriculture extensive. **-ly**, *adv.* **To use sth. e.**, se servir beaucoup de qch.; faire un usage considérable de qch.

extensor [iks'tensər], *s. Anat:* (Muscle) extenseur *m.*

extent [iks'tent], *s.* Étendue *f.* **What is the e. of the park?** jusqu'où va le parc? **E. of the damage,**

importance *f* du dommage. **To a certain e.**, jusqu'à un certain point; dans une certaine mesure. **To a great e., to a large e.**, dans une large mesure. **To such an e. that . . .**, à tel point que. . . . **To some slight e.**, quelque peu. **To the full e. of his power**, de tout son pouvoir.

extenuate [eks'tenjueit], *v.tr.* **To e. an offence**, atténuer, minimiser, une faute. **extenuating**, *a.* **E. circumstance**, circonstance atténuante.

extenuation [eks,tenju'eiʃ(ə)n], *s.* Atténuation *f* (d'une faute). **To plead sth. in e. of a crime**, alléguer qch. pour atténuer un crime.

exterior [eks'tiəriər]. **1.** *a.* Extérieur (to, à); en dehors (to, de). *Geom:* **E. angle**, angle externe. **2.** *s.* Extérieur *m*, dehors *mpl.* **On the e.**, à l'extérieur.

exteriorize [eks'tiəriəraiz], *v.tr. Phil: Psychics:* Extérioriser.

exterminate [eks'tə:mineit], *v.tr.* Exterminer. **exterminating**, *a.* Exterminateur, -trice.

extermination [eks,tə:mi'neiʃ(ə)n], *s.* Extermination *f.*

exterminator [eks'tə:mineitər], *s.* Exterminateur, -trice.

external [eks'tə:nl]. **1.** *a.* (*a*) Externe. *Med:* **For e. application**, pour l'usage externe. (*b*) Extérieur; du dehors. **E. walls**, murs extérieurs. **E. events**, affaires du dehors. **2.** *s.* (*Usu. in pl.*) Extérieur *m.* **To judge by externals**, juger les choses d'après les apparences. **-ally**, *adv.* Extérieurement; à l'extérieur.

externalize [eks'tə:nəlaiz], *v.tr. Phil: Psychics:* Extérioriser.

extinct [iks'tiŋ(k)t], *a.* (*a*) (*Of volcano, passion*) Éteint. (*b*) (*Of race*) Disparu; (*of title*) aboli, tombé en désuétude.

extinction [iks'tiŋ(k)ʃ(ə)n], *s.* Extinction *f* (d'un incendie, d'une race, d'une dette). **Race threatened with e.**, race en passe de disparaître.

extinctive [iks'tiŋ(k)tiv], *a.* Extinctif.

extinguish [iks'tiŋgwiʃ], *v.tr. Lit:* Éteindre (le feu); souffler (la chandelle). *Jur:* Abolir (un droit). *Fin:* Amortir, éteindre (une dette). **To be extinguished by s.o.**, être surpassé, éclipsé, par qn. **extinguishing**, *a.* Extincteur, -trice.

extinguisher [iks'tiŋgwiʃər], *s.* (*a*) (Appareil) extincteur *m* (d'incendie). (*b*) (*For candle*) Éteignoir *m.*

extirpate ['ekstə:peit], *v.tr.* Extirper.

extirpation [,ekstə'peiʃ(ə)n], *s.* Extirpation *f.*

extirpator ['ekstəpeitər], *s.* **1.** (*Pers.*) Extirpateur, -trice. **2.** (*Machine*) Extirpateur *m.*

extol [iks'tol], *v.tr.* (**extolled**) Exalter, prôner. **To e. s.o. to the skies**, porter qn aux nues.

extort [iks'to:t], *v.tr.* Extorquer (une signature, etc.) (from, out of, s.o., à qn). **To e. money out of s.o.**, extorquer de l'argent à qn. **To e. a promise from s.o.**, arracher une promesse à qn.

extortion [iks'to:ʃ(ə)n], *s.* Extorsion *f*, exaction *f* (d'impôts); arrachement *m* (d'une promesse).

extortionate [iks'to:ʃnit], *a.* (Prix) exorbitant.

extortioner [iks'to:ʃnər], *s.* extortionist [iks'to:ʃənist], *s.* Extorqueur, -euse; exacteur *m.*

extra ['ekstrə]. **1.** *a.* (*a*) En sus, de plus; supplémentaire. **E. dish** (plat d')extra. **To make an e. charge**, percevoir un supplément. **E. pay**, surpaye *f*; *Mil: Navy:* supplément de solde. *Rail:* **To put on an e. coach**, rajouter une voiture. *Sch:* **E. subject**, matière facultative. (*b*) De qualité supérieure; superfin; *F:* extra. **Rope of e. strength**, corde extraforte. **2.** *adv.* (*a*) Plus que d'ordinaire; extra-. **E. strong binding**, reliure extra-solide. (*b*) En plus. **The wine is e.**, le vin est en plus. **Packing e.**, emballage non compris. **3.** *s.* (*a*) Supplément *m* (de menu); édition spéciale (d'un journal); numéro *m* supplémentaire (d'un programme). (*b*) *Cin:* Figurant, -ante. (*c*) *pl.* Extras, frais *m* ou dépenses *f* supplémentaires. *Sch:* Arts *m* d'agrément. *Typ:* Surcharge *f.* **Little extras**, les petits à-côtés.

extract[1] ['ekstrækt], *s.* Extrait *m.* (*a*) **Meat e.**, extrait, concentré *m*, de viande. (*b*) *Lit: Sch:* **Extracts**, morceaux choisis.

extract[2] [iks'trækt], *v.tr.* Extraire, tirer. **To e. a tooth**, extraire, arracher, une dent. **To e. a bullet from a wound**, retirer une balle d'une plaie. **To e. a confession from s.o.**, arracher un aveu à qn.

extraction [iks'trækʃ(ə)n], s. Extraction f. 1. E. of a tooth, arrachement m, extraction, d'une dent. E. of a nail, arrachement d'un clou. *Mill:* E. rate, taux de blutage. 2. Origine f. To be of English e., être d'origine anglaise.

extractor [iks'træktər], s. Extracteur m. *A:* Bullet e., tire-balle m, pl. tire-balles.

extraditable ['ekstrədaitəbl], a. 1. (*Of pers.*) Passible d'extradition. 2. E. crime, crime qui justifie l'extradition.

extradite ['ekstrədait], v.tr. *Jur:* Extrader.

extradition [ekstrə'diʃ(ə)n], s. Extradition f.

extrajudicial ['ekstrədʒu(:)'diʃ(ə)l], a. Extrajudiciaire; en dehors des débats.

extramural ['ekstrə'mjuər(ə)l], a. (Quartier) extra-muros inv. E. studies, cours en dehors du programme des examens.

extraneous [eks'treinjəs], a. Étranger (to, à). To be e. to the matter in hand, n'avoir rien à voir avec l'affaire.

extraordinary [iks'trɔːdinri], a. (a) Extraordinaire. An e. meeting of the shareholders, une assemblée générale extraordinaire. (b) *F:* Prodigieux; invraisemblable. He has an e. capacity for drink, c'est inouï ce qu'il boit. -ily, adv. Extraordinairement.

extrapolate [ik'stræpəleit], v.tr. Extrapoler.

extrasensory ['ekstrə'sensəri], a. Extra-sensoriel, -elle.

extraterritoriality ['ekstrə,teri,tɔ:ri'æliti], s. Exterritorialité f, extra-territorialité f.

extravagance [iks'trævəgəns], s. Extravagance f, exagération f. 2. Folles dépenses; prodigalités fpl. A piece of e., une dépense inutile.

extravagant [iks'trævəgənt], a. 1. Extravagant. E. praise, éloges outrés. 2. (*Of pers.*) Dépensier. E. tastes, goûts dispendieux. 3. (*Of price*) Exorbitant. -ly, adv. 1. D'une façon extravagante. To talk e., dire des folies. 2. Excessivement; à l'excès. She dresses e., elle s'habille au-delà de ses moyens.

extravaganza [eks,trævə'gænzə], s. *Lit: Mus:* Œuvre f d'une extravagance bouffonne; histoire extravagante; fantaisie f.

extravasate [eks'trævəseit], v.i. (*Of blood*) S'extravaser, s'épancher.

extravasation [eks,trævə'seiʃ(ə)n], s. *Med:* Synovial e., épanchement m de synovie.

extravert ['ekstrəvə:t], s. = EXTROVERT.

extraversion [ekstrə'və:ʃ(ə)n], s. = EXTROVERSION.

extreme [iks'tri:m]. 1. a. Extrême. The e. penalty, le dernier supplice. *R.C.Ch:* E. unction, extrême-onction f. To hold e. opinions, être outrancier dans ses opinions; avoir des opinions extrémistes. E. old age, extrême vieillesse. E. youth, grande jeunesse. An e. case, un cas exceptionnel. 2. s. To go from one e. to the other, aller d'un extrême à l'autre. In the e., à l'excès; au dernier degré. To go to extremes, pousser les choses à l'extrême. To drive s.o. to extremes, pousser qn à bout. -ly, adv. Extrêmement; au dernier point. To be e. witty, avoir énormément d'esprit.

extremist [iks'tri:mist], s. Extrémiste mf.

extremity [iks'tremiti], s. 1. Extrémité f; point m extrême; bout m (d'une corde); sommité f (d'une plante, d'une branche). 2. pl. The extremities, les extrémités (du corps). 3. They are in great e., ils sont dans une grande gêne.

extricate ['ekstrikeit], v.tr. Dégager. To e. oneself from difficulties, se débrouiller, se dépêtrer.

extrinsic [eks'trinsik], a. Extrinsèque.

extrovert ['ekstrəvə:t], s. Extraverti, -ie, extroverti, -ie.

extroversion [ekstrə'və:ʃ(ə)n], s. *Psy:* Extraversion f. *Med:* Extroversion f.

extrude [eks'tru:d], v.tr. (a) Expulser, (faire) sortir, (from, de). (b) *Metalw:* Refouler (un métal).

exuberance [ig'zju:b(ə)r(ə)ns], s. Exubérance f.

exuberant [ig'zju:b(ə)r(ə)nt], a. Exubérant. In e. health, débordant de santé. -ly, adv. Avec exubérance.

exudation [eksju'deiʃ(ə)n], s. 1. Exsudation f (de la résine). 2. *Arb:* E. of sap, écoulement m de la sève.

exude [ig'zju:d], v.tr. & i. Exsuder.

exult [ig'zʌlt], v.i. 1. Exulter, se réjouir (at, in, de). 2. To e. over s.o., triompher de qn.

exultant [ig'zʌlt(ə)nt], a. Triomphant, exultant. To be e., exulter, jubiler. -ly, adv. D'un air de triomphe. He spoke e., il exultait.

exultation [egzʌl'teiʃ(ə)n], s. Exultation f.

ex-voto ['eks'voutou], s. *Ecc:* Ex-voto m inv.

eye¹ [ai], s. 1. Œil m, pl. yeux. (a) To have blue eyes, avoir les yeux bleus. To give s.o. a black e., pocher l'œil à qn. To lose an e., perdre un œil; devenir borgne. To put out s.o.'s eyes, crever les yeux à qn. To open one's eyes wide, ouvrir de grands yeux; écarquiller les yeux. *F:* That made him open his eyes, ça a été pour lui une révélation. To screw up one's eyes, faire les petits yeux. To do sth. with one's eyes open, faire qch. en connaissance de cause. To keep one's eyes open, *F:* skinned, avoir l'œil (ouvert); *F:* ne pas avoir les yeux dans sa poche. Keep your eyes open! ouvrez l'œil! ayez l'œil! (He was so sleepy that) he could not keep his eyes open, il dormait debout. To open s.o.'s eyes (to sth.), éclairer, désabuser, qn. To shut one's eyes to the faults of s.o., fermer les yeux sur les défauts de qn. To shut one's eyes to the truth, se refuser à l'évidence. To do sth. with one's eyes shut, faire qch. les yeux fermés. To be up to the eyes in work, avoir du travail par-dessus la tête. To show the whites of one's eyes, faire les yeux blancs. With tears in one's eyes, les larmes aux yeux. To look on with dry eyes, regarder d'un œil indifférent. *P:* My eye! mince (alors)! des clous! That's all my e. (and Betty Martin)! tout ça c'est de la blague. *Z:* Simple e., ocelle m, stemmate m. (b) To catch the e., frapper l'œil, attirer les regards. To catch s.o.'s e., attirer l'attention de qn. (*In Parliament*) To catch the Speaker's e., obtenir la parole. He has eyes at the back of his head, il a des yeux d'Argus. To set eyes on sth., apercevoir, voir, qch. Where are your eyes? êtes-vous aveugle? (c) To make eyes at s.o., *F: O:* to give s.o. the glad e., faire de l'œil à qn, lancer des œillades. To make sheep's eyes at s.o., faire les yeux doux à qn. To see e. to e. with s.o., voir les choses du même œil que qn. You can see that with half an e., cela saute aux yeux. *Mil:* Eyes right! tête (à) droite! Eyes front! fixe! (d) To give an e. to sth., veiller à qch. To keep a strict e. on s.o., surveiller qn de près. *Golf:* To keep one's e. on the ball, fixer la balle. Keep your e. on him! ne le quittez pas des yeux! Under the e. of . . ., sous la surveillance de. . . . To have one's e. on a situation, *F:* lorgner une place. To work with an e. to the future, travailler en vue de l'avenir. To be all eyes, être tout yeux. (e) To have an e. for a horse, s'y connaître en chevaux. *Sp:* To have one's e. well in, avoir l'œil exercé. (f) To be very much in the public e., occuper une position très en vue. (g) Private e., détective m, enquêteur m privé. 2. (a) Eyes in a peacock's tail, yeux, miroirs m, de la queue d'un paon. (b) *Hort:* (i) Œil, bourgeon m. (ii) (*In grafting*) Œilleton m. 3. (a) Chas m (d'une aiguille). To pass through a needle's e., passer par le trou d'une aiguille. (b) Piton m. *S.a.* HOOK¹ 1. 4. (a) *Phot: etc:* Œilleton m (de viseur clair). (b) *El.E:* Electric e., cellule f photo-électrique; œil électrique. Magic e., œil magique. 5. In the e. of . . ., dans la direction opposée à. . . . *Nau:* In the wind's e., dans le lit m du vent. 'eye-bath, s. *Med:* Œillère f; gondole f. 'eye-bolt, s. Piton m. 'eye-bud, s. *Hort:* Œilleton m. 'eye-catching, a. Accrocheur, -euse. An eye-c. title, un titre accrocheur. 'eye-glass, s. (a) (*Single*) Monocle m. (b) (Pair of) eye-glasses, binocle m, lorgnon m, pince-nez m inv. 'eye-opener, s. Révélation f; surprise f. 'eye-shade, s. Visière f. 'eye-strain, s. To suffer from e.-s., avoir les yeux fatigués. 'eye-tooth, s. (Dent) œillère f. 'eye-wash, s. 1. *Pharm:* Collyre m. 2. *F:* That's all e.-w., tout ça c'est du boniment, de la poudre aux yeux.

eye², v.tr. (eyed; eyeing) Regarder, observer (d'un œil jaloux, etc.); mesurer (qn) des yeux; *F:* reluquer (qn). To e. s.o. from head to foot, toiser qn (de haut en bas).

eyeball ['aibɔ:l], s. Globe m de l'œil; globe oculaire.

eyebrow ['aibrau], s. Sourcil m. To knit one's eyebrows, froncer le(s) sourcil(s). He never raised an e., il n'a pas sourcillé. *P:* He's hanging on by his eyebrows, il se maintient tout juste; il est dans une position périlleuse.

eyed [aid], a. 1. -eyed (*with adj. or numeral prefixed, e.g.*) A black-eyed boy, un garçon aux yeux noirs. 2. (Poinçon) à œil. 3. (*Of feather*) Ocellé.

eyeful ['aiful], s. I opened the bottle and got an e. of beer, j'ai ouvert la bouteille et j'ai reçu de la bière plein dans l'œil. *F:* It was an e.! Ce qu'on a pu se rincer l'œil, s'en mettre plein la vue!

eyehole ['aihoul], s. 1. Orbite *m* de l'œil. 2. Petite ouverture; judas *m* (d'une porte). 3. Œillet *m* (à lacet, etc.).

eyelash ['ailæʃ], s. Cil *m*.

eyelet ['ailit], s. Œillet *m*; (*in rope*) cosse *f*.

eyelid ['ailid], s. Paupière *f*.

eyepiece ['aipiːs], s. (*a*) Oculaire *m* (de télescope). (*b*) Viseur *m* (de théodolite).

eyesight ['aisait], s. Vue *f*. To have good e., avoir bonne vue, la vue bonne. My e. is failing, ma vue baisse.

eyesore ['aisɔːr], s. Ce qui blesse la vue. To be an e., offenser les regards. To be an e. to s.o., être la bête noire de qn.

eyewitness ['aiwitnis], s. Témoin *m* oculaire.

eyot [eit], s. [= AIT] Ilot *m*.

eyrie, eyry ['aiəri], s. Aire *f* (d'un aigle).

Ezekiel [i'ziːkjəl]. *Pr.n.m. B.Hist:* Ézéchiel.

F, f [ef], s. 1. (La lettre) F, f *f & m.* 2. *Mus:* Fa *m.* **F clef**, clef *f* de fa. *Tp:* F for Frederick, F comme François. **'f-hole**, s. Esse *f* (de violon).
fable ['feibl], s. 1. Fable *f*, conte *m.* **To sort out fact from f.**, séparer le réel de l'imaginaire. 2. *Lit:* Fable, apologue *m.*
Fabian ['feibiən], a. Fabien, -ienne. **F. Society**, Association fabienne (parti socialiste datant de 1884).
fabric ['fæbrik], s. 1. (a) Édifice *m*, bâtiment *m.* (b) *Ecc:* Fabrique *f.* 2. *Tex:* Tissu *m*; étoffe *f.* *Av:* Entoilage *m.* **Silk and woollen fabrics**, soieries *f* et lainages *m.* 3. Structure *f* (d'un édifice, d'un système).
fabricate ['fæbrikeit], v.tr. Inventer, fabriquer, forger.
fabrication [ˌfæbri'keiʃ(ə)n], s. (a) Invention *f.* (b) Contrefaçon *f.*
fabulist ['fæbjulist], s. Fabuliste *m.*
fabulous ['fæbˈuləs], a. 1. Fabuleux, -euse; (personnage) légendaire, mythique. 2. *F:* Prodigieux; mirifique. **A f. price**, un prix fabuleux, fou. **-ly**, adv. Fabuleusement; prodigieusement.
façade [fæˈsɑːd], s. *Arch:* Façade *f.*
face¹ [feis], s. 1. Figure *f*, visage *m*, face *f.* **Pretty little f.**, joli minois. **To strike s.o. in the f.**, frapper qn au visage. **I can never look him in the f. again**, je me sentirai toujours honteux devant lui. **He won't show his f. here again!** il ne se risquera pas à remettre les pieds ici! **To come f. to f. with s.o.**, se trouver nez à nez avec qn. **To bring the two parties f. to f.**, mettre les deux parties en présence. **To fall on one's f.**, tomber à plat ventre. **To set one's f. against sth.**, s'opposer résolument à qch. **In the f. of danger**, en présence du danger. **To fly in the f. of Providence**, porter un défi à la Providence. **I told him so to his f.**, *F:* je ne le lui ai pas envoyé dire. **In the f. of all men**, au vu et au su de tous. **Before my face**, sous mes yeux. 2. (a) Mine *f*, physionomie *f.* **To be a good judge of faces**, être psychologue. **To make, pull, faces (at s.o.)**, faire des grimaces (à qn). **To keep a straight f.**, garder son sérieux. **To put a good, a brave, f. on a bad business**, faire contre mauvaise fortune bon cœur. (b) Audace *f*, front *m.* **He had the f. to tell me so**, il a eu l'aplomb, le toupet, de me le dire. 3. Apparence *f*, aspect *m* (de qch.). **To save f.**, sauver la face; sauver les apparences. **On the f. of things**, à première vue. **His evidence is false on the f. of it**, son témoignage est manifestement faux. 4. Surface *f* (de la terre). 5. Surface frontale. (a) Face (d'une pièce de monnaie). (b) Devant *m*, façade *f* (d'un bâtiment); face (d'une falaise); paroi *f* (d'un rocher); parement *m* (d'un mur). **Min:** **Coal f.**, front *m* de taille (du charbon). (c) Cadran *m* (de montre). (d) *Typ:* Œil *m* (d'un caractère). **'face-ache**, s. Névralgie faciale. **'face-cream**, s. **Toil:** Crème *f* de beauté. **'face-flannel**, s. Gant *m* de toilette; *Fr.C:* débarbouillette *f.* **'face-lift(ing)**, s. Ridectomie *f*, lifting *m.* **'face-powder** s. Poudre *f* (de riz). **'face-towel**, s. Serviette *f* de toilette. **'face value**, s. **Fin:** Valeur nominale.
face², v.tr. 1. Affronter, faire face à, faire front à (un danger); envisager (les faits). **The problem that faces us**, le problème qui nous confronte. **To be faced with bankruptcy**, être acculé à la faillite. *F:* **To f. the music**, tenir tête à l'orage. 2. (a) v.tr. Faire face à, se tenir devant (qn, qch.). **Window that faces the garden**, fenêtre qui donne sur le jardin. **Hotel facing the square**, hôtel en façade sur la place. **The picture facing page 10**, la gravure en regard de la page 10. **Facing each other**, vis-à-vis l'un de l'autre. *Rail:* **Seat facing the engine**, place dans le sens de la marche. (b) v.i. **The house faces north**, la maison est exposée au nord. **F. this way!** tournez-vous de ce côté! *Mil:* **Right f.!** à droite, droite! 3. *Cards:* Retourner (une carte). 4. *Tchn:* (a) Faced surface, surface dressée, usinée. *Tex:* Faced cloth, drap fin. (b) Pa   ementer, revêtir (un mur). (c) Coat faced with silk, habit à revers de soie. **face about**, v.i. *Mil:* Faire volte-face; faire demi-tour. **face out**, v.tr. **To f. it out**,

payer d'audace. **face up**, v.i. **To f. up to s.o., a danger**, affronter qn, un danger. **To f. up to the facts**, envisager la situation. **facing**, s. 1. Surfaçage *m*; dressage *m* (d'une surface). 2. (a) Revers *m*, parement *m* (d'un habit). *Mil:* **Regimental facings**, parement (de la manche ou du col) qui sert à distinguer les différents corps. (b) Perré *m* (d'un talus); revêtement *m*, parement (d'un mur).
facer ['feisər], s. 1. *F: A:* Gifle *f* ou coup *m* au visage. 2. *P:* That's a f., ça, c'est une tuile!
facet¹ ['fæsit], s. Facette *f* (d'un diamant, *Ent:* de l'œil).
facet², v.tr. Facetter (un diamant).
facetious [fəˈsiːʃəs], a. Facétieux, plaisant, farceur, -euse; (style) bouffon. **-ly**, adv. Facétieusement.
facetiousness [fəˈsiːʃəsnis], s. Humeur facétieuse.
facial ['feiʃ(ə)l]. 1. a. (Nerf, etc.) facial, -aux. 2. s. *F:* Massage facial.
facile ['fæsail], a. *Usu.Pej:* 1. (Of work, etc.) Facile. 2. (Of pers.) Accommodant, complaisant.
facilitate [fəˈsiliteit], v.tr. Faciliter.
facility [fəˈsiliti], s. Facilité *f.* 1. (a) F. in speaking, facilité de parole. (b) To enjoy facilities for doing sth., avoir la facilité de faire qch. **To give full facilities . . .**, donner toutes facilités. . . . **There are no bathing facilities**, on ne peut pas s'y baigner. **Harbour facilities**, installations portuaires. **We don't have the facilities for it**, nous ne sommes pas équipés, outillés, pour cela. 2. Souplesse *f* de caractère; complaisance *f.*
facsimile [fækˈsimili], s. Fac-similé *m.* **F. signature**, signature autographiée.
fact [fækt], s. 1. Fait *m*, action *f.* 2. **To bow before the facts**, s'incliner devant les faits; se rendre à l'évidence. **To look facts in the face**, voir les choses telles qu'elles sont. **F. and fiction**, le réel et l'imaginaire. **To stick to facts**, s'en tenir aux faits. **To tell someone the facts of life**, enseigner aux enfants ne se font pas par l'oreille. **Owing to the f. that these things are rare**, du fait que ces choses sont rares. **It is a f. that . . .**, il est de fait que. . . . **To accept a statement as f.**, ajouter foi à une déclaration. **Apart from the f. that . . .**, hormis que. . . . **To know for a f. that . . .**, savoir pertinemment que. . . . **The f. is**, I have no money, c'est que je n'ai pas d'argent. **Is it a f. that . . .?** est-il vrai que. . . .? **In f.**, de fait. **In point of f.**, par le fait. **By the mere f. of that . . .**, par le, du seul, fait de, que . . . **As a matter of f.**, à vrai dire; en réalité.
faction ['fækʃ(ə)n], s. 1. Faction *f*, cabale *f.* 2. (Esprit *m* de) discorde *f.*
factious ['fækʃəs], a. Factieux.
factitive ['fæktitiv], a. *Gram:* Factitif, -ive (verbe, etc.).
factor ['fæktər], s. 1. (Pers.) (a) *Com:* Agent *m* (dépositaire). (b) *Scot:* Régisseur *m*; intendant *m* (d'un domaine). 2. (a) *Mth:* Facteur *m*, diviseur *m.* **Prime f.**, diviseur premier. **The greatest common f.**, le plus grand commun diviseur. (b) *Mec.E:* etc: **F. of safety**, facteur, coefficient *m*, de sûreté, de sécurité. 3. Facteur (concourant à un résultat). **The human f.**, l'élément humain.
factorial [fækˈtɔːriəl], s. *Mth:* Factorielle *f.*
factorize ['fæktəraiz], v.tr. *Mth:* Décomposer (une quantité) en facteurs.
factory ['fækt(ə)ri], s. 1. *Com:* Factorerie *f*, comptoir *m.* 2. *Ind:* Fabrique *f*, usine *f.* **F. inspector**, inspecteur du travail. **'factory-hand**, s. Ouvrier, -ière, d'usine.
factotum [fækˈtoutəm], s. Factotum *m*; homme *m* à tout faire.
factual ['fæktjuəl], a. Positif, -ive. **F. knowledge**, connaissance *f* des faits.
faculty ['fæk(ə)lti], s. 1. (a) Faculté *f.* **To be in possession of all one's faculties**, jouir de toutes ses facultés. (b) Facilité *f*, talent *m.* **To have the f. of observation**, savoir bien observer. 2. *Sch:* The four faculties, les

facultés des lettres, des sciences, de droit et de médecine. *Abs.* The (medical) F., la Faculté. *U.S:* The F., le corps enseignant. 3. Faculté, liberté *f* (to do sth., de faire qch.).

fad [fæd], *s.* Marotte *f*, dada *m*, manie *f*. To be full of fads, *F:* avoir un tas de marottes. It's just a f., c'est du snobisme.

faddist ['fædist], *s. F:* Maniaque *mf*; homme, femme, à marottes. Food f., partisan *m* d'un régime alimentaire.

faddy ['fædi], *a.* Capricieux, -euse, maniaque.

fade [feid]. 1. *v.i.* (a) Se faner, se flétrir; (*of colour*) passer; (*of material*) déteindre. Guaranteed not to f., garanti bon teint. To f. from memory, s'effacer de la mémoire. (b) To f. away, out, s'évanouir, s'affaiblir. Her smile faded away, son sourire s'éteignit. She was fading away, elle dépérissait. 2. *v.tr.* (a) Curtains faded by the sun, rideaux décolorés par le soleil. (b) *Cin:* To f. one scene into another, enchaîner deux scènes. **fading,** *s.* 1. Flétrissure *f* (d'une plante); décoloration *f* (d'une étoffe); affaiblissement *m* (de la lumière). 2. *W.Tel:* Fading *m.* 3. *Cin: T.V:* Fondu *m.* **fade in,** *v.i. Cin: T.V:* Apparaître progressivement, s'ouvrir, arriver dans un fondu. 'fade-in, *s. Cin: T.V:* Ouverture en fondu. **fade out,** *v.i. Cin: T.V:* Disparaître progressivement, se fermer, partir dans un fondu. 'fade-out, fading out, *s. Cin: W.Tel: T.V:* Fondu *m; Cin: T.V:* fermeture *f* en fondu. *W.Tel:* Fading *m.*

fader ['feidər], *s.* Potentiomètre *m.*

faecal ['fi:k(ə)l], *a.* Fécal, -aux.

faeces ['fi:si:z], *s. Med: Ch:* Fèces *fpl*, matières fécales.

fag[1] [fæg], *s.* 1. *F:* (a) Fatigue *f.* What a f.! quelle corvée! It's too much fag, ça prend trop de peine. (b) Surmenage *m.* 2. *Sch:* "Petit" attaché au service d'un grand. 3. *O: P:* Cigarette *f; P:* sèche *f.* 'fag-'end, *s. F:* 1. (a) Bout *m* (d'un morceau d'étoffe, d'un cordage); restes *mpl* (d'un gigot, etc.). (b) Queue *f* (de l'hiver). 2. Mégot *m.*

fag[2], *v.* (fagged) 1. (a) *v.i. & pron.* Trimer; *P:* s'échiner. To f. oneself out, s'éreinter. (b) *v.tr.* (*Of occupation*) Fatiguer, *F:* éreinter (qn). 2. *v.i. Sch:* To f. for a senior, être au service d'un grand. **fagging,** *s. Sch:* Système d'après lequel les jeunes élèves font le service des grands.

faggot ['fægət], *s.* 1. (a) Fagot *m. Fort:* Fascine *f.* (b) *Metall:* Faisceau *m* (de fer en barres). 2. *Cu:* Boulette *f* (de viande).

Fahrenheit ['færənhait], *a.* (Thermomètre) Fahrenheit. (Degrés F.—32) × ⅝ = degrés centigrades.

fail[1] [feil]. *Adv.phr.* Without f., (i) sans faute, (ii) immanquablement, à coup sûr.

fail[2]. 1. *v.i.* (a) Manquer, faillir, faire défaut. To f. in one's duty, manquer, faillir, à son devoir. To f. to do sth., négliger de faire qch. I shall not f. to do so, je n'y manquerai pas. He failed to come, il n'est pas venu. Things that cannot f. to be seen, choses qui ne sauraient échapper aux regards. To f. s.o., manquer à ses engagements envers qn. My strength is failing, mes forces m'abandonnent, me trahissent. His heart failed him, le cœur lui manqua. His memory often fails him, la mémoire lui fait souvent défaut. (b) Rester en panne; flancher. The engine failed, le moteur a eu une panne. (c) Baisser. His sight is failing, sa vue commence à baisser, à faiblir. His memory is failing, sa mémoire baisse. He is failing, sa santé baisse. (d) Ne pas réussir; échouer; manquer son coup, *F:* rater; (*of play*) être un four. I fail to see why . . ., je ne vois pas pourquoi. . . . *Sch:* To f. in an examination, être refusé, échouer, à un examen. (e) *Com:* Faire faillite. To f. for a million, faire une faillite d'un million. 2. *v.tr. Sch:* (a) Refuser, coller (un candidat). (b) To f. an examination, être recalé à un examen. **failing**[1], *s.* 1. (a) Manquement *m.* (b) Affaiblissement *m,* défaillance *f* (de forces, etc.); baisse *f* (de la vue, etc.). (c) Non-réussite *f*; échec *m.* 2. Faible *m*, faiblesse *f*, défaut *m.* **failing**[2], *prep.* A défaut de; faute de (paiement, etc.).

failure ['feiljər], *s.* 1. (a) Manque *m*, manquement *m*, défaut *m.* F. to observe a bye-law, to keep a promise, inobservation *f* d'un règlement de police, manquement à une promesse. F. to pay a bill, défaut de

paiement d'un effet. (b) Panne *f*, défaillance *f* (d'électricité, etc.). *S.a.* HEART-FAILURE. 2. (a) Insuccès *m*, non-réussite *f*; avortement *m* (d'un projet, etc.); échec *m* (à un examen, dans une entreprise). *Th:* Four *m*, fiasco *m*; chute *f* (d'une pièce). To court f., aller au-devant d'un échec. To be doomed to f., être voué à l'échec. (b) *Com:* Faillite *f*, déconfiture *f.* 3. (a) (*Of pers.*) Raté, -ée; *F:* fruit sec. (b) The play was a f., la pièce a été un four, est tombée à plat. Apples are a complete f. this year, cette année les pommes font absolument défaut.

fain [fein]. 1. *Pred.a. A. & Lit:* Contraint par la nécessité (to do sth., de faire qch.). 2. *adv. A. & Lit:* Volontiers.

faint[1] [feint], *a.* 1. F. heart, cœur pusillanime. 2. (a) Faible, affaibli, alangui. F. hope, faible espoir. F. voice, voix faible, éteinte. (b) (*Of colour*) Pâle, délavé; (*of sound, breeze, etc.*) léger, à peine perceptible; (*of idea, etc.*) vague, peu précis. I haven't the faintest idea, je n'en ai pas la moindre idée. 3. = FEINT[2]. 4. To feel f., se sentir mal; être pris d'une défaillance. -ly, *adv.* 1. Faiblement; d'une voix éteinte. 2. Légèrement; un peu. F. reminiscent of . . ., qui rappelle vaguement. . . . F. sarcastic tone, ton légèrement sarcastique. F. visible, à peine visible. faint-'hearted, *a.* Pusillanime, timide. faint-'heartedness, *s.* Pusillanimité *f*, timidité *f.*

faint[2], *s.* Évanouissement *m*, syncope *f*, défaillance *f.* To be in a (dead) f., être évanoui.

faint[3], *v.i.* S'évanouir, défaillir; se trouver mal; *F:* tourner de l'œil. **fainting,** *s.* Évanouissement *m*, défaillance *f.* F. fit = FAINT[2].

faintness ['feintnis], *s.* 1. (*Of voice*) Faiblesse *f*; (*of breeze*) légèreté *f.* 2. Malaise *m*, faiblesse.

fair[1] ['fɛər], *s.* Foire *f. Horse-f.,* foire aux chevaux. World f., exposition universelle. Fun f., fête foraine. 'fair-ground, *s.* Champ *m* de foire.

fair[2]. I. *a.* 1. Beau, *f.* belle. The f. sex, le beau sexe. 2. Spécieux, plausible. To put s.o. off with f. promises, faire patienter qn avec de belles promesses. 3. (*Of pers., hair*) Blond. 4. (a) Net, nette, sans tache. *S.a.* COPY[1] 2. (b) (*Intensive*) *P:* It's a f. swindle, c'est une pure, véritable, escroquerie. (c) Juste, équitable; loyal, -aux. F. play, jeu loyal, franc jeu. *F:* It's not f.! ce n'est pas juste! As is, was, only f., comme de juste. F. enough! ça va! d'accord! By f. means or foul, d'une manière ou d'une autre; de gré ou de force. *Jur:* F. and accurate report, compte rendu loyal et exact. 5. Passable; assez bon. A f. number of . . ., un nombre respectable de. . . . He has a f. chance of success, il a des chances de réussir. To obtain a f. mark (*in an exam, etc.*), obtenir une note passable. It is f. to middling, c'est entre les deux; c'est passable. 6. (a) (*Of wind, etc.*) Propice, favorable. *Nau:* F. wind, vent portant. (b) F. weather, beau temps. Set f., beau (temps) fixe. -ly, *adv.* 1. Impartialement, équitablement. 2. Honnêtement, loyalement, franchement. 3. *F:* We were f. caught in the trap, nous étions bel et bien pris (au piège). They f. screamed with delight, ce fut une véritable explosion de cris de joie. 4. Moyennement, passablement; assez (riche, habile, etc.). To do sth. f. well, s'acquitter assez bien de qch. It is f. certain that . . ., il est à peu près certain que. . . . II. fair, *adv.* 1. *A:* To speak (s.o.) f., parler courtoisement (à qn). 2. *F:* (Agir) loyalement, de bonne foi. To play f., jouer beau jeu. *S.a.* BID[2] 2. 'fair and 'square. 1. *a.* (a) Coup de marteau) au beau milieu. (b) Loyal, honnête. It's all f. and square, c'est de bonne guerre. 2. *adv.* (a) Struck fair(ly) and square(ly) by a shell, frappé au plein milieu par un obus. (b) Loyalement. 'fair-haired, *a.* Blond; aux cheveux blonds. *U.S: F:* F.-h. boy, favori *m.* 'fair-'minded, *a.* Équitable; impartial, -iaux. 'fair-'mindedness, *s.* Impartialité *f.* 'fair-'sized, *a.* Assez grand. 'fair-'spoken, *a. A:* (a) A la parole courtoise. (b) A la parole mielleuse. 'fair-weather, *attrib. a. F:* F.-w. friends, amis des beaux jours.

fairing ['fɛəriŋ], *s.* 1. *Av: Aut:* Profilage *m*; carénage *m.* 2. Entoilage *m.*

fairness ['fɛənis], *s.* 1. Couleur blonde (des cheveux); fraîcheur *f* (du teint). 2. Équité *f*, honnêteté *f*, impartialité *f.* In all f., en toute justice.

fairway ['fɛəwei], s. **1.** *Nau:* Chenal *m*, passe *f*, passage *m*. **2.** *Golf:* Parcours normal.

fairy ['fɛəri]. **1.** *s.* (*a*) Fée *f*. **The wicked f.**, la fée Carabosse. *Th:* F. play, féerie *f*. (*b*) *P:* Pédéraste *m*, *P:* tapette *f*. **2.** *a.* Féerique; de(s) fée(s). **F. godmother**, (i) marraine *f* fée; (ii) *F:* marraine gâteau. **F. footsteps**, pas légers. **'fairy-lamp, -light**, *s.* Lampion *m* (pour décorations). **'fairy-like**, *a.* Féerique. **'fairy-ring**, *s.* Cercle *m*, rond *m*, des fées (dessiné sur l'herbe par les champignons). **F.-r. mushroom**, mousseron *m*. **'fairy-tale**, *s.* **1.** Conte *m* de fées. **2.** (*a*) Conte invraisemblable. (*b*) Mensonge *m*; *F:* craque *f*.

fairyland ['fɛərilænd], *s.* (*a*) Le royaume des fées. (*b*) Féerie *f*.

fait accompli [,feitəkom'pli:], *s.* Fait accompli.

faith [feiθ], *s.* Foi *f*. **1.** (*a*) Confiance *f*, croyance *f*. **To have f. in s.o.**, avoir confiance en qn. **To have f. in God**, avoir foi en Dieu. **To pin one's f. on**, to, s.o., se fier aveuglément à qn. (*b*) **The Christian f.**, la foi chrétienne. **To belong to the same f.**, appartenir à la même communion. **To die in the f.**, faire une bonne mort. **Political f.**, credo *m* politique. **2.** (*a*) Fidélité *f* à ses engagements. **To keep f. with s.o.**, tenir ses engagements envers qn. **To break f. with s.o.**, manquer de foi, de parole, à qn. (*b*) **Good f.**, bonne foi, loyauté *f*. He acted in all good f., il a agi en tout bien, tout honneur; en toute bonne foi. **To allege, plead, one's good f.**, exciper de sa bonne foi. **Bad f.**, perfidie *f*, déloyauté *f*. **'faith-healing**, *s.* Thérapeutique fondée sur la prière et sur la suggestion.

faithful ['feiθful]. **1.** *a.* Fidèle. (*a*) Loyal, -aux. (*b*) (*Of copy, etc.*) Exact, juste, vrai. **2.** *s.pl. Ecc:* The f., les fidèles *m*; (*Islam*) les croyants *m*. **-fully**, *adv.* **1.** Fidèlement, loyalement. *Corr:* (**We remain**) yours f., agréez nos meilleures salutations. **He promised f. to come tomorrow**, il (nous) a donné sa parole qu'il viendrait demain. **2.** (*Traduire*) exactement, fidèlement.

faithfulness ['feiθfulnis], *s.* Fidélité *f*. **1.** Loyauté *f* (to, envers). **2.** Exactitude *f*.

faithless ['feiθlis], *a.* **1.** Infidèle; sans foi. **2.** Déloyal, -aux; perfide.

faithlessness ['feiθlisnis], *s.* **1.** Infidélité *f* (to, à). **2.** Déloyauté *f*.

fake¹ [feik], *s.* *F:* Article truqué; maquillage *m*. It's a f., c'est du trucage.

fake², *v.tr.* *F:* Truquer (des calculs); maquiller (un meuble, etc.); cuisiner (des nouvelles). **fake up**, *v.tr.* Inventer (une histoire); fabriquer (un appareil) de pièces et de morceaux; maquignonner (un cheval, etc.). **faking**, *s.* Trucage *m*, maquillage *m*.

faker ['feikər], *s.* Truqueur *m*; maquilleur *m*.

fakir [fæ'kiər, 'feikiər], *s.* Fakir *m*.

falcon ['fɔ:(l)kən], *s.* *Orn:* Faucon *m*. **Peregrine f.**, faucon pèlerin.

falconer ['fɔ:(l)kənər], *s.* Fauconnier *m*.

falconry ['fɔ:(l)kənri], *s.* Fauconnerie *f*.

fall¹ [fɔ:l], *s.* **1.** (*a*) Chute *f* (d'un corps); descente *f* (d'un marteau, etc.). *Th:* Chute, baisser *m* (du rideau). **To have a f.**, faire une chute; tomber. **To ride for a f.**, (i) aller en casse-cou; (ii) aller au-devant de la défaite; courir à un échec. (*b*) *Wr:* (i) Chute (d'un lutteur); (ii) reprise *f*. (*c*) **There has been a heavy f. of snow**, il est tombé beaucoup de neige. **2.** The f. of the year, le déclin de l'année. *U.S:* **The f.**, l'automne *m*. **3.** (*a*) *Usu. pl.* Chute (d'eau); cascade *f*, cataracte *f*. **The Victoria Falls**, les chutes Victoria. (*b*) *Hyd.E:* Hauteur *f* de chute (d'un barrage). **4.** (*a*) Décrue *f*, baisse *f* (des eaux); reflux *m*, jusant *m* (de la marée); diminution *f* (de poids, etc.); baisse, descente *f*, chute (du baromètre, etc.). (*b*) Dénivellation *f*; pente *f*, inclinaison *f* (d'un toit, etc.). (*c*) Baisse (des prix). *St.Exch:* **Dealing for a f.**, opération à la baisse. **5.** Perte *f*, ruine *f*. **F. from grace**, déchéance *f*. **The F.**, la chute de l'homme. **6.** Chute (d'une place forte); déchéance (d'un empire, etc.). **The f. of the Bastille**, la prise de la Bastille. **7.** Éboulement *m*, éboulis *m*, tombée *f* (de terre, de rochers). **8.** *Nau:* The falls, les garants *m* (des embarcations). **'fall-pipe**, *s.* *Const:* Descente *f* (de gouttière). **'fall-trap**, *s.* *Ven:* Assommoir *m*.

fall², *v.i.* (fell [fel]; fallen ['fɔ:lən]) Tomber. **1.** (*a*) **To f. to the ground** (*from high up*), tomber à terre. **To f. off a ladder**, tomber d'une échelle, à bas d'une échelle. **To f. on one's feet**, (i) (re)tomber sur ses pieds; (ii) *F:* avoir de la chance, de la veine. **To f. into a trap**, tomber, donner, dans un piège. **To let f.**, (i) laisser tomber (une assiette); (ii) baisser (le rideau); (iii) abaisser (une perpendiculaire); (iv) laisser échapper (une larme, un mot). **Night is falling**, la nuit tombe; il se fait nuit; le jour baisse. (*b*) **His hair fell to his shoulders**, ses cheveux lui pendaient, lui descendaient, jusqu'aux épaules. (*c*) **Christmas falls on a Thursday**, Noël tombe un jeudi. **2.** (*From standing position*) (*a*) **To f. to the ground**, tomber par terre. **To f. full length**, tomber de tout son long. **To f. on one's knees**, tomber à genoux. *O:* **To f. by the sword**, périr par l'épée. **To f. (to temptation)**, succomber à la tentation. (*b*) (*Of building*) Crouler, s'écrouler, s'effondrer; (*of horse, tree*) s'abattre. **To f. to pieces**, tomber en morceaux. (*c*) **When Liège fell**, lorsque Liège capitula. **The Government has fallen**, le Ministère est tombé, a été renversé. **3.** (*a*) (*Of tide, barometer*) Descendre, baisser; (*of wind*) tomber; (*of sea*) se calmer, *Nau:* calmir; (*of price, etc.*) baisser. **F: His stock is falling**, ses actions baissent. (*b*) (*Of ground*) Aller en pente; s'incliner; descendre, s'abaisser. *Mth:* (*Of curve*) Décroître. **His face fell**, sa figure s'allongea. (*c*) *Nau:* **To f. to leeward**, tomber sous le vent. (*d*) **To f. from one's position**, déchoir de sa position. **To f. in esteem**, déchoir dans l'estime (du public). **4.** (*a*) **The sunlight falls on the peaks**, le soleil donne sur les cimes. **A sound fell (up)on my ear**, un son frappa mon oreille. (*b*) **To f. upon s.o.'s neck**, on one's food, se jeter au cou de qn, sur la nourriture. **To f. (up)on the enemy**, fondre sur, attaquer, l'ennemi. **5.** (*a*) **To f. to s.o.'s share**, échoir (en partage) à qn. **The blame falls upon . . .**, le blâme retombe sur. . . . **The responsibility falls on me**, toute la responsabilité retombe sur moi. **It falls on me to . . .**, c'est à moi qu'incombe la tâche de. . . . **It fell to me to . . .**, le devoir m'échut de. . . . **This falls within article 10**, cela rentre dans, relève de, l'article 10. (*b*) (*Of pers.*) **To f. under suspicion**, se trouver, devenir, l'objet des soupçons; devenir suspect. **To fall on evil days**, connaître de mauvais jours. (*c*) **I soon fell into their ways**, (i) je me suis vite accoutumé à leur manière de faire; (ii) j'eus bientôt appris la routine. **To f. into a habit**, contracter une habitude. **To f. out of a habit**, perdre une habitude. **To f. into error**, être induit en erreur. **6.** *Pred.* (*a*) **To f. sick**, tomber malade. (*Of post*) **To fall vacant**, se trouver vacant. (*b*) **To f. a victim to . . .**, être victime de. . . . **7.** **To f. to sth.**, to doing sth., se mettre à qch., à faire qch. **They fell to work (again)**, ils se (re)mirent au travail. **fall away**, *v.i.* **1.** (*Of ground, etc.*) S'affaisser brusquement; s'abaisser. **2.** Faire défection. *Theol:* Apostasier. **fall back**, *v.i.* **1.** Tomber en arrière, à la renverse. **2.** (*Of outpost*) Se replier; reculer. (*b*) **To f. back on substitutes**, se rabattre sur des succédanés. **Sum put by to f. back upon**, somme en réserve comme en-cas. **fall behind**, *v.i.* Rester en arrière. *Rac:* Se laisser distancer. **fall down**, *v.i.* **1.** Tomber à terre, par terre. **To f. down before s.o.**, se prosterner devant qn. **2.** (*a*) (*Of building*) Crouler, s'écrouler, s'effondrer. (*b*) *U.S: F:* (*Of pers., plan*) Échouer. **fall for**, *v.i.* *F:* **1.** Tomber amoureux de (qn); adopter (un projet, etc.) avec enthousiasme. **2.** He fell for the trick, il s'y laissa prendre. **fall in**, *v.i.* **1.** (*a*) (*Of roof, etc.*) S'écrouler, s'effondrer; (*of trench*) s'ébouler. (*b*) (*Of cheeks*) Se creuser. (*c*) Tomber à l'eau. **2.** *Mil:* (*Of troops*) Former les rangs; (*of man*) rentrer dans les rangs. **F. in.!** Rassemblement! **3.** (*Of lease, etc.*) Expirer. **D.** (*Of debt*) Arriver à échéance. **4.** (*a*) **To f. in with s.o.**, rencontrer qn. (*b*) **To f. in with s.o.'s opinion**, se ranger, se conformer, à l'avis de qn. **To f. in with a proposal**, accepter une proposition. (*c*) (*Of plan, etc.*) **To f. in with . . .**, cadrer avec. . . . **'fall-in**, *s.* *Mil:* Rassemblement *m*. **'falling 'in**, *s.* **1.** Écroulement *m*, effondement *m*. **2.** *Mil:* Rassemblement *m*. **3.** Expiration *f* (d'un bail); échéance *f* (d'une dette). **4.**

(a) Rencontre f (**with s.o.**, avec qn). (b) Acquiescement m (**with**, à); acceptation f (**with**, de). **fall off**, v.i. 1. His hat fell off, son chapeau tomba. 2. Nau: Abattre sous le vent; arriver. 3. (Of followers) Faire défection. 4. (a) (Of profits) Diminuer; (of speed) ralentir, décroître; (of zeal) se relâcher. (b) Décliner; (of skill) baisser; (of beauty) passer. 'falling 'off, s. 1. Défection f (de partisans, etc.). 2. Diminution f, ralentissement m (des exportations, etc.). **fall out**, v.i. 1. Tomber dehors. 2. (Of hair) Tomber. 3. Mil: Quitter les rangs. 4. Se brouiller, se fâcher (**with**, avec). 5. Things fell out well, les choses se sont bien passées. It (so) fell out that . . ., il advint que . . que. . . . 'fall-out, s. Rad.A: Retombée f. **Fall-out shelter**, abri m antiatomique. **fall over**, v.i. 1. (Of pers.) Tomber à la renverse; (of thg) se renverser, être renversé. 2. To f. over an obstacle, trébucher sur un obstacle. Publishers were falling over each other for his new book, les éditeurs se disputaient avec acharnement son prochain livre. **fall through**, v.i. (Of scheme) Échouer, avorter, F: tomber à l'eau. **fall to**, v.i. (a) Se mettre à l'œuvre, au travail. (b) Entamer la lutte. (c) S'attaquer au repas. **fallen**, a. (a) F. leaves, feuilles tombées. (b) F. humanity, l'humanité déchue. 2. s. The f., les morts m (sur le champ de bataille). **falling**, a. Tombant. Ph: F. body, corps en chute. F. temperature, température en baisse. Com: F. market, marché orienté à la baisse.

fallacious [fə'leiʃəs], a. Fallacieux,-euse,trompeur,-euse.

fallaciousness [fə'leiʃəsnis], s. Fausseté f.

fallacy ['fæləsi], s. Log: Sophisme m; faux raisonnement. A current f., une erreur courante.

fallibility [fæli'biliti], s. Faillibilité f.

fallible ['fælibl], a. Faillible.

fallow[1] ['fælou]. Agr: 1. s. Jachère f, friche f. 2. a. (Of land) En friche; en jachère. To lie f., être en jachère; être, rester, en friche; chômer. Mind that lies f., esprit inculte.

fallow[2], a. See DEER.

false [fɔls], a. Faux, f. fausse. 1. F. report, F: canard m. To take a f. step, faire un faux pas. To be in a f. position, se trouver dans une position fausse. To put a f. interpretation on sth., interpréter qch. à faux. S.a. ALARM[1] 1. 2. Perfide, infidèle; (of promise) mensonger. F. balance-sheet, faux bilan. To be f. to one's husband, tromper son mari. F. witness, faux témoin. To bear f. witness, rendre faux témoignage. adv. To play s.o., trahir qn; faire une perfidie à qn. 3. (Of hair, etc.) Artificiel, postiche; (of action, tears) feint, prétendu, simulé; (of document, etc.) forgé; (of coin, seal) contrefait. F. teeth, fausses dents. F. bottom, double fond (d'une boîte). **-ly**, adv. Faussement. 1. To interpret sth. f., interpréter qch. à faux. 2. Perfidement.

falsehood ['fɔlshud], s. 1. To distinguish truth from f., distinguer le vrai d'avec le faux. 2. Mensonge m.

falseness ['fɔlsnis], s. 1. Fausseté f. 2. (a) Infidélité f (d'un amant, etc.). (b) Fourberie f.

falsetto [fɔl'setou], s. & attrib. Mus: Falsetto (voice), voix f de tête, de fausset.

falsies ['fɔlsiz], s.pl. F: Seins artificiels, P: Roberts mpl de chez Michelin.

falsification [ˌfɔlsifi'keiʃ(ə)n], s. Falsification f.

falsifier ['fɔlsifaiər], s. Falsificateur, -trice.

falsify ['fɔlsifai], v.tr. (falsified; falsifying) 1. Falsifier (un document); fausser (un bilan); dénaturer (des faits). 2. (a) Prouver la fausseté de (qch.). (b) Tromper (un espoir).

falsity ['fɔlsiti], s. Fausseté f (d'une doctrine).

falter ['fɔltər]. 1. v.i. (a) (Of voice) Hésiter, trembler, s'altérer. (b) (Of pers.) Vaciller, chanceler. (c) (Of pers. or courage) Défaillir; F: flancher. 2. v.tr. Dire (qch.) d'une voix hésitante, tremblante. **faltering**, a. 1. (Of voice, etc.) Hésitant, tremblant, troublé. 2. (Of legs) Vacillant, chancelant. 3. (Of courage, memory, etc.) Défaillant. **-ly**, adv. 1. (Parler) d'une voix tremblante, troublée. 2. (Marcher) d'un pas mal assuré.

fame [feim], s. Renom m, renommée f. To win f., se faire un grand nom. Of good, ill, f., bien, mal, famé.

famed [feimd], a. Célèbre, renommé, fameux. To be f. for sth., être renommé, bien connu, pour qch.

familiar [fə'miljər]. 1. a. (a) Familier, intime. To be f., on f. terms, with s.o., être familier, intime, avec qn. You are too f., vous vous croyez tout permis. (b) F. spirit, démon familier. (c) (Of thg) Familier; bien connu. In f. surroundings, en pays de connaissance. F. phrase, expression bien connue. To be on f. ground, être sur son terrain. His voice sounded f. to me, il me sembla reconnaître sa voix. (d) (Of pers.) To be f. with sth., être familier avec qch.; bien connaître qch. To make oneself f. with a language, se familiariser avec une langue. 2. s. Démon familier. **-ly**, adv. Familièrement, intimement.

familiarity [fəˌmili'æriti], s. Familiarité f. 1. Intimité f. Prov: F. breeds contempt, la familiarité engendre, fait naître, le mépris. 2. Connaissance f (**with**, de).

familiarize [fə'miljəraiz], v.tr. 1. Familiariser (qch.); rendre (qch.) familier. 2. To f. s.o. with sth., habituer qn à qch; faire connaître qch. à qn.

family ['fæm(i)li], s. Famille f. To be one of the f., être de la famille. Man of good f., homme de bonne famille. It runs in the f., cela tient de famille. A f. dinner, un dîner en famille. F. hotel, hôtel de famille. F. butcher, boucher qui livre à domicile. F. life, vie familiale. F. man, (i) père de famille; (ii) homme d'intérieur. Com: In family-size jar, en pot familial. F: She is in the f. way, elle est dans une condition intéressante. F. allowances, allocation familiale.

famine ['fæmin], s. (a) Famine f. To die of f., mourir de faim. (b) Disette f. At f. prices, à des prix de famine.

famished ['fæmiʃt], a. Affamé. F.-looking, (à l'aspect) famélique.

famishing ['fæmiʃiŋ], a. Qui a grand-faim. F: To be f., avoir une faim de loup.

famous ['feiməs], a. 1. Célèbre, renommé, fameux (for, pour, par). 2. F: O: That's f.! excellent! à la bonne heure! **-ly**, adv. F: Fameusement; à merveille.

fan[1] [fæn], s. 1. Husb: Tarare m. 2. (a) Éventail m. (b) Geog: Alluvial f., cône d'alluvions. (c) Arch: F. vaulting, voûtes f en éventail. F. tracery, nervures f en éventail. 3. Ventilateur (rotatif, à ailes). 'fan-light, s. Imposte f. 'fan-shaped, a. En éventail. 'fan-tail, s. Orn: Pigeon paon.

fan[2], v.tr. (fanned) 1. Husb: Vanner (le grain). 2. Éventer (qn). To f. (up) the fire, aviver le feu. To f. a quarrel, attiser, envenimer, une querelle. 3. Agiter (l'air). **fan out**, v.i. Se déployer, s'étaler en éventail.

fan[3], s. F: Passionné, -ée, enragé, -ée, fervent m (du sport, etc.). Film f., cinéphile mf. Football fans, les mordus du football. F. mail, courrier m des admirateurs et admiratrices (d'une vedette, etc.).

fanatic [fə'nætik], a. & s. Fanatique (m); illuminé, -ée.

fanatical [fə'nætik(ə)l], a. Fanatique. **-ally**, adv. Fanatiquement.

fanaticism [fə'nætisizm], s. Fanatisme m.

fancier ['fænsiər], s. Amateur, -trice (de fleurs, etc.). Dog f., (i) amateur de chiens; (ii) éleveur m de chiens. S.a. BIRD-FANCIER, PIGEON-FANCIER.

fanciful ['fænsiful], a. 1. (Of pers.) Capricieux, fantasque. (b) (Travail) fantaisiste. 2. (Projet) chimérique; (conte) imaginaire.

fancy[1] ['fænsi]. I. s. 1. (a) Imagination f, fantaisie f. The land of f., le pays des chimères. A: In f. I saw . . ., en esprit, en imagination, je voyais. . . . (b) It's only f.! c'est pure imagination! idées que tout cela! (c) Idée f. I have a f. that . . ., j'ai idée que. . . . 2. (a) Fantaisie, caprice m. Just as the f. takes me, comme ça me chante. (b) Fantaisie, goût m. To take a f. to sth., prendre goût à qch. To take a f. to s.o., prendre qn en affection; s'éprendre, s'enticher, de qn. It took my f. at once, cela m'a séduit du premier coup. F: That suits my f., cela me va. We must let her marry according to her f., il faut la laisser se marier à son idée. To have a (passing) f. for s.o., avoir un caprice, un petit béguin, pour qn. 3. A: The f. (a) The amateurs m de la boxe; (ii) la boxe. (b) Les éleveurs m d'animaux ou d'oiseaux d'agrément. II. **fancy**, a. (a) (Bouton, etc.) de fantaisie. (b) F. goods, nouveautés f. F. dress, travesti m, déguisement m. F.-dress ball, bal travesti. (b) F. dog, f. breed, chien, race, d'agrément, de luxe. 'fancy work, s. Ouvrage(s) m(pl) d'agrément; travaux mpl pour dames.

fancy[2], *v.tr.* **1.** (*a*) S'imaginer, se figurer (qch.). **He fancies he knows everything,** il se figure tout savoir. *P:* **F. now!** f. (that)! figurez-vous ça! conçoit-on! *P:* **F. meeting you!** je ne m'attendais guère à vous rencontrer! (*b*) Croire, penser. **I f. he is out,** je crois bien, j'ai (l')idée, qu'il est sorti. **He fancied he heard footsteps,** il crut entendre des pas. **2.** (*a*) **To f. sth.,** se sentir attiré vers qch. **I don't f. his offer,** son offre ne me dit rien. **Let him eat anything he fancies,** il peut manger tout ce qui lui dira. (*b*) *F:* **To f. s.o.,** se sentir attiré vers qn; être épris, entiché, de qn. (*c*) *F:* **To f. oneself,** être infatué de sa petite personne, *F:* se gober, s'en croire. **He fancies his tennis,** il se croit de première force au tennis, **fancied,** *a.* Imaginaire, imaginé.

fandango [fæn'dæŋgou], *s. Danc:* Fandango *m.*

fanfare ['fænfeər], *s.* Fanfare *f* (de cors); sonnerie *f* (de trompettes).

fang [fæŋ], *s.* **1.** (*a*) Croc *m* (de chien, etc.); défense *f* (de sanglier). (*b*) Crochet *m* (de vipère). **2.** Soie *f* (d'un outil). **3.** Racine *f* (d'une dent).

fantasia ['fæntə'zi:ə, fæn'teiziə], *s.* **1.** *Mus:* Fantaisie *f.* **2.** *Equit:* Fantasia *f.*

fantastic [fæn'tæstik], *a.* Fantasque, bizarre, excentrique; invraisemblable. **A f. tale,** un récit fantastique.

fantasy ['fæntəzi], *s.* **1.** Fantaisie *f.* (*a*) Imagination capricieuse. (*b*) Caprice *m.* **2.** (*a*) Vision *f*, idée *f*, bizarre, fantastique. (*b*) Idée fantasque.

far[1] [fɑ:r], *adv.* (**farther, -est, further, -est,** *q.v.*) Loin. **1.** (*a*) **To go f.,** aller loin. **'Not so 'f.,** pas si loin. (*Cp.* 2) **To advance f. into Africa,** pénétrer très avant dans l'Afrique. **To carry a canal as f. as the sea,** conduire un canal jusqu'à la mer. **How f. is it from . . . to . . .?** combien y a-t-il de . . . à . . .? **'So f. and no farther,** jusque-là et pas plus loin. **Thus f.,** jusqu'ici; jusque-là. **As f. as the eye can reach,** à perte de vue. **To live f. away, far off,** demeurer au loin. **F. and wide,** de tous côtés; partout. **Stake driven f. into the ground,** pieu enfoncé profondément dans la terre. **F. from . . .,** loin de. . . . **Not f. from . . .,** à peu de distance de . . .; non loin de. . . . (*b*) **That will go f. towards making up for our loss,** cela aidera beaucoup à nous dédommager. **To make one's money go f.,** faire bon usage de son argent. **To go so f. as to do sth.,** aller jusqu'à faire qch. **He has gone too f. to withdraw,** il est trop engagé pour reculer. **That is going too f.,** cela passe la mesure, les bornes. **To carry a joke too f.,** pousser trop loin une plaisanterie. **How f. have you got (in your reading, etc.)?** où en êtes-vous (de votre lecture, etc.)? **As f. as I know,** autant que je sache. **As f. as that goes . . .,** pour ce qui est de cela. . . . **I will help you as f. as I can,** je vous aiderai dans la mesure de mes moyens. **So f. so good,** c'est fort bien jusque-là; jusqu'ici ça va bien. **In so f. as . . .,** dans la mesure où . . .; pour autant que. . . . **To be f. from believing sth.,** être à cent lieues de croire qch. **F. from admiring him I loathe him,** bien loin de l'admirer je le déteste. **He is f. from happy,** il est loin d'être heureux. **F. from it,** tant s'en faut; loin de là. **Not f. from it,** peu s'en faut. **F. be it from me to put pressure on you!** loin de moi l'idée de vous influencer! **He is not f. off sixty,** il approche de la soixantaine. **By f. the best,** de beaucoup le meilleur. **2.** (*Of time*) **'So f.,** jusqu'ici. **Not 'so f.,** pas encore. (*Cp.* 1 (*a*).) **As f. back as I can remember,** aussi loin, du plus loin, qu'il me souvienne. **As f. back as 1900,** déjà en 1900. **As f. as I can tell,** autant que je puisse prévoir. **He did not look so f. into the future,** il ne regardait pas si avant (dans l'avenir). **F. into the night,** bien avant dans la nuit. **3.** (*With qualifying adjectives, adverbs, etc.*) Beaucoup, bien, fort. **It is f. better,** c'est beaucoup mieux, c'est bien préférable. **It is f. more serious,** c'est bien autrement sérieux. **F. and away the best,** de beaucoup le meilleur. **The night was f. advanced, f. spent,** la nuit était fort avancée. **'far-away,** *a.* Lointain, éloigné. **F.-a. look,** regard perdu dans le vague. **F.-a. voice,** voix éteinte. **'far be'tween,** *pred. a.* **Visits few and f. 'b.,** visites rares et espacées. **'far-'famed,** *a.* Dont la renommée s'est étendue au loin; célèbre. **'far-'fetched,** *a.* (*Of example, comparison*) Forcé, outré; tiré par les cheveux. **'far-flung,** *a.* (*Of empire, etc.*) Très étendu; vaste. **'far-'off,** *a.* = FAR-AWAY. **'far-'reaching,** *a.* De grande envergure, d'une grande portée. **'far-'seeing,** *a.* Prévoyant, clairvoyant, perspicace. **'far-'sighted,** *a.* **1.** = FAR-SEEING. **2.** Presbyte; hypermétrope. **far-'sightedness,** *s.* **1.** Prescience *f*; perspicacité *f.* **2.** Presbytie *f*; hypermétropie *f.*

far[2], *a.* (**farther, -est, further, -est,** *q.v.*) **1.** Lointain, éloigné, reculé. **2. At the f. end of the street,** à l'autre bout de la rue. **In the f. distance,** tout-à-fait au loin. **The f. side (of the road),** (i) le côté gauche (*in France*); (ii) le côté droit (*in England*). *S.a.* EAST, WEST.

farad ['færæd], *s. El.Meas:* Farad *m.*

faradaic [færə'deik], *a. El:* (Courant, etc.) faradique.

faradmeter ['færædmi:tər], **faradimeter** ['færə'dimitər], **faradometer** ['færæd'ɔmitər], *s. El:* Faradmètre *m.*

farandole [færən'doul], *s.* Farandole *f.*

farce [fɑ:s], *s. Th:* Farce *f. F:* **The exam was an absolute f.,** ça a été un examen pour rire.

farcical ['fɑ:sik(ə)l], *a.* Risible, bouffon, grotesque. vaudevillesque. **A f. examination,** un examen pour rire.

fare[1] ['feər], *s.* **1.** (*a*) Prix *m* du voyage, de la place; prix de la course (en taxi, etc.). **Single f.,** (prix du) billet simple. **Return f.,** aller (et) retour *m.* **Excess f.,** supplément *m.* (*In bus, etc.*) **Fares, please!** les places, s'il vous plaît! **Any more fares, please?** Tout le monde est servi? (*b*) (*In hired vehicle*) Client *m*; voyageur, -euse. **2.** Chère *f*, manger *m.* **Prison f.** régime *m* de prison. **To be fond of good f.,** aimer la table.

fare[2], *v.i.* **1.** *A. & Lit:* Voyager. **To f. forth,** partir. **2.** (*a*) **To f. well, ill,** aller bien, mal; se trouver dans une bonne, mauvaise, situation. **To f. alike,** partager le même sort. *A. & Poet:* **F. thee well!** adieu! (*b*) *A:* *Impers:* **How fares it (with you)?** Comment allez-vous? **3.** Manger, se nourrir. **We fared well,** nous avons fait bonne chère.

farewell ['feə'wel], *int. & s.* (*a*) *O:* Adieu (*m*). **To bid f. to s.o.,** dire adieu, faire ses adieux, à qn. (*b*) *attrib.* **A f. dinner,** un dîner d'adieu.

farinaceous [færi'neifəs], *a.* Farinacé, farineux. **F. food,** (aliments) farineux (*m*).

farm[1] [fɑ:m], *s.* (*a*) Ferme *f* (d'exploitation agricole). **Sheep-f.,** élevage *m* de moutons. *S.a.* BABY-FARM, MUSSEL-FARM, OYSTER-FARM, POULTRY-FARM, SEWAGE. (*b*) = FARM-HOUSE. **'farm-hand, -labourer,** *s.* Valet *m* de ferme; ouvrier *m* agricole. **'farm-house,** *s.* (Maison *f* de) ferme *f.* **'farmstead,** *s.* Ferme *f.* **'farmyard,** *s.* Cour *f* de ferme; basse-cour *f.*

farm[2], *v.tr.* **1. To f.** (out). (*a*) Donner à ferme, affermer (des impôts). (*b*) Mettre (des enfants) en nourrice. **2.** (*a*) Cultiver, faire valoir (une propriété). (*b*) *Abs.* Être fermier. **farming**[1], *a.* **F. communities,** (i) les peuples cultivateurs; (ii) les agglomérations rurales. **farming**[2], *s.* **1.** Affermage *m* (d'une propriété, des impôts). **2.** Exploitation *f* agricole; agriculture *f.* **Stock f.,** élevage *m.* **Mixed f.,** polyculture *f.* **Dry f.,** dry farming *m*, culture *f* à sec. **Mechanized f.,** motoculture *f.* **F. lease,** bail *m* à ferme. *S.a.* DAIRY-FARMING.

farmer ['fɑ:mər], *s.* **1.** *Hist:* **F. of revenues,** fermier *m* des impôts. **2.** Fermier, cultivateur *m.* **The f.'s wife,** la fermière. **Stock f.,** éleveur *m.* *S.a.* BABY-FARMER.

faro ['feərou], *s. Cards:* Pharaon *m.*

Faroe Islands ['feərou'ailəndz]. *Pr.n.pl.* Les îles *f* Féroé.

farrago [fə'reigou], *s. Pej:* Méli-mélo *m.*

farrier ['færiər], *s.* **1.** Maréchal (ferrant). **2.** *A:* Vétérinaire *m.*

farriery ['færiəri], *s.* **1.** Maréchalerie *f.* **2.** *A:* Art *m* vétérinaire.

farrow ['færou], *s.* Portée *f* (de cochons).

fart[1] [fɑ:t], *s. V:* Pet *m.* **Silent f.,** vesse *f.*

fart[2], *v.i. V:* Péter, faire un pet.

farther ['fɑ:ðər]. (*Comp.* of FAR) **1.** *adv.* (*a*) Plus loin (than, que). **F. off,** plus éloigné. **F. on,** plus en avant; plus loin; plus avancé. **Nothing is f. from my thoughts,** rien n'est plus éloigné de ma pensée. *F:* **To wish s.o. f.,** envoyer qn au diable. (*b*) *F.* **back,** plus en arrière. **2.** *a.* (*a*) Plus lointain, plus éloigné. **At the f. end of the room,** à l'autre bout de la salle; au fond de la salle. (*b*) **F. back,** antérieur (**than,** à).

farthermost ['fɑ:ðəmoust], *a.* Le plus lointain, le plus éloigné, le plus reculé.

farthest ['fɑ:ðist], (*Sup. of* FAR) **1.** *a.* (*a*) F. (off), le plus lointain, le plus éloigné. **In f. Siberia,** au fin fond de la Sibérie. (*b*) (*Of way, etc.*) Le plus long. **2.** *adv.* Le plus loin.

farthing ['fɑ:ðiŋ], *s.* Quart *m* d'un penny. **F: Not to have a f.,** n'avoir pas le sou. **To pay to the uttermost f.,** payer jusqu'au dernier sou. **F: I wouldn't give a brass f. for it,** je n'en donnerais pas un centime, **P:** un rond.

fascia, *pl.* **-iae** ['fæʃiə, -ii:], *s.* **1.** (*a*) *Arch:* Fasce *f*, bandelette *f*, bande *f*. (*b*) *Com:* Enseigne *f* en forme d'entablement. (*c*) *Attrib. Aut:* **F. board,** tableau *m* de bord. **2.** *Anat:* Fascia *m.*

fascicle ['fæsikl], **fascicule** ['fæsikjuːl], *s. Nat. Hist: Bookb: etc.* Fascicule *m.*

fascinate ['fæsineit], *v.tr.* (*a*) (*Of serpent*) Fasciner. (*b*) Fasciner, charmer, séduire. **fascinating,** *a.* Enchanteur, -eresse; séduisant.

fascination ['fæsi'neiʃ(ə)n], *s.* **1.** Fascination *f* (d'une proie). **2.** Fascination, charme *m,* attrait *m.*

fascine [fæ'si:n], *s.* Fascine *f.*

fascism ['fæʃizm], *s. Pol:* Fascisme *m.*

fascist ['fæʃist], *a. & s. Pol:* Fasciste (*mf*).

fashion[1] ['fæʃ(ə)n], *s.* **1.** Façon *f* (d'un habit, etc.); forme *f* (d'un objet); manière *f* (de faire qch.). (**In the**) **French f.,** à la française. **Everyone does it in his own f.,** chacun le fait à sa mode, à sa façon. **After the f. of . . .,** à la façon, à la manière, de . . . **After a f.,** tant bien que mal. **2.** Habitude *f,* coutume *f.* **3.** (*Of clothes, etc*) Mode *f,* vogue *f.* **In (the) f.,** à la mode, de mode, en vogue. **Out of f.,** passé de mode; démodé. **To bring sth. into f.,** mettre qch. à la mode; lancer la mode de qch. **To come into f.,** devenir la mode. **To. lead, set, the f.,** donner la note, le ton; fixer, mener, la mode. **A man of f.,** un élégant. **A woman of f.,** une élégante, une mondaine. **F. house,** maison *f* de haute couture. **'fashion-book,** *s.* Journal *m* de modes. **'fashion-plate,** *s.* Gravure *f* de modes. **'fashion show,** *s.* Présentation *f* de collections, défilé *m* de mannequins.

fashion[2], *v.tr.* Façonner, former (une poterie, etc.); confectionner (une robe, etc.). **fashioned,** *a.* **1.** (*Of wood, etc.*) Façonné, travaillé, ouvré. **2.** New-f., de nouvelle mode; à la mode (du jour). *S.a.* OLD-FASHIONED, FULLY.

fashionable ['fæʃ(ə)nəbl], *a.* A la mode, élégant, en vogue. **A f. jacket,** une veste à la mode. **The f. world,** le beau monde. **A f. resort,** un endroit mondain. **-ably,** *adv.* Élégamment; à la mode.

fast[1] [fɑ:st], *s.* Jeûne *m.* **To break one's f.,** (i) rompre le jeûne; (ii) déjeuner. **I have not yet broken my f.,** je suis encore à jeun. **'fast-day,** *s. Ecc:* Jour *m* de jeûne.

fast[2], *v.i.* (*a*) Jeûner; s'abstenir (**from,** de). *Med:* **'To be taken fasting,' "**à prendre le matin à jeun.**"** (*b*) *Ecc:* Jeûner. **fasting,** *s.* Jeûne *m.*

fast[3]. **I.** *a.* **1.** (*a*) Ferme, fixe, solide; (*of grip, hold*) tenace; (*of knot*) serré. **Feet f. in the mud,** pieds collés dans la boue. **To make a rope f.,** amarrer un cordage. **To have f. hold of sth.,** tenir qch. serré. **F. friends,** des amis sûrs, solides. (*b*) *Nau:* Amarré. **To make a boat f.,** amarrer un bateau. *Abs.* **To make f.,** prendre le corps-mort; s'amarrer. (*c*) (*Of door, etc.*) (Bien) assujetti; bien fermé. (*d*) (*Of colour*) Solide, résistant; bon teint *inv.* **2.** (*a*) Rapide, vite. *Fb:* **F. forwards,** avants très vites. *Rail:* **F. train,** express *m.* (*b*) **F. billiard-table,** billard qui rend bien. **C:** F: **That's a f. one!** c'est une roublardise! **3.** (*Of clock, watch*) **En avance. My watch is five minutes f.,** ma montre avance de cinq minutes. **4.** F: (*Of pers.*) (*a*) Dissipé; de mœurs légères. **O:** The f. set, les viveurs *m.* (*b*) (Trop) émancipé. **F. girl,** jeune fille d'allures très libres. **II. fast,** *adv.* **1.** Ferme, solidement. **To hold f.,** tenir ferme; tenir bon. **To stand f.,** tenir bon; rester inébranlable. **To stick f.,** (i) bien tenir; (ii) rester pris, rester collé. **To sleep f.,** dormir d'un profond sommeil. **F: To play f. and loose,** agir avec inconstance; jouer double jeu (**with s.o.,** avec qn). **2.** Vite, rapidement. **Not so f.!** pas si vite! doucement! **It is raining f.,** il pleut à verse. **He drew back as f. as I advanced,** (au fur et) à mesure que j'avançais il reculait.

fasten ['fɑ:sn]. **1.** *v.tr.* (*a*) Attacher (**to, on,** à). **To f. a boat to a post,** amarrer un bateau à un pieu. **To f. one's eyes on s.o.,** attacher son regard, fixer les yeux, sur qn. **To f. a crime on s.o.,** imputer un crime à qn. **To f. the responsibility on s.o.,** mettre, rejeter, la responsabilité sur le dos de qn. (*b*) Fixer, assurer, assujettir (la porte, etc.). **To f. (up) a garment,** agrafer, boutonner, un vêtement. **2.** *v.i.* S'attacher, se fixer. **His opponent fastened on to his leg,** son adversaire se cramponna à sa jambe. **To f. (up)on a pretext,** saisir un prétexte. **fasten down,** *v.tr.* Assujettir, fixer, (qch.) à terre ou en place. **fastening,** *s.* **1.** Attache *f*; assujettissement *m*; agrafage *m.* **2.** = FASTENER.

fastener ['fɑ:snər], *s.* Attache *f*; (*of garment*) agrafe *f*; (*of book, purse*) fermoir *m*; (*of window, etc.*) fermeture *f.* **Patent f., snap f.,** bouton *m* (à) pression. *S.a.* PAPER-FASTENER, ZIP[1] 3.

fastidious [fəs'tidiəs], *a.* Difficile (à satisfaire); délicat (**about sth.,** sur qch.). **-ly,** *adv.* D'un air de dégoût; dédaigneusement.

fastness ['fɑ:stnis], *s.* **1.** (*a*) Fermeté *f*, stabilité *f* (d'un pieu); solidité *f* (d'une couleur). (*b*) Rapidité *f,* vitesse *f.* (*c*) Légèreté *f* de conduite. **2.** *Lit:* Place forte. **Mountain f.,** repaire *m* (de brigands).

fat[1] [fæt], *a.* (fatter; fattest) **1.** Gras, *f.* grasse. **To get, grow, f.,** engraisser; prendre de l'embonpoint. **F: To give a f. laugh,** rire gras. **F: A f. lot of good it will do you!** cela vous fera une belle jambe! **F: A f. lot of difference it makes to you!** pour ce que ça vous coûte! **F: A f. lot you know about it!** comme si vous en saviez quelque chose! **F. volume,** gros tome. **F. wallet,** portefeuille bien garni. *Aut:* **F. spark,** étincelle nourrie. **F. coal,** houille grasse, bitumineuse. **2.** (*Of land*) Riche, fertile, gras. **F: F. salary, F. appointements,** de gros appointements. **'fat-head,** *s. F:* Imbécile *m,* nigaud *m.* **'fat-headed,** *a. F:* A l'esprit bouché; sot, *f.* sotte. **That f.-h. postman,** cet imbécile de facteur.

fat[2], *s.* **1.** Graisse *f.* Mutton f., suif *m* de mouton. *Cu:* **Frying f.,** (graisse de) friture. **Fats, matières grasses.** *Pharm:* Hog's f., axonge *f.* **F: The fat's in the fire,** le feu est aux poudres! gare la bombe! **F:** (*Of person*) **To put on f.,** engraisser. **2.** Gras *m* (de viande). **F: To live on the f. of the land,** vivre comme un coq en pâte; vivre grassement.

fat[3], *v.tr. & i. Husb:* = FATTEN. **fatted,** *a.* **A:** Engraissé. **To kill the f. calf,** tuer le veau gras.

fatal ['feit(ə)l], *a.* Fatal, -als. **1.** The f. hour, l'heure fatale; l'heure de la mort. **2.** (*a*) F. blow, coup fatal, mortel. **F. disease,** maladie mortelle. (*b*) **F. decision,** décision *f* funeste. **F. influence,** influence néfaste. **A f. mistake,** une faute capitale. **-ally,** *adv.* **1.** Fatalement, inévitablement. **2.** Mortellement (blessé, etc.).

fatalism ['feitəlizm], *s.* Fatalisme *m.*

fatalist ['feitəlist], *s.* Fataliste *mf.*

fatalistic ['feitə'listik], *a.* Fataliste.

fatality [fə'tæliti], *s.* **1.** (*Fate*) Fatalité *f.* **2.** Caractère *m* funeste, influence *f* néfaste (**of,** de). **3.** Accident mortel; sinistre *m.* **Bathing fatalities,** baignades tragiques.

fate [feit], *s.* Destin *m,* sort *m.* *Myth:* **The Fates,** les Parques *f.* **To leave s.o. to his f.,** abandonner qn à son sort. **He met his f. in 1915,** il trouva la mort en 1915.

fated ['feitid], *a.* **1.** (*Of day, occurrence*) Fatal, -als; inévitable. **2.** Destiné, condamné (**to do sth.,** à faire qch.). **3.** Voué à la destruction; condamné.

fateful ['feitful], *a.* **1.** (Voix, etc.) prophétique. **F. word,** parole fatidique. **2.** (Jour, etc.) décisif, fatal, -als. **3.** (Événement, etc.) fatal, inévitable.

father[1] ['fɑːðər], *s.* **1.** Père *m.* **From f. to son,** de père en fils. **Like a f.,** paternellement; en père. **F: To talk to s.o. like a f.,** sermonner qn. *Th:* Noble f., père noble. **2.** *pl.* **Our fathers,** nos ancêtres *m,* nos pères. **3.** (*a*) Père, fondateur *m,* créateur *m* (d'un art, etc.). (*b*) **The Fathers (of the Church),** les Pères de l'Église. **4.** *Theol:* **God the F.,** Dieu le Père. **5.** *Ecc:* (*a*) **The Holy F.,** le Saint-Père, le père des fidèles. **F. confessor,** père spirituel; directeur *m* (de conscience). (*b*) **F. O'Malley,** (i) le Père O'Malley; (ii) l'abbé O'Malley. **Yes, F.,** oui, mon Père. **The Capuchin fathers,** les pères capucins. **6.** Doyen *m* (d'une société, etc.). *Rom.Hist:* **The City Fathers,** les Édiles *m.* **'father-in-law,** *s.m.* Beau-père.

father², *v.tr.* **1.** Engendrer (un enfant); inventer, produire (qch.); concevoir (un projet). **2.** Adopter (un enfant). **3.** To f. a child, a book, (up)on s.o., attribuer à qn la paternité d'un enfant, d'un livre.
fatherhood ['fɑːðəhud], *s.* Paternité *f.*
fatherland ['fɑːðəlænd], *s.* Patrie *f.*
fatherless ['fɑːðəlis], *a.* Sans père; orphelin, -ine, de père.
fatherly ['fɑːðəli], *a.* Paternel.
fathom¹ ['fæðəm], *s. Nau:* Brasse *f* (= 1 m. 829).
fathom², *v.tr. Nau:* Sonder. To f. the mystery, approfondir, pénétrer, sonder. le mystère. **fathoming**, *s. Nau:* Sondage *m.*
fathomless ['fæðəmlis], *a.* (Abîme) sans fond, insondable.
fatigue¹ [fə'tiːg], *s.* **1.** (a) Fatigue *f.* (b) *Tchn:* Metal f., fatigue d'un métal. **2.** *Mil:* Corvée *f.* To be on f., être de corvée. F. party, (détachement *m* de) corvée. **fa'tigue-dress**, *s. Mil:* Tenue *f* de corvée; (jeu *m* de) treillis *m.*
fatigue², *v.tr.* **1.** Fatiguer, lasser (qn). **2.** *Tchn:* Fatiguer (un métal, un mât). **fatiguing**, *a.* Fatigant, épuisant.
fatness ['fætnis], *s.* **1.** Adiposité *f*; embonpoint *m*, corpulence *f.* **2.** Onctuosité *f* (de l'argile).
fatten ['fætn]. **1.** *v.tr.* To f. (up), engraisser (des moutons, etc.); empâter (la volaille). **2.** *v.i.* Engraisser. To f. on sth., s'engraisser de qch. **fattening¹**, *a.* (Of food, etc.) Qui fait grossir. **fattening²**, *s.* Engraissement *m.*
fatty ['fæti]. **1.** *a.* (a) Graisseux, onctueux, oléagineux. F. foods, aliments gras. *Ch:* F. acid, acide gras. (b) (Of tissue, etc.) Adipeux, -euse. *Med:* F. heart, dégénérescence graisseuse du cœur. **2.** *s. P:* Gros enfant; gros bonhomme.
fatuity [fæ'tjuː)iti], **fatuousness** ['fætjuəsnis], *s.* Sottise *f*; imbécillité *f.*
fatuous ['fætjuəs], *a.* Sot, imbécile, idiot; (sourire) béat. **-ly**, *adv.* Sottement; d'un air idiot.
fauces ['fɔːsiːz], *s. Anat:* Arrière-bouche *f.*
faucet ['fɔːsit], *s.* (a) *Dial:* Cannelle *f* (de tonneau). (b) *U.S:* Robinet *m.*
faugh [fɔː], *int.* Pouah!
fault¹ [fɔːlt], *s.* **1.** Défaut *m*, travers *f*; vice *m* de construction. In spite of all his faults, malgré tous ses travers. His f. is excessive shyness, il pèche par trop de timidité. Scrupulous to a f., scrupuleux à l'excès. To find f. with s.o., sth., trouver à redire contre qn, à qch. I can find no f. with him, je ne trouve rien à lui reprocher. **2.** Faute *f.* To be in f., at f., être en défaut; être fautif, coupable. Whose f. is it? à qui la faute? It is nobody's f. but your own, il ne faut vous en prendre qu'à vous-même. **3.** *Ten:* Faute. **4.** (a) *Ven:* (Of hounds) To bark at f., aboyer à faux. (b) To be at f., être en défaut. Memory at f., mémoire en défaut; mémoire défaillante. **5.** *Geol:* Faille *f.* **'fault-finder**, *s.* **1.** (*Pers.*) Censeur; éplucheur, -euse; mécontent *m.* **2.** *El.E:* (*Device*) Déceleur *m* de fuites. **'fault-finding**, *a.* Critiqueur, chicanier, -ière.
fault², *v.tr.* I can't f. him, je ne peux pas le prendre en faute.
faultiness ['fɔːltinis], *s.* Incorrection *f* (de style, etc.); défectuosité *f*, imperfection *f.*
faultless ['fɔːltlis], *a.* Sans défaut, sans faute; impeccable, irréprochable. **-ly**, *adv.* Parfaitement, irréprochablement. F. dressed, d'une mise impeccable.
faultlessness ['fɔːltlisnis], *s.* Perfection *f.*
faulty ['fɔːlti], *a.* (Of work, etc.) Défectueux, imparfait; (of style, etc.) incorrect; (of reasoning, etc.) erroné, inexact. *Gram:* F. construction, construction vicieuse.
faun [fɔːn], *s. Myth:* Faune *m.*
fauna ['fɔːnə], *s.* Faune *f* (d'un pays).
Fauve [fouv], *s. Art:* Fauve *m.*
Fauvism [fouvizm], *s. Art:* Fauvisme *m.*
faux-bourdon [fouˈbuːədɔn], *s. Mus:* Faux-bourdon *m.*
favour¹ ['feivər], *s.* Faveur *f.* **1.** Approbation *f*; bonnes grâces. To find f. with s.o., to gain s.o.'s f., gagner la faveur de qn; se faire bien voir de qn. To be in f. with s.o., être bien en cour auprès de qn;

jouir de la faveur de qn. To be restored, to return, to f., rentrer en grâce. To be out of f., (i) être mal en cour; (ii) (of fashion) n'être plus en vogue. To bring sth. into f., mettre qch. à la mode. **2.** Grâce *f*, bonté *f.* To ask a f. of s.o., solliciter une grâce, une faveur, de qn. To do s.o. a f., faire une faveur à qn; obliger qn. Will you do me a f.? voulez-vous me faire plaisir? As a f., à titre gracieux. *O:* (In letter) Your f. of the 15th, votre lettre, votre honorée, du 15. **3.** (a) Partialité *f*, préférence *f.* To show f. towards s.o., favoriser qn; accorder à qn un traitement de faveur. To administer justice without fear or f., rendre la justice sans distinction de personnes. (b) Appui *m*, protection *f.* Under f. of the night, à la faveur de la nuit. **4.** *Prep.phr.* In f. of . . ., en faveur de . . .; à l'avantage de. . . . To have everything in one's f., avoir tout pour soi. To decide in f. of s.o., in s.o.'s f., donner gain de cause à qn; donner raison à qn. To be in f. of sth., être partisan de qch.; tenir pour qch. **5.** Faveur *f*; nœud *m* de ruban.
favour², *v.tr.* Favoriser. **1.** Approuver, préférer. To f. a scheme, se prêter à un projet; approuver un projet; être pour un projet. I don't f. the idea, l'idée ne me sourit pas. **2.** Obliger (qn); accorder une grâce à (qn). To f. s.o. with an interview, accorder un rendez-vous à qn. To be favoured with an order, être honoré d'une commande. **3.** (a) Avantager (qn); montrer de la partialité pour (qn). (b) Faciliter (qch.). Favoured by fortune, secondé par le sort. Device that favours combustion, dispositif qui active la combustion. **4.** (Of fact) Confirmer (un rapport). **5.** *A:* Ressembler à (qn). **favoured**, *a.* (Of pers.) **1.** Favorisé. The few, les élus. **2.** Well-f., beau, *f.* belle. *S.a.* ILL-FAVOURED.
favourable ['feiv(ə)rəbl], *a.* Favorable, (of weather) propice; (of reception) bienveillant; (of terms) bon, avantageux; (of report) rassurant. To look on s.o. with a f. eye, regarder qn d'un œil favorable. *Com:* Specially f. rate, taux de faveur. **-ably**, *adv.* Favorablement, avantageusement. *S.a.* PROGRESS².
favourite ['feiv(ə)rit]. **1.** *s.* Favori, *f.* favorite. To be a f. with, of, s.o.; to be s.o.'s f., être bien vu, bien vue, de qn. He is a universal f., tout le monde l'aime. *Rac:* To back the f., jouer le favori. **2.** *a.* (Fils, auteur, etc.) favori, préféré. F. event, réunion (sportive) très courue.
favouritism ['feivritizm], *s.* Favoritisme *m.*
fawn¹ [fɔːn], *s. Z:* Faon *m.* **2.** *a. & s.* fauve *m.*
fawn², *v.ind.tr.* To f. (up)on s.o., (i) (of dog) caresser qn; se coucher devant qn; (ii) (of pers.) faire le chien couchant, le plat valet, auprès de qn; ramper devant qn. **fawning¹**, *a.* (Of dog) Caressant; (of pers.) servile; flagorneur, -euse. **fawning¹**, *s.* Flagornerie *f*; servilité *f.*
fawner ['fɔːnər], *s.* Adulateur, -trice; flagorneur, -euse.
fealty ['fiːlti], *s.* Féauté *f*; fidélité *f.*
fear¹ ['fiər], *s.* **1.** Crainte *f*, peur *f.* Deadly f., effroi *m.* To be, stand, go, in f. of s.o., redouter, craindre, qn. To go in f. of one's life, craindre pour sa vie. For f. of mistakes, of making a mistake, de crainte d'erreur. For f. we should forget, de peur que nous (n')oublions. To have fears for s.o., for s.o.'s safety, craindre pour qn. *F:* No f.! pas de danger! **2.** Respect *m*, crainte (de Dieu, etc.). *F:* To put the f. of God into s.o., faire à qn une semonce dont il se souviendra.
fear², *v.tr.* **1.** Craindre, avoir peur de, redouter. **2.** Appréhender, craindre (un événement). To f. for s.o., s'inquiéter au sujet de qn. I f. it is too late, j'ai peur, je crains, qu'il ne soit trop tard. I f. I'm late, je crois bien être en retard. I f. I don't know, je regrette, mais je ne sais pas.
fearful ['fiəful], *a.* **1.** Affreux, effrayant, redoutable. *F:* A f. mess, un désordre effrayant. **2.** Peureux, craintif, timide. **-fully**, *adv.* **1.** Affreusement, terriblement. **2.** Peureusement, craintivement, timidement.
fearfulness ['fiəfulnis], *s.* **1.** Caractère épouvantable, terrifiant (de qch.). **2.** Crainte *f*, timidité *f.*
fearless ['fiəlis], *a.* Intrépide, courageux; sans peur (of, de). **-ly**, *adv.* Intrépidement; sans peur, sans hésitation.

fearlessness ['fiəlisnis], *s.* Intrépidité *f*.
fearsome ['fiəsəm], *a.* Redoutable.
feasibility [fi:zi'biliti], **feasibleness** ['fi:ziblnis], *s.* 1. Praticabilité *f*, possibilité *f*. 2. Plausibilité *f*, vraisemblance *f*.
feasible ['fi:zibl], *a.* 1. Faisable, possible, praticable. 2. Vraisemblable, probable.
feast[1] [fi:st], *s.* 1. *Ecc: etc:* Fête *f*. Movable f., fête mobile. 2. Festin *m*, banquet *m*; régal *m*, -als. 'feast-day, *s.* (Jour *m* de) fête *f*; jour férié.
feast[2]. 1. *v.i.* Faire festin; banqueter, se régaler. 2. *v.tr.* Régaler, fêter (qn). To f. one's eyes on sth., repaître ses yeux de qch. **feasting,** *s.* Festoiement *m*; bonne chère.
feat [fi:t], *s.* 1. Exploit *m*, haut fait; prouesse *f*. F. of **arms,** fait d'armes. 2. (*a*) Tour *m* de force. (*b*) F. of skill, tour d'adresse.
feather[1] ['feðər], *s.* 1. Plume *f*; (*of tail, wing*) penne *f*. *F: O:* To show the white f., laisser voir qu'on a peur; *P:* caner, caler. I tried to smooth his ruffled feathers, j'ai essayé de le remettre de bonne humeur. *F:* You could have knocked me down with a f.!, j'ai pensé tomber de mon haut. *U.S:* Red f. campaign, collecte *f* d'œuvres de charité. 2. Plumage *m*. To be in full f., avoir tout son plumage. They are birds of a f., ils sont du même acabit. *Prov:* Birds of a f. flock together, qui se ressemble s'assemble. 3. *Mil:* Plumet *m*. *F:* That's a f. in his cap, c'est tout à son honneur, c'est qch. dont il peut être fier. 4. *Mec.E:* Clavette plate. 5. (*In gem*) Crapaud *m*. 'feather-'bed[1], *s.* 1. Lit *m* de plume. 2. *U.S:* Sinécure *f*, *F:* fromage *m*. 'feather-'bed[1]. 1. *v.i. U.S:* Gonfler les besoins de main-d'œuvre. 2. *v.tr. U.S:* Subventionner abusivement (une industrie). 'feather-brained, *a.* Écervelé, étourdi; à tête de linotte. 'feather-'brush, -'duster, *s.* Plumeau *m*. 'feather-stitch, *s. Needlew:* Point *m* d'épine. 'feather-weight, *s. Box:* Poids *m* plume.
feather[2]. 1. *v.tr.* (*a*) Empenner (une flèche); emplumer (un chapeau). *F:* To f. one's nest, faire sa pelote, ses choux gras; mettre du foin dans ses bottes. (*b*) *Row:* Ramener (l'aviron) à plat; *abs.* nager plat. (*c*) *Av:* Mettre en drapeau (une hélice). 2. *v.i.* (*Of young bird*) To f. (out), s'emplumer.
featherless ['feðəlis] *a.* 1. Sans plumes. 2. Déplumé.
feathery ['feðəri], *a.* Plumeux.
feature[1] ['fi:tʃər], *s.* 1. Trait *m* (du visage). The features, la physionomie. 2. (*a*) Trait, caractéristique *f*, particularité *f* (d'un paysage, d'un édifice). Main features, grands traits. Natural features (of a country) topographie *f* (d'un pays). (*b*) Shop that makes a f. of its China tea, boutique qui a pour spécialité les thés de Chine. *Cin:* The f. film, le grand film du programme.
feature[2], *v.tr.* 1. Caractériser, marquer, distinguer (qch.). 2. *Cin:* (i) Représenter (qn); tourner (un rôle). (ii) Film featuring Charlie Chaplin, film avec Charlot en vedette. 3. *Journ:* To f. a piece of news, mettre une nouvelle en manchette. -featured, *a.* Rugged-f., aux traits rudes. Pleasant-f., à la physionomie agréable.
febrifuge ['febrifju:dʒ], *s. Med:* Fébrifuge *m*.
febrile ['fi:brail]. *a.* Fébrile, fiévreux.
February ['februəri], *s.* Février *m*. In F., au mois de février. (On) the fifth of F., le cinq février.
feckless ['feklis], *a.* 1. Veule; sans énergie. 2. Incapable.
fecund ['fekənd], *a. Lit:* 1. Fécond. 2. Fécondant, fertilisant.
fecundate ['fekəndeit], *v.tr.* Féconder.
fecundation ['fekən'deiʃ(ə)n], *s.* Fécondation *f*.
fecundity [fe'kʌnditi], *s.* Fécondité *f*.
fed [fed]. *See* FEED[2].
federal ['fedərəl]. 1. *a.* Fédéral, -aux. 2. *s. U.S.Hist:* Fédéral *m*, nordiste *m*.
federalism ['fedərəlizm], *s.* Fédéralisme *m*.
federalist ['fedərəlist], *s.* Fédéraliste *mf*.
federate[1] ['fedərit], *a.* Fédéré.
federate[2] ['fedəreit]. 1. *v.tr.* Fédérer. 2. *v.i.* Se fédérer.
federation [fedə'reiʃ(ə)n], *s.* Fédération *f*.
federative ['fedərətiv], *a.* Fédératif, -ive.
fedora [fi'dɔ:rə], *s. U.S:* Chapeau mou.

fee [fi:], *s.* 1. (*a*) *Hist:* Fief *m*. (*b*) *Jur:* Propriété *f* héréditaire. 2. (*a*) Honoraires *mpl* (d'un avocat, etc.); cachet *m* (d'un précepteur, d'un acteur, etc.); jeton *m* de présence (d'un administrateur). To draw one's fees, toucher ses honoraires, ses cachets; (*of director*) toucher ses jetons. (*b*) School fees, rétribution *f* scolaire; frais *mpl* de scolarité. Boarding-school fees, pension *f*. Examination f., droit *m* d'examen. *Post:* Registration f., taxe *f* de recommandation. Late f., taxe supplémentaire. *S.a.* ENTRANCE-FEE. 'fee-simple, *s.* (Property held in) f.-s., propriété *f* sans conditions; bien *m* en toute propriété.
feeble [fi:bl], *a.* Faible, infirme, débile. F. pulse, pouls déprimé. F. work, travail médiocre. *F:* He's a f. type, c'est un garçon sans caractère. -bly, *adv.* Faiblement. 'feeble-'minded, *a.* D'esprit faible.
feebleness ['fi:blnis], *s.* Faiblesse *f*.
feed[1] [fi:d], *s.* 1. (*a*) Alimentation *f* (d'un animal). (*b*) Nourriture *f*, pâture *f*; fourrage *m* (pour les chevaux, etc.) To give the horse a f., donner à manger au cheval. *F:* To be off one's f., bouder sur la nourriture. (*c*) Mesure *f*, ration *f*. F. of oats, picotin *m* d'avoine. (*d*) *F:* Repas *m*, festin *m*. To have a good f., bien manger; faire bonne chère. 2. *Tchn:* (*a*) Alimentation *f* (d'une chaudière, etc.); avance *f* (d'une machine-outil). Gravity f., alimentation par (la) pesanteur. Pump f., alimentation par pression. Forced f., pressure f. (of oil), graissage *m* sous pression. (*b*) Conduit *m* (d'alimentation). feed-back, *s. El.E: W.Tel:* Rétroaction *f. Electronics:* Réaction *f.* 'feed-pipe, *s.* Tuyau *m* d'alimentation. 'feed-tank, *s. Mch:* Bâche *f* d'alimentation; réservoir *m* alimentaire. *I.C.E:* Nourrice *f.* 'feed-wire, *s. El.E:* Fil *m* d'amenée.
feed[2], *v.* (fed [fed]; fed) I. *v.tr.* 1. (*a*) Nourrir; donner à manger à (qn); alimenter (une famille, etc.); approvisionner (un pays, etc.); ravitailler (une armée); allaiter (un enfant); (*of mother bird*) embecquer, donner la becquée à (ses petits). To f. s.o. on, with, sth., nourrir qn de qch. (*b*) Field that feeds three cows, champ qui nourrit trois vaches. 2. (*a*) Alimenter (une machine, le feu); charger (un fourneau). *Mec.E:* To f. the tool to the work, faire avancer l'outil à la pièce. (*b*) *Fb:* To f. the forwards, alimenter les avants. (*c*) *Th:* To f. an actor, donner la réplique à un acteur; soutenir un acteur. II. *v.i.* Manger. (*Of cattle, sheep*) Paître, brouter. To f. (up)on sth., se nourrir, s'alimenter, se repaître, de qch. (*Of animal*) To f. out of s.o.'s hand, manger dans la main de qn. feed up, *v.tr.* Engraisser (une bête); suralimenter (qn). *F:* To be fed up, en avoir assez; en avoir soupé; en avoir plein le dos. feeding, *s.* 1. Alimentation *f.* Forcible f., gavage *m*. 2. *Mec.E:* Amenage *m*, avance *f*, avancement *m* (du travail à l'outil, etc.). 'feeding-bottle, *s.* Biberon *m*. 'feeding-cup, *s. Med:* Biberon, canard *m*.
feeder ['fi:dər], *s.* 1. (*a*) *Husb:* Nourrisseur *m* (de bestiaux). (*b*) = EATER. Heavy f., gros mangeur. 2. (*a*) Bavette *f*; bavoir *m*; serviette *f* d'enfant. (*b*) Biberon *m*. 3. *Hyd.E:* Canal *m* d'alimentation, d'amenée. *El.E:* F.(-cable), conducteur *m* alimentaire. 4. *ind:* Mechanical f., chargeur *m* mécanique.
feel[1] [fi:l], *s.* 1. Toucher *m*, tact *m*. Rough to the f., rude au toucher. He has the f. of his car, il a sa voiture bien en main. 2. (*a*) Toucher, manier *m*, main *f* (du papier, etc.). To know sth. by the f. (of it), reconnaître qch. au toucher. (*b*) Sensation *f.* The f. of his clammy hand, la sensation de sa main froide et moite.
feel[2], *v.* (felt [felt]; felt) 1. (*a*) *v.tr.* Toucher, palper (qch. avec la main); promener les doigts sur (qch.); tâter (le pouls, etc.); manier (une étoffe). (*b*) *v.tr. & i.* To f. (about) for sth., to f. after sth., chercher qch. à tâtons. To f. about in the dark, tâtonner dans l'obscurité. To f. one's way, (i) avancer, aller, marcher, à tâtons; (ii) sonder, explorer, le terrain. To f. in one's pockets for sth., chercher qch. dans ses poches. 2. (*a*) *v.tr.* Sentir (qch.). I felt the floor tremble, je sentis trembler le plancher. (*b*) *v.tr. & i.* (Res)sentir, éprouver (de la douleur, etc.). The effect will be felt, l'effet se fera sentir. To f. the heat, être incommodé par la chaleur. To f. the cold, être sensible au froid: être frileux. To make one's

authority felt, faire sentir son autorité. To f. an interest towards s.o., éprouver de la sympathie pour qn. I f. for him, il a toute ma sympathie, je le comprends. To f. for, with, s.o. in his sorrow, compatir à la douleur de qn. How did you f.? quels sentiments avez-vous éprouvés? (c) v.tr Avoir conscience de (qch.). I f. it in my bones that I shall succeed, quelque chose me dit que je réussirai. I felt it necessary to interfere, j'ai jugé nécessaire d'intervenir. 3. v.i. (Of pers.) (a) Pred. To f. cold, avoir froid. To f. ill, tired, se sentir malade, fatigué. To f. all the better for it, s'en trouver mieux. He doesn't f. quite himself, il n'est pas dans son assiette. To f. up to sth., to doing sth., se sentir (i) assez bien pour faire qch., (ii) de taille à faire qch. To f. certain that . . ., être certain que. . . . (b) I f. as if . . ., il me semble que. . . ., j'ai l'impression que . . ., j'ai l'impression de (+ inf). To f. like doing sth., être en humeur de faire qch. I felt like crying, j'avais envie de pleurer. If you f. like it, si le cœur vous en dit. I don't feel like it, ça ne me dit rien. Do you f. like cheese? aimeriez-vous un peu de fromage? I f. like a cup of tea, je prendrais bien une tasse de thé. 4. v.i. To f. hard, soft, être dur, doux, au toucher. The room feels damp, la salle donne une impression d'humidité. It feels like . . ., cela donne la sensation de. . . . feeling[1], a. 1. (Of pers.) Sensible. 2. (Of language, etc). Ému, -ly, adv. To speak f. of sth., parler (i) d'une voix émue, (ii) avec sympathie, (iii) avec chaleur, de qch. feeling[2], s. 1. Palpation f; maniement m. 2. (Sense of) f., toucher m, tact, m. To have no f. in one's arm, avoir le bras mort. 3. Sensation (douloureuse, etc.). 4. Sentiment m. (a) To have kindly feelings towards s.o., éprouver de la sympathie pour qn. The f. of the meeting, l'opinion f, le sentiment, de l'assemblée. Public f., le sentiment populaire. F. is running very high, les esprits sont très montés. Class f., esprit m de classe. No hard feelings! sans rancune! (b) I had a f. of danger, j'avais le sentiment d'être en danger. There is a general f. that . . ., l'impression règne dans le public que. . . . (c) Sensibilité f, émotion f. To have a f. for nature, avoir le sentiment de la nature. To have a f. for music, apprécier la musique. To have no feelings, être dépourvu de toute sensibilité; n'avoir point de cœur. To speak with f. parler (i) avec émotion, (ii) avec chaleur.
feeler ['fiːlər], s. 1. Antenne f; palpe f (d'un insecte); corne f (d'escargot); moustache f (d'un chat, etc.); tentacule m (d'un mollusque). 2. To throw out a f., lancer un ballon d'essai; tâter le terrain. 3. Mec.E: Feuille f d'épaisseur. A set of feelers, calibre m d'épaisseur (à lames).
feet, s.pl. See FOOT[1].
feign [fein]. 1. v.tr. Feindre, simuler. To f. surprise, affecter, jouer, la surprise. To f. death, faire le mort. 2. v.i. To f. sick, faire semblant d'être malade. feigned, a. Feint, simulé. feigning, s. Feinte f; (dis)simulation f.
feint[1] [feint], s. (a) Mil: Fausse attaque. (b) Box: Fenc: Feinte f. (c) To make f. of doing sth., feindre, faire semblant, de faire qch.
feint[2], v.i. (a) Mil: Faire une fausse attaque. (b) Box: Fenc: Feinter.
feint[3], a. & adv. Com: Paper with f. lines, f.-ruled paper, papier réglé (en bleu clair).
fel(d)spar ['fel(d)spɑːr], s. Miner: Feldspath m.
felicitations [fi,lisi'teiʃ(ə)nz], s.pl. Félicitations f.
felicitous [fi'lisitəs], a. Heureux. (a) (Of word, etc.) Bien trouvé; à propos. (b) (Of pers.) F. in his choice of words, heureux dans le choix de ses mots.
felicity [fi'lisiti], s. 1. Félicité f, bonheur m. 2. A-propos m, bien-trouvé m (d'une observation).
felidae ['fiːlidiː], s.pl. Z: Félidés m.
feline ['fiːlain]. 1. a. Félin. F. grace, grâce féline. 2. s. Félin m.
fell[1] [fel], s. 1. Fourrure f; peau f (de bête). 2. Toison f.
fell[2], s. (In N. of Eng.) Colline ou montagne rocheuse.
fell[3], v.tr. 1. (a) Abattre (un adversaire); assommer (un bœuf, etc.). (b) Abattre (un arbre). 2. Rabattre (une couture). felling, s. Abattage m.
fell[4], a. Lit: 1. Féroce, cruel. 2. (Of thg) Funeste (Now used in) At one f. swoop, d'un seul coup redoutable, sinistre.

fell[5]. See FALL[2].
fellah, pl. fellaheen ['felə, 'feləhiːn], s. Fellah m.
fellow ['felou], s. 1. Camarade m, compagnon m, confrère m, collègue m. F. sufferer, compagnon de misère. F. being, f. creature, semblable m. F. citizen, concitoyen, -enne. F. countryman, woman, compatriote mf, concitoyen, -enne. F. student, camarade mf d'études; condisciple m. F. worker, (i) compagnon (d'un ouvrier); (ii) collaborateur, -trice; (iii) confrère. 2. (Of pers.) Semblable m, pareil m; (of thg) pendant m. 3. (a) Sch: (i) Membre m de la corporation (d'une université); (ii) boursier chargé de cours. (b) Membre, associé, -ée (d'une société savante). 4. F: (a) Homme m, garçon m. A good f., un brave garçon, un brave type. He's a queer f., c'est un drôle de type. That old f., ce vieux bonhomme. (b) Pej: Individu m. Good-for-nothing f., mauvais sujet, propre m à rien. (c) O: Why can't you let a f. alone! laissez-moi donc tranquille! A f. doesn't like to be treated like that, on n'aime pas à être traité comme ça. fellow-'feeling, s. Sympathie f. 'fellow-'traveller, s. Communisant, -ante. The communists and their fellow-travellers, les communistes et leurs sympathisants.
fellowship ['felouʃip], s. 1. Communion f, communauté f. 2. (Good) f., amitié f, camaraderie f. 3. Association f, corporation f, (con)fraternité f. 4. (a) (i) Dignité f de membre (d'une corporation universitaire); (ii) bourse f universitaire (avec obligation de faire un cours, des recherches). (b) Titre m de membre, d'associé (d'une société savante).
felo-de-se ['fiːloudiː'siː], s. Jur: 1. Suicidé, -ée. 2. Suicide m.
felon ['felən], s. Jur: Criminel, -elle.
felonious [fi'lounjəs], a. Jur: Criminel. Accused of loitering with f. intent, accusé de vagabondage délictueux. -ly, adv. Criminellement.
felony ['feləni], s. Jur: Crime m.
felt[1] [felt], s. 1. Feutre m. Imitation f., feutrine f. 2. Roofing f., tarred f., feutre bitumé, goudronné.
felt[2]. 1. v.tr. (a) Tex: Feutrer. (b) Couvrir (un toit, etc.) de feutre bitumé. 2. v.i. (Of wool, etc.) Se feutrer. felting, s. Feutrage m.
felt[3]. See FEEL[2].
felucca [fe'lʌkə], s. Nau: Felouque f.
female ['fiːmeil]. 1. a. (a) (Of pers.) Féminin; (de) femme. F. child, enfant du sexe féminin. My f. relations, mes parentes. Male and f. candidates, candidats et candidates. Male and f. patients, malades hommes et femmes. F. education, l'éducation des filles. (b) (Of animals, plants, etc.) Femelle. 2. s.f. (a) Jur: (Of pers.) Femme. (b) (Of animals, plants) Femelle.
feminine ['feminin], a. Féminin. She is very f., elle est très femme Gram: In the f. (gender), au féminin.
feminism ['feminizm], s. Féminisme m.
feminist ['feminist], a. & s. Féministe (mf).
femoral ['femərəl], a. Anat: Fémoral, -aux.
femur, pl. femurs, femora ['fiːmər, -əz, 'femərə], s. Anat: Ent: Fémur m.
fen [fen], s. Marais m, marécage m. Geog: The Fens, les plaines marécageuses de l'Est de l'Angleterre.
fence[1] [fens], s. 1. L'escrime f. 2. Clôture f, barrière f, palissade f. Wire f., clôture en fil métallique. Sunk f., saut m de loup. Sp: To put a horse over the fences, mettre un cheval sur les obstacles. F: To sit on the f., ménager la chèvre et le chou; se réserver. 3. Ind: Garde f (d'une machine-outil, etc.); garde-corps m inv. 4. F: Receleur, -euse (d'objets volés).
fence[2]. 1. v.i. Faire de l'escrime; tirer des armes; abs. tirer. 2. v.tr. To f. (in), clôturer, palissader (un terrain). To f. off one corner of a field, séparer un coin d'un champ par une clôture. 3. Abs. P: Faire le recel. fencing, s. 1. Escrime f. 2. F. (in), clôture f (d'un terrain). 3. Clôture, barrière f, palissade f. 4. Ind: Garde-corps m inv (de machine); garde f. 'fencing-bout, s. Assaut m d'armes. 'fencing-master, s.m. Maître d'escrime, d'armes. 'fencing-match, s. Assaut m d'armes. 'fencing-school, s. Salle f d'armes.
fencer ['fensər], s. 1. Escrimeur m; tireur m (d'armes). 2. Cheval sauteur de haies.

fend [fend]. **1.** *v.tr.* To f. off, parer, détourner (un coup, etc.). **2.** *v.i.* To f. for oneself, se débrouiller; voler de ses propres ailes.

fender ['fendər], *s,* **1.** (*a*) *Aut: U.S:* (i) Pare-choc(s) *m inv;* (ii) aile *f. Nau:* Défense *f;* baderne *f.* (*b*) Bouteroue *f,* borne *f. Civ.E:* Éperon *m* (de pile de pont). **2.** *Furn:* Galerie *f* de foyer; garde-feu *m inv.* **3.** *Rail:* Chasse-pierres *m inv.*

fennel [fenl], *s. Bot:* Fenouil *m.* **2. Giant f.,** férule *f.*

ferment[1] ['fə:mənt], *s.* **1.** Ferment *m.* **2.** (*a*) Fermentation *f* (des liquides). (*b*) Agitation *f* (populaire). **The whole town was in a (state of) f.,** toute la ville était en effervescence *f.*

ferment[2] [fə'ment]. **1.** *v.i.* (*a*) Fermenter; (*of wine*) travailler; (*of cereals*) s'échauffer. (*b*) (*Of sedition, etc.*) Fermenter; (*of the people*) être en effervescence. **2.** *v.tr.* Faire fermenter (un liquide, etc.).

fermentation [ˌfə:men'teiʃ(ə)n], *s.* (*a*) Fermentation *f;* travail *m* (du vin); échauffement *m* (des céréales). (*b*) Effervescence *f.*

fern [fə:n], *s. Bot:* Fougère *f.* **'fern-owl,** *s. Orn:* Engoulevent *m.*

fernery ['fə:nəri], *s.* Fougeraie *f.*

ferocious [fə'rouʃ(ə)s], *a.* Féroce. **-ly,** *adv.* Férocement.

ferocity [fə'rɔsiti], *s.* Férocité *f.*

ferrate ['fereit], *s. Ch:* Ferrate *f.*

ferret[1] ['ferit], *s. Z:* Furet *m.*

ferret[2], *v.* (ferreted) **1.** *v.i.* Fureter; chasser au furet. **To f. about,** fureter, fouiner, partout. **2.** *v.tr.* Chasser, prendre, (les lapins) au furet. *F:* **To f. out (sth.),** dénicher (qch.). **ferreting,** *s.* Furetage *m;* chasse *f* au furet. **To go f.,** chasser au furet.

ferrety ['feriti], *a.* **1.** De furet. *Esp.* F. eyes, yeux de furet, de fouine. **2.** (*Of pers.*) Fureteur, -euse; *F:* fouinard.

ferric ['ferik], *a. Ch:* Ferrique.

ferro-chrome ['ferokroum], *s. Metall:* Ferrochrome *m.*

ferro-concrete ['fero'kɔnkri:t], *s.* Béton armé.

ferrocyanide ['fero'saiənaid], *s.* Ferrocyanure *m.*

ferro-magnetic ['feromæg'netik], *a.* Ferromagnétique.

ferro-manganese ['fero'mæŋgəni:z], *s. Miner:* Ferromanganèse *m.*

ferro-nickel ['fero'nikl], *s.* Ferronickel *m.*

ferrotype ['ferotaip], *s. Phot:* Ferrotypie *f.*

ferrous ['ferəs], *a.* (Oxyde) ferreux.

ferruginous [fi'ru:dʒinəs], *a.* Ferrugineux, -euse.

ferrule [ferəl, 'ferju:l], *s.* Virole *f,* frette *f* (d'un manche d'outil, etc.); bout ferré, embout *m* (de canne).

ferry[1] ['feri], *s.* **1.** Endroit *m* où l'on peut passer la rivière en bac; passage *m;* *F:* le bac. To cross the f., passer le bac. F. dues, droits de passage. **2.** Ferry-boat, *m;* bac. Chain f., toue *f.* Train f., transbordeur *m* de trains, ferry-boat *m.* **'ferry-boat,** *s.* Bac *m;* va-et-vient *m inv.*

ferry[2]. **1.** *v.i.* To f. across, over, the river, passer la rivière en bac. *v.tr.* (*a*) To f. the car across the river, passer la voiture en bac; transborder la voiture. Will you f. me across? voulez-vous me passer? (*b*) To f. an aircraft, livrer un avion (par air).

ferryman, *pl.* **-men** ['ferimən], *s.m.* Passeur.

fertile [fə:'tail], *a.* Fertile, fécond (in, en). **F. egg,** œuf fécondé, coché.

fertility [fə:'tiliti], *s.* Fertilité *f,* fécondité *f.*

fertilization [ˌfə:tilai'zeiʃ(ə)n], *s.* **1.** Fertilisation *f,* fécondation *f* (d'un œuf). *Bot:* Pollinisation *f.* **2.** Fertilisation, amendement *m* (du sol).

fertilize ['fə:tilaiz], *v.tr.* Fertiliser (le sol), féconder (un œuf). **fertilizing,** *a.* Fertilisant, fécondateur, -trice.

fertilizer ['fə:tilaizər], *s.* (*a*) Engrais *m,* fertilisant *m.* (*b*) Fécondateur, -trice.

fervency ['fə:v(ə)nsi], *s.* Ferveur *f* (d'une prière).

fervent ['fə:v(ə)nt], *a.* Ardent, fervent. **-ly,** *adv.* (Prier) avec ferveur.

fervour ['fə:vər], *s.* Passion *f,* ferveur *f,* ardeur *f;* zèle *m.*

fess(e) [fes], *s. Her:* Fasce *f.*

festal ['fest(ə)l], *a.* **1.** (Jour, air) de fête. **2.** (Gens) en fête, joyeux.

fester[1] ['festər], *s. Med:* Plaie suppurante.

fester[2]. **1.** *v.i.* (*a*) (*Of wound*) Suppurer, s'envenimer. (*b*) Se putréfier, pourrir. (*c*) (*Of resentment*) Couver. **2.** *v.tr.* (*a*) Envenimer (une plaie). (*b*) Putréfier. **festering**[1], *a.* (*a*) (*Of wound*) Ulcéreux, suppurant. (*b*) Putrescent, pourrissant. **festering**[2], *s.* (*a*) Suppuration *f,* ulcération *f.* (*b*) Putréfaction *f.*

festival ['festiv(ə)l], *s.* (*a*) Fête *f.* (*b*) *Mus:* Festival *m,* -als.

festive ['festiv], *a.* **1.** (Jour) de fête; (table) du festin. *F:* The f. season, les fêtes de Noël. F. air, air *m* de fête. **2.** To be in f. mood, avoir le cœur en fête.

festivity [fes'tiviti], *s.* Festivité *f,* réjouissance *f.*

festoon[1] [fes'tu:n], *s.* Feston *m,* guirlande *f.*

festoon[2], *v.tr.* (*a*) Festonner (with, de). (*b*) Disposer (des fleurs, etc.) en festons.

fetch [fetʃ], *v.tr.* **1.** (*a*) Aller chercher (qn, qch.). Go and f. him, allez le chercher. To f. water from the river, aller puiser de l'eau à la rivière. (*b*) Apporter (qch.); amener (qn). To f. and carry for s.o., (*of dog*) rapporter; (*of pers.*) faire les commissions de qn. **2.** Rapporter. It fetched a high price, cela se vendit cher. **3.** *F:* Faire de l'effet sur (le public, etc.). **4.** To f. a sigh, a groan, pousser un soupir, un gémissement. To f. one's breath, reprendre haleine. **5.** *F:* To f. s.o. a blow, flanquer un coup à qn. **6.** *Nau:* Gagner, atteindre (le rivage), gagner le port. *v.i.* To fetch into port, gagner le port. **fetch about,** *v.i. Nau:* Tirer des bordées. **fetch back,** *v.tr.* Ramener; rapporter. **fetch down,** *v.tr.* Faire descendre (qn); descendre (qch.). **fetch in,** *v.tr.* Rentrer (la lessive, etc.). **fetch up.** **1.** *v.tr.* (*a*) Faire monter. (*b*) *F:* Vomir (des aliments). **2.** *v.i. Nau:* To f. up at a port, parvenir, arriver à un port. **fetching,** *a.* (Sourire, air) séduisant, attrayant, *F:* aguichant. **There's something f. about her,** *F:* elle a de ça.

fête[1] [feit], *s.* Fête *f.* Village f., fête communale. Charity f., kermesse *f.*

fête[2], *v.tr.* Fêter (un événement); faire fête à (qn).

fetid ['fetid, 'fi:tid], *a.* Fétide, puant.

fetidity [fe'tiditi, fi:'tiditi], **fetidness** ['fetidnis, 'fi:tidnis] *s.* Fétidité *f,* puanteur *f.*

fetish ['fi:tiʃ, 'fe-], *s.* Fétiche *m.*

fetlock[1] ['fetlɔk], *s.* Fanon *m* (du cheval). F. joint, boulet *m.*

fetter[1] ['fetər], *s.* Lien *m;* *pl.* chaînes *f,* fers *m.* In fetters, dans les fers.

fetter[2], *v.tr.* Enchaîner (qn); charger (qn) de fers; entraver (un cheval, la pensée).

fettle ['fetl], *s.* Condition *f.* To be in fine, in good, f., être en forme, en train.

feud [fju:d], *s.* Inimitié *f* (entre familles, clans). Family blood f., vendetta *f.* Family feuds, dissensions *f* domestiques. To be at f. with s.o., être à couteaux tirés avec qn.

feudal ['fju:d(ə)l], *a.* Féodal, -aux.

feudalism ['fju:dəlizm], *s.* **1.** Le régime féodal; la féodalité.

fever ['fi:vər], *s. Med:* Fièvre *f.* High f., forte fièvre. Fièvre de cheval. To be in a f., avoir la fièvre. To throw s.o. into a f., donner la fièvre à qn. A f. of excitement, une agitation fébrile. **'fever-swamp,** *s.* Marécage à fièvres.

fevered ['fi:vəd], *a.* Enfiévré, fiévreux, -euse.

feverfew ['fi:vəfju:], *s. Bot:* Matricaire *f;* pyrèthre *m.*

feverish ['fi:v(ə)riʃ], *a.* **1.** (État) fiévreux, fébrile. To make s.o. f., donner la fièvre à qn. **2.** (*Of climate*) Fiévreux, malsain. **-ly,** *adv.* Fiévreusement, fébrilement.

feverishness ['fi:vriʃnis], *s.* État fiévreux.

few [fju:], *a.* **1.** (*a*) Peu de (personnes). He has (but) f. friends, il a peu d'amis. One of the f. people who . . ., une des rares personnes qui. . . . During the last (or next) f. days, ces jours-ci. With f. exceptions, à de rares exceptions près. Every f. days, tous les deux ou trois jours. (*b*) A f., quelques. A f. more, encore quelques-uns. In a f. minutes, dans quelques minutes. (*c*) (*Pred. use*) Peu nombreux. Our days are f., nos jours sont comptés. Such occasions are f., de telles occasions sont rares. **2.** (*With noun function*) (*a*) Peu (de gens, etc.). F. of them had travelled, peu d'entre eux avaient voyagé. There are very f. of us, nous sommes peu nombreux. The fortunate f., une minorité de gens heureux. (*b*) Quelques-uns,

-unes. **A f. thought otherwise,** quelques-uns pensaient autrement. **A f. of the survivors,** quelques-uns des survivants. *F:* **There were a good f. of them,** il y en avait pas mal.

fewer ['fjuːər], *a.* (*Comp. of* FEW) **1.** Moins (de). **2.** (*Pred. use*) Plus rares; moins nombreux.

fewest ['fjuːist], *a.* (*Sup. of* FEW) **1.** Le moins (de). **2.** **There are the houses are fewest,** c'est là que les maisons sont le moins nombreuses, le plus rares.

fey [fei]. *a. Scot:* **1.** (*a*) Destiné à mourir. (*b*) Qui est doué de seconde vue. **2.** Fou, *f.* folle.

fez [fez], *s. Cost:* Fez *m.*

fiancé, *f.* **-ée** [fiˈɑ̃(n)sei], *s.* Fiancé, -ée.

fiasco [fiˈæskou], *s.* Fiasco *m*; *F:* four *m.*

fiat ['faiæt], *s.* **1.** Consentement *m*, autorisation *f.* **2.** Décret *m.* ordre *m.*

fib[1] [fib], *s. F:* Petit mensonge; *F:* craque *f*, blague *f.*

fib[2], *v.i.* (**fibbed**) *F:* Blaguer; en conter (à qn).

fibre ['faibər], *s.* **1.** Fibre *f*; filament *m.* (*a*) **Muscle f.,** fibre musculaire. (*b*) *F:* **Our moral f.,** notre nature *f.* **2.** *Com:* **F. trunk,** malle en fibre. **Wood f.,** laine *f* de bois. **Glass f.,** laine *f*, fibre *f* de verre. *Tex:* **Staple f.,** fibran(n)e *f.*

fibril ['faibril], *s.* Fibrille *f.*

fibrin ['faibrin], *s. Ch: Physiol:* Fibrine *f.*

fibroid ['faibrɔid]. **1.** *a.* (Tumeur) fibroïde. **2.** *s.* Fibrome *m.*

fibroma, *pl.* **-as, -mata** [faiˈbroumə, -əs, faibroˈmɑːtə], *s. Med:* Fibrome *m.*

fibrositis ['faibroˈsaitis], *s. Med:* Fibromatose *f.*

fibrous ['faibrəs], *a.* Fibreux, -euse; filamenteux, -euse.

fibula ['fibjulə], *s.* **1.** *Rom.Ant:* Fibule *f.* **2.** *Anat:* Péroné *m.*

fickle ['fikl], *a.* Inconstant, volage, changeant.

fickleness ['fiklnis], *s.* Inconstance *f.*

fiction ['fikʃ(ə)n], *s.* **1.** Fiction *f*; création *f* de l'imagination. **It's pure f.!** c'est pure invention! *Jur:* **Legal f.,** fiction légale. **2.** (**Works of**) **f.,** romans *m*; ouvrages *m* d'imagination. **Light f.,** romans de lecture facile.

fictitious [fik tiʃəs], *a.* (*a*) Fictif. **F. being,** être imaginaire. (*b*) (*Of fight, etc.*) Simulé, feint. **-ly,** *adv.* Fictivement.

fid [fid], *s.* **1.** *Nau:* Clef *f* (de mât). **2.** Épissoir *m.* **3.** Cale *f*, coin *m* (pour caler ou obturer).

fiddle[1] ['fidl], *s.* **1.** *F:* (*a*) Violon *m*, *P:* crincrin *m.* (*b*) *F:* (Joueur *m* de) violon. *A:* **First f.,** premier violon. **Second f.,** *F:* sous-fifre *m.* **To play second f. (to s.o.),** jouer un rôle secondaire (auprès de qn); *Th:* jouer les utilités. **2.** *Nau:* Violon de mer; fiche *f* de roulis. **2.** *F:* **It's a f.!** c'est une combine! **'fiddle-block,** *s. Nau:* (Poulie *f* à) violon *m.*

fiddle[2],*v.i. F:* **1.** (i) Jouer du violon (ii) *Pej:* violoner; racler du violon. **2.** (*a*) S'amuser à des niaiseries, baguenauder, tripoter, bricoler, trifouiller. **Don't f. with the mechanism,** laissez le mécanisme tranquille. **He was fiddling about with his car,** il bricolait après sa voiture. **To f. away one's time,** passer son temps à des niaiseries. (*b*) **To f. the accounts,** maquiller la comptabilité. **fiddling**[1], *s. F:* Futile, insignifiant, sans importance. **fiddling**[2], *s. F:* Combine *f.*

fiddlededee ['fidldiˈdiː], *int. F: O:* Bah! turlututu! turlurette! quelle blague!

fiddle-faddle[1] ['fidlfædl]. **1.** *s.* **Bagatelles** *fpl*, balivernes *fpl*, niaiseries *fpl*. **2.** *a.* Chipotier, musard.

fiddle-faddle[2], *v.i.* Muser, musarder, baguenauder.

fiddler ['fidlər], *s. F:* (*a*) Joueur *m* de violon. (*b*) **Strolling f.,** ménétrier *m*, violoneux *m.* (*c*) **He's an awful f.!** c'est un fameux combinard!

fiddlestick ['fidlstik]. **1.** *s.* Archet *m* (de violon). *F:* **I don't care a f.,** je m'en moque comme d'une guigne. **2.** *int.* **Fiddlesticks!** Sornettes!

fidelity [faiˈdeliti, fi-], *s.* Fidélité *f*, loyauté *f.* (*Gramophones, etc.*) **High f.,** haute fidélité.

fidget[1] ['fidʒit], *s.* **1.** **To have the fidgets, to be in a f.,** ne pas tenir en place; se trémousser (sur sa chaise); avoir des impatiences dans les jambes; *F:* avoir la bougeotte **It gives me the fidgets,** cela m'énerve. **2.** **He's a f.,** c'est un agité.

fidget[2], *v.i.* (**fidgeted**) (*a*) **To fidget** (**about**), remuer continuellement; se trémousser. (*To child*) **Don't f.!**

tiens-toi tranquille! **To f. with one's keys,** tripoter ses clefs. (*b*) S'inquiéter, se tourmenter. **2.** *v.tr.* Agacer (qn). **fidgeting,** *s.* Agitation nerveuse; nervosité *f.* impatient.

fidgety ['fidʒiti], *a.* **1.** Remuant, agité. **2.** Nerveux, impatient.

fiduciary [faiˈdjuːʃiəri], *a.* Fiduciaire.

fie [fai], *int. A: F:* **F.** (**upon you**)! fi (donc)!

fief [fiːf], *s. Hist:* Fief *m.*

field[1] ['fiːld], *s.* **1.** Champ *m.* (*a*) **In the fields,** aux champs. **The beasts of the f.,** les bêtes sauvages. (*b*) District *m*, région *f. S.a.* GOLD-FIELD, MINEFIELD, OILFIELD. (*c*) *Mil:* **F. of battle,** champ de bataille. **To take the f.,** entrer en campagne. **To hold the f.** (i) *Mil:* se maintenir sur ses positions; (ii) (*Of theory, etc.*) être toujours en faveur; faire autorité. *Attrib.* **F. service,** service en campagne. **2.** *Cr: Fb:* (*a*) Terrain *m. Baseball:* Champ. (*b*) *Cr:* **To place the f.,** disposer l'équipe. **3.** *Turf:* **The f.,** les chevaux courants (à l'exception du favori). **There are already several books in the f. on this subject,** plusieurs livres ont déjà paru sur ce sujet. **To be first in the f.,** (i) être au premier rang; (ii) être le premier à faire qch. **4.** (*a*) Étendue *f*, espace *m.* (*b*) *Her:* Champ, sol *m.* **5.** (*a*) Théâtre *m*, champ (d'opération); domaine *m* (d'une science). **F. of conjecture,** champ des hypothèses. **To have a clear f.** (**before one**), avoir le champ libre. **In the political f.,** sur le plan politique. (*b*) *Com:* **There is a great f. for . . .,** il y a un excellent marché pour. . . . (*c*) **F. survey, f. study,** études *f* sur le terrain. **6.** (*a*) *Opt:* **F. of vision,** champ de vision. (*b*) *El: Magn:* Champ (magnétique). **field-ar'tillery,** *s.* Artillerie *f* de campagne. **'field-coil,** *s. El:* Bobine *f* de champ. **'field-day, s. 1.** *Mil:* Jour *m* de grandes manœuvres. **2.** *F:* Grande occasion; grand jour. **'field-'dressing, s. Mil:** **1.** Paquet (individuel) de pansement. **2.** Pansement *m* sommaire. **'field-events,** *s.pl.* épreuves *f* d'athlétisme. **'field-glass(es),** *s. Usu. pl.* Jumelle(s) *f.* **'field-gun,** *s.* Canon *m* de campagne. **'field-'hospital,** *s. Mil:* Ambulance *f* divisionnaire. **'field-ice,** *s.* Glace *f* de banquise. **'field-kitchen,** *s. Mil:* Cuisine roulante. **'field-'marshal,** *s.* Maréchal, *m, pl.* -aux. **'field-mouse,** *pl.* -**mice,** *s.* Mulot *m.* **'field-officer,** *s. Mil:* Officier supérieur. **'field-sports,** *s.pl.* Sports *m* au grand air; la chasse et la pêche. **field-'winding,** *s. El:* Bobinage inducteur. **field-work, s. 1.** *Mil:* Ouvrage de campagne, retranchement improvisé. **2.** Travaux pratiques, travaux sur le terrain.

field[2]. *Cr:* **1.** *v.i.* Tenir le champ (pour relancer la balle). **2.** *v.tr.* **To field the ball,** arrêter (et relancer) la balle.

fielder ['fiːldər], *s. Cr:* Membre *m* de l'équipe du lanceur.

fieldfare ['fiːldfɛər], *s. Orn:* Litorne *f.*

fiend [fiːnd], *s.* **1.** (*a*) Démon *m*, diable *m.* (*b*) Monstre *m* (de cruauté). **He's a perfect f.,** c'est un vrai suppôt de Satan. **2.** *F:* **Autograph f.,** coureur, -euse, d'autographes. **Examination f.,** bête *f* à concours. *S.a.* DRUG-FIEND.

fiendish ['fiːndiʃ], *a.* Diabolique, satanique. **-ly,** *adv.* Diaboliquement.

fiendishness ['fiːndiʃnis], *s.* Méchanceté *f* ou cruauté *f* diabolique.

fierce ['fiəs], *a.* (*a*) Féroce; (*of desire*) ardent; (*of battle*) acharné; (*of wind*) furieux, violent. **The weather has been f.,** il a fait un temps de chien. (*b*) *Aut:* **F. brake,** frein brutal. **-ly,** *adv.* **1.** Férocement. **2.** Violemment; avec acharnement.

fierceness ['fiəsnis], *s.* Violence *f*, véhémence *f* (de qn); férocité *f* (d'un animal); ardeur *f* (du feu); acharnement *m* (de la bataille); fureur *f* (du vent). *Aut:* Brutalité *f* (de l'embrayage).

fieriness ['faiərinis], *s.* **1.** Ardeur *f* (du soleil). **2.** Ardeur, fougue *f.*

fiery ['faiəri], *a.* **1.** Ardent, brûlant, enflammé. **F. red,** rouge ardent, rouge feu. **F. sky,** ciel embrasé. **F. taste,** saveur cuisante. *Cr:* **F. pitch, wicket,** terrain très sec. **2.** (*Of pers.*) (i) Fougueux, emporté, impétueux; (ii) colérique, bouillant. *Lit:* **F. steed,** cheval ardent, coursier fougueux. **3.** (*Of gas*) Inflammable; (*of mine*) grisouteux, à grisou.

fife [faif], *s. Mus:* Fifre *m.*

fifteen ['fif'ti:n], *num. a. & s.* Quinze (*m*). **A Rugby f.**, une équipe de rugby. *Rugby Fb:* **The French f.**, le quinze français.

fifteenth ['fif'ti:nθ]. **1.** *num. a. & s.* Quinzième. **Louis the F.**, Louis Quinze. **2.** *s.* (*Fractional*) Quinzième *m*.

fifth [fifθ]. **1.** *num. a. & s.* Cinquième. **Henry the F.**, Henri Cinq. **Charles the F.** (of Holy Roman Empire), Charles-Quint. *Sch:* **F. form,** (*approx.* =) classe *f* de seconde. **2.** *s.* (*a*) (*Fractional*) Cinquième *m*. (*b*) *Mus:* Quinte *f*. **Diminished f.**, fausse quinte. **-ly,** *adv.* Cinquièmement; en cinquième lieu. **'fifth-'rate,** *a.* De cinquième ordre.

fiftieth ['fiftiəθ], *num. a. & s.* Cinquantième.

fifty ['fifti], *num. a. & s.* Cinquante (*m*). **F.-f.-moitié-moitié. To go f.-f. with s.o.**, se mettre de moitié avec qn; mettre qn de compte à demi dans l'affaire. **About f. books,** une cinquantaine de livres. **She is in her fifties,** elle a passé la cinquantaine.

fig¹ [fig], *s.* Figue *f*. *F: A:* **A f. for Smith!** zut pour Smith! **'fig-tree,** *s.* Figuier *m*. **'fig-leaf,** *s.* **1.** Feuille *f* de figuier. **2.** *Art:* Feuille de vigne.

fig², *s.* *F:* **In full f.,** en grande tenue; en grande toilette.

fight¹ [fait], *s.* **1.** (*a*) Combat *m*, bataille *f*. **Sham fight,** petite guerre; simulacre *m* de combat. **They had a f.,** ils se sont battus. (*b*) *Box:* Assaut *m*. **Hand-to-hand f.**, corps-à-corps *m*. **F. to the death,** combat à outrance. **Free f.**, mêlée générale. **2.** (*a*) Lutte *f*. **To carry on a stubborn f. against s.o.**, soutenir une lutte opiniâtre contre qn. (*b*) **To show f.**, résister; *F:* montrer les dents, rouspéter. *Sp: etc:* **To put up a good f.**, se bien acquitter. **There was no f. left in him,** il était à bout de forces.

fight², *v.* (fought [fɔ:t]; fought) **1.** *v.i.* Se battre; combattre; lutter; (*in bull-ring*) toréer. **To f. against disease,** combattre la maladie. **To f. against sleep,** lutter contre le sommeil. **To f. for one's own hand,** défendre ses propres intérêts. **Two dogs fighting over a bone,** deux chiens qui se disputent un os. **They began to f.**, ils en vinrent aux mains. **To f. a battle,** livrer (une) bataille. **To f. one's way (out),** se frayer un passage (pour sortir). **To f. an action (at law),** se défendre dans un procès. **2.** *v.tr.* (*a*) **To f. s.o.**, se battre avec, contre, qn; combattre qn. **To f. a fire,** combattre un incendie. (*b*) **To f. one's ships (in battle),** manœuvrer ses vaisseaux. **fight down,** *v.tr.* Vaincre (une passion). **fight off,** *v.tr.* **1.** Résister à (une maladie). **2. To f. off the enemy,** repousser l'ennemi. **fight out,** *v.tr.* **To f. it out,** se battre jusqu'à une décision; lutter jusqu'au bout.

fighting¹, *a.* **F. men,** combattants *m*; *Mil:* hommes disponibles. **F. forces,** forces sous les armes.

fighting², *s.* Combat *m*. *Box:* Pugilat *m*, boxe *f*. **Close f.**, lutte *f* corps à corps. **F. line,** ligne de combat. **There's just a f. chance for his recovery,** il a une chance sur dix de s'en tirer. **'fighting-cock,** *s.* Coq *m* de combat. *F:* **To live like a f.-c.**, vivre comme un coq en pâte.

fighter ['faitər], *s.* **1.** Combattant *m*. **F. for an idea,** militant *m* d'une idée. **He's a fighter,** il est batailleur. **2.** *Av:* Avion *m* de chasse, chasseur *m*. **Rocket f.**, chasseur-fusée *m*. **'fighter-'bomber,** *s.* Chasseur-bombardier *m*, *pl.* chasseurs-bombardiers.

figment ['figmənt], *s.* Fiction *f*, invention *f*.

figuration [figju'reiʃ(ə)n], *s.* **1.** (*a*) Figuration *f* (d'une idée). (*b*) Configuration *f* (d'un objet). **2.** Représentation figurative.

figurative ['figərətiv], *a.* **1.** Figuratif, emblématique. **2.** (*Of language*) Figuré, métaphorique. **In the f. sense,** au figuré. **-ly,** *adv.* **1.** Figurativement, figurément. **2.** Au figuré; par métaphore.

figure¹ ['figər], *s.* **1.** (*a*) Figure *f*; forme extérieure. (*b*) (*Of pers.*) Taille *f*, tournure *f*. **To have a fine f.**, être bien fait de sa personne; (*esp. of woman*) être bien prise. **His commanding f.**, son port imposant. **To keep one's f.**, garder sa ligne. **To watch one's f.**, soigner sa ligne. **2.** (*a*) Personne *f*, être *m*; forme humaine, silhouette *f*. **A magnificent f. of a man,** un homme magnifique. **A fine f. of a woman,** une belle femme. **What a f. of fun!** quelle caricature! (*b*) Personnage *m*. **The central f.** (*of a drama*), le pivot de l'action. (*c*) Figure, apparence *f*. **To cut a sorry**

f., faire piètre figure. **3.** *Art:* **Lay f.**, mannequin *m*. **Anatomical f.**, pièce *f* d'anatomie. **4.** (*a*) **Geometrical f.**, figure géométrique. (*b*) Illustration *f* (dans un livre). **5.** (*a*) Chiffre *m*. **To work out the figures,** effectuer les calculs. **In round figures,** en chiffres ronds. **A mistake in the figures,** une erreur de calcul. **To be quick at figures,** calculer vite et bien. **To fetch a high f.**, se vendre cher. *P:* **What's the f.?** ça coûte combien? **Double figures,** nombre *m* de deux chiffres. **His income runs into five figures,** il a un revenu de plus de dix mille livres par an. *Tchn:* **Dimensional figures,** cotes *f* (d'une machine). *Med:* **F. of eight bandage,** bandage en huit de chiffre. (*b*) *pl.* **Figures,** détails chiffrés (d'un projet). **6. F. of speech,** (i) figure de rhétorique; métaphore *f*; (ii) façon *f* de parler. **'figure-head,** *s.* **1.** *N.Arch:* Figure *f* de proue. (*a*) Prête-nom *m*. (*b*) Personnage purement décoratif.

figure². **1.** *v.tr.* (*a*) Figurer, représenter. (*b*) **To f. sth.** (*to oneself*), se représenter, se figurer, qch. (*c*) *U.S:* *F:* Estimer, évaluer. (*d*) Brocher, gaufrer, ouvrager (la soie). *a. Tex:* **Figured (material),** (tissu) à impressions; façonné. (*e*) *Mus:* Chiffrer (la basse). **2.** *v.i.* (*a*) Chiffrer, calculer; faire des chiffres. (*b*) *U.S:* **To f. on a success,** compter sur un succès. (*c*) **His name figures on the list,** son nom figure sur la liste. **figure out. 1.** *v.i.* Se chiffrer. **The total figures out at £50,** le total se monte à cinquante livres. **2.** *v.tr.* **To f. out the expense,** calculer le montant de la dépense. **That's how I f. it out,** voilà mon calcul. **I can't f. it out,** ça me dépasse.

figurine ['figə'ri:n[, *s.* Figurine *f*.

filament ['filəmənt], *s.* **1.** Filament *m*, cil *m*, fibre *m*. *Bot:* Filet *m* (de l'étamine). **2.** *El:* Fil *m*, filament (d'une lampe). **3.** *Ph:* Filet (d'air, d'eau).

filamentous [filə'mentəs], *a.* Filamenteux, -euse.

filbert ['filbət], *s.* Aveline *f*.

filch [fil(t)ʃ], *v.tr.* *F:* Chiper, barboter, chaparder.

file¹ [fail], *s.* **1.** *Tls:* Lime *f*. **Three-cornered f.**, **triangular f.**, tiers-point *m*. *F:* **To gnaw, bite, a f.**, tomber sur un os. **2.** *F: O:* **He's a sly old f.**, c'est un fin matois.

file², *v.tr.* Limer (le métal, etc.). **To f. down,** enlever (une saillie, etc.) à la lime; adoucir (une surface) à la lime; *Farr:* raboter (le sabot d'un cheval). **To f. away, off,** enlever (une saillie) à la lime. **filing¹,** *s.* **1.** Limage *m* (d'un métal). **F. down,** adoucissement *m* à la lime. **2.** *pl.* **Filings,** limaille *f*. **'filing-machine,** *s.* Limeuse *f*.

file³, *s.* **1.** (*a*) **Bill f.**, **spike f.**, pique-notes *m inv.* (*b*) Classeur *m*, cartonnier *m*. **Card-index f.**, fichier *m*. **2.** Collection *f*, liasse *f* (de papiers). *Adm:* Dossier *m*. **'file-copy,** *s. Publ:* Exemplaire *m* des archives.

file⁴, *v.tr.* **1.** Classer (des fiches); ranger (des lettres, etc.). **2.** *Jur:* **To f. a petition,** enregistrer une requête. **To f. one's petition (in bankruptcy),** déposer son bilan. **filing²,** *s.* **1.** Classement *m*. **F.-cabinet,** classeur *m*. **F.-clerk,** archiviste *m*. **2.** *Jur:* Enregistrement *m* (d'une requête).

file⁵, *s.* File *f*. **In single, Indian, file,** en file indienne; *F:* à la queue leu leu. **To walk in single f.**, marcher à la file, en file indienne. *Mil:* **To form single f.**, dédoubler les rangs. **Blank f.**, file creuse. **'file-closer,** *s.* Serre-file *m inv.* **'file-leader,** *s. Mil:* Chef *m* de file.

file⁶, *v.i.* **To f. off,** défiler. **To f. past the war memorial,** défiler devant le monument aux morts. **To f. in, out,** entrer, sortir, un à un.

filial ['filiəl], *a.* Filial, -aux.

filiation [fili'eiʃ(ə)n], *s.* Filiation *f*.

filibuster¹ ['filibʌstər], *s.* **1.** *Hist:* Flibustier *m*. **2.** *Pol:* *U.S:* (*a*) Obstructionniste *m*. (*b*) Obstructionnisme *m*.

filibuster², *v.i.* **1.** *Hist:* Flibuster. **2.** *Pol:* *U.S:* Faire de l'obstruction. **filibustering,** *a.* *Pol:* *U.S:* Obstructionniste.

filigree ['filigri:], *s.* Filigrane *m*.

fill¹ [fil], *s.* **1.** **To have one's f. of sth.**, avoir sa suffisance, son content, de qch. **To eat one's f.**, manger à sa faim. **When he had taken his f. . . .**, quand il se fut rassasié. . . . **To drink one's f.**, boire à sa soif. **2.** Charge *f*, plein *m*. **A f. of tobacco,** une pipe de tabac.

fill². I. *v.tr.* **1.** (*a*) Remplir, emplir (**with,** de). **To f. s.o.'s glass,** verser à boire à qn; (*to the brim*) verser une rasade à qn. **To f. a truck,** charger un wagon. **To f. a lamp,** garnir une lampe. **To f. one's pipe,** bourrer sa pipe. **Well-filled pockets,** poches bien bourrées. **To f. (up) the boilers,** faire le plein des chaudières. (*b*) **To f. the air with one's cries,** remplir l'air de ses cris. **He is filled with despair,** il est en proie au désespoir. **2.** (*a*) Combler (une brèche, une lacune, etc.), obturer. **To fill a tooth,** plomber une dent. **To f. a tooth with gold,** aurifier une dent. (*b*) **To f. (up) a vacancy,** pourvoir à une vacance. **3.** Occuper. (*a*) **A post he has filled for some time,** un poste qu'il occupe depuis quelque temps. *Th:* **To f. a part,** remplir, tenir, un rôle. (*b*) **The thoughts that filled his mind,** les pensées qui occupaient son esprit. **4. To f. every requirement,** répondre à tous les besoins. *Com:* **To f. an order,** exécuter une commande. II. **fill,** *v.i.* **1.** Se remplir, s'emplir. **The hall is beginning to f.,** la salle commence à se garnir. **2.** *Nau:* (*Of sails*) S'enfler, porter. **fill in,** *v.tr.* **1.** Combler, remplir (un trou); condamner (une porte); remblayer (un fossé). **2.** Combler (des vides); remplir (une formule); libeller (un chèque). **To f. in the date,** insérer la date. **fill out. 1.** *v.tr.* (*a*) Enfler, gonfler (un ballon). (*b*) Étoffer (un discours). (*c*) *U.S:* Remplir (une formule). **2.** *v.i.* (*a*) S'enfler, se gonfler. (*b*) Prendre de l'embonpoint; se remplumer. **Her cheeks are filling out,** ses joues se remplissent. **fill up. 1.** *v.tr.* (*a*) Remplir jusqu'au bord; combler (une mesure). *Abs.* **To f. up with petrol,** faire le plein d'essence. (*b*) Boucher (un trou avec du mastic); condamner (une porte); remblayer (un fossé). (*c*) Remplir (une formule); libeller (un chèque). **2.** *v.i.* Se remplir, s'emplir, se combler. **filling¹,** *a.* (*Of food*) Rassasiant. **filling²,** *s.* **1.** (*a*) (R)emplissage *m* (d'une mesure); chargement *m* (d'un wagon). (*b*) Peuplement *m* (d'un étang). **2.** (*a*) Comblement *m* (d'une brèche); obturation. *Dent:* Plombage *m*. (*b*) **F. of a vacancy,** nomination *f* de quelqu'un à un poste. **3.** Occupation *f* (d'un poste). **4.** Matière *f* de remplissage. *Dent: Carp:* Mastic *m*. '**filling-station,** *s. Aut:* Poste *m* d'essence. **F.-s. attendant,** pompiste *m*.

filler ['filər], *s* (*a*) (*Pers.*) Remplisseur, -euse. (*b*) (*Thg*) Remplisseuse *f*.

fillet¹ ['filit], *s.* **1.** *Cost:* Filet *m*, bandelette *f* (pour maintenir les cheveux). **2.** *Cu:* (*a*) Filet (de bœuf). (*b*) Rouelle *f* (de veau). **3.** (*a*) *Arch:* Nervure *f*, filet. (*b*) *Join:* Baguette *f*, listel *m* (de panneau). (*c*) *Mec.E:* Bourrelet *m*, boudin *m* (sur un tuyau). *Metalw:* F.(-border), suage *m*. **4.** (*a*) *Her:* Filet. (*b*) *Bookb: Typ:* Filet.

fillet², *v.tr.* (**filleted**) **1.** Orner (qch.) d'un filet, d'une baguette. **2.** *Cu:* Détacher, lever, les filets (d'un). **Filleted sole,** filets de sole.

fillip¹ ['filip], *s.* **1.** Chiquenaude *f*; *F:* pichenette *f*. **2.** Coup de fouet (donné au système nerveux). **To give a f. to business,** stimuler les affaires.

fillip², *v.tr.* **1.** Donner une chiquenaude à (qn). **2.** Stimuler, fouetter (le sang).

filly ['fili], *s.* Pouliche *f*.

film¹ [film], *s.* **1.** (*a*) Pellicule *f*, couche *f* (de glace, d'huile); peau *f* (du lait bouilli). **F. over the eye,** taie *f* sur l'œil. (*b*) Voile *m* (de brume). **2.** *Phot:* (*a*) Pellicule, film *m*. (*b*) Couche sensible (de la plaque ou de la pellicule). **3.** *Cin:* (*a*) Film *m*, bande *f*. **Silent f.,** film muet. **Talking f.,** film parlant. **News f.,** film d'actualités. **3D(imensional) f.,** film à réfraction. **Colour f.,** film en couleurs. **Full-length f.,** long métrage. **Horror f.,** film *m* d'épouvante. **Supplementary f.,** hors-programme *m inv*. **To shoot a f.,** tourner un film; prendre les vues. **To act in a f.,** jouer dans, *F:* tourner, un film. (*b*) **The films,** le cinéma. **Silent films,** l'écran muet. **Sound films,** le cinéma sonore. **He acts for the films,** il fait du cinéma. **To have a f. face,** être photogénique. **F. library,** filmothèque *f*., cinémathèque *f*. **F. rights,** droits d'adaptation cinématographique. **F. star,** vedette *f* de l'écran, du cinéma. '**film-script,** *s.* Scénario *m*. '**film-strip,** *s.* Film *m* fixe (d'enseignement). '**film-stock,** *s.* Film(s) vierge(s).

film². **1.** *v.tr. Cin:* Filmer, tourner (une scène). **He films well,** il est photogénique. **2.** *v.t.* **To f. (over),** (i) (*of lake*) se couvrir d'une pellicule; (ii) (*of the eyes*) se couvrir d'une taie.

filmy ['filmi], *a.* **1.** (*a*) Couvert d'une pellicule; (*of eye*) couvert d'une taie. (*b*) Voilé (de brume). **2.** (*Of lace, cloud*) Léger, transparent.

filter¹ ['filtər], *s.* **1.** Filtre *m*; épurateur *m* (d'essence). **2.** *Phot:* Écran (coloré, orthochromatique). '**filter-paper,** *s.* Papier *m* filtre. '**filter-tip,** *s.* Bout filtrant (de cigarette).

filter². **1.** *v.tr.* Filtrer (l'eau); épurer, tamiser (l'air). **2.** *v.i.* (*a*) (*Of water*) Filtrer, s'infiltrer (**through,** à travers). (*b*) *Aut:* Déboîter.

filterable ['filtərəbl], *a.* (Virus) filtrant.

filth [filθ], *s.* **1.** (*a*) Ordure *f*; immondices *fpl.* (*b*) **To live in f.,** vivre dans la saleté. **2.** (*a*) Corruption morale. (*b*) **To talk f.,** dire des saletés.

filthiness ['filθinis], *s.* **1.** Saleté *f*. **2.** Corruption morale; obscénité *f*.

filthy ['filθi], *a.* **1.** Sale, immonde, dégoûtant. **A f. hovel,** un taudis infect. **2.** (*Of talk*) Ordurier, -ière; (*of pers.*) crapuleux, -euse.

filtrate ['filtreit], *s. Ch: etc:* Filtrat *m*.

filtration [fil'treiʃ(ə)n], *s.* Filtration *f*, filtrage *m*.

fin [fin], *s.* **1.** Nageoire *f* (d'un poisson); aileron *m* (d'un requin); palme *f* (pour natation sous-marine). **2.** Plan fixe vertical (d'un avion); aileron (d'automobile). **3.** (*a*) Ailette *f* (de radiateur d'automobile). (*b*) Bavure *f* (d'une pièce coulée). '**fin-back,** *s. Z:* Rorqual *m*, -als.

final ['fain(ə)l]. **1.** *a.* Final, -als. (*a*) Dernier. **To put the f. touches to sth.,** mettre la dernière main à qch. *Com:* **F. date (for payment),** terme fatal, de rigueur. (*b*) Définitif, décisif. *Jur:* **F. judgment,** jugement définitif; jugement souverain. **The umpire's decision is f.,** la décision de l'arbitre est sans appel. **Am I to consider that as f.?** c'est votre dernier mot? **Take this as f.,** tenez-le-vous pour dit. (*c*) *Phil:* **F. cause,** cause finale. *Gram:* **F. clause,** proposition finale. **2.** *s.* (*a*) *Sp:* **The finals,** les (épreuves) finales, la finale. (*b*) *Sch:* = Quatrième certificat de licence. **-ally,** *adv.* Finalement. **1.** Enfin. **2.** Définitivement. **3.** En somme, en définitive.

finale [fi'nɑ:li], *s.* **1.** *Mus:* Final(e) *m*. **2.** Conclusion *f*. *Th:* Grand f., apothéose *f*.

finalist ['fainəlist], *s. Phil: Sp:* Finaliste *mf*.

finality [fai'næliti], *s.* **1.** *Phil:* Finalité *f*. **2.** Caractère définitif; irrévocabilité *f*.

finalize ['fainəlaiz], *v.tr.* Mettre au point. **The matter has now been finalized,** c'est une affaire faite.

finance¹ [fai'næns, fi-], *s.* **1.** Finance *f*. **High f.,** la haute finance. **2.** *pl. F:* **His finances are low,** ses fonds sont bas, en baisse.

finance², *v.tr.* Financer, commanditer (une entreprise). **financing,** *s.* Financement *m* (d'une entreprise).

financial [fai'næns(ə)l, fi-], *a. Fin:* **F. statement,** état *m* des finances, bilan *m. Adm:* **F. year,** exercice (financier), année *f* budgétaire. **F. resources,** ressources fiscales.

financier [fai'nænsiər, fi-], *s.* **1.** Financier *m*. **2.** Bailleur *m* de fonds.

finch [fin(t)ʃ], *s. Orn:* Pinson *m*. **Thistle f., yellow f.,** chardonneret *m. S.a.* BULLFINCH, CHAFFINCH, GOLDFINCH.

find¹ [faind], *s.* **1.** Découverte *f*. **2.** Trouvaille *f*.

find², *v.tr.* (**found** [faund]; **found**) Trouver. **1.** (*a*) Rencontrer, découvrir. **It is found everywhere,** cela se trouve, se rencontre, partout. **To f. some difficulty in doing sth.,** éprouver quelque difficulté à faire qch. **The bullet found its mark,** la balle atteignit son but. (*b*) **To f. s.o. at home,** trouver qn chez lui. **To leave everything as one finds it,** tout laisser tel quel. **I found myself obliged to beg,** je me voyais obligé de mendier. **I found myself crying,** je me surpris à pleurer. **2.** (*By searching*) (*a*) **The (lost) key has been found,** la clef s'est retrouvée. **To try to f. sth.,** chercher qch. **He is not to be found,** il est introuvable. **To f. a leak in a main,** localiser une fuite dans une conduite. **To f. one's way home,** retrouver le chemin pour rentrer chez soi. **To f. oneself,** trouver sa voie. **I can't f. time to . . .,** je n'ai pas le temps de. . . . **He found**

courage to . . ., il eut le courage de. . . . To f. it in one's heart to do sth., avoir le cœur de faire qch. (b) Obtenir (une sûreté, une caution). (c) Abs. Ven: To f., découvrir le renard, etc. 3. (a) Constater. It has been found that . . ., on a constaté que. . . . I found she had left the house, j'appris, je vis, qu'elle avait quitté la maison. I f. it is time to go, je m'aperçois qu'il est temps de partir. This letter, I f., arrived yesterday, cette lettre, à ce que je vois, à ce que j'apprends, est arrivée hier. (b) They will f. it easy, cela leur sera facile. To f. it impossible to . . ., se trouver dans l'impossibilité de. . . . 4. Jur: (a) To f. s.o. guilty, déclarer qn coupable. (b) Rendre (un verdict). To f. for s.o., prononcer un verdict en faveur de qn. 5. (a) To f. the money for an undertaking, procurer les capitaux, fournir l'argent, pour une entreprise. X finds half the money, X baille les fonds pour moitié. (b) Wages £20, all found, gages £20, nourri, logé, chauffé, et blanchi; gages £20, tout fourni. A: To f. oneself, se pourvoir soi-même. A: To f. oneself in clothes, se vêtir à ses frais. find out, v.tr. (a) Deviner (une énigme); découvrir (un secret); constater (une erreur). Abs. To f. out about sth., se renseigner sur qch. What have you done with it?— F. out! qu'en avez-vous fait?—A vous de trouver. (b) To f. s.o. out, (i) découvrir le vrai caractère de qn, démasquer qn; (ii) trouver qn en défaut. finding, s. 1. (a) Découverte f (d'un pays); invention f (d'un système). (b) Fourniture f (de fonds). 2. Trouvaille f. 3. Verdict m. The findings of an official report, les conclusions f d'un procès-verbal.
finder ['faindər], s. 1. Trouveur, -euse; Jur: inventeur, -trice (d'un objet perdu). 2. (a) Opt: (Of telescope) Chercheur m. (b) Phot: View-f., viseur m; Cin: oculaire m. (c) El: Short-circuit f, détecteur m de courts-circuits.
fine¹ [fain], s. 1. In fine, enfin, finalement. 2. Jur: (a) Pas-de-porte (payé par un locataire à son prédécesseur. (b) Amende f. To impose a f. on s.o., infliger une amende à qn.
fine², v.tr. Condamner (qn) à une amende; frapper (qn) d'une amende.
fine³, a. 1. (a) Fin, pur. Gold twenty-two carats f., or à vingt-deux carats de fin. (b) Fin, subtil, raffiné. F. distinction, distinction subtile. 2. Beau, bel, belle, beaux. (a) F. woman, belle femme. The f. arts, les beaux-arts m. (b) F. sentiments, de beaux sentiments. To appeal to s.o.'s finer feelings, faire appel aux sentiments élevés de qn. 3. (a) Meat of the finest quality, viande de premier choix. (b) Excellent, magnifique. F. display, étalage superbe. F. piece of business, affaire d'or. F. future, bel avenir. We had a f. time, nous nous sommes bien amusés. That's f.! voilà qui est parfait. (c) Iron: That's all very f., but . . ., tout cela est bel et bon, est fort beau, F: tout ça, c'est bien joli, mais. . . . 4. Beau. When the weather is f., quand il fait beau. One of these f. days, un de ces beaux jours; un de ces quatre matins. 5. (a) (Of texture) Fin; (of dust) menu, subtil. To chop (meat) f., hacher menu. (b) Effilé; (of writing, thread) délié, mince. F. edge, tranchant affilé, aigu. F. nib, plume pointue. Not to put too f. a point on it . . ., pour parler franc, carrément. . . . 6. F: To cut it f., to run it f., faire qch. tout juste; réussir tout juste; arriver de justesse. It's no good cutting prices too f., il ne sert à rien de trop baisser les prix. Sp: To train a horse too f., pousser trop loin l'entraînement d'un cheval. -ly, adv. 1. Finement. (a) Habilement; on ne peut mieux. (b) Délicatement, subtilement. (c) F. powdered, finement pulvérisé. F. chopped, haché menu. 2. Admirablement, magnifiquement. 'fine-'drawn, a. 1. (a) Needlew: F.-d. seam, rentraiture f. (b) (Of wire) Finement étiré; (of thread) délié, ténu. 2. F.-d. arguments, arguments subtils. 'fine-'spun, a. Tex: Fil ténu, délié.
fineness ['fainnis], s. 1. Titre m, aloi m (de l'or). 2. Qualité supérieure, excellence f (d'un article). 3. Splendeur f, élégance f (d'un costume). 4. Finesse f (d'une étoffe); ténuité f (d'un fil); délicatesse f (des sentiments).
finery ['fainəri], s. Iron: Parure f; fanfreluches fpl. Decked out in all her f., parée de ses plus beaux atours.

finesse¹ [fi'nes], s. Finesse f, finasserie f.
finesse². 1. v.i. (a) Finasser. (b) Cards: Faire une impasse. 2. v.tr. Cards: To f. the queen, faire une impasse à la dame.
finger¹ ['fiŋgər], s. 1. Doigt m (de la main). First f., index m. Middle f., second f., médius m, doigt du milieu. Third f., ring f., annulaire m. Little f., petit doigt; auriculaire m. I forbid you to lay a f. on him, je vous défends de le toucher. To lay, put, one's f. on the cause of the evil, mettre le doigt sur la source du mal. He wouldn't lift a f. to help you, il ne remuerait pas le petit doigt pour vous aider. To point the f. of scorn at s.o., montrer qn au doigt. He has a f. in every pie, il est mêlé à tout. Let's keep our fingers crossed = touchons du bois. He is a Frenchman to the f. tips, il est Français jusqu'au bout des ongles. He has the whole business at his fingers' ends, at his f. tips, il est au courant de toute l'affaire. 2. Mec.E: Doigt (de guidage). 'finger-board, s. Mus: (a) Touche f (de violon). (b) Clavier m (de piano). 'finger-bowl, s. Rince-doigts m inv. 'finger-hold, s. Prise f pour les doigts. 'finger-marks, s. Traces f de mains sales. 'finger-nail, s. Ongle m (de la main). 'finger-plate, s. Plaque f de propreté (d'une porte). 'finger-print, s. Adm: Empreinte digitale. F.-p. identification, dactyloscopie f. 'finger-stall, s. Med: Doigtier m.
finger², v.tr. 1. Manier, tâter, palper, F: tripoter (qch.); feuilleter (des papiers). F: To f. s.o.'s money, palper l'argent de qn. 2. Mus: Doigter (un morceau). fingering, s. 1. (a) Maniement m. (b) Palpation f. 2. Mus: Doigté m.
finial ['finiəl], s. Arch: Fleuron m (de faîte), épi m.
finical ['finik(ə)l], finicking ['finikiŋ], finicky ['finiki], a. Méticuleux, vétilleux; (of pers.) fignoleur, -euse.
finis ['finis], s. (At end of book, story) Fin f.
finish¹ ['finiʃ], s. 1. Fin f. Sp: Arrivée f (d'une course), finish m. To fight (it out) to a f., se battre jusqu'à une décision. To be in at the f., (i) Sp: Turf: assister à l'arrivée; (ii) voir la fin de l'aventure. 2. (a) Fini m, achevé m (d'un travail); finesse f de l'exécution (d'un travail). (b) Apprêt m (d'un drap).
finish². 1. v.tr. Finir; terminer, achever. To f. doing sth., achever, finir, de faire qch. To f. off a piece of work, mettre la dernière main à un travail. To f. off a wounded beast, achever une bête blessée. He's finished! Il est fini; F: il est flambé! F. up your soup! finis ta soupe! 2. v.i. Cesser, se terminer. His engagement finishes this week, son engagement prend fin cette semaine. Tp: etc: Have you finished? terminé? (b) To f. in a point, se terminer, finir, en pointe. (c) He finished by calling me a liar, il finit par me traiter de menteur. (d) I have finished with it, je n'en ai plus besoin. F: I'm finished with it, j'en ai marre, je ne m'en occupe plus. F: I've finished with you! tout est fini entre nous! (e) F: Wait till I've finished with him! attendez que je lui aie réglé son compte! (f) To f. fourth, finir, arriver, quatrième (dans une course). finished, a. 1. (Article) fini, apprêté. 2. (Of appearance) Soigné, parfait. A f. speaker, un parfait orateur; un orateur accompli. A f. portrait, un portrait achevé. finishing, s. 1. (a) Achèvement m. (b) Tchn: Finissage m (d'un article de commerce); apprêtage m (des tissus). 2. Sp: F. line, ligne f d'arrivée. 'finishing-school, s. École f où l'on parachève l'éducation des jeunes filles (croit-on).
finisher ['finiʃər], s. Ind: Finisseur, -euse. Dressm: Retoucheuse f.
finite ['fainait], a. (a) Fini, limité, borné. (b) Gram: F. mood, mode fini. F. verb, verbe à un mode fini.
Finland ['finlənd]. Pr.n. Geog: La Finlande.
Finn [fin], s. Finlandais, -aise; Finnois, -oise.
finnan ['finən], s. F. (haddock), (variété de) haddock m.
finned [find], a. 1. Ich: A nageoires. 2. Tchn: A ailettes.
Finnish ['finiʃ]. 1. a. Finlandais. 2. s. Ling: Le finnois.
fiord [fjɔ:d], s. Geog: Fiord m, fjord m.
fir [fə:r], s. 1. F.(-tree), sapin m. Silver f., sapin blanc, argenté. Scotch f., pin m sylvestre; pin d'Écosse; sapin du nord. F. plantation, sapinière f. 2. (Bois m de) sapin. 'fir-cone, s. Pomme f, cône m, de pin; pigne f.

fire[1] ['faiər], s. **1.** Feu m. (a) **To light, make, a f.,** faire du feu. **To lay a f.,** préparer le feu. **To make up the f.,** arranger le feu. **To cook sth. on a slow f.,** faire cuire qch. à petit feu, à feu doux. (*Of cooking utensils, etc.*) **To stand the f.,** aller au feu F: **To keep the f. warm,** garder le coin du feu. **Before a roaring f.,** devant une belle flambée. **Open f.,** feu dans la cheminée, feu nu. **Electric f.,** radiateur m électrique. (b) Incendie m, sinistre m. **We have had a f.,** le feu s'est mis chez nous; nous avons eu un incendie. **F.!** au feu! **To catch f.,** prendre feu; s'enflammer. **Her dress caught f.,** le feu a pris à sa robe. **To set f. to sth., to set sth. on f.,** mettre le feu à qch. **On f.,** en feu, en flammes. **A chimney on f.,** un feu de cheminée. F: **To get on like a house on f.,** avancer à pas de géant. **To add fuel to the f.,** jeter de l'huile sur le feu. **There's no smoke without f.,** il n'y a pas de fumée sans feu. (c) **Greek f.,** feu grégeois. (d) Lumière f, éclat m. **The f. of a diamond,** les feux d'un diamant. *Nau:* **St Elmo's f.,** feu de Saint-Elme. **2.** Ardeur f, fougue f. **The f. of youth,** l'enthousiasme m de la jeunesse. **3.** *Mil:* Feu, tir m; coups mpl de feu. **To open f.,** ouvrir le feu. **Individual f.,** tir à volonté. **Rapid f. of questions,** feu roulant de questions. **To set f. to sth.,** essuyer le feu. **To be steady under f.,** être ferme au feu. **To be between two fires,** être pris entre deux feux. '**fire-alarm,** s. (Appareil) avertisseur m d'incendie. '**fire-arm,** s. Arme f à feu. '**fire-ball,** s. *Meteor:* (a) Bolide m. (b) Globe m de feu. '**fire-bar,** s. Barreau m de grille (de foyer). '**fire-basket,** s. Brasier m, braséro m. '**fire-belt,** s. Pare-feu m inv. (dans une forêt). '**fire-box,** s. Foyer m, boîte f à feu (d'une locomotive). '**fire-brand,** s. **1.** Tison m, brandon m. **2.** (*Pers.*). Brandon de discorde; boutefeu m. '**fire-brick,** s. Brique f réfractaire. '**fire-brigade,** s. (Corps m de) sapeurs-pompiers mpl; F: les pompiers. '**fire-bucket,** s. Seau m à incendie. '**fire-clay,** s. Argile f réfractaire. '**fire-control,** s. *Navy:* Direction f du tir. '**fire-damp,** s. *Min:* Grisou m; méthane m. '**fire-department,** s. *U.S:* = FIRE BRIGADE. '**fire-dog,** s. *Furn:* Chenet m; (*large*) landier m. '**fire-door,** s. (a) Porte de foyer. (b) Porte coupe-feu. '**fire-drill,** s. Exercises mpl de sauvetage. '**fire-eater,** s. **1.** (Saltimbanque) avaleur m de feu. **2.** Tranche-montagne m, matamore m. '**fire-engine,** s. Pompe f à incendie. '**fire-escape,** s. (a) Échelle f de sauvetage. (b) Escalier m de secours. '**fire-extinguisher,** s. Extincteur m d'incendie. '**fire-fighter,** s. Pompier m. '**fire-fighting,** s. Précautions fpl contre l'incendie; service m d'incendie. '**fire-float,** s. Ponton m d'incendie. '**fire-fly,** s. *Ent:* Luciole f; F: mouche f à feu. '**fire-guard,** s. **1.** Pare-étincelles m inv; garde-feu m inv. **2.** (*Pers.*) *U.S:* Guetteur m. '**fire-hose,** s. Tuyau m, manche f d'incendie. '**fire-hydrant,** s. Bouche f d'incendie; *Fr.C:* borne-fontaine f. '**fire-insurance,** s. Assurance f (contre l')incendie. '**fire-iron,** s. **1.** Ringard m (de fourneau). **2.** pl. **Fire-irons,** garniture f de foyer. '**fire-lighter,** s. Allume-feu m inv. '**fire-line,** s. *For:* Tranchée f garde-feu. '**fire-place,** s. Cheminée f, foyer m. '**fire-plug,** s. Prise f d'eau; bouche f d'incendie. '**fire-proof,** a. (a) Incombustible, ignifuge. **F.-p. door,** porte à revêtement calorifuge. **To make a door f.-p.,** ignifuger une porte. (b) *Cer:* Réfractaire. **F.-p. dish,** plat allant au feu. '**fire-proof,** v.tr. Ignifuger (un tissu). '**fire-quarters,** s.pl. *Nau:* Postes m d'incendie. '**fire-raiser,** s. Incendiaire mf. '**fire-raising,** s. *Jur:* Incendie m volontaire, par malveillance. '**fire-ranger,** s. (*In Canada*) Guetteur m. '**fire-resisting,** a. **1.** Ignifuge. **2.** *Cer:* Réfractaire. '**fire-screen,** s. (a) Devant m de cheminée. (b) Écran m ignifuge. '**fire-station,** s. Poste m d'incendie, caserne f de (sapeurs-) pompiers. '**fire-watcher,** s. Guetteur m. '**fire-wall,** s. Cloison m pare-feu.

fire[2], v. I. v.tr. **1.** (a) Mettre le feu à, incendier (une maison, etc.). (b) Enthousiasmer, F: emballer (qn); enflammer (les passions). **2.** Cuire (de la poterie). **3.** *Mch:* etc: Chauffer (une locomotive); allumer (une chaudière). **4.** (a) **To f. a mine,** faire jouer la mine. *I.C.E:* **To f. the mixture,** enflammer le mélange (gazeux). (b) **To f. a torpedo,** lancer une torpille. (c) *Abs.* **To f. at, on, s.o.,** tirer sur qn. **To f. a gun at s.o.,** lâcher un coup de fusil à qn. **To f. a question at s.o.,** poser à qn une question à brûle-pourpoint. **To f. (off) a gun,** tirer un canon; faire feu d'une pièce. (*With passive force*) **Guns were firing,** on tirait le canon. **Without firing a shot,** sans un coup de fusil. **5.** F: *Esp. U.S:* Renvoyer, F: flanquer à la porte (un employé, etc.). II. **fire,** v.i. (a) (*Of shot*) Partir. (b) *I.C.E:* (*Of mixture*) Exploser. **The engine fires evenly,** le moteur tourne régulièrement. **Engine firing badly,** moteur qui donne mal. **fire away,** v.tr. **1.** Gaspiller (ses munitions). **2.** *Abs.* F: **F. away!** allez-y! allez, racontez! **fire off,** v.tr. Tirer, faire partir (un coup de fusil). **fire up.** **1.** v.i. F: (*Of pers.*) S'emporter, F: monter comme une soupe au lait. **2.** v.tr. *Mch:* etc: (a) Allumer (une chaudière). (b) *Abs.* Activer la chauffe. **firing,** s. **1.** *Brickm: Cer:* Cuite f, cuisson f. **2.** Chauffage m, chauffe f (d'un four, d'une locomotive). **3.** (a) *Min:* Allumage m (d'un coup de mine). (b) *I.C.E:* Allumage. (c) *Mil:* etc: Tir m, feu m. *Artil:* Barrage f, tir de barrage. **F. party, squad,** peloton m d'exécution. **4.** Combustible m. '**firing-pin,** s. Percuteur m (de mitrailleuse); aiguille f (de fusil).

fireboat ['faiəbout], s. **1.** Bateau-pompe m, pl. bateaux-pompes.

firelight ['faiəlait], s. **By, in, the f.,** à la lumière du feu.

firelock ['faiələk], s. *Sm.a: A:* Fusil m à pierre.

fireman, pl. -men ['faiəmən], s.m. **1.** Chauffeur (d'une machine à vapeur). **2.** (Sapeur-)pompier.

fireside ['faiəsaid], s. **1.** Foyer m; coin m du feu. **F. chair,** coin-de-feu m, chauffeuse f.

firewood ['faiəwud], s. Bois de chauffage. **Bundle of f.,** fagotin m, margotin m.

firework ['faiəwə:k], s. **1.** Pièce f d'artifice. **2.** pl. **Fireworks,** feu m d'artifice.

firkin ['fə:kin], s. **1.** Tonnelet m, barillet m.

firm[1] [fə:m], s. *Com:* **1.** Raison sociale; firme f. **2.** Maison f (de commerce). **Name, style, of the f.,** raison sociale.

firm[2], a. Ferme. **1.** (*Of substance*) Consistant, compact; (*of post, nail*) solide, fixe; (*of touch*) vigoureux, assuré. **As f. as a rock,** inébranlable. **To rule with a f. hand,** gouverner d'une main ferme. **2.** (*Of friendship, etc.*) Constant; (*of intention*) résolu, déterminé; (*of character*) décidé, résolu. **F. chin,** menton qui dénote la fermeté. **To be f. as to sth.,** tenir bon sur qch. **To have a firm belief that . . .,** être fermement convaincu que. . . . **3.** *Com: Fin:* (*Of offer, sale*) Ferme. *St.Exch:* **These shares remain firm at . . .,** Ces actions f se maintiennent à . . . **4.** adv. **To stand f.,** tenir bon, tenir ferme. **-ly,** adv. **1.** Fermement, solidement. **To hold the reins f.,** tenir les rênes d'une main ferme. **2.** D'un ton ferme.

firmament ['fə:məmənt], s. Firmament m.

firmness ['fə:mnis], s. Fermeté f; solidité f.

first [fə:st]. I. a. **1.** Premier. (a) **The f. of April,** le premier avril. **The f. two acts,** les deux premiers actes. **To live on the f. floor,** (i) demeurer au premier (étage); (ii) *U.S:* demeurer au rez-de-chaussée. **Charles the F.,** Charles Premier. **The f. comers,** les premiers venus. **At f. sight,** de prime abord; au premier abord. **In the f. place,** d'abord; en premier lieu. **To succeed the very f. time,** réussir du premier coup. **To wear a new dress for the f. time,** étrenner une robe. **To fall head f.,** tomber la tête la première. **To come out f.,** être reçu premier (dans un examen). **I'll do it f. thing,** je vais m'y mettre tout de suite. **I'll do it to-morrow f. thing,** demain, je le ferai dès demain matin. *Th:* **F. night,** première f. *Typ:* **F. edition,** édition princeps; édition originale. *Aut:* **F. (gear),** première (vitesse). *S.a.* FORM[1] 5. (b) (*In importance, rank*) *Rail:* etc: **To travel f. (class),** voyager en première (classe). **F. Lord of the Admiralty** = Ministre m de la Marine. *U.S: Army:* **F. lieutenant,** lieutenant m. *U.S:* **F. lady,** femme du Président. **To put f. things f.,** mettre en avant les choses essentielles; commencer par le plus pressé. (c) **To have news at f. hand,** tenir une nouvelle de première main. **2. Twenty-f.,** vingt et unième. **Seventy-f.,** soixante et onzième. **-ly,** adv. Premièrement; en premier lieu. II. **first,** s. **1.** (Le) premier, (la) première. **He was among the very f.,** il est arrivé dans les tout premiers. **To come in an**

easy f., arriver bon premier. *Sch:* **To get a f.** = avoir une mention bien. **2.** Commencement *m*. **From f. to last**, depuis le début jusqu'à la fin. **From the f.**, dès le premier jour. **At f.**, au commencement; d'abord. **III. first**, *adv.* **1.** Premièrement, au commencement, d'abord. **F. of all, f. and foremost**, pour commencer; en premier lieu. *U.S:* **F. off**, de prime abord. **First and last**, en tout et pour tout. **To say f. one thing and then another**, *F:* dire tantôt blanc tantôt noir. **2.** Pour la première fois. **When I f. saw him**, la première fois que je l'ai vu. **When did you f. see him?** quand l'avez-vous vu pour la première fois? **3.** Plutôt. **I'd die f.**, plutôt mourir. **4. He arrived f.**, il arriva le premier. **You go f.!** allez devant! **F. come f. served**, premier arrivé, premier servi. **Ladies f.!** place aux dames! **Women and children f.!** les femmes et les enfants d'abord! '**first-'aid**, *s.* Premiers secours; soins *mpl* d'urgence. **F.-a. kit, outfit**, trousse *f* de première urgence. **F.-a. station, post**, poste de (premiers) secours. **Hints on f.-a.**, notions de secourisme. '**first-born**, *a. & s.* (Enfant) premier-né, *pl.* premiers-nés. '**first-class**, *a.* (Wagon) de première classe; (marchandises) de première qualité, de (premier) choix, *F:* extra *a. inv;* (hôtel) de premier ordre. **F.-c. dinner**, excellent dîner. **F.-c. player**, joueur de premier ordre, de première force. *Post: U.S:* **F.-c. mail**, lettre close; paquet clos. '**first-'hand**, *a.* (Nouvelle) de première main. '**first-'rate**, *a.* Excellent; de première classe, *F:* extra *a.inv.* **Of f.-r. quality**, de toute première qualité. **F.-r. dinner**, dîner soigné. **F.-r. idea**, fameuse idée. **He is a f.-r. man**, c'est un homme supérieur. *adv. F:* **It is going f.-r.**, ça marche à merveille. '**first-'rater**, *s. F:* As *m*.

firth [fə:θ], *s.* (*Scot.*) Estuaire *m*.

fiscal ['fisk(ə)l]. **1.** *a.* Fiscal, -aux. **F. year** (année d')exercice. **2.** *s. Scot:* = PROCURATOR-FISCAL.

fish¹, *pl.* **fishes**, *coll.* **fish** [fiʃ, -iz], *s.* **1.** Poisson *m*. **Fresh-water f.**, poisson d'eau douce. **Saltwater f.**, poisson de mer. **He is like a f. out of water**, il n'est pas dans son élément. **All is f. that comes to his net**, tout lui est bon. **I've other f. to fry**, j'ai d'autres chats à fouetter. *F:* **To feed the fishes**, (i) se noyer; (ii) avoir le mal de mer, *F:* donner à manger aux poissons. **Neither f., flesh nor fowl**, ni chair ni poisson. *F:* **He's a queer f.**, c'est un drôle de bonhomme, c'est un type à part. **2.** *Astr:* **The Fish(es)**, les Poissons. '**fish-ball**, *s. Cu:* Boulette *f* de poisson. '**fish-basket**, *s.* **1.** Panier *m* de pêche. **2.** Bourriche *f* à poissons. '**fish-bone**, *s.* Arête *f* (de poisson). '**fish-cake**, *s.* Croquette *f* de poisson. '**fish-eating**, *a.* Ichtyophage. '**fish-glue**, *s.* Colle *f* de poisson. '**fish-farm**, *s.* Établissement *m* piscicole. '**fish-farming**, *s.* Pisciculture *f*. '**fish-hawk**, *s.* Orfraie *f*. '**fish-hook**, *s.* Hameçon *m*. '**fish-kettle**, *s. Cu:* Poissonnière *f*. '**fish-market**, *s.* Marché *m* au poisson. '**fish-shop**, *s.* poissonnerie *f*. '**fish-slice**, *s.* Truelle *f* à poisson. '**fish-spear**, *s.* Foëne *f*, trident *m*. '**fish-train**, *s.* Train *m* de marée.

fish². **1.** *v.i.* Pêcher. **To f. for trout**, pêcher la truite. **To go fishing**, aller à la pêche. **To f. for compliments**, quêter, chercher, des compliments. **2.** *v.tr.* (a) **To f. up a dead body**, (re)pêcher un cadavre. (b) **To f. a river**, pêcher une rivière. *Abs.* **Don't f.**, trop de modestie! **fishing**, *s.* La pêche. **Trout-f.**, la pêche à la truite. **Deep-sea f.**, la grande pêche. **Pearl-f.**, la pêche des perles. **Underwater f.**, chasse, pêche, sous-marine. *P.N:* '**Private f.**,' "pêche réservée." '**fishing-boat**, *s.* Bateau *m* de pêche. '**fishing-ground**, *s.* Pêcherie *f*, lieu *m* de pêche. '**fishing-line**, *s.* Ligne *f* (de pêche). '**fishing-net**, *s.* Filet *m* de pêche. '**fishing-rod**, *s.* Canne *f* à pêche. '**fishing-smack**, *s.* Barque *f* de pêche. '**fishing-tackle**, *s.* Attirail *m* de pêche.

fish³, *pl.* **fishes**, *s. Rail: Const:* Éclisse *f*. '**fish-plate**, *s. Rail:* Éclisse *f*.

fisherman, *pl.* **-men** ['fiʃəmən], *s.m.* Pêcheur. '**fisher-man-'knit**, *a.* Fisherman-knit jersey, tricot *m* sport.

fishery ['fiʃəri], *s.* **1.** Pêche *f*. **Cod, whale, f.**, pêche à la morue, à la baleine. **Coral f.**, la pêche du corail. **High-sea(s) f.**, la grande pêche. **F.-protection vessel, garde-pêche** *m inv.* **2.** (*Fishing-ground*) Pêcherie *f*.

fishmonger ['fiʃmʌŋgər], *s.* Marchand *m* de poisson.

fishpond ['fiʃpɔnd], *s.* Vivier *m*.

fishwife, *pl.* **-wives** ['fiʃwaif, -waivz], *s.f.* Marchande de poisson; *F:* poissarde. **She swears like a f.**, elle jure comme un charretier.

fishy ['fiʃi], *a.* **1.** (Odeur, goût) de poisson. *F:* **F. eyes**, yeux ternes, vitreux. **2.** *F:* Véreux, -euse; louche. **It looks, sounds, f.**, ce n'est pas catholique.

fissile ['fisail], *a.* Fissile, lamellé.

fission ['fiʃ(ə)n], *s.* **1.** *Biol:* Fissiparité *f*. **2.** *Ph:* Fission *f*, division *f*. **Nuclear f.**, fission nucléaire.

fissiparous [fi'sipərəs], *a. Biol:* Fissipare.

fissure¹ ['fiʃər], *s.* Fissure *f*, fente *f*, crevasse *f*.

fissure². **1.** *v.tr.* Fissurer, fendre. **2.** *v.i.* (*Of rock*) Se fissurer, se crevasser.

fist [fist], *s.* Poing *m*. **To fight with one's fists**, se battre à coups de poing. **To shake one's f. at s.o.**, menacer qn du poing.

fistful ['fistful], *s.* Poignée *f* (d'argent, etc.).

fisticuffs ['fistikʌfs], *s.pl.* Coups *m* de poing. **To resort to f.**, se battre à coups de poing.

fistula ['fistjulə], *s. Med:* Fistule *f*.

fit¹ [fit], *s.* **1.** (a) Accès *m*, attaque *f* (de fièvre, etc.). **F. of madness**, accès de folie. **F. of coughing**, quinte *f* de toux. (b) **Fainting f.**, évanouissement *m*, syncope *f*. **To fall into a f.**, tomber en convulsions. *F:* **He will have a f. when he knows**, cela lui donnera un coup de sang quand il le saura. **To frighten s.o. into fits**, effrayer qn à lui donner des convulsions. **2.** Accès, mouvement *m* (de mauvaise humeur). **To answer in a f. of temper**, répondre sous le coup de la colère. **F. of crying**, crise *f* de larmes. **To be in fits of laughter**, avoir le fou rire. **To have sudden fits of energy**, avoir des élans d'énergie. **To work by fits and starts**, travailler par accès, par à-coups.

fit², *a.* (**fitter; fittest**) **1.** Bon, propre, convenable (for sth., à qch.). **F. to** + *inf.*, bon à, propre à + *inf.* **F. to drink**, buvable, potable. **F. to wear**, mettable. **I am not f. to be seen**, je ne suis pas présentable. **At a fitter moment**, à un moment plus opportun. **To think f.**, see f., to do sth., juger convenable, trouver bon. de faire qch. **Do as you think f.**, faites comme bon vous semblera. **She cried f. to break her heart**, elle pleurait à gros sanglots. **2.** (a) Capable. **F. for sth.**, en état de faire qch.; apte à qch. *Mil:* **F. for service**, bon pour le service. **To be f. for one's job**, être à la hauteur de sa tâche. **He is not f. to live**, il n'est pas digne de vivre. **He is f. for nothing**, il n'est propre à rien; c'est un propre à rien. (b) *F:* Disposé, prêt (à faire qch.). **I felt f. to drop**, je n'en pouvais plus. **3.** *Med: Sp:* **To be (bodily) f.**, être en bonne santé; être dispos. **To keep f.**, se maintenir en forme, s'entretenir. **To be as f. as a fiddle**, être en parfaite santé. **-ly**, *adv.* Convenablement.

fit³, *s.* (a) Ajustement *m*. **Your coat is a perfect f.**, votre pardessus est juste à votre taille. **My dress is a tight f.**, ma robe est très juste, un peu serrée. (*Of people in a room, etc.*). **It was a tight f.**, on tenait tout juste. (b) *Mec.E:* Ajustage *m* (d'un assemblage); frottement *m* (d'organes mobiles). **Easy f.**, frottement doux. **Tight f.**, ajustage serré.

fit⁴, *v.* (**fitted**) **I.** *v.tr.* **1.** (*Of clothes, etc.*) Aller à (qn); être à la taille de (qn). **Key that fits the lock**, clef qui va à la serrure. **Shoes that f. well**, souliers qui chaussent bien. **It fits you like a glove**, cela vous va comme un gant. **2.** (a) Adapter, ajuster, accommoder (sth. to sth., qch à qch.). **To make the punishment f. the crime**, proportionner le châtiment à la faute. **To f. a garment on s.o.**, ajuster un vêtement à qn. **To f. a handle to a broom**, emmancher un balai. **To f. the key in the lock**, engager la clef dans la serrure. (b) **To f. parts (together)**, monter, assembler, des pièces. **To f. sth. together**, préparer qch à qch. **4. To f. sth. with sth.**, garnir, munir, qch. de qch. **Fitted with two propellers**, pourvu de deux hélices. **II. fit**, *v.i.* (a) **To f. (together)**, s'ajuster, s'adapter, se raccorder. **To f. on sth.**, s'adapter sur qch. **To f. into sth.**, s'emboîter, s'enclaver, dans qch. (b) Frottement doux. **Your dress fits well**, votre robe (vous) va bien. **fit in. 1.** *v.tr.* (a) Emboîter (des tubes). (b) Faire concorder (des témoignages). **2.** *v.i.* (a) **To f. in between two things**, s'emboîter entre deux choses. (b) **To f. in with sth.**, être en harmonie avec qch. **Your plans do not f. in with mine**, vos projets ne cadrent pas avec les miens. **fit out,** *v.tr.* Équiper **(sth. with sth.,** qch. de qch.); garnir (un coffret); outiller (une usine); *Nau:* armer (un navire). **To f. s.o. out, (with clothing,** etc.), équiper qn. **' fit-out,** *s.* (*a*) Trousseau *m.* (*b*) Équipement *m.* **fit up,** *v.tr.* Monter (une machine, etc.). **fitted,** *a.* **1.** Ajusté, monté. F. carpet, tapis cloué, ajusté. **F. overcoat,** pardessus à taille. (*Of case, chest*) F. (up), garni. **2. He is f. for the post,** il est apte à occuper le poste. **fitting¹,** *a.* **1.** Convenable, bienséant; approprié **(to,** à). **F. remark,** remarque à propos. **2. Well-f. garment,** vêtement qui va bien. **-ly,** *adv.* Convenablement; à propos. **fitting²,** *s.* **1.** (*a*) Ajustage *m* (d'une pièce). F. **(up, together) of a machine,** montage *m* d'une machine. **F. on of a tyre,** montage d'un pneu. (*b*) **F. (on) (of clothes),** essayage *m*, ajustage (de vêtements). **F. room,** salon d'essayage. **2.** *Usu. pl.* Agencements *m,* installations *f* (d'un atelier); équipement *m;* garniture *f* (d'une chambre); appareillage *m* (pour lumière électrique). **Metal fittings,** ferrures *f.* **Brass fittings,** garnitures en cuivre.

fitful ['fitful], *a.* Irrégulier, capricieux; d'humeur changeante. **F. cough,** toux quinteuse. **-fully,** *adv.* Irrégulièrement; par à-coups.

fitness ['fitnis], *s.* **1.** Aptitude *f* **(for,** à, pour). *Aut:* **F. to drive,** aptitude à conduire. **2.** (*a*) A-propos *m,* justesse *f* (d'une remarque). (*b*) Convenance *f,* bienséance *f.* **3. Physical f.,** bon état *m* physique, bonne forme.

fitter ['fitər], *s.* **1.** *Mec.E:* *Aut:* Ajusteur *m,* monteur *m;* installateur *m.* **2.** *Tail:* Essayeur, -euse.

five [faiv], *num. a. & s.* Cinq (*m*). **A f.-pound note,** un billet de cinq livres. **F.-Year Plan,** Plan quinquennal. **F.-year period,** quinquennat *m.* (*For other phrases see* EIGHT.)

fivefold ['faivfould]. **1.** *a.* Quintuple. **2.** *adv.* Cinq fois autant; au quintuple.

fiver ['faivər], *s.* F: Billet *m* de cinq livres, *U.S:* de cinq dollars.

fives [faivz], *s. Games:* = Balle *f* au mur.

fix¹ [fiks], *s.* F: **1.** Embarras *m,* difficulté *f,* mauvais pas. **To be in a f.,** être dans une situation embarrassante; se trouver dans une impasse; être dans le pétrin. **To get into a f.,** se mettre dans le pétrin. **2.** *Nau: Av:* Position *f,* relèvement *m.*

fix², *v.tr.* Fixer. **1.** Caler, monter (une poulie, etc.); assujettir (une poutre); ancrer (un tirant); arrêter, assurer (une planche). **To f. a stake into the ground,** ficher un pieu en terre. **To f. sth. in one's memory,** se graver qch. dans la mémoire. **To f. one's eye(s) on s.o.,** fixer qn (du regard). **2.** (*a*) *Phot: etc:* Fixer (une épreuve, etc.). (*b*) *Med:* Stériliser (une préparation microscopique). **3.** Établir. **To f. a camp,** établir un camp. **4.** (*a*) Fixer (une limite, un jour, etc.). **On the date fixed,** à la date prescrite. **There is nothing fixed yet,** il n'y a encore rien de décidé. (*b*) **To f. (up)on sth.,** se décider pour qch. **5.** F: (*a*) Mettre (qn) dans l'impossibilité de nuire. **I've fixed him!** il a son compte! **I'll f. him yet,** je l'aurai au tournant. (*b*) Graisser la patte à (qn). **6.** (*a*) F: Réparer (qch.). (*b*) *U.S:* Préparer (un repas, etc.). **fix up,** *v.tr.* F: **1.** Placer, mettre, installer (qch.). **2.** Arranger, régler, conclure (une affaire). **I've fixed it up,** j'ai conclu l'affaire. **It is all fixed up,** c'est une affaire réglée. **3. To f. s.o. up with sth.,** pourvoir qn de qch. **I'll f. you up for the night,** je vous hébergerai pour la nuit. **fixed,** *a.* Fixe, arrêté. **1.** (Vitrage, etc.) dormant. F. **wheel,** roue calée. *Ind:* F. **plant,** matériel fixe. **2.** (*a*) Lever arm of f. length, bras de levier de longueur constante. *Com:* F. **prices,** prix fixes. F. **rule,** règle établie. **F. idea,** idée fixe. F. **smile,** sourire figé. (*b*) F. **point,** point fixe. *Astr:* F. **star,** étoile fixe. F. **assets,** immobilisations *f.* **3.** (*a*) *U.S:* **To be well f.,** avoir ce qu'il faut. (*b*) **How are we f. for time?** de combien de temps disposons-nous? **fixing,** *s.* **1.** Fixage *m,* pose *f* (de rails); fixage (d'une épreuve photographique); ancrage *m* (de crampons). **2.** *pl.* *U.S:* **Fixings,** garniture *f* (d'un plat). **'fixing-bath,** *s. Phot:* Bain *m* de fixage.

fixation [fiks'eiʃ(ə)n], *s.* Fixation *f.*

fixative ['fiksətiv], *s. Art: Toil:* Fixatif *m.*

fixedly ['fiksidli], *adv.* Fixement.

fixer ['fiksər], *s. Phot:* Bain *m* de fixage.

fixity ['fiksiti], *s.* Fixité *f.* **F. of purpose,** détermination *f.*

fixture ['fikstʃər], *s.* **1.** Appareil *m* fixe; partie *f* fixe (d'une machine, etc.); meuble *m* à demeure. **To make sth. a f.,** ancrer qch. en place. **2.** *Usu. pl.* Choses fixées à demeure; agencements *m* inamovibles. **3.** *Sp:* Engagement *m;* match (prévu). **List of fixtures,** programme *m*

fizz¹ [fiz], *s* **1.** Pétillement *m* (du champagne, etc.); crachement *m,* sifflement *m* (de la vapeur). **2.** *P: O:* Champagne *m.*

fizz², *v.i.* (*Of champagne, etc.*) Pétiller; (*of escape of steam*) fuser, siffler.

fizzle¹ ['fizl], *s.* Pétillement *m* (du champagne, etc.); sifflement *m;* grésillement *m* (de la graisse bouillante).

fizzle², *v.i.* (*Of wine, etc.*) Pétiller; (*of gas-burner*) siffler; (*of boiling fat*) grésiller. **fizzle out,** *v.i.* F: (*Of affair, etc.*) Avorter; faire fiasco; s'en aller en eau de boudin.

fizzy ['fizi], *a.* (*Of mineral water, etc.*) Gazeux, effervescent; (*of wine*) mousseux.

fjord [fjɔːd], *s.* Fiord *m,* fjord *m.*

flabbergast ['flæbəgɑːst], *v.tr.* F: Épater, abasourdir, ahurir (qn). **I was flabbergasted,** j'en suis resté éberlué, F: assis, baba. **flabbergasting,** *a.* Ahurissant, abasourdissant.

flabbiness ['flæbinis], *s.* Flaccidité *f,* manque *m* de fermeté (de la chair, etc.); avachissement *m,* mollesse *f* (de caractère).

flabby ['flæbi], *a.* (*Of muscles, etc.*) Flasque; mou, *f.* molle; (*of cheeks*) pendant; (*of pers., character*) mollasse, avachi. **-ily,** *adv.* Mollement.

flaccid ['flæksid], *a.* Mou, *f.* molle; (chair) flasque.

flag¹ [flæg], *s. Bot:* Iris *m.* **Water f.,** glaïeul *m* des marais.

flag², *s. Const:* **(Paving-)f.,** carreau *m* (en pierre); dalle *f.* **'flag-layer,** *s.* Dalleur *m.*

flag³, *v.tr.* Daller, carreler (un trottoir, etc.). **flagging¹,** *s.* Carrelage *m,* dallage *m.*

flag⁴, *s.* **1.** (*a*) Drapeau *m.* *Mil:* **Headquarters f.,** fanion *m* de commandement. **F. of truce, white f.,** drapeau parlementaire. **With flags flying,** enseignes déployées. (*b*) *Nau:* Pavillon *m.* **Black f.,** pavillon noir (des pirates). **To fly a f.,** (i) battre pavillon; (ii) arborer un pavillon. **To keep the f. flying,** maintenir l'honneur de la maison, etc. **To lower one's f.,** baisser pavillon. (*c*) Flags (*for dressing a ship*), pavois *m.* **To deck a ship with flags,** pavoiser un navire. **2.** *Ven:* (*Of dog*) Queue *f* (de setter). **3.** Drapeau (de taximètre). **Taxi with the f. up,** taxi libre. **'flag-captain,** *s. Navy:* Capitaine *m* de pavillon. **'flag-day,** *s.* Jour *m* de vente d'insignes pour une œuvre de bienfaisance. **'flag-lieutenant,** *s. Navy:* Officier *m* d'ordonnance. **'flag-officer,** *s. Navy:* Officier général. **'flag-wagger,** *s.* **1.** *Mil:* F: Signaleur *m.* **2.** F: Patriotard *m,* chauvin *m.* **'flag-wagging, -waving,** *s.* F: Chauvinisme *m;* patriotisme *m* de façade.

flag⁵, *v.tr.* **1.** Pavoiser (un vaisseau). **2.** Transmettre des signaux à (qn) au moyen de fanions.

flag⁶, *v.i.* (*Of plant*) Languir; (*of pers.*) s'alanguir; (*of conversation*) se ralentir, traîner; (*of attention*) faiblir, fléchir; (*of zeal*) se relâcher. **flagging²,** *s.* Amollissement *m* (du courage); ralentissement *m* (du zèle).

flagellate ['flædʒəleit], *v.tr.* Flageller; fouetter.

flagellation [flædʒe'leiʃ(ə)n], *s.* Flagellation *f.*

flageolet¹ ['flædʒəlet, flædʒə'let], *s. Mus:* Flageolet *m.*

flageolet², *s. Hort: Cu:* (Haricot *m*) flageolet *m.*

flagon ['flægən], *s.* **1.** Flacon *m.* *Ecc:* Burette *f.* **2.** Grosse bouteille ventrue.

flagrancy ['fleigrənsi], *s.* Énormité *f* (d'un crime, etc.).

flagrant ['fleigrənt], *a.* (*Of offence*) Flagrant, énorme. **A f. case,** un cas notoire. **-ly,** *adv.* Scandaleusement; d'une manière flagrante.

flagrante delicto [flə'græntidi'liktou]. *Lt. adv. phr.* En flagrant délit.

flagship ['flægʃip], *s.* (Navire *m*) amiral *m.*

flagstaff ['flægstɑːf], *s.* **1.** (i) Mât *m* de drapeau; (ii) lance *f,* hampe *f,* de drapeau. **2.** *Nau:* (*a*) Mât de pavillon. (*b*) Gaule *f* (d'enseigne).

flagstone ['flægstoun], s. = FLAG².
flail [fleil], s. *Husb:* Fléau m.
flair ['flɛər], s. Flair m, perspicacité f. **To have a f. for bargains**, avoir du flair pour les occasions.
flak [flæk], s. Tir m contre-avions, la D.C.A.
flake¹ [fleik], s. (a) Flocon m (de neige, etc.). (b) Flammèche f. (c) Écaille f, éclat m, paillette f (de métal, etc.).
flake², v.i. (a) (*Of snow, etc.*) Tomber en flocons. (b) (*Of metal, mineral, etc.*) **To f. (away, off)**, s'écailler, se feuilleter; (*of stone*) s'épaufrer.
flaky ['fleiki], a. 1. (*Of snow, etc.*) Floconneux. 2. (*Of metal, etc.*) Écailleux, lamellé, lamelleux. **F. pastry**, pâte feuilletée; feuilleté m.
flamboyant [flæm'bɔiənt], a. Flamboyant.
flame¹ [fleim], s. 1. Flamme f. **In flames**, en flammes, en feu. **To burst, break, into flame(s)**, s'enflammer brusquement. 2. *F:* (a) Passion f, ardeur f, flamme. (b) *O:* **An old f. of mine**, une de mes anciennes amours, *F:* un de mes anciens béguins. 'flame-arrester, -trap, s. *Ind:* Pare-flamme m. 'flame-thrower, s. *Mil: Hort:* Lance-flammes m inv. 'flame-'red, a. Rouge feu inv.
flame², v.i. (*Of fire, etc.*) Flamber, jeter des flammes; *F:* (*of passions, etc.*) s'enflammer. **Her cheeks flamed**, le rouge lui monta aux joues. **flame up**, v.i. (a) S'enflammer; flamboyer. (b) *F:* (*Of pers.*) S'emporter. **flaming¹**, a. 1. (Feu) flambant, flamboyant; (maison, etc.) en flammes. 2. **F. sun**, soleil ardent, flamboyant. **F. red**, rouge feu inv. 3. *P:* Sacré. **A f. liar**, un sacré menteur. **flaming²**, s. Flamboiement m, embrasement m.
flamenco [flə'meŋkou], s. *Danc:* Flamenco f.
flamingo [flə'miŋgou], s. *Orn:* Flamant m (rose).
flan [flæn], s. *Cu:* Tarte f aux fruits.
Flanders ['flɑːndəz]. *Pr.n. Geog:* La Flandre.
flange¹ [flændʒ], s. 1. Collet m, collerette f, saillie f; bride f, bourrelet m (d'un tuyau, etc.); boudin m, rebord m (d'une roue). **F. coupling, f. joint**, joint m ou raccordement m à brides. 2. **Cooling f.**, ailette f ou nervure f de refroidissement.
flange², v.tr. *Tchn:* Brider, faire une bride à (un tube, etc.). **To f. a plate**, border une tôle. **flanged**, a. (Tube, etc.) à bride(s); (roue, etc.) à boudin, à rebord. **F. plate**, tôle à bord tombé.
flank¹ [flæŋk], s. 1. (a) Flanc m. (b) *Cu:* Flanchet m (de bœuf). 2. (a) *F:* Côté m, flanc (d'une montagne, etc.). (b) *Mil:* **To take the enemy in f.**, prendre l'ennemi de flanc.
flank², v.tr. Flanquer. 1. **To f. sth. with, by, sth.**, flanquer qch. de qch. **The accused is flanked by two policemen**, le prévenu est encadré de deux gendarmes. 2. *Mil:* Prendre (l'ennemi) de flanc.
flannel ['flænl], s. (a) Flanelle f. **Face f.** = gant de toilette; *Fr.C:* débarbouillette f. *attrib.* **F. trousers**, pantalon m de flanelle. (b) pl. **Flannels**, pantalon de flanelle. **To wear flannels**, porter un pantalon de flanelle.
flannelette [ˌflænəl'et], s. Flanelle f de coton.
flap¹ [flæp], s. 1. (a) Battement m, coup m (d'aile, etc.); clapotement m, claquement m (d'une voile). (b) Coup léger (de la main); tape f. 2. (a) Patte f, rabat m (d'une enveloppe, d'une poche, etc.); rebras m (de la jaquette d'un livre); rabat m (d'une casquette). (b) Abattant m, battant m (de table); trappe f (de cave). *Phot:* **F.-shutter**, obturateur m à volet. (c) *Av:* Volet m. 3. *F:* Affolement m. **To get into a f.**, s'agiter, s'affoler, ne plus savoir où donner de la tête. 'flap-seat, s. 1. Strapontin m. 2. Abattant m (de cuvette de W.C.). 'flap-valve, s. (Soupape f à) clapet m.
flap², v. (flapped) 1. v.tr. (a) Battre (des ailes). **To f. one's arms about**, agiter les bras. (b) Frapper (qch.) légèrement. **To f. away the flies**, chasser les mouches. 2. v.i. (*Of sail, etc.*) Battre, fouetter, claquer; (*of wings, shutter*) battre. *F:* (*Of pers.*) S'agiter sans but, s'affoler.
flapdoodle [ˌflæp'duːdl], s. *F:* Balivernes fpl; boniments mpl oiseux.
flapper ['flæpər], s. 1. Balai m tue-mouches; tapette f. 2. (a) = FLIPPER 1. (b) *Crust:* Telson m. 3. *F: O:* Gamine f, jeunesse f.

flare¹ ['flɛər], s. 1. (a) Flamboiement irrégulier; flamme vacillante. (b) Feu m (de signal). *Mil:* Artifice éclairant; fusée éclairante. *Av:* **Landing f.**, feu d'atterrissage. (c) *Phot:* **F.(-spot)**, tache f par réflexion; spectre m secondaire. 2. Évasement m, godet m (d'une jupe); pavillon m (d'un entonnoir). 'flare-path, s. *Av:* Piste balisée.
flare². 1. v.i. (a) Flamboyer, vaciller. (b) (*Of skirt*) S'évaser. 2. v.tr. Évaser (une jupe, une embrasure). **flare up**, v.i. (a) S'enflammer brusquement; lancer des flammes. (b) *F:* (*Of pers.*) S'emporter; se mettre en colère. **How easily he flares up**, c'est une soupe au lait. flare-'up, s. (a) Flambée soudaine. (b) *F:* (i) Altercation f, scène f; (ii) bagarre f.
flash¹ [flæʃ], a. *F:* 1. Fastueux, voyant. 2. (*Of money*) Contrefait, faux. 3. *O:* **F. gentry**, les filous m, les escrocs m; la haute pègre.
flash², s. 1. Éclair m; éclat m (de flamme). *El:* **F. across the terminals**, jaillissement m d'étincelles entre les bornes. *F:* **A f. in the pan**, un feu de paille. **F. of wit**, saillie f, boutade f. *Journ:* **News f.**, flash m. **In a f.**, en un rien de temps; en un clin d'œil. *Mil:* Écusson m. 3. *F:* Faste m, ostentation f; *F:* tape-à-l'œil m. 'flash-bulb, s. *Phot:* Ampoule f flash. 'flash-lamp, s. 1. Lanterne f de signalisation. 2. Lampe électrique portative; lampe de poche. 3. *Phot:* Flash m. 'flash-light, s. 1. (*Of lighthouse*) Feu m à éclats. 2. *Phot:* Éclair m de magnésium; flash m. 3. Lampe f, torche f électrique. 'flash-point, s. = FLASHING-POINT.
flash³. 1. v.i. (a) Jeter des éclairs; lancer des étincelles; flamboyer; (*of diamonds*) éclater, briller, étinceler. **His eyes flashed fire**, ses yeux jetèrent des éclairs. (b) **To f. past**, passer comme un éclair. **It flashed across my mind that . . .**, l'idée me vint tout d'un coup que. . . . 2. v.tr. (a) Faire flamboyer (un sabre, etc.); faire étinceler (ses bijoux). (b) Projeter (un rayon de lumière). **He flashed his lantern on to . . .**, il dirigea les rayons de sa lanterne sur. . . . **He flashed a glance of hatred at me**, il darda sur moi un regard chargé de haine. (c) Répandre (une nouvelle) par le télégraphe ou par la radio. **flash back**, v.i. Avoir un retour de flamme. 'flash-back, s. 1. Retour m de flamme. 2. *Cin:* Scène f rétrospective, retour m en arrière. **flashing¹**, a. Éclatant, flamboyant. *Nau:* **F. light**, feu m à éclats. **flashing²**, s. Flamboiement m (du feu); éclat m, étincellement m (d'un diamant); clignotement m (d'un signal). 'flashing-point, s. Point m d'éclair, point d'ignition (d'une huile lourde).
flashiness ['flæʃinis], s. Éclat superficiel; faux brillant.
flashy ['flæʃi], a. (*Of speech, etc.*) (D'un éclat) superficiel; d'un faux brillant; (*of dress, etc.*) voyant, éclatant, tapageur. **-ily**, adv. **F.-dressed**, à toilette tapageuse.
flask [flɑːsk], s. (a) Flacon m; fiasque f; gourde f. (b) *Ch:* (i) Fiole f. (ii) Ballon m.
flat¹ [flæt], s. Appartement m. **Service-f.**, appartement avec service compris et repas à volonté. **Block of flats**, immeuble m; maison f de rapport.
flat². I. a. Plat. 1. (a) Horizontal, -aux; posé à plat. (b) (*Of curve, etc.*) Aplati. (c) Étendu à plat. **To fall f. on one's face**, tomber, se jeter, à plat ventre. **To fall f. on one's back**, tomber sur le dos. **To lie down f. on the ground**, s'aplatir par terre. **To place sth. f. against a wall**, mettre qch. à plat contre un mur. *Aut:* **To go f. out**, filer à toute allure. (d) (*Of surface*) Plat, uni. **F. nose**, nez épaté, aplati, camus. **F. tyre**, *U.S:* **s. flat**, pneu à plat. **To beat, make, sth. f.**, aplatir qch. *Sp:* **F. racing**, le plat. *Geom:* **F. projection**, plan géométral. *F:* **As f. as a pancake**, plat comme une galette. (e) *Paint:* **F. colour**, surface mate, couleur mate. 2. *F:* Net, f. nette; positif. **F. refusal**, refus net, catégorique. *F:* **That's f.!** voilà qui est net! 3. (a) Monotone, ennuyeux, -euse; (*of style, etc.*) fade, insipide. **F. voice**, voix terne, blanche. **I was feeling a bit f.**, je me sentais déprimé, à plat. *Com:* **F. market**, marché calme, languissant. *F:* **To fall f.**, (*of joke, etc.*) rater, manquer, son effet; (*of play*) faire four. (b) (*Of drink*) Éventé, plat. 4. Invariable, uniforme. **F. rate of pay**, taux uniforme de salaires. 5. (a) (Son, etc.) sourd. (b) *Mus:* Bémol

inv. **To sing f.**, chanter faux. **-ly,** *adv. F:* Nettement, carrément. **To deny sth. f.**, nier absolument qch. **To refuse f.**, refuser carrément. **F. opposed,** en contradiction directe. II. **flat,** *adv. F:* Nettement, positivement. **I'm f. broke,** je suis sans le sou. III. **flat,** *s.* 1. Plat *m* (d'un sabre, de la main, etc.). 2. *(a)* Plaine *f;* bas-fond *m;* marécage *m. (b) Nau:* Basfond. 3. *Rail:* **Track on the f.**, voie en palier. *Rac:* **On the f.**, sur le plat. 4. *(a) Nau: =* FLAT-BOAT. *(b) Th:* Châssis *m* ou ferme *f;* paroi *f* (d'une scène). 5. *Mus:* Bémol *m.* **'flat-boat,** *s. Nau:* Bateau plat; plate *f.* **'flat-'bottom(ed),** *a.* (Bateau) à fond plat. **'flat-fish,** *s. Ich:* Poisson plat. **'flat-foot,** *s.* 1. *Med:* Pied plat. 2. *P:* Agent *m* de police, *F:* flic *m.* **'flat-'footed,** *a.* 1. A pied plat, aux pieds plats. 2. *U.S:* Franc, franche; carré, brutal. **A f.-f. refusal,** un refus catégorique. 3. *U.S:* Au pied levé. **'flatiron,** *s. Laund:* Fer *m* à repasser. **'flat-top,** *s. U.S: & Navy:* Porte-avions *m inv.*

flatlet ['flætlit], *s.* Petit appartement; studio *m.* .

flatness ['flætnis], *s.* 1. Égalité *f* (d'une surface); manque *m* de relief. *Opt:* Absence *f* de distorsion (du champ d'une lentille). 2. Aplatissement *m* (d'une courbe, etc.). 3. Netteté *f* (d'un refus). 4. *(a)* Monotonie *f* (de l'existence, etc.); engourdissement *m,* langueur *f* (du marché, etc.); platitude *f,* insipidité *f* (du style, etc.). *(b) (Of beer, etc.)* Évent *m.*

flatten ['flætn]. 1. *v.tr. (a)* **To f.** (down, out), aplatir, aplanir, laminer (qch.). **To f. oneself against a wall,** se plaquer, se coller, contre un mur. *F:* **To f.** (out) s.o., aplatir, écraser, qn. *(b) Mus·* Bémoliser (une note). *(c)* Rendre mat; amatir, amortir (une couleur). 2. *v.i. (a)* S'aplatir, s'aplanir. *(b) Av:* **To f. out,** (i) se redresser (après un vol piqué); (ii) allonger le vol. **flattening,** *s.* 1. *(a)* Aplatissement *m,* aplatissage *m* (d'une courbe, etc.); affaissement *m,* écrasement *m* (en charge). *(b)* Amortissement *m* (d'une couleur). 2. *Av:* **F. out** (after dive), ressource *f,* redressement *m.*

flatter ['flætər], *v.tr.* 1. Flatter; louanger (qn). **To f. oneself on one's cleverness, on being clever,** se flatter de son habileté, d'être habile. 2. Charmer, flatter (les yeux, l'oreille). **flattering,** *a. (Of words, portrait)* Flatteur, -euse. **-ly.** *adv.* Flatteusement.

flatterer ['flætərər], *s.* Flatteur, -euse; flagorneur, -euse.

flattery ['flætəri], *s.* Flatterie *f;* adulation *f.*

flatulence ['flætjuləns], **flatulency** ['flætjulənsi], *s.* 1. *Med:* Flatulence *f,* flatuosité *f.* 2. *(a)* Prétention *f,* vanité *f. (b)* Emphase *f.*

flatulent ['flætjulənt], *a.* 1. *Med:* Flatulent. 2. *(a)* Bouffi d'orgueil. *(b)* (Style) emphatique.

flaunt [flɔːnt]. 1. *v.i. (a) (Of flag)* Flotter (fièrement). *(b) (Of pers.)* Se pavaner, s'afficher. 2. *v.tr.* **To f. one's wealth,** faire montre, faire étalage, de sa richesse; étaler son luxe.

flautist ['flɔːtist], *s. Mus:* Flûtiste *mf.*

flavour¹ ['fleivər], *s.* Saveur *f,* goût *m;* parfum *m* (d'une glace).

flavour². *v.tr.* Assaisonner, parfumer, aromatiser. **To f. a sauce with garlic,** relever une sauce avec de l'ail. **flavouring,** *s.* 1. Assaisonnement *m* (d'un mets). 2. Assaisonnement, condiment *m.*

flavourless ['fleivəlis], *a.* Sans saveur; insipide.

flaw [flɔː], *s.* 1. Défaut *m,* défectuosité *f,* imperfection *f; (in china, etc.)* fêlure *f; (in gem)* glace *f,* crapaud *m; (in wood, etc.)* fissure *f,* fente *f; (in metal)* paille *f,* soufflure *f. (In reputation, etc.)* Flétrissure *f,* tache *f.* **F. in a scheme,** point *m* faible d'un projet. 2. *Jur: (In deed, etc.)* Vice *m* de forme (entraînant la nullité).

flawed [flɔːd], *a.* Défectueux; *(of timber)* gercé; *(of iron)* pailleux; *(of gem)* glaceux, -euse.

flawless ['flɔːlis], *a.* Sans défaut; parfait; (technique) impeccable. **-ly,** *adv.* Parfaitement.

flax [flæks], *s. Bot:* Lin *m.* **F. field,** linière *f.*

flaxen ['flæks(ə)n], *a.* 1. (Toile, etc.) de lin. 2. *(Of hair)* Blond filasse *inv.* **'flaxen-haired,** *a. (Of pers.)* Aux cheveux très blonds; blondasse.

flay [flei], *v.tr. (a)* Écorcher (un animal, etc.). **To be flayed alive,** être écorché vif. *Fig: F:* Fouetter, rosser, étriller (qn); *(of critics)* éreinter (un auteur). *(b) F: (Of shop-keeper)* Écorcher (un client). **flaying,** *s.* Écorchement *m.*

flea [fliː], *s. Ent:* Puce *f. S a.* EAR¹ 1. **'flea-bag,** *s. Mil: P:* Sac *m* de couchage; *P:* pucier *m.* **'flea-bite,** *s.* 1. Morsure *f* de puce. 2. *F:* Vétille *f,* bagatelle *f,* rien *m.* **'flea-bitten,** *a.* 1. Mordu par les puces. 2. *(Of horse's coat)* Moucheté, truité. **'flea-market,** *s. F:* Marché *m* aux puces.

fleck¹ [flek], *s.* 1. Petite tache (de lumière, de rousseur); moucheture *f* (de couleur). 2. Particule *f* (de poussière, etc.).

fleck², *v.tr.* Tacheter, moucheter **(with, de).**

fled *See* FLEE.

fledged [fledʒd], *a.* (Oiseau) qui a toutes ses plumes.

fledg(e)ling ['fledʒliŋ], *s.* 1. Oisillon *m.* 2. Béjaune *m,* novice *mf.*

flee [fliː], *v.* (**fled** [fled]; **fled**) 1. *v.i. (a) (Of pers.)* Fuir, s'enfuir, se sauver. *(b)* **Time was fleeing (away),** le temps s'écoulait vite; le temps fuyait. 2. *v.tr.* S'enfuir de (qn, la ville, etc.); fuir, éviter (la tentation, etc.). **fleeing,** *a. (Of army, etc.)* En fuite.

fleece¹ [fliːs], *s.* 1. Toison *f.* 2. *Tex:* Molleton *m.*

fleece², *v.tr. F:* Tondre, écorcher, plumer. **I have been fleeced,** je me suis fait tondre; j'ai essuyé le coup de fusil. **fleecing,** *a.* Voleur, -euse. **fleecing,** *s.* Écorchage *m.*

fleecy ['fliːsi], *a. (Of wool)* Floconneux, -euse; *(of hair, etc.)* laineux; *(of cloud)* moutonné, cotonneux, -euse. **F. lined slippers,** pantoufles doublées de fourrure.

fleet¹ [fliːt], *s.* 1. Flotte *f* (de navires). **River f.,** batellerie fluviale. **Fishing f.,** flottille *f* de pêche. 2. Parc *m* (d'autobus, de locomotives). **A f. of coaches took the tourists to their hotel,** une caravane de cars a amené les touristes à leur hôtel. **Air f.,** flotte aérienne.

fleet², *a. Lit:* **F. of foot,** léger à la course; au pied léger. **'fleet-'footed,** *a. Lit:* Au pied léger.

fleet³, *v.i. (Of time, etc.)* Passer rapidement; s'enfuir. **fleeting,** *a. (Of time)* Fugitif, fugace; *(of beauty)* passager, éphémère. *Lit:* **The f. years,** les années qui passent. **To pay s.o. a f. visit,** faire une courte visite à qn.

fleetness ['fliːtnis], *s.* Vitesse *f,* rapidité *f* (à la course).

Fleming ['flemiŋ], *s.* Flamand, -ande.

Flemish [flemiʃ]. 1. *a.* Flamand. 2. *s. Ling:* Le flamand.

flesh [fleʃ], *s.* Chair *f.* 1. *(a)* **To make s.o.'s f. creep,** donner la chair de poule à qn. **To put on f.,** *(of animal)* prendre chair; *(of pers.)* grossir; prendre de l'embonpoint. **To lose f.,** maigrir. *(b) Occ.* Viande *f. Ecc:* **To eat f.,** faire gras. *S.a.* FISH¹, HORSE-FLESH. *(c)* Chair (d'un fruit). 2. **To mortify the f.,** mortifier, châtier, son corps. **It was he in the f., in f. and blood,** c'était lui en chair et en os. **His own f. and blood,** la chair de sa chair; les siens. **It is more than f. and blood can stand,** c'est plus que la nature humaine ne saurait endurer. **To go the way of all f.,** payer sa dette à la nature. *B:* **The Word was made f.,** le Verbe s'est fait chair. **The f. is weak,** la chair est faible. **'flesh-colour,** *s.* Couleur *f* (de) chair; *Art:* carnation *f.* **'flesh-coloured,** *a.* De couleur chair. **'flesh-eating,** *a. Z:* Carnassier, -ière. **'flesh-pink,** *a.* (Teint) carné; rose incarnat *inv.* **'flesh-pots,** *s.pl. B:* La bonne chère. **To sigh for the flesh-pots of Egypt,** regretter les oignons d'Egypte. **'flesh-tints,** *s.pl. Art:* Carnations *f,* chairs *f.* **'flesh-wound,** *s.* Blessure *f* dans les chairs.

fleshiness ['fleʃinis], *s.* État charnu (du corps, du nez, etc.).

fleshless ['fleʃlis], *a.* Décharné.

fleshy ['fleʃi], *a.* Charnu.

fletch [fletʃ], *v.tr.* Empenner (une flèche).

fletching ['fletʃiŋ], *s.* Empennage *m* (d'une flèche).

fleur-de-lis, *pl.* **fleurs-de-lis** ['flɜːdə'liː(s)], *s. Her:* Fleur *f* de lis.

flex¹ [fleks]. 1. *v.tr.* Fléchir (le bras). 2. *v.i. (Of spring)* Fléchir; *Geol: (of stratum)* se plier.

flex², *s. El:* Câble *m* souple; fil *m* souple, flexible *m.*

flexibility [ˌfleksi'biliti], *s.* Flexibilité *f;* élasticité *f;* souplesse *f.*

flexible ['fleksibl], *a.* Flexible, souple, pliant. *Aut:* **F. engine,** moteur souple, nerveux. **F. character,** caractère (i) liant, souple, (ii) complaisant. *El:* **F. wire,** cordon *m* souple; flexible *m.*

flexion ['flekʃ(ə)n], *s.* 1. Flexion *f,* courbure *f* (d'un ressort, etc.). 2. Courbe *f.* 3. *Gram: =* INFLEXION 2.

flexional ['flekʃən(ə)l], *a. Ling:* Flexionnel. **F. ending,** désinence *f.*

flick[1] [flik], *s.* 1. Petit coup (de fouet, etc.); (*with finger*) chiquenaude *f, F:* pichenette *f.* **At the f. of a switch,** en poussant un bouton. **A f. of the wrist,** un tour de main. **F. knife,** couteau *m* automatique. 2. *A:* F: **The flicks,** le ciné.

flick[2], *v.tr.* (*With whip,* etc.) Effleurer; (*with finger*) donner une chiquenaude (à). **To f. sth. away, off, with a duster,** faire envoler qch. d'un coup de torchon.

flicker[1] ['flikər], *s.* (*a*) Tremblotement *m.* **F. of the eyelids,** battement *m,* clignement *m,* de paupière. (*b*) **A f. of light,** une petite lueur tremblotante. (*c*) *Cin: T.V:* Scintillement *m,* papillotement *m.*

flicker[2], *v.i.* (*Of flame,* etc.) Trembloter, vaciller; (*of light*) papilloter, clignoter; (*of speedometer needle, etc.*) osciller. *Cin: T.V:* (*Of reproduction*) Scintiller, papilloter. **The candle flickered out,** la bougie vacilla et s'éteignit. **flickering,** *s.* (*a*) Tremblotement *m,* vacillement *m,* papillotement *m,* clignotement *m.* (*b*) *Cin: T.V:* Scintillement *m,* papillotement *m.*

flier ['flaiər], *s.* = FLYER.

flight[1] [flait], *s.* 1. (*a*) Vol *m* (d'un oiseau, d'un avion). *Av:* **Trial f.,** vol d'essai. *Av:* **Ligne** *f.* **Passengers for f. A to Brussels . . .,** les voyageurs pour Bruxelles ligne A . . . (*b*) Course *f* (d'un projectile, des nuages, etc.). **The f. of time,** le cours du temps. (*c*) Envol *m* (d'un oiseau, d'un avion). (*Of bird*) **To take its f.,** prendre son vol, son essor; s'envoler. **F. of fancy,** élan *m,* essor *m,* de l'imagination. (*d*) Migration *f* (d'oiseaux, d'insectes). 2. Volée *f,* distance parcourue (par un oiseau, etc.); trajectoire *f* (d'un projectile). 3. (*a*) **F. of stairs,** volée d'escalier; escalier *m.* (*b*) *Rac:* **F. of hurdles,** série *f* de haies. 4. (*a*) Bande *f,* vol, volée (d'oiseaux, etc.). *F:* **In the top f.,** parmi les tout premiers. (*b*) *Av:* Escadrille *f* (d'avions). '**flight-deck,** *s. Nav: Av:* Pont *m* d'envol. '**flight-lieutenant,** *s. Av:* Capitaine aviateur.

flight[2], *s.* Fuite *f.* **To take to f.** To **put the enemy to f.,** mettre l'ennemi en fuite, en déroute. **In full f.,** en pleine déroute.

flightiness ['flaitinis], *s.* Inconstance *f*; instabilité *f* (de caractère); légèreté *f,* étourderie *f.*

flighty ['flaiti], *a.* (*a*) Frivole, écervelé, étourdi. (*b*) Volage. **F. imagination,** imagination vagabonde.

flimsiness ['flimzinis], *s.* Manque *m* de solidité. (*a*) Légèreté *f* (d'une étoffe, du papier, etc.). (*b*) Futilité *f,* faiblesse *f* (d'une excuse).

flimsy ['flimzi]. 1. *a.* Sans solidité. (*a*) (*Of material, etc.*) Léger; peu résistant; peu solide; sans consistance. (*b*) (*Of excuse, etc.*) Pauvre. 2. *s.* (*a*) Papier *m* pellicule; papier pelure. (*b*) *P: O:* Billet *m* de banque.

flinch [flin(t)ʃ], *v.i.* 1. Reculer, fléchir, défaillir. 2. Faire une grimace; tressaillir (de douleur). **Without flinching,** sans broncher, sans sourciller.

fling[1] [fliŋ], *s.* 1. (*a*) Jet *m*; (*of horse*) ruade *f.* **To have a f. at s.o.,** (i) (*of horse*) lancer un coup de pied à qn; (ii) *F:* (*of pers.*) envoyer, lancer, un trait à qn. (*b*) *F:* Essai *m,* tentative *f.* 2. *Danc:* **Highland f.,** pas seul écossais. 3. *F:* **To have one's f.,** jeter sa gourme. **Youth will have its f.,** il faut que jeunesse se passe.

fling[2], *v.* (flung [flʌŋ]; flung) 1. *v.tr.* Jeter (qch.); lancer (une balle, etc.). **To f. one's money out of the window,** jeter son argent par la fenêtre. **To f. one's arms round s.o.'s neck,** se jeter, sauter, au cou de qn. **To f. abuse at s.o.,** lancer des injures, des sottises, à qn. 2. *v.i.* Se précipiter, s'élancer. **fling about,** *v.tr.* Jeter (des objets) de côté et d'autre. **To f. one's arms about,** gesticuler violemment. **To f. oneself about like a madman,** se démener comme un possédé. **fling aside,** *v.tr.* Rejeter (qch.); jeter (qch.) de côté. **fling away,** *v.tr.* Jeter de côté (qch.). **To f. away one's money,** prodiguer, gaspiller, son argent. **fling back,** *v.tr.* Repousser ou renvoyer violemment (qch.). **To f. back defiance,** riposter par un défi. **fling down,** *v.tr.* Jeter (qch.) à terre. **fling off,** *v.tr.* Jeter, se débarrasser de (ses vêtements, etc.); secouer (le joug). **fling open,** *v.tr.* Ouvrir toute grande (la fenêtre, etc.). **fling out. 1.** *v.tr.* (*a*) Jeter dehors; *F:* flanquer (qn) à la porte. (*b*) **To f. out one's arm,** étendre le bras d'un grand geste. 2. *v.i.* (*Of horse*) Lancer une ruade; ruer. *F:* **To f. out at**

s.o., faire une algarade à qn. **fling up,** *v.tr.* 1. Jeter (qch.) en l'air; ouvrir, relever, brusquement (la fenêtre). **To f. up one's hands,** lever les bras au ciel. (*Of horse*) **To f. up its heels,** ruer. 2. *F:* Abandonner, renoncer à (une tâche); lâcher (sa situation).

flint [flint], *s.* 1. *Miner:* Silex *m.* **Heart of f.,** cœur de pierre. 2. Pierre *f* à briquet; pierre à feu, à fusil. '**flint-glass,** *s. Glassm: Opt:* Flint(-glass) *m*; verre *m* de plomb. '**flint-lock,** *s. A:* Fusil *m* à pierre. '**flint-ware,** *s. Cer: U.S:* Grès fin.

flinty ['flinti], *a.* 1. (*a*) De silex. (*b*) Caillouteux, -euse, rocailleux, -euse. 2. *O:* (Cœur) dur, insensible.

flip[1] [flip], *s.* 1. Chiquenaude *f,* pichenette *f.* 2. Petite secousse vive. **F. of the tail,** coup *m* de queue. 3. *Av:* Petit tour de vol. 4. (Sorte de) boisson chaude. *S.a.* EGG-FLIP.

flip[2], *v.* (flipped) 1. *v.tr.* = FLICK[2]. 2. *v.i.* **To f. through a book,** feuilleter un livre.

flippancy ['flipənsi], *s.* Légèreté *f,* irrévérence *f,* désinvolture *f.*

flippant ['flipənt], *a.* Léger, désinvolte, irrévérencieux. **-ly,** *adv.* Légèrement, irrévérencieusement.

flipper ['flipər], *s.* 1. Nageoire *f* (de cétacé); aileron *m* (de requin); aile *f* (de pingouin); palme *f* (d'homme-grenouille). 2. *P:* Main *f*; *P:* patte *f,* pince *f.*

flirt[1] [flə:t], *s.* Flirteur *m*; (*woman*) coquette *f.*

flirt[2]. 1. *v.tr.* Jeter, lancer (qch.) (d'un mouvement sec); (*of bird*) agiter (les ailes, etc.). **To f. a fan,** jouer de l'éventail. 2. *v.i.* (*a*) S'agiter; (*of bird, etc.*) trémousser. (*b*) Flirter. **To f. with s.o.,** (*of woman*) coqueter, faire la coquette, avec qn; (*of man*) conter fleurette à (une jeune fille). **flirting,** *s.* Flirt *m.*

flirtatious [flə:'teiʃəs], *a. F:* (*Of man*) Flirteur; (*of woman*) coquette.

flirtation [flə:'teiʃ(ə)n], *s.* Flirt *m.* **To carry on a (little) f. with a woman,** faire un doigt de cour à une femme.

flit[1] [flit], *s. Scot:* Déménagement *m.* **Moonlight f.,** déménagement à la cloche de bois.

flit[2], *v.i.* (flitted) 1. **To f. (away),** partir. 2. *Scot:* Déménager. 3. (*Of pers., bird, etc.*) **To f. by,** passer comme une ombre. **To f. about, to f. to and fro,** aller et venir sans bruit. **To f. into the room,** se glisser (vivement) dans la salle. **A smile flitted across his face,** un sourire fugitif passa sur son visage. **flitting,** *s.* 1. Départ *m.* 2. *Scot:* Déménagement *m.* 3. Volettement *m,* voltigement *m.*

flitch [flitʃ], *s.* Flèche *f* (de lard).

flitter ['flitər], *v.i.* Voleter, voltiger. '**flittermouse,** *s. Z:* Chauve-souris *f, pl.* chauves-souris.

flivver ['flivər], *s. P:* Bagnole *f*; tacot *m.*

float[1] [flout], *s.* 1. (*a*) Train *m* (de bois). (*b*) Radeau *m.* 2. Flotteur *m* (de chaudière, de carburateur, d'hydravion). *Fish:* Flotteur, flotte *f,* bouchon *m.* 3. *Th:* (*Lighting*) **The float(s),** la rampe. 4. **F.(-board),** aube *f,* palette *f* (de roue hydraulique). 5. (*a*) Charrette basse à essieu brisé. (*b*) Wagon *m* en plate-forme; char *m* de cavalcade. '**float-chamber,** *s. I.C.E:* Chambre *f* du flotteur (du carburateur). '**float-needle,** *s. I.C.E:* Pointeau *m* (du carburateur).

float[2]. I. *v.i.* 1. (*a*) Flotter, nager (sur un liquide); surnager. (*b*) *Swim:* Faire la planche. 2. **The microscopic animals that f. about in the water,** les animaux microscopiques qui nagent dans l'eau. **Corpse that floats to the surface,** cadavre qui revient sur l'eau. **To f. about in the air,** planer dans l'air. **A rumour is floating about, around, that . . .,** le bruit court que. . . . II. **float,** *v.tr.* (*a*) Flotter (des bois, etc.). (*b*) **To f. a rumour,** faire circuler un bruit. (*c*) *Com:* Lancer, créer, fonder (une compagnie). *Fin:* **To f. a loan,** émettre un emprunt. (*d*) Mettre à flot (un navire). **float off. 1.** *v.i.* (*Of ship*) déséchouer. 2. *v.tr.* Renflouer, déséchouer (une épave). **floating off,** *s. Nau:* Renflouage *m,* renflouement *m.* **floating**[1], *a.* 1. Flottant, à flot. 2. (*a*) Libre, mobile. **F. ribs,** côtes flottantes. **F. population,** population flottante, instable. (*b*) *Pol:* **F. voter,** électeur indécis. (*c*) *Com:* **F. capital,** fonds *mpl* de roulement. **floating**[2], *s.* 1. (*a*) Flottement *m.* (*b*) *Swim:* La planche. 2. (*a*) Mise *f* à flot (d'un bateau). (*b*) Flottage *m* (à bûches perdues). (*c*) *Com:* Lancement *m* (d'une société commerciale, etc.). *Fin:* Émission *f* (d'un emprunt).

floatage ['floutidʒ], s. **1.** Flottage m (des bois). **2.** Flottabilité f. **3.** Œuvres mortes (d'un navire).
flo(a)tation [flou'teiʃ(ə)n], s. **1.** Nau: Flottaison f. **2.** Com: Lancement m (d'une compagnie); émission f (d'un emprunt).
floater ['floutər], s. **1.** Tchn: Flotteur m. **2.** St.Exch: Titre m de premier rang.
flocculate ['flɔkjuleit], v.i. Floculer.
flocculation [flɔkju'leiʃ(ə)n], s. Floculation
flocculent ['flɔkjulənt], a. Floconneux, -euse.
flock¹ [flɔk], s. Bourre f de laine.
flock², s. Bande f, troupe f (d'animaux); troupeau m (de moutons, d'oies). **Flocks and herds**, le menu et le gros bétail. **A pastor and his f.**, un pasteur et ses ouailles f. **Those who have strayed from the f.**, ceux qui se sont écartés du bercail. **They arrived in flocks**, ils arrivaient en bandes, en foule.
flock³, v.i. **To f. (together)**, s'attrouper, s'assembler. **To f. in**, entrer en masse.
floe [flou], s. Banc m de glace.
flog [flɔg], v.tr. (flogged) Fustiger, flageller; donner le fouet à (qn). **To f. a horse**, (i) fouetter, (ii) cravacher, un cheval. **To f. a dead horse**, se dépenser en pure perte. **To f. oneself**, s'éreinter. **To f. a competitor**, battre un concurrent à plate couture. P: **To f. one's watch**, lessiver sa montre. **flogging**, s. Fustigation f, flagellation f. Sch: La punition du fouet ou des verges.
flood¹ [flʌd], s. **1.** Nau: Flot m, flux m (de la marée); marée montante. **Ebb and f.**, flux et reflux. **2.** (a) Déluge m, inondation f. B: **The F.**, le Déluge. (b) **A f. of lights**, des flots de lumière. **Floods of tears**, un torrent de larmes. **A f. of letters**, une avalanche de lettres. (c) Crue f (d'une rivière). **'flood-gate**, s. Vanne f (de décharge); porte f d'écluse. **To open, close, the flood-gates**, lever, mettre, les vannes. **'flood-light¹**, s. **1.** Lumière f à grands flots. **2.** F.-l. **(projector)**, projecteur m à flots de lumière; phare m d'éclairage. **'flood-light²**, v.tr. Illuminer (un bâtiment, etc.) par projecteurs. **'flood-lighting**, s. Éclairage diffusé; illumination f par projecteurs (à flots de lumière). **'flood-'plain**, s. Geog: Lit majeur (d'une rivière); plaine f d'inondation. **'flood-tide**, s. Marée montante; flux m.
flood². **1.** v.tr. (a) Inonder, submerger. Agr: Irriguer, noyer (une prairie). (Of house, etc.) **To be flooded**, être envahi par l'eau. I.C.E: **To f. the carburettor**, noyer le carburateur. F: **To be flooded with letters**, être inondé, submergé, de lettres. (b) (Of rain, etc.) Faire déborder (une rivière). **2.** v.i. (a) (Of river, etc.) Déborder. I.C.E: (Of carburettor) Se noyer. (b) (Of river) Être en crue. **flooding**, s. **1.** Inondation f; irrigation f (d'une prairie). **2.** Débordement m (d'une rivière, etc.).
floodlit ['flʌdlit], a. Illuminé (par des projecteurs).
floor¹ ['flɔːr], s. **1.** (a) Plancher m, parquet m. **Tile(d) f.**, carrelage m. **To throw sth. on the f.**, jeter qch. par terre. P: **To wipe the f. with s.o.**, battre qn à plate couture. (b) N.Arch: Plafond m (de cale). **F.-frame, -timber**, varangue f. (c) Fond m (de l'océan); tablier m, aire f (d'un pont); sole f (d'une galerie de mine). (d) Parquet (à la Bourse); parquet, prétoire m (d'un tribunal); hémicycle m (du Parlement). U.S: **To have, take, the f.**, avoir, prendre, la parole. **2.** Étage m (de maison). **Ground f.**, U.S: **first f.**, rez-de-chaussée m. **House on two floors**, maison avec étage. **To live on the second f.**, (i) demeurer au second; (ii) U.S: demeurer au premier. **We live on the same f.**, nous habitons sur le même palier. **3.** Aire (d'une grange, etc.). **floor-board**, s. Lame f de parquet. **'floor-cloth**, s. **1.** O: P: Linoléum m. **2.** Serpillière f; torchon m à laver. **'floor-polish**, s. Encaustique f; cire f à parquet. **'floor-show**, s. Spectacle m de cabaret. **'floor-'waiter**, s. (In hotel) Garçon m d'étage. **'floor-'walker**, s. U.S: = SHOP WALKER.
floor², v.tr. **1.** Const: (i) Planchéier, (ii) parqueter, (iii) carreler (une pièce). **2.** (a) Terrasser (un adversaire). (b) F: Mettre, réduire, (qn) à quia; clouer le bec à (qn); aplatir (qn). Sch: Coller (un candidat, etc.). **flooring**, s. **1.** (a) (i) Planchéiage m, (ii) parquetage m, (iii) carrelage m, dallage m. (b) Renversement m (d'un adversaire). **2.** (a) Plancher m. (b) Carreau m; carrelage, dallage.

floorer ['flɔːrər], s. F: **1.** Coup m qui terrasse. **2.** (a) Nouvelle déconcertante. (b) (In examination) Colle f. (c) Argument m sans réplique. **That's a f. for you!** ça te la coupe!
flop¹ [flɔp], s. F: **1.** Coup mat; bruit sourd (d'un rat qui plonge, etc.). **2.** Four m, fiasco m.
flop², int. & adv. F: **1.** Plouf! patapouf! floc! **To fall f.**, faire patapouf. **2.** **To go f.**, (of play) faire four; (of business, etc.) aller à vau-l'eau; (of pers.) s'effondrer.
flop³, v.i. (flopped) F: **1.** **To f. (down)**, se laisser tomber; s'affaler. **To f. about**, faire des sauts de carpe. **2.** = **to go flop**, q.v. under FLOP² 2.
floppy ['flɔpi], a. (Of hat, etc.) Pendant, flasque, souple; (of garment) lâche, trop large; F: (of pers.) veule, mollasse.
flora ['flɔːrə], s. Flore f (d'une région).
floral ['flɔːrəl], a. Floral, -aux. **Dress with a bold f. design**, robe à grands ramages.
florescence [flɔː'res(ə)ns], s. Fleuraison f, floraison f.
floret ['flɔːrit], s. Bot: Fleuron m.
floribunda [ˌflɔːri'bʌndə], a. & s. F. **(rose)**, rosier m multiflore.
florid ['flɔrid], a. (Of style, etc.) Fleuri; orné à l'excès; (of architecture, etc.) flamboyant; (of countenance) rubicond, fleuri. **To have a f. complexion**, être haut en couleur.
florin ['flɔrin], s. Num: Florin m; pièce f de deux shillings.
florist ['flɔrist], s. Fleuriste mf.
floss [flɔs], s. F.(-silk), bourre f de soie; filoselle f; soie f floche.
flotation [flou'teiʃ(ə)n], s. = FLOATATION.
flotilla [flə'tilə], s. Flottille f.
flotsam ['flɔtsəm], s. Jur: F. **(and Jetsam)**, épave(s) flottante(s) (jetée(s) sur la côte).
flounce¹ [flauns], s. Mouvement, geste, vif (d'indignation, d'impatience).
flounce², v.i. **To f. in, out**, entrer, sortir, dans un mouvement d'indignation.
flounce³, s. Dressm: Volant m.
flounder¹ ['flaundər], s. Ich: Flet m.
flounder², v.i. **1.** Patauger, barboter, patouiller, s'embourber. **To f. about in the water**, se débattre dans l'eau. **To f. along**, avancer en trébuchant. F: **To f. in a speech**, patauger dans un discours. **2.** (Of horse) (a) Se débattre (par terre). (b) Faire feu des quatre fers (pour ne pas tomber). **floundering**, s. Barbotage m, cafouillage m, pataugeage m.
flour¹ ['flauər], s. Farine f. **Pure wheaten f.**, fleur f de farine. **Potato f.**, fécule f de pommes de terre. **To cover, dust, sth. with f.**, (en)fariner qch. **'flour-bin**, s. Huche f, maie f. **'flour-box, -dredger**, s. Saupoudroir m à farine. **'flour-mill**, s. Moulin m à farine; (large) minoterie f. **'flour-milling**, s. Minoterie f, meunerie f.
flour², v.tr. (En)fariner (qn, qch.); saupoudrer de farine.
flourish¹ ['flʌriʃ], s. **1.** (a) Trait m de plume, enjolivure f; (after signature) parafe m. (b) Fleur f (de rhétorique); fioriture f (de style). **2.** Geste prétentieux; brandissement m (d'épée). **3.** Mus: (a) Fanfare f (de trompettes). (b) Fioriture, ornement m.
flourish². **1.** v.i. (a) (Of plant) Bien venir. **To f. in a sandy soil**, se plaire dans un terrain sablonneux. (b) (Of pers., commerce, etc.) Être florissant; prospérer. (c) Être dans sa fleur, dans tout son éclat; battre son plein; (of arts) fleurir. **2.** v.tr. Brandir (une épée, un bâton). **To f. one's stick**, (i) agiter sa canne; (ii) faire des moulinets avec sa canne. **flourishing**, a. Florissant; (commerce) prospère.
floury ['flauəri], a. **1.** Enfariné. **2.** (Pommes de terre) farineuses.
flout [flaut], v.tr. Faire fi de (l'autorité de qn); se moquer (d'un ordre). **flouting**, s. Moquerie f, raillerie f.
flow¹ [flou], s. **1.** (a) Écoulement m. (b) Mch: Courant m, flux m de vapeur). (c) El: Passage m (du courant). El.E: **Parallel-f. condenser**, condensateur à courants dans le même sens. (d) Courant. (e) Arrivée f (d'air, I.C.E: d'essence, etc.) (f) F. **of the tide**, flot m, flux m, de la marée. S.a. EBB¹ 1. **2.** Volume m (de liquide débité). Hyd.E: Débit m (d'un lac, d'une pompe). **3.** Flux (de sang, de paroles, etc.). **To have a ready f. of language**, avoir de la faconde; être disert. **4.** Lignes tombantes (d'une robe); drapé m (d'un vêtement). **'flow-metre**, s. Débitmètre m.

flow², *v.i.* **1.** (*a*) Couler, s'écouler. (*Of river*) **To f. into the sea**, se jeter, se déverser, dans la mer. (*b*) (*Of tide*) Monter. (*c*) (*Of blood, electric current, etc.*) Circuler. (*d*) (*Of drapery, etc.*) Flotter. **2.** Dériver, découler, provenir (from, de). **3.** *Lit:* Abonder. **Land flowing with milk and honey**, pays ruisselant de lait et de miel. **flow away**, *v.i.* (*Of liquid*) S'écouler. **flow back**, *v.i.* Refluer. **flow in**, *v.i.* (*a*) (*Of liquid*) Entrer. (*b*) (*Of people, money*) Affluer. **flow out**, *v.i.* Sortir, s'écouler. **flowing**, *a.* **1.** Coulant; (*of tide*) montant. **2.** (*Of style, etc.*) Coulant, fluide, facile; (*of movement*) gracieux, aisé. **3.** (*Of draperies*) Flottant. **F. beard**, barbe longue, flottante. **-ly**, *adv.* D'une manière coulante; avec facilité.

flower¹ ['flauər], *s.* **1.** Fleur *f.* **Wild flowers**, fleurs sauvages. **Bunch of flowers**, bouquet *m.* **He had a f. in his buttonhole**, il avait la boutonnière fleurie. **To lay flowers on a grave**, fleurir une tombe. **'No flowers by request,'** "ni fleurs ni couronnes." **F. show**, exposition *f* horticole; floralie(s) *f(pl.)*. **2.** *pl.* Fleur(s) (de soufre, etc.). **3.** (*a*) *Typ:* Fleuron *m.* (*b*) **Flowers of speech**, fleurs de rhétorique. **4. Fine fleur**, élite *f* (de l'armée, etc.). **5.** Fleuraison *f.* **In f.**, en fleur. **In full f.**, en pleine épanouissement. **To burst into f.**, fleurir. *Lit:* **To be in the f. of one's age**, être dans la fleur de l'âge. **'flower-bearing**, *a.* Florifère. **'flower-bed**, *s.* Parterre *m*; plate-bande *f*, *pl.* plates-bandes. **'flower-garden**, *s.* Jardin *m* d'agrément. **'flower-piece**, *s.* Tableau *m* de fleurs. **'flower-pot**, *s.* Pot *m* à fleurs. **'flower-shop**, *s.* Boutique *f* de fleuriste. **'flower-stand**, *s.* Jardinière *f.*

flower², *v.i.* Fleurir. **flowered**, *a.* *Tex:* F. **material**, tissu à fleurs, à ramages. **flowering¹**, *a.* **1.** Fleuri; en fleur. **2. F. plant**, plante à fleurs. **flowering²**, *s.* Fleuraison *f.*

floweret ['flauərit], *s.* Fleurette *f.*

flowery ['flauəri], *a.* **1.** (Pré, etc.) fleuri; (tapis, etc.) orné de fleurs et de ramages. **2.** (*Of speech, style*) Fleuri.

flown *See* **FLY³, HIGH-FLOWN.**

flu [flu:], *s. Med: F:* = **INFLUENZA.**

fluctuate ['flʌktjueit], *v.i.* Fluctuer. **1.** (*Of conditions*) Varier; (*of markets, values*) osciller. **2.** (*Of pers.*) Flotter, vaciller, hésiter. **fluctuating**, *a.* (*Of temperature, etc.*) Variable; (*of prices, etc.*) oscillant.

fluctuation [flʌktju'eiʃ(ə)n], *s.* Oscillation *f*; variations *fpl* (de température); fluctuation *f* (du marché).

flue [flu:], *s.* **1.** Conduit *m*, tuyau *m*, de cheminée. **2.** *Mus:* Bouche *f* (de tuyau d'orgue). **'flue-brush**, *s.* Hérisson *m.* **'flue-pipe**, *s.* **1.** *Mus:* Tuyau *m* à bouche (d'un orgue). **2.** *Const:* Tuyau de poêle.

fluency ['flu:ənsi], *s.* Facilité *f* (de parole).

fluent ['flu:ənt], *a.* (*Of speech, etc.*) Coulant, facile, fluide. **To be a f. speaker**, avoir la parole facile; être disert. **He is a f. speaker of French**, il parle le français couramment. **-ly**, *adv.* Couramment; (s'exprimer) avec facilité.

fluff¹ [flʌf], *s.* **1.** Duvet *m* (d'étoffe); peluches *fpl.* (*Of cloth*) **To lose, shed, its f.**, pelucher. *F: O:* **A little bit of f.**, une petite femme, une jeunesse. **2.** Fourrure douce (d'un jeune animal). **3.** *Th: F:* Loup *m.*

fluff², *v.tr.* Lainer (un drap, etc.). **To f. (out) one's hair**, faire bouffer ses cheveux. **Bird that fluffs (up) its feathers**, oiseau qui hérisse ses plumes. **2.** *Th: F:* **To f. one's entrance**, louper, bouler, son entrée.

fluffy ['flʌfi], *a.* (Drap) pelucheux; (poussin, etc.) duveteux. **F. hair**, cheveux flous.

fluid ['flu:id]. **1.** *a. & s.* (*a*) Fluide (*m*). (*b*) Liquide (*m*). **F. measures**, mesures *f* pour les liquides. **2.** *a.* (*a*) (*Of style, etc.*) Fluide, coulant, facile. (*b*) (*Of opinions, etc.*) Inconstant, changeant; mouvant. **A f. situation**, une situation fluide.

fluidity [flu'iditi], *s.* **1.** Fluidité *f.* **2.** (*a*) Fluidité, facilité *f* (de style, etc.). (*b*) Caractère changeant; inconstance *f.*

fluke¹ [flu:k], *s. Vet:* F.(-worm), douve *f* (du foie).

fluke², *s. Nau:* Patte *f* (d'ancre). **2.** *pl.* Queue *f* (de baleine).

fluke³, *s.* (*a*) *Bill:* (Coup *m* de) raccroc *m.* **By a f.**, par raccroc. (*b*) *F:* Coup de veine, de hasard; chance *f.*

fluky ['flu:ki], *a.* (Coup, etc.) de raccroc; (jeu) hasardeux, incertain. **F. wind**, vent incertain.

flummox ['flʌməks], *v.tr.* *F:* Réduire (qn) à quia; démonter (qn). *Sch:* Coller (un élève). **To be flummoxed**, ne savoir sur quel pied danser.

flung *See* **FLING².**

flunk [flʌŋk]. *U.S: Sch: F:* **1.** *v.i.* Se faire recaler, se faire coller (à un examen). **2.** *v.tr.* Recaler, coller (qn).

flunkey ['flʌŋki], *s.* Laquais *m*, *F:* larbin *m.*

fluoresce [flu(:)ə'res], *v.i.* Émettre une fluorescence.

fluorescence [flu(:)ə'res(ə)ns], *s.* Fluorescence *f.*

fluorescent [flu(:)ə'res(ə)nt], *a.* Fluorescent. **F. lighting**, éclairage fluorescent, par fluorescence.

fluorine ['flu(:)ə'ri:n], *s. Ch:* Fluor *m.*

fluorspar ['flu:ə(:)spɑ:r], *s. Miner:* Spath *m* fluor.

flurry¹ ['flʌri], *s.* **1.** (*a*) *Nau:* Risée *f*, petit grain *m*; brise folle. (*b*) *U.S:* Rafale *f* de neige. **2. Agitation** *f*, bouleversement *m*, émoi *m.* **All in a f.**, tout effaré, tout en émoi. **3. The death f.**, les dernières convulsions (de la baleine expirante, etc.).

flurry², *v.tr.* Agiter, étourdir, effarer (qn). **To get flurried**, perdre la tête.

flush¹ [flʌʃ], *s. Ven:* Envolée *f* (d'oiseaux).

flush², *v.tr. Ven:* (Faire) lever, faire partir (des oiseaux).

flush³, *s.* **1.** *Hyd.E:* Chasse *f* (d'eau). **2. Accès** *m*, élan *m* (d'émotion, de passion, etc.). **In the first f. of victory**, dans l'ivresse de la victoire. **3.** (*a*) Éclat *m* (de lumière, de la beauté). **To be in the full f. of health**, jouir d'une santé florissante. (*b*) Rougeur *f*, afflux *m* de sang (au visage); (*in fever*) bouffée *f* de chaleur.

flush⁴, *v.* **1.** *v.tr.* **To f. (out) a drain**, donner une chasse à un égout; balayer un égout à grande eau. **To f. the lavatory**, tirer la chasse d'eau. **To f. away**, jeter à l'égout. **2.** *v.i.* S'empourprer; (*of pers.*) rougir; (*of blood*) monter (au visage). **His face flushed, he flushed up**, le sang, le rouge, lui monta au visage. **flushed**, *a.* (Visage) enfiévré, empourpré. **Face f. with drink**, visage allumé par la boisson. **F. with success**, grisé par le succès.

flush⁵, *s. Cards:* (At poker) Flush *m.*

flush⁶, *a.* **1.** (*a*) (*Of stream, etc.*) Très plein; débordant. (*b*) *F:* (*Of pers.*) **To be f.**, être en fonds, *P:* plein aux as. **2.** (*Of surfaces, etc.*) Ras; de niveau. **F. joint**, assemblage affleuré. **To be f. with sth.**, être à fleur, au ras, de qch. **Houses built f. with the pavement**, maisons bâties à même le trottoir.

Flushing ['flʌʃiŋ]. *Pr.n. Geog:* Flessingue *f.*

fluster¹ ['flʌstər], *s.* Agitation *f*, trouble *m.* **In a f.**, tout en émoi.

fluster². **1.** *v.tr.* Agiter, bouleverser (qn); faire perdre la tête à (qn). **To be, get, flustered**, se troubler; être démonté, effaré. **2.** *v.i.* S'agiter, s'énerver.

flute¹ [flu:t], *s.* **1.** Flûte *f.* **Concert f.**, grande flûte. **2. F.(-player)**, (joueur *m* de) flûte. **3.** (*a*) Rainure *f*; cannelure *f* (de colonne). (*b*) *Laund:* Tuyau *m.*

flute², *v.tr.* (*a*) Rainer, rainurer (une planche); canneler (une colonne). (*b*) *Laund:* Tuyauter, rucher, gaufrer. **fluted**, *a.* **1.** (*Of notes, voice*) Flûté. **2.** (*a*) A rainure(s); à cannelures; (*of column*) cannelé, strié. (*b*) (Linge) tuyauté, à godets. **fluting**, *s.* **1. F. machine**, machine *f* à canneler. *Laund:* **F. iron**, fer *m* à tuyauter. **2.** *Coll.* Rainures *fpl.* cannelures *fpl. Laund:* Tuyaux *mpl*, godrons *mpl.*

flutist ['flu:tist], *s. Mus:* (Joueur *m* de) flûte, flûtiste *m.*

flutter¹ ['flʌtər], *s.* **1.** Volètement *m*, voltigement *m*, trémoussement *m* (d'un oiseau); battement *m* (des ailes); palpitation *f* (du cœur); flottement *m*, voltigement (d'un drapeau). *Av:* Vibration *f* (de l'hélice). **2. Agitation** *f*, trouble *m*, émoi *m.* **To be (all) in a f.**, être tout troublé, tout en émoi. **3.** *Fin: F:* Petite spéculation. *Cards: Turf:* **To have a little f.**, risquer de petites sommes.

flutter². **1.** *v.i.* (*a*) (*Of birds*) Voleter, battre des ailes; (*of flag, ribbon, etc.*) flotter, s'agiter (au vent); (*of heart*) palpiter, battre; (*of pulse*) battre irrégulièrement. (*b*) (*Of pers.*) Trembler, frémir. **2.** *v.tr.* (*a*) Agiter, secouer (un drapeau, etc.); jouer de (l'éventail). (*Of bird*) **To f. its wings**, battre des ailes. *F:* Agiter, troubler (qn).

fluty ['flu:ti], *a.* (*Of voice, etc.*) Flûté.

fluvial ['flu:viəl], *a.* Fluvial, -aux.

fluvio-glacial ['flu:viou'gleiʃ(ə)l], *a. Geol:* Fluvio-glaciaire.

flux [flʌks], s. **1.** *Med:* Flux *m* (de sang, etc.); flux de ventre. **2.** (*a*) Flux; changement continuel. **To be in a state of f.**, être sujet à des changements fréquents. (*b*) *Ph:* Flux (magnétique, etc.). **3.** (*a*) *Metall:* Fondant *m*, flux. (*b*) *Metalw:* Décapant *m*; fondant de brasage.

fly¹, *pl.* **flies** [flai(z)], s. (*a*) *Ent:* Mouche *f*. **House f.**, mouche commune. **Spanish f., blister(ing) f.**, mouche d'Espagne; cantharide *f*. **Horse f.**, taon *m*. **Blow f.**, mouche à viande. **Black f.**, (*sg. & pl.*), thrips *m*. (*In S. Africa*) **The f.**, la tsétsé. *S.a.* GREEN-FLY. (*Of cow, horse, etc.*) **To whisk away the flies**, s'émoucher. **They died like flies**, on mourait dru, comme des mouches. *F:* **There's a f. in the ointment**, *F:* il y a un cheveu, une ombre au tableau. **That's the f. in the ointment**, voilà le chiendent. **To catch flies**, bayer aux corneilles. **There are no flies on him**, c'est un malin. *Box:* **F.-weight**, poids *m* mouche. (*b*) *Fish:* Mouche. **To rise to the f.**, mordre à l'appât. **'fly-blow**, s. **1.** Œufs *mpl* de mouche (dans la viande). **2.** *F:* Chiures *fpl* de mouche. **'fly-blown**, *a.* **1.** Couvert d'œufs de mouches; (viande) gâtée. *F:* (*Of reputation, etc.*) Souillé, entaché. **2.** *F:* Couvert de chiures de mouche. **'fly-catcher**, s. **1.** Piège *m* à mouches; attrape-mouche(s) *m*. **2.** *Orn:* Gobe-mouches *m inv.* **'fly-fishing**, s. *Fish:* Pêche *f* à la mouche. **'fly-paper**, s. Papier *m* attrape-mouche(s). **'fly-speck**, s. Chiure *f* de mouche. **'fly-swatter**, s. Tapette *f* à mouches.

fly², s. **1.** Vol *m*. **2.** *A:* (*pl. usu.* **flys**) Fiacre *m*; voiture *f* de place. **3.** (*a*) Patte *f* (d'habit); braguette *f*, brayette *f* (de pantalon). (*b*) Battant *m* (d'un drapeau). (*c*) Auvent (de tente). **4.** *pl. Th:* The flies, les cintres *m*, les dessus *m*. **5.** *Tchn:* Moulinet *m* (d'anémomètre, etc.); régulateur *m*, volant *m* (de sonnerie d'horloge). **'fly-bill**, s. **1.** Feuille volante; prospectus *m*. **2.** (*Poster*) Papillon *m*. **'fly-half**, s. *Rugby Fb:* Demi *m* d'ouverture. **'fly-leaf**, s. (Feuille *f* de) garde (d'un livre broché). **'fly-nut**, s. Écrou ailé, à oreilles; papillon *m*. **'fly-sheet**, s. Feuille volante, mobile. **'fly-wheel**, s. *Mec.E:* Volant *m*. **To act as a f.-w.**, faire volant.

fly³, *v.* (**flew** [flu:]; **flown** [floun]) I. *v.i.* **1.** (*a*) (*Of bird*) Voler. **To f. into the room**, entrer en volant dans la pièce. **To catch sth. flying**, saisir qch. au vol. *F:* **To find the birds flown**, trouver buisson creux. **To f. high**, (i) voler haut; (ii) *F:* avoir de hautes visées. (*b*) *Av:* Voler. **To f. to Paris**, se rendre à Paris en avion. **To f. over London**, survoler Londres. **2.** (*Of flag, etc.*) Flotter. **3.** (*a*) (*Of pers.*) Courir, aller à toute vitesse; (*of time*) fuir. **He flew into the room**, il est entré dans la pièce en coup de vent. **To f. to s.o.'s assistance**, voler à l'aide de qn. **To f. at s.o.**, (i) s'élancer sur qn; (ii) faire une algarade à qn; invectiver qn. **To f. at s.o.'s throat**, sauter à la gorge de qn. **To f. into a rage**, s'emporter; prendre la mouche. **The door flew open**, la porte s'ouvrit brusquement, en coup de vent. **The branch flew back**, la branche fit ressort. (*b*) (*Of cork, etc.*) Voler; sauter en l'air; (*of sparks*) jaillir. *F:* **To make the money f.**, prodiguer son argent. **To f. off the handle**, (i) *of axe-head, etc.*) se démancher, s'envoler; (ii) *P:* s'emporter; sortir de ses gonds. *F:* **To send s.o. flying**, envoyer rouler qn (sur le carreau). **To send a plate flying**, envoyer, lancer, une assiette à la volée. (*c*) **To f. in pieces**, voler en éclats. **4.** **To let f.**, lancer, décocher, (un projectile, une flèche). **To let f. at s.o.**, (i) tirer sur qn; (ii) *F:* flanquer un coup à qn; (of horse) détacher une ruade à qn; (iii) s'en prendre à qn. **5.** (= FLEE, *in pres. tenses only*) (*a*) Fuir, s'enfuir. **To send the enemy flying**, mettre l'ennemi en fuite. **To f. from a place**, s'enfuir d'un endroit. **To f. from danger**, fuir le danger, se dérober au danger. **To f. for one's life**, chercher son salut dans la fuite. (*b*) *v.tr.* **To f. the country**, s'enfuir du pays; émigrer. II. **fly**, *v.tr.* **1.** *Nau:* **To f. a flag**, battre un pavillon. **2.** *Ven:* Lancer, faire voler (un faucon, etc.). **3.** **To f. a kite**, faire voler un cerf-volant. **4.** *Av:* (*a*) Piloter (un avion). **To f. s.o. to Paris**, conduire qn en avion à Paris. (*b*) **To f. the Channel**, passer la Manche en avion; survoler la Manche. **Letters are flown to London**, le courrier est transporté à Londres par avion. **fly away**, *v.i.* **1.** (*Of bird, etc.*) S'envoler;

prendre son vol. **2.** (*Of pers.*) S'enfuir. **fly back**, *v.i.* **1.** Revenir (i) en volant, (ii) au plus vite. **2.** (*Of steel rod, etc.*) Faire ressort. **'fly by¹**, s. *U.S:* = FLY PAST¹. **fly by²**, *v.i.* Passer très rapidement, comme un éclair. **fly off**, *v.i.* **1.** (*Of bird, etc.*) = FLY AWAY 1. **2.** (*Of pers.*) S'en aller en coup de vent. (*Of button, etc.*) Sauter. **fly-over**, s. **1.** *Av:* Défilé *m* aérien (à basse altitude). **2.** *Civ.E:* Enjambement *m*, passage supérieur, saut-de-mouton *m*, *pl.* sauts-de-mouton. **'fly-past¹**, s. Défilé aérien. **fly-past²**, *v.i. Mil: Av:* Défiler (devant un général, etc.). **fly up**, *v.i.* Se projeter en l'air. **flying¹**, a. **1.** (Oiseau) volant. **F. hours**, heures de vol *m*. *Av:* **Flying officer**, lieutenant. **2.** (Voile, ruban) volant, flottant, léger. *S.a.* COLOUR¹ 4. **3.** (*a*) (Course, etc.) rapide. **F. column**, (i) *Mil:* colonne *f* mobile; camp volant; (ii) police *f* de la route, police routière. **To take a f. shot at sth.**, tirer (un oiseau, etc.) au vol. (*b*) Court, passager. **To pay a f. visit to London**, faire une visite éclair à Londres. (*c*) *Sp:* **F. start**, départ lancé. *Fb:* **F. kick**, coup de pied à la volée. **4. F. scaffold(ing)**, échafaudage volant. **5.** En fuite. **'flying-bomb**, s. *Mil:* Bombe volante. **'flying-boat**, s. Hydravion *m* à coque. **'flying-buttress**, s. *Arch:* Arc-boutant *m*, *pl.* arcs-boutants. **'flying-'fish**, s. *Ich:* Poisson volant. **flying²**, s. **1.** (*a*) Vol *m* (d'un oiseau, etc.). (*b*) Aviation *f*, vol. **Blind f.**, pilotage *m* sans visibilité. **Trick f.**, vol d'acrobatie. **F. boot**, botte *f* de vol. **F. ground**, terrain *m* d'aviation. **F. school**, école *f* de pilotage. **Flying sickness**, mal *m* de l'air. **2.** Sautage *m* (d'un rivet, etc.); jaillissement *m* (d'étincelles). **3.** Fuite *f*. **4.** (*a*) Lancement *m* (de pigeons, d'un cerf-volant). (*b*) Déploiement *m* (d'un drapeau). **'flying-club**, s. Aéro-club *m*. **'flying-height**, s. *Av:* Altitude *f*. **Maximum f.-h.**, (valeur *f* de) plafond *m*. **'fly-by-night**, s. *F:* **1.** Oiseau *m* de nuit; noctambule *mf*. **2.** Déménageur *m* à la cloche de bois.

fly⁴, *a. F:* Astucieux; *F:* ficelle.

flyer ['flaiər], s. **1.** (*a*) Oiseau *m*, insecte *m*, qui vole. (*b*) Aviateur, -trice. **2.** (*a*) Aile *f*, volant *m* (de moulin à vent). (*b*) Balancier *m* (de tournebroche, etc.).

foal¹ [foul], s. Poulain *m*; ânon *m*, bourriquet *m*. **Mare in, with, f.**, jument pleine.

foal², *v.tr.* (*Of mare, etc.*) Mettre bas (un poulain, etc.); *abs.* pouliner.

foam¹ [foum], s. **1.** Écume *f*; (*on beer*) mousse *f*. **His horse was in a f.**, son cheval écumait. **2.** (*a*) (*Slaver*) Bave *f*. (*b*) Écume (à la bouche). **foam(-)rubber**, s. Caoutchouc *m* mousse.

foam², *v.i.* (*Of sea, etc.*) Écumer, moutonner; (*of beer, etc.*) mousser. **To f. at the mouth**, avoir l'écume aux lèvres; (*of dog, etc.*) baver. *F:* **To f. with rage**, écumer; être furieux.

foamy ['foumi], *a.* Écumeux; (*of drink, etc.*) mousseux.

fob¹ [fob], s. Gousset *m* (de pantalon). **Fob-chain**, régence *f*.

fob², *v.tr.* (**fobbed**) *F:* **To f. s.o.** (**off**), tromper, duper qn. **To f. s.o. off with sth.**, to f. sth. off on s.o., *F:* refiler qch. à qn.

focal ['fouk(ə)l], *a.* Focal, -aux.

fo'c'sle ['fouksl], s. = FORECASTLE.

focus¹, *pl.* **foci, focuses** ['foukəs, 'fousai, -ki:, 'foukəsiz], s. **1.** Foyer *m* (de lentille, de miroir, de courbe). *Opt:* **In f.**, au point. **Out of f.**, (i) (*of image*) pas au point; brouillé; (ii) (*of head-lamp bulb, etc.*) mal centré ou mal réglé. **To bring sth. into f.**, mettre qch. au point. **2.** Siège *m*, foyer (d'une maladie, etc.); centre (d'un tremblement de terre, etc.).

focus², *v.tr.* (**focused** ['foukəst]) **1.** Concentrer (les rayons de lumière, l'observation, etc.) (in, on, dans, sur); faire converger (des rayons). *v.i.* (*Of light, sound, etc.*) Converger (on, sur). **All eyes were focused on him**, il était le point de mire de tous les yeux. **2.** Mettre au point (un microscope, un objet). **focusing**, s. **1.** Concentration *f*, convergence *f* (de rayons, etc.). **2.** Mise *f* au point (d'une jumelle, etc.). *Phot:* **F. screen**, verre dépoli.

fodder¹ ['fodər], s. Fourrage *m*; *P:* nourriture *f*. *S.a.* CANNON-FODDER.

fodder², *v.tr.* Affour(r)ager, affener.

foe [fou], s. *Lit:* Ennemi *m*, adversaire *m*.

foeman, pl. **-men** ['foumən], s.m. A. & Lit: Ennemi, adversaire.

foetal ['fi:tl], a. Physiol: Fœtal, -aux.

foetus, pl. **-uses** ['fi:təs, -əsiz], s. Fœtus m.

fog[1] [fɔg], s. (a) Brouillard m; Nau: brume f. F: I'm in a f., je ne sais plus où j'en suis. (b) Phot: (On negative) Voile m. 'fog-bound, a. Arrêté, paralysé, par le brouillard; pris dans la brume. 'fog-horn, s. Nau: Corne f de brume; sirène f. 'fog-lamp, s. Aut: Phare m antibrouillard. 'fog-signal, s. (a) Nau: Signal m, -aux, de brume, de brouillard. (b) Rail: Pétard m.

fog[2], v. (**fogged** [fɔgd]) 1. v.tr. (a) Embrumer (un endroit). F: Brouiller (les idées); embrouiller (qn). (b) Phot: Voiler (un cliché). 2. v.i. (Of negative) Se voiler. **fogging**, s. Phot: Voile m.

fogey ['fougi], s. = FOGY.

foggy ['fɔgi], a. 1. Brumeux. On a f. day, par un jour de brouillard. It is f., il y a, il fait, du brouillard. 2. (Of photograph. etc.) Voilé, brouillé; (esprit, etc.) confus. F: I haven't the foggiest (idea)! je n'en ai pas la moindre idée!

fogy ['fougi], s. F: Old f., vieille baderne, vieille barbe.

foible ['fɔibl], s. Côté m faible. point m faible; faible m (de qn).

foil[1] [fɔil], s. 1. Arch: Lobe m (d'un arc, etc.). 2. Metalw: (a) Feuille f, lame f (d'or, etc.); clinquant m. Brass f., oripeau m. S.a. SILVER-FOIL, TINFOIL. (b) Tain m (d'une glace). 3. To serve as a f. to s.o.'s beauty, servir de repoussoir m à la beauté de qn.

foil[2], v.tr. 1. Lap: Monter (un diamant sur un paillon). 2. Faire ressortir (qch.); servir de repoussoir à.

foil[3], s. Fenc: Fleuret m.

foil[4], s. Ven: Foulée f, piste f.

foil[5], v.tr. 1. Ven: Dépister (la meute). 2. Faire échouer, faire manquer (une tentative, etc.); déjouer (qn, un complot).

foiled [fɔild], a. Arch: (Arc, etc.) à lobes.

foist [fɔist], v.tr. Refiler (sth. on s.o., qch. à qn). To f. a bad coin on s.o., repasser une fausse pièce à qn. To f. oneself on s.o., s'implanter chez qn; s'imposer à qn, chez qn.

fold[1] [fould], s. 1. Sheep-f., parc m à moutons; bergerie f. 2. Sein m de l'Église; bercail m.

fold[2], v.tr. Husb: Parquer, emparquer (les moutons).

fold[3], s. (a) Pli m, repli m (du papier, d'un tissu, etc.). F. (of fat), bourrelet m. (b) Metalw: Repli, agrafe f (d'une tôle). (c) Battant m, vantail m, -aux (d'une porte); feuille f (de paravent). (d) Geol: Flexure f, plissement m. Recumbent f., nappe f de recouvrement.

fold[4]. 1. v.tr. (a) Plier (une feuille de papier. etc.). To f. back, rabattre (un col, etc.) To f. back, down, the blankets, retourner les couvertures. To f. sth. up (again), (re)plier qch. (b) To f. sth. in sth., envelopper qch. de, dans, qch. (c) To f. one's arms, (se) croiser les bras. To f. one's hands, (i) joindre les mains; (ii) F: rester sans rien faire. 2. v.i. Se (re)plier, se briser. To f. back, down, se rabattre. **folding**[1], a. Pliant, repliable, rabattable. F. camera, appareil pliant. F. chair, chaise pliante. F. ladder, échelle f double. F. steps, escabeau (pliant). **folding**[2], s. 1. (a) Pliage m (de l'étoffe, etc.). F. up, down, repliage m, repliement m, rabattement m. (b) Metalw: Agrafage m (de tôles). 2. Geol: Plissement m (du terrain).

foldable ['fouldəbl], a. Pliable.

folder ['fouldər], s. 1. (Pers.) Plieur, -euse (de journaux, etc.). 2. Tls: Bookb: Plioir m. 3. Com: Prospectus (plié); dépliant m. 4. (For papers, etc.) Chemise f.

foliage ['fouliidʒ], s. Feuillage m.

foliate ['fouliit, -eit], a. Bot: Feuillé, feuillu.

foliated ['foulieitid], a. Miner: Geol: etc: Feuilleté, lamellaire. Sculp: F. scroll, rinceau m.

foliation [fouli'eiʃ(ə)n], s. 1. Foliation f, frondaison f (d'une plante). 2. Foliotage m (d'un livre).

folio[1], pl. **-os** ['fouliou, -ouz], s. 1. (a) Folio m, feuille f, feuillet m (de manuscrit). (b) Typ: etc: Numéro m (d'une page); folio. 2. (Livre m) in-folio m.

folio[2], v.tr. Folioter, paginer (les feuilles d'un livre).

folk [fouk], s. 1. A: Race f; peuple m, nation f. 2. pl. **Folk(s)**, gens mf, personnes f. Country folk(s) campagnards m. My folk(s), les miens, ma famille. 'folk-dance, s. Danse villageoise, rustique. 'folk-song, s. chanson traditionnelle.

folklore ['fouklɔːr], s. Folklore m; traditions f populaires.

folkloric [fouk'lɔrik], a. Folklorique.

folksy [fouksi], a. U.S: F: Liant, sociable, populaire.

follow ['fɔlou]. I. v.tr. 1. Suivre. (a) To f. s.o. about, suivre qn partout. To f. s.o. in, entrer à la suite de, après, qn. To f. the hounds, chasser à courre. A: To f. the plough, être laboureur. F: To f. one's nose, aller tout droit devant soi. (b) To f. a road, suivre un chemin. Boat that follows the coast, bateau qui longe la côte. (c) Succéder à (qn, qch.). The years f. one another, les années se succèdent, se suivent. (Of action) To be followed by consequences, entraîner des conséquences. 2. Être le disciple, le partisan, de (qn). 3. Poursuivre (l'ennemi). 4. Suivre, se conformer à (la mode, etc.). To f. s.o.'s advice, example, suivre le conseil, l'exemple, de qn. 5. Exercer, suivre (une profession); embrasser, poursuivre (une carrière). To f. the sea, être marin. 6. (a) Suivre, comprendre (une explication, etc.). To f. s.o., suivre (un discours). 7. To f. a tragedy with a light comedy, faire suivre une tragédie d'une comédie légère. II. **follow**, v.i. 1. To f. (after), suivre; aller ou venir à la suite. As follows, comme suit. Our method is as follows, notre méthode est la suivante. 2. To f. in s.o.'s footsteps, marcher sur les traces de qn. To f. close behind s.o., emboîter le pas à qn. 3. S'ensuivre, résulter (from, de). Hence it follows that . . ., il s'ensuit que . . ., il suit de là que . . . It does not f. that . . ., ce n'est pas à dire que + sub. **follow on**, v.i. Continuer (dans la même direction). **follow out**, v.tr. Poursuivre (une idée, etc.) jusqu'à sa conclusion. **follow through**, v.i. Sp: etc. Suivre le coup. **follow up**, v.tr. 1. Suivre (qn, qch.) de près. 2. (a) Poursuivre (avec énergie). Com: Suivre, F: chauffer (une affaire). To f. up a clue, s'attacher à une piste. To f. up an advantage, poursuivre un avantage. (b) Donner suite immédiate à (une menace, etc.).

following[1], a. 1. Qui suit Please note the f., prière de noter ce qui suit. Nau: F. sea, mer f de l'arrière. 2. (a) Suivant. On the f. day, le jour suivant; le lendemain. (b) The f. resolution, la résolution énoncée ci-après, la résolution que voici. (c) Two days f., deux jours de suite. **following**[2], s. (a) Suite f (d'un prince). (b) Pol: etc: Parti m (d'un chef). He has a large f., il a beaucoup de partisans m, de disciples m. 'follow-'my-'leader, s. Games: Jeu m de la queue leu leu. Pol: F: F.-my-l. policy, politique f à la remorque.

follower ['fɔlouər], s. (a) Suivant -ante; serviteur m; satellite m, affidé, -ée. (b) Partisan m, disciple m, sectateur, -trice. (c) F: O: Amoureux m, admirateur m (d'une domestique, etc.).

folly ['fɔli], s. 1. Folie f, sottise f, déraison f. To pay for one's f., être victime de sa propre folie. 2. Édifice coûteux et inutile, folie.

foment [fo'ment], v.tr. Fomenter (une plaie, la discorde).

fomentation [foumen'teiʃ(ə)n], s. Fomentation f.

fomenter [fo'mentər], s. Fomentateur, -trice, fauteur, -trice (de troubles etc.).

fond [fɔnd], a. 1. A: Crédule, naïf. F. hope, espoir dont on se berce. 2. (a) (Parent) follement dévoué, trop indulgent. (b) Affectueux, tendre, aimant. 3. (a) To be f. of s.o., aimer, affectionner, avoir de l'attachement pour, qn. They are f. of each other, ils s'aiment. (b) To be f. of music, of novelty, être amateur de musique, de nouveauté. To be f. of sweets, friand de sucreries. To be f. of doing sth., aimer faire qch.; faire volontiers qch. -ly, adv. 1. Crédulement, naïvement. He f. hoped to . . ., il se flattait de. . . . 2. Tendrement, affectueusement.

fondant ['fɔndənt], s. Cu: Fondant m.

fondle ['fɔndl], v.tr. Caresser, câliner, F: chouchouter (qn); faire des mamours à (qn).

fondness ['fɔndnis], s. 1. Indulgence excessive (d'une mère, etc.). 2. Affection f, tendresse f (for, pour, envers). 3. Penchant m, prédilection f, goût m (for sth., pour qch.).

fondue ['fɔndjuː], s. Cu: Fondue f.

font [fɔnt], s. Fonts baptismaux.

food [fu:d], s. **1.** (a) Nourriture f; aliments mpl; vivres mpl. **To offer s.o. f.,** offrir à manger à qn. **F. and clothing,** le vivre et le vêtement. **Plain f.,** aliments simples. **Hotel where the f. is good,** hôtel où la cuisine, la table, est bonne. **To be off one's f.,** n'avoir pas d'appétit. **F.-stuffs, articles of f.,** comestibles m, denrées f alimentaires. **F. products,** produits m alimentaires. **F. value,** valeur nutritive. **Ministry of F.,** Ministère m du Ravitaillement. (b) **Aliment. Complete f.,** aliment complet. Toil: **Skin f.,** aliment pour la peau. (c) Husb: **Pâture** f (d'animaux); nourriture, mangeaille f (de volaille). **Soft f.** (for poultry), pâtée f. (d) **Mental, intellectual, f.,** nourriture de l'esprit. **To give s.o. f. for thought,** donner à penser, à réfléchir, à qn. **2. F. and drink,** le boire et le manger. **'food-processing,** s. The f.-p. industry, l'industrie f alimentaire. **'food-poisoning,** s. Intoxication f alimentaire.

fool[1] [fu:l], s. **1.** Imbécile mf; idiot, -ote; niais, -aise; sot, f. sotte. F: **To play, act the f.,** faire l'imbécile; faire des bêtises, des sottises. **To make a f. of oneself,** se rendre ridicule. **Silly f.!** P: espèce d'idiot! **Some f. of a politician,** U.S: some f. politician, quelque imbécile d'homme politique. **2. Fou** m, bouffon m. **To play the f.,** faire le pitre. (Cf. 1.) **3.** Dupe f. **To make a f. of s.o.,** berner qn, mystifier qn. **To go on a f.'s errand,** aller faire pour des prunes, se casser le nez. S.a. ALL FOOLS' DAY, APRIL, PARADISE. **'foolproof,** a. A l'épreuve des imbéciles; (mécanisme) indéréglable, indétraquable.

fool[2]. F: **1.** v.i. Faire la bête. **Stop fooling!** assez de bêtises! **To f. about, around,** flâner; baguenauder; gâcher son temps; courir la ville (with, avec). **2.** v.tr. Berner, mystifier, duper (qn); F: se payer la tête de (qn). **fooling,** s. **1.** Bouffonnerie f; (in school, etc.) dissipation f. **2.** Bernement m, duperie f (de qn).

fool[3], s. Cu: Marmelade f (de fruits) à la crème.

foolery ['fu:ləri], s. F: **1.** Sottise f, bêtise f. **2.** Bouffonnerie f; pitrerie f.

foolhardiness ['fu:lhɑ:dinis], s. Témérité f, imprudence f.

foolhardy ['fu:lhɑ:di], a. Téméraire, imprudent.

foolish ['fu:liʃ], a. **1.** (a) Insensé; fou, f. folle; étourdi. (b) Sot, f. sotte; bête. **2.** Absurde, ridicule. **To look f.,** avoir l'air penaud. **To feel f.,** rester tout bête. **-ly,** adv. **1.** Follement, étourdiment. **2.** Sottement, bêtement.

foolishness ['fu:liʃnis], s. **1.** Folie f, étourderie f. **2.** Sottise f, bêtise f.

foolscap ['fu:lskæp], s. Papier m ministre.

foot[1], pl. **feet** [fut, fi:t], s. **1.** Pied m. (a) **He gets under your feet,** il se met dans vos jambes. **To put one's best f. foreward,** (i) presser, allonger, le pas; (ii) pousser la besogne; faire de son mieux. **To sit at s.o.'s feet,** (i) s'asseoir aux pieds de qn; (ii) être le disciple de qn. **To set f. on an island,** mettre le pied sur une île. **To knock s.o. off his feet,** faire perdre l'équilibre à qn; renverser qn. **To carry s.o. off his feet,** transporter qn d'admiration, d'enthousiasme. **To keep one's feet,** (i) tenir pied, rester debout; (ii) F: tenir bon, tenir ferme. **To rise to one's feet (again),** se (re)lever; se (re)mettre debout. **To be on one's feet,** se tenir debout. **He is on his feet again,** il est de nouveau sur pied; le voilà remis. **To set s.o. on his feet again,** (i) (re)mettre qn sur pied, (r)établir qn; (ii) (re)lancer qn (dans les affaires, etc.). **To find one's feet,** voler de ses propres ailes; se débrouiller. **To put one's f. down upon sth.,** réprimer énergiquement (un abus); opposer un refus formel à (un projet, etc.). F: **To put one's f. down,** faire acte d'autorité. Aut: **Put your f. down!** allez-y! accélérez! **To get one's f. in,** s'implanter, s'impatroniser (chez qn, etc.). F: **To put one's f. in it,** mettre les pieds dans le plat. F: **To put one's feet up,** se reposer. F: **To have, get, cold feet,** caner, caponner. F: **To have a light f., a heavy f.,** avoir le pas léger, lourd. **Swift of f.,** léger à la course. (c) Adv.phr. **On f.** (i) A pied; (ii) en train. **To set negotiations on f.,** ouvrir des négociations. **Under f.,** sous les pieds. **To trample, tread, sth. under f.,** fouler qch. aux pieds. **2.** Pied (d'animaux à sabot); patte f (de chien, de chat,

d'insecte, d'oiseau). Equit: **The fore feet,** le bipède antérieur (du cheval). **3.** Coll. Mil: Infanterie f. **F. and horse,** infanterie et cavalerie. **4.** (a) Pied, semelle f (d'un bas). (b) Bas bout (d'une table); pied (d'un lit); extrémité inférieure (d'un lac). (c) Base f (de colonne, etc.); pied m (de verre à boire). (d) Bas m (d'échelle, de page); départ m (d'un escalier); fond (d'une voile). **At the f. of the page,** au bas de la page. **At the f. of the list, of the class,** à la queue de la liste, de la classe. **5.** (a) Pros: Pied. (b) Meas: Pied anglais (de 30 cm. 48). **foot-and-'mouth disease,** s. Fièvre aphteuse; F: cocotte f. **'foot-bath,** s. Bain m de pieds. **'foot-brake,** s. Frein m à pédale; frein au pied. **'foot-bridge,** s. Passerelle f. **'foot(-)control,** s. Mec.E: Commande f au pied. **'foot(-)fault,** s. Ten: Faute f de pied. **'foot-gear,** s. = FOOT-WEAR. **'foot-guards,** s.pl. Mil: Gardes m à pied; garde f à pied. **'foot-lathe,** s. Tls: Tour m à pédale. **'foot-muff,** s. Chancelière f. **'foot(-)note,** s. Note f au bas de la page; renvoi m en bas de page. **'foot-pace,** s. **To go, ride, at a f.-p.,** aller au pas. **'foot-passenger,** s. Piéton m. **'foot-plate,** s. Mch: Plate-forme f, tablier m (de locomotive). **'foot-race,** s. Course f à pied. **'foot-rest,** s. Cy: Cale-pied(s) m inv. **'foot-rot,** s. Vet: Fourchet m, piétin m. **'foot-rule,** s. Règle f (d'un pied). **'foot-work,** s. Sp: Jeu m de pieds, de jambes.

foot[2], v.tr. **1.** (a) A: Danser (un quadrille). (b) F: **To f. it,** faire le trajet à pied. **2.** F: **To f. the bill,** payer la note. **3.** U.S: **To f. (up) the account,** faire l'addition. **-footed,** a. **Flat-f.,** aux pieds plats. **Sure-f.,** au pied sûr. **footing,** s. **1.** (a) Fenc: Danc: etc: Pose f des pieds. (b) = FOOTHOLD. **To lose one's f.,** perdre pied. **I missed my f.,** le pied me manqua. **To miss one's f.,** faire un faux mouvement. **2.** (a) Situation sûre. **To gain a f.,** s'implanter, prendre pied. (b) Position f, condition f. **To be on a good f. with s.o.,** être en bons termes avec qn. **To be on an equal f.** (with . . .), être de pair, sur un pied d'égalité (avec . . .). (c) Admission f (à une société). **To pay one's f.,** payer sa bienvenue; Mil: arroser ses galons. **3.** Const: Empattement m.

football ['futbɔ:l], s. **1.** Ballon m. **2.** Le football. Rugby f., le rugby. **F. ground,** terrain m de football. **footballer** ['futbɔ:lər], s. Joueur m de football; footballeur m.

footfall ['futfɔ:l], s. (Bruit m de) pas m.

foothills ['futhilz], s.pl. Contreforts m (d'un massif); vallonnements m.

foothold ['futhould], s. Assiette f, prise f, pour le pied. **To get a f.,** prendre pied. **To keep one's f.,** garder l'équilibre. **To lose one's f.,** perdre pied.

footle ['fu:tl], v.i. F: **To f. about,** s'occuper à des bagatelles. **To f. away one's time,** gâcher son temps. **footling,** a. F: Insignifiant, futile.

footless ['futlis], a. **1.** Z: Apode; sans pieds, sans pattes. **2.** U.S: = FUTILE.

footlights ['futlaits], s.pl. Th: Rampe f.

footman, pl. **-men** ['futmən], s.m. Valet de pied; laquais.

footmark ['futmɑ:k], s. Empreinte f de pied.

footpad ['futpæd], s. A: Voleur m; détrousseur m de grand chemin.

footpath ['futpɑ:θ], s. Sentier m (pour piétons); (in street) trottoir m.

footprint ['futprint], s. Empreinte f de pas.

footsore ['futsɔər], a. Aux pieds endoloris.

footstep ['futstep], s. **1.** Pas m. **2. To follow, tread, walk, in s.o.'s footsteps,** emboîter le pas à qn; suivre les brisées, marcher sur les traces, de qn.

footstool ['futstu:l], s. Tabouret m.

footway ['futwei], s. = FOOTPATH.

footwear ['futwɛər], s. Com: Chaussures fpl.

foozle ['fu:zl], v.tr. & abs. Golf: **To f. (a shot),** rater, manquer, un coup.

fop [fɔp], s. A: Bellâtre m, fat m.

foppish ['fɔpiʃ], a. A: (Homme) bellâtre, fat.

foppishness ['fɔpiʃnis], s. O: Fatuité f.

for[1] [fɔ:r, unstressed fər], prep. Pour. **I. 1.** (a) (i) (Representing) **Member f. Liverpool,** député de Liverpool. Tp: **A f. Andrew,** A comme Anatole. (ii) (Instead of) **To act f. s.o.,** agir pour qn, au nom de qn. **He is writing f. me,** il écrit à ma place, de ma

part. (b) He wants her f. his wife, il la veut pour
femme. (c) To be paid f. one's services, être payé pour,
de, ses services. (d) To exchange one thing f. another,
échanger une chose contre une autre. To sell sth.
f. ten francs, vendre qch. dix francs. He'll do it f. a
fiver, il le fera pour cinq livres. 2. (a) (In favour of)
He is f. free trade, il est pour le libre-échange. The
exchange is f. us, le change nous est favorable. (b)
It is not f. you to blame him, ce n'est pas à vous de le
critiquer. 3. (a) What f.? pourquoi (faire)? What is it
f.? Quel en est l'objet? What's that gadget f.? à
quoi sert ce truc-là? Shoes f. men, chaussures pour
hommes. F. sale, à vendre. F. example, par exemple.
P: He's f. it ['fɔːrit], he's in for it ['infɔrit], son
affaire est bonne. (b) (i) To marry s.o. f. his money,
épouser qn pour son argent. To choose s.o. f. his
ability, choisir qn en raison de sa compétence. He
was gaoled f. six months f. breaking into our house, il
a attrapé six mois de prison pour avoir cambriolé
notre maison. P: He was had f. a mug, il s'est
laissé prendre. To jump f. joy, sauter de joie. (ii)
I've slept all day and feel all the better f. it, j'ai
dormi toute la journée et je m'en trouve mieux. 4.
(a) Ship bound for America, navire en partance pour
l'Amérique. The trains f. Orleans, les trains pour,
sur, Orléans. Train f. London, train direction de
Londres. Change here f. Bristol, direction de Bristol,
changez de train. (b) His feelings f. you, ses sentiments envers vous. 5. The road is lined with trees
f. two miles, la route est bordée d'arbres sur, pendant,
deux milles. 6. (a) (Future) I am going away f. a
fortnight, je pars pour quinze jours. He will be away
f. a year, il sera absent pendant un an. He won't be
back f. a week, il ne reviendra pas d'ici à huit jours.
(b) (Past) He was away f. a fortnight, il fut absent
pendant quinze jours. I have not seen him f. three
years, voilà, il y a, trois ans que je ne l'ai vu. (c) I
have been here f. three days, il y a trois jours que je
suis ici; je suis ici depuis trois jours. I had known
him f. years, je le connaissais depuis des années.
7. (a) This box is f. you, cette boîte est pour vous. A
cake had been set aside f. me, on avait mis de côté un
gâteau à mon intention. To make a name f. oneself,
se faire un nom. Here is news f. you! voici une
nouvelle qui vous intéressera! To write f. the papers,
écrire dans les journaux. (b) Sch: Your prep f.
tomorrow, votre devoir pour demain. 8. I don't care
f. her very much, je ne l'aime pas beaucoup. Fit f.
nothing, bon à rien. You're the man f. the job, vous
êtes mon homme. Oh! f. a house on the Riviera!
oh! si je pouvais avoir une maison sur la côte d'Azur!
Now f. it! allons-y! 9. (a) As f. him . . ., quant à
lui. . . . As for that . . ., pour ce qui est de cela. . . .
See f. yourself! voyez par vous-même! (b) For all
that, malgré tout; ce nonobstant. For all that, you
should have let me know, tout de même, vous auriez dû
me prévenir. (c) But for her I should have died, n'eût
été elle, sans elle, je serais mort. (d) Translate word
for word, traduisez mot à mot. For one enemy he has
a hundred friends, pour un ennemi il a cent amis. 10.
(To the amount of). To draw on s.o. f. £50, fournir
une traite de £50 sur qn. Put my name down f. £1,
inscrivez-moi pour £1. II. for introducing an infinitive
clause. 1. It is easy for him to come, il lui est facile de
venir. For this to be feasible, pour que cela se
puisse. It is too late f. us to start, il est trop tard
pour que nous partions. 2. I have brought it for you
to see, je l'ai apporté pour que vous le voyiez. It is
not for me to decide, ce n'est pas à moi de décider.
3. It's no good for Mr X to talk, M. X a beau dire.
4. He gave orders for the trunks to be packed, il donna
l'ordre de faire les malles. 5. To arrange for sth. to
be done, prendre des dispositions pour que qch. se
fasse. To wait for sth. to be done, attendre que qch.
se fasse. 6. The best plan will be for you to go away
for a time, le mieux sera que vous vous absentiez
pour quelque temps. It would be a disgrace for you
to back out now, vous retirer maintenant serait
honteux.
for², conj. Car.
forage¹ ['fɔridʒ], s. 1. Fourrage(s) m (pl). 2. To go on
the f., aller au fourrage. 'forage-cap, s. Mil:
Bonnet m de police; calot m.

forage². 1. v.i. Fourrager; aller au fourrage. F: To
f. for sth., fouiller pour trouver qch. 2. v.tr. (a)
Ravager, saccager, fourrager (un pays). (b) Donner
du fourrage à (un cheval, etc.).
forager ['fɔridʒər], s. Fourrageur m.
foramen, pl. -mina [fə'reimen, -minə], s. Anat:
Nat.Hist: Foramen m; orifice m.
forasmuch [fɔːrəz'mʌtʃ], adv. A: F. as . . ., d'autant
que, vu que, attendu que. . . .
foray¹ ['fɔrei], s. Razzia f, incursion f, raid m.
foray², v.i. Faire des incursions, des raids.
forbade [fɔː'bæd]. See FORBID.
forbear¹ ['fɔːbɛər], s. Aïeul, -eux m; ancêtre m.
forbear² [fɔː'bɛər], v. (p.t. forbore [fɔː'bɔːr]; p.p. forborne [fɔː'bɔːn]) 1. v.tr. S'abstenir de (qch.). 2. v.i. (a)
S'abstenir. To f. from doing sth.,s'abstenir de, se garder
de, faire qch. (b) To bear and f. ['fɔːbɛər], se montrer
patient et indulgent. forbearing, a. Patient, endurant.
forbearance [fɔː'bɛərəns], s. 1. F. from, of, sth.,
abstention f de qch. 2. Patience f, longanimité f.
forbid [fɔː'bid], v.tr. (forbade [fɔr'bæd]; forbidden) 1.
Défendre, interdire; Jur: prohiber. I am forbidden
tea, le thé m'est défendu. 'Smoking forbidden,'
"défense de fumer." Forbidden fruit, fruit défendu.
Forbidden subjects, sujets tabous. Mil: Forbidden
weapons, armes prohibées. To f. s.o. sth., défendre,
interdire, qch. à qn. To f. s.o. the house, interdire,
défendre, (l'entrée de) sa maison à qn. To f. s.o. to
do sth., défendre à qn de faire qch. 2. Empêcher
(qch.). My health forbids my coming, ma santé
m'empêche de venir. God f. (that . . .)! à Dieu ne
plaise (que + sub.)! forbidding, a. (Visage) sinistre,
rébarbatif; (ciel, temps) sombre, menaçant.
forbore, forborne. See FORBEAR².
force¹ [fɔːs], s. Force f. 1. (a) Violence f, contrainte f.
By sheer f., de vive force. By sheer f. of will, à force
de volonté. Owing to the force of circumstances, par
la force des choses. To resort to f., (i) faire appel à
la force; (ii) se porter à des voies de fait. To yield
to f., céder à la force. (b) Influence f, autorité f. 2.
(a) Énergie f; effort(s) m(pl), intensité f (du vent).
He argued with much f. that . . ., il a représenté avec
insistance que. . . . (b) Mec: Force, effort. F. of
gravity, (force de la) pesanteur. Impulsive f., force
d'impulsion. 3. Puissance f (militaire); force (au
service de l'État). The allied forces, les armées
alliées. Home forces, armée métropolitaine. Land
and sea forces, armées de terre et de mer. The police
f., F: the F., la force publique; la police. A strong
f. of police, un fort détachement de police. In (full)
f., en force. We turned out in full f., nous étions la
au grand complet, en force. 4. (a) Vertu f, efficacité
f (d'un remède, etc.). There is f. in what you say,
votre argument n'est pas sans valeur. (b) Signification f (d'un mot). Verb used with passive f., verbe
employé avec la valeur d'un passif. 5. (Of law) To
come into f., entrer en vigueur. The methods in f., les
méthodes appliquées actuellement. 'force-pump, s.
Hyd.E: Pompe (re)foulante.
force², v.tr. Forcer. 1. (a) To f. s.o.'s hand, forcer la
main à qn. To f. the pace, forcer l'allure. She forced
a smile, elle eut un sourire contraint. (b) Prendre
(qn, qch.) de force; violenter; fracturer (un coffre-
fort). To f. one's way, se frayer un chemin. To f.
one's way into a house, pénétrer de force dans une
maison. (c) To f. sth. into sth., faire entrer qch. de
force dans qch. (d) To f. a plant, forcer une plante.
Aut: etc: To f. the engine, trop pousser le moteur.
2. (a) Contraindre, obliger. The town was forced to
capitulate, la ville fut obligée de capituler. I am forced
to conclude that . . ., je suis forcé de conclure que.
. . . (b) To f. a nation into war, forcer une nation à
entrer en guerre. (c) To f. an action on the enemy,
contraindre l'ennemi à la bataille. (d) To f. sth. from
s.o., extorquer, arracher, (une promesse, etc.) à qn.
force back, v.tr. 1. Repousser; faire reculer. 2.
Refouler (l'air, l'eau). forced, a. Forcé. 1. Inévitable, obligatoire. F. loan, emprunt forcé. 2. Contraint. F. laugh, rire forcé. To give a f. laugh,
rire jaune. Mil: F. march, marche forcée. Forced
style, style m guindé. forcing, s. 1. Forcement m
(d'une serrure, etc.). 2. Hort: Forçage m; culture
forcée. 'forcing-house, s. Hort: Forcerie f.

forceful ['fɔːsful], *a.* (*Of pers., speech*) Plein de force; énergique. **-fully,** *adv.* Avec force.

forcemeat ['fɔːsmiːt], *s. Cu:* Farce *f*, hachis *m*. **F. ball,** boulette *f*.

forceps ['fɔːseps], *s. sg. & pl. Surg:* Pince *f. Obst:* Fers *mpl*, forceps *m. Dent:* Davier *m. Ent:* Pince (de forficule).

forcible ['fɔːsibl], *a.* 1. (Entrée) de force. 2. (Langage) énergique, vigoureux. **-ibly,** *adv.* 1. Par la force, de force. 2. Énergiquement.

ford¹ [fɔːd], *s.* Gué *m*.

ford², *v.tr.* Guéer, passer à gué (une rivière).

fordable ['fɔːdəbl], *a.* Guéable.

fore¹ ['fɔːr]. I. *a.* (*a*) Antérieur, -eure; de devant. (*b*) *Nau:* (De l')avant. II. **fore,** *s.* (*a*) *Nau:* Avant *m*. **At the f.,** au mât de misaine. (*b*) **To the f.,** (i) en vue, en évidence; (ii) présent. **To come to the f.,** passer au premier plan; commencer à être connu. **'fore(-) and(-)'aft,** *a. & adv. Nau:* De l'avant à l'arrière. **F.-and-a. sail,** voile *f* aurique. **'fore-cabin,** *s. Nau:* Cabine *f* de l'avant. **'fore-carriage,** *s.* Avant-train *m* (d'une voiture). **'fore-deck,** *s. Nau:* Plage *f* avant. **'fore-edge,** *s. Bookb:* Gouttière *f* (d'un livre). **'fore-foot,** *pl.* **-feet,** *s.* Pied antérieur; patte *f* de devant. **'fore(-)part,** *s.* Avant *m*, devant *m*; avant-corps *m inv* (d'un bâtiment); tête *f* (d'un train). **The f.-p. of the ship,** la partie avant du navire. **'fore-quarter,** *s.* Quartier *m* de devant (de bœuf). **Fore-quarters of a horse,** avant-main *m*, avant-train *m*, d'un cheval. **'fore-sail,** *s. Nau:* (Voile *f* de) misaine *f*. **'fore-stage,** *s. Th:* Avant-scène *f*. **'fore-tooth,** *pl.* **-teeth,** *s.* (Dent) incisive *f*; dent du devant.

fore², *int. Golf:* Attention devant! gare devant!

forearm ['fɔːrɑːm], *s.* Avant-bras *m inv*.

forearmed [fɔːrˈɑːmd], *a. See* FOREWARN.

forebode [fɔːˈboud], *v.tr.* 1. (*Of thg*) Présager, laisser prévoir (un malheur). 2. (*Of pers.*) Pressentir (un malheur). **foreboding,** *s.* 1. Présage *m* (de malheur). 2. (Sombre) pressentiment.

forebrain ['fɔːbrein], *Anat:* = Cerveau antérieur.

forecast¹ ['fɔːkɑːst], *s.* Prévision *f. Horse Rac:* (Pari) tiercé. **Racing f., betting f.,** pronostic *m*.

forecast, *v.tr.* (*p.t. & p.p.* forecast *or* forecasted) Calculer, prévoir (les événements). **To f. the weather,** prévoir le temps.

forecastle ['fouksl], *s. Nau:* 1. Gaillard *m* (d'avant). 2. (*In merchant vessel*) Poste *m* de l'équipage.

foreclose [fɔːˈklouz], *v.tr.* **To f. (the mortgage),** saisir l'immeuble hypothéqué.

foreclosure [fɔːˈklouʒər], *s. Jur:* Saisie *f* (d'une hypothèque).

forecourt ['fɔːkɔːt], *s.* Avant-cour *f*, *pl.* avant-cours.

foredoomed [fɔːˈduːmd], *a.* Condamné d'avance (to, à). **Plan f. to failure,** projet mort-né, voué à l'insuccès.

forefather ['fɔːfɑːðər], *s.* Aïeul *m*, ancêtre *m*. **Our forefathers,** nos aïeux.

forefinger ['fɔːfiŋgər], *s.* Index *m*.

forefront ['fɔːfrʌnt], *s.* Premier rang, premier plan.

foregather [fɔːˈgæðər], *v.i,* = FORGATHER.

forego [fɔːˈgou], *v.tr.* = FORGO.

foregoing [fɔːˈgouiŋ], *a.* Précédent, antérieur; déjà cité. **The f.,** ce qui précède.

foregone ['fɔːgɔn], *a.* (*Of conclusion*) Décidé d'avance; prévu.

foreground ['fɔːgraund], *s. Art: Phot:* Premier plan; avant-plan *m*. **In the f.,** au premier plan.

forehand ['fɔːhænd], *s.* **1.** *s.* (*Of horse*) Avant-main *m*. **2.** *a. Ten:* F. stroke, coup *m* d'avant-main; coup droit.

forehead ['fɔrid], *s. Anat:* Front *m*.

foreign ['fɔrin], *a.* Étranger. **1. F. to, from (sth.),** étranger à, éloigné de, sans rapport avec (qch.). *Med: etc:* **F. body,** corps étranger. **2.** Qui n'est pas du pays. (*a*) (*Situated abroad*) **F. countries, f. parts,** pays étrangers; l'étranger *m*. **He has been in f. parts,** il a été à l'étranger. **Our relations with f. countries,** nos rapports avec l'extérieur. (*b*) (*Dealing with foreign countries*) **F. trade,** commerce extérieur. *Nau:* **To be in the f. trade,** naviguer au long cours. **F. money order,** mandat international. **The F. Office** = le Ministère des Affaires étrangères. **The F. Secretary** = le Ministre des Affaires étrangères.

foreigner ['fɔrinər], *s.* Étranger, -ère.

foreknowledge ['fɔːˈnɔlidʒ], *s.* Préconnaissance *f*; prescience *f*.

foreland ['fɔːlənd], *s.* Cap *m*, promontoire *m*; pointe *f* (de terre); falaise *f* à pic.

foreleg ['fɔːleg], *s.* Jambe antérieure, de devant (d'un cheval); patte *f* de devant (d'un chien).

forelock ['fɔːlɔk], *s.* (*Of pers.*) Mèche *f* (de cheveux) sur le front; (*of pers., horse*) toupet *m*. **To take time by the f.,** saisir l'occasion aux cheveux.

foreman, *pl.* **-men** ['fɔːmən], *s.m.* **1.** *Jur:* Chef du jury. **2.** (*a*) *Ind:* Contremaître; chef d'équipe. **Works f.,** conducteur des travaux. (*b*) **Printer's f.,** prote *m*.

foremast ['fɔːmɑːst], *s.* Mât *m* de misaine; (arbre *m* de) trinquet *m*.

foremost ['fɔːrmoust]. **1.** *a.* Premier; le plus avancé. **In the f. rank,** au tout premier rang. **To come f.,** venir tout en tête. **2.** *adv.* **First and f.,** tout d'abord; d'abord et avant tout.

forenoon ['fɔːnuːn], *s.* (*esp. Scot. & Irish*) Matinée *f*.

forensic [fəˈrensik], *a.* (Éloquence) judiciaire, du barreau. **F. medicine,** médecine légale. **F. scientist,** expert *m* légiste.

forerunner ['fɔːrʌnər], *s.* Avant-coureur *m*, avant-courrier, -ière; précurseur *m*.

foresee [fɔːˈsiː], *v.tr.* (foresaw [fɔːˈsɔː]; foreseen [fɔːˈsiːn]) Prévoir, entrevoir (des difficultés, l'avenir). **foreseeable,** *a.* Prévisible. **foreseeing,** *a.* Prévoyant.

foreshadow [fɔːˈʃædou], *v.tr.* Présager, annoncer, laisser prévoir (un événement).

foreshore ['fɔːʃɔːr], *s.* **1.** Plage *f*. **2.** Partie *f* de la plage qui découvre à marée basse, laisse *f* de marée.

foreshorten [fɔːˈʃɔːtn], *v.tr. Art:* Dessiner, présenter, (un objet) en raccourci, en perspective. **foreshortened,** *a. Art:* Raccourci, en raccourci. **foreshortening,** *s. Art:* Raccourci *m*.

foresight ['fɔːsait], *s.* **1.** (*a*) Prévision *f* (de l'avenir). (*b*) Prévoyance *f*. **Want of f.,** imprévoyance *f*, imprévision *f*. **2.** *Sm.a:* Guidon *m*.

foreskin ['fɔːskin], *s. Anat:* Prépuce *m*.

forest ['fɔrist], *s.* Forêt *f*. **F. of timber trees, open f.,** forêt de haute futaie. **The national forests,** le domaine forestier. **'forest-guard,** **-'ranger,** *s.* Garde forestier. **'forest-tree,** *s.* Arbre forestier; arbre de haute futaie.

forestall [fɔːˈstɔːl], *v.tr.* Anticiper, devancer, prévenir (qn, un événement). **forestalling,** *s.* Anticipation *f* (des désirs de qn); devancement *m* (d'un concurrent).

forester ['fɔristər], *s.* (Garde) forestier *m*.

forestry ['fɔristri], *s.* Sylviculture *f*. **School of f.,** école forestière.

foretaste ['fɔːteist], *s.* Avant-goût *m*.

foretell [fɔːˈtel], *v.tr.* (foretold [fɔːˈtould]; foretold) **1.** (*Of pers.*) Prédire. **2.** Présager. **foretelling,** *s.* Prédiction *f*.

forethought ['fɔːθɔːt], *s.* **1.** Préméditation *f*. **2.** Prévoyance *f*.

foretold. *See* FORETELL.

foretop ['fɔːtɔp], *s. Nau:* Hune *f* de misaine.

forever [fərˈevər], *adv. See* EVER 2 (b).

forevermore [fərevəˈmɔːr], *adv. See* EVERMORE.

forewarn [fɔːˈwɔːn], *v.tr.* Prévenir, avertir. **Forewarned is forearmed,** un homme averti en vaut deux.

forewoman, *pl.* **-women** ['fɔːwumən, -wimin], *s.f.* Contremaîtresse; "première."

foreword ['fɔːwəːd], *s.* Avant-propos *m inv*, préface *f*; avis *m* au lecteur; avertissement *m*.

forfeit¹ ['fɔːfit], *a. Hist: Jur:* Confisqué; perdu.

forfeit², *s.* (*a*) Amende *f. Turf:* Forfait *m*. **F. clause** (of a contract), clause *f* de dédit. (*b*) *Games:* Gage *m*, punition *f*.

forfeit³, *v.tr.* **1.** Perdre (qch.) par confiscation. **To f. a right,** être déchu d'un droit; laisser périmer un droit. **2.** Perdre (qch.). **To f. one's life,** payer de sa vie. **To f. one's honour,** forfaire à l'honneur.

forfeiture ['fɔːfitʃər], *s.* Perte *f* (de biens) par confiscation; perte (de l'honneur, etc.). *Jur: Fin:* Déchéance *f*, forfaiture *f* (d'un droit).

forgather [fɔːˈgæðər], *v.i.* **1.** S'assembler; se réunir. **2. To f. with s.o.,** rencontrer qn.

forgave. *See* FORGIVE.

forge¹ [fɔːdʒ], s. Forge f.

forge², v.tr. 1. (a) Forger (un fer à cheval). (b) Metall: Forger, cingler (le fer). To f. hot, cold, forger à chaud, à froid. 2. Forger (une excuse); contrefaire (une signature). Abs. Commettre un faux. **forged,** a. 1. (Fer) forgé. 2. (Document) faux, falsifié. Jur· To produce a f. will, supposer un testament. **Production of f. documents,** supposition f. **forging,** s. 1. 'Metalw: Travail m de forge. 2. Pièce forgée. 3. Falsification f (de documents).

forge³, v.i. To f. ahead. (a) (Of ship) Courir sur son erre. (b) (i) Nau: Voguer à pleines voiles; (ii) gagner les devants; (iii) (in business) pousser de l'avant; Rac: foncer.

forger ['fɔːdʒər], s. 1. Metall: Forgeron m. 2. (Of signature) Faussaire mf; falsificateur, -trice.

forgery ['fɔːdʒəri], s. 1. Contrefaçon f (de billets de banque); falsification f (de documents); supposition f (de testament). Jur: Plea of f., (action en) inscription f de faux. 2. Faux m. The signature was a f., la signature était contrefaite.

forget [fə'get], v.tr. (forgot [fə'gɔt]; forgotten [fə'gɔtn]; forgetting) Oublier. 1. Perdre le souvenir de (qch.). To f. a fact, oublier un fait. To f. one's Latin, désapprendre son latin. F. about it! n'y pensez plus! F: And don't you f. it! faites-y bien attention! To f. how time goes, perdre la notion de l'heure, du temps. That is easily forgotten, cela s'oublie facilement. This is best forgotten, il vaut mieux ne plus en parler. Never to be forgotten, inoubliable. 2. (a) Omettre, oublier (un nom sur une liste, etc.). Don't f. to . . ., ne manquez pas de. . . . (b) Oublier (son mouchoir, etc.). (c) Négliger (son devoir, etc.). Mil: etc: To f. one's orders, F: manger la consigne. 3. F· To f. oneself, s'oublier. (a) Manquer à soi-même ou aux bienséances. To f. oneself so far as to . . ., s'oublier au point de. . . . (b) Ne plus penser à ce qu'on fait. I forgot myself! ça m'a échappé! **forgetting,** s. Oubli m. **for'get-me-not,** s. Bot: Myosotis m; F: ne m'oubliez pas m inv.

forgetful [fə'getful], a. 1. Oublieux (of, de). He is very f., il a très mauvaise mémoire. 2. Négligent.

forgetfulness [fə'getfulnis], s. 1. (a) Manque (habituel) de mémoire. (b) A moment of f., un moment d'oubli m. 2. Négligence f.

forgivable [fə'givəbl], a. Pardonnable.

forgive [fə'giv], v.tr. (forgave [fə'geiv]; forgiven [fə'giv(ə)n]). 1. (a) Pardonner (une injure, etc.). (b) To f. s.o. a debt, faire grâce d'une dette à qn. 2. To f. s.o., pardonner à qn. I have never been forgiven for this joke, on ne m'a jamais pardonné cette plaisanterie. **forgiving,** a. Indulgent; peu rancunier.

forgiveness [fə'givnis], s. 1. (a) Pardon m. (b) Remise f (d'une dette). 2. Indulgence f, clémence f.

forgo [fɔː'gou], v.tr. (forwent [fɔː'went]; forgone [fɔː'gɔn]) Renoncer à (qch.); s'abstenir de (qch.). **forgone,** a. It was a f. conclusion, on s'y attendait.

·**forgot, forgotten.** See FORGET.

fork¹ [fɔːk], s. 1. Agr: Fourche f. Two-pronged f., fourchet m. Hand f., déplantoir m. 2. Fourchette f (de table). 3. (a) (Prop) Poteau fourchu, fourchon m. 4. (a) Cy: Front fork(s), fourche de direction. Mec.E: Cardan f., chape f de cardan. (b) Mus: Tuning-f., diapason m. 5. (a) Bifurcation f, fourche (de routes). (b) Enfourchure f (de branches, des jambes).

fork². 1. v.i. (Of tree, etc.) Fourcher; (of road) fourcher, faire la fourche, (se) bifurquer. Aut: F. right for York, prenez à droite pour York. 2. v.tr. Remuer (le foin, le sol) à la fourche. **fork out, up,** v.tr. P: Allonger, abouler (de l'argent). Abs. S'exécuter, P: casquer. **forked,** a. Fourchu, bifurqué. F. lightning, éclair m en zigzags. **forking,** s. Bifurcation f.

forlorn [fə'lɔːn], a. Lit: 1. (Of undertaking) Désespéré. F. hope, aventure désespérée. 2. (a) Abandonné, délaissé. (b) appearance, mine triste, désolée.

form¹ [fɔːm], s. 1. (a) Forme f, conformation f, configuration f (d'un objet). Statistics in tabular f., statistique sous forme de tableau. (b) Figure f, silhouette f. In the f. of a dog, sous la forme d'un chien. The f. and the substance, la forme et le fond. 2. (a) Forme, formalité f. To go through the f. of

refusing, faire des simagrées de refuser. For f.'s sake, as a matter of f., pour la forme; par manière d'acquit. It is a mere matter of f., c'est une pure formalité. (b) Les convenances f; l'étiquette f. It is good f., c'est de bon ton. It is not good f., it is bad f., cela ne se fait pas, ne se dit pas. 3. (a) Formule f, forme. Correct f. of words, tournure correcte de phrase. It is only a f. of speech, ce n'est qu'une façon de parler. (b) Adm: Formule. Printed form, imprimé m. F. of tender, modèle m de soumission. Inquiry f., bulletin m de demande de renseignements. To fill in, fill up, a f., remplir une formule, un formulaire. You must fill in a f., F: il faut faire une demande (par écrit). 4. (a) Sp: (Of horse, athlete) Forme; état m, condition f. To be in f., out of f., être, ne pas être, en forme. (b) (Of pers.) To be in good f., être en verve, en train. To be in poor f., être en petite forme. Sp: Return to f., retour m en forme. 5. Sch: Classe f. First f., approx = classe de) sixième f. Sixth f., approx. = (classe de) première f. F. master, professeur principal. 6. Banc m, banquette f. 7. (a) Metall: Forme, moule m. (b) Typ: Forme. 8. Gîte m (du lièvre). **'form-room,** s. Sch: Salle f de classe; la classe.

form². I. v.tr. 1. Former, faire, façonner. To f. sth. from, out of, sth., faire qch. de qch. To f. a child's mind, façonner l'esprit d'un enfant. 2. (a) Former, organiser (une société). They formed themselves into a committee, ils se constituèrent en comité. (b) Former, contracter (une habitude). (c) Se former, se faire (une opinion). (d) Former, arrêter (un plan). 3. (a) The coastline forms a series of curves, le littoral dessine une série de courbes. Mil: To f. fours, se mettre par quatre. (b) To f. part of sth., faire partie de qch. The ministers who f. the cabinet, les ministres qui composent le gouvernement. II. form, v.i. Prendre forme; se former. His style is forming, son style se fait. Mil: To f. into line, se mettre, se former, en ligne. To f. into a square, former le carré.

formal ['fɔːm(ə)l], a. 1. Log: Theol: Formel. 2. (Of procedure) Formel, en règle; (of order) formel, positif. F. denial, démenti formel. F. contract, contrat en due forme. 3. Protocolaire; cérémonieux. F. bow, salut cérémonieux. A f. dinner, un grand dîner, un dîner d'apparat. F. style, style empesé. 4. (a) (Of pers.) Formaliste, cérémonieux, pointilleux. He is always very f., il est toujours très compassé. She is very f., elle est très collet monté. (b) (Style) conventionnel. -ally, adv. 1. Formellement. 2. Cérémonieusement.

formalin(e) ['fɔːməlin], s. Ch: Formol m.

formalism ['fɔːməlizm], s. Formalisme m.

formalist ['fɔːməlist], s. Formaliste mf.

formality [fɔː'mæliti], s. 1. Formalité f. A mere f., une pure formalité. 2. (a) Raideur (de maintien), compassement m (d'un discours). (b) Cérémonie f, formalité(s), formes fpl.

format ['fɔːmæt], s. Format m (d'un livre).

formation [fɔː'meiʃ(ə)n], s. 1. Formation f. 2. Formation, disposition f (des troupes). Battle f., formation de combat. Close f., ordre serré. Av: F. flying, vol m de groupe. To break f., décrocher. 3. Geol: Granite f., formation, terrain m, granitique.

formative ['fɔːmətiv], a. The f. years, les années de formation.

former¹ ['fɔːmər], a. 1. Antérieur, -eure, précédent, ancien, -ienne. My f. pupils, mes anciens élèves. His f. letters, ses lettres précédentes. F. times, le passé. In f. times, autrefois. He is a mere shadow of his f. self, il n'est plus que l'ombre de lui-même. 2. The f. (a) I prefer the f. alternative to the latter, je préfère la première alternative à la seconde. (b) pron. Celui-là, celle-là, ceux-là, celles-là. Of the two methods I prefer the f., des deux méthodes je préfère celle-là. -ly, adv. Autrefois, jadis.

former², s. Ind: Gabarit m, calibre m (de forme); matrice f. El.E: Winding f., gabarit de bobinage.

formic ['fɔːmik], a. F. acid, acide m formique.

formidable ['fɔːmidəbl], a. Formidable, redoutable. -ably, adv. Formidablement.

formless ['fɔːmlis], a. Informe.

formlessness ['fɔːmlisnis], s. Absence f de forme.

formula, pl. -as, -ae ['fɔːmjulə, -əz, -iː], s. Formule f.

formulate ['fɔːmjuleit], v.tr. Formuler.

fornicate ['fɔːnikeit], *v.i.* Forniquer.
fornication |fɔːni'keiʃ(ə)n], *s.* Fornication *f.*
forrader ['forədər], *adv. P:* I can't get any f., je peux pas aller plus loin.
forsake [fə'seik], *v.tr.* (forsook [fə'suk]; forsaken [fə'seikən]) 1. Abandonner, délaisser (qn). His confidence forsook him, la confiance lui fit défaut. 2. Renoncer à (une habitude).
forsooth [fə'suːθ], *adv. A. & Lit:* 1. En vérité. 2. *Iron:* Par exemple! ma foi!
forswear [fɔː'swɛər], *v.tr.* (forswore [fɔː'swɔːr]; forsworn [fɔː'swɔːn]) 1. Abjurer, renier (qch.). 2. To f. oneself, se parjurer. forsworn, *a.* Parjure.
forsythia [fɔː'saiθiə], *s. Bot:* Forsythia *m.*
fort [fɔːt], *s. Mil:* Fort *m.* Small f., fortin *m.*
forte¹ [fɔːt], *s.* Fort *m.* Singing is not his f., le chant n'est pas son fort.
forte² ['fɔːtei], *a., adv. & s. Mus:* Forte (*m inv*).
forth [fɔːθ], *adv.* 1. En avant. To go, sally, f., sortir; se mettre en route. To stretch f. one's hand, avancer la main. 2. From this time f., dès maintenant; désormais. 3. And so f., et ainsi de suite.
forthcoming [fɔːθ'kʌmiŋ], *a.* 1. (a) Qui arrive. Help is f., des secours sont en route. (b) Prochain, à venir. 2. (Livre) prêt à paraître. 3. *F:* He's f., il est ouvert. He's not very f., il est fermé, plutôt réticent.
forthright [fɔː'θrait]. *A. & Lit:* 1. *adv.* Tout droit; carrément. 2. *a.* ['fɔːθrait] = DOWNRIGHT 2 (a).
forthwith ['fɔːθ'wiθ], *adv.* Sur-le-champ; tout de suite.
fortieth ['fɔːtiiθ], *num. a. & s.* Quarantième.
fortification [fɔːtifi'keiʃ(ə)n], *s.* 1. (a) Fortification *f* (d'une ville); renforcement *m* (d'une barricade). (b) Fortification, affermissement *m* (du courage). 2. *pl.* Fortifications, fortifications.
fortify ['fɔːtifai], *v.tr.* 1. (a) Renforcer, fortifier (un navire, etc.). (b) Fortifier, affermir (qn). Courage fortified against dangers, courage armé contre les dangers. 2. Remonter (un vin) en alcool. 3. *Mil:* Fortifier (une place). Fortified area, camp retranché.
fortitude ['fɔːtitjuːd], *s.* Force *f* d'âme; courage *m.*
fortnight ['fɔːtnait], *s.* Quinzaine *f;* quinze jours. This day, today, f., d'aujourd'hui en quinze. To adjourn a case for a f., remettre une cause à quinzaine.
fortnightly ['fɔːtnaitli]. 1. *a.* Bimensuel. 2. *adv.* Tous les quinze jours.
fortress ['fɔːtris], *s.* Forteresse *f;* place forte.
fortuitous [fɔː'tju(:)itəs], *a.* Fortuit, imprévu. -ly, *adv.* Fortuitement, par hasard.
fortunate ['fɔːtʃənit], *a.* 1. Heureux, fortuné. To be f. avoir de la chance. 2. Propice, heureux. How f.! quel bonheur! quelle chance! -ly, *adv.* 1. Heureusement. 2. Par bonheur.
fortune ['fɔːtʃən], *s.* Fortune *f.* 1. (a) Hasard *m*, chance *f.* By good f., par bonheur. To try one's f., tenter la chance. F. favours him, la fortune lui sourit. (b) Destinée *f*, sort *m.* The f. of war, le sort des armes. To tell fortunes, dire la bonne aventure. To tell s.o.'s f. by cards, tirer les cartes à qn. 2. (a) Bonne chance; bonheur *m.* (b) Prospérité *f*, richesse *f.* A man of f., un homme riche. Born to f., né coiffé. (c) Richesses *fpl*, biens *mpl.* To make a f., faire fortune. To come into a f., hériter d'une fortune; faire un gros héritage. *F:* It has cost me a f., cela m'a coûté un argent fou. *F:* To marry a f., épouser une grosse dot. 'fortune-hunter, *s.* Coureur *m* de dots. 'fortune-teller, *s.* Diseur, -euse, de bonne aventure; (*with cards*) cartomancien, -enne. 'fortune-telling, *s.* La bonne aventure; (*with cards*) cartomancie *f.*
forty ['fɔːti], *num. a. & s.* Quarante (*m*). About f. guests, une quarantaine d'invités. She'll never see f. again, elle a passé la quarantaine. She's in the forties, elle a passé la quarantaine. To be in the late forties, friser la cinquantaine. The forties, les années quarante (1940-1949). *Ecc:* The F. Hours, les (prières *f* des) quarante heures. *Ind: etc:* F.-hour week, semaine *f* de quarante heures, *F:* les quarante heures. *S.a.* WINK. 'forty-'niner, *s.* Quelqu'un qui prit part à la première course à l'or en Californie en 1849.
forward¹ ['fɔːwəd]. I. *a.* 1. (a) De devant, d'avant. *Nau:* De l'avant, sur l'avant, avant. F. turret, tourelle *f* avant. (b) (Mouvement) progressif, en avant. F. motion, marche (en) avant. The f. journey, l'aller *m.* *Fb:*

F. pass, passe en avant. 2. (*Of plants, child*) Avancé; précoce. 3. (*Of opinions*) Avancé. 4. Effronté. 5. *Com:* (*Of price, delivery*) A terme. II. forward, *s. Fb:* (*Pers.*) Avant *m.* III. forward, *occ.* forwards ['fɔːwədz], *adv.* 1. (a) From that day f., à partir de ce jour-là. To look f. to sth., attendre qch. avec plaisir; se faire une fête de (faire) qch. (b) *Bank:* 'F.' rates, taux *m* pour les opérations à terme. 2. (a) En avant. To move f., avancer. To go straight f., aller tout droit. To rush f., se précipiter (en avant). F.! en avant! (b) (*Position*) A l'avant. The seat is too far f., la banquette est trop avancée. *Fb:* To play f., jouer comme avant. The crew's quarters are f., le logement de l'équipage est à l'avant. (c) *Com:* (Carried) f., à reporter; report *m.* 3. To come f., se proposer, s'offrir. To thrust, push, oneself f., se mettre en avant. 4. En avance. I want to get f. with tomorrow's work, je veux m'avancer pour demain.
forward², *v.tr.* 1. Avancer, favoriser, seconder (un projet). 2. (a) Expédier, envoyer (des marchandises). To f. sth. to s.o., faire parvenir qch. à qn. (b) 'To be forwarded,' 'please f.,' "prière de faire suivre"; "à faire suivre." forwarding, *s.* 1. Avancement *m* (d'une affaire). 2. (a) Expédition *f*, envoi *m* (d'un colis). (b) Transmission *f* (d'une lettre).
forwardness ['fɔːwədnis], *s.* 1. Avancement *m*, progrès *m* (d'un travail). 2. État avancé; précocité *f* (de la récolte, d'un élève). 3. Empressement *m.* 4. Hardiesse *f*, effronterie *f.*
fossa, *pl.* -ae ['fɔsə. -iː], *s. Anat:* Fosse (nasale).
fossil ['fɔsl]. 1. *s.* Fossile *m.* *F:* An old f., un vieux fossile, une vieille baderne, une croûte. 2. *a.* Fossile.
fossilize ['fɔsilaiz]. 1. *v.tr.* Fossiliser. 2. *v.i.* Se fossiliser. *F:* (*Of pers.*) S'encroûter.
foster¹ ['fɔstər], *v.tr.* 1. Élever, nourrir (un enfant). 2. Entretenir, nourrir (une idée). To f. friendship between peoples, développer, encourager, l'amitié entre les peuples.
foster-², *comb.fm.* Qui se rapporte à l'élevage, à l'alimentation. 'foster-brother, *s.m.* 1. Frère de lait. 2. Frère adoptif. 'foster-child, *s.* 1. Nourrisson, -onne. 2. Enfant adopté. 'foster-father, *s.m.* Père adoptif. 'foster-home, *s.* Placing of children in foster-homes, placement familial des enfants. 'foster-mother, *s.f.* 1. (Mère) nourricière; (mère) nourrice. 2. Mère adoptive. 'foster-sister, *s.f.* 1. Sœur de lait. 2. Sœur adoptive.
fought. See FIGHT.²
foul¹ [faul]. I. *a.* 1. (a) Infect, nauséabond, empesté; méphitique. F. air, air vicié. F. gas, gaz toxique. (b) (*Of thoughts*) Immonde, impur; (*of language*) ordurier. F. word, gros mot. (c) (*Of deed*) Noir, infâme. F. trick, crapulerie *f.* (d) *F:* What f. weather! quel sale temps! 2. (a) (Linge) sale. F. water, eau croupie. (b) (*Of sparking-plug*) Encrassé; (*of pump*) engorgé. *Nau:* (*Of ship*) F. bottom, carène *f* sale. 3. *Nau:* (a) (*Of anchor*) Engagé. F. cable, tour *m* de chaîne. To run f. of another ship, aborder, entrer en collision avec, un autre navire. *F:* To fall f. of s.o., se brouiller, se prendre de querelle, avec qn. To fall f. of the law, tomber sous le coup de la loi. (b) F. weather, gros temps. 4. *Sp: etc:* Déloyal, -aux; illicite. F. play, (i) *Sp:* jeu déloyal; (ii) malveillance *f.* Box: F. blow, coup bas. -lly, *adv.* 1. Salement. 2. Abominablement, méchamment. He was f. murdered, il fut ignoblement assassiné. II. foul, *s. Sp:* Faute *f;* coup illicite, déloyal. *Fb:* Poussée irrégulière. Box: Coup bas. III. foul, *adv.* Irrégulièrement, déloyalement. To fight f., se battre déloyalement, contre les règles. foul-'mouthed, *a.* (*Of pers.*) Mal embouché; grossier.
foul². I. *v.tr.* 1. (a) Salir, souiller (sa réputation). (b) Encrasser (un canon de fusil). 2. (a) Embarrasser, obstruer. *Nau:* Engager (une ancre). (b) *Nau:* (*Of ship*) Entrer en collision avec, aborder (un autre navire). II. foul, *v.i.* 1. (*Of gun-barrel*) S'encrasser; (*of pump*) s'engorger. 2. *Nau:* (*Of anchor*) To foul. to become fouled, s'engager.
foulard ['fuːlɑː(d)], *s. Tex: Cost:* Foulard *m.*
foulness ['faulnis], *s.* 1. (a) Impureté *f* (de l'air). (b) Saleté *f*, malpropreté *f.* 2. Obscénité *f* (de langage). 3. Infamie *f*, noirceur *f* (d'un acte).

found¹ [faund]. *See* FIND².

found², *v.tr.* (*a*) Fonder (un édifice, etc.), fonder, créer, établir (une institution, etc.). **To f. a family,** fonder une famille; faire souche. (*b*) Baser, fonder, appuyer (son opinion, etc.) (on, sur). (*Of novel*) **Founded on fact,** reposant sur des faits véridiques.

found³, *v.tr. Metall:* Fondre (les métaux); mouler (la fonte).

foundation [faun'deiʃ(ə)n], *s.* **1.** (*a*) Fondation *f* (d'une ville, etc.); établissement *m*, institution *f* (d'une maison de commerce, etc.). (*b*) Fondation (et dotation *f*) (d'une œuvre, etc.). **2.** (*a*) Fondement *m*, fondation (d'un édifice); assise *f* (d'un mur, d'une machine). *Civ.E:* Hérisson *m* (d'une route). **The foundations of a building,** les fondements d'un édifice. **To dig the foundations,** creuser les fondements. (*b*) **The foundations of music,** les bases *f* de la musique. **3.** (*a*) *Dressm:* Fond *m* (d'une robe, etc.). *Cost:* F. (garment), gaine *f*. (*b*) *Th: Toil:* (Make-up) f., fond *m* de teint. **4.** Fondement, base (d'une théorie, etc.). **5.** (*a*) Institution dotée; fondation. *Sch:* F. scholar, étudiant, -te, élève, boursier, -ière. (*b*) Capital légué (pour une œuvre), fondation. **foun'dation-stone,** *s. Constr:* Pierre fondamentale. **To lay the f.-s.,** poser la première pierre.

founder¹ ['faundər], *s.* Fondateur *m* (d'une institution); souche *f* (d'une famille).

founder², *s. Metall:* Fondeur *m*.

founder³, *v.i.* (*a*) (*Of building, etc.*) S'effondrer, s'écrouler; (*of cliff*) s'ébouler. (*b*) (*Of horse*) Se mettre à boiter, devenir fourbu. (*c*) *Nau:* (*Of ship*) Sombrer; couler bas. **foundered,** *a.* **1.** *Vet:* (Cheval) fourbu. **2.** (Navire) qui a sombré.

foundling ['faundliŋ], *s.* Enfant trouvé, -ée.

foundry ['faundri], *s. Metalw:* Fonderie *f.*

fount¹ [faunt], *s. Poet: Lit:* Source *f.* **He is a f. of knowledge,** c'est un puits de science.

fount², *s. Typ:* Fonte *f.* **Wrong f.,** lettre *f* d'un autre œil.

fountain ['fauntin], *s.* Fontaine *f.* (*a*) *A. & Lit:* Source *f. O:* **F. of wisdom,** source de sagesse. (*b*) Jet *m* d'eau. **'fountain-head,** *s.* Source *f* (d'une rivière). **To go to the f.-h. (for information, etc.),** puiser à la source. **'fountain-pen,** *s.* Stylo(graphe) *m.*

four [fɔːr], *num. a. & s.* Quatre (*m*). *Pol:* **The Big F.,** les Quatre Grands. **Scattered to the f. corners of the earth,** éparpillés aux quatre coins du monde. **He came down the stairs four at a time,** il a descendu l'escalier quatre à quatre. *Mil:* **(Move) to the right in fours!** à droite par quatre! **To run on all fours,** courir à quatre pattes. *F:* **To be on all fours with . . .,** aller de pair avec. . . . (*For other phrases see* EIGHT.) **four-'engined,** *a. Av:* Quadrimoteur. **F.-e. jet plane,** quadriréacteur *m.* **'four-figure,** *attrib.a.* **F.-f. number,** nombre *m* à quatre chiffres. **F.-f. logarithms,** logarithmes à quatre décimales. **'four-footed,** *a.* Quadrupède; à quatre pattes. **four-'handed,** *a.* **1.** (Singe) à quatre mains, quadrumane. **2.** (Jeu) à quatre (personnes). **'four-in-hand,** *s.* Attelage *m* à quatre. **2.** *adv.* **To drive f.-in-h.,** conduire à grandes guides. **'four-leaved,** *a. Bot:* Quadrifolié. **'four-letter,** *a.* **F.-l. word,** mot *m* obscène. **four-'master,** *s. Nau:* Quatre-mâts *m inv.* **'four-'part,** *a. Mus:* A quatre voix. **four-'poster,** *s.* Lit *m* à colonnes. **four-'seater,** *s. Aut:* Voiture *f* à quatre places. **'four-'square,** *a. & adv.* Solide(ment).

fourfold ['fɔːfould]. **1.** *a.* Quadruple. **2.** *adv.* Quatre fois autant; au quadruple.

fourscore ['fɔːskɔːr], *a. A. & Lit:* Quatre-vingts.

foursome ['fɔːs(ə)m]. **1.** *a.* A quatre. *Danc:* **F. reel,** "reel" dansé à quatre. **2.** *s. Golf:* Partie *f* (de) double, à deux contre deux.

fourteen ['fɔː'tiːn], *num. a. & s.* Quatorze (*m*).

fourteenth ['fɔː'tiːnθ], *num. a. & s.* Quatorzième. **Louis the F.,** (XIVth), Louis Quatorze (XIV).

fourth ['fɔːθ]. **1.** *num. a. & s.* Quatrième. **He arrived f. or fifth,** il est arrivé quatre ou cinquième. *Sch:* **The f. form,** *approx.* = la classe de troisième. *Cards:* **To make a f.,** faire le quatrième. **2.** *s.* (*a*) (*Fractional*) Quart *m.* (*b*) *Mus:* Quarte *f.* **-ly,** *adv.* Quatrièmement; en quatrième lieu.

fowl [faul], *s.* **1.** (*a*) *Lit:* Oiseau *m*; volatile *m.* **The fowl of the air,** les oiseaux des cieux. (*b*) *Coll:* Oiseaux. **Wild f.,** gibier *m* d'eau. **2.** (*a*) Poule *f*, coq *m*; volaille *f.* **To keep fowls,** élever de la volaille. **F. pest,** peste *f* aviaire. (*b*) *Cu:* **(Boiling) f.,** poule.

fowler ['faulər], *s.* Oiseleur *m.*

fowling ['fauliŋ], *s.* Chasse *f* aux oiseaux. **Wild f.,** chassé au gibier d'eau, à la sauvagine. **'fowling-piece,** *s.* Fusil *m* de chasse (à petit plomb).

fox¹ [fɔks], *s.* (*The female is* VIXEN, *q.v.*) Renard *m.* **She-fox,** renarde *f. Cost:* **F. fur,** (fourrure *f* en) renard. *F:* **A sly f.,** un madré, un fin matois. **'fox-cub,** *s.* Renardeau *m.* **'fox-hound,** *s. Ven:* Chien courant. **'fox-hunt,** *s.* Chasse *f* au renard. **'fox-hunter,** *s.* Chasseur *m* de renards. **'fox-hunting,** *s.* La chasse au renard. **fox-'terrier,** *s.* Fox *m.* **'fox-trot,** *s. Danc:* Fox-trot *m inv.*

fox². **1.** *v.tr.* (*a*) Maculer, piquer (une gravure). (*b*) *F:* Mystifier, tromper (qn). **2.** *v.i. F:* Feindre; ruser. **foxed,** *a.* (Livre, papier) piqué; (estampe) maculée. **foxing,** *s.* **1.** Décoloration *f*, piqûre *f* (du papier). **2.** Piqûres; macules *fpl* (d'une estampe).

foxglove ['fɔksglʌv], *s. Bot:* Digitale (pourprée).

foxiness ['fɔksinis], *s.* Astuce *f*, roublardise *f.*

foxtail ['fɔksteil], *s.* **1.** Queue *f* de renard. **2.** *Bot:* Vulpin *m.*

foxy ['fɔksi], *a.* **1.** Rusé, madré. **2.** (*Of hair, complexion*) Roux, *f* rousse.

foyer ['fwajei], *s. Th:* Foyer *m* (du public).

fraction ['fræk(ʃ)ən], *s.* **1.** Petite portion; fragment *m.* **He escaped death by a f. of a second, an inch,** il a été à deux doigts de la mort. **2.** *Mth:* Fraction *f*; nombre *m* fractionnaire. **Vulgar f.,** fraction ordinaire. **Improper f.,** expression *f* fractionnaire.

fractional ['frækʃən(ə)l], *a.* **1.** *Mth: etc:* Fractionnaire. **F. part,** fraction *f.* **2.** **F. distillation,** distillation fractionnée.

fractious ['frækʃəs], *a.* (*a*) Difficile de caractère; revêche. (*b*) **A f. baby,** un bébé pleurnicheur. (*c*) (Cheval) rétif; (vache) indocile.

fractiousness ['frækʃəsnis], *s.* (*a*) Humeur hargneuse; (*of a baby*) pleurnichage *m.* (*b*) Rétivité *f* (d'un animal).

fracture¹ ['fræktʃər], *s.* **1.** Fracture *f* (d'un os, etc.). *Surg:* **Compound f.,** fracture compliquée. **To set a f.,** réduire une fracture. **2.** *Miner:* Cassure *f*, fracture.

fracture². **1.** *v.tr.* Casser, briser (qch.). *Surg:* Fracturer (un os). **2.** *v.i.* Se casser, se briser; (*of limb*) se fracturer.

fragile ['frædʒail], *a.* Fragile; (*of pers.*) faible, chétif. *F:* **I'm feeling rather f.,** (i) je ne suis pas dans mon assiette, (ii) j'ai la gueule de bois.

fragility [frə'dʒiliti], *s.* Fragilité *f*; (*of pers.*) faiblesse *f*; délicatesse *f* (de santé).

fragment ['frægmənt], *s.* Fragment *m*, morceau *m* (de papier, etc.); éclat *m* (d'obus). **Smashed to fragments,** réduit en fragments; brisé en mille morceaux.

fragmentary ['frægmənt(ə)ri], *a.* Fragmentaire.

fragrance ['freigrəns], *s.* Parfum *m.*

fragrant ['freigrənt], *a.* Parfumé, odorant.

frail [freil], *a.* **1.** Fragile; frêle. **2.** (*a*) (*Of pers., health*) Faible, délicat. **She's getting very f.,** elle commence à se casser. (*b*) *A:* (Femme) de petite vertu.

frail², *s. Com:* Cabas *m*; panier *m* de jonc.

frailty ['freilti], *s.* Faiblesse morale; fragilité humaine.

framboesia [fræm'biːziə], *s. Med:* Pian *m.*

frame¹ [freim]. **1.** (*a*) Construction *f*, structure *f*, forme *f.* **F. of mind,** disposition *f* d'esprit. (*b*) Système *m*, forme (de gouvernement). (*a*) Ossature *f* (d'un animal). **Man of gigantic f.,** homme d'une taille colossale. **Sobs shook her f.,** des sanglots lui secouaient le corps. (*b*) Charpente *f* (d'un bâtiment); bâti *m* (d'un moteur); cadre *m* (d'une bicyclette); châssis *m* (d'une automobile); monture (d'un parapluie, de lunettes); carcasse *f* (d'un abat-jour); corps *m* (d'un filtre); armature *f* (d'une raquette). (*c*) *N.Arch:* Membrure *f*, carcasse d'un navire). **3.** (*a*) Cadre, encadrement *m* (d'un tableau). (*b*) Chambranle *m*, châssis (d'une fenêtre). (*c*) *Cin:* Image *f* (de film). *T.V:* Image. **4.** (*a*) Métier *m* (à broder, etc.); tambour *m* (à broder). (*b*) *Tex:* Métier (à filer). **5.** *Hort:* Châssis de couches. **'frame-house,** *s. U.S:* Maison *f* de bois. **'frame-saw,** *s. Tls:* Scie *f* à monture.

frame², *v.tr.* 1. Former, régler (ses pensées). *v.i.* He is framing well, il montre des dispositions. 2. (*a*) Projeter (un dessein); charpenter (un roman, etc.). (*b*) Articuler, prononcer (un mot). 3. (*a*) Imaginer, concevoir (une idée); se faire (une opinion). (*b*) Ourdir (un complot). F: To frame s.o., inventer une fausse accusation contre qn. 4. Encadrer (un tableau). **'frame-up**, *s.* F: Coup monté. **framing**, *s.* (*a*) Construction *f*, formation *f* (de qch.). (*b*) Composition *f* (d'un poème); conception *f* (d'une idée). (*c*) Articulation *f* (d'un mot). (*d*) Invention *f* (d'une fausse accusation). (*e*) Encadrement *m* (d'un tableau).

framer ['freimər], *s.* Auteur *m* (d'un projet), rédacteur, -trice (d'un traité). (**Picture-**)f., encadreur *m*.

framework ['freimwɔːk], *s.* (*a*) Charpente *f*, ossature *f*, carcasse *f*. (*b*) Construction *f* en cloisonnage; coffrage *m* (de travaux en béton). (*c*) Cadre *m*. Within the f. of the United Nations, dans le cadre des Nations Unies.

franc [fræŋk]. *s. Num:* Franc *m*.

France [frɑːns]. *Pr.n. Geog:* La France. In, to, F., en France. *Hist:* Free F., La France Libre.

Frances ['frɑːnsis] *Pr.n.f.* Françoise.

franchise ['fræntʃaiz], *s.* 1. *Hist: Jur:* Franchise *f*, privilège *m*. 2. *Pol:* Droit *m* de vote. 3. Droit de cité.

Francis ['frɑːnsis]. *Pr.n.m.* François.

Franco-American ['fræŋkouəˈmerikən], *s.* (*In Canada*) Franco-Américain, -aine.

francophile ['fræŋkofail], *a. & s.* Francophile (*mf*).

francophobe ['fræŋkofoub], *a. & s.* Francophobe (*mf*).

Franco-Prussian ['fræŋkouˈprʌʃ(ə)n], *a.* Franco-prussien, -ienne. The F.-P. War, la guerre franco-allemande de 1870.

frangible ['frændʒibl], *a.* Cassant, fragile.

Frank¹ [fræŋk], *s. Hist:* Franc, *f.* Franque.

frank², *a.* Franc, *f.* franche; sincère. To be quite f., parler franchement, à cœur ouvert. **-ly**, *adv.* Franchement; ouvertement.

frank³, *v.tr. Post:* Affranchir (une lettre). **frànking**, *s.* Affranchissement *m*. F. **machine**, machine à affranchir (les lettres).

Frank⁴. *Pr.n.m.* (*Dim. of Francis*) François.

frankfurter [fræŋkfɔːtər], *s. Cu:* Saucisse *f* de Francfort.

frankincense ['fræŋkinsens], *s.* Encens *m*.

Frankish ['fræŋkiʃ], *a. Hist:* Franc, franque.

frankness ['fræŋknis], *s.* Franchise *f*, sincérité *f*.

frantic ['fræntik], *a.* 1. Frénétique, forcené. F. efforts, efforts prodigieux. F. with joy, fou de joie. It drives him f., cela le met hors de lui. 2. *F:* F. toothache, mal de dents affreux. **-ally**, *adv.* Frénétiquement.

fraternal [frəˈtəːn(ə)l], *a.* Fraternel, -elle. **-ally**, *adv.* Fraternellement.

fraternity [frəˈtəːniti], *s.* 1. Fraternité *f*. 2. Confrérie *f*.

fraternization ['frætənaizˈeiʃ(ə)n], *s.* Fraternisation *f* (**with**, avec).

fraternize ['frætənaiz], *v.i.* Fraterniser (**with**, avec). **fraternizing**, *s.* Fraternisation *f* (**with**, avec).

fratricidal ['frætriˈsaid(ə)l], *a.* (Guerre) fratricide.

fratricide¹ ['frætrisaid], *s.* Fratricide *mf*.

fratricide², *s.* (Crime *m* de) fratricide *m*.

fraud [frɔːd], *s.* 1. (*a*) *Jur:* Fraude *f*, dol *m*. (*b*) Supercherie *f*, tromperie *f.* Pious f., pieux mensonge. 2. *F:* (*a*) Imposteur *m*. He's a (pious) f., c'est un fumiste. (*b*) Chose *f* qui ne répond pas à l'attente.

fraudulence ['frɔːdjuləns], *s.* (*a*) Caractère *m* frauduleux (d'une transaction). (*b*) Infidélité *f* (d'un dépositaire).

fraudulent ['frɔːdjulənt]. *a.* Frauduleux. F. **conversion**, carambouillage *m*. **-ly**, *adv.* Frauduleusement, en fraude.

fraught [frɔːt], *a.* 1. *A:* Pourvu, muni (**with**, de). 2. *Lit:* (*a*) Remarks f. with malice, observations pleines de méchanceté. (*b*) Decision f. with far-reaching consequences, décision grosse de conséquences.

fray¹ [frei], *s.* 1. Bagarre *f*, échauffourée *f*, mêlée *f*. 2. *Lit:* Combat *m*. Always ready for the f., toujours prêt à se battre.

fray². 1. *v.tr.* Érailler, effiler (un tissu). *F:* My nerves are frayed out, je suis à bout de nerfs. 2. *v.i.* (*Of tissue*) S'érailler, s'effiler

frazzle ['fræzl], *s. F:* To be worn to a f., être éreinté, complètement à plat. *P:* To beat s.o. to a f., battre qn à plates coutures.

freak [friːk], *s.* 1. Fantaisie *f*; lubie *f*. Freaks of fashion, caprices *m* de la mode. F. of fortune, jeu *m* de la fortune, du hasard. 2. F. (of nature), (i) *Nat. Hist:* variation sportive; (ii) *F:* phénomène *m*, curiosité *f* He's a f., c'est un drôle de numéro. 3. *Attrib. F:* F. religion, religion de fantaisie. A f. accident, un accident imprévisible.

freakish ['friːkiʃ], *a.* Capricieux, fantasque, bizarre. F. **notion**, fantaisie *f*. **-ly**, *adv.* Capricieusement, bizarrement.

freakishness ['friːkiʃnis], *s.* Caractère *m* fantasque, baroque, bizarre (de qch.).

freckle¹ ['frekl], *s.* Tache *f* de rousseur, *F:* tache de son.

freckle². 1. *v.tr,* Marquer (la peau) de taches de rousseur. 2. *v.i.* Se couvrir de taches de rousseur. **freckled**, *a.* Couvert de taches de rousseur.

free¹ [friː], *a. & adv.* 1. (*a*) Libre. *Nau:* Free port, port franc. Man is a f. agent, l'homme est libre. F. house, débit de boissons non lié à un fournisseur particulier. (*b*) En liberté. To set s.o. free, rendre la liberté à qn. Why is he allowed to go free? pourquoi est-il en liberté? To set a slave f., affranchir un esclave. To set a bird f., laisser envoler un oiseau. To set f. a prisoner, élargir un prisonnier. She offered to set him f., elle lui proposa de lui rendre sa parole. 2. (*Unoccupied*) Libre. F. day, jour *m* de liberté. Is this table free? est-ce que cette table est libre? *Tg: Tp:* F. line, ligne dégagée. 3. (*a*) F. speech, libre parole. F. love, amour libre. Right of f. entry, droit de passer librement les frontières. To have a f. hand, avoir ses coudées franches (**to**, pour). To give s.o. a f. hand, donner carte blanche à qn. You are f. to do so, libre à vous de le faire. He is not f. to act, il a les mains liées. Fishing is f., la pêche est autorisée. (*b*) (*Of touch, style, etc.*) Franc, *f.* franche; sans raideur; aisé. (*c*) *Mec.E:* F. motion of a piece, jeu *m* d'une pièce. (*d*) F. from sth., of sth., débarrassé, exempt, de qch. To be f. from care, être sans souci. Style f. from affectation, style dénué de toute recherche. At last I am f. of him, enfin je suis débarrassé de lui. To break f. from an influence, s'affranchir d'une influence. (*e*) Franc (of, de). *Cust:* F. of duty, duty-f., exempt de droits d'entrée. To import sth. f. of duty, faire entrer qch. en franchise. You may bring in half a bottle f. (of duty), il y a tolérance pour une demi-bouteille. F. list, liste d'exemptions. 4. (*a*) *Ch: etc:* (*Of gas, etc.*) (A l'état) libre, non combiné. F. gold, or à l'état natif. (*b*) (*Of power, energy*) Disponible. 5. (*a*) F. offer, offre spontanée. As a f. gift, en pur don. *Pros:* F. verse, vers libres. You are very f. in blaming others, vous blâmez volontiers les autres. (*b*) Libéral, généreux, large. To be f. with sth., donner largement. To be f. with one's money, ne pas regarder à l'argent. To be f. with one's hands, avoir la main leste. (*c*) (*Of pers., manner*) Franc, ouvert, aisé. F. and easy, sans façons; désinvolte, sans gêne. F. and easy tone, ton dégagé. To be f. and easy, prendre ses aises. (*d*) To make f. with sth., prendre des libertés avec qn. To make f. with sth., user librement de qch. (*e*) (*Of language*) Libre, licencieux. 6. To be f. of s.o.'s house, avoir ses entrées libres chez qn. 7. Gratuit; franco *inv.* Admission f., entrée gratuite, gratis. *Th: etc:* F. ticket, billet de faveur. *Com:* Delivery f., livré franco. Post f., franco de port. F. on rail, franco gare. F. alongside ship, franco quai. F. on board (*abbr.* f.o.b.), franco à bord. 8. *adv.* (*a*) Catalogue sent f. on request, catalogue franco sur demande. The gallery is open f. on Saturdays, l'entrée du musée est gratuite le samedi. (*b*) Vessel running f., navire courant largue. **-ly**, *adv.* 1. Librement, volontairement. To give f. to s.o., faire des libéralités à qn. 2. (Parler) franchement, à cœur ouvert. **'free-board**, *s. Nau:* Franc-bord *m*. **'Free 'Church**, *s.* Église *f* non-conformiste; Église libre. **'free-for-'all**, *s. F:* Mêlée générale. **'free-hand**, *a. & s.* F.-h. (drawing), dessin *m* à main levée. **free-'handed**, *a.* Généreux. **'free-lance**, *a. & s.* F.-l. (journalist), journaliste indépendant. **free-'spoken**, *a.* Franc, *f.* franche; qui a son franc-parler. **free-'thinker**, *s.* Libre penseur; esprit fort. **free-'thinking, free-'thought**, *s.* Libre pensée *f.* **free 'trade**, *s.* Libre-échange *m.* **F.-t. policy**, politique libre-échangiste. **free-'trader**, *s.* Libre-échangiste *m.* **'free 'wheel**, *s.* Cy: Roue *f* libre. **'free-'wheel**, *v.i.* 1. *Cy:* Faire roue libre. 2. *Aut:* Marcher, rouler, en roue libre. **'free 'will**, *s.* Libre arbitre *m.* Of one's own f. w., de son plein gré. F.-w. offering, don volontaire.

free², *v.tr.* (freed; freeing) (*a*) Affranchir (un peuple); libérer, élargir (un prisonnier). To f. oneself from **s.o.'s grasp**, se dégager des mains de qn. To f. oneself from one's commitments, se délier de tous ses engagements. (*b*) Débarrasser (from, of, de); dégager (un sentier). (*c*) *Mec.E:* Dégager (une pièce). (*d*) Décolmater, désobstruer (un filtre). (*e*) To f. a property (from mortgage), déshypothéquer une propriété.

freebooter ['fri:bu:tər], *s.* 1. *Hist:* Flibustier *m.* 2. *F:* Maraudeur *m*; pillard *m.*

freedom ['fri:dəm], *s.* 1. (*a*) Liberté *f*, indépendance *f.* (*b*) Liberté d'action; liberté d'agir, de penser. **F. of speech**, le franc-parler. 2. (*a*) Franchise *f*, aisance *f*, familiarité *f* (d'une conversation, du style). (*b*) Sans-gêne *m.* 3. (*Of action*) Facilité *f*, souplesse *f.* 4. (*a*) Exemption *f*, immunité *f* (from, de). **F. from hunger campaign**, campagne *f* contre la famine. (*b*) F. of the city, droit *m* de cité. 5. Jouissance *f*, libre usage *m* (de qch.).

freehold ['fri:hould]. 1. *a.* Tenu en propriété perpétuelle et libre. 2. *s.* Propriété foncière libre.

freeholder ['fri:houldər], *s.* Propriétaire foncier (à perpétuité).

freeman, *pl.* **-men** ['fri:mən], *s.m.* 1. Homme libre. 2. Citoyen. F. of a city = citoyen d'honneur.

freemason ['fri:meisn], *s.* Franc-maçon *m*, *pl.* francs-maçons.

freemasonry ['fri:meisnri], *s.* Franc-maçonnerie *f.*

freestone ['fri:stoun], *s.* Pierre *f* de taille.

freestyle ['fri:stail]. 1. *s.* Nage *f* libre. The 220 f., le 220 mètres (yards) en nage libre. 2. *a.* F. relay, course en nage libre.

freeze [fri:z], *v.* (froze [frouz]; frozen ['frouzn]) Geler. 1. *v.i.* (*a*) *Impers.* It is freezing hard, il gèle à pierre fendre. (*b*) (Se) geler; se congeler; prendre. **The river has, is, frozen** (up), la rivière est prise. *F:* **Till hell freezes** (over), jusqu'à la Saint Glinglin. **The wheels were frozen fast in the mud**, les roues étaient prises dans la boue glacée. **His fingers froze to his rifle**, le froid collait ses doigts à son fusil. *U.S: F:* To f. on to s.o., (i) se coller, se cramponner, à qn; (ii) s'attacher à qn. **The smile froze on his lips**, le sourire se figea sur ses lèvres. (*c*) I'm freezing, je gèle. To f. to death, mourir de froid. 2. *v.tr.* (*a*) Geler, congeler (qch.). **To f. the blood** (in one's veins), glacer le sang, le cœur. (*b*) *Fin:* Geler (des crédits, des devises). **To f. wages**, bloquer les salaires. *s.* **freeze, prices and wages f.**, blocage *m* des prix et des salaires. **freeze out**, *v.tr. F:* (*a*) Évincer (qn); supplanter (un rival). (*b*) Boycotter (qn). **freezing**, *s.* 1. Congélation *f*; gel *m.* *Ph:* **F. point**, point *m* de congélation. 2. Réfrigération *f.* **'freezing-mixture**, *s.* Mélange réfrigérant.

freight¹ [freit], *s.* 1. (*a*) Fret *m* (d'un navire). (*b*) Transport *m* (de marchandises). **Air f.**, transport *m* par avion. **F. plane**, avion *m* de transport. 2. (*a*) Fret, cargaison *f.* To take in f., prendre du fret. (*b*) *U.S: F.* train, train de marchandises. **F. car**, fourgon *m.* 3. Fret; prix *m* du louage d'un navire, d'un avion; du transport de marchandises.

freight², *v.tr.* Fréter, affréter (un navire).

freighter ['freitər], *s.* 1. Affréteur *m* (d'un bateau). 2. Transporteur *m*; transitaire *m.* 3. *Nau:* Cargo *m.*

French [fren(t)ʃ]. I. *a.* 1. (*a*) Français. **F. Canadian**, canadien français. **F. king**, roi de France. **F. emperor**, empereur des Français. (*b*) (*Of fashion, etc.*) A la française. **F. cleaning**, nettoyage *m* (à sec). *Cu:* **F. dressing**, vinaigrette *f.* *U.S:* **F. fried potatoes**, **F. fries**, pommes de terre frites, *F:* frites *fpl.* *Dressm:* **F. seam**, couture anglaise. *S.a.* BEAN, BREAD, HORN. (*c*) *Sch:* A F. lesson, une leçon de

français. **F. master**, professeur de français. 2. To take F. leave, filer à l'anglaise; brûler la politesse à qn. II. French, *s.* 1. Le français; la langue française. To speak F., parler français. Say it in F., dites-le en français. 2. *pl.* The F., les Français. **'french 'chalk**, *s.* Talc *m*; craie *f* de tailleur. **'french 'polish**, *s*, Vernis *m* au tampon, à l'alcool. **'french-'polish²**, *v.tr.* Vernir (un meuble) au tampon. **'French-speaking**, *a.* Francophone, d'expression française. **F.-s. Switzerland**, la Suisse romande. **'French 'window**, *s.* Porte-fenêtre *f*, *pl.* portes-fenêtres.

Frenchman, *pl.* **-men** ['fren(t)mən], *s.m.* Français.

Frenchwoman, *pl.* **-women** ['fren(t)ʃwumən, -wimin], *s.f.* Française.

frenzied ['frenzid], *a.* (*Of pers.*) Affolé, forcené; (*of joy*) frénétique, délirant.

frenzy ['frenzi], *s.* 1. Frénésie *f.* **F. of joy**, transport *m* de joie. **Poetic f.**, fureur *f* poétique. 2. *Med:* Délire *m.*

frequency ['fri:kwənsi], *s.* Fréquence *f.* *W.Tel:* **To change the f.**, changer la fréquence. **F. modulation**, modulation *f* de fréquence.

frequent¹ ['fri:kwənt], *a.* 1. (*a*) Nombreux, abondant. **It is quite a f. practice**, c'est une coutume assez répandue. (*b*) *Med:* F. pulse, pouls rapide. 2. Fréquent; qui arrive souvent. **-ly**, *adv.* Fréquemment.

frequent² [fri'kwent], *v.tr.* Fréquenter, hanter, courir (les théâtres). **A much frequented road**, une route très passante.

frequentation [,fri:kwen'teiʃ(ə)n], *s.* Fréquentation *f.*

frequenter [fri'kwentər], *s.* Habitué *m*, familier *m* (d'une maison).

fresco, *pl.* **-o(e)s** ['freskou(z)], *s.* *Art:* Fresque *f.* **To paint in f.**, peindre à fresque. **F. painting**, (peinture *f* à) fresque. **F. painter**, (peintre *m*) fresquiste *mf.*

fresh [freʃ]. I. *a.* 1. (*a*) Nouveau, *-vel*, *-elle*. **F. paragraph**, nouveau paragraphe. **To put f. courage into s.o.**, ranimer le courage de qn. **He has had a f. attack of gout**, il a la goutte d'un repris. (*b*) Frais, *f.* fraîche; récent. **It is still f. in my memory**, j'en ai le souvenir tout frais. **F. from London**, nouvellement arrivé de Londres. **The bread was f. from the oven**, le pain sortait du four. 2. Inexpérimenté, novice. 3. (*a*) (Beurre) frais, (légume) vert. (*b*) (Air) frais, pur. **F. water**, (i) (*newly drawn*) eau fraîche; (ii) (*not salt*) eau douce. **In the f. air**, au grand air, en plein air. 4. (*a*) (Teint) frais, fleuri. **As f. as a daisy**, frais comme une rose. (*b*) (*Of pers.*) Vigoureux, alerte; (*of horse*) fougueux. (*c*) *U.S: F:* Outrecuidant, effronté. 5. *Nau:* **F. breeze**, jolie brise. *adv.* **It blows f.**, il vente frais. 6. *F:* (*Of pers.*) Éméché; un peu gris. **-ly**, *adv.* (*a*) Fraîchement. (*b*) Nouvellement. (*c*) Vivement. II. **fresh**, *adv.* Fraîchement, nouvellement, récemment. **F.-cut flowers**, fleurs nouvellement cueillies. **F. shaven**, rasé de frais. **F. killed**, (bétail) fraîchement tué. **'fresh-'coloured**, *a.* (Visage) au teint frais.

freshen ['freʃ(ə)n]. 1. *v.i.* (*a*) (*Of temperature*) (Se) rafraîchir. (*b*) (*Of wind*) Fraîchir. 2. *v.tr.* Rafraîchir (la mémoire, etc.). *F:* **To f. s.o. up**, requinquer qn.

fresher ['freʃər], *s.* *F:* = FRESHMAN.

freshman, *pl.* **-men** ['freʃmən], *s.* (*At University*) Étudiant *m* de première année.

freshness ['freʃnis], *s.* 1. Caractère récent (d'un événement); nouveauté *f.* 2. Fraîcheur *f.* 3. (*Of pers.*) (*a*) Vigueur *f*, vivacité *f.* (*b*) Naïveté *f*, inexpérience *f.* (*c*) *U.S:* Effronterie *f*, toupet *m.*

freshwater ['freʃwɔ:tər], *attrib.a.* (Poisson) d'eau douce. *F:* **F. sailor**, marin d'eau douce.

fret¹ [fret], *s.* 1. *Arch:* (Greek) f., grecque *f*; frette *f.* 2. *Her:* Frette. **'fret-saw**, *s.* Scie *f* à découper.

fret², *s.* *Mus:* Touchette *f* (de guitare).

fret³, *s.* Irritation *f*; état *m* d'agacement. **To be in a f.**, se faire du mauvais sang; se tracasser.

fret⁴, *v.* (fretted) 1. *v.tr.* (*a*) Ronger (qch.). **Horse that frets its bit**, cheval qui ronge son mors. **Fretted rope**, cordage éraillé, mâché. **The stream has fretted a channel through the rock**, le ruisseau a creusé un chenal dans le roc. (*b*) Inquiéter, tracasser (qn). 2. *v.pr. & i.* To f. (oneself), se tourmenter; se faire du mauvais sang; ronger son frein. **Don't f.!** ne vous faites pas de bile! **Child fretting for its mother**, enfant qui demande sa mère. **To f. and fume**, s'impatienter, enrager.

fretful ['fretful], a. Chagrin; irritable. **F. old age,** vieillesse chagrine. **F. baby,** bébé agité. **-fully,** adv. D'un air chagrin, inquiet.
fretfulness ['fretfulnis], s. Irritabilité f.
fretwork ['fretwɔ:k], s. Woodw: Travail ajouré; découpages mpl.; bois découpé.
Freudian ['frɔidiən], a. Psy: Freudien, -ienne.
Freudianism ['frɔidiənizm], s. Psy: Freudisme m.
friability [ˌfraiə'biliti], **friableness** ['fraiəblnis], s. Friabilité f.
friable ['fraiəbl], a. Friable.
friar ['fraiər], s. Moine m, frère m, religieux m. **Grey F.,** Franciscain m. **Black F.,** Dominicain m. **White F.,** Carme m. **'friar's 'balsam,** s. Pharm: Baume m de benjoin.
friary ['fraiəri], s. Monastère m; couvent m (de moines).
fricassee[1] [frikə'si:], s. Cu: Fricassée f.
fricassee[2], v.tr. Fricasser.
friction ['frikʃ(ə)n], s. 1. Med: Toil: Friction f. 2. Frottement m (de deux corps). Av: **F. of the air,** frottement de l'air. 3. Désaccord m. **There is f. between them,** il y a du tirage entre eux. **'friction-clutch,** s. Mec.E: Embrayage m à friction.
Friday ['fraidi], s. Vendredi m. **He is coming on F.,** il viendra vendredi. **He comes on Fridays,** il vient le vendredi. **Good F.,** (le) Vendredi saint.
fridge [fridʒ], s. F: Réfrigérateur m, F: frigo m.
fried. See FRY[3].
friend [frend], s. 1. Ami, f. amie. **Bosom f.,** ami(e) intime; un(e) intime. **A schoolmaster f. of mine,** un professeur de mes amis. **To be friends with s.o.,** être lié (d'amitié) avec qn; F: être ami avec qn. **To make friends with s.o.,** se lier d'amitié avec qn. **You'd better remain friends with them,** vous ferez bien de ne pas vous brouiller avec eux. **He is no f. of mine,** (i) il n'est pas de mes amis; (ii) il ne me veut pas de bien. Prov: **The best of friends must part,** il n'est si bonne compagnie qui ne se sépare. **A f. in need is a f. indeed,** c'est dans le besoin qu'on connaît ses véritables amis. 2. Connaissance f. **A f. at court,** un ami en haut lieu. **To have friends at court,** avoir des protections, F: avoir du piston. **To dine with a few friends,** dîner en petit comité. **My f. Robinson,** mon ami Robinson. Parl: **My honourable f.,** Jur: **my learned f.,** mon (cher) confrère. 3. Ami, partisan m (de l'ordre, etc.); patron, -onne (des arts, etc.). 4. **The Society of Friends,** la Société des Amis; les Quakers.
friendless ['frendlis], a. Délaissé; sans amis.
friendliness ['frendlinis], s. Bienveillance f, bonté (to, towards, envers); dispositions amicales.
friendly ['frendli], a. 1. (Ton, sentiment) amical, -aux; sympathique. **To be f. with s.o.,** être ami avec qn. **In a f. manner,** amicalement. **To be on f. terms with s.o.,** être en bons rapports, en relations d'amitié, avec qn. Sp: **F. match,** match amical. 2. (Of pers.) Bienveillant, favorablement disposé; favorable. 3. **F. society,** amicale f, mutuelle f. 4. Geog: **The F. Islands,** les îles Amis, l'Archipel m de Tonga.
friendship ['frendʃip], s. Amitié f. **I did it out of f.,** je l'ai fait par amitié.
Friesian ['fri:ziən], a. & s. = FRISIAN. **F. cow,** vache frisonne.
Friesland ['fri:zlənd]. Pr.n. Geog: La Frise.
frieze[1] [fri:z], s. Tex: Frise f, ratine f.
frieze[2], s. 1. Arch: Frise f. 2. Bordure f (de papier peint).
frig [fridʒ], s. F: = FRIDGE.
frigate ['frigit], s. Navy: Frégate f. Orn: **F. bird,** petrel, pétrel m frégate.
fright [frait], s. 1. Peur f, effroi m. **I had an awful f.,** j'ai eu une belle peur, une peur bleue. **To escape with a bad f.,** en être quitte pour la peur. **To take f.,** s'effrayer, s'effarer (at, de); prendre peur. **To give s.o. a f.,** faire peur à qn. 2. F: (Esp. of woman) Épouvantail m, -ails. **What a perfect f. you look!** comme vous voilà fagoté(e)!
frighten ['fraitn], v.tr. Effrayer (qn); faire peur à (qn). F: **To f. s.o. out of his wits,** faire une peur bleue à qn. **I'm not going to be frightened into apologising,** on ne m'arrachera pas des excuses en essayant de m'intimider. **frighten away, off,** v.tr. **The dog frightened the thieves away,** le chien a fait décamper les voleurs. **Don't f. away the birds,** n'effarouchez pas les oiseaux. **frightened,** a. (Of pers., etc.) Apeuré, épeuré. **Easily f.,** peureux, poltron. **To be, feel, f.,** avoir peur. **To be f. to death,** mourir de peur. **To be f. at, of, sth.,** avoir peur de qch. **He was more f. than hurt,** il a eu plus de peur que de mal. **frightening,** a. Effrayant.
frightful ['fraitful], a. Terrible, effroyable, affreux, épouvantable. F: **To have a f. headache,** avoir un mal de tête affreux. **He was in a f. temper,** il était dans une colère terrible. **-fully** adv. Terriblement. effroyablement, affreusement. F: **I am f. sorry,** je regrette énormément.
frightfulness ['fraitfulnis], s. Horreur f, atrocité f (d'un crime, etc.).
frigid ['fridʒid], a. (a) Glacial, -als; (très) froid. (b) **F. person,** personne froide. **F. politeness,** politesse glaciale. (c) Physiol: Frigide. **-ly,** adv. Glacialement; très froidement.
frigidity [fri'dʒiditi], s. (a) Frigidité f; grande froideur. (b) Physiol: Frigidité, froideur (sexuelle).
frigorific [ˌfrigə'rifik], a. Frigorifique.
frill[1] [fril], s. (a) Cost: Volant m, ruche f. **Toby f.,** collerette plissée; fraise f. **Shirt f.,** jabot m. Cu: (Cutlet, ham) f., papillote f. (b) pl. **Façons** fpl, **affectations** fpl. **A plain meal without frills,** un repas simple sans présentation compliquée.
frill[2], v.tr. Plisser, froncer tuyauter (le linge).
fringe[1] [frindʒ], s. 1. Tex: Frange f. 2. (a) Bordure f, bord m. **The outer fringe(s) of London,** la grande banlieue de Londres. **To live on the f. of society,** vivre en marge de la société. T.V: **F. area,** zone f limitrophe. F: **F. benefits,** la gratte. (b) Haird: **To wear a f.,** être coiffé(e) à la chien.
fringe[2], v.tr. Franger (un tapis, etc.). **Eyes fringed with black lashes,** yeux bordés, frangés, de cils noirs. **fringing,** a. Marginal, -aux; (récif, etc.) en bordure.
frippery ['fripəri], s. Colifichets mpl.; camelote f; (of style, etc.) clinquant m.
Frisian ['frizian], a. & s. Geog: Frison, -onne.
frisk [frisk]. 1. v.i. **To f. (about),** (of lambs, etc.) s'ébattre; gambader, faire des cabrioles. 2. v.tr. (Of dog, etc.) **To f. its tail,** frétiller de la queue. (b) U.S: Fouiller (un suspect).
friskiness ['friskinis], s. Folâtrerie f, vivacité f.
frisky ['friski], a. Vif, folâtre; frétillant; (cheval) fringant. **-ily,** adv. Folâtrement, d'un air fringant.
fritillary [fri'tiləri], s. 1. Bot: Fritillaire f. 2. Ent: Damier m.
fritter[1] ['fritər], s. Cu: Beignet m.
fritter[2], v.tr. **To f. (sth.) away, down,** morceler (qch.); réduire (qch.) à rien. **To f. away one's money,** gaspiller son argent.
frivol ['friv(ə)l], v. (frivolled) F: 1. v.i. Baguenauder muser. 2. v.tr. **To f. away one's time,** passer son temps à des riens.
frivolity [fri'voliti], s. Frivolité f.
frivolous ['frivələs], a. Frivole; (of claim, etc.) vain, futile; (of pers.) baguenaudier, évaporé; futile. **-ly,** adv. Frivolement.
frizz [friz]. 1. v.tr. Crêper, bichonner (les cheveux). 2. v.i. (Of hair) Frisotter.
frizzle ['frizl]. 1. v.i. Grésiller. 2. v.tr. Cu: (a) Faire frire (le lard, etc.). (b) Griller (le lard, etc.).
frizzy ['frizi], a. (Of hair) Crépu.
fro [frou], adv. **To and f.,** see TO III. 2.
frock [frok], s. Cost: 1. Robe f (d'enfant, de femme). 2. (a) Froc (de moine). (b) A: Blouse f, sarrau m (de paysan, d'ouvrier). **'frock-'coat,** s, Redingote f.
frog[1] [frog], s. 1. Grenouille f. 2. Med: Aphte m. F: **To have a f. in one's throat,** avoir un chat dans la gorge. **'frog-march,** v.tr. Porter (un récalcitrant) à quatre, le derrière en l'air.
frog[2], s. Farr: Fourchette f (du sabot).
frog[3], s. Mil: etc: 1. Porte-épée m inv; porte-baïonnette m inv. 2. Cost: Soutache f, olive f. **Frogs and loops,** brandebourgs mpl.
frog[4], s. Rail: (Cœur m de) croisement m.
frogged [frogd], a. Cost: A brandebourgs.
frogman ['frogmən], s. Homme-grenouille m. **F.'s mask,** masque m sous-marin.

frolic[1] ['frɔlik], s. (a) Ébats mpl, gambades fpl. (b) Fredaine f, divertissement m.
frolic[2], v.i. (frolicked) Se divertir, batifoler, folâtrer. **frolicking**, s. Divertissement m, ébats mpl.
frolicsome ['frɔliksəm], a. Gai, espiègle, folâtre.
from [frɔm], prep. 1. De. To go f. home, partir de chez soi; quitter la maison. From . . . to . . ., de . . . à . . .; depuis . . . jusqu'à. . . . F. flower to flower, de fleur en fleur. F. side to side, d'un côté à l'autre. Wines f. one franc a bottle, vins depuis, à partir de, un franc la bouteille. 2. Depuis, dès, à partir de. F. the earliest records onwards, à partir des plus anciens documents. As f. . . ., à partir de. . . . F. his childhood, f. a child, depuis, dès son enfance. F. time to time, de temps en temps. 3. He is away, absent, f. home, il est absent, sorti, en voyage. Not far f. . . ., pas loin de. . . . 4. (a) De, à. Take that knife f. that child, ôtez ce couteau à cet enfant. He stole a pound f. her, il lui a volé une livre. To dissuade s.o. f. doing sth., dissuader qn de faire qch. (b) To shelter f. the rain, s'abriter contre la pluie. 5. (a) F. bad to worse, de mal en pis. The price has been increased f. sixpence to a shilling, on a porté le prix de six pence à un shilling. (b) D'avec, de. To distinguish the good f. the bad, distinguer le bon d'avec le mauvais. (c) To pick s.o. out f. the crowd, distinguer qn parmi la foule. To drink f. the brook, boire au ruisseau. He took a knife f. the table, il prit un couteau sur la table. He learned it f. a book, il l'a appris dans un livre. 6. (a) He is, comes, f. Manchester, il est natif, originaire de Manchester. Where are you f.? d'où êtes-vous? Air-lines to and f. the Continent, lignes aériennes à destination ou en provenance du Continent. Broadcast commentary (on the Derby) f. Epsom, radio-reportage en direct d'Epsom, depuis Epsom. A quotation f. Shakespeare, une citation tirée de Shakespeare. To draw a conclusion f. sth., tirer une conclusion de qch. To write f. s.o.'s dictation, écrire sous la dictée de qn. F. your point of view, à votre point de vue. (b) A letter f. my father, une lettre de mon père. The petition is f. . . ., la pétition émane de. . . . A dispatch f. the colonel, une dépêche de la part du colonel. Tell him that f. 'me, dites-lui cela de ma part. (On parcel) F. . . ., envoi de. . . . (On letter) Exp(éditeur, -trice). (c) Painted f. life, f. nature, peint d'après nature. 7. To act f. conviction, agir par conviction. To die f. fatigue, mourir de fatigue. F. what I heard . . ., d'après ce que j'ai entendu dire. F. what I can see . . ., à ce que je vois. . . . I know him f. seeing him at the club, je le reconnais pour l'avoir vu au cercle. 8. (With adv., prep.) F. above, d'en haut. I saw him f. afar, je l'ai vu de loin. F. henceforth, à partir d'aujourd'hui. To look at s.o. f. under, f. over, one's spectacles, regarder qn par-dessous, par-dessus, ses lunettes. F. of old, du temps jadis, du vieux temps. I know him f. of old, je le connais de longue date.
frond [frɔnd], s. Bot: 1. Fronde f (de fougère). 2. F: Feuille f (de palmier).
front[1] [frʌnt]. I. s. 1. (a) Front m, contenance f. F. to f., face à face. To put a bold f. on it faire bonne contenance. (b) To have the f. to do sth., avoir l'effronterie, le front, F: le toupet de faire qch. 2. Mil: Front (d'une armée). To present an unbroken f., présenter un front inentamé. At the F., au front, sur le front. Pol: United, common f., front commun. Popular f., front populaire. The home f., la politique intérieure. 3. (a) Devant m, partie antérieure; façade f, face f (d'un bâtiment); avant (d'une voiture); devant, plastron m (de chemise). To look at the f. of sth., regarder qch. de face. Fenc: To show less f., s'effacer. (b) = SEAFRONT. House on the f., maison faisant face à la mer. 4. To push one's way to the f., se frayer un chemin jusqu'au premier rang, F: se pousser (en avant). F: To come to the f., arriver au premier rang; percer; se faire connaître. 5. Adv.phr. In f., devant, en avant. To send s.o. on in f., envoyer qn en avant. Attacked in f. and rear, attaqué par devant et par derrière. In f. of, (i) en face de, vis-à-vis de; (ii) devant. Look in f. of you, regardez devant vous. II. front, a. Antérieur, de devant, d'avant, de face. F. seat, (i) siège au premier rang; (ii) Aut: siège avant. Rail: F.

carriage, voiture f de tête. In the f. part of the train, en tête du train. F. rank, premier rang. F.-line soldiers, soldats du front. 'front-brake, s. Cy: Frein m avant. 'front-'door, s. Porte f d'entrée (principale); porte sur la rue. 'front page, s. Journ: Première page, F: la une. 'front-'room, s. Chambre f sur le devant, sur la rue. 'front-'view, s. Vue f de face. Arch: Élévation f.
front[2]. 1. v.tr. & i. To f. sth.; to f. (up)on, to(wards), sth., faire face à qch.; être tourné vers qch. Windows that f. the street, fenêtres qui donnent sur la rue. 2. v.tr. To f. s.o. with s.o., confronter qn avec qn. 3. v.tr. House fronted with stone, maison avec façade en pierre. 4. Mil: (a) v.i. Faire front. (b) v.tr. Établir le front de (l'armée, etc.).
frontage ['frʌntidʒ], s. 1. Terrain m en bordure (d'une chaussée, etc.). 2. (a) Longueur f de façade (d'un édifice); devanture f (d'un magasin). (b) Façade f (sur la rue).
frontal ['frʌnt(ə)l], a. 1. Anat: Frontal, -aux. 2. Mil: (Attaque, etc.) de front. -ally, adv. De front.
frontier ['frʌntiər], s. Frontière f. F. town, ville f frontière. F: districts, régions frontalières, de la frontière. F. guard, garde-frontière f.
frontier(s)man, pl. -men ['frʌntiə(z)mən,] s.m. Frontalier.
frontispiece ['frʌntispiːs], s. Typ: Frontispice m.
fronton ['frʌntən], s. Arch: Fronton m.
frost[1] [frɔst], s. 1. (a) Gelée f, gel m. Ground f., white f., gelée blanche. F: Jack F., le bonhomme Hiver. Ten degrees of f., dix degrés de froid. (b) (Hoar) f., givre m; Lit: frimas m. Glazed f., verglas m. 2. F: Four m, fiasco m. The play was a dead f., ç'a été un four noir. 'frost-bite, s. 1. Med: Gelure f. 2. Agr: Hort: Brûlure f par la gelée. 'frost-bitten, a. 1. (Of nose, etc.) Gelé. 2. (Of plants) Brûlé par le froid. 'frost-hardy, a. Arb: Bot: Résistant au froid. 'frost-tender, a. Arb: Bot: Sensible au froid. 'frost-work, s. Fleurs fpl de givre.
frost[2], v.tr. 1. Geler (un arbre fruitier). 2. (a) Givrer (les vitres, etc.). (b) Glacer (un gâteau). 3. Dépolir (le verre). frosted, a. 1. Givré. 2. (Of glass) Dépoli. 3. (Of precious stones) Givreux, -euse.
frosty ['frɔsti], a. 1. Gelé; glacial, -als. F. day, jour de gelée. F. reception, accueil glacial. 2. (Carreaux) couverts de givre; (arbre) givré. -ily, adv. F: Glacialement.
froth[1] [frɔθ], s. 1. Écume f (du bouillon, aux lèvres); mousse f (du savon, de la bière); F: faux col f (d'un verre de bière). 2. F: Futilités fpl; paroles creuses; Fr.C: P: broue f.
froth[2], v.i. Écumer, mousser. To f. up, mousser fortement. To f. over, déborder (en moussant). He was frothing at the mouth, sa bouche écumait.
frothy ['frɔθi], a. Écumeux, écumant; mousseux.
frown[1] [fraun], s. Froncement m de sourcils; regard sévère, désapprobateur.
frown[2], v.i. (a) (Of pers.) Froncer les sourcils; se renfrogner. To f. at, (up)on, ε.o., regarder qn de travers, en fronçant les sourcils. To f. upon a suggestion, désapprouver une suggestion. (b) (Of thgs) Avoir l'air sombre, menaçant. frowning, a. (Of looks, face, etc.) Renfrogné; (of brow) sourcilleux; (of thgs) sombre, menaçant.
frowstiness ['fraustinis], s. F: Odeur f de renfermé.
frowsty ['frausti], a. F: Qui sent le renfermé.
frowzy ['frauzi], a. 1. Qui sent le renfermé. 2. (Of pers., clothes) Sale, mal tenu, peu soigné.
frozen ['frou:zn], a. Gelé, glacé. To f. death, mort de froid. F: I'm f. to death, je meurs de froid. Com: F. meat, viande frigorifiée. Frozen foods, aliments surgelés. Fin: F. assets, fonds m non liquides. F. capital, credits, capitaux, crédits, gelés. Geog: The F. North, le grand Nord.
fructification [ˌfrʌktifiˈkeiʃ(ə)n], s. Fructification f.
fructify ['frʌktifai], v.i. Fructifier.
frugal ['fruːɡ(ə)l], a. 1. (Of pers.) Frugal, -aux; économe. To be f. of sth., ménager qch. 2. (Of meal) Frugal, simple. F. eater, homme sobre. -ally, adv. Frugalement, sobrement.
frugality [fruːˈɡæliti], s. Frugalité f.

fruit [fruːt], s. Fruit m. **1. Stone f.**, fruit à noyau. **Eat more f.**, mangez plus de fruits. **Dried f.**, fruits secs. **Stewed f.**, compote f de fruits. **To bear f.**, (i) donner des fruits, porter fruit; (ii) être couronné de succès. **2. The fruits of the earth**, les fruits de la terre. **His knowledge is the f. of much study**, son savoir est le fruit de longues études. **'fruit-bearing,** a. Fructifère. **'fruit-cake**, s. Cake m. **'fruit-dish, -stand,** s. Compotier m. **'fruit-growing,** s. Arboriculture f fruitière. **'fruit-knife,** s. Couteau m à fruit(s). **'fruit-tree,** s. Arbre fruitier.
fruiterer ['fruːtərər], s. (Pers.) Fruitier, -ière.
fruitful ['fruːtfl], a. (Of tree, etc.) Fructueux, productif; (of soil, etc.) fertile, fécond. **Action f. of, in, consequences**, action fertile en conséquences. **-fully,** adv. Fructueusement, utilement.
fruitfulness ['fruːtflnis], s. Productivité f (d'un arbre, etc.); fertilité f (du sol, etc.).
fruition [fruː'iʃ(ə)n], s. **1.** Jouissance f (d'un bien). **2.** Réalisation f (d'un projet); fructification f (d'une idée). **To come to f.**, fructifier.
fruitless ['fruːtlis], a. (Of plant, work) Stérile, infructueux, -euse. **F. efforts**, vains efforts. **-ly,** adv. Vainement.
fruity ['fruːti], a. **1.** (a) (Goût, etc.) de fruit. (b) (O, oil) Fruité. **2.** F: (Scandale, etc.) corsé.
frump [frʌmp], s.f. F: Old f., vieille caricature, vieille toupie, vieux tableau.
frumpish ['frʌmpiʃ], **frumpy** ['frʌmpi], a. F: (Of woman) Fagotée; mal attifée. **A frumpish hat**, un chapeau pisseux.
frustrate [frʌs'treit], v.tr. (a) Faire échouer, faire avorter (un projet, etc.). **To f. s.o.'s hopes**, frustrer l'espoir de qn, désapppointer qn. (b) Contrecarrer (qn).
frustration [frʌs'treiʃ(ə)n], s. Anéantissement m (des projets de qn); frustration f (d'un espoir).
frustum, pl. **-ta, -tums** ['frʌstəm, -tə, -təmz], s. Tronc m (de cône, de prisme, etc.); tronçon m (d'une colonne).
fry¹ [frai], s. Coll. **1.** Ich: Frai m, fretin m, alevin m. **Small f.**, menu fretin. **2.** F: The small f., (i) le menu fretin, le menu peuple, les petites gens; (ii) les gosses m.
fry², s. Cu: **1.** Plat m de viande frite; friture f. **2.** Issues fpl; fressure f.
fry³, v. (fried [fraid]) **1.** v.tr. (Faire) frire (la viande, etc.). **Fried eggs**, œufs sur le plat. **2.** v.i. (Of meat, etc.) Frire. F: **To f. in one's own grease**, cuire dans son jus. **'frying-pan,** s. Poêle f (à frire); sauteuse f. F: **To jump out of the f.-p. into the fire**, tomber d'un mal dans un pire, de Charybde en Scylla.
fuchsia ['fjuːʃə], s. Bot: Fuchsia m.
fuddle ['fʌdl], v.tr. (a) Soûler, griser. **The wine had fuddled his brain**, le vin lui avait enfumé le cerveau. (b) Brouiller les idées de (qn). **fuddled,** a. F: **1.** Soûl; pris de vin; gris. **To get f.**, s'enivrer. **2.** Brouillé (dans ses idées); hébété.
fudge [fʌdʒ], s. **1.** Bêtise(s) f, sottise(s) f. **2.** Fondant (américain).
fuel¹ ['fjuəl], s. (a) Combustible m. **Patent f.**, compressed f., aggloméré(s) m(pl). **To add f. to the flame, to the fire,** jeter de l'huile sur le feu. (b) I.C.E: Carburant m. **'fuel-oil,** s. Fuel-oil, mazout m.
fuel², v.tr. (fuelled) (a) Charger (un fourneau, etc.) **Oil-fuelled,** alimenté au pétrole. (b) Ravitailler (la flotte, etc.) en combustibles. **fuelling,** s. Ravitaillement m en combustibles.
fug [fʌg], s. F: Forte odeur de renfermé; touffeur f.
fugacious [fjuː'geiʃəs], a. Fugace.
fugacity [fjuː'gæsiti] s. Fugacité f.
fugginess ['fʌginis], s. F: Touffeur f.
fuggy ['fʌgi], a. F: (Salle) qui sent le renfermé.
fugitive ['fjuːdʒitiv]. **1.** a. (a) Fugitif, en fuite. (b) (Of happiness, etc.) Fugitif, fugace, éphémère. **2.** s. (a) Fugitif, -ive; fuyard m. (b) Exilé, -ée; réfugié, -ée.
fugue [fjuːg], s. Mus: Med: Fugue f.
fulcrum, pl. **-cra** ['fʌlkrəm, -krə], s. Mec: (Point m, axe m, d')appui m, centre m, pivot m (d'un levier).
fulfil [ful'fil], v.tr. (fulfilled) **1.** (a) Accomplir (une prophétie); répondre à, remplir (l'attente de qn). (b) Satisfaire (un désir); exaucer (une prière). (c) Accomplir (une tâche). **To f. a duty**, s'acquitter d'un devoir; remplir un devoir. (d) Remplir (les conditions requises, etc.). (e) Obéir à (un commandement). **2.** Achever, compléter.

fulfilment [ful'filmənt], s. **1.** (a) Accomplissement m (d'un devoir, etc.). (b) Exaucement m (d'une prière); satisfaction (d'un désir). (c) Exécution f (d'une condition, d'un projet). **2.** Achèvement m (d'une période de temps, etc.).
fuliginous [fjuː'lidʒinəs], a. Fuligineux, -euse.
full¹ [ful]. I. a. **1.** Plein, rempli, comble. **To have one's pockets f. of money**, avoir de l'argent plein les poches. **F. to overflowing**, plein à déborder. **F. day,** jour chargé. **His heart was f.,** il avait le cœur gros, gonflé. **F. of holes**, tout troué. **Look f. of gratitude**, regard chargé de reconnaissance. **To be f. of hope,** avoir bon espoir. **2.** (Of bus, etc.) Plein, complet. **To be f. up**, avoir son plein. **F. up! F. house,** salle f comble. **F. session (of a committee, etc.)**, réunion, assemblée, plénière. **3. To be f. of one's own importance**, être pénétré de sa propre importance. **4.** (Of facts, etc.) Ample, abondant, copieux. **F. particulars,** tous les détails. **Until fuller information is available . . .**, jusqu'à plus ample informé. **5.** Complet, entier. (a) **F. meal,** repas complet. **F. price**, prix fort. **F. pay,** paye entière; solde entière. Th: **To pay f. price**, Rail: to pay f. fare, payer place entière. **F. weight, f. measure,** poids juste; mesure comble. **F. text,** texte intégral. Mil: **F. discharge,** congé définitif. **Battalion at f. strength,** bataillon au grand complet. (b) **In f. flower**, en pleine fleur. **In f. uniform**, en grande tenue. (c) **I waited two f. hours**, j'ai attendu deux bonnes heures, deux grandes heures. **It is a f. five miles from here**, c'est à au moins huit kilomètres d'ici. **6.** (a) (Of face) Plein; (of figure) rond, replet; (of chin) renflé. **F. lips**, lèvres grosses, fortes. (b) (Of sleeve, etc.) Ample, large, bouffant. (c) **F. voice**, voix pleine, ronde, étoffée. **7.** Nau: (Of sail) Plein, gonflé. **To keep her f.**, porter plein. **F. and by,** près et plein. **-lly,** adv. **1.** (a) Pleinement, entièrement, complètement, amplement. **F. armed,** armé de toutes pièces. **F. fashioned** (of stockings, etc.), entièrement diminué, proportionné. **I'll write to you more f.**, je vous écrirai plus longuement. **F. paid,** payé intégralement. (b) **To treat a subject, develop a negative, f.**, traiter un sujet, développer un cliché, à fond. **2. It takes f. two hours**, cela prend bien, au moins, deux heures. II. **full,** s. **1. The moon is at the f.**, la lune est dans son plein. **2.** adv.phr. (a) **In f. To publish a letter in f.**, publier une lettre intégralement. **Account given in f.**, compte rendu in extenso. Fin: **Capital paid in f.**, capital entièrement versé. **Name in f.**, (i) nom m et prénoms; (ii) nom en toutes lettres. (b) **To the f.**, complètement. **To indulge one's tastes to the f.**, donner libre carrière à ses goûts. III. **full,** adv. **1.** A. & Lit: **F. many a time**, bien des fois. **I know it f. well**, je le sais bien, parfaitement. **It is f. five miles from here**, c'est à au moins huit kilomètres d'ici. **2.** Précisément, en plein. **F. in the middle,** au beau milieu. **Hit f. in the face**, atteint en pleine figure. **They are working f. out**, ils travaillent à plein rendement. **'full-back,** s. Fb: Arrière m. **'full-'blooded,** a. **1.** (a) (Of brother, sister) Germain. (b) De race pure; (cheval) pur sang inv. **2.** Vigoureux; robuste. **3.** (Tempérament) sanguin. **'full-'blown,** a. **1.** (Of rose, etc.) Épanoui; en pleine fleur. **2.** F: **He is a f.-b. doctor**, il a (obtenu) tous ses diplômes, **'full-bodied,** a. **1.** Corpulent. **2.** (Vin) corsé, qui a du corps. **'full-bred,** a. De race pure; (cheval) pur sang inv. **'full-'cream,** a. **F.-c. milk**, lait entier, non écrémé. **'full-dress,** attrib.a. **F.-d. clothes**, tenue f de cérémonie. **F.-d. debate**, débat solennel. Th: **F.-d. rehearsal**, répétition générale, en costumes. **'full-fledged,** a. **1.** (Of bird) Qui a toutes ses plumes. **2.** F: = FULL-BLOWN 2. **'full-'grown,** a. Adulte. **'full-length,** a. (Portrait) en pied. **F.-l. evening dress**, robe (de soirée) longue. **F.-l. film**, long métrage. **'full-page,** attrib.a. (Illustration) hors texte. **'full-rigged,** a. Nau: Gréé en trois-mâts carré. **'full-size(d),** a. (Dessin, etc.) (i) de grandeur naturelle; (ii) Ind: à la dimension exacte, à la cote. **'full 'stop,** s. (In punctuation) Point (final). F: **He came to a f. s.**, il est resté court (dans son discours). **'full-'throated,** a. (Chant, etc.) à plein gosier, à pleine gorge. **'full-time.** Ind: **1.** a. **F.-t. employment**, emploi m à temps complet, à plein temps. **2.** adv. **To work f. t.**, travailler à pleines journées.

full², *v.tr.* Fouler (l'étoffe, le cuir). **fulling**, *s.* Foulage *m* (des draps).

fuller¹ ['fulər], *s. Tex:* Fouleur, -euse; foulon *m.* **F.'s earth**, terre savonneuse; terre à foulon. *Bot:* **F.'s teasel**, cardère *f* à foulon; chardon *m* à foulon.

fuller², *s. Tls:* Dégorgeoir *m.*

ful(l)ness ['fulnis], *s.* **1.** État plein (d'un récipient); plénitude *f* (de l'estomac). **Out of the f. of his heart, he told us . . .**, comme son cœur débordait il nous raconta. . . . **2.** Plénitude, totalité *f* (de la force, etc.). **In the f. of time**, quand les temps furent, seront, révolus. **3.** Ampleur *f* (d'un vêtement, d'un compte rendu); abondance *f* (de détail); rondeur *f* (de la forme); richesse *f* (du style, d'une couleur).

fulminate¹ ['fʌlmineit], *s. Ch:* Fulminate *m* (de mercure, etc.).

fulminate². **1.** *v.i.* Fulminer; faire explosion. **2.** *v.tr. & i. Ecc:* Fulminer (une excommunication). **To f. against s.o.**, fulminer contre qn.

fulness ['fulnis], *s. See* FUL(L)NESS.

fulsome ['fulsəm], *a.* (*Of praise, etc.*) Écœurant, excessif. **F. flattery**, flagornerie *f*, adulation *f.*

fulsomeness ['fulsəmnis], *s.* Bassesse *f*, platitude *f* (des louanges, etc.).

fulvous ['fʌlvəs], *a.* Fauve.

fumble ['fʌmbl]. **1.** *v.i.* Fouiller (au hasard); tâtonner. **To f. (in a drawer, etc.) for sth.**, (far)fouiller (dans un tiroir, etc.) pour trouver qch. **To f. for words**, chercher ses mots. **To f. with sth.**, manier qch. maladroitement. **2.** *v.tr.* Manier (qch.) maladroitement, gauchement; tripoter (qch.). *Sp:* **To f. the ball**, arrêter, attraper, la balle maladroitement. **fumbling**, *a.* Maladroit, gauche.

fumbler ['fʌmblər], *s.* Maladroit, -e, lourdaud, -e.

fume¹ [fju:m], *s.* **1.** Fumée *f*, vapeur *f*, exhalaison *f. Ind:* **Factory fumes**, fumée d'usine. **2.** *F:* **In a f.**, hors de soi; en rage. **'fume-chamber, -cupboard,** *s. Ch:* Sorbonne *f* (de laboratoire).

fume². **1.** *v.tr.* Exposer (qch.) à une vapeur, à un gaz. **Fumed oak**, chêne patiné. **2.** *v.i.* (*a*) Fumer; émettre de la fumée, des vapeurs. (*b*) (*Of smoke, vapour*) Monter, s'exhaler. (*c*) *F:* (*Of pers.*) Rager; *F:* fumer.

fumigate ['fju:migeit], *v.tr.* Exposer (qch.) à la fumée; désinfecter (un appartement) par fumigation; mécher (un tonneau).

fumigation [,fju:mi'geif(ə)n], *s.* Fumigation *f*; désinfection *f*; méchage *m.*

fumitory ['fju:mitəri], *s. Bot:* Fumeterre *f.*

fun [fʌn], *s.* Amusement *m*, gaieté *f*; plaisanterie *f*; *F:* rigolade. **To make f. of, poke f. at, s.o.**, se moquer, rire, de qn. *P:* charrier qn. **For f., in f.**, (i) pour rire; par plaisanterie; (ii) pour se distraire. **I did it for the f. of the thing**, je l'ai fait histoire de rire. **He's great f., full of f.**, il est très gai, il a toujours le mot pour rire. *F:* c'est un rigolo. **I don't see the f. of it**, je ne trouve pas ça drôle. **It's good, clean f.**, c'est d'un comique sain. **It was great f.**, c'était fort amusant. **To have f.**, s'amuser, se divertir. **It was only my f.**, c'était pour rire. **'fun fair**, *s.* (*a*) Foire, fête foraine. (*b*) Parc *m* d'attractions.

funambulist [fju:'næmbjulist], *s.* Funambule *mf*; danseur, -euse, de corde.

function¹ ['fʌŋ(k)ʃ(ə)n], *s.* **1.** Fonction *f.* **Vital functions**, fonctions vitales. **2.** (*a*) (*Of office-holder, etc.*) Fonction, charge *f.* **In his f. as a magistrate**, en sa qualité de magistrat. (*b*) *pl.* **To discharge one's functions**, s'acquitter de ses fonctions. **It is part of my functions to . . .**, c'est à moi qu'il appartient de. . . . **3.** (*a*) Réception *f*, soirée *f.* **Society f.**, réunion mondaine. (*b*) Cérémonie publique; solennité *f.* **4.** *Mth:* Fonction. **As a f. of . . .**, en fonction de. . . .

function², *v.i.* **1.** Fonctionner, marcher. *F:* **This gadget won't f.**, ce truc ne marche pas. **2. Adjective that functions as an adverb**, adjectif qui fait fonction d'adverbe.

functional ['fʌŋ(k)ʃən(ə)l], *a.* Fonctionnel.

functionalism ['fʌŋk'ʃənəlizm], *s.* Fonctionnalisme *m.*

functionary ['fʌŋ(k)ʃənəri], *s.* Fonctionnaire *m.*

fund¹ [fʌnd], *s.* **1.** Fonds *m* (d'érudition, etc.). **He has a rare f. of perseverance**, il a des trésors de persévérance. **2.** *Fin: etc:* (*a*) Fonds *m*, caisse *f.* **Old-**

age pension f., caisse des retraites pour la vieillesse. **To start a f.**, lancer une souscription. (*b*) *pl.* **Funds**, fonds, masse *f*; disponibilités *fpl.* **I can't do it, I haven't got the funds**, je ne peux pas le faire, je n'ai pas l'argent pour cela. (*Of company*) **To make a call for funds**, faire un appel de capital. **To be in funds**, être en fonds. *Bank:* 'No funds,' "défaut *m* de provision", "manque *m* de fonds", "pas d'encaisse". **To misappropriate public funds**, détourner les deniers de l'État, les deniers publics; (*c*) *pl.* **Funds**, la Dette publique; les fonds publics; la rente sur l'État.

fund², *v.tr. Fin:* **1.** Consolider (une dette publique). **2.** Placer (de l'argent) dans les fonds publics. **Funded property**, biens en rentes.

fundament ['fʌndəmənt], *s. Anat:* Fondement *m*; *F:* le derrière.

fundamental [,fʌndə'ment(ə)l]. **I.** *a.* **1.** (*a*) Fondamental, -aux; essentiel. **F. question**, question de fond. **F. qualities of s.o.**, qualités foncières de qn. (*b*) (*Of colours, etc.*) Primitif; original, -aux. **2.** *Mus:* (*Of note, etc.*) Fondamental. **-ally**, *adv.* Fondamentalement, foncièrement. **His argument is f. wrong**, son raisonnement pèche par la base. **II.** **fundamental**, *s.* **1.** *pl.* **Fundamentals**, principe *m*, partie essentielle (d'un système, etc.). **2.** *Mus:* Fondamentale; fondamentale *f.*

funeral ['fju:n(ə)rəl], *s.* **1.** Funérailles *fpl*; obsèques *fpl*; enterrement *m. F:* **That's your f.!** ça c'est votre affaire! **2.** *attrib.a.* **F. expenses**, frais funéraires, d'enterrement. **F. procession**, convoi *m* funèbre, cortège *m* funèbre. *F:* **At a f. pace**, à un pas d'enterrement.

funereal [fju:'niəriəl], *a.* **1.** *Poet:* Funèbre, funéraire. **2.** *F:* Lugubre, funèbre, triste; (*of voice*) sépulcral, -aux. **-ally**, *adv.* Funèbrement, lugubrement.

fungicide ['fʌndʒisaid], *s.* Fongicide *m.*

fungous ['fʌŋgəs], *a.* Fongueux, -euse, fongoïde.

fungus ['fʌŋgəs], *s.* **-uses, -i** ['fʌŋgəs, -əsiz -gai], *s. Bot:* Champignon *m.* **Edible f.**, champignon comestible. **Poisonous f.**, champignon vénéneux.

funicular [fju'nikjulər], *a. & s.* Funiculaire (*m*).

funk¹ [fʌŋk], *s. P:* **1.** Frousse *f*, trac *m*, trouille *f.* **To be in a (blue) f.**, avoir une peur bleue; avoir le trac, la frousse. **2.** Froussard, -arde; trouillard, -arde. **'funk-hole**, *s. F:* **1.** *Mil:* Abri enterré, *F:* cagna *f.* **2.** (*For shirkers*) Planque *f.*

funk², *v.tr. & i. P:* **To f. (it)**, caner, se dégonfler. **To f. s.o., sth., to f. doing sth., to f. at sth.**, avoir peur de qn, de qch., de faire qch.

funky ['fʌŋki], *a. P:* Froussard.

funnel ['fʌnl], *s.* **1.** (*a*) Entonnoir *m.* (*b*) *Ind:* (Charging, loading) f., trémie *f*, hotte *f.* **2.** (*a*) Tuyau *m* (d'aérage). (*b*) Cheminée *f* (de locomotive, de bateau à vapeur).

funniness ['fʌninis], *s.* **1.** Drôlerie *f.* **2.** Bizarrerie *f.*

funny¹ ['fʌni], *a.* Drôle. **1.** Comique, amusant, facétieux, -euse. **None of your f. tricks! I don't want any f. business!** (i) pas de blagues! (ii) je ne veux pas d'histoires. **He is trying to be f.**, il veut faire de l'esprit. **It was really too f.!** c'était tordant! *Th:* **F. man**, bouffon *m*, pitre *m.* **2.** Curieux, bizarre, *F:* marrant. **He was f. that way**, il était comme ça. **A f. idea**, une drôle d'idée. **This butter tastes f.**, ce beurre a un drôle de goût. *P:* **I came over all f.**, je me suis senti(e) tout(e) chose. **-ily**, *adv.* Drôlement. **1.** Comiquement. **2.** Curieusement. **F. enough . . .**, chose curieuse. . . . **'funny-bone**, *s. F:* Le "petit juif" (à l'articulation du coude).

funny², *s.* esp. *U.S:* (*a*) Dessin *m* humoristique; bande dessinée. (*b*) usu. *pl.* Pages *f* comiques.

fur¹ [fə:r], *s.* **1.** Fourrure *f*, pelleterie *f.* **F. coat**, manteau de fourrure. (*b*) Poil *m*, pelage *m* (de lapin, etc.). *F:* **To make the f. fly**, se battre avec acharnement. (*c*) *pl.* **Furs**, peaux *fpl* (d'animaux). **2.** *Her:* Fourrure. **3.** (*a*) (*In boiler, bottle, etc*) Incrustations *fpl*, tartre *m*, dépôt *m.* (*b*) *Med:* (*On tongue*) Enduit *m* (blanchâtre, noirâtre). **'fur-lined**, *a.* Doublé de fourrure; fourré. **'fur-trade**, *s.* Pelleterie *f.* **'fur-trader**, *s.* Pelletier *m.*

fur², *v.* (**furred**) **I.** *v.tr.* **1.** Entartrer, incruster (une chaudière, etc.). *Med:* Charger (la langue). **2.** Détartrer, piquer (une chaudière). **II.** **fur**, *v.i.* **To f. up.** (*of boiler, etc.*) s'incruster, s'entartrer; (*of tongue*) se charger, s'empâter. **furred**, *a.* **1.** (*a*) (*Of pers.*)

Habillé de fourrures. (b) (Animal) à poil. **2.** (Of boiler, etc.) Entartré, incrusté. Med: **F. tongue,** langue chargée. **furring,** s. **1.** (a) Entartrage m, incrustation f (d'une chaudière, etc.). (b) Détartrage m, décrassage m (des chaudières). **2.** (In boiler) Calcin m tartre m.

furbelow ['fə:bilou], s. **1.** A: Falbala m. **2.** F: **Furbelows,** fanfreluches f.

furbish ['fə:biʃ], v.tr. To f. (up). **1.** Fourbir, polir, astiquer. **2.** (Re)mettre à neuf, retaper (des meubles, etc.).

furcate ['fə:keit], a. (Of road, etc.) A bifurcation; (of hoof) fourchu.

furious ['fjuəriəs], a. Furieux, -euse; (of look) furibond; (of battle) acharné; (of wind) violent. **At a f. pace,** à une allure folle; (of horseman) à bride abattue. **F. at having failed,** furieux d'avoir manqué son coup. **To get f.,** entrer en fureur. **To be f. with s.o.,** être furieux contre qn. Aut: **F. driving,** (i) Jur: Excès de vitesse; (ii) train m d'enfer. **-ly,** adv. Furieusement; (combattre, etc.) avec acharnement, avec furie; (conduire) à une allure folle; (of horseman) (courir) à bride abattue.

furiousness ['fjuəriəsnis], s. Fureur f; acharnement m (d'un combat, etc.); violence f (du vent).

furl [fə:l], v.tr. (a) Nau: Serrer, ferler (une voile). (b) Rouler (un parapluie, etc.) Mil: (Of flag) **Furled and craped,** en berne.

furlong ['fə:lɔŋ], s. Meas: Huitième partie f du mille (220 yards = 201 mètres).

furlough ['fə:lou], s. Mil: Congé m, permission f. **To be, go, on f.,** être, aller, en permission.

furnace ['fə:nis], s. **1.** (a) Metall: etc: Fourneau m, four m. S.a. BLAST-FURNACE. (b) (Hot place) Fournaise f. **2.** (a) **Oil-fired f.,** brûleur m à mazout. (b) Mch: Foyer m (de chaudière).

furnish ['fə:niʃ], v.tr. **1.** (a) Fournir, donner (des renseignements, etc.); pourvoir (les fonds nécessaires, etc.); alléguer (des raisons, etc.). (b) **To f. s.o. with sth.,** fournir, pourvoir, munir, qn de qch. **2.** Meubler, garnir (une maison, etc.). **Furnished flat,** appartement meublé. **To live in furnished apartments,** loger en garni, en meublé. **furnishing,** s. **1.** (a) Ameublement m (action de meubler une maison). (b) **F. fabric,** tissu m d'ameublement. (c) Agencement m (d'un avion). **2.** pl. (a) **Furnishings,** ameublement m (d'une maison). (b) U.S: **Men's furnishings,** lingerie f pour hommes, chemiserie f.

furnisher ['fə:niʃər], s. Fournisseur m (of, de); esp. marchand m d'ameublement.

furniture ['fə:nitʃər], s. **1.** Meubles mpl, ameublement m, mobilier m; matériel m. **Piece of f.,** meuble. **Suite, set, of f.,** mobilier; A: meuble (de salon, etc.). **Antique f.,** meubles d'époque. **2.** Ferrures fpl (d'une porte, etc.). **'furniture-polish,** s. Encaustique f. **'furniture-remover,** s. Déménageur m; entrepreneur m de déménagements. **'furniture-shop,** s. Maison f d'ameublement. **'furniture-van,** s. Camion m de déménagement.

furrier ['fʌriər], s. Pelletier, -ière; fourreur m.

furriery ['fʌriəri], s. Pelleterie f.

furrow[1] ['fʌrou], s. **1.** (a) Agr: Sillon m. Lit: **To plough a lonely f.,** travailler en isolé; poursuivre seul une idée. (b) Lit: Sillage m (d'un navire). **2.** Cannelure f, rainure f. **3.** (On face, etc.) Ride profonde; sillon.

furrow[2], v.tr. **1.** Labourer (la terre); sillonner (les mers, etc.). **2.** Canneler, rainer (une planche, etc.). **3.** Rider profondément.

furry ['fə:ri], a. **1.** = FURRED. **2.** Qui ressemble à (de) la fourrure.

further[1] ['fə:ðər]. (Comp. of far) I. adv. **1.** = FARTHER 1. **2.** (a) Davantage, plus. **I did not question him any f.,** je ne l'interrogeai pas davantage. **Without troubling any f.,** sans plus se tracasser. **Until you hear f.,** jusqu'à nouvel avis. (b) **To go f. into sth.,** entrer plus avant dans qch. **To go no f. in the matter,** en rester là. **To go f. back,** remonter plus haut. (c) (In time) **Further back,** à une période plus reculée. (d) En outre, de plus, du reste. II. **further,** a. **1.** = FARTHER 2 (a). **2.** Nouveau, additionnel, supplémentaire. **To remand a case for f. enquiry,** remettre une affaire pour plus ample informé. **Without f. loss of time,** sans autre perte de temps. **Without f. ado . . .,** sans plus de cérémonie . . .; sans plus. . . . **Upon f. consideration,** (toute) réflexion faite. **One or two f. details,** encore un ou deux détails. Com: **F. orders,** commandes ultérieures. **Awaiting your f. orders,** dans l'attente de vos nouvelles commandes.

further[2], v.tr. (Faire) avancer, favoriser, servir (les intérêts de qn, etc.).

furtherance ['fə:ðərəns], s. Avancement m (d'un travail, etc.). **For the f. of, in f. of (sth.),** pour (faire) avancer (qch.).

furthermore ['fə:ðə'mɔ:r], adv. En outre, outre cela, de plus, bien plus, par ailleurs.

furthermost ['fə:ðəmoust], a. = FARTHERMOST.

furthest ['fə:ðist], a. & adv. = FARTHEST.

furtive ['fə:tiv], a. (Of action, etc.) Furtif; (of pers.) sournois. **-ly,** adv. Furtivement; à la dérobée.

furuncle ['fjuərʌŋkl], s. Med: Furoncle m.

fury ['fjuəri], s. **1.** Furie f, fureur f, emportement m; acharnement m (d'un combat). **To get into a f.,** entrer en fureur, en furie; s'emporter. F: **To work like f.,** travailler avec acharnement. **2.** pl. Myth: **The Furies,** les Furies f.

furze [fə:z], s. Bot: Ajonc m.

fuse[1] [fju:z], s. **1.** Fusée f (d'obus); amorce f. Min: (Safety-)f., étoupille f, cordeau m.

fuse[2], s. El.E: (Safety-)f., (coupe-circuit m à) fusible m; (in private house) plomb m. **'fuse-box,** s. Boîte f à fusibles. **'fuse-wire,** s. (Fil m) fusible (m).

fuse[3]. **1.** v.tr. (a) Fondre, mettre en fusion (un métal, etc.). (b) Fusionner, amalgamer, réunir (deux partis, etc.). **2.** v.i. (a) (Of metals, etc.) Fondre. F: **The light has fused,** les plombs ont sauté. (b) Fusionner; s'amalgamer.

fuselage ['fju:zəlɑ:ʒ], s. Av: Fuselage m.

fusel oil ['fju:z(ə)l ɔil], s. Huile f de fusel.

fusibility ['fju:zi'biliti], s. Fusibilité f.

fusible ['fju:zibl], a. Fusible.

fusiform ['fju:zifɔ:m], a. Fuselé.

fusilier ['fju:zəliər], s. Mil: Fusilier m.

fusillade [fju:zi'leid], s. Mil: Fusillade f.

fusion ['fju:ʒ(ə)n], s. **1.** Fusion f. **1.** (a) Fondage m, fonte f (d'un métal, etc.). (b) Atom.Ph: Fusion f. **2.** Fusionnement m (de plusieurs banques, etc.). Pol: Fusion (de deux partis, etc.).

fuss[1] [fʌs], s. **1.** Bruit exagéré. **A lot of f. over a trifle, about nothing,** bien du tapage pour peu de chose; beaucoup de bruit pour rien. **To make, kick up, a f.,** faire un tas d'histoires. **There's nothing to make a f. about,** il n'y a pas de quoi fouetter un chat. **2.** Embarras mpl; façons fpl. **To make a f.,** faire des cérémonies, des embarras, F: du, des, chichi(s). **To make a f. of s.o.,** (i) être aux petits soins pour qn; (ii) mettre en avant. **'fuss-pot,** s. F: Tatillon, -onne; faiseur, -euse, d'embarras; chichiteux, -euse.

fuss[2]. **1.** v.i. Tatillonner; faire des embarras; faire des histoires; se tracasser. **To f. about, to f. round,** faire l'affairé; s'affairer. **To f. over, around, s.o.,** être aux petits soins pour qn; faire l'empressé auprès de qn. **2.** v.tr. Tracasser, agiter (qn).

fussiness ['fʌsinis], s. Affairement m., embarras mpl.

fussy ['fʌsi], a. **1.** (Of pers.) Tatillon, -onne; méticuleux, -euse. **2.** (Of dress, etc.) Qui manque de simplicité. **-ily,** adv. (a) D'une manière tatillonne. (b) D'un air important; en faisant des embarras.

fustian ['fʌstjən], s. **1.** Tex: Futaine f. **2.** Grandiloquence f, emphase f.

fustigate ['fʌstigeit], v.tr. Hum: Fustiger (qn).

fustiness ['fʌstinis], s. **1.** Odeur f de renfermé. **2.** Caractère suranné, démodé.

fusty ['fʌsti], a. **1.** F. smell, odeur de renfermé. **F. ideas,** idées d'un autre âge.

futile ['fju:tail], a. **1.** Futile, vain. **2.** Puéril.

futility [fju:'tiliti], s. **1.** Futilité f. **2.** Puérilité f.

future ['fju:tʃər]. **1.** a. (Of life, etc.) Futur; (of events) à venir; (of prospects, etc.) d'avenir. **My f. wife,** ma future. **F. delivery,** livraison à terme. **2.** s. (a) Avenir m. **In (the) f., for the f.,** à l'avenir. **In the near f.,** dans un proche avenir; à brève échéance. **(Film, novel, etc.) about the f.,** (film, roman) d'anticipation. (b) Gram: (Temps) futur m. **Verb in the f.,** verbe au futur. (c) **To ruin one's f.,** briser son avenir.

futurist ['fju:tʃərist], *s.* *Art:* Futuriste *mf.*

futuristic [fju:tʃə'ristik], *a.* *Art:* Futuriste.

futurity [fju'tjuəriti], *s.* **1.** (*a*) L'avenir *m.* (*b*) Vie future. **2.** *pl.* Événements *m* à venir.

fuze [fju:z], *s.* = FUSE[1].

fuzz[1] [fʌz], *s.* **1.** (*On blankets*, *etc.*) Peluches *fpl*, bourre *f*, duvet *m.* **A f. of hair,** cheveux bouffants, crêpelus. **2.** *Phot:* Flou *m.*

fuzz[2], *v.* **To fuzz (out). 1.** *v.i.* (*Of hair*, *etc.*) Bouffer, frisotter. **2.** *v.tr.* Faire bouffer, frisotter (les cheveux).

fuzziness ['fʌzinis], *s.* **1.** Crêpelure *f* (des cheveux). **2.** *Art:* Flou *m.*

fuzzy ['fʌzi], *a.* **1.** (*Of hair*) (i) Bouffant, flou; (ii) crêpelu, frisotté, moutonné. **2.** (*a*) *Phot:* Flou. (*b*) *F: O:* Un peu ivre; gris, éméché.

fylfot ['filfət], *s.* Croix gammée; svastika *m.*

G, g [dʒiː], s. 1. (La lettre) G, g m. Tp: G for George, G comme Gaston. 2. Mus: Sol m. G clef, clef de sol. 3. G. suit, vêtement m anti-G.

gab [gæb], s. 1. Mec.E: Enclenche f. 2. Faconde f, F: bagou(t) m. Esp: To have the gift of the g., avoir la langue bien pendue; avoir de la faconde; F: avoir du bagout.

gabardine [ˌgæbə'diːn], s. Tex: Gabardine f.

gabble[1] ['gæbl], s. 1. Bredouillement m. 2. Caquet m, jacasserie f.

gabble[2]. 1. v.i. (a) Bredouiller. Don't g.! ne parlez pas si vite! (b) (Of pers., birds) Caqueter, jacasser. 2. v.tr. To g. out a speech, débiter un discours à toute vitesse. To g. off a mass, dire sa messe au galop.

gabbro ['gæbrou], s. Geol: Gabbro m.

gaberdine [ˌgæbə'diːn], s. = GABARDINE.

gable ['geibl], s. Arch: Const: Pignon m. G. roof, comble m sur pignon(s). Stepped g., pignon à redans. 'gable-'end, s. Pignon m.

gabled ['geibld], a. (Of house) A pignon(s); (of wall) en pignon; (of roof) sur pignon(s).

Gaboon [gə'buːn]. Pr.n. Geog: Le Gabon. G. (wood), okumé m.

gad[1] [gæd], v.i. (gadded) To gad (about), courir le monde, la ville, les rues.

Gad[2], int. A: (= GOD) (By) G.! ma foi! parbleu! sapristi!

gadabout ['gædəbaut], s. Coureur, -euse.

gad-fly ['gædflai], s. Ent: (a) Taon m. (b) Œstre m.

gadget ['gædʒit], s. F: (a) Accessoire m (de machine); dispositif m; système m. (b) Chose m, machin m, truc m, F: bidule m.

gadroon [gə'druːn], s. Arch: etc: Godron m.

Gaelic ['geilik]. 1. a. Gaélique. 2. s. Ling: Le gaélique.

gaff[1] [gæf], s. 1. Fish: Gaffe f. 2. Nau: Corne f. 'gaff-hook, s. Fish: Gaffeau m. 'gaff-sail, s. Nau: Voile f à corne.

gaff[2], v.tr. Gaffer (un saumon, etc.).

gaff[3], s. P: To blow the g., vendre la mèche.

gaffer ['gæfər], s. F: 1. A: L'ancien; F: le vieux. 2. Contremaître m; chef m d'équipe. 3. F: Le patron.

gag[1] ['gæg], s. 1. Bâillon m. 2. Parl: Clôture f (des débats). 3. Th: F: Interpolation faite par l'acteur; gag m. Esp. U.S: Plaisanterie f.

gag[2], v.tr. (gagged) 1. Bâillonner; mettre un bâillon à (qn). 2. Parl: F: Clôturer (un débat). 3. Th: F: To gag one's part, abs. to gag, enchaîner.

gaga ['gɑːgɑː], a. F: Gâteux, -euse.

gage[1] [geidʒ], s. 1. Gage m, garantie f. Jur: Nantissement m. To give sth. in g., donner qch. en gage. 2. G. of battle, gage de bataille, de combat. To throw down the g. to s.o., lancer un défi à qn.

gage[2], v.tr. Mettre, donner, (qch.) en gage.

gage[3], s. & v.tr. = GAUGE[1,3]

gaggle ['gægl], v.i. (Of goose) Cacarder.

gaiety ['geiəti], s. 1. Gaieté f. 2. Usu. pl. Amusement m, fête f, réjouissances fpl.

gaily, adv. See GAY.

gain[1] [gein], s. 1. Gain m, profit m, avantage m, bénéfice m. Ill-gotten gains, bien mal acquis. 2. Accroissement m, augmentation f.

gain[2], v.tr. Gagner. 1. Acquérir (une réputation, des faveurs). To g. strength, (re)prendre des forces. To g. a hearing, (i) obtenir une audience; (ii) se faire écouter. You will g. nothing by it, vous n'y gagnerez rien. To g. by doing sth., gagner à faire qch. 2. O: To g. (s.o.) over, gagner (qn) à sa cause; gagner (un partisan). 3. He is gaining (in) weight, il prend du poids. To g. in popularity, gagner de la popularité. 4. (a) To g. the day, gagner une bataille; remporter la victoire. To g. the upper hand, prendre le dessus. (b) (Of sea) To g. (ground) on the land, empiéter sur la terre. To g. (ground) on s.o., gagner (du terrain) sur qn. Sp: To g. on a competitor, prendre de

l'avance sur un concurrent. A bad habit gains on one, une mauvaise habitude s'impose, s'enracine, peu à peu. (c) O: To g. the further shore, gagner, atteindre, l'autre rive. (d) To g. time, gagner du temps. S.a. END[1] 4. 5. (Of clock) To g. five minutes a day, avancer de cinq minutes par jour. Abs. To g., avancer; prendre de l'avance.

gainer ['geinər], s. 1. Gagnant (d'une victoire). 2. To be the g. by sth., gagner à qch.

gainsay [gein'sei], v.tr. (gainsaid [gein'sed]) Contredire, démentir; nier (un fait). Facts that cannot be gainsaid, faits indéniables.

gait [geit], s. (a) Allure f, démarche f. Unsteady g., pas chancelant, mal assuré. To know s.o. by his g., reconnaître qn à son allure. His awkward g., sa dégaine. (b) Allures, train m (d'un cheval). To break up, ruin, a horse's g., détraquer un cheval.

gaiter ['geitər], s. 1. Guêtre f. 2. A: Guêtre, emplâtre m (pour pneu). (b) Aut: Spring g., gaine f de ressort.

gala ['gɑːlə], s. Fête f, gala m. Swimming g., grand concours de natation. G. day, jour de gala, de fête.

galactic [gə'læktik], a. Astr: Galactique.

galalith ['gæləliθ], s. Ind: Galalithe f.

galantine ['gælənˌtiːn], s. Cu: Galantine f.

galaxy ['gæləksi], s. 1. Astr: Galaxie f. The G., la Voie lactée. 2. O: Assemblée brillante (de belles femmes, etc.); constellation f (d'hommes illustres, etc.).

gale[1] [geil], s. 1. Nau: etc: Coup m de vent; grand vent, vent fort. Fresh g., brisk g., vent frais. Moderate g., forte brise. 2. Tempête f. (Of wind) To blow a g., souffler en tempête; faire rage. To encounter, weather a g., essuyer un coup de vent. There's a howling g., F: il fait un vent à décorner les bœufs.

gale[2], s. Bot: (Sweet) g., galé m; myrte m des marais.

galena [gə'liːnə], s. Miner: Galène f.

Galenism ['geilənizm], s. Hist. of Med: Galénisme m.

Galilean [gæli'liən], a. & s. B.Hist: Galiléen, -éenne.

Galilee ['gælili]. Pr.n. La Galilée.

Galileo [gæli'leiou]. Pr.n.m. Hist. of Astr: Galilée.

gall[1] [gɔːl], s. 1. Fiel m. (a) To vent one's g. on s.o., épancher sa bile contre qn. (b) U.S: Effronterie f. 2. Anat: Vésicule f biliaire. 'gall-bladder, s. Anat: Vésicule f biliaire. S.a. Med: Calcul m biliaire.

gall[2], s. Bot: Galle f. S.a. OAK-GALL, ROSE-GALL. 'gall-fly, s. Cynips m. 'gall-nut, s. Noix f de galle.

gall[3], s. (a) Écorchure, excoriation (causée par le frottement). (b) O: Froissement m, humiliation f; blessure (faite à l'amour-propre).

gall[4], v.tr. (a) Écorcher (par le frottement); mettre (le talon, etc.) à vif. (b) Irriter, exaspérer; froisser, blesser, humilier. galling, a. (Of restrictions) Irritant, exaspérant; (of remark) blessant, humiliant. G. experience, expérience amère.

gallant ['gælənt]. I. a. 1. (a) Brave; vaillant; chevaleresque. (b) (Of ship, etc.) Beau, f. belle; noble, fier, superbe. 2. [gə'lænt] Galant (auprès des femmes). -ly, adv. Galamment. 1. Bravement, vaillamment. 2. Élégamment, magnifiquement. 3. [gə'læntli] En homme galant; avec empressement (auprès d'une femme). II. gallant, s. 1. A: Galant m, élégant m. 2. [gə'lænt] A: Galant; amoureux m.

gallantry ['gæləntri], s. 1. Vaillance f, bravoure f. 2. Galanterie f (auprès des femmes).

galleon ['gæliən], s. A: Nau: Galion m.

gallery ['gæləri], s. 1. (a) Galerie f. Parl: Public g., strangers' g., tribune réservée au public; tribune publique. (b) The g., Th: la (troisième) galerie. Sp: etc: F: To play to the g., jouer pour la galerie; F: cabotiner. 2. Art g., (i) galerie; (ii) musée m (de peinture). 3. Min: Galerie.

galley ['gæli], s. 1. Nau: (a) A: Galère f. (b) Yole f (d'amiral). 2. Nau: Cuisine f, coquerie f. 3. Typ: Galée f. 'galley-proof, s. Épreuve f en placard. 'galley-slave, s. Galérien m.

Gallic¹ ['gælik], a. Gaulois.

gallic², a. Ch: (Acide) gallique.

Gallicanism ['gælikənizm], s. Ecc: Gallicanisme m.

gallicism ['gælisizm], s. Gallicisme m.

gallinaceae [ˌgæli'neisii:], s.pl. Orn: Gallinacés m.

gallinaceous [ˌgæli'neiʃəs], a. Orn: Gallinacé.

gallivant [ˌgæli'vænt], v.i. (a) Courir le monde, la ville. (b) Fréquenter la société des femmes; courir la pretentaine.

gallomaniac ['gælo'meiniæk], a. & s. Gallomane (mf).

gallon ['gælən], s. Gallon m (= 4 lit. 54, U.S: 3 lit. 78).

gallop¹ ['gæləp], s. 1. Galop m. (At) full g., au grand galop; à fond de train; (of horse) ventre à terre; (of rider) à bride abattue. To break into a g., prendre le galop. 2. To have, go for, a g., faire une galopade.

gallop², v. (galloped) 1. v.i. (a) (Of horse,) Galoper. (b) (Of rider) Aller au galop, à bride abattue. To g. away, partir, s'éloigner, au galop. To g. back, revenir au galop. 2. v.tr. Faire aller (un cheval) au (grand) galop; galoper (un cheval). **galloping**, a. 1. (Of horse, etc.) Au galop. 2. Med: A: G. consumption, phtisie galopante.

gallophile ['gælofail], a. & s. Gallophile (mf).

gallophobia [ˌgælo'foubiə], s. Gallophobie f.

Gallo-Roman ['gælou'roumən], a. Gallo-romain.

gallows ['gælouz], s. (Often with sg. const.) 1. Potence f, gibet m. To have a g. look, avoir une mine patibulaire; sentir la potence. 2. Portique m (de gymnastique). **'gallows-bird**, s. F: Gibier m de potence; pendard m. **'gallows-bitts**, s.pl. Nau: Potence f de drome. **'gallows-tree**, s. Gibet m; potence f.

Gallup ['gæləp]. Pr.n. G. poll, sondage m de l'opinion publique, F: gallup m.

galop ['gæləp], s. Danc: Galop m.

galore [gə'lo:r], s. & adv. F: En abondance, à foison, à profusion, F: à gogo.

galosh [gə'lɒʃ], s. 1. A: Galoche f. 2. Caoutchouc; couvre-chaussure m.

galumph [gə'lʌmf], v.i. F: Caracoler.

galvanic [gæl'vænik], a. Galvanique.

galvanism ['gælvənizm], s. Galvanisme m.

galvanization [ˌgælvənai'zeiʃ(ə)n], s. 1. Galvanisation f (du corps humain, etc.). 2. Metalw: Galvanisation; galvanisage m; (i) métallisation f électrique; (ii) zingage m au trempé.

galvanize ['gælvənaiz], v.tr. 1. Galvaniser (un cadavre, etc.). F: To g. sth. into life, donner à qch. une animation passagère; galvaniser qch. 2. Metalw: Galvaniser; (i) plaquer par galvanoplastie; (ii) zinguer. **Galvanized iron**, tôle galvanisée.

galvanometer [ˌgælvə'nɒmitər], s. Galvanomètre m.

galvanoplasty ['gælvənou'plæsti], s. Galvanoplastie f.

galvanoscope ['gælvənoskoup], s. Galvanoscope m.

Gambia ['gæmbiə]. Pr.n. Geog: Gambie f.

gambit ['gæmbit], s. Chess: Gambit m.

gamble¹ ['gæmbl], s. F: (a) Jeu m de hasard. (b) Pure g., pure spéculation; affaire f de chance.

gamble². 1. v.i. Jouer (de l'argent) To g. on a throw of the dice, miser sur un coup de dé(s). To g. on the Stock Exchange, agioter. To g. on a rise in prices, jouer à la hausse. 2. v.tr. To g. away, perdre (sa fortune, etc.) au jeu. **gambling**, s. Le jeu. G. debts, dettes f de jeu. G. den, house, maison f de jeu; tripot m.

gambler ['gæmblər], s. Joueur, -euse (pour de l'argent). G. on the Stock Exchange, spéculateur, -trice; agioteur, -euse.

gamboge [gæm'bu:ʒ, -'boudʒ], s. Gomme-gutte f.

gambol¹ ['gæmb(ə)l], s. (a) Gambade f, cabriole f. (b) pl. F: Ébats m.

gambol², v.i. (gambolled) (a) Gambader, cabrioler; faire des gambades. (b) S'ébattre.

game¹ [geim], s. 1. (a) Amusement m, divertissement m, jeu m. To make g. of s.o., se moquer de qn; se jouer de qn. (b) Jeu. G. of skill, of chance, jeu d'adresse, de hasard. Outdoor games, jeux de plein air. Sch: Games master, maître qui organise et surveille les sports. Olympic games, jeux olympiques. F: It's all in the g., c'est dans la règle du jeu. (c) To play a good g., être bon joueur. To play the g., jouer franc jeu; jouer, agir, loyalement. That's not

playing the g., ce n'est pas loyal; ce n'est pas de jeu. To play s.o.'s g., faire le jeu de qn. To beat s.o. at his own g., battre qn avec ses propres armes. Two can play at that g., à bon chat bon rat. To be off one's g., jouer moins bien qu'à l'ordinaire. (d) F: What's his g.? où veut-il en venir? quel but poursuit-il? I was watching their little g., j'observais leur manège. To spoil s.o.'s g., déjouer les plans de qn. The g.'s up, l'affaire est dans l'eau; il n'y a plus rien à faire. (e) Partie f (de cartes, de billard, etc.); manche f (d'une partie de cartes). To have, play, a g. of cricket, faire une partie de cricket. How's the g. going? (i) comment marche la partie? (ii) où en est la partie? To be g., avoir gagné la partie. The odd g., the deciding g., la belle. Ten: G., set, and match, jeu, set, et partie. To have, hold, the g. in one's hands, tenir le succès entre ses mains. 2. (a) Gibier m. Big g., (i) gros gibier; (ii) les grands fauves. Big g. shooting, la chasse aux grands fauves. Small g., menu gibier. F: Fair g., (gibier) de bonne prise. He is fair g., on a le droit de se moquer de lui. (b) Cu: Gibier. G. pie, pâté m de gibier. **'game-bag**, s. Carnassière f, gibecière f. **'game-cock**, s. Coq m de combat. **'game-licence**, s. Permis m de chasse. **'game-preserve**, s. Parc m à gibier; réserve f de chasse.

game². 1. v.i. Jouer (de l'argent). 2. v.tr. To g. away a fortune, dissiper une fortune au jeu. **gaming**, s. Jeu m. G. debt, dette de jeu. G. house = gambling house. G. losses, pertes au jeu. G.-table, table de jeu.

game³, a. Courageux, résolu. To be g., (i) avoir du cran; (ii) être d'attaque. He is g. for anything, il est prêt à tout, capable de tout. To die g., mourir crânement.

game⁴, a. G. arm, bras estropié. G. leg, jambe boiteuse, percluse. **game-'legged**. a. Estropié, boiteux.

gamekeeper ['geimki:pər], s. Garde-chasse m, pl. gardes-chasse(s).

gameness ['geimnis], s. Courage m, crânerie f.

gamete [gæ'mi:t], s. Biol: Gamète m.

gamma ['gæmə], s. 1. Gr.Alph: Gamma m. 2. Atom. Ph: G. rays, rayons m gamma.

gammon¹ ['gæmən], s. (a) Quartier m de derrière (du porc). (b) Quartier de lard fumé.

gammon², s. P: O: Blague f; bourrage m de crâne.

gammon³, v.tr. P: O: Blaguer (qn); monter un bateau à (qn).

gammy ['gæmi], a. F: = GAME⁴.

gamp [gæmp], s. F: Parapluie m, F: pépin m.

gamut ['gæmət], s. 1. Mus: (a) Gamme f. (b) Étendue f (de la voix). 2. Gamme (de couleurs, etc.).

gamy ['geimi], a. Cu: Faisandé, avancé.

gander ['gændər], s. 1. Jars m. S.a. SAUCE¹ 1. 2. F: Niais m, sot m, imbécile m. 3. U.S: F: To take a g. (at sth.), regarder (qch.).

gang¹ [gæŋ], s. 1. (a) Groupe m, troupe f (de personnes); équipe f, escouade f, atelier m (d'ouvriers). Civ.E: Itinerant g. (of roadmen), brigade ambulante. (b) Bande f, F: gang m (de voleurs, de faussaires, etc.). Pej: One of the g., un de la clique. The whole g., toute la bande. 2. (a) Série f (d'outils qui vont ensemble). (b) W.Tel: Two-g. condenser, condensateur à deux blocs. **'gang-plank**, s. Nau: Planche f à débarquer; appointement m.

gang², v.i. F: To g. up (with s.o.), faire bande (avec qn), s'allier (avec, à, qn). To g. up on s.o., attaquer qn de concert, se liguer contre qn. **ganged**, a. 1. (Outils) multiples ou montés ensemble. 2. W.Tel: G. condensers, condensateurs à blocs combinés.

ganger ['gæŋər], s. Rail: Chef m d'équipe. Civ.E: Chef m cantonnier.

Ganges (The) [ðə'gæn(d)ʒi:z]. Pr.n. Geog: Le Gange.

gangling ['gæŋgliŋ], a. Grand et maigre. A g. youth, F: une perche.

ganglion, -ia ['gæŋgliən, -iə], s. (a) Anat: Ganglion m. (b) F: Centre m. foyer m, d'activité.

ganglionary ['gæŋglionri], **ganglionic** [ˌgæŋgli'ɒnik], a. Anat: Ganglionnaire.

gangrene¹ ['gæŋgri:n], s. Med: Gangrène f.

gangrene². 1. v.tr. Gangrener, mortifier. 2. v.i. Se gangrener.

gangrenous ['gæŋgrinəs], a. Gangreneux, -euse.

gangster ['gæŋstər], s. F: Bandit m; gangster m.

gangsterism ['gæŋsterizm], s. F: Gangstérisme m.

gangway ['gæŋwei], s. **1.** Passage m; couloir central (d'autobus, etc.). F: **G., please!** Dégagez, s'il vous plaît, (laissez passer,) s'il vous plaît! **2.** Nau: (a) Passerelle f de service. (b) (Opening) Coupée f (dans la muraille). (c) (Fore-and-aft) g., passavant m.

gannet ['gænit], s. Orn: Fou m (de Bassan).

gantry ['gæntri], s. **1.** Chantier m (pour fûts); porte-fût(s) m inv. **2.** Ind: (a) Portique m; pont roulant (pour grue roulante). Rail: **Signal g.**, pont à signaux. (b) **G.(-crane),** grue f à portique.

gaol¹ [dʒeil], s. Prison f; maison f d'arrêt. **The County g.** = la maison centrale. **To be in g.**, être en prison. 'gaol-bird, s. F: Échappé, -ée, de prison; gibier m de potence. 'gaol-delivery, s. Levée f d'écrou (de prisonniers).

gaol², v.tr. Mettre (qn) en prison; écrouer (qn).

gaoler ['dʒeilər], s. Gardien m de prison; geôlier m.

gap [gæp], s. **1.** (a) Trou m; trouée f, ouverture f, vide m (dans une haie, etc.); brèche f (dans un mur, etc.); solution f de continuité (d'une surface). **To fill (in), fill up, a g.**; **to stop a g.**, boucher un trou, une brèche; combler un vide. S.a. STOP-GAP. (b) U.S: Col m (de montagne). (c) Interstice m; jour m (entre des planches, etc.); distance f, intervalle m (entre des électrodes). **To reduce the g. between . . .**, réduire l'écart entre. . . . **To bridge the g.**, faire la soudure. **G. between the curtains,** interstice entre les rideaux; bâillement m des rideaux. **Armature g.**, ouverture, entrefer m, d'induit. (d) Av: Écartement m (des plans). (e) Trou, lacune f, vide (dans des souvenirs, etc.). **2.** Mec.E: Coupure f, rompu m (d'un banc de tour). 'gap-toothed, a. Aux dents écartées.

gape¹ [geip], s. Bâillement m. F: O: **To give s.o. the gapes,** faire bâiller qn.

gape², v.i. **1.** (a) (Of pers.) (i) Ouvrir la bouche toute grande; (ii) bâiller (d'ennui). (b) (Of bird) Ouvrir un large bec. (c) (Of thg) **To g. (open),** s'ouvrir (tout grand); (of hole) être béant; (of seam, etc.) bâiller. **2.** (Of pers.) Être, rester, bouche bée; bayer aux corneilles. **To g. at s.o., sth.,** regarder qn, qch., bouche bée, d'un air hébété. **gaping¹,** a. Béant. **gaping²,** s. **1.** Contemplation f bouche bée. **2.** Bâillement m.

garage¹ ['gæra:ʒ], s. Aut: Garage m. **Lock-up g.**, box m. **G. keeper, proprietor,** garagiste m.

garage², v.tr. (i) Garer, (ii) remiser (une auto).

garb¹ [ga:b], s. Vêtement m, costume m. **In Turkish g.**, vêtu à la turque. **His usual g. of indifference,** ses dehors habituels d'indifférence.

garb², v.tr. Habiller, vêtir (in, de).

garbage ['ga:bidʒ], s. **1.** Tripaille f, issues fpl (de boucherie). **2.** Immondices fpl, détritus mpl; ordures (ménagères). **G. heap,** tas m d'ordures; voirie f. U.S: Dom.Ec: **G. disposal unit,** broyeur m d'ordures. **G. can,** poubelle, f. **G. truck** = dust-cart.

garbageman ['ga:bidʒmən], s. U.S: Boueur m.

garble ['ga:bl], v.tr. Tronquer, fausser (une citation, des comptes, etc.); dénaturer (les faits); mutiler, altérer (un texte). **Garbled account,** compte rendu mensonger.

garbler ['ga:blər], s. Mutilateur, -trice (d'un texte, etc.); faussaire m (de faits, etc.).

garden¹ ['ga:dn], s. (a) Jardin m. **Small g.,** jardinet m. **Kitchen g., vegetable g.,** (jardin) potager m. **Market g.,** jardin maraîcher. **Strawberry g.,** champ m de fraises. **Winter g.,** (i) jardin d'hiver; grande serre; (ii) (in hotel, etc.) hall vitré. **G. of remembrance** = cimetière m d'un crématorium. F: **To lead s.o. up the g. (path),** duper qn. S.a. BEAR-GARDEN, LANDSCAPE-GARDEN, ROCK-GARDEN, TEA-GARDEN. (b) pl. Jardin public, parc m. 'garden-'hose, s. Tuyau m d'arrosage. 'garden-'party, s. Réception (mondaine) en plein air; garden-party f. 'garden-'produce, -'stuff, s. Jardinage m; produits maraîchers; denrées potagères.

garden², v.i. Jardiner. **gardening,** s. Jardinage m; horticulture f.

gardener ['ga:dnər], s. Jardinier m. S.a. LANDSCAPE-GARDENER, MARKET-GARDENER, NURSERY-GARDENER.

gardenia [ga:'di:niə], s. Bot: Gardénia f.

gargantuan [ga:'gæntjuən], a. Gargantuesque.

gargle¹ ['ga:gl], s. Med: Gargarisme m.

gargle². 1. v.tr. Se gargariser. **2.** v.tr. **To g. one's throat,** se gargariser la gorge. **gargling,** s. Gargarisme m.

gargoyle [ga:goil], s. Arch: Gargouille f.

garish ['gɛəriʃ], a. **1.** (Of dress, etc.) Voyant; d'un luxe criard. **2. G. light,** lumière crue, aveuglante. **-ly,** adv. (Meublé, etc.) avec un luxe criard.

garishness ['gɛəriʃnis], s. **1.** Luxe criard; faste m. **2.** Éclat excessif; crudité f (d'une couleur).

garland¹ ['ga:lənd], s. Guirlande f; couronne f (de fleurs). **To hang sth. with garlands,** orner, parer, qch. de guirlandes.

garland², v.tr. (En)guirlander.

garlic ['ga:lik], s. Bot: Ail m, pl. ails or aulx. **Spanish g.,** rocambole f. **Clove of g.,** gousse f d'ail; caïeu m d'ail. **G. sauce,** aillade f.

garment ['ga:mənt], s. Vêtement m.

garner¹ ['ga:nər], s. Lit: Grenier m, grange f.

garner², v.tr. Lit: Mettre (le grain) en grenier, en grange; engranger, rentrer (le blé, etc.). **garnering,** s. Engrangement m (du blé, etc.).

garnet ['ga:nit], s. Miner: Grenat m.

garnish¹ ['ga:niʃ], s. Cu: etc: Garniture f.

garnish², v.tr. Garnir, orner, embellir (with, de). **garnishing,** s. **1.** Garnissage m, garnissement m. **2.** Garniture f (d'un plat).

garret ['gærət], s. Mansarde f, galetas m, soupente f. **From cellar to g.,** de la cave au grenier. 'garret-'window, s. (Fenêtre f en) mansarde f.

garrison¹ ['gærisn], s. Garnison f. **To be in g. in a town,** être en garnison dans une ville. Attrib. **G. duty,** service de place, de garnison. **G. troops,** troupes sédentaires. **G. artillery,** artillerie de place.

garrison², v.tr. **1. To g. a town,** (i) placer, mettre, une garnison dans une ville; (ii) (of troops) être en garnison dans une ville. **To g. a stronghold,** garnir une place de guerre. **2.** Mettre (des troupes) en garnison.

gar(r)otte¹ [gə'rɔt], s. **1.** Supplice m du garrot. **2.** Strangulation f.

gar(r)otte², v.tr. **1.** Garrotter (qn). **2.** Étrangler (qn); P: serrer le quiqui à (qn). **garrotting,** s. **1.** Garrottage m. **2.** Strangulation f.

garrotter [gə'rɔtər], s. Étrangleur m.

garrulity [gæ'ru:liti], **garrulousness** ['gæruləsnis], s. **1.** Loquacité f; garrulité f. **2.** Verbosité f (de style).

garrulous ['gæruləs], a. **1.** Loquace, bavard. **2.** (Discours, style) verbeux. **-ly,** adv. Avec volubilité; verbeusement.

garter ['ga:tər], s. (a) Jarretière f. U.S: Fixe-chaussette m, jarretelle f. **The Order of the G.,** l'Ordre m de la Jarretière. (b) Arm-g., bracelet m (pour retenir les manches de chemise). 'garter-stitch, s. Knitting: Tricot uni.

gas¹, pl. **gases** [gæs, 'gæsiz], s. **1.** Gaz m inv. (a) Ch: Ind: **Nitrogen g.,** gaz azote. (b) **Natural g.,** gaz naturel. **Coal g.,** gaz de houille. **The g. is laid on,** les conduites de gaz sont posées; F: le gaz est posé. **The g. is on,** le gaz est ouvert. **The g. industry,** l'industrie gazière. (c) Med: Dent: **Laughing g.,** F: gas, gaz hilarant. F: **To have g.,** se faire anesthésier. (d) Mil: **Asphyxiating g.,** F: poison-g., gaz asphyxiants, toxiques. **2.** U.S: F: = GASOLINE (b). S.a. STEP ON. **3.** P: Verbiage m, bavardage m. 'gas-bacillus, s. Med: Vibrion m septique. 'gas-bag, s. F: Grand parleur; vantard m. 'gas-burner, s. Bec m de gaz. 'gas-chamber, s. Chambre f à gaz. 'gas-coke, s. Coke m de gaz. 'gas(-)cooker, s. Cuisinière f à gaz, fourneau m à gaz. 'gas-engine, s. I.C.E: Moteur m à gaz; machine f à gaz. 'gas-filled, a. El.E: (Lampe) gazeuse. 'gas-'fire, s. Radiateur m à gaz. 'gas-fitter, s. Gazier m. 'gas-generator, s. Générateur m de gaz; gazogène m. 'gas-'heater, s. (a) Radiateur m à gaz. (b) Chauffe-eau m. 'gas-holder, s. Gazomètre m. 'gas-lamp, s. (In street) Bec m de gaz; réverbère m. 'gas(-)light, s. Lumière f du gaz. 'gas-lighter, s. Briquet m (à gaz). 'gas(-)lighting, s. Éclairage m au gaz. 'gas-main, s. (Tuyau m de) conduite f de gaz. 'gas-man, pl. -men, s.m. F: Employé du gaz; (i) le gazier; (ii) l'encaisseur (de la Compagnie). 'gas-mantle, s. Manchon m (de bec de gaz). 'gas-mask, s. Masque *m* à gaz, antigaz. 'gas-meter, *s.* Compteur *m* (à gaz). 'gas-oil, *s.* Gas-oil *m*, gaz-oil *m*. 'gas-oven, *s.* Four *m* à gaz. To put one's head in the g.-o., s'asphyxier, se suicider, au gaz. 'gas-pipe, *s.* Tuyau *m* à gaz; conduite *f* de, du, gaz. 'gas-ring, *s.* 1. *Cu:* Réchaud *m* à gaz à un feu. 2. (Brûleur *m* à) couronne *f*. 'gas-stove, *s.* 1. Cuisinière *f* à gaz. 2. *O:* = GAS-FIRE. 'gas-works, *s.pl.* (*Usu. with sg.const.*) Usine *f* à gaz.

gas², *v.* (gassed) 1. *v.tr.* (*a*) *Ch: Ind:* Passer (un produit) au gaz. (*b*) Asphyxier, intoxiquer. *Mil:* Gazer. To g. oneself, s'asphyxier. 2. *v.i. P:* Jaser; (*of public speaker, etc.*) pérorer.

Gascon ['gæskən], *a. & s. Geog:* Gascon, -onne.

Gascony ['gæskəni]. *Pr.n. Geog:* La Gascogne.

gaseous ['geisiəs], *a.* Gazeux, -euse.

gash¹ [gæʃ], *s.* Coupure *f*, entaille *f* (faite dans la chair); taillade *f*; (*on face*) balafre *f*.

gash², *v.tr.* Entailler, couper; balafrer (le visage).

gasification [gæsifi'keiʃ(ə)n], *s. Ch:* Gazéification *f*.

gasiform ['gæsifɔ:m], *a.* Gazéiforme.

gasify ['gæsifai], *v.tr.* Gazéifier.

gasket ['gæskit], *s.* 1. *Nau:* Garcette *f*, raban *m* (de ris, de ferlage). 2. *Mec.E:* Joint *m* métallo-plastique, en papier huilé, en étoupe, à l'amiante; *I.C.E:* obturateur *m* de joint.

gasogene ['gæsodʒi:n], *s.* Gazogène *m*.

gasolene, gasoline ['gæsoli:n], *s.* (*a*) Gazoline *f*. (*b*) *U.S: Aut:* Essence *f*.

gasometer [gæ'sɔmitər], *s.* Gazomètre *m*; réservoir *m* à gaz.

gasp¹ [gɑ:sp], *s.* Hoquet *m*, sursaut *m* (de surprise, etc.). To be at one's last g., agoniser. To defend sth. to the last g., défendre qch. jusqu'à son dernier souffle.

gasp², *v.i. & tr.* (*a*) Avoir un hoquet (de surprise, etc.). To g. with fright, with astonishment, sursauter. To make s.o. g., couper la respiration, le souffle, à qn. (*b*) To g. for breath, for air, haleter, suffoquer.

gasping, *s.* Halètement *m*.

gasper ['gɑ:spər], *s. P: A:* Cigarette *f* (de mauvaise qualité); *P:* sèche *f*.

gassy ['gæsi], *a.* 1. Gazeux, -euse; (*of wine*) mousseux, crémant. 2. *P:* Verbeux, -euse, bavard.

gast(e)ropod ['gæst(e)rəpod], *pl.* -ods, -opoda ['gæst(ə)rəpodə], *s. Moll:* Castéropode *m*.

gast(e)ropodous [gæs'trɔpədəs], *a. Moll:* Gastéropode.

gastrectomy [gæs'trektəmi], *s. Surg:* Gastrectomie *f*.

gastric ['gæstrik], *a.* Gastrique. G. trouble(s), embarras *m* gastrique. G. flu, grippe intestinale. G. ulcer, ulcère *m* d'estomac; gastrite ulcéreuse.

gastritis [gæs'traitis], *s. Med:* Gastrite *f*.

gastro-enteric ['gæstroen'terik], *a. Med:* Gastro-entérique.

gastro-enteris ['gæstro,entə'raitis], *s. Med:* Gastro-entérite. *f*.

gastro-intestinal ['gæstroin'testinl], *a. Med:* Gastro-intestinal, -aux.

gastronome ['gæstrənoum], gastronomer [gæs'trɔnəmər], *s.* Gastronome *m*.

gastronomic(al) [gæstrə'nɔmik(əl)], *a.* Gastronomique.

gastronomy [gæs'trɔnəmi], *s.* Gastronomie *f*.

gastrotomy [gæs'trɔtəmi], *s. Surg:* Gastrotomie *f*.

gate¹ [geit], *s.* 1. Porte *f* (d'une ville, etc.). Main gates (of exhibition, etc.), entrée principale. *U.S: P:* To give s.o. the g., congédier qn. 2. (*a*) (Wooden) g., barrière *f*; porte à claire-voie. (Wrought-iron) entrance g. (to grounds), grille *f* d'entrée. *Skiing:* Porte *f*. (*b*) *Sp:* (i) Le public (à un match); (ii) = GATE-MONEY. 3. *Aut:* G. (quadrant), grille (de changement de vitesse). 'gate-crasher, *s. F:* Resquilleur, -euse. 'gate-crashing, *s.* Resquillage *m*. 'gate-house, *s.* 1. Loge *f* de garde (à l'entrée d'un parc). 2. Corps-de-garde *m inv* (d'un château fort). 'gate-keeper, *s.* 1. Portier, -ière. 2. *Rail:* Garde-barrière *mf*, *pl.* gardes-barrière(s). 'gate-legged, *a.* G.-l. table, table à abattants. 'gate-money, *s. Sp:* Recette *f*; les entrées *f*. gate-post, *s.* Montant *m* (de barrière, de porte).

gate², *v.tr.* (*In universities*) Consigner (un étudiant).

gating, *s.* Consigne *f*.

gateway ['geitwei], *s.* 1. Porte *f*, entrée *f*. Carriage g., porte cochère. 2. Porte monumentale; portail *m*.

gather¹ ['gæðər]. I. *v.tr.* 1. (*a*) Assembler, rassembler (des personnes); rassembler, recueillir (des choses). To g. one's thoughts, se recueillir. To g. all one's strength in order to . . ., rassembler, ramasser, toutes ses forces pour. . . . (*b*) Ramasser (ses papiers, etc.). To g. (up) one's hair into a knot, tordre ses cheveux en chignon. To g. up one's skirts, retrousser ses jupes. *Fb:* To g. the ball, cueillir le ballon. To g. (in) the harvest, rentrer la récolte. To g. the strawberries, faire la cueillette des fraises. To g. sticks (for firewood), ramasser du bois. To g. taxes, rents, percevoir les contributions, les loyers. (*d*) To g. oneself, se mettre en boule. To g. (oneself) together for a spring, se ramasser pour sauter. 2. To g. speed, acquérir, prendre, de la vitesse. (*Of invalid*) To g. strength, reprendre des forces. To g. volume, croître en volume. 3. (*a*) Serrer. To g. the blankets around one, se serrer dans ses couvertures. (*b*) *Needlew:* To g. a skirt, froncer une jupe. 4. Conclure. I g. from the papers that he has . . ., à en croire les journaux il aurait. . . . As will be gathered from the enclosed letter, comme il ressort de la lettre ci-jointe. II. gather, *v.i.* 1. (*Of pers.*) (*a*) Se réunir, se rassembler. To g. round the fire, se grouper autour du feu. G. around! approchez-vous! faites cercle! (*b*) Affluer, s'attrouper (en foule). 2. (*Of thgs*) S'accumuler, s'amonceler, s'amasser. A storm is gathering, un orage se prépare. (*b*) In the gathering darkness, dans la nuit grandissante. The story gathered like a snowball, l'histoire faisait boule de neige. 3. *Med:* (*Of wound*) Abcéder. (*Of abscess*) To g. to a head, aboutir, mûrir. 4. *Needlew:* To g. in the waistline, blouser. gathered, *a.* (*a*) (Front) sourcilleux. (*b*) *Needlew:* (Volant, etc.) froncé, à fronces. (*c*) To have a g. finger, avoir un abcès au doigt.

gathering, *s.* 1. (*a*) Rassemblement *m*, attroupement *m* (d'une foule). (*b*) Accumulation *f* (de choses). (*c*) Cueillette *f* (des fruits, etc.). (*d*) (in) of the crop, (rentrage *m* de la) récolte. (*d*) Froncement *m* (des ¡sourcils). *Needlew:* Fronçure *f* (d'une robe, etc.). (*e*) Accumulation, amoncellement *m* (de nuages). (*f*) *Med:* Collection *f* (du pus). 2. (*a*) Assemblée *f*, réunion *f*, compagnie *f* (dans une salle); assemblage *m*, rassemblement, attroupement (dans les rues). Family g., réunion de famille. (*b*) *Needlew:* Froncis *m*, fronces *fpl.* (*c*) *Med:* Abcès *m*; *F:* bobo *m*.

gather², *s. Usu.pl. Dressm:* Gathers, fronces *f*.

gatherer ['gæðərər], *s.* (*Pers.*) (*a*) (R)amasseur, -euse. (*b*) Cueilleur, -euse (de fruits, etc.). Tax-g., percepteur *m* (des contributions).

gauche [gouʃ], *a.* Gauche.

gaucho ['gautʃou], *s.* Gaucho *m*.

gaudiness ['gɔ:dinis], *s.* Ostentation *f*; clinquant *m*.

gaudy ['gɔ:di], *a.* (*Of colours, etc.*) Voyant, criard, éclatant; (*of display, etc.*) fastueux, -euse. -ily, *adv.* De manière voyante; fastueusement; (peint) en couleurs criardes.

gauge¹ [geidʒ], *s.* 1. (*a*) Calibre *m* (d'un écrou, etc.); jauge *f* (d'une futaille. etc.). *Hosiery:* Jauge *f*. Fine g. stockings, bas *m* de fine jauge. Heavy g. stockings, bas de grosse jauge. To take s.o.'s g., mesurer les capacités, prendre la mesure, de qn. (*b*) *Rail:* G. (of the track), largeur *f*, écartement *m*, de la voie. Standard g., écartement normal, voie normale. Broad g. line, voie à grand écartement. 2. (*a*) (Appareil *m*) vérificateur *m*; calibre, jauge (pour mesurer qch.). *Mec.E:* Thickness-g., feeler-g., calibre d'épaisseur. Slide, sliding, g., (i) calibre à curseur; pied *m*, compas *m*, à coulisse; (ii) vernier *m*. Calliper g., calibre de précision. Cylindrical g., plug g., tampon vérificateur. *Rail:* Loading g., tunnel g., gabarit *m* de chargement. (*b*) *Carp:* (Marking) g., trusquin *m*. 3. Indicateur *m*, contrôleur *m*. (*a*) Vacuum g., indicateur, jauge, du vide. (*b*) *Mch: etc:* Water g., oil g., (indicateur de) niveau *m* d'eau, d'huile. *Aut:* Petrol g., jauge d'essence. *S.a.* PRESSURE-GAUGE, RAIN-GAUGE, TYRE-GAUGE. 4. *Const:* Dose *f* (de ciment). 5. *Nau:* (Often gage) Tirant *m* d'eau (d'un navire). *S.a.* LEE-GAUGE, WEATHER-GAUGE.

gauge², *v.tr.* **1.** Ca¹ibrer, étalonner (un écrou, etc.); jauger, mesurer (le vent, etc.). **To g. sth. by the eye,** mesurer qch. à l'œil, à la vue. **To g. s.o.'s capacities,** estimer, jauger, les capacités de qn. **2.** *Carp:* Trusquiner (le bois). **3.** Doser (le ciment). **4.** *Dressm:* **A:** Bouillonner (une jupe, etc.). **Gauged sleeves,** manches à bouillons. **gauging,** *s.* **1.** Calibrage *m*; étalonnage *m*; jaugeage *m*. **2.** Dosage *m* (du ciment). **3.** *Dressm:* **A:** Bouillon *m*.
Gaul [gɔ:l]. **1.** *Pr.n. A.Geog:* La Gaule. **2.** *s.* Gaulois, -oise.
Gaullism ['goulizm], *s. Pol:* Gaullisme *m*.
Gaullist ['goulist], *s. Pol:* Gaulliste *mf*.
gaumless ['gɔ:mlis], *a. F:* = GORMLESS.
gaunt [gɔ:nt], *a.* **1.** Maigre, décharné. **2.** *(a)* D'aspect redoutable, farouche. *(b)* Lugubre, désolé.
gauntlet¹ ['gɔ:ntlit], *s.* **1.** *Arm:* Gantelet *m*, gant *m*. **To throw down the g. to s.o.,** jeter le gant à qn. **To take up the g.,** relever le gant. **2. G. glove,** gant à crispins, à manchette; gant à la mousquetaire.
gauntlet², *s. Mil:* **A:** **To run the g.,** passer par les bretelles, par les baguettes. **To run the g. of adverse criticism,** soutenir un feu roulant de critiques adverses.
gauze [gɔ:z], *s. (a)* Gaze *f*. *(b)* **Wire g.,** toile *f* métallique, tissu *m* métallique.
gauzy ['gɔ:zi], *a.* Diaphane; léger.
gave. *See* GIVE².
gavel ['gævl], *s.* Marteau *m* (de commissaire-priseur, etc.).
gavotte [gə'vɔt], *s. Danc: Mus:* Gavotte *f*.
gawk¹ [gɔ:k], *s.* **G. of a man,** escogriffe *m*; grand dadais. **G. of a woman,** grande godiche; grande bringue.
gawk², *v.i.* = GAPE 2.
gawkiness ['gɔ:kinis], *s.* Gaucherie *f*.
gawky ['gɔ:ki], *a.* Dégingandé, gauche; *F:* empoté, godiche.
gay [gei], *a.* (gayest) **1.** *(a)* Gai, allègre. *(b)* **To lead a g. life,** mener une vie de plaisir(s). **To have a g. time,** s'amuser follement. *S.a.* DOG¹ 3. **2.** Gai, splendide, brillant. **Scene g. with lights,** scène égayée, resplendissante, de lumières. **gaily,** *adv.* **1.** Gaiement, allègrement. **2.** (Habillé) de couleurs gaies.
gaze¹ [geiz], *s.* Regard *m* fixe. **A horrible sight met his g.,** un spectacle horrible s'offrit à sa vue, à ses regards.
gaze², *v.i.* Regarder fixement. **To g. into space,** regarder dans le vide. **To g. at, on, upon, s.o.,** fixer, contempler, considérer, qn. **gazing,** *a. (Of crowd, etc.)* Curieux, -euse.
gazelle [gə'zel], *s. Z:* Gazelle *f*.
gazer ['geizər], *s.* Contemplateur, -trice (**at, upon,** de); curieux, -euse.
gazette¹ [gə'zet], *s.* **1.** *A:* Gazette *f*. **2.** Journal officiel. **To be, appear, in the G.,** figurer (à la *Gazette*) dans les déclarations de faillite.
gazette², *v.tr.* Annoncer, publier, (une faillite, une nomination, etc.) dans un journal officiel. **To be gazetted,** être à la *London Gazette* (= à l'Officiel).
gazetteer [gæzə'tiər], *s.* **1.** *(Pers.)* **A:** *(a)* Gazetier (officiel). *(b)* Nouvelliste *m*. **2.** Répertoire *m* géographique.
gean [gi:n], *s. Bot:* **1.** Merise *f*. **2. G.(-tree),** merisier *m*.
gear¹ [giər], *s.* **1.** *(a)* **A:** Accoutrement *m*. *(Still used in compounds)* **Foot-g.,** chaussures *fpl*. *(b)* Harnais *m*, harnachement *m* (de cheval de trait). **2.** *(a)* Effets (personnels). **Household g.,** ustensiles *m* de ménage. *(b)* Attirail *m*, équipement *m*, appareil *m*; *Nau:* apparaux *mpl*. **Fishing g.,** attirail de pêche. **Pump g.,** garniture *f*, équipement *m*, d'une pompe. **3.** *Mec.E:* *(a)* Appareil, mécanisme *m*. **Control g.,** les commandes *f*. *(b)* **(Driving-, transmission-)g.,** transmission *f*, commande *f*. **Wheel g.,** transmission, commande, par engrenage. **Belt g.,** commande par courroie. **Crank g.,** pédalier *m* (d'une bicyclette, etc.). **Train of gears,** train *m* d'engrenages. **Reversing g.,** (appareil de) changement *m* de marche; *Aut:* marche arrière. **In g.,** embrayé, en prise; *(ii)* *(of machine)* en action. **To come into g.,** s'enclencher **(with,** avec). **To throw (sth.) into g.,** embrayer, enclencher, engrener (les roues); mettre (une machine) en marche. **Out of g.,** *(i)* débrayé; *(ii)*

(of machine) hors d'action; *(iii)* hors de service; détraqué; *(iv)* *F:* *(of organization, etc.)* dérangé, déréglé. *(c)* *(i)* Multiplication *f*, démultiplication *f* (d'un engrenage, etc.). **Bicycle with a 66 inch g.,** bicyclette avec un développement de 5 m. 25, qui développe 5 m. 25. *(ii)* *Aut:* Vitesse *f*. **First, bottom,** *U.S:* **low g.,** première (vitesse). **Neutral g.,** point mort. **In top g.,** en prise (directe). **To change g.,** changer de vitesse. **gear-box,** *s.* **1.** *Mec.E:* Carter *m*. **2.** *Aut:* Boîte *f* de vitesses. **gear-case,** *s. Cy:* Carter *m*. **gear-change,** *s.* Changement *m* de vitesse. *Cy:* Dérailleur *m*. **gear-lever,** *s.* Levier *m* de changement de vitesse. **gear-ratio,** *s. Mec.E:* Rapport *m* d'engrenage; *(i)* multiplication *f*; *(ii)* (reduction) g.-r., démultiplication *f*. **gear-wheel,** *s.* *(a)* *Mec.E:* (Roue *f* d')engrenage *m*; roue dentée; rouage *m*. *(b)* *Cy:* Pignon *m*.
gear². **1.** *v.tr.* *(a)* Équiper (une machine). *(b)* Embrayer, enclencher, engrener (un pignon, etc.). **2.** *v.i.* S'embrayer, s'enclencher, s'engrener. **3.** *v.tr.* **To g. up, down,** multiplier, démultiplier (la vitesse de révolution). **4.** *v.tr.* **Salary geared to the cost of living,** salaire indexé au coût de la vie. **geared,** *a. Mec.E:* (Tour, etc.) à engrenage(s). **gearing,** *s.* **1.** *(a)* Engrenage *m*, embrayage *m*, enclenchement *m*. *(b)* **G. up,** multiplication *f*; *Cy:* développement *m*. **G. down,** démultiplication *f*, réduction *f*. **2.** Transmission *f*, commande *f*. **(Train of) g.,** système *m*, jeu *m*, train *m*, d'engrenages.
gearshift ['giəʃift], *s. Aut:* Changement *m* de vitesse.
gecko ['gekou], *s. Rept:* Gecko *m*. **Wall g.,** gecko des murailles.
gee¹ [dʒi:]. **1.** *Int:* **G.-up!** hue! huhau! **2.** *s.* = GEE-GEE.
gee², *int. U.S: F:* Ça alors! mince alors! oh là là! ah la vache!
gee-gee ['dʒi:dʒi:], *s. (Child's speech)* Cheval *m*; dada *m*.
geese [gi:s]. *See* GOOSE.
geezer ['gi:zər], *s. P:* **Old g.,** vieux type; *(of woman)* vieille toupie. **Funny old g.,** drôle de bonhomme.
Gehenna [gi'henə]. *Pr.n. B.Hist:* La Géhenne, l'Enfer.
Geiger counter ['gaigə,kauntər], *s. Atom.Ph:* Compteur *m* de Geiger, compteur à scintillations.
gel¹ [dʒel], *s. Ch:* Gel *m*.
gel², *v.i.* (gelled) *(Of colloid)* Se gélifier.
gelatine ['dʒelətiːn], *s.* *(a)* Gélatine *f*. *(b)* *Exp:* **Blasting g., explosive g.,** gélatine explosive; dynamite gomme *f*; plastic *m*.
gelatinize [dʒi'lætinaiz], *v.tr.* Gélatiner; gélatiniser.
gelatinous [dʒi'lætinəs], *a.* Gélatineux, -euse.
geld [geld], *v.tr.* Hongrer (un cheval).
gelding ['geldiŋ], *s.* Cheval *m* hongre.
gelignite ['dʒelignait], *s. Expl:* Gélignite *f*.
gem [dʒem], *s.* **1.** *(a)* Pierre précieuse; gemme *f*, joyau *m*. *(b)* **The g. of the collection,** le joyau de la collection. *(c)* *F: Sch:* (= *mistake*) Perle *f*. **2.** Pierre gravée; intaille *f*, camée *m*.
geminate ['dʒeminit], *a. (Of leaves, etc.)* Géminé, accouplé.
gemmed [dʒemd], *a.* Orné de pierres précieuses, de pierreries; gemmé.
gen [dʒen], *s. F:* Renseignements *mpl*.
gender ['dʒendər], *s.* **1.** *Gram:* Genre *m*. **2.** Sexe *m*.
gene [dʒi:n], *s. Biol:* Gène *m*.
genealogical [ˌdʒi:niə'lɔdʒik(ə)l], *a.* Généalogique. **-ally,** *adv.* Généalogiquement.
genealogist [ˌdʒi:ni'ælədʒist], *s.* Généalogiste *m*.
genealogy [ˌdʒi:ni'ælədʒi], *s.* Généalogie *f*.
genera. *See* GENUS.
general ['dʒen(ə)r(ə)l]. **I.** *a.* Général, -aux. **1. G. drawing, sketch,** dessin d'ensemble (d'une machine, etc.). **2.** *(a)* **G. meeting,** assemblée générale. **G. mathematics,** éléments *m* de mathématiques. *Adm:* **G. holiday,** fête publique; jour férié. *Mil:* **G. headquarters,** grand quartier général. *Ecc:* **G. confession,** confession en commun. *(b)* **The use of it is fairly g.,** l'usage en est assez répandu, assez général. **As a g. rule,** en règle générale. **In a g. way;** *F:* **as a g. thing,** d'une manière générale. **The g. public,** le grand public. **The g. reader,** le commun des lecteurs; le public (qui lit). *(c)* **G. knowledge,** connaissances générales. **G. store(s), shop,** épicerie-droguerie *f*,

pl. épiceries-drogueries; magasin *m* de village. *Publ:* **G. books,** livres *m* pour le grand public. **G. servant,** bonne *f* à tout faire. *(d)* **G. resemblance,** ressemblance générale, vague. **3. Inspector-g.,** inspecteur général, en chef. **4.** *adv.phr.* **In g.,** en général; généralement. **-ally,** *adv.* **1.** Généralement, universellement. **2.** Généralement; en général. **G. speaking,** (parlant) d'une manière générale; en général. **3. He g. comes on Thursdays,** en règle générale il vient le jeudi. **II. general,** *s.* **1. To argue from the g. to the particular,** raisonner du général au particulier. **2.** Général d'armée. **Lieutenant-g.,** général de corps d'armée. **Major-g.,** général de division. **G. Smith,** Monsieur le général Smith. **Yes, G.,** (i) oui, (monsieur le) général; (ii) *(from subordinate)* oui, mon général. *F:* **He's no g.,** il n'est pas tacticien, stratégiste. **3.** *Ecc:* Général (d'un ordre). **4.** *F:* Bonne à tout faire.

generalissimo [ˌdʒenər(ə)ʹlisimou], *s.* Généralissime *m*.

generality [ˌdʒenəʹræliti], *s.* Généralité *f.* (a) **G. of a statement,** portée générale d'une affirmation. (b) Considération générale. **To confine oneself to generalities,** s'en tenir aux généralités. (c) **The g. of mankind,** la généralité, la plupart, des hommes.

generalization [ˌdʒen(ə)rəlaiʹzeiʃ(ə)n], *s.* Généralisation *f*.

generalize [ʹdʒen(ə)rəlaiz], *v.tr.* **1.** Généraliser (des faits). **2.** Répandre, populariser (un usage, etc.). **generalizing**[1],*a.* Généralisateur, -trice; généralisant.

generalizing[2], *s.* Généralisation *f*.

generalship [ʹdʒen(ə)r(ə)lʃip], *s.* **1.** Généralat *m.* 2. Stratégie *f,* tactique *f*.

generate [ʹdʒenəreit], *v.tr.* **1.** *A:* Engendrer (des êtres vivants, des plantes, etc.). **2.** Produire (de la vapeur, de la chaleur, etc.). **3.** *Geom:* Engendrer (une surface, etc.). **4.** Amener, produire (un résultat). **generating,** *a.* Générateur, -trice. **G. station,** station, usine, génératrice; centrale *f* électrique.

generation [ˌdʒenəʹreiʃ(ə)n], *s.* Génération *f.* **1.** Production *f* (de chaleur, etc.). **2.** (a) **From g. to g.,** de génération en génération; de père en fils. *F:* **It is generations since anybody did such a thing,** on n'a pas fait une telle chose depuis des siècles. (b) **The rising g.,** la jeune, la nouvelle, génération, la génération qui monte.

generative [ʹdʒenəreitiv, -ətiv], *a.* Génératif; générateur, -trice; producteur, -trice.

generator [ʹdʒenəreitər], *s.* **1.** *(Pers.)* Générateur, -trice (d'une idée, etc.). **2.** *(Apparatus, plant)* (a) Générateur (de vapeur, de gaz, etc.); appareil producteur (de gaz). (b) *El.E:* Générateur; génératrice. *Aut:* Dynamo *f.* **3.** *Mus:* Son fondamental, son générateur (d'un accord).

generic(al) [dʒiʹnerik(əl)], *a.* Générique. **-ally,** *adv.* Génériquement.

generosity [ˌdʒenəʹrositi], *s.* Générosité *f.* (a) Magnanimité *f.* (b) Libéralité *f*.

generous [ʹdʒen(ə)rəs], *a.* Généreux. (a) Magnanime. (b) Libéral, -aux; donnant. (c) **G. soil,** sol généreux, fertile. **G. living,** bonne chère. **G. colour,** couleur riche. (d) *F:* **G. meal,** repas copieux, plantureux. **-ly,** *adv.* Généreusement. **1.** Avec magnanimité. **2.** Libéralement.

genesis [ʹdʒenisis], *s.* **1.** Genèse *f;* origine *f.* **2.** *B:* (The Book of) **G.,** la Genèse.

geneticist [dʒiʹnetisist], *s.* Généticien, -ienne, génétiste *mf*.

genetics [dʒiʹnetiks], *s.* Génétique *f*.

Geneva [dʒiʹniːvə]. *Pr.n. Geog:* Genève *f.* **The Lake of G.,** le lac Léman. *Attrib.* **G. gown,** robe noire (des prédicateurs calvinistes).

Genevan [dʒiʹniːvən], *a. & s.* Genevois, -oise.

genial [ʹdʒiːnjəl], *a.* **1.** (a) *(Of climate, etc.)* Doux, *f.* douce; clément; *(of fire, etc.)* réconfortant. (b) Plein de bienveillance; plein de bonne humeur; sympathique. **2.** Génial, -aux; de génie. **-ally,** *adv.* Affablement, cordialement.

geniality [ˌdʒiːniʹæliti], *s.* (a) Douceur *f,* clémence *f* (d'un climat). (b) Bienveillance *f;* bonne humeur.

genie, *pl. usu.* **genii** [ʹdʒiːni, ʹdʒiːniai], *s. Myth:* Djinn *m,* génie *m*.

genital [ʹdʒenitl]. **1.** *a.* Génital, -aux. **2.** *s.pl.* **Genitals,** organes génitaux externes; *F:* les parties.

genitive [ʹdʒenitiv], *a. & s. Gram:* Génitif (*m*).

genius [ʹdʒiːniəs], *s.* **1.** (a) *(Only in sg.)* Génie *m;* esprit *m* tutélaire. (b) *(With pl.* **genii** [ʹdʒiːniai]*)* Génie, démon *m,* esprit, djinn *m.* **2.** *(No pl.)* Génie particulier, esprit (d'une époque, etc.). **3.** *(No pl.) (Ability)* (a) Aptitudes naturelles. **To have a g. for mathematics,** avoir le don, *F:* la bosse, des mathématiques. **To have a g. for doing sth.,** avoir le don de faire qch. (b) **Man of g.,** homme de génie. **Work of g.,** œuvre géniale, de génie. **4.** *(Pers.) (pl.* **geniuses** [ʹdʒiːniəsiz]*)* **To be a g.,** être un génie. *F:* **He's no g.,** ce n'est pas un aigle.

Genoa [ʹdʒenouə]. *Pr.n. Geog:* Gênes.

genocide [ʹdʒenəsaid], *s.* Génocide *m*.

Genoese [ˌdʒenouʹiːz], *a. & s. Geog:* Génois, -oise.

genre [ʒaːnr], *s.* Genre *m. Art:* **G. painting,** peinture *f* de genre.

gent [dʒent], *s. P. & Com: =* GENTLEMAN. **Gents' footwear,** chaussures pour hommes. *(On door of public convenience)* **Gents,** hommes. *P:* **Where's the gents?** où sont les W.C.?

genteel [dʒenʹtiːl], *a. (Now usu. Iron:)* De bon ton; comme il faut. **G. tone of voice,** ton maniéré. *P:* **She's ever so g.,** elle est de la haute.

gentian [ʹdʒenʃ(i)ən], *s. Bot:* Gentiane *f*.

Gentile [ʹdʒentail], *a. & s. B.Hist:* Gentil. *Coll.* **The Gentiles,** la gentilité.

gentility [dʒenʹtiliti], *s. (Now usu. Iron:)* Distinction, bon ton. **Shabby g.,** la misère en habit noir.

gentle [ʹdʒentl]. **I.** *a.* **1.** (a) Bien né; *A:* gentil. **Of g. birth,** de bonne naissance; de bonne extraction. (b) *A:* **G. reader,** cher lecteur; aimable lectrice. **2.** Doux, *f.* douce. **G. as a lamb,** doux comme un agneau. **The gentle(r) sex,** le sexe faible. **G. exercise,** exercice physique modéré. **G. medicine,** médicament bénin. **-tly,** *adv.* **1.** *A:* **G. born,** bien né. **2.** Doucement. **G. (does it)!** allez-y doucement, *F:* en douceur. **II. gentle,** *s.* **1.** *pl. A:* **Gentles =** GENTLE-FOLK. **2.** *Fish:* Asticot *m*.

gentlefolk(s) [ʹdʒentlfouk(s)], *s.pl.* (a) Gens *m* comme il faut. (b) Personnes *f* de bonne famille. **Distressed g.,** les nouveaux pauvres.

gentleman, *pl.* **-men** [ʹdʒentlmən], *s.m.* **1.** *A:* Gentilhomme, *pl.* gentilshommes. **G. in waiting,** gentilhomme servant, de service (près du roi). **G.-at-arms,** gentilhomme de la garde. **2.** Galant homme; homme comme il faut. *Lit:* **A fine old English g.,** un gentleman de la vieille roche. *F:* **To be no g.,** être un goujat, un malotru. **G.'s agreement,** convention verbale, où l'on n'est engagé que la parole d'honneur des deux parties. **3.** (a) *Jur:* **G. (of independent means),** homme sans profession; rentier. *F:* **To be a g. of leisure,** vivre de ses rentes. (b) *Sp:* Amateur. **4.** Monsieur. *(To audience)* **Ladies and gentlemen!** mesdames et messieurs! mesdames, messieurs! **Young g.,** jeune homme, jeune monsieur. *F:* **The old g. (in black),** le diable. *Com:* **Gentlemen's hairdresser,** coiffeur pour hommes, d'hommes. **G.'s g.,** valet *m* de chambre. *P.N: (on door of public convenience)* **Gentlemen,** hommes, messieurs. **5.** *Danc:* Cavalier. *(Of a lady)* **To dance, take, g.,** faire le cavalier; conduire. **'gentleman-'farmer,** *s.m.* Gentleman-farmer, *pl.* gentlemen-farmers. **'gentleman-'usher,** *s.m. Hist:* Huissier (d'une grande maison).

gentlemanlike [ʹdʒentlmənlaik], *a. =* GENTLEMANLY.

gentlemanliness [ʹdʒentlmənlinis], *s.* Bonnes manières; savoir-vivre *m*.

gentlemanly [ʹdʒentlmənli], *a.* Comme il faut; bien élevé. **G. appearance,** (i) tenue convenable; (ii) air distingué.

gentleness [ʹdʒentlnis], *s.* **1.** *A:* Bonne naissance. **2.** Douceur *f*.

gentlewoman, *pl.* **-women** [ʹdʒentlwumən, -wimin], *s.f.* **1.** (a) Dame ou demoiselle bien née. (b) Personne comme il faut, tout à fait bien. (c) *Jur:* Dame sans profession, qui vit de ses rentes. **2.** *A:* Dame d'honneur; dame de compagnie (à la Cour).

gently [ʹdʒentli], *adv. See* GENTLE I.

gentry [ʹdʒentri], *s. Coll.* **1.** Petite noblesse. **The nobility and g.,** la haute et la petite noblesse. **2.** *Pej:* Gens *mpl;* individus *mpl.* **The light-fingered g.,** messieurs les voleurs à la tire.

genuflection, genuflexion [‚dʒenju(:)'flekʃ(ə)n], s. Génuflexion f.

genuine ['dʒenjuin]. a (a) Authentique, véritable. G. coin, pièce de bon aloi. A g. diamond, un diamant véritable. (b) Véritable, sincère; franc. f. franche. Com: G. purchaser, acheteur sérieux. -ly, adv. 1. Authentiquement. 2. Franchement véritablement.

genuineness ['dʒenjuinnis], s. 1. Authenticité f (d'un manuscrit, etc.); historicité f (d'un événement). 2. Sincérité f, loyauté f.

genus, pl. **genera** ['dʒiːnəs, 'dʒenərə], s. 1. Log: Genre m. 2. (a) Nat.Hist: Genre. (b) Genre, espèce f.

geocentric [‚dʒiː(:)o'sentrik], a. Astr: Géocentrique.

geode ['dʒiː(:)oud], s. Geol: Géode f.

geodesist [dʒiː'ɔdəsist], s. Géodésien m. géodésiste m.

geodesy [dʒiː(:)'ɔdisi], s. Mth: Géodésie f.

geographer [dʒiː'ɔgrəfər], s. Géographe m.

geographic(al) [‚dʒiːo'græfik(əl)], a. Géographique. -ally, adv. Géographiquement.

geography [dʒiː'ɔgrəfi], s. 1. Géographie f. F: To study the g. of the place, étudier la disposition des lieux. 2. (Traité m de) géographie.

geoid ['dʒiː(:)ɔid], s. Geog: Géoïde m.

geological [‚dʒiː:ə'lɔdʒik(ə)l], a. Géologique. -ally, adv. Géologiquement.

geologist [dʒiː'ɔlədʒist], s. Géologue m.

geology [dʒiː'ɔlədʒi], s. Géologie f.

geometer [dʒiː'ɔmitər], s. 1. Géomètre m. 2. Ent: (a) (Chenille) arpenteuse f. (b) (Moth) Géomètre f.

geometric(al) [‚dʒiːə'metrik(əl)], a. Géométrique. -ally, adv Géométriquement.

geometrician [‚dʒiːəme'triʃ(ə)n], s. Géomètre m.

geometry [dʒiː'ɔmitri], s. Géométrie f. Solid g., géométrie dans l'espace. Analytic, coordinate g., géométrie analytique.

geomorphology ['dʒiːoumɔ:'fɔlədʒi], s. Géomorphologie f.

geophysics ['dʒiː(:)o'fiziks], s.pl. Géophysique f.

geopolitics ['dʒiou'pɔlitiks], s. Géopolitique f.

georama [‚dʒiou'rɑ:mə], s. Géorama m.

George [dʒɔ:dʒ]. Pr.n.m. 1. Georges. F: O: By G.! sapristi! 2. s. Av: F: Pilote m automatique, George m.

georgette [‚dʒɔː'ʒet], s. Tex: Crêpe m georgette.

geothermal ['dʒiou'θəːm(ə)l], **geothermic** ['dʒiou-'θəːmik], a. Géothermique.

geranium [dʒi'reinjəm], s. Bot: Géranium m.

gerfalcon ['dʒɑ:fɔ:(l)kən], s. Orn: Gerfaut m.

geriatrics [dʒeri'ætriks], s. Med: Gériatrie f.

germ [dʒəːm], s. 1. Biol: Germe m (d'un organisme). 2. Med: Germe, microbe m (d'une maladie); bacille m. G. warfare, guerre f bactériologique. 'germ-carrier, s. Med: Porteur m de bacilles. 'germ-destroying, a. Germicide.

german¹ ['dʒəːmən], a. Germain.

German², a. & s. 1. Geog: Allemand, -ande. Hist: The G. Empire, l'empire allemand; l'empire germanique. 2. s. Ling: L'allemand m. S.a. MEASLES.

germander [dʒəː'mændər], s. Bot: Germandrée f.

germane [dʒəː'mein], a. 1. A: = GERMAN¹. 2. Approprié (to, à); en rapport (to, avec); se rapportant (to, à).

Germanic [dʒəː'mænik], a. 1. Allemand. 2. Hist: Germanique, germain.

Germanization [‚dʒəːm(ə)nai'zeiʃ(ə)n], s. Germanisation f

Germanophile [dʒəː'mænofil], a. & s. Germanophile.

Germanophobe [dʒəː'mænofoub], s. Germanophobe mf.

Germanophobia [‚dʒəːm(ə)no'foubiə], s. Germanophobie f.

Germanophobic [‚dʒəːm(ə)no'foubik], a. Germanophobe.

Germany ['dʒəːm(ə)ni]. Pr.n. Geog: L'Allemagne f. West, East, G., l'Allemagne de l'ouest, de l'est.

germicide ['dʒəːmisaid], s. Germicide m.

germinate ['dʒəːmineit]. 1. v.i. Germer. 2. v.tr. Faire germer.

germination [‚dʒəːmi'neiʃ(ə)n], s. Biol: Germination f.

gerontology [dʒerən'tɔlədʒi], s. Gérontologie f.

gerrymander¹ ['gerimændər], s. Truquage électoral; tripatouillage m.

gerrymander², v.tr. To g. an election, truquer. manigancer, une élection

gerund ['dʒerə)nd]. Gram Gérondit m.

gerundive [dʒi'rʌndiv] Gram. 1. a. Du gérondif. 2. s. Adjectif verbal.

Gestapo [ges'tɑ:pou], s. Hist. Gestapo f.

gestation [dʒes'teiʃ(ə)n], s. Physiol. Gestation f.

gesticulate [dʒes'tikjuleit]. 1. v.i. Gesticuler. 2. v.tr. Exprimer, manifester, (des sentiments, etc.) par des gestes

gesticulation [dʒes‚tikju'leiʃ(ə)n], s. Gesticulation f.

gesticulator [dʒes'tikjuleitər], s. Gesticulateur, -trice.

gesture¹ ['dʒestər], s. Geste m, signe m; mouvement m To make a g., faire un geste. By gestures, par gestes, à la muette.

gesture², 1. v.i. Faire des gestes 2 v.tr Exprimer (qch.) par gestes.

get [get], v. (p.t. got [gɔt]; p.p. got, A. & U.S: gotten [gɔtn]; pr p. getting) 1. v.tr 1. Procurer, obtenir. (a) To g. sth. (for oneself), se procurer qch. To g. sth. for s.o., to g. s.o. sth., procurer qch. à qn. To g. sth. to eat, (i) trouver de quoi manger; (ii) manger quelque chose (au buffet, etc.). Where can I g. . . .? où trouverai-je . . ? I got this horse cheap, j'ai eu ce cheval à bon marché. (b) Acquérir, gagner. To g. (oneself) a name, se faire un nom. To g. a wife, prendre femme. To g. the prize, gagner, remporter, avoir, le prix. To g. one's living, gagner sa vie. I will see what I can g. for it, je verrai ce qu'on m'en donnera. To g. nothing by it, out of it, n'y rien gagner. F: Don't you wish you may g. it! je vous en souhaite! (c) To g. leave (of, from, s.o.) to do sth., obtenir la permission (de qn) de faire qch. To g. one's own way, faire valoir sa volonté. S.a. WAY¹ 6. If I g. the time, si j'ai le temp- I'll switch on the radio to g. the time, je vais mettre la radio pour savoir l'heure. To g. a fine view of sth., avoir une belle vue de ch (d) W.Tel. We can't g Moscow, nous ne pouvons pas avoir Moscou Tp: I had some trouble in getting you, j'ai eu du mal à vous joindre. 2. (a) Recevoir (un cadeau, une lettre, etc.). He gets his timidity from his mother, il tient sa timidité de sa mère (b) Attraper (une maladie). To g. a blow, recevoir, attraper un coup. F: To g. religion, se convertir. He got ten years (in prison), il a été condamné à, F: il a attrapé, dix ans de prison. P: To g. it, en prendre pour son compte. 3. (a) Prendre, attraper (une bête fauve, etc.). F: We'll g. them yet! on les aura! The play didn't really g. me, la pièce ne m'a pas emballé. What's got him? qu'est-ce qu'il a? (b) F: I don't g. you, your meaning, je ne saisis pas bien. Got me? vous comprenez? 4. Aller chercher (son chapeau, un médecin). 5. (a) Faire parvenir. To g. s.o. home, conduire ou transporter qn chez lui. To g. s.o. upstairs, aider qn à monter l'escalier. To g. s.o. on to a subject, amener qn sur un sujet. (b) To g. lunch (ready), préparer le déjeuner. To g. s.o. into trouble, (i) attirer des histoires à qn; (ii) rendre (une femme) enceinte. F: That gets me down, ça me donne le cafard. 6. (a) To g. sth. done (by s.o.), faire faire qch. (à, par, qn). To g. the house painted, faire (re)peindre la maison. To g. oneself appointed, se faire nommer. (b) To g. one's work finished, finir son travail. To g. one's arm broken, se (faire) casser le bras. (c) To g. s.o. to do sth., faire faire qch. à qn. G. him to read it, faites-le-lui lire. To g. a plant to grow, réussir à faire pousser une plante. (d) F: That got him guessing, ça l'a intrigué. Aut: I must g. the engine running, il faut que je mette le moteur en marche. 7. F: (Only in perf.) Have got. (a) Avoir. I haven't got any, je n'en ai pas. What's that got to do with it? qu'est-ce que cela y fait? He's got measles, il a la rougeole. F: You've got it! vous avez deviné! vous y êtes! (b) (Obligation) You have got to do it, il faut absolument que vous le fassiez. It has got to be done, il faut que cela se fasse. II. get, v.i. 1. (a) Devenir (riche, gras, etc.). To g. old, devenir vieux, vieillir. To g. angry, se mettre en colère. Flowers are getting scarce, les fleurs se font rares. It is getting late, il se fait tard. (b) To g. dressed, s habiller. To g. married, (i) se marier; (ii) se faire épouser. To g.

killed, se faire tuer. **To g. drowned skating,** se noyer en patinant. **Everything gets known,** tout se sait. (c) *F:* **To g. doing sth.,** se mettre à faire qch. **To g. talking with s.o.,** entrer en conversation avec qn. *F:* **Let's g. cracking,** allons-y. 2. (a) Aller arriver, se rendre (to a place, etc., à un endroit, etc.). **He'll g. here tomorrow,** il arrivera (ici) demain. *F:* **To g. there,** arriver, réussir. *F:* **We're not getting anywhere, we're getting nowhere,** nous n'aboutissons à rien. **Where have you got to with your work?** où en êtes-vous dans votre travail? **Where has that book got to?** où est-ce que ce livre a passé? *U.S: P:* **G.!** Va-t-en! Fiche le camp! (b) Se mettre. **To g. behind a tree,** se mettre derrière un arbre. **To g. to work,** (i) se mettre à l'œuvre; (ii) arriver au bureau, à l'usine, etc. **I take the train to g. to work,** je prends le train pour me rendre au bureau, etc. **To g. to bed,** aller se coucher. (c) **To g. to do sth.,** finir par, en arriver à, faire qch. **To g. to know sth.,** apprendre qch. **When once one gets to know him,** quand on le connaît mieux. **get about,** *v.i.* 1. (*Of pers.*) Circuler. (*Of invalid*) **To g. a. again,** être de nouveau sur pied. 2. (*Of news*) Se répandre, circuler, s'ébruiter. **it's sure to g. a.,** cela se saura certainement. **get across.** 1. *v.i.* Traverser (une plaine); passer (une rivière). *Th: F:* **The play failed to g. a.** (the footlights), la pièce n'a pas passé la rampe. 2. *v.tr.* Faire passer (qn, qch.). *F:* **He couldn't get it across,** il n'a pas réussi à se faire comprendre. **get along.** 1. *v.i.* (a) S'avancer (dans son chemin). *F:* **G. a.** (with you)! (i) allez-vous-en! (ii) allons donc! (b) Faire des progrès; faire du chemin. **To g. a. without s.o., sth.,** se passer de qn, de qch. (c) **To g. a. with s.o.,** faire bon ménage avec qn. 2. *v.tr.* Faire avancer (qn, qch.). **get at,** *v.i.* 1. Parvenir à, atteindre (un endroit). **Difficult to g. at,** (endroit) peu accessible. **To g. at the root of the trouble,** trouver la racine du mal. *F:* **What are you getting at?** (i) où voulez-vous en venir? (ii) qu'est-ce que vous voulez insinuer? **Let me g. at him!** si jamais il me tombe sous les pattes! 2. (a) Accéder jusqu'à (qn). (b) *F:* **To g. at a witness,** suborner, travailler, un témoin. 3. *F:* Faire des sorties contre (qn). **Who are you getting at?** à qui, après qui, en avez-vous? **get away.** 1. *v.i.* (a) Partir, déloger. **To g. a. for the holidays,** partir en vacances. *F:* **G. a. with you!** allons donc! (b) (*Of prisoner, etc.*) S'échapper, se sauver. **To g. a. from one's environment,** échapper, se soustraire, à son entourage. *F:* **There's no getting away from it,** il n'y a pas à sortir de là; il faut bien l'admettre. (c) *Aut:* Démarrer. **Car that gets away quickly,** voiture qui a une bonne reprise. (d) **The burglars got away with £1000,** les cambrioleurs ont raflé £1000. *F:* **To g. a. with it,** faire accepter la chose. 2. *v.tr.* (a) Arracher (sth. from s.o., qch. à qn). (b) Éloigner (qn). **'get-away,** *s.* 1. Fuite *f.* **To make one's g.-a.,** s'enfuir, s'évader. 2. (a) *Rac:* Départ *m*; démarrage *m* (d'un coureur). (b) *Aut:* Démarrage. **get back.** 1. *v.i.* (a) Reculer. (b) Revenir, retourner. **To g. b. home,** rentrer chez soi. 2. *v.tr.* (a) Se faire rendre (qch.); rentrer en possession de (qch.); retrouver (un objet perdu); regagner (l'estime publique, etc.); recouvrer (ses biens); reprendre (ses forces). **I got my money back,** on m'a remboursé. **To g. one's own back,** (i) recouvrer ce qui vous appartient; (ii) *F:* prendre sa revanche. (b) Faire revenir (qn). **To g. sth. back into its box,** faire rentrer qch. dans sa boîte. **get beyond,** *v.i.* Dépasser (qch.). *F:* **This is getting beyond me,** cela me dépasse. **get by,** *v.i.* (a) Passer. (b) *F:* Se débrouiller. **get down.** 1. *v.i.* (a) Descendre (from, off, de). (*Child asks*) **Please may I g. d.?** est-ce que je peux quitter la table, s'il vous plaît? **To g. d. on one's knees,** se mettre à genoux. (b) *F:* **To g. d. to one's work,** se mettre à l'ouvrage pour de bon. **To g. d. to the facts,** en venir aux faits. (c) (*To dog*) **G. d.!** à bas les pattes! 2. *v.tr.* (a) Descendre (un livre d'un rayon, etc.); décrocher (son chapeau). *Nau:* Amener (une voile). (b) **To get sth. down** (on paper), noter qch. par écrit. (c) Avaler (une bouchée, etc.). **get in.** I. *v.i.* 1. *F:* = GET INTO 1 (a). 2. (a) Entrer; monter (en wagon, en voiture). **The water had got in everywhere,** l'eau avait pénétré partout. **If the** train gets in on time, si le train arrive à l'heure. **We got in at about eleven,** nous sommes rentrés vers onze heures. (b) **To g. in between two people,** s'introduire, se glisser, entre deux personnes. (c) *F:* **To g. in with s.o.,** s'insinuer dans les bonnes grâces de qn. (d) *Pol:* **To g. in for a constituency,** être élu député pour une circonscription. II. **get in,** *v.tr.* 1. Rentrer. **To g. in the crops,** rentrer la moisson. **To g. in debts,** recouvrer des dettes. **To get money in,** faire rentrer ses fonds. **To get a man in to mend the window,** faire venir un homme pour réparer la fenêtre. 2. **To get a blow in,** placer un coup. **To get a word in,** placer un mot. **If I can get it in (in the time),** si je trouve le temps nécessaire pour le faire. 3. **To get one's hand in,** se faire la main. 4. Planter, semer (des graines, etc.). **get into.** 1. *v.i.* (a) Entrer dans (une maison); pénétrer dans (un bois, etc.); monter dans (une voiture). **To g. i. a club,** se faire élire membre d'un club. **To g. i. bad company,** faire de mauvaises connaissances. (b) Mettre (ses habits). **To g. i. a rage,** se mettre en rage. **To g. i. a bad habit,** acquérir une mauvaise habitude. **To g. i. the way of doing sth.,** (i) apprendre à faire qch.; (ii) prendre l'habitude de faire qch. 2. *v.tr.* **To get sth. into sth.,** (faire) (r)entrer, enfoncer, qch. dans qch. **To get s.o. into the way of doing sth.,** faire prendre à qn l'habitude de faire qch. **get off.** I. *v.i.* 1. (a) Descendre de (la table). **The (bus) conductor will tell you where to g. o.,** le receveur vous dira où descendre. *P:* **I told him where to g. o.,** je lui ai dit ses vérités. (b) **To g. o. a duty,** se faire exempter d'une tâche. 2. (a) Se tirer d'affaire; être acquitté. **To g. o. with a fine,** en être quitte pour une amende. (b) *F:* (*Of girl*) **To get off,** (i) faire une conquête; (ii) attraper, décrocher, un mari. (c) *F:* Partir. **The train got off on time,** le train est parti à l'heure. *Av:* S'élever, décoller. (d) **To g. o. to sleep,** s'endormir. II. **get off,** *v.tr.* 1. **To g. o. one's clothes,** ôter ses vêtements. **To get a nut off,** desserrer un écrou. **To get stains off** (sth.), ôter, enlever, des taches (de qch.). 2. Expédier (un colis). 3. **To get sth. off one's hands,** se débarrasser de qch. **To get one's daughter off** (one's hands), marier, caser, sa fille. 4. Faire acquitter (un prévenu); tirer (qn) d'affaire. 5. Renflouer, déséchouer (un navire). **get on.** I. *v.tr.* 1. Mettre (ses souliers, etc.). 2. *F:* **To get a move on,** se dépêcher. 3. Faire faire des progrès à (un élève). II. **get on,** *v.i.* 1. Monter, se mettre, sur (une chaise, etc.); enfourcher (une bicyclette). **To g. on the train,** monter dans le train, en wagon. 2. (a) S'avancer (vers un endroit). **To be getting on for forty,** approcher de, friser, la quarantaine. **To be getting on (in years),** prendre de l'âge; avancer en âge. **Time is getting on,** allons, l'heure s'avance. **It is getting on for midnight,** il approche de minuit. **Getting on for 300 boys,** pas loin de 300 garçons. (b) Faire des progrès. **To g. on in life,** réussir dans la vie. **He will g. on (in the world),** il fera son chemin (dans le monde); il arrivera. **How to g. on,** le moyen de parvenir. **To g. on with the job,** pousser la besogne. **How are you getting on?** comment allez-vous? **How did you g. on in your examination?** comment votre examen a-t-il marché? (c) **To g. on without s.o., sth.,** se passer de qn, de qch. (c) **To g. on (well) with s.o.,** s'accorder, s'entendre, s'accommoder, avec qn. **Not to g. on with s.o.,** être en froid avec qn. **Easy to g. on with,** commode à vivre. (d) *P:* **G. on with you!** allons donc! (e) *U.S: F:* **To g. on to the racket,** découvrir le truc. **get out.** 1. *v.tr.* (a) Arracher (une dent); tirer, retirer (un bouchon); enlever, faire disparaître (une tache). **To get sth. out of sth.,** faire sortir, tirer, qch. de qch. **To get a secret out of s.o.,** arracher un secret à qn. **To get money out of s.o.,** tirer, *Pej:* soutirer, de l'argent à qn. *F:* **To get sth. out of it,** y gagner qch.; y trouver son compte. **To get s.o. out of a fix,** tirer qn d'embarras, d'un mauvais pas. **To get s.o. out of a habit,** défaire qn d'une, faire passer à qn une, habitude. (b) Sortir (ses outils). **To g. o. one's car,** (faire) sortir sa voiture. **To g. o. a boat,** mettre une embarcation à l'eau, à la mer. **To g. o. a book,** (i) (*of publisher*) publier un livre; (ii) (*of library-member*) emprunter un livre. **To g. o. a scheme,** préparer un devis. **To g. o. plans,** dresser, lever, des plans. **He could hardly**

g. o. a word, c'est à peine s'il a pu sortir un mot. *Com:* To g. o. a balance-sheet, établir, dresser, un bilan. (*c*) Résoudre (un problème). 2. *v.i.* (*a*) To g. o. of sth., sortir de qch. The lion got out of its cage, le lion s'échappa de sa cage. The secret got out, le secret perça. To g. o. of s.o.'s way, faire place, céder le pas, à qn. **G. o.** (of here)! fichez-moi le camp! **You must either do it or g. o.,** *F:* il faut passer par là ou par la porte. (*b*) **To g. o. of a difficulty,** se soustraire à une, venir à bout d'une, difficulté. **To g. o. of a duty, of doing sth.,** se faire exempter, se faire dispenser, d'une corvée, de faire qch. *Com: F:* **To g. o. without loss,** couvrir ses frais. (*c*) To g. o. of the habit of doing sth., perdre l'habitude de faire qch. *U.S: P:* **G. o.!** Mon œil! '**get-out,** *s. F:* Échappatoire *f.* **get over.** 1. *v.i.* (*a*) Franchir, escalader, passer par-dessus (un mur, etc.). *Th: F:* The play failed to g. o., la pièce n'a pas passé la rampe. (*b*) **To g. o. an illness,** se remettre, guérir, revenir, d'une maladie. **She cannot g. c. her loss,** elle est inconsolable de sa perte. **To g. o. one's shyness,** vaincre, revenir de, sa timidité. **To g. o. one's surprise,** revenir de sa surprise. **He can't g. o. it,** il n'en revient pas. 2. *v.tr.* (*a*) Faire passer (qch.) par-dessus (un mur, etc.). (*b*) To get sth. over, (i) en finir avec qch.; (ii) *F:* faire accepter ou comprendre qch. (à qn). **get round.** 1. *v.i.* (*a*) Tourner (un coin). **To g. r. to every boy in a class,** interroger, voir le travail de, chaque élève dans une classe. (*b*) = GET ABOUT 2. (*c*) Tourner (une difficulté, la loi). *F:* **To g. r. s.o.,** enjôler qn. **To know how to g. r. s.o.,** savoir prendre qn. (*c*) **To g. r. to doing sth.,** trouver le temps de faire qch. 2. *v.tr.* **To get s.o. round,** faire reprendre connaissance à, ranimer, qn. **get through.** I. *v.i.* 1. (*a*) Passer par (un trou); se frayer un chemin à travers (la foule). (*b*) Accomplir, arriver au bout de (sa tâche, etc.); achever (un livre). **To g. t. the day,** faire passer la journée. **To g. t. an examination,** être reçu, admis, à un examen. **I shall never g. t. this work,** je ne viendrai jamais à bout de ce travail. 2. (*a*) Parvenir (à franchir un obstacle). **The news got through to them,** la nouvelle leur est parvenue. (*b*) (*Of candidate*) Passer; être reçu. (*c*) *Pol:* Bill that will never g. t., projet de loi qui ne passera jamais. (*d*) *Tp:* **To g. t. (to s.o.),** obtenir la communication (avec qn). II. **get through,** *v.tr.* **To get a bill through (Parliament),** faire adopter un projet de loi. **To get sth. through the customs,** (faire) passer qch. à la douane. *Tp:* **To get s.o. through to s.o.,** donner à qn la communication avec qn. **get together,** 1. *v.i.* Se réunir, se rassembler. 2. *v.tr.* Rassembler, ramasser (des objets); rassembler, réunir (des amis, etc.). '**get-together.** *s. F:* Rassemblement *m,* réunion *f.* **get under.** 1. *v.i.* (i) **To g. u. sth.,** (i) passer par-dessous qch.; (ii) se mettre, se glisser, sous qch. 2. *v.tr.* Maîtriser (un adversaire, un incendie). **get up.** I. *v.i.* 1. **To g. u. a ladder,** monter à une échelle. 2. (*a*) **To g. up behind s.o.** (*on horse*), monter en croupe derrière qn. (*b*) **To g. up to s.o.,** arriver à la hauteur de qn. **Where have you got up to?** où en êtes-vous? (*c*) Se mettre debout; se lever. **Get up!** debout! levez-vous! (*d*) Se lever (du lit). (*e*) **To g. up to mischief,** faire des malices. (*f*) (*Of wind*) Se lever; (*of sea*) grossir. II. **get up,** *v.tr.* 1. **To get s.o. up a tree, up a hill,** faire monter qn à un arbre; faire gravir une colline à qn. 2. (*a*) Monter (une malle au grenier); relever (un navire coulé). *Rail: Aut:* **To g. up speed,** donner de la vitesse. (*b*) Faire lever (qn). (*c*) Organiser, arranger (une fête, etc.); monter (une pièce de théâtre); concerter (un complot); fomenter (une querelle). *Laund:* Apprêter (du linge). (*e*) **To g. oneself up,** se faire beau, belle; s'endimancher. '**get-up,** *s.* 1. Habillement *m,* toilette *f, Pej:* attifement *m.* 2. Apprêt *m* (de linge, etc.); facture *f,* façon *f,* présentation *f,* aspect *m* (d'un livre). '**got up,** *a.* (*Of pers.*) Attifé. **getting up,** *s.* 1. Lever *m.* The g.-up bell, la cloche du lever. 2. *Nau:* Gréage *m* (d'un mât). 3. Organisation *f* (d'une fête); montage *m* (d'une pièce de théâtre). **get-'at-able,** *a. F:* D'accès facile.

Gethsemane [geθ'semǝni]. *Pr.n. B:* Gethsémani *m.*

gewgaw ['gju:gɔ:], *s.* Bagatelle *f,* babiole *f.*

geyser ['gi:zǝr], *s.* 1. *Geol:* Geyser *m.* 2. **Chauffe-bain(s)** *m;* chauffe-eau *m inv.* à gaz.

Ghana ['gɑ:nǝ]. *Pr.n. Geog:* Le Ghana.

Ghanaian [gɑ:'neiǝn], *a. & s.* Ghanéen, -enne.

ghastliness ['gɑ:stlinis], *s.* 1. Horreur *f* (d'un crime). 2. Pâleur mortelle.

ghastly ['gɑ:stli]. 1. *a.* (*a*) Horrible, effroyable, affreux, -euse. *F:* **What a g. picture!** quelle peinture abominable! (*b*) Blême. **G. light,** lumière spectrale, blafarde. **G. smile,** sourire affreux à voir. 2. *adv.* (*a*) Horriblement, effroyablement, affreusement. (*b*) **G. pale,** blême.

Ghent [gent]. *Pr.n. Geog:* Gand *m.*

gherkin ['gǝ:kin], *s.* Cornichon *m.*

ghetto ['getou], *s.* Ghetto *m.*

Ghibelline ['gibilain], *s. Hist:* Gibelin *m.*

ghost[1] [goust], *s.* 1. *A:* Ame *f.* **To give up the g.,** rendre l'âme. 2. **The Holy G.,** le Saint-Esprit. 3. (*a*) Fantôme *m,* spectre *m,* revenant *m,* ombre *f,* apparition *f.* **To raise a g.,** évoquer un esprit. **To lay a g.,** conjurer, exorciser, un esprit. *Attrib.* **G. ship,** vaisseau fantôme. *T.V:* Écho *m.* (*b*) **To be the mere g. of one's former self,** n'être plus que l'ombre de soi-même. **Not the g. of a chance,** pas la moindre chance. 4. *F:* Nègre *m* (d'un auteur, etc.). '**ghost-story,** *s.* Histoire *f* de revenants.

ghost[2], *v.i.* Servir de nègre (à un auteur).

ghostlike ['goustlaik], *a.* 1. Spectral, -aux; de spectre. 2. *adv. Lit:* Comme un spectre.

ghostly ['goustli], *a.* 1. *A:* (Conseil, directeur) spirituel. 2. Spectral, -aux; de fantôme.

ghoul [gu:l], *s. Myth:* Goule *f,* vampire *m.*

ghoulish ['gu:lif], *a.* De goule; *F:* vampirique. **G. humour,** esprit *m* macabre.

giant ['dʒaiǝnt]. 1. *s.* Géant *m;* colosse *m.* 2. *a.* (Chêne, etc.) géant, gigantesque.

giantess ['dʒaiǝntes], *s.f.* Géante.

gibber[1] ['dʒibǝr], *s.* (*a*) Sons inarticulés. (*b*) Baragouin *m.*

gibber[2], *v.i.* (*a*) Produire des sons inarticulés (comme un singe, un idiot). (*b*) Baragouiner. **gibbering**[1], *a.* **G. idiot,** (i) idiot aphasique; (ii) *F:* espèce *m* d'idiot. **gibbering**[2], *s.* Baragouinage *m.*

gibberish ['gibǝrif], *s.* Baragouin *m.*

gibbet ['dʒibit], *s.* Gibet *m,* potence *f.*

gibbon ['gibǝn], *s. Z:* Gibbon *m.*

gibbose [gi'bous], **gibbous** ['gibǝs], *a.* 1. Gibbeux, -euse, convexe. 2. (*Of pers.*) Bossu.

gibbosity [gi'bɔsiti], *s.* Gibbosité *f,* bosse *f.*

gibe[1] [dʒaib], *s.* Raillerie *f;* moquerie *f;* sarcasme *m;* quolibet *m,* brocard *m.*

gibe[2], *v.tr. & i.* **To g. (at) s.o.,** railler qn; se moquer de qn. **gibing,** *a.* Railleur, moqueur.

giblets ['dʒiblits], *s.pl.* Abattis *m* (de volaille).

giddiness ['gidinis], *s.* 1. Étourdissement *m,* vertige *m.* 2. (*a*) Étourderie *f.* (*b*) Frivolité *f;* légèreté *f.*

giddy ['gidi], *a.* 1. (*a*) Étourdi. **To be, feel, turn, g.,** être pris de vertige. **I feel g.,** la tête me tourne. (*b*) Vertigineux, -euse; qui donne le vertige. 2. Frivole, étourdi, écervelé. **She's a g. young thing,** c'est une évaporée. **-ily,** *adv.* 1. D'une manière vertigineuse. 2. Étourdiment; à l'étourdie.

gift [gift], *s.* Don *m.* (*a*) **To make a g. of sth. to s.o.,** faire don de qch. à qn. *Jur:* **Deed of g.,** donation *f* entre vifs. **To acquire sth. by free g.,** acquérir qch. à titre gratuit. (*b*) Cadeau *m,* présent *m.* **It was a g.,** (i) on me l'a offert; (ii) *F:* c'était donné. *Com:* **Gifts,** pour offrir. *F:* **He thinks he is God's g. to mankind,** il se prend pour le nombril du monde. (*c*) (*On presentation of coupons*) Prime *f.* (*d*) **To have a g. for mathematics,** avoir le don, le génie, des mathématiques. '**gift-horse,** *s. Prov:* (You must) never look a g.-h. in the mouth, à cheval donné on ne regarde pas à la bride, à la bouche.

gifted ['giftid], *a.* Bien doué; (artiste) de valeur, de talent.

gig[1] [gig], *s.* 1. Cabriolet *m.* 2. *Nau:* Petit canot; yole *f.*

gig[2], *s. Fish:* Foëne *f,* foène *f.*

gigantic [dʒai'gæntik], *a.* Géant, gigantesque; (bâtiment, etc.) colossal, -aux. **-ally,** *adv.* Gigantesquement.

gigantism ['dʒaigæntizm], *s.* Gigantisme *m.*

giggle[1] ['gigl], *s.* (*Esp. of girls*) Petit rire nerveux; rire bébête.

giggle[2], *v.i.* (*Esp. of girls*) Rire nerveusement; pousser des petits rires. **giggling**, *s.* Rires nerveux; petits rires bébêtes.

gigolo ['dʒigəlou], *s.* P: Gigolo *m.*

gild [gild], *v.tr.* (*p.t.* **gilded**; *p.p.* **gilded**, *occ.* **gilt** [gilt]) Dorer. **To g. sth. over**, couvrir qch. d'une couche de dorure. **To g. the lily**, ajouter des ornements superflus, faire œuvre de superfétation. **gilded**, *a.* Doré. **gilt**[1], *a.* Doré. **gilt**[2], *s.* Dorure *f*, doré *m.* **Imitation gilt**, similor *m. S.a.* SILVER-GILT. **'gilt-'edged**, *a.* 1. (*Of book, card, etc.*) Doré sur tranche. 2. *Fin:* G.-e. stock, valeurs de tout repos, de premier ordre. **gilding**, *s.* Dorure *f.* **Leaf g.**, dorure à la feuille.

gill[1] [gil], *s.* 1. *Usu. pl.* Ouïe(s) *f*, branchie(s) *f* (de poisson). 2. *pl.* **Gills.** (*a*) Caroncules *f*, fanons *m* (d'un oiseau). (*b*) Lames *f*, lamelles *f* (d'un champignon). (*c*) F: Bajoues *f* (de qn). **To look green about the gills**, avoir le teint vert. 3. *Mch: Ind:* Ailette *f* (de cylindre, etc.). **'gill-cover**, *s. Ich:* Opercule (branchial).

gill[2] [dʒil], *s. Meas:* = 0,142 litre, *U.S:* 0,118 litre.

gilled [gild], *a.* 1. *Biol:* Pourvu de branchies, de caroncules, de lames. 2. *Mch: etc:* G. radiator, radiateur à ailettes.

gillie ['gili], *s. Scot:* 1. *Hist:* Suivant *m* (d'un chef). 2. *Ven:* Fish: Serviteur *m*, porte-carnier *m.*

gillyflower ['dʒililflauər], *s. Bot:* 1. (Clove-) g., œillet *m* giroflée. 2. *Dial:* = WALL-FLOWER 1.

gilt[1],[2] *a. & s. See* GILD.

gimcrack ['dʒimkræk], *a.* (Meubles, etc.) de pacotille; (maison) de carton; (bijoux) en toc.

gimlet ['gimlit], *s. Tls: Carp:* Vrille *f*; foret *m* à bois; perçoir *m. Attrib.* G. eyes, yeux perçants.

gimmick ['gimik], *s. F:* Machin *m*, truc *m*, bidule *m.* **Advertising g.**, artifice *m*, trouvaille *f*, publicitaire.

gin[1] [dʒin], *s.* 1. *Ven:* Piège *m*, trébuchet *m.* 2. *Mec.E: Ind:* Chèvre *f*, engin *m.*

gin[2], *s.* Genièvre *m*; gin *m. S.a.* SLOE. **'gin-soaked**, *a.* (*Of pers.*) Abruti par la boisson, par l'alcool.

ginger[1] ['dʒindʒər], *s.* 1. *s.* (*a*) Gingembre *m.* (*b*) *F:* Entrain *m*, énergie *f*, vitalité *f.* 2. *a.* (*Of hair*) Roux, *f.* rousse; *P:* rouquin. **ginger-'ale, -'beer**, *s.* Variétés de boissons gazeuses au gingembre. **'ginger-'haired**, *a.* Aux cheveux roux; rouquin. **'ginger-nut**, *s.* Biscuit *m* au gingembre.

ginger[2], *v.tr.* 1. Aromatiser (une boisson, etc.) au gingembre. 2. *F:* To g. s.o. up, mettre du cœur au ventre de qn; secouer, remonter, exciter, qn.

gingerbread ['dʒindʒəbred]. *s.* Pain *m* d'épice.

gingerly ['dʒindʒəli], *adv. & a.* In a g. fashion, g., délicatement, doucement, avec précaution.

gingival [dʒindʒaiv(ə)l], *a.* Gingival, -aux.

gingivitis [,dʒindʒi'vaitis], *s. Med:* Gingivite *f.*

gingham ['giŋəm], *s. Tex:* Guingan *m.*

Gioconda (la) [ɪɑːdʒ(i)ə'kəndə]. *Pr.n.f. Hist. of Art:* La Joconde. A G. smile, un sourire de Joconde.

gipsy ['dʒipsi], *s.* Bohémien, -ienne; nomade *mf*; romanichel, -elle. *Ent:* G. moth, zigzag *m.*

giraffe [dʒi'rɑːf, -'ræf], *s. Z:* Girafe *f.* Baby g., girafeau *m.*

girandole ['dʒir(ə)ndoul], *s.* 1. Girande *f.* 2. Girandole *f.*

gird[1] [gəːd], *v.tr.* (*p.t. & p.p.* **girded, girt** [gəːt]) *Lit:* 1. Ceindre. (*a*) **To g. up one's loins**, se ceindre les reins. **To g. oneself for the fray**, se préparer à la lutte. (*b*) **To g. s.o. with sth., to g. sth. on s.o.**, ceindre qn de qch.; ceindre qch. à qn. **To g. (on) one's sword**, ceindre son épée. 2. Entourer, encercler, ceindre (**with**, de).

gird[2], *s.* = GIBE[1].

gird[3], *v.i.* **To g. at s.o.**, railler qn; se moquer de qn.

girder ['gəːdər], *s.* Support *m.* (*a*) *Const:* Solive *f*, longrine *f* (de plancher). (*b*) Poutre *f.* **Plate-g.**, poutre à âme pleine. **Trussed g.**, poutre armée; ferme *f.*

girdle[1] [gəːdl], *s.* (*a*) *Cost:* Ceinture *f*; gaine *f.* **Dressing-gown g.**, cordelière *f* de robe de chambre. (*b*) *Anat:* Pelvic g., ceinture pelvienne.

girdle[2], *v.tr.* Ceinturer, ceindre, encercler.

girdle[3], *s.* Tôle circulaire sur laquelle on cuit des galettes. **'girdle-cake**, *s.* Galette *f.*

girl [gəːl], *s.f.* 1. Jeune fille. (*a*) **Little g., young g.**, fillette. **Girl's name**, prénom féminin. **Poor little g.**, pauvre petite. (*b*) Girls' school, école *f*, lycée *m*, de filles; pensionnat *m* de jeunes filles. Old g., ancienne élève. 2. Jeune personne, jeune femme, jeune fille. (*a*) His fiancée is a charming g., sa fiancée est une jeune fille charmante. (*Often best translated by* jeune.) A French g., une jeune Française. Blind g., jeune aveugle. The Smith girls, les demoiselles Smith. *Attrib.* G. typist, jeune dactylographe *f.* G. friend, (jeune) amie. (*b*) *P:* His (best) g., his g. friend, une petite amie. My dear g.! ma chère amie! (*c*) My eldest g., ma fille aînée, mon aînée. 3. Chorus g., girl *f.*

girlhood ['gəːlhud], *s.* Jeunesse *f* ou adolescence *f* (d'une femme). In her g., quand elle était (i) petite fille, (ii) jeune fille.

girlish ['gəːliʃ], *a.* 1. (*Of behaviour, figure, etc.*) De petite fille ou de jeune fille. 2. (*Of boy, etc.*) Mou, efféminé. **-ly**, *adv.* 1. En jeune fille, en petite fille. 2. Comme une petite fille.

girt. *See* GIRD[1].

girth [gəːθ], *s.* 1. *Harn:* Sangle *f*; sous-ventrière *f* (de harnais de trait). Saddle-g., sangle de selle. 2. Circonférence *f* (d'un arbre, etc.); tour *m* (de poitrine).

gist [dʒist], *s.* 1. *Jur:* Principal motif (d'une action). 2. Fond *m*, substance *f*, essence *f* (d'une conversation, etc.); point essentiel (d'une question).

give[1] [giv], *s. F:* Élasticité *f.*

give[2], *v.* (*p.t.* **gave** [geiv]; *p.p.* **given** ['givn]) I. *v.tr.* Donner. 1. (*a*) **To g. sth. to s.o., to g. s.o. sth.**, donner qch. à qn. **It was given to me**, on me l'a offert. **To g. alms**, faire l'aumône. **It is not given to all to achieve fame**, il n'appartient pas, il n'est pas donné, à tous de devenir célèbres. **G. me the good old days!** parlez-moi du bon vieux temps! (*b*) **To g. and take**, y mettre chacun du sien. **It's a case of g. and take**, c'est donnant donnant. 2. (*a*) **To g. s.o. sth. to eat, to drink**, donner à manger, à boire, à qn. **To g. a child a name**, donner un nom à un enfant. **To g. s.o. a job**, assigner une tâche, un rôle, à qn. (*b*) **To g. sth. into s.o.'s hands**, remettre qch. entre les mains de qn. (*c*) **To g. one's compliments to s.o.**, présenter ses compliments à qn. **G. him my love**, faites-lui mes amitiés. **Given these facts, explain . . .**, à partir de ces données, expliquez. . . . (*d*) Engager (son honneur, etc.). **To g. one's word**, donner sa parole. 3. **To g. a good price for sth.**, donner, payer, un bon prix pour qch. **What did you g. for it?** combien l'avez-vous payé? 4. **To g. one's life to God**, donner, consacrer, sa vie à Dieu. **To g. one's mind, oneself, to study**, s'adonner, s'appliquer, à l'étude. (*Of woman*) **To g. oneself**, se donner. 5. Faire (une action). **To g. a jump**, faire un saut; tressauter. **To g. a laugh**, laisser échapper un rire. **To g. a sigh**, pousser un soupir. **To g. s.o. a blow**, porter un coup à qn. **To g. s.o. a smile**, adresser un sourire à qn. **He gave a queer look**, il eut un regard singulier. **To g. orders**, (i) donner des ordres; (ii) (*at shop*) faire des commandes. 6. (*a*) **To g. s.o. one's hand**, donner, tendre, la main à qn. *O:* **She gave him her hand in marriage**, elle lui accorda sa main. (*b*) **To g. (one's) attention to s.o.**, faire attention à qn. **I will g. the matter every attention**, j'y mettrai tous mes soins. 7. (*a*) **To g. a decision**, (i) donner, fournir, des détails. **To g. a decision**, (i) faire, faire connaître, sa décision; (ii) *Jur:* prononcer, rendre, un arrêt. (*b*) **To g. no sign(s) of life**, ne donner aucun signe de vie. **To g. an average of . . .**, rendre une moyenne de. . . . (*c*) **To g. an example**, donner un exemple. *Mth: etc:* **Given any two points**, étant donné(s) deux points quelconques. (*d*) **To g. a recitation**, réciter; dire des vers. (*e*) **To g. a toast**, boire à la santé de qn. **I g. you our host**, je bois à la santé de notre hôte. 8. (*a*) That gave me **the idea of travelling**, cela me donna l'idée de voyager. (*b*) **To g. pain, pleasure**, faire, causer, de la peine, du plaisir. **To g. oneself trouble**, se donner du mal. (*c*) **To g. s.o. to suppose, believe, sth.**, faire supposer, faire croire, qch. à qn. **To g. s.o.**

to understand that . . ., donner à entendre à qn que. . . . (d) Rendre. Investment that gives 10%, placement qui rend, rapporte, 10%. 9. (a) P: To g. it (to) s.o., (i) semoncer vertement qn; P: laver la tête à qn; (ii) rosser qn. P: I gave him what for! je l'ai arrangé de la belle façon! (b) F: To g. as good as one gets, rendre coup pour coup. 10. To g. way. (a) (Also abs. to g.) Céder, fléchir; (of ladder, etc.) se casser. The ground gave way under our feet, le sol s'affaissa, se déroba, sous nos pieds; le sol nous manqua sous les pieds. To feel one's legs g. (way), beneath one, sentir ses jambes (se) fléchir, se dérober, sous soi. (b) Lâcher pied. To g. way to s.o., céder à qn. To g. way to despair, s'abandonner (au désespoir). To g. way to temptation, céder à la tentation. To g. way to one's emotions, s'abandonner, se laisser aller, à ses émotions. (c) Céder la place (to s.o., à qn). P.N: Aut: G. way = priorité à droite. (d) Fin: Com: (Of prices, shares) Fléchir; crouler. II. give, v.i. 1. (Of elastic, etc.) Prêter, donner. The rope has given, le cordage s'est relâché. 2. The window gives on to the garden, la fenêtre donne sur le jardin. give away, v.tr. 1. Donner (sth. to s.o., qch. à qn); se dénantir de (ses possessions). I would rather g. it away, je préférerais en faire cadeau. 2. To g. a. the bride, conduire, accompagner, la mariée à l'autel. 3. F: To g. s.o. away, trahir, vendre, dénoncer, qn. To g. oneself away, se trahir. To g. the show away, bavarder; vendre la mèche. give-away, s. F: Révélation f involontaire. give back, v.tr. Rendre, restituer; renvoyer (un écho). giving back, s. Restitution f. give forth, v.tr. 1. = GIVE OFF. 2. Rendre, émettre, faire entendre (un son). give in. 1. v.tr. To g. in one's name, donner son nom; se faire inscrire. To g. in a parcel (at the door), délivrer, remettre, un paquet. 2. v.i. Céder; se rendre, se soumettre. give off, v.tr. Dégager, exhaler (une odeur, etc.); répandre (de la chaleur). give out. 1. v.tr. (a) Distribuer (les vivres, etc.). (b) = GIVE OFF. (c) Annoncer (un cantique, etc.). To g. out a notice, lire une communication. To g. it out that . . . annoncer que. . . . To g. oneself out for an expert, se dire expert. 2. v.i. Manquer; faire défaut. My strength was giving out, j'étais à bout de forces. My brakes gave out, mes freins lâchèrent. give over, v.tr. 1. To g. sth. over to s.o., remettre qch. entre les mains de qn; abandonner qch. à qn. 2. F Cesser; finir. To be given over to despair, être abandonné, en proie, au désespoir. give up, v.tr. 1. (a) Rendre (sa proie); abandonner (ses biens, ses prétentions). To g. up one's seat to s.o., ceder sa place à qn. (b) Remettre (un billet) (to, à). 2. (a) Renoncer à (un projet, etc.); abandonner (un ami). To g. up the idea of doing sth., renoncer à faire qch. To g. up a newspaper, se désabonner à un journal. To g. up business, cesser, quitter, les affaires, se retirer. To g. up the game, the struggle, abandonner la partie. To g. up the race, etc., abs. to g. up, abandonner, lâcher, renoncer. (Of riddle) I g. it up, je donne ma langue au chat, aux chiens. To give s.o. up (as a bad job), y renoncer. (b) To give s.o. up (for lost), considérer qn comme perdu. I had given you up! je ne vous espérais plus! 3. (a) Livrer (qn à la justice, etc.); faire arrêter (qn) To g. oneself up, se constituer prisonnier. (b) To g. oneself up to sth., se livrer (à un vice, etc.); s'absorber (dans la lecture d'un livre); s'appliquer, s'adonner (à l'étude); s'abandonner (à la paresse). giving up, s. Remise f (d'un billet); abandon m (d'une habitude, etc.). given, a. 1. In a g. time, dans un délai donné, convenu, déterminé. At a g. point, à un point donné. U.S: G. name, nom de baptême; prénom. 2. Porté, enclin (to, à). G. to drink, adonné à la boisson. I am not g. that way, cela n'entre pas dans mes goûts, dans mes habitudes. giving, s. 1. Don m, donation f (d'un cadeau, etc.); administration f (d'une potion, etc.); remise f (de qch. entre les mains de qn, etc.); engagement m (de sa parole). 2. Prononciation f, prononcé m (d'un arrêt, etc.). 3. G. way, (i) affaissement m, fléchissement m (d'une poutre, etc.); altération f (de la santé, etc.); (ii) abandon m (à ses émotions). 'give-and-'take, a. G.-and-t. policy, politique d'accommodement, de concessions mutuelles.

giver ['givər], s. Donneur, -euse; donateur, -trice. St. Exch: G. of stock, reporté m.

gizzard ['gizəd], s. Gésier m. F: That sticks in my g., je ne peux pas avaler, digérer, ça.

glabrous ['gleibrəs], a. Nat.Hist: Glabre.

glacé ['glæs(e)i], a. (Cuir, etc.) Glacé. G. cherries, cerises cristallisées.

glacial ['gleisiəl], a. 1. Geol: Glaciaire. 2. (Vent, etc.) glacial, -als. 3. Ch: Cristallisé; en cristaux.

glaciation [glæsi'eiʃ(ə)n], s. Glaciation f.

glacier ['glæsiər], s. Geol: Glacier m.

glacis ['glæsis], s. Fort: Glacis m.

glad [glæd], a. (gladder) Heureux. 1. Bien aise; content. To be g. to hear sth., être heureux, bien content, d'apprendre qch. I'm very g. of it, j'en suis bien aise. He is only too g. to help you, il ne demande pas mieux que de vous aider. It makes my heart g. to hear him, cela me réjouit le cœur de l'entendre. 2. O: G. tidings, nouvelles joyeuses, heureuses; bonne nouvelle. 3. P: O: G. rags, habit m ou robe f de soirée. -ly, adv. (a) Avec plaisir, volontiers, de bon cœur. (b) Avec joie.

gladden [glædn], v.tr Réjouir.

glade [gleid], s. Clairière f, éclaircie f (dans une forêt).

gladiator ['glædieitər], s. Gladiateur m.

gladiolus, pl. -luses, -li [glædi'ouləs, -ləsiz, -lai], s. Bot: Glaïeul m.

gladness ['glædnis], s. Joie f, allégresse f.

glamorize ['glæməraiz], v.tr. Donner une beauté factice, un prestige factice (à qn, à qch.).

glamorous ['glæmərəs], a. Enchanteur, -eresse; charmeur, -euse, prestigieux, -euse.

glamour ['glæmər], s. 1. Enchantement m, charme m. To cast a g. over s.o., ensorceler qn. 2. Fascination f; prestige m (d'un nom, etc.); éclat m.

glance¹ [glɑːns], s. 1. Ricochet m. 2. Regard m; coup d'œil. At a g., d'un coup d'œil. At the first g., au premier coup d'œil. Angry g., regard irrité.

glance², v.i. 1. (a) (Of bullet, etc.) To g. aside, g. off, dévier, ricocher. (b) v.tr. To g. back the rays of light, réfléchir, refléter, les rayons de lumière. 2. To g. at s.o., at sth., jeter un regard sur qn, sur qch; lancer un coup d'œil à qn. To g. up, down, jeter un coup d'œil en haut, en bas. To g. through, over, sth., parcourir, feuilleter (un livre). glancing, a. (Of blow, etc.) Oblique.

gland¹ [glænd], s. Biol: Glande f. Swollen glands, (i) glandes engorgées; (ii) (in childhood) états m ganglionnaires de l'enfance.

gland², s. Mec.E: Mch: Couronne f, gland m, chapeau m

glandered ['glændəd], a. Vet: (Cheval) morveux, glandé.

glanders ['glændəz], s.pl. (With sg. const.) Vet: Med: Morve f (chez le cheval ou l'homme).

glandular ['glændjulər], a. Glandulaire.

glandulous ['glændjuləs], a. Glanduleux, -euse.

glare¹ ['gleər], s. 1. (a) Éclat m, clarté f, rayonnement m; lumière crue. In the full g. of the sun, au grand soleil. In the full g. of publicity, sous les feux de la rampe. (b) Éblouissement m, aveuglement m (d'un phare, etc.) 2. Clinquant m; faux éclat. 3. Regard fixe et irrité.

glare², v.i. 1. (Of sun, etc.) Briller d'un éclat éblouissant. 2. To g. at s.o., lancer un regard furieux, furibond, à qn. glaring, a. 1. (a) (Of light, etc.) Éblouissant, éclatant; (soleil) aveuglant. (b) (Of costume, etc.) Voyant, éclatant; (of colour) cru. 2. (Of fact, etc.) Manifeste, patent; (of injustice, etc.) flagrant. -ly, adv. 1. Avec un faux éclat ou avec trop d'éclat. 2. Manifestement.

glass [glɑːs], s. 1. Verre m. Pane of g., vitre f, carreau m. Wired g., verre grillagé, armé; cristal armé. Frosted g., ground g., verre dépoli. Ribbed g., verre strié. Window g., sheet g., verre à vitres. Plate g., verre laminé. Optical g., verre d'optique. Cut g., cristal taillé. Stained g., coloured g., verre de couleur. Stained g. window, vitrail (peint); verrière f. The (stained) g. of a church, les vitraux, les verrières, d'une église. Spun g., laine f, fil m, de verre. Aut: Safety g., verre de sûreté. 2. (a) (Drinking) g., verre (à boire). Wine g., verre à vin. G. of wine, verre de vin. Champagne g., flûte f, coupe f, à champagne.

Sherry g., verre à madère. **Stemmed** g., verre à pied. **A g. of brandy,** *etc.,* un petit verre. **To have had a g. too many,** avoir bu un coup de trop. *F:* **He's festive when he's had a** g., il a le vin gai. *(b) Coll.* **Table** g., verrerie *f* de table. **Oven** g., verrerie allant au four. **Hollow** g., gobeleterie *f.* **G. and china shop,** magasin de verrerie et porcelaine. 3. Vitre *f* (de fenêtre); glace *f* (de voiture); verre (de montre, de lampe). 4. *(a)* Lentille *f* (d'un instrument d'optique). *(b)* (Magnifying-, reading-) g., loupe *f;* verre grossissant. 5. (Looking-) g., glace, miroir *m.* 6. *pl.* **Glasses,** lunettes *f.* **To wear** g., porter des lunettes. 7. Longue-vue *f, pl.* longues-vues; lunette (d'approche); *pl.* jumelles *f.* 8. (Weather-)g., baromètre *m* (à cadran). **The g. is falling,** le baromètre baisse. 9. *Hort:* **Grown under g.,** cultivé sous verre. 10. **Musical glasses,** harmonica *m.* 11. *Attrib.* De, en, verre. **G. bottle,** bouteille de, en, verre. **G. door,** porte vitrée. **G. partition,** vitrage *m.* **G. rod,** baguette *f* de, en, verre. **G. roof,** verrière *f* (d'une gare, etc.). *Prov:* **People who live in g. houses shouldn't throw stones,** il faut être sans défauts pour critiquer autrui. **glass-blower,** *s.* Souffleur *m* (de verre); verrier *m.* **'glass-blowing,** *s.* Soufflage *m* (du verre). **'glass-'case,** *s.* Vitrine *f.* **To keep sth. in a g.-c.,** garder qch. sous verre. **'glass-cloth,** *s.* Essuie-verres *m inv.* **'glass-cutter,** *s. Tls:* Coupe-verre *m inv;* (circular) tournette *f.* **'glass-house,** *s. (a) Hort:* Serre *f. (b) F:* Prison *f* militaire, *P:* ours *m.* **'glass-lined,** *a. Ind:* G.-l. tank, cuve verrée. **'glass-making,** *s.* Verrerie *f.* **'glass-paper,** *s.* Papier de verre. **'glass-'wool,** *s.* Laine *f* de verre. **'glass-work,** *s.* 1. *(In church)* Vitrage *m.* 2. *pl.* **Glass-works,** verrerie *f;* glacerie *f.* **'glass-worker,** *s.* Verrier *m.*

glassful ['glɑːsful], *s.* (Plein) verre.

glassware ['glɑːswɛər], *s.* Articles *mpl* de verre; verrerie *f.*

glasswort ['glɑːswɔːt], *s. Bot: (a)* **Jointed** g., salicorne *f. (b)* **Prickly** g., soude *f.*

glassy ['glɑːsi], *a.* Vitreux, -euse.

Glaswegian [glæs'wiːdʒiən], *a. & s.* (Natif, originaire) de Glasgow.

glaucoma [glɔːˈkoumə], *s. Med:* Glaucome *m.*

glaucous ['glɔːkəs], *a.* Glauque.

glaze¹ [gleiz], *s.* 1. Glace *f.* lustre *m,* vernissure *f* (du drap). 2. *Cer:* Glaçure *f,* vernis (luisant), enduit *m.* 3. *Cu:* Glace; dorure *f.* 4. *Paint:* Glacis *m.* **glaze².** I. *v.tr.* 1. Vitrer (une fenêtre). 2. *(a)* Glacer, lustrer (une étoffe); vernir (le cuir); lisser (le papier). *Phot:* Glacer, émailler (une épreuve). *(b) Cer:* Vernir, émailler (la poterie); plomber (la vaisselle de terre); vitrifier (les tuiles). *(c) Cu:* Glacer, dorer. II. **glaze,** *v.i.* **To g. (over),** se glacer; *(of eye)* devenir vitreux, **glazed,** *a.* 1. *(Of roof, door)* Vitré. *(Of picture)* **Framed and g.,** encadré et sous verre. *Nau:* G.-in light, verrine *f.* 2. *(a)* (Tissu) glacé, lustré; (papier) brillant, satiné. *(b) Cer:* Glacé, émaillé; *(of brick)* vitrifié. *(c) Cu:* Glacé, doré. **glazing,** *s. (a)* Pose *f* des vitres. *(b)* Vernissage *m. Cer: etc:* Émaillage *m.*

glazer ['gleizər], *s.* 1. *(Pers.)* Vernisseur *m;* satineur *m.* 2. *(Instrument)* Glaceur *m,* satineur *m.*

glazier ['gleiziər], *s.* Vitrier *m.*

gleam¹ [gliːm], *s. (a)* Lueur *f;* rayon *m* (de lumière). **The first gleams of the sun,** les premières clartés du soleil. **G. of hope,** lueur d'espoir. *(b)* Reflet *m* (d'un couteau); miroitement *m* (d'un lac). **gleam²,** *v.i.* Luire, reluire; *(of water)* miroiter. **gleaming¹,** *a.* Luisant. **gleaming²,** *s.* Miroitement *m.*

glean [gliːn], *v.tr.* 1. Glaner (du blé, des renseignements). 2. *Vit:* Grappiller. **gleaning,** *s.* 1. *(a)* Glane *f. (b) Vit:* Grappillage *m.* 2. *pl.* **Gleanings,** glanure(s) *f.*

gleaner ['gliːnər], *s.* 1. Glaneur, -euse. 2. *Vit:* Grappilleur, -euse.

glebe [gliːb], *s.* 1. *Poet: A:* Glèbe *f.* 2. *Ecc:* Terre assignée à un bénéfice.

glee [gliː], *s.* 1. Joie *f,* allégresse *f.* 2. *Mus:* Petit chant à trois ou quatre parties.

gleeful ['gliːf(u)l], *a.* Joyeux, allègre. **-fully,** *adv.* Joyeusement; allégrement. **She g. pointed out his mistake,** elle lui indiqua son erreur avec un petit air de triomphe.

glen [glen], *s.* Vallée étroite; vallon *m.*

glengarry [glen'gæri], *s.* (Coiffure écossaise) Toque *f* (haute sur le devant).

glib [glib], *a. Pej: (a) (Of answer)* Spécieux, patelin. *(b) (Of speaker)* Qui a de la faconde. **To have a g. tongue,** avoir le débit facile. **-ly,** *adv. (a)* Spécieusement. *(b)* (Parler) avec aisance.

glibness ['glibnis], *s.* 1. Spéciosité *f* (d'une excuse). 2. Faconde *f; F:* bagout *m.*

glide¹ [glaid], *s.* 1. *(a)* Glissement *m. (b) Danc:* Glissade *f.* 2. *Av:* Vol plané. **G. path,** axe *m* de descente. 3. *Mus:* Port *m* de voix. 4. *Ling:* son *m* transitoire. **glide²,** *v.i. (a)* (Se) glisser, couler. **To g. past,** passer tout doucement. **The years g. past,** les années coulent. *(b) Av:* (i) Planer. (ii) Faire du vol à voile. **gliding,** *s. (a)* Glissement *m. (b)* Vol plané.

glider ['glaidər], *s. Av: (Machine)* Planeur *m.*

glimmer¹ ['glimər], *s.* Faible lueur *f* (d'une chandelle); miroitement *m* (de l'eau). **G. of hope,** lueur d'espoir. **Not the slightest g. of intelligence,** pas la moindre trace d'intelligence. **glimmer²,** *v.i.* Jeter une faible lueur; *(of water)* miroiter.

glimpse¹ [glim(p)s], *s.* Vision momentanée (de qch.). **G. of a subject,** aperçu *m* sur un sujet. **To catch a g. of sth.,** entrevoir, aviser, apercevoir, qch. **I only caught a g. of him,** je n'ai fait que l'entrevoir. **glimpse²,** *v.tr.* **To g. sth.,** avoir la vision fugitive de qch.; entrevoir qch.

glint¹ [glint], *s.* Trait *m,* éclair *m* (de lumière); reflet *m* (d'un couteau). **glint²,** *v.i.* Entreluire. étinceler.

glissade¹ [gli'saːd], *s.* Glissade *f.* **glissade²,** *v.i.* 1. *Danc:* Faire une glissade. 2. *Mount:* Filer en ramasse.

glisten ['glisn], *v.i.* Étinceler, reluire, scintiller.

glitter¹ ['glitər], *s.* Étincellement *m,* scintillement *m,* éclat *m,* brillant *m.* **glitter²,** *v.i.* Scintiller, étinceler, (re)luire; *(of sea)* brasiller. *Prov:* **All is not gold that glitters,** tout ce qui brille n'est pas or. **glittering,** *s.* Étincellement *m,* scintillement *m.*

gloaming ['gloumiŋ], *s.* Crépuscule *m* (du soir). **In the g.,** entre chien et loup; à la brune.

gloat [glout], *v.i.* **To g. over sth.,** faire des gorges chaudes de qch.; savourer (un spectacle). **To g. over one's victim,** couver du regard sa victime. **To g. over the news,** se réjouir (méchamment) de la nouvelle. **To g. over s.o.'s misfortune,** triompher du malheur de qn. **gloating,** *a.* (Œil) avide; (sourire) d'exultation méchante.

global ['gloubl], *a.* 1. Global, -aux (poids, etc.). 2. Mondial. **G. war(fare),** guerre mondiale.

globe [gloub], *s.* 1. Globe *m. (a)* Sphère *f. (b)* (La) terre. *(c) Sch:* Globe terrestre. *(d)* Globe (de lampe). *(e)* Bocal *m,* -aux (pour poissons rouges). **'globe-artichoke,** *s. Hort:* Artichaut *m.* **'globe-trotter,** *s.* Touriste *mf* qui court le monde, *F:* globe-trotter *m.*

globular ['globjulər], *a.* Globulaire, globuleux, -euse.

globule ['globjuːl], *s.* Globule *m,* gouttelette *f* (d'eau).

globulin ['globjulin], *s. Physiol:* Globuline *f.*

gloom [gluːm], *s.* 1. Obscurité *f,* ténèbres *fpl.* 2. Assombrissement *m.* mélancolie *f.* **To cast a g. over the company,** attrister l'assemblée.

gloominess ['gluːminis], *s.* 1. Assombrissement *m. (a)* Obscurité *f* (du temps). *(b)* Tristesse *f* (de qn).

gloomy ['gluːmi], *a.* 1. Sombre, obscur, ténébreux. 2. Lugubre, morne, sombre. **The weather is g.,** il fait sombre. **G. picture,** tableau poussé au noir. **To see the g. side of things,** voir (tout en) noir. **-ily,** *adv.* Sombrement, lugubrement.

glorification [ˌglɔːrifiˈkeiʃ(ə)n], *s.* Glorification *f.*

glorify ['glɔːrifai], *v.tr.* Glorifier, exalter, magnifier. *Theol:* Glorifié. 2. *F: (Of thg)* En plus grand; en mieux. **Their chapel is only a g. barn,** leur temple n'est guère qu'une grange.

glorious ['glɔːriəs], *a.* 1. *(Règne)* glorieux. **G. deed,** action éclatante. 2. *(a)* Resplendissant, radieux. **A g. day,** une journée radieuse. *(b)* Magnifique, superbe. **What g. weather!** quel temps magnifique! *Iron:* **A g. mess,** un joli gâchis. **-ly,** *adv.* 1. Glorieusement. 2. Magnifiquement.

glory[1] ['glɔ:ri], s. Gloire f. **1.** (a) Honneur m, renommée f. **To cover oneself with g.**, se couvrir de gloire. (b) **G. be to God!** gloire à Dieu! P: **G.(be)! grand Dieu!** (c) **The saints in g.**, les glorieux. O: **To go to g.**, (i) mourir; (ii) F: (of thg) aller à la ruine. **2.** Splendeur f, éclat m (d'un spectacle). **3.** U.S: F: **Old G.**, la bannière étoilée (des États-Unis). '**glory-hole**, s. F: Capharnaüm m; cambuse f, (chambre f de) débarras m.

glory[2], v.i. **To g. in sth.**, se glorifier de qch.; être fier de qch. **To g. in doing sth.**, se faire gloire, se faire un mérite, de faire qch.

gloss[1] [glɔs], s. **1.** Lustre m, vernis m. Tex: Cati m. attrib. **G. paint**, peinture f vernis. **To take the g. off sth.**, délustrer qch; Tex: décatir (une étoffe). **2.** F: **To put a g. on the truth**, farder la vérité.

gloss[2], v.tr. **1.** Lustrer, glacer. Tex: Catir (l'étoffe). **2.** F: **To g. over s.o.'s faults**, glisser sur les défauts de qn. **To g. over the facts**, farder les faits.

glossary ['glɔsəri], s. Glossaire m, lexique m.

glossiness ['glɔsinis], s. Lustre m, vernis m; éclat soyeux (des cheveux).

glossy ['glɔsi], a. Lustré, glacé, brillant, brillanté. Phot: **G. paper**, papier brillant. **G. print**, épreuve glacée. **G. magazine**, revue f de luxe.

glottal ['glɔtl], a. Ling: **G. stop**, coup m de glotte.

glottis ['glɔtis], s. Anat: Glotte f.

glove[1] [glʌv], s. Gant m. (a) **Suède gloves**, gants de suède. **Fur-lined gloves**, gants fourrés. **The g. counter** (in shop), la ganterie. El.E: **Wiring-gloves**, moufles f. **To put on one's gloves**, mettre ses gants; se ganter. **To take off one's gloves**, se déganter. Aut: **G. compartment**, boîte f à gants. (b) Box: (Boxing-)g., gant (de boxe). **To put on the gloves**, mettre les gants. F: **To handle s.o. with the gloves off**, traiter qn sans ménagement. '**glove-factory**, s. Ganterie f. '**glove-maker**, s. Gantier, -ière. '**glove-making**, s. Ganterie f. '**glove-shop**, s. Ganterie f. '**glove-stretcher**, s. Ouvre-gants m inv. '**glove-trade**, s. Ganterie f. '**glove-wear**, s. Ganterie f.

glove[2], v.tr. Ganter.

glover ['glʌvər], s. Gantier, -ière.

glow[1] [glou], s. **1.** Lueur f rouge; incandescence f. **In a g.**, (i) incandescent, chauffé au rouge; (ii) (of coal) embrasé. **2.** (a) Physiol: Sensation f de douce chaleur. F: **The exercise had put me all in a g.**, l'exercice m'avait fouetté le sang. (b) Ardeur f, chaleur f. **In the first g. of enthusiasm**, dans l'exaltation première. **3. The g. of health**, l'éclat du teint dû à la santé. '**glow-lamp**, s. El: Lampe f à incandescence. '**glow-worm**, s. Ent: Ver luisant; lampyre m.

glow[2], v.i. **1.** Rougeoyer, Lit: rutiler. **To (begin to) g.**, (i) (of metal) rougir; (ii) (of coal) s'embraser; (iii) El: (of lamp) s'allumer. **2.** (a) Rayonner. (b) His cheeks glowed, il avait les joues en feu. **3.** Sentir une douce chaleur (dans le corps). **glowing**, a. **1.** Incandescent, rougeoyant, Lit: rutilant. **2.** (Of coal) Embrasé. **3.** Rayonnant. **G. cheeks**, joues rouges, vermeilles. **G. with health**, éclatant de santé. **4.** (Of description, etc.) Chaleureux; (of pers.) ardent. **To paint sth. in g. colours**, présenter une affaire sous un jour des plus favorables. **To speak in g. terms of s.o.**, dire merveille de qn.

glower ['glauər], v.i. **To g. at s.o.**, regarder qn d'un air fâché ou menaçant.

gloxinia [glɔk'sinjə], s. Bot: Gloxinia f.

gloze [glouz], v.i. **To g. over (sth.)**, glisser sur, pallier (les défauts).

glucose ['glu:kous], s. Glucose m, sucre m de raisin.

glue[1] [glu:], s. Colle (forte). **Marine g.**, glu marine. '**glue-pot**, s. Pot m à colle.

glue[2], v.tr. (**glued**; **gluing**) (a) Coller (à la colle forte) (to, on, à). (b) F: **Her face was glued to the window**, son visage était collé à la vitre. **His eyes were glued on the door**, il ne détachait pas les yeux de la porte.

gluey ['glu(:)i], a. Gluant, poisseux.

glum [glʌm], a. (Visage) renfrogné, maussade. **To look g.**, se renfrogner. **-ly**, adv. D'un air maussade.

glume [glu:m], s. Bot: Glume f, balle f.

glumness ['glʌmnis], s. Air m sombre.

glut[1] [glʌt], s. **1.** (a) Rassasiement m (de l'appétit). (b) Excès m (de nourriture). **2.** Com: (a) Encombrement m (du marché). (b) Surabondance f (d'une denrée). **There is a g. of pears on the market**, le marché regorge de poires.

glut[2], v.tr. (**glutted**) (a) **To g. oneself**, se rassasier, se gorger. **Glutted with food**, soûl de manger. (b) Com: Encombrer, inonder (le marché).

gluten ['glu:tən], s. Gluten m.

glutinous ['glu:tinəs], a. Glutineux, -euse.

glutton ['glʌtn], s. **1.** (a) Gourmand, -ande; glouton, -onne; goulu, -e. (b) F: **He's a g. for work**, c'est un bourreau de travail. Box: **G. for punishment**, encaisseur m. **2.** Z: Glouton.

gluttonous ['glʌt(ə)nəs], a. Glouton, goulu. **-ly**, adv. Gloutonnement.

gluttony ['glʌt(ə)ni], s. Gloutonnerie f, gourmandise f.

glycemia [glai'si:miə], s. Glycémie f.

glycerin(e) ['glisərin, -i:n], s. Ch: etc: Glycérine f.

glycin(e) ['glisin], s. Ch: Glycine f.

glyph [glif], s. Arch: Glyphe f.

glyptics ['gliptiks], s. Engr: Glyptique f.

gnarl [nɑ:l], s. Loupe f, nœud m, broussin m (d'un arbre).

gnarled [nɑ:ld], a. **1.** (Of tree) (a) Noueux. (b) Tortu, tordu. **2.** (Mains) noueuses.

gnash [næʃ], v.tr. **To g. one's teeth**, grincer des dents. **gnashing**, s. Grincement m (des dents).

gnat [næt], s. Ent: Cousin m, moustique m.

gnaw [nɔ:], v.tr. & i. (p.t. **gnawed**; p.p. **gnawed, gnawn**) (a) **To g. (at, into) sth.**, ronger qch. F: **To g. one's fingers with impatience**, se mordre les poings d'impatience. (b) **Gnawed by hunger**, tenaillé par la faim. **gnawing**. **1.** (a) Rongement m. (b) **Gnawings of hunger**, tiraillements m de la faim.

gneiss [nais], s. Geol: Gneiss m.

gnome [noum], s. Myth: Gnome m.

gnomic ['noumik], a. (Poète) gnomique.

gnomon ['noumən], s. Gnomon m.

gnomonic [nou'mɔnik], a. Gnomonique.

gnosis ['nousis], s. Theol: Gnose f.

gnostic ['nɔstik], a. & s. Gnostique (mf).

gnosticism ['nɔstisizm], s. Gnosticisme m; gnose f.

gnu [nu:], s. Z: Gnou m.

go[1] [gou], s. (pl. **goes**) **1.** **To be always on the go**, être toujours à trotter, à courir. **To keep s.o. on the go**, faire trimer qn. **2. To be full of go**, to have plenty of go, être plein d'entrain; avoir de l'allant; avoir beaucoup de dynamisme. **3.** Coup m, essai m. **To have a go at sth.**, (i) tenter l'aventure; (ii) s'attaquer à (un rôti). **Let's have a go!** essayons le coup! F: **To make a go of it**, y réussir. Cards: etc: F: **It's your go**, c'est à vous de jouer. **At one go**, d'un (seul) coup; tout d'une haleine. **4.** F: **That was a near go!** nous l'avons échappé belle! **No go!** rien à faire! **5.** F: O: **It's all the go**, c'est la grande vogue.

go[2], v.i. (thou **goest**, he **goes**; p.t. **went** [went]; p.p. **gone** [gɔn]. The aux. is 'have,' occ. 'be.') Aller. **1.** (a) **To go to a place**, aller, se rendre, à un endroit. F: **To go places**, (i) sortir; (ii) voyager; (iii) réussir. **To go to France, to Japan**, aller en France, au Japon. **To go to church**, aller à l'église. **What shall I go in?** que vais-je mettre? **To go to prison**, être mis en prison. **To go to the window**, se mettre à la fenêtre. **To come and go**, aller et venir. **To go to s.o. for sth.**, aller trouver qn pour avoir, obtenir, qch. **To go (on) a journey**, faire un voyage. **To go (for) a walk**, faire une promenade. **To go on foot, on horse-back, by train, by car**, aller à pied, à cheval, par le chemin de fer, en auto. **There he goes!** le voilà qui passe! **Who goes there?** qui va là? qui vive? **To go the shortest way**, prendre par le plus court. **To go (at) ten miles an hour**, faire dix milles à l'heure. **You go first!** (i) partez en tête; (ii) à vous d'abord. **You go next!** à vous ensuite; à votre tour. (b) **This road goes to London**, cette route mène à Londres. (c) **To go to school**, (i) aller à l'école; (ii) fréquenter l'école. **To go on the stage**, monter sur les planches. **To go to sea**, se faire marin. **To go into the army**, F: O: **to go for a soldier**, se faire soldat; s'engager (dans l'armée). **Wine that goes to the head**, vin qui monte à la tête. (d) **To go hungry**, se serrer le ventre. (e) **To go one's own way**, faire à sa guise. (f) **The names**

go in alphabetical order, les noms sont rangés par ordre alphabétique. **Promotion goes by seniority,** l'avancement se fait à l'ancienneté 2. Marcher (a) **To go by steam.** marcher à la vapeur To be going, être en marche. To set a machine going, mettre une machine en marche We must keep industry going, il faut maintenir l'activité de l'industrie. To keep the fire going, entretenir le feu. To make things go, (i) faire marcher rondement les choses; (ii) mettre de l'entrain dans la réunion. F: **How goes it?** ça va bien? comment ça va? (Of play) **To go (well),** réussir. **The rehearsal went well,** la répétition a bien marché. **Things are not going well,** cela ne marche pas. **As things are going,** du train dont vont les choses. **When he gets going he never stops,** une fois lancé, il ne s'arrête plus. F: **What I say, goes,** c'est moi qui commande. (b) (i) **It has just gone twelve,** midi, minuit, vient de sonner. **It has gone six already,** il est déjà six heures passées. F: **The clock went eight,** huit heures sonnèrent. F: **To be gone forty,** avoir quarante ans sonnés, avoir dépassé la quarantaine. (ii) **To go bang,** faire pan. (c) **This is how the chorus goes,** voici les paroles du refrain. **I forget how the tune goes,** l'air m'échappe. (d) (Of contest) Aboutir. **I don't know how matters will go,** je ne sais pas comment cela tournera. **Judgment went for the plaintiff,** l'arrêt fut prononcé en faveur du demandeur. (e) F: **Vendre goes like descendre,** vendre se conjugue comme descendre. 3. (a) (Of time) Passer. **The time will soon go,** le temps passera vite. **Ten minutes gone and nothing done,** dix minutes de passées et rien de fait. (b) **As the saying goes,** comme dit l'autre. **That's not dear as things go,** ce n'est pas cher au prix où sont les choses. (c) **To go by a false name,** être connu sous un faux nom. (d) **That goes without saying,** cela va sans dire. 4. (a) Partir; s'en aller. **After I have gone,** après mon départ. **Don't go yet,** ne vous en allez pas encore. **Let me go!** laissez-moi partir! (Cp. 12 (a).) **Go,** A: **be gone!** allez-vous-en! Sp: **Go!** partez! F: **From the word go,** dès le commencement. (b) **A hundred employees will have to go,** cent employés vont recevoir leur congé. (c) Disparaître. **My hat has gone,** mon chapeau a disparu. **It has, is, all gone,** il n'y en a plus. **The wine is all gone,** le vin est épuisé. **That's the way the money goes,** voilà comme l'argent file. **Her sight is going,** elle est en train de perdre la vue. **His teeth are all gone,** il a perdu toutes ses dents. (d) (i) **The spring went,** le ressort s'est cassé. El: **A fuse went,** un plomb sauta. (ii) **This material goes at the folds,** ce tissu se coupe aux plis. (e) **These spoons are going for two francs each,** ces cuillers sont en vente, en solde, à deux francs pièce. **Going! going! gone!** une fois! deux fois! adjugé! (f) **If I hear of any job going,** si j'apprends qu'une situation se présente. (g) **To go the way of all things,** P: to go west, mourir; F: plier bagage. **She's gone,** elle n'est plus, F: elle est partie. 5. (a) **To go to see s.o.; to go and see s.o.,** aller voir qn; aller trouver qn. **Go and shut the door!** allez fermer la porte! P: **Now you've (been and) gone and done it!** vous en avez fait une belle! (b) (Merely purpose) **To go to do sth.,** aller pour faire qch. (c) (Determination) **I am going to have my own way,** je veux en faire à ma tête. (d) (Intention) **I'm going to spend my holidays abroad,** je compte passer mes vacances à l'étranger. (e) (Immediate future) **I am going to tell you a story,** je vais vous raconter une histoire. (f) **To go hunting, fishing,** aller à la chasse, à la pêche. F: **There you go again!** vous voilà reparti! 6. (a) **To go to law,** aller en justice. **To go to war,** se mettre en guerre. **He will not go to the trouble of . . .,** il ne veut pas prendre, se donner, la peine de. . . . (b) Cards: **To go two, three, no trumps,** annoncer deux, trois, sans atout. **To go one better,** renchérir. 7. (a) (i) **Trunk that will go under the berth,** malle qui se case sous la couchette. (ii) **Where does this book go?** où est la place de ce livre? (b) **Six into twelve goes twice,** douze divisé par six fait deux. 8. **His title will go to his eldest son,** son titre (de noblesse) passera à son fils aîné. **The proceeds will go to charity,** les profits iront à des œuvres de bienfaisance. 9. Contribuer (à qch.). **The qualities that go to make a great man,** les qualités qui constituent un grand

homme. **To go to prove sth.,** servir à prouver qch. 10. S'étendre. **The estate goes down to the river,** la propriété s'étend jusqu'à la rivière. **The report is accurate as far as it goes,** le rapport est exact quant à ce qu'il dit (mais il omet beaucoup de choses). 11 (a) Devenir. **To go mad,** devenir fou. Pol: **The town went labour,** la ville a fait volte-face et a voté socialiste. **To go white, red, etc.,** blanchir, rougir, etc. (See these adjectives). (b) (Of house) **To go to ruin,** tomber en ruine. **His son has gone to the bad,** son fils a mal tourné. 12. (a) **To let go,** lâcher prise. **To let go (one's hold of) sth.,** lâcher, laisser échapper (une corde). **Let me go!** lâchez-moi! (Cp. 4 (a).) Nau: **Let go forward!** larguez devant! (b) **To let oneself go,** se laisser aller. **To let oneself go on a subject,** s'étendre, s'emballer, sur un sujet. (c) **Well, let it go at that!** passons! **We'll let it go at that,** tenons-nous-en là. 13. P: (a) **To go it, to go the pace,** s'en donner à cœur joie; aller grand train. **He's going it!** il se lance! (b) **Go it!** vas-y, allez-y! allez toujours! **go about,** v.i. 1. (a) Aller çà et là; circuler. **There is a rumour going about that . . .,** le bruit court que. . . . **He goes about a great deal,** il sort beaucoup. (b) Nau: Virer de bord. 2. (a) **To go about the streets,** circuler dans les rues. (b) Se mettre à (une tâche). **How to go about it,** comment s'y prendre. (c) **In the morning I go about my work,** le matin je vaque à mes affaires. **go across,** v.i. Traverser, passer (la mer); franchir (le pont). **go after,** v.i. (a) Courir après (les femmes). (b) Solliciter, briguer (un emploi). **go against,** v.i. 1. **If fate goes against us,** si la fortune nous est contraire. **His appearance goes against him,** il ne paye pas de mine. 2. (a) **To go against the tide,** aller, avancer, contre la marée. (b) Aller à l'encontre de, heurter (l'opinion publique). **It goes against my conscience to . . .,** il me répugne de. . . . **go along,** v.i. 1. Passer par (une rue). 2. Passer, suivre, son chemin. **I make up my accounts and check the figures as I go along,** je fais mes comptes et vérifie les chiffres à mesure. F: **Go along with you!** (i) allez, filez! (ii) dites cela à d'autres! **go at,** v.i. S'attaquer à (qn, qch.). **To go at it hard,** y aller de tout son cœur. **go away,** v.i. (a) S'en aller, partir; s'absenter. (b) **To go away with sth.,** emporter, enlever, qch. **going away,** s. Départ m. attrib. G.-a. dress, robe de voyage de noces. **go back,** v.i. 1. (a) **To go back to one's native land,** retourner dans sa patrie. (b) Rebrousser chemin. **To go b. on one's steps,** revenir sur ses pas. (c) **To go b. two paces,** reculer de deux pas. (d) **To go b. to a subject,** revenir sur un sujet. **He went back to his reading,** il se replongea dans sa lecture. **To go b. to the beginning,** recommencer. 2. **To go b. to the Flood,** remonter (jusqu')au déluge. **We won't go b. to the past,** ne revenons pas sur le passé. **His family goes back to the crusaders,** sa famille remonte aux croisés. 3. (a) **To go b. on a promise,** revenir sur sa promesse; se dédire. (b) F: **To go b. on a friend,** lâcher un ami. **going back,** s. 1. (a) Retour m. (b) F: **There's no g. b.,** il n'y a pas à reculer. (b) **There's no g. b. on one's word,** manque m de parole. (b) **There's no g. b. on it,** il n'y a pas à y revenir. (c) F: **G. b. on a friend,** trahison f d'un ami. **go before,** v.i. 1. (a) Devancer, précéder (qn). (b) Primer. **Might went before right,** la force primait le droit. 2. (a) Partir en avant. (b) Marcher devant. **go behind,** v.i. (a) Revenir sur (une décision). (b) **To go b. s.o.'s back,** faire qch. derrière le dos de qn. **go by,** v.i. 1. Passer. **As the years go by,** à mesure que les années passent. **You must not let this chance go by,** il ne faut pas manquer cette occasion. 2. (a) **He went by the shop,** il est passé devant le magasin. (b) **To go by s.o.,** se régler sur qn. **To go by the directions,** suivre les instructions. **To go by appearances,** juger d'après les apparences. **That is nothing to go by,** on ne peut fonder là-dessus. **'go-by,** s. F: **To give s.o. the go-by.** 1. Dépasser, devancer, qn. 2. **He gave me the go-by yesterday,** hier il a fait semblant de ne pas me reconnaître. 3. Oublier qn. **To give s.o.'s orders the go-by,** ne pas tenir compte des ordres de qn. **go down,** v.i. 1. Descendre (l'escalier). 2. (a) Descendre. **To go d. to dinner,** descendre dîner. Sch: **To go d. (from the university),** (i) quitter l'université; (ii) partir en vacances. (b) F: **My dinner won't go d.,** mon dîner a du mal à passer. **That won't go d. with me,** ça ne prend pas avec moi. **To go d. well,** (i) (of drink) se laisser boire; (of food) se laisser manger; (ii) (of play, etc.) être bien reçu. F: **The idea didn't go d. too well with them,** ils ont eu du mal à l'avaler. (c) (Of sun) Se coucher. (d) (Of ship) Couler à fond; sombrer. **To go d. by the bows,** piquer de l'avant. (e) Tomber. **To go d. on one's knees,** se mettre à genoux. (f) (Of temperature) Baisser, s'abaisser. **The neighbourhood has gone down,** ce quartier a déchu. F: **He has gone down in the world,** il a connu des jours meilleurs. (g) (Of swelling) Désenfler; (of balloon, tyre, etc.) se dégonfler. (h) **To go d. to posterity,** passer à la postérité. **go for,** v.i. 1. Aller chercher (qn). 2. (a) F: Tomber sur, fondre sur (qn). (b) F: S'en prendre à (qn); chercher noise à (qn). **To go for s.o. in the papers,** attaquer qn dans les journaux. **go forward,** v.i. Avancer. Nau: Aller devant. **The work is going forward,** le travail avance. **go in,** v.i. 1. **The key goes in the lock,** la clef entre dans cette serrure. 2. (a) Entrer, rentrer. **I must go in to cook the dinner,** il faut que je rentre préparer le dîner. F: **Let's go in!** allons-y! **Shall we go in?** on y va? (b) (Of sun) Se cacher. (c) **To go in for (sth.),** s'occuper de, se mêler de (qch.). **To go in for a course of lectures,** s'inscrire à un cours; suivre un cours. **To go in for sports,** s'adonner aux sports; faire du sport. **To go in for teaching,** entrer dans l'enseignement. **To go in for an examination,** se présenter à un examen. **To go in for a competition,** prendre part à un concours. (d) **To go in with s.o. in an undertaking,** se joindre à qn dans une affaire. 3. Mil: F: Attaquer. 4. Cr: Aller au guichet. **go into,** v.i. 1. (a) Entrer dans (une maison). **To go i. society,** aller dans le monde. **To go i. the army,** entrer dans l'armée. (b) **To go i. a lengthy explanation of sth.,** entrer dans de longues explications. (c) **To go i. mourning,** prendre le deuil. **To go i. fits of laughter,** éclater de rire. **To go i. hysterics,** avoir une crise de nerfs. (d) Aut: **To go i. second (gear),** passer en seconde (vitesse). 2. Examiner, étudier (une question). **To go closely into a question,** approfondir une question. **go off,** v.i. 1. (a) Partir, s'en aller. Th: Quitter la scène. (b) **To go o. with sth.,** emporter qch. (c) (Of gun) Partir. (d) **To go o. to sleep,** s'endormir. **To go off (into a faint),** perdre connaissance; s'évanouir. (e) (Of feeling) Passer. (Of tennis player) Perdre de sa forme; baisser. (f) (Of wine, etc.) S'éventer; perdre; (of fish, meat) se gâter; (of milk) tourner. (g) **Everything went off well,** tout s'est bien passé. (h) Com: (Of goods) Se vendre. 2. (a) **To go o. the rails,** (i) (of train) dérailler; (ii) F: (of pers.) dérailler, déraisonner. **To go off the beaten track,** s'écarter du chemin battu. S.a. DEEP. (b) **I have gone off motoring,** je ne fais plus d'auto. **I've gone off eggs,** je ne mange plus d'œufs, j'ai perdu le goût des œufs. **'go-'off,** s. (At) first go-o., au premier essai, du premier coup. **go on,** v.i. 1. (a) (i) **Time goes on,** le temps marche. (ii) Continuer sa route; poursuivre sa course. (iii) **He is going on for forty,** il va sur la quarantaine. **It is going on for three o'clock,** il est près de trois heures. (b) Continuer (de faire qch.); reprendre la parole. **If you go on like this . . .,** si vous continuez. . . . **I've got enough to go on with,** j'ai de quoi marcher. (c) **I shall now go on to another matter,** je passe maintenant à une autre question. **He went on to give me all the details,** puis il me donna tous les détails. F: (Iron:) **Go on!** allons donc! dites ça à d'autres! (d) Marcher. **This has gone on for years,** cela dure depuis des années. **Preparations are going on,** les préparatifs se poursuivent. **What is going on here?** qu'est-ce qui se passe ici? **How are you going on?** comment cela marche-t-il? comment allez-vous? **To go on as before,** faire comme par le passé. (e) F: Se conduire. **I don't like the way she goes on,** je n'aime pas son manège. (f) F: **To go on at s.o.,** gourmander qn. P: **She went on dreadfully,** elle nous a fait une scène terrible. (g) Th: **To go on,** monter en scène; entrer en scène. 2. (a) **I went on that supposition,** je me suis fondé sur cette hypothèse. (b) **Those shoes won't go on,** ces souliers sont trop petits. **'goings-'on,** s.pl. F: Conduite f; manège

m. **go out,** v.i. 1. (a) Sortir. **Out you go!** hors d'ici! **She was dressed to go o.,** elle était en tenue de ville. **To go o. (on strike),** se mettre en grève. **I am going out to dinner,** je dîne en ville; je dîne chez des amis. **My heart went out to him,** je ressentis de la pitié pour lui. (b) Aller dans le monde; sortir. F: **He was going out with her for two years before they got married,** il l'a fréquentée pendant deux ans avant de se marier. (c) Être mis en circulation. **This communiqué should never have gone out,** on n'aurait pas dû publier ce communiqué. 2. **To go o. of fashion,** passer de mode. 3. Disparaître. **All the hatred had gone out of his voice,** toute la haine avait disparu de sa voix. 4. Pol: Quitter le pouvoir. 5. Games: **How many points do you need to go out?** combien de points vous faut-il pour gagner? 6. **To go o. of one's way,** s'écarter de son chemin. S.a. WAY[1] 2 (a). 7. Terminer. 8. (Of fire) S'éteindre; (of pers.) mourir. 9. (Of tide) Baisser. **going out,** s. 1. Sortie f. **To like g. o.,** aimer à sortir. 2. Baisse f (de la marée). **go over,** v.i. 1. (a) Traverser, passer (la mer). (b) **To go o. a drawing with ink,** passer un dessin à l'encre. (c) Examiner (un compte). **To go o. a house,** visiter une maison. **To go o. the ground,** reconnaître le terrain. (d) **To go o. sth. in one's mind,** repasser qch. dans son esprit. 2. **To go o. to the enemy,** passer à l'ennemi. **go round,** v.i. 1. (a) (i) Faire un détour, un circuit. **You'll have to go r.,** il faudra faire le tour. (ii) F: **To go r. to see s.o.,** rendre visite à qn. (b) (Of wheel) Tourner. **My head is going round,** la tête me tourne. (c) (Of rumour) Circuler, courir. (d) **There is not enough to go r.,** il n'y en a pas pour tout le monde. 2. **To go r. the town,** faire le tour de la ville. **go through,** v.i. 1. (a) Passer par (un trou); traverser (un pays). **A shiver went through me,** un frisson me parcourut. (b) Passer par, suivre en entier (un cours d'études). **To go t. one's apprenticeship,** faire son apprentissage. **To go t. the whole programme,** exécuter tout le programme. (c) **The book has gone through ten editions,** on a déjà tiré dix éditions de ce livre. (d) Remplir, accomplir (des formalités); subir, essuyer (de rudes épreuves). F: **I have gone through it,** j'ai passé par là. F: **He's gone through a lot,** il en a vu des vertes et des pas mûres. (e) Transpercer, percer. **This cold goes right through me,** ce froid me transit. (f) Examiner en détail. (i) Compulser (des documents). (ii) Fouiller dans (les poches de qn). (g) Manger (une fortune). 2. (a) **The bill has gone through,** on a voté le projet de loi. **The deal did not go through,** le marché n'a pas été conclu. (b) **To go t. with sth.,** aller jusqu'au bout (d'une épreuve). **We've got to go t. with it,** F: le vin est tiré, il faut le boire. (c) **To go t. with a divorce,** divorcer. **go together,** v.i. (a) (Of misfortunes) Marcher ensemble. (b) (Of colours) S'accorder; aller bien ensemble. (c) P: (Of man and woman) Être bien ensemble. **go under,** v.i. Succomber, sombrer. **go up,** v.i. 1. (a) Monter; aller en haut. **A cry went up from the crowd,** un cri s'éleva de la foule. Sch: **To go up a form,** monter d'une classe. (b) **To go up to the university,** entrer à l'université. **To go up to s.o.,** s'avancer vers qn; aborder qn. (c) (Of price, temperature) Monter, hausser. **Bread is going up (in price),** le pain renchérit. (d) (Of mine) Sauter. **To go up in flames,** se mettre à flamber. 2. Monter (une colline). **To go up a ladder,** monter à une échelle. **To go up a river,** remonter une rivière. Mil: **To go up the line,** monter en ligne. **go with,** v.i. 1. (a) Accompagner. P: **To go w. a girl,** faire la cour à, sortir avec, une jeune fille. (b) **Salary that goes with an office,** traitement applicable à une fonction. (c) **To go w. the times,** marcher avec son époque. 2. S'accorder avec (qch.); se marier avec (une teinte). **go without,** v.i. (a) (Do without) Se passer de (qch.). **To go w. food,** se passer de nourriture, F: se serrer le ventre; se mettre la ceinture. (b) (Be without) Manquer de (qch.). **gone,** a. 1. (a) Disparu, parti. **I won't be g. long,** je ne serai pas longtemps absent. (b) Mort. 2. **He is too far g. to speak,** (i) il est trop bas pour parler; (ii) F: il est dans un état d'ivresse trop avancé pour parler. F: **She's five months g.,** elle est enceinte de cinq mois. 3. F: **To be g. on s.o.,** être amoureux, épris, de qn. **going[1],** a. 1. Qui marche. **The business is a g. concern,** la maison est en pleine activité. **2. One of the best firms g.,** une des meilleures maisons qui soient. **going**[2], *s.* **1.** (*a*) **Comings and goings,** allées *f* et venues *f*. (*b*) **Eight miles in two hours, that's very good g.!** huit milles en deux heures, c'est bien marché! (*c*) **G. to law,** recours *m* à la justice. *Typ:* **G. to press,** mise *f* sous presse. **2.** Départ *m*. **3. Rough g.,** chemin rude. *F:* **To go while the g. is good,** profiter de ce que les circonstances sont favorables. **'go-ahead. 1.** *a.* Plein d'allant; entreprenant. **2.** *s. F:* **To give s.o. the go-a.,** donner à qn le feu vert. **'go-as-you-'please,** *attrib.a.* **1.** (Vie) libre. **2.** (Travail) sans méthode. **'go-between,** *s.* Intermédiaire *mf*; entremetteur, -euse. **'go-cart,** *s.* Chaise pliante, charrette pliante (pour enfants); trotteuse *f* (pour apprendre à marcher aux bébés). **'go-'getter,** *s. U.S:* Arriviste *m*. **'go-kart,** *s.* Kart *m*. **Go-k. racing,** karting *m*. **'go-'slow,** *a.* Go-s. (strike), travail *m* au ralenti, grève perlée.

goad[1] [goud], *s.* Aiguillon *m*.

goad[2], *v.tr.* Aiguillonner, piquer. **To g. s.o. on,** aiguillonner, inciter, qn.

goal [goul], *s.* **1.** But *m*. (*a*) **My g. is in sight,** j'approche de mon but. (*b*) *Fb:* **To score, kick, a g.,** marquer, réussir, un but. **To keep g.,** garder le but. **'goal-keeper,** *s. Fb: etc:* Gardien *m* de but; garde-but *m*, *F:* le goal. **'goal-line,** *s. Fb:* Ligne *f* de but. **'goal-mouth,** *s. Fb:* Entrée *f* du but. **'goal-post,** *s. Fb:* Montant *m* de but. **'goal-scorer,** *s. Sp:* Buteur *m*.

goat [gout], *s.* **1.** Chèvre *f*. **She-g.,** bique *f*, chèvre. **He-g.,** bouc *m*. **Old he-g.,** bouquin *m*. **Young g.,** chevreau, *f*. chevrette. *F:* **Don't play the g.,** ne faites pas l'imbécile. *F:* **He gets my g.,** il m'irrite. **2.** *Astr:* **The G.,** le Capricorne.

goatee [gou'ti:], *s.* Barbiche *f*, bouc *m*.

goatherd ['goutha:d], *s.* Chevrier, -ière.

goatskin ['goutskin], *s.* **1.** Peau *f* de chèvre; peau *f* de bique. **2.** (*Bottle*) Outre *f*.

goatsucker ['goutsʌkər], *s. Orn:* Engoulevent *m*; *F:* tête-chèvre *m*.

gob [gob], *s. P:* Bouche *f*, gueule *f*. **Shut your g.!** la ferme!

gobble[1] ['gobl], *v.tr.* **To g. (up) sth.,** avaler qch. goulûment.

gobble[2], *v.i.* (*Of turkey-cock*) Glouglouter.

gobbler ['goblər], *s.* Dindon *m*.

goblet ['goblit], *s.* **1.** *A:* (*a*) Gobelet *m*. (*b*) *Lit:* Coupe *f*. **2.** *Com:* Verre *m* à pied.

goblin ['goblin], *s.* Gobelin *m*, lutin *m*.

goby ['goubi], *s. Ich:* Gobie *m*.

god [god], *s.* **1.** (*a*) Dieu *m*. *F:* **Feast (fit) for the gods,** festin digne des dieux. **To make a (little tin) g. of s.o.,** se faire un dieu de qn. *F:* **O: Ye gods (and little fishes)!** grands dieux! (*b*) *Th:* **The gods,** le poulailler, le paradis. **2.** Dieu; *F:* le bon Dieu. **God willing,** s'il plaît à Dieu. **Would to God . . . ,** plût à Dieu. . . . *F:* **What in God's name are you doing?** que faites-vous là, grand Dieu! **G. Almighty!** Dieu tout-puissant! **Thank G.!** Dieu merci! grâce au ciel! **'god-child,** *pl.* **-children,** *s.* Filleul, *f*. filleule. **'god-daughter,** *s.f.* Filleule. **'god-for-saken,** *a. F:* **G.-f. place,** endroit perdu, *F:* trou. **What a g.-f. country!** quel fichu pays! **'god-parent,** *s.* Le parrain ou la marraine. **'God's 'acre,** *s.* Le cimetière. **god-'speed,** *s. O:* **To bid s.o. g.-s.,** souhaiter bon voyage à qn.

goddess ['godis], *s.f.* Déesse.

godfather ['godfɑ:ðər], *s.m.* Parrain.

godhead ['godhed], *s.* Divinité *f*. **The G.,** Dieu *m*.

godless ['godlis], *a.* Athée, impie.

godlessness ['godlisnis], *s.* Impiété *f*.

godliness ['godlinis], *s.* Piété *f*.

godly ['godli], *a.* Dévot, pieux, saint.

godmother ['godmʌðər], *s.f.* Marraine.

godsend ['godsend], *s.* Aubaine *f*, bénédiction *f*; bienfait *m* du ciel.

godship ['godʃip], *s.* Divinité *f*.

godson ['godsʌn], *s.m.* Filleul.

goer ['gouər], *s.* **1.** Celui, celle, qui part. **2.** (*Of horse*) **Good g., bad g.,** bon, mauvais, marcheur. **3.** *In compounds.* **Theatre g.,** habitué, -ée, des théâtres.

goffer[1] ['gofər, 'gou-], *s.* **1.** *Cost:* Godron *m*, tuyau *m*, plissé *m*. **2.** Fer *m* à tuyauter, à gaufrer.

goffer[2], *v.tr. Laund:* Gaufrer; tuyauter; plisser.

goffering, *s. Laund:* Gaufrage *m*; tuyautage *m*; plissage *m*. **G.-tongs, g.-iron(s),** fer *m* à tuyauter, à gaufrer.

goggle[1] ['gogl], *v.i.* (*a*) Rouler de gros yeux. (*b*) (*Of the eyes*) Être saillants.

goggle[2], *a.* (Yeux) à fleur de tête. *F:* **G. box,** télévision. **'goggle-eyed,** *a.* Qui a des yeux à fleur de tête, *F:* en boules de loto.

goggles ['goglz], *s.pl. Ind: Aut:* Lunettes (protectrices).

goitre ['goitər], *s. Med:* Goitre *m*.

gold [gould], *s.* (*a*) Or *m*. **G. in nuggets,** or brut. **Ingot g.,** en or en barres. *St.Exch:* **G. shares,** valeurs aurifères. **The Bank's g. reserve,** le stock d'or de la Banque. *U.S: P:* **To sell s.o. a g. brick,** escroquer, filouter, qn. (*b*) (Pièces *fpl* d'or). (*c*) **Dutch g.,** oripeau *m. Cost:* **Worked with g.,** lamé (d'or). (*d*) **Couleur *f* de l'or. Old-g. (colour),** vieil or *inv*. **'gold-bearing,** *a.* (Filon, etc.) aurifère. **'gold-beater,** *s.* Batteur, -euse, d'or. **gold-'cased,** *a.* Doublé d'or. **'gold-digger,** *s.* **1.** Chercheur *m* d'or. **2.** *F:* (*Of woman*) Exploiteuse *f* d'hommes riches. **'gold-digging,** *s.* (*a*) Exploitation *f* de quartz aurifère. (*b*) *pl.* **Gold-diggings,** placer *m*. **'gold-dust,** *s.* Poudre *f*, poussière *f*, d'or. **'gold-fever,** *s.* Fièvre *f* de l'or. **'gold-field,** *s.* Champ *m* aurifère. *pl.* **Gold-fields,** districts *m* aurifères, régions *f* aurifères. **'gold-fish,** *s.* Poisson *m* rouge. **'gold-foil,** *s.* Feuille *f* d'or. **gold-'laced,** *a.* Galonné d'or; chamarré d'or. **'gold-leaf,** *s.* Feuille *f* d'or; or *m* en feuille. **'gold-mine,** *s.* Mine *f* d'or. *F:* **A regular g.-m.,** une affaire d'or. **'gold-nibbed,** *a.* (Stylo) avec plume en or. **gold 'plate,** *s.* Vaisselle *f* d'or. **gold-'plated,** *a.* Doublé d'or. **'gold-rimmed,** *a.* (Monocle, etc.) cerclé d'or. **G.-r. spectacles,** lunettes à monture d'or. **'gold-rush,** *s.* Ruée *f* vers l'or. **'gold-tipped,** *a.* **A bout doré. 'gold-washer,** *s.* Orpailleur *m*.

golden ['gould(ə)n], *a.* D'or. (*a*) **The G. Fleece,** la Toison d'or. (*b*) **G. hair,** cheveux, chevelure, d'or d'un blond doré. (*c*) **G. rule,** règle par excellence, précieuse. **'golden-'rod,** *s. Bot:* Solidago *m*; verge *f* d'or. **'golden 'wedding,** *s.* Noces *fpl* d'or. **To celebrate one's g. w.,** célébrer la cinquantaine.

goldfinch ['gouldfin(t)ʃ], *s.* Chardonneret *m*.

goldsmith ['gouldsmiθ], *s.* Orfèvre *m*. **G.'s work,** orfèvrerie *f*.

golf[1] [golf], *s.* Golf *m*. **'golf-club,** *s.* **1.** Crosse *f* de golf; club *m*. **2.** Club de golf. **'golf-course,** *s.* **'golf-links,** *s.pl.* Terrain *m* de golf; *F:* un golf.

golf[2], *v.i.* Jouer au golf.

golfer ['golfər], *s.* Golfeur, -euse.

golly ['goli], *int. O:* Fichtre! mince (alors)!

golosh [gə'loʃ], *s.* = GALOSH.

gonad ['gonæd], *s. Biol:* Gonade *f*.

gondola ['gondələ], *s.* **1.** *Nau:* Gondole *f*. **2.** Gondole, nacelle *f* (d'un dirigeable). **3.** *U.S: Rail:* Wagon à marchandises ouvert.

gondolier [,gondə'liər], *s.* Gondolier *m*.

gone. *See* GO[2].

goner ['gonər], *s. P:* **1.** Homme mort, femme morte. **2.** Homme ruiné. **He's a g.,** c'en est fait de lui, *P:* il est foutu.

gong[1] [goŋ], *s.* (*a*) Gong *m*. (*b*) *Ind: Nau:* **Alarm g.,** timbre avertisseur. (*c*) *P:* Décoration *f* militaire, *P:* banane *f*.

gong[2], *v.tr. Aut:* **To be gonged,** se faire siffler, *F:* se faire épingler.

goniometer [,gouni'omitər], *s.* Goniomètre *m*.

goniometry [,gouni'omitri], *s.* Goniométrie *f*.

gonococcus, *pl.* **-cocci** [,gono'kokəs, -'kokai], *s. Bac: Med:* Gonocoque *m*.

gonorrhoea [,gonə'riə], *s. Med:* Gonorrhée *f*; blennorragie *f*.

goo [gu:], *s. F:* **1.** Substance collante. **2.** Sentimentalité *f* à l'eau de rose.

good [gud]. **I.** *a.* (**better, best**) Bon. **1.** (*a*) **G. wine,** bon vin; vin de bonne qualité. **G. handwriting,** belle écriture. **G. story,** bonne histoire. *F:* **That's a g. one!** en voilà une bonne! **G. to eat,** bon à manger. **Give me something g.**, donnez-moi quelque chose de bien, de bon. **I've had a g. life**, j'ai bien rempli ma vie; j'ai eu une vie agréable. *Pol: F:* **You've never had it so g.**, le pays n'a jamais été si prospère. **This is g. enough for me**, cela fera mon affaire. **That's not g. enough**, (i) je n'accepte pas cela; (ii) *F:* ça c'est un peu fort! **G. business men**, excellents hommes d'affaires. **In g. plain English**, en bon anglais. **To have g. sight**, avoir de bons yeux. *(b)* *(Of food)* **To keep g.**, rester bon; se conserver. *(c)* **G. reason, excuse**, raison, excuse, valable. **G. debt**, bonne créance. **Chit g. for ten shillings**, bon *m* de dix shillings. *F:* **How much is he g. for?** on peut compter sur lui pour combien? **Ticket g. for two months**, billet valable, bon, pour deux mois. **He is g. for another ten years**, il en a encore bien pour dix ans à vivre. *(d)* Avantageux. **G. marriage**, mariage avantageux; bon parti. **G. opportunity**, bonne occasion. **They are people of g. position**, ce sont des gens bien. **I thought g. to do so**, il m'a semblé bon d'en faire ainsi. **A g. day** (at the races), un jour de veine. **To make a g. thing out of sth.**, tirer bon parti de qch. **To earn g. money**, gagner largement sa vie. *(e)* Heureux. **G. news**, bonnes, heureuses, nouvelles. **It is too g. to be believed**, c'est trop beau pour y croire. **G. for you!** (i) tant mieux pour toi, pour vous! (ii) à la bonne heure! **G. (job)! that's a g. thing!** c'est bien heureux! tant mieux! à la bonne heure! bon! **Very g.!** très bien! **It was a g. thing she called on him**, bien lui (en) a pris d'aller le voir. **How g. it is to . . .**, comme il est agréable de. . . . *(f)* *(As salutation)* **G. morning! g. day! g. afternoon!** bonjour! **G. evening!** bonsoir! **G. night!** (i) bonsoir! (ii) *(on retirement to bed)* bonne nuit! **To wish s.o. g. night**, souhaiter (le) bonsoir à qn. *(g)* **Beer is not g. for me**, la bière ne me vaut rien. **To drink more than is g. for one**, boire plus que de raison. *(h)* **He's g. with his hands**, il est adroit, il est habile de ses mains. **G. for nothing**, bon à rien. **He is g. for nothing**, c'est un propre à rien. *(i)* **G. at Latin**, bon, fort, *F:* calé, en latin. **He is g. at all sports**, il excelle à tous les sports. *(j) F:* **To feel g.**, se sentir gaillard, bien en train. **2.** *(a)* **G. man**, homme de bien. **To lead a g. life**, vivre en homme de bien; mener une vie exemplaire. *O:* **The g. people**, les fées *f. s.* **The g. and the bad**, les bons et les méchants. **G. old John!** bravo Jean! *A. & Lit:* **The g. ship Arethusa**, l'Aréthuse *f.* *(b)* *(Of children)* Sage. **As g. as gold**, sage comme une image. **Be a g. child!** sois sage! *(c) O:* **Her g. man**, son mari. **His g. lady**, sa femme. *(d)* Aimable. **That's very g. of you**, c'est bien aimable à vous. **Will you be g. enough to** + *inf.*, je vous prie, puis-je vous demander, de vouloir bien + *inf.* **To be g. to animals**, être bon pour les animaux. **He is a g. sort**, c'est un brave garçon. *(e)* **G. Lord, deliver us!** Seigneur, délivrez-nous! *F:* **G. Lord! G. Heavens!** grand Dieu! par exemple! **3.** *(Intensive)* *(a)* **To wait two g. hours**, attendre deux grandes heures. **A g. long time, a g. while**, pas mal de temps. **You still have a g. way to go**, vous avez encore un bon bout de chemin à faire. **A g. deal**, beaucoup. **A g. many people, a g. few people**, beaucoup de gens; pas mal de gens. **After a g. cry . . .**, après avoir bien pleuré. . . . *(b) adv. F:* **To dress s.o. down g. (and proper)**, tancer qn de la belle manière. **4. As g. as.** **My family is as g. as his**, ma famille vaut bien la sienne. **To give s.o. as g. as one gets**, rendre la pareille à qn. **It is as g. as new**, c'est comme neuf. **It is as g. as done**, c'est une affaire faite ou autant vaut. **As g. as cured**, quasiment guéri. **5. To make g.** *(a)* Se rattraper de (ses pertes); remédier à (l'usure); réparer (une injustice). **I will make it g. to you**, je vous en dédommagerai. *(b)* Justifier (une affirmation); remplir (sa promesse). *(c)* Effectuer (sa retraite). **To make g. one's escape**, parvenir à s'échapper. *(d)* Assurer (sa position); faire prévaloir (ses droits). *(e) Abs.* (i) Prospérer. (ii) Racheter son passé. **II. good, s. 1.** Bien *m. (a)* **To do g.** (in the world), faire du bien. **He will never do any more good**, il ne fera plus jamais rien de bon. **He is up to no g.**, il prépare quelque mauvais coup. **There's some g. in him**, il a du bon. *(b)* **I did it for your g.**, je l'ai fait pour votre bien. **For the g. of one's**

health, en vue de sa santé. **To work for the common g.**, travailler pour le bien public. *F:* **Much g. may it do you!** grand bien vous fasse! *F:* **A (fat) lot of g. that will do you!** c'est ça qui vous fera une belle jambe! la belle avance! **That won't be much g.**, ça ne servira pas à grand-chose. **It is no g. saying . . .**, rien ne sert de dire. . . . **No g. talking about it**, inutile d'en parler. **He will come to no g.**, il tournera mal. **He's no g.**, il est nul; c'est une non-valeur. *(c)* **It is all to the g.**, c'est autant de gagné; tant mieux. *(d) Adv.phr.* **He is gone for g. (and all)**, il est parti définitivement, pour (tout) de bon. **2.** *pl.* **Goods.** *(a) Jur:* Biens, effets *m.* *(b)* (Comme singulier on emploie le mot COMMODITY.) Objets *m*, articles *m*; *Com:* marchandise(s) *f.* **To deliver the goods**, (i) livrer la marchandise (ii) *P:* remplir ses engagements. *U.S: P:* **To have the goods**, être capable. *F:* **That's the goods!** à la bonne heure! *U.S:* **To have the goods on s.o.**, (i) avoir l'avantage sur qn; (ii) avoir preuves de la culpabilité de qn. **Goods lift**, monte-charge *m inv.* **Goods train**, train *m* de marchandises. **Goods yard**, gare *f* aux marchandises. *S.a.* CONSUMER. **good 'feeling**, *s.* Bonne entente. **good-'fellowship**, *s.* Camaraderie *f.* **'good-for-nothing. 1.** *a. (Of pers.)* Qui n'est bon à rien; *(of thg)* sans valeur. **2.** *s. (a)* Propre *mf* à rien. *(b)* Vaurien, -ienne. **good-'hearted**, *a.* (Personne) qui a bon cœur. **good-'humoured**, *a.* (Personne) d'un caractère, facile, facile à vivre; (sourire) de bonne humeur; (plaisanterie) sans malice. **-ly**, *adv.* Avec bonhomie. **good-'looker**, *s. F:* Belle femme. **good-'looking**, *a.* Bien de sa personne; beau, *f.* belle; *(of girl)* jolie. **He is a g.-l. fellow**, il est beau garçon. **She is rather g.-l.**, elle n'est pas mal. **good 'nature**, *s.* Bon naturel; bonhomie *f.* **good-'natured**, *a. (Of pers.)* Au bon naturel; accommodant. **G.-n. smile**, sourire bon enfant. **-ly**, *adv.* Avec bonhomie. **'good-sized**, *attrib.a.* De belle taille. **good-'tempered**, *a.* De caractère facile, égal; facile à vivre.

good-bye [gud'bai], *int. & s.* Au revoir; *A:* & *Dial:* adieu. **G.-b. for the present**, à bientôt, à tantôt. **To say g.-b. to s.o.**, faire ses adieux à qn, dire au revoir à qn. **G.-b. to hope!** plus d'espoir! *F:* **I can say g.-b. to the Legion of Honour**, je peux faire mon deuil de la Légion d'Honneur.

goodies ['gudiz], *s.pl. A:* Bonbons *m*, friandises *f.*

goodish ['gudiʃ], *a.* **1.** Assez bon. **2. It's a g. step from here**, c'est à un bon bout de chemin d'ici.

goodly ['gudli], *a. Lit:* **1.** D'une belle apparence; beau, *f.* belle. **2.** *(Of portion)* Large, ample. **G. heritage**, bel héritage.

goodman, *pl.* **-men** ['gudmæn], *s.m. A. & Lit:* Maître (de la maison).

goodness ['gudnis], *s.* **1.** *(a)* Bonté *f* (de cœur). *(b)* Bonne qualité (d'un article). **2. To extract all the g. out of sth.**, extraire de qch. tout ce qu'il y a de bon. **3. G. gracious!** bonté divine! miséricorde! **My g.!** mon Dieu! **Thank g.!** Dieu merci! **G. (only) kno vs what I must do**, Dieu seul sait ce que je dois faire.

goodwife, *pl.* **-wives** ['gudwaif, -waivz], *s.f. A. & Scot:* Maîtresse (de la maison).

goodwill ['gud'wil], *s.* **1.** Bonne volonté; bienveillance *f* (**towards**, pour, envers). **To retain s.o.'s g.**, conserver les bonnes grâces de qn. **2.** *Com:* Clientèle *f*; achalandage *m*; pas *m* de porte.

goody ['gudi], *s.f. A:* **G. So-and-So**, la mère une telle.

goody(-goody) ['gudi(gudi)]. *Pej: (a)* (Personne) d'une vertu suffisante; (livre) édifiant. *(b) s.* **He's, she's, a little g.-g.**, c'est un petit saint (de bois); elle fait sa Sophie.

gooey ['gu:i], *a. F:* **1.** Gluant, collant. **2.** (Sentimentalité) à l'eau de rose.

goof [gu:f], *s. F:* Imbécile *m.*

goofy ['gu:fi], *a.* Idiot, imbécile.

goon [gu:n], *s. O:* Crétin *m.*

goosander [gu:'sændər], *s. Orn:* Grand harle *m.*

goose, *pl.* **geese** [gu:s, gi:s], *s.* **1.** *(a)* *(Female of gander)* Oie *f.* *(b)* *(Generic)* Oie. **Grey g.**, oie cendrée. **Green g.**, oison *m* (de moins de quatre mois). *F:* **All his geese are swans**, tout ce qu'il fait tient du prodige. **2.** *F:* Niais, *f.* niaise. **She's a little g.**, c'est une petite sotte. **'goose-flesh**, *s. F:* Chair *f* de poule. 'goose-foot, s. 1. Bot: (pl. goose-foots) Chénopode m; ansérine f. 2. Mec.E: Aer: (pl. goose-feet) Patte-d'oie, pl. pattes-d'oie. 'goose-girl, s.f. Gardeuse d'oies. 'goose-grass, s. Bot: 1. Grateron m. 2. Potentille f ansérine. 'goose-quill, s. Plume f d'oie. 'goose-step, s. Mil: Pas m de l'oie.

gooseberry ['guzb(ə)ri], s. 1. (a) Groseille f à maquereau, groseille verte. (b) G.(-bush), groseillier m (à maquereau). 2. Chinese g., actinidia m, souris végétale. Cape g., coqueret m du Pérou. 3. F: To play g., (i) faire le chaperon; (ii) se trouver en tiers (avec deux amoureux).

gooseherd ['gu:shə:d], s. Gardeur, -euse, d'oies.

Gordian ['gɔ:diən], a. A.Hist: Gordien. To cut the G. knot, trancher le nœud gordien.

gore¹ ['gɔ:r], s. 1. (a) Dressm: (i) Soufflet m, (ii) godet m. (b) Nau: Pointe f (de voile). 2. Aer: Fuseau m (d'un ballon). 3. U.S: Langue f de terre; enclave f.

gore², v.tr. 1. Tailler (du drap) en pointe. 2. Poser des soufflets à (une robe, etc.) Gored skirt, jupe f à godets, jupe en forme. 3. Four-gored skirt, jupe à quatre lés.

gore³, s. Lit: 1. Sang coagulé. 2. Sang versé. He lay in his g., il baignait dans son sang.

gore⁴, v.tr. (Of horned animal) Encorner, découdre (qn). Gored to death, tué d'un coup de corne.

gorge¹ [gɔ:dʒ], s. 1. A. & Lit: (a) Gorge f, gosier m. (b) My g. rises at it, cela me soulève le cœur. 2. Geog: Gorge, défilé m. 3. Mec.E: Gorge (de poulie). 4. Arch: Gorge (d'une moulure).

gorge². 1. v.i. To g. (oneself), se gorger; se rassasier; s'assouvir, F: se gaver, s'empiffrer (on, de). 2. v.tr. Assouvir, gorger, rassasier (qn); gaver (une oie). gorging, s. 1. Rassasiement m, F: gavage m. 2. Bâfrerie f.

gorgeous ['gɔ:dʒəs], a. (a) Magnifique, splendide. (b) F: O: Épatant, superbe. -ly, adv. Magnifiquement, splendidement.

gorgeousness ['gɔ:dʒəsnis], s. Splendeur f, magnificence f.

gorgon ['gɔ:gən], s. Gr.Myth: Gorgone f.

gorilla [gə'rilə], s. Z: Gorille m.

gormandize ['gɔ:məndaiz]. 1. v.tr. Manger goulûment. 2. v.i. Bâfrer. gormandizing, a. Glouton, goulu.

gormandizer ['gɔ:məndaizər], s. Glouton, -onne; F: bâfreur, -euse; goinfre m.

gormless ['gɔ:mlis], a. F: Mollasse; bouché. He's g., c'est une nouille.

gorse [gɔ:s], s. Bot: Ajonc(s) m(pl); F: landier m.

gory ['gɔ:ri], a. Sanglant, ensanglanté.

gosh [gɔʃ], int. F: O: (By) g.! sapristi!

goshawk ['gɔʃɔ:k], s. Orn: Autour m.

gosling ['gɔzliŋ], s. Oison m.

gospel ['gɔsp(ə)l], s. Évangile m. To preach the g., prêcher l'évangile. F: To take sth. for g., accepter qch. comme parole d'évangile, pour argent comptant. F: To preach the g. of economy, prêcher l'économie.

gossamer ['gɔsəmər]. 1. s. (a) Fils mpl de la Vierge; filandres fpl. (b) Tex: Gaze légère. 2. a. (Tissu) très léger.

gossip¹ ['gɔsip], s. 1. (Pers.) (a) A: Compère m, commère f. (b) Bavard, -arde. (c) (Ill-natured) Cancanier, -ière. 2. (a) Causerie f. Journ: Propos familiers. Social g. (column), chronique mondaine. To (have a) g. with s.o., bavarder avec qn. (b) (Ill-natured) Cancans mpl; commérage(s) m(pl). Piece of g., racontar m, ragot m.

gossip², v.i. (a) Bavarder, papoter, F: ragoter. (b) To g. about s.o., faire des cancans, des commérages, raconter des histoires, sur qn.

got. See GET.

Gothic ['gɔθik]. 1. a. (Race) gothique. G. architecture, architecture gothique. 2. s. Art: Ling: Le gothique.

gouache [gu'ɑ:ʃ], s. Art: Gouache f. To paint in g., peindre à la gouache.

gouge¹ [gaudʒ], s. Tls: Carp: Gouge f.

gouge², v.tr. 1. Gouger (le bois). 2. To g. out, creuser (une cannelure) à la gouge. Engr: Échopper. To g. out s.o.'s eye, faire sauter un œil à qn. 3. U.S: To g. s.o., exploiter qn.

gourd [guəd], s. 1. Bot: Courge f, gourde f. 2. (Bottle) Gourde, calebasse f.

gourmand ['guəmənd]. 1. a. Gourmand, glouton. 2. s. ['gurmɑ̃(d)] (a) = GOURMET. (b) Glouton m.

gourmet ['guəmei], s. Gourmet m, gastronome m.

gout [gaut], s. 1. Med: Goutte f; (of feet) podagre f. 2. A. & Lit: Goutte, caillot m (de sang).

gouty ['gauti], a. (Of pers., joint) Goutteux, -euse; (of pers.) podagre.

govern ['gʌvən], v.tr. 1. (a) Gouverner, régir (un État); administrer (une entreprise, une province). Abs. To g., gouverner. (b) Laws that g. chemical reactions, lois qui régissent les réactions chimiques. (c) Gram: To g. the accusative, gouverner, régir, l'accusatif. 2. Maîtriser, gouverner (ses passions). To g. one's temper, se maîtriser. governing¹, a. Gouvernant. G. body, conseil m d'administration (d'une société). governing², s. (a) Gouvernement m. (b) Maîtrise f (des passions). governable, a. Gouvernable.

governess ['gʌvənis], s.f. Institutrice (privée). S.a. NURSERY-GOVERNESS. 'governess-car, -cart, s. A: Veh: Tonneau m; (of wicker) panier m.

government ['gʌv(ə)nmənt], s. Gouvernement m. (a) Form of g., régime m. Monarchical g., régime monarchique. (b) attrib. G. offices, Ministères m. G. loan, emprunt public. (c) To form a g., former un ministère, un gouvernement. The G. party, le parti gouvernemental. Shadow g., gouvernement fantôme. Puppet g., gouvernement fantoche. S.a. LOCAL 1.

governmental [,gʌvən'mentl], a. Gouvernemental, -aux.

governor ['gʌv(ə)nər], s. 1. Gouvernant m. 2. (a) Gouverneur m (d'une colonie, d'une banque). (b) Membre m du conseil d'administration (d'une école). (c) P: The G., (i) le patron, le singe; (ii) père m; le vieux. 3. Mec.E: (Device) Régulateur m, modérateur m (de vitesse). G.-valve, soupape régulatrice. 'governor-'general, pl. governor-generals, s. Gouverneur général, pl. gouverneurs généraux.

gown¹ [gaun], s. 1. Robe f (de femme). 2. Robe, toge f (de magistrat). Judge in his g., juge en robe.

gown². 1. v.tr. Revêtir (qn) d'une robe, d'une toge. 2. v.i. (Of judge) Revêtir sa robe.

gownsman, pl. -men ['gaunzmən], s.m. Membre d'une université.

grab¹ [græb], s. 1. Mouvement vif de la main pour saisir qch. 2. Civ.E: Excavateur m, pelle f mécanique. 'grab-bag, s. U.S: = LUCKY DIP. 'grab-dredge(r), s. Grappin m.

grab², v.tr. & i. (grabbed) To g. (hold of) sth., s.o., saisir qch. (d'un geste brusque); se saisir de qch.; empoigner qn. He grabbed a revolver from the table, il saisit un revolver sur la table. To g. at so., s'agripper à qn.

grabber ['græbər], s. Accapareur, -euse.

Gracchi (the) [ðə'grækai]. Pr.n.m.pl. Rom.Hist: Les Gracques.

grace¹ [greis], s. Grâce f. 1. (a) To do sth. with g., mettre de la grâce à faire qch. (b) To do sth. with a good g., faire qch. de bonne grâce. He had the g. to be ashamed, il faut dire à son honneur qu'il se montra confus. (c) Gr.Myth: The Graces, les Grâces. 2. (a) Act of g., gracieuseté f, faveur f. By God's g., grâce à Dieu. To get into s.o.'s good graces, se mettre dans les bonnes grâces de qn. (b) Theol: The grace of God, la grâce de Dieu. Saving g., grâce sanctifiante. F: It has the saving g. that . . ., cela a au moins ce mérite que. . . . In the year of g. 1066, en l'an de grâce 1066. 3. (a) Jur: Grâce, pardon m. (Still so used in) Act of g., (i) lettres fpl de grâce; (ii) loi f d'amnistie. (b) Com: Days of g., délai m (accordé pour le paiement d'un effet). 4. G., (before meal) bénédicité m; (after meal) grâces 5. Your G., votre Grandeur. His G. the Duke of B., Monsieur le Duc de B. His G. the Archbishop of Canterbury, Monseigneur l'Archevêque de Cantorbéry. 'grace-note, s. Mus: Note f d'agrément.

grace², v.tr. (a) Honorer (with, de). (b) Embellir, orner.

graceful ['greisf(u)l], a. Gracieux. -fully, adv. Avec grâce; avec élégance.

gracefulness ['greisf(u)lnis], s. Grâce f, élégance f.

graceless ['greislĭs], a. (a) Sans grâce, gauche. (b) Theol: Pas en état de grâce. (c) Effronté, mauvais sujet. How's that g. nephew of yours getting on? que devient votre garnement m de neveu?

gracile ['græsil], a. Gracile, grêle.

gracious ['greiʃəs], a. 1. Gracieux, -euse, indulgent, bienveillant. 2. (Of God) Miséricordieux. 3. G. (me)! good(ness) g.! miséricorde! bonté divine! Good g., no! jamais de la vie! -ly, adv. 1. Avec bienveillance. 2. Miséricordieusement, avec miséricorde.

graciousness ['greiʃəsnis], s. 1. Grâce f. 2. Condescendance f, bienveillance f (to, towards, envers). 3. Bonté f, miséricorde f (de Dieu).

gradate [grə'deit]. 1. v.i. (Of colours) Se dégrader, se fondre. 2. v.tr. Dégrader (des teintes).

gradation [grə'deiʃ(ə)n], s. 1. (a) Gradation f. Aut: G. of speeds, échelonnement m des vitesses. (b) Art: (Dé)gradation f (des teintes). 2. Ling: (Vowel) g., alternance f de voyelles; apophonie f.

grade¹ [greid], s. 1. (a) Grade m, rang m, degré m. Sch: U.S: Classe f. G. school, école f primaire (parfois avec cours supérieur). (b) Qualité f; classe f. G. of ore, teneur f du minerai. 2. Civ.E: U.S: (a) Pente f, rampe f; montée f ou descente f (d'une voie ferrée). To make the g., (i) parvenir au sommet; (ii) F: réussir. (b) Niveau m. U.S: G. crossing, passage m à niveau.

grade², v.tr. & i. 1. Classer, trier (des marchandises). 2. (a) Graduer (des exercices). Graded tax, impôt progressif. (b) Art: Dégrader, fondre (des teintes). 3. Civ.E: Rail: (A)ménager, régulariser, la pente de (la voie). 4. Ling: (Of vowel) S'altérer par apophonie. grading, s. 1. Classement m, gradation f; triage m (du minerai). 2. (Dé)gradation f (des teintes). 3. (A)ménagement m (d'une pente).

gradient ['greidiənt], s. Civ.E: Rampe f, dénivellation f, pente f. Upward g., rampe. Downward g., pente. Angle of g., angle de déclivité. Rail: Steep gradients, lignes f à forte pente. Meteor: etc: (Barometric) g., gradient m. 'gradient-indicator, -meter, s. Aut: Av: Indicateur m de pente; clinomètre m.

gradual ['grædju(ə)l]. 1. a. Graduel; progressif. G. slope, pente douce. G. process, gradation f. 2. s. Ecc: Graduel m. -ally, adv. Graduellement; peu à peu.

graduate¹ ['grædjuit], s. Sch: Gradué, -ée, diplômé, -ée.

graduate² ['grædjueit]. 1. v.i. Sch: Prendre ses grades, ses diplômes; (in Fr.) être reçu(e) licencié(e). 2. v.tr. (a) Graduer (un thermomètre). Graduated in inches, gradué en pouces. (b) Graduer (des exercices). Graduated taxation, taxes imposées par paliers. Graduated income-tax, impôt progressif. (c) Dégrader (des teintes).

graduation [ˌgrædju'eiʃ(ə)n], s. 1. Sch: (a) Collation f des grades; remise de diplômes. (b) (By student) Réception f d'un grade, d'un diplôme. 2. Graduation f (d'un thermomètre). 3. Gradation f (d'exercices).

Gr(a)eco-Latin ['gri:kou'lætin], a. Ling: Gréco-latin.

graffiti [græ'fi:ti], s.pl. Graffiti mpl.

graft¹ [grɑːft], s. Arb: Surg: Greffe f.

graft², v.tr. (a) Arb: Surg: Greffer, enter. (b) Surg: Greffer, implanter. grafting, s. (a) Arb: Greffe f, greffage m. (b) Surg: Greffe (humaine); implantation f. Skin g., greffe épidermique. 'grafting-knife, s. Arb: Greffoir m, entoir m.

graft³, s. F: Corruption f, F: graissage m de patte, pots-de-vin m; F: gratte f.

grafter ['grɑːftər], s. F: Fonctionnaire, politicien, véreux, qui se fait de la gratte.

Grail [greil], s. Medieval Lit: The Holy G., le (Saint) Graal.

grain¹ [grein], s. 1. (a) Grain m (de blé). (b) Coll. G. crop, récolte de grains, de céréales. (c) (Brewers') grains, drêche f. 2. (a) Grain (de poivre). (b) Grain (de sel, de sable). Exp: Large g., small g, powder, poudre à gros grains, à grains fins. G. of consolation, brin m de consolation. Not a g. of common sense, pas un grain, pas un brin, pas l'ombre, de bon sens. (c) Meas: Grain (= 0 gr. 0648). 3. (a) Grain (du bois); texture f (de la fonte). Close g., grain fin,

dense. Man of coarse g., homme sans délicatesse. (b) Fil m (du bois, de la viande). Against, across, the g., contre le fil; à contre-fil. It goes against the g. for me to do it, c'est à contre-cœur que je le fais.

grain², v.tr. 1. Chagriner, grainer (le cuir, le papier). 2. Paint: Veiner (une surface) façon bois. 3. Tan: Rebrousser (le cuir). grained, a. (a) Granulé, grenu. (b) Paint: Veiné ou marbré. graining, s. 1. Leath: Rebroussement m; grenure f. 2. Veinage m (de la peinture).

gram¹ [græm], s. Meas: = GRAMME.

Gram². Pr.n. Bac: G.-positive, -negative, gram positif, négatif.

graminaceous [græmi'neiʃəs], gramineous [græ-'miniəs], a. Bot: Graminé. G. plants, graminées f.

Gramineae [grə'minii], s.pl. Bot: Graminées f.

grammalogue ['græmələg], s. (In shorthand) Sténogramme m.

grammar ['græmər], s. (a) Grammaire f. That's not (good) g., ce que vous dites là n'est pas grammatical. (b) (Livre m, traité m, de) grammaire. 'grammar-school, s. Lycée m; U.S: collège pour élèves d'environ 12 à 15 ans.

grammarian [grə'mɛəriən], s. Grammairien, -ienne.

grammatical [grə'mætik(ə)l], a. Grammatical, -aux. -ally, adv. Grammaticalement.

gramme [græm], s. Meas: Gramme m. (Poids en grammes × 0.035 = poids en onces.) 'gramme-calory, s. Ph: Petite calorie.

gramophone ['græməfoun], s. Phonographe m.

grampus ['græmpəs], s. 1. Z: Epaulard m, orque f. 2. F: Gros (bonhomme) poussif.

granary ['grænəri], s. Grenier m.

grand [grænd], a. 1. (In titles) Grand. The G. Vizier, le grand vizir. 2. (a) Grand; principal, -aux. The g. staircase, l'escalier d'honneur. (b) G. total, total global. 3. (a) G. display of fireworks, grand feu d'artifice. (b) A g. piano, F: a g., un piano à queue. 4. (a) Grandiose, magnifique. (b) The g. air, le grand air; le panache. 5. (a) F: Excellent; F: épatant. He's a g. fellow, c'est un type épatant. (b) F: I'm not very g., ça ne va qu'à moitié. 6. s. U.S: F: Mille dollars. -ly, adv. (a) Grandement, magnifiquement. (b) Grandiosement. 'Grand 'Cross, s. 1. Grand-croix f inv. 2. Knight G. C., grand-croix m, pl. grands-croix. 'grand-dad, s.m. F: Bon-papa, pl. bons-papas. 'grand-daughter, s.f. Petite-fille, pl. petites-filles. 'Grand-'ducal, a. Grand-ducal. 'Grand 'Duchess, s.f. Grande-duchesse, pl. grandesduchesses. 'Grand 'Duchy, s. Grand-duché m, pl. grands-duchés. 'Grand 'Duke, s.m. Grand-duc, pl. grands-ducs. 'grand-nephew, s.m. Petit-neveu, pl. petits-neveux. 'grand-niece, s.f. Petite-nièce, pl. petites-nièces.

grandchild, pl. -children ['græn(d)tʃaild, -tʃildrən], s. Petit-fils m ou petite-fille f, pl. petits-enfants m.

grandee [græn'di:], s. (a) Grand m (d'Espagne). (b) F: Grand personnage.

grandeur ['græn(d)ʒər], s. Grandeur f. (a) Noblesse f, éminence f. (b) Splendeur f. The g. of the landscape, la majesté du paysage.

grandfather ['græn(d)fɑːðər], s.m. Grand-père, pl. grands-pères; aïeul, pl. aïeuls.

grandiloquence [græn'diləkwəns], s. Grandiloquence f; emphase f.

grandiloquent [græn'diləkwənt], a. Grandiloquent; (ton) doctoral, -aux; (style) emphatique. -ly, adv. Avec emphase.

grandiose ['grændious], a. (a) Grandiose, magnifique. (b) Pompeux, -euse; qui vise à la majesté.

grandmamma, grandma ['græn(d)(mə)mɑː], s.f. Grand-maman, pl. grand-mamans.

grandmother ['græn(d)mʌðər], s.f. Grand-mère, pl. grand-mères; aïeule.

grandmotherly ['græn(d)mʌðəli], a. De grand-mère; F: (législation) méticuleuse, tatillonne.

grand(pa)pa ['græn(pə)pɑː], s.m. Grand-papa, pl. grands-papas, F: pépé, pépé.

grandparent ['græn(d)pɛər(ə)nt], s. Grand-père m, grand-mère f; aïeul, -e; pl. grands-parents m.

grandsire ['græn(d)saiər], s.m. Lit: 1. Grand-père m, pl. grands-pères. 2. Aïeul, pl. aïeux; ancêtre m.

grandson ['græn(d)sʌn], *s.m.* Petit-fils, *pl.* petits-fils.

grandstand ['grændstænd], *s. Sp:* Tribune *f* (d'honneur).

grange [grein(d)ʒ], *s.* 1. *A:* Grange *f.* 2. Manoir *m* (avec ferme); château *m.*

granite ['grænit], *s. Geol:* Granit(e) *m.* G. formation, formation graniteuse, granitique.

granitic [græ'nitik], *a.* Granitique, graniteux, -euse.

grannie, granny ['græni], *s.f. F:* Bonne-maman, *pl.* bonnes-mamans, mémé.

grant¹ [grɑ:nt], *s.* 1. (*a*) Concession *f,* octroi *m* (d'une permission). (*b*) *Jur:* Don *m,* cession *f* (d'un bien). Post in s.o.'s g., poste en la disposition de qn. (*c*) *Jur:* Acte *m* de transfert. 2. Aide *f* pécuniaire; subvention *f.* To receive a State g., être subventionné ou doté par l'État. To put in a claim for a g., demander une allocation.

grant², *v.tr.* 1. (*a*) Accorder, concéder, octroyer (un privilège, etc.). He was granted permission to . . ., il reçut la permission de. . . . Heaven g. that . . ., fasse le ciel que. . . . God g. that . . ., Dieu veuille que. . . . *P* I beg your pardon.—Granted! je vous demande pardon.—Il n'y a pas de quoi; mais comment donc! (*b*) Exaucer (une prière); accéder à (une requête). 2. Accorder (une subvention à qn). To g. a loan, consentir un prêt (to, à). 3. To g. sth. as a fact, admettre, reconnaître, qch. pour vrai. I g. that you may be right, je veux bien que vous ayez raison. Granted that you are right, admettons, *F:* mettons, que vous ayez raison. I g. you that he is a rogue, j'avoue que c'est un coquin. To take sth. for granted, considérer qch. comme allant de soi. He takes it for granted that he may . . ., il se croit permis de . . ., il ne se gêne pas pour. . . . You take too much for granted, vous présumez trop. I take it for granted you will come, c'est entendu que vous venez. **granting,** *s.* Concession *f;* octroi *m.* **'grant-'aided,** *a.* Subventionné. **'grant-in-'aid,** *s.* Subvention *f.*

granular ['grænjulər], *a.* (*a*) (*Of surface*) Granulaire, granuleux, -euse. (*b*) *Med:* (*Of fracture*) Grenu; (*of tumour*) granuleux.

granulate ['grænjuleit], *v.tr.* Granuler; grener, grainer (la poudre); cristalliser (le sucre); grenailler (un métal). **granulated,** *a.* (*a*) Granulé, grené; (métal) en grenaille; (sucre) cristallisé. *Tp:* G. carbon, grenaille *f* de charbon. (*b*) (*Of surface*) Grenu.

granulation [,grænju'leiʃ(ə)n], *s.* 1. Granulation *f;* grenaillement *m* (d'un métal). 2. *pl. Med:* Granulations, bourgeonnement *m.*

granule ['grænju:l], *s.* Granule *m. Tp:* Carbon granules, grenaille *f* de charbon.

granulous ['grænjuləs], *a.* Granuleux, -euse, granulaire.

grape [greip], *s.* (*a*) Grain *m* de raisin. (*b*) *pl.* Bunch of grapes, grappe *f* de raisin. Dessert grapes, raisin(s) de table. For dessert I'll have grapes, pour dessert je prendrai un raisin, du raisin. *F:* Sour grapes! ils sont trop verts! **'grape-gatherer,** *s.* Vendangeur, -euse. **'grape-gathering, -harvest,** *s.* Vendange *f.* **'grape-hyacinth,** *s. Bot:* Muscari *m.* **'grape-shot,** *s. Mil: A:* Mitraille *f.* **'grape-sugar,** *s.* Sucre *m* de raisin; glucose *m.*

grapefruit ['greipfru:t], *s.* Pamplemousse *f.*

grapevine ['greipvain], *s.* 1. Vigne *f.* 2. *F:* Téléphone *m* arabe.

graph¹ [græf, grɑ:f], *s.* 1. Graphique *m,* courbe *f,* tracé *m* (d'une équation, etc.). G. paper, papier quadrillé. 2. Abaque *m;* barème *m* graphique.

graph², *v.tr.* Tracer, figurer, (une courbe) graphiquement.

graphic ['græfik], *a.* 1. *Mth:* etc: Graphique. 2. (*Of description*) Pittoresque, vivant. **-ally,** *adv.* 1. (Résoudre un problème) graphiquement. 2. (Décrire) pittoresquement.

graphite ['græfait], *s.* Graphite *m;* mine *f* de plomb; plombagine *f.*

graphology [græ'fɔlədʒi], *s.* Graphologie *f.*

graphological [,græfə'lɔdʒikəl], *a.* Graphologique.

graphologist [græ'fɔlədʒist], *s.* Graphologue *m.*

graphometer [græ'fɔmitər], *s.* Graphomètre *m.*

grapnel ['græpnəl], *s. Nau:* Grappin *m. Hyd.E.:* Araignée *f. Aer:* Ancre *f* (de ballon).

grapple ['græpl], *v.i.* To grapple with s.o., en venir aux prises avec qn; saisir qn à bras le corps; colleter qn. To grapple with a difficulty, en venir aux prises avec, s'attaquer à, une difficulté.

grasp¹ [grɑ:sp], *s.* 1. (*a*) Poigne *f.* (*b*) Prise *f;* étreinte *f.* To escape from s.o.'s g., échapper à l'étreinte de qn. To have sth. within one's g., avoir qch. à sa portée; tenir (le succès) entre ses mains. Beyond one's g., hors d'atteinte. (*c*) Compréhension *f.* To have a good g. of modern life, avoir une profonde connaissance de la vie moderne. 2. Poignée *f* (d'un aviron, d'une épée).

grasp². 1. *v.tr.* (*a*) Saisir; empoigner (un outil); serrer (qch.) dans sa main; étreindre (qch.). To g. s.o.'s hand, serrer la main à qn. To g. the nettle, y aller franchement; prendre le taureau par les cornes. (*b*) S'emparer, se saisir, de (qch.). To g. the opportunity, saisir l'occasion au vol. *Prov:* G. all, lose all, qui trop embrasse mal étreint. 2. *v.tr.* Comprendre (une difficulté, etc.); se rendre compte de (l'importance de qch.). Argument difficult to g., raisonnement difficile à saisir. 3. *v.i.* To g. at sth. (*a*) Chercher à saisir qch. (*b*) Saisir avidement (une occasion). **grasping,** *a.* 1. (*Of claws*) Tenace. 2. To be g., être âpre au gain; *F:* avoir les dents longues.

grass¹ [grɑ:s], *s.* Herbe *f.* 1. (*a*) Blade of g., brin d'herbe. *F:* Not to let the g. grow under one's feet, ne pas perdre de temps; ne pas traîner en affaires. (*b*) *Bot:* The grasses, les graminées *f.* 2. (*a*) Herbage *m,* pâture *f.* To turn, put, a horse out to g., mettre un cheval à l'herbe, au vert. To put land under g., mettre du terrain en pré. (*b*) Gazon *m. P.N* 'Please keep off the g.', "défense de circuler sur le gazon." **'grass-green,** *a.* Vert pré *inv.* **'grass-grown,** *a.* Herbu, herbeux. **'grass-land,** *s.* Prairie *f,* pré *m,* herbage *m.* **'grass roots,** *s. U.S:* 1. Couche supérieure du sol. 2. (*a*) Les communes rurales et la campagne. (*b*) La population rurale. 3. Fondation *f,* source *f,* base *f.* **'grass-snake,** *s. Rept:* Couleuvre *f.* **'grass-'widow,** *s.f. F:* Femme dont le mari est absent, veuve à titre temporaire. **'grass-'widower,** *s.m.* Mari dont la femme est absente; veuf à titre temporaire.

grass², *v.tr.* 1. Mettre en herbe (un champ); gazonner (un terrain). 2. *Tex:* Blanchir au pré (le lin).

grasshopper ['grɑ:shɔpər], *s. Ent:* Sauterelle *f.*

grassy ['grɑ:si], *a.* Herbu, herbeux, -euse.

grate¹ [greit], *s.* 1. = GRATING¹ 1. 2. (i) Grille *f* (de foyer); (ii) *F:* foyer *m,* âtre *m. Mch:* Grille, grillage *m* (de foyer de chaudière). **'grate-polish,** *s.* Noir *m* à fourneaux.

grate², *v.tr.* Griller (une fenêtre, etc.). **grated,** *a* Grillé; à grille. **grating,**¹ *s.* 1. (*a*) Grille *f,* grillage *m* (de fenêtre, etc.); treillis *m;* (cloison *f* à) claire-voie *f. Hyd.E:* Crapaudine *f;* gril *m* (en amont d'une vanne). (*b*) *Nau:* Caillebotis *m.* 2. *Opt:* Diffraction g., réseau *m.*

grate³. I. *v.tr.* 1. Râper (de la muscade, etc.). Grated cheese, du râpé. 2. To g. one's teeth, grincer des dents. II. **grate,** *v.i.* (*a*) (*Of machinery*) Grincer (of chalk on blackboard) crisser. The door grated on its hinges, la porte cria sur ses gonds. (*b*) To g. on the ear, choquer, écorcher, l'oreille. To g. on the nerves, taper sur les nerfs; agacer les nerfs. **grating**², *a.* (*Of noise,* etc.) Discordant, grinçant; qui écorche l'oreille². G. sound, grincement *m,* crissement *m.* **grating²,** *s.* 1. (*a*) Râpage. *m.* (*b*) *pl.* Gratings râpure(s) *f(pl).* 2. Grincement *m,* crissement *m* (d'un gond, etc.).

grateful ['greitf(u)l], *a.* 1. (*Of pers.*) Reconnaissant. To be g. to s.o. for sth., savoir (bon) gré à qn de qch. I am g. to you for . . ., je vous suis très reconnaissant de. . . . 2. (*Of thg*) Agréable; (repos) réconfortant, bienfaisant. **-fully,** *adv.* Avec reconnaissance.

gratefulness ['greitf(u)lnis], *s.* Reconnaissance *f.*

grater ['greitər], *s.* Râpe *f* (à muscade, etc.).

gratification ['grætifi'keiʃ(ə)n], *s.* 1. Satisfaction *f,* plaisir *m.* To do sth. for one's own g., faire qch. pour son propre contentement. 2. Satisfaction, assouvissement *m* (des passions).

gratify ['grætifai], v.tr. 1. Faire plaisir, être agréable, à (qn). 2. Satisfaire, contenter (le désir de qn, etc.). To g. s.o.'s whims, flatter les caprices de qn. To g. one's fancy for sth., se passer la fantaisie de qch. **gratified**, a. Satisfait, content (with, de); flatté. **gratifying**, a. Agréable; flatteur. It is g. to learn that . . ., c'est un plaisir d'apprendre que. . . .

gratis ['greitis]. 1. a. Gratis, gratuit. 2. adv. Gratis, gratuitement, à titre gratuit.

gratitude ['grætitju:d], s. Gratitude f, reconnaissance f (to, envers).

gratuitous [grə'tju(:)itəs], a. 1. Gratuit; (service) bénévole. 2. F: G. insult, insulte injustifiée, gratuite. G. lie, mensonge sans motif. -ly, adv. Gratuitement; à titre bénévole, gratuit. 2. F: Sans motif.

gratuitousness [grə'tju:itəsnəs], s. Gratuité f; (of a remark, etc.) manque m d'à-propos, inopportunité f.

gratuity [grə'tju(:)iti], s. 1. Gratification f, F: pourboire m; pot-de-vin m. 'No gratuities,' "défense de donner des pourboires." 2. Mil: Navy: Prime f de démobilisation; pécule m.

gravamen, pl. -ina [grə'veimen, -inə], s. Jur: Fond m, fondement m (d'une accusation). G. of a charge, matière f d'un crime.

grave[1] [greiv], s. (a) Tombe f, tombeau m, fosse f. The Paupers' g., la fosse commune. To be in one's g., être enterré. He just escaped a watery g., il a failli être enseveli dans les flots. F: He must have turned in his g., il a dû se retourner dans sa tombe. To have one foot in the g., être au bord de la tombe. (b) From beyond the g., d'outre-tombe. 'grave-digger', s. Fossoyeur m. 'grave-digging', s. Fossoyage m.

grave[2], v.tr. (graved; graven, graved) A: Graver, tailler, échopper (une inscription, etc.). Lit: Graven on his memory, gravé dans sa mémoire. B: Graven image, image taillée.

grave[3], a. 1. (a) Grave, sérieux. To look g., avoir l'air sévère. (b) G. news, de graves nouvelles. To make a g. mistake, se tromper lourdement. G. symptoms, symptômes graves, inquiétants. 2. Gram: [grɑːv] G. accent, accent grave. -ly, adv. Gravement, sérieusement.

grave[4], v.tr. Radouber (un navire). **graving**, s. Radoub m. S.a. DOCK[3]. 'graving-beach, s. (Cale f d')échouage m.

gravel[1] ['græv(ə)l], s. 1. Gravier m. Fine g., gravillon m. 2. Med: Gravelle f; F: graviers, sable m. 'gravel-'path, s. Allée sablée, gravelée. 'gravel-pit, s. Gravière f, sablière f.

gravel[2], v.tr. (gravelled) 1. Graveler; sabler, gravillonner (un chemin). 2. F: O: Mettre, réduire, (qn) à quia; P: coller (qn). To be gravelled, être à quia. **gravelling**, s. Gravelage m.

gravelly ['grævəli], a. Graveleux.

graveness ['greivnis], s. Gravité f.

graver ['greivər], s. 1. (Pers.) Graveur m. 2. Tls: Échoppe f, burin m, gravoir m.

gravestone ['greivstoun], s. = TOMBSTONE.

graveyard ['greivjaːd], s. Cimetière m.

gravid ['grævid], a. (Of woman) Gravide, enceinte; (of animal) pleine.

gravitate ['græviteit], v.i. Graviter (towards, vers; round, autour de).

gravitation [.grævi'teiʃ(ə)n], s. Gravitation f. The Law of g., la loi de la pesanteur.

gravitational [.grævi'teiʃən(ə)l], a. Attractif. G. force, force f de gravitation. G. acceleration, accélération f de la pesanteur.

gravity ['græviti], s. Gravité f. 1. (a) To preserve, lose, one's g., garder, perdre, son sérieux, sa gravité. (b) Gravité (d'une situation, d'une blessure). 2. Ph: Gravité, pesanteur f. Centre of g., centre de gravité. Force of g., force de gravitation. Aut: G. feed, alimentation par la pesanteur, en charge. S.a. SPECIFIC 1. 'gravity-fed, a. Aut: etc: (Carburateur, etc.) alimenté par différence de niveau.

gravy ['greivi], s. 1. Cu: (a) Jus m (qui sort de la viande). (b) Sauce f (au jus). 2. U.S: F: Argent facilement gagné. G. train, assiette f au beurre. 'gravy-boat, s. Saucière f.

gray [grei], a. & s. = GREY.

grayling ['greiliŋ], s. Ich: Ombre m.

graze[1] [greiz]. 1. v.i. Paître, brouter. 2. v.tr. (a) Paître, faire paître, mener paître (un troupeau). (b) (Of cattle, etc.) Pâturer (un champ); paître (l'herbe). **grazing**, s. Pâturage m (de troupeaux); élevage m (de moutons). 'grazing-ground, -land, s. Pâturage m.

graze[2], s. Écorchure f, éraflure f.

graze[3], v.tr. 1. Écorcher, érafler (ses genoux, etc.). 2. Effleurer, raser, frôler. The bullet grazed his shoulder, his ribs, la balle lui rasa l'épaule, lui glissa sur les côtes. Nau: (Of ship) To g. the bottom, labourer le fond; toucher.

grazier ['greiziər], s. Herbager m.

grease[1] [griːs], s. (a) Graisse f. Mil: Rifle g., graisse d'armes. Mec.E: Belt-g., enduit m pour courroies. (b) Wool g., suint m. Wool in (the) g., laine en suint. 'grease-band, s. Arb: Bande enduite de glu horticole. 'grease-box, s. Mch: Boîte f, réservoir m, à graisse. 'grease-cap, -cup, s. (Godet) graisseur m. 'grease-cock, s. Mec.E: Robinet graisseur. 'grease-extractor, s. Mch: Dégraisseuse f. 'grease-gun, s. Mec.E: Aut: Pompe f à graisse. 'grease-paint, s. Th: Stick of g.-p., crayon gras (de maquillage). 'grease-proof, a. (Papier) parcheminé, sulfurisé. 'grease remover, s. Ind: Dégraisseur m.

grease[2] [griːs], v.tr. 1. Graisser, encrasser (ses habits). 2. Graisser, lubrifier (une machine); suiffer (un mât). To keep a mechanism well greased, entretenir un mécanisme au gras. S.a. PALM[2] 1. **greasing**, s. Graissage m; lubrification f. I.C.E: etc: Pressure g., graissage sous pression.

greaser ['griːsər], s. 1. (Pers.) Graisseur m. 2. = GREASE-CUP.

greasiness ['griːzinis, 'griːsinis], s. Onctuosité f, état graisseux.

greasy, a. 1. ['griːsi], (a) Graisseux, huileux. To taste g., sentir le graillon. (b) Taché d'huile, de graisse. 2. ['griːzi] Gras, f. grasse; (chemin) gras, glissant. G. pole, mât m de cocagne.

great [greit], a. Grand. (a) G. (big) man, homme de grande taille. A g. big lorry, un énorme camion. O: G. toe, gros orteil. Greater London, Montreal, l'agglomération londonienne, montréalaise; le grand Londres, Montréal. To grow greater (and greater), augmenter, s'agrandir, grandir (de plus en plus). (b) A g. deal, beaucoup, une quantité considérable (of, de). A g. many, beaucoup (de + pl.). There were not a g. many people there, il n'y avait pas grand monde. The g. majority, the greater part, la plupart, la majeure partie (of, de). To a g. extent, en grande partie. To reach a g. age, parvenir à un âge avancé. Of g. antiquity, de haute antiquité. (c) His greatest fault, son plus grand défaut; son défaut capital. To take g. care, prendre grand soin (of, de); prendre beaucoup de soin. G. difference, grande, forte, différence. With the greatest pleasure, avec le plus grand plaisir. The G. War, la Grande Guerre. (d) The great men (of the age), les grands hommes, les célébrités f (de l'époque). F: G. Scott! grands dieux! Alexander the G., Alexandre le Grand. (e) G. eater, grand, gros, mangeur. They are g. friends, ils sont grands amis. F: To be g. on dogs, être grand amateur de chiens. To be g. at tennis, être fort au tennis. (f) It is no g. matter, ce n'est pas une grosse affaire. To have no g. opinion of s.o., tenir qn en médiocre estime. The g. thing is that . . ., le grand avantage, le principal, c'est que . . . It was a g. joke, ça nous a joliment amusés. F: It's g.! fameux! c'est magnifique! (g) Nav: G. circle, grand cercle. -ly, adv. Grandement; beaucup. We were g. amused, cela nous a beaucoup amusés. G. irritated, très irrité; fortement irrité. It is g. to be feared that . . ., il est fort à craindre que. . . . 'great-aunt, s.f. Grand-tante. 'great-coat, s. Pardessus m. Mil: Capote f. great-'grandchild, pl. -children, s. Arrière-petit-fils m, arrière-petite-fille f, pl. arrière-petits-enfants m. great-'grand-daughter, s.f. Arrière-petite-fille, pl. arrière-petites-filles. great-'grand-father, s.m. Arrière-grand-père, pl. arrière-grands-pères; bisaïeul. great-'grandmother, s.f. Arrière-grand-mère, pl. arrière-grand-mères; bisaïeule. great-'grandparents, s.pl. Arrière-grands-parents mpl. inv.

'great-'grandson, s.m. Arrière-petit-fils, pl. arrière-petits-fils. 'great-great-'grandfather, s.m. Trisaïeul. 'great-great-'grandmother, s.f. Trisaïeule. 'Great 'Lakes (the), Pr.n. Geog: Les Grands Lacs. 'great-'hearted, a. Généreux; magnanime. great-'nephew, s.m. Petit-neveu, pl petits-neveux. great-'niece, s.f Petite-nièce, pl. petites-nièces. 'great-uncle, s.m Grand-oncle, pl. grands-oncles.

greatness ['greitnis], s. Grandeur f.

greave [gri:v], s. Arm: Jambière f.

greaves [gri:vz], s.pl. Cu: Cretons m, rillons m.

grebe [gri:b], s. Orn: Grèbe f.

Grecian ['gri:ʃ(ə)n]. a. Grec, f. grecque. In the G. style, dans le style grec; à la grecque.

Greece [gri:s]. Pr.n. Geog: La Grèce.

greed [gri:d], s. Avidité f, cupidité f.

greediness ['gri:dinis], s. 1. = GREED. 2. Gourmandise f, gloutonnerie f.

greedy ['gri:di], a. 1. Avide, cupide; âpre (au gain). 2. Gourmand; glouton, -onne; goulu. -ily, adv. 1. Avidement, cupidement. 2. Avec gourmandise, gloutonnement; (manger) à belles dents, goulûment.

Greek [gri:k]. 1. a. & s. Grec, f. grecque. Art: G. key pattern, G. border, grecque f. The G. Church, l'Église grecque; l'Église orthodoxe. 2. s. Ling: Le grec. F: It is all G. to me, c'est de l'hébreu pour moi.

green [gri:n]. 1. a. Vert. (a) As g. as grass, vert comme pré. To grow g., verdir; (of grass, etc.) verdoyer. S.a. SEA 2. (b) G. arbour, tonnelle de verdure. G. winter, hiver doux, clément. G.-stuff, légumes verts; fourrage m. Husb: G. food, g. meat, fourrages verts, frais, (c) G. old age, verte vieillesse. To keep s.o.'s memory g., entretenir, chérir, la mémoire de qn. Memories still g., souvenirs encore vivaces. (d) G. fruit, fruits verts. G. corn, blé en herbe. Tan: G. hide, peau verte; peau crue. G. bacon, lard salé et non fumé. (e) (Of complexion) Blême. To go, turn, g., blêmir. S.a. ENVY¹ 1. (f) (i) Jeune, inexpérimenté. (ii) Naïf, f. naïve. He 'is g.! il est bien de son village! He's not so g., il n'est pas né d'hier. (g) She has g. fingers, en jardinage elle a la main heureuse, elle a le pouce vert. 2. s. & a. (In Fr. a.inv.) Grass-g., vert pré m. Sage-g., vert cendré. S.a. BOTTLE-GREEN, OLIVE-GREEN. 3. s. The greens of a picture, les verts d'un tableau. (b) pl. Greens, légumes verts. (c) Pelouse f, gazon m. Village g., pelouse communale, place f du village. Golf: The (putting-) green, la pelouse d'arrivée. Turf: The green, la pelouse. 'green-bottle, s. Ent: Mouche verte (de la viande). 'green(-)fly, s. Ent: 1. Puceron m (du rosier); aphis m. 2. Coll. Aphididés mpl, aphidiens mpl. 'green-room, s. Th: Foyer m des artistes. 'green-stick, s. & attrib. Med: G.-s. (fracture), fracture incomplète, F: en bois vert. 'green-stone, s. Miner: Néphrite f.

greenback ['gri:nbæk], s. U.S: Billet m de banque.

greenery ['gri:nəri], s. Verdure f, feuillage m.

greenfinch ['gri:nfin(t)ʃ], s. Orn: Verdier m.

greengage ['gri:ngeidʒ], s. Reine-claude f, pl. reines-claudes.

greengrocer ['gri:ngrousər], s. Marchand, -ande, de légumes; fruitier, -ière. Greengrocer's shop, marchand de légumes; fruiterie f.

greenhorn ['gri:nhɔ:n], s. F: Blanc-bec m, pl. blancs-becs; F: bleu m, cornichon m, béjaune m.

greenhouse ['gri:nhaus], s. Hort: Serre f; esp. serre chaude.

greenish ['gri:niʃ], a. Verdâtre.

Greenland ['gri:nlənd]. Pr.n. Le Groenland. In G., au Groenland.

Greenlander ['gri:nləndər], s. Groenlandais, -aise.

greenness ['gri:nnis], s. 1. Verdeur f. (a) Couleur verte. (b) Immaturité f (d'un fruit, d'un projet, etc.). (c) (i) Inexpérience f; (ii) naïveté f. (d) Verdeur, vigueur f (d'un vieillard). 2. Verdure f (du paysage, etc.).

greensward ['gri:nswɔ:d], s. Lit: Pelouse f; (tapis m de) gazon m; tapis de verdure.

greet¹ [gri:t], v.tr. (a) Saluer, aborder, ou accueillir (qn) avec quelques paroles aimables. To g. a speech with cheers, saluer un discours d'acclamations. (b) O: g. the ear, the eye, frapper l'oreille, s'offrir aux regards. greeting, s. Salutation f, salut m. To send one's greetings to s.o., envoyer le bonjour à qn. New-year greetings, compliments m du jour de l'an. G. card, carte f (d'anniversaire, etc.).

greet², v.i. Scot: Pleurer.

gregarious [gri'gɛəriəs]. a. Grégaire. Men are g., les hommes aiment à vivre en société. -ly, adv. (Vivre) en troupes, par bandes.

gregariousness [gri'gɛəriəsnis], s. Grégarisme m.

Gregorian [gri'gɔ:riən], a. (Chant, etc.) grégorien.

Gregory ['gregəri], Pr.n.m. Grégoire. Pharm: Gregory('s) powder, rhubarbe f en poudre.

grenade [gri'neid], s. 1. Mil: Grenade. f S.a. HAND-GRENADE. 2. (Fire-)grenade, grenade extinctrice.

grenadier [grenə'diər]), s. Mil: Grenadier m.

grenadine ['grenədi:n], s. 1. Tex: Grenadine f. 2. (Syrup) Grenadine. Pharm: Sirop grenadin.

grew [gru:]. See GROW.

grey [grei]. 1. a. Gris. (a) G. sky, ciel gris. Anat: G. matter, substance, matière, grise (du cerveau). (b) (Of hair) Gris. To turn g., go g., grisonner. Grown g. in the service, F: in harness, blanchi sous le harnais. (c) (Of complexion) (Ashen) g., blême. To turn (ashen) g., blêmir. (d) (Of outlook, etc.) sombre, mélancolique, morne. 2. s. & a. (In Fr. a.inv.) Dull g., gris mat. To paint (sth.) g., peindre (qch.) en gris. S.a. BLUE-GREY, DAPPLE-GREY, etc. 3. s. (a) Gris m. Hair touched with g., cheveux grisonnants. (b) Cheval gris. 'grey-'haired, -'headed, a. Aux cheveux gris; grisonnant.

greybeard ['greibiəd], s. Grison m; vieille barbe; vieux barbon.

greyhound ['greihaund], s. Lévrier m; (bitch) levrette f. G.-racing, courses de lévriers. G.-racing track, cynodrome m.

greyish ['greiiʃ], a. Grisâtre.

greylag (goose) ['greilæg('gu:s)], s. Orn: Oie f sauvage, oie cendrée.

greyness ['greinis], s. Teinte grise. The g. of London, la grisaille, la tonalité grise, de Londres.

grid [grid], s. 1. (a) Grille f, grillage m. El: Accumulator g., grille, grillage, d'accumulateur. (b) W.Tel: Valve g., grille de lampe. G. battery, pile de polarisation. Double-g. valve, lampe bigrille. S.a. BIAS¹ 4, SCREENED 1. 2. = GRIDIRON. 3. Surv: Treillis m, graticule m. G.-map, carte quadrillée. 4. The g., le réseau électrique national.

gridded ['gridid], a. (Carte) quadrillée.

griddle ['gridl], s. Tôle circulaire sur laquelle on cuit des galettes. 'griddle-cake, s. Galette f.

gridiron ['gridaiən], s. 1. Cu: Gril m. Ph: G. pendulum, balancier à gril. 2. U.S: F: Terrain m de football.

grief [gri:f], s. Chagrin m, douleur f, peine f. To die of g., mourir de chagrin. To come to g., (i) se voir accablé de malheurs; (ii) (of plan) échouer, mal tourner; (iii) avoir un accident; faire une chute (de cheval, etc.). To bring s.o., sth., to g., faire échouer qn, qch. 'grief-stricken, a. Pénétré, accablé, de douleur.

grievance ['gri:v(ə)ns], s. 1. Grief m. To air one's grievances, conter ses doléances. 2. Injustice f. To redress a g., réparer un tort fait à qn.

grieve [gri:v]. 1. v.tr. Chagriner, affliger, peiner (qn); faire de la peine à (qn). 2. v.i. Se chagriner, s'affliger, se désoler (over, about, sth., de qch.). grieved, a. Chagriné, affligé, désolé (at, de). Deeply g., navré. We are most g. to learn . . ., nous apprenons avec peine. . . .

grievous ['gri:vəs], a. 1. Douloureux, pénible. G. loss, perte cruelle. 2. (Blessure) grave; (erreur) grave, lamentable. -ly, adv. 1. Douloureusement, péniblement. 2. Gravement; grièvement (blessé).

griffin ['grifin], griffon¹ ['grifən], s. Myth: Griffon m.

griffon² ['grifən], s. (Chien) griffon m.

griffon³, s. G.(-vulture), (vautour m) griffon m.

grill¹ [gril], s. 1. Cu: Grillade f. 2. G.(-room), grill-room m (de restaurant).

grill², s. Dom.Ec: Gril m.

grill³, v.tr. Cu: Griller, brasiller (la viande). U.S: P: To g. a prisoner, cuisiner un détenu. grilled, a. Grillé. G. steak, bifteck m sur le gril; grillade f.

grille [gril], *s.* Grille *f* (de couvent, etc.); judas *m* (de porte). *Aut:* **Radiator** g., calandre *f*.

griller ['grilər], *s.* Gril *m* (de fourneau); grilloir *m*.

grim [grim], *a.* Menaçant. sinistre; (sourire) de mauvais augure; (humour) macabre; (visage) sévère, rebarbatif; (tyran) farouche. **G. Death,** la Mort inexorable. **To hold on like a. death,** se cramponner avec acharnement. **G. determination,** volonté inflexible. *F:* **"How do you feel?"—"Pretty g.",** "comment ça va?"—"Plutôt mal." **-ly,** *adv.* Sinistrement, sévèrement; (se battre) avec acharnement.

grimace¹ [gri'meis], *s.* **1.** Grimace *f.* **To make a** g., faire la grimace; faire des mines. **2.** Grimacerie *f,* affectation *f.* **To make grimaces,** faire des façons, des simagrées.

grimace², *v.i.* **1.** Grimacer; faire la grimace. **2.** Faire des façons, des mines, des simagrées. **grimacing,** *a.* Grimaçant, grimacier.

grimalkin [gri'mælkin], *s.* *F:* (Cat) Mistigri *m.*

grime¹ [graim], *s.* Saleté *f;* poussière *f* de charbon, de suie (qui vous entre dans la peau); crasse *f.*

grime², *v.tr.* (Of coal-dust, etc.) Salir, noircir, encrasser (le visage, les mains).

grimness ['grimnis], *s.* Caractère *m* sinistre, aspect *m* redoutable (de qch.); sévérité *f* (de visage); acharnement *m* (d'un combat).

grimy ['graimi], *a.* Sale, encrassé, noirci; noir (de suie, etc.); (linge) crasseux; (visage) barbouillé.

grin¹ [grin], *s.* Large sourire; sourire épanoui. **To give a broad** g., sourire à belles dents.

grin², *v.i.* (grinned) Sourire à belles dents. **To g. at s.o.,** (i) adresser à qn un sourire de grosse gaieté; (ii) regarder qn avec un sourire narquois. **He grinned broadly,** son visage s'épanouit en un large sourire. **To g. and bear it,** faire bonne contenance, garder le sourire. **To g. like a Cheshire cat,** rire à se fendre la bouche.

grind¹ [graind], *s.* **1.** Grincement *m,* crissement *m* (de roues, etc.). **2.** *F:* Labeur monotone et continu; *P:* turbin *m.* **The daily** g., le boulot journalier; le train-train quotidien. **What a g.!** quelle corvée!

grind², *v.* (ground [graund]; ground) **1.** *v.tr.* (a) Moudre (du blé, du café); moudre, piler (du poivre); broyer (des couleurs); *U.S:* hacher (la viande). **To g. sth. (down) to dust,** pulvériser qch.; réduire qch. en poudre. **To g. sth. between one's teeth,** broyer qch. entre ses dents. **To g. sth. under one's heel,** écraser qch. sous ses pieds. **To g. the faces of the poor,** pressurer, opprimer, les pauvres. (b) Meuler (une pièce coulée); rectifier (une pièce) à la meule; dépolir (le verre); égriser (le marbre, le verre, etc.). *Mec.E:* **To g. (in) a valve,** roder une soupape. **To g. down a lens,** meuler une lentille. (c) Aiguiser, émoudre, affûter (un outil); repasser (un couteau, un outil) (sur la meule). *S.a.* AXE 1. (d) **To g. one's teeth,** grincer, crisser, des dents. (e) **To g. a barrel organ,** jouer d'un orgue de Barbarie. **To g. (out) a tune,** tourner, seriner, un air. **2.** *v.i.* (a) (Of wheels, etc.) Grincer, crisser. (b) *F:* Bûcher, turbiner; *Sch:* bachoter. **To g. for an exam.,** potasser un examen. **ground,** *a.* **1.** Moulu, broyé, pilé. *S.a.* ALMOND, RICE. **2.** (Acier) meulé; (verre) dépoli. **G. (glass) stopper,** bouchon *m* à l'émeri. **grinding¹.** **I. G. sound,** grincement *m,* crissement *m.* **2. G. poverty,** la misère écrasante. **grinding²,** *s.* **1.** Mouture *f* (du blé); broyage *m,* broiement *m* (des couleurs); pilage *m* (dans un mortier). **2.** Oppression *f,* écrasement *m* (du peuple). **3.** (a) Meulage *m;* rodage *m;* polissage *m* à la meule. **G. machine,** machine *f* à meuler. (b) Aiguisage *m,* affûtage *m,* émoulage *m,* repassage *m.* **4.** Grincement *m,* crissement *m.* **'grinding-wheel,** *s.* Roue *f* à meuler; meule *f* de rectification.

grinder ['graindər], *s.* **1.** (a) Pileur, -euse; broyeur, -euse. (b) Rémouleur *m* (de couteaux). **Itinerant knife** g., repasseur ambulant. **2.** (a) (Dent) molaire *f.* (b) *pl.* *F:* *O:* Grinders, dents *f.* **3.** (a) Appareil broyeur. **Coffee-g.,** moulin *m* à café. *U.S:* **Meat g.,** hachoir *m.* (b) *Mec.E:* Machine *f* à rectifier. (c) Machine à aiguiser; affûteuse *f.*

grindstone ['graindstoun], *s.* Meule *f* (en grès) à aiguiser. *Geol:* **G. grit,** (pierre) meulière *f.* *F:* **To keep one's nose to the** g., travailler sans relâche, sans désemparer.

grip¹ [grip], *s.* **1.** Prise *f,* serrage *m;* serrement *m* (d'un outil, de mains); étreinte *f* (des mains). **To have a strong** g., avoir une forte poigne. **To be at grips with the enemy,** être aux prises avec l'ennemi. **To come to grips,** en venir aux mains, aux prises (with, avec). **To get a g. on sth.,** agripper qch. *Com:* **With handy g.,** avec nervures de prehension. **To lose one's g.,** (i) lâcher prise; (ii) *F:* commencer a manquer de poigne; (ii) *F:* baisser (du point de vue mental). *F:* **In the g. of a disease,** en proie a une maladie. **The fever has him in its g.,** la fièvre le tient. **To have, get, a good g. of the situation,** avoir, prendre. la situation bien en main; *F:* empaumer l'affaire. **To have a good g. of a subject,** bien posséder un sujet. **2.** (a) Poignée *f* (d'aviron, etc.); crosse *f* (de pistolet). (b) *Ten:* Manchon *m,* couvre-manche *m* (pour raquette). *Cy:* Manchon, poignée (de guidon). **3.** *Mec.E:* Douille *f* (de serrage); pince *f;* griffe *f.* **4.** *U.S:* Sac *m* de voyage.

grip², *v.tr.* (gripped) (a) Saisir, empoigner, *F:* agripper (qch.); serrer, étreindre, (qch.) dans la main. **To g. sth. in a vice,** serrer, pincer, qch. dans un étau. (b) *Abs.* **The wheels are not gripping,** les roues n'adhèrent pas (sur la route). *Nau:* **The anchor grips,** l'ancre croche, mord. (c) **He was gripped by fear,** la peur le saisit. **Play that grips the audience,** pièce qui empoigne les spectateurs. **Story that grips you,** histoire passionnante.

gripe [graip]. **1.** *v.tr.* (a) Affliger (qn). (b) Donner la colique (à qn). **Griping pains,** colique *f,* tranchées *fpl.* **2.** *v.i.* *F:* Râler, ronchonner, grogner, rouspéter.

gripes [graips], *s.pl.* Colique *f,* tranchées *fpl.*

grisly ['grizli], *a.* *Lit:* (a) Affreux, effroyable. (b) Effrayant, macabre. **G. shadow,** ombre monstrueuse.

grist [grist], *s.* **1.** Blé *m* à moudre. **That brings g. to the mill,** ça fait venir l'eau au moulin. **All is g. that comes to his mill,** il fait profit de tout. **2.** Blé moulu.

gristle ['grisl], *s.* Cartilage *m,* croquant *m.*

gristly ['grisli], *a.* Cartilagineux, -euse.

grit¹ [grit], *s.* **1.** (a) Grès *m,* sable *m.* (b) *Mec.E: etc:* Corps étrangers; impuretés *fpl.* **2.** (Gritstone) Grès (dur). **Millstone g.,** grès à meule(s); (pierre) meulière *f.* **3.** Grain *m* (d'une pierre). **4.** *F:* Cran *m,* courage *m.* **Man who has plenty of g.,** homme qui a du cran.

grit², *v.* (gritted) **1.** *v.i.* Grincer, crisser. **2.** *v.tr.* **To grit one's teeth,** grincer des dents. **3.** *v.tr.* Sabler (une route glissante).

gritstone ['gritstoun], *s.* Grès (dur); pierre *f* de grès.

gritty ['griti], *a.* (Sol) sablonneux; (crayon, etc.) graveleux. **G. pear,** poire graveleuse.

grizzle¹ ['grizl], *v.tr. & i.* Grisonner. **grizzled,** *a.* (Of hair, pers.) Grisonnant. **G. beard,** barbe poivre et sel.

grizzle², *s.* *F:* **1. To have a good** g., raconter ses griefs. **2.** Pleurnicherie *f.*

grizzle³, *v.i.* *F:* **1.** Ronchonner; grognonner. **2.** Pleurnicher, geindre.

grizzler ['grizlər], *s.* *F:* **1.** Ronchonneur, -euse. **2.** Pleurnicheur, -euse.

grizzly ['grizli], *a.* **1.** = GRIZZLED. **2.** *Z:* **G. (bear),** grizzli *m,* grizzly *m.*

groan¹ [groun], *s.* Gémissement *m,* plainte *f.* (*At public meeting*) **Groans,** murmures *m* (de désapprobation).

groan², *v.i.* Gémir; se plaindre. **To g. in pain,** gémir de douleur. **groaning,** *s.* Gémissement(s) *m(pl).*

groat [grout], *s.* *Num:* *A:* Pièce *f* de quatre pence.

groats [grouts], *s.pl.* Gruau *m* d'avoine.

grocer ['grousər], *s.* Épicier, -ière. **You can get it at the grocer's,** vous aurez cela à l'épicerie, chez l'épicier, à l'alimentation.

grocery ['grousəri], *s.* **1. G. store,** grocery, épicerie *f,* alimentation *f.* **2.** *pl.* **Groceries,** (articles *m* d') épicerie.

grog [grɔg], *s.* Grog *m.* **'grog-blossom,** *s.* Bourgeon *m* (au nez d'un ivrogne).

groggy ['grɔgi], *a.* Chancelant, titubant, vacillant. **To feel** g., être peu solide sur ses jambes. *F:* **G. old table,** vieille table bancale.

grogram ['grɔgrəm], *s.* *Tex:* Gros-grain *m.*

groin [grɔin], *s.* **1.** *Anat:* Aine *f.* **2.** *Arch:* (a) G.(-rib), arête *f* (de voûte). (b) Nervure *f* (d'arête). **'groin-vault,** *s.* *Arch:* Voûte *f* d'arêtes.

groined [grɔind], *a. Arch:* (Voûte) à arêtes.

grom(m)et ['grɔmit], *s.* = GRUMMET.

groom¹ [gru:m], *s.m.* 1. Gentilhomme, valet (de la Chambre du Roi, etc.). 2. (*a*) Palefrenier; valet d'écurie. (*b*) Valet (dont on se fait suivre à cheval). 3. = BRIDEGROOM.

groom², *v.tr.* Panser (un cheval). **groomed,** *a.* Well-groomed, (i) (cheval) bien entretenu, bien pansé; (ii) (*of pers.*) bien soigné, bien peigné.

groomsman, *pl.* -men ['gru:mzmən], *s.m.* Garçon d'honneur (à un mariage).

groove¹ [gru:v], *s.* 1. Rainure *f*; rayure *f* (d'un canon); cannelure *f* (d'une colonne); creux *m* (d'une vis); gouttière *f* (d'une épée); *Anat:* sillon *m*, gouttière (d'un os); *Carp:* (*notch*) encoche *f*; (*rabbet*) feuillure *f*; *Mount:* dièdre m. **Thumb-nail g.** (of penknife), onglet *m*. **G.** for sliding part, coulisse *f*, glissière *f*. *Carp:* **G. and tongue joint,** assemblage à rainure et languette. *Gramophones:* **Sound g.,** sillon sonore. 2. *F:* **To get into a g.,** s'encroûter; devenir routinier. **To get out of the g.,** sortir de l'ornière.

groove², *v.tr.* Rainer; rayer (un canon); canneler (une colonne). **To g. and tongue,** assembler à rainure et languette. **grooved,** *a.* Rayé, rainé, cannelé; à rayures, à rainures, à cannelures; (colonne) cannelée, striée; (pneu) cannelé; (roue) à gorge; (rail) à gorge, à ornière. **'grooving-plane,** *s. Tls:* Bouvet *m*; guillaume *m*.

grope [group], *v.i.* Tâtonner. **To g. for, after, sth.,** chercher qch. à tâtons. **To g. one's way,** avancer à tâtons, à l'aveuglette. **To g. one's way in, out,** entrer, sortir, à tâtons. **groping,** *a.* Tâtonnant. **-ly,** *adv.* A tâtons; en tâtonnant.

groper ['groupər], *s.* 1. Tâtonneur, -euse. 2. = GROUPER.

grosbeak ['grousbi:k], *s. Orn:* Gros-bec *m*.

grosgrain ['grougrein], *s. Tex:* Gros-grain *m*.

gross¹ [grous], *s.inv.* Douze douzaines *f*; grosse *f*. **Great g.,** douze grosses.

gross², *a.* 1. Gras, *f.* grasse; gros, *f.* grosse; tout en chair. 2. Grossier. (*a*) **G. ignorance,** ignorance crasse, grossière. **G. injustice,** injustice flagrante. **G. mistake,** grosse faute; faute grossière. (*b*) (*Of story*) Grivois, graveleux. 3. (*Of amount*) Brut. *Nau:* **G. displacement,** déplacement global. **G. tonnage,** jauge brute. *Com:* **G. profit,** bénéfice brut. **-ly,** *adv.* Grossièrement. **G. exaggerated,** exagéré outre mesure.

grossness ['grousnis], *s.* Grossièreté *f*; énormité *f* (d'un crime, etc.); indécence *f* (d'une histoire).

grotesque [gro'tesk]. 1. *a. & s.* Grotesque (*m*). 2. *a. F:* Absurde; saugrenu.

grotesqueness [gro'tesknis], *s.* Caractère *m* grotesque.

grotto, *pl.* -o(e)s ['grotou, -ouz], *s.* Grotte *f* (pittoresque).

ground¹. See GRIND².

ground², *s.* 1. Fond *m* (de la mer). (*Of ship*) **To touch g.,** talonner. 2. *pl.* **Grounds,** marc *m*, fond, (du café); sédiment *m*. 3. (*a*) Fond, champ *m* (d'un tableau). *Paint:* **G. colour,** première couche. *Cin:* **G. noise,** bruit de fond. (*b*) *Art:* **The middle g.,** le second plan. 4. (*a*) Raison *f*, cause *f*, sujet *m*; base *f* (de soupçons, etc.). **G. for complaint,** grief *m*. **There are grounds for supposing that . . . ,** il y a lieu de supposer que. . . . **What grounds have you for saying that?** sur quoi vous fondez-vous pour affirmer cela? **I acted thus upon good grounds,** c'est à bon escient que j'ai agi de la sorte. **Upon what grounds?** à quel titre? **He has been retired on health grounds,** on l'a mis à la retraite pour raison de santé. **On legal grounds,** pour des raisons de droit. (*b*) *Jur:* **Grounds for divorce,** motifs *m* de divorce. **Grounds for appeal,** voies *f* de recours. 5. (*a*) Sol *m*, terre *f*. **To sit down on the g.,** s'asseoir par terre. **To sleep on the (bare) g.,** coucher sur la dure. **To fall to the g.,** (i) tomber à, par, terre; (ii) *F:* (*of scheme*) tomber à l'eau. **To dash s.o.'s hopes to the g.,** anéantir les espérances de qn. **Above g.,** sur terre; *Min:* au jour, à la surface. *F:* **He is still above g.,** il est toujours de ce monde. **Burnt down to the g.,** brûlé de fond en comble. *F:* **That suits me down to the g.,** (i) cela me va à merveille, comme un gant; (ii) ça m'arrange

le mieux du monde. *U.S:* **To begin again from the g. up,** recommencer à zéro. **To study a case from the g. up,** étudier un problème de A à Z. (*Of building*) **To rest on firm g.,** reposer sur un terrain solide. *F:* **To be on sure, firm, g.,** connaître le terrain; être sûr de son fait. **To cut the g. from under s.o.'s feet,** couper l'herbe sous le pied à qn. *Av:* **G. staff,** personnel non-navigant, *F:* personnel rampant. (*b*) *Ven:* (*Of fox*) **To run, go, to g.,** se terrer. (*c*) **Terrain** *m. Mil:* **Drill g., parade g.,** champ *m*, terrain, de manœuvres. **To find a common g. for negotiations,** s'accorder sur une base de négociation. **To change, shift, one's g.,** changer de terrain. **To gain g.,** gagner du terrain; (*of idea*) se répandre; prendre pied. **To give g.,** lâcher pied; (*of troops*) se replier. **To lose g.,** perdre, céder, du terrain. **To hold, stand, one's g.,** tenir bon, tenir ferme, tenir tête, tenir pied. **To tread on forbidden g.,** empiéter sur un terrain défendu. (*d*) *pl.* **Grounds,** terrains, parc *m*, jardin *m* (d'une maison). **'ground(-)bait,** *s. Fish:* Amorce *f* de fond. **'ground ivy,** *s. Bot:* Lierre *m* terrestre, rampant. **'ground landlord,** *s.* Propriétaire foncier. **'ground light,** *s.* Balise *f* (d'un aéroport). **'ground line,** *s. Fish:* Ligne *f* de fond; traînée *f*. **'ground(-)nut,** *s. Arachide f.* **'ground plan,** *s. Const:* Plan *m* de fondation; plan horizontal; projection horizontale. *Fort:* Tracé *m* (d'une œuvre). **'ground-rent,** *s.* Loyer *m* de la terre; (*as source of income*) rente foncière. **'ground swell,** *s. Nau:* Houle *f*, lame *f*, de fond.

ground³. 1. *v.tr.* (*a*) Fonder, baser, appuyer (on, in, sth., sur qch.). **To g. one's belief on . . . ,** asseoir sa conviction sur. . . . (*b*) **To g. a pupil in Latin,** bien débuter un élève en latin. (*c*) Mettre (qch.) à terre. *Golf:* **To g. one's club,** asseoir sa crosse sur le sol. *Mil:* **G. arms!** reposez armes! l'arme au pied! (*d*) *Nau:* Jeter (un navire) à la côte. (*e*) *Av:* **To g. an aircraft,** interdire de vol (un avion). (*f*) *El: U.S:* Mettre, relier, à la terre. 2. *v.i.* (*a*) (*Of ship*) (i) (S')échouer (on, sur). (ii) Talonner. (*b*) (*Of balloon, etc.*) Atterrir. **grounded,** *a.* 1. **Well-, ill-g. belief,** croyance bien, mal, fondée. 2. **To be well g. in Latin,** posséder à fond les premiers principes du latin. **grounding,** *s.* 1. (*a*) Assise *f* (d'un argument sur qch.). (*b*) *Nau:* (i) échouage *m*; (ii) talonnement *m*. (*c*) *Av:* Interdiction *f* de vol. 2. **To have a good g. in Latin,** avoir une connaissance solide des rudiments du latin. **He has a good g.,** il a une bonne base.

groundhog ['graundhog], *s. U.S: Z:* Marmotte *f* d'Amérique.

groundless ['graundlis], *a.* (Soupçon, bruit) mal fondé, sans fondement, immotivé. **My suspicions were g.,** mes soupçons n'étaient pas fondés. **-ly,** *adv.* (S'alarmer) sans cause.

groundsel¹ ['graun(d)s(ə)l], *s. Bot:* Séneçon *m*.

groundsel², *s. Const:* Sole *f*, semelle *f* (de cadre); seuil *m* (de dormant de porte).

groundsheet ['graundʃi:t], *s.* Tapis *m* de sol.

groundsman, *pl.* -men ['graundzmən], *s.m.* Préposé à l'entretien d'un terrain de jeux.

groundwork ['graundwə:k], *s.* 1. Fond *m* (de tapisserie, etc.). 2. (*a*) Fondement *m*; assise *f* (de la société, etc.). (*b*) Plan *m*, canevas *m* (d'un roman, etc.).

group¹ [gru:p], *s.* Groupe *m*; peloton *m* (de personnes). **In groups,** par groupes. **To form a g.,** se grouper. **Literary g.,** cercle *m*, cénacle *m*, littéraire. *Mil:* **Army g.,** groupe d'armées. *Pol:* **Pressure g.,** groupe de pression. **To arrange articles in groups,** grouper des articles.

group². 1. *v.tr.* Grouper, disposer en groupes, répartir par groupes; combiner (des idées). 2. *v.i.* Se grouper (round, autour de). **grouping,** *s.* Groupement *m* (de figures, etc.); combinaison *f* (de couleurs); agencement *m* (des figures d'un tableau).

grouper ['gru:pər], *s. Ich:* Mérou *m*.

grouse¹ [graus], *s. inv. Orn:* Tétras *m. Esp.* (Red) g., lagopède *m* rouge d'Écosse, grouse *f*.

grouse², *s. F:* 1. **He enjoys a good g.,** il aime à grogner. 2. **To have a good g.,** avoir bonne raison de se plaindre. **To have a g. against s.o.,** avoir un grief contre qn.

grouse³, *v.i. F:* Ronchonner, maronner, renauder, bougonner (at, about, contre). **grousing,** *s.* Grognonnerie *f*, bougonnement *m*.

grout[1] [graut], *s. Const:* Coulis *m*; mortier *m* liquide. Cement g., lait *m* de ciment. *Hyd: El:* G. hole, trou *m* d'injection. Coffee g., fond *m* du café.

grout[2], *v.tr. Const:* To grout (in) stones, liaisonner, jointoyer, des pierres (avec du mortier liquide). **grouting**, *s.* 1. Jointoiement *m* au mortier liquide; injection *f.* 2. = GROUT[1].

grove [grouv], *s.* Bocage *m*, bosquet *m*. Beech grove, hêtraie *f.* Orange grove, orangeraie *f.*

grovel ['grɔv(ə)l], *v.i.* (grovelled) Ramper. To g. in the dirt, se vautrer, se traîner, dans la boue. *F:* To g. to, before, s.o., ramper, se mettre à plat ventre, devant qn. **grovelling**, *a.* Rampant; *F:* vil, abject.

grow [grou], *v.* (grew [gru:]; grown [groun]) I. *v.i.* 1. (*a*) (*Of plant*) Croître, pousser. To g. again, repousser; (*of plant, hair*) revenir. (*Of nail*) To g. in, s'incarner. (*b*) (*Of seeds*) Germer. A feeling of hate grew (up) between them, un sentiment de haine naissait entre eux. This state grew out of a few small towns, cet État est né de, doit son origine à, quelques bourgades. 2. (*Of pers.*) Grandir. To g. tall, devenir grand; se faire grand; grandir. To g. into a woman, passer femme. To g. up, grandir; atteindre l'âge adulte. To g. out of one's clothes, devenir trop grand pour ses vêtements. He will g. out of it, cela passera avec l'âge. 3. (*a*) S'accroître, croître, augmenter, grandir. The crowd grew, la foule grossissait. The firm has grown considerably, la maison a pris une extension considérable. To g. in wisdom, croître en sagesse. (*b*) Habit that grows on one, habitude qui vous gagne. (*c*) That picture grows on me, plus je regarde ce tableau plus il me plaît, plus il me dit. 4. (*a*) Devenir. To g. old, devenir vieux; se faire vieux; vieillir. To g. alarmed, s'alarmer. To g. rarer, se faire plus rare. It is growing dark, il commence à faire sombre. (*b*) I have grown to think that . . ., j'en suis venu à penser que. . . . II. **grow**, *v.tr.* 1. Cultiver (des roses); planter (des choux); faire venir (du blé). 2. Laisser pousser (sa barbe, etc.). **grown**, *a.* 1. (Full-)g., grand; qui a fini sa croissance. G.(-up) man, homme fait. When you are g. up, quand tu seras grand. *s.* The g.-ups, les grandes personnes; les adultes. 2. Wall g. over with ivy, mur couvert de lierre. **growing**[1], *a.* 1. Croissant; qui pousse. G. crops, récoltes sur pied. 2. Grandissant. G. child, enfant en cours de croissance. G. debt, dette grossissante. There was a g. fear that . . ., on craignait de plus en plus que. . . . 3. Wheat-g. district, région à blé. **growing**[2], *s.* 1. Croissance *f.* The g. age, l'âge de croissance. 2. Culture *f* (de plantes).

grower ['grouər], *s.* Cultivateur, -trice (de roses, etc.). Rose g., rosiériste *m.* Vine g., viticulteur *m.*

growl[1] [graul], *s.* Grondement *m*, grognement *m* (d'un chien, etc.).

growl[2], *v.i. & tr.* 1. (*Of animal*) Grogner, gronder; (*of cat*) feuler. 2. *F:* (*Of pers.*) Grogner, grommeler; *F:* ronchonner. To g. out oaths, marmonner des jurons. **growling**, *s.* Grognement *m*, grondement *m*; (*of cat*) feulement *m.*

growler ['graulər], *s.* 1. (*Pers.*) Ronchonneur, -euse; grognon *mf.* 2. *A.Veh:* *F:* Fiacre *m.*

growth [grouθ], *s.* 1. Croissance *f*, venue *f.* To attain full g., (i) atteindre l'âge adulte; (ii) (*of plant, etc.*) arriver à maturité. 2. Accroissement *m*; augmentation *f* (en quantité); extension *f* (des affaires). 3. (*a*) Yearly g., pousse annuelle. (*b*) Poussée *f* (de cheveux, etc.). A week's g. on his chin, le menton couvert d'une barbe de huit jours. 4. *Med:* Grosseur *f*, tumeur *f.* Morbid g., excroissance *f* morbide.

groyne [grɔin], *s. Hyd.E:* Épi *m*; éperon *m* (brise-lames).

grub[1] [grʌb], *s.* 1. *Ent:* (*a*) Larve *f.* (*b*) *F:* Ver (blanc); asticot *m.* 2. *P:* Mangeaille *f*, boustifaille *f.*

grub[2], *v.* (grubbed) 1. *v.tr.* (*a*) Fouir, travailler superficiellement (la terre). (*b*) Défricher (un terrain). 2. *v.i.* Fouiller (dans la terre). **grub about**, *v.i.* Fouiller, farfouiller **grub up**, *v.tr.* Essoucher, essarter (un terrain); extirper (une racine); déraciner (une plante). **grubbing**, *s.* Fouillage *m.* *S.a.* MONEY-GRUBBING. **'grubbing-hoe**, *s. Tls:* Hoyau *m.*

grubbiness ['grʌbinis], *s.* Malpropreté *f*, saleté *f.*

grubby ['grʌbi], *a.* 1. (*Of plant*) Véreux, -euse, mangé des vers. 2. Sale, malpropre, crasseux. G. hands, mains douteuses.

grudge[1] [grʌdʒ], *s.* Rancune *f.* To bear, owe, s.o., a g.; to have, nurse, a g. against s.o., garder rancune à qn; en vouloir à qn.

grudge[2], *v.tr.* 1. Donner, accorder, (qch. à qn) à contre-cœur. To g. s.o. the food he eats, mesurer la nourriture à qn. He does not g. his efforts, il ne marchande pas sa peine. 2. To g. s.o. his pleasures, voir d'un mauvais œil les plaisirs de qn. **grudging**, *a.* 1. (*Of praise, gift*) Donné, accordé, à contre-cœur, en rechignant. 2. He is g. of praise, il est avare de louanges. -**ly**, *adv.* (Faire qch.) à contre-cœur, à son corps défendant, en rechignant. To praise s.o. g., marchander ses éloges à qn.

gruel ['gruəl], *s.* 1. *Cu:* Gruau *m* (d'avoine); (*thin*) brouet *m.* 2. *P:* To give s.o. his g., (i) battre qn comme plâtre; (ii) échiner, éreinter, qn. To take, get, one's g., avaler sa médecine; encaisser.

gruelling[1] ['gruəliŋ], *a.* Éreintant, épuisant; (match) âprement disputé.

gruelling[2], *s.* *F:* Raclée *f*; épreuve éreintante.

gruesome ['gru:səm], *a.* Macabre, affreux; qui donne le frisson.

gruff [grʌf], *a.* (Ton) bourru, revêche, rébarbatif, rude. G. voice, grosse voix. -**ly**, *adv.* D'un ton bourru, rébarbatif.

gruffness ['grʌfnis], *s.* Ton bourru, rébarbatif.

grumble[1] ['grʌmbl], *s.* (*a*) Grommellement *m*, grognement *m.* (*b*) Murmure *m* (de mécontentement). To obey without a g., obéir sans murmurer.

grumble[2], *v.i. & tr.* Grommeler, grogner, grognonner, murmurer; *F:* ronchonner, bougonner. To g. about the food, trouver à redire à la nourriture. To g. at s.o., dire son mécontentement à qn. **grumbling**[1], *a.* Grognon, bougon; grondeur, -euse. -**ly**, *adv.* En grommelant; en murmurant. **grumbling**[2], *s.* 1. Grognonnerie *f.* 2. (Murmures *m* de) mécontentement *m.*

grumbler ['grʌmblər], *s.* 1. Grognon, -onne, bougon, -onne. An old g., un vieux ronchon. 2. Mécontent, -ente.

grummet ['grʌmit], *s.* 1. *Nau:* Estrope *f*; erse *f*; anneau *m* de corde; bague *f* en corde. 2. *Mec.E:* (*a*) Bague *f* d'étoupe. (*b*) Virole *f*, rondelle *f.*

grumpy ['grʌmpi], *a.* Maussade, renfrogné, grincheux. -**ily**, *adv.* Maussadement; d'un ton maussade ou renfrogné.

Grundy ['grʌndi]. *Pr.n.* **Mrs Grundy**, personnification *f* du qu'en-dira-t-on, de la pudibonderie.

grunt[1] [grʌnt], *s.* Grognement *m.*

grunt[2], *v.i.* (*Of pig, F: of pers.*) Grogner. **grunting**, *s.* Grognement(s) *m*(*pl*).

grunter ['grʌntər], *s.* 1. Grogneur, -euse. 2. *F:* Porc *m.*

g-string ['dʒi:striŋ], *s.* Cache-sexe *m inv.*

guano ['gwa:nou], *s.* Guano *m.*

guarantee[1] [gærən'ti:], *s.* 1. Garant, -ante; caution *f.* To go g. for s.o., se rendre garant de qn, se porter caution pour qn. 2. Clock with g. for two years, pendule avec une garantie de deux ans. 3. To leave sth. as a g.. donner qch. pour caution, en garantie, en gage.

guarantee[2], *v.tr.* Garantir, cautionner (qn, qch.); se porter garant, caution, pour (qn, qch.); garantir (une dette). Watch guaranteed for two years, montre garantie pour deux ans. I g. his obedience, je réponds de son obéissance. *F:* He'll come, I guarantee, il viendra, je vous le garantis. **guaranteed**, *a.* *Com:* Avec garantie.

guarantor [gærən'tɔ:r], *s.* Garant, -ante; garantisseur *m*; caution *f*, répondant *m.* To stand as g. for s.o., appuyer qn de sa garantie; cautionner qn.

guaranty ['gærənti], *s.* = GUARANTEE[1] 2, 3.

guard[1] [ga:d], *s.* 1. Garde *f.* (*a*) Posture *f* de défense. *Fenc: Box:* To take one's g., se mettre en garde. On g.! en garde! (*b*) To be, stand, on one's g., être se tenir, sur ses gardes; se tenir pour averti. To be on one's g. against sth., se méfier de qch. To put s.o. on (his) g., mettre qn en garde (against, contre); donner l'éveil à qn. To throw s.o. off his g., tromper la surveillance de qn; endormir la vigilance de qn. **To be caught off one's g.**, être pris au dépourvu. (c) *Mil:* **To be on g.** (duty), être en faction; être de garde, de faction. **To go on g., to mount g.**, monter la garde. **To come off g.**, descendre de garde. **To keep g.**, faire la garde. **He was marched off under g.**, il fut emmené sous escorte. **To keep a prisoner under g.**, garder un prisonnier à vue. **2.** *Coll.* (a) *Mil:* Garde *f*. **Advanced g.**, avant-garde *f*. **New g., relieving g.**, garde montante. **Old g.**, garde descendante. *F:* **One of the old g.**, un vieux de la vieille. **To form a g. of honour**, faire, former, la haie. (b) **To set a g. on a house**, faire surveiller une maison. **3.** (a) *Rail:* Chef *m* de train. (b) *Mil:* **The Guards**, la Garde. **Frontier g.**, garde-frontière *m*, *pl.* gardes-frontière. (c) *U.S:* Gardien *m* (de prison). **4.** (a) Dispositif protecteur; protecteur *m* (d'une machine); carter *m* (d'engrenages). **Fire-g.**, garde-feu *m inv*, pare-étincelles *m inv*. (b) (**Hand-**)g. of a sword, garde *f*, coquille *f*, d'une épée. (c) *Bookb:* Onglet *m*. **5.** *Med:* Correctif *m* (d'un médicament). **'guard-house**, *s. Mil:* Corps de garde *m inv*. **'guard-rail**, *s.* Garde-corps *m*, garde-fou *m*. *Nau:* Filière *f*, main courante. **'guard-room**, *s. Mil:* **1.** Corps de garde *m inv*. **2.** Poste *m* de police.

guard². **1.** *v.tr.* (a) Garder. **To g. s.o. from, against, a danger**, garder, protéger, qn d'un danger. (b) **To g. one's tongue**, surveiller sa langue. (c) *Ind:* Protéger (une courroie, etc.); grillager (une machine-outil). (d) *Cards:* **To g. one's clubs**, se garder à trèfle. **My king is guarded**, j'ai la garde au roi. **Guarded king**, roi second. **Guarded queen**, dame troisième. (e) *Med:* Mêler un correctif à (un narcotique). **2.** *v.i.* **To g. against sth.**, se garder, se mettre à l'abri, de qch.; se précautionner contre qch.; parer à qch. **To g. against an error**, se méfier d'une erreur. **guarded**, *a.* (*Of speech, etc.*) Prudent, mesuré. **To be g. in one's speech**, surveiller ses paroles; ne parler qu'à bon escient. **-ly**, *adv.* Avec réserve, avec précaution.

guardian ['gɑːdjən], *s.* **1.** Gardien, -ienne. **2.** Tuteur, -trice, curateur, -trice (de mineur, etc.). **3.** *A:* **The (Board of) Guardians**, le comité d'administration de l'Assistance publique. **4.** *Attrib.* Gardien, tutélaire. **G. angel**, ange gardien.

guardianship ['gɑːdjənʃip], *s.* **1.** Garde *f*. **2.** *Jur:* Gestion *f* tutélaire; tutelle *f*, curatelle *f*. **Child under g.**, enfant en tutelle.

guardship ['gɑːdʃip], *s. Navy:* Stationnaire *m*.

guardsman, *pl.* **-men** ['gɑːdzmən], *s.m.* Soldat *m* ou officier de la Garde.

guava ['gwɑːvə], *s. Bot:* Goyave *f*. **G.(-tree)**, goyavier *m*.

gubernatorial [gʌbənə'tɔːriəl] *a. U.S:* Du gouverneur.

gudgeon¹ ['gʌdʒən], *s. Ich:* Goujon *m*.

gudgeon², *s.* **1.** *Mec.E:* Goujon *m*, tourillon *m*, axe *m*. **2.** *Const:* Goujon (pour pierres). **'gudgeon-pin**, *s.* **1.** *I.C.E:* Axe *m* de pied de bielle. **2.** *Mch:* Tourillon *m* de la crosse.

guelder rose ['geldə'rouz], *s. Bot:* Boule-de-neige *f*.

Guelph [gwelf], *s. Hist:* Guelfe *m*.

Guernsey ['gəːnzi]. *Pr.n. Geog:* Guernesey.

guer(r)illa [gə'rilə], *s. Mil:* **1.** Guérillero *m*. **2.** **G. warfare**, guerre *f* de guérillas, d'embuscades.

guess¹ [ges], *s.* Conjecture *f*, estimation *f*. **To give, have, make, a g.**, (i) hasarder une conjecture; (ii) tâcher de deviner. **I give you three guesses**, je vous le donne en trois. **It's pure g.-work**, c'est pure conjecture. **By g.(-work)**, à l'estime; au jugé; à vue de nez. *F:* **It's anybody's g.**, Dieu seul le sait; qui sait? **Your g. is as good as mine**, j'en sais autant que toi.

guess², *v.tr. & i.* **1. To g. at sth.**, (tâcher de) deviner, conjecturer, qch. **To g. (at) the length of sth.**, estimer la longueur de qch. **I guessed him to be twenty-five**, je lui donnai vingt-cinq ans. **To keep an opponent guessing**, mystifier un adversaire. **2. To g. right, wrong**, bien, mal, deviner. **To g. a riddle**, trouver le mot d'une énigme. **You've guessed it!** vous y êtes! **3.** *U.S:* Croire, penser. **You're right, I g.**, oui, il me semble que vous avez raison.

guest [gest]. *s.* **1.** Convive *mf*; invité, -ée; hôte, -esse. *attrib.* **G. room**, chambre *f* d'amis. **2.** (i) Pensionnaire *mf*, (ii) client, -ente (d'un hôtel). *S.a.* PAYING¹

1. 'guest-house, *s.* **1.** Hôtellerie *f* (d'un monastère). **2.** Pension *f* de famille.

guffaw¹ [gʌ'fɔː], *s.* Gros rire (bruyant); pouffement *m* (de rire).

guffaw², *v.i.* Pouffer de rire; partir d'un gros rire.

Guiana [gi'ɑːnə]. *Pr.n. Geog:* La Guyane.

Guianese [ˌgiə'niːz], *a. & s. Geog:* Guyanais, -aise.

guidance ['gaid(ə)ns], *s.* **1.** Direction *f*, gouverne *f*, conduite *f*. **I owe much to his g.**, je dois beaucoup à ses conseils. **This is for your g.**, ceci est à titre d'indication; ceci est pour votre gouverne. *Sch:* **Vocational g.**, orientation professionnelle. **2.** *Tchn:* Guidage *m*. **Command g.**, téléguidage *m* par ondes haute-fréquence.

guide¹ [gaid], *s.* **1.** (*Pers.*) (a) Guide *m*. **Alpine g.**, guide alpin. **G., philosopher and friend**, mentor *m*. **To take sth. as a g.**, prendre qch. pour règle. (b) (**Girl**) g., éclaireuse *f*; (*attached to Fr. R.C. Ch.*) guide *f* de France. **2.** **G.(-book)**, guide *m*; itinéraire *m*. **G. to Switzerland**, guide de la Suisse. **G. to photography**, introduction *f* à la photographie. **3.** (a) Indication *f*, exemple *m*. **Let this be a g. to you**, que ceci vous serve d'exemple. (b) *Mec.E:* **Belt-g.**, guide de courroie; guide-courroie *m*. *Mch:* (**Slipper-**)g., glissière *f*. *Tex:* **Thread-g.**, distributeur *m* du fil. *Mec.E:* **Guides, g.-rails**, guidage *m* (*of pile-driver, etc.*). (c) **G.-cards**, (*of card-index*), intercalaires *m*. **'guide-lines**, *s.pl.* Transparent (rayé) (pour écrire). **'guide-rope**, *s.* **1.** Câble *m* de guidage. **2.** *Aer:* Guide-rope *m*.

guide², *v.tr.* Guider, conduire, diriger. **To g. the way for s.o.**, guider qn. **All are guided by him**, tous se règlent sur lui. **guided**, *a.* (a) *Mount: etc:* Sous la conduite d'un guide. (b) (*Of missile*) Téléguidé. **guiding¹**, *a.* Qui sert de guide; directeur, -trice. **G. principle**, principe directeur. **G. star**, guide *m*. **guiding²**, *s.* Guidage *m*, conduite *f*, direction *f*.

guider ['gaidər], *s.f.* Cheftaine (de guides ou d'éclaireuses).

guild [gild], *s.* **1.** *Hist:* Corporation *f*. **Trade g.**, corps *m* de métier. **2.** Association *f*, confrérie *f*. **Church g.**, cercle *m* (catholique, etc.).

guilder ['gildər], *s. Num:* Gulden *m*.

guildhall ['gildhɔːl], *s.* Hôtel *m* de ville.

guile [gail], *s.* Artifice *m*, ruse *f*, astuce *f*. **She uses the g. of her sex**, elle use de la finesse de son sexe.

guileful ['gailful], *a.* Astucieux, artificieux, rusé; finassier, -ière.

guileless ['gaillis], *a.* **1.** Franc, *f* franche; sincère, loyal; sans malice. **2.** Candide, naïf. **-ly**, *adv.* **1.** Franchement, sincèrement. **2.** Candidement.

guilelessness ['gaillisnis], *s.* **1.** Franchise *f*, sincérité *f*. **2.** Candeur *f*, naïveté *f*.

guillemot ['gilimɔt], *s. Orn:* Guillemot *m*.

guillotine¹ [gilə'tiːn], *s.* **1.** Guillotine *f*. **2.** *Bookb:* Massicot *m*; presse *f* à rogner. **3.** *Parl:* Clôture *f* par tranches.

guillotine², *v.tr.* Guillotiner, décapiter (qn). **guillotining**, *s.* Guillotinement *m*; exécution *f*.

guilt [gilt], *s.* Culpabilité *f*. *S.a.* ADMIT 1.

guiltless ['giltlis], *a.* Innocent (of sth., de qch.).

guiltlessness ['giltlisnis], *s.* Innocence *f*.

guilty ['gilti]. *a.* Coupable. (a) **G. of theft**, coupable de vol. **G. person**, coupable *mf*. *Jur:* **To plead g.**, s'avouer coupable. **The accused pleads not g.**, l'accusé nie. **To find s.o. g.**, not g., prononcer qn coupable, innocent. **He was found g.**, il fut reconnu coupable. (b) **G. conscience**, mauvaise conscience. **G. look**, regard confus. **-ily**, *adv.* Coupablement; d'un air coupable.

Guinea ['gini]. **1.** *Pr.n. Geog:* La Guinée. **2.** *s. A:* (Pièce *f* d'or d'une) guinée (= 21 shillings) (encore usitée comme monnaie de compte). **'guinea-cock**, *s.m.* Pintade *f* mâle. **'guinea-fowl**, *s.* Pintade *f*. **'guinea-pig**, *s.* Cobaye *m*; cochon *m* d'Inde. *F:* **To be a g.-p.**, servir de cobaye.

Guinean ['giniən], *a. & s. Geog:* Guinéen, -enne.

guise [gaiz], *s.* **1.** *A:* Vêtements *mpl*, costume *m*. **In the g. of a pilgrim**, vêtu ou travesti en pèlerin. **2.** **She appeared in the g. of a nymph**, elle apparut sous la forme d'une nymphe. **Under, in, the g. of friendship**, sous l'apparence, sous le masque, de l'amitié.

guitar [gi'tɑːr], s. *Mus:* Guitare *f.* **G. player,** guitariste *m.*

gulch [gʌltʃ], s. *U.S:* Ravin *m* (aurifère).

gules [gjuːlz], s. *Her:* Gueules *m.*

gulf [gʌlf], s. **1.** *Geog:* Golfe *m.* **The G. Stream,** le Courant du Golfe, le Gulf-Stream. **2.** Gouffre *m*, abîme *m*; abysse *m* (de la mer).

gull¹ [gʌl], s. *Orn:* Mouette *f*, goéland *m.*

gull², s. *F: O:* Gogo *m*, jobard *m*, gobeur *m.*

gull³, *v.tr. F: O:* Jobarder, flouer, rouler (qn). **He is easily gulled,** il se laisse facilement rouler.

gullet ['gʌlit], s. Œsophage *m*; *F:* gosier *m.*

gullibility [gʌli'biliti], s. Jobarderie *f*, jobardise *f.*

gullible ['gʌlibl], a. Facile à duper; jobard; qui s'en laisse conter.

gully¹ ['gʌli], s. **1.** *Geol:* (Petit) ravin; couloir *m.* **2.** *Civ.E:* Caniveau *m*; rigole *f.* **'gully-hole,** s. Bouche *f* d'égout.

gully², *v.tr.* Raviner; creuser.

gulp¹ [gʌlp], s. Coup *m* de gosier. **At one g.,** (avaler qch.) d'un coup; (vider un verre) d'un (seul) trait, d'une lampée.

gulp². **1.** *v.tr.* (a) **To g. sth. down,** avaler qch. à grosses bouchées; ingurgiter, gober (une huître); avaler (un verre de vin) à pleine gorge. **He gulped it down,** il n'en fit qu'une bouchée; (of drink) il n'en fît qu'une gorgée. (b) *F:* **To g. down, back, one's tears,** avaler, refouler, ses larmes. **To g. down a sob,** ravaler un sanglot. **2.** *v.i.* Avoir un brusque serrement de gorge. **He gulped,** sa gorge se serra.

gum¹ [gʌm], s. **1.** Gomme *f* (soluble à l'eau). **2.** (Mucilage) Gomme, colle *f.* **3.** (a) **G. resin,** gomme-résine *f.* (b) **G. elastic,** *U.S:* gum, gomme élastique; caoutchouc *m.* **4.** (a) = CHEWING-GUM. (b) (Sweet-meat) Boule *f* de gomme. **5.** (Of eye) Chassie *f.* **6.** *Bot:* **G.(-tree),** gommier *m.* *P:* **To be up a g.-tree,** être dans le pétrin. **gum-'arabic,** s. Gomme *f* arabique. **'gum-boots,** *s.pl.* Bottes *f* de caoutchouc. **gum 'tragacanth,** s. *Com:* Gomme *f* adragante.

gum², *v.* (gummed) **1.** *v.tr.* (a) Gommer; encoller (le papier, la toile). (b) Coller (une page dans un livre, etc.). (c) **To gum (up),** gommer (un piston); encrasser (une lime). **2.** *v.i.* **To gum (up),** (of piston) (se) gommer; (of file) s'encrasser. **gummed,** a. **1.** (Of label, etc.) Gommé. **2.** **G. piston,** piston gommé. **G. oil,** huile goudronnée. **gumming,** s. Gommage *m.*

gum³, s. Gencive *f.*

gum⁴, *int. F:* (Euphemism for GOD) **By g.!** fichtre! mazette!

gumboil ['gʌmbɔil], s. Abcès *m* à la gencive; fluxion *f* (à la joue).

gummy ['gʌmi], a. **1.** Gommeux, gluant, visqueux. **G. oil,** huile goudronneuse. **2.** (Of eyes) Chassieux.

gumption ['gʌm(p)ʃ(ə)n], s. *F:* Jugeotte *f.* **He has plenty of g.,** c'est un débrouillard.

gun [gʌn], s. **1.** (a) *Artil:* Canon *m.* **Rifled g.,** canon rayé. **The guns,** le canon, l'artillerie *f.* **The big guns,** le gros canon. *Navy:* **Naval gun,** pièce *f* de bord. **Heavy g.,** grosse pièce. **After g.,** pièce de retraite. **To be going great guns,** marcher tambour battant. (b) **Salute of six guns,** salve de six coups de canon. **2.** (a) Fusil *m*; *esp.* fusil de chasse non rayé. (Cp. RIFLE² 2.) **Sporting g., shot-g.,** fusil de chasse. (b) **A party of six guns,** une bande de six chasseurs, de six fusils. **3.** *U.S:* Revolver *m*; pistolet *m.* **4.** *Paint:* Spray g., pistolet (vaporisateur). *S.a.* GREASE-GUN. **'gun-carriage,** s. *Artil:* Affût *m* (de canon); (at military funeral) prolonge *f* d'artillerie. **'gun-case,** s. Étui *m* à fusil. **'gun-cotton,** s. *Exp:* Coton nitré; fulmicoton *m*, coton-poudre *m.* **'gun-dog,** s. Chien *m* de chasse à tir, chien d'arrêt. **'gun-fodder,** s. *F:* Chair *f* à canon. **'gun-room,** s. *Navy:* Poste *m* des aspirants. **'gun-running,** s. Contrebande *f* d'armes.

gunboat ['gʌnbout], s. *(Chaloupe)* canonnière *f.*

gunfire ['gʌnfaiə], s. *Artill:* Canonnade *f*; feu *m* (des pièces).

gunman, *pl.* -men ['gʌnmən], s.m. *U.S:* Voleur armé; bandit *m.*

gunmetal ['gʌnmetl], s. **1.** Bronze *m* à canon. **2.** *Com: F:* Métal oxydé.

gunnel ['gʌn(ə)l], s. = GUNWALE.

gunner ['gʌnər], s. (a) Artilleur *m*, canonnier *m.* (b) **(Machine-)g.,** mitrailleur *m.*

gunnery ['gʌnəri], s. Artillerie *f*; tir *m* au canon.

gunpowder ['gʌnpaudər], s. Poudre *f* (à canon). *Hist:* **The G. Plot,** la Conspiration des Poudres (1605).

gunshot ['gʌnʃɔt], s. **1.** Coup *m* de fusil, de canon; coup de feu. **G. wound,** blessure par balle, par obus. **2. Within g.,** à (une) portée de fusil. **Out of g.,** hors de portée de fusil.

gunsmith ['gʌnsmiθ], s. Armurier *m.* **G.'s shop,** armurerie *f.*

gunwale ['gʌn(ə)l], s. *Nau:* Plat-bord *m.* (Of ship) **To roll g. under,** engager; rouler à faire cuiller.

gurgle¹ ['gəːgl], s. (a) (Of liquid) Glouglou *m*; gargouillis *m* (de l'eau qui tombe). (b) *F:* (Of pers.) Gloussement *m*, roucoulement *m.*

gurgle². **1.** *v.i.* (Of liquid) (a) Glouglouter; faire glouglou. (b) Gargouiller (en tombant). **2.** *v.i. & tr.* (Of pers.) Glousser, roucouler. **He gurgled with laughter,** il eut un rire gras. **gurgling,** s. **1.** (a) Glouglou *m.* (b) Gargouillement *m*, gargouillis *m.* **2.** *F:* Roucoulement *m.*

gurnard ['gəːnəd], **gurnet** ['gəːnit], s. *Ich:* Red g., grondin *m* rouge. **Grey g.,** grondin gris. **Flying g.,** rouget volant.

Guru ['guruː], s. *Hindu Rel:* Gourou *m.*

gush¹ [gʌʃ], s. **1.** Jaillissement *m*, effusion *f* (d'une source, de larmes). **2.** Jet *m*, flot *m* (de sang). **3.** Débordement sentimental.

gush², *v.i.* (a) **To gush (forth, out),** jaillir, saillir, couler à flots, déborder; (of torrent) bouillonner. **The blood was gushing out,** le sang sortait à gros bouillons. **The tears gushed into her eyes,** un flot de larmes lui monta aux yeux. (b) Faire de la sensiblerie; *F:* la faire au sentiment. **She gushed over their baby,** elle s'attendrissait sur leur bébé. **gushing¹,** a. **1.** (Of water) Jaillissant, vif; (of torrent) bouillonnant. **G. spring,** source d'eau vive. **2.** (Of pers.) Exubérant, expansif. **G. compliments,** compliments chaleureux. **-ly,** adv. Avec effusion. **gushing²,** s. = GUSH¹ 3.

gusher ['gʌʃər], s. Source jaillissante. (Mineral oil) **G.,** puits jaillissant.

gusset ['gʌsit], s. *Dressm: Tail:* Élargissure *f*, soufflet *m*; gousset *m* (de manche, etc.).

gust [gʌst], s, **G. of rain,** ondée *f*, giboulée *f.* **G. of wind,** coup *m* de vent; rafale *f*, bourrasque *f*, *Nau:* grain *m.* **G. of anger,** bouffée *f* de colère.

gustative ['gʌstətiv], a. Gustatif.

gustatory ['gʌstətəri], a. (Nerf, etc.) gustatif.

gusto ['gʌstou], s. **To eat sth. with gusto,** manger qch. savoureusement, en savourant. *F:* **To do sth. with g.,** faire qch. (i) avec plaisir, (ii) avec entrain, avec brio.

gusty ['gʌsti], a. (Vent) à rafales, qui souffle par rafales; (journée) de grand vent.

gut¹ [gʌt], s. **1.** *Anat:* Boyau *m*, intestin *m.* **Small g.,** intestin grêle. **2.** *pl.* **Guts.** (a) Boyaux, intestins, entrailles *f*; vidure *f* (de volaille). (b) *F:* **To have guts,** avoir du cran; avoir du cœur au ventre. **3.** Corde *f* à, de, boyau (pour violons, etc.). **4.** *Fish:* **Silkworm g., silk gut,** racine (anglaise). **5.** Goulet *m* (dans un port, etc.); boyau, étranglement *m* (dans une rue).

gut², *v.tr.* (gutted) Étriper (un animal); vider (un poisson, une volaille). **The fire gutted the house,** le feu n'a laissé que les quatre murs, la carcasse, de la maison.

gutta-percha ['gʌtə'pəːtʃə], s. Gutta-percha *f.*

gutter¹ ['gʌtər], s. **1.** (Eaves-)g., gouttière *f*, chéneau *m* (de toit). **2.** Ruisseau *m* (de rue); caniveau *m* (de chaussée). **Open g. (across road),** cassis *m.* **Born in the g.,** né dans le ruisseau. **He rose from the g.,** il est sorti de très bas, du ruisseau, il est parti de rien. **G. wit,** esprit gavroche. **3.** (a) Rigole *f*; sillon (creusé par la pluie). (b) Cannelure *f*, rainure *f* (dans une tôle, etc.). **'gutter(-)press,** s. *Journ:* Bas-fonds *mpl* du journalisme; la presse de bas étage. **'gutter-snipe,** s. Gamin, -ine, des rues; gavroche *m*; petit voyou, petite voyoute.

gutter². **1.** *v.tr.* Sillonner, raviner (la terre). **2.** *v.i.* (Of candle) Couler. **guttering,** s. *Coll.* Gouttières *fpl* (d'une maison).

guttural ['gʌtərəl]. **1.** a. Guttural, -aux. **2.** s. *Ling:* Gutturale *f.* **-ally,** adv. D'un ton guttural, d'une voix gutturale.

Guy¹ [gai]. **1.** *Pr.n.m.* Gui, Guy. **2.** *s.m.* (*a*) Effigie *f* burlesque de Guy Fawkes. (*b*) Épouvantail *m.* **She's a regular g.,** elle est ficelée comme quatre sous. **What a g.!** comme la voilà fagotée! **3.** *U.S: F:* Type *m,* individu *m.* **A big g.,** (i) un gros bonnet; (ii) un criminel de marque. **Tough g.,** dur *m.* **Wise g.,** donneur *m* de conseils.

guy², *v.tr.* (guyed) (*a*) Se moquer de (qn). (*b*) *Th:* Charger, travestir (un rôle).

guy³, *s. Nau: etc:* (Câble *m* de) retenue *f;* hauban *m,* gui *m,* étai *m.* **'guy-rope,** *s.* (*a*) Cordon *m* (de tente). (*b*) *Aer:* Corde *f* de manœuvre.

guy⁴, *v.tr.* Hauban(n)er (un mât, etc.).

Guyana [gai'ænə]. *Pr.n. Geog:* La Guyane.

guzzle¹ ['gʌzl], *s.* Bâfrée *f.*

guzzle², *v.tr. & i.* (*a*) Bâfrer, bouffer (la nourriture); s'empiffrer, goinfrer. (*b*) Boire avidement, lamper (la boisson). **guzzling,** *a.* Glouton, goulu.

guzzler ['gʌzlər], *s.* (*a*) Bâfreur, -euse; goinfre *m.* (*b*) Pochard, -arde; sac *m* à vin.

gym [dʒim], *s. F:* **1.** = GYMNASIUM. **2.** = GYMNASTICS. *S.a.* SHOE.

gymkhana [dʒim'kɑːnə], *s.* Gymkhana *m.*

gymnasium [dʒim'neiziəm], *s.* Gymnase *mf.*

gymnast ['dʒimnæst], *s.* Gymnaste *mf.*

gymnastic [dʒim'næstik]. **1.** *a.* Gymnastique. **2.** *s.pl.* (*Usu. with sg. const.*) **Gymnastics,** gymnastique *f.* **To do g.,** faire de la gymnastique.

gymnosophy [dʒim'nɔsəfi], *s.* Gymnosophie *f.*

gymnosophist [dʒim'nɔsəfist], *s.* Gymnosophiste *m.*

gymnotus, *pl.* **-i** [dʒim'noutəs, -ai], *s. Ich:* Gymnote *m.*

gynaeceum [ˌdʒaini'siəm], *s.* Gynécée *m.*

gynaecological [ˌgainikə'lədʒik(ə)l], *a.* Gynécologique.

gynaecologist [ˌgaini'kɔlədʒist], *s.* Gynécologiste *mf,* gynécologue *mf.*

gynaecology [ˌgaini'kɔlədʒi], *s.* Gynécologie *f.*

gyp¹ [dʒip], *s.m.* (*Cambridge & Durham Univ.*) Domestique (attaché au service des étudiants).

gyp², *s. P:* **To give s.o. g.,** (i) flanquer une raclée à qn; (ii) (*of toothache, etc.*) faire souffrir qn.

gyp³, *v.tr. U.S: P:* Filouter, escroquer (qn).

gypsophila [dʒip'sɔfilə], *s. Bot:* Gypsophile *m* or *f.*

gypsum ['dʒipsəm], *s. Miner:* Gypse *m;* pierre *f* à plâtre. **'gypsum-quarry,** *s.* Plâtrière *f.*

gypsy ['dʒipsi], *s.* = GIPSY.

gyrate [dʒaireit], *v.i.* Tourner; tournoyer.

gyration [dʒai'reiʃ(ə)n], *s.* Giration *f.*

gyratory [dʒai'reit(ə)ri, 'dʒairət(ə)ri], *a.* Giratoire.

gyro [dʒairou], *s. Av:* = GYROSCOPE. **Directional g.,** conservateur *m* de cap.

gyro-compass ['dʒairou'kʌmpəs], *s. Nau:* Gyrocompas *m.*

gyroplane ['dʒairoplein], *s. Av:* Giravion *m.*

gyroscope ['dʒairəskoup], *s.* Gyroscope *m.*

gyroscopic ['dʒairo'skɔpik], *a.* Gyroscopique.

gyrostabilizer ['dʒairo'steibilaizər], *s. Av:* Gyrostabilisateur *m.*

gyrostat ['dʒairəstæt], *s.* Gyrostat *m.*

H, h [eitʃ], s. 1. (La lettre) H, h *mf.* **Silent h,** h muette. **H aspirate,** h aspirée. **To drop one's h's** [ˈeitʃiz], ne pas aspirer les h. *Tp:* **H for Harry,** H comme Henri. 2. **H beam, H girder,** poutre en H, en double T. 3. *Mil:* **H-bomb,** bombe f à (l')hydrogène, bombe H.

ha¹ [hɑː], *int.* Ha! ah!

ha², *v.i. See* HUM² 1.

haberdasher [ˈhæbədæʃər], s. 1. Mercier m. 2. (*esp. U.S.*) Chemisier m.

haberdashery [ˈhæbədæʃəri], s. 1. Mercerie f. 2. (*esp. U.S.*) Chemiserie f.

habit [ˈhæbit], s. 1. Habitude f, coutume f. **To be in the h.,** **to make a h.,** **of doing sth.,** avoir coutume, avoir l'habitude, avoir pour habitude, de faire qch. **I don't make a h. of it,** ce n'est pas une habitude chez moi. **To get, grow, into the h. of doing sth.,** prendre, contracter, l'habitude de faire qch. **To get a dog into habits of obedience,** habituer un chien à obéir. **To fall out, get out, of a h.,** perdre une habitude; se défaire d'une habitude. **Out of (sheer) h.,** **from force of h.,** par habitude. 2. (a) **H. of body,** tempérament m; constitution f physique. (b) **H. of mind,** tournure f d'esprit. 3. *Cost:* (a) **Habit** m (de religieuse). (b) **(Lady's) riding-h.,** amazone f; habit de cheval. **'habit-forming,** a. (Stupéfiant, etc.) qui mène à la toxicomanie.

habitability [ˌhæbitəˈbiliti], **habitableness** [ˈhæbitəblnis], s. Habitabilité f.

habitable [ˈhæbitəbl], a. Habitable.

habitat [ˈhæbitæt], s. *Nat.Hist:* Habitat m.

habitation [ˌhæbiˈteiʃ(ə)n], s. 1. Habitation f (d'une maison). **Fit for h.,** en état (d'être habité). 2. Habitation, demeure f; lieu m de séjour.

habitual [həˈbitjuəl], a. 1. Habituel, d'habitude. 2. (Ivrogne) invétéré. **He is a h. liar,** le mensonge lui est familier. **-ally,** *adv.* Habituellement, d'habitude, par habitude.

habituate [həˈbitjueit], *v.tr.* **To h. s.o. to sth., to doing sth.,** habituer, accoutumer, qn à qch., à faire qch.

habitué [(h)əˈbitjuei], s. Habitué, -e.

hachure¹ [hæˈʃər, hæˈʃjuər], s. *Mapm:* Hachure f.

hachure², *v.tr.* Hachurer.

hack¹ [hæk], s. (a) Taillade f, entaille f. (b) *Fb:* Coup m de pied (sur le tibia). **'hack-saw,** s. Scie f à métaux.

hack², *v.tr. & i.* Hacher; *Surg: F:* charcuter (un malade). **To h. sth. to pieces,** tailler qch. en pièces. **To h. sth. down,** abattre qch. à coups de pioche. **Hacked out,** taillé à coups de serpe, à coups de hache. **To h. up the joint,** massacrer le rôti. **To h. one's way through,** se frayer un chemin. **To h. s.o. on the shins,** donner à qn des coups de pied sur le tibia. **hacking,** a. **H. cough,** toux sèche et pénible.

hack³, s. 1. (a) Cheval m de louage. (b) *F:* Rosse f, haridelle f. (c) Cheval de selle à toutes fins. (d) *U.S:* Voiture f de place, de louage. 2. Homme m de peine. **Literary h.,** écrivain m à la tâche. *Journ:* **H. writer,** écrivain besogneux. **To be a h. reporter,** *F:* faire la chronique des chiens écrasés. **'hack-work,** s. Travail m d'écrivain à gages; besogne f alimentaire.

hack⁴. 1. *v.tr.* (a) Banaliser (qch.). **To h. an argument to death,** ressasser un argument. (b) Louer (des chevaux). 2. *v.i.* (a) **To h. along the road,** cheminer à cheval. **To h. home** (after hunting), rentrer (chez soi) au petit trot. (b) Monter des chevaux de louage.

hackle¹ [ˈhækl], s. 1. *Tex:* Peigne m, sérançoir m. 2. *Orn:* Plume f du cou (des gallinacés). *pl.* **Hackles,** camail m. (Of pers.) **When his hackles are up,** quand il monte sur ses ergots.

hackle², *v.tr. Tex:* Peigner, sérancer (le lin, le chanvre).

hackney [ˈhækni], s. (a) Cheval m de louage. (b) Cheval de route; bidet m. (c) (Cheval) trotteur m (de course). **'hackney-'carriage,** s. Voiture f de place, de louage.

hackneyed [ˈhæknid], a. (Sujet) rebattu, usé, banal. **H. phrase,** expression devenue banale; cliché m.

had. *See* HAVE².

haddock [ˈhædək], s. *Ich:* Aiglefin m. *Cu:* **Smoked h.,** haddock m.

Hades [ˈheidiːz], s. *Gr.Myth:* Les Enfers m.

haematite [ˈhemətait, ˈhiː-], s. *Miner:* Hématite f.

haematologist [ˌhiːməˈtɔlədʒist], s. *Med:* Hématologue m.

haematology [ˌhiːməˈtɔlədʒi], s. *Med:* Hématologie f.

haematuria [ˌhiːməˈtjuəriə], s. *Med:* Hématurie f.

haemoglobin [ˌhiːmoˈgloubin], s. Hémoglobine f.

haemophilia [ˌhiːmoˈfiliə], s. *Med:* Hémophilie f.

haemophilic [ˌhiːmoˈfilik], a. Hémophile.

haemoptysis [hiːˈmɔptisis], s. *Med:* Hémoptysie f.

haemorrhage [ˈheməridʒ], s. Hémorragie f.

haemorrhagic [ˌheməˈrædʒik], a. *Med:* Hémorragique.

haemorrhoidal [heməˈrɔid(ə)l], a. *Med:* Hémorroïdal, -aux.

haemorrhoids [ˈhemərɔidz], *s.pl. Med:* Hémorroïdes f.

haemostat [ˈhiːmɔstæt], s. *Med:* Hémostatique m.

haft¹ [hɑːft], s. Manche m, poignée f (d'un poignard, d'un outil).

haft², *v.tr.* Emmancher, mettre un manche à (un outil, etc.).

hag¹ [hæg], s. (Vieille) sorcière. *F:* **Old h.,** vieille fée, *P:* vieille taupe, vieille rombière. **hag-ridden,** a. 1. *A:* Tourmenté de cauchemars. 2. **H.-r. by the fear of illness,** tourmenté par une terreur de la maladie.

hag², s. *esp. Scot:* (Moss-)h., fondrière f.

haggard [ˈhægəd]. 1. a. (a) Hâve; (visage) décharné. (b) (Visage) égaré, hagard, décomposé. 2. a. & s. *Ven:* (Faucon) hagard (m).

haggis [ˈhægis], s. *Cu:* Estomac de mouton bourré d'un hachis d'abats et de farine d'avoine. (Mets national écossais.)

haggish [ˈhægiʃ], a. (Femme) vieille et laide; (apparence) de vieille sorcière. *F:* **She looks pretty h.,** elle a l'air bien laide, bien moche.

haggle [ˈhægl], *v.i.* Marchander, *F:* lésiner, chipoter. **To h. about, over, the price (of sth.),** chicaner sur le prix de qch.; marchander qch.; débattre le prix.

hagiographer [ˌhægiˈɔgrəfər], s. Hagiographe m.

hagiographic(al) [ˌhægiəˈgræfik(əl)], a. Hagiographique.

hagiography [ˌhægiˈɔgrəfi], s. Hagiographie f.

Hague (the) [ðəˈheig]. *Pr.n.* La Haye.

ha-ha¹ [ˈhɑːhɑː], *int.* Ha, ha!

ha-ha² [ˈhɑːhɑː], s. Haha m inv, saut m de loup.

hail¹ [heil], s. Grêle f. **'hail-stone,** s. Grêlon m. **'hailstorm,** s. Orage accompagné de grêle.

hail², *v.i. & tr.* Grêler. *Impers:* **It is hailing,** il grêle. *F:* **Bullets were hailing on us,** les balles nous pleuvaient dru comme grêle.

hail³. 1. *int.* Salut! **The H. Mary,** la salutation angélique. **H. Mary, full of grace,** je vous salue, Marie, pleine de grâce. 2. s. Appel m. **Within h.,** à portée de voix. **To be h.-fellow-well-met with everyone,** traiter les gens de pair à compagnon; être à tu et à toi avec tout le monde.

hail⁴. 1. *v.tr.* (a) Saluer (qn). **To h. s.o. (as) king,** acclamer, saluer, qn roi. (b) Héler (qn, un navire). *Nau:* Arraisonner (un navire). **To h. a taxi,** appeler, héler, un taxi. **Within hailing distance,** à portée de voix. 2. *v.i.* **Ship hailing from London,** (i) navire qui dépend du port de Londres; (ii) navire en provenance de Londres. **hailing,** a. *Nau:* Arraisonneur. **The h. ship,** le navire arraisonneur.

hair [hɛər], s. 1. (Of head) (a) Cheveu m. *F:* **To split hairs,** fendre, couper, un cheveu en quatre; pointiller; vétiller. *S.a.* TURN² I. 2. (b) *Coll:* **The h.,** les cheveux, la chevelure. **Head of h.,** chevelure. **To do one's h.,** se coiffer; s'arranger les cheveux. **To wash one's h.,** se laver la tête. **To set one's h.,** se faire une mise en plis. **To have one's h. set,** se faire faire une mise en plis. **It was enough to make your h. stand on end,** c'était à faire dresser les cheveux sur la tête. *P:* **Keep your h. on!** ne vous emballez pas! **To let one's h. down,** (i) se mettre à son aise; (ii) se raconter (réciproquement) ses secrets intimes; (iii) s'amuser follement.

U.S: F: **To get in s.o.'s h.,** taper sur les nerfs de qn. **2.** (*a*) (*Of body*) (*Usu. coll. sg.*) Poil *m.* **To remove s.o.'s superfluous h.(s),** épiler qn. (*b*) *Coll.* (*Of animal*) Poil, pelage *m.* **Against the h.,** à contre-poil; à rebrousse-poil; à rebours. (*c*) Crin *m* (de cheval); soie *f* (de porc). **H.-mattress,** matelas de crin. **'hair-curler,** *s. Toil:* Épingle *f*, pince *f*, pincette *f*, à onduler; bigoudi *m.* **'hair-cut,** *s.* Taille *f*, coupe *f*, de cheveux. **To have a h.-c.,** se faire couper les cheveux. **'hair-do,** *s. F:* I'm going to have a h.-d., je vais me faire coiffer. **'hair-drier,** *s.* Séchoir *m* (électrique); sèche-cheveux *m.* **'hair-grip,** *s.* Pince-guiches *m inv;* barrette *f.* **'hair-line,** *s.* **1.** Délié *m.* **2.** *Typ:* H.-l. letter, capillaire *f.* **3.** *pl. Opt:* Fils croisés. **4.** *Haird:* (*a*) Naissance *f* des cheveux; (*b*) **The fashionable h.-l.** this year, la coiffure à la mode cette année. **'hair-net,** *s.* Résille *f;* filet *m* à cheveux. **'hair-raising,** *a.* Horripilant, horrifique. **'hair-restorer,** *s.* Régénérateur *m* des cheveux. **'hair's-breadth,** *s.* **To escape death by a h.-b.,** avoir été à deux doigts de la mort. **To be within a h.-b. of ruin,** être à un cheveu de la ruine. **'hair-set, -setting,** *s. Haird:* Mise *f* en plis. **'hair-'shirt,** *s.* Haire *f*, cilice *m.* **'hair-slide,** *s. Toil:* Barrette *f.* **'hair-space,** *s. Typ:* Espace *f* d'un point. **'hair-splitting,** *s.* Ergotage *m*, ergoterie *f;* distinctions subtiles. **'hair-spring,** *s. Clockm:* (Ressort) spiral *m.* **'hair-style,** *s.* Coiffure *f.* **'hair-stylist,** *s.* Coiffeur, -euse. **'hair-trigger,** *s. Sm.a:* Déclic *m* (de détente). **H.-t.** lock, platine *f* à double détente.

hairbreadth ['hɛəbredθ]. **1.** *s.* = HAIR'S-BREADTH. **2.** *Attrib.* To have a h. escape, l'échapper belle; échapper comme par miracle.

hairbrush ['hɛəbrʌʃ], *s.* Brosse *f* à cheveux.

haircloth ['hɛəklɔθ], *s.* **1.** *A:* Cilice *m*, haire *f.* **2.** Tissu *m* de crin; étamine *f* de crin; (*coarse*) thibaude *f.*

hairdresser ['hɛədresər], *s.* Coiffeur, -euse.

hairdressing ['hɛədresiŋ], *s.* Coiffure *f.* **Style of h.** coiffure.

-haired [hɛəd], *a.* **Long-h., black-h.,** (*of pers.*) aux cheveux longs, noirs; (*of animal*) à long pelage, à pelage noir.

hairiness ['hɛərinis], *s.* Aspect velu; pilosité *f.*

hairless ['hɛəlis], *a.* Sans cheveux; chauve; (*of animal*) sans poils. **H. face,** visage glabre. **H. hide,** peau pelée.

hairpin ['hɛəpin], *s.* Épingle *f* à cheveux. **H. bend** (*in road*), lacet *m*, (virage en) épingle à cheveux.

hairy ['hɛəri], *a.* **1.** Velu, poilu; (*of scalp*) chevelu. **2.** *Bot:* Velu.

hake [heik], *s. Ich:* Merluche *f;* colin *m.*

halation [hæ'leiʃ(ə)n], *s. Phot:* Halo *m.*

halberd ['hælbəd], **halbert** ['hælbət], *s.* Hallebarde *f.*

halberdier [hælbə'diər], *s.m.* Hallebardier.

halcyon ['hælsiən]. **1.** *s.* (*a*) *Myth:* Alcyon *m.* (*b*) *Orn:* Halcyon *m.* **2.** *Attrib.* **H. days,** jours sereins; jours de bonheur paisible.

hale [heil], *a.* (Vieillard) vigoureux, encore gaillard. **To be h. and hearty,** être frais et gaillard; avoir bon pied bon œil; se porter comme un charme.

half, *pl.* **halves** [hɑːf, hɑːvz]. **1.** *s.* (*a*) Moitié *f.* **H.** (**of**) **his men,** la moitié de ses hommes. **To take h. of sth.,** prendre la moitié de qch. **More than h.** (**of**) **the time,** les trois quarts du temps. To cut sth. in h., in halves, couper qch. par moitié, en deux. **To go halves with s.o.,** se mettre de moitié, de compte à demi, avec qn. **Bigger by h.,** plus grand de moitié. *F:* **He is too clever by h.,** il est beaucoup trop malin. **To do things by halves,** faire les choses à demi. (*b*) Demi *m*, demie *f.* **Two halves,** deux demis. **Three and a h.,** trois et demi. **I waited for two hours and a h.,** j'ai attendu pendant deux heures et demie. (*c*) *F:* **My better h.,** mon époux; ma (chère) moitié, mon épouse. (*d*) *Rail:* **Outward h., return h.** (of ticket), (billet *m* d') aller (*m*), (billet de) retour (*m*). (*e*) *Fb:* (i) **The first h.** (of the game), la première mi-temps. **The second h.,** la seconde mi-temps; la reprise (ii) = HALF-BACK. **Wing halves,** demis aile. **2.** *a.* Demi. **H. an hour,** une demi-heure. *F:* **In h. a second,** en moins de rien, d'un instant. **H. a dozen,** une demi-douzaine. **H. a cup,** une demi-tasse. **H. one thing and h. another,** mi- figue, mi- raisin. **3.** *adv.* (*a*) **He only h. understands,** il ne comprend qu'à moitié. **She h. got up,**

elle se releva à demi. **He is not h. so formidable,** il n'est pas de moitié si redoutable. **H. laughing, h. crying,** moitié riant, moitié pleurant. **H. done,** à moitié fait. **H. undressed,** à demi dévêtu. **H. asleep,** à moitié endormi. **I was h. afraid that . . .,** j'avais quelque crainte que + *sub. F:* **It isn't h. bad,** (i) ce n'est pas mauvais du tout; (ii) ce n'est pas si mal. (*Intensive*) *P:* **He hasn't h. changed!** Il a drôlement décollé! *P:* **She isn't h. smart!** elle est rien chic! **Not h.!** un peu! tu parles! (*b*) **It is h. past two,** il est deux heures et demie. **H. past twelve,** midi ou minuit et demi. (*c*) **H. as big,** moitié aussi grand. **I got h. as much, h. as many,** j'en ai reçu la moitié autant, (la) moitié moins. **H. as big again,** plus grand de moitié. **H. as much again,** moitié plus. **'half-'alive,** *a.* À demi mort. **'half-and-'half,** *adv.* Moitié l'un moitié l'autre. **How shall I mix them?** —H.-and-h., comment faut-il les mélanger?—A doses égales. **'half-'back,** *s. Fb:* Demi-arrière *m, pl.* demi-arrières; demi *m.* **'half-'baked,** *a.* **1.** A moitié cuit. **2.** *F:* (*a*) (*Of pers.*) (i) Inexpérimenté, à peine dégrossi; (ii) niais. (*b*) (Projet) bâclé, qui ne tient pas debout. **'half-belt,** *s. Tail:* Martingale *f.* **'half-binding,** *s. Bookb:* Demi-reliure *f* à petits coins. **'half-blood,** *s.* = HALF-CASTE. **'half-'boot,** *s.* Demi-botte *f, pl.* demi-bottes. **'half-bottle,** *s.* Demi-bouteille *f.* **'half-bred,** *a.* **1.** Métis, -isse. **2.** (Cheval) demi-sang *inv.* **'half-breed,** *s.* **1.** Métis, -isse. **2.** (Cheval *m*) demi-sang *inv.* **'half-brother,** *s.m.* Demi-frère, *pl.* demi-frères. **'half-'caste,** *a.* & *s.* Métis, -isse; sang-mêlé *m.inv.* **'half-'closed,** *a.* Entr'ouvert. **'half-'cock,** *a.* **At h.-c.,** (fusil) au repos, au cran de sûreté. *F:* **To go off at h.-c.,** mal partir, mal démarrer. **'half-'cooked,** *a.* À moitié cuit. **'half-commission,** *a. St.Exch:* **Half-commission man,** remisier *m.* **'half-'crown,** *s. Num:* Demi-couronne *f* (deux shillings six pence). **'half-cup,** *s.* Demi-tasse *f.* **'half-'dead,** *a.* À moitié mort; à demi mort. **H.-d., with fright,** plus mort que vif. **'half-'dozen,** *s.* Demi-douzaine *f.* **'half-'dressed,** *a.* A moitié vêtu; à demi vêtu. **'half-'empty¹,** *a.* A moitié vide. **half-'empty,²** *v.tr.* Vider à moitié. **'half-'fare,** *s. Rail: etc:* Demi-place *f.* **H.-f. ticket,** billet à demi-tarif. **'half-'hearted,** *a.* Tiède; sans entrain; (effort) timide. **-ly,** *adv.* Avec tiédeur; sans enthousiasme. **'half-'hogshead,** *s. Wine-m:* Demi-pièce *f, pl.* demi-pièces. **'half-'holiday,** *s.* Demi-congé *m.* **'half-'hose,** *s. Com:* Chaussettes *fpl* (d'hommes), mi-bas *m inv*, demi-bas *m inv.* **'half-'hour,** *s.* Demi-heure *f.* **'half-'hourly, 1.** *adv.* Toutes les demi-heures; de demi-heure en demi-heure. **2.** *a.* De toutes les demi-heures. **'half-'length,** *s. Sp: etc:* Demi-longueur *f, pl.* demi-longueurs. **H.-l. portrait,** portrait en buste, portrait à mi-corps. **'half-'light,** *s.* Demi-jour *m;* pénombre *f.* **'half-'mast,** *a.* **At h.-m.,** à mi-mât; (pavillon) en berne. **'half-'measure,** *s.* Demi-mesure *f.* **To have done with h.-measures,** trancher dans le vif. **'half-'monthly,** *a.* Semi-mensuel. **'half-'moon,** *s.* **1.** Demi-lune *f.* **2.** Lunule *f.* (des ongles). **'half-'mourning,** *s.* Demi-deuil *m.* **'half-'naked,** *a.* A demi nu. **'half-'open,** *v.tr.* Entr'ouvrir. **'half-'pay,** *s.* Demi-solde *f;* solde de non-activité. **On h.-p.,** en demi-solde, en disponibilité. **'half-'pint,** *s. Meas:* Chopine *f. F:* **He's a h.-p. size chap,** il est tout riquiqui. **'half-'point,** *s. Nau:* (*of the compass*) Demi-quart *m.* **'half-'price,** *s.* **To sell sth.** (at) **h.-p.,** vendre qch. à moitié prix. *Th: etc:* **Children h.-p.,** les enfants paient demi-place. **'half-'ration,** *s. Mil:* Demi-ration *f;* demi-portion *f* (de vivres) **'half-'roll,** *s. Av:* Demi-tonneau *m.* **'half-seas-'over,** *a. P:* A moitié ivre; éméché; paf. **'half-shaft,** *s. Aut:* Demi-arbre, *m, pl.* demi-arbres. **'half-'shut,** *a.* Entre-clos. **'half-'sister,** *s.f.* Demi-sœur. *pl.* demi-sœurs. **'half-'speed,** *s. Nau: etc:* (De)mi-vitesse *f.* **'half-'term,** *s. Sch:* Congé *m* de mi-trimestre. **'half-'tide,** *s. Nau:* Mi-marée *f.* **'half-'timbered,** *a.* **1.** *Constr: Min:* (Galerie *f*, etc.) à demi-boisage. **2.** *Arch:* **H.-t. house,** maison *f* en colombage, à pans de bois, aux poutres apparentes. **'half-'time,** *s.* **1.** **To work h.-t.,** travailler à mi-temps. **2.** *Fb:* (La) mi-temps. **'half-tint,** *s.* Demi-teinte *f.* **'half-title,** *s. Typ:* Faux titre¹ avant-titre *m* (d'un livre). **'half-'tone,** *s. Art:* Demi-teinte *f Phot.Engr* Similigravure *f* **'half-track,** *s.* Chenille *f attrib.* H.-t. **vehicle,** auto-chenille *f* half-track *m.* **'half-'truth,** *s.* Demi-vérité *f.* **'half-turn,** *s.* **1.** Demi-tour *m.* **2.** (*Of wheel*) Demi-révolution *f.* **'half-'volley,** *s. Ten:* Demi-volée *f pl* demi-volées. **half-'watt,** *a.* Demi-watt *inv* **'half-'way,** *adv* A moitié chemin; à mi-chemin **H.-w. to Paris,** à mi-chemin de Paris. **H.-w. up, down, the hill,** à mi-côte, à mi-pente. **H.-w. up, down, the street,** à la moitié de la rue. **To meet s.o. h.-'w.,** faire la moitié des avances; *F:* couper la poire en deux. **'half-wit,** *s.* (*a*) Idiot *m;* simple *m* d'esprit. (*b*) **You h.-w.!** Espèce d'imbécile! **'half-'witted,** *a.* Faible d'esprit; *F:* à moitié idiot. **'half-'year,** *s.* Semestre *m.* **half-'yearly 1.** *a.* Semestriel. **2.** *adv* Tous les six mois.

halfpenny ['heip(ə)ni], *s.* Demi-penny *m.* **1.** (*pl.* **halfpence,** *F:* **ha'pence** ['heipəns]) **It will cost you three halfpence,** cela vous coûtera un penny et demi. **2.** (*pl.* **halfpennies**) Pièce *f* d'un demi-penny.

halfpennyworth ['heipniwəθ, *F:* 'heipəθ], *s.* (*a*) Pour un demi-penny; pour un sou. (*b*) Trois fois rien.

halibut ['hælibət], *s. Ich.* (Grand) flétan.

halitosis [hæli'tousis], *s. Med:* Mauvaise haleine.

hall [hɔːl], *s.* **1.** Grande salle. (*a*) Dining-h., (i) salle à manger; (ii) (*of college*) réfectoire *m.* (*b*) **The servant's h.,** l'office *f;* la salle commune (des domestiques). (*c*) **Concert h.,** salle de concert. **Music-h.,** music-hall *m.* **2.** (*a*) Château *m,* manoir *m.* **Born in marble halls,** né sous des lambris dorés. (*b*) Maison *f* (d'un corps de métier, etc.). *S.a.* GUILDHALL, TOWN-HALL. (*c*) *Sch:* (i) Fondation *f* universitaire. (ii) **H. (of residence)** = cité *f* universitaire. **3.** (*a*) (Entrance-)h., vestibule *m* (d'une maison); hall *m* (d'un hôtel). **H. porter,** concierge *m.* (*b*) *U.S:* Corridor *m;* palier *m* (surtout dans une maison de rapport). **'hall-bedroom,** *s. U.S:* Petite chambre (au-dessus du vestibule, donc) pas chère. **'hall-mark¹,** *s.* Poinçon *m* (sur les objets d'orfèvrerie). **The h.-m. of genius,** le cachet, l'empreinte *f,* du génie. **Work bearing the h.-m. of genius,** ouvrage marqué au coin du génie. **'hall-mark²,** *v.tr.* Contrôler, poinçonner (l'orfèvrerie). **'hall-stand,** *s.* Porte-habit(s) *m inv.*

hallboy ['hɔːlbɔi], *s. U.S:* Chasseur *m* (d'hôtel).

hallelujah [hæli'luːjə], *int. & s.* Alléluia *m.*

halliard ['hæljəd], *s.* = HALYARD.

hallo [hə'lou], *int. & s.* (*a*) Holà! ohé! (*b*) Bonjour!

halloo¹ [hə'luː]: **1.** *s.* Cri *m* d'appel. *Ven.* Huée *f.* **2.** *int. Ven:* Taïaut!

halloo², *v.t.* (*a*) Crier, appeler. **To h. to s.o.,** appeler qn (à grands cris). (*b*) *Ven:* Huer; crier taïaut.

hallow ['hælou], *v.tr.* Sanctifier, consacrer. **Hallowed** ['hælou(i)d] **be thy name,** que ton nom soit sanctifié. **Hallowed** ['hæloud] **ground,** terre sainte.

Hallowe'en [hælou'iːn], *s. Scot:* Veille *f* de la Toussaint.

hallucinate [hə'luːsineit]. *v.tr.* Halluciner.

hallucination [hə,luːsi'neiʃ(ə)n], *s.* Hallucination *f,* illusion *f*

hallucinatory [hə,luːsin'eitri], *a.* Hallucinatoire.

hallway ['hɔːlwei], *s. U.S:* **1.** Vestibule *m* entrée *f.* **2.** Corridor *m,* palier *m,* d'étage.

halo¹, *pl.* -o(e)s ['heilou, -ouz], *s.* **1.** *Astr: Opt:* Halo *m;* auréole *f,* aréole *f* (de la lune). **2.** Auréole, nimbe *m* (d'un saint).

halo², *v.tr.* Auréoler, nimber.

halogen ['hælədʒin], *s. Ch:* Halogène *m.*

haloid ['hæloid], *a. & s. Ch:* Haloïde (*m*).

halt¹ [hɔlt], *s.* **1.** Halte *f,* arrêt *m.* **Ten minutes' h.,** dix minutes d'arrêt. **To come to a h.,** faire halte; s'arrêter. *P.N: Aut:* **H.! stop!** *Mil:* **At the h.,** de pied ferme. *S.a.* CALL² I. 1. **2.** *Rail:* (*Small station*) Halte.

halt², *v.i.* Faire halte; s'arrêter. *Mil:* **H.!** halte!

halt³, *s. A:* To walk with a h., boiter (en marchant). **To speak with a h.,** hésiter en parlant.

halt⁴, *a. A. & B:* Boiteux. *s.pl.* **The h.,** les estropiés.

halt⁵, *v.i. A. & Lit:* (*Of pers., verse, etc.*) Boiter, clocher. **halting,** *a.* (Discours) hésitant; (vers) qui boitent; (style) heurté. **-ly,** *adv.* En hésitant.

halter ['hɔːltər], *s.* **1.** Licou *m,* licol *m.* **H.** rope, longe *f* (pour chevaux). **2.** Corde *f* (de pendaison). **3.** *Dressm:* H.-neck, -top, corsage *m* bain-de-soleil.

halve [hɑːv], *v.tr.* **1.** (*a*) Diviser en deux; couper par (la) moitié: partager (qch. en deux). *Golf:* **Halved hole,** trou partagé. (*b*) Réduire (les dépenses, etc.) de moitié. **2.** *Carp:* **Halved joint,** assemblage *m* à mi-bois.

halves [hɑːvz], *s.pl. See* HALF.

halyard ['hæljəd], *s. Nau.* Drisse *f.*

ham [hæm], *s.* **1.** (*a*) *A:* Jarret *m.* (*b*) *pl. F:* **The hams,** les fesses *f,* le derrière. **2.** *Cu:* Jambon *m.* **H. and eggs,** œufs au jambon. *S.a.* SANDWICH. **3.** *Th:* (*Of play*) Navet *m.* **To act h.,** jouer comme un pied. **H. actor,** cabotin *m.* **'ham-'fisted,** *a. F:* Maladroit, brutal (dans sa façon de manier un outil, etc.).

Hamburg ['hæmbəːg]. *Pr.n.m. Geog:* Hambourg. *Cu:* **H. steak** = HAMBURGER 2 (*c*).

Hamburger ['hæmbəːgər], *s.* **1.** *Geog:* Hambourgeois, -oise. **2.** *s.m.* (*a*) Sorte de saucisse allemande. (*b*) Bifteck haché. (*c*) Bifteck haché entre deux morceaux de pain.

hamlet ['hæmlit], *s.* Hameau *m.*

hammer¹ ['hæmər], *s.* **1.** *Tls:* Marteau *m;* (*heavy*) masse *f. Mount:* Piton h., marteau-piolet. *F:* **To go at it h. and tongs,** y aller de toutes ses forces. *S.a.* CLAW-HAMMER, POWER-HAMMER, SLEDGE³, STEAM-HAMMER. **2.** Marteau (de commissaire-priseur). **To come under the h.,** passer sous le marteau; être mis aux enchères. **3.** Marteau (de piano). **4.** Chien *m* ou percuteur *m* (d'une arme à feu). **'hammer-beam,** *s. Arch:* Blochet *m* à mi-bois. **'hammer-drill,** *s. Constr. etc:* Marteau *m* pneumatique; marteau perforateur. **'hammer-'harden,** *v.tr. Metalw:* Écrouir (l'acier); marteler à froid. **'hammer-head,** (*a*) *s.* **1.** Tête *f* de marteau; pilon *m* (d'un marteau-pilon). (*b*) *a.* En forme de marteau. **H.-h. crane,** grue *f* marteau. **2.** *Ich:* H.-h. (shark), marteau *m.*

hammer². **1.** *v.tr.* (*a*) Marteler; battre (le fer); travailler (le fer) au marteau. **To h. sth. into shape,** (i) façonner qch. à coups de marteau; (ii) *F:* mettre (un projet) au point. *F:* (*Of boxer*) **To h. one's opponent,** cogner dur sur son adversaire. (*b*) *St.Exch:* **To h. a defaulter,** exécuter un agent. **2.** *v.i.* (*a*) Travailler avec le marteau. *F:* **To h. at, on, the door,** cogner à la porte à coups redoublés. **To h. away at sth.,** travailler d'arrache-pied à qch. *Mil: Av: etc:* **To h. at the enemy,** pilonner, s'acharner sur, l'ennemi. (*b*) (*Of machine part*) Tambouriner, cogner, marteler. **hammer down,** *v.tr.* Aplatir (un rivet); rabattre (une inégalité). **hammer in,** *v.tr.* Enfoncer (un clou) à coups de marteau. **hammer out,** *v.tr.* Étendre (l'or, etc.) sous le marteau. *F:* **To h. out lines of verse,** (i) (*of reciter*) marteler des vers; (ii) (*of poet*) forger des vers. **To h. out an excuse,** se forger une excuse. **hammering,** *s.* **1.** (*a*) Martelage *m,* martèlement *m;* battage *m* (du fer). (*b*) *P:* Dégelée *f* (de coups). **To give s.o. a good h.,** cogner dur sur qn; bourrer qn de coups. **2.** *Mec.E:* Tambourinage *m,* cognement *m,* martèlement *m. Hyd.E:* (Water-)h. in a pipe, coup *m(pl)* de bélier dans une conduite.

hammerless ['hæmərlis], *a.* (Fusil *m*) hammerless (*m*), fusil à percussion centrale.

hammerman, *pl.* -men ['hæməmən], **hammersmith** ['hæməsmiθ], *s.* Marteleur *m;* frappeur *m.*

hammock ['hæmək], *s.* Hamac *m.* **H.-chair,** chaise-longue *f* de pont.

hamper¹ ['hæmpər], *s.* Manne *f,* banne *f;* bourriche *f* (d'huîtres, etc.); (*small*) banneau *m,* bannette *f.*

hamper², *v.tr.* Embarrasser, gêner, empêtrer (qn). **To h. the progress of business,** entraver la marche des affaires. **To h. oneself with luggage,** s'empêtrer de colis.

hamster ['hæmstər], *s. Z:* Hamster *m.*

hamstring¹ ['hæmstriŋ], *s. Anat:* Tendon *m* du jarret.

hamstring², *v.tr* (*p.t. & p.p.* hamstringed *or* -strung) **1.** Couper les jarrets à (un cheval, etc.). **2.** *F:* Couper les moyens à (qn).

hand¹ [hænd], *s.* **1.** Main *f.* (*a*) **To go on one's hands and knees,** aller, marcher, à quatre pattes. **To vote by show of hands,** voter à main levée. **To hold (sth.) in one's h.,** tenir, avoir, (son chapeau) à la main, (des sous) dans la main, (le succès) entre les mains. **To take s.o.'s h.,** to lead s.o. **by the h.,** donner la main à qn. (*Of woman*) **To give one's h. to a suitor,** donner, accorder, sa main à un prétendant. **To take sth. with.**

in, both hands, prendre qch. à deux mains. To lay hands on sth., mettre la main sur qch.; s'emparer de qch. If anyone should lay a h. on you, si quelqu'un portait la main sur vous. Hands off! (i) n'y touchez pas! (ii) à bas les mains! Hands up! haut les mains! To act with a high h., agir en despote, de haute main. To rule with a firm h., gouverner d'une main ferme. Believers in the strong h., partisans de la manière forte. Fb: Hands, faute f de mains. (b) To set one's h. to a task, entreprendre, commencer, un travail. He can turn his h. to anything, c'est un homme à toute main. What can you turn your h. to? à quoi êtes-vous bon? He never does a h.'s turn, il ne fait jamais œuvre de ses dix doigts. To have a h. in sth., se mêler de qch.; tremper dans (un crime). To have a h. in it, il y est pour quelque chose. I had no h. in it, je n'y suis pour rien. To take a h. in sth., se mêler de qch.; se mettre de la partie. To lend, give, s.o. a h., aider qn; donner un coup de main, prêter la main, à qn. I got a friend to lend a h., give me a h., je me suis fait aider par un ami. (c) To have one's hands full, avoir fort à faire; avoir beaucoup de besogne sur les bras. To have sth. on one's hands, avoir qch. à sa charge, sur les bras. To get sth. off one's hands, se décharger de qch. She is off my hands, elle n'est plus à ma charge. Com: Goods left on our hands, marchandises invendues ou laissées pour compte. To change hands, (i) (of pers.) changer de main; passer qch. à l'autre main; (ii) (of thg) changer de propriétaire, de mains. To fall into enemy hands, tomber entre les mains de l'ennemi. To be in good hands, (i) être en bonnes mains; (ii) être à bonne école. To put oneself in s.o.'s hands, s'en remettre à qn. I am in your hands, je m'en remets entièrement à vous. To put a matter in the hands of a lawyer, confier une affaire à un homme de loi. My fate is in your hands, mon sort est entre vos mains. To have s.o. in the hollow of one's h., avoir qn sous sa coupe, à sa merci. 2. Adv.phrs. (a) To be (near) at h., être sous la main, à portée de la main. Spring is at h., voici venir le printemps. Christmas was (close) at h., Noël était tout proche. I have money at h., j'ai de l'argent tout prêt. (b) Made by h., fait à la main. To send a letter by h. envoyer une lettre par porteur. (c) In h. Hat in h., chapeau bas. Revolver in h., revolver au poing. To have so much money in h., avoir tant d'argent disponible. Stock in h., marchandises en magasin. S.a. CASH¹. (To catch a train) with five minutes in h., (prendre un train) avec cinq minutes de bon. I've got five minutes in h., j'ai encore cinq minutes. The matter in h., la chose en question, dont il s'agit. To take sth. in h., prendre qch. en main; se charger de qch. To have a piece of work in h., avoir du travail en chantier; une œuvre sur le métier. Horse, situation, well in h., cheval, situation, bien en main. To keep oneself well in h., se contenir. (d) Work on h., travail en cours. To take too much on h., trop entreprendre à la fois. Supplies on h., ressources existantes. (e) On the right h., du côté droit. On every h., on all hands, partout; de toutes parts. On the one h. . . . , d'une part. . . . On the other h. . . . , d'autre part . . . ; par contre. . . . (f) To do sth. out of h., faire qch. sur-le-champ. To shoot s.o. out of h., abattre qn sans autre forme de procès. To get out of h., perdre toute discipline. These children are quite out of h., on ne peut plus tenir ces enfants. (g) Com: Your parcel has come to h., votre envoi m'est parvenu. Your favour of 4th inst. to h., nous avons bien reçu votre lettre du 4 ct. The first excuse to h., le premier prétexte venu. (h) To be h. and glove, h. in glove, with s.o., être d'intelligence, P: de mèche, avec qn. (i) H. in h., la main dans la main. Here stock-raising goes h. in h. with arable farming, ici l'élevage va de pair avec l'agriculture. (j) H. over hand, hand over fist, main sur main (en grimpant). F· To make money h. over fist, faire des affaires d'or. (k) H. to h., (combattre) corps à corps. H.-to-h. fight, corps-à-corps m. (l) To live from h. to mouth, vivre au jour le jour. (m) Rac: To win hands down. gagner haut la main. 3. (Pers.) (a) Ouvrier, -ière; manœuvre m. To take on hands, embaucher de la main-d'œuvre. P.N: Hands wanted, on embauche. No hands wanted, pas d'embauche.

Nau: The ship's hands, l'équipage m; les hommes. All hands on deck! tout le monde sur le pont! (Of ship) To be lost with all hands, périr corps et biens. S.a. DECK-HAND, FACTORY-HAND, etc. (b) To be a good, a great, h. at doing sth., être adroit à faire qch.; avoir le talent de faire qch. She is a good h. at making an omelette, elle réussit bien une omelette. S.a. OLD 3. 4. (a) Écriture f. Round h., running h., écriture ronde, cursive. To write (in) a small h., écrire en petits caractères. He writes a good h., il a une belle main, une belle écriture. (b) To set one's h. to a deed, apposer sa signature à un acte. Under your h. and seal, signé et scellé de votre propre main. Note of h., billet à ordre. 5. Cards: (a) Jeu m. To have a good h., avoir beau jeu. I am holding my h., je me réserve. To throw in one's h., abandonner la partie. (b) Partie f. Let's have a h. at bridge, faisons une partie de bridge. 6. Farr: Horse fifteen hands high, cheval de quinze paumes f. 7. (a) Typ: Index m, ☞. (b) (Of sign-post) Indicateur m. (c) Indicateur (de baromètre, etc.); aiguille f (de montre). 8. (a) H. of pork, jambonneau m. (b) H. of bananas, régime m de bananes. 9. Attrib: H. luggage, bagages à main, colis à la main. H. tool, outil à main. H. lamp, lampe portative. 'hand-ball, s. Sp: 1. Balle f (pour jeux de plage, etc.). 2. (Game) Hand-ball m. 'hand-barrow, s. Civière f, bard m; charrette f à bras. 'hand-cart, s. Voiture f à bras, charrette f à bras. 'hand-gallop, s. Equit: Petit galop, galop de manège. 'hand-glass, s. 1. Loupe f. 2. Miroir m à main. 'hand-grenade, s. Mil: Grenade f (à main). 'hand-lever, s. Manette f. 'hand-'made, a. Fait, fabriqué, (à la) main. 'hand-operated, a. Actionné à la main. 'hand-'pick, v.tr. Trier à la main. Mil: Hand-picked troops, troupes d'élite, triées sur le volet. 'hand-rail, s. Garde-fou m, garde-corps m; rampe f, main courante (d'escalier). 'hand-sewn, -stitched, a. Cousu (à la) main. 'hand-written, a. Manuscrit.

hand², v.tr. 1. To h. a lady into a carriage, donner la main à une dame pour l'aider à monter en voiture. 2. Passer, remettre, donner (qch. à qn). To h. one's card to s.o., tendre sa carte à qn. 3. P: To h. it to s.o., reconnaître la supériorité de qn. For cheek, I must h. it to you! pour avoir du toupet, c'est vous qui prenez le pompon. hand about, v.tr. Faire passer (qch.) de main en main. hand down, v.tr. 1. Descendre (qch.) (et le remettre à qn). 2. (a) Transmettre (une tradition). (b) Clothes I handed down to my sister, des vêtements que j'ai passés à ma sœur. 'hand-me-down, s. & attrib. U.S: = REACH-ME-DOWN. hand in, v.tr. Remettre (un paquet, un télégramme). hand on, v.tr. Transmettre (une coutume). To h. on news, passer une nouvelle (to, à). 'hand out, v.tr. (a) Tendre, remettre (qch. à qn). (b) To h. out the wages, distribuer la paie. 'hand-out, s. 1. U.S: Aumône f. To live on hand-outs, vivre d'aumône. 2. Journ: Communiqué m à la presse. hand over, v.tr. Remettre (qch. à qn). (a) To h. s.o. over to justice, livrer, remettre, qn aux mains de la justice. (b) To h. over one's authority, transmettre ses pouvoirs (to, à). (c) To h. over one's property to s.o., céder son bien à qn. hand round, v.tr. Passer, faire passer, (les gâteaux, etc.); faire circuler (la bouteille).

handbag ['hændbæg], s. Sac m à main.
handbell ['hændbel], s. Sonnette f, clochette f.
handbill ['hændbil], s. Prospectus m; annonce f; programme m (de spectacle).
handbook ['hændbuk], s. 1. Sch: Manuel m (de sciences, etc.). 2. Guide m (du touriste); livret m (d'un musée). 3. Turf: U.S: Livre m de paris (d'un bookmaker).
handcuff ['hændkʌf], v.tr. Mettre les menottes à (qn). Handcuffed, menottes f aux mains.
handcuffs ['hændkʌfs], s.pl. Menottes f.
handful ['hændful], s. 1. Poignée f (de noisettes, etc.). To throw money away by the h., in handfuls, jeter l'argent à pleines mains, à poignées. There was only a h. there, il n'y avait là que quelques personnes. 2. F: That child is a h., c'est un enfant terrible. 3. Cards: To have a h. of trumps, avoir de l'atout plein les mains.

handgrip ['hændgrip], s. 1. Prise f. To come to hand-grips, en venir aux prises, aux mains. 2. Poignée de main.

handhold ['hændhould], s. 1. Prise f. Crag with no h., varappe où la main ne trouve pas de prise. 2. (On wall, etc.) Main f de fer.

handicap[1] ['hændikæp], s. (a) Sp: Handicap m. Weight h. (of racehorse), surcharge f. Time h., rendement m de temps. (b) Désavantage m. To be under a heavy h., être fort désavantagé.

handicap[2], v.tr. (handicapped) Sp: Handicaper. **handicapped**, a. 1. Handicapé. 2. Désavantagé (by, par suite de). (A) physically h. (person), un diminué physique.

handicraft ['hændikrɑːft], s. 1. Travail manuel; habileté manuelle. 2. Métier manuel. 3. Handi-crafts, produits mpl de l'industrie artisanale.

handicraftsman, pl. -men ['hændikrɑːftsmən], s.m. Artisan.

handiness ['hændinis], s. 1. Adresse f, dextérité f; habileté (manuelle). 2. (a) Commodité f (d'un outil). (b) Maniabilité f (d'un navire).

handiwork ['hændiwəːk], s. (a) Travail manuel. (b) Ouvrage m, œuvre f. That is his h., c'est le travail de ses mains; c'est son ouvrage.

handkerchief ['hæŋkətʃi(ː)f], s. (Pocket-)h., mouchoir m (de poche). Fancy h., pochette f.

handle[1] ['hændl], s. (a) Manche m (de balai, de couteau, etc.); anse f (d'un pinceau); balancier m, brimbale f (de pompe); brancard m (de civière); bras m (de brouette); queue f (de poêle); poignée f (de porte, de bicyclette, etc.); clef f (de robinet). El.E: Switch h., manette f d'interrupteur. F: To have a h. to one's name, avoir un titre (de noblesse). To give a h. to, for, calumny, donner prise à la calomnie. F: To fly off the h., s'emporter, sortir de ses gonds. (b) Anse f (de broc, de corbeille, de seau); portant m (de valise). (c) (Crank-handle) Manivelle f. Aut: (Starting-)h., manivelle (de mise en marche). 'handle-bar, m. Guidon m (de bicyclette). F: H.-b. moustache, moustaches f raides.

handle[2], v.tr. 1. Tâter des mains. To h. a material, tâter un tissu. 2. (a) Manier, manipuler (qch.). Ind: Manutentionner (des pièces lourdes). How to h. a gun, comment se servir d'un fusil. To h. a ship, manœuvrer, gouverner, un navire. (b) Manier (qn, une affaire). He is hard to h., il n'est pas commode. To h. s.o. roughly, malmener, rudoyer, qn. To h. a situation, prendre en main une situation. (c) To h. a lot of business, brasser beaucoup d'affaires. To h. a lot of money, remuer beaucoup d'argent. We don't h. those goods, nous ne tenons pas ces articles. Fb: To h. the ball, toucher le ballon. **handling**, s. (a) Maniement m (d'un outil); manutention f (de marchandises); manœuvre (d'un navire). (b) Traitement m (de qn, d'un sujet). Rough h., traitement brutal. (c) Maniement (de fonds). (d) Com: Distribution f.

handle[3], v.tr. Emmancher (un outil). Ivory-handled, à manche d'ivoire. Short-handled, à manche court.

handmaid(en) ['hændmeid(n)], s. A: & B: Servante f.

handsaw ['hændsɔː], s. Égoïne f; scie f à main.

handshake ['hændʃeik], s. Poignée f de main; serrement m de main.

handsome ['hænsəm], a. (a) Beau, f. belle. H. young man, jeune homme bien tourné, de belle mine. H. furniture, meubles élégants. H. residence, maison de belle apparence. (b) (Of conduct) Gracieux, généreux. Prov: H. is that h. does, la noblesse ne fait pas la noblesse. A h. apology, une réparation honorable. To do the h. (thing) by s.o., agir en galant homme à l'égard de qn, avec qn; F: se montrer chic. (c) H. fortune, belle fortune. H. gift, riche cadeau. To make a h. profit, réaliser de beaux bénéfices. -ly, adv. 1. (a) (S'habiller) élégamment, avec élégance. (b) (Agir) généreusement; (se conduire) en galant homme; (payer) libéralement. P: To come down h., ouvrir largement sa bourse. 2. Nau: Doucement.

handsomeness ['hænsəmnis], s. (a) Beauté f, élégance f. (b) Générosité f (d'une action); libéralité f (d'une récompense).

handspike ['hændspaik], s. (a) Nau: Anspect m; barre f de cabestan. (b) Artil: Levier m de manœuvre.

handstand ['hændstænd], s. Gym: To do a h., faire l'arbre fourchu, l'arbre droit, le poirier.

handwork ['hændwəːk], s. Travail m à la main, travail manuel.

handworker ['hændwəːkər], s. Ouvrier, -ière.

handwriting ['hændraitiŋ], s. Écriture f. This letter is in the h. of . . ., cette lettre a été écrite par . . ., est de la main de. . .

handy ['hændi]. a. 1. (Of pers.) Adroit (de ses mains); débrouillard. H. at doing sth., adroit à faire qch. To be h. with a tool, savoir se servir d'un outil. 2. (Of implement) Maniable; bien en main(s). H. ship, navire maniable. 3. Commode. That would come in very h., cela ferait bien l'affaire, viendrait bien à point. 4. A portée (de la main). To keep sth. h., tenir qch. sous la main. -ily, adv. 1. Adroitement. 2. (Placé) commodément, sous la main. 'handy(-) man, pl. -men, s.m. Homme à tout faire, à toute main.

hang[1] [hæŋ], s. 1. (a) Pente f, inclinaison f (d'une falaise) (b) Ajustement m (d'un costume); drapé m (d'un tissu). (c) F: To get the h. of sth., (i) attraper le coup, saisir le truc, pour faire qch.; (ii) saisir le sens de qch. When you have got the h. of things, quand vous serez au courant. 2. F: I don't care a h., je m'en moque. It's not worth a h., cela ne vaut pas tripette.

hang[2], v. (hung [hʌŋ]; hung) I. v.tr. 1. Pendre, accrocher, suspendre (on, from, à). To h. a picture, (i) suspendre un tableau; (ii) exposer un tableau (au salon, etc.) Three pictures by him have been hung, on a exposé trois de ses tableaux. To h. one's hat on a peg, accrocher son chapeau à une patère. To h. a door, monter une porte; mettre une porte sur ses gonds. Veh Hung on springs, monté sur ressorts. Aut: Low-hung axle, essieu surbaissé. 2. To h. (down) one's head, baisser la tête. 3. Cu: Faire faisander (le gibier). 4. (a) To h. a room with tapestries, tendre une salle de tapisseries. Windows hung with lace curtains, fenêtres garnies de rideaux en dentelle. (b) To h. wallpaper, coller du papier peint. 5. To h. fire, (i) (of fire-arms) faire long feu; (ii) F: (of plan) traîner (en longueur). 6. (p.t. & p.p. hanged, often F: hung) Pendre (un criminel). He hanged himself out of despair, il se pendit de désespoir. F: H. the fellow! que le diable l'emporte! O: That be hanged for a tale! quelle blague! (I'll be) hanged if I know! je n'en sais fichtre rien! H. it! sacristi! zut! H. the expense! je me fiche pas mal de la dépense! S.a. DOG[1] I. 7. Jur: U.S: To h. a jury, faire avorter les délibérations d'un jury, en refusant de se conformer à l'avis de la majorité. II. hang, v.i. 1. Pendre, être suspendu (on, from, à). Picture hanging on the wall, tableau pendu, accroché, au mur. Fruit hanging on a tree, fruits qui pendent à un arbre. To h. out of the window, (of pers.) se pencher par la fenêtre; (of thg) pendre à la fenêtre. 2. A thick fog hangs over the town, un épais brouillard plane, pèse, sur la ville. The danger hanging over our heads, le danger suspendu sur nos têtes. A heavy silence hung over the meeting, un silence pesait sur l'assemblée. 3. (a) To h. on s.o.'s arm, se pendre au bras de qn; se cramponner au bras de qn. To h. on s.o.'s words, boire les paroles de qn. (b) Everything hangs on his answer, tout dépend de sa réponse. 4. Responsibility hangs heavy upon him, la responsabilité pèse sur lui. Time hangs heavy on my hands, le temps me pèse. 5. He's always hanging around here, il est toujours à flâner, à rôder, par ici. To h. round a woman, tourner autour d'une femme. 6. (Of drapery) Tomber, se draper. Her hair hangs down her back, ses cheveux lui tombent dans le dos. His clothes h. loosely around him, il flotte dans ses vêtements. 7. (Of criminal) Être pendu. **hang about**, U.S: hang around, v.i. 1. Rôder, flâner. To keep s.o. hanging about, faire croquer le marmot à qn. 2. To h. about a neighbourhood, rôder dans un voisinage. I have a cold hanging about me, j'ai un rhume dòn je ne peux pas me débarrasser. **hang back**, v.i. 1. Rester en arrière. 2. F: Hésiter; montrer peu d'empressement. **hang down**, v.i. 1. Pendre 2. Pencher. **hang on**, v.i. Se cramponner, s'accrocher (to, à). H. on to your job, ne lâchez pas votre situation. He is always hanging on to his mother, il est toujours dans les jupons de sa mère. *Tp: F:* H. on! ne raccrochez pas! attendez une minute! **hang out. 1.** *v.tr.* Pendre (qch.) au dehors; étendre (le linge); arborer (un pavillon). *U.S:* To h.o. one's shingle, accrocher son enseigne *f*, ouvrir un magasin, un cabinet. *(Of dog)* To h. out its tongue, tirer la langue. **2.** *v.i.* Pendre (au dehors). *F:* Where do you h. out? où nichez-vous? où juchez-vous? **hang over,** *v.i.* Surplomber. **'hang-over,** *s.* **1.** Reste *m* (de superstition, d'une habitude). **2.** *P:* To have a h.-o., avoir la gueule de bois, avoir mal aux cheveux. **hang together,** *v.i.* **1.** Rester unis. **2.** *(Of statements)* S'accorder. **hang up,** *v.tr.* (*a*) Accrocher, pendre (son chapeau, un tableau). *P:* He wants to h. up his hat, il a envie de se marier. *Tp:* To h. up (the receiver), raccrocher (l'appareil). (*b*) Remettre (un projet) à plus tard. **Parcels hung up in transit,** colis en souffrance. We were hung up with a puncture, nous avons été retardés par une crevaison. **hanging¹,** *a.* **1.** (Pont) suspendu; (lustre) pendant; (échafaudage) volant. H. stair, escalier en encorbellement. H. door, porte battante. The h. gardens of Babylon, les jardins suspendus de Babylone. **2.** *Hist:* H. judge, juge qui condamne tous les accusés à la potence. **hanging²,** *s.* **1.** (*a*) Suspension *f*; montage *m* (d'une porte). (*b*) Pendaison *f* (d'un criminel). It's a h. matter, c'est un cas pendable. *F:* H. is too good for him, il n'est pas bon à jeter aux chiens. (*c*) H. wardrobe, penderie *f*. **2.** *pl.* Hangings, tenture *f*; tapisserie *f*. Bed hangings, rideaux *m* de lit. **'hang-dog,** *a.* H.-d. look, (i) air *m* en dessous; (ii) tête basse. **'hang-nail,** *s.* = AGNAIL.

hangar ['hæŋər], *s.* *Av:* Hangar *m*.

hanger ['hæŋər], *s.* **1.** (*Pers.*) Poseur *m* (de tapisseries). *S.a.* PAPER-HANGER **2.** Crochet *m* (de suspension). (Coat-)h., cintre *m*; porte-vêtements *m inv.* **3.** (*Pers.*) H.-on, *pl.* hangers-on, (i) dépendant *m*; (ii) *F:* écumeur *m* de marmites; écornifleur *m*. **Hanger-back,** *pl.* **hangers-back,** *P:* renâcleur *m*.

hangman, *pl.* -men ['hæŋmən], *s.m.* Bourreau.

hank [hæŋk], *s.* **1.** Écheveau *m* (de laine, etc.). **2.** *Nau:* Anneau *m*, cosse *f*, bague *f*.

hanker ['hæŋkər], *v.i.* To h. after sth., désirer ardemment qch.; être talonné par le désir de qch. To h. after praise, être affamé de louanges. **hankering,** *s.* Vif désir, grande envie (after, for, de). To have a h. for sth., soupirer après qch. H. after the stage, aspirations *fpl* à la scène. He had hankerings after the sea, (i) il avait la nostalgie de la mer; (ii) il avait des envies de se faire marin.

hanky-panky ['hæŋki'pæŋki], *s.* *F:* Supercherie *f*; finasseries *fpl.* That's all h.-p., tout ça c'est du boniment. To play h.-p. with s.o., (i) mettre qn dedans, (ii) finasser avec qn.

Hannibal ['hænib(ə)l]. *Pr.n.m.* *A.Hist:* Annibal.

Hansard ['hænsɑːd], *s.* Compte rendu officiel des débats parlementaires (en Angleterre).

Hanse [hæns], *s.* *Hist:* Hanse *f.* The H., la Ligue hanséatique.

Hanseatic [,hænsi'ætik], *a.* *Hist:* The H. League, la Ligue hanséatique.

hansom(-cab) ['hænsəm('kæb)], *s.* Cab (anglais).

ha'pence ['heipəns], *s.pl.,* **ha'penny** ['heipni], *s.* *F:* *See* HALFPENNY, KICK¹ I.

haphazard [hæp'hæzəd], **1.** *s.* At h., au hasard; au petit bonheur. **2.** *a.* H. arrangement, disposition fortuite. To choose in a h. way, choisir à l'aveuglette. **-ly,** *adv.* To live h., vivre à l'aventure.

hapless ['hæplis], *a.* Infortuné, malheureux.

ha'p'orth ['heipəθ], *s.* *F:* (= HALFPENNY-WORTH) He hasn't a h. of courage, il n'a pas pour deux sous de courage.

happen ['hæp(ə)n], *v.i.* **1.** Arriver. (*a*) Se passer, produire. An accident happens, un accident se produit; il arrive un accident. Don't let it h. again! que cela n'arrive plus! Just as if nothing had happened, comme si de rien n'était. Whatever happens, quoi qu'il advienne; quoi qu'il arrive. H. what may, advienne que pourra. How does it h. that . . ? d'où vient que . . . ? It might h. that . . ., il pourrait se faire que. . . . It so happened that . . ., le hasard a voulu que . . .; il se trouva que. . . . As it happens . . ., justement. . . . *F:* Worse things h. at sea, il y a pire. (*b*) What has happened to him? (i) qu'est-ce qui lui est arrivé? (ii) qu'est-ce qu'il est devenu? If anything happened to you, si vous veniez à mourir. Something has happened to him, il lui est arrivé quelque malheur. It can never h. here, cela ne nous arrivera pas, à nous. **2.** To h. to do sth., faire qch. accidentellement. A car happened to be passing, une voiture vint à passer. The house happened to be empty, la maison se trouvait vide. Do you h. to know whether . . .? sauriez-vous par hasard si . . .? If I do h. to forget, s'il m'advient, m'arrive, d'oublier. **3.** To h. upon sth., tomber sur qch.; trouver qch. par hasard. *U.S:* To h. in, entrer (chez qn) en passant. **happening,** *s.* Événement *m*.

happiness ['hæpinis], *s.* Bonheur *m*, félicité *f.*

happy ['hæpi], *a.* Heureux. **1.** (*a*) In happier circumstances, dans des circonstances plus favorables. In a h. hour, à un moment propice. (*b*) To be as h. as the day is long, as a king, as a sand-boy, être heureux et sans soucis; être heureux comme un roi; être heureux comme un poisson dans l'eau. H. party of children, bande joyeuse d'enfants. *A:* I was h. in a son, j'avais le bonheur de posséder un fils. To make s.o. h., (i) rendre qn heureux; (ii) faire la joie de qn. To be h. to do sth., être heureux, bien aise, content, de faire qch. **2.** H. phrase, expression heureuse, à propos. H. thought! bonne inspiration! **-ily,** *adv.* Heureusement. To live h., vivre heureux. H., he did not die, par bonheur il ne mourut pas. She smiled h., elle eut un sourire heureux.

happy-go-lucky ['hæpigou'lʌki], *attrib.a.* Sans souci; insouciant. To do sth. in a h.-go-l., fashion, faire qch. au petit bonheur.

hara-kiri ['hɑːrə'kiəri], *s.* Hara-kiri *m.*

harangue¹ [hə'ræŋ], *s.* Harangue *f.*

harangue². **1.** *v.tr.* Haranguer (la foule). **2.** *v.i.* Prononcer, faire, une harangue; discourir (en public).

harass ['hærəs]. *v.tr.* **1.** *Mil:* Harceler, tenir en alerte (l'ennemi). **2.** Harasser, tracasser, tourmenter (qn).

harassment ['hærəsmənt], *s.* **1.** Harcèlement *m* (de l'ennemi). **2.** Harassement *m*, tracasserie *f.*

harbinger ['hɑːbindʒər], *s.* Avant-coureur *m*; messager, -ère; annonciateur, -trice; précurseur *m.*

harbour¹ ['hɑːbər], *s.* **1.** (*a*) *A:* Abri *m*, asile *m.* (*b*) *Ven:* Lit *m* (d'un cerf). **2.** *Nau:* Port *m.* Inner h., arrière-port *m.* Outer h., avant-port *m.* Tidal h., port de, à, marée. To enter h., entrer au port, dans le port. To leave h., sortir du port. To clear the h., quitter le port. *attrib.* H. installations, installations portuaires. **'harbour-dues,** *s.pl.* *Nau:* Droits *m* de mouillage. **'harbour-master,** *s.* Capitaine *m* de port. **'harbour-station,** *s.* Gare *f* maritime.

harbour², *v.tr.* Héberger; donner asile à (qn); recéler (un criminel). H. dirt, retenir la saleté. To h. a grudge against s.o., garder rancune à qn. To h. suspicions, entretenir, nourrir, des soupçons.

harbourage ['hɑːbəridʒ], *s.* **1.** Refuge *m*, abri *m*, asile *m.* **2.** *Nau:* To give good h., offrir un bon mouillage, une rade sûre.

hard [hɑːd]. **I.** *a.* **1.** Dur. To get h., durcir. H. snow, neige durcie. H. muscles, muscles fermes. *F:* To be as h. as nails, (i) être en bonne forme; (ii) être impitoyable. *Med:* H. tissues, tissus scléreux. *Pol.Ec:* H. currency, devise forte. *Fin:* H. money, espèces sonnantes *pl.* **2.** Difficile; (tâche) pénible. To be h. to please, être exigeant, difficile. To be h. of hearing, être dur d'oreille. *I.C.E:* The engine is h. to start, le moteur est dur à lancer. I find it h. to believe that . . ., j'ai peine à croire que + *sub.* **3.** (*a*) *(Of pers.)* Dur, sévère, rigoureux (to, towards, envers). H. master, maître sévère, exigeant. To be h. on s.o., être sévère, user de rigueur, envers qn. To be h. on one's clothes, user rapidement ses vêtements. (*b*) To call s.o. h. names, qualifier durement qn. H. fact, fait brutal. Times are h., les temps sont rudes, durs. To have a h. time of it, en voir de dures. *F:* H. lines! h. luck! pas de chance! quelle guigne! (*c*) H. to the touch, rude au toucher. H. water, eau crue, dure; eau calcaire. *U.S:* H. liquor, boissons alcooliques. *Phot:* H. print, épreuve heurtée. H. paper, papier à contrastes. **4.** H. work, (i) travail assidu; (ii) travail ingrat. It is h. work for me to . . ., j'ai beaucoup de peine, bien du mal, à . . . H. drinker, grand buveur. H. fight, rude combat. H.

match, match vivement disputé. **It is a h. blow for him,** c'est un rude coup pour lui. **To try one's hardest,** faire tout son possible, faire l'impossible. *S.a.* LABOUR[1] 1. **5.** H. frost, forte gelée. H. winter, hiver rigoureux. **-ly,** *adv.* 1. (*a*) Sévèrement. **To deal h. with s.o.,** user de rigueur envers qn. (*b*) **H. contested,** vivement, chaudement, contesté. (*c*) Péniblement. **The victory was h. won,** la victoire a été remportée de haute lutte. **2.** (*a*) **A peine;** ne . . . guère. **She can h. read,** (c'est) à peine si elle sait lire. **He had h. escaped when . . .,** à peine s'était-il échappé que. . . . **You'll h. believe it,** vous aurez (de la) peine, du mal, à le croire. **I h. know,** je n'en sais trop rien. **I need h. say . . .,** point besoin de dire. . . . **H. anyone,** presque personne. **H. ever,** presque jamais. (*b*) **He could h. have said that,** il n'aurait sûrement pas dit cela. **II. hard,** *adv.* **1.** (*a*) **Pull the bell h.,** tirez fort la sonnette. **As h. as one can,** de toutes ses forces. **To throw a stone h.,** lancer une pierre avec raideur. **To hit h.,** cogner dur; frapper raide. **To bite h.,** mordre serré. **To beg h.,** prier instamment. **To look h. at s.o.,** regarder fixement qn. **To think h.,** réfléchir profondément. **To work h.,** travailler dur, ferme. **To be h. at work,** être en plein travail. **He is always h. at it,** il est toujours attelé à son travail. **He studies h.,** il étudie sans relâche. **It is raining h.,** il pleut à verse. **To freeze h.,** geler dur, ferme. **To snow h.,** neiger dru. (*b*) **It will go h. with him if . . .,** il lui en cuira si. . . . (*c*) *Nau:* H. over! la barre toute! **H. a-port!** tribord toute! (*d*) *F:* **To be h. up (for money),** être à court (d'argent), être dans la dèche. **To be h. up for sth.,** avoir grand besoin de qch. **2.** Difficilement; avec peine. **H.-earned wages,** salaire péniblement gagné. *S.a.* DIE[2] I. **3.** **H. by,** tout près, tout contre, tout à côté. **To follow h. (up)on, after, s.o.,** suivre qn de près. **It was h. on twelve,** il était bientôt minuit. **'hard and 'fast,** *a.* **To lay down a h. and f. rule,** poser une règle absolue, rigoureuse. **'hard-'bitten,** *a.* *F:* (*Of pers.*) Tenace; dur à cuire. **'hard,'boiled,** *a.* **1.** (Œuf) dur. **2.** = HARD-BITTEN. **hard-'faced, -'favoured, -'featured,** *a.* (Personne *f*) aux traits durs, sévères; au masque dur. **hard-'fisted,** *a.* *F:* (Homme) dur à la détente. **'hard-'fought,** *a.* Chaudement contesté; âprement disputé. **'hard-'headed,** *a.* (*Of pers.*) Positif, pratique. **'hard-'hearted,** *a.* Insensible, impitoyable, au cœur dur. **hard-'mouthed,** *a.* (Cheval) dur de bouche, sans bouche. **hard-'set,** *a.* **1.** (*Of pers.*) Fort embarrassé; aux abois. **2.** **When the cement is hard-set,** lorsque le ciment a bien pris, a durci. **hard-'solder,** *v.tr.* *Metalw:* Braser; souder au cuivre. **'hard-top,** *s.* *Aut:* Berline *f.* **hard-'wearing,** *a.* (Vêtement *m*) de bon usage, de bon service; (tissu *m*) durable. **'hard-'won,** *a.* **H.-w. trophy,** trophée chaudement disputé, remporté de haute lutte. **'hard-'working,** *a.* Laborieux; travailleur, -euse; assidu.

hardboard ['hɑːdbɔːd], *s.* *Constr:* Isorel *m* (R.t.m.).

harden ['hɑːdn]. **1.** *v.tr.* (*a*) Durcir, rendurcir; tremper (l'acier, les muscles); *Med:* indurer, scléroser. **To h. s.o. to fatigue,** aguerrir qn à, contre, la fatigue. **He hardened his heart,** il s'endurcit le cœur. (*b*) *Metall:* **To (case-)h.,** cémenter (l'acier). (*c*) *Phot:* Aluner (un cliché). **2.** *v.i.* (*a*) (*Of substance*) Durcir, s'affermir; (*of tissue*) s'ossifier. **His voice hardened,** sa voix devint dure. (*b*) (*Of shares*) **To h. (up),** se tendre. **Prices are hardening,** les prix sont en hausse. (*c*) **Scientific opinion has hardened to the view that . . .,** le monde savant est de plus en plus d'avis que. . . . **hardened,** *a.* Durci; (acier) trempé; (criminel) endurci. **To be h. against entreaties,** être endurci contre les supplications. **hardening,** *s.* (*a*) Durcissement *m*, affermissement *m. Metall:* Trempe *f.* **Air h.,** (i) prise *f*, durcissement, (du ciment, etc.) à l'air; (ii) *Metall:* trempe à l'air. **H. steel,** acier de trempe. (*b*) *Metall:* (Case-) h., cémentation *f* (de l'acier). (*c*) *Phot: Dy:* Alunage *m. S.a.* BATH[1] 3.

hardheartedly ['hɑːd'hɑːtidli], *adv.* Impitoyablement; sans pitié.

hardheartedness ['hɑːd'hɑːtidnis], *s.* Insensibilité *f*; dureté *f* de cœur.

hardihood ['hɑːdihud], *s.* Hardiesse *f*; (i) intrépidité *f*; (ii) audace *f*, effronterie *f.*

hardiness ['hɑːdinis], *s.* Robustesse *f*, vigueur *f.*

hardness ['hɑːdnis], *s.* **1.** (*a*) Dureté *f*; trempe *f* (de l'acier). (*b*) Tons heurtés (d'un cliché). (*c*) Crudité *f* (de l'eau). **2.** Tension *f*, raffermissement *m* (du marché). **3.** (*a*) Difficulté *f* (d'un problème, etc.). (*b*) H. of hearing, dureté d'oreille. **4.** Sévérité *f*, rigueur *f*, dureté.

hardship ['hɑːdʃip], *s.* Privation *f*, fatigue *f*; (dure) épreuve. **He has suffered great hardships,** il en a vu de dures.

hardware ['hɑːdwɛər], *s.* Quincaillerie *f.* **H. dealer,** quincaillier *m.* **H. shop,** quincaillerie. **Builders' h.,** serrurerie *f* de bâtiments.

hardwood ['hɑːdwud], *s.* Bois dur.

hardy ['hɑːdi], *a.* **1.** Hardi; audacieux, intrépide. **2.** (*a*) Robuste; endurci (à la fatigue). (*b*) *Bot:* Rustique, vivace; (plante) de pleine terre. **H. annual,** plante annuelle de pleine terre. **-ily,** *adv.* **1.** Hardiment, audacieusement. **2.** Vigoureusement.

hare[1] ['hɛər], *s.* **1.** Lièvre *m.* **Buck-h.,** bouquin *m.* **Doe-h.,** hase *f.* **Arctic, polar, h.,** lièvre des neiges. *Cu:* **Jugged h.,** civet *m* de lièvre. **To run with the h. and hunt with the hounds,** ménager la chèvre et le chou; nager entre deux eaux. **First catch your h.,** assurez-vous d'abord de l'essentiel. *Sp:* **H. and hounds** = PAPER-CHASE. **2.** *Z:* Belgian h., léporide *m.* **'hare-brained,** *a.* Écervelé, étourdi; (projet) insensé. **He's a h.-b. person,** c'est une tête de linotte, de moineau. **'hare-lip,** *s.* Bec-de-lièvre *m.* **'hare-lipped,** *a.* A bec-de-lièvre.

hare[2], *v.i.* *F:* **To h. back home,** regagner la maison à toutes jambes. **To h. off,** se sauver à toutes jambes.

harebell ['hɛəbel], *s.* *Bot:* (*a*) Jacinthe *f* des bois. (*b*) Campanule *f* à feuilles rondes.

harem [hɑːˈriːm], *s.* Harem *m.*

haricot ['hærikou], *s.* **1.** *Cu:* **H. mutton,** haricot *m* de mouton. **2.** *Bot:* **H. (bean),** haricot blanc.

hark [hɑːk], *v.i.* **1.** *O:* **To h. to a sound,** prêter l'oreille à, écouter, un son. **H.!** écoutez! **2.** *Ven:* **H. away!** taïaut! (*Of pers.*) **To h. back to sth.,** revenir à un sujet. **He's always harking back to that,** il y revient toujours.

harlequin ['hɑːlikwin], *s.* *Th:* Arlequin *m.* **H. coat,** habit bigarré ou mi-parti.

harlequinade [ˌhɑːlikwiˈneid], *s.* Arlequinade *f.*

harlot ['hɑːlət], *s.* *A:* Prostituée *f.*

harlotry ['hɑːlətri], *s.* *A:* Prostitution *f.*

harm[1] [hɑːm], *s.* Mal *m*, tort *m.* **To do s.o. h.,** faire du tort à qn; nuire à qn. **To see no h. in sth.,** ne pas voir de mal, de malice, à qch. **You will come to h.,** il vous arrivera malheur. **Out of harm's way,** à l'abri du danger; en sûreté, en lieu sûr. **It will do more h. than good,** cela fera plus de mal que de bien. **That won't do any h.,** cela ne gâte rien; cela ne nuira en rien. **There's no h. in saying so,** il n'y a pas de mal à le dire. *S.a.* MEAN[4] I.

harm[2]. **1.** *v.tr.* Faire du mal, du tort, à (qn); nuire à (qn); léser (les intérêts de qn). **2.** *v.i.* *O:* **He will not h. for a little privation,** un peu de privation ne lui fera pas de mal.

harmful ['hɑːmful], *a.* Malfaisant, pernicieux; nocif, nuisible (to, à). **-fully,** *adv.* Nuisiblement.

harmfulness ['hɑːmfulnis], *s.* Nocivité *f.*

harmless ['hɑːmlis], *a.* (Animal) inoffensif, pas méchant; (homme) sans malice; (passe-temps) innocent. **H. talk,** conversation anodine. **-ly,** *adv.* Sans (faire de) mal; (s'amuser) innocemment.

harmlessness ['hɑːmlisnis], *s.* Innocuité *f.*

harmonic [hɑːˈmɔnik]. **1.** *a.* Harmonique. **2.** *s.* Harmonique *f.* **-ally,** *adv.* Harmoniquement.

harmonica [hɑːˈmɔnikə], *s.* = MOUTH-ORGAN.

harmonious [hɑːˈmounjəs], *a.* Harmonieux. **1.** En bon accord. **2.** Mélodieux. **-ly,** *adv.* Harmonieusement; (vivre) en harmonie, en bon accord.

harmonist ['hɑːmənist], *s.* Harmoniste *mf.*

harmonium [hɑːˈmounjəm], *s.* Harmonium *m.*

harmonization [ˌhɑːmənaiˈzeiʃ(ə)n], *s.* Harmonisation *f.*

harmonize ['hɑːmənaiz]. **1.** *v.tr.* (*a*) Harmoniser (des idées); concilier, faire accorder (des textes); allier (des couleurs). (*b*) *Mus:* Harmoniser (une mélodie). **2.** *v.i.* (*Of colours, etc.*) S'harmoniser, s'allier, s'assortir; (*of facts, pers.*) s'accorder. **To h. with sth.,** s'adapter harmonieusement à qch.; s'accorder, se marier, avec qch. **harmonizing. 1.** *a.* Qui s'harmonise, qui s'accorde, qui s'assortit (with, avec). **2.** *s.* Harmonisation *f.*

harmony ['hɑːməni], s. 1. *Mus:* Harmonie f. 2. Harmonie, accord m. Colours in perfect h., assortiment parfait de couleurs. To live in perfect h., vivre en parfaite intelligence. In h. with . . ., en rapport, en accord, avec. . . . His tastes are in h. with mine, ses goûts sont conformes aux miens.

harness¹ ['hɑːnis], s. Harnais m, harnachement m. A set of h., un harnais. To get back into h., reprendre le collier. To die in h., mourir à la besogne, à la peine. To be out of h., être à la retraite. *Av:* Parachute h., ceinture f de parachute. 'harness-maker, s. Bourrelier m; harnacheur m; sellier m. 'harness-making, -trade, s. Bourrellerie f. 'harness-room, s. Sellerie f.

harness², v.tr. 1. Harnacher, enharnacher (un cheval). To h. a horse to a carriage, atteler un cheval à une voiture. 2. Aménager (une chute d'eau); mettre (une chute d'eau) en valeur.

harp¹ ['hɑːp], s. *Mus:* Harpe f. To play the h., pincer, jouer, de la harpe.

harp², v.i. Jouer de la harpe. *F:* To be always harping on the same string, rabâcher toujours la même chose; réciter toujours la même litanie. He is always harping on that, c'est toujours la même ritournelle.

harpist ['hɑːpist], s. *Mus:* Harpiste mf.

harpoon¹ [hɑːˈpuːn], s. Harpon m.

harpoon², v.tr. Harponner.

harpooner [hɑːˈpuːnər], s. Harponneur m.

harpsichord ['hɑːpsikɔːd], s. *Mus:* Clavecin m.

harpy ['hɑːpi], s.f. *Myth:* Harpie. *F:* Old h., vieille sorcière; vieille mégère, vieille harpie. 'harpy-eagle, s. *Orn:* Harpie f.

harquebus ['hɑːkwibʌs], s. *A.Arms:* Arquebuse f.

harridan ['hærid(ə)n], s.f. *F:* Vieille mégère; vieille chipie.

harrier¹ ['hæriər], s. *Orn:* Busard m.

harrier², s. *Sp:* 1. Harrier m, chien courant (anglais, pour la chasse au lièvre, en meute). 2. (a) Chasseur m au lièvre (à pied, avec une meute). (b) Crossman, m, pl. crossmen. Harriers, club de coureurs de cross.

harrow¹ ['hærou], s. *Agr:* Herse f. To be under the h., subir des tribulations, de dures épreuves.

harrow², v.tr. *Agr:* Herser (un terrain). To h. s.o., s.o.'s feelings, agir sur la sensibilité de qn; déchirer le cœur à qn. **harrowing. 1.** s. *Agr:* Hersage m. 2. a. (Conte, etc.) poignant, navrant; (cri) déchirant.

Harry¹ ['hæril]. *Pr.n.m.* 1. Henri. 2. *F:* Old H., le diable. The climate has played old H. with his health, le climat lui a détraqué la santé.

harry², v.tr. 1. Dévaster, mettre à sac (un pays). 2. Harceler (qn). To h. the enemy, ne laisser à l'ennemi aucun répit. To h. a debtor, pourchasser un débiteur.

harsh [hɑːʃ], a. Dur, rêche, rude (au toucher); âpre (au goût); aigre, strident (à l'oreille). H. voice, voix rude, rauque, éraillée. H. style, style dur. H. colour, couleur brutale. 2. (Caractère) dur, bourru; (maître, réponse) rude. To exchange h. words, échanger des propos durs. -ly, adv. (Répondre, etc.) avec dureté, avec rudesse, d'un ton bourru; (traiter qn) sévèrement, avec rigueur.

harshness ['hɑːʃnis], s. 1. Dureté f, rudesse f (au toucher); âpreté f (du vin); aigreur f (d'un son). asperité f (du style, de la voix). 2. Sévérité f, rudesse (d'une punition); rigueur f (du destin).

hart [hɑːt], s. Cerf m. H. of ten, cerf dix cors. 'hart's-tongue, s. *Bot:* Langue-de-cerf f.

harum-scarum ['hɛərəmˈskɛərəm], a. & s. *F:* Étourdi, écervelé. She's a h.-s., c'est une évaporée.

harvest¹ ['hɑːvist], s. 1. Moisson f (du blé); récolte f (des fruits); fenaison f (du foin); vendange f (du vin). To get in, win, the h., faire la moisson. 2. (Époque f de) la moisson. 'harvest-bug, -mite, s. Trombidion m, *F:* aoûtat m, rouget m. 'harvest-home, s. (i) Fin f de la moisson; (ii) fête f de la moisson. 'harvest-rash, s. Trombidiose f. 'harvest-spider, s. *Arach:* Faucheur m, faucheux m.

harvest², v.tr. Moissonner (les blés); récolter (les fruits). *Abs.* Rentrer, faire, la moisson; faire les blés.

harvester ['hɑːvistər], s. 1. (*Pers.*) Moissonneur, -euse. 2. (*Machine*) Moissonneuse f; esp. moissonneuse-lieuse. 3. = HARVEST-BUG.

has. *See* HAVE².

has-been ['hæzbiːn], s. *F:* Homme m vieux jeu; vieux ramolli.

hash¹ [hæʃ], s. 1. *Cu:* Hachis m. *U.S: P:* H. house, gargote f. 2. *F:* To make a h. of sth., gâcher un travail; faire un beau gâchis de qch. To make a h. of it, bousiller l'affaire. *P:* To settle s.o.'s h., (i) régler son compte à qn; faire son affaire à qn; (ii) rabattre le caquet à qn. 3. *F:* H.-up, réchauffé m, *P:* ripopée f (de vieux contes, etc.).

hash², v.tr. To h. (up) meat, hacher la viande. **hash over**, v.tr. *U.S: F:* Discuter qch.; discuter le coup.

hasheesh, hashish ['hæʃiːʃ], s. Hachich m.

hasp [hɑːsp], s. 1. (Staple-)h. (*for padlocking*), moraillon m. 2. (a) Loquet m (de porte). (b) Espagnolette f (de porte-fenêtre). (c) Fermoir m, agrafe f (d'album, etc.).

hassock ['hæsək], s. Agenouilloir m; carreau m, coussin m (pour les genoux ou les pieds).

hastate ['hæsteit], a. *Bot:* Hasté.

haste [heist], s. Hâte f, diligence f. To do sth. in h., (i) faire qch. à la hâte, en hâte; (ii) faire qch. à l'étourdie. In hot h., en toute hâte. To make h., se hâter, se dépêcher. Make h.! dépêchez-vous! More h. less speed, hâtez-vous lentement.

hasten ['heisn]. 1. v.tr. (a) Accélérer, hâter, presser (le pas, etc.); avancer (le départ de qn). This action hastened his fall, cette action précipita sa chute. (b) Activer (une réaction). 2. v.i. Se hâter, se dépêcher, se presser (to do sth., de faire qch.). We h. to assure you that . . ., nous nous empressons de vous assurer que. . . . To h. downstairs, se hâter de descendre. **hasten away**, v.i. Partir à la hâte. **hasten back**, v.i. Revenir en toute hâte. **hasten out**, v.i. Sortir à la hâte; se hâter de sortir.

hastiness ['heistinis], s. 1. Précipitation f, hâte f. 2. (*Of temper*) Emportement m, vivacité f.

hasty ['heisti], a. 1. (Départ) précipité; (croquis) fait à la hâte; (repas) sommaire. Let us not be over-h., ne précipitons rien. 2. (Aveu) irréfléchi. 3. Emporté, vif. To be h.-tempered, être d'humeur prompte, *F:* être soupe au lait. 4. (*Of growth*) Rapide. -ily, adv. 1. A la hâte; précipitamment. 2. (Parler) sans réflexion; (juger) à la légère.

hat [hæt], s. Chapeau m. Top h., silk h., chapeau haut de forme, haut-de-forme m. Soft felt h., chapeau mou. Paper h., coiffure f de cotillon. To raise one's h. to s.o., saluer qn (d'un coup de chapeau); donner à qn un coup de chapeau. H. in hand, chapeau bas. To put on one's h., mettre son chapeau; (*of man*) se couvrir. To keep on one's h., (*man*) rester couvert; (*woman*) garder son chapeau. To take off one's h., enlever son chapeau; (*of man*) se découvrir. To take off one's h., to s.o., reconnaître la supériorité de qn. *F:* To send, pass, the h. round, on s.o.'s behalf, faire la quête au profit de qn. *F:* My h.! (i) pas possible! (ii) pigez-moi ça! Keep it under your h., gardez ça pour vous. *a.phr. F:* Old h., vieux jeu. *S.a.* TALK² I. I. 'hat-block, s. Forme f à chapeaux. 'hat-box, s. (i) Carton m à chapeaux (de modiste). (ii) Boîte f à chapeau (de voyage). 'hat-lining, s. Coiffe f. 'hat-maker, s. (*For men*) Chapelier m. 'hat-peg, s. Patère f. 'hat-pin, s. Épingle f à chapeau. 'hat-shop, s. 1. (*For men*) Chapellerie f. 2. (*For women*) (Boutique f de) modiste (f). At the h.-s., chez la modiste. 'hat-stand, s. Porte-chapeaux m inv. 'hat trick, s. *Cr:* Mise f hors jeu de trois batteurs avec trois balles de suite.

hatband ['hætbænd], s. Ruban m de chapeau. Mourning h., crêpe m.

hatch¹ [hætʃ], s. 1. *Nau:* H.(way), descente f, écoutille f. H.(-cover), panneau m de descente. Under hatches, dans la cale. To close down the h., fermer le panneau. To (cover and) secure the hatches, condamner les descentes. *P:* Down the h.! à la vôtre! 2. Service h., buttery-h., passe-plats m inv; guichet m de dépense.

hatch² [hætʃ], s. *Husb:* 1. Éclosion f (d'un œuf). 2. Couvée f.

hatch³. 1. v.tr. (a) Faire éclore (des poussins). To h. out eggs, incuber, (faire) couver, des œufs. To h. a plot, ourdir, tramer, couver, un complot. (b) *Pisc:* Incuber (les œufs). 2. v.i. To h. (out), (*of chicks or eggs*) éclore. A plot is hatching, il se trame quelque chose. *S.a.* CHICKEN 1. **hatching¹**, s. 1. (a) Éclosion f (d'une couvée); *Pisc:* incubation f (des œufs). (b) Machination f (d'un complot). 2. Couvée f.

hatch⁴, v.tr. Engr: Mapm: Hacher, hachurer. **hatching**,² s. **1.** Engr: Mapm: Hachure f. **2.** Mapm: Liséré m (en couleur).

hatchery ['hætʃəri], s. **1.** Husb: Couvoir m, poussinière f. **2.** Pisc: Alevinier m.

hatchet ['hætʃit], s. Hachette f, cognée f; hache f à main. **To bury the h.**, enterrer la hache de guerre; faire la paix. **'hatchet-faced**, a. Au visage en lame de couteau.

hatchment ['hætʃmənt], s. Her: Écusson m funéraire.

hate¹ [heit], s. = HATRED. P: **I've got a h. on, against, him**, je le trouve détestable.

hate², v.tr. **1.** Haïr, détester, exécrer; avoir (qn) en haine, en horreur. **To h. s.o. like poison, like the plague**, haïr qn comme la peste. **2. To h. to do sth.**, détester (de) faire qch. **She hates to be contradicted**, elle ne peut pas souffrir qu'on la contredise. **I should h. to be late**, cela m'ennuierait fort d'être en retard. **I h. his going so far away**, cela me chagrine qu'il s'en aille si loin. **I h. to trouble you**, je suis désolé de vous déranger.

hateful ['heitful], a. Odieux, détestable. **-fully**, adv. Odieusement, détestablement.

hatefulness ['heitfulnis], s. Odieux m, nature f détestable (de qch.).

hath [hæθ]. See HAVE².

hatless ['hætlis], a. Sans chapeau, tête nue; (femme) en cheveux.

hatred ['heitrid], s. Haine f (of, de, contre). **To incur s.o.'s h.**, s'attirer la haine de qn. **Out of h. of sth.**, en haine de qch.

hatter ['hætər], s. Chapelier m.

hauberk ['hɔːbəːk], s. Arm: Haubert m.

haughtiness ['hɔːtinis], s. Hauteur f, morgue f.

haughty ['hɔːti], a. Hautain, altier, sourcilleux. **-ily**, adv. Hautainement; avec hauteur.

haul¹ [hɔːl], s. **1.** Amenée f; effort m (pour haler ou amener qch.). **2.** Fish: (a) **At one h. (of the net)**, d'un seul coup de filet. (b) Prise f, pêche f. **To make, get, a good h.**, ramener un fameux coup de filet. **3.** Trans: (a) Parcours m, trajet m (d'un objet traîné, remorqué). (b) Charge f; charretée f.

haul². **1.** v.tr. (a) Tirer; traîner (une charge); remorquer (un bateau, un train). Min: Ind: **To h. coal**, rouler le charbon; hercher. (b) Nau: **To h. the wind**, serrer le vent (de près). **2.** v.i. Nau: (a) **To h. on a rope**, haler sur une manœuvre. (b) **To h. upon the wind**, haler le vent; se haler dans le vent. **haul down**, v.tr. Nau: Haler bas, rentrer, affaler (les voiles, etc.); rentrer (un pavillon); amener (un signal). **haul in**, v.tr. Nau: Haler, rentrer (une manœuvre). **haul up**, v.tr. Nau: Hisser (un pavillon). **To h. up a boat**, (aboard ship) rentrer une embarcation; (on the beach) haler une embarcation à sec. **hauling**, s. (a) Traction f; Min: herchage m. (b) Nau: Halage m.

haulage ['hɔːlidʒ], s. **1.** (a) (Transport m par) roulage m, charriage m, camionnage m. **H. contractor**, entrepreneur m de transports. (b) Traction f, remorquage m, halage m. Min: Ind: Herchage m. **Man h.**, traction à bras. Min: Ind: **H. man**, rouleur m, hercheur m. **2.** Frais mpl de roulage, de transport.

hauler ['hɔːlər], s, **1.** Haleur, -euse. **2.** Min: Ind: = HAULIER 2.

haulier ['hɔːliər], s.m. **1.** Camionneur. **2.** Min: Hercheur, rouleur.

haulm [hɔːm], s. Bot: **1.** Fane f (de légume). **2.** Coll. Fanes, chaume m.

haunch [hɔːn(t)ʃ], s. (a) Anat: Hanche f. (b) Cu: Cuissot m, quartier m (de chevreuil). (c) pl. **Haunches**, arrière-train. **Dog sitting on his haunches**, chien assis sur son derrière. **'haunch-bone**, s. Anat: Os m iliaque.

haunt¹ [hɔːnt], s. Lieu fréquenté (par qn, un animal); repaire m (de bêtes féroces, de voleurs); liteau m (de loups). **An evil h.**, un mauvais lieu.

haunt², v.tr. (a) (Of pers., animal) Fréquenter, hanter (un endroit). (b) (Of ghost) Hanter (une maison). **This place is haunted**, il y a des revenants ici. (c) (Of thoughts) Obséder, poursuivre (qn); troubler (l'esprit). **Haunted by memories**, assiégé, obsédé, par des souvenirs. **haunting**, a. (Mélodie, etc.) qui vous hante, qui vous trotte dans la mémoire; (doute) obsédant.

haute couture ['outku'tjuːər], s. Dressm: Haute couture.

haute école ['outei'kɔl], s. Equit: Haute école.

Havana [hə'vænə]. **1.** Pr.n. Geog: La Havane. **2.** s. A H. (cigar), un havane.

Havanese ['hævəniz], a. & s. Geog: Havanais, -aise.

have¹ [hæv], s. **1.** The haves and the have-nots, les riches et les pauvres. **2.** P: (a) (Swindle) Attrape f; escroquerie f. (b) (Joke) Attrape.

have², v.tr. (pr.ind. have, hast, has, A. & B: hath, pl. have; pr. sub. have; past ind. & sub. had, hadst; pr.p. having; p.p. had) **1.** (a) Avoir, posséder. **He had no friends**, il n'avait pas d'amis. **All I h.**, tout ce que je possède, tout mon avoir. **He has a shop**, il tient un magasin. **My bag has no name on it**, ma valise ne porte pas de nom. **H. you any apples? If you h.**, avez-vous des pommes? Si vous en avez, . . . **I h. no words to express . . .**, les mots me manquent pour exprimer. . . . **I h. no Latin**, j'ignore le latin. **I h. it!** j'y suis! (b) We don't h. many visitors, nous ne recevons pas beaucoup de visites. **2. To h. a child**, avoir un enfant. **Our cat has had kittens**, notre chatte a fait des petits. **3.** (a) **There was no work to be had**, on ne pouvait pas obtenir, se procurer, de travail. **It is to be had at the chemist's**, cela se trouve chez le pharmacien. (b) **To h. news from s.o.**, recevoir des nouvelles de qn. **I h. it on good authority that . . .**, je tiens de bonne source que. . . . (c) **I must h. them by tomorrow**, il me les faut pour demain. **I will let you h. it for £5**, je vous le céderai pour cinq livres. **Let me h. the money tomorrow**, envoyez-moi l'argent demain. **Let me h. your keys**, donnez-moi, laissez-moi, vos clefs. **Let me h. an early reply**, répondez-moi sans retard. P: **I let him h. it**, (i) je lui ai dit son fait; (ii) je lui ai réglé son compte. P: **You've had it, chum!** (i) tu es fait, mon vieux! (ii) tu es foutu, mon vieux! P: **Don't get him up, you've had it**, pas besoin de s'en faire, c'est loupé. **4. To h. tea with s.o.**, prendre le thé avec qn. **What will you h.? What will you h., sir?**—I'll h. a chop, que prendra monsieur?—Donnez-moi une côtelette. **He is having his dinner**, il est en train de dîner. **I had some more**, j'en ai repris. **To h. a cigar**, fumer un cigare. P: **I'm not having any!** on ne me la fait pas! ça ne prend pas! **5.** (In verbal phrases: e.g.) (a) **To h. measles**, avoir la rougeole. **To h. an idea**, avoir une idée. **To h. a right to sth.**, avoir droit à qch. (b) **To h. a dream**, faire un rêve. **To h. a game**, faire une partie. (c) **To h. a lesson**, prendre une leçon. **To h. a bath, a shower**, prendre un bain, une douche. (d) **To h. a pleasant evening**, passer une soirée agréable. **I didn't h. any trouble at all**, cela ne m'a donné, ne m'a coûté, aucune peine. **We had a rather strange adventure**, il nous est arrivé une aventure assez étrange. **The only thing I ever had happen to me was . .**, la seule chose qui me soit jamais arrivée, c'est. . . . **6.** (a) **He 'will h. it that Hamlet is mad**, il soutient que Hamlet est fou. **Rumour has it that . .**, le bruit court que. . . . (b) **As Plato has it**, comme dit Platon. (c) **He will not h. it that she is delicate**, il n'admet pas qu'elle soit de santé délicate. **7.** (a) **To h. s.o. in one's power**, avoir qn en son pouvoir. **He had me by the throat**, il me tenait à la gorge. (b) **You h. me there!** voilà où vous me prenez en défaut! (c) F: (Outwit) Avoir, attraper (qn); mettre (qn) dedans. **You've been had!** on vous a eu! vous avez été refait! **I'm not to be had**, on ne me la fait pas; ça ne prend pas. **8.** (a) (Causative) **To h. sth. done**, faire faire qch. **To h. s.o. do sth.**, faire faire qch. à qn. **To h. one's hair cut**, se faire couper les cheveux. **H. it repaired**, faites-le réparer. **He 'would h. me come in**, il a voulu à toute force me faire entrer. (b) **He had his leg broken**, il s'est cassé la jambe. **I had my watch stolen**, je me suis fait, laissé, voler ma montre. (c) **I shall h. everything ready**, je veillerai à ce que tout soit prêt. **9.** Will h. (a) **Which one will you h.?** lequel voulez-vous? **She won't h. him**, elle ne veut pas de lui. **What more would you h.?** que vous faut-il de plus? **As ill-luck would h. it he arrived too late**, la malchance voulut qu'il arrivât trop tard. (b) **What would you h. me do?** que voulez-vous que je fasse? **I would h. you know that . .**, sachez que. . . . (c) **I will not h. such conduct**, je ne supporterai pas une pareille conduite. **I won't h.**

him teased, je ne veux pas qu'on le taquine. **10.** (*a*) **To h. to do sth.,** devoir faire qch.; être obligé, forcé, de faire qch. **We shall h. to walk faster,** il nous faudra marcher plus vite. **I don't h. to work,** moi je n'ai pas besoin de travailler. (*b*) **My shirt will h. to be ironed,** il va falloir me repasser ma chemise. **11.** (*Aux. use*) (*a*) **To h. been, to h. given,** avoir été, avoir donné. **To h. come, to h. hurt oneself,** être venu, s'être blessé. **When I had dined, I went out,** (i) quand j'avais dîné, je sortais; (ii) quand j'eus dîné, je sortis; (iii) quand j'ai eu dîné, je suis sorti. **I h. lived in London for three years,** voilà trois ans que j'habite Londres. (*Emphatic*) **Well, you 'h. grown!** ce que tu as grandi! (*b*) **You h. forgotten your gloves.—So I h.!** vous avez oublié vos gants.—En effet! Tiens, c'est vrai! **You haven't swept the room.—I h.!** vous n'avez pas balayé la chambre.—Si! Mais si! Si fait! **You h. been in prison before.—I haven't!** vous avez déjà fait de la prison.—C'est faux! **12.** (*Past sub.*) **I had better say nothing,** je ferais mieux de ne rien dire. **I had as soon,** *O:* **as lief, stay here,** j'aimerais autant rester ici. **I had much rather start at once,** j'aimerais bien mieux partir tout de suite. **have in,** *v.tr.* **To h. s.o. in to dinner,** (i) inviter qn à dîner; (ii) avoir qn à dîner. **I had them in for a cup of tea,** je les ai fait entrer pour prendre une tasse de thé. **I had the doctor in,** j'ai fait venir le médecin. **have on,** *v.tr.* **1.** (*a*) **To h. on a coat,** porter une veste. **To h. nothing on,** être nu; *F:* être à poil. (*b*) **This evening, I h. a lecture on,** ce soir, je dois (i) faire une conférence; (ii) assister à une conférence. **2.** *P:* Duper, faire marcher (qn). **3.** *F:* **I don't go racing, but I like to h. sth. on,** je n'assiste pas aux courses (de chevaux) mais j'aime faire quelques petits paris. *See* ON II. 1., 4. **have out,** *v.tr.* **1.** **To h. a tooth out,** se faire arracher unc dent. **2.** *F:* **To h. it out with s.o.,** vider une querelle avec qn; s'expliquer avec qn. **have up,** *v.tr.* *F:* (*a*) Citer, poursuivre, (qn) en justice. (*b*) (*Of magistrate*) Sommer (qn) de comparaître. **To be had up for an offence,** être cité devant les tribunaux pour un délit.

haven ['heiv(ə)n], *s.* (*a*) Havre *m*, port *m*. (*b*) Abri *m*, asile *m*. **H. of refuge,** port de salut.

haversack ['hævəsæk], *s.* **1.** *Mil:* Musette *f*. **2.** Havresac *m* (de tourisme).

havoc ['hævək], *s.* Ravage *m*, dégâts *mpl*; saccage *m*. **The frosts have wrought h. in, made h. of, played h. among, the vineyards,** les gelées ont fait de grands dégâts, des ravages, dans les vignobles.

haw¹ [hɔː], *s. Bot:* (*a*) Cenelle *f*. (*b*) = HAWTHORN.

haw², *v.i. See* HUM² I.

Hawaii [hə'waiiː]. *Pr.n. Geog:* Hawaï *m*.

Hawaiian [hə'waiən], *a. & s.* Hawaïen, -ïenne.

hawfinch ['hɔːfin(t)ʃ], *s. Orn:* Gros-bec *m*.

haw-haw¹ ['hɔː'hɔː], *s.* **1.** Rire bruyant; gros rire. **2.** Prononciation affectée.

haw-haw², *v.i.* Rire bruyamment, bêtement.

hawk¹ [hɔːk], *s.* **1.** *Orn:* Faucon *m*. **To have eyes like a h.,** avoir des yeux d'aigle. **2.** *F:* (*Of pers.*) Vautour *m*; homme *m* rapace. **'hawk-eyed,** *a.* Au regard d'aigle; qui a la vue perçante. **'hawk-moth,** *s. Ent:* Sphinx *m*; smérinthe *m*. **'hawk-nosed,** *a.* Au nez aquilin.

hawk², *v.i.* Chasser au faucon. (*Of bird or insect*) **To h. at the prey,** fondre sur la proie. **hawking¹,** *s.* Chasse *f* au faucon; fauconnerie *f*. **To go h.,** faire la chasse au faucon.

hawk³, *s. F:* Graillement *m*, expectoration *f*.

hawk⁴, *v.i. & tr. F:* Graillonner. **To h. up phlegm,** expectorer des mucosités.

hawk⁵, *v.tr.* Colporter, cameloter (des marchandises). **hawking²,** *s.* Colportage *m*.

hawk⁶, *s. Tls:* Taloche *f* (de plâtrier).

hawker ['hɔːkər], *s.* (*a*) Colporteur *m*, marchand ambulant, camelot *m*. (*b*) (*Of fruit, vegetables*) Marchand des quatre saisons.

hawkweed ['hɔːkwiːd], *s. Bot:* Épervière *f*.

hawse [hɔːz], *s.inv. Nau:* **1.** (*a*) **A:** = HAWSE-HOLE. (*b*) *pl.* **The h.,** les écubiers *m*. **2.** (*a*) Affourchage *m*, évitage *m*. (*b*) Clear, open, h., chaînes claires. **'hawse-hole,** *s.* Écubier *m*. **'hawse-pipe,** *s.* Manchon *m* d'écubier.

hawser ['hɔːzər], *s. Nau:* (*a*) Haussière *f*, aussière *f*, grelin *m*. (*b*) Amarre *f*. (*c*) Câble *m* de remorque.

hawthorn ['hɔːθɔːn], *s.* Aubépine *f*.

hay¹ [hei], *s.* **1.** Foin *m*. **To make h.,** faire les foins; faner. *Prov:* **To make h. while the sun shines,** battre le fer pendant qu'il est chaud. *F:* **To make h. of sth.,** embrouiller qch.; démolir (un argument). **2.** *U.S:* *P:* Lit *m*. **To hit the h.,** aller se coucher, *P:* se pagnoter. **'hay(-)fever,** *s. Med:* Rhume *m* des foins. **'hay-fork,** *s.* Fourche *f* à foin. **'hay-harvest,** *s.* Fenaison *f*. **'hay-rack,** *s.* **1.** Râtelier *m* d'écurie. **2.** (*On cart*) Fausse ridelle.

hay², *v.i.* Faire les foins. **haying,** *s.* Fenaison *f*.

haycock ['heikək], *s.* Meulette *f*, tas *m*, meulon *m*, de foin.

hayloft ['heilɔft], *s.* Fenil *m*; grenier *m* ou grange *f* à foin.

haymaker ['heimeikər], *s.* **1.** Faneur, -euse. **2.** (*Machine*) Faneuse *f*.

haymaking ['heimeikiŋ], *s.* Fenaison *f*.

hayrick ['heirik], **haystack** ['heistæk], *s.* Meule *f* de foin.

hayseed, *s.* **1.** Graine *f* de foin. **2.** *U.S:* *F:* Paysan *m*, rustaud *m*.

haywire ['heiwaiər], *a. F:* **He's gone h.,** il ne tourne plus rond. **His plans have gone h.,** c'est une affaire loupée.

hazard¹ ['hæzəd], *s.* **1.** (*a*) Hasard *m*. **Game of h.,** jeu de hasard. (*b*) Risque *m*, péril *m*. **At all hazards,** coûte que coûte. **2.** *Bill:* Coup *m* qui fait entrer une des billes dans la blouse. **To play a winning h.,** blouser la bille sur laquelle on vise. **To play a losing h.,** se blouser. **3.** *Golf:* Accident *m* de terrain.

hazard², *v.tr.* Hasarder, risquer, aventurer (sa vie, sa fortune); hasarder (une opinion).

hazardous ['hæzədəs], *a.* Hasardeux, chanceux, hasardé, risqué.

haze¹ [heiz], *s.* (*a*) Brume légère. **Heat h.,** brume de chaleur. (*b*) Obscurité *f*, incertitude *f* (de l'esprit).

haze², *v.tr.* **1.** Rendre brumeux, embrumer. **2.** *Nau:* Harasser (qn) de corvées. *U.S:* (i) *Sch:* Brimer (un nouvel élève). (ii) Conduire, pousser le bétail (comme font les cowboys, à cheval).

hazel ['heizl], *s.* **H.(-tree),** noisetier *m*, coudrier *m*. **H.-grove, -wood,** coudraie *f*. **H. eyes,** yeux couleur (de) noisette. **'hazel-nut,** *s.* Noisette *f*.

hazer ['heizər], *s. U.S:* Cowboy *m*.

haziness ['heizinis], *s.* État brumeux, nébuleux (du temps, de l'esprit). **The h. of his knowledge,** le vague, l'imprécision *f*, de son savoir.

hazy ['heizi], *a.* **1.** (*Of weather*) Brumeux, embrumé, gris. **2.** (*a*) (Contour, etc.) flou, estompé. (*b*) (*Of ideas*) Nébuleux, fumeux, vague. **-ily,** *adv.* Vaguement, indistinctement.

he [hi, hiː], *pers.pron.nom.m.* **1.** (*Unstressed*) Il. (*a*) **What did he say?** qu'a-t-il dit? (*b*) **Here he comes,** le voici qui vient. **He is an honest man,** c'est un honnête homme. **2.** (*Stressed*) (*a*) Lui. **He and I,** lui et moi. **I am as tall as he,** je suis aussi grand que lui. **It is he,** c'est lui. (*Emphatic*) **'He knows nothing about it,** il n'en sait rien, lui; lui n'en sait rien. (*b*) (*Antecedent to a rel. pron.*) (i) Celui. **He that, he who, believes,** celui qui croit. (ii) **It is he who said so,** c'est lui qui l'a dit. **3.** (*As substantive*) Mâle. *Attrib:* He-bear, ours mâle. He-goat, bouc. **'he-man,** *pl.* **-men,** *s.m.* *F:* Homme dominateur, homme viril.

head¹ [hed], *s.* **1.** Tête *f*. (*a*) **From h. to foot,** de la tête aux pieds, des pieds à la tête; (armé) de pied en cap. **To walk with one's h. (high) in the air,** marcher le front haut. **To sell a house over s.o.'s h.,** vendre une maison sans donner au locataire l'occasion de l'acheter. **He gives orders over my h.,** il donne des ordres sans me consulter. **H. down,** la tête baissée. **H. downwards,** la tête en bas. **H. first, h. foremost,** la tête la première. **To stand on one's h.,** se tenir sur sa tête. *F:* **I could do it on my h.,** c'est simple comme bonjour. **To go, turn, h. over heels,** faire la culbute. **To fall h. over heels in love with s.o.,** devenir éperdument amoureux de qn. **He is taller than his brother by a h.,** il dépasse son frère de la tête. *Turf:* (*Of horse*) **To win by a h.,** gagner d'une tête. **To win by a short h.,** gagner de justesse. **To give a horse its h.,** lâcher la bride, donner carrière, à un cheval. **His**

guilt be on his own h., puisse son crime retomber sur lui. **To strike off s.o.'s h.,** décapiter qn. *F:* **To talk s.o.'s h. off,** étourdir qn; rompre les oreilles à qn. **A fine h. of hair,** une belle chevelure. *Anthr:* (*Indian*) **H. shrinker,** (Indien) réducteur *m* de têtes. (*b*) (*Pers:*) **Crowned h.,** tête couronnée. (*c*) *Cu:* **Sheep's h.,** tête de mouton. **Boar's h.,** hure *f* de sanglier. **Potted h.,** fromage *m* de tête, de hure. (*d*) *Ven:* (*Antlers*) Bois *m*, tête (de cerf). **2.** (*a*) (*Intellect, mind*) **He has a good h. on his shoulders, his h. is screwed on the right way,** c'est une forte tête, un homme de tête, de bon sens. **To have a good h. for business,** avoir l'entente des affaires; s'entendre aux affaires. **Idea running through my h.,** idée qui me trotte dans la cervelle. **To reckon in one's h.,** calculer de tête. **To get sth. into one's h.,** se mettre qch. dans la tête, en tête, dans l'esprit. **I can't get that into his h.,** je ne peux pas lui enfoncer ça dans la tête, dans la cervelle. **He has got, taken, it into his h. that . . .,** il s'est mis dans la tête que. . . . **To take it into one's h. to do sth.,** s'aviser, se mettre en tête, de faire qch. **It never entered my h. that . . .,** il ne me vint pas à l'idée, à l'esprit, que. . . . **What put that into your h.?** où avez-vous pris cette idée-là? **To put ideas into s.o.'s h.,** donner des idées à qn. **His name has gone out of my h.,** son nom m'est sorti de la mémoire. **We laid, put, our heads together,** nous avons conféré ensemble; nous nous sommes concertés. *Prov:* **Two heads are better than one,** deux conseils, deux avis, valent mieux qu'un. **He gave an answer out of his own h.,** il a donné une réponse de son cru. **Wine that goes to one's h.,** vin *m* qui porte à la tête. **To have a good, strong, h. for drink,** avoir la tête solide, bien porter le vin. (*Of speech, etc.*) **To be over the heads of the audience,** dépasser (l'entendement de) l'auditoire. **To keep one's h.,** conserver sa tête. **To lose one's h.,** perdre la tête. **He is off his h.,** il est timbré, il déménage; il n'a plus sa tête à lui. **To go off one's h.,** devenir fou. **Weak in the h.,** faible d'esprit. (*b*) *F:* **To have a bad h., to have a h. on one,** avoir mal à la tête, un mal de tête. **3.** (*a*) Tête (d'arbre, de fleur, de laitue); pomme *f* (de chou); pointe *f* (d'asperge); pied *m* (de céleri); épi *m* (de blé). (*b*) (*Knob-shaped end*) Tête (de violon, d'épingle, de clou); pomme (de canne); champignon *m* (de rail). (*c*) (*Top section*) Tête (de volcan, etc.); haut *m* (de page); en-tête (de chapitre); chapiteau *m* (de colonne). *Nau:* **H. of a sail,** têtière *f,* (ii) envergure *f* (d'une voile). (*d*) Haut (de l'escalier). (*e*) Tête, culasse *f,* fond *m* (de cylindre); chapiteau (d'alambic). *Gramophones:* **Recording h.,** tête enregistreuse. *I.C.E:* **Combustion h.,** culasse, calotte *f. Aut:* **Car with a folding h.,** voiture décapotable. **Sliding h.,** toit ouvrant. (*f*) Chevet *m,* tête (de lit); haut bout (de la table); source *f* (d'une rivière). **At the h. of the lake,** à l'amont du lac. (*g*) (*Of abscess*) **To come to a h., to gather to a h.,** mûrir, aboutir. **To bring a matter to a h.,** faire aboutir une affaire. (*h*) **H. on beer,** mousse *f.* **4.** (*Category*) **On this h.,** sur ce chapitre, sur ce point, sur cet article. **Under separate heads,** sous des rubriques différentes. *Jur:* **Heads of a charge,** chefs *m* d'accusation. **5.** (*a*) Nez *m,* avant *m,* cap *m* (de navire, etc.). **H. of a jetty, of a pier,** musoir *m.* **To collide with a ship h. on** [hed'ɔn], aborder un navire par l'avant. **To be h. to sea, h. on to the sea,** présenter l'avant à la lame. **H. on to the wind,** cap au vent. **Ship (down) by the h.,** vaisseau sur le nez. **How is her h.?** où a-t-on le cap? où est le cap? (*b*) = HEAD-LAND **2. Beachy H.,** le cap Beachy. **6.** (*a*) (*Front or chief place*) **At the h. of a column** (of troops), of a procession, à la tête d'une colonne, d'un cortège. **To be at the h. of the list,** venir en tête de liste. (*b*) (*Pers.*) Chef *m* (de la famille, d'une maison de commerce); directeur, -trice (d'une école). **H. of a department, departmental h.,** chef de service; (*in stores*) chef de rayon. (*c*) *Attrib.* **H. clerk,** premier commis; chef de bureau; *Jur:* premier clerc. **H. agent,** agent principal. **H. gardener,** jardinier en chef. **H. office,** bureau central, bureau principal. *Sch:* **H. boy,** élève choisi parmi les grands pour maintenir la discipline, etc. **7.** (*a*) (*Unit*) *Usu. inv.* **Six h. of cattle,** six têtes, pièces *f,* de bétail. **Thirty h. of deer, of oxen,** trente cerfs, trente bœufs. (*b*) **To pay so much per h.,** so

much a h., payer tant par tête, par personne. **8. H. of a coin,** face *f.* **To toss heads or tails,** jouer à pile ou face. *F:* **I can't make h. or tail of this,** je n'y comprends rien. **9.** *Hyd.E: etc:* **H. of water,** colonne *f* d'eau; charge *f* d'eau. *Ph:* Hauteur *f* manométrique. **Hydraulic h.,** pression *f* en colonne d'eau. *Mch:* **H. of steam,** volant *m* de vapeur. **To gather h.,** (i) (*of flood*) monter; (ii) (*of discontentment*) augmenter, gagner de la force. **'head-cheese,** *s. Cu: U.S:* Hure *f,* fromage de tête, de hure. **'head-dress,** *s.* **1.** (*Hairdressing*) Coiffure *f.* **2.** = HEAD-GEAR. **'head-gear,** *s.* Garniture *f* de tête; coiffure *f;* chapeau *m.* **'head-hunter,** *s. Anthr:* Chasseur *m* de têtes. **'head(-)lamp, 'head(-)light,** *s.* Phare *m,* projecteur *m* (d'automobile, de locomotive); feu *m* d'avant (de locomotive). *Aut:* Feu de route. **Non-dazzle, anti-dazzle, dipped, h.-l.,** phare-code *m, pl.* phares-code, feu de croisement. **To dip the h. lights,** se mettre en code. **'head-noises,** *s.pl. Med:* Tintement *m* des oreilles; bourdonnement(s) *m.* **'head-on,** *a.* De front. **H.-o. collision,** collision frontale. **'head(-)phone,** *s. W.Tel: F:* (*a*) Écouteur *m.* (*b*) *pl.* **H.(-)phones,** casque *m* (téléphonique). **To listen-in with h.-phones,** écouter au casque. **Wearing h.-phones,** *F:* casqué. **'head-piece,** *s.* **1.** (*Helmet*) Casque *m.* **2.** *Typ:* Vignette *f* ou fleuron *m* de tête. **head(-)'quarters,** *s.pl.* **1.** *Mil:* Quartier général; état-major *m.* **H.(-)q. staff,** état-major du général en chef. **2.** Centre *m,* siège social, bureau principal (d'une administration, d'une banque, etc.). **'head-race,** *s. Hyd.E:* Canal *m* de prise, d'amenée, de dérivation; bief *m* d'amont (d'un moulin à eau); rayère *f* (d'une roue à auges). **'head-rest,** *s.* Appui-tête *m, pl.* appuis-tête; support *m* de tête. **'headroom,** *s.* **1.** *Arch:* Échappée *f* (d'un arc); tirant *m* d'air (sous un pont). **2.** *Mec.E: Mch:* Hauteur *f* libre. **3.** *P.N:* hauteur limite. **'head-rope,** *s.* Longe *f,* attache *f* (de cheval). **'head-splitting,** *a.* (Bruit) qui casse la tête. **H.-s. task,** casse-tête *m inv.* **'head-stall,** *s. Harn:* Têtière *f,* licou *m,* licol *m.* **'head voice,** *s. Mus:* Voix *f* de tête; (voix de) fausset *m.* **'head-wind,** *s. Nau:* Vent *m* contraire; vent debout. **'head-work,** *s.* **1.** Travail *m* de tête; travail intellectuel. **2.** *Fb:* Jeu *m* de tête.

head², *v.tr. & i.* **1. To h. (down) a tree,** étêter, écimer, un arbre. **2.** (*Put a head on*) (*a*) Entêter, mettre une tête à (une épingle, un clou, etc.). (*b*) **To h. a chapter with certain words,** mettre certains mots en tête d'un chapitre. **3.** (*a*) Conduire, mener (un cortège, un parti); être à la tête (d'un parti); venir en tête (d'un cortège). **To h. the poll,** venir en tête du scrutin. **To h. the list,** (i) s'inscrire en tête de la liste (de souscriptions, etc.); (ii) être, venir, en tête de (la) liste; ouvrir la liste. (*b*) (*Of thg*) Surmonter, couronner, coiffer. **4.** *Fb:* **To h. the ball,** jouer le ballon de la tête; renvoyer d'un coup de tête. **5.** *v.i.* **To h. for a place,** (i) *Nau:* piquer, gouverner, avoir le cap, mettre le cap, sur un endroit; (ii) s')avancer, se diriger, vers un endroit. **The State is heading for ruin,** l'État va tout droit vers la ruine, marche à la ruine. **6.** *v.i.* (*Of cabbage, etc.*) Pommer; (*of grain*) épier. **head back,** *v.tr.* Rabattre (le gibier); couper la retraite à (l'ennemi). **head off,** *v.tr.* Barrer la route à (qn); détourner, intercepter (des fugitifs); rabattre (le gibier, l'ennemi); couper la retraite à (l'ennemi); parer à (une question embarrassante). **headed,** *a.* **1.** Muni (i) d'une tête, (ii) d'un en-tête. **2.** (*a*) **Black-h.,** aux cheveux noirs, à la chevelure noire; (oiseau) à tête noire. (*b*) **Gold-h. cane,** canne à pomme d'or. **heading,** *s.* **1.** Écimage *m* (d'un arbre, d'une branche). **2.** *Fb:* Jeu *m* de tête. **3.** Intitulé *m* (d'un chapitre); rubrique *f* (d'un article); en-tête *m, pl.* en-têtes. *Book-k:* Poste *m,* rubrique. **To come under the h. of . . .,** ressortir à. . . .

headache ['hedeik], *s.* (*a*) Mal *m* de tête; maux de tête. **Sick h.,** migraine *f.* **To have a h.,** avoir mal à la tête. (*b*) *F:* (*Of problem, etc.*) Casse-tête *m.*

headachy ['hedeiki], *a.* **1.** (*Of pers.*) Qui souffre du mal de tête. **To feel h.,** avoir la tête lourde. **2.** (*Of occupation, etc.*) Qui vous donne mal à la tête. (*Of atmosphere, etc.*) Migraineux.

headband ['hedbænd], *s.* **1.** Bandeau *m.* **2.** *Bookb:* Tranchefile *f,* comète *f.*

header ['hedər], s. **1.** (a) **To take a h.**, (i) plonger (dans l'eau) la tête la première; faire le plongeon; piquer une tête; (ii) F: tomber (par terre) la tête la première; piquer une tête; faire panache. (b) Fb: Coup m de tête. **2.** Const: Boutisse f.

headiness ['hedinis], s. **1.** Emportement m, impétuosité f. **2.** Qualité capiteuse (d'un vin).

headland ['hedlənd], s. **1.** Agr: Tournière f, chaintre m or f. **2.** Geog: Cap m, promontoire m.

headline ['hedlain], s. Typ: Ligne f de tête; titre courant; en-tête m, pl. en-têtes. Journ: Titre ou sous-titre m (de rubrique). **Banner headlines**, titres flamboyants. **Sensational h.**, manchette f. **To hit the headlines**, défrayer la chronique.

headliner ['hedlainər], s. U.S: Th: Cin: etc: Vedette f. **He's a h.**, il est en vedette.

headlong ['hedlɔŋ]. **1.** adv. **To fall h.**, tomber la tête la première. **To rush h. into the fight**, se jeter tête baissée dans la mêlée. **2.** a. (a) **H. fall**, chute f la tête la première. (b) Précipité, irréfléchi, impétueux. **H. flight**, sauve-qui-peut m inv.; panique f.

headman, l. -men ['hedmən], s.m. Chef (d'une tribu).

headmaster ['hed'mɑːstər], s.m. Directeur (d'une école). (In Fr.) Principal (d'un collège); proviseur (d'un lycée).

headmastership [,hed'mɑːstəʃip], s. Directorat m; direction f.

headmistress ['hed'mistris], s.f. Directrice.

headsman, pl. -men ['hedzmən], s.m. Bourreau.

headstock ['hedstək], s. Mec.E: Poupée f (de tour, de machine-outil).

headstone ['hedstoun], s. **1.** Pierre tombale. **2.** Arch: (a) Clef f de voûte. (b) Pierre angulaire.

headstrong ['hedstrɔŋ], a. Volontaire, têtu, entêté, obstiné.

headway ['hedwei], s. **1.** Progrès m. Nau: Erre f; marche f avant; sillage m. **To make h.**, avancer; faire des progrès; (of ship) faire de la route. **The enquiry is making no h.**, l'enquête piétine. Nau: **To gather, fetch, h.**, prendre de l'erre. **2.** Civ.E: Hauteur f libre, échappée f (d'une voûte).

heady ['hedi], a. **1.** (Of pers., action) Impétueux, emporté. **2.** (Parfum, vin) capiteux, entêtant, qui monte au cerveau.

heal [hiːl]. **1.** v.tr. Guérir (qn); guérir, cicatriser (une blessure). **To h. the breach (between two people)**, amener une réconciliation (entre deux personnes). **2.** v.i. (Of wound) **To h. (up), (se)** guérir, se cicatriser, se refermer. **healing**[1], a. **1.** (Remède, etc.) curatif; (onguent) cicatrisant; (conseil) calmant, conciliateur. **2. H. sore**, plaie f qui se cicatrise, qui se referme. **healing**[2], s. **1.** Guérison f. **2.** Cicatrisation f (d'une plaie). **'heal-all**, a. **1.** Panacée f. **2.** Bot: Valériane f.

healer ['hiːlər], s. Guérisseur, -euse.

health [helθ], s. Santé f. **1.** (a) **To restore s.o. to h.**, rendre la santé à qn. **To regain h.**, recouvrer la santé. (b) **To be in good h.**, être en bonne santé, bien portant; se bien porter. **To be in bad h.**, se mal porter, être mal portant. F: **Businessmen don't work for their h.**, les hommes d'affaires ne travaillent pas pour leur bon plaisir. **Public h.**, Santé publique. **The Ministry of H.**, le Ministère de la Santé publique. **The National Health Service**, le Service de santé de la Sécurité Sociale. **H. Centre**, = Contrôle médical de la Sécurité Sociale. **Medical officer of h.**, médecin inspecteur m de santé publique. **H. insurance**, assurance f maladie. **H. certificate**, certificat médical. **H. resort**, station f climatique, (curative baths) station balnéaire; (thermal springs) station thermale; (springs generally) ville f d'eau. **2. To drink (to) the h. of s.o.**, to propose s.o.'s h., porter la santé, boire à la santé, de qn.

healthful ['helθful], a. (Air) salubre; (exercice) salutaire.

healthfulness ['helθfulnis], s. = HEALTHINESS.

healthiness ['helθinis], s. Salubrité f (d'un endroit, d'un climat).

healthy ['helθi], a. **1.** (a) (Of pers.) Sain; en bonne santé; bien portant. (b) (Of climate, food, etc.) Salubre. **To make healthier**, assainir (qch.). **2. H. appetite**, appétit robuste. **H. criticism**, critique vivifiante. -ily, adv. **1.** Sainement. **2.** Salubrement, salutairement.

heap[1] [hiːp], s. (a) Tas m, monceau m, amas m, amoncellement m. **In a h.**, en tas. F: (Of pers.) **To fall in a h.**, s'affaisser (sur soi-même); tomber comme une masse. **To be struck all of a h.**, en rester abasourdi, stupéfait, tout ébaubi, tout pantois. (b) F: **A h. of people**, un tas de gens. **She has heaps of children**, elle avait une ribambelle, P: une flopée, d'enfants. **Heaps of times**, bien des fois; très souvent. **Heaps of time**, grandement, largement, le temps.

heap[2], v.tr. **1.** (a) **To h. (up)**, entasser, amonceler; amasser. (b) **To h. praises, insults, on s.o.**, combler qn d'éloges; accabler, charger, qn d'injures. **2. To h. sth. with sth.**, combler qch. de qch. **She heaped my plate with cherries**, elle a rempli mon assiette de cerises. **Heaped measure**, mesure comble. **Heaped spoonful**, cuillère bien pleine; Cu: cuillère (à café, etc.) arrondie.

hear ['hiər], v.tr. (heard [həːd]; heard) **1.** Entendre. **I h. you**, je vous entends. **A groan was heard**, un gémissement se fit entendre. **I heard my name (mentioned)**, j'entendis prononcer mon nom. **To h. s.o. speak**, entendre parler qn. **I could hardly make myself heard**, je pouvais à peine me faire entendre. **He likes to h. himself talk**, il aime à s'entendre parler. **To h. sth. said (or told) to s.o.**, entendre dire qch. à qn. **To h. s.o. say sth.**, entendre dire qch. à qn, par qn. **I have heard it said**, O: **I have heard tell, that . . .**, j'ai entendu dire que. . . . **2.** (Listen to) (a) Écouter. **H. me out**, écoutez-moi, entendez-moi, jusqu'au bout. (At meetings) **H.! h.!** très bien! très bien! Bravo! Ecc: **To h. mass**, assister à la messe. Jur: **To h. a case**, entendre une cause. (b) Sch: **To h. a lesson**, écouter une leçon. **To h. a child's lesson**, faire réciter, faire répéter, sa leçon à un enfant. (c) **To h. a prayer**, exaucer, écouter, une prière. **3.** (Learn) **To h. a piece of news**, apprendre une nouvelle. **I have heard that . . .**, j'ai appris, on m'a appris, que. . . . **Have you heard the news?** Connaissez-vous la nouvelle? **4.** (a) **To h. from s.o.**, recevoir des nouvelles, une lettre, de qn. **You will h. from me**, je vous écrirai. (As a threat) **You will h. from me later on!** vous aurez de mes nouvelles! Com: **Hoping to h. from you**, dans l'attente de vous lire. (b) **To h. of, about, s.o.**, avoir des nouvelles de qn, entendre parler de qn. **The explorers were never heard of again**, on n'a plus retrouvé trace des explorateurs. **This is the first I have heard of it**, c'est la première fois que j'en entends parler; en voici la première nouvelle. **I never heard of such a thing!** a-t-on jamais entendu une chose pareille! c'est inouï! **I h. of nothing else**, j'en ai les oreilles rebattues. **Father won't h. of it**, mon père ne veut pas en entendre parler, s'y oppose absolument. **hearing,** s. **1.** (a) Audition f (d'un son). (b) Audition, audience f. **Give me a h.!** veuillez m'entendre! **To condemn s.o. without a h.**, condamner qn sans entendre sa défense. (c) Jur: **H. of witnesses**, audition des témoins. **H. of the case**, (i) l'audience; (ii) l'audition de la cause par le juge (sans jury). **2.** Ouïe f. **To be quick of h.**, to have a keen sense of h., avoir l'oreille, l'ouïe, fine; avoir l'oreille sensible. **Within h.**, à portée d'oreille, de la voix. **Out of h.**, hors de portée de la voix. **It was said in my h.**, on l'a dit devant moi, en ma présence. **'hearing-aid,** s. Appareil m de correction auditive, aide-ouïe m, aide auditif.

hearer ['hiərər], s. Auditeur, -trice. pl. Hearers, auditoire m.

hearsay ['hiəsei], s. Ouï-dire m inv. **I know it, have it only from h.**, je ne le sais que par ouï-dire.

hearse [həːs], s. **1.** Ecc: (Taper-)h., if m, herse f. **2.** Corbillard m; char m funèbre. A: **The pauper's h.**, le char des pauvres.

heart[1] [hɑːt], s. Cœur m. **1. With beating h.**, le cœur battant. **To have a weak h.**, être cardiaque. Med: **H. attack**, crise f cardiaque. **H. failure**, défaillance f cardiaque. Surg: **H. transplant**, greffe f du cœur. **Open-h. surgery**, opération f à cœur ouvert. S.a. HOLE[1]. F: **To have one's h. in one's mouth**, avoir un serrement de cœur; être angoissé. **To have one's h. in one's boots**, avoir une peur bleue; avoir un trac formidable. **To press, clasp, s.o. to one's h.**, serrer, presser, qn sur son cœur; étreindre qn. **To break s.o.'s h.**, briser le cœur à qn. **He died of a broken**

h., il est mort de chagrin; il mourut le cœur brisé. **To break one's h. over sth.**, se ronger le cœur au sujet de qch. **2.** (*a*) **H. of gold**, cœur d'or. **H. of steel**, cœur de fer; cœur impénétrable. **To have a h. of stone**, avoir un cœur de pierre. **His h. is in the right place**, il a le cœur bien placé. **Have a h.!** ayez un peu de cœur! **To wear one's h. on one's sleeve**, ne pas savoir cacher ses sentiments. (*Of thg*) **To do one's h. good**, réchauffer le cœur. **Set your h. at rest**, tranquillisez-vous; soyez tranquille. **His h. was full, heavy**, il avait le cœur gros. **With a heavy h.**, le cœur serré, navré. **Sight that goes to one's h., cuts one to the h.**, spectacle qui vous fend le cœur; spectacle navrant. **They were cut to the h.**, ils étaient navrés. **In my h. of hearts**, au plus profond de mon cœur; en mon for intérieur. **From the bottom of my h.**, de tout mon cœur. **At h. he is not a bad fellow**, au fond ce n'est pas un mauvais garçon. **Searchings of the h.**, inquiétudes *f* de l'âme. **To learn sth. by h.**, apprendre qch. par cœur. (*b*) **To love s.o. with all one's h.**, aimer qn de tout son cœur. **To give, lose, one's h. to s.o.**, donner son cœur à qn; s'éprendre de qn. **To win s.o.'s h.**, gagner le cœur de qn; faire la conquête de qn. **To have s.o.'s welfare at h.**, avoir à cœur le bonheur de qn. **He's a man after my own h.**, je le trouve très sympathique. **To take, lay, sth. to h.**, prendre qch. à cœur. (*c*) **To have set one's h. on sth., on doing sth.**, avoir qch. à cœur; avoir, prendre, à cœur de faire qch.; vouloir absolument avoir qch. **The thing he has set his h. on**, la chose qui lui tient à cœur. **To one's h.'s content**, à cœur joie, à souhait. **To eat, drink, to one's h.'s content**, manger, boire, tout son soûl, tout son content. (*d*) **To have one's h. in one's work**, avoir le cœur à l'ouvrage. **With all my h.**, du meilleur de mon cœur, de tout mon cœur. **With h. and hand**, de cœur et de main, de cœur et d'âme; de tout cœur. (*e*) **To put new h. into s.o.; to put s.o. in good h.**, donner du courage, du cœur, à qn; réchauffer le cœur à qn; ragaillardir, encourager, qn. **To pluck up, take, h.**, prendre, reprendre, courage. **To be of good h.**, avoir bon courage. **To lose h.**, perdre courage; se décourager, se rebuter. **Not to find it in one's h., not to have the h., to do sth.**, ne pas avoir le cœur, le courage, de faire qch.; ne pouvoir se décider à faire qch. **To be in good, strong, h.**, (i) (*Of pers.*), être de bonne humeur, être en train; (ii) *Agr*: (*Of soil*) être bien entretenu, d'un bon rapport. **3.** Cœur (d'un chou); fond *m* (d'artichaut); cœur, vif *m* (d'un arbre). **H. of oak**, homme courageux; cœur de chêne. **H. of a cable**, âme *f*, mèche *f*, d'un câble. **The h. of the matter**, le vif de l'affaire. **In the h. of ..**, au cœur (d'une ville), au (beau) milieu (d'une forêt), au (fin) fond (d'un désert). **4.** *Cards:* **Queen of hearts**, dame *f* de cœur. **Have you any hearts?** avez-vous du cœur? ′**heart(-)ache**, *s.* Chagrin *m*, peine *f* de cœur, douleur *f.* ′**heart(-)break**, *s.* Déchirement *m* de cœur; brisement *m* de cœur; chagrin poignant. ′**heart(-)breaking**, *a.* Navrant. **It was h.-b.**, c'était à fendre l'âme. ′**heart(-)broken**, *a.* **To be h.-b.**, avoir le cœur brisé; être navré. ′**heart′burning**, *s.* Dépit *m*; jalousie *f.* **To cause much h.-b.**, exciter bien des rancunes. ′**heart-case**, *s. Med:* (*Pers.*) Cardiaque *mf.* ′**heart-disease**, *s.* Maladie *f* de cœur. ′**heart(-)failure**, *s.* Arrêt *m* du cœur; syncope (mortelle). ′**heart(-)felt**, *a.* (*Vœu*) sincère; qui vient, part, du cœur. **H.-f. words**, paroles bien senties. **To make a h.-f. appeal**, mettre tout son cœur dans son plaidoyer. ′**heart-piercing, -rending**, *a.* (Soupir, nouvelle) à fendre le cœur, qui fend l'âme; (spectacle) navrant. **H.-r. cries**, cris déchirants. ′**heart-searching. 1.** *a.* (Question) qui sonde le cœur. **2.** *s.* Examen *m* de conscience. ′**heart's-ease**, *s. Bot:* Pensée *f* sauvage. ′**heart-shaped**, *a.* Cordiforme; en (forme de) cœur. ′**heart(-)sick**, *a.* Écœuré. **To be, feel, h.-s.**, être, se sentir, découragé; avoir la mort dans l'âme. ′**heart-strings**, *s.pl.* **1.** *A:* Fibres *f* du cœur. **2.** Tug at one's h.-s., serrement *m* de cœur. ′**heart-to ′heart**, *a. & adv.phr.* **H.-to-h. talk**, conversation intime. **To talk with s.o. h. to h.**, parler avec qn à cœur ouvert. ′**heart-whole**, *a.* **1.** Qui a le cœur libre; qui n'a pas d'amour en tête. **2.** **H.-w. affection**, affection

sincère, vraie. **3.** Qui a conservé tout son courage. ′**heart-wood**, *s. Arb:* Bois *m* de cœur; cœur *m* du bois.

heart², *v.i.* (*Of cabbage, lettuce*) **To h.** (up), pommer.

heartburn [′hɑːtbəːn], *s. Med:* Pyrosis *m*; *F:* aigreurs *fpl* (d'estomac); brûlures *fpl* d'estomac.

-hearted [′hɑːtid], *a.* **Evil-h.**, méchant; au cœur mauvais. **Big-h., great-h., fellow**, garçon de cœur. **True-h., open-h.**, sincère. **Warm-h.**, au cœur chaud, généreux. **Warm-h. welcome**, accueil chaleureux. **Whole-h.**, (qui vient) du cœur; sincère. **Whole-h. laugh**, rire épanoui. *S.a.* BROKEN-HEARTED, CHICKEN-HEARTED, HARD-HEARTED, etc.

hearten [′hɑːtn]. **1.** *v.tr.* **To h. s.o.** (up), ranimer, relever, le courage de qn; donner du cœur à qn. **2.** *v.i.* **To h. up**, reprendre courage.

hearth, *pl.* **-ths** [hɑːθ, -ðz], *s.* **1.** Foyer *m*, âtre *m.* **Without h. or home**, sans feu ni lieu. **2.** (*a*) *Metall:* Aire *f*, foyer, sole *f* (de four à réverbère); creuset *m* (de haut-fourneau). (*b*) **Smith's h.**, (foyer de) forge (*f*). ′**hearth-rug**, *s.* Tapis *m*, carpette *f*, de foyer; devant *m* de foyer.

hearthstone [′hɑːθstoun], *s.* **1.** Pierre *f* de la cheminée. **2.** *Dom.Ec:* Blanc *m* d'Espagne. **3.** *U.S:* = HEARTH 1.

heartiness [′hɑːtinis], *s.* Cordialité *f*, chaleur *f* (d'un accueil); vigueur *f* (de l'appétit). **The h. which he puts into his work**, l'ardeur *f* qu'il met à son travail.

heartless [′hɑːtlis], *a.* Sans cœur, insensible, sans pitié; (traitement, mot) dur, cruel. **You will not be so h. as to do that**, vous n'aurez pas le cœur de faire cela. **-ly**, *adv.* Sans cœur, sans pitié.

heartlessness [′hɑːtlisnis], *s.* Manque *m* de cœur.

hearty [′hɑːti], *a.* **1.** Cordial, -aux; (sentiment) sincère, qui part du cœur. **2.** (*a*) Vigoureux, robuste, bien portant. *S.a.* HALE. (*b*) (Repas) copieux, abondant, solide. **H. appetite**, gros, excellent appétit. **He is a h. eater**, il mange ferme; c'est un gros mangeur, une bonne fourchette. **3.** *s. Nau:* **Now then, my hearties!** allons, mes braves! **-ily**, *adv.* **1.** Cordialement; chaleureusement; (travailler, rire) de bon cœur; (se réjouir) sincèrement. **2.** (Dîner) copieusement; (manger) de bon appétit, avec appétit.

heat¹ [hiːt], *s.* **1.** (*a*) Chaleur *f*; ardeur *f* (du soleil, d'un foyer). **In the h. of the day**, au plus chaud de la journée. **The h. and the cold should be avoided**, le chaud et le froid sont à éviter. *Hort:* **To sow in h.**, semer sur couche. (*b*) *Ph: etc:* Chaleur, calorique *m.* **Specific h.**, chaleur spécifique. **H. efficiency**, rendement *m* calorifique. **H. constant**, constante *f* calorifique. (*c*) *Metall:* Chaleur, chaude *f.* **Red h.**, chaude rouge. **White h.**, chaleur d'incandescence; chaude blanche. **To raise iron to a white h., to a red h.**, chauffer le fer à blanc, au rouge. (*d*) *Cu:* Intensité *f* de chauffe; température *f.* **2.** (*Passion*) **To get into a h.**, s'échauffer, s'emporter. **To reply with some h.**, répondre avec une certaine vivacité. **H. of youth**, fougue *f* de la jeunesse. **In the h. of the moment**, dans la chaleur du moment. **3.** (*a*) *Med:* Rougeur *f* (sur la peau). *Esp:* **Prickly h.**, lichen *m* vésiculaire; miliaire *f*; bourbouille *f.* (*b*) *Vet:* (*Rut*) Rut *m*; chaleur *f.* **4.** *Sp: Rac:* Épreuve *f*, manche *f.* **Qualifying h.**, (épreuve) éliminatoire (*f*). **Dead h.**, manche nulle; course nulle. **To run a dead h.**, courir à égalité. ′**heat-absorbing**, *a.* Qui absorbe la chaleur. ′**heat-energy**, *s. Ph:* Énergie *f* thermique. ′**heat-insulating**, *a. & s.* (Produit *m*) calorifuge (*m*), isolant (*m*). ′**heat-insulation**, *s.* Calorifugeage *m*, isolation *f.* ′**heat-proof**, *a.* (Vernis *m*) résistant à la chaleur, (plat *m*) allant au four, au feu. ′**heat-pump**, *s.* Thermopompe *f.* ′**heat-rash**, *s. Med:* Échauffaison *f*, échauffure *f.* ′**heat-resisting**, *a.* **1.** Ignifuge, calorifuge. **2.** (Acier) indétrempable. **3.** Thermorésistant. ′**heat-sealing**, *s.* Thermocollage *m.* ′**heat-setting**, *s.* (Résine *f*) thermodurcissab'e. ′**heat-stroke**, *s. Med: Vet:* Coup *m* de chaleur. ′**heat-wave**, *s.* (*a*) *Ph:* Onde *f* calorifique. (*b*) *Meteor:* Vague *f* de chaleur.

heat². **1.** *v.tr.* (*a*) Chauffer. (*b*) (*Abnormally*) Échauffer (le sang, etc.); enflammer (l'esprit). **To h. oneself running**, s'échauffer à courir. **2.** *v.i.* (*a*) *Of water, etc.*) Chauffer. (*b*) (*Of bearing*) **To h.** (up), chauffer, s'échauffer. **heat up,** *v.tr.* (Faire) réchauffer (un plat). **heated,** *a.* **1.** Chaud, chauffé. **2.** (*a*) H. **bearing,** palier échauffé, qui chauffe. (*b*) (*Of pers.*) To get h., s'échauffer. H. **debate,** discussion chaude, animée. -**ly,** *adv.* Avec chaleur, avec emportement. **heating**[1], *a.* **1.** Échauffant. **2.** H. **action of the sun,** action calorifiante du soleil. **heating**[2], *s.* **1.** (*Making hot*) (*a*) Chauffage *m,* chauffe *f* (des chaudières, etc.). **Central h.,** chauffage central. H. **power,** puissance *f,* pouvoir *m,* calorifique; rendement *m* calorique. H. **apparatus,** calorifère *m.* (*b*) Réchauffage *m* (d'un plat, etc.). **2.** (*Becoming hot*) Échauffement *m* (d'un coussinet); échauffement, fermentation *f* (du foin).

heater ['hiːtər], *s.* Appareil *m* de chauffage, F: chauffage *m;* calorifère *m.* (*a*) Radiateur *m.* **Electric h.,** radiateur électrique. (*b*) **Gas (water-) h.,** chauffe-bains *m inv,* chauffe-eau *m inv* (à gaz). (*c*) **Car h.,** chauffage *m* (de voiture). (*d*) Réchaud *m.* (*e*) *U.S:* P: (*Revolver*) P: Rigolo *m,* seringue *f,* rigoustin *m.*

heath [hiːθ], *s.* **1.** Bruyère *f,* lande *f,* brande *f.* **2.** *Bot:* Bruyère, brande.

heathen ['hiːð(ə)n], *a. & s.* Païen, -ienne. *Coll.* The h., les païens. **2.** Barbare, grossier.

heather ['heðər], *s. Bot:* Bruyère *f,* brande *f.* **Scotch h., bell h.,** bruyère cendrée. **'heather-mixture,** *s. Tex:* Drap chiné bruyère, tweed *m.*

heathery ['heð(ə)ri], *a.* **1.** Couvert de bruyère. **2.** Ressemblant à la bruyère.

heave[1] [hiːv], *s.* Soulèvement *m.* **1.** Effort *m* (pour soulever). *Gym:* To do heaves, faire des tractions *f.* **2.** (*a*) Haut-le-cœur *m inv;* nausée *f.* (*b*) Palpitation *f* (du sein). **3.** *Nau:* H. of the sea, poussée *f,* ondulation *f,* des lames; houle *f.* **4.** *pl.* (*With sing. const.*) *Vet:* The heaves, la pousse.

heave[2], *v.* (*p.t. & p.p.* **heaved** or (*esp. Nau:*) **hove** [houv]) I. *v.tr.* **1.** (*Lift*) Lever, soulever (un fardeau), *Nau:* To h. (up) the anchor, *abs.* to h. up, déraper; lever l'ancre. **2.** Pousser (un soupir). **3.** (*a*) (*Pull, haul*) To h. coal, (i) porter, (ii) décharger, le charbon. (*b*) *Nau:* To h. the ship ahead, astern, virer le navire de l'avant, de l'arrière. **4.** (*Throw*) Lancer, jeter (sth. at s.o., qch. contre qn). *Nau:* To h. the lead, jeter la sonde, le plomb; sonder. **5.** *Sp:* To h. oneself up, faire un rétablissement. II. **heave,** *v.i.* **1.** (*a*) (*Swell*) (Se) gonfler, se soulever; (*of sea*) se soulever; (*of bosom*) palpiter. (*b*) (*Of pers.*) Avoir des haut-le-cœur. (*Of the stomach*) Se soulever, se retourner. (*c*) (*Of horse*) Battre du flanc. **2.** *Nau:* (*a*) To h. at a rope, haler sur une manœuvre. To h. (away) at the capstan, virer au cabestan. (*b*) To h. ahead, astern, virer de l'avant, de l'arrière. **3.** *Nau:* (*Of land, ship*) To h. in sight, paraître (à l'horizon); poindre. **heave in,** *v.tr. Nau:* Rentrer, virer (un cordage). To h. in the lines, rentrer les amarres. *Abs.* To h. in, virer au cabestan. **heave to,** *v.tr. & i. Nau:* (Se) mettre en panne, à la cape; prendre la panne; empanner. To be hove to, être en panne, à la cape. Hove to under bare poles, en panne sèche.

heaven ['hev(ə)n], *s.* Ciel *m, pl.* cieux. In h., au ciel. To go to h., aller au ciel, en paradis. Heavens above! Good Heavens! juste ciel! bonté divine! Thank H.! Dieu merci! For H.'s sake! pour l'amour de Dieu! To move h. and earth (to do sth.), remuer ciel et terre, se mettre en quatre (pour faire qch.). **'heaven-born,** *a.* Céleste; divin; **'heaven-sent,** *a.* Providentiel, -elle.

heavenly ['hevnli], *a.* Céleste; (don) du ciel. H. **body,** astre *m.* **Our H. Father,** notre Père céleste. *F:* What h. peaches! quelles pêches délicieuses!

heavenliness ['hevənlinis], *s.* Caractère *m* céleste (de qch.). **The h. of last summer's weather!** la perfection, la beauté incomparable, du temps qu'il a fait l'été passé!

heaviness ['hevinis], *s.* (*a*) Lourdeur, *f,* pesanteur *f;* poids *m* (d'un fardeau). (*b*) Engourdissement *m,* lassitude *f* (des membres, de l'esprit). H. of heart, serrement *m* de cœur; tristesse *f.*

heavy ['hevi], *a.* **1.** Lourd. (*a*) H. **parcel,** paquet lourd, pesant. To weigh h., peser lourd. To make a burden heavier, alourdir, appesantir, un fardeau. *Ph:* H. **bodies,** corps graves. *Av:* Heavier-than-air craft, appareil plus lourd que l'air. H. **blow,** (i) coup violent; (ii) rude coup (du sort, etc.). H. **wine,** gros vin; vin à forte teneur d'alcool. (*b*) H. **tread,** pas pesant, lourd. (*c*) (*Of animal*) H. **with young,** gravide. **2.** (*a*) H. **baggage,** gros bagages. H. **wire,** fil (de) grosse épaisseur. *Metall:* H. **castings,** grosses pièces. *Mil:* H. **guns,** artillerie lourde. H. **cavalry,** grosse cavalerie. *Navy:* H. **armament,** artillerie de gros calibre. (*b*) H. **features,** gros traits. H. **line,** gros trait. *Typ:* H. **type,** caractères gras. (*c*) H. **beard** forte barbe. H. **crop,** grosse récolte; récolte abondante. H. **meal,** repas copieux. *Mil:* H. **fire,** feu nourri; feu vif; feu intense. H. **shower,** grosse averse. H. **fog,** brouillard épais. H. **expenditure,** dépenses considérables; grosses dépenses. *El:* H. **current,** courant intensif, intense. H. **cold,** gros rhume, *F:* rhume carabiné. (*d*) H. **silence,** silence profond. H. **sleep,** profond sommeil. **3.** H. **odour,** odeur lourde. **Air h. with scent,** air chargé de parfums. *S.a.* HEART[1] 2. **4.** H. **eyes,** yeux battus. H. **(with sleep),** appesanti par le sommeil; accablé de sommeil. **5.** (*a*) (*Travail*) pénible, difficile, dur, laborieux. **He did the h. work,** c'est lui qui a fait le gros de la besogne. H. **day,** journée chargée. H. **soil, h. ground,** terrain lourd; sol gras; sol fort. (*b*) H. **weather,** gros temps. H. **sea,** forte mer, grosse mer. **A h. sea was running,** il faisait une mer houleuse. To ship a h. sea, embarquer un coup de mer. **6.** *Th:* H. **parts,** rôles sérieux, tragiques. H. **father,** père *m* noble. **7.** H. **eater,** gros mangeur. H. **drinker,** fort buveur. To be a h. sleeper, avoir le sommeil dur. -**ily,** *adv.* **1.** Lourdement. **Time hangs h. on his hands,** le temps lui pèse, lui dure. **He walked h.,** il avançait d'un pas pesant, à pas pesants. **2.** H. **underlined,** fortement souligné. To lose h., perdre une forte somme; *F:* perdre gros. To be h. taxed, être fortement imposé. **3.** To sigh h., soupirer profondément. To sleep h., dormir profondément. **4.** (Respirer, se mouvoir) péniblement; (se mouvoir) avec difficulté. **'heavy-'eyed,** *a.* Aux yeux battus. **'heavy-'handed,** *a.* **1.** A la main lourde. **2.** H.-h. government, gouvernement oppressif. **2.** Maladroit, gauche. **'heavy-'hearted,** *a.* Abattu; qui a le cœur gros. **'heavy-weight.** **1.** *s. Box:* Poids lourd. **2.** *a.* H.-w. **materials,** tissus lourds.

Hebraic [hiˈbreiik], *a.* Hébraïque.

Hebraism ['hiːbreiizm], *s.* Hébraïsme *m.*

Hebraist ['hiːbreiist], *s.* Hébraïsant *m,* hébraïste *m.*

Hebrew ['hiːbruː]. **1.** *B.Lit:* (*a*) *s.* Hébreu, *f.* Hébreue, Israélite *mf.* (*b*) *a.* Hébreu, *f.* hébraïque. **(The)** H. **(language),** l'hébreu *m.* To study H., hébraïser. **2.** (*Modern use*) *a. & s.* Hébraïque (*mf*); Israélite (*mf*).

hecatomb ['hekətuːm], *s. Gr.Ant:* Hécatombe *f.*

heck [hek], *s. & int. F:* **What the h. are you doing?** que diable faites-vous? H.! zut! flûte!

heckle ['hekl], *v.tr.* (*At public meetings*) Interpeller (un candidat politique). **heckling,** *s.* Interpellation, *f.*

heckler ['heklər], *s. Pol: etc:* Interpellateur, -trice, adversaire *m* qui cherche à embarrasser le candidat.

hectare ['hekteər], *s. Meas:* Hectare *m.*

hectic ['hektik], *a.* **1.** *Med:* (*a*) Hectique. (*b*) H. **cough,** toux de phtisique. **2.** *F:* Agité, fiévreux. H. **life,** existence trépidante. **We had a h. time,** (i) ç'a été à ne savoir où donner de la tête; (ii) on a fait une de ces noces!

hectogram(me) ['hektəgræm], *s. Meas:* Hectogramme *m, F:* hecto *m.*

hectolitre ['hektəliːtər], *s.* Hectolitre *m, F:* hecto *m.*

hectometre ['hektəmiːtər], *s.* Hectomètre *m.*

hector ['hektər], *v.tr. & i.* Faire de l'esbroufe; faire le matamore; intimider, rudoyer (qn). **hectoring,** *a.* (Ton, etc.) autoritaire, impérieux.

hectowatt ['hektəwɔt], *s. El:* Hectowatt *m.*

he'd [hiːd] = he had, he would.

heddles ['hedlz], *s.pl. Tex:* Lices *f* (du métier).

hedge[1] [hedʒ], *s.* **1.** Haie *f.* **Quickset h.,** haie vive. **Dead h.,** haie morte, sèche. **2.** Haie (d'agents de police, de troupes). **3.** *Attrib. Pej:* De bas étage; interlope. **H.-priest, h.-parson,** (i) prêtre ignorant; (ii) prêtre interlope. H. **lawyer,** avocat marron. **'hedge-hop,** *v.i. Av:* Voler en rase-mottes. **'hedge-hopping,** *s. Av: F:* Vol *m* à ras de terre; rase-mottes *m inv.*

hedge². 1. *v.tr.* To h. in, off, a piece of ground, mettre une haie autour d'un terrain; enfermer, enclore, un terrain. **Hedged in, hedged about, with difficulties**, entouré de difficultés. 2. *v.i.* (*a*) *Turf:* Parier pour et contre. *St.Exch: U.S:* Faire la contre-partie. (*b*) (*In discussion*) Chercher des échappatoires; se réserver; s'échapper par la tangente. **hedging**, *s.* 1. Entretien *m* des haies. 2. Bordure *f.* 3. *Turf:* Pari *m* pour et contre.

hedgehog ['hedʒ)hɔg], *s.* Hérisson *m.* *F:* **To curl up like a h.**, se mettre en boule. *Mil:* Hérisson.

hedger ['hedʒər], *s.* 1. (*a*) Planteur *m*, (*b*) réparateur *m*, de haies. 2. Personne *f* qui se réserve, qui évite de se décider.

hedgerow ['hedʒrou], *s.* Bordure *f* de haies, d'arbres ou d'arbustes formant une haie.

hedonism ['hi:dənizm], *s.* *Phil:* Hédonisme *m.*

hedonist ['hi:dənist], *s.* *Phil:* Hédoniste *mf.*

heed¹ [hi:d], *s.* Attention *f*, garde *f*, soin *m.* **To give, pay, h. to sth., to s.o.**, faire attention à qch.; prêter (son) attention à qn. **To take h.**, prendre garde. **To take no h. of sth.**, ne tenir aucun compte de qch. **To take h. to do sth.**, prendre garde, prendre soin, de faire qch.

heed², *v.tr.* Faire attention à, prendre garde à, tenir compte de (qch.).

heedful ['hi:dful], *a.* Vigilant, prudent. **H. of advice**, attentif aux conseils.

heedfulness ['hi:dfulnis], *s.* Attention *f* (of, à); soin *m* (of, de); vigilance *f*, prudence *f.*

heedless ['hi:dlis], *a.* 1. Étourdi, insouciant, imprudent. 2. **To be h. of** (sth.), être inattentif à (ce qui se passe); être peu soucieux de (l'avenir, etc.). -ly, *adv.* Étourdiment.

heedlessness ['hi:dlisnis], *s.* Inattention *f* (of, à); étourderie *f*, insouciance *f.*

hee-haw¹ ['hi:hɔ:], *s.* Hi-han *m*; braiment *m.*

hee-haw², *v.i.* Braire; faire hi-han.

heel¹ [hi:l], *s.* 1. (*a*) Talon *m* (du pied). **Achilles' h.**, talon d'Achille. **To be under the h. of the invader**, être sous la botte de l'envahisseur. **To tread on, be upon, s.o.'s heels**, marcher sur les talons de qn; être aux trousses de qn. **To be quick on s.o.'s heels**, suivre qn de près. **To show a clean pair of heels, to take to one's heels**, prendre la fuite; tourner les talons. **He showed us a clean pair of heels**, il nous a échappé. **To lay s.o. by the heels**, arrêter qn; *F:* pincer qn; mettre qn au bloc. *Nau:* **To have the heels of another ship**, dépasser, enganter, un autre navire. **To turn on one's h.**, faire demi-tour, *F:* tourner les talons (sans cérémonie). **To kick, cool, one's heels**, croquer le marmot; faire le pied de grue; *P:* faire le poireau; poireauter. **To come to h.**, (*of dog*) venir derrière à l'ordre; obéir à l'appel; (*of pers.*) se soumettre. **To bring s.o. to h.**, mater qn; mettre qn au pas. *S.a.* HEAD¹ 1. (*b*) Talon (d'un soulier, d'un bas). **High heels, low heels**, talons hauts, bas. **French heels**, talons Louis XV. **Stiletto h.**, talon aiguille. **Out at heels**, (bas) troués aux talons. *F:* (*Of pers.*) **To be out at heels**, (i) porter des bas percés; (ii) être dans la dèche. **To be down at h.**, (i) porter des souliers éculés; (ii) être dans la dèche. *Geog:* **The H. of Italy**, la Terre d'Otrante; le talon de la botte. (*c*) *U.S: P:* Canaille *f.* 2. Talon (d'outil, de crosse de golf). *Nau:* **H. of the rudder**, talon, talonnière *f*, du gouvernail. 3. (*a*) Éperon *m*, ergot *m* (de coq). (*b*) Talon *m* du sabot (d'un cheval, etc.). (*Of horse*) **To fling out its heels**, ruer. **'heel-tap**, *s.* 1. *Bootm:* Rondelle *f* en cuir (pour talon); hausse *f.* 2. *pl.* **Heel-taps**, fonds *m* de verre. **To leave no heel-taps**, *F:* faire cul sec.

heel². 1. *v.i.* Danser en frappant du talon. 2. *v.tr.* (*a*) (i) Mettre un talon à (un soulier, un bas). (ii) Réparer le talon (d'un soulier); refaire le talon (d'un bas). (*b*) *Golf:* Talonner (la balle). (*c*) *Rugby Fb:* **To h. (out)**, talonner. (*d*) *Hort:* Mettre en jauge (des plantes). **heeled**, *a.* A talons. **High-h. shoes**, souliers à hauts talons. **Low-h. shoes**, souliers plats. *U.S: P:* **To be well-h.**, être bien pourvu d'argent.

heel³, *s.* *Nau:* Bande *f*, gîte (d'un navire). **On the h.**, à la bande.

heel⁴, *v.* *Nau:* **To h. (over)**. 1. *v.i.* (*Of ship*) Avoir, donner, de la bande; prendre de la gîte. 2. *v.tr.* Mettre (un navire) à la bande.

hefty ['hefti], *a.* *F:* (Homme) fort, solide, *F:* costaud.

Hegelian [he'gi:liən], *a. & s.* *Phil:* Hégélien, -ienne.

hegemony [hi'geməni, hi'dʒeməni], *s.* Hégémonie *f.*

hegira [hi'dʒaiərə], *s.* *Moham. Rel:* Hégire *f.*

heifer ['hefər], *s.* Génisse *f.*

heigh [hei], *int.* 1. Hé! 2. Hé, là-bas!

height [hait], *s.* 1. (*a*) Hauteur *f*, élévation *f.* **Wall six feet in h.**, mur qui a six pieds de haut. (*b*) Taille *f*, grandeur *f*, stature *f* (de qn). **Full h.**, taille debout. **Of average h.**, de taille moyenne. 2. **H. above sea level**, altitude *f* au-dessus du niveau de la mer. 3. (*Hill*) Hauteur; éminence *f* (de terrain); colline *f.* 4. Apogée *m* (de la fortune, de la gloire); faîte *m* (des grandeurs); comble *m* (de la folie). **At the h. of the storm, of the action**, au (plus) fort de l'orage, du combat. **In the h. of summer**, au cœur, au milieu, au fort, de l'été; en plein été. **The season is at its h.**, la saison bat son plein. **In the h. of fashion**, à la dernière mode; du dernier cri.

heighten ['haitn]. 1. *v.tr.* (*a*) Surélever, surhausser, rehausser (un mur, un immeuble). (*b*) Accroître, augmenter (un plaisir); aggraver (un mal); accentuer (un contraste); relever, faire ressortir (la beauté de qch.). 2. *v.i.* S'élever; se rehausser; augmenter.

heinous ['heinəs], *a.* (Crime) odieux, atroce, abominable. -ly, *adv.* Odieusement, atrocement, abominablement.

heinousness ['heinəsnis], *s.* Énormité *f*, atrocité *f* (d'un crime).

heir ['ɛər], *s.* Héritier *m.* **To be h. to a relative, to an estate**, être l'héritier, le légataire, d'un parent, le légataire d'une propriété. *Jur:* **H. apparent**, héritier présomptif. **H.-at-law, rightful h.**, héritier légitime, naturel.

heiress ['ɛəres], *s.f.* Héritière.

heirloom ['ɛəlu:m], *s.* Meuble *m* ou bijou *m* de famille.

held. *See* HOLD².

Helen ['helin]. *Pr.n.f.* Hélène.

heliacal [hi:'laiəkəl], *a.* *Astr:* Héliaque.

helianthus [hi:li'ænθəs], *s.* *Bot:* Hélianthe *m*, tournesol *m.*

helical ['helik(ə)l], *a.* 1. *Conch:* **H. shell**, hélice *f*, coquille contournée. 2. *Mec.E:* (*Of gear, etc.*) Hélicoïdal, -aux; (*of spring*) hélicoïde, en hélice. **Double h. gear**, engrenage à chevrons. **-ally**, *adv.* En spirale, en hélice.

helicoid ['helikoid]. 1. *a.* Hélicoïde; hélicoïdal, -aux. 2. *s.* Hélicoïde *m.*

helicoidal [,heli'koid(ə)l], *a.* = HELICOID 1.

helicopter ['helikɔptər], *s.* *Av:* Hélicoptère *m.* **Pressure-jet h.**, hélicoptère à réaction. **H. station**, héligare *f.* **Transported by h., h.-borne**, héliporté.

heliograph¹ ['hi:liəgrɑ:f, -græf], *s.* 1. Héliographe *m*; héliostat *m.* 2. *Phot.Engr:* Héliogravure *f.*

heliograph², *v.tr.* 1. Communiquer (un message) par héliographe. 2. Reproduire (un dessin) par héliogravure.

heliogravure ['hi:liougrə'vjuər], *s.* Héliogravure *f*; photogravure *f.*

helioscope ['hi:liəskoup], *s.* *Astr:* Hélioscope *m.*

heliostat ['hi:liəstæt], *s.* Héliostat *m.*

heliotherapy ['hi:liou'θerəpi], *s.* Héliothérapie *f.*

heliotrope ['hi:liətroup]. 1. *s.* *Bot:* Héliotrope *m.* 2. *a.* Héliotrope *inv.*

heliport ['helipɔ:t], *s.* Héliport *m.*

helium ['hi:liəm], *s.* *Ch:* Hélium *m.*

helix, *pl.* **helices**, ['hi:liks, 'heliks, 'hi:lisi:z], *s.* 1. (*a*) *Geom:* Hélice *f.* (*b*) *Arch:* etc: Spirale *f*; volute *f.* 2. *Anat:* Hélix *m* (de l'oreille). 3. *Moll:* (*Snail*) Hélice, colimaçon *m.*

hell [hel], *s.* 1. *Myth:* Les enfers *m.* 2. L'enfer. (*a*) **In heaven and h.**, au ciel et en enfer. **H. is let loose**, les diables sont déchaînés. **It's h. on earth!** c'est infernal! **To raise h.**, faire une scène. **To ride h. for leather**, galoper à bride abattue, à toute bride; aller au triple galop. (*b*) *P:* **To make a h. of a noise**, faire un bruit d'enfer, un bruit infernal; *P:* un boucan infernal. **To catch h.**, prendre un savon. **To give s.o. h.**, (faire) passer un savon à qn; faire passer un mauvais quart d'heure à qn. **To h. with him!** qu'il aille au diable! **He'll be a h. of a good sailor**, il fera un marin du tonnerre (de Dieu). **To**

work like h., travailler avec acharnement. **What the h. do you want?** que diable désirez-vous? 3. (*Gambling-den*) Tripot *m*. 4. *Int*: Nom d'un nom, d'une pipe, d'un chien! 'hell-bent, *a*. *U.S*: (*a*) Casse-cou *inv*. (*b*) Acharné, têtu. (*c*) At h.-b. speed, à toute vitesse, à une allure infernale. 'hell-cat, *s.f*. Mégère *f*. 'hell-'fire, *s*. Feu *m*, tourments *mpl*, de l'enfer. 'hell-hound, *s*. Suppôt *m* de Satan.

he'll [hi:l] = *he will*.

hellebore ['helibɔ:r], *s*. *Bot*: Ellébore *m*.

Hellene ['heli:n], *s*. Hellène *mf*.

Hellenic [he'li:nik], *a*. (Race) hellène; (langue) hellénique.

Hellenism ['helinizm], *s*. Hellénisme *m*.

Hellenist ['helinist], *s*. Helléniste *mf*.

Hellenize ['helinaiz], *v.tr. & i*. Helléniser, gréciser.

hellish ['heliʃ], *a*. Infernal, -aux; d'enfer; diabolique. -ly, *adv*. D'une manière diabolique.

hellishness ['heliʃnis], *s*. Méchanceté *f* diabolique.

hello [he'lou], *int*. (*a*) (*Calling attention*) H. there, wake up! holà! debout! hé, là-bas, debout! (*b*) (*On the telephone*) Allô! (*c*) (*Indicating surprise*) H., is that you? tiens! c'est vous!

helm¹ [helm], *s*. *Arm: A:* Heaume *m*.

helm², *s*. *Nau:* Barre *f* (du gouvernail); gouvernail *m*, timon *m*. **The man at the h.,** (i) l'homme de barre; (ii) l'homme qui tient le gouvernail, qui dirige l'entreprise. **Down (with the) h.!** la barre dessous! **Up (with the) h.!** la barre au vent! **The h. of the State,** le timon de l'État.

helmet ['helmit], *s*. 1. Casque *m*. **Tropical h.,** casque colonial. 2.*Ph: Ch: Ind:* Chapiteau *m* (de cornue).

helmsman, *pl.* **-men,** ['helmzmən], *s.m. Nau:* Homme de barre; timonier.

helot ['helət, 'hi:-], *s*. *Gr.Hist:* Ilote *m*.

helotism ['helətizm], *s*. *Gr.Hist:* Ilotisme *m*.

help¹ [help], *s*. 1. Aide *f*, assistance *f*, secours *m*. **With the h. of a friend,** avec l'aide d'un ami. **Mutual h.,** entr'aide *f*, secours *m* réciproque. **With the h. of a rope,** à l'aide, au moyen, d'une corde. **With God's h.,** Dieu aidant. **To cry for h.,** crier au secours; appeler à l'aide. **Past h.,** perdu. **To lend one's h.,** prêter son concours. 2. **To come to s.o.'s h.,** venir au secours de qn; porter secours à qn. 3. **There's no h. for it,** il n'y a pas de remède; il n'y a rien à faire. 4. (*a*) **To be a h. to s.o.,** être d'un grand secours à qn, rendre grand service à qn. (*b*) (*Pers.*) Aide *mf*. *Esp. U.S:* Domestique *mf*, bonne *f*; femme *f* de journée. **Home h.,** aide ménagère. **Mother's h.,** travailleuse, aide, familiale. *Journ:* 'H. wanted,' = Offres *f* d'emploi.

help², *v.tr.* 1. (*a*) Aider, secourir, assister; venir en aide à (qn); venir à l'aide de (qn). **To h. s.o. to do sth.,** aider qn à faire qch. **That will not h. you,** cela ne vous servira à rien. **God h. you!** Dieu vous soit en aide! **So h. me God!** que Dieu me juge si je ne dis pas la vérité! **I got a friend to h. me,** je me suis fait aider par un ami. **Not to do more than one can h.,** (i) ne pas faire plus que de raison; (ii) faire le moins possible, *F:* ne pas se fouler la rate, *P:* ne pas se la fouler. **He knows how to h. himself,** il sait se tirer d'affaire, se débrouiller. *Prov:* **God helps him who helps himself,** aide-toi et le ciel t'aidera. **H.!** au secours! (*b*) Faciliter (la digestion, le progrès). **To h. s.o. down, in, out, up,** aider qn à descendre, à entrer, à sortir, à monter. **To h. s.o. out,** *F:* dépanner qn. 2. (*At table*) (*a*) Servir (qn). **To h. s.o. to soup,** servir du potage à qn. **To h. s.o. to wine,** etc., verser à boire à qn. **H. yourself,** servez-vous. (*b*) **To h. the soup, the fish,** servir le potage, le poisson. 3. (*With negation expressed or implied*) (*a*) Empêcher. **Things we cannot h.** (happening), choses qu'on ne saurait empêcher. **I can't h. it,** je n'y peux rien. **It can't be helped,** tant pis! c'est sans remède. (*b*) S'empêcher, se défendre (de faire qch.). **I can't h. laughing,** je ne peux m'empêcher de rire. **I can't h. it,** c'est plus fort que moi. (*c*) **Don't be away longer than you can h.,** tâchez d'être absent le moins de temps possible. 'help-your'self, *a*. **H.-y. store,** magasin *m* libre-service. **helping¹,** *a*. **To lend a h. hand,** prêter son aide; donner un coup d'épaule. **helping²,** *s*. Portion *f* (de nourriture). **I had two helpings,** j'en ai repris.

helper ['helpər], *s*. Aide *mf*.

helpful ['helpful], *a*. 1. (Personne) secourable, serviable. 2. (Livre, etc.) utile; (remède, etc.) salutaire. -fully, *adv*. Utilement; salutairement.

helpless ['helplis], *a*. 1. Sans ressource, sans appui, délaissé. 2. Faible, impuissant; réduit à l'impuissance. **I am h. in the matter,** je n'y puis rien. *F:* **She's quite h.,** elle n'a aucune initiative. -ly, *adv*. 1. Sans ressource. 2. Faiblement.

helplessness ['helplisnis], *s*. 1. Abandon *m*, délaissement *m*. 2. Faiblesse *f*; manque *m* d'énergie, manque d'initiative.

helpmate ['helpmeit], *s*. 1. Aide *mf*, collaborateur, -trice. 2. = HELPMEET.

helpmeet ['helpmi:t], *s*. Compagnon *m* ou compagne *f*; *esp*. épouse *f*.

helter-skelter ['heltə'skeltər]. 1. *adv*. (Courir, fuir) pêle-mêle, à la débandade. 2. *a*. **H.-s. flight,** fuite désordonnée; débandade *f*; sauve-qui-peut *m inv*.

helve [helv], *s*. Manche *m* (d'une hache, d'un marteau)

Helvetia [hel'vi:ʃə]. *Pr.n*. L'Helvétie *f*.

Helvetian [hel'vi:ʃ(ə)n], *a. & s*. Helvétien, -ienne; helvète.

Helvetic [hel'vetik], *a*. Helvétique.

hem¹ [hem], *s*. 1. Bord *m* (d'un vêtement). 2. Ourlet *m* (d'un mouchoir, etc.). 'hem(-)stitch¹, *s*. *Needlew:* Ourlet *m* à jour; ajour *m*. 'hem(-)stitch², *v.tr*. Ourler (un mouchoir) à jour; faire des ajours à, ajourer.

hem², *v.tr.* 1. *A:* Border, mettre un bord à (un vêtement). 2. Ourler (un mouchoir, du drap). 3. **To h. in,** entourer, cerner (l'ennemi); investir (une place).

hem³, *v.i.* 1. Faire hem, hum; tousser un coup; toussoter. 2. **To h. and haw** = to hum and haw, *q.v. under* HUM² 1.

hematologist [ˌhemə'tɔlədʒist, hi:mə'tɔlədʒist], *s*. Hématologue *m*.

hematology [ˌhemə'tɔlədʒi, ˌhi:mə'tɔlədʒi], *s*. *Med:* Hématologie *f*.

hematoma [ˌhi:mə'toumə], *s*. *Med:* Hématome *m*.

hemeralopia [hemərə'loupiə], *s*. *Med:* Nyctalopie *f*.

hemeralopic [hemərə'loupik], *a*. *Med:* Nyctalope.

hemicycle ['hemisaikl], *s*. *Arch:* Hémicycle *m*.

hemiplegia [ˌhemi'pli:dʒiə], *s*. *Med:* Hémiplégie *f*.

hemiplegic [ˌhemi'pli:dʒik], *a*. *Med:* Hémiplégique.

hemisphere ['hemisfiər], *s*. Hémisphère *m*.

hemispheric(al) [ˌhemi'sferik(əl)], *a*. Hémisphérique.

hemistich ['hemistik], *s*. *Pros:* Hémistiche *m*.

hemlock ['hemlɔk], *s*. *Bot:* 1. Ciguë *f*. 2. **H. fir, h. spruce,** sapin *m* du Canada; sapin-ciguë *m*.

hemorrhage ['heməridʒ], *s*. = HAEMORRHAGE.

hemp [hemp], *s*. 1. (*a*) *Bot:* Chanvre *m*. (*b*) *Tex:* Chanvre, filasse *f*. **H. cloth,** tissu *m* de chanvre. 2. *Pharm:* Hachisch *m*, bang(h) *m*. 'hemp-field, *s*. Chènevière *f*.

hempen ['hempən], *a*. (Étoffe, corde, fil) de chanvre. **H. collar,** corde *f* de potence.

hempseed ['hempsi:d], *s*. Chènevis *m*.

hen [hen], *s*. 1. Poule *f*. **Boiling hen,** poule à mettre au pot. *F:* **To take tea with a lot of old hens,** prendre le thé avec un tas de vieilles dindes. 2. Femelle *f* (d'oiseau, etc.). **H.-bird,** oiseau *m* femelle. **H.-lobster,** homard *m* femelle. 'hen-coop, *s*. Cage *f* à poules; mue *f*. 'hen-house, *s*. Poulailler *m*. 'hen-party, *s*. *F:* Réunion *f* entre femmes. 'hen-peck, *v.tr*. (*Of wife*) Gouverner (son mari); mener (son mari) par le bout du nez. 'hen-pecked, *a*. H.-p. husband, mari dont la femme porte la culotte, que sa femme mène par le bout du nez. 'hen-roost, *s*. (*a*) Juchoir *m*, perchoir *m*. (*b*) Poulailler *m*.

henbane ['henbein], *s*. *Bot:* Jusquiame *f*.

hence [hens], *adv*. 1. *A. & Lit:* (From) h., d'ici. **(Get thee) h.!** hors d'ici! 2. (*Of time*) Dorénavant, désormais; à partir d'aujourd'hui. **Five years h.,** dans cinq ans (d'ici). 3. H. his anger, de là sa fureur.

henceforth [hens'fɔ:θ], **henceforward** ['hens'fɔ:wəd], *adv*. Désormais, dorénavant, à l'avenir.

henchman, *pl.* **-men** [henʃmən], *s.m*. (*a*) *Hist:* Écuyer; homme de confiance. (*b*) Partisan, acolyte.

hendecagon [hen'dekəgən], *s*. *Geom:* Hendécagone *m*.

hendecasyllabic ['hendekəsi'læbik], *a*. *Pros:* Hendécasyllabe.

hendecasyllable ['hendekæ'silǝbl], s. Pros: Hendéca-syllabe m.

henna¹ ['henǝ], s. Bot: etc: Henné m.

henna², v.tr. Teindre au henné.

Henrietta [henri'etǝ]. Pr.n.f. Henriette.

Henry ['henri]. 1. Pr.n.m. Henri. 2. El. Meas: Henry m, pl. henrys.

hepatic [hi'pætik], a. & s. Anat: Pharm: Hépatique (mf).

hep [hep], a. U,S: F: (Individu m) averti, au courant, à la page, affranchi. To get h., se dessaler, se mettre à la coule.

hepcat ['hepkæt], s. U.S: F: Fanatique m de la musique de danse dernier cri.

hepatism ['hepǝtizm], s. Med: Hépatisme m.

hepatite ['hepǝtait], s. Miner: Hépatite f.

hepatitis [hepǝ'taitis], s. Med: Hépatite f.

heptachord ['heptǝkɔ:d], s. Mus: Heptacorde m.

heptagon ['heptǝgǝn], s. Heptagone m.

heptagonal [hep'tægǝn(ǝ)l], a. Heptagone; heptagonal, -aux.

heptameter [hep'tæmǝtǝr], s. Pros: Heptamètre m.

heptarchy ['heptɑ:ki], s. Heptarchie f.

Heptateuch (the) [ðǝ'heptǝtju:k], s. B.Hist: L'Heptateuque m.

her¹ [hǝr, hǝ:r], pers. pron. f., objective case. 1. (Unstressed) (a) (Direct) La, (before a vowel sound) l'; (indirect) lui. Have you seen h.? l'avez-vous vue? I obey h., je lui obéis. Look at h., regardez-la. Tell h., dites-lui. (b) I am thinking of h., je pense à elle; je ne l'oublie pas. I remember h., je me souviens d'elle. (c) (Refl.) Elle. She took her parcel away with h., elle emporta son paquet avec elle. 2. (Stressed) (a) Elle. I found him and h. at the station, je les ai trouvés lui et elle à la gare. H. I can never forgive, je ne lui pardonnerai jamais à elle. I am thinking of 'h., c'est à elle que je pense. (b) To h. who should take offence at this I would say. . ., à celle qui s'en offenserait je dirais. . . . 3. F: It's h., c'est elle. That's h.! la voilà!

her², poss.a. (denoting a f. possessor) Son, f sa, pl ses. H. friend, h. friends, son ami, f. son amie; ses amis, f. ses amies. The date and place of h. birth, ses date et lieu de naissance. She has hurt h. hand, elle s'est fait mal à la main. (Emphatic) 'H. idea would be to . . ., son idée f à elle serait de. . . .

herald¹ ['herald], s. (a) Héraut m. (b) Avant-coureur m, précurseur m; avant-courrier m, messager m.

herald², v.tr. Annoncer, proclamer.

heraldic [he'rældik], a. Héraldique. H. bearing, armoirie f, blason m.

heraldist ['heraldist], s. Héraldiste m.

heraldry ['heraldri], s. 1. L'art m, la science, héraldique; le blason. 2. Pompe f héraldique.

herb [hǝ:b], s. Bot: (a) Herbe f. (b) Herbs (for seasoning), fines herbes. Medicinal herbs, herbes, plantes, médicinales; simples m. H.-shop, herboristerie f. H. seller, h.-woman, herbière f.

herbaceous [hǝ:'beiʃǝs], a. Bot: Herbacé. H. border, bordure herbacée.

herbage ['hǝ:bidʒ], s. Herbes fpl; herbage(s) m.

herbal ['hǝ:b(ǝ)l]. 1. s. Herbier m. 2. a. (Breuvage) fait avec des herbes; (infusion, tisane) d'herbes.

herbalist ['hǝ:bǝlist], s. Herboriste mf.

herbarium [hǝ:'beǝriǝm], s. Herbier m.

herbivora [hǝ:'bivǝrǝ], s.pl. Z: Herbivores m.

herbivorous [hǝ:'bivǝrǝs], a. Z: Herbivore.

herborist ['hǝ:bǝrist], s. = HERBALIST.

herborization [hǝ:bǝrai'zeiʃ(ǝ)n], s. Herborisation f.

herborize ['hǝ:bǝraiz], v.i. Herboriser, botaniser.

herborizer ['hǝ:bǝraizǝr], s. Herborisateur, -trice.

Herculean [hǝ:kju'liǝn], a. (Travail, effort) herculéen; (taille) d'Hercule.

Hercules ['hǝ:kjuli:z]. 1. Pr.n.m. Hercule. 2. s. Homme d'une grande force; hercule m.

herd¹ [hǝ:d], s. (a) Troupeau m (de gros bétail, de porcs); harde f (de cerfs); troupe f, bande f (de chevaux, de baleines, etc.). The h. instinct, (i) l'instinct grégaire; (ii) l'instinct qui gouverne le troupeau. S.a. FLOCK². (b) F: Troupeau, foule f (de gens). The common, vulgar, h., la foule, le commun des hommes.

herd², v.i. (a) (Of animals) To h. together, (i) vivre en troupeaux; (ii) s'assembler en troupeau. (b) (Of pers.) To h. with . . ., s'associer à, aller avec, fréquenter (un parti, une société).

herd³, s. Pâtre m, gardien m (de bêtes). H.-boy, jeune pâtre, aide-bouvier m. See GOOSEHERD, SHEPHERD, SWINE-HERD, etc.

herd⁴, v.tr. Garder, surveiller, soigner (les bestiaux, les oies, etc.).

herdsman, pl. -men ['hǝ:dzmǝn], s.m. Bouvier, pâtre.

here [hiǝr], adv. 1. (a) Ici. Stay h., restez ici. In h., ici. Come in h., please, venez par ici, s'il vous plaît. Up to h., down to h., jusqu'ici. About h., par ici. Near h., près d'ici. From h. to there, d'ici là. Between h. and London, d'ici à Londres. Christmas is h.! voici Noël! I must have it h. and now, il me le faut sur-le-champ, séance tenante. H. goes! allons-y! (b) Ci. (Only in) This one h. and that one there, celui-ci et celui-là. H. lies . . ., ci-gît. . . . (c) (At roll-call) Présent! (d) H. below, ici-bas. 2. H.'s your hat, voici votre chapeau. H. I am, me voici! S.a. AGAIN 1. H. you are! (i) vous voici! (ii) tenez! (ceci est pour vous). 3. (In drinking a health) H.'s to you! à votre santé! F: à la vôtre! 4. My friend h. will tell you, mon ami que voici vous le dira. 5. (Exclamatory) H.! I want you! pst! venez ici! 6. (a) H. and there, par-ci par-là; çà et là. (b) H., there, and everywhere, un peu partout. (c) F: That's neither h. nor there, cela ne fait rien (à l'affaire); cela ne fait ni chaud ni froid.

hereabout(s) ['hiǝrǝbaut(s)], adv. Près d'ici, par ici, dans ces parages, dans les environs.

hereafter [hiǝr'ɑ:ftǝr]. 1. adv. (a) (Of position) (In book, writings, etc.) Ci-après, ci-dessous. (b) (Of time) Dorénavant, à l'avenir, désormais. (c) Dans la vie à venir; dans l'autre monde. 2. s. L'au-delà m; l'autre monde m.

hereby [hiǝ'bai, 'hiǝbai], adv. Jur: Par ces présentes. The council h. resolve, resolve h., that . . ., le conseil déclare par le présent acte que. . . .

hereditable [hi'reditǝbl], a. (Of property) Dont on peut hériter.

hereditament [heri'ditǝmǝnt], s. Jur: 1. Bien transmissible par héritage. Esp. pl. Hereditaments, biens composant la succession; terres f et immeubles m. 2. = INHERITANCE 1.

hereditary [hi'redit(ǝ)ri], a. Héréditaire. -ily, adv. Héréditairement.

heredity [hi'rediti], s. Hérédité f.

herein [hiǝr'in], adv. 1. Ici, dans ce livre, dans ce lieu. The letter enclosed h., la lettre ci-incluse. 2. (In this matter) En ceci, sur ce point.

hereof [hiǝr'ov], adv. A: De ceci.

heresy ['herǝsi], s. Hérésie f. (Of opinion) To smack of h., F: sentir le roussi, le fagot.

heretic ['herǝtik], s. Hérétique mf. Lapsed h., relaps, f. relapse.

heretical [hi'retik(ǝ)l], a. Hérétique.

hereto [hiǝ'tu:], adv. Jur: Annexed h., ci-joint.

heretofore ['hiǝtu'fɔ:r], adv. Jadis, autrefois; jusqu'ici. As h., comme auparavant.

hereunder [hiǝr'ʌndǝr], adv. Ci-dessous.

hereupon [hiǝrǝ'pon], adv. Là-dessus; sur ce.

herewith [hiǝ'wið], adv. Avec ceci. Com: I am sending you h. . . ., je vous envoie ci-joint, sous ce pli. . . .

heritable ['heritǝbl], a. 1. Biol: Héréditaire. 2. Jur: (a) (Droit) héréditaire; (propriété) héritable. (b) (Of pers.) Capable d'hériter.

heritage ['heritidʒ], s. Héritage m, patrimoine m.

heritor ['heritǝr], s. Jur: Héritier, -ière.

hermaphrodism [hǝ:'mæfrǝdizm], hermaphroditism [hǝ:'mæfrǝdi:tizm], s. Biol: Hermaphrodisme m.

hermaphrodite [hǝ:'mæfrǝdait], a. & s. Hermaphrodite m.

Hermes ['hǝ:mi:z]. Pr.n.m. Gr.Myth: Hermès.

hermetic [hǝ:'metik], a. Hermétique. 1. H. philosophy, science, l'alchimie f. 2. H. sealing, bouchage m hermétique. -ally, adv. (Scellé) hermétiquement.

hermit ['hǝ:mit], s. Ermite m. H.-crab, bernard-l'ermite m.

hermitage ['hǝ:mitidʒ], s. Ermitage m.

hernia ['hə:niə], s. Hernie f. **Strangulated h.**, hernie étranglée. **Suffering from h.**, hernieux.
hernial ['hə:niəl], **herniary** ['hə:niəri], a. Herniaire.
herniated ['hə:nieitid], a. (Intestin) hernié.
hero, pl. **-oes** ['hiərou, -ouz], s.m. Héros. **To die like a h.**, se faire tuer en brave, en héros. **'hero-worship**, s. Culte m des héros.
Herod ['herəd]. Pr.n.m. Hist: Hérode. **To out-H. H.**, être plus royaliste que le roi.
heroic(al) [hi'rouik(əl)]. **1.** a. Héroïque. **H. deed**, action d'éclat. **H. remedy**, remède héroïque. **H. poem**, poème épique. **H. verse**, vers décasyllabe, vers héroïque. **2.** s. (Usu. pl.) F: **Heroics**, déclamation f de sentiments outrés; grandiloquence f. **-ally**, adv. Héroïquement.
heroin ['herouin], s. Pharm: Héroïne f.
heroine ['herouin], s.f. Héroïne.
heroism ['herouizm], s. Héroïsme m.
heron ['herən], s. Orn: Héron m. **Young h.**, héronneau m.
heronry ['herənri], s. Héronnière f.
herpes ['hə:pi:z], s. Med: Herpès m; dartres fpl.
herpetic [hə:'petik], a. Med: Herpétique; dartreux.
herring ['heriŋ], s. Ich: Hareng m. **Red h.**, (i) hareng saur; (ii) F: diversion f. **To draw a red h. across the track**, (i) dépister la meute; (ii) faire dévier la conversation. **'herring-boat**, s. Harenguier m, trinquart m, touque f. **'herring-bone**, s. Arête f de hareng. **H.-b. pattern**, dessin m ou tracé m en arête de hareng, en chevrons, à chevrons, à brin de fougère. **H.-b. flooring**, parquet m à bâtons rompus. Needlew: **H.-b. stitch**, point m de chausson. **'herring-fisher**, s. Harenguier m. **'herring-harvest**, s. Harengaison f. **'herring-market**, s. Harengerie f. **'Herring-pond (the)**, s. F: L'Atlantique m; F: La Mare aux Harengs.
hers [hə:z], poss.pron. Le sien, la sienne, les siens, les siennes. **She took my pen and h.**, elle prit ma plume et la sienne. **This book is h.**, ce livre est à elle, lui appartient; c'est son livre à elle. **A friend of h.**, un(e) de ses ami(e)s; un(e) ami(e) à elle. **That pride of h.**, cet orgueil dont elle ne peut se défaire.
herself [hə(:)'self], pers.pron. See SELF 4.
hertz [hə:ts], s. El.E: Hertz m.
Hertzian ['hə:tsiən], a. El: Hertzien. **H. waves**, ondes hertziennes.
he's [hi:z] = he is, he has.
hesitancy ['hezitənsi], s. Hésitation f, incertitude f.
hesitant ['hezitənt], a. Hésitant, irrésolu.
hesitate ['heziteit], v.i. Hésiter. **To h. for a word**, hésiter pour trouver un mot. **To h. between two courses**, hésiter, balancer, entre deux partis. **He hesitates at nothing**, il n'hésite pas, ne recule, devant rien. **To h. to do sth.**, hésiter à faire qch. **hesitating**, a. Hésitant, incertain. **-ly**, adv. Avec hésitation; en hésitant.
hesitation [,hezi'teiʃ(ə)n], s. Hésitation f. **There's no room for h.**, il n'y a pas à hésiter. **Without (the slightest) h.**, sans (la moindre) hésitation; sans balancer.
Hesperus ['hespərəs]. Pr.n. Poet: Vesper m; Vénus; l'étoile f du soir; F: l'étoile du berger.
Hessian [hesiən]. **1.** a. & s. Geog: Hessois, -oise. A. Mil. Cost: **H. boots**, Hessiens, bottes f à la Souvarov. **2.** s. Tex: Étoffe grossière de chanvre, toile f d'emballage. **3.** s. U.S: Mercenaire m.
het [het], a. F: **H. up**, (i) chauffé, survolté; (ii) fâché. **Don't get h. up about it**, ne t'en fais pas.
heteroclite ['het(ə)rəklait], a. Hétéroclite.
heterodox ['het(ə)rədɔks], a. Hétérodoxe.
heterodoxy ['het(ə)rədɔksi], s. Hétérodoxie f.
heterodyne ['het(ə)rədain], a. & s. W.Tel: (Récepteur) hétérodyne (m).
heterogeneity [,het(ə)rodʒi'ni:iti], s. Hétérogénéité f.
heterogeneous ['het(ə)rə'dʒi:niəs], a. Hétérogène.
heteroplasty ['het(ə)rəplæsti], s. Surg: Hétéroplastie f.
hevea ['hi:viə], s. Bot: Hévéa m.
hew [hju:], v.tr. (p.t. hewed; p.p. hewed, hewn [hju:n]) Couper, tailler, (avec une hache, etc.). **To h. a stone**, tailler, dresser, équarrir, une pierre. **To h. coal**, piquer la houille. **To h. one's way**, se frayer, se tailler, un passage (à coups de hache). **hew away, down, off**, v.tr. Abattre. **hew out**, v.tr. **1.** Taillor,

façonner (un trou, un passage). **2. To h. out a statue**, ciseler une statue. **To h. out a career for oneself**, se faire, se tailler, une carrière. **hewing**, a. Abattage m (d'un arbre); taille f, coupe f, équarrissage m (de pierres, de bois); piquage m (de la houille).
hewer ['hju(:)ər], s. **1.** Tailleur m (de pierre). Min: Piqueur m (de houille); haveur m. B: **To be hewers of wood and drawers of water**, (i) B: être employés à couper le bois et à puiser l'eau; (ii) mener une vie de forçat, de galérien. **2.** Abatteur m (d'arbres).
hewn [hju:n]. See HEW.
hex[1] [heks], s. U.S: **1.** Sortilège m, (mauvais) sort; F: guigne f, guignon m. **2.** Sorcière f.
hex[2], v. U.S: **1.** v.i. Être sorcière f; pratiquer la sorcellerie. **2.** v.tr. Jeter un sort, un maléfice, sur qn, sur qch.
hexachord ['heksəkɔ:d], s. Mus: Hexacorde m.
hexad ['heksæd], a. & s. Ch: (Corps simple, ou radical) hexavalent.
hexagon ['heksəgən], s. Geom: Hexagone m.
hexagonal [hek'sægən(ə)l], a. Hexagone, hexagonal, -aux. S.a. NUT 2.
hexahedral [,heksə'hi:drəl], a. Geom: Hexaèdre, hexaédrique.
hexahedron [,heksə'hi:drən], s. Geom: Hexaèdre m.
hexameter [hek'sæmitər], s. Pros: Hexamètre m.
hexametric(al) [,heksə'metrik(əl)], a. Hexamètre.
hey [hei], int. **1.** Hé! holà! **2.** Hein? **3. H. presto!** passez muscade!
heyday ['heidei], s. Apogée m, beaux jours (de ses forces, de la prospérité). **To be in the h. of youth**, of life, être en pleine jeunesse, dans la fleur de l'âge, au midi de la vie.
Hezekiah [,hezi'kaiə]. Pr.n.m. B: Ézéchias.
hi [hai], int. **1.** Hé, là-bas! ohé! **2.** U.S: F: Salut! Bonjour!
hiatus, pl. **-uses** [hai'eitəs, -əsiz], s. **1.** Lacune f (dans une série, un récit, etc.). **2.** Med: Gram: Hiatus m.
hibernal [hai'bə:n(ə)l], a. Hivernal, -aux; (sommeil) hibernal.
hibernate ['haibəneit], v.i. (a) Z: (Of animals) Hiberner, hiverner. (b) (Of pers.) (To winter) Hiverner.
hibernation [,haibə'neiʃ(ə)n], s. Hibernation f.
Hibernian [hai'bə:niən], a. & s. Hibernien, -ienne; irlandais, -aise.
Hibernianism [hai'bə:niənizm], **Hibernicism** [hai'bə:nisizm], s. Ling: Locution irlandaise; tour de phrase irlandais.
hibiscus [hi'biskəs], s. Bot: Ketmie f, hibiscus m.
hiccough[1], **hiccup**[1] ['hikʌp], s. Hoquet m. **To have (got) the hiccups**, avoir le hoquet.
hiccough[2], **hiccup**[2]. **1.** v.i. Avoir le hoquet; hoqueter. **2.** v.tr. **He hiccuped out an apology**, il s'excusa entre deux hoquets.
hick [hik], a. & s. U.S: Rustaud (m), paysan (m), rustre (m).
hickory ['hikəri], s. Noyer (blanc) d'Amérique; hickory m.
hidalgo [hi'dælgou], s. Hidalgo m.
hide[1] [haid], v. (p.t. hid; p.p. hid, hidden [hidn]) **1.** v.tr. (a) Cacher (from, à); enfouir (qch. dans la terre). F: **Where has he gone and hidden himself?** où est-il allé se fourrer? **To h. one's face**, se cacher la figure, se voiler la face. **I did not know where to h. my head**, je ne savais où me fourrer, où me mettre. **To h. sth. from s.o.**, (i) cacher qch. à qn; (ii) taire qch. à qn. **To h. (away) a treasure**, mettre un trésor dans une cache. (b) **To h. sth. from sight**, dérober, soustraire, qch. aux regards. **Clouds hid the sun**, des nuages voilaient le soleil. **Small house hidden in a wood**, petite villa tapie, nichée, dans un bois. Carp: etc: **Hidden joint**, joint dérobé. F: **Hidden hand**, influence f occulte. **2.** v.i. Se cacher; (i) se tenir caché; se blottir (dans un coin, etc.); (ii) aller se cacher. **I didn't know where to h.**, je ne savais où me fourrer. **hide out**, v.i. U.S: Se cacher (de la police, etc.). **'hide-out**, s. F: Planque f. **hiding**[1], s. Dissimulation f (de la joie, etc.). Jur: Recel m (d'un criminel). **To go into h.**, se cacher; se soustraire aux regards. **To come out of h.**, se tenir caché. **'hiding-place**, s. Cachette f; (lieu m de) retraite f. **'hide-and-'seek**, **U.S: 'hide-and-go-'seek**, s. Games: Cache-cache m.

hide², s. Peau f, dépouille f (d'un animal). *Com:* Cuir m. **H. rope**, corde en cuir. *F:* **To save one's h.**, sauver sa peau. *F:* **To take the h. off (s.o.)**, tanner le cuir (à qn). **'hide-bound**, a. *F:* Aux vues étroites; plein de préjugés. **H.-b. opinions**, idées étroites. **H.-b. etiquette**, étiquette rigide.

hiding² ['haidiŋ], s. *F:* Raclée f, rossée f, volée f.

hideous ['hidiəs], a. **1.** Hideux, affreux, effroyable; (crime) horrible, odieux. **2.** D'une laideur repoussante. **-ly**, adv. Hideusement, affreusement.

hideousness ['hidiəsnis], s. Hideur f, laideur f, horreur f.

hie [hai], v.i. & pr. A: & Lit: **To h. to a place**, se hâter de se rendre dans un lieu.

hierarch ['haiərɑːk], s. *Ecc:* Hiérarque m; grand prêtre.

hierarchic(al) [haiə'rɑːkik(əl)], a. Hiérarchique. **In h. order**, par ordre hiérarchique. **-ally**, adv. Hiérarchiquement.

hierarchy ['haiərɑːki], s. Hiérarchie f.

hieroglyph ['haiərəglif], s. Hiéroglyphe m.

hieroglyphic(al) [haiərə'glifik(əl)], a. Hiéroglyphique.

hieroglyphics [haiərə'glifiks], s.pl. Hiéroglyphes m; signes m hiéroglyphiques.

hi-fi ['hai'fai]. *F:* **1.** s. *Gramophones: etc:* Haute fidélité. **2.** a. Hi-fi inv.

higgle ['higl], v.i. Marchander.

higgledy-piggledy ['higldi'pigldi], adv. Sans ordre, en pagaïe, pêle-mêle.

high [hai]. **I.** a. Haut. **1.** (a) **H. mountain**, haute montagne. **The highest point of the range**, le point culminant de la chaîne. **Wall six feet h.**, mur haut de six pieds; mur qui a six pieds de haut, de hauteur. **How h. is that tree?** quelle est la hauteur de cet arbre? (b) *Cost:* (Corsage, col) montant. **2.** Élevé. (a) **The sun is getting higher (with the lengthening days)**, le soleil remonte. **Glory to God in the Highest**, gloire à Dieu au plus haut des cieux. **Higher up the river**, en amont. **To walk with one's head h.**, marcher tête haute. **To hold one's head h.**, porter la .tête haute, porter haut la tête. *Equit:* **H. action**, allure relevée (d'un cheval). (b) **To be h. in office**, avoir un poste élevé, une haute situation. **H. official**, haut fonctionnaire. **Higher posts**, postes supérieurs. *Sch:* **The h. table**, la table des professeurs (au réfectoire); la table d'honneur. **H. and mighty**, haut et puissant. *F:* **To be h. and mighty**, faire le grand seigneur; se donner de grands airs; le prendre de haut. s. **The Most High(est)**, le Très-Haut, le Tout-Puissant. **H. and low**, les grands et les petits. (c) **H. thoughts**, grandes pensées. **H. mind**, esprit élevé, noble. **H. art**, le grand art. (d) **H. rate of interest**, taux élevé; gros intérêt. **It fetches a h. price**, cela se vend cher. **To buy at a h. figure**, acheter cher. **To set a h. value on sth.**, estimer qch. haut. **To play for h. stakes**, jouer gros (jeu). **H. percentage of moisture**, forte proportion d'humidité. **H. temperature**, (i) température élevée; (ii) forte fièvre. **H. speed**, grande vitesse. **Anthracite with a h. ash content**, anthracite à teneur en cendres élevée. (e) **In the highest degree**, au suprême degré, au plus haut degré; par excellence. **In the highest sense of the word**, dans toute l'acception du mot; par excellence. **H. respect**, respect profond. **H. fever**, forte fièvre; grosse fièvre. **H. wind**, vent fort, violent; grand vent; gros vent. **A h. sea is running**, la mer est grosse, houleuse. (f) **To have a h. opinion of s.o.**, tenir qn en haute estime. (g) **H. colour**, (i) couleur vive; (ii) vivacité f du teint. *Art:* **H. lights**, (i) hautes lumières; rehauts m; accents m, clairs m (d'un tableau); (ii) *Phot:* blancs m (de l'image); grands noirs (du cliché). **The h. spot of the match**, le point culminant du match. **H. diet, h. feeding**, forte nourriture. (h) **H. voice**, (i) voix élevée, haute; (ii) voix grêle. **3.** *Sch:* **The higher forms**, les classes supérieures; *F:* les grandes classes. **Higher mathematics**, mathématiques supérieures. **The higher animals**, les animaux supérieurs. **4.** (*Principal*) **The H. Street**, la Grand-rue, la Grande rue. *Ecc:* **H. mass**, la grand-messe, la grande messe. **5.** **H. day**, jour de fête. **6.** (a) **H. noon**, plein midi. **It is h. time he went to school**, il est grand temps, grandement temps, qu'il aille à l'école. (b) *Cu:* (*Of meat*) Avancé, gâté; (*of game*) faisandé. **H. butter**, beurre fort. *F:* **He's rather h.**,

il est paf, un peu parti, éméché, gai. **7.** *Nau:* (*Of ship*) **H. and dry**, (échoué) à sec (sur le sable, sur la plage). *F:* **To leave s.o. h. and dry**, laisser qn en plan. **8.** **On h.**, en haut; dans le ciel. **From on h.**, d'en haut; de là-haut. **-ly**, adv. **1.** (a) **H. placed official**, haut fonctionnaire. (b) **To be h. descended**, être de haute naissance. **2.** **His services are h. paid**, ses services sont largement rétribués. **To think h. of s.o.**, avoir une haute opinion de qn. **3.** Fort, très, bien, fortement. **H. amusing**, fort, très, amusant. **H. coloured**, (tableau, style) haut en couleur; (récit) coloré. **II.** high, adv. **1.** Haut; en haut. **Higher and higher**, de plus en plus haut. **Higher up**, plus haut. **To aim, fly, h.**, viser, voler, haut; avoir de hautes visées. **To rise h. in public esteem**, monter très haut dans l'estime publique. **To hunt h. and low for sth.**, chercher qch. de haut en bas, de la cave au grenier. **2.** **To go as h. as £2000**, aller jusqu'à 2000 livres. *Cards: etc:* **To play, stake, h.**, jouer gros jeu. **3.** Fort, fortemeni, très. (*Of wind*) **To blow h.**, souffler avec violence, en tempête. **To run h.**, (i) (*of the sea*) être grosse, houleuse; (ii) (*of feeling, words*) s'échauffer; (iii) (*of prices*) être élevé. **4.** **This question was h.**, **on the agenda**, cette question figurait dans les premières à l'ordre du jour. **III.** high, s. **1.** *Meteor:* Zone f de haute pression. **2.** *F:* **All-time h.**, record le plus élevé. **'high-born**, a. De haute naissance. **'high-bred**, a. **1.** (a) De famille noble, de haute naissance. (b) (Cheval) de race. **2.** Parfaitement élevé; élevé dans le grand monde. **'high-'chair**, s. Chaise haute (pour enfants). **'high-class**, a. De premier ordre, de première qualité. **'high-'coloured**, a. Haut en couleur. **'high-fi'delity**, a. *Gramophones: etc:* Haute fidélité. **'high-flown**, a. (Style, discours) ampoulé. **To write in a h.-f. style**, écrire avec emphase, dans un style ambitieux. **'high-'flyer**, s. *F:* Ambitieux, -ieuse. **high-'frequency**, attrib.a. *El:* (Courant) à haute fréquence. **'high-grade**, attrib.a. **1.** (Minerai, etc.) à haute teneur, d'un haut titre. **2.** **H.-g. petrol** supercarburant m; *F:* super m. **'high-'handed**, a. (Action) arbitraire; (autorité) tyrannique. **-ly**, adv. Arbitrairement; tyranniquement. **'high-'hat**. **1.** s.m. *U.S: F:* Gommeux, faraud, rupin. **2.** attrib.a. Snob, dédaigneux. **high-'minded**, a. A l'esprit élevé; aux sentiments nobles. **high-'mindedness**, s. Élévation f d'esprit; grandeur f d'âme. **'high-necked**, a. **H.-n. dress**, robe montante. **high(-)'octane**, attrib.a. *Aut: Av:* **H.(-)o. petrol**, supercarburant m. **'high-pitched**, a. **1.** (*Of sound*) Aigu, -uë. **2.** **H.-p. roof**, comble à forte inclinaison, à forte pente. **'high-'power(ed)**, a. (a) (Auto) de haute puissance. (b) (Jumelles) à fort grossissement. **'high-'pressure**, attrib.a. (Machine) à haute pression. **'high-'priced**, a. De grand prix; cher. **'high-'priest**, s.m. Grand-prêtre, pl. grands-prêtres. **'high-'souled**, a. Magnanime. **'high-sounding**, a. Pompeux, prétentieux. **'high-speed**, attrib.a. (a) (Locomotive) à grande vitesse. (b) *Ind:* (Machine) à mouvement accéléré, à bon rendement. **'high-'spirited**, a. Intrépide; plein d'ardeur, de feu; (cheval) fougueux, vif. **'high-'strung**, a. (Tempérament) nerveux, exalté. **'high-'toned**, a. **1.** (Livre m, journal m) d'un ton élevé. **2.** *U.S:* (i) Aux principes élevés; qui a de bons principes. (ii) *Often Iron:* slightly Pej: Supérieur, élégant.

highball ['haibɔːl], s. *U.S:* (i) Whisky m à l'eau; (ii) whisky-soda m.

highbinder ['haibaindər], s. *U.S: F:* **1.** (a) Gangster m; assassin m; bandit m. (b) Assassin chinois à gages (qui opère dans les quartiers chinois des cités américaines). **2.** (a) Escroc m, filou m. (b) Politicien corrompu.

highboy ['haibɔi], s. *U.S: Furn:* = TALLBOY.

highbrow ['haibrau], s. *F:* **1.** Intellectuel, -elle. *Pej:* **She's a h.**, elle a des prétentions (intellectuelles). **2.** attrib. **H. literature**, littérature pour les intellectuels.

highfalutin(g) ['haifə'luːtin, -iŋ], a. *F:* (Style) ampoulé, prétentieux.

highland ['hailənd]. **1.** s.pl. **Highlands**, pays montagneux, hautes terres. *Geog:* **The Highlands**, la Haute Écosse. **2.** attrib.a. (a) Des montagnes; montagnard. (b) De la Haute Écosse.

highlander ['hailəndər], *s.* **1.** Montagnard *m.* **2.** A H., un Highlander; un montagnard écossais; un habitant de la Haute Écosse.

highlight[1] ['hailait], *s.* *F:* Clou *m.* **The h. of the fête,** of the performance, le clou de la fête, de la représentation.

highlight[2], *v.tr.* Mettre en vedette.

highness ['hainis], *s.* **1.** (*a*) Élévation *f* (des prix, etc.). (*b*) Grandeur *f* (d'âme). **2.** (*Title*) Altesse *f.*

highroad ['hairoud], *s.* Grande route, route nationale.

highway ['haiwei], *s.* (*a*) Chemin *m* de grande communication; grande route, grand-route *f.* **Highways and by-ways,** chemins et sentiers. **The King's H.,** le grand chemin. **To be on the h. to success, to ruin,** être en bonne voie de réussir; être sur la pente fatale de la ruine. (*b*) *Adm:* Voie publique. **The H. Code,** le Code de la route. (*c*) *U.S:* Dual h., route jumelée, à double piste. **H. patrolman,** motard *m.*

highwayman, *pl.* **-men** ['haiweimən], *s.m.* Voleur de grand chemin, bandit, brigand.

hijack ['haidʒæk], *v.tr.* *F:* (*a*) S'emparer de force d'articles de contrebande. (*b*) Arrêter (un camion) pour le voler.

hijacker ['haidʒækər], *s.* *F:* (*a*) Bandit armé qui s'attaque aux contrebandiers. (*b*) Bandit armé qui s'empare d'un camion.

hike[1] [haik], *s.* *F:* **1.** Vagabondage *m.* **To be on the h.,** vagabonder; être sur le trimard. **2.** Excursion *f* à pied.

hike[2]. **1.** *v.i.* *F:* (*a*) Vagabonder, trimarder. (*b*) Faire du tourisme à pied. **To h. it,** faire le trajet à pied. **2.** *v.tr.* *F:* *esp.* *U.S:* Traîner, *P:* trimbaler (qch. quelque part). **To h. up one's trousers,** se remonter le pantalon. **hiking,** *s.* Excursions *fpl* à pied.

hiker ['haikər], *s.* Excursionniste *mf* à pied; *F:* randonneur, -euse (à pied).

hilarious [hi'lɛəriəs], *a.* Gai, joyeux, hilare. **-ly,** *adv.* Gaiement, joyeusement, *F:* en rigolant.

hilariousness [hi'lɛəriəsnis], **hilarity** [hi'læriti], *s.* Hilarité *f,* gaieté *f.*

Hilary ['hiləri]. *Pr.n.m. or f.* Hilaire. *Jur:* H. term, session *f* de la Saint-Hilaire (commençant en janvier).

hill [hil], *s.* **1.** (*a*) Colline *f,* coteau *m.* **Up h. and down dale,** over h. and dale, par monts et par vaux. **H. country,** pays de montagne(s). (*b*) Éminence *f;* monticule *m.* *See* ANT-HILL, MOLEHILL. **2.** (*On road*) Côte *f;* (i) montée *f;* (ii) descente *f.* *Aut:* **Speed up h.,** vitesse en côte. **To go down the h.,** (i) descendre la colline; (ii) *F:* baisser, décliner. **hill(-)side,** *s.* Flanc *m* de coteau; coteau *m.*

hillbilly ['hilbili]. *U.S:* *F:* **1.** *a.* **H. songs,** chansons montagnardes. **H. farmers,** fermiers, exploitants, montagnards. **2.** *s.* Montagnard; paysan des pays montagneux des États du S.-E.

hilliness ['hilinis], *s.* Caractère montagneux, accidenté (d'un paysage).

hillock ['hilək], *s.* Petite colline; monticule *m,* butte *f,* tertre *m;* (*rounded*) mamelon *m.* **Sand hillocks,** buttes de sable.

hilly ['hili], *a.* **1.** Montagneux; (terrain) accidenté. **2.** (Chemin) montueux, à fortes pentes.

hilt [hilt], *s.* **1.** Poignée *f,* garde *f* (d'épée). **Up to the h.,** jusqu'à la garde. *F:* **Right up to the h.,** jusqu'à la gauche. **To prove an assertion up to the h.,** démontrer surabondamment une assertion. **2.** Manche *m* (de dague, etc.); crosse *f* (de pistolet).

hilum ['hailəm], *s.* *Bot:* *Anat:* Hile *m.*

him [him], *pers.pron.m.,* *objective case.* **1.** (*Unstressed*) (*a*) (*Direct*) Le, (*before a vowel sound*) l'; (*indirect*) lui. **Do you love h.?** l'aimez-vous? **I obey h.,** je lui obéis. **I shall tell h. so,** je le lui dirai. (*b*) (*Refl.*) Lui, soi. **He took his luggage with h.,** il prit ses bagages avec lui. (*c*) (*Refl.*) *A.* & *Lit:* **He laid h. down to sleep,** il se coucha pour dormir. **2.** (*Stressed*) (*a*) Lui. **I found h. and his friend in the park,** je les ai trouvés, lui et son ami, dans le parc. **H. I admire,** lui je l'admire. (*b*) **The prize goes to h. who comes in first,** le prix est pour celui qui arrivera le premier. **3.** *F:* **It's h.,** c'est lui. **That's h.!** le voilà!

Himalaya [himə'leiə]. *Pr.n. Geog:* **The Himalayas,** les monts *m* Himalaya; l'Himalaya *m.*

Himalayan [himə'leiən], *a.* & *s.* *Geog:* Himalayen, -enne.

himself [him'self], *pers.pron.* *See* SELF 4.

hind[1] [haind], *s.* Biche *f.*

hind[2], *s.* *A:* **1.** Valet *m* de ferme. **2.** (*a*) Paysan *m.* (*b*) Rustre *m.*

hind[3], **hinder**[1] ['haindər], *a.* **1.** (*Usu.* hinder) Hinder part, partie postérieure, partie arrière. **2.** (*Always* hind) H. legs, feet, jambes, pattes, de derrière. *F:* **To get on one's h. legs,** se mettre debout. **H. quarters** (of a horse), arrière-main *f,* arrière-train *m.*

hindbrain ['hain(d)brein], *s.* *Anat:* = Cerveau postérieur.

hinder[2] ['hindər], *v.tr.* **1.** Gêner, embarrasser (qn); retarder, entraver (qch.); faire obstacle à (un mouvement). **2.** (*Prevent*) Empêcher, retenir, arrêter (s.o. from doing sth., qn de faire qch.).

hindermost ['haindəmoust], *a.* = HINDMOST.

Hindi ['hindi:], *s.* *Ling:* Le Hindî.

hindmost ['haindmoust], *a.* Dernier. **Everyone for himself and the devil take the h.,** sauve qui peut.

hindrance ['hindrəns], *s.* Empêchement *m,* obstacle *m.* **Without (let or) h.,** sans entrave(s); en toute liberté.

hindsight [haindsait], *s.* **1.** *Arms:* Hausse *f* (à curseur) (d'une carabine). **2.** *Iron:* Sagesse *f* en rétrospective, *F:* sagesse d'après coup.

Hindu [hin'du:], *a.* & *s.* *Rel:* Hindou, -oue.

Hinduism ['hinduizm], *s.* *Rel:* Hindouisme *m.*

Hindustan [hindu'stɑːn]. *Pr.n. Geog:* Hindoustan *m.*

Hindustani [hindu'stɑːni], *s.* *Ling:* *A:* Hindoustani *m;* hindî *m,* ourdou *m.*

hinge[1] [hindʒ], *s.* **1.** (*a*) Gond *m* (de porte); paumelle *f.* **Hook and h.,** penture *f* et gond. **Door off its hinges,** porte hors de ses gonds. *Philately:* (**Stamp)** h., charnière *f.* (*b*) (**Butt-)h.,** charnière *f.* **Pin h.,** charnière à fiche, à broche. **2.** Pivot *m* (d'une entreprise); point principal, nœud *m* (d'un argument). **'hinge-pin,** *s.* Broche *f,* cheville *f,* de charnière.

hinge[2]. **1.** *v.tr.* (i) Monter (une porte, etc.) sur ses gonds; (ii) mettre les charnières à (une boîte, etc.). **2.** *v.i.* (*a*) Tourner, pivoter (on, autour de). (*b*) **Everything hinges on his answer,** tout dépend de sa réponse. **hinged,** *a.* (Couvercle) à charnière(s). **H. flap** (*of counter*), battant *m* relevable. **H. girder,** poutre articulée.

hinny[1] ['hini], *s.* *Z:* Bardot *m,* bardeau *m.*

hinny[2], *v.i.* (*Of horse*) Hennir.

hint[1] [hint], *s.* **1.** (*a*) Insinuation *f;* allusion indirecte, voilée. **Broad h.,** (i) allusion évidente; (ii) avis peu voilé. **To give, drop, s.o. a (gentle) h.,** toucher un mot à qn (tout doucement). **To drop, let fall, a h. that . . . ,** donner à entendre que. . . . **To know how to take a h.,** entendre (qn) à demi-mot. **I can take a h.,** je comprends. (*b*) (*Sign*) Signe *m,* indication *f,* suggestion *f.* **Not the slightest h. of . . . ,** pas le moindre soupçon de. . . . **A h. of a Belgian accent,** une pointe d'accent belge. **2.** Hints for housewives, conseils *m* aux ménagères. **Maintenance hints and tips,** conseils et indications pour l'entretien (d'un appareil, etc.).

hint[2], *v.tr.* & *i.* Insinuer (qch.); suggérer, dire, (qch.) à mots couverts. **To h. to s.o. that . . . ,** faire entendre à qn que. . . . **To h. at sth.,** laisser entendre qch.

hinterland ['hintəlænd], *s.* Hinterland *m;* arrière-pays *m.*

hip[1] [hip], *s.* **1.** *Anat:* Hanche *f.* *Dressm:* *Tail:* **H. measurement,** tour *m* de hanches. **To smite s.o. h. and thigh,** anéantir qn. **2.** *Const:* **H.(-piece, -rafter),** arêtier *m,* arête *f.* **'hip-bone,** *s.* Os *m* de la hanche; os iliaque. **'hip-disease,** *s.* Coxalgie *f.* **'hip-flask,** *s.* Flacon *m* de (poche). **'hip-joint,** *s.* Articulation *f* de la hanche. **'hip-pocket,** *s.* Poche *f* revolver. **'hip-roof,** *s.* *Arch:* Comble *m* en croupe. **'hip-shot,** *a.* *Vet:* (Cheval) déhanché, éhanché.

hip[2], *s.* *Bot:* Cynorhodon *m;* *F:* gratte-cul *m inv.*

hip[3], *int.* H.! h.! (h.!) hurrah! hip! hip! hip! hourra!

hip[4], *a.* *U.S:* *F:* **1.** A la page, dans le vent. **2.** Fanatique de jazz.

hippocras ['hipəkræs], *s.* Hypocras *m.*

hippocratic [hipə'krætik], *a.* Hippocratique.

hippodrome ['hipədroum], *s.* Hippodrome *m.*

hippopotamus, *pl.* **-muses,** **-mi** [hipə'potəməs, -məsiz, -mai], *s.* *Z:* Hippopotame *m.*

hircine ['hɔːsain], a. Hircin.
hire¹ ['haiər], s. 1. Louage m (d'un domestique, d'une voiture); U.S: embauchage m (de main-d'œuvre); location f (d'une maison). **To let sth. (out) on h.**, louer qch. 2. A: & U.S: Salaire m, gages mpl. **'hire-'purchase**, s. Vente f à crédit.
hire², v.tr. 1. (a) Louer, engager (un domestique). **Hired assassin**, assassin m à gages. U.S: **Hired man, hired girl**, domestique mf, bonne f. (b) Louer (une voiture, etc.). **Hired carriage**, voiture f de remise. **2. To h. out**, louer, donner en location (une voiture, etc.).
hireling ['haiəliŋ], s. & a. Mercenaire (m).
hirer ['haiərər], s. 1. Locataire m (d'une charrette, etc.). 2. H. out, loueur, -euse.
hirsute ['hɔːsjuːt], a. Hirsute, velu.
his¹ [hiz], poss.a. (denoting a m. possessor) Son, f sa, pl. ses. **One of h. friends**, un de ses amis. **The date and place of h. birth**, ses date et lieu de naissance. **He fell on h. back**, il tomba sur le dos. (Emphatic) 'H. idea would be to . . ., son idée à lui serait de. . . .
his², poss.pron. (denoting a m. possessor) Le sien, la sienne, les siens, les siennes. **He took my pen and h.**, il prit ma plume et la sienne. **This book is h.**, ce livre est à lui, lui appartient; c'est son livre à lui. **A friend of h.**, un de ses amis. **That pride of h.**, cet orgueil dont il ne peut se défaire.
Hispanic [his'pænik], a. Hispanique.
Hispano-American [hi'spænouə'merikən], a. & s. Hispano-américain, -aine.
Hispano-Moorish [hi'spænou'muəriʃ], **Hispano-Moresque** [hi'spænoumə:'resk], a. Hispano-moresque.
hispid ['hispid], a. Nat.Hist: Hispide.
hiss¹ [his], s. 1. (a) Sifflement m (du gaz). (b) Th: etc: Sifflet m. 2. Ling: Sifflante f.
hiss². 1. v.i. (Of serpent, steam, etc.) Siffler; (of arclamp) bruire; (of steam, gas) chuinter. 2. v.tr. **To h. an actor**, siffler un acteur.
hist [hist], int. 1. (To enjoin silence) Chut! 2. (To attract attention) Pst!
histological [ˌhistə'lədʒik(ə)l], a. Biol: Histologique.
histology [his'tələdʒi], s. Biol: Histologie f.
historian [his'tɔːriən], s. Historien m.
historiated [his'tɔːriːeitid], a. (Manuscrit) historié.
historic [his'tɔrik], a. Historique; (événement) marquant. **Place of h. interest**, monument m historique.
historical [his'tɔrik(ə)l], a. 1. (Fait) historique, de l'histoire. 2. H. painting, painter, tableau, peintre, d'histoire. **H. novel**, roman historique. **-ally**, adv Historiquement.
historiographer [his,tɔːri'ɔgrəfər], s. Historiographe m.
historiography [his,tɔːri'ɔgrəfi], s. Historiographie f.
history ['hist(ə)ri], s. 1. L'histoire f. **We are making h.**, ce que nous faisons en ce moment restera, marquera, dans l'histoire, fera date. F: **That's ancient h.**, c'est de l'histoire ancienne; c'est (du) vieux. **To know the inner h. of a matter**, connaître les dessous d'une affaire. **H.-book**, manuel m, livre m, d'histoire. 2. **Natural h.**, histoire naturelle. 3. Mil: Navy: H. sheet, feuille f matriculaire.
histrion ['histriən], s. Pej: Histrion m, cabotin m.
histrionic(al) [ˌhistri'ɔnik(əl)], a. 1. Théâtral, -aux. 2. Pej: Histrionique; (effusions) de cabotin.
histrionics [ˌhistri'ɔniks], s.pl. 1. L'art m du théâtre. 2. Pej: Démonstrations peu f sincères; "la comédie."
hit¹ [hit], s. 1. (a) Coup m. F: **To have a sly h. at s.o.**, donner un coup de patte à qn. **That's a h. at you**, c'est vous qui êtes visé; c'est une pierre dans votre jardin. (b) Fenc: Touche f, coup. **To score a h.**, toucher. (c) Hockey: Coup de crosse. **Free h.**, coup franc. (d) Baseball: Coup de batte; frappe f. 2. (a) Coup réussi; succès m. **Lucky h.**, (i) coup heureux; (ii) trouvaille f. **To make a h.**, (of thg) réussir. **To make a big h.**, décrocher le grand succès. (b) Th: Pièce f à succès. **It is a great h.**, c'est un succès fou. **'hit-tune**, s. Air m à succès.
hit². (p.t. & p.p. hit; pr.p. hitting) 1. v.tr. (a) Frapper. **To h. s.o. a blow**, porter, donner, un coup à qn. (b) v.i. **To h. against sth.**, s'attraper à qch.; se cogner contre qch. **His head h. against the pavement**, sa tête a porté, a donné, sur le trottoir. (c) Atteindre. Aut: P: **To h. the hundred mark**, taper le 160. **He couldn't h. an elephant, a haystack**, il raterait un éléphant dans

un couloir. Fenc: Bill: Toucher. **To h. the mark**, atteindre le but; frapper juste. **To be h. by a bullet**, être atteint par une balle. F: **To be h. in one's pride**, être blessé dans son orgueil. (Of allusion, etc.) **To h. home**, porter (coup); piquer (qn) au vif. F: **To be hard h.**, être gravement atteint (par ses pertes, etc.). **The strike hits several factories**, la grève affecte plusieurs usines. (d) adj. & adv.phr. **To attempt sth. h. or miss**, tenter qch. vaille que vaille. **To strike out h. or miss**, frapper au hasard. 2. v.tr. & i. **To h. (up)on sth.**, découvrir, trouver (un moyen); rencontrer (un indice, etc.). **You've h. it!** vous avez deviné juste! vous y êtes! **hit back**, v.tr. & i. Se défendre; rendre coup pour coup (à qn). **hit off**, v.tr. F: 1. (a) **To h. off a likeness**, attraper une ressemblance. **You have h. him off to a T**, P: c'est lui tout craché. (b) **To h. s.o. off**, donner un portrait satirique de qn; charger qn. 2. **To h. it off with s.o.**, s'accorder avec qn. **hit out**, v.i. **To h. out at s.o.**, décocher un coup à qn. **'hit-and-'run**, attrib.a. **H.-and-r. driver**, chauffard m.
hitch¹ [hitʃ], s. 1. Saccade f, secousse f. **To give one's trousers a h.**, remonter son pantalon. 2. Nau: Nœud m; amarrage m à demi-clefs; clef f. 3. Anicroche f, contretemps m. **There is a h. somewhere**, il y a quelque chose qui cloche. **Without a h.**, sans à-coup; sans accroc. W.Tel: T.V: **A technical h.**, une panne d'émission, un incident technique.
hitch², v.tr. 1. Remuer (qch.) par saccades. **To h. (up) one's trousers**, remonter son pantalon. 2. Accrocher, attacher, fixer. **To h. one's wagon to a star**, attacher son char à une étoile. F: **To h. a ride**, voyager en auto-stop. **hitch up**, v.i. U.S: Atteler (les chevaux). P: **To get hitched up**, se marier. **'hitch-hike**, v.i. Faire de l'auto-stop. **'hitch-hiker**, s. Auto-stoppeur, -euse. **'hitch-hiking**, s. Auto-stop m.
hither ['hiðər]. 1. adv. Ici (exprimant la venue). **H. and thither**, çà et là. 2. a. Le plus rapproché. A.Geog: **H. Gaul**, la Gaule citérieure.
hitherto ['hiðə'tuː], adv. Jusqu'ici. **As h.**, comme par le passé.
Hitlerism ['hitlərizm], s. Hitlérisme m.
Hitlerite ['hitlərait], a. Hitlérien.
hitter ['hitər], s. Frappeur m. Box: Cogneur m.
Hittite ['hitait], a. & s. Hist: Hittite (mf).
hive¹ [haiv], s. 1. Ruche f. 2. (Swarm) Essaim m.
hive². 1. v.tr. Mettre (des abeilles) dans une ruche; (re)cueillir (un essaim). 2. v.i. (Of swarm) Entrer dans la ruche. **hive off**. 1. v.i. Essaimer. 2. v.tr. Com: Donner (un travail) à un sous-traitant.
hives [haivz], s.pl. Med: Urticaire f.
ho [hou], int. 1. (Expressing surprise, mirth, etc.) Ho! 2. (To attract attention) Hé! ohé!
hoar [hɔːr], s. H.(-frost), gelée blanche; givre m, Lit: frimas m.
hoard¹ [hɔːd], s. Amas m, accumulation secrète (de vivres, etc.). **H. of money**, trésor m, F: magot m.
hoard², v.tr. Amasser (le blé, etc.); accumuler (de l'argent). **To h. up treasure**, abs. **to h.**, thésauriser (des capitaux); encoffrer (un trésor, etc.). **hoarding**¹, s. Resserre f, amassage m (de provisions); thésaurisation f (de capitaux).
hoarder ['hɔːdər], s. Amasseur, -euse. **H. of money**, thésauriseur, -euse. **H. of provisions, etc.**, spéculateur m.
hoarding² ['hɔːdiŋ], s. Clôture f en planches; palissade f (de chantier). (Advertisement) h., panneau-réclame m, pl. panneaux-réclame.
hoarse [hɔːs], a. Enroué, rauque. **To shout oneself h.**, s'enrouer à force de crier. **-ly**, adv. D'une voix rauque, enrouée.
hoarsen [hɔːs(ə)n]. 1. v.tr. Enrouer (la voix). 2. v.i. Devenir enroué; s'enrouer.
hoarseness ['hɔːsnis], s. Enrouement m.
hoary ['hɔːri], a. 1. (Of hair) Blanchi, chenu. 2. Vénérable, séculaire. **Of h. antiquity**, de la plus haute antiquité.
hoax¹ [houks], s. Mystification f, supercherie f, farce f; attrape f, F: canular(d) m. **To play a h. on s.o.**, (i) mystifier qn; (ii) faire une farce à qn.
hoax², v.tr. Mystifier, attraper (qn); F: faire marcher (qn); P: monter un bateau à (qn). **hoaxing**, s. Mystification f.

hob [hɔb], s. **1.** Plaque f de côté (d'une grille de cheminée, où l'on peut tenir les aliments au chaud). **2.** = HOBNAIL.

hobble[1] ['hɔbl], s. **1.** Boitillement m, clochement m. **2.** (a) Entrave f (pour chevaux, etc.). (b) F: Embarras m. 'hobble-skirt, s. A: Cost: Jupe étroite.

hobble[2]. **1.** v.i. Boitiller, clocher, clopiner. To h. along, avancer clopin-clopant; traîner la jambe. **2.** v.tr. Entraver (un cheval, etc.).

hobbledehoy ['hɔbldi'hɔi], s. Jeune homme gauche; grand dadais.

hobby ['hɔbi], s. **1.** A: Bidet m; petit cheval de selle. **2.** Passe-temps favori; violon m d'Ingres. To paint as a h., se distraire à faire de la peinture. My h. is carpentry, mon violon d'Ingres, c'est la menuiserie. 'hobby-horse, s. Dada m; cheval m de bois.

hobgoblin ['hɔbgoblin], s. Lutin m, farfadet m.

hobnail ['hɔbneil], s. Caboche f; clou m à ferrer (les souliers).

hobnailed ['hɔbneild], a. (Soulier) ferré, à gros clous. Med: F: H. liver, foie m cirrhotique.

hobnob ['hɔbnɔb], v.i. (hobnobbed) To h. with s.o., être de pair à compagnon avec qn; être à tu et à toi avec qn. To h. with the great, frayer avec les grands.

hobo ['houbou], s. U.S: (a) Ouvrier ambulant. (b) F: Chemineau m, trimardeur m, clochard m.

Hobson ['hɔbsn]. Pr.n.m. F: It's (a case of) H.'s choice, il n'y a pas d'alternative.

hock[1] [hɔk], s. Jarret m (de quadrupède).

hock[2], s. Vin m du Rhin.

hock[3], s. U.S: P: Gage m. In h., (i) (Of watch, etc.) au mont-de-piété, au clou, chez ma tante. (ii) (Of pers.) en prison. To be in h. to s.o., être endetté envers qn.

hock[4], v tr. U.S: P: Engager (sa montre, etc.); F: mettre (sa montre) au clou.

hockey ['hɔki], s. (Jeu m de) hockey m. Ice-h., U.S: h., hockey sur glace. H. stick, crosse f, stick m. (Ice-)h. player, hockeyeur m.

hocus ['houkəs], v.tr. (hocussed) **1.** Attraper (qn); F: monter un bateau à (qn). **2.** Narcotiser, droguer (une boisson).

hocus-pocus[1] ['houkəs'poukəs], s. Tromperie f, supercherie f.

hocus-pocus[2], v.tr. (-pocussed) Berner, mystifier (qn).

hod [hɔd], s. **1.** Oiseau m, auge f, hotte f (de maçon). **2.** Seau m à charbon.

hodful ['hɔdful], s. Hottée f.

hodman, pl. -men ['hɔdmən], s. Aide-maçon m, pl. aides-maçons.

hoe[1] [hou], s. Hort: Houe f, binette f. Two-pronged h., binochon m. Mechanical, motor, h., motobineuse f.

hoe[2], v.tr. (hoed; hoeing) Houer, biner (le sol); sarcler (les mauvaises herbes). F: A hard row to h., une tâche difficile, ingrate.

hoecake ['houkeik], s. U.S: Cu: Galette f de maïs.

hoer ['houər], (Pers.) Bineur, -euse.

hog[1] [hɔg], s. **1.** (a) Porc châtré. (b) (esp. U.S:) Porc, cochon m, pourceau m. F: To go the whole h., aller jusqu'au bout. U.S: H.-raising, l'industrie porcine. **2.** (Pers.) F: Goinfre m, glouton m; F: pourceau. **3.** Nau: (Brush) Goret m. 'hogcholera, s. Vet: U.S: Peste porcine. 'hog mane, s. Crinière (coupée) en brosse, anglaisée. 'hog's back, s. = HOGBACK. hog-tie, v.tr. U.S: Lier ensemble les quatre pattes (d'un animal). F: To h.-t. a prisoner, lier les poignets d'un prisonnier à ses chevilles. 'hog-wash, s. (a) Eaux grasses (que l'on donne aux porcs). (b) F: Rinçures fpl, lavasse f. (c) F: It's all h.-w., P: c'est de la foutaise. 'hog-wild, a. U.S: H.-w. enthusiasm, enthousiasme délirant, outré, exagéré, excessif.

hog[2], v. (hogged; hogging) **1.** v.i. P: (i) Se conduire comme un cochon. (ii) O: Dormir; roupiller. He spent the afternoon hogging, il a passé l'après-midi à roupiller. (iii) Aut: To come hogging round the corner, prendre le virage à une allure de chauffard. **2.** v.tr. (a) Couper en brosse, anglaiser (la crinière d'un cheval). (b) P: To h. (sth.), se réserver le monopole (de qch.), monopoliser (qch.). He hogs the limelight, il accapare la vedette. (c) P: Manger, boire, goulûment.

hogback ['hɔgbæk], s. Ph.Geog: Dos m d'âne; ligne f de crête; route f formant ligne de crête.

hogbacked ['hɔgbækt], a. (Pont, etc.) en dos d'âne.

hogged [hɔgd], a. **1.** (Navire) arqué, cassé. **2.** (Crinière de cheval) en brosse, anglaisée.

hoggish ['hɔgiʃ], a. F: (Individu) glouton, grossier.

hoggishness ['hɔgiʃnis], s. F: Gloutonnerie f; grossièreté f; malpropreté f.

Hogmanay [,hɔgmə'nei], s. Scot: La Saint-Sylvestre.

hogpen ['hɔgpen], s. U.S: Porcherie f, étable f à porcs.

hogshead ['hɔgzhed], s. Tonneau m, barrique f.

hogweed ['hɔgwi:d], s. (a) Berce commune. (b) Centinode f; (renouée f) traînasse f.

hoi(c)k[1] [hɔik], s. Coup sec; saccade f.

hoi(c)k[2], v.tr. F: (a) Lever, tirer, d'un coup sec. (b) Faire monter (un avion) en chandelle. (c) Redresser (l'avion).

hoist[1] [hɔist], s. **1.** (a) Coup m de treuil. To give sth. a h., hisser qch. (b) To give s.o. a h. (up), aider qn à monter. **2.** (a) Appareil m de levage; treuil m. (b) (For goods) Monte-charge m inv; ascenseur m (de marchandises).

hoist[2], v.tr. To h. (up), hisser, guinder. To h. a boat out, mettre un canot à la mer. F: To h. s.o. on to his horse, hisser qn sur son cheval. He was h. with his own petard, il fut pris à son propre piège. **hoisting**, s. Levage m; hissage m. Min: Remontée f, remonte f (du charbon). Nau: H. in (of boat), embarquement m. Mil: H. the colours, lever m des couleurs. Hoisting gear, tackle, engine, appareil m de hissage, de levage.

hoity-toity ['hɔiti'tɔiti]. **1.** A: & Hum: int. Ta, ta, ta! taratata! **2.** a. (a) Qui se donne des airs. (b) Qui se froisse facilement. Don't be so h.-t.! prenez-le sur un autre ton!

hold[1] [hould], s. **1.** (a) Prise f, étreinte f. To have h. of s.o., sth., tenir qn, qch. To catch, lay, take, h. of sth., saisir, empoigner, qch.; mettre la main sur qch. Where did you get h. of that? où vous êtes-vous procuré cela? F: où avez-vous pêché ça? To keep h. of sth., ne pas lâcher qch. To keep tight h. of, a firm h. on, sth., tenir qch. serré. To relax one's h., relâcher son étreinte. To leave, lose, h. of sth., lâcher qch. To lose, let go, one's h., lâcher prise. (b) To have a h. on, over, s.o., avoir prise sur qn. To gain a firm h. over s.o., acquérir un grand empire, un grand pouvoir, sur qn. (c) Box: Tenu m. Wr: Prise. **2.** Soutien m; point m d'appui.

hold[2], v. (held [held]; held) I. v.tr. **1.** Tenir. (a) To h. sth. tight, serrer qch.; tenir qch. serré. To h. s.o. fast, tenir solidement qn. To h. hands, se donner la main. To h. one's sides with laughter, se tenir les côtes de rire. To h. views, professer des opinions. (b) To h. the key to the puzzle, tenir le mot de l'énigme. **2.** (a) To h. sth. in position, tenir qch. en place. (b) To h. s.o. in check, tenir qn en échec. To h. s.o. prisoner, tenir, garder, qn prisonnier. To h. oneself ready, in readiness, se tenir prêt. To h. s.o. to his promise, obliger, contraindre, qn à tenir sa promesse. **3.** To h. one's ground, tenir bon, tenir ferme. To h. one's own against all comers, maintenir sa position envers et contre tous. He can h. his own, il sait se défendre. To h. one's drink, avoir la tête solide, bien porter le vin. F: To h. the fort, assurer la permanence (en l'absence des chefs). To h. the stage, (i) (of actor) retenir l'attention de l'auditoire; (ii) (of play) tenir l'affiche (pendant longtemps). Nau: To h. the course, tenir la route. Aut: Car that holds the road well, voiture f qui tient bien la route. Tp: H. the line! ne quittez pas! **4.** To h. one's head high, porter la tête haute. To h. oneself upright, se tenir droit. **5.** (a) Contenir, renfermer (une quantité de qch.). Car that holds six people, voiture à six places. This car cannot h. five (people), on ne tient pas cinq dans cette voiture. (b) What the future holds, ce que l'avenir nous réserve. **6.** Tenir (une séance); avoir (une consultation); célébrer (une fête). The Motor Show is held in October, le Salon de l'automobile se tient au mois d'octobre. To h. a conversation with s.o., s'entretenir avec qn. **7.** Retenir, arrêter, empêcher. (a) To h. (in) one's breath, retenir son haleine. There was no holding him, il n'y avait pas moyen de l'arrêter, de l'empêcher. H. your hand! arrêtez! F: H. your horses! arrêtez! attendez! une minute! Abs. H. (hard)! arrêtez! halte là! (b) To h. water, (i) (of cask, etc.) tenir l'eau, être étanche; (ii) F: (of theory, etc.) tenir debout. (c) Retenir (l'attention). To h. the floor, accaparer la conversation. (d) Mil: To h. the enemy, contenir l'ennemi. 8. Avoir, posséder (un emploi); détenir (une charge); occuper (une terre). To h. shares, détenir des actions. 9. (a) To h. sth. lightly, faire peu de cas de qch. This is held to be true, ceci passe pour vrai. To h. s.o. responsible, tenir qn responsable. F: To h. the baby, être responsable, se rendre, se trouver, responsable (d'un événement, d'un malheur, etc.); F: payer les pots cassés. To h. s.o. in respect, avoir du respect pour qn. (b) Avoir, professer (une opinion). He holds that . . ., il est d'avis que. . . . 10. (Sustain) Mus: To h. (on) a note, tenir, prolonger, une note. II. hold, v.i. 1. (Of rope, nail, etc.) Tenir (bon); être solide. To h. tight, firm, fast, tenir bon, tenir ferme. 2. (a) Durer, persister; continuer; (of weather) se maintenir. (b) To h. on one's way, suivre son chemin. 3. To h. (good, true), être vrai, valable. Promise that still holds good, promesse qui est toujours valable. The objection holds, cette objection subsiste. 4. To h. to a belief, rester attaché à une croyance. To h. by, to, one's opinion, adhérer à son opinion. hold back. 1. v.tr. (a) Retenir (qn, ses larmes). (b) Cacher, dissimuler (la vérité). 2. v.i. Rester en arrière; hésiter. To h. back from doing sth., se retenir de faire qch. To h. back for sth., se réserver pour qch. hold down, v.tr. 1. (a) To h. a man down, maintenir un homme à terre. (b) Opprimer (qn, le peuple). 2. Occuper (un emploi). hold forth, v.i. Disserter pérorer. To h. forth to the crowd, haranguer la foule. hold in, v.tr. Serrer la bride à (un cheval); réprimer (ses désirs); maîtriser (une passion). To h. oneself in, se contenir, se retenir. hold off. 1. v.tr. Tenir (qn, qch.) à distance. 2. v.i. (a) Se tenir à distance (from, de). (b) The rain is holding off, jusqu'ici il ne pleut pas. (c) S'abstenir; se réserver. hold on. 1. v.tr. Maintenir. 2. v.i. (a) To h. on to sth. (i) S'accrocher, se cramponner, à qch. (ii) Ne pas lâcher, ne pas abandonner, qch. H. on! (i) tenez bon! tenez ferme! (ii) Tp: ne quittez pas! (iii) (attendez) un instant! How long can you h. on? combien de temps pouvez-vous tenir? (b) F: H. on (a bit)! pas si vite! hold out, v.tr. Tendre, offrir, présenter (la main, etc.). F: To h. out a hand to s.o., tendre la perche à qn. 2. v.i. Durer. To h. out against an attack, soutenir une attaque; tenir bon contre une attaque. To h. out to the end, tenir jusqu'au bout. hold over, v.tr. Remettre (à plus tard). hold together. 1. v.tr Maintenir (deux choses) ensemble. To h. one's staff together, assurer la cohésion de son personnel. 2. v.i. Tenir (ensemble); garder de la cohésion. We must h. together, il faut rester unis. F: The story won't h. together, l'histoire ne tient pas debout. hold up. 1. v.tr. (a) Soutenir (qn, qch.). (b) Lever (qch.) (en l'air). To h. up one's head (again), relever redresser, la tête. To h. sth. up to the light, (i) exposer qch. à un bon jour; (ii) tenir qch. à contre-jour. (c) To h. s.o. up as a model, citer, offrir, proposer, qn comme modèle. To h. s.o. up to ridicule, tourner qn en ridicule. (d) Arrêter (un train, etc.); entraver, gêner (la circulation); immobiliser (l'ennemi). Goods held up at the customs, marchandises en consigne, en souffrance, à la douane. 2. v.i. (a) Se soutenir. (b) (Of weather) Se maintenir. (c) Ne pas tomber. 'hold-up, s. 1. (a) Arrêt m, embarras m (de voitures); suspension f de la circulation. (b) Panne f (du métro, etc.). 2. Attaque f; coup m à main armée; hold-up m. hold with, v.i. To h. with s.o., tenir pour qn; être du parti de qn. F: I don't hold with such behaviour, je désapprouve une telle conduite. holding, s. 1. (a) Tenue f (d'une plume, etc.). (b) Tchn: Fixation f; serrage m. (c) Mil: H. of a captured position, conservation f d'une position. (d) Tenue (d'une séance, etc.). (e) Possession f (de terres); tenure f. 2. (a) Agr: Terre affermée; ferme f. Small(-)holding, closerie f; petite propriété. Division (of land) into small(-)holdings, morcellement m des terres. (b) Fin: Avoir m (en actions); fournissement m (en actions); effets mpl en portefeuille; dossier m; holding m. 'hold-all, s. (Sac m) fourretout m inv.

hold³, s. Nau: Cale f. The goods in the h., les marchandises à fond de cale.
holder ['houldər], s. 1. (Pers.) (a) Teneur, -euse (de qch.). Metalw: H.-on, -up, teneur de tas. (b) Détenteur, -trice (Fin: de titres, d'une lettre de change); porteur, -euse (Fin: de titres, d'un effet); titulaire mf (d'un droit); tenancier, -ière (d'une ferme); propriétaire mf (d'une terre). Small(-)h., petit propriétaire. 2. (Device) (a) Support m, monture f, patte f. (b) (Expressed by porte-, e.g.) Drill-h. bit-h., porte-foret m. Pen-h., porte-plume m inv. Tooth-brush holder, (i) (fixture) porte-brosses à dents, (ii) étui à brosse à dents. 3. Récipient m. Gas-h., cloche f à gaz; gazomètre m. 4. Poignée f.
holdfast ['houldfɑːst], s. Crampon m; serre-joint m. Bench h., valet m.
hole¹ [houl], s. Trou m. 1. (a) Creux m, cavité f. F: To be, find oneself, in a h., être, se trouver, dans l'embarras, dans le pétrin, dans une impasse. To get s.o. out of a h., tirer qn d'un mauvais pas. (b) Terrier m (de lapin); trou (de souris, de rat). (c) F: (House) taudis m, bicoque f; (town, etc.) trou. What a rotten h., quel sale trou. Dead and alive h., petit trou mort. 2. Orifice m, ouverture f; lumière f (de pinnule, etc.). Med: H. in the heart, (i) communication f inter-ventriculaire; (ii) communication inter-auriculaire. Holes in a strap, points m d'une courroie. Mec.E: Inspection h., orifice de visite; regard m (d'un fourneau, etc.). To bore a h., percer un trou. To wear a h. in a garment, trouer un vêtement. (Of garment) To wear, go, into holes, se trouer. Stockings in holes, full of holes, bas tout troués. To make a h. in sth., (i) faire un trou à qch.; (ii) F: faire une brèche à (son avoir). To knock holes in an argument, démolir un argument. To pick holes in (a theory, an argument), relever les points faibles (d'une théorie, d'un raisonnement). 'hole-and-'corner, attrib.a. Clandestin, secret. H.-a.-c. deal, affaire conclue en sous-main. 'hole-proof, a. (Bas m, chaussette f) inusable, introuable; (vêtement m, tissu m) indécirable.
hole². 1. v.tr. (a) Trouer, percer (qch.); pratiquer, faire, un trou dans (qch.). (b) Golf: To h. the ball, abs. to h. (out), poter (la balle); mettre la balle dans le trou. 2. v.i. Se trouer, se percer. To h. up, v.i. U.S: Se terrer, se cacher. Fr.C: S'encabaner.
holiday¹ ['holidi, -dei], s. (a) (Jour m de) fête (religieuse); jour m de fête. National, public, h., fête légale. To keep, make, h., faire fête. (b) (Jour de) congé m; jour de sortie. To take a h., prendre un congé; chômer. (c) The holidays, les vacances. A month's h., un mois de vacances. Holidays with pay, congé payé. To be on h., on one's holidays, (i) être en congé, en vacance(s); (ii) être en villégiature. 'holiday-maker, s. 1. Fêteur, -euse. 2. Villégiaturiste mf, vacancier, -ière; estivant, -ante.
holiday², v.i. Used mainly in compound tenses. F: Passer les vacances. He is holidaying at Nice, il passe ses vacances à Nice.
holiness ['houlinis], s. Sainteté f.
Holland ['holənd]. 1. Pr.n. La Hollande. 2. s. Toile f de Hollande; toile bise, toile écrue.
holler ['holər], v.i. P: Chialer; brailler.
hollow¹ ['holou]. I. a. 1. Creux, caverneux, évidé. H. eyes, yeux caves, enfoncés. F: To feel h., avoir un creux dans l'estomac; avoir faim. 2. (Son) sourd. In a h. voice, d'une voix caverneuse. 3. F: (Of friendship, etc.) Faux, f. fausse; trompeur, -euse; vain. II. hollow, adv. 1. To sound h., sonner creux. 2. To beat s.o. h., battre qn à plate couture. III. hollow, s. (a) Creux m (de la main, etc.); cavité f (d'une dent); excavation f. (b) Enfoncement m, dépression f (du sol). Ph.Geog: Bas-fond m. hollow-'cheeked, a. Aux joues creuses. hollow-'eyed, a. Aux yeux caves, enfoncés. 'hollow-ware, s. 1. Boissellerie f. 2. Articles mpl de vaisselle, de cuisine, en faïence ou en métal. Glass h.-w., gobeleterie f.
hollow². 1. v.tr. To h. (out), creuser, évider. 2. v.i. Se creuser; s'évider.
hollowness ['holənis], s. 1. Creux m, concavité f. 2. Timbre caverneux (de la voix). 3. Manque m de sincérité (d'une promesse, etc.); fausseté f (de cœur).

holly ['hɔli], s. Bot: Houx m. H. grove, plantation, houssaie f.

hollyhock ['hɔlihɔk], s. Rose trémière.

holm-oak ['houmouk], s. Bot: Yeuse f; chêne vert.

holocaust ['hɔləkɔːst], s. Holocauste m.

holograph ['hɔləgrɑːf]. 1. a. (Document) olographe. 2. s. Olographie f; testament m olographe.

holothurian [ˌhɔlo'θjuəriən], s. Echin: Holothurie f; F: concombre m de mer.

holster ['houlstər], s. Fonte f (de selle); étui m de revolver (de selle ou de ceinturon).

holy ['houli]. 1. a. (holiest) (a) Saint, sacré. The H. Ghost, le Saint-Esprit. The H. Father, le Saint-Père. H. Writ, les Écritures saintes. H. bread, water, pain bénit, eau bénite. To keep the Sabbath day h., sanctifier le dimanche. To swear by all that is h., jurer ses grands dieux. (b) (Of pers.) Saint, pieux. 2. s. The H. of Holies, le saint des saints. -ily, adv. Saintement.

holystone¹ ['houlistoun], s. Nau: Brique f à pont.

holystone², v.tr. Nau: Briquer (le pont).

homage ['hɔmidʒ], s. Hommage m. To pay, do, h. to s.o., rendre, faire, hommage à qn.

home¹ [houm]. I. s. 1. (a) Chez-soi m inv; logis m; foyer (familial, domestique); domicile m; intérieur m. The few houses near his h., les quelques maisons voisines de chez lui. Hamlet of fifty homes, hameau de cinquante feux. The Ideal H. Exhibition = le Salon des arts ménagers. To have a h. of one's own, avoir un chez-soi. To give s.o. a h., to make a h. for s.o., recueillir qn; recevoir qn chez soi. It's a h. from h., c'est un second chez-soi. To go to one's last h., partir pour sa dernière demeure. (b) Le chez-soi, la maison, le foyer. Be it ever so humble there's no place like h., il n'y a pas de petit chez-soi; à tout oiseau son nid est beau. At h., (i) à la maison, chez soi; (ii) Sp: (jouer) sur le terrain du club. Jeweller working at h., bijoutier en chambre. To stay at h., garder la maison. Is Mr X at h.? M. X est-il chez lui? est-ce que monsieur y est? Mrs X is not at h. to-day, Mme X (i) est sortie, (ii) ne reçoit pas, aujourd'hui. She is at h. on Tuesdays, elle reçoit le mardi; son jour est le mardi. To be 'not at h.' to anyone, consigner la porte à tout le monde. To feel at h. with s.o., se sentir à l'aise avec qn. He is at h. on, in, with, any topic, tous les sujets lui sont familiers. To make oneself at h., faire comme chez soi. To be (away, absent) from h., ne pas être à la maison. To go from h., (i) partir, aller, en voyage; faire un voyage; (ii) sortir. To leave h., (i) partir (définitivement); (ii) quitter sa famille. Patrie f; pays (natal); terre natale. At h. and abroad, chez nous, dans notre pays, et à l'étranger. Adm: Mil: Navy: Service at h., le service dans la métropole. 3. Nearer h. To take an example nearer h . . . ., sans aller chercher si loin. . . . When the question comes nearer h., they will think differently, quand la question les touchera de plus près, ils changeront d'avis. 4. (a) Nat.Hist: Habitat m. (b) Greece was the h. of fine arts, la Grèce fut la patrie des beaux-arts. 5. Asile m, refuge m. Sailors' h., foyer, abri m, du marin. H. for the blind, hospice m d'aveugles. Rest h., maison de repos. H. for old people, maison de retraite; hospice. Children's h., home m d'enfants; hospice. S.a. MENTAL, NURSING HOME. 6. (a) (In games) Le but. (b) Rac: L'arrivée f. II. home, adv. (Indique mouvement vers . . ., ou arrivée à. . . .) 1. (a) A la maison; chez soi. To go, come, h., (i) rentrer (à la maison); (ii) rentrer dans sa famille. The train is h., le train pour rentrer, le train du soir. To get h., regagner la maison, son chez-soi. (b) To go, come, h., retourner au pays; (of soldier, etc.) rentrer dans ses foyers. To send s.o. h. (from abroad), rapatrier (qn). To come h. (from abroad), se rapatrier. (c) To be h., être de retour. 2. (a) (Of bullet, etc.) To go h., porter (coup). The reproach went h., le reproche le toucha au vif; le reproche porta (coup). To strike h., frapper juste; porter coup. To bring sth. h. to s.o., faire sentir qch. à qn. To bring a charge h. to s.o., prouver une accusation contre qn. (b) To screw a piece h., visser, serrer, une pièce à fond, à bloc. III. home, attrib.a. 1. (a) H. circle, cercle de famille. H. training, éducation familiale. To enjoy h. life, avoir des goûts d'intimité; F: être pot-au-feu. H. address, adresse personnelle. (b) Ven: The h. coverts, les fourrés les plus près du château. (c) The h. counties, les comtés avoisinant Londres. Sp: H. ground, terrain du club. The h. side, l'équipe f qui reçoit. The h. backs, les arrières locaux. (d) H. journey, voyage de retour. S.a. TRUTH. 2. H. trade, commerce intérieur. H. products, produits nationaux, du pays. H. news, nouvelles de l'intérieur. The H. Fleet, la flotte métropolitaine. The H. Office = le Ministère de l'Intérieur. The H. Secretary = le Ministre de l'Intérieur. 'home-baked, a. (Pain, gâteau) fait à la maison. 'home-bird, U.S: -body, s. F: (Of pers.) Casanier, -ière. 'home-'bred, a. (a) Élevé au pays, indigène. (b) Élevé à la maison. (c) With a h.-b. courtesy, avec une courtoisie naturelle, rustique. 'home-brewed, a. (Bière) brassée, fabriquée, à la maison; (cidre) de ménage. 'home-coming, s. Retour m au foyer, à la maison. home de'fence, s. Défense nationale. 'home farm, s. Ferme attachée au domaine. 'home-folk(s), s. O: (i) Parents mpl, famille f; (ii) les gens m du village, de chez nous, F: de notre patelin. 'home-grown, a. (Denrée) du pays; (produit) indigène; (vin) du cru. Home-Guard (the), a. Mil: = Milice f. 'home-'made, a. Fait à la maison. Pol: H.-m. bomb, bombe f de fabrication artisanale. 'home-thrust, s. (a) Fenc: Botte f; grand coup. (b) F: Pointe f, critique f, qui va droit au but. That was a h.-t., cela l'a touché au vif. 'home-work, s. Sch: Devoirs mpl (et leçons f) du soir. H.-w. book, cahier m de textes. 'home-'worker, s. Ind: Ouvrier m, travailleur m en chambre.

home², v.i. 1. (Of pigeon) Revenir au colombier. 2. Av: Ball: (Of rocket, missile) Revenir par auto-guidage. homing¹, a. 1. H. pigeon, pigeon voyageur. 2. Av: Ball: H. eye, cellule f d'auto-guidage. H. head, tête chercheuse, tête de guidage. homing², s. Av: (Retour m par) auto-guidage m.

homeless ['houmlis], a. Sans foyer; sans feu ni lieu.

homelike ['houmlaik], a. Qui rappelle le chez-soi. Their living-room is h., leur salle f de séjour est (une pièce) intime.

homeliness ['houmlinis], s. 1. Simplicité f (de manières). 2. U.S: Manque m de beauté; laideur f.

homely ['houmli], a. 1. (Nourriture) simple, ordinaire; (goûts) bourgeois, modestes; (gens) tout à fait simples. 2. U.S: (Of pers.) Sans beauté; plutôt laid.

Homer¹ ['houmər]. Pr.n.m. Homère.

homer², s. 1. Orn: Pigeon voyageur. 2. Sp: Shoot m au but.

Homeric [ho'merik], a. Homérique.

homesick ['houmsik], a. Nostalgique. It makes me h., F: ça me donne le cafard. He's h., il a le mal du pays.

homesickness ['houmsiknis], s. Mal m du pays; nostalgie f.

homespun ['houmspʌn]. 1. a. (a) (Tissu m de laine) de fabrication domestique. H. linen, toile f de ménage. (b) Simple, sans apprêt. 2. s. Tissu fait à la maison.

homestead ['houmsted], s. Ferme f (avec dépendances).

homeward ['houmwəd]. 1. a. Qui se dirige (i) vers sa maison, vers sa demeure; (ii) (from abroad) vers son pays. 2. adv. = HOMEWARDS. 'homeward-'bound, a. (Vaisseau) à destination de son port d'attache; (cargaison) de retour.

homewards ['houmwədz], adv. Vers sa maison, vers sa demeure; (from abroad) vers son pays. To hasten h., se presser de rentrer. Cargo h., cargaison de retour.

homey ['houmi], a. F: = HOMELIKE.

homicidal [ˌhɔmi'said(ə)l], a. Homicide, meurtrier.

homicide¹ ['hɔmisaid], s. (Pers.) Homicide mf, meurtrier m.

homicide², s. (Crime) Homicide m. Jur: Felonious h., homicide prémédité; assassinat m. Justifiable h., homicide par légitime défense.

homily ['hɔmili], s. Homélie f. To read s.o. a h., sermonner qn.

hominy ['hɔmini], s. U.S: Cu: Bouillie f de farine de maïs; semoule f de maïs.

homo ['houmou], *s. P:* Homosexuel, -elle.
homocentric [,homo'sentrik], *a.* Homocentrique.
homoeopath ['houmiopæθ], *s. Med:* Homéopathe *m.*
homoeopathic [,houmio'pæθik], *a.* (Traitement) homéopathique; (médecin) homéopathe.
homoeopathy [,houmi'opəθi], *s. Med:* Homéopathie *f.*
homogeneity [,homodʒi'ni:iti], *s.* Homogénéité *f.*
homogeneous ['homo'dʒi:niəs], *a.* Homogène.
homogenization [ho,modʒənai'zeiʃ(ə)n], *s.* Homogénéisation *f.*
homogenize [ho'modʒənaiz], *v.tr.* Homogénéiser.
homogenizer [ho'modʒənaiz(ə)r], *s.* Homogénéiseur *m.*
homograph ['homəgræf, -'gra:f], *s.* Homographe *m.*
homologous [ho'mələgəs], *a.* Homologue.
homology [ho'mələdʒi], *s.* Homologie *f.*
homonym ['homənim], *s.* Homonyme *m.*
homonymous [ho'monimə s], *a.* Homonyme.
homosexual ['homo'sek-uəl, 'houmo-], *a. & s.* Homosexuel, -elle; pédéraste *m.*
homosexuality ['homouseksju'æliti], *s.* Homosexualité *f.*; pédérastie *f.*
homy ['houmi], *a. F:* = HOMELIKE.
hone¹ [houn], *s.* Pierre *f* à aiguiser, à affiler, pierre à rasoir.
hone² *v.tr.* Aiguiser, affiler; repasser (un rasoir).
honest ['onist], *a.* 1. (*a*) (*Of pers.*) Honnête, probe; loyal, -aux (en affaires); (juge) intègre. (*b*) Vrai, sincère. **The h. truth,** la pure vérité. **Honest-to-God working-man,** ouvrier *m,* travailleur *m,* sincère, de bonne foi. **Tell us your h. opinion,** dites-nous de bonne foi votre opinion. *F: O:* **H. Injun!** vrai de vrai! (*c*) **H. means,** moyens légitimes. **To give h. weight,** donner bon poids. 2. (*a*) *A:* (*Of woman*) Honnête, chaste. **To make an h. woman of s.o.,** rendre l'honneur à une femme (en l'épousant). (*b*) (*Respectable*) **They are h. folk,** ce sont de braves gens. **-ly,** *adv.* (*a*) Honnêtement, loyalement. (*b*) Sincèrement. **H. speaking,** à vrai dire.
honesty ['onisti], *s.* 1. (*a*) Honnêteté *f,* probité *f*; loyauté *f* (en affaires); intégrité *f.* (*b*) Véracité *f,* sincérité *f*; franchise *f.* **In all h.,** en toute sincérité. 2. *Bot:* Lunaire *f*; monnaie *f* du pape.
honey ['hʌni], *s.* 1. (*a*) Miel *m.* **Clear h.,** miel liquide. **Comb h.,** miel en rayon. (*b*) Douceur *f* (de mots, de caresses). **He was all h.,** il a été tout sucre et tout miel. 2. *F:* Chéri, *f.* chérie; mon petit chou. **'honey--bee,** *s. Ent:* Abeille *f* domestique; *F:* mouche *f* à miel. **'honey-cake,** *s.* Pain *m* d'épice au miel; nonnette *f.* **'honey-dew,** *s.* 1. Miellée *f,* miellure *f.* 2. Tabac sucré à la mélasse; honey-dew *m.* **'honey-eating,** *a. Z:* Mellivore. **'honey-mouthed, 'tongued,** *a.* (*Of pers.*) Aux paroles mielleuses; mielleux.
honeycomb¹ ['hʌnikoum], *s.* Rayon *m* de miel. *attrib. Tex:* H.-weave towel, serviette *f* nid d'abeilles.
honeycomb². 1. *v.tr.* Cribler (de petits trous). **The army was honeycombed with disaffection,** la désaffection ravageait l'armée. 2. *v.i.* (*Of metal*) Se cribler, se chambrer. **honeycombed,** *a.* 1. Alvéolé. 2. (Métal) chambré, crevassé.
honeyed ['hʌnid], *a.* (*a*) (En)miellé; couvert de miel. (*b*) **H. words,** paroles douceureuses, mielleuses.
honeymoon ['hʌnimu:n], *s.* Lune *f* de miel. **H. trip,** voyage *m* de noces.
honeymooner ['hʌnimu*n*ər], *s.* Nouveau marié.
honeysuckle ['hʌnisʌkl], *s.* Chèvrefeuille *m.*
honied ['hʌnid], *a.* = HONEYED.
honk¹ [hoŋk], *s. Aut:* Cornement *m* (de l'avertisseur). **H.! h.!** couin! couin!
honk², *v.i. Aut:* Corner.
honky-tonk ['hoŋki'toŋk], *s. U.S: F:* Bouge *m,* cabaret *m* borgne, bastringue *m. attrib.* **H.-t. music,** musiquette *f* de bastringue.
honorarium, *pl.* **-ia, -iums** [,onə'reəriəm, -iə, -iəmz], *s.* Honoraires *mpl.*
honorary ['onərəri], *a.* (*a*) (Emploi, service) honoraire, non rétribué, bénévole. (*b*) **H. member,** membre honoraire. (*c*) **H. degree,** grade honorifique, grade honoris causa.
honorific [onə'rifik], *a.* (Épithète) honorifique.
honour¹ ['onər], *s.* Honneur *m.* 1. **To hold s.o. in great h.,** honorer qn. **The seat of h.,** la place d'honneur.

To put up a statue in h. of s.o., ériger une statue à la gloire de qn. **To pay, do, h. to s.o.,** faire honneur à qn. **All h. to him!** honneur à lui! *Prov:* **H. where h. is due,** à tout seigneur tout honneur; à chaque saint sa chandelle. 2. (*a*) **To consider it an h. to do sth.,** tenir à honneur de faire qch. **To whom have I the h. of speaking?** à qui ai-je l'honneur de parler? *Com:* **I have the h. to submit to you . . .,** j'ai l'avantage de vous soumettre, de vous offrir. . . . (*b*) *Games:* **To have the h.,** (*at bowls*) avoir la boule; (*at golf*) avoir l'honneur. 3. **To lose one's h.,** perdre son honneur; se déshonorer. **To make (it) a point of h. to do sth.,** se piquer d'honneur de faire qch. **To be in h. bound to . . .,** être obligé par l'honneur à. . . . **He is the soul of h.,** il est l'honneur incarné, personnifié; il est la probité même. **I cannot in h. accept this money,** je ne peux pas, en tout honneur, accepter cet argent. **To state on one's h. that . . .,** déclarer sur l'honneur que. . . . **Word of h.,** parole *f* d'honneur. **To be on one's h.,** être engagé d'honneur. 4. **Distinction** *f* honorifique. **Academic honours,** distinctions académiques. **To carry off the honours,** remporter la palme. *Sch:* **Honours list,** palmarès *m.* 5. *Sch:* **Honours degree** = licence *f* (ès lettres, ès sciences, en droit). **To take honours in mathematics,** = obtenir sa licence de mathématiques. 6. (*a*) *Usu. pl.* **To receive s.o. with full honours,** recevoir qn avec tous les honneurs qui lui sont dus. **To do the honours (of one's house),** faire les honneurs (de sa maison). (*b*) *pl. Cards:* **Honours are even,** (i) les honneurs sont partagés; (ii) *F:* nous sommes à deux de jeu. 7. (*Of pers.*) (*a*) **To be an h. to one's country,** faire honneur à sa patrie. **An h. to his native town,** la gloire de sa ville natale. (*b*) **Your H., his H.,** Monsieur le juge, Monsieur le président. 8. *Com:* **Acceptance for h.,** acceptation *f* par honneur, sous protêt; intervention *f* à protêt.
honour², *v.tr.* 1. (*a*) Honorer. **I h. you for it,** cela vous fait honneur. (*b*) **To h. s.o. with one's confidence,** honorer qn de sa confiance. 2. **To h. one's signature,** faire honneur à sa signature. *Com:* **To h. a bill,** faire honneur à un effet. **honoured,** *a.* Honoré. **To bear an h. name,** porter un grand nom, un nom honorable.
honourable ['onərəbl], *a.* 1. (Conduite, famille) honorable. 2. **The H.,** *abbrev.* the Hon., l'honorable. . . . **The Hon. member for Caithness,** l'honorable membre représentant Caithness. **The Most H.,** le très honorable. **The Right H.,** le très honorable. **-ably,** *adv.* Honorablement.
hooch [hu:tʃ], *s. U.S: P:* Gnôle *f* (de contrebande).
hood [hud], *s.* 1. *Cost:* (*a*) Capuchon *m* (de moine); cagoule *f* (de pénitent); capeline *f* (de femme, d'enfant). (*b*) *Sch:* = Épitoge *f.* (*c*) *Nat.Hist:* Capuchon (de cobra). 2. (*a*) *Veh: etc:* (Folding, extensible) h., capote *f. U.S:* = BONNET 2. (*b*) *Phot:* Parasoleil *m* (d'objectif). (*c*) Hotte *f,* auvent *m* (de forge); chapeau *m* (de lampe). 3. *U.S:* = HOODLUM.
hooded ['hudid], *a.* (*a*) (*Of pers.*) Encapuchonné. (*b*) (Vêtement, fleur) à capuchon.
hoodlum ['hu:dləm], *s. U.S: P:* Voyou *m,* chenapan *m.*
hoodoo ['hu:du:], *s.* (*Of pers., thing*) Porteur, -euse de malheur, *F:* de guigne.
hoodwink ['hudwiŋk], *v.tr. F:* Tromper, donner le change à (qn).
hoof¹, *pl.* **-s, hooves** [hu:f, -s, hu:vz], *s.* (*a*) Sabot *m* (de cheval). **Beef on the h.,** bétail *m* sur pied. (*b*) *F:* Pied *m.*
hoof², *v.tr. & i. P:* 1. **To h. (it),** aller à pied, à pattes. 2. *v.tr.* **To h. s.o. out,** chasser qn à coups de pied.
hoofed [hu:ft], *a. Z:* Ongulé; à sabots.
hoo-ha ['hu:ha], *s. F:* **What's (all) the h.-h. about?** qu'est-ce qu'il y a de cassé? qu'est-ce qui se passe?
hook¹ [huk], *s.* 1. Crochet *m,* croc *m* griffe *f.* (*a*) **Chimney h.,** crémaillère *f.* **Hat and coat h.,** patère *f.* **H. nail,** (i) clou *m* à croc, à crochet; (ii) clou barbelé. (*b*) **Bench h.,** crochet d'établi. *Mec.E:* **Pawl h.,** croc à déclic. *Av: Nav:* **Arrester h.,** crosse *f* d'appontage. **Catapulting h.,** crochet de catapultage. *F:* **By h. or (by) crook,** d'une manière ou d'une autre. *S.a.* BOAT-HOOK. (*c*) *Cost:* Agrafe *f.* **H. and eye,** agrafe et œillet *m*; crochet et porte *f.* (*d*) **H. and**

hinge, gond *m* et penture *f.* 2. (Fish-)h., hameçon *m.* Blind h., hameçon sans œillet. *F:* To swallow sth. h. line and sinker, gober le morceau. 3. (Reaping-)h., faucille *f.* 4. (*a*) *Box:* Right h., left h., crochet du droit, du gauche. (*b*) *Golf:* Cr: Coup tourné à gauche; *Golf:* coup tiré. 5. Cap *m*; pointe *f* de terre. 6. *P:* To sling, take, one's h., décamper; plier bagage. 'hook-ladder, *U.S:* 'hook-and-ladder, *s. Fire-Fighting:* Échelle *f* à crochets, de sauvetage, à incendie. 'hook-nose, *s.* 1. Nez crochu. 2. Nez busqué, aquilin.

hook², *v.tr.* 1. Courber (le doigt). 2. To h. sth. (on, up) to sth., accrocher qch. à qch. *El.E: W.Tel: etc:* Assembler (les pièces d'un appareil); brancher (la radio). *F:* I hooked my arm in his, je lui ai pris le bras. 3. To h. up a curtain, agrafer un rideau. Dress that hooks up at the back, robe qui s'agrafe par derrière. 4. Crocher, gaffer (un objet flottant). 5. (*a*) *Fish:* Prendre (un poisson) à l'hameçon; accrocher, hameçonner (un poisson). (*b*) *F:* Amorcer, attraper (un mari, etc.). 6. *P:* To h. it, filer, décamper. 'hook-up, *s. T.V: W.Tel:* Conjugaison *f* de postes émetteurs (pour une émission spéciale). hooked, *a.* 1. Crochu, recourbé. 2. Muni de crochets, d'hameçons.

hookah ['hukə], *s.* Narguilé *m.*

hooker ['hukər], *s. Rugby Fb:* Talonneur *m.*

hookey ['huki], *s. Esp: U.S: F:* To play h., faire l'école buissonnière; prendre la clef des champs.

hooligan ['hu:ligən], *s.* Voyou *m*; gouape *f.*

hooliganism ['hu:ligənizm], *s.* Voyouterie *f.*

hoop¹ [hu:p], *s.* 1. (*a*) Cercle *m* (de tonneau). (*b*) Cercle, cerceau *m* (de mât, etc.); frette *f* (de pieu); virole *f* (de moyeu, etc.) (*c*) Jante *f*, bandage *m* (de roue). 2. Cerceau (d'enfant, de cirque). To trundle, drive, a h., faire courir, faire rouler, un cerceau. 3. (*Half-hoop*) (*a*) Cerceau (de tente de voiture, etc.). (*b*) *Croquet:* Arceau *m*, arche *f.* 'hoop-iron, *s.* Fer feuillard; fer plat. 'hoop-net, *s.* (*For fish*) Truble *f*, verveux *m*, pantène *f*, pantenne *f*; (*for birds*) nasse *f.*

hoop², *v.tr.* (*a*) *Coop:* Cercler (un tonneau). (*b*) Fretter, cercler (un canon, un mât, etc.).

hoop³,⁴, *int., s., & v.i.* = WHOOP¹,².

hoop-la ['hu:plɑ:], *s.* 1. (*At fairs*) Jeu *m* des anneaux. 2. (*Esp. U.S:*) *F:* Brouhaha joyeux, tapage *m, F:* boucan *m.*

hoopoe ['hu:pou], *s. Orn:* Huppe *f.*

hoosegow ['hu:s'gau], *s. U.S: P:* Prison *f; P:* violon *m*, taule *f*, tôle *f.*

hoot¹ [hu:t], *s.* 1. Ululation *f*, (h)ululement *m* (de hibou). 2. (*Of pers.*) Huée *f.* 3. (*a*) *Aut:* Cornement *m*, klaxonnement *m.* (*b*) Coup *m* de sirène (de bateau).

hoot². 1. *v.i.* (*a*) (*Of owl*) (H)ululer, huer. (*b*) (*Of pers.*) Huer. To h. after s.o., conspuer qn. (*c*) *Aut:* Corner; (*of driver*) donner un coup de klaxon, klaxonner. (*d*) (*Of siren*) Mugir; (*of ship*) lancer un coup de sirène. 2. *v.tr.* Huer, conspuer (qn); siffler (une pièce de théâtre). To h. s.o. down, faire taire qn (par des huées). To h. a play off the stage, faire tomber une pièce. hooting, *s.* 1. (H)ululement *m* (de hibou). 2. (*Of pers.*) Huées *fpl.* 3. (*a*) *Aut:* Cornement *m*; coups *mpl* de klaxon. (*b*) Mugissement *m* (d'une sirène).

hootch [hu:tʃ], *s.* = HOOCH.

hooter ['hu:tər], *s.* 1. *Nau: Ind:* Sirène *f*; sifflet *m.* 2. *Aut:* Avertisseur *m*; klaxon *m.*

Hoover¹ ['hu:vər], *s. R.t.m:* Aspirateur-batteur *m* Hoover; *F:* aspirateur *m.*

hoover², *v.tr.* Passer l'aspirateur (sur qch.).

hooves [hu:vz], *s.pl. See* HOOF¹.

hop¹ [hɔp], *s. Bot:* Houblon *m.* 'hop-field, -garden, *s.* Houblonnière *f.* 'hop-grower, *s.* Houblonnier *m.* 'hop-kiln, *s.* Four *m* à houblon. 'hop-picker, *s.* Cueilleur, -euse, de houblon. 'hop-picking, *s.* Cueillette *f* du houblon. *F:* 1. Perche *f* à houblon. 2. *F:* (*Pers.*) Grande perche.

hop², *v.* (hopped [hɔpt]; hopping) 1. *v.tr.* Houblonner (la bière). 2. *v.i.* Cueillir le houblon. To go hopping, faire la cueillette du houblon. 3. *U.S: P:* To be hopped up, être sous l'influence d'un stupéfiant, *F:* dopé, *P:* gonflé à bloc.

hop³, *s.* 1. (*a*) Petit saut; sautillement *m.* (*b*) Saut à cloche-pied. He went off with a h., skip and a jump, il s'en alla en gambadant. *F:* To catch s.o. on the h., prendre qn au pied levé. (*c*) *Av:* Flight in five hops, voyage avec quatre escales, en cinq étapes. 2. *F:* (*Dance*) Sauterie *f*; bal *m* musette.

hop⁴. (hopped) 1. *v.i.* (*a*) Sauter, sautiller. To h. away, (i) s'éloigner à cloche-pied; (ii) (*of sparrow*) s'éloigner en sautillant. *F:* To h. off, filer; ficher le camp. (*b*) To h. over a ditch, sauter un fossé. *F:* To h. over to Paris, ne faire qu'un saut jusqu'à Paris. To h. out of bed, sauter à bas de son lit. 2. *v.tr. F:* Sauter (un obstacle). *P:* To h. it, filer; ficher le camp; se débiner. H. it! allez, ouste! allez hop! va-t'en! 3. *U.S: P:* To h. a ride, a train, voyager (en chemin de fer) sans payer. 'hop-off, *s. U.S: Av: F:* Décollage *m.* hopping, *s.* Sautillement *m*, sauts *mpl.* 'Hop-o'-my-'thumb. *Pr.n.* Le Petit Poucet.

hope¹ [houp], *s.* 1. (*a*) Espérance *f*, espoir *m.* To be full of h., avoir bon espoir. Past all h., perdu sans espoir. To put one's h. in the future, compter sur l'avenir. To set all one's hopes on s.o., mettre tout son espoir en qn. *Geog:* The Cape of Good H., le cap de Bonne Espérance. (*b*) In the h. of . . ., dans l'attente de . . ., dans l'espoir de. . . . To be, live, in h. of doing sth., avoir l'espoir de faire qch. 2. He is the h. of his country, il est l'espoir de son pays. My last h., ma dernière planche de salut. *S.a.* FORLORN 1. To have hopes of sth., of doing sth., avoir qch. en vue; avoir l'espoir de faire qch. To live, be, in hopes that . . ., caresser l'espoir, avoir l'espoir, que. . . . *Iron:* P: What a h.! si vous comptez là-dessus! 'hope chest, *s. U.S:* Trousseau *m.*

hope². 1. *v.i.* Espérer. To h. against hope, espérer contre toute espérance. To h. for sth., espérer qch. Hoped-for victory, victoire attendue. To h. in God, mettre son espoir en Dieu. 2. *v.tr.* I h. and expect that . . ., j'espère avec confiance que. . . . I only h. you may get it! je vous en souhaite! *Corr:* Hoping to hear from you, dans l'espoir de vous lire. You've done your work, I hope? tu as fait ton travail, au moins?

hopeful ['houpful], *a.* 1. Plein d'espoir. To be h. that . . ., avoir bon espoir que. . . . 2. (*a*) (*Aviner*) qui donne de belles espérances, qui promet. A h. lad, un garçon plein d'avenir. (*b*) The situation looks more h., la situation s'annonce meilleure. 3. *s. F:* (*Usu. Iron:*) The young h., l'espoir de la famille. Young h. was spending a lot of money, le fils à papa dépensait pas mal d'argent. -fully, *adv.* (Travailler, etc.) avec bon espoir, avec confiance.

hopefulness ['houpfulnis], *s.* 1. Bon espoir; confiance *f.* 2. Bons indices (de la situation, etc.).

hopeless ['houplis], *a.* 1. Sans espoir; désespéré. 2. (*a*) Qui ne permet aucun espoir; (maladie, etc.) incurable; (situation) désespérée, sans issue. It's a h. job, c'est désespérant. To give sth. up as h., renoncer à faire qch. (*b*) H. drunkard, ivrogne incorrigible. -ly, *adv.* 1. (Vivre) sans espoir; (regarder qn) avec désespoir. 2. (Vaincu) irrémédiablement. H. drunk, soûl perdu.

hopelessness ['houplisnis], *s.* État désespéré.

hophead ['hɔphed], *s. U.S: P:* Toxicomane *mf*; drogué *m; P:* camé *m.*

hopper¹ ['hɔpər], *s.* 1. Sauteur, -euse. 2. Trémie *f*, huche *f*, hotte *f* (de moulin). 3. *Nau:* H.(-barge), marie-salope *f*, *pl.* maries-salopes; chaland *m* à vase. *Rail:* H. car, wagon *m* tombereau.

hopper², *s. F:* = HOP-PICKER.

hopscotch ['hɔpskɔtʃ], *s. Games:* La marelle.

horde [hɔːd], *s.* Horde *f.*

horehound ['hɔːhaund], *s. Bot:* Marrube *m.*

horizon [hə'raiz(ə)n], *s.* Horizon *m.* On the h., à l'horizon. *Av:* Artificial h., horizon gyroscopique.

horizontal ['hɔri'zɔnt(ə)l], *a.* Horizontal, -aux. -ally, *adv.* Horizontalement.

horizontality [,hɔrizɔn'tæliti], *s.* Horizontalité *f.*

hormonal [hɔː'moun(ə)l], *a. Physiol: Med:* Hormonal.

hormone ['hɔːmoun], *s. Physiol:* Hormone *f.*

hormonotherapy [,hɔːmounou'θerəpi], *s. Med:* Hormonothérapie *f.*

horn H : 27 **hospital**

horn [hɔːn], s. 1. (a) Corne f. Horns of a stag, bois m
d'un cerf. (Of stag) To shed, cast, its horns, muer.
(b) Nat.Hist: Antenne f (de cerf-volant); corne, F:
antenne (d'un limaçon). F: To draw in one's horns,
(i) rentrer les cornes; (ii) rabattre (de) ses prétentions; en rabattre. (c) Corne (d'un croissant);
antenne (de mine sous-marine). (d) On the horns of
a dilemma, enfermé dans un dilemme. 2. (Horny
matter) Corne. H. comb, peigne en corne. 3. Mus:
(a) Cor m. French h., cor d'harmonie. Hunting h.,
cor, trompe f, de chasse. Coach h., buccin m de mail-
coach. (b) English h. (tenor oboe), cor anglais. 4.
Aut: Avertisseur m (sonore); klaxon m. To sound,
blow, one's h., corner, klaxonner. 5. A: Drinking h.,
corne à boire. H. of plenty, corne d'abondance.
Cu: Cream h., cornet m de pâtissier. 'horn-handled,
a. (Couteau) à manche de corne. 'horn-owl, s. Orn:
Duc m. Great h.-o., grand-duc m, pl. grands-ducs.
'horn-player, s. Mus: Corniste m, cor m. 'horn-
rimmed, a. (Lunettes) à monture en corne.
hornbeam ['hɔːnbiːm], s. Bot: Charme m; hêtre
blanc.
hornbill ['hɔːnbil], s. Orn: Calao m.
hornblende ['hɔːnblend], s. Miner: Hornblende f.
horned ['hɔːnid, 'hɔːnd], a. (a) (Animal) à cornes,
encorné, cornu. (b) Orn: H. owl, duc m. Great h.
owl, grand-duc m.
hornet ['hɔːnit], s. Ent: Frelon m. F: To bring a h.'s
nest about one's ears, donner, se fourrer, dans un
guêpier.
horniness ['hɔːninis], s. (a) Nature cornée (d'une
substance). (b) Callosité f (des mains).
hornpipe ['hɔːnpaip], s. Danc: Matelote f.
horny ['hɔːni], a. (a) Corné; en corne. (b) (Of hand,
etc.) Calleux. H.-handed, aux mains calleuses.
horology [hɔ'rɔlədʒi], s. 1. Horlogerie f. 2. Horo-
métrie f.
horoscope ['hɔrəskoup], s. Horoscope m. To cast
s.o.'s h., tirer l'horoscope de qn.
horrible ['hɔrəbl], a. Horrible, affreux. -ibly, adv.
Horriblement, affreusement.
horrid ['hɔrid], a. 1. Horrible, affreux. 2. F: To be
h. to s.o., être méchant envers qn. Don't be h.! (i)
ne dites pas des horreurs pareilles! (ii) ne faites pas
le vilain! You h. thing! oh, le vilain! oh, la vilaine!
-ly, adv. 1. Affreusement. 2. F: Méchamment,
abominablement.
horrific [hɔ'rifik], a. Horrifique.
horrify ['hɔrifai], v.tr. (a) Horrifier (qn); faire
horreur à (qn). (b) F: Scandaliser (qn). To be
horrified, être saisi, pénétré, d'horreur. horrifying,
a. Horrifiant; horripilant.
horror ['hɔrər], s. 1. Horreur f. To have a h. of s.o.,
of sth., of doing sth., avoir horreur de qn, de qch., de
faire qch. H. film, film m d'épouvante. 2. (a) Chose
horrible, affreuse; horreur. Chamber of Horrors,
Chambre f des Horreurs (d'un musée). (b) F: To
have the horrors, grelotter de peur. It gives me the
horrors, cela me donne le frisson; ça me met les
nerfs en pelote. (c) F: (Of child) A little h., un petit
diable. 'horror-stricken, -struck, a. Saisi d'horreur;
pénétré, glacé, frappé, d'horreur.
hors concours ['ɔːkɔŋ'kuər], prep. phr. Hors concours.
hors-d'œuvre [ɔː'dəːvr], s. (pl. hors-d'œuvres) Cu:
Hors-d'œuvre m inv.
horse [hɔːs], s. 1. Cheval m, -aux. (a) Draught-h.,
cheval de trait. To mount, get on, a h., monter,
enfourcher, un cheval. To h.! à cheval! To fall off
one's h., faire une chute de cheval. F: To ride the
high h., to get on one's high h., monter sur ses grands
chevaux. S.a. ONE-HORSE. To talk h., parler chevaux;
parler courses. Prov: It's a good h. that never
stumbles, il n'y a si bon cheval qui ne bronche. To
back the wrong h., miser sur le mauvais cheval. To
eat like a h., manger comme un loup. That's a h. of
another colour, ça c'est une autre paire de manches.
(b) Breed: Cheval entier. To take a mare to h., faire
couvrir une jument. (c) Nau: White horses, vagues
f à crêtes d'écume; moutons m. 2. Coll. Mil:
Cavalerie f; troupes montées. Light h., cavalerie
légère. 3. (a) Wooden h., (i) (toy) cheval de bois; (ii)
Ind: chevalet m de montage. (b) Gym: (Vaulting)
h., cheval de bois; cheval d'arçons. (c) = HORSE-

POWER. 4. Towel h., porte-serviette(s) m inv (mobile).
Clothes h., séchoir m. 'horse-artillery, s. Artillerie
montée. 'horse-block, s. Montoir m. 'horse-box,
s. (a) Rail: Wagon m à chevaux. (b) Veh: Fourgon
m (pour le transport des chevaux); van m. 'horse-
breaker, s. Dresseur m de chevaux. 'horse-
butcher, s. Boucher m chevalin. H.-butcher's,
boucherie chevaline. 'horse-chestnut, s. 1. Marron
m d'Inde. 2. (Tree) Marronnier m d'Inde. 'horse-
cloth, s. Couverture f de cheval. 'horse-coper,
-dealer, s. Maquignon m. 'horse-doctor, s. F:
Vétérinaire m. 'horse-drawn, a. (Véhicule) hippo-
mobile. 'horse(-)flesh, s. 1. Viande f de cheval;
boucherie chevaline. 2. Coll: Horses mpl. To be
a judge of h., s'y connaître en chevaux. 'horse-fly,
s. Ent: 1. Taon m. 2. Œstre m. 'horse-gear, s.
Manège m (actionnant une machine). horse-girl,
sf. F: Palefrenière. 'Horse Guards, s.pl. The
(Royal) H. G., la Garde du corps (à cheval). 'horse-
hide, s. Peau f, cuir m, de cheval. 'horse-laugh,
-laughter, s. Gros rire bruyant. 'horse-marines,
s.pl. Hum: He's in the h.-m., c'est un amiral suisse.
'horse-opera, s. U.S: Cin: etc: Western m.
'horse-path, s. = BRIDLE-PATH. 'horse-ristol, s.
Pistolet m d'arçon. 'horse(-)play, s. Jeu brutal, jeu
de main(s). 'horse-pond, s. Abreuvoir m. 'horse(-)
power, s. (Abbr. h.p.) Mec: (i) Puissance f en
chevaux; (ii) Meas: cheval-vapeur m (britannique =
1,0139 ch.-v. français). A twelve h.-p. car, une automobile de douze chevaux; F: une douze chevaux.
'horse-race, s. Course f de chevaux. 'horse-
racing, s. Hippisme m; courses fpl de chevaux.
'horse-radish, s. Bot: Raifort m. 'horse-sense,
s. F: Gros bon sens. 'horse-show, s. Concours m
hippique. 'horse-tail, s. 1. Queue f de cheval. 2.
Bot: Prêle f (des marais). 'horse-trade, s. U.S:
Maquignonnage m. 'horse-trough, s. Abreuvoir m;
auge f (à chevaux).
horseback ['hɔːsbæk], s. On h., à (dos de) cheval. O:
A beggar on h., un parvenu. Cu: Angels on h.,
friture f d'huîtres au lard.
horsehair ['hɔːshɛər], s. Crin m (de cheval).
horseman, pl. -men ['hɔːsmən], s.m. Cavalier, écuyer.
horsemanship ['hɔːsmənʃip], s. Équitation f; hippo-
techr ie f; talent m d'écuyer.
horseshoe ['hɔːsʃuː], s. (a) Fer m à cheval. (b) attrib.
(Table, etc.) à fer à cheval.
horsewhip¹ ['hɔːswip], s. Cravache f.
horsewhip², v.tr. (horsewhipped) Cravacher, sangler
(qn). horsewhipping, s. Cravachée f.
horsewoman, pl. -women ['hɔːswumən, -wimin], s.f.
Amazone, cavalière, écuyère.
horsiness ['hɔːsinis], s. (Of pers.) Hippomanie f;
affectation f du genre jockey, du genre palefrenier.
horsy ['hɔːsi], a. (Of pers.) Hippomane; qui affecte le
langage, le costume, des grooms et des jockeys.
horticultural [hɔːti'kʌltʃ(ə)r(ə)l], a. (Outil) horticole.
H. show, exposition d'horticulture, horticole.
horticulture ['hɔːtikʌltʃər], s. Horticulture f.
horticulturist ['hɔːti'kʌltʃərist], s. Horticulteur m.
hose¹ [houz], s. 1. Coll. pl. (a) A: (i) Chausses fpl. (ii)
Haut-de-chausses m, pl. hauts-de-chausses. (b) Com:
Bas mpl. 2. (pl. hoses) Manche f à eau; tuyau m.
Rubber h., tuyau en caoutchouc. 'hose-pipe, s.
Tuyau m (de lavage, d'incendie, etc.). 'hose-reel, s.
Hort: Tambour-dévidoir m, dévidoir m.
hose², v.tr. 1. Laver (qch.) à grande eau. To h. (down)
the car, laver la voiture. 2. Arroser. To h. the lawn,
arroser le gazon (au jet d'eau).
hosier ['houʒiər], s. Bonnetier, -ière.
hosiery ['houʒiəri], s. Bonneterie f.
hospice ['hɔspis], s. 1. A: Hospice m (pour voyageurs). 2. Hospice; maison f de charité; asile m
(pour vieillards, etc.).
hospitable ['hɔspitəbl], a. Hospitalier; accueillant. -ably,
adv. Hospitalièrement; d'une manière accueillante.
hospital ['hɔspitl], s. 1. Hôpital m, -aux. Isolation
h., hôpital m d'isolement. Patient in h., hospitalisé,
-ée. O: (Of medical student) To walk the hospitals,
assister aux leçons cliniques; faire les hôpitaux. H.
nurse, infirmière f. H. train, train sanitaire. H. ship,
navire hôpital. 2. (a) Hist: Hospice m (des hospitaliers). (b) Occ: Asile m, hospice.

hospitalization [ˌhɔspitlaiˈzeiʃ(ə)n], s. Hospitalisation f (des malades).
hospitalize [ˈhɔspitlaiz], v.tr. Hospitaliser.
hospitality [ˌhɔspiˈtæliti], s. Hospitalité f. **To show s.o. h.**, héberger qn; faire à qn un accueil hospitalier.
hospital(l)er [ˈhɔspitələr], s. Hist: Hospitalier m. **Knights Hospitallers**, chevaliers hospitaliers.
host[1] [houst], s. (a) A. & Poet: Armée f. **The Lord God of Hosts**, le Dieu des armées. (b) O: **A (whole) h. of servants**, (tõute) une foule, (toute) une armée, de domestiques. **A h. of gnats**, une légion, une nuée, de moucherons.
host[2], s. (a) Hôte m. (b) Hôtelier m, aubergiste m. F: **To reckon without one's h.**, compter sans son hôte. (c) Biol: Hôte (porteur d'un parasite, etc.). **H.-plant**, hôte.
host[3], s. Ecc: Hostie f.
hostage [ˈhɔstidʒ], s. Otage m. **As (a) h.**, en otage, pour otage.
hostel [ˈhɔstəl], s. 1. A: Hôtellerie f. 2. (a) Pension f, foyer m (sous la direction d'une œuvre sociale); maison f universitaire. (b) **Youth Hostels**, auberges f de la jeunesse.
hosteller [ˈhɔstələr], s. (Youth) h., ajiste mf.
hostelling [ˈhɔstəliŋ], s. (Youth) h., ajisme m.
hostelry [ˈhɔstəlri], s. A. & Lit: Hôtellerie f.
hostess [ˈhoustis], s.f. (a) Hôtesse. (b) Hôtelière, aubergiste f. S.a. AIR-HOSTESS.
hostile [ˈhɔstail], a. (a) Hostile, ennemi. (b) Hostile, opposé (to, à); ennemi (to, de). **To be h. to s.o.**, être hostile à, envers, qn. -ely, adv. Hostilement.
hostility [hɔsˈtiliti], s. 1. Hostilité f (to, contre); animosité f. 2. pl. **Hostilities**, hostilités; état m de guerre.
hot[1] [hɔt], a. (hotter) 1. (a) Chaud. **Boiling h.**, (tout) bouillant. **Burning h.**, brûlant. **To be very h.**, (of thg) être très chaud; (of pers.) avoir très chaud; (of weather) faire très chaud. **To get h.**, (i) (of thg) devenir chaud; chauffer; (ii) (of weather) commencer à faire chaud; (iii) (of pers., contest) s'échauffer. **H. fire**, feu vif. **To be in h. water**, être dans le pétrin, dans l'embarras. **To get into h. water**, s'attirer, se créer, des ennuis. **To let off h. air**, parler pour ne rien dire, raconter des balivernes f. **It was h. work**, on s'y échauffait. **To blow h. and cold**, (i) souffler le chaud et le froid; (ii) parler, agir, de façons contra-dictoires. F: **To get all h. and bothered**, s'échauffer; se faire du mauvais sang. **To go h. and cold all over**, avoir le frisson. (b) Brûlant, cuisant. **H. tears**, larmes cuisantes. (c) (Poivre) cuisant; (moutarde) piquante; (assaisonnement) épicé. F: **He's h. stuff at tennis**, au tennis c'est un as. U.S: **H. spot**, boîte f de nuit. **H. music**, le jazz, le swing. (d) Atom.Ph: Radio-actif. **H. laboratory**, laboratoire m de re-cherches radio-actives. 2. (a) **News h. from the press**, nouvelles sortant tout droit de la presse. Pol: **H. line, telephone**, (i) ligne f, téléphone m, rouge (U.S.A. to Kremlin); (ii) ligne verte, téléphone vert (Elysée to Kremlin). (b) Ven: **H. trail**, voie chaude. **To be h. on the scent, on the trail**, être sur la bonne piste. Games: **You are getting h.**, tu brûles. 3. (a) Violent. **To have a h. temper**, s'emporter facilement. (b) Acharné. **H. contest**, chaude dispute. **At the hottest of the fray**, au plus fort du combat. **To be in h. pur-suit of s.o.**, presser qn de près. Adv.phr. **They went at it h. and strong**, ils y allaient avec acharnement, de toutes leurs forces. Turf: **H. favourite**, grand favori. F: **H. tip**, tuyau m increvable. 4. **To make a place too h. for s.o.**, rendre la situation intenable à qn (dans un endroit). **To make things too h. for s.o.**, rendre la vie intolérable, intenable, à quelqu'un. P: **H. car**, voiture volée. **To give it (to) s.o. h.**, laver la tête à qn; semoncer qn d'importance. **We are going to have a h. time**, il va y avoir du grabuge; ça va chauffer. 5. Fin: **H. money**, capitaux flottants. -ly, adv. 1. (Répondre, protester) vivement, avec chaleur. 2. (Poursuivi) avec acharnement, de près. **'hot-'blooded**, a. Emporté, ardent, passionné. **'hot dog**, s. Petit pain fourré d'une saucisse chaude. **'hot-'foot**, adv. A toute vitesse, en (toute) hâte; précipitamment. **'hot-'headed**, a. 1. Exalté, impétueux. 2. Emporté, violent; qui a la tête près du bonnet. **'hot-plate**, s. Dom.Ec: 1. Chauffe-

assiette(s) m. 2. Plaque chauffante. **'hot-pot**, s. Cu: Hochepot m. **'hot-press**, s. Calandre f. **'hot rod**, s. U.S: Aut: P: Bolide f (de course). **'hot-spot**, s. I.C.E: 1. Point m d'inflammation. 2. Réchauffeur m (des gaz). **'hot-'tempered**, a. Colérique; em-porté, vif. **hot-'water bottle**, s. (a) Bouillotte f (en caoutchouc, etc.). (b) Cruchon m.
hot[2], v.tr. F: **To h. sth. up**, (i) chauffer qch.; (ii) faire réchauffer (du potage etc.). **The cold war is hotting up**, la guerre froide se réchauffe. Aut: F: **Hotted-up engine**, moteur gonflé.
hotbed [ˈhɔtbed], s. 1. Hort: Couche f (de fumier). 2. **H. of corruption**, foyer (ardent) de corruption.
hotchpotch [ˈhɔtʃpɔtʃ], s. 1. Cu: Hochepot m, salmi-gondis m. **Vegetable h.**, macédoine f de légumes. 2. F: Mélange confus; méli-mélo m.
hotel [houˈtel], s. 1. Hôtel m (pour voyageurs). **H. de luxe**, palace m. **Private h.**, hôtel de famille. **Residential h.**, pension f de famille, pension bour-geoise. **H.-keeper**, hôtelier, -ière. 2. attrib. a. **The h. trade**, l'industrie hôtelière.
hotelier [(h)ouˈtelie], s. Hôtelier m.
hothead [ˈhɔthed], s. (Pers.) Tête chaude; impétueux, -euse.
hothouse [ˈhɔthaus], s. Serre chaude. **H. plant**, (i) plante de serre chaude; (ii) F: personne qui pense toujours à sa petite santé. **H. grapes**, raisin m de serre.
hotness [ˈhɔtnis], s. 1. Chaleur f, fougue f (des passions, du tempérament, etc.). 2. Force f (d'un assaisonne-ment).
hound[1] [haund], s. Chien m de meute, chien courant. **The (pack of) hounds**, la meute, l'équipage m. **Master of hounds**, maître d'équipage. **To ride to hounds**, chasser à courre. S.a. HARE[1] 1. F: A: (Of pers.) **You miserable h.!** misérable! Tex: **H.'s-tooth check**, pied-de-poule m.
hound[2], v.tr. 1. **To h. s.o. down**, poursuivre qn avec acharnement, sans relâche; traquer qn. **Hounded from place to place**, pourchassé d'un lieu à l'autre. 2. **To h. the dogs on**, exciter les chiens à la poursuite.
hour [ˈauər], s. Heure f. 1. **An h. and a half**, une heure et demie. **Half an h.**, une demi-heure. **A quarter of an h.**, un quart d'heure. **H. by h.**, d'heure en heure. **To pay s.o. by the h.**, payer qn à l'heure. **Five miles an h.**, cinq milles à l'heure. Ind: **Output per h.**, puissance horaire. F: **To take hours over sth.**, mettre un temps interminable à faire qch. **Eight-hour day**, journée f de huit heures. **Office hours**, heures de bureau. **After hours**, après l'heure de fermeture. **To work long hours**, faire de longues journées (de travail). 2. (a) **At the h. stated**, à l'heure dite. O: **At the h. of seven**, à sept heures. **The questions of the h.**, les questions de l'heure (actuelle); les actualités f. **In the h. of need**, à l'heure du besoin. **In a happy h.**, à un moment heureux. **The h. has come**, le moment est venu; il est l'heure. (b) **In the small hours (of the morning)**, fort avant dans la nuit. **To keep late hours**, (i) rentrer à des heures indues; (ii) veiller tard. (c) Ecc: **Book of Hours**, livre d'heures. **'hour-glass**, s. Sablier m. **'hour-hand**, s. Petite aiguille (de montre, de pendule).
hourly [ˈauəli]. 1. a. (a) De toutes les heures; (service de trains, etc.) à chaque heure. (b) (Rendement) par heure, à l'heure; (salaire) à l'heure. (c) De chaque instant. **His h. dread of death**, sa crainte perpétuelle de la mort. 2. adv. (a) Toutes les heures; d'heure en heure. (b) **We expect him h.**, nous l'attendons d'un moment à l'autre.
house[1], pl. -ses [haus, ˈhauziz], s. 1. Maison f, logis m, demeure f. **Town h.**, hôtel (particulier). **Country h.**, château m; maison de campagne. **Small h.**, maison-nette f. **Private h.**, maison particulière. **At, to, in, my h.**, chez moi. **To keep (to) the h.**, rester chez soi; garder la maison. **To keep h. for s.o.**, tenir le ménage de qn; tenir, diriger, la maison de qn. **To keep h. together**, faire ménage ensemble. **To set up h.**, entrer, se mettre, en ménage. **To move h.**, déménager. **To keep a good h.**, vivre bien; faire bonne chère. **To keep open h.**, tenir table ouverte. **H. of cards**, château de cartes. Attrib. **H. telephone**, téléphone intérieur. **H. coal**, charbon de ménage. S.a. DOG[1] 1. 2. (a) **The h. of G.**, la maison de Dieu. **H. of prayer**,

église *f*, temple *m*. **The H. of Commons,** la Chambre des Communes. (*b*) **Business h.,** maison de commerce. (*c*) *F:* **The H.** (i) *Parl:* La Chambre des Communes ou des Lords. **Bill before the H.,** loi en cours de vote. **To make a h.,** réunir le quorum. (ii) *Fin:* La Bourse. (*d*) *Sch:* = BOARDING-HOUSE 2. (*e*) **Public h.,** café *m*, cabaret *m*, débit *m* de boissons. **To have a drink on the h.,** prendre une consommation aux frais du cabaretier, de la maison. 3. (*a*) **Coach h.,** remise *f*. **Fowl-h.,** poulailler *m*. *S.a.* GATE-HOUSE, GLASS-HOUSE, *etc*. (*b*) *Tchn:* Cabine *f*, guérite *f* (d'une grue). *Nau:* Rouf *m* (sur le pont); kiosque *m* (de la barre, etc.). (*c*) *Com: Ind:* Salle *f*, bâtiment *m*. *S.a.* COUNTING-HOUSE. 4. (*a*) (*Members of household*) Maison, *F:* maisonnée *f*. (*b*) Famille *f*, maison, dynastie *f*. **The H. of Bourbon,** les Bourbons *m*, la Maison des Bourbons 5. *Th:* Auditoire *m*, assistance *f*. **A good h.,** une salle pleine. **To play to an empty h.,** jouer devant les banquettes. *Cin:* **The first h.,** la première séance. ʼhouse-agency, *s.* Agence immobilière. ʼhouse-agent, *s.* Courtier *m* en immeubles; agent immobilier. ʼhouse-arrest, *s.* **Under h.-a.,** en résidence surveillée. ʼhouse-boat, *s.* Péniche (aménagée en habitation). ʼhouse-charge, *s.* (*Au restaurant*) Couvert *m*. ʼhouse-flag, *s. Nau:* Pavillon *m* de compagnie. ʼhouse-fly, *s.* Mouche *f* domestique. ʼhouse-party, *s.* Les invités réunis dans une maison de campagne. ʼhouse-phyʼsician, *s.* Interne *m* en médecine (d'un hôpital). ʼhouse-porter, *s.* Concierge *m*. ʼhouse-property, *s.* Immeubles *mpl*. ʼhouse-room, *s.* Place *f* (pour loger qn, qch.); logement *m*. ʼhouse-shoe, *s.* Chaussure *f* d'intérieur. ʼhouse-surgeon, *s.* Interne *m* en chirurgie (d'un hôpital). ʼhouse-to-house, *attrib.a.* = door to door, *q.v. under* DOOR 1. ʼhouse-top, *s.* Toit *m*. *F:* **To proclaim sth. from the h.-tops,** crier qch. sur les toits. ʼhouse-train, *v.tr.* Dresser (un chiot, un enfant) (aux habitudes de propreté domestique). ʼhouse-trained, *a.* **A h.-t. puppy,** un chiot dressé (à la propreté). ʼhouse-warming, *s.* Pendaison *f* de la crémaillère. **To have a h.-w.** (party), pendre la crémaillère.

house² [hauz], *v.tr.* (*a*) Loger, héberger (qn); pourvoir au logement de (la population). (*b*) Faire rentrer (les troupeaux); rentrer, engranger (le blé). (*c*) Mettre à l'abri, à couvert (une locomotive, etc.); garer (une voiture); loger, caser (un ustensile). (*d*) Enchâsser (un essieu, etc.). *Nau:* Caler (un mât). **housing¹,** *s.* 1. (*a*) Logement *m*. **The h. problem, shortage,** la crise du logement. (*b*) Rentrée *f* (des troupeaux, du blé, etc.). (*c*) Mise *f* à l'abri; garage *m* (d'une auto). 2. Enchâssure *f* (d'un essieu, etc.). *Nau:* Calage *m* (d'un mât). 3. *Mch: Mech.E: etc:* Logement, bâti *m*, cage *f*; carter *m*, boîte *f*. **Chain h.,** logement de chaîne. **Flexible h.,** gaine *f* flexible.

housebreak [ʼhausbreik], *v.* 1. *v.tr. U.S:* Dresser (un chien, un enfant) (aux habitudes de propreté). 2. *v.i.* Cambrioler (une maison, etc.).

housebreaker [ʼhausbreikər], *s.* 1. Cambrioleur *m*. 2. *Const:* Démolisseur *m*. **H.'s yard,** chantier *m* de démolitions.

housebreaking [ʼhausbreikiŋ], *s.* 1. Effraction *f*, cambriolage *m*. 2. Démolition *f*.

housecoat [ʼhauskout], *s. Cost:* Peignoir *m*; robe *f* d'intérieur, déshabillé. **Quilted h.,** douillette *f*.

houseful [ʼhausful], *s.* Maisonnée *f*; pleine maison (d'invités, etc.).

household [ʼhaushould], *s.* 1. (Membres *mpl* de) la maison; le ménage; la famille. *attrib.* **H. expenses,** frais de ménage. **H. bread,** pain de ménage. *S.a.* SOAP¹. **H. gods,** dieux domestiques. **H. word,** mot d'usage courant. 2. (*a*) Les domestiques. **To have a large h.,** avoir une nombreuse domesticité. (*b*) **The h.,** la Maison du roi.

householder [ʼhaushouldər], *s.* 1. Chef *m* de famille, de maison. 2. *Adm:* (i) Propriétaire *mf*, (ii) locataire *mf* (d'une maison).

housekeeper [ʼhauski:pər], *s.* 1. Homme ou femme chargé(e) du soin d'un bâtiment; concierge *mf*. 2. Femme *f* de charge; gouvernante *f* (d'un prêtre, etc.); intendante *f* (d'un lycée etc.). 3. **My wife is a good h.,** ma femme est bonne ménagère, s'entend bien aux affaires du ménage.

housekeeping [ʼhauski:piŋ], *s.* 1. Le ménage. **To set up h.,** se mettre, entrer, en ménage. 2. Économie *f* domestique; les soins *m* du ménage. **H.-book,** carnet *m* de dépenses.

houseleek [ʼhausli:k], *s. Bot:* Joubarbe *f*.

houseless [ʼhauslis], *a*, Sans domicile, sans abri.

housemaid [ʼhausmeid], *s.f.* Bonne; femme de chambre. *F:* **H.'s knee,** épanchement *m* de synovie.

housemaster [ʼhausmɑːstər], *s.m. Sch:* (*Eng.*) Professeur chargé de la surveillance d'un internat.

housewife, *pl.* -wives. 1. *s.f.* [ʼhauswaif, -waivz], Maîtresse de maison; ménagère; femme *f* d'intérieur. 2. *s.* [ʼhʌzif, -vz] Trousse *f* de couture; nécessaire *m* à ouvrage.

housewifery [ʼhauswif(ə)ri], *s.* Économie *f* domestique; soin *m* du ménage.

housework [ʼhauswəːk], *s.* Travaux *mpl* domestiques, de ménage. **To do the h.,** faire le ménage.

housing² [ʼhauziŋ], *s. Usu. pl.* Housse *f* de cheval. Ceremonial housings, caparaçon *m*.

hove [houv]. *See* HEAVE².

hovel [ʼhɔv(ə)l], *s.* Taudis *m*, bouge *m*, masure *f*; *F:* baraque *f*, cahute *f*, bicoque *f*.

hover [ʼhɔvər], *v.i.* 1. (*Of bird, etc.*) Planer. **A smile hovered over her lips,** un sourire pointait, errait, sur ses lèvres. 2. (*Of pers.*) (*a*) **To h. about s.o.,** errer, rôder, autour de qn. (*b*) **To h. between two courses,** hésiter entre deux partis. **hovering,** *s. Av:* Vol *m* stationnaire.

hovercraft [ʼhɔvəˌkraːft], *s.* Aéroglisseur *m*.

hoverplane [ʼhɔvəplein], *s. F:* Hélicoptère *m*.

how [hau], *adv.* 1. Comment. **Tell me h. he did it,** dites-moi comment il l'a fait. **Look h. he holds his bow,** regardez de quelle façon il tient son archet. **H. are you?** comment allez-vous? **H. is it that . . .?** comment se fait-il que . . .? d'où vient que . . .? **H. so? h.'s that?** *U.S:* **h. come?** comment ça? **Mary answered him, and h.!** c'est Marie qui lui a répondu, et comment! **I see h. it is,** je vois ce qui en est. **I fail to see h. this affects you,** je ne vois pas en quoi cela vous intéresse. **H. could you!** vous n'avez pas eu honte? **To learn h. to do sth.,** apprendre à faire qch. **I know h. to swim,** je sais nager. **I enquired h. to send a postal order,** je me suis renseigné sur la manière d'envoyer un mandat. 2. (*a*) **H. much, h. many,** combien (de). **You see h. little he cares,** vous voyez combien peu il s'en soucie. **You can imagine h. angry I was,** songez si j'étais furieux! **H. wide?** de quelle largeur? **H. long is this room?** quelle est la longueur de cette pièce? **H. old are you?** quel âge avez-vous? **H. about my friends?** alors, et mes amis? *S.a.* FAR¹ 1, LONG¹ III. 1, OFTEN, SOON 1. (*b*) **H. pretty she is!** comme elle est jolie! qu'elle est jolie! **H. kind!** comme c'est aimable! **H. she has changed!** ce qu'elle a change! **You know h. I love you,** vous savez si je vous aime. **H. I wish I could!** si seulement je pouvais! **how-d'y(e)-do** [ʼhaudiˈduː], *s. F:* **Here's a (pretty) h.-d.-d.!** en voilà une affaire! en voilà du joli!

howbeit [hauˈbiːit], *adv. A:* Néanmoins; quoi qu'il en soit.

however [hauˈevər], *adv.* 1. (*a*) **H. he may do it,** de quelque manière qu'il le fasse. **H. that may be,** quoi qu'il en soit. (*b*) **H. artful she may be,** (i) si rusée qu'elle soit; (ii) toute rusée qu'elle est. **H. good his work is,** quelque excellent que soit son ouvrage. **H. much he may admire you,** si fort qu'il vous admire. **H. much money you spend,** quelque argent que vous dépensiez. **H. little,** si peu que ce soit. 2. Toutefois, cependant, d'ailleurs, pourtant. **The scheme h. failed,** pourtant le projet échoua. **If h. you don't agree,** si toutefois cela ne vous convient pas.

howitzer [ʼhauitsər], *s. Artil:* Obusier *m*.

howl¹ [haul], *s.* (*a*) Hurlement *m*; mugissement *m* (du vent). **To give a h. of rage,** pousser un hurlement de rage. (*b*) Huée *f*.

howl², *v.i. & tr.* 1. Hurler; pousser des hurlements; (*of wind*) mugir, rugir. *F:* **To h. with laughter,** rire à gorge déployée. 2. *W.Tel:* Brailler, hurler. **howl down,** *v.tr.* Faire taire (un orateur) en poussant des huées. **howling¹,** *a.* 1. Hurleur, -euse. **H. tempest,** tempête furieuse. 2. *F:* (*Intensive*) **H. mistake,** bourde *f* énorme. **H. success,** succès fou. **H. injustice,** injustice criante. **howling²,** *s.* Hurlement *m*; mugissement *m* (du vent).

howler ['haulər], s. 1. (a) Hurleur, -euse. (b) Z: (Monkey) Hurleur m. 2. F: Grosse gaffe, bourde f énorme. Schoolboy h., bourde d'écolier; bévue f risible; F: perle f.

howsoever [,hausou'evər], adv. = HOWEVER 1.

hoy [hɔi], int. Hé! ohé! holà!

hoyden ['hɔidn], s.f. Jeune fille à allures de garçon. She's a regular h., c'est un garçon manqué.

hoydenish ['hɔid(ə)niʃ], a. (Of manner, etc.) Garçon-r.ier, -ière.

hub [hʌb], s. 1. Moyeu m (de roue). 2. Centre m d'activité. The h. of the universe, le pivot, le centre, de l'univers. 'hub-cap, s. Couvre-moyeu m. Aut: Chapeau m de moyeu; enjoliveur m.

hubbub ['hʌbʌb], s. Remue-ménage m, vacarme m, tohu-bohu m. H. of voices, brouhaha m de voix.

hubby ['hʌbi], s. P: Mari m.

huckaback ['hʌkəbæk], s. H. (linen), (grosse) toile ouvrée; toile à grain d'orge.

huckleberry ['hʌklberi], s. Bot: U.S: Airelle f myrtille.

huckster¹ ['hʌkstər], s. 1. (a) A: Revendeur, -euse. (b) Colporteur m. (c) Publicitaire m. 2. Mercanti m; profiteur m. Political h., trafiquant m politique.

huckster². 1. v.i. (a) Marchander. (b) Trafiquer. 2. v.tr. (a) Revendre. (b) Colporter. (c) Faire l'article de ɕch. (d) Faire trafic de (son influence, etc.). **huckstering**, s. 1. Marchandage m. 2. Political h., politicailleries fpl.

huddle¹ ['hʌdl], s. Tas confus; fouillis m, ramassis m. A h. of roofs, un enchevêtrement de toits. A h. of people, une foule confuse. F: To go into a h., tenir une séance secrète.

huddle², v.tr. & i. 1. Entasser pêle-mêle, sans ordre. Houses huddled together in the valley, maisons serrées dans la vallée. Passengers huddled on the after-deck, passagers entassés sur l'arrière-pont. To h. together, se tasser; se serrer les uns contre les autres. 2. To h. (oneself) up, se pelotonner. Huddled (up) in bed, couché en chien de fusil. Huddled (up) in a corner, blotti dans un coin. Huddled over one's work, penché, blotti, sur son travail. 3. To h. on one's clothes, s'habiller à la hâte, à la va-vite.

hue¹ [hju:], s. Teinte f, nuance f.

hue² and cry ['hju:ən(d)'krai], s. Clameur f de haro. To raise a h. and c. against s.o., crier haro sur qn; crier tollé contre qn.

-hued [hju:d], a. (With a. prefixed, e.g.) Dark-h., light-h., de couleur foncée, claire.

huff¹ [hʌf], s. 1. To be in a h., être froissé, fâché. O: To take (the) h., s'offusquer; prendre la mouche. 2. Draughts: Soufflage m (d'un pion).

huff². 1. v.i. Souffler, haleter. 2. v.tr. (a) Froisser (qn). To be, feel, huffed, être froissé, fâché. (b) Draughts: Souffler (un pion).

huffiness ['hʌfinis], s. 1. Susceptibilité f. 2. Mauvaise humeur.

huffy ['hʌfi], a. 1. Susceptible. In a h. tone of voice, d'un ton pincé. 2. Fâché, vexé. He was very h. about it, il a très mal pris la chose. -ily, adv. Avec (mauvaise) humeur; d'un ton de dépit.

hug¹ [hʌg], s. Étreinte f. To give s.o. a h., étreindre qn.

hug², v.tr. (hugged) 1. (a) Étreindre, embrasser (qn); serrer (qn) entre ses bras, sur son cœur. (b) (Of bear) Étouffer, enserrer (sa victime). (c) Chérir (ses défauts); choyer, tenir à (un préjugé). 2. (a) Nau: To h. the shore, serrer la terre (de près); raser, ranger, longer, la côte. To h. the wind, serrer, pincer, le vent. (b) To h. the wall, raser, longer, serrer, le mur. Aut: To h. the kerb, serrer le trottoir. F: To h. the chimney-corner, se blottir au coin du feu.

huge [hju:dʒ], a. Énorme, vaste; (succès) immense, formidable, colossal, -aux. -ly, adv. Énormément; immensément.

hugeness ['hju:dʒnis], s. Énormité f, immensité f.

hugger-mugger ['hʌgəmʌgər]. 1. s. Désordre m, confusion f. To live in a h.-m. fashion, vivre dans le désordre matériel. 2. adv. En désordre, confusément, pêle-mêle.

Huguenot ['hju:gənət, -nou], s. Hist: Huguenot, -ote.

hulk [hʌlk], s. 1. Nau: (a) Carcasse f de navire; ponton m. Mooring-h., ponton d'amarrage. (b) pl. A: Hulks, bagne flottant; pontons. 2. F: (Of pers.) Gros pataud.

hulking ['hʌlkiŋ], a. Gros, lourd. Big h. creature, gros pataud.

hull¹ [hʌl], s. 1. Cosse f, gousse f (de pois, de fève); coquille f, écale f (de noix). 2. Coque f (de navire, d'hydroplane). Nau: H. down, coque noyée (sous l'horizon).

hull², v.tr. Écosser (des pois); écaler (des noix); décortiquer (le riz). Hulled barley, orge mondé. **hulling**, s. Décorticage m.

hullabaloo [,hʌləbə'lu:], s. Tintamarre m, vacarme m. To make a h., faire du vacarme.

hullo [hʌ'lou], int. (a) (Calling attention) Ohé! holà! H. you! hé, là-bas! (b) (Expressing surprise) H., old chap! tiens, c'est toi, mon vieux! H.! that's curious! tiens! tiens! c'est curieux. (c) H. everybody! salut à tous! (d) Tp: Allô!

hum¹ [hʌm], s. Bourdonnement m (d'abeille); ronflement m (de machine, de toupie); ronron m (d'un moteur); vrombissement m (d'un avion). W.Tel: Ronronnement m, ronflement. H. of conversation, brouhaha m de conversation.

hum², v. (hummed) 1. v.i. (a) (Of insect) Bourdonner; (of top) ronfler, brondir; (of aircraft) vrombir. W.Tel: Ronfler. F: To make things h., faire marcher rondement les choses. (b) (Of pers.) To h and ha(w), (i) toussoter (en commençant un discours); F: bafouiller; (ii) tourner autour du pot; barguigner. 2. v.tr. Fredonner, chantonner (un air). Mus: Hummed accompaniment, accompagnement (de voix) en sourdine; accompagnement à bouche fermée. 'humming-bird, s. Oiseau-mouche m, pl. oiseaux-mouches; colibri m.

hum³, v.i. (hummed; humming) P: Puer, empester, cocoter, fouetter.

human ['hju:mən]. 1. a. Humain. H. nature, la nature humaine. S.a. BEING² 2. 2. s. Être humain. Humans, les humains. -ly, adv. Humainement; en être humain. H. speaking, humainement parlant.

humane [hju:'mein], a. (a) Humain, compatissant. H. task, œuvre humanitaire. (b) Clément; qui évite de faire souffrir. -ly, adv. Humainement; avec humanité.

humaneness [hju:'meinnis], s. Bonté f, humanité f.

humanism ['hju:mənizm], s. Lit: Phil: Humanisme m.

humanist ['hju:mənist], s. Humaniste m.

humanitarian [hju:(:)mæni'teəriən], a. & s. Humanitaire (mf).

humanitarianism [hju:(:)mæni'teəriənizm], s. Humanitarisme m.

humanity [hju:(:)'mæniti], s. Humanité f. 1. (a) Nature humaine. (b) Le genre humain. 2. To treat s.o. with h., traiter qn avec humanité. 3. pl. Lit: Sch: The humanities, les humanités, les lettres f.

humanization [,hju:mənai'zeiʃ(ə)n], s. Humanisation f.

humanize ['hju:mənaiz], v.tr. Humaniser.

humankind ['hju:mən'kaind], s. Le genre humain.

humanness [hju:'mænnis], s. Qualité humaine (d'un animal, etc.). The h. of my dog's eyes, le regard vraiment humain de mon chien.

humble¹ ['hʌmbl], a. Humble. 1. H. prayer, humble prière. In my h. opinion, à mon humble avis. H.-hearted, au cœur humble. S.a. SERVANT 1. 2. Modeste. To spring from h. stock, être de modeste souche, d'humble extraction. -bly, adv. 1. (Parler) humblement, avec humilité. Most h., en toute humilité. 2. (Vivre) modestement. H. clad, pauvrement vêtu.

humble², v.tr. Humilier, mortifier (qn). To h. oneself, s'abaisser, F: s'aplatir (before, devant). To h. s.o.'s pride, (r)abattre, rabaisser, l'orgueil de qn.

humble-bee ['hʌmblbi:], s. Ent: = BUMBLE-BEE.

humbleness ['hʌmblnis], s. = HUMILITY.

humble pie ['hʌmbl'pai], s. F: To eat h.p., s'humilier (devant qn); se rétracter; faire amende honorable. To make s.o. eat h. p., forcer qn à se rétracter.

humbug¹ ['hʌmbʌg], s. 1. Charlatanisme m; F: blagues fpl. There's no h. about him, c'est un homme franc et sincère. (That's all) h.! tout cela c'est de la blague! balivernes! 2. (Pers.) (a) Charlatan m; blagueur m. (b) Enjôleur, -euse. 3. Comest: = Bêtise f de Cambrai.

humbug², v.tr. (humbugged) Conter des blagues à (qn); enjôler (qn); mettre (qn) dedans; mystifier (le public). Abs. Blaguer.

humdrum ['hʌmdrʌm], a. (Travail, existence) monotone; banal, -als; peu intéressant, ennuyeux. H. daily life, le train-train quotidien.

humeral ['hju:mər(ə)l], a. Anat: Huméral, -aux.

humerus, pl. -i ['hju:mərəs, -ai], s. Anat: Humérus m.

humid ['hju:mid], a. Humide; (of heat, skin) moite.

humidification [,hju(:)midifi'keiʃ(ə)n], s. Humidification f.

humidifier [hju:'midifaiər], s. Humidificateur m.

humidify [,hju(:)'midifai], v.tr. Humidifier (l'air, etc.).

humidity [hju(:)'miditi], s. Humidité f. H.-proof, résistant, étanche, à l'humidité.

humidor ['hju:midɔ:r], s. 1. Tex: Humidificateur m. 2. Boîte f à cigares (pourvue d'un humidificateur).

humiliate [hju(:)'milieit], v.tr. Humilier, mortifier. **humiliating**, a. Humiliant, mortifiant.

humiliation [hju(:),mili'eiʃ(ə)n], s. Humiliation f, affront m, mortification f.

humility [nju(:)'militi], s. Humilité f. With all h., en toute humilité.

hummock ['hʌmək], s. 1. Tertre m, mamelon m (de terre); monticule m. 2. Monticule de glace; hummock m.

humorist ['hju:mərist], s. 1. Farceur m, plaisant m. 2. (At concert) Comique m; diseur, -euse, de chansonnettes. 3. Écrivain m humoristique; humoriste m.

humorous ['hju:m(ə)rəs], a. (Of pers.) Plein d'humour; comique, drôle; (of writer) humoriste, humoristique, **-ly**, adv. Plaisamment, drôlement, comiquement, humoristiquement; plein d'humour.

humorousness ['hjum(ə)rəsnis], s. Humeur facétieuse; drôlerie f.

humour[1] ['hju:mər], s. 1. (a) A.Med: Humeur f. (b) Anat: Aqueous h., vitreous h., humeur aqueuse, vitrée (de l'œil). 2. Humeur, disposition f. To be in the h. to do sth., être en humeur de faire qch., être disposé à faire qch. Good h., bonne humeur. To be in a good, bad, h., être de bonne, de mauvaise, humeur; être bien, mal, disposé. To be in no laughing h., ne pas se sentir d'humeur à rire. To be out of h., être maussade. 3. (a) Humour m. Broad h., grosse gaieté. (b) The h. of the situation, le côté plaisant, le comique, de la situation. (c) To be lacking in h., n'avoir pas le sens de l'humour.

humour[2], v.tr. To h. s.o., se prêter aux caprices de qn; ménager qn; céder, se soumettre, aux exigences de qn. To h. s.o.'s fancy, passer une fantaisie à qn.

humourless ['hju:məlis], a. Dépourvu d'humour.

humoursome ['hju:məsəm], a. 1. Capricieux, fantasque. 2. D'humeur incertaine.

hump[1] [hʌmp], s. 1. Bosse f (de bossu, de chameau). To have a h., être bossu. 2. F: To have the h., avoir le cafard; broyer du noir. That gives me the h., cela m'embête.

hump[2], v.tr. To h. the back, arquer, bomber, le dos; faire le gros dos. To h. up one's shoulders, rentrer la tête dans les épaules. **humped**, a. (Dos, animal) bossu; (dos) voûté; (toit) en bosse.

humpback ['hʌmpbæk], s. Bossu, -ue.

humpbacked ['hʌmpbækt], a. Bossu. H. bridge, pont en dos d'âne.

humus ['hju:məs], s. Hort: Humus m; terreau m; terre végétale. **humus-bearing**, a. Humifère.

Hun [hʌn], s. Pej: Boche m.

hunch[1] [hʌnʃ], s. 1. Bosse f. 2. F: To have a h. that . . ., soupçonner que. . . .

hunch[2], v.tr. Arrondir (le dos); voûter (les épaules). To sit hunched up, se tenir accroupi le menton sur les genoux.

hunchback ['hʌn(t)ʃbæk], s. = HUMPBACK.

hunchbacked ['hʌn(t)ʃbækt], a. = HUMPBACKED.

hundred ['hʌndrəd], num. a. & s. Cent (m). A h. and one, cent un. About a h. houses, une centaine de maisons. Two h. apples, deux cents pommes. Two h. and one pounds, deux cent une livres. In nineteen h., en dix-neuf cent. To live to be a h., atteindre la centaine. They died in hundreds, in hundreds of thousands, ils mouraient par centaines, par centaines de mille. Hundreds and thousands of people, des milliers m de gens. To have nine h. a year, avoir neuf cents livres de rente. A h. per cent, cent pour cent. Com: A h. eggs, un cent d'œufs. To sell by the h., vendre au cent.

hundredfold ['hʌndrədfould]. 1. a. Centuple. 2. adv.phr. A h., cent fois autant. To be repaid a h., être payé au centuple.

hundredth ['hʌndrədθ], num.a. & s. Centième (m).

hundredweight ['hʌndrədweit], s. (a) Poids m de 112 livres, = 50 kg 802; (approx. =) quintal m. (b) U.S: Poids de 100 livres, = 45 kg 359.

hung [hʌŋ]. See HANG[2].

Hungarian [hʌŋ'gɛəriən], a. & s. Hongrois, -oise.

Hungary ['hʌŋgəri]. Pr.n. Geog: La Hongrie.

hunger[1] ['hʌŋgər], s. Faim f. H. is the best sauce, il n'est sauce que d'appétit. Pang of h., fringale f. H. for sth., ardent désir de qch.; soif f de qch. 'hunger-march, s. Marche f de la faim. 'hunger-marcher, s. Marcheur m de la faim. 'hunger-strike, s. Grève f de la faim. 'hunger-striker, s. Gréviste mf de la faim.

hunger[2], v.i. (a) Avoir faim. (b) To h. after, for, sth., être affamé de, avoir soif de, qch.; désirer ardemment qch. **hungering**, s. Faim f, soif f (after, for, de).

hungry ['hʌŋgri], a. 1. Affamé. To be, feel, h., avoir faim; sentir la faim. To remain h., rester sur sa faim. To be ravenously h., h. as a hunter, U.S: as a bear, avoir une faim de loup. To make s.o. h., donner faim à qn. To go h., souffrir de la faim. It's no use preaching to a h. man, ventre affamé n'a pas d'oreilles. To look h., avoir l'air famélique. 2. (Regard, œil) avide. **-ily**, adv. Avidement, voracement; (regarder) d'un œil avide.

hunk [hʌŋk], s. Gros morceau (de fromage); quignon m (de pain).

hunkers [hʌŋkə:z], s.pl. (Used only in) On one's h., à croupetons, accroupi.

hunks [hʌŋks], s. F: Stingy old h., vieil avare; grippe-sou m, pl. grippe-sou(s); ladre m.

hunky, pl. -ies [hʌŋki, -iz], s. U.S: P: Immigrant m de l'Europe Centrale.

hunky-dory [hʌŋki'dɔ:ri], a. U.S: F: Excellent.

hunt[1] [hʌnt], s. 1. (a) Chasse f; esp. chasse à courre, aux fauves. Tiger-h., chasse au tigre. (b) Équipage m de chasse. 2. Recherche f. There was a h. for the missing book, on cherchait le livre qui manquait.

hunt[2]. 1. v.i. (a) Ven: Chasser au chien courant; chasser à courre. (b) To h. (about) for sth., chercher (à découvrir) qch. To h. through the shops, courir les magasins. (c) (Of engine, alternator) Pomper; s'affoler par instants. 2. v.tr. (a) Chasser (le cerf, etc.). To h. whales, pêcher la baleine. (b) To h. a thief, poursuivre un voleur. (c) Parcourir, battre (un terrain). (d) To h. a horse, monter un cheval à la chasse. To h. the pack, diriger la meute. **hunt down**, v.tr. Traquer (une bête); mettre (qn) aux abois, à l'accul. **hunt out**, v.tr. Déterrer, dénicher (qch.) (à force de recherches). **hunt up**, v.tr. 1. Déterrer (des faits). 2. Aller relancer (qn). **hunting**, s. 1. (a) Chasse f (à courre). Fox-h., chasse au renard. To go h., aller à la chasse. H. knife, couteau de chasse. H. terms, termes de vénerie. (b) Bargain-h., chasse aux soldes. To go house-h., se mettre en quête d'un domicile; F: faire la chasse au logement. 2. Mch: Mouvement m de galop (de locomotive). Magn: Affolement m (de l'aiguille aimantée). 'hunting-box, s. Pavillon m de chasse. 'hunting-ground, s. 1. Terrain m de chasse. 2. A happy h.-ground for collectors (of curios), un endroit propice aux collectionneurs, un paradis pour les collectionneurs. 'hunting-horn, s. Cor m de chasse. 'hunt-the-'slipper, s. Games: Jeu m du furet.

hunter ['hʌntər], s. 1. (a) Chasseur m; tueur m (de lions, etc.). (b) Pourchasseur m (of, de). Curio-h., dénicheur m d'antiquités. 2. Cheval m de chasse. 3. (Montre f à) savonnette f.

huntress ['hʌntris], s.f. Chasseuse; Poet: chasseresse.

huntsman, pl. -men ['hʌntsmən], s.m. 1. Chasseur (à courre). 2. Veneur, piqueur.

hurdle[1] ['hə:dl], s. 1. Claie f. 2. Sp: Barrière f, obstacle m. Turf: Haie f. 'hurdle-race, s. Sp: Course f d'obstacles. Turf: Course de haies.

hurdle[2]. 1. v.tr. Garnir, entourer, (qch.) de claies. 2. v.i. Sp: Courir une course d'obstacles; Turf: courir une course de haies. **hurdling**, s. Sp: Saut m d'obstacles, de haies.

hurdler ['həːdlər], s. **1.** Fabricant m de claies. **2.** Sp: Sauteur m d'obstacles; Turf: jockey m, cheval m, de courses à obstacles.

hurdy-gurdy ['həːdigəːdi], s. **1.** A: Vielle f. **2.** F: Orgue m de Barbarie.

hurl [həːl], v.tr. Lancer (qch.) avec violence (at, contre). The explosion hurled them far and wide, l'explosion les projeta au loin. To h. oneself at s.o., se ruer sur qn. To h. oneself into the fray, se jeter à corps perdu dans la mêlée. Hurled into the chasm, précipité dans le gouffre. To h. reproaches at s.o., cribler, accabler, qn de reproches. **hurl back**, v.tr. Refouler, rejeter (l'ennemi); rétorquer (une accusation). **hurl down**, v.tr. Précipiter; jeter bas.

hurly-burly ['həːlibəːli], s. Tohu-bohu m.

Huron ['hjuərən]. **1.** a. & s. Ethn: Huron, -onne. H. country, Huronie f. **2.** Lake H., le lac Huron.

hurrah¹ [hu'rɑː], **hurray** [hu'rei], int. & s. Hourra (m). H. for the holidays! vive(nt) les vacances!

hurrah², v.i. Pousser un hourra, des hourras.

hurricane ['hʌrikən], s. Ouragan m, tornade f; Nau: tempête f; (West Indies) hurricane m. It was blowing a h., le vent soufflait en tempête. To let loose a h. of abuse, déchaîner une tornade d'injures. 'hurricane-lamp, s. Lanterne-tempête f. pl. lanternes-tempête.

hurriedness ['hʌridnis], s. Précipitation f (des préparatifs, etc.).

hurry¹ ['hʌri], s. Hâte f, précipitation f. To write in a h., écrire à la hâte. To be in a h. to do sth., avoir hâte de faire qch. To be in a h., être pressé. To be always in a h., F: avoir le feu au derrière. To be in no h., ne pas être pressé; avoir le temps. F: What's your h.? qu'est-ce qui vous presse? Is there any h.? est-ce pressé? est-ce que cela presse? There's no (special) h., rien ne presse. F: I shan't do it again in a h., on ne m'y reprendra pas de sitôt.

hurry². **1.** v.tr. (a) Hâter, presser, bousculer (qn). To h. oneself, se hâter, se dépêcher, se presser. (b) Hâter, activer (le travail). Work that cannot be hurried, travail qui demande du temps. (c) Troops were hurried to the spot, on amena au plus vite, en toute hâte, des troupes sur les lieux. **2.** v.i. (a) Se hâter, se presser; se dépêcher. To h. through, over, one's lunch, expédier son déjeuner. Don't h., ne vous pressez pas. (b) Presser le pas. To h. to a place, se rendre en toute hâte à un endroit. She hurried home, elle se dépêcha, s'empressa, de rentrer. (c) To h. into one's clothes, passer ses vêtements en toute hâte. **hurry along, 1.** v.tr. Entraîner (qn) précipitamment. **2.** v.i. Marcher d'un pas pressé. **hurry away, off. 1.** v.tr. Emmener (qn) précipitamment. **2.** v.i. Partir précipitamment. I must h. away, il faut que je me sauve. **hurry back**, v.i. Revenir à la hâte; se presser de revenir. **hurry on. 1.** v.tr. Faire hâter le pas à (qn); activer, pousser (la besogne); presser (le départ de qn). **2.** v.i. Presser le pas; continuer sa route à vive allure. **hurry out**, v.i. Sortir vivement, précipitamment. **hurry up**, v.i. Se dépêcher, se hâter. H. up! dépêchez-vous! plus vite que ça! P: grouillez-vous! **hurried**, a. (Pas) pressé, précipité; (ouvrage) fait à la hâte. On Mondays, I'm always h., le lundi, c'est toujours une bousculade. A few h. words, quelques paroles dites à la hâte. To take a h. luncheon, déjeuner à la hâte. -ly, adv. A la hâte, en toute hâte; précipitamment, vivement.

hurry-scurry¹ ['hʌriskʌri]. **1.** adv. Pêle-mêle, en désordre. **2.** s. Confusion f, désordre m, bousculade f.

hurry-scurry², v.i. Faire les choses à la hâte; courir à la débandade.

hurt¹ [həːt], s. Mal m. **1.** Blessure f. To do s.o. a h., faire du mal à qn; blesser qn. **2.** Tort m, dommage m. What h. can it do you? en quoi cela peut-il vous nuire?

hurt², v.tr. (hurt; hurt) **1.** Faire (du) mal à, blesser (qn). To h. oneself, se faire (du) mal. To h. one's foot se blesser au pied. To get h., être blessé; recevoir une blessure. My wound hurts (me), ma blessure me fait mal. That hurts, ça fait mal. **2.** Faire de la peine à (qn). To h. s.o.'s feelings, blesser, froisser, peiner, qn. **3.** (Of thg) Nuire à, abîmer (qch.). To h. s.o.'s interests, léser les intérêts de qn.

hurtful ['həːtf(u)l], a. **1.** (a) Nuisible, nocif. (b) Préjudiciable (to, à). It is h. to my interests, cela porte atteinte à mes intérêts. **2.** H. to the feelings, froissant, blessant. -fully, adv. **1.** D'une manière nuisible, préjudiciable. **2.** D'une manière mortifiante, blessante.

hurtle ['həːtl], v.i. Se précipiter, s'élancer (avec bruit, comme un bolide). (Of car, etc.) To h. along, dévorer la route. The rocks hurtled, came hurtling, down, les rochers dévalaient avec fracas.

husband¹ ['hʌzbənd], s. Mari m, époux m. H. and wife, les (deux) époux, les conjoints m. To live as h. and wife, vivre maritalement.

husband², v.tr. **1.** A: Cultiver (la terre, etc.). **2.** Ménager, épargner, économiser (son argent), ses forces); bien gouverner (ses ressources).

husbandman, pl. **-men** ['hʌzbən(d)mən], s.m. **1.** Cultivateur; exploitant. **2.** Laboureur; ouvrier agricole.

husbandry ['hʌzbəndri], s. **1.** Agronomie f; industrie f agricole. **Animal h.**, élevage m. **2.** Good h., bonne gestion; sage administration f (de son bien).

hush¹ [hʌʃ], s. Silence m, calme m. The h. before the storm, l'accalmie f avant la tempête.

hush². **1.** v.tr. (a) Apaiser, faire taire (un enfant); imposer silence à (qn). All nature is hushed, toute la nature se tait. (b) Hushed conversation, conversation étouffée, discrète. **2.** v.i. Se taire; faire silence. **hush up**, v.tr. Étouffer (un scandale). 'hush-money, s. Argent donné à qn pour acheter son silence; pot-de-vin m. Extortion of h.-m., chantage m.

hush³, int. Chut! silence! 'hush-hush, a. F: Secret, -ète. Pol: Mil: The latest type of h.-h. deterrent, la plus récente des armes de dissuasion secrètes.

husk¹ [hʌsk], s. Cosse f, gousse f (de pois, etc.); brou m, écale f (de noix); bogue f (de châtaigne); coque f (de grain de café); tégument m, balle f (de grain). Rice in the h., riz non décortiqué.

husk², v.tr. Décortiquer; écosser (des pois etc.); écaler, cerner (des noix); écorcer, perler, monder (le riz, l'orge); vanner (le grain).

huskiness ['hʌskinis], s. Enrouement m, empâtement m (de la voix).

husky¹ ['hʌski], a. **1.** H. voice, (i) voix enrouée, voilée; (of drunkard) voix de rogomme; (ii) voix altérée (par l'émotion). **2.** a. & s. F: (Homme) fort, costaud. -ily, adv. (Parler) d'une voix enrouée (par la fatigue), d'une voix altérée, voilée (par l'émotion, la colère).

husky², s. Chien m esquimau, chien de traîneau.

hussar [hu'zɑːr], s. Mil: Hussard m.

hussy ['hʌzi], s.f. F: O: **1.** Coquine, friponne. You little h.! petite effrontée! **2.** Drôlesse, garce.

hustle¹ ['hʌsl], s. **1.** Bousculade f. **2.** Hâte f; activité f énergique.

hustle². **1.** v.tr. (a) Bousculer, pousser, presser (qn). To h. things on, pousser le travail; F: mener les choses tambour battant. (b) To h. s.o. into a decision, forcer qn à se décider sans lui donner le temps de respirer. (c) (Of pickpocket) Bousculer (qn); voler (qn) à l'esbroufe. **2.** v.i. Se dépêcher, se presser. **hustling**, s. **1.** = HUSTLE¹. **2.** Vol m à l'esbroufe.

hustler ['hʌslər], s. **1.** (a) Bousculeur, -euse. (b) Esbroufeur m. **2.** U.S: Débrouillard m; brasseur d'affaires; abatteur m de besogne.

hut [hʌt], s. Hutte f, cabane f. Mil: Baraquement m. Alpine h., chalet-refuge m, pl. chalets-refuges.

hutch [hʌtʃ], s. **1.** Coffre m, huche f. **2.** (Rabbit-)h., clapier m, lapinière f. **3.** (a) (Baker's) h., pétrin m, huche. (b) Min: Benne (roulante); wagonnet m.

hutments ['hʌtmənts], s.pl. Mil: etc: Baraquements m; camp m de baraques.

hyacinth ['haiəs(i)nθ], s. **1.** Lap: Hyacinthe f. **2.** Bot: Jacinthe f. Wood, wild, h., jacinthe des prés. **3.** a. & s. (Colour) (a) Rouge orangé inv (de l'hyacinthe). (b) Bleu jacinthe inv.

hyacinthine [,haiə'sinθain], a. = HYACINTH 3.

hyaena [hai'iːnə], s. = HYENA.

hyaline ['haiəlin], a. Hyalin, transparent.

hyaloid ['haiəlɔid], a. Anat: etc: Hyaloïde m.

hybrid ['haibrid], a. & s. Biol: Ling: etc: Hybride (m). H. plant, plante hybride, métisse. Ling: H. character, caractère m, hybridité f.

hybridism ['haibridizm], **hybridity** [hai'briditi], s. Hybridisme m, hybridité f.

hybridization [ˌhaibridai'zeiʃ(ə)n], s. Biol: Hybridation f.
hybridize ['haibridaiz], v.tr. Hybrider.
hydra ['haidrə], s. Hydre f. **H.-headed**, à têtes d'hydre, à sept têtes.
hydrangea [hai'drein(d)ʒə], s. Bot: Hortensia m.
hydrant ['haidrənt], s. Prise f d'eau; bouche f d'eau. Esp. Fire-h., bouche d'incendie.
hydrarthrosis [ˌhaidrɑː'θrousis], s. Med: Hydarthrose f.
hydrate[1] ['haidreit], s. Ch: Hydrate m.
hydrate[2] [hai'dreit], v.tr. Ch: Hydrater.
hydration [hai'dreiʃ(ə)n], s. Ch: Hydratation f.
hydraulic [hai'drɔːlik], a. Hydraulique. **H. engineering**, hydraulique f. **H. engineer**, hydrauliste m. adv. **-ally**, Hydrauliquement.
hydraulician [ˌhaidrɔː'liʃ(ə)n], s. Hydrauliste m, ingénieur m en hydraulique.
hydraulics [hai'drɔːliks], s.pl. Hydraulique f.
hydric ['haidrik], a. Ch: -hydrique. **H. chloride**, acide m chlorhydrique.
hydride ['haidraid], s. Ch: Hydrure m.
hydro ['haidrou], s. F: = HYDROPATHIC 2.
hydrobromide ['haidro'broumaid], s. Ch: Bromhydrate m.
hydrocarbon ['haidro'kɑːbən], s. Ch: Hydrocarbure m; carbure m d'hydrogène.
hydrocephalic ['haidrose'fælik], **hydrocephalous** ['haidro'sefələs], a. Med: Hydrocéphale.
hydrocephalus ['haidro'sefələs], **hydrocephaly** [hai-dro'sefəli], s. Med: Hydrocéphalie f.
hydrochlorate ['haidro'klɔreit], s. Ch: Chlorhydrate m.
hydrochloric ['haidro'klɔrik], a. Ch: (Acide) chlorhydrique.
hydrochloride ['haidro'klɔːraid], s. Ch: Chlorhydrate m.
hydrocyanic ['haidrosai'ænik], a. Ch: Cyanhydrique.
hydrodynamic(al) ['haidrodai'næmik(əl)], a. Hydrodynamique.
hydrodynamics ['haidrodai'næmiks], s. Hydrodynamique f.
hydro(-)electric ['haidroi'lektrik], a. Hydro-électrique. **H.-e. power**, énergie f hydraulique, houille blanche.
hydro(-)electricity ['haidro'elektrisiti], s. El.E: Hydroélectricité f.
hydrofluoric ['haidroflu(:)'ɔrik], a. Ch: Fluorhydrique.
hydrofoil ['haidrofɔil], s. Nau: Hydrofoil m.
hydrogen ['haidridʒ(ə)n], s. Ch: Hydrogène m. **Heavy h.**, hydrogène lourd, deutérium m. **H. bomb**, bombe f à (l')hydrogène, bombe H.
hydrogenate [hai'drədʒineit], **hydrogenize** [hai'drədʒinaiz], v.tr. Hydrogéner.
hydrograph ['haidrogræf], s. Courbe f de débit d'un fleuve.
hydrographer [hai'drɔgrəfər], s. (Ingénieur) hydrographe m.
hydrographic(al) ['haidro'græfik(əl)], a. Hydrographique.
hydrography [hai'drɔgrəfi], s. Hydrographie f.
hydrology [hai'drɔlədʒi], s. Hydrologie f.
hydrolysis [hai'drɔlisis], s. Ch: Hydrolyse f.
hydromechanics ['haidromi'kæniks], s.pl. (Usu. with sg. const.) Hydromécanique f.
hydrometer [hai'drɔmitər], s. Ph: Aréomètre m; hydromètre m. **Acid h.**, pèse-acide m inv, acidimètre m.
hydrometric(al) ['haidro'metrik(l)], a. Hydrométrique.
hydrometry [hai'drɔmitri], s. Ph: Hydrométrie f.
hydropath ['haidropæθ], s. Med: Hydropathe m.
hydropathic ['haidro'pæθik], a. Med: 1. a. (a) (Établissement) hydrothérapique. (b) (Médecin) hydropathe. 2. s. Établissement m hydrothérapique; établissement thermal.
hydropathist [hai'drɔpəθist], s. Med: = HYDROPATH.
hydropathy [hai'drɔpəθi], s. Med: Hydropathie.
hydrophobia ['haidrə'foubiə], s. Med: Hydrophobie f; F: la rage.
hydrophobic ['haidrə'foubik], a. Hydrophobe. **H. patient**, hydrophobe mf.
hydroplane[1] ['haidroplein], s. 1. O: Av: Hydravion m; hydroplane m. 2. (Motor boat) Hydroglisseur m. 3. pl. Barres f de plongée (d'un sous-marin).

hydroplane[2], v.i. Hydroplaner.
hydroponics [ˌhaidro'pɔniks], s.pl. Culture f hydroponique.
hydroquinone ['haidrokwi'noun], s. Phot: Hydroquinone f.
hydrosol ['haidrosɔl], s. Ch: Hydrosol m.
hydrosphere ['haidrəsfiər], s. Hydrosphère f.
hydrostatic(al) ['haidro'stætik(əl)], a. Hydrostatique.
hydrostatics ['haidro'stætiks], s.pl. Hydrostatique f.
hydrosulphide ['haidro'sʌlfaid], s. Ch: Sulfhydrate m.
hydrosulphite ['haidro'sʌlfait], s. Ch: Hydrosulfate m.
hydrosulphuric ['haidrosʌl'fjuːrik], a. Ch: Sulfhydrique.
hydrotherapeutic ['haidro,θerə'pjuːtik], a. Med: Hydrothérapique.
hydrotherapeutics ['haidro,θerə'pjuːtiks], s.pl., **hydrotherapy** ['haidro'θerəpi], s. Med: Hydrothérapie f.
hydrous ['haidrəs], a. Ch: Hydrique, hydraté, aqueux, -euse.
hyena [hai'iːnə], s. Z: Hyène f.
hygiene ['haidʒiːn], s. Hygiène f.
hygienic [hai'dʒiːnik], a. Hygiénique. **-ally**, adv. Hygiéniquement.
hygroma [hai'groumə], s. Med: Hygroma m.
hygrometer [hai'grɔmitər], s. Ph: Hygromètre m.
hygrometric(al) ['haigro'metrik(əl)], a. Hygrométrique.
hygrometry [hai'grɔmitri], s. Hygrométrie f.
hygroscope ['haigrəskoup], s. Ph: Hygroscope m.
hygroscopic(al) ['haigrə'skɔpik(əl)], a. Hygroscopique.
hymenoptera ['haimen'ɔptərə], s.pl. Ent: Hyménoptères m.
hymn [him], s. Ecc: Hymne f, cantique m. **'hymnbook**, s. Recueil m de cantiques; hymnaire m.
hymnal ['himnəl], s. Recueil m de cantiques; hymnaire m.
hyoid ['haiɔid], a. & s. Anat: (Os m) hyoïde m.
hyoscine ['haiosain], s. Ch: Hyoscine f.
hyper-accurate ['haipər'ækjurit], a. D'une précision outrée.
hyperacid ['haipər'æsid], a. Hyperacide.
hyperacidity ['haipə(r)ə'siditi], s. **Gastric h.**, hyperchlorhydrie f.
hyper-active ['haipər'æktiv], a. D'une activité outrée.
hyperaesthesia ['haipərəs'θiːziə], s. Hyperesthésie f.
hyperbaton [hai'pəːbətən], s. Rh: Hyperbate f.
hyperbola [hai'pəːbələ], s. Geom: Hyperbole f.
hyperbole [hai'pəːbəli], s. Rh: Hyperbole f.
hyperbolic(al) ['haipə(:)'bɔlik(əl)], a. Geom: Rh: Hyperbolique. **-ally**, adv. Hyperboliquement.
hyperbolism [hai'pəːbəlizm], s. Hyperbolisme m.
hyperborean [ˌhaipə(:)bɔː'ri(:)ən], a. Hyperboréen, -enne.
hypercritical ['haipə(:)'kritik(ə)l], a. Qui outre la critique. **To be h.**, (i) chercher la petite bête; (ii) se montrer d'un rigorisme exagéré.
hyperfocal ['haipə(:)'fouk(ə)l], a. Phot: Hyperfocal, -aux.
hypergol ['haipəgɔl], s. Rockets: Hypergol m.
hypermetropia ['haipə(:)me'troupiə], s. Med: Hypermétropie f.
hypermetropic ['haipə(:)me'trɔpik], a. Med: Hypermétrope.
hypersensitive ['haipə(:)'sensitiv], a. Hypersensible.
hypertension ['haipə(:)'tenʃ(ə)n], s. Med: Hypertension (artérielle, etc.).
hypertensive ['haipə'tensiv], a. **H. patient**, hypertendu, -e.
hyperthyroidism ['haipə(:)'θairɔidizm], s. Med: Hyperthyroïdie f.
hypertrophic [ˌhaipə'trɔfik], a. Med: Hypertrophique.
hypertrophy[1] ['haipə(:)'trofi], s. Med: Hypertrophie f.
hypertrophy[2], v.i. S'hypertrophier.
hyphen[1] ['haif(ə)n], s. Trait m d'union.
hyphen[2], **hyphenate** ['haifəneit], v.tr. Mettre un trait d'union à (un mot). **Hyphenated word**, mot à trait d'union. U.S: **Hyphenated American**, immigrant m (soupçonné d'avoir des loyautés contradictoires).
hypnology [hip'nɔlədʒi], s. Med: Hypnologie f.
hypnosis [hip'nousis], s. Hypnose f.
hypnotic [hip'nɔtik], a. Hypnotique. **H. state**, état m d'hypnose; somnambulisme provoqué.

hypnotism ['hipnətism], *s.* Hypnotisme *m.*
hypnotist ['hipnətist], *s.* Hypnotiste *mf.*
hypnotize ['hipnətaiz], *v.tr.* Hypnotiser.
hypo ['haipou], *s.* **1.** *Phot: F:* = HYPOSULPHITE. **2.** *U.S: F:* (*a*) = HYPOCHONDRIAC. (*b*) (i) = HYPO-DERMIC; (ii) piqûre *f.*
hypoacidity [ˌhaipouə'siditi], *s.* *Med:* **Gastric h.,** hypochlorhydrie *f.*
hypochondria [ˌhaipo'kɔndriə], *s.* Hypocondrie *f.*
hypochondriac [ˌhaipo'kɔndriæk], *a. & s.* Hypocondriaque (*mf*); *s.* hypocondre *mf.*
hypocrisy [hi'pɔkrisi], *s.* Hypocrisie *f.*
hypocrite ['hipokrit], *s.* Hypocrite *mf*; *F:* tartufe *m.*
hypocritical [ˌhipo'kritik(ə)l], *a.* Hypocrite. **-ally,** *adv.* Hypocritement.
hypodermic [ˌhaipo'də:mik], *a.* *Med:* **H. syringe,** seringue *f* hypodermique, seringue de Pravaz.
hypogastric [ˌhaipo'gæstrik], *a.* *Anat:* Hypogastrique.
hypogastrium [ˌhaipo'gæstriəm], *s.* *Anat:* Hypogastre *m.*
hypogeum, -a [ˌhaipo'dʒi:əm, -ə], *s.* *Archeol:* Hypogée *m.*
hypoglyc(a)emia [ˌhaipouglai'si:miə], *s.* *Med:* Hypoglycémie *f.*
hypophosphate [ˌhaipo'fɔsfeit], *s.* *Ch:* Hypophosphate *m.*
hypophosphite [ˌhaipo'fɔsfait], *s.* *Ch:* Hypophosphite *m.*
hypophysis [hai'pɔfisis], *s.* *Anat:* Hypophyse *f.*
hypostasis [hai'pɔstəsis], *s.* *Phil: Theol:* Hypostase *f.*
hypostatic [ˌhaipo'stætik], *a.* *Phil: Theol:* Hypo statique.
hypostyle ['haipostail], *a.* *Arch:* Hypostyle.

hyposulphite [ˌhaipo'sʌlfait], *s.* *Ch:* Hyposulfite *m.* *Phot:* **H. of soda,** *F:* **hypo,** hyposulfite de soude; *F:* fixateur *m.*
hypotension ['haipo'tenʃ(ə)n], *s.* *Med:* Hypotension *f.*
hypotensive ['haipo'tensiv], *a.* **H. patient,** hypotendu, -e.
hypotenuse [hai'pɔtinju:z], *s.* *Geom:* Hypoténuse *f.*
hypothesis [hai'pɔθisis], *s.* Hypothèse *f.*
hypothesize [hai'pɔθisaiz], *v.i. & tr.* Supposer (une notion); faire des hypothèses; admettre comme hypothèse (**that,** que).
hypothetic(al) [ˌhaipo'θetik(ə)l], *a.* Hypothétique, supposé. **-ally,** *adv.* Par hypothèse.
hypothyroidism ['haipo'θairoidizm], *s.* *Med:* Hypothyroïdisme *m.*
hypsography [hip'sɔgrəfi], *s.* Hypsographie *f.*
hypsometer [hip'sɔmitər], *s.* *Surv:* Hypsomètre *m.*
hypsometric(al) [ˌhipso'metrik(ə)l], *a.* Hypsométrique.
hypsometry [hip'sɔmitri], *s.* *Surv:* Hypsométrie *f.*
hyssop ['hisəp], *s.* *Bot:* Hysope *f.*
hysterectomy [ˌhistə'rektəmi], *s.* *Surg:* Hystérectomie *f.*
hysteresis [ˌhistə'ri:sis], *s.* Hystérèse *f* (magnétique); traînée *f* magnétique.
hysteria [his'tiəriə], *s.* *Med:* Hystérie *f.*
hysterical [his'terik(ə)l], *a.* **1.** *Med:* Hystérique. **2.** (*a*) Sujet à des attaques de nerfs. **H. sobs,** sanglots convulsifs. **H. laugh,** rire nerveux, énervé. (*b*) **To become h.,** avoir une attaque de nerfs. **-ally,** *adv.* **To weep h.,** avoir une crise de larmes. **To laugh h.,** rire nerveusement; avoir le fou rire.
hysterics [his'teriks], *s.pl.* (*a*) Attaque *f* de nerfs; crise *f* de nerfs. **To go, fall, into h.,** avoir une crise de nerfs. (*b*) Fou rire.
hysterotomy [ˌhistə'rɔtəmi], *s.* *Surg:* Hystérotomie *f.*

I¹, i [ai], s. (La lettre) I, i m. **To dot one's i's**, mettre les points sur les i. *Tp:* **I for Isaac**, I comme Irma.
I², *pers. pron.* (a) Je, j'. **I sing**, je chante. **I accuse**, j'accuse. **Here I am**, me voici. **What have I said?** qu'ai-je dit? (b) Moi *mf.* **He and I are great friends**, lui et moi, nous sommes de grands amis. **It is I**, c'est moi. **I too**, moi aussi. *(Stressed)* **'I'll see you home**, c'est moi qui vais vous reconduire.
iamb [ˈaiæm(b)], s. = IAMBUS.
iambic [aiˈæmbik]. *Pros:* **1.** *a.* Iambique. **2.** *s.* Vers *m* ïambique; ïambe *m.*
iambus [aiˈæmbəs], s. *Pros:* Iambe *m.*
Iberia [aiˈbiəriə]. *Pr.n. A.Geog:* L'Ibérie *f.*
Iberian [aiˈbiəriən]. **1.** *a.* (Péninsule) ibérique; (peuple) ibérien. **2.** *s.* Ibérien, -ienne. **The Iberians**, les Ibères *m.*
ibex [ˈaibeks], s. *Z:* Bouquetin *m*, ibex *m.*
ibis [ˈaibis], s. *Orn:* Ibis *m.*
ice¹ [ais], s. Glace *f.* **1. The i. age**, la période, l'époque *f* glaciaire. **Granular i.**, névé *m.* **Mass of i.**, glacière *f.* **I. cave**, glacière naturelle. *Ind:* **Dry i.**, neige *f* carbonique. **My feet are like i.**, j'ai les pieds glacés. **To break the i.**, rompre la glace; (i) faire cesser la contrainte; (ii) entamer un sujet, une affaire. **To skate over thin i.**, toucher à un sujet délicat. **To cut no i. with s.o.**, ne faire aucune impression sur qn. **2.** *Cu:* **Strawberry i.**, glace à la fraise. **Mixed i.**, glace panachée. **'ice-axe**, s. Piolet *m.* **'ice-bag**, s. *Med:* Vessie *f*, sac *m*, à glace. **'ice-blue**, *a.* Bleu glacier. **'ice-bound**, *a.* (i) (Navire) retenu par les glaces, pris dans les glaces; (ii) (port) fermé, bâclé, par les glaces. **'ice(-)box**, (-)chest, *s.* (i) Glacière *f* (domestique); *U.S:* réfrigérateur *m*, (ii) sorbetière *f.* **'ice-breaker**, *s. Nau:* Brise-glace *m inv.* **'ice-brick**, *s. Cu:* Esquimau *m.* **'ice-bucket**, *s.* Seau *m* à glace, à champagne, à rafraîchir. **ice-'cream**, *s. Cu:* Glace. **I.-c. man**, glacier *m.* **'ice-field**, *s.* Champ *m* de glace. **'ice-floe**, *s.* Banquise *f*; banc *m* de glace. **'ice-hockey**, *s. Sp:* Hockey *m* sur glace. **Ice-hockey player**, hockeyeur *m.* **'ice-house**, *s.* Glacière *f.* *F:* **This room is like an i.-h.**, on gèle dans cette salle; c'est une glacière ici. **'ice-pack**, *s.* **1.** (a) Embâcle *m.* (b) Banquise *f.* **2.** *Med:* **To put an i.-p. on a patient's head**, mettre de la glace sur la tête d'un malade. **'ice-pick**, *s.* Pique *f* à glace (d'alpiniste). **'ice-plant**, *s.* **1.** *Bot:* (Ficoïde) glaciale *f.* **2.** *Ind:* Fabrique *f* de glace, glacerie *f.* **ice-'pudding**, *s. Cu:* Bombe glacée. **'ice-rink**, *s.* Salle *f*, stade *m*, de patinage sur glace (artificielle). **'ice-sailing**, *s.* Yachting *m* sur glace; course *f* à voile sur patins. **'ice-skate**, *s.* Patin *m* (à glace). **'ice-skating**, *s.* Patinage *m* (sur glace). **'ice-water**, *s.* **1.** Eau glacée, frappée. **2.** Eau de glace fondue.
ice², *v.tr.* **1.** Congeler, geler. **The pond was soon iced over**, l'étang eut, fut, bientôt gelé d'un bout à l'autre. **2.** Rafraîchir (l'eau, etc.) avec de la glace; frapper (du champagne). **3.** Glacer (un gâteau). **ice up**, *v.i. Av:* Givrer; se givrer, **icing up**, *s. Av:* Givrage *m.* **iced**, *a.* **1.** (Crème) glacée, à la glace; (melon) rafraîchi; (champagne) frappé. **I. coffee**, café glacé. **2. I. cake**, gâteau glacé. **icing**, *s.* (a) Congélation *f.* (b) Frappage *m* (du champagne, etc.). (c) (i) Glaçage *m*, surglaçage *m.* (ii) Glace, glacé *m* (d'un gâteau). (d) Givrage *m.*
iceberg [ˈaisbə:g], s. Iceberg *m.*
Iceland [ˈaislənd]. *Pr.n. Geog:* L'Islande *f.*
Icelander [ˈaisləndər], s. Islandais, -aise.
Icelandic [aisˈlændik]. **1.** *a.* Islandais; d'Islande. **2.** *Ling:* L'islandais *m.*
ichneumon [ikˈnju:mən], s. **1.** *Z:* Ichneumon *m*; *F:* rat *m* de Pharaon. **2.** *Ent:* **I.**(-fly), ichneumon.
ichnography [ikˈnɔgrəfi], s. Ichnographie *f.*
ichthyol [ˈikθiɔl], s. *Pharm: R.t.m:* Ichtyol *m.*
ichthyologic(al) [ˌikθiəˈlɔdʒik(əl)], a. Ichtyologique.
ichthyology [ˌikθiˈɔlədʒi], s. Ichtyologie *f.*
ichthyophagous [ˌikθiˈɔfəgəs], a. Ichtyophage.
ichthyophagy [ˌikθiˈɔfədʒi], s. Ichtyophagie *f.*

ichthyosaurus [ˌikθiəˈsɔ:rəs], s. *Paleont:* Ichtyosaure *m.*
icicle [ˈaisikl], s. Petit glaçon; chandelle *f* de glace.
iciness [ˈaisinis], s. **1.** Froid glacial. **2.** Froideur glaciale (d'un accueil).
icon [ˈaikən], s. *Ecc:* Icone *f.*
iconoclasm [aiˈkɔnoklæzm], s. Iconoclasie *f*, iconoclasme *m.*
iconoclast [aiˈkɔnoklæst], s. Iconoclaste *mf.*
iconoclastic [aiˌkɔnoˈklæstik], a. Iconoclaste.
iconographer [aikoˈnɔgrəfər], s. Iconographe *mf.*
iconographic(al) [ˈaikonoˈgræfik(əl)], a. Iconographique.
iconography [ˌaikoˈnɔgrəfi], s. Iconographie *f.*
iconometer [ˌaikoˈnɔmitər], s. *Phot:* Iconomètre *m.*
iconoscope [aiˈkɔnoskoup], s. *T.V:* Iconoscope *m.*
icteric(al) [ikˈterik(əl)], a. *Med:* Ictérique.
icterus [ˈiktərəs], s. Ictère *m*, jaunisse *f.*
ictus [ˈiktəs], s. *Pros: Med:* Ictus *m.*
icy [ˈaisi], a. **1.** Couvert de glace; glacial, -als. **I. road**, route verglacée. **2.** (Vent, accueil) glacial. **I. hands**, mains glacées. **This room is i. cold**, on gèle dans cette salle. **-ily**, *adv.* Glacialement, d'un air glacial.
idea [aiˈdiə], s. Idée *f.* **What a funny i.!** quelle drôle d'idée! **To give a general i. of a book**, donner un aperçu d'un livre. **I can't bear the i.**, l'idée m'en est trop pénible. **To hit upon the i. of doing sth.**, avoir la bonne inspiration, avoir l'idée, de faire qch. **I have an i. that . . .**, j'ai idée que. . . . **I had no i. that . . .**, j'étais loin de me douter que . . .; j'ignorais absolument que . . .; je n'avais aucune idée que. . . . **He has some i. of chemistry**, il a des notions de chimie. **I've an i. that I've seen him before**, j'ai l'impression de l'avoir déjà vu. *F:* **What's the big i.?** Qu'est ce qui vous prend? Quelle mouche vous pique? **To get ideas into one's head**, se faire des idées. *F:* **What an i.!** en voilà une idée! y pensez-vous? **The i.!** quelle idée! par exemple!
ideal [aiˈdi:əl]. **1.** *a.* Idéal, -aux. **It is i.!** c'est le rêve! **2.** *s.* Idéal *m*, -aux, -als. **The i. of beauty**, le beau idéal, la beauté idéale. **-ally**, *adv.* Idéalement (beau, etc.).
idealism [aiˈdi:əlizm], s. Idéalisme *m.*
idealist [aiˈdi:əlist], s. Idéaliste *mf.*
idealistic [ˌaidiəˈlistik], a. Idéaliste.
ideality [aidiˈæliti], s. Idéalité *f.*
idealization [aiˌdiəlaiˈzeiʃ(ə)n], s. Idéalisation *f.*
idealize [aiˈdi:əlaiz], *v.tr.* Idéaliser. **idealizing**, *s.* Idéalisation *f.*
identical [aiˈdentik(ə)l], a. Identique (**with**, à). **Our tastes are i.**, nous avons les mêmes goûts. **-ally**, *adv.* Identiquement.
identifiable [ai,dentiˈfaiəbl], a. Identifiable.
identification [ai,dentifiˈkeiʃ(ə)n], s. Identification *f.* *Aut:* **I. plate**, plaque *f* minéralogique, plaque d'immatriculation, *F:* de police. *Av:* **I. light**, feu *m* d'identification.
identify [aiˈdentifai], *v.tr.* **1.** Identifier (**sth. with sth.**, qch. avec qch.). **To i. oneself, become identified, with a party**, s'identifier à, avec, s'assimiler à, un parti. **2. To i. s.o.**, constater, établir, l'identité de qn.
identity [aiˈdentiti], s. Identité *f.* **I. card**, carte *f* d'identité. **Mistaken i.**, erreur *f* sur la personne. **To prove one's i.**, établir son identité.
ideogram [ˈidiogræm], **ideograph** [ˈidiogrɑ:f], s. Idéogramme *m.*
ideography [ˌidiˈɔgrəfi], s. Idéographie *f.*
ideologic(al) [ˌaidiəˈlɔdʒik(əl)], a. Idéologique.
ideologist [ˌaidiˈɔlədʒist], **ideologue** [ˈaidiəlɔg], s. Idéologue *mf.*
ideology [ˌaidiˈɔlədʒi], s. Idéologie *f.*
ides [aidz], *s.pl. Rom.Ant:* Ides *f.*
idiocy [ˈidiəsi], s. **1.** Idiotie (congénitale). **2.** Bêtise *f*, stupidité *f.*
idiom [ˈidiəm], s. **1.** (a) Dialecte *m*; idiome *m* (d'une région). (b) Langue *f*, idiome (d'un pays). **2.** Idiotisme *m.*
idiomatic [ˌidioˈmætik], a. **1.** Idiomatique. **I. phrase**, idiotisme *m.* **2.** Qui appartient à la langue courante. **-ally**, *adv.* (S'exprimer) d'une façon idiomatique.

idiosyncrasy [ˌidio'siŋkrəsi], s. **1.** Idiosyncrasie f. **2.** Habitude f propre à qn; petite manie; particularité f (de style).

idiot ['idiət], s. (a) Med: Idiot, -ote; imbécile mf. **The village i.**, l'innocent m du village. (b) Imbécile. F: **You i.!** espèce d'imbécile, d'idiot! **To play the i.**, faire l'idiot, l'innocent. F: **The i. box**, la télévision.

idiotic [ˌidi'ɔtik], a. Bête. **That's i.**, c'est stupide, c'est bête. **Don't be i.!** ne fais pas l'imbécile! **-ally**, adv. Bêtement; (se conduire) en imbécile.

idle[1] ['aidl], a. **1.** (a) (Of pers.) Inoccupé, oisif, -ive; désœuvré. **In my i. moments**, à mes heures perdues. (b) (Of machinery, workmen) Qui chôme, en chômage; (of machine) au repos. **Factory standing i.**, usine qui chôme. **To run i.**, (i) (of machine) marcher à vide; (ii) Aut: (of engine) tourner au ralenti. **Capital lying i.**, fonds dormants, inemployés. (c) Mec.E: **I. motion**, mouvement perdu. **I. period** (in cycle, etc.), temps mort. El: **I. current**, courant déwatté. (d) Mec.E: **I. wheel**, roue folle, décalée. **2.** (Of pers.) Paresseux, fainéant. **The i. rich**, les riches désœuvrés. **3.** Inutile, oiseux, futile. **I. wish**, vain désir. **I. threats**, menaces en l'air. **Out of, through, i. curiosity**, par simple curiosité. **idly**, adv. **1.** Sans travailler. **To stand i. by**, rester là à ne rien faire. **2.** Inutilement; (parler) en l'air. **3.** Paresseusement. **idle-'pulley**, s. Mec.E: **1.** Poulie-guide f. **2.** Galet m de renvoi.

idle[2], v.i. **1.** Fainéanter; paresser. **To i. about the streets**, flâner dans les rues. v.tr. **To i. one's time away**, perdre son temps à ne rien faire, à paresser, à flâner. **2.** Aut: (Of engine) **To i. (over)**, tourner au ralenti.

idleness ['aidlnis], s. **1.** Oisiveté f, désœuvrement m; inaction f. **2.** Futilité f (d'une menace, etc.). **3.** (Of pers.) Paresse f, fainéantise f. **To live in i.**, vivre dans l'oisiveté.

idler ['aidlər], s. **1.** (a) Oisif, -ive; désœuvré, -ée; flâneur, -euse. (b) Fainéant, -ante; paresseux, -euse. **2.** Mec.E: (a) Roue folle; pignon m libre. (b) (Pignon de) renvoi m. (c) Poulie f de tension.

idol ['aidl], s. Idole f.

idolater [ai'dolətər], f. **idolatress** [ai'dolətris], s. **1.** Idolâtre mf. **2.** Adorateur, -trice, fanatique mf (of, de).

idolatrous [ai'dolətrəs], a. Idolâtre.

idolatry [ai'dolətri], s. Idolâtrie f.

idolize ['aidəlaiz], v.tr. Idolâtrer, adorer (qn, qch.); faire une idole (de l'argent).

idyll ['aidil, 'id-], s. Lit: Idylle f.

idyllic [ai'dilik, id-], a. Idyllique. **-ally**, adv. D'une façon idyllique; en idylle.

if [if], conj. Si. **1.** (a) If I wanted him, I rang, si j'avais besoin de lui, je sonnais. **If I am late I apologise**, si je suis en retard je fais mes excuses. (b) If he does it, he will be punished, s'il le fait, il sera puni. **If he did it, he would be punished**, s'il le faisait, il serait puni. **If the weather is fine and (if) I am free, I shall go out**, s'il fait beau et si je suis libre, je sortirai. **If it is fine, and (if it is) not too windy, we shall go for a walk**, s'il fait beau et qu'il ne fasse pas trop de vent, nous irons nous promener. **If they are to be believed, nobody was saved**, à les en croire, personne n'aurait survécu. **If you hesitate (at all)**, pour peu que vous hésitiez. (If (it is) necessary, s'il est nécessaire; s'il le faut; au besoin. **If (it be) so**, s'il en est ainsi. **The water was warm, if anything**, l'eau était plutôt tiède. **He will give you a shilling for it, if that**, il vous en donnera un shilling, et encore! **If not**, sinon; si ce n'est. . . . **Go and see him, if only to please me**, allez le voir, ne fût-ce, ne serait-ce, que pour me faire plaisir. S.a. ANY I. 1, EVER 1. (c) **If I were you . . .**, si j'étais vous . . .; à votre place. . . . **Even if he did say so**, quand même il l'aurait dit. (Even) if I were given a hundred pounds, I would not do it, on me donnerait cent livres que je ne le ferais pas; quand même on me donnerait cent livres je ne le ferais pas. (d) (Exclamatory) If I had only known! si seulement je l'avais su! **If only he comes in time!** pourvu qu'il vienne à temps! F: **Well, if she hasn't taken my book!** Allons bon, voilà qu'elle m'a pris mon livre! (e) **As if**, comme si; comme. **He talks as if he were drunk**, il parle comme s'il était ivre. **He stood as if**

thunderstruck, il demeurait comme foudroyé. **As if by chance**, comme par hasard. **As if I would allow it!** comme si je le permettrais! S.a. LOOK[2] 3. **2.** (Concessive) If they are poor, they are at any rate happy, s'ils sont pauvres, du moins sont-ils heureux. **Pleasant weather, if rather cold**, temps agréable, bien qu'un peu froid, encore qu'un peu froid. **3.** (= WHETHER 1.) **Do you know if he is at home?** savez-vous s'il est chez lui? **4.** s. **Your ifs and buts**, vos si et vos mais.

igloo ['iglu:], s. Igloo m.

igneous ['igniəs], a. **I. rock**, roche éruptive, ignée.

igniferous [ig'nifərəs], a. Ignifère.

ignite [ig'nait], **1.** v.tr. Mettre le feu à (qch.); enflammer (un mélange explosif). **2.** v.i. Prendre feu; s'enflammer.

igniter [ig'naitər], s. Dispositif m d'allumage; Artil: Min: allumeur m.

ignition [ig'niʃ(ə)n], s. **1.** Ignition f, inflammation f (d'une charge de mine). **2.** I.C.E: Allumage m. **I. coil, circuit**, bobine f, circuit m, d'allumage. **I. key**, clef f de contact m.

ignitron ['ignitron], s. El: Ignitron m.

ignoble [ig'noubl], a. **1.** A: Plébéien, roturier. **2.** Ignoble; infâme, vil, indigne.

ignominious [ˌigno'miniəs], a. Ignominieux, -euse; honteux, -euse. **-ly**, adv. Ignominieusement; avec ignominie.

ignominiousness [ˌigno'miniəsnis], s. Caractère honteux, ignominieux (de qch.).

ignominy ['ignomini]. Ignominie f, honte f.

ignoramus [ˌigno'reiməs], s. Ignorant, -ante; ignare mf.

ignorance ['ign(ə)r(ə)ns], s. Ignorance f. **To keep s.o. in i. of sth.**, laisser ignorer qch. à qn. **I am in complete i. of his intentions**, j'ignore tout de ses intentions. **I. of the law is no excuse**, nul n'est censé ignorer la loi.

ignorant ['ign(ə)r(ə)nt], a. (a) Ignorant. **To be i. of a fact**, ignorer un fait. **He is i. of the world**, il ne connaît pas le monde. (b) An i. question, une question qui trahit l'ignorance. **-ly**, adv. **1.** (Se tromper) par ignorance. **2.** (Parler) avec ignorance.

ignore [ig'no:r], v.tr. **1.** Ne tenir aucun compte de (qch.); passer (qch.) sous silence. **To i. s.o., s.o.'s existence**, ne pas vouloir reconnaître qn; feindre de ne pas voir qn. **To i. the facts**, méconnaître les faits. **To i. an invitation**, ne pas répondre à une invitation. **To i. a rule**, sortir d'une règle. **To i. a prohibition**, passer outre à une interdiction. **You cannot afford to i. this**, il est nécessaire que vous teniez compte de cela. **2.** Jur: **To i. a bill**, prononcer un non-lieu. **To i. a complaint**, rejeter une plainte.

iguana [i'gwɑːnə], s. Rept: Iguane m.

ike [aik], s. U.S: T.V: P: = ICONOSCOPE.

ikon ['aikon], s. = ICON.

ileum ['iliəm], s. Anat: Iléon m, iléum m.

ilex, pl. **-exes** ['aileks, -eksiz], s. Bot: Ilex m. **1.** Yeuse f; chêne vert. **2.** Ilicacées fpl; (famille des) houx m.

iliac ['iliæk], a. Anat: Iliaque.

Iliad (the) [ði'iliəd], s. Gr.Lit: L'Iliade f.

ilium ['iliəm], s. Anat: Ilion m; os m iliaque.

I'll [ail] = I will, I shall.

ill [il]. **I.** a. (worse; worst, q.v.) **1.** (a) Mauvais. **I. effects**, effets pernicieux. Prov: **It's an i. wind that blows nobody good**, à quelque chose malheur est bon. **To do s.o. an i. turn**, desservir qn. **2.** (a) Méchant, mauvais. **House of i. repute**, maison mal famée. **2.** Malade; souffrant. **To be, feel, i.**, être malade; se sentir souffrant. **To fall i., be taken i.**, tomber malade. **illy**, adv. U.S: = ILL III. **II. ill**, s. **1.** Mal m. **To do i.**, faire le mal. **To speak i. of s.o.**, dire du mal de qn. **2.** (a) Dommage m, tort m. (b) pl. Maux m, malheurs m. **To suffer great ills**, souffrir de grands maux, de grandes misères. **III. ill**, adv. (worse, worst) Mal. **1.** **To take sth. i.**, prendre qch. en mauvaise part; savoir mauvais gré à qn de qch. **It will go i. with them**, il leur en cuira. **2.** **I can i. afford the expense**, je peux difficilement supporter cette dépense. **It i. becomes you to . . .**, il vous sied mal, il vous messied, de. . . . **3.** **To be i. at ease**, (i) être mal à l'aise; (ii) être inquiet. **ill-ad'vised**, a. **1.** (Of pers.) Malavisé. **2.** (Of action) Peu judicieux, impolitique. **-ly** [ˌiləd'vai-zidli], adv. Impolitiquement. **ill-as'sorted**, a. Mal assorti; inassorti; disparate. **ill-'bred,** *a.* Mal élevé; malappris. **ill-'breeding,** *s.* Manque *m* de savoir-vivre. **ill-con'ditioned,** *a.* (*a*) De mauvaise mine. (*b*) En mauvais état. **ill-con'sidered,** *a.* Peu réfléchi. **I.-c. measures,** mesures hâtives. **ill-de'fined,** *a.* Mal défini; indéfini. **ill-de'served,** *a.* Peu mérité. **ill-dis'posed,** *a.* 1. Malintentionné, malveillant. **I.-d. towards s.o.,** mal disposé envers qn. **2. To be i.-d. to do sth.,** être peu disposé à faire qch. **ill-'fated,** *a.* (Prince) infortuné; (effort) malheureux; (jour) fatal, néfaste. **ill-'favoured,** *a.* (*Of pers.*) Laid; de mauvaise mine. **He's an i.-f. fellow,** il ne paye pas de mine. **ill-'feeling,** *s.* Ressentiment *m*, rancune *f.* **No i.-f.!** sans rancune! **ill-'founded,** *a.* (*Of rumour*) Mal fondé, sans fondement. **ill-'gotten,** *a.* (Bien) mal acquis. *S.a.* GAIN¹. **ill-'health,** *s.* Mauvaise santé; manque *m* de santé. **ill-'humoured,** *a.* De mauvaise humeur; maussade, grincheux. **ill-in'formed,** *a.* 1. Mal renseigné. 2. Peu instruit; ignorant. **ill-in'tentioned,** *a.* Malintentionné (**towards,** envers). **'ill(-)'luck,** *s.* Mauvaise fortune; malchance *f*; *F:* guigne *f.* **By i.-l., as i.-l. would have it,** par malheur, par malchance; le malheur a voulu que + *sub.* **ill-'mannered,** *a.* Malhonnête, grossier, malappris. **ill-'matched,** *a.* Mal assorti; inassorti; disparate. **ill(-)'nature,** *s.* Méchant caractère; méchanceté *f.* **ill-'natured,** *a.* D'un mauvais caractère; méchant; désagréable. **-ly,** *adv.* Méchamment; avec méchanceté. **ill-'omened,** *a.* De mauvais présage; de mauvais augure. **ill-'pleased,** *a.* Mécontent. **ill-'qualified,** *a.* Incompétent; peu qualifié (pour faire qch.). **ill(-)re'pute,** *s.* Mauvaise réputation. **Man of i.(-)r.,** homme taré. **ill-'sounding,** *a.* Malsonnant. **ill-'starred,** *a.* Né sous une mauvaise étoile; (prince) infortuné; (jour) malheureux, néfaste. **I.-s. adventure,** entreprise vouée à l'insuccès. **ill(-)'temper,** *s.* Mauvais caractère; humeur *f* acariâtre. **ill-'tempered,** *a.* De mauvais caractère; maussade, grincheux, de mauvaise humeur. **ill-'timed,** *a.* Mal à propos; malencontreux. **I.-t. arrival,** arrivée inopportune, intempestive. **ill-'treat,** *v.tr.* Maltraiter, brutaliser. **ill-'treatment, ill-'usage,** *s.* Mauvais traitements. **ill-'use,** [ju:z], *v.tr.* (*a*) Maltraiter (un enfant); malmener (un adversaire). (*b*) Mal agir envers (qn); faire une injustice à (qn). **ill-'will,** *s.* Mauvais vouloir; malveillance *f*, rancune *f.* **To bear s.o. i.-w.,** garder rancune, en vouloir, à qn.

illegal [i'li:g(ə)l], *a.* Illégal, -aux. **I. entry,** violation *f* de domicile. **-ally,** *adv.* Illégalement.

illegality [ili(:)'gæliti], *s.* Illégalité *f.*

illegibility [i,ledʒə'biliti], *s.* Illisibilité *f.*

illegible [i'ledʒibl], *a.* Illisible. **-ibly,** *adv.* Illisiblement.

illegitimacy [,ili'dʒitiməsi], *s.* Illégitimité *f.*

illegitimate [,ili'dʒitimit], *a.* Illégitime. **-ly,** *adv.* Illégitimement.

illiberality [ilibə'ræliti], *s.* Illibéralité *f.* (*a*) Petitesse *f*, étroitesse *f* (d'esprit). (*b*) Manque *m* de générosité.

illicit [i'lisit], *a.* Illicite. **I. betting,** paris clandestins. **I. street vendor,** vendeur *m* à la sauvette. *adv.* **-ly.** Illicitement; à la sauvette.

illimitable [i'limitəbl], *a.* Illimitable, illimité; sans bornes.

illiteracy [i'lit(ə)rəsi], *s.* Manque *m* d'instruction; analphabétisme *m.*

illiterate [i'lit(ə)rit], *a.* & *s.* Illettré, -ée, analphabète (*mf*).

illness ['ilnis], *s.* Maladie *f.* **To have a long i.,** faire une longue maladie.

illogical [i'lodʒik(ə)l], *a.* Illogique; peu logique. **-ally,** *adv.* Illogiquement.

illogicality [i,lodʒi'kæliti], **illogicalness** [i'lodʒikəlnis], *s.* Illogisme *m.*

illuminate [i'lju:mineit], *v.tr.* 1. Éclairer (une salle, l'esprit). 2. Illuminer (un édifice à l'occasion d'une fête). **Illuminated sign,** enseigne lumineuse. 3. Enluminer (un manuscrit). **Illuminated capital,** lettrine *f.* 4. Éclairer, élucider (un sujet). **illuminating¹,** *a.* I. Éclairant. 2. I. talk, entretien éclaircissant. **illuminating²,** *s.* 1. = ILLUMINATION 1. 2. Illumination *f* (d'un édifice, etc.). 3. Enluminement *m* (d'un manuscrit, etc.). 4. Élucidation *f* (d'une question).

illumination ['ilju:mi'neiʃ(ə)n], *s.* 1. (*a*) Éclairage *m.* (*b*) Illumination *f* (d'un édifice). 2. (*a*) To go out to see the illuminations, sortir voir les illuminations. (*b*) *pl.* Enluminures *f* (d'un manuscrit). 3. *Opt:* Éclat *m* (d'un objectif).

illuminator [i'lju:mineitər], *s.* 1. (*Pers.*) (*a*) Illuminateur *m.* (*b*) *Art:* Enlumineur, -euse. 2. Dispositif *m* d'éclairage.

illusion [i'lu:ʒ(ə)n], *s.* Illusion *f*; tromperie *f.* (**Practice of**) **i.,** illusionnisme *m.* **Optical i.,** (i) illusion d'optique; (ii) truc *m* d'optique. **To be under an i.,** être le jouet d'une illusion. **I have no illusions, I am under no illusions, on this point,** je ne me fais aucune illusion sur ce point.

illusionist [i'lu:ʒənist], *s.* Prestidigitateur *m*, illusionniste *mf.*

illusive [i'lu:siv], *a.* Illusoire, trompeur, mensonger.

illusory [i'lu:s(ə)ri], *a.* Illusoire; sans effet.

illustrate ['iləstreit], *v.tr.* 1. Éclairer, expliquer, démontrer par des exemples (une règle). 2. Illustrer; orner de gravures, de dessins (le texte d'un livre). **Illustrated paper,** (journal) illustré (*m*).

illustration [,iləs'treiʃ(ə)n], *s.* 1. Explication *f*, exemple *m* (d'une règle). **By way of i.,** à titre d'exemple. 2. Illustration *f*, gravure *f*, image *f.* **Text i.,** vignette *f.*

illustrative ['iləstreitiv], *a.* Qui sert à éclaircir ou à expliquer. **I. of sth.,** qui fournit un exemple de qch.

illustrator ['iləstreitər], *s.* Illustrateur *m* (d'un ouvrage).

illustrious [i'lʌstriəs], *a.* Illustre, célèbre. **-ly,** *adv.* Avec éclat.

illy ['ili], *adv. See* ILL I, III.

image ['imidʒ], *s.* Image *f.* 1. Image sculptée; représentation *f* (d'un dieu); idole *f.* 2. *Opt:* **Real i.,** image réelle. **Virtual i.,** image virtuelle. 3. *B:* **God created man in his own i.,** Dieu créa l'homme à son image. **He is the living i. of his father,** c'est le portrait vivant de son père; *F:* c'est son père tout craché. 4. Image (d'un parti politique, etc.). 5. **To speak in images,** s'exprimer par métaphores.

imagery ['imidʒri], *s.* 1. *Coll.* Images sculptées; idoles *fpl.* 2. Figures *fpl* de rhétorique; images. **Style full of i.,** style imagé.

imaginable [i'mædʒinəbl], *a.* Imaginable. **The finest thing i.,** la plus belle chose qu'on puisse imaginer; tout ce qu'on peut imaginer de plus beau.

imaginary [i'mædʒin(ə)ri], *a.* Imaginaire.

imagination [i,mædʒi'neiʃ(ə)n], *s.* Imagination *f.* **To see one's youth in i.,** revoir sa jeunesse en imagination, en idée. **It's your i.!** vous l'avez rêvé!

imaginative [i'mædʒ(i)nətiv], *a.* 1. (*Of pers.*) Imaginatif, -ive. 2. **I. poem,** poème d'imagination.

imagine [i'mædʒin], *v.tr.* 1. (*a*) Imaginer, concevoir (qch.); se figurer, se représenter (qch.). **Try to i. our position,** essayez de vous faire une idée de notre position. **I. yourself in Paris, as a soldier,** supposez-vous à Paris, figurez-vous que vous soyez soldat. **As may (well) be imagined,** comme on peut (se) l'imaginer. **Just i. my despair,** figurez-vous, imaginez(-vous) un peu, mon désespoir. **You can i. how angry I was!** pensez, songez, si j'étais furieux! **You can't i. it!** on ne s'en fait pas idée! (*b*) **I i. them to be fairly rich,** je les crois assez riches. **I know something about it, I i.!** j'en sais quelque chose, peut-être! **Do not i. that I am satisfied,** n'allez pas croire que je sois satisfait. 2. **To be always imagining things,** se faire des imaginations, des idées. **I imagined I heard a knock at the door,** j'ai cru entendre frapper à la porte.

imago [i'meigou], *s. Ent:* Imago *f*; insecte parfait.

Imam [i'ma:m], *s. Moham.Rel:* Iman *m.*

imbecile ['imbisail, -si:l]. 1. *a.* Imbécile; faible d'esprit; d'une stupidité crasse. 2. *s.* Imbécile *mf. F:* You i.! espèce d'idiot!

imbecility [,imbi'siliti], *s.* Imbécillité *f*; faiblesse *f* d'esprit.

imbibe [im'baib], *v.tr.* (*a*) Absorber, s'assimiler (des connaissances). (*b*) Boire, avaler (une boisson); absorber (de la bière); aspirer (l'air frais). (*c*) (*Of thg*) Imbiber (qch.); s'imprégner, se pénétrer, de (créosote, etc.).

imbricate¹ ['imbrikeit], *v.tr.* Imbriquer.

imbricate², *-ated ; a.* Imbriqué; (structure) à écailles.

imbrication [,imbri'keiʃ(ə)n], *s.* Imbrication *f*, chevauchement *m.*

imbroglio [im'brouliou], *s.* Imbroglio *m.*
mbrue [im'bru:], *v.tr. Lit:* **Imbrued in, with, blood,** ensanglanté.
imbue [im'bju:], *v.tr.* **To i. s.o. with an idea,** pénétrer qn d'une idée. **Imbued with prejudices,** imbu de préjugés. **Imbued with false principles,** imprégné de faux principes.
imitable ['imitəbl], *a.* Imitable.
imitate ['imiteit], *v.tr.* (a) Imiter, copier. (b) Contrefaire (le cri d'un oiseau).
imitation [,imi'teiʃ(ə)n], *s.* 1. Imitation *f.* **In i. of sth.,** à l'imitation de qch. 2. (a) Copie *f,* imitation. *Com:* **Beware of imitations,** méfiez-vous des contrefaçons *f.* (b) *attrib.* Factice; simili-. **I. morocco,** genre maroquin. **I. gold,** similor *m.* **I. marble,** similimarbre *m.* **I. jewellery,** bijo uterie fausse; bijoux *mpl* en faux, en toc.
imitative ['imiteitiv, -tətiv], *a.* 1. (Son) imitatif. 2. (Of pers.) Imitateur, -trice.
imitator ['imiteitər], *s.* (a) Imitateur, -trice. (b) *Com:* Contrefacteur *m.*
immaculate [i'mækjulit], *a.* 1. Immaculé; sans tache. *Theol:* **The I. Conception,** l'Immaculée Conception. 2. (Of dress) Irréprochable, impeccable. -**ly,** *adv.* 1. Sans tache; sans défaut. 2. (Vêtu) irréprochablement.
immanence ['imənəns], **immanency** ['imənənsi], *s. Phil:* Immanence *f.*
immanent ['imənənt], *a. Phil:* Immanent.
immaterial [,imə'tiəriəl], *a.* 1. (Esprit) immatériel. 2. (a) Peu important. **That is quite i. to me,** cela m'est indifférent. (b) **I. to the subject,** qui n'a aucun rapport avec la question.
immaterialism [,imə'tiəriəlizm]. *Phil: s.* Immatérialisme *m.*
immaterialist [,imə'tiəriəlist]. *Phil: s.* Immatérialiste *mf.*
immateriality [,imətiəri'æliti], *s.* Immatérialité *f.*
immaterialize [,imə'tiəriəlaiz], *v.tr.* Immatérialiser.
immature [,imə'tjuər], *a.* (a) (Qui n'est) pas mûr. **Although she is nineteen she is still very i.,** quoiqu'elle ait dix-neuf ans elle est toujours très jeune. (b) **The project is i.,** le projet n'est pas suffisamment mûri.
immatureness [,imə'tjuənis], **immaturity** [,imə'tjuəriti], *s.* Immaturité *f.*
immeasurable [im'meʒ(ə)rəbl], *a.* (Espace) incommensurable; (temps) immesurable, immense. **To my i. delight,** à ma joie infinie, -**ably,** *adv.* Démesurément; outre mesure.
immediate [i'mi:djət], *a.* Immédiat. 1. (a) Sans intermédiaire; direct. **My i. object,** mon premier but. **The i. future,** le proche avenir. **In the i. future,** dans un avenir immédiat, dans l'immédiat. (b) **In the i. vicinity,** dans le voisinage immédiat. 2. Instantané; sans retard. **'For i. delivery,'** "à livrer de suite." 3. (Besoin) pressant, urgent. -**ly.** 1. *adv.* Immédiatement. (a) **It does not affect me i.,** cela ne me touche pas directement. (b) Tout de suite. **Please answer i.,** veuillez nous répondre incessamment. **I. on his return I wrote to him,** dès son retour je lui ai écrit. **I. after,** aussitôt après. 2. *conj.* **I. he received the money,** he paid me, dès qu'il eut reçu l'argent il me paya.
immemorial [,imə'mɔːriəl], *a.* Immémorial, -aux. **From time i.,** de temps immémorial, de toute éternité.
immense [i'mens], *a.* (Étendue) immense, vaste; (quantité) énorme. *F:* **An i. appetite,** un appétit féroce. -**ly,** *adv.* Immensément. *F:* **To enjoy oneself i.,** s'amuser énormément.
immensity [i'mensiti], *s.* Immensité *f.*
immensurable [i'menʃurəbl], *a.* Immensurable.
immerse [i'məːs], *v.tr.* 1. Immerger, submerger, plonger (qn, qch.) (dans un liquide). 2. **To be immersed in one's work,** être absorbé dans son travail.
immersion [i'məːʃ(ə)n], *s.* 1. Immersion *f,* submersion *f.* *El:* **I. heater,** (i) chauffe-eau *m* électrique; (ii) élément chauffant. **Baptism by i.,** baptême par immersion. 2. Absorption *f* (d'esprit) (in, dans).
immigrant ['imigrənt], *a. & s.* Immigrant, -ante; immigré, -ée.
immigrate ['imigreit], *v.i.* Immigrer.
immigration [,imi'greiʃ(ə)n], *s.* Immigration *f.* **I. officer,** agent *m* du service de l'immigration.

imminence ['iminəns], *s.* Imminence *f,* proximité *f* (of, de).
imminent ['iminənt], *a.* (Danger) imminent. -**ly,** *adv.* D'une manière imminente.
immiscible [i'misibl], *a.* Immiscible; qui ne peut être mélangé.
immitigable [i'mitigəbl], *a.* 1. Implacable. 2. Que l'on ne saurait adoucir.
immixture [i'mikstʃər], *s.* Mélange *m.*
immobile [i'moubail, -biːl], *a.* 1. Fixe; à demeure. 2. Immobile.
immobility [,imo'biliti], *s.* Immobilité *f.*
immobilization [i,moubilai'zeiʃ(ə)n], *s.* 1. (a) Immobilisation *f* (d'un bras cassé, etc.). (b) Immobilisation, arrêt *m* (de la circulation). 2. *Fin:* Immobilisation (de capitaux).
immobilize [i'moubilaiz], *v.tr.* 1. Immobiliser, arrêter (une armée). 2. *Fin:* **To i. capital, specie,** rendre des capitaux indisponibles; immobiliser des espèces (monnayées).
immoderate [i'mɔd(ə)rit], *a.* Immodéré, intempéré, extravagant. **I. thirst,** soif démesurée. -**ly,** *adv.* Immodérément.
immoderateness [i'mɔd(ə)ritnis], **immoderation** [i,mɔdə'reiʃ(ə)n], *s.* Immodération *f,* excès *m,* extravagance *f.*
immodest [i'mɔdist], *a.* Immodeste, impudique.
immodesty [i'mɔdisti], *s.* Immodestie *f,* impudeur *f.*
immolate ['imoleit], *v.tr.* Immoler.
immolation [,imo'leiʃ(ə)n], *s.* Immolation *f.*
immolator ['imoleitər], *s.* Immolateur, -trice.
immoral [i'mɔrəl], *a.* Immoral, -aux. (Of pers.) Dissolu. **I. conduct,** débauche *f. Jur:* **I. offence,** attentat *m* aux mœurs. -**ally,** *adv.* Immoralement.
immorality [imo'ræliti], *s.* Immoralité *f;* débauche *f.*
immortal [i'mɔːtl], *a. & s.* Immortel (*m*). **The immortals,** les (dieux) immortels.
immortality [,imɔː'tæliti], *s.* Immortalité *f.*
immortalize [i'mɔːtəlaiz], *v.tr.* Immortaliser.
immortelle [,imɔː'tel], *s. Bot:* Immortelle *f.*
immovability [i,muːvə'biliti], *s.* 1. Fixité *f* (d'une machine, etc.). 2. Immuabilité *f* (de la volonté).
immovable [i'muːvəbl], *a.* 1. Fixe; à demeure. 2. (Volonté) inébranlable. 3. (Visage) impassible. -**ably,** *adv.* 1. Sans bouger. 2. Immuablement, inébranlablement. 3. Sans s'émouvoir.
immune [i'mjuːn], *a. Med:* **I. from contagion,** à l'abri de la contagion. **I. against a poison,** immunisé contre un poison. *F:* **To have become i. to the drawbacks of the job,** être blindé, cuirassé, vacciné, contre les désagréments du métier.
immunity [i'mjuːniti], *s.* 1. Exemption *f* (from, de). 2. **I. from a disease,** immunité *f* contre une maladie.
immunization [,imjunai'zeiʃ(ə)n], *s. Med:* Immunisation *f* (from, contre).
immunize ['imjunaiz], *v.tr. Med:* Immuniser. **To i. against diphtheria,** vacciner contre la diphtérie.
immunochemistry [i'mjuːnou'kemistri], *s.* Immunochimie *f.*
immure [i'mjuər], *v.tr.* Enfermer, cloîtrer (qn).
immutability [i,mjuːtə'biliti], *s.* Immu(t)abilité *f.*
immutable [i'mjuːtəbl], *a.* Immuable; inaltérable. -**ably,** *adv.* Immuablement.
imp [imp], *s.* (a) Diablotin *m,* lutin *m.* (b) *F:* (Of child) Petit diable; polisson, -onne.
impact ['impækt], *s.* Choc *m,* impact *m.*
impaction [im'pækʃ(ə)n], *s. Surg:* Impaction *f. Med:* **I. of the bowel,** occlusion intestinale.
impair [im'peər], *v.tr.* Affaiblir (la vue, l'esprit); altérer, abîmer (la santé); diminuer (les forces); ébrécher (sa fortune). **Impaired digestion,** estomac délabré.
impairment [im'peəmənt], *s.* Affaiblissement *m;* altération *f* (de la santé); délabrement *m* (de l'estomac).
impale [im'peil], *v.tr.* 1. *Her:* Accoler (deux blasons). 2. Empaler (un criminel).
impalement [im'peilmənt], *s. Hist:* Supplice *m* du pal.
impalpability [im,pælpə'biliti], *s.* 1. Impalpabilité *f.* 2. Intangibilité *f.*
impalpable [im'pælpəbl], *a.* Impalpable.
impanel [im'pænl], *v.tr.* = EMPANEL.

impart [im'pɑːt], *v.tr.* **1.** (*a*) Donner (du courage); communiquer (un mouvement) (to, à). (*b*) **Body that imparts heat**, corps qui transmet de la chaleur. **2.** Communiquer (des connaissances); faire connaître (une nouvelle) (to, à).

impartial [im'pɑːʃ(ə)l], *a.* (*Of pers., conduct*) Impartial, -aux. **-ally,** *adv.* Impartialement.

impartiality ['im,pɑːʃi'æliti], *s.* Impartialité *f*.

impassable [im'pɑːsəbl], *a.* Infranchissable; (chemin) impraticable.

impasse ['ɛ̃pɑːs, æm'pɑːs], *s.* **To be in an i.**, se trouver dans une impasse, une situation sans issue; *F:* se trouver coincé.

impassibility [im,pæsi'biliti], *s.* Impassibilité *f*.

impassible [im'pæsibl], *a.* Impassible. **1.** Insensible (i) à la douleur, (ii) à la pitié. **2.** (Visage) composé. **-ibly,** *adv.* Impassiblement.

impassion [im'pæʃ(ə)n], *v.tr.* Passionner. **impassioned,** *a.* (Discours) passionné, exalté.

impassive [im'pæsiv], *a.* Impassible; (visage) composé. **-ly,** *adv.* Sans s'émouvoir.

impassiveness [im'pæsivnis], **impassivity** [impæ'siviti], *s.* Impassibilité *f*; insensibilité *f*.

impaste [im'peist], *v.tr. Art:* Empâter.

impasto [im'pæstou], *s. Art:* Empâtement.

impatience [im'peiʃ(ə)ns], *s.* (*a*) Impatience *f*. (*b*) **I. of sth.,** intolérance *f* de qch. (*c*) **I. to do sth.,** désir impatient de faire qch.

impatient [im'peiʃ(ə)nt], *a.* (*a*) Impatient. **To get, grow, i.,** s'impatienter. (*b*) **To be i. of advice,** souffrir difficilement les conseils. (*c*) **To be i. to do sth.,** être impatient de faire qch. **-ly,** *adv.* Avec impatience; impatiemment.

impeach [im'piːtʃ], *v.tr.* **1.** (*a*) Attaquer, mettre en doute (la probité de qn). (*b*) *Jur:* Révoquer (un témoignage) en doute. **2.** *Jur:* **To i. s.o. for high treason,** accuser qn de haute trahison.

impeachable [im'piːtʃəbl], *a.* **1.** (*a*) (*Of motive*) Attaquable; susceptible de blâme. (*b*) (Témoin, témoignage) sujet à caution. **2.** *Jur:* (*Of pers.*) Susceptible d'être mis en accusation.

impeachment [im'piːtʃmənt], *s.* (*a*) Accusation *f*. (*b*) *Hist:* Mise *f* en accusation (d'un ministre, etc.) par la Chambre des Communes.

impeccability [im,pekə'biliti], *s.* Impeccabilité *f*.

impeccable [im'pekəbl], *a.* Impeccable **-ably,** *adv.* De façon irréprochable.

impecuniosity [,impikjuːni'ɔsiti], *s.* Manque *m.* d'argent.

impecunious [,impi'kjuːniəs], *a.* Impécunieux, -euse, besogneux, -euse.

impedance [im'piːdəns], *s. El:* Impédance *f*.

impede [im'piːd], *v.tr.* Mettre obstacle à, empêcher, entraver, gêner (le progrès). **To i. the traffic,** entraver la circulation.

impediment [im'pedimənt], *s.* **1.** (*a*) Entrave *f*, empêchement *m*, obstacle *m* (to, à). (*b*) **I. of speech,** empêchement de la langue. **2.** *pl.* = IMPEDIMENTA.

impedimenta [im,pedi'mentə], *s.pl.* Impedimenta *mpl*; *F:* bagages *m*.

impel [im'pel], *v.tr.* (**impelled**) **1.** Pousser, forcer (s.o. to do sth., qn à faire qch.). **2.** Pousser (en avant). **Ship impelled by the wind,** navire chassé par le vent. **impelling,** *a.* Impulsif; moteur, -trice. **I. need,** besoin harcelant.

impend [im'pend], *v.i.* **1.** Être suspendu (over, sur). **2.** **War was impending,** la guerre était imminente. **impending,** *a.* (Danger) imminent, menaçant. **Her i. arrival,** son arrivée prochaine.

impenetrability [im,penitrə'biliti], *s.* Impénétrabilité *f*.

impenetrable [im'penitrəbl], *a.* Impénétrable (to, by, à). **I. mystery,** mystère insondable. **-ably,** *adv.* Impénétrablement.

impenitence [im'penit(ə)ns], *s.* Impénitence *f*.

impenitent [im'penit(ə)nt], *a. & s.* Impénitent, -ente. **-ly,** *adv.* Sans contrition.

imperative [im'perətiv]. **1.** *a. & s. Gram:* **In the i. (mood),** à l'impératif *m*, au mode impératif. **2.** *a.* (*a*) Impérieux, péremptoire. (*b*) Urgent, impérieux. **Discretion is i.,** la discrétion s'impose. **It is i. for us to . . .,** il nous incombe à tous de. . . . **-ly,** *adv.* Impérativement; impérieusement.

imperativeness [im'perətivnis], *s.* Urgence *f*.

imperceptibility [,impəsepti'biliti], *s.* Imperceptibilité *f*.

imperceptible [,impə'septəbl], *a.* Imperceptible; (bruit) insaisissable. **An i. difference,** une différence insensible. **I. to the eye,** inappréciable à l'œil. **-ibly,** *adv.* Imperceptiblement, insensiblement.

imperfect [im'pəːfikt]. **1.** *a.* Imparfait, incomplet, défectueux. **2.** *a. & s. Gram:* **I. (tense),** (temps) imparfait *m*. **-ly,** *adv.* Imparfaitement.

imperfectibility [,impəfektə'biliti], *s.* Imperfectibilité *f*.

imperfectible [,impə'fektəbl], *a.* Imperfectible.

imperfection [,impə'fekʃ(ə)n], *s.* **1.** Imperfection *f*, défectuosité *f*. *Bookb:* **Imperfections,** *pl.* défets *mpl*. **2.** État incomplet.

imperial [im'piəriəl]. **1.** *a.* (*a*) Impérial, -aux. (*b*) (Poids et mesures) qui ont cours légal dans le Royaume-Uni. (*c*) Majestueux, auguste. **2.** *s.* (Papier) grand jésus. **-ally,** *adv.* Impérialement; majestueusement.

imperialism [im'piəriəlizm], *s.* Impérialisme *m*; colonialisme *m*.

imperialist [im'piəriəlist], *s.* Impérialiste *mf*; colonialiste *mf*.

imperialistic [im,piəriə'listik], *a.* Impérialiste; colonialiste.

imperil [im'peril], *v.tr.* (**imperilled**) Mettre en péril, en danger.

imperious [im'piəriəs], *a.* **1.** Impérieux, arrogant. **2.** Urgent. **-ly,** *adv.* Impérieusement.

imperiousness [im'piəriəsnis], *s.* **1.** Arrogance *f*; ton, air, impérieux. **2.** Urgence *f*.

impermeability [im,pəːmiə'biliti], *s.* Imperméabilité *f*.

impermeable [im'pəːmiəbl], *a.* Imperméable, étanche.

impersonal [im'pəːsnl], *a.* **1.** (Style) impersonnel. **2.** *Gram:* **I. verb,** verbe impersonnel, unipersonnel. **-ally,** *adv.* Impersonnellement.

impersonate [im'pəːsəneit], *v.tr.* **1.** Personnifier (qch.). **2.** (*a*) *Th:* Représenter (qn). (*b*) Se faire passer pour (qn).

impersonation [im,pəːsə'neiʃ(ə)n], *s.* **1.** Personnification *f*. **2.** *Th:* (*a*) Création *f*, interprétation *f* (d'un rôle). (*b*) **To give impersonations of the actors of the day,** donner des imitations *f* des acteurs du jour. **3.** *Jur:* Supposition *f* de personne.

impersonator [im'pəːsəneitər], *s.* **1.** Personnificateur, -trice (of, de). **2.** *Th:* (*a*) Créateur, -trice, interprète *mf* (d'un rôle). (*b*) Imitateur, -trice (des vedettes, etc.). **3.** Celui, celle, qui se se fait passer pour un(e) autre.

impertinence [im,pəːtinəns], *s.* **1.** (*a*) Impertinence *f*, insolence *f*. **It's the height of i.,** c'est se moquer du monde. (*b*) **An i., a piece of i.,** une impertinence. **2.** *Jur:* Manque *m* de rapport avec la question.

impertinent [im'pəːtinənt], *a.* **1.** Impertinent, insolent. **An i. boy,** *Pej:* fellow, un impertinent. **To be i. to s.o.,** être insolent envers qn. **2.** *Jur:* Hors de propos; sans rapport avec la cause. **-ly,** *adv.* **1.** Avec impertinence; d'un ton insolent. **2.** *Jur:* (Répondre) en dehors de la question.

imperturbability [,impə(ː)təːbə'biliti], *s.* Imperturbabilité *f*; flegme *m*; sang-froid *m*.

imperturbable [,impə(ː)'təːbəbl], *a.* Imperturbable. **-ably,** *adv.* Imperturbablement; sans se déconcerter.

impervious [im'pəːviəs], *a.* **1.** (*a*) Impénétrable. (*b*) **I. (to water),** imperméable, étanche. **2.** **Person i. to reason,** personne inaccessible, fermée, à la raison. **To be i. to a joke,** ne pas comprendre une plaisanterie. **To have become i. to the drawbacks of the job,** être vacciné contre les désagréments du métier.

imperviousness [im'pəːviəsnis], *s.* (*a*) Impénétrabilité *f*. (*b*) **I. to damp,** imperméabilité *f*; étanchéité *f* (à l'humidité).

impetigo [,impi'taigou], *s. Med:* Impétigo *m*; *F:* (*in children*) gourme *f*.

impetuosity [im,petju'ɔsiti], **impetuousness** [im'petjuəsnis], *s.* Impétuosité *f*.

impetuous [im'petjuəs], *a.* Impétueux. **-ly,** *adv.* Impétueusement.

impetus ['impitəs], *s.* Vitesse acquise; élan *m*. **To give an i. to sth.,** donner l'impulsion à qch.

impiety [im'paiəti], *s.* Impiété *f*.

impinge [im'pin(d)ʒ], *v.ind.tr.* (*a*) **To i. on sth.,** entrer en collision avec qch.; se heurter à qch. (*b*) **To i. on s.o.'s authority,** empiéter sur l'autorité de qn.

impingement [im′pin(d)ʒmənt], s. (a) Collision f, heurt m. (b) Empiétement m.
impious [′impiəs], a. Impie. -ly, adv. Avec impiété.
impish [′impiʃ], a. De petit diable. I. laughter, rire espiègle, malicieux. -ly, adv. En espiègle; comme un petit diable.
impishness [′impiʃnis], s. Espièglerie f.
implacability [im,plækə′biliti], s. Implacabilité f.
implacable [im′plækəbl], a. Implacable (towards, à, pour). -ably, adv. Implacablement.
implant[1] [′implɑːnt], s. Med: etc: Implant m.
implant[2] [im′plɑːnt], v.tr. 1. To be implanted, être implanté (in, dans). 2. Implanter, inculquer (an idea in s.o., une idée dans la tête de qn). To i. in s.o.'s mind the desire to . . ., inspirer à qn le désir de. . . .
implantation [,implɑːn′teiʃ(ə)n], s. 1. Implantation f. 2. Med: Implant m.
implement[1] [′implimənt], s. Outil m, instrument m, ustensile m. Implements of war, matériel m de guerre.
implement[2] [impli′ment], v.tr. Rendre effectif (un contrat); exécuter, remplir (un engagement). To i. one′s promise, accomplir sa promesse. **implementing**, s. Exécution f (d′un engagement); mise f en œuvre (d′un accord).
implementation [,implimen′teiʃ(ə)n], s. = IMPLEMENTING.
implicate [′implikeit], v.tr. Impliquer. To i. s.o. in a crime, impliquer qn dans un crime. Without implicating anyone, sans mettre personne en cause.
implication [,impli′keiʃ(ə)n], s. 1. By i., implicitement. He did not realize the full i. of these words, il ne se rendait pas compte de la portée de ces paroles. 2. Insinuation f. 3. Jur: Implication f (in, dans).
implicit [im′plisit], a. 1. (Condition) implicite. I. recognition of . . ., reconnaissance tacite de. . . . 2. I. faith, confiance aveugle, sans réserve (in, dans). I. obedience, obéissance absolue. -ly, adv. 1. Implicitement, tacitement. 2. To obey i., obéir aveuglément.
implore [im′plɔːr], v.tr. Implorer. I implored his forgiveness, je le suppliai de me pardonner. To i. s.o. to do sth., conjurer, supplier, qn de faire qch. **imploring**, a. (Regard) suppliant; implorant. -ly, adv. D′un tou implorant, suppliant.
imply [im′plai], v.tr. 1. Impliquer. That implies courage on his part, cela lui suppose du courage. The questions implied, les questions en jeu. 2. Do you mean to i. that . . .? est-ce à dire que . . .? You seem to i. that . . ., ce que vous dites fait supposer que. . . . **implied**, 2. (Consentement) implicite, tacite.
impolite [,impə′lait], a. Impoli (to, towards, envers). I. answer, réponse malhonnête. -ly, adv. (Répondre) impoliment.
impoliteness [,impə′laitnis], s. Impolitesse f.
impolitic [im′politik], a. Impolitique; peu politique.
imponderability [im,pondə(ə)rə′biliti], s. Impondérabilité f.
imponderable [im′pond(ə)rəbl], a. & s. Impondérable (m).
import[1] [′impɔːt], s. 1. Sens m, signification f (d′un mot); teneur f (d′un document). 2. I had not grasped the full i. of these words, je ne m′étais pas rendu compte de toute la portée de ces mots. Matter of great i., affaire de haute importance. 3. Com: I. duty, droit m d′entrée. (Usu. pl.) Imports, (i) articles m d′importation; (ii) importations f.
import[2] [im′pɔːt], v.tr. 1. Com: Importer (des marchandises). Imported goods, importations f. 2. Indiquer. (a) Signifier; vouloir dire. (b) Déclarer, faire savoir (that, que). **importing**[1], a. Importateur, -trice. **importing**[2], s. Importation f (de marchandises).
importance [im′pɔːt(ə)ns], s. (a) Importance f. To give i. to a word, mettre un mot en valeur. To be of i., avoir de l′importance. Question of first, capital, i. question d′importance primordiale, capitale. It is of i. to . . ., il importe de. . . . It is of no great i., cela importe peu. To attach the greatest i. to a fact, tenir le plus grand compte d′un fait. (b) (Of pers.) Importance; conséquence f. People of i., personnages importants.

important [im′pɔːt(ə)nt], a. (a) Important. It is i. for you to know that . . ., il importe que vous sachiez que. . . . (b) (Of pers.) Important; plein d′importance. To look i., prendre, se donner, des airs d′importance. -ly, adv. (a) D′une manière importante. (b) D′un air, d′un ton, d′importance.
importation [,impɔː′teiʃ(ə)n], s. Importation f.
importer [im′pɔːtər], s. Importateur, -trice.
importunate [im′pɔːtjunət], a. (Créancier) importun; (visiteur) ennuyeux. -ly, adv. Importunément.
importune [impɔː′tjuːn, im′pɔːtjuːn], v.tr. Importuner (qn).
importunity [,impɔː′tjuːniti], s. Importunité f.
impose [im′pouz]. 1. v.tr. Typ: Imposer (une feuille); mettre (la matière) en pages. 2. v.tr. (a) To i. conditions (up)on s.o., imposer des conditions à qn. (b) To i. a tax on sugar, imposer, taxer, le sucre; frapper le sucre d′un impôt. To i. a penalty on s.o., infliger une peine à qn; frapper qn d′une peine. 3. v.i. To i. (up)on s.o., en imposer à qn; en faire accroire à qn; abuser de l′amabilité de qn. To (let oneself) be imposed upon, se laisser duper, F: se laisser monter le coup (par qn). **imposing**, a. (Air, ton) imposant; (spectacle) grandiose. -ly, adv. D′une manière imposante.
imposition [,impə′ziʃ(ə)n], s. 1. (a) Typ: Imposition f (d′une feuille). (b) Imposition (d′une tâche). 2. Imposition, impôt m; pl. contributions f. 3. Abus m de la bonne volonté de qn. 4. Sch: O: Pensum m. 5. Tromperie f, imposture f.
impossibility [im,posə′biliti], s. 1. Impossibilité f (de qch.). 2. Chose f impossible. Physical i., chose matériellement impossible. No one is expected to perform impossibilities, à l′impossible nul n′est tenu.
impossible [im′posəbl]. 1. a. (a) Impossible. To make it i. for s.o. to do sth., mettre qn dans l′impossibilité de faire qch. (b) (Histoire, récit) invraisemblable. I. person, personne difficile à vivre. You are i.! vous êtes impossible! vous êtes ridicule! I. hat, chapeau m impayable, grotesque, invraisemblable. 2. s. The i., l′impossible m.
impost[1] [′impoust], s. 1. Impôt m; taxe f. 2. Turf: Handicap m; surcharge f.
impost[2], s. Arch: Imposte f, sommier m.
impostor [im′postər], s. Imposteur m.
imposture [im′postʃər], s. Imposture f, supercherie f, tromperie f.
impotence [′impət(ə)ns], **impotency** [′impətənsi], s. (a) Impuissance f. (b) Faiblesse f, impotence f.
impotent [′impət(ə)nt], a. (a) Impuissant. (b) Impotent, décrépit. -ly, adv. Sans force; en vain.
impound [im′paund], v.tr. 1. (a) Mettre (une bête) en fourrière. (b) Hyd.E: Endiguer, capter (les eaux). 2. Jur: Confisquer, saisir.
impoverish [im′pov(ə)riʃ], v.tr. Appauvrir.
impoverishment [im′pov(ə)riʃmənt], s. Appauvrissement m (d′un pays, du sang); dégradation f (du sol).
impracticability [im,præktikə′biliti], s. Impraticabilité f, impossibilité f.
impracticable [im′præktikəbl], a. 1. Infaisable, impraticable. I. ideas, idées f irréalisables. 2. (Of pers.) Intraitable.
imprecation [,impri′keiʃ(ə)n], s. Imprécation f, malédiction f.
imprecatory [′imprikeitəri], a. Imprécatoire.
imprecise [,impri′sais], a. Imprécis.
imprecision [,impri′siʒ(ə)n], s. Imprécision f.
impregnable [im′pregnəbl], a. (Forteresse) imprenable, inexpugnable. -ably, adv. D′une façon inattaquable; dans une situation inexpugnable; invinciblement.
impregnate [′impregneit], v.tr. 1. Biol: Imprégner, féconder. 2. Imprégner, imbiber (sth. with sth., qch. de qch.).
impregnation [,impreg′neiʃ(ə)n], s. 1. Biol: Fécondation f. 2. Imprégnation f.
impresario [,impre′sɑːriou], s. Impresario m.
imprescriptible [,impris′kriptəbl], a. Jur: (Droit) imprescriptible.
impress[1] [′impres], s. (a) Impression f, empreinte f. (b) Marque distinctive; cachet m. Work that bears the i. of genius, œuvre qui porte le cachet du génie.

mpress² [im'pres], *v.tr.* **1.** (*a*) To i. a seal upon wax, imprimer un sceau sur la cire. (*b*) To i. motion (up)on a body, imprimer un mouvement à un corps. **2.** To i. sth. upon s.o., faire bien comprendre qch. à qn. I must i. upon you that . . ., mettez vous bien dans la tête que. . . . **3.** To i. s.o. with the idea that . . ., pénétrer qn de l'idée que. . . . **4.** (*a*) He impressed me favourably, il m'a fait une impression favorable. *F:* I'm not terribly impressed by him, il ne m'emballe pas. (*b*) To i. s.o., faire impression sur qn; impressionner qn. His firmness impressed them, sa fermeté leur en a imposé. *F:* I am not impressed, cela me laisse froid.

mpress³ [im'pres], *v.tr.* (*a*) Réquisitionner (des hommes en âge de servir). *Esp. Navy: A:* Presser, enrôler de force (des marins). (*b*) Réquisitionner (des vivres).

mpression [im'preʃ(ə)n], *s.* **1.** Impression *f* (d'un cachet sur la cire). *Typ:* Impression (d'un livre). **2.** Empreinte *f*, impression (d'un cachet). **3.** *Typ:* Empreinte (des caractères sur le papier); foulage *m.* **4.** *Publ:* Tirage *m*, édition *f* (d'un livre). Second i., deuxième tirage. **5.** (*a*) To make a good, bad, i. on s.o., faire une bonne, une mauvaise, impression sur qn. His speech created a great i., son discours fit une grande impression. (*b*) I am under the i. that . . ., j'ai l'impression que . . ., j'ai dans l'idée que. . . .

mpressionability [im,preʃnə'biliti], *s.* Impressionnabilité *f.*

mpressionable [im'preʃnəbl], *a.* Impressionnable, sensible. To be i., avoir la fibre sensible.

mpressionism [im'preʃənizm], *s. Art:* Impressionnisme *m.*

mpressionist [im'preʃənist], *s.* Impressionniste *mf.*

mpressionistic [im,preʃə'nistik], *a.* Impressionniste.

mpressive [im'presiv], *a.* (Spectacle) impressionnant. I. silence, silence impressionnant, solennel. -ly, *adv.* D'une manière impressionnante; (parler) d'un ton émouvant.

mprimatur [,impri'meitər], *s. Publ:* Imprimatur *m inv.*

mprint¹ ['imprint], *s.* **1.** Empreinte *f* (d'un cachet). **2.** Publisher's i., firme *f*, rubrique *f*, de l'éditeur.

mprint² [im'print], *v.tr.* Imprimer. To i. sth. on sth., imprimer, empreindre, qch. sur qch.

mprison [im'prizn], *v.tr.* Emprisonner. To keep s.o. imprisoned, tenir qn en prison.

mprisonment [im'priznmənt], *s.* Emprisonnement *m.* Ten days' i., dix jours de prison. To serve a sentence of i., faire de la prison.

mprobability [im,probə'biliti], *s.* Improbabilité *f*; invraisemblance *f.*

mprobable [im'probəbl], *a.* Improbable; (histoire) invraisemblable. -ably, *adv.* Improbablement; invraisemblablement. Not i., très probablement.

mpromptu [im'prom(p)tju:]. **1.** *adv.* (Faire qch.) sans préparation; (à l')impromptu. **2.** *a.* (Discours) impromptu *inv.*, improvisé. To get up an i. dance, improviser un bal. **3.** *s. Lit: Mus:* Impromptu *m.*

mproper [im'propər], *a.* **1.** (Partage) incorrect; (expression) impropre; (terme) inexact. *S.a.* FRACTION 2. **2.** Malhonnête, inconvenant; (conte) scabreux. There's nothing i. in the play, la pièce n'a rien d'inconvenant. **3.** Déplacé. -ly, *adv.* **1.** (Se servir d'une expression) improprement. Word i. used, mot employé abusivement. **2.** (Se conduire) d'une manière malséante; incongrûment, malhonnêtement. **3.** Contrairement à la bonne règle. *Aut:* To overtake i., dépasser contrairement au règlement.

mpropriety [,imprə'praiəti], *s.* (*a*) Impropriété *f* (de langage). (*b*) Inconvenance *f* (de conduite).

mprove [im'pru:v]. **1.** *v.tr.* (*a*) Améliorer (qch.); perfectionner (une invention). *Agr:* Bonifier, amender (le sol); abonnir (un terrain). To i. the appearance of sth., embellir qch. (*b*) To i. the occasion, saisir the shining hour, tirer parti de l'occasion. (*c*) *v.ind.tr.* To i. (up)on sth., améliorer qch.; remédier aux imperfections de qch. *Com:* To i. on s.o.'s offer, enchérir sur l'offre de qn. **2.** *v.i.* S'améliorer; (*of wine*) se bonifier, s'abonnir. To i. with use, s'améliorer à l'usage. He has greatly improved, il a fait de grands progrès. Business is improving, les affaires reprennent. She has greatly improved in looks, elle a beaucoup

embelli, elle est beaucoup embellie. **improved,** *a.* **1.** (*Of situation, position*) Amélioré; (*of invention, method*) perfectionné. *Agr:* I. land, terrain amendé. **improving,** *a.* **1.** (*a*) Améliorant; qui rend meilleur. (*b*) (Livre) instructif, édifiant. **2.** (Santé) en voie de rétablissement.

improvement [im'pru:vmənt], *s.* **1.** Amélioration *f* (de la situation); perfectionnement *m* (d'une invention); embellissement *m* (d'une ville). Open to i., susceptible d'amélioration. **2.** (*a*) (*Usu. pl.*) Improvements, améliorations, embellissements. All these so-called improvements, tous ces prétendus progrès. (*b*) To be an i. on sth., surpasser qch.; valoir mieux que qch. My new car is a great i. on the old one, ma nouvelle voiture est bien supérieure à l'ancienne.

improvidence [im'providəns], *s.* Imprévoyance *f.*

improvident [im'providənt], *a.* (*a*) Imprévoyant. (*b*) Prodigue. -ly, *adv.* Sans prévoyance.

improvisation [,improvai'zeiʃ(ə)n], *s.* Improvisation *f.*

improvise ['improvaiz], *v.tr.* Improviser (des vers, de la musique, un abri).

improviser ['improvaizər], *s.* Improvisateur, -trice.

imprudence [im'pru:d(ə)ns], *s.* Imprudence *f.*

imprudent [im'pru:d(ə)nt], *a.* Imprudent. How i. of you! quelle imprudence de votre part! -ly, *adv.* Imprudemment.

impudence ['impjud(ə)ns], *s.* Impudence *f*, effronterie *f*, audace *f.* To have the i. to say sth., avoir l'aplomb de dire qch. A piece of i., une insolence.

impudent ['impjud(ə)nt], *a.* Effronté, insolent. -ly, *adv.* Effrontément.

impugn [im'pju:n], *v.tr.* Attaquer, contester (une proposition); mettre en doute (la véracité de qch.). *Jur:* To i. a piece of evidence, récuser un témoignage.

impugnment [im'pju:nmənt], *s.* Mise *f* en doute (d'une affirmation). *Jur:* Récusation *f* (d'un témoin).

impulse ['impʌls], *s.* **1.** (*a*) Impulsion *f*; poussée motrice. (*b*) To give an i. to sth., donner une impulsion, de l'impulsion (au commerce, etc.). **2.** Impulsion; mouvement spontané; élan *m.* His first i. was to . . ., son premier mouvement fut de. . . . Rash, sudden i., coup *m* de tête. To yield to i., céder à l'entraînement du moment.

impulsion [im'pʌlʃ(ə)n], *s.* Impulsion *f*; *Mec.E: etc:* force impulsive.

impulsive [im'pʌlsiv], *a.* **1.** I. force, force impulsive. **2.** (*Of pers., action*) Impulsif; velléitaire; primesautier. I. action, coup *m* de tête. -ly, *adv.* (Agir) par impulsion.

impulsiveness [im'pʌlsivnis], *s.* Caractère impulsif.

impunity [im'pju:niti], *s.* Impunité *f.* With i., impunément.

impure [im'pjuər], *a.* Impur.

impurity [im'pjuəriti], *s.* **1.** Impureté *f* I. in the blood, vice *m* du sang. **2.** *pl.* Impurities, saletés *f*; corps étrangers.

imputability [im,pju:tə'biliti], *s.* Imputabilité *f.*

imputable [im'pju:təbl], *a.* Imputable, attribuable (to, à).

imputation [,impju(:)'teiʃ(ə)n], *s.* Imputation *f.* (*a*) Attribution *f* (d'un crime à qn). (*b*) Chose imputée à qn.

impute [im'pju:t], *v.tr.* Imputer.

in [in]. I. *prep.* **1.** (*Of place*) (*a*) En, à, dans. In Europe, en Europe. In Japan, au Japon. In India, dans l'Inde, aux Indes. (*Before names of islands that never take an article*) In Ceylon, à Ceylan. In Madagascar, à Madagascar. In Newfoundland, à Terre-Neuve. In such and such a latitude, sous telle ou telle latitude. Our conversations in Rome, nos conversations de Rome. In Paris, à Paris. The streets in Paris, les rues de Paris. To be in town, être en ville. To spend a week in town, passer une semaine à la ville. In the country, à la campagne. *Mil:* In the field, en campagne. In the press, sous presse. In prison, en prison. In school, in church, à l'école, à l'église. In bed, au lit. In one's house, chez soi. In the second chapter, au deuxième chapitre. My fate is in your hands, mon sort est entre vos mains. I have nothing in your size, je n'ai rien à votre taille. In the distance, au loin. In your place, à votre place. Wounded in the shoulder, blessé à l'épaule. (*b*) (*Among*) In the crowd, dans la foule. It is not done in our circle, cela ne se fait pas parmi nous. He is in the sixties, il a passé la soixantaine. 2. (In respect of) Blind in one eye, aveugle d'un œil. Strong in logic, fort en logique. Two feet in length, long de deux pieds. The books, three in number, ces livres, au nombre de trois. 3. (Of ratio) One in ten, un sur dix. To pay two shillings in the pound, payer deux shillings par livre sterling. Once in ten years, une fois tous les dix ans. 4. (Of time) (a) In those days, en ce temps-là. In the reign of Queen Victoria, sous la règne de la reine Victoria. In the night, pendant la nuit; de nuit. In the afternoon, dans l'après-midi. At four o'clock in the afternoon, à quatre heures de l'après-midi. In the evening, le soir, pendant la soirée. In summer, autumn, winter, en été, en automne, en hiver. In spring, au printemps. In August, au mois d'août, en août. In the future, à l'avenir. In the past, dans le passé. Never in my life, jamais de ma vie. (b) To do sth. in three hours, faire qch. en trois heures. He'll be here in three hours, il sera là dans trois heures. In a little while, sous peu. (c) In crossing the river, en traversant la rivière. 5. In good health, en bonne santé. In tears, en larmes. In despair, au désespoir. Any man in his senses, tout homme jouissant de son bon sens. 6. (Clothed in) In his shirt, en chemise. In slippers, en pantoufles. Dressed in white, habillé de blanc. 7. To go out in the rain, sortir par la pluie. To work in the rain, travailler sous la pluie. In the sun, au soleil. In the dark(ness), dans l'obscurité. 8. To be in the car industry, être dans l'industrie automobile. 9. In my opinion, à mon avis. In justice, en toute justice. 10. (a) (Of manner) In a gentle voice, d'une voix douce. In the French style, à la française. To be in (the) fashion, être à la mode. (b) To write in French, écrire en français. To write in ink, écrire à l'encre. In writing, par écrit. To talk in whispers, parler en chuchotant. (c) To walk in groups, se promener par groupes. To stand in a row, se tenir en ligne. In alphabetical order, par ordre alphabétique. Packed in dozens, en paquets de douze. (d) (Of material) Dress in green velvet, robe en velours vert. (e) In the form of . . ., sous forme de. . . . (f) To die in hundreds, mourir par centaines. In part, en partie. In places, par endroits. 11. (a) This product is not a poison in itself, ce produit n'est pas un poison en lui-même. (b) A peculiarity in young people, une particularité chez les jeunes gens. (c) His rivals are not in the same class as him, ses rivaux ne sont pas de sa taille. He's not in the running, il n'a aucune chance. II. in, adv. 1. (a) (At home) A la maison, chez soi. Mr Smith is in, M. Smith y est. (b) The harvest is in, la moisson est rentrée. (c) The train is in, le train est en gare, à quai. (d) Is the fire still in? est-ce que le feu brûle encore? (e) In with it! rentrez-le! 2. (a) The Labour Party was in, le parti travailliste était au pouvoir. (b) Strawberries are in, c'est la saison des fraises. (c) My hand is in, je suis bien en train. (d) To be (well) in with s.o., être en bons termes avec qn. (e) My luck is in, je suis en veine. F: To be in on something, être dans le coup. 3. We are in for a storm, nous aurons sûrement de l'orage. F: He is in for it! son affaire est bonne! le voilà dans de beaux draps! F: We are in for coming back on foot, on est bon pour rentrer à pied. 4. Phrases. (a) Day in, day out, tout le long du jour. (b) All in. (i) The prices quoted are all in, les prix cotés s'entendent tous frais compris. (ii) F: I'm absolutely all in, je suis absolument éreinté. III. in, s. To know the ins and outs of a matter, connaître tous les coins et recoins d'une affaire. U.S: F: To have an in with the Senator, avoir l'oreille du Sénateur, avoir ses entrées chez le Sénateur. 'in-fighting, s. Box: Corps à corps m. 'in-going, a. Qui entre; entrant. In-g. tenant, nouveau locataire. in-'laws, s.pl. F: Belle-famille f; les beaux-parents. 'in-patient, s. (Malade) hospitalisé, -ée.

inability [ˌinə'biliti], s. Incapacité f (to do sth., de faire qch.); impuissance f (to do sth., à faire qch.).

inaccessibility ['inæk,sesə'biliti], s. Inaccessibilité f.

inaccessible [ˌinæk'sesəbl], a. Inaccessible (to, à); (personne) inabordable.

inaccuracy]in'ækjurəsi], s. Inexactitude f, imprécision f.

inaccurate [in'ækjurit], a. (Calcul) inexact; (espri imprécis; (sens) incorrect. -ly, adv. (Calcule inexactement; (citer) incorrectement.

inactinic [ˌinæk'tinik], a. Ph: Inactinique.

inaction [in'ækʃ(ə)n], s. Inaction f.

inactive [in'æktiv], a. Inactif, -ive; (esprit) inerte.

inactivity [ˌinæk'tiviti], s. Inactivité f; inertie f passivité f. Masterly i., sage politique f de laisse faire.

inadaptability [ˌinədæptə'biliti], s. Incapacité f d s'adapter (to, à).

inadequacy [in'ædikwəsi], s. Insuffisance f (d'u revenu); imperfection f (de notre langage).

inadequate [in'ædikwit], a. Inadéquat, insuffisan (Of thg) To be i. to do sth., être insuffisant pour fair qch. -ly, adv. Insuffisamment.

inadmissibility [ˌinədmisə'biliti], s. Inadmissibilité (d'une supposition, d'une preuve); irrecevabilité Jur: Non-recevabilité f (d'une réclamation, etc.)

inadmissible [ˌinəd'misəbl], a. (Prétention) inadmis sible; (témoignage) irrecevable.

inadvertence [ˌinəd'vəːt(ə)ns], inadvertency [ˌin əd'vəːtənsi], s. Inadvertance f, étourderie f.

inadvertent [ˌinəd'vəːt(ə)nt], a. Commis par inadver tance, par mégarde. -ly, adv. Par inadvertance, pa mégarde; par étourderie.

inadvisability ['inəd,vaizə'biliti], s. Imprudence f, inop portunité f (d'une action).

inadvisable [inəd'vaizəbl], a. = UNADVISABLE.

inalienability [in,eiliənə'biliti], s. Jur: Inaliénabilité indisponibilité f (d'un bien, d'un don).

inalienable [in'eiliənəbl], a. (Bien, droit) inaliénable.

inamorato, f. -ta [inæmo'raːtou, -tə], s. Amant, -te amoureux, -euse.

inane [i'nein], a. Inepte, stupide. I. remark, ineptie f -ly, adv. Bêtement, stupidement.

inanimate [in'ænimit], a. Inanimé.

inanition [ˌinə'niʃ(ə)n], s. Inanition f.

inanity [i'næniti], s. Inanité f, niaiserie f.

inappeasable [ˌinə'piːzəbl], a. Inapaisable.

inapplicability ['in,æplikə'biliti], s. Inapplicabilité f (tc à).

inapplicable [in'æplikəbl, inə'plikəbl], a. Inapplicabl (to, à).

inapposite [in'æpəzit], a. (Citation, titre) sans rappor (to, avec); inapplicable (to, à); (réponse) faite mal propos, hors de propos.

inappreciable [ˌinə'priːʃəbl], a. Inappréciable (à l'œil

inapprehensible [ˌinæpri'hensibl], a. (Sentiment m signification f) insaisissable, incompréhensible.

inappropriate [ˌinə'prouupriit], a. Qui ne convient pa (to, à); (of word) impropre. -ly, adv. D'une faço impropre.

inapt [in'æpt], a. Inapte. 1. (a) Incapable. (b) Inhabile inexpert. 2. Peu approprié (to, à). -ly, adv. Impro prement.

inaptitude [in'æptitjuːd], s. Inaptitude f (for, à).

inarticulate [ˌinaː'tikjulit], a. 1. Nat.Hist: Inarticulé sans articulations. 2. (a) (Son) inarticulé, impar faitement prononcé. (b) Muet, -ette; incapable d parler. I. with rage, bégayant de colère. -ly, adv Indistinctement.

inartistic [ˌinaː'tistik], a. Peu artistique; sans valeu artistique; (of pers.) dépourvu de sens artistique -ally, adv. Sans art.

inasmuch as [ˌinəz'mʌt(ə)z], conj.phr. 1. Attendu que vu que. 2. A: Dans la mesure que; en tant que.

inassimilable [ˌinə'siməbl], a. Inassimilable.

inattention [ˌinə'tenʃ(ə)n], s. Inattention f. (a) Dis traction f. (b) I. to business, négligence f de se affaires. (c) Manque m de prévenances (to(wards s.o., à l'égard de qn).

inattentive [ˌinə'tentiv], a. 1. Inattentif, distrait. 2 Négligent (to, de). -ly, adv. Sans attention; dis traitement.

inaudibility [in,ɔːdə'biliti], s. Insaisissabilité f (d'u son); faiblesse f (de la voix).

inaudible [in'ɔːdəbl], a. (Son) imperceptible. I. voice voix faible. -ibly, adv. Sans bruit; (parler) d manière à ne pas être entendu.

inaugural [i'nɔːgjur(ə)l], a. Inaugural, -aux. I. address discours d'inauguration.

naugurate [i'nɔ:gjureit], v.tr. Inaugurer (un monument); inaugurer, commencer (une ère nouvelle); mettre en application (un nouveau système).

nauguration [i,nɔ:gju'reiʃ(ə)n], s. Inauguration f; mise f en application (d'un nouveau système).

nauspicious [,inɔ:s'piʃəs], a. Peu propice, impropice; néfaste. At an i. moment, à un moment malencontreux.

nborn ['in'bɔ:n], a. 1. (Instinct) inné, infus. 2. Med: I. weakness, faiblesse congénitale.

nbred ['in'bred], a. 1. Inné, naturel. 2. Breed: (Of horse, etc.) Consanguin.

nbreeding ['in'bri:diŋ], s. Biol: (Of animals, plants) Croisement consanguin.

nca ['iŋkə], s. Hist: Inca m.

ncalculable [in'kælkjuləbl], a. 1. Incalculable. 2. I. temper, humeur sur laquelle on ne peut compter. -ably, adv. Incalculablement.

ncandescence [,inkæn'des(ə)ns], s. Incandescence f; Metall: chaleur blanche.

ncandescent [,inkæn'des(ə)nt], a. Incandescent. I. light, lumière à incandescence.

ncantation [,inkæn'teiʃ(ə)n], s. Incantation f, conjuration f, charme m.

ncapability [in,keipə'biliti], s. Incapacité f. Jur: Inéligibilité f.

ncapable [in,keipəbl], a. 1. Incapable (of, de). I. of speech, incapable de parler. I. of proof, non susceptible de preuve. I. of pity, inaccessible a la pitié. 2. (Homme) incapable, incompétent. Jur: To be declared i. of managing one's own affairs, être en état d'incapacité légale.

ncapacitate [,inkə'pæsiteit], v.tr. 1. Rendre (qn) incapable (from, for, de). 2. Jur: Frapper (qn) d'incapacité.

ncapacitation ['inkə,pæsi'teiʃ(ə)n], s. 1. Jur: Privation f de capacité légale. 2. (a) I. for work, incapacité f de travail. (b) Mil: Invalidité f.

ncapacity [,inkə'pæsiti], s. 1. Incapacité f, incompétence f. Jur: The i. of the staff, la nullité du personnel. 2. Jur: Incapacité légale; inhabilité f (to inherit, à succéder).

ncarcerate [in'kɑ:səreit], v.tr. Incarcérer, mettre en prison, emprisonner.

ncarceration [in,kɑ:sə'reiʃ(ə)n], s. Incarcération f, emprisonnement m.

ncarnadine [in'kɑ:nədain], a. (a) Incarnadin; incarnat; couleur (de) chair. (b) Rouge sang inv.

ncarnate¹ [in'kɑ:neit], a. (a) (Of Christ) To become i., s'incarner. (b) A devil i., un démon incarné.

ncarnate² [in'kɑ:neit], v.tr. Incarner (une idée).

ncarnation [,inkɑ:'neiʃ(ə)n], s. Incarnation f (du Christ, d'une idée). 2. (Of pers.) To be the i. of wisdom, être la sagesse incarnée.

ncautious [in'kɔ:ʃəs], a. Imprudent; inconsidéré. -ly, adv. Imprudemment; sans réflexion.

ncendiarism [in'sendjərizm], s. Incendie m volontaire.

ncendiary [in'sendjəri]. 1. a. (Matériel) incendiaire. I. bomb, bombe f incendiaire. 2. s. Incendiaire m.

ncense¹ ['insens], s. Encens m. 'incense-bearer, s. Ecc: Thuriféraire m. 'incense-burner, s. 1. (Pers.) Brûleur, -euse, d'encens. 2. Ecc: Encensoir m.

ncense² [in'sens], v.tr. Exaspérer, courroucer. incensed, a. Enflammé de colère; courroucé.

ncentive [in'sentiv]. 1. a. (a) Provocant, excitant. (b) Stimulant. 2. s. Stimulant m, aiguillon m, encouragement m. Unemployment is an i. to crime, le chômage pousse au crime.

nception [in'sepʃ(ə)n], s. Commencement m, début m (d'une entreprise, etc.).

ncessant [in'sesnt], a. (Bruit) incessant, continuel. -ly, adv. Sans cesse; incessamment.

ncest ['insest], s. Inceste m.

ncestuous [in'sestjuəs], a. Incestueux, -euse.

nch [in(t)ʃ], s. Meas: Pouce m (= 1/36 du yard; = 2 centimètres 54). He couldn't see an i. before him, il n'y voyait pas à deux pas devant lui. To be within an i. of death, être à deux doigts de la mort. Not to give way an i., ne pas reculer d'une semelle. By inches, i. by i., peu à peu, petit à petit. I know every i. of the neighbourhood, je connais la région comme ma poche. To kill s.o. by inches, tuer qn à petit feu. Give him an i. and he'll take an ell, donnez-lui-en grand comme le doigt et il en prendra long comme le bras Knitting: I've still several inches to do, il m'en reste quelques doigts à faire.

incidence ['insid(ə)ns], s. 1. Incidence f (d'un impôt). 2. Opt: Angle d'i., angle m d'incidence. 3. The i. of tuberculosis has increased, les cas de tuberculose se sont multipliés.

incident¹ ['insid(ə)nt], s. Incident m. Journey full of incidents, voyage mouvementé. The different incidents of a novel, les épisodes, les incidents, d'un roman.

incident², a. 1. Qui appartient, qui tient (to, à). Dangers i. to travel, dangers que comporte un voyage. 2. Opt: (Rayon) incident.

incidental [,insi'dentl]. 1. a. (a) (Événement) fortuit, accidentel; (of observation) incident; (of circumstances, etc.) incidentel, -elle. I. expenses, faux frais. Gram: I. clause, incidente f, incise f. (b) I. to sth., qui est inséparable de qch. Fatigues i. to a journey, fatigues que comporte un voyage. 2. s. Chose fortuite; éventualité f. -ally, adv. 1. Accessoirement. 2. Soit dit en passant, entre parenthèses.

incinerate [in'sinəreit], v.tr. Incinérer, réduire en cendres, carboniser.

incineration [in,sinə'reiʃ(ə)n], s. Incinération f.

incinerator [in'sinəreitər], s. Incinérateur m.

incipient [in'sipiənt], a. Naissant; qui commence. I. beard, barbe naissante.

incise [in'saiz], v.tr. 1. Inciser, faire une incision dans (qch.). 2. Art: Graver en creux.

incision [in'siʒ(ə)n], s. Incision f, entaille f.

incisive [in'saisiv], a. Incisif, tranchant; (ton) mordant; (esprit, jugement) pénétrant. -ly, adv. Incisivement.

incisiveness [in'saisivnis], s. Ton incisif, tranchant.

incisor [in'saizər], s. (Dent) incisive f.

incite [in'sait], v.tr. Inciter, aiguillonner, pousser (to sth., à qch.). To i. s.o. to revolt, exciter qn à la révolte. To i. s.o. to work, stimuler qn au travail. inciting, a. Incitateur, -trice.

incitement [in'saitmənt], s. 1. Incitation f, excitation f (to, à). 2. Stimulant m, aiguillon m.

incivility [,insi'viliti], s. Incivilité f, malhonnêteté f. Piece of i., incivilité.

inclemency [in'klemənsi], s. Inclémence f, rigueur f (de climat). I. of weather, intempérie f.

inclement [in'klemənt], a. (Juge) inclément; (climat) rigoureux, rude.

inclination [,inkli'neiʃ(ə)n], s. 1. Inclination f (de la tête). 2. Inclinaison f, pente f (d'un coteau); dévers m (d'un mur). 3. (a) Inclination, penchant m (to, for, à, pour). To follow one's own i., F: en faire à sa tête. To do sth. from i., faire qch. par goût. (b) I. to stoutness, tendance f à l'embonpoint.

incline¹ ['inklain], s. Pente f, déclivité f, inclinaison f (du terrain). Civ.E: (Acclivity) Rampe f.

incline² [in'klain], v. Incliner. 1. v.tr. (a) Pencher (la tête). (b) B: I. our hearts to keep this law, inclinez nos cœurs à garder ce commandement. 2. v.i. (a) Incliner, pencher (to, towards, à, vers). Inclined at an angle of 45°, incliné à un angle de 45°. (b) Avoir un penchant (to, pour qch., à faire qch.); être enclin, porté (to, à). To i. to pity, incliner à la pitié. (c) Avoir une tendance à. (d) Mil: To i. to the left, obliquer à gauche. inclined, a. 1. (Plan) incliné. 2. Enclin, porté (to, à). To be i. to do sth., avoir de l'inclination à faire qch. He is i. to put on weight, il a une tendance à l'embonpoint. If you feel i., si le cœur vous en dit. If ever you should feel so i., si jamais l'envie vous en prenait. She is always i. to be grumpy at first, elle a le premier mouvement désagréable. I am i. to think that way i., il penche dans ce sens. Prices are i. to fall, les prix m tendent à baisser.

inclinometer [,inkli'nɔmitər], s. Av: etc: Clinomètre m, inclinomètre m.

include [in'klu:d], v.tr. Comprendre, renfermer, embrasser, comporter. He included them all in his contempt, il les englobait tous dans son mépris. His property was sold, his house included, ses biens furent vendus, y compris sa maison. We were six including our host, nous étions six y compris notre hôte. Up to and including 31st December, jusqu'au 31 décembre inclus.

inclusion [in'klu:ʒ(ə)n], s. Inclusion f.

inclusive [in'klu:siv], a. Qui comprend, qui renferme. **I. sum**, somme globale. **I. terms** (*at hotel*), conditions f tout compris, F: le tout compris. **-ly**, adv. Inclusivement.

incoercible [,inko'ə:sibl], a. Incoercible.

incognito [in'kɔgnitou]. **1.** adv. Incognito. **2.** s. To preserve one's i., garder l'incognito m.

incoherence [,inkou'hiər(ə)ns], **incoherency** [,inkou'hiər(ə)nsi], s. Incohérence f.

incoherent [,inkou'hiər(ə)nt], a. Incohérent. **I. style**, style décousu. **-ly**, adv. Sans cohérence, sans suite.

incohesive [,inkou'hi:siv], a. Incohésif, -ive.

incombustibility [,inkombʌstə'biliti], s. Incombustibilité f.

incombustible ['inkəm'bʌstəbl], a. Incombustible.

income ['inkəm], s. Revenu m, revenus mpl. **Private i.**, rente(s) f(pl). **To live up to one's i.**, dépenser (i) tout ce qu'on gagne, (ii) tout son revenu. '**income-tax**, s. Impôt m sur le revenu. **I.-t. return**, déclaration f de revenu. F: **The i.-t. people**, les gens du fisc.

incoming[1] ['inkʌmiŋ], a. Qui entre, qui arrive; (locataire) entrant. **I. tide**, marée montante.

incoming[2], s. **1.** Entrée f, arrivée f. **2.** pl. **Incomings**, recettes f, revenus m.

incommensurability ['inkə,menʃ(ə)rə'biliti], s. Incommensurabilité f.

incommensurable [,inkə'menʃ(ə)rəbl], a. *Mth:* (a) Incommensurable (with, avec). (b) **I. number**, nombre irrationnel.

incommensurate [,inkə'menʃ(ə)rit], a. Pas en rapport, pas en proportion (with, avec); disproportionné (with, à).

incommode [,inkə'moud], v.tr. Incommoder, gêner.

incommodious [,inkə'moudiəs], a. Incommode; (appartement) où l'on est à l'étroit.

incommunicable [,inkə'mju:nikəbl], a. Incommunicable.

incommunicado ['inkəmju:ni'kɑ:dou], a. Tenu au secret.

incomparable [in'kɔmp(ə)rəbl], a. Incomparable (to, with, à). **I. artist**, artiste hors ligne. **-ably**, adv. Incomparablement.

incomparableness [in'kɔmp(ə)rəblnis], s. Incomparabilité f.

incompatibility [,inkəmpætə'biliti], s. Incompatibilité f; inconciliabilité f (de deux théories). **I. of temper**, incompatibilité d'humeur.

incompatible [,inkəm'pætibl], a. **1.** Incompatible, inconciliable, inassociable (with, avec); (of ideas, etc.) inalliable. **2.** (Of metals, etc.) Non, peu, alliable (with, avec); *Pharm:* (médicaments m) incompatibles. **-ibly**, adv. Incompatiblement.

incompetence [in'kɔmpit(ə)ns], **incompetency** [in'kɔmpit(ə)nsi], s. **1.** *Jur:* Incompétence f, incapacité f (d'une personne). **I. to succeed**, inhabilité f à succéder. **2.** Incompétence (de qn); manque m de capacité.

incompetent [in'kɔmpit(ə)nt], a. **1.** *Jur:* Incompétent. **I. to make a will**, inhabile à tester. **I am i. to act**, je n'ai pas qualité pour agir. **2.** Incapable, incompétent. s. **To weed out the incompetents**, éliminer les incapables.

incomplete [,inkəm'pli:t], a. Incomplet, -ète; inachevé. **-ly**, adv. Incomplètement.

incompleteness [,inkəm'pli:tnis], s. Imperfection f, inachèvement m.

incomprehensibility [in,kɔmprihensə'biliti], s. Incompréhensibilité f.

incomprehensible [in,kɔmpri'hensəbl], a. Incompréhensible; indéchiffrable. **-ibly**, adv. Incompréhensiblement.

incomprehension [,inkɔmpri'henʃ(ə)n], s. Manque m de compréhension; incompréhension f.

incomprehensive [,inkɔmpri'hensiv], a. **1.** Incomplet, -ète; non inclusif, -ive. **2.** Incompréhensif, -ive.

incomputable [,inkəm'pju:təbl], a. (Somme f d'argent, nombre m etc.) incalculable.

inconceivable [,inkən'si:vəbl], a. Inconcevable. **-ably**, adv. Inconcevablement.

inconclusive [,inkən'klu:siv], a. Peu concluant. **-ly**, adv. D'une manière peu concluante.

incondensable [,inkən'densəbl], a. (Gaz, etc.) non con densable.

incongruity [,inkɔŋ'gruiti], s. **1.** Désaccord m; manqu m d'harmonie (with, avec). **I. of terms**, disconvenanc f de mots. **2.** Absurdité f, incongruité f. **3.** Incon venance f.

incongruous [in'kɔŋgruəs], a. **1.** Inassociable (with avec); sans rapport (to, with, avec). **I. colours** couleurs disparates. **2.** (Of remark) Incongru déplacé. **-ly**, adv. Sans harmonie; incongrûment.

inconsequence [in'kɔnsikwəns], s. Inconséquence f.

inconsequent [in'kɔnsikwənt], a. Inconséquent, il logique. **-ly**, adv. Inconséquemment.

inconsequential [in,kɔnsi'kwenʃ(ə)l], a. **1.** = INCONSE QUENT. **2.** (Affaire f) sans importance. **-ally**, ad Inconséquemment.

inconsiderable [,inkən'sid(ə)rəbl], a. Peu considérable insignifiant.

inconsiderate [,inkən'sid(ə)rit], a. **1.** Inconsidéré étourdi. **I. opinion**, opinion peu réfléchie. **2.** (Pe sonne) sans égards pour les autres. **It was most i. o you**, vous avez manqué d'égards. **-ly**, adv. **1.** San considération, sans réflexion. **2.** **To behave i. to s.o** manquer d'égards envers qn.

inconsiderateness [,inkən'sidərətnis], s. **1.** Irréflexio f, étourderie f, imprudence f. **2.** Manque d'égard (to, towards, envers).

inconsistency [,inkən'sist(ə)nsi], s. **1.** Inconsistance contradiction f. **2.** Inconséquence f, illogisme m.

inconsistent [,inkən'sist(ə)nt], a. **1.** Incompatible, e contradiction (with, avec); contradictoire (with, à) **His words are i. with his conduct**, il y a désaccor entre ses paroles et sa conduite. **2.** (Of pers.) Incor sistant, inconséquent, incohérent. **To be i. in one' replies**, varier dans ses réponses. **3.** (Histoire) qui n tient pas debout. **-ly**, adv. D'une manière inconsé quente; illogiquement.

inconsolable [,inkən'souləbl], a. Inconsolable. **-abl** adv. Inconsolablement.

inconspicuous [,inkən'spikjuəs], a. Peu en vue; pe apparent; peu frappant; effacé. **-ly**, adv. D'un manière discrète, discrètement.

inconstancy [in'kɔnstənsi], s. Inconstance f; ir stabilité f (du temps).

inconstant [in'kɔnstənt], a. Inconstant, volage. **-l** adv. Inconstamment.

incontestability ['inkən,testə'biliti], s. Incontes tabilité f.

incontestable [,inkən'testəbl], a. (Preuve) inconte table, indéniable. **-ably**, adv. Incontestablement.

incontinence [in'kɔntinəns], s. Incontinence f.

incontinent [in'kɔntinənt], a. Incontinent.

incontinently [in'kɔntinəntli], adv. Sur-le-champ incontinent.

incontrovertible [in,kɔntrə'və:təbl], a. (Vérité) incor testable; (preuve) irrécusable. **-ibly**, adv. San contredit.

inconvenience[1] [,inkən'vi:njəns], s. (a) Incommodité contretemps m. **I am putting you to a lot of i.**, je vou donne beaucoup de dérangement. **Without th slightest i.**, sans le moindre inconvénient. (b) **The of living so far from town**, les inconvénients qu'il y à vivre si loin de la ville.

inconvenience[2], v.tr. Déranger, incommoder, gêne (qn).

inconvenient [,inkən'vi:njənt], a. Malcommode, (c time) inopportun. **It is very i.**, c'est très gênant. **If** is not i. for you, si cela ne vous dérange pas. **-ly**, ad Incommodément.

inconvertible [,inkən'və:təbl], a. (a) *Fin:* Impe mutable. (b) *Log:* Inconversible, inconvertible.

incorporate [in'kɔ:pəreit]. **1.** v.tr. (a) Incorporer, un (with, à, avec). (b) *Com:* Constituer (une associatio en société commerciale. **2.** v.i. S'incorporer (wit others, avec, à, d'autres). **incorporated**, a. **1.** Incor poré; faisant corps (with others, avec d'autres). **2** *Com:* **I. company**, (i) société constituée; (ii) *U.S* société anonyme.

incorporation [in,kɔ:pə'reiʃ(ə)n], s. **1.** Incorporation (in, with, into, à, avec, dans). **2.** *Com:* Constitutio f (d'une association) en société commerciale.

incorporeal [,inkɔ:'pɔ:riəl], a. Incorporel, -elle.

incorrect [ˌinkə'rekt], *a.* **1.** (*a*) (*Of statement*) Inexact. Events have proved us i., les événements nous ont donné tort. (*b*) **I. expression**, locution vicieuse; incorrection *f* de langage. (*c*) **I. text**, texte fautif. **2.** (*Of behaviour*) Incorrect. It is i. to . . ., il est de mauvais ton de. . . . -**ly**, *adv.* **1.** Inexactement. **Letter i. addressed**, lettre mal adressée. **I. printed**, imprimé fautivement. **2.** Incorrectement.
incorrectness [ˌinkə'rektnis], *s.* **1.** Inexactitude *f* (d'un calcul). **2.** Incorrection *f.*
incorrigibility [in,kɔridʒə'biliti], *s.* Incorrigibilité *f.*
incorrigible [in'kɔridʒəbl], *a.* Incorrigible; irréformable. -**bly**, *adv.* Incorrigiblement.
incorrodible [ˌinkə'roudəbl], *a.* Inattaquable (par les acides, aux acides).
incorruptible [ˌinkə'rʌptəbl], *a.* Incorruptible.
increase[1] ['inkriːs], *s.* (*a*) Augmentation *f* (de prix); accroissement *m* (de vitesse); surcroît *m* (de besogne); redoublement *m* (d'efforts). **I. in the cost of living**, renchérissement *m* (du coût) de la vie. **The i. in crime**, la multiplication des crimes. **I. in value** (of property), plus-value *f.* (*b*) *Adv. phr.* **To be on the i.**, être en augmentation; aller (en) croissant. **Unemployment is on the i.**, le chômage s'accentue.
increase[2] [in'kriːs]. **1.** *v.i.* (*a*) Augmenter; grandir, s'agrandir; croître, s'accroître. **The rain increased**, la pluie redoubla. **To i. in price**, renchérir. **To go on increasing**, aller toujours (en) croissant. (*b*) Se multiplier. **The population increases**, la population grossit, se multiplie. **2.** *v.tr.* Augmenter (la production); grossir (le nombre); accroître (sa fortune). **To i. the cost of goods**, renchérir des marchandises. **To i. s.o.'s salary**, augmenter (les appointements de) qn. **To i. speed**, forcer la vitesse. *Nau:* **To i. speed to twenty knots**, pousser l'allure à vingt nœuds. **To i. one's vigilance**, redoubler de vigilance. **Increased cost of living**, renchérissement *m* de la vie. **increasing**, *a.* Croissant. *Mth:* **I. series**, progression ascendante. -**ly**, *adv.* De plus en plus (difficile).
incredibility [in,kredi'biliti], *s.* Incrédibilité *f.*
incredible [in'kredəbl], *a.* Incroyable. -**ibly**, *adv.* Incroyablement.
incredulity [ˌinkri'djuːliti], *s.* Incrédulité *f.*
incredulous [in'kredjuləs], *a.* Incrédule. **I. smile**, sourire d'incrédulité. -**ly**, *adv.* Avec incrédulité.
increment ['inkrimənt], *s.* **1.** Augmentation *f. Mth:* **I. of a function**, accroissement *m* d'une fonction. **2.** Profit *m.* **Unearned i.** (*of land*), plus-value *f.*
incriminate [in'krimineit], *v.tr.* **1.** Incriminer (qn). **2.** Impliquer (qn) (dans une accusation). **Incriminating documents**, pièces *f* à conviction.
incrimination [in,krimi'neiʃ(ə)n], *s.* Incrimination *f*, accusation *f* (de qn).
incrustation [ˌinkrʌs'teiʃ(ə)n], *s.* **1.** (*a*) Incrustation *f*; action *f* d'incruster. (*b*) *Mch:* Entartrage *m* (des chaudières). **2.** (*a*) Incrustation (de nacre). (*b*) *Mch:* Tartre *m.*
incubate ['inkjubeit]. **1.** *v.tr.* Couver, incuber (des œufs). **2.** *v.i.* (*Of eggs, of disease*) Couver.
incubation [ˌinkju'beiʃ(ə)n], *s.* Incubation *f. Med:* **I. period**, période *f* d'incubation, d'invasion (d'une maladie). *Husb:* **Artificial i.**, accouvage *m.*
incubator ['inkjubeitər], *s.* Incubateur *m*, couveuse *f; Husb:* éleveuse *f.*
incubus ['inkjubəs], *s.* **1.** *Myth:* Incube *m.* **2.** (*a*) (*Of pers.*) **To be an i. on s.o.**, être un cauchemar pour qn. (*b*) Fardeau *m*, poids *m* (des impôts).
inculcate ['inkʌlkeit]. *v.tr.* Inculquer (une leçon).
inculcation [ˌinkʌl'keiʃ(ə)n], *s.* Inculcation *f.*
inculpate ['inkʌlpeit], *v.tr.* **1.** Inculper, incriminer (qn). **2.** = INCRIMINATE 2.
inculpation [ˌinkʌl'peiʃ(ɔ)n], *s.* Inculpation *f.*
incumbency [in'kʌmbənsi], *s. Ecc:* **1.** (*a*) Possession *f* d'un bénéfice. (*b*) Charge *f.* **2.** Période *f* d'exercice (d'une charge).
incumbent[1] [in'kʌmbənt], *s. Ecc:* Bénéficier *m*; titulaire *m* (d'une charge).
incumbent[2], *a. Lit:* **To be i. on s.o. to do sth.**, incomber, appartenir, à qn de faire qch.
incumbrance [in'kʌmbrəns], *s.* = ENCUMBRANCE.
incunabulum, *pl.* -**a** [ˌinkju(:)'næbjuləm, -ə], *s.* Incunable *m.*

incur [in'kəːr], *v.tr.* (**incurred**) Courir (un risque); encourir (un blâme); s'attirer (le courroux de qn); contracter (des dettes); subir (une perte). **To i. ridicule**, s'exposer au ridicule. **To i. expenses**, encourir des frais.
incurability [in,kjuərə'biliti], **incurableness** [in'kjuərəblnis], *s.* Incurabilité *f.*
incurable [in'kjuərəbl], *a. & s.* Incurable. -**ably**, *adv.* **To be i. lazy**, être d'une paresse incurable.
incurious [in'kjuəriəs], *a.* Incurieux; sans curiosité. -**ly**, *adv.* Avec indifférence.
incursion [in'kəːʃ(ə)n], *s.* Incursion *f.*
incursive [in'kəːsiv], *a.* Incursif, -ive.
indebted [in'detid], *a.* **1.** Endetté. **2.** Redevable (**to s.o. for sth.**, à qn de qch.).
indebtedness [in'detidnis], *s.* **1.** Dette(s) *f(pl).* **2.** **Our i. to Greece**, notre dette envers la Grèce.
indecency [in'diːsnsi], *s.* Indécence *f*, inconvenance *f.*
indecent [in'diːsnt], *a.* Peu décent, indécent, inconvenant. -**ly**, *adv.* Indécemment.
indecipherable [ˌindi'saif(ə)rəbl], *a.* Indéchiffrable.
indecision [ˌindi'siʒ(ə)n], *s.* Indécision *f*, irrésolution *f.*
indecisive [ˌindi'saisiv], *a.* **1.** (*Of argument*) Indécisif, -ive, peu concluant; (*of battle*) indécis. **2.** (Homme) indécis, irrésolu. -**ly**, *adv.* D'une façon indécisive; sans aboutir à une conclusion.
indecisiveness [ˌindi'saisivnis], *s.* **1.** Manque *m* de décision. **2.** Caractère indécis (d'un combat, etc.).
indeclinable [ˌindi'klainəbl], *a. Gram:* Indéclinable.
indecorous [in'dekərəs], *a.* Inconvenant; peu convenable. -**ly**, *adv.* D'une manière peu convenable.
indecorousness [in'dekərəsnis], *s.* (*a*) Inconvenance *f.* (*b*) Manque *m* de décorum, de maintien.
indeed [in'diːd], *adv.* **1.** (*a*) En effet; vraiment. **One may i. say so**, on peut bien le dire. **Praise which i. was well deserved**, éloges qui de fait étaient bien mérités. (*b*) (*Intensive*) **I am very glad i.**, je suis très très content. **Thank you very much i.**, merci infiniment. (*c*) **I may i. be wrong**, il se peut toutefois que j'aie tort. **2.** Même; à vrai dire. **I think so, I am sure of it**, je le pense et même j'en suis sûr. **I forget his name, if i. I ever knew it**, son nom m'échappe, si tant est que je l'aie jamais su. **3.** (*a*) **Yes i.!** (i) mais certainement! *F:* pour sûr! (ii) (*contradicting*) si fait! (*b*) **I have lived in Paris.—I.?** j'ai vécu à Paris.—Vraiment?
indefatigable [ˌindi'fætigəbl], *a.* Infatigable, inlassable. -**ably**, *adv.* Infatigablement.
indefeasible [ˌindi'fiːzəbl], *a.* (*Droit*) irrévocable, imprescriptible. -**ibly**, *adv.* Irrévocablement.
indefectibility [ˌindi,fektə'biliti], *s. Theol:* Indéfectibilité *f.*
indefectible [ˌindi'fektəbl], *a. Theol:* Indéfectible.
indefensible [ˌindi'fensəbl], *a.* (Théorie) indéfendable; (argument) insoutenable. -**ibly**, *adv.* D'une manière inexcusable.
indefinable [ˌindi'fainəbl], *a.* **1.** Indéfinissable. **2.** (Sentiment) vague (de . . .). -**ably**, *adv.* **1.** D'une manière indéfinissable. **2.** Vaguement.
indefinite [in'definit], *a.* Indéfini. **1.** (Idée) vague. **2.** (*a*) (Nombre) indéterminé. **I. leave**, congé illimité. (*b*) *Gram:* **I. pronoun**, pronom indéfini. -**ly**, *adv.* **1.** (Promettre) vaguement. **2. To postpone sth. i.**, remettre qch. indéfiniment.
indelible [in'delibl], *a.* **1.** Indélébile, ineffaçable. **I. pencil**, crayon *m* à copier; crayon à encre indélébile. -**ibly**, *adv.* Ineffaçablement.
indelicacy [in'delikəsi], *s.* (*a*) Indélicatesse *f*; manque *m* de délicatesse. (*b*) Inconvenance *f*, grossièreté *f.*
indelicate [in'delikit], *a.* (*a*) Indélicat; qui manque de tact; peu délicat. **I. action**, indélicatesse *f.* (*b*) Inconvenant.
indemnification [in,demnifi'keiʃ(ə)n], *s.* **1.** Indemnisation *f*, dédommagement *m* (**for**, de). **2.** Indemnité *f.*
indemnify [in'demnifai], *v.tr.* **1.** Garantir (qn) (**from, against**, contre). **2.** Indemniser, dédommager (qn) (**for a loss**, d'une perte).
indemnity [in'demniti], *s.* **1.** Garantie *f*, assurance *f* (contre une perte, etc.). *Com:* (**Letter of**) **i.**, cautionnement *m*, décharge *f.* **2.** Indemnité *f*, dédommagement *m.*
indent[1] ['indent, in'dent], *s.* (*a*) *Adm:* Ordre *m* de réquisition (pour approvisionnements). (*b*) *Com:* Commande *f* de marchandises (reçue de l'étranger).

indent² [in'dent]. **1.** *v.tr.* (*a*) Denteler, découper (le bord de qch.). (*b*) *Typ:* Renfoncer, (faire) rentrer (une ligne). **2.** *v.i.* To i. for sth., (i) réquisitionner qch. (de qn); (ii) passer une commande (à qn) pour (une marchandise). indented, *a.* **1.** (Bord) dentelé; (littoral) échancré. **2.** *Typ:* I. line, ligne en alinéa, en retrait.

indent³ [in'dent], *v.tr.* Empreindre (en creux); bosseler, bossuer.

indentation [ˌinden'teiʃ(ə)n], *s.* **1.** Impression *f*, foulage *m* (du sable par les roues, etc.). **2.** Dentelure *f*; découpure *f*; échancrure *f* (du littoral). **3.** Empreinte creuse.

indention [in'denʃ(ə)n], *s.* *Typ:* Renfoncement *m* (d'une ligne).

indenture¹ [in'dentʃər], *s.* *Jur:* (*a*) Contrat *m* synallagmatique. To be bound by an i., être lié par un engagement. (*b*) *pl.* Indentures, contrat d'apprentissage.

indenture², *v.tr.* Mettre (qn) en apprentissage (to s.o., chez qn).

independence [ˌindi'pendəns], *s.* Indépendance *f* (of, à l'égard de); autonomie *f* (d'un état). Ghana achieved i. in 1957, le Ghana est devenu indépendant en 1957. The American War of I., la Guerre de l'Indépendance (des États-Unis). *U.S:* I. Day, le quatre juillet (fête nationale). To show i., faire preuve d'indépendance.

independent [ˌindi'pendənt], *a.* (*a*) Indépendant; (état) autonome. *Pol:* I. candidate, candidat indépendant. To be i., être son propre maître. To become i., s'affranchir. I. witness, témoin indépendant. *Mil:* I. firing, tir à volonté. An i. force, une armée autonome. I. school = école *f* libre. (*b*) A man of i. means, un rentier. To be of i. means, vivre de ses rentes. (*c*) (Caractère, air) indépendant. (*d*) I. (front wheel) suspension, roues (avant) indépendantes. -ly, *adv.* **1.** Indépendamment (of, de). They found their pleasure i., ils s'amusaient séparément. **2.** Avec indépendance; d'un air indépendant.

indescribable [ˌindis'kraibəbl], *a.* Indescriptible; (joie) indicible. -ably, *adv.* Indescriptiblement; indiciblement.

indestructibility ['indis,trʌktə'biliti], **indestructibleness** [ˌindis'trʌktəblnis], *s.* Indestructibilité *f*.

indestructible [ˌindis'trʌktəbl], *a.* Indestructible. -ibly, *adv.* Indestructiblement.

indeterminable [ˌindi'tə:m(i)nəbl], *a.* **1.** (Distance) indéterminable. **2.** (Dispute) qu'on ne saurait terminer.

indeterminate [ˌindi'tə:m(i)nit], *a.* Indéterminé; (of thought) vague. *Mth:* I. quantity, quantité indéterminée. I. problem, problème indéterminé, qui comporte plusieurs solutions.

indetermination ['indi,tə:mi'neiʃ(ə)n], *s.* Indétermination *f*, irrésolution *f*. *Mth:* Absence de solution.

index¹, *pl.* **indexes, indices** ['indeks, 'indeksiz, 'indisi:z], *s.* **1.** (*pl.* indexes) Index *m*; premier doigt. **2.** *Tchn:* (*pl.* indexes) Aiguille *f* (de balance). I. correction, correction du zéro. **3.** (*pl.* indices) Indice *m*; signe (indicateur). **4.** (*a*) (*pl.* indexes) Index, table *f* alphabétique, répertoire *m* (d'un livre). I. book, livre *m* répertoire. I. card, fiche *f*. (*b*) *R.C.Ch:* To put a book on the I., mettre un livre à l'Index. **5.** (*pl.* indices) (*a*) *Alg:* Exposant *m*. (*b*) *Opt:* I. of refraction, indice de réfraction. (*c*) *Pol.Ec:* Weighted i., index pondéré. Cost of living i., index du coût de la vie. 'index-finger, *s.* Index *m*. 'index-number, *s.* (*a*) *Com:* Chiffre indicateur. (*b*) *Pol.Ec:* Nombre *m* indice (du coût de la vie).

index², *v.tr.* **1.** (*a*) Faire, dresser, l'index (d'un livre). (*b*) Indexer, répertorier, classer (un article). **2.** *R.C.Ch:* Mettre (un livre) à l'Index.

India ['indjə]. *Pr.n.* L'Inde *f*. *Hist:* British I., l'Inde anglaise. The East I. Company, la Compagnie anglaise des Indes. India paper, *s.* Papier *m* bible. **india-'rubber**, *s.* See RUBBER¹ 3.

Indiaman, *pl.* -men ['indjəmən], *s.* *Hist:* Navire *m* qui faisait le service des Indes orientales.

Indian ['indjən]. **1.** (*a*) *a.* De l'Inde; des Indes; indien. The I. Ocean, la mer des Indes; l'océan Indien. *S.a.* INK¹ 1, TEA 1. (*b*) *s.* Indien, -ienne. **2.** (*a*) *a. & s.* Indien, -ienne (d'Amérique). Red Indians, (les) Peaux-Rouges *m*. (*b*) *a.* I. summer, l'été *m* de la St. Martin. *U.S: F:* I. gift, cadeau-

hameçon *m*. I. giver, donneur, -euse de cadeaux-hameçons. *S.a.* CLUB¹ 1, CORN¹ 2, FILE⁵.

indicate ['indikeit], *v.tr.* **1.** (*a*) Indiquer, montrer. (*b*) At the hour indicated, à l'heure dite, indiquée. (*c*) *Med:* Case in which a certain treatment is indicated, cas pour lequel un certain traitement est indiqué. **2.** Indiquer, dénoter (qch.). Expression that indicates energy, expression *f* qui dénote l'énergie.

indication [ˌindi'keiʃ(ə)n], *s.* **1.** Indication *f* (de qch. à qn). **2.** (*a*) Indice *m*, signe *m*. Not the least i. of . . ., aucune apparence de. . . . There are many indications that . . ., tout porte à croire que. . . . To give clear i. of one's intentions, faire connaître clairement ses intentions.

indicative [in'dikətiv]. **1.** *a. & s.* *Gram:* I. (mood), (mode) indicatif *m*. **2.** *a.* Indicatif (of, de).

indicator ['indikeitər], *s.* (*a*) Table *f* d'orientation. (*b*) Index *m*, aiguille *f* (de baromètre). (*c*) Pressure i., indicateur *m* de pression. *Av:* Turn and bank i., indicateur de virage et de pente latérale. (*d*) *El.E: etc:* I. (board), tableau indicateur; *Tp:* annonciateur *m*. I. switch, culbuteur *m*. Rail: Train i., tableau indicateur du service des quais.

indicatory ['indikeitəri], *a.* **1.** Indicateur, -trice; qui indique. **2.** (Symptôme) indicatif (of, de).

indices ['indisi:z], *s.pl.* See INDEX¹.

indict [in'dait], *v.tr.* Accuser, inculper (qn) (for, de); mettre (qn) en accusation; traduire, poursuivre, (qn) en justice (for, pour).

indictable [in'daitəbl], *a.* **1.** (Personne) attaquable, traduisible, en justice. **2.** (Action) qui tombe sous le coup de la loi. I. offence, délit *m*.

indictment [in'daitmənt], *s.* *Jur:* **1.** Accusation *f*; (*by public prosecutor*) réquisitoire *m*. I. for theft, inculpation *f* de vol. **2.** To draw up an i., rédiger un acte d'accusation.

Indies (the) [ði'indiz]. *Pr.n.pl.* Les Indes *f*. The East I., les Indes (orientales), les Grandes Indes. The West I., les Antilles *f*.

indifference [in'difr(ə)ns], *s.* **1.** Indifférence *f*, manque *m* d'intérêt (to, towards, sth., s.o., pour qch., à l'égard de qn). It is a matter of perfect i. to me, cela m'est parfaitement indifférent. **2.** Médiocrité *f* (de talent, etc.).

indifferent [in'difr(ə)nt], *a.* **1.** Indifférent (to, à). His praise is i. to me, ses éloges ne me font ni chaud ni froid. He is i. to everything, tout lui est indifférent, égal. **2.** Médiocre, passable. Very i. quality, qualité très médiocre. To be an i. painter, peindre pauvrement. **3.** To converse on i. topics, causer de choses sans importance. -ly, *adv.* **1.** Indifféremment; avec indifférence. **2.** Médiocrement.

indifferentism [in'difr(ə)ntizm], *s.* *Rel.H: Pol:* Indifférentisme *m*.

indigence ['indidʒ(ə)ns], *s.* Indigence *f*, pauvreté *f*.

indigenous [in'didʒinəs], *a.* Indigène (to, à); du pays.

indigent ['indidʒ(ə)nt], *a. & s.* Indigent, pauvre; nécessiteux, -euse.

indigestibility ['indi,dʒesti'biliti], *s.* Indigestibilité *f*.

indigestible [ˌindi'dʒestəbl], *a.* Indigeste.

indigestion [ˌindi'dʒestʃ(ə)n], *s.* Dyspepsie *f*; mauvaise digestion. An attack of i., une indigestion.

indignant [in'dignənt], *a.* (Air) indigné; (cri) d'indignation. To be, feel, i. at sth., être indigné, s'indigner, de qch. To make s.o. i., indigner qn. -ly, *adv.* Avec indignation; d'un air indigné.

indignation [ˌindig'neiʃ(ə)n], *s.* Indignation *f*. I. meeting, meeting *m*, réunion *f*, de protestation.

indignity [in'digniti], *s.* Indignité *f*; affront *m*.

indigo ['indigou], *s.* *Dy: Com:* Indigo *m*. 'indigo-'blue, *a. & s.* (Bleu) indigo *m inv.* 'indigo-plant, *s.* Indigotier *m*.

indirect [ˌindi'rekt], *a.* **1.** Indirect. *Gram:* I. speech, object, discours, complément, indirect. **2.** (Moyen, etc.) détourné, oblique. -ly, *adv.* Indirectement; par des voies détournées.

indiscernible [ˌindi'sə:nəbl], *a.* **1.** Indiscernable. **2.** Imperceptible.

indiscipline [in'disiplin], *s.* Indiscipline *f*.

indiscreet [ˌindis'kri:t], *a.* **1.** Indiscret, -ète. **2.** Peu judicieux; imprudent, inconsidéré. -ly, *adv.* **1.** Indiscrètement. **2.** Imprudemment; sans considération.

indiscretion [ˌindisˈkreʃ(ə)n], s. 1. (a) Manque m de discrétion. (b) Indiscrétion f. 2. (a) Action inconsidérée; imprudence f. (b) Écart m de conduite; faux pas. Youthful **indiscretions**, erreurs fpl de jeunesse.

indiscriminate [ˌindisˈkriminit], a. (Charité, admirateur) aveugle. I. **blows**, coups frappés à tort et à travers. -**ly**, adv. Sans faire de distinction; au hasard; (admirer) aveuglément.

indiscrimination [ˈindisˌkrimiˈneiʃ(ə)n], s. Manque m de discernement.

indispensability [ˈindisˌpensəˈbiliti], **indispensableness** [ˌindisˈpensəblnis], s. Indispensabilité f.

indispensable [ˌindisˈpensəbl], a. 1. (Loi, devoir) obligatoire. 2. Indispensable, de première nécessité (to s.o., à qn). To make oneself i. to s.o., se rendre indispensable à qn. -**ably**, adv. Indispensablement.

indispose [ˌindisˈpouz], v.tr. 1. To i. s.o. **towards** s.o., indisposer, prévenir, qn contre qn. 2. To i. s.o. **for** sth., for doing sth., rendre qn incapable, hors d'état, de faire qch. **indisposed**, a. 1. Peu enclin, peu disposé (to do sth., à faire qch.). 2. To be, feel, i., être indisposé, souffrant; ne pas être dans son assiette.

indisposition [ˌindispəˈziʃ(ə)n], s. 1. Manque m d'inclination (to do sth., à faire qch.). 2. Indisposition f, malaise m.

indisputability [ˈindispjutəˈbiliti], s. Indiscutabilité f, incontestabilité f, caractère m incontestable (d'un fait).

indisputable [indisˈpjutəbl], a. Incontestable, indiscutable. -**ably**, adv. Indiscutablement, incontestablement.

indissolubility [ˈindisəljuˈbiliti], s. Indissolubilité f (d'une union).

indissoluble [ˌindisˈsɔljubl], a. (Union) indissoluble. -**bly**, adv. Indissolublement.

indistinct [ˌindisˈti(ŋ)kt], a. (Objet) indistinct; (bruit) confus; (souvenir) vague. -**ly**, adv. (Voir, parler) indistinctement; (sentir) vaguement.

indistinctive [ˌindisˈti(ŋ)ktiv], a. Sans individualité; qui manque de caractère; sans particularité.

indistinctness [ˌindisˈti(ŋ)ktnis], s. Manque m de netteté.

indistinguishable [ˌindisˈtiŋgwiʃəbl], a. 1. Indistinguible, indiscernable (from, de). 2. (Bruit) insaisissable. I. to the naked eye, imperceptible à l'œil nu.

individual [ˌindiˈvidju(ə)l]. 1. a. (a) Individuel. I. **sounds**, sons isolés. (b) Particulier. 2. s. Individu m. -**ally** adv. 1. Individuellement. 2. Personnellement.

individualism [ˌindiˈvidjuəlizm], s. Individualisme m.

individualist [ˌindiˈvidjuəlist], s. Individualiste mf.

individualistic [ˌindividjuəˈlistik], a. Individualiste.

individuality [ˌidividjuˈæliti], s. Individualité f.

individualize [ˌindiˈvidjuəlaiz], v.tr. Individualiser, distinguer, considérer (qn, qch.) isolément.

indivisibility [ˈindiˌviziˈbiliti], s. Indivisibilité f.

indivisible [ˌindiˈvizibl], a. Indivisible. -**ibly**, adv. Indivisiblement.

Indo-China [indouˈtʃainə]. Pr.n. L'Indochine f.

Indo-Chinese [indoutʃainˈiːz], a. & s. Geog: Indochinois, -oise.

indocile [inˈdousail], a. Indocile.

indocility [ˌindouˈsiliti], s. Indocilité f.

indoctrinate [inˈdɔktrineit], v.tr. Endoctriner.

indoctrination [inˈdɔktrineiʃ(ə)n], s. Endoctrinement m.

Indo-European [ˌindoujuərəˈpiːən], a. & s. Ethn: Ling: Indo-européen, -enne.

Indo-Germanic [ˌindoudʒəˈmænik], a. Ethn: Ling: Indo-germanique.

indolence [ˈindoləns], s. Indolence f, paresse f.

indolent [ˈindolənt], a. Indolent, paresseux. -**ly**, adv. Indolemment, paresseusement.

indomitable [inˈdɔmitəbl], a. Indomptable. -**ably**, adv. Indomptablement.

Indonesia [ˌindəˈniːziə]. Pr.n. Geog: L'Indonésie f.

Indonesian [ˌindəˈniːziən], a. & s. Geog: Ethn: Indonésien, -ienne.

indoor [ˈindɔːr], a. (Robe) d'intérieur; d'appartement. I. **games**, jeux de salon. I. **sanitation**, W.C. dans la maison. I. **swimming pool**, piscine fermée.

indoors [inˈdɔːz], adv. A la maison. To go i., entrer, rentrer (dans la maison). She is obliged to stay i. on account of her health, elle est obligée de rester à la maison à cause de sa santé.

indorse, v.tr. indorsement, s. = ENDORSE, etc.

indubitable [inˈdjuːbitəbl], a. Indubitable; incontestable. -**ably**, adv. Indubitablement; incontestablement.

induce [inˈdjuːs], v.tr. 1. To i. s.o. to do sth., persuader à qn de faire qch.; décider qn à faire qch. 2. (a) Amener, produire, occasionner. To i. sleep, provoquer le sommeil. To i. the belief, the hope that . . ., porter à croire, faire espérer, que. . . . (b) El: etc: Amorcer (un courant, etc.); induire (un courant). 3. Induire, conclure (que . . .). **induced**, a. I. **draught**, tirage induit par aspiration; tirage par induction. El: I. **current**, courant induit. **inducing**, a. El: (Of wire, etc.) Inducteur, -trice.

inducement [inˈdjuːsmənt], s. Motif m, mobile m, raison f, cause f, qui encourage qn à faire qch. I. to sleep, provocation f au sommeil. To hold out an i. to s.o. to do sth., encourager qn à faire qch. (par des offres attrayantes).

induct [inˈdʌkt], v.tr. 1. Ecc: Installer (un ecclésiastique) dans sa paroisse. 2. U.S: Mil: etc: Incorporer (dans les forces armées).

inductance [inˈdʌktəns], s. El: 1. Inductance f; coefficient m de self-induction. 2. I. (-coil), (bobine f de) self(-induction) f.

inductee [indʌkˈtiː], s. U.S: (Conscrit) incorporé (dans l'armée, etc.).

inductile [inˈdʌktail], a. Metall: Inductile.

induction [inˈdʌkʃ(ə)n], s. 1. Installation f (d'un ecclésiastique, d'un fonctionnaire). 2. I. **of facts**, énumération f des faits; apport m de preuves. 3. Log: Mth: Induction f. 4. El: Induction. S.a. SELF-INDUCTION. 5. Mch: I.C.E: Admission f, entrée f (de la vapeur, des gaz); aspiration f (des gaz). in'duction-coil, s. El: Bobine f d'induction. in'duction-pipe, s. I.C.E: Tuyau m d'admission.

inductive [inˈdʌktiv], a. 1. Log: I. **reasoning**, raisonnement par induction. 2. El: (a) (Of current, etc.) Inducteur, -trice. (b) (Of charge, etc.) Inductif, -ive. -**ly**, adv. Log: El: Par induction.

inductor [inˈdʌktər], s. 1. Ecc: Installateur m (d'un ecclésiastique). 2. El: Inducteur m.

indulge [inˈdʌldʒ]. 1. v.tr. (a) Avoir, montrer, trop d'indulgence pour (qn); gâter (qn). To i. oneself, s'écouter; ne rien se refuser. To i. s.o. in sth., permettre qch. à qn. (b) S'abandonner à (une fantaisie); se laisser aller à (un penchant); nourrir (un espoir). 2. v.i. To i. in a practice, s'adonner, se livrer, à une habitude. To i. too freely in sth., faire abus de qch., abuser de qch. To i. in tobacco, être adonné au tabac. To i. in a cigar, se permettre un cigare.

indulgence [inˈdʌldʒ(ə)ns], s. 1. Indulgence f, complaisance f (to, envers). 2. R.C.Ch: Indulgence.

indulgent [inˈdʌldʒ(ə)nt], a. Indulgent (to s.o., envers, pour, qn). -**ly**, adv. Avec indulgence.

industrial [inˈdʌstriəl], a. Industriel, -elle. I. **injuries**, accidents du travail. I. **disputes**, conflits ouvriers. I. **unrest**, agitation ouvrière. -**ally**, adv. Industriellement.

industrialism [inˈdʌstriəlizm], s. Industrialisme m.

industrialist [inˈdʌstriəlist], s. Industriel m.

industrialization [inˌdʌstriəlaiˈzeiʃ(ə)n], s. Industrialisation f.

industrialize [inˈdʌstriəlaiz], v.tr. Industrialiser.

industrious [inˈdʌstriəs], a. Travailleur, -euse, assidu, industrieux, -euse. -**ly**, adv. Industrieusement, assidûment.

industriousness [inˈdʌstriəsnis], s. Assiduité f (au travail), application f.

industry [ˈindəstri], s. 1. Application f; assiduité f au travail; diligence f, zèle m. 2. Industrie f. Cottage i., artisanat m. The heavy, light, industries, les industries lourdes, légères, The (motor) car i., l'industrie automobile.

inebriate[1] [inˈiːbriit], s. Ivrogne, f. ivrognesse; alcoolique mf.

inebriate[2] [inˈiːbrieit], v.tr. Enivrer, griser. **inebriated**, a. Ivre, gris. I. **by success**, grisé par son succès.

inebriation [iˌniːbriˈeiʃ(ə)n], s. 1. Enivrement m. 2. Ivresse f.

inebriety [‚ini(:)'braiəti], s. 1. Ivresse f, ébriété f. 2. Ivrognerie f, alcoolisme m.

inedible [in'edibl], a. 1. Immangeable. 2. Non comestible.

inedited [in'editid], a. 1. (Roman m, etc.) inédit. 2. (Of memoirs etc.) Publié (i) intégralement, (ii) sans notes.

ineffability [in‚efə'biliti], s. Ineffabilité f.

ineffable [in'efəbl], a. Ineffable, indicible. -ably, adv. Ineffablement, indiciblement.

ineffaceable [‚ini'feisəbl], a. Ineffaçable, indélébile. -ably, adv. Ineffaçablement, indélébilement.

ineffective ['ini'fektiv], a. 1. Inefficace, sans effet, sans résultat. 2. (Architecture) qui manque d'effet artistique. I. reply, réplique qui ne porte pas. I. style, style plat, terne. 3. (Of pers.) Incapable. -ly, adv. Inefficacement, vainement.

ineffectiveness [‚ini'fektivnis], s. 1. Inefficacité f. 2. Manque m de force (d'un argument, etc.).

ineffectual [‚ini'fektju(ə)l], a. 1. (a) (Effort, raisonnement) inefficace. (b) Qui donne une impression de faiblesse; terne. 2. I. person, personne incapable; velléitaire mf. -ally, adv. Inefficacement.

ineffectualness [‚ini'fektju(ə)lnis], s. Inefficacité f.

inefficacious [‚inefi'keiʃəs], a. (Remède) inefficace, sans effet.

inefficacy [in'efikəsi], s. Inefficacité f.

inefficiency [‚ini'fiʃ(ə)nsi], s. 1. Inefficacité f (des mesures qu'on avait prises, etc.). 2. Incapacité (professionnelle); incompétence f, insuffisance f.

inefficient [‚ini'fiʃ(ə)nt], a. 1. (Of a measure, etc.) Inefficace. 2. (Of pers.) Incapable, incompétent. -ly, adv. 1. Inefficacement. 2. Sans compétence.

inelastic [‚ini'læstik], a. Inélastique; raide; qui ne prête pas.

inelasticity [‚inilæs'tisiti], s. 1. Inélasticité f. 2. Raideur f (d'esprit, de caractère).

inelegance [in'eligəns], s. Inélégance f.

inelegant [in'eligənt], a. 1. Inélégant; sans élégance 2. (Goût, etc.) peu délicat, fruste. -ly, adv. Sans élégance.

ineligibility [in‚elidʒə'biliti], s. 1. Inéligibilité f (d'un candidat, etc.). 2. Caractère m inacceptable, peu désirable.

ineligible [in'elidʒəbl], a. (a) (Candidat) inéligible. Mil: I. for military service, inapte au service militaire. (b) Indigne d'être choisi; peu acceptable, peu désirable, inacceptable.

ineluctable [‚ini'lʌktəbl], a. Inéluctable, inévitable. -ably, adv. Inéluctablement.

inept [i'nept], a. 1. Déplacé; mal à propos. 2. (Of remark, etc.) Inepte, absurde. 3. (Of pers.) He's hopelessly i., il est de la dernière stupidité. -ly, adv. Ineptement; stupidement.

ineptitude [i'neptitju:d], s. 1. Manque m de justesse, d'à-propos (d'une observation). 2. I. for sth., to do sth., inaptitude f à qch., à faire qch. 3. Ineptie f, sottise f.

ineptness [i'neptnis], s. = INEPTITUDE 1, 2.

inequality [‚ini(:)'kwɔliti], s. Inégalité f; irrégularité f.

inequitable [in'ekwitəbl], a. Inéquitable; peu équitable. -ably, adv. Inéquitablement, injustement.

inequity [in'ekwiti], s. Injustice f.

ineradicable [‚ini'rædikəbl], a. Indéracinable, inextirpable.

inert [i'nə:t], a. 1. Inerte; inexcitable. 2. Ch: (Gaz) inactif, inerte.

inertia [i'nə:ʃiə], s. 1. Ph: (a) Inertie f. Moment of i., moment m d'inertie. (b) Force f d'inertie. 2. (Of pers.) Inertie; paresse f.

inertness [i'nə:tnis], s. Inertie f, inactivité f.

inescapable [‚inis'keipəbl], a. Inéluctable, inévitable.

inestimable [in'estiməbl], a. Inestimable, incalculable, inappréciable. -ably, adv. Inestimablement, incalculablement.

inevitability [in‚evitə'biliti], **inevitableness** [in'evitəblnis], s. Inévitabilité f.

inevitable [in'evitəbl], a. (a) Inévitable, inéluctable. (b) Fatal, -als; obligé. The i. hour, l'heure fatale. -ably, adv. Inévitablement, inéluctablement; fatalement.

inexact [‚inig'zækt], a. Inexact. -ly, adv. Inexactement.

inexactitude [‚inig'zæktitju:d], s. 1. Inexactitude f. 2. Erreur f.

inexcusable [‚iniks'kju:zəbl], a. Inexcusable; sans excuse; impardonnable. -ably, adv. Inexcusablement.

inexhaustible [‚inig'zɔ:stəbl], a. Inépuisable; inexhaustible; (source) intarissable. -ibly, adv. Inépuisablement, intarissablement.

inexorability [in‚eks(ə)rə'biliti], s. Inexorabilité f (du sort, etc.).

inexorable [in'eks(ə)rəbl], a. Inexorable. -ably, adv. Inexorablement.

inexpedience [‚iniks'pi:diəns], **inexpediency** [‚iniks'pi:diənsi], s. Inopportunité f (of, de).

inexpedient [‚iniks'pi:diənt], a. Inopportun, malavisé.

inexpensive [‚iniks'pensiv], a. Peu coûteux; bon marché; (qui ne coûte) pas cher. -ly, adv. (A) bon marché; à bon compte; à peu de frais.

inexpensiveness [‚iniks'pensivnis], s. Bon marché, bas prix (de qch.).

inexperience [‚iniks'piəriəns], s. Inexpérience f.

inexperienced [‚iniks'piəriənst], a. 1. Inexpérimenté. I. in doing sth., qui n'a pas l'habitude de faire qch. 2. Inaverti. I. eye, œil inexercé.

inexpert [in'ekspə:t], a. Inexpert, maladroit; peu habile (in, à). -ly, adv. Maladroitement.

inexpiable [in'ekspiəbl], a. Inexpiable.

inexplicable [in'eksplikəbl, ineks'plikəbl], a. Inexplicable. -ably, adv. Inexplicablement.

inexplorable [‚iniks'plɔ:rəbl], a. Inexplorable.

inexpressible [‚iniks'presəbl], a. Inexprimable; (charme) indicible. -ibly, adv. Indiciblement.

inexpressive [‚iniks'presiv], a. (Geste, mot) inexpressif; sans expression; (visage) fermé.

inexpugnable [‚iniks'pʌgnəbl], a. (Forteresse) inexpugnable.

inextinguishable [‚iniks'tiŋgwiʃəbl], a. Inextinguible.

inextricable [in'ekstrikəbl, ineks'trikəbl], a. Inextricable. -ably, adv. Inextricablement.

infallibility [in‚fælə'biliti], s. Infaillibilité f.

infallible [in'fæləbl], a. Infaillible. -ibly, adv. I ailliblement.

infamous ['infəməs], a. 1. Infâme; (conduite) abominable; (homme) noté d'infamie. 2. Jur: Infamant.

infamy ['infəmi], s. Infamie f.

infancy ['infənsi], s. 1. (a) Première enfance; bas âge. (b) Débuts mpl, première période, enfance (d'un art). 2. Jur: Minorité f.

infant ['infənt], s. 1. Enfant mf en bas âge; tout(e) petit(e) enfant; nourrisson m. Newly-born i., nouveau-né m, nouveau-née f. I. mortality, mortalité infantile. Sch: Infants school, école pour enfants de 5 à 8 ans. 2. Jur: Mineur, -eure.

infanticide¹ [in'fæntisaid], s. (Pers.) Infanticide mf.

infanticide², s. (Crime m d')infanticide m.

infantile ['infəntail], a. 1. (Esprit) d'enfant; (raisonnement) enfantin. 2. (Maladie) infantile. I. paralysis, paralysie f infantile, poliomyélite f.

infantilism [in'fæntilizm], s. Infantilisme m.

infantry ['infəntri], s. Coll: Infanterie f. Four hundred i., quatre cents fantassins.

infantryman, pl. -men ['infəntrimən], s.m. Soldat d'infanterie; fantassin.

infarct [in'fɑ:kt], **infarction** [in'fɑ:kʃ(ə)n], s. Med: Infarctus m.

infatuate [in'fætjueit], v.tr. 1. Affoler (qn). 2. Enticher, engouer (qn) (with, de). infatuated, a. Entiché. To become, be, i. with s.o., s'engouer, s'enticher, de qn; être épris de qn; F: avoir un béguin pour qn.

infatuation [in‚fætju'eiʃ(ə)n], s. Engouement m.

infect [in'fekt], v.tr. 1. Infecter, corrompre, empester, vicier (l'air, les mœurs, etc.). 2. Med: Contaminer, contagionner. Infected with the plague, atteint de la peste.

infection [in'fekʃ(ə)n], s. Infection f, contagion f; Med: contamination f. Med: Liable to i., en état de réceptivité.

infectious [in'fekʃəs], a. 1. (Air) infect, pestilentiel. 2. (a) (Of disease) Infectieux. (b) I. laughter, rire contagieux, communicatif.

infectiousness [in'fekʃəsnis], s. Nature infectieuse (d'une maladie); contagion f (du rire, etc.).

infective [in'fektiv], a. 1. Med: (Germe) infectieux. 2. Contagieux, -euse.

infelicitous [ˌinfi'lisitəs], a. (Of event, expression, etc.) Malheureux, -euse; fâcheux, -euse.

infelicity [ˌinfi'lisiti], s. 1. (a) Infélicité f (d'un événement). (b) Mauvaise fortune. 2. Manque m de justesse, d'à-propos (d'une expression); gaffe f.

infer [in'fəːr], v.tr. (inferred) 1. To i. sth. from sth., inférer, déduire, arguer, qch. de qch. It is inferred that . . ., on suppose que. . . . 2. Impliquer.

inference ['inf(ə)r(ə)ns], s. Log: 1. Inférence f. By i., par induction. 2. Déduction f, conclusion f. To draw an i. from sth., tirer une conclusion, une conséquence, de qch.

inferential [ˌinfə'ren(ʃ)(ə)l], a. Déductif.

inferior [in'fiəriər]. 1. a. Inférieur. I. piece of work, ouvrage m de second ordre. Greatly i. to . . ., très inférieur à . . ., bien au-dessous de. . . . To be in no way i. to s.o., ne le céder en rien à qn. Typ: I. letter, petite lettre inférieure. 2. s. (a) Inférieur m. (b) Adm: etc: Subordonné, -ée; subalterne m.

inferiority [inˌfiəri'ɔriti], s. Infériorité f (to, par rapport à). I. in numbers, infériorité numérique, en nombre. Psy: I. complex, complexe m d'infériorité.

infernal [in'fəːnl], a. 1. Infernal, -aux; des enfers. The i. regions, les régions infernales; l'enfer m. 2. F: (a) Infernal, abominable, diabolique. (b) (Intensive) (Chaleur, etc.) d'enfer. I. row, bruit infernal. -ally, adv. F: It's i. hot, il fait une chaleur d'enfer.

inferno, pl. -os [in'fəːnou, -ouz], s. Enfer m.

infertile [in'fəːtail], a. (a) (Terrain) infertile, infécond; (esprit) stérile. (b) (Œuf) clair.

infertility [ˌinfə'tiliti], s. Infertilité f, infécondité f, stérilité f.

infest [in'fest], v.tr. (Of vermin, etc.) Infester (with, de).

infestation [ˌinfes'teiʃ(ə)n], s. Invasion f (de parasites).

infidel ['infidəl], a. & s. 1. Hist: Infidèle (mf). 2. Pej: Incroyant, -ante.

infidelity [ˌinfi'deliti], s. 1. Incroyance f (en matière de religion). 2. Infidélité f, déloyauté f (d'un serviteur, etc.). Conjugal i., infidélité conjugale.

infiltrate ['infiltreit]. 1. v.tr. (a) Infiltrer (un fluide) (into, dans). (b) (Of liquid) Infiltrer, imprégner (une substance); pénétrer dans (une substance). (c) Pol: Noyauter. 2. v.i. S'infiltrer.

infiltration [ˌinfil'treiʃ(ə)n], s. 1. Infiltration f (through, à travers). (Of troops, etc.) To advance, progress, by, i., s'infiltrer. 2. Pol: Noyautage m (par les communistes, etc.).

infinite ['infinit]. 1. a. Infini. (a) Illimité; sans bornes. Mth: I. series, série infinie. (b) To have i. trouble in doing sth., avoir une peine infinie, infiniment de peine, à faire qch. (c) [in'fainait] Gram: Verb i., formes substantives du verbe. 2. s. The I., l'infini m. -ly, adv. Infiniment.

infinitesimal [ˌinf(i)ni'tesim(ə)l], a. Infinitésimal, -aux. I. calculus, calcul infinitésimal. I. majority, majorité infime. -ally, adv. I. small, infiniment petit.

infinitive [in'finitiv], a. & s. Gram: I. (mood), (mode) infinitif (m). In the i., à l'infinitif.

infinitude [in'finitjuːd], s. = INFINITY 1.

infinity [in'finiti], s. 1. Infinité f, infinitude f (de l'espace, etc.). 2. Mth: etc: Infini m. To i., à l'infini.

infirm [in'fəːm], a. 1. (Of pers.) Infirme, débile. 2. (Esprit) irrésolu, flottant. O: To be i. of purpose, avoir une volonté flottante, débile.

infirmary [in'fəːməri], s. 1. Infirmerie f (d'une école, etc.). 2. Hôpital m, -aux.

infirmity [in'fəːmiti], s. 1. (a) Infirmité f, débilité f. (b) Infirmité; affection particulière. 2. I. of purpose, faiblesse f de caractère; irrésolution f.

inflame [in'fleim], v.tr. 1. Mettre le feu à, enflammer; allumer (les désirs). Med: Enflammer, irriter (une plaie). Inflamed wound, plaie irritée. 2. v.i. (a) S'enflammer; prendre feu. (b) Med: S'enflammer.

inflammability [inˌflæmə'biliti], s. Inflammabilité f.

inflammable [in'flæməbl], a. (a) Inflammable. (b) (Of pers., crowd) Prompt à s'échauffer. (c) U.S: Ignifuge.

inflammation [ˌinflə'meiʃ(ə)n], s. 1. (a) Inflammation f (d'un combustible). (b) Inflammation, excitation f (des esprits). 2. Med: Inflammation. I. of the lungs, fluxion f de poitrine. To reduce an inflammation, désenflammer (une plaie, etc.).

inflammatory [in'flæmət(ə)ri], a. 1. Med: Inflammatoire. 2. (Discours) incendiaire, inflammatoire. 3. (Projectile, etc.) incendiaire.

inflate [in'fleit], v.tr. 1. Gonfler (un pneu, un ballon). 2. (a) Com: Grossir, charger (un compte). (b) Hausser, faire monter (les prix). (c) Pol.Ec: To i. the currency, recourir à l'inflation. inflated, a. 1. (Ballon, etc.) gonflé. (Of pers.) I. with pride, bouffi, gonflé, d'orgueil. 2. (Prix) exagéré. 3. Lit: (Style) ampoulé.

inflation [in'fleiʃ(ə)n], s. (a) Gonflement m; insufflation f. (b) Hausse f (des prix). (c) I. (of the currency), inflation f fiduciaire.

inflationary [in'fleiʃənri], a. (Politique f) d'inflation.

inflationism [in'fleiʃənizm], s. Fin: Inflationnisme m.

inflationist [in'fleiʃənist], s. Fin: Inflationniste m.

inflect [in'flekt], v.tr. 1. Fléchir, courber (en dedans). To i. a ray, infléchir un rayon. 2. Gram: Donner des inflexions à (un mot). 3. (a) Moduler (la voix). (b) Mus: Altérer (une note).

inflection [in'flekʃ(ə)n], s. = INFLEXION.

inflexibility [inˌfleksə'biliti], s. Inflexibilité f.

inflexible [in'fleksəbl], a. Inflexible; (courage) inébranlable; (morale) rigide. -ibly, adv. Inflexiblement, rigidement.

inflexion [in'flekʃ(ə)n], s. 1. Inflexion f; fléchissement m (du corps, d'un ressort). 2. Gram: Inflexion, flexion f (d'un mot). 3. (a) Inflexion (de la voix). (b) Mus: Altération f (d'une note).

inflexional [in flekʃən(ə)l], a. (Of language) Flexionnel.

inflict [in'flikt], v.tr. To i. a wound on s.o., faire une blessure à qn. To i. suffering on s.o., faire subir, occasionner, du chagrin à qn. Jur: To i. a punishment, a fine, on s.o., infliger une punition, une amende, à qn. To i. oneself, one's company, on s.o., imposer sa compagnie à qn.

infliction [in'flikʃ(ə)n], s. 1. Jur: Infliction f (d'une peine). 2. (a) Peine infligée; châtiment m. (b) Vexation f; calamité f.

inflorescence [ˌinflɔ'resns], s. Bot: 1. Inflorescence f. 2. (a) Floraison f. (b) Fleurs fpl (d'un arbre, etc.).

inflow ['inflou], s. = INFLUX. I. pipe, arrivée f d'eau, tuyau m d'adduction (d'eau).

inflowing ['inflo[uin], a. Entrant; qui entre. I. waters, eaux affluentes.

influence[1] ['influəns], s. (a) Influence f (upon, sur). To exert an i., to bring i. to bear, on s.o., exercer une influence sur qn; agir sur qn. To bring every i. to bear, mettre tout en jeu (in order to, pour). To have great i. over s.o., avoir beaucoup d'influence sur qn. (Of thg) To have an i. on sth., agir, influer, sur qch. Under the i. of fear, sous le coup de la peur. Under the i. of drink, sous l'empire de la boisson. Jur: Undue i., intimidation f. (b) (Of pers.) To have i., (i) avoir de l'influence, de l'autorité; (ii) avoir de la protection, du crédit. To have far-reaching i., avoir le bras long. Man of i., homme influent. (c) Ph: Atom Ph: etc: Rayonnement m.

influence[2], v.tr. (Of pers.) Influencer (qn); (of thg) influer sur (qch.).

influential [ˌinflu'enʃ(ə)l], a. Influent. To be i., avoir de l'influence; avoir le bras long. To have i. friends, avoir des amis en haut lieu; avoir de belles relations.

influenza [ˌinflu'enzə], s. Med: Grippe f; influenza f. Gastric i., grippe gastro-intestinale. I. cold, catarrhe grippal.

influenzal [ˌinflu'enz(ə)l], a. Med: Grippal, -aux.

influx ['inflʌks], s. (a) Entrée f, affluence f (d'un cours d'eau, etc.). (b) Affluence (de gens); invasion f (d'idées nouvelles).

inform [in'fɔːm]. 1. v.tr. (a) To i.s.o. of sth., informer, avertir, aviser, qn de qch.; faire savoir qch. à qn; faire part de qch. à qn. To keep s.o. informed of what is happening, tenir qn au courant de ce qui se passe. To i. the police, avertir la police. I regret to have to i. you that . . ., j'ai le regret de vous annoncer, de vous faire savoir, que. . . . (b) To i. s.o. on, about, sth., renseigner qn sur qch. Until we are better informed, jusqu'à plus ample informé. 2. v.i. Jur: To i. against s.o., dénoncer qn. informed, a. I. public opinion considers that . . ., l'opinion publique bien renseignée, bien au courant, considère que. . . . S.a. ILL-INFORMED, WELL INFORMED.

informal [in'fɔ:məl], a. 1. (a) Jur: En dehors des règles; irrégulier. (b) (Réunion, séance) non officiel, en dehors des statuts; (renseignement) officieux. 2. (Dîner, etc.) sans cérémonie, en famille. -ally, adv. 1. (a) En dehors des règles; irrégulièrement. (b) A titre non-officiel. 2. Sans cérémonie; sans formalités.

informality [ˌinfɔ'mæliti], s. Absence f de formalité, de cérémonie.

informant [in'fɔ:mənt], s. 1. Informateur, -trice. Who is your i.? De qui tenez-vous cela? I have it from a reliable i., je le tiens de bonne source. 2. Jur: Adm: Déclarant, -ante.

information [ˌinfɔ'meiʃ(ə)n], s. 1. Renseignements mpl, informations fpl. I. processing, informatique f. To give s.o. i. on sth., renseigner qn sur qch. I am sending you for your i. . . ., je vous envoie à titre d'information. . . . To get i. about sth., se renseigner sur qch. Piece of i., indication f, renseignement. I. bureau, bureau de renseignements. Adm: Central Office of I., Commissariat m à l'Information. The Ministry of I., le Ministère de l'Information. 2. Instruction f, savoir m, connaissances fpl. 3. Jur: Dénonciation f (against s.o., contre qn); délation f (de qn). To lay an i. against s.o. with the police, dénoncer qn à la police; informer contre qn.

informative [in'fɔ:mətiv], **informatory** [in'fɔ:mət(ə)ri], a. Instructif, -ive. Cards: Informatory bid, annonce f d'indication.

informer [in'fɔ:mər], s. Dénonciateur, -trice. Jur: Common i., délateur, -trice. To turn i., dénoncer ses complices.

infra-black ['infrə'blæk], a. T.V: Infra-noir.

infraction [in'frækʃ(ə)n], s. 1. Infraction f (d'un droit); transgression f. I. of the law, violation f de la loi, infraction à la loi. 2. Surg: Fêlure f.

infra dig ['infrə'dig], adj.phr. F: Au-dessous de la dignité de (qn); au-dessous de soi.

infrangible [in'fræn(d)ʒibl], a. Infrangible; incassable.

infra-red ['infrə'red], a. Opt: Infra-rouge.

infrasonic ['infrə'sɔnik], a. Infrasonore. I. vibration, infrason m.

infrastructure ['infrəˌstrʌktʃər], s. Pol.Ec: Adm: Infrastructure f.

infrequency [in'fri:kwənsi], s. Rareté f, infréquence f.

infrequent [in'fri:kwənt], a. Rare; peu fréquent. -ly, adv. Rarement.

infringe [in'frindʒ]. 1. v.tr. Enfreindre, violer (une loi, un serment); transgresser (une règle). To i. a patent, (i) contrefaire un objet breveté; (ii) empiéter sur un brevet. 2. v.ind.tr. To i. upon s.o.'s rights, empiéter sur les droits de qn.

infringement [in'frindʒmənt], s. 1. Infraction f (d'un règlement); violation f (d'une loi, d'un droit). 2. I. of a patent, of copyright, contrefaçon f.

infuriate [in'fjuərieit], v.tr. Rendre furieux. **infuriated**, a. Furieux, -euse; en fureur.

infuse [in'fju:z], v.tr. 1. To i. courage into s.o., infuser du courage à qn. 2. Infuser, faire infuser (le thé, des herbes).

infuser [in'fju:zər], s. (Device) Infusoir m. Tea i., œuf m, boule f, à thé.

infusibility [inˌfju:zə'biliti], s. Infusibilité f.

infusible [in'fju:zəbl], a. Infusible; non fusible.

infusion [in'fju:ʒ(ə)n], s. (a) Infusion f (d'une tisane). (b) Tisane f, infusion.

ingenious [in'dʒi:njəs], a. ingénieux. -ly, adv. Ingénieusement.

ingeniousness [in'dʒi:njəsnis], **ingenuity** [ˌindʒi'njuiti], s. Ingéniosité f.

ingénue [ɛ̃:nʒei'nju], s.f. Th: Ingénue.

ingenuous [in'dʒenjuəs], a. 1. Franc, f. franche; sincère. 2. Ingénu, candide; naïf, f. naïve. -ly, adv. 1. Franchement, sincèrement. 2. Ingénument, naïvement.

ingenuousness [in'dʒenjuəsnis], s. Ingénuité f, naïveté f, candeur f.

ingest [in'dzest], v.tr. Physiol: Ingérer (un aliment).

ingestion [in'dʒestʃ(ə)n], s. Physiol: Ingestion f.

ingle ['iŋgl], s. Lit: Foyer m (domestique). The i.-nook, le coin du feu.

inglorious [in'glɔ:riəs], a. (Combat) honteux; in-glorieux, -euse. -ly, adv. Inglorieusement.

ingot ['iŋgət], s. Lingot m (d'or); saumon m (d'étain). I. mould, lingotière f.

ingrained [in'greind], a. (a) Hands i. with coal-dust, mains encrassées de charbon. I. dirt, saleté en-crassée. (b) I. prejudices, préjugés enracinés. I. habits, habitudes invétérées.

ingratiate [in'greiʃieit], v.tr. To i. oneself with s.o., s'insinuer dans les bonnes grâces de qn. **ingratiating**, a. Insinuant, prévenant. -ly, adv. D'une manière insinuante.

ingratiatory [in'greiʃiətəri], a. (Sourire, ton) insinuant.

ingratitude [in'grætitju:d], s. Ingratitude f.

ingredient [in'gri:diənt], s. Ingrédient m; élément m.

ingress ['ingres], s. Entrée f. Jur: Free i., droit m de libre accès.

ingrowing[1] ['ingrouiŋ], a. (Ongle) incarné.

ingrowing[2], s. Med: Incarnation f (des ongles).

ingrown ['ingroun], a. 1. (Ongle) incarné. 2. (Préjugé) invétéré.

ingurgitate [in'gə:dʒiteit], v.tr. Ingurgiter, avaler.

ingurgitation [ˌingə:dʒiteiʃ(ə)n], s. Ingurgitation f.

inhabit [in'hæbit], v.tr. Habiter, habiter dans (une maison).

inhabitable [in'hæbitəbl], a. Habitable.

inhabitant [in'hæbit(ə)nt], s. Habitant, -ante.

inhalant [in'heilənt], s. Pharm: Inhalation f.

inhalation [ˌin(h)əleiʃ(ə)n], s. (a) Inhalation f. (b) Aspiration f.

inhale [in'heil], v.tr. (a) Med: Inhaler. (b) Aspirer, humer (un parfum); avaler (la fumée d'une cigarette).

inhaler [in'heilər], s. (Device) Inhalateur m.

inharmonic [inhɑ:'mɔnik], a. Mus: Inharmonique.

inharmonious [inhɑ:'mounjəs], a. Inharmonieux, -euse; peu harmonieux, -euse.

inherence [in'hiər(ə)ns], **inherency** [in'hiər(ə)nsi], s. Inhérence f (in, à).

inherent [in'hiər(ə)nt], a. Inhérent, naturel (in, à) I. defect, vice propre. -ly, adv. Par inhérence. I. lazy, né paresseux.

inherit [in'herit], v.tr. (a) Hériter de (qch.); succéder à (une fortune). (b) To i. sth. from s.o., hériter qch. de qn. To i. a characteristic from one's father, tenir un trait caractéristique de son père. Inherited taint, tache héréditaire.

inheritable [in'heritəbl], a. (a) (Titre) dont on peut hériter. (b) (Maladie) transmissible à ses descendants.

inheritance [in'herit(ə)ns], s. 1. Succession f. Law of i., droit successif. 2. Patrimoine m, héritage m.

inheritor [in'heritər], s. Héritier m.

inhibit [in'hibit], v.tr. 1. (a) Jur: To i. s.o. from doing sth., interdire, défendre, à qn de faire qch. (b) Ecc: Suspendre, interdire (un prêtre). 2. Psy: Inhiber (un sentiment).

inhibition [inhi'biʃ(ə)n], s. 1. (a) Jur: Défense expresse; prohibition f. (b) Ecc: Interdiction f (d'un prêtre). 2. Psy: Inhibition f. 3. Med: I. of blood, absorption f de sang.

inhibitory [in'hibit(ə)ri], a. 1. (Mandat) prohibitif, inhibitoire. 2. Psy: Physiol: (a) Inhibitoire. (b) I. reflex, réflexe inhibiteur, inhibitif.

inhospitable [inhɔs'pitəbl], a. Inhospitalier, -ière.

inhospitality [inˌhospi'tæliti], s. Inhospitalité f.

inhuman [in'hju:mən], a. Inhumain; brutal, -aux. -ly, adv. Inhumainement.

inhumanity [ˌinhju(:)'mæniti], s. Inhumanité f, cruauté f.

inhumation [ˌinhju(:)'meiʃ(ə)n], s. Inhumation f; enterrement m.

inhume [in'hju:m], v.tr. Inhumer, enterrer.

inimical [i'nimik(ə)l], a. (a) Ennemi, hostile. (b) Défavorable, contraire (to, à). -ally, adv. Hostile-ment; en ennemi.

inimitable [i'nimitəbl], a. Inimitable. -ably, adv. D'une manière inimitable.

iniquitous [i'nikwitəs], a. Inique. -ly, adv. Iniquement.

iniquity [i'nikwiti], s. Iniquité f.

initial[1] [i'niʃ(ə)l]. 1. a. (a) Initial, -aux; premier, -ière. Disease in the i. stages, maladie au début de son évolution. (b) Typ: I. letter, lettre initiale; (ornamental) lettrine f. 2. s. (Usu. pl.) Initials, initiales f; paraphe m; (of supervisor, etc.) visa m. The U.N.E.S.C.O. initials, le sigle de l'U.N.E.S.C.O. -ally, adv. Au commencement; au début; initiale-ment.

initial[2], v.tr. (initialled) Parapher (une correction); viser (un acte, etc.).

initiate[1] [i'niʃiit], *a. & s.* Initié, -ée.

initiate[2] [i'niʃieit], *v.tr.* **1.** Commencer, ouvrir (des négociations); lancer, amorcer (une mode). **To i. a reform,** prendre l'initiative d'une réforme. *Jur:* **To i. proceedings against s.o.,** instituer des poursuites contre qn. **2.** Initier. **To i. s.o. into a secret,** initier qn à un secret.

initiation [i,niʃi'eiʃ(ə)n], *s.* **1.** Commencement(s) *m*, début(s) *m* (d'une entreprise). **2.** Initiation *f* (**into,** à).

initiative [i'niʃiətiv], *s.* Initiative *f*. **To take the i. in doing sth.,** prendre l'initiative pour faire qch. **To do sth. on one's own i.,** faire qch. de sa propre initiative, par soi-même.

initiator [i'niʃieitər], *s.* Initiateur, -trice; lanceur, -euse (d'une mode, etc.).

initiatory [i'niʃiət(ə)ri], *a.* (*Of rite*) Initiateur, -trice.

inject [in'dʒekt], *v.tr.* Injecter.

injection [in'dʒekʃ(ə)n], *s.* (*a*) Injection *f*. **To give s.o. an i.,** faire à qn une injection sous-cutanée, une piqûre. **To give oneself an i.,** se piquer. **Intra-muscular, intravenous i.,** injection intramusculaire, intraveineuse. **Rectal i.,** lavement *m*. (*b*) *Geol:* Injection. (*c*) *I.C.E:* **(Direct) i. engine,** moteur *m* à injection (directe).

injector [in'dʒektər], *s.* *Mch:* Injecteur *m*; appareil *m* alimentaire.

injudicious [,indʒu(:)'diʃəs], *a.* Peu judicieux; malavisé. **-ly,** *adv.* Injudicieusement. **You have acted i.,** vous avez agi d'une façon peu judicieuse.

injunction [in'dʒʌŋ(k)ʃ(ə)n], *s.* **1.** Injonction *f*, ordre *m*, recommandation *f*. **To give s.o. strict injunctions to do sth.,** enjoindre strictement, formellement, à qn de faire qch. **2.** *Jur:* Arrêt *m* de suspension; arrêt de sursis.

injure ['indʒər], *v.tr.* **1.** Nuire à, faire tort à (qn); endommager (la réputation de qn); léser (qn). **To i. s.o.'s interests,** compromettre, léser, les intérêts de qn. **2.** (*a*) Blesser (qn); faire mal à (qn). **To i. one-self,** se blesser; se faire du mal. **Fatally injured,** blessé mortellement. (*b*) Endommager, gâter (qch.). *Com:* Avarier (des marchandises). **injured,** *a.* **1.** (*Of pers.*) Offensé. **The i. party,** l'offensé, -ée; *Jur:* **the injured party,** la partie lésée. **In an i. tone (of voice),** d'une voix offensée. **2.** (Bras, etc.) blessé ou estropié. *s.* **The i.,** les blessés *m*; (*from accident*) les accidentés *m*.

injurious [in'dʒuəriəs], *a.* **1.** Nuisible, pernicieux (**to,** à). **I. to the health,** nocif; nuisible à la santé. **2.** (Langage) injurieux, offensant.

injuriousness [in'dʒuəriəsnis], *s.* Nocivité *f*.

injury ['in(d)ʒ(ə)ri], *s.* **1.** Tort *m*, mal *m*. *Jur:* Lésion *f*. **To do s.o. an i.,** faire tort à qn; nuire à qn; faire i. of s.o., au détriment de qn. **2.** (*a*) Blessure *f* (au corps). *Med:* Lésion. **To do oneself an i.,** se blesser; se faire du mal. **There were no personal injuries,** il n'y a pas eu d'accident de personne. **Industrial injuries,** accidents *mpl* du travail. (*b*) Dommage *m*, dégât *m*; *Nau:* avarie *f*.

injustice [in'dʒʌstis], *s.* **1.** Injustice *f*. **Flagrant cases of i.,** des injustices flagrantes. **2. You do him an i.,** vous êtes injuste envers lui.

ink[1] [iŋk], *s.* **1.** Encre *f*. **Copying i.,** encre à copier. **Printing i., printer's i.,** encre d'imprimerie. **Indian i.,** encre de Chine. **Written in i.,** écrit à l'encre. **2.** Encre (de seiche); sépia *f*. '**ink-bag,** *s. Moll:* Glande *f*, poche *f*, du noir (de la seiche). '**ink-bottle,** *s.* Bouteille *f* à encre. '**ink-fish,** *s. F:* Seiche *f*; calmar *m*. '**ink-pad,** *s.* Tampon encreur.

ink[2], *v.tr.* **1.** Noircir d'encre; tacher d'encre. **2.** *Typ:* Encrer (les lettres). **ink in, over,** *v.tr.* Tracer à l'encre (des lignes faites au crayon). **inking,** *s. Typ:* Encrage *m* (des rouleaux). **Inking roller,** rouleau encreur.

inkiness ['inkinis], *s.* Noirceur *f* (d'encre).

inkling ['iŋkliŋ], *s.* Soupçon *m*. **To give s.o. an i. of sth.,** faire pressentir qch. à qn. **He had an i. of the truth,** il entrevit, entrevoyait, la vérité. **Without having the least i. of . . .,** sans se douter le moins du monde de . . . .

inkpot ['iŋkpɔt], *s.* Encrier *m*.

inkstand ['iŋkstænd], *s.* Grand encrier (avec pose-plumes).

inkwell ['iŋkwel], *s.* Encrier *m* (pour pupitre).

inky ['iŋki], *a.* **1.** Taché d'encre; (doigt) barbouillé d'encre. **2.** Noir comme (de) l'encre.

inlaid. *See* INLAY[2].

inland ['inlænd, -lənd]. **1.** *s.* (L')interieur *m* (d'un pays). **2.** *attrib.* Intérieur. **I. sea,** mer intérieure, mer fermée. **I. trade,** commerce intérieur. **I. postage rates** (tarif d') affranchissement en régime intérieur. **I. money order,** mandat sur l'intérieur. **The I. Revenue,** le fisc. **I. Revenue stamp,** timbre fiscal. **3.** *adv.* ['in'lænd] Vers l'intérieur. **To go, march i.,** pénétrer dans les terres.

inlay[1] ['inlei], *s.* **1.** Incrustation *f* (de nacre, etc.). **Marquetry i.,** marqueterie *f*. **2.** *Bookb:* Encartage *m*.

inlay[2] ['in'lei], *v.tr.* (**inlaid**) **1.** Incruster (**with,** de); marqueter (une table, etc.). *Metalw:* Damasquiner (une épée, etc.). **2.** *Bookb:* Encarter (des illustrations). **inlaid,** *a.* **1.** Incrusté, marqueté; (plancher) parqueté. **I. work,** marqueterie *f*. **I. enamel work,** nielle *f*, niellure *f*. *Bookb:* **I. leather,** reliure *f* mosaïque. **2.** *Bookb:* Encarté.

inlet ['inlet], *s.* **1.** Arrivée *f*, admission *f* (de vapeur, *I.C.E:* d'essence, etc.). **I. valve,** soupape *f* d'admission. **2.** Orifice *m* d'admission (de vapeur, etc.); ouïe *f* (de ventilateur). **3.** *Geog:* Crique *f*, anse *f*.

inmate ['inmeit], *s.* (*a*) Habitant, -ante (d'une maison). (*b*) Pensionnaire *mf*, hôte *m* (d'un hospice, etc.). (*c*) Détenu, -e (dans une prison).

inmost ['inmoust], *a.* Le plus profond. **Our i. thoughts,** nos pensées les plus secrètes. **Our i. being,** le tréfonds de notre être.

inn [in], *s.* **1.** (*a*) Auberge *f*; (*fashionable hotel*) hostellerie *f*. (*b*) = Café *m*. **2.** *Jur:* **Inns of Court,** les (quatre) Écoles de droit de Londres qui seules confèrent le droit d'être avocat.

innards ['inədz], *s.pl. P:* Entrailles *fpl.*, viscères *fpl.*

innate ['in'neit], *a.* Inné, infus; (bon sens) foncier, naturel.

inner ['inər]. **1.** *a.* Intérieur; (écorce, etc.) interne, de dedans. **On the i. side,** à l'intérieur, en dedans. **I. harbour,** arrière-port *m*, *pl.* arrière-ports. **I. dock,** arrière-bassin *m*, *pl.* arrière-bassins. *Aut:* **I. tube,** chambre *f* à air. *Anat:* **I. ear,** oreille *f* interne. **I. meaning,** sens intime (d'un passage). **To belong to the i. circle,** compter parmi les initiés. *F:* **The i. man,** l'estomac *m*. **2.** *s.* Premier cercle autour de la mouche (d'une cible).

innermost ['inəmoust], *a.* = INMOST.

innings ['iniŋz], *s.sg.* (*pl. inv.*) *Cr:* Tour *m* de batte. **He had a long i.,** (i) il est resté longtemps au guichet; (ii) *F:* il a fourni une longue carrière. *F:* **My innings now!** à mon tour!

innkeeper ['inkiːpər], *s.* Aubergiste *mf*; hôtelier, -ière.

innocence ['inəsns], *s.* (*a*) Innocence *f* (d'un accusé). (*b*) Naïveté *f*, innocence, candeur *f*. **To pretend i.,** faire l'innocent.

innocent ['inəsnt], *a.* **1.** (*a*) Innocent; pas coupable. (*b*) Dépourvu, vierge (**of,** de). **2.** (*a*) Pur; sans péché; innocent. *s.* **The Holy Innocents,** les (Saints) Innocents. (*b*) Naïf, *f.* naïve; sans malice; innocent. **To put on an i. air,** faire l'innocent. **-ly,** *adv.* Innocemment.

innocuity [,inə'kju(ː)iti], **innocuousness** [i'nɔkjuəsnis] *s.* Innocuité *f*.

innocuous ['inɔkjuəs], *a.* Inoffensif. **-ly,** *adv.* Inoffensivement.

innovate ['inoveit], *v.i.* Innover (**in,** à, en, dans). **innovating,** *a.* Innovateur, -trice.

innovation [,ino'veiʃ(ə)n], *s.* Innovation *f*, changement *m*. **To make innovations in sth.,** apporter des changements à qch.

innovator ['inoveitər], *s.* (In)novateur, -trice.

innuendo, *pl.* **-oes** [,inju(ː)'endou, -ouz], *s.* Allusion (malveillante).

innumerable [i'njuːm(ə)rəbl], *a.* Innombrable; sans nombre.

inobservance [,inəb'zəːv(ə)ns], *s.* **1.** Inattention *f*. **2.** Inobservance *f* (d'une loi, etc.); inobservation *f* (d'une promesse).

inoculable [i'nɔkjuləbl], *a. Med:* Inoculable.

inoculate [i'nɔkjuleit], *v.tr. Med:* (*a*) **To i. s.o. with a germ, to i. a germ into s.o.,** inoculer un germe à qn. (*b*) **To i. s.o. (against a disease),** inoculer, vacciner, qn (contre une maladie).

inoculation [i,nɔkju'leiʃ(ə)n], *s. Med:* Inoculation *f*. **Preventive i.,** vaccination préventive, immunisante. **Curative i.,** inoculation curative.

inoculator [i'nɔkjuleitər], s. Inoculateur, -trice.
inodorous [in'oudərəs], a. (Gaz, etc.) inodore.
inoffensive [,inə'fensiv], a. Inoffensif, -ive. **-ly**, adv. Inoffensivement.
inoperable [in'ɔp(ə)rəbl], a. Surg: (Malade mf, cancer m) inopérable.
inoperative [in'ɔp(ə)rətiv], a. Jur: etc: Inopérant.
inopportune [in'ɔpətjuːn], a. Inopportun; intempestif; (propos) hors de saison. **-ly**, adv. Inopportunément; mal à propos. **To come i.**, tomber mal.
inopportuneness [in'ɔpətjuːnnis], **inopportunity** [in,ɔpə'tjuːniti], s. Inopportunité f.
inordinate [i'nɔːdinit], a. **1.** Démesuré, excessif, immodéré. **2. To keep i. hours**, rentrer à des heures indues. **-ly**, adv. Démesurément, excessivement.
inorganic [,inɔː'gænik], a. Inorganique.
inoxidizable [in,ɔksi'daizəbl], a. Inoxydable.
input ['input], s. **1.** Mch: I. of steam, prise f de vapeur. **2.** Énergie ou puissance absorbée; consommation f (d'une machine).
inquest ['inkwest], s. Enquête f. Esp. (Coroner's) i., enquête judiciaire par-devant jury (en cas de mort violente ou suspecte).
inquire [in'kwaiər], v.tr. & i. **1. To i. the price of sth.**, s'informer du prix de qch. **To i. the way of s.o.**, demander son chemin à qn. P.N: 'I. within,' "s'adresser ici." **2. To i. about sth.**, s'enquérir de, se renseigner sur, qch. **To i. after s.o.**, after s.o.'s health, s'informer de la santé de qn; demander des nouvelles de qn. **To i. for s.o.**, demander qn, demander si qn est là. **To i. into sth.**, faire des recherches, des investigations, sur qch.; examiner (une question); Jur: enquêter, faire une enquête, sur (une affaire).
inquiring, a. Investigateur, -trice; curieux. **An i. glance**, un coup d'œil interrogateur. **-ly**, adv. D'un air, d'un ton, interrogateur. **To glance i. at s.o.**, interroger qn du regard.
inquiry [in'kwaiəri], s. **1.** Enquête f. **To conduct, hold, an i.**, procéder à une enquête. **To set up an i. regarding sth.**, ouvrir une enquête sur qch. **To open a judicial i.**, = ouvrir une instruction. **Public i.**, enquête de commodo et incommodo. **To remand a case for further i.**, renvoyer une affaire à plus ample informé. **2.** Demande f de renseignements. **To make inquiries**, aller aux informations, aux renseignements. **To make inquiries about s.o.**, s'informer de, se renseigner sur, qn. **To make inquiries after s.o.**, s'enquérir de qn. **I. office, 'Inquiries'**, bureau m de renseignements. Tp: etc: **Inquiries**, renseignements mpl.
inquisition [,inkwi'ziʃ(ə)n], s. (a) Recherche f, investigation f. (b) Hist: **The I.**, l'Inquisition f.
inquisitive [in'kwizitiv], a. Curieux; questionneur, -euse. **-ly**, adv. Avec curiosité.
inquisitiveness [in'kwizitivnis], s. (a) Curiosité indiscrète. (b) **I. of mind**, curiosité f d'esprit.
inquisitor [in'kwizitər], s. Rel.H: Inquisiteur m.
inquisitorial [in,kwizi'tɔːriəl], a. Inquisitorial, -aux.
inroad ['inroud], s. (a) Mil: Incursion f, invasion f, irruption f. (b) Empiétement m (sur la liberté, les droits, de qn). **To make inroads into one's capital**, entamer, ébrécher, son capital.
inrush ['inrʌʃ], s. Irruption f (d'eau, de voyageurs, etc.); entrée soudaine (d'air).
insalubrious [,insə'luːbriəs], a. Insalubre; malsain.
insalubrity [,insə'luːbriti], s. Insalubrité f.
insane [in'sein], a. **1.** (Of pers.) Fou, f. folle; (esprit) dérangé, aliéné. **To become i.**, tomber en démence; perdre la raison. **2.** F: (Désir, etc.) insensé, fou. **3.** s.pl. **The i.**, les aliénés m. **-ly**, adv. Follement; comme un insensé.
insanitary [in'sænit(ə)ri], a. Insalubre; malsain; antihygiénique.
insanity [in'sæniti], s. Med: Folie f, démence f, aliénation mentale.
insatiability [in,seiʃiə'biliti], **insatiableness** [in'seiʃiəblnis], s. Insatiabilité f.
insatiable [in'seiʃiəbl], a. Insatiable. **-ably**, adv. Insatiablement.
inscribable [in'skraibəbl], a. Geom: Inscriptible(in,dans).
inscribe [in'skraib], v.tr. **1.** Inscrire, graver. **2.** Dédier (une œuvre littéraire). **3.** Geom: Inscrire (un polygone) (**in**, dans). **4.** Fin: **Inscribed stock**, rente inscrite (au Grand-Livre).

inscription [in'skripʃ(ə)n], s. **1.** Inscription f (sur un monument, etc.); légende f (d'une pièce de monnaie). **2.** Dédicace f (d'un livre, etc.).
inscrutability [in,skruːtə'biliti], s. Inscrutabilité f, impénétrabilité (d'un mystère, d'un visage).
inscrutable [in'skruːtəbl], a. (Dessein) impénétrable, inscrutable; (visage) fermé.
insect ['insekt], s. Insecte m. 'insect-eater, s. Z: Insectivore m. 'insect-powder, s. Poudre f insecticide.
insecticidal [in,sekti'saidl], a. Insecticide.
insecticide [in'sektisaid], a. & s. Insecticide (m).
insectivora [,insek'tivərə], s.pl. Z: Insectivores mpl.
insectivorous [,insek'tivərəs], a. Insectivore.
insecure ['insi'kjuər], a. **1.** (Verrou, etc.) peu sûr; (glace, etc.) peu solide; (pont) mal affermi; (espoir) incertain. **2.** Exposé au danger. **-ly**, adv. Peu solidement; sans sûreté; sans sécurité.
insecurity [,insi'kjuəriti], s. Insécurité f.
inseminate [in'semineit], v.tr. **1.** Husb: Semer (des graines). **2.** Biol: Breed: Inséminer.
insemination [in,semi'neiʃ(ə)n], s. **Artificial i.**, fécondation artificielle; insémination (artificielle).
insensate [in'senseit], a. **1.** (Corps) insensible. **2.** (Désir) insensé.
insensibility [in,sensə'biliti], s. **1.** Défaillance f. **2.** Insensibilité f (to, à); indifférence f (to, pour).
insensible [in'sensəbl], a. **1.** Insensible, imperceptible. **2.** Sans connaissance. **3.** Insensible, indifférent (à la douleur, etc.). **-ibly**, adv. Insensiblement, imperceptiblement; petit à petit; peu à peu.
insensitive [in'sens(i)tiv], a. Insensible (to, à).
insensitiveness [in'sensitivnis], **insensitivity** [,insensi'tiviti], s. Insensibilité f.
inseparability [in,sep(ə)rə'biliti], s. Inséparabilité f.
inseparable [in'sep(ə)rəbl], a. Inséparable (from, de). **-ably**, adv. Inséparablement.
insert [in'səːt], v.tr. **1.** Insérer. **To i. a clause in an act**, insérer, introduire, une clause dans un acte. El.E: **To i. a condenser in the circuit**, intercaler un condensateur dans le circuit. **2.** Introduire, enfoncer (la clef dans la serrure). Typ: **To i. a line**, intercaler une ligne.
insertion [in'səː'ʃ(ə)n], s. **1.** Insertion f, introduction f (de qch. dans qch.). **2.** (a) Typ: Insertion. **I. mark**, renvoi m. (b) Needlew: Entre-deux m inv. entretoile f (de dentelle, etc.). (c) Dressm: Incrustation f.
inset¹ ['inset], s. **1.** Flux m (de la marée). **2.** Bookb: (a) Carton m (de 4 ou 8 pages). (b) (Leaf) Encartage m. **3.** Typ: Gravure f hors texte; hors-texte m inv; médaillon m (en coin de page). Mapm: Carton m. **4.** Dressm: Incrustation f.
inset² ['in'set], v.tr. (p.p. & p.t. inset; insetting) **1.** Bookb: Encarter (des feuillets). **2.** Typ: Insérer en cartouche, en médaillon. 'I. map (in corner of larger one), carton m, papillon m. 'I. portrait (in corner of larger illustration), portrait en médaillon. **3.** Dressm: Insérer (une pièce d'étoffe, etc.). **4.** Typ: Renfoncer (les lignes, un alinéa).
inshore. 1. a. ['in'ʃəːr] Côtier. **I. wind**, vent m de mer. **2.** adv. [in'ʃəːr] **To sail i.**, naviguer près de la côte.
inside [in'said]. **1.** s. (a) Dedans m, (côté) intérieur m (d'un habit, etc.). **The door opens from the i.**, la porte s'ouvre de dedans. **On the i.**, en dedans, au dedans. **To walk on the i. of the pavement**, prendre le haut du trottoir. **To turn sth. i. out**, retourner qch. comme un gant. **To turn everything i. out**, mettre tout sens dessus dessous. **The wind has blown my umbrella i. out**, le vent a retourné mon parapluie. F: **To know sth. i. out**, savoir qch. à fond; connaître qch. comme sa poche. (b) Intérieur (d'une maison, etc.). (c) F: **To have pains in one's i.**, avoir mal au ventre ou à l'estomac. (d) Fb: **The insides**, les centres m. **2.** a. ['insaid] Intérieur, d'intérieur; (mesure, etc.) dans œuvre. Rac: **To be on the i. track**, tenir la corde. Fb: **I. left**, intérieur, F: inter m, gauche. **I. information**, renseignements privés. **I speak with i. knowledge**, ce que je dis, je le sais de bonne source. **3.** adv. [in'said] (a) Intérieurement; (fermé) en dedans. **There is nothing i.**, il n'y a rien dedans. **I. and out** ['insaid-ənd'aut], au dedans et au dehors. (b) F. & U.S: **To do sth. i. of three hours**, faire qch. en moins de trois heures. (c) P: **To be i.**, être en taule. **4.** prep. [in'said] A l'intérieur de; dans l'intérieur de; dans.

insidious [in'sidiəs], *a.* Insidieux, -euse; (raisonnement) captieux, astucieux. **An i. wine,** un petit vin traître. **-ly,** *adv.* Insidieusement, astucieusement.

insidiousness [in'sidiəsnis], *s.* Caractère insidieux (d'une maladie, etc.); astuce *f* (d'une question, etc.).

insight ['insait], *s.* **1.** Perspicacité *f*; pénétration *f*. **2.** Aperçu *m.* **To get an i. into sth.,** prendre un aperçu de qch.

insignia [in'signiə], *s.pl.* Insignes *m* (de la royauté, etc.).

insignificance [,insig'nifikəns], *s.* Insignifiance *f*.

insignificant [,insig'nifikənt], *a.* Insignifiant; de peu d'importance; (personne) sans importance.

insincere [,insin'siər], *a.* (*a*) Peu sincère; insincère; de mauvaise foi. (*b*) (*Of smile, etc.*) Faux, *f.* fausse. **-ly,** *adv.* Sans sincérité.

insincerity [,insin'seriti], *s.* Manque *m* de sincérité; fausseté *f*.

insinuate [in'sinjueit], *v.tr.* Insinuer. **1. To i. oneself into s.o.'s favour,** s'insinuer dans les bonnes grâces de qn. **2.** Donner adroitement à entendre, à comprendre (que); laisser entendre (que); laisser sousentendre (que).

insinuation [in,sinju'eiʃ(ə)n], *s.* Insinuation *f*.

insinuative [in'sinjueitiv], *a.* Insinuant.

insipid [in'sipid], *a.* Insipide, fade; (sourire) bête. **-ly,** *adv.* Insipidement, fadement.

insipidity [,insi'piditi], *s.* Insipidité *f*; fadeur *f*.

insist [in'sist], *v.i.* Insister. **1. To i. (up)on a point,** insister, appuyer, sur un point. **To i. upon one's innocence,** affirmer son innocence avec insistance; protester (hautement) de son innocence. **He insisted that it was so,** il maintenait, soutenait, qu'il en était ainsi. **To i. on doing sth.,** insister pour faire qch.; vouloir absolument faire qch. **To i. that s.o. shall do sth.,** on s.o.'s doing sth., exiger de qn qu'il fasse qch. **He insists on your coming,** il insiste pour que vous veniez. **I i. upon it,** je le veux absolument. **I i. on obedience,** je veux être obéi.

insistence [in'sist(ə)ns], **insistency** [in'sist(ə)nsi], *s.* Insistance *f.* (*a*) **His i. upon his innocence,** ses protestations *f* d'innocence. (*b*) **I. in doing sth.,** insistance à faire qch.

insistent [in'sist(ə)nt], *a.* Qui insiste, insistant; obsédant; (créancier) importun, pressant. **Don't be too i.,** n'appuyez pas trop, n'insistez pas trop. **-ly,** *adv.* Instamment; avec insistance.

insobriety [,insɔ'braiəti], *s.* Insobriété *f*.

insolate ['insoleit], *v.tr.* Insoler, exposer (qn, qch.) au soleil.

insolation [,inso'leiʃ(ə)n], *s.* **1.** *Ph: etc:* Insolation *f*. **2.** *Med:* (*a*) Coup *m* de soleil; insolation. (*b*) Héliothérapie *f*; cure *f*, bain *m*, de soleil.

insolence ['insə(ə)ns], *s.* Insolence *f* (to, envers).

insolent ['insə(ə)lənt], *a.* Insolent (to, envers). **-ly,** *adv.* Insolemment.

insolubility [in,sɔlju'biliti], *s.* **1.** Insolubilité *f* (d'un sel, d'un produit chimique); indissolubilité *f* (du mariage religieux, etc.). **2.** Insolubilité (d'un problème).

insoluble [in'sɔljubl], *a.* **1.** (Sel) insoluble; (lien, etc.) indissoluble. **2.** (Problème) insoluble, irrésoluble.

insolvency [in'sɔlvənsi], *s.* (*a*) Insolvabilité *f*. (*b*) Déconfiture *f*; faillite *f*.

insolvent [in'sɔlvənt]. **1.** *a.* (Débiteur) insolvable, en (état de) faillite. **To become i.,** faire faillite. **To declare oneself i.,** *Com:* déposer son bilan. **2.** *s.* Débiteur *m* insolvable; *Com:* failli *m*.

insomnia [in'sɔmniə], *s.* Insomnie *f*.

insomuch [,insou'mʌtʃ], *adv. Lit:* **1. I. as =** INASMUCH AS. **2. I. that . . .,** à un tel point que. . . .

insouciance [in'su:sjəns, ɛ̃susjɑ̃s], *s.* Insouciance *f*.

insouciant [in'su:sjənt, ɛ̃susjɑ̃], *a.* Insouciant, -ante.

inspan [in'spæn], *v.tr.* (*In S. Africa*) Atteler (un wagon, une paire de bœufs).

inspect [in'spekt], *v.tr.* **1.** Examiner de près (qch.); inspecter (une école, une fabrique); contrôler (les livres d'un négociant); vérifier, inspecter (une machine, etc.). **2.** Faire l'inspection (d'un régiment); passer (un régiment) en revue.

inspection [in'spekʃ(ə)n], *s.* **1.** Inspection *f*; vérification *f*, examen *m* (de documents); contrôle *m* (de billets). **To subject sth. to a close i.,** soumettre qch.

à un examen minutieux. **I. hole,** orifice *m* de visite. **I. chamber,** regard *m. Publ:* **I. copy,** spécimen *m. Jur:* **Right of i.,** droit *m* de regard. **2.** *Mil:* Revue *f*. **Kit i.,** revue d'effets, de détail.

inspector [in'spektər], *s.* Inspecteur *m* (des écoles, de police, etc.). **Woman i.,** inspectrice *f*. **I. of weights and measures,** vérificateur *m* des poids et mesures. **I. general,** inspecteur général. *S.a.* FACTORY, TICKET-INSPECTOR.

inspectorate [in'spekt(ə)rit], *s.* Corps *m* d'inspecteurs; inspectorat *m*; *F:* l'inspection *f*.

inspectorship [in'spektəʃip], *s.* Inspectorat *m*.

inspiration [,inspə'reiʃ(ə)n], *s.* **1.** Aspiration *f*, inspiration *f* (d'air). **2.** Inspiration. **Divine i.,** inspiration divine. **To do sth. by i.,** faire qch. d'inspiration. **To take one's i. from s.o.,** s'inspirer de qn. **To have a sudden i.,** avoir une inspiration subite.

inspiratory [in'spaiərət(ə)ri], *a. Anat: etc:* Inspirateur, -trice; (souffle *m*) aspiratoire. **The i. muscles,** les muscles inspirateurs.

inspire [in'spaiər], *v.tr.* **1.** Aspirer, inspirer (l'air, etc.). **2. To be inspired to do sth.,** être inspiré de faire qch. **To i. a feeling in, into, s.o.,** inspirer un sentiment à qn. **To i. s.o. with confidence, with fear,** inspirer (de la) confiance, de la terreur, à qn. **To i. s.o. with respect,** imposer le respect à qn. **To i. respect,** inspirer le respect. **inspired,** *a.* Inspiré. *Journ:* **I. paragraph,** note *f* d'origine officieuse. **To make an i. guess,** tomber juste.

instability [,instə'biliti], *s.* Instabilité *f*.

install [in'stɔ:l], *v.tr.* **1.** Installer (un évêque, qn dans une fonction). **To i. oneself in a place,** s'installer dans un endroit. **2.** (*a*) Installer (l'électricité, etc.). (*b*) Monter (un atelier, etc.).

installation [,instə:'leiʃ(ə)n], *s.* **1.** Installation *f* (d'un évêque, etc.). **2.** Installation (de l'électricité, de l'eau); montage *m* (d'un poste de télévision, etc.).

instalment [in'stɔ:lmənt], *s.* **1.** Acompte *m*; versement partiel. **To pay an i.,** verser un acompte, faire un versement. **To pay in, by, instalments,** échelonner les paiements. **To buy on the i. system,** acheter à tempérament, à crédit. **I. plan,** système *m* de crédit. **2.** (*a*) **I. of a publication,** livraison *f*, fascicule *m*, d'un ouvrage. **Instalment selling,** vente *f* par fascicules. (*b*) Feuilleton *m*.

instance [in'stəns], *s.* **1. At the i. of . . .,** sur l'instance de . . ., à la demande de. . . . **2.** Exemple *m*, cas *m*. **An isolated i.,** un cas isolé. **In many instances,** dans bien des cas. **For i.,** par exemple. **As an i. of his honesty, I may mention . . .,** en témoignage de son intégrité je pourrais citer. . . . **3. In the first i.,** en (tout) premier lieu. **In the present i., in this i.,** dans le cas actuel; dans cette circonstance.

instancy ['instənsi], *s.* Urgence *f* (d'un besoin); imminence *f* (du danger).

instant¹ ['instənt], *a.* **1.** Instant, pressant, urgent. **2.** (*Abbr.* **inst.**) Courant; de ce mois. **On the 5th inst.,** le 5 courant. **3.** (*a*) Immédiat. **This calls for i. remedy,** il faut y remédier sur-le-champ. (*b*) Imminent. **-ly,** *adv.* Tout de suite; sur-le-champ; à l'instant.

instant², *s.* Instant *m*, moment *m*. **Come this i.,** venez à l'instant, sur-le-champ. **The i. he arrived,** (i) au moment où il arriva; (ii) dès, aussitôt, qu'il fut arrivé.

instantaneous [,inst(ə)n'teinjəs], *a.* Instantané. *Phot:* **I. exposure,** instantané *m.* **-ly,** *adv.* Instantanément.

instantaneousness [,inst(ə)n'teinjəsnis], *s.* Instantanéité *f*.

instead [in'sted]. **1.** *Prep.phr.* **I. of sth.,** au lieu de qch. **To stand i. of sth.,** tenir lieu de qch. **I. of s.o.,** à la place de qn. **I. of doing sth.,** au lieu de faire qch. **I. of (our) having profited by it . . .,** au lieu d'y avoir gagné quelque chose. . . . **2.** *adv.* Au lieu de cela. **If he can't come, take me i.,** s'il ne peut pas venir, emmenez-moi à sa place.

instep ['instep], *s.* **1.** Cou-de-pied *m*, *pl.* cous-de-pied. **2.** *Bootm:* Cambrure *f* (d'un soulier).

instigate ['instigeit], *v.tr.* **1.** Inciter, provoquer (**to do sth.,** à faire qch. de mal). **2. To i. revolt,** provoquer, susciter, la révolte.

instigation [,insti'geiʃ(ə)n], *s.* Instigation *f*, incitation *f*. **At, by, the i. of s.o.,** à l'instigation de qn.

instigator ['instigeitər], s. 1. Instigateur, -trice (d'un meurtre, etc.). 2. Fomentateur, -trice, auteur m (de troubles).

instil(l) [in'stil], v.tr. (**instilled**) 1. Instiller (un liquide) (**into**, dans). 2. Faire pénétrer (goutte à goutte). **To i. an idea into s.o.**, infiltrer une idée dans l'esprit de qn.

instillation [,insti'leiʃ(ə)n], s. 1. Instillation f (d'un liquide). 2. Inspiration f (d'une idée); inculcation f (d'une vertu).

instinct ['instiŋ(k)t], s. Instinct m. **By i., from i.**, par instinct. Psy: **Unsatisfied instincts**, inassouvissement m.

instinctive [in'stiŋ(k)tiv], a. Instinctif, -ive. **-ly,** adv. D'instinct; instinctivement. **To act instinctively**, agir par pur instinct.

institute[1] ['institjuːt], s. Institut m.

institute[2], v.tr. 1. Instituer, établir. **Newly instituted office**, poste de création récente. 2. Jur: Ordonner, instituer (une enquête); procéder à (une enquête). **To i. (legal) proceedings, an action, against s.o.**, intenter un procès à qn.

institution [,insti'tjuːʃ(ə)n], s. 1. Institution f, établissement m (d'une loi, etc.). 2. Institution; chose établie. **Television has become an i.**, la télévision est passée dans les mœurs. 3. **Charitable i.**, institution, établissement, d'intérêt public (qui ne paie pas d'impôts).

institutional [,insti'tjuːʃnl], a. Institutionnel, -elle.

instruct [in'strʌkt], v.tr. 1. Instruire (qn). **To i. s.o. in sth., how to do sth.**, instruire qn en, dans, qch.; enseigner qch. à qn. 2. (a) **To i. s.o. of a fact, of what is going on**, instruire qn d'un fait, de ce qui se passe. (b) Jur: **To i. a solicitor**, donner ses instructions à un avoué. 3. **To i. s.o. to do sth.**, charger qn de faire qch.

instruction [in'strʌkʃ(ə)n], s. 1. Instruction f, enseignement m. Mil: Nav: Av: **School of I.**, École f d'application. Aut: **Driving i.**, leçons fpl de conduite. 2. Usu. pl. Indications f, instructions, ordres m; (to sentry, etc.) consigne f. **Instructions for use**, mode f d'emploi. Aut: etc: **I. book**, manuel m d'entretien. **To go beyond one's instructions**, aller au-delà des ordres reçus. Mil: **To act according to instructions**, se conformer à la consigne. Adm: etc: **(Book of) standing instructions**, règlement m; F: guide-âne m.

instructional [in'strʌkʃənl], a. (École f) d'application. Cin: **I. film**, (film) éducatif.

instructive [in'strʌktiv], a. Instructif, -ive. **-ly,** adv. D'une manière instructive.

instructor [in'strʌktər], s. Maître (enseignant). Mil: Instructeur m. Aut: **Driving i.**, moniteur m de conduite. Sp: Moniteur. **Swimming i.**, professeur m de natation. Sch: U.S: Chargé m de cours.

instrument[1] ['instrumənt, 'instrəmənt], s. Instrument m. 1. (Agent) Instrument, intermédiaire m. 2. (a) Instrument, appareil m, mécanisme m. Av: **I. flying**, vol m sans visibilité f, vol aux instruments. (b) **Musical i.**, instrument de musique. **Wind, stringed i.**, instrument à vent, à cordes. 3. (a) Jur: Acte m juridique; instrument; document officiel. (b) Com: **Negotiable i.**, effet m de commerce; titre m au porteur.

instrument[2] ['instrəmənt], v.tr. Mus: Orchestrer, instrumenter (un opéra, etc.).

instrumental [,instru'mentl], a. 1. Contributif, -ive (to, à). **To be i. to a purpose, in doing sth.**, contribuer à un but, à faire qch. 2. **I. music**, musique instrumentale. **I. performer**, instrumentiste m. **-ally,** adv. 1. (a) (Se servir de qch.) comme instrument. (b) (Agir) en qualité d'intermédiaire. 2. (a) Au moyen d'un instrument (scientifique). (b) Mus: Pour orchestre, par orchestre.

instrumentalist [,instru'mentəlist], s. Mus: Instrumentiste m.

instrumentality [,instrumen'tæliti], s. **Through the i. of s.o.**, avec le concours de qn, par l'intermédiaire de qn, à l'aide de qn.

instrumentation [,instrumen'teiʃ(ə)n], s. Mus: Instrumentation f.

insubordinate [,insə'bɔːdinit], a. Insubordonné, insoumis; mutin.

insubordination ['insə,bɔːdi'neiʃ(ə)n], s. Insubordination f, insoumission f.

insubstantial [,insəb'stænʃ(ə)l], a. Insubstantiel, -elle. 1. Imaginaire. 2. (Corps) immatériel.

insubstantiality ['insəbstænʃi'æliti], s. Manque m de substance; irréalité f.

insufferable [in'sʌf(ə)rəbl], a. Insupportable, intolérable. **-ably,** adv. Insupportablement, intolérablement.

insufficiency [,insə'fiʃ(ə)nsi], s. Insuffisance f.

insufficient [,insə'fiʃ(ə)nt], a. Insuffisant. **-ly,** adv. Insuffisamment.

insufflate ['insʌfleit], v.tr. Insuffler (une vessie, Med: un asphyxié, etc.).

insufflation [,insʌ'fleiʃ(ə)n], s. Med: Insufflation f.

insufflator ['insʌfleitər], s. Med: (Device) Insufflateur m.

insular ['insjulər], a. (a) (Climat) insulaire. (b) D'insulaire. **I. mind**, esprit étroit, borné, rétréci.

insularism ['insjulərizm], **insularity** [,insju'læriti], s. Étroitesse f de vues.

insulate ['insjuleit], v.tr. Isoler. (a) El: Isoler (un fil, etc.). (b) Calorifuger (une chaudière). (c) Cin: Insonoriser (la camera). **insulating**, a. 1. El: Isolant; isolateur, -trice. **I. tape**, chatterton m. 2. Mch: etc: (Enveloppe) isolant, calorifuge.

insulation [,insju'leiʃ(ə)n], s. 1. Isolement m (from, de). 2. El: (a) Isolement, isolation f (des câbles). (b) Isolant m. 3. **Heat i.**, isolation calorifuge, calorifugeage m. 4. Cin: Insonorisation f (de la camera, etc.).

insulator ['insjuleitər], s. 1. El: (a) (Material) Isolant m. (b) (Device) Isolateur m. 2. **Heat i.**, matière isolante, calorifuge.

insulin ['insjulin], s. Med: Insuline f.

insult[1] ['insʌlt], s. Insulte f, affront m, indignité f. **To suffer, pocket, an i.**, boire un affront; F: avaler une couleuvre. **To add i. to injury**, doubler ses torts d'un affront.

insult[2] [in'sʌlt], v.tr. Insulter (qn); faire (une) insulte à (qn); faire affront, faire injure, à (qn). **insulting**, a. Offensant, injurieux, -euse. **To use i. language to s.o.**, dire des injures, lancer des insultes, à qn.

insuperability [in,sjuːp(ə)rə'biliti], s. (Nature f, caractère m) insurmontable (d'un obstacle, d'une difficulté).

insuperable [in'sjuːp(ə)rəbl], a. (Difficulté, etc.) insurmontable; (obstacle) infranchissable.

insupportable [,insə'pɔːtəbl], a. Insupportable, intolérable. **-ably,** adv. Insupportablement, intolérablement.

insurable [in'ʃuərəbl], a. Assurable.

insurance [in'ʃuərəns], s. 1. (a) Assurance f. **Life i.**, assurance sur la vie; assurance-vie f. **Third-party i.**, assurance au tiers. **Comprehensive i.**, assurance tous risques. **Employers' liability i.**, assurance des patrons contre les accidents du travail. **Unemployment i.**, assurance f chômage. **Workmen's compensation i.**, assurance f contre les accidents du travail. **I. book**, portefeuille f d'assurances. **Car i.**, assurance automobile. **I. broker**, courtier m d'assurance. **Burglary i.**, assurance-vol f. **Fire i.**, assurance contre l'incendie, assurance-incendie. **To effect an i.**, passer une assurance (on, sur). **To take out an i.**, se faire assurer (against, contre). **I. company**, compagnie f, société f, d'assurance(s). (b) F: Prime f d'assurance. 2. Adm: **National I.**, assurances sociales. (**Employer's**) **Social i., contributions**, charges sociales.

insure [in'ʃuər], v.tr. 1. (i) Assurer, (ii) faire assurer (un navire, un mobilier). **To i. one's life**, s'assurer, se faire assurer, sur la vie. 2. (a) Garantir, assurer (le succès, etc.). (b) **To i. against a danger**, parer à un danger. **insured**, a. Adm: **I. person**, assuré(e). **I. parcel**, colis m avec valeur déclarée.

insurer [in'ʃuərər], s. Com: Assureur m.

insurgent [in'sɜːdʒ(ə)nt], a. & s. Insurgé, -ée, révolté, -ée. U. S. Hist: **The insurgents**, les Insurgents m (de la Guerre de l'Indépendance).

insurmountable [,insə(ː)'mauntəbl], a. Insurmontable; (obstacle) infranchissable.

insurrection [,insə'rekʃ(ə)n], s. Insurrection f, soulèvement m, émeute f.

insurrectional [,insə'rekʃnl], **insurrectionary** [,insə'rekʃnəri], a. Insurrectionnel, -elle.

insurrectionist [,insə'rekʃənist], s. Émeutier m, insurgé, -ée.

insusceptible [ˌinsə'septəbl], *a.* Insensible (to, à). A mind i. to flattery, un esprit insensible à la flatterie.
intact [in'tækt], *a.* Intact.
intaglio [in'tɑ:liou], *s. Lap:* Intaille *f;* (gravure) en creux.
intake ['inteik], *s.* 1. Prise *f*, appel *m* (d'air); prise (d'eau, *El:* de courant); adduction *f*, admission *f* (de vapeur). I. valve, soupape *f* d'admission. 2. Consommation *f. Physiol:* Caloric i., ration *f* calorique. Food i., ration alimentaire. 3. *Mil:* Contingent *m.*
intangibility [inˌtæn(d)ʒə'biliti], *s.* Intangibilité *f.*
intangible [in'tæn(d)ʒəbl], *a.* Intangible, impalpable; imperceptible. *Com:* I. assets, valeurs immatérielles. *Jur:* I. property, biens incorporels.
integer ['intidʒər], *s. Mth:* Nombre entier.
integral ['intəgrəl]. 1. *a.* (a) Intégrant. To be an i. part of sth., faire corps avec qch. To form an i. part of . . ., s'intégrer dans. . . . (b) *Mth:* I. calculus, calcul intégral. (c) *Mec.E:* (Tige, etc.) solidaire (with, de). Forged i. with . . ., forgé d'une seule pièce avec. . . . 2. *s. Mth:* Intégrale *f.* **-ally,** *adv.* Intégralement; en totalité.
integrate¹ ['intigrit], *a.* Intégral, -aux; entier, -ière.
integrate² ['intigreit]. 1. *v.tr.* (a) Compléter, rendre entier (qch. d'incomplet). (b) *Mth:* Intégrer (une fonction). 2. *v.i. Pol:* To i., to become integrated, s'intégrer (dans un milieu social, racial).
integration [ˌinti'greif(ə)n], *s.* 1. *Mth:* Intégration *f.* 2. *Pol:* Intégration (raciale).
integrity [in'tegriti], *s.* Intégrité *f.* 1. In its i., en entier. 2. Honnêteté *f*, probité *f.*
intellect ['intəlekt], *s.* Intelligence *f*, esprit *m.* Man of i., homme intelligent, à l'esprit éclairé.
intellectual [ˌintə'lektjuəl], *a. & s.* Intellectuel, -elle. **-ally,** *adv.* Intellectuellement.
intellectualism [ˌinti'lektjuəlizm], *s.* Intellectualisme *m.*
intellectuality ['intəˌlektjuˌæliti], *s.* Intellectualité *f.*
intelligence [in'telidʒəns], *s.* 1. Intelligence *f.* (a) Entendement *m*, sagacité *f.* (b) *Psy: Sch: Ind:* I. test, test *m* d'habilité mentale. I. quotient, quotient intellectuel. 2. Renseignement(s) *m(pl)*, avis *m*, nouvelle(s) *f(pl). Journ:* Latest i., dernières nouvelles; informations *fpl* de (la) dernière heure. Shipping i., mouvement *m* maritime. *Mil:* I. service = Deuxième Bureau.
intelligent [in'telidʒənt], *a.* Intelligent; avisé. **-ly,** *adv.* Intelligemment; avec intelligence.
intelligentsia [inˌteli'dʒentsiə], *s. Coll:* Intelligentsia *f;* élite intellectuelle.
intelligibility [inˌtelidʒi'biliti], *s.* Intelligibilité *f.*
intelligible [in'telidʒəbl], *a.* Intelligible. **-ibly,** *adv.* Intelligiblement.
intemperance [in'tempərəns], *s.* 1. Intempérance *f.* 2. Alcoolisme *m.*
intemperate [in'tempərit], *a.* 1. (*Of pers.*) Intempérant, immodéré. 2. Adonné à la boisson. **-ly,** *adv.* (Rire) immodérément; (boire) à l'excès.
intend [in'tend], *v.tr.* 1. (a) To i. doing sth., to do sth., to i. sth., avoir l'intention de faire qch. We intended no harm, nous l'avons fait sans mauvaise intention. Was that intended? était-ce fait avec intention, à dessein? (b) I i. to be obeyed, je veux être obéi. 2. To i. sth. for sth., destiner qch. à qch. Book intended for students, livre destiné à l'usage des étudiants. We i. our son to be a schoolmaster, nous destinons notre fils au professorat. Our son intends to become a schoolmaster, notre fils se destine au professorat. This remark is intended for you, c'est à vous que cette observation s'adresse. 3. (a) I intended it for a compliment, mon intention était de vous faire un compliment. (b) Vouloir dire; entendre. **intended,** *a.* 1. (a) (Voyage, etc.) projeté. *s. P:* My i., mon fiancé, ma fiancée, *P:* mon futur, ma future. (b) The i. effect, l'effet voulu. 2. Intentionnel; fait avec intention. **intending,** *a.* I. purchasers, acheteurs éventuels.
intense [in'tens], *a.* (a) Vif, *f.* vive; fort, intense. (b) I. expression, expression d'intérêt profond. (c) D'un sérieux exagéré. **-ly,** *adv.* (a) Excessivement. I. blue eyes, yeux d'un bleu très vif. To hate s.o. i., haïr qn profondément. (b) (Vivre, regarder) avec intensité; intensément.

intenseness [in'tensnis], *s.* Intensité *f* (du froid); force *f* (d'une passion); violence *f* (d'une douleur).
intensification [inˌtensifi'keif(ə)n], *s.* Intensification *f;* renforcement *m*, renforçage *m.*
intensify [in'tensifai]. 1. *v.tr.* Intensifier, augmenter; rendre plus fort, plus vif (un son); renforcer (une couleur). *Phot:* Renforcer (un cliché faible). 2. *v.i.* Devenir plus intense.
intensity [in'tensiti], *s.* 1.= INTENSENESS. 2. *Ph: El: etc:* Intensité *f*, puissance *f* (de son, de courant). *Phot:* I. of a negative, densité *f* d'un cliché. 3. With i., intensément.
intensive [in'tensiv], *a.* Intensif, -ive. **-ly,** *adv.* Intensivement.
intent¹ [in'tent], *s.* Intention *f*, dessein *m*, but *m.* With good i., dans une bonne intention. With i. to defraud, dans l'intention, dans le but, de frauder. To do sth. with i., with specific i., faire qch. de propos délibéré, dans une intention arrêtée. To all intents and purposes, virtuellement; en fait.
intent², *a.* 1. To be i. on sth., être tout entier à qch., être absorbé par qch. To be i. on doing sth., être résolu, déterminé, à faire qch. 2. Mind i. on learning, esprit acharné à l'étude. I. gaze, regard profond. **-ly,** *adv.* (Écouter) attentivement; (regarder) avec une attention soutenue.
intention [in'ten∫(ə)n], *s.* Intention *f.* 1. (a) Dessein *m.* I have not the slightest i. to . . ., je n'ai pas la moindre intention de . . . With the i. of being . . ., dans l'intention d'être. . . . To do sth. with the best (of) intentions, faire qch. dans la meilleure intention. (b) But *m.* With the i. of . . ., dans le but de. . . . (c) *pl. O:* To court a woman with honourable intentions, courtiser une femme pour le bon motif. To make known one's intentions, se déclarer. *Surg:* Healing by the first, second, i., réunion *f* par première, deuxième, intention.
intentional [in'ten∫ən(ə)l], *a.* Intentionnel, -elle, voulu; fait exprès. **-ally,** *adv.* A dessein; exprès; intentionnellement; de propos délibéré.
intentness [in'tentnis], *s.* Contention *f* d'esprit; tension *f* d'esprit; attention soutenue (du regard).
inter [in'tə:r], *v.tr.* (interred) Enterrer, ensevelir (un mort).
interact [intə'rækt], *v.i.* Réagir réciproquement. **interacting,** *a.* À action réciproque; à action conjuguée.
interaction [ˌintər'æk∫(ə)n], *s.* Action *f* réciproque.
interallied [ˌintər'ælaid], *a.* Interallié.
interbedded [ˌintər'bedid], *a. Geol:* Lardé (with, de).
interbreed [ˌintə'bri:d]. 1. *v.tr.* Croiser, entrecroiser (des races). 2. *v.i.* S'entre-croiser.
intercalate [in'tə:kəleit], *v.tr.* Intercaler.
intercalation [ˌintəkə'lei∫(ə)n], *s.* Intercalation *f.*
intercede [ˌintə'si:d], *v.i.* To i. (with s.o.) for s.o., intercéder (auprès de qn) en faveur de qn, pour qn; demander grâce pour qn.
intercellular [ˌintə'seljulər], *a.* Intercellulaire. *Bot:* I. space, méat *m* intercellulaire.
intercept [ˌintə'sept], *v.tr.* Intercepter (la lumière, une lettre); arrêter (qn) au passage. *Tg: Tp:* Capter, intercepter (un message).
interception [ˌintə'sep∫(ə)n], *s.* Interception *f. Tg: Tp:* Captation *f* (de messages).
interceptor [ˌintə'septər], *s.* 1. *Civ.E:* Siphon *m* d'égout. 2. *Av:* Intercepteur *m.* **interceptor-'fighter,** *s. Av:* Intercepteur *m.*
intercession [ˌintə'se∫(ə)n], *s.* Intercession *f.*
intercessor [ˌintə'sesər], *s.* Intercesseur *m.*
interchange¹ [intə'tfeindʒ], *s.* 1. Échange *m* (de compliments); communication *f* (d'idées). 2. Succession alternative, alternance *f* (du jour et de la nuit, etc.).
interchange² [ˌintə'tfeindʒ], *v.tr.* Échanger (des parties d'une machine, etc.). To i. the position of two things, changer deux choses de place; mettre l'une à la place de l'autre.
interchangeability ['intətfeindʒə'biliti], *s.* Interchangeabilité *f*, permutabilité *f.*
interchangeable [ˌintə'tfeindʒəbl], *a.* Interchangeable, permutable.
intercom ['intə'kəm], *s.* Intercom *m.*
intercommunicate [ˌintəkə'mju:nikeit], *v.i.* Communiquer. The prisoners i., les prisonniers communiquent entre eux.

intercommunication ['intəkəmju:ni'keiʃ(ə)n], s. Inter-communication f. I. system, intercom m.

intercommunion [,intəkə'mju:njən], s. 1. Rapports m intimes (between, entre). 2. Ecc: Intercommunion f (de plusieurs églises).

interconnected [,intəkə'nektid], a. 1. (Chambres, etc.) en communication réciproque. 2. (Faits) intimement liés.

intercontinental [,intəkɔnti'nent(ə)l], a. Intercontinental, -aux. I. ballistic missile, fusée intercontinentale, engin intercontinental.

intercostal [,intə'kɔst(ə)l], a. Anat: Intercostal, -aux.

intercourse ['intəkɔ:s], s. (a) Commerce m, relations fpl, rapports mpl. Human i., relations humaines. (b) Sexual i., rapports sexuels.

intercross [,intə'krɔs]. 1. v.tr. Entrecroiser; entrelacer. 2. v.i. S'entrecroiser; s'entrelacer.

interdepartmental ['intə'di:pɑ:t'ment(ə)l], a. Inter-départemental.

interdepend [,intədi'pend], v.i. Dépendre l'un de l'autre; être solidaires (l'un de l'autre).

interdependence [,intədi'pendəns], s. Interdépendance f; solidarité f.

interdependent [,intədi'pendənt], a. Solidaire (with, de).

interdict¹ ['intədikt], s. 1. Jur: Défense f, interdiction f. 2. Ecc: Interdit m. To lay a priest under an i., frapper d'interdit, d'interdiction, un prêtre.

interdict² [,intə'dikt], v.tr. 1. Jur: Interdire, prohiber. To i. s.o. from doing sth., interdire à qn de faire qch. 2. Ecc: Frapper d'interdiction, interdire (un prêtre).

interdiction [,intə'dikʃ(ə)n], s. Interdiction f.

interest¹ ['intrest], s. Intérêt m. 1. Com: etc: (a) Participation f. To have an i. in the profits, participer aux bénéfices. To have a financial, a money, i. in sth., avoir des capitaux, être intéressé, dans qch. To give s.o. a joint i. in a business, cointéresser qn dans une affaire. (b) The shipping i., les armateurs m; le commerce maritime. The Conservative i., le parti conservateur. The landed i., les propriétaires terriens. 2. Avantage m, profit m. To act for, in, one's own interest(s), agir dans son intérêt. To act in s.o.'s interest(s), agir pour le compte de qn. To promote s.o.'s i., prendre les intérêts de qn. 3. A: Crédit m, influence f. 4. To take, feel, an i. in s.o., in sth., s'intéresser à qn; prendre de l'intérêt à qch. To take no (further) i. in sth., se désintéresser de qch. Questions of public i., questions d'intérêt public. 5. Fin: To bear i., fructifier. To bear i. at 5%, porter intérêt à cinq pour cent. Simple, compound, i., intérêts simples, composés. Shares that yield high i., actions à gros rendement. To repay an injury with i., rendre le mal avec usure.

interest², v.tr. 1. Intéresser (s.o. in a business, qn à, dans, une affaire). 2. Éveiller l'intérêt de (qn). To i. oneself, to be interested, in s.o., in doing sth., s'intéresser à qn, à qch. To be i. in painting, in music, s'intéresser à la peinture, à la musique. I should be interested to hear the end of the story, je serais curieux d'apprendre la fin de l'histoire. **interested**, a. 1. The i. parties, les parties intéressées; les intéressés m. Jur: I. party, ayant droit, m, pl. ayants droit. 2. I. motives, motifs intéressés. 3. With an i. look, avec un regard d'intérêt; d'un air intéressé. -ly, adv. Avec intérêt. **interesting**, a. Intéressant. -ly, adv. D'une manière intéressante.

interfere [,intə'fiər], v.i. 1. (a) (Of pers.) S'ingérer, s'immiscer, intervenir (dans une affaire); s'interposer (dans une querelle). Don't i. with, in, what doesn't concern you, ne vous mêlez pas de ce qui ne vous regarde pas; F: mêlez-vous de vos affaires! (b) Toucher (with, à). Don't i. (with it)! n'y touchez pas! Don't i. with the children! laissez les enfants tranquilles! (c) (Of thg) To i. with (sth.), gêner (la circulation, etc.). Nothing must i. with the course of justice, rien ne doit entraver le cours de la justice. It interferes with my plans, cela dérange mes plans. 2. Ph: (Of light-waves, etc.) Interférer. W.Tel: Brouiller. **interfering**, a. 1. (a) (Of pers.) Importun, qui se mêle de tout. (b) He is so i.! il fourre son nez partout! 2. Ph: (Of rays, etc.) Interférent.

interference [,intə'fiərəns], s. 1. Intervention f; intrusion f, ingérence f (in sth.). 2. Ph: Interférence f. W.Tel: Effet m parasitaire, parasites mpl; brouillage m. Tp: Friture f.

interim ['intərim]. 1. adv. Entre-temps; en attendant. Ad i., par intérim, provisoirement. 2. s. Intérim m. In the i., dans l'intérim; sur ces entrefaites. 3. a. (Rapport, professeur) intérimaire. S.a. DIVIDEND.

interior [in'tiəriər]. 1. a. Intérieur. Geom: I. angle, angle interne. 2. s. (a) Intérieur m (du pays, des terres). (b) Art: (Tableau m d')intérieur.

interject [,intə'dʒekt], v.tr. Lancer (une remarque).

interjection [,intə'dʒekʃ(ə)n], s. Interjection f.

interlace [,intə'leis]. 1. v.tr. (a) Entrelacer; entrecroiser (des fils). T.V: Interlaced scanning, entrelacement m. (b) Entremêler (with, de). 2. v.i. S'entrelacer, s'entrecroiser. **interlacing**, s. Entrelacement m.

interlard [,intə'lɑ:d], v.tr. (Entre)larder, entremêler (un discours, ses récits) (with, de).

interleaf, pl. -leaves ['intəli:f, -li:vz], s. Feuille blanche (intercalée dans un livre); page interfoliée.

interleave [,intə'li:v], v.tr. Interfolier (un livre).

interline [,intəlain], v.tr. 1. (a) Interligner, entre-ligner. (b) Écrire (une traduction, etc.) entre les lignes. 2. Tail: Mettre une doublure intermédiaire à (un vêtement, etc.). **interlining**, s. 1. Interlinéation f; intercalation f (de mots, de lignes dans un texte). 2. Tail: Doublure f intermédiaire.

interlinear [,intə'liniər], a. (Traduction) interlinéaire.

interlink [intə'liŋk]. 1. v.tr. Enchaîner, relier, rattacher (with, à). 2. v.i. Se relier; s'agrafer. **interlinking**, s. Raccordement m; jonction f.

interlock [,intə'lɔk]. 1. v.tr. Emboîter. Rail: Enclencher (des aiguilles). 2. v.i. (a) S'entremêler, s'entrelacer, s'entrecroiser. (b) Mec.E: S'enclencher; s'emboîter. **interlocking**, s. Enclenchement m, emboîtement m; engrènement m.

interlock² ['intəlɔk], (a) s. Tex: Tissu m interlock. (b) attrib.a. Tex: I. machine, interlock m.

interlocution [,intəlo'kju:ʃ(ə)n], s. Interlocution f.

interlocutor [,intə'lɔkjutər], s. Interlocuteur m.

interlocutory [,intə'lɔkjutəri], a. Jur: (Arrêt) inter-locutoire, préjudiciel.

interlocutress [,intə'lɔkjutris], **interlocutrix** [,intə'lɔk-jutriks], s.f. Interlocutrice.

interlope [,intə'loup], v.i. 1. Com: etc: Faire du commerce interlope. 2. Se mêler des affaires d'autrui.

interloper ['intəloupər], s. (a) Intrus, -use. (b) Commerçant m marron.

interlude ['intəlju:d], s. Th: Intermède m. Musical i., interlude m.

intermarriage [,intə'mæridʒ], s. Intermariage m; mariage consanguin.

intermarry [,intə'mæri], v.i. (a) Épouser qn d'une race, d'une religion, différente. (b) Se marier entre parents.

intermediary [,intə'mi:djəri], a. & s. Intermédiaire (m).

intermediate¹ [,intə'mi:diit], a. Intermédiaire. Sch: I. course, cours moyen (d'algèbre, etc.). Sch: I. examination, examen m intermédiaire.

intermediate² [,intə'mi:djeit], v.i. S'entremettre; servir de médiateur (between, entre).

interment [in'tə:mənt], s. Enterrement m, inhumation f.

intermezzo [,intə'metsou], s. Mus: Intermezzo m.

interminable [in'tə:minəbl], a. Interminable; sans fin. -ably, adv. Interminablement; sans fin.

intermingle [,intə'miŋgl]. 1. v.tr. Entremêler; mélanger. 2. v.i. S'entremêler, se mêler, se confondre (with, avec).

interministerial ['intəminis'ti:riəl], a. Interministériel, -elle.

intermission [,intə'miʃ(ə)n], s. 1. Interruption f, trêve f. Med: Intermission f (de la fièvre). 2. Th: U.S: Entracte m.

intermit [,intə'mit], v. (intermitted) 1. v.tr. Interrompre, suspendre (ses travaux, etc.). 2. v.i. Med: (Of pulse etc:) Avoir des intermittences.

intermittence [,intə'mit(ə)ns], s. 1. Intermittence f (d'une source, etc.). 2. Pause f; arrêt momentané.

intermittent [,intə'mit(ə)nt], a. Intermittent. -ly, adv. Par intervalles, par intermittence.

intermolecular ['intəmo'lekjulər], a. Intermoléculaire.

intermuscular [,intə'mʌskjulər], a. (Tissu m, etc.) intermusculaire.

intern¹ [in'tə:n], v.tr. Interner.

intern² ['intə:n], s. U.S: Interne m (des hôpitaux).

internal [in'tə:n(ə)l], a. 1.(Puits, circuit) intérieur; (angle, maladie) interne. 2. (a) (Valeur) intrinsèque; (preuve) intime. (b) Secret, intime. 3. I. trade, commerce intérieur. U.S: 1. revenue, le fisc. -ally, adv. Intérieurement. Pharm: 'Not to be taken i.', pour usage externe.

international [intə'næʃ(ə)n(ə)l]. 1. a. International, -aux. I. law, droit international. 2. s. Sp: (Joueur) international. -ally, adv. Internationalement.

Internationale (the) [ði:,intənæʃən'ɑ:l], s. L'Internationale f.

internationalism [intə'næʃ(ə)nəlizm], s. Internationalisme m.

internationalist [intə'næʃ(ə)nəlist], a. & s. Internationaliste.

internationality ['intənæʃə'næliti], s. Internationalité f.

internationalize [intə'næʃ(ə)nəlaiz], v.tr. Internationaliser (un territoire, etc.).

internee [intə:'ni:], s. Interné, -ée.

internment [in'tə:nmənt], s. Internement m.

internship [in'tə:nʃip], s. U.S: Med: Internat m.

interoceanic ['intər,osi'ænik], a. Interocéanique.

interpenetrate ['intə'penitreit], v.tr. Pol.Ec: S'interpénétrer.

interpenetration [intəpeni'treiʃ(ə)n], s. Interpénétration f.

interphone ['intəfoun], s. Interphone m, téléphone intérieur.

interplanetary [intə'plænit(ə)ri], a. Interplanétaire.

interplay ['intəplei], s. Effet m réciproque; réaction f.

Interpol ['intəpɔl], s. Interpol m.

interpolar [intə'poulər], a. El: (Circuit m) interpolaire.

interpolate [in'tə:pəleit], v.tr. Interpoler, intercaler.

interpolation [in,tə:pə'leiʃ(ə)n], s. Interpolation f.

interpolator [in'tə:pəleitər], s. Interpolateur, -trice.

interpose [intə(:)'pouz]. 1. v.tr. Interposer. 2. v.i. S'interposer, intervenir.

interposition [intə:po'ziʃ(ə)n], s. 1. Interposition f. 2. Intervention f.

interpret [in'tə:prit], v.tr. 1. Interpréter, expliquer (un texte); déchiffrer (des signaux). 2. Th: Mus: Interpréter (un rôle, une composition). 3. Interpréter, traduire. Abs. Faire l'interprète.

interpretation [in,tə:pri'teiʃ(ə)n], s. Interprétation f.

interpreter [in'tə:pritər], s. Interprète mf.

interpretership [in'tə:pritəʃip], s. Interprétariat m.

interprofessional [intəprə'feʃənl], a. Interprofessionnel, -elle.

interregnum, pl. **-ums, -a** [intə'regnəm, -əmz, -ə], s. Interrègne m.

interrelated ['intə(:)ri'leitid], a. (Faits) intimement reliés, en relation mutuelle, en corrélation.

interrelation ['intə(:)ri'leiʃ(ə)n], s. Relation mutuelle; corrélation f.

interrogate [in'terogeit], v.tr. Interroger, questionner (qn).

interrogation [in,tero'geiʃ(ə)n], s. Interrogation f; interrogatoire m (d'un prévenu). I. mark, point m d'interrogation.

interrogative [intə'rogətiv], a. Interrogateur, -trice. I. pronoun, pronom interrogatif. -ly, adv. D'un air interrogateur.

interrogator [in'terogeitər], s. Interrogateur, -trice; questionneur, -euse.

interrogatory [intə'rogət(ə)ri]. 1. a. Interrogateur, -trice. 2. s. Jur: Interrogatoire m.

interrupt [intə'rʌpt], v.tr. 1. Interrompre; couper la parole à (qn). Abs. Don't i.! n'interrompez pas! 2. Interrompre (la circulation, un circuit électrique); rompre (la cadence).

interrupter [intə'rʌptər], s. 1. (Pers.) Interrupteur, -trice. 2. El: Interrupteur m; coupe-circuit m inv; (switch) disjoncteur m.

interruption [intə'rʌpʃ(ə)n], s. Interruption f; dérangement m (de qn). To work six hours without i., travailler six heures d'affilée.

inter-school [intə(:)'sku:l], a. (Match m, etc.) interscolaire.

intersect [intə(:)'sekt]. 1. v.tr. Entrecouper, intersecter, entrecroiser (with, by, de). 2. v.i. (Of lines) Se couper, se croiser.

intersection [intə'sekʃ(ə)n], s. 1. Geom: Intersection f. 2. Carrefour m; croisement m de chemins.

interspace ['intə'speis], v.tr. Espacer (ses visites).

intersperse [intə(:)'spə:s], v.tr. Entremêler (between, among, parmi; with, de). Pages interspersed with witty sayings, pages émaillées de bons mots.

interstellar [intə(:)'stelər], a. Interastral, -aux; intersidéral, -aux; interstellaire.

interstice [in'tə:stis], s. (a) Interstice m. (b) Alvéole m (de grillage d'accu, etc.).

intertwine [intə(:)'twain]. 1. v.tr. Entrelacer. 2. v.i. S'entrelacer, s'accoler.

interurban [intər'ə:bən], a. Interurbain.

interval ['intəv(ə)l], s. Intervalle m. 1. (a) At intervals, par intervalles; par à-coups. Meetings held at short intervals, séances très rapprochées. Meteor: Bright intervals, belles éclaircies. Short i. of fine weather, échappée f de beau temps. (b) Sch: Récréation f. (c) Th: Entracte m. Fb: etc. La mi-temps. 2. I. between beams, écartement m de deux poutres. To place objects at regular intervals, échelonner des objets.

intervene [intə(:)'vi:n], v.i. 1. Intervenir, s'interposer. 2. (Of event) Survenir, arriver. 3. Ten years intervened, dix ans s'écoulèrent. intervening, a. 1. (Of pers.) Intervenant. 2. (Événement) survenu. 3. (Époque f, distance f) intermédiaire.

intervention [intə(:)'venʃ(ə)n], s. Intervention f.

interventionism [intə'venʃ(ə)nizm], s. Pol: etc: Interventionnisme m.

interventionist [intə(:)'venʃənist], s. Pol: etc: Interventionniste m.

intervertebral [intə'və:tibrəl], a. Anat: Intervertébral, -aux. I. disk, disque intervertébral.

interview[1] ['intəvju:], s. 1. Entrevue f. Adm: To invite s.o. to an i., convoquer qn. 2. Journ: Interview f.

interview[2], v.tr. 1. Avoir une entrevue avec (qn). 2. Journ: Interviewer (qn).

interviewer ['intəvju:ər], s. Interviewe(u)r m; enquêteur, -trice.

inter-vivos [intə'vi:vous, -'vaivous], a. Jur: Entre-vifs.

inter-war ['intə'wɔ:r], a. The i.-w. years, l'entre-deux-guerres mf, l'interguerre m.

interweave [intə(:)'wi:v], v. (p.t. interwove [intə(:)-'wouv]; p.p. interwoven ['intə(:)'wouvn]) 1. v.tr. (a) Tisser ensemble (des fils d'or et de laine, etc.); entrelacer (des branches). (b) Entremêler (des idées, etc.). 2. v.i. S'entrelacer, s'entremêler. **interwoven**, a. Entrecroisé, intercroisé.

intestacy [in'testəsi], s. Jur: Fait m de mourir intestat; absence f de testament.

intestate [in'testeit], a. 1. To die i., mourir intestat inv. 2. I. estate, succession ab intestat.

intestinal [in'testinl, intes'tainəl], a. Anat: Intestinal, -aux. The i. tube, le conduit intestinal.

intestine [in'testin], s. Anat: Intestin m. The large i., le gros intestin. The small i., l'intestin grêle.

intimacy ['intiməsi], s. 1. Intimité f; familiarité f. 2. Jur: Relations charnelles.

intimate[1] ['intimit]. 1. a. Intime. (a) To become i. with s.o., se lier (d'amitié) avec qn. (b) To have an i. knowledge of sth., avoir une connaissance approfondie de qch. I. connexion, rapport intime, étroit. 2. s. His intimates, ses intimes mf, ses familiers m. -ly, adv. Intimement; à fond. I know Paris i., je connais Paris comme (le fond de) ma poche.

intimate[2] ['intimeit], v.tr. 1. To i. sth. to s.o., signifier, notifier, qch. à qn. 2. Donner à entendre, indiquer (que).

intimation [inti'meiʃ(ə)n], s. 1. Avis m (de décès, etc.). 2. Avis à mots couverts; suggestion f.

intimidate [in'timideit], v.tr. Intimider. Easily intimidated, timide, peureux. **intimidating**, a. Intimidateur, -trice; intimidant.

intimidation [in,timi'deiʃ(ə)n], s. Intimidation f; Jur: menaces fpl. I. of witnesses, subornation f de témoins.

intimidator [in'timideitər], s. Intimidateur, -trice.

intimity [in'timiti], s. 1. (Sentiment m d')intimité f. 2. La vie privée; le privé.

into ['intu, 'intə], prep. Dans, en. 1. To go i. a house, entrer dans une maison. To go i. France, passer en France. To fall i. the hands of the enemy, tomber entre les mains de l'ennemi. To work far i. the night, travailler bien avant dans la nuit. To look i. the future, voir dans l'avenir. 2. To change sth. i. sth., changer qch. en qch. To grow i. a man, devenir un homme. To divide i. four, diviser en quatre. To burst i. tears, fondre en larmes.

intolerability [in,tɔl(ə)rə'biliti], **intolerableness** [in'-tɔl(ə)rəblnis], s. Intolérabilité f (d'une douleur, d'une situation).
intolerable [in'tɔl(ə)rəbl], a. Intolérable, insupportable. **-ably,** adv. Insupportablement.
intolerance [in'tɔlər(ə)ns], s. Intolérance f (of, de). Religious i., intolérantisme m.
intolerant [in'tɔlər(ə)nt], a. 1. Intolérant. 2. Med: To be i. of a drug, ne pas supporter un médicament. **-ly,** adv. Avec intolérance.
intonation [,intə'neiʃ(ə)n], s. Intonation f, ton m, modulation f (de la voix).
intone [in'toun], v.tr. Ecc.Mus: 1. Psalmodier (les litanies). 2. Entonner (le chant).
intoxicant [in'tɔksikənt]. 1. a. Enivrant, grisant, capiteux, -euse. 2. s. Boisson f alcoolique.
intoxicate [in'tɔksikeit], v.tr. Enivrer, griser. **intoxicated,** a. Ivre; gris; pris de boisson. Jur: En état d'ébriété. I. with praise, grisé d'éloges. **intoxicating,** a. Enivrant, grisant. I. liquors, boissons f alcooliques.
intoxication [in,tɔksi'keiʃ(ə)n], s. 1. Med: Intoxication f. 2. (a) Ivresse f. (b) Griserie f, enivrement m (du plaisir, etc.).
intractability [in,træktə'biliti], **intractableness** [in'-træktəblnis], s. Indocilité f.
intractable [in'træktəbl], a. (Enfant, animal) intraitable, insoumis, indocile; (maladie) opiniâtre; (bois, etc.) difficile à travailler; (terrain, matériau) ingrat. **-ably,** adv. D'une façon intraitable.
intrados [in'treidɔs], s. Arch: Intrados m.
intramural [intrə'mjuər(ə)l], a. Intra-muros inv.
intramuscular [intrə'mʌskjulər], a. Med: (Piqûre f) intramusculaire.
intransigency [in'trænsidʒ(ə)nsi], s. Intransigeance f.
intransigent [in'trænsidʒ(ə)nt], a. & s. Intransigeant, -e.
intransitive [in'traːns(i)tiv], a. Gram: Intransitif. **-ly,** adv. Intransitivement.
intransmissible [,intrænz'misəbl], a. Intransmissible.
intravenous [intrə'viːnəs], a. Med: Intraveineux, -euse.
intrepid [in'trepid], a. Intrépide. **-ly,** adv. Intrépidement.
intrepidity [,intri'piditi], s. Intrépidité f.
intricacy [in'trikəsi], s. Complexité f (d'un mécanisme, d'un problème). The intricacies of the law, les dédales m de la loi.
intricate [in'trikit], a. (a) (Mécanisme) compliqué. (b) (Of statements) Embrouillé, confus. I. details, détails compliqués. I. style, style compliqué.
intrigue¹ [in'triːg], s. Intrigue f.
intrigue². 1. v.i. Intriguer; mener des intrigues. To i. against s.o., travailler contre qn. 2. v.tr. Intriguer (qn); éveiller, piquer, la curiosité de (qn). **intriguing¹,** a. 1. (Politicien, etc.) intrigant. 2. All this is very i., tout cela nous intrigue beaucoup. **intriguing²,** s. Machinations fpl, intrigues fpl.
intriguer [in'triːgər], s. Intrigant, -ante.
intrinsic [in'trinsik], a. Intrinsèque. **-ally,** adv. Intrinsèquement.
introduce [,intrə'djuːs], v.tr. 1. Introduire. (a) Faire entrer. To i. a subject, a question, amener un sujet, une question. (b) To i. s.o. into s.o.'s presence, introduire qn auprès de qn. (c) Établir, faire adopter (un usage). (d) To introduce a Bill (before Parliament), déposer un projet de loi. 2. To i. s.o. to s.o., présenter qn à qn. To i. oneself to s.o., se présenter à qn. 3. To i. s.o. to a process, initier qn à un procédé. It was I who introduced him to Greek, c'est moi qui lui ai fait faire la connaissance du grec.
introducer [,intrə'djuːsər], s. Introducteur, -trice.
introduction [,intrə'dʌkʃ(ə)n], s. 1. Introduction f. 2. Présentation f (of s.o. to s.o., de qn à qn). To give s.o. an i. to s.o., donner à qn une lettre de recommandation auprès de qn. 3. Avant-propos m inv; introduction (d'un livre); prélude m (d'une symphonie). 4. Manuel m élémentaire; introduction (to, à).
introductive [,intrə'dʌktiv], **introductory** [,intrə-'dʌkt(ə)ri], a. Introductoire. After a few i. words, après quelques mots d'introduction.
introit ['intrɔit], s. Ecc: Introït m.
introspection [,intro'spekʃ(ə)n], s. Introspection f.

introspective [,intro'spektiv], a. Introspectif, -ive.
introversion [,intro'vəːʃ(ə)n], s. 1. Recueillement m (de l'esprit); Psy: introversion f. 2. Surg: Invagination f. I. of the eyelid, entropion m.
introvert ['introvəːt], s. Psy: Introverti, -ie.
introverted [intro'vəːtid], a. (Esprit) recueilli. Psy: Introverti.
intrude [in'truːd]. 1. v.tr. (a) To i. sth. into sth., introduire qch. de force dans qch. To i. oneself into a business, s'ingérer dans une affaire. (b) To i. sth. on upon, s.o., imposer qch. à qn. 2. v.i. Faire intrusion (on s.o., auprès de qn). I am afraid of intruding, je crains de vous être importun, d'être de trop. I don't want to i. into your affairs, je ne voudrais pas m'ingérer dans vos affaires.
intruder [in'truːdər], s. Intrus, -use. Av: Chasseur m de pénétration.
intrusion [in'truːʒ(ə)n], s. 1. Intrusion f. I hope I am not guilty of an i., j'espère que je ne suis pas indiscret. 2. Geol: Intrusion, injection f (volcanique).
intrusive [in'truːsiv], a. Importun, indiscret. **-ly,** adv. Importunément; en importun.
intrusiveness [in'truːsivnis], s. Indiscrétion f; importunité f.
intuition [,intjuː'iʃ(ə)n], s. Intuition f. To have an i. of sth., avoir l'intuition de qch.
intuitional [,intjuː'iʃ(ə)nl], a. Intuitif, -ive.
intuitive [in'tjuːitiv], a. Intuitif, -ive. **-ly,** adv. Intuitivement; par intuition.
intumescence [,intjuː'mesns], s. Intumescence f; enflure f; boursouflure f.
intumescent [,intjuː'mesnt], a. Intumescent; boursouflé; enflé.
inundate ['inʌndeit], v.tr. Inonder (with, de). To be inundated with requests, être débordé de requêtes.
inundation [,inʌn'deiʃ(ə)n], s. Inondation f.
inure [i'njuər], v.tr. Accoutumer, habituer, rompre, endurcir (to, à). Inured to hardships, to fatigue, habitué aux privations; dur à la fatigue.
inurement [i'njuərmənt], s. Aguerrissement m, endurcissement m, (to, à); accoutumance f (à l'opium, etc.); habitude f (de l'opium, etc.).
invade [in'veid], v.tr. 1. Envahir. To i. s.o.'s house, faire invasion chez qn. To i. s.o.'s privacy, violer la retraite de qn. 2. Empiéter sur (les droits de qn).
invader [in'veidər], s. Envahisseur m.
invagination [in,vædʒi'neiʃ(ə)n], s. Surg: Invagination f.
invalid¹ [in'vælid], a. Jur: (Mariage) invalide; (arrêt) nul et non avenu. **-ly,** adv. Sans validité; illégalement.
invalid² ['invəlid, -liːd], a. & s. (Suffering from illness) Malade (mf); (from infirmity or disability) infirme (mf); (from ill-health) valétudinaire (mf). Helpless i., invalide impotent, grand invalide. I. chair, (i) fauteuil m de malade; (ii) voiture f d'infirme.
invalid³ [in'væliːd], v.tr. (a) Rendre malade ou infirme. (b) To i. a man out of the army, réformer un homme.
invalidate [in'vælideit], v.tr. Jur: 1. Invalider, rendre nul (un testament); vicier (un contrat). 2. Casser, infirmer (un jugement). **invalidating,** a. Jur: Infirmatif, -ive.
invalidation [in,væli'deiʃ(ə)n], s. Jur: 1. Invalidation f (d'un document). 2. Infirmation f (d'un jugement).
invalidity [,invə'liditi], s. 1. Invalidité f (d'un contrat, d'un passeport). 2. Valétudinarisme m; invalidité f.
invaluable [in'væljuə)bl], a. Inestimable, inappréciable; (trésor) d'un prix incalculable.
invariability [in,veəriə'biliti], **invariableness** [in'veə-rieblnis], s. Invariabilité f.
invariable [in'veəriəbl], a. Invariable. **-ably,** adv. Invariablement, immanquablement.
invasion [in'veiʒ(ə)n], s. 1. Invasion f, envahissement m. I. by the enemy, envahissement par l'ennemi. Mil: I. barge, péniche f de débarquement. These invasions of my privacy, ces intrusions f dans mon intimité. 2. Med: Invasion, début m (d'une maladie). 3. I. of s.o.'s rights, violation f des droits, atteinte f aux droits, de qn.
invective [in'vektiv], s. Invective f. Coll. A torrent of i., un flot d'invectives, d'injures f.
inveigh [in'vei], v.i. Invectiver, tonner, fulminer (against, contre).

nveigle [in'vi:gl, in'veigl], v.tr. Attirer, séduire, enjôler (qn). To i. s.o. into doing sth., entraîner qn à faire qch.

nveiglement [in'vi:glmənt, -'veig-], s. 1. Séduction f, enjôlement m. 2. Leurre m.

nveigler [in'vi:glər, -'veig-], s. Séducteur, -trice; enjôleur, -euse.

nvent [in'vent], v.tr. Inventer. Newly invented process, procédé d'invention récente.

nvention [in'venʃ(ə)n], s. Invention f. A story of his own i., une histoire de son cru.

nventive [in'ventiv], a. Inventif, -ive.

nventiveness [in'ventivnis], s. Fécondité f d'invention; don m d'invention; imagination f.

nventor [in'ventər], s. Inventeur, occ. f. -trice.

nventory ['invəntri], s. Com: Inventaire m. To take, draw up, an i., faire, dresser, un inventaire.

nverse ['invə:s]. 1. a. Inverse. In i. order, en sens inverse. In i. ratio, en raison inverse (to, de). 2. s. Inverse m, contraire m (of, de). -ly, adv. Inversement.

nversion [in'və:ʃ(ə)n], s. 1. Renversement m. I. of values, renversement des valeurs. 2. Gram: Inversion f (du sujet, etc.). 3. El: Pole i., inversion des pôles. 4. Psy: Sexual i., inversion sexuelle; homosexualité f.

nversive [in'və:siv], a. Inversif, -ive.

nvert [in'və:t], v.tr. 1. Renverser, retourner (un objet) (le haut en bas). Mus: To i. a chord, renverser un accord. 2. Invertir, intervertir, renverser (l'ordre, les positions). 3. Retourner; mettre à l'envers. inverted, a. Dressm: Inverted pleat, pli creux, double pli, pli inverti.

nvertebrate [in'və:tibrit, -breit], a. & s. Z: Invertébré (m).

nvest [in'vest], v.tr. 1. Revêtir (with, in, de). 2. To i. with an office, investir qn d'une fonction. 3. Mil: Investir, cerner (une place forte). 4. Fin: Placer, investir (des fonds). To i. money, faire des placements. To i. one's money in real estate, mettre son argent en biens-fonds. Abs: To i. in house property, faire des placements en immeubles. To i. in a new piece of furniture, se payer un nouveau meuble.

nvestigate [in'vestigeit], v.tr. Examiner, étudier, sonder (une question). To i. a crime, faire une enquête sur un crime; informer sur un crime. Investigating committee, commission f d'enquête.

nvestigation [in,vesti'geiʃ(ə)n], s. Investigation f; enquête f (of, sur). Question under i., question à l'étude. Preliminary investigations with a view to . . ., études f préparatoires en vue de. . . . Scientific i., enquête scientifique. On further i. . . ., en poursuivant mes recherches. . . .

nvestigator [in'vestigeitər], s. Investigateur, -trice; enquêteur, -euse.

nvestiture [in'vestitʃər], s. (a) Investiture f (d'un évêque, etc.). (b) Remise f de décorations.

nvestment [in'ves(t)mənt], s. 1. Mil: Investissement m (d'une place forte). 2. Fin: Placement m (de fonds); mise f de fonds. Investments, portefeuille m. Safe i., valeur f de tout repos.

nvestor [in'vestər], s. Actionnaire mf, capitaliste mf. Small investors, petits capitalistes, petits rentiers, petits épargnants.

nveteracy [in'vet(ə)risi], s. Caractère invétéré (d'un mal, etc.).

nveterate [in'vet(ə)rit], a. (a) Invétéré. (b) (Of smoker, etc.) Obstiné, acharné. I. hatred, haine implacable, vivace. -ly, adv. (a) Dans le fond; foncièrement. (b) Avec acharnement, opiniâtrement.

nvidious [in'vidiəs], a. 1. Haïssable, odieux. I. task, tâche ingrate. 2. (a) Qui excite l'envie, la haine. (b) Qui suscite la jalousie. I. comparison, comparaison désobligeante. -ly, adv. Odieusement, désobligeamment.

nvidiousness [in'vidiəsnis], s. Caractère m haïssable, blessant (de qch.); odieux m, injustice f (d'une mesure).

nvigilate [in'vidʒileit], v.i. Sch: Surveiller les candidats (à un examen).

nvigilation [invidʒi'leiʃ(ə)n], s. Sch: Surveillance f (des candidats).

nvigilator [in'vidʒileitər], s. Sch: Surveillant, -ante (d'un examen).

invigorate [in'vigəreit], v.tr. (a) Fortifier (qn); donner de la vigueur à (qn). (b) (Of the air, etc.) Vivifier, tonifier. invigorating, a. (Of food, etc.) Fortifiant; (of air, etc.) vivifiant, tonifiant.

invincibility [in,vinsi'biliti], s. Invincibilité f.

invincible [in'vinsəbl], a. Invincible. -ibly, adv. Invinciblement.

inviolability [in,vaiələ'biliti], s. Inviolabilité f.

inviolable [in'vaiələbl], a. Inviolable. -ably, adv. Inviolablement.

inviolate [in'vaiəlit], a. Invi lé.

invisibility [in,vizə'biliti], invisibleness [in'vizəblnis], s. Invisibilité f.

invisible [in'vizəbl], a. Invisible. I. ink, encre sympathique. S.a. MENDING. -ibly, adv. Invisiblement.

invitation [,invi'teiʃ(ə)n], s. Invitation f (to do sth., à faire qch.). To come at s.o.'s i., venir sur l'invitation de qn. invi'tation-card, s. Carte f d'invitation.

invite [in'vait], v.tr. 1. Inviter; convier (des amis à dîner). To i. s.o. in, prier qn d'entrer. 2. Engager, inviter, appeler (s.o. to do sth., qn à faire qch.). 3. Provoquer (le malheur, la critique). inviting, a. Invitant, attrayant; (mets) appétissant. Not very i., peu ragoûtant. -ly, adv. D'une manière attrayante, tentante.

invocation [,invo'keiʃ(ə)n], s. Invocation f.

invocatory [in'vəkətəri], a. (Formule f) invocatoire.

invoice[1] ['invois], s. Com: Facture f (d'achat). As per i., suivant la facture. I. clerk, facturier, -ière.

invoice[2], v.tr. Facturer (des marchandises). invoicing, s. I. of goods, facturation f (de marchandises).

invoke [in'vouk], v.tr. 1. (a) Invoquer (Dieu). (b) To i. s.o.'s aid, appeler qn à son secours. 2. Évoquer (un esprit) par des incantations.

invoker [in'voukər], s. Invocateur, -trice.

involucre ['invəlu:kər], s. Bot: Involucre m.

involuntary [in'vələnt(ə)ri], a. Involontaire. -ily, adv. Involontairement.

involute ['invəlu:t]. 1. a. (a) Bot: (Feuille) involutée, involutive. (b) (Arc) de développante; (engrenage) à développante. 2. s. Geom: Développante f.

involution [,invə'lu:ʃ(ə)n], s. 1. (a) Complication f; tours mpl et détours. (b) Enchevêtrement m, embrouillement m. 2. Nat.Hist: etc: Involution f.

involve [in'vəlv], v.tr. 1. (a) Lit: Envelopper, entortiller. To get involved with a rope, s'empêtrer dans un cordage. (b) Compliquer, entortiller (un récit). 2. To i. s.o. in a quarrel, engager qn dans une querelle. To i. s.o. in a charge, impliquer qn dans une accusation. He involved his friend in his ruin, il entraîna son ami dans sa ruine. To i. oneself in trouble, se créer des ennuis. To be involved in a failure, être enveloppé, entraîné, dans une faillite. He is involved in the plot, il est compromis, il a trempé, dans le complot. The vehicle involved, le véhicule en cause (dans l'accident). His honour is involved, son honneur est engagé. The forces involved, les forces en jeu. 3. Comporter, entraîner. To i. much expense, nécessiter, entraîner, de grands frais. It would i. living in London, cela nécessiterait que j'aille vivre à Londres. involved, a. 1. (Style) embrouillé, compliqué, touffu. 2. (Domaine) grevé de dettes.

involvement [in'vəlvmənt], s. 1. Empêtrement m; implication f (de qn, dans une affaire).

invulnerability [in,vʌln(ə)rə'biliti], s. Invulnérabilité f.

invulnerable [in'vʌln(ə)rəbl], a. Invulnérable.

inward ['inwəd]. 1. a. (a) Intérieur, interne. (b) Vers l'intérieur. 2. s.pl. P: Inwards ['inədz], entrailles f, viscères m. 3. adv. = INWARDS. -ly, adv. En dedans; intérieurement.

inwardness ['inwədnis], s. Essence f, signification f intime (de qch.).

inwards ['inwədz], adv. Vers l'intérieur; en dedans.

iodate[1] ['aiədeit], s. Ch: Iodate m.

iodate[2], v.tr. Med: Phot: Ioder, iodurer.

iodic [ai'ɔdik], a. Ch: (Acide m) iodique.

iodide ['aiədaid], s. Ch: Iodure m.

iodine ['aiədi:n], s. Iode m. Tincture of i., teinture f d'iode.

iodize ['aiədaiz], v.tr. Ioder, iodurer.

iodoform [ai'ɔdəfɔ:m], s. Pharm: Iodoforme m.

ion ['aiən], s. El: Ph: Ch: Ion m. Attrib.a. **I. rocket,** moteur-fusée m ionique. **I. propulsion,** propulsion f ionique.
Ionian [ai'ounjən], a. & s. Geog: Ionien, -ienne.
Ionic¹ [ai'ɔnik], a. Arch: Ionique.
ionic², a. El: Ph: Ch: Ionique.
ionization [,aiənai'zeiʃ(ə)n], s. El: Ph: Ionisation f.
ionize ['aiənaiz]. **1.** v.tr. El: Ph: Ioniser (l'air, un gaz). **2.** v.i. (Of acid, etc.) S'ioniser.
ionosphere [ai'ɔnəsfiər], s. Ionosphère f.
ionospheric [ai'ɔnəs'ferik], a. Ionosphérique. **I. recorder,** enregistreur m ionosphérique.
iota [ai'outə], s. **1.** Gr.Alph: Iota m. **2.** Not one i., pas un iota.
ipecacuanha [,ipikækju'ænə], F: **ipecac** ['ipikæk], s. Bot: Ipécacuana m, F: ipéca m.
Irak, Iraq [i'rɑːk]. Pr.n. Geog: L'Irak m.
Iraki [i'rɑːki], a. & s. Geog: Irakien, -ienne.
Iran [i'rɑːn]. Pr.n. Geog: L'Iran m.
Iranian [i'reinjən], a. & s. Geog: Iranien, -ienne.
Iraqi [i'rɑːki], a. & s. Geog: Irakien, -ienne.
irascibility [iræsi'biliti], s. Irascibilité f.
irascible [i'ræsibl], a. (Homme) irascible, coléreux; (tempérament) colérique.
irate [ai'reit], a. Courroucé; en colère.
ire ['aiər], s. Lit: Courroux m, ire f, colère f.
Ireland ['aiələnd]. Pr.n. L'Irlande f.
iridescence [,iri'desns], s. Irisation f, iridescence f; chatoiement m (d'un plumage, etc.).
iridescent [,iri'desnt], a. Irisé, iridescent; chatoyant.
iridioplatinum [i'ridiou'plætinəm], s. Metall: Platine iridié.
iridium [i'ridiəm], s. Ch: Iridium m.
iridize ['iridaiz], v.tr. Iridier (une pointe de vis, etc.).
Iris ['aiəris]. **1.** Pr.n.f. Myth: Iris. **2.** s. (pl. **irides** ['airidiːz]) Anat: Iris m (de l'œil). **3.** s. (pl. **irises** ['airisiz]) Bot: Iris m. **Yellow i.,** iris jaune, iris des marais. **4.** s. (pl. **irises**) Reflets irisés; chatoiement m. **'iris-'diaphragm,** s. Phot: Diaphragme m iris.
Irish ['aiəriʃ]. **1.** a. Irlandais; (toile) d'Irlande. S.a. STEW¹ **2. 2.** s. (a) Ling: L'irlandais m. (b) pl. **The I.,** les Irlandais m. **'Irish Free 'State (the).** Pr.n. Hist: L'État m libre d'Irlande.
Irishman, pl. **-men** ['aiəriʃmən], s.m. Irlandais.
Irishwoman, pl. **-women** ['aiəriʃwumən, -wimin], s.f. Irlandaise.
irk [əːk], v.tr. A: Ennuyer. Impers. **It irks me to . . .,** cela m'est pénible de . . .; il m'en coûte de. . . .
irksome ['əːksəm], a. (Travail) ennuyeux, ingrat. **-ly,** adv. D'une manière ennuyeuse.
irksomeness ['əːksəmnis], s. Caractère ennuyeux, ingrat (d'une tâche, etc.).
iron¹ ['aiən], s. **1.** (a) Metall: Fer m. **Iron and steel industry,** industrie f sidérurgique. **Cast i.,** fonte f (de fer). **Pig i.,** fonte en saumon, en gueuse(s). **Wrought i.,** fer forgé. Com: **Bar i.,** fer marchand, fer méplat. **Corrugated i.,** tôle ondulée. **Old i.,** ferraille f. (b) Attrib. **I. mounting, fitting,** ferrure f. **I. ore,** minerai de fer. **Red i. ore,** hématite f rouge. **I. will,** volonté de fer. **To have an i. constitution,** avoir une santé de fer. **Man of i.,** homme dur, sans pitié; cœur m de fer. S.a. LUNG 1. **2.** (a) Haird: O: Curling i., fer à friser. **To have too many irons in the fire,** mener trop d'affaires de front; courir trop de lièvres à la fois. (b) Tls: **Plane i.,** fer de rabot. **3.** Golf: (Crosse f en) fer. **4.** Dom.Ec: (Flat-)i., laundry i., fer à repasser. **Electric i.,** fer électrique. **5.** pl. (a) Fers, chaînes f. Nau: etc: **To put a man in irons,** mettre un homme aux fers. (b) (Of ship) **To be in irons,** faire chapelle. **'iron-'filings,** s.pl. Limaille f de fer. **'iron-foundry,** s. Fonderie f de fonte; usine f métallurgique. **'iron-'grey,** a. & s. Gris (de) fer (m inv). **'iron-holder,** s. Dom.Ec: (a) O: Poignée f (de fer à repasser). (b) Repose-fer m, pl. repose-fers. **'iron-mould,** s. Tache f de rouille. **'iron-shod,** a. Ferré.
iron², v.tr. Repasser (le linge). **To i. out a crease** (in a dress, etc.), faire disparaître un faux pli au fer chaud. **To i. out difficulties,** aplanir des difficultés. **ironing,** s. Repassage m. S.a. BOARD¹ 1. **'iron(ing)-stand,** s. Dom.Ec: Repose-fer m, pl. repose-fers.
ironclad ['aiənklæd]. **1.** a. (Navire) cuirassé; (puits) blindé. **2.** s. Navy: A: Cuirassé m.

ironer ['aiənər], s. Repasseur, -euse.
ironic(al) [ai'rɔnik(əl)], a. Ironique. **-ally,** adv. Ironiquement; par ironie.
ironmaster ['aiənmɑːstər], s.m. Maître de forges; métallurgiste.
ironmonger ['aiənmʌŋgər], s. Quincaillier m.
ironmongery ['aiənmʌŋg(ə)ri], s. Quincaillerie f.
ironware ['aiənwɛər], s. Ferronnerie f; articles mp en fer (forgé).
ironwork ['aiənwəːk], s. **1.** (a) Serrurerie f; (travail m de) ferronnerie f. (b) **Heavy i., constructional i.** charpente f en fer, grosse serrurerie, profilés mpl pour constructions. (c) (Parts made of iron) Ferrure(s) f(pl). **2.** pl. **Ironworks,** usine f sidérurgique; forges fpl.
ironworker ['aiənwəːkər], s. **1.** (In wrought iron) (Ouvrier) serrurier m; ferronnier m. **2.** (In heavy iron) Charpentier m en fer.
irony ['aiərəni], s. Ironie f.
irradiance [i'reidiəns], s. Rayonnement m, éclat m.
irradiant [i'reidiənt], a. Rayonnant.
irradiate [i'reidieit], v.tr. **1.** (Of light, heat) Irradier, rayonner sur (la terre); (of light rays) illuminer (une surface). **2.** Émettre comme des rayons. **3.** Lit: **Good humour irradiated his face,** la bonne humeur faisait rayonner son visage. **irradiated,** a. Rayonnant. Ph: **I. heat,** chaleur rayonnante.
irradiation [i,reidi'eiʃ(ə)n], s. **1.** Irradiation f. **2.** Rayonnement m (d'une source de lumière).
irrational [i'ræʃnl], a. (a) Dépourvu de raison. (b) Déraisonnable, absurde. (c) Mth: (Nombre) irrationnel. **-ally,** adv. Déraisonnablement; irrationnellement.
irrationality [i,ræʃə'næliti], s. Irrationalité f.
irreclaimable [i'ri'kleiməbl], a. **1.** Incorrigible; (ivrogne) invétéré. **2.** (Terrain) incultivable.
irreconcilability [i,rekənsailə'biliti], s. **1.** Irréconciliabilité f (de deux personnes). **2.** Inconciliabilité f (de deux croyances).
irreconcilable [,irekən'sailəbl], a. **1.** (Ennemi) irréconciliable; (haine) implacable. **2.** (Croyance) incompatible, inconciliable (with, avec). **-ably,** adv. **1.** Irréconciliablement. **2.** Inconciliablement.
irrecoverable [i,ri'kʌv(ə)rəbl], a. (Créance) irrécouvrable; (perte) irréparable. **-ably,** adv. Irréparablement; (ruiné) à tout jamais.
irrecusable [i'ri'kjuːzəbl], a. (Témoignage) irrécusable
irredeemable [i'ri'diːməbl], a. **1.** Irrachetable. **I. bonds,** obligations non amortissables. **2.** (a) (Désastre) irrémédiable. (b) (Of person) incorrigible. **-ably,** adv. (Condamné) sans recours.
irreducible [i'ri'djuːsəbl], a. (Fraction, hernie) irréductible.
irreformable [i'ri'fɔːməbl], a. Irréformable.
irrefrangible [i'ri'fræn(d)ʒəbl], a. Opt: Irréfrangible
irrefutability [i,rifjutə'biliti, 'iri,fjutə'biliti], s. Irréfutabilité f.
irrefutable [i'ri'fjuːtəbl, i'ri'fjuːtəbl], a. Irréfutable (témoignage) irrécusable. **-ably,** adv. Irréfutablement.
irregular [i'regjulər], a. Irrégulier. **1.** (a) Contraire aux règles. **I. life,** vie déréglée. (b) Nat. Hist: Anormal, -aux. **2.** Asymétrique; (of surface) inégal, -aux. **3.** Mil: **I. troops,** s.pl. **irregulars,** troupes irrégulières; irréguliers m. **-ly,** adv. Irrégulièrement.
irregularity [i,regju'læriti], s. (a) Irrégularité f (de conduite, etc.). (b) Adm: Com: **To commit irregularities,** commettre des irrégularités.
irrelevance [i'relivəns], **irrelevancy** [i'relivənsi], s. **1.** Inapplicabilité f (to, à). **2.** Manque m d'à-propos. **Speech full of irrelevancies,** discours rempli de hors de propos.
irrelevant [i'relivənt], a. Non pertinent; (of remark etc.) hors de propos. **To make i. remarks,** divaguer. **That is i.,** cela n'a rien à voir avec la question. **-ly,** adv. Mal à propos; hors de propos.
irreligion [i'ri'lidʒ(ə)n], s. Irréligion f.
irreligious [i'ri'lidʒəs], a. Irréligieux, -euse. **-ly,** adv. Irréligieusement.
irremediable [i'ri'miːdiəbl], a. Irrémédiable; sans remède. **-ably,** adv. Irrémédiablement; sans remède
irremissible [i'ri'misəbl], a. (Faute) irrémissible (péché) impardonnable.

irremovable [ˌiri'muːvəbl], a. (a) Qu'on ne saurait déplacer, fixe. (b) (Fonctionnaire) inamovible. -ably, adv. Fermement, fixement, inébranlablement.

irreparable [i'repərəbl], a. Irréparable; (perte) irrémédiable, irrécupérable. -ably, adv. Irréparablement, irrémédiablement.

irreplaceable [ˌiri'pleisəbl], a. (Trésor m, ami m) irremplaçable.

irrepressible [ˌiri'presəbl], a. (Bâillement) irrésistible, irréprimable; (force) irrépressible. I. child, enfant qui a le diable au corps. -ibly, adv. Irrésistiblement.

irreproachable [ˌiri'proutʃəbl], a. Irréprochable; (vêtement) impeccable. -ably, adv. Irréprochablement.

irresistibility ['iriˌzistə'biliti], s. Irrésistibilité f.

irresistible [ˌiri'zistəbl], a. Irrésistible. -ibly, adv. Irrésistiblement.

irresolute [i'rezəljuːt], a. 1. Indécis. 2. (Caractère) irrésolu; (esprit) vacillant, hésitant. -ly, adv. Irrésolument.

irresoluteness [i'rezəljuːtnis], irresolution [iˌrezə'ljuːʃ(ə)n], s. Indécision f (de caractère); irrésolution f.

irresolvable [ˌiri'zɔlvəbl], a. 1. Insoluble. 2. (Corps) indécomposable, irréductible.

irrespective [ˌiri'spektiv]. 1. a. Indépendant (of, de). 2. qdv. I. of sth., indépendamment, sans tenir compte, de qch.

irresponsibility ['iriˌspɔnsə'biliti], s. Étourderie f; manque m de sérieux; irréflexion f.

irresponsible [ˌiri'spɔnsəbl], a. (a) (Of pers.) Étourdi, irréfléchi; évaporé; à la tête légère. (b) (Of action) Irréfléchi. -ibly, adv. Étourdiment. To act i., agir à l'étourdie, à la légère.

irresponsive [ˌiri'spɔnsiv], a. (Of pers.) Flegmatique, froid; (visage) fermé. I. to entreaties, sourd aux prières.

irresponsiveness [ˌiri'spɔnsivnis], s. Flegme m, réserve f, froideur f.

irretrievable [ˌiri'triːvəbl], a. Irréparable, irrémédiable. -ably, adv. Irréparablement; irrémédiablement.

irreverence [i'rev(ə)rəns], s. Irrévérence f; manque m de respect (towards, envers, pour).

irreverent [i'rev(ə)rənt], a. 1. (In religious matters) Irrévérent. 2. (In social intercourse) Irrévérencieux. -ly, adv. 1. Irrévérement. 2. Irrévérencieusement.

irreversibility [ˌirivəːsə'biliti], s. Irréversibilité f; irrévocabilité f (d'une décision).

irreversible [ˌiri'vəːsəbl], a. 1. (Décision) irrévocable. 2. Irréversible. The course of history is i., le cours de l'histoire est irréversible.

irrevocability [iˌrevəkə'biliti], s. Irrévocabilité f.

irrevocable [i'revəkəbl], a. Irrévocable. Jur: Irréformable. -ably, adv. Irrévocablement.

irrigable ['irigəbl], a. (Terre) irrigable.

irrigate ['irigeit], v.tr. (a) Agr: Irriguer (des champs). (b) (Of river) Arroser (une région).

irrigation [ˌiri'geiʃ(ə)n], s. Irrigation f. Med: Colonic i., irrigation du côlon.

irrigator ['irigeitər], s. 1. Agr: (a) (Pers.) Arroseur m. (b) (Machine, device) Arroseuse f. 2. Med: Irrigateur m; bock m.

irritability [ˌiritə'biliti], irritableness ['iritəblnis], s. Irritabilité f.

irritable ['iritəbl], a. 1. Irritable, irascible. 2. Biol: (Nerf m, protoplasme m) irritable, -ably, adv. D'un ton de mauvaise humeur.

irritant ['iritənt], a. & s. Med: Irritant (m).

irritate ['iriteit], v.tr. 1. Irriter, agacer. 2. Med: Irriter (un organe); aviver, envenimer (une plaie). irritating, a. 1. Irritant, agaçant; F: empoisonnant. 2. Med: Irritant, irritatif, -ive. -ly, adv. D'une façon agaçante.

irritation [ˌiri'teiʃ(ə)n], s. 1. Irritation f; agacement m. Nervous i., énervement m. 2. Med: Irritation.

irruption [i'rʌpʃ(ə)n], s. Irruption f.

is. See BE.

Isaiah [ai'zaiə]. Pr.n.m. B.Hist: Isaïe.

isatin ['aisətin], s. Ch: Dy: Isatine f.

isba(h) ['izbə], s. Isba f.

isinglass ['aizinglɑːs], s. (a) Colle f de poisson; ichtyocolle f. (b) Gélatine f (pour gelées, etc.).

Islam ['izlɑːm, -ləm, -læm], s. Islam m (religion ou peuple). To go over to I., embrasser l'islamisme.

Islamic [iz'læmik], a. Islamique.

Islamism ['izləmizm], s. Islamisme m.

Islamist ['izləmist], Islamite ['izləmait], Islamite mf.

island ['ailənd], s. 1. Ile f. Small i., îlot m. Volcanic i., île volcanique. 2. (Street-)i., refuge m (pour piétons). 3. Nau: (esp. aircraft-carriers) Superstructure f, îlot m.

islander ['ailəndər], s. Insulaire mf. The Channel Islanders, les habitants des Iles de la Manche.

isle [ail], s. Ile f. Esp. Pr.n. The British Isles, les Iles britanniques. The I. of Man, l'île de Man.

islet ['ailit], s. Ilot m.

isobar ['aisobɑːr], s. Meteor: Isobare f.

isobaric [ˌaiso'bærik], a. (Ligne) isobare; (carte) isobarique, isobarométrique.

isochromatic [ˌaisokro'mætik], a. Isochromatique.

isochronal [ai'sokrənl], isochronic ['aiso'krɔnik], isochronous [ai'sokrənəs], a. Mec: Isochrone, isochronique.

isochronism [ai'sokrənizm], s. Mec: Isochronisme m.

isoclinal ['aisou'klainl], a. & s. Surv: etc: Isocline (f); isoclinal (m).

isodynamic ['aizodai'næmik], a. Mec: (Courbe f, ligne f,) isodynamique. (Dietetics) Isodyname.

isolable ['aisələbl], a. Ch: etc: Isolable.

isolate ['aisəleit], v.tr. 1. (a) Isoler (un malade)(from, de, d'avec); cantonner (des bestiaux). (b) Faire le vide autour de (qn). 2. (a) Ch: Isoler, dégager (un corps simple). (b) El: = INSULATE 2. isolated, a. (Hameau) isolé, écarté. I. instance, cas isolé.

isolation [ˌaisə'leiʃ(ə)n], s. 1. (a) Isolement m (d'un malade). I. hospital, hôpital d'isolement; hôpital de contagieux. (b) = INSULATION 2. 2. Isolement, solitude f.

isolationism [ˌaisə'leiʃ(ə)nizm], s. Pol: Isolationnisme m.

isolationist [ˌaisə'leiʃ(ə)nist], a. & s. Isolationniste mf.

isolator ['aisəleitər], s. El: = INSULATOR.

isomer ['aisomər], s. Ch: Isomère m.

isomeric [ˌaiso'merik], a. Ch: Isomère, isomérique.

isomerism [ai'somərizm], s. Ch: Isomérisme m.

isometric(al) [ˌaiso'metrik(l)], a. 1. Geom: I. perspective, perspective f isométrique. 2. Cryst: Isométrique.

isomorph ['aisomɔːf], s. Cryst: Isomorphe m.

isomorphic [ˌaiso'mɔːfik], isomorphous [ˌaiso'mɔːfəs], a. Isomorphe.

isomorphism [ˌaiso'mɔːfizm], s. Ch: Miner: Isomorphisme m.

isosceles [ai'sosiliːz], a. (Triangle) iso(s)cèle.

isotherm ['aisoθəːm], s. Meteor: Isotherme f.

isothermal [ˌaiso'θəːm(ə)l], a. (Ligne) isotherme.

isothermic [ˌaiso'θəːmik], a. Isothermique.

isotopes ['aisotoups], s.pl. Ch: (Composés) isotopes m.

Israel ['izrei(ə)l]. Pr.n.m. B.Hist: Israël. Pol: (L'État d') Israël.

Israeli [iz'reili], a. & s. Geog: Israélien, -ienne.

Israelite ['izriəlait], a. & s. Israélite (mf).

issue[1] [isjuː, 'iʃu], s. 1. Écoulement m. Med: O: Épanchement m, perte f, décharge f, saillie f (de sang, etc.); décharge (de pus). 2. Issue f, sortie f, débouché m (out of, de). To find an i. out of . . ., trouver un moyen de sortir de. . . . 3. Issue, résultat m, dénouement m. To await the i., attendre la fin, le résultat. In the i. . . ., à la fin . . ., en fin de compte. . . . To bring a matter to an i., faire aboutir une question; en finir avec une question. Favourable i., unfavourable i., bon, mauvais, succès. 4. Progéniture f, descendance f, postérité f. To die without i., mourir sans enfants. 5. Jur: I. (of fact, of law), (i) question f de fait, de droit; (ii) conclusion f. Main i. of a suit, fond m d'un procès. S.a. SIDE[1] 6. To join i., accepter les conclusions. To join i. with s.o. about sth., discuter l'opinion, le dire, de qn au sujet de qch. The point at i., la question pendante, en litige. The questions at i., les questions f en jeu. To be at i. with s.o., être (i) en désaccord, (ii) en contestation, avec qn. To obscure, confuse, the i., (i) obscurcir la question; (ii) faire du camouflage autour de la question, brouiller les cartes. To evade the i., user de faux-fuyants. 6. (a) Fin: Émission f (de billets de banque, d'actions). I. price, prix d'émission. Adm: Émission (de timbres-poste). (b) Publication f (d'un livre);

lancement *m* (d'un prospectus, etc.). (*c*) Délivrance *f* (de billets, de passeports). (*d*) (*In public library*) Communication *f* (de livres). (*e*) *Mil:* Distribution *f*, versement *m* (de vivres, etc.). **I. shirt,** chemise réglementaire, d'ordonnance. **7.** Édition *f* (d'un livre); édition, numéro *m* (d'un journal).

issue². 1. *v.i.* (*a*) To i. (out, forth), (*of pers.*) sortir; (*of blood*) jaillir, s'écouler (from, de); (*of smell, gas*) se dégager (from, de). (*b*) Provenir, dériver (from, de). 2. *v.tr.* (*a*) Émettre, mettre en circulation (des billets de banque, etc.). (*b*) Publier, donner (une nouvelle édition); lancer (un prospectus, etc.). *Jur:* To i. a warrant for the arrest of s.o., décerner, lancer, un mandat d'arrêt contre qn. *Mil:* To i. an order, publier, donner, un ordre. (*c*) Verser, distribuer (des provisions, etc.); délivrer (des passeports, etc.); communiquer (des livres). (*d*) To i. the ship's company with rum, distribuer du rhum à l'équipage. Each man will be issued with two uniforms, chaque homme touchera deux tenues.

issueless ['isjuːlis, 'iʃuːlis], *a.* Sans enfants; sans postérité; sans descendance.

Istambul [ˌistæm'buːl]. *Pr.n. Geog:* Istamboul *m.*

isthmus, *pl.* -uses ['is(θ)məs(iz)], *s. Geog: Anat:* Isthme *m.*

it [it], *pers.pron.* 1. (*a*) (*Nom.*) Il, *f.* elle. The house is small but it is my own, la maison est petite mais elle est à moi. (*b*) (*Acc.*) Le, *f.* la. He took her hand and pressed it, il lui prit la main et la serra. And my cake, have you tasted it? et mon gâteau, y avez-vous goûté? (*c*) (*Dat.*) Lui *mf.* Bring the kitten and give it a drink, amenez le chaton et donnez-lui à boire. (*d*) (*Reflexive*) The Committee has devoted great care to the task before it, le comité a donné beaucoup d'attention à la tâche qui lui incombait. (*e*) *F:* He thinks he's it [hiːz'it], il se croit sorti de la cuisse de Jupiter. This book is absolutely 'it! c'est un livre épatant! She's got 'it, elle a du sex-appeal. 2. To face it, faire front. Hang it! zut! I haven't got it in me to . . ., je ne suis pas capable de . . . Now for it! et maintenant allons-y! There is nothing for it but to run, il n'y a qu'une chose à faire, c'est de filer. To have a bad time of it, en voir de dures. The worst of it is that . . ., le plus mauvais de la chose c'est que. . . . 3. Ce, cela, il. Who is it? qui est-ce? This is it! ça y est! on est fait! That's it, (i) c'est ça; (ii) ça y est! It doesn't matter, cela ne fait rien. It is raining, il pleut. It is Monday, c'est aujourd'hui lundi. 4. It only remains to thank the reader, il ne me reste qu'à remercier le lecteur. It's nonsense talking like that, c'est absurde de parler comme ça. It makes one shudder to look down, cela vous fait frémir de regarder en bas. How is it that . . .? d'où vient que . . .? It is said that . . ., on dit que. . . . It is written that . . ., il est écrit que. . . . The fog made it difficult to calculate the distance, le brouillard rendait difficile l'estimation des distances. I thought it well to warn you, j'ai jugé bon de vous avertir. 5. At it, in it, to it, y. To consent to it, y consentir. To fall in it, y tomber. Above it, over it, au-dessus; dessus. Below it, under(neath) it, au-dessous; dessous. For it, en; pour lui, pour elle, pour cela. I feel the better for it, je m'en trouve mieux. From it,

en. Far from it, tant s'en faut, il s'en faut. Of it, en. Give me half of it, donnez-m'en la moitié. On it, y, dessus.

Italian [i'tæljən]. 1. *a.* Italien, d'Italie. 2. *s.* (*a*) Italien, -ienne. (*b*) *Ling:* L'italien *m.*

Italianize [i'tæljənaiz], *v.tr.* Italianiser.

Italic [i'tælik]. 1. *a. A.Geog:* Italique. 2. *s. Typ: Usu. pl.* To print in italic(s), imprimer en italique *m.* The italics are mine, c'est moi qui souligne.

italicize [i'tælisaiz], *v.tr. Typ:* Imprimer, mettre en italique.

Italy ['itəli]. *Pr.n.* L'Italie *f.*

itch¹ [itʃ], *s.* 1. Démangeaison *f. F:* To have an i. to do sth., avoir une démangeaison de faire qch.; brûler de faire qch. 2. *Med: Vet:* Gale *f.* '**itch-mite,** *s.* Sarcopte *m* de la gale; acare *m.*

itch², *v.i.* 1. Démanger; (*of pers.*) éprouver des démangeaisons. My hand itches, la main me démange. 2. *F:* To i. to do sth., brûler, griller d'envie, de faire qch. I was itching to speak, la langue me démangeait. He's itching for trouble, la peau lui démange. **itching,** *s.* Démangeaison *f.*

itchiness ['itʃinis], *s.* Démangeaison *f*, picotement *m* (à la peau).

itchy ['itʃi], *a.* 1. *Med:* Galeux. 2. Qui démange.

item ['aitəm]. 1. *adv.* Item; de plus. . . . 2. *s. Com: etc:* Article *m*; détail *m*; rubrique *f. Book-k:* Écriture *f*, poste *m.* **Expense i.,** chef *m* de dépense. To give the items, donner les détails. **Items of expenditure,** articles de dépense. **News items (in a paper),** faits divers; échos *m.* **Items on the agenda,** questions *f* à l'ordre du jour. **The last i. on the programme,** le dernier numéro du programme.

itemize ['aitəmaiz], *v.tr.* Détailler (un compte, etc.). **Itemized account,** compte spécifié.

iterate ['itəreit], *v.tr.* Réitérer.

iteration [ˌitə'reiʃ(ə)n], *s.* (Ré)itération *f.*

iterative ['itərətiv], *a.* Itératif.

itineracy [ai'tinərəsi, i'tin-], **itinerancy** [ai'tinərənsi, i'tin-], *s.* Vie ambulante.

itinerant [ai'tinərənt, i'tin-], *a.* 1. (Musicien) ambulant. **I. vendor,** marchand forain. 2. (Prédicateur) itinérant.

itinerary [ai'tinərəri, i'tin-], *a. & s.* Itinéraire (*m*).

itinerate [ai'tinəreit], *v.i. O:* Voyager.

its [its], *poss.a.* Son; *f.* sa, (*before vowel sound*) son; *pl.* ses. I cut off its head, je lui ai coupé la tête.

it's [its]. *F:* = it is; it has.

itself [it'self], *pers.pron. See* SELF 4.

I've, *F:* = I have.

ivied ['aivid], *a.* Couvert de lierre.

ivorine ['aivərin], *s. Com:* Ivorine *f.*

ivory ['aiv(ə)ri], *s.* 1. (*a*) Ivoire *m.* **Raw i., live i.,** ivoire vert. **Worker in i.,** ivoirier *m.* (*b*) (Objet *m* d')ivoire. (*c*) *pl. F:* **Ivories.** (i) *Bill:* Billes *f.* (ii) Dés *m.* (iii) Dents *f.* (iv) *Mus:* Touches *f* d'un piano. 2. *Attrib.* (*a*) D'ivoire, en ivoire. (*b*) *Geog:* **The I. Coast Republic,** la (République de la) Côte-d'Ivoire. '**ivory-'black,** *s.* Noir *m* d'ivoire. '**ivory-'white,** *s.* Blanc d'ivoire.

ivy ['aivi], *s. Bot:* 1. Lierre *m.* 2. **Poison i.,** sumac vénéneux, *Fr.C:* herbe *f* à la puce. *S.a.* GROUND-IVY.

izard ['izəd], *s. Z:* Isard *m*, izard *m.*

J, j [dʒei], s. (La lettre) J, j m. Tp: **J for Jack,** J comme Joseph.

jab¹ [dʒæb], s. 1. Coup m (du bout de quelque chose); coup de pointe. Med: F: Piqûre f. **Have you had your jabs?** Tu les a eues, tes piqûres? 2. Box: Coup sec.

jab², v.tr. & i. (jabbed) To j. (at) s.o. with sth., piquer qn. (du bout de qch.). **To j. s.o.'s eye out with an umbrella,** crever un œil à qn avec un parapluie. Med: F: **To j. s.o.,** faire une piqûre à qn.

jabber¹ ['dʒæbər], s. 1. Baragouin m, baragouinage m. 2. Bavardage m, jacasserie f.

jabber². 1. v.i. (a) Bredouiller, baragouiner. (b) Jacasser. 2. v.tr. Baragouiner (le français).

jabot ['ʒæbou], s. Cost: Jabot m.

jacaranda [dʒækə'rændə], s. Bot: Jacaranda m.

jacinth ['dʒæsinθ], s. Miner: Lap: Jacinthe f.

Jack¹ [dʒæk]. I. Pr.n.m. (Dim. of John) 1. Jeannot. F: **He was off before you could say J. Robinson,** il est parti sans qu'on ait le temps de faire ouf, de dire ouf. **J. Ketch,** le bourreau (= M. Deibler). 2. (Sailor) **When J. is ashore . . .,** quand le marin tire une bordée. . . . S.a. EVERY, FROST 1. II. **jack,** s. 1. (Pers.) (a) (i) Valet m; (ii) manœuvre m. (b) **Cheap-j.,** camelot m. **J. in office,** bureaucrate m (qui fait l'important). **J. of all trades,** touche-à-tout m inv. 2. Cards: Valet. 3. Clockm: Jaquemart m. 4. Ich: Brocheton m. 5. (a) (Indique le mâle de l'espèce) **J.-hare,** bouquin m. (b) (Indique les petites espèces) **J.-snipe,** bécassin m. III. **jack,** s. (Outil, dispositif) 1. **(Roasting-) j.,** tournebroche m. 2. (a) **Sawyer's j.,** chevalet m (de scieur). (b) Cric m, vérin m. **Wheel j.,** lève-roue m inv. **(Car) j.,** cric (pour autos). (c) See BOOT-JACK. 3. U.S: **Black j.,** matraque f, assommoir m. 4. El.E: Tp: Jack m; fiche femelle. 5. Games: (At bowls) Cochonnet m. 6. P: Flic m. **'jack-boots,** s.pl. Bottes f de cavalier. **'jack-in-the-box, s.** 1. Toys: Diable m (à ressort); diablotin m. 2. F: (Of pers.) Fantoche m. **'jack-knife¹, s.** 1. Couteau m de poche; couteau pliant. 2. Swim: **J.-k. dive,** saut m de carpe. **jack-knife²,** 1. v.tr. U.S: P: Suriner (qn). 2. v.i. (a) Se plier en deux (pour entrer, sortir de, quelque part). (b) Swim: Faire un saut de carpe. **jack(-)o'(-)lantern,** s. Feu follet. **'jack-plane,** s. Tls: Riflard m; demi-varlope f. **'jack(-)pot,** s. Gambling: Gros lot. Poker: (Jack-)pot m. **'jack-shaft,** s. Aut: Arbre m secondaire, arbre de renvoi. **'jack(-)tar,** s.m. Marin; loup de mer.

jack² up, v.tr. (a) Soulever (une voiture, etc.) avec un cric, avec un vérin. (b) F: Hausser (les prix).

jack³, s. Nau: Pavillon m de beaupré. S.a. UNION JACK. **'jack(-)staff,** s. Nau: Mât m, bâton m, de pavillon de beaupré.

jack⁴, s. Hist: 1. Cost: Jaque f, hoqueton m. 2. Broc m en cuir.

jackal ['dʒækɔ:l], s. Chacal m, -als.

jackanapes ['dʒækəneips], s. 1. A: Singe m. 2. F: (a) Impertinent m, fat m. (b) Petit vaurien.

jackass ['dʒækæs], s. 1. (a) Z: Ane (mâle) m; baudet m. (b) F: Idiot m, imbécile m. **Orn: Laughing j.,** martin-pêcheur géant d'Australie.

jackdaw ['dʒækdɔ:], s. Choucas m (des tours), corneille f d'église.

jacket¹ ['dʒækit], s. 1. (a) Cost: Veston m (d'homme); jaquette f (de femme); veste f (de garçon de café); casaque f (de jockey). **Bed-j.,** liseuse f. **Single-breasted j.,** veston droit. **Double-breasted j.,** veston croisé. **Sheepskin j.,** canadienne f. **Lumberman's j.,** lumber j., blouson m. S.a. BLUEJACKET, DINNER-JACKET, ÉTON JACKET, STRAIT 1. (b) Robe f (d'un animal); pelure f (de fruit, etc.). **Potatoes cooked in their jackets,** pommes de terre en robe de chambre. 2. (a) Chemise f (de documents). (b) Jaquette f, liseuse f (de livre). S.a. DUST-JACKET, I.C.E: etc: **Water-j.,** cooling-j., chemise d'eau; manchon m de refroidissement.

jacket², v.tr. Garnir, envelopper, (une chaudière, etc.) d'une chemise. **jacketing,** s. Chemisage m (d'un cylindre, etc.).

jackstay ['dʒækstei], s. Nau: Filière f d'envergure.

Jacob ['dʒeikəb]. Pr.n.m. Jacob. **J.'s ladder,** l'échelle f de Jacob.

Jacobean [,dʒækə'biən], a. (a) Eng.Arch: De l'époque de Jacques Ier. (b) Furn: En chêne patiné; de style Jacques Ier.

Jacobin ['dʒækəbin], a. & s. Rel.Hist: Fr.Hist: Jacobin, -ine.

Jacobite ['dʒækəbait], a. & s. Eng.Hist: Jacobite (mf); partisan m de Jacques II, des Stuarts (après 1688).

jaconet ['dʒækənit], s. Tex: 1. Jaconas m. 2. **Glazed j.,** brillanté m (pour doublures).

Jacquard ['dʒækɑ:d]. Tex: (a) **J. loom,** jacquard m. (b) **J. cloth,** tissu jacquard. **J. woven,** à la Jacquard.

jade¹ [dʒeid], s. 1. (Of horse) Rosse f, haridelle f. 2. O: (Of woman) (a) Drôlesse f. (b) **You little j.!** petite coquine! petite effrontée! **She's a fickle j.,** c'est un oiseau volage.

jade², s. Miner: 1. Jade m. 2. **J.(-green),** vert m de jade.

jaded ['dʒeidid], a. Surmené, éreinté, F: esquinté, crevé. **J. palate,** goût blasé.

jag¹ [dʒæg], s. Pointe f, saillie f, dent f (de rocher).

jag², v.tr. (jagged [dʒægd]) Déchiqueter (une robe, etc.); denteler (le bord d'une étoffe); ébrécher (un couteau). **jagged¹** ['dʒægid], a. Déchiqueté, dentelé, ébréché; (feuille) découpée. **J. stone,** pierre aux arêtes vives.

jag³, s. Esp. U.S: Petit fardeau; petite charge (de bois, etc.). F: **To go on the j.,** faire la bombe, la noce; se soûler; P: prendre une cuite.

jagged² ['dʒægd], a. U.S: F: Soûl; parti (pour la gloire).

jaguar ['dʒægjuər], s. Jaguar m.

jail [dʒeil], s. **jailer** ['dʒeilər], s. = GAOL¹, GAOLER.

jalap ['dʒæləp], s. Bot: Pharm: Jalap m.

jalop(p)y [dʒə'lɔpi], s. F: Vieux tacot.

jam¹ [dʒæm], s. 1. (a) Foule f, presse f (de gens). (b) **Traffic j.,** embouteillage m (de la circulation); embarras m de voitures. F: **To be in a j.,** être dans le pétrin. (c) Embâcle m (de glaçons, de bûches, dans une rivière).

jam², v. (jammed) 1. v.tr. (a) Serrer, presser. **To j. sth. into a box,** fourrer, enfoncer de force, qch. dans une boîte. (b) **To get one's finger jammed,** avoir le doigt coincé, écrasé. **To j. one's hat on one's head,** enfoncer son chapeau sur sa tête. **To j. on the brakes,** freiner brusquement; serrer les freins à bloc. (c) Coincer, caler (une machine, etc.); enrayer (une roue, etc.). **To get jammed,** (se) coincer; (of machine-gun) s'enrayer. (d) W.Tg: Brouiller (un message). 2. v.i. (Of machine part) (Se) coincer, s'engager; (of rifle) s'enrayer; (of wheel) se caler; (of brake) se bloquer. **jamming¹,** a. W.Tel: **J. station,** (poste) brouilleur (m). **jamming²,** s. W.Tel: Brouillage m.

jam³. 1. pred.a. Serré. **To stand j. (up) against the wall,** se tenir collé au mur. 2. adv. **The bus was j. full,** l'autobus était comble. **To screw up a nut j. tight,** serrer un écrou à refus.

jam⁴, s. Confiture(s) f(pl). P: **Bit of j.,** coup m de veine. **It's money for j.,** c'est de l'argent facile; c'est donné. **jam-jar, -pot,** c. Pot m à confitures. **'jam-'puff,** s. Cu: Puits m d'amour.

Jamaica [dʒə'meikə]. Pr.n. La Jamaïque.

Jamaican [dʒə'meik(ə)n], a. & s. Jamaïquain, -aine.

jamb [dʒæm], s. Jambage m, montant m, chambranle m (de porte, de cheminée); battée f (de porte).

jamboree [,dʒæmbə'ri:], s. Jamboree m.

James [dʒeimz]. Pr.n.m. Jacques.

Jane [dʒein]. Pr.n.f. Jeanne. s. **A plain J.,** un (petit) laideron.

Janet ['dʒænit]. Pr.n.f. (Dim. of Jane) Jeannette.

jangle¹ ['dʒæŋgl], s. 1. A: Chamaille f, chamaillerie f. 2. Sons discordants; bruit m de ferraille.

jangle². **1.** v.i. (a) A: Se chamailler. (b) Rendre des sons discordants; cliqueter; s'entre-choquer. **2.** v.tr. Faire entre-choquer (des clefs, etc.). **Jangled nerves**, nerfs en pelote. **jangling**, a. Aux sons discordants; cacophonique.

janissary ['dʒænisəri], s. Janissaire m.

janitor, f. **-tress** ['dʒænitər, -tris], s. Portier, -ière, concierge mf.

Jansenism ['dʒæns(ə)nizm], s. Rel.Hist: Fr.Lit: Jansénisme m.

Jansenist ['dʒæns(ə)nist], s. Rel.Hist: Fr.Lit: Janséniste m.

January ['dʒænjuəri], s. Janvier m. **In J.**, en janvier. **(On) the first, the seventh, of J.**, le premier, le sept, janvier.

Jap [dʒæp], s. F: Pej: Japonais, -aise. **J. silk**, pongé m du Japon.

Japan¹ [dʒə'pæn]. **1.** Pr.n. Le Japon. **In J.**, au Japon. **2.** s. (a) Laque m (de Chine); vernis japonais. (b) **Black j.**, vernis à l'asphalte.

japan², v.tr. (japanned) Laquer (un métal, etc.); vernir avec du laque. **Japanned leather**, cuir verni.

Japanese [ʒæpə'ni:z]. **1.** a. & s. Japonais, -aise; nippon, -onne. **J. curio**, japonerie f, japonaiserie f. **2.** s. Ling: Le japonais. **Student of J. (language, etc.)**, japonisant, -ante.

Japhet ['dʒeifit]. Pr.n.m. B.Hist: Japhet.

japonica [dʒə'pɔnikə], s. Bot: **1.** Cognassier m du Japon. **2. (Camellia) j.**, camélia m; rose f du Japon.

jar¹ [dʒɑ:r], s. **1.** Son discordant. **2.** (a) Ébranlement m; choc m; secousse f. **Jars of a machine**, à-coups m, secousses, battements m, d'une machine. **His fall gave him a nasty j.**, sa chute l'a fortement ébranlé. **J. to the nerves**, secousse nerveuse. (b) Manque m d'accord; choc (d'intérêts, etc.).

jar², v. (jarred) **1.** v.i. (a) Rendre un son discordant, dur. (b) Heurter, cogner. **To j. on s.o.'s feelings**, froisser, choquer, les sentiments de qn. **The noise jarred on my nerves**, le bruit me portait sur les nerfs; le bruit me crispait les nerfs; le bruit me tapait sur les nerfs. (c) (Of window, etc.) Vibrer, trembler; (of machine) marcher par à-coups. (d) Être e désaccord (with sth., avec qch.). **Colours that j.**, couleurs qui jurent (with, avec). (e) Mus: (Of note) Détonner. **2.** v.tr. (a) Faire vibrer. **Machine that jars the whole house**, machine qui ébranle toute la maison. (b) Choquer (l'oreille, etc.); agacer (les nerfs, etc.). **jarring**, a. **1.** (Of sound) Discordant, dur. **2.** (Of blow, etc.) Qui ébranle tout le corps; (of incident, etc.) qui produit une impression désagréable. **3.** (Of door, window, etc.) Vibrant, tremblant. **4.** En désaccord; opposé. **J. colours**, couleurs disparates.

jar³, s. **1.** Récipient m; pot m (à confitures, etc.); bocal m, -aux. **2.** El: Verre m, vase m (de pile). **Leyden j.**, bouteille f de Leyde.

jar⁴, s. O: Used only in the phr. **On the j.**, (porte) entrouverte, entrebâillée.

jargon ['dʒɑ:gən], s. **1.** Jargon m, langage m (d'une profession, etc.). **2.** Baragouin m (inintelligible); charabia m.

jasmin(e) ['dʒæzminl. s. Bot: Jasmin m. **Winter j.**, jasmin d'hiver.

jasper ['dʒæspər], s. Miner: Jaspe m.

jaundice ['dʒɔ:ndis], s. Med: Jaunisse f, ictère m.

jaundiced ['dʒɔ:ndist], a. Med: Ictérique, bilieux. **To look on things with a j. eye**, (i) voir tout en noir; (ii) tout regarder d'un œil envieux.

jaunt [dʒɔ:nt], s. Petite excursion, balade f, sortie f, randonnée f.

jauntiness ['dʒɔ:ntinis], s. (a) Désinvolture f, insouciance f. (b) Air effronté; suffisance f.

jaunty ['_lʒɔ:nti], a. **1.** (a) Insouciant, désinvolte. (b) Effronté, suffisant. **2.** Enjoué, vif. **J. gait**, démarche vive. **-ily**, adv. **1.** Avec insouciance; cavalièrement. **2.** D'un air effronté, suffisant.

Java ['dʒɑ:və]. Pr.n. Geog: Java.

Javanese [ˌdʒɑ:və'ni:z], a. & s. Javanais, -aise.

javelin ['dʒævlin], s. Arm: Sp: Javelot m. **J. throwing**, lancement m du javelot.

jaw¹ [dʒɔ:], s. **1.** (a) Mâchoire f. **The jaws**, la mâchoire, les mâchoires. **P: I'll break your j.**, je vais te casser la gueule! **Jaws of a chasm**, gueule f d'un gouffre. (b) Tchn: Mâchoire, mors m, (d'un étau, etc.);

bec m (d'une clef anglaise). **2.** P: (a) Caquet m, bavardage m. **Hold your j.!** ferme ça! ta gueule! (b) Causette f, conversation f. (c) Discours (édifiant); Sch: F: laïus m. (d) Sermon m, semonce f; P: engueulade f. **'jaw-bone**, s. Os m maxillaire; mâchoire f. **'jaw-breaker**, s. F: Mot m à vous décrocher la mâchoire.

jaw². **1.** v.i. P: (a) Caqueter, bavarder, jaser. (b) Sch: F: Laïusser; piquer un laïus. **2.** v.tr. P: Sermonner, chapitrer; P: engueuler (qn).

-jawed [dʒɔ:d], a. Heavy-j., à forte mâchoire. S.a. LANTERN-JAWED.

jay [dʒei], s. **1.** Orn: Geai m. **2.** P: Jobard m, P: gogo m. **'jay-walk**, v.i. Traverser (la rue) en dehors du passage clouté. **'jay-walker**, s. Piéton imprudent; piéton qui traverse (la rue) en dehors du passage clouté.

jazz¹ [dʒæz], s. (a) Jazz m. (b) Tex: Tissu bariolé. **'jazz-'band**, s. Jazz-band m.

jazz². **1.** v.i. Danser le jazz. **2.** v.tr. **To j. (up) a tune**, tourner une mélodie en jazz.

jealous ['dʒeləs], a. **1.** Jaloux, -ouse (of, de). **To be j. of, for, one's good name**, être jaloux de sa réputation. **2. J. care**, soin jaloux. **-ly**, adv. **1.** Jalousement. **2.** Soigneusement.

jealousy ['dʒeləsi], s. Jalousie f.

Jean¹ [dʒi:n]. Pr.n.f. Jeanne.

jean², s. **1.** Tex: Coutil m, treillis m. **2.** pl. Cost: **Jeans**, (i) jeu m de treillis; (ii) blue-jeans mpl.

jeep¹ [dʒi:p], s. Aut: Mil: Jeep f.

jeep². Esp. U.S: Aut: Mil: **1.** v.tr. Transporter (qch.) en jeep. **2.** v.i. Voyager en jeep.

jeepable ['dʒi:pəbl], a. (Route) praticable (seulement) en jeep.

jeer¹ ['dʒiər], s. **1.** Raillerie f, gausserie f. **2.** Huée f.

jeer², v.i. **1. To j. at sth.**, se moquer de qch. **2. To j. at s.o.**, (i) se moquer de qn; F: se gausser de qn; (ii) huer, conspuer, qn. **jeering¹**, a. Railleur, -euse, moqueur, -euse. **jeering²**, s. Raillerie f, moquerie f.

Jehovah [dʒi'houvə]. Pr.n.m. Jéhovah.

Jehu ['dʒi:hju:]. **1.** Pr.n.m. Jéhu. **2.** s. O: Cocher m, (by extension) automobiliste mf, qui va un train d'enfer.

jejune [dʒi'dʒu:n], a. Stérile, aride.

jell [dʒel], v.i. **1.** = JELLY² **2.** F: **My idea didn't j.**, mon idée n'a pas cristallisé.

jellaba [dʒe'lɑ:bə], s. Cost: Djellaba f.

jelly¹ ['dʒeli], s. **1.** Cu: Gelée f. F: **To pound s.o. to a j.**, réduire qn en marmelade. **2.** (a) Hectograph j., pâte f à copier. (b) Exp: Plastic m. **'jelly-bag**, s. Cu: Chausse f (à filtrer la gelée). **'jelly-fish**, s. Coel: Méduse f.

jelly². **1.** v.tr. Faire prendre (un jus) en gelée. **Cold jellied chicken**, chaud-froid m de poulet. **2.** v.i. Se prendre en gelée.

jemmy ['dʒemi], s. (Burglar's) j., pince-monseigneur f, pl. pinces-monseigneur.

jennet ['dʒenit], s. **1.** (Horse) Genet m. **2.** Anesse f.

Jenny ['dʒeni]. **1.** Pr.n.f. (Dim. of Jane) Jeannette. **2.** s. (a) **J. wren**, troglodyte mignon, roitelet m. (b) (Indicating the female) **J. owl**, hibou m femelle. **J.** (-ass), ânesse f. **3.** s. Tex: (Spinning-) j., machine f à filer.

jeopardize ['dʒepədaiz], v.tr. Exposer au danger; mettre en péril. **To j. one's life**, compromettre sa vie. **To j. one's business**, laisser péricliter ses affaires.

jeopardy ['dʒepədi], s. Danger m, péril m. **To be in j.**, (of life) être en danger; (of happiness) être compromis; (of business) péricliter.

jerboa [dʒɑ:'bouə], s. Z: Gerboise f.

jeremiad [ˌdʒeri'maiæd], s. Jérémiade f, plainte f.

Jeremiah ['dʒeri'maiə]. **1.** Pr.n.m. Jérémie. **2.** s.m. Geigneur, geignard; prophète de malheur.

Jericho ['dʒerikou]. Pr.n.m. Jéricho O: **To send s.o. to J.**, envoyer promener, envoyer paître, qn. **Go to J.!** va t'asseoir! fiche-moi le camp!

jerk¹ [dʒə:k], s. **1.** Saccade f, secousse f (d'une corde). **With one j.**, tout d'une tire. **To move by jerks**, avancer par saccades, par à-coups. P: **Put a j. in it!** grouille-toi! **2.** Med: Réflexe tendineux. **Knee-j.**, réflexe rotulien. **3.** U.S: F: **He's just a j.**, c'est un type complètement nul, c'est un zéro.

jerk². **1.** *v.tr.* (a) Donner une secousse, une saccade, des saccades, à (qch.); tirer (qch.) d'un coup sec. **He jerked himself free,** il se dégagea d'une secousse. (b) Lancer brusquement (une pierre). **2.** *v.i.* Se mouvoir soudainement, par saccades.

jerk³, *v.tr.* Charquer (la viande). **jerked,** *a.* (*Of meat*) Charqué.

jerkin ['dʒəːkin], *s.* A.Cost: Justaucorps *m.*

jerky ['dʒəːki], *a.* Saccadé; (*of style*) haché. **-ily,** *adv.* Par saccades; par à-coups.

jerrican ['dʒerikæn], *s.* Jerricane *f.*

Jerry ['dʒeri]. **1.** *Pr.n.m.* Jérémie. **2.** *s.* P: (a) Boche *m*, Fritz *m*, Fridolin *m*, doryphore *m*, chleuh *m.* (b) Pot *m* de chambre, P: Jules. 'jerry-builder, *s.* Constructeur *m* de maisons de carton, de camelote. **jerry-built,** *a.* J.-b., house, maison *f* de carton, de camelote. 'jerry-can, *s.* Jerricane *f.*

Jersey ['dʒəːrzi], *s.* **1.** *Pr.n. Geog:* (Île de) Jersey. **2.** *Cost:* Jersey *m*; tricot *m* (de laine). **Sailor's j.,** vareuse *f.* **Football j.,** maillot *m.* **3. J.** (**cloth**), jersey *m.*

Jerusalem [dʒəˈruːsələm]. *Pr.n. Geog:* Jérusalem. *S.a.* ARTICHOKE 2.

jessamine ['dʒesəmin], *s.* = JASMIN(E).

jest¹ [dʒest], *s.* **1.** Raillerie *f*, plaisanterie *f*, badinage *m*; F: blague *f.* **To say sth. in j.,** dire qch. en plaisantant. **Half in j., half in earnest,** moitié plaisantant, moitié sérieux. **2.** Bon mot; facétie *f.*

jest², *v.i.* Plaisanter (about sth., sur qch.); badiner. **jesting,** *s.* Raillerie *f*, plaisanterie *f*, badinage *m.*

jester ['dʒestər], *s. Hist:* Bouffon *m.*

Jesuit ['dʒezjuit], *s.* Jésuite *m.*

Jesuitical [dʒezjuˈitik(ə)l], *a.* Jésuitique.

Jesuitism ['dʒezjuitizm], **Jesuitry** ['dʒezjuitri], *s.* Jésuitisme *m.*

Jesus ['dʒiːzəs]. *Pr.n.m.* Jésus.

jet¹ [dʒet], *s. Miner:* Jais *m.* 'jet-'black, *a.* Noir comme du jais.

jet², *s.* **1.** Jet *m* (d'eau, de vapeur). **2.** (a) Ajutage *m*, jet (de tuyau d'arrosage). (b) I.C.E: (**Carburetter**) j., gicleur *m.* (c) Brûleur *m* (à gaz, de foyer à mazout). **3.** *Av: etc:* Jet *m*, tuyère *f*, gicleur *m.* **J. engine,** moteur *m* à réaction, réacteur *m*, turboréacteur *m.* **J. (plane), j.-propelled aircraft,** réacteur *m*, avion *m* à réaction. 'jet-'fighter, *s.* Chasseur *m* à réaction. **J. liner,** avion de ligne à réaction. **Power j.,** turboréacteur *m.* **Propeller j.,** turbopropulseur *m*, turbine *f* à hélice. 'jet-deflector, *s.* Déviateur *m* de jet. 'jet-pipe, *s. Av:* Tuyère *f.* 'jet-stream, *s. Meteor:* Jet-stream *m.*

jet³, *v.* (**jetted; jetting**). **1.** *v.i.* (*Of fluid, gas*) S'élancer en jet; gicler. **2.** *v.tr.* Émettre un jet (de fluide, de gaz).

jetsam ['dʒetsəm], *s. Jur:* **1.** Marchandise jetée à la mer (pour alléger le navire). **2.** Épaves jetées à la côte.

jettison ['dʒetis(ə)n], *v.tr.* (**jettisoned**) *Nau:* **To j. the cargo,** jeter (la cargaison) à la mer, par-dessus bord; se délester de la cargaison. *Av:* Larguer (des bombes, etc.).

jetty ['dʒeti], *s.* Jetée *f*, digue *f*; (*on piles*) estacade *f*, appontement *m.* 'jetty-'head, *s.* Musoir *m* (de jetée).

Jew¹ [dʒuː], *s.m.* Juif; (en Afrique du Nord) youdi *m.* **The wandering J.,** le Juif errant. **Jew-baiting,** *s.* Persécution *f* des Juifs. 'Jew's-'harp, *s.* Guimbarde *f.*

jew², *v.tr.* F: Pej: Duper, frauder (qn); mettre (qn) dedans.

jewel ['dʒuəl], *s.* **1.** (a) Bijou *m*, joyau *m.* **She's a j.,** c'est une perle. (b) *pl.* Pierres précieuses; pierreries *f.* **2.** *Clockm:* Rubis *m.* 'jewel-case, *s.* Coffret *m* à bijoux; écrin *m.*

jewelled ['dʒuəld], *a.* **1.** Orné de bijoux. **2.** *Clockm:* Monté sur rubis.

jeweller ['dʒuələr], *s.* Bijoutier *m*, joaillier *m.*

jewel(le)ry ['dʒuəlri], *s.* (*Trade or jewels*) Bijouterie *f*, joaillerie *f.* **Costume j.,** bijoux *mpl* de fantaisie.

Jewess ['dʒu(ː)es], *s.f.* Juive.

Jewish ['dʒu(ː)iʃ], *a.* Juif, *f.* juive.

Jewry ['dʒuəri], *s.* La Juiverie.

Jezebel ['dʒezəbel]. *Pr.n.f.* **1.** *B.Hist:* Jézabel. **2.** (a) Femme éhontée. (b) O: **Painted J.,** vieille femme fardée; F: vieux tableau.

jib¹ [dʒib], *s.* **1.** *Nau:* Foc *m.* **Main j.,** grand foc. **Flying j.,** clinfoc *m.* F: **I know him by the cut of his j.,** je le reconnais à sa tournure. **2.** *Mec.E:* (**Crane-**)j., derrick-j., volée *f*, flèche *f*, potence *f* (de grue). 'jib-'boom, *s. Nau:* Bout-dehors *m* de foc. **Flying j.-b.,** baïonnette *f* de clinfoc.

jib², *v.i.* (**jibbed**) (a) (*Of horse*) Refuser; se dérober. (b) (*Of pers.*) Regimber. **To j. at doing sth.,** rechigner à faire qch. **jibbing,** *a.* (Cheval) quinteux.

jibe [dʒaib], *s. & v.* = GIBE¹,².

Jibuti [dʒiˈbuːti]. *Pr.n.Geog:* See DJIBUTI.

jiffy ['dʒifi], *s.* F: **In a j.,** en, dans, un instant; en un clin d'œil.

jig¹ [dʒig], *s.* **1.** *Danc: Mus:* Gigue *f.* **2.** *Mec.E:* Calibre *m*, gabarit *m* (de réglage, d'usinage). **3.** *Min:* Plan automoteur (de crible à minerai); jig *m.*

jig², *v.* (**jigged**) **1.** *v.i.* (a) Danser la gigue. (b) **To j. up and down,** se trémousser (en dansant). **2.** *v.tr. Min:* Sasser (le minerai); laver (le minerai) au jig. 'jig-saw, *s.* Scie *f* à chantourner. **Games: J.-s. puzzle,** puzzle *m.*

jigger¹ ['dʒigər], *s.* **1.** (a) *Bill:* Chevalet *m.* (b) *El: W.Tel:* Transformateur *m* d'oscillations. (c) *Golf:* Fer *m* à face renversée. (d) F: Machin *m*, chose *f.* **2.** *Nau:* (*Sail*) Tapecul *m.*

jigger², *v.tr.* F: **1.** O: **I'm jiggered if I'll do it,** du diable si je le fais. **Well, I'm jiggered!** pas possible! zut alors! **2.** (a) **To j. sth up,** bousiller (une montre, etc.). (b) O: **To be jiggered up,** être éreinté, fourbu.

jiggery-pokery ['dʒigəriˈpoukəri], *s.* F: **1.** Manigances *f.* **2.** Eau bénite de cour.

jilt¹ [dʒilt], *s.f.* Coquette; lâcheuse.

jilt², *v.tr.* Laisser là, F: planter (là), plaquer (un amoureux).

Jim [dʒim], **Jimmy** ['dʒimi]. *Pr.n.m.* (*Dim. of James*) Jim, Jimmy. 'jim-'crow, *s.* U.S: Pej: Nègre *m.*

jingle¹ ['dʒingl], *s.* Tintement *m* (d'un grelot); bruit *m* d'anneaux; cliquetis *m.* Com: **J.** (*of advertisement*), ritournelle *f* publicitaire.

jingle². **1.** *v.i.* (*Of bells*) Tinter; (*of keys*) cliqueter. **2.** *v.tr.* Faire tinter (des grelots); faire sonner (son argent, ses clefs). **jingling,** *s.* Tintement *m* (de clochettes); cliquetis *m* (de clefs).

jingo ['dʒingou]. **1.** *int.* A· (a) **By j.!** nom de nom! (b) **By j., you're right!** tiens! mais vous avez raison! **2.** *s.* (*pl.* **jingoes**) Chauvin, -ine.

jingoism ['dʒingouizm], *s.* Chauvinisme *m.*

jingoistic [dʒingouˈistik], *a.* Chauviniste.

jink [dʒink], *v.i. Sp: Av:* S'esquiver, se dérober.

jinks [dʒinks], *s.pl.* F: **High j.,** (i) A: soirée *f* folâtre; (ii) O: folichonneries *fpl.*

jinnee, *pl.* **jinn,** F: **jinns** ['dʒiniː, dʒin, dʒinz], *s.* Djinn *m.*

jinricksha [dʒinˈrikʃə], *s.* Pousse-pousse *m inv.*

jinx¹ [dʒinks], *s. esp. U.S:* F: **1.** Porte-malheur *m inv.* **2.** Maléfice *m.*

jinx², *v.tr. U.S:* F: **1.** Porter malheur (à qn). **2.** Jeter un sort (sur qn).

jitter¹ ['dʒitə], *s.* P: **The jitters,** la frousse. **To give s.o. the jitters,** flanquer la trouille (à qn).

jitter², *v.i.* P: Se démener; s'exciter; se trémousser.

jitter³, *v.tr.* P: Flanquer la trouille (à qn).

jitterbug ['dʒitəbʌg], *s.* **1.** Danseur désordonné. **2.** F: Défaitiste *m*, paniquard *m.*

jittery ['dʒitəri], *a.* F: **To be j.,** avoir la venette; P: serrer les fesses.

jiu-jitsu [dʒuːˈdʒitsuː], *s. Sp:* Jiu-jitsu *m.*

jive¹ [dʒaiv], *s. Danc:* Jive *m.*

jive², *v.i.* U.S: F: Faire du jive.

Joan [dʒoun]. *Pr.n.f.* Jeanne.

job [dʒɔb], *s.* **1.** (a) Tâche *f*, besogne *f*, travail *m.* **To do a j.,** exécuter un travail. **I have a little j., a j. of work, for you,** j'ai de quoi vous occuper un peu. F: **To be on the j.,** travailler avec acharnement. **Odd jobs,** petits travaux. **To do odd jobs,** bricoler. **Odd-j. man,** homme à tout faire. **To work by the j.,** travailler à la tâche, à la pièce. **To make a (good) j. of sth.,** réussir qch. F: **My new car is a lovely j.,** ma nouvelle voiture, c'est du beau travail. **You've made a lovely j. of that,** vous vous en êtes tiré à merveille, F: vous avez fait du bon boulot. **To do a j.,** cela fait juste l'affaire. P: **The blonde j. sitting near the bar,** la petite blonde assise près du bar. **It's a good j.**

that . . ., il est fort heureux que. . . . **That's a good j.!** ce n'est pas malheureux! à la bonne heure! It's a bad j.! c'est une triste affaire! **To give sth. up as a bad j.,** y renoncer. (b) Tâche difficile; corvée f. **I had a j. to do it,** j'ai eu du mal à le faire. **It's quite a j. to get there,** c'est toute une affaire que d'y aller. (c) F: **The pill did its j.,** la pilule a rempli son office. **2.** F: Emploi m. **He has a fine j.,** il a une belle situation. **He likes his j.,** F: il aime son boulot. F: **To find a cushy j.,** trouver F: une prébende, P: une bonne planque. F: **With the Labour Government there was a rush to find jobs for the boys,** ce fut une ruée pour la distribution des planques, vers l'assiette au beurre, quand les Socialistes sont venus au pouvoir. **To be out of a j.,** être sans ouvrage; chômer. **To look for a j.,** chercher du travail, de l'embauche f. **This trade is not anybody's j.,** ce métier n'est pas l'affaire de tout le monde. **He knows his j.,** il connaît son affaire. **Every man to his j.,** chacun son métier. **3.** Intrigue f, tripotage m. **'job-line,** s. Com: Solde(s) m(pl); marchandises fpl d'occasion. **'job 'lot,** s. Com: (Lot m de) soldes mpl. **To buy a j. lot of books,** acheter des livres en vrac. **'job-master,** s. O: Loueur m de chevaux et de voitures. **'job-printer,** s. Typ: Imprimeur m de travaux de ville. **'job-work,** s. (a) Travail m à la pièce, aux pièces, à la tâche. (b) Travail à forfait.

jobber ['dʒɔbər], s. **1.** = JOB-MASTER. **2.** Intermédiaire m revendeur. **3.** St.Exch: (Stock-)j., marchand m de titres. **4.** Pej: Tripoteur m.

jobbery ['dʒɔbəri], s. **1.** F: Maquignonnage m; tripotages mpl; prévarication f. **2.** St.Exch: Agiotage m.

jobbing¹ ['dʒɔbiŋ], a. **J. workman,** ouvrier à la tâche. **J. tailor,** tailleur m à façon. **J. gardener,** jardinier m à la journée.

jobbing², s. **1.** Louage m de voitures, de chevaux. **2.** Ind: Com: Commerce m d'intermédiaire.

jobless ['dʒɔblis], a. Sans travail. **The j.,** les chômeurs.

jockey¹ ['dʒɔki], s. Jockey m.

jockey², v.tr. **To j. s.o. out of sth.,** soutirer, escamoter, qch. à qn. **To j. s.o. out of a job,** évincer qn. **To j. for position,** manigancer, manœuvrer, pour se caser. **To j. s.o. into doing sth.,** amener sournoisement qn à faire qch.

jocose [dʒɔ'kous], a. Facétieux, -euse, goguenard, gouailleur, -euse. **-ly,** adv. Facétieusement; d'un ton goguenard; en plaisantant.

jocoseness [dʒɔ'kousnis], **jocosity** [dʒɔ'kɔsiti], s. Humeur joviale; jovialité f.

jocular ['dʒɔkjulər], a. Facétieux, -euse; enjoué. **With a j. air,** d'un air rieur. **-ly,** adv. Facétieusement; jovialement.

jocularity [,dʒɔkju'læriti], s. Jovialité f.

jocund ['dʒɔkənd], a. Lit: Jovial, -aux; enjoué.

jodhpurs ['dʒɔdpə:z], s.pl. Cost: Jodhpurs mpl.

jog¹ [dʒɔg], s. **1.** (a) Coup m (de coude). **To give s.o.'s memory a j.,** rafraîchir la mémoire de qn. (b) Secousse f, cahot m. **2.** Petit trot. **'jog-trot,** s. Petit trot. **At a j.-t.,** au petit trot.

jog², v. (jogged) **1.** v.tr. **To j. s.o.'s elbow,** pousser le coude à qn. **To j. s.o.'s memory,** rafraîchir la mémoire à qn. **2.** v.i. **To j. along,** aller son petit bonhomme de chemin. **We are jogging along,** les choses vont leur train. F: 'How are things?' 'Jogging along', Comment ça va? On se maintient, on se défend.

jogger ['dʒɔgə], s. F: **Memory j.,** pense-bête m, pl. pense-bêtes.

joggle¹ ['dʒɔgl], v.tr. F: Secouer légèrement.

joggle², s. **1.** Joint m à goujon, à embrèvement. **2.** Carp: etc: Goujon m.

joggle³, v.tr. Carp: (a) Goujonner (deux pièces). (b) Embrever (deux pièces).

John [dʒɔn]. **1.** Pr.n.m. Jean. **St J. the Baptist,** saint Jean-Baptiste. **2.** U.S: F: Les cabinets. S.a. BARLEY-CORN, DORY.

Johnnie, Johnny ['dʒɔni]. **2.** Pr.n.m. Jeannot. Mil: P: **J. Raw,** bleu m, morveux m. **2.** s. P: O: Type m, individu m. **3.** s. Orn: F: Manchot m. **4.** U.S: F: = JOHN 2.

join¹ [dʒɔin], s. Joint m, jointure f; ligne f de jonction (de deux feuilles d'une carte, etc.).

join². **I.** v.tr. **1.** (a) Joindre, unir, réunir. **To j. (together) the broken ends of a cord,** (re)nouer les bouts cassés d'un cordon. **To j. sth. with sth.,** réunir qch. à qch. **To j. hands (with s.o.),** s'unir à qn, se joindre à qn (pour faire qch.); se donner la main. **To j. forces with s.o., to j. company with s.o.,** se joindre à qn. (b) Ajouter. **To j. threats with, to, remonstrances,** ajouter les menaces aux remontrances. (c) **Straight line that joins two points,** droite f qui joint deux points. **2.** (a) Se joindre à, s'unir à (qn); rejoindre (qn). **He joined us on our way,** il nous a rejoints en route. **Will you j. us, j. our party?** voulez-vous vous mettre des nôtres? **To j. the procession,** se mêler au cortège. (b) Mil: **To j. one's unit,** rallier son unité. Navy: **To j. one's ship,** rallier le bord. (c) Entrer dans (un club, un régiment). **To j. a party,** s'affilier à un parti. **3.** Se joindre, s'unir, à (qch.). **The footpath joins the road,** le sentier rejoint la route. **II.** join, v.i. Se (re)joindre, s'unir (with, à). **To j. together,** (of bone) se souder; (of people) se réunir. **join in,** v.i. **1.** **To j. in the protests,** prendre part, joindre sa voix, aux protestations. **2.** Se mettre de la partie. **join up.** **1.** v.tr. (a) Assembler (deux choses); embrancher (des tuyaux). (b) El: Connecter, (ac)coupler (des piles). **2.** v.i. Mil: F: S'engager; entrer au service. **joining,** s. **1.** Jonction f, assemblage m; liaison f (de sons). **2.** Entrée f (dans un club); engagement m (dans l'armée).

joiner ['dʒɔinər], s. Menuisier m. **J.'s shop,** menuiserie f.

joinery ['dʒɔinəri], s. Menuiserie f.

joint¹ [dʒɔint], s. **1.** (a) Joint m, jointure f. **To find the j. in the armour,** trouver le défaut de la cuirasse. **Soldered j.,** soudure f. **Universal j., Cardan j.,** joint articulé; joint de Cardan. (b) Bookb: Mors m. (c) Carp: etc: Assemblage m. **Mortise-and-tenon j.,** assemblage à tenon et (à) mortaise; assemblage à emboîtement. **Scarf-j.,** assemblage à mi-bois. **2.** Anat: Joint, jointure (du genou). **Elbow-j.,** articulation f du coude. **Rheumatism in, of, the joints,** rhumatisme articulaire. **Out of j.,** (bras) disloqué, déboîté. **3.** (a) Partie f entre deux articulations; phalange f (du doigt). **Three-j. fishing-rod,** canne à pêche à trois corps. (b) Cu: Morceau m, quartier m, pièce f, de viande. **Cut off the j.,** tranche f de rôti. **4.** U.S: P: Boîte f (louche). **Gambling j.,** tripot m.

joint², v.tr. **1.** (a) Joindre, assembler (des pièces de bois etc.); emmancher (des tuyaux, etc.). **2.** Découper, dépecer (une volaille). **3.** Const: Jointoyer (un mur). **jointed,** a. Articulé; jointif, -ive. Mec.E: **J. coupling,** accouplement m à articulation.

joint³, a. **1.** (En) commun; combiné. **J. action,** action collective. **J. commission,** commission mixte. **J. undertaking,** entreprise en participation. Jur: **J. estate of husband and wife,** biens communs, de communauté. Fin: **J. shares,** actions indivises. **J. stock,** capital social. **J.-stock bank,** société f de dépôt. **2.** Co-, associé. **J. author,** coauteur m, -trice. **J. heir,** cohéritier, -ière. **J. guardian,** cotuteur, -trice. **J. manager, manageress,** codirecteur, -trice, cogérant, -ante. **J. management,** codirection f. **J. owner,** copropriétaire mf. **J. ownership,** copropriété f. **J. partner,** coassocié, -ée. **J. purchaser,** coacquéreur m. **J. tenant,** colocataire mf. **-ly,** adv. Ensemble, conjointement. **To manage (business, etc.) jointly,** cogérer (une affaire). Jur: Indivisément. **J. liable, responsible,** solidaire. **J. and severally liable,** responsables conjointement et solidairement.

jointure ['dʒɔintʃər], s. Douaire m.

joist [dʒɔist], s. Const: Solive f, poutre f, poutrelle f.

joke¹ [dʒouk], s. (a) Plaisanterie f, farce f, F: blague f. **I did it for a j.,** je l'ai fait histoire de rire. **The j. is that . . .,** le comique de l'histoire, c'est que . . . . F: **It will be no j. to . . .,** ce ne sera pas une petite affaire (que) de. . . . F: **It's no j.,** cela n'est pas amusant. **Practical j.,** mystification f, farce. **That's a good j.!** en voila une bonne! **He knows how to take a j.,** il entend la plaisanterie. (b) Bon mot; facétie f, plaisanterie. **He must have his little j.,** il aime à plaisanter.

joke², *v.i.* Plaisanter, badiner. **To j. at, about, sth.,** plaisanter de qch. **I was only joking,** je l'ai dit histoire de rire. **You're joking!** vous voulez rire! **I'm not joking,** je ne plaisante pas. **joking¹,** *a.* (Ton, air) moqueur, de plaisanterie. **-ly,** *adv.* En plaisantant; pour rire. **joking²,** *s.* Plaisanterie *f,* badinage *m,* F: blague *f.*

joker ['dʒoukər], *s.* 1. Farceur, -euse; plaisant *m;* F: loustic *m.* **Practical j.,** mauvais plaisant. 2. P: Esp. Iron: Type *m,* individu *m.* 3. Cards: Joker *m.* 4. U.S: Jur: Pol: Clause ambiguë (dans un projet de loi, un contrat); échappatoire *f.*

jollification [ˌdʒɔlifi'keiʃ(ə)n], *s.* F: Partie *f* de plaisir; rigolade *f.*

jollity ['dʒɔliti], *s.* 1. Gaieté *f.* 2. Réjouissance *f.*

jolly¹ ['dʒɔli]. 1. *a.* Joyeux, gai, gaillard. **To have a j. evening,** passer une soirée joyeuse. (b) F: Éméché; légèrement pris de boisson. (c) O: J. **little room,** gentille petite chambre. 2. *adv.* P: Rudement, fameusement, drôlement. **J. glad,** rudement content. **I'll take j. good care,** je ferai rudement attention.

jolly², *v.tr.* Plaisanter (qn). **To j. s.o. along,** flatter, plaisanter, faire marcher (qn) (pour en obtenir qch.).

jolly-boat ['dʒɔlibout], *s.* Nau: (Petit) canot (à bord d'un navire).

jolt¹ [dʒoult], *s.* (a) Cahot, *m* secousse *f.* (b) Mec.E: A-coup *m, pl.* à-coups.

jolt². 1. *v.tr.* Cahoter, secouer. 2. *v.i.* (a) (Of veh.) Cahoter, tressauter. (b) Mec.E: Avoir, donner, des à-coups, des coups de raquette.

Jonah ['dʒounə]. 1. Pr.n.m. B.Hist: Jonas. 2. *s.* F: Guignard *m,* porte-malheur *inv.*

jonquil ['dʒɔŋkwil], *s.* Bot: 1. Narcisse *m* des poètes. 2. Jonquille *f.*

Jordan ['dʒɔːd(ə)n]. Pr.n. Geog: 1. (Country) La Jordanie. 2. (River) Le Jourdain. **This side of J.,** de ce côté de la tombe.

jorum ['dʒɔːrəm], *s.* Bol *m,* bolée *f* (de punch).

josh [dʒɔʃ], *v.tr.* U.S: F: Plaisanter, railler (qn); se moquer de (qn); taquiner (qn).

Joshua ['dʒɔʃjuə]. Pr.n.m. B.Hist: Josué.

joss [dʒɔs], *s.* (In China) Idole *f.* **'joss-house,** *s.* Temple *m.* **'joss-stick,** *s.* Bâton *m* d'encens.

josser ['dʒɔsər], *s.* P: O: Type *m,* individu *m.* **Old j.,** vieille baderne.

jostle ['dʒɔsl]. 1. *v.i.* Jouer des coudes. **To j. against s.o. in the crowd,** bousculer qn dans la foule. 2. *v.tr.* (a) Bousculer, coudoyer (qn). **To be jostled about,** être houspillé. (b) Rac: Serrer (un concurrent).

jostling, *s.* 1. Bousculade *f.* 2. Rac: Action *f* de serrer un concurrent.

jot¹ [dʒɔt], *s.* **Not a j., not one j. or tittle,** pas un iota. **Not a j. of truth,** pas un atome de vérité. **I don't care a j.!** je m'en fiche royalement!

jot², *v.tr.* (jotted) **To j. sth. down,** noter qch.; prendre note de qch.; jeter qch. sur le papier. **jotting,** *s.* 1. **J. down (of a note),** prise *f* (d'une note). 2. *pl.* Jottings, notes *f.*

jotter ['dʒɔtər], *s.* Bloc-notes *m, pl.* blocs-notes.

journal ['dʒəːn(ə)l], *s.* 1. Journal *m,* -aux. Nau: Journal de bord; livre *m* de loch. Book-k: (Livre) journal. Publ: Revue savante. 2. Mec.E: Tourillon *m* (d'arbre). **Main journals of the crank-shaft,** portées *fpl* du vilebrequin. **'journal-box,** *s.* Mec.E: Boîte *f* des coussinets.

journalese [ˌdʒəːnə'liːz], *s.* F: Style *m* de journaliste, de journal.

journalism ['dʒəːnəlizm], *s.* Journalisme *m.*

journalist ['dʒəːnəlist], *s.* Journaliste *mf.*

journalistic [ˌdʒəːnə'listik], *a.* (Style *m*) journalistique.

journalize ['dʒəːnəlaiz]. 1. *v.tr.* (a) Tenir un journal (des événements de sa vie quotidienne). (b) Book-k: Porter (un article) au journal. 2. *v.i.* Faire du journalisme.

journey¹, *pl.* **-eys** ['dʒəːni, -iz], *s.* Voyage *m;* trajet *m.* **Return j.,** voyage *m* de retour. **J. there and back,** voyage aller et retour. **To set out on one's j.,** se mettre en route. **On a j.,** en voyage. **He talked the whole j.,** il a parlé pendant tout le parcours. **The j. across the Sahara, across Europe,** la traversée du Sahara, de l'Europe.

journey², *v.i.* (journeyed) Voyager.

journeyman, *pl.* **-men** ['dʒəːnimən], *s.* 1. J. **carpenter,** compagnon charpentier. **J. baker,** ouvrier boulanger, F: mitron *m.* 2. Homme *m* de peine.

joust¹ [dʒaust], *s.* A. & Lit: Joute *f.*

joust², *v.i.* A. & Lit: Jouter.

Jove [dʒouv]. Pr.n.m. Jupiter. **J.'s thunderbolts,** les traits *m* de Jupiter. F: **By J.!** Bon sang! **By J., it is cold!** bigre, qu'il fait froid!

jovial ['dʒouvjəl], *a.* Jovial, -aux. **-ally,** *adv.* Jovialement.

joviality [ˌdʒouvi'æliti], *s.* Jovialité *f,* gaieté *f.*

jowl [dʒaul], *s.* (a) Mâchoire *f.* (b) Joue *f,* bajoue *f* (d'homme, de porc); hure *f* (de sanglier). S.a. CHEEK¹ 1. (c) Hure, tête *f* (de saumon).

joy [dʒɔi], *s.* Joie *f,* allégresse *f.* **To leap for j.,** sauter de joie. **To wish s.o. j. (of sth.),** féliciter qn (de qch.). **The joys of the countryside,** les charmes *m* de la campagne. **'joy-bells,** *s.pl.* Carillon *m* (de fête). **The j.-b. were ringing,** les cloches carillonnaient. **'joy-ride,** *s.* F: Balade *f* en auto (faite à l'insu du propriétaire). 2. Promenade *f* agréable. **'joy-stick,** *s.* Av: F: Levier *m* de commande; F: manche *m* à balai.

joyful ['dʒɔif(u)l], *a.* Joyeux, -euse, heureux, -euse. **-fully,** *adv.* Joyeusement.

joyfulness ['dʒɔifulnis], *s.* Joie *f,* allégresse *f.*

joyless ['dʒɔilis], *a.* Sans joie; triste.

joylessness ['dʒɔilisnis], *s.* Absence *f* de joie; tristesse *f.*

joyous ['dʒɔiəs], *a.* Lit: Joyeux, -euse, heureux, -euse. **-ly,** *adv.* Joyeusement.

joyousness ['dʒɔiəsnis], *s.* Joie *f,* allégresse *f.*

jubilant ['dʒuːbilənt], *a.* (a) (Of pers.) Réjoui (at sth., de qch.); dans la jubilation. (b) (Cri) joyeux. **J. face,** visage épanoui. **-ly,** *adv.* Avec joie; dans la jubilation.

jubilate ['dʒuːbileit], *v.i.* Se réjouir; exulter, F: jubiler.

jubilation [ˌdʒuːbi'leiʃ(ə)n], *s.* (a) Joie *f,* allégresse *f;* jubilation *f.* (b) Réjouissance *f,* fête *f.*

jubilee ['dʒuːbiliː], *s.* Jubilé *m;* cinquantenaire *m.* **Silver j.,** fête *f* du vingt-cinquième anniversaire. **Golden j.,** fête du cinquantenaire. **Diamond j.,** fête du soixantième anniversaire. **J. year,** année *f* jubilaire.

Judaea [dʒuː'diə]. Pr.n. B.Hist: Judée *f.*

Judaic(al) [dʒuː'deiik(əl)], *a.* Judaïque.

Judaism ['dʒuːdeiizm], *s.* Judaïsme *m.*

Judaize ['dʒuːdeiaiz], *v.i.* Judaïser.

Judas ['dʒuːdəs]. 1. Pr.n.m. B.Hist: Judas. **J. kiss,** baiser *m* de Judas. 2. *s.* **J.(-hole, -trap),** judas *m* (dans une porte). 3. **J. tree,** arbre *m* de Judée.

judge¹ [dʒʌdʒ], *s.* 1. Juge *m.* **Presiding j.,** président *m* du tribunal. **As solemn as a j.,** sérieux comme un pape. 2. Sp: etc: Arbitre *m,* juge. 3. Connaisseur, -euse. **To be a good j. of wine,** s'y connaître en vins.

judge², *v.tr.* 1. (a) Juger (un prisonnier, une affaire). **A man is judged by his actions,** un homme se juge par ses actions. (b) **To j. others by oneself,** mesurer les autres à son aune. **Judging by . . .,** à en juger par. . . . (c) Arbitrer (à un comice agricole, etc.). 2. Apprécier, estimer (une distance). 3. **To j. it necessary to do sth.,** juger nécessaire de faire qch. **It is for you to j.,** c'est à vous d'en juger. 4. *v.ind.tr.* **J. of my surprise!** jugez de ma surprise!

judg(e)ment ['dʒʌdʒmənt], *s.* Jugement *m.* 1. (a) **The Last J.,** le jugement dernier. **To sit in j. on s.o.,** se poser en juge de qn. (b) Décision *f* judiciaire; arrêt *m,* sentence *f.* **J. by consent,** jugement d'accord. **To pronounce, deliver, j.,** rendre un arrêt; statuer sur une affaire. **It is a j. on you,** c'est un châtiment de Dieu. 2. Opinion *f,* avis *m.* **To give one's j. on sth.,** exprimer son avis, son sentiment, sur qch. **Against our better j.,** contrairement à notre opinion, à notre jugement délibéré. 3. Bon sens; discernement *m.* **To have sound, good, j.,** avoir le jugement sain. **To use j. in sth.,** faire preuve de discernement. **'judg(e)ment-day,** *s.* (Jour *m* du) jugement dernier.

judgeship ['dʒʌdʒʃip], *s.* Fonctions *fpl,* dignité *f,* de juge.

judicature ['dʒuːdikətʃər], *s.* 1. Judicature *f.* 2. Coll. La magistrature.

judicial [dʒu(:)'diʃ(ə)l], a. 1. (a) Juridique. **J. enquiry**, enquête judiciaire. **J. proof**, preuves en justice. *S.a.* SEPARATION 1. (b) To be invested with **j. powers**, être investi de pouvoirs judiciaires. 2. **J. faculty**, faculté judiciaire; sens critique. -ally, *adv.* 1. Judiciairement. 2. Impartialement.

judiciary [dʒu(:)'diʃiəri]. 1. a. Judiciaire. 2. s. = JUDICATURE 2.

judicious [dʒu(:)'diʃəs], a. Judicieux, -euse. -ly, *adv.* Judicieusement.

judiciousness [dʒu(:)'diʃəsnis], s. Discernement m; bon sens.

judo ['dʒu:dou], s. Judo m.

judoka [dʒu:'doukə], s. Judoka mf.

jug[1] [dʒʌg], s. 1. Cruche f, broc m; (for milk) pot m. **Small jug**, cruchon m. 2. P: Prison f, P: taule f.

jug[2], v.tr. (jugged) 1. Cu: Étuver; faire cuire en civet. *Esp.* **Jugged hare**, civet m de lièvre. 2. P: Emprisonner, P: coffrer (qn).

jugful ['dʒʌgful], s. Cruchée f; plein pot (of, de). *U.S:* P: Not by a j., tant s'en faut.

juggins ['dʒʌginz], s. F: Niais m, jobard m.

juggle[1] ['dʒʌgl], s. 1. (a) Jonglerie f. (b) Tour m de passe-passe, d'escamotage. 2. F: Supercherie f, fourberie f. **Financial j.**, tripotage financier.

juggle[2]. 1. v.i. (a) Jongler (avec des boules). (b) Faire des tours de passe-passe. **To j. with figures**, jongler avec les chiffres. **To j. with s.o.'s feelings**, jouer avec les sentiments de qn. 2. v.tr. **To j. sth. away**, escamoter qch. **juggling**, s. = JUGGLERY.

juggler ['dʒʌglər], s. (a) Jongleur, -euse; bateleur m. (b) Escamoteur, -euse; prestidigitateur m.

jugglery ['dʒʌgləri], s. 1. (a) Jonglerie f. (b) Tours mpl de passe-passe; escamotage m. 2. F: Fourberie f; mauvaise foi.

jugular ['dʒʌgjulər], a. & s. Anat: Jugulaire (f).

jugulate ['dʒʌgjuleit], v.tr. 1. Égorger. 2. (a) Étrangler. (b) Juguler (une maladie, une épidémie).

juice [dʒu:s], s. 1. Jus m, suc m (de la viande, d'un fruit). *Physiol:* **Gastric j.**, suc m gastrique. *S.a.* STEW[2] 2. 2. P: (a) Aut: Essence f, P: jus. (b) El.E: Courant m, P: jus.

juiciness ['dʒu:sinis], s. Succulence f.

juicy ['dʒu:si], a. (a) Succulent, juteux; plein de jus. F: **J. pipe**, pipe qui supe. (b) F: (Histoire) risquée.

jujube ['dʒu:dʒu:b], s. 1. Bot: Jujube f. **J.(-tree)** jujubier m. 2. Boule f de gomme.

juke-box ['dʒu:kbɔks], s. Phonographe m à sous.

julep ['dʒu:lep], s. Pharm: Julep m. *U.S:* **Mint j.**, whisky frappé à la menthe.

Julian ['dʒu:ljən], a. Julien; de Jules César. *Chr:* **J. year**, année julienne.

julienne [dʒu:li'en], s. Cu: (Potage m à la) julienne.

Juliet ['dʒu:liət]. Pr.n.f. Juliette.

Julius ['dʒu:ljəs]. Pr.n.m. Jules.

July, pl. -s [dʒu'lai, -aiz], s. Juillet m. **In J.**, in the month of J., en juillet, au mois de juillet.

jumble[1] ['dʒʌmbl], s. Méli-mélo m, fouillis m, fatras m, embrouillamini m. **'jumble-sale**, s. Vente f d'objets usagés, etc. (pour une œuvre de charité).

jumble[2], v.tr. Brouiller, mêler. **To j. everything up**, F: tout mettre en salade.

jumbo ['dʒʌmbou], s. 1. F: Éléphant m. 2. Metall: Manchon m de refroidissement (de tuyère).

jump[1] [dʒʌmp], s. 1. (a) Saut m, bond m. **To take a j.**, faire un saut; sauter. *Sp:* **High j.**, saut en hauteur. F: **He's for the high j.**, qu'est-ce qu'il va prendre! **Long j.** *U.S:* **broad j.**, saut en longueur. **J. in prices**, saute f dans les prix. (b) Lacune f, vide m (dans une série). 2. Sursaut m, haut-le-corps m inv. **That gave me a j.**, cela m'a fait sursauter. F: **To keep s.o. on the j.**, ne pas laisser le temps de souffler à qn. 3. Turf: Equit: Obstacle m. **To put a horse over a j.**, faire sauter un obstacle à son cheval. **Race-course with jumps**, piste f à obstacles.

jump[2]. 1. v.i. 1. Sauter, bondir. **To j. off a wall**, sauter à bas d'un mur. **To j. down s.o.'s throat**, rembarrer, rabrouer, qn. **To j. at an offer**, saisir une occasion; s'empresser d'accepter une offre. **To j. to a conclusion**, conclure à la légère. (a) Sursauter, tressauter. **The price mentioned made me j.**, l'énoncé du prix me fit sauter. (b) (Of tool) Brouter. (c) (Of

gun) Se cabrer. II. **jump**, v.tr. 1. Franchir, sauter (une haie). **To j. a flight of stairs**, sauter du haut en bas d'un escalier. *Rail:* (Of engine, etc.) **To j. the metals**, sortir des rails; dérailler. (Of gramophone needle) **To j. the sound-groove**, dérailler. 2. (a) **To j. a horse**, faire sauter un cheval. (b) Bill: **To j. a ball off the table**, faure sauter une bille. 3. Saisir (qch.) à l'improviste. *Min:* U.S: **To j. a claim**, s'emparer d'une concession (en l'absence de celui qui l'a délimitée). **To j. the queue**, passer avant son tour, F: resquiller. F: **To j. the gun**, (i) Sp: voler le départ; partir en balance; (ii) commencer à faire quelque chose avant son tour, prématurément, prendre les devants. **jump about**, v.i. Sautiller. **jump across**, v.tr. Franchir (qch.) d'un bond. **jump in**, v.i. 1. Entrer d'un bond. Aut: Rail: **J. in!** montez vite! 2. Se jeter à l'eau (pour sauver qn). **jump out**, v.i. Sortir d'un bond. **To j. out of bed**, sauter à bas du lit. F: **I nearly jumped out of my skin**, cela m'a fait sursauter. **jump up**, v.i. 1. Sauter sur ses pieds. Bondir. **jumped-up**, a. F: (Bourgeois) parvenu. **jumping**, s. 1. Saut(s) m(pl); bond(s) m(pl). El: Jaillissement (d'une étincelle). *Mec.E:* Broutement m (d'un outil). 2. Franchissement m (d'une haie). *Equit:* Jumping m. *Sp:* Hurdle j., saut de haie. *Rail:* **J. of the metals**, déraillement. **'jumping-bar**, s. Sp: Sautoir m. **jumping-'off place**, s. Base avancée (d'une expédition, d'un raid aérien). **'jumping-pole**, s. Sp: Perche f à sauter.

jumper[1] ['dʒʌmpər], s. Sauteur, -euse. *Sp:* **High j.**, sauteur en hauteur. *Equit:* (i) Cheval m à obstacles; (ii) hunter m.

jumper[2], s. Cost: 1. Vareuse f, chemise f (de marin). 2. Tricot m (de femme); pull-over m, F: pull m. 3. *U.S:* (i) Robe f à bretelles, Fr.C: jumper m; (ii) barboteuse f (pour enfant).

jumpiness ['dʒʌmpinis], s. Nervosité f, agitation f.

jumpy ['dʒʌmpi], a. F: Agité, nerveux, -euse. **To be j.**, avoir les nerfs à vif.

junction ['dʒʌŋ(k)ʃ(ə)n], s. 1. Jonction f (de deux routes); raccordement m (de tuyaux). Anat: Bot: etc: **Line of j.**, commissure f. 2. (a) (Point m de) jonction; (em)branchement m, bifurcation f (de route, de voie de chemin de fer). (b) Rail: Gare f de bifurcation, d'embranchement.

juncture ['dʒʌŋ(k)tʃər], s. 1. Jointure f (de deux plaques). 2. Conjoncture f (de circonstances). **At this j.**, à ce moment critique.

June [dʒu:n], s. Juin m. **In J.**, in the month of J., en juin, au mois de juin.

jungle ['dʒʌŋgl], s. Jungle f.

junior ['dʒu:njər], a. & s. 1. Cadet, -ette; plus jeune. **He is my j. by three years**, il est plus jeune que moi de trois ans. **W. Smith J.** (abbr. Jun.), W. Smith (i) le jeune, (ii) fils. Sch: **The juniors**, the j. school, les petits. Sp: **J. event**, épreuve f des cadets. 2. Moins ancien; subalterne (m). Jur: **J. counsel**, avocat m en second.

juniper ['dʒu:nipər], s. Bot: Genévrier m, genièvre m. **'juniper-berry**, s. Baie f de genièvre.

junk[1] [dʒʌŋk], s. 1. (a) Vieux cordages; vieux filin; étoupe f. (b) Com: Piece of j., (i) camelote f; (ii) rossignol m. 2. Nau: Bœuf salé. **'junk-dealer**, s. Marchand m de ferraille, de chiffons; fripier m. **'junk-heap**, s. Dépotoir m; décharge publique. **'junk-market**, s. Marché m aux puces. **'junk-shop**, s. Boutique f de marchand de ferraille, brocanteur m; friperie f.

junk[2], s. Nau: Jonque f.

junket[1] ['dʒʌŋkit], s. 1. Cu: (Lait) caillé (m). 2. Festin m, bombance f. 3. Esp. U.S: Voyage officiel aux frais de la princesse.

junket[2], v.i. 1. Faire bombance; festoyer. 2. Esp. U.S: Voyager aux frais de la princesse. **junketing**, s. Bombance f, F: ripaille f.

Juno ['dʒu:nou]. Pr.n.f. Myth: Junon.

junta ['dʒʌntə], s. 1. Hist: Junte f. 2. = JUNTO.

junto, pl. -os ['dʒʌntou, -ouz], s. Cabale f, faction f.

Jupiter ['dʒu:pitər]. Pr.n.m. Myth: Jupiter.

Jura ['dʒuərə]. Pr.n.Geog: The J. (Mountains), le Jura.

Jurassic [dʒuə'ræsik], a. Geol: Jurassique.

juratory ['dʒuərət(ə)ri], a. Juratoire.

juridical [dʒuə'ridik(ə)l], a. Juridique.
jurisconsult ['dʒuəriskɔn,sʌlt], s. Jurisconsulte m, juriste m.
jurisdiction [,dʒuəris'dikʃ(ə)n], s. Juridiction f. Area within the j. of . . ., territoire soumis à la juridiction de . . ., territoire relevant de. . . . To come within the j. of a court, rentrer dans la juridiction d'une cour; être du ressort d'une cour. This matter does not come within our j., cette matière n'est pas de notre compétence.
jurisdictional [,dʒuəris'dikʃən(ə)l], a. Juridictionnel, -elle.
jurisprudence [,dʒuəris'pru:d(ə)ns], s. Jurisprudence f. Medical j., médecine légale.
jurist ['dʒuərist], s. Juriste m, légiste m.
juror ['dʒuərər], s. Juré m; membre m du jury. Panel of jurors, liste f du jury.
jury¹ [dʒuəri], s. Jury m; jurés mpl. To serve on the j., être du jury. Foreman of the j., chef m du jury. Gentlemen of the j.! messieurs les jurés! 'jury-box, s. Banc(s) m(pl) du jury.
jury², a. Nau: Improvisé. J.-mast, -rudder, mât m, gouvernail m, de fortune.
juryman, pl. -men ['dʒuərimən], jurywoman, -women ['dʒuəriwumən, -wimin], s. = JUROR.
just [dʒʌst], I. 1. a. (a) Juste, équitable. It is only j., ce n'est que justice. As was only j., comme de juste. To show j. cause for . . ., donner une raison valable de. . . (b) A j. remark, une observation juste, judicieuse. 2. s.pl. To sleep the sleep of the j., dormir du sommeil du juste. -ly, adv. Justement. 1. Avec justice. To deal j. with s.o., traiter qn équitablement. Famous and j. so, célèbre à juste titre. 2. Avec justesse; avec juste raison. II. just, adv. 1. (a) Juste, justement. J. here, juste ici. J. by the gate, tout près de la porte. Not ready j. yet, pas encore tout à fait prêt. J. how many are there? combien y en a-t-il au juste? I thought you were French.—That's j. what I am, je pensais que vous étiez Français.—Je le suis précisément. That's j. it, (i) c'est bien cela; (ii) justement! J. so! c'est bien cela! parfaitement! Very j. so, très correct. It's j. the same, c'est tout un; F: c'est tout comme. He did it j. for a joke, il l'a fait simplement histoire de rire. J. when the door was opening, au moment même où la porte s'ouvrait. (b) J. as, (i) I can do it j. as well as he, je peux le faire tout aussi bien que lui. It would be j. as well if he came, il y aurait avantage à ce qu'il vienne. He told me not to pay him back, which was just as well because I did not have any money, il m'a dit de ne pas lui rendre l'argent, ce qui était pour le mieux puisque je n'en avais pas. J. as you please! comme vous voudrez! à votre aise! Leave my things j. as they are, laissez mes affaires telles quelles. J. as . . . so . . ., de même que . . . de même. . . . (ii) J. as he was starting out, au moment où il partait. (c) J. now. (i) Business is bad j. now, actuellement les affaires vont mal. (ii) I can't do it j. now, je ne peux pas le faire pour le moment. (iii) I saw him j. now, je l'ai vu tout à l'heure. (d) It was j. splendid, c'était ni plus ni moins que merveilleux. P: Won't you j. catch it! tu (ne) vas rien écoper! F: You remember?—Don't I j.! vous vous en souvenez?—Si je m'en souviens! 2. (a) J. before I came, immédiatement avant mon arrivée. (b) He has j. written to you, il vient de vous écrire. He has (only) j. come, il ne fait que d'arriver. I have only j. heard of it, je l'apprends à l'instant même. I have j. dined, je sors de table. J. cooked, fraîchement cuit. (Of book) J. out, vient de paraître. 3. He was j. beginning, il ne faisait que (de) commencer. I was j. finishing my dinner, j'achevais de dîner. I am j. coming! j'arrive! He is j. going out, il est sur le point de sortir. 4. He j. managed to do it, c'est à peine s'il a pu le faire. I was only j. saved from drowning, j'allais me noyer quand on m'a repêché. I've only j. enough to live on, j'ai tout juste de quoi vivre. You are j. in time to . . ., vous arrivez juste à temps pour. . . . They j. missed the train, ils ont manqué de peu le train. 5. (a) Seulement. J. once, rien qu'une fois. J. one, un seul. J. a little bit, un tout petit peu. J. give her a pair of gloves, donnez-lui tout simplement une paire de gants. I j. told him that . . ., je lui ai dit tout bonnement que. . . . (b) J. sit down, please, veuillez donc vous asseoir. J. listen! écoutez donc! J. look! regardez-moi ça!
justice ['dʒʌstis], s. 1. Justice f. (a) To dispute the j. of a sentence, contester le bien-fondé, la justice, d'un jugement. (b) I am bound in j. to . . ., je suis obligé, pour être juste, de . . . Poetical j., justice idéale. The portrait did not do him j., le portrait ne l'avantageait pas. To do j. to one's talent, faire valoir son talent. To do j. to a meal, faire honneur à un repas. (c) To bring s.o. to j., traduire qn en justice. 2. Magistrat m. (a) Juge m. The Lord Chief J., le président du Tribunal du Banc du Roi. (b) The Justices, les juges (du tribunal d'instance).
justifiability [,dʒʌstifaiə'biliti], s. Caractère m justifiable (d'une accusation, etc.).
justifiable ['dʒʌstifaiəbl], a. (Crime) justifiable; (colère) légitime. J. refusal, refus motivé. -ably, adv. Justifiablement, légitimement.
justification [,dʒʌstifi'keiʃ(ə)n], s. 1. Justification f. 2. Typ: Justification.
justificative [dʒʌstifi'keitiv], **justificatory** [,dʒʌstifi'keitəri], a. Justificatif, -ive; justificateur, -trice.
justify ['dʒʌstifai], v.tr. 1. Justifier (qn, sa conduite); légitimer, motiver (une action). 2. Typ: (a) Justifier (une ligne). (b) Parangonner (des caractères de corps différents). **justified**, a. Justifié. Fully j. decision, décision bien fondée. To be j. in doing sth., être fondé, justifié, à faire qch. He was j. in the event, l'événement lui donna raison.
justness ['dʒʌstnis], s. 1. Justice f (d'une cause). 2. Justesse f (d'une observation).
jut¹ [dʒʌt], s. Saillie f, projection f (d'un toit, etc.).
jut², v.i. (jutted) To j. (out), être en saillie, faire saillie, (s')avancer. To j. out over sth., surplomber qch. **jutting(-out)**, a. Saillant; en saillie.
jute [dʒu:t], s. Bot: Tex: Jute m.
juvenile ['dʒu:vənail]. 1. a. Juvénile. J. books, livres pour la jeunesse. J. literature, littérature enfantine. J. court, tribunal m pour enfants et adolescents. J. delinquency, délinquance f juvénile. J. offender, accusé mineur. 2. s. Jeune mf.
juxtapose [,dʒʌkstə'pouz], v.tr. Juxtaposer. **juxtaposed**, a. Juxtaposé; en juxtaposition.
juxtaposition [,dʒʌkstəpə'ziʃ(ə)n], s. Juxtaposition f. To be in j., se juxtaposer.

K, k [kei], s. (La lettre) K, k m. Tp: K for king, K comme Kléber.

Kaffir ['kæfər], a. & s. Ethn: Cafre (mf).

kail [keil], s. = KALE.

kainite ['kainait], s. Miner: Kaïnite f.

kale [keil], s. 1. Curly k., chou frisé. Scotch k., chou rouge. 2. Scot: Soupe f aux choux.

kaleidoscope [kə'laidəskoup], s. Kaléidoscope m.

kaleidoscopic(al) [kə,laidə'skɔpik(əl)], a. Kaléidoscopique; toujours changeant.

kalends ['kælindz], s.pl. = CALENDS.

kangaroo [,kæŋgə'ru:], s. Z: Kangourou m.

Kantian ['Kæntiən]. 1. a. Kantien, kantiste. 2. s. Kantiste.

Kant(ian)ism ['kænt(iən)izm], s. Phil: Kantisme m.

kaolin ['keiəlin], s. Geol: Kaolin m.

kapok ['keipɔk,], s. Capoc m, kapok m.

karite ['kæriti], s. Bot: Karité m. K.nu‧ butter, beurre m de karité.

kart [kɑːt], s. Sp: Aut: Kart m. **Kart-racing,** karting m.

Kashmir [kæʃ'miər]. Pr.n. Le Cachemire.

Katherine ['kæθrin]. Pr.n.f. Catherine.

katydid ['keitidid], s. U.S: Ent: Sauterelle verte d'Amérique.

kauri ['kauəri], s. K. (pine), kauri m.

kayak ['kaiæk], s. Kayac m, kayak m.

keck [kek], v.i. F: Avoir envie de vomir; avoir des haut-le-cœur.

kedge¹ [kedʒ], s. Nau: K.(-anchor), ancre f de touée; ancre à jet.

kedge², v.tr. Nau: Haler (un navire) sur une ancre à jet.

keel¹ [ki:l], s. 1. (a) N.Arch: Quille f. Even k., tirant d'eau égal. On an even k., sans différence de calaison; sans roulis ni tangage. (b) Aer: (Quille de) dérive f. 2. Poet: Navire m. 3. Nat.Hist: Carène f (de pétale). **'keel-blocks,** s.pl. N.Arch: Tins m (de cale sèche).

keel². 1. v.tr. To k. over a ship, faire chavirer un navire. 2. To k. over, v.i. faire le tour, chavirer.

keen [ki:n], a. 1. (Couteau) affilé, aiguisé. K. edge, fil tranchant. 2. (Froid, vent) vif, perçant. 3. K. pleasure, vif plaisir. K. appetite, appétit dévorant. K. satire, satire mordante. 4. (a) Ardent, zélé. K. golfer, enragé m de golf. F: He is as k. as mustard, il brûle de zèle. F: To be k. on sth., être enthousiaste de qch.; être emballé pour qch. He is not k. on it, il n'y tient pas beaucoup. I'm not very k. on it, ça ne me dit pas grand-chose. (b) K. competition, concurrence acharnée. Com: K. prices, prix très étudiés. 5. (Œil, regard) perçant, vif. To have a k. eye for a bargain, être prompt à reconnaître une bonne affaire. To have a k. ear, avoir l'ouïe fine. 6. (Esprit) fin, pénétrant. -ly, adv. Aprement, avidement. To be k. interested in . . ., s'intéresser vivement à. . . . **'keen-'set,** a. Qui se sent de l'appétit (for, pour). **'keen-'sighted,** a. A la vue perçante. **'keen-'witted,** a. A l'esprit vif.

keenness ['ki:nnəs], s. 1. Finesse f, acuité f (du tranchant d'un outil). 2. Apreté f (du froid). 3. Ardeur f, zèle m, mordant m (des troupes, etc.). K. on doing sth., grand désir de, empressement à, faire qch. 4. K. of sight, acuité, visuelle, de la vision. K. of hearing, finesse de l'ouïe. 5. Pénétration, finesse (d'esprit).

keep¹ [ki:p], s. 1. Hist: Donjon m, réduit m (du château fort). 2. Nourriture f; frais mpl de subsistance. To earn one's k., (i) gagner de quoi vivre; (ii) en faire pour son argent. Ten francs a day and his k., dix francs par jour logé et nourri. He isn't worth his k., il ne gagne pas sa nourriture. 3. F: For keeps, pour de bon; à tout jamais.

keep², v. (kept [kept]; kept) I. v.tr. 1. Observer, suivre (une règle); tenir (une promesse). To k. an appointment, ne pas manquer à un rendez-vous. 2. Célébrer (une fête). To k. Lent, observer le Carême. 3. Garder,

protéger, préserver (du mal, du froid); défendre (une forteresse). 4. (a) Garder (des moutons). Sp: To k. (the) goal, garder le but. (b) Entretenir (une route, un jardin). (c) Tenir (un journal, des comptes). (d) Subvenir aux besoins de (qn), faire vivre, nourrir (qn). To k. s.o. in clothes, fournir le vêtement à qn. He has his parents to k., il a ses parents à sa charge. (e) Avoir (une voiture); élever (des volailles). To k. a mistress, entretenir une maîtresse. (f) Tenir (une pension, une boutique, un article). S.a. HOUSE¹ 1. 5. To k. order, maintenir l'ordre. To k. one's countenance, garder son sérieux. 6. (Detain) Tenir, retenir. To k. s.o. for dinner, retenir qn à dîner. To k. a boy at school, laisser un enfant au collège. Don't let me k. you, que je ne vous retarde pas! 7. (Restrain) Retenir. I don't know what kept me from slapping his face, je ne sais (pas) ce qui m'a retenu de le gifler. The noise keeps him from sleeping, le bruit l'empêche de dormir. 8. (Reserve) Garder, réserver. Is this place being kept? Cette place est-elle retenue? 9. Garder (des provisions, etc.). The place where I k. my clothes, l'endroit où je mets mes vêtements. To k. the archives, veiller à la conservation des archives. 10. (Retain) Garder, conserver, retenir (l'attention de qn). This child can't k. a thing in his head, cet enfant ne retient rien. To k. one's figure, garder la ligne. To k. in view, ne pas perdre de vue. 11. K. this to yourself, gardez cela pour vous. To k. sth. from s.o., cacher qch. à qn. 12. To k. one's course, poursuivre sa route. To k. the middle of the road, garder le milieu de la route. 13. To k. the stage, tenir la scène. To k. one's seat, rester assis. 14. (a) To k. sth. clean, tenir qch. propre. To k. oneself warm, (i) se tenir au chaud; (ii) se vêtir chaudement. To k. s.o. waiting, faire attendre qn. (b) F: To k. s.o. at it, serrer les côtes à qn. Naut: K. her so! Gouvernez comme ça! II. keep, v.i. 1. Rester, se tenir. To k. standing, rester debout. To k. smiling, rester souriant; F: garder le sourire. How are you keeping? comment allez-vous? 2. Continuer. (a) To k. at work, continuer son travail. F: To k. at it, travailler, F: piocher, sans relâche. To k. straight on, suivre tout droit. (b) To k. doing sth., ne pas cesser de faire qch. 3. (Of food, etc.) Se garder, se conserver. Butter that will k., beurre conservable. My revenge will k., il ne perdra rien pour attendre. **keep away.** 1. v.tr. Éloigner; tenir éloigné. 2. v.i. Se tenir éloigné; se tenir à l'écart. **keep back.** 1. v.tr. (a) Arrêter (une armée); contenir, retenir (la foule). (b) Retarder. (c) To k. back ten shillings from a servant's wages, retenir dix shillings sur les gages d'un domestique. To k. things back (from s.o.), faire des cachotteries (à qn). 2. v.i. Se tenir en arrière ou à l'écart. K. back! n'avancez pas! **keep down.** 1. v.tr. (a) Empêcher (qch.) de monter. (b) She kept her head down, elle restait la tête baissée. (c) Contenir, réprimer (une révolte). (d) To k. prices down, maintenir les prix bas, enrayer la hausse. 2. v.i. Se tapir. **keep from,** v.i. S'abstenir de (faire qch.). **keep in.** 1. v.tr. (a) Retenir (qn) à la maison. Sch: To k. a pupil in, mettre un élève en retenue; consigner un élève. (b) Contenir (sa colère). (c) Entretenir (le feu). (d) F: To k. one's hand in, s'entretenir la main. 2. v.i. (a) Garder la maison. (b) (Of fire) Rester allumé. (c) F: To k. in with s.o., rester bien avec qn; cultiver qn. **keep off.** 1. v.tr. (a) Ne pas mettre (son chapeau). (b) K. your hands off! n'y touchez pas! (c) Éloigner (qn, la foule). The wind will k. the rain off, le vent empêchera la pluie. 2. v.i. (Of pers.) Se tenir éloigné. If the rain keeps off, si nous n'avons pas de pluie. **keep on.** 1. v.tr. (a) Garder (son chapeau). K. your hat on, restez couvert. I hope I'll be kept on, j'espère garder ma place. 2. v.i. (a) Buttons that do not k. on, boutons qui ne tiennent pas. (b) Avancer; aller toujours. (c) To k. on doing sth., continuer de, à, faire qch.; ne pas cesser de faire qch. The dog keeps on barking, le chien ne fait qu'aboyer.

He keeps on hoping, il s'obstine à espérer. F: To k. on at s.o., harceler qn; être toujours sur le dos de qn. **keep out. 1.** (a) v.tr. Empêcher d'entrer. (b) v.i. Se tenir dehors. **2.** To k. out of, v.i. to k. out of a quarrel, ne pas se mêler d'une querelle. F: You k. out of this! Mêlez-vous de ce qui vous regarde! To k. out of danger, se tenir à l'abri du danger. **keep to.** (a) v.tr. To k. s.o. to his promise, exiger de qn qu'il tienne sa promesse. (b) v.i. S'en tenir à (une résolution). To k. to the pattern, se conformer au modèle. To k. to one's bed, garder le lit. To k. to the left, tenir la gauche. They k. to themselves, ils font bande à part. **keep together. 1.** v.tr. Tenir ensemble, unir (des personnes). **2.** v.i. (a) Rester ensemble. (b) Rester unis. **keep under,** v.tr. Tenir (qn) dans la soumission; maîtriser (ses passions); contenir (un incendie). **keep up. 1.** v.tr. (a) Empêcher de tomber; soutenir (qn). (b) Tenir (la tête) haute. (c) To k. prices up, maintenir les prix. (d) Entretenir (un bâtiment, une route); maintenir (une maison) en bon état. (e) Conserver (un usage); entretenir (une correspondance, son grec). To k. up the pace, conserver l'allure. F: K. it up! allez toujours! continuez! (f) Soutenir (l'intérêt). K. up your courage! haut les cœurs! To k. up appearances, sauver les apparences. (g) To k. s.o. up (at night), faire veiller qn. **2.** v.i. (a) Ne pas se laisser abattre; (of weather) se maintenir. (b) I can't k. up with you, je ne peux pas vous suivre. F: To k. up with the Joneses, rivaliser avec le voisin. To k. up with the times, F: être de son temps, se maintenir à la page. **keeping,** s. **1.** (a) Observation f (d'une règle). (b) Célébration f (d'une fête). K. of the Sabbath, sanctification f du dimanche. **2.** Garde f. To be in s.o.'s k., être sous la garde de qn. **3.** Tenue (d'une boutique, d'une comptabilité, etc.). **4.** In k. with . . ., en accord, en rapport, avec. . . . Their action was in k., ils se sont conduits à l'avenant. Out of k. with . . ., en désaccord avec. . . . **5.** K. up, entretien m (d'un bâtiment); conservation f (d'un usage).

keeper ['kiːpər], s. **1.** Garde m, gardien m; surveillant m; conservateur m (de musée). Park-k., lighthouse-k., gardien de parc, de phare. K. of the Seal = le Garde des Sceaux. (b) = GAMEKEEPER. (c) Boarding-house k., patron, -onne, d'une pension de famille. **2.** Bague f de sûreté (portée au doigt).

keepsake ['kiːpseik], s. Souvenir (donné à qn).

keg [keg], s. Caque f (de harengs); barillet m (d'eau-de-vie). Nau: Tonnelet m (d'eau potable).

kelp [kelp], s. Varech m.

kelpie ['kelpi], s. Scot: (Water-)k., esprit m des eaux.

ken [ken], s. Within, out of, s.o.'s k., (i) à portée de, hors de, la vue de qn; (ii) dans, hors de, la compétence de qn. That's beyond my k., cela dépasse mes connaissances.

kennel ['kenl], s. **1.** Chenil m (de chiens de chasse). **2.** Niche f (de chien de garde). **3.** pl. Kennels, (a) établissement m d'élevage de chiens. (b) Pension f pour chiens et chats.

kentledge ['kentlidʒ], s. Nau: Lest m en gueuses.

Kenya ['kiːnjə]. Pr.n. Geog: Kenya m.

kept [kept]. See KEEP².

kerb [kəːb], s. **1.** Bord m, bordure f, rebord m du trottoir. Aut: To strike the k., heurter le trottoir. **2.** Furn: Garde-feu m inv. 'kerb-side, s. Bord m du trottoir. kerb-stone, s. Bordure f du trottoir. St.Exh: The k.-s. market, le marché hors cote; la coulisse.

kerchief ['kəːtʃif], s. **1.** (a) (For head) Fanchon f; mouchoir m de tête. (b) Fichu m. **2.** Poet: = HANDKERCHIEF.

kerf [kəːf], s. **1.** trait m de scie; voie f de scie. **2.** Bout coupé (d'une branche).

kermes ['kəːmiz], s. (a) Ent: Dy: Kermès m. (b) Bot: K. (oak), chêne m kermès.

kernel ['kəːn(ə)l], s. (a) Amande f (de noisette); pignon m de pomme de pin. (b) Grain m (de céréale).

kerosene ['kerəsiːn], s. Ch: Kérosène m; U.S: pétrole lampant; pétrole.

kestrel ['kestrəl], s. Orn: Crécerelle f; émouchet m.

ketch [ketʃ], s. Nau: **1.** Ketch m. **2.** Fish: Dundee m.

ketchup ['ketʃəp], s. Sauce piquante (en bouteille) à base de tomates, de champignons.

kettle ['ketl], s. (a) Bouilloire f. (b) Mil: Camp-k., marmite f. Mess-k., gamelle f. F: Here's a pretty k. of fish! en voilà une belle besogne, une jolie affaire, un beau gâchis! 'kettle-drum, s. Mus: Timbale f. 'kettle-holder, s. Poignée f de bouilloire (en drap).

key¹ [kiː], s. **1.** Clef f, clé f (de serrure). Under lock and k., sous clef. To leave the k. in the door, laisser la clef sur la porte. **2.** (a) Clef (d'une énigme). I hold the k. to the puzzle, je tiens le mot de l'énigme. (b) Légende f (d'une carte). K. numbers (on a squared map), numéros m de repérage. (c) Sch: Corrigé m; livre m du maître; solutions fpl (des problèmes). **3.** Mus: Major k., ton majeur. The k. of C, le ton d'ut. To speak in a high k., parler sur un ton haut. **4.** (a) Touche f (de piano). To touch the right k., toucher la corde sensible. (b) Touche (de machine à écrire). Tg: Morse, sending, k., manipulateur m. (c) Clef (d'instrument à vent). **5.** (a) Clef à écrous. (b) Remontoir m (de pendule, de locomotive d'enfant). **6.** (a) Clavette f, cale f, coin m. (b) El: Fiche f. **7.** Bot: Samare f (de frêne, d'érable). 'key-industry, s. industrie f clef. 'key-man, s. Homme indispensable. 'key-money, s. Denier m à Dieu, pas m de porte. 'key-note, s. (a) Mus: Tonique f. (b) Note dominante (d'un discours). 'key-po'sition, s. Poste m, position f, clef. 'key-ring, s. Anneau brisé (pour clefs); porte-clefs m inv. 'key-'signature, s. Mus: Armature f (de la clef). 'keyway, s. **1.** Entrée f de serrure. **2.** Rainure f de clavette, de clavetage. 'keyword, s. Mot-clé m, pl. mots-clés.

key² [kiː], v.tr. Mec.E: Clavet(t)er, caler (a pulley on a spindle, une poulie sur un arbre). **2.** Mus: To k. (up), accorder (un piano). F: To k. s.o. up, mettre du cœur au ventre à qn. To be keyed up, F: être gonflé à bloc. Crowd keyed up for the match, foule tendue dans l'attente du match.

key³, s. Geog: Caye f, îlot m à fleur d'eau.

keyboard ['kiːbɔːd], s. **1.** Clavier m (de piano). **2.** (In hotel) Porte-clefs m inv; tableau m.

keyhole ['kiːhoul], s. Trou m de (la) serrure. K. saw, scie à guichet.

keystone ['kiːstoun], s. Clef f de voûte; claveau m.

khaki ['kɑːki]. **1.** s. Tex: Kaki m. F: To get into k., se faire soldat. **2.** a. Kaki inv.

kibosh ['kaibɔʃ], s. P: **1.** Bêtises fpl. **2.** To put the k. on s.o., on sth., faire son affaire à qn; mettre fin à qch.

kick¹ [kik], s. **1.** Coup m de pied. Fb: Free k., coup de pied franc. O: To get more kicks than ha'pence, recevoir plus de coups que de pain, que de caresses. **2.** (a) F: He has no k. left in him, il est à plat. (b) F: A drink with a k. in it, une boisson qui vous remonte. **3.** (a) Recul m (d'un fusil), réaction f. (b) I.C.E: Retour m (de manivelle). 'kick-start(er), s. Motor Cy: Démarreur m au pied; F: kick m.

kick². 1. v.i. (a) Donner un coup de pied; F: gigoter; (of animals) ruer. (b) (Of pers.) To k. at, against, sth., regimber contre qch., se rebiffer. (c) (Of gun) Reculer, donner du recul; repousser. **2.** v.tr. (a) Donner un coup de pied à (qn); pousser (qn) du pied; (of horse) détacher un coup de sabot à (qn). I felt like kicking myself, je me serais donné des claques. To k. s.o. downstairs, faire dégringoler l'escalier à qn. F: To k. s.o.'s bottom, botter (le derrière à) qn. P: To k. the bucket, casser sa pipe. (b) The gun kicked my shoulder, j'ai reçu le recul du fusil sur l'épaule. (c) Fb: To k. the ball, botter le ballon. To k. a goal, marquer un but. **kick about. 1.** v.i. F: (Of books, etc.) To lie kicking about the house, traîner partout dans la maison. **2.** v.tr. They were kicking the ball about, ils se relançaient le ballon. **kick away,** v.tr. Repousser (qch.) du pied. **kick back. 1.** v.i. I.C.E: (Of engine) Donner des retours en arrière. **2.** v.tr. Fb: Relancer (le ballon). **kick in. 1.** v.tr. (a) Faire entrer à coups de pied. (b) Enfoncer un coup de pied. **2.** v.i. U.S: F: Payer sa part. **kick off,** v.tr. **1.** Enlever (qch.) d'un coup de pied. **2.** Abs. Fb: Donner le coup d'envoi. 'kick-off, s. Fb: Coup d'envoi. 'kick-out, s. Fb: Renvoi m. **kick out. 1.** v.i. Lancer des ruades. **2.**

(a) F: Chasser à coups de pied. (b) Fb: Renvoyer (le ballon). **kick up**, v.tr. Soulever (la poussière, etc.) en marchant. S.a. ROW⁴ 1. **kicking**, s. 1. Coups mpl de pied; (of animal) ruades fpl. 2. Recul m, repoussement m (d'un fusil).

kid¹ [kid], s. 1. (a) Z: Chevreau m, f. chevrette. **Goat in kid**, chèvre pleine. (b) (Peau f de) chevreau. N. gloves, gants (en peau) de chevreau. F: **To handle s.o. with k. gloves**, ménager qn. 2. F: Mioche mf, gosse mf; P: loupiot m. attrib. **My k. brother**, mon frérot, mon petit frère.

kid², v. (**kidded**; **kidding**). 1. v.tr. (Of goat) Mettre bas (un chevreau). 2. v.i. (Of goat) Chevroter, biqueter; mettre bas.

kid³, s. P: Blague f.

kid⁴, v.tr. P: En conter à (qn); faire marcher (qn). **No kidding!** sans blague! **To k. oneself that . . .**, se faire accroire que. . . .

kiddy ['kidi], s. Petit(e) gosse.

kidnap ['kidnæp], v.tr. (**kidnapped**) Enlever (qn) de vive force; voler (un enfant); kidnapper. **kidnapping**, s. Enlèvement m, vol m (d'enfant); Jur: (délit m de) rapt m.

kidnapper ['kidnæpər], s. Auteur m de l'enlèvement; voleur, -euse, ravisseur, -euse (d'enfant).

kidney ['kidni], s. 1. (a) Anat: Rein m. (b) F: **Two people of the same k.**, deux personnes du même acabit. 2. Cu: Rognon m. **'kidney-bean**, s. (a) Haricot nain. (b) Haricot d'Espagne. **'kidney-po'tato**, s. Vitelotte f, saucisse f. **'kidney-shaped**, a. (Table, etc.), en forme de haricot. Nat.Hist: Réniforme. **'kidney-stone**, s. Geol: Rognon m de silex.

kill¹ [kil], s. Ven: (a) Mise f à mort (du renard, etc.). (b) Gibier tué; le tableau.

kill², v.tr. 1. (a) Tuer, faire mourir; abattre (une bête). **K. or cure remedy**, remède héroïque, F: de cheval. **To be hard to k.**, avoir la vie dure. **To k. two birds with one stone**, faire d'une pierre deux coups. **To k. s.o. with kindness**, faire du mal à qn par excès de bonté. **You are killing me by inches**, vous me faites mourir à petit feu. **He was laughing fit to k. himself**, il crevait de rire. **To be out to k.**, prendre un air conquérant. F: **To be dressed to k.**, porter une toilette irrésistible; être en grand tralala. (b) (Of butcher) Abattre, tuer (un bœuf). 2. **To k. time**, tuer le temps. **To k. a bill**, couler, faire échouer, un projet de loi. 3. (a) Amortir (le son). (b) **To k. lime**, éteindre la chaux. 4. Ten: Tuer, massacrer (la balle). **kill off**, v.tr. Exterminer. **killing¹**, a. 1. (a) Meurtrier. F: **K. glance**, œillade assassine. (b) (In compounds) Germ-k., microbicide. 2. (Travail) tuant, assommant, écrasant. 3. Tordant, F: crevant. F: **It is too k. for words**, c'est à mourir de rire. **killing²**, s. 1. Tuerie f, massacre m, abattage m (d'animaux). 2. Meurtre. m. **'kill-joy**, s. Rabat-joie m inv.

killer ['kilər], s. 1. (a) Tueur, -euse; meurtrier m. (b) **K.-whale**, épaulard m. 2. Vermin-k., insecticide m.

kiln [kiln], s. (a) Four m (céramique). (b) Séchoir m, étuve f. **kiln-dry**, v.tr. Sécher au four.

kilocycle ['kiləsaikl], s. Ph: El.E: Kilohertz m.

kilogram(me) ['kiləgræm], s. Kilogramme m, F: kilo m.

kilometre ['kiləmi:tər, ki'ləmitər], s. Kilomètre m. Rail: Adm: **Passenger kilometres**, kilomètres voyageurs. **Ton kilometres**, tonnes-kilomètres.

kilometric [kilə'metrik], a. Kilométrique.

kilovolt ['kiləvoult], s. Kilovolt m. **K. ampere**, kilovolt-ampère m.

kilowatt ['kiləwɔt], s. El.Meas: Kilowatt m. **'kilowatt-hour**, s. kilowatt-heure m.

kilt¹ [kilt], s. Cost: Kilt m.

kilt², v.tr. 1. O: **To kilt (up) one's skirts**, retrousser ses jupes. 2. Plisser (l'étoffe).

kimono [ki'mounou], s. Cost: Kimono m.

kin [kin], s. (a) Parents mpl. **His k.**, ses parents, sa parenté. (b) **To be of k. to s.o.**, être apparenté avec qn. **To inform the next of k.**, prévenir la famille.

kind¹ [kaind], s. 1. (Race) Espèce f, genre m. **The human k.**, le genre humain. 2. (a) (Sort) Genre, espèce, sorte f. **Book of the best k.**, livre du meilleur aloi. **He is the k. of man who will hit back**, il est homme à se défendre. **Perfect of its k.**, parfait dans son genre. **Something of the k.**, quelque chose de semblable, de ce genre. **Nothing of the k.**, rien de la sorte. **Do nothing of the k.**, gardez-vous-en bien! n'en faites rien! **Coffee of a k.**, quelque chose qui pouvait passer pour du café. **In a k. of a way**, en quelque façon. **That's the k. of thing I mean**, c'est à peu près ce que je veux dire. **He felt a k. of compunction**, il ressentait comme des remords. **She was with them as a k. of maid**, elle était comme qui dirait leur bonne. **He is a k. of fool**, c'est une espèce d'imbécile. (b) F: **These k. of men**, ce genre d'hommes; les hommes de cette sorte. F: **I k. of expected it**, je m'en doutais presque. 3. **In kind**. (a) **Discovery new in k.**, découverte d'un genre entièrement nouveau. **They differ in k.**, ils diffèrent en nature. **Difference in k.**, différence spécifique. (b) **Payment in k.**, paiement en nature. **To repay s.o. in k.**, (i) rembourser qn en nature; (ii) rendre à qn la monnaie de sa pièce.

kind², a. Bon, aimable, bienveillant. **They are k. people**, ce sont de braves gens. **To give s.o. a k. reception**, faire bon accueil à qn. **Give him my k. regards**, faites-lui mes amitiés. **To be k. to s.o.**, se montrer bon pour, envers, qn. **It is very k. of you**, c'est bien aimable à vous. **Be so k. as to . . .**, voulez-vous être assez aimable pour . . .; voulez-vous avoir l'amabilité de. . . . **-ly**, adv. Avec bonté, avec bienveillance, avec douceur. **He spoke very k. of you**, il m'a dit des choses très obligeantes à votre égard. **To be k. disposed towards s.o.**, être plein de bienveillance pour qn. **Will you k. . . .?** voulez-vous avoir la bonté de . . ., je vous prie de bien vouloir. **. . . Com:** **K. remit by cheque**, prière de nous couvrir par chèque. **To take sth. k.**, prendre qch. en bonne part. **To take k. to s.o., sth.**, prendre qn en amitié; s'adonner volontiers à qch. **kind-'hearted**, a. Bon, bienveillant.

kindergarten ['kindəga:tn], s. Jardin m d'enfants; école maternelle. **K. mistress**, jardinière f d'enfants.

kindle ['kindl], 1. v.tr. (a) Allumer; enflammer, embraser. (b) Allumer, faire naître, susciter (les passions); enflammer (les désirs); embraser (le cœur); exciter (le zèle). 2.v.i. S'allumer, s'enflammer, prendre feu. **kindling**, s. 1. Allumage m, embrasement m. 2. Petit bois (pour allumer); bois d'allumage; margotin(s) m.

kindliness ['kaindlinis], s. 1. Bonté f, bienveillance f. 2. Douceur f (de climat).

kindly¹ ['kaindli], adv. See KIND².

kindly², a. (a) Bon, bienveillant. **K. feeling**, de la sympathie. (b) (Climat) doux.

kindness ['kaindnis], s. 1. Bonté f (towards s.o., pour qn); bienveillance f, amabilité f (envers); prévenance f. **Will you have the k. to . . .?** voulez-vous avoir la bonté de . . .? 2. A k., un service (rendu). **To do s.o. a k.**, rendre service à qn. **To shower kindnesses on s.o.**, combler qn de bontés.

kindred ['kindrid]. 1. s. (a) (i) Parenté f. **The ties of k.**, les liens m du sang. (ii) Affinité f (**with**, avec). (b) Coll. Parents mpl. 2. a. (a) De la même famille, apparenté. (b) De (la) même nature; analogue. **K. souls**, âmes f sœurs.

kine [kain], s.pl. A: See COW¹.

kinematic [kini'mætik], a. Mth: Cinématique.

kinematics [kini'mætiks], s.pl. Mth: Cinématique f.

kinetic [ki'netik], a. Cinétique.

kinetics [ki'netiks], s.pl. Cinétique f.

king [kiŋ], s. 1. Roi m. (a) **K. Albert**, le roi Albert. B: **K. of Kings**, Roi des rois. B: **The three Kings**, les (trois) Rois Mages. **Dish fit for a k.**, morceau m de roi. (b) Magnat m (de la finance, etc.). **One of the oil kings**, un des rois du pétrole. 2. (a) (At chess, cards) Roi. (b) (At draughts) Dame f. **'king-bolt**, s. Cheville ouvrière; pivot central. **'king(-)cup**, s. Bot: Bouton m d'or. **King-of-'Arms**, s. Her: Roi m d'armes. **'king-pin**, s. 1. = KING-BOLT. 2. F: Gros bonnet. **K.-p. of a firm**, cheville ouvrière d'une entreprise. **'king-post**, 2. a. (of wall) Const: Poinçon m (d'une ferme de comble). **'king-size(d)**, a. Com: Géant.

kingdom ['kiŋdəm], s. 1. Royaume m. **The United K.**, le Royaume-Uni. 2. Biol: Règne (animal, végétal). 3. Theol: Règne. **Thy k. come**, que votre règne arrive. **'kingdom-come**, s. F: Le paradis.

kingfisher ['kiŋfiʃər], s. Orn: Martin-pêcheur m.

kinglike ['kiŋlaik]. 1. a. De roi. 2. adv. En roi.

kingly ['kiŋli], *a.* De roi; royal, -aux.
kingship ['kiŋʃip], *s.* Royauté *f.*
kink[1] [kiŋk], *s.* (*a*) Nœud *m*, tortillement *m* (dans une corde); faux pli (dans le fil de fer); *Nau:* Coque *f* (dans un cordage). (*b*) Crampe *f*; (*in the neck*) torticolis *m.* (*c*) *F:* Lubie *f.* He's got a k., il est un peu timbré.
kink[2]. 1. *v.i.* (*Of rope*) Se nouer, se tortiller; *Nau:* former une coque. 2. *v.tr.* Faire une coque à (un cordage).
kinkajou ['kiŋkədʒuː], *s. Z:* Kinkajou *m.*
kinky [kiŋki], *a.* 1. Noué; (of hair) crépu. 2. *F:* Bizarre.
kinsfolk ['kinzfouk], *s.pl.* Parents et alliés *mpl*; famille *f.*
kinship ['kinʃip], *s.* Parenté *f.*
kinsman, *pl.* -men ['kinzmən], *s.m.* Parent.
kinswoman, *pl.* -women ['kinzwumən, -wimin], *s.f.* Parente.
kiosk ['kiɔsk], *s.* Kiosque *m.*
kip[1] [kip], *s. P:* Lit *m, P:* plumard *m*, pieu *m.*
kip[2], *v.i. P:* To k. down, se pieuter.
kipper ['kipər], *s.* Hareng ouvert, légèrement salé et fumé; kipper *m.*
kirk [kəːk], *s. Scot:* Église *f.*
kirkyard ['kəːkjɑːd], *s. Scot:* Cimetière *m.*
kismet ['kizmit], *s.* Le sort, le destin.
kiss[1] [kis], *s.* 1. Baiser *m*; accolade *f.* To give s.o. a k., donner un baiser à qn. To blow s.o. a k., envoyer un baiser à qn du bout des doigts. 2. *Bill:* Contre-coup *m.* 'kiss-curl, *s.* Accroche-cœur *m.*
kiss[2]. 1. *v.tr.* Donner un baiser à, embrasser (qn); baiser (le front, la main, de qn). They kissed (each other), ils se sont embrassés. *F:* To k. and be friends, se réconcilier. To k. the Pope's toe, baiser la mule du Pape. *Lit:* To k. the dust, mordre la poussière. To k. one's hand to s.o., envoyer un baiser à qn. 2. *v.i. Bill:* (*Of balls*) Se frapper par contre-coup.
kissing [kisiŋ], *s.* Baisers; embrassade(s). K. of hands, baisemain *m.*
kit [kit], *s.* 1. (*a*) *Mil: Navy:* Petit équipement; fourniment *m; F:* fourbi *m.* K. inspection, revue *f* de détail. To pack up one's k., plier bagage, *F:* ramasser son barda. (*b*) Sac *m* (de marin). (*c*) *F:* Effets *mpl* (de voyageur). 2. *Tchn:* Trousseau *m*, trousse *f* (d'outils). Repair k., nécessaire *m* de réparation. 'kit-bag, *s.* 1. Sac *m* (de voyage). 2. *Mil:* Ballot *m*, musette *f. Navy:* Sac (de marin).
kitchen ['kitʃən], *s.* 1. Cuisine *f.* Communal k., soup k., fourneau *m* économique; "soupe" *f* populaire. Thieves' kitchen, repaire *m* de voleurs. 2. *Attrib.* De cuisine, cuisinier, -ière. K. table, table de cuisine. K. towel, essuie-mains *m* pour la cuisine. K. utensils, k. equipment, batterie *f* de cuisine. 'kitchen-garden, *s.* Jardin potager. 'kitchen-maid, *s.f.* Fille de cuisine. 'kitchen-range, *s.* Fourneau *m* de cuisine, cuisinière *f.* 'kitchen-unit, *s.* Bloc-cuisine *m.* 'kitchen-ware, *s.* Faïence *f*, vaisselle *f* de cuisine.
kitchener ['kitʃənər], *s.* 1. Cuisinier (de monastère). 2. Fourneau *m* de cuisine; cuisinière *f.*
kitchenette [,kitʃən'et], *s.* Petite cuisine.
kite [kait], *s.* 1. *Orn:* Milan *m.* 2. (*a*) Cerf-volant *m*, *pl.* cerfs-volants. *Fin:* Effet *m* de complaisance. To fly, send up, a k., (i) lancer, enlever, un cerf-volant; (ii) *F:* tâter le terrain; lancer un ballon d'essai. (iii) *Fin:* Tirer en l'air; tirer en blanc. *Whence:* (*b*) *Fin:* Cerf-volant; traite *f* en l'air; billet *m* de complaisance. 3. *Av: F:* (*aircraft*) Taxi *m.*
kith [kiθ], *s. A:* Amis *mpl*, voisins *mpl* et connaissances *fpl.* *Used in* Our k. and kin, nos amis et parents, nos proches.
kitten ['kitn], *s.* Chaton *m*; petit(e) chat(te). *F:* To have kittens, se tracasser, faire des histoires.
kittenish ['kitəniʃ], *a.* (*Of girl*) (*a*) Coquette, aguichante. (*b*) Enjouée.
kittiwake ['kitiweik], *s. Orn:* Mouette *f* tridactyle.
kitty[1] ['kiti], *s. F:* = KITTEN.
kitty[2] ['kiti], *s.* (*a*) Cagnotte *f.* (*b*) *F:* Magot *m.*
Kitty[3]. *Pr.n.f.* (*Dim. of Catherine*) Catherine.
kiwi ['kiːwiː], *s.* 1. *Orn:* Aptéryx *m*; kiwi *m.* 2. *Av: F:* Rampant *m.*
kleptomania [,kleptə'meiniə], *s.* Kleptomanie *f.*
kleptomaniac [,kleptə'meiniæk], *a. & s.* Kleptomane (*mf*).

klystron ['klistrən], *s. W.Tel:* Klystron *m.*
knack [næk], *s.* Tour *m* de main; *F:* truc *m.* To have the k. of doing sth., a k. for doing sth., avoir le talent, *F:* le chic, pour faire qch. To acquire, get into, the k. of sth., attraper le coup pour faire qch. He has a happy k. of saying the right thing, il a le don de l'à-propos.
knacker ['nækər], *s.* 1. Équarrisseur *m.* 2. Entrepreneur *m* de démolitions.
knag [nag], *s.* Nœud (dans le bois).
knapsack ['næpsæk], *s.* (*a*) Havresac *m*; sac alpin. (*b*) *Mil:* Havresac, sac *m, F:* as *m* de carreau.
knapweed ['næpwiːd], *s. Bot:* Centaurée (noire).
knave [neiv], *s.* 1. Fripon *m*, coquin *m.* 2. *Cards:* Valet *m.*
knavery ['neivəri], *s.* Friponnerie *f*, coquinerie *f.*
knavish ['neiviʃ], *a.* De fripon; fourbe, malin. K. trick, tour *m* de coquin.
knead [niːd], *v.tr.* 1. Pétrir, malaxer, travailler (la pâte, l'argile). 2. *Med:* Masser, pétrir (les muscles).
kneading, *s.* 1. Pétrissage *m* (de la pâte); malaxage *m* (de l'argile, etc.). 2. *Med:* Massage *m.* 'kneading-trough, *s.* Pétrin *m.*
knee [niː], *s.* 1. (*a*) Genou *m*, -oux. To bend, bow, the k. to, before, s.o., mettre un genou en terre devant qn. On one's (bended) knees, à genoux. On one knee, un genou à terre. To go down, fall, drop, on one's knees, s'agenouiller; se mettre, se jeter, à genoux. To go down on one's knees to s.o., se jeter aux genoux de qn. To bring s.o. to his knees, (i) forcer qn à s'agenouiller; (ii) obliger qn à capituler. To learn sth. at one's mother's k., apprendre qch. auprès de sa mère. (*b*) *Med: F:* Housemaid's k., épanchement *m* de synovie. *Vet:* (*Of horse*) Broken knees, couronnement *m.* To break its knees, se couronner. (*c*) *F:* 'Knees' (*in trousers*), poches *f*, ronds *m* aux genoux. 2. *Mec.E: Const:* Genou, équerre *f.* knee-bracket, console-équerre *f.* 'knee-breeches, *s.pl.* Culotte courte. 'knee-cap, *s. Anat:* Rotule *f.* 'knee-'deep, *a.* Jusqu'aux genoux; à hauteur du genou. 'knee-hole, *s.* Trou *m* (dans un bureau) pour l'entrée des genoux. K.-h. writing-table, bureau *m* ministre. 'knee-holly, *s. Bot:* Fragon épineux, petit houx. 'knee-joint, *s.* 1. Articulation *f* du genou. 2. *Mec.E:* Joint articulé; rotule *f.* 'knee-pad, *s.* Genouillère *f* (de parqueteur, etc.). 'knee-pipe, *s.* Genou *m*, coude *m* (de tuyau).
-kneed [niːd], *a.* 1. (*With adj. prefixed, e.g.*) Weak-k., faible des genoux, du jarret. *S.a.* KNOCK-KNEED. 2. *Tchn:* Coudé.
kneel [niːl], *v.i.* (*p.t. & p.p.* knelt) [nelt] To k. (down), s'agenouiller; se mettre à genoux. To k. to s.o., se mettre à genoux devant qn. kneeling[1], *a.* Agenouillé; à genoux. kneeling[2], *s.* Agenouillement *m.*
kneesies ['niːziz], *s.pl. F:* To play k., faire du genou.
knell [nel], *s.* Glas *m.* To toll the k., sonner le glas.
knelt. *See* KNEEL.
knew. *See* KNOW[2].
knickerbockers ['nikəbɔkəz], *s.pl.* Culotte (bouffante).
knickers ['nikəz], *s.pl.* Pantalon *m*, culotte *f* (de femme).
knick-knack ['niknæk], *s.* Colifichet *m*, bibelot *m.*
knife[1], *pl.* **knives** [naif, naivz], *s.* 1. (*a*) Couteau *m.* Table-k., couteau de table. Carving-k., couteau à découper. Cook's k., tranchelard *m.* To lay a k. and fork for s.o., mettre un couvert pour qn. (*b*) Pocket-k., couteau de poche; *P:* Flick k., couteau automatique. *S.a.* CLASP-KNIFE, JACK-KNIFE[1]. (*c*) Couteau, poignard *m; P:* surin *m.* War to the k., guerre à couteaux tirés, à outrance. *F:* To have one's k. in s.o., s'acharner après, contre, sur, qn. 2. Couteau, lame *f* (d'un hache-paille, etc.); couperet *m* (de la guillotine). 3. *Surg:* The k., le bistouri, le scalpel. To resort to the k., porter le fer; trancher dans le vif. 'knife-board, *s.* Planche *f* à couteaux. 'knife-edge, *s.* 1. (*a*) Arête *f* en lame de couteau. (*b*) *Ph:* Couteau *m* de balance. 2. (*a*) *W.Tel:* K.-e. tuning, réglage *m* à sélectivité très poussée. (*b*) *Attrib:* Trousers with a k.-e. crease, pantalon au pli cassant. 'knife-grinder, *s.* Rémouleur *m*; repasseur *m* de couteaux. 'knife-rest, *s.* Porte-couteau *m.* 'knife-switch, *s. El:* Interrupteur *m* à couteaux.

knife², v.tr. Donner un coup de couteau à (qn); poignarder (qn); P: suriner (qn).

knight¹ [nait], s. 1. Chevalier m. K. of the Garter, Chevalier de (l'ordre de) la Jarretière. 2. (At chess) Cavalier m. **knight-'errant**, pl. **knights-'errant**, s.m. Chevalier errant; paladin m. **knight-'errantry**, s. Chevalerie errante.

knight², v.tr. 1. Hist: Armer chevalier (un écuyer, etc.). 2. Faire, créer, (qn) chevalier; donner l'accolade à (qn).

knighthood ['naithud], s. 1. Chevalerie f. 2. Titre m de chevalier.

knightly ['naitli], a. Chevaleresque; de chevalier.

knit¹ [nit], v. (p.t. & p.p. **knitted** or **knit**; pr.p. **knitting**) 1. v.tr. (a) Tricoter. (b) K. two, purl two, deux (mailles) à l'endroit, deux à l'envers. (c) To k. one's brows, froncer les sourcils. (d) Joindre, unir, lier. 2. v.i. (a) (Of bones) Se souder. (b) To k. (together), (of persons) se lier. **knit²**, **knitted**, a. 1. **Knitted scarf**, écharpe tricotée; écharpe de, en, tricot. **Knitted wear**, tricot m. s. **Fisherman k.**, tricot sport. **Knit(ted) goods**, bonneterie f. 2. **Knitted eyebrows**, sourcils froncés. 3. **Closely k. sentences**, phrases d'une structure serrée. **knitting**, s. 1. (a) Tricotage m. (b) Union f. (c) Soudure f (des os). 2. Tricot m. **Plain k.**, tricot à l'endroit. **'knitting-machine**, s. Machine f à tricoter, tricoteuse f. **'knitting-needle**, s. Aiguille f à tricoter.

knitter ['nitər], s. Tricoteur, -euse.

knob [nob], s. 1. (a) Bosse f, protubérance f; (on tree) nœud m. (b) Pomme f (de canne); bouton m, olive f (de porte, de tiroir); bouton de réglage, de mise en marche, etc.). 2. Morceau m (de charbon, de sucre). **knobb(l)y** ['nob(l)i], a. Noueux.

knock¹ [nok], s. 1. Coup m, heurt m, choc m. To give s.o. a k. on the head, (i) porter à qn un coup à la tête; (ii) assommer qn. To get a nasty k., attraper un vilain coup. 2. (a) K. at the door, coup à la porte; coup de marteau. There was a k. (at the door), on frappa à la porte. He heard a k., il entendit frapper. (b) K., k.! toc, toc! pan, pan! 3. I.C.E: (Engine) k., cognement m du moteur. 4. F: Cr: = INNINGS.

knock². 1. v.tr. (a) Frapper, heurter, cogner. To k. s.o. on the head, (i) frapper qn sur la tête; (ii) assommer qn. To k. one's head against sth., (i) se cogner la tête contre qch.; (ii) F: se heurter à un obstacle. To k. sth. out of s.o.'s hand, faire tomber, faire sauter, qch. de la main de qn. (b) To k. a hole in, through, sth., faire un trou dans qch.; percer qch. (c) To k. s.o. endways, sideways, épater, renverser (qn). (d) U.S: F: Critiquer, éreinter (qn, qch.). 2. v.i. (a) Frapper, heurter (at, à); taper (at, sur). (b) To k. against sth., se donner un coup, se heurter, se cogner, contre qch. (c) I.C.E: (Of engine) Cogner, pilonner. **knock about**. 1. v.tr. Bousculer, maltraiter, malmener (qn). Ship that has been terribly knocked about, vaisseau affreusement ravagé. 2. v.i. To k. about (the world), parcourir le monde; rouler sa bosse; Nau: bourlinguer. **'knock-about**, attrib.a. (a) (Jeu, etc.) violent, bruyant. Th: K.-about comedian, bateleur m; clown m. (b) K.-about life, vie errante; F: vie de bâton de chaise. (c) (Habits) de tous les jours. **'knock-'back**, v.tr. 1. P: To k. b. a drink, s'enfiler un pot, s'envoyer un verre. 2. P: O: My car knocked me back thirty pounds, ma voiture m'a coûté trente livres. **knock down**, v.tr. 1. Renverser; jeter (qch.) par terre; étendre (qn) par terre d'un coup de poing; abattre (une muraille, des pommes, etc.), démonter (une baraque, etc.). He was knocked down by a motor car, il a été renversé par une voiture. 2. (At auction) To k. sth. down to s.o., adjuger qch. à qn. 3. Baisser, faire baisser considérablement (le prix de qch.). **'knock-down**, attrib.a. 1. K.-down blow, coup d'assommoir. 2. K.-down price, (i) (at auction) prix minimum; (ii) Com: prix de réclame. **knock in**, v.tr. 1. (R)enfoncer (un clou). **knock off**, I. v.tr. 1. (Prep. use) (a) To k. the book off the table, faire tomber le livre de la table. (b) To k. the handle off the jug, faire sauter l'anse de la cruche. (b) To k. something off the price, rabattre quelque chose du prix. 2. (Adv. use) (a) Faire tomber (le chapeau de qn, etc.). To k. s.o.'s head, P: block, off, (i) flanquer une taloche à

qn; (ii) battre qn à plates coutures. (b) Achever (un travail), expédier (une besogne). (c) To k. off the odd pence, rabattre les quelques sous d'appoint. II. 'knock off, v.i. Ind: F: (Of workman) Débrayer. **'knock-on**, s. Atom. Ph: Collision f de neutrons. **knock out**, v.tr. 1. Faire sortir (qch.); chasser, repousser (un rivet); secouer (sa pipe). To k. s.o.'s brains out, faire sauter la cervelle à qn. 2. Box: To k. s.o. out, mettre (l'adversaire) knock-out; knock-outer qn. 3. (a) F: Supprimer (un mot d'un passage, etc.). (b) Ten: To be knocked out in a tournament, être éliminé. **'knock-out**. 1. Attrib.a. (a) (Coup) de grâce. (b) (Prix) imbattable. 2. s. (a) Box: Knockout m. (b) U.S: P: Type formidable; chose épatante. (c) (At auction sale) (i) entente entre brocanteurs; (ii) (membre de) la bande noire. (d) Sp: Élimination progressive des concurrents ou des équipes. **knock over**, v.tr. Faire tomber, renverser (qn, qch.). **knocking over**, s. Renversement m. **knock up**. 1. v.tr. (a) To k. s.o.'s hand up, écarter la main de qn. (b) To k. up the ball, faire une chandelle. Ten: F: To k. up the balls, faire quelques balles avant la partie. (c) Cr: To k. up a century, totaliser cent points. (d) Construire (un édifice) à la hâte. (e) Réveiller, faire lever (qn). (f) Éreinter, épuiser, échiner (qn); mettre (un cheval, qn) sur le flanc. I'm completely knocked up, je n'en peux plus; je suis complètement éreinté. 2. v.i. (a) To k. up against sth., se heurter contre qch. F: To k. up against s.o., rencontrer qn par hasard, tomber sur qn. (b) S'effondrer (de fatigue, etc.). **knocking**, s. 1. Coups mpl. 2. (Of engine) Pilonnage m; cognement m. **'knock-'kneed**, a. Cagneux. **'knock-knees**, s.pl. Genoux m en dedans, cagneux.

knocker ['nokər], s. (Door-)k., marteau m (de porte); heurtoir m.

knoll [noul], s. Tertre m, monticule m, butte f, mamelon m.

knot¹ [not], s. 1. (a) Nœud m. To tie a k., faire un nœud. To untie a k., défaire un nœud. Running k., slip-k., nœud coulant. Granny's k., nœud mal fait; nœud de vache, d'ajust. (b) Nœud (de rubans). Sailor's k., nœud régate. (c) K. of hair, chignon m. 2. Nau: (a) Nœud, division f, de la ligne de loch. (b) (Of ship) To make ten knots, filer dix nœuds. 3. Nœud (d'un problème). 4. The marriage k., les nœuds du mariage; le lien conjugal. 5. Nœud (d'une tige, du bois). K.-hole, trou m provenant d'un nœud (dans le bois). 6. Groupe m (de personnes, d'objets). K. of trees, bouquet m d'arbres. **'knot-grass**, s. Bot: Renouée f des oiseaux; F: herbe f aux cent nœuds.

knot², v. (knotted) 1. v.tr. Nouer; faire un nœud, des nœuds, à (une ficelle). To k. together two ropes, attacher deux cordages ensemble. 2. v.i. Se nouer; faire des nœuds. **knotted**, a. 1. (Corde, fouet) à nœuds. 2. = KNOTTY 3.

knottiness ['notinis], s. 1. Nodosité f (d'une plante). 2. Difficulté f, complexité f (d'un problème).

knotty ['noti], a. 1. (Of rope, etc.) Plein de nœuds. 2. F: K. point, question difficile, épineuse. 3. (a) (Of plank, etc.) Noueux, raboteux. (b) K. hands, mains noueuses.

knout¹ [naut], t. Knout m.

knout², v.tr. Knouter, donner le knout.

know¹ [nou], s. F: To be in the k., être au courant; être dans le secret (des dieux). Those who are in the k., les initiés.

know², v.tr. (knew [nju:]; known [noun]) 1. (a) Reconnaître. I knew him by his walk, je l'ai reconnu à son allure, à sa démarche. I knew him for a German, je l'ai reconnu comme Allemand. (b) Distinguer (from, de, d'avec). To k. good from evil, connaître le bien d'avec le mal. You wouldn't k. him from an Englishman, vous le prendriez pour un Anglais. 2. (a) Connaître (qn, un lieu). To get, come, to k. s.o., faire la connaissance de qn. To get to k. s.o. better, faire plus ample connaissance avec qn. To be in surroundings one knows, être en pays de connaissance. (b) He knows no fear, il ne sait pas ce que c'est que d'avoir peur. His zeal knows no bounds, son zèle ne connaît pas de bornes. 3. Connaître, fréquenter (qn). They are neighbours of ours but we do not k. them, ils sont nos voisins, mais nous ne les fréquentons pas. 4. Savoir, connaître, posséder (un sujet). To k. sth. by heart, savoir qch. par cœur. To k. how to do sth., savoir faire qch. To k. how to read, savoir lire. 5. (a) To k. more than one says, en savoir plus long qu'on n'en dit. I k. that well enough, je ne le sais que trop. As far as I k., for all I k., autant que je sache. Not to k. sth., ne pas savoir qch.; ignorer qch. Is his father rich?—I don't k., son père est-il riche?—Je n'en sais rien. How do I k.? est-ce que je sais? He knows his own mind, il sait ce qu'il veut. I would have you k. that . . ., sachez que. . . Jur: Be it known that . . . il est fait assavoir que. . . . I don't k. that he understands much about it, je doute qu'il y entende grand-chose. I knew (that) he had talent, je lui connaissais, savais, du talent. He didn't quite k. what to say, il ne savait trop que dire. F: He knows a good thing when he sees it, il sait ce qui est bon, c'est un connaisseur. He knows what he is talking about, F: he knows what's what, il est sûr de son fait. P: What do you k.?(!) (i) quoi de nouveau? (ii) sans blague! I k. not what, je ne sais quoi. (b) I k. him to be a liar, je sais que c'est un menteur. I have known it (to) happen, c'est une chose que j'ai vue se produire. Have you ever known me (to) tell a lie? m'avez-vous jamais entendu dire un mensonge? He had never been known to laugh, on ne l'avait jamais vu rire. 6. To get to k. sth., apprendre qch. I knew it yesterday, je l'ai appris hier; je l'ai su hier. Please let us k..whether . . ., veuillez nous faire savoir si. . . . Everything gets known, tout se sait. 7. F: Don't I k. it! à qui le dites-vous! Not if I k. it! pour rien au monde! 8. To k. better than to . . ., se bien garder de. . . . I k. better (than that), (i) je le sais le contraire; (ii) je suis plus malin que ça. He knows better than to do that, il est trop fin, trop avisé, pour faire cela. You ought to k. better at your age, vous devriez avoir plus de sagacité à votre âge. You ought to have known better, vous auriez dû être plus prudent. You k. best, vous en êtes le meilleur juge. F: I wouldn't k., je ne saurais dire. . . . F: Not that I know of, pas que je sache. 9. Iron: He knows better! Il s'y connaît! They k. no better, ils ne peuvent faire mieux. know about, v.i. To k. about sth., être informé de qch.; être au courant. He knows all about it, (i) il sait tout; (ii) il est renseigné; (ii) il s'y entend. I don't k. about that! je n'en suis pas bien sûr! I k. nothing about it, je n'en sais rien, je n'en sais pas un mot. know-all, s. Un je-sais-tout. 'know-how, s. Tour m de main, savoir-faire m, méthode f, technique f, manière f (de s'y prendre). know of, v.i. To k. of s.o., connaître qn de réputation. I k. of a good watchmaker, je connais un bon horloger. To get to k. of sth., apprendre qch. known, a. Connu, reconnu, su. Such are the k. facts, tels sont les faits constatés. A k. thief, un voleur avéré. (Of news, etc.) To become k. to s.o., arriver à la connaissance, aux oreilles, de qn. To make sth. k. to s.o., porter qch. à la connaissance de qn. To make s.o.'s presence k., divulguer la présence de qn. To make one's wishes k., faire connaître ses volontés. It is k. to all that . . ., il est notoire que. . . . He is k. to everyone, k. everywhere, il est connu partout, tout le monde le connaît. K. as . . ., connu sous le nom de. . . . This is what is k. as . . ., c'est ce qu'on appelle. . . . (Of author, etc.) To become k. sortir de l'obscurité. knowing¹, a. Fin, malin, rusé. A k. smile, un sourire entendu. To put on a k. look, faire l'entendu. -ly, adv. 1. Sciemment; à bon escient. 2. Finement, habilement; d'un air rusé. knowing², s. 1. Compréhension f, connaissance f (of,

de). 2. There is no k. (how . . ., why . . .), il n'y a pas moyen de savoir (comment . . ., pourquoi . . .).

knowable ['nouəbl], a. 1. Connaissable. 2. Reconnaissable (by, à).

knowledge ['nɔlidʒ], s. 1. (a) Connaissance f (d'un fait, d'une personne). To get k. of sth., apprendre qch. I had no k. of it, je ne le savais pas; je l'ignorais. Lack of k., ignorance f (of, de). It is a matter of common k. that . . ., il est notoire que. . . . To the k. of everyone, to everyone's k., au su de tout le monde. To my k., to the best of my k., as far as my k. goes, à ma connaissance; autant que je sache. Not to my k., pas que je sache. Without my k., à mon insu. To speak with full k. (of the facts), parler en connaissance de cause. (b) He had grown out of all k., il était tellement grandi qu'on ne le reconnaissait plus. 2. Savoir m, science f, connaissances f. To have a k. of several languages, connaître plusieurs langues. To have a thorough k. of a subject, connaître, posséder, un sujet à fond His wide k., son savoir étendu; ses vastes connaissances (of, en). K. of the world, of the heart, la science du monde, du cœur. K. is power, savoir c'est pouvoir. The advance of k., les progrès m de la science.

knowledgeable ['nɔlidʒəbl], a. F: Intelligent; bien informé.

knuckle¹ ['nʌkl], s. 1. Articulation f, jointure f, du doigt. To rap s.o. over the knuckles, donner sur les ongles à qn. 2. Cu: Souris (d'un gigot). K. end, côté du manche (d'un gigot). K. of veal, jarret m de veau. K. of ham, jambonneau m. F: O: That's getting rather near the k., cela frise l'indécence. 'knuckle-bone, s. 1. = KNUCKLE¹ 1. 2. Osselet m. To play at k.-bones, jouer aux osselets. 'knuckle-duster, s. Coup-de-poing américain. 'knuckle-'joint, s. 1. = KNUCKLE¹ 1. 2. Mec.E: Articulation f à genouillère.

knuckle², v.i. To k. down, s'y mettre sérieusement. To k. under, se soumettre; céder; mettre les pouces; filer doux. I won't k. down to him, il ne va pas me faire la loi.

knur(r) [nə:r], s. Nœud m (dans un tronc d'arbre).

knurl¹ [nə:l], s. 1. Nœud m (du bois). 2. (a) Tls: Molette f. (b) Molet(t)age m.

knurl², v.tr. Molet(t)er, godronner.

koala [kou'ɑ:lə], s. Z: Koala m.

kohlrabi [koul'ræbai], s. Bot: Chou-rave m, pl. choux-raves.

kola ['koulə], s. Bot: Cola m, kola m.

kolkhoz ['kɔlkɔz], s. Kolkhoze m, ferme collective.

kommandatura [kə'mændə'tjuərə], s. Mil.Adm: Commandature f, kommandatur f.

Koran (the) [ðɔkɔ:'rɑ:n], s. Le Koran, le Coran.

Korea [kə'riə]. Pr.n. Geog: La Corée.

Korean [kə'riən], a. & s. Coréen, -enne. The K. war, la guerre de Corée.

kosher ['kouʃər], a. Jew.Rel: Cachir inv; cacher, -ère.

ko(w)tow [kou'tau], v.i. 1. Se prosterner, se courber (à la chinoise) (to, devant). 2. F: To k. to s.o., s'aplatir devant qn; courber l'échine devant qn.

kraft [krɑ:ft], s. Paperm: Kraft m.

Krakow ['krɑ:kəf]. Pr.n. Geog: Cracovie f.

kudos ['kju:dɔs], s. F: La gloriole.

Kurd [kə:d], a. & s. Ethn: Kurde.

Kurdish ['kə:diʃ]. 1. a. Kurde. 2. s. Ling: Le kurde.

Kurdistan ['kə:dis'tɑ:n]. Pr.n. Le Kurdistan.

kyle [kail], s. Scot: Détroit m, pertuis m.

L, l [el], s. **1.** (La lettre) L, l m or f. Tp: L for Lucy, L comme Louis. **2.** (Abbr. of Lat. libra, pound) Livre f sterling. F: It is not merely a question of L.S.D., ce n'est pas simplement une question d'argent.

la [lɑ:], s. Mus: **1.** (Fixed la) La m. **2.** (Movable la) La sus-dominante.

laager¹ [ˈlɑːgər], s. (In S. Africa) Laager m; campement m avec rempart de chars à bœufs.

laager². **1.** v.tr. Former (les chars à bœufs) en laager; mettre (les gens) en laager. **2.** v.i. Se former en laager; former le camp.

lab [læb], s. F: Labo m.

label¹ [ˈleibl], s. **1.** Étiquette f. Gummed l., étiquette gommée. Stick-on l., étiquette adhésive. **2.** Com: Marque f, label m. **3.** Arch: = DRIP-STONE.

label², v.tr. (labelled) Étiqueter. Luggage labelled for London, bagages enregistrés pour Londres. Labelled as . . ., désigné sous le nom de . . .

labial [ˈleibiəl]. **1.** a. Labial, -aux. **2.** s. Ling: Labiale f.

labiate [ˈleibiit]. Bot: **1.** a. Labié. **2.** s. Labiée f.

laboratory [læˈbərətri, occ. ˈlæbərətri], s. Laboratoire m. L. assistant, assistant m de laboratoire; préparateur, -trice; laborantin, -ine.

laborious [ləˈbɔːriəs], a. Laborieux, -euse. **1.** Travaillleur, -euse. **2.** Pénible, fatigant. -ly, adv. Laborieusement, péniblement.

labour¹ [ˈleibər], s. **1.** (a) Travail m, labeur m, peine f. Material and l., tissu m et façon f. Manual l., travail manuel. (b) Jur: Hard l., réclusion criminelle. **2.** (a) Ind: Main-d'œuvre f; travailleurs mpl. Skilled l., main-d'œuvre spécialisée. Capital and l., le capital et la main-d'œuvre. L. troubles, conflits entre ouvriers et patrons; agitation ouvrière. (b) Coll. Pol: Les travaillistes m. The L. party, le parti travailliste. **3.** The twelve labours of Hercules, les douze travaux d'Hercule. L. of love, (i) travail gratuit; (ii) travail fait avec plaisir. **4.** Med: Travail; couches fpl. Premature l., accouchement m avant terme. Woman in l., femme en couches. 'labour-exchange, s. Bourse f du Travail. 'labour-saving, a. Qui allège le travail. Dom.Ec: L.-s. device, appareil ménager.

labour². **1.** v.i. (a) Travailler, peiner. To l. at, over sth., travailler à qch.; peiner sur qch. (b) To l. along, marcher, avancer, péniblement. To l. up a hill, gravir péniblement une côte. (c) To l. under a burden, être courbé sous un fardeau. To l. under a sense of injustice, nourrir un sentiment d'injustice. To l. under a delusion, être (la) victime d'une illusion; se faire illusion. (d) (Of engine) Fatiguer, peiner. (Of ship) Bourlinguer, fatiguer. (Of car) To l. uphill, peiner en côte. **2.** v.tr. Travailler (son style). I will not l. the point, je ne m'étendrai pas là-dessus. laboured, a. **1.** (Style) travaillé, qui sent l'huile. **2.** (Respiration) pénible. labouring, a. O: L. man, ouvrier m. The l. class, la classe ouvrière.

labourer [ˈleibərər], s. (a) Travailleur m. Prov: The l. is worthy of his hire, toute peine, tout travail, mérite salaire. (b) Ind: Manœuvre m; homme m de peine. S.a. DAY-LABOURER. (c) Agricultural l., ouvrier m agricole.

laburnum [ləˈbəːnəm], s. Bot: Cytise m; faux ébénier.

labyrinth [ˈlæbirinθ], s. Labyrinthe m, dédale m.

lac [læk], s. Gomme f laque; laque f.

lace¹ [leis], s. **1.** Lacet m (de corset, de soulier); cordon m (de soulier). **2.** Gold l., galon m, ganse f, passement m d'or. **3.** Dentelle f, point m. Bobbin l., pillow l., dentelle aux fuseaux; guipure f. Alençon l., point d'Alençon. 'lace-maker, s. **1.** Fabricant, -ante, de dentelles. **2.** Dentellière f. 'lace-making, s. Dentellerie f. 'lace-work, s. (a) Dentelles fpl; dentellerie f. (b) Passementerie f.

lace², v.tr. **1.** To l. (up) one's shoes, lacer ses chaussures. A: To l. oneself in, se lacer. L.-up shoes, chaussures à lacets. **2.** To l. sth. with sth., entrelacer qch. de, avec, qch. **3.** Garnir, border, de dentelles. **4.** Glass of milk laced with rum, lait m au rhum. lacing, s. **1.** Lacement m, laçage m. **2.** (a) Lacet m. (b) Galon m, passement m.

lacerate [ˈlæsəreit], v.tr. Lacérer; déchirer (la chair, le cœur).

laceration [ˌlæsəˈreiʃ(ə)n], s. **1.** Lacération f, déchirement m. **2.** Med: Déchirure f.

lachrymal [ˈlækrim(ə)l], a. Lacrymal, -aux.

lachrymatory [ˈlækrimət(ə)ri], a. **1.** (Urne) lacrymatoire. **2.** (Gaz) lacrymogène.

lachrymose [ˈlækrimous], a. Larmoyant.

lack¹ [læk], s. Manque m, absence f, défaut m (of, de). L. of money, pénurie f d'argent. For l. of . . ., faute de. . . .

lack², v.tr. & i. To l. (for) sth., manquer de qch.; ne pas avoir qch. lacking, a. Qui manque; manquant. Money was l., l'argent manquait, faisait défaut. He is l. in courage, il manque de courage. L. in meaning, dépourvu, dénué, de sens. F: He's a bit l. (in the top storey), il est un peu simplet. 'lack-lustre, attrib.a. (Œil) terne, éteint.

lackadaisical [ˌlækəˈdeizik(ə)l], a. Affecté, affété, minaudier; languissant.

lackey [ˈlæki], s. Laquais m.

laconic [ləˈkɔnik], a. Laconique. -ally, adv. Laconiquement.

lacquer¹ [ˈlækər], s. **1.** Vernis-laque m inv; vernis m de Chine; laque m. Gold l., batture f. **2.** Peinture laquée. Cellulose l., laque cellulosique.

lacquer², v.tr. **1.** Laquer. **2.** Vernir (des meubles, etc.).

lacrosse [ləˈkrɔs], s. Games: Crosse canadienne.

lactation [lækˈteiʃ(ə)n], s. Lactation f.

lacteal [ˈlæktiəl], a. Lacté; (suc) laiteux.

lactic [ˈlæktik], a. Ch: Lactique.

lactiferous [lækˈtifərəs], a. (Conduit, etc.) lactifère.

lactometer [lækˈtɔmitər], s. Lactomètre m, pèse-lait m inv.

lacuna, pl. -ae, -as [ləˈkjuːnə, -iː, -əz], s. Lacune f; hiatus m.

lacustrine [ləˈkʌstrin], a. (Plante, habitation) lacustre.

lad [læd], s.m. (a) Jeune homme; (jeune) garçon. Now then, my lads, allons, mes garçons! allons, les gars! (b) F: He's a bit of a lad! ça c'est un gars!

ladder¹ [ˈlædər], s. **1.** Échelle f. The social l., l'échelle sociale. To be at the top of the l., être au haut de l'échelle. **2.** Hyd.E: L. of locks, suite f de biefs. **3.** I've a l. in my stocking, j'ai une maille qui file. To mend a l., rem(m)ailler un bas. 'ladder-mender, s. Remailleuse f (femme ou instrument). 'ladder-proof, a. (Bas) indémaillable.

ladder², v.i. (Of stocking) Se démailler, filer.

laddie [ˈlædi], s.m. Scot: F: (a) = LAD. (b) Mon petit gars.

lade [leid], v.tr. (laded; laden) Nau: (a) Charger (un navire) (with, de). (b) Embarquer (des marchandises). laden, a. Chargé. Fully l. ship, navire en pleine charge. Well-l. tree, arbre chargé de fruits. lading, s. Chargement m (d'un navire). S.a. BILL⁴ 4.

la-di-da [ˈlɑːdiˈdɑː], a. F: La-di-da manner, air affecté.

ladle¹ [ˈleidl], s. **1.** Cuiller f à pot. Soup l., louche f. **2.** (a) Ind: Puisoir m, pucheux m. (b) Metall: Foundry l., poche f de fonderie, de coulée.

ladle², v.tr. To l. (out) the soup, servir le potage.

ladleful [ˈleidlful], s. Pleine cuiller à pot, pleine louche (of, de).

lady [ˈleidi], s.f. Dame. **1.** (a) L.-in-waiting, dame d'honneur. (b) (usu. O: or P:) Dame, femme bien élevée. P: She's a real l., vraiment, c'est une dame. She's no l., c'est une personne commune, vulgaire. (c) (Woman) A l. and a gentleman, un monsieur et une dame. An old l., une vieille dame. O: Young l., jeune fille; jeune femme. (To child) And how are you, young l.? et comment allez-vous, ma petite demoiselle? Com: The young l. will attend to you, la vendeuse s'occupera de vous. I'm sorry, this l. was before you, je m'excuse, mais cette dame était là avant vous. Com: P: Here you are, l.! voilà madame, P: ma petite dame. (At public meeting, etc.) Ladies and gentlemen! Mesdames, mesdemoiselles, messieurs! (On public convenience) Ladies, dames. (d) The l. of the house, la maîtresse de maison. *P:* (*Referring to employer*) My l., la patronne. (*e*) **Lady's watch,** montre *f* de dame. **Ladies' tailor,** tailleur pour dames. **A ladies', lady's, man,** un homme galant. *Com:* **L. cashier,** caissière. *Becoming P:* (*now usu.* **woman-**) **L. doctor,** femme médecin, doctoresse. 2. *Ecc:* **Our L.,** Notre-Dame, la Sainte Vierge. 3. (*As title, no Fr. equivalent*) **Lady,** *F:* milady. **My l.,** madame (la comtesse, etc.). *Hist:* **The l. of the manor,** la châtelaine. 4.*P:* **My young l.,** (i) ma bonne amie; (ii) ma future. **'lady-bird,** *s. Ent:* Coccinelle *f; F:* bête *f* à bon Dieu. **'lady chapel,** *s. Ecc:* Chapelle *f* de la Vierge. **'Lady day,** *s. Ecc:* La fête de l'Annonciation. **'lady-killer,** *s.m.* Tombeur *m* (de femmes). **'lady's 'slipper,** *s. Bot:* Sabot *m* de la Vierge, de Vénus.

ladylike ['leidilaik], *a. O:* (Air) distingué, de dame; (*of pers.*) comme il faut; bien élevée.

ladyship ['leidiʃip], *s.* Her l., your l., madame (la comtesse, etc.).

lag¹ [læg], *s. Ph:* Retard *m*; décalage *m* (entre deux opérations). **Magnetic l.,** retard d'aimantation; hystérésis *f.* **L. of the brushes,** décalage des balais (d'une dynamo, etc.). **Phase l.,** retard de phase; déphasage *m* en arrière.

lag², *v.i.* (**lagged**) 1. (*Of pers.*) To l. (**behind**) rester en arrière; traîner. 2. *Tchn:* (*Of tides, etc.*). Retarder. *El.E:* (*Of current*) Être déphasé en arrière.

lag³, *s. P:* Condamné *m*, forçat *m.* **An old l.,** un repris de justice; un récidiviste, *F:* un cheval de retour.

lag⁴, *v.tr.* Garnir, envelopper, revêtir, (une chaudière) d'un calorifuge. **Air-lagged,** à chemise d'air. **lagging,** *s.* 1. Garnissage *m.* 2. Enveloppe isolante, chemise *f*, revêtement *m* calorifuge (d'une chaudière).

lager ['lɑːgər], *s. L.* (beer), bière blonde allemande.

laggard ['lægəd]. 1.*a.* Lent, paresseux. 2.*s.* Traînard *m*; lambin, -ine.

lagoon [lə'guːn], *s.* 1. Lagune *f.* 2.*s.* Lagon *m* (d'atoll).

laicism ['leiisizm], *s.* Laïcisme *m.*

laicization [ˌleiisai'zeiʃ(ə)n], *s.* Laïcisation *f.*

laicize ['leiisaiz], *v.tr.* Laïciser.

laid. See LAY⁴.

lain. See LIE³.

lair ['lɛər], *s.* Tanière *f*, repaire *m* (de bête fauve); lit *m* (du cerf); bauge *f* (du sanglier). **Brigands' l.,** repaire, caverne *f*, de brigands.

laird ['lɛəd], *s. Scot:* Propriétaire (foncier). **The l.,** le seigneur du village.

laissez-faire ['leisei'fɛər], *s.* Laisser-faire *m inv.* **L.-f. policy,** politique *f* du laisser-faire.

laity ['leiiti], *s. Coll.* Les laïques *m.*

lake¹ [leik], *s.* Lac *m.* **Ornamental l.,** bassin *m*; pièce d'eau décorative. *P:* **Go jump in the l.,** va te faire pendre. *Eng.Lit:* **The L. poets,** les lakistes *mpl.* **'lake(-)dwelling,** *s.* Habitation *f* lacustre.

lake², *s. Paint:* Laque *f.* **Crimson l.,** laque carminée.

lam [læm], *v.tr. & i.* (**lammed**) *P:* To l. (**into**) s.o., rosser, étriller, qn.

lama ['lɑːmə], *s. Buddhist Rel:* Lama *m.*

lamb¹ [læm], *s.* Agneau *m.* **Ewe with l.,** brebis pleine. **Ewe lamb,** agnelle *f. F:* **My one ewe l.,** mon seul trésor. *Theol:* **The L.** (of God), l'Agneau (de Dieu). *F:* **He took it like a l.,** il n'a pas protesté. *Cu:* **L. chop, cutlet,** côtelette *f* d'agneau. **'lamb-like,** *a.* Doux, *f.* douce, comme un agneau. **'lamb's 'lettuce,** *s. Bot:* Mâche *f.* **'lambs' 'tails,** *s.pl. Bot:* Chatons *m* (du noisetier).

lamb², *v.i.* (*Of ewe*) Agneler, mettre bas. **lambing,** *s.* Agnelage *m.*

lame¹ [leim], *a.* 1. (*a*) Boiteux; (*through accident*) estropié; *F:* éclopé. **To be l. of, in, one leg,** boiter d'une jambe. **To walk l.,** boiter, clocher; traîner la jambe. **I have walked myself l.,** j'ai tant marché que je traîne la patte. **To go l.,** se mettre à boiter. (*b*) *Pros:* **L. verses,** vers boiteux; vers qui clochent. 2. **L. excuse,** piètre, pauvre, excuse. **L. story,** histoire qui ne tient pas debout. **-ly,** *adv.* 1. (Marcher) en boitant. 2. (S'excuser, etc.) imparfaitement, faiblement.

lame², *v.tr.* (*a*) (*Of pers.*) Rendre (qn) boiteux; écloper (qn, un cheval); (*of blister, etc*) faire boiter (qn). (*b*) Estropier.

lamella, *pl.* **-ae** [lə'melə, -iː], *s.* Lamelle *f.*

lamellar [lə'melər], *a.* Lamellaire.

lamellate ['læmələit], *a.* Lamellé, feuilleté.

lameness ['leimnis], *s.* 1. (*a*) Claudication *f*; boitement *m.* (*b*) Boiterie *f* (d'un cheval). 2. Faiblesse *f* (d'une excuse, etc.).

lament¹ [lə'ment], *s.* 1. Lamentation *f.* 2. *Mus: A:* Complainte *f.*

lament², *v.tr. & i.* To l. (for, over) sth.,s.o., se lamenter sur qch.; pleurer qch., qn. **lamented,** *a.* **The late l. X,** le regretté X.

lamentable ['læməntəbl], *a.* (Perte) lamentable, déplorable. **-ably,** *adv.* Lamentablement, déplorablement.

lamentation [ˌlæmən'teiʃ(ə)n], *s.* Lamentation *f.*

lamina, *pl.* **-ae** ['læminə, -iː], *s.* Lame *f*, lamelle *f*, feuillet *m. Bot:* Limbe *m.*

laminar ['læminər], *a.* Laminaire.

laminate¹ ['læmineit]. 1.*v.tr.* (*a*) Laminer. (*b*) Diviser en lamelles; feuilleter. (*c*) *Bookb:* Plastifier. 2. *v.i.* Se feuilleter. **laminated,** *a.* 1. (Ressort, etc.) feuilleté, à feuilles, à lames. 2. (Bois) contre-plaqué. 3. **L. plastic,** lamifié *m*, plastique *f* en feuilles. *Bookb:* **L. jacket,** jaquette plastifiée, acétatée.

laminate² ['læminit], *a. Nat.Hist:* Lamineux, -euse; à lamelles.

lamination [ˌlæmi'neiʃ(ə)n], *s.* 1. (*a*) Laminage *m. Bookb:* Plastification *f.* (*b*) Feuilletage *m.* 2.Lamelle *f.*

Lammas ['læməs], *s. Scot:* L.(-day,-tide),le premier août.

lammergeyer ['læməgaiər], *s. Orn:* Gypaète barbu.

lamp [læmp], *s.* 1. (*a*) Lampe *f.* **Portable l., inspection l.** (of garage, etc.), baladeuse *f.* **Pocket l.,** torche *f*; lampe de poche. *Min:* **Safety l.,** lampe de sûreté. (*b*) *Aut:* **Head-l.,** phare *m.* **Side lamps,** feux *m* de position. 2. **Table l.,** lampe de table; lampe portative. **Standard l.,** lampadaire *m.* **Wall l.,** applique *f.* **Ceiling l.,** plafonnier *m. S.a.* GAS-LAMP, READING-LAMP, STREET-LAMP. 3. *El:* (*Bulb*) Lampe, ampoule *f. S.a.* ARC-LAMP. **'lamp-black,** *s.* Noir *m* de fumée. **'lamp-bracket,** *s.* Applique *f.* **'lamp-holder,** *s. El:* Douille *f* (de lampe); porte-ampoule *m inv.* **'lamp-oil,** *s.* 1. Huile *f* d'éclairage; huile lampante. 2. Pétrole lampant. **'lamp-post,** *s.* (*In street*) Réverbère *m.* **'lamp-shade,** *s.* Abat-jour *m inv.*

lamplight ['læmplait], *s.* Lumière *f* de la lampe. **To work by l.,** travailler à la lampe.

lamplighter ['læmplaitər], *s. A:* Allumeur *m* de réverbères.

lampoon¹ [læm'puːn], *s.* Pasquinade *f*, libelle *m*, satire *f*, brocard *m.*

lampoon², *v.tr.* Lancer des satires, des libelles, des brocards, contre (qn); chansonner (qn).

lampooner [læm'puːnər], **lampoonist** [læm'puːnist], *s.* Libelliste *m*, satiriste *m.*

lampoonery [læm'puːnəri], *s.* Satire *f*; esprit *m* satirique.

lamprey ['læmpri], *s. Ich:* Lamproie *f.*

Lancaster ['læŋkəstər]. *Pr.n. Geog:* Lancastre.

Lancastrian [læŋ'kæstriən], *a. & s. Hist:* Lancastrien, -ienne.

lance¹ [lɑːns], *s.* 1. Lance *f.* 2. (*Pers.*) *Hist:* Lance. *S.a.* FREE LANCE. **'lance-'corporal,** *s. Mil:* Soldat *m* de première classe; sous-brigadier *m* (de police). **'lance-'sergeant,** *s. Mil:* (*a*) Caporal-chef *m*, *pl.* caporaux-chefs. (*b*) (*Mounted arms*) Brigadier-chef *m*, *pl.* brigadiers-chefs.

lance², *v.tr. Med:* Donner un coup de bistouri, de lancette, à (un abcès); percer, inciser (un abcès).

lanceolate ['lɑːnsiouleit, 'læn-], *a. Bot:* Lancéolé; en fer de lance.

lancer ['lɑːnsər], *s.* 1. *Mil:* Lancier *m.* 2. *pl.* Lancers, (quadrille *m* des) lanciers.

lancet ['lɑːnsit], *s.* 1. *Med:* Lancette *f*, bistouri *m.* 2. *Arch:* (Ogive *f* à) lancette.

lancinating ['lɑːnsineitiŋ], *a.* Lancinant. **L. pains,** élancements *m.*

land¹ [lænd], *s.* 1. (*a*) (*Opposed to sea*) Terre *f.* **Dry l.,** terre ferme. **To travel by l.,** voyager par voie de terre. **By l. and sea,** sur terre et sur mer. **To see how the l. lies,** (i) *Nau:* prendre le gisement de la côte; (ii) sonder, tâter, le terrain. **To make, sight, l.,** atterrir; arriver en vue de la terre. **To touch l.,**

toucher terre; aborder, atterrir. (*b*) (*Soil*) Terre, terrain *m*, sol *m*. Back to the l., le retour aux champs, à la terre. Waste l., terre inculte; terrain vague. The l. question, la question agraire. 2. Terre, pays *m*, contrée *f*. Distant lands, pays lointains. The Holy L., la Terre Sainte. Theatre l., le quartier des spectacles. 3. Terre(s); fonds *m* de terre; 'land-act, *s*. *Jur:* Loi *f* agraire. 'land-agency, *s*. 1. Gérance *f* (de domaine). 2. Agence foncière. 'land-agent, *s*. 1. Intendant *m*, régisseur *m*, d'un domaine. 2. Courtier *m* en immeubles. 'land-breeze, *s*. *Meteor:* Brise *f* de terre. 'land-girl, *s.f.* Travailleuse agricole. 'Land's End, *Pr.n. Geog:* La pointe de Cornouailles. 'land-surveying, *s*. Arpentage *m*; géodésie *f*. 'land-surveyor, *s*. *See* SURVEYOR 1. 'land warfare, *s*. Guerre *f* sur terre. 'land-worker, *s*. Travailleur *m* agricole.

land². 1. *v.tr.* (*a*) Mettre, faire descendre, (qn) à terre; mettre (qch.) à terre, décharger (qch.); débarquer (qn, qch.). To l. an aircraft, atterrir un avion. (*b*) To l. a fish, amener un poisson à terre. *F:* To l. a prize, remporter un prix. (*c*) Amener. *F:* That will l. you in prison, cela vous vaudra de la prison. You have landed us in a nice fix! vous nous avez mis dans de beaux draps! I was landed with an encyclopaedia I didn't want, je me suis trouvé empêtré d'une encyclopédie dont je n'avais que faire. (*d*) *F:* To l. s.o. a blow in the face, allonger, porter, flanquer, à qn un coup au visage. 2. *v.i.* (*Of pers.*) Descendre à terre; débarquer; (*of aircraft*) atterrir; faire escale (at, à). *Av:* To 'l.' on the sea, amerrir. *Navy: Av:* To l. on deck of aircraft carrier, Apponter. To l. on the moon, alunir. (*b*) Tomber (à terre). (*c*) (*After jumping*) Retomber. To l. on one's feet, retomber sur ses pieds; retomber d'aplomb. *F:* He always lands on his feet, il retombe toujours sur ses pieds, il se tire toujours d'affaire. landed, *a*. L. property, propriété foncière; bien-fonds *m, pl.* biens-fonds. L. proprietor, propriétaire terrien. landing¹, *a*. L. force, troupes *fpl* de débarquement. landing², *s*. 1. (*a*) *Nau:* Débarquement *m*; mise *f* à terre. (*b*) *Mil: Navy:* Descente *f*. (*c*) *Av:* (i) Atterrissage *m*; (ii) (*on sea*) amerrissage *m*; (iii) *Av:* (*on flight-deck of aircraft carrier*) appontage *m*; (iv) (*on the moon*) alunissage *m*. Parachute l., parachutage *m*. Wheels-up l., belly l., atterrissage sur le ventre. Heavy l., atterri·sage brutal. Intermediate l., escale *f*. L. officer, officier d'appontage. L. area, aire *f* d'atterrissage. 2. (*a*) *Cons]:* Palier *m* (de repos) (d'un escalier); repos *m*, carré *m*. (*b*) *Min:* Recette *f*. 'landing-barge, *s*. Péniche *f* de débarquement. 'landing-craft, *s*. Bâtiment *m* de débarquement. Tank landing-craft, chaland transporteur de tanks. 'landing-ground, *s*. *Av:* Terrain *m* d'atterrissage. 'landing-net, *s*. *Fish:* Épuisette *f*. 'landing-stage, *s*. Débarcadère *m*, embarcadère *m* (flottant); ponton *m*. 'landing-strip, *s*. *Av:* Piste *f* d'atterrissage.

landau ['lændɔ:], *s*. *A: Veh:* Landau *m*, -aus.

landfall ['lændfɔ:l], *s*. *Nau: Av:* Arrivée *f* en vue de terre. To make a l., arriver en vue de terre.

landlady ['lændleidi], *s.f.* 1. Propriétaire *f* (d'un immeuble). 2. Logeuse (en garni). 3. Hôtelière, hôtesse; *F:* patronne.

landlocked ['lændlɔkt], *a*. *Geog:* Enfermé entre les terres; entouré de terre. L. sea, mer intérieure.

landlord ['lændlɔ:d], *s*. 1. Propriétaire (d'un immeuble). 2. Aubergiste *m*, hôtelier *m*, hôte *m*.

landlubber ['lænd,lʌbər], *s*. *F:* Marin *m* d'eau douce.

landmark ['lændmɑːk], *s*. 1. Borne *f* limite. 2. (*a*) (Point *m* de) repère *m*. *Nau:* Amer *m*. (*b*) Point coté (sur une carte, etc.). 3. Point décisif, événement marquant (dans l'histoire, etc.). (*Of event*) To be a l., faire époque.

landowner ['lændounər], *s*. Propriétaire foncier.

landscape ['lændskeip], *s*. Paysage *m*. L. design, architecture *f* de paysage. 'landscape-'garden, *s*. Jardin *m* à l'anglaise. 'landscape-'gardener, *s*. Jardiniste *m*; architecte *m*, jardinier *m* paysagiste. 'landscape-'painter, *s*. Paysagiste *m*.

landslide ['lændslaid], *s*. 1. Éboulement *m* (de terrain). 2. *Pol:* Débâcle *f*, défaite accablante (aux élections); raz de marée électoral.

landslip ['lændslip], *s*. Éboulement *m*, glissement *m*, de terrain.

landsman, *pl.* -men ['lændzmən], *s.m.* Terrien.

landward ['lændwəd]. 1. *adv.* Du côté de la terre; vers la terre. 2. *a.* (Côté) de la terre.

landwards ['lændwədz], *adv.* Du côté de la terre; vers la terre.

lane (lein), *s*. 1. (*In country*) Chemin (vicinal, rural). O: (in town) ruelle *f*, passage *m*. (*Of troops, etc.*) To form a l., faire la haie. 2. (*In ice-field*) Fissure *f*, passage. 3. *Nau:* Route *f* (de navigation). *Av:* Voie (aérienne). 4. *Adm:* Traffic l., voie *f*. Four l. highway, route à quatre voies.

lang syne ['læŋ'sain]. *Scot:* 1. *adv.* Autrefois, jadis. 2. *s*. Le temps jadis. *S.a.* AULD.

language ['læŋgwidʒ], *s*. 1. Langue *f* (d'un peuple). Dead, living, languages, langues mortes, vivantes. Modern languages, langues vivantes. Source l., langue de départ. Target l., langue d'arrivée. 2. Langage *m*. Strong l., langage violent, expressions vives. Bad l., langage grossier; gros mots.

languid ['læŋgwid], *a*. Languissant, langoureux; mou, *f*. molle. To be l. about sth., avoir peu d'enthousiasme pour qch. L. voice, voix traînante. -ly, *adv.* Languissamment, langoureusement; mollement, sans animation.

languidness ['læŋgwidnis], *s*. Langueur *f*, mollesse *f*.

languish ['læŋgwiʃ], *v.i.* Languir. To l. after, for, s.o., sth., languir après, pour, qn, qch. languishing, *a*. Languissant, langoureux, -euse.

languor ['læŋgər], *s*. Langueur *f*.

languorous ['læŋgərəs], *a*. Langoureux, -euse. -ly, *adv.* Langoureusement.

laniard ['lænjəd], *s*. = LANYARD.

laniferous [læ'nifərəs], lanigerous [læ'nidʒərəs], *a*. Lanifère, lanigère.

lank [læŋk], *a*. 1. (*Of pers.*) Maigre; sec, *f*. sèche; (*of animal*) efflanqué. 2. L. hair, cheveux plats.

lankiness ['læŋkinis], *s*. Aspect efflanqué.

lanky ['læŋki], *a*. Grand et maigre; grand et sec. A great l. fellow, un grand maigre; un grand efflanqué.

lantern ['læntən], *s*. 1. (*a*) Lanterne *f*, falot *m*. *Nau:* Fanal *m*, -aux. Dark l., bull's-eye l., lanterne sourde. Chinese l., lanterne vénitienne. (*b*) *A:* Magic l., lanterne magique; lanterne à projections. 2. *Arch:* Lanterne, lanterneau *m* (de dôme). 'lantern-jawed, *a*. Aux joues creuses; à la figure émaciée. 'lantern-jaws, *s.pl.* Joues creuses.

lanyard ['lænjəd], *s*. 1. *Nau:* Aiguillette *f*; ride *f* (de hauban); (*of knife, etc.*) corde *f*. 2. *Artil:* (Cordon *m*) tire-feu *m inv.*

lap¹ [læp], *s*. 1. *A:* Pan *m*, basque *f* (d'un vêtement). 2. Genoux *mpl*; giron *m*. To sit in, on, s.o.'s lap, s'asseoir sur les genoux de qn. It is in the lap of the gods, Dieu seul le sait. *S.a.* LUXURY. 'lap-dog, *s*. Chien *m* de salon, d'appartement, de manchon.

lap², *s*. 1. *Const:* Chevauchement *m*, recouvrement *m* (des ardoises, etc.). 2. *El:* Guipage *m* (de coton); couche isolante. 3. (*a*) Tour *m* (d'une corde autour d'un cylindre, etc.). (*b*) *Sp:* Tour (d'une piste); boucle *f*, circuit *m*; étape *f*. To cover a lap in six minutes, boucler le circuit en six minutes. 'lap-joint¹, *s*. 1. *Carp: etc:* Assemblage *m* à recouvrement. 2. *Metalw:* Ourlet *m*. 'lap-joint², *v.tr.* 1. (*a*) Assembler (des planches) à clin. (*b*) Assembler (des poutres) (i) à mi-fer, (ii) à mi-bois. 2. Ourler (une tôle). 'lap-jointed, *a*. A recouvrement, à clin.

lap³, *v*. (lapped [læpt]) 1. *v.tr.* (*a*) To lap sth. round sth., enrouler qch. autour de qch. (*b*) *Const:* Enchevaucher (des planches). (*c*) *El.E:* Guiper (un câble, etc.). 2. *v.i.* To lap over sth., retomber, se rabattre, sur qch.; dépasser, chevaucher, qch. lapped, *a*. 1. *Carp: Mec.E: etc:* (Joint) à recouvrement. L. tiles, tuiles chevauchées. 2. *El.E:* Single-l. wire, double-l. wire, fil à guipage simple, double. lapping, *s*. 1. Recouvrement *m*, chevauchement *m*. 2. *El:* (i) Guipage *m*, (ii) guipure *f* (d'un câble, etc.).

lap⁴, *s*. 1. Gorgée *f* (de lait, etc.). 2. Clapotement *m*, clapotis *m* (de vagues).

lap⁵. 1. *v.tr.* (*Of animal*) To lap (up) milk, laper du lait. *F:* He laps up everything you tell him, il avale, gobe, tout ce qu'on lui dit. 2. *v.i.* (*Of waves*) Clapoter.

laparotomy [ˌlæpəˈrɔtəmi], *s. Surg:* Laparotomie *f.*
lapel [ləˈpel], *s. Tail:* Revers *m* (d'un habit).
lapelled [ləˈpeld], *a. Tail:* A revers.
lapidate [ˈlæpideit], *v.tr.* Lapider.
lapidation [ˌlæpiˈdeiʃ(ə)n], *s.* Lapidation *f.*
lapis lazuli [ˈlæpisˈlæzjulai], *s. Miner:* Lazulite *m*; lapis(-lazuli) *m inv.*
Lapland [ˈlæplænd]. *Pr.n.* La Laponie.
Laplander [ˈlæplændər], *s.* Lapon, -one.
Lapp [læp]. **1.** *a. & s.* Lapon, -one. **2.** *s. Ling:* Le lapon.
lapse[1] [læps], *s.* **1.** (*a*) (*Mistake*) Erreur *f,* faute *f.* **L. of the tongue,** lapsus *m* linguæ. **Lapse of memory,** défaillance *f,* lapsus, de mémoire. (*b*) Faute; faux pas; écart *m* de conduite. **L. from one's duty,** manquement *m* à son devoir. **2.** *Jur:* Déchéance *f* (d'un droit). **3.** Cours *m,* marche *f* (du temps); laps *m* de temps. **After a l. of three months,** après un délai de trois mois; au bout de trois mois.
lapse[2], *v.i.* **1.** (*a*) **To l. from duty,** manquer au devoir; s'écarter de son devoir. **To l. (back) into idleness,** (re)tomber dans la paresse. **To l. into obscurity,** rentrer dans l'ombre. (*b*) *Abs.* Manquer à ses devoirs; être coupable d'un écart de conduite; faire un faux pas. **2.** *Jur:* (*Of right, of law, etc.*) (Se) périmer; tomber en désuétude; cesser d'être en vigueur. (*Of right, estate, etc.*) **To l. to s.o.,** passer à qn. **lapsed,** *a.* **1.** Déchu. **L. catholic,** catholique (i) déchu; (ii) non pratiquant. **2.** (Billet) périmé. *Jur:* (Droit) périmé; (legs) tombé en dévolu; (contrat) caduc, *f.* caduque.
lapwing [ˈlæpwiŋ], *s. Orn:* Vanneau *m.*
lar, *pl.* **lares** [lɑːr, ˈlɛəriːz], *s. Rom.Ant:* Lare *m. Esp. pl.* Dieux lares.
larboard [ˈlɑːbəd], *s. Nau: A:* = PORT[3].
larceny [ˈlɑːsəni], *s.* Larcin *m. Jur:* **Petty l.,** vol simple.
larch [lɑːtʃ], *s. Bot:* Mélèze *m.* **L.-wood,** (bois *m* de) mélèze.
lard[1] [lɑːd], *s.* (*a*) Saindoux *m*; graisse *f* de porc; panne *f.* (*b*) *Pharm: Ind:* Axonge *f.*
lard[2], *v.tr. Cu:* Larder, piquer (la viande). **Larding-needle, -pin,** lardoire *f.* *F:* **To l. one's writings with quotations,** larder, entre-larder, ses écrits de citations.
larder [ˈlɑːdər], *s.* Garde-manger *m inv.*; placard *m* aux provisions.
large [lɑːdʒ]. **I.** *a.* (*a*) De grandes dimensions; grand; gros, fort. **L. book, parcel,** gros livre; gros paquet; paquet volumineux. **The largest room,** la pièce la plus vaste. **To grow l., larger,** grossir, grandir. **As l. as life,** (*of statue, etc.*) grandeur nature. *F:* **He turned up the next day as l. as life,** il reparut le lendemain comme si de rien n'était. (*b*) **A l. sum,** une grosse, forte, somme; une somme considérable. **L. fortune,** grande, belle, fortune. **L. family,** famille nombreuse. **L. meal,** repas copieux. **In a l. measure,** en grande partie. **Criminal on a l. scale,** criminel de grande envergure. **L. scale business,** grosse entreprise. **To do things on a l. scale,** faire les choses en grand. **-ly,** *adv.* **1.** En grande partie; pour une grande part. **They come very l. from round about Birmingham,** ils viennent pour la plupart des environs de Birmingham. **2.** **That is l. sufficient,** cela suffit grandement. **II. large,** *adv. Nau:* **To sail l.,** courir largue; naviguer vent largue. *S.a.* BY II. 1. **III. large,** *s.* (*a*) **To set a prisoner at l.,** élargir, relaxer, un prisonnier. **To be at l.,** être libre, en liberté. (*b*) **Society, the people, at l.,** le grand public. **'large-'hearted,** *a.* **1.** Magnanime. **2.** Généreux. **'large-'heartedness,** *s.* **1.** Magnanimité *f.* **2.** Générosité *f.* **'large-'sized,** *a.* De grandes dimensions; (livre) de grand format.
largeness [ˈlɑːdʒnis], *s.* (*a*) Grosseur *f* (du corps). (*b*) Importance *f* (d'une majorité); ampleur *f* (d'un repas).
largess(e) [ˈlɑːdʒes], *s. A. & Lit:* Largesse *f.*
lariat [ˈlæriət], *s.* **1.** Corde *f* à piquet. **2.** Lasso *m.*
lark[1] [lɑːk], *s. Orn:* Alouette *f.* **To rise with the l.,** se lever au chant du coq. **She sings like a l.,** elle chante comme un rossignol.
lark[2], *s. F:* Farce *f,* rigolade *f,* blague *f.* **To do sth. for a l.,** faire qch. pour rire, histoire de rigoler.
lark[3], *v.i. F:* Faire des farces; folichonner, rigoler.
larkspur [ˈlɑːkspəːr], *s. Bot:* Pied-d'alouette *m.*

larrikin [ˈlærikin], *s. F:* (*In Austr.*) Gavroche *m*; gamin *m* (des rues).
larva, *pl.* **-vae** [ˈlɑːvə, -viː], *s.* Larve *f.*
larval [ˈlɑːv(ə)l], *a.* **1.** *Ent:* Larvaire. **2.** (*Of disease*) Latent, larvé.
laryngeal [ˌlærinˈdʒiəl], *a.* **1.** (Muscle, nerf) laryngé. **2. L. cavity,** cavité laryngienne.
laryngectomy [ˌlærinˈdʒektəmi], *s. Med:* Laryngectomie *f.*
laryngitis [ˌlærinˈdʒaitis], *s. Med:* Laryngite *f.*
laryngologist [ˌlærinˈgɔlədʒist], *s. Med:* Laryngologue *mf,* laryngologiste *mf.*
laryngology [ˌlærinˈgɔlədʒi], *s. Med:* Laryngologie *f.*
laryngoscope [ləˈriŋgəskoup], *s. Med:* Laryngoscope *m.*
larynx [ˈlæriŋks], *s. Anat:* Larynx *m.*
lascar [ˈlæskər], *s.* Lascar *m.*
laser [leizər], *s. Ph:* Laser *m.*
lascivious [ləˈsiviəs], *a.* Lascif, -ive. **-ly,** *adv.* Lascivement.
lasciviousness [ləˈsiviəsnis], *s.* Lasciveté *f.*
lash[1] [læʃ], *s.* **1.** (*a*) Coup *m* de fouet; cinglon *m.* (*b*) Lanière *f* (de fouet). (*c*) (The penalty of) the l.,** le supplice du fouet. **To be under the l. of criticism,** être exposé aux coups de la critique; être flagellé par la critique. **2.** *Mec.E:* Jeu *m.* **Side l.,** jeu latéral. *S.a.* BACK-LASH. = EYELASH.
lash[2], *v.tr. & i.* **1.** (*a*) Fouailler, cingler (un cheval, etc.). (*Of rain*) **To l. (against) the windows, the face,** fouetter les vitres, cingler le visage. *F:* **To l. oneself into a fury,** entrer dans une violente colère. (*b*) (*Of animal*) **To l. its tail,** se battre les flancs avec la queue. **2.** *v.i. Mec.E:* (*Of running part*) Fouetter. **lash out,** *v.i.* **1.** (*Of horse*) Ruer. (*Of pers.*) **To l. out at s.o.,** (i) lâcher un coup (de poing, etc.) à qn; (ii) invectiver qn. **2.** (*a*) Décocher un coup de fouet (à un cheval). (*b*) **To l. out into expenditure,** se livrer à de folles dépenses. **lashing**[1], *a.* (*Of rain*) Cinglant; (*of criticism*) acéré, cinglant. **lashing**[2], *s.* **1.** (*a*) Coups *mpl* de fouet; le fouet. (*b*) Fouettée *f.* (*c*) *Mec.E:* Fouettement *m.* **2.** *pl. F:* **Lashings,** des tas *mpl* (of, de).
lash[3], *v.tr.* Lier, attacher; *Nau:* amarrer; saisir (l'ancre). **To l. down the load on a trailer,** lier, brider, bréler, la charge sur une remorque. *Nau:* **To l. a pulley,** aiguilleter une poulie. **lashing**[3], *s. Nau:* **1.** Amarrage *m,* aiguilletage *m.* **2.** Amarre *f*; point *m* d'amarrage; aiguillette *f.*
lass [læs], *s.f.* **lassie** [ˈlæsi], *s.f. Esp. Scot:* Jeune fille; bonne amie.
lassitude [ˈlæsitjuːd], *s.* Lassitude *f.*
lasso[1] [læˈsuː], *s.* Lasso *m.*
lasso[2], *v.tr.* Prendre au lasso.
last[1] [lɑːst], *s. Bootm:* Forme *f* (à chaussure). *Prov:* Let the shoemaker stick to his l., à chacun son métier.
last[2]. **I.** *a.* Dernier. **1.** (*a*) **The l. two, the two l.,** les deux derniers. **She was the l. to arrive,** elle arriva la dernière. **The l. but one, the next to l.,** l'avant-dernier. **I should be the l. to believe it,** je serais le dernier à le croire. **L. but not least,** enfin et surtout. **That's the l. thing that's worrying me,** c'est le dernier, le cadet de mes soucis. **In the l. resort, as a l. resource,** en dernier ressort; en désespoir de cause. **To have the l. word,** avoir le dernier mot. **He has said the l. word on the matter,** il a dit le mot final là-dessus. *F:* **The l. word in hats,** chapeau dernier cri. **L. thing at night,** tard dans la soirée. *v. U.S:* **The l. of the week, month, year, etc.,** le dernier jour, la fin, de la semaine, du mois, de l'année, etc. (*b*) **A matter of the l. importance,** une affaire de la plus haute importance, de la dernière importance. **2. L. Tuesday, Tuesday l.,** mardi dernier. **L. week,** la semaine dernière; la semaine passée. **L. evening, here (au) soir. L. night,** (i) la nuit dernière; (ii) hier soir. **I saw him the night before l.,** je l'ai vu avant-hier (au) soir. **It rained the night before l.,** avant-hier il a plu pendant la nuit. **I have not seen him for the l. four days,** il y a quatre jours que je ne l'ai vu. **In the l. fifty years,** dans les cinquante ans qui viennent de s'écouler. **This day l. week,** il y a aujourd'hui huit jours. **This day l. year,** l'an dernier à pareil jour. **-ly,** *adv.* Pour finir . . .; en dernier lieu. **II. last. 1. This l.,** ce dernier, cette dernière. **2.** (*a*) **We shall never hear the l. of it,** on ne nous le laissera pas oublier. **We haven't heard the l. of it,** tout n'est pas dit. **That is the l. I saw of him,** je

ne l'ai pas revu depuis. **This is the l. of it,** c'est la fin. (*b*) **To, till, the l.,** jusqu'au bout, jusqu'à la fin, jusqu'au dernier moment. *S.a.* FIRST II. 2. (*c*) **At l., at long l.,** enfin; à la fin (des fins). (*d*) **To look one's l. on sth.,** jeter un dernier regard sur qch.; voir qch. pour la dernière fois. (*e*) **To be near one's l.,** toucher à sa fin. III. **last,** *adv.* (*a*) **When I saw him l.,** la dernière fois que je l'ai vu. **When did you eat l.,** quand avez-vous pris votre dernier repas? (*b*) **He spoke, came, l.,** il a parlé, est arrivé, le dernier. **'last-'ditcher,** *s. Pol:* Jusqu'au-boutiste *mf.*

last³. 1. *v.i.* Durer, se maintenir. **It's too good to l.,** c'est trop beau pour durer. **How long does your leave l.?** quelle est la durée de votre congé? **The supplies will not l. (out) two months,** les vivres ne feront pas deux mois. **Material that will not l. long,** tissu qui ne tiendra pas. **Dress which will l. me two years,** robe qui me fera deux ans. **It will l. me a lifetime,** j'en ai pour la vie. *F:* **He won't l. (out) long,** il n'ira pas loin, il ne fera pas long feu. **2.** *v.tr.* **To l. s.o. out,** (*of pers.*) survivre à qn; (ii) (*of thg*) durer autant que qn. **My overcoat will l. the winter out,** mon pardessus fera encore l'hiver. **lasting,** *a.* Durable; (*of material, etc.*) résistant, de bon usage. **L. peace,** paix durable.

Lastex ['læsteks], *s. R.t.m.* Lastex *m.*

latch¹ [lætʃ], *s.* (*a*) Loquet *m*, clenche *f.* (*b*) Serrure *f* de sûreté. **To leave the door on the l.,** fermer la porte au loquet. **'latch-key,** *s.* Clef *f* de maison.

latch², *v.tr.* Fermer (la porte) au loquet.

latchet ['lætʃit], *s. A:* Cordon *m* (de soulier).

late [leit]. **I.** *a.* (later; latest; *see also* LATTER *and* LAST²) **1.** (*a*) En retard. **To be l. (for sth.),** être en retard (pour qch.); se faire attendre. **I don't want to make you l.,** je ne veux pas vous mettre en retard. **The train is l.,** is ten minutes l., le train a du retard, a dix minutes de retard. (*b*) (*Delayed*) Retardé. **2.** (*a*) Tard. **It is getting l.,** il se fait tard. **I was too l.,** je ne suis pas arrivé à temps. **It is l. in the day to change your mind,** il est un peu tard pour changer d'avis. **I was l. (in) going to bed,** je me suis couché tard. **At a l. hour (in the day),** très avant, fort avant, dans la journée. **A l. party,** une réunion qui commence ou qui finit tard. **In the l. afternoon,** tard dans l'après-midi. **In the l. summer, in l. autumn,** vers la fin de l'été, de l'automne. **Later events proved that . . .,** la suite des événements a démontré que. . . . **At a later meeting,** dans une séance ultérieure. **In later life,** plus tard dans la vie. **Later generations,** les générations futures, la postérité. **What is the latest you can come?** à quel moment pouvez-vous venir au plus tard? **The latest I can come,** le plus tard que je puisse venir. **It is twelve o'clock at (the) latest,** c'est tout au plus s'il est midi. *Com:* **Latest date,** date *f* limite, délai *m* de rigueur; *Jur:* terme fatal. (*b*) **In the l. eighties,** dans les années approchant 1890. **3.** (Fruit, etc.) tardif, -ive. **L. frosts,** gelées tardives, printanières. **4.** (*a*) Ancien, -ienne, ex-. **The l. minister,** l'ancien ministre, l'ex-ministre. (*b*) **My l. father,** feu mon père, mon père décédé. **The l. queen,** feu la reine, la feue reine. *Com:* **Smith l. Jones,** Smith successeur de Jones. **5.** Récent, dernier. **Of l. years,** (dans) ces dernières années; depuis quelques années. **Of l.,** dernièrement; depuis peu. **This author's latest work,** le dernier ouvrage de cet auteur. **Latest novelties,** dernières nouveautés. *Journ:* **Latest intelligence, latest news,** informations *fpl* de la dernière heure; dernières nouvelles. **That is the latest,** (i) c'est ce qu'il y a de plus nouveau; (ii) *F:* ça c'est le comble! **X's latest,** (i) la dernière plaisanterie de X; (ii) le dernier exploit de X; (iii) la dernière conquête de X. **-ly,** *adv.* Dernièrement, récemment; il y a peu de temps; depuis peu. **Till l.,** jusqu'à ces derniers temps. **As l. as yesterday,** hier encore; pas plus tard qu'hier. **II. late,** *adv.* (later; latest; *see also* LAST²) **1.** En retard. **To arrive too l.,** arriver trop tard. *Prov:* **Better l. than never,** mieux vaut tard que jamais. **2.** Tard. **Early and l.,** à toute heure du jour; du matin au soir. **Early or l., sooner or late,** tôt ou tard. **To keep s.o. l.,** attarder qn. **Very l. at night,** bien avant, fort avant, dans la nuit. **L. into the night,** jusqu'à une heure avancée de la nuit. **L. in the afternoon,** vers la fin de l'après-midi.

L. in life, à un âge avancé, sur le tard. **As l. as yesterday,** no later than yesterday, hier encore; pas plus tard qu'hier. **A moment later,** l'instant d'après. **This happened later (on),** cela est arrivé après, plus tard. **A few days later,** à quelques jours de là. *F:* **See you later!** à plus tard! à tout à l'heure! **3.** (*Formerly*) **L. of London,** dernièrement domicilié, établi, à Londres. **'late-comer,** *s.* Retardataire *mf.*

lateen [lə ti:n], *a. Nau:* **L. sail,** voile latine. **L. yard,** antenne *f.*

lateness ['leitnis], *s.* **1.** Arrivée tardive (de qn); tardiveté *f* (d'un fruit). **2.** **The l. of the hour,** l'heure avancée.

latent ['leit(ə)nt], *a.* Latent; caché. *Ph:* **L. heat,** chaleur latente.

lateral ['læt(ə)rəl], *a.* Latéral, -aux. **-ally,** *adv.* Latéralement.

laterite ['lætərait], *s. Geol:* Latérite *f.*

latex ['leiteks], *s. Bot:* Latex *m.*

lath¹ [lɑ:θ, *pl.* lɑ:ðz], *s.* **1.** *Const:* (*a*) Latte *f.* **L. and plaster partition,** cloison lattée et plâtrée. (*b*) **Slate-l.,** volige *f.* **2.** (*Of Venetian blind*) Lame *f.* **3.** Batte *f*, latte (d'Arlequin).

lath², *v.tr.* (*a*) Latter (une cloison). (*b*) Voliger (un toit).

lathe [leið], *s. Tls:* Tour *m.* **1.** Treadle l., tour à pédale. **Power l.,** tour mécanique. **Bench l.,** tour à banc. **Gap l.,** tour à banc rompu. **Screw-cutting l.,** tour à fileter, à décolleter. **Capstan l., turret l.,** tour (à) revolver. **Polishing l.,** touret *m* à polir. **Made on the l.,** fait au tour. **2.** **Potter's l.,** tour de potier. **'lathe-bed,** *s.* Banc *m* de tour; bâti *m* de tour. **'lathe-'centre,** *s.* Pointe *f* (de tour). **lathe-'head,** *s.* Poupée *f.* **'lathe-turned,** *a.* Fait au tour; tourné.

lather¹ ['læðər], *s.* **1.** Mousse *f* de savon. **2.** (*On horse*) Écume *f.* **Horse all in a l.,** cheval couvert d'écume.

lather². 1. *v.tr.* (*a*) Savonner. (*b*) *F:* Rosser (qn). **2.** *v.i.* (*a*) (*Of soap*) Mousser. (*b*) (*Of horse*) Jeter de l'écume. **lathering,** *s.* **1.** Savonnage *m.* **2.** *F:* Rossée *f.*

Latin ['lætin]. **1.** *a. & s.* Latin, -ine. **2.** (*a*) *s. Ling:* Le latin. **Low, vulgar, L.,** bas latin. **Classical L.,** latin classique. **Late L.,** latin de la décadence. (*b*) *a.Typ:* **L. characters,** lettres romaines. *S.a.* DOG-LATIN.

Latinist ['lætinist], *s.* Latiniste *mf.*

latish ['leitiʃ], *a. & adv.* (*a*) Un peu en retard. (*b*) Un peu tard. **At a l. hour,** à une heure assez avancée; sur le tard.

latitude ['lætitju:d], *s.* **1.** **To allow s.o. the greatest l.,** laisser à qn la plus grande latitude, la plus grande liberté d'action. **2.** *Geog: Nau:* Latitude *f.* **In the l. of . . .,** sous, par, la latitude de. . . . **In l. 30° north,** par 30° (de) latitude nord. **In these latitudes,** sous ces latitudes.

latrines [lə'tri:nz], *s.pl.* Latrines *f.*

latter ['lætər], *a.* **1.** Dernier (des deux). **The l.,** ce, le, dernier; celui-ci, ceux-ci. **2.** **The l. half of June,** la seconde quinzaine de juin. **L. end,** (i) fin *f* (d'une époque); (ii) mort *f*, fin (de qn). **-ly,** *adv.* **1.** (*a*) Dans les derniers temps. (*b*) Dans la suite. **2.** = LATELY. **'latter-day,** *attrib.a.* Récent, moderne, d'aujourd'hui. **L.-d. saints,** Mormons *mpl.*

lattice¹ ['lætis], *s.* Treillis *m*, treillage *m.* **L. frame, l. girder,** poutre *f* en treillis, à croisillons. **L. mast,** (i) pylône *m* métallique; (ii) *Navy:* Mât-treillis. **'lattice-'window,** *s.* **1.** Fenêtre treillagée. **2.** Fenêtre *f* à losanges. **'lattice-work,** *s.* Treillage *m*, treillis *m*; (*metal*) grillage *m.*

lattice², *v.tr.* Treillager, treillisser.

Latvia ['lætviə]. *Pr.n.* La Lettonie.

Latvian ['lætviən], *a. & s.* **1.** *Geog:* Letton, -one. **2.** *s. Ling:* Le lette.

laud [lɔ:d], *v.tr.* Louer; chanter les louanges de (qn).

laudable ['lɔ:dəbl], *a.* Louable; digne d'éloges. **-ably,** *adv.* Louablement.

laudanum ['lɔd(ə)nəm], *s.* Laudanum *m.*

laudatory ['lɔ:dət(ə)ri], *a.* Élogieux, -euse; louangeur, -euse.

laugh¹ [lɑ:f], *s.* Rire *m.* **To burst into a l.,** éclater de rire. **To force a l.,** to give a forced l., rire du bout des dents; rire jaune. **With a l.,** en riant. **To raise a l.,** faire rire. **To raise a general l.,** provoquer l'hilarité générale. **To have the l. of s.o.,** mettre les rieurs de son côté. **To have the l. on one's side,** avoir les rieurs de son côté. **To do sth. for a l.,** faire qch. histoire de rire.

laugh². **1.** *v.i.* Rire. (*a*) To l. heartily, rire de bon cœur. To l. immoderately, uproariously, rire à gorge déployée. To l. till one cries, rire (jusqu')aux larmes. To l. to oneself, rire tout seul; rire tout bas. To l. up one's sleeve, rire sous cape, en dedans. To l. in s.o.'s face, rire au nez de qn. *F:* I soon made him l. on the wrong side of his face, je lui ai bientôt fait passer son envie de rire. (*b*) To l. at, over, sth., rire de qch. There is nothing to l. at, il n'y a pas de quoi rire. To l. at s.o., se moquer, (se) rire, de qn. I'm afraid of being laughed at, j'ai peur qu'on se moque de moi. *F:* Don't make me l.! laisse(z)-moi rire! **2.** *v.tr.* (*a*) *With cogn.acc.* He laughed a bitter l., il eut un rire amer. (*b*) We laughed him out of it, nous nous sommes tellement moqués de lui qu'il y a renoncé. To l. down a proposal, tuer une proposition par le ridicule. To l. s.o. out of court, se moquer des prétentions de qn. To l. s.o. to scorn, accabler qn de ridicule. He laughed the matter off, il tourna la chose en plaisanterie. **laughing¹**, *a.* Riant; rieur. **-ly**, *adv.* En riant. **laughing²**, *s.* Rires *mpl.* I'm in no l. mood, je n'ai pas le cœur à rire. It is no l. matter, il n'y a pas de quoi rire. **'laughing gas**, *s.* Gaz hilarant. **'laughing-stock**, *s.* Risée *f.* To make a l.-s. of oneself, se faire moquer de soi.

laughable ['lɑ:fəbl], *a.* Risible, ridicule. L. offer, offre dérisoire. **-ably**, *adv.* Risiblement.

laugher ['lɑ:fər], *s.* Rieur, -euse.

laughter ['lɑ:ftər], *s.* Rire(s) *m(pl).* He made us cry with l., il nous a fait rire aux larmes. To be convulsed, to shake, with l., se tordre de rire; se tenir les côtes de rire. To roar with l., rire aux éclats; rire à gorge déployée. Uncontrollable fit of l., (accès *m* de) fou rire. *F:* To split, die, with l., crever de rire.

launch¹ [lɔ:ntʃ], *s.* Chaloupe *f.* Motor l., canot *m* automobile; vedette *f* à moteur.

launch², *s.* = LAUNCHING 1.

launch³. **1.** *v.tr.* (*a*) Lancer (un projectile, un coup). (*b*) *Nau:* Lancer (un navire); mettre (une embarcation) à l'eau, à la mer. To l. a torpedo, lancer une torpille. (*c*) Lancer (qn, une affaire). *Mil:* To l. an offensive, déclencher une offensive. **2.** *v.i.* (*a*) To l. out at, against, s.o., (i) lancer un coup à qn; (ii) faire une sortie à, contre, qn. (*b*) To l. out, mettre à la mer. To l. out, forth, on an enterprise, se lancer dans une affaire. Once he is launched on this subject . . ., une fois lancé sur ce sujet. . . . To l. out (into expense), se lancer dans la dépense; se mettre en frais. **launching**, *s.* **1.** *Nau:* Lancement *m*, mise *f* à l'eau (d'un navire). **2.** Lancement (d'une affaire). **3.** Lancement (d'une fusée). L. pad, aire *f* de lancement. L. silo, puits *m* de lancement.

launder ['lɔ:ndər], *v.tr.* Blanchir (le linge). **laundering**, *s.* Blanchissage *m.*

launderer ['lɔ:ndərər], *s.* Blanchisseur *m.*

launderette ['lɔ:ndərɛt], *s.* Blanchisserie *f*, laverie *f*, automatique.

laundress ['lɔ:ndris], *s.f.* Blanchisseuse.

laundry ['lɔ:ndri], *s.* **1.** L.(-works), blanchisserie *f.* **2.** Linge blanchi ou à blanchir. L. list, liste *f* de blanchissage.

laureate ['lɔ:riit], *a. & s.* Lauréat, -ate. Poet l., poète lauréat.

laurel ['lɔrəl], *s.* *Bot:* Laurier *m.* Noble l., laurier commun. Crowned with laurel(s), couronné, ceint, de lauriers. To rest on one's laurels, se reposer sur ses lauriers.

Laurentian [lɔ:'renʃ(ə)n], *a.* *Geog:* Laurentien, -ienne. The L. Shield, le bouclier canadien.

lava ['lɑ:və], *s.* Lave *f.* Cellular l., scories *f* volcaniques. L. flow, coulée *f* de lave, nappe éruptive.

lavatory ['lævətri], *s.* **1.** Cabinet *m* de toilette; lavabo *m.* **2.** Water-closet *m*, cabinets *mpl*; (*on train*) toilette *f.* Public lavatories, W.C. publics, lieux payants.

lave [leiv], *v.tr.* **1.** *Lit:* Laver (les mains, etc.); (*of stream*) baigner, laver (un pré). **2.** *Med:* Bassiner (une plaie).

lavender ['lævindər]. **1.** *s.* Lavande *f.* French l., spike l., lavande commune, mâle; *F:* aspic *m*, spic *m.* Sea l., statice *m.* **2.** *a.* (*Colour*) Lavande *inv.* **'lavender-water**, *s.* Eau *f* de lavande.

lavish¹ ['læviʃ], *a.* **1.** Prodigue (in, of, de). To be l. in, of, praise, prodiguer des louanges; se prodiguer en éloges. **2.** Somptueux; abondant. L. meal, repas plantureux. L. expenditure, dépenses folles. **-ly**, *adv.* Avec prodigalité. To spend l., dépenser de l'argent à profusion, à pleine(s) main(s).

lavish², *v.tr.* Prodiguer, répandre (son argent). To l. sth. on s.o., prodiguer qch. à qn.

lavishness ['læviʃnis], *s.* Prodigalité *f.*

law [lɔ:], *s.* **1.** Loi *f.* Outline l., loi-cadre *f.* The laws in force, la législation en vigueur. L. of nature, loi de la nature. **2.** The l., la loi. To keep the l., observer la loi. To break the law(s), enfreindre la loi, les lois. As the l. at present stands, en l'état actuel de la législation. His word is l., sa parole fait loi. To lay down the l., faire la loi (to s.o., à qn). He thinks he's above the l., il se croit tout permis. To be a l. unto oneself, n'en faire qu'à sa tête. **3.** Droit *m.* Civil l., le droit civil. Common l., (i) le droit commun; (ii) le droit civil. Criminal l., le droit criminel, pénal. Commercial l., mercantile l., le droit commercial; le code de commerce. L. of Contract = droit des obligations. To read, study, l., étudier le droit; faire son droit. To practise l., exercer une profession juridique. L. student, étudiant en droit. Doctor of Laws, docteur en droit. **4.** Court of l., cour *f* de justice; tribunal *m*, -aux. To go to l., avoir recours à la justice. *F:* aller en justice. To settle a matter without going to l., arranger une affaire à l'amiable. To go to l. with s.o., *P:* to have the l. on s.o., citer, poursuivre, qn en justice. To come under the l., tomber sous le coup de la loi. Action at l., action *f* en justice. To be at l., être en procès. To take the l. into one's own hands, se faire justice (à soi-même). *Adm:* L. department, service du contentieux, le contentieux. **'law-abiding**, *a.* Respectueux des lois; ami de l'ordre. **'law-breaker**, *s.* Transgresseur *m*, violateur *m*, de la loi. **'law-lord**, *s.m.* *Pol:* Membre juriste de la Chambre des Lords.

lawful ['lɔ:f(u)l], *a.* **1.** Légal, -aux. Permis, licite; loisible. **2.** (Droit, enfant) légitime; (contrat) valide. L. currency, cours légal. **3.** (Revendication, etc.) juste. **-fully**, *adv.* Légalement, légitimement.

lawgiver ['lɔ:givər], *s.* Législateur *m.*

lawless ['lɔ:lis], *a.* **1.** Sans loi; (temps) d'anarchie. **2.** Déréglé, désordonné.

lawlessness ['lɔ:lisnis], *s.* Dérèglement *m*, désordre *m*, anarchie *f.*

lawn¹ [lɔ:n], *s.* *Tex:* Batiste *f*; (*fine*) linon *m.*

lawn², *s.* Pelouse *f*; (parterre *m* de) gazon *m.* **'lawn-mower**, *s.* Tondeuse *f* (de gazon). **'lawn-'tennis**, *s.* *See* TENNIS 1.

Lawrence ['lɔrəns]. *Pr.n.m.* Laurent. *Geog:* The (River) St. L., le (fleuve) Saint-Laurent. The St. L. Seaway, la voie maritime du Saint Laurent.

lawsuit ['lɔ:sju:t], *s.* Procès *m*; *F:* affaire *f.* To bring a l. against s.o., intenter un procès à qn.

lawyer ['lɔ:jər], *s.* **1.** Homme *m* de loi; juriste *m*; jurisconsulte *m.* Common-l., jurisconsulte en droit coutumier. **2.** = (i) SOLICITOR, (ii) BARRISTER.

lax [læks], *a.* **1.** (*a*) (*Of conduct*) Relâché; (*of pers.*) négligent, inexact; (gouvernement) mou. L. morals, morale *f* facile. L. conscience, *F:* conscience *f* élastique. To be l. in (carrying out) one's duties, être inexact à remplir ses devoirs. L. attendance, irrégularité *f* de présence. To become l., se relâcher. (*b*) Vague; peu exact. L. use of a word, emploi peu précis d'un mot. **2.** (*Limp*) Mou, *f.* molle; flasque. **3.** *Med:* (Ventre) lâche, relâché.

laxative ['læksətiv], *a. & s.* Laxatif (*m*).

laxity ['læksiti], *s.* (*a*) Relâchement *m* (des mœurs); inexactitude *f* à remplir ses devoirs. (*b*) Vague *m*, imprécision *f* (de langage, etc.).

lay¹ [lei], *s.* **1.** Lai *m*, chanson *f.* **2.** Poème *m* (lyrique); chant *m.*

lay², *a.* Laïque, lai. (*a*) *Ecc:* L. brother, frère lai, frère convers. L. sister, sœur converse. L. clerk, chantre *m.* (*b*) To the l. mind . . ., aux yeux du profane. . . .

lay³, *s.* **1.** Commettage *m* (d'un cordage). **2.** L. of the land, configuration *f* du terrain. **3.** *Typ:* To mark the l. on a page, repérer une page. L.-mark, repère *m.*

lay⁴, *v.tr.* (**laid** [leid]; **laid**) **1.** Coucher. (*a*) To l. s.o. low, flat, (i) coucher, étendre, qn (par terre); (ii) terrasser, abattre, qn. To l. low an empire, mettre à bas un empire. (*b*) (*Of wind*) Coucher, verser (le blé). **2.** (*a*) Abattre (la poussière, les vagues, etc.). (*b*) Exorciser, conjurer (un esprit). To l. s.o.'s fears, dissiper les craintes de qn. **3.** Mettre, placer, poser (**sth. on sth.,** qch. sur qch.). To l. one's hand on s.o.'s shoulder, mettre la main sur l'épaule de qn. To l. one's head on the pillow, mettre, poser, sa tête sur l'oreiller. To have nowhere to l. one's head, n'avoir pas où reposer la tête. To l. s.o. to rest, in the grave, mettre qn au tombeau. **4.** (*Of bird*) Pondre (un œuf). **5.** Faire (un pari); parier (une somme); mettre (un enjeu). To l. so much on a horse, mettre, parier, miser, tant sur un cheval. To l. that . . ., parier que. . . . **6.** (*a*) To l. a ship alongside (the quay), amener, accoster, un navire le long du quai. (*b*) *Artil:* Pointer (un canon). **7.** Soumettre (une demande). *Jur:* To l. a complaint, déposer une plainte; porter plainte. To l. a matter before the court, saisir le tribunal d'une affaire. To l. an information, présenter une information. *S.a.* CLAIM¹ 2. **8.** (*a*) Imposer (une peine, une charge) (**upon s.o.,** à qn); infliger (une amende, etc.). (*b*) To l. a tax on sth., mettre un impôt sur qch.; frapper qch. d'un impôt. (*c*) To l. a stick on s.o.'s back, *P:* to l. into s.o., taper ferme sur qn. To l. about one, frapper de tous côtés; frapper, taper, comme un sourd. **9.** (*a*) Poser, jeter, asseoir (des fondements); ranger (des briques); poser, immerger (un câble). To l. the table, the cloth, mettre, dresser, le couvert, mettre la table; mettre la nappe. To l. for three, mettre trois couverts. To l. a carpet, poser un tapis. To l. the fire, préparer le feu. *Navy:* To l. a mine, poser, mouiller, une mine. (*b*) Dresser, tendre (un piège, une embuscade). (*c*) Ourdir, tramer (un complot). To l. a scheme to do sth., combiner qch. (*d*) *Th:* The scene is laid in Paris, la scène se passe à Paris. (*e*) *Nav:* To l. the course, tracer, donner, la route. **10.** *Ropem:* Commettre (un cordage). **lay aside,** *v.tr.* Enlever, quitter (un vêtement); se dépouiller de (ses vêtements, ses préjugés); se départir de (sa fierté); abandonner, mettre de côté (un travail); écarter (un papier); épargner (de l'argent); déposer (la couronne). **lay away,** *v.tr.* Mettre (qch.) de côté; ranger, serrer (qch.). **lay by,** *v.tr.* Mettre (qch.) de côté; réserver (qch.). She had laid by a considerable sum, elle avait fait sa petite pelote. **'lay-by,** *s.* (*On road*) Garage *m,* refuge *m,* terre-plein *m* de stationnement. **lay down,** *v.tr.* **1.** (*a*) Déposer, poser (qch.). To l. down one's arms, mettre bas, rendre, les armes. *Cards:* To l. down one's hand, étaler, abattre, son jeu. (*b*) Coucher, étendre (qn). To l. oneself down, se coucher. (*c*) Quitter, se démettre de, résigner (ses fonctions). (*d*) To l. down one's life, donner, sacrifier, sa vie (**for,** pour). **2.** (*a*) To l. down a ship, mettre un navire en chantier. To l. down mains, a cable, poser une canalisation, un câble. (*b*) Poser, imposer, établir, instituer (un principe, une règle); fixer (des conditions); tracer, prescrire (une ligne de conduite). To l. it down (as a principle) that . . ., poser en principe que. . . . To l. down that . . ., stipuler que . . .; spécifier que. . . . To l. down conditions to s.o., imposer des conditions à qn. **3.** Mettre (du vin) en cave. **lay in,** *v.tr.* (*a*) Faire provision, s'approvisionner, de (qch.). (*b*) *Nau:* To l. in the oars, rentrer les avirons. **lay off,** *v.tr.* **1.** Licencier, congédier (des ouvriers). **2.** *Nau:* To l. off a bearing, porter un relèvement (sur la carte). **3.** *Turf: etc:* To l. off a bet, faire la contre-partie d'un pari. **4.** *v.i. U.S:* Se reposer; chômer. **lay on,** *v.tr.* **1.** Mettre (des impôts). **2.** Étendre, appliquer (un enduit). *F:* To l. it on thick, with a trowel, (i) flatter qn grossièrement; (ii) exagérer, y aller fort. **3.** (*a*) To l. on the lash, appliquer le fouet. (*b*) *Abs.* He laid on with a will, il frappait, il y allait, de bon cœur. **4.** (*a*) Installer (le gaz, l'électricité). Bedroom with water laid on, chambre avec eau courante. (*b*) *F:* Arranger, préparer, organiser. **lay out,** *v.tr.* **1.** Arranger, disposer (des objets); étaler, déployer (des marchandises). **2.** (*a*) Faire la toilette (d'un mort). (*b*) *F:* Étendre (qn) d'un coup; coucher (qn) par terre, sur le carreau.

Box: Envoyer au tapis. **3.** Dépenser, débourser (de l'argent). **4.** Dresser, tracer, aligner (un camp); dessiner, disposer (un jardin); tracer (une courbe); faire le tracé (d'une route). **5.** To l. oneself out to please, chercher à plaire; se mettre en frais pour plaire. **'lay-out,** *s.* Tracé *m* (d'une ville, etc.); dessin *m* (d'un jardin); disposition *f* typographique (d'une page, etc.); agencement *m* (d'une boîte de vitesses). **lay to. 1.** *v.tr.* *Nau:* Mettre (un navire) à la cape. **2.** *v.i.* (*Of ship*) Prendre la cape. **lay up,** *v.tr.* **1.** Mettre (qch.) en réserve; accumuler, amasser (des provisions, etc.). To l. up trouble for oneself, s'apprêter bien des ennuis. **2.** Désarmer (un navire). To l. up a car, remiser une voiture. **3.** To be laid up, être alité, au lit. **laid,** *a.* **1.** *Paperm:* Vergé. Cream-l. paper, vergé blanc. **2.** *Nau:* Cable-l. rope, cordage commis en grelin. **laying¹,** *a.* L. hen, poule pondeuse. **laying²,** *s.* **1.** Pose *f* (de rails, de tuyaux, de câbles, etc.); assise *f* (de fondements); commettage *m* (d'un cordage); mouillage *m* (d'une mine). **2.** Ponte *f* (des œufs). **3.** *Artil:* Pointage *m* (d'un canon). **'lay-days,** *s.pl.* *Com:* *Nau:* Jours *m* de planche, estarie *f.* **'lay-shaft,** *s.* *Mec.E:* *Aut:* Arbre *m* intermédiaire (de changement de vitesse); arbre de renvoi.

lay⁵. See LIE⁴.

layer¹ ['leiər], *s.* **1.** (*a*) Poseur *m* (de tuyaux, etc.); tendeur *m* (de pièges). (*b*) *Artil:* Pointeur *m.* **2.** (*Of hen*) Good l., bonne pondeuse. **3.** Couche *f* (de peinture, etc.); *Const:* assise *f,* lit *m* (de béton, etc.). **4.** *Hort:* Marcotte *f.*

layer², *v.tr.* (*a*) Poser, disposer, en couches. (*b*) *Hort:* Marcotter.

layette [lei'et], *s.* Layette *f.*

lay-figure ['leifigər], *s.* *Art:* Mannequin *m* (en bois, etc.).

layman, *pl.* **-men** ['leimən], *s.* **1.** *Ecc:* Laïque *m,* séculier *m.* **2.** Profane *m.*

lazaret(to) [,læzə'ret(ou)], *s.* *Nau:* Lazaret *m* (de quarantaine).

laze [leiz], *v.tr. & i.* To l. (about); to l. away one's time, paresser, fainéanter.

laziness ['leizinis], *s.* Paresse *f,* fainéantise *f.*

lazy ['leizi], *a.* **1.** Paresseux, fainéant, *F:* flemmard. **2.** L. moments, moments de paresse. *Nau:* L. guy, sheet, fausse écoute. **-ily,** *adv.* Paresseusement. **'lazy-bones,** *s.* Paresseux, -euse; fainéant, -ante, *F:* flemmard, -arde. **'lazy-tongs,** *s.pl.* *Tls:* Pince *f* à zigzags.

lea [li:], *s.* *Poet:* Prairie *f,* pâturage *m.*

leach [li:tʃ]. **1.** *v.tr.* Filtrer (un liquide). **2.** *v.i.* (*Of liquid*) Filtrer (**through,** à travers). **leaching,** *s.* (*a*) Filtration *f.* (*b*) Lessivage *m* (du sol).

lead¹ [led], *s.* **1.** Plomb *m.* (*a*) Sheet l., plomb laminé, en feuilles. *Sm.a:* L.-shot, grenaille *f* de plomb; petit plomb. (*b*) White l., blanc *m* de plomb; céruse *f.* Yellow l., massicot *m.* Red oxide of l., red l., minium *m.* *S.a.* BLACK-LEAD 1. (*c*) Window-leads, plombs de vitrail; plombure *f.* **2.** Mine *f* (de crayon). **3.** *Nau:* (Plomb de) sonde *f.* *F:* To swing the l., tirer au flanc. **4.** *Typ:* Interligne *f.* **'lead-poisoning,** *s.* Saturnisme *m.* **'lead-works,** *s.pl.* Fonderie *f* de plomb; plomberie *f.*

lead² [led], *v.tr.* (**leaded** ['ledid]; **leading** ['lediŋ]) (*a*) Plomber (un toit); couvrir, garnir, (un objet) de plomb. (*b*) *Fish:* Plomber, lester (une ligne, un filet). (*c*) *Typ:* Interligner (des lignes). To l. out matter, donner de l'air à, blanchir, la composition. **leading¹,** *s.* (*a*) Plombage *m.* (*b*) *Coll.* Plombs *mpl.* **leading out,** *s.* *Typ:* Interlignage *m.*

lead³ [li:d], *s.* **1.** Conduite *f* (action de conduire). (*a*) To follow s.o.'s l., se laisser conduire par qn; suivre l'exemple de qn. To give the l., montrer la voie (à suivre); *F:* donner le ton. To give s.o. a l., (i) amener qn (sur un sujet); (ii) mettre qn sur la voie. To take the l., (i) prendre la tête; (ii) prendre la direction. To take the l. of, over, s.o., prendre le pas, gagner les devants, sur qn. To have one minute's l. over s.o., avoir une minute d'avance sur qn. **2.** *Cards:* To have the l., jouer le premier; avoir la main. Your l.! à vous de jouer (le premier). To return a l., renvoyer de la couleur demandée; jouer dans la couleur de qn. **3.** *Th:* Premier rôle *m.* (*a*) Premier (rôle) de vedette *f.* To play juvenile leads, jouer les jeunes premiers, les jeunes premières. **4.** (*a*) *Mec.E:* Hauteur *f* du pas (d'une vis). (*b*) *Mch:* *I.C.E:* Avance *f* (du tiroir, de l'allumage, etc.). (c) *El.E:* (Angle of) l. of **brushes,** décalage *m* en avant, avance, des balais. **5.** (*For dog*) Laisse *f.* On a l., en laisse. **6.** *El.E:* Câble *m*, branchement *m*, de canalisation. **Battery l.,** connexion *f* de batterie.

lead⁴ [li:d], *v.* (led [led]; led) I. *v.tr.* **1.** (*a*) Mener, conduire, guider. **To l. s.o. into temptation,** induire qn en tentation. (*b*) **To l. the way, to l. the van,** montrer le chemin; marcher en tête; aller devant. **2.** Conduire, guider (un aveugle) par la main; mener (un cheval) par la bride; tenir (un chien) en laisse. **He is easily led,** il va comme on le mène. **To l. a woman to the altar,** conduire une femme à l'autel. **3.** Induire, porter, pousser (s.o. to do sth., qn à faire qch.). **That leads us to believe that . . .,** cela nous mène à croire que. . . . **I was led to the conclusion that . . .,** je fus amené à conclure que. . . . **4.** (*a*) Mener (une vie heureuse ou misérable). (*b*) **To l. s.o. a wretched life,** a dog's life, faire une vie d'enfer, une vie de chien, à qn. **5.** (*a*) Commander (une armée). (*b*) Diriger, mener. **To l. a movement,** être à la tête d'un mouvement. **6.** (*In race, etc.*) **To l. the field,** *Abs.* **to l.,** mener le champ; tenir la tête. **7.** *Cards:* **To l. clubs,** jouer, attaquer, trèfle. *Abs.* **To l.,** ouvrir le jeu; jouer le premier. *S.a.* SUIT⁴ 6. II. **lead,** *v.i.* **1.** (*Of road*) Mener, conduire (to, à). **Which street leads to the station?** quel est le chemin de la gare? **Door that leads to the garden,** porte qui donne accès au jardin. **2. To l. to a good result,** aboutir à un bon résultat; produire un heureux effet. **To l. to a discovery,** mener à une découverte. **Everything leads to the belief that . . .,** tout porte à croire que. . . . **This incident led to a breach,** cet incident amena une rupture. **To l. to nothing,** n'aboutir, ne mener, à rien. **lead away,** *v.tr.* **1.** Emmener. **2.** Entraîner, détourner (qn). *Esp. in passive.* **To be led away,** se laisser entraîner (from, de). **lead back,** *v.tr.* Ramener, reconduire. **lead in,** *v.tr.* **1.** Faire entrer, introduire (qn). **2.** *El.E:* Amener (le courant). **lead-'in,** *s.* (*a*) *W.Tel:* Tp: Fil d'entrée de poste. (*b*) *W.Tel:* Descente *f* d'antenne. **lead off. 1.** *v.tr.* Emmener, entraîner (qn). **2.** *v.i.* Commencer, débuter (with, par). **lead on,** *v.tr.* Conduire, entraîner (qn); montrer le chemin à (qn). **L. on!** en avant! **To l. s.o. on to talk,** encourager qn à parler. *F:* **To l. s.o. on,** (i) aider qn à s'enferrer; (ii) aguicher qn; entraîner qn. **lead out,** *v.tr.* Emmener, reconduire, faire sortir (qn); conduire (qch.) dehors. **lead up. 1.** *v.tr.* (*a*) Faire monter (qn); conduire (qn) en haut. (*b*) Amener, faire avancer (qn). **2.** *v.i.* (*a*) (*Of ladder, etc.*) Conduire, donner accès (au toit, etc.). (*b*) **To l. up to a subject,** amener un sujet. **leading,²** **1.** *v.tr.* *Jur:* **L. question,** question tendancieuse. **L. cases,** cas d'espèce qui font autorité. (*b*) *Mus:* **L. note,** note sensible. **2.** (*Chief*) Premier; principal, -aux. **A l. man,** un homme important; une notabilité. **The l. surgeon in Manchester,** le premier chirurgien de Manchester. **A l. shareholder,** un gros actionnaire. **L. idea,** idée dominante, directrice, maîtresse (d'une œuvre, etc.). *Journ:* **L. article** = LEADER 4. *Th:* **L. part,** premier rôle. **L. man, lady,** premier rôle; vedette *f.* **To play a l. part in a business,** jouer un rôle prépondérant dans une affaire. *Mus:* **L. violin,** premier violon. **3. L. car,** voiture de tête. *Navy:* **L. ship,** chef *m* de file. *Mil:* **L. wing,** aile marchante. **leading²,** *s.* **1.** Conduite *f* (de chevaux, etc.). *Harn:* **L.-rein,** longe *f.* **2.** (*a*) *Mil:* Commandement *m.* (*b*) Direction *f* (d'une entreprise, etc.). **'leading-strings,** *s.pl.* Lisières *f.* **To keep s.o. in l.-s.,** tenir, mener, qn en laisse.

leaden ['ledn], *a.* (Teint, ciel) de plomb. **L.-eyed,** aux yeux ternes. **L.-footed,** à la démarche pesante.

leader ['li:dər], *s.* **1.** (*a*) Conducteur, -trice; guide *m.* (*b*) Chef *m* (d'un parti, etc.); directeur *m*; meneur *m* (d'une émeute); (*c*) *Pol: F:* Leader *m.* *Mus:* Chef d'attaque. **2.** Cheval *m* de volée, de tête. **3.** Observation faite pour orienter la conversation. **4.** *Journ:* Article de fond, de tête; éditorial, -aux *m*, *F:* leader. **'leader-writer,** *s.* Éditorialiste *m.*

leaderless ['li:dəlis], *a.* Sans chef, sans guide.

leadership ['li:dəʃip], *s.* **1. To be under s.o.'s l.,** être sous la conduite de qn. **2.** (*a*) *Mil:* Commandement *m.* (*b*) Fonctions *fpl* de chef; direction *f.*

leadsman, *pl.* **-men** ['ledzmən], *s.m.* *Nau:* Sondeur; homme de sonde.

leaf¹, *pl.* **leaves** [li:f, li:vz], *s.* **1.** (*a*) Feuille *f.* (*Of tree*) **To shed its leaves,** s'effeuiller. **In l.,** (arbre) couvert de feuilles, en feuilles. **The trees are coming into l.,** les arbres se couvrent de feuilles. **Fall of the l.,** chute *f* des feuilles. (*b*) *F:* Pétale *m* (de fleur). **2.** (*a*) Feuillet *m* (de livre). **To turn over the leaves of a book,** feuilleter un livre. **To turn over a new l.,** changer de conduite; faire peau neuve. **To take a l. out of s.o.'s book,** prendre exemple sur qn. (*b*) **Counterfoil and l.,** talon *m* et volant *m* (d'un carnet de chèques, etc.). **3.** Feuille (d'or, etc.). **4.** Battant *m*, vantail *m*, -aux (de porte); feuille (de paravent); lame *f*, feuille, feuillet (de ressort). **L. of a table,** (*inserted*) (r)allonge *f*; (*hinged*) battant. **'leaf-insect,** *s.* *Ent:* Phyllie *f.* **'leaf-mould,** *s.* *Hort:* Terreau *m* de feuilles.

leaf², *v.i.* (Se) feuiller; pousser des feuilles.

leafless ['li:flis], *a.* Sans feuilles; dépourvu de feuilles.

leaflet ['li:flit], *s.* **1.** *Bot:* Foliole *f.* **2.** Feuillet *m* (de papier); feuille volante, feuille mobile; papillon *m* (de publicité); tract *m*, prospectus *m.*

leafy ['li:fi], *a.* Feuillu; couvert de feuilles.

league¹ [li:g], *s.* *Meas:* Lieue *f.*

league², *s.* Ligue *f.* **To form a l. against s.o.,** se liguer contre qn. **He was in l. with them,** il était ligué, de connivence, avec eux. *Hist:* **The Hanseatic L.,** la Hanse. **The L. of Nations,** la Société des Nations. *Fb:* **L. matches,** les matchs de championnat.

league³, *v.i.* **To l. (together),** se liguer.

leak¹ [li:k], *s.* **1.** (*a*) Fuite *f*, écoulement *m* (d'un liquide). (*b*) Infiltration *f*, rentrée *f* (d'eau, etc.). *Nau:* Voie *f* d'eau. (*Of ship*) **To spring a l.,** faire une voie d'eau. **To stop a l.,** (i) aveugler, boucher, une voie d'eau; (ii) remédier à, étancher, une fuite (d'eau, etc.). **2.** *W.Tel:* Grid-l. resistor, résistance *f* de polarisation automatique. **'leak-detector,** *s.* *El:* Indicateur *m* de pertes à la terre; déceleur *m* de fuites.

leak², *v.i.* **1.** (*Of tank, etc.*) Avoir une fuite, fuir, (*of liquid*) fuir, couler. **My shoes l.,** mes souliers prennent l'eau. **The roof leaks,** le toit laisse entrer la pluie. **To l. away,** se perdre. **2.** (*Of ship*) Faire eau. **leak out,** *v.i.* (*Of news, etc.*) S'ébruiter, transpirer. **3.** *v.tr.* (*a*) *abs:* Perdre; avoir une fuite. (*b*) *F:* Laisser filtrer (des nouvelles, etc.).

leakage ['li:kidʒ], *s.* **1.** (*a*) Fuite *f* (d'eau, de gaz); perte *f*, fuite, déperdition *f* (d'électricité). (*b*) Fuites, pertes, coulage *m* (dans une maison de commerce). **2. L. of official secrets,** fuite de secrets officiels.

leakiness ['li:kinis], *s.* Manque *m* d'étanchéité.

leaky ['li:ki], *a.* (*a*) (Tonneau) qui coule, qui perd, qui fuit. **L. shoes,** souliers qui prennent l'eau. (*b*) (Bateau) qui fait eau.

leal [li:l], *a.* *Scot:* Loyal, -aux; fidèle. **Land of the l.,** royaume *m* des cieux.

lean¹ [li:n]. **1.** *a.* Maigre. (*a*) Amaigri, décharné; (*of animal*) efflanqué. (*b*) **L. meat,** viande maigre. (*c*) **L. years,** années maigres, déficitaires, de disette. **L. diet,** régime frugal. **2.** *s.* Maigre *m* (de la viande).

lean², *s.* Inclinaison *f.*

lean³, *v.* (*p.t. & p.p.* leant [lent]). **1.** *v.i.* (*a*) S'appuyer (against, on, sth., contre, sur, qch.). **To l. on one's elbow(s),** s'accouder. **To l. (up) against the wall, with one's back against the wall;** **to l. back against the wall,** s'adosser au mur, contre le mur. **To l. on s.o.** (for aid), s'appuyer sur qn. (*b*) Se pencher (over, sur); (*of wall, etc.*) incliner, pencher. (*c*) **To l. towards, mercy,** incliner à la clémence. (*d*) *F:* **To l. over backwards to . . .,** (i) mettre tout en œuvre pour . . .; (ii) aller aux concessions extrêmes pour . . . **2.** *v.tr.* **To l. a ladder against the wall,** appuyer une échelle contre le mur. **To l. sth. (with its back) against sth.,** adosser qch. à qch. **lean back,** *v.i.* Se pencher en arrière. **To l. back in one's chair,** se renverser dans son fauteuil. **lean forward. 1.** *v.i.* Se pencher en avant. **2.** *v.tr.* Pencher (la tête) en avant. **lean out,** *v.i.* Se pencher au dehors. **To l. out of the window,** se pencher à, par, la fenêtre. **leaning¹,** *a.* Penché. **The L. Tower of Pisa,** la tour penchée de Pise. **leaning²,** *s.* **1.** Inclinaison *f* (d'une tour, etc.). **2.** Inclination *f* (towards, pour); penchant *m* (towards, pour, vers); tendance *f* (towards, à). **'lean-'to. 1.** *Attrib.a.* En appentis. **2.** *s.* Appentis *m.*

leanness ['li:nnis], s. Maigreur f.

leant. See LEAN³.

leap¹ [li:p], s. 1. Saut m, bond m. To take a l., faire un saut. **To take a l. in the dark,** faire un saut dans l'inconnu. **His heart gave a l.,** son cœur bondit. **To advance by leaps and bounds,** progresser par bonds, à pas de géant. 2. Obstacle m (à sauter); saut. '**leap-frog,** s. Games: Saute-mouton m. Swim: Passade f. '**leap-year,** s. Année f bissextile.

leap², v. (p.t. & p.p. **leaped** [li:pt] or **leapt** [lept]) 1. v.i. (a) Sauter, bondir. **To l. to one's feet,** se lever brusquement, être sur pied d'un bond. **To l. over the ditch,** sauter le fossé; franchir le fossé (d'un bond). F: **To l. at an offer,** sauter sur une offre. **To l. for joy,** sauter de joie. **To l. up with indignation,** sursauter d'indignation. (b) (Of flame, etc.) **To l. (up),** jaillir. 2. v.tr. Sauter (un fossé); franchir (un fossé) d'un saut.

leaper ['li:pər], s. Sauteur, -euse.

leapt. See LEAP².

learn [lə:n], v.tr. (p.t. & p.p. **learnt** [lə:nt] or **learned** [lə:nt]) 1. Apprendre. **To l. to read,** apprendre à lire. **To l. by heart,** apprendre par cœur. **He has learnt his lesson;** (i) Sch: il a appris sa leçon; (ii) il a eu sa leçon. **I have learnt better since then,** je sais à quoi m'en tenir maintenant. **I have to l. why,** j'ignore encore pourquoi. Prov: **It is never too late to l.;** live and l., on apprend à tout âge. 2. Apprendre (une nouvelle, etc.). **To l. sth. about s.o.,** apprendre qch. sur le compte de qn. **learned** ['lə:nid], a. Savant, instruit, érudit, docte. -ly, adv. Savamment. **learning,** s. 1. Étude f. 2. Science f, instruction f, érudition f. **Seat of l.,** centre intellectuel. **Man of great l.,** érudit m; homme d'un grand savoir. S.a. BOOK-LEARNING.

learnedness ['lə:nidnis], s. Érudition f.

learner ['lə:nər], s. 1. **To be a quick l.,** apprendre facilement. 2. Débutant, -ante. Aut: **Learner's car** = voiture f école.

lease¹ [li:s], s. Jur: (a) Bail m, pl. baux. **L. of a farm, of ground, of land,** bail à ferme. **To take land on l.,** louer une terre à bail; affermer une terre. **To take a new l. of a house,** renouveler le bail d'une maison. F: **To take (on) a new l. of life,** renaître, se reprendre, à la vie; faire corps neuf. (b) Concession f (d'une source d'énergie, etc.). '**lease-'lend,** s. Pol.Ec: Prêt-bail m (no pl.).

lease², v.tr. 1. **To l. (out),** louer; donner (une maison) à bail; affermer (une terre). 2. Prendre (une maison) à bail; louer (une maison); affermer (une terre). **leasing,** s. Location f à bail; affermage m.

leasehold ['li:should]. 1. s. (a) Tenure f à bail. (b) Propriété f, immeuble m, loué(e) à bail. 2.a. Tenu à bail.

leaseholder ['li:shouldər], s. Locataire mf; affermataire mf.

leash¹ [li:ʃ], s. 1. Laisse f, attache f. **On the l.,** (chien) en laisse, à l'attache. **To strain at the l.,** (i) tirer sur la laisse; (ii) (of pers.) F: ruer dans les brancards. 2. (a) Ven: Harde f (de trois chiens, etc.). (b) **A l. of . . .,** un trio de. . . .

leash², v.tr. 1. Mettre (un chien) à l'attache; attacher la laisse à (un chien). 2. Ven: Harder. **Leashed hounds,** chiens à l'accouple.

least [li:st]. 1. a. (a) (The) l., (le, la) moindre; (le) plus petit, (la) plus petite. (b) Le moins important. **This was not the l. of his services,** ce n'est pas le moindre des services qu'il nous a rendus. **That is the l. of my cares,** ça c'est le dernier, le cadet, de mes soucis. 2. s. (The) l., (le) moins. **To say the l. (of it),** pour ne pas dire plus; pour ne pas dire mieux. **At l., (tout) au moins. I can at l. try, je peux toujours essayer. It would at l. be advisable to . . .,** il conviendrait pour le moins de. . . . **A hundred pounds at the (very) l.,** cent livres au bas mot. **Not in the l. (degree),** pas le moins du monde; pas du tout. **It does not matter in the l.,** cela n'a pas la moindre importance. Prov: (The) l. said (the) soonest mended, moins on parle mieux ça vaut. **That's the very l. I could do,** c'est la moindre des choses. 3. adv. (The) l., (le) moins. **The l. unhappy,** le moins malheureux. **He deserves it l. of all,** il le mérite moins que tous les autres, moins que personne. **L. of all would I . . .,** je ne voudrais surtout pas. . . .

leastways ['li:stweiz], adv. Dial. & P: En tout cas . . .; ou du moins. . . .

leat [li:t], s. Hyd.E: Canal m d'amenée; (canal de) dérivation f; bief m.

leather¹ ['leðər], s. 1. Cuir m. **Russia l.,** cuir de Russie. **L. bottle,** outre f; gourde f. **L. shoes,** chaussures en cuir. **Fancy l. goods,** maroquinerie f. Mil: O: **L. equipment,** buffleterie f. 2. (a) Cuir (de pompe, de soupape, etc.). **Hand-l.,** manique f (de cordonnier); Nau: paumelle f (de voilier). **Upper l. (of shoe),** empeigne f. Sp: F: **The l.,** Cr: la balle; Fb: le ballon. (b) = STIRRUP-LEATHER. 3. **Artificial l.,** similicuir m. '**leather-jacket,** s. Ent: Larve f de la tipule. '**leather-work,** s. 1. Travail m en cuir; travail du cuir. 2. (a) Cuirs (d'une carrosserie, etc.). (b) Fancy l.-w., maroquinerie f.

leather², v.tr. 1. Garnir (qch.) de cuir. 2.P: Tanner le cuir à (qn); étriller, rosser (qn). **leathering,** s. P: To give s.o. a l., tanner le cuir à qn.

leatherette [,leðə'ret], s. Similicuir m.

leathern ['leðən], a. De cuir; en cuir.

leathery ['leðəri], a. Qui ressemble au cuir; (of food) coriace. **A l. steak,** F: de la semelle de chaussures.

leave¹ [li:v], s. 1. Permission f, autorisation f, permis m. **To beg l. to do sth.,** demander la permission de faire qch.; demander à faire qch. **By your l., with your l.,** avec votre permission; si vous le voulez bien; ne vous en déplaise. 2. (a) Mil: etc: L. (of absence), (in months) congé m; (in days) permission f. **Shore l.,** sortie f à terre; permission d'aller à terre. **To be on l.,** être (i) en permission, (ii) en congé. **Sick l.,** congé de maladie. **Soldier, sailor, on l.,** permissionnaire m. **Absence without l.,** absence illégale. **To break l.,** s'absenter sans permission. (b) **Release of prisoner on ticket of l.,** libération conditionnelle. **To break one's ticket of l.,** rompre son ban, être en rupture de ban. 3. **To take one's l.,** prendre congé; faire ses adieux. **To take l. of s.o.,** prendre congé de qn. **To take French l.,** filer à l'anglaise. '**leave-taking,** s. Adieux mpl.

leave², v.tr. (left [left]; left) 1. Laisser. (a) F: **Take it or l. it,** c'est à prendre ou à laisser. (b) **To l. a wife and three children,** laisser une femme et trois enfants. **She had been left a widow at thirty,** elle était restée veuve à trente ans. **To be left well, badly, off,** être laissé dans l'aisance, dans la gêne. (c) **To l. one's money to s.o.,** laisser, léguer, sa fortune à qn. (d) **To l. the door open,** laisser la porte ouverte. **To l. a page blank,** laisser une page en blanc. **Left to oneself,** livré à soi-même. **L. him to himself,** laissez-le faire. **Let us l. it at that,** demeurons-en là. (e) **To l. hold,** F: l. go, of sth., lâcher qch. (f) **To l. one's bag in the cloak-room,** déposer sa valise à la consigne. **Left-luggage office,** consigne. **Left-luggage ticket,** bulletin m de consigne. **To l. sth. with s.o.,** déposer qch. entre les mains de qn; confier qch. à qn. (g) **To l. s.o. to do sth.,** laisser à qn le soin de faire qch. **I l. it to you,** je m'en remets à vous. **L. it to me,** remettez-vous-en à moi; laissez-moi faire. **L. it to time,** laissez faire au temps. **I l. it to you whether I am right or wrong,** je vous laisse à juger si j'ai tort ou raison. (h) **To be left,** rester. **There are three bottles left,** il reste trois bouteilles. **I have none left,** il ne m'en reste plus. **To stake what money one has left,** jouer le reste de son argent. **Nothing was left to me but to . . .,** il ne me restait qu'à. . . . (i) **Three from seven leaves four,** trois ôté de sept reste quatre. 2. (a) Quitter (un endroit, qn). **He has left London,** il est parti de Londres; il a quitté Londres. **I l. home at eight o'clock,** je pars de la maison à huit heures. **To l. the room,** sortir (de la salle). **To l. one's bed,** quitter le lit. **You may l. us,** vous pouvez nous laisser; vous pouvez vous retirer. **To l. the table,** se lever de table. **To l. one's employment,** quitter son emploi. **On leaving school,** au sortir du collège. Nau: **To l. harbour,** sortir du port. **We l. tomorrow,** nous partons demain. **He has just left,** il sort d'ici. (Just) **as he was leaving, on leaving,** au moment de son départ. (b) Abandonner. **To l. one's wife,** quitter sa femme; se séparer d'avec sa femme. (c) (Of train) **To l. the track, the rails,** dérailler. **leave about,** v.tr. Laisser traîner (des objets, etc.). **leave behind,** v.tr.

1. Laisser, oublier (son parapluie); partir sans (qn). **2.** Laisser (des traces, etc.). **3.** Devancer, distancer, laisser en arrière (un rival). **leave off, 1.** *v.tr.* (a) Cesser de porter, ne plus mettre (un vêtement); quitter (un vêtement d'hiver). **Left-off clothing,** vieilles frusques; friperie *f.* (b) Quitter, renoncer à (une habitude). **To l. off smoking,** renoncer au tabac. (c) To l. off work, cesser le travail. To l. off crying, cesser de pleurer. **2.** *v.i.* Cesser, s'arrêter; en rester là. **Where did we l. off?** où en sommes-nous restés (de notre lecture)? *P:* L. off! cessez donc! finissez! **leave out,** *v.tr.* **1.** Exclure (qn). **2.** (a) Omettre (qch.). (b) Oublier. **To l. out a line (in copying),** sauter une ligne. (c) *Mus:* To l. out notes, croquer des notes. **leave over,** *v.tr.* **1.** Remettre (une affaire) à plus tard. **2. To be left over,** rester. **left overs,** *s.pl.* (a) Restes *mpl* (de repas). (b) *Com:* Surplus *m.* **leaving,** *s.* **1.** Départ *m. Sch: A:* L. **certificate,** = certificat *m* d'études (secondaires). **2.** *pl.* Leavings, restes *m*; débris *m.*

leaved [li:vd], *a.* **1.** Thick-l., aux feuilles épaisses. **Three-l.,** (volet, paravent) à trois feuilles. **2.** (Porte) à deux battants; (table) à rallonges.

leaven¹ ['lev(ə)n], *s.* Levain *m.*

leaven², *v.tr.* **1.** Faire lever (le pain, la pâte). **2.** Imprégner; transformer (with, de, par).

leaves [li:vz]. *See* LEAF¹.

Lebanese [,lebə'ni:z], *a. & s.* Libanais, -aise.

Lebanon ['lebənən]. *Pr.n. Geog:* Le Liban.

lecherous ['letʃərəs], *a.* Lascif, lubrique, débauché, paillard. **-ly,** *adv.* Lascivement.

lecherousness ['letʃərəsnis], **lechery** ['letʃəri], *s.* Lascivité *f,* lubricité *f,* paillardise *f.*

lectern ['lektə:n], *s. Ecc:* Lutrin *m,* aigle *m.*

lecture¹ ['lektʃər], *s.* **1.** Conférence *f* (on, sur); *Sch:* cours *m* (on, de). **To give, deliver, a l.,** faire une conférence. **To attend lectures,** (i) suivre un cours; (ii) assister à une série de conférences. *Sch:* L. **notes,** notes *fpl* sur un cours. **2.** *F:* Sermon *m,* semonce *f,* mercuriale *f.* **To read s.o. a l.,** sermonner qn; chapitrer qn. **'lecture-hall, -room,** *s.* Salle *f* de conférences, amphithéâtre *m.*

lecture². **1.** *v.i.* Faire une conférence, des conférences; faire un cours. **To l. on Napoleon,** (i) faire un cours, (ii) donner une conférence, sur Napoléon. **2.** *v.tr. F:* Sermonner, semoncer, réprimander (qn); faire la morale à (qn). **lecturing,** *s.* Cours *mpl;* conférences *fpl.*

lecturer ['lektʃərər], *s.* **1.** Conférencier, -ière. **2.** (*With permanent appointment*) Maître *m* de conférences; (*temporary*) chargé *m* de cours.

lectureship ['lektʃəʃip], *s. Sch:* Maîtrise *f* de conférences.

led. *See* LEAD⁴.

ledge [ledʒ], *s.* **1.** Rebord *m;* saillie *f;* (*on building*) corniche *f,* épaulement *m,* projecture *f.* **2.** Banc *m* de récifs.

ledger ['ledʒər], *s.* **1.** (a) *Book-k:* Grand livre. (b) *U.S:* Registre *m.* **2.** L.(-stone), dalle *f* tumulaire; pierre tombale. **'ledger-line,** *s. Mus:* Ligne *f* supplémentaire.

lee [li:], *s.* (a) *Nau:* Côté *m* sous le vent. **Under the l. of the land,** sous le vent de la terre. (b) Abri *m* (contre le vent). **Under the l.,** à l'abri du vent. **'lee-board,** *s. Nau:* Dérive *f.* **'lee-ga(u)ge,** *s. Nau:* Dessous *m* du vent. **To have the l.-g. of a ship,** être sous le vent d'un navire. **'lee-shore,** *s. Nau:* Terre *f* sous le vent.

leech¹ [li:tʃ], *s.* **1.** Sangsue *f.* **2.** *F:* (a) Extorqueur, -euse, sangsue. (b) Importun *m,* crampon *m.*

leech², *s. Nau:* Chute *f* arrière (de voile).

leek [li:k], *s.* Poireau *m.*

leer¹ ['liər], *s.* (a) Œillade *f* en dessous; mauvais regard de côté. (b) Regard paillard, polisson.

leer², *v.i.* **To l. at s.o.,** (i) lorgner, guigner, (qn) d'un air méchant; (ii) lancer des œillades à qn.

lees [li:z], *s.pl.* Lie *f* (de vin, etc.). **The l. of society,** le rebut, la lie, de la société.

leeward ['li:wəd, 'lu(:)əd]. *Nau:* **1.** *a. & adv.* Sous le vent. *Geog:* **The L. Islands,** les Isles Sous-le-Vent. **2.** *s.* Côté *m* sous le vent. **To drop, fall, to l.,** tomber sous le vent. **To (the) l. of . . . ,** sous le vent de. . . .

leeway ['li:wei], *s. Nau:* Dérive *f.* **He has considerable l. to make up,** il a un fort retard à rattraper.

left¹ [left]. **1.** *a.* Gauche. **On my l. hand,** à ma gauche. **2.** *adv. Mil:* Eyes l.! tête (à) gauche! **3.** *s.* (a) (i) (*Left hand*) Gauche *f.* **On the l., to the l.,** à gauche. (ii) *Box:* To feint with the l.,** feinter du gauche. (b) (*Left wing*) *Mil:* Gauche *f;* l'aile *f* gauche. (c) *Pol:* The L., les gauches *m;* la gauche. **'left-hand,** *attrib.a.* **On the l.-h. side,** à gauche. **The l.-h. drawer,** le tiroir de gauche. **left-'handed,** *a.* (a) (*Of pers.*) Gaucher, -ère. (b) *F:* L.-h. compliment, compliment douteux. **left-'handedness,** *s.* Habitude *f* de se servir de la main gauche. **left-'hander,** *s.* **1.** (*Pers.*) Gaucher, -ère. **2.** *Box:* Coup *m* du gauche.

left². *See* LEAVE².

leftism ['leftizm], *s.* Politique *f* de gauche.

leftist ['leftist], *a. Pol:* De gauche. *s.* Homme *m* de gauche.

leg¹ [leg], *s.* **1.** Jambe *f;* patte *f* (de chien, d'oiseau, d'insecte). *F:* Show a l.! lève-toi! *F:* To take to one's legs, prendre ses jambes à son cou. I ran as fast as my legs would carry me, j'ai couru à toutes jambes. To stand on one l., se tenir sur un pied. To jump on one l., sauter à cloche-pied. To be on one's legs, être debout, être sur pied. To get on one's legs again, (i) se relever; (ii) se rétablir. To set s.o. on his legs again, (i) relever qn; remettre qn debout; (ii) rétablir qn dans ses affaires; tirer qn d'affaire. To be on one's last legs, tirer vers sa fin; être à bout de ressources. To walk s.o. off his legs, exténuer qn à force de le faire marcher. To be carried off one's legs, être emporté; perdre pied. To feel, find, one's legs, (i) se trouver en état de se tenir debout; (ii) prendre conscience de ses forces; (iii) se faire une clientèle. To keep one's legs, se maintenir debout. To give s.o. a l. up, (i) faire la courte échelle à qn; (ii) aider qn à monter en selle; (iii) *F:* donner à qn un coup d'épaule. *F:* To pull s.o.'s l., se payer la tête de qn; faire marcher qn. **2.** *Cu:* L. of chicken, cuisse *f* de poulet. L. of beef, jarret *m,* gîte *m.* L. of veal, cuisseau *m.* L. of pork, jambon *m.* Roast l. of pork, jambon frais rôti (façon anglaise). L. of mutton, gigot *m. A: Cost: F:* L.-of-mutton sleeves, manches à gigot. *Nau:* L.-of-mutton sail, voile triangulaire. **3.** Jambe (de pantalon); tige *f* (de bas). **4.** Pied *m* (de table); branche *f* (de compas); jambage *m,* montant *m* (de chevalet). To set a chair on its legs (again), relever une chaise. **5.** *Nau:* Bordée *f.* **'leg-pull,** *s. F:* Mystification *f,* carotte *f.* **'leg-puller,** *s. F:* Farceur, -euse, mystificateur, -trice.

leg², *v.tr.* (legged) *F:* To l. it, (i) faire la route à pied; *P:* prendre le train onze; (ii) marcher ou courir rapidement; jouer des jambes.

legacy ['legəsi], *s.* Legs *m.* To leave a l. to s.o., faire un legs à qn. To come into a l., faire un héritage. This desk is a l. from my predecessor, j'ai hérité ce bureau de mon prédécesseur. **'legacy-duty,** *s.* Droits *mpl* de succession. **'legacy-hunter,** *s.* Coureur, -euse, d'héritages.

legal ['li:g(ə)l], *a.* **1.** Légal, -aux; licite. **2.** (a) Légal; judiciaire, juridique. By l. process, par voies de droit. L. security, caution *f* judiciaire. L. document, acte *m* authentique. (*Of corporation*) To acquire l. status, acquérir la personnalité juridique, civile, morale. (b) L. year, année civile. L. department (of bank, etc.), service *m* du contentieux. To go into the l. profession, se faire une carrière dans le droit. L. practitioner, homme de loi. To take l. advice, consulter un avocat. L. term, terme de pratique. The l. mind, l'esprit juridique. **-ally,** *adv.* Légalement. (i) licitement; (ii) judiciairement, juridiquement. L. responsible, responsable en droit.

legality [li(:)'gæliti], *s.* Légalité *f.*

legalize ['li:gəlaiz], *v.tr.* Rendre (un acte) légal; légaliser, authentiquer (un document).

legate ['legit], *s.* Légat *m.*

legatee [,legə'ti:], *s.* Légataire *mf.* Residuary l., légataire (à titre) universel.

legation [li'geiʃ(ə)n], *s.* Légation *f.*

legend ['ledʒənd], *s.* **1.** Légende *f,* fable *f.* **2.** (a) Inscription *f,* légende (sur une médaille, etc.). (b) Explication *f,* légende (d'une carte, etc.).

legendary ['ledʒənd(ə)ri], *a.* Légendaire.

legerdemain ['ledʒədə'mein], *s.* (Tours *mpl* de) passe-passe *m;* prestidigitation *f.*

leggings ['legiŋz], *s.pl. Cost:* Jambières *f*; guêtres *f*; leggings *m*, leggins *m*.

leggy ['legi], *a.* Aux longues jambes; dégingandé.

Leghorn ['legɔːn]. **1.** *Pr.n. Geog:* Livourne *f*. **2.** *s.* L. (hat), chapeau *m* de paille d'Italie. **3.** (*usu.* [le'gɔːn]) *Husb:* (White) L., leghorn *f*.

legibility [ˌledʒi'biliti], *s.* Lisibilité *f*, netteté *f* (d'une écriture).

legible ['ledʒibl], *a.* (Écriture) lisible, nette. **-ibly,** *adv.* Lisiblement.

legion ['liːdʒ(ə)n], *s.* Légion *f*. **British L.,** association (anglaise) des anciens combattants. *Mil.Hist:* **Foreign L.,** la Légion étrangère. **Their name is l.,** ils sont innombrables; ils s'appellent légion.

legionary ['liːdʒənəri], *a. & s.* Légionnaire (*m*).

legislate ['ledʒisleit], *v.i.* Faire les lois; légiférer.

legislation [ˌledʒis'leiʃ(ə)n], *s.* Législation *f*.

legislative ['ledʒislətiv], *a.* Législatif, -ive.

legislator ['ledʒisleitər], *s.* Législateur *m*.

legislature ['ledʒislətʃər], *s.* Législature *f*; corps législatif.

legist ['liːdʒist], *s.* Légiste *m*.

legitimacy [li'dʒitiməsi], *s.* Légitimité *f*.

legitimate[1] [li'dʒitimit], *a.* **1.** (*a*) (Enfant, autorité, etc.) légitime. (*b*) **The l. stage,** le vrai théâtre. **2.** (Raisonnement, etc.) légitime. **-ly,** *adv.* Légitimement.

legitimate[2] [le'dʒitimeit], *v.tr.* Légitimer (un enfant).

legitimation [li,dʒiti'meiʃ(ə)n], *s.* Légitimation *f*.

legless ['leglis], *a.* Sans jambes. **L. cripple,** cul-de-jatte *m*, *pl.* culs-de-jatte.

legume ['legjuːm], *s.*, **legumen** [le'gjuːmen], *s.* **1.** Fruit *m* d'une légumineuse. **2.** *pl.* Légumes *m*.

leguminous [le'gjuːminəs], *a.* Légumineux, -euse. **L. plant,** légumineuse *f*.

leisure ['leʒər], *s.* Loisir(s) *m(pl)*. **To have l. for reading,** l. **to read,** avoir le loisir, le temps, de lire. **To be at l.,** être de loisir; ne pas être occupé. **To do sth. at (one's) l.,** faire qch. à loisir, à tête reposée. **People of l.,** les désœuvrés *m*. **In my l. moments,** à mes moments perdus.

leisured ['leʒəd], *a.* De loisir; désœuvré. **The l. classes,** les désœuvrés *m*.

leisureliness ['leʒəlinis], *s.* Absence *f* de hâte; lenteur *f* (in doing sth., à faire qch.).

leisurely ['leʒəli]. **1.** *a.* (*Of pers.*) Qui n'est jamais pressé. **L. pace,** allure mesurée, posée, tranquille. **L. journey,** voyage par petites étapes. **To do sth. in a l. fashion,** faire qch. sans se presser. **2.** *adv.* (*a*) A tête reposée. (*b*) Posément; sans se presser.

leitmotiv ['laitmoutiːf], *s.* Leitmotiv *m*.

lemming ['lemiŋ], *s.* *Z:* Lemming *m*.

lemon[1] ['lemən]. **1.** *s.* *Bot:* (*a*) Citron *m*, limon *m*. (*b*) = LEMON-TREE. **2.** *a.* Jaune citron *inv*. **'lemon-cheese, -curd,** *s.* *Cu:* Gelée composée d'œufs, de beurre et de jus de citron. **'lemon-drop,** *s.* Bonbon acidulé. **'lemon 'squash,** *s.* = Limonade (non-gazeuse). **'lemon-squeezer,** *s.* Presse-citrons *m inv*. **'lemon-tree,** *s.* *Bot:* Citronnier *m*, limonier *m*. **'lemon-ver'bena,** *s.* *Bot:* Verveine *f* citronnelle.

lemonade [ˌlemə'neid], *s.* (*a*) Limonade *f*. (*b*) (Still) l., (i) citronnade *f*; (ii) limonade non-gazeuse.

lemon[2], *s.* *Ich:* L. **sole,** plie *f* sole. **L. dab,** limande *f* sole.

lemur ['liːmər], *s.* *Z:* Lémur *m*.

lend [lend], *v.tr.* (lent [lent]; lent) **1.** Prêter. **2. To l. s.o. a(helping) hand,** prêter aide, prêter secours, à qn. **To l. an ear, one's ear(s), to . . .,** prêter l'oreille à. . . . **3.** *v.tr.* **To l. oneself, itself, to sth.,** se prêter à qch. **Spot that lends itself to meditation,** lieu propice à la méditation. **lending[1],** *a.* Prêteur, -euse. **lending[2],** *s.* Prêt *m*; *Fin:* prestation *f* (de capitaux). **L. library,** bibliothèque *f* de prêt. **'lend-'lease,** *Pol.Ec:* Prêt-bail *m* (*no pl.*).

lender ['lendər], *s.* Prêteur, -euse.

length [leŋθ], *s.* **1.** Longueur *f*. **Overall l.,** longueur totale. **To be two feet in l.,** avoir deux pieds de longueur; être long de deux pieds. **L. of stroke,** course *f* (d'un outil); *Mch:* parcours *m* (du piston). (*Of ship. etc.*) **To turn in its own l.,** virer sur place. *Row: etc:* **To win by a l.,** gagner d'une longueur. **Throughut the l. and breadth of the country,** dans toute l'étendue du pays. **To go the l. of the street,** aller jusqu'au bout de la rue. **I fell full l. (on the ground),** je suis tombé de tout mon long. **2. Stay of some l.,** séjour assez prolongé, d'une certaine durée. **L. of service,** ancienneté *f*. **For some l. of time,** pendant quelque temps. **To recite sth. at (full) l.,** réciter qch. tout au long, d'un bout à l'autre. **To speak at some l. on a subject,** parler assez longuement sur un sujet. **He lectured me at great l.,** il m'a fait une longue semonce. **To recount sth. at greater l.,** raconter qch. plus en détail. **At l. he gave his consent,** enfin, à la fin, il consentit. **3. To go to the l. of asserting . . .,** aller jusqu'à prétendre. . . . **He would go to any lengths,** rien ne l'arrêterait; il ne reculerait devant rien (to, pour). **To go to great lengths,** aller bien loin, pousser les choses bien loin. **To go the whole l.,** aller jusqu'au bout; se porter aux dernières extrémités (against s.o., sur, contre, qn). **4.** *Pros:* Longueur (d'une voyelle, d'une syllabe). **5.** Morceau *m*, bout *m* (de ficelle, etc.); pièce *f*, coupon *m* (de tissu); tronçon *m* (de tuyau). *Dressm:* **Dress l.,** coupon de robe. **What l. of material do you require?** quel métrage vous faut-il?

lengthen ['leŋθən]. **1.** *v.tr.* Allonger, rallonger; prolonger (la vie, etc.). **2.** *v.i.* S'allonger, se rallonger; augmenter, croître, grandir. **His face lengthened,** son visage s'allongea. **lengthening,** *s.* Allongement *m*, rallongement *m*; prolongation *f* (d'un séjour, etc.).

lengthiness ['leŋθinis], *s.* Longueurs *fpl*; prolixité *f* (d'un discours).

lengthways ['leŋθweiz], *adv.* Longitudinalement; en longueur; en long.

lengthwise ['leŋθwaiz]. **1.** *adv.* = LENGTHWAYS. **2.** *a.* (Coupe) en long, en longueur.

lengthy ['leŋθi], *a.* (Discours) qui traîne en longueur, prolixe. **-ily,** *adv.* (Parler) longuement, avec prolixité; (raconter) tout au long.

leniency ['liːnjənsi], *s.* Clémence *f*; douceur *f*, indulgence *f* (to, towards, pour).

lenient ['liːnjənt], *a.* Clément; doux, *f.* douce; indulgent (to, towards, envers, pour). **-ly,** *adv.* Avec clémence, avec douceur.

lenitive ['lenitiv]. **1.** *a. & s.* *Med:* Lénitif (*m*); adoucissant (*m*). **2.** *s.* Palliatif *m*, adoucissement *m*.

lens [lenz], *s.* **1.** *Opt:* (*a*) Lentille *f*; verre *m* (de lunettes). (*b*) *Phot:* Objectif *m*. **Coated l.,** objectif bleuté. **Wide-angle l.,** objectif grand angulaire. **Supplementary l.,** bonnette *f*. **Electron l.,** lentille électronique. **2.** *Anat:* Crystalline l., cristallin *m* (de l'œil). **'lens-holder,** *s.* *Phot:* Porte-objectif *m inv*. **'lens-hood,** *s.* Parasoleil *m* (d'objectif).

Lent[1] [lent], *s.* *Ecc:* Le carême. **To keep L.,** faire carême.

lent[2]. *See* LEND.

lenten ['lentən], *a.* De carême.

lenticular [len'tikjulər], *a.* Lenticulaire, lenticulé, lentiforme.

lentil ['lentil], *s.* *Hort:* Lentille *f*.

leonine ['liː(ə)nain], *a.* De lion(s); léonin.

leopard ['lepəd], *s.* Léopard *m*. **American l.,** jaguar *m*.

leopardess ['lepədis], *s.* Léopard *m* femelle.

leper ['lepər], *s.* Lépreux, -euse.

lepidopter, *pl.* **-ters, -tera** [ˌlepi'dɔptər, -təz, -tərə], *Ent:* Lépidoptère *m*; papillon *m*. **The Lepidoptera,** les lépidoptères.

leporine ['lepərain], *a.* De lièvre.

leprechaun [leprə'kɔːn], *s.* *Irish Myth:* Farfadet *m*, lutin *m*.

leprosy ['leprəsi], *s.* *Med:* Lèpre *f*.

leprous ['leprəs], *a.* Lépreux, -euse.

Lesbian ['lezbiən]. **1.** *a. & s. Geog:* Lesbien, -ienne. **2.** *s.f.* Lesbienne, femme homosexuelle.

lèse-majesté ['leiz'mæʒəstei], *s.* Lèse-majesté *f*.

lesion ['liːʒ(ə)n], *s.* Lésion *f*.

less [les]. **1.** *a.* (*a*) Moindre. **Of l. value,** d'une moindre valeur; de moindre valeur. **In a l. degree,** à un moindre degré, à un degré inférieur. **Quantities, sums, l. than . . .,** quantités, sommes, au-dessous de. . . **To grow l.,** s'amoindrir. (*b*) **Eat l. meat,** mangez moins de viande. **With a few l. windows the house would be warmer,** avec quelques fenêtres de moins la maison serait plus chaude. (*c*) *A:* Moins important. **James the L.,** Jacques le Mineur. **2.** *prep.* **Purchase price l. 10%,** prix d'achat moins 10%, sous déduction de 10%. **3.** *s.* Moins *m*. **In l.**

than an hour, en moins d'une heure. **So much the l. to do**, d'autant moins à faire. **I can't let you have it for l.**, je ne peux pas vous le laisser à moins **(than, de)**. 4. *adv.* **L. known**, moins connu. **One man l.**, un homme de moins. **L. than six**, moins de six. **L. and l.**, de moins en moins. **I was (all) the l. surprised as . . .**, j'en ai été d'autant moins surpris que. . . . **Still l., even l.**, moins encore. **He continued none the l.**, il n'en continua pas moins. **None the l. he came in first**, néanmoins il arriva premier. 5. *(a)* **Nothing l. than.** (i) Rien (de) moins que. **It is nothing l. than monstrous**, c'est absolument monstrueux. (ii) Rien moins que. **He resembled nothing l. than a demagogue**, il ne ressemblait à rien moins qu'à un démagogue. *(b)* **No less.** (i) **To fight with no l. daring than skill**, se battre avec autant d'habileté que de courage. **No l. good**, également bon. (ii) **They have no l. than six servants**, ils n'ont pas moins de six domestiques. (iii) **It was no l. a person than the duke**, ce n'était rien moins que le duc. (iv) **He fears it no l. than I**, il ne le craint pas moins que moi (je ne le crains). **He fears him no l. than me**, il a aussi peur de lui que de moi.

lessee [le'siː], *s.* 1. Locataire *mf* (à bail) (d'un immeuble, etc.); tenancier, -ière (d'un casino, etc.); preneur (d'une terre, etc.). 2. Concessionnaire *mf*.

lessen ['les(ə)n]. 1. *v.i.* S'amoindrir, diminuer; *(of symptoms, etc.)* s'atténuer; *(of receding object)* (se) rapetisser. 2. *v.tr.* Amoindrir, diminuer; rapetisser; atténuer; ralentir (son activité). *Artil:* **To l. the range**, raccourcir le tir. **lessening**, *s.* Amoindrissement *m*, diminution *f*; atténuation *f*, rapetissement *m*.

lesser ['lesər], *attrib.a.* 1. Petit. *Ph:* **L. calory**, petite calorie. 2. **To choose the l. of two evils, the l. evil**, de deux maux choisir le moindre.

lesson ['les(ə)n], *s.* Leçon *f*. 1. **Dancing lessons**, leçons de danse; cours *m* de danse. **To give, take, lessons in French**, donner, prendre, des leçons de français. **Object l.**, (i) *Sch: A:* leçon de choses; (ii) exemple *m*. **To draw a l. from sth.**, tirer enseignement, tirer une leçon, de qch. *F:* **Let that be a l. to you!** que cela vous serve d'exemple, de leçon! *O:* **To read s.o. a l.**, faire la leçon à qn. 2. *Ecc:* **The first, second, l.**, la première, la seconde, lecture prise dans la Bible (office anglican).

lessor [le'sɔːr], *s.* Bailleur, -eresse.

lest [lest], *conj.* 1. De peur, de crainte, que . . . (ne) + *sub.* **L. we forget**, de peur que nous n'oublions. 2. *O:* **I feared l. he should fall**, je craignais qu'il (ne) tombât. **I feared l. I should fall**, j'avais peur de tomber; je craignais de tomber.

let[1] [let], *s.* 1. *A:* Empêchement *m*. *S.a.* HINDRANCE. 2. *Ten:* **L. (ball)**, coup *m* à remettre; balle *f* de filet.

let[2], *s.* Location *f*. **When I get a l. for the season**, quand je loue ma maison, etc. pour la saison.

let[3], *v.* *(p.t. & p.p.* **let**; *pr.p.* **letting**) I. *v.tr.* 1. *(a)* Permettre; laisser. **To let s.o. do sth.**, laisser qn faire qch.; permettre à qn de faire qch. **To l. oneself be guided**, se laisser guider. **L. me tell you that . . .**, permettez-moi de vous dire que. . . . *S.a.* FALL[2] 1, SLIP[2] I. 3, GO[2] 12. **When can you l. me have my coat?** quand pourrai-je avoir mon manteau? *S.a.* ALONE 2, FLY[3] I. 4, HAVE[2] 3, LOOSE[1] 1. *(b)* **To l. s.o. know sth.**, about sth., faire savoir, faire connaître, qch. à qn; faire part de qch. à qn. **L. me hear the story**, racontez-moi l'histoire. *(c)* **The police would not l. anyone along the street**, la police ne laissait passer personne. **To l. s.o. through**, laisser passer qn. *(d)* *A.Med:* **To l. blood**, pratiquer une saignée; saigner qn. 2. Louer (sa maison, etc.). **House to l.**, maison à louer. II. **let**, *v.aux.* (supplying 1st & 3rd pers. of imperative) **Let's make haste!** dépêchons-nous! **L. us pray**, prions. **Don't l. us start yet**, ne partons pas encore. *B:* **L. there be light**, que la lumière soit. **So l. it be!** soit! *Ecc:* ainsi soit-il! **L. there be no mistake about it!** qu'on ne s'y trompe pas! **L. ABC be any angle**, soit ABC un angle quelconque. **L. me see!** voyons! attendez un peu! **L. them all come!** qu'ils viennent tous! *F:* **Just l. me catch you at it again!** que je vous y reprenne! **let down**, *v.tr.* 1. *(a)* Baisser (la glace); descendre (une barrique à la cave). *(b)* Baisser (un store); défaire, dénouer (ses cheveux). *(c)* Allonger (une robe, etc.). 2. *(a)* **The chair l. him down**, la chaise

s'affaissa sous lui. *(b)* *F:* **To l. s.o. down gently, lightly**, user de tact pour faire comprendre à qn qu'il est dans son tort, pour lui refuser qch. *(c)* *F:* (i) Laisser (qn) en panne; faire faux bond à (qn); (ii) faire un affront à (qn). **I won't l. you down**, vous pouvez compter sur moi. 3. Détendre, débander (un ressort); dégonfler (un pneu). **'let-down**, *s.* *F:* Désappointement *m*, déception *f*. **let in**, *v.tr.* 1. *(a)* Laisser entrer (qn); faire entrer (qn); admettre (qn); laisser entrer (l'air, la pluie). **Shoes that l. in water**, souliers qui prennent l'eau. *(b)* *F:* **To l. s.o. in on a secret**, initier qn à un secret. 2. Encastrer (une plaque). *Dressm: Tail:* Ajouter, introduire (une pièce). 3. *F:* *(a)* Mettre (qn) dedans; rouler, duper (qn). **I've been l. in for a thousand**, j'y suis de mille livres. *(b)* **I didn't know what I was letting myself in for**, je ne savais pas à quoi je m'engageais. **let into**, *v.tr.* *(a)* **To l. s.o. into the house**, laisser entrer qn dans la maison. **To l. s.o. into a secret**, mettre qn dans le secret. *(b)* **To l. a slab into a wall**, encastrer une plaque dans un mur. **To let a piece into a skirt**, mettre une pièce à une jupe. **let off**, *v.tr.* 1. Tirer, faire partir (un feu d'artifice); décocher (une flèche). *S.a.* STEAM[1]. 2. *(a)* **To l. s.o. off from sth., from doing sth.**, décharger qn d'une corvée, etc.; dispenser qn de faire qch. *(b)* **To l. s.o. off**, faire grâce à qn. **To be l. off with a fine**, en être quitte pour une amende. **let on**, *v.i. & tr.* *F:* **To l. on about sth. to s.o.**, rapporter qch. à qn. **Don't l. on that I was there**, n'allez pas dire que j'y étais. **let out**, *v.tr.* 1. Laisser sortir (qn); ouvrir la porte à (qn); laisser échapper (un oiseau); élargir (un prisonnier). **To l. out the air from sth.**, laisser échapper l'air de qch.; dégonfler (un ballon, etc.). *F:* **To l. out a yell**, laisser échapper un cri. 2. *(a)* Rélargir (un vêtement). **To l. a strap out one hole**, (re)lâcher une courroie d'un cran. *(b)* *Nau:* Lâcher (un cordage); larguer (une voile). 3. **To l. chairs out (on hire)**, louer des chaises. 4. **To l. out a secret**, révéler un secret. 5. *v.i.* *F:* **To l. out at s.o. with one's foot**, décocher un coup de pied à qn. **let up**, *v.i. esp. U.S:* *(Of rain, pressure of business, etc.)* Diminuer; *(of frost, etc.)* s'adoucir. **Once he is started he never lets up**, une fois lancé il ne s'arrête plus. **To l. up on a pursuit**, abandonner une poursuite, lâcher. **'let up**, *s.* *Esp. U.S:* Diminution *f* (in, de); changement (du temps). **There will be no l. up in our endeavours**, nous ne relâcherons pas nos efforts. **To work fifteen hours without a l. up**, travailler quinze heures d'affilée. **letting**, *s.* Louage *m*. **L. value**, valeur locative.

lethal ['liːθ(ə)l], *a.* Mortel. **L. weapon**, arme meurtrière. **L. chamber**, salle *f* d'asphyxie (d'une fourrière); chambre *f* à gaz.

lethargic(al) [le'θɑːdʒik(əl)], *a.* Léthargique. **-ally**, *adv.* Lourdement, paresseusement.

lethargy ['leθədʒi], *s.* Léthargie *f*.

Lett [let], *s.* 1. *Ethn:* Letton, -one. 2. *Ling:* Le lette, le letton.

letter[1] ['letər], *s.* 1. Lettre *f*, caractère *m*. *Engr:* **Proof before letters**, épreuve *f* avant la lettre. *S.a.* BLACK LETTER, RED-LETTER. **To obey to the l.**, obéir à la lettre, au pied de la lettre. *Sp: U.S:* **To win one's l.**, être choisi comme membre de la première équipe. *S.a.* DEAD I. 1. 2. *(a)* Lettre, missive *f*. **To open the letters**, dépouiller le courrier. *(b)* *Jur:* **Letters of administration**, autorisation *f* nommant un administrateur à la succession d'un défunt intestat. 3. *pl.* **Letters**, lettres; belles-lettres; littérature *f*. **Man of l.**, homme de lettres. **'letter-box**, *s.* Boîte *f* aux lettres. **'letter-card**, *s.* Carte-lettre *f*, *pl.* cartes-lettres. **'letter-file**, *s.* Classeur *m* de lettres. **'letter-opener**, *s.* Ouvre-lettres *m inv.* **'letter-pad**, *s.* Bloc *m* de papier à lettres. **'letter-paper**, *s.* Papier *m* à lettres. **'letter-perfect**, *a.* To be l.-p. in one's part, savoir son rôle par cœur. **'letter-scales**, *s.pl.* Pèse-lettres *m inv.* **'letter-writer**, *s.* Épistolier, -ière.

letter[2], *v.tr.* Marquer (un objet) avec des lettres; graver des lettres sur (un objet); estampiller. **lettered**, *a.* 1. Marqué avec des lettres. 2. (Homme) lettré. **lettering**, *s.* 1. Lettrage *m*; estampillage *m*. *Typ:* **L. by hand**, repoussage *m*. 2. Lettres *fpl*; inscription *f*.

letter,³ s. Loueur -euse.
letterpress ['letəpres], s. **1.** *Typ:* Impression f typographique. **2.** Texte m (accompagnant une illustration).
Lettish ['letiʃ]. **1.** *a. & s. Ethn: Geog:* Letton, -one. **2.** s. *Ling:* Le lette, le letton.
lettuce ['letis], s. Laitue f, F: salade (verte). **Cabbage l.,** laitue pommée. *S.a.* COS, LAMB'S LETTUCE.
leucocyte ['lju:kosait], s. Leucocyte m.
leukaemia [lju:'ki:miə], s. *Med:* Leucémie f.
Levant¹ [li'vænt]. *Geog:* **1.** *Pr.n.* The L., le Levant. **2.** *attrib.* Du Levant; levantin.
levant², v.i. *F:* Partir sans payer; (*esp. of bookmaker*) décamper sans payer, *F:* lever le pied.
Levantine [lə'væntain], a. *& s. Geog:* Levantin, -ine.
levee¹ ['levi], s. (a) *Hist:* Lever m (du roi). (b) Réception royale (tenue l'après-midi et pour hommes seulement).
levee² [lə'vi:, 'levi], s. *Geog: Civ.E:* Levée f, digue f.
level¹ ['lev(ə)l]. **I.** s. **1.** *Tls:* (a) Niveau m (de charpentier, etc.). **Plumb l.,** niveau de maçon. *S.a.* SPIRIT-LEVEL. (b) *Mch:* Water-l., niveau d'eau. (a) Niveau (de la mer, etc.); niveau, étage m (de la société). **Difference of l. between two objects,** dénivellation f de deux objets. **At a higher l.,** en contrehaut (**than,** de). **At eye l.,** à la hauteur de l'œil; à hauteur des yeux. **On a l. with sth.,** de niveau avec qch.; à la hauteur de qch. **Drawing-room on a l. with the garden,** salon de plain-pied avec le jardin. **To be on a l. with s.o.,** être au niveau de qn; être l'égal de qn. **To come down to s.o.'s l.,** se mettre au niveau, à la portée, de qn. **At ministerial l.,** à l'échelon ministériel. (b) (*Of billiard-table, etc.*) **Out of l.,** dénivelé. **3.** (a) Surface f de niveau; terrain m de niveau. *Aut: Rail:* Palier m. **On the l.,** (i) à plat, sur le plat; (ii) *F:* (*of pers.*) loyal, -aux; de bonne foi; (iii) *F:* en toute honnêteté, en toute sincérité. *Aut:* **Speed on the l.,** vitesse en palier. (b) *Min:* (i) Niveau, étage; (ii) galerie f (de niveau). (c) Bief m (d'un canal). **II.** level, a. **1.** (a) (*Not sloping*) (Terrain) de niveau, à niveau; horizontal, -aux (route, etc.) en palier. (b) (*Flat*) Égal, -aux; uni. (c) **L. with . . .,** de niveau avec . . .; au niveau de . . .; à (la) hauteur de . . .; affleurant. . . . **L. with the water,** à fleur de l'eau; à fleur d'eau; au ras de l'eau. **L. with the ground,** à fleur du sol; à ras de terre. **To lay a building l. with the ground,** raser un édifice. **To be l.,** être de niveau. **L. crossing,** passage m à niveau. *Sp:* **To draw l. with . . .,** arriver à (la) hauteur de. . . . **2. L. tone,** ton soutenu. **To keep a l. head,** garder sa tête, son sang-froid. **To do one's l. best,** faire tout son possible. **'level-'headed,** a. Qui a la tête bien équilibrée; pondéré; d'aplomb. **level-'headedness,** s. Sens rassis; pondération f.
level², v.tr. (**levelled**) **1.** (a) Niveler; mettre (un billard, etc.) de niveau. **To l. (a town, house) to the ground,** raser (une ville, une maison). (b) Niveler, aplanir, égaliser (une surface). **2.** Pointer (un fusil), bracquer (un canon), diriger (une longue-vue) (at, sur). **To l. one's gun at, against, s.o.,** coucher, mettre, qn en joue. **To l. accusations against s.o.,** lancer des accusations contre qn. **To l. a blow at s.o.,** porter un coup à qn. **level down,** v.tr. **1.** Araser (un mur). **2.** Abaisser (qn, qch.) à son niveau. **3.** Niveler par le bas, au plus bas. **level out,** v.tr. Égaliser. **level up,** v.tr. **1. To l. sth. up to . . .,** élever qch. au niveau de. . . . **2.** Égaliser (le terrain, etc.). **3.** Niveler au plus haut. **levelling,** s. **1.** Nivellement m; (i) mise f à niveau, de niveau; (ii) aplanissement m (d'une surface). *Civ.E:* Régalement m (d'un terrain, etc.). **2.** Pointage m, braquage m (d'une arme à feu).
leveller ['lev(ə)lər], s. (*Pers.*) (a) Niveleur, -euse. (b) *Pol:* Égalitaire m.
lever¹ ['li:vər], s. *Mec:* Levier m. *Aut:* **Gear l.,** levier des vitesses. **Control l.** (*on steering column*), manette f. **'lever 'watch,** s. *Clockm:* Montre f à ancre, à échappement.
lever², **1.** v.i. Manœuvrer un levier. (*Of part, etc.*) **To l. against sth.,** faire levier sur qch. **2.** v.tr. **To l. sth. up,** soulever qch. au moyen d'un levier.
leverage ['li:vərid3], s. **1.** (a) Force f, puissance f, de levier. (b) **To bring l. to bear on** (a door, etc.), exercer des pesées f sur (une porte, etc.). **2.** Système m de leviers.

leveret ['levərit], s. Levraut m.
leviathan [li'vaiəθ(ə)n], s. **1.** *B:* Léviathan m. **2.** Navire m, etc. monstre.
Leviticus [li'vitikəs], s. *B:* Le Lévitique.
levity ['leviti], s. Légèreté f; manque m de sérieux.
levy¹ ['levi], s. **1.** (a) Levée f (d'un impôt). (b) *Mil:* Levée (de troupes); réquisition f (de chevaux, etc.). **2.** Impôt m, contribution f. *S.a.* CAPITAL² II. 1.
levy², v.tr. **1.** Lever, percevoir (un impôt); imposer (une amende). **To l. a fine on s.o.,** frapper qn d'une amende. **2.** *Mil:* Lever (des troupes). (b) Mettre en réquisition, réquisitionner (des denrées, etc.). **3.** (a) *Jur:* **To l. execution on s.o.'s goods,** faire une saisie-exécution sur les biens de qn. (b) **To l. war on s.o.,** faire la guerre à, contre, qn. **To l. blackmail,** faire du chantage.
lewd [lju:d], a. **1.** Impudique, lascif, -ive. **2.** *A. & B:* Bas, vil, ignoble. **-ly,** adv. Impudiquement, lascivement.
lewdness ['lju:dnis], s. **1.** Impudicité f, lasciveté f. **2.** Luxure f, débauche f.
Lewis ['luis]. *Pr.n.m.* Louis. **'Lewis gun,** s. *Mil:* Fusil mitrailleur.
lexicographer [‚leksi'kogrəfər], s. Lexicographe m.
lexicography [‚leksi'kogrəfi], s. Lexicographie f.
lexicology [‚leksi'kolədʒi], s. Lexicologie f.
lexicon ['leksikən], s. Lexique m.
Leyden ['laid(ə)n]. *Pr.n. Geog:* Leyde f. *S.a.* JAR³.
liability [‚laiə'biliti], s. **1.** *Jur:* Responsabilité f. **Joint l.,** responsabilité conjointe. **Several l.,** responsabilité séparée. **Joint and several l.,** responsabilité (conjointe et) solidaire. **2.** pl. *Com: Fin:* Liabilities, ensemble m des dettes; engagements mpl, obligations fpl; (*in bankruptcy*) masse passive. **Assets and liabilities,** actif m et passif m. **To meet one's liabilities,** faire face à ses engagements, à ses échéances. **3.** (a) **L. to a fine,** risque m d'(encourir une) amende. (b) Disposition f, tendance f (to sth., to do sth., à qch., à faire qch.). (c) (*Of product, etc.*) **L. to explode,** danger m d'explosion. **4.** *F:* **He's a l.,** c'est un poids mort.
liable ['laiəbl], a. **1.** *Jur:* Responsable (**for,** de). **2. L. to a tax,** assujetti à un impôt; passible d'un impôt. **Dividends l. to income-tax,** dividendes soumis à l'impôt sur le revenu. **L. to a fine,** passible d'une amende. **L. to military service,** astreint au service militaire. **3.** Sujet, exposé (**to,** à). **Car l. to overturn,** voiture sujette à capoter. **To be l. to catch cold,** avoir une disposition à s'enrhumer. **4. Difficulties are l. to occur,** des difficultés sont susceptibles de se présenter. **Plan l. to modifications,** projet qui pourra subir des modifications.
liaise [li'eiz], v.i. *Mil: F:* Faire, effectuer, la liaison.
liaison [li'eizən], s. Liaison f. **1.** *Mil:* **Poor l. between units,** mauvaise liaison entre les troupes. **L. officer,** officier m de liaison. **2.** Union f illicite. **3.** *Ling:* **To make a l.,** faire la liaison (entre deux mots).
liana [li'ɑːnə], s. *Bot:* Liane f.
liar ['laiər], s. Menteur, -euse.
lias ['laiəs], s. *Geol:* **1.** (*Rock*) Liais m. **2.** (*Stratum*) Lias m.
libation [lai'beiʃ(ə)n], s. Libation f.
libel¹ ['laibl], s. (a) Diffamation f, calomnie f. (b) *Jur:* Diffamation par écrit; écrit m diffamatoire; libelle m. **To bring an action for l. against s.o.,** intenter un procès en diffamation à qn.
libel², v.tr. (**libelled**) *Jur:* Diffamer (qn) (par écrit); calomnier (qn).
libeller ['laibələr], s. Diffamateur, -trice.
libellous ['laibələs], a. (Écrit) diffamatoire, calomnieux. **-ly,** adv. Calomnieusement.
liberal ['libərəl], a. **1.** (a) Libéral, -aux. **The l. arts,** les arts libéraux. (b) (*Of pers.*) D'esprit large; sans préjugés. **In the most l. sense of the word,** au sens le plus large du mot. **2.** (a) Libéral, généreux, -euse. **L. of advice,** prodigue de conseils. **L. offer,** offre généreuse. (b) Abondant. **L. provision of . . .,** ample provision de. . . . **3.** a. & s. *Pol:* Libéral (m). **-ally,** adv. Libéralement.
liberalism ['libərəlism], s. *Pol: etc:* Libéralisme m.
liberality [‚libə'ræliti], s. Libéralité f. **1.** Largeur f (de vues). **2.** Générosité f.

liberate ['libəreit], *v.tr.* **1.** Libérer; mettre en liberté; lâcher (des pigeons); délivrer (**from**, de). **2.** *Ch:* To **l. a gas**, dégager un gaz. **3.** *Fin:* To **l. capital**, mobiliser des capitaux. **liberating**, *a.* Libérateur, -trice.

liberation [ˌlibə'rei∫(ə)n], *s.* **1.** Libération *f*; mise *f* en liberté. **2.** *Ch: Ph:* L. of heat, dégagement *m* de chaleur. **3.** *Fin:* L. of capital, mobilisation *f* de capitaux.

liberator ['libəreitər], *s.* Libérateur, -trice.

libertinage ['libətinidʒ], **libertinism** ['libətinizm], *s.* Libertinage *m*; débauche *f*.

libertine ['libəti:n], *a. & s.* Libertin (*m*); débauché (*m*).

liberty ['libəti], *s.* Liberté *f*. (*a*) L. of conscience, liberté de conscience. At l., (i) en liberté; *Navy:* en permission; (ii) libre, disponible. To be at l. to do sth., être libre de faire qch. You are at l. to believe me or not, libre à vous de ne pas me croire. *O:* This is L. Hall, vous êtes ici comme chez vous. Statue of L., statue *f* de la Liberté. (*b*) To take the l. of doing sth., se permettre de faire qch. (*c*) To take liberties with s.o., prendre des libertés, se permettre des privautés, avec qn. He takes a good many liberties, il se permet bien des choses. **'liberty-boat**, *s. Navy:* Vedette *f* des permissionnaires. **'liberty-man**, *pl.* **-men**, *s.m. Navy:* Permissionnaire.

libidinous [li'bidinəs], *a.* Libidineux, -euse.

libido [li'bi:dou], *s.* Libido *f*.

librarian [lai'brɛəriən], *s.* Bibliothécaire *mf*.

library ['laibrəri], *s.* Bibliothèque *f* (collection de livres ou salle de lecture). Lending, circulating, l., bibliothèque de prêt (payante). Reference l., bibliothèque d'ouvrages de référence. Public l., bibliothèque municipale. Mobile l., bibliobus *m*. Photographic l., photothèque *f*. Record l., discothèque *f*. L. edition, édition grand format. *F:* He's a walking l., c'est une encyclopédie vivante.

librettist [li'bretist], *s. Th:* Librettiste *m*.

libretto, *pl.* **-i, -os**, [li'bretou, -i:, -ouz], *s.* Libretto *m*, livret *m* (d'opéra).

Libya ['libiə]. *Pr.n.* La Libye.

Libyan ['libiən], *a. & s.* Libyen, -enne. The L. Desert, le désert de Libye.

lice. *See* LOUSE.

licence ['lais(ə)ns], *s.* **1.** (*a*) Permission *f*, autorisation *f*. Under l. from the author, avec l'autorisation de l'auteur. (*b*) *Adm:* Permis *m*, autorisation; patente *f*, privilège *m*. Import l., licence *f* d'importation. L. to sell alcoholic drinks, licence de débit de boissons. Printer's l., brevet *m* d'imprimeur. Trades subject to a l., requiring a l., métiers patentables. Theatre l., tobacco l., wireless l., autorisation d'exploiter une salle de spectacles, un débit de tabac, d'avoir un poste de radio. Marriage l., dispense *f* de bans. Gun l., permis de port d'armes. To take out a l., se faire inscrire à la patente. L. holder, patenté, -ée. *Aut:* Car l. = carte grise. Driving l., permis de conduire. **2.** (*a*) Licence *f*. Poetic l., licence poétique. (*b*) = LICENTIOUSNESS.

license ['lais(ə)ns], *v.tr.* Accorder un permis, une patente, à (qn); patenter (qn). To be licensed to sell sth., avoir l'autorisation de vendre qch. To l. a play, autoriser la représentation d'une pièce. Licensed dealer, patenté. Licensed house, débit *m* de boissons. Licensed (to sell beer), *Fr.C:* licencié. *Av:* Licensed pilot, pilote breveté.

licensee [ˌlais(ə)n'si:], *s.* Patenté, -ée; détenteur *m* d'une patente ou d'un permis; (*of public house*) gérant, -ante ou propriétaire *mf*.

licentiate [lai'sen∫iit], *s.* Diplômé, -ée.

licentious [lai'sen∫əs], *a.* Licencieux, -euse, dévergondé.

licentiousness [lai'sen∫əsnis], *s.* Licence *f*, dérèglement *m*, dévergondage *m*.

lichen ['laikən], ['lit∫ən], *s.* Lichen *m*.

lichgate ['lit∫geit], *s.* Porche d'entrée de cimetière surmonté d'un petit toit (pour abriter le cercueil en attendant l'arrivée du prêtre).

licit ['lisit], *a.* Licite. **-ly**, *adv.* Licitement.

lick[1] [lik], *s.* **1.** Coup *m* de langue. *F:* To give oneself a l. and a promise, se faire un brin de toilette. **2.** *F:* At full l., à toute vitesse.

lick[2]. **1.** *v.tr.* Lécher. To l. one's lips, *F:* one's chops se (pour)lécher les babines. *F:* To l. s.o.'s boots, lécher les bottes à qn. To l. a recruit into shape, dégrossir une recrue. The cat licked up the spilt milk, le chat a léché, lapé, le lait répandu. **2.** *v.tr. F:* Battre, rosser (qn); rouler (un concurrent). This licks me, ça me dépasse. **3.** *v.i. F:* As hard as he could l., à toute vitesse. **lick off**, *v.tr.* Enlever (qch.) avec la langue. **licking**, *s.* **1.** Léchage *m*. **2.** *F:* (*a*) Raclée *f*, roulée *f*. To give s.o. a good l., rosser qn d'importance. (*b*) Défaite *f*.

lictor ['liktər], *s. Rom.Ant:* Licteur *m*.

lid [lid], *s.* **1.** Couvercle *m*. *F:* That puts the l. on it! ça c'est le comble! il ne manquait plus que ça! **2.** = EYELID. **3.** *Nat.Hist:* Opercule *m*.

lie[1] [lai], *s.* (*a*) Mensonge *m*. White l., mensonge innocent, pieux mensonge. It's a pack of lies! pure invention tout cela! To tell lies, mentir. (*b*) To give s.o. the l. (direct), donner un démenti (formel) à qn; démentir qn. **'lie-detector**, *s.* Machine à déceler le mensonge.

lie[2], *v.i.* (lied; lying) Mentir (to s.o., à qn). **lying**[1], *a.* Menteur, -euse; faux, *f* fausse; (récit) mensonger. **lying**[2], *s.* Le mensonge.

lie[3], *s.* **1.** Disposition *f. Geol:* Gisement *m* (d'une couche). *Civ.E:* Tracé (d'une route). L. of the land, configuration *f*, disposition, du terrain. To study the l. of the land, s'orienter; tâter le terrain. *Nau:* To know the l. of the coast, connaître le gisement de la côte. *Civ.E:* L. of the ground, site *m*. **2.** *Golf:* Position *f*, assiette *f* (de la balle). **3.** *Ven:* Retraite *f*, gîte *m* (d'une bête).

lie[4], *v.i.* (lay [lei]; lain [lein]; lying) **1.** (*a*) Être couché (à plat). To l. on the ground, être couché sur le sol. He was lying (helpless) on the ground, il gisait sur le sol. To l. asleep, être endormi. To l. at the point of death, être à l'article de la mort. To l. dead, être (étendu) mort. The body was lying in state, le corps reposait sur son lit de parade. (*On gravestone*) Here lies. . ., ci-gît. . . . (*b*) Être, rester, se tenir. To l. in bed, rester au lit. To l. in ambush, se tenir en embuscade. To l. still, rester tranquille. To l. under a charge, être sous le coup d'une accusation. To l. under suspicion, être soupçonné. *Mil:* A large force lay to the south, une forte armée se trouvait au sud. **2.** (*Of thg.*) Être, se trouver. His clothes were lying on the ground, ses habits gisaient par terre. Let it l. there! laissez-le là! The snow lies deep, la neige est épaisse. To l. open, être ouvert. The obstacles that l. in our way, les obstacles dont notre chemin est jonché. *Nau:* Ship lying at her berth, navire mouillé ou amarré à son poste. (*Of money*) To l. at the bank, être déposé à la banque. The snow did not l., la neige n'est pas restée. *S.a.* IDLE[1] 1. Time lies heavy on my hands, le temps me pèse. The onus of proof lies upon, with, them, c'est à eux qu'incombe le soin de faire la preuve. Town lying in a plain, ville située dans une plaine. His house lies on our way, sa maison se trouve sur notre chemin. *Nau:* The coast lies east and west, la côte s'étend à l'est et à l'ouest. To know how the coast lies, connaître le gisement de la côte. The island lies N.N.E., l'île gît N.N.E. *S.a.* LAND[1] 1. The difference lies in this, that . . ., la différence réside en ceci que. . . . The fault lies with you, la faute en est à vous. As far as in me lies, autant qu'il m'est possible, qu'il est en mon pouvoir. A vast plain lay before us, une vaste plaine s'étendait devant nous. A brilliant future lies before him, un brillant avenir s'ouvre devant lui. Our road lay along the valley, notre route longeait la vallée. **3.** *Jur:* It was decided that the action would not l., l'action fut jugée non recevable. No appeal lies against the decision, la décision ne souffre pas d'appel. **lie about**, *v.i.* Traîner. To leave one's papers lying about, laisser traîner ses papiers. **lie back**, *v.i.* Se laisser retomber; se renverser (dans un fauteuil, etc.). **lie by**, *v.i.* To have sth. lying by, avoir qch. en réserve. **lie down**, *v.i.* **1.** Se coucher, s'étendre. L. down for a little, couchez-vous un peu. **2.** *F:* He took it lying down, il n'a pas dit mot; *F:* il a filé doux. He won't take it lying down, il ne se laissera pas faire; il va se rebiffer. **lie in**, *v.i.* (*a*) *O:* Être en couches. (*b*) *F:* I want to l. in tomorrow morning, j'ai envie de faire la grasse matinée demain. **lying in,** *s.* Accouchement *m. O:* L.-in hospital, maternité *f.* **lie off,** *v.i.* 1. *Nau: (Of ship)* Rester au large. 2. *Ind:* Cesser de travailler; chômer. **lie over,** *v.i.* Rester en suspens. The motion was allowed to l. o., la motion a été ajournée. To let a bill l. o., différer l'échéance d'un effet. **lie to,** *v.i. Nau:* Être à la cape; tenir la cape. **lie up,** *v.i.* 1. *F:* Garder le lit. 2. *(Of ship)* Être désarmé. **lying²,** *a.* Couché, étendu.

lief [li:f], *a. & adv. A: Lit:* Volontiers. *(Used in)* I would, had, as l. . ., j'aimerais autant. . . . I would liefer have died, j'aurais préféré mourir.

liege [li:dʒ], *a. & s. Hist:* 1. (Vassal *m*) lige. 2. L. lord, suzerain *m.*

lien [li(:)ən], *s. Jur:* Privilège *m* (sur un meuble). L. on goods, droit *m* de rétention de marchandises.

lieu [lju:], *s.* In l. of . . ., au lieu de . . .; au lieu et place de. . . To stand in l. of . . ., tenir lieu de. . .

lieutenancy [lef'tenənsi], *s.* 1. *Hist:* Lieutenance *f.* 2. *Mil:* Grade *m* de lieutenant.

lieutenant [lef'tenənt], *s.* Lieutenant *m. Navy:* Lieutenant de vaisseau. **Second l.,** sous-lieutenant *m.* **lieu'tenant-'colonel,** *s.* Lieutenant-colonel *m.* **lieu'tenant-com'mander,** *s. Navy:* Capitaine *m* de corvette. **lieu'tenant-'general,** *s.* Général *m* de division. **'lieutenant-'governor,** *s. Fr.C:* Lieutenant-gouverneur *m.*

life, *pl.* lives [laif, laivz], *s.* 1. Vie *f.* To have l., être en vie; vivre. To come to l., s'animer. It is a matter of l. and death, c'est une question de vie ou de mort. L.-and-death struggle, lutte désespérée. To take s.o.'s l., tuer qn. To take one's own l., se suicider. To save s.o.'s l., sauver la vie à qn. To sell one's l. dearly, vendre cher sa peau. He was carrying his l. in his hands, il risquait sa vie. Without accident to l. or limb, sans accident personnel. To escape with one's l., s'en tirer la vie sauve. Many lives were lost, beaucoup de personnes ont péri; les morts ont été nombreux. To fly, run, for one's l., for dear l., s'enfuir à toutes jambes. Run for your lives! sauve qui peut! I cannot for the l. of me understand . . ., je ne comprends absolument pas. . . . *F:* Not on your l.! jamais de la vie! To have as many lives as a cat, avoir la vie dure. To give l. to . . ., animer (la conversation). To put new l. into . . ., ranimer, *F:* galvaniser (qn, une entreprise). He is the l. and soul of the party, c'est le boute-en-train de la compagnie. *F:* Put some l. into it.! Activez! *F:* mets-y du nerf! To draw from l., dessiner sur le vif; dessiner d'après nature. True to l., (roman) vécu, senti. His acting is absolutely true to l., son jeu est tout à fait naturel. *S.a.* LARGE I. 1. Animal, vegetable, l., la vie animale, végétale. Bird l., les oiseaux. The water swarms with l., la vie pullule dans l'eau. *Art:* Still l., nature morte. 2. *(a)* Vie, vivant *m* (de qn). Never in (all) my l., jamais de la vie. At my time of l., à mon âge. Early l., enfance *f.* Tired of l., las de vivre. Appointed for l., nommé à vie. L. annuity, rente viagère. Penal servitude for l., travaux forcés à perpétuité. L. senator, sénateur inamovible. *(b) Ins:* To be a good l., être bon sujet d'assurance. *(c)* Biographie *f.* *(d)* Durée *f* (d'une lampe, etc.). 3. *(a)* To depart this l., quitter ce monde; mourir. *(b) Manner of* l., manière *f* de vivre; train de vie. L. is pleasant here, il fait bon vivre ici. *F:* What a l.! quelle vie! quel métier? *F:* Well, how's l.? et alors, que devenez-vous? Such is l.! c'est la vie! He has seen l., il a beaucoup vécu. **'life-belt,** *s.* Ceinture *f* de sauvetage. **'life-blood,** *s. (a) Lit:* Sang *m* (de qn). *(b)* Ame *f* (d'une entreprise). **'life-buoy,** *s.* Bouée *f* de sauvetage. **'life estate,** *s.* Propriété viagère, en viager. **'life-giving,** *a.* Vivifiant. **'Life Guards (The),** *s.pl. Mil:* (British Army) Les cavaliers appartenant à la Maison du souverain. *S.a.* LIFE-GUARD. **'Life Guardsman,** *s.m. Mil:* Cavalier qui appartient aux *Life Guards.* **'life interest,** *s.* Usufruit *m* (in an estate, d'un bien). **'life(-)jacket,** *s.* Gilet *m* de sauvetage. **'life-line,** *s. (a)* Ligne *f* de sauvetage. *(b) (Aboard ship)* Sauvegarde *f.* *(c)* Corde *f* de communication (de scaphandrier). **'life-preserver,** *s.* Casse-tête *m inv*; assommoir *m.* **'life(-)saver,** *s. (Pers.)* Sauveteur *m.* **'life(-)saving,** *s.*

Sauvetage *m.* **'life-size,** *a. (Portrait)* de grandeur naturelle, de grandeur nature. **'life-table,** *s.* Table de mortalité. **'life-work,** *s.* Travail de toute une vie.

lifeboat ['laifbout], *s. Nau:* Canot *m* de sauvetage. L. Institution = société de sauvetage des naufragés.

lifeguard ['laifgɑːd], *s. Esp.U.S: (At seaside, etc.)* Sauveteur *m*; maître-nageur *m.*

lifeless ['laiflis], *a.* Sans vie; (i) mort; (ii) sans vigueur; (style) mou; (soirée) sans entrain.

lifelessness ['laiflisnis], *s.* (i) Absence *f* de vie; (ii) manque *m* d'animation; mollesse (de style, etc.)

lifelike ['laiflaik], *a.* (Portrait) vivant.

lifelong ['laiflɔŋ], *a.* (Amitié) de toute la vie. A l. friend, un ami de toujours.

lifer ['laifər], *s. F:* Forçat *m* à perpétuité.

lifetime ['laiftaim], *s.* Vie *f.* In his l., de son vivant. It is the labour of a l., c'est le travail de toute une vie.

lift¹ [lift], *s.* 1. Haussement *m*; levée *f. Aut: F:* May I give you a l.? puis-je vous conduire quelque part? I'll give you a l. (so far), je vais vous conduire (un bout de chemin). To get a l. up in the world, monter un degré de l'échelle sociale. 2. L. of a crane, hauteur *f* de levage d'une grue. *Hyd.E:* L. of a canal-lock, (hauteur *f*) de chute *f* d'un bief. 3. *Aer:* Effort sustentateur, poussée *f* (de l'avion). L. per unit of area, portance *f.* 4. Ascenseur *m.* Goods l., monte-charge *m inv.* Dinner l., service l., monte-plats *m inv.* **'lift-attendant, -boy, -girl, -man,** *s.* Liftier, -ière.

lift². I. *v.tr.* 1. *(a)* Lever, soulever (un poids); lever (les yeux). The tide will l. the boat, la marée soulèvera le bateau. To l. one's hand against s.o., lever la main sur qn. To l. s.o. up, (i) aider qn à se relever, à se mettre sur son séant; (ii) prendre (un enfant) dans ses bras. To l. up one's head, redresser la tête. To l. up one's hands to heaven, lever les bras au ciel. To l. up one's voice, élever la voix. To l. sth. down *(from a shelf),* descendre qch. She lifted the child out of bed, elle prit l'enfant dans son lit. He lifted the spoon to his mouth, il porta la cuiller à sa bouche. *(b)* The church lifts its spire to the skies, l'église dresse sa flèche vers le ciel. 2. *(a) Agr:* Lever, arracher (les pommes de terre). *(b) Com:* (Goods) Enlever. 3. *Cr: Golf:* Donner de l'essor à (la balle). 4. *F:* Voler, lever (qch.). To l. cattle, voler du bétail. To l. a passage from an author, plagier un auteur. 5. Lever (un embargo). II. lift, *v.i.* 1. *(Of fog)* Se lever; se dissiper. 2. *Nau: (Of vessel)* S'élever à la lame.

lifting, *s.* 1. Levage *m*, relevage *m*, soulèvement *m* (d'un poids). L. power, capacity, puissance *f* de levée (d'une grue). *Av:* L. force, force de sustentation, force ascensionnelle, force sustentatrice. 2. Arrachage *m*, récolte *f* (des pommes de terre). 3. *F:* Vol *m* (action de dérober qch.). **'lifting-gear,** *s.* Appareil *m* de levage. **'lifting-magnet,** *s.* Aimant *m* de suspension. **'lifting-platform,** *s. Aut:* Pont élévateur.

lifter [liftər], *s.* 1. *(Pers.)* Souleveur *m.* 2. *(a) I.C.E:* Exhaust (-valve) l., décompresseur *m.* *(b) Mec.E:* Came *f*, levée *f.*

ligament ['ligəmənt], *s. Anat:* Ligament *m.*

ligature¹ ['ligətʃər], *s.* 1. *Surg: Typ:* Ligature *f.* 2. *Mus:* Liaison *f.*

ligature², *v.tr. (a) Surg:* Ligaturer (une artère). *(b)* Lier.

light¹ [lait], *s.* 1. Lumière *f.* *(a)* By the l. of the sun, of the moon, à la lumière du soleil; au clair de (la) lune, à la clarté de la lune. Artificial l., lumière artificielle. *Ph:* L. wave, onde lumineuse. *(b)* The l. of day, le jour. The first l. of dawn, les premières lueurs, blancheurs, de l'aube. It is l., il fait jour. I was beginning to see l., le jour se faisait dans mon esprit. *(Of crime, etc.)* To come to l., se découvrir. Some curious facts have come to l., quelques faits curieux se sont révélés. To bring (sth.) to l., révéler (un crime); déterrer, exhumer (des objets anciens). *(c)* Éclairage *m.* This lamp gives a bad l., cette lampe n'éclaire pas. Sitting against the l., assis à contre-jour. To stand in s.o.'s l., cacher le jour à qn. To stand in one's own l., (i) tourner le dos à la lumière; (ii) ne pas se faire valoir. I do not look upon it in that l., ce n'est pas ainsi que j'envisage la chose. He does not see the matter in the right l., il ne voit pas al question sous son vrai jour. **His action appeared in the l. of a crime,** son action avait l'apparence d'un crime. (d) **To throw, shed, l. on sth.,** jeter le jour sur qch.; éclairer qch. **To act according to one's lights,** agir selon ses lumières. **2.** (a) Lumière, lampe f, bougie f. **To show s.o. a l.,** éclairer qn. **Bring in a l.,** apportez de la lumière. *Aut:* **Dash-board l.,** lampe f de bord, de tablier. *El.E: Ind:* **Warning l.,** lampe f témoin. *S.a.* NAKED 2. *F:* **One of the leading lights of the party,** une des lumières, un des hommes marquants, du parti. (b) **The l., the lights,** la lumière, l'éclairage; l'électricité f. (c) Feu m, phare m. *Mil:* **Lights out,** (sonnerie f de) l'extinction f des feux. *Nau:* **Navigation lights,** feux de route. **Riding lights,** feux de position. **To steam without lights,** naviguer à feux masqués, tous feux éteints. *Adm:* **Traffic lights,** signaux lumineux (de croisement). **Green l., red l.,** feu vert, feu rouge. *F:* **To see the red l.,** se rendre compte du danger. *F:* **To give s.o. the green l.,** donner le feu vert à qn. *Aut:* **Rear l., tail l.,** feu rouge. **Side lights,** feux de position. **Parking lights,** feux de stationnement. **Charged with driving without lights,** inculpé d'avoir circulé avec absence totale d'éclairage. *Av:* **Boundary l.,** feu, borne f, de balisage. **Navigation lights,** feux de bord. **Identification l.,** feu d'identification. *S.a.* LANDING² 1. (d) = LIGHTHOUSE. **The Portland l.,** le phare de Portland. **3.** (a) **Give me a l., please,** pourriez-vous, s'il vous plaît, me donner du feu? **To set l. to sth.,** mettre le feu à qch. *S.a.* STRIKE² I. 2. (b) Feu, éclat m (du regard). **I caught a l. in his eye,** je vis passer une lueur dans ses yeux. **4.** (a) Fenêtre f; lucarne f. *Aut:* Glace f. **Rear l.,** lunette f. (b) *Jur:* **Right of l.,** droit de vues (et de jours). **Ancient lights,** servitude f de vue. **5.** *Art: Phot:* Lumière, clair m. **L. effects,** effets de lumière. **L. and shade,** les clairs et les ombres. **The high lights,** les rehauts mpl. *Mus:* **Lights and shades (of expression),** nuances f. 'light-**filter,** s. *Phot:* Écran m orthochromatique. 'light-**meter,** s. *Phot:* Posemètre m. 'light-spot, s. (Of recording apparatus) Spot lumineux. 'light-year, s. *Astr:* Année-lumière f.

light², v. (p.t. & p.p. lighted or lit) **1.** v.tr. (a) Allumer. **L. a fire in my room,** faites du feu dans ma chambre. *Abs.* **To l. up,** (i) allumer; mettre la lumière; (ii) *Mch: Nau:* mettre les feux; (iii) *F:* allumer sa pipe. (b) Éclairer, illuminer (une pièce, les rues). (c) **To l., the way for s.o.,** éclairer qn. (d) **A smile lighted (up) her face,** un sourire illumina son visage. **2.** v.i. (a) S'allumer; prendre feu. **The match will not l.,** l'allumette ne prend pas. (b) S'éclairer, s'illuminer. **Her face lit up,** son visage s'éclaira. *F:* **Lit up,** un peu gris; éméché. **lighting,** s. **1.** Allumage m. **2.** Éclairage m. **Overhead l.,** éclairage vertical. *Adm:* **L. up time,** heure f d'éclairage. *Th:* **L. effects,** jeux m de lumière.

light³, a. **1.** Clair; (bien) éclairé. **2.** (Of hair) Blond; (of colour) clair. **L. blue,** bleu clair inv. 'light-**coloured,** a. Clair.

light⁴, a. **1.** (a) Léger. **L. as a feather,** aussi léger qu'une plume. **Lighter than air,** de moindre densité que l'air. **L. soil,** terre meuble. **To be l. on one's feet,** avoir le pas léger. **L. breeze,** brise faible, molle. **L. wine,** vin léger. (b) (Deficient) **L. weight,** poids faible. *S.a.* LIGHT-WEIGHT. **2.** (a) **L. cannon,** canon de petit calibre. **L. castings,** petites pièces. *Mil:* **L. cavalry, infantry,** cavalerie, infanterie, légère. *Typ:* **L. face,** œil léger. *S.a.* DRAUGHT¹ I. 5, RAILWAY 1. (b) Non chargé. **To travel l.,** voyager avec peu de bagages. *Rail:* **L. engine,** locomotive haut-le-pied. (c) **To be a l. sleeper,** avoir le sommeil léger. **3.** (a) **L. punishment,** peine légère. (b) **L. task,** tâche facile; travail peu fatigant. **4.** **L. comedy,** comédie légère. **L. reading,** lecture(s) amusante(s). **L. talk,** propos frivoles, légers. **To make l. of sth.,** traiter qch. à la légère. **To make l. of dangers,** mépriser les dangers. **5.** adv. **To sleep l.,** avoir le sommeil léger. -**ly,** adv. **1.** **Lightly clad,** vêtu légèrement, à la légère. **To walk, step, l.,** (i) marcher d'un pas léger; (ii) étouffer son pas. **To touch l. on a delicate matter,**

glisser sur un point délicat. **His hand ran l. over the strings (of the harp),** sa main effleura les cordes. **His responsibilities sit l. upon him,** ses responsabilités ne lui pèsent pas. **2.** **To get off l.,** s'en tirer à bon compte, **3.** **To speak l. of sth.,** parler de qch. à la légère. **light-'fingered,** a. **1.** Aux doigts agiles. **2.** **The l.-f. gentry,** messieurs les pickpockets; les voleurs à la tire. **light-'footed,** a. Agile, leste; au pied léger. **light-'headed,** a. **1.** **To be l.-h.,** avoir le délire. **2.** Étourdi, écervelé. **light-'hearted,** a. Au cœur léger; allègre. -**ly,** adv. Gaiement; de gaieté de cœur. **light-'minded,** a. Léger, étourdi, frivole. 'light-weight. **1.** s. *Box:* Poids léger. **2.** attrib. Léger.

light⁵, v.i. (p.t. & p.p. lit or lighted) (a) (Of bird) S'abattre, se poser; (of thg) s'abattre, tomber. (b) **To l. on one's feet,** tomber debout; retomber sur ses pieds. (c) **To l. (up)on sth.,** rencontrer qch.; trouver qch. par hasard. **To l. upon an interesting fact,** tomber sur un fait intéressant.

lighten¹ ['laitn]. **1.** v.tr. Alléger (un navire); réduire le poids de (qch.). **To l. a sorrow,** alléger, soulager, une douleur. **2.** v.i. **My heart lightened,** mon cœur fut soulagé. **lightening,** s. Allégement m.

lighten². **1.** v.tr. (a) Éclairer (le visage). (b) Éclaircir (une couleur). **2.** v.i. (a) S'éclairer, s'illuminer. **His eyes lightened (up),** son regard s'éclaira. (b) **It's lightening,** il fait des éclairs.

lighter¹ ['laitər], s. *Nau:* Allège f, péniche f, chaland m.

lighter², s. **1.** (Pers.) Allumeur, -euse. **2.** (Device) Allumeur, allumoir m (de becs de gaz). **Cigarette l.,** briquet m.

lighterage ['laitəridʒ], s. *Nau:* **1.** Déchargement m par allèges; transport m par chalands; acconage m. **2.** Droits mpl ou frais mpl d'acconage.

lighterman, pl. -men, ['laitəmən], s.m. *Nau:* Gabarier, acconier.

lighthouse ['laithaus], s. *Nau:* Phare m. 'lighthouse-**keeper,** s. Gardien m de phare.

lightness ['laitnis], s. Légèreté f.

lightning ['laitniŋ], s. Éclairs mpl, foudre f. **A flash of l.,** un éclair. **The l. has struck . . .,** la foudre est tombée sur. . . . **Struck by l.,** frappé de, par, la foudre. **As quick as l.,** with lightning speed, *F:* **like greased l.,** rapide comme l'éclair. **L. progress,** progrès foudroyants. *I.C.E:* **L. pick-up,** reprise foudroyante. **L. blow,** coup m raide comme (une) balle. *Ind:* **L. strike,** grève f surprise. *Th:* **L. change,** travestissement m rapide. 'lightning-**ar'rester,** s. Parafoudre m. 'lightning-con'ductor, s. Paratonnerre m. 'lightning-rod, s. Tige f de paratonnerre; paratonnerre m.

lights [laits], s.pl. *Cu:* Mou m (de bœuf, etc.).

lightship ['laitʃip], s. *Nau:* Bateau-feu m, bateau-phare m.

lightsome ['laitsəm], a. *Poet:* **1.** Léger, gracieux. **2.** Au cœur léger, gai.

ligneous ['ligniəs], a. Ligneux, -euse.

lignite ['lignait], s. *Miner:* Lignite m.

lignum vitae ['lignəm'vaiti:], s. *Bot:* (Bois m de) gaïac m.

like¹ [laik]. **I.** a. Semblable, pareil, tel. **1.** (a) **Two plants of l. species,** deux plantes de même espèce. *Prov:* **L. father, l. son,** tel père tel fils. (b) **The portrait is very l.,** le portrait est très ressemblant. **They are as l. as two peas,** ils se ressemblent comme deux gouttes d'eau, à s'y méprendre. **2.** (a) **I want to find one l. it,** je veux trouver le pareil, la pareille. **A critic l. you,** un critique tel que vous. **He is rather l. you,** il a de votre air. **She's l. nobody else,** elle est à part. **Whom is he l.;** *F:* **who is he l.?** à qui ressemble-t-il? **What is he l.?** comment est-il? **What's the weather l.?** qu'est-ce que dit le temps? **He was l. a father to me,** il m'a servi de père. **Old people are l. that,** les vieilles gens sont ainsi faits. **I never saw anything l. it,** je n'ai jamais rien vu de pareil. **The sum amounts to something l. ten pounds,** la somme s'élève à quelque dix livres. **Rather l. . . .,** un peu dans le genre de. . . . **Very much l. . . .,** tout à fait dans le genre de. . . . *F:* **That's something l. rain!** voilà qui s'appelle pleuvoir! *F:* **That's something l.!** à la bonne heure! **There is nothing l. health,** rien de tel que la santé. **There's nothing l. speaking frankly,** (il n'y a) rien de tel que de parler franchement. **She is nothing l. so pretty as you,** elle est bien loin d'être aussi jolie que vous. *S.a.* FEEL[2] 3, LOOK[2] 3. (*b*) **That's just l. a woman!** voilà bien les femmes! **That's l. his impudence!** voilà bien son toupet! **That's just l. me!** je me reconnais bien là! c'est bien de moi! II. **like,** *prep.* Comme. **I think l. you,** je pense comme vous. **Just l. anybody else,** tout comme un autre. *F:* **He ran l. anything, l. blazes, l. the (very) devil, l. mad,** il courait comme un dératé. **Don't talk l. that,** ne parlez pas comme ça, de la sorte. *P:* **L. hell I will!** jamais de la vie! **He stood there l. a statue,** il se tenait debout telle une statue. **To hate s.o. l. poison,** détester qn comme la peste. III. **like,** *adv.* 1. *F:* **L. enough, very l.;** (as) l. as not, probablement, vraisemblablement. IV. **like,** *s.* Semblable *mf*; pareil, -eille. **We shall never look upon his l. again,** nous ne reverrons plus son pareil. *P:* **It is too good for the likes of me,** c'est trop bon pour des gens comme moi. **I never heard the l.** (of it), je n'ai jamais entendu chose pareille. **To do the l.,** en faire autant; faire de même.

like[2], *s.* (*Usu. pl*) Goût *m*, préférence *f*. **Likes and dislikes,** sympathies *f* et antipathies *f*.

like[3], *v.tr.* 1. Aimer (qch.); avoir de la sympathie pour (qn). **I l. him,** je l'aime bien; il me plaît. **Do you l. him?** vous plaît-il? **I came to l. him,** il me devint sympathique. **I don't l. his looks,** sa figure ne me revient pas. **How do you l. him?** comment le trouvez-vous? **I should l. time to consider it,** j'aimerais avoir le temps d'y réfléchir. **As much as ever you l.,** tant que vous voudrez. **How do you l. your tea?** (i) comment prenez-vous votre thé? (ii) comment trouvez-vous votre thé? **Your father won't l. it,** votre père ne sera pas content. **Whether he likes it or not,** qu'il le veuille ou non; bon gré, mal gré. **These plants don't l. damp,** ces plantes craignent l'humidité. *F:* **I l. your impudence!** j'admire votre toupet! **I l. that!** en voilà une bonne! par exemple! 2. (*a*) **I l. to see them,** j'aime à les voir. **I l. to be obeyed,** j'aime qu'on m'obéisse. **Your going out so often isn't liked,** on trouve à redire à ce que vous sortiez si souvent. **Would you l. to smoke?** voulez-vous fumer? **I should l. to be able to help you,** je souhaiterais (de) pouvoir vous aider. **I should l. to have been there,** j'aurais bien voulu m'y trouver. (*b*) **As you l.,** comme vous voudrez. **I can do as I l. with him,** je fais de lui ce que je veux. **He is free to act as he likes,** il est libre d'agir à sa guise, comme il lui plaira. **To do just as one likes,** en faire à sa tête. **When I l.,** quand je veux. **When you l.,** quand il vous plaira. **I should l. nothing better,** je ne demande pas mieux. **He thinks he can do anything he likes,** se croit tout permis. **People may say what they l. . . .,** on a beau dire. . . .

liking, *s.* Goût *m*, penchant *m*. **To one's l.,** à souhait. **Is it to your l.?** cela est-il à votre goût? **His l. for me,** son penchant pour moi. **To have a l. for s.o.,** se sentir de l'attrait pour qn; affectionner qn. **I have taken a l. to it,** j'y ai pris goût. **I have taken a l. to him,** il m'est devenu sympathique.

likeable ['laikəbl], *a.* Agréable, sympathique.

likelihood ['laiklihud], *s.* Vraisemblance *f*, probabilité *f*. **There is little l. of his succeeding,** il y a peu de chances qu'il réussisse. **In all l.,** selon toute probabilité, toute apparence; vraisemblablement.

likely ['laikli]. I. *a.* 1. Vraisemblable, probable. *F:* **That's a l. story!** en voilà une bonne! **It is very l. to happen,** c'est très probable. **Is he l. to come?** est-il probable, y a-t-il des chances, (pour) qu'il vienne? **He is not l. to betray you,** ce n'est pas un homme à vous trahir. **He is hardly l. to succeed,** il a peu de chances de réussir. **He is quite l. to do it,** il est dans le cas de le faire. 2. **Incident l. to lead to a rupture,** incident susceptible d'entraîner une rupture. **This**

plan is most l. to succeed, ce projet offre toutes chances de succès. **The likeliest place for camping,** l'endroit le plus propre au camping. **The most l. candidates,** les candidats qui ont le plus de chances. 3. (*a*) *U.S:* **A l. child,** un bel enfant. (*b*) *O:* **A l. young man,** un jeune homme qui promet (beaucoup). II. **likely,** *adv.* **Most l., very l.,** vraisemblablement; très probablement. **As l. as not . . . ,** (pour) autant que je sache. . . . **He will succeed as l. as not,** il se pourrait bien qu'il réussisse. *P:* **Not l.!** pas de danger!

likemindedness ['laik'maindidnis], *s.* Communauté *f* de vues.

liken ['laik(ə)n], *v.tr. Lit:* Comparer, assimiler (**to, with,** à, avec).

likeness ['laiknis], *s.* 1. Ressemblance *f* (**to,** à). **Close l.,** ressemblance étroite. 2. Apparence *f*. 3. Portrait *m*, image *f*. **The picture is a good l.,** le portrait est très ressemblant.

likewise ['laikwaiz], *adv.* 1. De plus, également, aussi. 2. **To do l.,** faire de même; en faire autant.

lilac ['lailək]. 1. *s.* Lilas *m.* 2. *a.* Lilas *inv.*

Lilliputian [,lili'pju:ʃ(ə)n], *a. & s.* Lilliputien, -ienne.

lilt[1] [lilt], *s.* 1. Chant (joyeux). 2. Rythme *m*, cadence *f* (des vers).

lilt[2], *v.tr. & i.* Chanter mélodieusement, gaiement.

lily ['lili], *s. Bot:* 1. Lis *m. S.a.* GILD, ORANGE-LILY, TIGER-LILY, WATER-LILY. 2. **L. of the valley,** muguet *m.* 3. *U.S:* P: Homosexuel *m,* P: tapette *f.* **'lily-white,** *a.* Blanc, *f.* blanche, comme le lis; d'une blancheur de lis.

limb[1] [lim], *s.* 1. Membre *m.* **To tear an animal l. from l.,** mettre un animal en pièces. *S.a.* LIFE 1. 2. (*a*) **L. of Satan,** suppôt *m* de Satan. (*b*) *F: O:* Enfant *m* terrible; polisson *m.* 3. (Grosse) branche (d'un arbre); bras *m* (d'une croix). *F:* **Out on a l.,** en plan, le bec dans l'eau.

limb[2], *s. Astr: Bot: Mth:* Limbe *m*; bord *m.*

-limbed [limd], *a.* **Large-limbed, strong-limbed,** membru; bien membré.

limber[1] ['limbər], *s. Artil:* Avant-train *m.*

limber[2], *v.tr. Artil:* Atteler à l'avant-train. *Abs:* **To l. up,** (i) *Artil:* amener l'avant-train; (ii) se chauffer les muscles; se dégourdir.

limber[3], *a.* Souple, agile.

limbo ['limbou], *s. Theol:* Les limbes *m.* **To descend into l.,** tomber dans l'oubli.

lime[1] [laim], *s.* 1. = BIRD-LIME. 2. Chaux *f.* **Slaked l.,** chaux éteinte. *S.a.* QUICKLIME. **'lime-burner,** *s.* Chaufournier *m,* chaulier *m.* **'lime-kiln,** *s.* Four *m* à chaux. **'lime-pit,** *s.* Carrière *f* de pierre à chaux. **'lime-twig,** *s.* Gluau *m,* pipeau *m.* **'lime-water,** *s.* Eau *f* de chaux.

lime[2], *v.tr.* 1. Gluer (des ramilles). **To l. birds,** prendre des oiseaux à la glu. 2. *Agr:* Chauler (un terrain).

lime[3], *s. Bot:* Lime *f.* **Sweet l.,** limette *f.* **Sour l.,** limon *m,* citron *m.* **'lime-juice,** *s.* Jus *m* de lime douce, de citron doux.

lime[4], *s.* **L.-(tree),** tilleul *m.*

limelight ['laimlait], *s.* Lumière *f* oxhydrique. **In the l.,** sous les feux de la rampe; très en vue.

limerick ['limərik], *s.* Poème *m* en cinq vers, toujours comique et absurde, aux rimes a a b b a.

limestone ['laimstoun], *s. Miner:* Pierre *f* à chaux. *Geol:* Calcaire *m.*

limey ['laimi], *s. P:* 1. *U.S:* (*a*) Matelot anglais. (*b*) Un Anglais. 2. (*In Austr.*) Anglais nouveau débarqué.

limit[1] ['limit], *s.* 1. Limite *f,* borne *f.* **Within a three-mile l.,** dans un rayon de trois milles. **It is true within limits,** c'est vrai dans une certaine limite. **Without l.,** sans bornes. **Age l.,** limite d'âge. *F:* **That's the l.!** ça c'est le comble! ça c'est par trop fort! **He's the l.!** il est étonnant! il est impayable! *F:* il est marrant! 2. *Mec.E:* Tolérance *f.* **L. gauge,** calibre *m* de tolérance.

limit[2], *v.tr.* Limiter, borner, restreindre. **To l. oneself to . . . ,** se borner à. . . . **Limited intelligence,** intelligence bornée. **People of limited views,** gens bornés dans leurs vues, qui ont des œillères. *Publ:* **Limited edition,** édition à tirage restreint. *U.S:* **Limited train,** train *m* de luxe; rapide *m. S.a.* COMPANY[1] 4. **Limiting clause,** article limitatif.

limitation [ˌlimiˈteiʃ(ə)n], s. 1. Limitation f, restriction f. He has his limitations, ses connaissances, ses capacités, sont bornées. 3. Jur: Prescription (extinctive). Time l. (in a suit), péremption f.
limitless [ˈlimitlis], a. Sans bornes; illimité.
limousine [ˈlimuziːn], s. Aut: Limou— e f.
limp[1] [limp], s. Boitement m, clochement m, claudication f. To walk with a l., boiter.
limp[2], v.i. Boiter, clocher, clopiner. To l. along, (s'en) aller clopin-clopant. **limping**, a. Boiteux, -euse.
limp[3], a. Mou, f. molle; flasque. Bookb: L. binding, cartonnage m souple. F: To feel as l. as a rag, se sentir mou comme une chiffe. -ly, adv. Mollement; sans énergie.
limpet [ˈlimpit], s. Moll: Patelle f, bernique f.
limpid [ˈlimpid], a. Limpide, clair.
limpidity [limˈpiditi], s. Limpidité f, clarté f.
limpness [ˈlimpnis], s. Mollesse f.
linchpin [ˈlin(t)ʃpin], s. Veh: Esse f; clavette f de bout d'essieu.
linden(-tree) [ˈlindən(-triː)], s. Lit: & U.S: Tilleul m.
line[1] [lain], s. Nau: etc: Ligne f, corde f. Heaving-l., passeresse f, touline f. (b) Ligne (de pêche). To give a fish plenty of l., donner de la ligne, du mou, à un poisson. (c) Tg: Tp: Ligne, fil m. Tp: Shared, party, l., ligne partagée. S.a. HOLD[2] I. 3. (d) Const: Surv: Cordeau m. (e) F: It's hard lines, c'est dur; c'est de la malchance. It's hard lines on you, c'est bien malheureux pour vous. Hard lines! pas de chance! 2. Electric l., canalisation f électrique. 3. (a) Ligne, trait m, raie f. Oblique l., oblique f. Continuous l., trait plein. To draw a l., tirer, tracer, une ligne. Straight l., ligne droite. Broken l., trait discontinu. S.a. SIDELINE, TOE[2] 2. (b) Ph: Lines of the spectrum, spectrum lines, raies du spectre. The lines on his forehead, les rides f de son front. (c) Geog: The l., la Ligne (équatoriale); l'équateur m. (d) Ph: L. of force, ligne de force. (e) Art: Picture hung on the l., tableau pendu sur la cimaise. (f) To give s.o. a l. on sth., tuyauter qn sur qch. (g) Ligne (de l'horizon); contours mpl (du rivage). The hard lines of his face, ses traits durs. N.Arch: Lines of a ship, formes f d'un navire. Clean lines, formes fines. Art: Boldness of l., fermeté f des lignes. The general lines of a party's policies, les directives f politiques d'un parti. To be working on the right lines, être en bonne voie. (h) Ligne de démarcation. F: One must draw the l. somewhere, il y a limite à tout. I draw the l. at . . ., je ne vais pas jusqu'à (mentir, etc.), jusqu'au (mensonge, etc.). 4. (a) Ligne, rangée f (de personnes, d'objets). Const: To project beyond the building l., dépasser l'alignement. To stand in a l., se tenir en ligne, alignés. March in l., marche de front. I must try to fall into l. with your ideas, je vais essayer de me conformer à vos idées. To fall out of l., se désaligner. (b) File f; queue f. Ten cars in a l., dix voitures à la file. L. of moving traffic, colonne f de véhicules en marche. To stand in a l., (i) se tenir à la file; (ii) faire queue. (c) Mil: Nau: L. of battle, ligne de bataille. The front lines, le front. The back lines, l'arrière m. Navy: Ship of the l., vaisseau de ligne. (d) First l. of a paragraph alinéa m. (In dictating) 'Next l.' "à la ligne." L. for l. translation, traduction f linéaire. F: To drop s.o. a l., envoyer un (petit) mot à qn. L. of poetry, vers m. F: Marriage lines, acte m de mariage. 5. Ligne, compagnie f (de paquebots, etc.). Shipping l., compagnie de navigation. Air line, compagnie de transports aériens. 6. Ligne de descendants. In direct l., en ligne directe. 7. Rail: Voie f, ligne. Up l., voie descendante, paire. Down l., voie montante, impaire. Main l., grande ligne. 8. L. of thought, suite f d'idées. L. of argument, raisonnement m. The l. to be taken, la conduite à tenir, la marche à suivre. 9. (a) Genre m d'affaires; métier m. What is his l. (of business)? quel est son genre d'affaires? quelle est sa spécialité? F: That's not in my l., ce n'est pas (de) mon métier, mon rayon; ce n'est pas de mon ressort. That's more in his l., c'est plus dans son genre, dans ses cordes. (b) Com: L. of goods, série f d'articles; article m. Leading l., article (de) réclame. F: A rice pudding or something in that l., du riz au lait ou quelque chose dans ce genre-là. 'line drawing, s. Dessin m au trait. 'line engraving, s. Gravure

f au trait. 'line-fishing, s. Pêche f à la ligne. 'line-space, s. Typ: Typwr: Entre-ligne m, interligne m. 'line-spacer, s. Typwr: Levier m d'interligne.
line[2], v.tr. 1. Ligner, régler (une feuille de papier). (Of face) To become lined, se rider. 2. To l. a walk with poplars, border une allée de peupliers. The troops lined the streets, les troupes formaient la haie. line up. 1. v.tr. Aligner; mettre en ligne. 2. v.i. S'aligner. To l. up for the theatre, faire queue devant le guichet (du théâtre).
line[3], v.tr. 1. Doubler (un vêtement) (with, de). 2. Garnir à l'intérieur (with, de). A membrane lines the stomach, une membrane tapisse l'estomac. Nest lined with moss, nid garni de mousse. Walls lined with wooden panelling, murs revêtus de boiseries. S.a. POCKET[1] 1. **lined**, a. (Habit) doublé; (gant) fourré. Felt-l., garni de feutre. F: Well-l. purse, bourse bien garnie. **lining**, s. 1. Doublage m, garnissage m. 2. (a) Doublure f (de robe); coiffe f (de chapeau). (b) Garniture f, fourrure f (de frein); chemise f (de fourneau).
lineage [ˈliniidʒ], s. Lignée f, lignage m. To boast of an ancient l., se vanter d'une longue généalogie.
lineal [ˈliniəl], a. Linéal, -aux. L. descendant, descendant en ligne directe. -ally, adv. En ligne directe.
lineament [ˈliniəmənt], s. Usu.pl. Trait m, linéament m.
linear [ˈliniər], a. Linéaire.
lineman, pl. -men [ˈlainmən], s.m. = LINESMAN 1, 2.
linen [ˈlinin], s. 1. Toile f (de lin). L. sheets, draps en toile de fil. L. trade, commerce des toiles. L. warehouse, magasin m de blanc. 2. Linge m, lingerie f. Table l., body l., linge de table, de corps. A piece of l., a l. rag, un linge. F: Don't wash your dirty l. in public, il faut laver son linge sale en famille. 'linen-draper, s. Marchand de blanc, de nouveautés. 'linen-press, s. Armoire f à linge. 'linen-room, s. Lingerie f.
liner[1] [ˈlainər], s. Nau: Paquebot m; Transatlantique m.
liner[2], s. I.C.E: Chemise f (de cylindre).
linesman, pl. -men [ˈlainzmən], s.m. 1. (a) Rail: Cantonnier m. 2. Tg: Tp: Poseur de lignes. 2. Fb: Ten: Arbitre de lignes; Fb: arbitre, juge, de touche.
ling[1] [liŋ], s. Ich: Lingue f, morue longue.
ling[2], s. Bot: Bruyère commune.
linger [ˈliŋgər], v.i. (a) Tarder, s'attarder. To l. behind the others, traîner derrière les autres. To l. over a meal, prolonger un repas. A doubt still lingered in his mind, un doute subsistait encore dans son esprit. (b) (Of invalid) To l. (on), languir, traîner. **lingering**, a. 1. L. look, regard prolongé. L. doubt, doute qui subsiste encore. 2. L. death, mort lente.
lingerer [ˈliŋgərər], s. Traînard m; retardataire mf.
lingerie [ˈlɛ̃ːʒəriː], s. Lingerie f (pour femmes).
lingo [ˈliŋgou], s. (pl. lingoes [ˈliŋgouz]) F: (i) La langue du pays; (ii) baragouin m, jargon m.
lingua franca [ˈliŋgwəˈfræŋkə], s. Ling: Sabir m.
lingual [ˈliŋgwəl], a. Lingual, -aux.
linguiform [ˈliŋgwifɔːm], a. Linguiforme.
linguist [ˈliŋgwist], s. Linguiste mf. To be a good l. être doué pour les langues.
linguistic [liŋˈgwistik], a. Linguistique.
linguistics [liŋˈgwistiks], s.pl. Linguistique f.
liniment [ˈlinimənt], s. Liniment m.
link[1] [liŋk], s. 1. (a) Chaînon m, maillon m, anneau m (d'une chaîne). (b) Sleeve-links, cuff-links, boutons (de manchettes) jumelés, à chaînettes. 2. (a) Mec.E: Tige f d'assemblage. (b) W.Tel: Radio l., faisceau hertzien. 3. Lien m, trait m d'union (between, entre). Missing l., (i) lacune f; (ii) Biol: forme intermédiaire disparue; F: (le) pithécanthrope. Air l., liaison aérienne. 'link-lever, s. Mch: Levier m de changement de marche. 'link-pin, s. Goujon m de chaîne.
link[2]. 1. v.tr. Enchaîner, (re)lier, attacher (with, to, à). Line that links (up) two towns, ligne (de chemin de fer) qui relie deux villes. Closely linked facts, faits étroitement unis. To l. arms, se donner le bras. 2. v.i. To l. on to sth., s'attacher, s'unir, à qch.
links [liŋks], s.pl. (a) Scot: Dunes grises. (b) Terrain m de golf.
linnet [ˈlinit], s. Orn: Linotte f, linot m. Green l., verdier m.
lino [ˈlainou], s. F: 1. = LINOLEUM. 2. = LINOTYPE.
linocut [ˈlainoukʌt], s. F: Lino m.

linoleum [li'nouljəm], *s.* Linoléum *m.*

linotype ['lainotaip], *s. Typ:* Linotype *f.* **Setting by l.,** linotypie *f.* **L. operator,** linotypiste *m.*

linotypist ['lainotaipist], *s.* Linotypiste *mf.*

linseed ['linsi:d], *s.* Graine *f* de lin. **L. oil,** huile *f* de lin.

lint [lint], *s. Med:* Tissu de coton (employé en Angleterre pour les pansements).

lintel ['lint(ə)l], *s.* Linteau *m,* sommier *m* (de porte ou de fenêtre). *Arch:* **L. course,** plate-bande *f.*

lion ['laiən], *s.* **1.** (*a*) Lion *m.* **Lion's cub, whelp,** lionceau *m.* **The l.'s share,** la part du lion; la part léonine. (*b*) **Mountain l.,** puma *m,* couguar *m.* **2.** *F:* Personnage marquant; lion. **To make a l. of s.o.,** faire une célébrité de qn. **3. The Gulf of Lions,** le golfe du Lion. **'lion-hearted,** *a.* Au cœur de lion.

lioness ['laiənes], *s.f.* Lionne *f.*

lionize ['laiənaiz], *v.tr. F:* Faire une célébrité de (qn).

lip [lip], *s.* **1.** (*a*) Lèvre *f;* babine *f* (d'un animal). **Lower l.,** lèvre inférieure. **Upper l.,** lèvre supérieure. **To keep a stiff upper l.,** rester impassible, faire bonne contenance. **A cigar between his lips,** un cigare aux lèvres. **With parted lips,** les lèvres entrouvertes. **To bite one's lip(s),** se mordre les lèvres. **To smack one's lips over sth.,** se lécher les babines. **He never opened his lips,** il n'a pas desserré les dents. **No complaint ever passes his lips,** jamais il ne se plaint. **L. consonant,** consonne labiale; labiale *f.* (*b*) *P:* Insolence *f.* **None of your l.!** en voilà assez! (*c*) Lèvre (d'une plaie). **2.** (*a*) Bord *m,* rebord *m* (d'une tasse). (*b*) **Pouring l.,** bec *m* (de vase, d'éprouvette). (*c*) Rebord, saillie *f.* **'lip-read,** *v.i.* (*Of the deaf*) Lire sur les lèvres. **'lip-reading,** *s.* Lecture *f* sur les lèvres. **'lip-service,** *s.* **To pay l.-s. to s.o.,** rendre à qn des hommages peu sincères, servir en paroles.

lipoids ['lipoidz], *s.pl.* Lipides *mpl.*

lipped [lipt], *a.* **1. Thin-l.,** aux lèvres minces. **2.** (Tuyau) à rebord; (cruche) à bec.

lipsalve ['lipsɑ:v], *s.* Pommade *f* pour les lèvres.

lipstick ['lipstik], *s. Toil:* Bâton *m* de rouge; rouge *m* à lèvres. **Pink l.,** rouge à lèvres rose.

liquefaction [,likwi'fæk∫(ə)n], *s.* Liquéfaction *f.*

liquefiable ['likwifaiəbl], *a.* Liquéfiable.

liquefy ['likwifai]. **1.** *v.tr.* Liquéfier. **2.** *v.i.* (*a*) (*Of gas*) Se liquéfier. (*b*) (*Of oil*) Se défiger.

liqueur [li'kjuər], *s.* Liqueur *f.* **L. brandy,** fine *f.*

liquid ['likwid]. **1.** *a.* (*a*) Liquide. **To reduce sth. to a l. state,** liquéfier qch. (*b*) (Œil) limpide. (*c*) (Son) doux. (*d*) *Fin:* **L. assets,** valeurs *f* disponibles; liquidités *f;* disponibilités *f.* (*e*) *Ling:* (Consonne) liquide. **2.** *s.* Liquide *m.* **L. measure,** mesure de capacité pour les liquides.

liquidate ['likwideit], *v.tr. Com:* Liquider (une société, une dette). *F:* **To l. s.o.,** liquider qn.

liquidation [,likwi'dei∫(ə)n], *s. Com:* Liquidation *f.* **To go into l.,** entrer en liquidation.

liquidator ['likwideitər], *s.* Liquidateur *m.*

liquidity [li'kwiditi], *s. Fin:* Liquidité *f.*

liquor ['likər], *s.* **1.** Boisson *f* alcoolique. **Spirituous liquors,** spiritueux *m.* **F: To be in l., the worse for l.,** être ivre; être pris de boisson. **2.** ['laikwɔ:r] *Ch: Pharm:* Solution *f,* liqueur *f.*

liquorice ['likəris], *s.* Réglisse *f.*

Lisbon ['lizbən], *Pr.n. Geog:* Lisbonne *f.*

lisle [lail], *a.* **L. thread,** fil *m* d'Écosse. **L. stockings,** bas *mpl* de fil.

lisp¹ [lisp], *s.* Zézayement *m,* blésement *m.* **To speak with a l.,** zézayer.

lisp², *v.i. & tr.* Zézayer; bléser, *F:* zozoter. **lisping,** *a.* Blèse. *s.* Blésité *f.*

lissom(e) ['lisəm], *a.* Souple, agile, leste.

list¹ [list], *s.* **1.** *Tex:* Lisière *f.* **2.** *pl. A:* **Lists,** lice *f;* champ clos. **To enter the l.,** entrer en lice (contre qn); descendre dans l'arène *f.*

list², *s.* Liste *f,* rôle *m,* tableau *m,* état *m.* **Alphabetical l.,** répertoire *m* alphabétique. **The Civil L.,** la liste civile. **L. of names,** état nominatif. **Wine l.,** carte *f* des vins. **Waiting l.,** liste *f* des candidats, des postulants, liste d'attente. *Com:* **Mailing l.,** liste d'envoi, liste des abonnés. **Free l.,** (i) *Cust:* liste de franchise; (ii) *Th:* liste des personnes à qui l'entrée est gratuite. (*In hospitals*) **To be on the danger l.,** être dans un état grave. **Black l.,** liste noire. **F: Person on the black l.,** personne notée; suspect *m.* **St.Exch: Official l.,** cote officielle. *S.a.* ACTIVE 4, HONOUR¹ 4.

list³. **1.** *v.tr.* Cataloguer (des articles). **2.** *v.i.* *A:* = ENLIST 2.

list⁴, *s. Nau:* Faux bord; bande *f,* gîte *f.* **To have, take, a l.,** donner de la bande; prendre de la gîte.

list⁵, *v.i. Nau:* Donner de la bande; avoir un faux bord; prendre de la gîte.

listel ['list(ə)l], *s. Arch:* Listel *m, pl.* listeaux.

listen ['lisn], *v.ind.tr.* **1.** Écouter. **To l. to sth.,** écouter qch. **To l. attentively to s.o.,** prêter une oreille attentive à qn. **2.** Faire attention; écouter. **He would not l. (to us),** il a refusé de nous entendre. **listen in,** *v.i.* **1.** *Tg: Tp:* Capter un message. **2.** *W.Tel:* Se mettre à l'écoute; écouter la radio. **listening,** *s.* Écoute *f. Mil: Tp:* **L.-post,** poste *m* d'écoute; écoute. **L. table** (*used by police for tapping conversations*), table d'écoute.

listener ['lisnər], *s.* (*a*) (i) Auditeur, -trice; (ii) (*usu. Pej.*) écouteur, -euse. **He is a good l.,** il sait écouter. *Prov:* **Listeners never hear good of themselves,** qui écoute aux portes entend plus qu'il ne désire. (*b*) *Mil:* Écouteur.

listless ['listlis], *a.* Nonchalant, distrait; apathique. **-ly,** *adv.* Nonchalamment.

listlessness ['listlisnis], *s.* Nonchalance *f,* apathie *f;* indifférence *f.*

lit [lit]. *See* LIGHT².

litany ['litəni], *s. Ecc:* Litanies *fpl.*

literacy ['litərasi], *s.* Degré *m* d'instruction.

literal ['litərəl], *a.* **1.** (*a*) Littéral, -aux. **In the l. sense of the word,** au sens propre du mot. **To take sth. in a l. sense,** prendre qch. au pied de la lettre. (*b*) (*Of pers.*) Positif; prosaïque. **2.** (*a*) *Alg:* (Coefficient) littéral. (*b*) *Typ:* **L. error,** *s.* literal, coquille *f.* **-ally,** *adv.* Littéralement. **To take sth. l.,** interpréter qch. à la lettre. **L. speaking** à proprement parler.

literary ['litərəri], *a.* Littéraire. **L. man,** homme *m* de lettres. **L. agent,** agent *m* littéraire.

literate ['litərit], *a.* (*a*) Qui sait lire et écrire. (*b*) Lettré.

literature ['litrət∫ər], *s.* **1.** Littérature *f.* (*a*) La carrière des lettres. (*b*) Œuvres *f* littéraires. **Light l.,** lectures amusantes. **2.** (*a*) **The l. of a subject,** les écrits traitant d'un sujet. (*b*) Prospectus *mpl,* brochures *fpl,* documentation *f.*

lithe [laið], *a.* Souple, agile.

litheness ['laiðnis], *s.* Souplesse *f;* agilité *f.*

lithium ['liθiəm], *s. Ch:* Lithium *m.*

lithograph¹ ['liθəgræf, -grɑ:f], *s.* Lithographie *f;* image lithographiée.

lithograph², *v.tr.* Lithographier.

lithographer [li'θəgrəfər], *s.* Lithographe *m.*

lithographic [,liθə'græfik], *a.* Lithographique.

lithography [li'θəgrəfi], *s.* Lithographie *f;* procédés *m* lithographiques.

lithotomy [li'θɔtəmi], *s. Surg:* Lithotomie *f.*

Lithuania [,liθju'einiə], *Pr.n.* La Lithuanie.

Lithuanian [,liθju'einiən], *a. & s.* Lithuanien, -ienne.

litigant ['litigənt], *s.* Plaideur, -euse.

litigate ['litigeit], *v.i.* Plaider; être en procès.

litigation [,liti'gei∫(ə)n], *s.* Litige *m.*

litigious [li'tidʒəs], *a.* **1.** (Cas) litigieux, contentieux. **2.** (Homme) litigieux, processif, procédurier.

litmus ['litməs], *s.* Tournesol *m.* **L. paper,** papier *m* (de) tournesol. **L. solution,** teinture *f* de tournesol.

litotes [lai'touti:z], *s. Rh:* Litote *f.*

litre ['li:tər], *s. Meas:* Litre *m.*

litter¹ ['litər], *s.* **1.** (*a*) *Veh:* Litière *f.* (*b*) Civière *f* (pour le transport des blessés). **2.** *Husb:* (*a*) Litière (de paille). (*b*) Fumier *m* (d'écurie). **3.** (*a*) Papiers *m* et objets *m* malpropres (qui jonchent les rues). (*b*) Fouillis *m,* désordre *m.* **4.** Portée *f,* mise-bas *f* (d'un animal).

litter², *v.tr.* **1.** Mettre en désordre (une chambre). **Room littered with books,** chambre où des livres traînent partout. **Table littered with papers,** table encombrée de papiers. **2.** (*Of animals*) Avoir une portée.

little ['litl]. **I.** *a.* (*Comp. and sup.* less, least, smaller, smallest) **1.** Petit. **L. boy,** petit garçon; garçonnet *m.* **L. girl,** petite fille; fillette *f. O:* **L. ones,** enfants *m.* **The l. people,** les fées *f. O:* (*To child*) **Come here, my l. man,** viens ici, mon petit. *F:* **A tiny l. house,** une toute petite maison. **Wait a l. while!** attendez un petit moment! **The l. finger,** le petit doigt. **2.** Peu (de). **L. money,** peu d'argent. **A l. money,** un peu d'argent. **She knows a l. music,** elle sait quelque peu de musique. **I took very l. of it,** j'en ai pris moins que rien. **Be it ever so l.,** si peu que ce soit. **3.** (Esprit) mesquin. **A l. mind,** un petit esprit. **II. little,** s. (*Comp. and sup.* less, least) **1.** Peu *m.* **To eat l. or nothing,** manger peu ou point. **He knows very l.,** il ne sait pas grand-chose. **I had l. to do with it,** j'y ai été pour peu de chose. **I see very l. of him,** je ne le vois guère. **To think l. of sth.,** faire peu de cas de qch. **L. by l.,** petit à petit; peu à peu. *Prov:* **Every l. helps,** tout fait nombre; il n'y a pas de petites économies. **2. A l.** (*a*) A l. more, encore un peu. **A l. makes us laugh,** un rien nous fait rire. **For a l.** (while), pendant un certain temps. (*b*) **I was a l. afraid,** j'avais un peu peur. **III. little,** *adv.* Peu. **L. more than an hour ago,** il n'y a guère plus d'une heure.

littleness ['litlnis], s. Petitesse *f*; mesquinerie *f*.

littoral ['litərəl]. **1.** *a.* Littoral, -aux; du littoral. **2.** s. Littoral *m.*

liturgic(al) [li'tə:dʒik(əl)], *a.* Liturgique.

liturgy ['litədʒi], s. Liturgie *f*.

live¹ [laiv], *a.* **1.** (*a*) Vivant; en vie. *F:* **A real l. burglar,** un cambrioleur en chair et en os. (*b*) **L. coals,** charbons ardents. (*c*) **L. broadcast,** émission *f* en direct. **2.** (*a*) **L. cartridge,** cartouche chargée. (*b*) *El.E:* **L. wire,** fil sous tension. *F:* **He's a (real) l. wire,** il est très entreprenant, dynamique; il a de l'allant. **3.** *Tchn:* **L. weight,** poids utile. **'live-'bait,** s. *Fish:* Amorce vive. **To fish with l.-b.,** pêcher au vif. **'live'oak,** s. *Bot:* *U.S:* Chêne vert. **'live-stock,** s. *Husb:* Bétail *m,* bestiaux *mpl. Jur:* Cheptel *m.*

live² [liv]. **1.** *v.i.* Vivre. (*a*) **Is he still living?** vit-il encore? **While my father lives, lived,** du vivant de mon père. *F:* **Long l. the king!** vive le roi! **He hasn't a year to l.,** *F:* il n'en a pas pour un an. **He will l. to be a hundred,** il atteindra la centaine. **As long as I l.,** tant que je vivrai. **He cannot l. through the winter,** il ne passera pas l'hiver. *Prov:* **L. and learn,** (i) on apprend à tout âge; (ii) qui vivra verra. **L. and let l.,** il faut que tout le monde vive. (*b*) Durer. **His name will l.,** son nom vivra, durera. (*c*) **To l. on vegetables,** se nourrir de légumes. **To l. on hope,** vivre d'espérance. **He earns, gets, enough to l. on,** il gagne de quoi vivre. **To l. on one's capital,** manger son capital. **He lives by his pen,** il vit de sa plume. (*d*) **To l. honestly,** vivre honnêtement. **To l. in style,** mener grand train. **To l. well,** faire bonne chère. **To l. up to one's reputation,** faire honneur à sa réputation. (*e*) **Where do you l.?** où demeurez-vous? **To l. in the country,** demeurer à, habiter, la campagne. **I l. at number 36, Wilson Street,** je demeure rue Wilson, numéro 36. **House not fit to l. in,** maison inhabitable. (*f*) **He is living with his grandparents,** il habite chez ses grands-parents. **2.** *v.tr.* (*a*) **To l. a happy life,** mener, couler, une vie heureuse. (*b*) *Th:* **To l. a part,** entrer dans la peau d'un personnage. **live down,** *v.tr.* **To l. down a scandal,** faire oublier un scandale à la longue. **live in,** *v.i.* **The employees l. in,** les employés sont logés et nourris. **live on,** *v.i.* Continuer à vivre. **living¹,** *a.* Vivant, vif; en vie. **A l. man,** un homme vivant. **While he was l.,** de son vivant. **L. or dead,** mort ou vif. **Not a l. soul is to be seen,** on ne rencontre pas âme qui vive. **No l. man could do better,** personne au monde ne pourrait mieux faire. s. **The l.,** les vivants. **He is still in the land of the l.,** il est toujours vivant, encore de ce monde. **A l. death,** une vie pire que la mort. **living²,** s. **1.** Vie *f*. **L. space,** espace vital. **Style of l.,** train *m* de vie. **Standard of l.,** niveau *m* de vie. **To be fond of good l.,** aimer la bonne chère. **2. To earn one's l.,** gagner sa vie. **To work for one's l.,** travailler pour vivre. **To make a l.,** gagner de quoi vivre. **L. wage,** salaire minimum vital; salaire de base. **3.** *Ecc:* Bénéfice *m,* cure *f*. **'living-room,** s. Salle *f* de séjour, living-room *m*; *Fr.C:* vivoir *m*.

livelihood ['laivlihud], s. Vie *f*; moyens *mpl* d'existence; gagne-pain *m.inv.* **To make a l.,** gagner sa vie.

liveliness ['laivlinis], s. Vivacité *f*, animation *f*, entrain *m,* vie *f*.

livelong ['livlɔŋ], *a.* **The l. day,** toute la (sainte) journée; tout le long du jour.

lively ['laivli], *a.* **1.** (*Lifelike*) **To give a l. idea of sth.,** exposer qch. d'une manière vivante. **2.** (*a*) Vif, animé; plein d'entrain. **L. imagination,** imagination vive. **L. conversation,** conversation animée. (*b*) *F:* **Things are getting l.,** ça chauffe. **To have a l. time of it,** en voir de toutes les couleurs. (*c*) **To take a l. interest in sth.,** s'intéresser vivement à qch. **3. As l. as a cricket,** gai comme un pinson.

liven ['laiv(ə)n]. **1.** *v.tr.* **To l. (up),** animer. **2.** *v.i.* **To l. up,** s'animer.

liver¹ ['livər], s. *Anat:* Foie *m.* **Chicken livers,** foies de volaille. *F:* **To have a l.,** (i) être malade du foie; (ii) être de mauvaise humeur. **L. and white spaniel,** épagneul *m* foie et blanc *inv.*

liver², s. Personne *f* qui vit (de telle ou telle façon). **Loose l., evil l.,** libertin *m,* dissolu *m,* débauché *m.*

liveried ['livərid], *a.* En livrée.

liverish ['livəriʃ], *a.* *F:* Qui a le foie dérangé. **To feel l.,** se sentir mal en train.

liverwort ['livəwə:t], s. *Bot:* Hépatique *f*.

livery ['livəri], s. **1.** (*a*) Livrée *f.* (*b*) **L. company,** corporation *f* d'un corps de métier. **2. To take, keep, horses at l.,** prendre, avoir, des chevaux en pension. **'livery-horse,** s. Cheval de louage. **'livery-stable,** s. Écuries *fpl* de (chevaux de) louage. **L.-s. keeper,** loueur *m* de chevaux; remiseur *m.*

lives. See **LIFE.**

livid ['livid], *a.* (Teint) livide, blême; (ciel) plombé. **To become l. with anger,** devenir blême de colère.

lividity [li'viditi], s. Lividité *f*.

Livy ['livi]. *Pr.n.m.* Tite-Live.

lizard ['lizəd], s. Lézard *m.*

llama ['lɑ:mə], s. *Z:* Lama *m.*

lo [lou], *int.* *A. & Lit:* Voyez, voilà (que . . .).

loach [loutʃ], s. *Ich:* Loche *f*; barbotte *f*.

load¹ [loud], s. **1.** (*a*) Fardeau *m.* (*b*) Charge *f* (d'un camion). *Av:* **Commercial l.,** charge utile. **Flight l.,** charge en vol. **Touch-down l.,** charge imposée à l'impact. (*c*) **-load.** A lorry-l. of potatoes, un camion de pommes de terre. **A plane-l. of troops,** un avion rempli de soldats. **2.** *Mec.E:* Charge. **L. per unit area,** taux *m* de charge. *El:* **To shed the l.,** délester. **3.** Charge (d'une arme à feu). **4. To have a l. on one's conscience,** avoir un poids sur la conscience. **That's a l. off my mind!** quel soulagement! **5.** *pl.* *F:* **Loads of . . . ,** des tas *m,* des quantités *f,* de. . . . **We've loads of time,** nous avons largement le temps. **'load-shedding,** s. *El:* Délestage *m.*

load². **1.** *v.tr.* (*a*) Charger (un camion, etc.). **To be loaded up with . . . ,** être encombré de. . . . (*b*) **To l. s.o. with favours,** combler qn de faveurs. **Loaded with cares,** accablé de soucis. (*c*) Charger (un fusil). *Aut:* **To l. the grease-gun,** armer le graisseur. **2.** *v.i.* (*Of ship*) **To l. (up),** charger, prendre un chargement. **loaded,** *a.* **1.** (Camion, etc.) chargé. **2. L. dice,** dés pipés, chargés. **3.** *Ins:* **L. premium,** prime majorée; surprise *f.* **loading,** s. Chargement *m.* **Bulk l.,** chargement en vrac.

loadstone ['loudstoun], s. Aimant naturel, magnétite *f.*

loaf¹, *pl.* **loaves** [louf, louvz], s. Pain *m*; miche *f* (de pain). **Cottage l.,** = pain de ménage. **Sandwich l.,** pain de mie. **Tin l.,** pain moulé. *Prov:* **Half a l. is better than no bread,** faute de grives on mange des merles. **loaf-'sugar,** s. Sucre *m* en pains.

loaf², *v.i.* **To l. (about),** flâner, fainéanter, baguenauder. **loafing,** s. Flânerie *f,* fainéantise *f.*

loafer ['loufər], s. Flâneur *m*; *F:* baguenaudier *m.* **Young l.,** voyou *m.*

loam [loum], s. **1.** *Agr:* Terre grasse, végétale. **2.** *Metall:* Glaise *f*; potée *f*. **3.** Torchis *m,* pisé *m.*

loan¹ [loun], s. **1.** Prêt *m*; avance *f* (de fonds). **Short l.,** prêt à court terme. **L. without security,** prêt à fonds perdus. **L. bank,** caisse *f* de prêts. **On l. from . . . ,** prêté par . . . **2.** Emprunt *m.* **May I have the l. of . . .?** puis-je vous emprunter . . .? *Fin:* **To raise a l.,** contracter un emprunt. **'loan-word,** s. *Ling:* Mot d'emprunt (à une autre langue).

loan², *v.tr.* *U.S:* Prêter.

loath [louθ], *a.* **To be l. to do sth.,** répugner à faire qch.; faire qch. à contre-cœur. **To be l. for s.o. to do sth.,** ne pas vouloir que qn fasse qch. **He did it nothing l.,** il l'a fait très volontiers.

loathe [louð], v.tr. Détester, exécrer, F: abominer. I **l. doing it,** il me répugne de le faire. **He loathes being praised,** il a horreur des éloges. **loathing,** s. Dégoût m, répugnance f (for, pour).

loathsome ['louðsəm], a. Repoussant, écœurant, dégoûtant, répugnant. **-ly,** adv. D'une manière répugnante.

loaves. See LOAF¹

lob¹ [lɔb], s. Sp: Lob m; (balle envoyée en) chandelle (f). Ten: **To play a l.** (against s.o.), lober (qn).

lob², v.tr. Sp: Envoyer (une balle, etc.) en chandelle; lober (une balle); abs. lober. Ten: Renvoyer des chandelles.

lobate ['loubeit], a. Nat.Hist: Lobé, lobaire.

lobby ['lɔbi], s. (a) Vestibule m; promenoir m (d'un tribunal). (b) Parl: **The l. of the House,** la salle des pas perdus; les couloirs de la Chambre.

lobby², v.tr. & i. Pol: Faire les couloirs (de la Chambre). **lobbying,** s. Pol: Intrigues mpl de couloirs.

lobe [loub], s. Arch: Nat.Hist: Lobe m.

lobed [loubd], a. Nat.Hist: Lobé.

lobelia [lə'biːlia], s. Bot: Lobélie f.

lobster ['lɔbstər], s. Homard m. **Spiny l., rock ·l.,** langouste f. **Norway l.,** langoustine f. **'lobster-pot,** s. Casier m à homards.

lobular ['lɔbjulər], a. Lobulaire.

lobule ['lɔbjuːl], s. Physiol: Lobule m.

lob-worm ['lɔbwəːm], s. Arénicole m des pêcheurs; F: ver rouge.

local ['louk(ə)l]. **1.** a. Local, régional; de la localité. **L. colour,** couleur locale. **L. authorities,** autorités locales. **L. railway,** chemin de fer d'intérêt local. **L. road,** route vicinale, chemin vicinal. **L. government** = administration départementale, communale. (b) (On addresses) **'Local,'** en ville, "E.V." (c) **L. anaesthetic,** anesthésique local. **2.** s. (a) Habitant, -ante, de l'endroit. **The locals,** les gens du pays. (b) F: **The l.,** le bistrot du coin. **-ally,** adv. Localement. **Staff engaged l.,** personnel engagé sur place. **He is well known l.,** il est bien connu dans la région.

locale [lou'kɑːl], s. Scène f, théâtre m (des événements).

locality [lo'kæliti], s. **1.** (a) Caractère local. (b) Psy: (Sense of) **l.,** localisation f (d'un stimulus). (c) F: **To have the bump of l.,** avoir la bosse de l'orientation. **2.** Localité f. (a) Région f (d'une faune). (b) Endroit m, voisinage m. **In this l.,** dans cette région, dans ces parages.

localization [,loukəlai'zeiʃ(ə)n], s. Localisation f.

localize ['loukəlaiz], v.tr. Localiser (une épidémie, etc.).

locate [lo'keit], v.tr. **1.** Localiser (qch.); situer (qch.); découvrir, repérer (le siège du mal). El: **To l. a fault,** repérer, localiser, un dérangement. **2. To be located in a place,** être situé dans un endroit. **locating,** s. Détermination f (d'une fuite de gaz, etc.); relève f (d'un défaut dans un appareil). Artil: etc: Repérage m (d'une batterie, etc.).

location [lo'keiʃ(ə)n], s. **1.** = LOCATING. **2.** (a) Établissement m (de qn) dans un lieu. (b) Situation f, emplacement m. (c) Cin: Extérieurs mpl. **On l. sur les lieux. 3.** (S. Africa) Réserve f indigène.

locative ['lɔkətiv], a. & s. Gram: Locatif (m). **In the l.,** au locatif.

loch [lɔx], s. Scot: **1.** Lac m. **2. Sea l.,** bras m de mer.

lock¹ [lɔk], s. **1.** (a) Mèche f, boucle f (de cheveux). (b) pl. **His scanty locks,** ses rares cheveux. **2.** Flocon m (de laine).

lock², s. **1.** Serrure f, fermeture f. **Double l.,** serrure à double tour. **Double-sided l.,** serrure bénarde. **To pick a l.,** crocheter une serrure. **Under l. and key,** sous clef; (of pers.) sous les verrous. **2.** (a) Enrayure m (de roue). (b) Verrouillage m; verrou m, -ous. Rail: **L. and block system,** système m à bloc enclenché. **3.** Platine f (de fusil). F: **L. stock, and barrel,** tout sans exception, P: tout le tremblement. **4.** Wr: Étreinte f, clef f. **5.** Aut: (Steering) **l.,** angle m de braquage. **6.** Hyd.E: Écluse f. **To pass a barge through a l.,** écluser un chaland. **'lock-'gate,** s. Porte f d'écluse. **'lock(-)jaw,** s. Med: (i) Trismus m; (ii) F: tétanos m. **'lock-keeper,** s. Gardien m d'écluse; éclusier m. **'lock-nut,** s. **1.** Contre-écrou ṁ, pl. contre-écrous. **2.** Écrou m indesserrable. **'lock-stitch,** s. Point m de piqûre.

lock³. I. v.tr. **1.** (a) Fermer à clef; donner un tour de clef à (la porte). **The door locks on the inside,** la serrure joue à l'intérieur. (b) **To l. s.o. in a room,** enfermer qn dans une chambre. **2.** (a) Enrayer, caler (les roues); enclencher (les pièces d'un mécanisme); Sm.a: verrouiller (la culasse). **Wheel rigidly locked with another,** roue solidaire d'une autre. (b) (of pers.) **To be locked (together)** in a struggle, être engagés corps à corps dans une lutte. **To be locked in each other's arms,** se tenir étroitement embrassés. **3.** Hyd.E: **To l. a boat,** écluser, sasser, un bateau. **II. lock,** v.i. (a) (Of wheels, etc.) S'enrayer, se bloquer. (b) (Of machine parts) S'enclencher. **lock in,** v.tr. Enfermer (qn) à clef; mettre (qn) sous clef. **lock out,** v.tr. (a) Mettre (qn) dans l'impossibilité de rentrer (en fermant la porte à clef). **To find oneself locked out,** trouver porte close. (b) Ind: Fermer les ateliers (au personnel); **lock-outer** (le personnel). **'lock-out,** s. Ind: Lock-out m inv. **lock up,** v.tr. **1.** (a) Mettre, serrer (qch.) sous clef; enfermer, encoffrer (qch.). (b) **To l. s.o. up,** enfermer qn; écrouer qn au dépôt; F: coffrer qn. (c) **To l. up a house,** fermer une maison à clef. (d) Typ: **To l. up the forms,** serrer les formes. **2.** Fin: Immobiliser, bloquer, engager (des capitaux). **'lock-up,** s. **1.** Hangar m, etc., fermant à clef. **L.-up garage,** (i) box m (dans un garage); (ii) garage m (dans un immeuble). attrib. **L.-up shop, desk,** magasin, pupitre, fermant à clef. **2.** F: Poste m de police. F: violon m. **locking,** s. **1.** Fermeture f à clef. **2.** Mec.E: Immobilisation f, verrouillage m, blocage m, enclenchement m; enrayement m (des roues). **3.** Hyd.E: Éclusage m (d'un bateau).

locker ['lɔkər], s. **1.** Armoire f, coffre m (fermant à clef). **2.** Nau: (a) Caisson m, coffre. (b) Soute f.

locket ['lɔkit], s. Médaillon m (porté en parure).

locksmith ['lɔksmiθ], s. Serrurier m.

locomotion [,loukə'mouʃ(ə)n], s. Locomotion f.

locomotive [,loukə'moutiv]. **1.** a. Locomotif, locomobile. **2.** s. Locomotive f.

locum(-tenens) ['loukəm('tenenz)], s. Remplaçant, -ante (d'un médecin). **To act as l.-t. for a doctor,** faire l'intérim m d'un médecin, faire un remplacement.

locus, pl. loci ['loukəs, 'loukai], s. Geom: Lieu m géométrique.

locust ['loukəst], s. Criquet m; F: sauterelle. **Migratory l.,** criquet pèlerin. **2.** Bot: **L.(-bean),** caroube f. **'locust-tree,** s. Bot: **1.** Caroubier m. **2.** Robinier m; faux acacia.

locution [lo'kjuːʃ(ə)n], s. Locution f.

lode [loud], s. Min: Filon m, veine f, gisement m.

lodestar ['loudstɑːr], s. **1. The l.,** l'étoile f polaire. **2.** Point m de mire (de l'attention).

lodestone ['loudstoun], s. = LOADSTONE.

lodge¹ ['lɔdʒ], s. **1.** (a) Loge f (de concierge, etc.). (b) **Keeper's l.,** maison f de garde-chasse. **(Gate-)l.,** pavillon m d'entrée (d'une propriété). **2.** Shooting l., pavillon de chasse. **3.** Loge, atelier m (des francs-maçons). **'lodge-keeper,** s. Concierge m.

lodge². I. v.tr. **1.** Loger (qn dans un endroit); héberger; avoir (qn) comme locataire (en garni). **2.** (a) **To l. money with s.o.,** déposer de l'argent chez qn, confier de l'argent à qn. (b) **To l. a bullet on the target,** loger une balle dans la cible. (c) **To l. a complaint,** porter plainte (against, contre). S.a. APPEAL¹ 1. **II. lodge,** v.i. **1.** (Of pers.) (Se) loger (quelque part). **To l. with s.o.,** (i) demeurer chez qn (comme locataire en garni); (ii) être en pension chez qn. **2.** (Of thg) Rester, se loger. **The bullet has lodged in the lung,** la balle s'est logée dans le poumon. **lodging,** s. **1.** (a) Hébergement m. (b) Dépôt m, consignation f (d'argent, etc.). **2. A night's l.,** le logement pour la nuit. S.a. BOARD¹ 2. **3.** (Usu. in pl.) Logement, logis m, appartement meublé. **To let lodgings,** louer des chambres, des appartements. **To let furnished lodgings,** louer en garni, tenir un meublé. **To live, be, in (furnished) lodgings,** loger, habiter, en garni, en hôtel meublé. **To take lodgings,** louer un appartement meublé; louer une chambre, des chambres. **'lodging-house,** s. **1.** Hôtel garni; maison meublée. **2.** O: (Common) **l.-h.,** dépôt m de mendicité.

lodger ['lɔdʒər], s. Locataire *mf* (en meublé) ou pensionnaire *mf* (à la semaine, au mois). **To take (in) lodgers,** tenir un meublé; prendre des pensionnaires.

loess ['loues], s. *Geol:* Lœss *m.*

loft[1] ['lɔft], s. **1.** Grenier *m,* soupente *f.* **2.** (a) Pigeonnier *m,* colombier *m.* (b) **A l. of pigeons,** un vol de pigeons. **3.** Galerie *f,* tribune *f* (dans une église, etc.). **4.** *Ind:* Atelier *m. N.Arch:* **Drawing l.,** salle *f* de gabarits.

loft[2], *v.tr. Golf:* Donner de la hauteur à (la balle).

loftiness ['lɔftinis], s. **1.** Hauteur *f,* élévation *f* (d'une salle). **2.** Hauteur; ton hautain. **3.** Élévation (des sentiments, du style).

lofty ['lɔfti], a. **1.** Haut, élevé. **2.** (a) (Of pers.) Hautain, altier. (b) (Air) condescendant, protecteur. **3.** (a) **L. soul,** grande âme. (b) (Of style) Élevé, relevé, soutenu. **-ily,** adv. **1.** (Situé) en haut. **2.** Fièrement, altièrement.

log[1] [lɔg], s. **1.** Grosse bûche; rondin *m,* tronçon *m* de bois. **Chopping l.,** billot *m.* **Timber in the l.,** bois *m* en grume. **To stand like a l.,** rester (là) comme une souche. **To fall like a l.,** tomber comme une masse. **A King l.,** un roi soliveau. **2.** *Nau:* Loch *m.* **Patent l.,** loch enregistreur, à hélice; sillomètre *m.* **To heave, stream, the l.,** jeter, filer, le loch. **3.** *Nau:* = LOG-BOOK l. *Mil:* **L. of a listening-post,** journal *m* d'écoute. **'log-book,** s. **1.** *Nau:* **Ship's l.**(-book), journal *m* de mer, journal de bord. **2.** (a) *Aut: etc:* (i) Carnet *m* de route. (ii) *F:* = Carte grise. (b) *Av:* Carnet de vol. (c) *Ind:* Journal de travail (d'une machine); registre *m. W.Tel:* Carnet d'écoute. **'log-'cabin, -house, -'hut,** s. Cabane *f* en rondins. **'log-line,** s. *Nau:* Ligne *f* de loch. **'log-rolling,** s. **1.** Transport *m* des billes à la rivière. **2.** *U.S:* (a) Alliance *f* politique dans un but intéressé. (b) Battage *m* littéraire, camaraderie *f* littéraire.

log[2], *v.tr.* **1.** (a) *Nau:* Porter (un fait) au journal. (b) *Ind:* Noter (des résultats, etc.) sur le registre. **2.** *W.Tel:* Repérer, étalonner (une station).

log[3], s. *F: Mth:* = LOGARITHM.

loganberry ['lougənberi], s. Ronce-framboise *f, pl.* ronces-framboises.

logan(-stone) ['lougən(stoun)], s. Rocher branlant.

logarithm ['lɔgəriθm], s. Logarithme *m.*

logarithmic [ˌlɔgə'riθmik], a. **1.** Logarithmique. **2. L. table,** table *f* de logarithmes.

logger ['lɔgər], s.m. *U.S:* Bûcheron.

loggerhead ['lɔgəhed], s. **To be at loggerheads with s.o.,** être en bisbille, en désaccord, être brouillé, avec qn. **To come to loggerheads with s.o.,** entrer en conflit avec qn. **To set people at loggerheads,** mettre la discorde, semer la dissension, entre les gens; brouiller les gens.

loggia ['lɔdʒiə], s. *Arch:* Loge *f,* loggia *f.*

logic ['lɔdʒik], s. Logique *f.*

logical ['lɔdʒik(ə)l], a. **1.** Logique. **2.** (Of pers.) Qui a de la logique; qui a de la suite dans les idées. **-ally,** adv. Logiquement.

logician [lɔ'dʒiʃ(ə)n], s. Logicien, -ienne.

logistics [lɔ'dʒistiks], s.pl. **1.** *Mth:* Logistique *f.* **2.** *Mil:* Logistique.

logogriph ['lɔgəgrif], s. Logogriphe *m.*

logwood ['lɔgwud], s. (Bois *m* de) campêche *m.*

loin [lɔin], s. **1.** *pl.* **Loins,** reins *m. Anat:* Lombes *m. A:* **To gird up one's loins,** se ceindre les reins. **2.** *Cu:* Filet *m* (de mouton, de veau); longe *f* (de veau); aloyau *m* et faux-filet *m* (de bœuf). **loin-'chop,** s. Côtelette *f* de filet. **'loin-cloth,** s. Bande-culotte *f, pl.* bandes-culottes; pagne *m.*

loiter ['lɔitər], v.i. **1.** Flâner, traîner. **To l. on the way,** s'attarder en route; s'amuser en chemin. **2.** *Jur:* Rôder (d'une manière suspecte). **loitering**[1], a. Flâneur, -euse; traînard. **loitering**[2], s. **1.** Flânerie *f.* **2.** Vagabondage délictueux. **No l.!** défense de stationner! (said by police) Circulez!

loiterer ['lɔitərər], s. **1.** Flâneur, -euse. **2.** Rôdeur, -euse.

loll [lɔl], v. **1.** *v.tr.* (Of dog) **To l. out its tongue,** laisser pendre la langue. **2.** *v.i.* (a) (Of tongue) **To l. out,** pendre. (b) (Of pers.) Être étendu (F: comme un veau). **To l. (back) in an arm-chair,** se renverser nonchalamment, se prélasser, dans un fauteuil. (c) **To l. about,** flâner, fainéanter.

lollie ['lɔli], s. *F:* Sucette *f.*

lollipop ['lɔlipɔp], s. (a) Sucrerie *f;* sucre *m* d'orge. **Lollipops,** bonbons *m.* (b) Sucette *f.*

lolly ['lɔli], s. *F:* **1.** = LOLLIE. **Ice(d) l.,** sucette glacée. **2.** Argent *m, F:* pognon *m.*

Lombardy ['lɔmbədi]. *Pr.n.* La Lombardie.

London ['lʌndən]. *Pr.n.* Londres. **Greater L.,** le Grand Londres. **'London 'pride,** s. *Bot:* Désespoir *m* des peintres.

Londoner ['lʌndənər], s. Londonien, -ienne.

lone [loun], a. Solitaire, seul. **To play a l. hand,** agir tout seul.

loneliness ['lounlinis], s. **1.** Solitude *f,* isolement *m.* **2.** Sentiment *m* d'abandon.

lonely ['lounli], a. Solitaire, isolé. **To feel very l.,** se sentir bien seul.

lonesome ['lounsəm], a. *F:* Solitaire, seul.

long[1] [lɔŋ]. **I.** a. Long, *f.* longue. **1. To be six feet l.,** avoir six pieds de long, de longueur; être long de six pieds. **How l. is the table?** quelle est la longueur de la table? de quelle longueur est la table? **To make sth. longer,** allonger, rallonger, qch. **To take the longest way round,** prendre par le plus long; prendre le chemin des écoliers. **The best by a l. way,** de beaucoup le meilleur. **Two l. miles,** deux bons milles. **He pulled a l. face,** il a fait la grimace; son nez s'est allongé. **Face as l. as a fiddle,** figure longue d'une aune, figure d'enterrement. **To have a l. tongue,** avoir la langue trop longue. **To be l. in the arm,** avoir les bras longs. **2.** (In time) **How l. are the holidays?** quelle est la durée des vacances? **The l. vacation,** les grandes vacances. **The days are getting longer,** les jours augmentent, rallongent. **It will take a l. time,** cela prendra longtemps; ce sera long. **They are a l. time, a l. while, (in) coming,** ils se font attendre. **To be a l. time doing sth.,** mettre longtemps à faire qch. **It is a l. time since I saw him,** il y a longtemps que je ne l'ai vu. **A l. time ago,** il y a (bien) longtemps. **It will be a l. time before the agitation dies down,** l'agitation n'est pas près de se calmer. **To wait for a l. time,** attendre longtemps. **For a l. time he was thought to be dead,** pendant longtemps on le crut mort. **For a l. time past he had been contemplating this step,** depuis longtemps il méditait cette démarche. **It will not happen for a l. time,** cela ne se fera pas de longtemps, de si tôt. **Three days at the longest,** trois jours (tout) au plus. *Mil: Navy:* **L. service men,** engagés à long terme. **3. L. price,** grand prix, prix élevé. **L. bill,** grand compte. **L. purse,** bourse bien garnie. *Com:* **L. hundred,** grand cent, cent vingt. **4. L.-stemmed,** longicaule. **L.-leaved,** longifolié. **II. long,** s. **1.** (a) **He knows the l. and the short of the matter,** il connaît l'affaire à fond. **The l. and the short of it is that . . .,** le fin mot de l'affaire c'est que. . . . (b) *Pros:* **Longs and shorts,** longues *f* et brèves. **2. Before l.,** *Poet:* ere l., avant peu; sous peu. **For l.,** pendant longtemps. **I haven't l. to live,** je n'ai pas longtemps à vivre. **It will not take l.,** cela ne prendra pas longtemps. **I had only l. enough to . . .,** je n'ai eu que le temps de . . . **III. long,** adv. **1.** (a) Longtemps. **Have you been here l.?** y a-t-il longtemps que vous êtes ici? **He has been gone so l.,** il y a beau temps qu'il est parti. **L. live the King!** vive le roi! **Stay as l. as you like,** restez aussi longtemps que vous voudrez. **As l., so l., as I live,** tant que je vivrai. **You may do as you like so l. as you leave me alone,** faites tout ce que vous voudrez pourvu que vous me laissiez tranquille. **To be l. (in) doing sth.,** mettre longtemps à faire qch.; tarder à faire qch. **He was not l. in, about, over, setting up a ladder,** il eut bientôt fait de dresser une échelle. **You aren't l. about it,** vous allez vite en besogne. **He won't be l.,** il ne tardera pas. **Now we shan't be l.!** (i) nous n'en avons plus pour longtemps; (ii) *F:* voilà qui va bien! **It will be l. before we see his like,** de longtemps on ne verra son pareil. **It is l. since I saw him,** il y a longtemps que je l'ai vu. *F:* **So l.!** au revoir, à bientôt! (b) Depuis longtemps. **I have l. been expecting him,** je l'attends depuis longtemps. (c) **How l.?** combien de temps? **How l. have you been here?** depuis combien de temps êtes-vous ici? depuis quand êtes-vous ici? **How l. will it be until . . .?** combien de temps faudra-t-il pour que . . .? **How l. does your leave last?** quelle est la durée de votre congé? **2. L. before, after,** longtemps avant, après. **Not l. before, after,**

peu de temps avant, après. **He died l. ago,** il est mort depuis longtemps. **He died not l. ago,** il n'y a pas longtemps qu'il est mort; il est mort depuis peu. **He is not l. for this world,** il ne fera pas de vieux os. **3. All day l.,** tout le long du jour; pendant toute la journée. **His life l.** (toute) sa vie durant. **4. I could no longer see him,** je ne pouvais plus le voir. **I could not wait any longer,** je ne pouvais pas attendre plus longtemps. **How much longer will it last?** combien (de temps) cela durera-t-il encore? **5. L. felt want,** besoin senti depuis longtemps. **'long a'go.** **1.** *a.* D'autrefois, de jadis. **2.** *s.* Le temps jadis. **In the days of l.-a.,** autrefois; au temps jadis. **'long-boat,** *s. Nau:* Grand canot; chaloupe *f.* **'long bow,** *s. A.Arms:* Arc *m* d'homme d'armes. *F:* **To draw the l.-b.,** exagérer, *F:* galéjer. **'long-'clothes,** *s.pl. O:* Cache-maillot *m inv* (de bébé). **I was still in l.-c. when . . .,** j'étais encore au maillot quand. . . **'long-'dated,** *a. Fin:* A longue échéance. **'long-'distance,** *attrib.a. Tp:* **L.-d. telephone,** l'inter(urbain) *m. Sp:* **L.-d. runner,** coureur *m* de fond. **'long-'drawn(-'out),** *a.* **L.-d.(-o.) sigh,** long soupir; soupir prolongé. **'long-hand,** *s.* Écriture ordinaire, courante. **'long-'headed,** *a.* **1.** A (la) tête allongée; dolichocéphale. **2.** Perspicace, avisé, *F:* qui a le nez creux. **'long-'legged,** *a.* A longues jambes; *(of bird)* à longues pattes. **'long-'lived,** *a.* *(a)* Qui a la vie longue; *Nat.Hist:* vivace. *(b)* **L.-l. error,** erreur persistante, vivace. **'long-'lost,** *a.* Perdu depuis longtemps. **'long-'playing,** *a.* **L.-p. record,** microsillon *m.* **'long-'range,** *a.* A longue portée. *Av:* **L.-r. aircraft,** avion à grand rayon d'action. **'long-'sighted,** *a.* **1.** *Med:* *(a)* Presbyte. *(b)* Hypermétrope. **2.** Prévoyant. **long-'sightedness,** *s.* **1.** *Med:* *(a)* Presbytie *f.* *(b)* Hypermétropie *f.* **'long-'standing,** *attrib.a.* Ancien; de longue date. **'long-'suffering. 1.** *s.* *(a)* Patience *f,* endurance *f.* *(b)* Longanimité *f,* indulgence *f.* **2.** *a.* *(a)* Patient, endurant. *(b)* Longanime, indulgent. **'long-'term,** *attrib.a.* **L.-t. policy,** une politique à longue échéance, de longue haleine. **L.-t. transaction,** opération *f* à long terme. **'long-'winded,** *a.* *F:* **1.** (Histoire) de longue haleine, interminable. **2.** *(Of speaker)* Verbeux, intarissable.

long², *v.i.* **To l. for sth.,** désirer qch. fortement, ardemment; avoir grande envie de qch.; soupirer pour, après, qch. **To l. for home,** avoir la nostalgie du foyer. **To l. to do sth.,** avoir bien envie de faire qch.; être impatient de faire qch.; brûler, rêver, de faire qch. **I l. to go,** il me tarde d'y aller. **longing¹,** *a.* Qui désire ardemment, qui attend impatiemment. **-ly,** *adv.* Avec envie. **To look l. at sth.,** couver qch. des yeux. **longing²,** *s.* Désir ardent, grande envie **(for, after,** de). *Med:* Envie (de femme enceinte).

longanimity [lɔŋgə'nimiti], *s. Lit:* Longanimité *f.*

longevity [lɔn'dʒeviti], *s.* Longévité *f.*

longish ['lɔniʃ], *a.* Assez long, plutôt long.

longitude ['lɔndʒitju:d], *s.* Longitude *f.* **In l. 20°,** par 20° de longitude. **In the l. of . . .,** sous, par, la longitude de. . . .

longitudinal [lɔndʒi'tju:din(ə)l], *a.* Longitudinal, -aux; en long. **L. beam, girder,** longrine *f,* longeron *m.*

longshoreman, *pl.* -men ['lɔnʃɔ:mən], *s.m. Nau:* Homme qui travaille dans le port ou sur la côte; débardeur; ramasseur de varech, etc.

longways ['lɔnweiz], **longwise** ['lɔnwaiz], *adv.* En long, en longueur.

loo (the) [ðə'lu:], *s. F:* les cabinets *m.*

loofah ['lu:fə], *s. Toil:* Loofa(h) *m,* luffa *m;* éponge végétale.

look¹ [luk], *s.* **1.** Regard *m.* **To have a l. at sth.,** jeter un coup d'œil sur qch.; regarder qch. **To take a good l. at s.o.,** (i) scruter qn du regard; (ii) dévisager qn. **To have, take, a l. round the town,** faire un tour de ville. **2.** *(a)* Aspect *m,* air *m,* apparence *f* (de qn, de qch.); mine *f* (de qn). **By her l. one can see that . . .,** à sa mine on voit que. . . **To judge by looks,** juger d'après les apparences. **I don't like his looks, the l. of him,** sa figure ne me revient pas. **I don't like the l. of the thing,** cela me paraît louche; cela ne me dit rien de bon. **By the look(s) of it,** d'après l'apparence. **The portrait has a l. of your mother,** le portrait ressemble un peu à votre mère. *(b) pl.* **(Good) looks,** belle mine, bonne mine, beauté *f.*

look², *v.i. & tr.* **1.** *v.i.* Regarder. *(a)* **To l. through, out of, the window,** regarder par la fenêtre. **To l. in at the window,** regarder à la fenêtre. **To l. down a list,** parcourir une liste. **To l. the other way,** (i) regarder de l'autre côté; (ii) détourner les yeux. **To l. in s.o.'s face,** (i) regarder qn; (ii) dévisager qn. *(b)* **L. (and see) what time it is, what the time is,** regardez quelle heure il est. *(c) O:* **I had looked to find a stern master,** je m'attendais à trouver un maître sévère. *(d)* **Which way does the house l.?** quelle est l'exposition de la maison? **2.** *v.tr.* *(a)* **To l. s.o. (full, straight) in the face, in the eyes,** regarder qn bien en face, dans le blanc des yeux; dévisager qn. **I can never l. him in the face again,** je me sentirai toujours honteux devant lui. **To l. s.o. up and down,** toiser qn. *(b)* **To l. one's last on sth.,** jeter un dernier regard sur qch. **3.** *Pred.* Avoir l'air, paraître, sembler. **To l. happy,** avoir l'air heureux, avoir la mine heureuse. **She looks tired,** elle a l'air bien fatigué(e). **He looks young for his age,** il ne paraît pas son âge. **She looks her age,** elle paraît bien son âge. **To l. ill,** avoir l'air malade; avoir mauvaise mine. **To l. well,** (i) *(of pers.)* avoir bonne mine; (ii) *(of thg)* faire bien; faire bon effet. **It doesn't l. well,** (i) cela manque de cachet; (ii) *(of conduct, etc.)* cela fait mauvais effet. **Things are looking bad, black, nasty, ugly,** les choses prennent une mauvaise tournure, une mauvaise allure. **How did he l.?** quel air avait-il? quelle mine a-t-il faite? **How does my hat l.?** comment trouvez-vous mon chapeau? **He looks as if, as though, he wanted to . . .,** il a l'air de vouloir. . . . **It looks as if he wouldn't go,** il semble qu'il ne veuille pas y aller, il n'a pas l'air de vouloir y aller. **It does not l. to me as if . . .,** il ne me semble pas que + *sub.* **What does he l. like?** comment est-il? à quoi ressemble-t-il? **The rock looks like granite,** la roche ressemble à du granit. **This looks to me like a way in,** ceci m'a l'air d'une entrée. **He looks a rascal,** il a une mine de coquin, de fripon. **He looks the part,** il a le physique de l'emploi. **To l. like doing sth.,** paraître vouloir faire qch. **He looks like it,** il en a l'air. **It looks like it,** cela en a l'air; on le dirait. **It looks like rain,** on dirait qu'il va pleuvoir. **4.** *F:* **L. here!** écoutez donc! dites donc! **look about,** *v.i.* **1. To l. about one,** regarder autour de soi. **2. To l. about for s.o.,** chercher qn des yeux. **look after,** *v.ind.tr.* Sɔigner (qn, qch.); s'occuper de, avoir soin de (qn, qch.); veiller sur (qn, qch.). **He is able to l. after himself,** il est capable de se débrouiller; il se débrouillera bien seul. **To l. after one's interests, one's rights,** veiller à ses intérêts, à ses droits. **I l. after the car myself,** j'entretiens l'auto moi-même. **look at,** *v.ind.tr.* **1.** Regarder, considérer (qn, qch.). **What are you looking at?** qu'est-ce que vous regardez? **Just l. at this!** voyez donc, *F:* regardez-moi ça! **To l. at one's watch,** regarder sa montre. *F:* **She will not l. at a man,** elle dédaigne les hommes; les hommes lui sont indifférents. **To l. at him one would say . . .,** à le voir on dirait. . . . **What sort of a man is he to l. at?** quel air a-t-il? **The hotel is not much to l. at,** l'hôtel ne paye pas de mine. **2. L. at the result,** voyez, considérez, le résultat. **Way of looking at things,** manière *f* de voir les choses. **look away,** *v.i.* Détourner les yeux. **look back,** *v.i.* *(a)* Regarder en arrière; se retourner, tourner la tête **(at sth.,** pour regarder qch.). *(b)* **To l. back upon the past,** faire un retour sur le passé. **What a day to l. back to!** quelle journée à se rappeler plus tard! **look down,** *v.i.* Regarder en bas, par terre; baisser les yeux. **Standing here you l. down on the whole plain,** de ce point on domine toute la plaine. *F:* **To l. down on s.o.,** regarder qn de haut; dédaigner qn. **look for,** *v.ind.tr.* **1.** Chercher (qn, qch.). **To go and l. for s.o.,** aller à la recherche de qn. **To l. for a job,** être à la recherche d'un emploi. **2.** S'attendre à (qch.). **look forward,** *v.i.* **To l. forward to sth.,** (i) s'attendre à qch.; (ii) envisager qch. avec plaisir, se réjouir d'avance de qch. **look in,** *v.i.* **To l. in on s.o., at s.o.'s house,** entrer chez qn en passant; dire un petit bonjour à qn. **To l. in at the office,** prendre l'air du bureau. **I shall l. in again to-morrow,** je repasserai demain. **'look-in,** *s. F:* **1. To give s.o. a l.-in,** passer chez qn; faire une petite visite à qn. **2.** *Sp: etc:* **He won't get a l.-in,** il n'a pas la moindre chance.

look into, *v.ind.tr.* (a) Examiner, étudier (une question); prendre (une question) en considération. I will l. into it, j'en prendrai connaissance. (b) Feuilleter, parcourir (un livre). **look on.** 1. (a) = LOOK UPON. (b) (Of building, etc.) To l. on (to) . . ., donner sur. . . . 2. Être spectateur; faire galerie. Suppose you helped me instead of looking on, si vous m'aidiez au lieu de me regarder faire. **look out.** 1. *v.i.* (a) Regarder au dehors. (b) Room that looks out on the yard, pièce qui donne, qui a vue, sur la cour. (c) Veiller. To l. out for s.o., être à la recherche de qn; guetter qn. (d) F: Prendre garde; être sur ses gardes. **L. out!** attention! prenez garde! 2. *v.tr.* Chercher (qch.). To l. out a train in the time-table, chercher un train dans l'indicateur. **look-'out,** *s.* 1. Guet *m*, surveillance *f*; Nau: veille *f*. To keep a l.-o., avoir l'œil au guet. To keep a sharp l.-o., guetter d'un œil attentif; faire bonne garde; avoir l'œil. To be on the l.-o., (i) être en observation; Nau: être de veille; (ii) être sur ses gardes; être sur le qui-vive. To be on the l.-o. for s.o., être à l'affût de qn; guetter qn. 2. (a) Mil: (post), poste *m* d'observation. (b) L.-o. (man), (i) Mil: guetteur *m*; (ii) Nau: homme *m* de veille, de bossoir; vigie *f*. 3. Perspective *f*. F: That's a bad l.-o. for him, c'est une triste perspective. That's his l.-o.! ça c'est son affaire! **look over,** *v.tr.* 1. Jeter un coup d'œil sur (qch.); parcourir (qch.) des yeux; examiner (qch.). To l. over a house, visiter une maison. To l. over some papers, parcourir des papiers. To l. over an account (again), repasser un compte. To l. s.o. all over, toiser qn. 2. To l. over one's neighbour's newspaper, lire le journal par-dessus l'épaule de son voisin. (At cards) He is looking over your hand, il regarde votre jeu. **look round,** *v.i.* 1. Regarder autour de soi. To l. round for s.o., chercher qn du regard. 2. Se retourner (pour voir); tourner la tête. Don't l. round! ne regardez pas en arrière! **look through,** *v.tr.* 1. Parcourir, examiner (des papiers, etc.); repasser (une leçon). 2. To l. s.o. through and through, transpercer qn du regard. **look to,** *v.i.* (a) To l. to sth., s'occuper de qch.; voir à qch. L. to it that . . ., veillez, faites attention, à ce que + *sub.* To l. to the future, envisager l'avenir. (b) To l. to s.o. to do sth., compter sur qn pour faire qch. I l. to you for protection, je compte sur votre protection. **look up.** 1. *v.i.* (a) Regarder en haut; lever les yeux. (b) To l. up to s.o., respecter, considérer, qn. (c) F: Business is looking up, les affaires reprennent. Things are looking up with him, ses affaires vont mieux. 2. *v.tr.* (a) To l. up the time-table, consulter l'indicateur. To l. up a word in the dictionary, (re)chercher un mot dans le dictionnaire. (b) F: To l. s.o. up, aller voir qn. **look upon,** *v.ind.tr.* 1. Regarder (qn, qch.). A: Fair to l. upon, de belle apparence. 2. To l. upon s.o. favourably, voir qn d'un œil favorable. L. upon that as done, tenez cela pour fait. I do not l. upon it in that light, ce n'est pas ainsi que j'envisage la chose. **-looking,** *a.* Good-l., beau, *f.* belle; joli; de bonne mine. Queer-l., à l'air bizarre; d'un aspect singulier. Serious-l., d'apparence sérieuse. **'looking-glass,** *s.* Miroir *m*, glace *f.* Bot: Venus's l.-g., miroir de Vénus. **'look-see,** *s.* F: Coup *m* d'œil.

looker ['lukər], *s.* 1. L.-on, *pl.* **lookers-on,** spectateur, -trice (at, à); assistant *m* (at, à). To be a l.-on, faire galerie. 2. F: Good l., bel homme, belle femme.

loom[1] [lu:m], *s.* Tex: Métier *m* à tisser.

loom[2], *v.i.* Apparaître indistinctement; se dessiner, s'estomper, dans le lointain ou dans le brouillard. A ship loomed up out of the fog, un navire surgit, sortit, du brouillard. Dangers looming ahead, dangers qui menacent, qui paraissent imminents. (Of event) To l. large, paraître imminent, occuper le premier plan.

loon [lu:n], *s.* Orn: (Grand) plongeon.

loony ['lu:ni], *a. & s.* F: Fou, *f.* folle; timbré, maboul. **'loony-bin,** *s.* P: Maison *f* de fous.

loop[1] [lu:p], *s.* 1. Boucle *f* (de ruban, etc.); boucle, œil *m*, ganse *f* (d'un cordage); boucle (de lettre écrite). Running l., boucle à nœud coulant. Curtain-l. embrasse *f* de rideau. Cost: Epaulette l., bride *f*, attente *f* (d'épaulette). Overcoat l., attache *f* de par-

dessus. 2. (a) Méandre *m*, sinuosité *f*, boucle (de rivière). (b) Tour *m*, spire *f* (de spirale, de bobine). (c) Ph: Ventre *m*; antinœud *m* (d'une onde). (d) Rail: L.(-line), boucle, (voie *f* d')évitement *m*, (voie de) raccordement *m*.

loop[2]. 1. *v.tr.* (a) Boucler (un ruban, etc.). (b) En rouler (sth. with sth., qch. de qch.). (c) To l. up the hair, retrousser, relever, les cheveux. To l. back a curtain, retenir un rideau avec une embrasse. (d) Av: etc: To l. the loop, boucler la boucle, faire un looping. 2. *v.i.* Faire une boucle; boucler.

loophole ['lu:phoul], *s.* 1. (a) Fort: Meurtrière *f*, créneau *m*. (b) Trou, *m*, ouverture. *f* 2. To find a l., trouver une échappatoire; se ménager une issue.

loopy ['lu:pi], *a.* P: Toqué, dingo, loufoque, louftingue.

loose[1] [lu:s], *a.* 1. (a) Mal assujetti; branlant; (of page) détaché; (of knot) défait, délié. L. horseshoe, fer qui lâche. L. tooth, dent qui branle, qui remue. El: L. connection, raccord déconnecté, desserré. To come l., to get l., se dégager, se détacher; (of knot) se défaire, se délier; (of screw) se desserrer. (Of machine parts) To work l., prendre du jeu. (Of chisel, etc.) To be l. in the handle, branler dans le manche. (b) (Of animal) Déchaîné, échappé, lâché. To let a dog l., lâcher, détacher, un chien. To let l. a torrent of abuse, lâcher, déchaîner, un torrent d'injures. S.a. BREAK LOOSE. (c) Non assujetti; mobile. L. sheets (of paper), feuilles volantes. Mec.E: L. wheel, roue folle, décalée. L. piece, pièce rapportée, pièce de rapport. L. end (of rope), bout pendant. F: To be at a l. end, se trouver désœuvré, sans occupation; avoir une heure à perdre. (Of rope, etc.) To hang l., pendre, flotter. (d) The money was l. in his pocket, l'argent était à même sa poche. L. cash, menue monnaie. Com: L. goods, marchandises en vrac. 2. (Slack) (a) L. rope, câble mou, détendu. L. knot, nœud lâche. (Of shoe-lace) To come l., se relâcher. L. draperies, draperies flottantes. (b) Man of l. build, homme dégingandé. Med: L. cough, toux grasse. L. bowels, ventre *m* lâche. 3. L. earth, soil, terre *f* meuble; terrain *m* sans consistance. Mil: L. order, ordre dispersé. 4. Vague, peu exact; (style) lâche, décousu. L. translation, traduction approximative. 5. Dissolu, débauché, libertin. L. living, mauvaise vie; inconduite *f.* L. morals, mœurs relâchées. L. woman, femme de mauvaise vie. *s.* F: To be on the l., être en bordée; mener une vie de polichinelle. To go on the l., aller en vadrouille, vadrouiller. **-ly,** *adv.* 1. (Tenir qch.) sans serrer. L. clad, habillé dans des vêtements amples. 2. Vaguement, inexactement. Word l. employed, mot employé abusivement. 3. (Se conduire) d'une manière dissolue. **'loose box,** *s.* Box *m* (d'écurie). **'loose-fitting,** *a.* Non ajusté; (vêtement) ample, large. **'loose-jointed, -limbed,** *a.* Démanché; dégingandé. **'loose-leaf,** *attrib.a.* (Album, etc.) à feuilles mobiles.

loose[2], *v.tr.* 1. Délier, détacher. To l. s.o. from his bonds, libérer qn. To l. one's hold, lâcher prise. To l. hold of sth., lâcher qch. 2. Dénouer, défaire (un nœud, etc.); dénouer (ses cheveux). Nau: Larguer (une amarre). 3. Décocher (une flèche).

loosen ['lu:s(ə)n]. 1. *v.tr.* (a) Relâcher (un nœud); desserrer (un écrou, etc.); détendre (une corde, un ressort); ameublir (la terre). To l. s.o.'s bonds, dénouer les liens de qn. To l. one's grip, relâcher son étreinte. F: To l. s.o.'s tongue, délier, dénouer, la langue à qn. Mec.E: To l. a bearing, dégripper un palier. Med: To l. the bowels, relâcher le ventre. To l. the cough, dégager la toux. (b) Détacher (sth. from sth., qch. de qch.). (c) Relâcher (la discipline). 2. *v.i.* (Of knot, etc.) Se délier, se défaire; (of screw, etc.) se desserrer; (of guy-rope, etc.) se relâcher; (of machinery, etc.) prendre du jeu. Med: (Of cough) Se dégager.

looseness ['lu:snis], *s.* 1. (a) Etat branlant (d'une dent); jeu *m* (d'une cheville, etc.). (b) Flaccidité *f* (de la peau). 2. (a) Relâchement *m* (d'une corde); ampleur *f* (d'un vêtement). (b) Med: L. of the bowels, relâchement du ventre. 3. Inconsistance *f* (du terrain). 4. (a) Vague *m* (d'une pensée); imprécision *f* (de terminologie); décousu *m* (du style). (b) Relâchement *m* (de la discipline). (c) Licence *f* (de conduite).

loosestrife ['luːsstraif], s. Bot: (a) Lysimachie f, lysimaque f. (b) Salicaire f.

loot[1] [luːt], s. 1. Pillage m. **On the l.,** en maraude. 2. Butin m.

loot[2], v.tr. 1. Piller, saccager (une ville, etc.). 2. Voler (du bétail, etc.). **looting,** s. Pillage m; sac m (d'une ville, etc.).

looter ['luːtər], s. Pillard m.

lop[1] [lɔp], v.tr. (**lopped** [lɔpt]) (a) Élaguer, tailler, émonder (un arbre). **To l. away,** l. **off, a branch,** couper, élaguer, une branche. (b) **To lop off a head,** abattre une tête. **lopping,** s. 1. Élagage m (d'un arbre). 2. pl. **Loppings,** émondes fpl.

lop[2], v.i. **To l. (over),** retomber; pendre flasque. **'lop-ear,** s. 1. Oreille pendante. 2. Lapin m aux oreilles pendantes. **'lop-eared,** a. (Lapin, etc.) aux oreilles pendantes.

lope[1] [loup], s. Pas de course allongé.

lope[2], v.i. **To l. along,** courir à petits bonds.

lopsided [lɔp'saidid], a. Qui penche trop d'un côté; déjeté, déversé; de guingois; bancal.

lopsidedness ['lɔp'saididnis], s. Manque m de symétrie; déjettement m.

loquacious [lo'kweiʃəs], a. Loquace. **-ly,** adv. Avec loquacité.

loquaciousness [lo'kweiʃəsnis], **loquacity** [lo'kwæsiti], s. Loquacité f.

loquat ['loukwæt], s. Nèfle f du Japon.

lord[1] [lɔːd], s.m. 1. Seigneur, maître. Hist: **L. of the manor,** seigneur (foncier); châtelain. 2. Ecc: **L. God Almighty,** Seigneur Dieu Tout-puissant. **The L.,** le Seigneur; Dieu. **In the year of our L. . . . ,** en l'an de grâce. . . . **The L.'s Day,** le jour du Seigneur; le dimanche. F: **(Good) L.!** Seigneur (Dieu)! 3. (a) Lord m (titre des barons, vicomtes, comtes, et marquis). F: **To live like a l.,** mener une vie de grand seigneur. **My l.,** (i) monsieur le baron, le comte, etc.; (ii) (to bishop) monseigneur; (to judge) monsieur le juge; M. le président. (b) **L. High Constable,** grand connétable. **L. Mayor,** lord-maire m. **'lords and 'ladies,** s. Bot: Arum maculé; gouet m; pied-de-veau m.

lord[2], v.i. **To l. it,** faire l'important; trancher du grand seigneur. **To l. it over s.o.,** vouloir en imposer à qn; le prendre de haut avec qn.

lordliness ['lɔːdlinis], s. 1. (a) Dignité f. (b) Magnificence f (d'un château, etc.). 2. Hauteur f, orgueil m, morgue f.

lordling ['lɔːdliŋ], s. Petit seigneur, hobereau m.

lordly ['lɔːdli], a. 1. De grand seigneur; noble, majestueux; magnifique. 2. Hautain, altier.

lordship ['lɔːdʃip], s. 1. Suzeraineté f (over, de). 2. **Your l.,** votre Seigneurie; (to nobleman) monsieur le comte, etc.; (to bishop) monseigneur.

lore [lɔːr], s. Science f, savoir m. **Bird-l.,** ornithologie f.

lorgnette [lɔː'njet], **lorgnon** ['lɔːnjɔn], s. 1. Face-à-main m. 2. Jumelle f (de théâtre) à manche.

lorn [lɔːn], a. Poet: Délaissé, solitaire.

lorry ['lɔri], s. Veh: Camion m. **Heavy l.,** poids lourd. Adm: **Articulated l.,** véhicule articulé. **'lorry-borne,** a. Mil: Porté.

lose [luːz], v.tr. (**lost** [lɔst]; **lost**) 1. (a) Perdre, égarer (son parapluie, etc.). (b) Perdre (un droit, son argent, etc.). **To stand to l. nothing,** (i) n'avoir rien à perdre; (ii) être sûr de gagner de toute façon. **The incident did not l. in the telling,** en racontant l'histoire on en a rajouté. **To l. in value, in interest,** perdre de sa valeur, de son intérêt. Rac: etc: **To l. (ground) on a competitor,** perdre sur un concurrent. (c) **He has lost an arm,** il lui manque un bras. **He has lost his left arm,** il est manchot du bras gauche. **To l. one's voice,** avoir, attraper, une extinction de voix. **To l. one's reason,** perdre la raison. **To l. one's character,** se perdre de réputation. **To l. strength,** s'affaiblir. **The patient is losing strength,** le malade baisse. **To l. weight,** perdre de son poids. (d) Perdre (son père, etc.). (Of doctor) **To l. a patient,** (i) ne pas réussir à sauver un malade; (ii) perdre un client. **To be lost at sea,** périr en mer. **Both armies lost heavily,** les deux armées subirent de fortes pertes. 2. **To l. one's way, to l. oneself, to get lost,** perdre son chemin; se perdre, s'égarer. **To l. oneself, to be lost, in the crowd,** se perdre, se dissimuler dans, se mêler à, la foule. **To**

l. oneself in a book, s'absorber dans la lecture d'un livre. **To be lost in apologies,** se confondre en excuses. **To l. sight of s.o.,** perdre qn de vue. 3. Gaspiller, perdre (son temps); perdre (sa peine). F: **The joke was lost on him,** il n'a pas saisi la plaisanterie. 4. **Clock that loses five minutes a day,** pendule qui retarde de cinq minutes par jour. 5. (a) Manquer (le train, etc.). (b) **I lost several words of his answer,** plusieurs mots de sa réponse m'ont échappé. (c) **I lost the opportunity,** j'ai raté l'occasion. 6. Perdre (une partie, un procès). (In debate) **The motion was lost,** la motion a été rejetée. 7. Faire perdre (qch. à qn). **That mistake lost him the match,** cette faute lui coûta la partie. **lost,** a. Perdu. **L. property office,** service m des objets trouvés. **To give s.o. up for l.,** abandonner tout espoir de retrouver ou de sauver qn. **I gave myself up for l.,** je me crus perdu. **A l. soul,** un damné. **To wander like a l. soul,** errer comme une âme en peine. **He seems l., looks l.,** il a l'air dépaysé. **To be l. to all sense of shame,** avoir perdu tout sentiment de honte, toute honte. **losing,** a. Perdant. **L. game,** partie perdue d'avance. **To play a l. game,** (i) jouer un jeu à perdre; (ii) jouer à qui perd gagne; (iii) défendre une cause perdue.

loser ['luːzər], s. 1. **I am the l. by it,** j'y perds. 2. (a) **To be the l. of a battle,** perdre une bataille. (b) Sp: Perdant, -ante. **To be a bad l.,** être mauvais joueur.

loss [lɔs], s. 1. (a) Perte f (d'un parapluie); égarement m (d'un document). (b) **L. of sight,** perte, privation f, de la vue. **L. of voice,** extinction f de voix. **Without l. of time,** sans perte de temps; sans tarder. Jur: **L. of a right,** perte, déchéance f, d'un droit. **To meet with a l.,** subir une perte, F: boire un bouillon. **Dead l.,** perte sèche. Com: **To sell at a l.,** vendre à perte. F: **To cut one's losses,** faire la part du feu. **It is her l., the l. is hers,** c'est elle qui y perd. **He, it, is no l.,** la perte n'est pas grande. M.Ins: **Constructive total l.,** perte censée totale. 3. (a) Déperdition f (de chaleur, etc.). **L. in transit,** déchet m de route (d'un liquide, etc.). (b) Med: Écoulement m, perte. 4. **To be at a l.,** être embarrassé, désorienté. **I am quite at a l.,** je ne sais que faire. **To be at a l. to . . . ,** avoir de la peine à . . . ; être en peine de. . . . **To be at a l. what to do, what to say,** ne savoir que faire, que dire. **I am at a l. for words to express . . . ,** les mots me manquent pour exprimer. . . .

lost [lɔst]. See LOSE.

lot [lɔt], s. 1. **To draw, cast, lots for sth.,** tirer au sort pour qch.; tirer qch. au sort. **To throw in one's l. with s.o.,** partager le sort, la fortune, de qn; unir sa destinée à celle de qn. **Drawn by l. from amongst . . . ,** tiré au sort parmi. . . . Fin: **The debentures are redeemed by l.,** les obligations sont rachetées par voie de tirage. 2. (a) Sort, part f, partage m. **The l. fell upon him,** le sort tomba sur lui. **To fall to s.o.'s l.,** échoir, tomber, en partage à qn. **It fell to my l. to . . . ,** le sort voulut que je + sub. S.a. PART[1] I. 2. (b) Destin m, destinée f. 3. (a) (At auction) Lot m. (b) U.S: Lot (de terrain). Aut: **Parking l.,** parcage m, F: parking m. (c) Com: **In lots,** par parties. **To buy in one l.,** acheter en bloc. (d) F: **A bad l.,** une canaille; un mauvais garnement, un dévoyé. (e) F: **The l.,** le tout. **That's the l.,** c'est tout. **The whole l., all the l., of you,** tous tant que vous êtes. 4. F: (a) Beaucoup. **What a l.!** en voilà-t-il! **What a l. of people!** que de monde! que de gens! **Such a l.,** tellement. **I have quite a l.,** j'en ai une quantité considérable. **He knows quite a l. about you,** il en sait long sur votre compte. **I saw quite a l. of him when I was in Paris,** je l'ai vu assez souvent pendant mon séjour à Paris. **He would have given a l. to . . . ,** il aurait donné gros pour. . . . adv. **Times have changed a l.,** les temps ont bien changé. (b) pl. **Lots of good things,** un tas de bonnes choses. **Lots of people,** quantité de gens; des tas de gens. adv. **I feel lots better,** je me sens infiniment mieux.

lot[2], v.tr. (**lotted; lotting**) Diviser en lots.

Lot[3]. Pr.n.m. B.Hist: Loth.

Lothario [lo'θɑːriou]. Pr.n.m. **A gay L.,** un joyeux viveur, un Don Juan.

lotion ['louʃ(ə)n], s. Pharm: Lotion f.

lottery ['lɔtəri], s. Loterie f. **Life is a l.,** la vie est une loterie, est une affaire de chance.

lotus ['loutəs], s. 1. Gr.Myth: Lotus m. 2. Bot: (a) Lotus m, lotier m. (b) Egyptian l., nélombo m; lis m du Nil. 'lotus-eater, s. Gr.Myth: Lotophage m.

loud [laud]. 1. a. (a) Bruyant, retentissant. L. noise, l. cry, grand bruit, grand cri. L. laugh, gros rire. L. voice, voix forte. In a l. voice, à haute voix. L. cheers, vifs applaudissements. To be l. in one's praises of sth., louer qch. chaleureusement. (b) (Of pers., behaviour) Bruyant, tapageur. (c) (Of colour, etc.) Criard, voyant; (of costume) tapageur. 2. adv. (Crier) haut, à haute voix. -ly, adv. 1. (Crier) haut, fort, à voix haute; (rire) bruyamment. To call l. for sth., réclamer qch. à grands cris. L. dressed, à toilette tapageuse. loud-'mouthed, a. F: Fort en gueule. 'loud-'speaker, s. Haut-parleur m, pl. haut-parleurs.

loudness ['laudnis], s. 1. Force f (d'un bruit, etc.); grand bruit (d'une cataracte, etc.). 2. The l. of her dress, sa toilette tapageuse, criarde.

lough [lɔx], s. (Irish) 1. Lac m. 2. Bras m de mer.

lounge[1] [laundʒ], s. 1. O: (a) Flânerie f. (b) Allure nonchalante. 2. (a) Promenoir m; (in hotel) hall m; (in boarding-house) petit salon; (in house) salon. Sun l., véranda f. (b) Th: Foyer m (du public). 'lounge car, s. Rail: U.S: Voiture-bar (munie de fauteuils). 'lounge-chair, s. Chaise-longue f. 'lounge-suit, s. Complet veston m.

lounge[2], v.i. 1. Flâner. To l. about, F: tirer sa flemme. To l. along, avancer en se dandinant. 2. S'étaler, s'étendre paresseusement (sur un canapé, etc.). To l. against the wall, s'appuyer nonchalamment au mur.

lounger ['laundʒər], s. Flâneur, -euse.

lour ['lauər], s. & v.i. **louring** ['lauəriŋ], a. = LOWER[2],[3] LOWERING[3].

louse, pl. **lice** [laus, lais], s. Pou m, pl. poux.

lousewort ['lauswəːt], s. Bot: Pédiculaire f; herbe f aux poux.

lousy ['lauzi], a. 1. Pouilleux. 2. F: Sale, miteux, -euse, P: moche. L. trick, sale coup m; sale tour m, crasse f.

lout [laut], s. Rustre m, lourdaud m; paltoquet m.

loutish ['lautiʃ], a. Rustre, lourdaud.

louver, louvre ['luːvər], s. (a) Arch: Abat-vent m inv. abat-son m (de clocher). (b) Volet d'aération.

lovable ['lʌvəbl], a. Aimable; sympathique.

lovableness ['lʌvəblnis], s. Caractère m aimable.

lovage ['lʌvidʒ], s. Bot: Livèche f.

love[1] [lʌv], s. 1. Amour m. (a) Affection f, tendresse f. L. of, for, towards, s.o., amour de, pour, envers, qn. There is no l. lost between them, ils ne peuvent pas se sentir. For the l. of God, pour l'amour de Dieu. He learnt French for the love of it, il apprit le français par attrait m pour cette langue. To play for l., jouer pour l'honneur. To work for l., travailler pour rien, F: pour le roi de Prusse. Give my l. to your parents, faites mes amitiés à vos parents. F: It can't be had for l. nor money, on ne peut se le procurer à aucun prix. (b) (Between lovers) Amour (the pl. is fem. in Lit. & Poet. use). First l., les premières amours. L. at first sight, coup m de foudre. To be in l. with s.o., être amoureux, épris, de qn. Head over ears in l., éperdument amoureux. To fall in l. with s.o., s'éprendre, tomber amoureux, de qn. To make l. to s.o., faire la cour à qn. L. in a cottage, un cœur et une chaumière. To marry for l., faire un mariage d'inclination. 2. (Pers.) My l., mon amour; mon ami, mon amie. An old l. of mine, une de mes anciennes amours. 3. (At tennis, etc.) Zéro m, rien m. L. all, égalité f à rien. L. game, jeu blanc. 'love-bird, s. Orn: Agapornis m; inséparable m. 'love-child, s. Enfant naturel; enfant de l'amour. 'love-feast, s. Ecc.Hist: Agape f. 'love-in-a-'mist, s. Bot: Nigelle f (de Damas); cheveux mpl de Vénus. 'love-in-'idleness, s. Bot: Pensée f. 'love-knot, s. Lacs m d'amour. 'love-letter, s. Billet doux. 'love-lies-(a-)'bleeding, s. Bot: Amarante f queue de renard. 'love-lorn, a. Délaissé, abandonné. 'love-making, s. Cour (amoureuse). 'love-match, s. Mariage m d'amour, d'inclination. 'love-song, s. (a) Chant m d'amour. (b) Chanson f d'amour; romance f. 'love-story, s. Histoire f d'amour; roman m d'amour.

love[2], v.tr. 1. (a) Aimer, affectionner (qn). Prov: L. me love my dog, qui m'aime aime mon chien. F:

To play "she loves me, she loves me not," effeuiller la marguerite. (b) Aimer d'amour. 2. Aimer (passionnément) (son chez-soi, etc.). As you l. your life . . ., si vous tenez à la vie. . . . I l. horse-racing, les courses de chevaux me passionnent. I l. music, j'adore la musique. To l. to do sth., to l. doing sth., aimer à faire qch.; adorer faire qch. Will you come with me?—I should l. to, voulez-vous m'accompagner?—Je ne demande pas mieux; très volontiers. **loving**, a. 1. Affectueux, affectionné, tendre. 2. Money-l., qui aime l'argent. 3. L. cup, coupe f de l'amitié. -ly, adv. Affectueusement, affectionnément.

loveless ['lʌvlis], a. Sans amour. 1. Insensible à l'amour. 2. Pour qui personne ne ressent d'amour.

lovelessness ['lʌvlisnis], s. 1. Insensibilité f à l'amour. 2. Privation f d'amour.

loveliness ['lʌvlinis], s. Beauté f, charme m.

lovelock ['lʌvlɔk], s. Accroche-cœur m.

lovely ['lʌvli], a. (a) Beau f. belle; ravissant. A l. jewel, un amour de bijou. (b) F: It's been just l. seeing you again! ça a été charmant de vous revoir!

lover ['lʌvər], s. 1. (a) Amoureux m, prétendant m. (b) Fiancé m. 2. Her l., son amant, F: son bon ami. 3. Amateur m, ami(e) (de qch.). Music-l., mélomane mf. 'lovers' 'knot, s. = LOVE-KNOT.

lovesick ['lʌvsik], a. Féru d'amour. To be l., languir d'amour.

low[1] [lou]. I. a. 1. Bas, f. basse. L. wall, mur bas, peu élevé. L. stature, petite taille. Art: L. relief, bas-relief m. Light turned l., lumière en veilleuse. L. tide, l. water, marée basse; basse mer. My stocks are rather l., mes stocks sont un peu dégarnis. S.a. RUN[3] I, 10. 2. (a) L. ceiling, plafond bas, peu élevé. L. bow, profonde révérence. Geog: The L. Countries, les Pays-Bas. Aut: L. chassis, châssis surbaissé. (b) To bring s.o. l., humilier, abaisser, ravaler, qn. To lie l., (i) se tapir; se tenir accroupi; (ii) F: se tenir coi; faire le mort. S.a. LAY[4] 1. (c) Lower part, bas m (d'une échelle, etc.). The Lower Alps, les basses Alpes. The lower regions, les régions infernales. The lower jaw, la mâchoire inférieure. (d) L. German, le bas allemand. L. Latin, le bas latin. 3. (a) L. birth, basse naissance. There was something l. about her, elle avait un je ne sais quoi de peuple, de canaille. The lower orders, les basses classes; le bas peuple. Lower court, tribunal inférieur. Lower end of the table, bas bout de la table. Sch: Lower forms, petites classes. (b) The lower animals, les animaux inférieurs. L. comedy, le bas comique. (c) Bas, vil, trivial, canaille. The lowest of the l., le dernier des derniers. L. expression, expression vulgaire. That's a l. trick! ça c'est un sale coup! 4. L. diet, régime peu substantiel; régime débilitant. (Of invalid) To be very l., être bien bas. To feel low, to be in l. spirits, être abattu; F: avoir le cafard. 5. L. price, bas prix. At a l. price, à bon compte. The lowest price, le dernier prix. A hundred pounds at the very lowest, cent livres au bas mot, pour le moins. L. speed, petite vitesse, faible vitesse. L. fever, fièvre lente. L. latitudes, basses latitudes. Cards: The l. cards, les basses cartes. 6. L. note, note basse. L. sound, (i) son bas, grave; (ii) faible son. In a l. voice, à voix basse, à mi-voix. She has a l. voice, elle a une voix basse, au timbre grave. 7. Ecc: L. mass, messe basse. L. Sunday, Pâques closes, (dimanche de) la Quasimodo. -ly[1], adv. 1. L. born, (i) de basse naissance; (ii) de naissance modeste. 2. Humblement. II. low, adv. 1. (Pendre, viser) bas. To bow l., s'incliner profondément; saluer très bas. I cannot go so l. as to do that, je ne peux pas m'abaisser jusqu'à faire cela. Dress cut l. in the back, robe décolletée dans le dos. 2. The lowest paid employees, les employés les moins payés. 3. (a) (Parler) à voix basse. (b) Mus: I cannot get so l. as that, je ne peux pas descendre si bas (dans la gamme). To set (a song, etc.) lower, baisser (une chanson, etc.). III. low, s. All-time l., record le plus bas. 'low-born, a. 1. De basse naissance. 2. D'humble naissance. 'low-bred, a. Mal élevé; grossier. 'low-brow. F: 1. a. Terre à terre inv; peu intellectuel. 2. s. Bourgeois, -oise; philistin, -ine. 'low-built, a. Bas; peu élevé. Aut: L.-b. chassis, châssis surbaissé. 'low-class, a. De bas étage; vulgaire, inférieur. 'low-down[1], a. 1. Bas, f. basse;

près du sol. **2.** Bas, vil, ignoble, canaille. **L.-d. trick,** coup rosse. **'low-down²,** *s. F:* To give s.o. the l.-d., renseigner qn; tuyauter qn (on, sur). **'low-grade,** *attrib.a.* De qualité inférieure; (minerai) pauvre. **'low-level,** *attrib.a.* **1.** Bas, *f.* basse. **2.** En contrebas. **'low-'lying,** *a.* Situé en bas; (terrain) enfoncé. **'low-'necked,** *a.* (Robe) décolletée. **'low-'pitched,** *a.* **1.** (*a*) (Son) grave. (*b*) (Piano) accordé à un diapason bas. **2.** *Const:* (Comble) à faible pente; (chambre) à plafond bas. **'low-powered,** *a.* (Auto) de faible puissance. **'low-pressure,** *attrib.a.* (Cylindre, machine) à basse pression, à basse tension. **'low-'slung,** *a.* (Voiture) surbaissée. **'low-'spirited,** *a.* Abattu, triste, déprimé, découragé. **'low-'water,** *attrib. a.* **L.-w. mark,** (*of river*) étiage *m*; (*of sea*) (i) niveau *m* des basses eaux, (ii) laisse *f* de basse mer.
low², *s.* Meuglement *m* (d'une vache).
low³, *v.i.* (*Of cattle*) Meugler; (*occ. of bull*) beugler.
lower¹ ['louər], *v.tr.* (*a*) Baisser (la tête); abaisser (les paupières); abaisser, rabattre (son voile). (*b*) To l. s.o. on a rope, affaler, (faire) descendre, qn au bout d'une corde. To l. a ladder, descendre une échelle. *Nau:* L. away! laissez aller! To l. a boat, amener une embarcation; mettre une embarcation à la mer. (*c*) Abaisser (qch.); diminuer la hauteur de (qch.). (*d*) Baisser, rabaisser (un prix); réduire, abaisser (la pression); baisser (la lumière); amoindrir (un contraste). (*e*) Baisser (la voix, le ton). To l. the enemy's morale, déprimer le moral de l'ennemi. (*f*) (R)abaisser, faire baisser, (r)abattre (l'orgueil). To l. oneself s'abaisser, se rabaisser, se ravaler (to, à); s'avilir.
lowering¹, *a.* **1.** (*Of conduct*) Abaissant. **2.** *Med:* (Régime) débilitant. **lowering²,** *s.* **1.** (*a*) Abaissement *m*; baissement *m* (de la tête, etc.). (*b*) Descente *f* (d'une échelle dans un puits, etc.); mise *f* à la mer, (d'une embarcation). (*c*) Abaissement, diminution *f* de la hauteur de (qch.). **2.** Diminution (des prix); réduction *f* (de la pression).
lower² ['lauər], *s. O:* **1.** Air renfrogné, menaçant. **2.** Assombrissement *m* (du ciel); menace *f* (de la tempête).
lower³ ['lauər], *v.i.* **1.** (*Of pers.*) Se renfrogner; froncer les sourcils. **2.** (*Of sky*) s'assombrir, se couvrir; (*of clouds*) s'amonceler; (*of storm*) menacer. **lowering³,** *a.* **1.** (Air) renfrogné, menaçant; (front) sombre. **2.** (Ciel) sombre, menaçant, orageux. **-ly,** *adv.* **1.** (Regarder) d'un air renfrogné, menaçant. **2.** The clouds gathered l., les nuages menaçants s'amoncelaient.
lowermost ['louəmoust], *a.* Le plus bas.
lowland ['loulənd], *s.* (*a*) Plaine basse; terre *f* en contre-bas. (*b*) *pl.* **Lowlands,** terres basses; pays plat. *Geog:* The Lowlands, la Basse-Écosse.
lowliness ['loulinis], *s.* Humilité *f.*
lowly² ['louli], *a. A. & Lit:* Humble, modeste, sans prétention. *s.pl.* The l., les humbles m.
lowness ['lounis], *s.* **1.** Manque *m* de hauteur; petitesse *f* (d'un arbre, etc.). **2.** (*a*) Gravité *f* (d'un son). (*b*) Faiblesse *f* (d'un bruit); peu *m* d'élévation (de la température); modicité *f* (de prix). **3.** Bassesse *f* (de conduite). **4.** L. (of spirits), abattement *m*, découragement *m.*
loxodromic [,lɔksə'drɔmik], *a. Nau:* (Navigation, etc.) loxodromique.
loyal ['lɔiəl], *a.* **1.** (Ami, etc.) fidèle, dévoué (to, à); loyal, -aux (to, envers). **2.** Fidèle au souverain, à la famille royale. To drink the l. toast, porter le toast au souverain. **-ally,** *adv.* Fidèlement.
loyalism ['lɔiəlizm], *s. Pol:* Loyalisme *m.*
loyalist ['lɔiəlist], *s.* Loyaliste *mf.*
loyalty ['lɔiəlti], *s.* **1.** *A:* Fidélité *f* à sa promesse, à son serment. **2.** Fidélité à la Couronne, loyalisme *m.* L. to one's party, fidélité à son parti.
lozenge ['lɔzindʒ], *s.* **1.** *Geom: Her:* Losange *m.* **2.** *Pharm:* Pastille *f*, tablette *f.*
lubber ['lʌbər], *s.* (*a*) Lourdaud *m.* (*b*) *Nau:* Maladroit *m*, empoté *m.*
lubberliness ['lʌbəlinis], *s.* Gaucherie *f.*
lubberly ['lʌbəli]. **1.** *a.* Lourdaud; empoté, gauche. **2.** *adv.* Lourdement, gauchement.
lubricant ['lju:brikənt], *a. & s.* Lubrifiant (*m*).
lubricate ['lju:brikeit, 'lu:-], *v.tr.* Lubrifier; graisser. **Lubricating oil,** huile *f* de graissage. *U.S: F:* He's a bit lubricated, il est un peu gris, ivre.

lubrication [,lju:bri'keiʃ(ə)n, ,lu:-], *s.* Lubrification *f*, graissage *m.*
lubricator ['lju:brikeitər, 'lu:-], *s.* Graisseur *m.* Cap l., graisseur à chapeau. Drop l., graisseur compte-gouttes.
lubricity [lju(:)'brisiti, lu(:)-], *s.* **1.** Onctuosité *f.* **2.** Lubricité *f.*
Lucca ['lʌkə]. *Pr.n. Geog:* Lucques *f.* L. oil, huile *f* d'olives de Lucques.
lucency ['lu:sənsi], *s.* Brillance *f*, luminosité *f.*
lucent ['lu:sənt], *a.* **1.** Brillant, lumineux. **2.** Clair, transparent.
lucern(e)¹ [lu(:)'sə:n], *s. Bot:* Luzerne *f.*
Lucerne² [lu(:)'sə:n]. *Pr.n. Geog:* Lucerne *f.* The Lake of L., le lac des Quatre-Cantons.
lucid ['lu:sid], *a.* **1.** Brillant, lumineux. **2.** (*a*) (Esprit, style) lucide, clair. (*b*) *Med:* L. interval, intervalle *m* de lucidité. (*c*) *Poet:* Clair, transparent. **-ly,** *adv.* Lucidement.
lucidity [lu:'siditi], *s.* **1.** (*a*) Luminosité *f.* (*b*) Transparence *f.* **2.** Lucidité *f* (d'esprit); clarté *f* (de style).
luck [lʌk], *s.* **1.** Hasard *m*, chance *f*, fortune *f.* Good l., bonne chance, heureuse fortune, bonheur *m.* Ill l., bad l., malchance *f*, mauvaise fortune, malheur *m*; *F:* déveine *f*, guigne *f.* To be down on one's l., avoir de la déveine, être dans la déveine, *F:* avoir la guigne, *P:* la poisse. To try one's l., tenter sa chance. To bring s.o. good, bad, l., porter bonheur, porter malheur, à qn. Better l. next time! ça ira mieux, vous ferez mieux, une autre fois. Just my l.! c'est bien ma veine! Worse l.! tant pis! Hard l.! pas de chance! As l. would have it . . ., le hasard voulut que + *sub.* **2.** Bonheur *m*, bonne fortune, (bonne) chance. To have the l. to . . ., avoir la chance de . . ., être assez heureux pour. . . To keep sth. for l., garder qch. comme porte-bonheur. Bit, piece, stroke, of l., coup *m* de chance, coup de veine. To be in l., avoir de la chance, être en veine. To be out of l., jouer de malheur. My l.'s in! quelle veine! As l. would have it . . ., par bonheur. . . .
luckless ['lʌklis], *a.* **1.** (*Of pers.*) Malheureux, -euse, malchanceux, -euse. **2.** L. day, jour malencontreux.
lucky ['lʌki], *a.* (*a*) (*Of pers.*) Heureux, fortuné; (*of pers.*) chanceux, -euse. He was born l., *F:* il est né coiffé. *F:* L. dog! veinard que vous êtes! To be l., avoir de la chance, *F:* être verni. (*b*) L. hit, shot, coup de veine. L. day, jour faste, de veine. At a l. moment, au bon moment. How l.! quelle chance! It's l. that . . ., c'est une chance que . . . (+ *sub*). (*c*) (*Of thg*) To be l., porter bonheur. L. pig, petit cochon porte-bonheur. **-ily,** *adv.* Heureusement; par bonheur. **'lucky-bag, -dip, -tub,** *s.* Baquet rempli de son où l'on plonge la main pour retirer une surprise (à une vente de charité, etc.).
lucrative ['lju:krətiv, 'lu:-], *a.* Lucratif. **-ly,** *adv.* Lucrativement.
lucre ['lu:kər], *s.* Lucre *m.* To do sth. for (filthy) l., agir par amour du gain, du lucre.
ludicrous ['lju:dikrəs, 'lu:-], *a.* Risible, grotesque. **-ly,** *adv.* Risiblement, grotesquement.
ludicrousness ['lju:dikrəsnis, 'lu:-], *s.* Côté *m* comique (d'un incident); absurdité *f* (d'une réclamation, etc.).
luff¹ [lʌf], *s. Nau:* Lof *m*, ralingue *f* du vent (d'une voile). (*Of sail*) To tear from l. to leech, se déchirer dans toute sa loungeur, dans toute sa largeur.
luff², *v.i. Nau:* Lof(f)er.
lug¹ [lʌg], *s.* L.(-worm) = LOB-WORM.
lug², *s.* **1.** *Scot: F:* (*Ear*) Oreille *f.* **2.** (*a*) Oreillette *f* (de casquette). **2.** *Tchn:* Oreille, tenon *m*, bossage *m*, ergot *m.* Fixing l., patte *f* d'attache. **'lug-hole,** *s. P:* Oreille *f*, *P:* esgourde *f.*
lug³, *s.* Traction violente, subite.
lug⁴, *v.tr.* (lugged) Traîner, tirer (qch. de pesant). To l. sth. along, away, entraîner qch. To l. sth. about with one, promener, trimbaler, qch. avec soi.
luggage ['lʌgidʒ], *s.* Bagage(s) *m(pl)*. Heavy l., gros bagages. L. in advance, bagages non accompagnés. To take out, to check out, one's l., (from cloakroom) retirer ses bagages (de la consigne). **'luggage-label,** *s.* Étiquette *f* à bagages. **'luggage-rack,** *s.* (*a*) *Rail:* Porte-bagages *m inv.* (*b*) *Aut:* Galerie *f.* **'luggage-ticket,** *s.* Bulletin *m* (d'enregistrement) de bagages. **luggage-van,** *s. Rail:* Fourgon *m* (aux bagages).

lugger ['lʌgər], s. Nau: Lougre m.

lugsail ['lʌgseil, 'lʌgsl], s. Nau: Voile f à bourcet; taille-vent m inv.

lugubrious [lju'gu:briəs, lu-], a. Lugubre. **-ly,** adv. Lugubrement.

Luke [lu:k]. Pr.n.m. Luc.

lukewarm ['lu:kwɔ:m], a. Tiède. **To become l.,** s'attiédir, tiédir.

lull¹ [lʌl], s. Moment m de calme. Nau: Accalmie f; bonace f (avant une tempête).

lull². 1. v.tr. (a) Bercer, endormir (qn). (b) Endormir (les soupçons); calmer (une douleur). (c) Calmer, apaiser (la tempête). 2. v.i. (Of tempest) Se calmer, s'apaiser.

lullaby ['lʌləbai], s. Mus: Berceuse f.

lumbago [lʌm'beigou], s. Med: Lumbago m.

lumbar ['lʌmbər], a. Lombaire.

lumber¹ ['lʌmbər], s. 1. Vieux meubles; fatras m. 2. U.S: Bois m de charpente; bois en grume. **'lumber-jack,** s. U.S: Bûcheron m. **'lumber-jacket,** s. Blouson m; canadienne f. **'lumber-mill,** s. U.S: Scierie f. **'lumber-room,** s. Cabinet m, chambre f, de débarras; F: capharnaüm m. **'lumber-yard,** s. U.S: Chantier m de bois.

lumber², v.tr. (a) Encombrer, embarrasser (un lieu) (b) Entasser (des objets) pêle-mêle.

lumber³, v.i. To l. **along, in,** avancer, entrer, à pas pesants, lourdement. **lumbering,** a. Lourd, pesant.

lumberman, pl. **-men** ['lʌmbəmən], s.m. U.S: (a) Exploitant forestier. (b) Bûcheron.

Luminal ['lu:min(ə)l], s. Pr.n.Pharm: R.t.m: Gardénal m.

luminary ['lju:minəri, 'lu:-], s. 1. Corps lumineux; luminaire m, astre m. 2. F: (Of pers.) Lumière f; flambeau m (de la science, etc.).

luminescence [,lju:mi'nes(ə)ns, ,lu:-], s. Luminescence f.

luminescent [,lju:mi'nes(ə)nt, ,lu:-], a. Luminescent.

luminous ['lju:minəs, 'lu:-], a. Lumineux. **Watch with l. hands,** montre f (au) radium.

luminousness ['lju:minəsnis, 'lu:-], s. 1. Luminosité f. 2. Clarté f (d'une explication).

lump¹ [lʌmp], s. 1. (a) Gros morceau, bloc m (de pierre); motte f (d'argile); morceau (de sucre); masse f (de plomb, etc.); (in porridge, etc.) grumeau m. **To sell sth. in the l.,** vendre qch. en bloc, en gros. **L. sum,** (i) somme globale; (ii) prix à forfait. **To have a l. in one's throat,** avoir un serrement de gorge; se sentir le cœur gros. (b) Bosse f (au front, etc.). (c) Med: etc: Grosseur f. 2. F: (Of pers.) Empoté m, pataud m, lourdaud m. **Big l. of a girl,** grosse dondon.

lump². 1. v.tr. (a) Mettre en bloc, en masse, en tas. (b) To l. **things together,** réunir des choses ensemble. 2. v.i. (a) (Of earth) Former des mottes. (b) To l. **along,** marcher lourdement, à pas pesants.

lump³, v.tr. P: In the phr. If he doesn't like it, he can l. it, si cela ne lui plaît pas, qu'il s'arrange, c'est le même prix.

lumper ['lʌmpər], s. Nau: Déchargeur m, débardeur m.

lumpish ['lʌmpiʃ], a. 1. Lourd, pataud, godiche. 2. A l'esprit lent; à l'intelligence peu ouverte.

lumpishness ['lʌmpiʃnis], s. 1. Lourdeur f. 2. Stupidité f.

lumpy ['lʌmpi], a. (a) (Of earth) Rempli de mottes; (of sauce, etc.) grumeleux. (b) N. sea, mer courte, clapoteuse. (c) Couvert de protubérances.

lunacy ['lu:nəsi], s. Aliénation mentale; folie f; Jur: démence f. **It's sheer l.,** c'est de la folie.

lunar ['lu:nər], a. Lunaire; de (la) lune. **L. month,** mois lunaire.

lunate ['lu:neit], a. Nat.Hist: Luné, en forme de croissant.

lunatic ['lu:nətik]. 1. a. De fou(s), d'aliéné(s). **L. behaviour,** conduite folle, extravagante. **L. fringe,** les extrémistes, les originaux, F: les cinglés. 2. s. Fou, f. folle; aliéné, -ée; Jur: dément, -ente.

lunch¹ [lʌn(t)ʃ], s. Déjeuner m; U.S: casse-croûte m inv. **Quick l.,** petit repas, casse-croûte m inv (à un bar, etc.).

lunch². 1. v.i. Déjeuner. 2. v.tr. F: Donner à déjeuner à (qn); faire déjeuner (qn).

luncheon ['lʌn(t)ʃ(ə)n], s. Déjeuner m. **We take, have, l. at noon,** nous déjeunons à midi. Rail: Second l., deuxième service m. **L.-basket,** (i) panier m à provisions; (ii) Rail: panier-repas m, pl. paniers-repas. **'luncheon-'voucher,** s. Chèque-repas m, pl. chèques-repas.

lune [lu:n], s. Geom: Lunule f, croissant m.

lung [lʌŋ], s. Poumon m. **Inflammation of the lungs,** congestion f pulmonaire; F: fluxion f de poitrine. **L. trouble,** maladie f pulmonaire, esp. phtisie f. Iron l., poumon m d'acier.

lunge¹ ['lʌndʒ], s. Equit: Longe f.

lunge², v.tr. Equit: Faire trotter (un cheval) à la longe. **Lunging-rein,** longe f.

lunge³, s. 1. Fenc: Botte f; coup droit. 2. (a) Mouvement (précipité) en avant. (b) With each l. of the ship, chaque fois que le navire tanguait.

lunge⁴, v.i. 1. (a) Fenc: Se fendre. To l. at the adversary, porter une botte à l'adversaire. (b) To l. at s.o. with one's walking-stick, lancer un coup de pointe à qn avec sa canne. To l. out at s.o., (i) (of pers.) allonger un coup de poing à qn; (ii) (of horse) lancer une ruade à qn. 2. To l. forward, se précipiter en avant; se jeter en avant.

lungwort ['lʌŋwɔ:t], s. Bot: Pulmonaire f; herbe f aux poumons.

lunule ['lu:nju:l], s. Anat: Geom: etc: Lunule f.

lupin ['lu:pin], s. Bot: Lupin m.

lupine ['lu:pain], a. Lupin, de loup.

lupus ['lu:pəs], s. Med: Lupus m.

lurch¹ [lə:tʃ], s. **To leave s.o. in the l.,** laisser qn en plan; planter là qn; laisser qn le bec dans l'eau.

lurch², s. 1. Embardée f, coup m de roulis (d'un navire). 2. Cahot m, embardée (d'une voiture). 3. Pas titubant (d'un ivrogne); titubation f.

lurch³, v.i. 1. (a) (Of ship) Faire une embardée; embarder. (b) (Of vehicle, etc.) Faire une embardée, avoir un fort cahot. 2. (Of pers.) To l. **along,** marcher en titubant. To l. **in, out,** entrer, sortir, en titubant.

lurcher ['lə:tʃər], s. Lévrier bâtard; chien de braconnier.

lure¹ ['ljuər, 'luər], s. 1. Ven: Fish: Leurre m. 2. (a) Piège m. He fell a victim to her lures, il se laissa séduire. (b) Attrait m, attirance f (de la mer, etc.).

lure², v.tr. 1. Leurrer (un faucon, un poisson, etc.). 2. Attirer, séduire, allécher. To l. s.o. **away from a duty,** détourner qn d'un devoir. To be lured on to destruction, être entraîné à sa perte.

lurid ['ljuərid, 'lu-], a. 1. (Ciel, teint) blafard. **L. light,** lueur blafarde, sinistre. 2. (a) Cuivré. **L. flames,** flammes rougeoyantes. (b) F: Corsé; (langage) haut en couleur. **-ly,** adv. 1. Avec une lueur blafarde; sinistrement. 2. (a) En rougeoyant. (b) En corsant les effets.

lurk [lə:k], v.i. Se cacher; rester tapi (dans un endroit). **lurking,** a. Caché; secret, -ète. A l. suspicion, un vague soupçon.

luscious ['lʌʃəs], a. 1. Succulent, savoureux. 2. Pej: (a) (Vin) liquoreux, trop sucré. (b) (Style) trop fleuri.

lusciousness ['lʌʃəsnis], s. 1. Succulence f. 2. Pej: Douceur affadissante.

lush [lʌʃ], a. (Of grass) Plein de sève.

lushness ['lʌʃnis], s. Surabondance f, luxuriance f (de l'herbe, etc.).

lust¹ [lʌst], s. 1. (a) Theol: Appétit m (coupable); convoitise f. **Lusts of the flesh,** concupiscence f. (b) Luxure f; désir (libidineux). 2. Lit: Soif f (des richesses, du pouvoir).

lust², v.ind.tr. Lit: 1. (a) To l. **for, after, sth.,** convoiter qch. (b) To l. **after a woman,** désirer une femme. 2. To l. **for riches,** avoir soif de richesses.

lustful ['lʌstful], a. Lit: Lascif, -ive, libidineux, -euse; luxurieux, -euse. **-fully,** adv. Lascivement, libidineusement.

lustiness ['lʌstinis], s. Vigueur f.

lustre¹ ['lʌstər], s. 1. Éclat m, brillant m, lustre m. **To shed l. on a name,** rendre un nom illustre. 2. (a) Pendeloque f (de lustre). (b) Lustre (de plafond). **'lustre-ware,** s. Cer: Poterie f à reflets métalliques; poterie lustrée.

lustre², v.tr. Tex: Lustrer, catir (un tissu).

lustre³, s. Rom.Ant: Lustre m (espace de cinq ans).

lustreless ['lʌstələs], *a.* Mat, terne.
lustrine ['lʌstriːn], *s. Tex:* Lustrine *f.*
lustrous ['lʌstrəs], *a.* Brillant, éclatant; (*of material*) lustré.
lusty ['lʌsti], *a.* Vigoureux, fort, robuste; *F:* puissant (de corps). -**ily**, *adv.* Vigoureusement, de toutes ses forces; (chanter) à pleine poitrine, à pleine gorge.
lute[1] [l(j)uːt], *s. Mus:* Luth *m.* '**lute-maker**, *s.* Luthier *m.*
lute[2], *s.* Lut *m*, mastic *m.*
lute[3], *v.tr.* Luter, mastiquer.
Lutheran ['l(j)uːθərən], *a. & s.* Luthérien, -ienne.
luxation [lʌk'seiʃ(ə)n], *s.* Luxation *f*; déboîtement *m.*
Luxembourg ['lʌksəmbəːg]. *Pr.n. Geog:* (*a*) (Grand-Duché de) Luxembourg *m.* (*b*) Le Luxembourg (province belge).
luxuriance [lʌg'zjuəriəns], *s.* Exubérance *f*, luxuriance *f.*
luxuriant [lʌg'zjuəriənt], *a.* Exubérant, luxuriant. -**ly**, *adv.* Avec exubérance; en abondance.
luxuriate [lʌg'zjuərieit], *v.i.* 1. (*Of vegetation*) Croître avec exubérance. 2. (*Of pers.*) (*a*) To l. in idleness, se livrer avec délices à la paresse.
luxurious [lʌg'zjuəriəs], *a.* (Appartement) luxueux, somptueux. -**ly**, *adv.* Luxueusement; dans le luxe.
luxuriousness [lʌg'zjuəriəsnis], *s.* Luxe *m*; somptuosité *f.*

luxury ['lʌkʃəri], *s.* 1. Luxe *m.* To live in (the) lap of l., vivre dans le luxe, au sein du luxe. 2. (Objet *m* de) luxe. **L. article**, objet de luxe. **Table luxuries**, friandises *f.* It is quite a l. for us, c'est du luxe pour nous.
Lyceum [lai'siəm], *s. Gr.Ant:* The L., le Lycée.
lych-gate ['litʃgeit], *s.* = LICHGATE.
lychnis ['liknis], *s. Bot:* Lychnide *f*, lychnis *m.*
lye [lai], *s.* Lessive *f* (de soude, de potasse).
lying[1,2,3] ['laiiŋ], *a. & s.* See LIE[2,4].
lymph [limf], *s.* 1. *Physiol:* Lymphe *f.* 2. *Med:* Vaccin *m.*
lymphatic [lim'fætik], *a.* Lymphatique.
lynch [lin(t)ʃ], *v.tr.* Lyncher. **lynching**, *s.* Lynchage *m.*
lynx [liŋks], *s. Z:* Lynx *m*; loup-cervier *m*, *pl.* loups-cerviers.
Lyons ['laiənz]. *Pr.n. Geog:* Lyon *m.*
lyre ['laiər], *s. Mus:* Lyre *f.* '**lyre-bird**, *s. Orn:* Ménure *m*; oiseau-lyre *m.*
lyric ['lirik]. 1. *a.* Lyrique. **L. poet**, (poète) lyrique. 2. *s.* Poème *m* lyrique. *Th:* Chanson *f*, couplet *m.*
lyrical ['lirik(ə)l], *a.* Lyrique.
lyricism ['lirisizm], *s.* 1. Lyrisme *m.* 2. *F:* (Faux) lyrisme.
lyricist ['lirisist], *s.* Poète *m* lyrique; *Th:* parolier *m.*
lysergic [li'səːdjik], *a.* **L. acid diethylamide**, acide *m* lysergique (synthétique diéthylamine), L.S.D.
lysol ['laisəl], *s. Pharm:* Lysol *m.*

M, m [em], s. (La lettre) M, m. m. Tp: **M for Mary, M** comme Marcel.

ma [mɑ:], s. P: = MAMMA.

ma'am [mæm], s. = MADAM.

mac [mæk], s. F: Imper m.

macabre [məˈkɑ:br, mæˈkɑ:br], a. Macabre.

macadam [məˈkædəm], s. Civ.E: Macadam m. Tar m., macadam au goudron; tarmacadam m.

macadamize [məˈkædəmaiz], v.tr. Civ.E: Empierrer, macadamiser (une route).

macaque [məˈkɑːk], s. Z: Macaque m, magot m.

macaroni [ˌmækəˈrouni], s. Cu: Macaroni m. **M. cheese,** macaroni au gratin.

macaronic [ˌmækəˈrɔnik], a. Macaronique.

macaroon [ˌmækəˈruːn], s. Cu: Macaron m.

Macassar [məˈkæsər]. Pr.n. Geog: Macassar. **M. oil,** huile de Macassar.

mace[1] [meis], s. 1. Hist: Masse f d'armes. 2. (a) Masse (portée par le massier devant un fonctionnaire). (b) = MACE-BEARER. 'mace-bearer. s. Massier m; appariteur m.

mace[2], s. Bot: Cu: Macis m; fleur f de muscade.

Macedonia [ˌmæsiˈdouniə]. Pr.n. Geog: La Macédoine.

Macedonian [ˌmæsiˈdouniən], a. & s. Geog: Hist: Macédonien, -ienne.

macerate [ˈmæsəreit], v.tr. & i. Macérer.

maceration [ˌmæsəˈreiʃ(ə)n], s. Macération f.

Mach [mætʃ], s. Aerodynamics: M. (number), (nombre m de) Mach.

Machiavelli [ˌmækiəˈveli]. Pr.n.m. Machiavel.

Machiavellian [ˌmækiəˈveliən], a. Machiavélique.

Machiavellism [ˌmækiəˈvelizm], s. Machiavélisme m.

machicolation [mæˌtʃikoˈleiʃ(ə)n], **machicoulis** [ˈmæʃiˈkuːli], s. Mâchicoulis m.

machinate [ˈmækineit], v.i. Comploter; tramer des complots.

machination [ˌmækiˈneiʃ(ə)n], s. Machination f, complot m, intrigue f.

machine[1] [məˈʃiːn], s. Machine f, appareil m. (Of pers.) To be a mere m., n'être qu'un automate. **Reaping-m.,** moissonneuse f. **Rivet(t)ing-m.,** riveuse f. **M.-winding,** bobinage mécanique. **The party m.,** l'organisation f politique du parti. **Penny-in-the-slot (gambling) m.,** machine à sous. Typewr: **Four-bank m.,** machine à quatre rangs de touches. ma'chine-gun[1], s. Mitrailleuse f. **ma'chine-gun**[2], v.tr. Mitrailler. ma'chine-gunner, s. Mitrailleur m. **ma'chine-made,** a. (Fait) à la mécanique, à la machine. **ma'chine-minder,** s. Surveillant m, soigneur m, de machines. Typ: Conducteur m (de presse). **ma'chine-shop,** s. 1. Atelier m de construction mécanique. 2. Atelier d'usinage. 3. Atelier des machines. **ma'chine-tool,** s. Machine-outil f, pl. machines-outils. **ma'chine-turned,** a. Fait au tour.

machine[2], v.tr. 1. Ind: (a) Façonner (une pièce). (b) Usiner, ajuster. 2. Dressm: Coudre, piquer, à la machine. **machining,** s. 1. Usinage m; ajustage m mécanique. 2. Typ: Tirage m à la machine. 3. Couture f, piquage m, à la machine.

machinery [məˈʃinəri], s. 1. Mécanisme m; machines fpl, machinerie f. 2. **The intricate m. of government,** les rouages m de la machine gouvernementale. 3. Lit: Th: Le merveilleux.

machinist [məˈʃiːnist], s. 1. Machiniste m; mécanicien m. 2. Ind: (At sewing-machine) Mécanicienne f.

Machmeter [ˈmætʃmiːtr], s. Aerodynamics: Mach-mètre m.

mackerel [ˈmæk(ə)rəl], s. Ich: Maquereau m. 'mackerel-sky, s. Ciel pommelé.

mackintosh [ˈmækintɔʃ], s. 1. (Manteau m en) caoutchouc m; imperméable m; mackintosh m. 2. Tissu caoutchouté.

mackle[1] [ˈmækl], s. Typ: Bavochure f.

mackle[2], v.tr. Typ: Bavocher. **mackled,** a. Bavocheux, -euse.

macle [ˈmækl], s. Cryst: Miner: Macle f.

macrocosm [ˈmækrokɔzm], s. Macrocosme m.

macrophotography [ˌmækrofəˈtɔgræfi], s. Macro-photographie f.

macula, pl. **-ae** [ˈmækjulə, -iː], s. Astr: Med: Macule f. Anat: **M. (lutea),** tache f jaune.

macular [ˈmækjulər], a. Med: Maculeux, -euse.

maculation [mækjuˈleiʃ(ə)n], s. Maculation f, maculage m.

mad [mæd], a. (**madder**) 1. Fou, f. folle; dément. **Raving m.,** fou furieux. **As m. as a hatter, as m. as a March hare,** fou à lier. **To drive s.o. m.,** rendre qn fou. **To go m.,** devenir fou, être pris de folie, Imperialism gone m., impérialisme forcené. **M. with pain,** fou de douleur. **A m. plan,** un projet insensé. **A m. gallop,** un galop furieux, effréné. F: **Like m.,** comme un enragé, comme un perdu. 2. **M. for revenge,** assoiffé de revanche. F: **To be m. about, on,** s.o., sth., être fou, raffoler, de qn, qch. **He is m. on fishing,** c'est un pêcheur enragé. 3. F: **To be m. with s.o.,** être furieux contre qn. **It made me m. only to see him,** rien que de le voir me rendait furieux. 4. **M. bull,** taureau furieux. **M. dog,** chien enragé. **-ly,** adv. 1. Follement; comme un fou. 2. (Aimer) à la folie, éperdument. 3. Furieusement.

Madagascan [ˌmædəˈgæskən], a. Malgache.

Madagascar [ˌmædəˈgæskər]. Pr.n. Geog: Madagascar m. Pol: La République malgache.

madam [ˈmædəm], s.f. 1. Madame, mademoiselle. (In letters) **Dear M.,** Madame, Mademoiselle. 2. F: O: **She's a bit of a m.,** elle aime à le prendre de haut.

madcap [ˈmædkæp], a. & s. Écervelé, -ée.

madden [ˈmæd(ə)n], v.tr. Rendre fou; exaspérer. **maddening,'**a. A rendre fou; exaspérant, F: rageant.

madder [ˈmædər], s. Bot: Dy: Garance f. 'madder-root, s. Garance f.

madding [ˈmædiŋ], a. **Far from the m. crowd,** loin de la foule et du bruit.

made [meid]. See MAKE[2].

Madeira [məˈdiərə]. Pr.n. Geog: Madère f. **M. (wine),** vin m de Madère; madère m. **M. cake =** gâteau m de Savoie.

madhouse [ˈmædhaus], s. (a) A: Maison f de fous; asile m d'aliénés. (b) F: **The place is like a m.,** on se croirait à Charenton, chez les fous.

madman, pl. **-men** [ˈmædmən], s.m. Fou, aliéné. **To fight like a m.,** se battre comme un forcené.

madness [ˈmædnis], s. 1. Folie f; démence f. F: **It is sheer madness to go out in this weather,** c'est de la folie de sortir par le temps qu'il fait. **Midsummer m.,** le comble de la folie. **It's mere midsummer m.,** c'est une aberration qui passera. 2. (Of animals) Rage f; hydrophobie f.

madonna [məˈdɔnə], s.f. Madone.

madrepore [ˈmædripɔːr], s. Coel: Madrépore m.

madrigal [ˈmædrig(ə)l], s. Madrigal m, -aux.

madwort [ˈmædwɔːt], s. Bot: Alysse f, F: corbeille d'or.

Maecenas [miːˈsiːnæs]. Pr.n.m. Mécène.

Maelstrom [ˈmeilstroum], s. 1. Geog: (Le) Maelström. 2. Tourbillon m, gouffre m.

maenad [ˈmiːnæd], s.f. Gr.Myth: Ménade.

Mae West [ˈmei ˈwest], s. F: Gilet m de sauvetage, Mae West m.

magazine [ˌmægəˈziːn], s. 1. (a) Mil: Magasin m d'armes, de vivres, d'équipement; dépôt m de munitions. **Powder m.,** (i) Mil: poudrière f; (ii) Navy: soute f aux poudres. (b) Magasin (d'un fusil, etc.). **M. gun,** fusil à répétition. 2. Revue f, recueil m, périodique; périodique m.

Magdalen(e) [ˈmægdəli(:)n, B: -'liːni]. Pr.n.f. Madeleine. **Magdalen College** (Oxford) et **Magdalene College** (Cambridge) se prononcent [ˈmɔːdlinˈkɔledʒ].

Magdalenian [mægdəˈliːniən], a. Geol: Prehist: Magdalénien, -ienne.

magenta [məˈdʒentə], s. & a. (Colour) Magenta (m) inv.

Maggiore [mædʒiˈɔːri]. Pr.n. **Lake Maggiore,** le lac Majeur.

maggot ['mægət], *s.* Ver *m*, F: asticot *m*.
maggoty ['mægəti], *a.* Véreux, -euse.
magi, *s.pl. See* MAGUS.
magic ['mædʒik]. **1.** *s.* Magie *f*, enchantement *m*. As if by m., like m., comme par enchantement. **2.** *a.* Magique, enchanté. *S.a.* LANTERN 1.
magical ['mædʒik(ə)l], *a.* Magique. -ally, *adv.* Magiquement; comme par enchantement.
magician [mə'dʒiʃ(ə)n], *s.* Magicien, -ienne.
magisterial ['mædʒis'tiəriəl], *a.* **1.** (Air, ton) magistral, -aux; (air) de maître. **2.** De magistrat. -ally, *adv.* **1.** (*a*) Magistralement. (*b*) En maître. **2.** En qualité de magistrat.
magistracy ['mædʒistrəsi], *s.* Magistrature *f*.
magistrate ['mædʒistreit], *s.* Magistrat *m*, juge *m*.
magistrature ['mædʒistrətʃər], *s.* Magistrature *f*.
magma ['mægmə], *s. Geol:* Magma *m*.
Magna Carta ['mægnə'kɑːtə], *s. Eng.Hist:* La Grande Charte (de 1215).
magnanimity [mægnə'nimiti], *s.* Magnanimité *f*.
magnanimous [mæg'næniməs], *a.* Magnanime. -ly, *adv.* Magnanimement.
magnate ['mægneit], *s.* Magnat *m*, F: gros bonnet (de l'industrie). F: Oil m., roi *m* du pétrole.
magnesia [mæg'niːʃə], *s. Ch: Pharm:* Magnésie *f*.
magnesium [mæg'niːziəm], *s. Ch:* Magnésium *m*.
magnet ['mægnit], *s.* **1.** Aimant *m*. Bar m., barreau aimanté. Horse-shoe m., aimant en fer à cheval. **2.** Électro-aimant *m*. Compound m., faisceau aimanté.
magnetic [mæg'netik], *a.* **1.** Magnétique; aimanté. M. iron ore, aimant naturel, pierre *f* d'aimant. **2.** (*Of pers., power*) Magnétique, hypnotique. **3.** *s.pl.* **Magnetics**, magnétisme *m*. -ally, *adv.* Magnétiquement.
magnetism ['mægnitizm], *s.* **1.** Animal m., magnétisme animal; hypnotisme *m*. **2.** Aimantation *f*. Residual m., magnétisme rémanent.
magnetite ['mægnitait], *s. Miner:* Magnétite *f*.
magnetize ['mægnitaiz], *v.tr.* **1.** Magnétiser, attirer (qn). **2.** (*a*) Aimanter (une aiguille, etc.). (*b*) (*With passive force*) (*Of iron*) S'aimanter. **magnetizing**, *s.* **1.** Magnétisation *f* (de qn). **2.** Aimantation *f*.
magneto [mæg'niːtou], *s. I.C.E: etc:* Magnéto *f*.
magnetoscope [mæg'niːtouskoup], *s.* magnétoscope *m*.
magnification [mægnifi'keiʃ(ə)n], *s.* **1.** *Opt:* Grossissement *m*, amplification *f*. **2.** Exaltation *f* (de qn).
magnificence [mæg'nifis(ə)ns], *s.* Magnificence *f*.
magnificent [mæg'nifis(ə)nt], *a.* Magnifique; (repas) somptueux. -ly, *adv.* Magnifiquement.
magnifier ['mægnifaiər], *s.* Verre grossissant; loupe *f*.
magnify ['mægnifai], *v.tr.* Grossir, agrandir (une image); amplifier, renforcer (un son). **Magnifying glass**, loupe *f*; verre grossissant. *Opt:* **Magnifying power**, grossissement *m*. To m. an incident, grossir, exagérer, un incident.
magnitude ['mægnitjuːd], *s.* Grandeur *f*. *Astr:* Magnitude *f*.
magnolia [mæg'noulia], *s. Bot:* M.(-tree), magnolia *m*, magnolier *m*.
magnum ['mægnəm], *s.* Magnum *m* (de champagne, etc.).
magnum opus ['mægnəm'oupəs], *Lt.s.phr.* Grand ouvrage; chef-d'œuvre *m*.
magpie ['mægpai], *s. Orn:* Pie *f*; F: jacasse *f*.
magus, *pl.* -gi ['meigəs, -dʒai], *s.* Mage *m*. The Three Magi, les rois mages.
Magyar ['mægiɑːr], *a. & s. Ethn:* Magyar, -are.
maharaja(h) [mɑːhə'rɑːdʒə], *s.* Maharajah *m*.
maharanee [mɑːhə'rɑːni], *s.* Maharani *f*.
mahatma [mə'hætmə], *s.* Mahatma *m*.
mahogany [mə'həgəni], *s.* Acajou *m*.
Mahomet [mə'həmit], *Pr.n.m. Rel.H:* Mahomet.
Mahometan [mə'həmit(ə)n], *a. & s.* = MOHAMMEDAN.
mahout [mə'haut], *s.* Cornac *m*.
maid [meid], *s.f.* **1.** *Lit:* = MAIDEN 1 (*a*). **2.** *A. & Poet:* = MAIDEN 1 (*b*). The M. (of Orleans), la Pucelle (d'Orléans). **3.** Old m., vieille fille. **4.** Bonne, domestique, servante. Lady's m., camériste; femme de chambre. **5.** M. of honour, (i) demoiselle, dame d'honneur (de la reine); (ii) *U.S:* (*at wedding*) première demoiselle d'honneur. (iii) *Cu:* tartelette *f* aux amandes. 'maid-of-'all-work, *s.f. A:* Bonne à tout faire.

maiden ['meidn], *s.* **1.** (*a*) Jeune fille *f*. (*b*) Vierge *f*. **2.** *Attrib.* (*a*) M. aunt, tante non mariée. *O:* M. lady, demoiselle *f*. (*b*) M. name, nom de jeune fille. (*c*) M. voyage, m. trip, premier voyage, voyage inaugural (d'un navire). M. speech, discours de début (d'un député).
maidenhair ['meidnheər], *s. Bot:* M. (fern), capillaire *m*; *F:* cheveu *m* de Vénus.
maidenhood ['meidnhud], *s.* Célibat *m* (de fille); condition *f* de fille.
maidenlike ['meidnlaik], **maidenly** ['meidnli]. *O:* **1.** *a.* De jeune fille; virginal, -aux; modeste. **2.** *adv.* Avec modestie, avec pudeur.
maidservant ['meidsəːv(ə)nt], *s.f. Lit:* Servante; bonne.
mail[1] [meil], *s. Arm:* Mailles *fpl*.
mail[2], *s. Post:* **1.** Courrier *m*; *F:* la poste. To open the m., dépouiller le courrier. **2.** La poste. The Royal M. = le Service des postes. 'mail-bag, *s.* Sac postal. 'mail-boat, *s.* Courrier postal; paquebot-poste *m*, *pl.* paquebots-poste. 'mail box, *s. U.S:* Boîte *f* aux lettres. 'mail-coach, *s.* **1.** *A:* Malle-poste *f*. **2.** *Rail:* = MAIL-VAN 1. 'mail-order, *s. Com:* Commande *f* par poste; vente *f*, achat *m*, sur catalogue. 'mail-packet, *s.* = MAIL-BOAT. 'mail-train, *s.* Train-poste *m*, *pl.* trains-poste. 'mail-van, *s.* **1.** Wagon-poste *m*, *pl.* wagons-poste. **2.** Fourgon *m* des postes; fourgon postal.
mail[3], *v.tr. Esp. U.S:* Envoyer par la poste, expédier (des lettres, des paquets).
mailed [meild], *a.* Revêtu de mailles. To show the m. fist, employer la manière forte.
maim [meim], *v.tr.* Estropier, mutiler.
main[1] [mein], *s.* **1.** *Used only in the phr.* With might and m., de toutes mes, ses, forces. **2.** *Poet:* Océan *m*; haute mer. *S.a.* SPANISH 1. **3.** In the m., en général, en somme; à tout prendre. **4.** *Civ.E:* Canalisation maîtresse. Main(s) water, eau de la ville. *El:* Conducteur principal; câble *m* de distribution. *pl.* The mains, les fils *m* de la ligne. *El:* To take one's power from the mains, brancher sur le secteur.
main[2], *a.* **1.** By m. force, de vive force; à main armée. **2.** Principal, -aux; premier, essentiel. (*a*) The m. body, le gros (de l'armée, etc.). *Agr:* M. crop, culture principale. (*b*) The m. point, the m. thing, l'essentiel, le principal. M. idea, idée *f* mère (d'une œuvre). M. features of a speech, grands traits, points saillants, d'un discours. *Gram:* M. clause, proposition principale. *Cu:* M. dish, m. course, plat *m* de résistance. (*c*) M. road, m. highway, grande route; route à grande circulation. M. street, rue principale. *Rail: etc:* M. line, voie principale, grande ligne. (*d*) *Nau:* The m. masts, les mâts majeurs. M. boiler, chaudière principale. -ly, *adv.* **1.** Principalement, surtout. **2.** En grande partie. 'main-brace, *s. Nau:* Grand bras (de vergue). F: To splice the m.-b., donner une tournée de rhum supplémentaire. 'main-deck, *s. Nau:* Pont principal; premier pont. 'main-top, *s. Nau:* Grand-hune *f*. 'main-yard, *s. Nau:* Grand-vergue *f*.
mainland ['meinlænd], *s.* Continent *m*; terre *f* ferme.
mainmast ['meinmɑːst, -məst], *s. Nau:* Grand mât.
mainsail ['meinseil, 'meinsl], *s. Nau:* Grand-voile *f*.
mainspring ['meinspriŋ], *s.* **1.** Grand ressort; ressort moteur. **2.** Mobile essentiel, cheville ouvrière.
mainstay ['meinstei], *s.* **1.** *Nau:* Étai *m* de grand mât. **2.** Point *m* d'appui. He is the m. of his family, c'est le principal soutien de sa famille.
maintain [men'tein], *v.tr.* **1.** Maintenir (l'ordre); soutenir (un siège, la conversation); entretenir (des relations); conserver (la santé); garder, observer (une attitude, le silence); garder (son sang-froid). To m. s.o., sth., in a position, maintenir qn, qch., dans une position. The improvement is maintained, le mieux se maintient. **2.** Entretenir, soutenir, faire subsister (une famille, etc.); *Jur:* subvenir aux besoins de (sa famille). **3.** Entretenir (une armée, une route). **4.** Soutenir, défendre (une cause). To m. one's rights, défendre ses droits. **5.** Garder (un avantage). I m. my ground, je n'en démords pas. **6.** (S'obstiner à) soutenir (une opinion, un fait). To m. that . . ., maintenir, soutenir, prétendre, que. . . .
maintainable [men'teinəbl], *a.* **1.** (Position) tenable. **2.** (Opinion) soutenable.

maintenance [ˈmeintinəns], *s.* **1.** Maintien *m* (de l'ordre). **2.** (*a*) Entretien *m* (d'une famille, des routes). (*b*) (Moyens *mpl* de) subsistance *f*; *Jur:* pension *f* alimentaire. *Jur:* **M. order**, obligation *f* alimentaire, **3. M. of on.'s rights**, défense *f* de ses droits. **In m. of this opinion . . .,** à l'appui de cette opinion. . .

maisonnette [ˌmeizəˈnet], *s.* Appartement *m* à un ou deux étages, duplex *m*, appartement en duplex.

maize [meiz], *s.* Maïs *m*.

majestic(al) [məˈdʒestik(əl)], *a.* Majestueux, auguste. **-ally,** *adv.* Majestueusement, augustement.

majesty [ˈmædʒisti], *s.* Majesté *f*. **His M., Her M.,** Sa Majesté le Roi, Sa Majesté la Reine. **On His, Her, Majesty's Service,** *abbr.* O.H.M.S., (pour le) service de Sa Majesté (= service de l'État); *Post:* en franchise.

majolica [məˈdʒɔlikə], *s. Cer:* Majolique *f*.

major[1] [ˈmeidʒər], *s. Mil:* Commandant *m*; chef *m* de bataillon (d'infanterie); chef d'escadron(s) (de cavalerie). **ˈmajor-ˈgeneral,** *s.* Général *m* de division.

major[2]. **1.** *a.* (*a*) **The m. portion,** la majeure partie, la plus grande partie. *Geom:* **M. axis,** axe transverse, grand axe (d'une ellipse). *Mus:* **M. key,** ton majeur. *Aut:* **M. road,** route à priorité. *Cards:* (*At bridge*) **The m. suits,** les couleurs principales (pique et cœur). (*b*) *Sch:* **Smith m.,** Smith aîné. **2.** *s.* (*a*) *Jur:* (*Pers.*) Majeur, -eure; personne majeure. (*b*) *Log:* Majeure *f*.

major[3], *v.i. Sch: U.S:* **To m. in a subject** = *to take honours in a subject, q.v. under* HONOUR[1].

Majorca [məˈdʒɔːkə]. *Pr.n. Geog:* Majorque *f*.

major-domo, *pl.* **-os** [ˈmeidʒəˈdoumou, -ouz], *s.* Majordome *m*.

majority [məˈdʒɔriti], *s.* **1.** Majorité *f* (des voix). (*a*) **To be in a m., in the m.,** être en majorité, avoir la majorité. **Decision taken by a m.,** décision prise à la majorité (des voix). **By an overwhelming m.,** en nombre écrasant. *Attrib.* **M. party,** parti majoritaire. (*b*) La plus grande partie, le plus grand nombre, la plupart (des hommes, etc.). **2.** *Jur:* **To attain one's m.,** atteindre sa majorité; devenir majeur. **3.** *Mil:* Grade *m* de commandant.

make[1] [meik], *s.* **1.** (*a*) Façon *f*, fabrication *f* (d'une robe, etc.) (*b*) *Com: Ind:* Marque *f* (d'un produit). **Of French m.,** de fabrication française, de construction française. **2.** Taille *f* (de qn). **Man of slight m.,** homme plutôt mince. **F:** **To be on the m.,** être âpre au gain, chercher à faire fortune à tout prix. **4.** *El.E:* Fermeture *f* (du circuit).

make[2], *v.* (**made** [meid]; **made**) I. *v.tr.* **1.** Faire; construire (une machine, etc.); façonner (un vase, etc.); fabriquer (du papier, etc.); confectionner (des vêtements). **You are made for this work,** vous êtes fait pour ce travail. **F:** **He's as sharp as they m. 'em,** c'est un malin s'il en est. **What is it made of?** en quoi est-ce? **To m. a friend of s.o.,** faire de qn son ami. **I don't know what to m. of it, I can m. nothing of it,** je n'y comprends rien. **What do you m. of it?** Et vous, qu'en pensez-vous? **To show what one is made of,** donner sa mesure. **To m. milk into butter,** transformer le lait en beurre. **To m. one's will,** faire son testament. *Fin:* **To m. a promissory note, a bill of exchange,** souscrire un billet à ordre; libeller une lettre de change. **To m. the bed, the tea,** faire le lit, le thé. *Cards:* **To m. (the cards),** battre les cartes. **To m. trouble,** causer, occasionner, des désagréments. **To m. a noise,** faire du bruit. **To m. peace,** faire, conclure, la paix. **To make a speech,** faire un discours. **To m. a mistake,** faire, commettre, une erreur, se tromper. **To m. war,** faire la guerre. **To m. one's escape,** s'échapper, se sauver. **We made the whole distance in ten days,** nous avons couvert toute la distance en dix jours. **F:** **I just made my train,** j'ai eu mon train tout juste. **2.** (*a*) Établir, assurer (a connection between . . .), le raccordement (a . . .). *El:* **To m. the circuit,** fermer le circuit. (*b*) **Two and two m. four,** deux et deux font, égalent, quatre, **This book makes pleasant reading,** ce livre est d'une lecture agréable. **To m. a good husband, a good wife,** se montrer bon époux, bonne épouse. **Will you m. one of the party?** voulez-vous être des nôtres? **3. To m. twenty pounds a week,** gagner, se faire, vingt livres

par semaine. **To m. a fortune, one's fortune,** faire fortune; gagner une fortune. **F:** **To m. a bit,** se faire un peu d'argent. **F:** **To m. a bit on the side,** se faire de la gratte, faire danser l'anse du panier. **To m. a name,** se faire un nom. **To m. profits,** réaliser des bénéfices. **What will you m. by it?** qu'est-ce que vous en tirerez? *Cards:* **To m. a trick,** faire une levée. **To m. one's contract,** réussir son contrat. *Abs.* (*Of card*) **To m.,** faire la levée. **F:** **To m. it,** réussir; y arriver. **Do you think he'll m. the university?** Pensez-vous qu'il sera admis à l'université? **4. Faire la fortune de** (qn). **This book made him,** ce livre lui assura la célébrité, la renommée. **5.** *Pred.* **To m. s.o. happy,** rendre qn heureux. **To m. s.o. hungry, sleepy,** donner faim, sommeil, à qn. **To m. a dish hot,** (faire) chauffer un plat. **To m. s.o. a judge,** nommer qn juge. **He was made a knight,** il fut fait chevalier. **To m. sth. known, felt, understood,** faire connaître, sentir, comprendre, qch. **To m. oneself heard,** se faire entendre. **To m. oneself comfortable,** se mettre à l'aise. **To m. oneself ill,** se rendre malade. **To m. it a rule, one's object, to . . .,** se faire une règle, avoir pour but, de. . . . **Can you come at six?—M. it half-past,** pouvez-vous venir à six heures?— Plutôt la demie. **6. The climate is not so bad as you m. out,** le climat n'est pas si mauvais que vous le dites. **What do you m. the time? What time do you m. it?** quelle heure avez-vous? **I m. it five miles,** j'estime la distance à cinq milles. **7. To m. s.o. speak,** faire parler qn. **You should m. him do it,** vous devriez le lui faire faire. **What made you go?** qu'est-ce qui vous a déterminé à partir? **What made you say that?** pourquoi avez-vous dit cela? **8.** *Nau:* (*a*) Arriver à (un port). **To m. a headland,** (i) arriver en vue d'un cap; (ii) doubler, franchir, une pointe. (*b*) (*Of ship*) **To m. twenty knots,** faire vingt nœuds; filer à vingt nœuds. **We made bad weather,** nous avons essuyé du mauvais temps. II. **make,** *v.i.* **1. To m. for, towards, a place,** se diriger vers un endroit. **He made for, after, me like a madman,** il s'élança, se précipita, sur moi comme un fou. *Nau:* **To m. for . . .,** faire route sur . . ., mettre le cap sur. . . . **To m. for the open sea,** prendre le large. **To m. for the anchorage,** se rendre au mouillage. **2. These agreements m. for peace,** ces accords tendent à maintenir la paix. **This fine weather makes for optimism,** ce beau temps porte à l'optimisme. **3. To m. as if, as though, to do sth.,** faire mine, faire semblant, de faire qch. **make away,** *v.i.* (*a*) S'éloigner. (*b*) **To m. away with sth.,** détruire, faire disparaître, enlever, qch.; dérober (de l'argent, etc.); gaspiller (sa fortune). **F:** **To m. away with s.o.,** mettre qn à mort; **F:** supprimer qn. **To m. away with oneself,** se suicider; se donner la mort. **make off,** *v.i.* Se sauver; décamper, filer. **To m. off with the cash,** filer avec l'argent; lever le pied. **make out,** *v.tr.* **1.** Faire, établir, dresser (une liste, etc.); établir, dresser, relever (un compte); faire, tirer (un chèque). **2.** (*a*) Établir, prouver (qch.). **How do you m. that out?** comment arrivez-vous à ce résultat, à cette conclusion? (*b*) **To m. s.o. out to be richer than he is,** faire qn plus riche qu'il ne l'est. **He is not such a fool as people m. out,** il n'est pas aussi bête qu'on le croit. **3.** (*a*) Comprendre (une énigme); démêler les raisons (de qn); déchiffrer (une écriture); débrouiller (une affaire). **I can't m. it out,** je n'y comprends rien. (*b*) Distinguer, discerner (qch.). *Nau:* **To m. out a light,** reconnaître un feu. **make over,** *v.tr.* Céder, transférer, transmettre (sth. to s.o., qch. à qn). **make up.** I. *v.tr.* **1.** Compléter, parfaire (une somme); combler, suppléer à (un déficit). **To m. up the even money,** faire l'appoint. **2. To m. up lost ground,** regagner le terrain perdu. **To m. it up to s.o. for sth.,** dédommager qn de qch.; indemniser qn. **3.** Faire un paquet). *Pharm:* Exécuter (une ordonnance); préparer (une potion). **4.** (*a*) Faire, confectionner, façonner (des vêtements). '**Customers' own material made up,**' "on travaille à façon"; "tailleur à façon." (*b*) Dresser (une liste). (*c*) Régler, établir, arrêter (un compte). (*d*) Inventer, forger (une histoire, des excuses). **5.** (*a*) Rassembler, réunir (une compagnie); rassembler (une somme d'argent). (*b*) **To m. up the fire,** ajouter du combustible au feu; (re)charger le poêle.

(c) *Typ:* To m. up, mettre en pages. 6. Former, composer (un ensemble). 7. To m. (oneself) up, se farder, se maquiller; *Th:* faire sa figure; (*of man*) se grimer. 8. To m. up one's mind, se décider; prendre son parti. 9. Arranger, accommoder (un différend). To m. it up (again), se réconcilier; se remettre bien ensemble. II. make up, *v.i.* 1. (*a*) To m. up for lost time, rattraper le temps perdu. To m. up for one's losses, se rattraper de ses pertes. That makes up for it, c'est une compensation. (*b*) To m. up for the want of sth., suppléer au manque de qch. 2. To m. up on a competitor, gagner sur un concurrent. 3. To m. up to s.o., (i) s'avancer vers qn, s'approcher de qn; (ii) *F:* faire des avances, faire la cour, à qn. 'make-up, *s.* 1. Composition *f* (de qch.). 2. *Toil: Th:* Maquillage *m*, fard *m. Th:* M.-up-man, maquilleur *m.* 3. *Typ:* Mise *f* en pages. 4. Invention *f*; histoire inventée (de toutes pièces). 5. Appoint *m.* M.-up length (of pipe, etc.), pièce jointive; pièce de raccordement. 'made-'up, *a.* Artificiel, factice; faux, *f.* fausse. M.-up story, histoire inventée de toutes pièces. making- up, *s.* 1. Compensation *f* (for losses, de pertes). 2. *Pharm:* Préparation *f*, composition *f* (d'un médicament). 3. (*a*) Confection *f*, façon *f* (de vêtements). (*b*) *Com: Fin:* Confection (d'un bilan); arrêté *m*, clôture *f* (des comptes). *St.Exch:* M.-up price, cours *m* de compensation. (*d*) Invention (d'une histoire). 4. *Typ:* M. up and imposing, mise *f* en pages. 5. Composition, formation *f* (d'un ensemble). 6. *Th: etc:* Fardage *m*, maquillage *m.* 7. Arrangement *m*, raccommodement *m* (d'un différend). made, *a.* 1. Fait, fabriqué, confectionné. Foreign-m., fait à l'étranger. French-m. articles, articles de fabrication française. 2. *F:* He is a m. man, le voilà arrivé; son avenir est assuré; sa fortune est faite. making, *s.* 1. (*a*) Fabrication *f*; confection *f*, façon *f* (de vêtements); construction *f* (d'un pont); composition *f* (d'un poème). The marriage was none of her m., ce n'était pas elle qui avait arrangé le mariage. This incident was the m. of him, c'est à cet incident qu'il dut sa fortune. tout son succès. History in the m., l'histoire en train de se faire. The m. of English, la formation de l'anglais. (*b*) You have the makings of . . ., avoir tout ce qu'il faut pour devenir. . . . He has the makings of a state-man, il y a en lui l'étoffe d'un homme d'État. I have not the makings of a hero, je n'ai rien de héros. 2. *pl.* Makings, recettes *f*; petits profits. 'make-and-'break, *s. El:* Conjoncteur-disjoncteur *m*; trembleur *m*, vibreur *m.* M.-and-b. coil, bobine *f* à rupteur, à trembleur. 'make-believe¹. 1. *s.* Semblant *m*, feinte *f*, trompe-l'œil *m.* The land of m.-b., le pays des chimères. 2. *a.* M.-b. soldiers, soldats pour rire. make-be'lieve², *v.i.* (made-believe) (*Of children*) Jouer à faire semblant; faire semblant. 'make-do, *attrib.a.* M.-do expedient, moyen *m* de fortune. 'make-weight, *s.* Complément *m* de poids; supplément *m.* As a m.-w., (i) pour parfaire le poids; (ii) pour faire nombre.
maker ['meikər], *s.* 1. Faiseur, -euse. *Com: Ind:* Fabricant *m*; constructeur *m* (de machines). 2. Our M., the M. of all, le Créateur.
makeshift ['meikʃift], *s.* Pis-aller *m*, expédient *m*; moyen *m* de fortune. A m. government, un gouvernement, des gouvernants, de rencontre.
maladjusted [ˌmælə'dʒʌstid], *a. & s.* Inadapté.
maladjustment [ˌmælə'dʒʌs(t)mənt], *s.* Ajustement défectueux; dérèglement *m*; inadaptation *f.* Emotional m., déséquilibre émotif.
maladministration ['mælədˌminis'treiʃ(ə)n], *s.* Mauvaise administration; mauvaise gestion (des affaires publiques, etc.). *Jur:* Forfaiture *f*, prévarication *f.*
maladroit [ˌmælə'drɔit], *a.* Maladroit. -ly, *adv.* Maladroitement.
maladroitness [ˌmælə'drɔitnis], *s.* Maladresse *f.*
malady ['mælədi], *s.* Maladie *f*, mal *m.*
Malagasy [ˌmælə'gæsi], *a. & s. Geog: Ling:* Malgache.
malapropism ['mæləprɔpizm], *s.* Emploi *m* de mots savants déformés ou hors de propos; incongruité *f.*
malaria [mə'lɛəriə], *s. Med:* Malaria *f*; paludisme *m.*
malarial [mə'lɛəriəl], *a.* (*Of infection, etc.*) Paludéen.
malarious [mə'lɛəriəs], *a.* (Marécage) impaludé.
Malay [mə'lei]. 1. *a. & s. Geog:* Malais, -aise. The M. Archipelago, la Malaisie. 2. *s. Ling:* Le malais.

Malaya [mə'leiə]. *Pr.n. Geog:* La Malaisie.
Malayan [mə'leiən], *a. Geog:* Malais.
malcontent ['mælkəntent], *a. & s.* Mécontent, -ente.
male [meil]. 1. *a.* Mâle. M. sex, sexe masculin. M. child, enfant mâle. A m. friend, un ami. 2. *s.m.* Mâle.
malediction [ˌmæli'dikʃ(ə)n], *s.* Malédiction *f.*
maledictory [ˌmæli'dikt(ə)ri], *a.* De malédiction.
malefactor ['mælifæktər], *s.* Malfaiteur, -trice.
malefic [mə'lefik], *a.* Maléfique.
maleficence [mə'lefisns], *s.* Malfaisance *f.*
maleficent [mə'lefisnt], *a.* 1. Malfaisant (to, envers). 2. (*Of pers.*) Criminel.
malevolence [mə'levələns], *s.* Malveillance *f* (towards, envers).
malevolent [mə'levələnt], *a.* Malveillant. -ly, *adv.* Avec malveillance.
malfeasance [mæl'fi:z(ə)ns], *s.* 1. *Jur:* Agissements *m* coupables; malversation *f.* 2. Méfait *m.*
malformation ['mælfɔ:'meiʃ(ə)n], *s.* Malformation *f*; difformité *f*; défaut *m*, vice *m*, de conformation.
malice ['mælis], *s.* 1. Malice *f*, malveillance *f*, méchanceté *f.* Out of m., par malice, par méchanceté. To bear m. to, towards, s.o.; to bear s.o. m., en vouloir à qn; avoir de la rancune contre qn. 2. *Jur:* Intention criminelle ou délictueuse. With, of, m. prepense, with m. aforethought, avec intention criminelle; avec préméditation.
malicious [mə'liʃəs], *a.* 1. (*a*) Méchant, malveillant. (*b*) Rancunier. 2. *Jur:* Fait avec intention criminelle ou délictueuse; criminel. -ly, *adv.* 1. (*a*) Avec méchanceté, avec malveillance. (*b*) Par rancune. 2. *Jur:* Avec intention criminelle; avec préméditation.
malign¹ [mə'lain], *a.* Pernicieux, nuisible.
malign², *v.tr.* Calomnier, diffamer.
malignancy [mə'lignənsi], *s.* 1. Malignité *f*, méchanceté *f*, malveillance *f.* 2. *Med:* Malignité, virulence *f* (d'une maladie).
malignant [mə'lignənt], *a.* 1. Malin, *f.* maligne; méchant. 2. *Med:* Malin. -ly, *adv.* Avec malignité; méchamment.
maligner [mə'lainər], *s.* Calomniateur, -trice; diffamateur, -trice.
malignity [mə'ligniti], *s.* = MALIGNANCY.
malinger [mə'lingər], *v.i. Mil: etc:* Faire le malade; *P:* tirer au flanc. **malingering**, *s.* Simulation *f* (de maladie); *P:* tirage *m* au flanc.
malingerer [mə'lingərər], *s. Mil: etc:* Faux malade, simulateur *m*; *P:* tireur *m* au flanc.
mall [mɔ:l], *s.* (*a*) Mail *m*, promenade publique. (*b*) The M., le Mall (à Londres).
mallard ['mæləd], *s.* Malard *m*; col-vert *m*, colvert *m*; canard *m* sauvage.
malleability [ˌmæliə'biliti], *s.* Malléabilité *f.*
malleable ['mæliəbl], *a.* Malléable; forgeable.
mallet ['mælit], *s.* 1. *Tls:* Maillet *m*, mailloche *f.* 2. *Games:* Maillet (de croquet, de polo).
malmsey ['mɑ:mzi], *s.* (Vin *m* de) Malvoisie (*f*).
malnutrition ['mælnju:'triʃ(ə)n], *s.* 1. Sous-alimentation *f.* 2. Alimentation défectueuse; mauvaise hygiène alimentaire; déficience *f.*
malodorous ['mæ'loudərəs], *a.* Malodorant; nauséabond.
malpractice [mæl'præktis], *s.* 1. Méfait *m.* 2. *Jur:* (*a*) Négligence *f* (d'un médecin). (*b*) Malversation *f.*
malt [mɔ:lt], *s.* Malt *m.* 'malt-house, *s. Brew:* Malterie *f.*
Malta ['mɔ:ltə]. *Pr.n. Geog:* Malte *f.*
malted ['mɔ:ltid], *a.* M. milk, farine lactée.
Maltese [mɔ:l'ti:z], *a. & s. Geog: Ethn:* Maltais, -aise. *Her: Mec.E:* M. cross, croix *f* de Malte.
malthusian [mæl'θju:ziən], *a.* Malthusien, -ienne.
malthusianism [mæl'θju:ziənizm], *s.* Malthusianisme *m.*
malting ['mɔltin], *s.* 1. Maltage *m.* 2. = MALT-HOUSE.
Maltese [mɔ:l'ti:z], *a. Geog: Ethn:* Maltais, -aise. *Her: Mec.E:* M. cross, croix *f* de Malte.
maltose ['mɔ:ltous], *s. Ch: Ind:* Maltose *m.*
maltreat [mæl'tri:t], *v.tr.* Maltraiter, malmener.
maltreatment [mæl'tri:tmənt], *s.* Mauvais traitement.
malvaceae [mæl'veisii:], *s.pl. Bot:* Malvacées *f.*
malvaceous [mæl'veiʃəs], *a. Bot:* Malvacé.
malversation [ˌmælvə'seiʃ(ə)n], *s.* 1. Malversation *f.* 2. Mauvaise administration; gestion *f* coupable.

mamilla [mə'milə], s. 1. *Anat:* Bout *m* de sein. 2. *Anat: Bot:* Mamelon *m*.

mamillary [mæ'miləri], a. 1. Mamillaire. 2. = MAMMIFORM.

mamillate(d) ['mæmileit(id)], a. Mamelonné.

mamma [mə'mɑ:], s.f. F: Maman.

mammal ['mæm(ə)l], s. Z: Mammifère *m*.

mammary ['mæməri], a. *Anat:* Mammaire.

mammiform ['mæmifɔ:m], a. Mammiforme.

mammoth ['mæməθ]. 1. s. Mammouth *m*. 2. *Attrib.a. F:* Géant, monstre.

mammy ['mæmi], s.f. 1. A. & P: Maman. 2. *U.S:* Négresse bonne d'enfants.

man[1], pl. men [mæn, men], s.m. 1. (a) (*Human being*) Homme. The man in the street, le Français (Anglais, etc.) moyen. Every man, tout le monde; tous; chacun. Any man, quelqu'un; n'importe qui. No man, personne. No man's land, "no man's land" *m*; (i) terrains *m* vagues; (ii) *Mil:* zone *f* neutre (entre les premières lignes). Some men, quelques personnes, quelques-uns, certains. Few men, peu de gens. Men say that . . ., on dit que. . . . A man has a right to speak! on a bien le droit de parler! Solitude changes a man, la solitude, ça vous change. (b) (*Mankind*) L'homme. Man proposes, God disposes, l'homme propose et Dieu dispose. (c) *Theol:* The old, the new, man, le vieil homme, le nouvel homme. *F. & Hum:* To satisfy the inner man, se refaire, se restaurer. 2. (*Adult male*) Homme. (a) May I speak to you as man to man? puis-je vous parler d'homme à homme? They were killed to a man, ils furent tués jusqu'au dernier. To show oneself a man, montrer qu'on est un homme. To make a man of s.o., faire un homme de qn. To bear sth. like a man, supporter qch. virilement. A dangerous man, un esprit dangereux. He is not the man for that, il n'est pas fait pour cela. He is not the man (to refuse, etc.), il n'est pas homme à (refuser, etc.). I'm your man, (i) je suis votre homme; (ii) cela me va! He is just the man for me, c'est mon homme. A man's man, un vrai homme. *F:* Come here, young man! viens ici, mon petit bonhomme! Good man! bravo! Good-bye, old man! adieu, mon vieux! (b) (*Often not translated*) An old man, un vieillard. The dead man, le mort. *F:* Dead man, cadavre *m* (bouteille vide). He's an important man, *F:* a big man, c'est une personnalité, *F:* c'est quelqu'un. The man Smith, le nommé Smith, le dit Smith. That man Smith, (i) Smith que voilà; (ii) ce chenapan de Smith. (c) The men of Somerset, les habitants, les natifs, du Somerset. *Sch:* He's an Oxford man, (i) c'est un étudiant d'Oxford; (ii) il a fait ses études à l'Université d'Oxford. (d) *Attrib:* Man cook, cuisinier. (e) Ice-cream man, marchand *m* de glaces. A small m., un petit commerçant. 3. (a) *F:* Her man, son mari, *P:* son homme. (b) Man and wife, mari et femme. (c) *P:* My young man, (i) mon bon ami; (ii) mon futur, mon fiancé. 4. (a) Domestique *m*, valet *m*. (b) *Adm: Com:* Employé *m*, garçon *m*. (c) *Ind:* The employers and the men, les patrons et les ouvriers. (d) (*Delivery*) m., livreur *m*. (e) *Mil: Nau:* (*Usu. pl.*) Homme. Officers, N.C.O.'s, and men, officiers, sous-officiers, et hommes de troupe. (f) *Sp:* Joueur *m*. 5. (*At chess*) Pièce *f*; (at draughts) pion *m*. 'man-at-'arms, s.m. (pl. men-at-arms) *A:* Homme d'armes. 'man-child, s.m. Enfant du sexe masculin. 'man-eater, s. (pl. man-eaters) 1. (*Of pers.*) Anthropophage *m*, cannibale *mf*. 2. (*Of animal*) Mangeur *m* d'hommes. 'man-eating, a. 1. (Tribu, etc.) anthropophage. 2. (Tigre, etc.) mangeur d'hommes. 'man-hater, s. Misanthrope *m*. She's a m.-h., elle déteste les hommes. 'man-hole, s. Trou *m* d'homme (de chaudière); trou de visite; regard *m*. Man-hole cover, (i) plaque d'égout; (ii) *Mch:* autoclave *m* d'un trou d'homme. 'man-hour (pl. man-hours), s. F: Heure *f* de main-d'œuvre. 'man hunt, s. chasse *f* à l'homme. 'man-of-'war, s. (pl. men-of-war) *Nau:* Vaisseau *m* de guerre; vaisseau de ligne. 'man-power, s. 1. *Ind:* Main d'œuvre *f*. 2. *Coll.* (a) *Ind:* Main d'œuvre *f*. (b) Effectifs *mpl*. 'man-servant, s.m. (pl. men-servants) Domestique; valet (de chambre). 'man-trap, s. Piège *m* à hommes, à loups.

man[2], v.tr. (manned) Garnir d'hommes. (a) To man a fort, mettre une garnison dans un fort; garnir un fort. (b) *Nau:* Armer, équiper (un canot). Fully manned boat, canot à armement complet. (*In salute*) To man ship, faire passer (l'équipage) à la bande. To man a rope, se mettre à, sur, une manœuvre. To man the yards, monter les vergues.

manacle[1] ['mænəkl], s. *Usu.pl.* Manacles, menottes *f*.

manacle[2], v.tr. Mettre les menottes à (qn).

manage ['mænidʒ], v.tr. 1. Manier (un outil); diriger, manœuvrer (un navire). 2. Conduire (une entreprise, etc.); diriger, gérer (une affaire, une banque, etc.); régir (une propriété); mener (une affaire). To m. s.o.'s affairs, gérer les affaires de qn. To m. jointly, cogérer. 3. Gouverner, mater (qn); tenir (des enfants, etc.); maîtriser, dompter (un animal). To know how to m. s.o., savoir prendre qn. 4. Arranger, conduire (une affaire). To m. to do sth., arriver, parvenir, à faire qch.; trouver moyen de faire qch. I shall m. it, j'en viendrai à bout. How do you m. not to dirty your hands? comment faites-vous pour ne pas vous salir les mains? A hundred pounds is the most that I can m., cent livres, c'est tout ce que je peux faire (pour vous). If you can m. to see him, si vous pouvez vous arranger pour le voir. *F:* Can you m. a few more cherries? pouvez-vous manger encore quelques cerises? 5. *Abs.* She manages well, (i) elle sait s'y prendre; (ii) elle est bonne ménagère. M. as best you can, arrangez-vous comme vous pourrez. He'll m. all right, il saura bien se retourner; il se débrouillera. How will you m. about the children? et pour les enfants, comment ferez-vous? managing, a. Directeur, -trice; gérant. M. director, administrateur délégué; administrateur gérant.

manageable ['mænidʒəbl], a. 1. Maniable; (canot) manœuvrable. 2. (*Of pers.*) Traitable, facile à mener. 3. Praticable, faisable.

management ['mænidʒmənt], s. 1. (a) Maniement *m* (d'un outil, des hommes). (b) Direction *f*, conduite *f* (d'une affaire); gérance *f*, gestion *f* (d'une propriété). 'Under new m.,' "changement de propriétaire." 2. Adresse *f*; savoir-faire *m*. 3. *Coll.* Les administrateurs *m*; l'administration *f*, la direction.

manager ['mænidʒər], s. 1. Directeur *m*, administrateur *m*; gérant *m*; régisseur *m* (d'une propriété) Joint m., cogérant *m*. *Com:* Sales m., directeur commercial. Department m., chef de service. Personnel, staff, m., chef *m*, directeur, du personnel. *Rail: etc:* Traffic m., chef du mouvement. *Ind:* Works m., chef du service; directeur d'usine. Business m., (i) directeur commercial; (ii) *Journ:* administrateur; (iii) *Th:* imprésario *m* (d'une actrice, etc.). *Cin: Sp:* Manager *m*. 2. She is a good m., elle est bonne ménagère, bonne maîtresse de maison.

manageress ['mænidʒəres], s.f. Directrice, gérante. Joint m., cogérante.

managerial [mænə'dʒiəriəl], a. Directorial, -aux.

managership ['mænidʒəʃip], s. Direction *f*, gérance *f*.

manatee [mænə'ti:], s. Z: Lamantin *m*.

Manchuria [mæn'tʃuəriə]. *Pr.n.* La Mandchourie.

Manchurian [mæn'tʃuəriən], a. & s. Mandchou, -oue, pl. -ous, -oues.

mandarin[1] ['mændərin], s. Mandarin *m*.

mandarin[2], mandarine ['mændəri:n], s. Bot: Mandarine *f*.

mandatary ['mændət(ə)ri], s. *Jur:* Mandataire *mf*.

mandate[1] ['mændeit], s. 1. *Lit:* Commandement *m*, ordre *m*. 2. *Pol: Hist:* Mandat *m*.

mandate[2] [mæn'deit], v.tr. *Hist:* To m. a country to one of the Powers, attribuer sous mandat un pays à une des Puissances. Mandated territories, territoires sous mandat.

mandatory ['mændət(ə)ri]. 1. a. (a) M. writ, mandement *m*. (b) *Hist:* M. states, états mandataires. 2. s. = MANDATARY.

mandible ['mændibl], s. 1. Z: Mandibule *f*. 2. *Anat:* Mâchoire inférieure.

mandolin(e) ['mændəlin], s. Mandoline *f*.

mandrake ['mændreik], s. *Bot:* Mandragore *f*.

mandrel ['mændril], mandril ['mændril], s. *Mec.E:* 1. Mandrin *m*, arbre *m* (de tour). 2. Mandrin (pour évaser les tubes).

mandrill ['mændril], *s. Z:* Mandrill *m.*

mane [mein], *s.* Crinière *f.*

manes ['mɑːneiz], *s.pl. Rom.Ant:* Mânes *m.*

manful ['mænf(u)l], *a.* Vaillant, hardi, viril. **-fully,** *adv.* Vaillamment, hardiment.

manfulness ['mænf(u)lnis], *s.* Vaillance *f;* hardiesse *f,* virilité *f.*

manganate ['mæŋgənit], *s. Ch:* Manganate *m.*

manganese [,mæŋgə'niːz], *s.* **1.** *Miner:* (Oxyde noir de) manganèse *m.* Grey m. ore, manganite. **2.** *Ch:* Manganèse. *Metall:* M. steel, acier au manganèse.

manganite ['mæŋgənait], *s. Miner:* Manganite.

mange [mein(d)ʒ], *s.* Gale *f* (du chien, etc.).

mangel-wurzel ['mæŋgl'wəːzl], *s.* Betterave fourragère.

manger ['mein(d)ʒər], *s.* Mangeoire *f,* crèche *f;* auge *f* d'écurie. *F:* He is a dog in the m., il fait comme le chien du jardinier.

mangle[1] ['mæŋgl], *s. Laund:* Essoreuse *f* (à rouleaux).

mangle[2], *v.tr.* Essorer (le linge).

mangle[3], *v.tr.* **1.** Déchirer, lacérer, mutiler; charcuter, massacrer (une volaille). **2.** Mutiler, déformer (un mot); estropier (une citation). **mangling,** *s.* Lacération *f;* mutilation *f.*

mango, *pl.* **-oes** ['mæŋgou, -ouz], *s. Bot:* **1.** Mangue *f.* **2.** Manguier *m.*

mangrove ['mæŋgrouv], *s. Bot:* Manglier *m,* palétuvier *m.* **M. swamp,** mangrove *f.*

mangy ['mein(d)ʒi], *a.* **1.** Galeux. **2.** *(a) F: (Of furniture, etc.)* Minable, miteux. *(b) P:* Sale, moche.

manhandle ['mænhændl], *v.tr.* **1.** Manutentionner (des marchandises, etc.). **2.** *F:* Maltraiter, malmener (qn).

manhood ['mænhud], *s.* **1.** Humanité *f;* nature humaine. **2.** Age *m* d'homme; âge viril.

mania ['meiniə], *s.* **1.** *Med:* (i) Manie *f;* folie *f;* délire *m;* (ii) folie furieuse. **2.** Manie, passion *f* (de qch.). To have a m. for sth., for doing sth., avoir la passion de qch.

maniac ['meiniæk]. **1.** *a. & s.* Fou furieux, folle furieuse. **2.** *s.* Enragé, -ée (de qch.).

manicure[1] ['mænikjuər], *s.* **1.** Soin *m* des mains. M. set, trousse *f* de manucure; onglier *m.* **2.** = MANICURIST.

manicure[2], *v.tr.* **1.** Soigner les mains de (qn). **2.** Soigner (les mains). To m. one's nails, se faire les ongles.

manicurist ['mænikjuərist], *s.* Manucure *mf.*

manifest[1] ['mænifest], *a.* Manifeste, évident, clair. **-ly,** *adv.* Manifestement.

manifest[2], *s. Nau:* Manifeste *m* (de sortie).

manifest[3], *v.tr.* *(a)* Manifester, témoigner (qch.). *(b) Nau:* Déclarer, faire figurer sur le manifeste.

manifestation [,mænifes'teiʃ(ə)n], *s.* Manifestation *f.*

manifesto [,mæni'festou], *s. Pol:* Manifeste *m,* proclamation *f.*

manifold[1] ['mænifould]. **1.** *a.* *(a)* Divers, varié; de diverses sortes. *(b)* Multiple, nombreux. **2.** *s. (a) Com: etc:* Polycopie *f.* M. paper, papier à copies multiples. *(b) I.C.E:* etc: Tubulure *f,* tuyauterie *f;* collecteur *m.* **Exhaust m.,** tubulure d'échappement.

manifold[2], *v.tr.* Polycopier, autocopier.

manifoldness ['mænifouldnis], *s.* Multiplicité *f,* diversité *f.*

manikin ['mænikin], *s.* **1.** Petit bout d'homme; homoncule *m,* nabot *m.* **2.** *Art: etc:* Mannequin *m.*

Manil(l)a [mə'nilə]. *Pr.n. Geog:* Manille *f.* M. rope, cordage *m* en manille; manille *f.* M. paper, papier *m* bulle.

manille [mæ'nil], *s. Cards:* Manille *f.*

manioc ['mæniok], *s. Bot:* Manioc *m.*

manipulate [mə'nipjuleit], *v.tr.* **1.** Manipuler (un objet); manœuvrer, actionner (un dispositif mécanique). **2.** *F:* To m. accounts, tripoter, cuisiner, des comptes.

manipulation [mə,nipju'leiʃ(ə)n], *s.* **1.** Manipulation *f.* **2.** Manœuvre *f.* **3.** *Pej:* Tripotage *m.*

manipulator [mə'nipjuleitər], *s.* **1.** Manipulateur *m.* **2.** *Pej:* Tripoteur *m.*

mankind, *s.inv.* **1.** [mæn'kaind]. Le genre humain; l'homme *m.* **2.** ['mænkaind]. *(opp. to* womankind) Les hommes.

manliness ['mænlinis], *s.* Caractère mâle, viril; virilité *f.*

manly ['mænli], *a.* D'homme; mâle, viril.

manna ['mænə], *s.* **1.** *B:* Manne *f.* **2.** *Pharm:* Manne du frêne.

mannequin ['mænikin], *s. (Pers.)* Mannequin *m.*

manner ['mænər], *s.* **1.** Manière *f,* façon *f* (de faire qch.).. In, after, this m., de cette manière, de cette façon; ainsi. The m. in which . . ., la manière dont . . . After his own m., à sa façon. In like m., de la même manière; de même. In such a. m. that . . ., de manière que, de sorte que + *ind. or sub.* In the same m. as . . ., de la même manière que . . ., de même que . . . In a m. (of speaking), en quelque sorte; pour ainsi dire. It is a m. of speaking, c'est un façon de parler. Novel in the m. of Dickens, roman à la manière de Dickens. **2.** *A. & Lit:* Manière, coutume *f,* habitude *f.* After the m. of the kings of old à l'instar des anciens rois. As (if) to the m. born, comme si de sa vie il n'avait fait que cela. **3.** *pl.* Mœurs *f,* usages *m* (d'un peuple). **Manners change with the times,** autres temps, autres mœurs. **4.** Maintien *m,* tenue *f,* air *m.* I do not like his m. to his teachers, je n'aime pas son attitude envers ses professeurs. **5.** *pl. (a)* Manières. Bad manners, mauvaises manières; manque *m* de savoir-vivre. It is bad manners to stare, c'est mal élevé de dévisager les gens. *(b)* (Good) manners, bonnes manières, savoir-vivre *m,* politesse *f.* To teach s.o. manners, donner à qn une leçon de politesse. To forget one's manners, oublier les convenances; s'oublier. Where are your manners, Tommy? voyons, Tommy, est-ce comme ça qu'on se tient? *Aut:* Road manners, politesse de la route. **6.** Espèce *f,* sorte *f.* What m. of man is he? quel genre d'homme est-ce? All m. of people, of things, toutes sortes de gens, de choses. No m. of doubt, aucune espèce de doute, aucun doute.

mannered ['mænəd], *a.* **1.** Rough-m., aux manières rudes; (homme) brusque. **2.** Maniéré; affecté; (style) recherché, précieux.

mannerism ['mænərizm], *s.* **1.** Maniérisme *m,* affectation *f.* **2.** Particularité *f* (d'un écrivain, etc.).

mannerless ['mænəlis], *a.* Sans éducation; qui manque de savoir-vivre.

mannerliness ['mænəlinis], *s.* Courtoisie *f;* politesse *f.*

mannerly ['mænəli], *a.* Poli; courtois; (enfant) bien élevé.

mannish ['mæniʃ], *a.* **1.** Qui caractérise l'homme. **2.** *(Of woman)* Hommasse. M. ways, façons garçonnières.

manœuvrability [mə,nuːvrə'biliti], *s.* Maniabilité *f,* manœuvrabilité *f;* capacité *f* manœuvrière.

manœuvre[1] [mə'nuːvər], *s.* **1.** *Mil: Navy:* Manœuvre *f.* **2.** *(a)* A clever, a false, m., une manœuvre habile, une fausse manœuvre. *(b) pl. Mil:* (Underhand) manœuvres, menées *f,* intrigues *f. Pol:* Vote-catching manœuvres, manœuvres électorales.

manœuvre[2]. **1.** *v.tr.* Manœuvrer, faire manœuvrer (une armée, une flotte). To m. s.o. into a corner, acculer qn dans un coin; amener adroitement qn dans une impasse. **2.** *v.i.* Manœuvrer; *(of ship)* évoluer.

manometer [mə'nomitər], *s.* Manomètre *m.*

manometric(al) [,mæno'metrik(əl)], *a. Ph:* Manométrique.

manor ['mænər], *s. Hist:* Seigneurie *f.* **'manor-(house),** *s.* Château seigneurial; manoir *m*: gentilhommière *f.*

manorial [mə'nɔːriəl], *a.* Seigneurial, -aux.

mansard [,mænsɑːd], *s.* M. (roof), toit *m,* comble *m,* en mansarde.

manse [mæns], *s. Esp. Scot:* = Presbytère *m* (résidence du pasteur).

mansion ['mænʃ(ə)n], *s.* **1.** *(In country)* Château *m;* *(in town)* hôtel (particulier). **2.** The M. House, la résidence officielle du Lord Maire de Londres (dans la City).

manslaughter ['mænslɔːtər], *s. Jur:* *(a)* Homicide *m* involontaire, par imprudence. *(b)* Homicide sans préméditation.

mantelpiece ['mæntlpiːs], *s.* **1.** Manteau *m,* chambranle *m,* de cheminée. **2.** Dessus *m,* tablette *f,* de cheminée.

mantelshelf ['mæntlʃelf], *s.* = MANTELPIECE 2.

mantilla [mæn'tilə], *s. Cost:* Mantille *f.*

mantis ['mæntis], *s. Ent:* Mante *f.* **Praying m.,** mante religieuse.

mantissa [mæn'tisə], *s. Mth:* Mantisse *f* (d'un logarithme).

mantle¹ ['mæntl], s. 1. (a) Manteau m (sans manches); cape f. (b) Mante f, pèlerine f (de femme). 2. Manteau (de neige, de lierre); voile m (de brume). 3. Manchon m (de bec de gaz à incandescence).

mantle². 1. v.tr. (a) Couvrir, vêtir, envelopper, (qn) d'un manteau. (b) Jeter un manteau sur (qch.); voiler (qch.). (c) Couvrir, envelopper (with, de). 2. v.i. (Of blush) Se répandre (over the cheeks, sur les joues); (of face, cheeks) rougir, s'empourprer.

Mantua ['mæntjuə]. Pr.n. Geog: Mantoue f.

manual ['mænju(ə)l]. 1. a. (a) Manuel. M. labour, travail manuel; travail de manœuvre. M. fire-engine, pompe f à bras. S.a. SIGN-MANUAL. (b) Mil: M. exercise, maniement m d'armes. 2. s. (a) Manuel m; aide-mémoire m inv. (b) Mus: Clavier m (d'un orgue). Great-m., clavier du grand orgue. -ally, adv. Manuellement; à la main.

manufactory [,mænju'fækt(ə)ri], s. O: Fabrique f, usine f, manufacture f.

manufacture¹ [,mænju'fæktʃər], s. 1. (a) Fabrication f, élaboration f (d'un produit industriel); confection f (de vêtements, etc.). (b) Industrie f. 2. Produit manufacturé.

manufacture², v.tr. (a) Fabriquer, manufacturer (un produit industriel); confectionner (des vêtements, etc.). **Manufacturing town**, ville industrielle. (b) Forger, fabriquer (des nouvelles).

manufacturer [,mænju'fækt(ə)rər], s. Fabricant m, industriel m, manufacturier m, usinier m.

manumission [,mænju'miʃ(ə)n], s. Hist: Manumission f, affranchissement m.

manumit [,mænju'mit], v.tr. (manumitted) Hist: Affranchir, émanciper.

manure¹ [mə'njuər], s. Engrais m. **Farmyard m.**, fumier m (d'étable). **Fish m.**, engrais de poisson. **Artificial m.**, fumier artificiel. **Liquid m.**, purin m. **M. heap**, tas m de fumier; F: fumier.

manure², v.tr. Fumer, engraisser (la terre). **manuring**, s. Fumage m, fumure f, engraissement m.

manuscript ['mænjuskript]. 1. s. Manuscrit m. 2. a. Manuscrit; écrit à la main.

Manx [mæŋks]. 1. a. Geog: Mannois; manx(ois). M. cat, chat sans queue de l'île de Man. 2. s. Ling: Le mannois.

Manxman, pl. -men ['mæŋksmən], s. Mannois.

many ['meni]. 1. a. & s. (more, most, q.v.) Un grand nombre (de); beaucoup (de); bien des; plusieurs, maint. **M. a time, m. and m. a time**, mainte(s) fois; mainte et mainte fois. **M. a man, m. a one**, bien des gens. **Before m. days have passed**, avant qu'il soit longtemps. **Of m. kinds**, de toutes sortes. **In m. instances**, dans bien des cas. **For m. years**, pendant de longues années. **Ever so m. times**, je ne sais combien de fois. **He made m. mistakes**, il a fait de nombreuses fautes, beaucoup de fautes. **M. of us**, beaucoup, un grand nombre, d'entre nous. **M. have seen it**, beaucoup de personnes l'ont vu. **They were so m.**, ils étaient si nombreux; il y en avait tant. **So m. men, so m. minds**, autant d'hommes, autant d'avis. **He told me in so m. words that . . .**, il m'a dit en propres termes que. . . . **Too m. people**, trop de monde. **Three of you are none too m. for the job**, vous n'êtes pas trop de trois pour ce travail. **A card too m.**, une carte de trop. **How m. horses have you? combien de chevaux avez-vous? I have as m. books as you**, j'ai autant de livres que vous. **As m. again**, twice as many, deux fois autant, encore autant. **As m. as ten people saw it**, il y a bien dix personnes qui l'ont vu. **A great m. people**, un grand nombre de personnes. **A good m. things**, un assez grand nombre de choses; pas mal de choses. **There are a good m.**, il y en a pas mal. 2. **The m.**, la multitude; la foule, la masse. 3. Comb.fm. **M.-voiced**, aux voix nombreuses. **M.-flowered** -lobed, multiflore, multilobé. **many-'coloured**, a. Multicolore. **many-'sided**, a. 1. (Figure) à plusieurs côtés. 2. (Problème) complexe. 3. (Personne) aux talents variés.

map¹ [mæp], s. Carte f (géographique). **Map of a town**, plan m d'une ville. **Sketch map**, carte-croquis f; F: topo m. **Map of the world**, mappemonde f. **The building of the atomic pile will put our village on the m.**, la construction de la pile atomique va mettre notre village en vedette. **Our village is really off the**

m., notre village est vraiment au bout du monde. **'map-case**, **'map-holder**, s. Porte-carte m, pl. porte-cartes. **'map-maker**, s. Cartographe m. **'map-making**, s. Cartographie f.

map², v.tr. (mapped) 1. Dresser une carte, un plan, de (la région, etc.). 2. **To map out a route**, tracer un itinéraire. **To map out a course of action**, se tracer un plan d'action. **mapping**, s. Cartographie f.

maple ['meipl], s. (a) Érable m. **English m., common maple**, érable champêtre, petit érable. **Sugar m., rock maple**, érable à sucre. **M. grove**, érablière f. **M. syrup**, Sirop m de sucre d'érable. (b) **Great m.**, érable blanc; (érable) faux platane; sycomore m.

maquis ['mæki:], s. Geog: Pol: Maquis m. Pol: **To take to the m.**, prendre le maquis. **Member of the m.**, maquisard m.

mar [mɑːr], v.tr. (marred) Gâter, gâcher (le plaisir de qn); troubler (la joie de qn); déparer (la beauté de qn). **To make or mar s.o.**, faire la fortune ou la ruine de qn.

marabou ['mærəbu:], s. 1. Orn: Marabout m; cigogne f à sac. 2. Duvet m de marabout.

marabout ['mærəbu:t], s. Rel: Marabout (musulman).

maraschino [,mærəs'ki:nou], s. Marasquin m.

marathon ['mærəθən], s. Sp: Marathon m.

maraud [mə'rɔːd]. 1. v.i. Marauder; aller en maraude. 2. v.tr. Piller (un village, etc.). **marauding¹**, a. Maraudeur, -euse. **marauding²**, s. Maraude f; Jur: maraudage m. **To go m.**, aller à la maraude.

marauder [mə'rɔːdər], s. Maraudeur, -euse.

marble¹ ['mɑːbl], s. 1. Marbre m. (a) **Clouded m.**, marbre tacheté, moucheté. **Imitation m.**, similimarbre m. **M. pavement**, dallage m en marbre. **M. cutter, m. mason**, marbrier m. **M. quarry**, marbrière f. (b) Art: **The Elgin marbles**, les marbres d'Elgin. 2. Games: Bille f. **To play marbles**, jouer aux billes. **'marble-'edged**, a. Bookb: Marbré sur tranche.

marble², v.tr. Marbrer (une boiserie, etc.). Bookb: Marbrer, raciner (les plats). **marbled**, a. 1. Marbré. Bookb: (Of cover) Raciné, marbré; (of edge) jaspé. 2. (Salle, etc.) à revêtement de marbre. **marbling**, s. Marbrure f. Bookb: Racinage m (des plats); jaspage m, jaspure f (des tranches).

marcasite ['mɑːkəsait], s. Miner: Marcassite f.

March¹ [mɑː(t)ʃ], s. Mars m. **In M.**, au mois de mars. **(On) the fifth of M.**, le cinq mars.

march², s. Hist: (Often in pl.) Marche f; frontière f militaire. **'march-land**, s. Marches fpl; pays m frontière.

march³, v.i. (Of country, domain) **To m. upon, with . . .**, confiner à, être limitrophe de. . . .

march⁴, s. 1. Mil: (a) Marche f. **On the m.**, en marche. **To do a day's m.**, faire, fournir, une étape. **M. past**, défilé m (de revue, etc.). Mil: **Route m.**, marche d'entraînement. (b) Pas m, allure f. **Slow m.**, parade m., pas de parade. **Quick m.**, pas cadencé, accéléré. **Double m.**, pas gymnastique. 2. Marche, progrès m (des événements). 3. Mus: Marche.

march⁵. 1. v.i. Mil: etc: Marcher. **Quick m.!** en avant, marche! **M. at ease!** pas de route! **M. at attention!** pas cadencé, marche! **To m. along**, marcher, avancer. **To m. to, towards, a place**, s'acheminer sur, vers, un endroit. **To m. in**, entrer. **To m. out**, sortir. **To m. away**, partir. **To m. off**, (i) se mettre en marche; (ii) F: décamper; plier bagage. **To m. by, past (s.o.)**, défiler (devant qn). 2. v.tr. (a) Faire marcher (des troupes). (b) **He was marched off, away, to gaol**, il a été emmené en prison. **marching**, s. Mil: Marche f. **M. orders**, feuille f de route. F: **To give s.o. his m. orders**, signifier son congé à qn. **M. song**, chanson f de route.

marchioness ['mɑːʃənes], s.f. Marquise.

mare ['mɛər], s. Jument f. **The discovery turned out to be a m.'s nest**, la découverte s'est avérée illusoire. **'mare's-tail**, s. 1. Bot: (a) Pesse f d'eau. (b) Prêle f. 2. Meteor: (Nuage m en) queue-de-chat f; cirrus m en panaches.

Margaret ['mɑːg(ə)rit]. Pr.n.f. Marguerite.

margarine [,mɑːdʒə'riːn, mɑːgə'riːn], s. Com: Margarine f.

marge [mɑːdʒ], s. P: = MARGARINE.

margin[1] ['mɑ:dʒin], s. **1.** (a) Marge f; lisière f (d'un bois); bord m, rive f (d'une rivière). (b) Marge, écart m. **To allow s.o. some m.,** accorder quelque marge à qn. **To allow a m. for mistakes,** faire la part des erreurs possibles, calculer large. (c) Com: Marge, couverture f, provision f. St.Exch: Acompte (versé au courtier). (d) Mec.E: etc: M. (of error), tolérance f, limite f. **Safety m.,** marge de sécurité. **2.** Marge, blanc m (d'une page). Phot: Liséré m (d'une épreuve). **On, in, the m.,** en marge. Typewr: **M. release,** déclanche-marge m. **M. stop,** margeur m; régulateur m de marges.

margin[2], v.tr. **1.** Annoter en marge (un livre). **2.** **Pages insufficiently margined,** pages à marges insuffisantes. **3.** St.Exch: Fournir une couverture pour (une commande).

marginal ['mɑ:dʒinl], a. Marginal, -aux; en marge. **M. note,** note marginale; manchette f. Agr: **M. land,** terres f d'un faible rendement. Pol: **M. seat,** siège chaudement disputé.

margrave ['mɑ:greiv], s. Hist: Margrave m.

marguerite [ˌmɑ:gə'ri:t], s. Bot: (a) (Ox-eye daisy) Leucanthème m; grande marguerite. (b) (Paris daisy) Marguerite en arbre; anthémis f.

Maria [mə'raiə]. Pr.n.f. Maria. F: **Black M.,** la voiture cellulaire, P: panier m. à salade.

marigold ['mærigould], s. Bot: **1.** Souci m. **2.** French m., œillet m d'Inde. African m., rose f d'Inde. **3.** Corn m., field m., marguerite dorée.

marijuana [mæri'wɑ:nə], s. Marihuana f, marijuana f.

marinade [mæri'neid], s. Marinade f.

marinate ['mærineit], v.tr. Mariner.

marine [mə'ri:n]. **1.** a. (a) (Animal) marin. (b) **M. insurance,** assurance f maritime. (c) **M. forces,** troupes f de marine. (d) **M. engine,** moteur marin. **2.** s. (a) Marine f. **Mercantile m.,** marine marchande. (b) Mil: (i) Soldat m de l'infanterie de marine; (ii) fusilier marin. F: **Tell that to the (horse-)marines!** à d'autres! allez conter ça ailleurs!

mariner ['mærinər], s. Nau: Marin m (officier ou matelot).

marionette [ˌmæriə'net], s. Marionnette f.

marital ['mærit(ə)l], a. **1.** Marital, -aux. **2.** Matrimonial, -aux. **-ally,** adv. Maritalement.

maritime ['mæritaim], a. Maritime. Geog: **The M. Provinces,** les (Provinces) Maritimes.

marjoram ['mɑ:dʒ(ə)rəm], s. Bot: Origan m, marjolaine f.

mark[1] [mɑ:k], s. **1.** (a) But m, cible f. **To hit the m.,** atteindre le but; frapper juste; F: mettre dans le noir, dans le mille. **To miss the m.,** manquer le but, F: frapper à côté. **Beside the m.,** à côté de la question; hors de propos. **To be wide of the m.,** être loin de la réalité, la vérité, loin de compte. **You little know how near you are to the m.,** vous ne croyez pas si bien dire. (b) F: **He's an easy m.,** c'est un jobard, P: une poire. (c) Box: **Blow to the m.,** coup au creux de l'estomac. **2.** Nau: Marque f; amer m; (on buoy) voyant m. **3.** Marque, preuve f, signe m, témoignage m. **As a m. of my esteem,** en témoignage de mon estime. **4.** (a) Marque, tache f, signe, empreinte f. **Marks of a blow,** marques d'un coup. **Marks of old age,** marques, stigmates m, de la vieillesse. **To leave one's m. upon sth.,** laisser sa marque, son empreinte, sur qch. **To make one's m.,** se faire une réputation; arriver, percer. **(God) save the m.!** Dieu me pardonne! passez-moi le mot! (b) **The m. of a foot,** la marque, l'empreinte, d'un pied. Fb: **To make a m., one's m.,** faire une marque. **5.** (a) Marque, signe. **He cannot write; he makes his m.,** il ne sait pas écrire; il fait une croix. **Punctuation marks,** signes de ponctuation. **Interrogation, question, m.,** point m d'interrogation. (b) Sch: **Point** m; **note** f d'appréciation. **Good m., bad m.,** bon, mauvais, point. **Examination marks,** notes d'examen. **6.** (a) Marque, repère m, trace f. **Guiding m., guide-m., reference m.,** (point m de) repère. (b) Nau: **Plimsoll m.,** ligne f Plimsoll. F: (Of pers.) **To be up to the m.,** (i) (in ability) être à la hauteur; (ii) (in health) être dans son assiette; être en train. **I am not up to the m.,** je ne suis pas dans mon assiette. (Of thg) **To be, to come, up to the m.,** répondre à l'attente; être à la hauteur. **It is hardly up to the m.,** cela laisse à

désirer. **Close to the thousand m.,** tout près du millier. (c) For: (Blaze) Blanchi(s) m. (d) Sp: **Ligne de départ.** (Of motor car) **To be quick off the m.,** démarrer vivement, F: (Of person) être dégourdi, piger vite. Sp: **On your marks! Get set! Go!** à vos marques! Prêts! Partez! **7. Man of m.,** homme marquant.

mark[2], v.tr. **1.** (a) Marquer, chiffrer (du linge); estampiller (des marchandises). **To m. the cards,** biseauter, piper, piquer, maquiller, les cartes. (b) (Usu. passive) **To be marked with spots, stripes,** être marqué de taches, de raies. **2.** (a) **To m. (the price of) an article,** marquer le prix d'un article. (b) Sch: **To m. an exercise,** corriger, noter, coter, un devoir. **3.** **To m. s.o., sth., as . . .,** désigner, choisir, qn, qch., pour. . . . **If we are marked to die,** si nous sommes destinés à mourir. **4.** (a) Marquer, repérer, indiquer. **To m. the points in a game, to mark the game,** marquer les points du jeu. (b) **Stream that marks the limits of the estate,** ruisseau qui marque la limite de la propriété. **Post marking the course,** poteau indicateur de piste. (c) Indiquer. **Signs which mark the trend of public opinion,** signes indicateurs de l'opinion publique. **5.** (a) **To m. one's approval, one's displeasure (by . . .),** manifester, montrer, son approbation, son mécontentement (par . . .; en faisant qch.). **To m. time,** (i) Mil: marquer le pas; (ii) piétiner sur place. **He had to m. time before entering university,** il a dû attendre avant d'entrer à l'université. (b) **His reign was marked by great victories,** son règne fut marqué, signalé, par de grandes victoires. **To mark an era,** faire époque. **6.** (a) Lit: Observer, regarder, guetter. (b) **To m. the fall of a shell,** repérer le point de chute d'un obus. (c) Observer, remarquer, noter (qch.). **M. me! m. you! m. my words!** écoutez-moi bien! **7.** Fb: Marquer (un adversaire). **mark down,** v.tr. **1.** **To m. down (the price of) an article,** baisser un article de prix; démarquer un article. **2.** Inscrire (un article à l'inventaire, etc.). **3.** Sch: **To m. d. (a paper),** baisser la note (d'une copie). **mark off,** v.tr. **1.** (a) Surv: **To m. off a line, a road,** bornoyer, jalonner, une ligne, une route. (b) **To m. off a distance on the map,** (i) prendre, mesurer, (ii) rapporter, une distance sur la carte. (c) Cocher (une liste). **2.** **To m. sth. off from . . .,** distinguer, séparer, qch. de. . . **mark out,** v.tr. **1.** Délimiter, tracer (des frontières); borner, bornoyer (un champ); jalonner (une concession minière). **2.** (a) **His neat appearance marked him out from the crowd,** sa mise soignée le distinguait de la foule. (b) **To m. s.o. out for . . .,** destiner qn à . . .; désigner qn pour. . . . **mark up,** v.tr. Augmenter, élever, le prix de (qch.). **marked,** a. **1.** M. card, carte marquée, biseautée. **2.** **He's a m. man,** (i) c'est un homme marqué (par ses ennemis); (ii) F: il est fichu. **3.** M. difference, différence marquée, prononcée. **M. improvement,** amélioration sensible. **Strongly m. features, traits fortement accusés. **The change is becoming more m.,** le changement s'accentue. **marking,** s. **1.** (a) Marquage m. (b) Mec.E: Repérage m (du point mort, etc.). **2.** pl. **Markings,** marques f; (on animal) taches f, rayures f. **'marking-board,** s. Games: Tableau m (pour marquer les points). **'marking-ink,** s. Encre f à marquer. **'marking-tool,** s. Rouanne f; pointe f à tracer.

mark[3], s. Num: Mark m, marc m. **Gold marks,** marks or.

Mark[4]. Pr.n.m. Marc.

markedly ['mɑ:kidli], adv. D'une façon marquée. **M. polite,** d'une politesse marquée.

marker ['mɑ:kər], s. **1.** (Pers.) (a) Marqueur, -euse (de linge, etc.). (b) (At games) Marqueur m, pointeur m; (at butts) marqueur. (c) Mil: Jalonneur m. **2.** (a) Ten: etc: (Machine) Court-m., marqueur à chaux. (b) Cards: Bridge m., carnet-bloc m (de bridge). (c) = BOOKMARKER. **3.** Marque f, jalon m, repère m. Av: Boundary m., feu m, borne f, de balisage. **Flush m. light,** plot lumineux d'atterrissage.

market[1] ['mɑ:kit], s. **1.** (a) Marché m. **Covered m.,** marché couvert; halle f, halles fpl. **The m. square,** la place du marché. **In the m.,** au marché, à la halle. (b) **Overseas markets,** marchés d'outre-mer. St.Exch: **Outside m.,** la coulisse. (Of pers.) **To be in the m.**

for sth., être acheteur de qch. (*Of thg*) To be on the m., to come into the m., être mis en vente, dans le commerce. To find a m. for sth., trouver un débouché, des acheteurs, pour qch. (*Of thg*) To find a ready m., être d'un débit facile; se placer facilement. The m. has risen, les cours *m* sont en hausse. Black m., marché *m* noir. *Pol.Ec:* Common m., marché commun. M. research, étude *f* du marché. 'market-day, *s.* Jour *m* de marché. 'market 'garden, *s.* Jardin maraîcher. 'market gardener, *s.* Maraîcher, -ère. 'market 'gardening, *s.* Culture maraîchère. 'market-price, *s. Com:* Prix courant. 'market-town, *s.* Ville *f* où se tient un marché; bourg *m*, bourgade *f*.

market², *v.* (marketed) 1. *v.i.* Faire son marché, faire ses emplettes. To go marketing, aller faire son marché; aller aux provisions. 2. *v.tr.* Trouver des débouchés pour (ses marchandises); lancer (un article) sur le marché. marketing, *s.* Étude *f*, organisation *f*, des marchés.

marketable ['mɑːkitəbl], *a.* 1. (*Of goods*) Vendable; d'un débit facile. 2. M. value, valeur marchande.

marksman, *pl.* -men ['mɑːksmən], *s.* Bon tireur; tireur d'élite.

marksmanship ['mɑːksmənʃip], *s.* Adresse *f*, habileté *f*, au tir.

marl¹ [mɑːl], *s. Agr:* Marne *f*. 'marl-pit, *s.* Marnière *f*.

marl², *v.tr. Agr:* Marner (le sol). marling, *s. Agr:* Marnage *m*.

marline ['mɑːlin], *s. Nau:* (*Two yarns*) Lusin *m*; (*three yarns*) merlin *m*.

marline-spike, marlinspike ['mɑːlinspaik], *s. Nau:* Épissoir *m*.

marly ['mɑːli], *a.* (Sol) marneux.

marmalade ['mɑːməleid], *s. Cu:* Confiture *f* d'oranges. Lemon m., confiture de citrons.

marmoreal [mɑːˈmɔːriəl], marmorean [mɑːˈmɔːriən], *a. Poet:* Marmoréen; de marbre.

marmoset [mɑːməˈzet], *s.* Ouistiti *m*, marmouset *m*.

marmot ['mɑːmət], *s. Z:* Marmotte *f*.

maroon¹ [məˈruːn]. 1. *a. & s.* (*Colour*) Marron pourpré *inv.* 2. *s. Pyr:* Marron *m*; fusée *f* à pétard.

maroon², *s.* Nègre marron, négresse marronne.

maroon³, *v.tr.* (*a*) Abandonner (qn) dans une île déserte. (*b*) Villagers marooned by the floods, villageois isolés par les inondations.

marquee [mɑːˈkiː], *s.* Grande tente.

Marquesas (The) [ðɑːmaˈkeisæs]. *Pr.n. Geog:* Les Marquises.

marquess, marquis ['mɑːkwis], *s.* Marquis *m*.

marquetry ['mɑːkitri], *s.* Marqueterie *f*.

marriage ['mærid3], *s.* Mariage *m*. To give s.o. in m., donner qn en mariage. To take s.o. in m., épouser qn. Offer of m., demande *f* en mariage. Uncle by m., oncle par alliance. Civil m., mariage civil. M. settlement, dispositions *fpl* entre époux. M.-certificate, *F:* m. lines, acte *m* de mariage. M. rate, nuptialité *m*. The m. service, la bénédiction nuptiale.

marriageable ['mærid3əbl], *a.* (*a*) (Fille) nubile. She is of m. age, elle est d'âge à se marier. (*b*) To have three m. daughters, avoir trois filles à marier.

marrow ['mærou], *s.* 1. (*a*) Moelle *f*. *Cu:* (Spinal) m., amourettes *fpl*. To be frozen to the m., être glacé jusqu'à la moelle, *F:* jusqu'aux moelles. (*b*) *F:* Moelle, essence *f* (de qch.). 2. *Hort:* Vegetable m., courge *f* à la moelle; courgette *f*.

marrowbone ['mæroubboun], *s.* Os *m* à moelle.

marrowfat ['mæroufæt], *s. Hort:* M. (pea), pois carré.

marry ['mæri], *v.tr.* 1. (*Of priest, parent*) Marier; unir (en mariage). She has three daughters to m. (off), elle a trois filles à marier, à caser. 2. (*a*) Se marier avec, à (qn); épouser (qn). To m. money, faire un mariage d'argent, *F:* épouser le sac. (*b*) *Abs.* To m., to get married, se marier. To m. again, a second time, se remarier. To m. into a family, s'allier, s'apparenter, à une famille. To m. beneath one, se mésallier. 3. *Nau:* Marier (deux cordages). married, *a.* 1. M. man, homme marié. A m. couple, un ménage. 2. M. name, nom *m* de femme mariée, de mariage. M. love, l'amour conjugal.

marsh [mɑːʃ], *s.* Marais *m*, marécage *m*. 'marsh-'fever, *s.* Paludisme *m*; fièvre paludéenne. 'marsh-'gas, *s.* Gaz *m* des marais. 'marsh-'hen, *s.* Poule *f* d'eau. 'marsh-'mallow, *s.* Guimauve *f*. 'marsh-'marigold, *s.* Souci *m* d'eau.

marshal¹ ['mɑːʃ(ə)l], *s.* 1. *Hist:* Maréchal, -aux. 2. (*a*) *Mil:* Field-m., maréchal. (*b*) *Mil. Av:* M. of the R.A.F. = Commandant en Chef des Forces aériennes. Air Chief M., général d'armée aérienne. Air-M., général (de corps aérien). 3. Maître *m* des cérémonies. 4. Judge's m., secrétaire d'un juge en tournée. 5. *U.S:* = Commissaire *m* de police.

marshal², *v.tr.* (marshalled) 1. (*a*) Placer (des personnes) en ordre, en rang. (*b*) *Mil:* Ranger (des troupes). (*c*) To m. facts, rassembler des faits et les mettre en ordre. (*d*) *Her:* To m. two coats of arms in one shield, disposer deux blasons sur un écu. (*e*) *Rail:* Classer, trier (des wagons). (*f*) To m. s.o. in, out, introduire, reconduire, qn cérémonieusement. marshalling, *s.* 1. Disposition *f* en ordre (de personnes, de choses). 2. *Rail:* Classement *m*, triage *m*, manœuvre *f* (des wagons). M. yard, gare *f* de triage.

marshiness ['mɑːʃinis], *s.* État marécageux (du terrain).

marshland ['mɑːʃlænd], *s.* Marécages *mpl*.

marshy ['mɑːʃi], *a.* Marécageux.

marsupial [mɑːˈsuːpiəl]. 1. *a.* (Repli, etc.) marsupial, -aux. 2. *s. Z:* Marsupial *m*.

mart [mɑːt], *s.* 1. (Auction-) m., salle *f* de vente. 2. *A:* Centre *m* de commerce.

marten ['mɑːtin], *s. Z:* Mart(r)e *f*. Beech-m., stone-m., fouine *f*. Pine-m., martre commune.

martial ['mɑːʃ(ə)l], *a.* Martial, -aux; guerrier. M. law, loi martiale. To declare m. law (in a town), proclamer l'état de siège. -ally, *adv.* Martialement; en guerrier.

Martian ['mɑːʃjən], *a. & s.* Martien.

Martin¹ ['mɑːtin]. *Pr.n.m.* Martin. St M.'s summer, l'été *m* de la Saint-Martin.

martin², *s. Orn:* Martinet *m*. House-m., hirondelle *f* de fenêtre.

martinet [,mɑːtiˈnet], *s.* Officier *m* à cheval sur la discipline. He is a regular m., c'est un vrai garde-chiourme, *F:* un pète-sec.

martingale ['mɑːtiŋgeil], *s. Harn: etc:* Martingale *f*.

Martinmas ['mɑːtinməs], *s.* La Saint-Martin.

martlet ['mɑːtlit], *s.* 1. *Orn:* Martinet *m*. 2. *Her:* Merlette *f*.

martyr¹ ['mɑːtər], *s.* Martyr, *f.* martyre. *F:* To be a m. to gout, être sujet à la goutte; être torturé par la goutte. He makes a perfect m. of himself, il se torture le cœur à plaisir.

martyr², *v.tr.* Martyriser.

martyrdom ['mɑːtədəm], *s.* Martyre *m*.

martyrize ['mɑːtəraiz], *v.tr.* Faire subir le martyre (à qn); martyriser (qn).

martyrology [,mɑːtərˈələdʒiː], *s.* 1. (*List*) Martyrologe *m*. 2. (*History*) Martyrologie *f*.

marvel¹ ['mɑːv(ə)l], *s.* 1. (*a*) Merveille *f*. (*b*) It is a m. to me that . . ., cela m'étonne beaucoup que. . . . To work marvels, accomplir des merveilles. 2. *A:* Émerveillement *m*. 3. *Bot:* M. of Peru, belle-de-nuit *f*.

marvel², *v.i.* (marvelled) [mɑːvld]) S'émerveiller, s'étonner (at, de); se demander (why, pourquoi).

marvellous ['mɑːv(ə)ləs], *a.* 1. Merveilleux, étonnant. 2. *s.* I don't believe in the m., je ne crois pas au merveilleux. -ly, *adv.* A merveille; merveilleusement.

Mary ['mɛəri]. *Pr.n.f.* 1. Marie. 2. *F:* Little M., l'estomac *m*.

marzipan ['mɑːzipæn], *s.* Massepain *m*.

mascara [mæsˈkɑːrə], *s. Toil:* Mascara *m*; cosmétique *m* pour cils et sourcils.

mascot ['mæskət], *s.* Mascotte *f*; porte-bonheur *m* inv.

masculine ['mæskjulin], *a.* 1. Masculin, mâle. 2. *Gram:* (Nom) masculin. In the m. (gender), au masculin.

maser ['meizər], *s. Ph:* Maser *m*.

mash¹ [mæʃ], *s.* 1. *Husb:* Mash *m* (pour chevaux). pâtée *f* (pour cochons et volaille). Bran-m., pâtée *f* de son. M. tub, (*a*) *Brew:* cuve matière *f*, brassin *m*. (*b*) *Husb:* Barbotière *f*. 2. *F:* Purée *f* de pommes de terre. 3. Mélange *m*; pâte *f*; bouillie *f*.

mash², *v.tr.* Brasser, broyer, écraser, qch. *Cu:* To m. potatoes, mettre en purée des pommes de terre. **Mashed potatoes**, purée *f* de pommes de terre; pommes *f* mousseline.

masher ['mæʃər], *s. Tchn:* Broyeur *m*; mélangeur *m. Dom. Éc:* Presse-purée *m.inv.*

mask¹ [mɑːsk], *s.* 1. (a) Masque *m*; (*silk or velvet*) loup *m.* Under the m. of devotion, of friendship, sous le masque, sous le voile, de la dévotion, de l'amitié. To throw off, drop, the m., lever le masque; se démasquer. With the m. off, à visage découvert. (b) Protective m., masque de protection. 2. *Ven:* Face *f* (de renard, etc.). 3. *See* DEATH-MASK. 4. *Phot:* Printing-m., cache *m*.

mask², *v.tr.* 1. Masquer. To m. one's face, se masquer. 2. *Mil:* Masquer (une batterie, une place forte). 3. *Phot:* Poser un cache à (un cliché). 4. Cacher, déguiser (ses pensées); voiler (un défaut). **masked**, *a.* 1. Masqué. M. ball, bal masqué. *Bot:* M. flower, fleur personée. 2. (a) M. dictatorship, dictature larvée. (b) *Med:* M. fever, fièvre larvée.

masochism ['mæsokizm], *s. Psy:* Masochisme *m*.

masochist ['mæsokist], *s. Psy:* Masochiste *m. & f.*

mason ['meisn], *s.* 1. Maçon *m.* 2. = FREEMASON.

masonic [mə'sɔnik], *a.* Maçonnique; de la franc-maçonnerie.

masonry ['meisnri], *s.* 1. Maçonnerie *f.* 2. = FREE-MASONRY.

masque [mɑːsk], *s. A:* Masque *m* (pantomime ou féerie).

masquerade¹ [mæskə'reid], *s.* Mascarade *f.*

masquerade², *v.i.* Se masquer; aller en masque. To m. as . . ., se déguiser en . . ., se faire passer pour. . . .

masquerader [mæskə'reidər], *s.* (a) Personne déguisée, masquée. (b) Imposteur *m.*

mass¹ [mæs], *s. Ecc:* Messe *f.* High m., la grand-messe. Low m., messe basse. Requiem m., messe de requiem. To say m., dire, célébrer, la messe.

mass², *s.* 1. (a) Masse *f*, amas *m*, agglomération *f*. (b) *Mec:* Masse (d'un corps). Power per unit of m., puissance *f* unitaire massique. (c) *Atom. Ph:* Critical m., masse critique. 2. (a) A m. of people, une foule, une multitude, des masses, de gens. To gather in masses, se masser. The exercise was a m. of mistakes le devoir était cousu de fautes. He was a m. of bruises, il était tout couvert de meurtrissures. M. executions, exécutions *f* en masse. (b) The great m. of the people, la plus grande partie de la population. The masses, les masses; la foule. M. observation, études et enquêtes sociales. M. protest, protestation *f* en masse. M. radiography, radiographie collective. 'mass meeting, *s.* Réunion *f* en masse; *F:* meeting *m* monstre. 'mass produce, *v.tr.* Fabriquer en (grande) série. 'mass pro'duction, *s.* Fabrication *f*, travail *m*, en (grande) série.

mass³. 1. *v.tr.* Masser (des troupes, etc.). 2. *v.i.* (*Of troops*) Se masser; (*of clouds*) s'amonceler.

massacre¹ ['mæsəkər], *s.* Massacre *m*, tuerie *f.*

massacre², *v.tr.* Massacrer.

massage¹ ['mæsɑːʒ], *s.* Massage *m*. Scalp m., friction *f.*

massage² [mæ'sɑːʒ], *v.tr. Med:* Masser (le corps); malaxer (les muscles).

masseur, *f.* **masseuse** [mæ'səːr, mæ'səːz], *s. Med:* Masseur, -euse.

massif ['mæsiːf], *s. Geog:* Massif *m.*

massive ['mæsiv], *a.* Massif, -ive.

massiveness ['mæsivnis], *s.* Caractère ou aspect massif (d'un monument, etc.).

mast¹ [mɑːst], *s.* 1. *Nau:* Mât *m.* Masts, mâts, mâture *f.* Lower m., bas-mât. To take down the masts of a ship, démâter un navire. Before the m., en avant du grand mât; sur le gaillard d'avant. To sail before the m., servir comme simple matelot. 2. Pylône *m* (de T.S.F., etc.). 'mast-'head, *s. Nau:* Tête *f*, ton *m*, de mât. (*Of pers.*) To be at the m.-h., être en vigie. 'mast-'heel, *s. Nau:* Pied *m* de mât.

mast². *v.tr.* Mâter (un bâtiment). Three-masted, four-masted, ship, navire à trois, à quatre, mâts.

mast³, *s. Husb:* Faines *fpl* (de hêtre); fainée *f*; glands *mpl* (de chêne); glandée *f.*

master¹ ['mɑːstər], *s.* 1. (*Man in control*) (a) Maître *m.* To be m. in one's own house, être maître chez soi. To be m. of oneself, être maître de soi; avoir de l'empire sur soi. To be one's own m., s'appartenir; ne dépendre que de soi-même. To be m. of the situation, être maître de la situation. To remain m. of the field, rester maître du champ de bataille. To meet one's m., trouver son maître. (b) (*Employer*) Maître, patron *m*, chef *m.* Like m., like man, tel maître tel valet. *O:* The m. is not at home, monsieur n'y est pas. (c) (*At Oxford and Cambridge*) Directeur *m*, principal *m*, -aux (de certains collèges). (d) *Nau:* Patron (d'un bateau de pêche); capitaine *m*, commandant *m* (d'un navire de commerce). (e) M. of foxhounds, maître d'équipage; grand veneur. M. of Ceremonies, maître des cérémonies. M. of the Rolls, = vice-président de la Cour de Cassation. 2. *Sch:* (a) Maître; professeur *m* instituteur *m.* Form m., professeur principal (d'une classe). (b) Fencing m., professeur d'escrime; maître d'armes. (c) M. of Arts = licencié ès lettres; diplômé d'études supérieures. M. of Science = licencié ès sciences; diplômé d'études supérieures. 3. (a) *A:* Artisan établi à son compte, travaillant en chambre. (b) M. of an art, maître d'un art. To be m. of a subject, posséder un sujet à fond. To make oneself m. of sth., se rendre maître de qch. *S.a.* PAST-MASTER. *Art:* An old m., (i) un maître, (ii) tableau *m* de maître. 4. (*As title*) (a) *A:* My masters, messieurs. (b) *O:* (*As title given to boys*) M. John, Monsieur Jean. 5. *Attrib.* (a) M. carpenter, maître charpentier. M. mariner, capitaine au long cours; capitaine marchand. (b) M. hand, main *f* de maître. He is a m. hand at (doing sth.), est passé maître dans l'art de (faire qch.). (c) M. mind, esprit supérieur; esprit dirigeant. *Cards:* M. card, carte maîtresse. *Cin: etc:* M. (print), copie originale. 'master-at-'arms, *s. Navy:* Capitaine *m* d'armes. 'master-key, *s.* Passe-partout *m inv.* 'master-stroke, *s.* Coup *m* de maître.

master², *v.tr.* 1. Dompter, maîtriser (qn, un cheval). 2. Maîtriser, dompter (ses passions); surmonter (sa colère); apprendre (un sujet) à fond. To m. a difficulty, surmonter une difficulté; venir à bout d'une difficulté. To have mastered a subject, posséder un sujet à fond.

masterful ['mɑːstəf(u)l], *a.* Impérieux, -euse, autoritaire.

masterly ['mɑːstəli], *a.* De maître; magistral, -aux. In a m. manner, magistralement.

masterpiece ['mɑːstəpiːs], *s.* Chef-d'œuvre *m.*

mastery ['mɑːst(ə)ri], *s.* 1. Maîtrise *f* (of, de); domination *f* (over, sur). To gain the m., avoir le dessus, l'emporter (over, sur). 2. Connaissance approfondie (d'un sujet).

mastic ['mæstik], *s.* 1. (*Resin*) Mastic *m.* 2. (*Cement*) Mastic. 'mastic(-tree), *s.* Lentisque *m.*

masticate ['mæstikeit], *v.tr.* Mâcher, mastiquer.

mastication [mæsti'keiʃ(ə)n], *s.* Mastication *f.*

masticator ['mæstikeitər], *s.* Masticateur, -trice.

masticatory [mæsti'keit(ə)ri], *a.* Masticateur, -trice.

mastiff ['mæstif], *s.* Mâtin *m*; dogue anglais.

mastodon ['mæstədɔn], *s. Paleont:* Mastodonte *m.*

mastoid ['mæstɔid], *a. & s. Anat:* Mastoïde. *Med:* Inflammation of the m., *F:* mastoids, mastoïdite *f.*

masturbate [mæstə'beit], *v.i.* Se masturber.

masturbation ['mæstə'beiʃ(ə)n], *s.* Masturbation *f.*

mat¹ [mæt], *s.* 1. (a) Natte *f* (de paille). (b) Paillasson *m.* Fibre mat, tapis-brosse *m.* (c) Carpette *f.* (d) *F:* To be on the m., être sur la sellette. He's been on the m., on lui a passé un savon. *S.a.* BATH-MAT. (d) Table-m., dessous de plat; rond *m* de table. 2. *Nau:* Collision m., paillet *m* d'abordage.

mat², *v.tr.* (matted) (a) Natter, tresser (le jonc). (b) Emmêler (les cheveux). (c) (*Of hair*) To m., s'emmêler, se coller ensemble. Matted hair, cheveux emmêlés. (*Of material*) To become matted, se feutrer. **matting**, *s.* Natte(s) *f (pl)*, paillassons *mpl.*

mat³, *a.* Mat. Mat complexion, teint mat. *Phot:* Mat paper, papier mat.

matador ['mætədɔːr], *s.* Matador *m.*

match¹ [mætʃ], s. 1. (a) (Of pers.) Égal, -ale; pareil, -eille. **To meet one's m.**, trouver à qui parler. **To meet more than one's m.**, s'attaquer à plus fort que soi. **To be a m. for s.o.**, être de force à lutter avec qn. (b) (Of thgs) **To be a (good) m.**, aller bien ensemble; être bien assortis. **Perfect m. of colours**, assortiment parfait de couleurs. 2. Sp: Lutte f, partie f, match m; Fr.C: joute f (de hockey). **Tennis m.**, partie de tennis. **Football m.**, match de football. **To win the m.**, gagner la partie. **To play a m.**, F: matcher (ζgainst, contre). 3. Mariage m, alliance f. **To make a good m.**, trouver un bon parti, faire un beau mar.age. **'match-maker**, s. Marieur, -euse. **She's a regular m.-m.**, c'est une marieuse acharnée. **'match-making**, s. Manie f d'arranger des mariages. **'match-play**, s. 1. Ten: Jeu m de match. 2. Golf: Partie f par trous.

match². 1. v.tr. (a) Égaler (qn); être l'égal de (qn); rivaliser avec (qn). **Evenly matched**, de force égale. (b) **To m. s.o. against s.o.**, opposer qn à qn. (c) Apparier (des gants); appareiller (des chevaux); assortir (des couleurs). **Com: Articles difficult to m.**, rassortiments m difficiles à obtenir. 2. v.i. S'assortir; s'harmoniser. **Colours to match**, couleurs assorties. **Dress with hat to m.**, robe avec chapeau assorti, pareil. **matching**, s. Assortiment m; appariement m. **'match-boarding**, s. Carp: Planches bouvetées. **'match-mark**, s. Ind: (Trait de) repère m.

match³, s. 1. Allumette f. **Safety m.**, allumette de sûreté, allumette suédoise. **To strike a m.**, frotter, craquer, une allumette. 2. A.Artil: Mèche f. **Slow-m.**, corde f à feu. **'match-box**, s. Boîte f à allumettes. **Match-box holder**, porte-allumettes m inv.

matchet ['mætʃit], **machete (knife)** [mə'tʃeiti(naif)], s. Machette f.

matchless ['mætʃlis], a. Incomparable, inimitable; sans égal, sans pareil.

matchwood ['mætʃwud], s. Bois m d'allumettes. **Smashed to m.**, mis en miettes.

mate¹ [meit], s. Chess: = CHECKMATE¹.

mate², v.tr. Chess: Faire (le roi) échec et mat.

mate³, s. 1. Camarade mf; compagnon, f. compagne. Ind: **Workman's m.**, compagnon. P: **I say, m.**, dis donc, mon vieux. 2. (Of birds) Mâle m ou femelle f; (of persons) époux, f. épouse. 3. Nau: (a) (On merchant vessel) Officier m. **First m.**, second m. **Second m.**, lieutenant m. (b) Navy: Second maître.

mate⁴. 1. v.tr. Accoupler (des oiseaux). 2. v.i. (Of birds) S'accoupler. **mating**, s. Accouplement m (d'oiseaux). **The m. season**, la saison des amours.

maté ['mɑːtei], s. Maté m; thé m du Paraguay.

mater ['meitər], s. F: O: The mater, ma mère; maman.

material [mə'tiəriəl]. I. a. 1. (a) Phil: Matériel. (b) Matériel, grossier, terre-à-terre. **To be engrossed in m. things**, être enfoncé dans la matière. (c) **To have enough for one's m. needs**, avoir de quoi vivre matériellement. 2. (a) Important, essentiel (to, pour). **It has been of m. service to me**, cela m'a rendu un réel service. (b) (Fait) pertinent. **-ally**, adv. 1. Matériellement, essentiellement. 2. Sensiblement. II. material, s. 1. (a) Matière f, matériaux mpl. **Raw materials** matières premières. **Building materials**, matériaux de construction; matériau m. **To provide m. for conversation**, fournir des sujets de conversation. (b) pl. **Materials**, fournitures f, accessoires m. **Writing m.**, de quoi écrire. 2. Tex: Étoffe f, tissu m. **'Customers' own m. made up,"** "on travaille à façon."

materialism [mə'tiəriəlizm], s. Matérialisme m.

materialist [mə'tiəriəlist], s. Matérialiste m.

materialistic [mətiəriə'listik], a. 1. Matérialiste. 2. (Of pleasures) Matériel.

materialize [mə'tiəriəlaiz]. 1. v.tr. Matérialiser. 2. v.i. (a) Psychics: Se matérialiser. (b) Se réaliser; (of plans) aboutir.

materia medica [mə'tiəriə 'medikə], s. Med: Matière médicale.

maternal 'mə'təːnl], a. Maternel, -elle. **-ally**, adv. Maternellement.

maternity [mə'təːniti], s. Maternité f. **Maternity hospital**, maternité. **M. dress**, robe f de grossesse.

mathematical [mæθi'mætik(ə)l], a. Mathématique, de mathématiques. **He is a m. genius**, c'est un mathématicien de génie. **-ally**, adv. Mathématiquement.

mathematician [mæθimə'tiʃ(ə)n], s. Mathématicien, -ienne.

mathematics [mæθi'mætiks], s.pl. Mathématiques fpl. **General m.**, éléments mpl de mathématiques. **Strong in m.**, fort en mathématiques; F: fort en math.

maths [mæθs], s.pl. F: Math fpl.

matinée ['mætinei], s. Th: Matinée f.

matins ['mætinz], s.pl. Ecc: Matines f.

matriarch ['meitriɑːk], s.f. (a) Ethn: Chef m de tribu (d'un matriarcat). (b) Douairière f, matrone f.

matriarchal [meitri'ɑːk(ə)l], a. Matriarcal, -aux.

matriarchy ['meitriɑːki], s. Matriarcat m.

matricide¹ ['mætrisaid], s. Matricide mf.

matricide², s. (Crime) Matricide m.

matriculate [mə'trikjuleit], v.i. Passer l'examen d'entrée à l'université (et prendre ses inscriptions).

matriculation [mətrikju'leiʃ(ə)n], s. 1. Immatriculation f, inscription f (comme étudiant). 2. A: Examen m qui donnait accès à l'université.

matrimonial [mætri'mouniəl], a. Matrimonial, -aux; conjugal, -aux.

matrimony ['mætrim(ə)ni], s. Le mariage; la vie conjugale. **Joined in holy m.**, unis par les saints nœuds du mariage.

matrix, pl. **-ixes**, **-ices** ['meitriks, 'meitriksiz, 'meitriːsiz, in sense 3 'mætriks, 'mætrisiːz], s. 1. Anat: Matrice f. 2. Geol: Miner: Matrice, gangue f. 3. Typ: etc: Matrice, moule m.

matron ['meitrən], s.f. 1. Matrone; mère de famille. 2. (a) Intendante (d'une institution). (b) Infirmière-major (d'un hôpital).

matronly ['meitrənli], a. **A matronly woman**, une grosse matrone.

matt [mæt], a. = MAT³.

matter¹ ['mætər], s. 1. Matière f; substance f. (a) Log: **Form and m.**, la forme et le fond. (b) Ph: **The indestructibility of m.**, l'indestructibilité de la matière. (c) Vegetable m., matières végétales. **Colouring m.**, matière colorante. 2. Med: Matière (purulente); pus m. 3. (a) Matière, sujet m (d'un discours). **Reading m.**, choses f à lire. (b) Typ: Matière, copie f. **Plain m.**, composition f en plein. S.a. PRINT² 2. 4. **It makes no m.**, n'importe; cela ne fait rien. **No m. how you do it**, de n'importe quelle manière que vous le fassiez. **No m. how fast you run, you will not catch him**, vous avez beau courir, vous ne le rattraperez pas. 5. Affaire f, chose, cas m. **The m. I am speaking of**, l'affaire dont je parle. **It is an easy m.**, c'est facile, F: ce n'est pas une affaire. **It is no great m.**, c'est peu de chose. **That's quite another m.**, c'est tout autre chose. **As matters stand**, au point où en sont les choses. **Money matters**, affaires d'intérêt. **Business matters**, affaires. **In the m. of . . .**, quant à . . .; en ce qui concerne. . . . **In this m. . . .**, à cet égard. . . . **In matters of . . .**, en matière de. . . . **M. of taste**, affaire de goût. **It will be a m. of ten days**, ce sera l'affaire de dix jours. **For that m., for the m. of that**, pour ce qui est de cela; quant à cela; d'ailleurs. **What is the m.?** qu'est-ce qu'il y a? qu'y a-t-il? **Something must be the m.**, il doit y avoir quelque chose. **As if nothing was the m.**, comme si de rien n'était. **What is the m. with you?** qu'est-ce que vous avez au doigt? **You don't like that book? what is the m. with it?** vous n'aimez pas ce livre? qu'est-ce que vous y trouvez à redire? S.a. COURSE¹ 1, FACT 2. **'matter-of-'course**, a. Naturel; qui va de soi. **'matter-of-'fact**, a. Pratique, positif, prosaïque.

matter², v.i. 1. Importer (to s.o., à qn); avoir de l'importance. **It does not m.**, n'importe; cela ne fait rien. **It doesn't m. whether . . .**, peu importe que + sub. **Nothing else matters**, tout le reste n'est rien. **What does it m. to you?** qu'est-ce que cela vous fait? **It matters a good deal to me**, cela a beaucoup d'importance pour moi. 2. Med: Suppurer.

Matterhorn (the) [ðə'mætəhɔːn]. Pr.n. Le Mont Cervin.

Matthew ['mæθjuː]. Pr.n.m. Mat(t)hieu.

mattock ['mætək], *s. Tls:* Hoyau *m*; pioche *f*.

mattress ['mætris], *s.* (*a*) Matelas *m*. **Down m.**, duvet *m*. (*b*) **Spring m.**, box m., sommier *m* élastique.

maturation [ˌmætjuˈreiʃ(ə)n], *s.* Maturation *f* (d'un fruit, d'un abcès); développement *m* (de l'intelligence).

mature[1] [məˈtjuər], *a.* 1. Mûr; mûri. **Person of m. years**, personne d'âge mûr. 2. *Fin:* (Papier) échu. **-ly**, *adv.* Mûrement.

mature[2]. 1. *v.tr.* Mûrir; affiner (le vin, le fromage). 2. *v.i.* (*a*) Mûrir. (*b*) *Fin:* (*Of bill*) Échoir; arriver à échéance.

maturity [məˈtjuəriti], *s.* 1. Maturité *f*. **The years of maturity**, l'âge mûr. 2. *Com:* (**Date of) maturity**, échéance *f* (d'une traite).

matutinal [məˈtjuːtinl, ˌmætjuːˈtainl], *a.* Matutinal, -aux.

maudlin ['mɔːdlin], *a.* 1. Larmoyant, pleurard. 2. Dans un état d'ivresse larmoyante.

maul[1] [mɔːl], *s. Tls:* Maillet *m*, mailloche *f*, masse *f*.

maul[2], *v.tr.* Meurtrir, malmener (qn). **To be mauled by a tiger**, être écharpé par un tigre.

maulstick ['mɔːlstik], *s. Art:* Appui-main *m*, *pl.* appuis-main.

maunder ['mɔːndər], *v.i.* **To maunder (on)**, divaguer, radoter.

Maundy Thursday ['mɔːndiˈθəːzdi], *s.* Le jeudi saint.

Mauritania [ˌmɔriˈteinjə]. *Pr.n. Geog:* **The Islamic Republic of M.**, la République islamique de Mauritanie.

Mauritius [məˈriʃəs]. *Pr.n.* L'île *f* Maurice.

mausoleum, *pl.* **-lea, -leums** [mɔːsəˈli(ː)əm, -ˈli(ː)ə, -ˈli(ː)əmz], *s.* Mausolée *m*.

mauve [mouv], *a. & s.* (*Colour*) Mauve (*m*).

maw [mɔː], *s.* 1. *Z:* Caillette *f*; *F:* estomac *m*. **To fill one's maw**, se remplir la panse. 2. Gueule *f* (du lion).

mawkish ['mɔːkiʃ], *a.* (*a*) Fade, insipide. (*b*) D'une sensiblerie outrée.

maxilla [mækˈsilə], *s. Anat:* Maxillaire supérieur.

maxillary [mækˈsiləri], *a.* Maxillaire.

maxim ['mæksim], *s.* Maxime *f*, dicton *m*.

maximum, *pl.* **-a** ['mæksiməm, -ə]. 1. *s.* Maximum *m*, *pl.* maximums, -a. **Maximum thermometer**, thermomètre *m* à maxima. 2. *a.* Maximum, *f. occ.* maxima. **M. price**, prix *m* maximum. **M. load**, charge *f* limite.

may[1] [mei], *v.aux.* (3rd pers. sing. he may; p.t. **might** [mait]; *no pres. or past participle*) 1. (*a*) **With luck I m. succeed**, avec de la chance je peux réussir. **He m. not be hungry**, il n'a peut-être pas faim. **He m. miss the train**, il se peut qu'il manque le train. **I m. (possibly) have done so**, j'ai pu le faire. (*b*) **How old might she be?** quel âge peut-elle bien avoir? **Who m. 'you be?** qui êtes-vous, sans indiscrétion? **Might it not be well to warn him?** est-ce qu'on ne ferait pas bien de l'avertir? (*c*) **It m., might, be that . . .**, il se peut, se pourrait, bien que + *sub.* **Be that as it m.**, quoi qu'il en soit. **That's as m. be**, c'est selon. **As you m. suppose**, comme vous (le) pensez bien. *S.a.* COST[2] 1. **Run as he might he could not overtake me**, il a eu beau courir, il n'a pas pu me rattraper. (*d*) **We m., might, as well stay where we are**, autant vaut, vaudrait, rester où nous sommes. *S.a.* WELL[3] I. 1. (*e*) **I say, you might shut the door!** dites donc, vous pourriez bien fermer la porte! **He might have offered to help**, il aurait bien pu offrir son aide. 2. **M. I?** vous permettez? **M. I come in?—You m.**, puis-je entrer?—Mais parfaitement. **If I m. say so**, si j'ose (le) dire. **The Council m. decide . . .**, il appartient, au besoin, au Conseil de décider. . . . 3. **I hope it m. be true**, pourvu que cela soit vrai! **I hope he m. succeed**, j'espère qu'il réussira. 4. **M. he rest in peace!** qu'il repose en paix! **Much good m. it do you!** grand bien vous fasse! **Long m. you live to enjoy it!** puissiez-vous vivre longtemps pour en jouir!

May[2], *s.* 1. **Mai** *m*. **In (the month of) M.**, en mai; au mois de mai. (**On) the first, the seventh, of M.**, le premier, le sept, mai. **Queen of the M., May queen**, reine *f* du premier mai. *Lit: A:* **M. and December**, une jeune fille qui épouse un vieillard. 2. *Bot:* **May (-bush, -tree)**, aubépine *f*. **May(-blossom)**, fleurs *fpl* d'aubépine. **'may-beetle, -bug**, *s.* Hanneton *m*.

'May(-)day, *s.* 1. Le premier mai. 2. *Av: Nau:* Signal de détresse, S.O.S. **'may-fly**, *s. Ent:* Éphémère *m* (vulgaire).

maybe ['meibi:], *adv.* Peut-être.

mayhem ['meihem], *s. Jur: U.S:* **To commit m. (on s.o.)**, se livrer à des voies de fait (contre qn).

mayonnaise [ˌme(i)əˈneiz], *s.* Mayonnaise *f*.

mayor ['meər], *s.m.* Maire. **Deputy mayor**, adjoint (au maire); (*in Belgium*) échevin.

mayoralty ['meərəlti], *s.* Mandat *m* de maire.

mayoress ['meəris], *s.f.* Femme du maire, mairesse.

maypole ['meipoul], *s.* 1. Mai *m*. **To set up a m.**, planter un mai. 2. *F:* (*Tall man*) Échalas *m*; (*woman*) grande perche.

maze [meiz], *s.* Labyrinthe *m*, dédale *m*. *F:* **To be in a m.**, ne savoir où donner de la tête.

mazurka [məˈzəːkə], *s.* Mazurka *f*.

me [mi, miː], *pers.pron., objective case.* 1. (*a*) **Me**, (*before a vowel sound*) m'; moi. **They see me**, ils me voient. **He saw you and me**, il nous a vu(e)s, vous et moi. **They hear me**, ils m'entendent. **Listen to me!** écoutez-moi! **Give me some!** donnez-m'en! (*b*) (*Refl.*) Moi. **I will take it with me**, je le prendrai avec moi. 2. (*Stressed*) Moi. **Come to me**, venez à moi. **He loves me alone**, il n'aime que moi. **He gave it to me, not to you**, il me l'a donné à moi, pas à toi. *F:* **No one ever thought of poor little me**, personne ne pensait à ma pauvre petite personne. 3. (*Stressed: as a nominative*) *F:* **It's me**, c'est moi. **He is younger than me**, il est plus jeune que moi. 4. (*In interjections*) **Ah me! poor me!** pauvre de moi! **Dear me!** mon Dieu! vraiment! par exemple!

mead[1] [miːd], *s.* Hydromel *m*.

mead[2], *s. Poet:* = MEADOW.

meadow ['medou], *s.* Pré *m*, prairie *f*. **'meadow-grass**, *s. Bot:* Pâturin *m*. **'meadow-land**, *s.* Prairie(s) *f(pl)*; pâturages *mpl*. **meadow-saffron**, *s. Bot:* Colchique *m* (d'automne), safran *m* des prés. **'meadow-sweet**, *'s. Bot:* (Spirée *f*) ulmaire *f*; reine *f* des prés.

meagre ['miːgər], *a.* Maigre; peu copieux. **M. attendance at a meeting**, assistance peu nombreuse. **-ly**, *adv.* Maigrement.

meal[1] [miːl], *s.* (*a*) Farine *f* (d'avoine, de seigle, de maïs); *Scot:* = OATMEAL. (*b*) Farine ou poudre *f* (de diverses substances). *S.a.* WHOLE-MEAL.

meal[2], *s.* Repas *m*. **Square meal, hearty m.**, repas copieux; ample repas. **To make a meal of it**, en faire son repas. **I like to rest after a m.**, j'aime à me reposer après manger. *Pharm:* **'To be taken after meals,'** "à prendre après les principaux repas." **'meal-time**, *s.* Heure *f* du repas. **At meal-times**, aux heures de(s) repas.

mealy ['miːli], *a.* 1. Farineux. **M. potatoes**, pommes de terre farineuses. 2. (*a*) Saupoudré de blanc; poudreux. (*b*) *F:* (*Visage*) terreux, de papier mâché. 3. **Mealy(-mouthed)**, doucereux, mielleux, patelin.

mean[1] [miːn], *s.* 1. (*a*) Milieu *m*; moyen terme. **The golden m., the happy m.**, le juste milieu. (*b*) *Mth:* Moyenne *f*. **Geometrical m.**, moyenne proportionnelle. 2. *pl.* **Means**, moyen(s) *m(pl)*, voie(s) *f(pl)*. **To find (a) means to do sth.**, trouver moyen de faire qch. **There is no means of doing it**, il n'y a pas moyen. **He has been the means of . . .**, c'est par lui que. . . . **By all (manner of) means!** mais certainement! mais faites donc! **Do it by all means**, que rien ne vous en empêche! **May I come in?—By all means!** puis-je entrer?—Mais, comment donc! **Not by any means**, jamais de la vie. **By no (manner of) means**, en aucune façon; pas du tout. **He is not by any means a hero**, il n'est rien moins qu'un héros. **By some means or other**, de manière ou d'autre. **By means of s.o.**, par l'entremise de qn. **By means of sth.**, au moyen, par le moyen, de qch. 2. *pl.* Moyens (de vivre); ressources *fpl*. **To live beyond one's means**, dépenser plus que son revenu. **This car is beyond my means**, cette voiture n'est pas dans mes moyens. **Private means**, fortune personnelle. **He is a man of means**, il a une belle fortune. *Com:* **He has ample means at his disposal**, il dispose de capitaux considérables. **Means test**, enquête sur la situation (de fortune).

mean[2], *a.* Moyen. **M. time**, temps moyen. *Mth:* **M. proportional**, moyenne proportionnelle.

mean³, *a.* 1. (*a*) Misérable, minable. M. street, rue à l'aspect misérable. The meanest citizen, le dernier des citoyens. That ought to be clear to the meanest intelligence, cela devrait être compris par l'esprit le plus borné. (*b*) He is no m. scholar, c'est un érudit estimable. He had no m. opinion of himself, il ne se croyait pas peu de chose. 2. Bas, méprisable, mesquin. A m. trick, un vilain tour; un sale coup. To take a m. revenge, se venger mesquinement. To take a m. advantage of s.o., exploiter indignement qn. 3. Avare, mesquin, chiche. -ly, *adv.* 1. Misérablement, pauvrement. To think m. of sth., avoir une piètre opinion de qch. 2. (Se conduire) bassement, platement. 3. (Récompenser qn) mesquinement, chichement. 'mean-'spirited, *a.* A l'âme basse; vil, abject; mesquin.

mean⁴, *v.tr.* (meant [ment]; meant) 1. (*a*) Avoir l'intention (to do sth., de faire qch.); se proposer (de faire qch.). What do you m. to do? que comptez-vous faire? He meant to do me a service, il voulait me rendre service. He means no harm, il n'y entend pas malice; il ne pense pas à mal. I m. him no harm, je ne lui veux pas de mal. He meant no offence, il n'avait nullement l'intention de vous offenser. He didn't m. (to do) it, il ne l'a pas fait exprès. Without meaning it, sans le vouloir. (*b*) He means well, il a de bonnes intentions. He meant well, il croyait bien faire. (*c*) I m. to be obeyed, j'entends qu'on m'obéisse. I m. to succeed, je veux réussir. 2. (*a*) I meant this purse for you, je vous destinais cette bourse. (*b*) The remark was meant for you, la remarque s'adressait à vous. He meant that for you, c'est pour vous qu'il a dit cela. (*c*) Do you m. me? est-ce de moi que vous parlez? This portrait is meant to represent Mr A., ce portrait est censé représenter Monsieur A. 3. (*a*) (*Of words, phrase*) Vouloir dire; signifier. What does that word mean? que signifie ce mot? The name means nothing to me, ce nom ne me dit rien. What is meant by . . .? que veut dire . . .? (*b*) (*Of pers.*) What do you m.? que voulez-vous dire? What do you m. by that? qu'entendez-vous par là? *F:* What do you m. by coming late? qu'est-ce que c'est que ces façons d'arriver en retard? Does he m. what he says? dit-il réellement ce qu'il pense? I meant the remark for a joke, j'ai dit cela par plaisanterie. He meant it as a kindness, il l'a fait par bonté. You don't m. it! vous voulez rire! vous plaisantez! I m. it, c'est sérieux. (*c*) His refusal means ruin for me, s'il refuse, c'est la ruine pour moi. Ten pounds means a lot to him! dix livres, c'est une somme pour lui! That means nothing, c'est sans importance. If you knew what it means to live alone! si vous saviez ce que c'est que de vivre seul! meaning¹, *a.* 1. (*With adv. prefixed, e.g.*) Well-meaning, bien intentionné. 2. (Regard) significatif; (sourire) d'intelligence. -ly, *adv.* D'un air, d'un ton, significatif. meaning², *s.* (*a*) Signification *f*, sens *m*, acception *f* (d'un mot). What is the m. of that word? que signifie, que veut dire, ce mot? *F:* What's the m. of this? qu'est-ce que cela signifie? que signifie? (*b*) You mistake my m., vous me comprenez mal. (*c*) Look full of m., regard significatif.

meander¹ [mi'ændər], *s.* Méandre *m*, repli *m*, sinuosité *f*.

meander², *v.i.* (*Of river*) Faire des méandres, serpenter. meandering, *a.* 1. (Sentier, etc.) sinueux. 2. (Discours) sans suite.

meaningful ['mi:niŋful], *a.* Significatif, -ive.

meaningless ['mi:niŋlis], *a.* Dénué de sens; qui ne signifie rien.

meanness ['mi:nnis], *s.* 1. Médiocrité *f*, pauvreté *f*, petitesse *f* (de qch.); bassesse *f* (d'esprit). 2. (*a*) Mesquinerie *f*, avarice *f*. (*b*) Vilenie *f*. A piece of m. (i) une mesquinerie; (ii) une vilenie.

meant [ment]. See MEAN⁴.

meantime ['mi:ntaim], meanwhile ['mi:nwail], *s. & adv.* (In the) meantime, (in the) meanwhile, dans l'intervalle; en attendant.

measles ['mi:zlz], *s.pl.* 1. Rougeole *f*. German m., rubéole *f*. 2. Ladrerie *f* (des porcs).

measly ['mi:zli], *a.* 1. *Vet:* (Porc) ladre. 2. *F:* Insignifiant, misérable.

measurable ['meʒ(ə)rəbl], *a.* Mesurable, mensurable· Within m. distance of success, à deux doigts de la réussite.

measure¹ ['meʒər], *s.* Mesure *f.* 1. (*a*) Linear m., mesure de longueur. Square m., mesure de surface. Cubic m., mesure de volume. Give me full, good, m., faites-moi bonne mesure. (*b*) To take the m. of a man, prendre la mesure d'un homme. Made to m., fait sur mesure. 2. (*Instrument for measuring*) (*a*) Mesure (à grain, etc.). (*b*) Mètre *m. S.a.* TAPE-MEASURE. 3. Mesure, limite *f.* Beyond m., outre mesure; démesurément. In some m., en partie; jusqu'à un certain point. 4. (*a*) Mesure, démarche *f.* As a precautionary m., par mesure de précaution. He took measures accordingly, il a pris ses mesures en conséquence. To take extreme measures, employer les grands moyens. (*b*) Projet *m* de loi. 5. *pl. Geol:* Coal measures, gisements houillers. 6. *Mus:* Mesure.

measure², *v.tr.* 1. (*a*) Mesurer; métrer (un mur); cuber (le bois); mensurer. To m. a piece of ground, faire l'arpentage d'un terrain. To be measured (for one's height), passer à la toise. To m. the tonnage of a ship, jauger un navire. *F:* To m. one's length (on the ground), s'étaler par terre; tomber de tout son long. (*b*) *Tail:* Mesurer (qn); prendre la mesure de (qn). (*c*) To m. one's strength with s.o., mesurer ses forces avec qn. (*d*) To m. one's words, peser ses mots. 2. This book measures six inches by four, ce livre a six pouces de long sur quatre de large. measure out, *v.tr.* 1. Mesurer (un terrain de tennis, etc.). 2. Distribuer (les parts qui reviennent à chacun); mesurer (du blé, etc.). measured, *a.* 1. Mesuré, déterminé. *Nau:* M. ton, tonneau *m* d'encombrement. *S.a.* MILE. 2. (*a*) (Pas) cadencé. (*b*) With m. steps, à pas comptés. 3. M. language, langage modéré. To speak in m. tones, parler avec mesure. 'measuring-chain, *s.* Chaîne *f* d'arpenteur. 'measuring-glass, *s.* Verre gradué.

measurement ['meʒəmənt], *s.* 1. Mesurage *m.* 2. Mesure *f*, dimension *f.* Head-m., hip-m., tour *m* de tête, de hanches. To take s.o.'s measurements, prendre les mesures de qn. *Const:* Inside m., outside m., mesure dans œuvre, mesure hors d'œuvre.

meat [mi:t], *s.* 1. Viande *f. Ecc:* To abstain from m., faire maigre. M. diet, régime carné. M. extract, concentré *m* de viande. *S.a.* OLIVE 3. 2. Aliment *m*, nourriture *f.* M. and drink, le manger et le boire. *F:* This was m. and drink to them, ils en faisaient des gorges chaudes. To get the m. out of a book, extraire la moelle d'un livre. *Prov:* One man's m. is another man's poison, ce qui guérit l'un tue l'autre. 3. Grace before m., bénédicité *m.* 'meat-'broth, *s. Cu:* Bouillon gras. 'meat-safe, *s.* Garde-manger *m inv.* 'meat-saw, *s. Tls:* Scie *f* de boucher.

meatless ['mi:tlis], *a.* (Repas) maigre.

meaty ['mi:ti], *a.* 1. Charnu. 2. (Style, sujet) étoffé, fourni, plein de substance.

Mecca ['mekə]. *Pr.n. Geog:* La Mecque.

mechanic [mi'kænik], *s.* 1. *A:* Artisan *m*, ouvrier *m.* 2. Mécanicien *m.* Motor m., mécanicien garagiste *m.*

mechanical [mi'kænik(ə)l], *a.* 1. Mécanique. 2. The six mechanical powers, les six machines simples. *S.a.* DRAWING 2, ENGINEER¹ 1. 3. (*Of personal actions*) Machinal, -aux; automatique. -ally, *adv.* 1. Mécaniquement. M. operated, à commande mécanique. 2. Machinalement.

mechanics [mi'kæniks], *s.pl.* La mécanique.

mechanism ['mekənizm], *s.* 1. Appareil *m*, dispositif *m*; mécanisme *m.* 2. *Z:* Defence m., système *m* de défense.

mechanization [,mekənai'zeiʃ(ə)n], *s.* Mécanisation *f.*

mechanize ['mekənaiz], *v.tr.* Mécaniser. Mechanized farming, motoculture *f.*

Mechlin ['meklin]. *Pr.n. Geog:* Malines *f.* M. lace, dentelle *f* de Malines; malines *f.*

medal ['medl], *s.* Médaille *f.* The reverse of the m., le revers de la médaille. To wear, sport, one's medals, mettre toutes ses décorations, *F:* sortir toute sa batterie de cuisine, *Mil:* toutes ses bananes.

medallion [mi'dæljən], *s.* Médaillon *m.*

medallist ['medəlist], *s.* 1. Médailleur *m*, médailliste *m* 2. Médaillé, -ée. Gold m., titulaire *mf* d'une médaille d'or.

meddle ['medl], *v.i.* **To meddle with sth.,** se mêler de qch. **To m. in sth.,** s'immiscer, s'ingérer, dans qch. **Don't m. with my tools!** ne touchez pas à mes outils! **meddling,** *s.* Intervention *f*, ingérence *f* (**in, with, a matter,** dans une affaire).

meddler ['medlər], *s.* Officieux, -euse; fâcheux *m*; intrigant, -ante; touche-à-tout *m inv.*

meddlesome ['medlsəm], *a.* Intrigant; qui se mêle de tout.

mediaeval [,medi'i:v(ə)l], *a.* **1.** Du moyen âge; médiéval, -aux. **2.** *F: Pej:* Moyenâgeux

mediaevalist [,medi'i:vəlist], *s.* Médiéviste *mf*; *F:* moyenâgiste *mf.*

medial ['mi:diəl]. **1.** *a.* (*Of letter*) Médial, -als, -aux. **2.** *s.* Médiale *f.* **-ally,** *adv.* Médialement.

median ['mi:diən]. **1.** *a.* Médian. **2.** *s.* (*a*) Nerf médian; veine médiane. (*b*) (Ligne) médiane *f.*

mediate ['mi:dieit], *v.i.* S'entremettre, s'interposer; servir de médiateur.

mediation [,mi:di'eiʃ(ə)n], *s.* Médiation *f*; intervention (amicale).

mediator ['mi:dieitər], *s.* Médiateur, -trice.

medical ['medik(ə)l]. **1.** *a.* Médical, -aux. **The m. profession,** (i) le corps médical; (ii) la profession de médecin. **M. school,** école *f* de médecine. **M. student,** étudiant *m* en médecine. **M. stores,** matériel *m* sanitaire. **M. man,** médecin *m.* **Medical officer,** médecin du travail; *Adm:* médecin-conseil; *Mil:* médecin militaire, *F:* major *m*; (*in hospital*) chef *m* de service. **M. officer of health,** directeur *m* de la santé. **M.-board,** commission médicale; conseil de santé; *Mil:* conseil de révision; conseil de réforme. **2.** *s.* *F:* (*a*) Étudiant(e) en médecine. (*b*) Examen médical. **-ally,** *adv.* **M. speaking,** du point de vue médical. **To be m. examined,** subir un examen médical.

medicament [me'dikəmənt], *s.* Médicament *m.*

medicate ['medikeit], *v.tr.* Médicamenter.

Medici ['meditʃi(:)]. *Pr.n.pl. Hist:* The M., les Médicis.

medicinal [me'disinl], *a.* Médicinal, -aux.

medicine ['meds(i)n], *s.* **1.** La médecine. **To study m.,** faire sa médecine. **2.** (*a*) Médicament *m*, médecine. *F:* **To give s.o. a dose of h¹s own m.,** rendre la pareille à qn. (*b*) *F:* **To take m.,** se purger. **To take one's m.,** avaler la pilule. **3.** (Chez lés Peaux-Rouges) (i) Sorcellerie *f*; (ii) charme *m.* **'medicine-chest,** *s.* Armoire *f* à pharmacie *f.* **'medicine-glass,** *s.* Verre gradué. **'medicine-man,** *s.* (Sorcier) guérisseur *m.*

medico ['medikou], *s.* *F:* (*a*) Médecin *m* ou chirurgien *m*; *F:* toubib *m.* (*b*) *F:* Carabin *m.*

medieval [,medi'i:v(ə)l] = MEDIAEVAL.

mediocre [,mi:di'oukər], *a.* Médiocre.

mediocrity [,mi:di'ɔkriti], *s.* Médiocrité *f.*

meditate ['mediteit]. **1.** *v.tr.* Méditer (un projet). **To m. doing sth.,** méditer de faire qch. **2.** *v.i.* (*a*) Méditer (on, upon, sur). (*b*) Se recueillir.

meditation [,medi'teiʃ(ə)n], *s.* Méditation *f* (upon, sur); recueillement *m.*

meditative ['mediteitiv], *a.* Méditatif, recueilli.

Mediterranean [,meditə'reiniən], *a.* Méditerranéen, -éenne. **The M.** (**Sea**), la (mer) Méditerranée.

medium, *pl.* **-a, -ums** ['mi:diəm, -ə, -əmz]. I. *s.* **1.** Milieu *m*; moyen terme (between, entre). **Happy m.,** juste milieu. **2.** Milieu, véhicule *m.* **Air is the m. of sound,** l'air est le véhicule du son. **3.** Intermédiaire *m*, entremise *f.* **Through the m. of the press,** par la voie des journaux. **Advertising m.,** organe *m* de publicité. **4.** *Psychics:* Médium *m.* II. **medium,** *a.* Moyen. **M.-sized,** de grandeur moyenne, de taille moyenne.

medlar ['medlər], *s.* *Bot:* (*a*) Nèfle *f.* (*b*) Néflier *m.*

medley ['medli], *s.* Mélange *m*, méli-mélo *m*, bariolage *m.* *Mus:* Pot-pourri *m.*

medulla [mə'dʌlə], *s.* *Anat:* Moelle (épinière). **M. oblongata,** moelle allongée.

medullary [me'dʌləri], *a.* Médullaire.

Medusa [mi'dju:zə]. **1.** *Pr.n.f. Gr.Myth:* Méduse. **2.** *s.* *Coel:* Méduse *f.*

meek [mi:k], *a.* Doux, *f.* douce; humble. **-ly,** *adv.* Avec douceur; humblement.

meekness ['mi:knis], *s.* Douceur *f* de caractère; soumission *f*, humilité *f.* **M. of spirit,** résignation *f.*

meerschaum ['miəʃəm], *s.* **1.** Magnésite *f*; écume *f* de mer. **2.** Pipe *f* en écume de mer.

meet¹ [mi:t], *a.* *A. & Lit:* Convenable; à propos. **As was m.,** comme il convenait.

meet², *s.* *Ven:* Rendez-vous *m* de chasse; assemblée *f* de chasseurs; rassemblement *m* de la meute.

meet³, *v.* (met [met]; met) I. *v.tr.* **1.** Rencontrer (qn); se rencontrer avec (qn). **To m. s.o. on the stairs,** croiser qn dans l'escalier. **He met his death at . . .,** il trouva la mort à. . . . **2.** (*a*) Rencontrer (qn en duel). (*b*) Affronter (la mort); faire face à (une difficulté). **3.** Rejoindre, se rencontrer avec (qn). **To go to m. s.o.,** aller au-devant de qn; aller à la rencontre de qn. **The bus meets all trains,** l'autobus est en correspondance avec tous les trains. **To arrange to m. s.o.,** donner (un) rendez-vous à qn. **4.** Faire la connaissance de (qn). *U.S:* **M. Mr Smith,** je vous présente M. Smith. *P:* **Pleased to m. you,** enchanté de faire votre connaissance. **5. The scene that met my eyes . . .,** le spectacle qui s'offrait à mes yeux. . . . **There is more in it than meets the eye,** on ne voit pas le dessous des cartes. **My eye met his,** nos regards se croisèrent. **I dared not m. his eye,** je n'osais pas le regarder en face. **6.** (*a*) **To m. s.o.'s views,** se conformer aux vues de qn. *F:* **To m. s.o.,** faire des concessions à qn. (*b*) Satisfaire, répondre, à (un besoin); faire face à (une demande). (*c*) *Com:* Honorer (un effet). (*d*) **To m. expenses,** faire face aux dépenses. II. **meet,** *v.i.* (*a*) Se rencontrer, se voir. **We have met before,** nous nous sommes déjà vus. **When shall we m. again?** quand nous reverrons-nous? **They met in 1960,** ils se sont connus en 1960. (*b*) Se réunir (in session). **The society meets at, . . .** la société tient ses réunions à. . . . (*c*) Se joindre. *Prov:* **Extremes m.,** les extrêmes se touchent. **When two cars m.,** lors d'un croisement. **Our eyes met,** nos regards se croisèrent. *F:* **To make both ends m.,** joindre les deux bouts. (*d*) **To m. with sth.,** rencontrer, trouver, qch. **To m. with a kindly reception,** être accueilli avec bienveillance. **To m. with difficulties,** éprouver des difficultés; rencontrer des obstacles. **To m. with losses,** éprouver des pertes. **To m. with a refusal,** essuyer un refus. **He has met with an accident,** il lui est arrivé un accident. *Nau:* **To m. with a gale,** essuyer un coup de vent. **meeting,** *s.* **1.** Rencontre *f* (de personnes); croisement (de voitures). **2.** (*a*) Assemblée *f*, réunion *f*; *Pol: Sp:* meeting *m.* **The m. to be held to-morrow,** la réunion prévue pour demain. **To hold a public m.,** se réunir en séance publique. **To call a m. of the shareholders,** convoquer les actionnaires. **Notice of m.,** avis *m* de réunion. **To address the m.,** prendre la parole. **To put a resolution to the m.,** mettre une résolution aux voix. (*b*) *Rel:* **To go to m.** (of Quakers), aller au temple. **'meeting-house,** *s.* Temple *m* (des Quakers). **'meeting-place,** *s.* Lieu *m* de réunion; rendez-vous *m.*

megacycle ['megəsaikl], *s.* *W.Tel: T.V:* Mégacycle *m.*

megalith ['megəliθ], *s.* Mégalithe *m.*

megalithic [,megə'liθik], *a.* Mégalithique.

megalomania [,megəlou'meiniə], *s.* Mégalomanie *f*; folie *f* des grandeurs.

megalosaurus ['megəlou'sɔ:rəs], *s.* *Paleont:* Mégalosaure *m.*

megaphone ['megəfoun], *s.* Porte-voix *m inv.* *Sp: etc:* Mégaphone *m.*

megaton ['megətʌn], *s.* Mégatonne *f.*

megohm ['megoum], *s.* *El.Meas:* Mégohm *m.*

megrim ['mi:grim], *s.* *A:* **1.** Migraine *f.* **2.** Lubie *f.* **3.** *pl.* **Megrims,** (i) le spleen; vapeurs *fpl.* (ii) *Vet:* le vertigo.

melancholia [,melən'kouliə], *s.* *Med:* Mélancolie *f.*

melancholic [,melən'kɔlik], *a.* Mélancolique.

melancholy ['melənkɔli]. **1.** *s.* Mélancolie *f.* **2.** *a.* (*a*) (*Of pers.*) Mélancolique; triste. (*b*) **M. news,** nouvelle attristante.

Melanesia [melə'ni:sjə, -zjə]. *Pr.n. Geog:* La Mélanésie.

mellifluous [me'lifluəs], *a.* Mielleux; doucereux. *Lit:* **M. eloquence,** éloquence mellifue.

mellow¹ ['melou], *a.* **1.** (Fruit) fondant, mûr; (vin) moelleux; (terre) riche. **2.** (*Of voice*) Moelleux, doux, *f.* douce. **3.** (Esprit) mûr. **To grow m.,** mûrir; s'adoucir; (*of colour*) prendre de la patine. **4.** (*Of pers.*) *F:* Un peu gris; *P:* mûr.

mellow². **1.** *v.tr.* (*a*) (Faire) mûrir (des fruits); donner du moelleux à (un vin). (*b*) Mûrir, adoucir (le caractère de qn). **2.** *v.i.* (*a*) (*Of fruit, wine*) Mûrir; (*of colour*) prendre de la patine. (*b*) (*Of character*) S'adoucir. **mellowing,** *s.* Maturation *f* (des fruits, du vin); adoucissement *m* (de la voix, des couleurs).

mellowness ['meloʊnis], *s.* Maturité *f* (des fruits); moelleux *m* (du vin); douceur *f* (du caractère); fondu *m* (de couleurs).

melodic [me'lɔdik], *a.* *Mus:* (Progression) mélodique. *S.a.* PASSAGE 5.

melodious [me'loʊdiəs], *a.* Mélodieux, harmonieux. **-ly,** *adv.* Mélodieusement.

melodist ['melodist], *s.* Mélodiste *m.*

melodrama ['meloʊdrɑːmə], *s.* Mélodrame *m.*

melodramatic [ˌmeloʊdrə'mætik], *a.* Mélodramatique. **-ally,** *adv.* D'un air, d'un ton, mélodramatique.

melody ['melodi], *s.* Mélodie *f,* air *m,* chant *m.* **M. writer,** mélodiste *m.*

melomania ['meloʊ'meiniə], *s.* Mélomanie *f.*

melon ['melon], *s.* **1.** Melon *m.* *S.a.* WATER-MELON. **2.** *Fin:* *U.S:* *F:* **To carve, cut up, the m.,** distribuer les bénéfices. **'melon-bed,** *s.* Melonnière *f.*

melt¹ [melt], *v.* (*p.t.* **melted**; *p.p.* **melted**; *p.p. adj.* **molten** ['moʊlt(ə)n]) **I.** *v.i.* **1.** Fondre; se fondre. **2. His heart melted with pity,** la pitié lui attendrissait le cœur. **To m. into tears,** fondre en larmes. **3.** (*Of solid in liquid*) Fondre, se dissoudre. **II. melt,** *v.tr.* **1.** (Faire) fondre. **2.** Attendrir, émouvoir (qn). **melt away,** *v.i.* Fondre (complètement); se dissiper; (*of crowd*) se disperser. **melt down,** *v.tr.* Fondre (de la ferraille). **molten,** *a. Metall: Glassm:* En fusion; fondu. **melting¹,** *a.* **1.** (*a*) (*Of snow*) Fondant. (*b*) (*Of voice*) Attendri. **M. mood,** attendrissement *m.* **2. M. sun,** soleil brûlant, torride. **melting²,** *s.* **1.** Fonte *f,* fusion *f.* **2.** Attendrissement *m* (des cœurs). **'melting-point,** *s.* Point *m* de fusion. **'melting-pot,** *s.* Creuset *m.* *F:* **Everything is in the m.-p.,** on est en train de tout refondre.

melt², *s.* Rate *f.*

member ['membər], *s.* Membre *m.* **1.** *Nat.Hist:* Organe *m.* **2.** (*a*) *Carp:* Pièce *f* (d'une charpente). (*b*) *Gram: Mth:* Membre (de la phrase, d'une équation). **3.** (*a*) Membre (d'une société, etc.); adhérent *m* (d'un parti). **He is a m. of the family,** il fait partie de la famille. **M. of the audience,** assistant, -ante. (*b*) **M. of Parliament (M.P.),** membre de la Chambre des Communes; (*in Fr.*) député *m.* **Our m.,** notre représentant (à la Chambre).

membership ['membəʃip], *s.* **1.** Qualité *f* de membre; adhésion *f* (à un parti). **Qualifications for m.,** titres *m* d'éligibilité (of, à). **M. card,** carte *f* de membre. **2.** (Nombre *m* des) membres (d'une société).

membrane ['membrein], *s.* Membrane *f.* **Investing m.,** enveloppe *f*; tunique *f* (d'un organe). **Mucous m.,** muqueuse *f.*

membraned ['membreind], *a.* (Doigt) membrané.

membranous ['membrənəs], *a.* Membraneux, membrané.

memento, *pl.* **-o(e)s** [me'mentou, -ouz], *s.* Mémento, *m,* souvenir *m.*

memo ['memou], *s.* *F:* = MEMORANDUM. **M. pad,** bloc-notes *m.*

memoir ['memwɑːr], *s.* (*a*) Mémoire *m,* étude *f* (scientifique, etc.). (*b*) Notice *f* biographique. (*c*) *pl.* **Memoirs,** mémoires.

memorable ['mem(ə)rəbl], *a.* Mémorable. **-ably,** *adv.* Mémorablement.

memorandum, *pl.* **-da, -dums** [ˌmemə'rændəm, -də, -dəmz], *s.* Mémorandum *m,* note *f.* *Com:* Bordereau *m.* **memo'randum-book,'** *s.* Carnet *m,* calepin *m,* agenda *m.*

memorial [mi'mɔːriəl]. **1.** *a.* Commémoratif. *U.S:* **M. Day,** fête chômée (le 30 mai) en mémoire des morts à la guerre. **2.** *s.* (*a*) Monument (commémoratif). **War m.,** monument aux morts. (*b*) Pétition (adressée à un gouvernement). (*c*) *Jur:* **M. of a deed,** extrait *m* pour enregistrement.

memorialist [mi'mɔːriəlist], *s.* **1.** Mémorialiste *m.* **2.** Pétitionnaire *mf.*

memorialize [mi'mɔːriəlaiz], *v.tr.* **1.** Commémorer. **2.** Pétitionner.

memorization [ˌmemərai'zeiʃ(ə)n], *s.* Mémorisation *f.*

memorize ['meməraiz], *v.tr.* Apprendre (qch.) par cœur.

memory ['meməri], *s.* **1.** Mémoire *f.* *F:* **M. like a sieve,** mémoire de lièvre, cervelle *f* de lièvre. **I have a bad m. for names,** je n'ai pas la mémoire des noms. **Loss of m.,** perte *f* de mémoire; amnésie *f.* **To the best of my m. . . .,** autant que je m'en souviens, que je m'en souvienne. . . . **Never within living m.,** jamais de mémoire d'homme. **To play sth. from m.,** jouer qch. de mémoire. **2.** Mémoire, souvenir *m.* **Childhood memories,** souvenirs d'enfance. **We shall keep his m.,** nous garderons son souvenir. **In m. of . . .,** en, à la, mémoire de . . ., en souvenir de. . . .

mem-sahib ['memsɑːb], *s.f.* *O:* (*In India*) Femme européenne; (*as title*) Madame.

men [men], *s.m.pl.* *See* MAN¹.

menace¹ ['menəs], *s.* Menace *f.* *F:* **He's an awful m.,** c'est un fâcheux; il me tape sur les nerfs.

menace², *v.tr.* Menacer (qn). **menacing,** *a.* Menaçant. **-ly,** *adv.* D'un air menaçant.

menagerie [mi'nædʒəri], *s.* Ménagerie *f.*

mend¹ [mend], *s.* **1.** (*In fabric*) Reprise *f,* raccommodage *m.* **2. To be on the m.,** être en voie de guérison. **Trade is on the m.,** les affaires reprennent.

mend². **I.** *v.tr.* **1.** Raccommoder (un vêtement); réparer (un outil). **To m. invisibly,** stopper (un vêtement). **2.** Rectifier, corriger. **To m. one's ways,** changer de conduite. **3.** (*a*) Réparer (une faute). *Prov:* **Least said soonest mended,** trop gratter cuit, trop parler nuit. (*b*) **To m. matters,** arranger les choses. **II. mend,** *v.i.* **1.** (*Of invalid*) Se remettre. **The weather is mending,** le temps se remet au beau. **2.** S'amender, se corriger. **3.** S'améliorer. **mending,** *s.* (*a*) Raccommodage *m.* **M. cotton,** coton à repriser. **Invisible m.,** stoppage *m.* (*b*) Vêtements *mpl* à raccommoder.

mendacious [men'deiʃəs], *a.* Menteur, mensonger. **-ly,** *adv.* Mensongèrement.

mendaciousness [men'deiʃəsnis], **mendacity** [men'dæsiti], *s.* **1.** Penchant *m* au mensonge. **2.** Fausseté *f.*

Mendelian [men'diːliən], *a.* *Biol:* Mendélien, -ienne.

Mendelism ['mend(ə)lizm, *a.* *Biol:* Mendélisme *m.*

mender ['mendər], *s.* Raccommodeur, -euse; ravaudeur, -euse (de vêtements); repriseuse *f* (de dentelles); réparateur (de bicyclettes, etc.). **Invisible mender,** stoppeur, -euse.

mendicancy ['mendikənsi], *s.* Mendicité *f.*

mendicant ['mendikənt]. **1.** *a.* Mendiant. *Ecc:* **M. orders,** ordres mendiants. **2.** *s.* Mendiant, -ante.

mendicity [men'disiti], *s.* = MENDICANCY.

menfolk ['menfouk], *s.m.pl.* Les hommes (de la famille).

menhir ['menhiər], *s.* *Prehist:* Menhir *m.*

menial ['miːniəl]. **1.** *a.* (*Of duties*) Servile; bas, *f.* basse. **2.** *s.* *Usu. Pej:* Domestique *mf*; laquais *m.*

meningitis [ˌmenin'dʒaitis], *s.* *Med:* Méningite *f.* **Spinal m.,** méningo-myélite *f.* **Cerebro-spinal m.,** méningite cérébro-spinale.

meniscus [mi'niskəs], *s.* *Ph:* *Anat:* Ménisque *m.*

menopause ['menopɔːz], *s.* *Med:* Ménopause *f.*

menorrhagia [ˌmeno'reidʒiə], *s.* *Med:* Ménorragie *f.*

menses ['mensiːz], *s.* *Physiol:* Menstrues *f,* règles *f.*

menstrual ['menstruəl], *a.* *Physiol:* Menstruel, -elle.

menstruate ['menstrueit], *v.i.* *Physiol:* Avoir ses règles.

menstruation [ˌmenstru'eiʃ(ə)n], *s.* *Physiol:* Menstruation *f.*

mensurable ['menʃurəbl], *a.* Me(n)surable.

mensuration [ˌmensju(ə)'reiʃ(ə)n, ˌmenʃu-], *s.* **1.** Mesurage *m.* **2.** *Geom:* Mensuration *f.*

mental ['mentl], *a.* Mental, -aux; de l'esprit. **M. reservation,** restriction mentale; arrière-pensée *f.* **M. arithmetic,** calcul *m* mental, de tête. **M. deficiency,** déficience mentale; idiotie *f.* **The m. defectives, the m. deficients,** les déficients *m*; les minus habens *m.* *P:* **He's m.!** il est fou! il déménage. **A m. case,** un(e) aliéné(e). **M. hospital, m. home,** maison *f* de santé; hôpital *m,* clinique *f,* psychiatrique. **M. specialist,** médecin *m* aliéniste; psychiatre *m.* **-ally,** *adv.* Mentalement. **M. defective, m. deficient,** anormal, à mentalité retardée.

mentality [men'tæliti], s. Mentalité f.

menthol ['menθɔl], s. Menthol m.

mentholated ['menθoleitid], a. Pharm: Mentholé.

mention[1] ['menʃ(ə)n], s. 1. Mention f (de qch.). M. may be made of three churches . . ., on peut citer trois églises. . . . 2. Sch: etc: Honourable m., mention (honorable); accessit m.

mention[2], v.tr. Mentionner, citer, faire mention de (qch.). We need hardly m. that . . ., il est bien entendu que. . . . You never mentioned it, vous ne m'en avez jamais rien dit. I shall m. it to him, je lui en toucherai un mot. It must never be mentioned again, il ne faut plus jamais en reparler. Too numerous to m., trop nombreux pour les citer. It isn't worth mentioning, cela est sans importance. I've no books worth mentioning on the subject, je n'ai presque pas de livres sur ce sujet. I've no money worth mentioning, je n'ai pour ainsi dire pas d'argent. Not to m. . . ., sans parler de . . .; sans compter. . . . I heard my name mentioned, j'entendis prononcer mon nom. He mentioned no names, il n'a nommé personne. To m. s.o. in one's will, coucher qn sur son testament. F: Don't m. it! (i) cela ne vaut pas la peine d'en parler! (ii) il n'y a pas de quoi!

mentor ['mentɔːr], s. Mentor m, guide m.

menu ['menjuː], s. Menu m. Menu card, menu, carte f.

Mephistophelian [,mefisto'fiːljən], a. Méphistophélique.

mercantile ['məːk(ə)ntail], a. 1. Mercantile, marchand. M. nation, nation commerçante. 2. Pol.Ec: The m. system, theory, le système mercantile, la théorie de l'argent source de richesse. 3. ef: Mercantile, intéressé.

Mercator [məː'keitɔːr]. Pr.n.m. Mercator. M. projection, projection f de Mercator.

mercenary ['məːsin(ə)ri]. 1. a. Mercenaire, intéressé. 2. s. (Soldier) Mercenaire m.

mercerize ['məːsəraiz], v.tr. Merceriser.

merchandise ['məːtʃ(ə)ndaiz], s. Marchandise(s) f(pl).

merchandising ['məːtʃ(ə)ndaiziŋ], s. Techniques marchandes.,

merchant ['məːtʃ(ə)nt]. 1. s. (a) Négociant, -e; commerçant, -e; marchand, -ande, en gros. The prince, prince m, magnat m, du commerce. (b) Scot. & U.S: Marchand, -ande; boutiquier, -ière. (c) P: Type m, individu m. 2. a. Marchand; de commerce, du commerce. M. ship, m. vessel, navire marchand; navire de commerce. 'merchant-'seaman, pl. -men, s.m. Marin du commerce. 'merchant-'service, s. Marine marchande.

merchantable ['məːtʃ(ə)ntəbl], a. 1. Vendable. 2. De débit facile, de bonne vente.

merchantman, pl. -men ['məːtʃ(ə)ntmən], s. Navire marchand, navire de commerce.

merciful ['məːsif(u)l], a. Miséricordieux (to, pour); clément (to, envers). B: Blessed are the m., bienheureux sont les miséricordieux. **-fully**, adv. Miséricordieusement; avec clémence.

mercifulness ['məːsif(u)lnis], s. Miséricorde f.

merciless ['məːsilis], a. Impitoyable; sans pitié. **-ly**, adv. Impitoyablement; sans merci.

mercilessness ['məːsilisnis], s. Caractère m impitoyable; manque m de pitié.

mercurial [məː'kjuəriəl], a. 1. (a) Vif, ingénieux. (b) Inconstant; d'humeur changeante. 2. Med: Pharm: Mercuriel.

mercurochrome [məː'kjuərokroum], s. Pharm: Mercurochrome m.

Mercury ['məːkjuri]. I. Pr.n.m. Myth: Astr: Mercure. II. mercury, s. 1. Ch: Mercure m. 2. Bot: Mercuriale f.

mercy ['məːsi], s. Miséricorde f, grâce f, merci f, pitié f. (a) He has no m., il est sans pitié. To have m. on s.o., avoir pitié de qn. To call, beg, for m., demander grâce. For m.'s sake, de grâce; par pitié. Int: F: M. (on us)! grand Dieu! miséricorde! (b) To be at s.o.'s m., être à la merci de qn. Lit: At the m. of the waves, au gré des flots; à la dérive. B: Through the tender mercies of our God, par la miséricorde de Dieu. F: I left him to the tender mercies of his brother, je l'ai livré au bon vouloir de son frère. (c) Thankful for small mercies, reconnaissant des moindres bienfaits m. What a m.! quel bonheur! quelle chance! (d) Sister of M., sœur de charité, (sœur) hospitalière.

mere[1] ['miər], s. Lac m, étang m.

mere[2], a. Simple, pur, seul; rien que. . . . Out of m. spite, par pure méchanceté. It's m. chance, c'est un pur hasard. The m. sight of her, sa seule vue. I shudder at the m. thought of it, je frissonne rien que d'y penser. He's a m. boy, ce n'est qu'un enfant. S.a. NOBODY 2, NOTHING II. 3. **-ly**, adv. Simplement, seulement; tout bonnement. The invitation is m. formal, l'invitation est de pure forme. He m. smiled, il se contenta de sourire. I said it m. as a joke, j'ai dit cela histoire de rire.

meretricious [,meri'triʃəs], a. (Style, etc.) factice, clinquant.

merganser [məː'gænsər], s. Orn: Harle m.

merge [məːdʒ]. 1. v.tr. Fondre, fusionner (deux systèmes). To m. sth. in, into, sth., fondre qch. dans qch.; amalgamer qch. avec qch. These states became merged in the Empire, ces États furent englobés dans l'Empire. 2. v.i. Se fondre, se perdre (in, into, dans); se confondre (in, into, avec); (of banks, etc.) s'amalgamer, fusionner.

merger ['məːdʒər], s. 1. Fin: Fusion f (de plusieurs sociétés). M. company, sociétés réunies. 2. Jur: Extinction f par consolidation ou fusion.

meridian [mə'ridiən]. 1. s. (a) Méridien m. (b) Point culminant (d'un astre). At the m. of his glory, à l'apogée de sa gloire. 2. a. (a) Méridien, -ienne. (b) Culminant.

meridional [mə'ridiənl], a. & s. Méridional, -aux; du midi.

meringue [mə'ræŋ], s. Cu: Meringue f.

merino [mə'riːnou], s. Husb: Tex: Mérinos m.

merit[1] ['merit], s. 1. (a) Mérite m. To treat s.o. according to his merits, traiter qn selon ses mérites. (b) Jur: The merits of a case, le bien-fondé d'une cause. To judge a proposal on its merits, juger une proposition au fond. To go into the merits of sth., discuter le pour et le contre de qch. 2. Valeur f, mérite. Book of great, considerable, m., livre de véritable valeur. Sch: Certificate of m., accessit m.

merit[2], v.tr. Mériter.

meritorious [,meri'tɔːriəs], a. (Of pers.) Méritant; (of deed) méritoire. **-ly**, adv. D'une façon méritoire.

merlin ['məːlin], s. Orn: Émerillon m.

mermaid ['məːmeid], s.f. Sirène.

merman, pl. -men ['məːmən], s.m. Triton.

Merovingian [,mero'vin(d)ʒiən], a. & s. Hist: Mérovingien, -ienne.

merriment ['merimənt], s. Gaieté f, hilarité f, réjouissance f, divertissement(s) m(pl).

merry ['meri], a. (merrier) 1. (a) Joyeux, gai. To be always m. and bright, être toujours plein d'entrain. To make m., s'amuser. (A) m. Christmas! joyeux Noël! Prov: The more the merrier, plus on est de fous, plus on rit. (b) F: To be m., être émécbé; être un peu gris. To be m. in one's cups, avoir le vin gai. 2. A: (a) The m. month of May, le gentil mois de mai. (b) Robin Hood and his m. men, Robin des Bois et sa troupe de gaillards. **-ily**, adv. Gaiement, joyeusement. 'merry-go-round, s. (Manège m de) chevaux mpl de bois; carrousel m. 'merry-maker, s. Fêtard m. 'merry-making, s. Réjouissances fpl, partie f de plaisir.

merrythought ['meriθɔːt], s. Lunette f, fourchette f (d'une volaille).

mesenteritis [mə,sentər'aitis], s. Med: Mésentérite f.

mesentery ['mes(ə)nt(ə)ri], s. Anat: Mésentère m.

mesh[1] [meʃ], s. 1. Maille f (d'un filet). M. stocking, bas m indémaillable. M. bag, (sac) filet m. To mend the meshes of a net, re(m)mailler un filet. 2. Mec.E: Prise f, engrenage m. Constant-m. gear, pignons constamment en prise. In m. with, en prise avec.

mesh[2]. 1. v.tr. Mec.E: Endenter, engrener (des roues dentées). 2. v.i. (Of teeth of wheel) (S')engrener; être en prise. **-meshed**, a. Wide-meshed, à larges mailles.

mesmerism ['mezmərizm], s. Mesmérisme m, hypnotisme m.

mesmerist ['mezmərist], s. Hypnotiseur m.

mesmerization [,mezmərai'zeiʃən], s. Magnétisation f.

mesmerize ['mezməraiz], v.tr. Magnétiser; hypnotiser.

mesmerizer ['mezməraizər], s. Magnétiseur m, hypnotiseur m.

mesocarp ['mezokɑːp], s. Bot: Mésocarpe m.
mesoderm ['mezodəːm], s. Biol: Mésoderme m.
Mesopotamia [ˌmes(ə)pə'teimjə]. Pr.n. La Mésopotamie.
meson ['miːzən], s. Atom.Ph: Méson m.
mesozoic [mezo'zouik], a. & s. Geol: (L'ère) mésozoïque.
mess¹ [mes], s. 1. (a) A: Plat m, mets m. B: M. of pottage = plat de lentilles. (b) Husb: (For animal) Pâtée f. 2. Saleté f. To make a m. of the tablecloth, salir la nappe. 3. Fouillis m, gâchis m. Everything is in a m., tout est en désordre. What a m.! voilà du propre! F: quel gâchis! (Of pers.) To get into a m., se mettre dans de beaux draps. To get s.o. out of a m., tirer à qn une épine du pied. To make a m. of it, tout gâcher. 4. Mil: Navy: (For officers) Table f, mess m, F: popote f; (for men) Mil: ordinaire m, Navy: plat m. M.-jacket, veste f de mess, spencer m. 'mess-kettle, s. Navy: Gamelle f. 'mess-room, s. 1. Mil: Salle f de mess. 2. Navy: Carré m (des officiers). 'mess-tin, s. Mil: Gamelle (individuelle).
mess². 1. v.tr. (a) Salir, souiller. The child has messed up her dress, l'enfant a sali sa robe. (b) To mess (up) a business, gâcher une affaire. 2. v.i. Mil: Navy: Faire popote F: faire gamelle. mess about, v.i. F: (a) Patauger (dans la boue). (b) Bricoler; gaspiller son temps. 'mess-up, s. F: 1. Gâchis m. 2. Embrouillamini m, malentendu m; F: cafouillage m.
message ['mesidʒ], s. 1. (a) Message m. To leave a message for s.o., laisser un mot pour qn. I'll give him the m., je lui ferai la commission. (b) Communication f (par téléphone). 2. Commission f, course f. To run messages, faire les commissions, les courses. 3. (a) Prédiction f; évangile m (d'un prophète). (b) Message, enseignement m (d'un écrivain).
messenger ['mesindʒər], s. 1. (a) Messager, -ère. (b) Commissionnaire m; garçon m de bureau. Hotel messenger, chasseur m. Telegraph messenger, facteur m des télégraphes; facteur-télégraphiste m. S.a. EXPRESS¹ 1. (c) Adm: King's, Queen's m., courrier m diplomatique. 2. (On kite-string) Postillon m. 3. Nau: Tournevire m.
Messiah [mi'saiə]. Pr.n. Messie m.
messianic [mesi'ænik], a. Messianique.
messianism [mi'saiənizm], s. Messianisme m.
messmate ['mesmeit], s. Camarade m de table; Navy: camarade de plat.
Messrs ['mesəz], s.m.pl. Com: etc: Messieurs, abbr. MM.
messuage ['meswidʒ], s. Jur: Maison avec dépendances et terres attenantes.
messy ['mesi], a. F: 1. (a) Sale, malpropre. (b) En désordre. 2. Qui salit; salissant.
met. See MEET³.
metabolism [me'tæbəlizm], s. Biol: Métabolisme m. Constructive m., anabolisme m. Destructive m., catabolisme m.
metacarpus [metə'kɑːpəs], s. Anat: Métacarpe m.
metacentre ['metəsentər], s. Métacentre m.
metal¹ ['metl], s. 1. Métal m, -aux. Base metal, métal commun. Sheet metal, tôle f. 2. Glassm: Verre m en fusion. 3. Civ.E: (Matériau m d')empierrement m; ballast m (de voie ferrée). Road m., cailloutis m, pierraille f. 4. Typ: Caractères mpl. Old m., vieille matière. 5. pl. Rail: (Of engine) To leave, jump, the metals, quitter les rails; dérailler. 'metal-bearing, a. Métallifère. 'metal-work, s. 1. Travail m des métaux; serrurerie f. 2. Métal ouvré.
metal², v.tr. (metalled) Empierrer, caillouter (une route).
metallic [mi'tælik], a. Métallique.
metalliferous [metə'lif(ə)rəs], a. Métallifère.
metallization [ˌmetəlai'zeiʃ(ə)n], s. Métallisation f.
metallize ['metəlaiz], v.tr. Métalliser (une surface).
metallography [metə'lɔgrəfi], s. Métallographie f.
metalloid ['metəlɔid], a. & s. Métalloïde (m).
metallurgic(al) [metə'ləːdʒik(əl)], a. Métallurgique.
metallurgist [me'tælədʒist], s. Métallurgiste m.
metallurgy [me'tælədʒi], s. Métallurgie f.
metamorphic [metə'mɔːfik], a. Métamorphique.
metamorphism [metə'mɔːfizm], s. Métamorphisme m.

metamorphose [ˌmetə'mɔːfouz], v.tr. Métamorphoser, transformer (to, into, en).
metamorphosis, pl. -oses [ˌmetə'mɔːfəsis, -siːz], s. Métamorphose f.
metaphor ['metəfər], s. Métaphore f; image f. Mixed metaphor, métaphore incohérente.
metaphoric(al) [ˌmetə'fɔrik(əl)], a. Métaphorique. -ally, adv. Métaphoriquement.
metaphysical [ˌmetə'fizik(ə)l], a. Métaphysique. -ally, adv. Métaphysiquement.
metaphysician [ˌmetəfi'ziʃ(ə)n], s. Métaphysicien m.
metaphysics [ˌmetə'fiziks], s.pl. La métaphysique.
metatarsus, pl. -i [ˌmetə'tɑːsəs, -ai], s. Anat: Nat.Hist: Métatarse m.
metathesis, pl. -eses [me'tæθesis, -siːz], s. 1. Ling: Surg: Métathèse f. 2. Ch: Substitution f.
metazoon, pl. -zoa [metə'zouən, -'zouə], s. Biol: Métazoaire m.
mete [miːt], v.tr. Lit: To mete (out) punishments, rewards, assigner des punitions; distribuer, décerner, des récompenses.
metempsychosis [ˌmetempsi'kousis], s. Métempsycose f.
meteor ['miːtiər], s. Météore m.
meteoric [ˌmiːti'ɔrik], a. 1. Météorique. Meteoric iron, sidérolithe f. M. rise in the social scale, ascension météorique de l'échelle sociale. 2. Atmosphérique.
meteorite ['miːtiərait], s. Météorite f; aérolithe m.
meteorological [ˌmiːtjərə'lɔdʒik(ə)l], a. Météorologique.
meteorologist [ˌmiːtjə'rɔlədʒist], s. Météorologiste m, météorologue m, F: météo m.
meteorology [ˌmiːtjə'rɔlədʒi], s. Météorologie f.
meter ['miːtər], s. Compteur m; jaugeur m. Electric m., compteur électrique. To turn off the gas at the m., fermer le compteur. Parking m., parcomètre m, Fr.C: compteur m de stationnement.
methane ['meθein], s. Ch: Méthane m.
method ['meθəd], s. 1. (a) Méthode f; manière f (of doing sth., de faire qch.); procédé m (pour faire qch.). Adm: Methods of payment, modalités f de paiement. Mil: Tactical methods, procédés de combat. (b) Man of m., homme d'ordre. There's m. in his madness, il n'est pas si fou qu'il en a l'air.
methodical [mi'θɔdik(ə)l], a. Méthodique. M. life, vie réglée, ordonnée. -ally, adv. Méthodiquement; avec méthode.
methodicalness [mi'θɔdik(ə)lnis], s. Esprit méthodique, esprit de suite.
Methodism ['meθədizm], s. Ecc: Méthodisme m.
Methodist ['meθədist], a. & s. Ecc: Méthodiste (mf).
methyl ['meθil], s. Ch: Méthyle m. M. alcohol, alcool méthylique, F: esprit-de-bois m.
methylate ['meθileit], v.tr. Ch: Méthyler. Methylated spirit, alcool dénaturé; alcool à brûler.
methylene ['meθiliːn], s. Ch: Méthylène m.
meticulosity [mi,tikju'lɔsiti], s. Méticulosité f.
meticulous [mi'tikjuləs], a. Méticuleux. -ly, adv. Méticuleusement. To be always m. accurate, avoir le souci de l'exactitude.
meticulousness [mi'tikjuləsnis], s. Méticulosité f.
metonymical [metə'nimik(ə)l], a. Rh: Métonymique.
metonymy [mi'tɔnimi], s. Rh: Métonymie f.
metre¹ ['miːtər], s. Pros: Mètre m, mesure f.
metre², s. Meas: Mètre m (= 39·37 inches). Square m., mètre carré. Cubic m., mètre cube.
metric¹ ['metrik], a. Meas: Métrique. The m. system, le système métrique.
metric²(al) ['metrik(əl)], a. (Poésie) métrique.
metrication [metri'keiʃ(ə)n], s. Adoption f du système métrique.
metronome ['metrənoum], s. Mus: Métronome m.
metropolis [mi'trɔpəlis], s. Métropole f.
metropolitan [metrə'pɔlit(ə)n], a. 1. Métropolitain. 2. s. Ecc: Métropolitain m, archevêque m.
mettle ['metl], s. 1. Ardeur f, courage m, feu m; (of horse) fougue f. To put s.o. on his m., piquer qn d'honneur; exciter l'émulation de qn. I was on my m., je m'étais piqué au jeu. 2. Caractère m, tempérament m. To show one's m., faire ses preuves.
mettlesome ['metlsəm], a. (Of pers.) Ardent, vif, f. vive; (of horse) fougueux, -euse.
mew¹ [mjuː], s. Orn: (Sea-)mew, mouette f, goéland (cendré).

mew², *s.* Mue *f*, cage *f* (pour les faucons).
mew³, *s.* (*Of cat, sea-gull*) Miaulement *m*.
mew⁴, *v.i.* (*Of cat, sea-gull*) Miauler. **mewing¹**, *a.*
Miauleur, -euse. **mewing²**, *s.* Miaulement *m*.
mews [mjuːz], *s.pl.* **1.** Écuries *fpl.* **2.** Impasse *f*, ruelle *f*
(sur laquelle donnaient des écuries). **M. flat**, apparte-
ment aménagé dans une ancienne écurie.
Mexican ['meksikən], *a. & s.* Mexicain, -aine.
Mexico ['meksikou]. *Pr.n.* Le Mexique.
mezzanine ['mezəniːn], *s. Arch:* **M. (-floor)**, mezzanine
f, entresol *m*.
mezzo-soprano, *pl.* -os, -i ['medzousə'prɑːnou, -ouz,
-iː], *s.* Mezzo-soprano *m*, *pl.* mezzo-sopranos,
-soprani.
mezzotint ['medzoutint], *s. Engr:* Mezzo-tinto *m*,
gravure *f* à la manière noire.
mi [miː], *s. Mus:* Mi *m*.
miaow¹ [mi(ː)'au], *s.* Miaulement *m*, miaou *m* (du chat).
miaow², *v.i.* (*Of cat*) Miauler.
miasma, *pl.* -ata, -as [mi'æzmə, miæz'mɑːtə, -əz], *s.*
Miasme *m*.
miasmal [mi'æzm(ə)l], **miasmatic** [miəz'mætik], *a.*
Miasmatique.
mica ['maikə], *s.* Mica *m*.
micaceous [mai'keiʃəs], *a.* Micacé.
mice [mais]. *See* MOUSE¹.
Michael ['maikl]. *Pr.n.m.* Michel.
Michaelmas ['miklməs], *s.* **1. M. (Day)**, la Saint-
Michel. **2.** *Bot:* **M. daisy**, marguerite *f* d'automne,
aster *m* œil-du-Christ.
Michelangelo [,maikəl'ændʒəlou]. *Pr.n.m.* Michel-Ange.
mickey ['miki], *s. F:* **To take the m. out of s.o.**, se payer
la tête de qn.
microanalysis ['maikrouən'æləsis], *s. Ch:* Micro-
analyse *f*.
microbe ['maikroub], *s.* Microbe *m*.
microbial [mai'kroubiəl], **microbic** [mai'krɔbik], *a.*
Microbien.
microbiologist ['maikroubai'ɔlədʒist], *s.* Micro-
biologiste *mf*.
microbiology ['maikroubai'ɔlədʒi], *s.* Microbiologie *f*.
microcephalous ['maikrou'sefələs], *a.* Microcéphale.
microchemistry ['maikrou'kemistri], *s.* Microchimie *f*.
microcosm ['maikrokɔzm], *s.* Microcosme *m*.
microfilm¹ ['maikroufilm], *s.* Microfilm *m*.
microfilm², *v.tr.* Microfilmer.
micrography [mai'krɔgrəfi], *s.* Micrographie *f*.
microgroove ['maikrougruːv], *s.* Microsillon *m*.
microhm ['maikroum], *s. El.Meas:* Microhm *m*.
micrometer [mai'krɔmitər], *s.* Micromètre *m*. **M.
screw**, vis *f* micrométrique. **M. balance**, micro-
balance *f*.
micrometric [,maikro'metrik], *a.* Micrométrique.
micron ['maikrɔn], *s. Meas:* Micron *m*; millième *m*
de millimètre.
micro-organism ['maikrou'ɔːgənizm], *s.* Micro-
organisme *m*.
microphone ['maikrəfoun], *s.* Microphone *m*. **Concealed m.**, espion *m*.
microphotograph ['maikrou'foutəgrɑːf], *s.* Micro-
photographie *f*.
microphotography ['maikroufə'tɔgrəfi], *s.* Micro-
photographie *f*.
microscope ['maikrəskoup], *s.* Microscope *m*. **Electron m.**, microscope *m* électronique. **Light m.**,
microscope optique. **Visible under the m.**, visible au
microscope.
microscopic ['maikrə'skɔpik], *a.* **1.** Microscopique.
2. M. examination, examen au microscope.
microscopy [mai'krɔskəpi], *s.* Microscopie *f*.
microtherm ['maikrɔθəːm], *s. Ph.Meas:* Microthermie *f*.
microtome ['maikrotoum], *s.* Microtome *m*.
microwave ['maikrouweiv], *s. Electronics:* Hyper-
fréquence *f*.
microzoa [,maikro'zouə], *s.pl. Biol:* Microzoaires *m*.
micturate ['miktjureit], *v.i. Med:* Uriner.
micturition [,miktju'riʃ(ə)n], *s. Med:* Miction *f*.
mid [mid], *a.* Du milieu; mi, moyen. **From m. June to
m. August**, de la mi-juin à la mi-août. **In m. air**, entre
ciel et terre; en plein ciel. **In m. Channel**, au milieu
de la Manche. **'mid-iron**, *s. Golf:* Fer moyen;
crosse moyenne en fer. **mid-'season**, *s.* Demi-
saison *f*.

midday ['middei, 'mid'dei], *s.* Midi *m*. **M. heat**,
chaleur de midi.
midden ['midn], *s.* Tas *m* de fumier.
middle ['midl]. **1.** *Attrib.a.* Du milieu; central, -aux;
moyen, intermédiaire. **To take a m. course**, prendre
un parti moyen. **M. size**, grandeur moyenne. *Box:*
M. weight, poids moyen. *Log:* **M. (term)**, moyen
terme. *S.a.* AGE¹ 1, DISTANCE¹ 1. **2.** *s.* (*a*) Milieu,
centre *m*. **The m. of life**, l'âge mûr. **In the m.
of . . .**, au milieu de. . . . **The ball hit him in the m.
of the back**, le ballon l'atteignit en plein dos.
About the m. of August, à la mi-août. **In the very m.
of . . ., right in the m. of . .**, au beau milieu de. . . .
I was in the m. of reading, j'étais en train de lire.
(*b*) Taille *f*, ceinture *f*. **The water came up to his m.**,
l'eau lui venait à mi-corps. **middle-'aged**, *a.* (*Of
pers.*) Entre deux âges; d'un certain âge. **middle
'class**, *s. & attrib.a.* **The m. class(es)**, la classe
moyenne; la bourgeoisie. **m.-class**, *a.* bourgeois.
'middle-of-the-'road, *a.* Modéré. **M.-of-the-r.
policy**, politique du juste milieu. **middle-'sized**, *a.*
De grandeur moyenne; de taille moyenne.
middleman, *pl.* -men ['midlmən], *s.m. Com:* Intermédiaire, revendeur.
middlemost ['midlmoust], *a.* Le plus au milieu;
central, -aux.
middling ['midliŋ]. **1.** *a.* (*a*) (i) Médiocre; (ii) passable,
assez bon. *F:* **How are you?—M.**, comment allez-
vous?—Pas mal; comme ci comme ça. *F:* couci-
couça. (*b*) **Of m. size**, de grandeur moyenne. (*c*)
Com: Bon ordinaire; de qualité moyenne. **2.** *adv.*
Assez bien; passablement; ni bien ni mal.
middy ['midi], *s.m. Nau: F:* = MIDSHIPMAN.
midge [midʒ], *s.* Moucheron *m*; cousin *m*.
midget ['midʒit], *s.* **1.** Nain, *f.* naine; nabot, -ote.
2. *Attrib.* Minuscule. **M. submarine**, sous-marin *m*
de poche.
midland ['midlənd]. **1.** *s.pl.* **The Midlands**, les comtés
centraux (de l'Angleterre). **2.** *a.* Des comtés du
centre.
midmost ['midmoust], *a.* Le plus près du milieu;
central, -aux.
midnight ['midnait], *s.* Minuit *m*. **To arrive about m.**,
arriver sur les minuit.
midriff ['midrif], *s. Anat:* Diaphragme *m*. **Blow on
the m.**, coup au creux de l'estomac.
midship ['midʃip], *s. N.Arch:* Milieu *m* du navire.
Esp. attrib. **M. frame**, maître couple *m*.
midshipman, *pl.* -men ['midʃipmən], *s.m. Nau:*
Aspirant (de marine), *F:* midship.
midst [midst]. **1.** *s.* (*a*) **In the m. of sth.**, au milieu de,
parmi (la foule, etc.). **In the m. of winter**, en plein
hiver; au cœur de l'hiver. **In the m. of all this**, sur
ces entrefaites. **I was in the m. of reading**, j'étais en
train de lire. (*b*) **In our m.**, au milieu de nous; parmi
nous. **2.** *prep. Poet:* = AMID(ST).
midstream ['mid'striːm], *s.* **1.** Ligne médiane (d'un
fleuve). **2. In m.**, au milieu du courant.
midsummer ['midsʌmər], *s.* (*a*) Cœur *m*, plein *m*,
m de l'été. (*b*) Le solstice d'été. **M. day**, la Saint-
Jean.
midway ['mid'wei], *adv.* **A mi-chemin**, à moitié
chemin. **M. between . . . and . . .**, à mi-distance
entre . . . et. . . .
midwife, *pl.* -wives ['midwaif, -waivz], *s.f.* Sage-
femme, *pl.* sages-femmes.
midwifery ['midwifri], *s.* Obstétrique *f*.
midwinter ['mid'wintər], *s.* (*a*) Milieu *m* de l'hiver,
fort *m* de l'hiver. (*b*) Le solstice d'hiver.
mien [miːn], *s. Lit:* Mine *f*, air *m*.
might¹ [mait], *s.* Puissance *f*, force(s) *f(pl)*. **To work
with all one's m.**, travailler de toutes ses forces.
M. against right, la force contre le droit. **M. is right**,
la force prime le droit; la raison du plus fort est
toujours la meilleure.
might², *v. See* MAY¹.
mightiness ['maitinis], *s.* Puissance *f*, force *f*; grandeur *f*.
mighty ['maiti]. **I.** *a.* (*a*) Puissant, fort. *S.a.* HIGH I.
2. (*b*) Grand, vaste, grandiose. (*c*) *F:* **You're in a
m. hurry**, vous êtes diablement pressé. **-ily**, *adv.* **1.**
Puissamment, fortement, vigoureusement. **2.** *F:*
Extrêmement, fameusement. **II. mighty**, *adv. F:*
Fort, extrêmement, rudement (content, etc.).

mignonette [ˌminjəˈnet], s. Réséda odorant.
migraine [ˈmiːgrein, miˈgrein], s. Med: Migraine f.
migrant [ˈmaigrənt]. 1. a. = MIGRATORY. 2. s. Migrateur, -trice.
migrate [maiˈgreit], v.i. Émigrer.
migration [maiˈgreiʃ(ə)n], s. Migration f.
migratory [ˈmaigrət(ə)ri], a. (Peuple) migrateur, nomade; (oiseau) migrateur, de passage.
Mikado [miˈkaːdou], s. Mikado m.
mike[1] [maik], s. F: Microphone m, F: micro m.
mike[2], v.i. Mil: P: Tirer au flanc.
Mike[3]. Pr.n.m. (Dim. of Michael) Michel. F: For the love of M. . . ., pour l'amour de Dieu. . . .
Milanese [ˌmiləˈniːz], a. & s. Geog: Milanais, -aise.
milch-cow [ˈmiltʃkau], s. Vache laitière; F: vache à lait.
mild [maild], a. 1. (Of pers., word) Doux, f. douce. 2. (Of rule) Doux, peu sévère, peu rigoureux. M. punishment, punition légère. 3. (Climat) doux, tempéré; (hiver) doux, bénin; (air) tiède. It is milder here, il fait meilleur ici. 4. (a) (Médicament) doux, bénin; (tabac) doux. M. beer, s. mild, bière brune (légère). F: Draw it m.! tout doux! n'exagérez pas! (b) A m. form of measles, une forme bénigne de la rougeole. 5. (Exercice) modéré; (amusement) innocent, anodin. 6. M. steel, acier doux. -ly, adv. 1. Doucement; avec douceur. 2. F: To put it m., pour ne pas dire plus.
mildew[1] [ˈmildjuː], s. 1. (a) Rouille f (sur le blé, etc.). (b) Mildiou m (sur les vignes, etc.). 2. Moisissure f; taches fpl d'humidité.
mildew[2], v.tr. (a) Rouiller, moisir (une plante). (b) (Of damp) Piquer (le papier, etc.). **mildewed**, a. Vit: Atteint de mildiou, mildiousé.
mildness [ˈmaildnis], s. 1. Douceur f, clémence f (de qn, du temps). 2. Bénignité f caractère bénin d'une maladie).
mile [mail], s. Mille m. Statute m., English m. (= 1760 yards = 1609 m. 31), mille anglais, mille terrestre. Nautical m., sea m. (= 2026 yards = 1852 m.), mile marin. Square m. (= 259 hectares), mille carré. Measured m., base f (pour essais de vitesse). F: Nobody comes within miles of him, personne ne lui monte à la cheville.
mileage [ˈmailidʒ], s. Distance f en milles; Fr.C: millage m. Daily m., parcours journalier (d'une locomotive, etc.). Car with very small m., auto qui a très peu roulé.
milestone [ˈmailstoun], s. 1. Borne milliaire, routière (= borne kilométrique). 2. Milestones in s.o.'s life, événements qui jalonnent la vie de qn.
milfoil [ˈmilfɔil], s. Bot: Mille-feuille f.
miliary [ˈmiliəri], a. Med: Miliaire.
militancy [ˈmilitənsi], s. Esprit militant; activisme m.
militant [ˈmilitənt], a. & s. Militant.
militarism [ˈmilitərizm], s. Militarisme m.
militarist [ˈmilitərist], s. Militariste m.
military [ˈmilit(ə)ri]. 1. a. Militaire. Of m. age, en âge de servir. M. law, le code (de justice) militaire. 2. s.pl. Coll. The m., les militaires m; l'armée f; la force armée. -ily, adv. Militairement.
militate [ˈmiliteit], v.i. Militer (in favour of, against, en faveur de, contre).
militia [miˈliʃə], s. Milice f; garde nationale. U.S: Hommes d'âge militaire.
militiaman, pl. -men [miˈliʃəmən], s.m. Milicien; garde national.
milk[1] [milk], s. 1. Lait m. New m., lait (encore) chaud; lait du jour. Malted m., farine lactée. M. diet, régime lacté. F: To come home with the m., rentrer au grand jour; F: arriver dès les chats. Land flowing with m. and honey, pays de cocagne. S.a. FLOW[2] 3. M. and water, (i) lait coupé (d'eau); (ii) discours ou littérature fade, insipide. Prov: It is no use crying over spilt m., inutile de pleurer, ça ne changera rien. 2. Lait, eau f (de noix de coco). M. of almonds, of lime, lait d'amandes, de chaux. ˈmilk bar, s. Milk-bar m. ˈmilk-can, s. Boîte f à lait. ˈmilk-float, s. Voiture f de laitier. ˈmilk-jug, s. Pot m à lait. ˈmilk ˈpudding, s. Cu: Riz m, semoule f, tapioca m, etc., au lait. ˈmilk-tooth, pl. -teeth, s. Dent f de lait.
milk[2], v.tr. 1. Traire (une vache, etc.). 2. F: Dépouiller, exploiter (qn). **milking**, s. Traite f (d'une vache, etc.).

milker [ˈmilkər], s. 1. (a) (Pers.) Trayeur, -euse. (b) Mechanical m., trayeuse mécanique. 2. (Of cow) Good m., bonne laitière.
milkiness [ˈmilkinis], s. Couleur laiteuse; lactescence f (d'un liquide, etc.).
milkmaid [ˈmilkmeid], s.f. 1. Laitière, crémière. 2. Trayeuse; fille de laiterie.
milkman, pl. -men [ˈmilkmən], s.m. Laitier, crémier.
milksop [ˈmilksɔp], s. F: Poule mouillée.
milkweed [ˈmilkwiːd], s. Bot: Laiteron m.
milky [ˈmilki], a. Laiteux; lactescent. Astr: The M. Way, la Voie lactée.
mill[1] [mil], s. 1. (a) (Flour-)m., moulin m (à blé); minoterie f. To go, pass, through the m., passer par de dures épreuves; passer par la filière. (b) Coffee-m., pepper-m., moulin à café, à poivre. (c) (Crushing-)m., (moulin) broyeur m, concasseur m. 2. Metalw: Rolling-m., laminoir m. 3. Tls: = MILLING-CUTTER. 4. Usine f; manufacture f. Cotton-m., filature f de coton. Sugar m., raffinerie f de sucre. ˈmill-course, s. Bief m de moulin. ˈmill-dam, s. Barrage m de moulin. ˈmill-dust, s. Folle farine. ˈmill-hand, s. (a) Ouvrier, -ière, d'usine, de fabrique, de filature. (b) Garçon meunier. ˈmill-owner, s. 1. Propriétaire m de moulin. 2. Industriel m; filateur m. ˈmill-pond, s. 1. Réservoir m de moulin; retenue f. 2. Sea as smooth as a m.-p., mer f d'huile. ˈmill-race, s. Bief m de moulin.
mill[2]. 1. v.tr. (a) Moudre (le blé). (b) Broyer (du minerai). (c) Fouler (le drap). (d) Fraiser (des engrenages, etc.). (e) Molet(t)er (la tête d'une vis). Num: Créneler (une pièce de monnaie). Milled edge (on coin), crénelage m, grènetis m. 2. v.i. Esp. U.S: (a) (Of cattle) Tourner en masse. (b) (Of crowd) Fourmiller; tourner en rond. **milling**[1], a. In the m. crowd, dans les remous de la foule. **milling**[2], s. 1. Meunerie f, minoterie f. 2. (a) Mouture f, moulage m (du drap). 3. Metalw: (a) Fraisage m. (b) Molet(t)age m (d'une tête de vis.) 4. F: Coups mpl de poing; raclée f, rossée f. ˈmilling-cutter, s. Mec.E: Fraise f; fraiseuse f.
millboard [ˈmilbɔːd], s. Carton-pâte m inv; fort carton; carton épais.
millefeuille [ˈmiːlfœːj], s. Cu: Millefeuille f.
millenary [miˈlenəri], a. & s. Millénaire (m).
millennial [miˈleniəl]. 1. a. Millénaire; qui dure depuis mille ans. 2. s. Millième anniversaire m.
millennium [miˈleniəm], s. 1. Rel.H: Millénium m. 2. Millénaire m; mille ans m.
millepede [ˈmilipiːd], s. Myr: Mille-pattes m inv, mille-pieds m inv.
miller [ˈmilər], s. 1. Meunier m; (of steam mill) minotier m. 2. Mec.E: (a) (Pers.) Fraiseur m. (b) (Machine) Fraiseuse f; machine f à fraiser.
miller's thumb, s. Ich: Chabot, cabot, meunier.
millet [ˈmilit], s. Bot: Millet m, mil m. African, Indian, m., sorgho m.
milliampere [ˌmiliˈæmpɛər], s. El.Meas: Milliampère m.
milliard [ˈmiliaːd], s. Milliard m.
millibar [ˈmilibaːr], s. Meteor.Meas: Millibar m.
milliary [ˈmiliəri], a. & s. Rom.Ant: M. (column), (borne f) milliaire.
milligram(me) [ˈmiligræm], s. Milligramme m.
millimetre [ˈmilimiːtər], s. Millimètre m.
milliner [ˈmilinər], s. Modiste f.
millinery [ˈmilinəri], s. (Articles mpl de) modes fpl. M. shop, magasin m de modes.
million [ˈmiljən], s. Million m. Two m. men, deux millions d'hommes.
millionaire [ˌmiljəˈnɛər], a. & s. Millionnaire (mf).
millionth [ˈmiljənθ], a. & s. Millionième (m).
millstone [ˈmilstoun], s. Meule f (de moulin). Upper m., meule courante. Lower m., A: nether m., meule gisante. M. grit, pierre meulière, meulière f. Lit: O: To be between the upper and the nether m., être entre l'enclume et le marteau. It will be a m. round his neck all his life, c'est un boulet qu'il traînera toute sa vie. ˈmillstone-quarry, s. Meulière f.
millwright [ˈmilrait], s. Installateur m de moulins.
milt [milt], s. 1. Rate f (des mammifères). 2. Laitance f, laite f (des poissons).
mime[1] [maim], s. Th: Mime m; mimodrame m.

mime². **1.** *v.tr.* Mimer (une scène). **2.** *v.i.* Jouer par gestes.

mimetic [mi′metik], *a.* **1.** D'imitation; imitatif. **2.** = MIMIC¹ 1. **3.** (Papillon, etc.) mimétique.

mimetism [′mimɛtizm], *s.* *Nat.Hist:* Mimétisme *m.*

mimic¹ [′mimik]. **1.** *a.* (*Of gesture, etc.*) Mimique; imitateur, -trice. **2.** *s.* (*a*) Mime *m.* (*b*) Imitateur, -trice.

mimic², *v.tr.* (**mimicked**) **1.** Imiter, mimer, contrefaire; *F:* singer (qn). **2.** Imiter, contrefaire (la nature, etc.).

mimicker [′mimikər], *s.* Imitateur, -trice; *F:* singe *m.*

mimicry [′mimikri], *s.* Mimique *f*, imitation *f.*

mimosa [mi′mouzə], *s.* *Bot:* Mimosa *m.*

minaret [‚minə′ret], *s.* Minaret *m.*

minatory [′minətəri] *a.* Menaçant; *Jur:* comminatoire.

mince¹ [mins], *s.* *Cu:* Hachis *m.*

mince², *v.tr.* **1.** Hacher (menu) (de la viande, etc.). **Minced meat**, hachis *m*, haché *m.* **2.** (*Always neg.*) **Not to m. matters, one's words,** ne pas mâcher ses mots; dire les choses carrément. **3.** **To m. (one's words),** parler du bout des lèvres; (*of woman*) minauder. **mincing,** *a.* (*a*) Affecté, minaudier, affété. (*b*) **To take m. steps,** marcher à petits pas.

mincemeat [′minsmiːt], *s.* *Cu:* Compote *f* de raisins secs, de pommes, d'amandes, etc., liée avec de la graisse et conservée avec du cognac. *F:* **To make m. of s.o.,** réduire qn en chair à pâté.

mince-pie [′mins′pai], *s.* *Cu:* Tartelette *f* contenant du *mincemeat.*

mincer [′minsər], *s.* *Dom.Ec:* Hachoir *m* (à viande, à légumes).

mind¹ [maind], *s.* **1.** (*Remembrance*) Souvenir *m*, mémoire *f.* **To bear, keep, sth. in m.,** (i) se souvenir de qch.; garder la mémoire de qch.; ne pas oublier qch.; (ii) tenir compte de qch. **Bear him in m.,** songez à lui. **Bear in m. that she is only a child,** n'oubliez pas que ce n'est qu'une enfant. **To bring, (re)call, sth. to s.o.'s m.,** rappeler qch. à la mémoire de qn. **To call sth. to m.,** évoquer le souvenir de qch. **To put s.o. in m. of s.o.,** rappeler qn a qn. **He puts me in m. of his father,** il me fait penser à son père. **To go, pass, out of m.,** tomber dans l'oubli. **It went out of my m.,** cela m'est sorti de l'esprit. **2.** (*a*) Pensée *f*, avis *m*, idée *f.* **To give s.o. a piece, a bit, of one's m.,** dire son fait, ses vérités, à qn. **To be of the same m. as s.o.,** être du même avis que qn. (*Of several pers.*) **To be of a m., of one m., of the same m.,** être du même avis; être d'accord. **To my m.,** à mon avis; pour moi. **It takes my m. off my work,** (i) cela me change les idées; (ii) cela me dérange quand je travaille. **Nothing is farther from my m.,** rien n'est plus éloigné de mes intentions. (*b*) **To know one's own m.,** savoir ce qu'on veut. **To make up ore's m.,** prendre (un) parti; se décider. **To make up one's m. to do sth.,** se décider, se résoudre, à faire qch. **To make up one's m. about sth.,** prendre une décision au sujet de qch. **To make up one's m. to sth.,** (i) se résigner à qch.; (ii) décider en faveur de qch. **She couldn't make up her m. what to choose,** elle ne pouvait se décider à choisir. **To be in two minds about sth.,** about doing sth., être indécis sur qch., pour faire qch., quant au parti à prendre. **To speak one's m.,** dire ce qu'on pense. **To change, alter, one's m.,** changer d'avis; se raviser. **I have a m., a good m., to . . .,** j'ai (grande) envie, j'ai bien envie, de . . . **To have half a m. to do sth.,** avoir presque envie de faire qch. **To have no m. to do sth.,** n'avoir aucun désir de faire qch. *O:* **Those who have a m. can go,** ceux qui le désirent peuvent y aller. (*c*) **To let one's m. run upon sth.,** songer à qch. **To set one's m. on sth.,** désirer qch. ardemment, tenir à qch. **To have set one's m. on doing sth.,** avoir à cœur de faire qch. **His m. turned to . . .,** il se mit à songer à . . . **To give one's m. to sth.,** s'adonner, s'appliquer, à qch. **To give one's whole m. to sth.,** appliquer toute son attention à qch. **To keep one's m. on sth.,** se concentrer sur qch. **To bring one's m. to bear on sth.,** porter son attention sur qch. **To have sth. in m.,** avoir qch. en vue. **To find sth. to one's m.,** trouver qch. à

son goût, à son gré. **3.** Esprit *m*, âme *f.* **State of m.,** état *m* d'âme. **Turn of m.,** tour *m* d'esprit, mentalité *f* (de qn). **He was not in a state of m. to . . .,** (i) il n'était pas disposé à . . .; (ii) il n'était pas en état de. . . . **Peace of m.,** tranquillité *f* d'esprit. **To disturb s.o.'s peace of m.,** troubler l'esprit de qn. **4.** (*a*) *Phil: Psy:* (*Opposed to body*) Ame; (*opposed to matter*) esprit; (*opposed to emotions*) intelligence *f.* (*b*) Esprit, idée. **It comes to my m. that . . .,** l'idée me vient que . . ., il me vient l'idée que . . ., il me vient à l'esprit que. . . . **She has something on her m.,** elle a quelque chose qui la préoccupe. **To take s.o.'s m. off his sorrow,** distraire qn de son chagrin. **To be easy, uneasy, in one's m.,** avoir, ne pas avoir, l'esprit tranquille. **To set one's m. to sth.,** réfléchir à qch. **To turn one's m. to a study,** s'appliquer à une étude. **That is a weight off my m.,** voilà qui me soulage l'esprit, c'est un souci de moins. **To get an idea fixed in one's m.,** se mettre qch. dans la tête, en tête. **Put it out of your m.,** n'y pensez plus. **I can't get that out of his m.,** je ne peux pas lui ôter cela de l'idée. (*c*) **A noble m.,** une belle âme. *Prov:* **Great minds think alike,** les beaux esprits, les grands esprits, se rencontrent. **5.** **To be out of one's m.,** avoir perdu la raison, la tête; n'avoir plus sa raison. **To go out of one's m.,** perdre la raison. **To be in one's right m.,** avoir toute sa raison. **Of sound m.,** sound in m. sain d'esprit. **′mind-picture,** *s.* Représentation mentale. **′mind-reader,** *s.* Liseur *m* de pensée. **′mind-reading,** *s.* Lecture *f* de pensée.

mind², *v.tr.* **1.** Faire attention, prêter (son) attention à (qn, qch.). **Never m. him,** ne faites pas attention à lui. **Never m. that,** qu'à cela ne tienne. **Never m. the money!** ne regardez pas à l'argent! **Never m. the rest,** je vous tiens quitte du reste. **M. my words!** écoutez bien ce que je vous dis! **M. you!** remarquez bien! **2.** S'occuper de, se mêler de (qch.). **M. your own business!** occupez-vous, mêlez-vous, de ce qui vous regarde! **3.** (*a*) **Would you m. shutting the door?** voudriez-vous bien fermer la porte? **Do you m. coming?** cela vous est-il égal de venir? **D'you m. if I open the window?** ça ne vous fait rien que j'ouvre la fenêtre? **You don't m. my keeping you waiting?** cela ne vous ennuie pas que je vous fasse attendre? **You don't m. my smoking?** la fumée ne vous gêne pas? **You don't m. my mentioning it?** cela ne vous froisse pas que je vous le dise? **If you don't m.,** si cela ne vous fait rien. **I don't m. trying,** je veux bien essayer. **I shouldn't m. that,** cela ne me déplairait pas. *F:* **I shouldn't m. a cup of tea,** je prendrais volontiers une tasse de thé. *P:* **A glass of wine?—I don't m.,** un verre de vin?—Ce n'est pas de refus. (*b*) **Don't m. them,** ne vous inquiétez pas d'eux. **Never m. the consequences!** ne vous souciez pas des conséquences! **Never m.!** (i) n'importe! peu importe! tant pis! (ii) ne vous inquiétez pas! **I don't m. what people say,** je me moque du qu'en-dira-t-on. **Who minds what he says?** qui s'occupe de ce qu'il dit? **I don't m. the cold,** le froid ne me gêne pas. **He doesn't m. expense,** il ne regarde pas à la dépense. **I don't m.,** cela m'est égal; peu (m')importe. **4.** **M. you're not late!** ayez soin de ne pas être en retard. **M. you write to him!** ne manquez pas de lui écrire! **M. what you're doing!** prenez garde à ce que vous faites! **M. your language!** surveillez votre langage! **M. you don't fall!** prenez garde de tomber! **M. the step!** attention à la marche! **M. yourself!** méfiez-vous! ayez l'œil! **M. your backs!** dégagez! **5.** Soigner, avoir l'œil sur (des enfants); garder (des animaux, etc.). **To m. the house, the shop, the door,** garder la maison; garder, tenir, la boutique.

minded [′maindid], *a.* **1.** (*a*) Disposé, enclin (to do sth., à faire qch.). **If you are so m.,** si le cœur vous en dit. (*b*) (*With advs.*) **Commercially m.,** à l'esprit commerçant. **2.** (*With sb. or adj. prefixed, e.g.*) **Feeble-, healthy-m.,** à l'esprit faible, sain. **The book-m. public,** le public liseur.

-mindedness [′maindidnis], *s.* **Strong-m.,** force *f* de caractère. **Narrow-m.,** étroitesse *f* de vues, d'esprit.

minder [′maindər], *s.* (*a*) Gardeur, -euse (de bestiaux); surveillant, -ante (d'enfants). (*b*) *Ind:* = MACHINE-MINDER.

mindful ['maindful], *a. O:* Attentif (of one's health, à sa santé); soigneux (*of*, de). **To be m. of one's good name**, soigner sa réputation. **He is always m. of others**, il pense toujours aux autres.

mindless ['maindlis], *a. O:* (*a*) Insouciant (of, de); indifférent (of, à). (*b*) Oublieux (of, de).

mine¹ [main], *s.* **1.** Mine *f* (de houille, d'or). **A m. of information**, une mine, un trésor, d'informations. **2.** *Mil:* Mine. **To spring, touch off, a m.**, faire jouer une mine. *Navy:* **Ground m.**, mine de fond; **mine dormante. Contact m.**, mine vigilante. **Floating m.**, mine flottante. **To lay a m.**, poser, mouiller, une mine. **M. clearance**, déminage *m.* **M. clearance squad**, équipe *f* de démineurs. **To clear (a field) of mines**, déminer (un champ). **'mine-detector**, *s. Mil: Navy:* Détecteur *m* de mines. **'mine-layer**, *s.* **'mine-laying**, *s. Navy:* Poseur *m*, mouilleur *m*, de mines. **'mine-laying**, *s. Navy:* Pose *f*, mouillage *m*, de mines. **'mine-shaft**, *s. Min:* Puits *m* de mine. **'mine-sweeper**, *s. Navy:* Dragueur *m* de mines. **'mine-thrower**, *s. Mil:* Lance-mines *m inv*, mortier *m* de tranchée.

mine², *v.tr. & i.* **1.** (*a*) **To m. (under) the earth**, fouiller (sous) la terre, creuser la terre. (*b*) *Mil:* Miner, saper (une muraille). (*c*) *Mil: Navy:* Miner, semer des mines dans, un port, un champ. **2.** *Min:* **To m. (for) coal**, exploiter, extraire, le charbon. **mining**, *s.* **1.** *Mil:* Sape *f.* **2.** *Mil: Navy:* Pose *f* de mines. **3.** *Min:* Exploitation minière, des mines; l'industrie minière. **M. village**, village minier. **M. engineer**, ingénieur *m* des mines.

mine³. 1. *poss.pron.* Le mien, la mienne, les miens, les miennes. **Your country and m.**, votre patrie et la mienne. **This letter is m.**, (i) cette lettre est à moi, m'appartient; (ii) cette lettre est de moi. **A friend of m.**, un(e) de mes ami(e)s; un(e) ami(e) à moi. **It is no business of m.**, ce n'est pas mon affaire. **No effort of m.**, aucun effort de ma part. **2.** *poss.a. A. & Poet:* Mon, *f.* ma, *pl.* mes.

minefield ['mainfi:ld], *s. Mil: Navy:* Champ *m* de mines.

miner ['mainər], *s.* (*a*) *Min:* (Ouvrier *m*) mineur *m*; ouvrier du fond. (*b*) *Mil:* Mineur, sapeur *m.*

mineral ['minərəl]. **1.** *a.* Minéral, -aux. **The m. kingdom**, le règne minéral. **M. waters**, (i) eaux minérales; (ii) (*also s.pl. F:* **minerals**) boissons gazeuses. **M. spring**, source minérale. **2.** *s.* (*a*) Minéral *m.* (*b*) *Min:* Minerai *m*; (*in coal-mining*) charbon *m*, houille *f.* **M. rights**, droits miniers.

mineralogical [minərəl'lɔdʒik(ə)l], *a.* Minéralogique.

mineralogist [minə'rælədʒist], *s.* Minéralogiste *m.*

mineralogy [minə'rælədʒi], *s.* Minéralogie *f.*

mingle ['miŋgl]. **1.** *v.tr.* Mêler, mélanger. **2.** *v.i.* (*a*) Se mêler, se mélanger, se confondre (with, avec). (*b*) **To m. with the crowd**, se mêler à, dans, la foule.

mini– [mini-], *a.* Mini–. **M.-skirt**, mini-jupe *f.*

miniature ['mini(ə)tʃər]. **1.** *s.* Miniature *f.* **To paint in m.**, peindre en miniature. **A Niagara in m.**, un Niagara en miniature, en petit. **M. painter**, peintre *m* de miniatures; miniaturiste *mf.* **2.** *a.* En miniature, en raccourci. (*a*) **A m. edition of a book**, une édition minuscule d'un livre. *Phot:* **M. camera**, appareil *m* de petit format. (*b*) *Ind:* **M. model**, maquette *f.*

miniaturist ['miniətjuərist], *s.* Miniaturiste *mf.*

minim ['minim], *s.* **1.** *Mus:* Blanche *f.* **2.** *Meas:* Goutte.

minimal ['miniməl], *a.* Minimal, -aux.

minimize ['minimaiz], *v.tr.* Réduire au minimum; minimiser.

minimum, *pl.* -a ['miniməm, -ə]. **1.** *s.* Minimum *m*, *pl.* minimums, minima. **To reduce sth. to a m.**, réduire qch. au minimum. **M. thermometer**, thermomètre à minima. **2.** *a.* Minimum, *f. occ.* minima. **M. price**, prix minimum. *Mth:* **M. value**, valeur minima.

minion ['minjən], *s.* **1.** *A:* Favori, -ite. **2.** *F: Iron:* Subordonné, -ée; domestique *mf.*

minister¹ ['ministər], *s.* **1.** *Adm:* Ministre *m.* **2.** *Ecc:* (*a*) Ministre, pasteur *m* (d'un culte réformé). (*b*) R.C.Ch: Ministre (des Jésuites). **M. general**, Ministre général.

minister², *v.i.* (*a*) **To m. to s.o., to s.o.'s needs**, soigner qn, pourvoir, subvenir, aux besoins de qn. (*b*) *Ecc:* **To m. to a parish**, desservir une paroisse. **ministering¹**, *a.* (Ange, etc.) secourable. **ministering²**, *s.* Soins *mpl*, service *m* (to, de).

ministerial [minis'tiəriəl], *a.* **1.** Exécutif. **2.** Accessoire, subsidiaire. **To be m. to ...**, contribuer à ...; aider à ... **3.** *Ecc:* (*Of duties, life, etc.*) De ministre; sacerdotal, -aux. **4.** *Pol:* Ministériel; gouvernemental, -aux; du Gouvernement.

ministration [minis'treiʃ(ə)n], *s.* **1.** Service *m*; ministère *m*, soins *mpl.* **2.** *Ecc:* **To go about one's ministrations**, vaquer à son ministère. **To receive the ministrations of a priest**, être administré par un prêtre.

ministry ['ministri], *s.* **1.** (*a*) *Pol:* Ministère *m*, gouvernement *m.* (*b*) *Adm:* Ministère, département *m.* **The Air M.**, le Ministère de l'Air. **2.** *Ecc:* **The m.**, le saint ministère. **He was intended for the m.**, il fut destiné à l'Église. **3.** Ministère, entremise *f* (of, de).

mink [miŋk], *s. Z:* Vison *m.*

minnow ['minou], *s. Ich:* Vairon *m.*

minor ['mainər]. **1.** *a.* (*a*) (*Lesser*) Petit, mineur. **M. planets**, petites planètes. *Ecc:* **M. orders**, ordres mineurs. (*b*) Petit, menu, peu important. **M. poet**, petit poète; poète mineur. **Of m. interest**, d'intérêt secondaire. **To play a m. part**, jouer un rôle subalterne, accessoire. *Med:* **M. operation**, opération bénigne, petite opération. (*c*) *Log:* **M. term**, *s.* **minor**, petit terme; mineure *f.* (*d*) *Mus:* **M. scale**, gamme mineure. **In the m.** (key), en mineur. **In A m.**, en la mineur. (*e*) *Sch:* **Jones m.**, le plus jeune des deux Jones. **2.** *s. Jur:* Mineur, -eure.

Minorca [mi'nɔ:kə]. *Pr.n. Geog:* Minorque *f.*

minority [mi'nɔriti, mai-], *s.* **1.** Minorité *f.* **To be in a m.**, **in the m.**, être en minorité. **To be in a m. of one**, être seul de son opinion. *attrib.* **M. party**, parti *m* minoritaire. **2.** *Jur:* Minorité (d'âge).

minster ['minstər], *s.* **1.** Cathédrale *f.* **2.** Église abbatiale.

minstrel ['minstrəl], *s.* **1.** (*a*) *Hist:* Ménestrel *m.* (*b*) Poète *m*, musicien *m*, chanteur *m.* **2. Nigger minstrels**, troupe *f* de chanteurs et de comiques déguisés en nègres.

minstrelsy ['minstrəlsi], *s.Coll:* Chants *mpl* (d'une nation).

mint¹ [mint], *s.* **1.** **The M.** = (l'Hôtel *m* de) la Monnaie. **Fresh from the m.**, tout battant neuf. (*Of medal, stamp, book, etc.*) **In m. state**, **in m. condition**, à l'état (de) neuf. *F:* **To be worth a m. of money**, (i) (*of pers.*) rouler sur l'or; (ii) (*of thg*) valoir une somme fabuleuse. **It costs a m. of money**, cela coûte les yeux de la tête. **2.** Source *f*, origine *f.*

mint², *v.tr.* **1.** (*a*) **To m. money**, (i) frapper de la monnaie, battre monnaie; (ii) *F:* amasser de l'argent à la pelle. (*b*) Monnayer (de l'or, etc.). **2.** Inventer, forger, fabriquer (un mot, une expression). **'minting-press**, *s.* Presse *f* monétaire.

mint³, *s. Bot:* Menthe *f.* **'mint-'sauce**, *s. Cu:* Vinaigrette *f* à la menthe.

minuet [minju(:)'et], *s. Danc:* Menuet *m.*

minus ['mainəs]. **1.** *prep.* Moins. **Ten m. eight leaves two**, dix moins huit égale deux. *F:* **I got out of it m. one eye**, je m'en tirai avec un œil en moins. **Bond m. its coupons**, titre démuni de coupons. **2.** *a. Mth:* **M. sign**, *s.* **minus**, moins *m.* **M. quantity**, quantité négative.

minuscule ['minəskju:l]. **1.** *a.* Minuscule. **2.** *s. Pal:* Minuscule *f.*

minute¹ ['minit], *s.* **1.** (*a*) Minute *f* (de temps). **Ten minutes to three, ten minutes past three**, trois heures moins dix; trois heures dix. (*b*) **A m.'s rest**, un moment de repos. **Wait a m.!** attendez un instant! **He has come in this (very) m.**, il rentre à l'instant (même); il vient (tout juste) de rentrer. **He was here a m. ago**, il sort d'ici. **I'll come in a m.**, j'arrive(rai) dans un instant. **I shan't be a m.**, j'en ai pour une seconde; je ne ferai qu'aller et (re)venir. **I haven't a free m.**, je n'ai pas une minute à moi. **On the m.**, to **the m.**, ponctuel, exact. **He appeared at nine to the m.**, *F:* il est arrivé à neuf heures tapant. **I expect him any m.**, je l'attends d'un moment à l'autre. **I'll send him to you the m. (that) he arrives**, je vous l'enverrai dès qu'il arrivera. **2.** *Geom: Astr:* Minute (de degré). **3.** Minute, projet *m* (d'un contrat, etc.). **4.** (*a*) Note *f.* **To make a m. of sth.**, prendre note de qch.; faire la minute (d'une transaction, etc.). (*b*) *pl.* **Minutes of a meeting**, procès-verbal *m* d'une séance. (*c*) **Treasury m.**, communiqué *m* de la Trésorerie. **'minute-book**, *s.* Registre *m* des procès-verbaux; registre des délibérations. **'minute-hand**, *s.* Grande aiguille (d'horloge, etc.).

minute², *v.tr.* (a) Faire la minute de, minuter (un contrat, etc.). (b) To m. (the proceedings of) a meeting, dresser le procès-verbal, le compte rendu, d'une séance.

minute³ [mai'nju:t], *a.* 1. (a) Tout petit; menu, minuscule, minime. (b) **The minutest particulars,** les moindres détails. 2. Minutieux, -euse; (compte rendu) détaillé. **-ly,** *adv.* Minutieusement; en détail; dans les moindres détails.

minuteness [mai'nju:tnis], *s.* 1. Petitesse *f*, exiguïté *f*. 2. Minutie *f*; exactitude minutieuse.

minx [miŋks], *s.f.* Friponne, coquine; petite espiègle.

mirabelle ['mirəbel], *s. Hort:* M. **(plum),** mirabelle *f*.

miracle ['mirəkl], *s.* 1. (a) Miracle *m*. **By a m.,** par miracle. (b) Miracle, prodige *m*. **It is a m. that . . .,** c'est (un) miracle que + *sub.* 2. *Lit.Hist:* M. **play,** miracle.

miraculous [mi'rækjələs], *a.* (a) Miraculeux, -euse. (b) Extraordinaire, merveilleux. **-ly,** *adv.* Miraculeusement; par miracle.

mirador ['mirədɔ:r], *s.* Mirador *m*.

mirage ['mirɑ:ʒ], *s.* Mirage *m*.

mire ['maiər], *s.* (a) Bourbier *m*; fondrière *f*. (b) Boue *f*, bourbe *f*, fange *f*; (river deposit) vase *f*. **To sink into the m.,** (i) s'enfoncer dans la boue; s'embourber; (ii) s'avilir; (iii) se mettre dans le pétrin. **To drag s.o.'s name into the m.,** traîner qn dans la boue.

mirror¹ ['mirər], *s.* Miroir *m*, glace *f*. **Hand m.,** glace à main. **Distorting m.,** miroir déformant. *Aut:* **Driving m.,** *U.S:* **rearview, rearvision** *m.,* rétroviseur *m*. **M. maker,** miroitier *m*.

mirror², *v.tr.* Refléter. **To be mirrored,** se mirer, se refléter.

mirth [mə:θ], *s.* Gaieté *f*, allégresse *f*; hilarité *f*.

mirthful ['mə:θful], *a.* 1. Gai, joyeux. 2. Amusant, désopilant.

mirthless ['mə:θlis], *a.* Sans gaieté; triste. **-ly,** *adv.* Sans gaieté; tristement.

miry ['maiəri], *a.* Fangeux, -euse, bourbeux, -euse, vaseux, -euse.

misadventure [,misəd'ventʃər], *s.* Mésaventure *f*; contretemps *m*.

misalliance [,misə'laiəns], *s.* Mésalliance *f*.

misanthrope ['misənθroup, 'miz-], *s.* Misanthrope *mf*.

misanthropic [,misən'θrɔpik, miz-], *a.* (Personne) misanthrope; (humeur) misanthropique.

misanthropist [mi'sænθrəpist, mi'zæn-], *s.* Misanthrope *mf*.

misanthropy [mi'sænθrəpi, mi'zæn-], *s.* Misanthropie *f*.

misapplication [,misæpli'keiʃ(ə)n], *s.* 1. Mauvaise application, mauvais usage (d'un mot, etc.). 2. Détournement *m* (de fonds).

misapply [,misə'plai], *v.tr.* 1. Mal appliquer (qch.); appliquer (qch.) mal à propos. 2. Détourner (des fonds).

misapprehend [,misæpri'hend], *v.tr.* Mal comprendre; se méprendre sur (les paroles de qn).

misapprehension [,misæpri'henʃ(ə)n], *s.* Malentendu *m*, méprise *f*; idée fausse (des faits). **To do sth. under a m.,** faire qch. par méprise.

misappropriate [,misə'prouprieit], *v.tr.* Détourner, distraire (des fonds).

misappropriation [,misəproupri'eiʃ(ə)n], *s.* Détournement *m*, déprédation *f* (de fonds); *Jur:* abus *m* de confiance.

misbecome [,misbi'kʌm], *v.tr. O:* (Conj. like BECOME) Messeoir à (qn). **misbecoming,** *a.* Malséant.

misbegotten [,misbi'gɔtn], *a.* 1. (Enfant) illégitime, bâtard. 2. *F:* Vil, misérable; (projet) biscornu.

misbehave [,misbi'heiv], *v.i. & pr.* **To m. (oneself),** se mal conduire.

misbehaviour [,misbi'heivjər], *s.* Mauvaise conduite; inconduite *f*; écart *m* de conduite.

misbelief [,misbi'li:f], *s.* (a) *Theol:* Fausse croyance. (b) Opinion erronée.

miscalculate [,mis'kælkjuleit], 1. *v.tr.* Mal calculer (une somme, etc.). 2. *v.i.* **To m. about sth.,** se tromper sur qch.

miscalculation [,mis,kælkju'leiʃ(ə)n], *s.* Faux calcul; erreur *f* de calcul; mécompte *m*.

miscall [mis'kɔ:l], *v.tr.* Mal nommer; attribuer un faux nom à (qn).

miscarriage [mis'kæridʒ], *s.* 1. Égarement *m*, perte *f* (d'une lettre). 2. (a) Avortement *m*, insuccès *m* (d'un projet). (b) *Jur:* M. **of justice,** erreur *f* judiciaire. 3. *Med:* Fausse couche.

miscarry [mis'kæri], *v.i.* 1. (Of letter) (i) S'égarer; (ii) parvenir à une fausse adresse. 2. (Of scheme) Avorter, échouer; manquer, rater, mal tourner. 3. *Med:* Faire une fausse couche.

miscellaneous [,misə'leiniəs], *a.* Varié, mêlé, mélangé, divers. **-ly,** *adv.* Avec variété; diversement; de diverses façons.

miscellaneousness [,misə'leiniəsnis], *s.* Variété *f*, diversité *f*.

miscellany [mi'seləni], *s.* 1. Mélange *m*; collection *f* d'objets variés. 2. *Lit:* (a) *pl.* **Miscellanies,** miscellanées *f*, mélanges *m*. (b) Mélange, recueil *m*.

mischance [mis'tʃɑ:ns], *s.* 1. Mauvaise chance; malchance *f*. 2. Malheur *m*, mésaventure *f*, accident *m*.

mischief ['mistʃif], *s.* 1. Mal *m*, tort *m*, dommage *m*, dégât(s) *m(pl)*. **To do s.o. a m.,** faire du mal ou du tort à qn; porter un mauvais coup à qn. **To mean m.,** chercher à nuire; méditer un mauvais coup; avoir de mauvaises intentions. **To make m.,** apporter le trouble; semer la discorde. **To make m. between two people,** brouiller deux personnes. 2. Malice *f*. **Out of pure m.,** par pure malice; (i) par pure espièglerie; (ii) par pure méchanceté. (Of child) **He is always getting into m.,** il est toujours à faire des siennes. **To keep s.o. out of m.,** empêcher qn de faire des sottises, des bêtises. **He is up to (some) m.,** (i) il médite une malice; (ii) il médite quelque mauvais tour, un mauvais coup. 3. (*Pers.*) Fripon, -onne; malin, -igne. **Little m.,** petit(e) espiègle, petit(e) coquin(e). **'mischief-maker,** *s.* Brandon *m* de discorde; mauvaise langue; trouble-ménage *m inv.*

mischievous ['mistʃivəs], *a.* 1. Méchant, malfaisant; (of thg) mauvais, nuisible, pernicieux. 2. (Enfant) espiègle, malicieux. **As m. as a monkey,** malin comme un singe. **-ly,** *adv.* 1. (a) Méchamment; par malveillance. (b) Nuisiblement. 2. Malicieusement; par espièglerie.

mischievousness ['mistʃivəsnis], *s.* 1. (a) Méchanceté *f*. (b) Nature *f* nuisible (de qch.). 2. Malice *f*, espièglerie *f*.

miscibility [,misi'biliti], *s.* Miscibilité *f*.

misconception ['miskən'sepʃ(ə)n], *s.* 1. Idée fausse. 2. Malentendu *m*.

misconduct¹ [mis'kɔndʌkt], *s.* 1. Mauvaise administration, mauvaise gestion (d'une affaire). 2. (Of pers.) Mauvaise conduite; inconduite *f*.

misconduct² [,miskən'dʌkt], *v.tr.* 1. Mal diriger, mal gérer (une affaire). 2. *O:* **To m. oneself,** se mal conduire.

misconstruction [,miskən'strʌkʃ(ə)n], *s.* Fausse, mauvaise, interprétation.

misconstrue [miskən'stru:], *v.tr.* Mal interpréter (qch.); prendre (qch.); prendre (qch.) à rebours. **You have misconstrued my words,** vous avez mal pris mes paroles.

miscopy ['mis'kɔpi], *v.tr.* Copier de travers.

miscount¹ [mis'kaunt], *s.* Erreur *f* d'addition; *Pol:* erreur dans le dépouillement du scrutin.

miscount², *v.tr.* Mal compter.

miscreant ['miskriənt], *s.* (a) Scélérat *m*, misérable *m*, gredin *m*. (b) Mécréant *m*, infidèle *m*.

mis-cue [mis'kju:], *v.i. Bill:* Faire fausse queue.

misdate ['mis'deit], *v.tr.* Mal dater (une lettre). **misdating,** *s.* Erreur *f* de date.

misdeal¹ [mis'di:l], *s. Cards:* Maldonne *f*.

misdeal², *v.tr.* **(misdealt** [mis'delt]) *Cards:* **To m. the cards,** *abs.* **to m.,** faire maldonne, maldonner.

misdeed [mis'di:d], *s.* Méfait *m*.

misdemeanant [,misdi'mi:nənt], *s. Jur:* Délinquant, -ante.

misdemeanour [,misdi'mi:nər], *s.* 1. *Jur:* Délit *m*, *F:* contravention *f*. 2. Écart *m* de conduite; méfait *m*.

misdirect ['misdi'rekt], *v.tr.* 1. Mal adresser (une lettre). 2. Mal diriger (un coup); nval viser avec (un revolver, etc.). 3. Mal diriger (une entreprise, etc.). 4. Mal renseigner (qn), mettre (qn) sur la mauvaise voie. 5. *Jur:* (Of judge) Mal instruire (le jury).

misdirection ['misdi'rekʃ(ə)n], s. 1. (On letter) Erreur f d'adresse; fausse adresse. 2. Indication erronée; renseignement erroné.
misdoing [mis'du(:)iŋ], s. Méfait m, faute f.
miser ['maizər], s. Avare mf.
miserable ['miz(ə)rəbl], a. 1. (Of pers.) Malheureux, triste. To make s.o.'s life m., rendre, faire, la vie dure à qn. 2. Misérable, déplorable. What m. weather! quel temps abominable! 3. Misérable, pauvre, piteux, -euse. M. pay, salaire dérisoire. -ably, adv. Misérablement. (a) Malheureusement, lamentablement. (b) Piètrement, pauvrement.
miserliness ['maizəlinis], s. Avarice f.
miserly ['maizəli], a. 1. (Of pers.) Avare, pingre, ladre. 2. (Of habits, etc.) Sordide.
misery ['mizəri], s. 1. Souffrance(s) f (pl), supplice m. To put an animal out of its m., achever un animal. 2. Misère f; détresse f.
misfire¹ [mis'faiər], s. (a) Sm.a: Artil: Raté m. (b) I.C.E: Raté d'allumage.
misfire², v.i. (a) (Of gun) Rater; faire long feu. (b) I.C.E: (Of engine) Avoir des ratés. (c) (Of joke, etc.) Manquer son effet, tomber à plat. The plan misfired, le projet a échoué.
misfit ['mis'fit, 'misfit], s. Vêtement manqué, mal réussi. Com: Laissé-pour-compte m. The (social) misfits, les inadapté(e)s.
misfortune [mis'fɔ:tʃ(ə)n], s. Infortune f, malheur m, calamité f. It is more his m. than his fault, il est plus à plaindre qu'à blâmer. Misfortunes never come singly, un malheur ne vient jamais seul.
misgive [mis'giv], v.tr. (misgave [mis'geiv]; misgiven [mis'givn]) My heart, my mind, misgives me, j'ai des inquiétudes. **misgiving**, s. Doute m, crainte f; pressentiment m. Not without misgivings, non sans hésitation.
misgovern [mis'gʌvən], v.tr. Mal gouverner.
misgovernment ['mis'gʌvənmənt], s. Mauvais gouvernement; mauvaise administration.
misguided [mis'gaidid], a. 1. (Of pers.) Dont l'enthousiasme porte à faux; qui se fourvoie. These m. people . . ., ces malheureux. . . . 2. (Of conduct) Peu judicieux, (of zeal) hors de propos; (of attempt) malencontreux. -ly, adv. Sans jugement.
mishandle [mis'hændl], v.tr. Malmener, maltraiter (qn); mal traiter, mal conduire (des affaires).
mishap ['mishæp], s. Mésaventure f, contretemps m.
misinform ['misin'fɔ:m], v.tr. Mal renseigner.
misinformation ['mis‚infə'meiʃ(ə)n], s. Faux renseignement(s).
misinterpret ['misin'tə:prit], v.tr. Mal interpréter.
misinterpretation ['misin‚tə:pri'teiʃ(ə)n], s. 1. Fausse interprétation. 2. (In translating) Contresens m.
misjudge ['mis'dʒʌdʒ], v.tr. Mal juger; se tromper sur le compte de (qn); méconnaître (qn). **misjudged**, a. (Of person) Mal compris.
misjudg(e)ment ['mis'dʒʌdʒmənt], s. Jugement erroné.
mislay [mis'lei], v.tr. (mislaid [mis'leid]; mislaid) Égarer (un parapluie, etc.).
mislead [mis'li:d], v.tr. (misled [mis'led]; misled) (a) Induire (qn) en erreur; tromper (qn). (b) Égarer, fourvoyer (qn). **misleading**, a. Trompeur, -euse; fallacieux, -euse.
mismanage ['mis'mænidʒ], v.tr. Mal conduire, mal administrer, mal gérer (une affaire).
mismanagement ['mis'mænidʒmənt], s. Mauvaise administration, mauvaise gestion.
misname ['mis'neim], v.tr. Mal nomraer; nommer improprement.
misnomer [mis'noumər], s. 1. Jur: Erreur f de nom. 2. Fausse appellation; nom mal approprié.
misogamist [mi'sogəmist], s. Misogame mf.
misogynist [mai'sodʒinist], s. Misogyne m.
misogyny [mai'sodʒini], s. Misogynie f.
misplace ['mis'pleis], v.tr. 1. Placer à faux (l'accent tonique, etc.). 2. Mal placer (sa confiance). 3. Déplacer (un livre, etc.). **misplaced**, a. 1. (Of confidence, etc.) Mal placé. 2. (Mot) déplacé; (observation) hors de propos.
misprint ['misprint], s. Faute f d'impression; erreur f typographique; F: coquille f.
mispronounce ['misprə'nauns], v.tr. Mal prononcer, estropier.

mispronunciation ['misprə‚nʌnsi'eiʃ(ə)n], s. Mauvaise prononciation, faute f de prononciation.
misquotation ['miskwo'teiʃ(ə)n], s. Citation inexacte.
misquote ['mis'kwout], v.tr. Citer (qch.) à faux, inexactement.
misread ['mis'ri:d], v.tr (misread ['mis'red]; misread) Mal lire, mal interpréter (un texte, etc.). To m. s.o.'s feelings, se tromper sur les sentiments de qn.
misrepresent ['mis‚repri'zent], v.tr. Mal représenter; dénaturer, travestir (les faits).
misrepresentation ['mis‚reprizen'teiʃ(ə)n], s. Faux rapport, présentation erronée des faits. Jur: (i) Fausse déclaration; (ii) réticence f.
misrule¹ ['mis'ru:l], s. Mauvaise administration; désordre m, confusion f.
misrule², v.tr. Mal gouverner.
miss¹ [mis], s. Coup manqué; coup perdu. Bill: Manque m à toucher. F: To give (s.o., sth) a m., passer le tour de (qn); négliger de voir, de visiter (un monument); ne pas assister (à une conférence).
miss², v.tr. 1. (a) Manquer, F: rater (le but). To m. one's mark, one's aim, manquer son coup, son but; frapper à faux, à vide. Abs. He never misses, il ne manque jamais son coup. To m. the point, ne pas comprendre. Bill: To m., manquer à toucher; manquer de touche. Th: (Of actor) To m. one's entrance, rater, louper, son entrée. To m. one's cue, perdre le fil. (b) To m. one's way, se tromper de route. He missed his footing, le pied lui manqua. (c) Ne pas trouver, ne pas rencontrer (qn). (d) Manquer, F: rater (un train). To m. the train by three minutes, manquer le train de trois minutes. (e) Manquer, laisser échapper, F: rater (une occasion). An opportunity not to be missed, une occasion à saisir. F: You haven't missed much! ce n'était pas bien intéressant, F: vous n'avez pas raté grand-chose. To m. the market, laisser échapper le moment favorable pour la vente. (f) Ne pas se voir décerner (une récompense). I missed my holiday this year, je n'ai pas eu de vacances cette année. (g) Manquer (une conférence, un rendez-vous); F: sécher (un cours). I never m. going there, je ne manque jamais d'y aller. (h) He narrowly missed, just missed, being killed, il a failli se faire tuer. (i) To m. a remark, a joke, ne pas saisir une observation, une plaisanterie, ((i) ne pas l'entendre; (ii) ne pas la comprendre). You can't m. the house, vous ne pouvez pas manquer de reconnaître la maison. 2. (Omit) To m. (out) a word, passer, sauter, un mot. (At dinner) To m. (out) the fish course, ne pas prendre de poisson. 3. (a) Remarquer l'absence de (qn, qch.). I missed my spectacles, je ne trouvais plus mes lunettes. It will never be missed, on ne se rendra jamais compte que ça manque. (b) Regretter (qn); regretter l'absence de (qn). I m. you, vous me manquez. They will m. one another, ils se manqueront. **missing**, a. Absent; perdu; disparu, manquant. One man is m., il manque un homme. s.pl. Mil: etc: The m., les disparus.
miss³, s.f. 1. M. Smith, pl. the Misses Smith, mademoiselle Smith, Mlle Smith; les demoiselles Smith; (on address) Mademoiselle Smith, Mesdemoiselles Smith. Thank you, M. Smith, merci, mademoiselle. 2. Com: (To child) What can I get you, m.? qu'y a-t-il pour votre service, mademoiselle? Yes, M.; three whiskeys, M., oui, mademoiselle; trois whiskys, mademoiselle.
missal ['mis(ə)l], s. Ecc: Missel m.
missel(-thrush) ['mis(ə)l(θrʌʃ)], s. Draine f.
misshapen ['mis'ʃeip(ə)n], a. Difforme, contrefait; (of hat, figure, etc.) déformé; (of building, mind) biscornu.
missile ['misail], s. Projectile m; engin m, fusée f (engin). Guided m., missile m, engin, téléguidé. Intermediate range ballistic m., missile balistique de moyenne portée. Ground-to-air m., projectile terre-à-avion. Air-to-ground m., projectile avion-à-terre.
mission ['miʃ(ə)n], s. Mission f. (a) To be sent on a m. to s.o., être envoyé en mission auprès de qn. (b) Ecc: Foreign missions, missions étrangères. M. (station), mission. (c) She thinks her m. in life is to help lame dogs, elle croit avoir mission de secourir les malheureux.

missionary ['miʃn(ə)ri]. **1.** *a.* (Prêtre) missionnaire; (société) de missionnaires. **The m. field,** les missions (étrangères). **2.** *s.* (*a*) Missionnaire *m.* (*b*) **Police-court m.** = assistante sociale auprès des tribunaux.
missis ['misiz], *s.f. P:* (*a*) I say, M.! eh dites donc, la petite mère! (*b*) **The m., my m.,** ma femme; *P:* ma légitime, la bourgeoise. **Your m.,** votre dame.
missive ['misiv], *s.* Lettre *f,* missive *f.*
misspell ['mis'spel], *v.tr.* (misspelt ['mis'spelt]; **mis-spelt**) Mal épeler, mal orthographier. **misspelling,** *s.* Faute *f* d'orthographe.
misspent ['mis'spent], *a.* **A m. youth,** (i) une jeunesse mal employée; (ii) une jeunesse passée dans la dissipation.
misstate ['mis'steit], *v.tr.* Rapporter (qch.) incorrectement; altérer (des faits).
misstatement ['mis'steitmənt], *s.* Rapport inexact; erreur *f* de fait.
missus ['misəs], *s.f. P:* = MISSIS.
missy ['misi], *s.f. P:* Mademoiselle.
mist[1] [mist], *s.* **1.** Brume *f.* **Scotch m.,** bruine *f,* crachin *m,* brouillasse *f.* **Lost in the mists of time,** perdu dans la nuit des temps. **2.** Buée *f* (sur une glace, etc.); voile *m* (devant les yeux). **To see things through a m.,** voir trouble.
mist[2]. **1.** *v.tr.* Couvrir (une glace, etc.) de buée. **2.** *v.i.* **To m. over,** (i) (*of landscape*) disparaître sous la brume; (ii) (*of windscreen*) se couvrir de buée.
mistakable [mis'teikəbl], *a.* Sujet à méprise; facile à confondre (for, avec).
mistake[1] [mis'teik], *s.* Erreur *f,* méprise *f,* faute *f.* **M. in calculating,** erreur de calcul. **Grammatical mistakes,** fautes de grammaire. **To make a m.,** faire une faute; être dans l'erreur; se méprendre, se tromper. **You made me make a m.,** vous m'avez fait tromper. **To make the m. of doing sth.,** avoir le tort de faire qch. **To do sth. by m.,** faire qch. par erreur. **To labour under a m.,** être dans l'erreur. **To acknowledge one's m.,** avouer (être dans) son tort. **There is some m.!** il y a erreur! **There is, can be, no m. about that,** il n'y a pas à s'y tromper, c'est bien le cas de le dire. **Let there be no m. about it;** make no m., que l'on ne s'y trompe pas. *F:* **I am unlucky and no m.!** décidément je n'ai pas de chance! **To take s.o.'s umbrella in m. for one's own,** se tromper de parapluie.
mistake[2], *v.tr.* (mistook [mis'tuk]; mistaken [mis'teik(ə)n]) **1.** Mal comprendre (les paroles de qn); se méprendre sur (les intentions de qn). **To m. the time, one's way,** se tromper d'heure, de route. **To m. the way,** faire fausse route. **There is no mistaking the facts,** il n'y a pas à se tromper à cet égard. **2. To m. s.o. for s.o.,** prendre qn pour qn. **mistaken,** *a.* **1.** (*Of pers.*) **To be mistaken,** se tromper; faire erreur. **If I am not m.,** si je ne m'abuse; sauf erreur. **That is just where you are m.!** c'est justement ce qui vous trompe. **2. M. opinion,** opinion erronée. **M. zeal,** zèle mal entendu, hors de propos. **3. M. identity,** erreur *f* sur la personne. **M. statement,** (i) déclaration mal comprise; (ii) déclaration erronée. **-ly,** *adv.* Par erreur.
mister ['mistər], *s.* **1.** (*Always abbreviated to* Mr) **Mr Smith,** monsieur Smith; **M. Smith;** (*on address*) Monsieur Smith. **Mr Chairman,** monsieur le président. **2.** *P:* **What's the time, mister?** quelle heure est-il, monsieur?
mistime ['mis'taim], *v.tr.* **1.** Faire (qch.) à contre-temps. **2.** Mal calculer (un coup).
mistiness ['mistinis], *s.* (*a*) État brumeux. (*b*) **Owing to the m. of the windscreen . . .,** à cause de la buée qui obscurcissait le pare-brise. . . .
mistletoe ['misltou], *s. Bot:* Gui *m.*
mistook. *See* MISTAKE[2].
mistranslate ['mistrɑːns'lei, -træns-], *v.tr.* Mal traduire.
mistranslation ['mistrɑːns'leiʃ(ə)n, -træns-], *s.* Traduction inexacte; erreur *f* de traduction; contresens *m inv.*
mistress ['mistris], *s.f.* **1.** (*a*) Maîtresse (qui exerce l'autorité). **To be one's own m.,** être indépendante. **To be m. of oneself,** être maîtresse de soi; avoir de l'empire sur soi. **She is m. of her subject,** elle possède son sujet à fond. (*b*) **M. of a household,** maîtresse de maison. *O:* (*To servant*) **Is your m. at home?** madame

y est-elle? **The m. is not at home,** madame n'y est pas. (*c*) *Com:* Patronne. (*d*) Institutrice, maîtresse (d'école primaire); professeur *m* (de lycée). **The French m.,** le professeur de français. **Kindergarten m.,** jardinière *f* d'enfants. **2.** Maîtresse, amante. **Kept m.,** femme entretenue. **3.** (*In titles*) (*a*) *A:* **M. Quickly, Madame Quickly.** (*b*) (*Now always* Mrs ['misiz]) **Mrs Smith, Madame Smith,** Mme Smith,
mistrust[1] ['mis'trʌst], *s.* Méfiance, *f,* défiance *f* (of, in, de); soupçons *mpl* (of, in, à l'endroit de); manque *m* de confiance.
mistrust[2]. *v.tr.* Se méfier de (qn, qch.), ne pas avoir confiance en (qn).
mistrustful [mis'trʌstful], *a.* Méfiant, soupçonneux (of, à l'endroit de). **-fully,** *adv.* Avec méfiance.
misty ['misti], *a.* Brumeux, embrumé. **It is m.,** le temps est brumeux. **M. outlines,** contours vagues, flous. **M. eyes,** yeux voilés, embués, de larmes. **M. recollection,** souvenir vague, confus.
misunderstand ['misʌndə'stænd], *v.tr.* (misunderstood ['misʌndə'stud]; misunderstood) **1.** Mal comprendre; se méprendre sur (qch.); mal interpréter (une action). **If I have not misunderstood . . .,** si j'ai bien compris. **. . . We misunderstood each other,** il y a eu malentendu. **2.** Méconnaître (qn); se méprendre sur le compte de (qn). **misunderstood,** *a.* **1.** Mal compris. **2.** (*Of pers.*) Incompris. **misunderstanding,** *s.* **1.** Malentendu *m,* quiproquo *m.* **2.** Mésintelligence *f,* mésentente *f,* brouille *f.*
misuse[1] ['mis'juːs], *s.* Abus *m;* mauvais usage, mauvais emploi. **M. of authority,** abus d'autorité. **M. of words,** confusion *f* de mots. **Fraudulent m. of funds,** détournement *m* de fonds, abus *m* de confiance.
misuse[2] ['mis'juːz], *v.tr.* **1.** Faire (un) mauvais usage, (un) mauvais emploi, de (qch.); abuser de (son autorité). **To m. a word,** employer un mot incorrectement. **2.** Maltraiter, malmener (qn).
mite [mait], *s.* **1.** (*a*) **The widow's m.,** le denier de la veuve. *O:* **To offer one's m.,** donner son obole. (*b*) **There's not a m. left,** il n'en reste plus une miette. **2.** Mioche *mf,* bambin, -ine. **Poor little m.!** pauvre petit! pauvre petite! **3.** *Arach:* Acarien *m;* mite *f.* **Cheese m.,** mite du fromage.
mitigate ['mitigeit], *v.tr.* **1.** Adoucir, atténuer (la souffrance, un mal); amoindrir (un mal); mitiger, atténuer (la sévérité d'une peine). **2.** Tempérer (la chaleur); adoucir (le froid). **3.** Atténuer (un crime, une faute). **Mitigating circumstances,** circonstances atténuantes.
mitigation [miti'geiʃ(ə)n], *s.* Adoucissement *m;* amoindrissement *m* (d'un mal); mitigation *f,* atténuation *f* (d'une peine). *Jur:* **Plea in m. of damages,** demande *f* en réduction de dommages-intérêts.
mitre[1] ['maitər], *s. Ecc:* Mitre *f.*
mitre[2], *s. Carp:* **1.** M.(-joint), (assemblage *m* à) onglet *m.* **2.** = MITRE SQUARE. **'mitre-block, -board, -box,** *s. Carp:* Boîte *f* à onglet(s). **'mitre-gear,** *s. Mec.E:* Engrenage *m* à onglet, à 45°. **'mitre square,** *s. Tls:* Équerre *f* (à) onglet. **'mitre-wheel,** *s. Mec.E:* Roue *f* d'angle, roue (dentée) conique.
mitre[3], *v.tr.* **1.** Tailler (une pièce) à onglet. *Bookb:* **To m. the fillets,** biseauter les filets. **2.** Assembler (deux pièces) à onglet.
mitred ['maitəd], *a.* **M. abbot,** abbé mitré.
mitt [mit], *s. P:* = MITTEN.
mitten ['mitn], *s.* **1.** *Cost:* (*a*) Mitaine *f.* (*b*) Moufle *f. F: O:* **To give a suitor the m.,** éconduire un soupirant. **To get the m.,** (i) être éconduit; (ii) (*of employee, etc.*) recevoir son congé, *F:* être saqué. **2.** *pl. Box: F:* **The mittens,** les gants, *F:* les mitaines.
mix [miks]. **1.** *v.tr.* (*a*) Mêler, mélanger; allier (des métaux) (*b*) Préparer, composer (un breuvage, etc.). (*c*) Brasser (des billets de loterie, etc.); malaxer (le mortier, etc.). **To m. the salad,** retourner, *F:* fatiguer, la salade. (*d*) Confondre (des faits). **2.** *v.i.* Se mêler, se mélanger (with, à, avec); (*of fluids*) s'allier. (*Of colours, etc.*) **To m. well,** aller bien ensemble. **To m. in society, with people,** fréquenter la société, les gens. **mix up,** *v.tr.* **1.** Mêler, mélanger; embrouiller (ses papiers, etc.). **2.** I was mixing you up with your brother, je vous confondais avec votre frère. **3.** To

be **mixed up in an affair,** être mêlé à une affaire.
4. Embrouiller (qn). **I was getting all mixed up,** je ne savais plus où j'en étais. **'mix-up,** s. 1. Confusion f, embrouillement m; emmêlement m, F: embrouillamini m, pagaille f. 2. F: Bagarre f. **mixed,** a. 1. Mêlé, mélangé, mixte. **M. sweets,** bonbons assortis. **M. ice, m. salad,** glace, salade, panachée. **M. company,** compagnie mêlée; milieu m hétéroclite. **Person of m. blood,** sang-mêlé mf inv. **M. marriage,** mariage mixte. **M. feelings,** sentiments mixtes, divers. **To act from m. motives,** agir pour des motifs complexes. Mth: **M. number,** nombre fractionnaire. S.a. METAPHOR. 2. **M. school,** école mixte. Ten: **M. double,** double m mixte. 3. (Of pers.) **To get m.,** s'embrouiller; perdre la tête. **mixing,** s. Mélange m, brassage m; Glassm: maclage m; Cin: F: mixage m. Ind: **M. mill,** broyeur m.
mixer ['miksər], s. 1. (Pers.) Cin: Opérateur m des sons. 2. (Machine) (a) Ind: Malaxeur m, agitateur m. Dom.Ec: (Electric) m., batteur m (électrique). (b) I.C.E: Diffuseur m. 3. **Good, bad, m.,** personne qui sait, qui ne sait pas, s'adapter à son entourage. **He's a good m.,** il est très sociable, il se lie facilement.
mixture ['mikstʃər], s. 1. Mélange m. 2. Pharm: Mixtion f, mixture f. 3. Mus: **M.-stop,** (jeu m de) fourniture f (d'un orgue).
miz(z)en ['mizn], s. Nau: Miz(z)en(-sail), artimon m. **'miz(z)en-mast,** s. Mât m d'artimon. **'miz(z)en-top'gallant,** attrib.a. **M.t. sail,** perruche f. **'miz(z)en-'topsail,** s. Perroquet m de fougue.
mnemonic [ni'mɔnik], a. Mnémonique.
mnemonics [ni'mɔniks], s.pl. Mnémonique f, mnémotechnie f.
mnemotechnic ['ni:mo'teknik], a. Mnémotechnique.
mo [mou], s. P: = MOMENT 1. **Half a mo!** une seconde!
moan[1] [moun], s. Gémissement m, plainte f.
moan[2]. 1. v.i. Gémir; pousser des gémissements; se lamenter; (of wind) gémir. 2. v.tr. Dire (qch.) en gémissant. **moaning,** s. Gémissement m.
moat [mout], s. Fossé m, douve f (de fortifications).
moated ['moutid], a. (Château) entouré d'un fossé, de fossés.
mob[1] [mɔb], s. 1. **The m.,** la populace; le bas peuple, P: le populo. **M. rule,** voyoucratie f. 2. Foule f, cohue f; bande f d'émeutiers. **To form a m., to gather into a m.,** s'ameuter. **The army had become a m.,** l'armée n'était plus qu'une cohue.
mob[2], v. (mobbed) 1. v.tr. (a) (Of angry crowd) Molester, attaquer, malmener (qn). (b) (Of admiring crowd) Assiéger (qn); faire foule autour de (qn). 2. v.i. S'attrouper; former un rassemblement.
mob-cap ['mɔbkæp], s. A.Cost: Charlotte f.
mobile ['moubail], a. 1. Mobile. 2. (Of pers., character) Changeant, versatile. 3. s. Art: Mobile m.
mobility [mo'biliti], s. Mobilité f; capacité f de marche.
mobilization [,moubilai'zeiʃ(ə)n], s. Mobilisation f (de troupes, de capitaux).
mobilize ['moubilaiz]. 1. v.tr. Mobiliser (des troupes, Pol.Ec: le capital). 2. v.i. (Of army) Entrer en mobilisation.
moccasin ['mɔkəsin, mə'kæsin], s. Mocassin m.
mocha[1] ['moukə], s. Pierre de f Moka; agate mousseuse.
mocha[2], s. (Café m) moka m. Cu: **M. (cake),** (gâteau m) moka.
mock[1] [mɔk], attrib.a. D'imitation; feint, contrefait; faux, f. fausse. **M. tortoise-shell,** écaille imitation. **M. modesty,** fausse modestie. **M. tragedy,** tragédie burlesque. **M. trial,** simulacre m de procès. **M. fight,** simulacre de combat; petite guerre. **mock-he'roic,** a. Héroï-comique; burlesque. **'mock 'turtle,** s. Cu: **M. t. soup,** consommé m (à la) fausse tortue; consommé à la tête de veau.
mock[2], s. **To make a m. of s.o.,** se moquer de qn; tourner qn en ridicule.
mock[3]. 1. v.tr. & i. **To m. (at) s.o., sth.,** se moquer de qn, de qch.; railler qn, qch. 2. v.tr. (a) Narguer (qn). (b) Se jouer de, tromper (qn). (c) Imiter, contrefaire, singer (qn, qch.). **mocking,**[1] a. 1. Moqueur, -euse, railleur, -euse, narquois. **M. irony,** ironie gouailleuse. 2. (Ton) d'imitation, de singerie. **-ly,** adv. D'un ton moqueur, railleur; par moquerie, par dérision. **'mocking-bird,** s. Orn: U.S: Moqueur m. **mocking,**[2] s. Moquerie f, raillerie f.

mocker ['mɔkər], s. Moqueur, -euse.
mockery ['mɔkəri], s. 1. Moquerie f, raillerie f. 2. Sujet m de moquerie, de raillerie; objet m de risée, de dérision. 3. Semblant m, simulacre m (of, de).
mock-up ['mɔk'ʌp], s. Ind: Maquette f (d'un avion, etc.).
modal ['moudl], a. Modal, -aux, Log: **M. proposition,** modale f.
modality [mou'dæliti], s. Modalité f.
mode [moud], s. 1. (Manner) Mode m, méthode f, manière f. **M. of life,** façon f de vivre; manière de vivre, train m de vie. 2. (Fashion) Mode f. 3. Mus: Mode m. **Major, minor, m.,** mode majeur, mineur. 4. Log: Phil: Mode m.
model[1] ['mɔdl], s. 1. (a) Modèle m. **To make a m. of a monument,** etc., faire la maquette d'un monument, etc. **Scale m.,** modèle réduit, à petite échelle. **Demonstration m.,** (i) maquette (pour l'enseignement); (ii) appareil m de démonstration. **M. maker,** modéliste m; maquettiste m & f. (b) N.Arch: Gabarit m. 2. (a) Art: **Drawn from the m.,** dessiné d'après le modèle. **Anatomical m.,** écorché m. (b) On the m. of s.o., à l'imitation de qn. **To take s.o. as one's m.,** prendre modèle sur qn. (c) Art: (Pers.) Modèle m. **He married one of his models,** il a épousé un de ses modèles. 3. Dressm: (a) Modèle m, patron m. (b) Mannequin m. 4. Attrib. (a) **Model farm,** ferme modèle. **M. husband,** époux modèle; le modèle des époux. (b) **M. aeroplane,** modèle réduit (d'avion).
model[2], v.tr (modelled ['mɔd(ə)ld]) Modeler. **To m. sth. after, upon, sth.,** modeler qch. sur qch. **To m. oneself on s.o.,** se modeler sur qn; prendre exemple sur qn. **To m. (fashions),** être mannequin. **modelling,** s. 1. (a) Art: Modelage m. (b) Facture f sur modèle, sur gabarit. 2. Création f de modèles.
modeller ['mɔdlər], s. Modeleur m.
moderate[1] ['mɔd(ə)rit], a. Modéré; moyen, ordinaire, raisonnable; (résultat) médiocre. **M. in one's desires,** modéré dans ses désirs. **M. drinker,** buveur plutôt sobre. **M. language,** langage mesuré. **M. price,** prix modéré, modique. **M. capacities,** talents ordinaires, moyens. **M. size,** grandeur moyenne. **M. opinions,** opinions modérées. **M. meal,** repas sobre. **-ly,** adv. Modérément; avec modération; sobrement; médiocrement. **'moderate-'sized,** a. De grandeur moyenne.
moderate[2] ['mɔdəreit]. 1. (a) v.tr. Modérer; tempérer (l'ardeur du soleil). **To m. one's pretensions,** rabattre de ses prétentions, F: en rabattre. (b) v.i. (Of storm, etc.) Se modérer. 2. v.i. Ecc: (Esp. Scot:) Présider (une assemblée).
moderateness ['mɔd(ə)ritnis], s. 1. Modération f, modicité f (de prix). 2. Médiocrité f.
moderation [,mɔdə'reiʃ(ə)n], s. 1. Modération f. mesure f, retenue f; sobriété f (de langage). **With m.,** mesurément. **In m.,** modérément. 2. pl. Sch: (At Oxford) **Moderations,** F: Mods, premier examen pour le grade de Bachelor of Arts.
moderator ['mɔdəreitər], s. (Esp. Ecc: Scot:) Président m (d'une assemblée).
modern ['mɔd(ə)n], a. Moderne. **To build in the m. style,** bâtir à la moderne. **M. times,** le temps présent, les temps modernes. **M. languages,** langues vivantes. s. **The ancients and the moderns,** les anciens m et les modernes m.
modernism ['mɔdə(:)nizm], s. 1. Modernisme m. 2. (a) Nouveauté f. (b) Néologisme m.
modernist ['mɔdə(:)nist], s. Moderniste m. & f.
modernity [mɔ'də:niti], s. Modernité f.
modernize ['mɔdə(:)naiz], v.tr. Moderniser; rénover; mettre (ses idées, etc.) à jour, à la page.
modest ['mɔdist], a. Modeste. (a) **To be m. about one's achievements,** avoir un succès modeste. (b) (Of woman) Pudique, honnête, chaste. (c) **To be m. in one's requirements,** être peu exigeant. **M. fortune,** fortune modeste. (d) Sans prétentions. **-ly,** adv. 1. Modestement; avec modestie. 2. Pudiquement, chastement. 3. Modérément. 4. Sans prétentions; sans faste.
modesty ['mɔdisti], s. 1. Modestie f. **With all due m.,** soit dit sans vanité. 2. Pudeur f; honnêteté f (chez une femme). **To offend m.,** commettre un outrage à la pudeur. Cost: **M.-front, -vest,** plastron m. 3. Modération f (d'une demande, etc.); modicité f (d'une dépense). 4. Absence f de prétention; simplicité f.

modicum ['mɔdikəm], s. A m. of . . ., une petite portion, une faible quantité, de. . .

modification [ˌmɔdifi'keiʃ(ə)n], s. 1. Modification f. To make modifications to sth., apporter des modifications à qch. 2. Atténuation f.

modify ['mɔdifai], v.tr. 1. (a) Modifier; apporter des modifications à (qch.). (b) Mitiger, atténuer (une peine). To m. one's demands, rabattre de ses prétentions. 2. Modifier (le verbe, une voyelle).

modulate ['mɔdjuleit]. 1. v.tr. (a) Moduler (sa voix). W.Tel: Cin: Modulated output power, puissance modulée. (b) Ajuster, approprier (to, à). 2. v.i. Mus: To m. from one key (in)to another, passer d'un ton dans un autre; moduler. **modulating**, a. Mus: El: Modulateur, -trice.

modulation [ˌmɔdju'leiʃ(ə)n], s. Modulation f.

modulator ['mɔdjuleitər], s. El: Modulateur m.

module ['mɔdjul], s. (Lunar) m., module m (lunaire).

modulus, pl. -i ['mɔdjuləs, -ai], s. Mth: Mec: Module m, coefficient m. Mec: Young's m., m. of elasticity, module, coefficient, d'élasticité.

Mogul ['mougʌl], s. The Great, Grand, M., le Grand Mogol.

mohair ['mouhɛər], s. Tex: Mohair m.

Mohammedan [mou'hæmid(ə)n], a. & s. Musulman, -ane.

moiety ['mɔiəti], s. A. & Jur: 1. Moitié f. 2. Part f, ˜ demi-portion f.

moil [mɔil], v.i. Peiner. In the phr. To toil and m., q.v. under TOIL².

moire [mwɑ:r], s. Tex: Moire f.

moiré ['mwɑ:rei], a. & s. Moiré (m).

moist [mɔist], a. (Climat, chaleur) humide; (peau, main, chaleur) moite. Eyes m. with tears, yeux mouillés de larmes. To grow m., s'humecter, se mouiller.

moisten ['mɔisn]. 1. v.tr. (a) Humecter, mouiller; moitir (la peau); arroser (la pâte, etc.). Tchn: Humidifier. (b) To m. a rag, a sponge, with . . ., imbiber un chiffon, une éponge, de. . . . 2. v.i. S'humecter, se mouiller.

moistening ['mɔis(ə)niŋ], s. Humidification f.

moistness ['mɔistnis], s. Humidité f; moiteur f (de la peau).

moisture ['mɔistʃər], s. Humidité f; buée f (sur une glace, etc.). M.-proof, à l'épreuve de l'humidité, hydrofuge.

moke [mouk], s. F: Bourricot m, bourrique f.

molar¹ ['moulər]. 1. a. (Dent) molaire. 2. s. Molaire f.

molar², a. Qui se rapporte à la masse; (concrétion) molaire.

molasses [mo'læs], s. Geol: Mol(l)asse f.

molasses [mə'læsiz], s.pl. Mélasse f.

mole¹ [moul], s. (a) Grain m de beauté. (b) Nævus m.

mole², s. Z: Taupe f. **'mole-catcher**, s. Taupier m; preneur m de taupes. **'mole-trap**, s. Taupière f, piège m à taupes.

mole³, s. Môle m; brise-lames m inv; digue f; jetée f.

molecular [mo'lekjulər], a. Moléculaire; Ph: (motion) brownien, -ienne.

molecule ['mɔlikju:l], s. Ch: Molécule f.

molehill ['moulhil], s. Taupinière f, taupinée f.

moleskin ['moulskin], s. 1. (Peau f de) taupe f. M. coat, manteau en taupe. 2. (a) Tex: Velours m de coton. (b) pl. A.Cost: Moleskins, pantalon m en velours de coton (de garde-chasse, etc.).

molest [mo'lest], v.tr. 1. A. & Jur: Molester, inquiéter (qn). 2. Rudoyer; se livrer à des voies de fait contre (qn).

molestation [ˌmoules'teiʃ(ə)n], s. 1. Molestation f. 2. Voies fpl de fait.

mollification [ˌmɔlifi'keiʃ(ə)n], s. Apaisement m, adoucissement m.

mollify ['mɔlifai], v.tr. To m. s.o., adoucir, apaiser, qn, la colère de qn.

mollusc ['mɔləsk], s. Mollusque m.

mollusca [mɔ'lʌskə], s.pl. Les mollusques m.

Molly ['mɔli]. Pr.n.f. (Dim. of Mary) Mariette, Manon. **'molly-coddle¹**, s. F: (a) Petit chéri à sa maman. (b) (Homme) douillet m. (c) Poule mouillée. **'molly(-coddle)²**, v.tr. Dorloter (un enfant); élever (un enfant) dans du coton.

molten ['moult(ə)n]. See MELT.

Molucca [mo'lʌkə]. Pr.n. The Moluccas, the M. Islands, les Moluques f.

molybdenum [mə'libdənəm], s. Ch: Molybdène m.

moment ['moumənt], s. 1. Moment m, instant m. Wait a m.! one m.! half a m.! just a m.! une minute! un moment! un instant! attendez une seconde! One m., please! (i) Tp: ne quittez pas! (ii) W.Tel: ne quittez pas l'écoute! To expect s.o. (at) any m., attendre qn d'un moment à l'autre, d'un instant à l'autre. To interrupt at every m., interrompre à tout bout de champ. His entry was timed to the m., son entrée était calculée à la minute. I have just this m., only this m., heard of it, je l'apprends à l'instant. I saw him a m. ago, je l'ai vu il y a un instant. I came the (very) m. I heard of it, je suis venu aussitôt que je l'ai appris. The m. I saw him I recognized him, je ne l'eus pas plus tôt vu que je le reconnus. From the m. when . . ., dès l'instant où. . . At this m., at the present m., en ce moment; actuellement. I am busy at the m., je suis occupé pour le moment. At the last m., à la dernière minute. The book appeared just at the right m., le livre parut à point nommé. I will come in a m., je viendrai dans un instant. It was all over in a m., cela s'est fait en un clin d'œil. I want nothing for the m., je n'ai besoin de rien pour le moment. Not for a m.! jamais de la vie! pour rien au monde! 2. Mec: Moment (d'une force); couple moteur. M. of inertia, moment d'inertie. Bending m., effort m de flexion. (Of piece) To carry the bending m., travailler à la flexion. 3. (Of fact, event) To be of m., être important. Of great, little, m., de grande importance, de peu d'importance.

momentary ['moumənt(ə)ri], a. Momentané, passager. **-ily**, adv. Momentanément, passagèrement.

momentous [mo'mentəs], a. Important. M. decision, décision capitale.

momentousness [mo'mentəsnis], s. Importance f (d'un événement, etc.).

momentum, pl. -ta [mo'mentəm, -tə], s. 1. Mec: Ph: Force vive; quantité f de mouvement. 2. (Impetus) Vitesse acquise. To lose m., perdre son élan. Carried away by my own m., emporté par mon propre élan.

monac(h)al ['mɔnək(ə)l], a. Monacal, -aux.

monachism ['mɔnəkizm], s. Monachisme m.

monad ['mɔnæd], s. Phil: Biol: Monade f.

monadelphous [ˌmɔnə'delfəs], a. Bot: Monadelphe.

monandrous [mɔ'nændrəs], a. Bot: Monandre.

monarch ['mɔnək], s. Monarque m.

monarchic(al) [mɔ'nɑ:kik(ə)l], a. Monarchique.

monarchism ['mɔnəkizm], s. Monarchisme m.

monarchist ['mɔnəkist], s. Monarchiste m.

monarchy ['mɔnəki], s. Monarchie f.

monastery ['mɔnəstri], s. Monastère m.

monastic [mə'næstik], a. Monastique; monacal, -aux; claustral, -aux.

monasticism [mə'næstisizm], s. Monachisme m.

monaural [mɔn'ɔ:r(ə)l], a. W.Tel: etc: Monaural, -aux.

Monday ['mʌndi], s. Lundi m. To take M. off, prolonger le weekend jusqu'au mardi. (For other phrases cf. FRIDAY.)

monetary ['mʌnit(ə)ri], a. Monétaire.

monetize ['mʌnitaiz], v.tr. Monétiser, monnayer.

money ['mʌni], s. 1. (a) Monnaie f, numéraire m, espèces monnayées; argent m. Piece of m., pièce de monnaie. Silver m., monnaie d'argent. Paper m., papier-monnaie m. Current m., monnaie qui a cours. Counterfeit m., base m., fausse monnaie. To throw good m. after bad, s'enfoncer davantage dans une mauvaise affaire. Ready m., argent comptant, argent liquide. To pay in ready m., payer comptant. M. payment, paiement en numéraire. (b) I bought it with my own m., je l'ai acheté de mes propres deniers Fin: M. is scarce, l'argent est rare, les capitaux m sont rares. Bank: M. at call, dépôts mpl à vue. To make m., faire, gagner, de l'argent. F: To be coining m., être en train de faire fortune. To come into m., hériter d'une fortune. To be made of m., être cousu d'or. He has pots of m., il a des écus, P: il est plein aux as. To be rolling in m., rouler sur l'or. To part with one's m., débourser. I want to get my m. back je voudrais rentrer dans mes fonds. *F:* He's the man for my m., c'est juste l'homme qu'il me faut. There's m. in it, c'est une bonne affaire. It will bring in big m., cela rapportera gros. You have had your m.'s worth, vous en avez eu pour votre argent. M. makes, begets, m., un sou amène l'autre. Your m. or your life! la bourse ou la vie! M. interest, intérêt pécuniaire. 2. *pl. A. & Jur:* Moneys, monies, argent, fonds *mpl.* Moneys paid out, versements opérés. Moneys paid in, recettes effectuées. Public moneys, deniers publics. Sundry monies owing to him, diverses sommes à lui dues. '**money-bag**, *s.* Sacoche *f.* '**money-belt**, *s.* Ceinture *f* à porte-monnaie. '**money-bill**, *s.* Loi *f* de finance(s). '**money-box**, *s.* 1. Tirelire *f.* 2. Caisse *f*, cassette *f.* '**money-changer**, *s.* Changeur *m*, cambiste *m.* '**money-grubber**, *s. F:* Grippe-sou *m*, *pl.* grippe-sous. '**money-grubbing**[1], *a. F:* Cupide, avare. '**money-grubbing**[2], *s. F:* Thésaurisation *f.* '**money-lender**, *s.* 1. Prêteur *m* d'argent, prêteur sur gages. 2. *Com:* Bailleur *m* de fonds. '**money-market**, *s.* Marché monétaire, financier; bourse *f.* '**money-wort**, *s. Bot:* Nummulaire *f*; herbe *f* aux écus.

moneyed ['mʌnid], *a.* 1. Riche; qui a de l'argent. The m. classes, les classes possédantes. 2. The m. interest, les capitalistes *m*, les puissances *f* d'argent.

monger ['mʌŋgər], *s.* (*Chiefly in combination*) 1. Marchand, -ande. **Cheesem.**, **fishm.**, marchand de fromage, de poisson. **Ironm.**, quincaillier *m.* 2. *Pej:* News-m., colporteur *m* de nouvelles. **Slanderm.**, mauvaise langue; médisant, -ante. *S.a.* PANIC-MONGER, SCANDALMONGER, WARMONGER.

Mongol ['mɔŋgɔl], 1. *a. & s. Ethn:* Mongol, -ole. 2. *a. Med:* Mongolien, -ienne.

Mongolia [mɔŋ'gouljə]. *Pr.n.* La Mongolie.

Mongolian [mɔŋ'gouljən]. 1. (*a*) *a. & s. Geog:* Mongol, -ole. The M. People's Republic, la République populaire de Mongolie. (*b*) *s. Ling:* Le mongol. 2. *a. & s. Med:* Mongolien, -ienne.

mongolism ['mɔŋgəlizm], **mongolianism** [mɔŋ'gouljənizm], *s. Med:* Mongolisme *m.*

mongoloid ['mɔŋgɔlɔid], *a. Ethn:* Mongoloïde.

mongoose [mʌŋ'guːs, 'mɔŋ-], *s. Z:* Mangouste *f.*

mongrel ['mʌŋgrəl]. 1. *s.* Métis, -isse; (*of dog*) bâtard, -arde. 2. *a.*(Animal) métis; (plante) métisse.

monied ['mʌnid], *a.* = MONEYED.

monism ['mɔnizm], *s. Phil:* Monisme *m.*

monition [mɔ'niʃ(ə)n], *s.* 1. (*a*) Avertissement *m.* (*b*) *Ecc:* Monition *f.* 2. *Jur:* Citation *f* (à comparaître).

monitor[1] ['mɔnitər], *s.* 1. Moniteur, -trice. *W.Tel:* Opérateur *m* d'interception. *Cin:* Projection-room m., haut-parleur *m* de cabine, de contrôle. **M. speaker**, haut-parleur témoin. '**monitor room**, *s. Cin:* Salle *f*, cabine *f*, d'écoute, cabine de contrôle.

monitor[2], *v.tr. W.Tel:* Contrôler.

monitoring ['mɔnitəriŋ], *s. W.Tel:* Interception *f* (des émissions), monitoring *m.* **M. station**, station *f*, centre *m*, d'écoute. **News m.**, service *m* des écoutes *f* radiotéléphoniques.

monitory ['mɔnit(ə)ri], *a.* (*a*) (Mot) d'admonition, d'avertissement. (*b*) *Ecc:* Monitoire; monitorial, -aux.

monk [mʌŋk], *s.m.* Moine, religieux. '**monk's-hood**, *s. Bot:* Aconit *m* (napel), *F:* casque de Jupiter.

monkey[1] ['mʌŋki], *s.* 1. *Z:* Singe *m.* **Female m.**, she-m., guenon *f. F:* You young m.! petit polisson! petit garnement! petit(e) espiègle! As artful as a cartload of monkeys, malin comme un singe. *P:* To put s.o.'s m. up, mettre qn en colère; faire sortir qn de ses gonds. *P:* To get one's m. up, se fâcher, *F:* piquer une colère. *F:* I won't stand any m. business! vous n'allez pas me la faire! 2. *Civ.E:* Mouton *m* (de sonnette). 3. *P:* (Somme *f* de) cinq cents livres, *U.S:* cinq cents dollars. '**monkey-house**, *s.* Singerie *f*; pavillon *m* des singes. '**monkey-jacket**, *s. Nau:* Veston court, veste courte, spencer *m.* '**monkey-like**, *a.* Simiesque. '**monkey nut**, *s.* = PEANUT. '**monkey-puzzle**, *s. Bot:* Araucaria *m.* '**monkey-tricks**, *s.pl.* Singeries *f*, chinoiseries *f*, espiègleries *f.* '**monkey-wrench**, *s.* Clé, clef, anglaise; clé à molette. To throw a m.-w. into the works, mettre des bâtons dans les roues.

monkey[2], *v.i.* (*a*) Faire des singeries. (*b*) *P:* To m. (about) with sth., tripoter qch.; toucher à qch. (qu'il faut laisser tranquille).

monkish ['mʌŋkiʃ], *a.* De moine; monacal, -aux.

mono ['mɔnou], *a. F:* = MONAURAL.

monobasic ['mɔnə'beisik], *a. Ch:* Monobasique.

monocarp ['mɔnoukɑːp], *s. Bot:* Plante monocarpienne.

monochromatic [mɔnəkro'mætik], *a.* (Éclairage) monochromatique.

monochrome ['mɔnəkroum]. *Art:* 1. *a.* Monochrome. 2. *s.* Peinture *f* monochrome; monochrome *m.*

monocle ['mɔnəkl], *s.* Monocle *m.*

monocotyledon ['mɔnə,kɔti'liːd(ə)n], *s. Bot:* Monocotylédone *f.*

monoculture ['mɔnəkʌltʃər], *s. Agr:* Monoculture *f.*

monocycle ['mɔnəsaikl], *s. Biol:* Monocycle *m.*

monogamic [ˌmɔnoˈgæmik], *a.* 1. (*Of rule, custom*) Monogamique. 2. (*Of pers.*) = MONOGAMOUS.

monogamist [mɔ'nəgəmist], *s.* Monogame *mf.*

monogamous [mɔ'nəgəməs], *a.* Monogame.

monogamy [mɔ'nəgəmi], *s.* Monogamie *f.*

monogram ['mɔnəgræm], *s.* Monogramme *m*, chiffre *m.*

monograph ['mɔnəgrɑːf, -græf], *s.* Monographie *f.*

monographic ['mɔnə'græfik], *a.* Monographique.

monolith ['mɔnoliθ], *s.* Monolithe *m.*

monolithic [mɔnə'liθik], *a.* Monolithe.

monologue ['mɔnələg], *s.* Monologue *m.*

monomania ['mɔnə'meiniə], *s.* Monomanie *f.*

monomaniac ['mɔnə'meiniæk], *s.* Monomane *mf*, monomaniaque *mf.*

monomaniacal ['mɔnəmə'naiəkl], *a.* Monomane, monomaniaque.

monomial [mɔ'noumiəl], *a. & s. Mth:* Monôme (*m*).

monophase ['mɔnəfeiz], *a. El.E:* (Courant) monophasé, uniphasé.

monoplane ['mɔnəplein], *s. Av:* Monoplan *m.*

monopolist [mɔ'nəpəlist], *s.* Monopolisateur *m*; accapareur, -euse.

monopolistic [mɔˌnəpə'listik], *a.* Monopolisateur, -trice.

monopolization [mɔˌnəpəlai'zeiʃ(ə)n], *s.* Monopolisation *f.*

monopolize [mɔ'nəpəlaiz], *v.tr.* 1. Monopoliser, accaparer (une denrée). 2. Accaparer; s'emparer de (la conversation).

monopoly [mɔ'nəpəli], *s.* Monopole *m.*

monorail [mɔ'nəreil], *a. & s.* Monorail (*m*).

monoshell ['mɔnəʃel], *a. Aut:* Monocoque.

monosyllabic ['mɔnəsi'læbik], *a.* Monosyllabe, monosyllabique.

monosyllable ['mɔnə'siləbl], *s.* Monosyllabe *m.*

monotheism ['mɔnəθi:izm], *s.* Monothéisme *m.*

monotheist ['mɔnəθi:ist], *s. & a.* Monothéiste.

monotonous [mɔ'nɔt(ə)nəs], *a.* Monotone; fastidieux. **-ly**, *adv.* Monotonement; fastidieusement.

monotony [mɔ'nɔt(ə)ni], *s.* Monotonie *f.*

Monotremata ['mɔnə'tri:mətə], *s.pl. Z:* Monotrèmes *m.*

monotreme ['mɔnətri:m], *a. & s. Z:* Monotrème (*m*).

monotype ['mɔnətaip], *s. Typ:* Monotype *f.*

monovalence, -valency ['mɔnə'veiləns, -'veilənsi], *s. Ch:* Monovalence *f*, univalence *f.*

monovalent ['mɔnə'veilənt], *a. Ch:* Monovalent, univalent.

monoxide [mɔ'nɔksaid], *s. Ch:* Protoxyde *m.* **Carbon m.**, oxyde *m* de carbone.

monsoon [mɔn'su:n], *s. Meteor:* Mousson *f.*

monster ['mɔnstər]. 1. *s.* Monstre *m.* 2. *a. F:* Monstre; colossal, -aux; énorme.

monstrance ['mɔnstrəns], *s. Ecc:* Ostensoir *m.*

monstrosity [mɔn'strɔsiti], *s.* Monstruosité *f.* 1. Monstre *m.* 2. Énormité *f* (d'un crime).

monstrous ['mɔnstrəs], *a.* Monstrueux. (*a*) Contre nature. (*b*) Odieux. *F:* It is perfectly monstrous that..., c'est monstrueux que+*sub.* (*c*) Énorme; colossal,-aux.

montbretia [mɔnt'bri:ʃə, mɔm'b-], *s. Bot:* Montbrétia *m.*

month [mʌnθ], *s.* Mois *m.* **Calendar m.**, mois du calendrier; mois civil. **Lunar m.**, mois lunaire. In the m. of August, au mois d'août; en août. **Current m.**, mois en cours. At the end of the current m., fin courant. **What day of the m. is it?** quel jour du mois, le combien, sommes-nous? **This day m.**, dans un mois, jour pour jour. **To hire sth. by the m.**, louer

qch. au mois. **Once a m.,** une fois par mois; mensuellement. **To receive one's m.'s pay,** toucher son mois. *Fin:* **Bill at three months,** papier à trois mois (d'échéance).
monthly¹ ['mʌnθli]. **1.** *a.* (*a*) Mensuel. *Com:* **M. instalment,** mensualité *f.* (*b*) *Rail:* **M. return ticket,** billet d'aller et retour valable pour un mois. (*c*) *Physiol:* F: **M. period,** règles *fpl.* **2.** *s.* F: Revue mensuelle; publication mensuelle.
monthly², *adv.* Mensuellement; une fois par mois; tous les mois.
Montreal [,mɔntri'ɔːl]. *Pr.n.Geog:* Montréal.
monument ['mɔnjumənt], *s.* **1.** Monument *m.* **To be scheduled as an ancient m.,** être classé comme monument historique. **2.** Monument funéraire; pierre tombale.
monumental [,mɔnju'mentl], *a.* **1.** Monumental, -aux. F: **M. ignorance,** ignorance monumentale, prodigieuse. **2.** **M. mason,** entrepreneur *m* de monuments funéraires; marbrier *m.*
moo¹ [muː], *s.* Meuglement *m,* beuglement *m.*
moo², *v.i.* (**mooed**) Meugler, beugler; mugir.
moo³, *int.* Meuh!
mooch [muːtʃ], *v.i.* F: **To m. about,** flâner, traîner; se balader.
mood¹ [muːd], *s. Gram: Log: Mus:* Mode *m.*
mood², *s.* **1.** Humeur *f,* disposition *f.* **To be in a good, bad, m.,** être bien, mal, disposé; être de bonne, mauvaise, humeur, *F:* de bon, de mauvais, poil. **To be in a generous m.,** être en veine de générosité. **To feel in the m. to write,** se sentir en disposition d'écrire. **To be in the m. for reading, in a reading m.,** être en humeur de lire. **To be in no m. for laughing, in no laughing m.,** ne pas avoir le cœur à rire; n'avoir aucune envie de rire; ne pas être d'humeur à rire. **2.** *pl.* **To have moods,** être lunatique, avoir des lunes.
moodiness ['muːdinis], *s.* **1.** Humeur chagrine; morosité *f.* **2.** Humeur changeante.
moody ['muːdi], *a.* **To be m.,** (i) être maussade; (ii) être mal luné; (iii) avoir des lunes, être lunatique. **-ily,** *adv.* D'un air chagrin, morose; maussadement.
moon¹ [muːn], *s.* **1.** Lune *f.* **New m.,** nouvelle lune. **Full m.,** pleine lune. **There is a m. to-night,** il fait clair de lune, il y a de la lune, ce soir. **To land on the m.,** alunir. **Landing on the m.,** alunissage *m.* *F:* **To cry for the m., to ask for the m.,** demander la lune. **Once in a blue m.,** tous les trente-six du mois; une fois par extraordinaire. **2.** Lunule *f* (d'ongle). **'moon-fish,** *s.* Môle *f*; poisson-lune *m.*
moon², **1.** *v.i.* **To m. about,** muser, musarder. **2.** *v.tr.* **To m. away two hours,** passer deux heures à musarder.
moonbeam ['muːnbiːm], *s.* Rayon *m* de lune.
moonless ['muːnlis], *a.* (Nuit, etc.) sans lune.
moonlight ['muːnlait], *s.* Clair *m* de lune. **In the m., by m.,** au clair de (la) lune; à la clarté de la lune.
moonlit ['muːnlit], *a.* Éclairé par la lune.
moonrise ['muːnraiz], *s.* Lever *m* de (la) lune.
moonshine ['muːnʃain], *s.* **1.** Clair *m* de lune. **2.** *F:* Balivernes *fpl;* contes *mpl* en l'air. **That's all m.,** tout ça c'est de la blague. **3.** *U.S:* F: Alcool *m* de contrebande.
moonstone ['muːnstoun], *s.* *Lap:* Feldspath nacré; pierre *f* de lune.
moonstruck ['muːnstrʌk], *a.* **1.** (*a*) A l'esprit dérangé; *F:* toqué. (*b*) Halluciné. **2.** F: Abasourdi, sidéré.
moor¹ [muər], *s.* **1.** Lande *f,* bruyère *f.* (*b*) *Scot:* Chasse réservée. **'moor-cock,** *s.* *Orn:* Lagopède *m* d'Écosse mâle. **'moor-hen,** *s.* *Orn:* **1.** Poule *f* d'eau. **2.** Poule lagopède d'Écosse.
moor², *v.* *Nau:* **1.** *v.tr.* Amarrer (un navire); mouiller (une bouée, une mine). **To m. a ship alongside (the quay),** accoster un navire le long du quai. **2.** *v.i.* S'amarrer; prendre le corps-mort. **mooring,** *s.* **1.** Amarrage *m* (d'un navire); mouillage *m* (d'une bouée). **M. ring,** anneau *m* d'amarrage; organeau *m.* **M. rope,** amarre *f*; aussière *f.* **2.** *pl.* **Ship at her moorings,** navire sur ses amarres. **To pick up one's moorings,** prendre son coffre.
Moor³, *s.* Maure *m,* Mauresque *f.*
moorage ['muəridʒ], *s.* *Nau:* **1.** Amarrage *m,* mouillage *m.* **2.** (Droits *mpl* d') ancrage *m.*
Moorish ['muəriʃ], *a.* Mauresque, moresque, maure. **A M. woman,** une Mauresque.

moorland ['muələnd], *s.* = MOOR¹ (*a*).
moose [muːs], *s.* *Z:* (*a*) American m., orignal *m,* élan *m* du Canada. (*b*) Eurasiatic m., élan. **'moose-caller,** *Fr.C:* bourgot *m.*
moot¹ [muːt], *s.* *Hist:* Assemblée *f* (du peuple).
moot², *a.* (*Of question*) Sujet à controverse; discutable. **M. point,** (i) point *m* discutable; (ii) *Jur:* point de droit.
moot³, *v.tr.* Soulever (une question). **This question is mooted again,** cette question est remise sur le tapis.
mop¹ [mɔp], *s.* **1.** (*a*) Balai *m* à laver, balai éponge; balai à franges. (Dish-)m., lavette *f* (à vaisselle). (*b*) *Nau:* Faubert *m,* vadrouille *f.* **2.** F: **M. of hair,** tignasse *f.*
mop², *v.tr.* (**mopped**) Éponger, essuyer (le parquet). *Nau:* Fauberder (le pont). **To m. one's brow,** s'éponger, se tamponner, le front (avec son mouchoir). *S.a.* FLOOR¹ 1. **mop up,** *v.tr.* (*a*) Éponger (de l'eau); essuyer (la transpiration, etc.). (*b*) Rafler, absorber (tous les bénéfices). **'mopping 'up,** *s.* Épongeage *m*; essuyage *m.* *Mil:* Nettoyage *m.*
mope [moup], *v.i.* Être triste, mélancolique; s'ennuyer; *F:* broyer du noir.
moped ['mouped], *s.* F: Cyclomoteur *m.*
moquette [mə'ket], *s.* *Tex:* Moquette *f.*
moraine [mə'rein], *s.* *Geol:* Moraine *f.* End m., moraine frontale. Lateral m., moraine latérale.
moral ['mɔr(ə)l]. **I.** *a.* Moral, -aux. **1.** **M. philosophy,** la morale, l'éthique *f.* **To raise the m. standard of the community,** relever les mœurs de la société. **2.** Conforme aux bonnes mœurs. **To live a m. life,** avoir de bonnes mœurs. **3.** **M. courage,** courage moral. **M. victory,** victoire morale. **4.** **M. certainty,** (i) certitude morale; (ii) *Turf: F:* gagnant sûr; certitude. **-ally,** *adv.* Moralement. **II.** *s. moral,* *s.* **1.** Morale *f,* moralité *f* (d'un conte). *S.a.* POINT¹ I. 2. **2.** *pl.* **Morals,** moralité, mœurs *fpl.* **Man of loose morals,** homme de moralité douteuse. **3.** = MORALE.
morale [mə'raːl], *s.* (*No pl.*) Moral *m* (d'une personne, d'un groupe).
moralism ['mɔrəlizm], *s.* Moralisme *m.*
moralist ['mɔrəlist], *s.* Moraliste *mf.*
morality [mə'ræliti], *s.* **1.** (*a*) Moralité *f*; principes moraux; sens moral. (*b*) Bonnes mœurs. **2.** Réflexion morale; moralité. **3.** *Lit.Hist:* M.-play, moralité.
moralization [,mɔrəlai'zeiʃ(ə)n], *s.* Moralisation *f.*
moralize ['mɔrəlaiz]. **1.** *v.i.* Moraliser, faire de la morale (on, sur). **2.** *v.tr.* Moraliser, donner un sens moral à (qch.). **moralizing¹,** *a.* Moralisateur, -trice. **moralizing²,** *s.* F: Stop your m.! pas de morale!
moralizer ['mɔrəlaizər], *s.* Moraliseur *m.*
morass [mə'ræs], *s.* Marais *m*; fondrière *f.*
moratorium [,mɔrə'tɔːriəm], *s.* (*a*) *Fin:* Moratoire *m.* (*b*) Trève *f.*
morbid ['mɔːbid], *a.* **1.** Morbide. **M. curiosity,** curiosité malsaine, maladive. **2.** *Med:* M. anatomy, anatomie *f* pathologique. **-ly,** *adv.* Morbidement, maladivement.
morbidity [mɔː'biditi], **morbidness** ['mɔːbidnis], *s.* (*a*) Morbidité *f*; état maladif. (*b*) Tristesse maladive (des pensées).
mordacity [mɔː'dæsiti], **mordancy** ['mɔːd(ə)nsi], *s.* Mordacité *f,* causticité *f,* mordant *m* (d'une critique).
mordant ['mɔːd(ə)nt]. **1.** *a.* Mordant, caustique. **2.** *s.* *Dy:* etc: Mordant *m.*
more [mɔːr]. **1.** *a.* Plus (de). **He has m. patience than I,** il a plus de patience que moi. **M. than ten men,** plus de dix hommes. **One m.,** un de plus; encore un. **One or m.,** un ou plusieurs. (Some) m. bread, please! encore du pain, s'il vous plaît! **To have some m. wine,** reprendre du vin. **Is there any m.?** y en a-t-il encore? en reste-t-il? **Do you want any m.,** some m.? en voulez-vous encore? A little m., encore un peu. **Have you any m. books?** avez-vous d'autres livres? **A few m. days,** quelques jours de plus. **Many m.,** beaucoup d'autres; encore beaucoup. **As many m.,** encore autant. **2.** *s. or indef. pron.* I cannot give m., je ne peux donner davantage. **That's m. than enough,** c'est plus qu'il n'en faut (to, pour). **That hat costs m. than this one,** ce chapeau-là coûte plus cher que celui-ci. **What m. can you ask?** qu'est-ce que vous voulez de plus? **This incident, of which m. anon . . .,** cet incident, sur lequel nous

reviendrons. . . What is m. . . ., qui plus est. . . She was m. of a tie than a companion, c'était une attache plutôt qu'une compagne. 3. *adv.* (*a*) Plus, davantage. M. easily, plus facilement. M. and m., de plus en plus. You are rich but he is m. so, vous êtes riche mais il l'est davantage. He was m. surprised than annoyed, il était plutôt surpris que fâché. His total debts are m. than covered by his assets, le chiffre de ses dettes est couvert et au-delà par son actif. M. or less, plus ou moins. (*b*) Once m., encore une fois, une fois de plus. Never m., jamais plus, plus jamais. If I see him any m., si jamais je le revois. 4. The m. (*a*) *a.* He only does the m. harm, il n'en fait que plus de mal. (The) more's the pity, c'est d'autant plus malheureux. (*b*) *s.* The m. one has the m. one wants, plus on a, plus on désire avoir; *Prov:* l'appétit vient en mangeant. (*c*) *adv.* All the m. . . ., à plus forte raison . . .; d'autant plus. . . . (as, que). It makes me all the m. proud, je n'en suis que plus fier. The m. he drank the thirstier he got, plus il buvait, plus il avait soif. 5. No m., not any m. (*a*) *a.* I have no m. money, je n'ai plus d'argent. No m. soup, thank you, plus de potage, merci. (*b*) *s.* I have no m., je n'en ai plus. To say no m., ne pas en dire davantage. Let us say no m. about it, qu'il n'en soit plus question; n'en parlons plus. (*c*) *adv.* (i) The house is no m., la maison n'existe plus. I shall see her no m., je ne la verrai jamais plus. (ii) He is no m. a lord than I am, il n'est pas plus (un) lord que moi. He thought you didn't want to see him.—No m. I do, il a pensé que vous ne vouliez pas le voir.—Effectivement. I can't make out how it has come about.—No m. can I, je ne m'explique pas comment c'est arrivé.—(Ni) moi non plus.

morel(le) [mɔ'rel], *s. Fung: Cu:* Morille *f.*

morello [mɔ'relou], *s. Hort:* M. (cherry), griotte *f.*

moreover [mɔ:'rouvər], *adv.* D'ailleurs; du reste; et qui plus est; bien plus.

Moresque [mɔ'resk], *a. & s.f.* Mauresque, moresque.

morganatic [,mɔ:gə'nætik], *a.* Morganatique. **-ally,** *adv.* Morganatiquement.

morgue[mɔ:g],*s. Esp. U.S:* Morgue *f*; dépôt *m* mortuaire.

moribund ['mɔribʌnd], *a.* Moribond.

Mormon ['mɔ:mən], *a. & s.* Mormon, -one.

Mormonism ['mɔ:mənizm], *s.* Mormonisme *m.*

morn [mɔ:n], *s. Poet:* = MORNING.

morning ['mɔ:niŋ], *s.* 1. (*a*) Matin *m.* I saw him this m., je l'ai vu ce matin. To-morrow m., demain matin. The next m., the m. after, le lendemain matin. *F:* The m. after (the night before), le lendemain de cuite, de bombe. The m. before, la veille au matin. Every Monday m., tous les lundis matins. Four o'clock in the m., quatre heures du matin. First thing in the m., dès le matin; à la première heure. Early in the m., matinalement; de grand matin. What do you do in the m.? que faites-vous le matin? Good m., bonjour. (*b*) Matinée *f.* In the course of the m., dans, au cours de, la matinée. M. off, matinée de congé. A morning's work, une matinée de travail. 2. *attrib.* Matinal, -aux; du matin. Early m. tea, tasse de thé prise avant de se lever. 'morning-room, *s.* Petit salon.

Moroccan [mɔ'rɔkən], *a. & s.* Marocain, -aine.

Morocco [mɔ'rɔkou]. 1. *Pr.n. Geog:* Le Maroc. 2. *s.* M. (leather), maroquin *m.*

mor'on ['mɔ:rɔn], *s.* 1. (Homme, femme) faible d'esprit. 2. *F:* Idiot, -ote, minus habens *m inv.*

moronic [mɔ'rɔnik], *a.* 1. Faible d'esprit. 2. *F:* Idiot, bête; bouché.

morose [mə'rous], *a.* Chagrin, morose. **-ly,** *adv.* D'un air chagrin, morose.,

moroseness [mə'rousnis], *s.* Morosité *f*; humeur chagrine.

Morpheus ['mɔ:fjəs]. *Pr.n.m.* Morphée. In the arms of M., dans les bras de Morphée.

morphia ['mɔ:fjə], **morphine** ['mɔ:fi:n], *s.* Morphine *f.* M. addict, morphinomane *mf.*

morphi(n)omania ['mɔ:fi(n)o'meiniə], *s.* Morphinomanie *f.*

morphi(n)omaniac ['mɔ:fi(n)o'meiniæk], *a. & s.* Morphinomane (*mf*).

morphology [mɔ:'fɔlədʒi], *s.* Morphologie *f.*

morris dance ['mɔrisdɑ:ns], *s.* (Sorte de) danse *f* folklorique.

morrow ['mɔrou], *s. A. & Lit:* Lendemain *m.* On the m., le lendemain. *A:* Good m., bonjour.

Morse [mɔ:s]. *Pr.n.m. Tg:* The M. code, le morse.

morsel ['mɔ:s(ə)l], *s.* Petit morceau. Choice m., dainty m., morceau friand, de choix. Not a m. of bread, pas une bouchée de pain.

mort [mɔ:t], *s. Ven:* Hallali *m.*

mortadella ['mɔ:tə'delə], *s. Cu:* Mortadelle *f.*

mortal ['mɔ:tl], *a.* Mortel. 1. M. remains, dépouille mortelle. *s.* The mortals, les mortels. *F: O:* She's a queer m., c'est une drôle de femme. 2. (*a*) Funeste; fatal, -als (to, à). M. blow, coup mortel. (*b*) M. sin, péché mortel. 3. M. enemy, ennemi mortel. M. combat, combat à outrance, à mort. 4. (*a*) To be in m. anxiety, avoir la mort dans l'âme. To be in m. fear of . . ., avoir une peur mortelle de. . . . (*b*) *F: O:* Two m. hours, deux mortelles heures; deux heures interminables. (*c*) *F:* Any m. thing, n'importe quoi. **-ally,** *adv.* Mortellement. M. wounded, blessé à mort.

mortality [mɔ:'tæliti], *s.* Mortalité *f.* Infant m. rate, taux *m* de mortalité infantile.

mortar[1] ['mɔ:tər], *s.* 1. (*a*) Mortier *m.* (*b*) *Artil:* Mortier, lance-bombes *m inv.* 2. *Const:* (*a*) Mortier. (*b*) Clay and straw m., bauge *f*, torchis *m.* 'mortar-board, *s.* 1. *Const:* Planche *f* à mortier. 2. *Cost:* Toque universitaire anglaise.

mortar[2], *v.tr. Const:* Lier (les pierres) avec du mortier.

mortgage[1] ['mɔ:gidʒ], *s.* Hypothèque *f.* Loan on m., prêt *m* hypothécaire. To raise a m., prendre une hypothèque. To secure a debt by m., hypothéquer une créance. To pay off, redeem, a m., purger, lever, une hypothèque. M. deed, contrat *m* hypothécaire.

mortgage[2], *v.tr.* Hypothéquer, grever (une terre, des titres). **Mortgaged estate,** domaine affecté d'hypothèques. *F:* I've already mortgaged my month's salary, j'ai déjà engagé, mangé, mon mois.

mortgageable [,mɔ:'gidʒəbl],*a.*Hypothécable; affectable.

mortgagee [,mɔ:gə'dʒi:], *s.* Créancier *m* hypothécaire.

mortgagor ['mɔ:gədʒər], *s.* Débiteur *m* hypothécaire.

mortician [mɔ:'tiʃ(ə)n], *s. U.S:* Entrepreneur *m* de pompes funèbres.

mortification [,mɔ:tifi'kei(ʃ)(ə)n], *s.* 1. Mortification (corporelle). 2. Mortification, déconvenue *f.* 3. *Med:* Mortification, sphacèle *m*, gangrène *f.*

mortify ['mɔ:tifai]. 1. *v.tr.* Mortifier. (*a*) Châtier (son corps). To m. one's flesh, se macérer. (*b*) Humilier (qn). (*c*) *Med:* Gangrener. 2. *v.i. Med:* Se gangrener, se mortifier.

mortise[1]['mɔ:tis], *s. Carp:* Mortaise *f.* 'mortise gauge,*s. Tls:* Trusquin *m.* 'mortise lock, *s.* Serrure encastrée.

mortise[2], *v.tr.* Mortaiser. **mortised,** *a.* Assemblé à mortaise. **mortising,** *s.* Mortaisage *m.* M. axe, besaiguë *f.*

mortmain ['mɔ:tmein], *s. Jur:* Mainmorte *f.*

mortuary ['mɔ:tjuəri]. 1. *a.* Mortuaire. 2. *s.* (*a*) Dépôt *m* mortuaire; dépositoire *m*; salle *f* mortuaire (d'hôpital). (*b*) Morgue *f.*

mosaic[1] [mə'zeiik]. 1. *a.* M. flooring, dallage *m* en mosaïque. 2. *s.* Mosaïque *f. T.V:* Photoelectric m., mosaïque *f* photoélectrique.

Mosaic[2], *a. B.Hist:* (Loi) mosaïque, de Moïse.

Moscow ['mɔskou]. *Pr.n.* Moscou *m.* The inhabitants of M., les Moscovites. *Hist:* The retreat from M., la retraite de Russie. *attrib. Pol:* The M. government, le gouvernement de Moscou.

Moses ['mouziz]. *Pr.n.m.* Moïse. *P: O:* Holy Moses! Oh! Seigneur Dieu!

Moslem ['mɔzlem], *a. & s.* Mahométan, -ane, musulman, -ane. **Strict M.,** musulman de stricte obédience.

mosque [mɔsk], *s.* Mosquée *f.*

mosquito, *pl.* **-oes** [mɔs'ki:tou, -ouz], *s. Ent:* Moustique *m.* M. bite, piqûre *f* de moustique. mos'quito craft, *s. Coll. Navy:* Bâtiments légers. mos'quito-net, *s.* Moustiquaire *f.*

moss [mɔs], *s.* 1. *Scot:* Marais *m*, marécage *m.* (Peat-)m., tourbière *f.* 2. *Bot:* Mousse *f. S.a.* ROLLING[1] 1. 'moss-grown, *a.* Couvert de mousse; moussu. 'moss-hag, *s. Scot:* Tourbière épuisée; fondrière *f.* 'moss rose, *s. Bot:* Rose moussue. 'moss stitch, *s. Knitting:* Point *m* de riz.

mossy ['mɔsi], *a.* Moussu.

most [moust]. **1.** *a.* *(a)* You have made (the) m. mistakes, c'est vous qui avez fait le plus de fautes. *(b)* **M. men**, la plupart des hommes. **For the m. part**, (i) pour la plupart, en majeure partie; (ii) le plus souvent. **2.** *s. & indef. pron.* *(a)* **Do the m. you can**, faites le plus que vous pourrez. **At (the) (very) m.**, au maximum; (tout) au plus. **To make the m. of sth.**, (i) tirer le meilleur parti possible de qch.; faire valoir (son argent); bien employer (son temps); ménager le plus possible (ses provisions, etc.); (ii) représenter qch. sous son plus beau jour ou sous son plus vilain jour. *(b)* **M. of the work**, la plupart, la plus grande partie, la majeure partie, du travail. **M. of them have forgotten him**, la plupart d'entre eux l'ont oublié. **3.** *adv.* *as sup. of comparison.* **What I desire m.**, ce que je désire le plus, surtout, par-dessus tout. **The m. intelligent child**, l'enfant le plus intelligent. **The m. beautiful woman**, la plus belle femme. **Those who have answered m. accurately**, ceux qui ont répondu le plus exactement. **4.** *adv.* *(Intensive)* Très, fort, bien. **M. likely**, très probablement. **A m. expensive car**, une voiture des plus coûteuses. **He has been m. rude**, il a été on ne peut plus grossier. **It is m. remarkable**, c'est tout ce qu'il y a de plus remarquable. **The M. Honourable . . .**, le Très Honorable. **. . . -ly**, *adv.* **1.** Pour la plupart; principalement. **2.** Le plus souvent; (pour) la plupart du temps.

mote [mout], *s.* Atome *m* de poussière. *B:* **To behold the m. in one's brother's eye**, voir la paille dans l'œil du prochain.

motel [mou'tel], *s.* Motel *m.*

moth [mɔθ], *s.* *Ent:* Lépidoptère *m.* **1.** *(a)* (Clothes-)m., mite *f;* teigne *f* des draps. *(b) Coll.* **Fur coat ruined by m.**, manteau de fourrure abîmé par les mites. **2.** Papillon *m* nocturne, de nuit; phalène *f.* **Emperor m.**, paon *m* de nuit. **Death's-head m.**, sphinx *m* tête de mort. '**moth-balls**, *s.pl.* Boules *f* de naphtaline. '**moth-eaten**, *a.* Mangé des mites, des vers; mité. *F:* (*Of pers.*) Miteux, -euse. **To become m.-e.**, se miter. '**moth-killer**, *s.* Anti-mites *m.* '**moth-proof**[1], *a.* Anti-mites, à l'épreuve des mites. '**moth-proof**[2], *v.tr.* Antimiter.

mother[1] ['mʌðər], *s.f.* **1.** Mère. **She is the m. of six**, elle est mère de six enfants. **Unmarried m.**, fille-mère. *F:* **Every m.'s son**, tous sans exception. **Mother's day**, la fête des mères. *attrib.* **M. hen**, mère poule. **2.** *A. & F:* **Old M. Brown**, la mère Brown. **M. Goose stories**, contes de ma mère l'Oie. **3.** *Ecc:* **The M. Superior**, la Mère supérieure. **4.** **M.** (of vinegar), mère (de vinaigre). **M. rock**, roche *f* mère. '**mother 'country**, *s.* Mère-patrie *f;* métropole *f* (d'une colonie). '**mother 'earth**, *s.* La terre notre mère, la terre nourricière. '**mother-in-law**, *s.f.* Belle-mère (mère du mari ou de la femme de qn). '**mother 'naked**, *a.* Nu comme un ver, comme la main. '**mother of 'pearl**, *s.* Nacre *f.* '**mother 'ship**, *s. Navy:* Ravitailleur *m.* '**mother 'tongue**, *s.* Langue maternelle. '**mother 'wit**, *s.* Bon sens; sens commun.

mother[2], *v.tr.* **1.** *(a)* Donner des soins maternels à (qn); servir de mère à (qn). *(b)* Dorloter, pouponner (qn). **2.** **To m. a young wolf upon a bitch**, faire élever un louveteau par une chienne. **mothering**, *s.* Soins maternels. *attrib.* **M. Sunday**, la fête des mères.

mothercraft ['mʌðəkrɑːft], *s.* Puériculture *f.*

motherhood ['mʌðəhud], *s.* Maternité *f.*

motherland ['mʌðəlænd], *s.* Patrie *f;* pays natal.

motherless ['mʌðəlis], *a.* Sans mère; orphelin (de mère).

motherly ['mʌðəli], *a.* Maternel, -elle.

motion[1] ['mouʃ(ə)n], *s.* **1.** Mouvement *m,* déplacement *m.* **In m.**, en mouvement; en marche. **To put, set, (sth.) in m.**, imprimer un mouvement à (qch.); mettre (qn) en mouvement, en jeu, en marche; faire mouvoir (qch.); faire agir (la loi). **2.** Signe *m,* geste *m.* **To make motions to s.o. to do sth.**, faire signe à qn de faire qch. **To go through the motions of doing sth.**, faire semblant de faire qch. **3.** *(a)* **To do sth. of one's own m.**, faire qch. de sa propre initiative. *(b)* Motion *f,* proposition *f.* **To propose, bring forward, a m.**, faire une proposition; présenter une motion. **The m. was carried**, la motion fut adoptée. *(c) Jur:* Demande *f,* requête *f.* **4.** *(a)* Mécanisme *m.* **Planetary m.**, engrenage *m* planétaire. *(b)* Mouve-

ment (d'une montre). **5.** *Med:* Évacuation *f,* selle *f.* '**motion picture**, *s. Cin: Esp.U.S:* Film *m.*

motion[2], *v.tr. & i.* **To m. (to) s.o. to do sth.**, faire signe à qn de faire qch. **He motioned me to a chair**, d'un geste il m'invita à m'asseoir.

motionless ['mouʃ(ə)nlis], *a.* Immobile; immobilisé; sans mouvement.

motivate ['moutiveit], *v.tr.* Motiver (une action).

motivation [mouti'veiʃ(ə)n], *s.* Motivation *f.*

motive ['moutiv]. **1.** *a.* *(a)* Moteur, -trice. **M. power**, force motrice. *(b)* **M. energy**, énergie cinétique. **2.** *s.* *(a)* Motif *m* (**for acting**, d'action). **From a religious m.**, poussé par un sentiment religieux. *(b)* Mobile *m* (d'une action). **Interest is a powerful m.**, l'intérêt est un puissant ressort.

motivity [mou'tiviti], *s.* **1.** Motilité *f.* **2** Énergie *f* cinétique. **3.** *Biol:* Motricité *f.*

motley ['mɔtli]. **1.** *a.* *(a)* Bariolé, bigarré. *(b)* Divers, mêlé. **M. crowd**, foule bigarrée, mélangée. **2.** *s.* Couleurs bigarrées; mélange *m* (de choses disparates).

motor[1] ['moutər]. **1.** *a.* Moteur, -trice. **2.** *s.* *(a)* Moteur *m.* **Driven by a clockwork m.**, entraîné par un mouvement d'horlogerie. *(b) El.E:* **M. generator**, groupe générateur. *(c) I.C.E:* **Four-stroke, two-stroke, m.**, moteur à quatre, à deux, temps. **Outboard m.**, moteur hors-bord. *(d)* **M. vehicle**, voiture *f* automobile. **M. car**, automobile *f,* auto *f,* voiture. **M. show**, salon *m* de l'automobile. '**motor boat**, *s.* Canot *m* automobile; vedette *f* à moteur. '**motor boating**, *s.* Motonautisme *m.* '**motor bus**, *s.* Autobus *m.* '**motor coach**, *s.* Autocar *m;* car *m; Rail:* motrice *f.* '**motor cycle**, *F:* '**motor bike**, *s.* Motocyclette *f,* F: moto *f.* **Lightweight m.-c.**, vélomoteur *m.* *Sp:* **Motor-bike steeplechase**, motocross *m.* '**motor-cycling**, *s.* Motocyclisme *m.* '**motor cyclist**, *s.* Motocycliste *mf.* '**motor lorry**, *s. O:* Camion *m;* (*light*) camionnette *f.* '**motor(-)pump**, *s.* Motopompe *f.* '**motor-road**, *s.* Route ouverte à la circulation automobile. '**motor-scooter**, *s.* Scooter *m.* **M.-s. rider**, scootériste *mf.*

motor[2]. **1.** *v.i.* Aller, voyager, en auto(mobile). **2.** *v.tr. O:* Conduire (qn) en auto(mobile). **motoring**, *s.* Automobilisme *m;* tourisme *m* automobile. **School of m.**, auto-école *f.*

motorail ['moutoureil], *s.* train *m* (à autos-couchettes).

motorcade ['moutəkeid], *s. Esp. U.S:* Défilé *m* d'automobiles, de voitures.

motorist ['moutərist], *s.* Automobiliste *mf.* **A veteran m.**, un vieux, un vétéran, du volant.

motorization [,moutərai'zeiʃ(ə)n], *s.* Motorisation *f.*

motorize ['moutəraiz], *v.tr.* Motoriser (une voiture, l'armée). **Motorized bicycle**, vélomoteur *m.*

motorway ['moutəwei], *s.* Autoroute *f.*

motory ['moutəri], *a. Anat:* Moteur, -trice.

motte [mɔt], *s.* *a.* *(a)* Monticule *m,* butte *f.* *(b)* Motte *f* (d'un château).

mottle[1] ['mɔtl], *s.* **1.** Tache *f,* moucheture *f.* **2.** Marbrure *f,* diaprure *f.*

mottle[2], *v.tr.* Tacheter, diaprer, marbrer; moirer (le métal); jasper (des outils, etc.). **The cold mottles the skin**, le froid marbre la peau. **mottled**, *a.* Truité, marbré, pommelé; (savon) marbré; (bois) madré; (tissu) chiné.

motto, *pl.* **-oes** ['mɔtou, -ouz], *s.* Devise *f.*

moujik ['muːʒik], *s.* Moujik *m.*

mould[1] [mould], *s.* Terre franche. **Vegetable m.**, terreau *m,* humus *m.*

mould[2], *s.* **1.** (*Template*) Calibre *m,* profil *m.* *N.Arch:* Gabarit *m.* **2.** *(a) Art: Cer:* Moule *m.* **To be cast in heroic m.**, être de la pâte dont on fait les héros. *Cu:* **Jelly m.**, moule à gelée. *(b) Metall:* **Casting m.**, moule à fonte. **Box m.**, châssis *m* à mouler. *(c) Typ:* Matrice *f.* **3.** *Cu:* **Rice m.**, gâteau *m* de riz.

mould[3], *v.tr.* **1.** Mouler; pétrir, former, façonner (le caractère de qn). **2.** *Bak:* Mettre (le pain) en forme. **3.** *N.Arch:* Gabarier (la quille, etc.). **4.** *Typ:* **To m. a page**, prendre l'empreinte d'une page. **moulding**, *s.* **1.** *(a)* Moulage *m.* *(b) N.Arch:* Gabariage *m.* *(c)* Formation *f* (du caractère). **2.** Moulure *f,* moulage. **Plain m.**, listeau *m,* listel *m.* **Grooved m.**, moulure à gorge. *Com: Ind:* **Mouldings**, profilés *m* (en fer, etc.). '**moulding-plane**, *s.* Rabot *m* à moulures; mouchette *f.*

mould⁴, s. Moisi m, moisissure f.
mould⁵, v.i. Moisir. **Blue-moulded cheese**, fromage bleu.
moulder¹ ['mouldər], v.i. Tomber en poussière; s'effriter. **To m. in idleness**, s'encroûter dans l'oisiveté.
moulder², s. Cer: Metall: Mouleur m.
mouldiness ['mouldinis], s. État de moisi; moisissure f.
mouldy ['mouldi], a. Moisi. **To go m.**, (se) moisir. **To smell m.**, sentir le moisi. P: **I feel (really) m.**, je me sens mal en train; j'ai le cafard.
moult¹ [moult], s. Mue f.
moult². 1. v.i. (Of bird, reptile) Muer. 2. v.tr. Perdre (ses plumes, sa peau, sa carapace). **moulting¹**, a. En mue. **moulting²**, s. Mue f. **M.-time**, mue.
mound [maund], s. (a) Tertre m, monticule m, butte f; motte f (d'un château). Civ.E: Remblai m. Prehist: **Burial m.**, tumulus m. (b) Monceau m, tas m (de pierres, etc.).
mount¹ [maunt], s. Mont m, montagne f. **M. Sinai**, le mont Sinaï.
mount², s. 1. (a) Montage m, support m; monture f (d'une lentille); armement m (d'une machine); affût m, pied m (de télescope). **Brass mounts**, ferrures f en cuivre. (b) **Picture m.**, carton m de montage. (c) **Stamp m.** (in album), charnière f. 2. Monture f (d'un cavalier). **My m. was a camel**, j'étais monté sur un chameau. 3. Turf: Monte f.
mount³. I. v.i. 1. Monter (en haut d'une colline, etc.). 2. Equit: Se mettre en selle; monter, sauter, à cheval. 3. (Of bill, etc.) Se monter, s'élever (to so much, à tant). II. mount, v.tr. & i. 1. **To m. (on, upon) a chair**, monter sur une chaise. **To m. the pulpit**, monter en chaire. (Of car, etc.) **To m. the pavement**, monter sur le trottoir. 2. **To m. (on, upon) a horse, a bicycle**, monter sur, enfourcher, un cheval, une bicyclette. III. mount, v.tr. 1. Monter, gravir (l'escalier, une colline). **To m. a ladder**, monter à une échelle. 2. **To m. s.o. (on a horse)**, (i) hisser qn sur un cheval; (ii) pourvoir (un soldat, etc.) d'un cheval. **Mounted police**, agents à cheval. 3. (a) Artil: Affûter, armer (une pièce). (b) **Ship mounting twenty guns**, navire armé de vingt canons. (c) **To m. guard**, monter la garde (over, auprès de). 4. (a) Monter (un diamant, une scie, un hameçon); installer (une machine); entoiler, encoller (une carte). **Diamonds mounted in platinum**, diamants montés sur platine, sertis de platine. (b) Th: Monter, mettre (une pièce) à la scène. **mount up**, v.i. (Of costs) Croître, monter, augmenter. **mounting**, s. 1. (a) Montage m, installation f (d'une machine). (b) Entoilage m, encollage m. 2. (a) Monture f, garniture f (de fusil, etc.). Iron m., ferrure f; garniture de fer. (b) Affût m (de canon, de mitrailleuse). **Tripod m.**, affût-trépied m. (c) = MOUNT² 1. **'mounting-block**, s. Equit: Montoir m.
mountain ['mauntin], s. Montagne f. **To make mountains out of molehills**, se noyer dans un verre d'eau; s'embarrasser d'un rien. **M. stream**, torrent m. **M. flower**, fleur de (haute) montagne. **M. tribe**, tribu montagnarde. **M. cure**, cure f d'altitude. **'mountain 'ash**, s. Bot: Sorbier m des oiseleurs, des oiseaux. **'mountain 'range**, s. Chaîne f de montagnes.
mountaineer¹ [,maunti'niər], s. Alpiniste mf, ascensionniste mf.
mountaineer², v.i. Faire des ascensions en montagne; faire de l'alpinisme. **mountaineering**, s. Alpinisme m.
mountainous ['mauntinəs], a. (Pays) montagneux. **M. seas**, mer démontée.
mountebank ['mauntibæŋk], s. (a) Saltimbanque m, bateleur m. (b) Charlatan m. **Political m.**, polichinelle m de la politique.
mounter ['mauntər], s. Monteur, -euse (de diamants, de machines, etc.); metteur m en œuvre (de diamants, etc.).
Mountie, Mounty ['maunti], s. F: Membre m de la *Royal Canadian Mounted Police*.
mourn [mɔːn], v.i. & tr. Pleurer, se lamenter, s'affliger. **To m. (for, over) sth.**, pleurer, déplorer, qch. **To m. for s.o.**, pleurer (la mort de) qn. **His death was universally mourned**, sa mort fut un deuil général.
mourning, s. 1. Affliction f, deuil m. 2. (a) House

of m., maison endeuillée. (b) Habits mpl de deuil. **In deep m.**, en grand deuil. **To go into m.**, se mettre en deuil; prendre le deuil. **To be in m. for s.o.**, être en deuil, porter le deuil, de qn. **'mourning-band**, s. Crêpe m; brassard m de deuil.
mourner ['mɔːnər], s. 1. Affligé, -ée. 2. Personne qui suit le cortège funèbre. **The mourners**, le convoi; le cortège funèbre. **To be chief m.**, mener, conduire, le deuil.
mournful ['mɔːnf(u)l], a. Lugubre, mélancolique; (figure) d'enterrement; (voix) funèbre. **-fully**, adv. Lugubrement, mélancoliquement.
mouse¹, pl. **mice** [maus, mais], s. Souris f. **Young m.**, souriceau m. **'mouse-colour**, s. (Couleur f) gris m (de) souris. **'mouse-ear**, s. Bot: Oreille f de souris. **'mouse-hole**, s. Trou m de souris.
mouse² [maus, mauz]. 1. v.i. (Of cat, etc.) Chasser aux souris; chasser les souris. 2. v.tr. Nau: Moucheter, aiguilleter (un croc). **mousing**, s. 1. Chasse f aux souris. 2. Nau: Aiguilletage m.
mouser ['mausər], s. Souricier m. **Good m.**, chat bon souricier.
mousetrap ['maustræp], s. (a) Souricière f, tapette f (à souris). (b) F: Pej: Fromage m de qualité inférieure.
mousy ['mausi], a. (a) Qui ressemble à une souris; timide. (b) (Couleur) gris (de) souris. **M. hair**, cheveux de couleur indéterminée.
moustache [məs'taːʃ], s. Moustache(s) f(pl).
mouth¹ [mauθ], s. (pl. mouths [mauðz]) 1. (Of pers.) Bouche f. **To make s.o.'s m. water**, faire venir l'eau à la bouche à qn. **To put words into s.o.'s m.**, attribuer des paroles à qn. P: **I'll stop your m. for you!** je te fermerai la gueule! 2. Bouche (de cheval, d'âne, de bœuf, de mouton, d'éléphant, de poisson); gueule f (de chien, d'animaux carnassiers, de gros poissons). Equit: **Horse with a hard m.**, cheval fort en bouche, sans bouche. **Soft m.**, bouche tendre, sensible. 3. (a) Bouche (de puits, de volcan); goulot m (de bouteille); pavillon m (d'entonnoir); guichet m (de boîte à lettres); gueule (de four, de canon); ouverture f, entrée f (de tunnel, de caverne); bief m (de bief). (b) Embouchure f (de fleuve). **'mouth-organ**, s. Harmonica m. **'mouth-wash**, s. Eau f dentifrice; collutoire m.
mouth² [mauð]. 1. v.tr. **To m. one's words**, déclamer ses phrases. 2. v.i. (a) Grimacer; faire des grimaces. (b) Déclamer. **mouthing**, s. Emphase f (dans le discours).
-mouthed ['mauðd], a. 1. (a) **Single-m.**, à une seule bouche. (b) (Of pers.) **Cruel-m.**, à la bouche cruelle. **Foul-m.**, au langage grossier. 2. **Well-m. horse**, cheval bien embouché.
mouthful ['mauθful], s. 1. Bouchée f. **To swallow sth. at one m.**, ne faire qu'une bouchée de qch. **To swallow a m. of water (while swimming)**, F: to get a m., boire une, la, tasse. **M. of wine**, gorgée f de vin. 2. F: Mot long d'une aune.
mouthpiece ['mauθpiːs], s. 1. (a) Embouchure f (de chalumeau, etc.); embout m (de porte-voix). (b) Mus: Bec m, embouchure (de clarinette); bocal m (de basson). (c) Tp: Microphone m. 2. Pol: **To be the m. of a party**, être le porte-parole inv d'un parti.
movable ['muːvəbl]. 1. a. (a) Mobile. **M. feast**, fête mobile. Typ: **M. type**, caractère(s) m mobile(s). (b) Jur: Mobilier, meuble. **M. effects**, effets mobiliers. 2. s.pl. **Movables**. (a) Mobilier m; agencements m amovibles. (b) Jur: Biens mobiliers, biens meubles.
move¹ [muːv], s. 1. (a) Chess: etc: Coup m. **Knight's m.**, marche f du cavalier. **To have first m.**, avoir le trait. **To make a m.**, jouer. **Whose m. is it?** c'est à qui de jouer? **Your m.**, à vous (de jouer). (b) Coup, démarche f. **What is the next m.?** qu'est-ce qu'il faut faire maintenant? **He must make the first m.**, c'est à lui de faire le premier pas. F: **He is up to every m. (in the game)**, il sait parer à tous les coups. 2. Mouvement m. F: **We must make a m.**, il faut partir. **To be always on the m.**, (i) être toujours en mouvement; (ii) être toujours en voyage, être toujours par monts et par vaux. F: **To get a m. on**, se dépêcher; P: se grouiller. 3. Déménagement m.

move². I. *v.tr.* 1. (*a*) Déplacer (un meuble, des troupes, etc.). To m. one's chair, changer sa chaise de place. *Sch:* To be moved up, passer dans la classe supérieure. *Chess:* To m. a piece, jouer une pièce. (*b*) To m. house, *abs.* to m., déménager. To m. into the country, aller s'installer à la campagne. 2. (*a*) Remuer, bouger (la tête, etc.). Not to m. a muscle, ne pas sourciller. The wind moving the trees, le vent qui agite les arbres. (*b*) Mouvoir, animer (qch.); mettre (qch.) en mouvement; mettre en marche (une machine). (*c*) *Med:* To m. the bowels, relâcher le ventre. 3. (*a*) Faire changer d'avis à (qn). He is not to be moved, il est inébranlable. (*b*) To m. s.o. to do sth., pousser, inciter, qn à faire qch. I will do it when the spirit moves me, je le ferai quand le cœur m'en dira. (*c*) Émouvoir, toucher, affecter (qn). Easily moved, émotionnable. To m. s.o. to anger, provoquer la colère de qn. To m. s.o. to laughter, faire rire qn. To m. s.o. to tears, émouvoir qn jusqu'aux larmes. To m. s.o. to pity, exciter la pitié de qn; attendrir qn. Tears will not m. him (to pity), les larmes le laisseront insensible. 4. To m. a resolution, proposer une motion; mettre aux voix une résolution. To m. that . . ., proposer que + *sub.* II. **move,** *v.i.* (*a*) Se mouvoir, se déplacer. Keep moving! circulez! *Com: F:* This article is not moving, cet article ne se vend pas. (*Of pers.*) To m. in high society, fréquenter la haute société. (*b*) To m. (about), faire un mouvement; bouger, (se) remuer. Don't m.! ne bougez pas! *Mec.E:* (*Of part*) To m. freely, jouer librement. (*c*) Marcher, aller; s'avancer. To m. towards a place, se diriger vers un endroit. He moved with dignity, il avait une démarche digne. *F:* It is time we were moving, il est temps de partir. *Chess:* The bishop moves diagonally, le fou marche diagonalement. **move about.** 1. *v.tr.* Déplacer (qch.). 2. *v.i.* Aller et venir. **move away.** 1. *v.tr.* Écarter, éloigner (qch.). 2. *v.i.* S'éloigner, s'en aller, se retirer. They've moved away from here, ils n'habitent plus ici. **move back.** 1. *v.tr.* (*a*) Faire reculer. (*b*) Ramener (qch.) en arrière. 2. *v.i.* (*a*) (Se) reculer. (*b*) Revenir en arrière. **move forward.** 1. *v.tr.* Avancer (un outil, etc.); faire avancer, porter en avant (des troupes). 2. *v.i.* (S')avancer; (*of troops*) se porter en avant. **move in,** *v.i.* (*a*) Entrer, pénétrer (dans un endroit). (*b*) Emménager. **move off,** *v.i.* S'éloigner, s'en aller; (*of army, train*) se mettre en marche, s'ébranler; (*of car*) démarrer. **move on,** *v.i.* (*a*) Avancer; continuer son chemin. M. on, please! circulez, s'il vous plaît! (*b*) Se remettre en route. **move out.** 1. *v.tr.* (*a*) Sortir (qch.), faire sortir (qn). (*b*) Déménager (ses meubles). 2. *v.i.* (*a*) Sortir. (*b*) Déménager. **move over.** 1. *v.tr.* Déplacer, écarter. 2. *v.i.* S'écarter, se déplacer. **moving,** *a.* 1. (*a*) En mouvement; en marche. (*b*) Mobile. M. staircase, escalier roulant. M. coil, bobine *f* mobile (de haut-parleur). 2. (*Of force, etc.*) Moteur, -trice. The m. spirit, l'âme *f* (d'une entreprise). 3. Émouvant, touchant, attendrissant.

movement ['mu:vmənt], *s.* Mouvement *m.* 1. (*a*) Déplacement *m.* Oblique m., oblique *m.* There was a general m. towards the door, tout le monde se dirigea vers la porte. (*b*) *pl.* To study s.o.'s movements, épier les allées et venues de qn. *Journ:* Movements of ships, déplacements. 2. To make a m. of impatience, avoir un geste d'impatience. 3. Popular m., mouvement populaire. 4. Transport *m* (de marchandises). 5. Clockwork m., mouvement d'horlogerie. 6. *Mus:* Symphony in three movements, symphonie *f* en trois mouvements.

mover ['mu:vər], *s.* 1. Moteur *m.* Prime m., premier moteur, premier mobile. 2. Auteur *m* (d'une motion).

movie ['mu:vi], *s. F: esp. U.S:* Film *m.* The movies, le cinéma.

mow [mou], *v.tr.* (mowed; mown) 1. Faucher, moissonner. To m. down the enemy, faucher l'ennemi. 2. Tondre (le gazon). 'mowing, *s.* 1. Fauchage *m.* 2. Tonte *f* (du gazon). 'mowing-machine, *s.* 1. Faucheuse *f.* 2. Tondeuse *f* (de gazon).

mower ['mouər], *s.* 1. (*Pers.*) Faucheur, -euse. 2. (Lawn) m., tondeuse *f* (de gazon).

Mozarab [mə'zærəb], *s.* Mozarabe *mf.*

Mozarabic [mə'zærəbik], *a.* Mozarabe.

Mr ['mistər]. *See* MISTER 1.

Mrs ['misiz]. *See* MISTRESS 3 (*b*).

mu [mju:], *s. Gr.Alph:* Mu *m.*

much [mʌtʃ]. 1. *a.* (*a*) Beaucoup (de); bien (du, de la, des). M. care, beaucoup de soin; bien des soins. (*b*) How m. bread? combien de pain? How m. is it? c'est combien? 2. *adv.* Beaucoup, bien. (Very) m. better, beaucoup mieux. M. worse, bien pis. It doesn't matter m., cela ne fait pas grand-chose. He is not m. richer than I, il n'est guère plus riche que moi. So m. more intelligent, infiniment plus intelligent. M. the largest, de beaucoup le plus grand. Thank you very m. (for . . .), merci bien; je vous remercie infiniment (de . . .). M. of an age, à peu près du même âge. It is pretty m. the same thing, c'est à peu près la même chose. M. to my astonishment, à mon grand étonnement. I don't want two, much less three, il ne m'en faut pas deux, encore moins trois. *P:* Not m.! je t'en fiche! 3. *s.* (*a*) M. still remains to be done, il reste encore beaucoup à faire. M. of the paper is damaged, une bonne partie du papier est avariée. Do you see m. of one another? vous voyez-vous souvent? M. happened while you were away, il s'est passé bien des choses en votre absence. There is not m. to see, il n'y a pas grand-chose à voir. To have m. to be thankful for, avoir tout lieu d'être reconnaissant. *F:* It is not up to m., cela ne vaut pas grand-chose; ce n'est pas fameux; c'est quelconque. *F:* He wasn't m. of a teacher, il ne valait pas grand-chose comme professeur. I am not m. of a playgoer, je ne vais guère au théâtre. Not m. of a dinner, un pauvre dîner. *Iron:* M. he knows about it! Comme s'il y connaissait quelque chose! (*b*) This m., autant que ceci. That m. too big, trop grand de cela. Cut that m. off, coupez-en long comme ça. This m. is certain, that . . ., il y a ceci de certain que. . . . (*c*) To make m. of sth. (i) faire grand cas de qch.; (ii) vanter qch. *F:* To make m. of s.o., (i) faire fête à qn; (ii) câliner, choyer (un enfant, etc.). I don't think m. of it, j'en fais peu de cas; ça ne me dit pas grand-chose. I don't think m. of him, je ne l'estime pas beaucoup. 4. (*a*) M. as. M. as I like him . . ., quelle que soit mon affection pour lui. . . . M. as I dislike it . . ., si peu que cela me dise . . . (*b*) As m., autant (de). As m. again, encore autant. Give me half as m. again, donnez-m'en la moitié en plus, *F:* moitié plus. Twice as m. water, deux fois autant d'eau. *F:* thought as m., je m'y attendais; je m'en doutais bien. (*c*) As m. as . . ., autant que. . . . I have three times as m. as I want, j'en ai trois fois plus qu'il ne m'en faut. He hates you as m. as you like him, autant vous l'aimez, autant il vous déteste. It is a m. as he can do to read, c'est tout juste s'il sait lire. He looked at me as m. as to say . . ., il me regarda avec l'air de vouloir dire. . . ., comme pour dire . . . (*d*) As m. (as), so m. (as), tant (que), autant (que). He does not like me as m. as her, il ne m'aime pas autant qu'il l'aime, elle. Oceans do not so m. divide the world as unite it, les océans ne divisent pas tant le monde qu'ils l'unissent. I haven't so m. as my fare, je n'ai pas même, pas seulement, le prix de mon voyage. (*e*) So m., tant (de); autant (de). So m. money, tant d'argent. So m. exaggerated, tellement exagéré. So m. the better, tant mieux. It will be so m. the less to pay, ce sera autant de moins à payer. So m. so that . . ., à ce point, à tel point que. . . . So m. for his friendship! et voilà ce qu'il appelle l'amitié! So m. for that! Voilà pour cela! *F:* et d'une! (*f*) So m. per cent, tant pour cent. (*g*) Too m., trop (de). Ten pounds too m., dix livres de trop. Too m. by half, moitié de trop. To make too m. of sth., attacher trop d'importance à qch. They were too m. for him, il n'était pas de taille à leur résister. 'much-admired, *a.* Admiré de tous, très admiré. 'much-loved, *a.* Bien-aimé.

muchness ['mʌtʃnis], *s.* It's much of a m., c'est bonnet blanc et blanc bonnet; *F:* c'est kif-kif.

mucilage ['mju:silidʒ], *s.* Mucilage *m.*

mucilaginous [,mju:si'lædʒinəs], *a.* Mucilagineux, -euse.

muck[1] [mʌk], *s.* **1.** (a) Fumier *m.* (b) Fange *f*; (*from street*) crotte *f*, ordures *fpl.* *F:* To be all in a m., être crotté jusqu'à l'échine. **2.** *F:* Choses dégoûtantes; saletés *fpl.* '**muck-heap,** *s.* Tas *m* d'ordures; fumier *m.* '**muck-rake,** *s.* Racloir *m* à boue; râteau *m* à fumier. '**muck-spreader,** *s.* *Agr:* Épandeur *m* (de fumier).

muck[2]. **1.** *v.tr.* (a) To m. (out) a stable, nettoyer une écurie. (b) Salir, crotter. (c) *F:* To m. (up) a job, *F:* cochonner, saloper, un travail. **2.** *v.i.* *F:* To m. about, flâner, flânocher. muck in, *v.i.* *P:* To m. in with s.o., (i) chambrer avec qn; (ii) prendre ses repas avec qn.

muckiness ['mʌkinis], *s.* Saleté *f*, malpropreté *f.*
mucky ['mʌki], *a.* *F:* Sale, crotté, souillé, malpropre.
mucosity [mju(:)'kɔsiti], *s.* Mucosité *f.*
mucous ['mju:kəs], *a.* Muqueux, -euse.
mucus ['mju:kəs], *s.* Mucus *m*, mucosité *f*, glaire *f.*
mud [mʌd], *s.* (a) Boue *f*, bourbe *f*; *Lit:* fange *f.* (River) m., vase *f.* (Of ship) To sink in the m., s'envaser. To drag s.o.'s name in the m., traîner qn dans la boue. To fling, throw, m. at s.o., déblatérer contre qn. M. hut, hutte *f* de terre. M. wall, mur en torchis, en pisé. (b) *Mch:* Boue; tartres boueux. '**mud-bank,** *s.* Banc *m* de vase. '**mud-barge,** *s.* Marie-salope *f.* '**mud-bath,** *s.* *Med:* Bain *m* de boues. '**mud-cock,** *s.* *Mch:* Purgeur *m*; robinet *m* d'ébouage. '**mud-flat,** *s.* Plage *f* de vase. '**mud-pack,** *s.* *Toil:* Emplâtre *m* de boues. '**mud-slinging,** *s.* *F:* Calomnies *fpl*; médisance *f.*
muddied ['mʌdid], *a.* Crotté; couvert de boue.
muddiness ['mʌdinis], *s.* **1.** Saleté *f.* **2.** Turbidité *f*, aspect trouble (d'un liquide).
muddle[1] ['mʌdl], *s.* Confusion *f*, emmêlement *m*, fouillis *m*, embrouillamini *m.* To be in a m., (i) (of thgs) être en désordre, en pagaille; (ii) (of pers.) avoir les idées brouillées. The whole thing is in a hopeless m., c'est la bouteille à l'encre. To get into a m., s'embrouiller. '**muddle-headed,** *a.* À l'esprit confus; brouillon. **M.-h.** ideas, idées confuses, embrouillées.
muddle[2], *v.tr.* (a) Embrouiller, brouiller (qch.); emmêler (une histoire). To m. things (up), embrouiller les choses; *F:* brouiller les fils. (b) Brouiller l'esprit à (qn); embrouiller (qn). **muddle through,** *v.i.* Se débrouiller; se tirer d'affaire tant bien que mal.
muddler ['mʌdlər], *s.* Brouillon, -onne.
muddy ['mʌdi], *a.* **1.** (a) Boueux, fangeux, bourbeux; (cours d'eau) vaseux, limoneux. *Nau:* M. bottom, fond *m* de vase. (b) (Vêtement) crotté, couvert de boue. **2.** (a) (Liquide) trouble. M. ink, encre pâteuse. (b) (Couleur) sale, enfumée. M. complexion, teint brouillé, terreux.
mudguard ['mʌdgɑːd], *s.* *Veh:* Garde-boue *m inv*, pare-boue *m inv.*
mudlark ['mʌdlɑːk], *s.* Gamin *m* des rues.
muezzin [mu'ezin], *s.* Muezzin *m.*
muff[1] [mʌf], *s.* **1.** *Cost:* Manchon *m.* **2.** *Mec.E:* Manchon d'accouplement. '**muff-coupling,** *s.* Accouplement *m* à manchon.
muff[2], *s.* *F:* *O:* **1.** (Pers.) Empoté *m*; *F:* andouille *f.* **2.** *Sp:* Coup raté.
muff[3], *v.tr.* *F:* *O:* Rater, bousiller, louper. *Sp:* To m. a shot, manquer, rater, un coup.
muffin ['mʌfin], *s.* Petit pain mollet (plat et rond; se mange à l'heure du thé, beurré à l'intérieur et rôti).
muffle[1] ['mʌfl], *s.* Mufle *m* (de bœuf, de vache).
muffle[2], *s.* *Metall:* *Cer:* Moufle *m.* **M.-furnace,** (four *m* à) moufle.
muffle[3], *v.tr.* **1.** Emmitoufler (in, de). To m. oneself up, s'emmitoufler. **2.** Envelopper (qch., pour amortir le son); assourdir (une cloche); étouffer (un son). **Muffled drums,** tambours voilés.
muffler ['mʌflər], *s.* **1.** Cache-nez *m inv.* **2.** *I.C.E:* *esp. U.S:* Pot *m* d'échappement; silencieux *m.*
mufti[1] ['mʌfti], *s.* *Moham. Rel:* Mufti *m.*
mufti[2], *s.* *Mil:* *F:* Tenue civile. In m., en civile, *F:* en pékin.
mug[1] [mʌg], *s.* (For beer) Chope *f*, pot *m*; (for tea) (grosse) tasse. Tin m., timbale *f*, gobelet *m.*
mug[2], *s.* *P:* **1.** Jobard *m*, nigaud *m.* He looks a bit of a m., il a l'air d'une poire. **2.** Andouille *f.*

mug[3], *v.tr.* (mugged) *Sch:* *F:* To m. up a subject bûcher, potasser, piocher, *P:* chiader un sujet.
mug[4], *s.* *P:* (Face) Binette *f*, fiole *f*, trogne *f.* **Ugly m.,** sale binette; vilain museau, drôle de gueule *f.*
mugger ['mʌgər], *s.* *Z:* Crocodile *m* des marais, de l'Inde.
muggy ['mʌgi], *a.* **1.** (Temps) mou, lourd. **2.** (Salle) qui sent le renfermé.
mulatto [mju(:)'lætou]. **1.** *a.* (a) Mulâtre. (b) (Teint) basané. **2.** *s.* Mulâtre, -esse.
mulberry ['mʌlb(ə)ri], *s.* *Bot:* **1.** Mûre *f.* **2.** Mûrier *m.*
mulch[1] [mʌltʃ], *s.* *Hort:* Paillis *m.*
mulch[2], *v.tr.* *Hort:* Pailler.
mulct[1] [mʌlkt], *s.* Amende *f.*
mulct[2], *v.tr.* **1.** *Jur:* Frapper (qn) d'une amende. **2.** Priver (s.o. of sth., qn de qch.).
mule[1] [mju:l], *s.* **1.** (He-)m., mulet *m.* (She-)m., mule *f.* On a m., à dos de mulet. **2.** Métis, -isse; hybride *m.* **3.** *Tex:* Mule-jenny *f*; renvideur *m.* **Self-acting m.,** renvideur automatique. '**mule-driver,** *s.* Muletier *m.* '**mule-train,** *s.* Équipage muletier.
mule[2], *s.* (Slipper) Mule *f.*
muleteer [ˌmju:li'tiər], *s.* Muletier *m.*
mulish ['mju:liʃ], *a.* **1.** De mulet. **2.** Entêté, têtu, comme un mulet. **-ly,** *adv.* Avec entêtement.
mull[1] [mʌl], *s.* Mousseline *f.*
mull[2], *v.tr.* Chauffer (du vin ou de la bière) avec des épices. **Mulled wine,** vin chaud épicé.
mull[3], *s.* *Scot:* Cap *m*, promontoire *m.*
mullein ['mʌlin], *s.* *Bot:* Molène *f*, *F:* bouillon-blanc *m.*
muller ['mʌlər], *s.* Molette *f*, porphyre *m* (de broyeur de couleurs).
mullet ['mʌlit], *s.* *Ich:* **1.** Muge *m.* Grey m., mulet *m.* **2.** Red m., rouget *m*; surmulet *m.*
mulligatawny [ˌmʌligə'tɔːni], *s.* Potage *m* au curry.
mullion ['mʌliən], *s.* *Arch:* Meneau (vertical).
mullioned ['mʌliənd], *a.* (Fenêtre) à meneau(x).
multicoloured ['mʌlti,kʌləd], *a.* Multicolore.
multifarious [ˌmʌlti'fɛəriəs], *a.* Extrêmement varié, divers; multiple.
multiflorous [ˌmʌlti'flɔːrəs], *a.* *Bot:* Multiflore.
multiform ['mʌltifɔːm], *a.* Multiforme.
multilateral [ˌmʌlti'læt(ə)r(ə)l], *a.* Multilatéral, -aux.
multimillionaire ['mʌlti,miljə'nɛər], *a.* & *s.* Multimillionnaire (*mf*), milliardaire (*mf*), archimillionnaire (*mf*).
multiparous [mʌl'tipərəs], *a.* *Biol:* Multipare.
multiphase ['mʌltifeiz], *a.* *El:* Multiphasé.
multiple ['mʌltipl]. **1.** *a.* Multiple. M. store, maison *f* à succursales (multiples). **2.** *s.* Multiple *m.* *Ar:* Lowest common m., plus petit commun multiple.
multiplex ['mʌltipleks], *a.* (Télégraphe) multiplex.
multipliable ['mʌltiplaiəbl], *a.* Multipliable.
multiplicand [ˌmʌltipli'kænd], *s.* *Mth:* Multiplicande *m.*
multiplication [ˌmʌltipli'keiʃ(ə)n], *s.* Multiplication *f.*
multiplicity [ˌmʌlti'plisiti], *s.* Multiplicité *f.*
multiplier ['mʌltiplaiər], *s.* *Mth:* *El:* Multiplicateur *m.*
multiply ['mʌltiplai]. **1.** *v.tr.* Multiplier. **2.** *v.i.* (Of species, etc.) Se multiplier.
multipolar [ˌmʌlti'poulər], *a.* Multipolaire.
multitude ['mʌltitjuːd], *s.* **1.** Multitude *f*, multiplicité *f* (de raisons, etc.). **2.** Multitude, foule *f.*
multitudinous [ˌmʌlti'tjuːdinəs], *a.* **1.** Nombreux, innombrable. **2.** De toutes sortes; multiple.
multivalence [ˌmʌlti'veiləns], *s.* *Ch:* Polyvalence *f.*
multivalent [ˌmʌlti'veilənt], *a.* *Ch:* Polyvalent.
mum[1] [mʌm], *int.* & *a.* Chut! Mum's the word! motus! To keep m. (about sth), ne pas souffler mot (de qch.); *F:* ne pas piper.
mum[2], *s.* *P:* Maman *f.*
mum[3], *s.* *P:* Madame *f.*
mumble ['mʌmbl], *v.tr.* Marmotter, marmonner, mâchonner. *Abs:* Manger ses mots. He mumbled a few words, il prononça quelques mots entre ses dents.
mumbler ['mʌmblər], *s.* Marmotteur, -euse.
mumbo-jumbo ['mʌmbou 'dʒʌmbou], *s.* (a) Culte superstitieux. (b) Baragouin *m.*
mummer ['mʌmər], *s.* Acteur *m* de pièces folkloriques; mime *m.*
mummification [ˌmʌmifi'keiʃ(ə)n], *s.* Momification *f.*

mummify ['mʌmifai], *v.tr.* Momifier. **To become mummified**, se momifier.
mummy[1] ['mʌmi], *s.* Momie *f.* '**mummy-cloth**, *s.* Bandelette *f* de momie.
mummy[2], *s. F:* Maman *f.*
mumps [mʌmps], *s.pl. Med:* Oreillons *mpl.*
munch [mʌn(t)ʃ], *v.tr.* Mâcher, mâchonner.
mundane ['mʌndein], *a.* Mondain. 1. Terrestre. 2. **M. pleasures**, plaisirs mondains.
municipal [mju(:)'nisip(ə)l], *a.* Municipal, -aux. **M. buildings**, = hôtel *m* de ville.
municipality [mju(:),nisi'pæliti], *s.* Municipalité *f.*
munificence [mju(:)'nifisns], *s.* Munificence *f.*
munificent [mju(:)'nifisnt], *a.* Munificent, généreux, -euse, libéral, -aux.
munition[1] [mju(:)'niʃ(ə)n], *s.* **Munition(s) of war**, munitions *f* de guerre. **M. factory**, usine *f* de guerre.
munition[2], *v.tr.* Approvisionner; ravitailler en munitions; armer (un vaisseau).
muraena [mju(:)'ri:nə], *s. Ich:* Murène *f.*
mural ['mjuərəl], *a.* Mural, -aux. **M. paintings**, *s.* murals, peintures murales.
murder[1] ['mə:dər], *s.* Meurtre *m.* **Premeditated m.**, assassinat *m.* **To commit (a) m.**, commettre un meurtre, un assassinat. **M.!** au meurtre! à l'assassin! **To cry m.**, crier à l'assassin. *Prov:* **M. will out**, tôt ou tard la vérité se fait jour.
murder[2], *v.tr.* 1. Assassiner. 2. *F:* Estropier (un vers); massacrer (une chanson); écorcher (le français).
murderer ['mə:d(ə)rər], *s.m.* Meurtrier, assassin.
murderess ['mə:d(ə)ris], *s.f.* Meurtrière.
murderous ['mə:d(ə)rəs], *a.* Meurtrier, assassin. **With m. intent**, dans une intention homicide.
murk [mə:k], *s. Scot:* Obscurité *f*, ténèbres *fpl.*
murkiness ['mə:kinis], *s.* Obscurité *f*; fuliginosité *f.*
murky ['mə:ki], *a.* Fuligineux, ténébreux; (ciel) brouillé. *F:* **M. past**, passé obscur, ténébreux.
murmur[1] ['mə:mər], *s.* 1. (*a*) Murmure *m*; bruissement *m.* (*b*) *Med:* **Cardiac m.**, murmure, bruit *m*, cardiaque). 2. Murmure (d'approbation ou d'improbation).
murmur[2], *v.i. & tr.* 1. Murmurer, susurrer. 2. **To m. at sth., against s.o.**, murmurer contre qch., contre qn.
muscat ['mʌskət], *a. & s.* **M. (grape)**, (raisin *m*) muscat *m.* **M. (wine)**, (vin *m*) muscat.
muscatel [,mʌskə'tel], *s.* 1. *Vit:* = MUSCAT. 2. **M. raisins**, *s.* muscatels, raisins secs de Malaga.
muscle ['mʌsl], *s.* Muscle *m.* **Oblique m.**, oblique, *m.*
Muscovite ['mʌskovait]. 1. *a. & s. Geog:* Moscovite (*mf*). 2. *s. Ch:* Muscovite *f.*
Muscovy ['mʌskəvi], 1. *Pr.n.A. Geog:* La Moscovie 2. *attrib.* **M. duck**, canard musqué de Barbarie.
muscular ['mʌskjulər], *a.* 1. (Tissu, force) musculaire. 2. (Homme) musculeux, musclé, bien découplé.
Muse[1] [mju:z], *s.f.* Muse.
muse[2], *v.i.* Méditer, rêver, rêvasser. **To m. on, about, sth.**, méditer sur qch.; réfléchir à qch. **musing**[1], *a.* Rêveur, -euse, -ly, *adv.* D'un air songeur, rêveur. **musing**[2], *s.* Rêverie *f* (on, à); méditation *f* (on, sur). **Idle musings**, rêvasseries *f.*
museum [mju(:)'ziəm], *s.* Musée *m* (d'antiquités, d'arts et métiers). **M. piece**, pièce *f* de musée.
mush [mʌʃ], *s.* 1. *F:* (*a*) Bouillie *f*, panade *f.* (*b*) *W.Tel:* Cafouillage *m*; (bruits *mpl* de) friture *f.* *T.V:* Brouillard *m* de fond. 2. *P:* Bêtises *fpl*, niaiseries *fpl*; sensibleries *fpl.*
mushroom[1] ['mʌʃrum], *s.* 1. Champignon *m* (comestible, de couche). *F:* **Fairy ring m.**, mousseron *m.* **M. bed**, champignonnière *f.* **M. spawn**, blanc *m* de champignon. **M. town**, ville champignon. **M. cloud**, nuage en forme de champignon. *Cu:* **M. ketchup**, sauce *f* aux champignons. 2. Darning m., œuf m, boule *f* à repriser. '**mushroom-'anchor**, *s. Nau:* Ancre *f* à champignon. '**mushroom-grower**, *s.* Champignonniste *m.*
mushroom[2], *v.i.* 1. Faire la cueillette des champignons, aller aux champignons. 2. (*Of bullet, etc.*) Faire champignon; s'aplatir. 3. *F:* Champignonner.
mushy ['mʌʃi], *a.* 1. (*Of food, ground*) Détrempé; (*of fruit*) blet, *f.* blette. 2. *F:* **M. sentimentality**, sensiblerie *f.*
music ['mju:zik], *s.* Musique *f.* **To set verses to m.**, mettre des vers en musique. **M. while you work**,

travail *m* en musique. **Programme m.**, musique de genre. **Hot m.**, jazz *m.* **To face the m.**, tenir tête à l'orage. *A:* **The m. of the spheres**, l'harmonie *f* céleste. '**music-case**, *s.* Porte-musique *m inv.* '**music-hall**, *s.* Music-hall *m.* '**music-lover**, *s.* Amateur, -trice, de musique. '**music-rest**, *s.* Tablette *f* de piano. '**music-roll**, *s. O:* 1. (*Carrier*) Rouleau *m* à musique. 2. Rouleau perforé, bande perforée (pour piano mécanique). '**music-stand**, *s.* Pupitre *m* à musique. '**music stool**, *s.* Tabouret *m* de piano.
musical ['mju:zik(ə)l], *a.* 1. Musical, -aux. **M. instrument**, instrument *m* de musique. **M. box**, boîte *f* à musique. 2. (*Of pers.*) (*a*) (Bon) musicien, (bonne) musicienne. (*b*) Amateur, -trice, de bonne musique. 3. (*Of sounds, verses*) Harmonieux, mélodieux, chantant. 4. *s.* Opérette *f.*
musician [mju:'ziʃ(ə)n], *s.* Musicien, -ienne.
musk [mʌsk], *s.* Musc *m.* **To perfume with m.**, musquer. '**musk-deer**, *s. Z:* Musc *m.* '**musk-duck**, *s.* Canard de Barbarie; canard musqué. '**musk ox**, *s. Z:* Bœuf musqué. '**musk-rat**, *s. Z:* Rat musqué. '**musk-rose**, *s.* 1. Rose musquée. 2. (*Bush*) Rosier musqué.
muskeg ['mʌskeg], *s.* Fondrière *f* de mousse.
muskellunge ['mʌskə'lʌndʒ], *s. Ich: Fr.C:* Maskinongé *m.*
musket ['mʌskit], *s. Sm.a:* Mousquet *m.*
musketeer [,mʌski'tiər], *s. A:* Mousquetaire *m.*
musketry ['mʌskitri], *s. Mil:* Tir *m*; mousqueterie *f.* **M. instruction**, exercices *mpl* de tir; école *f* de tir.
musky ['mʌski], *a.* Musqué. **M. smell**, odeur de musc.
Muslim ['mʌzlim], *a. & s.* = MOSLEM.
muslin ['mʌzlin], *s.* Mousseline *f.*
musquash ['mʌskwəʃ], *s.* 1. *Z:* Rat musqué. 2. *Com:* Castor *m* du Canada.
mussel ['mʌsl], *s. Moll: Cu:* Moule *f.* '**mussel-bed**, -**farm**, *s.* Banc *m* de moules; moulière *f*; parc *m* à moules.
must[1] [mʌst], *s. Vit:* Moût *m*; vin doux.
must[2], *s.* Moisi *m*; moisissure *f.*
must[3], *modal aux. v.* (*pr.t. & p.t.* must *in all persons; no infin., pr.p., p.p., or future*) 1. (*a*) (*Obligation*) You m. be ready at four o'clock, vous devrez être prêt, il faut, faudra, que vous soyez prêt, à quatre heures. You m. hurry up, il faut vous dépêcher. Plant that m. have continual attention, plante qui demande, qui réclame, des soins continuels. Cars m. slow down when crossing the bridge, les automobiles sont tenues de ralentir en passant sur le pont. They 'm. have new clothes, il leur faut absolument de nouveaux habits. He simply 'm. come, il faut absolument qu'il vienne. Do so if you m., faites-le s'il le faut. He is failing, I m. say, il faut avouer qu'il baisse. (*b*) (*Probability*) There's a ring, it m. be the doctor, on sonne, ce doit être le médecin. He m. have missed the train, il aura manqué le train. I m. have made a mistake, je me serais trompé. You 'm. know him, vous n'êtes pas sans le connaître. 2. (*Past Tense*) (*a*) I saw that I m. appear guilty, je me rendais compte que je ne pouvais que paraître coupable. I saw that he m. have suspected something, je vis bien qu'il avait dû se douter de quelque chose. Had he attempted the task he m. have failed, s'il avait tenté l'affaire il aurait forcément échoué. (*b*) As we were starting what m. he do but cut his finger! au moment de partir ne voilà-t-il pas qu'il s'est coupé le doigt!
must[4], *s. F:* Chose obligatoire It's a m., c'est une nécessité. This book is a m., c'est un livre qu'il faut lire.
mustang ['mʌstæŋ], *s. Z:* Mustang *m.*
mustard ['mʌstəd], *s. Bot: Cu:* Moutarde. **Wild m.**, moutarde des champs. *Hort:* **M. and cress**, moutarde blanche et cresson alénois. '**mustard-'bath**, *s. Med:* Bain sinapisé. '**mustard-'gas**, *s. Mil:* Yperite *f*; gaz *m* moutarde. '**mustard-'plaster**, *s. Med:* Sinapisme *m*; papier Rigollot. '**mustard-pot**, *s.* Moutardier *m*, pot *m* à moutarde. '**mustard-'poultice**, *s.* Cataplasme sinapisé; cataplasme à la (farine de) moutarde. '**mustard seed**, *s.* Graine *f* de moutarde. *B:* **Grain of m. seed**, grain *m* de moutarde.

muster¹ ['mʌstər], s. **1.** (a) Rassemblement m (d'une tribu, etc.). (b) Mil: Revue f. **To take a m. of the troops**, passer les troupes en revue. F: **To pass m.**, passer; être passable; être à la hauteur. (c) Nau: Appel m. **2.** Assemblée f, réunion f. **To turn out in full m.**, se présenter au grand complet. **'muster-roll,** s. Feuille f d'appel. Mil: Contrôles mpl. Nau: Rôle m de l'équipage.

muster², **1.** v.tr. (a) Rassembler (ses partisans, etc.). Society that musters a hundred (members), association qui compte cent membres. (b) Mil: Passer (des troupes) en revue. (c) Nau: Faire l'appel (des hommes). (d) To m. (up) one's strength, rassembler toutes ses forces. **2.** v.i. Se réunir, se rassembler.

mustiness ['mʌstinis], s. Goût m ou odeur f de moisi; relent m; remugle m.

musty ['mʌsti], a. **1.** (Goût, odeur) de moisi. **M. smell,** remugle m. **To smell m.,** sentir le moisi; (of room) sentir le renfermé. **2.** F: Suranné. **M. old laws,** vieilles lois désuètes.

mutability [,mju:tə'biliti], s. Mutabilité f.

mutable ['mju:təbl], a. **1.** Muable, variable. **2.** Ling: Sujet à la mutation.

mutage ['mju:tidʒ], s. Vit: Mutage m.

mutation [mju:'teiʃ(ə)n], s. Mutation f.

mute¹ [mju:t]. **I.** a. **1.** Muet, -ette. Jur: **To stand m.** (of malice), refuser de plaider ou de répondre. **2.** Ling: (a) **H m.,** h muet. (b) **M.** consonant, consonne sourde. **II. mute,** s. **1.** (Pers.) (a) Muet, -ette. (b) Employé m des pompes funèbres; croque-mort m. (c) Th: Personnage muet. **2.** Ling: Consonne sourde. **3.** Mus: Sourdine f. **With the m. on,** en sourdine.

mute², v.tr. **1.** Amortir, étouffer, assourdir (un son). **2.** Mus: Mettre la sourdine à (un violon, etc.). **muted,** a. Mus: (Violon) en sourdine; (corde) sourde.

mute³, v.tr. Vit: Muter.

muteness ['mju:tnis], s. Mutisme m.

mutilate ['mju:tileit], v.tr. Mutiler, estropier (qn); mutiler (une statue); tronquer (un passage).

mutilation [,mju:ti'leiʃ(ə)n], s. Mutilation f.

mutineer [,mju:ti'niər], s. Mil: Nau: Révolté m, mutiné m, mutin m.

mutinous ['mju:tinəs], a. Rebelle, mutiné, mutin; (équipage) en révolte.

mutiny¹ ['mju:tini], s. Mil: Nau: Révolte f, mutinerie, f. Hist: **The Indian M.,** la Révolte des cipayes.

mutiny², v.i. Se révolter, se mutiner (**against**, contre).

mutism ['mju:tizm], s. Mutisme m.

mutt [mʌt], s. F: Imbécile m, corniaud m, andouille f. **You silly m.!** espèce d'imbécile!

mutter ['mʌtər], v.tr. & i. Marmonner, marmotter. **To m. an oath,** grommeler, maronner, un juron. **muttering,** s. Marmottage m; murmures mpl.

mutton ['mʌt(ə)n], s. Cu: Mouton m. **Leg of mutton,** gigot m. **'mutton-'chop,** s. Cu: Côtelette f de mouton. F: **M.-c. whiskers,** favoris mpl en côtelette.

mutual ['mju:tjuəl], a. **1.** Mutuel, réciproque. **Transaction on m. terms,** marché stipulant un échange de services. **M. benefit society,** société f de secours mutuels. **2.** M. friend, ami commun. **-ally,** adv. Mutuellement, réciproquement.

mutuality [,mju:tju'æliti], s. Mutualité f.

muzzle¹ ['mʌzl], s. **1.** Museau m (d'un animal). **2.** Bouche f, gueule f (d'une arme à feu). **3.** Muselière f (pour chiens); bâillon m (pour chevaux). **'muzzle-ve'locity,** s. Ball: Vitesse f initiale.

muzzle², v.tr. Museler (un chien); F: museler, bâillonner (la presse).

muzzy ['mʌzi], a. (a) (Of pers.) Brouillé dans ses idées; au cerveau fumeux. (b) (Of ideas) Confus, vague; (of outline) flou, estompé. (c) (Of weather) Brumeux, embrumé.

my [mai], poss.a. Mon; f. ma, pl. mes. **One of my friends,** un de mes amis; Lit: un mien ami. **I have broken my arm,** je me suis cassé le bras. (Emphatic) **'My idea would be to . . .,** mon idée à moi serait de. . . . P: **My!** sapristi! par exemple!

myalgia [mai'ældʒiə], s. Med: Myalgie f, myodynie f.

mycologist [mai'kɔlədʒist], s. Mycologue m.

mycology [mai'kɔlədʒi], s. Bot: Mycologie f.

myelitis [,maiə'laitis], s. Med: Myélite f.

myocarditis [,maiouka:'daitis], s. Med: Myocardite f.

myocardium [,maio'ka:diəm], s. Anat: Myocarde m.

myology [mai'ɔlədʒi], s. Anat: Myologie f.

myopia [mai'oupiə], s. Med: Myopie f.

myopic [mai'ɔpik], a. Myope.

myosotis [,maiə'soutis], s. Bot: Myosotis m.

myriad ['miriəd]. **1.** s. Myriade f. **2.** a. Poet: Innombrable.

myriapod ['miriəpɔd], a. & s. Z: Myriapode (m); F: mille-pattes m inv.

Myriapoda [,miri'æpədə], s.pl. Z: Myriapodes m.

myrrh [məːr], s. Myrrhe f.

Myrtaceae [məː'teisii:], s.pl. Bot: Myrtacées f.

myrtle ['məːtl], s. Bot: **1.** Myrte m. **2.** Bog myrtle, myrica m.

myself [mai'self], pers.pron. See SELF 4.

mysterious [mi'stiəriəs], a. Mystérieux. **-ly,** adv. Mystérieusement.

mystery ['mistəri], s. **1.** Mystère m. **To make a m. of sth.,** faire mystère de qch. **It is a m. to me,** c'est lettre close pour moi. **2.** A.Th: M.(-play), mystère.

mystic ['mistik]. **1.** a. (a) (Of rites, arts) Ésotérique, mystique. (b) (Of power) Occulte; (of formula) magique. **2.** a. & s. Theol: Mystique (mf).

mystical ['mistik(ə)l], a. Mystique.

mysticism ['mistisizm], s. Mysticisme m.

mystification [,mistifi'keiʃ(ə)n], s. **1.** Mystification f. **2.** Embrouillement m, désorientation f (de l'esprit de qn).

mystify ['mistifai], v.tr. **1.** Mystifier (qn). **Mystified by . . .,** intrigué par. . . . **2.** Embrouiller, désorienter, dérouter.

myth [miθ], s. Mythe m.

mythical ['miθik(ə)l], a. Mythique.

mythological [,miθə'lɔdʒik(ə)l], a. Mythologique.

mythology [mi'θɔlədʒi], s. Mythologie f.

mythomania [,miθo'meiniə], s. Mythomanie f.

mythomaniac [,miθo'meiniæk], a. Mythomane; mythomaniaque.

myxoedema [,miksi'di:mə], s. Med: Myxœdème m.

myxomatosis [,miksoumə'tousis], s. Myxomatose f.

myxomycetes [,miksoumai'si:ti:z], s.pl. Fung: Myxomycètes m.

N, n [en], s. (a) (La lettre) N, n m. Tp: N for Nellie, N comme Nicolas. (b) Mth: To the nth (power), à la nième puissance. (c) Typ: N(-quadrat), demi-cadratin m.

nab [næb], v.tr. (nabbed) P: 1. (a) Saisir, arrêter, P: pincer, cueillir (qn). The police nabbed the lot, la police les a ratissés. To get nabbed, se faire pincer. (b) Prendre (qn) sur le fait, la main dans le sac. 2. Escamoter, chiper, chaparder (qch.).

nabob ['neibɔb], s. Nabab m.

nacelle [nə'sel], s. Aer: Nacelle f.

nacre ['neikər], s. Nacre f.

nacreous ['neikriəs], a. Nacré.

nadir ['neidiər], s. Astr: Nadir m.

naevus, pl. -i ['niːvəs, -ai], s. Nævus m, pl. nævi.

nag¹ [næg], s. F: Petit cheval (de selle); bidet m.

nag², v.tr. & i. (nagged) Quereller (qn); gronder (qn) sans cesse. To be always nagging (at) s.o., être toujours sur le dos de qn. nagging, a. 1. (Of pers.) Querelleur, -euse, grondeur, -euse, hargneux, -euse. 2. (Of pain) Agaçant, énervant.

naiad ['naiæd], s. Myth: Naïade f; nymphe f des eaux.

nail¹ [neil], s. 1. Ongle m (de doigt, d'orteil). 2. Clou m, pl. clous. Brass-headed n., clou doré. To hit the n. on the head, frapper juste, tomber juste; mettre le doigt dessus. 3. F: To pay on the n., payer argent comptant; payer rubis sur l'ongle. 'nail-brush, s. Toil: Brosse f à ongles. 'nail-claw, -drawer, -wrench, s. Tls: Arrache-clou(s) m inv; tire-clou(s) m inv; pied-de-biche m. 'nail-file, s. Toil: Lime f à ongles. 'nail-hole, s. 1. (a) (In horseshoe, etc.) Étampure f. (b) Clouure f; trou fait par un clou. 2. (On penknife) Onglet m. 'nail-scissors, s.pl. Toil: Ciseaux m à ongles; ongliers m. 'nail varnish, s. Toil: Vernis m à ongles.

nail², v.tr. 1. Clouer. To n. (up) a notice to a wall, clouer une affiche au mur. S.a. COLOUR¹ 4. 2. Clouter (des chaussures, une porte). nail down, v.tr. 1. Clouer (le couvercle d'une boîte). 2. To n. s.o. down to his promise, obliger qn à tenir sa promesse. nail up, v.tr.: (a) Clouer (une caisse); condamner (une porte). (b) Palisser (un arbre fruitier). nailed, a. 1. (a) Cloué. (b) Clouté; garni de clous. Heavily n. door, porte garnie de gros clous. 2. Pourvu d'ongles. Long-n., aux ongles longs.

nainsook ['neinsuːk], s. Tex: Nansouk m.

naïve [naːˈiːv], a. Naïf, f. naïve; ingénu. -ly, adv. Naïvement, ingénument.

naïveté, naïvety [naːˈiːvti], s. Naïveté f.

naked ['neikid], a. Nu. 1. (a) (Of pers.) Sans vête-ments; P: à poil. Stark n., mother n., tout nu; F: nu comme un ver, comme la main. (b) (Dos) dé-couvert, nu. The toga left the right arm n., la toge laissait à découvert, à nu, le bras droit. (c) (Mur) nu, dégarni, sans ornement; (pays) dénudé, pelé; (arbre) dépouillé de ses feuilles. 2. (a) N. sword, épée nue, sans fourreau. To fight with n. fists, se battre sans gants. N. light, feu nu; Min: lampe f à feu libre. (b) Visible to the n. eye, visible à l'œil nu. (c) The n. truth, la vérité toute nue, sans fard. N. facts, faits bruts.

nakedness ['neikidnis], s. Nudité f.

namby-pamby ['næmbi'pæmbi]. 1. a. (Of style) Affété, mignard, fade; (of pers.) maniéré, affecté; mignard, minaudier; gnangnan inv. 2. s. F: (O, pers.) Poule mouillée.

name¹ [neim], s. 1. Nom. m. (a) Full n., nom et prénoms. Christian, first, n., U.S: given n., prénom m; nom de baptême. My n. is . . ., je m'appelle. . . . N. of a firm, raison sociale (d'une maison de commerce). A man, X by n., un homme du nom de X; Jur: le dénommé X. To go by the n. of . . ., être connu sous le nom de. . . . To know s.o. (only) by n., (ne) connaître qn (que) de nom. F: To mention no names, ne nommer personne. (To caller) What n. shall I say? qui dois-je annoncer? To send in one's n., (i) se faire inscrire (dans un concours); (ii) se

faire annoncer. To put one's n. down (for sth.), (i) poser sa candidature; (ii) s'inscrire (pour qch.). List of names, liste nominative. F: (Of police) To take s.o.'s n. and address = dresser une contravention à qn. In the n. of . . ., au nom de . . ., de la part de. . . . In the n. of the king, de par le roi. F: What in the n. of goodness are you doing? que diable faites-vous là? (b) Terme m. Endearing names, termes d'amitié. S.a. CALL² I. 3. 2. Réputation f, renom-mée f. To get a bad n., se faire un mauvais renom. S.a. DOG¹ 1. He has a n. for honesty, il passe pour honnête. To make a name for oneself, to make one's n., se faire un grand nom; se faire une réputation. S.a. MUD. 'name-plate, s. Plaque f (pour porte, etc.); écusson m, médaillon m (avec le nom).

name², v.tr. 1. Nommer; dénommer (un nouveau produit). He was named Peter, (i) on lui a donné le nom de Pierre; (ii) il s'appelait, se nommait, Pierre. A person named Jones, un nommé Jones. To n. s.o. after, U.S: for s.o., donner à qn le nom de qn. To n. s.o. to an office, nommer qn à un poste. 3. Désigner (qn, qch.) par son nom. N. the kings of England, donnez les noms des rois d'Angleterre. Jur: The last-named, celui-ci, celle-ci. 4. (a) Citer (un exemple). (b) Fixer (le jour, l'heure). S.a. DAY 3.

nameless ['neimlis], a. 1. Sans nom; inconnu. 2. Anonyme. A lady who shall be nameless, une dame dont je tairai le nom. 3. (a) (Of dread, etc.) Indicible, inexprimable. (b) (Vice, etc.) innommable.

namely ['neimli], adv. (A) savoir; c'est-à-dire.

namesake ['neimseik], s. Homonyme m (de qn). He is my n., il s'appelle comme moi.

nankeen [næn'kiːn], s. 1. Tex: Nankin m. 2. A: pl. Nankeens, pantalon m de nankin.

nanny ['næni], s.f. Bonne f d'enfant, nurse; (in child's speech) Nounou. 'nanny(-goat), s.f. Chèvre; F: bique.

nap¹ [næp], s. Petit somme. Afternoon n., sieste f. To take, have, a n., faire un petit somme; (after midday meal) faire la sieste.

nap², v.i. (napping) Sommeiller. F: To catch s.o. napping, (i) surprendre la vigilance de qn; prendre qn au dépourvu; (ii) prendre qn en faute.

nap³, s. (Of velvet, cloth, felt) Poil m; (of cloth) duvet m. Cloth with raised n., étoffe molletonnée. Short-n. velvet, velours ras. Against the n., à contre-poil, à rebrousse-poil. His overcoat had lost its n., son pardessus était râpé, élimé.

nap⁴, v.tr. Tex: Garnir, gratter, lainer, rebrousser (le drap, etc.); molletonner (la laine, le coton).

nap⁵, s. 1. Cards: Napoléon m; nap m. F: To go n. on a horse, jouer son va-tout sur un cheval. To deal oneself a n. hand, se donner un beau jeu. 2. Turf: Tuyau sûr.

napalm ['neipɑːm], s. Napalm m. N. bomb, bombe f au napalm.

nape [neip], s. The n. of the neck, la nuque.

napery ['neipəri], s. A. & Scot: Linge m de table.

naphtha ['næfθə], s. (Huile f de) naphte m.

naphthalene ['næfθəliːn], s. Naphtaline f.

napierian [nei'piəriən], a. Mth: (Logarithme) népérien.

napkin ['næpkin], s. 1. (a) (Table-)n., serviette f (de table). N. ring, rond m de serviette. (b) (To protect tablecloth) Napperon m. (c) Ecc: (For consecrated bread) Tavaiole f. 2. (a) (For infant) Couche f. (b) U.S: Sanitary n., serviette hygiénique.

Napoleon [nə'poulian]. Pr.n.m. Napoléon.

Napoleonic [næpouli'ɔnik], a. Napoléonien, -ienne.

nappy ['næpi], s. F: = NAPKIN 2.

narcissism ['naːsizism], s. Psy: Narcissisme m.

Narcissus [naːˈsisəs]. 1. Pr.n.m. Myth: Narcisse. 2. s. (pl. narcissi [naːˈsisai]) Bot: Narcisse m.

narcosis [naːˈkousis], s. Med: Narcose f. (Diving) Nitrogen n., narcose, ivresse f des profondeurs.

narcotic [naːˈkɔtik], a. & s. Narcotique (m), stupéfiant (m).

narcotize ['nɑ:kətaiz], *v.tr.* Donner un narcotique à (qn).

nard [nɑ:d], *s. Bot:* Nard *m.*

narghile, nargileh ['nɑ:gilei], *s.* Narghileh *m*, narguilé *m.*

nark [nɑ:k], *s. P:* Mouchard *m.*

nark, *v. P:* **1.** *v.i.* Faire l'espion; moucharder. **2.** *v.tr.* (a) Irriter (qn). (b) N. it, fous-nous la paix.

narrate [nə'reit], *v.tr.* Narrer, raconter, relater (qch.).

narration [nə'reiʃ(ə)n], *s.* **1.** Narration *f* (d'une histoire, etc.). **2.** = NARRATIVE[1].

narrative[1] ['nærətiv], *s.* Récit *m*, narration *f.*

narrative[2], *a.* Narratif.

narrator [nə'reitər], *s.* (a) Narrateur, -trice. (b) (*In oratorio*) Récitant *m.*

narrow[1] ['nærou]. **1.** *a.* (a) (Chemin) étroit; (vallon) serré, resserré, encaissé; (passage) étranglé; (jupon) étriqué. To grow n., se rétrécir. N.-gauge railway, chemin de fer à voie étroite. *Nau:* The n. seas, la Manche et la mer d'Irlande. (b) De faibles dimensions, de peu d'étendue; (esprit) étroit, borné. N. limits, limites restreintes. In the narrowest sense, dans le sens le plus étroit. (c) (Examen) minutieux, méticuleux. (d) A n. majority, une faible majorité; une majorité bien juste. *S.a.* ESCAPE[1] 1, SHAVE[1] 2. **2.** *s.pl.* Narrows, passe étroite (entre deux terres); goulet *m* (d'un port); étranglement *m* (de rivière). **-ly,** *adv.* **1.** (a) (Interpréter) strictement, étroitement, rigoureusement. (b) (Examiner) minutieusement, de près. **2.** Tout juste. He n. missed being run over, il faillit être écrasé. **narrow-'minded,** *a.* Borné; à l'esprit étroit. **N.-m. ideas,** idées étroites, mesquines. **narrow-'mindedness,** *s.* Étroitesse *f*, petitesse *f*, d'esprit.

narrow[2], **1.** *v.tr.* (a) Resserrer, rétrécir. Narrowed eyelids, paupières mi-closes. (b) Restreindre, limiter, borner; rétrécir (un espace, les idées). **2.** *v.i.* Devenir plus étroit; se resserrer, se rétrécir; (*of channel*) s'étrangler.

narrowness ['nærounis], *s.* **1.** (a) Étroitesse *f*; manque *m* de largeur. (b) Petitesse *f*, exiguïté *f* (d'un espace); limitation *f*, circonscription *f* (de la vie, de l'intelligence). N. of mind, étroitesse d'esprit. **2.** Minutie *f* (d'un examen).

narthex ['nɑ:θeks], *s. Ecc.Arch:* Narthex *m.*

narwhal ['nɑ:wəl], *s. Z:* Narval *m*, -als.

nasal ['neiz(ə)l]. **1.** *a.* Nasal, -aux. N. accent, accent nasillard. **2.** *s.* (a) *Arm:* Nasal *m* (de casque). (b) *Ling:* Nasale *f.*

nasality [nei'zæliti], *s.* Nasalité *f.*

nasalize ['neizəlaiz], *v.tr.* Nasaliser (une syllabe).

nascent ['næs(ə)nt], *a.* Naissant; *Ch:* à l'état naissant.

nastiness ['nɑ:stinis], *s.* **1.** Mauvais goût; odeur *f* désagréable. **2.** Méchanceté *f.* **3.** *Esp. U.S:* Saleté *f*, malpropreté *f.* **4.** Obscénité *f.*

nasturtium [nə'stə:ʃəm], *s. Hort:* Capucine *f.*

nasty ['nɑ:sti], *a.* **1.** (a) Désagréable, dégoûtant. To smell n., sentir mauvais. (b) N. weather, sale vilain, temps. N. job, besogne difficile, dangereuse. N. corner, tournant dangereux. N. accident, accident sérieux. To receive a n. blow, recevoir un mauvais coup. *F:* That's a n. one! quelle tuile! Cheap and n., bon marché et de mauvais aloi. **2.** (*Of pers.*) Méchant, désagréable; *P:* rosse. To turn n., prendre un air méchant. *F:* He's a n. piece of work, c'est un sale type. N. trick, vilain tour; rosserie *f.* **3.** (a) *Esp. U.S:* Sale, malpropre. (b) (*Of book, etc.*) Ordurier, malpropre. (c) To have a n. mind, avoir l'esprit mal tourné; voir des obscénités où il n'y en a pas. **-ily,** *adv.* **1.** Désagréablement. **2.** (a) *Esp. U.S:* Malproprement. (b) Indécemment.

natality [nə'tæliti], *s.* Natalité *f.*

natation [nə'teiʃ(ə)n], *s.* Natation *f.*

natatory ['neitət(ə)ri], *a. Nat.Hist:* Natatoire.

nation ['neiʃ(ə)n], *s.* **1.** Nation *f.* The nations of Europe, les nations de l'Europe; les peuples européens. People of all nations, des gens de toutes les nationalités. *Pol:* The United Nations, les Nations Unies. **2.** The whole n. rose in arms, tout le pays se souleva. The voice of the n. la voix du peuple. **'nation(-)wide,** *a.* Répandu dans tout le pays.

national ['næʃ(ə)n(ə)l]. **1.** *a.* National, -aux; de l'État. *Adm:* N. status, nationalité *f. Mil:* N. service, service *m* militaire. *Nau:* N. flag, pavillon *m* de nation. *Pol:* N. Socialism, national-socialisme *m.* **2.** *s.pl.* Nationals, nationaux *m*, ressortissants *m* (d'un pays). **-ally,** *adv.* Nationalement; du point de vue national.

nationalism ['næʃ(ə)nəlizm], *s.* Nationalisme *m.*

nationalist ['næʃ(ə)nəlist], *a. & s.* Nationaliste (*mf*). N. China, la Chine nationaliste.

nationalistic [ˌnæʃ(ə)nə'listik], *a.* Nationaliste.

nationality [ˌnæʃə'næliti], *s.* Nationalité *f.*

nationalization [ˌnæʃ(ə)nəlai'zeiʃ(ə)n], *s.* Nationalisation *f.*

nationalize ['næʃ(ə)nəlaiz], *v.tr.* **1.** Nationaliser. **2.** Naturaliser (un étranger).

native ['neitiv]. **I.** *s.* **1.** Natif, -ive (d'un pays, d'une ville); indigène *mf* (d'un pays). N. of Australia, Australien de naissance. He speaks English like a n., il parle l'anglais comme un Anglais. *F:* (*Of a white man*) To go n., s'encanaquer. **2.** (a) (*Of plant, animal*) Indigène. The elephant is a n. of Asia, l'éléphant est originaire de l'Asie. (b) *pl.* Natives, huîtres *f* du pays. **II. native, a. 1.** (*Of qualities, etc.*) Naturel, inhérent, inné. N. to s.o., inhérent à qn. N. wit, bon sens natif. **2.** (a) (*Of place*) Natal, -als; de naissance. N. language, langue maternelle. N. land, terre natale; patrie *f*, pays *m.* (b) (Costume, huîtres) du pays. **3.** (*Of mineral*) A l'état natif. **4.** (*Of plant, pers.*) Indigène, originaire (to, de).

nativity [nə'tiviti], *s.* **1.** *Ecc:* Nativité *f.* **2.** *Astrol:* Nativité, horoscope *m.* To cast s.o.'s n., tirer l'horoscope de qn. **na'tivity play,** *s. Th:* Mystère *m* de la Nativité.

Nato ['neitou], *s.* L'Otan *m.*

natter ['nætər], *v.i. F:* Bavarder; jacasser.

natty ['næti], *a.* **1.** (*Of pers., dress*) Pimpant; coquet, -ette. **2.** (a) (*Of pers.*) Adroit. (b) Habilement exécuté.

natural ['nætʃər(ə)l]. **I.** *a.* Naturel. **1.** N. law, loi de la nature. N. size, grandeur nature; de grandeur normale. In the n. state, à l'état de nature. To die from n. causes, mourir de sa belle mort. *F:* To die a n. death, (d'un projet, etc.) échouer; tomber dans l'oubli. *Tex:* N. wool, laine beige. **2.** (a) Natif, inhérent, inné. N. goodness, bonté foncière. It comes n. to him, c'est un don chez lui. It comes n. to him to . . ., il a une facilité innée pour. . . . *Ph:* N. oscillation, oscillation propre. (b) It is n. that . . ., il est (bien) naturel que + *sub.* As is n., comme de raison. **3.** N. child, enfant naturel, illégitime. **-ally,** *adv.* **1.** (a) N. lazy, paresseux de sa nature, par tempérament. N. curly hair, cheveux qui frisent naturellement. (b) (Parler) naturellement, sans affectation. He writes n., son style coule de source. (c) To die n., mourir de sa belle mort. **2.** He n. does not wish . . ., naturellement, comme de raison, il ne veut pas. . . . Did you answer him?—N., lui avez-vous répondu?—Naturellement. **II. natural, s. 1.** *A:* Idiot, -ote (de naissance). **2.** As an actor, he's a n., c'est un acteur né. **3.** *Mus:* (a) Note naturelle. (b) (*Sign*) Bécarre *m.*

naturalism ['nætʃərəlizm], *s.* Naturalisme *m.*

naturalist ['nætʃərəlist], *s.* Naturaliste *mf.*

naturalistic [ˌnætʃ(ə)rə'listik], *a.* **1.** Naturaliste. **2.** *Art: Lit:* Naturiste.

naturalization [ˌnætʃərəlai'zeiʃ(ə)n], *s.* **1.** Naturalisation *f* (d'un étranger). N. papers, lettres *f* de naturalisation. **2.** *Biol:* Acclimatation *f.*

naturalize ['nætʃərəlaiz], *v.tr.* (a) Naturaliser (un étranger, un mot). To become a naturalized Frenchman, se faire naturaliser Français. (b) Acclimater (une plante, un animal).

naturalness ['nætʃərəlnis], *s.* **1.** Caractère naturel (d'une action, etc.). **2.** Naturel *m*; absence *f* d'affectation.

nature ['neitʃər], *s.* Nature *f.* **1.** (a) (*Of thg*) Essence *f*, caractère *m.* It is in the nature of things that . . ., il est dans l'ordre des choses que. . . . (b) (*Of pers.*) Naturel *m*, caractère, tempérament *m.* It is not in his n. to . . ., il n'est pas de sa nature de. . . . By n., par tempérament; naturellement. It comes to him by n., cela lui vient tout naturellement. **2.** Espèce *f*, sorte *f*, genre *m.* Something in the n. of a . . ., une espèce, une sorte, de. . . . 3. (a) (La) nature. The laws of n., les lois de la nature. N. study, histoire naturelle. To draw from n., dessiner d'après nature. Return to n., retour à l'état de nature. (b) Human n., la nature humaine. 'nature-worship, s. Adoration f des phénomènes naturels.

naturism ['neitʃərizm], s. Naturisme m.

naturist ['neitʃərist], s. Naturiste mf.

naturistic [neitʃər'istik], a. Naturiste.

naught [nɔːt], s. 1. Rien m, néant m. To come to n., échouer; n'aboutir à rien. To set the law at n., ne tenir aucun compte de la loi; passer outre à la loi. 2. Ar: Zéro m.

naughtiness ['nɔːtinis], s. 1. Mauvaise conduite (d'un enfant). 2. F: Caractère risqué, grivois.

naughty ['nɔːti], a. 1. (Of child) Vilain, méchant. You n. child! petit méchant! oh, le laid! 2. F: (Conte) risqué, grivois. -ily, adv. To behave n., ne pas être sage; être méchant.

nausea ['nɔːsiə], s. 1. (a) Nausée f; soulèvement m de cœur. To be overcome with n., avoir mal au cœur; avoir des nausées. (b) Mal m de mer. 2. Dégoût m, nausée, écœurement m.

nauseate ['nɔːsieit]. 1. v.tr. (a) Prendre (qch.) en dégoût. (b) Écœurer, dégoûter (qn); donner des nausées à (qn). ·2. v.i. Avoir la nausée (de qch.). **nauseating**, a. Nauséabond, dégoûtant, écœurant. It is n., cela soulève le cœur.

nauseous ['nɔːsiəs, -jəs], a. = NAUSEATING.

nautical ['nɔːtik(ə)l], a. Nautique, marin. Sch: N. school, école f de navigation (de la marine marchande). N. chart, carte marine. N. term, terme de navigation, de marine. N. almanac, almanach m nautique; éphémérides fpl.

nautilus, pl. -uses, -i ['nɔːtiləs, -əsiz, -ai], s. Moll: Nautile m. Paper n., argonaute m.

naval ['neiv(ə)l], a. Naval, -als; de marine (de guerre). N. forces, marine f (de guerre, militaire); armée navale. N. engagements, combats sur mer. N. base, port m de guerre. N. officer, officier de marine. N. college, école navale.

nave[1] [neiv], s. Moyeu m (de roue).

nave[2], s. Nef f (d'église).

navel ['neiv(ə)l], s. Anat: Nombril m, ombilic m. 'navel orange, s. Hort: Orange navel. 'navel-string, s. Cordon ombilical. 'navel-wort, s. Bot: Ombilic m; nombril m de Vénus.

navicert ['nævisɔːt], s. Navicert m.

navigability [nævigə'biliti], s. Navigabilité f.

navigable ['nævigəbl], a. (Fleuve) navigable. Ship in n. condition, navire en état de navigabilité.

navigate ['nævigeit]. 1. v.i. Naviguer. 2. v.tr. (a) Parcourir (les mers); naviguer sur (les mers); voyager dans (les airs). (b) Gouverner, diriger (un navire).

navigation [nævi'geiʃ(ə)n], s. Navigation f; conduite f (d'un navire). The N. Laws, le Code maritime. High seas n., navigation hauturière, au long cours. Inland n., navigation fluviale. S.a. LIGHT[1] 2.

navigator ['nævigeitər], s. Navigateur m.

navvy ['nævi], s. (Pers.) Terrassier m.

navvying ['næviiŋ], s. Travaux mpl de terrassier, de terrassement.

navy ['neivi], s. 1. Marine f de guerre, marine militaire. The Royal Navy = la marine de l'État. The merchant n., la marine marchande. U.S: Secretary for the N. = Ministre m de la marine. 2. F: = NAVY BLUE. 'navy 'blue, s. Bleu marine inv; bleu foncé inv. attrib. A n.b. suit, un costume bleu marine.

nay [nei]. 1. adv. (a) A. & Lit: Non. (b) Lit: Pour mieux dire. 2. s. A: Non m. I cannot say him n., je ne peux pas le lui refuser.

Nazarene [næzə'riːn], a. & s. B.Hist: Nazaréen, -enne.

naze [neiz], s. Promontoire m, cap m, pointe f.

Nazi ['nɑːtsi], s. Pol. Hist: Nazi mf.

nazify [nɑːtsifai], v.tr. Nazifier.

Nazism ['nɑːtsizm], s. Pol. Hist: Nazisme m.

Neanderthal [ni'ændətɑːl]. Pr.n.Geog: Le Néanderthal. Ethn: The N. man, l'homme m de Néanderthal.

neap[1] [niːp], a. & s. N. tides, [F: neaps, mortes eaux, marées de morte eau, de quadrature.

neap[2]. 1. v.i. (Of tides) Décroître. 2. v.tr. (Of ship) To be neaped, être retenu par manque d'eau; être amorti.

Neapolitan [niə'pɔlit(ə)n], a. & s. Napolitain, -aine. N. ice-cream, tranche napolitaine.

near[1] [niər]. I. adv. 1. (a) Près, proche. To come n., draw n., s'approcher (to, de). He drew nearer, il s'approcha davantage. N. at hand, à proximité, tout près, à portée de la main. Keep n. to me, restez près de moi. (b) They are n. of kin, ce sont de proches parents. Those n. and dear to him, ceux qui lui touchent de près. 2. As n. as I can remember, autant que je puisse m'en souvenir; autant qu'il m'en souvienne. I came n. to crying, je fus sur le point de pleurer. II. near, prep. 1. Près de, auprès de. The houses n. the mountains, les maisons dans le voisinage des montagnes. Bring your chair near(er) to fire, (r)approchez votre chaise du feu. 2. N. death, près de mourir; sur le point de mourir. To be n. the end, toucher à la fin. He came near being run over, il a failli être écrasé. III. near, a. 1. (Of relative) Proche; (of friend) intime, cher. Our n. relations, nos proches (parents). 2. The n. side, (of horse) côte (du) montoir; Aut: (en Angleterre) le côté gauche, (en France) le côté droit, d'une voiture. P.N: Keep to the n. side (lane), (en Angleterre) serrez à gauche, (en France) serrez à droite. 3. The nearest inn, l'auberge la plus voisine, la plus proche. The hour is n., l'heure est proche. To the nearest milligramme, à un milligramme près. 4. To go by the nearest road, prendre par le plus court. 5. N. translation, traduction serrée. N. resemblance, grande ressemblance. N. guess, conjecture à peu près juste. N. offer, offre approchante. It was a n. thing, nous l'avons échappé belle; P: il était moins cinq. 6. (Of pers.) Chiche, parcimonieux. -ly, adv. 1. (De) près. We are n. related, nous sommes proches parents. Nat.Hist: Nearly allied species, espèces voisines. 2. (a) Presque, à peu près, près de. It is n. midnight, il est bientôt minuit. N. the whole of our resources, la presque totalité de nos ressources. It is the same thing or n. so, c'est la même chose ou peu s'en faut. Is he dead?—Pretty n., est-il mort?—Il ne s'en faut guère. Very n., peu s'en faut. I n. caught them, j'ai été près de les attraper. I n. fell, je faillis tomber, j'ai manqué de tomber. (b) She is not n. so old, as you, elle est loin d'être aussi âgée que vous. 'near-'by[1], a. Voisin, proche. 'near 'by[2], adv. & prep. Tout près (de); tout proche (de). near-'sighted, a. Myope.

near[2], v.tr. (S')approcher de (qch.). The road is nearing completion, la route est près d'être achevée. We are nearing the goal, nous touchons au but.

nearness ['niənis], s. 1. (a) (Of time, place) Proximité f; (of place) voisinage m. (b) (Of translation) Fidélité f, exactitude f. 2. Parcimonie f.

neat [niːt], a. 1. (Of spirits) Pur; sans eau. To drink one's whisky n., boire son whisky sec. 2. (a) Simple et de bon goût; (of room, drawer) bien rangé, en ordre; (of garden) bien tenu, coquet. N. handwriting, écriture nette. N. ankles, chevilles fines. His n. attire, sa mise soignée. As n. as a new pin, tiré à quatre épingles. (b) (Of style) Élégant, choisi; (of phrase) bien tourné, adroit. 3. (Of pers.) Ordonné; qui a de l'ordre. -ly, adv. 1. (Ranger) avec ordre. N. dressed, habillé avec goût, avec soin. 2. Adroitement. N. turned compliment, compliment bien tourné.

neatness ['niːtnis], s. 1. Simplicité f, bon goût (dans la mise); apparence soignée (d'un jardin); netteté f (d'écriture); bon ordre (d'un tiroir, etc.); finesse f (de la cheville); tournure adroite (d'une phrase). 2. (Of pers.) (a) Ordre m. (b) Adresse f, dextérité f.

Nebuchadnezzar [nebjukəd'nezər]. Pr.n.m. B.Hist: Nabuchodonosor.

nebula, pl. -ae ['nebjulə, -iː], s. Astr: Nébuleuse f.

nebular ['nebjulər], a. Nébulaire.

nebulosity [nebju'lɔsiti], s. Nébulosité f.

nebulous ['nebjuləs], a. Nébuleux, -euse. N. character, personnage flou.

necessary ['nesəs(ə)ri]. 1. a. (a) Nécessaire, indispensable (to, for, à). It is n. to (do sth.), il est nécessaire de (faire qch.); il faut (faire qch.). I shall do everything n. to . . ., je ferai tout ce qu'il faudra pour. . . .

To make all n. arrangements, prendre toutes dispositions utiles. To make it n. for s.o. to do sth., mettre qn dans la nécessité de faire qch. If n., s'il le faut; s'il y a lieu; au besoin; en cas de besoin. Not to do more than is absolutely n., ne faire que le strict nécessaire, l'indispensable. (b) (Résultat) inévitable, inéluctable. 2. s. (a) Usu. pl. Ce qui est nécessaire à l'existence; le nécessaire. (b) P: The n., de l'argent P: du fric. F: To do the n., faire le nécessaire; esp. payer la note. -ily, adv. Nécessairement, de (toute) nécessité. What he says is not n. what he thinks, ce qu'il dit n'est pas forcément ce qu'il pense.

necessitate [ni'sesiteit], v.tr. Nécessiter (qch.); rendre (qch.) nécessaire. Process that necessitates very high pressures, procédé qui comporte des pressions très élevées.

necessitous [ni'sesitəs], a. Nécessiteux, besogneux. To be in n. circumstances, être dans le besoin.

necessity [ni'sesiti], s. 1. Nécessité f. (a) Obligation f, contrainte f. Dire n. compels me to . . ., la dure nécessité me force à. . . . By, out of, n., par nécessité. Of n., de (toute) nécessité, nécessairement. To be under the n. of doing sth., être dans la nécessité, se trouver dans l'obligation, de faire qch. Case of absolute n., cas de force majeure. S.a: VIRTUE. (b) Besoin m. The n. for sth., le besoin de qch. In case of n., au besoin, en cas de besoin. There is no n. for you to come, vous n'avez pas besoin de venir. 2. = NECESSARY 2 (a). Bare necessities, le strict nécessaire. A car is a n. nowadays, de nos jours une voiture est indispensable. 3. Nécessité, indigence f.

neck [nek], s. 1. (a) Cou m. To have a stiff n., avoir un, le, torticolis. F: To be up to one's n. in work, avoir du travail par-dessus la tête. F: He's in it up to his n., il trempe dans le bain. To fling one's arms round s.o.'s n., sauter, se jeter, au cou de qn. To break one's n., se casser le cou. F: To save one's n., sauver sa peau. F: To talk through the back of one's n., dire des bêtises. P: It gives me a pain in the n., ça me débecte. He's a pain in the n., c'est un casse-pieds. P: To get it in the n., écoper. Rac: To win by a n., gagner par une encolure. To finish n. and n., arriver à égalité. F: N. and crop, tout entier; à corps perdu. It is n. or nothing, il faut jouer le tout pour le tout. (b) Cu: Collet m (de mouton); collier m (de bœuf). Best end of n., côtelettes premières de mouton. (c) Dressm: Encolure f (de robe). High n., col montant. Low n., décolleté m. Square n., décolleté carré. V n., décolleté en pointe. 2. (a) Goulot m (de bouteille); col (d'un vase); goulet m (d'un port); rétrécissement m, étranglement m (de tuyau); manchon m (de ballon). (b) Langue f (de terre); collet (de vis, etc.); manche m (de violon). 'neck-band, s. Tour-de-cou m (de chemise). 'neck-line, s. Dressm: Encolure f, échancrure f; (low) décolletage m, décolleté m. Boat n.-l., décolleté bateau. 'neck-tie, s. Cost: Cravate f. 'neck-wear, s. Com: Cols mpl, cravates fpl, foulards mpl, etc.

neck², v. F: 1. v.tr. Pinter, lamper (la bière, etc.). 2. (a) v.tr. Bécoter, peloter (qn), faire des mamours à (qn). (b) v.i. (Of couple) Se faire des mamours. **necking**, s. F: Caresses fpl, pelotage m, papouilles fpl.

-necked [nekt], a. 1. (Of pers.) Bull-n., au cou de taureau. Short-n., à col court. 2. (Of dress) Square-n., V-n., à décolletage carré, en pointe.

necklace ['neklis], s. Collier m (de diamants, etc.).

necklet ['neklit], s. Collier m (de perles, de fourrure, etc.).

necrological [nekro'lɔdʒik(ə)l], a. Nécrologique.

necrology [ne'krɔlədʒi], s. 1. Nécrologe m (d'une église, etc.). 2. Nécrologie f.

necromancer ['nekrɔmænsər], s. Nécromancien, -ienne.

necromancy ['nekrɔmænsi], s. Nécromancie f.

necrophagous [ne'krɔfagəs], a. Z: Nécrophage.

necropolis [ne'krɔpəlis], s. Nécropole f.

necrosis [ne'krousis], s. Med: Nécrose f; gangrène f des os.

nectar ['nektər], s. Nectar m.

nectarine ['nektərin, -i:n] s. Brugnon m; nectarine f.

nectary ['nectəri], s. Bot: Nectaire m.

née [nei], a.f. Née.

need¹ [ni:d], s. 1. Besoin m. (a) If need(s) be, in case of n., en cas de besoin, au besoin; si besoin est. There is no n. to . . ., il n'est pas nécessaire, il n'est pas besoin de. . . . What n. is there to send for him? à quoi bon le faire venir? No n. to say that . . ., inutile de dire que. . . . To have n. (to) do sth., avoir besoin de, devoir, faire qch. You had no n. to speak, vous n'aviez que faire de parler. (b) To have n., stand in n., be in n., of sth., avoir besoin de qch.; manquer de qch. Premises badly in n. of repairs, local qui a grand besoin de réparations. I have no n. of your assistance, je n'ai que faire de votre aide. 2. (a) Adversité f; embarras m. In times of n., aux moments difficiles. (b) Besoin, indigence f, dénuement m. To be in n., être dans le besoin. 3. pl. My needs are few, peu me suffit. To supply the needs of s.o., pourvoir aux besoins de qn.

need². 1. v.tr. (3rd pers. sg. pr. ind. needs; p.t. & p.p. needed) (a) (Of pers.) Avoir besoin de (qn, qch.); (of thg) réclamer, exiger, demander (qch.). This will n. some explanation, ceci demande à être expliqué. These facts n. no comment, ces faits se passent de commentaire. To n. a lot of asking, se faire prier. A much needed lesson, une leçon dont on avait grand besoin. (b) To n. to do sth., être obligé, avoir besoin, de faire qch. They n. to be told everything, il faut qu'on leur dise tout. You only needed to ask, vous n'aviez qu'à demander. 2. Modal aux, (3rd pers. sg. pr. ind. need; p.t. need) N. he go? a-t-il besoin, est-il obligé, d'y aller? He needn't go, n. he? il n'est pas tenu d'y aller, n'est-ce pas? You n. not wait, inutile d'attendre. I n. hardly tell you . . ., point n'est besoin de vous dire. . . . Why n. he bother us? qu'a-t-il besoin de nous déranger? 3. Impers. It needed the horrors of war to open our eyes, il a fallu les horreurs de la guerre pour nous ouvrir les yeux.

needful ['ni:df(u)l], a. Nécessaire (to, for, à, pour). As much as is n., autant qu'il est besoin, autant qu'il en faut. s. F: To do the n., faire le nécessaire. To supply the n., fournir l'argent nécessaire; P: casquer.

needle ['ni:dl], s. Aiguille f. 1. Aiguille à coudre, à tricoter, etc. To look for a n. in a haystack, chercher une aiguille dans une botte de foin. 2. Tchn: (a) Aiguille (de phonographe). I.C.E: Pointeau m de carburateur, de soupape). Sm.a: Firing n., percuteur m. Art: Engraving n., pointe f pour taille-douce, pointe sèche. (b) Aiguille (de boussole, etc.); aiguille, languette f (de balance); Geog: aiguille (rocheuse). 3. Cleopatra's N., l'Obélisque m de Cléopâtre. 'needle-case, s. Étui m à aiguilles; aiguillier m. 'needle-gun, s. Sm.a.: Fusil m à aiguille. 'needle-holder, s. Surg: Porte-aiguille m.inv. 'needle-lace, s. Dentelle f à l'aiguille. 'needle-valve, s. I.C.E: Soupape f à pointeau.

needle, v.tr. F: Chiner (qn); être (toujours) sur le dos de (qn); empoisonner (qn).

needleful ['ni:dlful], s. Aiguillée f (de fil).

needless ['ni:dlis], a. Inutile, peu nécessaire, superflu. (It is) n. to say that . . ., (il est) inutile de dire que . . ., point n'est besoin de dire que. . . . She is n. to say very pleased, il va sans dire qu'elle est très contente.

needlewoman, pl. -women ['ni:dlwumən, -wimin], s.f. 1. Femme d'aiguille. She is a good n., elle travaille adroitement à l'aiguille. 2. Couturière à la journée; (in institution) lingère.

needlework ['ni:dlwə:k], s. Travaux mpl à l'aiguille; ouvrages mpl de dames; (as school subject) couture f. Bring your n., apportez votre ouvrage.

needs [ni:dz], adv. (Used only with 'must') (a) Nécessairement. If n. must, s'il le faut. Lit: I must n. obey, I n. must obey, (i) force m'est d'obéir; (ii) force me fut d'obéir. N. must when the devil drives, nécessité n'a pas de loi. (b) He had no money but she must n. marry him, il était sans le sou mais il a fallu qu'elle l'épouse!

needy ['ni:di], a. Nécessiteux, -euse, besogneux, -euse.

ne'er [neər], adv. Poet: = NEVER. 'ne'er-do-well, a. & s. Propre à rien.

nefarious [ni'feəriəs], a, Infâme, scélérat.

negate [ni'geit], v.tr. 1. Nier; nier l'existence de . . . 2. Nullifier (une loi).

negation [ni'geiʃ(ə)n], s. Négation f.

negative[1] ['negətiv]. I. a. Négatif. El: N. electrode, cathode f. Mth: N. sign, (signe m) moins (m). -ly, adv. Négativement. II. negative, s. 1. (a) Négative f. Gram: Négation f. To answer in the negative, répondre par la négative. The answer is in the n., la réponse est négative, est non. (b) Valeur négative. Mth: Quantité négative. 2. (a) Phot: Négatif m, cliché m. (b) (Of gramophone record) Matrice f. (c) El: Plaque négative (de pile).

negative[2], v.tr. 1. S'opposer à, rejeter (un projet); repousser (un amendement). 2. Réfuter (une hypothèse); contredire, nier (un rapport); annuler (un signal). 3. Neutraliser (un effet).

negatron ['negətrɔn], s. Ph: Négaton m.

neglect[1] [ni'glekt], s. 1. (a) Manque m d'égards (of, envers, pour). (b) Manque de soin(s). To die in total n., mourir complètement abandonné. (c) Mauvais entretien (d'une machine). 2. Négligence f, inattention f. From n., par négligence. N. of one's duties, inobservance de ses devoirs.

neglect[2], v.tr. 1. (a) Manquer d'égards envers (qn). (b) Manquer de soins pour (qn); ne prendre aucun soin de (ses enfants). 2. Négliger, oublier (ses devoirs, un avis). To n. an opportunity, laisser échapper une occasion. To n. to do sth., négliger, omettre, de faire qch. **neglected,** a. (Of appearance, etc.) Négligé. N. garden, jardin mal tenu, à l'abandon. N. wife, épouse délaissée.

neglectful [ni'glektful], a. Négligent. To be n. of sth., négliger qch. N. of his interests, insoucieux de ses intérêts.

négligé(e) ['negliʒei], s. (a) Cost: Négligé m. (b) O: In n., en déshabillé.

negligence ['neglidʒəns], s. 1. Négligence f, incurie f; manque m de soins. Through n., par négligence. S.a. CONTRIBUTORY. 2. Nonchalance f, insouciance f.

negligent ['neglidʒənt], a. 1. Négligent. To be n. of sth., négliger qch. 2. (Air, ton) nonchalant, insouciant. N. attire, tenue négligée. -ly, adv. Négligemment; avec négligence.

negligible ['neglidʒibl], a. Négligeable.

negotiable [ni'gouʃiəbl], a. 1. Fin: (Effet, titre) négociable. Not n., non-négociable. (of military pension, etc.) incessible. S.a. INSTRUMENT[1] 3. 2. (Barrière) franchissable; (chemin) praticable.

negotiate [ni'gouʃieit]. 1. v.tr. (a) Négocier (une affaire, un emprunt). (b) To n. a bill, négocier un effet. To n. a treaty, (i) négocier, (ii) conclure, un traité. (c) Franchir (un obstacle); surmonter (une difficulté). Aut: To n. a bend, prendre un virage. 2. v.i. To be negotiating with s.o. for . . ., être en pourparlers avec qn pour. . . . To n. for peace, entreprendre des pourparlers de paix.

negotiation [ni,gouʃi'ei(ə)n], s. 1. Négociation f (d'un traité, d'un emprunt). Under n., en négociation. By n., par voie de négociations. Price a matter for n., prix à débattre. To be in n. with s.o., être en pourparler(s) avec qn. To enter into, upon, negotiations with s.o., engager, entamer, des négociations avec qn. 2. Franchissement m (d'un obstacle); prise f (d'un virage).

negotiator [ni'gouʃieitər], s. Négociateur, -trice.

Negress ['niːgres], s.f. Ethn: & Pej: Négresse.

Negro, pl. -oes ['niːgrou, -ouz], a. & s. Ethn: & Pej: Nègre (m). The n. race, la race nègre.

negroid ['niːgrɔid], a. Ethn: Négroïde.

neigh[1] [nei], s. Hennissement m.

neigh[2], v.i. Hennir. **neighing,** s. Hennissement m.

neighbour ['neibər], s. 1. Voisin, -ine. My right-, left-hand n., mon voisin de droite, de gauche. 2. B: Prochain m. One's duty towards one's n., le devoir envers son prochain, envers autrui.

neighbourhood ['neibəhud], s. 1. Voisinage m, proximité f (of, de). To live in the n. of . . ., demeurer, habiter, à proximité de. . . . F: Something in the n. of ten pounds, une somme dans les dix livres. 2. (a) Alentours mpl, environs mpl (d'un lieu). In the n. of the town, aux alentours de la ville. (b) Voisinage, quartier m. The fruit grown in that n., les fruits cultivés dans cette localité. All the youth of the n., toute la jeunesse du voisinage.

neighbouring ['neibəriŋ], a. Avoisinant, voisin; proche.

neighbourliness ['neibəlinis], s. Bons rapports sentre voisins.

neighbourly ['neibəli], a. (Of pers.) Obligeant; amical, -aux. To act in a n. fashion, agir en bon voisin.

neither ['naiðər, 'niːðər]. 1. adv. & conj. (a) N. . . . nor . . ., ni . . . ni . . . . He will n. eat nor drink, il ne veut ni manger ni boire. (b) Non plus. If you do not go, n. shall I, si vous n'y allez pas, je n'irai pas non plus. (c) = NOR 1. 2. a. & pron. Ni l'un(e) ni l'autre; aucun(e). N. (of them) knows, ils ne le savent ni l'un ni l'autre; ni l'un ni l'autre ne le sait. On n. side, ni d'un côté ni de l'autre.

nematode ['nemətoud], s. Ann: Nématode m.

nem. con. ['nem'kɔn]. Lt.adv.phr. (nemine contradicente) Unanimement; à l'unanimité; (voter une loi) sans opposition.

nenuphar ['nenjufɑːr], s. Bot: Nénuphar m.

neo-classicism [niːou'klæsisizm], s. Néo-classicisme m.

neo-impressionism [niːouim'preʃənizm], s. Art: Néo-impressionisme m.

neolithic [niːo'liθik], a. Néolithique.

neologism [ni'ɔlədʒizm], s. Néologisme m.

neomycin ['niou'maisin], s. Pharm: Néomycine f.

neon ['niːɔn], s. Ch: Néon m. El.E: N. lighting, éclairage m au néon.

neophyte ['niːofait], s. Néophyte mf; débutant, -ante.

neoplasticism ['niːou'plæstisizm], s. Art: Néo-plasticisme m.

nephew ['nevju:], s.m. Neveu.

nephrite ['nefrait], s. Miner: Néphrite f.

nephritic [ni'fritik], a. Med: Néphrétique.

nephritis [ni'fraitis], s. Med: Néphrite f.

nepotism ['nepətizm], s. Népotisme m.

Nereid ['niəriid], s. Myth: Néréide f.

Nero ['niərou]. Pr.n.m. Rom.Hist: Néron.

nervate ['nəːveit], a. Bot: Nervé.

nerve[1] [nəːv], s. 1. (a) Anat: Nerf m. F: Fit of nerves, crise de nervosité. To be in a state of nerves, être énervé; avoir ses nerfs. To get on s.o.'s nerves, porter, donner, taper, sur les nerfs à qn. To kill the n. of a tooth, dévitaliser une dent. (b) Courage m, assurance f. To lose one's n., perdre son sang-froid; avoir le trac. (c) F: Audace f, aplomb m. To have the n. to . . ., avoir l'aplomb de. . . . P: You have got a n.! tu en as un toupet! 2. Bot: Arch: Nervure f. 3. (a) A: Tendon m. To strain every n. to do sth., déployer tous ses efforts pour faire qch. (b) Force f (musculaire). 4. attrib.a. N. specialist, neurologue m. 'nerve-cell, s. Anat: Cellule nerveuse. 'nerve-racking, a. Énervant, horripilant.

nerve[2], v.tr. Fortifier; donner du nerf, de la force, à (son bras); donner du courage à (qn). To n. oneself to do sth., s'armer de courage, faire appel à tout son courage, pour faire qch.; s'enhardir (à parler).

nerveless ['nəːvlis], a. 1. Inerte, sans force; (style) sans vigueur, mou. 2. (a) Anat: Z: Sans nerfs. (b) Bot: Sans nervures.

nervelessness ['nəːvlisnis], s. Inertie f; manque m de force, d'énergie.

nerviness ['nəːvinis], s. F: Nervosité f; énervement m.

nervous ['nəːvəs], a. 1. (Of pers.) (a) Excitable, irritable. (b) Inquiet, -ète; ému. (c) Timide, peureux. To feel n. in s.o.'s presence, se sentir intimidé en présence de qn. To get n., s'intimider. I was n. on his account, j'avais peur pour lui. To be n. of doing sth., éprouver une certaine timidité à faire qch. (c) It makes me n., cela m'intimide. To be n. that, craindre, avoir peur, que. 2. A: (Style) nerveux, énergique. 3. Anat: The n. system, le système nerveux. S.a. BREAK-DOWN 2, WRECK[1] 1. -ly, adv. 1. Timidement. 2. Craintivement.

nervousness ['nəːvəsnis], s. (a) Nervosité f, état nerveux, état d'agitation. (b) Timidité f.

nervy ['nəːvi], a. F: (a) Énervé, irritable. To feel n., être dans un état d'agacement, d'énervement; avoir les nerfs agacés, en pelote. She is n., elle est très nerveuse. (b) (Mouvement) nerveux, sec, saccadé.

nescience ['nesiəns], s. Nescience f; ignorance (of, de).

nest[1] [nest], s. 1. (a) Nid m. (b) Repaire m, nid (de brigands). 2. Nichée f (d'oiseaux, etc.). 3. Série f, jeu m (d'objets). N. of tables, table f gigogne. N. of drawers, chiffonnier m; (for office) classeur m (à tiroirs). N. of shelves, casier m. Mil: N. of machine-guns, nid de mitrailleuses. 'nest-box, s. Pondoir m. 'nest-egg, s. 1. Nichet m; œuf m en faïence. 2. Argent mis de côté; pécule m. To have a nice little n.-e., avoir un bas de laine bien garni.

nest². 1. *v.i.* (*a*) (*Of bird, etc.*) (Se) nicher; faire son nid. (*b*) = BIRD'S-NEST². 2. *v.tr.* Emboîter (des tubes, etc.) les uns dans les autres. **nesting¹**, *a.* (Oiseau) nicheur. **nesting²**, *s.* 1. N. time, époque *f* de la couvaison. 2. Emboîtage *m.*

nestful ['nestful], *s.* Nichée *f.*

nestle ['nesl], *v.i.* Se nicher. To n. (down) in an armchair, se blottir, se pelotonner, dans un fauteuil. To n. close (up) to s.o., se serrer contre qn. Village nestling in a valley, in a wood, village blotti, tapi, dans une vallée, niché dans un bois.

nestling ['nes(t)liŋ], *s.* Oisillon *m;* petit oiseau (encore au nid).

net¹ [net], *s.* 1. (*a*) *Fish: etc:* Filet *m.* **Cast(ing) net**, épervier *m.* **Shrimp(ing) n.**, filet à crevettes; bichette *f.* **Butterfly n.**, filet à papillons. (*b*) *Ven:* (**Game**) **n.**, rets *m;* panneau *m;* filet. 2. (*a*) **Hair n.**, filet, résille *f*, réseau *m* (pour cheveux). (*b*) *Ten:* Filet. To go up to the n., monter au filet. **N. play**, jeu au filet. 3. *Tex:* Tulle *m.* **Foundation n.**, mousseline forte. '**net-fishing**, *s.* Pêche *f* au filet.

net², *v.* (netted) 1. *v.tr.* (*a*) Prendre (des poissons, etc.) au filet. (*b*) Tendre des filets dans (une rivière). (*c*) Couvrir de filets (un groseillier). (*d*) *Sp:* Envoyer (le ballon, la balle) dans le filet. 2. *v.i.* Faire du filet. **netted**, *a.* 1. Couvert d'un filet, d'un réseau. 2. (*Of veins, paths*) En lacis, en réseau. 3. (Oiseau, etc.) pris au filet. **netting**, *s.* 1. Fabrication *f* du filet. 2. (*a*) Pêche *f* au filet. (*b*) Pose *f* de filets, de rets; chasse *f* au filet. 3. (*a*) Tulle *m.* (*b*) *Nau:* Nettings, bastingages *mpl.*

net³, *a.* (*Of weight, price*) Net, *f.* nette. '**Terms strictly n. cash**,' "sans déduction"; "payable au comptant."

net⁴, *v.tr.* (netted) 1. (*Of pers.*) Toucher net (tant de bénéfices). 2. (*Of enterprise*) Rapporter net (une certaine somme).

netball ['netbɔːl], *s.* *Sp:* = Basket-ball *m.*

nether ['neðər], *a.* Inférieur, bas. The n. lip, la lèvre inférieure. The n. regions, l'enfer *m.*

Netherlands (the) [ðə'neðələndz]. *Pr.n.pl.* Les Pays-Bas *m.*

nethermost ['neðəmoust], *a.* Le plus bas; le plus profond.

nett [net], *a.* = NET³.

nettle¹ ['netl], *s.* Ortie *f.* **Stinging n.**, ortie brûlante. *S.a.* GRASP² 1. Dead n., ortie blanche; lamier (blanc). **Hedge n.**, épiaire *m.* '**nettle-rash**, *s.* *Med:* Urticaire *f.* '**nettle-tree**, *s.* Micocoulier *m.*

nettle², *v.tr.* (*a*) Piquer, irriter (qn). **Greatly nettled by, at, this remark**, piqué au vif par cette parole. (*b*) Piquer (qn) d'honneur.

network ['netwəːk], *s.* 1. Ouvrage *m* en filet. **Wire n.**, treillis *m* métallique. 2. Réseau *m* (de veines, de voies ferrées); lacis *m* (de nerfs, de tranchées). **Road n.**, réseau routier.

neuralgia [njuə'rældʒə], *s.* Névralgie *f.*

neuralgic [njuə'rældʒik], *a.* Névralgique.

neurasthenia [ˌnjuərəs'θiːniə], *s.* Neurasthénie *f.*

neurasthenic [ˌnjuərəs'θenik], *a. & s.* Neurasthénique (*mf*).

neuritis [njuə'raitis], *s.* Névrite *f.*

neurologist [njuə'rɔlədʒist], *s.* *Med:* Neurologue *m.*

neurology [njuə'rɔlədʒi], *s.* *Med:* Neurologie *f.*

neuropath ['njuərɔpæθ], *s.* Névropathe *mf.*

neurosis, *pl.* **-es** [njuə'rousis, -iːz], *s.* *Med:* Névrose *f.*

neurotic [njuə'rɔtik]. 1. *a.* Névrosé, neurotique. 2. *s.* Névrosé, -ée.

neuter¹ ['njuːtər]. 1. *a.* (*a*) *Gram:* Neutre. This word is n., ce mot est du neutre. (*b*) *Biol:* Neutre, asexué. N. bee, abeille neutre. 2. *s.* (*a*) *Gram:* (Genre) neutre *m.* In the n., au neutre. (*b*) Animal châtré.

neuter², *v.tr.* *F:* Châtrer (un chat, etc.).

neutral ['njuːtrl]. 1. *a.* (*a*) *Pol: etc:* Neutre. To remain n., garder la neutralité. (*b*) Neutre; moyen, indéterminé; *Ch:* (sel) neutre, indifférent. *s.* Teinte *f* neutre. (*c*) *Aut:* In n., au point mort. 2. *s.* *Pol:* Neutre *m.* **Rights of neutrals**, droits des neutres.

neutralism ['njuːtrəlizm], *s.* Neutralisme *m.*

neutralist ['njuːtrəlist], *a. & s.* Neutraliste *mf.*

neutrality [njuː'træliti], *s.* *Pol: Ch:* Neutralité *f.*

neutralization [ˌnjuːtrəlai'zeiʃ(ə)n], *s.* Neutralisation *f.*

neutralize ['njuːtrəlaiz], *v.tr.* Neutraliser. (*Of forces*) To n. one another, se détruire.

neutron ['njuːtrɔn], *s.* *El:* Neutron *m.*

névé ['neivei], *s.* *Geog:* Névé *m.*

never ['nevər], *adv.* (*a*) (Ne . . .) jamais. I n. go there, je n'y vais jamais. N. again, jamais plus; plus jamais (. . . ne). He n. came back, il ne revint plus. The thing had n. been seen before, jusqu'alors la chose ne s'était jamais vue. I have n. yet seen . . ., je n'ai encore jamais vu. . . . N. shall I forget it, jamais je ne l'oublierai. N. in (all) my life, jamais de la vie. (*b*) (*Emphatic negative*) I n. expected him to come, je ne m'attendais aucunement à ce qu'il vînt. He n. said a word to him about it, il ne lui en a pas dit le moindre mot. You (surely) n. left him all alone! ne me dites pas que vous l'avez laissé tout seul! *P:* Well I n.! par exemple! c'est formidable! (*c*) N. mind! ne vous en faites pas! never-'ceasing, *a.* Incessant, continuel. N.-c. complaints, plaintes sempiternelles. never-'ending, *a.* Perpétuel, éternel; qui n'en finit plus. never-'failing, *a.* 1. (Remède) infaillible. 2. (Source) intarissable. 'never-'never, *s.* *F:* To buy sth. on the n.-n., acheter qch. à crédit, à tempérament. 'never-to-be-forgotten, *a.* Inoubliable; qui ne s'oubliera jamais.

nevermore ['nevə'mɔːr], *adv.* (Ne . . .) plus jamais; (ne . . .) jamais plus.

nevertheless [ˌnevəðə'les], *adv.* Néanmoins, quand même, toutefois, pourtant. It n. makes me anxious, cela ne laisse pas (que) de m'inquiéter; toujours est-il que cela m'inquiète.

new [njuː], *a.* 1. (*a*) Nouveau, -elle. N. fashion, nouvelle mode; mode nouvelle. Here's something n., (i) voici quelque chose de nouveau; (ii) *F:* voici du nouveau! N. ideas, idées nouvelles, idées neuves. N. ground, terre vierge. A district quite n. to me, une région qui est toute nouvelle pour moi. That has made a n. man of him, cela a fait de lui un autre homme. N. batteries cost a shilling, les piles de rechange coûtent un shilling. *Mil:* The n. guard, la garde montante. *Sch:* The n. boys, les nouveaux. (*b*) (*Of pers.*) To be n. to business, être nouveau, neuf, aux affaires. I was n. to that kind of work, je n'étais pas fait, je n'étais pas habitué, à ce genre de travail. 2. Neuf, *f.* neuve; non usagé. (Brand)n. garment, vêtement neuf. To be dressed in n. clothes, être habillé de neuf. *Com:* As n., à l'état (de) neuf. To make sth. like n., remettre qch. à neuf. The subject is quite n., ce sujet est neuf, n'a pas encore été traité. 3. (Pain) frais; (vin) nouveau, jeune. N. potatoes, pommes de terre nouvelles. *S.a.* MILK¹ 1. -ly, *adv.* Récemment, nouvellement. N. shaven, rasé de frais. The n.-elected members, les députés nouveaux élus. N.-painted wall, mur fraîchement peint. N.-formed friendship, amitié de fraîche date, de date récente. 'newly-weds, *s.pl.* Nouveaux mariés. 'new blown, *a.* (*Of flower*) Fraîs éclos, *f.* fraîche éclose; frais épanoui, *f.* fraîche épanouie. 'new-born, *a.* Nouveau-né. N.-b. children, enfants nouveau-nés. N.-b. daughter, fille nouveau-née. 'New 'Brunswick. *Pr.n.Geog:* Le Nouveau-Brunswick. 'New 'England. *Pr.n.Geog:* La Nouvelle-Angleterre. 'New Cale-'donia. *Pr.n.Geog:* La Nouvelle-Calédonie. 'new-comer, *s.* Nouveau venu, nouvel arrivé, *f.* nouvelle venue, etc. The new-comers, les nouveaux venus. 'new-found, *a.* Récemment découvert ou inventé. New 'Guinea. *Pr.n.* La Nouvelle-Guinée. 'new-laid, *a.* (Œuf) frais pondu, du jour. 'new-made, *a.* De facture récente; nouvellement construit. New Or'leans. *Pr.n.* La Nouvelle-Orléans. 'New South 'Wales. (*a*) *Pr.n.* La Nouvelle-Galles du Sud. (*b*) *attrib.a.* Néo-gallois. 'New South 'Welshman, *s.* Néo-Gallois. 'New 'Year, *s.* Nouvel an; nouvelle année. New-Year's Day, le jour de l'an. New-Year's Eve, la Saint-Sylvestre. To see the New Year in, faire la veillée, le réveillon, de la Saint-Sylvestre; réveillonner. To wish s.o. a happy New Year, souhaiter la bonne année à qn. New-Year's gift, étrennes *fpl;* cadeau *m* de jour de l'an. 'New 'York. 1. *Pr.n.* New York. 2. *attrib.a.* New-yorkais. 'New 'Yorker, *s.* New-yorkais, -aise. New 'Zealand. *Pr.n.* La Nouvelle-Zélande. New 'Zealander, *s.* Néo-Zélandais, -aise.

newel ['njuəl], *s.* 1. Noyau *m* (d'escalier tournant). 2. N.(-post), pilastre *m* (de rampe d'escalier).

newfangled [ˌnjuːˈfæŋgld], *a. Pej:* D'une modernité outrée.

Newfie [ˈn(j)uːfi], *s. U.S:* F: Terre-neuvien, -ienne.

Newfoundland [ˈnjuːfəndlænd, njuːˈfaundlənd]. 1. *Pr.n. Geog:* Terre-Neuve. In N., à Terre-Neuve. The N. fishermen, the N. fishing-boats, les terre-neuviens *m.* 2. *s.* [njuːˈfaundlənd] (*Dog*) Terre-neuve *m inv.*

Newfoundlander [ˈnjufəndlændər, njuːˈfaundləndər], *s.* Terre-neuvien, -ienne.

newness [ˈnjuːnis], *s.* 1. (*a*) Nouveauté *f* (d'une mode, d'une idée). (*b*) Inexpérience *f* (d'un employé). 2. État neuf (d'un vêtement). 3. Manque *m* de maturité (du vin, du fromage).

news [njuːz], *s.* Nouvelle(s) *f.* 1. What (is the) n.? quelles nouvelles? qu'est-ce qu'il y a de nouveau, de neuf? A sad piece of n., une triste nouvelle. To break the n. to s.o., faire part d'une mauvaise nouvelle à qn. No n. is good n., point de nouvelles, bonnes nouvelles. 2. (*a*) *Journ:* Financial n., chronique financière. 'The Sporting N.', "la Gazette du Turf." N. in brief = faits divers. *F:* To be in the n., être en vedette, avoir les honneurs de la presse, défrayer la chronique. *F:* To make n., faire sensation. The cold war is very much in the n., la guerre froide est à l'ordre du jour. The n., *W.Tel:* les informations *fpl; Cin:* actualités *fpl.* N. cinema, ciné-actualités *m.* N. film, reel, film *m* d'actualités, actualités *fpl* (*b*) Sujet *m* propre au reportage. A public house brawl isn't n., une rixe de cabaret est sans intérêt pour le public. **'news-agency,** *s.* Agence *f* d'informations. **'news(-)agent,** *s.* Marchand *m* de journaux; dépositaire *m* de journaux. **'news(-)print,** *s.* Papier *m* de journal. **'news(-)stand,** *s.* Kiosque *m* (où l'on vend des journaux).

newscast [ˈnjuːzkɑːst], *s. W.Tel:* F: Les informations *fpl.*

newsmonger [ˈnjuːzmʌŋgər], *s.* Colporteur, -euse, de nouvelles.

newspaper [ˈnjuːspeɪpər], *s.* Journal *m*, -aux. Daily n., (journal) quotidien *m.* Weekly n., (journal) hebdomadaire *m.* N. rack., porte-journaux *m inv.* Newspaper man, (i) marchand *m* de journaux; (ii) journaliste *m.*

newt [njuːt], *s. Amph:* Triton *m;* salamandre *f* aquatique; *F:* lézard *m* d'eau.

newton [ˈnjuːt(ə)n], *s.Ph:* Newton *m.*

next [nekst]. I. *a.* 1. (*Of place*) Prochain; le plus proche. The n. room, la chambre voisine. Her room is n. to mine, sa chambre est à côté de la mienne. The garden n. to mine, le jardin attenant au mien. Seated n. to me, assis à côté de moi. The n. house, la maison d'à côté. The n. house but one, la deuxième maison à partir d'ici. 2. (*a*) (*Of time*) Prochain, suivant. The n. day, le jour (d')après; le lendemain. The n. day but one, le surlendemain. The n. three days, les trois jours suivants. (The) n. morning, le lendemain matin. The n. instant, l'instant d'après. (*Future time*) N. year, l'année prochaine. By this time n. year, dans un an d'ici. The year after n., dans deux ans. On Friday n., n. Friday, vendredi prochain. (*b*) (*Of order*) The n. chapter, le chapitre suivant. *Journ:* Continued in the n. column, la suite à la colonne suivante. To be continued in our n., la suite au prochain numéro. The n. time I see him, la première fois que je le reverrai. *F:* What n.! par exemple! (*In shop*) What n., please? et avec cela? et ensuite? *Sch:* N. (boy) please! au suivant! Who comes n.? à qui le tour? (*c*) The n. size (*in shoes, etc.*) la pointure au-dessus. The n. best thing would be to . . ., à défaut de cela, le mieux serait de. . . . *F:* I got it for n. to nothing, je l'ai eu pour presque rien. There is n. to no evidence, il n'y a pour ainsi dire pas de preuves. There was next to nobody at the meeting, il n'y avait presque personne à la réunion. 3. *Jur:* N. friend, ami le plus proche. 4. *U.S:* F: To get n. to s.o., faire la connaissance de qn. *S.a.* KIN. II. **next,** *adv.* 1. Ensuite, après. What shall we do n.? qu'est-ce que nous allons faire maintenant, après cela? 2. La prochaine fois. When you are n. that way, la prochaine fois que vous passerez par là. When I n. saw him, quand je le revis. III. **next,** *prep.* Auprès de, à côté de. The carriage n. (to) the engine, la première voiture près de la locomotive.

'next 'door. 1. *s.* The girl from n. d., la jeune fille (de la maison) d'à côté. 2. *adv.phr.* (*a*) He lives n. d. (to us), il habite dans la maison voisine; il habite à côté (de chez nous). (*b*) Flattery is n. d. to lying, de la flatterie au mensonge il n'y a qu'un pas. Ideas n. d. to madness, idées qui avoisinent, qui frisent, la folie. 3. *adv.* The people n. d., les gens d'à côté. 4. *Attrib.* N.-d. neighbours, voisins d'à côté.

nib [nib], *s.* 1. (Bec *m* de) plume *f.* Broad n., grosse plume; plume à gros bec. 2. *See* COCOA-NIB.

nibbed [ˈnibd], *a.* Hard-n. pen, plume à bec dur; plume dure. *S.a.* GOLD-NIBBED.

nibble¹ [ˈnibl], *s.* 1. (*a*) Grignotement *m.* To have a n. at the cake, grignoter le gâteau. (*b*) *Fish:* Touche *f.* I didn't have a n. all day, ça n'a pas mordu de toute la journée. 2. Juste de quoi grignoter; petit morceau (de biscuit). (*for sheep*) de quoi brouter.

nibble², *v.tr. & i.* Grignoter, mordiller (qch.); (*of sheep*) brouter (l'herbe). To n. (at) a biscuit, grignoter un biscuit. He nibbles at his food, il mange du bout des dents, des lèvres. (*Of fish, F: of pers.*) To n. (at the bait), mordre à l'hameçon. To n. at an offer, se sentir tenté par une offre (sans pouvoir se décider).

niblick [ˈniblik], *s. Golf:* Niblick *m.*

nibs [nibz], *s. F:* His n., sa seigneurie, sa majesté.

nice [naɪs], *a.* 1. *Lit:* (*a*) (*Of pers.*) (i) Difficile, délicat, exigeant; (ii) *O:* scrupuleux, méticuleux. To be n. about, in, the choice of words, avoir des scrupules dans le choix des mots. (*b*) (*Of question, etc.*) Délicat; (*of distinction*) subtil, fin; (*of ear, eye*) sensible, juste. That's a very n. point, voilà une question délicate. 2. *F:* (*a*) (*Of pers.*) Gentil, *f.* gentille; sympathique. He was as n. as could be, il s'est montré aimable au possible. To be n. to s.o., se montrer gentil, aimable, avec qn. It is n. of you to . . ., vous êtes bien aimable de. . . . (*b*) (*Of thg*) Joli; bon. N. dinner, bon dîner. N. evening, soirée agréable. N. car, jolie auto. A n. little sum, une somme rondelette. It is n. here, il fait bon ici. (*c*) (*Intensive*) It is n. and cool, le temps est d'une fraîcheur agréable. They are n. and warm in their cots, ils sont bien au chaud dans leurs petits lits. The tea was n. and sweet, le thé était bien sucré. (*d*) N. people, des gens bien. Not n., pas tout à fait convenable. (*e*) *Iron:* We are in a n. mess! nous voilà dans de beaux draps! That's a n. way to behave! voilà une jolie conduite! -ly, *adv.* 1. *Lit:* Scrupuleusement, méticuleusement. 2. Joliment, gentiment, bien. N. situated house, maison agréablement située. Those will do n., ceux-là feront très bien l'affaire. *F:* He's getting on n., (i) (*of invalid*) il fait du progrès; (ii) ses affaires ne marchent pas mal.

Nicene [ˈnaɪsiːn], *a.* The N. creed, le symbole de Nicée.

niceness [ˈnaɪsnis], *s.* 1. *Lit:* Scrupulosité *f*, méticulosité *f*; minutie *f*; sensibilité *f.* 2. *F:* Gentillesse *f*, (de qn); goût *m* agréable (d'un aliment).

nicety [ˈnaɪsiti], *s.* 1. (*a*) Justesse *f*, précision *f* (d'un calcul). To a n., exactement, à la perfection, à merveille. (*b*) Subtilité *f*, délicatesse *f* (d'une question, etc.). 2. *pl.* Niceties, minuties *f.* Niceties of a craft, finesses *f* d'un métier.

niche [nitʃ], *s.* Niche *f* (pour statue, etc.). To make a n. for oneself, se caser.

Nicholas [ˈnikələs]. *Pr.n.m.* Nicolas.

Nick¹ [nik]. *Pr.n.m.* (*Dim. of*) Nicolas. *F:* Old N., le diable.

nick², *s.* 1. (*a*) Entaille *f*, encoche *f*, cran *m;* (*in tally-stick*) coche *f*, hoche *f*; (*in screw-head*) fente *f.* (*b*) Saignée *f* (de graissage); onglet *m* (de lame de couteau). 2. (*Just*) in the n. of time, à point nommé; juste à temps, juste à point. You have come just in the n. of time, vous tombez à pic.

nick³. 1. *v.tr.* (*a*) Entailler, encocher (un bâton, etc.); biseauter (les cartes). (*b*) Anglaiser (la queue d'un cheval). 2. *v.tr.* (*a*) Deviner (la vérité, etc.). (*b*) *F:* Arrêter, *F:* pincer (un malfaiteur). 3. *v.i. Rac:* To n. in, couper son concurrent; s'insinuer.

nickel¹ [ˈnikl], *s.* 1. Nickel *m.* 2. *U.S:* Pièce *f* de cinq cents. *S.a.* **'nickel-bearing,** *a. Miner:* Nickélifère. **nickel-'plate,** *v.tr.* Nickeler.

nickel², *v.tr.* (nickelled) Nickeler. **nickelling,** *s.* 1. (*Action*) Nickelage *m.* 2. Nickelure *f.*

nick-nack [ˈniknæk], *s.* = KNICK-KNACK.

nickname¹ ['nikneim], *s.* Surnom; sobriquet *m.*
nickname², *v.tr.* Surnommer (qn); donner un sobriquet à (qn). **He was nicknamed the Hunchback,** il était connu sous le sobriquet du Bossu.
nicotine ['nikəti:n], *s. Ch:* Nicotine *f.* **N. poisoning,** nicotinisme *m,* tabagisme *m.*
nic(ti)tate ['nik(ti)teit], *v.i.* Cligner les yeux; ciller; (*of horse*) nicter. *Z:* **Nictitating membrane,** membrane nictitante; *F:* onglet *m* (d'oiseau, etc.).
nic(ti)tation [,nik(ti)'teiʃ(ə)n], *s.* Nic(ti)tation *f.*
niece [ni:s], *s.f.* Nièce *f.*
niellist [ni'elist], *s.* Nielleur, -euse.
niello [ni'elou], *s. Metalw:* Nielle *m.* **To inlay with n.** nieller. **N-work,** niellure *f.*
nife [naif], *s. Geol:* Nifé *m.*
niff¹ [nif], *v.i. P:* Puer, *P:* schlinguer, cocoter.
niff², *s. P:* Puanteur *f*; odeur infecte.
nifty ['nifti], *a. P:* 1. Coquet, pimpant. 2. Puant.
niggard ['nigəd], *s.* Grippe-sou *m,* pingre *m.*
niggardliness ['nigədlinis], *s.* Ladrerie *f,* pingrerie *f*; mesquinerie *f.*
niggardly ['nigədli], *a.* (*Of pers.*) Chiche, ladre, pingre; mesquin; (*of sum, portion*) mesquin.
nigger ['nigər], *s. F: Pej:* Nègre *m, f.* négresse, noir, -e. **A little n. boy,** un négrillon. *F:* **There's a n. in the wood-pile,** il y a (quelque) anguille sous roche. *S.a.* MINSTREL², WORK² 1. **'nigger-'brown,** *a. Pej: in U.S:* (*Colour*) Tête-de-nègre *inv.*
niggle ['nigl], *v.i. Vétiller*; tatillonner. *Art:* Fignoler, pignocher. **To n. over trifles,** s'attarder à des vétilles.
niggling, *a.* (*Of details*) Insignifiant; de rien du tout; (*of work*) fignolé, léché; (*of pers.*) tatillon, -onne.
nigh [nai], *a., adv. & prep. Poet: Dial:* = NEAR. **N. unto death,** à l'article de la mort. *S.a.* WELL-NIGH.
night [nait], *s.* 1. (*a*) Nuit *f,* soir *m.* **Last n.,** la nuit dernière; hier (au) soir. **The n. before last,** avant-hier (au) soir. **The n. before,** la veille (au soir). **To-morrow n.,** demain soir. **Ten o'clock at n.,** dix heures du soir. **To be accustomed to late nights,** être accoutumé aux veilles. **To have a good, a bad, night('s rest),** bien, mal, dormir. **Good n.!** bonsoir! (*when retiring*) bonne nuit! **The maid's n. out,** le soir de sortie de la bonne. **At n.,** la nuit, à la nuit. **In the n.,** (*pendant*) la nuit. **By n.,** de nuit. **The n. boat,** le bateau de nuit. (*b*) *Th:* **First n.,** première *f.* **Wagner n.,** soirée musicale consacrée à Wagner. 2. Obscurité *f,* ténèbres *fpl.* **N. is falling,** il commence à faire nuit, la nuit tombe. *attrib.* **N. driving is dangerous,** conduire la nuit est dangereux. **'night-a'ttire,** *s.* = NIGHT-CLOTHES. **'night-bird,** *s.* (*a*) Oiseau *m* de nuit; (*oiseau*) nocturne. (*b*) *F:* Noctambule *mf.* **'night-blindness,** *s.* Héméralopie *f.* **'night-cap,** *s.* 1. *A:* Bonnet *m* de nuit (de femme); bonnet de coton (d'homme). 2. *F:* Boisson *f* (alcoolique) (prise avant de se coucher). **'night-clothes,** *s.pl.* Vêtements *m* de nuit. **'night-club,** *s.* Établissement *m* de nuit; *F:* boîte *f* de nuit. **'night(-)dress, (-)gown,** *U.S:* (-)robe, *s.* Chemise *f* de nuit (de femme), *Fr.C: F:* jaquette *f.* **'night-flowering,** *a. Bot:* Noctiflore. **'night-light,** *s.* Veilleuse *f.* **'night-shift,** *s. Ind:* Équipe *f* de nuit. **To be on n.-s.,** être de nuit. **'night-shirt,** *s.* Chemise *f* de nuit (d'homme). **'night-soil,** *s. Hyg:* Matières *fpl* de vidange; vidanges *fpl.* **'night-stick,** *s. U.S:* Matraque *f* (d'agent de police). **'night-time,** *s.* La nuit. **'night-watch,** *s.* (*a*) Garde *f* de nuit; veille *f.* (*b*) *Nau:* Quart *m* de nuit. **'night-watchman,** *pl.* **-men,** *s.m. Ind:* Veilleur, gardien, de nuit. **'night-wear,** *s.* = NIGHT-CLOTHES.
nightfall ['naitfɔ:l], *s.* Tombée *f* du jour, de la nuit. **At n.,** à la nuit tombante; à nuit close.
nightie ['naiti], *s. F:* = NIGHT-DRESS.
nightingale ['naitiŋgeil], *s. Orn:* Rossignol *m.*
nightjar ['naitdʒɑ:r], *s. Orn:* Engoulevent *m.*
nightly ['naitli]. 1. *a.* (*a*) (*Happening at night*) De nuit, du soir, nocturne. (*b*) **N. performance,** représentation (de) tous les soirs; soirée quotidienne. 2. *adv.* Tous les soirs, toutes les nuits.
nightmare ['naitmeər], *s.* Cauchemar *m.* **To have (a) n.,** avoir le cauchemar. *F:* **The prospect was a n. to me,** cette perspective me donnait le cauchemar.
nightmarish ['naitmeəriʃ], *a.* Cauchemardesque.

nightshade ['naitʃeid], *s. Bot:* **(Black) n.,** morelle noire; raisin *m* de loup. **Woody n.,** douce-amère *f.* **Deadly n.,** belladone *f.*
nihilism ['nai(h)ilizm], *s.* Nihilisme *m.*
nihilist ['nai(h)ilist], *s.* Nihiliste *mf.*
nil [nil], *s.* Rien *m*; (*on report-sheet, etc.*) néant *m. Sp:* Zéro *m.* **The balance is nil,** le solde est nul.
Nile (the) [ðə'nail]. *Pr.n. Geog:* Le Nil.
nilgai ['ni:lgai], *s. Z:* Nilgau(t) *m.*
nimble ['nimbl], *a.* (*Of pers.*) Agile, leste, preste; (*of mind, etc.*) délié, subtil, prompt. (*Of old pers.*) **Still n.,** encore ingambe. **-bly,** *adv.* Agilement; lestement, prestement. **nimble-'footed,** *a.* Aux pieds agiles.
nimbus, *pl.* **-i, -uses** ['nimbəs, -ai, -əsiz], *s.* 1. (*a*) *Art:* Nimbe *m,* auréole *f,* gloire *f.* (*b*) *Meteor:* Auréole *f* (autour de la lune). 2. *Meteor:* Nimbus *m.*
nincompoop ['niŋkəmpu:p], *s. F:* Benêt *m,* nigaud, -e, niais, -e.
nine [nain]. 1. *Num. a. & s.* Neuf (*m*). **To have n. lives** (like a cat), avoir l'âme chevillée au corps. **N. times out of ten,** neuf fois sur dix; en général. 2. *s. Sp: U.S:* Équipe de baseball. *S.a.* DRESS UP. (*For other phrases see* EIGHT.)
ninefold ['nainfould]. 1. *a.* Multiplié par neuf. 2. *adv.* Neuf fois autant.
ninepin ['nainpin], *s.* 1. *pl.* **Ninepins,** (jeu *m* de) quilles *fpl.* 2. Quille. *F:* **To go down like ninepins,** tomber comme des capucins de cartes.
nineteen ['nain'ti:n], *num. a. & s.* Dix-neuf (*m*). *S.a.* DOZEN. (*For other phrases see* EIGHT.)
nineteenth ['nain'ti:nθ], *num. & s.* Dix-neuvième.
ninetieth ['naintiiθ], *num. a. & s.* Quatre-vingt-dixième.
ninety ['nainti], *num. a. & s.* Quatre-vingt-dix. **N.-one, n.-nine,** quatre-vingt-onze, quatre-vingt-dix-neuf. *Med:* **Say ninety-nine** = dites quarante-quatre, dites trente-trois. **The nineties,** les années entre 1890 et 1900. (*Of person*) **To be in one's nineties,** être nonagénaire.
ninth [nainθ], *num. a. & s.* Neuvième (*m*). (*For other phrases see* EIGHTH.)
nip¹ [nip], *s.* 1. Pincement *m.* **To give s.o. a n.,** pincer qn. 2. Morsure *f* (de la gelée, du froid); *Hort:* coup *m* de gelée. **There was a n. in the air,** l'air était piquant; l'air piquait.
nip², *v.* (**nipped**) I. *v.tr.* 1. Pincer. **He nipped his finger,** il s'est pincé le doigt. *Aut:* **To n. an inner tube,** pincer, cisailler, une chambre à air. *Nau:* **To n. a cable,** étriver, étrangler, un cordage. 2. *Hort:* Pincer (des bourgeons). *F:* **To n. in the bud,** écraser dans l'œuf; étouffer dans le germe; étrangler au nid. 3. (*Of cold*) (*a*) Pincer, piquer, mordre (les doigts, etc.). (*b*) Brûler (les bourgeons). **Frost-nipped,** brûlé par la gelée. II. **nip,** *v.i. F:* **Just n. round to the baker's and get a loaf,** cours vite chez le boulanger prendre un pain. **To n. in and out of the traffic,** se faufiler adroitement parmi les voitures. **nip off.** 1. *v.tr.* Enlever, couper, (qch.) en le pinçant. *Hort:* Pincer (un bourgeon). 2. *v.i.* Filer, s'esquiver.
nipping, *s.* 1. Pincement *m. Aut:* Cisaillement *m* (de la chambre à air). 2. *Nau:* Étrive *f,* étranglement *m* (d'un cordage). 3. *Hort:* Pincement, pinçage *m.*
nip³, *s. F:* Goutte *f,* doigt *m* (d'eau-de-vie, etc.). **To take a n.,** boire une goutte.
nip⁴, *v.i.* (**nipped**) *F:* Boire la goutte; siroter.
Nip⁵, *s. P: Pej:* Japonais *m.*
nipper ['nipər], *s.* 1. (Pair of) **nippers.** (*a*) Pince(s) *f(pl)* (de serrage); pincette(s) *f(pl),* tenaille(s) *f(pl).* **Spring nippers,** brucelles *f.* (*b*) Cisaille(s) *f(pl)*; pince(s) coupante(s). 2. Pince (d'un homard, etc.). 3. *F:* Gamin *m,* gosse *m.* **My little n.,** mon mioche.
nipple ['nipl], *s.* 1. (*a*) *Anat:* Mamelon *m*; bout *m* de sein. (*b*) Tétine *f* (de biberon). 2. *Tchn:* Raccord *m* (d'une conduite de vapeur, etc.). *Cy: Aut:* Douille *f,* écrou *m* (d'un rayon de roue). **Grease n.,** raccord de graissage; embout *m.*
nippy ['nipi], *a. F:* 1. Alerte, vif. *P:* **Tell him to be n. about it,** dites-lui de se grouiller. 2. (Vent) coupant, âpre.
nisi ['naisai], *Lt.conj. Jur:* (*Of decree, order*) Provisoire; (*of decision*) rendu sous condition.
nit¹ [nit], *s.* Lente *f*; œuf *m* de pou.
nit², *F:* Crétin *m,* andouille *f.*

nitrate[1] [ˈnaitreit], *s. Ch:* Nitrate *m*, azotate *m*.
nitrate[2], *v.tr.* Nitrer; traiter (une matière) à, par, l'acide nitrique.
nitre [ˈnaitər], *s.* Salpêtre *m*.
nitric [ˈnaitrik], *a. Ch:* N. **acid**, acide *m* nitrique, azotique; *Com:* eau-forte *f*.
nitro-cellulose [ˈnaitroˈseljulous], *s.* Nitrocellulose *f*.
nitro-compound [ˈnaitroˈkɔmpaund], *s. Ch:* Dérivé nitré; composé nitré.
nitrogen [ˈnaitrɔdʒən], *s. Ch:* Azote *m*. **To add n.** (to sth.), azoter (qch.). *S.a.* NARCOSIS.
nitrogenous [naiˈtrɔdʒənəs], *a. Ch:* Azoté.
nitroglycerin(e) [ˈnaitroˈglisəriːn], *s. Exp:* Nitroglycérine *f*.
nitrous [ˈnaitrəs], *a.* Nitreux, -euse, azoteux, -euse.
nitwit [ˈnitwit], *s. F:* Imbécile *mf*; crétin *m*; andouille *f*.
nitwitted [ˈnitwitid], *a. F:* Pauvre d'esprit.
nix [niks]. **1.** *s. P:* Rien (du tout). **2.** *int.* Pet! vingt-deux!
nix(ie) [ˈniks(i)], *s. Myth:* Ondine *f*, nixe *f*.
no [nou]. **I.** *a.* **1.** Nul, pas de, point de, aucun (*with* ne *expressed or understood*). **He made no reply**, il ne fit aucune réponse. **He spared no pains**, il n'est sorte de soins qu'il n'ait pris. **I have no room to write more**, la place me manque pour vous en écrire davantage. **It is no distance**, ce n'est pas loin. **No two men are alike**, il n'y a pas deux hommes qui se ressemblent. **Details of no interest**, détails de peu d'intérêt. **No surrender!** on ne se rend pas! **No nonsense!** pas de bêtises! *P.N:* **No admittance**, entrée interdite, défense d'entrer. **No smoking**, défense de fumer. **2.** Peu; ne . . . pas (du tout). (*a*) **The task is no easy one**, ce n'est pas une tâche facile. *S.a.* SUCH I. 1. (*b*) **He is no artist**, il n'est pas artiste. **He was no general**, il n'avait aucune des qualités d'un général. **King or no king, he has no right to interfere**, qu'il soit roi ou non, il n'a pas le droit d'intervenir. (*c*) (*With gerund*) **There is no pleasing him**, il n'y a pas moyen de le satisfaire. **There is no getting out of it**, impossible de s'en tirer. **3. No one** = NOBODY 1 (*a*). **II. no**, *adv.* **1. Or no**, ou non. **Whether or no**, que cela soit ou non; dans tous les cas. **Whether you want it or no**, que tu le veuilles ou non. **2.** (*With comp.*) **I am no richer than he (is)**, je ne suis pas plus riche que lui. **He is no longer here**, il n'est plus ici. *S.a.* LESS 5 (*b*), MORE 5, SOON 2. **III. no. 1.** *adv.* (*a*) Non. **Have you seen him?**—No, l'avez-vous vu?—Non. **No, no, you are mistaken!** mais non, mais non, vous vous trompez! (*b*) **One man could not lift it, no, not half a dozen**, un homme seul ne saurait le soulever, ni même six, pas même six. **2.** *s.* (*pl.* **noes**) Non *m inv.* **Not to take no for an answer**, ne pas admettre de refus. (*In voting*) **Ayes and noes**, voix pour et contre. **The noes have it**, les non l'emportent; le vote est contre.
no-ʹload, *attrib.a. Ind: Mec.E:* (Marche) à vide. **No-load release**, (i) déclenchement *m* à vide; (ii) interrupteur *m* à vide, à zéro.
Noah [ˈnouə]. *Pr.n.m. B.Hist:* Noé.
nob[1] [nɔb], *s. P:* Tête *f*; boule *f*, caboche *f*.
nob[2], *s. P:* Aristo *m*. **The nobs**, les rupins *m*.
nobble [ˈnɔbl], *v.tr. F:* **1.** (*a*) Écloper (un cheval). (*b*) Donner un narcotique (à un cheval, avant la course). **2.** Soudoyer, acheter (qn, un journal). **3.** Voler, chiper (qch.). **4.** Pincer (un voleur). **5.** Aborder (qn).
nobelium [noˈbiːliəm], *s. Ch:* Nobélium *m*.
nobiliary [noˈbiliti], *a.* Nobiliaire.
nobility [noˈbiliti], *s.* **1.** Noblesse *f* (de rang, de cœur). **2.** *Coll:* Noblesse; (la classe des) nobles *m. A:* **The n. and gentry**, la haute et la petite noblesse.
noble [ˈnoubl]. **1.** *a.* (*a*) Noble. **To be of n. birth**, être noble de naissance. (*b*) (Sentiment) noble, sublime, relevé. (*c*) (*Of monument, etc.*) Empreint de grandeur. **2.** *s.* Noble *m.* **-bly**, *adv.* **1.** Noblement. **N. born**, noble de naissance. **2.** Magnifiquement, superbement.
nobleman, *pl.* **-men** [ˈnoublmən], *s.m.* Noble; gentilhomme, *pl.* gentilshommes.
nobody [ˈnoubədi]. **1.** *pron.* (*a*) Personne *m*, nul *m*, aucun *m* (*with* ne *expressed or understood*). **N. spoke to me**, personne ne m'a parlé. **Who is there?**—Nobody, qui est là?—Personne. **N. is perfect**, nul n'est parfait. **N. is more expert at it than he is**, il s'y connaît comme personne, comme pas un. **There is n. better informed**, il n'y a personne de mieux renseigné.

There was nobody else on board, personne (d')autre n'était à bord. **N. who was there heard anything**, aucun de ceux qui étaient là n'a rien entendu. **There was nobody about**, il n'y avait pas âme qui vive; l'endroit était désert. (*b*) *F:* **I knew him when he was nobody**, j'ai été en relations avec lui alors qu'il était encore inconnu. **2.** *s.* (*Pers.*) (i) Nullité *f*, zéro *m*; (ii) parvenu, -ue. **They are (mere) nobodies**, ce sont des gens de rien.
noctambulism [nɔkˈtæmbjulizm], *s.* **1.** Noctambulisme *m.* **2.** Somnambulisme *m*.
noctambulist [nɔkˈtæmbjulist], *s.* **1.** Noctambule *mf*. **2.** Somnambule *mf*.
nocturnal [nɔkˈtəːn(ə)l], *a.* Nocturne.
nocturne [ˈnɔktəːn], *s. Mus:* Nocturne *m*.
nocuous [ˈnɔkjuəs], *a.* Nocif, nuisible.
nod[1] [nɔd], *s.* Inclination *f* de la tête. **1.** (*a*) Signe de tête affirmatif. **To answer with a n.**, répondre d'une inclination de tête. *U.S: F:* **To get sth. when he was nodding**, (*b*) Signe de tête (impératif). **2.** **He gave me a n.**, il me fit un petit signe de la tête (en guise de salut). **3. The land of N.**, le pays des rêves.
nod[2], *v.tr. & i.* (nodded) **1. To n.** (one's head), faire un signe de tête; incliner la tête. **To n. to s.o.**, (i) faire un signe de tête à qn (en guise d'ordre ou pour exprimer son consentement); (ii) saluer qn d'une inclination de tête. **To n. assent**, faire signe que oui; opiner de la tête. **2.** Dodeliner (de) la tête; somnoler, sommeiller. (**Even**) **Homer sometimes nods**, Homère lui-même se trompe quelquefois. **3.** (*Of plumes, etc.*) Danser, ballotter. **nodding**[1], *a.* (Vieillard, etc.) à la tête dodelinante, branlante; (fleur, panache) qui se balance (au vent, etc.). **nodding**[2], *s.* Inclination *f* de tête. **To have a n. acquaintance with s.o.**, connaître qn vaguement.
nodal [ˈnoud(ə)l], *a. Ph: Opt:* Nodal, -aux.
noddle [ˈnɔdl], *s. F:* Tête *f*; *P:* boule *f*, caboche *f*.
node [noud], *s.* **1.** *Astr: Ph: Geom:* Nœud *m. El:* **Potential n.** (*in circuit, aerial*), nœud de potentiel, de tension. **2.** Nœud, nodosité *f* (d'un tronc d'arbre, etc.). *Bot:* Nœud, articulation *f* (des graminées).
nodosity [noˈdɔsiti], *s.* Nodosité *f*.
nodule [ˈnɔdjuːl], *s. Geol: Med: Bot:* Nodule *m.* **Flint n.**, rognon *m* de silex.
nog[1] [nɔg], *v.tr.* (nogged) *Const: Min:* Hourder (une cloison, un mur). **nogging**, *s. Const:* Hourdage *m*, hourdis *m*.
nog[2], *s. A:* Bière forte. *S.a.* EGG-NOG.
noggin [ˈnɔgin], *s.* **1.** (Petit) pot (en étain, etc.). **2.** *Approx: Meas:* Quart *m* de pinte.
nohow [ˈnouhau], *adv. F:* En aucune façon.
noise[1] [nɔiz], *s.* Bruit *m.* **1.** Tapage *m*, vacarme *m*, fracas *m.* **To make a n.**, faire du bruit, du tapage. *P:* **The big n.**, le grand manitou (de l'entreprise). **2.** Son *m. Tp:* Friture *f.* **Tinkling n.**, tintement *m.* **Hammering n.**, bruit de marteau. **To have noises in the ears**, avoir des bourdonnements *m* d'oreilles. *W.Tel:* (Background) n., bruit de fond. *Gramophones:* **Surface n.**, bruissement *m* de l'aiguille. *Th:* (*pers.*) **Noises off**, bruiteur *m*.
noise[2], *v.tr.* **To n. sth. abroad**, ébruiter, *F:* corner (une nouvelle); publier, crier, qch. sur les toits.
noiseless [ˈnɔizlis], *a.* Sans bruit; (appareil) silencieux. **With n. tread**, à pas feutrés. **-ly**, *adv.* Silencieusement; sans bruit, à petit bruit.
noisiness [ˈnɔizinis], *s.* **1.** Vacarme *m*, tintamarre *m.* **2.** Turbulence *f* (des enfants, etc.).
noisome [ˈnɔisəm], *a.* **1.** *A:* Nocif, -ive, nuisible. **2.** (*Of smell, etc.*) Fétide, infect, méphitique. **3.** *F:* N. task, tâche désagréable, répugnante.
noisy [ˈnɔizi], *a.* Bruyant, tapageur; tintamarresque; (enfant) turbulent; (*of street*) tumultueux. (*Of pers.*) **To be n.**, faire du bruit, du tapage. **-ily**, *adv.* Bruyamment; à grand bruit.
nomad [ˈnoumæd], *a. & s.* Nomade (*mf*).
nomadic [noˈmædik], *a.* Nomade.
no man's land [ˈnoumænzˌlænd], *s.* (i) Terrains *mpl* vagues; no man's land *m*; (ii) *Mil:* no man's land, zone *f* neutre, terrain contesté; (iii) *Nau:* Trou *m* de la drome, parc *m*.
nomenclature [nouˈmenklətʃər], *s.* Nomenclature *f*.
nom de plume [ˈnɔmdəˈpluːm], *s.* (*pl.* noms de plume) Pseudonyme *m* (d'un auteur).

nominal ['nɔmin(ə)l], a. Nominal, -aux. 1. Qui n'a que le nom. To be the n. head, n'être chef que de nom. N. value, valeur nominale, fictive. N. rent, loyer purement nominal, insignifiant. 2. *Mil: etc:* N. roll, état nominatif. -ally, adv. 1. Nominalement; de nom. 2. Nominativement.

nominate ['nɔmineit], v.tr. (a) Nommer, choisir, désigner (qn). To n. s.o. to, for, a post, nommer qn à un emploi. (b) Proposer, présenter (un candidat).

nomination [,nɔmi'nei∫(ə)n], s. 1. (a) Nomination f (de qn à un emploi). (b) Droit m de nommer qn à un poste. 2. Présentation f; investiture f (d'un candidat).

nominative ['nɔminətiv]. *Gram:* (a) a. & s. Nominatif (m). In the n. (case), au nominatif, au cas sujet. (b) s. Sujet m (de la phrase).

nominator ['nɔmineitər], s. Présentateur m (d'un candidat).

nominee [nɔmi'ni:], s. 1. (For an annuity, etc.) Personne dénommée. 2. (For a post) Candidat désigné, choisi.

non- [nɔn], pref. 1. Non-. Non-admission, non-admission. 2. In-. Non-compliance, insoumission. 3. Sans. Non-alcoholic, sans alcool.

non-acceptance ['nɔnək'septəns], s. *Com:* Non-acceptation f, refus m d'acceptation (d'un effet).

nonage ['nounidʒ], s. Minorité f. To be still in one's n., être encore mineur.

nonagenarian [,nounədʒi'nɛəriən], a. & s. Nonagénaire (mf).

non-aggression ['nɔnə'gre∫(ə)n], s. N.-a. pact, pacte m de non-agression.

non-alignment ['nɔnə'lainmənt], s. *Pol:* Neutralisme m.

non-alloyable ['nɔnə'lɔiəbl], a. *Metall:* Incompatible.

non-appearance ['nɔnə'piərəns], s. *Jur:* Défaut m (de comparution); non-comparution f.

non-arrival ['nɔnə'raiv(ə)l], s. Non-arrivée f.

non-attendance ['nɔnə'tendəns], s. Absence f.

non-belligerency ['nɔnbi'lidʒər(ə)nsi], s. Non-belligérance f.

nonce [nɔns], s. For the n., pour l'occasion. 'nonce-word, s. Mot créé, forgé, pour l'occasion; mot de circonstance.

nonchalance ['nɔn∫ələns], s. Nonchalance f.

nonchalant ['nɔn∫ələnt], a. Nonchalant; indifférent. -ly, adv. Nonchalamment; avec nonchalance.

non-com. ['nɔn'kɔm], s. *Mil: F:* Sous-off m.

non-combatant ['nɔn'kɔmbətənt], a. & s. *Mil:* Non-combattant (m).

non-commissioned ['nɔnkə'mi∫(ə)nd], a. *Mil:* Sans brevet. N.-c. officer, sous-officier m; gradé m.

non-committal ['nɔnkə'mit(ə)l], a. (Of answer, etc.) Qui n'engage à rien, diplomatique. To be n.-c. (in answering, etc.), observer une prudente réserve.

non-completion ['nɔnkəm'pli:∫(ə)n], s. Non-achèvement m (d'un travail); non-exécution f (d'un contrat).

non compos mentis ['nɔn'kɔmpɔs'mentis], *F:* non compos. *Lt.-phr.* Aliéné, fou.

non-condensing ['nɔnkən'densiŋ], a. (Machine) sans condensation, à échappement libre.

non-conducting ['nɔnkən'dʌktiŋ], a. *Ph:* Non-conducteur, -trice; mauvais conducteur; (heat) calorifuge; (electricity) isolant.

non-conductor ['nɔnkən'dʌktər], s. *Ph:* Non-conducteur m, mauvais conducteur; (of heat) calorifuge m; (of electricity) isolant m.

nonconformist ['nɔnkən'fɔ:mist], s. & a. *Ecc:* Dissident, -ente.

non-content ['nɔnkən'tent], s. *Parl:* Voix f contre (à la Chambre des Lords).

non-contributory ['nɔnkən'tribjuteri], a. N.-c. pension scheme, caisse de retraite sans versement de la part des bénéficiaires.

non-dazzle ['nɔn'dæzl], a. *Aut:* Non-aveuglant; anti-éblouissant.

non-delivery ['nɔndi'livəri], s. Non-livraison f; défaut m de livraison; non-remise f (de lettres).

nondescript ['nɔndiskript], a. Indéfinissable, inclassable; (costume) hétéroclite, quelconque.

non-detachable ['nɔndi'tæt∫əbl], a. Inamovible.

none [nʌn]. 1. pron. (a) Aucun. N. of them is, are, known to us, nous n'en connaissons aucun. N. of you can tell me . . ., personne d'entre vous, aucun

d'entre vous, ne peut me dire. . . . N. of this concerns me, rien de ceci ne me regarde. No news today?—None, pas de nouvelles aujourd'hui?—Aucune(s). Strawberries! there are none, des fraises! il n'y en a pas. N. at all, pas un seul, une seule. Any occupation is better than n. at all, une occupation quelle qu'elle soit est préférable à pas d'occupation du tout. N. of your impudence! pas d'insolences de votre part! His nature is n. of the calmest, sa nature n'est pas des plus calmes. (b) N. can tell, personne ne le sait; nul ne le sait. He is aware, none better, that . . ., il sait mieux que personne que. . . . N. but he knew of it, lui seul le savait. The visitor was none other than the king, le visiteur n'était autre que le roi. (c) (In schedules, etc.) 'N.,' "néant." 2. a. A: Money I had n., d'argent je n'en avais point. Sounds there were n., save the barking of a dog, de sons aucun, sauf les aboiements d'un chien. Village there was n., de village point. 3. adv. (a) He is n. the happier for his wealth, pour être riche, il n'en est pas plus heureux. I like him n. the worse for that, je ne l'en aime pas moins. S.a. LESS 4, WORSE 1. (b) He was n. too soon, il arriva juste à temps. They love each other n. too well, ils ne sont pas fort épris l'un de l'autre. The evening passed n. too gaily, la soirée fut peu gaie. His position is n. too secure, sa position n'est rien moins qu'assurée.

nonentity [nɔn'entiti], s. Personne insignifiante, de peu d'importance; non-valeur f; nullité f.

non-essential, ['nɔni'sen∫(ə)l], a. = UNESSENTIAL.

non-existence ['nɔnig'zist(ə)ns], s. Non-existence f; non-être m.

non-existent ['nɔnig'zist(ə)nt], a. Non-existant; inexistant.

non-explosive ['nɔniks'plousiv], a. Inexplosible.

non-fading ['nɔn'feidiŋ], a. (Of colour) Résistant à la lumière, au soleil; bon teint.

non-ferrous ['nɔn'fərəs], a. Non-ferreux.

non-freezing ['nɔn'fri:ziŋ], a. Incongelable.

non-fulfilment ['nɔnful'filmənt], s. Non-exécution f, inexécution f.

non-glare ['nɔn'glɛər], a. N.-g. goggles, lunettes anti-éblouissantes.

non-inflammable ['nɔnin'flæməbl], a. Ininflammable, ignifuge.

non-intervention ['nɔnintə'ven∫(ə)n], s. Non-intervention f; non-interventionnisme m; laisser-faire m.

non-iron ['nɔn'aiən], a. *Dom.Ec:* Ne nécessitant, n'exigeant, aucun repassage.

non-juring ['nɔn'dʒuəriŋ], a. *Hist:* (Prêtre) inassermenté, non assermenté.

non-ladder ['nɔn'lædər], a. (Bas) indémaillable.

non-member ['nɔn'membər], s. (At club) Invité, -ée. Open to non-members, ouvert au public.

non-observance ['nɔnəb'zə:v(ə)ns], s. Inobservance f (des lois).

nonpareil ['nɔnpə'rel], s. (a) *Typ:* Nonpareille f; corps m six. (b) (Apple) Nonpareille.

non-payment ['nɔn'peimənt], s. Non-paiement m; défaut m de paiement.

non-performance ['nɔnpə'fɔ:məns], s. Non-exécution f, inexécution f (d'un contrat, etc.).

nonplus [nɔn'plʌs], v.tr. (nonplussed) Embarrasser, interdire, interloquer (qn); mettre, réduire, (qn) à quia. To be nonplussed, être désemparé.

non-resident ['nɔn'rezid(ə)nt], a. & s. 1. Non-résident (m). Non-r. landowner, propriétaire forain. 2. *Sch:* Externe (mf). (Hotel) Hôte m de passage. Open to non-residents, repas servis aux voyageurs de passage.

non-returnable ['nɔnri'tə:nəbl], a. Perdu. N.-r. packing, emballage perdu, non repris, non consigné.

non-reversible ['nɔnri'və:səbl], a. *Mec.E:* Irréversible.

non-satisfaction ['nɔn,sætis'fæk∫(ə)n], s. Inassouvissement m.

nonsense ['nɔns(ə)ns], s. 1. Non-sens m 2. (a) Absurdité f, déraison f. A piece of n., une bêtise, une absurdité. To talk n., déraisonner; dire des bêtises, des inepties. This passage makes n., ce passage est inintelligible. N.! pas possible! à d'autres! quelle blague! It is n. to think that . . ., il est absurde de penser que. . . . Now, no n.! allons, pas de bêtises! S.a. STUFF¹ 1. (b) attrib.a. N. verse, vers amphigouriques.

nonsensical [nɔn'sensik(ə)l], a. 1. Absurde; qui n'a pas le sens commun. 2. **Don't be n.!** ne dites pas de bêtises, d'absurdités.

non sequitur [nɔnsekwitər], s. Illogicité f.

non-skid(ding) ['nɔn'skid(iŋ)], a. Aut: etc: (Bandage) antidérapant.

non-smoker ['nɔn'smoukər], s. 1. (Pers.) Non-fumeur m. 2. Rail: F: Compartiment dans lequel il est interdit de fumer.

non-smoking ['nɔn'smoukiŋ], a. Rail: N.-s. compartment, compartiment dans lequel il est interdit de fumer.

non-stop ['nɔn'stɔp]. 1. Attrib.a. N.-s. train, train faisant le trajet sans arrêt; train direct. Av: N.-s. flight, vol sans escale. 2. adv. Sans arrêt; (voler) sans escale.

nonsuit[1] ['nɔn'sju:t], s. Jur: Débouté m; ordonnance f de non-lieu.

nonsuit[2], v.tr. Débouter (un plaideur) (de son appel); renvoyer (qn) de sa demande.

non-union ['nɔn'ju:njən], attrib.a. (Ouvrier) non-syndiqué.

non-unionist ['nɔn'ju:njənist], s. Non-syndiqué(e).

non-violence ['nɔn'vaiələns], s. Non-violence f.

noodle ['nu:dl], s. F: 1. Niais, -aise, nigaud, -aude; benêt m, andouille f. 2. U.S: Tête f.

noodles ['nu:dlz], s.pl. Cu: Nouilles f.

nook [nuk], s. (a) Coin m, recoin m. **Nooks and corners, nooks and crannies,** coins et recoins. (b) Renfoncement m (dans une salle).

noon [nu:n], s. Midi m. **The sun at n.,** le soleil de midi. **Shadow at n.,** ombre méridienne.

noonday ['nu:ndei], **noontide** ['nu:ntaid], s. Midi m; plein jour. **The n. sun,** le soleil de midi.

noose[1] [nu:s], s. (a) Nœud coulant; (for catching hares, etc.) lacet m, lacs m, collet m. (b) **Hangman's n.,** corde f (de potence).

noose[2], v.tr. 1. Faire un nœud coulant à (une corde). 2. Prendre (un lièvre) au lacet.

nopal ['noup(ə)l], s. Bot: Nopal m, -als; cochenillier m.

nor [nɔ:r], conj. 1. (Ne, ni . . .) ni. **Neither you n. I know,** ni vous ni moi ne le savons. **He shall not go n. you either,** il n'ira pas, ni vous non plus. 2. I do not know, n. can I guess, je n'en sais rien et je ne peux pas le deviner. **N. does it seem that . . .,** il ne semble pas non plus que . . ., d'ailleurs il ne semble pas que . . .

nor' [nɔ:r]. Nau: **Nor'east, nor'west** = NORTH-EAST, NORTH-WEST.

Nordic ['nɔ:dik], a. Ethn: Nordique, scandinave.

noria ['nɔ:riə], s. Noria f; (pompe f à) chapelet m.

norm [nɔ:m], s. Norme f.

normal ['nɔ:m(ə)l]. 1. a. (a) Geom: Normal, -aux, perpendiculaire (to, à). (b) Normal, régulier, ordinaire. **N. speed,** vitesse de régime. Med: **N. temperature,** température moyenne, normale. (c) U.S: **N. school** = école normale. 2. s. (a) Geom: Normale f, perpendiculaire f. (b) Condition normale; état normal. **Temperature above (the) n.,** température au-dessus de la normale. **-ally,** adv. Normalement.

normality [nɔ:'mæliti], s. Normalité f.

Norman ['nɔ:mən], a. & s. Normand, -ande. **N. architecture,** (i) l'architecture normande; (ii) l'architecture romane (anglaise).

Normandy ['nɔ:məndi]. Pr.n. La Normandie.

Norse [nɔ:s]. 1. a. (a) Norvégien. (b) Hist: Nordique. 2. s. Ling: Les langues f scandinaves; esp. le norvégien.

Norseman, pl. **-men** ['nɔ:smən], s. Hist: **The Norsemen,** les Normands.

north [nɔ:θ]. 1. s. Nord m. **On the n., to the n. (of)** au nord (de). **To live in the n. of England,** habiter dans le nord de l'Angleterre. **The Frozen N. (of Canada),** le grand Nord (canadien). 2. adv. Au nord. **To travel n.,** voyager vers le nord. 3. a. Nord inv; septentrional, -aux; (pays) du nord; (mur) exposé au nord. **The n. wind,** le vent du nord; Lit: la bise. **N. Britain,** l'Écosse f. **'North-'African,** a. & s. Nord-africain, -aine. **'North-Am'erican,** a. & s. Nord-Américain, -aine. **'North 'Cape (the),** s. Le Cap Nord. **'North 'Country (the),** s. L' Angleterre du nord. **north-'east.** 1. s. Nord-est m.

2. (a) (Du) nord-est inv. 3. adv. Vers le nord-est. **'north-'easter,** Nau: nor'easter, s. Vent du nord-est. **north-'easterly,** a. Du nord-est. **north-'eastern,** a. (Du) nord-est inv. **'North 'Sea (the),** s. La mer du Nord. **north-'west.** 1. s. Nord-ouest m. 2. a. (Du) nord-ouest inv. 3. adv. Vers le nord-ouest. **north-'wester,** Nau: nor'wester, s. Vent du nord-ouest, noroît m. **north-'westerly,** a. Du nord-ouest. **north-'western,** a. (Du) nord-ouest inv.

northerly ['nɔ:ðəli], a. (Of wind) Du nord; (of district) (du, au) nord; (of direction) vers le nord. **N. aspect,** exposition au nord.

northern ['nɔ:ðən], a. (Du) nord; septentrional, -aux. **N. Ireland,** l'Irlande du nord. **N. lights,** aurore boréale.

northerner ['nɔ:ðənər], s. Habitant, -ante, originaire mf, du nord.

northward ['nɔ:θwəd]. 1. s. To the n., au nord. 2. a. Au, du nord; du côté du nord.

northwards ['nɔ:θwədz], adv. Vers le nord.

Norway ['nɔ:wei]. Pr.n. Geog: La Norvège.

Norwegian [nɔ:'wi:dʒ(ə)n]. 1. a. & s. Norvégien, -ienne. 2. s. Ling: Le norvégien.

nose[1] [nouz], s. 1. (Of pers., animal) Nez m; (of many animals) museau m. **To blow one's n.,** se moucher. **To hold one's n.,** se boucher le nez. **To speak through the n.,** nasiller; parler du nez. F: **The parson's n.,** le croupion (d'une volaille); F: as m de pique. **I did it under his (very) n.,** je l'ai fait à son nez, à sa barbe. **To poke one's n. into everything,** fourrer son nez partout. **To look down one's n. at s.o.,** regarder qn de haut en bas. **To lead s.o. by the n.,** mener qn par le bout du nez. 2. Odorat m. **Dog with a good n.,** chien qui a du flair, du nez. (Of pers.) **To have a n. for sth.,** avoir un, du, flair pour qch. 3. Tchn: Nez (d'un bateau, d'un avion); nez, bec m (d'un outil); ajutage m (d'un tuyau). (Of vehicles) **N. to tail,** pare-choc à pare-choc. Mil: Pointe f (d'une balle). Navy: Cône m de choc (d'une torpille). Ball: **N. cone,** ogive f (d'une fusée). **'nose-bag,** s. Musette f (de cheval); sac m à fourrages. **'nose-band,** s. Harn: Muserolle f. **'nose-bleeding,** s. Saignement m du nez. **'nose-dive**[1], s. Av: Vol piqué; piqué m. **'nose-dive**[2], v.i. Av: Piquer du nez; descendre en piqué. **'nose-piece,** s. Ajutage m, bec m (de tuyau d'arrosage, etc.); buse f, tuyère f (de soufflet); porte-objectifs m inv. (de microscope). **'nose-ring,** s. 1. Husb: Anneau nasal, nasière f (de taureau, etc.). 2. Anthr: Anneau porté au nez.

nose[2]. 1. v.tr. Flairer, sentir (qch.). 2. v.i. **To n. at sth.,** flairer qch. **Tò n. about, (a)round,** fureter, fouiner; fourrer le nez partout. **The ship nosed (her way) through the fog,** le navire s'avançait à l'aveuglette à travers le brouillard. **nose out,** v.tr. (Of dog) **To n. out the game,** flairer le gibier. F: **To n. out a secret,** découvrir, éventer, un secret. **To n. s.o. out,** dépister, dénicher, qn. **-nosed,** a. **Red-nosed,** au nez rouge. S.a. FLAT-NOSED, etc. **nosing,** a. (a) (Of stair-tread) Nez m, profil m. (b) Arch: Arête f (de moulure).

nosebleed ['nouzbli:d], s. F: A n., un saignement du nez.

nosegay ['nouzgei], s. Bouquet m (de fleurs odorantes).

nostalgia [nɔs'tældʒiə], s. Nostalgie f.

nostalgic [nɔs'tældʒik], a. Nostalgique.

nostril ['nɔstril], s. (Of pers.) Narine f; (of horse, etc.) naseau m.

nostrum ['nɔstrəm], s. Drogue f, orviétan m; remède m de charlatan.

nosy ['nouzi], a. P: Fouinard; fureteur, -euse. **A n. parker,** un indiscret, F: un fouinard.

not [nɔt], adv. (Ne) pas, (ne) point. 1. A. & Lit: **I know n.,** je ne sais pas. **Fear n.,** n'ayez point de crainte. 2. (a) **He will n., won't, come,** il ne viendra pas. **She is n., isn't, there,** elle n'est pas là. **Do n., don't, move,** ne bougez pas. **You understand, do you n., don't you?** vous comprenez, n'est-ce pas? **He is here, isn't he, is he n.?** il est ici, n'est-ce pas? (b) (Stressed) **I am 'not ready.—You are 'not ready,** je suis prêt.—Non, vous n'êtes pas prêt. (c) **What is she like?—N. pretty,** comment est-elle?—Pas jolie. **Are you ill?—N. at all,** êtes-vous malade?—Pas du tout. F: **Thank you so much!—N. at all!** mille mercis!—De rien (monsieur, madame)! P: **N. if I know it!** jamais de la vie! **If**

fine, we shall go out, if n., n., s'il fait beau nous sortirons, sinon, pas. **Why** n.? pourquoi pas? I **wish it were** n. (so), je voudrais bien que non, que cela ne soit pas. I **don't care whether he comes or** n., qu'il vienne ou non, cela m'est égal. I **think** n., je crois que non. **N. even in France**, (non) pas même en France. **N. negotiable**, non-négociable. **3. N. wishing to be seen**, I drew the curtain, ne désirant pas être vu, comme je ne désirais pas être vu, je tirai le rideau. **N. including . . .**, sans compter. . . . He begged me **n. to move**, il me pria de ne pas me déranger. *F:* **N. to worry!** ne vous en faites pas! **4. N. that . . .**, ce n'est pas que . . ., ce n'est point à dire que. . . **N. that I fear him**, non (pas) que je le craigne. **5.** *(With pronoun)* **Are you going to tell him?—N. I!**, allez-vous le lui dire?—Moi? Bien sûr que non! **N. everybody can be a Milton**, il n'est pas donné à tout le monde d'être un Milton. **6.** *(In litotes)* **There were n. a few women amongst them**, il y avait pas mal de femmes parmi eux. **The news caused n. a little surprise**, grande fut la surprise à cette nouvelle. **An air of dignity** n. **unmingled with shyness**, un air digne qui n'allait pas sans une certaine timidité. *P:* **N. half! beaucoup!** tu parles! **7. N. a murmur was heard**, pas un murmure ne se fit entendre.

notability [ˌnoutəˈbiliti], s. **1.** *(Pers.)* Notabilité *f*, célébrité *f*, notable *m*; personnalité *f*. **2.** Notabilité, caractère *m* notable (d'un fait).

notable [ˈnoutəbl], a. **1.** (a) Notable, considérable, insigne; *(of pers.)* éminent. (b) s. Notable *m*. **2.** *Ch:* *(Of quantity, etc.)* Perceptible, sensible. **-ably**, adv. **1.** Notablement, remarquablement. **2.** Notamment, particulièrement.

notary [ˈnoutəri], s. *Jur:* N. (public) = notaire *m*.

notation [noˈtei(ə)n], s. Notation *f*. *Ar:* Decimal n., numération décimale.

notch¹ [nɔtʃ], s. **1.** (a) Entaille *f*, encoche *f*, cran *m*. *Mec.E:* Stop-n., cran d'arrêt. *Sm.a.:* Sight n., sighting n., cran de mire. (b) Brèche *f* (dans une lame, etc.). **2.** *U.S:* Défilé *m*, gorge *f* (de montagne).

notch², v.tr. (a) Entailler, encocher (un bâton, etc.). (b) Ébrécher (une lame, etc.).

note¹ [nout], s. **1.** (a) Note *f*; caractère *m* de musique. (b) Touche *f* (d'un piano). (c) Note, son *m*. To sing, play, a false n., faire une fausse note. There was a n. of impatience in his voice, son ton indiquait une certaine impatience. Speech that hits the right n., discours dans la note voulue. **2.** Marque *f*, signe *m*, indice *m*. *Typ:* N. of exclamation, point *m* d'exclamation. **3.** (a) Note, mémorandum *m*. To make, take (down), notes, prendre des notes. To make a n. of sth., noter qch.; prendre note de qch. (b) Note, annotation *f*, remarque *f* (sur un texte). Notes on Tacitus, commentaire *m* sur Tacite. (c) Billet *m*; petite lettre. I wrote off a n. to her at once, je lui ai tout de suite écrit un mot, un billet. (d) Diplomatic n., note diplomatique, mémorandum. **4.** *Com:* (a) Billet, bordereau *m*. N. of hand, reconnaissance *f* (de dette). Credit n., note, facture *f*, de crédit. Advice n., note, lettre, d'avis. (b) (Bank) n., billet (de banque). Ten-franc notes, coupures *f* de dix francs. **5.** (a) Man of n., homme marquant, de renom, de marque. (b) It is worthy of n. that . . ., il convient de noter que. . . Nothing of n., rien d'important. To take n. of sth., retenir qch. dans sa mémoire; remarquer qch. *S.a.* COMPARE² 1. ˈnote-book, s. Carnet *m*, calepin *m*; (for shorthand, etc.) bloc-notes *m*. ˈnote-case, s. Porte-billets *m* inv. ˈnote-paper, s. Papier *m* à lettres, à écrire.

note², v.tr. **1.** Noter, constater, remarquer, prendre note de (qch.); relever (une erreur). We duly n. that . . ., nous prenons bonne note (de ce) que. . . . It is worth noting that . . ., il convient de remarquer que. . . . **2.** To n. sth. (down), écrire, inscrire, qch. noted, a. *(Of pers.)* Distingué, éminent, illustre; *(of thg)* célèbre, remarquable (for sth., par qch.). He was n. for his kindness, il était connu pour sa gentillesse.

noteworthy [ˈnoutwəːði], a. Remarquable; digne d'attention, de remarque.

nothing [ˈnʌθiŋ]. **I.** s. or pron. Rien *(with ne expressed or understood)*. (a) I see n. that I like, je ne vois rien qui me plaise. N. could be simpler, rien de plus

simple; c'est tout ce qu'il y a de plus simple. You can't live on n., on ne peut pas vivre de rien. *S.a.* NEXT I. **2.** *F:* I feel like n. on earth, je ne suis pas dans mon assiette. To say n. of . . ., sans parler de. . . . There's n. in these rumours, ces bruits sont sans fondement. He was n. if not discreet, il était discret avant tout. To create an army out of n., créer une armée de toutes pièces. (b) *(Followed by adj.)* N. new, rien de nouveau. That's n. unusual, cela n'a rien d'anormal. There is n. heroic about him, il n'a rien d'un héros. N. much, pas grand-chose. There is n. more to be said, il n'y a plus rien à dire. (c) To have n. to do with sth., n'avoir rien à faire, n'avoir aucun rapport, avec qch.; n'avoir rien à voir à qch. I have n. to do with it, je n'y suis pour rien. That is n. to do with you, ce n'est pas votre affaire; cela ne vous regarde pas. N. doing! rien à faire! There is n. to cry about, il n'y a pas de quoi pleurer. (d) He is n. of a scholar, ce n'est pas du tout un savant. *S.a.* KIND¹ 2, SORT¹ 1. (e) N. else, rien d'autre. N. else could be done, (i) on ne pouvait rien faire de plus; (ii) on ne pouvait faire autrement. N. but the truth, rien que la vérité. He does n. but go in and out, il ne fait qu'entrer et sortir. There is n. for it but to submit, il n'y a qu'à se soumettre. There was n. for it but to wait, force nous fut d'attendre. You walked back?—There was n. else for it, vous êtes revenu à pied?—Il a bien fallu. (f) It is not for n. that . . ., ce n'est pas sans raison que. . . . All that goes for n., tout cela ne compte pas. *F:* I got n. out of it, j'en suis pour mes frais. (g) She is n. to him, elle lui est indifférente. It is n. to me whether he comes or not, qu'il vienne ou non, cela m'est égal. (h) To make, think, n. of sth., n'attacher aucune importance à qch.; ne faire aucun cas de qch. He makes n. of walking twenty miles, il se fait un jeu de faire vingt milles à pied. He thinks n. of borrowing from the till, il ne se fait pas scrupule d'emprunter à la caisse. **II.** nothing, s. **1.** *Ar:* Zéro *m*. **2.** Néant *m*; rien. To come to n., ne pas aboutir; *(of hopes, etc.)* s'anéantir. **3.** A hundred francs? A mere n.! cent francs? Une misère! To punish a child for a mere n., punir un enfant pour une vétille. *S.a.* SWEET I. 5. **III.** nothing, adv. Aucunement, nullement; pas du tout. N. loath, volontiers, sans hésiter. *S.a.* DAUNT. He is n. the worse for it, il ne s'en porte pas plus mal. It was n. (like) so wonderful as one imagined, ce n'était nullement aussi merveilleux que l'on se le figurait. N. near so large, loin d'être aussi grand. It is n. less than madness, c'est de la folie ni plus ni moins.

nothingness [ˈnʌθiŋnis], s. Néant *m*.

notice¹ [ˈnoutis], s. **1.** (a) Avis *m*, notification *f*. N. of receipt, avis de réception. (b) Préavis *m*, avertissement *m*. To give s.o. n. of sth., prévenir qn de qch. I must have n., il faudra m'en avertir. *Pol:* I must have n. of that question, je demande que cette interpellation soit inscrite à l'ordre du jour. Without n. (given), he sold the house, sans avis préalable, sans en aviser personne, il a vendu la maison. To give out a n., lire une communication; faire l'annonce de qch. N. is hereby given that . . ., le public est avisé que . . .; on fait savoir que. . . . Public n., avis au public. Until further n., jusqu'à nouvel avis, ordre; jusqu'à avis contraire. (c) Avis formel, instructions formelles. To give s.o. n. to do sth., aviser qn de faire qch. *Jur:* To receive n. to do sth., être mis en demeure de faire qch. N. to pay, avertissement. To serve a n. on s.o., signifier un arrêt à qn. (d) At short n., à court délai. Ready to start at short n., at a day's n., prêt à partir à l'instant, du jour au lendemain. At a moment's n., à la minute, à l'instant; (renvoyer qn) sans avertissement préalable. To give six months' n. of sth., donner avis de qch. six mois d'avance; donner un préavis de six mois. *Com:* Can be delivered at three days' n., livrable dans un délai de trois jours. (e) N. to quit, congé *m*; avis de congé. *Jur:* intimation *f* de vider les lieux. To give a tenant n. to quit, donner congé, signifier son congé, à un locataire. To give n. to an employee, donner, signifier, son congé à un employé. *(Of master or servant)* To give s.o. a week's notice, donner ses huit jours à qn. To give n. (to one's employer), donner sa démission. **2.** (a) Affiche *f*; indication *f*, avis (au public); (on card) écriteau m. N. of sale by auction, publication de vente aux enchères. (b) (In newspaper) Annonce f. To put a n. in the papers, faire passer une note dans les journaux. (c) Revue f (d'un ouvrage). 3. (a) To take n. of sth., tenir compte, prendre connaissance, de qch. To take no n. of sth., ne faire aucune attention à qch.; passer outre à (une objection). I have never taken any n. of it, je n'y ai jamais pris garde. The fact came to his n. that . . ., son attention fut attirée par le fait que. . . . To attract n., se faire remarquer. To avoid n., se dérober aux regards. To bring, call, a matter to s.o.'s n., porter une affaire à la connaissance de qn; faire observer qch. à qn. (b) F: To sit up and take n., se réveiller, dresser l'oreille. 'notice-board, s. (On house to let, etc.) Écriteau m; (in school, club, etc.) tableau m d'annonces; porte-affiches m inv.

notice², v.tr. Observer, remarquer, s'apercevoir de, tenir compte de, prendre garde à (qn, qch.); faire la remarque de (qch.). I have never noticed it, je n'y ai jamais pris garde. I noticed her wipe away a tear, je vis qu'elle essuyait une larme. To get oneself noticed, attirer l'attention (sur soi).

noticeable ['noutisəbl], a. 1. Digne d'attention, de remarque. To be n. on account of sth., se faire remarquer par qch. 2. Perceptible, sensible. It is not n., cela ne se voit, ne se remarque, pas. -ably, adv. Perceptiblement, sensiblement.

notifiable ['noutifaiəbl], a. (Maladie) dont la déclaration aux autorités est obligatoire.

notification [‚noutifi'keiʃ(ə)n], s. Avis m, notification f, annonce f; déclaration f (de naissance, etc.).

notify ['noutifai], v.tr. Annoncer, notifier (qch.); déclarer (une naissance). To n. s.o. of sth., avertir, aviser, qn de qch. To n. the police of sth., signaler qch. à la police.

notion ['nouʃ(ə)n], s. (a) Notion f, idée f. To form a true n. of sth., se former une idée exacte de qch. To have no n. of sth., n'avoir pas la moindre notion de qch. (b) Opinion f, pensée f. I have a n. that . . ., j'ai dans l'idée que . . .; je me suis mis en tête que. . . . (c) Caprice m. As the n. takes him, selon son caprice. To have a n. to do sth., s'aviser de faire qch. (d) pl. U.S: Notions, mercerie f.

notoriety [‚noutə'raiəti], s. Notoriété f de mauvais aloi.

notorious [no'tɔ:riəs], a. D'une triste notoriété; (menteur) insigne; (malfaiteur) reconnu comme notoire; (endroit) mal famé. -ly, adv. Notoirement. N. cruel, connu pour sa cruauté.

notwithstanding ['nɔtwiθ'stændiŋ]. 1. prep. Malgré; en dépit de. This n., ce nonobstant. This rule n., par, en, dérogation à cette règle. 2. adv. Quand même, tout de même; néanmoins, pourtant.

nougat ['nu:gɑ:], s. Nougat m.

nought [nɔ:t], s. = NAUGHT.

noun [naun], s. Gram: Substantif m, nom m. N. clause, proposition substantive.

nourish ['nʌriʃ], v.tr. 1. Nourrir (qn, une plante); alimenter (qn); sustenter (le corps); entretenir (le cuir). To n. s.o. on, with, sth., nourrir qn de qch. 2. O: Nourrir, entretenir (un espoir). nourishing, a. Nourrissant, nutritif, -ive. Milk is n., le lait nourrit.

nourishment ['nʌriʃmənt], s. 1. Alimentation f, nourriture f. 2. Nourriture, aliments mpl.

nous [naus], s. 1. Phil: Intellect m, esprit m. 2. F: Intelligence f; F: jugeotte f.

nouveau riche, pl. nouveaux riches ['nu:vou'ri:ʃ], s. Nouveau riche m.

Nova Scotia ['nouvə'skouʃiə]. Pr.n. Geog: La Nouvelle-Écosse.

novel¹ ['nɔv(ə)l], s. Lit: Roman m.

novel², a. Nouveau, -elle; original, -aux; singulier, -ière. That's a n. idea! voilà qui est original!

novelette [nɔvə'let], s. Roman m sans valeur littéraire, roman de quatre sous.

novelist ['nɔvəlist], s. Romancier, -ière.

novelty ['nɔvəlti], s. 1. Chose nouvelle; innovation f. Com: (Article m de) nouveauté f. 2. Nouveauté (de qch.). The charm of n., le charme de la nouveauté.

November [no'vembər], s. Novembre m. In N., en novembre, au mois de novembre. (On) the fifth of N., le cinq novembre.

novena [no'vi:nə], s. Ecc: Neuvaine f.

novice ['nɔvis], s. 1. Ecc: Novice mf. 2. (a) Novice, apprenti, -ie, débutant, -ante. To be a n. in, at, sth., être novice dans, à, qch. He is no n., il n'en est pas à son coup d'essai. (b) (At horse-show, etc.) Cheval (etc.) qui n'a jamais gagné un prix.

noviciate [no'viʃieit], s. (a) Ecc: Noviciat m. To go through one's n., faire son noviciat. (b) Maison des novices, noviciat.

now [nau]. I. adv. 1. Maintenant. (a) En ce moment, actuellement, à l'heure actuelle. The n. reigning emperor, l'empereur qui règne actuellement. N. or never! allons-y! risquons le coup! N. or never, is the time to . . ., c'est le cas ou jamais de. . . . (b) He won't be long n., il ne tardera plus guère. I cannot n. very well refuse, dans ces circonstances je ne peux guère refuser. (c) Tout de suite. It's going to begin n., ça va commencer tout de suite. Now I'm ready, me voilà prêt. U.S: Right n., tout de suite. (d) (In narrative) Alors; à ce moment-là. All was n. ready, dès lors tout était prêt. He was even n. on his way, il était déjà en route. I saw him just n., je l'ai vu il y a un instant. (e) (Every) n. and then, (every) n. and again, de temps en temps, de temps à autre; de loin en loin; par moments. N . . ., n . . ., tantôt . . . tantôt. . . . Even n., même à cette heure tardive. S.a. JUST II. 1. 2. (Without temporal significance) (a) B: N. Barabbas was a robber, or Barabbas était un brigand. N. this was little enough, but . . ., c'était déjà peu, mais. . . . (b) N. what's the matter with you? qu'avez-vous donc? voyons, qu'est-ce que vous avez? Come n.! stop quarrelling! voyons, voyons! assez de querelles! Well n.! eh bien! N. then, (i) attention! (ii) voyons! allons! II. now, conj. Maintenant que, à présent que. N. I am older I think otherwise, maintenant que je suis plus âgé je pense autrement. III. now, s. I shall see you between n. and then, je vous verrai d'ici là. In three days from n., d'ici trois jours. By n., à l'heure qu'il est. He ought to be here by n., il aurait dû être arrivé avant n. Until n., up to n., jusqu'ici, jusqu'à présent. From n. (on), dès maintenant, à présent, à partir de maintenant.

nowadays ['nauədeiz], adv. Aujourd'hui; de nos jours; à l'heure actuelle; F: à l'heure qu'il est.

nowhere ['nouwɛər]. 1. adv. Nulle part; en aucun lieu. He is n. near as tall as you, il n'est pas à beaucoup près aussi grand que vous; il s'en faut de beaucoup qu'il soit aussi grand que vous. Rac: My horse was n., mon cheval est arrivé dans les choux. 2. s. Le néant. A man in uniform appeared from n., un homme en uniforme apparut soudain.

nowise ['nouwaiz], adv. En aucune façon.

noxious ['nɔkʃəs], a. Nuisible, nocif, -ive; malfaisant, malsain; (plante) vireuse; (gaz) délétère; (air) contagieux.

nozzle ['nɔzl], s. Ajutage m; jet m, lance f (de tuyau); canule f (de seringue); bec m, tuyau m, buse f (de soufflet); ventouse f, buse aspiratrice (d'aspirateur); Av: injecteur m. Spray-n., (i) ajutage d'arrosage; (ii) I.C.E: gicleur m.

nuance ['nju:ã(n)s], s. Nuance f.

nub [nʌb], s. 1. Petit morceau (de charbon, etc.). N. sugar, sucre concassé. 2. L'essentiel m (de l'affaire).

nubile ['nju:bail], a. Nubile.

nubility [nju:'biliti], s. Nubilité f.

nuclear ['nju:kliər], a. Nucléaire. N. aircraft, avion à propulseur atomique. N. power, énergie f atomique. N. radiation, rayonnement m atomique. N. reaction, réaction f nucléaire. N. war(fare), guerre f atomique. N. collision, collision f nucléaire.

nucleon ['nju:klion], s. Atom. Ph: Nucléon m.

nucleonics [nju:kli'oniks], s.pl. Atom.Ph: Nucléonique f.

nucleus, pl. -ei ['nju:kliəs, -iai], s. Noyau m (de cellule, de comète, etc.). The n. of a library, un commencement de bibliothèque.

nude [nju:d]. 1. a. Nu. Art: To paint n. figures, peindre des nus. 2. s. Art: Nudité f; figure nue. To draw from the n., dessiner d'après le nu. A study from the n., une académie; un nu. In the n., nu, F: dans le costume d'Adam.

nudge¹ [nʌdʒ], s. Coup m de coude.

nudge², v.tr. Pousser (qn) du coude; donner un coup de coude à (qn) (en guise d'avertissement).

nudism ['nju:dizm], s. Nudisme m.
nudist ['nju:dist], s. Nudiste mf.
nudity ['nju:diti], s. Nudité f.
nugget ['nʌgit], s. Pépite f (d'or).
nuisance ['nju:s(ə)ns], s. **1.** Jur: Dommage m; atteinte portée aux droits du public. P.N: **Commit no n.**, défense d'uriner; défense de déposer des immondices. **2.** (a) F: Peste f, fléau m. **He is a perfect n.**, il est assommant. **Go away, you're a n.!** va-t'en, tu m'embêtes. (b) Désagrément m. **Long skirts are a n.**, les jupes longues sont gênantes. **That's a n.!** voilà qui est bien ennuyeux! **What a n.!** quel ennui! F: **que c'est embêtant!** Attrib.a. **It has a certain n. value**, cela sert au moins, sinon à autre chose, à embêter les gens.
null [nʌl], a. Jur: Nul, f. nulle; (of legacy) caduc, f. caduque. **N. and void**, nul et de nul effet, nul et sans effet, nul et non avenu.
nullify ['nʌlifai], v.tr. Annuler, nullifier; infirmer (un acte).
nullity ['nʌliti], s. **1.** Jur: Nullité f, invalidité f (d'un mariage, etc.). **2.** (Pers.) **A n.**, une non-valeur; un homme nul.
numb[1] [nʌm], a. Engourdi. **Hands n. with cold**, mains engourdies par le froid.
numb[2], v.tr. Engourdir. **Senses numbed with terror**, sens glacés d'effroi.
number[1] ['nʌmbər], s. **1.** (a) Ar: Nombre m. **Whole n.**, nombre entier. (b) **The greater n. are of this opinion**, le plus grand nombre est de cette opinion. **Given equal numbers we should be the stronger**, à nombre égal nous serions les plus forts. **To swell the n.**, faire nombre. **They were six in n.**, ils étaient au nombre de six. **They are few in n.**, ils sont en petit nombre, peu nombreux. **Books without n.**, des livres innombrables. (c) **A (certain) n. of persons**, un certain nombre de personnes; plusieurs personnes. **A (large) n. of men, numbers of men, were killed**, de nombreux hommes furent tués. F: **Any n. of . . .**, un grand nombre de . . . ; bon nombre de . . . . (d) pl. **Numbers. In small numbers**, en petit nombre. **To win by (force of) numbers**, l'emporter par le nombre. **To be overpowered by numbers**, succomber sous le nombre. (e) **One of their n.**, (l')un d'entre eux. (f) pl. B: **Numbers**, Les Nombres. **2.** Chiffre m. **To write the n. on a page**, numéroter une page. **3.** Numéro m (d'une maison, d'une auto, etc.); (numéro) matricule m (d'un soldat, d'un fusil). **I live at n. forty**, je demeure au numéro quarante. Tp: **You've got the wrong n.**, vous vous êtes trompé de numéro. Mil: **N. one (uniform)**, tenue numéro un. F: **To take care of n. one**, prendre soin de sa petite personne. **A car with the registration n. SPF 342**, une voiture immatriculée SPF 342. F: **His n. is up**, son affaire est faite; F: il est fichu, flambé. **4.** Gram: Nombre. **5.** (a) Th: Numéro (du programme). **Vocal n.**, tour m de chant. (b) Publ: Numéro (d'un journal); livraison f, fascicule m (d'un ouvrage qui paraît par fascicules). **6.** Mus: **Soft numbers**, doux accords.
number[2], v.tr. **1.** Compter, dénombrer. **His days are numbered**, il n'a plus longtemps à vivre; ses jours sont comptés. **To n. s.o. among one's friends**, compter qn parmi ses amis. **The army numbers thirty thousand**, l'armée compte trente mille hommes. **They n. several thousand**, ils sont au nombre de plusieurs mille; leur nombre se chiffre par milliers. **2.** (a) Numéroter (les maisons, etc.). (b) v.i. Mil: **To n. (off)**, se numéroter. 'numbering-machine, -stamp, s. Numéroteur m.
numberless ['nʌmbəlis], a. Innombrable; sans nombre.
numbness ['nʌmnis], s. Engourdissement m; torpeur f (de l'esprit).
numeral ['nju:mərl]. **1.** a. Numéral, -aux. **2.** s. (a) Chiffre m, nombre m. (b) **The cardinal numerals**, les nombres cardinaux.
numeration [ˌnju:mə'reiʃ(ə)n], s. Ar: Numération f.
numerator ['nju:məreitər], s. Mth: Numérateur m.
numerical [nju:'merik(ə)l], a. Numérique. -ally, adv. Numériquement.
numerous ['nju:mərəs], a. Nombreux, -euse.
numismatic [ˌnju:miz'mætik], a. Numismatique.
numismatics [ˌnju:miz'mætiks], s.pl. La numismatique.

numismatist [nju:'mizmətist], s. Numismate m.
numskull ['nʌmskʌl], s, F: Nigaud, -aude; F: buse f; idiot, -ote.
nun [nʌn], s.f. Ecc: Religieuse, nonne. **He was nursed by the nuns**, il a été soigné par les (bonnes) sœurs. 'nun's 'veiling, s. Tex: Flanelle f mousseline.
nunciature ['nʌnʃiətʃər], s. Ecc: Nonciature f.
nuncio ['nʌnʃiou], s. Papal n., nonce m du Pape.
nunnery ['nʌnəri], s. Couvent m (de religieuses).
nuptial ['nʌpʃəl]. **1.** a. Nuptial, -aux. **2.** s.pl. **Nuptials**, noces f.
nurse[1] [nə:s], s. **1.** (a) (Wet-)n., nourrice f. **To put a baby out to n.**, mettre un bébé en nourrice. **(b)** See DRY-NURSE. (c) Bonne f (d'enfants). **2.** (Sick-)n., garde-malade f, pl. gardes-malades. **Hospital n.**, infirmière f. **Male n.**, garde-malade m; infirmier m. **District n.** = infirmière f d'hygiène sociale. **Nursery n.**, puéricultrice f.
nurse[2], v.tr. **1.** Allaiter (un enfant). **To be nursed in luxury**, être élevé dans le luxe. **2.** Soigner (un malade). **She nursed him back to health**, elle lui fit recouvrer la santé grâce à ses soins. **To n. a cold**, soigner un rhume. **3.** (a) Soigner, abriter (des plantes, etc.); ménager (un cheval, etc.) en vue du dernier effort à donner. **To n. one's public**, soigner sa popularité. Pol: **To n. a constituency**, cultiver, soigner, les électeurs. (b) Nourrir, entretenir (un chagrin, etc.); mitonner, mijoter (un projet). **4.** Bercer (un enfant); tenir (qn, qch.) dans ses bras.
nursing[1], a. **1.** N. **mother**, (i) mère allaitante; (ii) (mère) nourrice f. **2.** (In hospital) The n. **staff**, le personnel infirmier. **nursing**[2], s. **1.** Allaitement m. **2.** Culture assidue (des plantes, etc.); ménagement m, soin m (d'une affaire); entretien m (d'un sentiment). **3.** (a) Soins mpl (d'une garde-malade). (b) Profession f de garde-malade, d'infirmière. **To go in for n.**, se faire infirmière. 'nursing home, s. (For mental cases) Maison f de santé; (for surgical cases) clinique f; hôpital privé.
nursemaid ['nə:smeid], s.f. Bonne d'enfants.
nursery ['nə:s(ə)ri], s. **1.** (a) Chambre f des enfants; nursery f. **Night n.**, dortoir m des enfants. **N. rhyme**, chanson f de nourrice. (b) Crèche f; garderie f. **Resident n.**, pouponnière f. **N. school**, maternelle f. **2.** (a) Pépinière f. (b) Pisc: Vivier m. 'nursery-'gardener, s. Pépiniériste mf. 'nursery-'governess, s.f. Gouvernante pour jeunes enfants.
nurseryman, pl. **-men** ['nə:s(ə)rimən], s.m. Pépiniériste.
nursling ['nə:sliŋ], s. Nourrisson m.
nurture[1] ['nə:tʃər], s. Nourriture f. **1.** Éducation f; soins mpl. **N. of the mind**, nourriture de l'esprit. **2.** Aliments mpl.
nurture[2], v.tr. **1.** Nourrir (les enfants, etc.) (on, de). **2.** Élever, faire l'éducation de (qn).
nut [nʌt], s. **1.** (a) Noix f. **Hazel-n.**, noisette f, aveline f. F: **Tough, hard, n. to crack**, (i) problème m difficile à résoudre; os bien dur à ronger; (ii) personne difficile, peu commode. **He can't sing for nuts**, il ne sait pas chanter du tout. **To be dead nuts on s.o., on sth.**, raffoler de qn, de qch. S.a. BEECH-NUT, GROUND-NUT, etc. (b) P: Tête f; P: ciboulot m, boule f, caboche f. **To be off one's nut**, être timbré, toqué, loufoque; avoir perdu la boule. **He's nuts**, il est cinglé, il travaille du chapeau. **2.** Écrou m. **Wing-n., butterfly-n.**, écrou à oreilles, à ailettes. **Hexagonal n.**, écrou à six pans. S.a. CASTLE-NUT, CHECK-NUT. **3.** Mus: (a) Sillet m (de violon). (b) Hausse f (d'archet). **'At, with, the n.'** "du talon." **4.** Com: **N. coal, nuts**, gailletin m. 'nut-brown, a. (Couleur) noisette inv. **N.-b. hair**, cheveux châtains. 'nut-cracker, s. (Pair of) nut-crackers, casse-noisette(s) m inv, casse-noix m inv. **N.-c. chin**, menton en casse-noisette, en galoche. 'nut-tree, s. Noisetier m; coudrier m.
nuthatch ['nʌthætʃ], s. Orn: (Sittelle f) torchepot (m); casse-noisette m inv.
nutmeg ['nʌtmeg], s. (Noix f) muscade f.
nutria ['nju:triə], s. Fourrure f de coypou; Com: loutre f d'Amérique; nutria m; ragondin m.
nutriment ['nju:trimənt], s. Nourriture f; aliments nourrissants.
nutrition [nju:'triʃ(ə)n], s. Nutrition f.
nutritionist [nju:'triʃənist], s. Diététicien, -ienne.

nutritious [njuːˈtriʃəs], *a.* Nutritif, -ive, nourrissant.

nutritive [ˈnjuːtritiv], *a.* Nutritif, -ive, nourrissant.

nutshell [ˈnʌtʃel], *s.* Coquille *f* de noix. **That's the whole thing in a n.**, voilà toute l'affaire (résumée) en un mot, en deux mots.

nutting [ˈnʌtiŋ], *s.* Cueillette *f* des noisettes.

nux vomica [ˈnʌksˈvomikə], *s.* Noix *f* vomique. **N. v. tree**, vomiquier *m.*

nuzzle [ˈnʌzl], *v.i.* **1.** (*Of pig, etc.*) Fouiller avec le groin. **2. To n. against s.o.'s shoulder**, (*of dog, horse*) fourrer son nez contre l'épaule de qn; (*of pers.*) se blottir sur l'épaule de qn.

nyctalope [ˈniktəloup]. **1.** *s.* Héméralope *mf.* **2.** *a.* Héméralopique.

nyctalopia [niktəˈloupiə], *s.* Héméralopie *f.*

nylon [ˈnailon], *s. Tex:* Nylon *m.* **N. stockings**, bas *mpl* nylon. **Crêpe n. socks**, chaussettes crêpe *m* mousse.

nymph [nimf]. **1.** *s.f. Myth:* Nymphe. **Wood-nymph**, hamadryade. **2.** *s. Ent:* Nymphe *f.*

nymphomania [nimfoˈmeiniə], *s. Med:* Nymphomanie *f.*

nymphomaniac [nimfoˈmeiniæk], *s.f. Med:* Nymphomane.

O¹, o, *pl.* **o's, oes** [ou, ouz], *s.* **1.** (La lettre) O, o *m. Tp:* O for Oliver, O comme Oscar. **2.** *Tp:* (*Nought*) Zéro *m.* **3.** Cercle *m,* rond *m.*

O², *int. Lit:* O, oh. O how tired I am! ah! que je suis fatigué! O for a glass of water! que ne donnerais-je pas pour un verre d'eau! O to be in England! que ne suis-je en Angleterre!

oaf, *pl.* **-s,** *A:* **oaves** [ouf, -s, ouvz], *s.* (*a*) Lourdaud *m,* ours mal léché. (*b*) Bon m à rien.

oafish ['oufiʃ], *a.* Lourdaud, stupide; rustre.

oak [ouk], *s.* (*a*) *Bot:* O. (-tree), chêne *m.* **Evergreen o.,** holm-o., yeuse *f;* chêne vert. **O. plantation,** chênaie *f.* (*b*) (Bois *m* de) chêne. **Dark o.,** (couleur) vieux chêne. *attrib.* **O. furniture,** meubles *m* de, en, chêne. (*c*) (*At universities*) To sport one's o., défendre sa porte. **'oak-apple, -gall,** *s.* Noix *f* de galle; pomme *f* de chêne. **'oak-mast,** *s.* Glands *mpl* de chêne; glandée *f.*

oakum ['oukəm], *s.* Étoupe *f,* filasse *f.* **To pick o.,** (i) tirer de l'étoupe; faire de la filasse; (ii) *F:* (*as prison task =*) casser des cailloux.

oar ['ɔːr], *s.* (*a*) Aviron *m,* rame *f.* **To ply the oars, to pull at the oars,** tirer à la rame; *Nau:* souquer ferme. *Nau:* Oars! lève rames! **To rest on one's oars,** (i) lever les avirons; (ii) s'accorder un moment de répit. *F:* **To stick one's o. in,** intervenir (mal à propos). (*b*) (*Opposed to scull*) Aviron de pointe. (*c*) (*Oarsman*) Good o., bon rameur.

-oared ['ɔːd], *a.* **Four-o.,** à quatre rames. **Eight-o. boat,** huit *m* de pointe.

oarlock ['ɔːlək], *s.* *U.S:* = ROWLOCK.

oarsman, *pl.* **-men** ['ɔːzmən], *s.m.* Rameur; tireur d'aviron; *Nau:* nageur.

oasis, *pl.* **oases** [ou'eisis, -iːz], *s.* Oasis *f.*

oast(-house) ['oust(haus)], *s.* Séchoir *m* (à houblon); four *m* à houblon.

oat [out], *s.* (*a*) *Bot:* Avoine commune. **Wild oat(s),** folle avoine. **To sow one's wild oats,** faire des fredaines; jeter sa gourme. (*b*) *Agr:* *pl.* **Oats,** avoine. **A field of oats,** un champ d'avoine. (*Porridge*) oats, flocons *mpl* d'avoine. (*Of horse, F: of pers.*) **To be off its, his, oats,** refuser de manger; être malade. **'oat-grass,** *s.* Folle avoine.

oatcake ['outkeik], *s.* *Cu:* Galette *f* d'avoine.

oaten ['outn], *a.* (De farine) d'avoine.

oath, *pl.* **oaths** [ouθ, ouðz], *s.* **1.** Serment *m.* **To take the o.,** prêter serment. **I'll take my o. on it,** j'en jurerais; *F:* j'en lève la main. **To put s.o. on his o., to administer, tender, the o. to s.o.,** faire prêter serment à qn; déférer le serment à qn. **On o.,** sous (la foi du) serment. **To break one's o.,** se parjurer; fausser, rompre, son serment. **2.** Juron *m;* gros mot.

oatmeal ['outmiːl], *s.* Farine *f* d'avoine.

obduracy ['ɔbdjurəsi], *s.* **1.** (*a*) Endurcissement *m* (de cœur); opiniâtreté *f,* entêtement *m.* (*b*) Inflexibilité *f.* **2.** *Theol:* Impénitence *f.*

obdurate ['ɔbdjurit], *a.* **1.** (*a*) Endurci; têtu, opiniâtre. (*b*) Inexorable, inflexible. **2.** Impénitent. **-ly,** *adv.* (*a*) Avec entêtement. (*b*) Inexorablement.

obedience [o'biːdjəns], *s.* **1.** Obéissance *f* (to, à). **To enforce o. to the law,** faire respecter la loi. **To compel o.,** se faire obéir. *S.a.* SERVANT. **2.** (*a*) *Ecc:* Obédience *f.* (*b*) *Pol:* **Countries of the Communist o.,** pays d'obédience communiste.

obedient [o'biːdjənt], *a.* Obéissant, soumis, docile. **To be o. to s.o.,** obéir à qn. **-ly,** *adv.* Avec obéissance, avec soumission.

obeisance [ou'beis(ə)ns], *s.* **1.** *A. & Lit:* Salut *m,* révérence *f.* **To make (an) o. to s.o.,** s'incliner devant qn. **2.** Obéissance *f,* hommage *m.* **To pay o. to s.o.,** rendre hommage à qn.

obelisk ['ɔbilisk], *s.* **1.** *Archeol:* Obélisque *m.* **2.** (*a*) *Pal:* Obèle *m.* (*b*) *Typ:* Croix *f;* obèle *m.*

obelus, *pl.* **-li** ['ɔbiləs, -lai], *s.* = OBELISK 2.

obese [ou'biːs], *a.* Obèse.

obesity [ou'biːsiti], *s.* Obésité *f.*

obey [o'bei], *v.tr.* Obéir à (qn, un ordre). *Abs.* Obéir, être obéissant. **To make oneself obeyed,** se faire obéir. **The orders must be obeyed,** il faut obéir aux ordres. **I must o. instructions,** je ne connais que la consigne. **To o. the law,** obéir, se plier, aux lois. *Jur:* **To o. a summons,** obtempérer à une sommation. **To o. the dictates of one's conscience,** écouter sa conscience.

obfuscate ['ɔbfʌskeit], *v.tr.* Obscurcir (la vue, le jugement).

obiter ['ɔbitər], *Lt.adv.* En passant. *Jur:* **O. dictum,** opinion judiciaire incidente.

obituary [o'bitjuəri], *a. & s.* **O.** (-list), nécrologe *m,* obituaire *m.* **O. notice,** notice nécrologique. *Journ:* **O. column,** nécrologie *f.*

object¹ ['ɔbdʒikt], *s.* **1.** (*a*) Objet *m,* chose *f.* (*b*) **O. of, for, pity,** objet, sujet *m* de pitié. **To be an o. of ridicule,** être en butte au ridicule. *F:* **Did you ever see such an o.?** A-t-on jamais vu une telle horreur? **2.** (*a*) But *m,* objectif *m,* objet. **With this o. (in view) . . ., dans ce but . . .;** à cette fin . . . **What is the o. of all this?** à quoi vise tout cela? **There's no o. in doing that,** cela ne sert à rien de faire cela. (*b*) (*In applying for post*) **Salary no o.,** les appointements importent peu. **Expense is no o.,** on ne regarde pas à la dépense. **3.** *Gram:* Complément *m,* régime *m,* objet. **O. clause,** proposition complétive. **'object-glass, -lens,** *s.* *Opt:* Objectif *m.* **Photomicrographic o.-g.,** micro-objectif *m.* **'object-plate, -slide,** *s.* Porte-objet *m inv* (de microscope).

object² [əb'dʒekt]. **1.** *v.tr.* **To o. sth. to s.o.,** objecter qch. à qn. **It was objected that . . .,** on a objecté que . . .; on a fait valoir que. . . . **2.** *v.i.* **To o. to sth.** faire objection, élever une objection, trouver à redire, à qch.; désapprouver qch. **To o. to s.o.,** avoir des objections à faire contre qn; récuser (un témoin). **To o. to doing sth.,** se refuser à faire qch. **I o. to his doing it,** je m'oppose à ce qu'il le fasse. **Do you o. to my smoking?** la fumée vous gêne-t-elle? *F:* **I don't o. to a glass of wine,** un verre de vin ne serait pas de refus.

objection [əb'dʒek(ʃ)(ə)n], *s.* **1.** Objection *f.* **To raise an o.,** soulever, formuler, une objection. **The o. has been raised that . . .,** on a objecté que. . . . **To find, make, an o. to sth.,** trouver un empêchement à qch. **To take o. to sth.,** (i) faire des objections à qch.; (ii) se fâcher de qch. **To make no o. to sth.,** ne rien objecter contre qch. **I have no o. to his doing so,** je ne m'oppose pas à ce qu'il le fasse. **I have a strong o. to doing that,** il me répugne (fortement) de faire cela. **If you have no o.,** si cela ne vous fait rien. **Conscientious o.,** objection de conscience. **2.** Obstacle *m,* inconvénient *m.* **There is no o. to your leaving at once,** il n'y a pas d'obstacle à ce que vous partiez immédiatement. **I see no o. (to it),** je n'y vois pas d'inconvénient.

objectionable [əb'dʒekʃnəbl], *a.* **1.** A qui, à quoi, on peut trouver à redire; répréhensible; inacceptable, inadmissible. **2.** Désagréable. **Idea that is most o. to me,** idée qui me répugne. **He's a most o. person,** c'est un homme que personne ne peut souffrir. **To use o. language,** tenir des propos choquants; cire des grossièretés.

objective [əb'dʒektiv]. **1.** *a.* (*a*) *Phil:* Objectif. (*b*) *Gram:* **O. case,** cas régime, cas objectif. **2.** *s.* (*a*) But *m,* objectif *m.* (*b*) *Opt:* Objectif.

objectivity [əbdʒek'tiviti], *s.* Objectivité *f.*

objector [əb'dʒektər], *s.* Protestataire *mf.* *S.a.* CONSCIENTIOUS 2.

objet d'art [əbʒei'dɑː], *s.* Objet *m* d'art.

objurgate ['ɔbdʒəːgeit], *v.tr.* Accabler (qn) de reproches.

objurgation [ɔbdʒəː'geiʃ(ə)n], *s.* Objurgation *f.*

oblate¹ ['ɔbleit], *s.* *Ecc:* Oblat, -ate.

oblate² ['ɔbleit, o'bleit], *a.* *Geom:* (Ellipsoïde, etc.) aplati (aux pôles).

oblation [o'bleiʃ(ə)n], *s.* *Ecc:* Oblation *f.*

obligation [əbli'geiʃ(ə)n], *s.* Obligation *f.* (*a*) To put, lay, s.o. under an o. to do sth., imposer à qn l'obligation de faire qch. To be under an o. to do sth., être dans l'obligation de, être astreint à, être tenu de, faire qch. I am under no o. to go with them, rien ne m'oblige à les accompagner. *Ecc:* Day of o., fête *f* d'obligation. *Jur:* Perfect o., obligation légale. Imperfect o., obligation morale. (*b*) Dette *f* de reconnaissance. To be under an o. to s.o., devoir de la reconnaissance à qn. To lay, put, s.o. under an o., obliger qn; créer une obligation à qn. You are laying me under an o., c'est à charge de revanche. (*c*) *Com:* To meet, to fail to meet, one's obligations, faire honneur, manquer, à ses engagements. *Com:* Without o., sans engagement. *P.N:* No o. to buy = entrée libre.

obligatory [o'bligət(ə)ri], *a.* Obligatoire; de rigueur. To make it o. (up)on s.o. to do sth., imposer à qn l'obligation de faire qch.

oblige [ə'blaidʒ], *v.tr.* 1. Obliger, astreindre (qn à faire qch.). To be obliged to do sth., être obligé, tenu, de faire qch. I was obliged to obey, je fus contraint d'obéir; force me fut d'obéir. 2. (*a*) To oblige a friend, rendre service à un ami. You would greatly o. (me) by sending me . . ., vous m'obligeriez beaucoup en m'envoyant. . . . Can you o. me with a light? auriez-vous l'amabilité de me donner du feu? He did it to o. (us), il l'a fait par pure complaisance. In order to o. you . . ., pour vous être agréable. . . . An answer by bearer will o., prière de vouloir bien confier la réponse au porteur. *P:* A lady I used to oblige, une dame chez laquelle je faisais le ménage. (*b*) To be obliged to s.o., être obligé à qn. I am much obliged to you for your kindness, je vous suis bien reconnaissant de votre bonté. obliging, *a.* Obligeant, complaisant, serviable. -ly, *adv.* Obligeamment, complaisamment.

obligingness [ə'blaidʒiŋnis], *s.* Obligeance *f*, complaisance *f*.

oblique[1] [o'bliːk], *a.* (*a*) (Ligne, angle) oblique; (regard) de biais. *Mil:* O. fire, tir d'écharpe. (*b*) O. ways, moyens indirects, détournés. (*c*) *Gram:* O. case, cas indirect, oblique. -ly, *adv.* Obliquement, de biais, en biais. *Carp:* En mouchoir.

oblique[2], *v.i. Mil: etc:* Obliquer.

obliquity [o'blikwiti], *s.* Obliquité *f.*

obliterate [o'blitəreit], *v.tr.* 1. (*a*) Faire disparaître, effacer (des chiffres, etc.). (*b*) Oblitérer, composter (un timbre). 2. *Med:* Oblitérer, obstruer (un conduit, etc.).

obliteration [o,blitə'reiʃ(ə)n], *s.* 1. (*a*) Effaçage *m*; grattage *m.* (*b*) Rature *f.* 2. Oblitération *f* (d'un timbre).

oblivion [o'bliviən], *s.* (État *m* d')oubli *m.* To sink into o., tomber dans l'oubli.

oblivious [o'bliviəs], *a.* Oublieux, -euse (of, de). *F:* To be totally o. of sth., ignorer tout à fait qch.

oblong [ɔblɔŋ]. 1. *a.* Oblong, -ongue; (sphéroïde) allongé. 2. *s.* Rectangle *m.*

obloquy [ɔbləkwi], *s.* (*a*) Calomnie *f.* To cover s.o. with o., cribler qn d'attaques malveillantes. Held up to public o., exposé à la vindicte publique. (*b*) Honte *f*, opprobre *m.*

obnoxious [əb'nɔkʃəs], *a.* Haïssable, odieux, -euse; détestable, exécrable; antipathique (to s.o., à qn). (*b*) O. smell, odeur repoussante, désagréable.

oboe ['oubou], *s.* Hautbois *m.*

oboist ['oubouist], *s.* Hautboïste *mf*, hautbois *m.*

obscene [ɔb'siːn], *a.* Obscène. -ly, *adv.* D'une manière obscène. To talk o., dire des obscénités.

obscenity [ɔb'siːniti, ɔb'seniti], *s.* Obscénité *f.*

obscurantism [ɔbskjuə'ræntizm], ̩*s.* Obscurantisme *m.*

obscurantist [ɔbskjuə'ræntist], *a. & s.* Obscurantiste (*mf*).

obscuration ['ɔbskju(ə)'̩eiʃ(ə)n], *s.* 1. Obscurcissement *m.* 2. Obscuration *f* (d'un astre).

obscure[1] [əb'skjuər], *a.* 1. Obscur, ténébreux, sombre. *Ph:* O. rays, rayons invisibles. 2. (Discours, livre) obscur; (argument) peu clair. 3. O. birth, naissance obscure. O. author, (i) auteur peu connu, obscur auteur; (ii) auteur obscur (= *abstruse*). -ly, *adv.* Obscurément.

obscure[2], *v.tr.* 1. Obscurcir. To o. sth. from s.o.'s view, cacher qch. à qn. Clouds obscured the sun, des nuages voilaient le soleil. *Nau:* To o. the lights, masquer les feux. *S.a.* ISSUE[1] 5. 2. Éclipser, surpasser.

obscurity [əb'skjuəriti], *s.* Obscurité *f* (de la nuit, de style, de naissance); hermétisme *m* (d'un texte, etc.). To lapse into o., tomber dans l'obscurité. To live in o., vivre dans l'obscurité. To rise from o., sortir de l'obscurité.

obsequies ['ɔbsikwiz], *s.pl.* Obsèques *f*, funérailles *f.* To attend the o., suivre le convoi.

obsequious [əb'siːkwiəs], *a.* Obséquieux, -euse. -ly, *adv.* Obséquieusement.

obsequiousness [əb'siːkwiəsnis], *s.* Obséquiosité *f.*

observable [əb'zəːvəbl], *a.* 1. (Cérémonie, etc.) à observer. 2. Visible; (changement) perceptible, sensible. 3. Remarquable; digne de remarque, d'attention. -ably, *adv.* Sensiblement, perceptiblement.

observance [əb'zəːv(ə)ns], *s.* 1. (*a*) Observation *f*, observance *f* (de la loi, etc.); observance (du dimanche). (*b*) Règle *f*, observance (d'un ordre religieux). 2. Religious observances, pratiques religieuses.

observant [əb'zəːv(ə)nt], *a.* 1. Observateur, -trice (of a rule, d'une règle). *O:* He is always o. of his duty, il est toujours très attentif à son devoir. 2. O. mind, esprit observateur. He is very o., rien ne lui échappe.

observation [ˌɔbzə(ː)'veiʃ(ə)n], *s.* Observation *f.* 1. (*a*) To keep s.o. under o., tenir qn en observation; surveiller qn. To come under s.o.'s o., tomber sous les yeux de qn. To escape o., se dérober aux regards. *Mil:* O. post, poste *m* d'observation; observatoire *m. Med:* O. ward, salle *f* des malades en observation. *Rail:* O. car, voiture *f* panoramique. (*b*) *Astr: Surv: etc:* Coup *m* de lunette; sondage *m.* To take an o., prendre, faire, une observation; *Nau:* faire le point. 2. Remarque *f.*

observatory [əb'zəːvətri], *s.* Observatoire *m.*

observe [əb'zəːv], *v.tr.* 1. Observer (la loi, un jeûne); se conformer à (un ordre). To o. silence, observer le silence. To o. care in doing sth., apporter des précautions à faire qch. To o. the Sabbath, observer, respecter (i) le sabbat, (ii) le dimanche. 2. Observer, regarder (les étoiles, etc.). To o. the enemy, surveiller l'ennemi. 3. Apercevoir, remarquer, noter (un fait). I observed him draw the curtains, je le vis tirer les rideaux. 4. (*a*) Dire. I observed (to him) that . . ., je lui fis remarquer, je lui fis l'observation, que. . . . (*b*) *Abs.* No one has observed on this fact, personne n'a commenté ce fait. observing, *a.* = OBSERVANT.

observer [əb'zəːvər], *s.* Observateur, -trice. He had come as an o., il était venu en curieux. *Pol:* United Nations o., observateur des Nations Unies.

obsess [əb'ses], *v.tr.* Obséder. To be obsessed with an idea, être obsédé, hanté, par une idée; être en proie à une idée.

obsession [əb'seʃ(ə)n], *s.* Obsession *f:* idée fixe.

obsidian [əb'sidiən], *s. Miner:* Obsidienne *f*, obsidiane *f.*

obsolescence [ˌɔbso'lesəns], *s.* Vieillissement *m*; tendance *f* à tomber en désuétude.

obsolescent [ˌɔbso'lesnt], *a.* Qui tombe en désuétude. This word is o., ce mot a vieilli.

obsolete ['ɔbsoliːt], *a.* Désuet, -ète; hors d'usage; tombé en désuétude; (of fashion, car) suranné; (of ship) déclassé. To grow o., passer de mode; tomber en désuétude.

obstacle ['ɔbstəkl], *s.* Obstacle *m*, empêchement *m.* To put obstacles in s.o.'s way, dresser, susciter, des obstacles à qn. To be an o. to sth., faire obstacle à qch. *Sp:* O. race, course *f* d'obstacles.

obstetric(al) [əb'stetrik(əl)], *a.* Obstétrical, -aux; obstétrique.

obstetrician [ˌɔbste'triʃ(ə)n], *s.* Accoucheur, -euse.

obstetrics [əb'stetriks], *s.pl.* Obstétrique *f.*

obstinacy ['ɔbstinəsi], *s.* Obstination *f*, entêtement *m*, opiniâtreté *f. Med:* Persistance *f* (d'une maladie). To show o., s'obstiner.

obstinate ['ɔbstinit], *a.* Obstiné (in doing sth., à faire qch.); opiniâtre. O. as a mule, entêté, têtu, comme un mulet. O. contest, combat acharné. -ly, *adv.* Obstinément, opiniâtrement.

obstreperous [əb'strep(ə)rəs], *a.* Bruyant, tapageur; turbulent. (*Of arrested drunkard, etc.*) To be o., *F:* rouspéter.

obstreperousness [əb'strep(ə)rəsnis], *s.* Tapage *m*; turbulence *f.*

obstruct [əb'strʌkt], *v.tr.* (*a*) Obstruer; encombrer (la rue); engorger, boucher (un tuyau). *Med:* Engouer. 'Do not o. the gangway,' "n'encombrez pas la passerelle." To o. the view, incommoder, gêner, la vue. (*b*) Gêner, entraver (les mouvements de qn). *Parl:* To o. a bill, faire de l'obstruction. (*c*) To o. the traffic, embarrasser, entraver, la circulation.

obstruction [əb'strʌkʃ(ə)n], *s.* 1. (*a*) Engorgement *m* (d'un tuyau). *Med:* Encombrement *m.* O. (of the bowels), occlusion, obstruction, intestinale. (*b*) Empêchement *m* (de qn dans ses affaires). (*c*) *Parl:* To practise o., faire de l'obstruction. 2. Encombrement *m*, embarras *m* (dans la rue); entrave *f* (à la navigation). *Rail:* An o. on the line, un obstacle sur la voie.

obstructionism [əb'strʌkʃənizm], *s.* *Pol:* Obstructionnisme *m.*

obstructionist [əb'strʌkʃənist], *s.* *Pol:* Obstructionniste *m.*

obstructive [əb'strʌktiv], *a.* Obstructif; *Pol:* obstructionniste. O. tactics, o. measures, tactique d'obstruction; mesures vexatoires.

obtain [əb'tein]. 1. *v.tr.* Obtenir; se procurer (des provisions, etc.). To o. sugar from beet, retirer du sucre de la betterave. He obtained the appointment through merit, son mérite lui a valu sa nomination. To o. first place, remporter la première place (dans un concours). 2. *v.i.* Avoir cours; prévaloir. Practice that obtains among civil servants, pratique établie, qui règne, chez les fonctionnaires. System now obtaining, régime actuellement en vigueur.

obtainable [əb'teinəbl], *a.* Procurable. Where is that o.? où cela s'obtient-il? où peut-on se procurer cela?

obtrude [əb'tru:d], *v.tr. & i.* Mettre (qch.) en avant. To o. oneself, s'imposer à l'attention. To o. (oneself) on s.o., importuner qn.

obtrusion [əb'tru:ʒ(ə)n], *s.* Intrusion *f*; importunité *f.*

obtrusive [əb'tru:siv], *a.* 1. Importun; indiscret, -ète. 2. O. smell, odeur pénétrante.

obtrusiveness [əb'tru:sivnis], *s.* Importunité *f.*

obturate ['ɔbtjureit], *v.tr.* Boucher, obturer. **obturating,** *a.* Obturateur, -trice.

obturation [ɔbtju'reiʃ(ə)n], *s.* Obturation *f.*

obturator ['ɔbtjureitər], *s.* Obturateur *m.*

obtuse [əb'tju:s], *a.* 1. Obtus, émoussé. *Geom:* O. angle, angle obtus. 2. (Esprit) obtus, peu intelligent. **ob'tuse-angled,** *a.* Obtusangle.

obtuseness [əb'tju:snis], *s.* 1. Manque *m* de tranchant, de pointe. 2. Stupidité *f*, manque de compréhension.

obverse ['ɔbvə:s], *a. & s.* (*a*) Obverse (side) of a medal, a coin, avers *m*, obvers(e) *m*, face *f*, d'une médaille, d'une monnaie. (*b*) O. of a truth, opposé *m* d'une vérité.

obviate ['ɔbvieit], *v.tr.* Éviter, parer à, obvier à (une difficulté); prévenir (des scrupules).

obvious ['ɔbviəs], *a.* Évident, clair, manifeste; de toute évidence. O. fact, fait patent, qui crève les yeux. It's o., c'est évident. It was the o. thing to do, c'était la chose à faire, c'est ce qu'il fallait faire, c'était tout indiqué, cela s'imposait. An o. remark, une vérité évidente, une vérité de La Palisse. -ly, *adv.* Évidemment, manifestement. She is o. wrong, il est clair qu'elle a tort.

obviousness ['ɔbviəsnis], *s.* Évidence *f*, clarté *f*, caractère *m* manifeste (of, de).

occasion [ə'keiʒ(ə)n], *s.* 1. Cause *f*, occasion *f.* You have no o. to be alarmed, il n'y a pas lieu de vous inquiéter. I have no o. for complaint, je n'ai aucun sujet de me plaindre. To give o. for scandal, donner occasion à la médisance. There's no o. to crow, il n'y a pas de quoi chanter victoire. Should the o. arise, s'il y a lieu; le cas échéant. 2. *pl.* To go about one's lawful occasions, vaquer à ses affaires (dans le cadre de la loi). 3. (*a*) Occasion, occurrence

f. On the o. of . . ., à l'occasion de . . .; lors de. . . . On one o., une fois. On several occasions, à plusieurs reprises. On such an o., en pareille occasion. On occasion, de temps à autre, de temps en temps. As o. requires, suivant l'occasion; au besoin. Play written for the o., pièce de circonstance. (*b*) Cérémonie *f.* 4. (*Opportunity*) I'll speak to him on the first o., je lui parlerai à la prochaine occasion.

occasion², *v.tr.* Occasionner, entraîner, provoquer, donner lieu à (qch.); faire naître (qch.).

occasional [ə'keiʒənl], *a.* 1. (*a*) O. verse, vers de circonstance. (*b*) O. table, petite table de salon. 2. An o. visitor, un visiteur qui vient de temps en temps. O. showers, averses éparses. 3. *Phil:* O. cause, cause occasionnelle. -lly, *adv.* De temps en temps; par occasion; par intervalles.

occident ['ɔksidənt], *s.* Occident *m.*

occidental ['ɔksi'dentl], *a.* Occidental, -aux.

occipital [ɔk'sipitl], *a.* Occipital, -aux.

occiput ['ɔksipʌt], *s.* *Anat:* Occiput *m.*

occlude [ɔ'klu:d], *v.tr.* Fermer, boucher (un conduit, etc.); occlure (les rayons de lumière).

occlusion [ɔ'klu:ʒ(ə)n], *s.* Occlusion *f*, bouchage *m*, fermeture *f* (d'un conduit, etc.).

occult¹ [ɔ'kʌlt], *a.* Occulte.

occult². 1. *v.tr.* *Astr:* Occulter (une planète, etc.). 2. *v.i.* *Nau:* (*Of light*) S'éclipser.

occultation [ɔkʌl'teiʃ(ə)n], *s.* *Astr:* Occultation *f.*

occultism ['ɔk(ə)ltizm], *s.* Occultisme *m.*

occupancy ['ɔkjupənsi], *s.* Occupation *f*, habitation *f* (d'un immeuble). *Jur:* Possession *f* à titre de premier occupant.

occupant ['ɔkjupənt], *s.* 1. Occupant, -ante (de terres); locataire *mf* (d'une maison); titulaire *mf* (d'un emploi). 2. The occupants of the car, les voyageurs *m.*

occupation [ɔkju'peiʃ(ə)n], *s.* Occupation *f.* 1. (*a*) To be in o. of a house, occuper une maison. House fit for o., maison habitable. 2. (*a*) To give s.o. o., donner de l'occupation à qn. To do sth. for lack of o., faire qch. par désœuvrement. (*b*) Métier *m*, emploi *m.* What is his o.? quel est son métier? *Mil: Adm:* To be in a reserved o., être affecté spécial, avoir une affectation spéciale.

occupational [ɔkju'peiʃən(ə)l], *a.* O. disease, maladie professionnelle. O. therapy, thérapie rééducative. O. hazards, risques *mpl* du métier.

occupier ['ɔkjupaiər], *s.* Occupant, -ante; locataire *mf*; habitant, -ante (d'une maison).

occupy ['ɔkjupai], *v.tr.* 1. Occuper. (*a*) Habiter (une maison). (*b*) Remplir (un emploi). (*c*) Garnir (une place de guerre); s'emparer (d'un point stratégique). *Mil:* In occupied territory, en territoire occupé. 2. Remplir (un espace); occuper (une place, le temps). The table occupies half the floor space, la table tient la moitié de la pièce. Is this seat occupied? est-ce que cette place est libre? To o. one's time in doing sth., remplir, occuper, son temps à faire qch. 3. Occuper (qn); donner du travail à (qn). To keep one's mind occupied, s'occuper l'esprit.

occur [ə'kə:r], *v.i.* (occurred) 1. (*Of event*) Avoir lieu; survenir, arriver; se produire. Should the case o., le cas échéant. If another opportunity occurs, si une autre occasion se présente. This seldom occurs, ce fait est assez rare. Don't let it o. again! que cela n'arrive plus! 2. Se rencontrer, se trouver. This word occurs twice in the letter, ce mot se rencontre deux fois dans la lettre. 3. It occurs to me that . . . il me vient à l'esprit, que . . .; l'idée me vient que. . . . Such an idea would never have occurred to me, une pareille idée ne me serait jamais venue à l'esprit.

occurrence [ə'kʌr(ə)ns], *s.* 1. To be of frequent o., arriver souvent; se produire, se renouveler, fréquemment. 2. Événement *m*, occurrence *f.* An everyday o., un fait journalier.

ocean ['ouʃ(ə)n], *s.* Océan *m.* O. currents, courants océaniques. O. floor, le fond sous-marin. **'ocean-going,** *a.* (Navire) au long cours, long-courrier. **'ocean-'lane,** *s.* *Nau:* Route *f* de navigation.

Oceania [ouʃi'einiə]. *Pr.n.* *Geog:* L'Océanie *f.*

oceanic [ˌouʃiˈænik], a. (a) Océanique. (b) (Of fauna) Pélagique.

oceanographer [ˌouʃiənˈɔgrəfər], s. Océanographe mf.

oceanography [ˌouʃiənˈɔgrəfi], s. Océanographie f.

ocellus, pl. -i [oˈseləs, -ai], s. Nat.Hist: Ocelle m.

ocelot [ˈousilət], s. Z: Ocelot m.

ochre[1] [ˈoukər], s. Miner: Ocre f. Red o., ocre rouge. Yellow o., jaune m d'ocre.

ochre[2], v.tr. Ocrer.

o'clock [əˈklɔk], adv.phr. See CLOCK[1] 2.

octagon [ˈɔktəgən], s. Geom: Octogone m.

octagonal [ɔkˈtægənl], a. Octogonal, -aux; (écrou) à huit pans.

octahedral [ˌɔkteˈhiːdr(ə)l], a. Octaèdre, octaédrique.

octahedron [ˌɔkteˈhiːdr(ə)n], s. Octaèdre m.

octane [ˈɔktein], s. Ch: Octane m. O. number, indice m d'octane.

octave [ˈɔktiv, ˈɔkteiv], s. 1. Octave f. 2. Pros: Huitain m.

octavo [ɔkˈteivou], a. & s. Typ: In-octavo (m).

octet(te) [ɔkˈtet], s. Mus: Octuor m.

October [ɔkˈtoubər], s. Octobre m. In O., au mois d'octobre. (On) the fifth of O., le cinq octobre.

octogenarian [ˈɔktodʒiˈnɛəriən], a. & s. Octogénaire (mf).

octopus [ˈɔktəpəs], s. Poulpe m, pieuvre f.

octoroon [ɔktoˈruːn], s. Ethn: Octavon, -onne.

octosyllabic [ˈɔktosiˈlæbik], a. Octosyllabe, octosyllabique.

octuple [ˈɔktjupl], a. Octuple.

ocular [ˈɔkjulər]. 1. a. Oculaire. 2. s. Opt: Oculaire m (de microscope, etc.).

oculist [ˈɔkjulist], s. Oculiste m.

odalisque [ˈoudəlisk], s. Odalisque f.

odd [ɔd], a. 1. (a) (Nombre) impair. O. or even, pair ou impair. (b) A hundred o. sheep, une centaine de moutons. Fifty o. thousand, cinquante à soixante mille. Fifty thousand o., cinquante mille et quelques centaines. A hundred o. yards, cent et quelques mètres. Twenty pounds o., vingt livres et quelques shillings. The o. three halfpence, les trois sous de reste. To be o. man (out), rester en surnombre. O.day (of leap year), bissexte m. (At cards, etc.) The o. game, la belle. To make up the o. money, faire l'appoint m. 2. (a) (Of one of a set) Dépareillé; (of one of a pair) déparié. O. stockings, bas qui ne vont pas ensemble. (b) O. moments, moments de loisir, moments perdus. At o. times, par-ci par-là. O. (job) man, homme à toute faire. S.a. JOB 1. Com: O. lot, solde m. 3. (a) Com: O. size, dimension spéciale, non courante. (b) Singulier, drôle; (of pers.) excentrique, original, -aux. The o. thing about it is that ..., le curieux de l'affaire, c'est que.... Well, that's o.! voilà qui est singulier! c'est bizarre! -ly, adv. Bizarrement, singulièrement. O. enough nobody knew anything about it, chose curieuse, personne n'en savait rien.

oddball [ˈɔdbɔːl], s. F: U.S: Drôle m d'oiseau.

oddity [ˈɔditi], s. 1. (a) Singularité f, bizarrerie f. (b) He has some little oddities, il a quelques petites manies. 2. (a) Personne excentrique; original, -ale. (b) Chose f bizarre; curiosité f.

oddments [ˈɔdmənts], s.pl. 1. Com: Fonds m de boutique; fins f de série. 2. = ODDS AND ENDS (see ODDS 3).

oddness [ˈɔdnis], s. 1. Imparité f. 2. Singularité f, bizarrerie f.

odds [ɔdz], s.pl. (Occ. with sg. const.) 1. (a) Avantage m; chances fpl. The o. are ag..inst him, les chances sont contre lui. To fight against (great, long) o., (i) lutter contre des forces supérieures; (ii) avoir affaire à plus fort que soi. (b) Différence f. What's the o.? qu'est-ce que ça fait? It makes no o., ça ne fait rien. (c) Turf· O. on, against a horse, cote f d'un cheval. Long o., forte cote. Short o., faible cote. To give, take, o., faire un pari inégal. The o. are that . . ., there's an odds on chance that . . ., il y a gros à parier que. . . . (d) Sp: To give s.o. o., concéder des points à qn. 2. To be at o. with s.o., (i) ne pas être d'accord avec qn; (ii) être brouillé avec qn. 3. O. and ends, petits bouts; bribes f et morceaux m; restes mpl.

ode [oud], s. Lit: Ode f.

odious [ˈoudjəs], a. Odieux, -euse (to, à); détestable. -ly, adv. Odieusement, détestablement.

odiousness [ˈoudjəsnis], s. Caractère odieux, l'odieux m (d'une action).

odium [ˈoudiəm], s. Réprobation f; détestation f. To bring o. upon s.o., rendre qn odieux.

odoriferous [ˌoudəˈrifərəs], a. Odoriférant, parfumé.

odorous [ˈoudərəs], a. Odorant.

odour [ˈoudər], s. 1. (a) Odeur (bonne ou mauvaise). (b) Parfum m. 2. To be in good, bad, o., être en bonne, mauvaise, odeur; être, ne pas être, en faveur (with s.o., auprès de qn). To die in (the) o. of sanctity, mourir en odeur de sainteté.

odourless [ˈoudəlis], a. Inodore; sans odeur.

Odyssey [ˈɔdisi], s. Odyssée f.

œcumenical [iːkjuˈmenik(ə)l], a. = ECUMENICAL.

œdema [iːˈdiːmə], s. Œdème m.

Oedipus [ˈiːdipəs]. Pr.n.m. Œdipe. O. complex, complexe m d'Œdipe.

œnometer [i(ː)ˈnɔmitər], s. Pèse-vin m inv.

o'er [ɔər], prep. Poet: = OVER I.

œsophagus [iːˈsɔfəgəs], s. Œsophage m.

œstrus [ˈiːstrəs], s. Ent: Œstre m.

of strong form [ɔv], weak forms [əv, v, f], prep. De. 1. (a) (Separation) South of, au sud de. Free of, libre de. U.S: Five minutes of one, une heure moins cinq. (b) (i) (Origin) To buy sth. of s.o., acheter qch. à, chez, qn. The works of Shakespeare, les œuvres de Shakespeare. (For 'beg of,' 'inquire of,' etc., see the verbs.) (ii) (Cause) Of necessity, par nécessité. To die of a wound, mourir (des suites) d'une blessure. (For 'to smell of,' 'to taste of,' etc., see the verbs.) 2. (Agency) (a) A: Beloved of all, aimé de tout le monde. (b) It is very kind of you, c'est bien aimable de votre part. 3. (Material) Made of wood, fait de, en, bois. 4. (a) (Introducing ind. obj. of verb) To think of s.o., penser à qn. Judge of my surprise, jugez de ma surprise. (b) (After adjs) Guilty of, coupable de. (c) Doctor of medicine, docteur en médecine. Master of arts = licencié(e)-ès-lettres. (d) F: Well, what of it? eh bien, et après? 5. (Descriptive genitive) (a) (i) Name of Jones, nom de Jones. The city of Rome, la cité de Rome. Trees of my planting, arbres que j'ai plantés moi-même. People of foreign appearance, gens à l'air étranger. Child of ten, enfant (âgé) de dix ans. U.S: His wife of twenty years, la femme qu'il a épousée il y a vingt ans. (ii) Swift of foot, aux pieds légers. Hard of heart, au cœur dur. Hard of hearing, (un peu) sourd. (b) A palace of a house, une maison qui est un vrai palais. That fool of a sergeant, cet imbécile de sergent. (c) All of a sudden, tout d'un coup. F: All of a tremble, tout tremblant. 6. (a) (Subjective genitive) The love of a mother, l'amour d'une mère. (b) (Objective genitive) The fear of God, la crainte de Dieu. Hope of relief, espoir de secours. 7. (Partitive) (a) How much of it do you want? combien en voulez-vous? Two of them died, deux d'entre eux moururent. There were several of us, nous étions plusieurs. He's one of us, il est des nôtres. Of the twenty only one was bad, sur les vingt un seul était mauvais. (b) (After superlative) The best of men, le meilleur des hommes. The one he loved most of all, celui qu'il aimait entre tous. (c) (Out of) He, of all men, should have been grateful, lui entre tous aurait dû se montrer reconnaissant. The one thing of all others that I want, ce que je désire par-dessus tout, avant tout. (d) (Intensive) A fool of fools, un triple sot. He is a radical of radicals, c'est un ultra-radical. The virtue of all virtues is success, la vertu qui prime toutes les autres, c'est de réussir. 8. (Possession or dependence) (a) The widow of a barrister, la veuve d'un avocat. The first of the month, le premier du mois. The first of June, le premier juin. (b) (+ possessive) He is a friend of mine, of my father's, c'est un de mes amis; c'est un ami de mon père. It's no business of yours, ce n'est pas votre affaire, cela ne vous regarde pas. 9. (In temporal phrases) F: What do you do of a Sunday? que faites-vous le dimanche?

off [ɔf]. I. *adv.* **1.** (*Away*) (*a*) **House a mile o.,** maison à un mille de distance. **To keep s.o. o.,** empêcher qn d'approcher. *S.a.* HOLD OFF, KEEP OFF. (*b*) (*Departure*) **To go o.,** s'en aller, partir. **I'm o. to Mass, to London,** je pars à la messe, je pars pour Londres. **It's getting late, I'm o.,** il se fait tard, je me sauve, je file. **Be o.! allez-vous-en! filez! They're o.!** les voilà partis! **O. we go!** (i) en route! (ii) nous voilà partis! **To go o. to sleep,** s'endormir. (*c*) *Nau:* Au large. (*d*) *Th:* A la cantonade; derrière la toile. **2.** (*a*) (*Removal*) **To take o. one's coat,** ôter son manteau. **Hats o.!** chapeaux bas! **O. with your shoes!** ôtez vos souliers! **To cut s.o.'s head o.,** décapiter qn. (On gas, electric, equipment, etc.) **'Off,'** fermé. *I.C.E:* **The ignition is o.,** l'allumage est coupé. (*In restaurant*) **Chicken is o.,** il n'y a plus de poulet. **The deal, the concert is o.,** le marché ne se fera pas; le concert n'aura pas lieu. (*b*) **Qui n'est plus frais. Meat that is slightly o.,** viande un peu avancée. *F:* **This beer's o.,** cette bière est éventée. (*c*) (Idée d'achèvement) **To finish o. a piece of work,** parachever un travail. **3. To be well o.,** *see* WELL OFF. **To be badly, poorly, o.,** être dans la gêne. **To be badly o. for sth.,** avoir grand(ement) besoin de qch. **He is better o. where he is,** il est bien mieux, dans une meilleure situation, où il est. **He is worse o.,** sa situation a empiré. **4.** *Adv.phr.* **O. and on; on and o.,** par intervalles; à différentes reprises. **Right o., straight o.,** immédiatement; tout de suite. II. **off,** *prep.* **1.** (*a*) *Usu.* De. **To fall o. sth.,** tomber de qch. **To fall o. one's horse,** tomber de son cheval. **To chase the cat o. the flower-bed,** chasser le chat du parterre. **Door o. its hinges,** porte *f* qui est hors de ses gonds. **To take sth. (from) o. a table,** prendre qch. sur une table. **To eat o. silver plate,** manger dans des assiettes d'argent. **To dine o. a leg of mutton,** dîner d'une tranche de gigot. **To take sth. o. the price,** rabattre qch. du prix. *adv.* **To allow 2½% o. for ready money,** faire une remise de 2½% pour paiement comptant. (*b*) Écarté de, éloigné de. **A yard o. me,** à un mètre de moi. **Street o. the main road,** (i) rue qui donne sur la grande route; (ii) rue éloignée de la grande route. *Fb:* **Player o. side,** joueur hors jeu. *S.a.* POINT[1] I. 3. (*e*) *F:* **To be o. one's food,** n'avoir pas d'appétit. *F:* **To be o. colour,** ne pas être dans son assiette. *U.S:* *F:* **An o. colour joke,** une plaisanterie grivoise, grossière. **I am o. that work now,** je ne fais plus ce travail. **To have time o. (work),** avoir du temps de libre. **To have a day o.,** avoir un jour de congé. **2.** *Nau:* (*a*) **O. the Cape,** à la hauteur du Cap; au large du Cap. **O. Calais,** devant Calais. (*b*) **To sail o. the wind,** naviguer vent largue. **3. O.-white,** blanc légèrement teinté. III. **off,** *a.* **1.** (*a*) *Equit: etc:* **O. rein,** rêne du dehors. *Aut: etc:* **The o. side,** le côté extérieur; le côté droit; *U.S:* le côté gauche; *Equit:* le côté hors montoir. (*b*) *Bookb:* **O. side,** verso *m.* **2.** Subsidiaire; (rue) secondaire. **3. O. day,** (i) jour de chômage, de liberté; (ii) jour où l'on n'est pas en train. **O. season,** morte-saison *f.* **4. O. consumption** (*of intoxicants*), consommation *f* à domicile. **off-'hand.** **1.** *adv.* (*a*) Sans préparation; au pied levé. **To speak o.-h.,** parler impromptu. (*b*) Sans cérémonie, sans façon; d'un air dégagé. **2.** *a.* (*a*) Spontané. **'O.-h. speech,** discours impromptu, improvisé. (*b*) Brusque, cavalier; dégagé, désinvolte. **To treat s.o. in an 'o.-h. manner,** traiter qn à la cavalière, avec désinvolture. **off-'handed,** *a.* = OFF-HAND 2 (*b*). **-ly,** *adv.* = OFF-HAND 1 (*b*). **off-'handedness,** *s.* Brusquerie *f,* sans-façon *m,* désinvolture *f.*; sans-gêne *m.* **'off-licence,** *s.* (*a*) Licence permettant exclusivement la vente des boissons à emporter. (*b*) Débit *m* où on vend des boissons à emporter. **'off-'peak,** *a.* **O.-p. hours,** heures creuses. *Av: El: etc:* **O.-p. tariff,** tarif *m* de nuit. **'off-print,** *s. Typ:* Tirage *m* à part, tiré-à-part *m.* **'off(-)'shore.** *Nau:* **1.** *adv.* Au large. **2.** *a.* (*a*) Du côté de la terre. (*b*) Éloigné de la côte. **offal** ['ɔf(ə)l], *s.* **1.** (*a*) Rebut *m,* restes *mpl,* déchets *mpl.* (*b*) Ordures *fpl.* **2.** Déchets *d'abattage* (de boucherie); abats *mpl.*; *F:* tripaille *f.*
off beat ['ɔf'biːt], *s. Mus:* Temps *m* faible.
offbeat ['ɔf'biːt], *a. F:* Original, -aux; qui sort de l'ordinaire.

offence [ə'fens], *s.* **1.** Blessure faite à la susceptibilité de qn; sujet *m* de déplaisir. **To take o. (at sth.),** se formaliser, se froisser (de qch.); *F:* prendre la mouche. **To give o. to s.o.,** offenser, blesser, froisser, qn. **I meant no o.,** je ne voulais offenser personne. **2.** (*a*) Offense *f,* faute *f.* **Serious o.,** faute grave. **To commit an o. against the law,** against propriety, commettre une infraction à la loi; faire outrage aux convenances. (*b*) *Jur:* **Indictable o.,** crime *m* ou délit *m*; acte délictueux. **Minor o.,** contravention *f.* **Second o.,** récidive *f.*
offend [ə'fend]. **1.** *v.i.* **To o. against the law,** violer, enfreindre, la loi. **To o. against the laws of courtesy,** pécher contre la politesse. **2.** *v.tr.* (*a*) Offenser, blesser, froisser (qn). **To be offended at, with, by, sth.,** se piquer, se fâcher, de qch. **To be easily offended,** être très susceptible. (*b*) (*Of thg*) **To o. the eye,** choquer les regards, la vue; offusquer l'œil. **Word that offends the ear,** mot qui sonne mal. **It offends our sense of justice,** cela outrage notre sentiment de la justice. **offending,** *a.* Offensant, fautif, -ive.
offender [ə'fendər], *s.* **1.** *Jur:* Délinquant, -ante, contrevenant, -ante. **A first o.,** un délinquant primaire. **An old, a hardened, o.,** un récidiviste, un repris de justice. **The chief o.,** le grand coupable. **2.** Offenseur *m.*
offensive [ə'fensiv]. **1.** *a.* (*a*) *Mil: etc:* Offensif. (*b*) Offensant, choquant; (spectacle) désagréable, repoussant; (odeur) nauséabonde. (*c*) (*Of pers.*) **To be o. to s.o.,** insulter qn; injurier qn; dire des grossièretés à qn. **2.** *s. Mil:* **To take the o.,** prendre l'offensive *f.* **-ly,** *adv.* **1.** *Mil: etc:* Offensivement. **2.** (*a*) Désagréablement; d'une manière choquante. (*b*) D'un ton injurieux.
offer[1] ['ɔfər], *s.* Offre *f*; proposition *f.* **To make an o. of sth. to s.o.,** faire offre de qch. à qn. *Com:* **To make an o. for sth.,** faire une offre pour qch. **That is the best o. I can make,** c'est le plus que je puis offrir. **O. of marriage,** demande *f* en mariage.
offer[2]. **1.** *v.tr.* (*a*) **To o. s.o. sth., sth. to s.o.,** offrir qch. à qn. **To o. (up) prayers to God,** adresser des prières à Dieu. **To o. oneself for a post,** s'offrir, se présenter, à un emploi. **To o. goods for sale,** offrir des marchandises en vente. **House offered for sale,** maison mise en vente. **To o. one's flank to the enemy,** prêter le flanc à l'ennemi. **To o. battle,** inviter le combat. **To o. to do sth.,** offrir de, s'offrir à, faire qch. (*b*) **To o. a remark, an opinion,** faire une remarque; avancer une opinion. (*c*) Essayer, tenter. **To o. resistance,** faire (de la) résistance. *O:* **He offered to strike me,** il fit mine de me frapper; il voulut, essaya de, me frapper. *Th:* **'Offers to go,'** "fausse sortie." **2.** *v.i.* S'offrir, se présenter. **If a good occasion offers,** s'il s'offre une belle occasion. **offering,** *s.* **1.** (*Action*) Offre *f.* **2.** (*Thg offered*) Offre; *Ecc:* offrande *f.* **Burnt o.,** holocauste *m.*
offertory ['ɔfət(ə)ri], *s. Ecc:* **1.** Offertoire *m.* **2.** Quête *f* (de l'offrande).
office ['ɔfis], *s.* **1.** (*a*) Office *m,* service *m.* **Through the good offices of . . .,** grâce aux bons offices de . . ., par les soins de. . . . (*b*) **Last offices (to the dead),** derniers devoirs (rendus à un mort). **2.** (*a*) Fonctions *fpl.* **Public offices,** administrations (publiques). **It is my o. to . . .,** il est de mon devoir de . . .; il rentre dans mes fonctions de. . . . (*b*) **Charge** *f,* emploi *m.* **To be in o., to hold o.,** (i) remplir un emploi; (ii) (*of government*) être au pouvoir. **To take o.,** (i) entrer en fonctions; (ii) **To come into o.** (*of government*) prendre le pouvoir. **To leave o.,** se demettre (de ses fonctions). **3.** *Ecc:* **O. for the Dead,** office des morts. **4.** (*a*) Bureau *m*; (*lawyer's*) étude *f*; *U.S:* (*doctor's*) cabinet *m* de consultation. **Head o.,** registered offices (*of company*), bureau central; siège (social). **O. supplies,** articles *m* de bureau. **This will be very good o. space,** ceci fera d'excellents bureaux. (*b*) **Private o.,** cabinet particulier. (*c*) **The Home O.** = le ministère de l'Intérieur. **The Foreign O.** = le ministère des Affaires Etrangères. (*d*) *pl.* **Offices (of a house),** communs *m* et dépendances *f.* **The usual offices,** (i) cuisine *f,* salle *f* de bains, etc.; (ii) les lieux *m* d'aisance. **'office-boy,** *s.m.* Coursier *m,* garçon *m* de courses. **'office-holder,** *s. U.S:* Fonctionnaire *m.* **'office-work,** *s.* Travail *m* de bureau.

officer¹ ['ɔfisər], s. 1. (a) Fonctionnaire m, officier m. Police o., agent m de police, de la sûreté. Sheriff's o., huissier m. (b) Officers of a society, membres m du bureau d'une société. 2. (a) Mil: Regimental o., officier de corps, de troupe. Staff o., officier d'état-major. Sch: Officers' training corps, bataillon m scolaire. Mil.Av: Acting pilot o., aspirant m. Pilot o., sous-lieutenant (aviateur). Flying o., lieutenant (aviateur). (In women's services, W.R.A.F.) Pilot o., troisième classe f. Flying o., deuxième classe f. Flight o., première classe f. Squadron o., hors classe f. Warrant o., deuxième catégorie f. (b) Navy: Executive o., deck o., officier de pont. Engineer o., officier mécanicien. S.a. NAVAL, PETTY 3. 3. High o., (of an order), grand dignitaire.

officer², v.tr. Mil: Fournir des officiers à (un corps); encadrer (un bataillon). A well-officered battalion, un bataillon bien commandé.

official [ə'fiʃ(ə)l]. 1. a. (a) Officiel. O. seal, cachet m réglementaire, de service. To act in one's o. capacity, agir dans l'exercice de ses fonctions. O. style, style administratif. (b) O. news, nouvelles authentiques, officielles. (c) The o. organist, le titulaire de l'orgue. 2. s. Fonctionnaire m. Minor officials, petits fonctionnaires. Higher officials, hauts fonctionnaires. Railway o., employé m des chemins de fer. -ally, adv. Officiellement. O. confirmed, homologué. O. recognised record, record homologué.

officialdom [ə'fiʃ(ə)ldəm], s. 1. L'administration f. 2. Bureaucratie f, fonctionnarisme m.

officialese [ə'fiʃə'li:z], s. F: Jargon administratif.

officialism [ə'fiʃəlizm], s. Bureaucratie f, fonctionnarisme m.

officiate [ə'fiʃieit], v.i. 1. Ecc: To o. at a service, officier à un office. To o. at a church, desservir une église. Officiating minister, officiant m. 2. To o. as host, remplir, exercer, les fonctions d'hôte.

officinal [ɔfi'sainl], a. Pharm: Officinal, -aux.

officious [ə'fiʃəs], a. 1. Empressé; trop zélé. 2. (Unofficial) Adm: Officieux, -euse.

officiousness [ə'fiʃəsnis], s. Excès m de zèle.

offing ['ɔfiŋ], s. Nau: The o., le large; la pleine mer. In the o., au large. To get an o., gagner au large. F: I have a job in the o., j'ai une place en perspective.

offset¹ ['ɔfset], s. 1. Occ: = OUTSET. 2. Hort: Rejeton m, œilleton m, stolon m. 3. Repoussoir m. To serve as an o. to s.o.'s beauty, faire ressortir la beauté de qn. 4. Compensation f, dédommagement m. As an o. to my losses, en compensation de mes pertes. 5. (a) Arch: Ressaut m, saillie f. (b) Mec.E: Désaxage m, décalage m, déport m. 6. Surv: Perpendiculaire f. 7. (a) Typ: Maculage m. (b) Phot.Engr: O. process, offset m.

offset², v. (Conj. like SET) 1. v.tr. (a) Compenser (ses pertes, etc). (b) Mec.E: Désaxer, décentrer (une roue); déporter, décaler (un organe). 2. v.i. (a) Hort: (Of plant) Pousser des rejetons. (b) Typ: Faire du maculage. **offset**², a. Mec.E: Désaxé, déporté; Const: en porte-à-faux.

offshoot ['ɔfʃu:t], s. 1. Rejeton m (d'un arbre, d'une famille). 2. Geol: Caprice m (d'un filon).

offspring ['ɔfspriŋ], s. 1. Coll. Progéniture f, descendance f; descendants mpl. 2. Descendant, rejeton m.

oft [ɔft], adv. Poet: Souvent. Many a time and oft, mainte(s) et mainte(s) fois. **'oft-times**, adv. A: Poet: Souvent, A: souventefois.

often ['ɔfn], adv. Souvent, fréquemment, mainte(s) fois. I see him o., I o. see him, je le vois souvent. How o.? (i) combien de fois? (ii) tous les combien? As o. as..., toutes les fois, chaque fois, que.... As o. as not, more o. than not, le plus souvent. It cannot be too o. repeated..., on ne saurait trop répéter.... I don't see him very o. now, je ne le vois plus guère. Every so o., de temps en temps, de temps à autre.

ogee ['oudʒi:], s. Arch: O. (-moulding), doucine f, cimaise f. O. arch, arc m en accolade. Tls: O. plane, doucine.

ogival [ou'dʒaiv(ə)l], a. Ogival, -aux.

ogive ['oudʒaiv], s. Ogive f.

ogle¹ ['ougl], s. Œillade (amoureuse); lorgnade f.

ogle². 1. v.tr. Lorgner, guigner (qn); lancer des œillades à (qn); reluquer (qn); P: faire de l'œil à (qn). 2. v.i. Jouer de la prunelle.

Ogpu ['ɔgpu:], s. Russian Adm: Le Guépéou.

ogre, f. **ogress** ['ougər, 'ougris], s. Ogre, f. ogresse.

oh [ou], int. = O².

ohm [oum], s. El.Meas: Ohm m.

ohmmeter ['oum,mi:tər], s. Ohmmètre m.

oil¹ [ɔil], s. 1. Huile f. 1. Ecc: The holy o., les saintes huiles. Tchn: Lubricating o., huile de graissage. Lamp o., (i) huile à brûler; huile lampante; (ii) pétrole lampant. Engine o., huile de machine. Aut: To change the o., faire la vidange. F: To burn the midnight o., travailler fort avant dans la nuit. To pour o. on troubled waters, apaiser les esprits. Vegetable oil, huile végétale. Fried in oil, frit à l'huile. Vegetable-oil industry, industrie f oléicole. Linseed oil, huile de (graine de) lin. Painting in oil(s), peinture à l'huile. S.a. CASTOR OIL, OLIVE-OIL, etc. 2. Mineral o., huile minérale, pétrole m. Paraffin o., pétrole (lampant). Fuel o., crude o., mazout m. O. gas, gaz m de pétrole. The oil industry, l'industrie pétrolière. O. shares, valeurs f pétrolières, pétroles. 3. Essential o., huile essentielle; essence f. O. of cloves, huile de girofle. **'oil-bath**, s. Mec.E: Bain m d'huile. **'oil-bearing**, a. 1. Bot: Oléagineux, -euse, oléifère. 2. Geol: Pétrolifère. **'oil-can**, s. 1. Bidon m à huile. 2. = OILER 2. **'oil-colour**, s. Couleur f à l'huile. **'oil-cooling**, s. Refroidissement m par l'huile. **'oil-duct**, s. Mec.E: Conduite f d'huile. **'oil-engine**, s. Moteur m à pétrole. **'oil-field**, s. Geol: Gisement m pétrolifère. **'oil-fired**, a. (Of engine, etc.) Chauffé au mazout. **'oil-gauge**, s. Jauge f de niveau d'huile. **'oil-groove**, s. Saignée f de graissage. **'oil-heating**, s. Chauffage m au mazout. **'oil-hole**, s. Trou m de graissage. **'oil-lamp**, s. Lampe f à huile ou à pétrole. **'oil-merchant**, s. = OIL-MAN 1. **'oil-mill**, s. Huilerie f. **'oil-paint**, s. = OIL-COLOUR. **'oil-painting**, s. 1. Peinture f à l'huile. 2. Tableau peint à l'huile. **'oil-press**, s. Pressoir m à huile. **'oil-producing**, a. = OIL-BEARING 1. **'oil-ring**, s. 1. Mec.E: Anneau graisseur. 2. Cartel m du pétrole. **'oil-seed**, s. Oléagineux m. **'oil-stove**, s. Réchaud m ou fourneau m à pétrole. **'oil-tanker**, s. Pétrolier m. **'oil-tracks**, s.pl. Mec.E: Araignée f (d'un palier). **'oil-varnish**, s. Vernis m à l'huile; vernis gras. **'oil-well**, s. Puits m pétrolifère; puits de, à, pétrole.

oil². 1. v.tr. (a) Huiler, graisser, lubrifier (une machine, etc.). To o. the wheels, graisser les roues; F: faciliter les choses. (b) To o. a pool (against mosquitoes), pétroler une mare. 2. v.i. Nau: Faire le plein de mazout. To oil up, v.tr. (a) Encrasser (d'huile). (b) (With passive force) S'encrasser (d'huile). **oiled**, a. (a) Graissé; huilé. To keep one's tools slightly o., tenir ses outils un peu gras. F: Well-o. tongue, langue bien pendue. F: He's well o., il est un peu parti, (un peu) éméché. (b) O. silk, taffetas m imperméable. **oiling**, s. 1. (a) Graissage m, huilage m, lubrification f. (b) Onction f (d'un athlète). 2. Pétrolage m (d'une mare).

oilcake ['ɔilkeik], s. Tourteau m (pour bétail).

oilcloth ['ɔilklɔθ], s. 1. (For waterproofs, etc.) Tissu huilé. 2. (For tables, etc.) Toile cirée. 3. (For floors) Linoléum imprimé.

oiler ['ɔilər], s. 1. (Pers.) Graisseur m. 2. Burette f à huile; burette de graissage.

oiliness ['ɔilinis], s. État ou aspect graisseux; onctuosité f.

oilman, pl. -men ['ɔilmən], s.m. 1. (a) Huilier; marchand d'huile. (b) Marchand de couleurs; droguiste. 2. Graisseur (de machines). 3. Expert pétrolier.

oilskin ['ɔilskin], s. 1. Toile cirée, vernie, huilée. 2. Nau: etc: (Suit of) oilskins, blouse f et pantalon m en toile huilée; ciré m.

oilstone ['ɔilstoun], s. Tls: Pierre f à huile (pour affûter); pierre à morfiler, à repasser; affiloire f.

oily ['ɔili], a. 1. Huileux, -euse; gras, f. grasse; graisseux, -euse. 2. F: (Of manner) Onctueux.

ointment ['ɔintmənt], s. Onguent m, pommade f. Zinc o., pommade à l'oxyde de zinc. A fly in the o., une ombre au tableau.

O.K.¹ ['ou'kei]. F: (a) int. Très bien! ça va! d'accord! O.K.! (b) a. That's O.K., ça colle. Everything's O.K., tout est en règle. (On document) Vu et approuvé; vérifié; Typ: bon à tirer, F: O.K.

O.K.², s. F: Approbation f. **We'll have to get an O.K.**, il faut qu'on nous donne le feu vert.

O.K.³, v.tr. **(O.K'd)** F: Passer, approuver (une commande).

okapi [o'ka:pi], s. Z: Okapi m.

okay¹·²·³ ['ou'kei], a., s., & v.tr. = O.K.¹·²·³

old [ould], a. **1.** (a) (Aged) Vieux, f. vieille; âgé. **My o. friend**, mon vieil ami, mon vieux ami. **To be growing o.**, tirer sur l'âge; se faire vieux; vieillir. **To make oneself look old(er)**, se vieillir. **To give oneself out as older than one is**, se vieillir. **A man is as o. as he feels**, on a l'âge de ses artères. **An o. man**, un homme âgé, un vieillard, F: un vieux. **O. as Methuselah**, vieux comme Hérode. **An o. woman**, une vieille femme, une vieille. **O. John**, le père Jean. **O. Mrs Brown**, la vieille Madame Brown, la mère Brown. **O. folk(s)**, les vieux. **O. wives' tale**, conte de bonne femme. s.pl. **O. and young**, grands et petits. **O. age**, la vieillesse. **To die at a good o. age**, mourir à un âge avancé, à un bel âge. **To live to be o.**, vivre vieux, vieille. (b) **O. clothes**, vieux habits. **O. wine**, vin vieux. **2.** (S.a. ELDER¹ 1, ELDEST.) **How o. are you?** quel âge avez-vous? **To be five years o.**, avoir cinq ans. **He is older than I**, il est plus âgé que moi; il est mon aîné. **To be ten years older than ...**, avoir dix ans de plus que ...; être plus âgé de dix ans que.... **A two-year-o. (child)**, un enfant (âgé) de deux ans. **To be o. enough to do sth.**, être d'âge à faire qch.; être en âge de faire qch. **3.** (a) (Long-established) Vieux, ancien; (famille) de vieille souche; (dette) d'ancienne date. **He's an o. friend of mine**, c'est un de mes vieux amis. **That's an o. dodge**, c'est un coup classique. **That's as o. as the hills**, c'est vieux comme le Pont-Neuf, comme Hérode, comme les rues. **It's as o. as Adam**, cela remonte au déluge. (b) **O. hand**, ouvrier expérimenté; Nau: etc: vétéran m. **He's an o. hand (at it)**, il possède la pratique du métier; il n'en est pas à son coup d'essai. **4.** (Former) Ancien. (a) **O. boy, pupil**, ancien élève. **O. girl, pupil**, ancienne élève. **O. customs**, anciennes coutumes. **We used to do it in the o. days**, nous l'avons fait dans le temps. **O. French**, l'ancien français. (b) **The O. World**, l'ancien monde; l'ancien continent. **The O. Country**, la mère-patrie. **The O. Testament**, l'Ancien Testament. **5.** F: (a) **Any o. thing**, la première chose venue; n'importe quoi. **Take any o. hat**, prenez un chapeau quelconque. (b) **O. man, o. chap**, mon vieux. P: **The o. man**, (i) papa; (ii) le patron, P: le singe. P: **My o. man**, mon homme. **My o. woman**, ma femme; la bourgeoise. **6.** Of o. (a) Adj. phr. Ancien, d'autrefois. **The knights of o.**, les chevaliers de jadis. (b) Adv.phr. (i) Jadis, autrefois. (ii) **I know him of o.**, je le connais depuis longtemps.

'old-'clothes-man, pl. **-men**, s.m. Marchand d'habits; fripier, F: marchand de puces. **'old-'clothes-shop**, s. Boutique f d'habits d'occasion; friperie f. **'old-'clothes-woman**, pl. **-women**, s.f. Marchande d'habits; fripière. **old-es'tablished**, a. Ancien; établi depuis longtemps. **old-'fashioned**, a. **1.** (i) A l'ancienne mode; (ii) démodé; passé de mode; suranné. **2.** (i) (Of pers.) Partisan des anciens usages; (of manner) de l'ancien temps; (ii) (of ideas) arriéré, vieillot, vieux jeu. **3.** F: **An o.-f. look**, un regard de travers. **old-'maidish**, a. (Façons) de vieille fille. **'old-'time**, a. **O.-t. dances**, danses fpl du bon vieux temps. **'old-'timer**, s. Vieux copain. **'old-'world**, attrib.a. **1.** De l'ancien temps. **2.** Du temps jadis. **O.-w. appearance**, aspect m d'antan.

olden ['ouldən], a. **In olden time(s)**, au temps jadis; autrefois.

oldish ['ouldiʃ], a. Vieillot, -otte.

oleaginous [ouli'ædʒinəs], a. Oléagineux, -euse, huileux, -euse.

oleander [ouli'ændər], s. Bot: Oléandre m; laurier-rose m.

oleiferous [ouli'ifərəs], a. Oléifère, oléagineux, -euse.

olfactive [ɔl'fæktiv], **olfactory** [ɔl'fæktəri], a. Olfactif.

oligarchic(al) [ɔli'gɑ:kik(əl)], a. Oligarchique.

oligarchy ['ɔligɑ:ki], s. Oligarchie f.

oliphant ['ɔlifənt], s. Mediev. Lit: Olifant m; cor m d'ivoire.

olive ['ɔliv], s. **1.** O.(-tree), olivier m. B.Hist: **The Mount, Garden, of Olives**, le Mont, le Jardin, des Oliviers. **2.** Olive f. **O. oil**, huile f d'olive. **Pickled o.**, picholine f. **3.** Cu: (Meat-)o., paupiette f. **4.** a. inv. Olive; (teint, etc.) olivâtre. **'olive-branch**, s. Rameau m d'olivier. **To hold out the o.-b.**, se présenter l'olivier à la main; faire les premières avances (pour une réconciliation). **'olive-'green**, a. (Couleur d')olive inv; olivacé. **O.-g. ribbons**, rubans olive. **'olive-grove, -plantation**, s. Olivette f, olivaie f. **'olive-grower**, s. Oléiculteur m. **'olive-growing**, a. Oléicole.

Oliver ['ɔlivər]. Pr.n.m. Olivier.

olympiad [o'limpiæd], s. Olympiade f.

Olympian [o'limpiən], a. & s. Olympien, -ienne. **The O. gods**, les dieux de l'Olympe.

Olympic [o'limpik], a. **The O. games**, F: the Olympics, les jeux olympiques.

Olympus [o'limpəs]. Pr.n. L'Olympe m.

ombre ['ɔmbər], s. A. Cards: Hombre m.

omelet(te) ['ɔmlit], s. Cu: Omelette f. **Ham o.**, omelette au jambon.

omen¹ ['oumen], s. Présage m, augure m. **To take sth. as a good o.**, prendre qch. à bon augure. **Bird of ill o.**, oiseau de sinistre présage, de mauvais augure; porte-malheur m inv.

omen², v.tr. Augurer, présager. **Ill-omened**, de mauvais augure.

ominous ['ɔminəs], a. De mauvais augure; menaçant; sinistre; inquiétant. **An o. silence**, un silence lourd de menaces. **-ly**, adv. Sinistrement; d'une façon menaçante, inquiétante.

omission [o'miʃ(ə)n], s. **1.** Omission f. **2.** Négligence f. **To rectify an o.**, réparer un oubli. Theol: **Sin of o.**, péché m, faute f, d'omission. **3.** Typ: Bourdon m.

omit [o'mit], v.tr. (omitted) **1.** (a) Omettre; passer sous silence. (b) Typ: Bourdonner (un mot). **2. To o. to do sth.**, oublier, omettre, de faire qch. **Not to o. to do sth.**, ne pas manquer de faire qch.

omnibus, pl. **omnibuses** ['ɔmnibəs, -əsiz]. **1.** s. A: Autobus m. **2.** a. **O. volume**, gros recueil (de contes, etc.). **O. bill**, projet de loi embrassant des mesures diverses.

omnipotence [ɔm'nipotəns], s. Omnipotence f; toute-puissance f.

omnipotent [ɔm'nipotənt], a. Omnipotent; tout-puissant, pl. tout-puissants; f. toute-puissante.

omnipresence ['ɔmni'prez(ə)ns], s. Omniprésence f; toute-présence f.

omnipresent ['ɔmni'prez(ə)nt], a. Omniprésent.

omniscient [ɔm'nisiənt], a. Omniscient.

omnivore ['ɔmnivɔ:r], s. Omnivore mf. pl. **Omnivora**, les omnivores.

omnivorous [ɔm'niv(ə)rəs], a. Omnivore.

on [ɔn]. **I.** prep. **1.** (a) Usu. Sur. **To tread on sth.**, marcher sur qch. **Do not tread on it**, ne marchez pas dessus. **On the Continent**, sur le Continent. **On the high seas**, en haute mer. **Dinner on the train**, dîner dans le train. **The room on the second floor**, la chambre du second, U.S: du premier. **An hotel on the left bank**, un hôtel de la rive gauche. **Is she on the (tele)phone?** (i) est-ce qu'elle a le téléphone chez elle? est-elle abonnée au téléphone? (ii) F: est-ce qu'elle parle au téléphone? (b) **On shore**, à terre. **On foot**, à pied. **On horseback**, à cheval. (c) **To be on the committee**, être membre du comité. **To be on the staff**, faire partie du personnel. **2.** (a) **Hanging on the wall**, pendu au mur, contre le mur. **On the ceiling**, au plafond. **Shoes on his feet**, des souliers aux pieds. **His hat on his head**, son chapeau sur la tête. **Have you any money on you?** avez-vous de l'argent (sur vous)? **He played it on his violin**, il l'a joué sur son violon. **On page four**, à la page quatre. Journ: **Continued on page four**, la suite en quatrième page. (b) (Proximity) (i) **House on the main road**, maison sur la grande route. U.S: **He lives on X. street**, il habite la rue X. (ii) **Just on a year ago**, il y a près d'un an. **3.** (a) **On (to)**, sur à. **To drift on to the shore**, dériver sur la terre, vers la terre. (b) **On the right, left**, à droite, à gauche. **On this side**, de ce côté. (c) **To march on London**, avancer vers, sur, Londres. **To smile on s.o.**, sourire à qn. (d) **To serve a writ on s.o.**, signifier un arrêt à qn. **To leave one's card on s.o.**, déposer une carte chez qn. **4.** Based on a fact, fondé sur un fait. To have sth. on good authority, savoir qch. de source certaine, de bonne part. Arrested on a charge of murder, arrêté sous l'inculpation de meurtre. On pain, penalty, of death, sous peine de mort. On an average, en moyenne. To borrow money on security, emprunter de l'argent sur nantissement. To retire on a pension of £500 a year, prendre sa retraite avec une pension de cinq cents livres par an. Dependent on circumstances, qui dépend des circonstances. On condition that..., à condition que.... To buy sth. on good terms, acheter qch. à d'excellentes conditions. **5.** (a) On Sunday, dimanche (prochain ou dernier). On Sundays, le(s) dimanche(s). On the following day, le lendemain. On April 3rd, le trois avril. On the evening of the first of June, le premier juin au soir. (b) On a warm day like this, par une chaleur comme celle-ci. On a fine day in June, par une belle journée de juin. On certain days, à (de) certains jours. On and after the fifteenth, à partir, à dater, du quinze. On or about the twelth, vers le douze. On that occasion, à, dans, cette occasion. On his majority, à, lors de, sa majorité. On my arrival, à mon arrivée. On application, sur demande. On examination, après examen. On delivery of the letter, lors de la remise de la lettre. (c) On (my) entering the room..., à, dès, mon entrée dans la salle.... **6.** (With adjs) On the cheap, à bon marché. On the sly, en sourdine, en catimini. **7.** On sale, en vente. On tap, en perce. **8.** (Concerning) A lecture on history, une conférence d'histoire. Inquiry on sth., enquête sur qch. Hume Brown on John Knox, l'appréciation f de John Knox par Hume Brown. To congratulate s.o. on his success, féliciter qn de son succès. F: Mad on s.o., fou, entiché, de qn. **9.** I am here on business, je suis ici pour affaires. On tour, en tournée. On holiday, en congé, en vacances. To be (working) on sth., travailler à qch. **10.** To have pity on s.o., avoir pitié de qn. Attack on s.o., attaque contre qn. F: This round (of drinks) is on me, c'est moi qui paie cette tournée. F: To have one on the house, prendre une consommation aux frais du patron (de l'établissement). U.S: F: I have nothing on him, je n'ai rien contre lui. **11.** To live on one's (private) income, vivre de ses rentes. Many live on less than that, beaucoup vivent avec moins que ça. **12.** (Added to) Disaster on disaster, désastre sur désastre. **13.** Turf: To put money on a horse, parier sur un cheval. **II.** on, adv. **1.** (a) To put on the cloth, mettre la nappe. To put the kettle on, mettre la bouilloire à chauffer. Th: (Of actor) To be on, être en scène. F: It's simply not on, il n'y a pas moyen. (b) To put on one's clothes, mettre ses habits. To put on one's gloves, se ganter. To have one's boots on, avoir ses bottes aux pieds; être chaussé. What did he have on? qu'est-ce qu'il portait? On with your coat! mettez votre veston! To have nothing on, être tout(e) nu(e). **2.** To fly on, go on, ride on, work on, continuer son vol, son chemin, sa chevauchée, son travail. To crawl on, drive on, talk on, wander on, continuer à ramper, à rouler, à parler, à errer. Go on! (i) continuez! allez toujours! (ii) P: pas vrai! Lit: On, Stanley, on! en avant, Stanley, en avant! To toil on and on, peiner sans fin. And so on, et ainsi de suite. **3.** Nau: To be broadside on to the shore, présenter le côté à la terre. **4.** (a) Later on, plus tard. From that day on, à dater de ce jour. S.a. NOW III. Well on in April, fort avant dans le mois d'avril. Well on in years, d'un âge avancé. (b) P: To have s.o. on, monter un bateau à qn. **5.** To turn on the tap, ouvrir le robinet. 'On,' "ouvert"; (of electric circuit) "fermé." The engine was on, le moteur était en marche. The brakes are on, les freins sont serrés. The performance is now on, la représentation est commencée. On with the show! que le spectacle commence! What is on (at the theatre) just now? qu'est-ce qui se joue actuellement? I see Hamlet is on again, je vois qu'on redonne Hamlet. This film was on last week, ce film a passé la semaine dernière. What's on to-night? (i) qu'est-ce qui se passe ce soir? (ii) que fait-on ce soir? Have you anything on this evening? êtes-vous occupé, invité,

ce soir? **6.** F: (a) I'm on! ça me va! (b) To be on to sth., comprendre, saisir, qch. They were on to him at once, ils ont tout de suite vu clair dans son jeu. (c) I was on to him on the phone this morning, je lui ai parlé au téléphone ce matin. The police are on to him, la police est sur sa piste. (d) He is always on at me, il s'en prend toujours à moi. **7.** On and off. See OFF I. 4. **'on-coming**, a. (a) Approchant (en sens inverse); (danger) imminent. On-c. traffic, véhicule venant en sens inverse. (b) Ind: On-coming shift poste entrant. **'on-shore**, a. (Vent) du large.

onager ['ɔnədʒər], s. Z: Onagre m.

once [wʌns], adv. **1.** (a) Une fois. O. only, une seule fois. O. a week, tous les huit jours. O. more, o. again, encore une fois. O. in a while, une fois en passant. O. (and) for all, une (bonne) fois pour toutes. O. a flirt, always a flirt, qui a flirté flirtera (b) (If) o...., (when) o...., dès que..., pour peu que.... O. grasp this fact and everything become plain, comprenez bien cela et tout s'éclaircit. **2** Autrefois. O. (upon a time) there was..., il était une fois..., il y avait une fois, jadis.... I knew him o., je l'ai connu autrefois, dans le temps. A collar that had o. been white, un faux col jadis blanc. O. when I was young..., il arriva un jour quand j'étais petit(e), que.... **3.** At o. (a) Tout de suite; à l'instant; sur-le-champ. (b) Don't all speak at o., ne parlez pas tous à la fois, en même temps. At o. a food and a tonic, à la fois un aliment et un fortifiant. To do a great deal at o., faire beau coup (i) en une fois, (ii) à la fois. S.a. ALL I. 3 **'once-over**, s. F: To give sth. the o.-o., s'assurer d'un coup d'œil que tout est bien.

one [wʌn]. **I.** num.a. **1.** (a) Un. Twenty-o. apples vingt et une pommes. A hundred and o., cent un A thousand and o., mille un. The Thousand and o Nights, les Mille et une Nuits. (b) He comes o. day out of two, il vient un jour sur deux. That's o. way of doing it, c'est une manière comme une autre de le faire. That's o. comfort, c'est déjà une consolation S.a. ANOTHER 4. **2.** (a) Seul, unique. My o. and only collar, mon seul et unique faux col. The o way to do it, le seul moyen de le faire. No 'o. man can do it, il n'y a pas d'homme qui puisse le faire à lui seul. (b) They cried out with o. voice, ils s'écrièrent d'une seule voix, d'une commune voix. To advance like o. man, avancer comme un seul homme. (c) Même. All in o. direction, tous dans la même direction. O. and the same thought came into our minds, une seule et même pensée nous vint à l'esprit. F: It's all o., cela revient au même; c'est tout un. It's all o. to me, cela m'est égal; cela ne me fait ni chaud ni froid. (d) God is o., Dieu est un. O: To become o., to be made o., s'unir; se marier. To be o. with sth., ne faire qu'une pièce avec qch.: faire corps avec qch. **II.** one, s. **1.** Eleven is written with two ones, onze s'écrit avec deux un. Chapter o., chapitre un, chapitre premier. Number o., (i) numéro un; (ii) F: soi-même. Mil: Number o. (uniform), tenue f numéro un. F: To look after number o., soigner sa petite personne; mettre ses intérêts en premier lieu. **2.** (a) There is only o. left, il n'en reste qu'un. The last but o., l'avant-dernier, -ière. The topmost stair but o., l'avant-dernière marche. S.a. LAST² I. 1, NEXT I. 1, 2. Goods that are sold in ones, marchandises qui se vendent à la pièce. Garment all in o., vêtement en une pièce. To be at o. with s.o., être d'accord avec qn. (b) O. and sixpence, un shilling (et) six pence. O. (o'clock), une heure. P: I fetched, landed, him o., je lui ai flanqué un marron. F: To call at the pub for a quick o., entrer au café pour s'en enfiler une. F: He's had o. too many, il a bu un verre de trop. That is o. up for us! et d'un dans nos filets! Knitting: Knit o., make o., une (maille) à l'endroit, faire une augmentation. **III.** one, dem.pron. (a) This o., celui-ci, f. celle-ci. That o., celui-là, f. celle-là. Which o do you prefer? lequel, laquelle, préférez-vous? The o. on the table, celui, celle, qui est sur la table. She is the o. who helped Louise, c'est elle qui a aidé Louise. (b) To pick the ripe plums and leave the green ones, cueillir les prunes mûres et laisser les vertes. The portraits on the walls, especially the full-length ones..., les portraits pendus aux murs, surtout les portraits en pied.... That's a good o.! en voilà une bonne! He's a sharp o., c'est un malin. *P:* He's a o.! quel type! Our dear ones, ceux qui nous sont chers. The little ones, les petits enfants; *(of animals)* les petits. The Evil O., le Malin, l'Esprit malin. IV. one, *indef.a.* O. day, un jour. O. stormy evening in January, par une soirée tempêtueuse de janvier. V. one, *indef. pron* 1. *(pl.* some, any) I haven't a pencil, have you got o.? je n'ai pas de crayon, en avez-vous un? The idea is o. which occurs in primitive societies, cette idée est de celles que l'on rencontre dans les sociétés primitives. O. of them, (i) l'un d'entre eux; l'un d'eux; (ii) *P:* un homosexuel. He is o. of the family, il fait partie de la famille; il est de la famille. Will you make o. of us? voulez-vous vous mettre de la partie? voulez-vous être des nôtres? Any o. of us, l'un quelconque d'entre nous; n'importe lequel d'entre nous. *S.a.* EVERY (c). Not o. (of them), *A:* never a o., pas un. O. and all, tous sans exception. (The) ... the other, l'un ... l'autre. You can't have o. without the other, l'un ne va pas sans l'autre. O. after the other, l'un après l'autre. To come in o. or other of the doors, entrer par l'une ou l'autre des portes. O. another, *see* ANOTHER 4. O. by o., un à un, une à une. 2. I want the opinion of o. better able to judge, je voudrais avoir l'opinion de quelqu'un qui soit plus capable de juger. He looked like o. dead, il avait l'air d'un mort. To o. who can read between the lines, it is evident that..., à qui sait lire entre les lignes, il est évident que... O. Mr Jenkins, un certain M. Jenkins; un nommé Jenkins. I for o. shall come, quant à moi, je viendrai. I am not (the) o. to..., je ne suis point homme à..., je ne suis pas de ceux qui.... *F:* I'm not much of a o. for chocolate, je ne suis pas grand amateur de chocolat. 3. *(a) (Nom.)* On. O. cannot always be right, on ne peut pas toujours avoir raison. *(b) (Acc.)* Vous. It is enough to kill o., il y a de quoi vous faire mourir. 4. One's, son, *f.* sa, *pl.* ses; votre, *pl.* vos. To give one's opinion, donner son avis. When o. is allowed to see one's friends, quand il nous est permis de voir nos amis. To cut one's finger, se couper le doigt. 'one-armed, *a.* A un seul bras; *(of pers.)* manchot. *F:* One-arm(ed) bandit, *F:* tire-pognon *m, pl.* tire-pognons. 'one-celled, *a.* Biol: Unicellulaire. 'one-cylinder, *attrib.a. I.C.E:* (Moteur) à cylindre unique, monocylindrique. 'one-eyed, *a. (a) Z:* Unioculé. *(b) (Of pers.)* Borgne. 'one-horse, *attrib.a. esp. U.S: F:* A o.-h. show, (i) un spectacle de deux sous; (ii) une affaire de quatre sous. O.-h. town, petit bourg de rien du tout. 'one-legged, *a.* Qui n'a qu'une jambe; amputé de la jambe; unijambiste; *Z:* monopode. 'one-'price, *attrib.a.* (Article, magasin) à prix unique; (magasin) uniprix. 'one-'sided, *a.* 1. *(Of contract)* Unilatéral, -aux. 2. *(Of shape)* Asymétrique. 3. *(a) (Of bargain)* Inégal, -aux; inéquitable. *(b) (Of judgment)* Partial, -aux; injuste. 'one-storied, *a.* (Maison) sans étage. 'one-time, *F: (a) a.* Ancien, -ienne. *(b) adv.* Autre fois. 'one-track, *a. F:* O.-t. mind, esprit obsédé par une seule idée. 'one-'upmanship, *s. F:* L'art *m* de surpasser les autres. 'one-way, *attrib.a.* O.-w. street, rue à sens unique. O.-w. traffic, circulation en sens unique.

onerous ['ɔnərəs], *a.* 1. Onéreux, -euse; (tâche) pénible. 2. *Jur:* (Scot.) (Contrat) à titre onéreux.

oneself [wʌn'self], *pron. See* SELF 4.

onion ['ʌnjən], *s.* Oignon *m.* Spring o., ciboule *f*; petit oignon. O. stew, fricassée *f* aux oignons. O. sauce, sauce blanche à l'oignon. *F:* To know one's onions, connaître son affaire. String of onions, chapelet *m* d'oignons. 'onion skin, *s.* 1. Pelure *f* d'oignon. 2. *Com:* Papier *m* pelure.

onlooker ['ɔn,lukər], *s.* Spectateur, -trice. The onlookers, l'assistance *f*; les assistants *m.*

only ['ounli]. I. *a.* Seul, unique. O. son, fils unique. His one and o. hope, son seul et unique espoir. His o. answer was to burst out laughing, pour toute réponse il éclata de rire. He was the o. one who noticed it, il fut le seul à s'en apercevoir. You are

not the o. one, vous n'êtes pas le seul; il n'y a pas que vous. II. only, *adv.* Seulement, ne... que. I have o. three,—O. three? je n'en ai que trois.— Que trois? *P.N:* Ladies o., dames seules. Staff o., réservé au personnel. O. he can say, lui seul saurait le dire. O. the binding is damaged, il n'y a que la reliure d'abîmée. I o. touched it, je n'ai fait que le toucher. He has o. to ask for it, il n'a qu'à le demander. I shall be o. too pleased to..., je ne serai que trop heureux de... I will o. say..., je me bornerai à dire.... O. to think of it, rien que d'y penser. If o., ne fût-ce que, ne serait-ce que. If o. I knew where he is! si seulement je savais où il est! Not o. ... but also..., non seulement... mais aussi, mais encore.... O. yesterday, hier encore; pas plus tard qu'hier. *S.a.* JUST II. 2, 4. III. only, *conj.* Mais. The book is interesting, o. rather too long, le livre est intéressant, mais un peu trop long, seulement un peu long. I would do it only (that)..., je le ferais (si ce) n'était que.... 'only-be'gotten, *a. Ecc:* (Fils) unique.

onomatopoeia [ɔnomæto'pi(:)ə], *s.* Onomatopée *f.*

onrush ['ɔnrʌʃ], *s.* Ruée *f*; attaque *f.* The o. of water, l'eau qui se précipite.

onset ['ɔnset], *s.* 1. Assaut *m*, attaque *f.* To withstand the o. of the enemy, soutenir le choc de l'ennemi. 2. At the (first) o., d'emblée, de prime abord, au premier abord. From the o., dès l'abord.

onslaught ['ɔnslɔːt], *s.* = ONSET 1. To make a savage o. on the Prime Minister, attaquer véhémentement le Premier ministre.

Ontarian [ɔn'teeriən], *s.* Habitant, -ante, de l'Ontario, Ontarien, -ienne.

onto ['ɔntu(:), 'ɔntə], *prep.* = on to, *q.v. under* ON I. 3.

ontogenesis [ɔnto'dʒenisis], *s. Biol:* Ontogenèse *f.*

ontological [ɔnto'lɔdʒik(ə)l], *a.* Ontologique.

ontology [ɔn'tɔlədʒi], *s.* Ontologie *f.*

onus ['ounəs], *s.* Responsabilité *f*, charge *f. Jur:* O. probandi [pro'bændai], charge de la preuve.

onward ['ɔnwəd]. 1. *adv.* = ONWARDS. 2. *a.* En avant; progressif, -ive.

onwards ['ɔnwədz], *adv. (a)* En avant. *(b)* From tomorrow o., à partir de demain. From this time o., désormais, dorénavant.

onyx ['ɔniks], *s.* 1. *Miner:* Onyx *m.* Black o., jais artificiel. 2. *Vet:* Ongle *m* (à l'œil).

oodles ['uːdlz], *s.pl. F:* Une grande quantité (of, de). O. of money, de l'argent à gogo.

oof [uːf], *s. O: F:* De l'argent; *P:* pognon *m.*

oolite ['ouolait], *s. Miner: Geol:* Oolithe *m.*

oolitic [ouo'litik], *a. Miner: Geol:* Oolithique.

oomph [umf], *s. F:* Sex-appeal *m.*

ooze[1] [uːz], *s.* 1. Vase *f*, limon *m.* 2. Suintement *m*, dégouttement *m* (d'un liquide).

ooze[2], *v.i. (a)* Suinter; dégoutter. His courage is oozing away, son courage l'abandonne. *(b) (With cogn. acc.)* Suer, suinter (de l'eau, etc.); laisser dégoutter (l'eau). He oozes self-conceit, il sue l'orgueil par tous les pores. **oozing,** *s.* Suintement *m*, fuite *f* (de l'eau, etc.).

op [ɔp], *s. F:* 1. *Med:* Opération (chirurgicale). 2. *Mil:* Combined op(s), opération (i) amphibie, (ii) interarmées.

opacity [ou'pæsiti], *s.* 1. Opacité *f.* 2. Lourdeur *f* (d'intelligence); esprit obtus.

opal ['oup(ə)l], *s.* 1. *Lap:* Opale *f.* 2. *Glassm:* O. glass, verre opalin; verre opale.

opaline ['oupəliːn], *a.* Opalin.

opalescence [oupə'lesns], *s.* Opalescence *f.*

opalescent [oupə'lesnt], *a.* Opalescent.

opaque [ou'peik], *a.* 1. Opaque. 2. *(Of pers.)* Peu intelligent; à l'esprit épais, obtus.

opaqueness [ou'peiknis], *s.* = OPACITY.

open[1] ['oup(ə)n], *a.* Ouvert. 1. *(a)* O. window, fenêtre ouverte. To push the door o., ouvrir la porte d'une poussée. Half o., entrouvert, entrebâillé. *S.a.* WIDE OPEN. To keep o. house, o. table, tenir table ouverte. *(b) (Of box)* Ouvert; *(of parcel)* défait. O. grave, tombe qui attend son cercueil. *El:* O. circuit, circuit ouvert, coupé. To break o., smash o., a box, éventrer une boîte. To cut o., couper, ouvrir. *(c)* O. to the public, ouvert, accessible, au public. *(d)* In (the) o. court, en plein tribunal. **O. trial**, jugement public. (*e*) Posts o. to all, charges accessibles à tout le monde. (*f*) *Sp:* = Accessible à tous. *Turf:* **O. race**, omnium *m*. **2.** Sans limites; sans bornes. **In the o. air**, *s.* in the o., au grand air, en plein air. **To sleep in the o.** (air), coucher à la belle étoile. **O. country**, pays découvert. **In the o. country**, en pleine campagne, en rase campagne. **The house stands in the o.**, la maison est située en pleine campagne. **The o. sea**, la haute mer; le large. **In the o. sea**, en pleine mer. **3.** (*a*) **O. car**, voiture découverte. **O. boat**, bateau non ponté. **O. light**, feu nu. (*b*) *Nau:* **O. roadstead**, rade foraine. **O. field**, champ *m* sans enclos. (*c*) **O. to every wind**, exposé à tous les vents. (*d*) **O. to criticism**, prêter le flanc, donner prise, à la critique. **O. to ridicule**, qui prête au ridicule. **O. to doubt**, exposé au doute. (*e*) **To be o. to conviction**, être accessible à la conviction. **To be o. to advice**, être tout prêt à accueillir des conseils. **Invention o. to improvement**, invention susceptible d'amélioration. **4.** (*a*) Manifeste; public, -ique. **O. secret**, secret de Polichinelle. **O. letter**, lettre ouverte (communiquée à la presse). **Fact o. to all**, fait patent. (*b*) *Franc.* **O. admiration**, franche admiration. **O. enemy of the Government**, ennemi déclaré du Gouvernement. **To be o. with s.o.**, parler franchement à qn; ne rien cacher à qn. (*c*) *s.* **To come out into the o.**, venir au grand jour, se dévoiler. **5. Open wound**, plaie (i) béante, (ii) non cicatrisée. **Dress o. at the neck**, robe échancrée au col. **O. pores**, pores dilatés. *Ling:* **O. vowel**, voyelle ouverte. **6.** Non serré. *Mil:* **To attack in o. order**, attaquer en ordre dispersé. **O. fence**, clôture à claire-voie. **O. tissue**, tissu à jour. **7.** (*a*) Non obstrué. **O. road**, chemin libre. *Rail:* **O. signal**, signal effacé. **O. view**, vue dégagée. *Aut:* **O. corner**, virage découvert. **To keep the bowels o.**, tenir le ventre libre. *Mus:* **O. string**, corde à vide. **O. town**, (i) *Mil:* ville non fortifiée; (ii) *U.S: P:* ville où la police se montre indulgente en matière de vice. (*b*) **To keep a day o. for s.o.**, réserver un jour pour qn. **The job is still o.**, la place est toujours vacante. **Two courses are o. to us**, deux moyens s'offrent à nous. **It is o. to you to object**, il vous est permis, loisible, de faire des objections. **8.** Non résolu. **O. question**, question discutable, indécise. **To keep an o. mind on sth.**, rester sans parti pris; réserver son opinion sur qch. *S.a.* VERDICT 1. **9.** *Com:* **O. account**, compte ouvert; compte courant. **O. credit**, crédit à découvert; crédit en blanc. **O. cheque**, chèque ouvert, non barré. **-ly**, *adv.* Ouvertement, franchement, en toute franchise; au vu (et au su) de tous. **To act o.**, agir à découvert; jouer franc jeu. **'open-air**, *attrib.a.* Au grand air, en plein air. **O.-a. life**, la vie des champs. **O.-a. meeting**, assemblée en plein vent. **'open-'cast**, *a.* **O.-c. mining**, exploitation *f.* à ciel ouvert. **open-'eyed**, *a.* **1.** Qui voit clair; qui ne se laisse pas duper. **2. To look at s.o. with o.-e. astonishment**, regarder qn les yeux écarquillés de surprise. **open-'handed**, *a.* Libéral, -aux; généreux. **-ly**, *adv.* Libéralement. **open-'handedness**, *s.* Libéralité *f.* **open-'hearted**, *a.* **1.** Franc, *f.* franche; expansif. **2.** Au cœur tendre, compatissant. **open-'minded**, *a.* Qui a l'esprit ouvert, large; impartial, -aux. **To be o.-m. (on a subject)**, n'avoir pas de parti pris, d'idée préconçue, avoir l'esprit libre (sur un sujet). **open-'mouthed**, *a.* **To remain o.-m.**, rester bouche bée. **open-'necked**, *a.* A col ouvert. **'open-work**, *s.* (*a*) Ouvrage *m* à jour. **O.-w. stockings**, bas ajourés, à jour. (*b*) Ajours *mpl*, jours *mpl*.

open². I. *v.tr.* **1.** (*a*) Ouvrir (une porte, etc.); baisser (une glace). **To half o. the door**, entrebâiller, entrouvrir, la porte. *S.a.* DOOR 1. (*b*) Déboucher, entamer (une bouteille); écailler (une huître); décacheter (une lettre); défaire (un paquet); lâcher (une écluse). **To o. the mail**, dépouiller le courrier. *El:* **To o. the circuit**, (inter)rompre, couper, le courant. *Med:* **To o. the bowels**, relâcher les intestins. (*c*) **To o. a new shop**, ouvrir, fonder, monter, un nouveau magasin. **To o. a road (to traffic)**, livrer une route à la circulation. (*d*) Inaugurer (une fête, un établissement). **2.** Écarter (les jambes); ouvrir

(la main, etc.). **I have not opened my mouth all day**, je n'ai pas desserré les dents de la journée. **To half o. one's eyes**, entrouvrir les yeux. *S.a.* EYE¹ 1. **3.** **To o. a hole in a wall**, pratiquer, percer, un trou dans un mur. **To o. a road**, ouvrir, frayer, un chemin (*Cp.* 1 (*c*).) **4.** Découvrir, exposer, révéler. **To o. one's heart, to o. oneself**, (i) épancher son cœur (ii) ouvrir son cœur, s'ouvrir (to s.o., à qn). **5.** Commencer; entamer, engager (une conversation, un débat). *Com:* **To o. an account in s.o.'s name**, ouvrir un compte en faveur de qn. *Jur:* **To o. the case**, ouvrir l'affaire; exposer les faits. *Cards:* **To o. clubs**, attaquer trèfle; entamer trèfle. **6.** *U.S: P:* Cambrioler. **II. open**, *v.i.* S'ouvrir. **1.** (*a*) (*Of door, etc.*) **To half o., to o. a little**, s'entrebâiller, s'entrouvrir. **Door that opens into, on to, the garden**, porte qui donne sur, dans, le jardin, qui ouvre sur le jardin. **The exits o. on to the street**, les sorties donnent accès à la rue. (*b*) **The bank opens at ten**, la banque ouvre, ouvre ses portes, à dix heures. **As soon as the season opens**, dès l'ouverture de la saison. **2.** (*a*) (*Of view, etc.*) S'étendre. (*b*) (*Of flower*) S'épanouir, s'ouvrir. **3.** Commencer. **Play that opens with a brawl**, pièce qui débute par une rixe. *St.Exch:* **Rubber opened firm**, le caoutchouc a ouvert ferme. **open out**. **1.** *v.tr.* (*a*) Ouvrir, déplier (une feuille de papier, etc.). (*b*) Développer (une entreprise, etc.). (*c*) Élargir, agrandir (un trou); évaser (un tuyau). **2.** *v.i.* (*a*) (*Of view, etc.*) S'ouvrir, s'étendre. (*b*) *Aut:* Mettre, ouvrir, les gaz. **open up**. **1.** *v.tr.* Ouvrir (une mine, etc.); exposer, révéler (une perspective); frayer, pratiquer (un chemin). **To o. up a country to trade**, ouvrir un pays au commerce. **2.** *v.i.* (*a*) *Com:* Ouvrir une succursale (dans un endroit); entamer des affaires (dans un pays). (*b*) *F:* **To make s.o. o. up**, délier la langue de qn. (*c*) Ouvrir le feu. (*d*) = OPEN OUT 2(*b*). **opening**, **1.** (*a*) Ouverture *f*; débouchage *m* (d'une bouteille); dépouillement *m* (du courrier). (*b*) Formal o. inauguration *f*. *Jur:* **The o. of the courts**, la rentrée des tribunaux. (*c*) Commencement *m* (d'une conversation, etc.). *Jur:* Exposition *f* des faits. (*d*) *Cards:* Attaque *f*. **Chess openings**, débuts *m* de partie. **2.** Trou *m*, ouverture, orifice *m*; embouchure *f* (d'un sac); percée *f* (dans une forêt, un mur); éclaircie *f* (dans les nuages); clairière *f* (dans un bois). **3.** Occasion *f* favorable. *Com:* Débouché *m* (pour une marchandise). **Fine o. for a young man, beau débouché pour un jeune homme. **To give an adversary an o.**, prêter le flanc à un adversaire. **4.** Épanouissement *m* (d'une fleur); commencement, début *m* (d'une pièce de théâtre). **5.** *Attrib.* D'ouverture, inaugural, -aux. **O. sentence**, phrase de début. *St.Exch:* **O. price**, cours de début, d'ouverture; premier cours. *Cards:* (*At bridge*) **O. bid**, annonce d'entrée. **opener** ['oup(ə)nər], *s.* **1.** (*Pers.*) Ouvreur, -euse. **2.** (*Device*) *See* CASE-OPENER, EYE-OPENER, TIN-OPENER. **openness** ['oupənnis], *s.* **1.** Situation exposée (d'une côte); aspect découvert (du terrain). **2.** Franchise *f*; ouverture *f* de cœur. **opera** ['op(ə)rə], *s.* Opéra *m*. **Grand o.**, grand opéra. **'opera-glass(es)**, *s.(pl.)* Jumelle(s) *f* (de théâtre). **'opera-hat**, *s.* (Chapeau *m*) claque *m*; gibus *m*. **'opera-house**, *s.* (Théâtre *m* de l')opéra *m*. **operable** ['op(ə)rəbl], *a. Surg:* Opérable. **operate** ['opəreit]. I. *v.i.* **1.** (*a*) Opérer. (*Of medicine*) Agir; produire son effet. (*b*) *Mch: U.S:* Fonctionner. **2.** *St. Exch:* **To o. for a rise, for a fall**, jouer, spéculer, à la hausse, à la baisse. **3. To o. on s.o., on an appendix**, opérer qn, un appendice. **To o. (on s.o.) for appendicitis**, opérer (qn) de l'appendicite, faire une appendicectomie. **To be operated (up)on**, subir une opération. II. **operate**, *v.tr.* **1.** Opérer, effectuer, accomplir (une guérison, etc.). *Tg:* Manipuler. **2.** (*a*) *Esp. U.S:* Diriger. Faire manœuvrer (une machine); faire jouer (un mécanisme). (*b*) (*Of part of machine*) **To o. another part**, commander, actionner, attaquer, un autre organe. **'operating-lever**, *s.* *U.S:* Levier *m* de manœuvre, de commande. **'operating-table**, *s. Surg:* Table *f* d'opération. **'operating-theatre** *s. Surg:* Salle *f* d'opération.

operatic [ˌɔpəˈrætik]. **1.** *a.* D'opéra. **O. singer,** chanteur dramatique d'opéra. **2.** *s.pl. F:* **Operatics,** opéra *m* d'amateurs.

operation [ˌɔpəˈreiʃ(ə)n], *s.* **1.** Fonctionnement *m,* action *f.* *(Of law)* **To come into o.,** entrer en vigueur. **To be in o.,** fonctionner, jouer. **In full o.,** en pleine activité. **Restrictions at present in o.,** restrictions actuellement en vigueur. **Mode of o.,** mode *m* opératoire. **The machine is in o.,** la machine est en marche. **2.** *Mth: Mil: etc:* Opération. *Mil:* **Combined operation,** opération combinée ((i) opération amphibie, (ii) opération interarmées). *U.S:* **Operations research,** recherche opérationnelle. *St. Exch: pl.* Opérations sur les valeurs. **3.** *Surg:* Opération *f,* intervention chirurgicale.

operational [ˌɔpəˈreiʃ(ə)nl], *a.* Opérationnel, -elle. **O. duties,** service *m* en campagne. **O. training,** entraînement *m* de guerre.

operative [ˈɔp(ə)rətiv]. **1.** *a.* (a) Opératif, -ive, actif, -ive. *(Of law, etc.)* **To become o.,** entrer en vigueur; prendre effet. *Jur:* **O. clause,** clause essentielle. **The o. word,** le mot qui compte, le mot pivot. (b) *Surg:* **O. field,** champ opératoire; champ d'opération. **2.** (a) *a. & s.* Ouvrier, -ière; artisan *m.* (b) *s. U.S:* Détective *m.*

operator [ˈɔpəreitər], *s.* **1.** Opérateur, -trice. *Tg:* Télégraphiste *mf.* **Wireless o.,** radio *m* (à bord d'un navire, etc.). *Tp:* **To call the o.,** appeler le, la standardiste. *St.Exch:* **O. for a fall, for a rise,** opérateur, joueur *m,* à la baisse, à la hausse. **3.** *Surg:* Opérateur. **4.** *U.S: F:* = SWINDLER.

operetta [ˌɔpəˈretə], *s. Mus:* Opérette *f.*

ophidia [ɔˈfidiə], *s.pl. Rept:* Ophidiens *m.*

ophidian [ɔˈfidiən], *a. & s. Rept:* Ophidien (*m*).

ophite [ˈɔfait], *s. Miner:* Ophite *m;* marbre serpentin.

ophthalmia [ɔfˈθælmiə], *s. Med:* Ophtalmie *f.*

ophthalmic [ɔfˈθælmik], *a.* **1.** Ophtalmique. **2.** (Hôpital) ophtalmologique, pour les maladies des yeux.

ophthalmologist [ˌɔfθælˈmɔlədʒist], *s.* Ophtalmologue.

ophthalmology [ɔfθælˈmɔlədʒi], *s.* Opthalmologie *f.*

ophthalmoscope [ɔfˈθælmɔskoup], *s. Med:* Ophtalmoscope *m.*

opiate [ˈoupiit], *s. Pharm:* Opiacé *m,* opiat *m,* narcotique *m.*

opine [ɔˈpain]. *O:* **1.** *v.tr.* (a) Être d'avis (that, que). (b) Émettre l'avis (that, que). **2.** *v.i.* Opiner.

opinion [əˈpinjən], *s.* (a) Opinion *f,* avis *m.* **In my o.,** à, selon, mon avis; à mon sens. **In the o. of experts,** de l'avis, au dire, au jugement, des experts. **To be of (the) o. that . . .,** être d'avis, estimer, que. . . . **To be entirely of s.o.'s o.,** abonder dans le sens de qn. **Matter of o.,** affaire d'opinion. **To give one's o.,** dire son opinion. **To ask s.o.'s o.,** se référer à qn; consulter qn. **To form an o. on sth.,** se faire une opinion sur, de, qch. **What is your o. of him?** que pensez-vous de lui? **To have, hold, a high o. of s.o.,** tenir qn en haute estime. **To have a high o. of oneself,** s'estimer beaucoup. **To have no o. of sth.,** ne pas faire grand cas de qch. **Public o.,** l'opinion (publique). (b) Consultation *f* (de médecin, etc.). *Jur:* Counsel's o., avis motivé. **To take counsel's o.,** consulter un avocat.

opinionated [əˈpinjəneitid], *a.* Opiniâtre; entier (dans ses opinions); imbu de ses opinions.

opium [ˈoupjəm], *s.* Opium *m.* **O. extract,** extrait *m* thébaïque. **'opium-addict,** *s. F:* Opiomane *mf.* **'opium den,** *s.* Fumerie *f* d'opium. **'opium-smoker,** *s.* Fumeur *m* d'opium.

Oporto [ɔˈpɔːtou]. *Pr.n. Geog:* Porto *m.*

opossum [əˈpɔsəm], *s. Z:* Opossum *m;* sarigue *mf* de Virginie.

opponent [əˈpounənt], *s.* Adversaire *m,* antagoniste *mf* (**of,** de).

opportune [ˈɔpətjuːn], *a.* *(Of time)* Opportun, convenable, commode; *(of action)* à propos. **You have come at an o. moment,** vous tombez bien. **This cheque is most o.,** ce chèque tombe à merveille. **-ly,** *adv.* Opportunément, en temps opportun, à propos. **It happens most o.,** cela arrive à point (nommé).

opportuneness [ˈɔpətjuːnnis], *s.* Opportunité *f;* à-propos *m.*

opportunism [ˈɔpətjuːnizm], *s.* Opportunisme *m.*

opportunist [ˈɔpətjuːnist], *s.* Opportuniste *mf.*

opportunity [ˌɔpəˈtjuːniti], *s.* **1.** Occasion *f* (favorable); possibilités *fpl.* **A golden o.,** une occasion magnifique. **At the first, earliest, o.,** à la première occasion. **When the o. occurs, offers,** à l'occasion. **If I get an o. . . .,** si l'occasion se présente. . . . **To take the o. to do sth.,** profiter de l'occasion pour faire qch. **To miss an o.,** laisser passer une occasion. **To make an o. of doing sth.,** se ménager une occasion de faire qch. **2.** = OPPORTUNENESS.

oppose [əˈpouz], *v.tr.* **1.** Opposer (deux choses); mettre (deux couleurs) en opposition. **2.** S'opposer à (qn, qch.); aller au contraire de (qch.); mettre obstacle, opposition, à (qch.); résister à (qn, qch.). **To o. the motion,** soutenir la contre-partie; parler contre. **opposed,** *a.* **1.** Opposé, hostile. **2. What he says is o. to all reason,** ce qu'il dit est le rebours, l'envers, du bon sens. **Country life as o. to town life,** la vie à la campagne, par opposition à, par contraste avec, la vie dans les grandes villes. **3.** *Mec:* Horizontally **o. cylinders,** cylindres opposés. **opposing,** *a.* *(Of armies, characters, etc.)* Opposé; *(of party, etc.)* opposant.

opposer [əˈpouzər], *s.* **1.** Opposant *m,* contradicteur *m.* **2.** = OPPONENT.

opposite [ˈɔpəzit]. **1.** *a.* (a) Opposé (to, à); vis-à-vis (to, de); en face (to, de). **See the diagram on the o. page,** voir la figure ci-contre. **Text with illustration on the o. page,** texte avec illustration en regard. **The house o.,** la maison (d')en face. *Mil: Navy: etc:* **O. number,** correspondant *m* en grade; *F:* homologue *m.* (b) Contraire (to, from, à). **The o. sex,** l'autre sexe. *Magn:* **O. poles,** pôles contraires, de nom contraire. **To take the o. course, the o. view, to . . .,** prendre le contre-pied de. . . . **In the o. direction,** en sens inverse; dans le sens opposé. **Ships going in o. directions,** navires allant à contre-bord. **2.** *s.* Opposé *m;* le contre-pied. **Just the o. of what he says,** tout le contraire de ce qu'il dit. **3.** *adv.* Vis-à-vis; en face. **4.** *prep.* En face de, vis-à-vis (de). **To stand, sit, o. s.o.,** faire vis-à-vis à qn. **Stop o. number 128,** arrêtez-vous à la hauteur du numéro 128. *Th: Cin:* **He, she, played o. X,** il, elle, a joué avec X, avec X pour partenaire. *Th:* **She played o. Irving,** elle a donné la réplique à Irving.

opposition [ˌɔpəˈziʃ(ə)n], *s.* Opposition *f.* (a) **To act in o. to public opinion,** agir contrairement à l'opinion publique. **Parties in o.,** partis qui se combattent. (b) Résistance *f.* (c) (Le) camp adverse. *Pol:* **The party in o., the o.,** (le parti de) l'opposition. **The o. spokesman,** le porte-parole de l'opposition. (d) *Com:* **To start up (shop) in o. to s.o.,** ouvrir un magasin en concurrence avec qn.

oppress [əˈpres], *v.tr.* (a) Opprimer. (b) Oppresser, accabler (l'esprit).

oppression [əˈpreʃ(ə)n], *s.* (a) Oppression *f.* *Jur:* Abus *m* d'autorité. (b) Accablement *m* (de l'esprit, etc.); resserrement *m* (de cœur).

oppressive [əˈpresiv], *a.* **1.** *(Of law, etc.)* Oppressif, -ive, opprimant, tyrannique. **2.** (a)(*Of atmosphere,etc.*) Lourd, étouffant. (b) *(Of mental burden)* Accablant. **-ly,** *adv.* **1.** Tyranniquement. **2.** D'une manière accablante.

oppressiveness [əˈpresivnis], *s.* **1.** Caractère oppressif (d'un gouvernement, etc.). **2.** Lourdeur *f* (du temps).

oppressor [əˈpresər], *s.* (a) Oppresseur *m.* (b) **Oppressors and oppressed,** les opprimants *m* et les opprimés *m.*

opprobrious [əˈproubriəs], *a.* Injurieux, -euse, outrageant. **-ly,** *adv.* Injurieusement.

opprobrium [əˈproubriəm], *s.* Opprobre *m.*

opt [ɔpt], *v.i.* Opter (**for,** pour; **between,** entre). **To o. out of sth.,** décider de ne pas s'affilier à qch.

optative [ˈɔptətiv], *a. & s. Gram:* Optatif (*m*).

optic [ˈɔptik], *a.* **O. nerve,** nerf optique.

optical [ˈɔptik(ə)l], *a.* **1.** Optique. **2.** (Instrument) d'optique. **O. illusion,** illusion d'optique.

optician [ɔpˈtiʃ(ə)n], *s.* Opticien *m.*

optics [ˈɔptiks], *s.pl.* L'optique *f.*

optimism [ˈɔptimizm], *s.* Optimisme *m.*

optimist [ˈɔptimist], *s.* Optimiste *mf.*

optimistic [ˌɔptiˈmistik], *a.* Optimiste. **-ally,** *adv.* Avec optimisme.

optimum ['ɔptiməm]. **1.** *s.* *Biol:* Optimum *m.* **2.** *a.* Optimum, optimal, -aux.

option ['ɔpʃ(ə)n], *s.* **1.** Option *f*, choix *m.* (*a*) To make one's o., faire son choix; opter (**between**, entre). **Lease renewable at the o.** of the tenant, bail renouvelable au gré du locataire. (*b*) To have the o. of doing sth., avoir la faculté, le choix, de faire qch. **To have no o. but to . . .**, ne pouvoir faire autrement que de . . ., ne pas avoir d'autre alternative que de . . . *Jur:* **Imprisonment without the o.** of a fine, emprisonnement sans substitution d'amende. **2.** (*a*) **To take an o. on sth.**, prendre une option sur qch. (*b*) *St.Exch:* Option; (marché *m* à) prime *f.* **O. dealing(s)**, opérations *fpl* à prime.

optional ['ɔpʃənl], *a.* Facultatif, -ive. **It is o.** for you to go or stay, vous avez le choix de partir ou de rester. *Sch:* **O. subjects**, matières *f* à option. **Evening dress is o.**, l'habit *m*, la tenue de soirée, n'est pas de rigueur.

optometrist [ɔp'tɔmətrist], *s.* *Opt:* *U.S:* Réfractionniste *m.*

optometry [ɔp'tɔmətri], *s.* *Opt:* Optométrie *f.*

opulence ['ɔpjuləns], *s.* Opulence *f*, richesse *f.*

opulent ['ɔpjulənt], *a.* Opulent. **-ly,** *adv.* Avec opulence.

opus ['oupəs], *s.* *Mus:* Opus *m.*

opuscule [ə'pʌskjuːl], *s.* Opuscule *m.*

or [ɔːr], *conj.* (*a*) Ou; (*with neg.*) ni. **Will you have beef or ham?** voulez-vous du bœuf ou du jambon? **Either one or the other**, soit l'un soit l'autre; l'un ou l'autre. *S.a.* ELSE 1. **Either you or he has done it**; he or you have done it, c'est vous ou (c'est) lui, c'est l'un de vous deux, qui l'a fait. **I cannot (either) read or write**, je ne sais ni lire ni écrire. **Without money or luggage**, sans argent ni bagages. **In a day or two**, dans un ou deux jours. **A mile or so**, environ un mille. (*b*) **Don't move, or I'll shoot**, ne bougez pas, sinon je tire.

oracle ['ɔrəkl], *s.* Oracle *m.* **To pronounce an o.**, rendre un oracle. *F:* **To work the o.**, (i) faire agir certaines influences; (ii) arriver à ses fins; soutirer de l'argent à qn.

oracular [ɔ'rækjulər], *a.* Équivoque, obscur; (réponse, etc.) en style d'oracle.

oral ['ɔːr(ə)l], *a.* **1.** Oral, -aux. *Sch:* **O. examination**, *s.* *F:* oral, (examen) oral *m.* **2.** (*a*) **O. cavity**, cavité orale, buccale. **O. vaccine**, vaccin buccal. (*b*) **O. administration** (of a drug), administration par la bouche, par voie buccale. **-ally,** *adv.* **1.** Oralement; de vive voix. **2.** *Med:* Par la bouche; par voie buccale.

orange ['ɔrin(d)ʒ], *s.* **1.** Orange *f.* **Bitter o., Seville o.**, orange amère; bigarade *f.* **Blood o.**, orange sanguine *Cu:* **O. marmalade**, confiture *f* d'oranges. *Hort:* **Cox's o.** (pippin), (pomme) reinette *f.* **2.** O.(-tree), oranger *m.* **3.** *a. & s.* (*Colour*) Orangé (*m*); orange (*m*) *inv.* **'orange-blossom**, *s.* Fleurs *fpl* d'oranger. **'orange-flower**, *s.* Fleur *f* d'oranger. **O.-f. water**, eau *f* de fleur(s) d'oranger. **'orange-grove**, *s.* Orangeraie *f.* **'orange-house**, *s.* Orangerie *f.* **'orange-lily**, *s.* *Bot:* Lis orange. **'orange-plantation**, *s.* Orangeraie *f.* **'orange-stick**, *s.* *Toil:* Bâtonnet *m*; bâton *m* d'oranger.

orangeade ['ɔrin(d)ʒeid], *s.* Orangeade *f.*

Orangeman, *pl.* **-men** ['ɔrin(d)ʒmən], *s.m.* Orangiste (du parti protestant de l'Irlande du Nord).

orangery ['ɔrin(d)ʒəri], *s.* Orangerie *f.*

orang-(o)utang ['ɔːræŋ'uːtæŋ], *s.* *Z:* Orang-outan(g) *m*, *pl.* orangs-outan(g)s.

orate [ɔ'reit], *v.i.* *Pej:* Pérorer.

oration [ɔ'reiʃ(ə)n], *s.* Allocution *f*, discours *m*; morceau *m* oratoire; *Pej:* harangue *f*; *Sch:* *F:* laïus *m.* **Funeral o.**, oraison *f* funèbre.

orator ['ɔrətər], *s.* Orateur *m.* *F:* **Soap-box o.**, orateur de carrefour.

Oratorian [ˌɔrə'tɔːriən], *s.* *Ecc:* Oratorien *m*, père *m* de l'Oratoire.

oratorical [ˌɔrə'tɔrik(ə)l], *a.* **1.** (*a*) (Style) oratoire. (*b*) (Discours) verbeux, ampoulé. **2.** (*Of pers.*) (*a*) Grand parleur; disert. (*b*) Phraseur.

oratorio [ˌɔrə'tɔːriou], *s.* *Mus:* Oratorio *m.*

oratory[1] ['ɔrət(ə)ri], *s.* L'art *m* oratone; l'éloquence *f.*

oratory[2], *s.* *Ecc:* **1.** Oratoire *m*; chapelle privée. **2.** L'Oratoire, les pères de l'Oratoire.

orb [ɔːb], *s.* Orbe *m.* (*a*) Globe *m*, sphère *f.* **The orb of the sun**, le globe du soleil. (*b*) *Poet:* Corps *m* céleste; astre *m.* (*c*) (*Of regalia*) Globe.

orbit[1] ['ɔːbit], *s.* **1.** Orbite *f* (d'une planète). **To put a satellite, a man, into o.**, mettre un satellite, un homme, en orbite. **2.** *Anat:* Orbite. (de l'œil); fosse *f* orbitaire. **3.** *Pol:* Orbite **Hungary is drawn into the Russian o.**, la Hongrie est attirée dans l'orbite de la Russie. **The Russian o.**, la sphère *f* d'influence soviétique.

orbit[2], *v.tr.* Décrire une orbite (autour d'une planète).

orc [ɔːk], *s.* *Z:* Épaulard *m*; orque *m.*

orchard ['ɔːtʃəd], *s.* Verger *m.*

orchestra ['ɔːkistrə], *s.* **1.** Orchestre *m.* **O. stalls**, fauteuils *m* d'orchestre. **2. String o.**, orchestre d'archets, à cordes.

orchestral [ɔː'kestr(ə)l], *a.* Orchestral, -aux.

orchestrate ['ɔːkestreit], *v.tr.* *Mus:* Orchestrer, instrumenter.

orchestration [ˌɔːkes'treiʃ(ə)n], *s.* Orchestration *f*, instrumentation *f.*

orchid ['ɔːkid], *s.* Orchidée *f.* **Wild o.**, orchis *m.*

orchis ['ɔːkis], *s.* *Bot:* Orchis *m.*

ordain [ɔː'dein], *v.tr.* Ordonner. **1.** *Ecc:* Conférer les ordres à (un prêtre). **To o. s.o. deacon**, ordonner qn diacre. **To be ordained**, recevoir les ordres. **2.** (*Of the Deity, of fate*) (*a*) Destiner. **Ordained of God to be judge**, destiné de Dieu pour être juge. (*b*) Ordonner, fixer. (*c*) (*Of pers.*) Prescrire, décréter (une mesure). **To o. that . . .**, statuer que + *ind.*

ordeal [ɔː'diːl], *s.* **1.** *Hist:* Épreuve *f* judiciaire; *A:* ordalie *f*; jugement *m* de Dieu. **O. by fire**, épreuve du feu. **2. To go through a terrible o.**, passer par une rude épreuve.

order[1] ['ɔːdər], *s.* Ordre *m.* **1.** (*a*) **Talents of the first o.**, of a high o., talents du premier ordre, d'un ordre élevé. (*b*) *pl.* *Ecc:* **Holy orders**, ordres sacrés, ordres majeurs. **Minor orders**, ordres mineurs. **To take (holy) orders**, prendre les ordres; recevoir les ordres, entrer dans les ordres. **To be in holy orders**, être prêtre. (*c*) *Monastic o.*, ordre religieux; communauté *f.* **O. of knighthood**, ordre de chevalerie. **The O. of the Garter**, l'ordre de la Jarretière. *S.a.* BOOT[1] 1. (*d*) **To be wearing all one's orders**, porter tous ses ordres, toutes ses décorations. (*e*) *Arch:* **Ionic o., Doric o.**, ordre ionique, ordre dorique. (*f*) *Nat.Hist:* Ordre. **2.** Succession *f*, suite *f.* **In alphabetical o.**, par ordre alphabétique. **In chronological o.**, par ordre de dates. **In o. of age**, par rang d'âge. **Out of (its) o.**, hors de son rang. *I.C.E:* **O. of firing**, rythme *m* d'allumage. **3.** *Mil:* (*a*) **Close o.**, ordre serré. **O. of battle**, *Mil:* ordre de bataille; *Navy:* ordre tactique. (*b*) **In marching o.**, en tenue de route. **In review o., in gala o.**, en grande tenue. **4. The old o.** (of things), l'ancien régime. **The present o.** of things, le régime actuel. **5.** (*a*) **To put a matter in o.**, mettre une question en règle; mettre ordre à une affaire. **The matter is now in o.**, l'affaire est dès maintenant en règle. **To set one's house in o.**, (i) remettre de l'ordre dans son ménage; (ii) remettre de l'ordre dans ses affaires. **Is your passport in o.?** votre passeport est-il en règle? **Cargo received in good o.**, chargement reçu en bon état. **Machine in good (working) o.**, machine en bon état (de fonctionnement). *S.a.* WORKING[2] 3. **Out of o.**, en mauvais état; en panne; (*of room, business affairs*) en désordre; (*of machinery*) détraqué; *Tp:* *El:* en dérangement. **To get out of o.**, se dérégler, se détraquer. (*b*) *Parl:* etc: **In o.**, dans les règles. **It is not in o.**, ce n'est pas réglementaire. **To rule a question out of o.**, statuer qu'une interpellation n'est pas dans les règles, n'est pas pertinente. **To rise to (a point of) o.**, se lever pour demander le rappel à l'ordre. **To call s.o. to o.**, rappeler qn à l'ordre. **O.! o.!** à l'ordre! **O. of the day**, ordre du jour. **6. Law and o.**, l'ordre public. **To keep o. in a town, in a classroom**, maintenir, assurer, l'ordre dans une ville; maintenir la discipline dans une classe. **To keep the children in o.**, (i) soumettre les enfants à la discipline; (ii) avoir les enfants bien en main. **7.** *Ecc:* **O. of service**, office *m.* **8.** *Mil:* **Arms at the o.**, l'arme au pied. **9. In o.** to do sth., afin de, pour, faire qch. **In o. that . . .,** afin que, pour que, + *sub.* **10.** (*a*) Commandement *m*, instruction *f*. *Mil: Navy:* Consigne *f*. **To give orders for** sth. **to be done,** that sth. **should be done,** ordonner qu'on fasse qch., que qch. se fasse. **He gave me orders to do it,** il m'a donné (l')ordre de le faire. **Orders are orders,** je ne connais que la consigne. **Standing orders,** ordres permanents; règlement(s) *m*. **Until further orders,** jusqu'à nouvel ordre; sauf avis *m* contraire. **By o. of . . .,** par ordre de. . . . **By o. of the king,** de par le roi. (*b*) *Com:* **Pay to the o. of . . .,** payez à l'ordre de. . . . **Pay X or o.,** payez à X ou à son ordre. **Bill to o.,** billet à ordre. **Cheque to o., o. cheque,** chèque à ordre. (*c*) *Com:* Commande *f*. (*Of tradesman*) **To call for orders,** passer prendre les commandes. **To place an o. with** s.o., **to give an o. to** s.o., (i) faire, confier, passer une commande à qn; (ii) commander qch. à qn. **To put goods on o.,** commander des marchandises; mettre des marchandises en commande. **By o. and for account of . . .,** d'ordre et pour compte de. . . . **Made to o.,** fabriqué sur commande, à la demande. **Suit made to o.,** complet fait sur mesure. *F:* **That's** (rather) **a tall, large, o.!** ça c'est une grosse affaire! c'est demander un peu trop! **11.** (*a*) **Written o.,** ordre par écrit. **O. to view** (**a house**), permis *m* de visiter (une maison). *Adm:* **General o.,** arrêt *m*. **Departmental o.,** arrêté ministériel. **O. to pay, o. for payment,** ordonnance *f* de paiement. **O. in Council** = décret présidentiel, arrêté ministériel; décret-loi *m*, *pl.* décrets-lois. *Jur:* **Judge's o.,** ordonnance. **Deportation o.,** arrêté d'expulsion. **O. of the court,** injonction *f* de la cour. *Mil:* **Regimental orders,** décisions *f*. **Mention in orders,** citation *f* (à l'ordre du jour). *Navy:* **Sailing orders,** instructions *f* pour la marche. **To be under sailing orders,** avoir reçu l'ordre d'appareiller. **Sealed orders,** ordres cachetés; pli secret. *S.a.* MARCHING. (*b*) **O. on a bank,** mandat *m* sur une banque. **Money o., postal order,** = mandat-poste, *pl.* mandats-poste; mandat-carte, *pl.* mandats-cartes; mandat-lettre, *pl.* mandats-lettres. **Foreign, international, money o.,** mandat-poste international, sur l'étranger. **'order-book,** *s.* Carnet *m* de commandes.

order², *v.tr.* **1.** (*a*) Arranger, ranger, ordonner (des papiers, des meubles); régler (sa vie). (*b*) *Mil:* **O. arms!** reposez armes! **2.** = ORDAIN 2. **3.** (*a*) **To o.** s.o. **to do** sth., ordonner, commander, à qn de faire qch. **They ordered him to be hanged,** ils ordonnèrent qu'on le pendît. *Jur:* **To be ordered to pay costs,** être condamné aux dépens. **To o. an officer to Plymouth,** désigner un officier pour Plymouth. (*b*) *Med:* Prescrire, ordonner (un traitement, un remède, à qn). *F:* **The very thing, just what the doctor ordered,** tout à fait ce qu'il faut pour l'occasion. (*c*) *Com:* Commander, commissionner (qch.); mettre (qch.) en commande. **To o. a suit of clothes,** commander un complet; se faire faire un complet. **To o. a taxi,** faire venir un taxi. **order about,** *v.tr.* Envoyer (qn) de côté et d'autre, à droite et à gauche; *F:* faire marcher, faire aller (qn). **order off,** *v.tr.* Ordonner à (qn) de s'éloigner, de s'en aller. *Fb:* **To order a player off (the field),** ordonner à un joueur de quitter la partie (pour brutalité). **ordering,** *s.* Mise *f* en ordre; agencement *m* (d'un appartement, etc.); disposition *f* (de troupes, de sa maison, etc.); règlement *m*.

orderliness ['ɔːdəlinis], *s.* **1.** Bon ordre; méthode *f*. **2.** Habitudes *fpl* d'ordre. **3.** Discipline *f*; calme *m*.

orderly ['ɔːdəli]. **1.** *a.* (*a*) Ordonné, méthodique; (*of life*) réglé, rangé, régulier. (*Of pers.*) **To be very o.,** avoir beaucoup de méthode, beaucoup de soin. (*b*) (*Of crowd, etc.*) Tranquille, discipliné. (*c*) *Mil:* **O. officer,** officier *m* de service; officier de semaine. **2.** *s. Mil:* Planton *m*. **Mounted o.,** estafette *f*. **Hospital o.** *Mil:* infirmier *m*, ambulancier *m*; *Med:* aide-infirmier, -ière.

ordinal ['ɔːdinl], *a. & s.* Ordinal, -aux.

ordinance ['ɔːdinəns], *s.* **1.** Ordonnance *f*, décret *m*, règlement *m*. **Police o.,** ordonnance, arrêté *m*, de police. **2.** *Ecc:* Rite *m*, cérémonie *f* (du culte).

ordinand ['ɔːdinænd], *s. Ecc:* Ordinand *m*.

ordinary ['ɔːdin(ə)ri]. **I.** *a.* **1.** (*a*) Ordinaire; (*of routine, etc.*) coutumier, -ière; normal, -aux; courant. *Dipl:* **O. ambassador,** ambassadeur ordinaire. *Fin:* **O. share,** action ordinaire. *S.a.* SEAMAN 1. (*b*) **O. Englishman,** Anglais moyen, typique. **The o. reader,** le commun des lecteurs. **2.** *Pej:* **A very o. kind of man,** un homme tout à fait quelconque. **A small and very o. room,** une petite chambre banale. **-ily,** *adv.* Ordinairement, normalement; d'ordinaire, d'habitude; à l'ordinaire. **II. ordinary,** *s.* **1.** Ordinaire *m*. **Out of the o.,** exceptionnel, -elle; peu ordinaire. **Physician-in-o.** **to the king,** médecin ordinaire du roi. **2.** *A:* (*In restaurant*) Table *f* d'hôte; ordinaire *m*. **3.** *Her:* Pièce *f* honorable. **4.** (*Pers.*) (*a*) (*Scot.*) Juge *m*. (*b*) *Ecc:* Ordinaire (archevêque ou évêque). **5.** *Ecc:* **The O.** (**of the mass**), l'ordinaire (de la messe).

ordinate ['ɔːdineit], *s. Mth:* Ordonnée *f*.

ordination [ˌɔːdi'neiʃ(ə)n], *s.* **1.** Arrangement *m*; classification *f* (des plantes, etc.). **2.** Ordonnance *f* (de Dieu). **3.** *Ecc:* Ordination *f*.

ordnance ['ɔːdnəns], *s.* **1.** Artillerie *f*. **Piece of o.,** bouche *f* à feu; pièce *f* d'artillerie. **2.** *Mil:* (*a*) Service *m* du matériel, des dépôts. **O. and supplies,** ravitaillement *m*. (*b*) **O. Survey,** (i) service topographique, cartographique; (ii) corps *m* des ingénieurs-géographes.

ordure ['ɔːdjuər], *s.* Ordure *f*. (*a*) Excrément *m*. (*b*) Immondice *f*, saleté *f*.

ore ['ɔːr], *s.* Minerai *m*. **Iron o.,** minerai de fer.

organ ['ɔːɡən], *s.* **1.** *Mus:* (*a*) Orgue *m*, orgues *fpl*. **Grand o.** (*in organ-loft*), grand orgue; grandes orgues. **To be, preside, at the o.,** tenir l'orgue, les orgues. (*b*) **American o.,** harmonium *m*. (*c*) **Street o., orgue de Barbarie.** (*d*) **Theatre o.,** orgue *m* de cinéma. **2.** (*a*) Organe *m* (de la vue, etc.). **O. of hearing,** organe de l'ouïe. **The vocal organs,** l'appareil vocal. **Reproductive organs,** les organes reproducteurs. (*b*) Journal *m*, bulletin *m*, organe, porte-parole *m* *inv* (d'un parti politique, etc.). **'organ-blower,** *s.* **1.** Souffleur *m* (d'orgue). **2.** La soufflerie. **'organ-builder,** *s.* Facteur *m* d'orgues. **'organ-case,** **-chest,** *s.* Buffet *m* d'orgue. **'organ-grinder,** *s.* Joueur *m* d'orgue de Barbarie. **'organ-loft,** *s.* Tribune *f* (de l'orgue). **'organ-pipe,** *s.* Tuyau *m* d'orgue. **'organ-screen,** *s.* Jubé *m* (formant tribune d'orgue). **'organ-stop,** *s.* Jeu *m* d'orgue.

organdie ['ɔːɡəndi], *s. Tex:* Organdi *m*.

organic [ɔːˈɡænik], *a.* **1.** (Maladie, fonction) organique. **2.** (*a*) **O. beings,** êtres organisés. **The law of o. growth,** la loi de croissance organisée. (*b*) **O. chemistry,** chimie organique. **-ally,** *adv.* **1.** Organiquement. **2.** Foncièrement.

organism ['ɔːɡənizm], *s.* Organisme *m*.

organist ['ɔːɡənist], *s.* Organiste *m*.

organization [ˌɔːɡənaiˈzeiʃ(ə)n], *s.* **1.** Organisation *f*. **2.** Organisme *m* (politique, etc.). **Charity o.,** œuvre *f* de charité. **Youth o.,** mouvement *m* de jeunesse.

organize ['ɔːɡənaiz], *v.tr.* **1.** Organiser. **2.** Arranger (un concert); aménager (ses loisirs). **organized,** *a.* Organisé. **O. labour,** les syndicats (ouvriers).

orgasm ['ɔːɡæzm], *s.* Orgasme *m*.

organizer ['ɔːɡənaizər], *s.* Organisateur, -trice.

orgiastic [ɔːdʒiˈæstik], *a.* Orgiaque.

orgy ['ɔːdʒi], *s.* Orgie *f*; *F:* bacchanale *f*. **O. of colour,** orgie, profusion *f*, de couleurs.

oriel ['ɔːriəl], *s.* (i) Fenêtre *f* en saillie; (ii) fenêtre en encorbellement.

orient ['ɔːriənt], *s.* (*a*) Orient *m*. *Geog:* **The O.,** l'Orient. (*b*) **Pearl of a fine o.,** perle d'un bel orient.

oriental [ˌɔːriˈentl]. **1.** *a.* Oriental, -aux; d'Orient. **2.** *s.* Indigène *mf* de l'Orient; Oriental, -ale.

orientate ['ɔːrienteit], *v.tr.* Orienter.

orientation [ˌɔːrienˈteiʃ(ə)n], *s.* Orientation *f*.

orientator ['ɔːrienteitər], *s. Av: Surv:* (*Instrument*) Orientateur *m*.

orifice ['ɔrifis], *s.* Orifice *m*, ouverture *f*, trou *m*.

origanum [ɔˈriɡənəm], *s. Bot:* Origan *m*.

origin ['ɔridʒin], *s.* Origine *f*. **1.** **The o. of the universe,** la genèse des mondes. **2.** **Word of Greek o.,** mot d'origine grecque. (*Of pers.*) **To be of noble, humble, o.,** être d'origine illustre, d'humble extraction *f*. *Com:* **Country of o.,** pays de provenance. *Cust:* **Certificate of o.,** certificat d'origine.

original [ə'ridʒənl]. **1.** *a.* (*a*) Originaire, primordial, -aux, primitif, -ive. **O. meaning of a word**, sens premier d'un mot. **O. idea of a work**, idée mère d'une œuvre. **O. member of a club**, membre originaire d'un club. *Theol:* **O. sin**, péché originel. (*b*) **O. edition**, édition princeps. **The o. picture is at . . .**, le tableau original est au musée de. . . . (*c*) (Style, ouvrage) original; (spectacle, etc.) inédit. **The scheme is not an o. one**, ce projet n'est pas inédit. **2.** *s.* Original *m* (d'un tableau, d'une facture). **To read the classics in the o.**, lire les classiques dans l'original. **3.** *s.* Personne originale; original, -ale; *F:* un type à part; un type. **-ally**, *adv.* **1.** (*a*) Originairement; à l'origine, dans l'origine. (*b*) Originellement; dès l'origine. **2.** Originalement.

originality [əridʒi'næliti], *s.* Originalité *f.*

originate [ə'ridʒineit]. **1.** *v.tr.* Faire naître, donner naissance à, être l'auteur de (qch.). **2.** *v.i.* Tirer son origine, dériver, provenir (**from, in,** de); avoir son origine (dans). **The fire originated under the floor**, le feu a pris naissance sous le plancher.

origination [əridʒi'neiʃ(ə)n], *s.* (*a*) Source *f*, origine *f.* (*b*) Création *f* (d'un projet). (*c*) Naissance *f* (d'une rumeur).

originator [ə'ridʒineitər], *s.* Créateur, -trice; auteur *m*; initiateur, -trice; promoteur *m* (d'une industrie).

Orinoco (the) [ðiːəri'noukou]. *Pr. n. Geog:* L'Orénoque *m.*

oriole ['ɔːrioul], *s. Orn:* Loriot *m.*

orison ['ɔrizən], *s. A:* Oraison *f*, prière *f.*

Orkneys (the) [ðiː'ɔːkniz]. *Pr.n.pl. Geog:* Les Orcades *f.*

Orleans [əː'liːənz]. *Pr.n. Geog:* Orléans. **New O.**, la Nouvelle-Orléans.

orlop ['ɔːlɔp], *s. Nau:* Faux-pont *m.*

ormolu ['ɔːmɔluː], *s.* **1.** Or moulu. **O. clock**, pendule en or moulu. **2.** Chrysocale *m.*

ornament¹ ['ɔːnəmənt], *s.* Ornement *m.* **The altar ornaments**, le parement d'autel.

ornament² [ɔːnə'ment], *v.tr.* Orner, ornementer, décorer; agrémenter (une robe).

ornamental [ɔːnə'mentl], *a.* Ornemental, -aux; d'ornement, d'agrément. **-ally**, *adv.* **1.** Pour servir d'ornement. **2.** Décorativement.

ornamentation [ɔːnəmen'teiʃ(ə)n], *s.* **1.** Ornementation *f*, embellissement *m*, décoration *f.* **2.** Les ornements *m.*

ornate [ɔː'neit], *a.* Orné; surchargé d'ornements. **O. style**, style imagé, fleuri. **-ly**, *adv.* Avec une surabondance d'ornements; en style trop fleuri.

ornithological [ɔːniθə'lɔdʒik(ə)l], *a.* Ornithologique.

ornithologist [ɔːni'θɔlədʒist], *s.* Ornithologue *m*, ornithologiste *m.*

ornithology [ɔːni'θɔlədʒi], *s.* Ornithologie *f.*

ornithorhynchus [ɔːniθə'riŋkəs], *s. Z:* Ornithorynque *m.*

orography [ɔ'rɔgrəfi], *s.* Orographie *f.*

orographic(al) [ɔrə'græfik(l)], *a.* Orographique.

orphan¹ ['ɔːf(ə)n]. **1.** *s.* Orphelin, -ine. **To be left an o.**, rester, devenir, orphelin. **2.** *a.* **An o. child**, un(e) orphelin(e).

orphan², *v.tr.* Rendre orphelin, -ine. **He was orphaned by an earthquake**, il a perdu ses parents dans un tremblement de terre.

orphanage ['ɔːfənidʒ], *s.* **1.** État *m* d'orphelin. **2.** Orphelinat *m.*

Orpheus ['ɔːfjuːs]. *Pr.n.m.* Orphée.

orpiment ['ɔːpimənt], *s. Miner:* Orpiment *m*, orpin *m*; sulfure *m* jaune d'arsenic.

orrery ['ɔrəri], *s. Astr:* Planétaire *m.*

orris ['ɔris], *s. Bot:* Iris *m. Pharm:* **O. root**, racine *f* d'iris. **O. powder**, poudre *f* d'iris.

orthocentre [ɔːθo'sentər], *s. Geom:* Orthocentre *m.*

orthochromatic ['ɔːθokro'mætik], *a.* Orthochromatique.

orthodox ['ɔːθədɔks], *a.* Orthodoxe. **O. Church**, l'Église *f* orthodoxe.

orthodoxy ['ɔːθədɔksi], *s.* Orthodoxie *f*; conformisme *m.*

orthogonal [ɔː'θɔgənl], *a. Geom:* Orthogonal, -aux; orthographique. **-ally**, *adv.* Orthogonalement; à angle droit.

orthographic(al) [ɔːθo'græfik(əl)], *a.* **1.** *Gram:* Orthographique. **2.** *Geom:* = ORTHOGONAL. **3.** *Geog:* **Orthographic projection**, projection orthographique, orthogonale.

orthography [ɔː'θɔgrəfi], *s.* **1.** *Gram:* Orthographe *f.* **2.** *Geom:* Coupe *f* perpendiculaire; projection orthogonale.

orthopaedic [ɔːθo'piːdik], *a.* Orthopédique.

orthopaedics [ɔːθo'piːdiks], *s.* Orthopédie *f.*

orthopaedist [ɔːθo'piːdist], *s.* Orthopédiste *m.*

orthopaedy ['ɔːθopiːdi], *s.* Orthopédie *f.*

ortolan ['ɔːtəlæn], *s. Orn:* Ortolan *m.*

Oscar ['ɔskər]. *Pr.n.m.* (*a*) Oscar. (*b*) *Cin: etc:* Oscar *m.*

oscillate ['ɔsileit]. **1.** *v.i.* Osciller. (*Of indicator needle*) **To o. violently**, s'affoler. **2.** *v.tr.* Balancer; faire osciller. **oscillating**, *a.* (*a*) Oscillant. (*b*) *El:* **O. current**, courant oscillatoire. (*c*) *W.Tel:* **O. coil**, bobine oscillatrice, bobinage oscillateur.

oscillation [ɔsi'leiʃ(ə)n], *s. Ph: etc:* Oscillation *f* (d'un pendule, etc.). *W.Tel: etc:* **Damped oscillations, sustained oscillations**, oscillations amorties, entretenues.

oscillator ['ɔsileitər], *s. W.Tel:* (*a*) Oscillateur *m*; bobine oscillatrice. (*b*) Lampe oscillatrice. *Cin:* **Mirror o. (for registering sound track)**, miroir oscillant (pour enregistrement de la piste sonore).

oscillatory ['ɔsileitəri], *a.* Oscillatoire. *El:* **O. discharge**, décharge oscillante. *W.Tel:* **O. circuit**, circuit *m* vibratoire.

oscillograph [ɔ'siləgraːf], *s. Ph: El:* Oscillographe *m.*

oscilloscope [ɔ'siləskoup], *s.* Oscilloscope *m. T.V:* **Cathode-ray o.**, oscillographe *m* cathodique.

osculate ['ɔskjuleit], *v.i.* **1.** *Geom:* (*Of curve*) **To o. with a line**, avoir un contact d'ordre supérieur avec une ligne. **2.** *Nat. Hist:* Avoir des traits en commun (avec).

osculation [ɔskju'leiʃ(ə)n], *s. Geom:* Osculation *f.*

osculatory ['ɔskjulətri], *a. Geom:* Osculateur, -trice.

osier ['ouziər], *s.* Osier *m.* **Common o.**, velvet o., osier blanc, vert; saule *m* des vanniers. **'osier-bed**, *s.* Oseraie *f.*

osmium ['ozmiəm], *s. Ch:* Osmium *m.*

osmosis [ɔz'mousis], *s. Ph:* Osmose *f.*

osmotic [ɔz'mɔtik], *a. Ph:* (Pression) osmotique.

osprey ['ɔspri], *s.* **1.** *Orn:* Orfraie *f*, pygargue *m.* **2.** *Cost:* Aigrette *f.*

osseous ['ɔsiəs], *a.* Osseux, -euse.

ossicle ['ɔsikl], *s. Anat:* Osselet *m*; ossicule *m.*

ossification [ɔsifi'keiʃ(ə)n], *s.* Ossification *f.*

ossify ['ɔsifai]. **1.** *v.i.* S'ossifier. **2.** *v.tr.* Ossifier (un cartilage).

ossuary ['ɔsjuəri], *s.* Ossuaire *m.*

Ostend [ɔs'tend]. *Pr.n. Geog:* Ostende.

ostensible [ɔs'tensəbl], *a.* Prétendu; qui sert de prétexte; soi-disant; feint. **He went out with the o. object of . . .**, il est sorti sous prétexte de. . . . **-ibly**, *adv.* En apparence; censément.

ostensory [ɔs'tensəri], *s. Ecc:* Ostensoir *m.*

ostentation [ɔsten'teiʃ(ə)n], *s.* Ostentation *f*, faste *m*, apparat *m*, parade *f*; braverie *f.*

ostentatious [ɔsten'teiʃəs], *a.* Fastueux, -euse; ostentatoire; plein d'ostentation, qui fait de l'ostentation; (luxe) affichant. **-ly**, *adv.* Avec ostentation; avec faste.

osteology [ɔsti'ɔlədʒi], *s.* Ostéologie *f.*

osteopath ['ɔstiəpəθ], *s.* Chiropracteur *m.*

osteopathy [ɔsti'ɔpəθi], *s. Med:* Chiropractie *f*, chiropraxie *f.*

ostler ['ɔslər], *s.m. A:* Valet d'écurie; garçon d'écurie; palefrenier.

ostracism ['ɔstrəsizm], *s.* Ostracisme *m.*

ostracize ['ɔstrəsaiz], *v.tr.* **1.** *Gr.Ant:* Ostraciser, exiler, bannir. **2.** Ostraciser; mettre (qn) au ban de la société.

ostreiculture ['ɔstriiˌkʌltər], *s.* Ostréiculture *f.*

ostrich ['ɔstritʃ], *s.* Autruche *f.* **Young o.**, autruchon *m.* **O. farm**, autrucherie *f.* **'ostrich-feather**, *s.* Plume *f* d'autruche. **'ostrich-plume**, *s.* Plume *f* ou plumes d'autruche.

otalgia [o'tældʒiə], *s. Med:* Otalgie *f.*

other ['ʌðər]. **1.** *a.* Autre. *(a)* **The o. one**, l'autre. **I saw him the o. day**, je l'ai vu l'autre jour. *S.a.* EVERY. **The o. world**, l'autre monde; **l'au-delà** *m.* *S.a.* HAND¹ 2. *F:* **If he doesn't like it he can do the o. thing**, si cela ne lui plaît pas, tant pis pour lui. *(b)* **The o. four**, les quatre autres. **Potatoes and (all) o. vegetables**, les pommes de terre et autres légumes. **O. things being equal**, toutes choses égales (d'ailleurs). *(c)* **Potatoes and (some) o. vegetables**, les pommes de terre et d'autres légumes. **O. people have seen it**, d'autres l'ont vu. **O. people's property**, le bien d'autrui. **No one o. than he knows it**, nul autre que lui, personne d'autre, ne le sait; lui seul à le savoir. *S.a.* SOME I. 1. *(d) (Different)* **I do not wish him o. than he is**, je ne le souhaite pas autre qu'il n'est. **2.** *pron.* Autre. *(a)* **One after the o.**, l'un après l'autre. *S.a.* EACH 2, ONE V. 1. *(b) pl.* **The others**, les autres, le reste. *(c)* **Some . . . others . . .**, les uns . . . les autres. . . . **Have you any others?** (i) en avez-vous encore? (ii) en avez-vous d'autres? **There are three others**, (i) il y en a encore trois; (ii) il y en a trois autres. **I have no o.**, je n'en ai pas d'autre. **For this reason if for no o.** . . . pour cette raison à défaut d'une autre . . . **One or o. of us will see to it**, l'un de nous s'en occupera. **This day of all others**, ce jour entre tous. *S.a.* SOMETHING I. 1. *(d) pl. (Of pers.)* **Others**, d'autres; *(in oblique cases autrui)* autrui *m.* **The happiness of others**, le bonheur d'autrui. *(e)* **I could not do o. than . . .**, I could do no o. than . . ., (i) je n'ai pu faire autrement que . . . ; (ii) je n'ai pu m'empêcher de. . . . **3.** *adv.* Autrement. **To see things o. than they are**, voir les choses autrement qu'elles ne sont.

otherwise ['ʌðəwaiz], *adv.* **1.** Autrement (**than**, que). **He could not do o. than obey**, il n'a pu faire autrement que d'obéir. **Should it be o.**, dans le cas contraire. **If he is not o. engaged**, s'il n'est pas occupé à autre chose. **Except where o. stated . . .**, sauf indication contraire. . . . **Poquelin, o. Molière**, Poquelin, (autrement) dit Molière. **2.** Autrement; sans quoi, sans cela; dans le cas contraire. **Work, o. you shall not eat**, travaille, sans quoi tu ne mangeras pas. **3.** Sous d'autres rapports; par ailleurs. **O. he is quite sane**, à d'autres égards, *F:* à part ça, il est complètement sain d'esprit.

otherworldly ['ʌðə'wə:ldli], *a.* Détaché de monde.

otic ['outik], *a. Anat:* **O. bone**, os pétreux; rocher *m.* **The o. bones**, les osselets *m* de l'oreille.

otiose ['outious, 'ouʃious], *a.* Inutile, superflu, oiseux, -euse. **O. epithet**, épithète oiseuse.

otology [ou'tolədʒi], *s. Med:* Otologie *f.*

otter ['otər], *s. Z:* Loutre *f.* **'otter-skin**, *s.* Loutre *f.*

Otto ['otou]. *Pr.n.m.* Othon.

Ottoman¹ ['otəmən], *a.&s.* Ottoman,-ane; turc, *f.* turque.

ottoman², *s. Furn:* Divan *m*, ottomane *f.* **2.** *Tex:* Ottoman *m.*

ought¹ [ɔːt], *v.aux. (With present and past meaning: inv. except for A:* **oughtest** *or* **oughtst**) *(Parts of)* devoir, falloir. **1.** *(Obligation)* **One o. never to be unkind**, il ne faut, on ne doit, jamais être malveillant. **To behave as one o.**, se conduire comme il convient. **I thought I o. to let you know about it**, j'ai cru devoir vous en faire part. **2.** *(Vague desirability or advantage)* **You o. to go and see the Exhibition**, vous devriez aller voir l'Exposition. **You o. not to have waited**, vous n'auriez pas dû attendre. **You o. to have said so**, il fallait le dire. **You o. to know**, vous êtes bien placé pour le savoir. **You ought to have seen it!** il fallait voir ça! **3.** *(Probability)* **Your horse o. to win**, votre cheval a de grandes chances de gagner. **That o. to do**, je crois que cela suffira.

ought², *s. =* AUGHT.

ought³, *s. F: =* NAUGHT.

ounce¹ [auns], *s. Meas:* Once *f.* **1. Avoirdupois o. =** 28,35 g; **Troy o. =** 31,1035 g. **He hasn't an o. of courage**, il n'a pas pour deux sous de courage. **2. Fluid o.**, once liquide (**=** 28,4 cm³).

ounce², *s. Z:* Once *f*; léopard *m* des neiges.

our ['auər], *poss.a.* Notre, *pl.* nos. **O. house and garden**, notre maison et notre jardin. **O. friends**, nos ami(e)s. **It's one of o. books**, (i) c'est un livre à nous; (ii) c'est un livre que nous avons écrit; (iii) c'est un livre publié par notre maison. *Com:* **Our Mr Jones**, M. Jones de notre maison.

ours ['auəz], *poss.pron.* Le nôtre, la nôtre, les nôtres. **Your house is larger than o.**, votre maison est plus grande que la nôtre. **This is o.**, ceci est à nous; ceci nous appartient. **This book is one of o.**, (i) ce livre nous appartient, est à nous; (ii) c'est nous qui avons écrit ce livre; (iii) ce livre est de notre maison. **A friend of o.**, un(e) de nos ami(e)s; un(e) ami(e) à nous.

ourself [,auə'self], *pers.pron. (Of monarch, editor)* Nous-même. *(Cf.* WE 2.)

ourselves [,auə'selvz], *pers.pron.pl.* See SELF 4.

oust [aust], *v.tr.* **1.** *(a) Jur:* Déposséder, évincer (qn) (**of, de**). *(b)* **To o. s.o. from his post**, déloger qn de son poste. **2.** Prendre la place de (qn); évincer, supplanter (qn).

out [aut]. **I.** *adv.* **1.** Dehors. *(a) (With motion)* **To go o., walk o.**, sortir. **To run o.**, sortir en courant. **O. you go!** hors d'ici! **Put him o.!** **o. with him!** mettez-le dehors! emmenez-le! **My daughter goes o. a great deal**, ma fille sort beaucoup. *Nau:* **The voyage o.**, l'aller *m.* **To insure a ship o. and home**, assurer un navire pour l'aller et le retour. *S.a.* CALL OUT, DRIVE OUT, GO OUT, SHOW OUT, etc. *(b) (Without motion)* **My father is o.**, mon père est sorti. **My daughter is o. a great deal**, ma fille sort beaucoup. **He is o. and about again**, il est de nouveau sur pied. **Day o.**, jour de sortie (d'une domestique). *F:* **To have a night o.**, passer la nuit à faire la bombe. **The workmen are o.**, les ouvriers sont en grève. **The troops are o.**, les troupes sont sur pied. **He does not live far o. (of the town)**, il ne demeure pas loin de la ville. **O. at sea**, en mer, au large. **Four days o. from Liverpool**, à quatre jours de Liverpool. **O. there**, là-bas. **The tide is o.**, la marée est basse. *Fish: Nau:* **Our lines were o.**, nos lignes étaient dehors. **2.** *(a)* **To turn one's toes o.**, tourner les pieds en dehors. *S.a.* INSIDE 1. *(b)* **To lean o. (of the window, etc.)**, se pencher au dehors. *S.a.* HANG OUT, HIT OUT, STICK OUT, etc. **3.** *(a)* **O. in the open air**, au clair; découvert, exposé; *(of bird)* éclos; *(of sword)* tiré, au clair. **The sun is o.**, il fait du soleil. **The book is o., is already o., is just o.**, le livre est paru, a déjà paru, vient de paraître. **The secret is o.**, le secret est connu, éventé. *(b) (With motion)* **To whip o. a revolver**, tirer, sortir, vivement un revolver. *F:* **O. with it!** achevez donc! allons, dites-le! expliquez-vous! *S.a.* GIVE OUT 1, MURDER¹, TRUTH. *(c) (Of sail, etc.)* Déployé; *(of flower, etc.)* épanoui. **The may is o.**, l'aubépine est en fleur. *(d) F:* **To be o. after s.o.**, être à la recherche de qn. **I am not o. to reform the world**, je n'ai pas entrepris, je n'ai pas à tâche, de réformer le monde. **To go all o. for sth.**, mettre toute son énergie à, se donner corps et âme pour, faire aboutir qch.; mettre tout en œuvre pour obtenir qch. **An all-o. attack**, une attaque à fond, avec tous ses moyens. *(e) Sp: Aut: etc:* **All o.**, à toute vitesse, à toute allure; à plein rendement. *(f)* **O. loud**, tout haut, à haute voix. **To tell s.o. sth. straight o., right o.**, dire qch. à qn carrément, franchement, sans détours, sans ambages. *S.a.* CALL OUT 2, CRY OUT, SHOUT OUT. **4. Shoulder o. (of joint)**, épaule luxée. **I'm (quite) out of pocket**, je n'ai plus le sou; je suis rouillé. **To be £50 o. of pocket**, être en perte de £50. *Pol:* **The Conservatives are out**, les Conservateurs ne sont plus au pouvoir. *Cr: (Of batsman)* **O.**, hors jeu. *(Of boxer)* **To be o. for seven seconds**, rester sur le plancher pendant sept secondes. *S.a.* KNOCK OUT 2. *F:* **To be o. on one's feet**, tituber de fatigue. **5. To be o. in one's calculations**, être loin de compte; avoir dépassé ses prévisions. **He is five pounds o. (in his accounts)**, il a une erreur de cinq livres dans ses comptes. **I was not far o.**, je ne me trompais pas de beaucoup. **You've put me o.**, vous m'avez dérouté. **6.** **The fire, gas, is out**, le feu, le gaz, est éteint. *Mil:* **Lights o.**, extinction *f* des feux. **7.** *(a)* **A bout**; achevé. **My pipe is smoked o.**, j'ai fini ma pipe. **Before the week is o.**, avant la fin de la semaine; avant que la semaine soit achevée. *S.a.* DIE OUT, GIVE OUT 2, YEAR. *(b)* Jusqu'au bout. **Hear me o.**, entendez-moi, écoutez-moi, jusqu'à la fin, jusqu'au bout. **To have one's sleep o.**, dormir tout son soûl; finir de dormir. *F:* **That's o.!** ça, c'est vieux jeu! *S.a.* FIGHT OUT, HAVE OUT 2, *etc.* (*c*) **These two projects are now definitely o.**, il n'est plus possible de considérer ces deux projets. **8.** *Prep.phr.* **From out.** **From o.** the open window came bursts of laughter, par la fenêtre ouverte arrivaient des éclats de rire. **9. Out of.** (*a*) Hors de, au dehors de, en dehors de. **That is o.** of our power, cela n'est pas en notre pouvoir. **O. of danger,** (i) hors de danger; (ii) à l'abri du danger. **O. of sight,** hors de vue. *S.a.* MIND[1] 1, SIGHT[1] 2. **To live o. of the world,** vivre retiré du monde. **He is well o. of the whole business,** il en est quitte, il s'en est tiré, à bon marché. **To be o. of it,** (i) ne pas être de la partie (de plaisir, de chasse, etc.); (ii) ne pas être de connivence; (iii) être laissé à l'écart. **To feel o. of it,** se sentir dépaysé; se sentir de trop. *S.a.* PLACE[1] 2, REACH[1] 2. (*b*) **O. of season,** hors de saison. *S.a.* SEASON[1] 2. **Times o. of number,** maintes et maintes fois. **O. of measure,** outre mesure. **To be o. of one's mind,** avoir perdu la raison. *S.a.* MIND[1] 5. **O. of spirits,** mal en train. **It's o. of the question,** c'est impossible, jamais de la vie! (*c*) (*With motion*) **To go o. of the house,** sortir de la maison. **To throw sth. o. of the window,** jeter qch. par la fenêtre. **To turn s.o. o. of the house,** mettre, *F:* flanquer, qn à la porte. **To get money o. of s.o.,** obtenir de l'argent de qn; soutirer, extorquer, de l'argent à qn. (*d*) Dans, à, par. **To drink o. of a glass,** boire dans un verre. **To drink o. of the bottle,** boire à (même) la bouteille. **To eat o. of the same dish,** manger au même plat. **To copy sth. o. of a book,** copier qch. dans un livre. **To look o. of the window,** regarder par la fenêtre. (*e*) Parmi, d'entre. **Choose one o. of these ten,** choisissez-en un parmi les dix. **One o. of every three,** un sur trois; de trois l'un. (*f*) **Hut made o. of a few old planks,** cabane faite de quelques vieilles planches. (*g*) **O. of respect for you,** par respect pour vous. **To do sth. o. of friendship, o. of curiosity,** faire qch. par amitié, par curiosité. (*h*) **To be o. of, to have run o. of, tea,** ne plus avoir de thé; être démuni, dépourvu, à court, de thé; manquer de thé. *Com:* **This article is o. of stock, I am o. of this article,** je suis démuni de cet article. **Publ:** This book is o. of stock, ce livre manque, est temporairement épuisé. (*i*) *Breed:* **Gladiator by Monarch o. of Gladia,** Gladiator par Monarch et Gladia. *S.a.* BREATH, POCKET[1] 1, WORK[1] 4. **II. out,** *s.* **1. Ins and outs.** *See* IN III. **2.** *Typ:* Bourdon *m.* **To make an o.,** sauter un mot. **'out and 'out. 1.** *adv.phr.* Complètement, absolument, sans restriction. **2.** *a.* **O. a. o. liar,** menteur fieffé, achevé. **O. a. o. nationalist,** nationaliste intransigeant. **'out-bound,** *a.* *Nau:* (Navire) sortant. **'out-building,** *s.* Bâtiment extérieur; annexe *f.* **Out-buildings,** communs *m,* dépendances *f.* **'out-of-'date,** *adj.phr.* **1.** Suranné, vieilli; passé de mode; démodé; dépassé. *S.a.* DATE[2]. **2.** (Billet, passeport) périmé. **'out of 'pocket,** *attrib. a.* **O. of p. expenses,** débours *mpl.* **'out-of-'school,** *a.* Extra-scolaire. **O.-of-s. activities,** activités *f* extra-scolaires. **'out-of-the-'way,** *a.* **1.** (*Of house, etc.*) Écarté. **2.** Peu ordinaire, peu commun. **The price is not o.-of-t.-w.,** le prix n'est pas exorbitant. **'out-patient,** *s.* Malade qui vient consulter à l'hôpital, à la clinique. **Out-patients' department** (*of hospital*), service *m* de consultations externes.

outback ['autbæk], *s.* (*In Austr.*) L'intérieur *m.*

outbid ['aut'bid], *v.tr.* (*p.t.* **outbade, outbid;** *p.p.* **outbid, -bidden**) **1.** (*At auction*) (R)enchérir, surenchérir, sur (qn). **2.** Surpasser.

outboard ['autbɔːd]. **1.** *a.* *Esp. Nau:* (*Of rigging, etc.*) Extérieur. **O. motor,** moteur hors-bord. **O. motor boat,** hors-bord *m inv.* **2.** *adv. Esp. Nau:* Au dehors; hors bord.

outbreak ['autbreik], *s.* **1.** Éruption *f;* début *m,* ouverture *f* (des hostilités, etc.); débordement *m* (des sentiments). **O. of temper,** explosion *f,* bouffée *f,* accès *m,* de colère. **O. of an epidemic,** première manifestation d'une épidémie. **O. of pimples,** poussée *f* de boutons; éruption. **O. of fire,** incendie *m.* **New o.,** recrudescence *f* (d'une épidémie, du feu, etc.). **2.** Révolte *f,* émeute *f.*

outburst ['autbəːst], *s.* Éruption *f,* explosion *f;* éclat *m* (de rire, etc.); élan *m* (de générosité); déchaînement *m* (de colère).

outcast ['autkɑːst], *a. & s.* Expulsé, -ée, exilé, -ée, proscrit, -ite, banni, -ie. **Social outcasts,** le rebut *m* de la société.

outcaste ['autkɑːst]. **1.** *a.* Qui n'appartient à aucune caste; hors-caste. **2.** *s.* Hors-caste *mf inv;* paria *m.*

outclass [aut'klɑːs], *v.tr. Sp:* Surclasser.

outcome ['autkʌm], *s.* Issue *f,* résultat *m,* conséquence *f,* aboutissement *m,* dénouement *m.*

outcrop[1] ['autkrɔp], *s. Geol:* Affleurement *m.*

outcrop[2], *v.i.* (**outcropped**) *Geol:* (*Of seam*) Affleurer.

outcry ['autkrai], *s.* (*a*) Cri *m,* cris (de réprobation, d'indignation); clameur *f.* **To raise an o. against s.o.,** crier haro sur qn. (*b*) Réclamations indignées (against, contre).

outdistance [aut'distəns], *v.tr.* Distancer, dépasser (un concurrent).

outdo [aut'duː], *v.tr.* (*p.t.* **outdid** [aut'did]; *p.p.* **outdone** [aut'dʌn]) Surpasser (**s.o. in sth.,** qn en qch.); l'emporter sur (qn).

outdoor ['autdɔːr], *a.* **1.** Extérieur, -eure; au dehors; (vie, jeux) au grand air, en plein air. **I must put on my o. clothes,** il faut que je m'habille pour sortir. **2.** *Adm:* **O. relief,** secours *mpl* à domicile.

outdoors [aut'dɔːz], *adv.* Dehors; hors de la maison; en plein air. **To sleep o.,** coucher à la belle étoile.

outer ['autər]. **1.** *a.* Extérieur, -eure; externe. **The o. side of . . .,** le côté extérieur, externe, de . . . **O. space,** l'espace intersidéral. **O. garments,** vêtements de dessus. *S.a.* PORT[1]. **2.** *s.* (*In range-shooting*) Balle *f* hors zone.

outermost ['autəmoust], *a.* **1.** Le plus à l'extérieur; le plus en dehors. **2.** Le plus écarté; extrême.

outface [aut'feis], *v.tr.* Dévisager, décontenancer (qn).

outfall ['autfɔːl], *s.* Déversoir *m,* déchargeoir *m,* débouché *m* (d'un égout).

outfit ['autfit], *s.* **1.** Équipement *m,* équipage *m;* attirail *m* (de chasse, etc.). *Nau:* Armement *m* (d'un navire). **Tool o.,** jeu *m* d'outils; outillage *m.* **First aid o.,** trousse *f* de premiers secours. **Repair o.,** nécessaire *m,* trousse, de réparation, à réparations. **2.** (*Of clothes*) Trousseau *m;* effets *mpl; Mil:* équipement *m.* **3.** *F:* Organisation *f.* **What's he doing in that o.?** que diable fait-il dans cette galère?

outfitter ['autfitər], *s. Com:* Marchand *m* de confections, confectionneur *m.*

outfitting ['autfitiŋ], *s.* **1.** Équipement *m;* armement *m* (d'un navire). **2.** *Com:* **O. department,** rayon de confection *f.*

outflank [aut'flæŋk], *v.tr.* (*a*) *Mil:* Déborder, tourner (l'ennemi, etc.). (*b*) Circonvenir (qn).

outflow ['autflou], *s.* Écoulement *m,* dépense *f* (d'eau, de gaz, etc.); coulée *f* (de lave, etc.); décharge *f* (d'un égout, d'un bief, etc.).

outgoing[1] ['autgouiŋ], *a.* (*Of tenant, etc.*) Sortant; (*of train*) en partance. **O. tide,** marée descendante. **O. ministry,** ministère démissionnaire. **O. mail,** courrier à expédier.

outgoing[2], *s.* **1.** **O. inventory,** inventaire *m* de sortie (lorsqu'on quitte un immeuble). **2.** *pl.* **Outgoings,** dépenses *f,* débours *m;* sorties *fpl* de fonds.

outgrow [aut'grou], *v.tr.* (**outgrew** [aut'gruː]; **outgrown**) **1.** Croître plus vite, devenir plus grand, que (qn, qch.). **2.** (*a*) Devenir trop grand pour (ses vêtements, etc.). (*b*) **To o. a habit,** perdre une habitude avec le temps, en grandissant.

outgrowth ['autgrouθ], *s.* Excroissance *f.*

out-Herod [aut'herəd], *v.tr.* **To o.-H. Herod,** être plus royaliste que le roi; dépasser les bornes.

outhouse ['authaus], *s.* (*a*) Dépendance *f.* (*b*) Appentis *m,* hangar *m.* (*c*) *U.S:* Lieux *mpl* d'aisance.

outing ['autiŋ], *s.* (*a*) Promenade *f.* (*b*) Excursion *f,* sortie *f.*

outlandish [aut'lændiʃ], *a.* (*a*) (*Of manner, costume*) Baroque, bizarre, étrange; (langage) barbare. (*b*) (*Of place*) Retiré, écarté.

outlast [aut'lɑːst], *v.tr.* Durer plus longtemps que (qch.); survivre à (qch.).

outlaw[1] ['autlɔː], *s.* Hors-la-loi *m inv;* proscrit; banni.

outlaw[2], *v.tr.* Mettre (qn) hors la loi; proscrire (qn).

outlawry ['autlɔːri], *s.* Mise *f* hors la loi; proscription *f.*

outlay ['autlei], s. Débours mpl, frais mpl, dépenses fpl. Ind: etc: First o., initial o., première mise de fonds; frais de premier établissement. **To get back, recover, one's o.**, rentrer dans ses débours. Capital o., dépenses fpl d'établissement.

outlet ['autlet], s. 1. Orifice m d'émission; issue f (de tunnel, etc.); sortie f, départ m (d'air, de gaz); échappement m (de vapeur); débouché m (de tuyau); déversoir m, issue (pour son trop-plein d'énergie). **To give sth. an o.**, donner issue à q⌐h. 2. Com: Débouché (pour marchandises).

outline[1] ['autlain], s. 1. Outline(s), contour(s) m, profil m (d'une colline, etc.); configuration f (de la terre); silhouette f (d'un édifice). 2. Dessin m au trait; tracé m; argument m, canevas m (d'une pièce, d'un roman). **Main outlines, general o., broad outlines, of a scheme,** grandes lignes, données générales, aperçu m, d'un projet. **Outlines of astronomy,** éléments m d'astronomie. 3. (Shorthand) Sténogramme m.

outline[2], v.tr. 1. Contourner, silhouetter (le profil de qch.). 2. Exposer à grands traits, dans ses lignes générales (une théorie, etc.); esquisser (un roman, un projet); ébaucher, indiquer (un plan d'action). 3. Draw: Esquisser à grands traits.

outlive [aut'liv], v.tr. Survivre à (qn, une défaite).

outlook ['autluk], s. 1. Guet m. **To be on the o. for sth.,** guetter qch. 2. Vue f, perspective f; point m de vue. **The o. is none too promising,** la perspective n'est pas des plus rassurantes. **Breadth of o.,** largeur f de vues.

outlying ['autlaiiŋ], a. Éloigné, écarté. **O. quarter, area,** quartier excentrique.

outmanœuvre ['autmə'nu:vər], v.tr. L'emporter sur (l'ennemi) en tactique; déjouer (qn, les plans de qn).

outmoded [aut'moudid], a. Démodé; passé de mode.

outmost ['autmoust], a. = OUTERMOST.

outnumber [aut'nʌmbər], v.tr. L'emporter en nombre sur, surpasser en nombre, être plus nombreux que (l'ennemi, etc.).

outpace [aut'peis], v.tr. Dépasser, devancer, distancer (un concurrent, etc.); gagner (qn) de vitesse.

outpost ['autpoust], s. Avant-poste m, poste avancé.

outpouring ['aut,pɔːriŋ], s. Épanchement m, effusion f (de sentiments); débordement m (d'injures).

output ['autput], s. 1. Rendement m (d'une machine, etc.); production f (d'une mine); débit m (d'un générateur, d'une pompe). **Literary o.,** production f littéraire. 2. W.Tel: **O. valve,** lampe f de sortie.

outrage[1] ['autreidʒ], s. (a) Outrage m, atteinte f. **To commit an o. on, against, s.o.,** faire outrage à qn. (b) **Plastic bomb o.,** attentat m au plastic.

outrage[2], v.tr. Outrager, faire outrage à (la religion, etc.); violenter (une femme).

outrageous [aut'reidʒəs], a. (a) Immodéré, indigne; (of price) excessif, -ive, exorbitant. (b) (Of statement, accusation) Outrageant, outrageux, -euse. (of conduct, etc.) outrageux, atroce, indigne. (c) F: **O. fashion,** mode f impossible. **-ly,** adv. (a) Immodérément; outre mesure. **O. expensive,** horriblement cher. (b) D'une façon scandaleuse, indigne.

outride [aut'raid], v.tr. (outrode [aut'roud]; **outridden** [aut'ridn]). 1. Chevaucher plus vite que (qn); dépasser, devancer, (qn) à cheval. 2. Nau: Étaler (une tempête).

outrider ['autraidər], s. Piqueur m (de carrosse).

outrigger ['autrigər], s. 1. Row: (a) Porte-nage m inv en dehors; porte-en-dehors m inv; dame f de nage. (b) (Boat) Outrigger m. 2. Nau: Balancier m (d'un prao).

outright [aut'rait]. I. adv. 1. (a) Complètement. **To buy sth. o.,** acheter qch. comptant, à forfait. (b) Du premier coup; sur le coup. **To kill s.o. o.,** tuer qn raide. 2. Sans ménagement; franchement, carrément. **To laugh o. (at s.o.),** partir d'un franc rire (au nez de qn); éclater de rire. II. outright, a. (attrib. ['autrait]) 1. **O. sale,** vente f à forfait. **O. purchase,** marché m forfaitaire. 2. (Of manner) Franc, f. franche; carré.

outrun [aut'rʌn], v.tr. (p.t. outran [aut'ræn]; p.p outrun ['aut'rʌn]; pr.p. outrunning) 1. Dépasser; gagner (qn) de vitesse; distancer (un concurrent). 2. His zeal outruns his discretion, son ardeur l'emporte sur son jugement.

outset ['autset], s. Commencement m. **At the o.,** au début; tout d'abord. **From the o.,** dès le début, dès l'origine, dès l'abord.

outshine ['aut'ʃain], v.tr. (outshone ['aut'ʃɔn]; outshone) Surpasser en éclat; dépasser, éclipser.

outside [,aut'said]. 1. s. (a) Extérieur m, dehors m (d'une maison, d'un livre). **On the o. of sth.,** à l'extérieur de qch. **To open a door from the o.,** ouvrir une porte du dehors. **The window opens to the o.,** la fenêtre s'ouvre en dehors. **To turn a skin o. in,** retourner une peau (de lapin, etc.). (b) **At the o.,** tout au plus; au maximum. (c) A: Impériale f (d'un autobus); banquette f (d'une diligence). 2. attrib.a. ['autsaid] (a) Du dehors; extérieur, -eure. **O. seat,** (i) A: (on bus) banquette de l'impériale; (ii) (of a row of seats) place du bout. (b) **O. porter,** commissionnaire messager. **O. worker,** ouvrier, -ière, à domicile. (c) **To get an o. opinion,** obtenir un avis du dehors, un avis étranger. (d) **O. prices,** les plus hauts prix; prix maximum. (e) F: **It was an o. chance,** il y avait tout juste une chance (de réussite). 3. adv. Dehors, à l'extérieur, en dehors. **I've left my dog o.,** j'ai laissé mon chien dehors, à la porte. **To put s.o. o.,** mettre qn dehors. **Seen from o.,** vu de dehors. A: **To ride o.,** voyager sur l'impériale. 4. prep. En dehors de, hors de, à l'extérieur de. **O. my bedroom,** (i) à la porte de, (ii) sous les fenêtres de, ma chambre. **Garden lying o. my grounds,** jardin extérieur à ma propriété. **That's o. the question,** c'est en dehors du sujet. (Of artist) **To go o. his range,** sortir de son talent.

outsider [aut'saidər], s. F: 1. Étranger, -ère; profane mf; outsider m. **He's an o.,** (i) il n'est pas du métier, de la partie; (ii) il n'est pas de notre monde; c'est un intrus. 2. St.Exch: Courtier marron. 3. Turf: Cheval non classé; outsider m; toquard m.

outsize ['autsaiz], s. Com: Dimension f, pointure f, hors série; taille exceptionnelle. **O. dress,** robe en taille exceptionnelle. **For outsizes,** pour les grandes tailles. **An o. packet,** un paquet géant.

outskirts ['autskə:ts], s.pl. Abords m; lisière f (d'une forêt); faubourgs mpl (d'une ville); banlieue f (d'une grande ville); approches fpl (d'une ville).

outspan ['autspæn], v. (outspanned) (In S. Africa) 1. v.i. (a) Dételer. (b) Camper à l'étape. 2. v.tr. Dételer (les bœufs).

outspoken [aut'spoukən], a. (Of pers.) Franc, f. franche; carré, rond. **To be o.,** avoir son franc-parler. **-ly,** adv. Carrément, rondement.

outspokenness [aut'spoukənnis], s. Franchise f un peu brusque; franc-parler m.

outspread [aut'spred], a. Étendu, étalé. **With o. wings,** les ailes déployées.

outstanding [aut'stændiŋ], a. 1. (Of detail, feature, etc.) Saillant; (of pers., incident) marquant; (of artist, etc.) hors ligne, éminent. **O. success,** succès éclatant. 2. (Affaire) en suspens, en cours de règlement; (compte) impayé, dû; (paiement) arriéré, en retard; (intérêt) échu. Fin: **O. coupons,** coupons en souffrance. **-ly,** adv. Éminemment.

outstare [aut'stɛər], v.tr. Fixer (qn) jusqu'à ce qu'il détourne son regard; faire baisser les yeux à (qn).

outstay [aut'stei], v.tr. 1. Rester plus longtemps que (qn). 2. **To o. one's welcome,** lasser l'amabilité de ses hôtes.

outstretched ['aut'stretʃt], a. Déployé, étendu; (bras) tendu. **With o. arms,** les bras ouverts.

outstrip [aut'strip], v.tr. (outstripped) (a) Devancer, dépasser (qn à la course); gagner (qn) de vitesse. (b) Surpasser.

outvie ['aut'vai], v.tr. Surpasser (qn en splendeur, etc.); l'emporter sur (un concurrent).

outward ['autwəd]. 1. a. (a) En dehors. Nau: Pour l'étranger. **The o. and the homeward voyages** l'aller et le retour. Rail: **O. half (of ticket),** billet m d'aller. (b) Extérieur; de dehors. **O. form,** extérieur m, dehors m. Pharm: For o. application, pour l'usage externe. 2. adv. = OUTWARDS. **-ly,** adv. 1. À l'extérieur, au dehors. 2. En apparence.

'outward-'bound, a. Nau: 1. (Navire) en partance, sortant. 2. (Navire) faisant route pour l'étranger.

outwards ['autwədz], adv. Au dehors; vers l'extérieur. **To turn one's feet o.,** tourner les pieds en dehors.

outvote ['aut'vout], v.tr. Obtenir une majorité sur, l'emporter sur (qn). **To find oneself outvoted,** être mis en minorité.

outwear ['aut'wɛər], v.tr. (outwore ['aut'wɔːr]; outworn ['aut'wɔːn]) 1. User complètement. 2. Durer plus longtemps que (qch.); faire plus d'usage que (qch.).
outweigh ['aut'wei], v.tr. 1. Peser plus que (qch.). 2. Avoir plus d'influence, plus de poids, que (qn); l'emporter sur (qch.).
outwit [aut'wit], v.tr. (outwitted) 1. Circonvenir (qn); déjouer les intentions, les menées, de (qn); duper (qn). 2. Dépister (les chiens, la police).
outwork ['autwɔːk], s. Fort: Ouvrage avancé. Arch: Hors-d'œuvre m inv.
ouzel ['uːzl], s. Orn: 1. (a) Ring o., merle m à plastron. (b) Water o., merle d'eau. 2. A. & Lit: = BLACKBIRD.
oval ['ouv(ə)l]. 1. a. Ovale; en ovale. 2. s. Ovale m.
ovalize ['ouvəlaiz]. Mec.E: 1. v.tr. Ovaliser. 2. v.i. (Of cylinder, etc.) S'ovaliser.
ovary ['ouvəri], s. Ovaire m.
ovate ['ouveit], a. Nat.Hist: Ové.
ovation [o'veiʃ(ə)n], s. Ovation f. To give s.o. an o., faire une ovation à qn.
oven ['ʌv(ə)n], s. 1. Dom.Ec: Four m. In the o., au four. To cook sth. in a slow o., cuire qch. à (un) feu doux. F: This room is a regular o., cette salle est une fournaise. S.a. GAS-OVEN. 2. Drying o., étuve f.
ovenware ['ʌvənwɛər], s. Vaisselle f allant au four.
over ['ouvər]. I. prep. 1. (a) Sur, dessus, par-dessus. To spread a cloth over sth., étendre une toile sur, par-dessus, qch. (b) All o. the north of England, sur toute l'étendue du nord de l'Angleterre. Famous all o. the world, célèbre, connu, dans le monde entier, par tout le monde. Measured o. its widest part, mesuré sur la partie la plus large. S.a. OVERALL. F: To be all o. s.o., faire l'empressé auprès de qn. (c) O. (the top of) sth., par-dessus (qch.). To throw something o. the wall, jeter qch. par-dessus le mur. We heard voices o. the wall, nous entendîmes des voix de l'autre côté du mur. To fall o. a cliff, tomber du haut d'une falaise. To stumble, trip, o. sth., buter contre qch.; trébucher sur qch. 2. (a) Jutting out o. the street, faisant saillie sur la rue, au-dessus de la rue. His name is o. the door, il a son nom au-dessus de la porte. Hanging o. our heads, suspendu au-dessus de, sur, nos têtes. With his hat o. his eyes, le chapeau enfoncé jusqu'aux yeux. His hat o. one ear, le chapeau sur l'oreille. To be o. one's ankles in water, avoir de l'eau par-dessus la cheville. S.a. EAR¹ 1, HAND¹ 2. (b) To have an advantage o. s.o., avoir un avantage sur qn. To reign o. a country, régner sur un pays. He is o. me, il est au-dessus de moi. (c) Bending o. his work, courbé sur son travail. How long will you be o. it? cela vous prendra combien de temps? quand l'aurez-vous fini? Sitting o. the fire, assis tout près du feu; F: couvant le feu. 3. (Across) (a) The house o. the way, la maison d'en face; la maison vis-à-vis. O. the border, au delà de la frontière. To live o. the river, demeurer de l'autre côté de la rivière. (b) The bridge o. the river, le pont qui traverse la rivière. 4. (In excess of) Numbers o. a hundred, numéros au-dessus de cent. O. fifty pounds, plus de cinquante livres. O. five (years of age), au-dessus de cinq ans. He is o. fifty, il a (dé)passé la cinquantaine. He receives tips o. and above his salary, il reçoit des pourboires en sus de ses gages. 5. O. the last three years wages have increased, au cours des trois dernières années les salaires ont augmenté. Can you stay o. Sunday? pouvez-vous rester jusqu'à lundi? II. over, adv. 1. (a) Sur toute la surface. To be all o. dust, être tout couvert de poussière. To ache all o., avoir mal partout; souffrir de partout. F: That's you all o.! je vous reconnais bien là! (b) To read a letter o., lire une lettre en entier. I have had to do it all o. again, j'ai dû la refaire d'un bout à l'autre. S.a. GO OVER 1, LOOK OVER. (c) (Repetition) Ten times o., dix fois de suite. Twice o., à deux reprises. O. and o. (again), à plusieurs reprises; maintes et maintes fois. 2. (a) Par-dessus (qch.). To look o. into a garden, regarder dans un jardin par-dessus le mur. The milk boiled o., le lait s'est sauvé. (b) To lean o., (i) (of pers.) se pencher (à la fenêtre, etc.); (ii) (of thg) pencher. 3. (a) To fall o., (i) (of pers.) tomber (par terre); (ii) (of thg) se renverser; être renversé. To knock sth. o., renverser qch.

(b) Please turn o., voir au dos; tournez, s'il vous plaît. To turn sth. o. and o., tourner et retourner qch. S.a. TURN OVER. To bend sth. o., replier qch. (c) Hard o.! (i) Nau: la barre toute! (ii) Aut. Braquez (jusqu'à la dernière limite)! 4. To cross o. (i) traverser (la rue, etc.); (ii) faire la traversée (de la Manche, etc.). O. there, o. yonder, là-bas. O. here, ici; de ce côté. O. against sth., vis-à-vis de qch.; en face de qch. He is o. from France, il vient de France. Our friends are coming o. tomorrow, nos amis vont venir nous voir demain. W.Tel: O. (to you), à vous. S.a. GET OVER, GIVE OVER, etc. 5. En plus, en excès. (a) Children of fourteen and o., les enfants qui ont quatorze ans et davantage, et au delà. Three into seven goes twice and one o., sept divisé par trois donne deux, (et il) reste un. He is six foot and a bit over, il a six pieds et le pouce. (b) You will keep what is (left) o., vous garderez l'excédent, le surplus. I have a card o., j'ai une carte de trop, en trop. And o. and above, he is younger than you, et en outre, et d'ailleurs, il est moins âgé que vous. (c) (Till later) To hold o. a decision, ajourner une décision. The question is held o., la question est différée. (d) (Compounded with adjs. and advs.) Trop; à l'excès. O.-abundant, surabondant. To be o.-particular, être (par) trop exigeant, trop méticuleux. O.-scrupulous, scrupuleux (jusqu')à l'excès. Not o.-gay, peu gai. (e) (Compounded with a noun) Excès de. O.-confidence, excès de confiance. (f) (Compounded with a verb) (i) Trop, sur-. To over-stretch a spring, trop tendre, surtendre, un ressort. (ii) To overpass, overstep, outrepasser. 6. Fini, achevé. The storm, danger, is o., l'orage est passé, est dissipé; le danger est passé. It is all o., c'est fini; tout est fini. It is all o. with me, c'en est fait de moi. S.a. GIVE OVER 2. III. over, s. 1. Cr: Série f (de six ou huit balles). 2. (a) Typ: Overs, main f de passe; simple passe f. Double overs, double passe. (b) Publ: Overs, exemplaires de passe. 3. Knitting: Single over, double over, jeté m simple, jeté double. 'over-'bold, a. 1. Téméraire. 2 Présomptueux, -euse. 'over-'confidence, s. 1. Confiance exagérée (in, en). 2. Suffisance f, présomption f, témérité f. 'over-'confident, a. 1. Trop confiant (in s.o., en qn). 2. Suffisant, présomptueux -euse, téméraire. 'over(-)de'velop, v.tr. Développer à l'excès. Phot: Over-developed negative, négatif trop poussé. over-elaborate [ouvəri'laborét] a. Trop compliqué; (of literary style) trop fouillé, tourmenté. over(-)estimate¹ [ouvər'estimet], s. Surestimation f; surévaluation f. over-estimate² [ouvər'estimeit], v.tr. Surestimer; surévaluer; exagérer (le danger, etc.). 'over(-)ex'pose, v.tr. Phot: Surexposer; donner trop de pose à (un négatif, etc.). 'over(-)ex'posure, s. Phot: Surexposition f; excès m de pose. 'over-fa'miliar, a. To be o.-f. with s.o., se montrer trop familier avec qn; prendre des libertés, des privautés, avec qn. 'over-'fond, a. An o.-f. mother, une mère abusive. 'over-in'dulge. 1. v.tr. (a) Montrer trop d'indulgence envers (qn); gâter (qn). (b) Se laisser aller trop librement à (une passion, etc.). 2. v.i. To o.-i. in metaphor, faire abus des métaphores. 'over-in'dulgence, s. 1. Indulgence excessive (of s.o. envers qn). 2. Abus m, excès m (in wine, etc., de vin, etc.). 'over-'nice, a. Trop exigeant; renchéri. O.-n. distinction, distinction f vétilleuse. 'over-par'ticular, a. Exigeant. 'over-'populated, a Surpeuplé. 'over(-)print¹, s. Surcharge f (de timbre-poste). 'over(-)print², v.tr. 1. Surcharger (un timbre-poste). 2. Typ: Tirer trop d'exemplaires de (qch.). 3. Phot: Trop pousser (une épreuve). 'over-'printing, s. Surimpression f. 'over-proof, attrib.a (Of spirits) Au-dessus de preuve. 'over-re'finement s. (a) Affèterie f, affectation f. (b) Alambiquage m, préciosité f (du style). 'over-'ripe, a. Trop mûr (of cheese) trop fait; (of fruit) blet, f. blette. 'over-'sensitive, a. Hypersensible. 'over-'sensitiveness s. Hypersensibilité f. 'over(-)sub'scribe, v.tr. Fin Surpasser (une émission). 'over-'train, v.tr. & i Sp: (S')épuiser par un entraînement trop sévère "claquer." 'over-'zealous, a. Trop zélé. To be o.-z., pécher par excès de zèle.

overact ['ouvər'ækt], *v.tr. Th:* Outrer, charger (un rôle).

overall ['ouvərɔːl]. **1.** *a.* Total, global, d'ensemble. **O. length,** longueur hors tout. **2.** *s.* (*a*) Blouse *f* sarrau *m,* -aus, -aux; (*b*) *Ind: etc:* **Overalls,** salopette *f;* combinaison *f; F:* bleus *mpl.*

overarm ['ouvərɑːm], *attrib.a.* (*a*) *Swim:* **O. stroke,** brasse indienne; nage (à l')indienne. (*b*) *Ten:* **To serve o.,** servir par le haut.

overawe [,ouvər'ɔː], *v.tr.* Intimider; en imposer à (qn).

overbalance ['ouvə'bæləns]. **1.** *v.tr.* (*a*) Peser plus que (qch). (*b*) Surpasser, l'emporter sur (qch.). (*c*) Renverser (qch.). **2.** *v.i. & pr.* **To o.** (oneself), perdre l'équilibre. **3.** *v.i.* (*Of thg*) Se renverser; tomber.

overbear ['ouvə'bɛər], *v.tr.* (*Conj. like* BEAR) **1.** Renverser, terrasser (son adversaire). **2.** (*a*) **To o. s.o.,** **s.o.'s will,** passer outre aux volontés de qn. (*b*) Intimider (qn). **overbearing,** *a.* Arrogant, impérieux, -euse, autoritaire.

overbid ['ouvə'bid], *v.tr.* (*Conj. like* BID) Enchérir sur (qn). *Cards:* Forcer sur l'annonce de qn.

overboard ['ouvəbɔːd], *adv. Nau:* Hors du bord; par-dessus (le) bord. **To fall o.,** tomber à la mer. **Man o.!** un homme à la mer!

overbuild ['ouvə'bild], *v.tr.* Surbâtir. **over'built,** *a.* **O. areas,** localités trop denses.

overburden [,ouvə'bə:d(ə)n], *v.tr.* Surcharger, accabler (**with,** de). *F:* **He's not overburdened with brains,** *F:* ce n'est pas l'intelligence qui l'écrase.

overcall ['ouvə'kɔːl], *v.tr. Cards:* Forcer sur l'annonce de qn. **To o.** (one's hand), annoncer au-dessus de ses moyens.

overcapitalization ['ouvəkæpitəlai'zeiʃ(ə)n], *s. Fin:* Surcapitalisation *f.*

overcast ['ouvəkɑːst], *v.tr.* (overcast; overcast) **1.** Obscurcir, assombrir (le ciel, l'esprit); couvrir (le ciel). **2.** *Needlew:* Surjeter, surfiler. **overcast,** *a.* **1.** (*a*) Obscurci, assombri, couvert (**with,** de). (*b*) **O. sky,** ciel couvert, sombre. **O. weather,** temps bouché. **2.** *Needlew:* **O. stitch,** (point *m* de) surjet *m. S.a.* SEAM¹ **1.**

overcharge¹ ['ouvətʃɑːdʒ], *s.* **1.** Surcharge *f* (d'un accumulateur, etc.). **2.** (*a*) Prix excessif; prix surfait. (*b*) Majoration *f* (d'un compte).

overcharge² ['ouvə'tʃɑːdʒ], *v.tr.* **1.** Surcharger. **2.** **To o. goods,** surfaire les marchandises. **To o. s.o.,** faire payer trop cher un article à qn; *F:* écorcher qn.

overcloud [,ouvə'klaud]. **1.** *v.tr.* (*a*) Couvrir de nuages. (*b*) Obscurcir, assombrir. **2.** *v.i.* (*Of sky*) Se couvrir de nuages.

overcoat ['ouvəkout], *s.* Pardessus *m; Mil:* capote *f.*

overcome [,ouvə'kʌm], *v.tr.* (overcame ['ouvə'keim]; overcome) Triompher de, vaincre (ses adversaires, etc.); venir à bout de, avoir raison de (qn, qch.); dominer, maîtriser, surmonter (son émotion, etc.). **overcome,** *a.* **To be o. with, by** (sth.), être accablé de (douleur, etc.); être transi de (peur); être gagné par (le sommeil, les larmes). **To be o. by a spectacle,** être fortement ému par un spectacle. **To be o. by the heat, by emotion,** succomber à la chaleur, à l'émotion.

overcrowd [,ouvə'kraud], *v.tr.* (*a*) Trop remplir (un autobus, etc.). **To o. a shelf with ornaments,** surcharger une planche d'ornements. (*b*) Surpeupler (une ville, une forêt). **overcrowded,** *a.* (*a*) Trop rempli (**with,** de); (appartement, autobus) bondé (**with people,** de monde). (*b*) (Ville) surpeuplée; (forêt) trop dense, surpeuplée. **overcrowding,** *s.* **1.** Encombrement *m.* **2.** Surpeuplement *m.*

overdo [,ouvə'duː], *v.tr.* (*Conj. like* DO) **1.** Outrer (les choses); charger (un rôle, etc.). **Type of advertisement that has been overdone,** genre d'annonce dont on a abusé. **2.** **To o. it, to** surmener. *Iron:* **Don't o. it!** pas de zèle! **3.** *Cu:* Trop cuire (la viande).

overdose ['ouvədous], *s.* Trop forte dose; dose (i) nuisible, (ii) mortelle.

overdraft ['ouvədrɑːft], *s. Bank:* Découvert *m;* solde débiteur.

overdraw ['ouvə'drɔː], *v.tr.* (*Conj. like* DRAW) **1.** Charger (le portrait de qn); trop colorer (un récit). **2. To o. one's account,** mettre son compte à découvert; tirer à découvert. **Overdrawn account,** compte découvert.

overdress ['ouvə'dres], *v.tr.* Habiller avec trop de recherche. **She is rather overdressed,** sa toilette manque de simplicité et de bon ton.

overdrive¹ ['ouvə'draiv], *v.tr.* (*Conj. like* DRIVE) Surmener, *F:* éreinter (un cheval); surmener, fatiguer (une machine, etc.).

overdrive² ['ouvədraiv], *s. Aut:* (Vitesse) surmultipliée.

overdue ['ouvə'djuː], *a.* (*a*) (*Of account*) Arriéré, échu, en retard, en souffrance. (*b*) **Train ten minutes o.,** train en retard de dix minutes.

overeat ['ouvər'iːt], *v.pr. & i.* **To overeat** (oneself), trop manger. **overeating,** *s.* Excès *mpl,* de table.

overexcite ['ouvərik'sait], *v.tr.* Surexciter.

overexcitement ['ouv(ə)rik'saitmənt], *s.* Surexcitation *f.*

overexertion ['ouvərig'zə:ʃ(ə)n], *s.* Surmenage *m;* abus *m* de ses forces.

overfeed ['ouvə'fiːd], *v.* (overfeed; overfed) **1.** *v.tr.* Suralimenter, (on, de). **2.** *v.i. & pr.* Trop manger. **overfed,** *a.* **1.** Suralimenté. **2.** *F:* Pansu, ventru.

overflow¹ ['ouvəflou], *s.* **1.** (*a*) Débordement *m,* épanchement *m* (d'un liquide). (*b*) Inondation *f.* **2.** Trop-plein *m inv.* **O.-pipe,** (tuyau *m* de) trop-plein; déversoir *m* (d'une citerne). *Civ.E:* **O. channel,** émissaire *m.* **3.** **O. meeting,** réunion *f* supplémentaire (pour ceux qui en arrivant ont trouvé salle comble).

overflow² [,ouvə'flou]. **1.** *v.tr.* (*a*) (*Of liquid*) Déborder de (la coupe, etc.). (*b*) (*Of river, etc.*) Inonder (un champ). **The river overflowed its banks,** la rivière est sortie de son lit. **2.** *v.i.* (*a*) (*Of cup, heart, etc.*) Déborder. **Room overflowing with people,** salle qui regorge de monde. (*b*) (*Of liquid*) Déborder, s'épancher; (*of gutter, stream*) dégorger. **overflowing¹,** *a.* Débordant; plein à déborder; (*of kindness*) surabondant. **overflowing²,** *s.* Débordement *m.* **Full to o.,** plein à déborder.

overfree ['ouvə'friː], *a.* Trop familier (**with,** avec). **To be o. in one's conduct,** se conduire trop librement.

overgarment ['ouvəgɑːmənt], *s.* Vêtement *m* de dessus.

overgrow ['ouvə'grou], *v.tr.* (*Conj. like* GROW) (*Of plants, etc.*) Couvrir, recouvrir (un mur, etc.); envahir (un terrain, etc.). **overgrown,** *a.* **1.** Couvert (**with sth.,** de qch.). **Garden, road, o. with weeds,** jardin envahi par les mauvaises herbes; route mangée d'herbes. **2.** (*Of child*) Qui a grandi trop vite.

overgrowth ['ouvəgrouθ], *s.* **1.** Surcroissance *f;* croissance excessive. **2.** Couverture *f* (d'herbes, de ronces, de poils, etc.).

overhang¹ ['ouvəhæn], *s.* Surplomb *m;* porte-à-faux *m inv,* saillie *f.*

overhang² ['ouvə'hæn], *v.tr.* (overhung ['ouvə'hʌn]; overhung) Surplomber; faire saillie au-dessus de, pencher sur (qch.). **overhung,** *a.* **1.** En surplomb; en saillie; surplombant; en porte-à-faux. **2.** *Cu:* (*Of game*) Trop faisandé. **overhanging,** *a.* Surplombant, en surplomb, en porte-à-faux.

overhaul¹ ['ouvəhɔːl], *s.* (*a*) Examen détaillé (d'un malade, etc.); révision *f* (d'une machine, etc.); visite *f* (pour réparations). (*b*) Remise *f* en état.

overhaul² [,ouvə'hɔːl], *v.tr.* **1.** Examiner en détail (un malade, une machine); réviser, remettre en état, réparer, réfectionner. *Nau:* Radouber (un navire). **2.** *Nau:* Rattraper, dépasser (un autre navire).

overhead ['ouvə'hed]. **1.** *adv.* Au-dessus (de la tête); en haut, en l'air. **2.** *Attrib.a.* ['ouvəhed] (*a*) **O. cable,** câble aérien. (*b*) **O.** (**cable**) **transport,** transport *m* par trolley; téléphérage *m. S.a.* CRANE¹ **2.** (*b*) *I.C.E:* **O. valves,** soupapes en dessus, en tête. *S.a.* ENGINE **3.** (*c*) *Com:* **O. expenses,** *s. F:* **overhead(s),** frais généraux; dépenses générales. (*d*) *Art: Phot:* **O. lighting,** éclairage vertical.

overhear [ouvə'hiər], *v.tr.* (*Conj. like* HEAR) Surprendre (une conversation, etc.).

overheat ['ouvə'hiːt], *v.tr.* (*a*) Surchauffer, trop chauffer. (*b*) **To o. oneself,** s'échauffer (trop). **overheated,** *a.* (*Of engine, etc.*) Surchauffé. **To get o.,** (i) (*of pers.*) s'échauffer, prendre chaud; (ii) (*of engine, brakes*) chauffer.

overink ['ouvə'ink], *v.tr. Typ:* Empâter. **Overinking,** *s.* Empâtement *m.*

overjoyed [ˌouvə'dʒɔid], a. Transporté de joie. To be overjoyed, être au comble de la joie, rempli de joie. To be o. to see s.o., être ravi de voir qn.

overladen ['ouvə'leidn], a. Surchargé (with, de).

overland [ˌouvə'lænd]. 1. adv. Par voie de terre. 2. Attrib.a. ['ouvəlænd] Qui voyage par voie de terre. O. route, voie f de terre.

overlap[1] ['ouvəlæp], s. Recouvrement m; chevauchement m; (of slates, etc.) chevauchure f, imbrication f. Carp: O. joint, joint à recouvrement.

overlap[2] [ˌouvə'læp], v.tr. & i. (overlapped [-'læpt]) 1. Recouvrir (partiellement). (Of tiles, slates) To o. (one another), chevaucher; imbriquer. 2. Dépasser, outrepasser (l'extrémité de qch.). 3. (Of categories, etc.) Se chevaucher; faire double emploi avec qch. **overlapping**, s. 1. Recouvrement m, chevauchement m. 2. Double emploi m.

overlay[1] ['ouvəlei], s. 1. Furn: Matelas m. 2. Typ: Hausse f.

overlay[2] [ˌouvə'lei], v.tr. (Conj. like LAY) 1. Recouvrir, couvrir (with, de). Overlaid with mud, enduit (d'une couche) de boue. 2. Typ: Mettre des hausses sur (le tympan).

overlay[3]. See OVERLIE.

overleaf ['ouvə'li:f], adv. Au dos, au verso (de la page). 'See o.,' "voir au verso."

overlie [ˌouvə'lai], v.tr. (overlay; overlain) Recouvrir, couvrir. **overlying**, a. Superposé.

overload[1] ['ouvəloud], s. 1. Poids m en surcharge; surcharge f. 2. Mch: O. running, marche f en surcharge.

overload[2] ['ouvə'loud], v.tr. 1. Surcharger. 2. Surmener (une machine).

overlook ['ouvə'luk], v.tr. 1. Avoir vue sur (qch.); (of building) dominer, commander (un vallon, etc.); (of window) donner sur (la rue). 2. (a) Oublier, laisser passer (l'heure, etc.); négliger, laisser échapper (une occasion). I overlooked the fact, ce fait m'a échappé. (b) Fermer les yeux sur (qch.); passer sur (qch.); laisser passer (une erreur). O. it this time, passez-le-moi cette fois. 3. Surveiller (un travail).

overlord ['ouvələ:d], s. Suzerain m.

overly ['ouvəli], adv. U.S: Excessivement, (beaucoup) trop.

overmantel ['ouvəmæntl], s. Étagère f de cheminée.

overmaster [ˌouvə'ma:stər], v.tr. Maîtriser, subjuguer. **overmastering**, a. (a) (Of will) Dominateur, -trice. (b) (Of passion) Irrésistible.

overmuch ['ouvə'mʌtʃ]. adv. (Par) trop; à l'excès; outre mesure.

overnight ['ouvə'nait]. 1. adv. (a) La veille (au soir). (b) (Pendant) la nuit. He became famous o., il devint célèbre du jour au lendemain. (Of food) To keep o., se conserver jusqu'au lendemain. 2. ['ouvənait], a. De la veille. O. stay, séjour m d'une seule nuit. O. bag, sac m de voyage. O. case, mallette f.

overpass[1] [ˌouvə'pa:s], v.tr. 1. Surmonter, vaincre (un obstacle). 2. Surpasser (s.o. in sth., qn en qch.). 3. Outrepasser (les bornes de . . .).

overpass[2], s. Civ.E: U.S: Enjambement m., passage supérieur.

overpayment ['ouvə'peimənt], s. 1. Surpaie f; paiement m en trop. Fin: Trop-perçu m. 2. Rétribution excessive.

overplay [ouvə'plei], v.tr. To o. one's hand, viser trop haut.

overpower [ˌouvə'pauər], v.tr. Maîtriser, dominer, vaincre, accabler. Overpowered with grief, accablé de douleur. **overpowering**, a. (Of emotion) Accablant; (of desire) tout-puissant, irrésistible. O. heat, chaleur accablante. F: I find her o., c'est une femme imposante.

overpraise ['ouvə'preiz], v.tr. Trop louer.

overproduce ['ouvəprə'dju:s], v.tr. Produire trop de (qch.); Abs: surproduire.

overproduction ['ouvəprə'dʌkʃ(ə)n], s. Surproduction f.

overrate ['ouvə'reit], v.tr. Surestimer, surfaire; faire trop de cas de (qch.). To o. one's strength, trop présumer de ses forces. An overrated restaurant, un restaurant surfait.

overreach [ˌouvə'ri:tʃ], v.tr. 1. Dépasser. 2. Tromper, duper (qn). 3. To o. oneself, (i) se donner un effort; (ii) être victime de sa propre fourberie.

override ['ouvə'raid], v.tr. (Conj. like RIDE) 1. (a) Outrepasser (ses ordres, etc.); fouler aux pieds (les droits de qn). (b) Avoir plus d'importance que (qch.). Considerations that o. all others, considérations qui l'emportent sur toutes les autres. 2. Surmener (un cheval). 3. v.i. (Of ends of fractured bone, of the toes, etc.) Chevaucher. **overriding**, a. O. principle, principe auquel il ne saurait être dérogé. Jur: O. clause, clause dérogatoire.

overrider ['ouvə'raidər], s. Aut: Sabot m (de parechoc), barrette (verticale).

overrule [ˌouvə'ru:l], v.tr. 1. Gouverner, diriger (avec une autorité supérieure). 2. (a) Décider contre (l'avis de qn). (b) Jur: Annuler, casser (un arrêt); rejeter (une réclamation). (c) Passer outre à (une difficulté); passer à l'ordre du jour sur (une objection).

overrun ['ouvə'rʌn], v. (Conj. like RUN) I. v.tr. 1. (a) (Of invaders) (i) Se répandre sur, envahir (un pays); (ii) dévaster, ravager (un pays). (b) These eastern towns are o. with soldiers, ces villes de l'est grouillent de soldats. House o. with mice, maison infestée de souris. 2. Dépasser, aller au delà de (la limite). 3. Surmener, fatiguer (une machine); El: survolter (une lampe). 4. Typ: Reporter (un mot) à la ligne ou à la page suivante. II. overrun, v.i. (Of liquid, river) Déborder. Typ: Chasser. **overrunning**, s. Typ: Remaniage m.

overseas ['ouvə'si:z], adv. Par delà les mers. Visitors from o., visiteurs d'outre-mer. attrib.a. D'outre-mer.

oversee ['ouvə'si:], v.tr. (Conj. like SEE) Surveiller, F: avoir l'œil sur (un atelier, etc.).

overseer ['ouvəsiər], s. Surveillant, -ante; inspecteur, -trice; Ind: contremaître, -tresse; chef m d'atelier.

oversew ['ouvəsou], v.tr. (p.p. oversewn ['ouvəsoun]) Needlew: Surjeter; assembler au point de surjet.

overshadow [ˌouvə'ʃædou], v.tr. 1. Ombrager; couvrir de son ombre. 2. Éclipser (qn); surpasser en éclat.

overshoe ['ouvəʃu:], s. Couvre-chaussure m; galoche f. Rubber overshoes, caoutchoucs m.

overshoot[1] ['ouvəʃu:t], s. Av: Présentation trop longue, remise f de gaz.

overshoot[2] ['ouvə'ʃu:t], v.tr. (Conj. like SHOOT) 1. Dépasser, outrepasser (le point d'arrêt, etc.); (of shot, gun) porter au delà de (qch.). Av: Se présenter trop long (sur la piste), remettre les gaz. To o. the mark, dépasser le but. 2. Trop chasser sur (une terre); dépeupler (une chasse). **overshot**, a. Hyd.E: O. wheel, roue (à augets) en dessus.

oversight ['ouvəsait], s. 1. Oubli m, omission f, inadvertance f. Through, by, an o., par mégarde; par inadvertance. 2. Surveillance f.

oversize ['ouvəsaiz], s. (a) Mec.E: etc: Surépaisseur f. (b) Dimensions fpl (i) au-dessus de la moyenne, (ii) Mec.E: au-dessus de la cote. O. tyre, bandage surprofilé. I.C.E: O. piston, piston à cote de réalésage.

oversleep ['ouvə'sli:p], v.i. & pron. (Conj. like SLEEP) To o. (oneself), dormir trop longtemps.

oversleeve ['ouvəsli:v], s. Fausse manche f.

overspill ['ouvəspil], s. An o. of population, un déversement de population.

overspread [ˌouvə'spred], v.tr. (Conj. like SPREAD) 1. Couvrir (with, de). 2. Se répandre, s'étendre sur (qch.); (of floods, light, etc.) inonder.

overstate ['ouvə'steit], v.tr. Exagérer (les faits, etc.). **overstated**, a. Outré.

overstatement ['ouvə'steitmənt], s. 1. Exagération f. 2. Récit exagéré.

overstay ['ouvə'stei], v.tr. Dépasser (son congé, etc.). S.a. WELCOME[2].

oversteer [ouvə'stiər], v.i. Aut: Survirer.

overstep ['ouvə'step], v.tr. (Conj. like STEP) Outrepasser, dépasser (les bornes).

overstock ['ouvə'stɔk], v.tr. (a) Encombrer (le marché, etc.) (with, de). (b) Trop meubler (une ferme) de bétail; surcharger (un étang) de poissons.

overstrain[1] ['ouvəstrein], s. 1. Tension excessive. 2. Surmenage m.

overstrain[2] ['ouvə'strein], v.tr. 1. Surtendre (un câble). 2. (a) Surmener. (b) To o. an argument, pousser trop loin un argument.

overstress[1] ['ouvəstres], s. Mec.E: Surcharge f.

overstress² ['ouvə'stres], *v.tr.* **1.** *Mec.E:* Surcharger (une transmission). **2.** Trop insister sur (un détail).

overt [ou'və:t], *a.* Patent, évident. *Jur:* O. act, acte manifeste. **Market o.**, marché public.

overtake [,ouvə'teik], *v.tr.* (*Conj. like* TAKE) **1.** (*a*) Rattraper, atteindre (qn). (*b*) Doubler, dépasser, gagner de vitesse (un concurrent, une voiture, un bateau). *Aut:* To o. three abreast, doubler en troisième position. *P.N:* Do not o., défense de doubler. **2.** (*Of accident*) Arriver à (qn); (*of misfortune, etc.*) s'abattre sur (qn). Overtaken by a storm, surpris par un orage. **overtaking**, *s.* *Aut:* Dépassement *m. P.N:* No overtaking, défense de doubler.

overtax ['ouvə'tæks], *v.tr.* (*a*) Pressurer (le peuple). (*b*) Trop exiger de (qn). To o. one's strength, se surmener; abuser de ses forces.

overthrow¹ ['ouvəθrou], *s.* Renversement *m* (d'un empire); ruine *f*, défaite *f* (de qn, d'un projet).

overthrow² [,ouvə'θrou], *v.tr.* (*Conj. like* THROW) **1.** Renverser. **2.** Défaire, vaincre (qn); mettre à bas (un empire); renverser, culbuter (un ministère, etc.); ruiner, réduire à néant (les projets de qn).

overtime ['ouvətaim]. **1.** *s.* *Ind:* Heures *f* supplémentaires (de travail). **2.** *adv.* To work o., faire des heures supplémentaires.

overtone ['ouvətoun], *s.* *Mus:* Harmonique *m.*

overtop ['ouvə'tɔp], *v.tr.* (overtopped) **1.** Dépasser en hauteur. **2.** Surpasser (qn).

overtrump ['ouvə'trʌmp], *v.tr.* *Cards:* Surcouper. **overtrumping**, *s.* Surcoupe *f.*

overture ['ouvətjuər], *s.* **1.** Ouverture *f*, offre *f.* To make overtures to s.o., faire des ouvertures à qn. **2.** *Mus:* Ouverture.

overturn ['ouvə'tə:n]. **1.** *v.tr.* Renverser; mettre (qch.) sens dessus dessous; faire verser (une voiture); (faire) chavirer (un canot). **2.** *v.i.* (*a*) Se renverser; (*of boat*) chavirer. **3.** *Aut: Av:* Capoter.

overvaluation ['ouvə,vælju'eiʃ(ə)n], *s.* Surestimation *f*, surévaluation *f.*

overvalue ['ouvə'vælju(:)], *v.tr.* **1.** *Com:* Surestimer, surévaluer. **2.** Faire trop de cas de (qch.).

overvoltage ['ouvə'voultidʒ], *s.* *El:* Surtension *f.*

overweening [,ouvə'wi:niŋ], *a.* Outrecuidant, présomptueux, -euse, suffisant.

overweight ['ouvəweit]. **1.** *s.* (*a*) Surpoids *m*; excédent *m* (de poids). (*b*) Excédent (de bagages). **2.** *a.* Parcel two pounds o., colis qui excède, dépasse, de deux livres le poids réglementaire. **He's rather o.**, il a de l'embonpoint.

overwhelm [,ouvə'(h)welm], *v.tr.* **1.** Ensevelir (une ville dans la lave, etc.); submerger. **2.** (*a*) Écraser, accabler (l'ennemi, etc.). (*b*) To be overwhelmed with work, être accablé, débordé, de travail. (*c*) Combler (qn de bontés); confondre (qn de honte). I am overwhelmed by your kindness, je suis confus de vos bontés. Overwhelmed with joy, au comble de la joie. **overwhelming**, *a.* Irrésistible; accablant. O. majority, majorité écrasante.

overwork¹ ['ouvəwə:k, 'ouvə'wə:k], *s.* **1.** Travail *m* en plus. **2.** Surmenage *m.*

overwork² ['ouvə'wə:k]. **1.** *v.tr.* (*a*) Surmener; surcharger (qn) de travail. *F:* He doesn't exactly o., il ne se fatigue pas les méninges; il ne se foule pas la rate. (*b*) To o. a device, abuser d'un truc. **2.** *v.i.* Se surmener; travailler outre mesure.

overwrought ['ouvə'rɔ:t], *a.* (*a*) (*Of pers.*) Excédé (de fatigue); surmené. (*b*) O. senses, sens surexcités.

ovibos ['ouvibɔs], *s.* Ovibos *m*; bœuf musqué.

oviduct ['ouvidʌkt], *s.* Oviducte *m.*

oviform ['ouvifɔ:m], *a.* Oviforme, ovoïde.

ovine ['ouvain], *a.* (Race *f*) ovine.

oviparous [ou'vipərəs], *a.* Ovipare.

ovoid ['ouvɔid], *a.* Ovoïde.

ovolo, *pl.* -li ['ouvolou, -li], *s.* *Arch:* Boudin *m* (de base de colonne); quart *m* de rond.

ovule ['ouvju:l], *s.* *Biol:* Ovule *m.*

ovum, *pl.* ova ['ouvəm, 'ouvə], *s.* *Biol:* Ovule *m*; œuf *m.*

owe [ou], *v.tr.* (owed [oud]) Devoir. **1.** (*a*) To o. s.o. sth., to o. sth. to s.o., devoir qch. à qn. *Abs.* I still o. you for the petrol, je vous dois encore l'essence. (*b*) To o. respect to one's father, devoir du respect à son père. To o. allegiance to s.o., devoir obéissance à qn. I o. it to my friends to spare them this sorrow,

je dois à mes amis de leur éviter ce chagrin. **2.** I o. my life to you, je vous dois la vie. He owes his ability to his mother, il tient sa capacité de sa mère. To what do I o. this honour? qu'est-ce qui me vaut cet honneur? **owing. 1.** *Pred.a.* Dû, *f.* due. All the money o. to me, tout l'argent qui m'est dû. **2.** *Prep.phr.* O. to, à cause de, par suite de. O. to a recent bereavement . . ., en raison d'un deuil récent. . . . All this is o. to your carelessness, tout cela vient de votre négligence.

owl [aul], *s.* *Orn:* Hibou *m*, -oux. The o., le hibou. Little o., chouette *f* chevêche. Brown o., wood o., tawny o., chat-huant *m*; chouette des bois; chouette hulotte. Barn o., screech owl, chouette effraie. Horn(ed) o., duc *m.* *F:* Drunk as an o., saoul comme une bourrique.

owlet ['aulit], *s.* *Orn:* Jeune hibou. 'owlet moth, *s.* *Ent:* Noctuelle *f.*

owlish ['auliʃ], *a.* De hibou. He looks o., il a des yeux de hibou; il a l'air de tomber de la lune.

own¹ [oun], *v.tr.* **1.** Posséder. Who owns this land? quel est le propriétaire de cette terre? **2.** Reconnaître. (*a*) To o. a child, reconnaître un enfant. Dog nobody will o., chien que personne ne réclame. (*b*) Avouer (qch.); convenir de (qch.). I o. I was wrong, j'ai eu tort, je l'avoue, j'en conviens. To o. oneself beaten, s'avouer vaincu. (*c*) Reconnaître l'autorité de (qn). **3.** *v.ind.tr.* To o. to a mistake, reconnaître, avouer, une erreur; convenir d'une erreur. She owns (up) to (being) thirty, elle accuse trente ans. To o. up to a crime, faire l'aveu d'un crime. To o. up to having done sth., avouer avoir fait qch. *Abs.F:* To o. up, faire des aveux.

own². 1. *a.* (*a*) *attrib.* Propre. Her o. money, son propre argent; son argent à elle. O. brother, sister, frère germain, sœur germaine. I had my o. table, j'avais ma table à part. I do my o. cooking, je fais la cuisine moi-même; jc fais ma propre cuisine. (*b*) *Pred.* Le mien, le tien, etc.; à moi, à toi, etc. The house is my o., la maison est à moi; la maison m'appartient (en propre). My time is my own, mon temps est à moi; je suis libre de mon temps. **2.** *s.* My o., his o., *etc.* (*a*) Le mien, le sien, etc. I have money of my o., j'ai de l'argent à moi. He has a copy of his o., il a un exemplaire à lui, en propre. For reasons of his o., pour des raisons particulières, à lui connues. A style all one's o., un style original. May I have it for my o.? est-ce que je peux l'avoir pour moi seul? To come into one's o., rentrer en possession de son bien. (*b*) To do sth. on one's o., faire qch. (i) de sa propre initiative, de son chef; (ii) indépendamment, à soi tout seul. I am (all) on my o. to-day, je suis seul aujourd'hui.

owner ['ounər], *s.* Propriétaire *mf*, possesseur *m*; patron, -onne (d'une maison de commerce). Joint owners, copossesseurs. Cars parked here at owner's risk, garage pour autos aux risques et périls de leurs propriétaires. *Aut:* O.-driver, conducteur *m* propriétaire.

ownerless ['ounəlis], *a.* Sans propriétaire. O. dog, chien *m* sans maître, *Adm:* chien épave.

ownership ['ounəʃip], *s.* (Droit *m* de) propriété *f*; possession *f.* Bare o., nue propriété. *P.N:* (*On shop, etc.*) Under new o., changement *m* de propriétaire.

ox, *pl.* oxen [ɔks, 'ɔks(ə)n], *s.* Bœuf *m.* Wild oxen, bovidés *m* sauvages. Ox team driver, pique-bœuf *m.* 'ox-bow, *s.* **1.** Collier *m* de bœuf. **2.** *Geog:* Ox-bow lake, bras mort (d'un cours d'eau). 'ox-cart, *s.* Char *m* à bœufs. 'ox-eye, *s.* *Bot:* Ox-e. daisy, grande marguerite; œil-de-bœuf *m*, *pl.* œils-de-bœuf. 'ox-pecker, *s.* *Orn:* Pique-bœuf *m.* 'ox-tail, *s.* *Cu:* Queue *f* de bœuf. Oxtail soup, crème *f* de queue de bœuf. 'ox-tongue, *s.* Langue *f* de bœuf.

oxalate ['ɔksəleit], *s.* *Ch:* Oxalate *m.*

oxalic [ɔk'sælik], *a.* *Ch:* Oxalique.

oxalis ['ɔksəlis], *s.* *Bot:* Oxalide *f*, oxalis *f.*

Oxford ['ɔksfə:d]. *Pr.n.Geog:* Oxford. *attrib.* O. blue, (i) bleu foncé; (ii) étudiant (de l'Université d'Oxford) qui a reçu une distinction sportive. O. shoes, *s.* oxfords, (chaussures) richelieus *mpl.* He's an O. man, (i) il a fait, (ii) il fait, ses études à Oxford.

oxherd [ˈɔkshəːd], s. Bouvier m.
oxhide [ˈɔkshaid], s. Cuir m de bœuf.
oxidant [ˈɔksidənt], s. Ch: Oxydant m; Rockets: comburant m.
oxide [ˈɔksaid], s. Ch: Oxyde m.
oxidizable [ˈɔksidaizəbl], a. Ch: Oxydable.
oxidization [ɔksidaiˈzeiʃ(ə)n], s. Ch: Oxydation f. Metall: Calcination f.
oxidize [ˈɔksidaiz]. 1. v.tr. Ch: Oxyder. Metall: Calciner. 2. v.i. S'oxyder. **oxidizing**, s. Oxydation f.
oxidizer [ˈɔksidaizər], s. Ch: Oxydant m.
oxlip [ˈɔkslip], s. Primevère f à grandes fleurs.
Oxonian [ɔkˈsounjən]. 1. a. Oxonien, -ienne. 2. s. Membre m de l'Université d'Oxford.
oxyacetylene [ˈɔksiəˈsetiliːn], attrib.a. Metalw: Oxy-acétylénique. O. **cutting out**, F: découpage m au chalumeau. O. **cutting torch**, chalumeau m de découpage. S.a. WELDING.
oxygen [ˈɔksidʒen], s. Ch: Oxygène m. O. **cylinder**, bouteille f d'oxygène. O. **tent**, tente f à oxygène.
oxygenate [ɔkˈsidʒineit], v.tr. Ch: Oxygéner.
oxyhaemoglobin [ˈɔksihiːmoˈgloubin], s. Physiol: Oxyhémoglobine f.

oxyhydrogen [ˈɔksiˈhaidridʒ(ə)n], attrib.a. (Of blow-pipe, light) Oxhydrique.
oyes! oyez! [ouˈjes], int. Oyez!
oyster [ˈɔistər], s. Huître f. Pearl o., huître perlière, à perle. He's as close as an o., il sait garder un secret. ˈoyster-bed, s. Huîtrière f. (a) Banc m d'huîtres. (b) Parc m à huîtres. ˈoyster-breeder, s. Ostréiculteur m. ˈoyster-breeding, s. Ostréiculture f. ˈoyster-catcher, s. Orn: Huîtrier-pie m. oyster-dealer, s. Écailler, -ère; marchand, -ande, d'huîtres. ˈoyster-farm, s. Parc m à huîtres; clayère f. ˈoyster-farming, s. L'industrie huîtrière, ostréicole. ˈoyster-knife, s. Ouvre-huîtres m inv. ˈoyster-shell, s. Écaille f d'huître.
oysterpiece [ˈɔistəpiːs], s. Cu: Sot-l'y-laisse m.
ozocerite [ouˈzɔsərait], **ozokerit(e)** [ouˈzoukərit], s. Miner: Ozocérite f, ozokérite f; cire minérale.
ozone [ˈouzoun], s. Ch: Ozone m.
ozonization [ouzonaiˈzeiʃ(ə)n], s. Ch: Ozonisation f.
ozonize [ˈouzonaiz], v.tr. Ch: Ozoniser.
ozonizer [ˈouzonaizər], s. Ch: Ozoniseur m.
ozonosphere [ouˈzounɔsfiːər], s. Meteor: Ozonosphère f.

P, p [piː], s. (La lettre) P, p m. **To mind one's P's and Q's,** (i) se surveiller; (ii) faire bien attention. *Tp:* P for Peter, P comme Pierre.

pa [pɑː], s.m. *F:* Papa.

pace¹ [peis], s. 1. Pas m. **Ten paces off,** à dix pas de distance. 2. (a) **Paces of a horse,** allures f d'un cheval. **To put s.o. through his paces,** mettre qn à l'épreuve. (b) (*Speed*) Vitesse f, train m, allure. **To gather p.,** prendre de la vitesse. **At a good, a smart, p.,** à vive allure. **At a walking p.,** au pas. **At a rapid p.,** d'un pas rapide. **To quicken one's p.,** hâter, presser, le pas. *Sp:* **To set, make, the p.,** mener le train. **To keep p. with s.o.,** marcher de pair avec qn. *F:* **To go the p.,** (i) mener la vie à grandes guides; (ii) mener un train d'enfer. 3. *Equit:* Amble m. **'pace(-)maker,** s. *Sp:* (a) Entraîneur m. (b) Meneur m de train. *Cy:* Pacemaker.

pace². 1. *v.i.* (a) Aller au pas; marcher à pas mesurés. **To p. up and down,** faire les cent pas. (b) *Equit:* Ambler; aller l'amble. 2. *v.tr.* (a) Arpenter (la rue, etc.). (b) **To p. (off) a distance,** mesurer une distance au pas. (c) *Sp:* Entraîner (un cycliste, etc.).

-paced ['peist], a. **Even-p.,** à l'allure égale. **Easy-p. horse,** cheval au train doux.

pachyderm ['pækidəːm], s. Pachyderme m.

pachydermatous [ˌpækiˈdəːmətəs], a. Pachyderme; à la peau épaisse.

pacific [pəˈsifik], a. 1. (a) Pacifique. (b) Paisible. 2. *Geog:* **The P. (Ocean),** l'océan m Pacifique; le Pacifique.

pacification [ˌpæsifiˈkeiʃ(ə)n], s. Pacification f; apaisement m.

pacifier ['pæsifaiər], s. 1. Pacificateur, -trice. 2. *U.S:* Sucette f (pour bébés).

pacifism ['pæsifizm], s. Pacifisme m.

pacifist ['pæsifist], s. & a. Pacifiste (mf).

pacify ['pæsifai], v.tr. Pacifier (une foule, un pays); apaiser, calmer (qn). **pacifying,** a. Pacificateur, -trice.

pack¹ [pæk], s. 1. (a) Paquet m; balle f (de coton); ballot m (de colporteur); bât m (de bête de charge). *Mil:* Paquetage m; sac m d'ordonnance. (b) *F: Pej:* **P. of lies,** tissu m, tas m, de mensonges. 2. (a) Bande f (de loups, de voleurs). **P. of fools,** tas d'imbéciles. (b) *Rugby Fb:* **The p.,** le pack. (c) *Ven:* **P. of hounds,** meute f. 3. Jeu m (de cartes, de dominos). 4. (Ice-)p., embâcle m (de glaçons); pack. 5. (a) *Med:* **Cold p., wet p.,** enveloppement froid, humide. (b) *Toil:* Emplâtre m. **'pack-animal,** s. Bête f de charge, de somme. **'pack-cloth,** s. Toile f d'emballage. **'pack-drill,** s. *Mil:* Punition f de l'exercice en tenue de route. **'pack-'full,** a. Plein à déborder. **'pack-horse, -mule,** s. Cheval m, mulet m, de bât, de somme. **'pack-ice,** s. Glace f de banquise; pack m. **'pack-road,** s. Chemin muletier. **'pack-saddle,** s. Bât m. **'pack-trail,** s. Piste muletière. **'pack-train,** s. Convoi m de bêtes de somme. **'pack-wool,** s. Laine f en balles.

pack² (packed [pækt]). I. *v.tr.* 1. (a) Emballer, empaqueter. *Abs.* **To p.,** faire ses malles, *P:* faire son baluchon. **To p. up,** (i) plier bagage, *F:* prendre ses cliques et ses claques; (ii) cesser; (iii) (*of engine*) flancher. *P:* **P. it up!** (i) cesse de faire ça! (ii) ta gueule! la ferme! **Tent that packs (up) easily,** tente qui est facile à emballer. (b) *Com:* Conserver (la viande) en boîtes; embariller (des harengs). 2. Tasser (de la terre dans un trou, etc.); serrer (des voyageurs dans une voiture). **Packed (in) like herrings, like sardines (in a box),** serrés comme des harengs en caque. 3. Remplir, bourrer (sth. with sth., qch. de qch.). **To p. one's trunk,** faire sa malle. **The train was packed (with people),** le train était bondé. **Packed hall,** salle comble. **Book packed with facts,** livre bourré de faits. 4. *Mch:* Garnir (un gland, un piston); étouper (un gland). 5. (a) **To p. a jury,** se composer un jury favorable. **To p. a meeting,** s'assurer un nombre prépondérant de

partisans à une réunion. **Packed meeting,** salle faite d'avance. (b) *Cards:* Apprêter (les cartes). 6. (a) **To p. a child off to bed,** envoyer un enfant au lit. (b) *F:* **To send s.o. packing,** envoyer promener qn. 7. *U.S:* **To p. a pistol,** porter un revolver. II. **pack,** *v.i.* 1. (*Of earth, etc.*) Se tasser. 2. (*Of people*) S'attrouper. **They packed round the speaker,** ils se pressaient autour de l'orateur. **packing,** s. 1. (a) Emballage m, empaquetage m. **Non-returnable p.,** emballage perdu. **To do one's p.,** faire ses malles. (b) Conservation f (de la viande, etc.). 2. Tassement m, agglomération f (de la terre, etc.). 3. *Mch:* Garnissage m; étoupage m (d'un gland). 4. (a) Matière f pour garnitures, pour emballage. (b) *Mch:* Garniture f (d'un piston, etc.). **'packing-case,** s. Caisse f, boîte f, d'emballage. **'packing-needle,** s. Carrelet m; aiguille f d'emballage, d'emballeur. **'packing-paper,** s. Papier m d'emballage; papier gris. **'packing-ring,** s. 1. *Mec.E:* Rondelle f, bague f, de garniture. 2. *Mch:* Segment m, bague, garniture f (de piston). **'packing-sheet,** s. Drap m d'emballage.

package¹ ['pækidʒ], s. 1. Empaquetage m, emballage m. 2. Paquet m, colis m, ballot m. **'package deal,** s. *Pol. Ec: Ind: Com:* Contrat global. **'package store,** s. *U.S:* Magasin m vendant les boissons alcooliques pour consommation à domicile. **'package tour,** s. Voyage organisé.

package², *v.tr. Com:* Conditionner (des marchandises). **packaged,** a. *Com:* Préconditionné. **packaging,** s. *Com:* Conditionnement m.

packager ['pækidʒər], s. *Com:* Conditionneur, -euse.

packer ['pækər], s. Emballeur, -euse. *Com:* Conditionneur, -euse.

packet ['pækit], s. 1. (a) Paquet m; pochette f (de papier etc.). **P. of needles,** sachet m d'aiguilles. (b) Colis m; article m de messagerie. **Postal p.,** colis postal. 2. **P. (-boat),** paquebot m.

packman, pl. **-men** ['pækmən], s.m. *A:* Colporteur, porteballe.

packthread ['pækθred], s. Fil m d'emballage.

pact [pækt], s. Pacte m, convention f, contrat m. **To make a p. with s.o.,** faire, signer, un pacte avec qn; *Pej:* pactiser (avec qn).

pad¹ [pæd], s. 1. *Dial: P:* Chemin m, route f. **To be on the p.,** être sur le trimard. *S.a.* FOOTPAD. 2. Bruit sourd des pas (d'un loup etc.).

pad², *v.tr. & i.* (padded) (a) *F:* Aller à pied. *O:* **To p. it, to p. the hoof,** trimarder. (b) (*Of wolf, etc.*) **To p. (along),** trotter à pas sourds. (*Of pers.*) **To p. about the room,** aller et venir à pas feutrés, à pas de loup.

pad³, s. 1. (a) Bourrelet m, coussinet m. *Fb:* **Ankle-p.,** protège-cheville m inv. (b) Tampon m (d'ouate, etc.). **Stamp p.,** tampon à timbrer. **Inking p.,** tampon encreur. **Engraver's p.,** tapette f. (c) *Toil:* **Hair-p.,** crêpé m. (d) *Harn:* Sellette f (de cheval de trait). **Collar p.,** coussin m de collier. (e) *Fenc:* Plastron m. 2. (a) Pelote digitale; pulpe f (du doigt, de l'orteil). (b) Patte f (de lapin, de chameau, etc.). 3. (a) Bloc m (de papier). **Note-p.,** bloc-notes m. (b) Sous-main m. *S.a.* BLOTTING-PAD, WRITING-PAD. 4. *Tls:* (a) Mandrin m (de vilebrequin). (b) Manche m porte-outils. (c) *Aut:* Plaquette f (d'un frein à disque). 5. Support m, amortisseur m; cale f de support; tampon amortisseur. *Ball:* **Launching p.,** base f de lancement (pour engins).

pad⁴, *v.tr.* (padded) 1. Rembourrer (un coussin); matelasser (une porte); capitonner (un meuble); ouater (un vêtement). *Tail:* Garnir (les épaules d'un vêtement). **Padded cell,** cellule matelassée; cabanon m. 2. *F:* **To p. (out) a chapter,** tirer à la ligne. **To p. a speech,** délayer un discours. **padding,** s. 1. (a) Remplissage m, rembourrage m. (b) Délayage m (d'un discours); *F:* bla-bla-bla m. 2. (a) Ouate f, bourre f; coussin m de collier de cheval. (b) Remplissage (dans une œuvre littéraire).

paddle[1] ['pædl], s. 1. Pagaie f. 2. (a) Aube f, pale f, palette f, jantille f (de roue hydraulique). (b) = PADDLE-WHEEL. 3. Nageoire f (de cétacé, de tortue); aileron m (de requin). 'paddle-boat, s. Bateau m à aubes, à roues. 'paddle-wheel, s. Roue f à aubes, à palettes.

paddle[2], s. Row: (a) Allure douce. (b) Promenade f (en canot) à allure douce.

paddle[3]. (a) v.tr. Pagayer. F: To p. one's own canoe, conduire seul sa barque; se débrouiller tout seul. (b) v.i. Row: Tirer en douce. (c) U.S: Donner une fessée à, fesser, un enfant.

paddle[4], v.i. Barboter, F: grenouiller (dans l'eau); patauger (dans l'eau, la boue). 'paddling-pool, s. Bassin m à patauger; F: grenouillère f (pour les enfants).

paddler ['pædlər], s. 1. Pagayeur, -euse. 2. pl. Cost: Paddlers, barboteuse f (d'enfant).

paddock ['pædək], s. (a) Parc m, enclos m (pour chevaux). To put a horse in the p., parquer un cheval. (b) Turf: Pesage m, paddock m.

paddy[1] ['pædi], s. Com: Paddy m (riz non décortiqué). P.-field, rizière f.

Paddy[2]. 1. Pr.n.m. (Dim. of Patrick) (a) Patrice. (b) s.m. F: Un Irlandais. (c) U.S: P: Agent m de police. 2. s. P: To be in a p., être en colère. 3. U.S: F: P. wagon, panier m à salade (de la police).

padlock[1] ['pædlɔk], s. Cadenas m.

padlock[2], v.tr. Cadenasser; fermer (une porte) au cadenas.

padre ['pɑːdri], s.m. Aumônier (militaire).

paean ['piːən], s. Gr.Ant: Péan m.

paederast ['pedəræst], s. Pédéraste m.

paederasty ['piːdəræsti], s. Pédérastie f.

paediatrician [piːdiə'triʃ(ə)n], **paediatrist** [‚piːdi'ætrist], s. Med: = PEDIATRICIAN, PEDIATRIST.

paediatrics [‚piːdi'ætriks], **paediatry** [‚piːdi'ætri], s. Med: = PEDIATRICS, PEDIATRY.

pagan ['peigən], a. & s. Païen, -ienne.

paganism ['peigənizm], s. Paganisme m.

page[1] [peidʒ], s. 1. (a) A: Petit laquais. (b) Page m. P. of honour, page du roi, de la reine. 2. (i) P.(-boy), petit groom (d'hôtel); chasseur m. (ii) attrib: Haird: P.-b. bob, style, coiffure f à l'ange.

page[2], v.tr. 1. Faire chercher, appeler (qn) par un chasseur. 2. O: Servir (qn) comme page.

page[3], s. Page f. Right-hand p., recto m. Left-hand p., verso m. On p. 6, à la page 6. 'page-proof, s. Typ: Épreuve f en pages.

page[4], v.tr. 1. Numéroter (les feuilles); paginer (un livre); folioter (un registre). 2. Typ: Mettre (la composition) en pages. **paging**, s. 1. Pagination f, foliotage m. 2. Typ: Mise f en pages.

pageant ['pædʒ(ə)nt], s. 1. Spectacle pompeux. 2. Grand spectacle historique donné en costume.

pageantry ['pædʒ(ə)ntri], s. Apparat m, pompe f.

paginate ['pædʒineit], v.tr. Paginer; folioter.

pagination [‚pædʒi'neif(ə)n], s. Pagination f.

pagoda [pə'goudə], s. Pagode f.

pah [pɑː], int. Pouah!

paid. See PAY[1].

pail [peil], s. 1. Seau m; (wooden) seille f. Nau: Baille f. 2. A p. of water, un seau d'eau.

pailful ['peilful], s. (a) (Plein) seau (de lait, etc.).

pain[1] [pein]. 1. (a) Douleur f, souffrance f; (mental) peine f. To give s.o. p., (i) (of tooth, etc.) faire mal à qn, faire souffrir qn; (ii) (of incident, etc.) faire de la peine à qn. To be in great p., souffrir beaucoup. To put a wounded animal out of its p., achever un animal blessé. (b) A p. in the side, une douleur dans le côté; un point de côté. To have a p., pains, in one's head, souffrir de la tête. Shooting pains, douleurs lancinantes, élancements mpl. F: He is, gives me, a p. in the neck, il me tape sur le système, il est enquiquinant. 2. pl. Pains, peine. To take pains, be at great pains, to do sth., prendre, se donner, de la peine pour faire qch.; se donner du mal pour faire qch. To take pains over sth., s'appliquer à qch.; y mettre tous ses soins. To take pains to grow old gracefully, mettre une certaine coquetterie à vieillir. To have one's labour for one's pains, en être pour sa peine, pour ses frais. 3. A: Châtiment m. Still so used in On p. of death, sous peine de mort. 'pain-

killer, 'pain-reliever, s. Anodin m, antalgique m, analgésique m, calmant m.

pain[2], v.tr. Faire souffrir (qn); (physically) faire mal à (qn); (mentally) faire de la peine à (qn); peiner, affliger (qn). It pains me to say so, cela me coûte à dire; il m'en coûte de le dire. **pained**, a. Attristé, peiné (at). To look p., avoir l'air blessé, froissé.

painful ['peinf(u)l], a. 1. (Of wound) Douloureux. (Of limb, etc.) To become p., s'endolorir. My knee was getting p., mon genou commençait à me faire mal. 2. (Of spectacle, effort) Pénible. P. to behold, pénible à voir. It is p. to hear him, cela fait peine de l'entendre. **-fully**, adv. Douloureusement; péniblement.

painfulness ['peinfulnis], s. Caractère douloureux, pénible (of, de).

painless ['peinlis], a. 1. (Extraction, etc.) sans douleur. 2. P. tumour, tumeur indolente, indolore.

painlessness ['peinlisnis], s. Absence f de douleur.

painstaking ['peinz‚teikiŋ], 1. a. Soigneux, assidu; (élève) travailleur, appliqué; (travail) soigné. 2. s. Soin m. With a little p. you will manage it, en vous donnant un peu de peine vous y arriverez.

paint[1] [peint], s. (a) Peinture f. Gloss(y) p., peinture vernis. Mat(t) p., peinture mate. Coat of p., couche f de peinture. Give it a coat of p., passez-y une couche (de peinture). 'Mind the p.!' 'Wet p.!' "attention à la peinture!" (b) Box of paints, boîte de couleurs. 'paint-brush, s. Pinceau m. **paint**(-) **roller**, s. Rouleau m à peinture. 'paint-sprayer, s. Pistolet m à peindre; pulvérisateur m (de peinture).

paint[2], v.tr. 1. (a) To p. a portrait in oils, peindre un portrait à l'huile. To p. a sunset, peindre un coucher de soleil. (b) Abs. Faire de la peinture. 2. Dépeindre. What words can p. the scene? comment dépeindre cette scène? 3. (a) Enduire de peinture; peinturer. To p. a door green, peindre une porte en vert. Th: To p. the scenery for a play, brosser les décors d'une pièce. P: To p. the town red, faire une noce à tout casser; F: faire la nouba. (b) To p. one's face, se farder; F: Pej: se plâtrer (le visage). (c) Med: Badigeonner (la gorge, etc.). To p. with iodine, badigeonner à la teinture d'iode. **painting**, s. Peinture f. 1. (a) To study p., étudier la peinture. (b) Med: Badigeonnage m. (c) (Ornamental) p., décoration f (en bâtiment, etc.). 2. Tableau m (à l'huile ou à l'aquarelle).

painter[1] ['peintər], s. 1. (a) Art: Peintre m. The p. of the picture, l'auteur m du tableau. She was a famous p., elle fut un peintre célèbre. S.a. PORTRAIT-PAINTER, SCENE-PAINTER, etc. (b) Coloriste mf (de jouets, etc.). 2. (House-)p., peintre en bâtiments; peintre décorateur.

painter[2], s. Nau: Amarre f. To slip the p., (i) filer son amarre, son nœud; (ii) F: mourir. To cut the p., couper, trancher, l'amarre.

paintwork ['peintwəːk], s. (House-building) Les peintures f.

pair[1] [peər], s. 1. (a) Paire f. Arranged in pairs, arrangés deux par deux, par paires. The p. of you, vous deux. F: Another p. of shoes, une autre paire de manches. (b) A p. of trousers, un pantalon. (c) Carriage and p., voiture f à deux chevaux. P. of oxen, paire de bœufs. (d) (Man and wife) Couple m. P. of pigeons (cock and hen), couple m de pigeons. (e) These two pictures are a p., ces deux tableaux se font pendant. (f) Where is the p. of this glove? où se trouve l'autre gant de cette paire? (g) Row: Deux m. 2. O: P. of stairs, escalier m (en deux volées); étage m. To lodge on the three-p. front, back, loger au troisième (étage) sur la rue, sur la cour. P. of steps, escabeau m.

pair[2]. 1. v.tr. (a) Appareiller, apparier, assortir (des gants, etc.). (b) Accoupler, apparier (des oiseaux, etc.). 2. v.i. (a) Faire la paire (with sth., avec qch.). Two vases that p., deux vases qui (se) font pendant. (b) (Of birds, etc.) S'accoupler, s'apparier. (c) Parl: To p. (off), s'absenter après entente avec un adversaire qui désire aussi s'absenter. **pair off.** 1. v.tr. Arranger, distribuer, deux par deux. 2. v.i. S'en aller, défiler, deux par deux. **paired**, a. En couples; deux par deux. Artil: Guns p. on turret, canons conjugués. **pairing**, s. (a) Appariement m (de chaussures etc.); conjugaison *f* (de machines, des canons d'une tourelle); appareillement *m* (de bœufs pour le joug.) (*b*) Appariement *m*, accouplement *m* (d'animaux mâle et femelle). (*c*) *T.V:* Pairage *m*.

pair³. *Used in the a. phr.* au pair. An au p. student, un étudiant, une étudiante, au pair.

pajamas [pə'dʒɑːməz], *s.pl. U.S:* = PYJAMAS.

Pakistan [pɑːkis'tɑːn], *Pr.n. Geog:* Le Pakistan.

Pakistani [pɑːkis'tɑːni], *a. & s.* Pakistanais, -aise.

pal¹ [pæl], *s. P:* Camarade *mf; P:* copain, *f.* copine.

pal², *v.i.* (**palled** [pæld]) *P:* To p. up with s.o., se lier (d'amitié) avec qn; *P:* devenir copain avec qn.

palace ['pæləs], *s.* Palais *m.* **Bishop's p.,** évêché *m;* palais épiscopal.

paladin ['pælədin], *s.* Paladin *m.*

pal(a)eographer [,pæli'ogrəfər], *s.* Paléographe *m;* archiviste *m.*

pal(a)eographic(al) [,pæliə'græfik(l)], *a.* Paléographique.

pal(a)eography [,pæli'ografi], *s.* Paléographie *f.*

pal(a)eolithic [,pæliə'liθik], *a.* Paléolithique. **The p. age,** l'âge de la pierre taillée.

pal(a)eontologist [,pælion'tolədʒist], *s.* Paléontologiste *mf,* paléontologue *mf.*

pal(a)eontology [,pælion'tolədʒi], *s.* Paléontologie *f.*

pal(a)eozoic [,pæliə'zouik], *a. Geol:* Paléozoïque.

palais de danse [,pæleidə'dɑːns], *s.* Dancing *m.*

palanquin [,pælən'kiːn], *s.* Palanquin *m.*

palatable ['pælətəbl], *a.* (*a*) Agréable au palais, au goût. (*b*) (*Of doctrine, etc.*) Agréable (to, à).

palatal ['pælətl], *Ling:* 1. *a.* Palatal, -aux. **P. l, l mouillé.** 2. *s.* Palatale *f.*

palatalization ['pælətəlai'zeiʃ(ə)n, pə'læt-], *s. Ling:* Palatalisation *f.*

palatalize ['pælətəlaiz, pə'læt-], *v.tr. Ling:* Mouiller (un l, la combinaison gn).

palate ['pælit], *s.* (*a*) *Anat:* (Hard) p., palais *m.* Soft p., voile *m* du palais. Cleft p., palais fendu. (*b*) To have a delicate p., avoir le palais fin.

palatial [pə'leiʃ(ə)l], *a.* (Édifice) qui ressemble à un palais; magnifique, grandiose.

palatinate [pə'lætinit], *Hist:* The P., le Palatinat.

palatine ['pælətain], *a. & s.* 1. *Hist:* Palatin, -ine. 2. *A.Geog:* The P. (Hill), le (mont) Palatin.

palaver¹ [pə'lɑːvər], *s.* 1. Palabre *f.* 2. *F:* (*a*) Cajoleries *fpl;* flagornerie *f.* (*b*) Embarras *mpl.* None of your p.! pas tant d'histoires! (*c*) Bavardages *mpl.*

palaver², *v.i.* Palabrer.

pale¹ [peil], *s.* 1. Pieu *m* (de clôture). 2. *A:* Bornes *fpl,* limites *fpl.* Still so used in Outside the p. of society, beyond the p., au ban de la société. Within the p. of the Church, dans le giron, dans le sein, de l'Église. 3. *Her:* Pal *m.* party per p., parti.

pale², *a.* (*a*) Pâle, blême. Deadly p., ghastly p., pâle comme la mort, comme un mort; d'une pâleur mortelle. To grow, turn, p., pâlir. (*b*) (*Of colour*) P. blue dress, robe d'un bleu pâle; robe bleu clair. By the p. light of the moon, à la lumière blafarde de la lune. 'pale-face, *s.* Blanc, *f.* blanche (dans le parler des Peaux-Rouges). 'pale-faced, *a.* Au visage pâle, blême.

pale³, *v.i.* (*a*) Pâlir, blêmir. (*b*) My adventures p. beside yours, before yours, mes aventures pâlissent auprès des vôtres.

paleness ['peilnis], *s.* Pâleur *f.*

Palestine ['pæləstain]. *Pr.n.* La Palestine.

palette ['pælit], *s. Art:* Palette *f.* To set the p., faire, charger, sa palette.

palfrey ['pɔːlfri], *s. Lit:* Palefroi *m.*

palimpsest ['pælimpsest], *a. & s.* Palimpseste (*m*).

palindrome ['pælindroum], *s.* Palindrome *m.*

paling(s) ['peiliŋ(z)], *s.(pl.)* Clôture *f* à clairevoie; palissade *f,* palis *m.*

palisade¹ [,pæli'seid], *s.* Palissade *f.*

palisade², *v.tr.* Palissader.

palish ['peiliʃ], *a.* Un peu pâle; pâlot, -otte.

pall¹ [pɔːl], *s.* 1. *Ecc:* Poêle *m;* drap *m* mortuaire. 2. Manteau *m* (de neige, etc.); voile *m* (de fumée, etc.). 'pall-bearer, *s.* Porteur *m* d'un cordon du poêle.

pall², *v.i.* S'affadir; devenir fade, insipide (on s.o., pour qn). These pleasures p., on se blase de ces

plaisirs. **Food, literature, that palls,** nourriture, littérature, fastidieuse. **It never palls on you,** on ne s'en dégoûte jamais.

palladium [pə'leidiəm], *s. Ch:* Palladium *m.*

pallet ['pælit], *s.* (*a*) Paillasse *f.* (*b*) Grabat *m.*

palliasse [pæl'jæs], *s.* Paillasse *f.*

palliate ['pælieit], *v.tr.* Pallier (une faute, une maladie); atténuer (un vice). **Palliating circumstances,** circonstances atténuantes.

palliation [,pæli'eiʃ(ə)n], *s.* Palliation *f* (de la misère, d'une maladie); atténuation *f* (d'une faute).

palliative ['pæliətiv], *a. & s.* Palliatif (*m*), lénitif (*m*), anodin (*m*).

pallid ['pælid], *a.* (*a*) Pâle, décoloré. (*b*) (*Of light*) Blafard. (*c*) (*Of face*) Blême.

pallidness ['pælidnis], **pallor** ['pælər], *s.* Pâleur *f.* Deathly, deadly, p., pâleur mortelle.

pally ['pæli], *a. P:* 1. Qui se lie facilement (d'amitié); liant. 2. To be p. with s.o., être lié, être copain, avec qn.

palm¹ [pɑːm], *s.* 1. (*Tree*) Palmier *m.* Dwarf p., palmette *f.* 2. (*Branch*) Palme *f. Ecc:* Rameau *m.* P. Sunday, le dimanche des Rameaux. To bear the p., remporter la palme. To yield the p. to s.o., céder la palme à qn. 'palm-'cabbage, *s.* Chou-palmiste *m.* 'palm-grove, *s.* Palmeraie *f.* 'palm-house, *s.* Serre *f* de palmiers. 'palm-oil, *s.* Huile *f* de palme, de palmier.

palm², *s.* 1. Paume (de la main). *F:* To grease, oil, s.o.'s p., graisser la patte de, à, qn. 2. *Nau:* Patte, oreille *f* (d'ancre). (*b*) *Tls:* Paumelle *f* (de voilier). 3. *Ven:* Empaumure *f* (de bois de cerf). 'palm-greasing, *s. F:* Graissage *m* de patte.

palm³, *v.tr.* To p. a card, escamoter une carte; filer la carte. palm off, *v.tr.* Faire passer, *P:* refiler (sth. on s.o., qch. à qn). To p. off a bad coin on s.o., (re)passer une fausse pièce à qn.

palmate ['pælmeit], *a. Nat.Hist:* Palmé.

palmer ['pɑːmər], *s. A:* Pèlerin *m* de retour de la Terre Sainte.

palmetto [pæl'metou], *s. Bot:* (*a*) Palmier nain; palmette *f.* (*b*) Chou-palmiste *m.*

palmiped ['pælmiped], *a. & s. Orn:* Palmipède (*m*).

palmist ['pɑːmist], *s.* Chiromancien, -ienne.

palmistry ['pɑːmistri], *s.* Chiromancie *f.*

palmy ['pɑːmi], *a. P:* days, jours heureux; époque florissante (d'une nation, etc.).

palp [pælp], *s. Nat.Hist:* Palpe *f.*

palpability [,pælpə'biliti], **palpableness** ['pælpəblnis], *s.* 1. Palpabilité *f.* 2. Évidence *f* (d'un fait, etc.).

palpable ['pælpəbl], *a.* 1. Palpable; que l'on peut toucher. 2. Palpable, manifeste, clair, évident; (différence) sensible. -ably, *adv.* 1. Palpablement. 2. Manifestement; sensiblement; évidemment.

palpate ['pælpeit], *v.tr. Med:* Palper.

palpitate ['pælpiteit], *v.tr.* Palpiter. **palpitating,** *a.* Palpitant. *F:* A p. novel, un roman palpitant (d'intérêt).

palpitation [,pælpi'teiʃ(ə)n], *s.* Palpitation *f.*

palsied ['pɔːlzid], *a.* Paralysé, paralytique.

palsy ['pɔːlzi], *s. Med:* Paralysie *f.* Cerebral p., paralysie spasmodique.

palter ['pɔːltər], *v.i.* To p. (with s.o.), biaiser (avec qn). To p. with one's honour, transiger sur, avec, l'honneur. **paltering,** *s.* Compromission *f;* faux-fuyants *mpl.*

paltriness ['pɔːltrinis], *s.* Mesquinerie *f* (d'un cadeau).

paltry ['pɔːltri], *a.* Misérable, mesquin. I had lost a p. five-franc piece, j'avais perdu une malheureuse pièce de cinq francs. P. excuses, plates excuses; pauvres excuses.

paludal ['pæljudl], *a. Med:* (*Of marsh, fever*) Paludique; paludéen, -enne.

paludism ['pæljudizm], *s. Med:* Paludisme *m.*

pampa ['pæmpə], *s. Geog:* Pampa *f.* **The Pampa(s),** la Pampa. 'pampas-grass, *s.* Gynérion argenté; *F:* herbe *f* des pampas.

pamper ['pæmpər], *v.tr.* Choyer, dorloter, mignoter (un enfant).

pamphlet ['pæmflit], *s.* Brochure *f;* (*literary, scientific*) opuscule *m;* (*scurrilous*) pamphlet *m.*

pamphleteer [,pæmfli'tiər], *s.* Auteur *m* de brochures; (*scurrilous*) pamphlétaire *m.*

pan¹ [pæn], s. 1. (a) Cu: Casserole f, poêlon m. Frying-p., poêle f. Baking-p., plat m à rôtir. Pots and pans, batterie f de cuisine. (b) Earthenware p., cocotte f en terre cuite. Art: Moist colours in pans, couleurs moites en godets. 2. (a) (i) Plateau m, (ii) bassin m (d'une balance). (b) Hyg: Lavatory p., cuvette de W.C. 3. A: (Priming-)p., bassinet m (d'un fusil). S.a. FLASH² 1, ³ 1. 4. Geol: Cuvette. S.a. SALT-PAN.

pan², v. (panned) 1. v.tr. Gold-min: To p. (out), laver (le gravier) à la bat(t)ée. 2. v.i. F: Things did not p. out as he intended, les choses ne se sont pas passées comme il l'aurait voulu.

pan³, v.tr. Esp.U.S: F: Rabaisser, exécuter (qn, qch.).

pan⁴, v.tr. (panned, panning) Cin: F: Panoramiquer (une vue). panning, s. Cin: Survol m, panoramiquage m.

Pan⁵. Pr.n.m. Myth: (Le dieu) Pan. Pan's pipes, P.-pipe, flûte f de Pan.

panacea [ˌpænəˈsiə], s. Panacée f; remède universel.

pan-African [ˈpænˈæfrikən], a. Panafricain, -aine.

Panama [ˈpænəˈmɑː]. 1. Pr.n. Geog: Le Panama. 2. s. P. (hat), panama m.

pan-American [ˈpænəˈmerikən], a. Panaméricain.

pan-Americanism [ˈpænəˈmerikənizm], s. Panaméricanisme m.

pan-Arabism [ˈpænˈærabizm], s. Panarabisme m.

pancake¹ [ˈpænkeik], s. 1. Cu: Crêpe f. P. day, mardi gras. Av: P. landing, atterrissage m sur le ventre. S.a. FLAT² I 1. 2. Nau: P. ice, gâteaux mpl de glace. 3. W.Tel: P. coil, galette f.

pancake², v.i. Av: To p. (to the ground), asseoir l'appareil; descendre à plat; (se) plaquer.

panchromatic [ˈpænkrouˈmætik], a. Phot: Panchromatique.

pancreas [ˈpæŋkriəs], s. Anat: Pancréas m.

pancreatic [ˌpæŋkriˈætik], a. Pancréatique.

panda [ˈpændə], s. Z: Panda m.

pandemonium [ˌpændiˈmounjəm], s. Pandémonium m. It's p., c'est une vraie tour de Babel. To kick up a fearful p., faire un bruit infernal. In five minutes there was p., au bout de cinq minutes ce fut une scène de désordre indescriptible.

pander¹ [ˈpændər], s. Entremetteur m, proxénète m, P: maquereau m.

pander², v.tr. & i. Servir de proxénète à (qn). To p. to a vice, encourager, se prêter à, un vice. To p. to a taste, flatter bassement un goût.

pane [pein], s. Vitre f, carreau m (de fenêtre).

panegyric [ˌpæniˈdʒirik], a. & s. Panégyrique (m).

panegyrical [ˌpæniˈdʒirikl], a. Élogieux, -euse.

panegyrist [ˌpæniˈdʒirist], s. Panégyriste m; glorificateur, -trice.

panel¹ [ˈpænl], s. 1. (a) Panneau m (de porte); caisson m (de plafond). Sunk p., panneau en retrait. Aut: Av: Instrument p., tableau m de bord. (b) Dressm: Panneau, (shaped) volant m. (c) Arch: Civ.E: Entre-deux m inv. 2. (a) Jur: Tableau, liste f, du jury. Jur: T.V: etc: The p., le jury. (b) Scot: Commission f (d'enquête, etc.). 'panel-beater, s. Aut: Tôlier m. 'panel-doctor, s. Adm: A: Médecin désigné pour le service des assurances sociales.

panel², v.tr. (panelled) 1. (a) Diviser (un mur, etc.) en panneaux. (b) Recouvrir de panneaux; lambrisser (une paroi); plaquer (une surface). 2. Dressm: Garnir (une robe) de panneaux. panelled, a. Boisé, lambrissé, revêtu de boiseries. Oak-p., à panneaux de chêne; lambrissé de chêne. P. door, porte à panneaux. panelling, s. 1. (a) Division f (d'un mur) en panneaux. (b) Lambrissage m (d'une salle). 2. Lambris m, boiserie f. Oak p., panneaux mpl de chêne.

panful [ˈpænful], s. Terrinée f, bassinée f, poêlée f.

pang [pæŋ], s. Angoisse subite; douleur f; serrement m de cœur. The pangs of death, les affres fpl, les angoisses, de la mort. To feel a p., sentir une petite pointe au cœur. To feel the pangs of hunger, entendre crier ses entrailles.

pan-Germanism [ˈpænˈdʒəːmənizm], s. Pangermanisme m.

panhandle¹ [ˈpænhændl], s. U.S: Geog: Projection étroite d'un territoire dans un autre; enclave f.

panhandle², v.i. U.S: Mendier, P: mendigoter.

panhandler [ˈpænˈhændlər], s. U.S: Mendiant m, P: mendigot m.

panic¹ [ˈpænik], a. & s. P. (terror), (terreur f) panique f; affolement m. To throw the crowd into a p., affoler la foule. They fled in a p., pris de panique ils s'enfuirent. Journ: P. press, presse f alarmiste. 'panic-monger, s. Semeur, -euse, de panique; F: paniquard m. 'panic-stricken, a. Pris de panique; affolé.

panic², v. (panicked [ˈpænikt]) 1. v.tr. Remplir de panique; affoler (la foule, etc.). 2. v.i. Être pris de panique; s'affoler.

panic³(-grass) [ˈpænik(grɑːs)], s. Panic m (d'Italie); millet m des oiseaux.

panicky [ˈpæniki], a. F: (Of pers.) Sujet à la panique; (of newspaper, etc.) alarmiste. Don't get p., ne vous impressionnez pas.

panicle [ˈpænikl], s. Bot: Panicule f.

pan-Islamism [ˈpænˈizlɑːmizm], s. Panislamisme m.

panjandrum [pænˈdʒændrəm], s. F: Gros bonnet; grand personnage. Esp. Grand, Great, P., grand manitou.

pannier [ˈpæniər], s. 1. (a) (Basket) Panier m. (b) Panier de bât (d'une bête de somme). (c) Hotte f (de vendangeur). 2. A.Cost: Dress with panniers, robe à paniers.

pannikin [ˈpænikin], s. Écuelle f, gobelet m (en fer blanc).

panoply [ˈpænəpli], s. Panoplie f.

panorama [ˌpænəˈrɑːmə], s. Panorama m.

panoramic [ˌpænəˈræmik], a. Panoramique. P. table, table f d'orientation.

pansy [ˈpænzi], s. 1. Bot: Pensée f. 2. P: Pédéraste m, P: tapette f.

pant [pænt], v.i. 1. (a) Panteler; (of animal) battre du flanc; (of heart) palpiter. (b) Haleter. To p. for breath, chercher à reprendre haleine. 2. To p. to do sth., désirer ardemment faire qch. To p. for, after, sth., soupirer après qch. panting, s. (a) Essoufflement m, halètement m. (b) Palpitation f (du cœur).

pantagruelic [ˌpæntəgruˈelik], a. (Repas, etc.) pantagruélique.

pantechnicon [pænˈteknikən], s. Camion m de déménagement.

pantees [ˈpæntiːz], s.pl. Cost: Slip m.

pantheism [ˈpænθi(ː)izm], s. Panthéisme m.

pantheist [ˈpænθi(ː)ist], s. Panthéiste m.

pantheistic(al) [ˌpænθi(ː)ˈistik(əl)], a. Panthéiste.

pantheon [ˈpænθi(ː)ən], s. Panthéon m.

panther [ˈpænθər], s. Z: 1. Panthère f. 2. U.S: Couguar m, puma m.

panties [ˈpæntiz], s.pl. Cost: Slip m.

pantile [ˈpæntail], s. Tuile flamande, en S; panne f.

pantograph [ˈpæntəgrɑːf], s. 1. Draw: Pantographe m. 2. El.E: Pantographe (de locomotive électrique, etc.).

pantomime¹ [ˈpæntəmaim], s. Th: 1. Rom.Ant: (Pers) Pantomime m, mime m. 2. (a) (Dumb show) Pantomime f. (b) Revue-féerie f à grand spectacle.

pantomime². 1. v.tr. Mimer (un rôle, qn, qch.). 2. v.i. S'exprimer en pantomime.

pantry [ˈpæntri], s. 1. Garde-manger m inv, placard m aux provisions. 2. Butler's p., office f.

pants [pænts], s.pl. Cost: F: (Pair of) p., (i) U.S: pantalon m, (ii) Com: caleçon m. Long p., caleçon long. Short p., under-p., caleçon court, slip m (d'homme). F: A kick in the p., un coup de pied au derrière. V: au cul. P: To be caught with one's p. down, se trouver pris dans une position fort embarrassante, en mauvaise posture.

pap¹ [pæp], s. A. & Dial: Mamelon m, tétin m, bout m de sein.

pap² [pæp], s. (a) Bouillie f. (b) Pulpe f, pâte f (très liquide).

papa [pəˈpɑː], s.m. F: Papa; petit père.

papacy [ˈpeipəsi], s. 1. Papauté f. 2. Pej: Papisme m.

papal [ˈpeip(ə)l], a. Papal, -aux. P. legate, légat du Pape.

paper¹ [ˈpeipər], s. 1. Papier m. (a) Note-p., papier à lettres. Art p., coated p., papier couché. Brown p., papier gris. Cigarette p., papier à cigarettes. Phot: Glossy p., papier brillant. Blue-print p., papier autocopiste. **Cambric p.**, papier (à lettres) toile. **Carbon p.**, papier carbone, carboné. **Super-royal, long royal p.**, papier jésus. **Dull-finish p.**, papier mat, non satiné. **Greaseproof p.**, papier beurre, jambon, parcheminé, sulfurisé. *S.a.* BLOT-TING-PAPER, EMERY, *etc.* (*b*) **To put sth. down on p.**, coucher qch. par écrit. **The scheme is a good one on p.**, ce projet est excellent en théorie. **P. profits**, profits fictifs. 2. (Morceau *m* de) papier. *A:* **Curl-p.**, papillote *f*. 3. (*a*) Écrit *m*, document *m*, pièce *f*. **My private papers**, mes papiers. **Family papers**, documents de famille. **Old papers**, paperasse(s) *f(pl)*. *Mil:* **Call-up papers**, ordre *m* d'appel. (*Of officer*) **To send in one's papers**, donner sa démission. **Ship's papers**, papiers du bord. (*b*) *Com:* **Valeurs** *fpl*, papier(s). **Negotiable p.**, papier(s) négociable(s). (*c*) **Voting-p.**, bulletin *m* de vote. 4. *Sch:* (**Examination-)p.** (*a*) Composition *f* (d'examen); épreuve (écrite). **History p.**, composition en histoire. **To set a p.**, choisir les sujets de composition. **To correct papers**, corriger l'écrit. (*b*) **To do a good mathematics p.**, rendre une bonne copie de mathématiques. 5. Étude *f*, mémoire *m* (sur un sujet scientifique, etc.). **To read a p.**, (i) faire une communication (à une société savante, etc.); (ii) faire une conférence, un exposé, *F:* lire un papier. 6. Journal *m*, -aux. **Weekly p.**, hebdomadaire *m*. **Fashion p.**, journal de modes. **To write in the papers**, faire du journalisme. 7. *Attrib:* **P. industry**, industrie papetière. **P. bag**, sac *m*, poche *f*, en papier. **P. parcel**, paquet enveloppé de papier. '**paper-back**, *s.* Livre *m* de poche. '**paper-backed**, *a.* *Bookb:* Broché. '**paper boy**, *s.m.* Garçon, (i) vendeur de journaux; (ii) qui livre les journaux à domicile. '**paper-chase**, *s.* *Sp:* Rallye-paper *m*. '**paper-clamp**, *s.* Pince-notes *m inv*, pince-feuilles *m inv*. '**paper-fastener**, *s.* Attache *f* métallique (à tête). *S.a.* CLIP¹ 1. '**paper-hanger**, *s.* Colleur *m*, poseur *m* de papiers peints. '**paper-hanging**, *s.* Collage *m*, pose *f*, de papiers peints. '**paper-knife**, *s.* 1. Coupe-papier *m inv*; couteau *m* à papier. 2. Plioir *m*. '**paper-mill**, *s.* Fabrique *f* de papier; papeterie *f*. '**paper-trade**, *s.* Papeterie *f*. '**paper-weight**, *s.* Presse-papiers *m inv*.

paper², *v.tr.* 1. Tapisser (une chambre). **Room papered in blue**, pièce tapissée de bleu, tendue de (papier) bleu. 2. *Th: P:* Remplir (la salle) de billets de faveur.

papier mâché ['pæpjei'mæʃei], *s.* Carton-pâte *m*.

Papilionaceae [pæ,pilio'neisii:], *s.pl.* *Bot:* Papilionacées *f*.

papilla, *pl.* -ae [pə'pilə, -i:], *s.* *Nat.Hist:* Papille *f*.

papillary [pə'piləri], *a.* Papillaire.

papism ['peipizm], *s.* Papisme *m*.

papist ['peipist], *s.* Papiste *mf*.

papistic(al) [pə'pistik(əl)], *a.* *Pej:* Qui sent le papisme; papiste.

papistry ['peipistri], *s.* *Pej:* Papisme *m*.

pappus ['pæpəs], *s.* *Bot:* Pappe *m*, aigrette *f*.

paprika ['pæprikə], *s.* *Cu:* Paprika *m*.

papula, *pl.* -ae ['pæpjulə, -i:], *s.* *Med: Bot:* Papule *f*.

papyraceous [pæpi'reiʃəs], *a.* Papyracé.

papyrus, *pl.* -ri [pə'paiərəs, -rai], *s.* Papyrus *m*.

par¹ [pɑːr], *s.* Pair *m*, égalité *f*. (*a*) **To be on a p. with s.o.**, être au niveau de, aller de pair avec, qn. (*b*) *Fin:* **P. of exchange**, pair du change. **Above p., below p.**, au-dessus, au-dessous, du pair. **Exchange at p.**, change à (la) parité. (*c*) **Below p.**, au-dessous de la moyenne; médiocre. **To feel below p.**, ne pas être dans son assiette; être mal en train.

par², *F:* (*Paragraph*) 1. *Journ:* Entrefilet *m*; fait-divers *m*. **P. writer**, courriériste *m*, échotier *m*. 2. Paragraphe *m*; alinéa *m*.

parable ['pærəbl], *s.* Parabole *f*. **To speak in parables**, parler par, en, paraboles.

parabola [pə'ræbələ], *s.* *Geom:* Parabole *f*.

parabolic(al) [pærə'bolik(əl)], *a.* Parabolique. **P. velocity**, vitesse *f* de libération (de l'attraction terrestre).

parachute¹ ['pærəʃuːt], *s.* 1. *Av:* Parachute *m*. **Seat-type p.**, parachute à siège. **P. skirt**, bord *m* de parachute. **P. drop, landing**, parachutage *m*. **P. flare**, fusée-parachute *f*. 2. *Attrib:* Parachutiste *m*. **P. Regiment**, régiment *m* de parachutistes.

parachute², *v.i. & v.tr.* *Av:* Parachuter. **To p. down**, descendre en parachute. **parachuting**, *s.* Parachutage *m*.

parachutist ['pærəʃuːtist], *s.* Parachutiste *mf*, *F:* para *m*.

Paraclete ['pærəkliːt], *s.* *Theol:* Le Paraclet.

parade¹ [pə'reid], *s.* 1. Parade *f*. **To make a p. of one's poverty**, faire parade, étalage, de sa pauvreté; afficher sa pauvreté. 2. *Mil:* (*a*) Rassemblement *m*. (*b*) Exercice *m*. **On p.**, à l'exercice. **To go on p.**, parader. **P.-ground**, terrain *m* de manœuvres; place *f* d'armes. (*c*) *Fenc:* Parade. 3. Défilé *m* (de troupes, etc.). **Mannequin p.**, défilé de mannequins. **Fashion p.**, présentation *f* de collection. 4. Esplanade *f*; promenade publique; boulevard *m* (le long de la plage).

parade². 1. *v.tr.* (*a*) Faire parade, ostentation, étalage, de (ses richesses, etc.). **To p. one's poverty**, afficher sa pauvreté. (*b*) *Mil:* Faire l'inspection (des troupes); faire parader, faire défiler (les troupes). 2. *v.i.* (*a*) *Mil:* Faire la parade; parader (pour l'exercice, pour l'inspection). (*b*) **To p. (through) the streets**, défiler dans les rues.

paradigm ['pærədaim], *s.* *Gram:* Paradigme *m*.

paradise ['pærədais], *s.* Paradis *m*. 1. **The Earthly P.**, le Paradis terrestre. **An earthly p.**, un paradis sur terre. 2. **To go to p.**, aller en paradis. **To live in a fool's p.**, se bercer d'un bonheur illusoire, de douces illusions. **Bird of p.**, oiseau *m* de paradis, paradisier *m*.

paradisiac(al) [pærə'diziæk(əl)], **paradisial** [pærə'di:-si:əl], *a.* Paradisiaque.

paradox ['pærədɔks], *s.* Paradoxe *m*.

paradoxical [pærə'dɔksik(ə)l], *a.* Paradoxal, -aux. **-ally**, *adv.* Paradoxalement.

paraffin¹ ['pærəfin], 1. *Ch:* Paraffine *f*. *Pharm:* **Liquid p.**, huile *f* de paraffine. 2. *Com:* **P. (oil)**, pétrole (lampant), kérosène *m*, kérosine *f*. **paraffin 'lamp**, *s.* Lampe *f* à pétrole. **paraffin 'wax**, *s.* Paraffine *f* (solide).

paraffin², *v.tr.* 1. Paraffiner. 2. Pétroler (un marais, etc.).

paragon ['pærəgən], *s.* 1. Modèle *m* (de vertu, etc.). 2. Diamant *m*, perle *f*, sans défaut. **This diamond is a p.**, ce diamant est un parangon.

paragraph¹ ['pærəgrɑːf, -græf], *s.* 1. Paragraphe *m*, alinéa *m*. **To begin a new p.**, aller à la ligne. '**New p.**,' "à la ligne." *Typ:* **P. (mark)**, pied *m* de mouche. 2. *Journ:* Entrefilet *m*.

paragraph², *v.tr.* Diviser (une page) en paragraphes, en alinéas.

paragrapher ['pærəgrɑːfər, -græf-], **paragraphist** ['pærəgrɑːfist, -græf-], *s.* *Journ:* Échotier *m*.

parakeet ['pærəkiːt], *s.* *Orn:* Perruche *f*.

parallax ['pærəlæks], *s.* Parallaxe *f*.

parallel¹ ['pærəlel]. I. *a.* Parallèle (with, to, à). 1. **In a p. direction with sth.**, parallèlement à qch. *El:* **P. connection**, accouplement *m* en parallèle. **Cells in p.**, piles en parallèle, en quantité, en dérivation. *S.a.* FLOW¹ 1. 2. Pareil, semblable; (cas) analogue (to, with, à). II. **parallel**, *s.* 1. (*a*) (Ligne *f*) parallèle *f*. (*b*) *Geog:* Parallèle *m* (de latitude). 2. Parallèle *m*, comparaison *f*. **To draw a p. between two things**, établir un parallèle entre deux choses. **Wickedness without a p.**, méchanceté sans pareille. 3. *El.E:* Dynamos out of p., dynamos déphasées, hors de phase.

parallel², *v.tr.* (**paralleled**) 1. Mettre (deux choses) en parallèle. 2. Égaler (qch.); être égal, pareil, à (qch.). 3. *El.E:* Synchroniser (deux dynamos, etc.).

parallelism ['pærəlelizm], *s.* Parallélisme *m*.

parallelogram [pærə'leləgræm], *s.* Parallélogramme *m*.

paralyse ['pærəlaiz], *v.tr.* Paralyser. **Paralysed in one leg**, paralysé d'une jambe. **Paralysed with fear**, transi de peur; médusé. **paralysing**, *a.* Paralysant; paralysateur, -trice.

paralysis [pə'rælisis], *s.* *Med:* Paralysie *f*. **Creeping p.**, paralysie progressive. **P. agitans**, paralysie agitante. **Infantile p.**, = POLIOMYELITIS.

paralytic [pærə'litik], 1. *a.* Paralytique. **To have a p. stroke**, tomber en paralysie. *F:* **He's positively p.**, il est soûl comme un Polonais. 2. *s.* Paralytique *mf*.

parameter [pə'ræmitər], s. *Mth:* Paramètre *m*.
paramilitary [pærə'militri], a. Paramilitaire.
paramount ['pærəmaunt], a. 1. Éminent, souverain. **Lord p., suzerain** *m*. 2. **Of p. importance,** d'une suprême importance. **Duty is p. (to everything) with him,** chez lui le devoir l'emporte (sur tout).
paramour ['pærəmuər], s. *A: & Lit:* (i) Amant *m*; (ii) maîtresse *f*, *Lit:* amante *f*.
paranoia [,pærə'nɔiə], s. *Med:* Paranoïa *f*.
paranoiac [pærə'nɔiæk], a. & s. *Med:* Paranoïaque (*mf.*).
parapet ['pærəpit], s. 1. *Fort:* Parapet *m*; berge *f* (de tranchée). (b) *Civ.E:* Parapet; garde-fou *m*, garde-corps *m inv* (d'un pont, etc.). 'parapet-'walk, s. *Fort: Arch:* Chemin *m* de ronde.
paraph ['pæræf], s. Paraphe *m*, parafe *m*.
paraphernalia [,pærəfə'neiliə], s.pl. *F:* (a) Effets *m*; affaires *f*. **All the p.,** tout le bataclan. (b) Accessoires *mpl* (de toilette). (c) Attirail *m*, appareil *m* (de pêche, etc.).
paraphrase[1] ['pærəfreiz], s. Paraphrase *f*.
paraphrase[2], v.tr. Paraphraser.
paraplegia [pærə'pli:dʒiə], s. *Med:* Paraplégie *f*.
paraplegic ['pærə'pli:dʒik], a. *Med:* Paraplégique.
parasite ['pærəsait], s. Parasite *m*; (of pers.); pique-assiette *m inv*.
parasitic [,pærə'sitik], a. (Of insect, etc.) Parasite (on, de). **P. disease,** maladie parasitaire.
parasitism ['pærəsitizm], s. Parasitisme *m*.
parasitology [pærəsi'ɔlədʒi], s. Parasitologie *f*.
parasol [,pærə'sɔl], s. Ombrelle *f*, parasol *m*.
parathyroid [,pærə'θairɔid], *Physiol:* 1. a. **P. glands,** les glandes parathyroïdes. 2. s.pl. **The parathyroids,** les parathyroïdes *fpl*.
paratrooper ['pærə,tru:pər], s. (Soldat) parachutiste *m*.
paratroops ['pærətru:ps], s.pl. (Soldats) parachutistes *mpl*.
paratyphoid [,pærə'taifɔid], s. *Med:* Paratyphoïde *f*.
paravane ['pærəvein], s. *Navy:* Paravane *m*; pare-mines *m inv*.
parboil ['pɑ:bɔil], v.tr. *Cu:* Faire cuire, faire bouillir (de la viande, etc.) légèrement; blanchir (des légumes).
parcel[1] ['pɑ:s(ə)l], s. 1. (a) A: Partie *f*. *S.a.* PART[1] I. 1. (b) Morceau *m*, parcelle *f* (de terrain). (c) *St.Exch: etc:* **P. of shares,** paquet *m* d'actions. **P. of goods,** (i) lot *m*, (ii) envoi *m*, de marchandises. *Pej:* **P. of lies,** tas *m* de mensonges. 2. Paquet, colis *m*. **Parcels office,** bureau *m* de(s) messageries. 'parcel(s) de'livery, s. Service *m* de messageries; remise *f* de colis à domicile; factage *m*. 'parcel 'post, s. Service *m* des colis postaux; service de messageries. **To send sth. by p. p.,** envoyer qch. comme, par, colis postal.
parcel[2], v.tr. (parcelled) (a) **To p. (out),** parceller, partager (un héritage); morceler (into, en); lotir (des terres, etc.). (b) Empaqueter (du thé, etc.). **To p. up a consignment of books,** mettre en paquets, emballer, un envoi de livres.
parch [pɑ:tʃ]. 1. v.tr. (a) Rôtir, griller, sécher (des céréales). (b) (Of fever) Brûler (qn). **Grass parched (up) by the wind,** herbe desséchée par le vent. **To be parched with thirst,** avoir une soif ardente, dévorante. 2. v.i. Se dessécher.
parchment ['pɑ:tʃmənt], s. (a) Parchemin *m*. (b) **P. paper, vegetable p.,** papier parchemin; papier parcheminé.
pard [pɑ:d], s. A: & Poet: Léopard *m*.
pardon[1] ['pɑ:d(ə)n], s. 1. Pardon *m*. **I beg your p.!** je vous demande pardon! **I beg your p.?** plaît-il? pardon? 2. *Ecc:* Indulgence *f*. 3. *Jur:* (a) Free p., grâce *f*. **To receive the King's, Queen's p.,** être gracié. **General p.,** amnistie *f*. (b) Lettré *f* de grâce.
pardon[2], v.tr. 1. Pardonner (une faute, etc.). **P. my contradicting you,** pardonnez(-moi) si je vous contredis. 2. (a) **To p. s.o.,** pardonner à qn. *U.S: & P:* **P. me!** mille pardons! (b) **To p. s.o. sth.,** pardonner qch. à qn. 3. *Jur:* Faire grâce à (qn); gracier, amnistier.
pardonable[1] ['pɑ:dnəbl], a. 1. Pardonnable, excusable. 2. *Jur:* Graciable.

pare [peər], v.tr. 1. Rogner (ses ongles, etc.); ébarber (la tranche d'un livre). *Leath:* Doler (les peaux). 2. Éplucher; peler (un fruit). **pare down,** v.tr Rogner (ses ongles, les dépenses); amenuiser (un bâton). **paring,** s. 1. (a) Rognage *m*, rognement *m*; ébarbage *m* (d'un livre). *Leath:* Dolage *m* (des peaux). (b) Épluchage *m*. 2. *Usu.pl.* Rognures *f*. **Parings of metal,** cisaille *f*. (b) Épluchures *f*, pelures *f* (de légumes, etc.). *S.a.* CHEESE-PARING 'paring-knife, s. Rognoir *m*. *Bootm:* Tranchet *m*.
paregoric [,pæri'gɔrik], a. & s. *Pharm:* Parégorique (*m*).
parent ['peərənt], s. 1. Père *m*, mère *f*; pl. parents *m*, les père et mère. **Parents and relations,** les ascendants directs et les collatéraux. 2. **P. rock,** roche mère. **P. state** (of ex-colonies), mère patrie, métropole *f*. *Com:* **P. establishment,** maison mère. (Welding) **P. metal,** métal *m* de base. 'parent-'ship, s. *Nav:* **Submarine p.-s.,** ravitailleur *m* de sous-marins.
parentage ['peərəntidʒ], s. Origine *f*, naissance *f*. **Born of humble p.,** né de parents humbles.
parental [pə'rent(ə)l], a. (Autorité, etc.) des parents, des père et mère; (pouvoir) paternel.
parenthesis, pl. **-theses** [pə'renθəsis, -θəsi:z], s. Parenthèse *f*. **In parentheses,** entre parenthèses.
parenthetic(al) [,pærən'θetik(əl)], a. 1. Entre parenthèses. 2. *Gram:* **P. clause,** incidente *f*. **-ally,** adv. Par parenthèse.
pareo [pə'reiou], s. *Cost:* Paréo *m*.
parfait ['pɑ:fei], s. *Cu:* **Coffee p.,** parfait *m* au café.
parhelion, pl. **-ia** [pɑ:'hi:liən, -iə], s. Par(h)élie *m*; faux soleil.
pariah ['pæriə], s. Paria *m*.
parietal [pə'raiət(ə)l], a. *Anat:* Pariétal, -aux.
pari passu ['pæri'pæsju:]. *Lt.phr.* **To go p. p. with . . .,** marcher de pair avec. . . .
Paris ['pæris]. *Pr.n. Geog:* Paris *m*. *Com:* **P. white,** blanc *m* de Paris. *Dressm:* **P. binding,** extra-fort *m*. *S.a.* PLASTER[1] 2.
parish ['pæriʃ], s. (a) *Ecc:* Paroisse *f*. **P. church,** église paroissiale. **P. priest,** (i) curé *m*; (ii) pasteur *m*. **P. hall,** salle *f* d'œuvres. (b) Civil p., commune *f*. **P. Council** = conseil municipal. A: **P. school,** = école communale. A: **To come, go, on the p.,** tomber à la charge de la commune.
parishioner [pə'riʃənər], s. Paroissien, -ienne.
Parisian [pə'riziən], a. & s. Parisien, -ienne.
parisyllabic [,pærisi'læbik], a. Parisyllabe; parisyllabique.
parity ['pæriti], s. 1. (a) Égalité *f* (de rang, etc.); parité *f*. (b) **P. of reasoning,** raisonnement *m* analogue; analogie *f* de raisonnement. 2. **Exchange at p.,** change à (la) parité; change au pair.
park[1] [pɑ:k], s. 1. (a) Parc (clôturé). **Deer-p.,** parc (clôturé) à cerfs. (b) **National p.,** parc national. **Public p.,** jardin public; parc. 2. **Car p.,** parc de stationnement pour autos, à voitures; stationnement autorisé; *F:* parking *m*. *Mil:* **Artillery-p.,** parc d'artillerie.
park[2], v.tr. 1. (a) Enfermer (des moutons) dans un parc. (b) Mettre (de l'artillerie) en parc. 2. (a) Parquer, garer (une auto). (b) *Abs. Aut:* Stationner. (c) *F:* **P. it over there!** mets-le là! **To p. oneself,** s'installer, *P:* se planquer (quelque part). **parking,** s. Parcage *m*. *P.N: Aut:* **No p. here,** défense de stationner; stationnement interdit. **P. place,** *U.S:* **p. lot,** parc *m* de stationnement, *F:* parking *m*. **P. meter,** compteur *m* de stationnement, *Fr.C:* parcomètre *m*. **P. attendant,** gardien *m* d'autos. **P. lights,** feux *m* de position, de stationnement.
parkerize ['pɑ:kəraiz], v.tr. *Metalw:* Parkériser. **parkerizing,** s. *Metalw:* Parkérisation *f*.
Parkinson ['pɑ:kins(ə)n], *Pr.n. Med:* **Parkinson's disease,** paralysie agitante, maladie *f* de Parkinson.
parlance ['pɑ:ləns], s. Langage *m*, parler *m*. **In common p.,** en langage ordinaire. **In legal p.,** en termes de pratique.
parley[1] ['pɑ:li], s. Conférence *f*. *Mil:* Pourparlers *mpl* (avec l'ennemi). **To hold a p.,** parlementer (with, avec).
parley[2], v.i. Être, entrer, en pourparlers; parlementer; entamer des négociations (avec l'ennemi).

parliament ['pɑ:ləmənt], s. Le Parlement; (in Fr.) = les Chambres f. The Houses of P., le palais du Parlement. In p., au parlement.

parliamentarian [,pɑ:ləmən'tɛəriən]. **1.** s. Parlementaire m; membre m du Parlement. **2.** a. Parlementaire.

parliamentary [,pɑ:lə'ment(ə)ri], a. Parlementaire. P. election, élection législative. **P. government**, parlementarisme m. P. eloquence, éloquence de la tribune.

parlour ['pɑ:lər], s. Petit salon; parloir m (d'un couvent, etc.). Bar p., arrière-salle f de la taverne. P. games, jeux de salon, de société. F: P. tricks, (i) arts m d'agrément; (ii) talents m de société. 'parlo(u)r-car, s. Rail: U.S: Wagon-salon m, pl. wagons-salons. 'parlour-maid, s.f. Bonne (affectée au service de table).

parlous ['pɑ:ləs], a. Lit: Périlleux, -euse; précaire. The p. state of the finances, l'état alarmant des finances.

Parmesan [,pɑ:mi'zæn], s. P. (cheese), parmesan m.

Parnassian [pɑ:'næsiən], a. & s. Parnassien, -ienne.

Parnassus [pɑ:'næsəs]. Pr.n. Le Parnasse.

parochial [pə'roukiəl], a. (a) Ecc: Paroissial, -aux. The p. hall, la salle d'œuvres de la paroisse. U.S: P. school, école confessionnelle. (b) (Of civil parish) Communal, -aux. (c) Pej: Provincial, -aux. P. spirit, esprit de clocher.

parochialism [pə'roukiəlizm], s. Esprit m de clocher.

parodist ['pærədist], s. Parodiste m.

parody¹ ['pærədi], s. Parodie f, pastiche m.

parody², v.tr. Parodier, pasticher.

parole¹ [pə'roul], s. Esp.Mil: Parole f (d'honneur). Prisoner on p., prisonnier sur parole. To be put on p., être libéré sur parole. To break one's p., manquer à sa parole.

parole², v.tr. Libérer un prisonnier (i) sur parole, (ii) conditionnellement.

parotid [pə'rɔtid], a. & s. Anat: (Glande f) parotide (f).

paroxysm ['pærəksizm], s. (a) Med: Paroxysme m (d'une fièvre). (b) Crise f (de fou rire, de larmes); accès m (de fureur). P. of toothache, rage f de dents.

parpen ['pɑ:pin], s. Const: Parpaing m. P. wall, mur de parpaing(s).

parquet ['pɑ:kei], s. 1. P. (floor), parquet m (en parquetage). P. flooring, parquetage m. 2. Th: U.S: Premiers rangs du parterre.

parquetry ['pɑ:kitri], s. Parquetage m, parqueterie f.

parr [pɑ:r], s. Ich: Saumoneau m.

parricidal [,pæri'said(ə)l], a. Parricide.

parricide¹ ['pærisaid], s. (Pers.) Parricide mf.

parricide², s. (Crime m de) parricide m.

parrot ['pærət], Orn: Perroquet m. Hen-p., perruche f.

parry¹ ['pæri], s. Fenc: Box: Parade f.

parry², v.tr. (a) Parer, détourner (un coup); tourner, éviter (une difficulté); parer (une question). (b) Abs. To p. with the riposte, riposter du tac au tac.

parse [pɑ:z], v.tr. Faire l'analyse (grammaticale) (d'un mot). parsing, s. Analyse grammaticale.

parsec ['pɑ:sek], s. Astr. Meas: Parsec m.

Parsee [pɑ:'si:], a. & s. Parsi, -ie.

parsimonious [,pɑ:si'mouniəs], a. Parcimonieux, -euse. (a) Économe, épargnant, F: regardant. (b) Pej: Pingre. -ly, adv. Parcimonieusement.

parsimony ['pɑ:siməni], s. Parcimonie f. (a) Épargne f. (b) Pej: Pingrerie f.

parsley ['pɑ:sli], s. Bot: Persil m.

parsnip ['pɑ:snip], s. Panais m.

parson ['pɑ:s(ə)n], s. Ecc: **1.** Titulaire m d'un bénéfice. **2.** F: Prêtre m; pasteur m. S.a. NOSE¹ 1.

parsonage ['pɑ:sənidʒ], s. = Presbytère m, cure f.

part¹ [pɑ:t]. **I.** s. **1.** Partie f. (a) P. of the paper is damaged, une partie du papier est avariée. Good in parts, bon en partie. The funny p. (about it) is that . . . le comique de l'histoire, ce qu'il y a de comique, c'est que. . . . The greater p. of the inhabitants, la plus grande partie, la plupart, des habitants. In my p. of the world . . ., par chez moi. . . . To be, form, p. of sth., faire partie de qch. It is p. and parcel of . . ., c'est une partie intégrante, essentielle, de. . . . It is no p. of my intentions to . . ., il n'entre pas dans mes intentions de. . . . In (a) great p. due to . . ., dû en grande partie à. . . . To pay in p., payer partiellement. S.a. MOST 1. Ten parts of water to one of milk, dix parties d'eau pour

une (partie) de lait. Results accurate to one p. in ten million, résultats justes à un dix-millionième près. Three parts drunk, aux trois quarts ivre. (b) Ind: Pièce f, organe m. Machine p., élément m de machine. Spare parts, pièces de rechange, pièces détachées. (c) Gram: Parts of speech, parties du discours. Principal parts (of a verb), temps principaux. (d) Fascicule m, livraison f (d'une œuvre littéraire). **2.** Part f. (a) To take (a) p. in sth., prendre part à, participer à, qch. To take p. in the conversation, se mêler à la conversation. To have neither p. nor lot in sth., n'avoir aucune part dans (une affaire, etc.). I had no p. in it, je n'y suis pour rien. Each one did his p., chacun s'acquitta de sa tâche. (b) Th: Rôle m, personnage m. Small parts, utilités f. To play heroes' parts, jouer les héros. He is playing a p., il joue la comédie; c'est une comédie qu'il nous fait. To play one's p., remplir son rôle. In all this imagination plays a large p., dans tout ceci l'imagination entre pour beaucoup. It is not my p. to speak about it, ce n'est pas à moi d'en parler. It is the p. of prudence to . . ., c'est agir avec sagesse que de. . . . (c) Orchestral parts, parties d'orchestre. To sing in parts, chanter à plusieurs parties, à plusieurs voix. **3.** (a) pl. You don't belong to these parts? vous n'êtes pas de ces parages? vous n'êtes pas de ce pays? On the one p. . . ., on the other p. . . ., d'un côté . . ., de l'autre . . .; d'une part . . ., d'autre part. . . . (c) To take s.o.'s p., prendre le parti de qn; prendre fait et cause pour qn. (d) An indiscretion on the p. of . . ., une indiscrétion de la part de. . . . For my p. . . ., quant à moi, pour ma part. . . . **4.** To take sth. in good p., prendre qch. en bonne part, du bon côté. **5.** pl. Man of (good) parts, homme de valeur, de talent; homme bien doué. **II.** part, adv. P. eaten, partiellement mangé; mangé en partie. Material p. silk p. cotton, étoffe mi-soie et mi-coton. P. one and p. the other, moitié l'un moitié l'autre. 'part-'owner, s. Copropriétaire mf. 'part-song, s. Chanson f à plusieurs voix. 'part-time, s. & attrib.a. P.-t. employment, emploi m à temps incomplet, à mi-temps. To be on p.-t., être en chômage partiel.

part². **1.** v.tr. (a) Séparer en deux; fendre (la foule). To p. one's hair, se faire une raie. Her: Shield parted per pale, écu mi-parti. (b) Séparer (from, de). (c) Rompre (une amarre, etc.). Nau: To p. one's cable, casser sa chaîne. **2.** v.i. (a) (Of crowd, etc.) Se diviser; se ranger de part et d'autre. (b) (Of two pers.) Se quitter, se séparer; (of roads) diverger. Prov: The best of friends must p., il n'y a si bonne compagnie qui ne se sépare. (c) (Of cable, etc.) (Se) rompre; partir, céder. part with, v.i. Céder (qch.); se dessaisir, se départir, de (qch.). Jur: Aliéner (un bien). He hates to p. with his money, il n'aime pas à débourser. parting¹, a. **1.** P. line, ligne de séparation. **2.** A: Partant. Poet: The p. day, le jour qui tombe. parting², s. **1.** (a) Séparation f; (of water) partage m. To be at the p. of the ways, être au carrefour. (b) Départ m. P. kiss, baiser d'adieu. A few p. directions, quelques dernières recommandations. **2.** Rupture f (d'un câble, etc.). **3.** (Of the hair) Raie f; (of horse's mane) épi m.

partake [pɑ:'teik], v.i. (partook [pɑ:'tuk]; partaken) To p. in, of, sth., prendre part, participer, à qch. O: To p. of a meal, (i) partager le repas de qn; (ii) prendre un repas. Ecc: To p. of the Sacrament, s'approcher des sacrements.

partaker [pɑ:'teikər], s. Participant, -ante (in sth., à qch.). Ecc: To be a regular p. of the Sacrament, fréquenter les sacrements.

parthenogenesis ['pɑ:θino'dʒenisis], s. Biol: Parthénogénèse f.

Parthian ['pɑ:θiən], a. & s. A.Geog: Parthe (mf). A P. shaft, shot, la flèche du Parthe.

partial ['pɑ:ʃ(ə)l], a. **1.** (a) (Of judge) Partial, -aux; injuste. (b) F: To be p. to sth., avoir un faible, une prédilection, pour qch. I am p. to a pipe after dinner, je fume volontiers une pipe après dîner. **2.** Partiel, -elle; en partie. P. board, demi-pension f. -ally, adv. **1.** Partialement; avec partialité. **2.** Partiellement; en partie.

partiality [ˌpɑːʃiˈæliti], s. 1. (a) Partialité f (for, to, pour, envers); injustice f. (b) Favoritisme m. A mother's p. for her children, la faiblesse d'une mère pour ses enfants. 2. To have a p. for sth., marquer de la prédilection pour qch. A p. for the bottle, un penchant pour la boisson.

participant [pɑːˈtisipənt], a. & s. Participant, -ante (in, à).

participate [pɑːˈtisipeit], v.i. (a) To p. in sth., prendre part, participer, s'associer, à qch. (b) (Of thg) Participer, tenir (de qch.).

participation [pɑːtisiˈpeiʃ(ə)n], s. Participation f (in, à).

participator [pɑːˈtisipeitər], s. Participant,-ante (in, de).

participial [ˌpɑːtiˈsipiəl], a. Gram: Participial, -aux.

participle [ˈpɑːtisipl], s. Gram: Participe m.

particle [ˈpɑːtikl], s. 1. Particule f, parcelle f (de sable, etc.); paillette f (de métal). There is not a p. of truth in this story, il n'y a pas l'ombre de vérité dans ce récit. Not a p. of evidence, pas la moindre preuve, pas un semblant de preuve. 2. Gram: Particule.

parti-coloured [ˈpɑːtikʌləd], a. 1. Mi-parti. 2. Bigarré, bariolé, panaché.

particular [pəˈtikjulər]. I. a. 1. Particulier, -ière; spécial, -aux. A p. object, un objet déterminé. My own p. sentiments, mes propres sentiments; mes sentiments personnels. To take p. care over sth., faire qch. avec un soin particulier. For no p. reason, sans raison précise, sans raison bien définie. In p., en particulier; notamment. 2. (Of pers.) Méticuleux, -euse, minutieux, -euse; pointilleux, -euse, vétilleux, -euse. To be p. about one's food, être difficile, exigeant, sur la nourriture. To be p. about one's dress, soigner sa mise. P. on points of honour, délicat sur le point d'honneur. Don't be too p., ne vous montrez pas trop exigeant. He is not p. to a few pounds, il n'y regarde pas à quelques livres près. I am not p. about it, je n'y tiens pas plus que ça. -ly, adv. Particulièrement. Notice p. that..., notez en particulier que.... I want this (most) p. for tomorrow, il me le faut absolument pour demain. I p. asked him to be careful, je l'ai prié instamment de faire attention. II. particular, s. Détail m, particularité f. Alike in every p., semblables en tout point. To give particulars of sth., donner les détails de qch. He asked me for particulars about her, il m'a demandé des renseignements à son sujet, sur elle. For further particulars apply to..., pour plus amples renseignements s'adresser à.... Cust: etc: Particulars of a car, signalement m d'une voiture.

particularism [pəˈtikjulərizm], s. Pol: Theol: Particularisme m.

particularity [pəˌtikjuˈlæriti], s. 1. Particularité f. 2. Méticulosité f; minutie f (d'une description).

particularization [pəˌtikjuləraiˈzeiʃ(ə)n], s. Particularisation f.

particularize [pəˈtikjuləraiz], v.tr. (a) Particulariser, spécifier. (b) Abs. Entrer dans les détails; préciser.

partisan[1] [ˈpɑːtizæn, ˌpɑːtiˈzæn], s. Partisan m. To act in a p. spirit, faire preuve (i) d'esprit de parti, (ii) de parti pris.

partisan[2] [ˈpɑːtizæn], s. A: Arms: Pertuisane f.

partisanship [ˌpɑːtiˈzænʃip], s. Partialité f; esprit m de parti.

partition[1] [pɑːˈtiʃ(ə)n], s. 1. Partage m (d'un pays); morcellement m (d'une terre). Hist: The p. of Poland, le partage de la Pologne. 2. (a) Cloison f, cloisonnage m. Internal p., mur m de refend. Wooden p., pan m de bois. Glass p., vitrage m. (b) Compartiment m (de cale, etc.).

partition[2], v.tr. 1. Morceler (un domaine); partager, démembrer (un pays vaincu). 2. To p. (off) a room, cloisonner une pièce. **partitioning**, s. 1. = PARTITION[1] 1. 2. Cloisonnage m, compartimentage m.

partitive [ˈpɑːtitiv], a. & s. Gram: Partitif (m).

partly [ˈpɑːtli], adv. Partiellement; en partie. P. by force, p. by persuasion, moitié de force, moitié par persuasion.

partner[1] [ˈpɑːtnər], s. (a) Associé, -ée. P. in life, époux, épouse; conjoint, -e. Com: Senior p., associé principal. Full p., associé à part entière.

Sleeping, U.S: silent, p., (associé) commanditaire m. (b) Games: Partenaire mf. (c) Danc: (Woman's p.) Cavalier m. (Man's p.) Cavalière f.

partner[2], v.tr. 1. (a) Etre associé, s'associer, à (qn). (b) Games: Être le partenaire de (qn). (c) Danc: Mener (une dame). 2. To p. s.o. with s.o., donner qn à qn comme associé, comme partenaire, comme cavalier.

partnership [ˈpɑːtnəʃip], s. 1. (a) P. in crime, association f dans le crime. (b) Com: To enter, go, into p. with s.o., entrer en association avec qn; s'associer avec qn. To take s.o. into p., prendre qn comme associé. To give s.o. a p. in the business, intéresser qn dans son commerce. 2. Com: Ind: Société f. General p., société en nom collectif. Limited p., (société en) commandite f.

partridge [ˈpɑːtridʒ], s. (a) Perdrix f. Brace of partridges, couple de perdrix. Young p., p. poult, perdreau m. (b) Cu: Perdreau.

parturition [ˌpɑːtjuˈriʃ(ə)n], s. Parturition f.

party [ˈpɑːti], s. 1. Political parties, partis m politiques. The Labour p., le parti travailliste. P. leader, chef m de parti. P. warfare, guerre f de partis. P. quarrels, querelles partisanes. 2. (a) (Pleasure) p., partie f de plaisir. Will you join our p.? voulez-vous être des nôtres? We are a small p., nous sommes peu nombreux. I was one of the p., j'étais de la partie. (b) Private p., réunion f intime; réception f. Evening p., soirée f. To give a p., recevoir du monde; donner une (petite) fête. To go to a p., aller en soirée. Children's p., goûter m d'enfants. P. dress, toilette f de fête. F: He's caught the p. spirit, il s'est abandonné aux joies de la fête. U.S: P. girl, (i) entraîneuse f; (ii) prostituée f. 3. (a) Bande f, groupe m (de voyageurs, etc.). (b) Brigade f, équipe f (de mineurs, etc.); atelier m (d'ouvriers). Rescue p., équipe de secours. (c) Mil: Détachement m. The advance p., les éléments m d'avant-garde. Firing p., peloton m d'exécution. 4. (a) Jur: P. to a dispute, partie f. To be p. to a suit, être en cause. (b) Com: To become a p. to an agreement, signer un contrat. A third p., un tiers, une tierce personne. Third-p. insurance, assurance f au tiers. (c) To be (a) p. to a crime, être complice d'un crime; tremper dans un crime. To be no p. to sth., ne pas s'associer à qch.; n'être pour rien dans qch. (d) P: A p. of the name of Jones, un individu du nom de Jones. **'party line**, s. 1. Pol: To follow the p. l., obéir aux directives f du parti. 2. Tp: Ligne partagée. **'party 'spirit**, s. Esprit m de parti. **'party-'wall**, s. Mur mitoyen.

parvenu [ˈpɑːvənjuː], s. Parvenu, -e.

parvis [ˈpɑːvis], s. Parvis m (d'une cathédrale).

paschal [ˈpɑːsk(ə)l], a. Pascal, -aux.

pasha [ˈpɑːʃə, ˈpæʃə], s. Pacha m.

pasque-flower [ˈpɑːskflauər], s. (Anémone f) pulsatille f; fleur f de Pâques; coquelourde f; passe-fleur f.

pass[1] [pɑːs], s. 1. Col m, défilé m (de montagne). To hold the p., tenir la clef d'une position. To sell the p., trahir son pays, son parti. 2. Nau: Passe f (entre des hauts-fonds).

pass[2], s. 1. (a) A. & Lit: To come to p., arriver, avoir lieu. S.a. BRING. (b) Things have come to a pretty p., les choses sont dans un bel état. 2. Sch: To obtain a p., passer tout juste. P.-mark, moyenne f. 3. (a) Passe f (de prestidigitateur). (b) Fenc: Passe, botte f. F: To make a p. at s.o., faire des avances amoureuses à qn. 4. Laissez-passer m inv, permission f. (Free) p., (i) Rail: titre m, carte f, de circulation; (ii) Th: billet m de faveur. Police p., coupe-file m inv. 5. Fb: Passe. 6. Cards: Pass! parole! **'pass-book**, s. Carnet m de banque. **'pass-key**, s. (Clef f) passe-partout m inv.

pass[3], v. (p.p. (in compound tenses) passed, (as adj.) past [pɑːst]) I. v.i. Passer. 1. (a) Words passed between them, il y eut un échange d'injures. Mil: P. friend! avance à l'ordre! (b) The procession passed (by) slowly, le cortège défila lentement. Everyone smiles as he passes, chacun sourit à son passage. To let s.o. p., livrer passage à qn. Let it p.! passe pour cela! Be it said in passing, (ceci) soit dit en passant. 2. (Of time) To p. (by), (se) passer, s'écouler. When five minutes had passed, au bout de cinq minutes. How time passes! comme le temps passe vite! 3. **To p. (away)**, disparaître; *(of clouds)* se dissiper. 4. **To come to p.**, arriver. 5. *(a)* Coin that passes in England, pièce qui a cours en Angleterre. That won't p.! (i) c'est inacceptable! (ii) ça ne prend pas! *(b)* She passes for a great beauty, elle passe pour une beauté. 6. *Jur:* *(Of verdict)* Être prononcé (for, en faveur de). II. **pass**, *v.tr.* 1. *(a)* Passer devant, près de (la fenêtre). **To p. s.o.** on the stairs, croiser qn dans l'escalier. *(b)* *Rail:* **To p. a station**, ne pas s'arrêter à une gare; *F:* brûler une gare. *(c)* *(Of company)* **To p. a dividend**, conclure un exercice sans payer de dividende. *(Cp.* II. 2 *(a)*.*)* *(d)* Passer, franchir (la frontière). *(e)* Dépasser (le but); outrepasser (les bornes de qch.). That passes my comprehension, cela me dépasse. *(f)* Surpasser (qn); gagner (qn) de vitesse; dépasser, rattraper (qn). *Sp:* Devancer (un concurrent). *Aut:* Doubler. *(g)* **To p. a test**, subir une épreuve avec succès. *(h)* **To p. an examination**, être reçu à un examen; réussir à un examen. *(i)* *Abs.* If the bill passes, si le projet de loi est voté. *(j)* **To p. the censor**, être accepté par la censure. 2. Approuver. *(a)* *Adm:* **To p. an item of expenditure**, allouer une dépense. *(Of company)* **To p. a dividend of 5%**, approuver un dividende de 5%. *(Cp.* II. 1 *(c)*.*)* *(b)* *Sch:* **To p. a candidate**, recevoir un candidat. *(c)* *Parl:* **To p. a bill**, voter, adopter, un projet de loi. 3. *(a)* Transmettre, donner. **To p. sth. from hand to hand**, passer qch. de main en main. *Fb:* **To p. the ball**, *abs.* **to p.**, passer le ballon; faire une passe. *F:* **To p. the buck**, se débrouiller sur le voisin. *(b)* (Faire) passer, écouler (un faux billet de banque). 4. **To p. one's hand between the bars**, glisser, passer, sa main à travers les barreaux. **To p. a sponge over sth.**, passer l'éponge sur qch. *Cu:* **To p. vegetables through a sieve**, passer les légumes. 5. *Mil:* **To p. troops in review**, passer les troupes en revue. 6. **To p. the spring abroad**, passer le printemps à l'étranger. **To p. (away) the time**, passer le temps. 7. *(a)* *Jur:* **To p. sentence**, prononcer le jugement. *(b)* *F:* **To p. remarks on sth.**, faire des observations sur qch. *S.a.* TIME[1] 6. 8. *Hyg: Med:* Évacuer. 9. *Abs. Cards: etc:* Passer (son tour). *(At dominoes)* Bouder. **pass across**, *v.i.* Traverser (la rue). **pass along**. 1. *v.i. (a)* Passer par (la rue). *Rail:* P. along the car! dégagez la portière! *(b)* P. along! (i) circulez! (ii) passez votre chemin! 2. *v.tr.* Faire passer (qch.) de main en main. **pass away**. 1. *v.i. (a)* *See* PASS[3] I. 3. *(b)* Mourir, *P:* passer. He passed away in the night, il est mort pendant la nuit, 2. *v.tr. See* PASS[3] II. 6. **passing away**, *s.* Mort *f.* **pass down**, *v.i.* Passer par, descendre (la rue). P. d. the car! dégagez la portière! **pass off**. 1. *v.i. (a)* *(Of pers.)* Se passer; disparaître. *(b)* Everything passed off smoothly, tout s'est bien passé. 2. *v.tr. (a)* **To p. sth. off on s.o.**, repasser qch. à qn. *(b)* **To p. oneself off for an artist**, se faire passer pour artiste. *(c)* **To p. sth. off as a joke**, (i) prendre qch. en riant; (ii) dire que cela a été fait pour rire. **pass on**. 1. *v.i.* Passer son chemin; passer outre. **To p. on to a new subject**, passer à un nouveau sujet. 2. *v.tr.* Read this and p. it on, lisez ceci et faites circuler. *F:* We have passed it on, on ne l'est dit. **passing on**, *s.* Transmission *f* (d'un ordre). **pass out**, *v.i.* 1. *(a)* Sortir (d'une salle). *(b)* *Sch:* *(Of pupils, after final examination)* Sortir. *Mil:* Cadets passing out, promotion sortante. 2. *(a)* *F:* S'évanouir; se trouver mal; *F:* tomber dans les pommes. *(b)* *F:* Mourir. 3. *v.tr.* **To p. sth. out of the window**, sortir qch. par la fenêtre. **pass-'out check**, *s.* *Th:* Contremarque *f* de sortie. **pass'over**. 1. *v.i.* 1. *(a)* **To p. over a river**, traverser, franchir, une rivière. 2. Passer (qch.) sous silence. **P. over the details**, vous pouvez omettre les détails. 2. *(a)* **To p. o. to the enemy**, passer à l'ennemi. *(b)* *(Of storm)* Se dissiper, finir. II. **pass over**, *v.tr.* 1. Donner, transmettre (qch. à qn). 2. **To p.s.o. over** *(in making a promotion)*, passer au-dessus le dos à qn. **pass round**. 1. *v.i. (a)* Contourner (un obstacle). *(b)* The bottle passes round, la bouteille circule de main en main. 2. *v.tr.* **To p. round the wine**, faire circuler le vin. *S.a.* HAT. **pass through**, *v.i.* 1. **To p. through a country**, traverser un pays. **To p. through a gateway**, franchir

un portail. 2. **To p. through a crisis**, traverser une crise. **pass up**, *v.tr.* 1. Monter, faire monter qch. 2. *U.S:* Négliger, laisser passer (une occasion, etc.). **To p. up ministerial office**, refuser un portefeuille. **passing**[1]. 1. *a. (a)* *(Of pers.)* Passant. A p. cyclist, un cycliste qui passait par là. P. events, actualités *f.* P. remark, remarque en passant. *(b)* Passager, éphémère. The p. hour, l'heure fugitive. 2. *adv. Lit:* Extrêmement, fort (riche). P. fair, de toute beauté. **passing**[2], *s.* 1. *(a)* Passage *m* (d'un train). *(b)* Dépassement *m*, doublement *m* (d'une autre voiture). *Aut:* *U.S:* No p., défense de doubler. 2. *(a)* Écoulement *m* (du temps). *(b)* Mort *f.* **'passing-bell**, *s.* Glas *m.* **'passing-note**, *s. Mus:* Note *f* de passage.

passable ['pɑːsəbl], *a.* 1. (Rivière) traversable; (route) praticable. P. by vehicles, carrossable. 2. Passable; assez bon. **-ably**, *adv.* Passablement, assez.

passage ['pæsidʒ], *s.* 1. *(a)* Passage *m.* P. of birds, passe *f* d'oiseaux. Bird of p., oiseau passager, migrateur. *(b)* Air, sea, p., prix *m* du billet par avion, par bateau. *Nau:* To have a bad p., faire une mauvaise traversée. To work one's p., gagner son passage. *(c)* *Pol:* The p. of a bill, adoption *f* d'un projet de loi. 2. *(a)* Couloir *m*, corridor *m.* *(b)* Passage, ruelle *f.* 3. *(a)* *Mec.E:* Air p., conduit *m* à air. *(b)* *Med:* *F:* The p., (i) l'urètre *m*; (ii) le rectum. 4. Passage of arms, (i) *A:* *Mil:* passe *f* d'armes; (ii) échange *m* de mots vifs. 5. Passage (d'un texte). The love passages, les scènes amoureuses (de la comédie). Selected passages, morceaux choisis. *Mus:* Melodic p., trait *m.* 6. *Equit:* Passège *m*, passage *m.* **'passage-way**, *s.* 1. To leave a p.-w., laisser le passage libre. 2. Passage, ruelle *f.*

passant ['pæsənt], *a. Her:* Passant. Lion p. gardant, lion léopardé.

passé ['pɑːsei], *a. (a)* Qui n'est plus à la mode. *(b)* Défraîchi; fané.

passenger ['pæs(ə)ndʒər], *s.* 1. Voyageur, -euse; *(by sea or air)* passager, -ère. 2. *Sp: Ind:* Non-valeur *f.* **'passenger coach**, *s. Rail:* Wagon *m*, voiture *f*, à voyageurs. **'passenger train**, *s.* Train *m* de voyageurs.

passe-partout ['pæspaːˈtuː], *s.* 1. (Clef *f*, cadre *m*) passe-partout *m inv.* 2. P.-p. framing, encadrement *m* en sous-verre.

passer(-by) ['pɑːsə(ˈbai)], *s.* Passant, -ante.

passerine ['pæsərain]. *Orn:* 1. *a.* Des passereaux. 2. *s.* Passereau *m.*

passion ['pæʃ(ə)n], *s.* 1. The P. (of Christ), la Passion. 2. Passion. Ruling p., passion dominante. To have a p. for painting, avoir la passion de la peinture. P. for work, acharnement *m* au travail. 3. Colère *f*, emportement *m.* Fit of p., accès de colère. To be in a p., être furieux. 4. Amour *m*, passion. To conceive a p. for s.o., se prendre d'amour pour qn. 5. She burst into a p. of tears, elle eut une crise de larmes terrible. **'passion-flower**, *s.* Fleur *f* de la Passion, passiflore *f.* **'passion-play**, *s. Lit.Hist:* Mystère *m* de la Passion.

passionate ['pæʃənit], *a.* 1. Emporté; (discours) véhément. 2. Passionné. P. embrace, étreinte ardente. **-ly**, *adv.* 1. Passionnément. To be p. in love with s.o., aimer qn à la folie. To be p. fond of sth., être passionné de qch. A p. interesting job, travail, métier, passionnant. 2. Avec colère, avec emportement.

passive ['pæsiv]. 1. *a.* Passif. P. resistance, résistance passive, inerte. 2. *a. & s. Gram:* The p. (voice), la voix passive; le passif. **-ly**, *adv.* Passivement.

passiveness ['pæsivnis], **passivity** [pæˈsiviti], *s.* Passivité *f*; inertie *f.*

Passover ['pɑːsouvər], *s.* La Pâque.

passport ['pɑːspɔːt], *s. (a)* Passeport *m.* *(b)* Ship's p., permis *m* de navigation.

password ['pɑːswɔːd], *s.* Mot *m* de passe.

past[1] [pɑːst]. 1. *a. (a)* Passé, ancien. Those days are p., ces jours sont passés. In times p., autrefois; au temps jadis. P. chairman, (i) président sortant; (ii) ancien président. *(b)* *Gram:* P. participle, participe passé. Verb in the p. tense, verbe au passé. *(c)* The p. few years, ces dernières années. For some time p., depuis quelque temps. 2. *s.*

Passé m. (a) In the p., au temps passé; autrefois. To live in the p., vivre du passé. As in the p., comme par le passé. The old plan is a thing of the p., l'ancien projet (i) n'existe plus, (ii) est périmé. (b) Town with a p., ville historique. (c) (Of pers.) To have a (murky) p., avoir des antécédents mpl. 'past-'master, s. 1. A: Maître passé (d'un corps de métier). He is a p.-m. at it, il est expert dans la matière. 2. Ancien maître (d'une loge de francs-maçons).

past². 1. prep. Au delà de. (a) A little (way) p. the bridge, un peu plus loin que le pont. To walk p. s.o., passer qn, passer devant qn. The train ran p. the signal, le train brûla, dépassa, le signal. (b) Plus de. He is p. eighty, il a quatre-vingts ans passés. A quarter p. four, quatre heures un quart. (c) P. all understanding, hors de toute compréhension. P. endurance, insupportable. That is p. all belief, cela n'est pas à croire. To be p. one's work, n'être plus en état de travailler. To be p. caring for sth., être revenu de qch. F: I wouldn't put it p. him, il en est bien capable. S.a. PRAY 1. 2. adv. To walk, go, p., passer. To march p., défiler.

pasta ['pæstə], s. Cu: Pâtes fpl (alimentaires).

paste¹ [peist], s. 1. Cu: Pâte f (de pâtisserie). 2. Pâte. Tooth paste, pâte dentifrice. Bloater, anchovy, p., beurre m de harengs, d'anchois. Starch p., colle f d'amidon. S.a. SCISSOR¹. 3. Lap: Stras(s) m; faux brillants; F: du toc.

paste², v.tr. 1. Coller. To p. (up) a poster, coller une affiche. 2. F: To p. s.o., flanquer une raclée à (qn). pasting, s. 1. Collage n (d'affiches, etc.). 2. F: Rossée f raclée f. Mil: Av: To give the enemy a good p., bombarder l'ennemi à plat.

pasteboard ['peistbɔːd], s. 1. (a) Carton m. (b) F: O: (i) Carte de visite; (ii) cartes à jouer. 2. U.S: = PASTRY-BOARD.

pastel¹ ['pæst(ə)l], s. Art: Pastel m; crayon m pastel. P. drawing, (dessin m au) pastel. P. shades, (i) couleurs tendres; (ii) Com: tons pastels.

pastel², s. Bot: Dy: = WOAD.

pastern ['pæstən], s. Anat: Vet: Paturon m (d'un cheval). P.-joint, boulet m.

pasteurization [,pæstərai'zeiʃ(ə)n], s. Pasteurisation f.

pasteurize ['pæstəraiz], v.tr. Pasteuriser; stériliser.

pastiche [pæs'tiːʃ], s. Art: Lit: Mus: Pastiche m.

pastille [pæs'tiːl], s. Comest: Pharm: Pastille f. Fruit pastilles, pâtes f de fruits.

pastime ['pɑːstaim, pæs-], s. Passe-temps m inv, amusement m, distraction f, divertissement m.

pastor ['pɑːstər], s. Ecc: (a) Pasteur m, ministre m. (b) U.S: Prêtre m, ecclésiastique m.

pastoral ['pɑːstərəl], 1. a. Pastoral, -aux. (a) P. tribes, tribus pastorales; peuples pasteurs. (b) Ecc: P. letter, s. pastoral, (lettre) pastorale (f). 2. s. Pastorale f. Lit: Poème pastoral; bergerie f. Mus: P. song, dance, pastourelle.

pastry ['peistri], s. 1. Pâtisserie f. 2. Pâte f. 'pastry(-)board, s. Planch: f à pâtisserie. 'pastry-cook, s. Pâtissier, -ière. 'pastry-making, s. Pâtisserie f.

pasturage ['pɑːstjuridʒ], s. 1. Pâturage m, pacage m (du cheptel). 2. = PASTURE¹ 1.

pasture¹ ['pɑːstjər], s. 1. Lieu m de pâture; pâturage m, pacage m. 2. = PASTURAGE 1. 'pasture-land, s. Pâturages mpl.

pasture². 1. v.i. (Of animals) Paître, pacager. 2. v.tr. (Of shepherd) (Faire) paître (les bêtes). pasturing, s. Pacage m.

pasty¹ ['peisti], a. 1. Pâteux, -euse. 2. P. face, visage terreux; F: figure en papier mâché. 'pasty-faced, a. Au teint brouillé, terreux.

pasty² ['pæsti], s. Cu: (Petit) pâté (en croûte).

pat¹ [pæt], s. 1. (a) Coup léger; petite tape f. (b) Caresse f. F: P. on the back, éloge m; mot m d'encouragement. 2. (a) Rondelle f, pelote f, médaillon m, coquille f, (de beurre). (b) Motte f, pain m (de beurre).

pat², v.tr. (patted) (a) Taper, tapoter. (b) Caresser. To p. a dog on the back, flatter le dos d'un chien. To p. s.o. on the back, encourager qn. To p. oneself on the back over sth., s'applaudir de qch. patting, s. Tapotement m; caresses fpl.

pat³. 1. adv. A propos. He answered p., his answer came p., il répliqua sur-le-champ. 2. a. Apte; à propos. He always has an excuse p., il a toujours une excuse toute prête.

Pat⁴. Pr.n.m. or f. (Dim. of Patrick, Patricia) Patrice; Patricia.

patch¹ [pætʃ], s. 1. (a) Pièce f (pour raccommoder). F: Not to be a p. on s.o., ne pas aller à la cheville de qn. (b) Pièce rapportée; Nau: placard m (de voile). 2. (a) Aut: etc: (Rubber) p., (for inner tube) pastille f. (b) Eye-p., couvre-œil m. (c) Toil: Mouche f. 3. Tache f (de couleur). P. of blue sky, échappée f de ciel bleu. P. of snow on the mountain, flaque f de neige sur la montagne. P. of ice, plaque f de glace. F: To strike a bad p., être en guigne, en déveine. 4. (a) Morceau m, parcelle f (de terre). (b) Carré m, plant m (de légumes).

patch², v.tr. Rapiécer, raccommoder (un vêtement); poser une pastille à (une chambre à air). patch up, v.tr. Rapetasser (de vieux vêtements); rafistoler (une machine). Patched-up peace, paix fourrée. patching, s. Rapiéçage m (d'un vieux vêtement); raccommodage m.

patchiness ['pætʃinis], s. Manque m d'harmonie (d'un paysage, etc.).

patchwork ['pætʃwəːk], s. Ouvrage fait de pièces et de morceaux. P. of fields, campagne bigarrée.

patchy ['pætʃi], a. Inégal, -aux.

pate [peit], s. F: Tête f, caboche f.

pâté ['pæteij], s. Pâté m. Liver p., pâté de foie. I'll take some of your special p., je prendrai du pâté maison.

patella [pə'telə], s. 1. Anat: Rotule f (du genou). 2. Rom.Ant: Moll: Patelle f.

paten ['pæt(ə)n], s. Ecc: Patène f.

patent¹ ['peit(ə)nt, 'pæt(ə)nt]. I. a. 1. Letters p., lettres patentes; (i) brevet m d'invention; (ii) lettres de noblesse. 2. Breveté. P. medicine, spécialité pharmaceutique. P. leather, cuir verni. S.a. LOG¹ 2. 3. (Fait) patent, manifeste. -ly, adv. Manifestement; clairement. II. patent, s. 1. P. of nobility, lettres de noblesse. 2. (a) Brevet m d'invention. To take out a p., prendre un brevet, faire breveter (une invention). Infringement of a p., contrefaçon f. P. agent, agent en brevets (d'invention), P. office, bureau des brevets. P.-rights, propriété industrielle. (b) Invention ou fabrication brevetée.

patent², v.tr. Faire breveter (une invention). patenting, s. Brevetage m.

patentee [,peitn'tiː], s. Breveté m.

paternal [pə'təːn(ə)l], a. Paternel, -elle. -ally, adv. Paternellement.

paternalism [pə'təːnəlizm], s. Paternalisme m.

paternalist [pə'təːnəlist], a. Paternaliste.

paternity [pə'təːniti], s. (a) Paternité f. (b) Origine f. Of doubtful p., de paternité douteuse.

paternoster ['pætə'nɔstər], s. Patenôtre f; pater m.

path, pl. paths [pɑːθ, pɑːðz], s. 1. Chemin m; sentier m; (in garden) allée f. The p. of glory, le chemin de la gloire. S.a. DOWNWARD 1. 2. Course f (d'un corps en mouvement); route f (du soleil). 'path-finder, s. Pionnier m.

pathetic [pə'θetik], a. (a) Pathétique, touchant, attendrissant. F: Isn't it p.? c'est tout de même triste! She's a p. creature, c'est une créature pitoyable. s. The p., pathétique m; pathétisme m. (b) Qui a rapport aux émotions. -ally, adv. Pathétiquement.

pathless ['pɑːθlis], a. Sans chemin (frayé).

pathological [,pæθə'lɒdʒik(ə)l], a. Pathologique.

pathologist [pæ'θɒlədʒist], s. (a) Pathologiste m. (b) Médecin m légiste.

pathology [pæ'θɒlədʒi], s. Pathologie f.

pathos ['peiθɒs], s. Pathétique m. Told with p., raconté d'une façon touchante.

pathway ['pɑːθwei], s. (a) Sentier m. (b) Accotement m (de grand chemin).

patience ['peiʃ(ə)ns], s. 1. Patience f. To try, tax, s.o.'s p., éprouver, exercer, la patience de qn. My p. is exhausted, je suis à bout de patience. To have p. with s.o., prendre patience avec qn. I have no p. with him, il m'impatiente, F: il m'enquiquine. To possess one's soul in p., patienter. 2. Cards: Réussite f. To play p., faire des réussites.

patient ['peiʃ(ə)nt]. I. *a.* Patient, endurant. To be p., patienter. -ly, *adv.* Patiemment. To wait p. for s.o., attendre qn avec patience. II. **patient,** *s.* Malade *mf*; (*surgical case*) patient, -ente; (*operated upon*) opéré, -ée. A doctor's patients, les clients *m* d'un médecin.

patina ['pætinə], *s.* Patine *f.*

patio ['pætiou], *s. Arch:* Patio *m.*

patriarch ['peitriɑ:k], *s.* Patriarche *m.*

patriarchal [ˌpeitri'ɑ:k(ə)l], *a.* Patriarcal, -aux.

patriarchate ['peitriɑ:keit], *s. Ecc:* Patriarcat *m.*

patriarchy ['peitriɑ:ki], *s.* Patriarcat *m*; régime social patriarcal.

patrician [pə'triʃ(ə)n], *a. & s.* Patricien, -ienne.

patricide[1] ['pætrisaid], *s. U.S:* (*Pers.*) Parricide *mf.*

patricide[2], *s. U.S:* (*Crime*) Parricide *m.*

Patrick ['pætrik]. *Pr.n.m.* Patrice.

patrimonial [ˌpætri'mounjəl], *a.* Patrimonial, -aux.

patrimony ['pætriməni], *s.* 1. Patrimoine *m.* 2. Biens-fonds *mpl*, revenu *m*, d'une église.

patriot ['peitriət, 'pæ-], *s.* Patriote *mf.*

patriotic ['pætri'ɔtik], *a.* 1. (*Of pers.*) Patriote. 2. (Discours, chanson) patriotique. -ally, *adv.* Patriotiquement; en patriote.

patriotism ['pætriətizm, 'pæ-], *s.* Patriotisme *m.*

patrol[1] [pə'troul], *s.* Patrouille *f.* (a) To go on p., faire la patrouille; faire une ronde. (b) Mounted p., patrouille à cheval. *Mil:* Member of a p., patrouilleur *m.* P. leader, chef *m* de patrouille. (c) *Scouting:* Troupe *f.* P. leader, chef de troupe. pa'trol-boat, -ship, *s.* Patrouilleur *m.* pa'trol-car, *s.* Voiture *f* de liaison, de reconnaissance, policière. pa'trol-wagon, *s. U.S:* Voiture *f* cellulaire; *F:* panier *m* à salade.

patrol[2], *v.* (patrolled) 1. *v.i.* Patrouiller; faire une ronde. 2. *v.tr.* Faire la patrouille dans (un quartier).

patrolman, *pl.* -men [pə'trolmən], *s.m. U.S:* 1. Patrouilleur. 2. = POLICEMAN.

patron ['peitrən]. 1. *s.m.* (a) Protecteur (des arts); patron (d'une œuvre de charité). (b) *Ecc:* P. saint, patron, -onne. (c) *Ecc:* Patron, présentateur (d'un bénéfice). 2. *s.m. & f. Com:* Client, -ente (d'un magasin); habitué, -ée (d'un cinéma). The patrons of the drama, le public du théâtre.

patronal [pə'trounl], *a.* Patronal, -aux.

patronage ['pætrənidʒ], *s.* 1. (a) Protection *f*, encouragement *m* (des arts); patronage *m.* To extend one's p. to s.o., accorder sa protection à qn. Concert under the p. of . . ., concert honoré d'une souscription de. . . . (b) *Pej:* Air protecteur (of, envers). 2. Clientèle *f* (d'un hôtel, etc.). 3. *Ecc:* Droit *m* de présentation (of a living, à un bénéfice).

patroness ['peitrənes], *s.* *f* Protectrice (des arts); (dame) patronnesse (d'une œuvre de charité).

patronize ['pætrənaiz], *v.tr.* 1. (a) Patronner, protéger (un artiste). (b) Traiter (qn) d'un air protecteur. 2. Accorder sa clientèle à (une maison). **patronizing,** *a.* (a) Protecteur, -trice. (b) P. tone, ton de condescendance. To become p., prendre un air protecteur. -ly, *adv.* D'un air protecteur.

patronymic [ˌpætro'nimik]. 1. *a.* Patronymique. 2. *s.* Nom *m* patronymique, patronyme *m.*

patter[1] ['pætər], *s.* 1. (a) Argot *m.* (b) Boniment *m* (de charlatan); bagou(t) *m.* (c) *F:* Bavardage *m*, jaserie *f.* 2. Parlé *m* (dans une chansonnette).

patter[2]. 1. *v.tr.* Bredouiller (ses prières). 2. *v.i.* Bavarder sans arrêt, jaser, caqueter.

patter[3], *s.* Petit bruit (de pas précipités); fouettement *m* (de la pluie).

patter[4], *v.i.* (a) Trottiner, marcher à petits pas rapides; (*of hail, rain*) crépiter, fouetter. (b) (*Of pers.*) To p. about, trottiner çà et là.

pattern ['pæt(ə)n], *s.* 1. Modèle *m*, type *m.* To take s.o. as a p., se modeler sur qn; s'inspirer de qn. 2. (a) Modèle, dessin *m.* Garments of different patterns, vêtements de coupes différentes. (b) *Dressm: etc:* Patron *m* (en papier). To take a p., relever un patron. (c) *Metall:* Casting p., gabarit *m*, calibre *m.* 3. Échantillon *m.* 4. Dessin, motif *m* (de papier peint, etc.). *Tex:* Broché *m* (d'un tissu). *T.V.* Test p., mire *f.* **pattern bombing,** *s. Mil.Av:* Bombardement *m* en masse. **'pattern-book,** *s. Com:* Livre *m* d'échantillons. **'pattern-shop,** *s. Ind:* Atelier *m* de modelage.

patty ['pæti], *s. Cu:* = Bouchée *f* à la reine.

paucity ['pɔ:siti], *s.* Manque *m*, disette *f*; rareté *f.* P. of new plays, indigence *f* de la production théâtrale. There is a p. of news, il y a disette de nouvelles. P. of money, manque d'argent, rareté de l'argent. P. of words, sobriété *f* de mots.

Paul [pɔ:l]. *Pr.n.m.* Paul. 'Paul 'Jones, *s. Danc:* Boulangère *f.*

paunch [pɔ:n(t)ʃ], *s.* (a) Panse *f*, ventre *m*, *F:* bedaine *f* (de qn). (b) Panse, rumen *m* (des ruminants).

pauper ['pɔ:pər], *s.* 1. *Adm:* Indigent, -ente. *A:* P. children, enfants assistés. *S.a.* GRAVE[1]. 2. Pauvre, -esse; mendiant, -ante.

pauperism ['pɔ:pərizm], *s.* Paupérisme *m.*

pauperization [ˌpɔ:pərai'zeiʃ(ə)n], *s.* Réduction *f* à l'indigence.

pauperize ['pɔ:pəraiz], *v.tr.* Réduire (qn) à l'indigence.

pause[1] [pɔ:z], *s.* 1. (a) Pause *f*, arrêt *m.* There was a p. in the conversation, il y eut un silence. (b) To give p. to s.o., faire hésiter qn. 2. *Pros:* Repos *m.* 3. *Mus:* Point *m* d'orgue. 4. *Typ:* P. dots, points *mpl* de suspension.

pause[2], *v.i.* 1. Faire une pause; pauser; s'arrêter un instant; marquer un temps. 2. Hésiter. To make s.o. p., donner à réfléchir à qn. 3. To p. (up)on a word, s'arrêter sur un mot.

pavane [pæ'vɑ:n], *s. Danc: Mus:* Pavane *f.*

pave [peiv], *v.tr.* Paver (une rue); carreler (une cour). To p. the way, préparer le terrain; frayer la voie. **paving,** *s.* 1. Pavage *m*, dallage *m*, carrelage *m.* 2. Pavé *m*, dalles *fpl.* **'paving-block, -stone,** *s.* Pierre *f* à paver; pavé *m.*

pavement ['peivmənt], *s.* (a) Pavé *m*, pavage *m*, dallage *m.* (b) Trottoir *m.* (c) *U.S:* Chaussée *f.* **'pavement-artist,** *s.* Barbouilleur *m* de trottoir. **'pavement-glass, -light,** *s.* Dallage *m* en verre.

pavilion [pə'viljən], *s.* 1. *A:* Pavillon *m*, tente *f.* 2. *Sp:* Pavillon. 3. *Arch:* Pavillon.

paviour ['peiviər], *s.* Paveur *m*, carreleur *m.*

paw[1] [pɔ:], *s.* (a) Patte *f* (d'animal onguiculé). (b) *P:* Main *f*; *P:* patte (de qn). *P:* Paws off! à bas les pattes!

paw[2], *v.tr.* 1. (a) Donner des coups de patte à (qn, qch.). (b) (*Of horse*) To p. the ground, *abs.* to p., piaffer; gratter (la terre) du pied. 2. (*Of pers.*) *F:* Tripoter, patouiller (qn, qch.); *P:* peloter (une femme).

pawkiness ['pɔ:kinis], *s. Scot:* 1. Malice *f*, finasserie *f.* 2. Humour *m* de pince-sans-rire.

pawky ['pɔ:ki], *a. Scot:* 1. Rusé, malicieux, -euse, finaud. 2. A p. answer, une réponse normande. -ily, *adv.* Avec un grain de malice.

pawl [pɔ:l], *s. Mec.E:* Linguet *m* (de cabestan); cliquet *m* (d'arrêt), chien *m* (d'arrêt).

pawn[1] [pɔ:n], *s.* 1. Gage *m*, nantissement *m.* 2. In p., en gage. To put one's watch in p., engager sa montre. To take sth. out of p., dégager qch. **'pawn-ticket,** *s.* Reconnaissance *f* (de dépôt de gage).

pawn[2], *v.tr.* Mettre (qch.) en gage; engager (qch.). **pawning,** *s.* Mise *f* en gage.

pawn[3], *s. Chess:* Pion *m.* *F:* To be s.o.'s p., être le jouet de qn.

pawnbroker ['pɔ:nbroukər], *s.* Prêteur, -euse, sur gage(s); commissionnaire *m* au crédit municipal.

pawnshop ['pɔ:nʃəp], *s.* Bureau *m* de prêt sur gage(s); maison *f* de prêt; caisse *f* de crédit municipal.

pax [pæks]. 1. *s. Ecc:* Paix *f.* 2. *int. Sch:* Pouce!

pay[1] [pei], *s.* Paie *f*, salaire *m* (d'un ouvrier, d'un employé); gages *mpl* (d'un domestique); traitement *m* (d'un fonctionnaire). *Mil: Navy:* Solde *f.* Unemployed p., solde de non-activité. Holidays with p., congés payés. To be in s.o.'s p., être à la solde, aux gages, de qn. **'pay-day,** *s.* Jour *m* de paie, de paiement; *P:* la Sainte-Touche; **'pay-desk,** *s.* Caisse *f*; comptoir-caisse *m.* **'pay-dirt,** *s. Gold-Min:* Alluvion *f* exploitable. **'pay(-)load,** *s.* Charge payante, commerciale. *Av:* Poids *m* utile. **'pay-office,** *s.* Caisse *f*, guichet *m.* **'pay-roll, -sheet,** *s.* Feuille *f* de paie. *Adm:* Feuille d'émargement. *Mil:* État *m* de solde. He is on the p.-r., il émarge au budget. **'pay station,** *s. Tp: U.S:* Cabine *f* téléphonique (automatique).

pay², *v.tr.* (*p.t. & p.p.* **paid** [peid]) **1.** (*a*) To p. s.o. ten francs, payer, compter, dix francs à qn. To p. s.o. an annuity, servir une rente à qn. (*Income tax*) P. as you earn, *U.S:* p. as you go = retenue *f* de l'impôt à la base, à la source. *F:* What's to p.? c'est combien? *Abs.* To p. ready money, cash down, payer (argent) comptant. To p. in advance, payer d'avance. 'P. at the gate,' "entrée payante." *F:* To p. through the nose, payer un prix excessif. We had to p. through the nose, on nous a salés. *S.a.* DEVIL¹ 1. (*b*) Payer (un domestique); solder (des troupes); rétribuer (un employé). (*c*) To p. s.o. to do sth., payer qn pour faire qch. **2.** (*a*) Payer (une dette). To p. a bill, solder, régler, un compte. (*On receipted bill*) 'Paid,' "pour acquit." *F:* To put paid to s.o.'s account, régler son compte à qn. To p. the duty on sth., acquitter les droits sur qch. *S.a.* WAY¹ 2. (*b*) To p. honour to s.o., faire honneur à qn. To p. one's respects to s.o., présenter ses respects à qn. To p. s.o. a visit, faire, rendre, une visite à qn. *F:* To p. a visit, aller faire pipi. *S.a.* COMPLIMENT¹, COURT¹ 2. **3.** To p. money into an account, verser une somme à un compte. **4.** It will p. you to... , vous y gagnerez à.... It doesn't p., on n'y trouve pas son compte; ce n'est pas rentable. *Prov:* It pays to advertise, la publicité rapporte. **pay away**, *v.tr.* Dépenser (de l'argent). **pay back**, *v.tr.* **1.** Rendre, restituer (de l'argent emprunté). **2.** Rembourser (qn). *F:* To p. s.o. back (in his own coin), rendre la pareille à qn. **pay down**, *v.tr.* (*a*) Payer (qch.) comptant. (*b*) To p. something down, verser une provision; donner des arrhes. **pay for**, *v.tr.* **1.** (*a*) To p. (s.o.) for sth., payer qch. (à qn). What do you p. for tea? combien payez-vous le thé? I had paid for his schooling, j'avais subvenu aux frais de ses études. To p. for services, rémunérer des services. To p. s.o. for his trouble, dédommager qn de sa peine. (*b*) To p. dear(ly) for one's happiness, payer cher son bonheur. He paid for it up to the hilt, il a expié durement sa faute. He paid for his rashness with his life, il a payé sa témérité de sa vie. I'll make him p. for this! il me le paiera! **2.** He likes to invite people and to p. for them, il aime à inviter les gens à ses frais. **pay in**, *v.tr.* To p. in a cheque, donner un chèque à l'encaissement. *Abs.* To p. in to a fund, contribuer à une caisse. **'paying(-)in**, *s.* Versement *m* (d'argent à la banque, etc.) *Bank:* P.-in slip, bordereau *m*, feuille *f*, fiche *f*, de versement. **pay off**, *v.tr.* **1.** Solder, régler, acquitter (une dette); s'acquitter de (ses dettes). **2.** (*a*) Rembourser (un créancier); donner son compte à (un employé). (*b*) Congédier (un domestique); licencier (des troupes); désarmer (un navire). **3.** *Nau:* To p. o. the ship's head, laisser arriver le navire. **4.** *v.i. esp. U.S:* The business paid off well, le commerce se montra très rentable. The years of work paid off at last, les années de travail furent enfin couronnées de succès. **pay out**, *v.tr.* **1.** Payer, débourser, décaisser. To be always paying out, avoir toujours la main à la poche. **2.** I'll p. you out for that! je vous revaudrai cela! **3.** *Nau:* (Laisser) filer (un câble). **'paying-out**, *s. Com:* Décaissage *m*, décaissement *m*. **pay up**, *v.tr.* **1.** To p. up one's debts, *abs.* to p. up, se libérer (de ses dettes). P. up! payez! **2.** *Fin:* Libérer (des actions). Fully paid-up share, action libérée. **paying¹**, *a.* **1.** (Élève, etc.) payant. P. guest, pensionnaire *mf.* **2.** (*Of business*) Rémunérateur; qui rapporte. **paying²**, *s.* **1.** Paiement *m*, versement *m* (d'argent); remboursement *m* (d'un créancier). **2.** Règlement *m*, acquittement *m* (d'une dette).

payable ['peiəbl], *a.* Payable, acquittable. Taxes p. by the tenant, impôts à la charge du locataire. *Com:* P. at sight, payable à vue. To make a bill p. to s.o., faire un billet à l'ordre de qn. To make a cheque p. to bearer, souscrire un chèque au porteur.

payee [pei'i:], *s.* Preneur, -euse, bénéficiaire *mf* (d'un mandat-poste, etc.).

payer ['peiər], *s.* Payeur, -euse, payant, -ante.

paymaster ['peimɑːstər], *s.* Payeur *m. Mil:* Trésorier *m. Navy:* Commissaire *m.*

payment ['peimənt], *s.* (*a*) Paiement *m*; versement *m*; règlement *m.* On p. of ten francs, moyennant paiement de dix francs. To stop p. of a cheque, frapper un chèque d'opposition. (*Of bank*) To stop p., cesser les paiements. Method of p., mode *m* de règlement. Cash p., paiement comptant. P. on account, versement à compte; acompte *m.* P. in full, liquidation *f* (d'un compte). P. of interest, service *m* de l'intérêt. 'P. received,' "pour acquit." (*b*) Rémunération *f.* As p. for your services, en rémunération de vos services.

payoff ['peiɔf], *F:* *U.S:* **1.** *a.* The p. test, le test final, décisif. **2.** *s.* (*a*) Paiement *m* versement *m*; rémunération *f.* (*b*) Facteur décisif. (*c*) le fin mot (de l'histoire).

pea [piː], *s.* **1.** *Hort:* Pois *m. Cu:* Green peas, petits pois. Split peas, pois cassés. To jump about like a p. on a drum, se démener comme un diable dans un bénitier. *S.a.* LIKE¹ I. 1. **2.** *Bot:* Sweet p., pois de senteur. 'pea-'green, *a. & s.* Vert feuille (*m*) *inv. F:* He turned p.-g., il devint blême. 'pea-pod, *s.* Cosse *f*, gousse *f*, de pois. 'pea-'shooter, *s.* Sarbacane *f* de poche. 'pea-'soup, *s.* Soupe *f*, potage *m*, crème *f*, aux pois (cassés); (*thick*) purée *f* de pois. 'pea-'souper, *s. F:* Brouillard *m* (jaune) à couper au couteau.

peace [piːs], *s.* **1.** (*a*) Paix *f.* Country at p. with its enemies, pays en paix avec ses ennemis. To make (one's) p. with s.o., faire la paix, se réconcilier, avec qn. To sue for p., demander la paix. P. with honour, une paix honorable. (*b*) P.(-treaty), traité *m* de paix. **2.** P. and order, la paix et l'ordre public. P. prevails in the town, la paix règne dans la ville. To keep the p., (i) ne pas troubler l'ordre public; (ii) veiller à l'ordre public. To break, disturb, the p., troubler, violer, l'ordre public. Justice of the p., = juge *m* d'instance (à titre bénévole). **3.** (*a*) Tranquillité *f* (de l'âme). To live in p. (and quietness), vivre en paix. You may sleep in p., vous pouvez dormir tranquille. To give s.o. no p., ne donner ni paix ni trêve à qn. God rest his soul in p.! que Dieu donne le repos à son âme! (*b*) To hold one's p., se taire; garder le silence. 'peace-ioving, *a.* Pacifique. 'peace-offering, *s.* **1.** *Jew.Rel:* Sacrifice *m* de propitiation. **2.** Cadeau *m* de réconciliation.

peaceable ['piːsəbl], *a.* **1.** Pacifique, qui aime la paix. P. man, homme de paix. **2.** = PEACEFUL 2. **-ably**, *adv.* **1.** Pacifiquement. **2.** En paix.

peaceful ['piːsful], *a.* **1.** Paisible, calme, tranquille. The p. countryside, les campagnes paisibles. **2.** Pacifique, qui ne trouble pas la paix. **-fully**, *adv.* **1.** Paisiblement. **2.** Pacifiquement.

peacefulness ['piːsfulnis], *s.* Tranquillité *f*, paix *f.*

peacemaker ['piːsmeikər], *s.* Pacificateur, -trice, conciliateur, -trice. *B:* Blessed are the peacemakers, bienheureux les pacifiques.

peach¹ [piːtʃ], *s. Hort:* **1.** (*a*) Pêche *f.* (*b*) *F:* It's a p., c'est une perle. **2.** P.(-tree), pêcher *m.* 'peach-blossom, *s.* Fleur *f* de pêcher.

peach², *v.i. O:* *F:* Cafarder, moucharder. He peached to the boss, il a rapporté ça au patron.

pea-chick ['piːtʃik], *s. Orn:* Paonneau *m.*

peacock ['piːkɔk], *s. Orn:* Paon *m.* 'peacock-'blue, *a. & s.* Bleu paon (*m*) *inv.*

peafowl ['piːfaul], *s.* Paon *m*, paonne *f.*

peahen ['piːhen], *s.* Paonne *f.*

pea-jacket ['piːdʒækit], *s. Nau:* Vareuse *f*, caban *m.*

peak [piːk], *s.* **1.** (*a*) Visière *f* (de casquette). (*b*) Bec *m* (d'une ancre). (*c*) Pointe *f* (de toit, etc.). Widow's p., pointe *f* de cheveux sur le front. **2.** *Nau:* (*a*) Coqueron *m* (de la cale). (*b*) Pic *m* (de voile). With the flag at the p., le pavillon à la corne. **3.** (*a*) Pic, cime *f* (de montagne). The highest peaks, les plus hauts sommets. (*b*) *Med:* (*Of fever*) Pointe. *Mec: etc:* Pointe, apogée *m* (d'une courbe, d'une charge). *Ph:* Sommet (d'une onde). *El.E:* P. power, puissance *f* de crête. P. load, charge maximum (d'un générateur). *Ind:* P. output, record *m* (de production). *Rail: etc:* P. hours, heures de pointe; heures d'affluence. 'peak-'halyard, *s. Nau:* Drisse *f* de pic.

peaked [piːkt], *a.* (*a*) (Casquette) à visière. (*b*) High-p. **hat**, chapeau (haut et) pointu. (*c*) *F:* P. **features**, traits tirés, fatigués, hâves.

peaky ['piːki], *a. F:* **To look p.**, avoir les traits tirés, hâves; (*of child*) être pâlot.

peal[1] [piːl], *s.* **1.** P. **of bells**, carillon *m.* **2.** (*a*) **To ring a p.**, carillonner. (*b*) **Full p. of the bells**, volée *f* de cloches. **3.** Retentissement *m*; grondement *m* (du tonnerre); coup *m* (de tonnerre). **4.** P. **of laughter**, éclat *m* de rire.

peal[2]. **1.** *v.i.* (*a*) (*Of bells*) Carillonner. (*b*) (*Of thunder*) Retentir, gronder. (*c*) (*Of laughter*) Résonner. **2.** *v.tr.* Sonner (les cloches) à toute volée.

peanut ['piːnʌt], *s. Bot:* Arachide *f.* P. **oil**, huile *f* d'arachide. P. **butter**, beurre *m* d'arachide. **Roasted peanuts**, cacahuètes *fpl. U.S: Th: F:* P. **gallery**, poulailler *m. F:* P. **politics**, politicailleries *fpl. Esp. U.S: F:* **Peanuts**, une bagatelle, un rien. **This salary's peanuts compared with . . .**, ces appointements sont dérisoires à côté de . . .

pear [peər], *s.* **1.** Poire *f. S.a.* PRICKLY 1. **2.** P.(-**tree**), poirier *m* 'pear-**shaped**, *a.* En forme de poire; piriforme.

pearl[1] [pəːl], *s.* **1.** Perle *f.* (**Real) p.**, perle fine. **Cultured p.**, perle cultivée, perle japonaise. **String of pearls**, fil *m* de perles. **2.** (*Mother-of-pearl*) Nacre *f* (de perle). P. **button**, bouton de nacre. 'pearl-'**barley**, *s.* Orge perlé. 'pearl-**diver**, -**fisher**, *s.* Pêcheur *m* de perles. 'pearl-**fishery**, *s.* Pêcherie *f* de perles. 'pearl-'**grey**, *a. & s.* Gris perle (*m*) *inv.* 'pearl-**shell**, *s.* Coquille nacrée. 'pearl-'**white**. **1.** (*a*) D'une blancheur de perle. **2.** *s. Com:* Blanc de perle.

pearl[2]. *v.i.* (*Of moisture*) Perler; former des gouttelettes; (*of sugar*) faire la perle.

pearly ['pəːli], *a.* Perlé; nacré. P. **teeth**, dents de perle; dents perlées. P. **king**, marchand *m* des quatre saisons de Londres qui porte aux jours de fête un costume couvert de boutons de nacre.

peasant ['pez(ə)nt], *s.* Paysan, -anne; campagnard, -arde.

peasantry ['pez(ə)ntri], *s.* **The p.**, les paysans *m*; les campagnards *m. Coll:* Paysannerie f; paysannat *m.*

pease [piːz], *s. A:* Pois *mpl.* 'pease-**flour**, -**meal**, *s.* Farine *f* de pois cassés. 'pease-**pudding**, *s.* Purée *f* de pois (cassés).

peat [piːt], *s.* **1.** *Coll.* Tourbe *f.* **To dig, cut, p.**, extraire de la tourbe. **2.** (*Turf, sod, block, of*) p. motte *f* de tourbe. 'peat-**bog**, *s.* Tourbière *f.* 'peat-**moss**, *s.* **1.** = PEAT-BOG. **2.** *Bot:* Sphaigne *f.*

peaty ['piːti], *a.* **1.** Tourbeux, -euse. P. **soil**, sol tourbeux, tourbier. **2.** (Goût *m*) de fumée de tourbe.

pebble[1] ['pebl], *s.* **1.** (*a*) Caillou *m*; (*on sea-shore*) galet *m.* **You're not the only p. on the beach**, vous n'êtes pas unique au monde. (*b*) **Scotch p.**, agate *f* (des ruisseaux d'Écosse). **2.** *Opt:* (*a*) Cristal *m* de roche. (*b*) Lentille *f* en cristal de roche. **3.** *Leath:* Maroquinage (communiqué au cuir). **4.** *Tex:* P. **weave**, granité *m.* 'pebble-**dash**, *s. Const:* Crépi (moucheté). P.-d. **finish**, crépissure *f.*

pebble[2], *v.tr. Leath:* Crépir, maroquiner (le cuir).

pebbly ['pebli], *a.* Caillouteux, -euse; (plage) à galets.

pecan ['piːkæn], *s.* Pacanier *m.* P. **nut**, pacane *f.*

peccadillo [,pekə'dilou], *s.* Peccadille *f*; vétille *f.*

peccary ['pekəri], *s. Z:* Pécari *m.*

peck[1] [pek], *s.* (*a*) Coup *m* de bec. (*b*) *F:* (*Kiss*) Bécot *m.* **To give s.o. a p.**, bécoter qn.

peck[2], *v.tr.* **1.** (*a*) (*Of bird*) Picoter, becqueter (qch.); donner un coup de bec à (qn). (*b*) *F:* (*Kiss*) Bécoter, baisoter (qn). **2.** *Abs. F:* Manger du bout des dents. **peck at**, *v.ind.tr.* (*a*) Picoter; donner des coups de bec à (qn, qch.). (*b*) *F:* Pignocher, mangeotter (un plat). **peck out**, *v.tr.* Crever (les yeux) à coups de bec. **pecking**, *s.* Becquetage *m.*

peck,[3] *s. Meas:* **1.** (*a*) *Approx.* = Quart de boisseau *m.* (*b*) Picotin *m* (d'avoine). **She's had a p. of trouble**, elle a eu bien des malheurs.

pecker ['pekər], *s. F:* Courage *m*; cran *m. Mainly in the phr.* **To keep one's p. up**, ne pas se laisser abattre.

peckish ['pekiʃ], *a. F:* **To be, feel, p.**, se sentir le ventre creux.

pectin ['pektin], *s. Ch:* Pectine *f.*

pectoral ['pektərəl]. **1.** *a.* Pectoral, -aux. **2.** *s. Jew.Rel: Anat: Pharm:* Pectoral *m.*

peculate ['pekjuleit], *v.i.* Détourner des fonds.

peculation [,pekju'leiʃən], *s.* Péculat *m*, déprédation *f*; détournement *m* de fonds. *Jur:* Vol public; prévarication *f.*

peculator ['pekjuleitər], *s.* Concussionnaire *m*, prévaricateur *m.*

peculiar [pi'kjuːliər], *a.* (*a*) Particulier. **The condor is p. to the Andes**, le condor est particulier aux Andes. (*b*) Spécial, -aux; particulier. **Of p. interest**, d'un intérêt tout particulier. (*c*) (*Of thg*) Étrange; (*of pers.*) bizarre, singulier. **He, she, is a little p.**, c'est un(e) excentrique. **To be p. in one's dress**, s'habiller singulièrement. **-ly**, *adv.* (*a*) Personnellement. (*b*) Particulièrement. (*c*) Étrangement; singulièrement.

peculiarity [pi,kjuː'li'æriti], *s.* **1.** Trait distinctif; particularité *f.* (*On passport*) **Special peculiarities**, signes particuliers. **2.** Bizarrerie *f*, singularité *f.* **We all have our little peculiarities**, nous avons tous nos petites manies.

pecuniary [pi'kjuːniəri], *a.* Pécuniaire. P. **difficulties**, ennuis *m* d'argent.

pedagogic(al) [,pedə'gɔdʒik(ə)l], *a.* Pédagogique.

pedagogue ['pedəgɔg], *s. Pej:* Pédagogue *m*; magister *m*; pédant *m.*

pedagogy ['pedəgɔdʒi], *s.* Pédagogie *f.*

pedal[1] ['ped(ə)l], *s.* **1.** *a) Mec.E:* Pédale *f. Aut:* **Clutch p.**, pédale d'embrayage. (*b*) *Cy:* Pédale. **2.** (*a*) (*Of piano*) **Soft p.**, petite pédale. **Loud p.**, grande pédale. (*b*) (*Of organ*) **Swell p.**, pédale expressive. (*c*) P. **note**, pédale. 'pedal-**bin**, *s.* Poubelle *f* à pédale. 'pedal-**board**, *s.* Pédalier *m* (d'un orgue). 'pedal-**car**, *s.* Vélocar *m.* 'pedal **craft**, pédalo *m.*

pedal[2] ['ped(ə)l], *v.i.* (**pedalled**) **1.** *Cy:* Pédaler. **2.** (*Piano*) Mettre la pédale.

pedant ['ped(ə)nt], *s.* Pédant, -ante.

pedantic [pi'dæntik], *a.* Pédant, pédantesque. **-ally**, *adv.* Pédantesquement; en pédant.

pedantry ['ped(ə)ntri], *s.* Pédantisme *m*, pédanterie *f.*

peddle [pedl]. **1.** *v.i.* Faire le colportage. **2.** *v.tr.* Colporter (des marchandises). **To p. drugs**, faire le trafic des stupéfiants. **peddling**, *s.* Colportage *m.*

pederast ['pedəræst], *s.* = PAEDERAST.

pedestal ['pedist(ə)l], *s.* **1.** Piédestal *m*, -aux; socle *m*; (*small, for bust, etc.*) piédouche *m.* **To put s.o. on a p.**, mettre qn sur un piédestal. **2.** (*a*) Socle (de pompe); support *m*, colonne *f.* (*b*) *Mec.E:* Palier *m*, chevalet *m* (de coussinet). **3.** P. **writing-table**, bureau ministre. 'pedestal-'**table**, *s.* Guéridon *m.*

pedestrian [pi'destriən]. **1.** *a.* (*a*) Pédestre; (voyage) à pied. (*b*) (Style) prosaïque, terre à terre. **2.** *s.* Piéton *m*; voyageur, -euse, à pied. *attrib. Adm:* P. **crossing**, passage clouté, passage à piétons.

pediatrician [,piːdiæ'triʃ(ə)n], **pediatrist** [,piːdi'ætrist] *s. Med:* Pédiatre *m.*

pediatrics [,piːdi'ætriks], *s. Med:* Pédiatrie *f.*

pediatry [,piːdi'ætri], *s. Med:* Pédiatrie *f.*

pedicular [pe'dikjulər], *a. Med:* (Maladie) pédiculaire.

pedicure ['pedikjuər], *s.* Pédicure *mf.*

pedigree ['pedigriː], *s.* **1.** Arbre *m* généalogique. **2.** (*a*) Ascendance *f*, généalogie *f* (de qn). (*b*) *Breed:* Certificat *m* d'origine, pedigree *m* (d'un chien, etc.). P. **dog**, chien de (pure) race, de bonne souche.

pediment ['pedimənt], *s. Arch:* Fronton *m.*

pedlar ['pedlər], *s.* Colporteur *m*, porteballe *m.* **Drug p.**, trafiquant *m* en stupéfiants.

pedology [pe'dɔlədʒi], *s. Geol:* Pédologie *f.*

pedometer [pe'dɔmitər], *s.* Podomètre *m*, compte-pas *m inv.*

peduncle [pe'dʌŋkl], *s. Bot:* Pédoncule *m.*

pee[1] [piː], *v.i. F:* Faire pipi.

pee[2], *s. F:* Pipi *m.*

peek[1] [piːk], *s.* = PEEP[2].

peek[2], *v.i.* = PEEP[4].

peel[1] [piːl], *s.* Pelure *f* (de pomme); écorce *f*, peau *f*, *Cu:* zeste *m* (de citron). **Candied p.**, zeste confit.

peel[2]. **1.** *v.tr.* (*a*) Peler (un fruit); éplucher (des pommes de terre); écorcer (un bâton). *Cu:* **To p. the outer skin off a lemon**, zester un citron. (*b*) *Sp: F:* **To p.**, se dépouiller de ses vêtements. **2.**

v.i. (*a*) To p. (off), (*of paint*) s'écailler; (*of skin*) se desquamer. *Av:* To p. off, se détacher. (*b*) (*Of the nose, etc.*) Peler; (*of tree*), se décortiquer; (*of wall*) se décrépir; (*of tyre*) se déchaper. **peeling,** *s.* 1. (*a*) Épluchage *m*; écorçage *m*. (*b*) P. (off), écaillement *m*; *Med:* desquamation *f.* 2. *pl.* Peelings, épluchures *f.*

peeler ['pi:lər], *s. Tls:* 1. *Dom.Ec:* Éplucheur *m.* Vegetable p., rasoir *m* à légumes. *S.a.* POTATO-PEELER. 2. *Ind: etc:* Épluchoir *m.* **Orange-, lemon-peeler,** zesteuse *f.*

peen [pi:n], *s. U.S:* Panne *f* (de marteau). '**peen-hammer,** *s. Tls:* Marteau *m* à panne. **Ball-p. hammer,** marteau à panne ronde; marteau de mécanicien.

peep¹ [pi:p], *s.* Piaulement *m*, pépiement *m* (d'oiseau); cri *m* (de souris).

peep², *v.i.* (*Of bird*) Piauler, pépier; (*of mouse*) crier.

peep³, *s.* 1. Coup d'œil (furtif). To get a p. at sth., entrevoir qch. 2. Filtrée *f* (de lumière); petite flamme (de gaz). At p. of day, au point du jour; dès l'aube. '**peep-bo,** *int.* Coucou! '**peep-hole,** *s.* 1. Judas *m.* 2. *Mec.E:* (Trou *m* de) regard *m.* 3. *Sm.a:* Œilleton *m* (d'une hausse).

peep⁴, *v.i.* 1. To p. at sth., regarder qch. à la dérobée. To p. round the corner, risquer un coup d'œil au coin de la rue. Peeping Tom, curieux *m*, indiscret *m.* 2. To p. (out), se laisser entrevoir, se montrer.

peer¹ [pi:ər], *s.* 1. Pair *m*; pareil, -eille. 2. P. of the realm, pair du Royaume-Uni.

peer², *v.i.* (*a*) To p. at s.o., sth., scruter qn, qch., du regard. (*b*) To p. over the wall, risquer un coup d'œil par-dessus le mur.

peerage ['piəridʒ], *s.* 1. Pairie *f.* 2. *Coll.* The p., (i) les pairs *m*; (ii) la noblesse. 3. Almanach *m* nobiliaire.

peeress ['piəris], *s.f.* Pairesse.

peerless ['piəlis], *a.* Sans pareil, sans pair. *Lit:* P. beauty, beauté *f* incomparable.

peeved [pi:vd], *a. F:* Fâché, irrité, ennuyé.

peevish ['pi:viʃ], *a.* Irritable, geignard; maussade. **-ly,** *adv.* Maussadement; avec humeur.

peevishness ['pi:viʃnis], *s.* Maussaderie *f*; mauvaise humeur; hargne *f.*

peewit ['pi:wit], *s. Orn:* Vanneau (huppé).

peg¹ [peg], *s.* 1. (*a*) Cheville *f* (en bois); fiche *f.* **He's a square p. in a round hole,** il n'est pas dans son emploi. To take s.o. down a p. (or two), remettre qn à sa place; *F:* rabattre le caquet de qn. To come down a p., baisser d'un cran; *F:* en rabattre. *S.a.* CLOTHES-PEG. (*b*) (Hat-)p., patère *f. F:* To buy clothes off the p., acheter un tailleur, un complet, de confection. P. to hang a grievance on, prétexte *m* de plainte. (*c*) Piquet *m* (de tente, etc.). (At croquet) Finishing p., piquet d'arrivée. 2. (*a*) Pointe *f*, fer *m*, (de toupie); pied *m*, pique *f* (de violoncelle). *P: A:* Jambe *f*; *P:* quille *f.* 3. Doigt *m* (de whisky, etc.). To mix oneself a stiff p., se faire un grog bien tassé. '**peg-leg,** *s. F: O:* Jambe *f* de bois. '**peg-top,** *s.* Toupie *f.*

peg², *v.tr.* (pegged) 1. Cheviller (un assemblage). To p. clothes on the line, accrocher du linge sur la corde. *Bootm:* Pegged soles, semelles chevillées. 2. *Games:* Marquer (des points). 3. *Fin:* To p. the exchange, stabiliser le cours du change. *Pol. Ec:* To p. prices, indexer les prix. 4. *v.i. F:* To p. away (at sth.), travailler ferme (à qch.), *F:* piocher (un sujet). **peg down,** *v.tr.* Fixer (une tente), assujettir (un filet), avec des piquets. **peg out.** 1. *v.tr.* To p. out a claim, piqueter, jalonner, une concession. 2. *v.i.* (*a*) *Croquet:* Toucher le piquet final (et se retirer de la partie). (*b*) *P:* Mourir; *P:* casser sa pipe. **pegging,** *s.* 1. Chevillage *m.* 2. *Sp: Games:* It's still level p., ils sont encore à égalité. 3. *Fin:* Stabilisation *f* (du marché, de la livre sterling). *Pol.Ec:* P. of prices, indexation *f.*

Pegasus ['pegəsəs]. *Pr.n. Gr.Myth:* Pégase *m.*

pejorative ['pedʒərətiv, pi'dʒɔr-], *a. & s.* Péjoratif (*m*).

peke [pi:k], *s. Z: F:* = PEKIN(G)ESE 2.

Pekin(g) [pi:'kin,-iŋ], *Pr.n. Geog:* Pékin. *Anthr:* P. man, sinanthrope *m.*

Pekinese, Pekingese ['pi:ki'ni:z, -kiŋ'i:z], 1. *a. & s. Geog:* Pékinois, -oise. 2. *s.* (Chien) pékinois.

pelagian [pi'leidʒiən], **pelagic** [pe'lædʒik], *a. Oc:* Pélagien, pélagique.

pelargonium [,pelə'gounjəm], *s. Bot:* Pélargonium *m*, *F:* géranium *m.*

pelf [pelf], *s. Pej:* Richesses *fpl*, lucre *m.*

pelican ['pelikən], *s.* Pélican *m.*

pelisse [pe'li:s], *s. A: Cost:* Pelisse *f.*

pellagra [pe'lægrə, pe'leigrə], *s. Med:* Pellagre *f.*

pellet ['pelit], *s.* (*a*) Boulette *f* (de papier); pelote *f* (d'argile). (*b*) *Sm.a:* Grain *m* de plomb. (*c*) *Pharm:* Pilule *f.* (*d*) *Husb:* Granulé *m.* (*e*) *Metall: Ch:* Boulette.

pellicle ['pelikl], *s.* (*a*) Pellicule *f.* (*b*) Membrane *f.*

pellicular [pe'likjulər], *a.* (*a*) Pelliculaire. (*b*) Membraneux, -euse.

pellitory ['pelitəri], *s. Bot:* 1. P. of Spain, pyrèthre *m.* 2. Wall-p., pariétaire *f.*

pell-mell ['pel'mel]. 1. *adv.* Pêle-mêle. 2. *a.* En confusion, en désordre.

pellucid [pe'lju:sid], *a.* (*a*) Pellucide, transparent. (*b*) (Style) lucide, limpide. (*c*) (Esprit) clair.

pelmet ['pelmit], *s. Furn:* Lambrequin *m.*

pelota [pe'loutə], *s. Games:* Pelote *f* basque. P. player, pelotari *m.*

pelt¹ [pelt], *s.* 1. Peau *f*, fourrure *f* (de mouton). 2. *Tan:* Peau verte.

pelt², *s.* 1. Grêle *f* (de pierres). 2. (At) full p., (courir) à toute vitesse.

pelt³. 1. *v.tr.* To p. s.o. with stones, lancer une volée de pierres à qn. 2. *v.i.* (*a*) (*Of rain*) To p. (down), tomber à verse, tomber à seaux. **Pelting rain,** pluie battante. (*b*) *F:* He was off as fast as he could p., il se sauva à toutes jambes.

peltry ['peltri], *s.* Pelleterie *f*; peaux *fpl.*

pelvic ['pelvik], *a. Anat:* Pelvien, -enne.

pelvis ['pelvis], *s. Anat:* Bassin *m.* **False p.,** pelvis *m.*

pen¹ [pen], *s.* 1. Parc *m*, enclos *m* (à moutons). *U.S:* Hog p., porcherie *f. Bullfighting:* Bull p., toril *m.* 2. *Navy:* Submarine p., abri *m*, nid *m*, de sous-marins.

pen², *v.tr.* (penned) To p. (up, in), parquer (des moutons); (r)enfermer, confiner (qn dans une pièce).

pen³, *s.* 1. Plume *f* (pour écrire). *S.a.* FOUNTAIN-PEN. Mapping p., plume à dessin, à dessiner. **Ball-point p., F:** ball-p., stylo *m* à bille. Stroke of the p., trait *m* de plume. To put one's p. to paper, mettre la main à la plume. To have a ready p., avoir la plume facile. To make a living by one's p., vivre de sa plume. To run one's p. through sth., biffer, rayer, qch. (d'un trait de plume). **P.-and-ink drawing,** dessin à la plume. 2. P.(-nib), (bec *m* de) plume. '**pen-friend,** *s.* Correspondant, -ante. '**pen-name,** *s.* Pseudonyme *m.* '**pen-pusher,** *s. F:* Plumitif *m*; rond-de-cuir *m.* '**pen-tray,** *s.* Plumier (plat).

pen⁴, *v.tr.* (penned) *O:* Écrire (une lettre).

pen⁵, *s. Orn:* Cygne *m* femelle.

penal ['pi:n(ə)l], *a.* (*Of laws*) Pénal, -aux; (*of offence*) qui comporte, entraîne, une pénalité. **P. servitude,** travaux forcés, *F:* bagne *m.* *A:* P. colony, p. settlement, colonie *f* pénitentiaire. **-ally,** *adv.* Pénalement.

penalization [,pi:nəlai'zeiʃ(ə)n], *s.* Infliction *f* d'une peine. *Sp: Games:* Pénalisation *f.*

penalize ['pi:nəlaiz], *v.tr.* 1. Sanctionner (un délit) d'une peine. 2. (*a*) Infliger une peine à (qn). (*b*) *Games:* Pénaliser (un joueur). (*c*) *Sp:* Handicaper.

penalty¹ ['penəlti], *s.* 1. (*a*) Peine *f*, pénalité *f. Com:* Amende *f* (pour retard de livraison). *Adm:* Sanction (pénale). P. clause (*in contract*), clause pénale (de dommages-intérêts). **The death p.,** la peine de mort. (Up)on, under, p. of death, sous peine de mort. *F:* To pay the p. of one's foolishness, être puni de sa sottise. (*b*) Désavantage *m.* To pay the p. of fame, payer la rançon de la gloire. 2. *Sp:* (*a*) Pénalisation *f*, pénalité *f.* *Golf:* P. stroke, coup d'amende. *Fb:* P. kick, shot, coup de pied de réparation; penalty *m*, *pl.*, penaltys. P. area, surface *f*, zone *f* de pénalisation, de pénalité. (*b*) Handicap *m.*

penalty², *a. U.S.: Post:* P. mail, courrier en franchise (au service de l'État). P. envelope, enveloppe réservée au service de l'État.

penance ['penəns], *s.* Pénitence *f.* To do p. for one's sins, faire pénitence de, pour, ses péchés.

Penates [pe'neiti:z], *s.pl. Rom.Ant:* Pénates *m.*

pence [pens], *s.pl. See* PENNY 2.

pencil[1] ['pens(i)l], *s.* **1.** Crayon *m.* (*a*) **Lead p.,** crayon à mine de plomb. **Coloured p.,** crayon de couleur. **Indelible p.,** crayon à encre indélébile. **Propelling p.,** porte-mine *m inv* (à vis). **Written in p.,** écrit au crayon. **P. drawing,** dessin *m* au crayon; crayonnage *m.* (*b*) **Slate p.,** crayon d'ardoise. *Toil:* Eyebrow p., crayon à sourcils. **2.** (*a*) *Opt:* **P. of light-rays, light p.,** faisceau lumineux. (*b*) *Ball:* **P. of trajectories,** gerbe *f* de trajectoires. **'pencil-arm,** *s.* Branche *f* porte-mine (de compas). **'pencil-box,** *s.* Plumier *m.* **'pencil-cap,** *s.* Protège-mine *m inv,* protège-pointe(s) *m inv.* **'pencil-case,** *s.* **1.** (*a*) Porte-crayon *m.* (*b*) Porte-mine *m inv.* **2.** Plumier *m*; trousse *f* d'écolier. **'pencil-holder,** *s.* Porte-crayon *m.* **'pencil-mark,** *s.* Trait *m* au crayon. **'pencil-sharpener,** *s.* Taille-crayon *m.*

pencil[2], *v.tr.* (**pencilled**) **1.** (*a*) Marquer (qch.) au crayon. (*b*) Dessiner au crayon. (*c*) (i) To p. one's eyebrows, se faire les sourcils (au crayon). (ii) **Delicately pencilled eyebrows,** sourcils d'un tracé délicat. **2.** To p. a note, crayonner un billet.

pendant ['pendant], *s.* **1.** Pendentif *m* (de collier); pendeloque *f* (de lustre). *Arch:* Cul-de-lampe *m.* *Furn:* **Electric light p.,** lustre *m*; (lampe *f* à) suspension *f.* **2.** *Nau:* (*Rope*) Martinet *m.* **3.** (*Also* [pɑ̃dɑ̃]) Pendant *m* (d'un tableau).

pendent ['pendant], *a.* **1.** (*Of plant*) Pendant; (*of draperies*) retombant. **2.** *Jur:* (Procès) pendant, en instance.

pendentive [pen'dentiv], *s.* *Arch:* Pendentif *m.*

pending ['pendiŋ]. **1.** *a.* = PENDENT 2. **2.** *prep.* En attendant (le retour de qn, la fin d'une affaire, etc.). **P. the negotiations,** en attendant la conclusion des négociations.

pendulous ['pendjuləs], *a.* **1.** (*Of lip*) Pendant. **2.** Balançant, oscillant; (mouvement) pendulaire.

pendulum ['pendjuləm], *s.* Pendule *m,* balancier *m.* *S.a.* SWING[1] 2.

peneplain ['piːniplein], *s.* *Geol:* Pénéplaine *f.*

penetrability [ˌpenitrə'biliti], *s.* Pénétrabilité *f.*

penetrable ['penitrəb], *a.* Pénétrable.

penetrate ['penitreit]. **1.** *v.tr.* Pénétrer, percer. **The shell penetrated the hull,** l'obus a pénétré la coque. **2.** *v.i.* **The bayonet penetrated to the lung,** la baïonnette pénétra jusqu'au poumon. **The water is penetrating everywhere,** l'eau s'introduit partout. **penetrating,** *a.* **1.** (Vent) pénétrant; (son) mordant. **2.** (Esprit) clairvoyant, pénétrant.

penetration [ˌpeni'treiʃ(ə)n], *s.* (*a*) Pénétration *f.* (*b*) Pénétration (de l'esprit); perspicacité *f.*

penetrative ['penitreitiv], *a.* Pénétrant.

penguin ['pengwin, 'peŋgwin], *s.* *Orn:* Manchot *m*; pingouin *m.* **King p.,** pingouin royal. **Emperor p.,** pingouin impérial.

penholder ['penhouldər], *s.* Porte-plume *m inv.*

penicillin [ˌpeni'silin], *s.* Pénicilline *f.*

peninsula [pə'ninsjulə], *s.* *Geog:* Péninsule *f*; presqu'île *f.*

peninsular [pə'ninsjulər], *a.* Péninsulaire. *Hist:* **The P. War,** la guerre d'Espagne.

penis ['piːnis], *s.* *Anat:* Pénis *m.*

penitence ['penit(ə)ns], *s.* Pénitence *f,* contrition *f.*

penitent ['penit(ə)nt]. **1.** *a.* Pénitent, contrit. **2.** *s.* Pénitent, -ente. **-ly,** *adv.* D'un air contrit.

penitential [ˌpeni'tenʃ(ə)l], *a.* Pénitentiel, -ielle.

penitentiary [ˌpeni'tenʃəri]. **1.** *a.* *Ecc:* **P. priest,** pénitencier *m.* **2.** *s.* *U.S:* Prison *f.*

penknife ['pennaif], *s.* Canif *m.*

penmanship ['penmənʃip], *s.* **1.** L'art *m* d'écrire. **2.** Calligraphie *f.*

pennant ['penənt], *s.* **1.** *Nau:* (*Flag*) Flamme *f,* guidon *m.* **2.** = PENNON 1. **3.** *U.S: Sp:* Banderole *f* du championnat.

pennate ['peneit], *a.* *Nat.Hist:* Penné, pinné.

penniless ['penilis], *a.* Sans le sou; sans ressources. **To be p.,** ne pas avoir le sou. **To leave oneself p.,** se dépouiller de ses biens.

pennon ['penən], *s.* **1.** Flamme *f,* banderole *f.* *Sp:* Fanion *m.* **2.** *Nau:* = PENDANT 2 (*b*).

penn'orth ['penəθ], *s.* *P:* = PENNYWORTH.

Pennsylvania [ˌpensil'veinjə], *Pr.n. Geog:* La Pennsylvanie.

penny ['peni], *s.* **1.** (*Coin*) (*pl.* **pennies**) = Deux sous; *A:* gros sou. **They haven't a p. (to bless themselves with),** ils n'ont pas le sou. **To look twice at every p.,** prendre garde à chaque sou. 'A p. for your thoughts,' "A quoi pensez-vous?" **To come back like a bad p.,** revenir comme un mauvais sou. *F:* He's a bad p., c'est un mauvais sujet. *F:* **The penny's dropped,** j'y suis, il y est, voilà qu'il comprend. **2.** (*pl.* **pence**) (*a*) (*Value*) **Nobody was a p. the worse,** cela n'a fait de tort à personne. **I'm not a p. the wiser,** je n'en sais pas plus qu'avant. *Prov:* **In for a p. in for a pound,** qui a dit A doit dire B. **In p. numbers,** en petites quantités. *S.a.* SPEND 1. (*b*) *Coll. Prov:* **Take care of the pence and the pounds will take care of themselves,** il n'y a pas de petites économies. **3.** **That will cost a pretty p.,** cela coûtera cher. **A thousand pounds is a pretty p.,** mille livres, c'est un beau denier. **He makes a pretty p.,** il fait un beau bénéfice. **To earn an honest p.,** gagner honnêtement de l'argent. **4.** *B:* Denier *m.* **'penny-a-'liner,** *s.* *F: O:* Journaliste *m* à deux sous la ligne; *Pej:* écrivassier *m.* **penny 'dreadful,** *s.* Roman *m* à sensation. **'penny-'farthing,** *s.* *Cy: A:* Vélocipède *m.* **'penny'piece,** *s.* Used esp. in phr. **I haven't a p.p.,** je n'ai pas un sou vaillant. **'penny-'post,** *s. Hist:* **Post:** = Affranchissement *m* à deux sous. **'penny-'whistle,** *s.* Flûteau *m.* **'penny-wise,** *a.* Qui fait des économies de bouts de chandelle; lésineur, -euse. **To be p.-w. and pound-foolish,** économiser les sous et prodiguer les louis.

pennyroyal ['peni'rɔiəl], *s. Bot:* Pouliot *m.*

pennyweight ['peniweit], *s. Meas: Approx.* = Un gramme et demi.

pennyworth ['peniwəːθ, 'penəθ], *s.* = De la valeur d'un sou. **Not a p. of food in the house,** pas une miette de nourriture dans la maison.

pension[1] ['penʃ(ə)n], *s.* **1.** Pension *f* (somme annuelle). **Old age p.,** retraite *f* de vieillesse. **Retiring p.,** pension de retraite; *Mil:* solde *f* de retraite; *F:* retraite. **To retire on a p.,** prendre sa retraite. **To be discharged with a p.,** être mis à la retraite. **2.** [pɑ̃sjɔ̃] Pension de famille.

pension[2], *v.tr.* Pensionner (qn). **To p. s.o. off,** mettre qn à la retraite.

pensionable ['penʃ(ə)nəbl], *a.* **1.** (*Pers.*) Qui mérite une pension; qui a droit à sa retraite. **2.** (*Of injury etc.*) Qui donne droit à une pension. **P. age,** âge *m* de la mise à la retraite.

pensioner ['penʃənər], *s.* Titulaire *mf* d'une pension; retraité, -ée; pensionné, -ée. *Army p.,* (i) militaire retraité; (ii) (*in institution*) invalide *m.* **State p.,** pensionnaire *mf* de l'État.

pensive ['pensiv], *a.* Pensif, -ive, songeur, -euse. **-ly,** *adv.* Pensivement; d'un air pensif.

pensiveness ['pensivnis], *s.* Air pensif; songerie *f.*

pent [pent], *a.* **1.** P. (in, up), renfermé; parqué. **2.** **P. up emotion,** émotion refoulée, contenue. **To be p. up,** être sous pression.

pentagon ['pentəgən], *s.* Pentagone *m.* *Mil:* **The P.,** le Pentagone.

pentahedron [ˌpentə'hiːdrən], *s.* Pentaèdre *m.*

pentameter [pen'tæmitər], *s. Pros:* Pentamètre *m.*

pentane ['pentein], *s. Ch:* Pentane *m.*

pentasyllabic [ˌpentəsi'læbik], *a.* Pentasyllabe.

Pentateuch (the) [ðə'pentətjuːk], *s. B:* Le Pentateuque.

pentathlon [pen'tæθlən], *s. Sp:* (*Olympic Games*) Pentathle *m,* pentathlon *m.*

pentavalent [pen'tævələnt], *a. Ch:* Pentavalent.

Pentecost ['pentikɔst], *s.* La Pentecôte.

penthouse ['penthaus], *s. Const:* (*a*) Appentis *m*; hangar *m.* (*b*) (*Over door*) Auvent *m.* (*c*) *U.S:* Appartement entouré d'une terrasse et construit sur le toit d'un building.

pentode ['pentoud], *s. W.Tel:* Lampe *f* à cinq électrodes; lampe pent(h)ode.

Pentothal ['pentəθæl], *s. Pharm: R.t.m:* Pentothal *m.*

pent-roof ['pentruːf], *s.* Comble *m* en appentis.

penult [pe'nʌlt], **penultimate** [pe'nʌltimit]. **1.** *a.* Pénultième; avant-dernier, -ière. **2.** *s.* Avant-dernière syllabe; pénultième *f.*

penumbra [pe'nʌmbrə], *s.* Pénombre *f.*

penurious [pe'njuəriəs], *a.* **1.** Pauvre. **2.** (*a*) Parcimonieux. (*b*) Mesquin. **-ly,** *adv.* **1.** Pauvrement. **2.** (*a*) Parcimonieusement. (*b*) Mesquinement.

penury ['penjuri], s. Pénurie f. 1. Indigence f; dénuement m, misère f. 2. Manque m, pauvreté f (of, de).

peony ['pi(:)əni], s. Bot: Pivoine f.

people¹ ['pi:pl], s. 1. (pl. peoples) Peuple m, nation f. II. people (Coll. with pl. const.) 1. (a) Peuple, habitants mpl (d'une ville). The country p., les populations rurales. (b) The King and his p., le roi et ses sujets. (c) F: Parents mpl. My p. are abroad, mes parents sont à l'étranger. 2. (a) Pol: Citoyens mpl (d'un état). Government by the p., gouvernement par le peuple. Pol: People's democracy, démocratie f populaire. The p. at large, le grand public. (b) The (common) p., la populace; le (bas, menu, petit) peuple. A man of the p., un homme sorti du peuple. 3. (a) Gens m or fpl., monde m. Young p., jeunes gens. Old p., les vieilles gens, les vieux. Society p., gens du monde. All p. who are honest, tous ceux qui sont honnêtes. What do you p. think? qu'en pensez-vous, vous autres? (b) Personnes fpl. One thousand p., mille personnes. (c) (Nom.) On; (obl. cases) vous. P. say, on dit. That's enough to alarm p., il y a de quoi vous alarmer.

people², v.tr. Peupler (with, de).

pep¹ [pep], s. F: Entrain m, fougue f. Full of p., plein de sève, d'allant. Aut: Engine full of p., moteur nerveux. P. pill, excitant m. P. talk, petit discours d'encouragement.

pep², v.tr. (pepped) F: To p. s.o. up, ragaillardir qn. To p. up a dance, donner de l'entrain à un bal. To p. up a play, corser une pièce.

pepper¹ ['pepər], s. 1. Poivre m. S.a. CAYENNE 2. 2. Bot: Black p., poivrier m. 'pepper-and-'salt, a. (Tissu) marengo inv; (cheveux) poivre et sel. 'pepper-box, -pot, s. 1. Poivrier m. 2. Arch: F: P.-box (turret), poivrière f. 'pepper-castor, s. Poivrière f. 'pepper-mill, s. Moulin m à poivre.

pepper², v.tr. 1. Poivrer. 2. Cribler (l'ennemi) de balles.

peppercorn ['pepəkɔːn], s. Grain m de poivre. P. rent, loyer nominal.

peppermint ['pepəmint], s. 1. Menthe poivrée; menthe anglaise. 2. P. (-drop, -lozenge), pastille f de menthe.

peppery ['pepəri], a. 1. Poivré. 2. (Of pers.) Irascible, colérique.

pepsin ['pepsin], s. Pepsine f.

peptic ['peptik], 1. a. Physiol: (Digestion f) peptique, gastrique. P. glands, glandes f gastriques. 2. s. Pharm: Digestif m.

peptone ['peptoun], s. Peptone f.

per [pəːr], prep. 1. (a) Par. Sent p. carrier, envoyé par messageries. P. Messrs Smith and Co., par l'entremise de MM. Smith et Cie. (b) As p. invoice, suivant facture. As p. sample, conformément à l'échantillon. (c) One franc p. pound, un franc la livre. Sixty miles p. hour, soixante milles à l'heure. P. day, par jour. 2. P. annum, par an. P. cent(um), pour cent. Credited as p. contra, crédité ci-contre, en contre-partie.

peradventure [pərəd'ventʃər], adv. A: 1. Par aventure, par hasard. 2. Peut-être. P. he is mistaken, il a pu se tromper. 3. s. Beyond p. il n'en pas douter.

perambulate [pə'ræmbjuleit], v.tr. 1. Parcourir, se promener dans (son jardin). 2. Visiter, inspecter (une propriété, une forêt); délimiter (la commune, un terrain).

perambulation [pəræmbju'leiʃ(ə)n], s. 1. Promenade f, tournée f. 2. Visite f, inspection f; délimitation f.

perambulator [pə'ræmbjuleitər], s. Voiture f d'enfant; landau m.

perceivable [pə'siːvəbl], a. (Of sound, etc.) Percevable (à l'oreille); perceptible. No p. difference, aucune différence sensible. -ably, adv. Perceptiblement, sensiblement.

perceive [pə'siːv], v.tr. 1. Percevoir (la vérité). 2. Percevoir (un son). 3. S'apercevoir de (qch.). He perceived that he was being watched, il s'aperçut qu'on l'observait. 4. To p. s.o., apercevoir qn.

percentage [pə'sentidʒ], s. 1. Pourcentage m. To allow a p. on all transactions, allouer un tantième sur toutes opérations. Only a small p. of the pupils were successful, la proportion des élèves admis a été faible. 2. P. of acid, teneur f en acide. P. of alcohol in a wine, proportion f d'alcool dans un vin.

perceptibility [pə,septi'biliti], s. Perceptibilité f.

perceptible [pə'septibl], a. (a) Perceptible (à l'esprit). P. difference, différence sensible. (b) P. to the eye, visible. -ibly, adv. Sensiblement.

perception [pə'sep(ə)n], s. (a) Perception f. (b) Sensibilité f (aux impressions extérieures).

perceptive [pə'septiv], a. Perceptif, -ive.

perceptivity [,pəːsep'tiviti], s. Perceptivité f; faculté perceptive.

perch¹ [pəːtʃ], s. 1. Perchoir m; (in cage) bâton m. F: To knock s.o. off his p., déjucher qn. 2. Meas: Perche f (de 5½ yards, approx. = 5 m.).

perch². (a) v.i. (Of bird, F: of pers.) (Se) percher (on, sur); jucher. (b) v.pr. Se percher, se jucher (on, sur). perching, a. (Oiseau) percheur.

perch³, s. Ich: Perche f.

perchance [pə'tʃɑːns], adv. A: = PERADVENTURE.

percipient [pə'sipiənt]. 1. a. Percepteur, -trice (de sensations); conscient. 2. s. Sujet m télépathique.

percolate ['pəːkəleit]. 1. v.i. S'infiltrer; (of coffee) filtrer. 2. v.tr. To p. the coffee, passer le café.

percolation [,pəːkə'leiʃ(ə)n], s. 1. Infiltration f. 2. Filtration f, filtrage m.

percolator ['pəːkəleitər], s. (a) Filtre m; esp. filtre à café. (b) Cafetière f automatique, cafetière russe.

percuss [pə'kʌs], v.tr. (a) Taper, percuter. (b) Med: Percuter (la poitrine).

percussion [pə'kʌʃ(ə)n], s. 1. Percussion f; choc m. Mus: P. instruments, instruments m de, à, percussion; batterie f. Sm.a: P. cap, amorce f. 2. Med: Percussion (d'un organe). per'cussion-fuse, s. Artil: Fusée percutante. per'cussion-pin, s. Artil: Rugueux m (de fusée).

percussive [pə'kʌsiv], a. Percutant; Mus: tympanique.

percutaneous [,pəːkjuː'teiniəs], a. Med: (Of injection, etc.) Hypodermique; sous-cutané. P. reaction, percuti-réaction f.

perdition [pəː'diʃ(ə)n], s. Perte f, ruine f; Theol: perdition f.

peregrination [,perigri'neiʃ(ə)n], s. Pérégrination f, voyage m.

peregrine ['perigrin], a. Ven: P. (falcon), (faucon) pèlerin (m).

peremptoriness [pə'rem(p)trinis], s. Caractère péremptoire, absolu (d'un ordre etc.); intransigeance f.

peremptory [pə'rem(p)təri], a. Péremptoire. (a) (Of refusal) Absolu, décisif, -ive. P. necessity, nécessité absolue. (b) (Of tone) Tranchant, impératif, -ive, absolu. -ily, adv. (a) Péremptoirement, absolument. (b) Impérieusement.

perennial [pə'renjəl]. 1. a. (a) Éternel, perpétuel. (b) Bot: Vivace, persistant. 2. s. Plante f vivace. -ally, adv. A perpétuité; éternellement.

perfect¹ ['pəːfikt]. 1. a. (a) Parfait; (ouvrage) achevé. P. specimen, spécimen parfait. To be p., avoir toutes les perfections. To have a p. knowledge of sth., savoir qch. à fond. His English is p., son anglais est impeccable. (b) F: P. idiot, parfait imbécile. She is a p. fright, c'est un véritable épouvantail. He is a p. stranger to me, il m'est parfaitement inconnu. 2. (a) Mth: P. square, carré parfait. (b) Mus: P. fourth, quarte f juste. 3. Nat.Hist: (plant, insect) Complet, -ète. 4. Gram: The p. tense, s. the p., le parfait. Future p., futur antérieur. Verb in the p., verbe au parfait. -ly, adv. Parfaitement.

perfect² [pə'fekt, 'pəːfikt], v.tr. 1. Achever, parachever (une besogne). 2. Rendre parfait, parfaire (une méthode). To p. an invention, mettre une invention au point. 3. Typ: Imprimer (une feuille) en retiration. perfecting, s. 1. Achèvement m, accomplissement m. 2. Perfectionnement m. 3. Typ: (Impression f en) retiration f.

perfectibility [pə,fekti'biliti], s. Perfectibilité f.

perfectible [pə'fektibl], a. Perfectible.

perfection [pə'fek(ə)n], s. Perfection f. 1. (a) Achèvement m, accomplissement m (d'une tâche). (b) Perfectionnement m (d'un projet). 2. (a) To succeed to p., réussir à souhait. With rare p., dans une rare perfection. P. of detail, achevé m (d'un objet d'art). In, to, p., à la perfection. S.a. COUNSEL¹ 2. (b) Développement complet (d'une plante).

perfervid [pə'fəːvid], *a.* Ardent, exalté. **-ly,** *adv.* Avec exaltation.

perfidious [pə'fidjəs], *a.* Perfide; traître, -esse. **-ly,** *adv.* Perfidement, traîtreusement.

perfidiousness [pə'fidiəsnis], **perfidy** ['pəːfidi], *s.* Perfidie *f,* traîtrise *f.*

perforate ['pəːfəreit]. 1. *v.tr.* Percer, transpercer; *Techn: Med: Surg:* perforer. **Perforating machine,** machine *f* à perforer; *Surg: etc:* perforateur *m; Mec.E: Min: etc:* perforatrice *f; Cin:* perforeuse *f.* 2. *v.i.* Pénétrer (**into,** dans). **perforated,** *a.* Perforé, troué, ajouré.

perforation [pəːfə'reiʃ(ə)n], *s.* Perforation *f.* 1. Perçage *m,* percement *m.* 2. (*a*) Petit trou. (*b*) *Coll:* Trous *mpl,* perforation.

perforator ['pəːfəreitər], *s.* 1. Machine *f* à perforer; perforateur *m. Min:* Perforatrice *f.* 2. *Surg:* Tréphine *f.*

perforce [pə'fɔːs], *adv. Lit:* Forcément.

perform [pə'fɔːm], *v.tr.* 1. Exécuter (un mouvement); accomplir (une tâche); effectuer (une addition); célébrer (un rite); s'acquitter de, remplir (son devoir). 2. (*a*) Jouer, représenter (une pièce de théâtre); exécuter (une danse); remplir (un rôle). (*b*) *Abs.* To p. **in a play,** jouer, tenir un rôle, dans une pièce. To p. **on the flute,** jouer de la flûte. **Performing dogs,** chiens savants. **performing,** *s.* 1. Accomplissement *m* (of, de). 2. *Th:* Représentation *f* (d'une pièce).

performance [pə'fɔːməns], *s.* 1. Exécution *f* (d'un opéra); accomplissement *m* (d'une tâche); célébration *f* (d'un rite). 2. (*a*) Acte *m,* exploit *m.* (*b*) Marche *f,* fonctionnement *m* (d'une machine). *Av: Aut:* Rendement *m.* (*c*) *Sp: Aut:* Performance *f* (d'un coureur, d'une voiture). To put up a good p., bien s'acquitter. 3. Représentation *f* (d'une pièce); séance *f* (de cinéma, etc.). **Evening p.,** soirée *f.* **Afternoon p.,** matinée *f.* **No p. tonight,** ce soir relâche.

performer [pə'fɔːmər], *s.* Artiste *mf.* 1. *Mus:* Exécutant, -ante. 2. *Th:* Acteur, -trice.

perfume[1] ['pəːfjuːm], *s.* 1. Parfum *m.* (*a*) Odeur *f* agréable. (*b*) Bottle of p., flacon *m* de parfum.

perfume[2] [pə'fjuːm], *v.tr.* Parfumer.

perfumer [pə'fjuːmər], *s.* Parfumeur, -euse.

perfumery [pə'fjuːməri], *s.* Parfumerie *f.*

perfunctoriness [pə'fʌŋktrinis], *s.* Négligence *f;* manque *m* de soin (à faire qch.).

perfunctory [pə'fʌŋkt(ə)ri], *a.* 1. (*Of examination*) Fait pour la forme. P. **glance,** coup d'œil superficiel. P. **enquiry,** enquête peu poussée; renseignements pris par manière d'acquit. 2. (*Of pers.*) Négligent; peu zélé. **-ily,** *adv.* Par manière d'acquit; superficiellement; pour la forme.

perfusion [pə'fjuːʒ(ə)n], *s. Med:* Perfusion *f.*

pergola ['pəːgələ], *s.* Treille *f* à l'italienne; pergola *f;* tonnelle *f.*

perhaps [pə'hæps, præps], *adv.* Peut-être. P. **so,** p. **not,** peut-être (bien) que oui, que non. P. I have it, il se peut que je l'aie. I am giving up this work, but may p. resume it later, j'abandonne ce travail, quitte à le reprendre plus tard.

peri ['piəri], *s. Myth:* Péri *mf.*

perianth ['periænθ], *s. Bot:* Périanthe *m.*

pericarditis [perikaː'daitis], *s. Med:* Péricardite *f.*

pericardium [peri'kaːdiəm], *s. Anat:* Péricarde *m.*

pericarp ['perikaːp], *s. Bot:* Péricarpe *m.*

pericranium [peri'kreiniəm], *s. Anat:* Péricrâne *m.*

perigee ['peridʒiː], *s. Astr:* Périgée *m.*

perihelion [peri'hiːlion], *s. Astr:* Périhélie *m.*

peril ['peril], *s.* Péril *m,* danger *m.* In p. **of one's life,** en danger de mort. To do sth. **at one's** (**own**) p., faire qch. à ses risques et périls. **Touch him at your p.,** gare à vous si vous le touchez.

perilous ['periləs], *a.* Périlleux, -euse, dangereux, -euse. **-ly,** *adv.* Périlleusement, dangereusement.

perimeter [pe'rimitər], *s. Geom: Mil:* Périmètre *m. Attrib. Sp. etc:* P. **track,** piste *f* périphérique.

perineum [peri'niː(ː)əm], *s. Anat:* Périnée *m.*

period ['piəriəd], *s.* Période *f.* 1. (*a*) Durée *f,* délai *m. Sch:* Heure *f* de cours. **Within the agreed p.,** dans le délai fixé. **Deposit for a fixed p.,** dépôt à terme fixe. (*b*) *Astr: etc:* P. **of planet's revolution,** cycle

m, période, de la révolution d'une planète. (*c*) *Med:* **Periods of a disease,** stades *m,* phases *f,* d'une maladie. (*d*) *Met:* Fair p., éclaircie *f.* 2. Époque *f,* âge *m. Cost:* P. **dress,** robe de style. P. **furniture,** meubles *m* de style. 3. (*a*) *Rh:* Phrase *f.* **Well rounded periods,** phrases, périodes, bien tournées. (*b*) *Mus:* Phrase complète. 4. *Gram: Typ:* Point *m* (de ponctuation). *F: Esp: U.S:* 'He's no good at maths'—'He's no good, p.' "Il est nul en math." — "Il est nul, tout court." 5. *Physiol: F:* Règles *fpl.*

periodic [piəri'ɔdik], *a.* 1. Périodique. 2. *Lit:* P. **style,** style riche en périodes; style ample.

periodical [piəri'ɔdik(ə)l]. 1. *a.* Périodique. 2. *s.* Publication *f* périodique; périodique *m.* **-ally,** *adv.* Périodiquement.

periosteum [peri'ɔstiəm], *s. Anat:* Périoste *m.*

periostosis [periɔs'tousis], *s. Med:* Périostose *f.*

peripatetic [peripə'tetik], *a.* (*a*) *A.Phil:* Péripatéticien, -ienne, péripatétique. (*b*) P. **teacher,** professeur qui dessert plusieurs écoles.

peripheral [pe'rifərəl], *a.* Périphérique, périmétrique. P. **speed,** vitesse circonférentielle.

periphery [pe'rifəri], *s.* Périphérie *f,* pourtour *m.*

periphrasis, *pl.* **-es** [pe'rifrəsis, -iːz], *s.* Périphrase *f;* circonlocution *f.*

periphrastic [peri'fræstik], *a.* Périphrastique.

periscope ['periskoup], *s.* 1. Périscope *m.* 2. *Phot:* Objectif *m* périscopique.

periscopic [peri'skɔpik], *a.* Périscopique.

perish ['periʃ]. 1. *v.i.* (*a*) Périr, mourir. **I shall do it or p. in the attempt,** je le ferai ou j'y perdrai la vie. *Lit:* P. **the thought!** loin de nous cette pensée! *F:* I'm perishing with cold, je meurs de froid. (*b*) (*Of rubber, etc.*) Se détériorer. 2. *v.tr.* (*a*) Détériorer. (*b*) (*Of frost*) Faire mourir, brûler (la végétation). **perished,** *a.* 1. (*Of rubber*) Détérioré. 2. *F:* To be p. **with cold,** être transi de froid. **My feet are p.,** j'ai les pieds gelés. **perishing,** *a.* (*a*) It's absolutely p., il fait un froid de tous les diables. (*b*) *P:* P. **idiot,** sacré idiot.

perishable ['periʃəbl]. 1. *a.* (*a*) Périssable; sujet à s'altérer. (*b*) De courte durée; éphémère. 2. *s.pl.* **Perishables,** marchandises *f* périssables.

peristaltic [peri'stæltik], *a. Physiol:* Péristaltique.

peristyle ['peristail], *s. Arch:* Péristyle *m.*

peritoneum [peritə'niː(ː)əm], *s. Anat:* Péritoine *m.*

peritonitis [peritə'naitis], *s. Med:* Péritonite *f.*

periwig ['periwig], *s. A:* Perruque *f.*

periwinkle[1] ['periwiŋkl], *s. Bot:* Pervenche *f.*

periwinkle[2], *s. Moll:* Bigorneau *m.*

perjure ['pəːdʒər], *v.pr.* To p. **oneself,** (i) se parjurer; (ii) commettre un parjure; violer son serment. **perjured,** *a.* (*Of pers.*) Parjure.

perjurer ['pəːdʒərər], *s.* Parjure *mf.*

perjury ['pəːdʒəri], *s.* 1. (*As a moral offence*) Parjure *m.* 2. *Jur:* (*a*) To commit p., faire un faux serment. (*b*) Faux témoignage.

perk [pəːk]. 1. *v.i.* To p. (**up**), redresser la tête; se ranimer. 2. *v.tr.* (*a*) To p. **up one's head,** redresser la tête. (*b*) To p. **s.o. up,** (i) parer, requinquer, qn; (ii) (*of drink, etc.*) ravigoter qn.

perkiness ['pəːkinis], *s.* 1. Allure(s) dégagée(s). 2. Air éveillé, alerte; ton guilleret.

perks [pəːks], *s.pl. F:* See PERQUISITE.

perky ['pəːki], *a.* (*a*) Éveillé, guilleret. (*b*) (Ton) dégagé, désinvolte. **-ily,** *adv.* (*a*) D'un air éveillé. (*b*) D'un air dégagé.

perm[1] [pəːm], *s. F: Hairdr:* (Ondulation) permanente *f,* indéfrisable *f.*

perm[2], *v.tr. F:* To have one's hair permed, se faire faire une permanente.

permanence ['pəːmənəns], *s.* Permanence *f;* stabilité *f.*

permanency ['pəːmənənsi], *s.* 1. = PERMANENCE. 2. Emploi permanent.

permanent ['pəːmənənt], *a.* Permanent. P. **post,** place inamovible; poste fixe. P. **establishment,** établissement à demeure. P. **address,** résidence fixe. *Rail:* The p. **way,** la voie ferrée. P.-**way man,** ouvrier *m* de la voie. *Hairdr:* P. **wave,** (ondulation) permanente (*f*). **-ly,** *adv.* D'une façon permanente. To be p. **appointed,** être nommé à titre définitif; être titularisé.

permanganate [pəˈmæŋgənit], *s. Ch:* Permanganate *m.*

permeability [ˌpəːmiəˈbiliti], *s.* Perméabilité *f*, pénétrabilité *f.*

permeable [ˈpəːmiəbl], *a.* Perméable, pénétrable.

permeate [ˈpəːmieit], *v.tr. & i.* To p. (through) sth., filtrer à travers qch. **Water permeates everywhere,** l'eau s'insinue partout. **The soil was permeated with water,** le sol était saturé d'eau.

permeation [ˌpəːmiˈeiʃ(ə)n], *s.* Pénétration *f*, infiltration *f.*

permissible [pəˈmisəbl], *a.* Tolérable, permis. **Would it be p. to say that . . .?** serait-on reçu à dire que . . .?

permission [pəˈmiʃ(ə)n], *s.* Permission *f.* (a) **To give s.o. p. to do sth.,** donner à qn la permission de faire qch. **With your (kind) p.,** si vous voulez bien (me) le permettre. (b) Permis *m*, autorisation *f.*

permissive [pəˈmisiv], *a.* 1. Qui permet. **P. legislation,** législation facultative. 2. Permis, toléré.

permit¹ [ˈpəːmit], *s.* 1. (For pers.) Permis *m*, autorisation *f.* **To take out a p.,** se faire délivrer un permis. 2. *Cust:* (For goods) (a) Passavant *m*; acquit-à-caution *m, pl.* acquits-à-caution. (b) Export p., autorisation d'exporter.

permit² [pəˈmit]. 1. *v.tr.* (permitted) Permettre. **To p. s.o. to do sth.,** permettre à qn de faire qch. **I was permitted to visit the works,** j'ai été autorisé à visiter l'usine. **P. me to tell you the truth,** souffrez que je vous dise la vérité. 2. *v.ind.tr.* **Tone which permitted of no reply,** ton qui n'admettait pas, ne souffrait pas, de réplique.

permutable [pəˈmjuːtəbl], *a.* Permutable.

permutation [ˌpəːmjuˈteiʃ(ə)n], *s. Mth: Ling:* Permutation *f.*

permute [pəˈmjuːt], *v.tr. Mth:* Permuter. *Ling:* **Permuted consonants,** consonnes permutées.

pernicious [pəˈniʃəs], *a.* Pernicieux, -euse; malsain, délétère. **-ly,** *adv.* Pernicieusement.

pernickety [pəˈnikəti], *a. F:* 1. Vétilleux, -euse, pointilleux, -euse. **P. old fool!** espèce de vieux tatillon! **P. about one's food,** difficile au sujet de sa nourriture. 2. (Of task) Délicat, minutieux, -euse.

perorate [ˈperəreit], *v.i.* Pérorer; discourir longuement.

peroration [ˌperəˈreiʃ(ə)n], *s.* Péroraison *f.*

peroxide¹ [pəˈrɔksaid], *s. Ch:* Peroxyde *m.* **Hydrogen p.,** eau oxygénée. *Ind:* **Red p. of iron,** colcotar *m. attrib.* **P. blonde,** (blonde) décolorée.

peroxide², *v.tr. F:* Décolorer (ses cheveux) à l'eau oxygénée; oxygéner. **Peroxided hair,** cheveux oxygénés.

peroxidize [pəˈrɔksidaiz], *v.tr. Ch:* Peroxyder.

perpendicular [ˌpəːpənˈdikjulər]. 1. *a.* (a) Perpendiculaire; (of cliff) vertical, -aux. (b) *Arch:* (Style) perpendiculaire. 2. *s.* (a) Fil *m* à plomb. (b) *Geom:* perpendiculaire *f.* (c) Out of (the) p., hors d'aplomb; hors d'équerre. **-ly,** *adv.* Perpendiculairement; verticalement.

perpetrate [ˈpəːpitreit], *v.tr.* Commettre, perpétrer (un crime).

perpetration [ˌpəːpiˈtreiʃ(ə)n], *s.* 1. Perpétration *f* (d'un crime). 2. Péché *m*, crime *m.*

perpetrator [ˈpəːpitreitər], *s.* Auteur *m* (d'un crime). **The p. of the joke,** l'auteur de la farce.

perpetual [pəˈpetjuəl], *a.* (a) Perpétuel, éternel. (b) Sans fin; continuel. **-ally,** *adv.* (a) Perpétuellement. (b) Sans cesse.

perpetuate [pəˈpetjueit], *v.tr.* 1. Perpétuer, éterniser. 2. **This invention has perpetuated his name,** cette invention a préservé son nom de l'oubli.

perpetuation [pəˌpetjuˈeiʃ(ə)n], *s.* 1. Perpétuation *f*, éternisation *f.* 2. Préservation *f* de l'oubli.

perpetuity [ˌpəːpiˈtjuː(ː)iti], *s.* 1. Perpétuité *f.* **In, to, for, p.,** à perpétuité. 2. Rente perpétuelle.

perplex [pəˈpleks], *v.tr.* Embarrasser (qn); mettre (qn) dans la perplexité. **perplexed,** *a.* 1. (Of pers.) Perplexe, embarrassé. 2. (Air) confus, perplexe.

perplexing, *a.* Embarrassant, troublant.

perplexedly [pəˈpleksidli], *adv.* D'un air embarrassé, perplexe; avec perplexité.

perplexity [pəˈpleksiti], *s.* Perplexité *f*, embarras *m.*

perquisite [ˈpəːkwizit], *s.* (a) Casuel *m.* (b) *pl.* **Perquisites,** *F:* perks, *F:* gratte *f.* **These are the perquisites of the trade,** c'est le revenant-bon du métier.

---

perry [ˈperi], *s.* Poiré *m*; cidre *m* de poire.

persecute [ˈpəːsikjuːt], *v.tr.* 1. Persécuter (les hérétiques). 2. Tourmenter; harceler.

persecution [ˌpəːsiˈkjuːʃ(ə)n], *s.* Persécution *f. Psy:* **P. mania,** délire de (la) persécution.

persecutor [ˈpəːsikjuːtər], *s.* Persécuteur, -trice.

perseverance [ˌpəːsiˈviərəns], *s.* Persévérance *f*; constance *f* (dans le travail).

persevere [ˌpəːsiˈviər], *v.i.* Persévérer. **To p. with one's work,** persévérer dans son travail. **persevering,** *a.* Persévérant, assidu (in doing sth., à faire qch.); constant (dans le travail). **-ly,** *adv.* Avec persévérance.

Persia [ˈpəːʃə]. *Pr.n. Geog:* La Perse.

Persian [ˈpəːʃ(ə)n]. 1. *a. & s. Geog:* (i) Persan, -ane; (ii) *A.Hist:* perse. (iii) **The P. Gulf,** le Golfe Persique. *Com:* **P. carpet,** tapis *m* de Perse. *Z:* **P. cat,** (chat) persan. 2. *s. Ling:* Le persan.

persimmon [pəːˈsimən], *s. Bot:* 1. Plaquemine *f.* **Chinese p.,** kaki *m.* 2. **P.(-tree),** plaqueminier *m.*

persist [pəˈsist], *v.i.* Persister. 1. **To p. in one's opinion,** s'obstiner dans son opinion. **To p. in doing sth.,** persister, s'obstiner, à faire qch. 2. Continuer. **The fever persists,** la fièvre persiste.

persistence [pəˈsist(ə)ns], **persistency** [pəˈsist(ə)nsi], *s.* Persistance *f.* 1. Obstination *f.* 2. Continuité *f.* **P. of matter,** permanence *f* de la matière.

persistent [pəˈsist(ə)nt], *a.* 1. Persistant; tenace. 1. **P. rain,** pluie qui s'obstine. 2. Continu. *Com:* **P. demand for . . .,** demande suivie pour . . . . **-ly,** *adv.* Avec persistance, avec ténacité.

person [ˈpəːs(ə)n], *s.* Personne *f.* 1. (a) Individu *m; pl.* gens *m.* **Private p.,** simple particulier *m.* **To be no respecter of persons,** ne pas faire cas des personnalités *f. Jur:* **Some p. or persons unknown,** un certain quidam. *Pol:* **Displaced p.,** personne déplacée. (b) **In (one's own) p.,** en (propre) personne. **'To be delivered to the addressee in p.,' "**à remettre en mains propres." (c) **To have a commanding p.,** posséder un extérieur imposant. (d) *Th: Lit:* Personnage (d'un drame). 2. *Gram:* **Verb in the first p.,** verbe à la première personne.

personable [ˈpəːs(ə)nəbl], *a.* Bien (fait) de sa personne; présentant bien.

personage [ˈpəːsənidʒ], *s.* 1. Personnage *m*, personne *f*, personnalité *f.* **He's an important p.,** c'est une personnalité. 2. *Th:* Personnage.

personal [ˈpəːsən(ə)l], *a.* Personnel. 1. (a) **P. liberty,** liberté individuelle. **P. rights,** droits du citoyen. **This is p. to myself,** cela m'est propre. **To give a p. touch to sth.,** personnaliser (qch.). *Cust:* **Articles for p. use,** effets usagers. *Journ:* **P. column,** petite correspondance. (b) **Don't be p.,** ne faites pas de personnalités. (c) **To make a p. application,** se présenter en personne. **I have p. knowledge of this kind of life,** j'ai connu cette existence par moi-même. 2. *Jur:* **P. property,** biens mobiliers. 3. *Gram:* **P. pronoun,** pronom personnel. **-ally,** *adv.* Personnellement. **P., I think . . .,** quant à moi, je pense . . . . **P., I am willing,** moi, je veux bien. **Don't take that remark p.,** ne prenez pas cette remarque pour vous. **To deliver sth. to s.o. p.,** remettre qch. à qn en main(s) propre(s).

personality [ˌpəːsəˈnæliti], *s.* 1. (a) Personnalité *f*, personnage *m.* (b) Caractère *m* propre (de qn). **To be lacking in p.,** manquer de personnalité. **He's quite a p.,** *F:* c'est vraiment quelqu'un. **He has a strong p.,** il a une personnalité marquante. 2. **To indulge in personalities,** dire des personnalités (à qn).

personalize [ˈpəːsənalaiz], *v.tr.* (a) Personnifier. (b) *F: Com:* **Personalized sales technique,** publicité personnalisée. *Esp. U.S:* **A personalized shirt,** une chemise personnalisable.

personalty [ˈpəːsən(ə)lti], *s. Jur:* 1. Objet mobilier. 2. Biens meubles; fortune mobilière.

personification [pəːˌsɔnifiˈkeiʃ(ə)n], *s.* Personnification *f.*

personify [pəˈsɔnifai], *v.tr.* Personnifier; personnaliser. **He is avarice personified,** il est, c'est, l'avarice même.

personnel [ˌpəːsəˈnel], *s. Ind: Mil: etc:* Personnel *m.* **Sea-going, flying, p.,** personnel navigant. **P. department,** service *m* du personnel. **P. manager,** chef *m* du personnel.

perspective [pə'spektiv]. **1.** *s.* (*a*) Perspective *f*. To see a matter in its true p., voir une affaire sous son vrai jour. *Th:* Stage p., optique *f* du théâtre. (*b*) **A fine p.** opened out before his eyes, une belle perspective, une belle vue, s'ouvrit devant ses yeux. **2.** *a.* (Dessin) perspectif, en perspective.

perspicacious [,pə:spi'keiʃəs], *a.* Perspicace. He is very p., *F:* il a du nez.

perspicacity [,pə:spi'kæsiti], *s.* Perspicacité *f*, pénétration *f*, clairvoyance *f*, discernement *m*.

perspicuity [,pə:spi'kju(:)iti], *s.* Clarté *f*, netteté *f*, lucidité *f* (de l'expression).

perspicuous [pə'spikju(:)əs], *a.* (*Of style*) Clair, lucide; (*of reason*) évident.

perspiration [,pə:spə'reiʃ(ə)n], *s.* (*a*) Transpiration *f*. To break into p., entrer en moiteur. (*b*) Sueur *f*. Bathed in p., trempé de sueur; *F:* en nage.

perspire [pə'spaiər], *v.i.* Transpirer, suer. **perspiring**, *a.* En sueur.

persuade [pə'sweid], *v.tr.* (*a*) To p. s.o. of sth., persuader, convaincre, qn de qch.; persuader qch. à qn. To p. s.o. that he ought to do sth., persuader à qn qu'il doit faire qch. (*b*) To p. s.o. to do sth., persuader à qn de faire qch.; amener qn à faire qch. P. your brother to come! déterminez, décidez, votre frère à venir! (*c*) He persuaded me not to, il m'en a dissuadé.

persuasion [pə'sweiʒ(ə)n], *s.* **1.** Persuasion *f*. (*a*) The art of p., l'art de persuader. (*b*) Conviction *f*. It is my p. that he is mad, je suis convaincu, j'ai la conviction, qu'il est fou. (*c*) He wants to collectivize agriculture by p., il veut collectiviser l'agriculture par la douceur. **2.** (*a*) (Religious) p., religion *f*, confession *f*. They are both of the same p., ils ont la même religion. (*b*) The Methodist p., la secte méthodiste.

persuasive [pə'sweisiv], *a.* Persuasif, -ive; persuadant. **-ly,** *adv.* D'un ton persuasif.

pert [pə:t], *a.* Mutin; effronté, hardi. **-ly,** *adv.* Avec mutinerie; d'un air effronté.

pertain [pə'tein], *v.i.* Appartenir (to sth., à qch.). Subjects pertaining to religion, sujets qui ont rapport à la religion. This does not p. to my office, cela n'est pas de mon ressort.

pertinacious [,pə:ti'neiʃəs], *a.* Obstiné, entêté, opiniâtre. **-ly,** *adv.* Obstinément, opiniâtrement.

pertinaciousness [,pə:ti'neiʃəsnis], **pertinacity** [,pə:ti-'næsiti], *s.* Obstination *f*, opiniâtreté *f*, entêtement *m* (in doing sth., à faire qch.).

pertinence ['pə:tinəns], **pertinency** ['pə:tinənsi], *s.* Pertinence *f* (d'une raison); à-propos *m*, justesse *f* (d'une observation).

pertinent ['pə:tinənt], *a.* (*a*) Pertinent, à propos, juste. (*b*) Books p. to the question, livres qui ont rapport à la question. **-ly,** *adv.* D'une manière pertinente; à propos.

pertness ['pə:tnis], *s.* Mutinerie *f*, effronterie *f*, irrespect *m*.

perturb [pə'tə:b], *v.tr.* Troubler, inquiéter, agiter, perturber.

perturbation [,pə:tə:'beiʃ(ə)n], *s.* Agitation *f*, inquiétude *f*, trouble *m* (de l'esprit).

Peru [pə'ru:]. *Pr.n. Geog:* Le Pérou.

perusal [pə'ru:z(ə)l], *s.* Lecture *f*. To give sth. a careful p., lire qch. attentivement.

peruse [pə'ru:z], *v.tr.* Lire attentivement, prendre connaissance de (qch.).

Peruvian [pə'ru:viən], *a. & s.* Péruvien, -ienne.

pervade [pə:'veid], *v.tr.* S'infiltrer dans (qch.). The religious feeling that pervades the book, le sentiment religieux qui anime tout ce livre. To become pervaded, se pénétrer (with, de). (All-) pervading, qui se répand partout; régnant, dominant.

pervasive [pə:'veisiv], *a.* Qui se répand partout; pénétrant.

perverse [pə'və:s], *a.* (*a*) Pervers, méchant. (*b*) Entêté dans le mal. (*c*) Contrariant. (*d*) Revêche. **-ly,** *adv.* (*a*) Perversement; avec perversité. (*b*) D'une manière contrariante.

perverseness [pə'və:snis], *s.* (*a*) Perversité *f*. (*b*) Esprit *m* contraire. (*c*) Caractère *m* revêche.

perversion [pə'və:ʃ(ə)n], *s.* Perversion *f*. A p. of the truth, un travestissement de la vérité.

perversity [pə'və:siti], *s.* = PERVERSENESS.

pervert[1] ['pə:və:t], *s.* **1.** (*a*) Perverti, -ie. (*b*) Apostat *m*. **2.** *Psy:* Inverti, -ie.

pervert[2] [pə'və:t], *v.tr.* **1.** Détourner (qch. de son but). **2.** Pervertir (qn); dépraver (le goût). **3.** Fausser (les faits).

perverter [pə'və:tər], *s.* Pervertisseur, -euse.

pervious ['pə:viəs], *a.* Perméable (à l'eau, etc.).

perviousness ['pə:viəsnis], *s.* Perméabilité *f* (to, à).

pessimism ['pesimizm], *s.* Pessimisme *m*.

pessimist ['pesimist], *s.* Pessimiste *mf*.

pessimistic [,pesi'mistik], *a.* Pessimiste. To feel p. about a matter, augurer mal d'une affaire. **-ally,** *adv.* Avec pessimisme.

pest [pest], *s.* (*a*) Insecte *m* ou plante *f* nuisible. Here the rabbits are a p., ici les lapins sont un fléau. (*b*) *F:* Peste *f*, fléau. That child is a perfect p.! quelle peste, quel casse-pieds, que cet enfant! **'pest-destroying,** *a.* Pesticide.

pester ['pestər], *v.tr.* **1.** Tourmenter, importuner; *F:* empoisonner. *F:* He pesters me to death, il me casse les pieds. To p. s.o. with questions, assommer qn de (ses) questions. To p. s.o. to do sth., importuner qn pour lui faire faire qch. **2.** House pestered with rats, maison infestée de rats.

pesticide ['pestisaid], *s.* Pesticide *m*, antiparasite *m*.

pestiferous [pes'tifərəs], *a.* (*a*) (*Of air*) Pestifère. (*b*) (*Of insects, etc.*) Nuisible. (*c*) *F:* (*Of doctrine*) Pernicieux.

pestilence ['pestiləns], *s.* Peste *f*.

pestilent ['pestilənt], *a.* Pestilent. (*a*) Malsain, nocif, -ive. (*b*) (*Of doctrine, etc.*) Pernicieux, -euse; corrupteur, -trice.

pestilential [,pesti'lenʃ(ə)l], *a.* Pestilentiel, -elle. (*a*) (*Of disease*) Contagieux, -euse, pestifère. (*b*) (*Of doctrine, etc.*) Pernicieux, -euse, corrupteur, -trice. (*c*) *F:* Assommant, empoisonnant, rasoir.

pestle[1] ['pesl], *s.* Pilon *m* (pour mortier).

pestle[2], *v.tr.* Piler, broyer (au mortier).

pet[1] [pet]. **1.** *s.* (*a*) Animal familier, favori. To make a p. of an animal, choyer un animal. 'No pets,' "pas de bêtes." (*b*) He is his mother's p., c'est l'enfant gâté de sa mère. My p.! mon chouchou! **2.** *attrib.* Choyé, favori; de prédilection. He's on his p. subject again, le revoilà sur son dada. P. name, diminutif *m*; nom *m* d'amitié. *S.a.* AVERSION 2. **'pet-shop,** *s.* Magasin *m*, boutique *f* aux petites bêtes (chiots, chatons, cobayes, etc.).

pet[2], *v.tr.* (petted) **1.** Choyer, mignoter, chouchouter. **2.** *Esp. U.S:* Caresser, câliner (qn); *F:* peloter (qn). **petting,** *s. Esp. U.S:* Bécotage *m*; *F:* pelotage *m*.

pet[3], *s. O:* Accès *m* de mauvaise humeur. To take the p., prendre la mouche. To be in a p., bouder; être de mauvaise humeur.

petal ['petl], *s. Bot:* Pétale *m*. (*Of flower*) To shed its petals, s'effeuiller.

petard [pe'tɑ:d], *s.* **1.** *Mil: A:* Pétard *m*. *S.a.* HOIST[2]. **2.** *Pyr:* Pétard.

Peter[1] ['pi:tər]. **1.** *Pr.n.m.* Pierre. *R.C.Ch:* Peter's pence, le denier de Saint-Pierre. **2.** *s. Nau:* Blue P., pavillon *m* de partance.

peter[2] out [pi:tə'raut], *v.i. F:* **1.** (*a*) *Min:* (*Of seam*) Mourir; s'épuiser. (*b*) (*Of stream*) Disparaître (sous terre); se perdre dans les sables. **2.** (*Of scheme*) Tomber dans l'eau; s'en aller en fumée. **3.** *Aut:* (*Of engine*) S'arrêter (faute d'essence).

petersham ['pi:təʃəm], *s.* **1.** Gros drap (à pardessus); ratine *f*. **2.** P. ribbon, ruban *m* gros grain.

petiole ['petioul], *s. Bot:* Pétiole *m*.

petite [pə'ti:t], *a.* (*Of woman*) Petite (et svelte).

petition[1] [pi'tiʃ(ə)n], *s.* (*a*) Prière *f* (à Dieu). (*b*) Pétition *f*, supplique *f*, requête *f*. (*c*) *Jur:* P. for a reprieve, recours *m* en grâce. P. for a divorce, demande *f* en divorce. P. in bankruptcy, (i) requête des créanciers; (ii) requête du négociant insolvable. *S.a.* FILE[4] 2.

petition[2], *v.tr.* Adresser, présenter, une pétition, une requête, à (la cour, un souverain). To p. the court for sth., réclamer qch. au tribunal.

petitioner [pi'tiʃənər], *s.* Pétitionnaire *mf*, solliciteur, -euse; demandeur, -euse. *Jur:* Requérant, -ante.

petrel ['petrəl], *s. Orn:* Pétrel *m*. Stormy p., (i) pétrel des tempêtes; (ii) émissaire *m* de discorde.

petrifaction [‚petri′fækʃ(ə)n], s. Pétrification f.
petrify [′petrifai]. 1. v.tr. (a) Pétrifier (le bois). (b) Pétrifier, méduser (qn de peur). 2. v.i. Se pétrifier. **petrified**, a. (a) Pétrifié. (b) Paralysé de terreur. **petrifying**, a. (a) Pétrifiant; incrustant. (b) Terrifiant.
petrography [pe′trɔgrəfi], s. Geol: Pétrographie f.
petrol [′petr(ə)l], s. Aut: Essence f. High-grade, brand-d, premium-grade, p., supercarburant m, F: super m. Car heavy on p., voiture qui consomme beaucoup. ′petrol-can, s. Bidon m à essence. ′petrol-lorry, s. F: Camion-citerne m, pl. camions-citernes. S.a. PUMP¹, COUPON.
petrolatum [‚petro′leitəm], s. U.S: 1. Pharm: Vaseline officinale. 2. Ind: Graisse verte.
petroleum [pi′trouliəm], s. Pétrole m. The p. industry, l'industrie pétrolière. P. wharf, bassin m, quai m à pétrole. Pharm: P. jelly, vaseline f.
petrology [pe′trɔlədʒi], s. Pétrologie f.
petticoat [′petikout], s. (a) A: Jupe f, cotillon m. P. government, régime m de cotillons. He is under p. government, c'est sa femme qui porte la culotte. (b) Jupe de dessous; jupon m.
pettifog [′petifog], v.i. (pettifogged) Avocasser. Pettifogging lawyer, homme de loi de bas étage.
pettiness [′petinis], s. Petitesse f, mesquinerie f.
pettish [′petiʃ], a. De mauvaise humeur; maussade; irritable. -ly, adv. Avec humeur.
pettishness [′petiʃnis], s. Mauvaise humeur; irritabilité f; maussaderie f.
petty [′peti], a. 1. (a) Petit, insignifiant, sans importance. P. monarch, roitelet m. P. expenses, menus frais. S.a. LARCENY, SESSION 4. (b) P.(-minded), mesquin. 2. Com: P. cash, petite caisse. 3. Navy: P. officer, officier marinier; F: gradé m. The p. officers, la maistrance. petty-′mindedness, s. = PETTINESS.
petulance [′petjuləns], s. Irritabilité f, vivacité f. Outburst of p., mouvement m d'humeur.
petulant [′petjulənt], a. Irritable, susceptible, vif. -ly, adv. Avec irritation.
petunia [pi′tjuːnjə], s. Bot: Pétunia m.
pew [pjuː], s. Banc m d'église.
pewit [′piːwit], s. Orn: Vanneau (huppé).
pewter [′pjuːtər], s. 1. Étain m, potin m. P. ware, vaisselle f d'étain. 2. Pot m d'étain.
phagocyte [′fægəsait], s. Biol: Phagocyte m.
phalanges [fæ′lændʒiːz], s.pl. See PHALANX 2.
phalanstery [′fælənst(ə)ri], s. Hist. of Pol. Ec: Phalanstère m.
phalanx [′fælæŋks], s. 1. Gr.Ant: (pl. usu. phalanxes [′fælæŋksiz]) Phalange f. 2. Anat: Bot: (pl. usu. phalanges [fə′lændʒiːz]) Phalange.
phallic [′fælik], a. Phallique. P. symbol, emblème phallique.
phallus [′fæləs], s. Phallus m.
phanerogam [′fænərougæm], s. Bot: Phanérogame f.
phantasm [′fæntæzm], s. 1. Chimère f, illusion f, fantasme m. 2. (a) Med: Phantasme m. (b) Psychics: Apparition f.
phantasmagoria [‚fæntæzmə′gɔriə], s. Fantasmagorie f.
phantasmagoric [‚fæntæzmə′gɔrik], a. Fantasmagorique.
phantasmal [fæn′tæsml], **phantasmic** [fæn′tæsmik], a. Fantomatique, spectral, -aux.
phantom [′fæntəm], s. Fantôme m, spectre m.
Pharaoh [′fɛərou], s. A.Hist: Pharaon m.
Pharisaic(al) [‚færi′seiik(əl)], a. Pharisaïque. -ally, adv. Pharisaïquement; en pharisien.
Pharisee [′færisiː], s. Pharisien m.
pharmaceutic(al) [‚faːmə′sjuːtik(əl)], a. Pharmaceutique.
pharmaceutics [‚faːmə′sjuːtiks], s.pl. La pharmaceutique; la pharmacie.
pharmacology [‚faːmə′kɔlədʒi], s. Pharmacologie f.
pharmacopœia [‚faːməkə′piːə], s. (a) Pharmacopée f; codex m. (b) (Medicine chest) Pharmacie f.
pharmacy [′faːməsi], s. 1. Pharmacie f. 2. Esp. U.S: Pharmacie; boutique f de pharmacien.
pharyngeal [fæ′rindʒiːəl], a. Anat: Pharyngien, -ienne.
pharyngitis [‚færin′dʒaitis], s. Med: Pharyngite f.
pharynx [′færiŋks], s. Anat: Pharynx m.

phase¹ [feiz], s. 1. Phase f. Phases of an illness, phases, périodes f, d'une maladie. 2. El.E: Phase. Three-p., triphasé.
phase², v.tr. (a) El.E: etc: Mettre en phase; caler en phase. (b) Développer (un projet) en phases successives.
pheasant [′feznt], s. (Cock-)p., faisan m. Hen-p. faisane f. P. preserve, faisanderie f.
phenacetin [fi′næsitin], s. Phénacétine f.
phenobarbital [′fiːno′baːbitl], **phenobarbitone** [′fiːno′baːbitoun], s. Pharm: Barbiturique m, barbital m, phénobarbital m.
phenol [′fiːnɔl], s. Ch: Phénol m, acide m phénique.
phenomena [fi′nɔminə], s.pl. See PHENOMENON.
phenomenal [fi′nɔminl], a. Phénoménal, -aux. 1. Phil: Aperceptible. 2. Extraordinaire, prodigieux. -ally, adv. Phénoménalement.
phenomenon, pl. -ena [fi′nɔminən, -ənə], s. 1. Phénomène m. Atmospheric p., phénomène météorologique. 2. Phénomène; chose f remarquable; (of pers.) prodige m.
phenyl [′fiːnil], s. Ch: Phényle m.
phew [fjuː], int. 1. Pouf! 2. (Disgust) Pouah!
phial [′faiəl], s. Fiole f, flacon m; topette f.
philander [fi′lændər], v.i. Flirter. To p. with s.o., conter fleurette à (une femme).
philanderer [fi′lændərər], s. Flirteur m; galant m.
philanthropic(al) [‚filən′θrɔpik(əl)], a. Philanthropique; (of pers.) philanthrope.
philanthropist [fi′lænθrəpist], s. Philanthrope mf.
philanthropy [fi′lænθrəpi], s. Philanthropie f.
philatelic [‚filə′telik], a. Philatélique, philatéliste.
philatelist [fi′lætəlist], s. Philatéliste mf.
philately [fi′lætəli], s. Philatélie f, philatélisme m.
philharmonic [‚filɑː′mɔnik], a. (Société, etc.) philharmonique.
Philip [′filip]. Pr.n.m. Philippe.
philippic [fi′lipik], s. (a) A.Lit: The Philippics, les Philippiques f. (b) Philippique.
Philippines (The) [ðə′filipiːnz], Pr.n.Geog: Les Philippines fpl.
Philistine [′filistain], a. & s. (a) B.Hist: Philistin (m). (b) Philistin; affreux bourgeois.
Philistinism [′filistinizm], s. Philistinisme m; esprit bourgeois.
philological [‚filə′lɔdʒik(ə)l], a. Philologique. -ally, adv. Philologiquement.
philologist [fi′lɔlədʒist], s. Philologue m.
philology [fi′lɔlədʒi], s. Philologie f.
philosopher [fi′lɔsəfər], s. Philosophe m. Moral p., moraliste m. The philosophers' stone, la pierre philosophale.
philosophical [‚filə′sɔfik(ə)l], a. 1. Philosophique. 2. (Of pers.) Philosophe, calme, modéré. -ally, adv. Philosophiquement.
philosophize [fi′lɔsəfaiz], v.i. Philosopher.
philosophy [fi′lɔsəfi], s. Philosophie f. Moral p., la morale.
philtre [′filtər], s. A: Philtre m.
phiz [fiz], s. F: O: Visage m, F: binette f.
phlebitis [fli′baitis], s. Med: Phlébite f.
phlegm [flem], s. 1. Flegme m. To cough up p., tousser gras. 2. Flegme, calme m.
phlegmatic [fleg′mætik], a. Flegmatique. -ally, adv. Flegmatiquement.
phlegmon [′flegmon], s. Med: Phlegmon m.
phlox [flɔks], s. Bot: Phlox m.
phobia [′foubiə], s. Phobie f.
Phoebus [′fiːbəs], Pr.n.m. Myth: Phébus.
Phœnicia [fi′niːʃiə], Pr.n. A.Geog: La Phénicie.
Phœnician [fi′niːʃiən], a. & s. Phénicien, -ienne.
phœnix [′fiːniks], s. Phénix m.
phone¹ [foun], s. F: Téléphone m. He's on the p., (i) il a le téléphone (chez lui); (ii) il parle au téléphone. P. box, cabine f téléphonique. ′phone-tapping, s. Tp: (By the police) Emploi m de la table d'écoute.
phone², v.tr. & i. F: To p. s.o. (up), téléphoner à qn. To p. for sth., for s.o., demander qch., qn, par téléphone. To p. for a taxi, appeler un taxi.
phonetic [fo′netik], a. Phonétique. P. spelling, écriture f phonétique. -ally, adv. Phonétiquement.
phonetician [‚founi′tiʃ(ə)n], s. Phonéticien, -ienne.

honetics [fo'netiks], *s.pl.* Phonétique *f*.

honey ['founi]. **1.** *a.* F: Faux, *f.* fausse; (bijouterie) en toc. That's a p. story, cette histoire, c'est de la blague. The p. war, (1939–40) la drôle de guerre. **2.** *s.* F: Imposteur *m*, charlatan *m*.

honiatrics [,founi'ætriks], *s.pl.*, **phoniatry** [,founi-'ætri], *s. Med:* Phoniatrie *f*.

honic ['founik, 'fɔnik], *a.* Phonique.

honograph ['founəgræf, -grɑ:f], *s. U.S:* Phonographe *m*.

honology [fə'nɔlədʒi], *s. Ling:* Phonologie *f*.

hosgene ['fɔzdʒi:n], *s. Ch:* Phosgène *m*.

hosphate ['fɔsfeit], *s. Ch:* Phosphate *m*.

hosphene ['fɔsfi:n], *s. Physiol:* Phosphène *m*.

hosphide ['fɔsfaid], *s. Ch:* Phosphure *m*.

hosphine ['fɔsfi:n], *s. Ch:* Phosphine *f*.

hosphorescence [,fɔsfə'resns], *s.* Phosphorescence *f*.

hosphorescent [,fɔsfə'resnt], *a.* Phosphorescent.

hosphoric [fɔs'fɔrik], *a. Ch:* (Acide) phosphorique.

hosphorous ['fɔsf(ə)rəs], *a.* Phosphoreux, -euse.

hosphorus ['fɔsf(ə)rəs], *s. Ch:* Phosphore *m*. Yellow p., phosphore blanc.

hosphuretted ['fɔsfjuretid], *a.* Phosphuré. P. hydrogen, hydrogène phosphoré.

hoto ['foutou], *s.* F: = PHOTOGRAPH[1].

hotocell ['foutou'sel], *s.* Cellule *f* photo-électrique.

hotochemistry [foutou'kemistri], *s.* Photochimie *f*.

hotocopy ['foutou'kɔpi], *s.* Photocopie *f*.

hoto(-)electric [,foutoui'lektrik], *a.* (Cellule) photo-électrique. P.-e. current, photo-électricité *f*.

hoto-engraver ['foutouin'greivər], *s.* Photograveur *m*.

hoto-engraving ['foutouin'greiviŋ], *s.* Photogravure industrielle.

hoto-finish ['foutou'finiʃ], *s. Sp:* Photo *f* à l'arrivée, décision *f* par photo. P.-f. camera, photo-finish *f*.

hotogenic [,foutou'dʒenik], *a.* Photogénique.

hotograph[1] ['foutəgræf, -grɑ:f], *s.* Photographie *f*. To take a p., prendre une photo(graphie) de qn, qch.; photographier (qn, qch.). To have one's p. taken, se faire photographier.

hotograph[2], *v.tr.* **1.** Photographier; prendre une photo(graphie) de (qn). **2.** (*With passive force*). To p. well, être photogénique.

hotographer [f(ə)'tɔgrəfər], *s.* Photographe *m*. Street p., photostoppeur *m*.

hotographic [,foutə'græfik], *a.* Photographique. P. library, photothèque *f*. -ally, *adv.* Photographiquement.

hotography [f(ə)'tɔgrəfi], *s.* Photographie *f*; prise *f* de vue(s). Colour p., photographie en couleurs.

hotogravure [,foutəgrə'vjuər], *s.* Héliogravure *f*.

hotolysis [fou'tɔlisis], *s. Biol:* Photolyse *f*.

hotomacrography ['foutoumə'krɔgrəfi], *s.* Macrophotographie *f*.

hotomap ['foutoumæp], *s.* Carte-photographie aérienne.

hotometer [fou'tɔmitər], *s.* Photomètre *m*. Shadow p., photomètre de Rumford. Grease-spot p., photomètre à tache d'huile; photomètre de Bunsen.

hotometry [fou'tɔmitri], *s.* Photométrie *f*.

hotomicrograph ['foutou'maikrəgræf, -grɑ:f], *s.* Photomicrographie *f*.

hotomicrography ['foutoumai'krɔgrəfi], *s.* Photomicrographie *f* (le procédé).

hoton ['foutɔn], *s. Ph:* Photon *m*.

hoto-reconnaissance [,foutoure'kɔnisəns], *s. Av:* Reconnaissance *f* photographique.

hotosphere ['foutousfiər], *s. Astr:* Photosphère *f*.

hotostat ['foutoustæt], *s.* Photocopie *f*; photostat *m*.

hotostat[2], *v.tr.* Photocopier.

hotosynthesis ['foutou'sinθisis], *s. Biol: Ch:* Photosynthèse *f*.

hototelegraphic ['foutou,teli'græfik], *a.* Téléphotographique.

hototelegraphy ['foutouti'legrəfi], *s.* Téléphotographie *f*, phototélégraphie *f*.

hototherapy ['foutou'θerəpi], *s.* Photothérapie *f*.

hototype ['foutoutaip], *s.* Phototype *m*; (*from tracing*) photocalque *m*.

hototypography ['foutoutai'pɔgrəfi], *s.* Phototypographie *f*.

phrase[1] [freiz], *s.* **1.** (*a*) Locution *f*, expression *f*; tour *m* de phrase. Technical p., locution technique. As the p. goes, comme on dit, F: comme dit l'autre. (*b*) Felicity of p., bonheur *m* d'expression. (*c*) *Gram:* Locution; membre *m* de phrase. **2.** *Mus:* Phrase *f*, période *f*. 'phrase-book, *s.* Recueil *m* de locutions, d'expressions.

phrase[2], *v.tr.* **1.** Exprimer (sa pensée). Well-phrased letter, lettre bien rédigée, bien tournée. That is how he phrased it, voilà comment il s'est exprimé. **2.** *Mus:* Phraser.

phraseology [,freizi'ɔlədʒi], *s.* Phraséologie *f*.

phrenologist [fri'nɔlədʒist], *s.* Phrénologiste *m*.

phrenology [fri'nɔlədʒi], *s.* Phrénologie *f*.

Phrygia ['fridʒiə]. *Pr.n. A.Geog:* La Phrygie.

phthisis ['θaisis], *s. A: Med:* Phtisie *f*; tuberculose *f* pulmonaire.

phut [fʌt], *adv.* F: To go p., (*of electric lamp*) griller; (*of one's business, an engine*) claquer.

phylactery [fi'læktəri], *s. Jew. Rel:* Phylactère *m*.

phylloxera [fi'lɔksərə], *s. Ent: Vit:* Phylloxéra *m*.

phylum *pl.* -a ['failəm, -ə], *s. Nat.Hist:* Embranchement.

physic ['fizik], *s. O:* Médecine *f*, médicaments *mpl*, F: drogues *fpl*.

physical ['fizik(ə)l], *a.* Physique. **1.** P. impossibility, impossibilité matérielle. **2.** (Piece of) p. apparatus, appareil *m* de physique. **3.** P. force, force physique. *Gym:* P. exercises, exercices physiques; exercices d'assouplissement. *S.a.* DEFECT 2. -ally, *adv.* Physiquement. Thing p. impossible, chose matériellement impossible. A p.-handicapped person, un diminué physique.

physician [fi'ziʃ(ə)n], *s.* Médecin *m*.

physicist ['fizisist], *s.* Physicien, -ienne.

physics ['fiziks], *s.pl.* La physique.

physiocrat ['fiziəkræt], *s.* Physiocrate *m*.

physiognomist [,fizi'ɔnəmist], *s.* **1.** Physionomiste *mf*. **2.** Physiognomoniste *mf*.

physiognomy [,fizi'ɔnəmi], *s.* **1.** Physionomie *f*. **2.** Physiognomonie *f*.

physiological [,fiziə'lɔdʒik(ə)l], *a.* Physiologique. *Bio.Ch:* P. salt solution, solution *f*, sérum *m*, physiologique.

physiologist [,fizi'ɔlədʒist], *s.* Physiologiste *mf*, physiologue *mf*.

physiology [,fizi'ɔlədʒi], *s.* Physiologie *f*.

physiotherapist [,fizio'θerəpist], *s.* Physiothérapiste *mf*, physiothérapeute *mf*.

physiotherapy ['fiziou'θerəpi], \s. *Med:* Physiothérapie *f*.

physique [fi'zi:k], *s.* **1.** Physique *m* (de qn). To have a fine p., avoir un beau physique. To be of poor p., être d'apparence malingre; être peu robuste. **2.** Structure *f* du corps.

phytozoon, *pl.* -zoa [faito'zouən, -'zouə], *s.* Zoophyte *m*; phytozoaire *m*.

pi[1] [pai], *s. Gr.Alph:* Pi *m*.

pi[2], *a. P:* Pieux, -euse.

pia mater ['paiə'meitər], *s. Anat:* Pie-mère *f*.

pianist ['piənist], *s.* Pianiste *mf*.

piano[1] ['pjɑ:nou], *adv. Mus:* Piano (signe d'expression).

piano[2] [pi'ænou], *Mus:* Piano *m*. (Concert) grand p., piano à queue. Baby-grand p., F: crapaud *m*. Upright p., piano droit. To play (on) the p., jouer du piano. pi'ano-maker, *s.* Facteur *m* de pianos. pi'ano-stool, *s.* Tabouret *m* de piano. pi'ano-tuner, *s.* Accordeur *m* de pianos. pi'ano-wire, *s.* Corde *f* à piano.

pianola [pjæ'noulə], *s. Mus: R.t.m:* Pianola *m*.

piastre [pi'æstər], *s. Num:* Piastre *f*.

piazza [pi'ætsə], *s.* **1.** (*a*) Place publique (en Italie). (*b*) *Town P:* Place publique interdite aux véhicules. **2.** *U.S:* Véranda *f*.

pibroch ['pi:brɔx, -ɔk], *s.* Pibroch *m* (air de cornemuse avec variations, martial ou funèbre).

pica ['paikə], *s. Typ:* Cícéro *m*; corps *m* 12. Double p., gros parangon; corps 22.

picador ['pikədɔ:r], *s.* (*Bullfighting*) Picador *m*.

Picardy ['pikədi]. *Pr.n.* La Picardie.

picaresque [,pikə'resk], *a.* (Roman *m*) picaresque.

piccalilli ['pikəlili], *s. Cu:* Pickles *mpl* à la moutarde.

piccaninny ['pikənini], *s. Pej:* Négrillon, -onne. F: Mioche *mf*; bambin, -ine.

piccolo ['pikəlou], *s. Mus:* Piccolo *m*, petite flûte.

pick¹ [pik], s. Pic m, pioche f. Min: Rivelaine f. **P. and shovel man,** terrassier m. **P. and shovel work,** (i) travail fatigant, pénible; (ii) recherche (scientifique) patiente et laborieuse. **'pick-hammer,** s. Picot m.

pick², s. Choix m, élite f. **The p. of the basket, of the bunch,** le dessus du panier. **The p. of the army,** la (fine) fleur de l'armée.

pick³, v.tr. 1. (a) Piocher (la terre). (b) F: **To p. holes in sth.,** trouver à redire à qch.; F: chercher la petite bête. (c) F: **Why p. on me?** pourquoi m'accuser, moi? 2. **To p. one's teeth,** se curer les dents. 3. Éplucher (des groseilles). **To p. a bone,** ôter, enlever, la chair d'un os. F: **To have a bone to p. with s.o.,** avoir maille à partir avec qn. 4. (Of birds) Picoter, becqueter (le blé). F: (Of pers.) **To p. (at) one's food,** manger du bout des dents, des lèvres. 5. (a) Choisir. **To p. one's steps,** marcher avec précaution. **To p. and choose,** se montrer difficile. Games: **To p. sides,** tirer les camps. S.a. QUARREL². (b) Trier (du minerai). 6. (a) Cueillir (des fleurs, des fruits). (b) **To p. rags,** chiffonner. (c) **To p. acquaintance with s.o.,** lier connaissance avec qn. 7. (a) **To p. pockets,** pratiquer le vol à la tire. (b) Crocheter (une serrure). (c) **To p. s.o.'s brains,** exploiter l'intelligence, les connaissances, de qn. 8. Défaire, détisser effilocher (des chiffons). S.a. OAKUM, PIECE¹ 1. **pick off,** v.tr. 1. Enlever, ôter; égrener (des raisins). 2. **A sniper picked off the three officers,** un tireur descendit un à un les trois officiers. **pick out,** v.tr. 1. (a) Extirper, enlever (qch.). (b) Faire le tri de (qch.); choisir. **P. out the best!** choisissez les meilleurs! **To p. s.o. out from the crowd,** repérer qn parmi la foule. 2. Paint: Réchampir. **Picked out in gold,** à filets d'or. **pick over,** v.tr. Trier (un panier de fruits). **pick up. I.** v.tr. 1. Prendre; (off the ground) ramasser, relever. **To p. up a shilling,** (i) ramasser un shilling (par terre); (ii) se faire, gagner, un shilling. **To p. s.o. up in passing,** prendre qn en passant. **I will p. you up at Basle,** je vous rejoindrai à Bâle. **To p. up shipwrecked men,** recueillir des naufragés. Nau: **To p. up an anchor,** relever une ancre. Knitting: **To p. up a stitch,** relever une maille. Cards: **To p. up a trick,** ramasser les cartes. 2. Apprendre (un tour). 3. Trouver, retrouver. **To p. up sth. cheap,** acheter qch. à bon marché. **It is a curio that I picked up,** c'est un bibelot de rencontre. **To p. up a livelihood,** gagner péniblement sa vie. 4. (a) (Of searchlight) **To p. up an aircraft,** repérer un avion. (b) El: Prendre, capter (le courant). W.Tel: Capter (un message). **To p. up Paris,** avoir Paris. 5. **That will p. you up,** voilà qui vous requinquera. 6. (a) I.C.E: (Of engine) **To p. up speed,** abs. **to p. up,** reprendre. (b) (Of pers.) **To p. up strength,** reprendre des forces. **II. pick up,** v.i. 1. Retrouver ses forces; se rétablir. 2. F: **To p. up with s.o.,** faire la connaissance de qn. '**pick-up,** s. 1. Connaissance f de rencontre. 2. I.C.E: Reprise f (du moteur). 3. Gramophones: Pick-up m inv. 4. W.Tel: Captage m (des ondes). 5. Electronics: Capteur m. 6. Veh: Pick-up. **picking,** s. 1. (a) Épluchage m (d'une salade). (b) Picotage m (du fruit par les oiseaux). (c) Choix m (de ses mots); triage m (du minerai). (d) Cueillage m, cueillette f (de fruits). (e) **P. and stealing,** grappillage m. (f) Crochetage m (d'une serrure). 2. pl. **Pickings.** (a) Épluchures f, rognures f. (b) F: Bénéfices m, gratte f. '**pick-me-up,** s. F: Cordial m, -aux; réconfortant m; remontant m. **That's a rare p.-me-up!** voilà qui vous remonte!

pick-a-back ['pikəbæk], adv. (Porter qn) sur le dos, sur les épaules.

pickax(e) ['pikæks], s. Tls: Pioche f. Min: Hoyau m.

picker ['pikər], s. 1. Cueilleur, -euse (de fleurs, etc.); récolteur, -euse (de fruits). **Grape-p.,** vendangeur, -euse. 2. Crocheteur m (de serrures).

picket¹ ['pikit], s. 1. (a) Piquet m. Mil: **Alignment p.,** jalon m. (b) Piquet d'attache (pour chevaux). 2. (a) Mil: etc: Piquet, poste m (d'hommes). **Fire p.,** piquet d'incendie. **Outpost p.,** avant-poste m, pl. avant-postes. (b) Ind: **Strike pickets,** piquets de grève. '**picket-boat,** s. Vedette f. '**picket-fence,** s. Palis m, palissade m.

picket², v.tr. (picketed) 1. Mettre (des chevaux) au(x) piquet(s). 2. Ind: **To p. a factory,** installer de piquets de grève. **picketing,** s. 1. Mise f (de chevaux) au piquet. 2. Ind: Constitution f d piquets de grève.

pickle¹ ['pikl], s. 1. Marinade f; saumure f c vinaigre m. **In p.,** en train de mariner. S.a. ROD 2. pl. **Pickles,** pickles mpl, conserves f au vinaigre Fr.C: marinades fpl. 3. F: (a) **To be in a (nic sorry) p.,** être dans de beaux draps. **What a p. you're in!** vous voilà bien! (b) Enfant mf terrible 4. Metalw: Solution f de décapage.

pickle², v.tr. 1. Mariner; conserver (au vinaig ou à la saumure). 2. Metalw: Décaper. **pickled a.** 1. Mariné, salé, saumuré; confit (au vinaigre **P. cabbage,** chou m rouge au vinaigre. 2. F: lvre gris, parti.

picklock ['piklɔk], s. 1. (Pers.) Crocheteur m d serrures. 2. Crochet m (de serrurier); rossignol r (de cambrioleur).

pickpocket ['pik,pɔkit], s. Voleur m à la tire; pick pocket m.

picky ['piki], a. F: Difficile, délicat.

picnic¹ ['piknik], s. Pique-nique m, pl. pique-niques **We'll take a p. (meal) with us,** nous emporterons ui pique-nique. F: **The Korean campaign was no p.** la campagne de Corée n'a guère été une partie de plaisir.

picnic², v.i. (picnicked) Faire un pique-nique; pique niquer.

picnicker ['piknikər], s. Pique-niqueur m.

picrate ['pikrit], s. Ch: Picrate m.

picric ['pikrik], a. Ch: (Acide m) picrique.

Pict [pikt], s. Ethn: Hist: Picte m.

pictograph ['piktəgræf, -grɑːf], s. Pictographe m.

pictography [pik'tɔgrəfi], s. Pictographie f.

pictorial [pik'tɔːriəl], a. 1. (a) (Écriture) en images (b) (Périodique) illustré. (c) (Description) pit toresque. 2. s. (Magazine, journal) illustré (m) **-ally,** adv. Au moyen d'illustrations.

picture¹ ['piktʃər], s. 1. Image f, tableau m; peinture f, gravure f. **He is the p. of his father,** c'est le portrai de son père. **He is the p. of health,** il respire la santé **She is a perfect p.,** elle est à peindre. **To draw mental p. of sth.,** se représenter qch. (Of pers., thg F: **To be in the p.,** être à la page; être tout à fait au courant. Jur: **Composite p., mind p.,** portrait robot. 2. Th: **Living pictures,** tableaux vivants. 3. Cin: Film m. F: **The pictures** le cinéma. '**picture-book,** s. Livre m d'images '**picture-card,** s. Cards: Figure f. '**picture palace,** s. O: Cinéma m. '**picture postcard,** s. Carte postale (illustrée). '**picture-rail,** s. Moulure f pour accrocher les tableaux (au mur).

picture², v.tr. 1. Dépeindre, représenter (qn, qch.). 2. **To p. to oneself,** s'imaginer, se figurer (qch.).

picturesque [,piktʃə'resk], a. Pittoresque. **P. phrases** expressions qui font image. **-ly,** adv. Pittoresquemen

picturesqueness [,piktʃə'resknis], s. Pittoresque m.

piddle ['pidl], v.i. F: Faire pipi.

piddling ['pidliŋ], a. F: Sans importance.

pidgin ['pidʒin], s. 1. **P. English,** jargon commercial anglo-chinois, anglo-ouest-africain, etc., (S. Pacific area) bichlamar m. F: **To talk p. =** parler petit nègre. 2. F: **That's my p.,** ça c'est mon affaire.

pie¹ [pai], s. Orn: = MAGPIE.

pie², s. (a) **Meat p. =** pâté m en croûte. **Shepherd's p.** hachis m aux pommes de terre. S.a. FINGER¹ 1 HUMBLE PIE. (b) **Fruit p.,** tourte f. '**pie-dish,** s. (a) (For covered pies) Cocotte f (à rebords); plat m allant au four, plat à four. (b) (For open pies tarts) Tourtière f; moule f, tôle f, à tarte.

pie³, s. Typ: (Composition tombée en) pâte f; pâté m. '**pie-eyed,** a. F: Éméché.

piebald ['paibɔːld], a. & s. 1. (a) (Cheval) pie m. (b) F: Bigarré, disparate.

piece¹ [piːs], s. Pièce f. 1. (a) Morceau m (de pain); bout m (de ruban); parcelle f (de terrain). (b) Fragment m. **To come, fall, go, to pieces,** s'en alle en morceaux. **Garment falling to pieces,** vêtemen qui ne tient plus (ensemble). F: **He went to pieces in the second set,** il s'est écroulé au second set. **To fly in, into, to, pieces,** voler en éclats. F: **To**

pick s.o. to pieces, déchirer qn à belles dents. To pull, tear, to pieces, déchirer, défaire (qch.). F: To tear an argument to pieces, démolir un argument. F: To pull s.o. to pieces, critiquer qn sévèrement; éreinter qn. 2. Partie f (d'une machine). To take a machine to pieces, démonter une machine. To take a dress to pieces, défaire une robe. 3. Com: Pièce (de drap); rouleau m (de papier peint). To pay workmen by the p., payer des ouvriers à la pièce, à la tâche. 4. All in one p., tout d'une pièce. F: They are all of a p., ils sont tous du même acabit. 5. (a) A p. of my work, un échantillon de mon travail. P. of water, pièce d'eau. P. out of a book, passage m d'un livre. (b) P. of folly, acte m de folie. P. of wit, trait m d'esprit. (c) A p. of advice, un conseil. A p. of carelessness, une étourderie. A ridiculous p.of affectation, une affectation ridicule. A p. of (good) luck, une chance (heureuse). A p. of news, une nouvelle. A p. of luggage, une valise, un colis. A p. of furniture, un meuble. A p. of clothing, un vêtement. 6. (a) (i) Artil: Pièce (d'artillerie). (ii) To load one's p., charger son fusil. (b) Pièce (de monnaie). Five-shilling p., pièce de cinq shillings. 7. Morceau (de musique, de poésie); pièce (de théâtre). 8. Chess: Pieces and pawns, pièces et pions. 'piece-work, s. Travail m à la tâche, à la pièce. 'piece-worker, s. Ouvrier, -ière, à la tâche, à la pièce.

piece², v.tr. 1. Rapiécer, raccommoder. 2. To p. ropes, joindre, assembler, des cordages. piece together, v.tr. Joindre, unir, rassembler (des fragments). To p. facts together, coordonner des faits.

piecemeal ['piːsmiːl], adv. Par morceaux; pièce à pièce. To find sth. out p., apprendre qch. par bribes.

piecrust ['paikrʌst], s. Croûte f, chapeau m, de pâté.

pied [paid], a. Mi-parti; bariolé, bigarré.

Piedmont ['piːdmənt]. Pr.n. Geog: Le Piémont.

Piedmontese [ˌpiːdmənˈtiːz], a. & s. Geog: Piémontais, -aise.

pieman, pl. -men ['paimən], s.m. O: Marchand de petits pâtés.

pier ['piər], s. 1. (a) (Of stone) Jetée f, digue f. (b) (On piles) Estacade f. (Landing) p., quai m. P. dues, droits m de quai. (c) (At seaside resort) Jetée promenade f. 2. Civ.E: Pilier m (de maçonnerie). 3. Arch: (a) Pilastre m, pied-droit m (de porte). (b) Trumeau m. 'pier-glass, s. Furn: Trumeau m. 'pier-head, s. Extrémité f de la jetée; musoir m.

pierce [piəs]. 1. v.tr. Percer, transpercer, pénétrer. A thorn pierced his finger, une épine lui est entrée dans le doigt. Wall pierced with loop-holes, mur troué de meurtrières. (Of light) To p. the darkness, percer les ténèbres. 2. v.i. To p. through the enemy's lines, pénétrer les lignes de l'ennemi. pierce through, v.tr. Transpercer. To p. through and through, percer de part en part. piercing, a. (Cri) aigu, perçant; (froid) pénétrant. piercingly, adv. D'une manière perçante, pénétrante. To fix one's eye p. on s.o., fixer qn d'un regard perçant.

pierrot ['piərou], s.m. Th: Pierrot.

pietism ['paiətizm], s. 1. Rel.H. Piétisme m. 2. Bigoterie f.

piety ['paiəti], s. Piété f. Filial p., piété filiale.

piezometer [piˈzəmitər], s. Ph: Piézomètre m.

piffle¹ ['pifl], s. O: F: Futilités fpl, balivernes fpl. To talk p., dire des futilités.

piffle², v.i. O: F: 1. Dire des niaiseries, des sottises. 2. S'occuper à des futilités. piffling, a. F: Futile.

pig¹ [pig], s. 1. (a) Porc m, cochon m, pourceau m. Suck(l)ing p., cochon de lait. pl. Pigs (in general), les porcins mpl. To eat like a p., manger gloutonnement. P. farm, porcherie f. P. breeding, l'élevage des porcs. F: To buy a p. in a poke, acheter chat en poche. To bleed like a stuck p., saigner comme un bœuf. S.a. CLOVER. (b) P: (i) Grossier personnage. (ii) You dirty little p.! petit sale! (iii) To make a p. of oneself, manger gloutonnement. (iv) Don't be a p.! voyons, sois chic! 2. Metall: Gueuse f (de fonte); saumon m (de plomb). Converter p., fonte f d'affinage. 'pig-eyed, a. A petits yeux (de porc). 'pig-iron, s. Metall: Fer m en fonte, en gueuse. 'pig-bucket, -pail, -tub, s. Seau m aux déchets (de cuisine), aux eaux grasses.

pig², v.i. (pigged) 1. (Of sow) Mettre bas. 2. (a) F: To p. (it), vivre comme dans une étable. (b) P: To p. together, partager la même chambre.

pigeon ['pidʒin], s. 1. Pigeon m. Domestic p., pigeon domestique. Hen-p., pigeonne f. Young p., pigeonneau m. P.-club, société f colombophile. Sp: Clay p., pigeon artificiel. F: That's my p., ça c'est mon affaire. S.a. CAPE², STOOL PIGEON. P: Pigeon, dupe f. 3. = PIDGIN. 'pigeon-breasted, -chested, a. A la poitrine bombée, saillante. 'pigeon-fancier, s. Colombophile mf. 'pigeon-hole¹, s. Case f, alvéole m (de bureau). 'pigeon-hole², v.tr. (a) Caser, classer (des papiers). (b) Adm: Classer (une réclamation). 'pigeon-house, -loft, s. Colombier m, pigeonnier m. 'pigeon-shooting, s. Sp: Tir m aux pigeons. 'pigeon-toed, a. Qui marche les pieds tournés en dedans.

piggery ['pigəri], s. (a) Porcherie f. (b) F: Endroit m sale; vraie bauge.

piggish ['pigiʃ], a. (a) Sale, malpropre, grossier. (b) Goinfre. (c) Égoïste, désagréable.

piggishness ['pigiʃnis], s. (a) Saleté f, malpropreté f. (b) Goinfrerie f.

piggy ['pigi], s. F: = PIGLET. 'piggy-bank, s. F: Tirelire f (en forme de cochon).

pigheaded ['pig'hedid], a. Têtu comme un âne, obstiné, entêté.

pigheadedness ['pig'hedidnis], s. Obstination f, entêtement m.

piglet ['piglit], pigling ['piglin], s. Cochonnet m, cochon m de lait, porcelet m.

pigman, pl. -men ['pigmən], s.m. Porcher.

pigment ['pigmənt], s. 1. Art: Matière colorante; colorant m. 2. Physiol: etc: Pigment m. 'pigment-cell, s. Cellule f pigmentaire.

pigment², [pig'ment], v.tr. Pigmenter.

pigmentary ['pigməntəri], a. Physiol: etc: Pigmentaire.

pigmentation [ˌpigmənˈteiʃ(ə)n], s. Pigmentation f.

pigmy ['pigmi], s. = PYGMY.

pigskin ['pigskin], s. 1. Peau f de porc. Imitation p., cuir m façon porc. 2. F: (a) Rac: Selle f. (b) Fb: Ballon m.

pigsticker ['pig,stikər], s. 1. (a) Chasseur m de sangliers (à courre avec épieu). (b) Égorgeur m, saigneur m, de porcs. 2. F: Gros couteau; eustache m.

pigsticking ['pig,stikin], s. 1. Chasse f au sanglier (à courre, avec épieu). 2. Égorgement m de porcs.

pigsty ['pigstai], s. 1. Porcherie f; étable f à porcs. 2. F: Bauge f; (sale) taudis m.

pigswill ['pigswil], s. = SWILL¹ 2, PIGWASH.

pigtail ['pigteil], s. 1. Tabac m en corde. 2. Queue f, natte f (de cheveux).

pigwash ['pigwoʃ], s. 1. Pâtée f pour les porcs; eaux grasses. 2. P: Lavasse f.

pike¹ [paik], s. A. Arms: Pique f.

pike², s. Ich: Brochet m.

pike³, s. A: Barrière f de péage. S.a. TURNPIKE.

pikestaff ['paiksta:f], s. Bois m, hampe f, de pique. S.a. PLAIN I. 1.

pilaff ['pi:læf, pi'la:f], s. Cu: = PILAU.

pilaster [pi'læstər], s. Arch: Pilastre m.

pilau, pilaw [pi'lau, -'lɔ:], s. Cu: Pilau m, pilaf m.

pilchard ['piltʃəd], s. Ich: Sardine f.

pile¹ [pail], s. Pieu m, pilot m. Row of piles, pilotis m. To drive in a p., enfoncer un pieu. Built on piles, bâti sur pilotis. 'pile-driver, s. Civ.E: Sonnette f. 'pile-dwelling, s. Archeol: Habitation f lacustre.

pile², s. 1. (a) Tas m, monceau m; pile f (d'obus). (b) El: Voltaic p., pile de Volta. Atomic p., pile atomique. (c) Mil: Faisceau m (d'armes). El: F: Magot m. To make one's p., faire fortune; faire sa pelote. 2. (a) Masse f (d'un édifice). (b) Édifice.

pile³. 1. v.tr. (a) To p. (up), (i) entasser, amonceler; amasser (une fortune); (ii) empiler (du bois). Ship piled up on the rocks, vaisseau échoué sur les rochers. F: To p. on the agony, accumuler les détails pénibles. To p. it on, exagérer, P: charrier. (b) Mil: To p. arms, former les faisceaux. 2. v.i. To p. up, s'amonceler, s'entasser.

pile⁴, s. Tex: Poil m (d'un tapis). P. fabrics, tissus peluchés.

pile⁵, *s. Med: usu. pl.* Piles, hémorroïdes *f.*
pilewort ['pailwə:t], *s. Bot:* Ficaire *f.*
pilfer ['pilfər], *v.tr.* Chaparder, chiper (sth. from s.o., qch. à qn). *Abs.* Chaparder; grappiller. **pilfering¹**, *a.* (Enfant) voleur, -euse. **pilfering²**, *s.* Petits vols; chapardage *m;* larcin *m.*
pilferer ['pilfərər], *s.* Chapardeur, -euse, chipeur, -euse; grappilleur, -euse.
pilgrim ['pilgrim], *s.* 1. Pèlerin, -ine. 2. *Hist:* The P. Fathers, les Pèlerins (colons anglais qui fondèrent New Plymouth).
pilgrimage ['pilgrimidʒ], *s.* Pèlerinage *m.*
piliferous [pai'lifərəs], *a. Bot:* Pilifère.
pill [pil], *s.* Pilule *f.* It is a bitter p., la dragée est amère. **'pill-box**, *s.* 1. Boîte *f* à pilules. 2. *Mil:* Réduit *m* en béton pour mitrailleuse. **'pill-bug**, *s. U.S: Ent:* = WOODLOUSE.
pillage¹ ['pilidʒ], *s.* Pillage *m.*
pillage², *v.tr.* Piller, saccager. *Abs.* Se livrer au pillage. **pillaging¹**, *a.* Pillard. **pillaging²**, *s.* Pillage *m.*
pillager ['pilidʒər], *s.* Pilleur, -euse; pillard, -arde; saccageur, -euse; rapineur, -euse.
pillar ['pilər], *s.* 1. Pilier *m;* colonne *f.* He is a p. of the Church, c'est un pilier d'église. To drive s.o. from p. to post, renvoyer qn de Caïphe à Pilate. (*a*) *Mec.E:* Colonne, montant *m* (d'une machine). (*b*) *N.Arch:* Épontille *f*, étançon *m.* **'pillar-box**, *s.* (*In street*) Boîte *f* aux lettres. P.-b. red, rouge drapeau (*m*).
pillion ['piliən], *s.* 1. *Harn:* Coussinet *m* de cheval. To ride p., monter en croupe. 2. *Motor Cy:* P. (-seat), siège *m* arrière; tansad *m.* To ride p., monter derrière. **P.-rider**, passager, -ère (de derrière).
pillory¹ ['piləri], *s.* Pilori *m.*
pillory², *v.tr.* (pilloried) Mettre, clouer, (qn) au pilori.
pillow¹ ['pilou], *s.* 1. (*a*) Oreiller *m. O:* To take counsel of one's p., consulter son chevet; prendre conseil de son oreiller. Take counsel of your p., dormez là-dessus. (*b*) Lace-p., coussin *m* (pour dentelle). 2. *Mec.E:* Coussinet *m.* **'pillow-block**, *s. Mec.E:* Palier *m* (d'arbre). **'pillow-case, -slip**, *s.* Taie *f* d'oreiller. P.-c., 'housewife' style, taie portefeuille. **'pillow-lace**, *s.* Dentelle *f* aux fuseaux.
pillow², *v.tr.* To p. one's head on one's arms, reposer sa tête sur ses bras.
pilose, pilous ['pailous], *a. Nat.Hist:* Pileux, -euse, poilu.
pilot¹ ['pailət], *s.* 1. (*a*) Pilote *m.* Deep-sea p., pilote hauturier. Coast p., in-shore p., branch-p., pilote côtier; lamaneur *m.* (*b*) Guide *m*, mentor *m.* (*c*) *Av:* Pilote (aviateur). Ferry p., pilote convoyeur, pilote de convoyage. Test p., pilote d'essais. Second p., copilote *m.* Air-line p., pilote de ligne. P. officer, sous-lieutenant aviateur. Automatic p., pilote automatique, *F:* Georges. 2. *Rail:* (*a*) = PILOT-ENGINE. (*b*) *U.S:* Chasse-pierres *m inv;* chasse-bestiaux *m inv.* 3. P.(-lamp), lampe *f* témoin. **'pilot-balloon**, *s.* Ballon m d'essai; ballon pilote; ballon de sondage. **'pilot-boat**, *s.* Bateau *m* pilote. **'pilot-coat**, *s. Nau:* Vareuse *f*, caban *m.* **'pilot-engine**, *s. Rail:* Locomotive *f* estafette. **'pilot-factory**, *s.* Usine *f* pilote. **'pilot-fish**, *s. Ich:* Pilote *m* (de requin). **'pilot-flame**, *s.* Veilleuse *f* (d'un appareil à gaz). **'pilot-jet**, *s. Aut:* Gicleur *m* de ralenti. **'pilot-light**, *s.* (i) = PILOT-JET. (ii) *El:* Lampe *f* témoin. **'pilot-'plant**, *s. U.S:* = PILOT-FACTORY.
pilot², *v.tr.* (*a*) Piloter (un navire, un avion). (*b*) Mener, conduire (qn à travers des obstacles). **piloting**, *s.* Pilotage *m.*
pilotage ['pailətidʒ], *s.* 1. Pilotage *m.* 2. P. (dues), (droits m, frais m, de) pilotage.
pilotless ['pailətlis], *a.* Sans pilote. P. plane, avion *m* robot.
pilule ['pilju:l], *s.* Petite pilule.
pimento [pi'mentou], *s. Bot: Cu:* Piment *m;* poivron *m.*
pimp¹ [pimp], *s.* Entremetteur *m;* proxénète *m; P:* maquereau *m*, maq *m.*
pimp², *v.i.* Faire le proxénète, *V:* le maquereau.
pimpernel ['pimpənəl], *s. Bot:* Mouron *m.* Scarlet p., mouron rouge, mouron des champs.

pimple ['pimpl], *s.* Pustule *f*, bouton *m.* To come out in pimples, avoir une poussée de boutons.
pimply ['pimpli], *a.* Pustuleux, -euse, boutonneux, -euse.
pin¹ [pin], *s.* 1. (*a*) Épingle *f.* Tie-p., épingle de cravate. *S.a.* BROOCH, DRAWING-PIN, HAIRPIN, SAFETY-PIN. You could have heard a p. drop, on aurait entendu trotter une souris. For two pins I would box his ears, pour un peu je lui flanquerais une gifle. He doesn't care two pins, il s'en moque comme de l'an quarante; *F:* il s'en fiche; *P:* il s'en fout. To be on pins and needles, être sur des charbons. (*b*) Pins and needles, fourmillements *m.* 2. (*a*) Goupille *f*, cheville *f.* Axle p., clavette *f* d'essieu. Split p., goupille fendue. *Mil:* Safety p., (*of fuse*) goupille de sureté. (*b*) Centre p., pivot central (de plaque tournante). (*c*) Fiche *f* (d'une charnière). *El:* Fiche de prise de courant. (*d*) *Nau:* Thole-p., tolet *m*, dame *f.* 3. *Cu:* Rolling-p., rouleau *m* à pâte. 4. (*a*) *Surv:* Fiche de jalonneur. (*b*) *Golf:* Drapeau *m* de trou. 5. (*a*) (*At ninepins*) Quille *f.* (*b*) *pl. P:* Jambes *f*, P: guibolles *f*, quilles, pinceaux *m.* **'pin-feather**, *s. Orn:* Plume naissante. **'pin-fire**, *attrib.a. Sm.a:* (Cartouche, fusil) à broche. **'pin-head**, *s.* 1. Tête *f* d'épingle. P.-h. grey, drap *m* gris pointillé. 2. *U.S: P:* Idiot *m*, crétin *m.* What a p.-h.! Quelle andouille! **'pin-hole**, *s.* (*a*) Trou *m* d'épingle. (*b*) *Opt:* Très petite ouverture (dans un écran). *Phot:* Sténopé *m.* **'pin-money**, *s. O:* (*a*) Argent (donné à une femme) pour ses frais de toilette. (*b*) Argent de poche (d'une jeune fille). **'pin-point**, *s.* To turn down the gas to a p.-p., mettre le gaz en veilleuse. **pin-point²**, *v.tr.* Indiquer exactement, mettre le doigt sur. *Mil:* To p.-p. the enemy position, indiquer exactement l'emplacement de l'ennemi. **'pin-pool**, *s. Bill:* Partie de quilles (sur table). **'pin-prick**, *s.* Piqûre *f* d'épingle. *pl. F:* P.-pricks, tracasseries *f.* Policy of p.-pricks, politique *f* de coups d'épingle. **'pin-stripe**, *s. Tex:* Rayure *f*, filet *m* (de couleur dans un tissu). *attrib.* P.-s. trousers, pantalon rayé. **'pin-table**, *s.* (Sorte de) billard chinois automatique. **'pin-wheel**, *s.* 1. *Clockm:* Roue *f* des chevilles. 2. *Mec.E:* Roue à fuseaux. 3. *Pyr:* Soleil *m.*
pin², *v.tr.* (pinned) 1. (*a*) Épingler; attacher avec une épingle. To p. clothes on a line, épingler du linge sur une corde. To p. the paper to the board, fixer le papier sur la planchette (avec des punaises). (*b*) *Mec.E:* Cheviller, goupiller. 2. Fixer, clouer. To p. s.o.'s arms to his sides, (i) immobiliser le bras à qn; (ii) ligoter qn. To be pinned (down) under a fallen tree, se trouver pris sous un arbre déraciné. To p. s.o. (down) to facts, obliger qn à s'en tenir aux faits, à reconnaître les faits. *Mil:* To be pinned down by enemy fire, rester cloué au sol par le feu de l'ennemi. *Chess:* To p. a piece, clouer une pièce. 3. Étayer, étançonner (un mur). **pin on**, *v.tr.* Épingler (qch.), attacher (qch.) avec une épingle (to sth., à qch.). **pin up**, *v.tr.* Épingler (ses cheveux, une couture). To p. sth. up on the wall, pendre, attacher qch. au mur. **'pin-up girl**, *s.f. P:* Pin-up *f inv.*
pinafore ['pinəfɔ:r], *s.* Tablier *m* (d'enfant).
pinaster [pai'næstər], *s. Bot:* Pinastre *m;* pin *m* maritime.
pinball ['pinbɔ:l], *s. U.S:* P. machine, game, jeu *m* de foire automatique.
pincers ['pinsəz], *s.pl.* 1. (Pair of) p., pince *f*, tenaille *f* (*pl*). 2. Pince (de crustacé). 3. *attrib. Mil:* Pincer(s) movement, manœuvre *f* en tenailles.
pinch¹ [pin(t)ʃ], *s.* 1. (*a*) Action *f* de pincer; pinçade *f.* To give s.o. a p., pincer qn. (*b*) The p. of poverty, la gêne. The p. of hunger, la morsure de la faim; la faim. To feel the p., tirer le diable par la queue. (*c*) *F:* At a p., au besoin. 2. Pincée *f* (de sel, etc.). To take a p. of snuff, humer une prise.
pinch², *v.tr.* 1. Pincer. *Cy:* Pinched inner tube, chambre à air cisaillée. *Prov:* Everyone knows best where the shoe pinches, chacun sait où le soulier le blesse. 2. Serrer, gêner. To p. oneself, *abs.* to p., se priver (du nécessaire). To p. and scrape for one's children, se saigner aux quatre veines pour ses enfants. 3. *P:* (*a*) Chiper, choper, chaparder. Someone has pinched my matches, on m'a chauffé mes allumettes.

My watch has been pinched, on m'a refait ma montre. (b) Arrêter (un malfaiteur). **To get pinched,** se faire pincer. **pinch off,** v.tr. Hort: **To p. off a bud,** épincer un bourgeon. **pinched,** a. 1. (Of face) Tiré, hâve, amaigri. **Face p. with hunger,** traits tirés par la faim. 2. Étroit. **P. for money,** à court d'argent; dans la gêne. **To be p. for room,** être à l'étroit. **pinching,** s. 1. Pinçure f, pincement m; cisaillement (d'une chambre à air, etc.). 2. Parcimonie f. 3. P: Chapardage m.

inchbeck ['pin(t)ʃbek], s. 1. Chrysocale m, similor m. 2. Attrib. (a) En chrysocale, en similor. (b) F: En toc.

incushion ['pinku(ə)n], s. Pelote f à épingles.

ine¹ [pain], s. 1. P.(-tree), pin m. **Norway p.,** pin sylvestre; pin suisse. **Parasol p., stone-p.,** pin pignon; pin (en) parasol. **Maritime p.,** pin maritime. 2. (Bois m de) pin. **'pine-cone,** s. Pomme f de pin. **'pine-grove,** s. Pinière f, pineraie f, pinède f. **'pine-kernel,** s. Pigne f, pignon m. **'pine-wood,** s. 1. (Bois m de) pin m. 2. Pinière f, pinède f, pineraie f, bois de pins.

ine², v.i. 1. **To p. (away),** languir, dépérir. 2. **To p. for s.o., for sth.,** languir pour, après, qn, qch. **He is pining for home,** il a la nostalgie du foyer.

ineal ['piniəl], a. Anat: Pinéal, -aux.

ineapple ['painæpl], s. Ananas m.

inetum [pai'ni:təm], s. Pineraie f, pinède f.

ing¹ [pin], s. Cinglement m, fouettement m, sifflement m (d'une balle de fusil).

ing², v.i. (Of bullet) Cingler, fouetter, siffler.

ing-pong ['pinpon], s. Sp: R.t.m. Ping-pong m inv.

inion¹ ['pinjən], s. 1. (a) Bout m d'aile; aileron m. (b) Poet: Aile f. 2. Penne f, rémige f.

inion², v.tr. 1. Rogner les ailes à (un oiseau). 2. **To p. s.o.'s arms to his sides,** lier les bras de qn, ligoter qn.

inion³, s. Mec.E: Pignon m. **Sliding p.,** pignon baladeur. **P. wheel,** roue à pignon.

ink¹ [pink]. I. s. (a) Bot: Œillet m. **Garden p.,** (œillet) mignardise f. **Sea p.,** œillet maritime. (b) **The p. of perfection,** la perfection même. O: **The p. of politeness,** la fine fleur de la politesse. **In the p. (of condition),** en excellente condition; en parfaite santé. II. a. & s. (a) Rose (m); couleur f de rose. **P. cheeks,** joues roses. **The p. eyes of the albinos,** les yeux rouges des albinos. (b) Ven: **To wear p.,** porter la tunique rouge, écarlate.

ink², v.tr. 1. Toucher (son adversaire avec l'épée). 2. Dressm: **To p. (out),** (i) denteler les bords de (qch.); (ii) travailler (du cuir) à jour. 3. **To p. out,** orner, parer.

ink³, v.i. I.C.E: (Of engine) Cliqueter. **pinking,** s. Cliquetis m.

inkish ['pinkiʃ], a. Rosé, rosâtre.

inkness ['pinknis], s. Couleur f rose; rose m.

innace ['pinis], s. Navy: Grand canot, pinasse f.

innacle ['pinəkl], s. 1. Arch: (a) Pinacle m, clocheton m. (b) Couronnement m (de faîte). 2. (a) Cime f (d'une montagne); pic m. (b) Rock p., gendarme m. 3. **The p. of glory,** le faîte de la gloire. **On the highest p. of fame,** à l'apogée de la gloire.

innate ['pineit], a. Nat.Hist: Penné, pinné.

inny ['pini], s. F: = PINAFORE.

int [paint], s. Meas: Pinte f (0 litres 568). **A p. of beer** = une canette de bière.

intail ['pinteil], s. Orn: (Canard) pilet m.

intle ['pintl], s. (a) Pivot central; goujon m (d'une charnière). Veh: Cheville ouvrière. (b) Nau: Aiguillot m (de gouvernail).

ioneer [paiə'niər], s. Pionnier m. **To do p. work in a subject,** défricher un sujet. Lit: Art: etc: **Pioneers,** hommes m d'avant-garde.

ious ['paiəs], a. (a) Pieux, -euse. (b) **P. deeds,** œuvres f pies. **-ly,** adv. Pieusement; avec piété.

ip¹ [pip], s. Pépie f (de la volaille). F: **To give s.o. the p.,** donner le cafard à qn.

ip², s. 1. Point m (d'une carte, d'un dé). 2. Mil: F: = galon m (d'officier), F: ficelle f. **He's just got his third p.** = il vient de recevoir sa troisième ficelle. 3. W.Tel: F: Top m. **The pips,** le signal horaire, F: les tops.

ip³, v.tr. (pipped) P: 1. Vaincre, battre (qn). 2. Atteindre (qn) d'une balle.

pip⁴, s. Pépin m (de fruit).

pip⁵, s. Mil. Tg. & Tp: (La lettre) **P. P. emma** (= p.m.), (six heures, etc.) du soir.

pipe¹ [paip], s. 1. (a) Tuyau m, tube m, conduit m. **To lay pipes,** poser des tuyaux; canaliser. (b) Anat: Tube; esp. tube respiratoire. S.a. WINDPIPE. (c) Forure f, canon m (d'une clef). 2. (a) Mus: Pipeau m, chalumeau m. **(Bag)pipes,** cornemuse f. S.a. PAN⁴. (b) Nau: Sifflet m (du maître d'équipage). 3. Filet m de voix; chant m (d'oiseau). 4. Pipe f. **I am a p.-smoker,** je fume la pipe. **P. of peace,** calumet m de paix. **To smoke the p. of peace with s.o.,** fumer le calumet de paix avec qn. P: **Put that in your p. and smoke it!** mettez cela dans votre poche et votre mouchoir dessus! mettez ça dans votre pipe! O: **To put s.o.'s p. out,** faire échouer qn. **'pipe-clay,** s. Terre f de pipe; blanc m de terre à pipe (pour astiquage). **'pipe-cleaner,** s. Cure-pipe m (pour fumeurs); nettoie-pipe m inv. **'pipe-dream,** s. Rêve m; projet m illusoire. **'pipe-key,** s. Clef forée. **'pipe-lighter,** s. Briquet m (à essence, à gaz). **'pipe-'major,** s. Mil: Mus: Cornemuse-chef m. **'pipe-organ,** s. Mus: Grand orgue. **'pipe-rack,** s. Râtelier m à pipes. **'pipe-stopper,** s. Bourre-pipe m. **'pipe-wrench,** s. Plumb: etc: Clef f à tubes.

pipe². I. v.i. (a) (i) Poet: Jouer du chalumeau ou de la flûte. (ii) Jouer du fifre ou de la cornemuse. (b) (Of wind) Siffler. (c) Nau: Donner un coup de sifflet. II. **pipe,** v.tr. 1. (a) Jouer (un air) (sur le fifre ou sur la cornemuse). (b) Navy: Siffler (un commandement). **To p. all hands down,** siffler en bas tout le monde. 2. F: **To p. one's eye,** pleurer, pleurnicher. 3. Dressm: etc: Lisérer, ganser. 4. Hort: Bouturer (des œillets). 5. Canaliser (l'eau, le gaz, le pétrole, etc.). **pipe down,** v.i. F: (i) Changer de ton. (ii) P: La boucler. **Pipe down!** boucle-la! (iii) Mettre une sourdine, filer doux. **pipe up.** 1. v.i. F: **Here a little voice piped up,** à ce moment une petite voix se fit entendre. 2. v.tr. Navy: Appeler (la bordée) au son du sifflet. **piped,** a. A tuyau(x); à tube(s). **piping¹,** a. 1. Lit: **P. times of peace,** heureuse époque de paix. 2. **P. hot,** tout chaud, tout bouillant. **piping²,** s. 1. (a) Son m du chalumeau, du fifre, de la cornemuse. (b) Sifflement m (du vent); gazouillement m (d'oiseaux). (c) Navy: Commandement m au sifflet. 2. (a) Canalisation f (de l'eau). (b) Coll. Tuyauterie f, conduites fpl. 3. Laund: Tuyautage m. 4. Dressm: (a) Lisérage m. **P. cord,** ganse f. (b) Passepoil m; (on trousers) baguette f. 5. Cu: **P. bag,** poche f à douille. **P. nozzle,** douille f.

pipe³, s. Pipe f (de vin); grande futaille.

pipeful ['paipful], s. Pipe f (de tabac).

pipeline ['paiplain], s. 1. Conduite f, canalisation f; (for petroleum) oléoduc m, pipe-line m, pl. pipe-lines; (for gas) gazoduc m; feeder m.

piper ['paipər], s. Joueur m de chalumeau, de cornemuse; cornemuseur m. **To pay the p.,** payer les violons. **He who pays the p. calls the tune,** qui paye a bien le droit de choisir.

pipette [pi'pet], s. Ch: Pipette f. Pharm: Compte-gouttes m inv.

pipistrelle [,pipi'strel], s. Z: Pipistrelle f.

pipit ['pipit], s. Orn: Pipi m, pipit m. **Meadow p.,** Pipi, pipit, des prés.

pippin ['pipin], s. (Pomme f) reinette f.

pip-squeak ['pipskwi:k], s. F: Petit personnage de rien du tout; bonhomme riquiqui.

piquancy ['pi:kənsi], s. 1. Goût piquant (d'un mets). 2. Sel m, piquant m (d'un conte). **The p. of the situation,** le piquant de l'affaire.

piquant ['pi:kənt], a. (Of flavour, etc.) Piquant. **-ly,** adv. D'une manière piquante.

pique¹ [pi:k], s. Pique f, ressentiment m. **In a fit of p.,** dans un accès de pique. **Feeling of p.,** sentiment m de rancune.

pique², v.tr. 1. Piquer, dépiter (qn). 2. Piquer, exciter (la curiosité de qn). 3. **To p. oneself on sth.,** se piquer de qch.

piquet [pi'ket], s. Cards: Piquet m.

piracy ['paiərəsi], s. 1. Piraterie f. 2. Contrefaçon f (d'un livre); pillage m (des idées).

Piraeus [pai'ri:əs]. *Pr.n. Geog:* Le Pirée.
pirate[1] ['paiərət], *s.* 1. Pirate *m*, forban *m*, flibustier *m*. 2. Contrefacteur *m* (d'un ouvrage littéraire); voleur *m* (d'idées). 3. *attrib. W.Tel:* P. **station**, poste *m* pirate.
pirate[2], *v.tr.* Contrefaire, démarquer (un livre); s'approprier (une invention).
piratical [pai'rætik(ə)l], *a.* 1. De pirate. 2. De contre-facteur; de contrefaçon.
pirogue [pi'roug], *s.* Pirogue *f*.
pirouette[1] [ˌpiru'et], *s. Danc:* Pirouette *f*.
pirouette[2], *v.i.* Pirouetter; faire la pirouette.
piscatorial [ˌpiskə'tɔːriəl], **piscatory** ['piskət(ə)ri], *a.* Qui se rapporte à la pêche.
piscicultural [ˌpisi'kʌltʃər(ə)l], *a.* Piscicole.
pisciculture ['pisikʌltʃər], *s.* Pisciculture *f*.
piscina, *pl.* **-as, -ae** [pi'si:nə, -əz, -i:], *s.* 1. *Rom. Ant: Ecc:* Piscine *f*. 2. Vivier *m*.
piscivorous [pi'sivərəs], *a.* Piscivore.
pish [piʃ], *int. O:* Fi! zut! bah!
piss[1] [pis], *s. P:* Urine *f*; (*of animals*) pissat *m*.
piss[2]. *P:* 1. *v.i.* Uriner, pisser; *F:* faire pipi. 2. *v.tr.* Pisser (du sang, etc.).
pistachio [pis'tɑ:ʃiou], *s.* 1. (*Nut*) Pistache *f*. 2. (*Tree*) Pistachier *m*. 3. *a.* P.(**-green**), (vert) pistache (*m*).
pistil ['pistil], *s. Bot:* Pistil *m*.
pistol ['pistl], *s.* 1. *Sm.a:* Pistolet *m*. *A.Arms:* Duelling-**pistols**, pistolets de combat. 2. *Tls:* Pistolet (d'un outil pneumatique). **pistol-shot**, *s.* Coup *m* de pistolet.
piston ['pistən], *s.* Piston *m* (d'une machine à vapeur, *Mus:* d'un cornet à pistons); sabot *m* (de pompe). **piston-ring**, *s. I.C.E:* Segment *m* de piston. **piston-rod**, *s.* Tige *f*, verge *f*, de piston. **piston-stroke**, *s.* 1. Coup *m* de piston. 2. Course *f* du piston.
pit[1] [pit], *s.* 1. (*a*) Fosse *f*, trou *m*. *Aut: etc:* Inspection p., fosse (à réparations). *Mil:* Gun-p., emplacement *m* de pièce. (*b*) *Lit:* The p., l'enfer *m*, les enfers. (*c*) Trappe *f*, piège *m* (à animaux). To dig a p. for s.o., tendre un piège à qn. (*d*) (i) Carrière *f* (à chaux). (ii) Puits *m* (d'une mine de charbon). (iii) Mine *f* (de charbon). 2. (*a*) *Th:* Parterre *m*. (*b*) *U.S:* The (Chicago) wheat p., la Bourse des blés. 3. (*a*) Petite cavité, piqûre *f* (dans un métal). (*b*) *Med:* Cicatrice *f* (de la petite vérole). 4. *Anat:* The p. **of the stomach**, le creux de l'estomac. *S.a.* ARMPIT.
pit-head, *s. Min:* Bouche *f* de puits; carreau *m* (de la mine). **P.-h. price**, prix (du charbon) sur le carreau. **P.-h. baths**, bains *mpl*, douches *fpl* (à proximité de la mine). **pit-prop**, *s. Min:* Poteau *m*, étai *m*, de mine. Pit-props, bois *m* de soutènement. **pit-saw**, *s. Tls:* Scie *f* de long.
pit[2], *v.tr.* (pitted) 1. (*a*) *A.Sp:* Mettre (deux coqs) en parc. (*b*) To p. s.o. **against** s.o., opposer qn à qn, To pit oneself **against** s.o., se mesurer contre qn. 2. (*a*) (*Of acids*) Piquer, trouer (le métal). (*b*) *Med:* (*Of smallpox*) Grêler, marquer (le visage). **pitted**, *a.* 1. (*Of metal*) Piqué (par un acide). 2. (*Of pers.*) Grêlé (par la petite vérole).
pit[3], *s. U.S: Bot:* Noyau *m* (d'une drupe).
pit-(a-)pat ['pit(ə)pæt], *adv.* To go p.-a-p., (*of rain*) crépiter; (*of feet*) trottiner; (*of the heart*) battre, palpiter.
pitch[1] [pitʃ], *s.* Poix *f*; brai *m*; bitume *m*; asphalte minéral; goudron *m* à calfater. **pitch-'black**, *a.* 1. Noir comme poix. 2. = PITCH-DARK. **pitch-'dark**, *a.* It is p.-d., il fait nuit noire; il fait noir comme dans un four, noir comme poix. **pitch-pine**, *s.* Pitchpin *m*; faux sapin.
pitch[2], *v.tr.* Brayer; enduire (qch.) de brai.
pitch[3], *s.* 1. Lancement *m*, jet *m* (d'une pierre, etc.). The stone came full p. at my head, la pierre vint droit à ma tête. 2. *Nau:* Tangage *m*. 3. (*a*) Place *f* (dans un marché); place habituelle (d'un camelot). *S.a.* QUEER[2]. (*b*) *Cr:* Terrain *m* entre les guichets. *Fb:* Terrain (de jeu). 4. (*a*) *Arch:* Hauteur *f* sous clef (d'un arc). (*b*) *Mus:* Hauteur (d'un son); diapason *m* (d'un instrument). To give the orchestra the p., donner l'accord à l'orchestre. Voice, instrument, that is going off p., voix, instrument, qui déraille. (*c*) Degré *m* (d'élévation). To excite s.o.'s interest to the highest p., porter l'intérêt de qn à son comble. To such a p. that . . ., à tel point que. . . . 5. Degré de

pente (d'un toit, etc.). 6. (i) Avancement *m*, pas ? (d'une vis); (ii) espacement *m*, pas, de la dentu— (d'une roue); (iii) angle *m* des dents (d'une scie (iv) (*Helicopter*) Collective p., pas collectif. **Cyclic p** pas cyclique. **'pitch-pipe**, *s. Mus:* Diapason *r* de bouche.
pitch[4]. I. *v.tr.* 1. Dresser (une tente; *Cr:* les guichets *Abs.* Camper. 2. *Civ.E:* (i) Empièrrer, (ii) pave (une chaussée). 3. *Mus:* To p. one's voice highe— lower, hausser, baisser, le ton de sa voix. To p. one' **aspirations too high**, viser trop haut. 4. Lancer (un balle). *Cr:* Full-pitched ball, balle à toute volé— To be pitched off one's horse, être désarçonné. *F:* To p. a yarn, débiter une histoire. To p. it strong exagérer; y aller fort. II. pitch, *v.i.* 1. To p. o one's head, tomber sur la tête. 2. (*Of ship*) Tanguer 3. To p. (up)on sth., arrêter son choix sur qch. **pitc in**, *v.i. F:* Se mettre à la besogne. **pitch into**, *v.*— *F:* 1. (*a*) (i) Taper sur (qn); s'attaquer à (qn (ii) Dire son fait à qn. (*b*) To p. into the work s'attaquer au travail, *F:* au boulot. 2. Tombe— la tête la première dans (la mare, etc.). **pitched** *a.* **P. battle**, bataille rangée. **pitching**[1], *a. Nau* **P. ship**, navire qui tangue. **pitching**[2], *s.* 1. Dressag *m* (d'une tente). 2. (*a*) Pavage *m*, empierrement *m* (*b*) Pavé *m*. 3. Lancement *m* (d'une pierre, d'un balle). 4. *Nau:* Tangage *m*. **'pitch-and-'toss** *s.* Jeu *m* de pile ou face.
pitchblende ['pitʃblend], *s. Miner:* Pechblende *f*.
pitcher[1] ['pitʃər], *s.* 1. Cruche *f* (de grès); broc *m* 2. *Bot:* Ascidie *f*. **'pitcher-plant**, *s.* Népenthès *m*
pitcher[2], *s.* (*At baseball*) Lanceur *m* (de la balle).
pitchfork[1] ['pitʃfɔ:k], *s.* Fourche *f* (à foin).
pitchfork[2], *v.tr.* 1. Lancer (une gerbe) avec la fourche 2. *F:* Bombarder (qn dans un poste).
piteous ['pitiəs], *a.* Pitoyable, piteux, -euse. **-ly** *adv.* Pitoyablement.
piteousness ['pitiəsnis], *s.* État piteux, misérabl— (d'une personne, etc.).
pitfall ['pitfɔ:l], *s.* Trappe *f*, fosse *f*; piège *m*. Th— **pitfalls of the law**, les traquenards *m* de la procédure
pith [piθ], *s.* 1. (*a*) Moelle *f*. (*b*) Peau blanche (d'un orange). 2. (*a*) Vigueur *f*, sève *f*, ardeur *f*. (*b* Moelle, essence *f* (d'un livre).
pithecanthropus [ˌpiθi'kænθroupəs], *s. Paleont* Pithécanthrope *m*.
pithiness ['piθinis], *s.* Concision *f*; style nerveux.
pithy ['piθi], *a.* 1. (*Of stem*) Plein de moelle. 2 (*Of style*) (i) Nerveux, -euse, concis, vigoureux -euse; (ii) substantiel, -elle. **-ily**, *adv.* En un styl— condensé; avec concision.
pitiable ['pitiəbl], *a.* Pitoyable, piteux, -euse; (o **appearance**) minable. **-ably**, *adv.* Pitoyablement à faire pitié.
pitiful ['pitiful], *a.* 1. Compatissant; plein de pitié 2. (*a*) Pitoyable, lamentable. It is p. to see him il fait pitié. (*b*) *Pej:* Lamentable. **-fully**, *adv.* 1 Avec compassion. 2. (*a*) Pitoyablement. To cry p. pleurer à fendre l'âme. (*b*) *Pej:* Lamentablement.
pitiless ['pitilis], *a.* Impitoyable; sans pitié; (froid cruel. **-ly**, *adv.* Sans pitié.
piton ['pitɔ], *s. Mount:* Piton *m*.
pittance ['pit(ə)ns], *s.* Maigre salaire *m*. To b— reduced to a mere p., être réduit à la portion congrue
pitter-patter ['pitəpætər], *s.* = PATTER[3].
pituitary [pi'tju:itəri], *a. Anat:* Pituitaire. **P. gland** glande *f* pituitaire.
pity[1] ['piti], *s.* Pitié *f*. (*a*) Compassion *f*, apitoiement *m*. To take p. on s.o., prendre pitié de qn. To feel p. for s.o., s'apitoyer sur qn. To move s.o. to p. exciter la compassion de qn; apitoyer qn. To do sth out of p. for s.o., faire qch. par pitié pour qn. Fo pity's sake, par pitié; de grâce. (*b*) What a p.! quel dommage! It is a great p., c'est bien dommage *S.a.* MORE 4.
pity[2], *v.tr.* Plaindre (qn); avoir pitié de, s'apitoye— sur (qn). He is to be pitied, il est à plaindre. **pitying** *a.* Compatissant; (regard) de pitié. **pityingly**, *adv* Avec compassion, avec pitié.
pivot[1] ['pivət], *s.* Pivot *m*; tourillon *m*; axe *m* (de rotation). **Ball p.**, pivot à rotule. This man is th— p. of the enterprise, cet homme est le pivot de l'entre prise.

pivot², v. (pivoted) 1. v.tr. (a) Monter (une pièce) sur pivot. (b) To p. a fleet, faire pivoter une flotte. 2. v.i. Pivoter, tourner. **pivoting**, a. Pivotant; à pivot. **'pivot-bridge**, s. Civ.E: Pont tournant, pivotant.

pixie, pixy ['piksi], s. (i) Lutin m, farfadet m; (ii) fée f.

pixil(l)ated ['piksileitid], a. 1. A: Égaré, désorienté (par les fées etc). 2. F: esp. U.S: Loufoque, un peu fou. 3. esp. U.S: F: Légèrement gris.

pizzicato [ˌpitsiˈkɑːtou], a., adv. & s. Mus: Pizzicato (m), pincé (m).

placard¹ ['plækɑːd], s. Écriteau m; affiche f.

placard², v.tr. 1. Couvrir (un mur) d'affiches. 2. Placarder, afficher (une annonce).

placate [pləˈkeit], v.tr. Apaiser, calmer (qn).

place¹ [pleis], s. 1. (a) Lieu m, endroit m, localité f. To come to a p., arriver dans un lieu. This is the p., c'est ici. A native of the p., quelqu'un du pays. Fortified p., place forte. P. of refuge, lieu de refuge. Watering p., ville f d'eaux; station f balnéaire. A small country p., un petit coin rustique. From p. to p., de-ci de-là. To move from p. to p., se déplacer souvent. Books all over the p., des livres dans tous les coins. In another p., autre part; ailleurs. This is no p. for you, vous n'avez que faire ici. F: To go places, (i) sortir; (ii) voyager; (iii) réussir. S.a. HOME I. 1. (b) P. of amusement, lieu de divertissement. P. of worship, édifice m du culte. P. of business, maison f de commerce; établissement m. P. of residence, demeure f, résidence f. F: Come and lunch at our p., venez déjeuner chez nous. A low p., un endroit mal fréquenté. In high places, en haut lieu. (c) (In street names) (i) Cour f, ruelle f. (ii) Place f. (d) Market p., place du marché. 2. Place. To put a book back in its p., remettre un livre à sa place. To lay a p. (at table), mettre un couvert. To change places with s.o., changer de place avec qn. If I were in your p., I should go, à votre place, j'irais. In (the) p. of ..., au lieu de.... Out of (its) p., (volume) déplacé; (fiche) déclassée. Remark out of p., observation hors de propos, déplacée. (Of pers.) To look (sadly) out of p., avoir l'air dépaysé. To take p., avoir lieu; se passer; arriver. The marriage will not take p., le mariage ne se fera pas. While this was taking p., sur ces entrefaites. 3. Place, rang m. (a) To attain to a high p., atteindre à un rang élevé. To put s.o. in his p., remettre qn à sa place. To keep one's p., observer les distances. In the first p., d'abord. In the second p., en second lieu. In the next p...., ensuite..., puis.... Rac: To back a horse for a p., jouer un cheval placé. (b) Mth: Answer to three places of decimals, solution f à trois décimales. 4. Place, poste m, emploi m, situation f. To take, fill, s.o.'s p., remplacer qn. To lose one's p., perdre son emploi, sa situation. It is not my p. to do it, ce n'est pas à moi de le faire. 5. (a) Weak p. in a beam, endroit défectueux d'une poutre. (b) To find one's p. (in a book), se retrouver. To lose one's p., ne plus retrouver où on en est resté. To laugh at the right p., rire au bon endroit. **'place-kick**, s. Fb: Coup m d'envoi. **'place-mat**, s. Napperon individuel. **'place-name**, s. Nom m de lieu.

place², v.tr. 1. Placer, mettre; poser. (a) To p. a book on the table, mettre un livre sur la table. To be awkwardly placed, se trouver dans une situation difficile. I explained to him how I was placed, je lui ai exposé ma situation. The house is well placed, la maison est bien située. (b) To p. a book with a publisher, faire accepter un livre par un éditeur. Com: Difficult to p., de vente difficile. Fin: To p. a loan, négocier un emprunt. (c) To p. a matter in s.o.'s hands, remettre une affaire entre les mains de qn. To p. an order (for goods), passer (une) commande. To p. a child under s.o.'s care, mettre un enfant sous la garde de qn. S.a. CONTRACT¹ 2. (d) Rugby: To p. a goal, marquer un but sur coup de pied placé. 2. Donner un rang à (qn). To be well placed (on a class list), avoir une bonne place. Sp: To be placed third, se classer troisième. Turf: To be placed, être placé. 3. F: I can't p. him, je ne le remets pas.

placebo [pləˈsiːbou], s. Med: Remède m factice.

placenta [pləˈsentə], s. Bot: Obst: Placenta m.

placental [pləˈsentl], a. Bot: Anat: Obst: Placentaire.

Placentalia [ˌplæsenˈteiliə], spl. Z: Placentaires mpl.

placentary [pləˈsentəri], a. Bot: Anat: Obst: Placentaire.

placer ['pleisər], s. Geol: Min: Placer m; gisement m aurifère.

placid ['plæsid], a. Placide, calme, tranquille, serein. -ly, adv. Avec calme; tranquillement.

placidity [plæˈsiditi], s. Placidité f, calme m, tranquillité f.

placket(-hole) ['plækit(houl)], s. Dressm: Fente f de jupe.

plagiarism ['pleidʒiərizm], s. 1. Plagiat m; démarquage m. 2. Plagiat m.

plagiarist ['pleidʒiərist], s. Plagiaire m; démarqueur m.

plagiarize ['pleidʒiəraiz], v.tr. Plagier (un auteur); faire un plagiat à, contrefaire (une œuvre).

plague¹ [pleig], s. 1. Fléau m. The ten plagues of Egypt, les dix plaies f d'Égypte. What a p. the child is! quelle petite peste que cet enfant! 2. Peste f. Cattle p., peste bovine. A: A p. on him! la (male) peste soit de lui! **'plague-spot**, s. 1. Lésion, tache, occasionnée par la peste. 2. Foyer m d'infection. **'plague-stricken**, a. 1. (Pays) frappé de la peste. 2. (Of pers.) Pestiféré.

plague², v.tr. F: Tourmenter, harceler (qn); F: embêter, raser (qn). To p. s.o.'s life out, empoisonner l'existence de qn, F: casser les pieds à qn. To p. s.o. with questions, assommer qn de questions.

plaguy ['pleigi], a. F: A: Fâcheux, -euse, assommant.

plaice [pleis], s. Ich: Carrelet m; plie f.

plaid [plæd], s. 1. Plaid m. 2. Tex: Tartan m, écossais m.

plain [plein]. I. a. 1. Clair, évident. To make sth. p. to s.o., faire comprendre qch. à qn. It is as p. as a pikestaff, as p. as daylight, c'est clair comme le jour; cela saute aux yeux. To make one's meaning perfectly p., bien se faire comprendre. In p. English ..., pour parler clairement.... Goods marked in p. figures, articles marqués en chiffres connus. Tg: etc: Message in p., message en clair. 2. (a) P. style, style simple. In p. clothes, en civil; Adm: en costume de ville. P.-clothes policeman, agent en civil. Under p. cover, sous pli discret. P. paper, papier non réglé. Knitting: P. stitch, maille à l'endroit. P. and purl, mailles endroit, mailles envers. S.a. SAILING² 1. (b) Uni, lisse. P. material, étoffe unie. (c) P. cooking, cuisine simple. (d) P. truth, vérité pure, simple. He was called p. John, il s'appelait Jean tout court. P. answer, réponse carrée. P. speech, le franc-parler; la rondeur. To be p. with s.o., être franc avec qn. To use p. language, parler franchement. P. dealing, procédés m honnêtes. P. country-folk, de simples villageois. 3. (Of pers.) To be p., manquer de beauté. Our p. sisters, nos sœurs déshéritées. She looks plainer than ever, elle a enlaidi. -ly, adv. 1. Clairement, manifestement, évidemment. I can see it p., cela saute aux yeux. P. I was not wanted, il était évident que j'étais de trop. 2. (a) Simplement. To dress p., s'habiller sans recherche. (b) Franchement, carrément. To put it p., you refuse, pour parler clair, vous refusez. To speak p., user du franc-parler. II. plain, adv. Clairement, distinctement. I can't speak any plainer, je ne peux pas m'exprimer plus clairement. III. plain, s. Plaine f. In the open p., en rase campagne. **'plain-'speaking**, s. Franchise f; franc-parler m. **'plain-'spoken**, a. Qui a son franc-parler; franc, franche; carré, rond. To be very p.-s. with s.o., user d'une franchise brutale avec qn.

plainness ['pleinnis], s. 1. Clarté f (des objets lointains). 2. (a) Simplicité f (de vie, etc.). (b) Franchise f (de langage). 3. Manque m de beauté.

plainsong ['pleinsɔŋ], s. Mus: Plain-chant m.

plaint [pleint], s. 1. Jur: Plainte f. 2. Poet: Plainte, lamentation f.

plaintiff ['pleintif], s. Jur: Demandeur, -eresse; plaignant, -ante.

plaintive ['pleintiv], a. Plaintif, -ive. -ly, adv. Plaintivement; d'un ton plaintif.

plait[1] [plæt], *s.* Natte *f*, tresse *f* (de cheveux).
plait[2], *v.tr.* Natter, tresser. *Hatm:* Ourdir (la paille).
plan[1] [plæn], *s.* **1.** (*a*) Plan *m* (d'une maison); cadre *m*, plan (d'une œuvre littéraire). **To draw a p.**, tracer un plan. (*b*) *Mth: Arch:* Plan, projection *f. Surv:* Levé *m* (d'un terrain). **2.** Projet *m*, plan; *F:* combinaison *f.* **P. of campaign**, plan de campagne. **Preliminary p.**, avant-projet *m.* **To draw up a p.**, dresser un plan. **To change one's plans**, prendre d'autres dispositions. **To have no fixed plans**, ne pas être fixé. **To upset s.o.'s plans**, déranger les combinaisons de qn. **Everything went according to p.**, tout a marché selon les prévisions. **The best plan would be to . . .**, le mieux serait de. . . .
plan[2], *v.tr.* (**planned**) **1.** (*a*) Faire, tracer, le plan de (qch.). (*b*) Arrêter le plan (d'un roman). **2.** Projeter, se proposer (un voyage); combiner (une attaque); tramer, ourdir (un complot). **To p. for the future**, songer à l'avenir. **To p. to do sth.**, se proposer, former le projet, de faire qch. **planned**, *a.* **Well p.**, bien conçu. *Pol.Ec:* **P. economy**, dirigisme *m* économique. **planning**, *s.* **1.** Tracé *m* (d'un plan). **Town p.**, urbanisme *m.* **Country p.**, aménagement *m* des campagnes, du territoire. **2.** Organisation *f* (d'un complot, etc.). **3.** *Pol.Ec:* Dirigisme *m*, planification *f. Ind:* Planning *m. attrib.* **The p. mania**, la folie planiste. **4.** **Family p.**, limitation *f*, contrôle *m*, des naissances, planning familial.
planchette [plɑ:nʃet], *s. Psychics:* Planchette *f.*
plane[1] [plein], *a.* (*a*) Plan, uni; plat. (*b*) *Geom:* Plan. *S.a.* TRIGONOMETRY. **'plane-table**, *s. Surv:* Planchette *f.*
plane[2], *s.* **1.** (*a*) Plan *m* (d'un cristal, etc.). **Horizontal p.**, plan horizontal. *Art:* **Planes that build up the face**, méplats *m* du visage. *Arch:* **Curved p.**, rampe hélicoïdale (d'accès). (*b*) **A high p. of intelligence**, un niveau élevé de capacité intellectuelle. **2.** *Mec:* **Inclined p.**, plan incliné. **3.** *Av:* (*a*) Plan, aile *f*; surface portante. (*b*) *F:* Avion *m.*
plane[3], *v.i. Av:* **To p. down**, descendre en vol plané.
plane[4], *s. Tls:* Rabot *m.* **Long p.**, varlope *f.* **To run the p. over a plank**, passer le rabot sur une planche. **'plane-iron**, *s.* Fer à rabot. **'plane-stock**, *s.* Fût *m* de rabot.
plane[5], *v.tr.* Raboter (le bois); aplanir, planer (le bois, le métal). **To p. a board even**, araser une planche. **To rough-p.**, corroyer. **To p. down a board**, menuiser une planche. **planing**, *s.* Rabotage *m*; aplanissage *m.* **Rough-p.**, corroyage *m.* **'planing-machine**, *s. Carp: Metalw:* Raboteuse *f*, planeuse *f*; *Carp:* varlopeuse *f.*
plane[6], *s.* **P.(-tree)**, platane *m.*
planet ['plænit], *s. Astr:* Planète *f.* **'planet-gear**, *s. Mec.E:* (**Sun-and-)p.-gear**, engrenage *m* planétaire. **'planet-pinion, -wheel**, *s.* (Roue *f*) satellite *m.*
planetarium [ˌplæniˈtɛəriəm], *s. Astr:* Planétarium *f.*
planetary ['plænit(ə)ri], *a. Astr:* (Système) planétaire.
planetoid ['plænitɔid], *s. Astr:* Planétoïde *m.*
planimeter [plæˈnimitər], *s.* Planimètre *m.*
planish ['plæniʃ], *v.tr.* **1.** Dresser au marteau, aplanir (le métal). **2.** Polir. *Phot:* Satiner (une épreuve).
planisphere ['plænisfiər], *s.* Planisphère *m*; mappe-monde *f* céleste.
plank[1] [plæŋk], *s.* Planche (épaisse); madrier *m.* **Timber in planks**, bois méplat. *Nau: A:* **To walk the p.**, passer à la planche.
plank[2], *v.tr.* Planchéier (un plancher). **plank down**, *v.tr. P:* Jeter, déposer. **To p. down the money**, allonger l'argent. **To p. oneself down on a seat**, se camper sur un banc. **planking**, *s.* **1.** Planchéiage *m.* **2.** *Coll.* Planches *fpl.*; revêtement *m.*
plankton ['plæŋktən], *s. Oc:* Plancton *m*, plankton *m.*
planner ['plænər], *s.* Projeteur, -euse; auteur *m* (d'un crime). *Pol.Ec:* Planificateur *m.*
plant[1] [plɑ:nt], *s.* **1.** Plante *f.* **P. life**, (i) la vie végétale; (ii) flore *f* (d'une région). **Indoor pot p., house p.**, plante *f* d'appartement. **Bedding p.**, plant *m* à repiquer. **2.** *Ind:* (*a*) Appareil(s) *m(pl)*; installation *f* (d'éclairage); matériel *m*, outillage *m* (d'une usine). **The p.**, la machinerie. **Heavy p.**, grosses machines. (*b*) Usine *f.* **3.** *P:* Coup monté. **4.** *P:* (*Pers.*) Mouchard *m.* **'plant-louse**, *pl.* **-lice**, *s. Ent:* Aphis *m*, puceron *m.*

plant[2], *v.tr.* **1.** Planter (un arbre); enterrer (de oignons). **To p. a field with corn**, mettre une terre e blé. *Nau:* Mouiller (une mine). **2.** (*a*) Planter (u piquet dans la terre). **To find oneself planted on desert island**, se trouver délaissé sur une île déserte **To p. an idea in s.o.'s mind**, implanter une idée dan l'esprit de qn. **To p. a bomb**, poser, déposer, un bombe. (*b*) *F:* **To p. a bullet in the target**, loge une balle dans la cible. **A well-planted blow**, un cou bien asséné. *F:* **To p. oneself in front of** s.o se planter, se camper, devant qn. *F:* **To p. onesel on** s.o., s'implanter chez qn. **3.** *F:* (*a*) Planter aposter (un espion). (*b*) **To p. incriminating evidenc on** s.o., substituer les preuves d'un délit sur u tiers. (*c*) Mettre en sûreté, planquer (des objet volés). **4.** *F:* Planter là (un ami, etc.); plaquer (un femme). **plant out**, *v.tr. Hort:* Repiquer, dépote (des semis); décaisser (un arbuste, etc.). **'plantin 'out**, *s.* Repiquage *m*; dépotage *m*; décaissage *m* **planting**, *s.* **1.** *Hort: Agr:* Plantage *m*, plantatio *f* (d'un arbre, etc.). **P. bed**, planche *f* de semis. **2** *Nau:* Mouillage *m* (d'une mine). **3.** Apostement *m* (d'un espion).
plantain[1] ['plæntin], *s. Bot:* Plantain *m.*
plantain[2], *s. Bot:* **1.** Banane *f* des Antilles. **2.** **P.(-tree)** bananier *m* (du paradis).
plantation [plɑ:ˈnteiʃ(ə)n, plæn-], *s.* (*a*) For Plantation *f*, pépinière *f*, peuplement *m* (d'arbres (*b*) Plantation (de coton, de café, etc.).
planter ['plɑ:ntər], *s.* (*a*) Planteur *m* (de choux etc.). (*b*) Planteur (de coton, de café, etc.); proprié taire *m* d'une plantation.
plantigrade ['plæntigreid], *a. & s. Z:* Plantigrad (*m*).
plaque [plɑ:k], *s.* Plaque *f* (de bronze, etc.).
plash[1] [plæʃ], *s. Lit:* Clapotement *m* (des vagues) babillement *m* (d'un ruisseau).
plash[2], *v.i. Lit:* Clapoter; (*of stream*) babiller.
plasm ['plæzm], *s. Biol:* Protoplasme *m.*
plasma ['plæzmə], *s.* **1.** *Biol:* (*a*) Plasma *m* (du sang) (*b*) = PLASM. **2.** *Miner:* Calcédoine *f* vert foncé.
plaster[1] ['plɑ:stər], *s.* **1.** *Med:* Emplâtre *m.* **Adhesive** *F:* **sticking, p.**, sparadrap *m.* **Mustard p.**, sinapism *m.* **2.** Plâtre *m.* **Wall-p.**, enduit *m* de mur. **P. o Paris**, plâtre de moulage. *attrib.* **P. cast**, moulage *r* au plâtre. *S.a.* CAST[1] 4. LATH[1] 1. **P. work**, plâtrag *m*, plâtrerie *f.* **P. works, factory**, plâtrière *f.*
plaster[2], *v.tr.* **1.** *Med:* Mettre un emplâtre su (une plaie). **2.** **To p. (over) a wall**, plâtrer, ravale un mur. **Wall plastered with advertisements**, mu tapissé d'affiches. **To be plastered (over) with mud** être tout couvert de boue. **Plastered with decorations** chamarré de décorations. **plaster down**, *v.tr.* (*hair*) Aplatir, s'aplatir. **Hair plastered down on th forehead**, cheveux plaqués, gominés, sur le front **plaster up**, *v.tr.* Plâtrer, boucher (une fente)
plastered, *a.* **1.** Plâtré. **2.** *P:* Ivre, gris, soûl **plastering**, *s.* **1.** (*a*) *Med:* Pose *f* d'un emplâtre (*b*) Plâtrage *m* (d'un mur, etc.). (*c*) Travaux *mp* de plâtrerie. **2.** Enduit *m* de plâtre; plâtrage. **3** *F:* Volée *f* de coups.
plasterer ['plɑ:stərər], *s. Const:* Plâtrier *m*, ravaleur *m*
plastic ['plæstik], *a.* **1.** (Art) plastique. **P. surgery** chirurgie plastique. **P. surgeon**, chirurgien *n* plastique. **2.** Plastique; qui se laisse mouler o modeler. **P. clay**, terre *f* à modeler. **P. mind** esprit malléable. **3.** *a. & s. Ind:* (Matière) plastiqu (*m*). **A p. cup**, une tasse en (matière) plastique **Laminated p.**, laminé *m.* **4.** **P. bomb**, explosive plastic *m*, plastique *m.*
plasticine ['plæstisi:n], *s. R.t.m.* = Pâte à modeler **P. set**, boîte de modelage.
plasticity [plæsˈtisiti], *s.* Plasticité *f.*
plasticize ['plæstisaiz], *v.tr.* Plastifier
plasticizer ['plæstisaizər], *s.* Plastifian. *m.*
plastron ['plæstr(ə)n], *s. Fenc:* Plastron *m.*
plate[1] [pleit], *s.* **1.** Plaque *f*, lame *f*, feuille *f* (de métal **2.** (*a*) **P. iron**, tôlerie *f*, tôle *f.* *Mch:* **Bottom plates** tôles, plaques, de fond (de chaudière). (*b*) *Plate r* (de machine); platine *f* (de serrure); paumelle *f* (de gond de porte). *Dom.Ec:* **Hot p.**, plaqu (chauffante) (de cuisinière électrique). *Aut:* **Clutch p.**, plateau d'embrayage. *El:* **Terminal p.**, socle *m*

tablette f, à bornes. **Accumulator p.**, plaque d'accumulateur. *W.Tel:* **Valve p.**, plaque, anode f, de lampe. **P. battery**, batterie de plaque. (c) *Aut:* **Number p.**, plaque d'immatriculation; plaque minéralogique. **Door, name, plate**, plaque de porte. (d) *Dent:* Dentier m; prothèse f dentaire. **3.** (a) Plaque de verre. (b) *Phot:* Plaque. **Sensitive p.**, plaque sensible. **Full, whole, p.**, format m 16 cm 5 × 21 cm 5. **Half p.**, format 12 cm × 16 cm. **4.** (a) *Engr:* Planche f. (b) *Engr:* Gravure f, estampe f. **Full-page p.**, gravure hors texte. (c) *Typ:* (Stereotype) **p.**, cliché m. **5.** *Const:* Roof p., sablière f de comble. **6.** (a) Orfèvrerie f; vaisselle f d'or, d'argent. (b) It's only p., c'est seulement de l'argenté. (c) *Rac:* Coupe donnée en prix. **7.** (a) Assiette f. **Dinner p.**, assiette plate. **Soup p.**, assiette creuse. *F:* **To have a lot on one's p.**, avoir du pain sur la planche. (b) *Ecc:* (Collection) **p.**, plateau m de quête. **To take round the p.**, faire la quête. **'plate-armour, s. 1.** (a) Plaque f de blindage. (b) Blindage m. **2.** *A: Arm:* Armure f à plates. **'plate-clutch, s.** *Aut:* Embrayage m à disques. **'plate-'glass, s.** Glace de vitrage; verre m à glaces. **'plate(-)layer, s.** *Rail:* (a) Poseur m de rails, de la voie. (b) Ouvrier m de la voie. **Foreman p.-l.**, piqueur m de la voie. **'plate-laying, s.** *Rail:* Pose f de voies. **'plate-mark, s. 1.** = HALL-MARK[1]. **2.** *Engr: Phot:* Coup m de planche. **'plate-rack, s.** *Dom.Ec:* Porte-assiettes m inv; égouttoir m. **'plate-warmer, s.** Chauffe-assiettes m inv; réchaud m.

plate[2], v.tr. **1.** (a) Blinder; recouvrir, garnir (qch.) de plaques. (b) Plaquer. **To p. with gold, silver**, dorer, argenter. **2.** *Typ:* Clicher (les pages). **plated**, a. **1.** Recouvert, garni, de plaques; blindé. **2. Gold-p.**, doublé d'or. **Nickel-p.**, nickelé. **Chromium p.**, chromé. *Com:* **P. ware**, plaqué m. **plating, s. 1.** (a) Revêtement m en tôle. (b) Tôles fpl. **Steel-p.**, blindage m. **2.** Placage m. **3.** *Typ:* Clichage m.

Plate[3], *Pr.n.* *Geog:* The (river) P., le Rio de la Plata.

plateau, pl. -x, -s ['plætou, -z], s. *Ph.Geog:* Plateau m.

plateful ['pleitful], s. Assiettée f.

platelet ['pleitlit], s. **Blood platelets**, plaquettes sanguines, hématoblastes m.

platen ['plæt(ə)n], s. **1.** Plateau m, table f (de machine-outil). **2.** (Of printing-press) Platine f. **3.** *Typewr:* Rouleau m porte-papier.

plater ['pleitər], s. **1.** *Metalw:* Plaqueur m. **2.** *Turf:* (a) Cheval m à réclamer. (b) Cheval de second ordre.

platform ['plætfɔ:m], s. **1.** Terrasse f. *Fort:* Plate-forme f (en terre). **2.** (a) Plate-forme; tablier m (de bascule). **Entrance p.** (of a bus), plate-forme d'entrée. *Aut:* **P. wagon**, *U.S:* **p. truck**, camion-plate-forme m. *Artil:* **Loading p.**, plateau chargeur. (b) *Nau:* **Engine-room p.**, parquet m de la machine. (c) *Rail:* Quai m. **Departure p.**, (quai de) départ m. **Arrival platform**, (quai d') arrivée. **From what p. does the train start?** de quel quai part le train? *S.a.* TICKET[1] 1. **3.** (a) Estrade f, tribune f (de réunion publique). (b) *Pol:* Plate-forme, programme m (d'un parti). **4.** *Cin:* **Travelling p.**, travelling m.

platinize ['plætinaiz], v.tr. Platiner.

platinotype ['plætinotaip], s. *Phot:* Platinotypie f.

platinum ['plætinəm], s. Platine m. **P. foil**, platine laminé. **platinum(-)black, s.** *Ch:* Noir m de platine. **'platinum-'blond, a.** (Cheveux mpl) platinés s. **A p.-blonde**, une blonde platinée. **'platinum-'plated, a.** Platiné. **'platinum-point, s.** Grain platiné.

platitude ['plætitju:d], s. **1.** Platitude f, insipidité f (d'un discours). **2.** Platitude; lieu commun.

platitudinize [plæti'tju:dinaiz], v.i. Débiter des platitudes, des banalités.

Plato ['pleitou], *Pr.n.m.* Platon.

Platonic [plə'tɔnik], a. (a) (Philosophe) platonicien. (b) (Amour) platonique.

Platonism ['pleit(ə)nizm], s. *Phil:* Platonisme m..

platoon [plə'tu:n], s. *Mil:* Section f (de combat).

platter ['plætər], s. **1.** *A: & U.S:* Plat m, écuelle f. **2.** *U.S: F:* Disque m (de phonographe).

platypus ['plætipəs], s. Ornithor(h)ynque m.

plaudits ['plɔ:dits], s.pl. (Salve f d')applaudissements mpl.

plausibility ['plɔ:zi'biliti], s. Plausibilité f.

plausible ['plɔ:zibl], a. **1.** (a) Plausible, vraisemblable. (b) Spécieux, -euse. **2.** (Of pers.) Enjôleur, -euse; aux belles paroles. **-ibly**, adv. Plausiblement.

play[1] [plei], s. **1.** (a) Jeu m (de lumière). **P. of light on a jewel**, chatoiement m d'un bijou. (b) Jeu, maniement m (d'armes). (c) Jeu, activité f. **To come into p.**, entrer en jeu. **To call sth. into p.**, mettre qch. en jeu, en œuvre. **In full p.**, en pleine activité. **To give full p. to one's imagination**, donner libre cours à son imagination. *U.S:* **To make a p. for sth.**, mettre tout en œuvre, jouer le grand jeu, pour obtenir qch. (d) Jeu, fonctionnement m (d'une pièce de mécanisme). (e) *Mec.E: etc:* Jeu. **2.** (a) Jeu, amusement m. **Schoolboys at p.**, élèves en récréation. (b) **To say sth. in p.**, dire qch. pour plaisanter. **P. on words**, calembour m, jeu m de mots. **3.** (a) *O:* Jeu (de hasard). **To be ruined by p.**, s'être ruiné au jeu. (b) *Games:* **P. began at one o'clock**, la partie a commencé à une heure. **Ball in p., out of p.**, balle f en jeu; balle hors jeu. **4.** (a) *Th:* Pièce f de théâtre. **Shakespeare's plays**, le théâtre de Shakespeare. (b) Spectacle m. **To go to the p.**, aller au spectacle, au théâtre. **'play-acting, s.** = ACTING[2] (b), (c). **'play-actor, s. -actress, s.** *Pej:* Cabotin, -ine. **'play-bill, s.** Affiche f (de théâtre); annonce f de spectacle. **'play-boy, s.** *F:* Luron m; farceur m; bon vivant; *F:* fils à papa. **'play-pen, s.** Parc m pour enfants. **'play-room, s.** Salle f de jeux, de récréation.

play[2]. **I.** v.i. **1.** Se mouvoir vivement; (of animals) gambader, folâtrer; (of light) jouer, chatoyer. **The sun plays on the water**, le soleil se joue sur l'eau. **2.** (a) (Of fountain) Jouer. (b) **The organ is playing**, les orgues donnent. v.tr. **The band played the troops past**, la musique accompagna le défilé des troupes. (c) (Of part of mechanism) Jouer; fonctionner librement. **3.** (a) Jouer, s'amuser, se divertir. **Run away and p.!** va-t'en jouer (et laisse-moi tranquille)! (b) **To p. with fire**, jouer avec le feu. **He's not a man to be played with**, ce n'est pas un homme avec qui on plaisante. (c) **To p. at soldiers**, jouer aux soldats. **To (only) p. at doing sth.**, faire qch. en amateur. **II.** play, v.tr. or ind.tr. **1.** **To p. (at) billiards, chess**, jouer au billard, aux échecs. **P.! y êtes-vous?** *Ten:* play! **To p. fair**, jouer franc jeu; agir loyalement. **To p. for one's own hand**, jouer un jeu intéressé. **To p. into the hands of s.o.**, faire, jouer, le jeu de qn. **They p. into each other's hands**, ils sont d'intelligence. *S.a.* TIME[1] 2. **2.** **To p. the piano, the flute**, jouer du piano, de la flûte. **She was playing the organ**, elle tenait les orgues. **Won't you p. for us?** voulez-vous nous faire un peu de musique? **III.** play, v.tr. **1.** *Th:* (a) **To p. a part**, jouer un rôle. **To p. Macbeth**, tenir le rôle de Macbeth. *F:* **To p. the idiot**, faire l'imbécile. **To p. the man**, se conduire en homme. *F:* **To p. the fool**, faire des sottises. *S.a.* TRUANT. (b) **To p. a tragedy**, jouer, représenter, une tragédie. (With passive force) **Production now playing at . . .**, pièce qu'on donne actuellement à. . . . **2.** **To p. a joke, a trick, on s.o.**, jouer un tour à qn. **3.** (a) *Cards:* **To p. a card**, jouer une carte. (b) *Games:* **To p. the ball too high**, renvoyer la balle trop haut. *Abs.* **Who plays first?** à qui d'entamer? *Bowls:* à qui la boule? *Golf:* à qui l'honneur? **4.** (a) **To p. a game of tennis**, faire une partie de tennis. *S.a.* GAME[1]. **To p. a match**, disputer un match. (b) **To p. s.o. at chess**, faire une partie d'échecs avec qn. **I'll p. you for the drinks**, je vous joue les consommations. (c) *Sp:* Inclure (qn) dans son équipe. **5.** **To p. s.o. false**, trahir qn. **6.** **To p. a fish**, manœuvrer, épuiser, un poisson. **7.** **To p. water on the fire**, diriger de l'eau sur l'incendie. *Abs.* **The fire-engine played on the house**, la pompe à incendie donna contre la maison. **To p. on s.o.'s feelings**, agir sur les sentiments de qn. **To p. on s.o.'s credulity**, abuser de la crédulité de qn. **play back, v.tr.** Faire repasser (la bande) (d'un Magnétophone). **P. b. the last sentence**, faites repasser la dernière phrase. **'play-back, s.** Play-back m; lecture f sonore. **play down, v.tr.** Minimiser (l'importance de qch.). **play off, v.tr. 1.** **To p. off s.o. against s.o.**, opposer qn à qn. **2.** *Sp:* Rejouer (un match nul). **play on, v.i.** Continuer de jouer. **play out, v.tr. 1.** Jouer (une pièce de théâtre) jusqu'au bout. **2.** The organ played the people out, l'orgue a joué la sortie. **3.** *F:* To be played out, être à bout de forces. This theory is played out, cette théorie a fait son temps. **play up. 1.** *v.i.* (*a*) Faire de son mieux. **P. up!** allez-y! (*b*) To p. up to s.o., (i) *Th:* donner la réplique à qn; (ii) *F:* flatter, aduler, qn. **2.** *v.tr.* *F:* (*a*) To play s.o. up, agacer qn, chahuter qn. She plays him up, elle le fait marcher. (*b*) My back's playing me up, mon dos me donne du tracas. (*c*) Exploiter (un incident, un scandale). **playing,** *s.* **1.** Jeu *m.* **2.** *Th:* Interprétation *f* (d'un rôle); jeu (d'un acteur). **3.** *Mus:* Exécution *f* (d'un morceau). **'playing-card,** *s.* Carte *f* à jouer. **'playing-field,** *s.* Terrain *m* de jeux, de sports.

player ['pleiər], *s.* Joueur, -euse. **1.** *Mus:* Exécutant, -ante. **2.** *Th:* Acteur, -trice. **3.** *Sp:* (*a*) Équipier *m.* (*b*) **Gentlemen versus players,** amateurs contre professionnels. **4.** *Cards:* First p., premier en cartes. **'player-piano,** *s.* Piano *m* mécanique (à rouleau).

playfellow ['pleifelou], *s.* *O:* Camarade *mf* de jeu.
playful ['pleiful], *a.* Enjoué, badin, folâtre. **-fully,** *adv.* Gaiement; en badinant.
playfulness ['pleifulnis], *s.* Enjouement *m,* badinage *m,* folâtrerie *f.*
playgoer ['pleigouər], *s.* Habitué, -ée, des spectacles; amateur de théâtre.
playground ['pleigraund], *s.* *Sch: etc:* Cour *f,* terrain *m,* de récréation. **Covered p.,** préau *m.*
playhouse ['pleihaus], *s.* *A:* Théâtre *m.*
playlet [pleilit], *s.* Saynète *f.*
playmate ['pleimeit], *s.* *O:* = PLAYFELLOW.
plaything ['pleiθiŋ], *s.* Jouet *m;* *F:* joujou *m.*
playtime ['pleitaim], *s.* *Esp.* *Sch:* (Heure *f* de la) récréation; heures de loisir.
playwright ['pleirait], *s.* Auteur *m* dramatique; dramaturge *m.*

plea [pli:], *s.* **1.** *Jur:* (*a*) A. & *Scot:* Procès *m.* (*b*) Défense *f.* P. in bar, special p., exception *f* péremptoire; fin *f* de non-recevoir. **To submit the p. that . . .,** plaider que + *ind.* **2.** (*a*) Excuse *f,* prétexte *m.* **On the p. of . . .,** sous prétexte de. . . . (*b*) P. for mercy, appel *m* à la clémence.
plead [pli:d]. **1.** *v.i.* Plaider (for, pour; against, contre). **To p. guilty,** s'avouer coupable. **To p. not guilty,** nier sa culpabilité. **2.** *v.tr.* (*a*) Plaider (une cause). **To p. s.o.'s cause with s.o.,** intercéder pour qn auprès de qn. (*b*) Invoquer, alléguer (une excuse). **To p. ignorance,** prétexter l'ignorance. **pleading**[1], *a.* Implorant. **-ly,** *adv.* D'un ton suppliant. **To look (at s.o.) p.,** jeter un regard implorant (à qn). **pleading**[2], *s.* **1.** L'art *m* de plaider. **2.** (*a*) Plaidoirie *f.* (*b*) **Special p.,** arguments spécieux. **3.** Prières *fpl,* intercession *f* (for, en faveur de).
pleader ['pli:dər], *s.* Avocat (plaidant); défenseur *m.*
pleasant ['plez(ə)nt], *a.* **1.** Agréable, charmant, aimable. **Story that makes p. reading,** histoire agréable à lire. **P. breeze,** brise douce. **Life is p. here,** il fait bon vivre ici. **Good night, p. dreams,** bonne nuit, faites de beaux rêves. **2.** (*Of pers.*) Affable. **To make oneself p. (to s.o.),** faire l'agréable (auprès de qn). **-ly,** *adv.* **1.** Agréablement. **2.** Avec affabilité.
pleasantness ['plez(ə)ntnis], *s.* **1.** Agrément *m,* charme *m* (d'un endroit). **2.** (*Of pers.*) Affabilité *f.*
pleasantry ['plez(ə)ntri], *s.* *Lit:* Plaisanterie *f.*
please [pli:z], *v.tr.* **1.** (i) Plaire à (qn); faire plaisir à (qn); (ii) contenter (qn). **To be easily pleased,** s'arranger de tout. **There is no pleasing him,** il n'y a pas moyen de lui plaire. **He is hard to p.,** il est difficile. **In order to p. s.o.,** pour faire plaisir, pour être agréable, à qn. **The plan pleases him,** le projet lui sourit. **Music that pleases the ear,** musique qui flatte l'oreille. **P. yourself!** faites à votre guise. *Abs.* **To lay oneself out to p.,** se mettre en frais. **2.** (*a*) *Impers.* **P. God!** plaise à Dieu! Dieu le veuille! (*b*) (If you) p., s'il vous plaît. **P. don't cry,** de grâce, ne pleurez pas. **P. tell me . . .,** veuillez me dire. . . . **May I?—P. do!** vous permettez?— Je vous en prie! **P. sit down,** veuillez (donc) vous asseoir. **P. return this book,** prière de retourner ce livre. **3.** *Abs.* **To do as one pleases,** agir à sa guise. **Do as you p.,** faites comme vous voudrez, comme bon vous semblera. **He will do just as he pleases,** il n'en fera qu'à sa tête. **pleased,** *a.* **1.** Satisfait,

content. **To be p. with sth.,** être satisfait de qch. **He is very p. with himself,** il est fort satisfait de sa petite personne. **I am p. at the news,** je suis heureux d'apprendre cette nouvelle. **To be anything but p.,** n'être pas du tout content. *F:* He is as p. as Punch, il est heureux comme un roi; il est aux anges. **I shall be p. to come,** j'aurai grand plaisir à venir. **He will be very p. to do it,** il le fera volontiers. *Com:* **I am p. to inform you that . . .,** je m'empresse de vous aviser que. . . . **2.** His, Her, Majesty has been graciously p. to . . .,** il a plu à sa gracieuse Majesté de. . . . **pleasing,** *a.* Agréable. **P. expression,** expression agréable (du visage).
pleasurable ['pleʒərəbl], *a.* Agréable. **-ably,** *adv.* Agréablement.
pleasure ['pleʒər], *s.* **1.** Plaisir *m.* **To take, find, p. in doing sth.,** éprouver du plaisir à faire qch. **I have much p. in informing you that . . .,** je suis très heureux de vous faire savoir que. . . . **It would afford us great p. to . . .,** nous aurions grand plaisir à. . . . **Mrs X requests the p. of Mrs Y's company at . . .,** Mme X prie Mme Y de lui faire le plaisir d'assister à. . . . **With p.,** avec plaisir; volontiers. **2.** Plaisir(s), jouissances *fpl.* A life of p., vie adonnée au plaisir. **P. trip,** voyage d'agrément. **3.** Volonté *f;* bon plaisir. **At p.,** à volonté. **At s.o.'s p.,** au gré de qn. **Office held during p.,** emploi amovible. **'pleasure-boat,** *s.* Bateau *m* de plaisance. **pleasure-ground(s),** *s.* Parc *m,* jardin *m,* d'agrément. **'pleasure-loving,** *a.* Qui aime le plaisir.
pleat[1] [pli:t], *s.* *Dressm: etc:* Pli *m.* **Knife pleats,** plis couchés, plats. **Inverted pleats,** pli creux, double pli, pli inverti, plis rentrés. *pl.* Pleats, plissure *f.*
pleat[2], *v.tr.* Plisser (une jupe). **Permanently pleated skirt,** jupe indéplissable. **pleating,** *s.* Plissage *m.*
plebeian [plir'bi(:)ən], *a.* Plébéien, -ienne; du peuple; roturier, -ière.
plebiscite ['plebisit, -sait], *s.* Plébiscite *m.* **To vote by p.,** plébisciter.
plebs (the) [plebz], *s.* La plèbe; le peuple.
plectrum ['plektrəm], *s.* *Mus:* Plectre *m,* médiator *m.*
pledge[1] [pledʒ], *s.* **1.** (*a*) Gage *m,* nantissement *m.* (*b*) To put sth. in p., mettre qch. en gage. **To take sth. out of p.,** dégager qch. **2.** P. of good faith, garantie *f* de bonne foi. **3.** (*a*) Promesse *f,* vœu *m;* parole *f* d'honneur. **I am under a p. of secrecy,** j'ai fait vœu de garder le secret. (*b*) To take, sign, the p., promettre de s'abstenir d'alcool; faire vœu de tempérance.
pledge[2], *v.tr.* **1.** Mettre (qch.) en gage; engager (une montre). **To p. one's property,** engager son bien. **2.** Engager (sa parole). **To be pledged to do sth.,** avoir pris l'engagement de faire qch. **To p. one's allegiance to the king,** vouer obéissance au roi. **3.** *A:* Boire à la santé de (qn); porter un toast à (qn).
Pleiad, *pl.* -ads, -ades ['plaiəd, -ədz, -ədi:z]. *Pr.n.* **1.** *pl.* *Astr:* Les Pléiades *f.* **2.** *Fr.Lit:* (La) Pléiade.
pleistocene ['plaistosi:n], *a.* & *s.* *Geol:* Pléistocène (*m*).
plenary ['pli:nəri], *a.* Complet, -ète; entier, -ière. **P. powers,** pleins pouvoirs. **P. assembly,** assemblée plénière. *R.C.Ch:* **P. indulgence,** indulgence plénière.
plenipotentiary [ˌplenipə'tenʃ(ə)ri], *a.* & *s.* Plénipotentiaire (*m*).
plenitude ['plenitju:d], *s.* Plénitude *f.*
plenteous ['plentiəs], *a.* *Poet:* **1.** Abondant, copieux, -euse. **2.** Fertile, riche (in, en). **-ly,** *adv.* En abondance.
plenteousness ['plentiəsnis], *s.* *Lit:* Abondance *f.*
plentiful ['plentif(u)l], *a.* Abondant, copieux, -euse. **-fully,** *adv.* Abondamment; copieusement.
plenty ['plenti]. **1.** *s.* Abondance *f.* (*a*) He has p. of everything, il a de tout en suffisance. **P. of money,** une ample provision d'argent. **To have p. of courage,** ne pas manquer de courage. **You have p. of time,** vous avez largement le temps. **To have p. to live on,** avoir grandement de quoi vivre. (*b*) To live in p., vivre à l'aise, grassement. **Land of p.,** pays de cocagne. **2.** *adv.* *F:* P. big enough, bien assez gros.
plenum ['pli:nəm], *s.* *Ph:* Plein *m.* **P. fan,** ventilateur positif, soufflant.

pleonasm ['pliːənæzm], s. Pléonasme m.
pleonastic [ˌpli(ː)ə'næstik], a. Pléonastique, redondant. **-ally**, adv. Par pléonasme.
plesiosaurus, pl. **-ri** [pliːsiə'sɔːrəs, -rai], s. Palæont: Plésiosaure m.
plethora ['pleθərə], s. 1. Med: Pléthore f. 2. Pléthore, surabondance f (de bien, etc.).
plethoric [ple'θɔrik], a. Pléthorique.
pleura, pl. **-ae** ['pluərə, -iː], s. Anat: Plèvre f.
pleural ['pluər(ə)l], a. Anat: Pleural, -aux.
pleurisy ['pluərisi], s. Med: Pleurésie f. **Dry p.**, pleurite f. **Wet p.**, pleurésie purulente.
pleuritic [pluə'ritik], a. Pleurétique.
pleuro-pneumonia ['pluərɔnju(ː)'mounjə], s. Med: Pleuropneumonie f.
plexiglass ['pleksiglaːs], s. R.t.m. Plexiglas m.
plexus ['pleksəs], s. Anat: Plexus m, réseau m (de nerfs, etc.).
pliability [ˌplaiə'biliti], s. (a) Flexibilité f. (b) Docilité f, souplesse f (de caractère).
pliable ['plaiəbl], a. 1. (a) Flexible; (cuir) souple. (b) (Voix) flexible. 2. (Caractère) docile, complaisant.
pliancy ['plaiənsi], s. = PLIABILITY.
pliant ['plaiənt], a. = PLIABLE.
pliers ['plaiəz], s.pl. Tls: Pince(s) f(pl); tenaille(s) f(pl). **Insulated p.**, pince isolante.
plight¹ [plait], s. Condition f, état m. **To be in a sorry p.**, (i) F: être dans de beaux draps; (ii) être dans un triste état.
plight², v.tr. Lit: **To p. one's troth**, promettre, engager, sa foi. **Plighted word**, parole engagée.
Plimsoll ['plimsəl]. 1. Pr.n. Nau: **P. line**, ligne f de Plimsoll; ligne de flottaison en charge. 2. s.pl. O: **Plimsolls** = souliers m de gymnastique.
plinth [plinθ], s. Arch: Plinthe f; socle m (d'une colonne).
Pliny ['plini]. Pr.n.m. Lt.Lit: Pline.
pliocene ['plaiəsiːn], a. & s. Geol: Pliocène (m).
plod [plɔd], v.i. (**plodded**) 1. Marcher lourdement, péniblement. **To p. along**, cheminer d'un pas pesant. **To p. on**, persévérer. **To p. (away)**, travailler laborieusement (at, à). **plodding¹**, a. (a) (Pas) pesant, lourd. (b) Persévérant. **plodding²**, s. Labeur assidu.
plodder ['plɔdər], s. Travailleur persévérant (mais peu doué).
plonk¹ [plɔnk]. 1. s. Bruit sourd. 2. adv. Avec un bruit sourd.
plonk², v.tr. F: Poser (qch.) bruyamment et sans façons.
plonk³, s. Austr: P: Vin m ordinaire, pinard m.
plop¹ [plɔp], s., adv. & int. 1. Flac (m), plouf (m) (de qch. tombant dans l'eau). 2. **He sat down p.**, il s'est affalé (dans un fauteuil, etc.).
plop², v.i. (**plopped** [plɔpt]) 1. Faire flac, plouf. 2. Tomber en faisant pouf.
plosive ['plousiv], a. & s. Ling: (Consonne) plosive.
plot¹ [plɔt], s. 1. (Parcelle f, lot m, de) terrain m; lopin m (de terre). **Building p.**, terrain à bâtir; lotissement m. (In a garden) **The vegetable p.**, le coin des légumes. 2. Intrigue f, action f, affabulation f (d'une pièce, d'un roman). **The p. thickens**, l'intrigue se noue; F: l'affaire f se corse. **Unravelling of the p.**, dénouement m. 3. Mth: etc: Tracé m, graphique m. 4. Complot m, conspiration f. **To hatch a p.**, ourdir un complot.
plot², v.tr. (**plotted**) 1. (a) Relever (un terrain, etc.) (b) Tracer, rapporter (un levé de terrain). **To p. a diagram**, relever un diagramme. 2. Mth: **To p. the graph of an equation**, tracer le graphique d'une équation. 3. (a) Comploter, conspirer, tramer (la ruine de qn). (b) Abs. Comploter, conspirer (against s.o., contre qn). **plotting**, s. 1. Levé m (d'un terrain). 2. Tracé m, graphique m. 3. Complots mpl, machinations fpl.
plotter ['plɔtər], s. 1. (Pers.) Traceur m (d'un cadastre). 2. Conspirateur, -trice; conjuré, -ée.
plough¹ [plau], s. 1. Charrue f. **Tractor-driven p.**, charrue tractée. **Trenching p.**, défonceuse f. **To put, set, one's hand to the p.**, mettre la main à la pâte. 2. Astr: **The P.**, le Chariot. 3. Bookb: Rognoir m. **'plough-horse**, s. Cheval, -aux m, de labour. **'plough(-land)**, s. (a) Terre f de labour; labours mpl. (b) Terre arable.

plough², v.tr. 1. (a) Labourer (un champ); tracer, creuser (un sillon). Abs. **To p.**, labourer la terre. **Ploughed lands**, labours m. S.a. FURROW¹ 1. (b) (Of ship) Fendre, sillonner (les flots). 2. Bookb: Rogner (le papier). 3. Sch: F: Refuser, retoquer, recaler (un candidat). **To be ploughed**, échouer (à un examen); être refusé. **Ploughed in the oral (examination)**, collé à l'oral. 4. Com: Fin: **Profits ploughed back into the business**, bénéfices reversés dans l'affaire. **Ploughing back of profits**, autofinancement m. **plough in**, v.tr. Enterrer, enfouir, (le fumier, etc.) dans le sol en labourant. **plough through**, v.tr. i. **To p. (one's way) t. the mud**, avancer péniblement dans la boue. **plough up**, v.tr. 1. (a) Faire passer la charrue dans (un champ). **To p. up waste land**, défricher (un terrain). (b) (Of shells) Effondrer, défoncer (le terrain). 2. Extirper (des mauvaises herbes, etc.) avec la charrue. **ploughing**, s. Labourage m, labour m.
ploughboy ['plaubɔi], s.m. Valet de charrue.
ploughman, pl. **-men** ['plaumən], s.m. Laboureur.
ploughshare ['plauʃɛər], s. Soc m de charrue.
plover ['plʌvər], s. 1. Orn: Pluvier m. 2. Cu: **Plovers' eggs**, œufs m de vanneau.
plow [plau], s. & v. U.S: = PLOUGH.
ploy [plɔi], s. 1. Scot: Occupation f; passe-temps m inv. 2. Démarche f.
pluck¹ [plʌk], s. 1. **To give a p. at sth.**, tirer qch. d'un petit coup sec. 2. Cu: Fressure f (de veau). 3. Courage m, cran m.
pluck², v.tr. 1. Arracher (des plumes); cueillir (une fleur); épiler (les sourcils). 2. (a) **To p. s.o. by the sleeve**, tirer qn par la manche. (b) **To p. a guitar**, pincer de la guitare. 3. Sch: F: = PLOUGH² 3. 4. Plumer (une volaille). **pluck off**, v.tr. Détacher (une feuille d'une plante). **pluck out**, v.tr. Arracher (des cheveux). **pluck up**, v.tr. **To p. up (one's) courage**, s'armer de courage.
plucky ['plʌki], a. Courageux, -euse. F: crâne. **To be p.**, F: avoir du chien, du cran. **-ily**, adv. Courageusement; sans se laisser abattre.
plug¹ [plʌg], s. 1. (a) Tampon m, bouchon m, bonde f, soupape f (d'une baignoire, d'un réservoir). **P. of a boat**, bouchon de nable d'une embarcation. (b) Med: Tampon d'ouate. Surg: Bourdonnet m. 2. (a) Cheville f. El: Fiche f. **Two-pin p.**, fiche à deux broches. **Wall p.**, prise f de courant. (b) I.C.E: **Sparking p.**, bougie f (d'allumage). 3. (a) Fire-hydrant p., touche f d'incendie. (b) Plumb: Chasse f d'eau (du W.C.). **To pull the p.**, tirer, faire fonctionner, la chasse d'eau (du W.C.). 4. (a) = PLUG-TOBACCO. (b) **P. of tobacco**, chique f de tabac. 5. U.S: F: (a) Vieux cheval; rosse f. (b) Réclame f, battage m. (c) F: hat, chapeau haut de forme; chapeau melon. 6. P: Coup m de poing. **A p. on the ear**, un pain sur l'oreille. **'plug-hole**, s. Bonde f; trou m d'écoulement (de baignoire); Nau: nable m (d'embarcation). **'plug-to'bacco**, s. Tabac m en carotte. **'plug-'ugly**, pl. plug-uglies, s. U.S: F: Gangster m; voyou m.
plug², v. (**plugged**) I. v.tr. 1. **To p. (up) an opening**, boucher, tamponner, une ouverture. **To p. a wound**, tamponner une plaie. 2. P: (a) Flanquer une balle dans la peau à (qn). (b) Flanquer un coup à (qn). 3. Faire une campagne de publicité enragée (pour qch.). II. plug, v.i. 1. **To p. away**, persévérer, s'acharner; bûcher. plug in, v.tr. El: Brancher.
plum [plʌm], s. 1. Prune f. **P. tree**, prunier m. 2. A: Raisin sec. Still so used in PLUM-CAKE, PLUM-DUFF, PLUM-PUDDING. 3. F: Fin morceau; morceau de choix. **The plums**, les meilleurs postes; F: les filons. **'plum(-)'cake**, s. Cu: Cake m. **'plum-'duff**, s. Cu: Pudding m aux raisins. **'plum-'pudding**, s. Cu: Plum-pudding m (de Noël).
plumage ['pluːmidʒ], s. Plumage m.
plumb¹ [plʌm], s. 1. Plomb m (de fil à plomb). 2. Aplomb m. **Out of p.**, hors d'aplomb; (mur) qui porte à faux. 3. Nau: (Ligne f de) sonde f. **'plumb-bob**, s. Plomb m (de fil à plomb). **'plumb-line**, s. 1. Fil m à plomb. 2. Nau: Ligne f de sonde. **'plumb-rule**, s. Niveau vertical; niveau à plomb.

plumb², *v.tr.* **1.** Sonder (la mer). **To p. the depths of poverty,** sonder l'abîme de la misère. **2.** Vérifier l'aplomb de (qch.). **3.** *Plumb:* Plomber (une canalisation). **plumbing,** *s.* **1.** Plomberie *f.* **2.** *Coll.* Tuyauterie *f.* *F:* **To have a look at the p.,** aller faire pipi.

plumb³. **1.** *a.* Droit; vertical, -aux; d'aplomb. **2.** *adv.* *F:* **P. in the centre,** juste au milieu. *U.S:* *F:* **P. crazy,** complètement fou.

plumbago [plʌm'beigou], *s.* **1.** *Miner:* Plombagine *f.* **2.** *Bot:* Plombago *m,* dentellaire *f.*

plumber ['plʌmər], *s.* Plombier *m.*

plume¹ [plu:m], *s.* **1.** *A. & Lit:* Plume *f.* **2.** Panache *m,* aigrette *f;* plumet *m* (de casque).

plume². **1.** *v.tr.* Orner de plumes. **Black-plumed,** aux plumes noires. **2.** *v.pr.* (*a*) (*Of bird*) **To p. itself,** se lisser les plumes. (*b*) (*Of pers.*) **To p. oneself on sth.,** se glorifier, se piquer, se targuer, de qch.

plummer-block, -box ['plʌməblɔk, -bɔks], *s.* *Mec.E:* Palier *m.*

plummet ['plʌmit], *s.* **1.** Plomb *m* (de fil à plomb). **2.** *Nau:* Sonde *f.*

plump¹ [plʌmp], *a.* (*Of pers.*) Rebondi, grassouillet, rondouillard, dodu; (*of chicken or pers.*) bien en chair.

plump². **1.** *s.* Bruit sourd (de chute). **2.** *adv.* **To fall p. into the mud,** tomber dans la boue avec un floc.

plump³. **1.** *v.tr.* (*a*) Jeter brusquement; flanquer. **To p. oneself into an armchair,** se laisser tomber dans un fauteuil. (*b*) **To p. up (a pillow),** secouer, brasser (un oreiller). **2.** *v.i.* (*a*) Tomber lourdement; faire plouf. (*b*) **To p. for sth.,** choisir qch., être tout entier pour qch. **To p. for a candidate** (*in municipal elections*), voter pour un seul candidat.

plumpness ['plʌmpnis], *s.* Embonpoint *m,* rondeur *f.*

plunder¹ ['plʌndər], *s.* **1.** Pillage *m* (d'une ville). **2.** (*a*) Butin *m.* (*b*) Petits bénéfices; *F:* gratte *f.*

plunder², *v.tr.* Piller, dépouiller (un pays).

plunderer ['plʌndərər], *s.* Pillard *m,* ravisseur, -euse; saccageur, -euse; rapineur, -euse.

plunge¹ [plʌn(d)ʒ], *s.* Plongeon *m.* **To take the p.,** sauter le pas; faire le plongeon. **To be about to take the p.,** être sur le tremplin.

plunge². **1.** *v.tr.* Plonger, immerger (le linge dans la lessive). **Plunged in darkness,** plongé dans l'obscurité. **2.** *v.i.* (*a*) Plonger, piquer une tête (dans l'eau, etc.); s'enfoncer (dans un bois); se jeter (à corps perdu) (dans une affaire). (*b*) **To p. forward,** s'élancer en avant. (*c*) (*Of horse*) (Se cabrer et) ruer. (*d*) (*Of ship*) Tanguer; piquer du nez. (*e*) *Gaming:* Jouer ou parier sans compter. *St.Exch:* Risquer de grosses sommes. **plunging¹,** *a.* Plongeant. *Artil:* (Feu) fichant. *Cost:* **P. neckline,** décolleté plongeant. **plunging²,** *s.* **1.** Plongée *f,* plongement *m.* **2.** Tangage *m* (d'un bateau).

plunger ['plʌn(d)ʒər], *s.* **1.** *F:* Joueur effréné. *St. Exch:* (Spéculateur) risque-tout *m inv.* **2.** (*a*) Plongeur (de pompe). **P.-piston,** (piston) plongeur. **Grease-gun p.,** piston compresseur de pompe de graissage. (*b*) *Husb:* Batte *f* à beurre (de baratte). (*c*) *Navy:* **P. of a mine,** plongeur.

plunk¹ [plʌnk], *s.* *U.S:* **1.** Son aigu. **2.** *F:* Coup sec.

plunk², *v.tr.* *U.S:* **1.** Jeter (qch) bruyamment. **2.** *P:* Flanquer une balle dans la peau (de qn).

pluperfect [plu:'pə:fikt], *a. & s.* *Gram:* Plus-que-parfait (*m*).

plural ['pluər(ə)l]. **1.** *a. & s.* *Gram:* Pluriel (*m*). **In the p.,** au pluriel. **2.** *a.* *Pol:* **P. vote,** vote plural.

pluralism ['pluərəlizm], *s.* **1.** (*Esp.Ecc:*) Cumul *m* de fonctions. **2.** *Phil:* Pluralisme *m.*

plurality [pluə'ræliti], *s.* **1.** Pluralité *f.* **2.** **P. of offices,** cumul *m* de fonctions. **3.** *U.S:* *Pol:* Majorité relative.

plus [plʌs]. **1.** *prep.* Plus. **Courage p. sense,** le courage plus le bon sens. **2.** *a.* (*Of quantity*) Positif. (*b*) **On the p. side of the account,** à l'actif du compte. (*c*) *Sp:* **P. player,** joueur qui rend des points. **3.** *s.* (*pl.* **plusses** ['plʌsiz]) (*a*) Plus *m;* signe *m* de l'addition. (*b*) Quantité positive. **'plus-'fours,** *s.pl.* *Cost:* Culotte *f* de golf, knickerbocker *m.*

plush [plʌʃ]. *s.* **1.** *Tex:* Peluche *f,* panne *f.* **2.** *a.* (*a*) Peluché. (*b*) *P:* Rupin.

plushy ['plʌʃi], *a.* (*a*) Peluché. (*b*) *P:* Rupin.

plutocracy [plu:'tɔkrəsi], *s.* Ploutocratie *f.*

plutocrat ['plu:tɔkræt], *s.* Ploutocrate *m.*

plutocratic [,plu:tɔ'krætik], *a.* Ploutocratique.

Plutonic [plu:'tɔnik], *a.* *Geol:* Plutonien, -ienne.

plutonium [plu:'touniəm], *s.* *Ch:* Plutonium *m.*

pluvial ['plu:viəl], *a.* *Geol:* Pluvial, -aux.

pluviometer [,plu:vi'ɔmitər], *s.* Pluviomètre *m.*

ply¹ [plai], *s.* **1.** (*a*) Pli *m* (de tissu en plusieurs plis). (*b*) Pli, épaisseur *f* (de contre-plaqué). **Five-p. wood,** contre-plaqué *m* en cinq épaisseurs. **2.** Brin *m,* fil *m* (de corde, de laine); toron *m* (de corde). **Three-p. wool,** laine trois fils.

ply². **1.** *v.tr.* (*a*) Manier vigoureusement. **To p. the oars,** (i) manier les avirons; (ii) faire force de rames. (*b*) *O:* **To p. a trade,** exercer un métier. (*c*) **To p. s.o. with questions,** presser qn de questions. **To p. s.o. with drink,** verser force rasades à qn. **2.** *v.i.* (*a*) (*Of bus*) Faire le service, le parcours, la navette, le va-et-vient (**between** . . . **and** . . ., entre . . . et . . .). (*b*) **To p. for hire,** faire un service de taxi.

plywood ['plaiwud], *s.* (Bois) contre-plaqué *m.*

pneumatic [nju:'mætik], *a.* Pneumatique. **P. tyre,** pneumatique *m,* pneu *m.* **P. pick, drill, hammer,** pic *m,* foreuse *f,* marteau *m,* pneumatique.

pneumatics [nju:'mætiks], *s.* *Ph:* Pneumatique *f.*

pneumococcus ['nju:mo'kɔkəs], *s.* *Bac:* Pneumocoque *m.*

pneumonia [nju:'mouniə], *s.* *Med:* Pneumonie *f;* fluxion *f* de poitrine.

pneumothorax ['nju:mo'θɔ:ræks], *s.* *Med:* Pneumothorax *m.*

po [pou], *s.* *F:* Pot *m* de chambre, vase *m* de nuit.

poach¹ [poutʃ], *v.tr.* *Cu:* Pocher (des œufs).

poach², *v.tr.* (*a*) Braconner dans (un bois). (*b*) Braconner (le gibier). (*c*) *Abs.* Braconner. **To p. on s.o.'s preserves,** (i) chasser sur les terres de qn; (ii) empiéter sur les prérogatives de qn; piquer dans l'assiette de qn. (*d*) *Ten:* **To p. a ball,** chiper une balle à son partenaire. **poaching,** *s.* Braconnage *m.*

poacher ['poutʃər], *s.* Braconnier *m.* *Tail:* **P.'s pocket,** poche *f* carnier (de costume de chasse), poche à soufflet.

pochard ['poutʃəd], *s.* *Orn:* Milouin *m.*

pochette [pɔ'ʃet], *s.* (Sac *m* à main) pochette (*f*) (de dame).

pock [pɔk], *s.* *Med:* Pustule *f* (de la petite vérole). **'pock-marked,** *a.* **P.-m. face,** visage grêlé, variolé.

pocket¹ ['pɔkit], *s.* **1.** (*a*) Poche *f* (de vêtement). **Trouser-p.,** poche de pantalon. **Waistcoat-p.,** gousset *m.* **Hip p.,** poche revolver. **Patch pockets,** poches rapportées, appliquées. **To have empty pockets,** avoir la poche vide. *F:* **To line one's pockets,** faire sa pelote. *F:* **To have s.o. in one's p.,** avoir qn dans sa manche. **I have him in my p.,** je sais le faire marcher. *S.a.* BURN² 1, PICK³ 7. *Typ:* **P. edition,** édition de poche. *Navy:* **P. battleship,** cuirassé *m* de poche. (*b*) **He always has his hand in his p.,** il est toujours à débourser. **To be in p.,** être en bénéfice. **I am out of p. by it,** j'y suis de ma poche. **2.** (*a*) Sac *m* (de houblon). (*b*) *Bill:* Blouse *f.* (*c*) *Aut:* (In door). Poche intérieure. (*d*) **Pockets under the eyes,** poches sous les yeux. **4.** *(a)* *Min:* Poche, sac (de minerai). (*b*) Cavité remplie d'eau, de gaz. (*c*) *Av:* Trou *m* d'air. *Hyd.E:* Poche d'air. **'pocket-book,** *s.* (*a*) Carnet *m* de poche; calepin *m.* (*b*) *Esp.U.S:* Porte-billets *m inv,* portefeuille *m.* (*c*) Livre *m* de poche. **'pocket-comb,** *s.* Peigne *m* de poche. **pocket-'handkerchief,** *s.* Mouchoir *m* de poche. **'pocket-knife,** *s.* Couteau *m* de poche. **'pocket-money,** *s.* Argent *m* de poche. **'pocket-picking,** *s.* Vol *m* à la tire. **'pocket 'veto,** *s.* *U.S:* *Pol:* *Adm:* Veto indirect, imposable par un haut fonctionnaire aux États-Unis, qui peut garder, sans le signer, un acte de la Législature jusqu'après la dissolution de celle-ci.

pocket², *v.tr.* (pocketed) **1.** (*a*) Empocher; mettre (qch.) dans sa poche. *U.S:* *Pol:* *Adm:* Imposer un veto indirect à un acte de la Législature. (*b*) *Pej:* Soustraire (de l'argent); chiper (qch.). **2.** Avaler (un affront). **3.** Refouler (sa colère). **To p. one's pride,** mettre son orgueil dans sa poche. **4.** *Bill:* Blouser (la bille). **pocketed,** *a.* Électrode, soupape) en retrait.

pocketful ['pɔkitful], s. Pleine poche; pochée f.
pod¹ [pɔd], s. (a) Cosse f, gousse f (de fèves); écale f (de pois). (b) **Senna pods**, follicules m de séné.
pod², v. (**podded**) **1.** v.i. (Of plant) Former des cosses. **2.** v.tr. Écosser, écaler (des pois, etc.).
podginess ['pɔdʒinis], s. F: Embonpoint m, rondeur f.
podgy ['pɔdʒi], a. F: Boulot, -otte, replet, -ète. **P. fingers**, doigts boudinés, rondelets.
poem ['pouim], s. Poème m; (short) poésie f.
poet ['pouit], s. Poète m.
poetaster [,poui'tæstər], s. Rimailleur m; versificateur m.
poetess ['pouitis], s.f. Femme poète; poétesse.
poetic(al) [pou'etik(əl)], a. Poétique. S.a. JUSTICE 1. **-ally**, adv. Poétiquement.
poetics [pou'etiks], s.pl. L'art m poétique.
poetry ['pouitri], s. Poésie f. **To write p.**, écrire des vers.
pogrom ['pɔgrəm], s. Pogrom m.
poignancy ['pɔinənsi], s. (a) Piquant m (d'une sauce); mordant m (d'une satire). (b) Violence f (d'une émotion); acuité f (d'une douleur).
poignant ['pɔinənt], a. (a) Piquant, âpre. (b) (Of emotion) Poignant, vif, vive; (of thought) angoissant. **-ly**, adv. D'une façon poignante.
point¹ [pɔint], s. I. **Point** m. **1.** Decimal p., virgule f. **Three p. five** (3·5), trois virgule cinq (3,5). **2.** (a) **P. of departure**, point de départ. Astr: The **cardinal points**, les points cardinaux. **At all points**, sous tous rapports; en tout point. Av: **P. of no return**, point limite de retour. **Critical p.**, point critique. (b) **P. of view, view-p.**, point de vue. **To consider sth. from all points of view**, considérer qch. sous tous ses aspects. **3.** (a) Point, détail m (d'un raisonnement). **Figures that give p. to his argument**, chiffres qui ajoutent du poids à sa thèse. **To differ on a p.**, ne pas être d'accord sur un point, sur un détail. **On that p. we disagree**, là-dessus nous ne sommes pas d'accord. **To pursue one's p.**, poursuivre son idée. **To make a p.**, faire ressortir un argument. **Points to be remembered**, considérations f à se rappeler. **A p. of conscience**, un cas de conscience. **To make a p. of doing sth.**, se faire un devoir de faire qch; s'obliger à faire qch. **P. of grammar**, question de grammaire. **In p. of fact**, par le fait. S.a. CARRY² 4, HONOUR¹ 3, POSSESSION 1, STRETCH² 1. (b) **The p.**, le sujet, la question. **Here is the p.**, voici ce dont il s'agit. **Off the p.**, étranger à la question, hors de propos. **On this p.**, à cet égard. **This is very much to the p.**, c'est bien parlé; c'est bien dit. **Your remark is not to the p.**, votre observation manque d'à-propos. **Let us get back to the p.**, revenons à nos moutons. (c) **What would be the p. of (doing sth.)?** à quoi bon (faire qch.)? **I don't see the p. of the story**, je ne vois pas où cette histoire veut en venir. **I see no p. in relating . . .**, je juge, j'estime, inutile de raconter . . ., **There is no p. in denying that . . .**, cela ne servirait à rien de nier que . . . S.a. MISS¹ 1. (d) **P. of interest**, détail intéressant. **To have one's good points**, avoir ses qualités. S.a. STRONG 2. **4.** (a) **To be on the p. of doing sth.**, être sur le point de faire qch. **I was on the p. of jumping**, j'allais sauter. (b) **Matters are at such a p. that . . .**, les choses en sont là que. . . . **Up to a p.**, jusqu'à un certain point, dans une certaine mesure. **To come to the p.**, arriver au fait. **Severe to the p. of cruelty**, sévère jusqu'à la cruauté. **5.** Games: **To score so many points**, marquer, faire, tant de points. **What points shall we play?** (i) en combien jouons-nous la partie? (ii) à combien le point? Box: **To win on points**, gagner aux points. **To give points to s.o.**, donner des points à qn. **6.** (a) **The thermometer went up two points**, le thermomètre est, a, monté de deux divisions. St.Exch: **To rise a p.**, hausser d'un point. (b) Typ: **Point. Set up in twelve-p. (body)**, composé en corps douze. II. **point**, s. **Pointe** f. **1.** (a) Pointe, extrémité f (d'une épingle); bec m (d'une plume à écrire). Box: **Blow to the p.**, coup sur la pointe de la mâchoire. **Five-p. star**, étoile à cinq rayons. **P. of a joke**, piquant m, sel m, d'une plaisanterie. S.a. FINE³ 5. (b) Vet: **Bay horse with black points**, cheval bai aux extrémités noires. **To describe the points of a hound**, décrire les caractéristiques d'un chien courant. (c)

pl. Ven: **Buck of ten points**, cerf dix cors. (d) Geog: Pointe, promontoire m. Nau: **To double a p.**, doubler une pointe. **2.** Tls: Pointe, poinçon m. **3.** El: (a) **Platinum (contact) p.**, contact platiné, vis platinée. (b) (Point de) prise f de courant (sur le secteur). **4.** Rail: **Points**, aiguillage m; aiguille f de raccordement. **To throw over the points**, aiguiller; changer l'aiguille. **5. P. of the compass**, aire f de vent. Nau: **To alter (the) course two points to the west**, changer la route de deux quarts vers l'ouest. **6.** Lacem: = POINT-LACE. **7.** Cr: Station f à droite dans le prolongement du guichet. III. **point**, s. Ven: **Dog making a p.**, chien qui tombe en arrêt.
'point-'blank. 1. a. (a) Ball: (Tir) direct, sans corrections. (b) (Question) de but en blanc; (refus) net. **2.** adv. **To fire p.-b. at s.o.**, tirer sur qn à bout portant. **He asked me p.-b. whether . . .**, il m'a demandé à brûle-pourpoint si. . . . **To refuse p.-b.**, refuser catégoriquement, (tout) net. **'point-duty**, s. **Policeman on p.-d.**, agent m de service, agent à station fixe. **To be on p.-d.**, être de service à poste fixe. **'point-'lace**, s. Dentelle f à l'aiguille; guipure f. **'point-to-'point**, a. & s. **P.-to-p. (race)**, (i) A: course f au clocher; (ii) (en Angleterre) steeple-chase m, F: steeple m (pour chevaux de chasse).
point². **I.** v.tr. **1.** (a) Marquer (qch.) de points. (b) Gram: Ponctuer (la phrase). **2.** (a) Tailler en pointe (un bâton, etc.); aiguiser (un outil). (b) Donner du piquant à (des remarques). **To p. a moral**, inculquer une leçon (en soulignant la conclusion de l'histoire). **3. To p. a gun, a telescope**, braquer un canon, une longue-vue (at, sur). S.a. FINGER¹ 1. **4. To p. the way**, indiquer, montrer, le chemin. **5.** Const: Jointoyer (un mur). **6.** Abs. Ven: (Of hound) Tomber en arrêt. **II. point**, v.i. **1. To p. at s.o.**, montrer qn du doigt, etc. **2.** (a) **The magnetic needle always points north**, l'aiguille aimantée est toujours tournée vers le nord. **The clock pointed to ten**, la pendule marquait dix heures. (b) **This points to the fact that . . .**, cette circonstance (i) laisse supposer que . . ., (ii) fait ressortir que. . . . **Everything seems to p. to success**, tout semble annoncer le succès. **Everything points to him as the culprit**, tout indique que c'est lui le coupable. **point out**, v.tr. **1. To p. out sth. to s.o. (with one's finger)**, désigner, montrer, qch. du doigt à qn. **2. To p. out sth. to s.o.**, signaler, faire remarquer, qch. à qn. **To p. out the mistakes**, signaler les erreurs. **To p. out a fact**, faire ressortir un fait. **To p. out to s.o. the advantages of . . .**, représenter à qn les avantages de. . . . **Might I p. out that . . .**, permettez-moi de vous faire observer que. . . . **pointed**, a. **1.** Pointu; à pointe. **P. beard**, barbe en pointe. S.a. ARCH¹ 1. **2.** (a) (Réplique) mordante. (b) (Allusion) peu équivoque. **-ly**, adv. (a) Sarcastiquement; d'un ton mordant. (b) Explicitement, nettement. (c) D'une manière marquée. **pointing**, s. **1.** Ponctuation f (de la phrase). **2.** Taillage m en pointe, affûtage m. **3.** Braquage m (d'un canon, d'une longue-vue). **4.** Constr: Jointoiement m (d'un mur). **5.** Arrêt m (d'un chien). **'pointing-trowel**, s. Constr: Fiche f (de maçon).
pointedness ['pointidnis], s. **1.** Mordant m (d'une remarque). **2.** Caractère m explicite (d'une allusion).
pointer ['pointər], s. **1.** Ven: Chien m d'arrêt, pointer m. **2.** (a) Aiguille f, index m (d'une balance). (b) Sch: Baguette f (du tableau noir). **3.** pl. Astr: **The Pointers**, les Gardes f (de la Grande Ourse). **4.** F: Renseignement m; F: tuyau m.
pointillism ['pwæntilizm], s. Art: Pointillisme m.
pointillist ['pwæntilist], s. Art: Pointilliste m.
pointless ['pointlis], a. **1.** Épointé, émoussé. **2.** (a) (Plaisanterie) fade, sans sel. (b) (Observation) qui ne rime à rien.
pointlessness ['pointlisnis], s. Fadeur f; manque m de propos.
pointsman, pl. **-men** ['pointsmən], s.m. Rail: Aiguilleur.
poise¹ [pɔiz], s. **1.** (Equal, even, just) p., équilibre m, aplomb m. **A man of p.**, un homme pondéré. **2.** Port m (de la tête, du corps).
poise². **1.** v.tr. (a) Équilibrer. (b) Balancer (un javelot). **To p. sth. in the hand**, soupeser qch. **2.** v.i. **To p. in the air**, planer en l'air.

poison[1] ['pɔizn], *s.* Poison *m*, toxique *m*. **Rank p.,** (i) poison violent; (ii) un vrai poison. **To take p.,** s'empoisonner. **To die of p.,** mourir empoisonné. *S.a.* HATE[2] 1, MEAT 2. **'poison-'gas,** *s.* Gaz toxique, asphyxiant. **'poison-gland,** *s. Z:* Glande *f* à venin. **'poison-'pen,** *a. & s.* Auteur *m* d'une lettre anonyme. **P.-p. letter,** lettre *f* anonyme.

poison[2], *v.tr.* (a) Empoisonner, intoxiquer. **Poisoned wound,** plaie envenimée. (b) Corrompre, pervertir (l'esprit). **poisoning,** *s.* (a) Empoisonnement *m*; intoxication *f.* (b) Corruption *f* (de l'esprit).

poisoner ['pɔiznər], *s.* Empoisonneur, -euse.

poisonous ['pɔiznəs], *a.* Toxique, intoxicant; empoisonné; (of animal) venimeux, -euse; (of plant) vénéneux, -euse. **P.** doctrine, doctrine pernicieuse. **She has a p. tongue,** elle a une langue de vipère.

poisonousness ['pɔiznəsnis], *s.* Toxicité *f*; caractère pernicieux (d'une doctrine).

poke[1] [pouk], *s.* Poussée *f*; coup *m* de coude; coup du bout du doigt; coup de tisonnier; coup du bout de sa canne. **To give s.o. a p. in the ribs,** enfoncer son doigt, son coude, dans les côtes de qn.

poke[2]. I. *v.tr.* 1. Pousser (qn, qch.) du bras, du coude; piquer (qch.) du bout d'un bâton. **To p. s.o. in the ribs,** donner une bourrade (amicale) à qn. **To p. a hole in sth.,** faire un trou dans qch.; crever qch. (avec le doigt, etc.). 2. Tisonner, attiser, fourgonner (le feu); ringarder (un fourneau). **To p. up the chimney, down the pipe,** passer qch. dans la cheminée, dans un tuyau. **To p. one's head round the corner,** porter la tête en avant pour regarder au coin; passer la tête au coin de la rue. *S.a.* NOSE[1] 1. 4. **To p. rubbish into a corner,** fourrer des saletés dans un coin. 5. **To p. fun at s.o.,** (i) plaisanter amicalement qn; (ii) tourner qn en ridicule; se moquer de qn; *F:* se payer la tête de qn. II. *poke, v.i.* 1. **To p. at sth. with one's umbrella,** tâter, tourmenter, qch. du bout de son parapluie. 2. **To p. (about) in every corner,** fouiller, farfouiller, fureter, dans tous les coins. **To p. into other people's business,** fourrer son nez dans les affaires d'autrui. **poke out,** *v.tr.* (a) **To p. s.o.'s eye out,** éborgner qn. **To p. the fire out,** (i) éteindre le feu à coups de tisonnier; (ii) éteindre le feu à trop le tisonner. (b) **To p. one's head out (of the window),** passer, sortir, la tête par la fenêtre.

poke[3], *s. O:* Sac *m*, poche *f. S.a.* PIG.

poker[1] ['poukər], *s.* 1. Tisonnier *m*, attisoir *m*, attisonnoir *m*; *Ind:* fourgon *m*; (for furnace) ringard *m*. **He looks as if he had swallowed a p.,** il est raide comme un pieu; on dirait qu'il a avalé sa canne. 2. Pointe *f* métallique (pour pyrogravure). 3. *Bot:* Red-hot p., tritoma *m*. **'poker-work,** *s.* Pyrogravure *f.*

poker[2], *s. Cards:* Poker *m.* **'poker-face,** *s.* Visage impassible.

poky ['pouki], *a.* (Of room) Exigu; misérable; (of occupation) mesquin. **A p. little room,** une petite pièce de rien du tout.

Poland ['pouland]. *Pr.n.* La Pologne.

polar ['poulər]. 1. *a.* Polaire. **P. circle,** cercle polaire. **P. bear,** ours blanc. 2. *a. Mth:* Polaire *f.*

polarimeter [,poulə'rimitər], *s. Ph:* Polarimètre *m.*

polariscope [pou'læriskoup], *s. Ph:* Polariscope *m.*

polarity [pou'læriti], *s.* Polarité *f.*

polarization [,poulərai'zeiʃ(ə)n], *s. Ph:* Polarisation *f.*

polarize ['pouləraiz], *v.tr.* (a) Polariser (la lumière, une barre de fer, etc.). (b) (With passive force) Se polariser. **polarizing,** *a.* Polarisant, polarisateur, -trice.

polarizer ['pouləraizər], *s. Opt:* Polariseur *m.*

polder ['pouldər, 'pɔl-], *s. Geog:* Polder *m.*

pole[1] [poul], *s.* 1. (a) Perche *f*; échalas *m*; baliveau *m*, mât *m* (d'échafaudage); hampe *f* (d'un drapeau); balancier *m* (de danseur de corde). **Tent p.,** mât *m* de tente. **Telegraph p.,** poteau télégraphique. *F:* **To be up the p.,** (i) être timbré, piqué, maboul; (ii) être dans le pétrin. *S.a.* BARBER, GREASY 2. (b) Timon *m*, flèche *f* (de voiture); bras *m* (de civière). (c) **Curtain-p.,** monture *f*, tringle *f*, pour rideaux. (d) *Nau:* Flèche (de mât). *S.a.* BARE[1] 1. 2. *Meas:* Perche *f* (de 5½ yards, approx. = 5 m. 03). **'pole-jump(ing),** *s.* Saut *m* à la perche.

pole[2], *v.tr.* Conduire, pousser, (un bateau) à la perche.

pole[3], *s.* Pôle *m.* 1. *Geog:* **South P.,** Pôle sud. **North P.,** Pôle nord. **Magnetic p.,** pôle magnétique. **Their views are poles apart,** leurs opinions sont diamétralement opposées. *S.a.* STAR[1] 1. 2. *El:* **Positive p.,** anode *f*; électrode positive. **Negative p.,** cathode *f*; électrode négative. **Opposite poles,** pôles de noms contraires.

Pole[4], *s. Geog:* Polonais, -aise.

pole-ax(e)[1] ['poulæks], *s.* 1. *A.Arms:* Hache *f* d'armes. 2. Merlin *m*; assommoir *m* (de boucher).

pole-axe[2], *v.tr.* Assommer; abattre (une bête) avec le merlin.

polecat ['poulkæt], *s. Z:* Putois *m.*

polemic [pɔ'lemik]. 1. *a.* Polémique. 2. *s.* Polémique *f.*

polemics [pɔ'lemiks], *s.pl. Esp. Theol:* La polémique.

polemize ['pɔlimaiz], *v.i.* Polémiquer, polémiser.

police[1] [pɔ'li:s], *s. inv.* **The p.,** la police; (in country districts) = la gendarmerie. **P. superintendent** = commissaire de police principal. **P. inspector** = (i) commissaire *m* de police divisionnaire; (ii) officier *m* de police. **P. constable, officer** = (i) agent *m* de police; (ii) (in country districts) gendarme *m.* **P. station** = commissariat de police. **Sub p. station** = poste *m* de police. **The River P.,** la police fluviale. **P. dog,** chien policier. **P. van,** (i) voiture *f* cellulaire; (ii) car *m* de police. **The Royal Canadian Mounted P.,** la Gendarmerie royale du Canada. *F:* **The p. are after him,** la police est à ses trousses.

police[2], *v.tr.* Policer; maintenir l'ordre dans (le pays, etc.).

policeman, *pl.* **-men** [pɔ'li:smən], *s.m.* Agent *m* de police; (in country districts) gendarme *m.* **P. on point duty, traffic p.,** agent de la circulation.

policewoman, *pl.* **-women** [pɔ'li:swumən, -wimin], *s.f.* Femme-agent (de police), *pl.* femmes-agents.

policlinic [,poli'klinik], *s.* Policlinique *f.*

policy[1] ['pɔlisi], *s.* 1. Politique *f*; ligne *f* de conduite. **Foreign p.,** politique extérieure. **Our p. is to satisfy our customers,** notre seul but, notre objectif, est de satisfaire nos clients. *Jur:* **Public p.,** l'intérêt public. **Contrary to public p.,** contraire à l'ordre public. 2. Diplomatie *f.* **To deem it p. to . . .,** considérer comme de bonne politique, juger prudent, de. . . . 3. *Scot:* Domaine *m* (d'un château).

policy[2], *s.* 1. Police *f* (d'assurance(s)). **Floating p.,** police flottante; police d'abonnement. **To take out a p.,** prendre une police. 2. *U.S:* Loterie publique (dont des numéros gagnants sont tirés tous les jours); **P. slip,** billet *m* de loterie. **'policy-holder,** *s.* Titulaire *mf* d'une police d'assurance; assuré, -ée.

polio ['pouliou], *s. F:* Polio *f*, poliomyélite *f.*

poliomyelitis ['pouliou,maii'laitis], *s. Med:* Poliomyélite *f.*

polish[1] ['pɔliʃ], *s.* 1. Poli *m*, brillant *m*, lustre *m* (d'une surface, etc.); brunissure *f* (des métaux). **High p.,** poli brillant. **To lose its p.,** se dépolir. **To take the p. off sth.,** dépolir, ternir, qch. 2. *Com: Ind:* (Coll.) Household polishes, produits d'entretien ménagers. **Floor p.,** encaustique *f*; cire *f* à parquet. **Boot, shoe, p.,** (i) cirage *m*; (ii) crème *f*, pâte, pour chaussures. **Nail p.,** brillant, vernis *m*, pour les ongles. 3. Politesse *f*; belles manières. **To have a certain p.,** avoir l'usage du monde.

polish[2], *v.tr.* 1. Polir (le bois, le fer); brunir (l'or, l'argent); cirer (des chaussures); astiquer (le cuir); lisser (une pierre); encaustiquer, faire reluire (les meubles); cirer (le parquet). 2. Polir, civiliser (qn). **polish off,** *v.tr. F:* (i) Terminer vite, expédier, *F:* bâcler (un travail); (ii) vider, *F:* siffler (un verre); ne rien laisser (d'un plat); (iii) régler le compte de, en finir avec (qn). **polish up,** *v.tr.* 1. Faire reluire (qch.); astiquer, brunir (des objets en métal). 2. **To p. up one's French,** dérouiller son français. **To p. up a poem,** etc., polir un poème, etc. **To p. up one's style,** châtier son style. **polished,** *a.* 1. Poli, brillant. **P. oak,** chêne ciré. 2. **P. manners,** manières polies, distinguées. 3. **P. style,** style châtié, raffiné. **polishing,** *s.* Polissage *m*; cirage *m*; astiquage *m.* **P. cloth,** chiffon *m* à cirer. **P. brush,** brosse *f* à reluire.

Polish[3] ['pouliʃ], *a. Geog:* Polonais.

polisher ['pɔliʃər], s. 1. (Pers.) Polisseur, -euse; cireur, -euse (de parquet, de chaussures); astiqueur m (de cuivres). 2. Tls: Polissoir m; (for gold, silver) brunissoir m. Dom.Ec: Electric (floor-, furniture-) p., cireuse f.

polite [pə'lait], a. 1. P. society, (i) le beau monde; (ii) les gens instruits, cultivés. 2. Poli, courtois, civil, honnête (to s.o., envers, avec, qn). -ly, adv. Poliment; avec politesse.

politeness [pə'laitnis], s. Politesse f, courtoisie f, civilité f.

politic ['pɔlitik], a. 1. (Of pers., conduct) (a) Politique, avisé. (b) Adroit, habile. (c) Pej: Rusé, astucieux, -euse. 2. Lit: The body p., l'État.

political [pə'litik(ə)l], a. Politique. 1. Qui se rapporte au gouvernement de l'État. P. parties, partis politiques. P. manœuvring, p. jobbery, politicailleries fpl. 2. Qui se rapporte aux peuples. P. map, carte f politique. -ally, adv. Politiquement.

politician [ˌpɔli'tiʃ(ə)n], s. Homme politique.

politics ['pɔlitiks], s.pl. La politique. To talk p., parler politique. To study p., étudier la politique. To go into p., se lancer dans la politique. F: To dabble in p., politiquer. U.S: Peanut p., politicailleries fpl. Such a scheme is not practical p., un tel projet n'est pas d'ordre pratique. What are his p.? quelles sont ses opinions politiques ?

polity ['pɔliti], s. 1. Administration f politique. 2. (a) Constitution f politique; régime m. (b) État m.

polka ['pɔlkə], s. Polka f. 'polka-dot, s. Tex: Pois m. Blue p.-d. tie, cravate bleue à pois.

poll¹ [poul], s. 1. A: Dial: (a) Tête f (d'une personne, d'un animal). (b) Sommet m, haut m, de la tête; nuque f (d'un cheval). 2. (i) Votation f par tête; (ii) vote m (par bulletins); scrutin m. To go to the polls, aller aux urnes f. To declare the p., déclarer, proclamer, le résultat du scrutin. To head the p., venir en tête de liste. 3. Sondage m (d'opinion publique). Gallup p., (sondage m) Gallup m. 'poll-tax, s. Hist: Capitation f.

poll² [poul]. I. v.tr 1. (a) A: Tondre (qn). (b) = POLLARD². (c) Écorner, décorner (un taureau). 2. (a) (Of polling-clerk) Faire voter (qn); recueillir le bulletin de vote de (qn). (b) (Of candidate) Réunir (tant de voix). II. poll, v.i. Voter (à une élection). polled, a. (Of ox, etc.) 1. Sans cornes. 2. Décorné. polling, s. Vote m; élections fpl. 'polling-booth, s. Isoloir m. 'polling-station, s. Centre m de vote.

pollack ['pɔlək], s. Ich: Merlan m jaune, lieu m. Green-p., colin m.

pollard¹ ['pɔləd], s. (a) Arb: Têtard m; arbre étêté. (b) Animal m sans cornes.

pollard², v.tr. Arb: Étêter, écimer (un arbre).

pollen ['pɔlin], s. Bot: Pollen m.

pollinate ['pɔlineit], v.tr. Bot: Polliniser.

pollin(iz)ation [ˌpɔli'neiʃ(ə)n, ˌpɔlinai'zeiʃ(ə)n], s. Bot: Pollinisation f, fécondation f.

pollster ['poulstər], s. U.S: Enquêteur m, organisateur m d'un sondage (d'opinion publique).

pollute [pə'lu:t], v.tr. 1. Polluer, souiller, rendre impur, corrompre. 2. Profaner, violer (un lieu saint).

polluter [pə'lu:tər], s. 1. Corrupteur, -trice. 2. Profanateur, -trice (d'un temple).

pollution [pə'lu:ʃ(ə)n], s. 1. Pollution f, souillure f. 2. Profanation f.

polo ['poulou], s. 1. Sp: Polo m. P. stick, mallet, maillet m. S.a. WATER-POLO. 2. Cost: P. neck, col roulé.

polonaise [pɔlə'neiz], s. Mus: Polonaise f.

polonium [pə'louniəm], s. Ch: Polonium m.

polony [pə'louni], s. P. (sausage), (petit) saucisson; cervelas m (sans ail).

poltergeist ['pɔltəgaist], s. Esprit frappeur.

polyandrous [ˌpɔli'ændrəs], a. Anthr: Bot: Polyandre.

polyandry ['pɔliændri], s. Anthr: Polyandrie f.

polyanthus [ˌpɔli'ænθəs], s. 1. Primevère f des jardins. 2. attrib. (Fleur, narcisse) à bouquets.

polychromatic [ˌpɔlikro'mætik], **polychrome** ['pɔlikroum], a. Polychrome.

polychromy ['pɔlikroumi], s. Polichromie f.

polyclinic [ˌpɔli'klinik], s. Polyclinique f.

polyester [ˌpɔli'estər], s. Ch: Ind: Polyester m.

polygamist [pə'ligəmist], s. Polygame m.

polygamous [pə'ligəməs], a. Polygame.

polygamy [pə'ligəmi], s. Polygamie f.

polyglot ['pɔliglɔt], a. & s. Polyglotte (mf).

polygon ['pɔligən], s. Polygone m.

polygonal [pə'ligənl], a. Polygonal, -aux.

polygonum [pə'ligənəm], s. Bot: Renouée f.

polyhedral ['pɔli'hi:dr(ə)l], **polyhedric** ['pɔli'hi:drik], a. Polyédrique, polyèdre.

polyhedron ['pɔli'hi:dr(ə)n], s. Polyèdre m.

polymer ['pɔlimər], s. Ch: Polymère m.

polymeric [ˌpɔli'merik], a. Ch: Polymère.

polymerization [pɔˌliməraiˈzeiʃ(ə)n], s. Ch: Polymérisation f.

polymorphic [ˌpɔli'mɔ:fik], **polymorphous** [ˌpɔli'mɔ:fəs], a. Polymorphe.

polymorphism [ˌpɔli'mɔ:fizm], s. Polymorphisme m, polymorphie f.

Polynesia [ˌpɔli'ni:ziə]. Pr.n. La Polynésie.

Polynesian [ˌpɔli'ni:ziən], a. & s. Polynésien, -ienne.

polynomial [ˌpɔli'noumiəl], s. Alg: Polynôme m.

polyp ['pɔlip], s. Coel: Med: Polype m.

polypary ['pɔlipəri], s. Coel: Polypier m.

polypetalous [ˌpɔli'petələs], a. Bot: Polypétale.

polyphase ['pɔlifeiz], a. El.E: 1. P. current, courant polyphasé. 2. (Alternateur, etc.) à courant polyphasé.

polyphony [pə'lifəni], s. Mus: Ling: Polyphonie f.

polypod ['pɔlipəd], a. & s. Z: Polypode (m); à pattes multiples.

polypoid ['pɔlipɔid], a. Z: Med: Polypoïde.

polypous ['pɔlipəs], a. Med: Polypeux, -euse.

polypus ['pɔlipəs], s. Med: Polype m.

polysyllabic ['pɔlisi'læbik], a. Polysyllabe, polysyllabique.

polysyllable ['pɔli,siləbl], s. Polysyllabe m.

polytechnic [ˌpɔli'teknik], a. & s. Polytechnique; (école) d'enseignement technique.

polytheism ['pɔliθi:izm], s. Polythéisme m.

polytheist ['pɔliθi:ist], a. & s. Polythéiste m.

polythene ['pɔliθi:n], s. Ch: Ind: Polyéthylène m polythène m.

polyvalence [ˌpɔli'veiləns], **polyvalency** [ˌpɔli'veiлənsi], s. Ch: Polyvalence f.

polyvalent [pə'livələnt], a. Ch: Polyvalent.

polyvinyl [pɔli'vinil], s. Polyvinyle m.

pomade [pə'mɑ:d], **pomatum** [pə'meitəm], s. Toil: Pommade f.

pomegranate ['pɔm(i)grænit], s. Bot: 1. Grenade f. 2. P.(-tree), grenadier m.

Pomerania [pɔmə'reiniə], Pr.n. Geog: La Poméranie.

Pomeranian [pɔmə'reiniən], a. & s. (a) Poméranien, -ienne. (b) P. (dog), loulou m de Poméranie.

pommel¹ ['pʌml], s. 1. Pommeau m (d'épée). 2. Harn: Arçon m de devant; pommeau (de selle).

pommel², v.tr. (pommelled), Bourrer (qn) de coups.

pommie, pommy ['pɔmi], s. Austr: P: Immigrant anglais.

pomp [pɔmp], s. Pompe f, éclat m, faste m, splendeur f, appareil m, apparat m. To like p., aimer le cérémonial. P. and circumstance, grand apparat.

Pompeii [pɔm'peii:]. Pr.n. A.Geog: Pompéi.

pom-pom ['pɔmpɔm], s. Mil: O: Canon-revolver m, canon-mitrailleuse m (système Maxim).

pompom ['pɔmpɔm], s. 1. Cost: etc: Pompon m. 2. Hort: (a) Rose f pompon. (b) Chrysanthème, dahlia, nain.

pomposity [pɔm'pɔsiti], s. Emphase f; suffisance f.

pompous ['pɔmpəs], a. 1. O: Pompeux, -euse, fastueux, -euse. 2. (a) A p. man, un homme suffisant, qui fait l'important. (b) P. style, style emphatique, ampoulé. -ly, adv. Avec suffisance; d'un style ampoulé.

pompousness ['pɔmpəsnis], s. Suffisance f.

poncho ['pɔn(t)ʃou], s. Cost: Poncho m.

pond [pɔnd], s. Étang m; bassin m, pièce f d'eau (de parc); mare f, abreuvoir m (de village); vivier m, réservoir m (pour le poisson); réservoir (de moulin). P. life, vie f des eaux stagnantes.

ponder ['pɔndər]. 1. v.tr. Réfléchir sur (une question); considérer, peser (un avis); ruminer (une idée). 2. v.i. Méditer. To p. on, over, sth., réfléchir à, méditer sur, qch. pondering, s. Méditation f.

ponderability [ˌpɔnd(ə)rə'biliti], s. Pondérabilité f.

ponderable ['pɔnd(ə)rəbl], a. Pondérable; (gaz) pesant.

ponderous ['pɔnd(ə)rəs], *a.* **1.** Massif, -ive, lourd, pesant. **2.** (Style) lourd, pesant, ampoulé. **-ly,** *adv.* (Écrire, etc.) avec lourdeur.

Pondicherry ['pɔndi'tʃeri]. *Pr.n. Geog:* Pondichéry.

pondweed ['pɔndwi:d], *s. Bot:* Potamot *m.*

pong[1] [pɔŋ], *v.i. P:* Puer, schlinguer.

pong[2], *s. P:* Mauvaise odeur. **What a p.!** comme ça pue! comme ça schlingue!

pongee [pɔn'dʒi:], *s. Tex:* Pongée *m.*

pontiff ['pɔntif], *s.* Pontife *m. Ecc:* Évêque *m,* prélat *m. Esp.* **The sovereign p.,** le souverain pontife, le pape.

pontifical [pɔn'tifik(ə)l]. **1.** *a.* Pontifical, -aux; épiscopal, -aux. *Pej:* **P. airs,** airs de pontife. **2.** *s.* Pontifical *m* (livre du rituel des évêques). **3.** *s.pl.* **Pontificals,** vêtements sacerdotaux.

pontificate[1] [pɔn'tifikit], *s.* Pontificat *m.*

pontificate[2] [pɔn'tifikeit], *v.i.* (*a*) Pontifier; célébrer l'office en qualité de pontife ou d'évêque. (*b*) *Pej:* Faire l'important; parler avec emphase.

Pontius Pilate ['pɔnʃəs'pailət]. *Pr.n.m. B.Hist:* Ponce Pilate.

pontoon[1] [pɔn'tu:n], *s.* **1.** Ponton *m,* bac *m.* **2.** *Mil.E:* Ponton (de pont de bateaux). **pon'toon-'bridge,** *s.* Pont *m* de bateaux.

pontoon[2], *s. Cards:* Vingt et un.

pony ['pouni], *s.* **1.** Poney *m. Haird:* **P. tail,** queue *f* de cheval. **2.** *P: O:* Vingt-cinq livres sterling. **3.** Petit verre. **4.** *U.S: Sch: F:* Traduction *f* (d'auteur) (employée pour étudier une langue étrangère). **'pony-carriage,** *s. Veh:* Attelage *m* à poney. **'pony-skin,** *s. Com:* (Fourrure *f*) poulain *m.*

pooch [pu:tʃ], *s. F:* Chien *m,* toutou *m.*

poodle ['pu:dl], *s.* Caniche *mf.*

pooh [pu:], *int.* Bah! peuh! **P., is that all!** la belle affaire!

pooh-pooh ['pu:'pu:], *v.tr.* Traiter légèrement, ridiculiser (une idée, etc.); se moquer, faire peu de cas (d'un avertissement); repousser (un conseil) avec mépris.

pool[1] [pu:l], *s.* **1.** (*a*) (*Of running water*) Fontaine *f.* (*b*) (*Stagnant*) Mare *f.* (*c*) (*For swimming*) Piscine *f.* (*d*) Flaque *f* (d'eau); mare (de sang). **2.** (*a*) (*In river*) Trou *m* d'eau. (*b*) **The P.** (of London), le port de Londres en aval de London Bridge.

pool[2], *s.* **1.** (*a*) *Games:* Poule *f,* cagnotte *f.* (*b*) *Bill: Fenc:* Poule. (*c*) **Football p.,** concours *m* de pronostics sportifs. **2.** *Com:* (*a*) Fonds communs; masse commune; *Pol.Ec:* pool *m.* (*b*) *Com:* Syndicat *m* de placement (de marchandises); syndicat de répartition des commandes. (*c*) **Typing p.,** équipe *f* de dactylos.

pool[3], *v.tr.* (*a*) Mettre en commun (des capitaux, etc.). (*b*) *Com:* Mettre en syndicat (les commandes); *Rail:* répartir l'exploitation (des lignes, etc.).

poop[1] [pu:p], *s. Nau:* **1.** Poupe *f.* **2. P.** (**-deck**), (pont *m*) dunette *f.* **'poop-rail,** *s. Nau:* Rambarde *f,* garde-fou *m, pl.* garde-fous.

poop[2], *v.tr. Nau:* **1.** (*Of wave*) **To p. a ship,** balayer la poupe d'un navire. **To be pooped,** embarquer une vague par l'arrière. **2.** (*Of ship*) Recevoir, embarquer, (un paquet de mer) par l'arrière.

poor [puər], *a.* Pauvre. **1.** Besogneux, -euse, malheureux, -euse; *Adm:* indigent. **A p. man,** un pauvre. **The poorer classes,** les classes pauvres. **As p. as a church-mouse, as Job,** gueux comme un rat d'église, pauvre comme Job. (*b*) *s.pl.* **The p.,** les pauvres *m,* les malheureux, les indigents. **2.** De piètre qualité; médiocre. (*a*) **P. soil,** sol maigre, peu fertile. **P. cattle,** bétail maigre. **P. wine,** *F:* vin guinguet; piquette *f.* **P. blood,** sang vicié. (*b*) **P. excuse,** piètre excuse. **He sells p. stuff,** il vend de la camelote. **P. quality,** basse qualité; qualité inférieure. **P. health,** santé débile. **My p. memory,** mon peu de mémoire. **To have a p. opinion of s.o.,** avoir une pauvre, piètre, triste, opinion de qn. **To cut a p. figure,** faire piètre figure. **He is a p. driver,** il n'est pas fameux comme conducteur. **To be p. at mathematics,** être faible en mathématiques. **My Italian is very p.,** je ne suis pas très fort(e) en italien. **3. P. creature!** **p. thing!** pauvre petit! pauvre petite! **P. fellow!** le pauvre homme! le pauvre garçon! *Iron:* **P. you!** vous voilà bien malade! **-ly. 1.** *adv.* Pauvrement, médiocrement, piètrement, maigrement.

S.a. OFF I. **3. 2.** *pred.a.* **To be p.,** être souffrant, indisposé. **He is looking very p.,** il a bien mauvaise mine, *F:* il a l'air patraque. **'poor-box,** *s. Ecc:* Tronc *m* (pour les pauvres). **'Poor Law,** *s. A: O:* Lois *fpl* sur l'assistance publique. **P. L. administration,** l'assistance publique. **'poor-'spirited,** *a.* Pusillanime.

poorhouse ['puəhaus], *s. A:* Hospice *m;* asile *m* des pauvres.

poorness ['puənis], *s.* **1.** Pauvreté *f,* insuffisance *f.* **2.** Infériorité *f;* peu *m* de valeur.

pop[1] [pɔp]. **1.** *int.* Crac! pan! **To go p.,** éclater, crever. **2.** *s.* (*a*) Bruit sec, soudain (de bouchon qui saute, etc.). (*b*) Boisson pétillante, gazeuse, mousseuse. (*c*) *P:* (*Of jewelry, etc.*) **To be in p.,** être au clou, chez ma tante. **'pop-eyed,** *a. F:* (*a*) Aux yeux protubérants, saillants. (*b*) Aux yeux en boules de loto. **'pop-gun,** *s. Toys:* Pistolet *m* d'enfant, pétoire *f;* pistolet *m* à bouchon.

pop[2], *v.* (**popped**) **1.** *v.i.* Faire entendre une petite explosion; éclater, péter; (*of cork*) sauter, péter; (*of toy balloon*) crever. **2.** *v.tr.* (*a*) Crever (un ballon); faire sauter (un bouchon). *U.S:* **To p. corn,** faire éclater le maïs (devant le feu). (*b*) *P:* **To p. one's watch,** mettre sa montre au clou, chez ma tante. **3.** (*In familiar speech*) (*a*) (= '*come*' or '*go*') pop over, out, round, **to the grocer's,** faire un saut jusque chez l'épicier. (*b*) (= '*put*') **To p. sth. behind a screen,** fourrer qch. derrière un écran. **To p. one's head out of the window,** sortir (tout à coup) sa tête par la fenêtre. *F:* **To p. the question,** faire sa déclaration; faire la demande en mariage. **pop in,** *v.i. F:* Entrer à l'improviste; entrer en passant. **pop off,** *v.i.* (*a*) *F:* Filer, déguerpir. (*b*) *P:* Mourir subitement. (*c*) *F:* **To p. o. a gun,** lâcher un coup de fusil. **pop out,** *v.i. F:* Sortir. **I saw him p. o. of the house,** je l'ai vu sortir. **His eyes were popping out of his head,** les yeux lui sortaient de la tête. **pop up,** *v.i. F:* Apparaître, surgir. (*Of swimmer, etc.*) **To p. up out of the water,** émerger brusquement à la surface de l'eau.

pop[3], *s. Esp. U.S: F:* Papa *m.*

pop[4], *a. F:* (*Abbr. for '*popular*'*) Populaire. **P. art,** le pop'art. **P. music,** yé-yé *m.* **P. singer,** chanteur, -euse, de yé-yé. **P. song,** chanson *f* en vogue.

popcorn ['pɔpkɔ:n], *s.* Maïs éclaté.

pope[1] [poup], *s.* Pape *m;* le Saint-Père. **P. Joan,** (i) la papesse Jeanne; (ii) *Cards:* le nain jaune.

pope[2], *s. Ecc:* Pope *m* (de l'Église orthodoxe).

popery ['poupəri], *s. Pej:* Papisme *m.*

popinjay ['pɔpindʒei], *s. A:* **1.** Perroquet *m,* papegai *m.* **2.** Fat *m,* freluquet *m.*

popish ['poupiʃ], *a. Pej:* Papiste.

poplar ['pɔplər], *s. Bot:* Peuplier *m.* **White p., silver p.,** peuplier blanc; ypréau *m.* **Lombardy p.,** peuplier d'Italie.

poplin ['pɔplin], *s. Tex:* Popeline *f.*

poppet ['pɔpit], *s.* **1.** *F:* **My p.,** mon chéri; ma chérie. **2.** *Mec.E:* **P.(-head),** poupée *f* (de tour). **'poppet-valve,** *s. I.C.E:* Soupape soulevante, à déclic; clapet *m;* (soupape en) champignon *m.*

poppy ['pɔpi], *s.* Pavot *m.* **Corn p., field poppy,** coquelicot *m.* **Opium p.,** pavot somnifère; œillette *f.* **P.(-seed) oil,** huile *f* d'œillette. **'poppy-head,** *s.* **1.** Tête *f* de pavot. **2.** *Ecc.Arch:* Finial *m* (de stalle).

poppycock ['pɔpikɔk], *s. F:* Bêtises *fpl.;* fadaises *fpl.* **That's all p.,** *P:* tout ça, c'est de la foutaise.

populace ['pɔpjuləs], *s.* **The p.,** (i) le peuple, la foule; (ii) *Pej:* la populace, le bas peuple.

popular ['pɔpjulər], *a.* Populaire. (*a*) Du peuple. **P. insurrection,** insurrection du peuple; insurrection populaire. *Pol:* **P. Front,** front *m* populaire, coalition de gauche. (*b*) (Prédicateur, opéra) à la mode, en vogue; (prédicateur) très couru. **P. singer,** chanteur, -euse, de charme. (*c*) Compréhensible pour tout le monde. **P. book on rockets,** ouvrage de vulgarisation sur les fusées. (*d*) **P. error,** erreur courante. **-ly,** *adv.* **It is p. believed that . . .,** les gens croient que. . .

popularity [pɔpju'læriti], *s.* Popularité *f.*

popularization [pɔpjulərai'zeiʃ(ə)n], *s.* Popularisation *f;* vulgarisation *f* (d'une science, etc.).

popularize ['pɔpjulǝraiz], *v.tr.* Populariser, vulgariser (des connaissances, etc.).

populate ['pɔpjuleit], *v.tr.* Peupler. **Thickly, densely, populated,** très peuplé. **Sparsely populated areas,** des régions à faible peuplement *m.*

population [ˌpɔpjuˈleiʃ(ǝ)n], *s.* Population *f.* **Fall in p.,** décroissance *f* de la population; dépopulation *f.* **Excess p.,** surpopulation *f. Adm:* **Increase, decrease in p.,** accroissement *m,* décroissement *m,* démographique.

populous ['pɔpjulǝs], *a.* Populeux, -euse; très peuplé.

populousness ['pɔpjulǝsnis], *s.* Densité *f* de population (d'une région).

porcelain ['pɔːslin], *s.* Porcelaine *f.*

porch [pɔːtʃ], *s.* (*a*) Porche *m,* portique *m.* (*b*) Marquise *f* (d'hôtel, etc.). (*c*) **P. roof,** auvent *m.* (*d*) *U.S:* Véranda *f, Fr.C:* galerie *f.*

porcine ['pɔːsain], *a.* De porc; (race) porcine.

porcupine ['pɔːkjupain], *s.* **1.** *Z:* Porc-épic *m, pl.* porcs-épics. **2. P. fish,** hérisson *m* de mer.

pore[1] ['pɔːr], *s. Anat: Bot:* Pore *m.*

pore[2], *v.i.* **To p. over a book,** s'absorber dans la lecture, dans l'étude, d'un livre; être piongé dans un livre. **To p. over a subject,** méditer longuement un sujet.

pork [pɔːk], *s. Cu:* (Viande *f* de) porc *m.* **Salt p.,** petit salé. **P. chop,** côtelette *f,* côte *f,* de porc. **P. sausage** (*for frying*), saucisse *f;* (*cooked or smoked*) saucisson *m.* **pork-barrel,** *s.* **1.** Baril *m* de porc salé, saloir *m.* **2.** *U.S. F:* L'assiette *f* au beurre. **'pork-butcher,** *s.* Charcutier *m.* **'pork-'pie,** *s.* Pâté *m* de porc (en croûte). **'pork-rind,** *s.* Couenne *f.*

porker ['pɔːkǝr], *s.* Porc gras (destiné à la boucherie).

porkling ['pɔːkliŋ], *s.* Goret *m,* porcelet *m,* cochonnet *m.*

porky ['pɔːki], *a.* **1.** Qui tient du porc. **2.** *F:* Gras, obèse.

pornographer [pɔːˈnɔgrǝfǝr], *s.* Pornographe *m.*

pornographic [pɔːnǝˈgræfik], *a.* Pornographique.

pornography [pɔːˈnɔgrǝfi], *s.* Pornographie *f.*

porosity [pɔːˈrɔsiti], *s.* Porosité *f.*

porous ['pɔːrǝs], *a.* Poreux, -euse; perméable.

porphyry ['pɔːfiri], *s.* Porphyre *m.*

porpoise ['pɔːpǝs], *s. Z:* Marsouin *m.*

porridge ['pɔridʒ], *s.* Bouillie *f* d'avoine; porridge *m.*

port[1] [pɔːt], *s.* **1.** Port *m.* **River p.,** port fluvial. **Outer p.,** avant-port *m.* **Naval p.,** port militaire; port de guerre. **Commercial p., trading p.,** port marchand; port de commerce. **Free p.,** port franc. *Navy:* **Home p.,** port d'attache. **The home ports,** les ports de la métropole. **P. of registry,** port d'armement. **P. charges,** droits *m* de port. **To come into p.,** entrer au port. **To get safe into p., to reach p. safely,** arriver à bon port. **To put into p.,** relâcher; *Nau:* escaler, faire escale *f.* **To leave p.,** quitter le port. **Any p. in a storm,** nécessité n'a pas de loi. *Adj. use.* **P. installations,** installations *f* portuaires. *S.a.* CALL[1] 3. **port-'admiral,** *s.* = préfet *m* maritime.

port[2], *s.* **1.** *Nau:* Sabord *m.* **P. lid,** mantelet *m* de sabord. **Coaling p.,** sabord à charbon. **2.** *Mch:* Orifice *m,* lumière *f,* fenêtre *f* (de cylindre). **Inlet p.,** admission *f;* lumière d'admission.

port[3], *s. Nau:* Bâbord *m.* **The p. side,** le côté de bâbord. **On the p. side, to p.,** à bâbord. **Land to p.!** (la) terre par bâbord! **P. tack,** bâbord amures. **Hard a-p.!** à gauche toute!

port[4]. *Nau:* **1.** *v.tr.* **To p. the helm,** mettre la barre à bâbord. **2.** *v.i.* (*Of ship*) Venir sur bâbord.

port[5], *s.* Vin *m* de Porto; porto *m.*

portable ['pɔːtǝbl], *a.* Portatif, -ive; transportable; mobile. **A p. radio, s. a p.,** une radio portative, un portatif. *Nau:* **P. winch,** cabestan volant.

portage ['pɔːtidʒ], *s.* **1.** Transport *m,* port *m* (de marchandises). **2.** Frais *mpl* de port, de transport. **3.** Portage *m* (de bateaux entre deux cours d'eau, etc.)

portal[1] ['pɔːtl], *s.* (*a*) Portail *m* (de cathédrale). (*b*) Portique *m.*

portal[2], *a. Anat:* **P. vein,** veine *f* porte.

portcullis [pɔːtˈkʌlis], *s. A: Fort:* Herse *f.*

portend [pɔːˈtend], *v.tr.* Présager, augurer, annoncer, faire pressentir (qch.).

portent ['pɔːtent], *s.* **1.** Présage *m* de malheur. **2.** Prodige *m.*

portentous [pɔːˈtentǝs], *a.* **1.** De mauvais présage, de mauvais augure; sinistre. **2.** Monstrueux, -euse, prodigieux, -euse.

porter[1] ['pɔːtǝr], *s.* Portier *m,* concierge *m;* tourier *m* (d'un monastère). **P.'s lodge,** (i) loge *f* de concierge; (ii) maisonnette *f,* pavillon *m,* du portier.

porter[2], *s.* **1.** Portefaix *m;* chasseur *m,* garçon *m* (d'hôtel); garçon (de magasin); (*at railway station*) porteur *m.* **Market p.** = fort *m* de la Halle. **2.** Bière brune (anglaise); porter *m.*

porterage ['pɔːtǝridʒ], *s.* **1.** Transport *m,* manutention *f,* factage *m* (de marchandises, de colis). **2.** Prix *m* de transport; factage.

porterhouse ['pɔːtǝhaus], *s. A:* Taverne *f. Cu:* **P. steak,** filet *m* de bœuf grillé.

portfolio [pɔːtˈfouljou], *s.* **1.** (*a*) Serviette *f* (pour documents, etc.). (*b*) Chemise *f* de carton; carton *m* (à dessins). (*c*) **Minister's p.,** portefeuille *m* de ministre. **Minister without p.,** ministre sans portefeuille. (*d*) *Com:* Portefeuille d'assurances. **Securities in p.,** valeurs en portefeuille.

porthole [pɔːthoul], *s. Nau:* Hublot *m.*

portico, *pl.* -o(e)s ['pɔːtikou, -ouz], *s. Arch:* Portique *m.*

portion[1] ['pɔːʃ(ǝ)n], *s.* **1.** (*a*) Partie *f;* part *f* (dans un partage); lot *m* (de terre). **A p. of my money,** une partie de mon argent. (*b*) Portion *f,* ration *f* (de viande); quartier *m* (de gâteau). (*c*) *Jur:* **P. (of inheritance),** part d'héritage. (*d*) (**Marriage**) **p.,** dot *f.* (*e*) *Rail:* Rame *f,* tranche *f* (de wagons). **2.** Destinée *f,* destin *m,* sort *m.*

portion[2], *v.tr.* **1. To p. (out),** partager (un bien, etc.); répartir (une somme); distribuer (les parts). **2.** *O:* Doter (sa fille).

Portland ['pɔːtlǝnd]. *Pr.n. Geog:* Portland *m.* **P. cement,** (ciment *m* de) Portland. **P. stone,** calcaire portlandien.

portliness ['pɔːtlinis], *s.* **1.** *O:* Prestance *f,* port majestueux; air imposant. **2.** Corpulence *f,* embonpoint *m.*

portly ['pɔːtli], *a.* **1.** Majestueux, -euse; de noble prestance. **P. matron,** matrone imposante. **2.** Corpulent, ventru.

portmanteau [pɔːtˈmæntou], *s.* (*a*) *O:* Valise *f.* (*b*) **P. word,** mot formé de deux mots télescopés (*p.ex.* **smog** = smoke + fog).

portrait ['pɔːtrit], *s.* Portrait *m.* **Full-length, half-length, p.,** portrait en pied, en buste. **To sit for one's p.,** se faire faire son portrait. **'portrait-painter,** *s.* Portraitiste *m;* peintre *m* de portraits.

portraiture ['pɔːtritʃǝr], *s.* **1.** Portrait *m.* **2.** L'art du portrait. **3.** *Lit:* Description *f* (d'une société, etc.).

portray [pɔːˈtrei], *v.tr.* **1.** Peindre (qn); faire le portrait de (qn). **2.** Dépeindre, décrire (une scène, etc.). **To p. character,** peindre les caractères.

portrayal [pɔːˈtreiǝl], *s.* Peinture *f,* représentation *f,* description *f* (d'une scène).

portrayer [pɔːˈtreiǝr], *s. Lit:* Peintre *m* (des événements, etc.).

portress ['pɔːtris], *s.f.* Portière, tourière (de couvent).

Portugal ['pɔːtjug(ǝ)l]. *Pr.n.* Le Portugal.

Portuguese [ˌpɔːtjuˈgiːz]. **1.** *a. & s. inv.* Portugais, -aise. *Coel:* **P. man-of-war,** physalie *f.* **2.** *s. Ling:* Le portugais.

pose[1] [pouz], *s.* **1.** Pose *f,* attitude *f* (du corps). **2.** Pose, affectation *f.*

pose[2]. **I.** *v.tr.* **1.** Poser (une question). **2.** *Art:* Faire prendre une pose à (qn); poser (un modèle). **II.** **pose,** *v.i.* **1.** (*a*) Poser (comme modèle). (*b*) Poser; se donner des airs (affectés, prétentieux). **2. To p. as a Frenchman,** se faire passer pour Français. **I don't p. as a scholar,** je ne prétends pas être un savant. **posing,** *s.* Pose *f,* affectation *f.*

poser ['pouzǝr], *s.* Question embarrassante; *F:* colle *f.* **To give s.o. a p.,** poser une colle à qn.

posh[1] [pɔʃ], *a.* **P:** Chic, bath, chouette. **It looks p.,** ça fait riche.

posh[2], *v.tr.* **P: To p. oneself up,** se faire beau, belle. **All poshed up,** sur son trente et un.

position[1] [pǝˈziʃ(ǝ)n], *s.* **1.** (*a*) Posture *f,* position *f,* attitude *f* (du corps, etc.). **To bring a gun to the firing p.,** mettre une pièce en batterie. (*b*) Attitude, disposition *f* (de l'esprit). **To take up a p. on a question,**

prendre position sur une question. 2. Position. (a) Place f; situation f (d'un objet, d'une ville). **Vertical p.,** station verticale. **In p.,** en place. **Out of p.,** hors de sa place; déplacé, dérangé. **To place sth. in p.,** mettre qch. en place. Navy: **To take up p. ahead, astern,** prendre poste en tête, derrière. (b) Nau: **Ship's p.,** lieu m du navire. **To determine the ship's p., to fix one's p.,** faire le point. (c) **To storm the enemy's positions,** prendre d'assaut les positions de l'ennemi. **To manœuvre for p.,** manœuvrer pour s'assurer l'avantage. 3. (a) État m, condition f, situation. **Put yourself in my p.,** mettez-vous à ma place. **To be in a p. to do sth.,** être en état, à même, de faire qch. **You are in a better p. to judge,** vous êtes mieux placé que moi pour en juger. **Cash p.,** situation de (la) caisse. **Customer's p. at the bank,** situation en banque d'un client. (b) Rang social. **In a high p.,** haut placé; dans une haute situation. **To keep up one's p.,** tenir son rang. **Young man of good social p.,** fils de famille. (c) Sch: **P. in class,** place f dans la classe; rang, classement m. 4. Emploi m, place, situation (dans un bureau, etc.). **To occupy, hold, a p.,** remplir une fonction. **P. of trust,** poste m de confiance. 5. Post: etc: Guichet m. **'P. closed,' "guichet fermé." po'sition-light,** s. Nau: Feu m de position.

position², v.tr. Déterminer la position de (qch.); situer (un lieu sur la carte). **positioning,** s. Mise f en place. T.V: **P. (of aerial),** orientation f (de l'antenne).

positive ['pozitiv], a. 1. (a) Positif, -ive, affirmatif, -ive. **P. order,** ordre formel. **P. proof,** preuve positive, manifeste. (b) **A p. miracle,** un pur, vrai miracle. **It's a p. fact!** c'est un fait authentique, F: c'est positif! 2. (a) Convaincu, assuré, sûr, certain (of, de). **He is p. of his facts,** il est sûr de ses faits. **I am quite p. on that point,** là-dessus je n'ai aucun doute. (b) **P. tone of voice,** ton absolu, tranchant. **P. person,** personne qui tranche sur tout. (c) **P. turn of mind,** esprit positif. **P. philosophy,** philosophie positive. 3. (a) Mth: **P. quantity,** quantité positive. (b) El: **P. pole,** pôle positif. (c) Mec.E: **P. drive,** commande positive; connexion directe. (d) Opt: **P. optical system,** système optique convergent, positif. 4. a. & s. Phot: Positif (m). 5. Gram: **P. (degree),** (degré) positif (m). **-ly,** adv. 1. Positivement, affirmativement. 2. (a) Assurément, certainement, sûrement. **I can't speak p.,** je ne puis rien affirmer. (b) D'un ton tranchant, absolu. 3. Mec.E: **P. connected,** solidarisé; à liaison rigide.

positiveness ['pozitivnis], s. 1. Certitude f, assurance f. 2. Ton décisif, tranchant.

positivism ['pozitivizm], s. Phil: Positivisme m.

positivist ['pozitivist], a. & s. Phil: Positiviste (mf).

positivity [pozi'tiviti], s. El: Phil: Positivité f.

positron ['pozitron], s. Atom.Ph: Positon m.

posology [po'sɔlədʒi], s. Med: etc: Posologie f.

posse ['posi], s. (a) Détachement m (d'agents de police). (b) Troupe f, bande f (de personnes).

possess [pə'zes], v.tr. 1. (a) Posséder (un bien); être possesseur, être en possession, de (qch.). **All I p.,** tout mon avoir. (b) Avoir, posséder (une qualité, une faculté). **To be possessed of a quality,** être doué d'une qualité. 2. (a) **To p. oneself of sth.,** se rendre maître, s'emparer, de qch. (b) **To be possessed of a property,** posséder un bien. 3. **To p. oneself,** se posséder, se contenir. **To p. one's soul in patience,** se munir de patience. 4. (Of evil spirit) Posséder (qn). **To be possessed by the devil,** être possédé du démon. **Possessed by fear,** sous le coup le l'effroi. **Possessed with doubt,** en proie au doute. **What possessed you to do that?** qu'est-ce qui vous a pris de faire cela? **To be possessed with an idea,** être obsédé, coiffé, d'une idée. **To become possessed with an idea,** se pénétrer d'une idée.

possession [pə'ze∫(ə)n], s. 1. Possession f, jouissance f (of, de). **To have sth. in one's p.,** avoir qch. en sa possession. **To come, enter, into p. of an estate,** entrer en possession, en jouissance, d'un bien. **To take, get, p. of sth.,** s'emparer de qch. **To remain in p. of the field,** rester maître du champ de bataille. **To be in p. of a large fortune,** disposer d'une grande

fortune. **In p. of a passport,** nanti d'un passeport. **In full p. of his faculties,** en pleine possession de toutes ses facultés. **Vacant p.,** libre possession (d'un immeuble). **House to let with vacant p.,** maison à louer avec jouissance immédiate. Prov: **P. is nine points of the law,** possession vaut titre. 2. Possession (par le démon). 3. (a) Objet possédé; possession. **A valued p. of my father's,** un objet auquel mon père attachait beaucoup de prix. (b) pl. **Possessions,** (i) possessions, biens, avoir m; (ii) possessions, conquêtes f, colonies f.

possessive [pə'zesiv], a. 1. Qui désire posséder (qn, qch.) entièrement; accapareur, -euse. **A p. mother,** une mère abusive. 2. Gram: **P. adjective,** adjectif possessif. a. & s. **The p. (case),** le (cas) possessif.

possessor [pə'zesər], s. Possesseur m; propriétaire mf.

possibility [posə'biliti], s. 1. Possibilité f. **To consider the p. of an event,** considérer l'éventualité d'un événement. **The p. of severe penalties,** la perspective de peines graves. **There is no p. of my going there,** il n'est pas possible que j'y aille. **If by any p. I am not there,** si par hasard, par impossible, je n'y étais pas. **Within the range, the bounds, of p.,** dans l'ordre des choses possibles; dans la limite du possible. 2. Événement m possible; éventualité f. **To foresee all the possibilities,** envisager tout ce qui peut arriver, toutes les éventualités. **To allow for all possibilities,** parer à toute éventualité. **Life is full of possibilities,** tout est possible dans la vie. **The subject is full of possibilities,** c'est un sujet qui prête. **The plan has possibilities,** ce projet offre des chances de succès; c'est un projet qui promet.

possible ['posəbl]. 1. a. (a) Possible. **It is p.,** c'est possible; cela se peut bien. **It's just p.,** il y a une chance. **It is p. for you to . . .,** il vous est possible de . . . **It is p. that . . .,** il se peut que + sub. **Is it p. that you know nothing about it?** se peut-il que vous n'en sachiez rien? **How is it p. to get out of it?** le moyen d'en sortir? **To give as many details as p.,** donner le plus de détails possible. **To give all p. details,** donner tous les détails possibles. **To do the utmost p. to get sth.,** faire tout son possible pour obtenir qch. **What p. interest can you have in it?** quel diable d'intérêt cela peut-il avoir pour vous? **If p.,** (i) (if feasible) si possible; Lit: si faire se peut; (ii) (if imaginable) si c'est possible. **As far as p.,** dans la mesure du possible; Lit: autant que faire se peut. **As early as p.,** le plus tôt possible. (b) **P. in certain contingencies,** éventuel. **As a p. event,** à titre éventuel. **To insure against p. accidents,** s'assurer contre des accidents éventuels. (c) F: (Of pers.) Tolérable, acceptable. 2. s. (a) (Shooting) **To score a p.,** faire le maximum. (b) Sch: F: Candidat m médiocre (dont le succès est fort douteux). **-ibly,** adv. 1. **I cannot p. do it,** il ne m'est pas possible de le faire. **How can I p. do it?** le moyen de le faire? **It can't p. be!** pas possible! **I'll do all I p. can,** je ferai tout mon possible. **I come as often as I p. can,** je viens aussi souvent que possible. 2. Peut-être (bien). **P. he has heard of you,** peut-être a-t-il entendu parler de vous. **P.! c'est possible;** cela se peut.

possum ['posəm], s. F: = OPOSSUM. **To play p.,** faire le mort; se tenir coi.

post¹ [poust], s. 1. (a) Poteau m, pieu m, montant m, pilier m. F: **He stood there like a p.,** il était planté là comme une borne, comme un piquet. **He's as deaf as a p.,** il est sourd comme un pot. (b) Const: Chandelle f; montant, dormant m, jambage m. (c) Arbre m, fût m (de grue). 2. El: Borne f à vis. 3. Turf: (a) (Winning-)p., (poteau d')arrivée f; but m. **To win on the p.,** gagner de justesse. (Starting-)p., (poteau de) départ m; barrière f. **To go to the p.,** prendre part à la course. (Of horse) **To refuse to leave the p.,** rester au poteau. **To be left at the p.,** manquer le départ. (b) Jalon m (de la piste).

post², v.tr. 1. **To p. (up),** placarder, coller (des affiches, etc.); afficher (un avis, etc.). **The market rates are posted at the Town Hall,** les cours sont affichés à la mairie. P.N: **Post no bills,** défense f d'afficher. 2. Inscrire (un vaisseau) comme disparu. (At a club, etc.) **To p. a member,** afficher le nom d'un membre en défaut.

post³, *s.* 1. *A:* (Malle-)poste *f.* **To travel p.,** (i) voyager en poste; (ii) aller un train de poste. 2. Courrier *m.* **By return of p.,** par retour du courrier. **It is p.-time,** c'est l'heure du courrier. **To miss the p.,** manquer la levée, le courrier. **The p. has come,** le facteur est passé. **To open one's p.,** dépouiller son courrier. *Games:* **General p.,** chassé-croisé *m.* **There has been a general p. among the staff,** il y a eu un remaniement du personnel. 3. Poste *f.* **To send sth. by p.,** envoyer qch. par la poste. 4. = POST-OFFICE. **To take a letter to the p.,** porter une lettre à la poste. **'post-chaise,** *s.* *A:* Chaise *f* de poste. **'post-'free,** *attrib. a.* Franc de port; en franchise; franco *inv.* **'post-'haste,** *adv.* En toute hâte. **'post-horn,** *s.* Trompe *f* (de la malle-poste). **'post-house,** *s.* *A:* Maison *f* de relais (de la malle-poste). **'post office,** *s.* Bureau *m* de poste; *F:* la poste. **P.O. Savings Bank** = Caisse nationale d'épargne. **'post orderly,** *s.* *Mil:* Vaguemestre *m.* **'post-'paid,** *a.* Affranchi; port payé.

post⁴, 1. *v.i.* *A:* Voyager par relais; voyager en poste. (*b*) *Equit:* *esp.* *U.S:* Faire du trot enlevé. 2. *v.tr.* (*a*) Mettre (une lettre) à la poste; jeter (une lettre) à la boîte; poster (une lettre). **To p. sth. to s.o.,** envoyer qch. à qn (par la poste). (*b*) *Book-k:* **To p. the books,** passer les écritures. **To p. an entry,** passer écriture d'un article. **To p. up the ledger,** mettre le grand-livre au courant, à jour. **To p. s.o. up with sth.,** documenter qn sur qch.; mettre qn au courant de qch. **To p. oneself up on a matter,** se renseigner sur un sujet. **To keep s.o. posted (up),** tenir qn au courant.

post⁵, *s.* 1. (*a*) Poste *m* (de sentinelle, etc.). **Advanced p.,** poste avancé. *Mil:* **To be on p.,** être en faction. **Take p.! posts!** à vos postes! **To die at one's p.,** mourir à son poste. (*b*) Poste (occupé par des troupes). (*c*) Troupes *fpl* (occupant un poste). 2. *Hist:* **Trading-p.,** station *f* de commerce; comptoir *m* (aux Indes, etc.). 3. Poste, situation *f,* emploi *m.* **To take up one's p.,** entrer en fonctions.

post⁶, *v.tr.* 1. Poster, mettre en faction (une sentinelle); aposter (un espion). **To p. a sentry at a door,** mettre un planton, un factionnaire, à une porte. 2. *Mil: Navy:* **To be posted to a command, to a unit,** recevoir une affectation, être affecté, à un commandement, à une unité. *Navy:* **To be posted to a ship,** être affecté à un navire. **To p. s.o. as captain,** nommer qn capitaine de vaisseau.

post⁷, *s.* *Mil:* **Last p.,** (i) la retraite (au clairon); (ii) la sonnerie aux morts. **To sound the last p. (over the grave),** rendre les honneurs au mort (par une sonnerie).

postage ['poustidʒ], *s.* Port *m,* affranchissement *m* (d'une lettre, d'un paquet). **Rates of p.,** taxes *fpl* d'affranchissement. **Postages,** ports de lettres; frais *m* de port. **P. paid,** port payé. *S.a.* STAMP¹ 4.

postal ['poust(ə)l], *a.* Postal, -aux. **(International) P. Union,** Union postale universelle. **The p. authorities,** l'administration *f* des Postes, des P. et T. **The P. Services,** les Postes et Télécommunications. **Two-tier p. service,** courrier *m* à deux vitesses. *Com:* **P. charges,** frais *mpl* de port, ports *m* de lettres. *S.a.* ORDER¹ 11.

postcard ['pous(t)kɑːd], *s.* Carte postale. **Picture p.,** carte postale illustrée.

post-communion ['poustkə'mjuːniən], *s.* *Ecc:* Post-communion *f.*

post-date ['poust'deit], *v.tr.* Postdater (un chèque, etc.).

poster ['poustər], *s.* 1. (*Pers.*) Afficheur *m.* 2. Affiche murale; *esp.* affiche illustrée. **P. designer,** affichiste *mf.*

poste restante ['poust'restɑːnt], *s.* *Post:* Poste restante.

posterior [pɔsˈtiəriər], 1. *a.* Postérieur (to, à). 2. *s.* *F:* Postérieur *m,* derrière *m* (de qn). **To kick s.o.'s p.,** enlever le ballon à qn, botter le derrière de qn.

posteriority [pɔs,tiəriˈɔriti], *s.* Postériorité *f.*

posterity [pɔsˈteriti], *s.* Postérité *f.* 1. **To leave a large p.,** laisser une postérité nombreuse. 2. **P. will be grateful to him,** la postérité lui sera reconnaissante.

postern ['pɔstəːn], *s.* 1. *Fort:* Poterne *f.* 2. *A:* **P. (door),** porte *f* de derrière; porte dérobée.

post-glacial ['poust'gleisiəl], *a.* *Geol:* Post-glaciaire.

post-graduate [poust'grædjuit, -eit], *a.* **P.-g. student,** étudiant licencié(e) qui continue ses études. **P.-g. course,** études poursuivies après l'acquisition des titres universitaires.

posthumous ['pɔstjuməs], *a.* Posthume. **-ly,** *adv.* Posthumement; (paru) après la mort de l'auteur.

postil(l)ion [pɔs'tiljən], *s.* Postillon *m.*

post-impressionism ['poustim'preʃənizm], *s.* *Art:* Post-impressionnisme *m.*

postman, *pl.* **-men** ['poustmən], *s.m.* 1. Facteur, *Adm:* préposé *m* des postes. 2. *Navy: Mil:* Vaguemestre.

postmark ['poustmɑːk], *s.* Cachet *m* de la poste; timbre *m* de départ ou d'arrivée; (timbre d')oblitération *f.* **Letter bearing a London p.,** lettre timbrée de Londres, portant le cachet de Londres.

postmaster ['poustmɑːstər], *s.m.* Receveur (des Postes). **The P. General** = le ministre des Postes et Télécommunications.

postmeridian ['poustmə'ridiən], *a.* De l'après-midi, du soir.

post meridiem ['poustmə'ridiəm]. *Lt.phr.* (*Abbr:* **p.m.** ['piːˈem]) De l'après-midi, du soir. **At four p.m.,** à quatre heures de l'après-midi.

postmistress ['poust,mistris], *s.f.* Receveuse des Postes.

post-mortem ['poust'mɔːtem], *attrib. a. & s.* Après décès. **P.-m. rigidity,** rigidité cadavérique. **To hold a p.-m. (examination),** faire une autopsie (cadavérique), autopsier.

postnatal ['poust'neitl], *a.* Postnatal, -als.

postnuptial ['poust'nʌpʃ(ə)l], *a.* Postérieur au mariage.

post-obit ['poust'ɔbit], *attrib. a. & s.* **P.-o. (bond),** contrat *m* exécutoire, obligation *f* réalisable, après le décès d'un tiers.

postoperational [,poustɔpə'reiʃənl], *a.* *Surg:* Post-opératoire.

postpalatal ['poust'pælətl], *a.* Postpalatal, -aux; (consonne) vélaire.

postpone [poust'poun], *v.tr.* Remettre, ajourner, renvoyer à plus tard, reporter à plus tard, différer; reculer (un départ); arriérer (un paiement, etc.). **To p. a matter for a week,** remettre, renvoyer, une affaire à huitaine. **To p. a burial,** surseoir à une inhumation. **The sale has been postponed,** il a été sursis à la vente.

postponement [poust'pounmənt], *s.* Remise *f* à plus tard; renvoi *m* (d'une cause) (for a week, à huitaine); ajournement *m.*

postprandial [poust'prændiəl], *a.* *Now usu. Hum:* **P. eloquence,** éloquence après dîner, au dessert. **P. nap,** sieste après le repas.

postscript ['poustkript], *s.* (*Abbr.* **P.S.** ['piːˈes]) 1. Post-scriptum *m inv.* 2. Postface *f* (d'un écrit).

post-synchronization ['poustsiŋkrənai'zeiʃ(ə)n], *s.* *Cin:* Postsynchronisation *f.*

post-synchronize ['poust'siŋkrənaiz], *v.tr.* *Cin:* Post-synchroniser.

postulant ['pɔstjulənt], *s.* *Ecc:* Postulant, -ante.

postulate¹ ['pɔstjulit], *s.* *Geom: Log:* Postulat *m.*

postulate² ['pɔstjuleit]. 1. *v.tr. & i.* **To p. (for) sth.,** postuler, demander, réclamer, qch. 2. *v.tr.* Poser (qch.) en postulat; considérer (qch.) comme admis, comme établi.

posture¹ ['pɔstʃər], *s.* (*a*) Posture *f,* pose *f,* attitude *f* (du corps). **To assume an easy p.,** prendre une posture commode. (*b*) Position *f,* situation *f,* état *m* (des affaires, etc.).

posture². 1. *v.tr.* Mettre (qn) dans une certaine posture; poser (un modèle). 2. *v.i.* Prendre une posture, une pose.

post-war ['poustwɔːr], *attrib. a.* D'après guerre. **The p.-w. period,** l'après-guerre *m inv.*

posy ['pouzi], *s.* Bouquet *m* (de fleurs des champs); petit bouquet.

pot¹ [pɔt], *s.* 1. (*a*) Pot *m.* (**Flower-)p.,** pot à fleurs. **To drink a p. of beer,** boire un pot, un cruchon, de bière. **Chamber-p.,** pot de chambre; vase *m* de nuit. *S.a.* CHIMNEY-POT, COFFEE-POT, INKPOT, JAM-POT, TEAPOT. (*b*) Marmite *f.* **Pots and pans,** batterie *f* de cuisine. *P:* **To go to p.,** aller à la ruine, (s'en) aller à vau-l'eau, à la dérive. **He's gone to p.,** *P:* il est fichu. *Prov:* **The p. calls the kettle black,** la pelle se moque du fourgon. (*c*) *Metall:* (Melting-)p., creuset *m.* (*d*) *Sp: F:* Coupe (remportée en prix). **2.** *Fish:* Casier *m. S.a.* CRAB-POT, LOBSTER-POT. **3.** (*a*) *F:* **Pots of money,** des tas *m* d'argent; de l'argent tant et plus; un argent fou. **To make pots of money,** gagner gros. (*b*) *Cards:* **The p.,** la cagnotte. **4.** *F:* (*Of pers.*) **A big p.,** un gros bonnet; *P:* une grosse légume. **5.** = POT-SHOT. 'pot-bellied, *a.* Ventru, pansu. **You are getting p.-b.,** tu commences à bedonner. 'pot-belly, *s.* Panse *f,* bedon *m,* bedaine *f.* 'pot-boiler, *s.* Œuvre *f* d'un écrivain, d'un peintre, etc., besogneux, œuvre de littérature alimentaire. 'pot-bound, *a.* (Plante) dont le pot est trop petit. 'pot-herb, *s.* Herbe potagère. 'pot(-)hole, *s.* **1.** *Geol:* Marmite de géants; poche *f.* **2.** *F:* Trou *m,* flache *f* (dans une route), *F:* nid *m* de poule. **Road full of p.-holes,** chemin défoncé. 'pot-holer, *s. F:* Spéléologue *mf.* 'pot-holing, *s. F:* Spéléologie *f.* 'pot-house, *s. O:* Cabaret *m,* taverne *f,* bistrot *m.* 'pot-hunter, *s. Sp:* Personne *f* qui prend part à tous les concours dans le seul but de remporter un prix. 'pot 'luck, *s.* **To take p. l.,** manger (chez qn) à la fortune du pot. **Come and take p.-l. with us,** venez dîner chez nous sans cérémonie. 'pot-'plant, *s.* (i) Plante *f* en pot; (ii) plante d'appartement. 'pot-pour'ri, *s.* (*a*) *Mus:* Pot pourri *m.* (*b*) (*Perfume*) Pot pourri *m.* 'pot-roast, *s. Cu:* Rôti cuit à l'étouffée. 'pot(-)scourer, *s.* Lavette *f* métallique; gratte-casseroles *m inv,* cure-casseroles *m inv.* 'pot-shot, *s. F:* **To take a p.-s. at sth.,** (i) faire qch. au petit bonheur; (ii) lâcher au petit bonheur un coup de fusil à qch.

pot², *v.tr.* (**potted**) **1.** (*a*) Mettre en pot, conserver (la viande, etc.). (*b*) Mettre en pot, empoter (une plante). (*c*) *Bill:* Blouser (une bille). **2.** *F:* (*a*) Tirer, tuer, abattre (du gibier, etc.). (*b*) *v.i.* **To p. at** (**game,** etc.**),** lâcher un coup de fusil à (une pièce de gibier); tirailler contre (l'ennemi); canarder (l'ennemi). **To p. at small game,** giboyer. **potted,** *a.* **1.** En pot, en terrine. **2.** *F:* Abrégé.

potability [ˌpoutəˈbiliti], *s.* Potabilité *f.*

potable [ˈpoutəbl], *a.* Potable, buvable.

potash [ˈpotæʃ], *s.* **1.** (**Carbonate of**) **p.,** carbonate *m* de potasse; *F:* potasse *f.* **2.** **Caustic p.,** potasse caustique. **3.** **Sulphate of p.,** potasse sulfatée. **Permanganate of p.,** permanganate *m* de potasse.

potassic [pəˈtæsik], *a. Ch:* Potassique.

potassium [pəˈtæsiəm], *s. Ch:* Potassium *m.* **P. chlorate,** chlorate *m* de potasse. **P. carbonate,** carbonate *m* de potasse; *F:* potasse *f.* **P. permanganate,** permanganate *m* de potasse.

potation [pouˈteiʃ(ə)n], *s.* (*a*) Action *f* de boire; gorgée *f.* (*b*) *pl.* Libations *f.*

potato, *pl.* **-oes** [pəˈteitou, -ouz], *s.* **1.** Pomme *f* de terre. **Boiled potatoes,** pommes (de terre) à l'anglaise, à l'eau. **Baked, roast, potatoes,** pommes (de terre) au four. **Mashed potatoes,** purée de pommes (de terre), pommes mousseline. **Chipped, French fried, potatoes,** pommes (de terre) frites, *F:* frites *fpl.* **P. crisps,** *U.S:* **p. chips,** pommes chips. **P. straws,** pommes paille. (**Thick**) **P. soup,** crème *f,* potage *m,* parmentier. **2. Sweet p.,** patate *f.* **Indian p.,** igname *f.* po'tato-blight, *s. Agr:* Frisolée *f,* friselée *f.* po'tato-chipper, *s. Dom.Ec:* Coupe-frites *m inv.* po'tato-masher, *s. Dom.Ec:* Presse-purée *m inv.* po'tato-peeler, *s. Dom.Ec:* Éplucheur *m;* couteau *m* économe; (*electric*) éplucheuse *f.* po'tato-spirit, *s. Dist:* Alcool *m* amylique.

pot(h)een [pɒˈt(h)iːn], *s.* Whisky irlandais distillé en fraude.

potency [ˈpout(ə)nsi], *s.* **1.** Puissance *f,* autorité *f* (du monarque, etc.). **2.** Force *f,* puissance (d'un argument); efficacité *f* (d'un médicament); force (d'une boisson alcoolique). **3.** *Physiol:* Virilité *f.*

potent [ˈpout(ə)nt], *a.* **1.** *Lit:* Puissant. **2.** (*Of drug, etc.*) Efficace, puissant; (*of motive, etc.*) convaincant; plein de force. **P. drink,** boisson très forte. **P. poison,** poison violent. **-ly,** *adv.* Puissamment.

potentate [ˈpoutənteit], *s.* Potentat *m.*

potential [pəˈtenʃ(ə)l]. **1.** *a.* (*a*) En puissance; virtuel, -elle; latent. **P. danger,** danger possible, latent. (*b*) Potentiel. **The p. resources of Africa,** les ressources potentielles de l'Afrique. (*c*) *a. & s. Gram:* **The p.** (**mood**), le potentiel. **2.** *s.* Potentiel *m.* **P. drop,** chute *f* de potentiel. **Operating p.,** voltage *m* de régime; tension *f* de service. *Mil:* **The military p. of a country,** le potentiel militaire d'un pays. **-ally,** *adv.* Potentiellement, virtuellement, en puissance.

potentiality [pəˌtenʃiˈæliti], *s.* Potentialité *f.* **Military potentialities of a country,** potentiel *m* militaire d'un pays. **Situation full of potentialities,** (i) situation où tout devient possible; (ii) situation qui promet.

potentiometer [pəˌtenʃiˈɒmitər], *s. El:* Potentiomètre *m.*

pother [ˈpɒðər], *s.* **1.** *O:* Nuage *m* de fumée, de poussière. **2.** *F:* (*a*) Agitation *f,* confusion *f.* (*b*) Tapage *m,* tumulte *m,* vacarme *m.* (*c*) Tracas *m,* embarras *mpl.* **To make a p.,** faire des histoires. **All this p. about nothing!** tant d'histoires à propos de rien!

pothook [ˈpɒthuk], *s.* **1.** Crémaillère *f* (de foyer), **2.** *Sch:* A: Bâton *m,* jambage *m* (de premier modèle d'écriture).

potion [ˈpouʃ(ə)n], *s.* Potion *f;* dose *f* (de médecine). **A: Love-p.,** philtre *m* (d'amour).

potsherd [ˈpɒtʃəːd], *s.* **1.** *A:* Débris *m* (de pot cassé); fragment *m* de vaisselle. **2.** *Archeol:* **Potsherds found on a prehistoric site,** tessons trouvés dans un gisement préhistorique.

Pott [pɒt]. *Pr.n. Med:* **Pott's disease,** mal *m* de Pott.

pottage [ˈpɒtidʒ], *s. A:* (*a*) Potage *m.* (*b*) Potée *f. S.a.* MESS¹.

potter¹ [ˈpɒtər], *s.* Potier *m.* **P.'s clay,** terre *f* de potier; argile *f* plastique. **P.'s wheel,** (i) tour *m* de potier; (ii) disque *m* (du tour).

potter², *v.i.* **1.** S'occuper de bagatelles; s'amuser à des riens. **To p. about at odd jobs,** bricoler. **2.** Traîner, flâner. *Aut: etc:* **To p. along,** rouler à la papa; aller son petit bonhomme de chemin. **To p. about the house,** trottiner par la maison; s'occuper, bricoler dans la maison.

pottery [ˈpɒtəri], *s.* **1.** Poterie *f.* (*a*) L'art *m* du potier. (*b*) La fabrique. **The Potteries,** les Poteries (du Staffordshire). **2.** Vaisselle *f* de terre. **A piece of p.,** une poterie.

potty¹ [ˈpɒti], *a. F:* **1.** (*a*) Petit, insignifiant. **A p. little state,** un petit État de rien du tout. (*b*) (*Of job, etc.*) Facile, simple. **2.** (*a*) Toqué, timbré. (*b*) **To be p. about a girl,** être toqué d'une jeune fille.

potty², *s. F:* Pot *m* de chambre (d'enfant).

pouch¹ [pautʃ], *s.* **1.** Petit sac; bourse *f U.S:* **Diplomatic p.,** valise *f* diplomatique. *S.a.* TOBACCO-POUCH. **2.** *Nat.Hist:* Poche ventrale (des marsupiaux); abajoue *f* (de singe). **3.** Poche (sous les yeux).

pouch². **1.** *v.tr.* (*a*) Empocher. (*b*) (*Of fish, penguin, etc.*) Avaler. (*c*) *Dressm:* Faire bouffer (un vêtement). **2.** *v.i.* (*Of dress*) Former une poche; bouffer.

pouf(fe) [puːf], *s.* **1.** *Haird:* Cheveux postiches (féminins), *P:* chichis *mpl.* **2.** *Dressm:* Bouffant *m.* **3.** *Furn:* Pouf *m.*

poulp(e) [puːlp], *s. Moll:* Poulpe *m,* pieuvre *f.*

poult¹ [poult], *s.* Jeune volaille *f;* (*of pheasant*) faisandeau *m;* (*of turkey*) dindonneau *m.*

poult²(-de-soie) [ˈpuː(də)swɑː], *s. Tex:* Pou-, pout-, poult-de-soie, *pl.* poux-, pouts-, poults-de-soie.

poulterer [ˈpoultərər], *s.* Marchand *m* de volaille.

poultice¹ [ˈpoultis], *s.* Cataplasme *m. S.a.* BREAD-POULTICE, MUSTARD-POULTICE.

poultice², *v.tr.* Mettre, appliquer, un cataplasme sur (qch.).

poultry [ˈpoultri], *s. Coll.* Volaille *f.* 'poultry-farm, *s.* Exploitation *f* (agricole) pour l'élevage de la volaille. 'poultry-farmer, *s.* Aviculteur *m,* éleveur *m* de volailles. 'poultry-farming, *s.* Aviculture *f,* élevage *m* de volailles. 'poultry-house, *s.* Poulailler *m.* 'poultry-'market, *s.* Poulaillerie *f,* marché *m* aux volailles. 'poultry-show, *s.* Concours *m* d'aviculture. 'poultry-yard, *s.* Basse-cour *f, pl.* basses-cours.

pounce¹ [pauns], *s.* **To make a p. on sth.,** (i) fondre, s'abattre, sur (sa proie); (ii) (*of pers.*) s'élancer pour saisir qch.; se jeter sur qch.

pounce², *v.i.* (*a*) **To p. on the prey,** fondre, s'abattre, sur la proie. (*b*) *F:* Se précipiter, se jeter (on, sur),

pounce³, *s.* **1.** (Poudre *f* de) sandaraque *f.* **2.** Ponce *f.*
pounce⁴, *v.tr.* **1.** Poncer; polir, frotter, à la ponce. **2.** Copier, calquer (un dessin) à la ponce; poncer (un dessin). Pounced drawing, poncif *m.*

pound¹ [paund], *s.* **1.** (*Abbr.* lb.) Livre *f* (de 453 gr, 6). Coffee at seven shillings a p., café à sept shillings la livre. To sell sugar by the p., vendre le sucre à la livre. **2.** (*Symbol* £) P. sterling, livre sterling (de 20 shillings). P. note, billet *m* (de banque) d'une livre. (*Of bankrupt*) To pay ten shillings in the p., payer dix shillings par livre. A question of pounds, shillings and pence, F: a question of £. s. d. [eles′di:], une question de gros sous.

pound², *s.* **1.** Fourrière *f* (pour animaux errants). **2.** Parc *m* (à moutons, etc.). **3.** *Fish:* P. net, verveux *m.* **4.** *Hyd.E:* Bief *m*, retenue *f* (entre deux écluses).

pound³. **1.** *v.tr.* (*a*) Broyer, piler, concasser; égruger (du sucre); pilonner (la terre, une drogue). (*b*) Bourrer (qn) de coups de poing. *Mil:* To p. a position, pilonner, marteler, une position. (*c*) To p. sth. to atoms, réduire qch. en miettes. To p. out a tune on the piano, marteler un air sur le piano. **2.** *v.i.* (*a*) To p. at, on, sth.; to p. away at sth., cogner dur, frapper ferme, sur qch. To p. (away) at the door, frapper à la porte à coups redoublés. *Equit:* To p. in the saddle, F: piler (du poivre). To p. on the piano, cogner sur le piano. (*b*) To p. along, avancer d'un pas lourd; (*of steamer*) fendre les vagues avec difficulté. (*c*) *I.C.E:* (*Of engine*) Cogner, marteler. (*d*) The ship was pounding on the bottom, le navire talonnait. The hull was pounding on the rocks, la coque se broyait sur les récifs.

poundage¹ [′paundidʒ], *s.* **1.** (*a*) Commission *f*; remise *f* de tant par livre (sterling). (*b*) Part donnée au personnel sur les bénéfices réalisés. **2.** Taux *m* de tant par livre (de poids).

poundage², *s.* **1.** Mise *f* en fourrière. **2.** Frais *mpl* de fourrière.

pounder [′paundər], *s. Tls:* **1.** (i) = PESTLE. (ii) = MORTAR **2.** (Concrete-)p., pilon *m*, dame *f.* (Paviour's) p., demoiselle *f*, hie *f.*

-pounder [′paundər], *s.* (*With num. prefixed, e.g.*) **1.** Two-p., poisson, etc., de deux livres. **2.** *Artil:* Thirty-p., canon *m*, pièce *f*, de trente. Eight-p., pièce de huit. **3.** *A: F:* Thousand-p., billet *m* de banque de mille livres.

pour¹ [′pɔ:r], *s. Metall:* Quantité *f* de métal coulée; coulée *f.*

pour². **1.** *v.tr.* (*a*) Verser (into, dans). River that pours into the lake, rivière qui se jette, se déverse, dans le lac. (*b*) *Metall:* To p. the metal, couler le métal. **2.** *v.i.* (*a*) (*Of rain*) Tomber à torrents, à verse. It is pouring (with rain), il pleut à verse. The water was pouring into the cellar, l'eau entrait à flots dans la cave. The water was pouring from the roof, l'eau ruisselait du toit. (*b*) To p. into, out of, the theatre, entrer dans le théâtre, sortir du théâtre, en foule, à flots. pour down. **1.** *v.i.* The rain came pouring down, il pleuvait à verse, à torrents, F: à seaux. pour in. **1.** *v.tr.* To p. in a broadside, lâcher, envoyer, une bordée. **2.** *v.i.* To p. in, to come pouring in, entrer à flots, en foule; arriver de toutes parts. Invitations are pouring in on us, il nous pleut des invitations. Tourists p. in from all quarters, les touristes affluent de toutes parts. pour off, *v.tr.* Décanter. pour out. **1.** *v.tr.* (*a*) Verser (une tasse de thé, etc.). He poured me out another glass, il me versa encore à boire. *Abs.* To p. out, présider (à la table de thé). (*b*) Répandre, exhaler (sa colère); donner libre cours à (ses sentiments); émettre des flots de (musique, etc.); épancher (ses chagrins); décharger (son cœur). To p. out one's thanks, se confondre en remerciements. To p. out threats, se répandre en menaces. **2.** *v.i.* (*a*) Sortir à flots; ruisseler. (*b*) Sortir en foule. **pouring¹**, *a.* P. rain, pluie torrentielle; pluie battante. A p. wet evening, une soirée ruisselante. **pouring²**, *s. Metall:* Coulée *f.*

pourer [′pɔ:rər], *s.* **1.** Verseur *m*; verseuse *f.* This teapot is not a good pourer, cette théière verse mal. **2.** *Metall:* (*Pers.*) Couleur *m.*

pout¹ [paut], *s. Ich:* (Whiting-)p., tacaud *m.* (Eel-)p., lotte *f.*

pout², *s.* Moue *f.*

pout³, *v.i.* **1.** (*a*) Faire la moue, la lippe. *v.tr.* To p. the lips, faire la moue. (*b*) Bouder. **2.** (*Of pigeon*) Enfler le jabot; faire jabot.

pouter [′pautər], *s.* **1.** Pigeon *m* grosse-gorge; (pigeon) boulant *m.* **2.** *Ich:* Tacaud *m.*

poverty [′povəti], *s.* **1.** Pauvreté *f. Adm:* Indigence *f.* Extreme p., abject p., misère *f.* To live in p., vivre dans la gêne, dans la misère. *Prov:* P. is no sin, no vice, pauvreté n'est pas vice. **2.** Disette *f*, manque *m*, pénurie *f* (de denrées, etc.); stérilité *f*, pauvreté (du sol). P. of ideas, dénuement *m* d'idées. *I.C.E:* P. of the mixture, pauvreté du mélange. ′poverty-stricken, *a.* **1.** Miséreux, -euse; indigent; dans la misère. **2.** P.-s. district, quartier misérable.

powder¹ [′paudər], *s.* Poudre *f.* (*a*) To reduce sth. to p., (i) réduire qch. en poudre; pulvériser qch.; (ii) réduire qch. en poussière; anéantir qch. (*b*) *Sporting* p., poudre de chasse. To smell p. for the first time, recevoir le baptême du feu. It is not worth p. and shot, le jeu n'en vaut pas la chandelle. To waste one's p. and shot, tirer sa poudre aux moineaux. (*c*) Face-p., toilet-p., poudre (de riz). ′powder-box, -bowl, -compact, *s. Toil:* Poudrier *m.* ′powder-flask, -horn, *s. A:* Poire *f*, cornet *m*, à poudre. ′powder-magazine, *s.* Poudrière *f.* ′powder-mill, *s.* Poudrerie *f*; manufacture *f* de poudre à canon. ′powder-puff, *s. Toil:* Houppe *f*; (*small*) houpette *f.* ′powder-room, *s.* (*In hotel, etc.*) Toilette *f* pour dames.

powder², *v.tr.* **1.** Saupoudrer (with, de). **2.** Poudrer (à blanc) (les cheveux). To p. one's face, *abs.* to p., se poudrer (le visage). F: To p. one's nose, aller aux cabinets. **3.** Réduire en poudre; pulvériser.

powderiness [′paudərinis], *s.* Pulvérulence *f.*

powdery [′paudəri], *a.* (*a*) Poudreux, -euse. (*b*) Friable.

power¹ [′pauər], *s.* **1.** Pouvoir *m.* I will do all in my p., je ferai tout ce qui est en mon pouvoir. As far as lies within my p., dans la mesure où cela m'est possible, où cela me sera possible. To the utmost of my p., de tout mon pouvoir. It is beyond my p., cela ne m'est pas possible. It is beyond my p. to save him, je suis impuissant à le sauver. **2.** (*a*) Faculté *f*, capacité *f*, talent *m.* P. of speech, la parole. He has great powers of speech, (i) c'est un grand orateur; (ii) il a la parole facile, F: il a la langue bien pendue. Mental powers, facultés intellectuelles. His powers are failing, ses facultés baissent. (*b*) *Ph:* P. of absorption, capacité d'absorption. **3.** Vigueur *f*, force *f. F:* More p. to your elbow! (i) allez-y! (ii) puissiez-vous réussir! **4.** (*a*) Puissance *f* (d'une machine, d'un microscope); force (d'un aimant, d'une chute d'eau). Attractive p., force d'attraction. *Mil:* Fire p., puissance de feu. Magnifying p., pouvoir grossissant. *Mec:* P.-to-weight ratio, puissance massique (d'une machine). P. delivered, puissance développée. *S.a.* HORSE-POWER. (*b*) Énergie *f* (électrique, hydraulique). *El: F:* Force *f.* Motive p., force motrice. P. unit, unité motrice. Generation of p., production *f* d'énergie. P. consumption, énergie consommée. P. supplied by a motor, débit *m* d'un moteur. The car came in under its own p., l'auto est rentrée par ses propres moyens. *Nau:* To work the engines at half p., manœuvrer à petite vitesse. Under p., sous pression. (*c*) P. has revolutionized modern industry, le machinisme a transformé l'industrie moderne. **5.** (*a*) Pouvoir, influence *f*, autorité *f.* Assumption of p., prise *f* de pouvoir. Spain was then at the height of her p., l'Espagne était alors à l'apogée de sa puissance. Absolute p., le pouvoir absolu. Executive p., le pouvoir exécutif. Legislative p., pouvoir législatif. Judicial p., pouvoir judiciaire. To have s.o. in one's p., avoir qn sous sa coupe. To fall into s.o.'s p., tomber au pouvoir de qn. To come into p., arriver au pouvoir. P. of life and death, droit *m* de vie et de mort. (*b*) To act with full powers, agir de pleine autorité. This lies within his powers, cela rentre dans ses attributions. To exceed, go beyond, one's powers, outrepasser ses pouvoirs; sortir de sa compétence. (*c*) *Jur:* Procuration *f*, mandat *m*, pouvoir. To furnish s.o. with full powers, donner pleins pouvoirs à qn. *S.a.* ATTORNEY². **6.** (*a*) The powers that be, les autorités constituées. The powers of darkness, les puissances des ténèbres. (b) The Great Powers, les Grandes Puissances. 7. P: O: A p. of people, une quantité de gens. To make a p. of money, gagner énormément d'argent. To do a p. of work, abattre de l'ouvrage tant et plus. To do a p. of good in the world, faire un bien énorme, le plus grand bien possible, dans le monde. 8. Mth: Puissance (d'un nombre). Three to the fourth p., trois (à la) puissance quatre; trois à la quatrième puissance. To the nth p., à la nme puissance. The p. of x, l'exposant m de x. 'power-'axle, s. Essieu moteur. 'power-dive, s. Av: Vol piqué fait à plein gaz. 'power-driven, a. Mû par moteur. 'power-hammer, s. Marteau-pilon m. 'power-house, s. = POWER STATION. 'power-loom, s. Tex: Métier m mécanique. 'power-plant, s. 1. Mec.E: Av: etc: Bloc moteur. 2. El.E: Groupe générateur. 'power 'politics, s.pl. Politique f de force armée. 'power-rail, s. El.Rail: Rail conducteur; rail de contact. 'power-station, s. Station génératrice (d'électricité); centrale f électrique. Oil-fired p.-s., centrale alimentée au fuel. Thermal, nuclear, p.-s., centrale thermique, nucléaire. 'power-stroke, s. Mch: Temps moteur. 'power-tube, -valve, s. W.Tel: Lampe émettrice, génératrice.

power², v.tr. Actionner. Powered by two engines, actionné par deux moteurs. Powered vehicle, véhicule f à moteur.

-powered ['pauəd], a. High-p. car, low-p. car, voiture f de haute, de faible, puissance.

powerful ['pauəful], a. 1. (a) Puissant. To have to deal with a p. adversary, avoir affaire à forte partie. (b) Fort, vigoureux, -euse. P. remedy, remède énergique, efficace. 2. F: O: A p. lot of people, une masse de gens. -fully, adv. Puissamment; fortement. P. built man, homme puissamment charpenté.

powerless ['pauəlis], a. 1. Impuissant. To be p. to do sth., se trouver impuissant à faire qch. They are p. in the matter, ils n'y peuvent rien. 2. (Remède) inefficace, sans vertu.

powerlessness ['pauəlisnis], s. 1. Impuissance f. 2. Inefficacité f.

pow-wow¹ ['pauwau], s. 1. Sorcier guérisseur (chez les Peaux Rouges). 2. Assemblée f (des Peaux-Rouges). 2. F: (a) Conférence f, palabre f. (b) Réunion amicale.

pow-wow² ['pau'wau], v.i. 1. (Of N. American Indians) Tenir une assemblée. 2. Palabrer. To p.-w. about sth., discuter qch.

pox [poks], s. 1. Med: (a) Vérole f, syphilis f. (b) See CHICKEN-POX, SMALLPOX. 2. Cow-p., vaccine f; variole f des vaches.

practicability [,præktikə'biliti], s. Praticabilité f; viabilité f (d'une route).

practicable ['præktikəbl], a. 1. Praticable; faisable. This method is not so p., cette méthode n'est pas, du point de vue pratique, aussi satisfaisante. 2. (a) (Of road, ford) Praticable. (b) Th: P. window, fenêtre praticable.

practical ['præktik(ə)l], a. 1. Pratique. (a) P. mechanics, chemistry, mécanique, chimie, appliquée. Of no p. value, inutilisable dans la pratique. S.a. JOKE¹. (b) P. proposal, proposition d'ordre pratique. P. common sense, sens pratique. (c) Very p. little girl, petite fille très entendue. To have a p. mind, avoir l'esprit positif. 2. With p. unanimity, d'un consentement pour ainsi dire unanime, quasi unanime. -ally, adv. 1. Pratiquement, en pratique. 2. Pour ainsi dire. There has been p. no snow, il n'y a pas eu de neige pour ainsi dire. P. cured, presque guéri. P. the whole of the audience, la quasi-totalité de l'auditoire.

practicalness ['præktikəlnis], s. 1. Nature f, caractère m, pratique (d'un projet, etc.). 2. Sens m, esprit m, pratique.

practice ['præktis], s. 1. Pratique f. The p. of medicine, l'exercice m de la médecine. Doctor who is no longer in p., médecin qui ne pratique plus, qui n'exerce plus. Jur: The p. of the courts, la procédure, la pratique, du Palais. To put, carry, a principle into p., mettre un principe en action, en pratique. In p., en pratique, pratiquement. 2. (a) Habitude f, coutume f, usage m. To make it a p., one's p., to do sth.; to make a p.

of doing sth., se faire une habitude, une règle, de faire qch. It is the usual p., c'est de pratique courante, F: c'est courant; c'est l'usage. (b) Shop p., tours mp de main d'atelier; technique f d'atelier. 3. Exercice(s) Sp: Entraînement m. It can only be learnt by p., cela ne s'apprend que par l'usage. Stroke that needs a lot of p., coup qui demande beaucoup d'application, de travail. To be in p., être en forme. Out of p., rouillé. To do sth. for p., faire qch. pour s'exercer. Band p., choir p., répétition f. Mil: Target p., exercices de tir. Prov: P. makes perfect, c'est en forgeant qu'on devient forgeron; on se perfectionne par la pratique. Sp: P. match, match d'entraînement. Av: P. flight, vol m d'entraînement. 4. Pratique, clientèle f (de médecin); étude f, cabinet m (d'avoué). To buy a p., acheter une clientèle. 5. Esp. in pl. Pratiques, menées fpl, machinations fpl, intrigue f. 'practice-firing, s. Mil: Exercice m de tir.

practician [præk'tiʃ(ə)n], s. Praticien, -ienne.

practise ['præktis], v.tr. 1. Pratiquer (une vertu, etc.); suivre (une méthode); mettre en pratique, en action (un principe, une règle). To p. what one preaches, prêcher d'exemple. 2. Pratiquer, exercer (une profession). To p. medicine, exercer la médecine. 3. Étudier (le piano, etc.); s'exercer (au piano, sur la flûte, à l'escrime); répéter (un chœur, etc.). Abs. Mus: Faire des exercices. To p. a shot (at tennis, billiards), s'exercer à un coup. To p. one's French on s.o., essayer son français sur qn. practised, a. Exercé, expérimenté; (joueur, etc.) averti. P. in sth., versé, habile, dans qch.; rompu à qch. practising¹, a. 1. Qui exerce; praticien; (médecin) exerçant, traitant; (avoué) en exercice. 2. (Catholique) pratiquant. practising², s. 1. Pratique f, exercice m (d'une profession, d'une vertu); entraînement m (pour un sport); répétitions fpl (théâtrales, de chant, de musique). 2. Exploitation f (de qn).

practitioner [præk'tiʃ(ə)nər], s. Praticien, -ienne. Medical p., médecin m. General p., omnipraticien, -enne; médecin de médecine générale. Local p., médecin de quartier.

praetor ['priːtər], s. Rom.Hist: Préteur m.

praetorian [priː'tɔːriən], a. & s. Prétorien (m).

pragmatic [præg'mætik], a. 1. Hist: Phil: Pragmatique. 2. = PRAGMATICAL.

pragmatical [præg'mætik(ə)l], a. 1. (i) Suffisant, important, infatué de soi-même; (ii) dogmatique, positif. 2. Phil: Pragmatique. -ally, adv. 1. Phil: Pragmatiquement. 2. D'un ton suffisant, dogmatique; d'un ton positif.

pragmatism ['prægmətizm], s. 1. Phil: Pragmatisme m. 2. Pédanterie f.

pragmatist ['prægmətist], s. Phil: Pragmatiste m.

prairie ['prɛəri], s. usu.pl. The prairies, la prairie (de l'Amérique du Nord). 'prairie-dog, s. Z: Cynomys m; F: chien de prairie.

praise¹ [preiz], s. (i) (Deserved) Éloge(s) m(pl); (ii) (adulatory or of worship) louange(s) f(pl). In p. of s.o., of sth., à la louange de qn, de qch. To speak in p. of s.o., faire l'éloge de qn. To sound one's own praises, faire son propre éloge. To damn (s.o., sth.) with faint p., assommer (qn, une œuvre) avec des fleurs. I am not given to p., je ne suis pas enclin à la louange. To be loud, warm, in s.o.'s p., prodiguer les éloges à qn. I have nothing but p. for him, for his conduct, je n'ai qu'à me louer de lui, de sa conduite. Beyond all p., au-dessus de tout éloge. To the p. of God, à la louange de Dieu. P. be to God! Dieu soit loué!

praise², v.tr. 1. Louer, faire l'éloge de (qn). He was praised by everyone, il s'attira les éloges de tout le monde. 2. To p. God, glorifier Dieu; chanter les louanges de Dieu. 3. F: To p. up, vanter, prôner.

praiseworthy ['preiz,wəːði], a. Digne d'éloges; (travail) méritoire. -ily, adv. Louablement.

pram [præm], s. F: Voiture f d'enfant.

prance [prɑːns], v.i. 1. (Of horse) Fringuer; piaffer. To p. about, caracoler. To p. (about) with rage, trépigner de colère. 2. (Of pers.) Se pavaner. prancing, s. Allure fringante (d'un cheval); caracoles fpl.

prang [præŋ], v.tr. F: Av: Bousiller (son appareil).

prank¹ [præŋk], s. 1. Escapade f, folie f, frasque f, fredaine f. To play pranks, faire des joyeusetés f. To play one's pranks, faire des siennes. 2. Tour m, farce f, niche f, espièglerie f. To play pranks on s.o., jouer des tours à qn; faire des espiègleries, des niches, à qn.

prank². A: 1. v.tr. Parer, orner. Field pranked with flowers, champ émaillé de fleurs. To p. oneself out, up, se parer de ses plus beaux atours. 2. v.i. Se pavaner; prendre des airs.

prankish ['præŋkiʃ], a. Espiègle, lutin.

prate [preit], v.i. (a) Dire des riens, des absurdités (d'un air important); jaser, bavarder, jacasser. (b) Rapporter des potins; jaser. prating, a. Babillard, bavard; jaseur, -euse.

prater ['preitər], s. Bavard, -arde, babillard, -arde.

pratique [præ'ti:k], s. Nau: Libre pratique f. To admit a ship to p., donner libre pratique à un navire; lever la quarantaine.

prattle¹ ['prætl], s. (a) Babil m, babillage m (d'enfants); gazouillis (des oiseaux, etc.). (b) Bavardage m, F: papotage m, caquet m.

prattle², v.i. (a) Babiller. (b) Jaser, bavarder, F: papoter, caqueter. prattling¹, a. (a) (Enfant) babillard. P. brook, ruisseau m qui gazouille. (b) Bavard; jaseur, -euse. prattling,² s. (a) Babillage m, gazouillement m. (b) Bavardage m, F: caquetage m, papotage m.

prattler ['prætlər], s. (a) Babillard, -arde. (b) Jaseur, -euse; bavard, -arde.

prawn [prɔːn], s. Crust: Crevette f rose, rouge; bouquet m; (grande crevette) salicoque f. Dublin bay p., langoustine f. Fresh-water p., écrevisse f.

pray [prei], v.tr. & i. 1. Prier, implorer, supplier (s.o. to do sth., qn de faire qch.). To p. (to) God, prier Dieu. To p. for s.o., prier pour qn. To p. for sth., prier le Seigneur qu'il nous accorde qch. I p. that he may be safe, je prie Dieu qu'il soit sain et sauf. To p. for s.o.'s soul, prier pour (le repos de) l'âme de qn. To p. for s.o. (in sickness, etc.), prier à l'intention de qn. He's past praying for, (i) il est perdu sans retour; (ii) F: il est incorrigible, indécrottable. 2. O: (I) p. (you), je vous (en) prie; de grâce. What good will that do, p.? à quoi bon, je vous demande un peu? P. take a seat, veuillez (bien) vous asseoir. praying-insect, -mantis, s. Ent: = MANTIS.

prayer¹ [prɛər], s. 1. (a) Prière f (à Dieu); oraison f. The Lord's P., l'oraison dominicale; le Pater. P. for the dead, requiem m; prière pour les morts; oraison des trépassés. To put up a p., to offer p. faire une prière. To say one's prayers, faire ses dévotions. F: He didn't get that saying his prayers, il n'a pas gagné cela en disant son chapelet. To be at one's prayers, être en prières. To be at prayers, être à la prière (en commun). Ecc: Morning P., Evening P., office m du matin, du soir. Sch: Prayers, la prière du matin en commun. (b) O: Demande instante. He did it at my p., il l'a fait à ma prière. 2. (Thing prayed for) His p. was granted, sa prière a été exaucée. 'prayer-book, s. Livre m de prières; livre d'heures. Ecc: The P.-B., le rituel de l'Église anglicane. 'prayer mat, s. Tapis m à prière. 'prayer-meeting, s. Ecc: Service m de la semaine. 'prayer-stool, s. Prie-Dieu m inv. 'prayer-wheel, s. (Buddhism) Moulin m, cylindre m, à prières.

prayer² ['preiər], s. Suppliant, -ante.

preach [pri:tʃ], v. Prêcher. 1. To s.o., sermonner qn; prêcher qn. To preach at s.o., diriger un sermon contre qn (qui est présent, mais sans nommer personne). 2. v.tr. (a) To p. a sermon, prononcer un sermon. (b) To p. the gospel, prêcher, annoncer, l'Évangile. preaching¹, a. Prêcheur, -euse. preaching², s. 1. Prédication f. 2. Pej: Prêcherie f.

preacher ['pri:tʃər], s. 1. Prédicateur m. 2. Pej: Prêcheur, -euse.

preachify ['pri:tʃifai], v.i. F: Sermonner; faire de la morale. preachifying, s. Prêcherie f; prêchi-prêcha m.

pre-admission ['pri:əd'miʃ(ə)n], s. Mch: Admission prématurée (de la vapeur, etc.).

preamble ['pri:æmbl], s. 1. (a) Préambule m. (b) Préliminaires mpl (d'un traité, etc.). 2. Jur: Exposé m des motifs (d'un projet de loi).

prearrange [,pri:ə'reindʒ], v.tr. Arranger au préalable, d'avance. Prearranged declarations, déclarations concertées.

prebend ['prebənd], s. Prébende f.

prebendal [pri'bendl], a. Ecc: Attaché à la prébende. P. stalls, stalles canoniales.

prebendary ['preb(ə)nd(ə)ri], s. Prébendier m, chanoine m.

precarious [pri'kɛəriəs], a. 1. Jur: (Possession) précaire. 2. Précaire, incertain. To make a p. living, gagner sa vie précairement. -ly, adv. Précairement.

precariousness [pri'kɛəriəsnis], s. Précarité f, incertitude f (dans la possession); état m précaire (de la santé).

precast ['pri:kɑst], a. Préfabriqué. P. concrete block, parpaing m.

precaution [pri'kɔ:ʃ(ə)n], s. Précaution f. To take (one's) precautions against sth., prendre ses précautions, se mettre en garde, se précautionner, contre qch. Air-raid precautions, défense passive.

precautionary [pri'kɔ:ʃnəri], a. De précaution.

precede [pri(:)'si:d], v.tr. 1. (a) Précéder. Formalities that p. the debate, formalités préalables aux débats. For a week preceding this occasion, pendant une semaine avant cette occasion. (b) Faire précéder. To p. a lecture with a few words of welcome, préfacer une conférence de quelques mots de bienvenue. 2. Avoir le pas, la préséance, sur (qn). preceding, a. Précédent. The p. day, la veille. The p. year, l'année d'auparavant. In the p. article, dans l'article ci-dessus.

precedence ['presidəns, pri'si:d(ə)ns], s. (a) Préséance f; priorité f. To have, take, p. of s.o., avoir le pas, la préséance, sur qn; prendre le pas sur qn. Ladies take p., les dames passent avant. To yield p. to s.o., céder le pas à qn. (b) Droit m de priorité.

precedent ['president], s. 1. Précédent m. To set, create, a p., créer un précédent. According to p., conformément à la tradition. 2. Jur: Décision f judiciaire faisant jurisprudence.

precentor [pri'sentər], s. Ecc: 1. (a) Premier chantre. (b) Maître m de chapelle. 2. Chef m du chœur (dans l'église réformée).

precentorship [pri'sentəʃip], s. Ecc: Maîtrise f. The p. of a cathedral, la maîtrise d'une cathédrale.

precept ['pri:sept], s. 1. Précepte m; commandement m (de Dieu). 2. Jur: Mandat m.

preceptor, -tress [pri'septər, -tris], s. Précepteur, -trice.

precession [pri'seʃ(ə)n], s. Astr: Précession f (des équinoxes).

precinct ['pri:siŋ(k)t], s. 1. (a) Enceinte f, enclos m. Shopping p., centre commercial (fermé à la circulation automobile). (b) pl. Precincts, pourtour m (d'une cathédrale). 2. Limite f (du pourtour). 3. U.S: Adm: (a) Circonscription électorale. (b) Circonscription administrative urbaine.

preciosity [,preʃi'ɔsiti], s. Préciosité f, affectation f.

precious ['preʃəs]. 1. a. (a) Précieux, -euse; de grand prix. P. stones, pierres précieuses. (b) Iron: Fameux, -euse. A p. pair, une belle paire (de vauriens, etc.). A p. fool he is! c'est un fameux imbécile! (c) (Style) précieux, recherché, affecté. (d) She always worries about her p. health, elle s'inquiète toujours de sa petite santé. 2. s. My p.! mon trésor! mon amour! 3. adv. F: To take p. good care of sth., prendre un soin particulier de qch. There are p. few of them, il n'y en a guère.

preciousness ['preʃəsnis], s. 1. Haute valeur (de qch.). 2. Art: Lit: Préciosité f.

precipice ['presipis], s. Précipice m. To fall over a p., tomber dans un précipice.

precipitable [pri'sipitəbl], a. Ch: Précipitable.

precipitancy [pri'sipitənsi], precipitancy [pri'sipitənsi], s. Précipitation f; (i) empressement m; (ii) manque m de réflexion.

precipitant [pri'sipitənt], s. Ch: Précipitant m.

precipitate¹ [pri'sipitit, -teit], s. 1. Ch: Précipité m. To form a p., (se) précipiter. 2. Meteor: Eau f de condensation.

precipitate² [pri'sipitit], a. Précipité. 1. Fait à la hâte. They escaped by a p. flight, une fuite précipitée leur permit de s'échapper. 2. Trop empressé; irréfléchi. -ly, adv. Précipitamment; avec précipitation.

precipitate[8] [pri'sipiteit]. **1.** *v.tr.* (*a*) Précipiter (**into, dans**). **To p. a country into war**, précipiter un pays dans la guerre. (*b*) (i) *Ch:* Précipiter (une substance). (ii) *Meteor:* Condenser; faire tomber (la rosée). (*c*) Accélérer, hâter, précipiter (un événement). **To p. matters**, brusquer les choses. **2.** *v.i.* (*a*) *Ch: Ph:* (Se) précipiter. (*b*) *Meteor:* Se condenser.

precipitation [prisipi'teiʃ(ə)n], *s.* **1.** (*a*) *Ch: Ph:* Précipitation *f.* (*b*) *Meteor:* Précipitation. **2. To act with p.**, agir avec précipitation, précipitamment.

precipitous [pri'sipitəs], *a.* Escarpé, abrupt; **à pic. -ly**, *adv.* A pic.

precipitousness [pri'sipitəsnis], *s.* Raideur *f* (d'une pente).

précis ['preisi:], *pl.* **précis** ['preisi:z], *s.* Précis *m*, analyse *f*, résumé *m*, abrégé *m. Sch:* **P.-writing**, compte-rendu de lecture.

precise [pri'sais], *a.* **1.** (*a*) Précis; exact. **P. movements**, mouvements exécutés avec précision. **In order to be p. . . .**, pour préciser. . . . (*b*) **At the p. moment when . . .**, au moment précis où. . . . **2.** (*Of pers.*) Formaliste; pointilleux, -euse; méticuleux, -euse. **-ly**, *adv.* **1.** (*a*) Avec précision. **To state the facts p.**, préciser les faits. (*b*) **At six o'clock p.**, à six heures précises. **2. P.!** précisément! parfaitement!

preciseness [pri'saisnis], *s.* **1.** Précision *f.* **2.** (*a*) Méticulosité *f.* (*b*) Formalisme *m.*

precision [pri'siʒ(ə)n], *s.* Précision *f.* **Lack of p.**, imprécision *f.* **P. instruments**, instruments de précision.

preclude [pri'klu:d], *v.tr.* Empêcher, prévenir, exclure, écarter (une objection, un malentendu, etc.). **In order to p. any misunderstanding . . .**, pour prévenir tout malentendu. . . . **To be precluded from an opportunity**, être privé d'une occasion. **To be precluded from doing sth.**, être dans l'impossibilité de faire qch.

precocious [pri'kouʃəs], *a.* Précoce, hâtif, -ive; (enfant) précoce. **-ly**, *adv.* Précocement; avec précocité.

precociousness [pri'kouʃəsnis], **precocity** [pri'kɔsiti], *s.* Précocité *f.*

precognition ['pri:kɔg'niʃ(ə)n], *s. Phil: etc:* Préconnaissance *f*; connaissance antérieure.

precombustion ['pri:kəm'bʌstʃ(ə)n], *s.* Précombustion *f. attrib.a.* **P. engine**, moteur diesel à chambre de précombustion.

preconceive [pri:kən'si:v], *v.tr.* Préconcevoir. **Pre-conceived idea**, idée préconçue.

preconception ['pri:kən'sepʃ(ə)n], *s.* **1.** Préconception *f.* **2.** (*a*) Idée ou opinion préconçue. (*b*) Préjugé *m.*

preconcerted ['pri:kən'sɔ:tid], *a.* Arrangé, concerté, d'avance. **Following no p. plan**, sans plan arrêté.

preconstruction ['pri:kən'strʌkʃ(ə)n], *s.* Préconstruction *f.*

precursor [pri(:)'kə:sər], *s.* Précurseur *m*; devancier *m*, avant-coureur *m.*

precursory [pri:kə:səri], *a.* (*a*) Précurseur, -euse; (symptôme) avant-coureur. (*b*) **P. remarks**, observations préliminaires.

predacious [pri'deiʃəs], *a.* **1.** (Animal) rapace; (bête) de proie. **2. Dog with p. instincts**, chien qui a des instincts de bête de proie.

predate ['pri:'deit], *v.tr.* **1.** Antidater (un document). **2.** Venir avant (un fait historique, etc.).

predatory ['predət(ə)ri], *a.* **1.** (*a*) Rapace, pillard, prédateur, -trice. (*b*) **P. animals**, bêtes de proie, bêtes rapaces. **2. P. habits**, habitudes de pillage, de rapine.

predecease[1] ['pri:di'si:s], *s.* Prédécès *m.*

predecease[2], *v.tr.* Prédécéder; mourir avant (qn).

predecessor ['pri:disesər], *s.* **1.** Prédécesseur *m*; devancier, -ière. **2.** Ancêtre *m.*

predestinate[1] [pri(:)'destinit], *a. & s.* Prédestiné, -ée.

predestinate[2] [pri(:)'destineit], *v.tr.* Prédestiner (**to, à**).

predestination [pri(:),desti'neiʃ(ə)n], *s.* Prédestination *f* (**to, à**).

predestine [pri(:)'desti'n], *v.tr.* Destiner d'avance (**to, à**); *Theol:* prédestiner (à).

predetermination ['pri:ditə:mi'neiʃ(ə)n], *s.* **1.** Détermination prise d'avance. **2.** *Theol:* Prédétermination *f.*

predetermine ['pri:di'tə:min], *v.tr.* **1.** Déterminer, arrêter, d'avance. **2.** *Theol: Phil:* Prédéterminer, préordonner.

predicament [pri'dikəmənt], *s.* **1.** *Phil: Log:* Prédicament *m*, catégorie *f.* **2.** Situation difficile, fâcheuse. **To be in an awkward p.**, être en mauvaise passe. *Iron:* **We're in a fine p.!** nous voilà dans de beaux draps! nous voilà propres!

predicant ['predikənt], *a. Ecc:* (Frère) prêcheur; prédicant *m.*

predicate ['predikit], *s.* **1.** *Log:* Prédicat *m.* **2.** *Gram:* Attribut *m.*

predicative [pri'dikətiv], *a.* Affirmatif, -ive. *Gram: Log:* Prédicatif, -ive. **P. adjective**, adjectif attribut

predict [pri'dikt], *v.tr.* Prédire.

predictable [pri'diktəbl], *a.* Qui peut être prédit.

prediction [pri'dikʃ(ə)n], *s.* Prédiction *f.*

predictive [pri'diktiv], *a.* Prophétique.

predigested ['pri:di'dʒestid, -dai-], *a.* Prédigéré.

predilection [,pri:di'lekʃ(ə)n], *s.* Prédilection *f* (**for, pour**). **To have a p. for sth.**, affectionner, affecter, qch.

predispose ['pri:dis'pouz], *v.tr.* Prédisposer (**to, à**).

predisposition ['pri:,dispə'ziʃ(ə)n], *s.* Prédisposition *f* (**to, à**).

predominance [pri'dɔminəns], *s.* Prédominance *f.*

predominant [pri'dɔminənt], *a.* Prédominant. **-ly**, *adv.* D'une manière prédominante. **This race is p. blue-eyed**, chez cette race les yeux bleus prédominent.

predominate [pri'dɔmineit], *v.i.* **1.** Prédominer. **2.** L'emporter par le nombre, par la quantité.

pre-elect ['pri:i'lekt], *v.tr.* **1.** Choisir d'avance. **2.** *Ecc:* Prédestiner au salut.

pre-election[1] [pri:i'lekʃ(ə)n], *attrib.a.* Antérieur aux élections. **P. promises**, promesses *f* de candidature.

pre-election[2], *s. Ecc:* Prédestination *f* (au salut).

pre-eminence [pri'eminəns], *s.* Prééminence *f.*

pre-eminent [pri'eminənt], *a.* (*a*) Prééminent. (*b*) Remarquable (**in, par**). **-ly**, *adv.* (*a*) A un degré prééminent. (*b*) Souverainement; par excellence.

pre-empt [pri'em(p)t], *v.tr.* Acquérir (qch.) en usant d'un droit de préemption.

pre-emption [pri'em(p)ʃ(ə)n], *s.* (Droit *m* de) préemption *f.*

pre-emptive [pri'em(p)tiv], *a.* **1.** (Titre, etc.) préemptif. **2.** *Cards:* **P. bid**, ouverture préventive.

pre-emptor [pri'em(p)tər], *s.* Acquéreur, -euse, en vertu d'un droit de préemption.

preen [pri:n], *v.tr.* **1.** (*Of bird*) Lisser, nettoyer (ses plumes). **2. To p. oneself**, (i) se bichonner; (ii) prendre un air avantageux; (*of girl*) faire des grâces.

pre-establish ['pri:is'tæbliʃ], *v.tr.* Préétablir. **pre-established**, *a.* Préétabli.

pre-exist ['pri:ig'zist], *v.i.* Préexister.

pre-existence ['pri:ig'zistəns], *s.* Préexistence *f.*

pre-existent ['pri:ig'zist(ə)nt], *a.* Préexistant.

prefab ['pri:fæb], *s. F:* Maison préfabriquée.

prefabricate ['pri:'fæbrikeit], *v.tr.* Préfabriquer.

prefabrication ['pri:fæbri'keiʃ(ə)n], *s.* Préfabrication *f.*

preface[1] ['prefis], *s.* **1.** Préface *f*; avant-propos *m inv.* **2.** Introduction *f*, préambule *m* (d'un discours). **3.** *Ecc:* Préface.

preface[2], *v.tr.* **1.** Écrire une préface pour (un ouvrage); préfacer (un ouvrage). **2.** Préluder à (un discours).

prefatory ['prefət(ə)ri], *a.* Préliminaire.

prefect ['pri:fekt], *s.* **1.** *Rom.Ant: Fr.Adm:* Préfet *m. Sch:* Élève choisi(e) pour aider au maintien de la discipline.

prefectorial ['pri:fek'tɔ:riəl], **prefectoral** [pri(:)'fektər(ə)l], *a.* Préfectoral, -aux.

prefecture ['pri:fektjuər], *s. Rom.Ant: Fr.Adm:* Préfecture *f.*

prefer [pri'fə:r], *v.tr.* (**preferred**) **1.** Nommer, élever (qn à une dignité). **2. To p. a complaint**, déposer une plainte, porter plainte (**against, contre**). **To p. a petition**, adresser une pétition. **3.** (*a*) **To p. sth. to sth**, préférer qch. à qch. **I p. meat well done**, je préfère la viande bien cuite. **I would p. to go without**, j'aimerais mieux m'en passer. (*b*) *Fin:* **Preferred stock**, actions privilégiées; actions de priorité.

preferable ['pref(ə)rəbl], *a.* Préférable (**to, à**). **-ably**, *adv.* Préférablement, par préférence (**to, à**).

preference ['pref(ə)r(ə)ns], s. 1. Préférence f (for, pour) In p., préférablement (to, à). To give sth. p., donner, accorder, la préférence à qch. (over, sur). 2. Pol.Ec: Tarif m de faveur. P. clause, pacte m de préférence. 3. Fin: P. stock, actions privilégiées; actions de priorité.

preferential [,prefə'renʃ(ə)l], a. (Traitement, etc.) préférentiel; (tarif) de faveur; (créancier) privilégié.

preferment [pri'fə:mənt], s. Avancement m; promotion f.

prefiguration ['pri:(t),figju'reiʃ(ə)n], s. Préfiguration f.

prefigure [pri:'figər], v.tr. 1. Préfigurer. 2. Se figurer, se représenter (qch.) d'avance.

prefix¹ ['pri:fiks], s. 1. Gram: Préfixe m. 2. Titre m (précédant un nom propre).

prefix² [pri:'fiks], v.tr. 1. Mettre (qch.) comme introduction (à un livre). 2. Gram: Préfixer (une particule à un mot). prefixed, a. (Particule) préfixe.

pregnancy ['pregnənsi], s. 1. Grossesse f; (of animal) gestation f. 2. Lit: (a) Fécondité f (de l'esprit). (b) Richesse f de sens (d'un mot); grande portée (d'un événement).

pregnant ['pregnənt], a. 1. (a) (Femme) enceinte, grosse. (b) (Of cow, etc.) Pleine, gravide. 2. P. with consequences, gros de conséquences.

preheat ['pri:'hi:t], v.tr. I.C.E: Mch: Chauffer d'avance (un carburant, etc.); dégourdir (le moteur, le carburant). preheating, s. I.C.E: etc: Dégourdissage m. P. device, dégourdisseur m.

preheater ['pri:'hi:tər], s. I.C.E: etc: Réchauffeur m; dégourdisseur m.

prehensile [pri'hensail], a. Préhensile.

prehistorian [pri:his'tɔ:riən], s. Préhistorien, -ienne.

prehistoric ['pri:(h)is'tɔrik], a. Préhistorique.

prehistory [pri:'hist(ə)ri], s. Préhistoire f.

pre-ignition ['pri:ig'niʃ(ə)n], s. I.C.E: Allumage prématuré; auto-allumage m.

prejudge ['pri:'dʒʌdʒ], v.tr. 1. Préjuger (une question). 2. Condamner (qn) d'avance.

prejudg(e)ment ['pri:'dʒʌdʒmənt], s. 1. Jugement prématuré. 2. Préjugé m.

prejudice¹ ['predʒudis], s. 1. Préjudice m, tort m, dommage m. Jur: Without p. (to my rights), réservation faite de tous mes droits. (In correspondence, etc.) Without p., sous toutes réserves. To the p. of . . ., au préjudice de. . . 2. Préjugé m, prévention f, préconception f. To have a p. against sth., être prévenu contre qch.

prejudice², v.tr. 1. Nuire, porter préjudice, préjudicier, à (une réputation, etc.). 2. Prévenir, prédisposer (s.o. against s.o., qn contre qn). prejudiced, a. (i) Prévenu (against, contre); (ii) à préjugés, à préventions. To be p., avoir des préjugés, des préventions.

prejudicial [,predʒu'diʃ(ə)l], a. Préjudiciable, nuisible (to, à); Jur: dommageable.

prelacy ['preləsi], s. (a) Prélature f, épiscopat m. (b) Coll. les prélats m; l'épiscopat.

prelate ['prelit], s. Prélat m.

prelim [pri'lim], s. F: (a) Sch: Examen préliminaire. (b) Typ: Prelims, pages f de départ.

preliminary [pri'liminəri]. 1. a. Préliminaire, préalable. Jur: P. investigation, instruction f (d'une affaire). Typ: P. matter, feuilles f liminaires, F: pages f de départ. 2. s. (a) Prélude m (à une conversation, etc.). By way of p., à titre de mesure préalable. (b) pl. Preliminaries, préliminaires m (d'un traité, etc.). -ily, adv. (a) Préliminairement. (b) Préalablement; au préalable.

prelude¹ ['prelju:d], s. 1. Prélude m (to, de). 2. Mus: Prélude.

prelude², 1. v.i. Mus: etc: (a) Préluder. (b) Servir d'introduction, préluder (to, à). 2. v.tr. (a) Faire présager (un événement, etc.). (b) Précéder.

premature ['premətjuər, 'pri:-], a. Prématuré. S.a. BIRTH 1, LABOUR¹ 4. -ly, adv. Prématurément. Obst: avant terme.

prematureness ['premətjuənis], prematurity [,premə'tjuəriti], s. Prématurité f.

premeditate [pri'mediteit], v.tr. Préméditer. premeditated, a. Prémédité; (crime) réfléchi. P. insolence, insolence calculée.

premeditation [pri,medi'teiʃ(ə)n], s. Préméditation f.

premier ['premiər, 'pri:miər]. 1. a. Premier (en rang, en importance). 2. s. Premier ministre.

première ['premiɛər], s. Th: Première f (d'une pièce, d'un film).

premiership ['premiə:ʃip, 'pri:-], s. Pol: Adm: (i) Fonctions, (ii) rang, de premier ministre.

pre-military ['pri:'militri], a. P. training, instruction f, formation f, prémilitaire.

premise¹ ['premis], s. 1. Log: Prémisse f. 2. pl. The premises, le local, les locaux; l'immeuble m. On the premises, sur les lieux.

premise² [pri'maiz], v.tr. (a) Log: Poser en prémisse (that, que + ind.) (b) Poser en principe (that, que). 2. Faire remarquer, citer, (qch.) en guise d'introduction.

premium ['pri:miəm], s. 1. Prix m, récompense f. To put a p. on laziness, donner une prime à la paresse. 2. (a) Prix convenu, indemnité f (pour l'apprentissage d'une profession libérale). (b) Insurance p., prime d'assurance. Ins: Loaded p., surprime f. Low p. insurance, assurance à prime réduite. (c) Droit m, redevance f (à payer au début d'un bail). 3. Fin: (a) (Exchange) p., agio m; prix du change. (b) Prime. P. on redemption, prime de remboursement. P. bonds, (i) obligations à primes; (ii) bons m à lots. To sell at a p., vendre à prime. (Of stock, etc.) To be at a p., faire prime. Antiques are at a p., les antiquités, (i) sont très recherchées; (ii) se vendent au prix d'or. 4. a. P.-grade petrol, supercarburant m.

premolar [pri'moulər], s. Anat: (Dent f) prémolaire (f).

premonition [,pri:mə'niʃ(ə)n], s. Prémonition f; pressentiment m (de malheur, etc.).

premonitory [pri'mɔnitəri], a. Prémonitoire; prémoniteur, -trice, (signe) avant-coureur; (indice) précurseur; annonciateur, -trice.

prenatal [pri:'neit(ə)l], a. Prénatal, -als, -aux.

prentice ['prentis]. 1. s. A: = APPRENTICE¹. 2. attrib. P. hand, main de novice; main inexpérimentée.

prenuptial [pri:'nʌpʃəl], a. Prénuptial, -aux.

preoccupation [priɔkju'peiʃ(ə)n], s. (a) Préoccupation f (de l'esprit). (b) My greatest p., ma plus grande préoccupation; mon premier souci.

preoccupy [pri'ɔkjupai], v.tr. Préoccuper, absorber (l'esprit). preoccupied, a. Préoccupé; absorbé (par un souci).

pre-ordain ['pri:ɔ:'dein], v.tr. 1. Ordonner, régler, d'avance. 2. Préordonner, prédéterminer.

prep [prep], s. Sch: F: Étude f (du soir). P. room, salle d'étude. P. school, école préparatoire (pour élèves de 8 à 13 ans).

prepacked ['pri:'pækt], a. Com: Préconditionné.

prepaid ['pri:'peid], a. See PREPAY.

preparation [,prepə'reiʃ(ə)n], s. 1. Préparation f (de la nourriture, d'un médicament, etc.). To do sth. without any p., faire qch. sans apprêts, sans aucun préparatif. 2. Usu.pl. Préparatifs mpl, apprêts mpl. To make (one's) preparations for sth., prendre ses dispositions, faire des préparatifs, en vue de qch. 3. Sch: Étude f (du soir). 4. Pharmaceutical p., préparation pharmaceutique.

preparative [pri'pærətiv]. 1. a. (Action f) préparatoire. 2. s.pl. Preparatives, préparatifs m.

preparatory [pri'pærət(ə)ri]. 1. a. Préparatoire, préalable (to, à). P. school, école préparatoire (pour élèves de 8 à 13 ans). 2. adv. Préalablement (to, à).

prepare [pri'pɛər]. 1. v.tr. Préparer (un repas, etc.); accommoder, confectionner (un mets); apprêter (le cuir, etc.). To p. s.o. for a piece of bad news, préparer qn à une mauvaise nouvelle. To p. a surprise for s.o., ménager une surprise à qn. To p. the way for negotiations, amorcer des négociations. Great events are preparing, de grands événements se préparent. 2. v.i. Se préparer, se disposer, s'apprêter (for sth., to do sth., à qch., à faire qch.). To p. for departure, faire ses préparatifs de départ. To p. for an examination, préparer un examen. prepared, a. To be p. for anything, être prêt, s'attendre, à toute éventualité. Be p. to be coolly received, attendez-vous à être mal accueilli. (Scouting) Be p., soyez toujours sur le qui-vive.

preparedness [pri'pɛəridnis], s. État m de préparation contre toute éventualité. **Everything was in a state of p.,** (i) tout était prêt; (ii) on était paré. *Mil: etc:* State of p., état d'alerte préventive.

preparer [pri'pɛərər], s. Préparateur, -trice.

prepay ['pri:'pei], v.tr. (p.t. & p.p. **prepaid**) Payer (qch.) d'avance; affranchir (une lettre, etc.). *Tg:* Answer prepaid, réponse payée.

prepayment ['pri:'peimənt], s. Paiement m d'avance; affranchissement m (d'une lettre).

preponderance [pri'pɔndərəns], s. Prépondérance f (over, sur).

preponderant [pri'pɔndərənt], a. Prépondérant.

preponderate [pri'pɔndəreit], v.i. Peser davantage; emporter la balance, l'emporter (over, sur).

preposition [prepə'ziʃ(ə)n], s. Préposition f.

prepositional [prepə'ziʃən(ə)l], a. Prépositionnel, -elle, prépositif, -ive.

prepossess ['pri:pə'zes], v.tr. 1. To p. s.o. with an idea, pénétrer qn d'une idée. 2. (*Of idea, etc.*) Accaparer, posséder (qn); obséder (qn); prendre possession de l'esprit de (qn). 3. Prévenir (**in favour of,** en faveur de; **against,** contre). prepossessed, a. 1. Imbu, imprégné (with, de); pénétré (d'une opinion, etc.). 2. Prévenu (en faveur de qn, contre qn). prepossessing, a. (Visage) agréable, prévenant. Of p. appearance, de bonne mine, de mine avantageuse, avenante. P. person, personne f sympathique. **-ly,** adv. D'une manière prévenante, attrayante, engageante.

prepossession ['pri:pə'zeʃ(ə)n], s. Prévention f; préjugé m.

preposterous [pri'pɔst(ə)rəs], a. Contraire au bon sens; absurde.

preposterousness [pri'pɔst(ə)rəsnis], s. Absurdité f.

prepotency [pri'poutənsi], s. 1. Prédominance f. 2. Biol: Prépotence f.

prepotent [pri'poutənt], a. 1. Prédominant. 2. Biol: (Caractère) dominant.

prepandial ['pri:'prændiəl], a. Usu. Hum: Avant le déjeuner. To have a p. drink, prendre un apéritif.

prepuce ['pri:pju:s], s. Anat: Prépuce m.

Pre-Raphaelite ['pri:'ræfeielait], a. & s. Hist. of Art: Préraphaélite (m).

prerecorded ['pri:ri'kɔ:did], a. W.Tel: T.V: P. broadcast, émission f en différé.

pre-release ['priri'li:s], a. Cin: **P.-r. showing** (of a film), avant-première f, pl. avant-premières.

prerequisite [pri'rekwizit]. 1. a. Nécessaire au préalable. 2. s. Nécessité f préalable.

prerogative [pri'rɔgətiv], s. Prérogative f, privilège m, apanage m. **To exercise the royal p.,** faire acte de souverain.

presage¹ ['presidʒ], s. (a) Présage m. (b) Pressentiment m.

presage² ['presidʒ, pri'seidʒ], v.tr. (a) (*Of omen, etc.*) Présager, annoncer (une catastrophe, etc.). (b) (*Of pers.*) Augurer, prédire (qch.). **To p. sth. from sth.,** augurer qch. de qch.

presanctified ['pri:'sæŋ(k)tifaid], a. Ecc: Présanctifié. **The Mass of the P.,** la messe des présanctifiés.

presbyopia [,prezbi'oupiə], s. Med: Presbytie f.

presbyopic [,prezbi'ɔpik], a. Presbyte.

presbyter ['prezbitər], s. 1. Rel.Hist: Presbyterian Ch: Ancien m. 2. Episcopal Ch: Prêtre m.

Presbyterian [,prezbi'tiəriən], a. & s. Presbytérien, -ienne.

Presbyterianism [,prezbi'tiəriənizm], s. Presbytérianisme m.

presbytery ['prezbit(ə)ri], s. 1. Ecc.Arch: Sanctuaire m, chœur m. 2. R.C.Ch: Presbytère m, cure f. 3. Presbyterian Ch: Consistoire m.

prescience ['presiəns], s. Prescience f.

prescient ['presiənt], a. Prescient.

prescribe [pri'skraib], v.tr. (a) Prescrire, ordonner. Prescribed task, tâche imposée. **In the prescribed time,** dans le délai prescrit. (b) Med: **To p. sth. for s.o.,** prescrire, ordonner, qch. à qn. Abs. **To p. for s.o.,** (i) indiquer un traitement pour qn; (ii) rédiger une ordonnance pour qn.

prescription [pri'skripʃ(ə)n], s. Prescription f. 1. (a) Ordre m, précepte m. (b) Med: Ordonnance f. **To write (out), make out, a p. for s.o.,** rédiger une ordonnance pour qn. 2. Jur: **Positive p., acquisitive p.,** prescription acquisitive.

prescriptive [pri'skriptiv], a. Consacré par l'usage.

preselection ['pri:si'lekʃ(ə)n], s. Présélection f.

preselector ['pri:si'lektər], s. Présélecteur m. Aut: P. gears, boîte f de vitesse à présélection.

presence ['prez(ə)ns], s. Présence f. 1. (a) Your p. is requested at . . ., (i) vous êtes prié d'assister à . . .; (ii) Adm: vous êtes convoqué à. . . . In the p. of, en présence de. . . . (b) To be admitted to the P., être admis en présence du roi, etc. F: A: Saving your p., sauf votre respect. 2. P. of mind, présence d'esprit. To retain one's p. of mind, conserver sa tête, son sang-froid. To lose one's p. of mind, perdre la tête. 3. (*Of pers.*) Air m, mine f, extérieur m, maintien m. To have a good p., avoir du maintien, une certaine prestance. He is lacking in personal p., il ne représente pas bien; il manque de prestance. 'presence-chamber, s. Salle f d'audience; salle du trône.

present¹ ['preznt]. I. a. 1. Usu.pred. Présent (et non absent). To be p. at a ceremony, être présent, assister, à une cérémonie. All p. heard it, toute l'assistance l'a entendu. Nobody else was p., nul autre n'était là. S.a. COMPANY 2. 2. (a) Actuel. P. fashions, modes actuelles, d'aujourd'hui. P. year, année courante. At the p. time, à présent; (i) en ce moment; (ii) à l'époque actuelle; aujourd'hui. P. worth, p. value, valeur actuelle. (b) En question; que voici. The p. writer, l'auteur (c.-à-d. moi). Com: On receipt of the p. letter, au reçu de la présente. (c) Gram: The p. tense, s. the p., le (temps) présent. In the p., au présent. **-ly,** adv. (a) fu. Tout à l'heure; bientôt; dans un instant; tout de suite; plus tard. (b) U.S: Maintenant, actuellement. II. present, s. 1. The p., le présent; le temps présent. Up to the p., jusqu'à présent. At p., à présent; actuellement. As things are at p., (i) au point où en sont les choses; (ii) par le temps qui court. At p. (*referring to past time*), alors. As matters stood at p., dans l'état où en était alors la question. For the p., pour le moment. 2. Jur: Know all men by these presents that . . ., savoir faisons par ces présentes que. . . . 'present-day, attrib.a. Actuel; d'aujourd'hui.

present², s. Don m, cadeau m, présent m. To make s.o. a p. of sth., faire présent, faire cadeau, de qch. à qn; offrir qch. à qn. It's for a p., c'est pour offrir.

present³ [pri'zent], v.tr. Présenter. 1. (a) **To p. s.o. to s.o.,** présenter qn à qn. **To p. s.o. at court,** présenter qn à la cour. Th: **To p. a play,** présenter, donner, une pièce. **To p. oneself at, for, an examination,** se présenter à, pour, un examen. (b) Matter that presents some difficulty, affaire qui présente des difficultés. A good opportunity presents itself (for doing sth.), une bonne occasion se présente (de faire qch.). (c) **To p. a pistol at s.o.'s head,** présenter un pistolet à la tête de qn. 2. (a) **To p. sth. to s.o., to p. s.o. with sth.,** donner qch. à qn; faire présent, faire cadeau, de qch. à qn. (b) **To p. one's compliments to s.o.,** présenter ses compliments à qn. 3. (a) Com: **To p. a bill for payment,** présenter un billet à l'encaissement. (b) Parl: **To p. a bill,** présenter, introduire, un projet de loi. 4. To **p. a plan to a meeting,** soumettre un plan à une assemblée. 5. Mil: **To p. arms,** présenter les armes. **P. arms!** Présentez armes! 6. v.i. Obst: Se présenter. **The child presents badly,** l'enfant se présente mal.

presentable [pri'zentəbl], a. (*Of pers.*) Présentable; (of garment) portable. He is quite p., il fait bonne figure; il n'est pas mal.

presentation [,prezen'teiʃ(ə)n], s. 1. (a) Présentation f (d'une personne à la cour, etc.). Ecc: (Feast of) the P., la Présentation de la Vierge. (b) Présentation (de qn à un poste, Ecc: à un bénéfice). (c) Présentation f (d'une pièce à la scène). (d) Com: Payable on p. of the coupon, payable contre remise du coupon. 2. (a) Remise f, présentation (d'un cadeau à qn). (b) Souvenir (offert à un fonctionnaire, etc.). presen'tation copy, s. (a) Exemplaire envoyé gracieusement, à titre gracieux; spécimen (gratuit). (b) Exemplaire offert à titre d'hommage (par l'auteur).

presentient [pri'senʃiənt], a. Qui a un pressentiment (of, de).

presentiment [pri'zentimənt], s. Pressentiment m.

presentment [pri'zentmənt], *s.* **1.** (*a*) Présentation *f* (d'une idée); représentation (de qch.) (en peinture, d'une pièce de théâtre). *Com:* P. of a bill, présentation d'une traite. (*b*) Image *f* (de qch.); description *f.* **2.** (*a*) *Jur:* Déclaration *f* émanant du jury. (*b*) *Ecc:* Plainte faite au diocésain.

preservation [,prezə(:)'veiʃ(ə)n], *s.* **1.** Conservation *f*; naturalisation *f* (d'une fleur). In a state of good p., in a good state of p., en bon état de conservation. **2.** Préservation *f* (from, de).

preservative [pri'zə:vətv], **1.** *a.* Préservatif, -ive; préservateur, -trice. **2.** *s.* (*a*) Préservatif *m.* (contre un danger). (*b*) Antiseptique *m*; agent *m* de conservation.

preserve[1] [pri'zə:v], *s.* **1.** *Usu. pl.* (*a*) Confiture *f.* (*b*) Conserves *fpl.* **2.** (*a*) *For:* Réserve *f.* (*b*) **Game p.,** chasse gardée. **Salmon p.,** vivier *m* à saumons. **To trespass, poach, on s.o.'s preserves,** *F:* marcher sur les plate-bandes *f* de qn.

preserve[2], *v.tr.* **1.** Préserver, garantir (**from,** de). **2.** (*a*) Conserver (un bâtiment, etc.); maintenir (la paix); garder, observer (le silence). **To p. appearances,** sauver les apparences, les dehors. (*b*) Conserver, mettre en conserve (des fruits, etc.); confire (des fruits). (*c*) Naturaliser (un spécimen botanique). **3.** (*a*) Élever (du gibier) dans une réserve. (*b*) Garder (une chasse). **preserved,** *a.* **1.** Conservé; (*of fruit*) confit. **P. food,** conserves *fpl.* **P. meat,** conserve de viande. **2.** Well p., badly p., (bâtiment, etc.) en bon, mauvais, état de conservation. A well-p. woman, une femme bien conservée, qui ne marque pas son âge. **pre'serving-pan,** *s.* Bassine *f* à confitures.

preserver [pri'zə:vər], *s.* Préservateur, -trice.

pre-shrink ['pri:'ʃrink], *v.tr.* Rendre (un tissu) irrétrécissable.

preside [pri'zaid], *v.i.* Présider. (*a*) **To p. at, over, a meeting,** présider (à) une réunion. **To p. at the organ,** tenir l'orgue. (*b*) *Abs.* Exercer les fonctions de président; occuper le fauteuil présidentiel; présider (à table, etc.).

presidency ['prezid(ə)nsi], *s.* Présidence *f.*

president ['prezidənt], *s.* **1.** Président, -ente. **The P. of the Republic,** le Président de la République. **P. of the Board of Trade** = Ministre *m* du Commerce. *U.S: Com:* P. of a corporation, président d'une société anonyme. **2.** *U.S: Sch:* Directeur *m*, recteur *m* (d'une université).

presidential [,prezi'denʃ(ə)l], *a.* Présidentiel, -elle.

presignalization ['pri:'sign(ə)lin], *s. Aut: Adm:* Présignalisation *f.*

press[1] [pres], *s.* **1.** (*a*) Pression *f* (sur qch.); serrement *m* (de main). (*b*) **P. of business,** presse *f*, urgence *f*, des affaires. (*c*) Presse, foule *f.* **To force one's way through the p.,** fendre la foule. *A:* In the p. of the fight, dans la mêlée. **2.** Presse. (*a*) **Letter-p., copying-p.,** presse à copier. *Ten:* **Racket p.,** presse à raquette. (*b*) **Hydraulic p.,** presse hydraulique. (*c*) **Linen-p.,** armoire *f* à linge. **3.** *Typ:* **Printing-p.,** presse d'imprimerie à imprimer. **Rotary p.,** presse rotative. (*b*) Imprimerie *f.* (*c*) In time for p., à temps pour l'impression. **We are going to p.,** nous mettons sous presse. **Ready for p.,** prêt à mettre sous presse. **To pass a proof for p.,** donner le bon à tirer. In the p., at p., sur le marbre; sous presse. The p., la presse, les journaux *m.* **P. campaign,** campagne *f* de presse. **Liberty of the p.,** liberté de la presse. (*Of book*) **To have a good, bad, p.,** avoir une bonne, mauvaise, presse. **P. photographer,** photographe de la presse. **To write for the p.,** faire du journalisme. **'press-agency,** *s. Journ:* Agence *f* de presse, d'informations. **'press-agent,** *s.* Agent *m* de publicité. **'press-box,** *s. Sp:* Stand *m* de la presse. **'press-button,** *s.* **1.** Bouton *m* à pression; bouton fermoir (de gant). **2.** = PUSH-BUTTON 1. **'press-copy,** *s. Publ:* Exemplaire *m* de publicité. **'press-cutting,** *s.* Coupure *f* de journal, de presse. **P.-c. agency,** argus *m* de la presse. **'press-forged,** *a. Metalw:* Embouti. **'press-gallery,** *s.* Tribune *f* de la presse, des journalistes (à la Chambre, etc.). **'press(-)mark,** *s.* Cote *f* (d'un livre de bibliothèque). **'press-proof,** *s. Typ:* Épreuve *f* en bon à tirer. **'press release,** *s. Journ:* Communiqué *m* de presse. **'press-stud,** *s.* Bouton *m* (à) pression.

press[2]. **I.** *v.tr.* Presser. **1.** (*a*) Appuyer, peser, sur (qch.). **P. the button,** appuyez sur le bouton. **His face pressed close to the window,** son visage collé à la vitre. (*b*) Serrer. **To p. the juice from, out of, a lemon,** exprimer le jus d'un citron. **2.** (*a*) *Tchn:* Mettre (qch.) sous presse; emboutir (le métal); satiner, calandrer (le papier). (*b*) Pressurer (des pommes, etc.). (*c*) *Tail:* To p. a suit, donner un coup de fer à un complet. **3.** (*a*) To p. the enemy hard, serrer l'ennemi de près. *F:* To p. s.o. hard, mettre qn aux abois. **Pressed by one's creditors,** pressé, harcelé, par ses créanciers. (*b*) To p. s.o. to do sth., presser qn de faire qch. **He did not need too much pressing,** il ne se fit pas trop prier. **To p. for an answer,** insister pour avoir une réponse immédiate. (*c*) To p. a point, a claim, insister sur un point, sur une demande. **To p. one's advantage,** poursuivre son avantage. (*d*) To p. a gift on s.o., forcer qn à accepter un cadeau. **4.** *Abs.* **Time presses,** le temps presse. **II. press,** *v.i.* **1.** (*a*) Se serrer, se presser. **To p. close against s.o.,** se serrer contre qn. (*b*) To p. on one's pen, appuyer sur son stylo. **2. His responsibilities p. heavily upon him,** ses responsabilités lui pèsent. **press back,** *v.tr.* Refouler (l'ennemi, ses larmes, etc.). **press down,** *v.tr.* (*a*) *Aut:* To p. the pedal down, enfoncer la pédale. (*b*) To p. (down) a seam, rabattre une couture. **press forward, press on. 1.** *v.i.* Presser, forcer, le pas; brûler une étape. *F:* **P. on regardless!** Avançons toujours et tant pis pour les autres! **2.** *v.tr.* Activer, hâter (le travail). **pressed,** *a.* **1.** (*a*) Pressé, serré, comprimé. (*b*) *Metalw:* Embouti. **2. To be hard p.,** (i) être serré de près; (ii) être aux abois, à la dernière extrémité. **P. for space,** à court de place. **P. for time,** très pressé; à court de temps. **We are very p.,** nous sommes débordés (de commandes). **pressing**[1], *a.* (Danger) pressant; (travail) pressé, urgent. **The case is p.,** il y a urgence. **P. invitation,** invitation instante. **Since you are so p....,** puisque vous insistez.... **pressing**[2], *s.* **1.** (*a*) Pression *f* (sur qch.); pressurage *m* (des raisins); calandrage *m* (du papier, etc.). *Metalw:* Emboutissage *m.* **P. machine,** presse *f.* (*b*) *Tail:* Coup *m* de fer tailleur; repassage *m* (d'un complet) à la vapeur; pressing *m* (d'un complet). **2.** (*a*) *Metalw:* Pièce emboutie.

press[3], *s. A:* Presse *f* (de matelots); enrôlement forcé. **'press-gang,** *s.* (Détachement *m* de la) presse.

press[4], *v.tr.* (*a*) *A:* Enrôler de force (un matelot). (*b*) **To p. into service,** enrôler, faire appel à (qn); réquisitionner (qch.).

presser ['presər], *s.* **1.** *Ind:* (*Pers.*) Presseur, -euse. **2.** Presse *f* (à viande, etc.); pressoir *m* (aux raisins).

pressman, *pl.* **-men** ['presmən], *s.m.* **1.** *Typ:* Pressier. **2.** Journaliste.

pressure ['preʃər], *s.* **1.** (*a*) *Ph: Mec:* Pression *f*; poussée *f* (d'une charge, etc.). **High p.,** haute pression. **P. of ten lbs to the square inch,** pression de dix livres par pouce carré; pression de 0,68 atmosphères. **Water p.,** poussée de l'eau; charge *f* d'eau. **Water under p.,** eau *f* sous pression. **Atmospheric p.,** pression atmosphérique. *Aut:* Table of tyre pressures, tableau *m* de gonflages. *Mch:* **Test-p.,** surcharge *f* d'épreuve; timbre *m.* **At full p.,** sous toute pression. **Back p.,** pression inverse. **Boost p.,** pression de suralimentation. (*b*) *El.E:* Tension *f*; potentiel *m.* **Working p.,** tension de régime. (*c*) *Med:* **Blood p.,** tension artérielle (du sang). **High, low, blood p.,** hypertension, hypotension (artérielle). (*d*) *Sp:* **Sustained p.,** forcing *m.* **2. To bring p. to bear on s.o.,** exercer une pression sur qn; agir sur, influencer, qn. **Under the p. of necessity,** poussé par la nécessité. **To act under p.,** agir par contrainte. **P. of business,** presse *f*, urgence *f*, des affaires. **To work at high p.,** travailler fiévreusement. *Ind: etc:* **To work at full p.,** travailler à plein rendement. **'pressure-cooker,** *s. Cu:* Marmite *f* sous pression, cocotte *f* minute, autocuiseur *m*, *pl.* auto-cuiseurs. **'pressure-feed,** *s. Mec.E:* Alimentation *f* sous pression. **'pressure-gauge,** *s.* Manomètre *m*; jauge *f* de pression. *Mch:* **Steam p.-g.,** manomètre à vapeur. *Aut:* **Tyre p.-g.,** contrôleur *m* de pression. **'pressure-re'ducer,** *s.* Détendeur *m* (de bouteille à gaz).

pressurize ['preʃəraiz], *v.tr.* Pressuriser.

prestige [pres'ti:ʒ], s. Prestige m. **It would mean loss of p.**, ce serait déchoir, déroger.

presto ['prestou]. **1.** adv. Mus: Presto. **2.** int: **Hey p.!** passez muscade!

prestress¹ ['pri:'stres], s. Précontrainte f.

prestress², v.i. Appliquer le procédé de la précontrainte. **prestressed**, a. Précontraint. **P. concrete**, béton précontraint.

presumable [pri'zju:məbl], a. Présumable (of s.o., de la part de qn). **-ably**, adv. Probablement. **P. he will come**, il est à croire qu'il viendra.

presume [pri'zju:m]. **1.** v.tr. (a) Présumer. **To p. s.o. (to be) innocent**, présumer qn innocent, que qn est innocent. **I p. that . . .**, j'aime à croire que + ind. **You are Mr X, I p.**, vous êtes M. X, je suppose. (b) **To p. to do sth.**, prendre la liberté, présumer, de faire qch. **May I p. to advise you?** puis-je me permettre de vous conseiller? **2.** v.i. (a) **To p. too much**, trop présumer de soi. (b) Abs. Se montrer présomptueux. (c) **To p. on s.o.'s friendship**, abuser de l'amitié de qn. **To p. on one's birth**, se prévaloir de sa naissance. **presuming**, a. (a) Présomptueux, -euse. (b) Indiscret, -ète.

presumption [pri'zʌm(p)ʃ(ə)n], s. **1.** Présomption f. **The p. is that he is dead**, on présume, il est à présumer, qu'il est mort. **2.** Présomption, arrogance f. **Forgive my p.**, excusez mon audace.

presumptive [pri'zʌm(p)tiv], a. **P. evidence**, preuve f par présomption; présomption f. M.Ins: **The ship is a p. loss**, il y a présomption de perte. Jur: **Heir p.**, héritier présomptif.

presumptuous [pri'zʌm(p)tjuəs], a. Présomptueux, -euse, outrecuidant. **-ly**, adv. Présomptueusement.

presumptuousness [pri'zʌm(p)tjuəsnis], s. Présomption f, outrecuidance f.

presuppose [,pri:sə'pouz], v.tr. Présupposer.

presupposition [,pri:sʌpə'ziʃ(ə)n], s. Présupposition f.

pretence [pri'tens], s. **1.** (Faux) semblant; simulation f; prétexte m. **To make a p. of doing sth.**, faire semblant de faire qch. **Under the p. of friendship**, sous prétexte, sous couleur, d'amitié. **Under, on, the p. of consulting me**, sous prétexte de me consulter. Jur: **To obtain sth. by, on, under, false pretences**, obtenir qch. par fraude f, par des moyens frauduleux. **2.** (a) Prétention f, vanité f. (b) **He makes no p. to wit**, il n'a aucune prétention à l'esprit.

pretend [pri'tend]. **1.** v.tr. (a) Feindre, simuler (qch.). **To p. ignorance**, simuler l'ignorance; faire l'ignorant. **To p. to do sth.**, faire semblant, feindre, de faire qch. **Let's p. we are kings and queens**, jouons au roi et à la reine. (b) Prétendre. **He does not p. to be artistic**, il ne prétend pas être artiste. **I can't p. to advise you**, je n'ai pas la prétention de vous conseiller. **2.** v.ind.tr. **To p. to intelligence**, avoir des prétentions, prétendre, à l'intelligence. **3.** v.i. Faire semblant; jouer la comédie. **Please, stop pretending!** Finissez de jouer la comédie, je vous en prie! **pretended**, a. **1.** (Of quality, emotion, etc.) Feint, simulé, faux, f. fausse. **2.** (Of pers.) Soi-disant, supposé, prétendu.

pretender [pri'tendər], s. **1.** Simulateur, -trice. **2.** Prétendant m (to, à). Hist: **The Young P.**, le Jeune Prétendant (Charles Stuart).

pretension [pri'tenʃ(ə)n], s. **1.** Prétention f (to, à). **To have no pretensions to the first rank**, n'avoir aucune prétention au premier rang. **Man of no pretension(s)**, homme sans prétentions. **To have pretensions to literary taste**, se piquer de littérature. **2.** Droit m, titre m. **To have some pretensions to be considered a scholar**, revendiquer à bon droit le titre d'érudit.

pretentious [pri'tenʃəs], a. Prétentieux, -euse. **-ly**, adv. Prétentieusement.

pretentiousness [pri'tenʃəsnis], s. Prétention f; air prétentieux.

preterit(e) ['pretərit], a. & s. Gram: P. (tense), (temps) passé (m); prétérit m. **In the p.**, au passé, au prétérit.

preternatural [,pri:tə'nætjurəl], a. Qui est en dehors de la nature; surnaturel, -elle.

pretext¹ ['pri:tekst], s. Prétexte m. **To find a p. for refusing**, trouver prétexte à un refus. **Under, on, the p. of consulting me**, sous prétexte de me consulter.

pretext² [pri'tekst], v.tr. Alléguer (qch.) comme prétexte; prétexter (qch.).

prettify ['pritifai], v.tr. Pej: Enjoliver.

prettiness ['pritinis], s. (a) Gentillesse f. (b) Afféterie f, mignardise f (de style, etc.).

pretty ['priti]. **1.** a. (a) Joli; beau, f. belle; (of manner, etc.) gentil, -ille. Sweetly p., **p. as a picture**, joli comme un cœur; gentil, joli, à croquer. **My p. (girl)**, ma mignonne. F: **To be sitting p.**, être bien placé, avoir la bonne place. (b) Iron: **This is a p. state of affairs!** (i) c'est du joli! c'est du propre! (ii) nous voilà dans de beaux draps! **I have heard some p. tales about you**, j'en ai entendu de belles sur votre compte. **2.** adv. Assez, passablement. **I am p. well**, cela ne va pas trop mal. **P. much the same**, à peu près la même chose. **New or p. nearly so**, neuf ou à peu de chose près. **-ily**, adv. Joliment; gentiment; délicatement, avec délicatesse. **'pretty-pretty**, a. Affété, mignard.

pretzel ['pretzl], s. Cu: Bretzel m.

prevail [pri'veil], v.i. **1.** **To p. over, against, s.o.**, prévaloir sur, contre, qn; avoir l'avantage, l'emporter, sur qn. **The strong hand of the law prevailed**, force est restée à la loi. **2.** **To p. (up)on s.o. to do sth.**, amener, déterminer, décider, qn à faire qch.; obtenir de qn qu'il fasse qch. **He was prevailed upon by his friends to . . .**, il se laissa persuader par ses amis de. . . . **3.** Prédominer, régner. **Calm prevails**, le calme règne. **The conditions prevailing in France**, les conditions qui règnent en France. **prevailing**, a. **P. winds**, vents régnants, dominants. **P. fashion**, mode en vogue. **P. opinion**, opinion prédominante, courante. **The p. cold**, le froid qui sévit en ce moment.

prevalence ['prevələns], s. Prédominance f. **P. of bribery**, généralité f de la corruption. **P. of an epidemic**, fréquence d'une épidémie.

prevalent ['prevələnt], a. (Pré)dominant, répandu, général. **Disease that is p. in a place**, maladie qui est très répandue dans un lieu.

prevaricate [pri'værikeit], v.i. **1.** Équivoquer, biaiser, tergiverser. **2.** Mentir; altérer la vérité. **prevaricating**, a. Menteur, -euse.

prevarication [pri,væri'keiʃ(ə)n], s. **1.** Équivoques fpl; tergiversation f. **2.** Mensonge m.

prevaricator [pri'værikeitər], s. **1.** Tergiversateur, -trice; chicaneur, -euse. **2.** Menteur, -euse.

prevent [pri'vent], v.tr. **1.** Empêcher, mettre obstacle à (qch.). **To p. s.o. (from) doing sth.**, empêcher qn de faire qch. **To be unavoidably prevented from doing sth.**, être dans l'impossibilité matérielle de faire qch. **There is nothing to p. . . .**, il n'est pas exclu que. . . . **2.** (a) Prévenir, détourner (un malheur); parer à (un accident). **To p. any scandal**, pour obvier à tout scandale. (b) **You must p. the dog from getting out**, il faut éviter que le chien ne sorte.

preventable, -ible [pri'ventəbl], a. Évitable; qui peut être empêché.

prevention [pri'venʃ(ə)n], s. Empêchement m. **P. of accidents**, précautions fpl contre les accidents. **P. of disease**, prévention f de la maladie. **Rust p.**, protection f contre la rouille.

preventive [pri'ventiv]. **1.** a. (a) (Médicament) préventif. **P. measure**, mesure imposée à titre préventif. (b) Adm: **The P. Service**, le Service des gardes-côtes (douaniers). **2.** s. Empêchement m; mesure préventive. (b) Médicament préventif. (c) **Rust p.**, antirouille m.

preview ['pri:vju:; 'pri:'vju:], s. Exhibition f préalable; vue f préliminaire; Cin: avant-première f.

previous ['pri:viəs]. **1.** a. Préalable; antérieur, antécédent (to, à). **The p. day**, le jour précédent; la veille. **P. engagement**, engagement antérieur. Parl: **To move the p. question**, demander la question préalable. (b) F: **You're a bit (too) p.!** vous allez trop vite! **2.** adv. **P. to my departure**, antérieurement à mon départ; avant mon départ.**-ly**, adv.Préalablement au préalable; auparavant.

prevision [pri'viʒ(ə)n], s. Prévision f.

pre-war ['pri:'wɔ:r]. attrib.a. D'avant -guerre.

prey¹ [prei], s. Proie f. **Birds of p.**, oiseaux de proie, oiseaux prédateurs. **Beasts (or birds) of p.**, les grands prédateurs. **Beasts of p.**, carnassiers m. **To be a p. to sth.**, être en proie à, être dévoré, travaillé, par (la peur, etc.). **To fall a p. to temptation**, tomber en proie à la tentation.

prey², *v.i.* To p. upon sth., faire sa proie de qch. **Something is preying on his mind,** il y a quelque chose qui le travaille. **Mind preyed upon by care,** esprit rongé, miné, par le souci.

price¹ [prais], *s.* (*a*) Prix *m.* **Cost p.,** prix coûtant, prix de revient. **Cash p.,** prix au comptant. **To pay top p.,** payer la forte somme. **At a reduced p.,** au rabais. **Reserve p.,** prix minimum. *Com:* **Fixed p.,** prix fixe, prix imposé. **Contract p.,** prix forfaitaire. **P. ex works,** prix départ usine. *Publ:* **Published p.,** prix fort. (*Of goods*) **To advance, rise, in p.,** renchérir. **What is the p. of that article?** quel est le prix de cet article? **His pictures fetch huge prices,** ses tableaux se vendent à prix d'or. **Beyond p., without p.,** sans prix; hors de prix. **You can buy it at a p.,** vous pouvez l'acheter si vous y mettez le prix. **This must be done at any p.,** il faut que cela se fasse à tout prix, coûte que coûte. **Not at any p.,** pour rien au monde. **To set a high p. on sth.,** faire grand cas de qch. **To set a p. on s.o.'s head,** mettre à prix la tête de qn. (*b*) *Turf:* Cote *f.* **Long p., short p.,** forte, faible, cote. *P:* **What p. my new bike?** et ma nouvelle bécane, qu'est-ce que tu en dis? (*c*) *Bank: Fin:* **P. of money,** taux *m* d'escompte. **Issue p. of shares,** taux d'émission d'actions. *St.Exch:* **Market prices,** cours *m* du marché. **To make a p.,** fixer un cours. **'price-cutting,** *F:* **'price-slashing,** *s. Com:* Gros rabais. **'price-list,** *s.* Prix-courant *m;* tarif *m.*

price², *v.tr.* 1. Mettre un prix à (qch.). **The book is priced at ten shillings net,** le livre se vend au prix net de dix shillings. **To p. oneself out of the market,** perdre sa clientèle en demandant des prix inabordables. 2. Estimer, évaluer. **To p. sth. high, low,** faire grand, peu de, cas de qch. 3. S'informer du prix (de qch.). **priced,** *a.* 1. High-p., de haut prix. 2. **Everything in the window is p.,** à l'étalage tous les prix sont marqués.

priceless ['praislis], *a.* (*a*) Hors de prix; inestimable. (*b*) *F:* (*Of joke, pers.*) Impayable.

pricelessness ['praislisnis], *s.* Valeur *f* inestimable (of, de).

pricey ['praisi], *a. F:* Cher, *f.* chère, coûteux, -euse.

prick¹ [prik], *s.* 1. Piqûre *f* (d'aiguille, etc.). **Pricks of conscience,** remords *m* de conscience. 2. **To kick against the pricks,** regimber. **'prick-eared,** *a.* 1. (Chien) aux oreilles droites, pointues. 2. (*Of pers.*) Aux oreilles dressées; l'oreille aux aguets.

prick², *v.tr.* 1. (*a*) Piquer; faire une piqûre à (qch.); dégonfler (un ballon, la vanité de qn). **To p. a blister,** crever, ponctionner, une ampoule. **His conscience pricks him,** sa conscience l'aiguillonne, le tourmente. (*b*) **To p. a hole in sth.,** faire un trou d'épingle dans qch. **To p. (off) a design on sth.,** piquer un dessin sur (un tissu, etc.). 2. **To p. (off) names on a list,** piquer, pointer, des noms sur une liste. *Nau:* **To p. a bearing (on the chart),** porter un relèvement sur la carte. **To p. the chart,** pointer la carte; faire le point. 3. **To p. one's horse with the spur,** appuyer l'éperon à son cheval; (*lightly*) picoter son cheval. 4. *v.i.* (*Of the skin, nerves, etc.*) Avoir des picotements; picoter; fourmiller. **prick out,** *v.tr. Hort:* Repiquer (des plants). **prick (up),** *v.tr.* **To p. (up) one's ears,** (i) (*of animal*) dresser les oreilles; (ii) (*of pers.*) tendre, dresser, l'oreille. **With pricked ears,** l'oreille aux aguets. **pricking,** *s.* 1. (*a*) Piquage *m. Med:* Ponction *f* (d'une ampoule). (*b*) Pointage *m* (d'une liste, *Nau:* de la carte). 2. **Prickings of conscience,** remords *mpl* (de conscience).

pricker ['prikər], *s. Tls:* Poinçon *m,* pointe *f;* aiguille *f. Leath:* Tire-point *m. Metall: Mch:* Ringard *m,* fourgon *m,* pique-feu *m inv.*

pricket ['prikit], *s. Ven:* Brocard *m* (d'un an); daguet *m.*

prickle¹ ['prikl], *s.* Piquant *m* (de plante, d'animal); épine *f,* aiguillon *m* (de plante).

prickle², *v.tr.* 1. Piquer, picoter, aiguillonner. 2. *v.i.* (*of parts of the body*) Fourmiller. **prickling,** *s.* Picotement *m;* fourmillement *m.*

prickly ['prikli], *a.* 1. (*a*) Hérissé; armé de piquants; épineux, -euse. *Bot:* **P. pear,** (i) figuier *m* de Barbarie; raquette *f;* (ii) figue *f* de Barbarie. (*b*) (*Of pers., question*) Épineux, -euse. 2. (Sensation) de picotement. *S.a.* HEAT¹ 3.

pride¹ [praid], *s.* 1. Orgueil *m.* (*a*) Fierté *f,* morgue *f.* **Puffed up with p.,** bouffi d'orgueil. **False p.** vanité *f.* **To take an empty p. in sth.,** tirer vanité de qch.; faire vanité de qch. (*b*) **Proper p.,** orgueil légitime; amour-propre *m.* **To take (a) p. in sth., in doing sth.,** être fier de qch; mettre son orgueil à faire qch. 2. **He is the p. of the family,** il fait l'orgueil de la famille. 3. Comble *m,* apogée *m.* **May was in its p.,** le mois de mai était dans toute sa splendeur. **In the p. of years,** à la fleur de l'âge. 4. A p. of lions, une troupe, une bande, de lions.

pride², *v.pr.* **To p. oneself (up)on sth., (up)on doing sth.,** s'enorgueillir, se piquer, se vanter, de qch., de faire qch.

prie-Dieu ['pri:djə:], *s.* Prie-Dieu *m inv.*

prier ['praiər], *s.* Curieux, -euse; *F:* fureteur, -euse, fouineur, -euse.

priest [pri:st], *s.m.* Prêtre. **The priests,** le clergé. **Parish p. =** curé. **Assistant p.,** vicaire **P. in charge,** desservant (d'église succursale). **The priests of the Temple of Jupiter,** les prêtres du Temple de Jupiter.

priestess ['pri:stes], *s.f.* Prêtresse.

priesthood ['pri:sthud], *s.* 1. Prêtrise *f,* sacerdoce *m.* **To enter the p.,** se faire prêtre. 2. *Coll.* **The p.,** le clergé.

priestly ['pri:stli], *a.* Sacerdotal, -aux.

prig [prig], *s.* (*a*) Poseur *m;* homme suffisant. **Don't be a p.!** *P:* ne fais pas ta poire! (*b*) Poseur à la vertu; (*of boy*) petit saint de bois.

priggish ['prigiʃ], *a.* 1. Poseur, -euse, suffisant. 2. Collet monté *inv;* bégueule.

priggishness ['prigiʃnis], *s.* 1. Pose *f,* suffisance *f;* pédanterie *f.* 2. Bégueulerie *f.*

prim¹ [prim], *a.* (*a*) (*Of pers.*) Collet monté *inv;* (*of manner*) guindé, compassé. **P. smile,** sourire pincé. (*b*) **P. garden,** jardin tracé au cordeau. **-ly,** *adv.* D'un air collet monté.

prim², *v.tr.* (primmed) *O:* 1. **To p. (up) one's mouth,** *abs.* **to p. (up),** prendre un air pincé; faire la bouche en cœur. 2. **To p. oneself (up),** faire un brin de toilette.

primacy ['praiməsi], *s.* 1. Primauté *f.* 2. *Ecc:* Primatie *f.*

primaeval [prai'mi:v(ə)l], *a. =* PRIMEVAL.

prima facie ['praimə'feiʃii:], *adv. & a.* De prime abord, à première vue. *Jur:* **P. f. case,** affaire qui d'après les premiers témoignages paraît bien fondée.

primage ['praimidʒ], *s. Nau:* Primage *m.*

primary ['praiməri], *a.* 1. Premier, -ière, primitif, -ive, originel, -elle. **P. product,** produit de base; produit brut. *Gram:* **P. tenses,** temps primitifs. **P. colours,** couleurs primaires. **P. education,** instruction primaire. *Geol:* **P. era,** ère *f* primaire. **P. rocks,** roches primaires. *El:* **P. current,** courant primaire. *Pol: U.S:* **P. assembly,** *s.* **primary,** réunion *f* des votants d'un parti pour nommer des candidats. 2. Premier, principal, -aux, essentiel, -elle. **P. cause,** cause première. **-ily,** *adv.* 1. Primitivement; dans le principe. 2. Principalement, essentiellement.

primate ['praimit], *s. Ecc:* Primat *m;* archevêque *m.*

primates ['praimeits, prai'meiti:z], *s.pl. Z:* Primates *m.*

prime¹ [praim], *a.* 1. Premier, -ière; principal, -aux; de premier ordre. **Of p. importance,** de toute première importance. **P. necessity,** nécessité primordiale. **P. mover,** (i) *Mch:* source *f* d'énergie, (puissance) motrice; (ii) (*pers.*) initiateur, -trice (d'un mouvement, etc.). 2. De première qualité. **P. quality meat,** viande (de) surchoix. 3. Premier, originel, -elle, primitif, -ive. **P. cause,** cause première. *Mth:* **P. number,** nombre premier. *S.a.* FACTOR 2. **'Prime 'Minister,** *s.* Premier ministre.

prime², *s.* (*a*) Perfection *f.* **In the p. of life, in one's p.,** dans la force, dans la vigueur, de l'âge; à, dans, la fleur de l'âge. **To be past one's p.,** *F:* être sur le retour. (*b*) Le choix, le meilleur (d'un rôti, etc.). 2. Premiers jours; commencement *m.* 3. *Ecc:* Prime *f.* **To sing (the) P.,** chanter prime. 4. *Fenc:* Prime. 5. *Mth:* N p., n prime; n'.

prime³, *v.tr.* 1. Amorcer (une pompe, etc.). *Mch:* **To p. the boilers,** faire le plein des chaudières. 2. *F:* (*a*) Faire la leçon à (un témoin, etc.). **To p. s.o. with a speech,** mettre qn au fait de ce qu'il devra dire.

To be well primed with information, être bien au courant. (*b*) To p. s.o. with food, bourrer qn de nourriture. To be well primed (with liquor), être bien parti; avoir son plumet. 3. (*a*) *Paint:* Imprimer, apprêter (la surface à peindre). (*b*) Maroufler (la toile). **priming**, *s.* 1. (*a*) Amorçage *m* (d'une pompe). (*b*) Amorce *f* (de mine, etc.). *Mch:* Primage *m*. 2. (*a*) *Paint:* Apprêtage *m*, impression *f* (d'une toile sur châssis). (*b*) Couche *f* d'apprêt.

primer¹ ['praimər], *s.* 1. Apprêteur, -euse (de toiles d'artiste, de boiseries, etc.). 2. (*Coat of paint*) (Peinture *f* d')apprêt (*m*).

primer², *s.* 1. (*a*) Premier livre de lecture; alphabet *m*. (*b*) P. of geography, premier cours de géographie; premiers éléments de géographie. 2. *Typ:* Great p., gros romain; corps 16.

primeval [prai'miːv(ə)l], *a.* Primordial, -aux; des premiers âges (du monde). P. forest, forêt vierge.

primitive ['primitiv], *a.* (*a*) Primitif, -ive. (*b*) (*Of method, etc.*) Primitif, rude, grossier, -ière. (*c*) *s. Hist. of Art:* The Primitives, les primitifs *m*.

primitiveness ['primitivnis], *s.* Caractère primitif; rudesse *f* (d'un peuple, etc.).

primness ['primnis], *s.* (*a*) Air *m* collet monté. The p. of her manners, ses manières compassées. (*b*) Arrangement (trop) méticuleux (d'un jardin, etc.); ordre (trop) parfait.

primogenitor [ˌpraimo'dʒenitər], *s.* 1. Premier ancêtre. 2. *F:* Ancêtre; aïeul *m*, *pl.* aïeux.

primogeniture [ˌpraimo'dʒenit∫ər], *s.* Primogéniture *f*. Right of p., droit *m* d'aînesse.

primordial [prai'mɔːdiəl], *a.* Primordial, -aux.

primp [primp], *v.tr. & i. F: U.S:* = PRINK 3.

primrose ['primrouz], *s. Bot:* Primevère *f* à grandes fleurs. Evening p., onagre *f*; herbe *f* aux ânes. *Lit:* The p. path, le chemin de velours.

primula ['primjulə], *s. Bot:* Primevère *f*.

Primulaceae [ˌprimju'leisiiː], *s.pl. Bot:* Primulacées *fpl.*

Primus (stove) ['praiməs ('stouv)], *s. R.t.m.* Primus *m*.

prince [prins], *s.m.* (*a*) Prince. *S.a.* CROWN¹ 1. (*b*) The princes of this world, les grands de ce monde. The p. of darkness, le prince des ténèbres; le diable.

princeling ['prinsliŋ], *s.m.* Principicule.

princely ['prinsli], *a.* Princier; royal, -aux. A p. gift, un cadeau royal, magnifique.

princess [prin'ses], *s.f.* Princesse. P. royal, princesse royale. *Cost:* P. petticoat, combinaison *f*. P.(-style) dress, robe *f* princesse.

principal ['prinsip(ə)l], I. *a.* Principal, -aux. P. clerk, commis en chef; premier commis. *Com:* P. assistant, secrétaire *mf* de direction. *Cu:* P. dish, pièce *f* de résistance. P. branch of a stream, branche maîtresse d'un cours d'eau. *Gram:* P. clause, proposition principale. -ally, *adv.* Principalement. II. principal, *s.* 1. (*Pers.*) (*a*) Directeur *m* (de fabrique, d'école); chef *m*, patron *m* (d'une maison de commerce); (*woman*) directrice *f*; patronne *f*. *Adm:* Assistant principal = secrétaire *mf* d'administration. (*b*) (*In transaction*) Mandant *m*. *St.Exch:* Donneur m d'ordre. *Jur:* P. and agent, employeur et mandataire *m*; commettant *m* et préposé *m*. (*c*) *Jur:* Auteur *m* (d'un crime). (*d*) Principals in a duel, combattants *m*, adversaires *m*, dans un duel. (*e*) *Mus:* Soliste *mf*. (*f*) *Th:* Premier rôle, rôle principal. 2. *Com:* Capital *m*, principal *m* (d'une dette).

principality [ˌprinsi'pæliti], *s.* Principauté *f*.

principle ['prinsipl], *s.* Principe *m*. 1. First principles of geometry, premiers principes de la géométrie. To lay sth. down as a p., poser qch. en principe. 2. To have high principles, avoir des principes. Man of high principles, homme de haute moralité. Laxity of p., morale relâchée. To do sth. on p., to make it a matter of p. to do sth., avoir pour principe de faire qch.; faire qch. par principe. 3. *Ch:* Active p., principe, élément, actif.

principled ['prinsipld], *a.* High-p., low-p., qui a de bons, de mauvais, principes.

prink [priŋk]. 1. *v.tr.* (*Of bird*) To p. its feathers, se lisser les plumes. 2. *v.i.* Prendre des airs; *P:* faire de l'esbrouffe. 3. *v.i. & pr.* To p. (oneself) up, s'attifer; se parer, se pomponner.

print¹ [print], *s.* 1. (*a*) Empreinte *f*, impression *f*. *S.a.* FINGER-PRINT, FOOTPRINT. Thumb p., empreinte du pouce. (*b*) Butter p., moule *m* à beurre, moule-beurre *m inv.* 2. *Typ:* (*a*) Matière imprimée. He likes to see himself in p., il aime à se faire imprimer, à se voir imprimé. The book is in p., le livre est imprimé, a paru. Out of p., épuisé. (*b*) Large p., small p., gros, petits, caractères. (*c*) Édition *f*, impression. 3. Estampe *f*, gravure *f*, image *f*. 4. *Phot:* (*a*) Épreuve *f*; copie *f*. To take a p. from a negative, tirer une épreuve d'un cliché. (*b*) *Ind:* Blue p., dessin négatif; photocalque *m*; *F:* bleu *m*. 5. *Tex:* Indienne *f*, cotonnade *f*; imprimé *m*. P. dress, robe d'indienne. '**print-room**, *s.* Cabinet *m* d'estampes. '**print-seller**, *s.* Marchand d'estampes, de gravures.

print², *v.tr.* 1. Empreindre; imprimer; marquer (qch.) d'une empreinte. 2. (*a*) *Typ:* Imprimer. To p. (off) a newspaper, tirer un journal. (*Of author*) To p. a book, to have a book printed, faire imprimer un livre; livrer un ouvrage à l'impression. The book is now printing, le livre est à l'impression. *Post:* Printed matter, imprimés *mpl.* (*b*) Mouler (des lettres). To p. an address, écrire une adresse en lettres moulées. 3. *Phot:* To p. (off, out) a negative, tirer une épreuve d'un cliché. Negative that prints well, cliché qui rend bien. 4. *Tex:* Printed calico, indienne imprimée. **printing**, *s.* 1. (*a*) Impression *f*, tirage *m* (d'un livre). (*b*) (*Art of printing*) Imprimerie *f*, typographie *f*. 2. *Phot:* Tirage. '**printing-frame**, *s. Phot:* Châssis-presse *m*. '**printing-machine**, *s. Typ:* Machine *f* à imprimer; presse *f* mécanique. '**printing-office, -works**, *s.* Imprimerie *f*. '**printing-paper**, *s.* 1. *Typ:* Papier *m* d'impression. 2. *Phot:* (*a*) P.(-out) paper, papier sensible. (*b*) *Ind:* Papier héliographique. '**printing-press**, *s. Typ: See* PRESS¹ 3.

printable ['printəbl], *a.* Imprimable.

printer ['printər], *s.* 1. *Typ:* (i) Imprimeur *m* (typographique), typographe *m*; (ii) ouvrier *m* typographe. P.'s error, faute *f* d'impression; coquille *f*. P.'s reader, correcteur, -trice, d'épreuves. 2. *Tex:* Calico p., imprimeur d'indiennes.

printery ['printəri], *s. U.S:* Imprimerie *f* (i) typographique, (ii) pour textiles.

prior¹ ['praiər]. 1. *a.* Préalable, précédent; antérieur (to sth., à qch.). To have a p. claim, être le premier en date. 2. *adv.* P. to my departure, antérieurement à mon départ, avant mon départ; avant de partir.

prior², *s.m. Ecc:* Prieur.

prioress ['praiəris], *s.f. Ecc:* Prieure.

priority [prai'ɔriti], *s.* 1. Priorité *f*, antériorité *f*. P. of invention, antériorité d'invention. To have p. over s.o., avoir le pas, la priorité, sur qn. According to p., selon l'ordre de priorité. P. rights, droits de priorité. *Fin:* P. share, action privilégiée. *attrib.a.* Prioritaire. **pri'ority-holder**, *s.* Prioritaire *mf*.

priory ['praiəri], *s.* Prieuré *m* (le couvent).

prism ['priz(ə)m], *s.* 1. Prisme *m*. *Opt:* Erecting p., prisme redresseur. Reflecting p., prisme réflecteur. Polarizing p., nicol *m*. 2. (*a*) Spectre *m* (solaire). (*b*) *pl.* Prisms, couleurs *f* prismatiques. *S.a.* PRUNE¹. '**prism-bi'noculars**, *s.pl.* Jumelles *f* prismatiques.

prismatic [priz'mætik], *a.* Prismatique. *Opt:* P. sight, viseur à prisme.

prison ['priz(ə)n], *s.* Prison *f*; maison *f* d'arrêt. To send s.o. to p.; to put s.o. in p., mettre qn en prison; (faire) emprisonner qn. To be sent to p., être incarcéré. He has been in p., il a fait de la prison. P. camp, camp *m* de prisonniers (de guerre). '**prison-breaker**, *s.* Échappé de prison. '**prison-breaking**, *s.* Évasion *f* de prison, *Jur:* bris *m* de prison. '**prison-van**, *s.* Voiture *f* cellulaire. '**prison-'yard**, *s.* Préau *m*, cour *f*, de prison.

prisoner ['priz(ə)nər], *s.* 1. Prisonnier, -ière. They were taken p., ils furent faits prisonniers. To be a p. to one's room, être cloué à sa chambre. 2. *Jur:* (*a*) P. at the bar, prévenu, -ue; accusé, -ée; inculpé, -ée. (*b*) (*After sentence*) Détenu, -ue; coupable *mf*. 3. *Games:* Prisoners' base, jeu *m* de) barres *fpl.*

prissy ['prisi], *a. F:* = PRIM¹.

pristine ['pristain], *a.* Premier, -ière, primitif, -ive; d'antan.

prithee ['priði], *int. A:* Je te prie.

privacy ['praivəsi, 'priv-], *s.* **1.** The p. of one's home, l'intimité *f* du foyer. **To live in p.,** mener une vie privée; vivre dans la retraite. **In the p. of his room,** retiré dans sa chambre. **Desire for p.,** désir de se cacher aux regards indiscrets. **There's no p. here,** on est complètement exposé aux regards indiscrets; ça manque d'intimité; on n'est jamais seul ici. **2.** **Lack of p.,** manque de secret (dans une affaire).

private ['praivit]. I. *a.* Privé, particulier. **1.** **P. persons,** (simples) particuliers. **In p. life,** dans le particulier, dans l'intimité *f. Pol:* **P. member,** simple député. **2.** Secret. **To keep a matter p.,** empêcher qu'une affaire ne s'ébruite; tenir une affaire secrète. **P. entrance,** (i) entrée secrète, dérobée; (ii) entrée particulière. **3.** **P. study,** études particulières. **P. motives,** motifs personnels, particuliers. **In my p. opinion,** à mon avis personnel. **4.** **P. and confidential,** secret et confidentiel. **P. conversation,** conversation intime; aparté *m.* **P. interview,** entretien à huis clos. **P. arrangement,** accord à l'amiable. *Jur:* **P. agreement,** acte *m* sous seing privé. **5.** (*a*) (*Not business*) **P. house,** maison particulière. **P. car,** voiture particulière, privée. (*b*) **P. room** (in hotel, etc.), salon réservé. **P. office,** cabinet particulier. **P. chauffeur,** chauffeur *m* de maître. (*c*) **P. dance,** bal sur invitation. **P. theatricals,** comédie de salon. **P. sitting,** séance privée; séance à huis clos. **The funeral will be p.,** les obsèques auront lieu dans la plus stricte intimité. (*d*) **P. education,** enseignement par un précepteur. *S.a.* HOTEL, SCHOOL[1]. **6.** **P. property,** propriété privée. *P.N:* **P.,** entrée interdite au public, défense d'entrer. **P. fishing,** pêche réservée. **P. income,** rentes *fpl;* fortune personnelle. **7.** (*Of place*) Loin des regards indiscrets; retiré. **-ly,** *adv.* **1.** En simple particulier. **P. owned,** qui appartient à un particulier. **To speak to s.o. p.,** parler à qn en particulier. **To hear sth. p.,** entendre qch. à titre confidentiel. **P. sold,** vendu à l'amiable, de gré à gré. II. **private,** *s.* **1.** *Adv.phr.* **In p.** (*a*) **To dine in p.,** dîner en famille. **Married in p.,** marié dans l'intimité. (*b*) (*Of assembly*) **To sit in p.,** se réunir en séance privée, à huis clos. **To talk to s.o. in p.,** parler à qn sans témoins. **2.** *Mil:* Simple soldat *m,* soldat de 2ᵉ classe. **Fall out P. Smith!** soldat Smith, sortez des rangs!

privateer[1] [‚praivə'tiər], *s.* **1.** (Bâtiment armé en) corsaire *m.* **2.** (*Pers.*) Corsaire.

privateer[2], *v.i. Nau:* Faire la course. **privateering,** *s.* (Guerre *f* de) course *f.*

privation [prai'veiʃ(ə)n], *s.* Privation *f.* **To live in p.,** vivre de privations.

privet ['privit], *s, Bot:* Troène *m.*

privilege[1] ['privilidʒ], *s.* **1.** Privilège *m,* prérogative *f.* **To enjoy the p. of doing sth.,** jouir du privilège, avoir le privilège, de faire qch. **2.** Immunité *f* contre les poursuites en diffamation. **The P.,** la prérogative royale. **Parliamentary p.,** prérogative, immunité, parlementaire.

privilege[2], *v.tr.* Privilégier (qn). **To p. s.o. to do sth.,** accorder à qn le privilège de faire qch. **A privileged few,** quelques privilégiés. **To be privileged to do sth.,** jouir du privilège de faire qch.

privy ['privi]. I. *a.* **1.** **To be p. to sth.,** avoir connaissance de qch.; être instruit de qch.; tremper dans (un complot). **2.** Privé. **The P. Council,** le Conseil privé (du souverain). **Lord P. Seal** = Garde *m* du petit sceau. **The P. Purse,** la cassette du souverain. **-ily,** *adv.* En secret. II. **privy,** *s.* **1.** *Jur:* Partie intéressée; ayant droit *m.* **2.** *A:* Lieux *mpl* d'aisances; cabinets *mpl. U.S:* Cabinets (au fond du jardin).

prize[1] [praiz], *s.* **1.** Prix *m.* **The Nobel p.,** le prix Nobel. **To carry off the p.,** remporter le prix. *attrib.* **P. ox,** bœuf primé, médaillé. **2.** (*In a lottery*) Lot *m.* **To draw the first p.,** gagner le gros lot. **'prize-book,** *s. Sch:* Livre *m* de prix. **'prize-fighter,** *s.* Boxeur professionnel. **'prize-fighting,** *s.* Boxe professionnelle. **'prize-giving,** *s.* Distribution *f* de prix. **'prize-list,** *s.* Palmarès *m.* **'prize-money,** *s.* Prix *m* en espèces. **'prize-winner,** *s.* Lauréat, -ate. **'prize-winning,** *a.* Qui remporte le prix. **P.-w. novel,** roman primé.

prize[2], *v.tr.* Évaluer, estimer, priser. **To p. sth. highly,** faire grand cas de qch. **Prized possessions,** biens les plus chéris, les plus estimés, les plus prisés.

prize[3], *s.* **1.** (*a*) *Navy:* Prise *f,* capture *f.* **To be (a) lawful p.,** être de bonne prise. **P. crew,** équipage *m* de prise. **P. Court,** Cour *f* des prises. (*b*) Butin *m* de guerre. **2.** Aubaine *f.* **'prize-money[2],** *s. Navy: A:* Part *f* de prise.

prize[4], *s.* **1.** Force *f* de levier; pesée *f* (au moyen d'un levier). **2.** Point *m* d'appui (pour exercer une pesée).

prize[5]. **1.** *v.tr.* **To p. sth. up,** soulever qch. à l'aide d'un levier. **To p. a lid open,** forcer un couvercle avec un levier. **2.** *v.i.* **To p. against sth.,** faire levier sur qch.; exercer une pesée sur (une porte, etc.).

prizeman, *pl.* **-men** ['praizmən], *s. Sch:* Lauréat *m.*

pro[1] [prou]. *Lt.prep.* **1.** **P. forma,** pour la forme. **P. forma invoice,** facture simulée. **2.** **P. rata,** au prorata; au marc le franc. **3.** **P. tempore,** *F:* pro tem. (i) *Adv.phr.* Temporairement. (ii) *Adj.phr.* Temporaire. **4.** **P. and contra,** *F:* pro and con, pour et contre. **5.** *s.* **The pros and cons,** le pour et le contre.

pro[2], *s. Sp:* Professionnel, -elle.

pro- [prou], *pref.* **1.** (*Substitute for*) **P.-rector,** vice-recteur *m.* **2.** (*In favour of*) **P.-British,** anglophile. **P.-French,** francophile. **P.-Franco,** franquiste.

probability [‚prɔbə'biliti], *s.* Probabilité *f*; vraisemblance *f.* **In all p.,** selon toute probabilité, selon toute vraisemblance. **The p. is that . . .,** il est très probable que + ind.

probable ['prɔbəbl], *a.* **1.** Probable. **It is p. that . . .,** il est probable, vraisemblable, que + ind.; il est à croire que + ind. *Rac:* **P. starters,** partants *m* probables. **2.** **P. story,** histoire vraisemblable. **-ably,** *adv.* Probablement; vraisemblablement.

probate[1] ['proubeit, -bit], *s. Jur:* Validation *f,* homologation *f* (d'un testament). **To take out p. of a will,** faire homologuer un testament. **To grant p. of a will,** homologuer un testament. **'probate-duty,** *s.* Droits *mpl* de succession (par testament).

probate[2] ['proubeit], *v.tr. Jur: U.S:* **1.** Homologuer, valider (un testament). **2.** Mettre (un jeune condamné) en liberté sous surveillance.

probation [prə'beiʃ(ə)n], *s.* **1.** Épreuve *f,* stage *m. Ecc:* Probation *f* (d'un novice). **To be on p.,** être à l'épreuve; faire son stage. **Period of p.,** période *f* stagiaire; stage. **2.** Mise *f* en liberté sous surveillance (d'un jeune condamné). **P. officer,** délégué *m* à la liberté surveillée.

probationary [prə'beiʃn(ə)ri], *a.* (Période) d'épreuve, de stage, stagiaire.

probationer [prə'beiʃnər], *s.* **1.** Stagiaire *mf. Ecc:* Novice *mf.* **2.** Jeune condamné, -ée, qui bénéficie d'un sursis sous surveillance.

probative ['proubətiv], *a.* (*Of evidence, etc.*) Probant, probatoire.

probe[1] [proub], *s.* **1.** *Surg:* (*a*) Sonde *f.* (*b*) Coup *m* de sonde. **2.** *Esp: U.S:* Enquête *f.*

probe[2], *v.tr.* **1.** *Med:* Sonder, explorer; introduire une sonde dans (une plaie). **2.** (*a*) Sonder (qn). (*b*) Approfondir, fouiller (un mystère); scruter (des témoignages). **3.** *v.i.* **To p. into the past,** sonder le passé. **He has probed deep into the matter,** il a examiné l'affaire de près. **probing,** *a.* (*Of question, etc.*) Pénétrant; (interrogatoire) serré.

prober ['proubər], *s.* Sondeur, -euse (d'une plaie); fouilleur, -euse (d'un mystère, etc.). **P. of secrets,** sondeur de secrets.

probity ['proubiti], *s.* Probité *f.*

problem ['prɔbləm], *s.* Problème *m.* **The housing p.,** la crise du logement. **P. child,** enfant *mf* difficile, caractériel *m.* **It's a p. to know what to do,** c'est bien embarrassant de savoir quoi faire. *Th:* **P. play,** pièce à thèse. *Mil: etc:* **Tactical p.,** thème *m* tactique.

problematic(al) [‚prɔbli'mætik(əl)], *a.* **1.** Problématique, douteux, -euse, incertain. **P. gain,** profit aléatoire. **-ally,** *adv.* Problématiquement.

proboscis [prə'bɔsis], *s.* **1.** Trompe *f* (d'éléphant, d'insecte). **2.** *F:* Nez *m,* P: pif *m.*

procedure [prə'si:dʒər], *s.* **1.** Procédé *m.* **I don't like his p.,** je n'aime pas sa manière d'agir, ses procédés. **The correct p.,** la (vraie) marche à suivre; la bonne méthode. **2.** (Mode *m* de) procédure *f* (du Parlement, etc.). **Order of p.,** règles *fpl* de procédure.

proceed [prə′siːd], v.i. 1. (a) To p. (on one's way), continuer son chemin; poursuivre sa route. **Before we p. any farther,** avant d'aller plus loin. (b) To p. to(wards) a place, se rendre à un endroit; diriger ses pas, s'acheminer, vers un endroit. (Of ship) To p. at twenty knots, filer à vingt nœuds. (c) **To p. cautiously,** agir, procéder, avec prudence. **How shall we p.?** quelle est la marche à suivre? (d) To p. to do sth., se mettre à faire qch. **To p. to business,** se mettre à la besogne; passer aux affaires. **I will now p. to another matter,** je passe maintenant à une autre question. **To p. to blows,** en venir aux coups. **To p. to violence,** recourir à la violence. 2. (a) (Se) continuer, se poursuivre. **After that things proceeded quickly,** après cela les choses ont marché rondement. (b) **The negotiations (now) proceeding,** les négociations en cours. **Things are proceeding as usual,** les choses vont leur train, suivent leur cours. **To pay as the work proceeds,** payer au fur et à mesure de l'ouvrage. (c) **To p. with sth.,** poursuivre, continuer (ses études, etc.). 3. Jur: To p. against s.o., procéder contre qn; intenter un procès à qn. 4. **Sounds proceeding from a room,** sons qui sortent, proviennent, d'une pièce. **proceeding,** s. 1. Façon d'agir. 2. (a) Procédé m, action f; pl. faits et gestes m. **To note proceedings,** noter ce qui se passe. (b) pl. Débats m (d'une assemblée). **Proceedings of the Royal Society,** délibérations f, travaux m, de la Société Royale. **The proceedings will begin at eight p.m.,** la séance, la cérémonie, commencera à huit heures du soir. **The proceedings were orderly,** la réunion s'est déroulée dans le calme. (c) Jur: **To take, institute, proceedings against s.o.,** intenter un procès à qn; engager des poursuites contre qn. **To order proceedings to be taken against s.o.,** instrumenter contre qn.
proceeds [′prousiːdz], s.pl. Produit m, montant m, (d'une vente).
process¹ [′prouses], s. 1. (a) Processus m, développement m. **Processes of the mind,** opérations f de l'esprit. **It's a slow p.,** c'est un travail long; cela prend du temps. (b) Cours m, avancement m; marche f (des événements). **During the p. of dismantling,** au cours du démontage. **Building in p. of construction,** bâtiment en cours, en voie, de construction. **To be in the p. of moving,** être en train de déménager. **In the p. of disappearing,** on passe de disparaître. 2. Méthode f; procédé m (photographique); réaction f (chimique); opération (métallurgique). Ch: **Wet p., dry p.,** voie humide, sèche. 3. Jur: Action f en justice. **First p.,** introduction f d'instance. 4. Anat: Excroissance f, processus, procès m; (of bone) apophyse f. ′process-block, s. Cliché m en similigravure, en simili. ′process-engraver, s. Similigraveur m. ′process-engraving, s. Similigravure f, F: simili f. ′process-server, s. Jur: Huissier m. ′process-work, s. Typ: Art: Similigravure f; F: simili f.
process², v.tr. 1. Ind: Traiter, transformer (qch.); faire subir une opération à (qch.). Tex: Apprêter. 2. Typ: Reproduire (un cliché) par similigravure. **processing,** s. Traitement m d'une matière première. **P. industry,** industrie f de transformation. Food-p., l'industrie alimentaire. Automation: **Data p.,** traitement des informations. **Information p.,** informatique f.
procession [prə′seʃ(ə)n], s. Cortège m; défilé m; (religious) procession f. **To go, walk, in p.,** aller en cortège, en procession; défiler. **P. of cars,** défilé, file f, de voitures.
processional [prə′seʃənl], a. Processionnel, -elle.
proclaim [prə′kleim], v.tr. 1. a. Proclamer; déclarer (publiquement). **To p. s.o. king,** proclamer qn roi. **His face proclaims his guilt,** son visage crie, dénonce, sa culpabilité. (b) v.pr. **Hitler proclaimed himself dictator,** Hitler se proclama dictateur 2. Irish Hist: Mettre au ban, hors la loi.
proclaimer [prə′kleimər], s. Proclamateur, -trice.
proclamation [ˌprɔklə′meiʃ(ə)n], s. Proclamation f; déclaration (publique). **To make, issue, a p.,** faire une proclamation. **To make sth. known by public p.,** annoncer qch. à cri public.
proclitic [pro′klitik], a. & s. Ling: Proclitique (m).
proclivity [prə′kliviti], s. Penchant m, tendance f, inclination f (to sth., à qch.).

proconsul [prou′kɔnsəl], s. Rom. & Fr. Hist: Proconsul m.
proconsular [prou′kɔnsjulər], a. Proconsulaire.
proconsulate [prou′kɔnsjulit, -eit], s. Proconsulat m.
procrastinate [pro′kræstineit], v.i. Remettre les affaires au lendemain, à plus tard; temporiser.
procrastination [proˌkræsti′neiʃ(ə)n], s. Remise f des affaires à plus tard; temporisation f.
procrastinator [pro′kræstineitər], s. Temporisateur, -trice.
procreate [′proukrieit], v.tr. Procréer, engendrer.
procreation [ˌproukri′eiʃ(ə)n], s. Procréation f, engendrement m.
procreative [′proukrieitiv], a. Procréateur, -trice.
proctor [′prɔktər], s. 1. Sch: Membre exécutif du conseil de discipline (dans une université). U.S: Surveillant m d'examen ou de discipline. 2. Jur: **King's, Queen's, p.,** procureur m du roi, de la reine.
procumbent [pro′kʌmbənt], a. 1. (Of pers.) Couché sur le ventre, la face contre terre. 2. Bot: Rampant.
procurable [prə′kjuərəbl], a. Procurable.
procuration [ˌprɔkju′reiʃ(ə)n], s. 1. Jur: Procuration f. **To act by p.,** agir par procuration. 2. Acquisition f, obtention f (de qch. pour qn). 3. Proxénétisme m.
procurator [′prɔkju(ə)reitər], s. 1. Hist: Procurateur m. 2. Jur: Fondé m de pouvoir(s); procureur m. ′procurator-′fiscal, s. (Scot.) Procureur général.
procure [prə′kjuər], v.tr. 1. (a) Obtenir, procurer. **To p. sth. for s.o.,** procurer qch. à qn. (b) To p. sth. (for oneself), se procurer qch. **This book is very difficult to p.,** il est très difficile de se procurer ce livre. 2. (a) Embaucher (une fille) en vue de la prostitution. (b) Abs. Faire le métier de proxénète, d'entremetteur, d'entremetteuse. **procuring,** s. Proxénétisme m.
procurement [prə′kjuəmənt], s. 1. Obtention f, acquisition f (of, de). 2. = PROCURING.
procurer [prə′kjuərər], s. (i) Acquéreur, -euse; (ii) Personne f qui procure (qch. pour qn). 2. Entremetteur m, proxénète m.
procuress [prə′kjuəris], s.f. Entremetteuse, procureuse.
prod¹ [prɔd], s. Coup (donné avec qch. de pointu). **To give s.o. a p. with a bayonet,** donner un coup de baïonnette à qn. F: **Give him a p.,** aiguillonnez-le un peu.
prod², v.tr. (prodded) 1. To p. (at) sth. (with sth.) tâter, pousser, qch. (du bout d'un bâton, du bout du doigt). 2. F: Aiguillonner, stimuler, pousser (s.o. into doing sth., qn à faire qch.). **To p. s.o. on,** presser, stimuler, qn.
prodigal [′prɔdig(ə)l], a. & s. Prodigue (mf); gaspilleur, -euse. B: **The P. Son,** l'enfant prodigue. **To be p. of sth.,** être prodigue de qch; prodiguer qch. **-ally,** adv. Prodigalement, en prodigue. **To give p.,** donner à pleines mains.
prodigality [ˌprɔdi′gæliti], s. Prodigalité f.
prodigious [prə′didʒəs], a. Prodigieux, -euse; F: merveilleux, -euse, mirobolant. **-ly,** adv. Prodigieusement; F: merveilleusement, énormément.
prodigy [′prɔdidʒi], s. Prodige m; merveille f. **Infant p.,** enfant prodige.
produce¹ [′prɔdjuːs], s. 1. (a) Rendement m (d'un champ de blé, d'une mine, etc.). (b) Produit m (de son travail). 2. Coll. Denrées fpl, produits. **Farm p.,** produits agricoles.
produce² [prə′djuːs], v.tr. 1. (a) Présenter, exhiber (son passeport). Jur: Représenter (des documents). **I can p. the documents,** je peux fournir les documents. (b) Th: Cin: To p. a play, a film, mettre une pièce, un film, en scène. **Badly produced play,** pièce mal montée. W.Tel: T.V: Mettre en ondes. 2. (a) Créer. El: To p. a spark, faire jaillir une étincelle. **Current produced by a battery,** courant engendré par une pile. (b) Ind: Fabriquer. (c) Produire, éditer (un livre, un film). (d) Produire, causer, provoquer (un effet). **To p. a sensation,** faire sensation. 3. Rapporter, rendre (un profit, etc.). 4. Geom: Prolonger (une ligne).
producer [prə′djuːsər], s. 1. Producteur, -trice. Th: Metteur m en scène. Cin: Directeur m de productions. W.Tel: T.V: Metteur m en ondes. Cin: W.Tel: T.V: Réalisateur, -trice; F: producer m. 2. Ind: (Gas-)p., gazogène m.
producible [prə′djuːsəbl], a. Productible.

product ['prɔdʌkt], s. 1. Produit m. **Products of a country**, produits, denrées f, d'un pays. _Ind:_ Secondary p., sous-produit m. 2. _Mth:_ Produit.
production [prɔ'dʌkʃ(ə)n], s. 1. (a) Production f, représentation f, communication f (de documents); présentation f (de son billet). (b) _Th:_ Mise f en scène (d'une pièce). _W.Tel: T.V:_ Mise en ondes. _Cin: W.Tel: T.V:_ Réalisation f. 2. (a) Génération f (de la vapeur); production (d'un bruit, d'un effet, etc.). (b) Fabrication f (de marchandises). **Industrial p. of a country**, production industrielle d'un pays. **Cost of p.**, prix m de fabrique. _S.a._ MASS PRODUCTION. 3. _Geom:_ Prolongement m (d'une ligne). 4. (a) Produit m. **Productions of a country**, produits, denrées f, d'un pays. (b) Production, œuvre f (littéraire).
productive [prɔ'dʌktiv], a. 1. (a) Productif, -ive, générateur, -trice (of sth., de qch.); (of mine, etc.) en rapport. (b) (Of land) Fécond. 2. _Pol.Ec:_ (Travail) productif. **-ly**, adv. Profitablement, avec profit.
productiveness [prɔ'dʌktivnis], **productivity** [,prɔ-dʌk'tiviti], s. Productivité f. **Land in full p.**, terres en plein rapport, en plein rendement. _Ind: etc:_ **P. of an enterprise**, rapport m, rentabilité f, d'une entreprise.
pro-English ['prou'ingliʃ], a. Anglophile.
profanation [,prɔfə'neiʃ(ə)n], s. Profanation f.
profane[1] [prɔ'fein], a. Profane. (a) **Things sacred and p.**, le sacré et le profane. (b) (Of pers.) Non initié. (c) Païen, -enne, impie. (d) (Langage) impie, blasphématoire. **P. word**, juron m, blasphème m. **Don't be p.!** pas de jurons! **-ly**, adv. 1. D'une manière profane; avec impiété. 2. En jurant, en sacrant.
profane[2], v.tr. Profaner; polluer (une église). **To p. the Sabbath(-day)**, violer le repos dominical.
profaner [prɔ'feinər], s. Profanateur, -trice; violateur, -trice (of, de).
profanity [prɔ'fæniti], s. 1. (a) Nature f profane (d'un écrit). (b) Impiété f (d'une action). 2. **To utter profanities**, proférer des blasphèmes, des jurons.
profess [prɔ'fes], v.tr. 1. (a) Professer, faire profession de (sa foi, etc.). **To p. oneself satisfied**, se déclarer satisfait. (b) (Falsely) **To p.** (oneself) **to be a social reformer**, se dire, se faire passer pour, réformateur social. **I do not p. to be a scholar**, je ne prétends pas être savant. **She professes to be thirty**, elle se donne trente ans. 2. (a) Exercer (un métier, la médecine). (b) _Sch:_ Professer (l'histoire, etc.). **professed** [prɔ'fest], a. 1. (Of monk, nun) Profès, -esse. 2. (a) **P. enemy of the Government**, ennemi déclaré du gouvernement. (b) Prétendu, soi-disant.
professedly [prɔ'fesidli], adv. De son propre aveu; ouvertement. **He is p. ignorant on the subject**, il avoue son ignorance à ce sujet.
profession [prɔ'feʃ(ə)n], s. 1. Profession f, déclaration f. **P. of faith**, profession de foi. _Ecc:_ **To make one's p.**, faire profession (dans un ordre). 2. (a) Profession, métier m. **The (learned) professions**, les carrières libérales. **The medical, teaching, p.**, le corps médical, enseignant. **By p. he is a doctor**, il est médecin de profession. (b) **The p.**, (i) les gens m du métier; _esp._ (ii) _F:_ le théâtre. **To belong to the p.**, faire du théâtre.
professional [prɔ'feʃənl], a. 1. _a._ Professionnel, -elle. (a) **P. practices**, usages m du métier. **To take p. advice on a matter**, (i) consulter un homme du métier sur qch.; (ii) consulter un médecin, un avocat. (b) **The p. army**, l'armée de métier. **P. diplomatist**, diplomate de carrière. (c) Expert. (d) **The p. classes**, les membres m des professions libérales. **P. man**, intellectuel m. 2. _s._ (a) Expert m. **Professionals**, gens m de métier. (b) _Sp:_ Professionnel, -elle. **To turn p.**, passer professionnel. **-ally**, adv. Professionnellement. **To act p.**, agir dans l'exercice de sa profession.
professionalism [prɔ'feʃən(ə)lizm], s. 1. Caractère professionnel (de qch.). 2. _Esp. Sp:_ Professionnalisme m.
professionalize [prɔ'feʃən(ə)laiz], v.tr. (a) Faire un métier de (qch.). (b) Livrer (un sport) au professionnalisme.
professor [prɔ'fesər], s. Professeur m (de faculté). **P. Smith**, (Monsieur) le professeur Smith.

professorial [,prɔfe'sɔ:riəl], a. Professoral, -aux. **-ally**, adv. D'un ton professoral; d'une manière professorale.
professoriate [,prɔfe'sɔ:riit], s. 1. Le corps professoral. 2. = PROFESSORSHIP.
professorship [prɔ'fesəʃip], s. Professorat m. **To be appointed to a p.**, être nommé à une chaire.
proffer ['prɔfər], v.tr. (proffered) Offrir, présenter. _O:_ **To p. one's hand**, tendre la main (à qn).
proficiency [prɔ'fiʃənsi], s. Capacité f, compétence f (in a subject, en une matière).
proficient [prɔ'fiʃənt], a. Capable, compétent; versé (in, dans). **To be p. in Latin**, être fort en latin; posséder le latin à fond. **-ly**, adv. Avec compétence.
profile[1] ['proufail], s. 1. (a) (i) Profil m; (ii) silhouette f. **Drawn in p.**, esquissé de profil. _Journ:_ Portrait m. (b) _Arch: etc:_ Profil, coupe f perpendiculaire. **To project in p.**, projeter en profil. (c) _Arch: Carp: Ind:_ Moulure f; chantournement m. (d) _Th:_ Ferme f (de décor). 2. _Cer: etc:_ Calibre m (de tourneur, etc.).
profile[2], v.tr. 1. _Ind:_ Profiler, contourner, chantourner. _Carp:_ Moulurer. 2. **The trees are profiled against the horizon**, les arbres se profilent sur l'horizon. **profiling**, s. Profilage m, contournement m; _Carp:_ moulurage m, moulure f. _Metalw:_ **P. machine**, machine f à profiler.
profit[1] ['prɔfit], s. 1. Profit m, bénéfice m. (a) Avantage m. **To turn sth. to p.**, tirer profit de qch. (b) _Com:_ **Net p.**, bénéfice net. **To bring in, yield, show, a p.**, donner un bénéfice. **To sell sth. at a p.**, vendre qch. à profit, à bénéfice. **To make a p. on, out of, a transaction**, retirer un profit d'une affaire. **To make huge profits**, gagner gros. **P. and loss**, profits et pertes. **'profit-earning**, a. Rentable. **P.-e. capacity**, rentabilité f. **'profit-seeking**, a. (Gens) intéressés; (association f) à but lucratif. **'profit-sharing**, s. _Ind:_ Participation f aux bénéfices. **P.-s. scheme**, système m de participation; intéressement m.
profit[2], v. (profited) 1. v.tr. Profiter à (qn); être avantageux à (qn). _A:_ **What will it p. you to go there?** à quoi (cela) vous profitera-t-il d'y aller? 2. v.i. **To p. by sth.**, profiter, bénéficier, de qch. **To p. by s.o.'s advice**, mettre à profit l'avis de qn.
profitability [,prɔfitə'biliti], s. Rentabilité f.
profitable ['prɔfitəbl], a. Profitable, avantageux, -euse; lucratif, -ive, rémunérateur, -trice. **It is more p. to us to sell it**, nous avons plus d'avantage à le vendre. **-ably**, adv. Profitablement, avantageusement. **To study p.**, étudier avec fruit.
profitableness ['prɔfitəblnis], s. Nature avantageuse (of, de); profit m, avantage m; rentabilité f (d'une affaire).
profiteer[1] [,prɔfi'tiər], s. _F:_ Profiteur m, mercanti m.
profiteer[2], v.i. Faire des bénéfices excessifs; agir en mercanti. **profiteering**, s. Mercantilisme m.
profiterole [prɔ'fitəroul], s. _Cu:_ Profiterole f.
profitless ['prɔfitlis], a. Sans profit.
profligacy ['prɔfligəsi], s. 1. Débauche f, libertinage m; crapule f, dévergondage m, paillardise f. 2. Prodigalité f.
profligate ['prɔfligit], a. & s. 1. Débauché, -ée; libertin, -ine; dévergondé, -ée. 2. Prodigue. **-ly**, adv. (Vivre, etc.) dans la débauche; (vivre) sans mœurs.
profound [prɔ'faund], a. Profond. **P. secret**, secret absolu. **P. scholar**, érudit accompli, profond. **P. study of a subject**, étude approfondie d'un sujet. **-ly**, adv. Profondément.
profoundness [prɔ'faundnis], **profundity** [prɔ'fʌnditi], s. Profondeur f.
profuse [prɔ'fju:s], a. 1. **To be p. in one's apologies**, se montrer prodigue d'excuses; se confondre en excuses. **To be p. of praise**, prodiguer les louanges. 2. Profus, abondant, excessif. **P. bleeding**, hémorragie abondante. **-ly**, adv. Profusément, abondamment. **To apologize p.**, se confondre en excuses.
profuseness [prɔ'fju:snis], s. Profusion f.
profusion [prɔ'fju:ʒ(ə)n], s. Profusion f; abondance f. **Flowers in p.**, des fleurs à profusion, à foison.
progenitor [pro'dʒenitər], s. Aïeul m, pl. aïeux; ancêtre m.

progenitress [pro'genitris], **progenitrix** [pro'genitriks], *s.f.* Aïeule.

progeniture [pro'dʒenit∫ər], *s.* Progéniture *f.*

progeny ['prɔdʒini], *s.* **1.** Progéniture *f.* **2.** Descendants *mpl*, lignée *f*, postérité *f.*

prognathic [prɔg'næθik], **prognathous** ['prɔgnəθəs], *a. Anthr:* Prognathe.

prognosis, *pl.* -oses [prɔg'nousis, -ousi:z], *s. Med:* **1.** Pronostic *m.* To give a very serious p., pronostiquer au plus grave. **2.** (*The art*) Prognose *f.*

prognostic [prɔg'nɔstik]. **1.** *a. Med:* (Signe) pro(g)nostique. Signs p. of sth., signes qui pronostiquent, présagent, qch. **2.** *s.* (*a*) Pronostic *m*, présage *m.* (*b*) *Med:* Signe pronostique; symptôme *m.*

prognosticate [prɔg'nɔstikeit], *v.tr.* Pronostiquer, présager, prédire (qch.).

prognostication [prɔg‚nɔsti'kei∫(ə)n], *s.* **1.** (*a*) Pronostication *f*, prédiction *f.* (*b*) Pressentiment *m.* **2.** = PROGNOSTIC 2.

program(me)[1] ['prougræm], *s.* Programme *m.* Dance p., carnet *m* de bal. To arrange a p., arrêter un programme. *F:* What's the p. today? que faisons-nous aujourd'hui? *W.Tel: T.V:* P. editor, éditorialiste *mf.* Request p., programme des auditeurs. *Cin:* P. film, *F:* (film *m*) bouche-trou (*m*), *pl.* bouchetrous. 'programme-music, *s.* Musique *f* de genre. 'programme-seller, *s.* Vendeuse *f* de programmes.

program(me)[2], *v.tr.* **1.** *Computers:* Programmer. Programmed teaching, enseignement programmé. **2.** *F: T.V: etc:* Programmer. **programming**, *s.* **1.** *Computers:* Programmation *f.* **2.** *F: T.V: etc:* Programmation. **programmer**, *s.* **1.** *Computers:* (*a*) (*Pers.*) Programmeur, -euse. (*b*) (*Machine*) Programmateur *m.* **2.** *F: T.V: etc:* (*Pers.*) Programmateur, -trice.

progress[1] ['prougres], *s.* (*No pl.*) **1.** (*a*) Marche *f* en avant; avancement *m* (d'un travail, etc.). The p. of events, le cours des événements. In p. of time, avec le temps. The work now in p., le travail en cours. Harvesting in full p., moisson qui bat son plein. (*b*) Progrès *m.* To make p. in one's studies, faire des progrès dans ses études. To make slow p., n'avancer que lentement. Negotiations are making good p., les négociations sont en bonne voie. *Com: Ind:* P. report, état *m* périodique. **2.** (*a*) *A:* Voyage *m.* (*b*) Tournée *f* (d'un juge). Royal p., voyage d'apparat (du roi, de la reine).

progress[2] [prə'gres], *v.i.* **1.** (*a*) S'avancer. As the year progresses, au cours de l'année. (*b*) To p. with one's studies, faire des progrès, avancer, dans ses études. The patient is progressing favourably, le malade fait des progrès satisfaisants. **2.** *A:* (*Of official*) Faire une tournée.

progression [prə'gre∫(ə)n], *s.* **1.** Progression *f.* Mode of p., mode *m* de locomotion. **2.** *Mth:* Arithmetical p., progression arithmétique. **3.** *Mus:* Harmonic p., marche *f* harmonique.

progressist [prə'gresist], *s. Pol:* Progressiste *mf.*

progressive [prə'gresiv]. **1.** *a.* Progressif, -ive. (*a*) By p. stages, par degrés. (*b*) P. age, siècle de progrès. To be p., être ami du progrès. **2.** *s.* Progressiste *mf.* -ly, *adv.* Progressivement; au fur et à mesure.

progressiveness [prə'gresivnis], *s.* Progressivité *f.*

prohibit [prə'hibit], *v.tr.* **1.** Prohiber, défendre, interdire (qch.). *P.N:* Smoking (is) prohibited, défense de fumer. To p. s.o. from doing sth., défendre, interdire, à qn de faire qch. **2.** Empêcher (s.o. from doing sth., qn de faire qch.).

prohibition [‚prou(h)i'bi∫(ə)n], *s.* (*a*) Prohibition *f*, interdiction *f*, défense *f* (from doing sth., de faire qch.). (*b*) *U.S:* Régime sec.

prohibitionism ['prou(h)i'bi∫ənizm], *s.* Prohibitionnisme *m.*

prohibitionist [‚prou(h)'bi∫ənist], *a. & s.* Prohibitionniste (*mf*). P. countries, pays secs.

prohibitive [prə'hibitiv], *a.* P. price, prix prohibitif, inabordable. The price of peaches is p., les pêches sont hors de prix.

prohibitory [prə'hibitri], *a.* (*Of law, etc.*) Prohibitif, -ive.

project[1] ['prɔdʒekt], *s.* Projet *m.*

project[2] [prə'dʒekt]. I. *v.tr.* Projeter. **1.** To p. a journey, projeter un voyage. Projected buildings, édifices en projet. **2.** Projeter, lancer, (un corps) en avant. **3.** To p. a picture on the screen, projeter une image sur l'écran. *Art:* Projected shadow, ombre portée. II. **project**, *v.i.* Faire saillie, faire ressaut; (s')avancer. Balcony projecting over the pavement, balcon surplombant le trottoir. To p. beyond the building line, déborder, dépasser, l'alignement. **projecting**, *a.* Saillant, en saillie; hors d'œuvre, en porte-à-faux. P. teeth, dents saillantes.

projectile [prə'dʒektail], *a. & s.* Projectile (*m*).

projection [prə'dʒek∫(ə)n], *s.* **1.** (*a*) Lancement *m* (d'un projectile); projection *f* (d'un rayon de lumière). *Cin:* P. room, cabine *f* de projection. (*b*) Conception *f* (d'un projet, etc.). **2.** *Geom:* Projection. **3.** Saillie *f.* (*a*) Avancement *m* (en dehors). (*b*) *Arch:* Partie *f* qui fait saillie; ressaut *m*; porte-à-faux *m*, portée *f* (d'un balcon).

projectionist [prə'dʒek∫ənist], *s. Cin:* Projectionniste *m.*

projector [prə'dʒektər], *s.* Projecteur *m* (de rayons lumineux, etc.). *Phot:* (Slide) projector, projecteur (pour diapositives). *Cin:* Projecteur *m*, appareil *m* de projection.

prolapse[1] [prou'læps], *s. Med:* Prolapsus *m*; descente *f* (de matrice, de rectum).

prolapse[2], *v.i. Med:* (*Of organ*) Descendre.

prolate ['prouleit], *a. Geom:* (Ellipsoïde) allongé, prolongé.

proletarian [‚prouli'tεəriən]. **1.** *a.* Prolétarien, -ienne, prolétaire. **2.** *s.* Prolétaire *mf.*

proletarianism [‚prouli'tεəriəniz(ə)m], *s.* **1.** Prolétariat *m.* **2.** Opinions *f* politiques du prolétariat.

proletariat(e) [‚prouli'tεəriət], *s.* Prolétariat *m.*

proliferate [prə'lifəreit], *v.tr. & i.* Proliférer; se multiplier.

proliferation [prəlifə'rei∫(ə)n], *s.* Prolifération *f.*

proliferous [prə'lifərəs], *a. Nat.Hist:* Prolifère.

prolific [prə'lifik], *a.* Prolifique; fécond, fertile (in, of, en). -ly, *adv.* Abondamment.

prolix ['prouliks], *a.* Prolixe, diffus; (style) délayé.

prolixity [pro'liksiti], *s.* Prolixité *f.*

prologue ['proulɔg], *s.* Prologue *m* (to, de).

prolong [pro'lɔŋ], *v.tr.* Prolonger.

prolongation [‚proulɔŋ'gei∫(ə)n], *s.* Prolongation *f*; délai accordé.

prom [prɔm], *s. F:* **1.** (*At seaside*) Esplanade *f.* **2.** = PROMENADE CONCERT. **3.** *U.S:* Bal *m* d'étudiants.

promenade[1] [prɔmən'ɑːd], *s.* **1.** Promenade *f* (en grande toilette). **2.** (*a*) (Lieu *m* de) promenade; (*at seaside*) esplanade *f.* (*b*) *Th:* Promenoir *m*, pourtour *m* (du parterre). **3.** *U.S:* Bal *m* d'étudiants. 'promenade 'concert, *s.* Concert *m* où une partie de l'auditoire reste debout. 'promenade 'deck, *s. Nau:* Pont-promenade *m*, promenoir *m.*

promenade[2]. **1.** *v.i.* Se promener, parader (à pied, en voiture, etc.). **2.** *v.tr.* (*a*) Se promener dans (la salle); se promener sur (les boulevards). (*b*) Promener (qn).

promenader [‚prɔmə'nɑːdər], *s.* Promeneur, -euse.

prominence ['prɔminəns], *s.* **1.** Proéminence *f*; relief *m.* (*b*) Saillie *f*, protubérance *f.* **2.** Éminence *f.* To bring sth. into p., to give sth. p., faire ressortir qch. To come into p., (*of pers.*) percer; arriver à un rang éminent; (*of thg*) acquérir de l'importance.

prominent ['prɔminənt], *a.* **1.** Saillant; en saillie; proéminent; (*of ears*) décollé. P. nose, nez prononcé. **2.** (*a*) Saillant; remarquable; (*of theory, etc.*) en évidence, très en avant. The most p. object on the hill, la chose la plus en vue sur la colline. (*Of idea, etc.*) To be p., ressortir. In a p. position, très en vue. To play a p. part in an affair, jouer un rôle important dans une affaire. (*b*) Éminent. The p. figures of the period, les personnages remarquables de l'époque. -ly, *adv.* (*a*) Éminemment. (*b*) Goods p. displayed, marchandises bien en vue.

promiscuity [‚prɔmis'kju(:)iti], *s.* Promiscuité *f.*

promiscuous [prə'miskjuəs], *a.* **1.** (*a*) Confus, mêlé. P. crowd, foule hétérogène. (*b*) Sans distinction de sexe. **2.** Casuel, -elle. She is completely p., elle couche avec n'importe qui. -ly, *adv.* **1.** (*a*) Confusément, sans ordre; en promiscuité. (*b*) Sans distinction de sexe. **2.** Casuellement, fortuitement.

promise¹ ['prɔmis], s. Promesse f. (a) To make a p., faire une promesse. To keep one's p., tenir sa promesse. To break one's p., manquer à sa promesse; manquer de parole. To release s.o. from his p., rendre sa parole à qn. (b) Child full of p., enfant qui promet. To show great p., donner de belles espérances. To hold out a p. to s.o. of sth. faire espérer qch. à qn.

promise², v.tr. (a) To p. s.o. sth., to p. sth. to s.o., promettre qch. à qn. F: He promised her the moon, the earth, il lui a promis monts et merveilles. To p. s.o. one's daughter in marriage, promettre sa fille en mariage à qn. To p. (s.o.) to do sth., promettre (à qn) de faire qch. To p. oneself sth., se promettre qch. You will be sorry for it, I p. you, vous le regretterez, je vous le promets, je vous en réponds. B: The Promised Land, la Terre promise. (b) Action that promises trouble, action qui laisse prévoir des ennuis. Abs. The scheme promises well, le projet s'annonce bien; l'affaire promet. **promising**, a. Plein de promesses. P. young man, jeune homme qui promet. The harvest looks p., la moisson s'annonce bien. The future doesn't look (too) p., l'avenir s'annonce mal. -ly, adv. Qui promet, d'une manière pleine de promesses.

promissory ['prɔmisəri, prɔ'misəri], a. (Of oath) Promissoire. Com: P. note, billet m à ordre.

promontory ['prɔmənt(ə)ri], s. Promontoire m.

promote [prə'mout], v.tr. 1. Donner de l'avancement à (qn). To p. s.o. to an office, nommer qn à un poste. To be promoted, être promu; avancer; monter en grade. 2. (a) Encourager (les arts, un projet); favoriser (le succès); faciliter (le progrès); avancer (les intérêts de qn); amener, contribuer à (un résultat, etc.). To p. good feeling between nations, encourager l'amitié entre les nations. (b) To p. a company, lancer une société anonyme. (c) Ch: Ph: etc: To p. a reaction, amorcer, provoquer, une réaction. (d) Faire de la réclame pour (un article de commerce); F: chauffer (un produit, une affaire). **promoting**, s. 1. Promotion f, avancement m. 2. Encouragement m.

promoter [prə'moutər], s. Instigateur, -trice, auteur m (d'un projet, etc.). Company p., promoteur m, fondateur m, de sociétés anonymes.

promotion [prə'mouʃ(ə)n], s. Promotion f, avancement m. Mil: etc: Nomination f à un grade supérieur. To get p., obtenir de l'avancement.

prompt¹ [prɔm(p)t], a. 1. Prompt. (a) Vif, f. vive, rapide. (b) Immédiat. P. reply, réponse par retour du courrier. P. delivery, livraison immédiate. P. in repartee, prompt à la riposte. (c) adv. To arrive p. to the minute, arriver à l'heure exacte, F: à l'heure pile. 2. Com: (a) P. cotton, coton livrable sur-le-champ et comptant. (b) Délai m limite, terme m (de paiement). -ly, adv. Promptement. (a) Avec empressement. (b) Sur-le-champ, immédiatement. To pay p., (i) payer argent comptant; (ii) payer ponctuellement. She screamed, and p. dropped the tray, elle jeta un cri, et du coup laissa tomber le plateau.

prompt², s. (a) Suggestion f; F: inspiration f, tuyau m. (b) Th: To give an actor a p., souffler un acteur. attrib. Th: P. side, côté m de la scène à la droite des acteurs; côté jardin. 'prompt-book, s. Th: Exemplaire m du souffleur. 'prompt-box, s. Th: Trou m du souffleur.'prompt-'copy, s.Th: Exemplaire m du souffleur.

prompt³, v.tr. 1. To p. s.o. to sth., suggérer qch. à qn. To p. s.o. to do sth., inciter qn à faire qch. He felt prompted to speak, il se sentit poussé à prendre la parole. To be prompted by a feeling of pity, être mû, animé, par un sentiment de pitié. 2. Souffler (un acteur, un élève). To p. a witness, suggérer des jalons à un témoin. **prompting**, s. 1. Suggestion f; incitation f (to do sth., à faire qch.). 2. Th: Action f de souffler (un acteur). Sch: No p.! ne soufflez pas!

prompter [prɔm(p)tər], s. 1. Instigateur, -trice (to a crime, d'un crime); incitateur, -trice (to, à). 2. Souffleur, -euse. Th: Opposite p., côté m de la scène à la gauche des acteurs; côté cour. Prompter's box, trou m du souffleur.

promptitude ['prɔm(p)titju:d], **promptness** ['prɔm(p)tnis], s. Promptitude f, empressement m.

promulgate ['prɔmʌlgeit], v.tr. 1. Promulguer (une loi). 2. Disséminer, répandre (une idée); proclamer, répandre (une nouvelle).

promulgation [,prɔməl'geiʃ(ə)n], s. 1. Promulgation f (d'une loi). 2. Dissémination f (d'une idée); proclamation f (d'une nouvelle).

prone [proun], a. 1. (a) (Of hand, etc.) En pronation. (b) (Of pers., etc.) Couché sur le ventre. 2. To be p. to sth., to do sth., être enclin, porté, à qch., à faire qch. To be accident p., être prédisposé aux accidents.

proneness ['prounnis], s. Disposition f, inclination f (to, à). P. to accidents, prédisposition f aux accidents.

prong [prɔŋ], s. Fourchon m, dent f, branche f (de fourche); dent (de fourchette); Ven: pointe f (d'andouiller, etc.).

pronged [prɔŋd], a. A fourchons, à dents. Two-p., à deux dents.

pronominal [pro'nɔmin(ə)l], a. Gram: Pronominal, -aux. -ally, adv. Pronominalement.

pronoun ['prounaun], s. Gram: Pronom m.

pronounce [prə'nauns], v.tr. 1. (a) Déclarer. To p. the patient out of danger, déclarer que le malade est hors de danger. (b) Jur: Prononcer (une sentence, un jugement); rendre (un arrêt). 2. Abs. To p. on a subject, prononcer sur un sujet. To p. for s.o., in favour of s.o., se déclarer pour qn. 3. Prononcer; articuler (un mot, etc.). **pronounced**, a. Prononcé, marqué. P. taste of garlic, goût d'ail très fort. **pronouncing**, s. 1. Déclaration f. Jur: Prononciation f (d'un jugement). 2. Prononciation f (d'un mot). P. dictionary, dictionnaire m avec prononciation phonétique, figurée.

pronounceable [prə'naunsəbl], a. Prononçable.

pronouncedly [prə'naunsidli], adv. D'une manière prononcée, marquée.

pronouncement [prə'naunsmənt], s. Déclaration f.

pronto ['prɔntou], adv. F: Sur-le-champ, immédiatement, F: illico.

pronunciation [prə,nʌnsi'eiʃ(ə)n], s. Prononciation f.

proof¹ [pru:f], s. 1. Preuve f. Positive p., preuve patente. Cast-iron p., preuve rigide. To give p. of sth., faire preuve de (bon vouloir); annoncer (l'intelligence). To give, show, p. of goodwill, faire acte, témoigner, de bonne volonté. To give p. of one's gratitude to s.o., témoigner sa reconnaissance à qn. This is p. that he is lying, cela prouve qu'il ment. In p. of one's good faith, en preuve, en témoignage, de sa bonne foi. Capable of p., susceptible de preuve, de démonstration. To await p. of sth., attendre la confirmation de qch. To produce p. to the contrary, fournir la preuve contraire. The onus of p. lies with . . ., le soin de faire la preuve incombe à. . . . Jur: P. of a right, constatation f d'un droit. Proof of (one's) identity, justification f, preuve, d'identité. 2. (a) Épreuve f. To bring, put, sth. to the p., mettre qch. à l'épreuve. It has stood the p., cela a résisté à l'épreuve. (b) Teneur f en alcool (d'un spiritueux). 3. (a) Typ: Épreuve. Galley p., épreuve en placard. To pass the proofs, donner le bon à tirer. (b) Engr: P. before the letter, before letters, épreuve avant la lettre. 'proof-reader, s. Typ: Correcteur, -trice (d'épreuves). 'proof-reading, s. Typ: Correction f sur épreuves.

proof², a. P. against sth., résistant à qch.; à l'épreuve de qch.; à l'abri de qch. P. against damp, damp-p., étanche à l'eau, à l'humidité. Bullet-p., à l'épreuve des balles. To be p. against danger, against disease, être à l'abri du danger, immunisé contre la maladie. P. against temptation, against flattery, inaccessible, insensible, aux tentations, à la flatterie.

proof³, v.tr. 1. Typ: Engr: Tirer une épreuve de (la page, etc.). 2. (a) Imperméabiliser, caoutchouter (un tissu, etc.). (b) Rendre (qch.) étanche. (c) Rendre (qch.) résistant (aux acides, etc.). **proofing**, s. 1. Imperméabilisation f. 2. Enduit m imperméable.

prop¹ [prɔp], s. 1. Appui m, support m, soutien m, étai m. Const: etc: Chandelle f, étançon m. S.a. PIT-PROP. 2. Échalas m (de vigne, etc.); tuteur m (d'un plant). 3. One of the props of society, un des appuis, un des piliers, de la société.

prop², v.tr. (propped) (a) To p. (up), appuyer, soutenir. To p. a ladder (up) against the wall, appuyer une échelle contre le mur. To p. up a piece of furniture, placer des hausses sous les pieds d'un meuble. (b) Const: Étayer, étançonner (un mur, etc.). (c) Échalasser (des vignes, etc.); ramer (des haricots, des pois).

prop³, s. Av: Nau: F: = PROPELLER 2.
prop⁴, s. Th: Cin: Usu. pl. Accessoire m.
propædeutics [‚proupi′dju:tiks], s.pl. (Usu. with sing. constr.) Propédeutique f.
propaganda [‚prɔpə′gændə], s. Propagande f. P. film, film m à propagande.
propagandism [‚prɔpə′gændizm], s. Propagandisme m.
propagandist [‚prɔpə′gændist], s. Propagandiste mf.
propagandize [‚prɔpə′gændaiz]. 1. v.tr. Soumettre (qn) à la propagande; convertir (qn) par la propagande. 2. v.i. Faire de la propagande.
propagate [′prɔpəgeit]. 1. v.tr. (a) Propager, faire reproduire (des animaux, etc.). (b) To p. light, propager, répandre, la lumière. To p. ideas, répandre, disséminer, propager des idées. 2. v.pr. & i. (Of animal, plant) Se propager, se reproduire, se multiplier.
propagation [‚prɔpə′geiʃ(ə)n], s. 1. Propagation f, reproduction f. 2. Propagation (de la lumière, etc.); dissémination f (d'une doctrine).
propagator [′prɔpəgeitər], s. 1. Propagateur, -trice. 2. Hort: Germoir m.
propane [′proupein], s. Ch: Propane m.
propel [prə′pel], v.tr. (propelled) Propulser; pousser en avant; donner une impulsion à (qch.). Propelled by steam, by machinery, mû par la vapeur, par une machine. propelling, a. Propulsif, -ive, propulseur (no fem.), moteur, -trice. S.a. PENCIL¹ 1.
propellant, propellent [prə′pelənt]. 1. a. Propulseur (no fem.), propulsif, -ive. 2. s. Combustible m; propulseur m; esp. Rockets: propergol m.
propeller [prə′pelər], s. 1. Propulseur m. 2. Nau: Av: (Screw) p., hélice f. Variable pitch p., hélice f à pas variable. Feathered p., hélice en drapeau. pro′peller-blade, s. Aile f, pale f, branche f, d'hélice. pro′peller-shaft, s. 1. Arbre m de l'hélice. 2. Aut: etc: Arbre à cardan; arbre de propulsion, de transmission.
propensity [prə′pensiti], s. Propension f, penchant m, inclination f, tendance f (to, towards, sth., à, vers, qch.; for doing sth., à faire qch.).
proper [′prɔpər], a. Propre. 1. A: With my (own) p. eyes, de mes propres yeux. 2. (a) P. to sth., propre, particulier, à qch. (b) To put sth. to its p. use, utiliser rationnellement qch. (c) Gram: P. noun, nom propre. (d) Her: Lion p., lion au naturel. 3. (a) Vrai, juste, approprié. The p. word, le mot juste. In a p. sense..., au sens propre.... (b) Mth: P. fraction, fraction moindre que l'unité. 4. F: He's a p. fool, c'est un imbécile dans toute l'acception du mot. To get a p. hiding, recevoir une belle volée (de coups), une belle raclée. 5. (a) Convenable. At the p. time, en temps opportun; en temps utile. To deem it p., to think p. to..., juger à propos de...; juger bon de.... Do as you think p., faites comme bon vous semblera. To do the p. thing by s.o., agir loyalement avec qn. The p. way to do it, la meilleure manière de le faire. The p. tool to use, le bon outil; l'outil approprié. P. receipt, quittance régulière. To keep sth. in p. condition, tenir qch. en bon état. (b) Comme il faut; (of language) bienséant, correct. A very p. old lady, une vieille dame (i) très comme il faut, (ii) très digne. P. behaviour, conduite bienséante. -ly, adv. 1. (a) Word p. used, mot employé (i) correctement, (ii) au (sens) propre. P. so called, proprement dit. (b) Bien; de la bonne façon. Do it p. or not at all, faites-le comme il faut ou pas du tout. 2. F: (Intensive) He was p. drunk, il était absolument soûl. To tick s.o. off p., rembarrer vertement qn; arranger qn de la belle manière. 3. (a) Convenablement. To behave p., se conduire comme il faut. (b) He very p. refused, il a refusé, comme faire se devait.
property [′prɔpəti], s. 1. (Droit m de) propriété f. 2. (a) Propriété, biens mpl, avoir(s) m(pl). Public p., propriété publique, de l'état. U.S: Community p., biens communs, de communauté. Personal p., biens personnels, mobiliers. Landed p., biens fonciers. That's my p., cela m'appartient; ça c'est à moi. Lost p., objets trouvés. (b) Immeuble m, immeubles. P. for sale, immeuble, maison f, à vendre. 3. Th: Cin: (a) Accessoire m. P. sword, épée de scène; épée pour rire. P.-horse, cheval-jupon m, pl. chevaux-jupons. (b) Properties, réserve f de décors, de costumes, etc. 4. Propriété; qualité f

(propre). Drug with antifebrile properties, drogu qui a des propriétés fébrifuges. Inherent p., attribu m. ′property-man, pl. -men, s.m. ′property mistress, s.f. Th: Cin: Accessoiriste mf. ′pro perty-room, s. Th: Magasin m des accessoires ′property-tax, s. Impôt foncier.
prophecy [′prɔfisi], s. Prophétie f.
prophesy [′prɔfisai]. 1. v.i. Parler en prophète prophétiser; (usu. Pej:) vaticiner. 2. v.tr. Prophétiser prédire (un événement). prophesying, s. Prophétie fpl; prédiction f.
prophet [′prɔfit], s. Prophète m. Mohamm. Rel The P., le Prophète. Prov: No man is a p. in his ow country, nul n'est prophète en son pays.
prophetess [′prɔfitis], s.f. Prophétesse.
prophetic(al) [prə′fetik(əl)], a. Prophétique. -ally adv. Prophétiquement.
prophylactic [‚prɔfi′læktik], a. & s. Med: Prophy lactique (m).
prophylaxis [‚prɔfi′læksis], s. Med: Prophylaxie f.
propinquity [prə′piŋkwiti], s. 1. Proximité f (de lieu) voisinage m. 2. (Proche) parenté f.
propitiate [prə′piʃieit], v.tr. 1. Rendre propice favorable. 2. Apaiser, propitier (qn); se faire pardonner par (qn).
propitiation [prə‚piʃi′eiʃ(ə)n], s. 1. Propitiation f 2. Apaisement m (des dieux courroucés, etc.). 3 Expiation f.
propitiative [prə′piʃiətiv], a. Expiatoire.
propitiator [prə′piʃieitər], s. Propitiateur, -trice.
propitiatory [prə′piʃiətri], a. & s. Propitiatoire (m); expiatoire.
propitious [prə′piʃəs], a. Propice, favorable. -ly adv. D'une manière propice; favorablement.
propitiousness [prə′piʃəsnis], s. Nature f propice (du climat, etc.).
proportion¹ [prə′pɔ:ʃ(ə)n], s. 1. Partie f (d'une surface) portion f; part f. To divide expenses in equa proportions, répartir les frais par parts égales. P of an ingredient in a mixture, dose f d'un ingrédient dans un mélange. 2. Rapport m, proportion f (a) P. of the net load to the gross load, rapport du poids utile au poids mort. Ch: Law of multiple proportions, loi des proportions multiples. (b) In p as..., à mesure que.... Payment in p. to work done rémunération au prorata du travail accompli His expenses are out of p. to, with, his income, ses dépenses sont disproportionnées à son revenu. (c) Out of p., mal proportionné. To have an eye for p. avoir du coup d'œil. To lose all sense of p., ne garder aucune mesure. 3. pl. Proportions, proportions (d'un édifice); Ind: dimensions f (d'une machine, etc.).
proportion², v.tr. 1. Proportionner (la punition au crime, etc.). 2. Doser (des ingrédients). 3. Ind: (a) Déterminer les dimensions (d'une pièce). (b) Coter (un dessin). 4. Well-proportioned, bien proportionné; (taille) bien prise.
proportional [prə′pɔ:ʃən(ə)l]. 1. a. Proportionnel, -elle; en proportion (to, de); proportionné (to, à). Inversely p. to..., inversement proportionnel à...; en raison inverse de.... Pol: P. representation, représentation proportionnelle. 2. s. Mth: Proportionnelle f. -ally, adv. En proportion (to, de); proportionnément, proportionnellement (to, à).
proportionate [prə′pɔ:ʃənit], a. Proportionné (to, à). -ly, adv. = PROPORTIONALLY.
proposal [prə′pouz(ə)l], s. 1. (a) Proposition f, offre f. To make a p., faire, formuler, une proposition. (b) Demande f en mariage; offre de mariage. 2. Dessein m, projet m.
propose [prə′pouz], v.tr. 1. Proposer, poser (une question). 2. (a) To p. a course of action, proposer une ligne de conduite. (b) To p. a candidate, proposer un candidat. To p. a motion, proposer une motion. Will you p. me for your club? voulez-vous me présenter à votre cercle? To p. the health of s.o., porter un toast en l'honneur de qn. To p. a toast, porter un toast. (c) To p. to do sth., doing sth., se proposer, avoir l'intention, de faire qch. What do you p. to do now? what do you p. doing now? que comptez-vous faire maintenant? 3. Abs. Faire la demande en mariage; faire sa déclaration. To p. to a girl, demander sa main à une jeune fille.

roposer [prə'pouzər], s. Proposeur, -euse. **P. of a member**, parrain m d'un candidat (à un cercle).

roposition [ˌpropə'ziʃ(ə)n], s. 1. (a) = PROPOSAL 1 (a). (b) Affaire f. **Mining p.**, entreprise minière. **Paying p.**, affaire qui rapporte, affaire intéressante, rentable. **It's a tough p.**, c'est une question difficile à résoudre. F: **He's a tough p.**, on ne sait par où le prendre; il n'est pas commode. 2. Log: Geom: Proposition f.

ropound [prə'paund], v.tr. 1. Proposer (une énigme); émettre (une idée); poser (une question, un problème); exposer (un programme). 2. Jur: Soumettre (un testament) à la validation.

ropounder [prə'paundər], s. Personne qui pose (un problème); auteur m (d'une théorie).

roprietary [prə'praiət(ə)ri], a. (a) De propriété, de propriété. **The p. rights of the Crown**, les droits de propriété de la Couronne. (b) O: **P. classes**, classes possédantes. (c) Com: **P. article**, spécialité f; article, produit, breveté. **P. medicines**, spécialités pharmaceutiques.

roprietor [prə'praiətər], s. Propriétaire mf. **Landed p.**, propriétaire foncier. **Peasant p.**, petit propriétaire foncier. **Garage p.**, propriétaire d'un garage, garagiste m.

roprietorship [prə'praiətəʃip], s. 1. Droit m de propriété. 2. Propriété f, possession f.

roprietress [prə'praiətris], s.f. Propriétaire, patronne.

ropriety [prə'praiəti], s. 1. (a) Propriété f, justesse f, à-propos m (d'une expression, etc.); correction f (de langage); rectitude f (de conduite). (b) Opportunité f (d'une démarche). 2. (a) Bienséance f, décence f. **Breach, lack, of p.**, manque m de savoir-vivre. **To throw p. to the winds**, se moquer de toutes les convenances. (b) **To observe the proprieties**, observer les convenances.

ropulsion [prə'pʌlʃ(ə)n], s. Propulsion f.

ropulsive [prə'pʌlsiv], a. Propulsif, -ive; (effort) de propulsion.

rorogation [ˌprourə'geiʃ(ə)n, ˌpro-], s. Prorogation f.

rorogue [prə'roug, pro-], v.tr. Proroger (le Parlement). **proroguing**. 1. a. Prorogatif, -ive. 2. s. Prorogation f.

rosaic [pro'zeiik], a. (Style m) prosaïque; (esprit) positif, banal. **-ally**, adv. Prosaïquement.

rosaicness [pro'zeiiknis], s. Prosaïsme (de la vie, etc.); banalité f (de style).

roscenium [pro'siːniəm], s. Th: Avant-scène f. **P. arch**, manteau m d'Arlequin.

roscribe [pros'kraib], v.tr. Proscrire. 1. Mettre hors la loi; bannir. 2. Interdire, défendre (un usage, etc.).

roscript ['prouskript], s. Proscrit m; hors-la-loi m inv.

roscription [pros'kripʃ(ə)n], s. Proscription f; (i) mise f (de qn) hors la loi; (ii) interdiction f (d'une pratique).

roscriptive [pros'kriptiv], a. 1. (Lois, etc.) de proscription. 2. (Décret) prohibitif.

rose [prouz], s. 1. Prose f. 2. Sch: Latin p., Greek p., thème latin, grec. **'prose-'poem**, s. Poème m en prose. **'prose-writer**, s. Prosateur m.

rosecute ['prosikjuːt], v.tr. (a) Poursuivre (qn) (en justice répressive); engager, exercer des poursuites contre (qn). **To be prosecuted for exceeding the speed limit**, attraper une contravention pour excès de vitesse. (b) **To p. an action**, intenter une action. **To p. a claim**, poursuivre une réclamation.

rosecution [ˌprosi'kjuːʃ(ə)n], s. 1. Jur: (a) Poursuites fpl (en justice répressive); poursuites judiciaires. **To start a p. against …**, engager des poursuites contre…. (b) Accusation f; action publique. (c) **The P.**, les plaignants m; (in Crown case) le Ministère public. **Witness for the p.**, témoin à charge. 2. (a) Continuation f (d'études, etc.). (b) Exercice m (d'un métier, etc.).

rosecutor ['prosikjuːtər], s. Jur: 1. Plaignant m, poursuivant m, demandeur m. 2. **The Public P.**, (i) le procureur du Roi, de la République, etc. (ii) (department) le Ministère public.

rosecutrix ['prosiˌkjutriks], s.f. Jur: Plaignante; demanderesse.

roselyte¹ ['prosilait], s. Prosélyte mf.

roselyte², v.tr. & i. U.S: = PROSELYTIZE.

roselytism ['prosilitizm], s. Prosélytisme m.

proselytize ['prosilitaiz]. 1. v.tr. Convertir (qn). 2. v.i. Faire des prosélytes.

prosiness ['prouzinis], s. Prosaïsme m (d'une conversation, etc.); terre à terre m inv (du style); verbosité f (d'une personne).

prosodic(al) [prə'sodik(əl)], a. Prosodique.

prosodist ['prosodist], s. Prosodiste m.

prosody ['prosodi], s. Prosodie f; métrique f.

prospect¹ ['prospekt], s. 1. Vue f; point m de vue; perspective f. **Wide p.**, horizon très étendu. 2. (a) Perspective, expectative f. **To have sth. in p.**, avoir qch. en perspective, en vue. (b) **There is no p. of their leaving**, il n'y a rien qui fasse prévoir leur départ. **No p. of agreement**, aucune perspective d'accord. 3. pl. Avenir m, espérances fpl. **Future prospects of an undertaking**, perspectives d'avenir d'une entreprise. **The prospects of the harvest are excellent**, la récolte s'annonce excellente. **His prospects are brilliant**, un brillant avenir s'ouvre devant lui. 4. Min: (a) Prélèvement m d'essai (d'un terrain riche en minerais). (b) Teneur f en minerai du prélèvement. 5. Esp. U.S: Com: Acheteur éventuel.

prospect² [prə'spekt]. 1. v.i. Min: Prospecter. 2. v.tr. Prospecter (un terrain). **prospecting**, s. Recherche f (de gisements).

prospection [prə'spekʃ(ə)n], s. Prospection f.

prospective [prə'spektiv], a. En perspective; prospectif, -ive, à venir; futur. **P. visit**, prochaine visite. **A p. buyer**, un acheteur éventuel. **-ly**, adv. 1. Dans l'avenir. 2. En perspective.

prospector [prə'spektər], s. (Pers.) Chercheur m (d'or, etc.); prospecteur m. **Oil p.**, chercheur m de pétrole, pétrolier m.

prospectus [prə'spektəs], s. Prospectus m.

prosper ['prospər]. 1. v.i. Prospérer, réussir; venir à bien. **He will p.**, il fera son chemin; il arrivera. 2. v.tr. O: Faire prospérer, faire réussir; favoriser. **May God p. you!** Dieu vous fasse prospérer!

prosperity [pros'periti], s. Prospérité f.

prosperous ['prospərəs], a. 1. Prospère, florissant. 2. **P. winds**, vents favorables.

prosperousness ['prospərəsnis], s. Prospérité f.

prostate ['prosteit], s. Anat: Prostate f.

prostatic [pros'tætik], a. Anat: Prostatique.

prostatitis [ˌprostə'taitis], s. Med: Prostatite f.

prostitute¹ ['prostitjuːt], s.f. Prostituée. **Registered p.**, fille soumise.

prostitute², v.tr. Prostituer (son corps, son honneur, son talent). (b) **To p. oneself**, se prostituer.

prostitution [prosti'tjuːʃ(ə)n], s. Prostitution f.

prostrate¹ ['prostrit], a. 1. Prosterné; couché (à terre); étendu. 2. Abattu, accablé. Med: Prostré.

prostrate² [pros'treit], v.tr. 1. **To p. oneself before s.o.**, se prosterner devant qn. 2. Med: Abattre; mettre dans un état de prostration. **Prostrated by the heat**, accablé par la chaleur.

prostration [pros'treiʃ(ə)n], s. 1. Prosternation f, prosternement m. 2. Abattement m. Med: Prostration f, affaissement m. **Nervous p.**, énervation f, dépression nerveuse.

prosy ['prouzi], a. Prosaïque; (of pers.) verbeux, -euse, ennuyeux, -euse. **-ily**, adv. Fastidieusement.

protagonism [pro'tægənizm], s. Défense f (d'une doctrine, etc.).

protagonist [pro'tægənist], s. Protagoniste m.

protect [prə'tekt], v.tr. 1. (a) Protéger. **To p. s.o. from sth., against sth.**, protéger qn contre qch.; préserver, défendre, qn de qch. **To p. sth. from the weather**, abriter qch. contre les intempéries. **To p. s.o. from s.o.'s wrath**, soustraire qn à la colère de qn. (b) Sauvegarder (les intérêts de qn, etc.). 2. Patronner (qn); tenir (qn) en tutelle. 3. Pol.Ec: Protéger (une industrie). **protecting**, a. Protecteur, -trice; de protection, de garde.

protection [prə'tekʃ(ə)n], s. 1. (a) Protection f, défense f (**against the weather, etc.**), contre les intempéries, etc.); sauvegarde f (des intérêts de qn, etc.). (b) **Under s.o.'s p.**, sous la sauvegarde de qn. (c) Patronage m. 2. Pol.Ec: Protectionnisme m. 3. (a) Abri m, refuge m. (b) Blindage m. 4. Sauf-conduit m, pl. sauf-conduits. **pro'tection racket**, s. F: Chantage m, sous prétexte de protection garantie contre le gangstérisme.

protectionist [prə'tekʃənist], *a. & s. Pol.Ec:* Protectionniste (*mf*).
protective [prə'tektiv], *a.* Protecteur, -trice; préservatif, -ive. *Pol.Ec:* P. **tariff,** tarif protecteur, de protection. **-ly,** *adv.* D'une manière protectrice. *Pol.Ec:* Par des droits protecteurs.
protectiveness [prə'tektivnis], *s.* Qualité protectrice; puissance *f* de protection.
protector [prə'tektər], *s.* 1. (*Pers.*) (*a*) Protecteur *m.* (*b*) Patron *m.* 2. (Dispositif) protecteur (d'un appareil, etc.).
protectorate [prə'tektərit], *s.* Protectorat *m.*
protectress [prə'tektris], *s.f.* Protectrice; patronne (des arts, etc.).
protégé ['prɔteʒei], *s.* Protégé, -ée.
protein ['proutiːn], *s. Ch: Physiol:* Protéine *f.*
protest[1] ['proutest], *s.* 1. Protestation *f.* To make, set up, a p., protester; faire des représentations. To raise a strong p., élever des protestations énergiques. A day of p., une journée revendicative. Under p., (i) (signer, etc.) sous réserve; (ii) (faire qch.) à son corps défendant, en protestant. 2. *Com:* Protêt *m.* To make a p., lever protêt. 3. *Nau:* Ship's p., rapport *m* de mer; procès-verbal *m* des avaries.
protest[2] [prə'test]. 1. *v.tr.* (*a*) Protester. To p. one's innocence, protester de son innocence. (*b*) *Com:* To p. a bill, (faire) protester une lettre de change. (*c*) *U.S:* To p. sth., s'élever contre qch. 2. *v.i.* Protester, réclamer, s'élever (against, contre).
protestant ['protist(ə)nt], *a. & s. Rel.H:* Protestant, -ante.
protestantism ['protist(ə)ntizm], *s. Rel.H:* Protestantisme *m.*
protestation [,protes'teiʃ(ə)n], *s.*1. Protestation *f* (against, contre). 2. Protestation, déclaration *f* (de sa foi, etc.).
protester, protestor [prə'testər], *s.* Protestateur, -trice; protestataire *mf.*
protocol ['proutəkəl], *s. Dipl:* Protocole *m.*
protohistory ['prouto'histri], *s.* Protohistoire *f.*
proton[1] ['proutən], *s. Atom.Ph:* Proton *m.*
protoplasm ['proutəplæzm], *s.* Protoplasme *m,* protoplasma *m.*
prototype ['proutətaip], *s.* Prototype *m.*
protozoa [prouto'zouə], *s.pl.* Protozoaires *m.*
protozoic [,prouto'zouik], *a.* Protozoaire.
protract [prə'trækt], *v.tr.* 1. Prolonger, allonger; traîner (une affaire) en longueur. 2. *Surv:* Relever (un terrain).
protractile [prə'træktail], *a. Z:* Extensile.
protraction [prə'trækʃ(ə)n], *s.* 1. Prolongation *f* (d'un procès, etc.). 2. *Surv:* Relevé *m* (d'un terrain).
protractor [prə'træktər], *s. Geom:* Rapporteur *m.*
protrude [prə'truːd]. 1. *v.tr.* Faire sortir; pousser en avant. 2. *v.i.* S'avancer, faire saillie, déborder. **protruding,** *a.* En saillie; saillant. P. **forehead,** front bombé. P. **eyes,** yeux qui sortent de la tête. P. **teeth,** dents saillantes, *F:* dents de lièvre.
protrusion [prə'truːʒ(ə)n], *s.* 1. Saillie *f.* 2. Protubérance *f.*
protuberance [prə'tjuːbərəns], *s.* Protubérance *f.*
protuberant [prə'tjuːbərənt], *a.* Protubérant.
proud [praud], *a.* 1. (*a*) Fier, orgueilleux, -euse. As p. as Lucifer, as a peacock, fier comme Artaban. (*b*) To be p. of sth., of having done sth., être fier de qch., d'avoir fait qch. **House-p.,** orgueilleux, -euse, de sa maison. (*c*) To be p. to do sth., se faire honneur de faire qch. *F:* To do s.o. p., (i) faire beaucoup d'honneur à qn; (ii) se mettre en frais pour qn. *F:* To do oneself p., se bien soigner; ne se priver de rien. 2. *Poet:* Altier, hautain, superbe. 3. P. **flesh,** (i) *Med:* chair baveuse; fongosité *f*; (ii) *Surg: Vet:* bouillon *m.* **-ly,** *adv.* Fièrement, orgueilleusement; avec fierté.
provable ['pruːvəbl], *a.* Prouvable, démontrable.
prove [pruːv], *v.* (*p.p.* **proved,** *A:* **proven** [pruːvn, prouvn]) I. *v.tr.* 1. (*a*) *A. & Tchn:* Éprouver; mettre à l'épreuve; essayer (l'or, un cheval). **Proved remedy,** remède éprouvé. To be proved by adversity, passer par le creuset de l'adversité. (*b*) *Mth:* Vérifier (un calcul); faire la preuve (d'une opération). 2. (*a*) Prouver, démontrer, établir (la vérité, etc.). It remains to be proved, cela n'est pas encore prouvé. To p. my case..., comme preuve à l'appui....

All the evidence goes to p. that..., les témoignages concourent à prouver que.... *Jur:* (*Scot.*) Not **proven** [not'prouvn], (verdict de) culpabilité non avérée; non-lieu *m* faute de preuves. (*b*) *Jur:* Homologuer (un testament); établir la validité (d'un testament). (*c*) To p. **oneself,** faire ses preuves. II. **prove,** *v.i.* Se montrer, se trouver, être. To p. useful, se trouver, être reconnu, utile. The news proved false, la nouvelle s'est avérée fausse. Their rashness proved fatal to them, leur audace leur fut fatale. To p. unequal to one's task, se révéler, se montrer, au-dessous de sa tâche. **proving,** *s.* 1. (*a*) Épreuve *f,* essayage *m.* **Proving-ground,** terrain *m* d'essai; *Artil:* polygone *m.* (*b*) *Mth:* Vérification *f* (d'un calcul). *Min:* Reconnaissance *f* (d'un terrain). 2. (*a*) Preuve *f,* démonstration *f*; constatation *f* (d'un fait). (*b*) *Jur:* Homologation *f* (d'un testament).
provender ['provindər], *s.* Fourrage *m,* affourragement *m,* provende *f.*
proverb ['provəːb], *s.* Proverbe *m.*
proverbial [prə'vəːbiəl], *a.* Proverbial, -aux; passé en proverbe. **-ally,** *adv.* Proverbialement. They're p. mean, leur avarice est passée en proverbe.
provide [prə'vaid]. 1. (*a*) *v.i.* To p. **against sth.,** se pourvoir, se prémunir, contre (une attaque, etc.) To p. **against a danger,** parer à un danger. Expenses provided for in the budget, dépenses prévues au budget. *Com:* To p. for a bill, faire provision pour une lettre de change. (*b*) *v.tr.* Stipuler (that, que + *ind.*). 2. (*a*) *v.tr.* To p. s.o. with sth., fournir qch. à qn, pourvoir, munir, fournir, approvisionner, qn de qch. To p. **an exit,** (i) (*of passage*) fournir une sortie. (ii) (*of architect*) ménager une sortie. (*b*) *v.i.* To p. for s.o., (i) pourvoir aux besoins, à l'entretien, de qn. (ii) mettre qn à l'abri du besoin. To p. **for oneself,** se suffire. To be provided for, être bien nanti; être à l'abri du besoin. *Abs.* The Lord will p., Dieu nous viendra en aide. (*c*) *v.i.* He provided for everything, il a subvenu à tout. **provided.** 1. *a.* Pourvu, muni (with, de). P. **for all eventualities,** préparé à toute éventualité. 2. *conj.* P. (that)..., pourvu que + *sub.* à condition que + *ind. or sub.*
providence ['provid(ə)ns], *s.* 1. (*a*) Prévoyance *f*, prudence *f.* (*b*) Économie *f,* épargne *f.* 2. **Providence** (divine). 3. By a special p...., par une intervention providentielle. ...
provident ['provid(ə)nt], *a.* (*a*) Prévoyant. P. **society,** société de prévoyance. P. **schemes,** œuvres *f* de prévoyance. (*b*) Économe, frugal, -aux.
providential [,provi'denʃ(ə)l], *a.* Providentiel, -elle. **-ally,** *adv.* Providentiellement.
provider [prə'vaidər], *s.* Pourvoyeur, -euse; fournisseur, -euse.
province ['provins], *s.* 1. Province *f* (d'un pays, d'un archevêque). In the provinces, en province. 2. *Jur: etc:* Juridiction *f,* ressort *m,* compétence *f* (d'un tribunal). That is not (within) my p., ce n'est pas, cela sort, de mon domaine, de mon ressort, de ma compétence; cela ne rentre pas dans mes attributions *f.*
provincial [prə'vinʃ(ə)l], *a. & s.* 1. Provincial, -ale, *pl.* -aux, -ales. P. **theatre,** théâtre de province. 2. *s.m. Ecc:* Provincial.
provincialism [prə'vinʃəlizm], *s.* Provincialisme *m.*
provinciality [prə,vinʃi'æliti], *s.* Provincialité *f*; caractère provincial.
provision[1] [prə'viʒ(ə)n], *s.* 1. (*a*) P. **for sth., against sth.,** prise *f* des dispositions nécessaires pour assurer qch., pour parer à qch. To make p. for sth., pourvoir à qch. To make p. for one's family, (i) pourvoir aux besoins, (ii) assurer l'avenir, de sa famille. To make p. against sth., se pourvoir, prendre des mesures, contre qch. To make a p. for s.o., assurer une pension à qn. (*b*) P. of the necessities of life, fourniture *f* des nécessités de la vie. *Com:* P. of capital, prestation *f* de capitaux. 2. (*a*) *Com:* Provision *f,* réserve *f.* (*b*) **Provisions,** provisions (de bouche); vivres *m,* comestibles *m.* **Wholesale p. business,** maison *f* d'alimentation, d'épicerie, en gros. P. **merchant,** marchand de comestibles, épicier *m.* 3. (*a*) Article *m* (d'un traité); clause *f,* stipulation *f* (d'un contrat). There is no p. to the contrary, il n'y a pas de clause contraire. To come within the provision of the law, tomber sous le coup de la loi.

▶rovision² *v.tr.* Approvisionner; ravitailler.

▶rovisional [prə'viʒən(ə)l], *a.* Provisoire; intérimaire; temporaire. -ally, *adv.* Provisoirement, intérimairement. **Appointed p.**, nommé à titre provisoire.

▶roviso [prə'vaizou], *s.* Clause conditionnelle; condition *f* (d'un contrat); stipulation *f.* **With the p. that . . .**, à condition que. . . .

▶rovisory [prə vaizəri], *a.* **1.** (*Of clause, etc.*) Conditionnel, -elle. **2.** Provisoire. -ily, *adv.* Provisoirement.

▶rovocation [,prəvə'keiʃ(ə)n], *s.* Provocation *f.* **To act under p.**, agir sous le coup de la colère.

▶rovocative [prə'vɔkətiv], *a.* (*a*) Provocateur, -trice; provocant. (*b*) (Sourire, etc.) agaçant, aguichant.

▶rovoke [prə'vouk], *v.tr.* **1.** (*a*) Provoquer, pousser, inciter (s.o. to do sth., qn à faire qch.). **To p. s.o. to anger**, mettre qn en colère. (*b*) Irriter, fâcher, impatienter, contrarier, agacer, exaspérer (qn). **To p. the dog**, exciter le chien. **2.** (*a*) Exciter, faire naître (la curiosité, etc.); provoquer (la gaieté). **To p. a smile**, faire naître un sourire. (*b*) **To p. fermentation**, provoquer la fermentation. **provoking**, *a.* Irritant, contrariant, exaspérant. **How p.!** quel ennui! comme c'est agaçant! -ly, *adv.* D'une manière irritante, contrariante, exaspérante.

▶rovoker [prə'voukər], *s.* Provocateur, -trice.

▶rovost ['prɔvəst], *s.* **1.** (*a*) Principal *m* (de certains collèges universitaires). (*b*) (*Scot.*) Maire *m.* (*c*) *Hist:* Prévôt *m.* **2.** [prə'vou] *Mil:* **P.-marshal**, grand prévôt.

▶row [prau], *s.* Proue *f.*

▶rowess ['prauis], *s. Lit:* Prouesse *f*, vaillance *f.*

▶rowl¹ [praul], *s.* (*Of lion, etc.*) **To go on the p.**, partir en chasse. *F:* (*Of pers.*) **To be for ever on the p.**, être toujours à rôder. **'prowl-car**, *s. U.S: F:* Voiture *f* de patrouille (policière).

▶rowl², *v.i.* (*a*) (*Of beast*) Rôder en quête de proie. (*b*) **To p. about the streets**, rôder par la ville.

▶rowler ['praulər], *s.* Rôdeur, -euse.

▶rox. [prɔks], *adv. Com:* = PROXIMO.

▶roximate ['prɔksimit], *a.* **1.** Proche, prochain, immédiat. **2.** Approximatif, -ive.

▶roximity [prɔk'simiti], *s.* Proximité *f.* **In the p. of a town**, à proximité d'une ville. **In p. to the station**, à proximité de la gare.

▶roximo ['prɔksimou], *adv.* (*Abbr.* prox.) (Du mois) prochain.

▶roxy ['prɔksi], *s. Jur:* **1.** Procuration *f*; pouvoir *m*; mandat *m.* **To vote by p.**, voter par procuration. **2.** Mandataire *mf*; fondé *m* de pouvoir(s); délégué, -ée.

▶rude [pru:d], *s.f.* Prude; *F:* bégueule.

▶rudence ['pru:d(ə)ns], *s.* Prudence *f*, sagesse *f.*

▶rudent ['pru:d(ə)nt], *a.* Prudent, sage, judicieux, -euse. -ly, *adv.* Prudemment, sagement.

▶rudential [pru(:)'denʃ(ə)l], *a.* De prudence; dicté, commandé, par la prudence.

▶rudery ['pru:dəri], *s.* Pruderie *f*; *F:* pudibonderie *f*, bégueulerie *f.*

▶rudish ['pru:diʃ], *a.* Prude; *F:* pudibond, bégueule. -ly, *adv.* Avec pruderie; en prude.

▶rudishness ['pru:diʃnis], *s.* = PRUDERY.

▶rune¹ [pru:n], *s.* **1.** Pruneau *m.* *F:* **Prunes and prisms**, afféteries *f* de prononciation et de langage. **2.** *U.S: F:* (Individu) moche, laid, stupide.

▶rune², *v.tr.* **1.** (*a*) Tailler (un rosier); rafraîchir (les racines d'un arbre). (*b*) Émonder (un arbre forestier). (*c*) **To p. (off, away) a branch**, élaguer une branche. **2.** *Journ: etc:* Faire des coupures dans, élaguer (un article). **pruning**, *s.* (*a*) Taille *f* (d'un rosier, etc.). (*b*) Émondage *m.* (*c*) **P. (off, away) of a branch**, élagage *m* d'une branche. **'pruning-hook**, *s.* Émondoir *m*, ébranchoir *m.* **'pruning-knife**, *s.* Serpette *f.* **'pruning-shears**, *s.pl.* Cisailles *fpl*; taille-buissons *m inv.*

▶runus ['pru:nəs], *s. Bot:* Prunus *m.*

▶rurience ['pruəriəns], pruriency ['pruəriənsi], *s.* **1.** *A:* Démangeaison *f.* **2.** Lasciveté *f.*

▶rurient ['pruəriənt], *a.* Lascif, -ive.

▶russia ['prʌʃə], *s.* La Prusse.

▶russian ['prʌʃ(ə)n], *a. & s.* Prussien, -ienne. **P. blue**, bleu *m* de Prusse.

▶russic ['prʌsik], *a.* **P. acid**, acide *m* prussique.

pry¹ [prai], *s. Used in the expression:* **A Paul P.**, un furet, un fouineur.

pry², *v.i.* (pried) Fureter; fouiller, chercher à voir, *F:* fourrer le nez (into sth., dans qch.). **To p. into a secret**, chercher à pénétrer un secret. **prying**, *a.* Curieux, -euse, indiscret, -ète; fureteur, -euse.

pry³, *v.tr.* (pried) Soulever, mouvoir, à l'aide d'un levier. **To p. a door open**, exercer des pesées sur une porte. **The box had been pried open**, on avait forcé la serrure du coffre.

psalm [sɑːm], *s.* Psaume *m.*

psalmist ['sɑːmist], *s.* Psalmiste *m.*

psalmodic [sæl'mɔdik], *a.* Psalmodique.

psalmodize ['sɑːmodaiz], *v.i.* Psalmodier.

psalmody ['sɑːmədi], *s.* Psalmodie *f.*

psalter ['sɔːltər], *s.* Psautier *m.*

psaltery ['sɔːltri], *s. Mus:* Psaltérion *m.*

psephology [si:'fɔlədʒi], *s. Pol:* L'étude *f* des élections.

pseudo ['sjuːdou]. **1.** *Comb.form.* Pseudo-. **2.** *a. F:* Insincère, faux, *f.* fausse.

pseudo-archaic ['sjuːdouɑːˈkeiik], *a.* Pseudo-archaïque; (style *m*) à l'antique.

pseudo-membrane ['sjuːdou'membrein], *s. Med:* Pseudo-membrane *f*; fausse membrane.

pseudonym ['sjuːdənim], *s.* Pseudonyme *m.*

pshaw [(p)ʃɔː], *int.* Fi (donc)! peuh! allons donc!

psittacosis [,sitə'kousis], *s. Med:* Psittacose *f.*

psoriasis [(p)sɔ'raiəsis], *s. Med:* Psoriasis *m.*

Psyche ['saiki]. *Pr.n.f.* Psyché.

psychedelic [saikidelik], *a.* Psychédélique.

psychiatric [,saiki'ætrik], *a.* Psychiatrique.

psychiatrist [sə'kaiətrist], *s.* Psychiatre *m.*

psychiatry [sə'kaiətri], *s.* Psychiatrie *f.* **Child p.**, psychiatrie infantile.

psychic(al) ['saikik(əl)]. **1.** *a.* Psychique; métapsychique. **2.** *s.* Psychic, médium *m.*

psychics ['saikiks], *s.pl.* La métapsychique; la parapsychologie.

psychism ['saikizm], *s.* Psychisme *m.*

psychoanalyse ['saikou'ænəlaiz], *v.tr.* Psychanalyser (qn).

psychoanalysis ['saikouə'nælisis], *s.* Psychanalyse *f.*

psychoanalytic(al) ['saikou,ænə'litik(l)], *a.* Psychanalitique.

psychoanalyst ['saikou'ænəlist], *s.* Psychanalyste *m.*

psychological [,saikə'lɔdʒik(ə)l], *a.* Psychologique. **The p. moment**, le moment psychologique. -ally, *adv.* Psychologiquement.

psychologist [sai'kɔlədʒist], *s.* Psychologue *m.*

psychology [sai'kɔlədʒi], *s.* Psychologie *f.*

psychoneurosis ['saikounju'rousis], *s. Med:* Psychonévrose *f.*

psychopath ['saikopæθ], *s.* Psychopathe *mf.*

psychopathology ['saikoupə'θɔlədʒi], *s.* Psychopathologie *f.*

psychopathy [sai'kɔpəθi], *s.* Psychopathie *f.*

psychosis, *pl.* -oses [sai'kousis, -ousiːz], *s. Med:* Psychose *f.*

psychosomatic ['saikousə'mætik], *a. Med:* Psychosomatique.

psychotechnic(al) ['saikou'teknik(l)], *a.* Psychotechnique.

psychotechnology ['saikou,tek'nɔlədʒi], *s.* Psychotechnie *f*, psychotechnique *f.*

psychotherapeutics ['saikou,θerə'pjutiks], *s. pl.* (*Usu. with sing. constr.*) Psychothérapeutique *f.*

psychotherapist ['saikou'θerəpist], *s.* Psychothérapeute *m.*

psychotherapy ['saikou'θerəpi], *s.* Psychothérapie *f.*

psychrometer [sai'krɔmitər], *s. Meteor:* Psychromètre *m.*

ptarmigan ['tɑːmigən], *s. Orn:* Ptarmigan *m*, lagopède alpin.

pterodactyl [tero'dæktil], *s. Paleont:* Ptérodactyle *m.*

pterosaur ['terosɔːr], *s. Paleont:* Ptérosaurien *m.*

Ptolemy ['tɔləmi]. *Pr.n.m.* Ptolémée.

ptomaine ['toumein, to'mein], *s. Ch:* Ptomaïne *f.* **P. poisoning**, intoxication *f* alimentaire (par les ptomaïnes).

pub [pʌb], *s. F:* (= *public house*) = Bistrot *m.* **'pub-crawl¹**, *s. F:* Tournée *f*, des bistrots. **'pub-crawl²**, *v.i. F:* Faire la tournée des bistrots. **'pub-crawler**, *s. F:* Coureur *m* de bistrots; vadrouilleur *m.*

puberty ['pju:bəti], s. Puberté f.

pubes ['pju:bi:z], s. Anat: Pubis m.

pubescence [pju(:)'bes(ə)ns], s. 1. Bot: Pubescence f. 2. Physiol: = PUBERTY.

pubescent [pju(:)'bes(ə)nt], a. 1. Bot: Pubescent. 2. Physiol: Pubère.

pubis ['pju:bis], s. Anat: Pubis m.

public ['pʌblik]. 1. a. Public, f. publique. (a) P. holiday, fête légale. P. works, travaux publics. P. utility service, service public. At the p. expense, aux frais du contribuable. Industry under p. ownership, industrie nationalisée. (b) P. library, bibliothèque municipale, communale. (c) To make sth. p., rendre qch. public, officiel; publier (une nouvelle). To make a p. protest, protester publiquement. (d) P. life, vie publique. P. spirit, patriotisme m; civisme m. (c) P. enemy, (i) ennemi universel; (ii) bandit m. P. enemy number 1, ennemi public numéro 1. Jur: P. nuisance, atteinte portée aux droits du public. F: He's a p. nuisance, c'est un casse-pieds. 2. s. (a) Public m. The general p., the p. at large, le grand public. (b) In p., en public; publiquement. -ly, adv. Publiquement; en public; au grand jour. public 'house, s. = Débit m de boissons, café m, bistrot m. public-'spirited, a. Dévoué au bien public.

publican ['pʌblikən], s. 1. Rom.Hist: B: Publicain m. 2. = Débitant m de boissons, patron, -onne, de café, de bistrot.

publication [,pʌbli'keiʃ(ə)n], s. 1. (a) Publication f; apparition f (d'un livre). (b) Publication (d'une nouvelle, des bans); promulgation f (d'un décret). 2. Ouvrage publié; publication.

publicist ['pʌblisist], s. 1. Journaliste m, publiciste m. 2. Expert m en droit international. 3. (Agent m) publicitaire (m).

publicity [pʌb'lisiti], s. 1. Publicité f. 2. Com: Publicité, réclame f. The p. department, (i) Com: la publicité; (ii) Publ: le service de presse. P. man, publicitaire m.

publicize ['pʌblisaiz], v.tr. Faire connaître au public.

publish ['pʌbliʃ], v.tr. 1. (a) Publier (un édit, etc.). (b) Publier, révéler (une nouvelle); crier (une nouvelle) sur les toits. 2 Publier, faire paraître, sortir (un livre). Just published, (qui) vient de paraître. **publishing**, s. 1. Publication f (des bans, etc.). 2. (a) Publication, mise f en vente (d'un livre). (b) L'édition f. P. house, maison d'édition.

publisher ['pʌbliʃər], s. Éditeur m.

puce [pju:s], a. & s. (Couleur) puce m inv.

Puck[1] [pʌk]. 1. Pr.n.m. (Le lutin) Puck. 2. s. Lutin m, farfadet m.

puck[2], s. Palet m (en caoutchouc) (pour le hockey sur glace).

pucker[1] ['pʌkər], s. Ride f, pli m (du visage); fronce f, faux pli, godet m (d'un tissu).

pucker[2]. 1. v.tr. Rider (le visage); plisser, froncer, faire goder (un tissu). To p. (up) one's brows, one's lips, froncer les sourcils; plisser les lèvres. 2. v.i. (a) (Of garment) To p. (up), faire des plis, des fronces; se froncer; (of felt) grigner. (b) His face puckered up, sa figure se crispa. **puckering**, s. Plissement m; froncement m.

puckish ['pʌkiʃ], a. De lutin; malicieux, -euse, espiègle.

pudding ['pudiŋ], s. 1. Cu: (a) Pudding m, pouding m. (b) Milk p., entremets sucré au lait; crème f. Rice p., riz m au lait; gâteau m de riz. (c) Black p., boudin (noir). White p., boudin blanc. 2. Nau: (a) Embodinure f. (b) Bourrelet m de défense. 'pudding-face, s. F: Visage empâté; P: tête de lard. 'pudding-head, s. F: Nigaud m; P: cruche f. 'pudding-stone, s. Miner: Poudingue m, conglomérat m.

puddle[1] ['pʌdl], s. 1. (a) Flaque f d'eau, d'huile. (b) Petite mare. 2. Hyd.E: Corroi m, glaise f. To line with p., corroyer, glaiser (un bassin, etc.).

puddle[2]. 1. v.i. To p. (about), (i) patauger, barboter (dans la boue); (ii) faire du gâchis. 2. v.tr. (a) Corroyer, malaxer (l'argile). (b) Metall: Puddler, brasser, corroyer (le fer). **puddling**, s. 1. (a) Corroyage m (de l'argile). (b) Metall: Puddlage m, brassage m (du fer). 'puddling-furnace, s. Metall: Four m à puddler. 'puddle-ball, s. Metall: Loupe f. 'puddle-'steel, s. Acier puddlé.

---

puddly ['pʌdli], a. Rempli, couvert, de flaqu... d'eau.

pudgy ['pʌdʒi], a. Boulot, -otte.

puerile ['pjuərail], a. Puéril.

puerility [pjuə'riliti], s. Puérilité f.

puerperal [pju(:)'ə:pərəl], a. Med: Puerpéral, -aux.

puff[1] [pʌf], s. 1. Souffle m (de la respiration, d'air... bouffée f (d'air, de tabac); échappement soudai... (de vapeur). F: Out of p., essoufflé; à bout d... souffle. Onomat: Pf(u)t! 2. Cost: (a) Bouillon ... (de robe); bouffant m (d'une manche). P. sleeve... manches bouffantes, ballonnées. (b) Bouffette ... (de ruban); chou m, pl. choux. U.S: = QUILT... 3. Toil: Powder-p., houppe f, houppette f. 4. Cu... Gâteau feuilleté (fourré de confiture, etc.). ... F: Réclame (tapageuse). 'puff-adder, s. Vipèr... heurtante. 'puff-ball, s. (a) Fung: Vesse-de-lou... f. (b) Bot: Boule f, aigrette f, de pissenlit, ... chandelle f, voyageur m. 'puff-'pastry, s. Cu... Pâte feuilletée. 'puff-puff, s. (Child's word) = ... PUFFER 1.

puff[2]. 1. v.i. (a) Souffler. To p. and blow, halete... To p. (and blow) like a grampus, souffler comme u... phoque. (b) Lancer des bouffées (de fumée); émettr... des jets (de vapeur). To p. (away) at one's pip... tirer sur sa pipe. 2. v.tr. (a) To p. a cigar, fumer u... cigare par petites bouffées. (b) Gonfler (le riz, etc.... (c) F: Prôner, vanter, faire mousser (ses marchand... ses). **puff out.** 1. v.tr. (a) Gonfler (les joues,... faire ballonner (une manche). (b) Émettre, lanc... (des bouffées de fumée). 2. v.i. (Of skirt) Bouffe... **puff up,** v.tr. (a) Gonfler (les joues). (b) Bouffi... gonfler (d'orgueil). To p. oneself up, se rengorge... **puffed up,** a. 1. (a) (Visage) enflé, bouffi. (b... (Style, langage) boursouflé. 2. P. up with prid... bouffi, gonflé, d'orgueil. **puffed,** a. 1. (a) P. sleeve... manches bouffantes. (b) P. rice, riz gonflé. 2. F... (Of runner, etc.) Essoufflé; à bout de souffle.

puffer ['pʌfər], s. 1. F: (In nursery speech) Loco... motive f; teuf-teuf m inv. 2. Com: Compère ... allumeur m (à une vente aux enchères).

puffin ['pʌfin], s. Orn: Macareux m moine.

puffiness ['pʌfinis], s. Boursouflure f, enflure f. ... round the eyes, bouffissure f des yeux.

puffy ['pʌfi], a. 1. (Vent) qui souffle par bouffées. ... (Of pers.) (i) A l'haleine courte; (ii) hors d'haleine... (iii) F: poussif, -ive. 3. Bouffi, boursouflé. (Of dress... bouffant.

pug[1] [pʌg], s. 1. P.(-dog), carlin m; petit dogue... doguin m; roquet m. 2. P.(-engine), locomotive ... de manœuvre; coucou m. 'pug(-)'nose, s. Ne... épaté, nez camus. 'pug-'nosed, a. Au nez épat... camard.

pug[2], s. Brickm: etc: Argile malaxée; glaise f.

pug[3], v.tr. (pugged) 1. Malaxer, corroyer, pétrir (l'argile... 2. Const: Hourder (un plancher).

pug[4], s. Empreinte f de pas (d'un tigre, d'un chie... etc.). Just look at those p. marks on the sofa... Regardez-moi ces marques de pattes sur le canapé!

pug[5], s. F: = PUGILIST.

pugilism ['pju:dʒilizm], s. Pugilat m; la boxe.

pugilist ['pju:dʒilist], s. Pugiliste m; boxeur m.

pugnacious [pʌg'neiʃəs], a. Querelleur, -euse; ... nace; batailleur, -euse.

pugnaciousness [pʌg'neiʃəsnis], **pugnacity** [pʌg'næsit... s. Humeur querelleuse, batailleuse; pugnacité f.

puke [pju:k], v.tr. & i. Vomir; P: dégobiller, dégueu... ler. **puking**, s. Vomissement m; P: dégobillage m... dégueulage m.

pukka ['pʌkə], a. O: F: Vrai, authentique. A ... Englishman, un vrai Anglais d'Angleterre.

pule [pju:l], v.i. Piauler, piailler.

pull[1] [pul], s. 1. (a) Traction f, tirage m. To giv... p., tirer. (b) P. of a magnet, force f d'attraction d'u... aimant; appel m, sollicitation f, d'un aiman... (c) Effort m de traction. Up-hill p., effort à la monté... (d) Row: Coup m (d'aviron); palade f. 2. Avantag... m. To have a p., (i) avoir le bras long; (ii) F: avo... du piston (with s.o., chez qn). To have a p. over s.o... avoir l'avantage sur qn. 3. F: (a) Gorgée f, ... lampée f (de bière, etc.). (b) To take a pull at one'... pipe, tirer une bouffée de sa pipe. 4. Bell p., poign... de sonnette. 5. Typ: Engr: Première épreuve.

ull², v.tr. 1. (a) Tirer (les cheveux de qn, la sonnette, etc.). To p. the trigger, presser la détente. U.S: F: To p. a gun, sortir son revolver. Equit: Horse that pulls, cheval qui se braque. S.a. LEG¹ 1., STRING¹ 1., WIRE¹ 1. (b) Row: Manier (un aviron). Abs: Ramer. To p. hard, souquer ferme. To p. ashore, ramer jusqu'au rivage. S.a. WEIGHT¹ 1. (c) Turf: Retenir, tirer (un cheval) (pour l'empêcher de gagner). (d) v.i. To p. at a rope, tirer, agir, sur un cordage. To p. at one's pipe, tirer des bouffées de sa pipe. 2. (a) Traîner, tirer (une charrette, etc.). P. your chair near the fire, approchez votre chaise du feu. Horse that pulls well, cheval qui tire bien. Aut: e.c: The engine is pulling heavily, le moteur fatigue, peine. (Of pers., car, etc.) To p. slowly up the hill, gravir péniblement la colline. (b) Body pulled by a force, corps sollicité par une force. 3. To p. a face, faire une grimace. To p. a wry face, faire la grimace. 4. F: To p. a yarn, raconter, débiter une histoire peu vraisemblable. F: To p. a fast one, avoir qn. 5. Typ: Engr: Tirer (une épreuve). 6. To p. the ball, abs. to p., (i) Cr: renvoyer la balle d'un coup tiré à gauche; (ii) Golf: faire un coup tiré. pull about, v.tr. (a) Tirailler; traîner (qch.) çà et là. (b) F: Houspiller, malmener. pull ahead, v.i. Se détacher du peloton. pull apart, asunder, v.tr. Séparer; déchirer en deux. pull away, v.tr. 1. Arracher, décoller (qch.); entraîner (qn). 2. Abs. P. away! tirez ferme! Row: Avant! souquez! pull back, v.tr. 1. Ramener en arrière. 2. Empêcher (qn) de progresser. 'pull-back, s. (a) Dispositif m de rappel. Bill: Effet m rétrograde; rétro m. (b) Entrave f. pull down, v.tr. 1. Baisser, faire descendre (un store, etc.); rabattre (son voile). 2. (a) Démolir, abattre (une maison); raser (des fortifications); démonter (une cabane). (b) F: Renverser (un gouvernement). 3. (Of disease) Abattre, affaiblir (qn). To be pulled down, être abattu, affaibli, F: amolli, P: amoché. pulling down, s. Démolition f, abattage m (d'une maison); rasement m (des fortifications); renversement m (d'un gouvernement). pull in, 1. v.tr. (a) Rentrer (un filet, etc.). (b) Retenir (son cheval); tirer les rênes de (son cheval). (c) To p. oneself in, se serrer la taille. (d) (Of police) To p. in a suspect, a gang, arrêter un suspect, rafler un gang. 2. v.i. Rail: (Of train) Entrer en gare. Aut: To p. in to the kerb, se ranger près du trottoir. 'pull-in, s. 1. Parking m (près d'un café, etc.). 2. Café m, restaurant m (pour routiers). pull off, v.tr. 1. To p. sth. off sth., enlever, arracher qch. de qch. 2. (a) Retirer, ôter (son chapeau); enlever (son pardessus). (b) Sp: F: Gagner, remporter, F: décrocher (un prix). (c) F: Réussir à faire (qch.); venir à bout de (qch.). It's up to you to p. it off, c'est à vous d'enlever l'affaire. pull on, v.tr. Enfiler, mettre (des bas, etc.). 'pull-on, a. & s. (Vêtement m) qui s'enfile. pull out. 1. v.tr. (a) Sortir, (re)tirer. To p. s.o. out of sth., tirer de qch. To p. s.o. out of a hole, tirer qn du pétrin. (b) Arracher (une dent). 2. v.i. (a) (Of rower) Ramer vers le large. (b) (Of train) Sortir de la gare; démarrer. (c) Aut: To p. out from behind a vehicle, sortir de la file pour doubler. (d) U.S: F: Se dérober. pull over. 1. v.tr. (a) To p. one's hat over one's eyes, ramener son chapeau sur ses yeux. (b) Renverser (qch.) (en tirant dessus). 2. v.i. (Of car, etc.) To p. over to one side, se ranger. To p. o. to the left, right, again, reprendre sa gauche, droite. pull round. F: 1. v.tr. (a) Ranimer (qn). (b) (After illness) Remettre (qn) sur pied. 2. v.i. (a) (After fainting) Se ranimer. (b) (After illness) Se remettre. pull through. 1. v.tr. Tirer (qn) d'embarras, d'affaire; aider (qn) à surmonter une difficulté. To p. a thing through, mener une chose à bien. 2. v.i. Se tirer d'affaire; s'en tirer. He will never p. through, il ne guérira pas; il n'en reviendra pas. pull to, v.tr. Tirer, fermer (la porte). pull together, v.tr. 1. To p. oneself together, se reprendre, se ressaisir; reprendre ses esprits. Come, p. yourself together! voyons, remettez-vous! 2. Abs. Tirer ensemble; F: agir de concert; s'accorder. They are not pulling together, ils ne s'entendent pas. Nau: P. together! nage d'accord! pull up. 1. v.tr. (a) (Re)monter, hisser (qn, qch.). Aut: To p. up

the brake, serrer le frein (à main). (b) Hausser, lever (un store); retrousser, relever (sa jupe). To p. up one's socks, (i) remonter ses chaussettes; (ii) F: se dégourdir, s'activer; faire appel à toute son énergie. (c) Arracher, extirper (les mauvaises herbes). (d) Arrêter (un cheval); arrêter brusquement (sa voiture). (e) F: Réprimander, rembarrer (qn). Aut: I've been pulled up (by the police), je me suis fait arrêter, siffler (par l'agent). 2. v.i. (a) S'arrêter. To p. up at the corner, arrêter (la voiture) au coin. To p. up at the kerb, se ranger le long du trottoir. (b) Gym: To p. up to the bar, faire une traction. (c) Sp: We'll p. up, nous allons remonter ça. pull-'up, s. 1. Arrêt m (d'une voiture, etc.); Mil: à-coup m (dans une colonne, etc.). 2. Café m, restaurant m (pour routiers). 3. (a) Mount: Tirée f. (b) Gym: Rétablissement m. (c) Sp: A good p.-up, une belle remontée. pulling, s. (a) Tirage m. S.a. WIRE-PULLING. (b) Typ: Tirage, impression f (d'épreuves). (c) P. race, course f à l'aviron.

puller ['pulər], s. 1. (a) Tireur, -euse. S.a. WIRE-PULLER. (b) Rameur, -euse. 2. (a) (Of horse) To be a good p., tirer à plein collier. (b) Equit: Cheval fort en bouche, qui tire à la main. 3. Tls: Extracteur m (pour roulements à billes).

pullet ['pulit], s. Poulette f. Fattened p., poularde f, gelinotte f. Corn-fed p., poulet m de grain.

pulley ['puli], s. 1. Poulie f. Grooved p., poulie à gorge. Differential p., palan différentiel. S.a. TACKLE¹ 2. 2. Belt-p., poulie; roue f de courroie. Fixed p., poulie fixe. Loose p., dead p., poulie folle; galopin m. 'pulley-block, s. (a) Moufle f. Three-strand p.-block, moufle à trois brins. (b) Palan m. 'pulley-wheel, s. Réa m, rouet m.

Pullman ['pulmən], s. Rail: P. car, train, voiture f Pullman, train m de luxe.

pullover ['puluuvər], s. Cost: Pull-over m, F: pull m.

pullulate ['puljuleit], v.i. (a) (Of seed) Germer; (of bud) pousser. (b) (Of rats, heresy) Pulluler; (of opinions) proliférer. (c) (Of vermin) Grouiller.

pullulation [pulju'leiʃ(ə)n], s. (a) Germination f; pousse f (des bourgeons, etc.). (b) Pullulation f.

pulmonary ['pʌlmənəri], a. 1. Anat: Pulmonaire. P. complaint, maladie des poumons. 2. (Of pers.) Poitrinaire.

pulmonate ['pʌlməneit], a. Z: A poumons.

pulp¹ [pʌlp], s. Pulpe f (des doigts, dentaire); pulpe, chair f (des fruits). (Paper-)p., pâte f, pulpe, à papier. To reduce sth. to a p., réduire qch. en pulpe. Arm crushed to p., bras réduit en marmelade, en bouillie. 'pulp-fiction, s. U.S: Roman m de concierge, à deux sous.

pulp², v.tr. (a) Réduire en pulpe. To p. books, mettre des livres au pilon. (b) Décortiquer. pulping, s. Réduction f en pulpe, en pâte; pulpation f. P. machine, pilon m.

pulpit ['pulpit], s. 1. Chaire f (du prédicateur). To ascend, mount, the p., monter en chaire. 2. Nau: (On poop) Balcon m.

pulpy ['pʌlpi], a. 1. Pulpeux, -euse, charnu. 2. F: Mou, f. molle; flasque.

pulsate [pʌl'seit], v.i. (a) (Of heart, etc.) Battre. (b) Palpiter; vibrer.

pulsatilla [pʌlsə'tilə], s. Bot: Pulsatille f; F: passefleur f.

pulsation [pʌl'seiʃ(ə)n], s. Pulsation f, battement m.

pulsatory [pʌl'seitri], a. Pulsatoire, pulsatif, -ive.

pulse¹ [pʌls], s. 1. Pouls m. To feel s.o.'s p., tâter le pouls à qn. 2. Pulsation f, battement m du cœur, etc.); vibration f (d'une corde). 3. El: Radar: Pulse m. P. radar, radar m à impulsions.

pulse², v.i. Avoir des pulsations; battre; palpiter.

pulse³, s. Coll. (Plantes) légumineuses (fpl).

pulsimeter [pʌl'simitər], s. Med: Sphygmographe m.

pulso-jet ['pʌlsou'dʒet], s. Av: Pulso-réacteur m.

pulsometer [pʌl'səmitər], s. 1. Ind: Pulsomètre m. 2. = PULSIMETER.

pulverizable ['pʌlvəraizəbl], a. Pulvérisable.

pulverization [pʌlvərai'zeiʃ(ə)n], s. Pulvérisation f.

pulverize ['pʌlvəraiz]. 1. v.tr. (a) Pulvériser; réduire en poudre; broyer. To p. an argument, réduire un argument en miettes, à néant. To p. s.o., pulvériser (l'orateur, etc.). (b) Atomiser, vaporiser (de la peinture, l'essence, etc.). 2. v.i. (a) Tomber en poussière. (b) Se vaporiser.

pulverizer ['pʌlvəraizər], s. (Device) Pulvérisateur m, vaporisateur m, atomiseur m.

pulverulent [pʌl'verjulənt], a. Pulvérulent; poudreux, -euse.

puma ['pju:mə], s. Z: Puma m, couguar m.

pumice ['pʌmis], s. P.(-stone), (pierre f) ponce f.

pummel ['pʌm(ə)l], v.tr. (pummelled) Bourrer (qn) de coups de poing. **pummelling**, s. Volée f de coups. To give s.o. a good p., F: donner une bonne raclée à qn.

pump[1] [pʌmp], s. (a) Pompe f. Hand p., pompe à bras. Aut: Petrol pump, (i) (of engine) pompe à essence; (ii) (of service station) poste m d'essence. Aut: P. attendant, pompiste mf. P. water, eau f de pompe. F: (Hair) straight as a yard of p. water, (des cheveux) raides comme des baguettes de tambour. (b) Pressure p., force p., pompe foulante. Bicycle p., pompe à bicyclette. Foot p., pompe à pied. S.a. AIR-PUMP. 'pump-gear, s. Garniture f, armature f, de pompe. 'pump-'handle, s. Bras m de pompe. P.-h. handshake, poignée f de main en coup de pompe. 'pump-room, s. 1. Chambre f des pompes. 2. (At a spa) Le Pavillon (de la source).

pump[2]. 1. v.tr. (a) To p. water, (i) pomper, extraire, de l'eau; (ii) épuiser l'eau à la pompe. (b) To p. a well dry, assécher un puits. F: To p. s.o., sonder, faire causer, qn; F: tirer les vers du nez de, à, qn. To p. a prisoner, cuisiner un prisonnier. (c) Refouler (l'eau dans une chaudière, l'air dans une mine). To p. air into the lungs, insuffler de l'air dans les poumons. 2. v.i. (Of heart, machine) Pomper. pump out, v.tr. Dénoyer (une mine); épuiser l'eau (d'un puits); assécher (un puits). pump up, v.tr. 1. Faire monter (l'eau) en la pompant; pomper (l'eau). 2. Gonfler (un pneu). pumped, a. (Of athlete, etc.) Essoufflé, F: pompé. pumping, s. 1. Pompage m, extraction f (de l'eau). 2. F: Action d'arracher un secret à qn. 'pumping-engine, s. Machine f d'épuisement; pompe f d'extraction. 'pumping-station, s. Min: Station f d'épuisement.

pump[3], s. Escarpin m; chaussure f de bal (pour homme).

pumpkin ['pʌm(p)kin], s. Hort: Potiron m, citrouille f.

pun[1] [pʌn], s. Calembour m; jeu m de mots.

pun[2], v.i. (punned) Faire des calembours, des jeux de mots.

punch[1] [pʌnʃ], s. 1. Tls: (a) Poinçon m. (Centre-)p., pointeau m (de mécanicien). (b) Chasse-goupilles m inv, chasse-clavettes m inv. Nail-p., brad-p., chasse-clou(s) m inv. (c) (For piercing) Perçoir m. (d) Hollow p., emporte-pièce m inv, découpoir m. (e) Étampe f, poinçon m. 2. Poinçon (de contrôleur de chemin de fer); pince f de contrôle. 'punch-card, s. Carte perforée. 'punch-mark, s. Coup m de pointeau; repère m.

punch[2], s. 1. Coup m de poing; horion m. Box: Punch m. F: He didn't pull his punches, il n'a pas ménagé l'adversaire. 2. F: Force f, énergie f. Style with p. in it, style énergique; style à l'emporte-pièce. 'punch-ball, s. Box: Punching ball m, punching m. 'punch-'drunk, a. Esp. Box: F: Abruti, stupéfié (de coups). 'punch-line, s. Th: T.V: etc: Mot m de la fin.

punch[3], v.tr. 1. (a) Percer; découper (à l'emporte-pièce); poinçonner. (b) Poinçonner (un billet). (c) To p. an iron plate, estamper, étamper, une plaque de fer. 2. Donner un coup de poing à (qn); cogner sur (qn). To punch s.o.'s face, casser la figure à qn. F: He's got a face you'd like to punch, F: il a une tête à massacre. punch in, v.tr. Enfoncer (un clou, etc.) au poinçon. punch out, v.tr. 1. Découper à l'emporte-pièce. 2. Chasser (une goupille). punching, s. 1. (a) Perçage m, poinçonnage m; découpage m à l'emporte-pièce. (b) Poinçonnement m, poinçonnage (des billets). 2. Metalw: Pièce étampée. 3. U.S: (Cow-) m, le métier de cowboy. 'punching-ball, s. Box: Punching-ball m, punching m. 'punching-machine, s. 1. Poinçonneuse f; machine f à poinçonner. 2. Découpeuse f.

punch[4], s. (Beverage) Punch m. Milk p., lait m au rhum. 'punch-bowl, s. 1. Bol m à punch. 2. Cuvette f (entre collines).

Punch[5]. Pr.n.m. = Polichinelle; Guignol. P. an Judy show, (théâtre m de) guignol m.

punch[6], s. Husb: Suffolk p., cheval m de gros trait d· Suffolk.

puncheon ['pʌn(t)ʃ(ə)n], s. Tonneau m (de 72 à 12· gallons). P. of rum, pièce f de rhum.

puncher ['pʌn(t)ʃər], s. 1. (Pers.) (a) Poinçonneur m perceur m (de tôle, etc.); poinçonneur (de billets etc.). (b) Estampeur m, frappeur m. 2. Tls: (a Poinçonneuse f; perforateur m; emporte-pièc m inv. (b) Découpeuse f. 3. U.S: (Cow-)p., cowboy m

punctilio [pʌŋk'tiliou], s. 1. Formalisme exagéré. 2 Point m d'étiquette. To stand upon punctilios s'attacher à des vétilles.

punctilious [pʌŋk'tiliəs], a. 1. (a) Pointilleux, -euse méticuleux, -euse. (b) P. on the point of honour chatouilleux sur le point d'honneur. 2. To be very p. être à cheval sur le cérémonial; être très soucieu· du protocole. -ly, adv. 1. Pointilleusement; scrupu· leusement. 2. Cérémonieusement.

punctiliousness [pʌŋk'tiliəsnis], s. 1. Pointillerie f scrupule m des détails. 2. Souci m du protocole.

punctual ['pʌŋktjuəl], a. Ponctuel, -elle, exact. Alway p., toujours à l'heure. To be p. in one's payments, a· the office, être exact, régulier, dans ses paiements, a· bureau. -ally, adv. Exactement, ponctuellement.

punctuality [pʌŋktju'æliti], s. Ponctualité f, exacti tude f.

punctuate ['pʌŋktjueit], v.tr. Ponctuer (une phrase etc.); accentuer (une remarque).

punctuation [pʌŋktju'eiʃ(ə)n], s. Ponctuation f.

puncture ['pʌŋktʃər], s. 1. (a) Surg: Ponction f. (b Crevaison f, perforation f (d'un abcès, d'un pneu) 2. (Hole) Piqûre f, perforation.

puncture[2], v.tr. (a) Ponctionner (un abcès). (b Crever, perforer (un pneu). (c) (With passive force (Of tyre) Crever.

pundit ['pʌndit], s. 1. Pandit m. 2. F: Ponte m.

pungency ['pʌndʒənsi], s. 1. Goût piquant; odeu· forte (d'un parfum). 2. (a) O: Acuité f (d'un· douleur); âcreté f, aigreur f (de paroles). (b) Saveu· f (d'un récit); causticité f (d'une épigramme).

pungent ['pʌndʒənt], a. 1. O: (Of pain) Cuisant; aigu· -uë; (of sorrow, etc.) poignant. 2. (Of style, etc. Mordant, caustique. P. remarks, observation· pleines de saveur. 3. (Of smell, etc.) Fort, violen· âcre, piquant, irritant. -ly, adv. D'une manièr· piquante.

Punic ['pju:nik], a. Hist: (Guerre, etc.) punique. P· faith, la foi punique; perfidie f.

puniness ['pju:ninis], s. Chétiveté f.

punish ['pʌniʃ], v.tr. 1. Punir; châtier (qn); corrige· (un enfant). To p. s.o. for sth., punir qn de qch. 2 F: Taper dur, cogner, sur (qn); malmener (qn· Box: He was severely punished, il a encaissé. To p· s.o.'s cellar, ne pas épargner la cave de qn. To p. th· roast beef, taper sur le rôti. Aut: etc: To p. th· engine, fatiguer, forcer, le moteur. punishing[1], a· Qui frappe dur; (coup) violent. P. game, jeu rude· P. work, travail épuisant. punishing[2], s. Punition· correction f.

punishable ['pʌniʃəbl], a. Punissable. Jur: Délic· tueux, -euse. P. by a fine, passible d'amende.

punishment ['pʌniʃmənt], s. Punition f, châtiment m· Corporal p., châtiment corporel. Capital p., pein· capitale. As a p., par punition. Mil: Summary p· sanction f disciplinaire. Box: F: Man who stand· takes, punishment, homme dur à l'encaisse, qui sa· encaisser. To take one's p. like a man, avaler s· médecine en homme.

punitive ['pju:nitiv], **punitory** ['pju:nitəri], a. Puniti· -ive; répressif, -ive.

punk [pʌŋk]. 1. s. U.S: Amadou m. 2. s. F: Obj· m sans valeur, camelote f. 3. a. F: (Of thg) Mauvai· P: moche.

punner ['pʌnər], s. Tls: Hie f, pilon m, dame f.

punnet ['pʌnit], s. Maniveau m.

punster ['pʌnstər], s. Faiseur m de calembours.

punt[1] [pʌnt], s. (a) Bateau plat (conduit à la perche· (b) Bachot m. 'punt-gun, s. Canardière f. 'pun· pole, s. Gaffe f, perche f.

punt[2], v.tr. (a) Conduire (un bateau) à la perche. (· Transporter (qn) dans un bateau plat.

punt³, s. *Rugby Fb:* Coup m (de pied) de volée.
punt⁴, v.tr. *Rugby Fb:* Envoyer (le ballon) d'un coup de pied de volée.
punt⁵, v.i. 1. *Cards:* Ponter. 2.(a) *Turf:* Parier. (b) *St.Exch:* Boursicoter.
punter ['pʌntər], s. 1. *Cards:* Ponte m. 2. (a) *Turf:* Parieur m. (b) *St.Exch:* Boursicoteur m.
puny ['pju:ni], a. 1. (a) Petit, menu, grêle. (b) Mesquin. 2. (Of pers.) Chétif, -ive, faible, débile.
pup¹ [pʌp], s. 1. (a) Petit chien, jeune chien; chiot m. (Of bitch) In p., pleine. F: To sell s.o. a p., tromper, rouler, filouter, qn. (b) Jeune phoque m. 2. F: Jeune prétentieux, suffisant.
pup², v.tr. & abs. (pupped) (Of bitch, seal) Mettre b.as (des petits).
pupa, pl. -ae ['pju:pə, -i:], s. *Ent:* Nymphe f, chrysalide f.
pupil¹ ['pju:p(i)l], s. 1. *Jur:* Pupille mf. 2. *Sch:* Élève mf; écolier, -ière.
pupil², s. Pupille f (de l'œil).
pupil(l)age ['pju:pilidʒ], s. *Jur:* (a) Minorité f. (b) Pupillarité f. Child in p., enfant en pupille, en tutelle.
pupil(l)ary ['pju:piləri], a. 1. *Jur:* Pupillaire. *Sch: O:* D'élève, d'écolier. 2. *Anat:* Pupillaire.
puppet ['pʌpit], s. Marionnette f. (Of pers.) Mere p., pantin m. *Pol:* P. government, gouvernement fantoche. **'puppet-play**, s. = PUPPET-SHOW 1. **'puppet-show**, s. 1. Spectacle m de marionnettes. 2. Théâtre m de marionnettes.
puppeteer [,pʌpi'tiər], s. Marionnettiste m, montreur, -euse, de marionnettes.
puppy ['pʌpi], s. 1. Jeune chien; chiot m. P. love, premier amour. 2. (Of pers.) Jeune suffisant.
puppyfat ['pʌpifæt], s. Adiposité f d'enfance, d'adolescence.
puppyish ['pʌpiiʃ], a. F: (Of pers.) (a) Impertinent, suffisant. (b) Tapageur, -euse, turbulent.
purblind ['pə:blaind], a. 1. (a) Myope. (b) Presque aveugle. 2. A l'esprit épais, obtus.
purblindness ['pə:blaindnis], s. 1. (a) Myopie f; vue basse. (b) Quasi-cécité f. 2. Manque m d'intelligence, de vision.
purchasable ['pə:tʃəsəbl], a. Achetable, acquérable.
purchase¹ ['pə:tʃis], s. 1. Achat m, acquisition f. To make some purchases, faire des emplettes, des achats. S.a. HIRE-PURCHASE. 2. *Jur:* At so many years' p., moyennant tant d'années de loyer. 3. (a) Force f mécanique. (b) Prise f. To get, secure, a p. on sth., trouver prise à qch. (c) Point d'appui; appui m. To take p. on . . ., prendre appui sur. . . . 4. (a) (Block) Palan m, moufle f. (b) (Tackle) Appareil m (de levage). **'purchase-money, -price**, s. Prix m d'achat.
purchase², v.tr. Acheter, acquérir. *Abs.* Now is the time to p., c'est maintenant qu'il faut faire vos achats. purchasing, s. *Pol.Ec:* P. power, puissance f, pouvoir m d'achat (de la livre, du dollar, du franc).
purchaser ['pə:tʃisər], s. Acheteur, -euse, acquéreur, -euse.
purdah ['pə:dɑ:], s. *Moham.Rel:* (a) Rideau (destiné à soustraire les femmes à la vue); purdah m. (b) Système m qui astreint les femmes à une vie retirée. F: We're going into p. for a bit, nous allons vivre très retirés pendant quelque temps.
pure ['pjuər], a. Pur. P. gold, or pur. P. alcohol, alcool rectifié. A p. green, un vert franc. P. mathematics, les mathématiques pures. The p. and simple truth, la vérité pure et simple. P. air, air pur. P. silk, soie naturelle. -ly, adv. Purement. **'pure-blood**, attrib. a. & s., **'pure-'blooded**, a. (Personne f, animal m) de sang pur; (cheval m) de race. **'pure-'bred**, a. (Chien) de race. **'pure-'minded**, a. Pur d'esprit; chaste.
purée ['pjuərei], s. (a) Marmelade f. Apple p., marmelade de pommes. (b) Potato p., purée f de pommes de terre.
purgation [pə:'geiʃ(ə)n], s. Purgation f.
purgative ['pə:gətiv], a. & s. Purgatif (m).
purgatorial [,pə:gə'tɔ:riəl], a. *Theol:* (a) Du purgatoire. (b) D'expiation, de purification.
purgatory ['pə:gət(ə)ri], s. *Theol:* Le purgatoire. The souls in p., les âmes du purgatoire, les âmes en peine. F: It is p. to me, cela me fait souffrir les peines du purgatoire.

purge¹ [pə:dʒ], s. 1. *Med:* Purgatif m, purge f. 2. Purgation f. *Pol:* Purge f, nettoyage m, épuration f. 3. *Mch:* P.-cock, robinet m de vidange, robinet purgeur.
purge², v.tr. 1. Purger (un malade). 2. Nettoyer (un égout); purifier (le sang); clarifier (un liquide); épurer (les mœurs). To p. the finances of a country, assainir les finances d'un pays. To p. away, p. out, one's sins, purger ses péchés. 4. *Jur:* To p. oneself of a charge, se disculper, se justifier. 5. *Jur:* To p. an offence, purger sa peine. purging¹, a. Purgatif, -ive. purging², s. 1. Purge f, purgation f (du corps). 2. Nettoyage m; purification f.
purger ['pə:dʒər], s. 1. Purificateur, -trice. 2. (Device) (a) Purificateur. (b) Nettoyeur m.
purification [,pjuərifi'keiʃ(ə)n], s. Purification f; épuration f.
purifier ['pjuərifaiər], s. 1. (Pers.) Purificateur, -trice. 2. (Apparatus) Épurateur m, purgeur m (de gaz, etc.).
purify ['pjuərifai], v.tr. Purifier (l'air, etc.); épurer (le gaz, l'huile, la langue); dépurer (le sang). purifying¹, a. Purifiant, purificateur, -trice. P. tank (for water supply), purgeoir m. purifying², s. Purification f; épuration f; dépuration f (du sang, etc.).
purist ['pjuərist], s. Puriste mf.
Puritan ['pjuərit(ə)n], a. & s. Puritain, -aine.
puritanical [,pjuəri'tænik(ə)l], a. De puritain.
puritanism ['pjuəritənizm], s. Puritanisme m.
purity ['pjuəriti], s. Pureté f.
purl¹ [pə:l], s. 1. *Needlew:* (Of twisted metal) Cannetille f (à broder). 2. Picot m, engrêlure f (de dentelle). 3. *Knitting:* P. stitch, maille f à l'envers.
purl², v.tr. 1. Engrêler (la dentelle). 2. *Knitting:* Faire des mailles à l'envers. Knit one, p. one, une maille à l'endroit, une maille à l'envers.
purl³, s. *Lit:* Doux murmure, gazouillement m (d'un ruisseau).
purl⁴, v.i. *Lit:* (Of brook) Murmurer, gazouiller.
purler ['pə:lər], s. F: To come a p., piquer une tête; P: ramasser une bûche.
purlieu ['pə:lju:], s. 1. *Jur:* Confins mpl (d'une forêt) soumis au régime du domaine forestier. 2. Limites fpl, bornes fpl. 3. pl. Purlieus, alentours mpl, environs mpl, abords mpl (d'une gare, etc.).
purlin ['pə:lin], s. *Const:* Panne f, filière f. Eaves p., panne sablière. Ridge p., panne faîtière.
purloin [pə:'lɔin], v.tr. Soustraire, détourner; voler.
purple ['pə:pl]. I. a. (a) A: Pourpre, pourpré. (b) Violet (tirant sur le rouge); violacé. F: To get p. in the face (with anger, etc.), devenir cramoisi, pourpre. *Lit:* P. passages, p. patches, passages marquants; morceaux de bravoure, bravoure f. II. purple, s. 1. (a) Pourpre f. (b) Violet m. (c) *Lit:* Born in the p., né dans la pourpre; né sous des lambris dorés. (d) *Physiol:* Visual p., pourpre rétinien. 2. pl. Purples, (a) *Med:* A: Purpura m, pourpre m. (b) *Vet:* Rouget m (du porc). (c) *Agr:* Nielle f (du blé). **'purple-wood**, s. *Bot:* Palissandre m.
purplish ['pə:pliʃ], a. Violacé, violâtre; (of the face) cramoisi.
purport¹ ['pə:pət, -pɔ:t], s. (a) Sens m, signification f, teneur f (d'un document). (b) Portée f, valeur f, force f (d'un mot).
purport² [pə'pɔ:t], v.tr. 1. To p. to be sth., avoir la prétention d'être qch.; être donné, présenté, comme étant qch. His story purports to be an autobiography, son récit a la prétention d'être autobiographique. 2. Impliquer; tendre à démontrer, à établir (un fait). purported, a. Esp. U.S: A p. author, un soi-disant auteur. P. spy, espion soupçonné, -ly, adv. He was p. a spy, on le disait espion, on le soupçonnait d'être espion.
purpose¹ ['pə:pəs], s. 1. (a) Dessein m, objet m; but m, fin f, intention f. Fixed p., dessein bien arrêté. For, with, the p. of doing sth., dans le but de, dans l'intention de, faire qch. To do sth. on p., faire qch. exprès, à dessein, de propos délibéré. Of set p., de propos délibéré, de parti pris. For all practical purposes, pratiquement. (b) Résolution f. Infirmity of p., manque m de volonté. Infirm of p., irrésolu; sans caractère. Steadfastness of p., ténacité f de caractère; détermination f. 2. Destination f, fin (d'un bâtiment, d'un appareil). To answer, serve,

various purposes, servir à plusieurs usages, à plusieurs fins. **To answer the p.,** répondre au but. **For this, that, p.,** dans ce but, dans cette intention; à cet effet. **For all purposes,** à toutes fins, à tous usages. **To serve no p.,** ne servir à rien. **To retain a portion for purposes of analysis,** en prélever une partie aux fins d'analyse. *Jur:* **For the p. of this convention . . .,** pour l'application de la présente convention. . . . 3. **To speak to the p.,** parler à propos. **Not to the p.,** hors de propos. 4. **To work to good p.,** travailler avec fruit. **He worked to such good p. that . . .,** il fit tant et si bien que. . . . **To some p.,** utilement, avantageusement, efficacement. **To work to no p.,** travailler en vain, en pure perte, inutilement. **To talk to no p.,** parler en l'air.

purpose[2], *v.tr. A:* **To p.** doing sth., to do sth., se proposer, avoir l'intention, de faire qch.

purposeful ['pəːpəsful], *a.* (*a*) Prémédité; (acte) réfléchi. (*b*) (*Of pers.*) Avisé. (*c*) Tenace. **-fully,** *adv.* Dans un but réfléchi.

purposeless ['pəːpəslis], *a.* Sans but; inutile.

purposely ['pəːpəsli], *adv.* 1. (Insulter qn) à dessein, de propos délibéré. 2. Exprès. **I came p. to see him,** je suis venu exprès pour le voir.

purpura ['pəːpjurə], *s. Med:* Pourpre *m*, purpura *m*.

purr[1] [pəːr], *s.* 1. Ronron *m* (de chat). 2. (*Of engine*) Ronron, ronflement *m*; vrombissement *m*.

purr[2], *v.i.* (*Of cat, engine*) Ronronner; (*of cat*) faire ronron; (*of engine*) ronfler; vrombir. **purring,** *s.* = PURR[1].

purse[1] [pəːs], *s.* 1. (*a*) Bourse *f*, porte-monnaie *m inv.* **Well-lined p.,** bourse bien garnie. **Light p.,** bourse plate, légère. **To have a common p.,** faire bourse commune. **That car is beyond my p.,** cette voiture est au-delà de mes moyens. **You cannot make a silk p. out of a sow's ear,** on ne peut tirer de la farine d'un sac de son. (*b*) **The Public p.,** les finances *f* de l'État; le Trésor. *S.a.* PRIVY I. 2. (*c*) *Sp: esp. Box:* **To give, put up, a p.,** constituer, offrir, une bourse. 2. *Nat.Hist: etc:* Sac *m*, bourse, poche *f.* **'purse-proud,** *a.* Orgueilleux, -euse, de sa fortune. **'purse-strings,** *s.pl.* Cordons *m*, tirants *m*, de bourse. *F:* **She holds the p.-s.,** c'est elle qui tient les cordons de la bourse.

purse[2], *v.tr.* **To p. (up) one's lips,** pincer les lèvres; faire la moue.

purser ['pəːsər], *s. Nau:* Commissaire *m* (de la marine (marchande)).

pursership ['pəːsəʃip], *s. Nau:* Commissariat *m* (de la marine (marchande)).

purslane ['pəːslin], *s. Bot:* Pourpier *m*.

pursuable [pə'sjuːəbl], *a.* Poursuivable.

pursuance [pə'sjuː(ə)ns], *s. Jur: Com:* Action *f* de poursuivre. **In p. of your instructions, of our intention,** conformément à vos instructions; suivant notre intention. **In p. of this decree,** en vertu de ce décret.

pursuant [pə'sjuː(ə)nt], *adv. Jur: Com:* **P. to your instructions,** conformément à vos instructions.

pursue [pə'sjuː]. 1. *v.tr. & ind.tr.* **To p. s.o., sth.,** (*a*) poursuivre (qn); (*b*) rechercher (le plaisir); être à la poursuite (du bonheur). 2. *v.tr.* Continuer, suivre (son chemin); donner suite à, poursuivre (une enquête). **To p. a line of conduct,** suivre une ligne de conduite. **To p. a profession,** suivre, exercer, un métier.

pursuer [pə'sjuː(ə)r], *s.* 1. Poursuivant, -ante. 2. *Jur:* (*Scot.*) = PLAINTIFF.

pursuit [pə'sjuːt], *s.* 1. (*a*) Poursuite *f.* **Pack in eager, hot, p.,** meute acharnée à la poursuite. **To set out in p. of s.o.,** se mettre à la poursuite de qn. *Mil: Av:* **P. plane,** chasseur *m*, avion *m* de chasse. (*b*) Recherche *f* (des richesses, etc.). **In p. of happiness,** à la recherche, en quête, du bonheur. **In his p. of knowledge,** dans ses efforts pour s'instruire. 2. (*a*) Carrière *f*, profession *f.* **To engage in scientific pursuits,** s'adonner à des recherches scientifiques. **His literary pursuits,** ses travaux *m* littéraires. (*b*) Occupation *f.*

pursuivant ['pəːswiv(ə)nt], *s. Her:* Poursuivant *m* d'armes.

pursy[1] ['pəːsi], *a.* 1. Poussif, -ive. 2. Corpulent, bedonnant.

pursy[2], *a. F:* **P. mouth,** bouche pincée.

purulence ['pjuəruləns], *s. Med:* 1. Purulence *f.* 2. Pus *m*.

purulent ['pjuərulənt], *a. Med:* Purulent.

purvey [pə'vei], *v.tr.* Fournir (des provisions).

purveyance [pə'veiəns], *s.* Fourniture *f* de provisions; approvisionnement *m*.

purveyor [pə'veiər], *s.* Fournisseur, -euse; pourvoyeur, -euse (de provisions).

purview ['pəːvjuː], *s.* 1. *Jur:* Corps *m*, texte *m*, articles *mpl* (d'un statut). 2. (*a*) Limites *fpl*, portée *f* (d'un projet, d'un livre). (*b*) **To lie, come, within the p. of s.o.,** (i) être à portée de la vue de qn; (ii) être du ressort de qn, de la compétence de qn.

pus [pʌs], *s. Med:* Pus *m*; sanie *f.*

push[1] [puʃ], *s.* 1. Poussée *f*, impulsion *f.* **To give sth. a p.,** pousser qch. **At, with, one p.,** d'un seul coup. *F:* **To give s.o. the p.,** flanquer qn à la porte; donner son congé à qn. 2. (*a*) Effort *m.* (*b*) *Mil:* Attaque *f* en masse. (*c*) **To have plenty of p.,** avoir de l'entregent; avoir de l'initiative, du dynamisme; *Pej:* être un arriviste. 3. *F:* **At a p.,** dans une extrémité; au besoin; au moment critique. **When it comes to the p.,** quand on en vient au moment décisif. **'push-bicycle,** *F:* **'push-bike,** *s.* Bicyclette *f*, *F:* bécane *f.* **'push-button,** *s.* 1. *El:* Bouton *m* de contact; poussoir *m. W.Tel:* Bouton-poussoir *m, pl.* boutons-poussoirs. *F:* **P.-b. war,** la guerre presse-bouton. 2. Poussoir (d'une montre à répétition). **'push-cart,** *s.* 1. Charrette *f* à bras. 2. Charrette d'enfant; *F:* poussette *f.* **'push-chair,** *s.* Poussette *f* (d'enfant). **'push-pin,** *s. U.S:* (= *Drawing pin*) Punaise *f.* **'push-rod,** *s. I.C.E:* Poussoir *m* de soupape. **'push-stroke,** *s. Bill:* Coup queuté. **To play a p.-s.,** queuter.

push[2]. I. *v.tr.* Pousser. 1. **To p. the button,** appuyer sur le bouton. **To p. one's finger into s.o.'s eye,** fourrer, enfoncer le doigt dans l'œil de qn. 2. (*a*) **To p. s.o. into the room,** faire entrer qn d'une poussée. **Don't p. (me)!** ne (me) bousculez pas! (*b*) **To p. oneself (forward),** se mettre en avant; se pousser dans le monde. 3. (*a*) Poursuivre (son avantage). **To p. an attack home,** pousser à fond une attaque. (*b*) Pousser la vente de (sa marchandise); lancer (un article). (*c*) *St.Exch:* **To p. shares,** placer des valeurs douteuses. 4. **To p. s.o. for payment,** presser, importuner, qn pour se faire payer. **I am pushed for time,** le temps me manque; je suis très pressé. **To be pushed for money,** être à court d'argent. II. **push,** *v.i.* 1. Avancer (avec difficulté). **To p. (one's way) through the crowd,** se frayer, s'ouvrir, un chemin à travers la foule. 2. Pousser; exercer une pression. **push aside,** *v.tr.* Écarter (d'une poussée). **push away,** *v.tr.* Repousser, éloigner. **push back,** *v.tr.* Repousser; faire reculer. **push forward,** 1. *v.tr.* Pousser en avant, (faire) avancer. *S.a.* PUSH[2] I. 2. 2. *v.i.* Avancer; se porter en avant. **push in.** 1. *v.tr.* Enfoncer, refouler, repousser. 2. *v.i.* Entrer à toute force. **push off,** *v.i. Nau:* Pousser au large. *F:* **Time to p. o.,** il est temps de se mettre en route. **'push-off,** 1. Poussée *f* au large (d'un bateau). 2. *F:* Impulsion (donnée à une affaire). **push on,** *v.tr.* Pousser en avant; faire avancer. **To p. on the work,** pousser, hâter, activer, les travaux. 2. *v.i.* (*a*) **To p. on to a place,** pousser jusqu'à un endroit. (*b*) **It's time to p. on,** il est temps de nous remettre en route. **push out.** 1. *v.tr.* (*a*) Pousser dehors; faire sortir. (*b*) **To p. a boat out,** mettre une embarcation à l'eau. (*c*) (*Of plant*) Pousser (des racines, etc.). (*Of snail*) **To push out its horns,** sortir ses cornes. **push over,** *v.tr.* Faire tomber (qn, qch.). **'push(-)over,** *s. F:* 1. (*Pers.*) Blanc-bec *m, pl.* blancs-becs; gogo *m*. 2. **It's a p.(-)o.,** c'est donné, c'est du gâteau. **push through.** 1. *v.tr.* (*a*) Faire passer (qch.) à travers. (*b*) Mener à bien, terminer (un travail, etc.). 2. *v.i.* Se frayer un chemin à travers. **push to,** *v.tr.* Pousser, fermer (la porte). **push up,** *v.tr.* 1. Relever (ses lunettes sur son front, etc.). *P:* **He's pushing up the daisies,** il est mort (et enterré), il mange les pissenlits par les racines. 2. *F:* **He was pushed up,** il est arrivé à coups de piston. **pushing,** *a.* (*a*) Débrouillard, entreprenant. (*b*) **A p. man,** un arriviste, un ambitieux. (*c*) Indiscret.

pusher ['puʃər], *s.* 1. Personne *f* qui pousse (qch.). 2. *F:* Arriviste *mf.* 3. (Baby's) p., raclette *f.*

pushful ['puʃful], *a.* **He's a p. type,** il veut arriver; il fera son chemin; il est arriviste.

pushy ['puʃi], a. F: = 1. PUSHING. 2. PUSHFUL.

pusillanimity [ˌpjuːsiləˈnimiti], s. Pusillanimité f; manque m de cœur.

pusillanimous [ˌpjuːsiˈlænəməs], a. Pusillanime.

puss [pus], s. Minet m, minette f; mimi m. P. in Boots, le Chat botté. To play (at) p. in the corner, jouer aux quatre coins.

pussy ['pusi], s. 1. P.(-cat) = PUSS. 2. Bot: Chaton m.

pussyfoot ['pusifut], s. U.S: F: = PROHIBITIONIST.

pustule ['pʌstjuːl], s. Med: Pustule f.

pustulous ['pʌstjuːləs], a. Med: Pustuleux, -euse.

put¹ [put], s. St.Exch: P. (option), prime f pour livrer; prime vendeur; option f de vente.

put², v. (put; put; putting) I. v.tr. Mettre. 1. (a) P. it on the mantelpiece, mettez-le, placez-le, posez-le, sur la cheminée. To p. milk in one's tea, mettre du lait dans son thé. To p. one's lips to one's glass, tremper ses lèvres dans son verre. To p. s.o. in his place, remettre qn à sa place; rembarrer qn. S.a. SHADE¹ 1. To p. one's signature to sth., apposer sa signature sur, à, qch. To p. honour before riches, préférer l'honneur à l'argent. (b) To p. the matter right, arranger l'affaire. S.a. WISE¹ 2. To p. s.o. out of suspense, tirer qn de doute. To p. s.o. against s.o., monter qn contre qn. To p. the law into operation, appliquer la loi. To p. a field under wheat, mettre une terre en blé. St.Exch: To p. stock at a certain price, délivrer, fournir, des actions à un certain prix. (c) To p. a passage into Greek, mettre, traduire, un passage en grec. (d) To p. money into an undertaking, verser des fonds dans une affaire. To p. money on a horse, miser, parier, sur un cheval. To p. a question to s.o., poser, faire, une question à qn. To p. a resolution to the meeting, présenter une résolution à l'assemblée. I p. it to you whether . . ., je vous demande un peu si. . . . Jur: I p. it to you that . . ., n'est-il pas vrai que. . . .? P. it to him nicely, présentez-lui la chose gentiment. To p. the case clearly, exposer clairement la situation. To p. it bluntly, pour parler franc. As Horace puts it, comme dit Horace. If one may p. it in that way, si l'on peut s'exprimer ainsi. It can all be p. in two words, tout cela tient en deux mots. I don't know how to p. it, je ne sais comment dire. 3. To p. the population at 10,000, estimer, évaluer, la population à 10,000. 4. To p. an end, a stop, to sth., mettre fin à qch. 5. (a) He is p. to every kind of work, on lui fait faire toutes sortes de besognes. P. him to a trade, apprenez-lui un métier. To p. s.o. to bed, mettre qn au lit; coucher (un enfant). To p. a horse to, at, a fence, lancer un cheval sur une barrière. To p. s.o. through an ordeal, faire subir une rude épreuve à qn. F: To p. s.o. through it, faire passer un mauvais quart d'heure à qn. (b) To p. the enemy to flight, mettre l'ennemi en déroute. To p. s.o. to sleep, endormir qn. 6. (a) To p. one's fist through the window, enfoncer une fenêtre d'un coup de poing. To p. one's pen through a word, rayer, barrer, biffer, un mot. (b) Sp: To p. the weight, the shot, lancer le poids. II. put, v.i. Nau: To (out) to sea, mettre à la voile, à mer; prendre le large. To p. into port, relâcher; faire relâche. put about, v.tr. 1. Faire circuler (une rumeur). 2. (a) Déranger (qn). (b) O: Mettre (qn) en émoi. Don't p. yourself a., n'allez pas vous inquiéter. 3. To p. a ship a., abs. to p. a., virer de bord. put across, v.tr. F: To p. a deal a., boucler une affaire. You can't p. that a. me, on ne me la fait pas. put aside, v.tr. 1. (a) Mettre (qch.) de côté. (b) Se défaire de (qch.). put away, v.tr. 1. (a) Serrer, ranger (qch. dans une armoire, etc.); remiser (son auto). P. a. your books, rangez vos livres. (b) Mettre de côté (de l'argent). (c) F: (i) Mettre (qn) en prison; coffrer (qn). (ii) Mettre (qn) dans une maison de santé. (d) P: Mettre (qch.) au clou. F: Bouffer (de la nourriture); P: siffler (un verre de vin). 2. Écarter, chasser (une pensée). 3. F: Tuer, assassiner (qn); tuer (un animal). put back. 1. v.tr. (a) Remettre (un livre) à sa place. (b) Retarder (une horloge, l'arrivée de qn). (c) Mil: Ajourner (une recrue). 2. v.i. Nau: Retourner, revenir (to a port, à un port); rentrer au port. put by, v.tr. Mettre de côté (de l'argent); mettre en réserve (des provisions). To p. by for the future, économiser pour l'avenir. He is living on the money he has p. by, il vit de ses

économies. put down, v.tr. 1. Déposer, poser. P. it d.! laissez cela! (Of bus) To p. d. passengers, débarquer, déposer, des voyageurs. Mil: To p. d. a smoke-screen, faire un barrage de fumée. Nau: To p. d. a buoy, mouiller une bouée. S.a. FOOT¹ 1. 2. Supprimer, réprimer (une révolte); vaincre (l'opposition); faire cesser, mettre fin à (un abus). 3. Fermer (un parapluie). 4. (a) Noter (sur papier); coucher par écrit. To p. d. one's name, s'inscrire; se faire inscrire (for, pour). P. it d. to my account, inscrivez-le, mettez-le à mon compte. (b) To p. d. a number, poser un chiffre. (c) I p. him d. as, for, a Frenchman, je jugeai qu'il était Français. I should p. her d. as thirty-five, je lui donne trente-cinq ans. (d) To p. d. sth. to sth., attribuer, imputer, qch. à qch. (e) He was unable to p.d. the money, il ne pouvait par payer comptant. 5. Abs. Av: Atterrir. 6. F: Tuer, abattre (un animal). put forward, v.tr. 1. (a) Émettre, exprimer, avancer, proposer; mettre en avant, en évidence; faire valoir (une théorie). Pol: To p. f. a list of candidates, déposer une liste électorale. (b) To p. oneself f., se mettre en avant, en évidence; s'imposer; se pousser, se produire. (c) F: To p. one's best foot f., (i) presser le pas; (ii) se mettre en devoir de faire de son mieux. 2. Avancer (la pendule, etc.). put in. 1. v.tr. (a) To p. one's head in at the window, passer sa tête par la fenêtre. (b) Planter (un arbre). (c) F: To p. a word in, placer un mot (dans la conversation). To p. in a (good) word for s.o., dire un mot en faveur de qn. (d) Jur: Présenter, produire, fournir (un document, un témoin). S.a. CLAIM¹ 2. (e) To p. in an hour's work, faire, fournir, une heure de travail. To p. in one's time reading, passer son temps à lire. 2. v.i. (a) To p. in at a port, entrer, relâcher, dans un port; faire escale dans un port. (b) To p. in for a post, poser sa candidature à un poste. To p. in for two days' leave, demander une permission de 48 heures. put off. 1. v.tr. (a) Retirer, ôter. To p. o. the mask, déposer le masque. (b) Remettre, différer; ajourner, renvoyer. To p. o. doing sth., différer de faire qch.; tarder à faire qch. Jur: To p. o. a case for a week, renvoyer, ajourner, une affaire à huitaine. To p. o. one's guests, contremander ses invités. (c) To p. s.o. o. with an excuse, se débarrasser de qn, renvoyer qn, avec une excuse. He is not to be p. o. with words, il ne se paie pas de paroles. (d) Déconcerter, dérouter (qn). You p. me o., vous me faites tromper. His stern look p. me off, son regard sévère m'a intimidé. (e) To p. s.o. off doing sth., éloigner, dégoûter, décourager, qn de faire qch.; faire passer à qn l'envie de faire qch. The smell puts me off, l'odeur m'en dégoûte. The doctor has p. me off eggs, le docteur m'a défendu de manger des œufs. 2. v.i. Nau: Déborder du quai; pousser au large; démarrer. put on, v.tr. 1. (a) To p. the kettle on, mettre chauffer de l'eau. To p. on a dish, servir un plat. To p. on a record, a tape; to p. a record, a tape, on, passer un disque, une bande. (b) To p. a play on, mettre sur la scène, monter, une pièce de théâtre. To p. on a train, mettre un train en service. (c) Aut: To p. on the brake, freiner. 2. (a) Mettre (ses vêtements); revêtir (un pardessus); enfiler (son pantalon); chausser (ses pantoufles). To p. on one's shoes, chausser. (b) To p. on an innocent air, prendre, se donner, un air innocent. S.a. AIR¹ III. F: To p. it on, poser; afficher de grands airs; P: faire sa poire. 3. To p. on weight, grossir; prendre du poids. To p. on speed, prendre de la vitesse. 4. Avancer (la pendule). 5. To p. on the light, mettre la lumière; allumer. To p. on steam, mettre la vapeur. To p. on the radio, faire marcher la radio. 6. To p. s.o. on to a job, confier, donner, un travail à qn. 7. F: Who p. you on to it? qui est-ce qui vous a donné le tuyau? 8. Tp: P. me on to City 1380, donnez-moi City 13.80. put out, v.tr. 1. Avancer, tendre (la main); allonger, étendre (le bras). 2. (a) Mettre dehors. To p. s.o. out (of the room), mettre qn à la porte. (b) To p. the clothes o. to dry, mettre du linge à sécher. Nau: To p.o. a boat, mettre un canot à l'eau. (c) To p. one's tongue o., tirer la langue (at s.o., à qn). To p. one's head o. of the window, passer sa tête par la fenêtre; sortir la

tête à la fenêtre. (*Traffic signal*) To p. o. one's arm, étendre, sortir, le bras. 3. To p. o. (of joint), démettre, déboîter. To p. one's arm o., se démancher le bras. 4. (*a*) Éteindre (une bougie, le feu). (*b*) To p. s.o.'s eyes o., crever les yeux à qn. To p. s.o.'s eye o. with an umbrella, éborgner qn avec un parapluie. 5. (*a*) Déconcerter, interloquer (qn). He never gets p. o., il ne se démonte jamais; il ne s'émeut de rien. (*b*) Ennuyer, contrarier (qn). To be p. o. about sth., être contrarié de qch. (*c*) Incommoder, gêner (qn). To p. oneself o. for s.o., se déranger, se mettre en frais, pour qn. 6. To p. money o. (to interest), placer de l'argent (à intérêt). 7. Publier (un ouvrage). **put through**, *v.tr.* 1. Mener à bien (un projet). 2. *Tp:* To p. s.o. through to s.o., mettre qn en communication avec qn; brancher (qn). I'll put you through to his secretary, je vous passe sa secrétaire. **put to**, *v.tr.* 1. Atteler (un cheval); accrocher (une locomotive). 2. He was hard p. to it to find a substitute, il a eu fort à faire, il était très embarrassé, pour se faire remplacer. **put together**, *v.tr.* 1. Joindre; monter, assembler (une robe, une machine). 2. Rapprocher, comparer, (des faits). *S.a.* HEAD¹ 2, TWO. **put up**, *v.tr.* 1. (*a*) Relever (le col de son pardessus); ouvrir (un parapluie); dresser (une échelle); accrocher (un tableau); poser (un rideau). (*Of prisoner*) To p. up one's hands, lever, mettre, haut les mains. To p. up one's hair, se faire un chignon. (*b*) Apposer, coller (une affiche); afficher (un avis). 2. *Ven:* (Faire) lever (une perdrix, etc.). 3. Augmenter, (faire) hausser, majorer (les prix). 4. Offrir, faire (une prière); présenter (une pétition). 5. To p. up a candidate, proposer un candidat. *v.i.* (*Of candidate*) To p. up for a seat, poser sa candidature à un siège. 6. To p. sth. up for sale, mettre qch. en vente. 7. To p. up the money for an undertaking, faire les frais d'une entreprise. 8. *Com:* This cream is p. up in tubes, cette crème est présentée en tubes. 9. Remettre (l'épée) au fourreau; rengainer. 10. To p. up a stout resistance, se défendre vaillamment. *S.a.* FIGHT¹. 11. Offrir un lit à (qn); héberger (qn). *v.i.* To p. up at a hotel, (i) descendre, (ii) loger, à un hôtel. 12. *Abs.* To p. up with sth., s'accommoder, s'arranger, de qch.; se résigner à (des inconvénients); souffrir, endurer (les railleries). It's hard to p. up with, *F:* c'est dur à encaisser. 13. (*a*) *O:* To p. s.o. up to a thing, mettre qn au courant, au fait, de qch.; *F:* tuyauter qn. (*b*) To p. s.o. up to sth., to doing sth. pousser, inciter, qn à qch., à faire qch. 14. Construire, bâtir (une maison); ériger (un monument). '**put-up**, *attrib.* a. *F:* A p.-up job, une affaire machinée d'avance; un coup monté. **put upon**, *v.ind.tr.* *F:* To p. upon s.o., en imposer à qn.
putative ['pju:tətiv], *a.* *Jur:* Putatif, -ive. **-ly**, *adv.* *Jur:* Putativement.
putrefaction [ˌpju:tri'fækʃ(ə)n], *s.* Putréfaction *f.*
putrefactive [ˌpju:tri'fæktiv], *a.* Putréfactif, -ive. P. fermentation, fermentation putride.
putrefiable [ˌpju:tri'faiəbl], *a.* Putréfiable, pourrissable.
putrefy ['pju:trifai]. 1. *v.tr.* Putréfier, pourrir. 2. *v.i.* (*a*) (*Of carrion*) Se putréfier, pourrir. (*b*) (*Of living tissue*) (i) Suppurer, s'envenimer; (ii) se gangrener. **putrefying**, *a.* En pourriture; putrescent.
putrescence [pju:'tres(ə)ns], *s.* Putrescence *f.*
putrescent [pju:'tres(ə)nt], *a.* En putréfaction; putrescent.
putrid ['pju:trid], *a.* 1. Putride; en putréfaction; infect. 2. *P:* = ROTTEN 2.
putridness ['pju:tridnis], **putridity** [pju:'triditi], *s.* Putridité *f*, pourriture *f*, corruption *f.*
putt¹ [pʌt], *s.* *Golf:* Putt *m.*
putt², *v.tr.* *Golf:* Jouer sur le putting(-green). '**putting-green**, *s.* *Golf:* Putting(-green) *m*; le vert.
puttee ['pʌti], *s.* Bande molletière.
putter¹ ['pʌtər], *s.* *Golf:* 1. (*Club*) Putter *m.* 2. (*Pers.*) Good p., joueur qui réussit bien les putts.

putter², *v.i.* *U.S:* = POTTER².
putty¹ ['pʌti], *s.* 1. Mastic *m*, enduit *m.* Glazier's p., mastic à vitres. Plasterer's p., pâte *f* de chaux. P. coloured, couleur mastic. 2. Jeweller's p., p.-powder, potée *f* (d'étain). '**putty-knife**, *s.* Spatule *f* de vitrier.
putty², *v.tr.* To p. (up) a hole, mastiquer un trou; boucher un trou au mastic. **puttying**, *s.* Masticage *m.*
puzzle¹ ['pʌzl], *s.* 1. Embarras *m*; perplexité *f.* 2. Énigme *f.* Your friend is a real p. to me, votre ami est pour moi un vrai problème. 3. (*a*) Chinese p., casse-tête chinois. *S.a.* JIG-SAW. (*b*) Devinette *f*, problème *m.* Crossword p., (problème de) mots croisés.
puzzle². 1. *v.tr.* Embarrasser, intriguer. I was somewhat puzzled how to answer, j'étais assez embarrassé pour répondre. To p. s.o. with a question, poser à qn une question embarrassante. It puzzles me what his plans are, ses projets m'intriguent. 2. *v.i.* To p. over sth., se creuser la tête pour comprendre qch. **puzzle out**, *v.tr.* Débrouiller, éclaircir (un mystère); déchiffrer (une écriture, un rébus). **puzzling**, *a.* Embarrassant, intrigant.
puzzler ['pʌzlər], *s.* Question embarrassante; *Sch:* colle *f.*
pyelitis [ˌpaii'laitis], *s.* *Med:* Pyélite *f.*
pygmy ['pigmi]. 1. *s.* Pygmée *m.* 2. *Attrib.* Pygméen, pygmée.
pyjama [pi'dʒɑ:mə], *s.* P. suit, pyjamas, pyjama *m.* P.-cord, cordelière *f.*
pylon ['pailən], *s.* Pylône *m.*
pylorus [pai'lɔ:rəs], *s.* *Anat:* Pylore *m.*
pyorrhea [ˌpaiə'ri:ə], *s.* *Med:* Pyorrhée *f*; gingivite expulsive.
pyracanth ['paiərəkænθ], *s.* *Bot:* Pyracanthe *f*, *F:* buisson ardent.
pyralis ['piralis], *s.* *Ent:* Pyrale *f.*
pyramid ['pirəmid], *s.* Pyramide *f.* P.-shaped, en pyramide.
pyramidal [pi'ræmid(ə)l], *a.* Pyramidal, -aux.
pyre ['paiər], *s.* Bûcher *m* (funéraire).
Pyrenean [ˌpirə'ni:ən], *a.* Pyrénéen, -enne; des Pyrénées.
Pyrenees (the) [ðəˌpirə'ni:z]. *Pr.n.* Les Pyrénées *fpl.*
pyrethrum [paiə'ri:θrəm], *s.* Pyrèthre *m.* P. powder, poudre *f* de pyrèthre.
Pyrex ['paireks], *s.* *Glassm: Cu:* R.t.m: Pyrex *m.*
pyrexia [paiə'reksiə], *s.* *Med:* Pyrexie *f*; fièvre *f.*
pyrites [paiə'raiti:z], *s.* Pyrite *f.* Copper p., chalcopyrite *f.* Iron p., sulfure *m* de fer; fer sulfuré.
pyritic [paiə'ritik], *a.* *Miner:* Pyriteux, -euse.
pyrogallic ['paiərou'gælik], *a.* *Ch:* P. acid, acide *m* pyrogallique; pyrogallol *m.*
pyrolatry [paiə'rolətri], *s.* Pyrolâtrie *f.*
pyromania ['paiərou'meiniə], *s.* *Psy: Med:* Pyromanie *f.*
pyromaniac ['pairo'meiniæk], *s.* Pyromane *mf.*
pyrometer [pai'romitər], *s.* Pyromètre *m.*
pyrosis [paiə'rousis], *s.* *Med:* Pyrosis *m.*
pyrotechnic(al) [ˌpaiərə'teknik(əl)], *a.* Pyrotechnique.
pyrotechnics [ˌpaiərə'tekniks], *s.pl.* Pyrotechnie *f.*
pyrotechnist [ˌpaiərə'teknist], *s.* Pyrotechnicien *m.*
pyrotechny ['pairo'tekni], *s.* = PYROTECHNICS.
Pyrrhic¹ ['pirik], *a. & s.* (Danse) pyrrhique (*f*).
Pyrrhic², *a.* *Rom.Hist:* De Pyrrhus. P. victory, victoire à la Pyrrhus; victoire désastreuse.
Pythagoras [pai'θægəræs, -rəs], *Pr.n.m.* Pythagore. P.'s theorem, théorème *m* de Pythagore.
python¹ ['paiθ(ə)n], *s.* *Gr.Myth: Rept:* Python *m.*
python², *s.* Démon *m*; esprit familier.
pythoness ['paiθənes], *s.f.* Pythonisse.
pyx [piks], *s.* *Ecc:* Ciboire *m.* '**pyx-cloth**, *s.* *Ecc:* Custode *f.*
pyxidium [pik'sidiəm], *s.* *Bot:* Pyxide *f.*
pyxis, *pl.* **-ides** ['piksis, -idi:z], *s.* 1. = PYXIDIUM. 2. *Anat:* Cavité *f* cotyloïde.

Q, q [kju:], s. (La lettre) Q, q m. Tp: Q for Queenie, Q comme quintal. F: On the q.t. [kju:'ti:] (= quiet), discrètement; en confidence. On the strict q.t., en secret. S.a. P.

qua [kwei], Lt.adv. En tant que; considéré comme. Men q. men, les hommes en tant qu'hommes.

quack¹ [kwæk], s. & int. Couin-couin (m).

quack², v.i. (Of duck) Crier; faire couin-couin.

quack³. 1. s. (a) Q. (doctor), charlatan m. (b) P: The q., le toubib. 2. a. Q. remedy, remède m de charlatan.

quackery ['kwækəri], s. 1. Charlatanisme m. 2. Charlatanerie f, hâblerie f.

quackish ['kwækiʃ], a. Charlatanesque; digne d'un charlatan.

quad¹ [kwɔd], s. Sch: F: = QUADRANGLE 2.

quad², s. Typ: F: = QUADRAT.

quadragenarian [ˌkwɔdrədʒi'nɛəriən], a. & s. Quadragénaire (mf).

Quadragesima [ˌkwɔdrə'dʒesimə], s. Ecc: La Quadragésime. **quadragesimal**, a. Quadragésimal, -aux.

quadrangle ['kwɔdræŋgl], s. 1. Geom: Quadrilatère m; rectangle m. 2. Cour (carrée) (d'une école, etc.).

quadrangular [kwɔ'dræŋgjulər], a. Quadrangulaire.

quadrant ['kwɔdrənt], s. 1. Astr: Mth: Quart m de cercle; quadrant m. 2. Mec.E: Secteur denté. Nau: Steering q., secteur du gouvernail.

quadrat ['kwɔdrət], s. Typ: Cadrat m, quadrat m. Em-q., cadratin m. En-q., demi-cadratin m.

quadrate [kwɔ'dreit], v.tr. Réduire (une surface, une expression) au carré équivalent.

quadratic [kwɔ'drætik], a. 1. Q. equation, équation du second degré. 2. Cryst: Quadratique.

quadrature ['kwɔdrətʃər], s. Quadrature f.

quadrennial [kwɔ'drenjəl], a. Quadriennal, -aux, quatriennal, -aux. **quadrennially**, adv. Tous les quatre ans.

quadrifoliate ['kwɔdri'fouliit], a. Quadrifolié.

quadriga [kwɔ'drii:gə], s. Rom.Ant: Quadrige m.

quadrilateral ['kwɔdri'læt(ə)rəl]. 1. a. Quadrilatéral, -aux; quadrilatère. 2. s. Quadrilatère m.

quadrille [kwɔ'dril], s. 1. Danc: Cards: etc: Quadrille m. 2. (Bull-fighting) Quadrille mf.

quadrillion [kwɔ'driljən], s. 1. Quatrillion m, quadrillion m (10²⁴). 2. U.S: Mille billions (10¹⁵).

quadripartite ['kwɔdri'pɑːtait], a. Bot: Arch: Quadriparti, -e, quadripartite.

quadrisyllabic ['kwɔdrisi'læbik], a. Quadrisyllabique.

quadrisyllable ['kwɔdri'siləbl], s. Quadrisyllabe m.

quadroon [kwɔ'druːn], a. & s. Ethn: Quarteron, -onne.

quadruman(e), pl. **quadrumana** ['kwɔdrumein, kwɔ'druːmənə], Z: 1. a. Quadrumane. 2. s.pl. Les Quadrumanes, mpl; les Primates mpl.

quadruped ['kwɔdruped], a. & s. Quadrupède (m).

quadruple¹ ['kwɔdrupl], a. & s. Quadruple (m).

quadruple², v.tr. & i. Quadrupler.

quadruplets ['kwɔdruplits], s.pl. Quadruplé(e)s.

quadruplicate¹ [kwɔ'druːplikit], a. Quadruplé, quadruple. In q., en quatre exemplaires.

quadruplicate² [kwɔ'druːplikeit], v.tr. 1. Quadrupler. 2. Faire, tirer, quatre exemplaires (de qch.)

quadruplication [kwɔˌdruːpli'keiʃ(ə)n], s. Quadruplication f.

quads [kwɔdz], s. F: = QUADRUPLETS.

quaff [kwɑːf], v.tr. Lit: (a) Boire à longs traits, à plein verre. (b) Vider (une coupe) d'un trait; F: lamper (son vin).

quag [kwæg], s. = QUAGMIRE.

quagga ['kwægə], s. Z: Couagga m.

quaggy ['kwægi, 'kwɔgi], a. Marécageux, -euse.

quagmire ['kwægmaiər, 'kwɔg-], s. Fondrière f; marécage m.

quail¹ [kweil], s. inv. Orn: Caille f. They shot six q., ils ont abattu six cailles.

quail², v.i. (Of pers.) Fléchir, faiblir (before, devant). His heart quailed, son cœur défaillit.

quaint [kweint], a. (a) Étrange, bizarre, original, fantasque. (b) Qui a le pittoresque de l'ancienne

mode. Q. ideas, idées (i) un peu surannées, (ii) baroques. Q. style, (i) style singulier, original; (ii) style d'un archaïsme piquant. -ly, adv. Étrangement, bizarrement; d'une manière originale, cocasse.

quaintness ['kweintnis], s. Bizarrerie f, singularité f.

quake [kweik], v.i. 1. (Of thg) Trembler, branler. 2. (Of pers.) Trembler, frémir, frissonner (with fear, de crainte). He is quaking at the knees, les jambes lui flageolent. F: To q. in one's shoes, trembler dans sa peau. 'quaking¹, a. Tremblant. 'quaking², s. (a) Tremblement m (de la terre). (b) Tremblement, frémissement m (de qn). 'quaking-grass, s. Bot: Amourette f.

Quaker ['kweikər]. 1. s. Rel: Quaker m. 2. a. (a) Des Quakers. (b) U.S: Philadelphien, -ienne.

quakerish ['kweikəriʃ], a. F: De Quaker, des Quakers.

Quakerism ['kweikərizm], s. Quakerisme m.

qualification [ˌkwɔlifi'keiʃ(ə)n], s. Qualification f. 1. Réserve f, restriction f. To accept without q., accepter (i) sans réserve, (ii) sans conditions. 2. **Qualifications for an appointment**, titres m à un emploi. To have the necessary qualifications, avoir les qualités requises (pour un poste); avoir capacité (pour exercer un droit). Qualifications for membership of a club, titres d'éligibilité à un cercle.

qualificative ['kwɔlifikətiv], **qualificatory** ['kwɔlifiˌkeitəri], a. Qualificatif.

qualify ['kwɔlifai]. I. v.tr. 1. (a) To q. sth. as sth., qualifier qch. de qch. (b) Gram: Qualifier. 2. To q. s.o. for sth., to do sth., rendre qn apte, propre, à qch., à faire qch.; Jur: donner qualité à qn pour faire qch. To q. oneself for a job, acquérir les titres nécessaires pour remplir un emploi. 3. (a) Apporter des réserves à (un consentement, etc.); modifier, atténuer (une affirmation). (b) (Of circumstance) Modérer, diminuer (un plaisir). 4. Étendre, couper (une boisson). II. qualify, v.i. Acquérir les connaissances requises, se qualifier (for, pour). To q. as (a) doctor, être reçu médecin. Av: To q. as a pilot, passer son brevet de pilote. **qualifiable**, a. Qualifiable. **qualified**, a. 1. (a) To be q. to do sth., avoir les capacités pour faire qch.; avoir qualité pour faire qch. Q. expert, expert diplômé. Q. seaman, matelot breveté. (b) Autorisé. To be q. to vote, avoir qualité d'électeur. Jur: Q. to inherit, habile à succéder. 2. Restreint, modéré. Q. approval, approbation modérée. Com: Q. acceptance, acceptation conditionnelle, sous condition (d'une traite). **qualifying**, a. 1. Gram: (Adjectif) qualificatif; (adverbe) modificatif. 2. (a) Q. examination, (i) examen pour certificat d'aptitude; (ii) examen d'entrée (à une école). (b) Ten: etc: Q. round, série f éliminatoire. 3. Modificateur, -trice.

qualitative ['kwɔlitətiv], a. Qualitatif.

quality ['kwɔliti], s. Qualité f. 1. (a) Of good, high, poor, q., de bonne qualité; de qualité supérieure, inférieure. Of the best q., de première qualité; de premier choix. (b) Wine that has q., vin qui a de la qualité. Com: Q. goods, marchandises fpl. de qualité. Journ: Q. newspapers, journaux sérieux. 2. (a) (Of pers.) Qualité (distinctive). He has many good qualities, bad qualities, il a beaucoup de qualités, de défauts. (b) Heating q., qualities, of a combustible, pouvoir m, valeur f, calorifique d'un combustible. 3. A: People of q., gens de qualité; gens du monde. The q., la noblesse, P: la haute. 4. To act in the q. of . . ., agir en qualité, en caractère, de . . . . 5. Qualité, timbre m (d'un son).

qualm [kwɑːm, kwɔːm], s. 1. Soulèvement m de cœur; nausée f. 2. (a) Scrupule m, remords m. To feel some qualms (about what one has done), avoir des remords de conscience. To have no qualms about doing sth., ne pas se faire le moindre scrupule de faire qch. (b) Pressentiment m de malheur; inquiétude f.

qualmish ['kwɑːmiʃ, 'kwɔː-], a. 1. Sujet aux nausées. 2. Mal à l'aise.

qualmishness ['kwɑːmiʃnis, 'kwɔː-], s. 1. Soulèvement m de cœur. 2. Scrupules exagérés.

quandary ['kwɔndəri], s. Situation embarrassante; difficulté f. To be in a q., (i) se trouver dans une impasse; être dans l'embarras; (ii) ne trop savoir que faire.

quanta ['kwɔntə], s.pl. See QUANTUM.

quantitative ['kwɔntitətiv], a. Quantitatif. Ch: Q. analysis, analyse quantitative.

quantity [', kwɔntiti], s. 1. (a) Quantité f. A small q. of . . ., une petite quantité de . . .; F: un soupçon de . . . To buy sth. in large quantities, acheter qch. par quantités considérables. In (great) quantities, en grande quantité, en abondance. Cust: Q. permitted, quantité permise, tolérance f. (b) To survey a building for quantities, faire le toisé d'un immeuble. Bill of quantities, devis m. (c) El: Connected in q., couplé en quantité, en parallèle. 2. Mth: Quantité. Unknown q., inconnue f. Negligible q., quantité négligeable. He's a negligible q., il n'a pas la moindre importance. 'quantity-surveying, s. Toisé m; métrage m. 'quantity-surveyor, s. Métreur (vérificateur).

quantum, pl. -a ['kwɔntəm, -ə], s. Quantum m. Ph: The q. theory, la théorie des quanta. Mil: The q. of forces, les effectifs mpl.

quarantine¹ ['kwɔrəntiːn], s. Esp. Nau: Quarantaine f. To be in q., faire (la) quarantaine. To go into q., se mettre en quarantaine. To be out of q., avoir libre pratique. The q. flag, le pavillon de quarantaine; le pavillon Q.

quarantine², v.tr. Mettre (qn, un navire) en quarantaine.

quarrel¹ ['kwɔrəl], s. A: Arms: Carreau m (d'arbalète).

quarrel², s. (a) Querelle f, dispute f, brouille f. To pick a q. with s.o., faire (une) querelle à qn. To try to pick a q. with s.o., chercher querelle à qn. (b) I have no q. with, against, him, je n'ai rien à lui reprocher. I have no q. with his behaviour, je n'ai rien à redire à sa conduite. (c) To take up s.o.'s q., épouser, embrasser, la querelle, la cause, de qn. To fight s.o.'s quarrels for him, prendre fait et cause pour qn.

quarrel³, v.i. (quarrelled) 1. Se quereller, se disputer (with s.o. over, about, sth., avec qn à propos de qch.); se brouiller (avec qn). 2. To q. with s.o. for doing sth., reprocher à qn de faire qch. To q. with sth., trouver à redire à qch. **quarrelling¹**, a. Querelleur, -euse. **quarrelling²**, s. Querelle(s) f(pl), dispute(s) f(pl).

quarreller ['kwɔrələr], s. Querelleur, -euse.

quarrelsome ['kwɔrəlsəm], a. Querelleur, batailleur, Q. fellow, F: mauvais coucheur. **-ly**, adv. D'une manière querelleuse; d'un ton hargneux.

quarrelsomeness ['kwɔrəlsəmnis], s. Humeur querelleuse.

quarry¹ ['kwɔri], s. Ven: 1. Proie f; gibier (poursuivi à courre). 2. A: Curée f.

quarry², s. 1. Carrière f (de pierres, etc.). 2. Carreau m (de céramique, A: de verre). **'quarry-stone**, s. Moellon m.

quarry³, v.tr. (quarried) 1. Extraire, tirer, (la pierre) de la carrière. Abs. Exploiter une carrière. 2. Creuser une carrière dans (une colline). **quarrying**, s. Exploitation f de carrières. Q. of stone, extraction f, tirage m, de la pierre.

quarryman, pl. -men ['kwɔrimən], s.m. (Ouvrier) carrier.

quart [kwɔːt], s. Meas: Un quart de gallon; approx. = litre m. (= 1 litre 136; U.S.: = 0 litre 946.)

quart(e) [kɑːt], s. Fenc: Quarte f. To parry in q., parer en quarte.

quartan ['kwɔːt(ə)n], a. Med: A: Q. fever, q. ague, fièvre quarte.

quarter¹ ['kwɔːtər], s. 1. (a) Quart m. To divide sth. in(to) quarters, diviser qch. en quatre. Bottle one q. full, bouteille au quart pleine. It is (only) a q. as long, c'est quatre fois moins long. (b) (i) Cu: Quartier m (de bœuf, d'agneau). Fore-q., hind-q., quartier de devant, de derrière. (ii) pl. (Hind-)quarters, arrière-train m, train m de derrière (d'une bête); arrière-main m or f (du cheval). (c) Her: Quartier, partition f (de l'écu). (d) Nau: Hanche f. On the q., par la hanche. To fire on the q., tirer en retraite. (e) F: O: tranche f (d'orange, etc.). (f) To cut timber on the q., débiter un tronc d'arbre sur quartier, sur maille. 2.

(a) Nau: Quart de brasse. (b) Trimestre m; terme m (de loyer). A quarter's rent, un terme, un trimestre (de loyer). (c) Moon at the first q., lune au premier quartier. Moon in its last q., lune sur son décroît. (d) A q. to six, six heures moins le quart. A q. past six, six heures et quart. (e) Num: U.S: Pièce f de 25 cents. 3. (a) Nau: (i) Quart d'aire de vent (= 2° 48' 45"); (ii) aire f de vent. What q. is the wind in? de quel côté souffle le vent? The wind is in the right q., le vent vient du bon côté. (b) The four quarters of the globe, les quatre parties du globe. They arrived from all quarters, ils arrivaient de tous côtés, de toutes parts. I expect no more trouble from that q., je n'attends plus aucune difficulté de ce côté-là. In high quarters, en haut lieu. In responsible quarters, dans les milieux autorisés. (News) from all quarters, (nouvelles) de partout. 4. Quartier (d'une ville). 5. pl. (a) Living quarters, appartements m (domestiques). F: To shift one's quarters, changer de résidence f. (b) Mil: Quartier, cantonnement m, logement m. To take up one's quarters, (of troops) prendre ses quartiers; F: (of pers.) se loger, s'installer. To return to quarters, rentrer au quartier. Navy: Sailors' quarters, poste m d'équipage. 6. pl. Navy: Postes de combat. To beat, pipe, to quarters, battre, sonner, le branle-bas. All hands to quarters! tout le monde à son poste! 7. To give q., faire quartier. To ask for q., to cry q., demander quartier; crier merci. **'quarter-binding**, s. Demi-reliure f. **'quarter-cask**, s. Quartaut m; feuillette f. **'quarter-day**, s. Le jour du terme; F: le terme. **'quarter-deck**, s. 1. Nau: Gaillard m (d')arrière. Navy: Plage f arrière. 2. Coll. Navy: The q.-deck, les officiers m. **'quarter-final**, s. Sp: Quart de finale. **'quarter-'hourly**. 1. adv. Tous les quarts d'heure; de quart d'heure en quart d'heure. 2. a. De tous les quarts d'heure. **'quarter-note**, s. Mus: U.S: Noire f. **'quarter-plate**, s. Phot: Plaque f et format m 8.2 × 10.8 (cm.). **'quarter-section**, s. (In U.S., Canada) Quart d'un mille carré. **'quarter-'sessions**, s.pl. Jur: Assises trimestrielles. **'quarter-wind**, s. Nau: Vent grand largue.

quarter², v.tr. 1. (a) Diviser (une pomme) en quatre; diviser (un bœuf) par quartiers; équarrir (un bœuf). Quartered logs (of firewood), bois m de quartier. (b) A: Écarteler (un condamné). (c) Her: Écarteler (l'écu). 2. Mil: Cantonner, caserner, encaserner (des troupes). To q. the troops on the inhabitants, loger les troupes chez l'habitant. To be quartered with s.o., loger chez qn. **quartering**, s. 1. (a) Division en quatre; équarrissage m (d'un tronc d'arbre). (b) A: Écartèlement m (d'un malfaiteur). 2. (a) Mil: Logement m, cantonnement m, stationnement m (de troupes). (b) Navy: Désignation f des postes (de combat, etc.). 3. Her: Écartelure f. 4. Ven: (Of dogs) Quête f.

quarterly ['kwɔːtəli]. 1. a. Trimestriel. 2. s. Publication trimestrielle. 3. adv. Trimestriellement; par trimestre; tous les trois mois.

quartermaster ['kwɔːtəmɑːstər], s. 1. Nau: Maître m de timonerie. 2. Mil: Q. General, F: Q.M.G., intendant général d'armée. U.S. Mil: Q. Corps, Service m de l'Intendance. Q. sergeant, (artillery, cavalry) = maréchal m des logis chef; (infantry) = sergent, chef fourrier m.; (Women's Services, W.R.A.C.); troisième catégorie.

quartern ['kwɔːtən], s. Meas: Quart m (de pinte, de stone). Q. loaf, pain m de quatre livres.

quarterstaff ['kwɔːtəstɑːf], s. Sp: 1. Bâton m (à deux bouts). To fence with quarterstaffs, jouer du bâton. 2. Escrime f au bâton.

quartet(te) [kwɔː'tet], s. Mus: Quatuor m.

quarto ['kwɔːtou], s. In-quarto (m) inv.

quartz [kwɔːts], s. Miner: Quartz m; cristal m de roche.

quartzite ['kwɔːtsait], s. Geol: Quartzite f.

quasar ['kwazər], s. Astr: Quasar m.

quash [kwɔʃ], v.tr. 1. Casser, infirmer, annuler (un jugement); invalider (une élection). To q. an action, arrêter les poursuites. 2. Étouffer (un sentiment, une révolte).

quasi ['kwɑːzi], pref. Quasi, presque. Q.-contract quasi-contrat m. Q.-public, quasi-public.

quassia ['kwɔʃə], s. **1.** Q.(-tree), quassier *m*, quassia *m*. **2.** *Pharm:* Quassia.

quatercentenary ['kwætəsen'tiːnəri], s. Quatrième centenaire *m*.

quaternary [kwə'təːnəri], a. Quaternaire.

quatrain ['kwɔtrein], s. *Pros:* Quatrain *m*.

quatrefoil ['kætrəfɔil], s. *Arch: Her:* Quatre-feuilles *m. inv.*

quaver[1] ['kweivər], s. **1.** *Mus:* Croche *f*. **2.** (*a*) *Mus:* Trille *m*, tremolo *m*. (*b*) Tremblement *m*, chevrotement *m* (de la voix). 'quaver-rest, s. *Mus:* Demi-soupir *m*.

quaver[2], v.i. (*a*) (*Of singer*) Faire des trilles. (*b*) (*Of voice*) Chevroter, trembloter. **quavering**, *a.* Q. voice, voix tremblotante, chevrotante. **-ly,** *adv.* D'une voix mal assurée.

quay [kiː], s. Quai *m*; appontement *m*. **Alongside the q.,** à quai.

quayage ['kiːidʒ], s. **1.** Quayage *m*; droit(s) *m(pl)* de quai, de bassin. **2.** Quais *mpl*.

quean [kwiːn], s.f. **1.** *A:* Coquine, gueuse. **2.** *Scot:* Jeune fille; beau brin de fille.

queasiness ['kwiːzinis], s. **1.** Malaise *m*; nausées *fpl*. **2.** Scrupules *mpl* de conscience.

queasy ['kwiːzi], a. (*a*) Sujet à des nausées. **To feel q.,** *F:* avoir le cœur barbouillé. **Q. stomach,** estomac délicat. (*b*) **Q. conscience,** conscience scrupuleuse à l'excès.

Quebec [kwi'bek]. *Pr.n. Geog:* Québec *m*.

queen[1] [kwiːn], s.f. **1.** Reine. **Q. Anne,** la reine Anne. **Q. Anne is dead,** c'est vieux comme le Pont-Neuf. **She was q. to Henry VIII,** elle fut l'épouse de Henri VIII. **Beauty q.,** reine de beauté. **2.** (*a*) *Cards:* Dame *f*. (*b*) *Chess:* Dame, reine. (*Of pawn*) **To go to q.,** aller à dame. **3.** *Ent:* Reine (des abeilles, des fourmis). **4.** Chatte *f*. **5.** *V:* **An old queen,** une vieille pédale. **queen-'bee,** s. Abeille *f* mère; reine *f. F:* Présidente active; maîtresse femme. **'queen-'mother,** s.f. Reine-mère. **'queen-post,** s. *Const:* Faux poinçon. **Q.-p. truss,** arbalète *f* à deux poinçons.

queen[2]. **1.** *v.tr. Chess:* Damer (un pion). **2.** *v.i.* (*a*) *F:* **To q. it,** faire la reine. (*b*) *Chess:* (*Of pawn*) Aller à dame.

queenhood ['kwiːnhud], s. Dignité *f* de reine; souveraineté *f*.

queenlike ['kwiːnlaik], **queenly** ['kwiːnli], a. De reine; digne d'une reine.

queenliness ['kwiːnlinis], s. Majesté *f*.

queer[1] ['kwiər], a. **1.** (*a*) Bizarre, étrange, singulier. **A q.-looking chap,** une drôle de tête. *F:* **To be in Q. Street,** être dans une situation (financière) embarrassée. (*b*) Suspect. *P:* **On the q.,** par des moyens peu honnêtes; par des moyens louches. (*c*) *s. P:* **A queer,** un homosexuel, un anormal; *P:* une tapette. **2.** *F:* **I feel very q.,** je me sens tout chose, tout patraque. **-ly,** *adv.* Étrangement, bizarrement.

queer[2], v.tr. *F:* Déranger, détraquer. **To q. s.o.'s pitch,** bouleverser, faire échouer, les plans de qn; contrecarrer qn.

queerish ['kwiəriʃ], a. **1.** Un peu bizarre; assez drôle. **2.** *F:* **To feel q.,** se sentir plutôt patraque.

queerness ['kwiənis], s. Étrangeté *f*, bizarrerie *f*.

quell [kwel], v.tr. Calmer, apaiser (une émotion); dompter, étouffer (une passion); réprimer, étouffer (une révolte).

quench [kwenʃ], v.tr. **1.** *Lit:* Éteindre (un feu). **2.** *Metalw:* Éteindre, tremper, refroidir (le métal). **Quenched in oil,** refroidi à l'huile. **3.** (*a*) Réprimer, étouffer (un désir). (*b*) **To q. one's thirst,** apaiser, étancher, sa soif; se désaltérer. (*c*) *El:* (i) Étouffer (une étincelle). (ii) Amortir (des oscillations).

quencher ['kwenʃər], s. *F:* Boisson *f*, consommation *f*. **Let's have a q.,** *P:* on va se rincer la dalle.

quenchless ['kwenʃlis], a. Inextinguible.

quenelle [kə'nel], s. *Cu:* Quenelle *f*.

quern ['kwəːn], s. Moulin *m* à bras.

querulous ['kwer(j)uləs], a. Plaintif et maussade; chagrin, grognon. **Q. tone,** ton plaintif, dolent. **-ly,** *adv.* D'un ton plaintif.

querulousness ['kwer(j)uləsnis], s. Disposition *f* à, habitude *f* de, se plaindre; humeur chagrine; ton plaintif.

query[1] ['kwiəri], s. **1.** (*a*) Question *f*, interrogation *f*. (*b*) **Q . . .,** reste à savoir si . . . (*In margin of document, etc.*) **Q.: is this accurate?** S'assurer de l'exactitude de ce fait. **2.** *Typ:* Point *m* d'interrogation.

query[2], v.tr. **1.** To q. if, whether . . ., s'informer si. . . . **2.** (*a*) *Typ:* Marquer (qch.) d'un point d'interrogation. (*b*) Mettre (une affirmation) en question, en doute.

quest [kwest], s. (*a*) *Ven:* Quête *f* (par les chiens). (*b*) Recherche *f*. **To go in q. of s.o.,** se mettre à la recherche, en quête, de qn.

question[1] ['kwest(ə)n], s. Question *f*. **1.** *A:* (*Torture*) **To put s.o. to the q.,** mettre qn à la question; appliquer la question à qn. **2.** Mise *f* en doute. **Without q.,** sans aucun doute; sans contredit; sans conteste. **To obey without q.,** obéir aveuglément. **Beyond (all) q.,** past q., hors de doute; incontestable. **To call, bring, sth. in q.,** mettre qch. en question, en doute; révoquer qch. en doute. **There is no q. about it,** il n'y a pas de doute là-dessus. **3.** (*a*) **The matter in q.,** l'affaire en question; l'affaire dont il s'agit. **There was some q. of . .,** il a été question de. . . . **There is no q. of his returning so soon,** il n'est pas question qu'il revienne si promptement. (*b*) **That is not the q.,** il ne s'agit pas de cela. **The q. is whether . . .,** il s'agit de savoir si. . . . **It is out of the q.,** c'est impossible; il ne faut pas y songer. **It is not out of the q. that . . .,** il n'est pas exclu que. . . . (*At meeting*) **To move the previous q.,** demander la question préalable. **To put the q.,** mettre la question aux voix. (*c*) **A vexed q.,** une question souvent débattue. **Success is merely a q. of time,** le succès n'est qu'une question de temps. **4. To ask s.o. a q.,** to put a q. to s.o., poser, adresser, une question à qn. **Questions and answers,** demandes *f* et réponses. **'question-mark,** s. Point *m* d'interrogation. **'question-master,** s. *W.Tel: T.V:* Meneur de jeu *m*, de débats *m*.

question[2], v.tr. **1.** Questionner, interroger (qn). **To q. s.o. closely,** soumettre qn à un interrogatoire serré. **To be questioned,** subir un interrogatoire. **2.** Mettre (qch.) en question, en doute; révoquer (qch.) en doute. **I q. whether he will come,** je doute qu'il vienne. **It is not to be questioned that . . .,** il n'y a pas de doute que + *ind.* **questioning**[1], a. (*Regard,* etc.) interrogateur. **-ly,** *adv.* **To look questioningly at s.o.,** interroger qn du regard. **questioning**[2], s. Questions *fpl*, interrogation *f*; interrogatoire *m* (de prisonniers).

questionable ['kwestʃənəbl], a. **1.** Contestable, discutable; problématique. **2.** *Pej:* (*Of conduct,* etc.) Équivoque. **In q. taste,** d'un goût douteux. **questionably,** *adv.* **1.** D'une manière incertaine, contestable. **2.** *Pej:* D'une manière équivoque.

questionableness ['kwestʃənəblnis], s. **1.** Caractère douteux (of, de); contestabilité *f*. **2.** Caractère équivoque (of, de).

questioner ['kwestʃənər], s. Interrogateur, -trice.

questionless ['kwestʃənlis], a. Hors de doute, incontestable.

questionnaire [ˌkestjə'neər, ˌkwestʃə'neər], s. Questionnaire *m*.

quetzal ['ketsəl], s. **1.** *Orn:* Quetzal *m*, pl. quetzals. **2.** *Num:* Quetzal (de Guatemala).

queue[1] [kjuː], s. **1.** Queue *f* (de cheveux). **2.** Queue (de personnes, de voitures). **To form a q.,** to stand in a q., faire (la) queue.

queue[2], v.i. **To q. (up),** faire (la) queue; (*of cars*) prendre la queue.

quibble[1] ['kwibl], s. **1.** *A:* Calembour *m*; jeu *m* de mots. **2.** Argutie *f*; chicane *f* de mots; faux-fuyant *m*.

quibble[2], v.i. **1.** Chicaner sur les mots; user d'équivoque. **2.** (*Split hairs*) Chicaner, vétiller. **quibbling,** s. Arguties *fpl*, évasions *fpl*; chicane *f* de mots.

quibbler ['kwiblər], s. Ergoteur, -euse; chicaneur, -euse.

quick [kwik]. **1.** a. (*a*) Rapide. **Q. pulse,** pouls fréquent. **The quickest way there,** le chemin le plus court pour y arriver. **Q. sale,** prompt débit; vente facile. **To have a q. lunch,** déjeuner sur le pouce. **As q. as lightning,** comme un éclair; en un clin d'œil. **Be q. (about it)!** faites vite! dépêchez-vous! **Try to be a little quicker,** tâchez d'y aller un peu plus vite. (*b*) **A q. child,** un enfant vif, éveillé, qui a l'esprit prompt. **Q. wit,** esprit prompt à la repartie. **Q. ear,** oreille fine. **She has a q. temper,** elle s'emporte facilement; _F:_ elle a la tête près du bonnet. **Q. to act,** prompt à agir. **Q. to answer back,** prompt, vif, à répliquer. (c) _Mus:_ Animé. (d) _A:_ Vif, vivant. **Q. hedge,** haie vive. _s._ **The q. and the dead,** les vivants et les morts. **2.** _s._ Vif _m_; chair vive. **To bite one's nails to the q.,** ronger ses ongles jusqu'au vif. **To sting, cut, s.o. to the q.,** piquer, blesser, qn au vif. **3.** _adv._ Vite, rapidement. **To run quicker,** courir plus vite. **-ly,** _adv._ Vite, rapidement, vivement. 'quick-'acting, _a._ (Mécanisme) à action rapide, immédiate. _Med: etc:_ (Drogue, médicament) à réaction rapide. 'quick-'change, _attrib.a._ _Th:_ **Q.-c. artist,** acteur à transformations rapides. **Q.-c. part,** rôle à travestissements. 'quick-'firing, _a._ (Canon) à tir rapide. 'quick-'freeze, _v.tr._ Surgeler. 'quick-'freezing, _s._ Surgélation _f_, surcongélation, quick-freezing _m._ 'quick-'growing, _a._ _Bot: etc:_ A croissance rapide. 'quick-'setting, _a._ (Mortier _m_, etc.) à prise rapide. 'quick-'sighted, _a._ **1.** Aux yeux vifs, perçants. **2.** Perspicace; à l'esprit pénétrant. 'quick-tempered, _a._ Emporté, irascible; prompt à la colère. 'quick-'witted, _a._ A l'esprit prompt, d'esprit vif; vif, éveillé.

quicken ['kwik(ə)n]. **1.** _v.tr._ (a) _Lit:_ Donner la vie à, (r)animer, vivifier. (b) Exciter, stimuler, aiguiser (le désir, l'appétit); animer (la conversation). (c) _Med:_ Accélérer (le pouls). _Mus:_ **To q. the tempo,** presser la mesure. **2.** _v.i._ (a) _(Of nature, hope)_ S'animer, se ranimer; _(of offspring in womb)_ donner des signes de vie, bouger; _(of pregnant woman)_ sentir bouger. (b) _(Of pace, etc.)_ Devenir plus rapide; s'accélérer. **quickening¹,** _a._ **1.** Animateur, -trice. **2.** (a) Qui s'anime, qui se ranime. (b) (Pas) qui s'accélère. **quickening²,** _s._ **1.** Retour à la vie (de la nature, etc.). _Obst:_ Premiers mouvements du fœtus. **2.** Accélération _f_ (du pas, du pouls).

quickie [kwiki], _s._ **1.** _Cin: F:_ Court métrage _m_ (de qualité inférieure). **2.** _F:_ Consommation prise sur le pouce. **Have a q.?** Tu prendras vite qch.? **3.** _U.S: F:_ Qch. fait, fabriqué, à la hâte. **4.** _U.S: F:_ Grève soudaine et irrationnelle.

quicklime ['kwiklaim], _s._ Chaux vive.

quickness ['kwiknis], _s._ **1.** Vitesse _f_, rapidité _f_. **2.** Acuité _f_ (de vision); finesse _f_ (d'oreille); promptitude _f_, vivacité _f_ (d'esprit).

quicksand ['kwiksænd], _s._ Sable(s) mouvant(s) (du bord de la mer); lise _f_. **To get caught in a q.,** s'enliser.

quickset ['kwikset]. **1.** _s._ Bouture _f_ (d'aubépine, etc.). **2.** _a. & s._ **Q.** (hedge), haie vive.

quicksilver¹ ['kwiksilvər], _s._ Vif-argent _m_, mercure _m._ **To have q. in one's veins,** avoir du vif-argent dans les veines.

quicksilver², _v.tr._ Étamer (une glace). **quicksilvering,** _s._ **1.** Étamage _m_ (d'une glace). **2.** Tain.

quickstep ['kwikstep], _s._ _Mil:_ Pas accéléré; pas redoublé.

quid¹ [kwid], _s._ _inv._ _P:_ Livre _f_ (sterling). **Five quid,** cinq livres.

quid², _s._ Chique _f_ (de tabac).

quid pro quo ['kwidprou'kwou], _s._ (a) Équivalent _m_, compensation _f_. (b) **To return a q. p. q.,** rendre la pareille à qn.

quiescence [kwai'es(ə)ns], _s._ Repos _m_, quiétude _f_, tranquillité _f._

quiescent [kwai'es(ə)nt], _a._ En repos; tranquille.

quiet¹ ['kwaiət], _s._ Tranquillité _f_, repos _m_, quiétude _f_, calme, _m._

quiet², _a._ **1.** Tranquille, calme, silencieux. **Q. running of a machine,** marche silencieuse d'une machine. **To keep q.,** se tenir, rester, tranquille; se tenir coi. **Be q.!** taisez-vous! laissez-moi tranquille! **2.** **Q. disposition,** caractère doux, calme. **Q. horse,** cheval doux, sage. **3.** (a) _(Of dress, colours)_ Simple; discret, -ète; sobre. **Q. dinner,** dîner intime. **Q. wedding,** mariage célébré dans l'intimité. **To live in a q. way,** avoir un train modeste. (b) **Q. irony,** ironie voilée. **To have a q. dig at s.o.,** faire une allusion discrète à qn. _s._ _F:_ **To do sth. on the q.,** faire qch. en cachette, à la dérobée. **I am telling you that on the q.,** _F:_ je vous dis ça entre nous deux, et pas plus loin. **4.** (a)

Calme, tranquille, paisible. **To lead a q. life,** mener une vie calme. **He has had a q. sleep,** il a dormi tranquillement. _F:_ **Anything for a q. life!** Tout ce que tu voudras, mais laisse-moi la paix! _St.Exch:_ **Oil shares are q.,** les pétroles sont calmes. (b) **Q. conscience,** avoir la conscience tranquille. **You may be q. on that score,** quant à cela vous pouvez être tranquille. **-ly,** _adv._ **1.** (a) Tranquillement, doucement. (b) Silencieusement, sans bruit; sans tambour ni trompette. **2. Q. and neatly dressed,** vêtu avec une simplicité de bon goût. **To get married q.,** se marier dans l'intimité, sans éclat.

quiet³, _v._ (**quieted**) **1.** _v.tr._ (a) Apaiser, calmer; tranquilliser (qn, sa conscience); faire taire (un enfant). (b) Apaiser, calmer (un tumulte); dissiper (les craintes). **quieting¹,** _a._ Apaisant, calmant, tranquillisant. **quieting²,** _s._ Apaisement _m_; dissipation _f_ (des soupçons). **2.** _v.i._ **To q. down,** s'apaiser, se calmer.

quieten ['kwaiət(ə)n], _v.tr. & i._ = QUIET³. **quietening,** _a. & s._ = QUIETING _a. & s._

quietism ['kwaiətizm], _s._ _Rel.Hist:_ Quiétisme _m._

quietist ['kwaiətist], _s._ _Rel.Hist:_ Quiétiste _m._

quietness ['kwaiətnis], _s._ **1.** Tranquillité _f_, repos _m_, calme _m._ **2.** Sobriété _f_ (de tenue, etc.).

quietude ['kwaiətju:d], _s._ Quiétude _f._

quietus [kwai'i:təs], _s._ Coup _m_ de grâce.

quiff [kwif], _s._ **Q.** (of hair), toupet _m._

quill [kwil], _s._ **1.** (a) _Orn:_ Tuyau _m_ (de plume). (b) = QUILL-FEATHER. (c) = QUILL-PEN. **2.** Piquant _m_ (de porc-épic, etc.). 'quill-bark, _s._ _Com:_ Quinquina _m_ en tuyaux. 'quill-feather, _s._ _Orn:_ Penne _f._ 'quill-'pen, _s._ Plume _f_ d'oie (pour écrire).

quilt¹ [kwilt], _s._ Couverture piquée, ouatée; édredon piqué; couvre-pied(s) _m._

quilt², _v.tr._ Piquer, contre-pointer, capitonner, ouater (un vêtement). **quilting,** _s._ **1.** Piquage _m_, capitonnage _m._ **2.** Piqué _m_, ouatine _f._

quinary ['kwainəri], _a._ _Mth:_ Quinaire.

quince [kwins], _s._ **1.** Coing _m._ **Q. cheese,** pâte _f_ de coings. **2.** **Q.(-tree),** cognassier _m._

quincentenary ['kwinsen'ti:nəri]. **1.** _a._ De cinq siècles, cinq fois centenaire. **2.** _s._ Cinquième centenaire.

quincunx ['kwinkʌŋks], _s._ _Arb:_ Quinconce _m._

quinine [kwi'ni:n], _s._ Quinine _f._

quinquagenarian ['kwiŋkwadʒi'neəriən], _a. & s._ Quinquagénaire (mf).

Quinquagesima ['kwiŋkwə'dʒesimə], _s._ _Ecc:_ **Q. (Sunday),** (le dimanche de) la Quinquagésime.

quinquenniad [kwiŋ'kweniæd], _s._ Quinquennat _m._

quinquennial [kwiŋ'kweniəl], _a._ Quinquennal, -aux.

quinquennium [kwiŋ'kweniəm], _s._ Quinquennium _m._

quinquina [kiŋ'ki:nə, kwiŋ'kwainə], _s._ _Bot: Pharm:_ Quinquina _m._

quins [kwinz], _s._ _F:_ = QUINTUPLET, 2.

quinsy ['kwinzi], _s._ _Med:_ Angine (laryngée); amygdalite aiguë.

quintain ['kwintin], _s._ _A:_ Quintaine _f._ **To tilt at the q.,** courir la quintaine.

quintal ['kwint(ə)l], _s._ _Meas:_ **1.** Quintal, -aux _m_ (de 112 livres, _U.S:_ de 100 livres). **2.** Quintal (métrique) (de 100 kg.).

quintan ['kwintən], _a. & s._ _A. Med:_ (Fièvre _f_) quinte; quinte _f._

quinte [kɛ̃:t], _s._ _Fenc:_ Quinte _f._ **To parry in q.,** parer en quinte.

quintessence [kwin'tes(ə)ns], _s._ Quintessence _f_; _F:_ suc _m_, moelle _f_ (d'un livre).

quintessential [kwinti'senʃ(ə)l], _a._ Quintessenciel, quintessencié.

quintet(te) [kwin'tet], _s._ _Mus:_ Quintette _m._

quintillion [kwin'tiljən], _s._ **1.** Quintillion _m_ (10³⁰). **2.** _U.S:_ Trillion (10¹⁸).

quintuple¹ ['kwintjupl], _a. & s._ Quintuple (_m_).

quintuple², _v.tr. & i._ Quintupler.

quintuplet [kwin'tju:plit, 'kwintjuplit], _s._ **1.** Groupe _m_ de cinq. **2.** _pl._ **Quintuplets,** quintuplé(e)s.

quip [kwip], _s._ Sarcasme _m_, repartie _f_; raillerie _f_; mot piquant; _F:_ lardon _m._

quire ['kwaiər], _s._ **1.** **Q. of paper (24 sheets)** = main _f_ de papier (25 feuilles). **Quarter of a q.,** cahier _m._ **2.** _Typ:_ **In quires,** en feuilles.

quirk [kwə:k], s. **1.** = QUIP. **2.** Faux-fuyant m; équivoque f. **There's sure to be a q. in it,** on va encore être dupés. **3.** Bizarrerie f de caractère. **4.** (a) Trait m de plume; arabesque f, fioriture f. (b) Paraphe m. **5.** Arch: Gorge f.

Quisling ['kwizliŋ], s. F: Quisling m.

quit[1] [kwit], a. Quitte. **The others can go q.,** les autres peuvent se considérer comme quittes. **To be q. for a fine,** en être quitte pour une amende. **To be q. of s.o.,** être débarrassé de qn. **'quit-rent,** s. Redevance f (minime).

quit[2], v.tr. (quitted, Dial & U.S: quit) **1.** (a) Quitter (qn, un endroit). Abs. Vider les lieux; déménager. S.a. NOTICE[1] **1.** (b) F: **To q. one's job,** U.S: to q., quitter son emploi; démissionner. (c) U.S: **To q. doing sth.,** cesser de faire qch. **2.** A: & U.S: (Acquit) **Q. you like men,** comportez-vous vaillamment.

quitch(-grass) ['kwitʃ(gra:s)], s. Bot: = COUCH[3] (-GRASS).

quite [kwait], adv. **1.** Tout à fait; entièrement. **Q. new,** tout nouveau. **Q. recovered,** complètement rétabli. **It is q. five days ago,** il y a bien cinq jours de cela. **Q. as much,** tout autant. **Q. enough,** bien assez. **Q. right,** très bien; (of sum of money) parfaitement juste. **Q. so!** q.! parfaitement! d'accord! **I do not q. know what he will do,** je ne sais pas trop ce qu'il fera. **I q. understand,** j'ai bien compris; je me rends parfaitement compte. **2. It is q. interesting,** cela ne manque pas d'intérêt. **His story is q. a romance,** son histoire est tout un roman. **It was q. a surprise,** ce fut une véritable surprise. **I q. believe that . . .,** je veux bien croire que. . . . S.a. LOT **4.**

quits [kwits], pred.a. Quitte(s). **We'll cry q.! now we're q.!** nous voilà quittes! nous voilà quitte à quitte! **I am q. with you,** nous sommes quittes.

quittance ['kwit(ə)ns], s. Quittance f, décharge f, acquit m, reçu m.

quitter ['kwitər], s. U.S: F: Tire-au-flanc m inv; lâcheur, -euse.

quiver[1] ['kwivər], s. Carquois m.

quiver[2], s. Tremblement m; frisson m; (ii) frémissement m; (iii) palpitation f. **With a q. in his voice,** d'une voix frémissante. **Q. of the eyelid,** battement m de paupière.

quiver[3], v.i. Trembler; frémir, tressaillir, frissonner; (of voice, light) trembloter; (of flesh) palpiter. **Q. with fear,** frémir de crainte. **quivering**[1], a. Tremblant, frissonnant, frémissant, palpitant. **-ly,** adv. En tremblant, avec un frémissement. **quivering**[2], s. Tremblement m, frémissement m, frissonnement m. **Q. of the eyelids,** battement m de paupières.

qui vive ['ki:'vi:v], s. Used in the phr. **To be on the q.v.,** être sur le qui-vive.

Quixote (Don) ['dɒn'kwiksət]. Pr.n.m. Don Quichotte.

quixotic [kwik'sɔtik], a. (a) Exalté, visionnaire. (b) Par trop chevaleresque. **-ally,** adv. En Don Quichotte.

quixotism ['kwiksətizm], **quixotry** ['kwiksətri], s. (Don)quichottisme m.

quiz[1] [kwiz], s. **1.** Mystification f, farce f. **2.** (a) A: & U.S: Une drôle de figure; original m. (b) A: & U.S: Railleur, -euse.

quiz[2], v.tr. (quizzed) **1.** A: Railler, persifler (qn). **2.** A: Lorgner, reluquer (qn). **3.** Poser des colles (à qn).

quizzing[1], a. A: Railleur, -euse; persifleur, -euse.

quizzing[2], s. A: **1.** Raillerie f persiflage m. **2.** Lorgnerie f. **quizzing-glass,** s. A: **1.** Lorgnon m; face-à-main m, pl. faces-à-main. **2.** Monocle m.

quiz[3], s. **1.** Sch: F: Examen oral; colle f. **2.** esp. W.Tel: T.V: Devinette f.

quizzical ['kwizik(ə)l], a. **1.** Risible, cocasse. **2.** Railleur, -euse; plaisant.

quod [kwɔd], s. P: Prison f; P: boîte f, bloc m; taule f. **In q.,** au bloc; "à l'ombre."

quoin[1] [kɔin], s. **1.** Const: Pierre f d'angle; encoignure f. **2.** Mec.E: Coin m (pour caler). Artil: Coussin m; coin de mire. Typ: Coin, cale f. **'quoin-stone,** s. Const: Pierre f d'angle, d'arête.

quoin[2], v.tr. Caler, coincer. **To q. up,** soulever avec des cales.

quoit [kɔit], s. Games: Palet m. **To play (at) quoits,** jouer au palet.

quondam ['kwɔndæm], a. D'autrefois.

quorum ['kwɔːrəm], s. Quorum m; nombre voulu. **To form a q.,** constituer un quorum. **Not to have a q.,** ne pas être en nombre.

quota ['kwoutə], s. (a) Quote-part f, quotité f. **To contribute one's q.,** payer, apporter, sa quote-part. (b) Full q. of troops, immigrants, plein contingent de troupes, d'immigrants. (c) Electoral q., quotient électoral. (d) Cin: etc: **Q. system** (of distribution), contingentement m. **To fix quotas for an import,** contingenter une importation.

quotable ['kwoutəbl], a. **1.** Citable. **2.** St.Exch: Cotable.

quotation [kwo'teiʃ(ə)n], s. **1.** Citation (empruntée à un auteur). **2.** St.Exch: Cote f, cours m, prix m. **The latest quotations,** les derniers cours faits. **3.** Typ: Cadrat creux. **quo'tation-marks,** s.pl. Guillemets m.

quote[1] [kwout], s. F: **1.** = QUOTATION. **2.** pl. **Quotes** = QUOTATION-MARKS.

quote[2], v.tr. **1.** (a) Citer (un auteur, un passage). Abs. **To q. from an author,** tirer une citation d'un auteur. **To q. an instance of sth.,** fournir un exemple de qch. (b) Com: **In reply please q. this number,** prière de rappeler ce numéro. **2.** (a) Com: Établir, faire (un prix). **To q. s.o. a price for sth.,** fixer à qn un prix pour qch. (b) St.Exch: Coter (une valeur). **Shares quoted at 45/-,** actions qui se cotent à 45 shillings. **3.** Typ: Guillemeter (un passage). **Words quoted,** mots entre guillemets.

quoth [kwouθ], v.tr. def. A: 'No,' q. I, "non," dis-je.

quotidian [kwo'tidiən]. **1.** a. Quotidien, -enne, journalier. **2.** s. Med: (Fièvre) quotidienne.

quotient ['kwouʃ(ə)nt], s. Mth: Quotient m.

R, r [ɑːr], s. (La lettre) R, r f. **The three R's** (*Reading,* (*w*)*Riting and* (*a*)*Rithmetic*), l'enseignement *m* primaire. *Tp:* **R for Robert,** R comme Raoul.

rabbet¹ ['ræbit], s. *Carp:* Feuillure f, rainure f. **'rabbet-joint,** s. Assemblage *m* à feuillure.

rabbet², *v.tr.* (*a*) Faire une feuillure, une rainure, à (une planche). (*b*) Assembler (deux planches) à feuillure. **rabbeting,** s. Assemblage *m* à feuillure.

rabbi ['ræbai], s. *Jew.Rel:* Rabbin *m*; (*voc. case and title*) rabbi *m*. **Chief r.,** grand rabbin.

rabbinic(al) [ræ'binik(əl)], a. Rabbinique.

rabbinism ['ræbinizm], s. Rabbinisme *m*.

rabbinist ['ræbinist], s. Rabbiniste *m*.

rabbit¹ ['ræbit], s. 1. Lapin *m*. **Buck r.,** lapin mâle. **Doe r.,** lapine f. **Young r.,** lapereau *m*. **Albino r.,** lapin russe; lapin albinos. **Tame r.,** lapin domestique, lapin de clapier. **Wild r.,** lapin de garenne. **R. breeder,** éleveur *m* de lapins. **R. breeding,** élevage *m* de lapins. 2. *Cu:* (*a*) Stewed r., = civet *m* de lapin. (*b*) **Welsh r.,** fondue f au fromage sur canapé. 3. *F:* (*a*) Personne faible, malingre, sans caractère. (*b*) *Sp:* Mazette f; novice *mf*. **'rabbit-hole,** s. Terrier *m* de lapin. **'rabbit-hutch,** s. Clapier *m*; lapinière f. **'rabbit-punch,** s. *Box:* Coup *m* du lapin. **'rabbit-warren,** s. Garenne f; lapinière f.

rabbit², *v.i.* To go rabbiting, aller à la chasse au lapin.

rabbity ['ræbiti], a. 1. (Goût *m*, etc.) de lapin. 2. *F:* (*a*) (Personne) malingre; timide. (*b*) A profil de lapin. (*c*) *Sp:* (Jeu *m*, style *m*) de novice.

rabble ['ræbl], s. 1. Cohue f; foule f (en désordre). 2. **The r.,** la populace, la canaille. **'rabble-'rouser,** s. *Pol:* Agitateur, -trice, fomentateur, -trice. **'rabble-'rousing.** 1. *a.* Qui incite à la violence, au désordre. 2. *s.* Incitation f à la violence, au désordre.

Rabelaisian [ræbə'leiziən], a. Rabelaisien, -ienne.

rabid ['ræbid], a. 1. (*a*) Furieux, -euse, féroce. **To be a r. enemy of s.o.,** être acharné contre, après, qn. (*b*) (Démagogue, etc.) outrancier, à outrance. **He had become a r. free-trader,** il était devenu libre-échangiste enragé. 2. *Vet:* (*a*) (Chien) enragé. (*b*) **R. virus,** virus rabique.

rabidness ['ræbidnis], s. 1. Violence f (des passions, des opinions). 2. Rage f (d'un animal).

rabies ['reibiːz], s. *Med:* Rage f, hydrophobie f. **Dumb r.,** rage mue.

raccoon [rə'kuːn], s. *Z:* Raton laveur.

race¹ [reis], s. 1. (*In sea*) Raz *m*, ras *m*, de courant. 2. (*a*) *Hyd.E:* Canal *m*, bief *m*. (*b*) *Mch:* Fly-wheel r., puits *m*, fosse f (du volant). 3. *Mec.E:* (Ball-)r., (i) voie f, chemin *m*, de roulement; (ii) cage f à billes. 4. *Sp:* Course. **To run a r.,** disputer une course. **Long-distance r.,** course de (grand) fond; marathon *m*. **Foot r.,** course à pied. **Horse r.,** course de chevaux. **Point-to-point r.,** course au clocher; steeple-chase *m*, *F:* steeple *m*. **To go to the races,** aller aux courses. **Arms r.,** course aux armements. *B:* **Let us run with patience the r. that is set before us,** nous devons . . . courir avec patience l'épreuve qui nous est proposée. *S.a.* RAT(-)RACE. **'race-card,** s. *Turf:* Programme *m* des courses. **'race-meeting,** s. Réunion f de courses.

race². 1. *v.i.* (*a*) Lutter de vitesse, faire une course (with, avec). (*b*) **To r. along,** aller grand train; filer à toute vitesse. **To r. down the street,** dévaler la rue à toute vitesse. (*c*) (*Of engine*) S'emballer; (*of propeller*) s'affoler. (*d*) (*Of pulse*) Battre la fièvre. 2. *v.tr.* (*a*) Lutter de vitesse avec (qn). **I'll r. you home!** au premier arrivé de nous deux à la maison! *Abs.* **To r.,** monter en course. (*b*) Faire courir (un cheval); *abs.* faire courir. (*c*) *I.C.E:* **To r. the engine** (without a load), emballer le moteur (à vide). (*d*) *F: Pol:* **To r. a bill through the House,** faire voter une loi au grand galop. **race about,** *v.i.* Parcourir le pays, la ville, la maison, au grand galop. **racing,** s. 1. Courses *fpl.* **Road r.,** courses sur route. **Boat r.,** courses d'aviron. **Horse r.,** les courses (de chevaux). **R. stable,** écurie de courses. **R. yacht,** racer *m*, yacht *m* de course. **R. car,** voiture f de course. **R. bicycle,** vélo *m* de course. **R. track,** piste f. 2. Emballement *m* (d'un moteur); affolement *m* (d'une hélice).

race³, s. Race f. 1. **R. consciousness,** racisme *m*. **R. hatred,** haine raciale. **R. riot,** bagarre, émeute, raciale. **The human r.,** la race humaine. 2. (*a*) Descendance f. **Of noble r.,** de sang noble. (*Of horse, etc.*) **True to r.,** fortement racé. (*b*) Lignée f. **A long r. of seafaring men,** une longue lignée de marins.

race⁴, s. Racine f (de gingembre).

racecourse ['reiskɔːs], s. *Turf: etc:* Champ *m* de courses.

racegoer ['reisgouər], s. Turfiste *mf*.

racehorse ['reishɔːs], s. Cheval *m* de course; racer *m*.

raceme [rə'siːm], s. *Bot:* Racème *m*, grappe f.

racer ['reisər], s. 1. (*Pers.*) Coureur, -euse. 2. (*a*) Cheval *m*, -aux, de course, racer *m*. (*b*) Bicyclette f, *F:* vélo *m*, automobile f, voiture f, de course. (*c*) Yacht *m* de course, racer *m*.

racetrack ['reistræk], s. *Esp: U.S:* 1. = RACECOURSE. 2. Piste f (pour autos, vélos, motos, etc.).

rachidian [rə'kidiən], a. *Nat. Hist: Anat:* Rachidien, -ienne.

rachis, *pl.* -ides ['reikis, -idiːz], s. *Nat. Hist: Anat:* Rachis *m*.

rachitic [ræ'kitik], a. *Med:* Rachitique.

rachitis [ræ'kaitis], s. *Med:* Rachitisme *m*.

racial ['reiʃ(ə)l], a. De (la) race. **R. minorities,** les races en minorité. **-ally,** *adv.* Du point de vue de la race.

racialism ['reiʃəlizm], s. Racisme *m*.

racialist ['reiʃəlist], s. Raciste *mf*.

raciness ['reisinis], s. 1. (*Of wine, fruit*) Goût *m* de terroir; (*of wine*) bouquet *m*. 2. (*Of style*) Piquant *m*, verve f.

racism ['reisiz(ə)m], s. *Esp. U.S:* Racisme *m*.

racist ['reisist], s. *Esp. U.S:* Raciste *mf*.

rack¹ [ræk], s. *Lit:* (Cloud-)r., légers nuages chassés par le vent.

rack², s. *Only in the phr.* **To go to r. and ruin,** aller à la ruine; tomber en ruine.

rack³, s. 1. (*a*) *Husb:* Râtelier *m* (d'écurie). (*b*) *Arms* r., râtelier d'armes. **Tool-r.,** porte-outils *m inv*. **Music-r.,** classeur *m* à musique. **Hat-and-coat r.,** porte-manteau *m*, vestiaire *m*. *Av:* **Bomb r.,** lance-bombes *m inv*. *Rail:* **Luggage r.,** porte-bagages *m inv*; filet *m* (à bagages). *Aut:* **Roof r.,** galerie f. **Newspaper r.,** porte-journaux *m inv*, porte-revues *m inv*. (*c*) *Veh:* Ridelle f (de charrette). 2. *Mec.E:* **R. and pinion,** crémaillère f (et pignon). **'rack-'rail-way,** s. Chemin *m* de fer à crémaillère. **'rack-wheel,** s. Roue dentée.

rack⁴, s. *Hist:* Chevalet *m* (de torture). **To put, submit, s.o. to the r.,** mettre qn à la torture, à la question. **To be on the r.,** être à la torture au supplice; être sur des charbons ardents. **To keep s.o. on the r.,** faire mourir qn à petit feu.

rack⁵, *v.tr.* 1. (*a*) *Hist:* Faire subir le supplice du chevalet à (qn). (*b*) (*Of pain, etc.*) Tourmenter, torturer (qn); faire souffrir le martyre à (qn). **Racked by remorse,** tenaillé par le remords. *S.a.* BRAIN¹ 2. 2. (*a*) Extorquer (un loyer); pressurer (un locataire). (*b*) Épuiser (le sol). **racking¹,** a. 1. (*Of pain*) Atroce, déchirant. **R. headache,** mal de tête fou. 2. (Impôt) exorbitant. **'rack-rent,** s. Loyer exorbitant. **'rack-renter,** s. 1. Propriétaire *mf* qui extorque un loyer abusif. 2. Locataire *mf* qui paye un loyer exorbitant.

rack⁶, *v.tr.* **To r.** (off) wine, soutirer du vin.

racket¹ ['rækit], s. 1. (*a*) Raquette f (de tennis, etc.). (*b*) *pl. Games:* **Rackets,** la raquette. 2. Raquette (pour la marche sur la neige). **'racket-press,** s. *Sp:* Presse-raquette *m*, *pl.* presse-raquettes.

racket², s. *F:* 1. Tapage *m*, vacarme *m*, tintamarre *m*. **To kick up a r.,** faire du boucan. **To kick up no end of a r.,** faire un charivari de tous les diables. **To stand the r.,** (i) subir les conséquences; (ii) affronter la critique; (iii) subvenir aux dépenses. 2. Gaieté tapageuse; dissipation *f.* **To go on the r.,** (i) s'adonner au plaisir; (ii) faire la bombe; tirer une bordée. **3.** (*a*) Racket *m*; genre *m* d'affaires, spécialité *f* (d'un escroc). **It's a r.,** c'est une escroquerie, c'est du vol. (*b*) Entreprise *f* de gangsters; gang *m*, affaire véreuse. **Do you want to be in on this r.?** voulez-vous être de la bande, dans le coup? **The rum r.,** le gang de l'alcool. (*c*) Supercherie *f*.

racket², *v.i.* (racketed) *F:* **1. To r.** (about), faire du tapage, *P:* du boucan. **2.** Faire la vie, faire la noce, la bombe.

racketeer ['ræki'tiər], *s.* **1.** *O:* Noceur *m.* **2.** Gangster *m*; *F:* racketter *m*; combinard *m.*

rackety ['ræk iti], *a.* **1.** Tapageur, bruyant. **2.** Noceur, coureur; fêtard.

racoon [rə'ku:n], *s.* *Z:* Raton laveur.

racquet ['rækit], *s.* = RACKET¹.

racy ['reisi], *a.* **1. To be r.** of the soil, sentir le terroir. **2.** (*a*) R. anecdote, anecdote savoureuse, risquée, salée. (*b*) (*Of pers.*) Vif, *f.* vive, piquant. **R. style,** style plein de verve. **-ily,** *adv.* D'une façon piquante.

radar ['reida:r], *s.* Radar *m.* **R. operator,** radariste *mf.* **Navigation by r.,** radionavigation *f.* **R. station,** radar *m.* **Continuous wave r.,** radar à ondes entretenues. **Pulse r.,** radar à impulsions. **R. scanner,** antenne *f* (de) radar. **R. screen,** écran *m* (de radar).

raddle¹ ['rædl], *s.* Ocre *f* rouge.

raddle², *v.tr.* (*a*) Peindre, marquer, à l'ocre. (*b*) **Raddled face,** visage au maquillage grossier.

radial ['reidiəl], *a.* **1.** *Mec.E: etc:* Radial, -aux. *I.C.E:* **R. engine,** moteur en étoile. *Mec:* **R. force,** force centrifuge. *Aut:* **R.-ply tyre,** pneumatique à carcasse radiale. **2.** *Anat:* Radial, du radius.

radian ['reidiən], *s.* *Mth:* Radian *m.*

radiance ['reidjəns], *s.* **1.** Rayonnement *m*, splendeur *f.* **In the full r. of her beauty,** dans tout l'éclat de sa beauté. **2.** *Ph:* Rayonnement, radiation *f.*

radiant ['reidjənt]. **1.** *a.* (*a*) **R. heat,** *Ph:* chaleur rayonnante; *Med:* chaleur radiante. (*b*) (Soleil, etc.) radieux. **Face r. with smiles,** visage souriant et radieux. **2.** *s.* (*a*) *Ph:* Foyer *m* de rayonnement. (*b*) *Astr:* Radiant *m.* **-ly,** *adv.* D'un air radieux. **R. happy,** rayonnant de joie.

radiate¹ ['reidiət], *a.* *Nat.Hist:* Radié.

radiate² ['reidieit]. **1.** *v.i.* Rayonner; irradier. (*a*) Émettre des rayons. **Happiness radiates from her eyes,** ses yeux sont rayonnants de bonheur. (*b*) (*Of lines*) Partir d'un même centre. **2.** *v.tr.* Émettre, dégager (de la chaleur, etc.).

radiation ['reidi'eiʃ(ə)n], *s.* **1.** Irradiation *f*; rayonnement *m.* **2.** (*Of radium, etc.*) Radiation *f.* **Nuclear r.,** rayonnement nucléaire.

radiator ['reidieitər], *s.* **1.** (*a*) Radiateur *m* (pour chauffage); *Fr.C:* calorifère *m.* (*b*) *I.C.E:* Radiateur, refroidisseur *m.* **Fan-cooled r.,** radiateur soufflé. *Aut:* **R. cap,** bouchon *m* de radiateur. **R. muff,** couvre-radiateur *m.* **2.** *W.Tel:* Antenne *f* d'émission.

radical ['rædik(ə)l]. **1.** *a.* Radical, -aux. (*a*) **To make a r. alteration in sth.,** changer qch. radicalement. **R. diversity,** diversité radicale, foncière. (*b*) *Pol: Hist:* **The R. party,** le parti radical; les gauches *m.* **2.** *s. Ch: Ling: Mth:* Radical *m.* **-ally,** *adv.* Radicalement, foncièrement.

radicalism ['rædikəlizm], *s.* *Pol. Hist:* Radicalisme *m.*

radicle ['rædikl], *s.* *Bot:* (*a*) Radicule *f* (de l'embryon). (*b*) Radicelle *f*; petite racine.

radiesthesia [,rædies'θi:ziə], *s.* Radiesthésie *f.*

radio¹ ['reidiou], *s.* **1.** *W.Tel:* Télégraphie *f*, téléphonie *f* sans fil; *F:* la radio. **R. station,** poste émetteur de T.S.F. (set), poste (récepteur de réception), *F:* radio *f.* **R. news bulletin,** radio-journal *m.* **R. link,** faisceau hertzien. **R. car, taxi,** voiture-radio *f*, taxi-radio *m.* **2.** (*Radio-telegraphy*) Radio *m.* **3.** (i) Radiographie *f*, *F:* radio *f*; (ii) radiologie *f*, *F:* radio *f.* **4.** *Nau: Av: O:* **R. officer,** radionavigant *m.* '**radio-as'tronomy,** *s.* Radio-astronomie *f.* '**radio-'beacon,** *s.* *Av:* Radio-balise *f.* **R.-b. navigation,** radiobalisage *m.* '**radio-'compass,** *s.* *Av:* Radiocompas *m.* '**radio-control¹,** *s.* Téléguidage *m.* '**radio-control²,** *v.tr.* Téléguider. '**radio-di'rection,** *s.* *Av: Nau:* Radioguidage *m.* '**radio-'element,** *s.* *Ph:* Élément radio-actif.

radio², *v.tr.* **1.** Radiotélégraphier, radiotéléphoner (un message); envoyer (un message) par radio. **2.** *Med:* Radiographier (qn).

radioactive ['reidiou'æktiv], *a.* Radio-actif, -ive.

radioactivity ['reidiouæk'tiviti], *s.* Radio-activité *f.*

radiocommunication ['reidioukə,mju:ni'keiʃ(ə)n], *s.* Radiocommunication *f.*

radiodetection ['reidioudi'tekʃ(ə)n], *s.* Radiodétection *f.*

radioelectricity ['reidiouilek'trisiti], *s.* Radio-électricité *f.*

radiogoniometer ['reidiou,gouni'ɔmitər], *s.* Radio-goniomètre *m.*

radiogram ['reidiou'græm], *s.* **1.** *W.Tel:* Radiogramme *m.* **2.** = RADIOGRAPH¹. **3.** Combiné *m* (radio-phono).

radiogramophone ['reidiou'græməfoun], *s.* Combiné *m* (radio-phono).

radiograph¹ ['reidiogræf, -gra:f], *s.* *Med: etc:* Radio-gramme *m*, radiographie *f.*

radiograph², *v.tr.* *Med: etc:* Radiographier.

radiographer [,reidi'ɔgrəfər], *s.* Technicien, -ienne, assistant(-e) d'un radiologue.

radiographic ['reidio'græfik], *a.* Radiographique.

radiography [,reidi'ɔgrəfi], *s.* *Med:* Radiographie *f.* **Mass r.,** radiographie collective.

radioisotope ['reidiou'aisətoup], *s.* Radio-isotope *m.*

radiolocation ['reidioulo'keiʃ(ə)n], *s.* Radio-repérage *m.*

radiological ['reidio'lɔdʒik(ə)l], *a.* Radiologique.

radiologist [reidi'ɔlədʒist], *s.* *Med:* Radiologue *mf* radiologiste *mf.*

radiology [,reidi'ɔlədʒi], *s.* *Med:* Radiologie *f.*

radioscopic ['reidiou'skɔpik], *a.* Radioscopique.

radioscopy [,reidi'ɔskəpi], *s.* Radioscopie *f.*

radiosonde ['reidiou'sɔnd], *s.* Radiosonde *f.*

radiosondage ['reidiou'sɔndidʒ], *s.* Radiosondage *m.*

radiotelegram ['reidiou'teligræm], *s.* *W.Tel:* Radio-télégramme *m*; *F:* radio *m.*

radiotelegraphy ['reidiouta'legrəfi], *s.* Radiotélé-graphie *f*; *F:* radio *f.*

radiotelephony ['reidiouta'lefəni], *s.* Radiotéléphonie *f*, *F:* radio *f.*

radiotherapy ['reidiou'θerəpi], *s.* Radiothérapie *f.*

radish ['rædiʃ], *s.* Radis *m.* *S.a.* HORSE-RADISH.

radium ['reidiəm], *s.* Radium *m.* '**radium-'therapy,** *s.* Radiumthérapie *f.*

radius, *pl.* -**ii** ['reidiəs, -iai], *s.* **1.** (*a*) *Geom:* Rayon *m* (de cercle). (*b*) *Aut:* Steering r., rayon de braquage. **R. of action of an aircraft,** rayon d'action d'un avion. *Techn:* Cruising r., autonomie *f.* **Within a r. of three miles,** dans un rayon de trois milles. **2.** *Anat:* Radius *m* (de l'avant-bras).

radon ['reidən], *s.* *Ph: Med:* Radon *m*; émanation *f* du radium.

raffia ['ræfiə], *s.* *Bot:* Raphia *m.*

raffish ['ræfiʃ], *a.* *F:* (*a*) Bravache, esbrouffeur. (*b*) (Air, etc.) canaille. **-ly,** *adv.* D'un air canaille.

raffle¹ ['ræfl], *s.* Loterie *f* (à une vente de charité).

raffle², *v.tr.* Mettre (qch.) en loterie. **raffling,** *s.* Mise *f* en loterie (of qch.).

raft¹ [ra:ft], *s.* **1.** Radeau *m.* **2.** Timber r., *U.S:* lumber r., train *m* de bois, train de flottage. **3.** *Const:* Foundation r., radier *m.* '**raft-wood,** *s.* Bois flotté; bois de flottage.

raft². **1.** *v.tr.* Transporter (qch.) sur un radeau. **2.** *v.i.* **To r. down the river,** descendre le fleuve sur un radeau. **rafting,** *s.* Flottage *m* en train.

raft³, *s.* *U.S:* Grand nombre, tas *m* (de choses).

rafter ['ra:ftər], *s.* *Const:* Chevron *m* (d'un comble). **Main r.,** arbalétrier *m.*

raftsman, *pl.* -**men** ['ra:ftsmən], *s.m.* Flotteur (de bois).

rag¹ [ræg], *s.* **1.** Chiffon *m*; lambeau *m.* *F:* **To feel like a r.,** se sentir (mou) comme une chiffe. **2.** *pl.* **Rags (and tatters),** haillons *m*, guenilles *f*, loques *f.* **To be in rags,** être en guenilles, déguenillé. *F:* **To put on one's glad rags,** mettre ses plus beaux atours. *F:* **I haven't a r. to my back,** je n'ai rien à me mettre sur le dos. *P:* **To chew the r.,** tailler une bavette. **It's like a red r. to a bull,** c'est comme le rouge pour les taureaux. **3.** *Paperm:* R. pulp, pâte *f* de chiffons. *Tex:* **The r. trade,** l'industrie *f* de l'habillement. **4.**

Pej: (*a*) (*Newspaper*) Feuille *f* de chou. (*b*) Mouchoir *m*, drapeau *m*, etc.; loque *f*. 'rag-and-'bone, *attrib.a.* R.-and-b. man, chiffonnier *m*. 'rag-bag, *s.* Sac *m* aux chiffons. 'rag-merchant, *s.* Chiffonnier *m* en gros. 'rag-paper, *s.* Papier *m* de chiffons. 'rag-picker, *s.* Chiffonnier, -ière. 'rag(-)tag, *s.* F: The r.-t. (and bob-tail), la canaille. 'rag(-)time, *s.* A: Musique nègre syncopée.

rag², *s. Sch: F:* 1. Brimade *f*; mauvais tour; farce *f*. (Student) r., canular *m*. 2. Chahut *m*, bacchanal *m*.

rag³, *v.tr.* (ragged) [rægd] *F:* 1. Brimer (un camarade). 2. Chahuter (un professeur); chambarder les effets (d'un étudiant). *Abs.* To r., chahuter; faire du chahut.

ragamuffin ['rægəmʌfin], *s.* 1. (*a*) Gueux *m*; va-nu-pieds *m inv*; loqueteux *m*. (*b*) Mauvais garnement. 2. Gamin *m* des rues.

rage¹ [reidʒ], *s.* 1. Rage *f*, fureur *f*, emportement *m*. Fit of r., accès *m* de fureur. To fly into a r., se mettre en colère; s'emporter. A tearing r., une rage à tout casser. 2. Fureur, furie *f* (des vents). 3. Manie *f*, toquade *f*. To have a r. for sth., avoir la rage, la manie, de qch. (*Of thg*) To be all the r., faire fureur, faire rage; être du dernier cri.

rage², *v.i.* 1. To r. (and fume), être furieux; rager; être dans une colère bleue. To r. against, at, s.o., tempêter contre qn. 2. (*Of wind*) Faire rage; (*of epidemic*) sévir. 'raging¹, *a.* Furieux, -euse; en fureur. To be in a r. temper, être furieux. R. sea, mer déchaînée, démontée. R. fever, fièvre de cheval. R. thirst, soif ardente. R. headache, mal de tête fou. 'raging², *s.* 1. Rage *f*, fureur *f*. 2. Fureur, furie *f* (de la mer).

ragged ['rægid], *a.* 1. (*a*) En lambeaux, en loques. (*b*) (*Of pers.*) En haillons; déguenillé. 2. (*a*) (Nuage) déchiqueté; (rocher) ébréché. (*b*) *Mus:* The execution is r., l'exécution manque d'ensemble. *Mil:* R. fire, feu désordonné. (*c*) *Bot:* R. Robin, lychnide *f* des prés.

raggedness ['rægidnis], *s.* 1. Déguenillement *m* (de qn); délabrement *m* (d'un vêtement). 2. Inégalité *f* (d'un ouvrage); manque *m* d'ensemble (de l'exécution).

ragger ['rægər], *s.* 1. *F:* Chahuteur, -euse. 2. *P:* Chineur, -euse.

raglan ['ræglən], *s. & attrib.a. Tail:* R. (overcoat), raglan *m*. *Dressm:* R. sleeve, manche *f* raglan.

ragman, *pl.* -men ['rægmən], *s.m.* Marchand de chiffons; chiffonnier; *F:* biffin.

ragout ['rægu:], *s. Cu:* Ragoût *m*.

ragstone ['rægstoun], *s. Const:* Pierre bourrue; souchet *m* (de carrière).

ragwort ['rægwə:t], *s. Bot:* Jacobée *f*.

raid¹ [reid], *s.* (*a*) Razzia *f* (de bandits). (*b*) Police r., descente *f* de police; rafle *f*. (*c*) *Mil:* Raid *m*; coup *m* de main. Air r., bombardement aérien. *Av:* Intruder r., raid d'interception.

raid². 1. *v.i.* Faire une razzia; *Mil:* faire un raid. *Av:* Raiding aircraft, avion ennemi. 2. *v.tr.* (*a*) Razzier (une tribu); (*of police*) faire une descente, une rafle, dans (une boîte de nuit, un quartier). (*b*) To r. orchards, marauder les fruits dans les vergers.

raider ['reidər], *s.* 1. (*a*) Maraudeur *m*; pillard *m*. (*b*) Soldat *m* en razzia; aviateur *m* en raid. (*c*) *Nau: A:* Corsaire *m*. 2. (*a*) Avion *m* en raid. 'Raiders past' signal, signal *m* de fin d'alerte. (*b*) Navire *m* de course.

rail¹ [reil], *s.* 1. (*a*) Barre *f*, barreau *m* (de barrière); bâton *m* (de chaise). (*b*) Barre d'appui; garde-fou *m*, parapet *m* (de pont); balustrade *f* (de balcon); rampe *f* (d'escalier). (*c*) *Veh:* Ridelle *f* (de charrette). 2. *pl.* (*Iron*) Grille *f*; (*wood*) clôture *f*, palissade *f*, balustrade *f*. *Rac:* The rails, la corde. 3. *N.Arch:* (*a*) Lisse *f*. (*b*) *pl. F:* Bastingage *m* (d'un paquebot). 4. *Rail:* (*a*) Rail *m*. Live r., rail de contact. To leave the rails, dérailler. *F:* (*Of pers.*) To go off the rails, dérailler, être détraqué. (*b*) Chemin *m* de fer; voie ferrée. To travel by r., voyager en chemin de fer. *Com:* Price on r., prix sur le wagon. 'rail-car, *s. Rail:* Automotrice *f*; autorail *m*. 'rail-chair, *s. Rail:* Coussinet *m* de rail; chaise *f* de rail. 'rail-head, *s. Rail:* Tête *f* de ligne.

rail², *v.tr.* 1. To r. sth. in, fermer (un jardin) avec une grille, une palissade; griller, palissader (un enclos). To r. sth. round, entourer (une pelouse) d'une grille. Railed off from the road, séparé de la route par une grille. To r. off (a danger-spot), protéger (un endroit dangereux) avec un garde-fou, une barre d'appui. 2. Envoyer (des marchandises) par chemin. de fer. railed, *a.* R.(-in, -off) space, espace entouré d'une grille. 'railing(s), *s.(pl.)* 1. Clôture *f* à claire-voie; grille *f*, palissade *f*. 2. Garde-fou *m*, parapet *m* (de pont); balustrade *f* (de balcon); rampe *f* (d'escalier).

rail³, *s. Orn:* Râle *m*. Water-r., râle d'eau.

rail⁴, *v.i.* Se répandre en plaintes, en injures. To r. at, against, s.o., crier, invectiver, contre qn; s'en prendre à qn. To r. at fate, s'en prendre au sort. 'railing, *s.* Criailleries *fpl*; injures *fpl*, invectives *fpl*.

raillery ['reiləri], *s.* 1. Raillerie *f*.

railroad¹ ['reilroud], *s. U.S:* Chemin *m* de fer. R. pass, carte *f* de circulation.

railroad², *v.tr.* (*a*) *U.S:* Envoyer (des marchandises) par chemin de fer. (*b*) *F:* Faire voter en vitesse un projet de loi.

railroader ['reilroudər], *s. U.S:* Employé *m* des chemins de fer; cheminot *m*.

railway ['reilwei], *s.* 1. R. (line), (ligne *f* de) chemin *m* de fer; voie ferrée. The main r. lines, les grandes lignes ferroviaires. Light r., chemin de fer à voie étroite. *S.a.* SCENIC 2. R. system, réseau ferré. R. station, gare *f*. R. engine, locomotive *f*. R. engineer, ingénieur de la voie. R. cutting, (voie *f* en) déblai *m*; tranchée *f*. R. embankment, (voie en) remblai *m*. 2. *Ind:* Overhead r. (*for shop use*), pont roulant.

railwayman, *pl.* -men ['reilweimən], *s.m.* Employé des chemins de fer; cheminot.

raiment ['reimənt], *s. A. & Poet:* Habillement *m*; vêtement(s) *m(pl)*.

rain¹ [rein], *s.* Pluie *f*. 1. Pelting r., driving r., pluie battante. It looks like r., le temps est à la pluie, la pluie menace. A walk in the r., une promenade sous la pluie. Come in out of the r.! entrez donc, ne restez pas à la pluie! Golden r., (i) *Pyr:* pluie d'or; (ii) *Bot:* cytise *f*. *S.a.* RIGHT¹ I. 4. 2. *pl.* The rains, (*in tropics*) la saison des pluies. 'rain-band, *s. Ph: Meteor:* Bande *f* de la pluie (dans le spectre). 'rain-chart, *s.* Carte *f* pluviométrique. 'rain-cloud, *s.* Nimbus *m*. 'rain-gauge, *s.* Pluviomètre *m*. Recording r.-g., pluviographe *m*.

rain², *v.tr. & i.* 1. Pleuvoir. It rains, it is raining, il pleut; il tombe de la pluie. It is raining fast, il pleut à verse. It is raining cats and dogs, il pleut des hallebardes; il pleut à seaux. *Prov:* It never rains but it pours, un malheur, un bonheur, ne vient jamais seul. 2. Blows rained upon him, les coups pleuvaient sur lui. To r. blows on s.o., faire pleuvoir des coups sur qn.

rainbow ['reinbou], *s.* Arc-en-ciel *m*. R. trout, truite *f* arc-en-ciel.

raincoat ['reinkout], *s.* Imperméable *m*; *F:* imper *m*.

raindrop ['reindrop], *s.* Goutte *f* de pluie.

rainfall ['reinfɔ:l], *s. Meteor:* Précipitation *f* (atmosphérique). Area of heavy r., région pluvieuse.

rainproof¹ ['reinpru:f], *a.* Imperméable (à la pluie); hydrofuge.

rainproof², *v.tr.* Imperméabiliser (un tissu, etc.).

rainwater ['reinwɔ:tər], *s.* Eau *f* de pluie. R. butt, tonneau *m* pour l'eau de pluie.

rainwear ['reinwɛər], *s.* Vêtements *mpl* de pluie.

rainy ['reini], *a.* Pluvieux, -euse. R. season, saison des pluies; saison pluvieuse. The r. season has set in, les pluies ont commencé. We must put something by for a r. day, il faut garder une poire pour la soif.

raise¹ [reiz], *s.* (*a*) *U.S:* Augmentation *f* (de salaire, d'enjeu). (*b*) *Cards:* Relance *f*.

raise² ['reiz], *v.tr.* 1. (*a*) Dresser, mettre debout (une échelle, un mât); relever (qch. qui est tombé). To r. the standard of revolt, arborer l'étendard de la révolte. (*b*) To r. (up) s.o. from the dead, ressusciter qn d'entre les morts. (*c*) *Pyr:* R. game, lever du gibier. To r. the people, soulever, exciter, le peuple (against, contre). 2. Bâtir, élever (un palais); ériger (une statue). 3. Élever (une famille, du bétail); cultiver (des légumes); faire l'élevage (du bétail). 4. (*a*) Produire. To r. a bump, faire une bosse. To r. steam, produire de la vapeur; chauffer. **To r. a storm of laughter,** déchaîner une tempête de rires. *S.a.* WIND¹ 1. **To r. a smile,** provoquer un sourire. **To r. a hope,** faire naître une espérance. (*b*) **To r. a cry,** faire entendre, pousser, un cri. **No one raised his voice,** personne ne souffla mot. (*c*) **To r. an objection,** soulever une objection. 5. (*a*) Lever (le bras, les yeux); soulever (un poids). **To r. one's glass to one's lips,** porter son verre à ses lèvres. **To r. a ship,** relever, renflouer, un navire. *S.a.* DUST¹ 1, HAT. (*b*) Élever. **To r. s.o. to power,** élever qn au pouvoir. **To r. s.o.'s hopes,** exalter l'espoir de qn. **To r. s.o.'s spirits,** relever le courage de qn. 6. (*a*) Hausser, relever (un store). (*b*) **To r. camp,** lever le camp. **To r. one's voice,** élever, hausser, la voix. (*d*) **To r. the price of goods,** élever, (re)hausser, le prix des marchandises. **To r. production to a maximum,** porter la production au maximum. **To r. s.o.'s salary,** augmenter (les appointements de) qn. 7. (*a*) **To r. an army,** lever, mettre sur pied, une armée. (*b*) **To r. money,** se procurer de l'argent. **To r. funds by subscription,** réunir des fonds par souscription. **To r. money on an estate,** emprunter de l'argent sur une terre. (*c*) (*Of the State*) **To r. a loan,** émettre un emprunt. 8. **To r. a spirit,** évoquer un esprit. *S.a.* CAIN. 9. *Nau:* **To r. the land,** relever la terre. 10. **To r. a siege,** (i) lever, (ii) faire lever, un siège. **raise up,** *v.tr.* **To r. up enemies,** se faire des ennemis. **raised,** *a.* 1. (*a*) (*Of arm, etc.*) Levé; (*of head*) relevé. (*b*) R. deck, pont surélevé. 2. Saillant; en relief. **R. work,** ouvrage relevé en bosse. 3. **R. voice,** voix élevée. 4. *Cu:* R. **pie** = pâté en croûte.

raisin ['reizn], *s.* Raisin sec.

raj [rɑːdʒ], *s.* Souveraineté *f.* **Under the British r.,** sous l'empire anglais.

raja(h) ['rɑːdʒə], *s.m.* Raja(h).

rake¹ [reik], *s.* *Tls:* 1. Râteau *m.* F: **Thin as a r.,** sec comme une trique. 2. (Fire-)r. (*a*) Fourgon *m*, rouable *m* (de boulanger). (*b*) Crochet *m* à feu (de forgeron); râble *m*.

rake², *v.tr.* 1. Ratisser (les feuilles). **To r. the hay,** râteler le foin. 2. (*a*) Râteler (le sol); ratisser (une allée). **The police raked the district,** la police a ratissé tout le quartier. **To r. one's memory,** fouiller (dans) ses souvenirs. *Abs.* **To r. (about) among old documents,** fouiller, fureter, dans de vieux documents. (*b*) Gratter, racler (une surface). 3. **To r. a trench,** enfiler, prendre en enfilade, une tranchée. **To r. the enemy with machine-gun fire,** mitrailler l'ennemi. **rake in,** *v.tr.* (*a*) (*At casino*) Ratisser (les mises). (*b*) F: Amasser (de l'argent). (*c*) **To r. in** (manure), enfouir (du fumier) au râteau. **rake off,** *v.tr.* F: Prélever (une somme d'argent, un tantième). 'rake- off, *s.* F: Gratte *f.* **rake out,** *v.tr.* **To r. out the fire,** (i) retirer, enlever, les cendres du feu; (ii) *Mch:* faire tomber le feu. **rake over,** *v.tr.* 1. Égratigner (le sol). 2. **To r. over a path,** repasser une allée. **rake up,** *v.tr.* Rassembler, attiser (le feu). **To r. up the past,** revenir sur le passé. **To r. up s.o.'s past,** fouiller dans le passé de qn. **raking¹,** *a.* (Feu) d'enfilade; (tir) en enfilade. **raking²,** *s.* 1. Râtelage *m*, ratissage *m*. 2. *pl.* **Rakings,** râtelures *f*.

rake³, *s.* Viveur *m*, roué *m*, noceur *m*. **Old r.,** vieux marcheur.

rake⁴, *s.* 1. Inclinaison *f* (d'un mât). *Nau:* **R. of the stem, of the stern-post,** élancement *m* de l'étrave; quête *f* de l'étambot. 2. *Th:* Pente *f* (du parterre, du plateau).

rakeful ['reikful], *s.* Râtelée *f* (de foin, etc.).

raking³ ['reikiŋ], *a.* (Mât) incliné vers l'arrière.

rakish¹ ['reikiʃ], *a.* 1. Libertin, dissolu. 2. **R. appearance,** air bravache. **To wear one's hat at a r. angle,** porter son chapeau en casseur d'assiettes. **-ly,** *adv.* 1. En libertin; dissolument. 2. Crânement, effrontément. **Hat tilted r.,** chapeau sur l'oreille.

rakish², *a.* *N.Arch:* (Avant) élancé; (navire) à formes élancées.

rakishness ['reikiʃnis], *s.* 1. Libertinage *m*; mœurs déréglées. 2. Crânerie *f*, effronterie *f*.

rally¹ ['ræli], *s.* 1. (*a*) Ralliement *m* (de partisans). (*b*) *Scouting:* Réunion *f* (de scouts). (*c*) *Aut:* (Car) r., rallye *m* d'automobiles, rallye automobile. 2. (*a*) *Mil:* Reprise *f* en main. *Sp:* Dernier effort pour

gagner le match; retour *m* d'énergie. (*b*) (i) Reprise des forces; (ii) mieux momentané. (*c*) *Com:* Reprise (des prix). 3. *Box:* Reprise. 4. *Ten:* (Belle) passe de jeu.

rally². 1. *v.tr.* (*a*) Rallier (ses partisans) (round, autour de). (*b*) Battre le rappel de (ses partisans). 2. *v.i.* (*a*) (*Of troops*) Se reformer. (*b*) Se rallier (**to a party,** à un parti). **His partisans rallied round him,** ses partisans se sont groupés autour de lui. (*c*) Reprendre des forces. **To r. from an illness,** se remettre d'une maladie. (*d*) (*Of team*) Se reprendre. **rallying¹,** *s.* 1. Ralliement *m.* 2. Reprise *f* des forces, retour *m* à la santé.

rally³, *v.tr.* Railler (s.o. on sth., qn de qch.); se gausser de (qn). **rallying²,** *a.* Railleur, -euse; narquois. **-ly,** *adv.* En raillant; d'un ton moqueur, narquois. **rallying³,** *s.* Raillerie *f.*

Ralph [reif, rælf]. *Pr.n.m.* Raoul, Rodolphe.

ram¹ [ræm], *s.* 1. (*a*) *Z:* Bélier *m.* (*b*) *Astr:* **The R.,** le Bélier. 2. (*a*) (Battering-)r., bélier. (*b*) *Hyd.E:* Bélier hydraulique. (*c*) *Aer:* R. pressure, pression *f* dynamique. 3. *N.Arch:* Éperon *m* (d'étrave). 4. Piston plongeur (de pompe refoulante, de presse). 5. Mouton *m*, pilon *m* (de marteau-pilon). 6. = RAMMER 1. 'ram-pump, *s.* *Hyd.E:* 1. Pompe (re)-foulante, à plongeur.

ram², *v.tr.* (**rammed**) 1. (*a*) Battre, damer, tasser (le sol). (*b*) *Min:* **To r. the charge home,** bourrer, refouler, la charge. (*c*) Enfoncer, damer (un pieu). *S.a.* THROAT. 2. (*a*) *Nau:* Éperonner (un navire). (*b*) *Aut:* **To r. a car,** tamponner une voiture. (*c*) Heurter, cogner (against, contre). **ram down,** *v.tr.* 1. Tasser (la terre). 2. (R)enfoncer (un pieu). **To r. one's hat down on one's head,** enfoncer son chapeau sur la tête. **ram in,** *v.tr.* Enfoncer, renfoncer (un pieu).

Ramadan ['ræmə'dɑːn], *s.* *Mohamm. Rel:* Ramadan *m.*

ramble¹ ['ræmbl], *s.* 1. Promenade *f* (sans itinéraire bien arrêté). **To go for a r.,** F: faire une balade. 2. Discours incohérent.

ramble², *v.i.* (*a*) Errer à l'aventure. (*b*) Faire des excursions à pied. 2. Parler sans suite; (*in delirium*) battre la campagne. **To r. on,** dire mille inconséquences. **rambling¹,** *a.* 1. Errant, vagabond. 2. (Discours) décousu, sans suite. 3. **R. house,** maison pleine de coins et de recoins. **-ly,** *adv.* 1. En vagabondant. 2. En divaguant; (parler) d'une manière décousue; (causer) à bâtons rompus. **rambling²,** *s.* 1. Promenades *fpl* à l'aventure; excursions *fpl* à pied. 2. Divagations *fpl*, radotages *mpl*.

rambler ['ræmblər], *s.* 1. Promeneur, -euse, excursionniste *mf.* 2. Rosier sarmenteux, grimpant.

ramekin, ramequin ['ræmikin], *s.* *Dom.Ec:* Ramequin *m.*

ramification [,ræmifi'keiʃ(ə)n], *s.* Ramification *f.*

ramify ['ræmifai], *v.i.* Se ramifier.

ramjet ['ræmdʒet], *s.* *Av:* Statoréacteur *s.*

rammer ['ræmər], *s.* 1. Dame *f*, demoiselle *f*, pilon *m* (de paveur). 2. *Artil: A:* Refouloir *m.* 3. Mouton *m* (pour pieux).

ramose ['ræmous], *a.* *Nat.Hist:* Rameux, -euse, branchu.

ramp¹ [ræmp], *s.* (*a*) Rampe *f*; pente *f*, talus *m.* *P.N:* **Beware r.,** dénivellation! **Approach r. of a bridge,** rampe d'accès d'un pont. **Unloading r.,** rampe de débarquement. (*b*) *Aut:* **Garage repair r.,** ponton *m* de visite; pont élévateur.

ramp², *v.i.* (*Of pers.*) Rager, tempêter. **To r. and rave,** crier comme un énergumène, comme un fou.

ramp³, *s.* F: 1. Supercherie *f.* **It's a r.,** c'est un coup monté. 2. Majoration exorbitante des prix. **The housing r.,** le scandale des loyers.

rampage¹ [ræm'peidʒ], *s.* F: **To be on the r.,** ne pas décolérer; se comporter comme un fou.

rampage², *v.i.* F: **To r.** (about), se conduire en énergumène, comme un fou.

rampageous [ræm'peidʒəs], *a.* F: Violent, furieux, -euse; tapageur, -euse; rageur, -euse.

rampant ['ræmpənt], *a.* 1. *Her:* (Lion) rampant. 2. (*Of pers.*) Violent, effréné. **Vice is r.,** le vice s'étale. 3. (*Of plant*) Exubérant. 4. *Arch:* (*Of arch*) Rampant.

rampart ['ræmpɑːt], *s.* *Fort:* Rempart *m.* 'rampart-walk, *s.* Chemin *m* de ronde.

rampion ['ræmpiən], s. Bot: Raiponce f.
ramrod ['ræmrɔd], s. A: Baguette f (de fusil). Artil: Écouvillon m. S.a. STRAIGHT I 1.
ramshackle ['ræmʃækl], a. Délabré; qui tombe en ruines. R. old car, vieille guimbarde. R. furniture, meubles boiteux.
ran. See RUN².
ranch¹ [rɑːn(t)ʃ], s. U.S: Ranch m; prairie f d'élevage; ferme f d'élevage.
ranch², v.i. U.S: Faire de l'élevage.
rancher ['rɑːnʃər], s. Propriétaire m d'un ranch.
rancid ['rænsid], a. Rance. To smell r., sentir le rance. To grow r., rancir.
rancidity [ræn'siditi], **rancidness** ['rænsidnis], s. Rancidité f.
rancorous ['ræŋkərəs], a. Rancunier, -ière, haineux, -euse.
rancour ['ræŋkər], s. ʾRancune f, rancœur f.
rand [rænd], s. 1. Bord m, marge f; bande f. Bootm: Couche-point m, pl. couche-points. 2. (S. Africa) Geog: Châine f de collines. The R., le Rand. 3. Num: (S. Africa) Rand m.
random ['rændəm]. 1. s. At r., au hasard, à l'aventure. To speak at r., parler à tort et à travers. To hit out at r., lancer des coups à l'aveuglette. 2. a. Fait au hasard. R. shot, coup tiré au hasard.
ranee [rɑːˈniː], s.f. Rani (épouse du rajah); reine.
rang. See RING⁴.
range¹ [reindʒ], s. 1. (a) Rangée f (de bâtiments). (b) Châine f (de montagnes). 2. Direction f, alignement m. 3. (a) Champ m libre. He has free r. of the house, la maison lui est ouverte. (b) U.S: Grand pâturage (non clôturé). (c) Nat.Hist: Région f, zone f; habitat m (d'une plante). 4. (a) Étendue f, portée f, domaine m. R. of knowledge, étendue des connaissances. R. of action, champ d'activité. Av: Long-r. aircraft, avion m à grand rayon d'action. R. of vision, étendue de la vue. R. of a telescope, portée d'une lunette. The whole r. of politics, le champ entier de la politique. Within my r., à ma portée. R. of speeds, gamme f de vitesses. Av: Wide r. of speeds, grand écart de vitesse. R. of colours, gamme, dégradé m, de couleurs. Wide r. of patterns, ample assortiment m d'échantillons. Pol.Ec: Salary r., éventail m des salaires. (c) The whole r. of events, la série complète des événements. 5. Ball: (a) La distance. At a r. of . . ., à une distance de. . . . At long r., à longue portée. To correct the r., rectifier le tir. (b) Portée (d'une arme à feu)ˋ. Rifle that has a r. of a thousand yards, fusil qui porte à mille mètres. Within r., à portée de tir. Aircraft out of r., avion hors de portée, hors d'atteinte. 6. Shooting r., champ de tir. Experimental r., polygone m. 7. Dom.Ec: Fourneau m de cuisine. ʾrange-finder, s. Télémètre m. ʾrange-finding, s. Télémétrie f.
range². I. v.tr. 1. (a) Ranger, aligner (des troupes); disposer (des objets) en ordre, en ligne. (b) Ranger, classer. To r. oneself with s.o., se ranger du côté de qn. 2. Parcourir (l'horizon). 3. (a) Braquer (un télescope). (b) Abs. Artil: Régler le tir. II. range, v.i. 1. S'étendre (from one place to another, d'un endroit à un autre). 2. Courir, errer. To r. over the country, parcourir le pays. Research ranging over a wide field, recherches qui s'étendent sur un vaste terrain. 3. Temperatures ranging from ten to thirty degrees, températures comprises, s'échelonnant, entre dix et trente degrés. 4. These guns r. over six miles, ces pièces ont une portée de six milles.
ranger ['reindʒər], s. 1. Grand maître des parcs royaux. 2. pl. Mil: (a) The Rangers, Chasseurs (à cheval). (b) U.S: = Gendarmerie montée. 3. Scouting: Guide aînée.
rank¹ [ræŋk], s. 1. Mil: (a) Rang m. To close the ranks, serrer les rangs. To fall into r., se mettre en rangs. (b) pl. The (other) ranks, les (simples) soldats; les hommes (de troupe). To rise from the ranks, sortir du rang; passer officier. Reduction to the ranks, dégradation f militaire. Adm: The higher ranks of the civil service, les hauts fonctionnaires. (c) The r. and file, (i) Mil: les hommes de troupe (simples soldats et gradés); la troupe; (ii) le commun des mortels. The r. and file of union members, le commun

des syndiqués. 2. (a) Rang (social); classe f. Dance of the first r., danseuse de la première volée. (b) Mil: Navy: etc: Grade m. He had attained the r of captain, il était passé capitaine. Officer of high r. officier supérieur. Substantive r., grade effectif. Al ranks, officiers et troupe. 3. (Taxi-)r., station f (pour taxis); stationnement m (pour taxis).
rank². 1. v.tr. To r. s.o. among the great writers ranger, compter, qn parmi les grands écrivains. U.S. To r. s.o., occuper un rang supérieur à qn. 2. v.i. Se ranger, être classé (among, parmi). To r. among the best, compter parmi les meilleurs. To r. above s.o. occuper un rang supérieur à qn. Fin: Shares that r. first in dividend rights, actions qui priment en fait de dividende. The shares will r. for the July dividend les actions prendront part à la distribution de dividendes en juillet. ranking, a. U.S: 1. Éminent. 2. R. officer, supérieur m hiérarchique.
rank³, a. 1. (Trop) luxuriant; exubérant. R. vegetation, végétation luxuriante. Land too r. for wheat, sol trop fort pour le blé. 2. (a) Rance; fétide. To smell r., sentir fort. (b) Grossier, répugnant. 3. R. poison, (i) vrai poison; (ii) poison violent. R. lie, mensonge grossier. R. injustice, injustice criante. -ly, adv. 1. Fortement; avec exubérance. 2. Avec une odeur fétide. 3. Grossièrement.
ranker ['ræŋkər], s. 1. Simple soldat m. 2. Officier sorti du rang.
rankle ['ræŋkl], v.i. 1. (a) A: S'envenimer, s'ulcérer (b) The wound still rankles, c'est une plaie qui saigne encore. 2. To r. in s.o.'s mind, rester sur le cœur de qn. It rankled with him, il en était ulcéré. rankling, a. 1. (a) A: Envenimé, enflammé. (b) (Of hatred) Envenimé. 2. Qui a laissé une rancœur.
rankness ['ræŋknis], s. 1. Luxuriance f, exubérance f (des mauvaises herbes). 2. Goût fort et désagréable. 3. Grossièreté f (d'une insulte).
ransack ['rænsæk], v.tr. 1. Fouiller (un tiroir); fouiller dans (sa mémoire). 2. Saccager, piller (une maison, etc.).
ransom¹ ['rænsəm], s. 1. Rachat m (d'un captif). To hold s.o. to r., mettre qn à rançon; rançonner qn. 2. Rançon f. To pay r., payer rançon. To cost a king's r., coûter un prix fou, impossible; être hors de prix.
ransom², v.tr. 1. (a) Racheter (qn); payer la rançon de (qn). (b) Racheter, expier (qch.). 2. Mettre (qn) à rançon; rançonner (qn). ransoming, s. 1. Rachat m. 2. Mise f à rançon; rançonnement m.
rant¹ [rænt], s. 1. Déclamation extravagante (d'un acteur, d'un orateur). 2. Discours creux; discours d'énergumène.
rant², v.i. Faire l'énergumène; déclamer avec extravagance; F: tempêter, tonitruer. ranting¹, a. Déclamatoire. ranting², s. = RANT¹.
ranter ['ræntər], s. Déclamateur, -trice; énergumène mf.
Ranunculaceae [rəˌnʌŋkjuˈleisiiː], s.pl. Bot: Renonculacées f.
ranunculus, pl. -uses, -i [rəˈnʌŋkjuləs, -əsiz, -ai], s. Bot: Renoncule f.
rap¹ [ræp], s. Petit coup sec et dur. To give s.o. a r. on the knuckles, donner sur les doigts à qn; remettre qn à sa place. A r. at the door, un coup à la porte. F: To take the r., payer les pots cassés.
rap² [ræp], v. (rapped) 1. v.tr. Frapper (qch.); donner un coup sec à (qch.). To r. s.o. over the knuckles, donner sur les doigts à qn. 2. v.i. To r. at the door, frapper un coup à la porte. Psychics: Rapping spirits, esprits frappeurs. rap out, v.tr. To r. out an oath, lâcher un juron. To r. out one's words, parler sec. rapping, s. Coups frappés.
rap³, s. A: Sou m, liard m. F: I don't care a r., je m'en fiche éperdument. It isn't worth a r., ça ne vaut pas tripette.
rapacious [rəˈpeiʃəs], a. Rapace. -ly, adv. Avec rapacité.
rapaciousness [rəˈpeiʃəsnis], **rapacity** [rəˈpæsiti], s. Rapacité f.
rape¹ [reip], s. 1. Poet: Rapt m, ravissement m. The r. of the Sabines, l'enlèvement m des Sabines. 2. Jur: Viol m.
rape², v.tr. 1. Poet: Ravir, enlever de force (une femme). 2. Jur: Violer.

rape³, s. *Bot:* **1.** (Summer) r., colza m. **2.** Navette f. **'rape-oil**, s. Huile f de colza; (huile de) navette f. **'rape-seed**, s. Graine f de colza.

rapid ['ræpid], a. & s. Rapide (m). **-ly**, adv. Rapidement; à grands pas.

rapidity [rə'piditi], s. Rapidité f.

rapier ['reipiər], s. Rapière f.

rapine ['ræpain], s. Rapine f.

rapscallion [ræp'skæljən], s. Homme m de rien; canaille f, vaurien m, propre m à rien.

rapt [ræpt]. **1.** p.p. (a) Ravi, extasié (by, par). (b) Absorbé (**in**, dans). **R. in contemplation**, plongé dans la contemplation; recueilli. **2.** a. (Of attention, interest) Profond.

raptores [ræp'tɔ:ri:z], s.pl. *Orn:* Rapaces m.

rapture ['ræptʃər], s. Ravissement m, extase m. **To be in raptures**, être ravi, enchanté (with, over, de). **To go into raptures**, s'extasier (over, sur).

rapturous ['ræptʃərəs], a. (Cris) de ravissement, d'extase. **R. applause**, applaudissements frénétiques. **-ly**, adv. Avec transport, avec frénésie.

rare¹ ['rɛər], a. **1.** (Atmosphère) rare, peu dense. **2.** R. occurrence, événement rare. **3.** P: Fameux, -euse. **You gave me a r. fright**, tu m'as fait une rude peur. **-ly**, adv. Rarement.

rare², a. Peu cuit; (bifteck) saignant.

rarebit ['ræbit], s. Welsh r., fondue f au fromage sur canapé.

rarefaction [rɛəri'fækʃ(ə)n], s. Raréfaction f.

rarefy ['rɛərifai], v.tr. Raréfier (l'air). **rarefied**, a. (Air) raréfié. **To become r.**, se raréfier.

rareness ['rɛənis], s. Rareté f (de l'atmosphère, d'un objet).

rarity ['rɛəriti], s. **1.** = RARENESS. **2.** Objet m rare; événement m rare.

rascal ['rɑ:sk(ə)l], s. Coquin m, fripon m; mauvais sujet. **That r. of a nephew of mine**, mon polisson de neveu.

rascally ['rɑ:skəli], a. De coquin; (homme de loi) retors. **R. trick**, méchant tour.

rase [reiz], v.tr. = RAZE.

rash¹ [ræʃ], s. *Med:* Éruption f; exanthème m. S.a. NETTLE-RASH.

rash², a. Téméraire; irréfléchi, impétueux, -euse. **R. words**, paroles inconsidérées, imprudentes. **R. act**, coup m de tête. **-ly**, adv. Témérairement; inconsidérément. **To speak r.**, parler à la légère. **To act r.**, agir à l'étourdie.

rasher ['ræʃər], s. *Cu:* Tranche f de lard.

rashness ['ræʃnis], s. Témérité f; étourderie f. **To pay for one's r.**, payer sa témérité.

rasp¹ [rɑ:sp], s. **1.** *Tls:* Râpe f. **2.** Bruit m de râpe; grincement m.

rasp². **1.** v.tr. (a) Râper (le bois). (b) Racler (une surface); écorcher (la peau). **Wine that rasps the throat**, vin qui racle, écorche, le gosier. **2.** v.i. Grincer, crisser. **3.** v.tr. **To r. out an insult**, lâcher une insulte d'une voix âpre. **rasp away, off**, v.tr. Enlever (qch.) à la râpe. **rasping**, a. **R. sound**, son grinçant, crissement m. **R. voice**, voix âpre; F: voix de crécelle.

raspberry ['rɑ:zb(ə)ri], s. **1.** Framboise f. **R. bush**, framboisier m. **2.** P: **To give** (s.o.) **a r.**, (i) faire nargue à (qn); (ii) engueuler (qn). **To get the r.**, (i) essuyer une rebuffade; (ii) se faire engueuler.

rat¹ [ræt], s. **1.** *Z:* Rat m. Sewer r., rat d'égout. Water r., rat d'eau, campagnol m. She-r., rate f. **R. extermination**, dératisation f. **R. poison**, raticide m, mort f aux rats. **R. trap**, ratière f. F: **To smell a r.**, soupçonner anguille sous roche. **To die like a r. in a hole**, mourir dans son trou, sans secours. F: **Rats!** (in disbelief) allons donc! **2.** (a) Pol: Transfuge m, renégat m. (b) *Ind:* Jaune m; renard m. **'rat-catcher**, s. **1.** Preneur m de rats. **2.** Cost: Veston m d'équitation en tweed. **'rat-catching**, a. Chasse f aux rats; dératisation f. **'rat(-)race**, s. F: Curée f des places, foire f d'empoigne, la course au bifteck. **'rat-tail(ed)**, a. Effilé.

rat², v.i. (ratted) **1.** (Of dog, etc.) **To r., go ratting**, faire la chasse aux rats. **2.** F: (a) Tourner casaque; revirer; abandonner son parti. (b) *Ind:* Faire le jaune; faire le renard. (c) **To r. on a friend**, vendre un copain.

ratafia [ˌrætə'fiə], s. Ratafia m.

ratchet ['rætʃit], s. **1.** Encliquetage m à dents. **2.** Cliquet m, rochet m. **'rachet-brace**, s. Vilebrequin m, foret m, à rochet. **'rachet-drill**, s. *Tls:* Drille f à rochet. **'ratchet-wheel**, s. Roue f à cliquet.

rate¹ [reit], s. **1.** Nombre proportionnel, quantité proportionnelle. **R. per cent**, pourcentage m. **Birth, death, r.**, (taux m de la) natalité, mortalité. **2.** (a) Taux, raison f. **R. of speed**, degré m de vitesse. **R. of growth**, taux d'accroissement. **At the present r. of consumption**, à raison de la consommation actuelle. El: **R. of charging**, taux, régime m, de chargement (d'un accumulateur). (b) Allure f, vitesse f, train m. **At the r. of . . .**, à la vitesse de. . . . *Nau:* **At the r. of twenty knots**, à l'allure de vingt nœuds. **He was going at a tremendous r.**, il allait d'un train d'enfer. (c) Taux, cours m; tarif m. **R. of interest**, taux d'intérêt. **The Bank r.**, le taux de la Banque; taux d'escompte. **Market r.**, taux (de l'escompte) hors banque; taux du cours libre (du change). *Ind:* **R. of wages**, taux du salaire. *Com:* **Market rates**, cours du marché. **Insurance r.**, prime f de l'assurance. **Harbour rates**, droits m de port. **Freight r.**, fret m maritime. **Advertising rates**, tarif de publicité. **To pay s.o. at the r. of . . .**, payer qn sur le pied de. . . . **R. of living**, train m de vie. **At that r.**, sur ce pied-là; à ce compte-là. **At any r.**, dans tous les cas, en tout cas. **3.** *Adm:* Impôt local; contribution foncière. **Rates and taxes**, impôts et contributions. **Borough rates**, taxes municipales. **4.** Estimation f, évaluation f. **To value sth. at a low r.**, faire peu de cas de qch. **'rate-collector**, s. Percepteur m des impôts locaux; receveur municipal. **R.-collector's office**, recette municipale; recette régionale.

rate². **1.** v.tr. (a) Estimer, évaluer (qch.). **To r. sth. high**, assigner une haute valeur à qch.; faire grand cas de qch. (b) Considérer, regarder (as, comme). (c) Taxer (s.o. at a certain sum, qn à raison d'une certaine somme). (d) Classer, classifier (une auto); *Nau:* classer (un navire). **2.** v.i. Être classé (as, comme). **rating¹**, s. **1.** (a) Estimation f, évaluation f. **Engine r.**, calcul m de la puissance des moteurs. (b) Répartition f des impôts locaux. (c) Classement m, classification f. **2.** (a) *Mec.E:* Cheval nominal. (b) *Sp:* Classe f, catégorie f, série f. **3.** *Navy:* (a) Spécialité f, classe f (d'un homme de l'équipage). (b) pl. **The ratings**, les matelots et gradés.

rate³, v.tr. Tancer, semoncer (qn) (for doing sth., d'avoir fait qch.), F: flanquer un savon à (qn); P: engueuler (qn). **rating²**, s. Semonce f; verte réprimande; P: engueulade f.

rateable ['reitəbl], a. **1.** Évaluable. **2.** Imposable. **R. value** = valeur locative imposable (d'un immeuble); évaluation cadastrale (d'un terrain).

ratel ['reitel], s. *Z:* Ratel m.

ratepayer ['reitpeiər], s. Contribuable mf.

rather ['rɑ:ðər], adv. **1.** Plutôt. **Or r.**, ou plutôt; pour mieux dire. **2.** Un peu; quelque peu; assez. **R. pretty**, assez joli. **R. plain**, plutôt laid. **R. a lot**, un peu trop. **Do I look ill?**—Well, you do r., est-ce que j'ai l'air malade?—Si, tout de même. **I r. think you know him**, je crois bien que vous le connaissez. **3.** Plutôt (than, que); de préférence (than, à). **Anything r. than . . .**, tout plutôt que. . . . **I would r. be loved than feared**, j'aime mieux être aimé qu'être craint. **I had r. suffer than tell a lie**, plutôt souffrir que mentir. **I'd r. not**, veuillez m'excuser. **I'd much r. you came**, je préférerais de beaucoup que vous veniez. **4.** F: **Do you know him?**—R.! le connaissez-vous?—Pour sûr!

ratification [ˌrætifi'keiʃ(ə)n], s. Ratification f.

ratify ['rætifai], v.tr. Ratifier, entériner (un décret, etc.). **To r. a contract**, approuver un contrat. **ratifying¹**, a. Ratificatif, -ive. **ratifying²**, s. Ratification f, validation f.

ratio ['reiʃiou], s., pl. -os ['reiʃiou, -ouz], s. Raison f, rapport m, proportion f. **Arithmetical r.**, raison, proportion, arithmétique. **In the r. of . . .**, dans le rapport de . . . **In direct r. to . . .**, en raison directe de. . . .

ration¹ ['ræʃ(ə)n], s. *Mil: etc:* Ration f. **Emergency**, F: **iron rations**, vivres m de réserve. **To put on (short) rations**, rationner (une garnison). *Adm:* **Off the r.**, sans tickets, en vente f libre. **'ration-book**, s. War Adm: Carte f d'alimentation, de ravitaillement, de rationnement.

ration², v.tr. **1.** Rationner (qn); mettre (qn) à la ration. **2.** To r. **bread**, rationner le pain. **rationing**, s. Rationnement m.

rational ['ræʃən(ə)l], a. **1.** (a) Raisonnable; doué de raison. To be quite r., avoir toute sa tête. (b) Raisonné; conforme à la raison. R. **belief**, croyance fondée sur la raison. **2.** Mth: Ph: Rationnel. **-ally**, adv. Raisonnablement.

rationalism ['ræʃənəlizm], s. Phil: Rationalisme m.

rationalist ['ræʃənəlist], a. & s. Phil: Rationaliste (mf).

rationality [ˌræʃə'næliti], s. **1.** Rationalité f. **2.** Faculté f de raisonner.

rationalization [ˌræʃənəlai'zeiʃ(ə)n], s. Rationalisation f.

rationalize ['ræʃənəlaiz], v.tr. Rationaliser.

ratlin(e) ['rætlin], s. Nau: Enfléchure f.

rat(t)an [rə'tæn], s. Bot: Rotin m; jonc m d'Inde. R. **walking-stick**, (canne f de) jonc.

rat(-tat)-tat ['ræt(ə)'tæt]. Toc, toc.

ratter ['rætər], s. **1.** (Chien) ratier m. **2.** Preneur m de rats. **3.** F: Lâcheur m.

rattle¹ ['rætl], s. **1.** (a) Hochet m (d'enfant). (b) Crécelle f (d'alarme). (c) pl. Rept: Rattles, sonnettes f (d'un crotale). **2.** (a) Bruit m, fracas m (d'une voiture); tapotis m (d'une machine à écrire); trictrac m (de dés); crépitement m (d'une fusillade). (b) Med: Râle m. (c) Bavardage m.

rattle². **1.** v.i. (a) (Of arms) Cliqueter; (of car) ferrailler; (of hail) crépiter; (of window) trembler, branler. To make the **windows** r., faire trembler les vitres. Aut: The body rattles, la carrosserie fait du bruit. (Of vehicle) To r. **along**, rouler avec fracas, à toute vitesse. (c) Med: Râler. **2.** v.tr. (a) Agiter (des chaînes) avec bruit; faire cliqueter (des clefs); faire sonner (son argent). To r. the dice, agiter les dés (dans le cornet). (b) F: Consterner, bouleverser (qn). He never gets rattled, il ne s'épate jamais; il ne se laisse pas démonter. **rattle off**, v.tr. Réciter rapidement (la prière); expédier (un travail). **rattle on**, v.i. Continuer à bavarder. **rattling¹**, a. **1.** Bruyant; crépitant. **2.** F: At a r. **pace**, au grand trot. **3.** F: O: Épatant. **rattling²**, s. = RATTLE¹ 2.

rattler ['rætlər], s. **1.** U.S: = RATTLESNAKE. **2.** Klaxon m d'alarme. **3.** F: O: Personne, chose, épatante.

rattlesnake ['rætlsneik], s. Serpent m à sonnettes; crotale m.

rattletrap ['rætltræp], s. Aut: F: Vieille guimbarde; tapecul m; patache f; vieille bagnole.

ratty ['ræti], a. F: **1.** Infesté de rats. **2.** Fâché; en rogne. **3.** U.S: P: Moche; mal soigné; délabré.

raucous ['rɔːkəs], a. Rauque. **-ly**, adv. D'une voix rauque, éraillée.

raucousness ['rɔːkəsnis], s. Raucité f (de la voix).

ravage¹ ['rævidʒ], s. Ravage m. The ravage(s) made **by torrents**, les dévastations f des torrents.

ravage², v.tr. Ravager, dévaster. **ravaging¹**, a. Ravageur, -euse. **ravaging²**, s. Ravagement m.

ravager ['rævidʒər], s. Ravageur m, dévastateur, -trice.

rave¹ [reiv], s. F: U.S: **1.** Béguin m, toquade f. **2.** Journ: etc: Éloge m enthousiaste. R. **review**, critique f dithyrambique.

rave², v.i. (a) Être en délire; F: battre la campagne. F: You're raving! vous divaguez! (b) To r. **and storm**, tempêter. To r. **at, against**, s.o., pester contre qn. **Raving lunatic**, fou furieux. (c) (Of wind) Être en furie. (d) F: To r. **about** sth., s'extasier sur qch. **raving**, s. **1.** Délire m, divagation f. **2.** pl. Ravings, paroles incohérentes.

ravel¹ ['ræv(ə)l], s. **1.** Emmêlement m. Threads in a r., fils enchevêtrés, emmêlés. **2.** Effilochure f.

ravel², v. (ravelled) **1.** v.tr. Embrouiller, emmêler (un écheveau). **2.** v.i. (Of skein) S'embrouiller, s'enchevêtrer. **ravelling**, s. **1.** Effilochage m. **2.** Effilochure f, effilure f.

raven¹ ['reiv(ə)n], s. Orn: (Grand) corbeau. a. D'un noir de jais.

raven² ['ræv(ə)n]. **1.** v.i. Faire des ravages; (of animal) chercher sa proie. **2.** v.tr. Dévorer (la proie). **ravening**, a. Vorace, rapace.

ravenous ['ræv(ə)nəs], a. **1.** (Animal) vorace. **2.** (a) R. **appetite**, appétit vorace, féroce. (b) F: To be r., avoir une faim de loup. **-ly**, adv. Voracement. To **eat** r., manger gloutonnement.

ravenousness ['ræv(ə)nəsnis], s. **1.** Voracité f. **2.** Faim f de loup; faim dévorante.

ravine [rə'viːn], s. Ravin m.

ravioli [rævi'ouli], s. Cu: Ravioli m.

ravish ['ræviʃ], v.tr. **1.** (a) Ravir; enlever (qn, qch.) de force. (b) O: Violer (une femme). **2.** Ravir (d'admiration); enchanter (qn). **ravishing**, a. **1.** Ravissant. O: R. **wolves**, loups dévorants. **2.** R. **sight**, spectacle enchanteur. **-ly**, adv. D'une manière ravissante.

ravisher ['ræviʃər], s. (a) Ravisseur m. (b) F: What a r.! Quelle femme ravissante!

ravishment ['ræviʃmənt], s. **1.** Enlèvement m, rapt m. **2.** Ravissement m; transports mpl (de joie).

raw [rɔː]. **I.** a. **1.** Cru. R. **meat**, viande crue. **2.** (a) R. **material(s)**, matière(s) première(s). R. **silk**, soie grège. R. **metal**, sugar, métal, sucre, brut. (b) R. **colouring**, coloris cru. **3.** Sans expérience; inexpérimenté. A r. **hand**, un novice; F: un bleu. R. **troops**, troupes non aguerries. S.a. RECRUIT¹. **4.** A vif. R. **wound**, plaie vive. My **nerves are** r. **today**, j'ai les nerfs à fleur de peau aujourd'hui. **5.** R. **weather**, temps gris et froid. R. **winds**, vents aigres. **II. raw**, s. To **touch** s.o. on the r., piquer qn au vif. **'raw(-)'boned**, a. Maigre, décharné; (cheval) efflanqué.

rawhide ['rɔːhaid]. **1.** a. De, en, cuir vert. R. **whip**, fouet m de cuir vert. **2.** s. Cuir vert, cuir, peau f, en poil.

rawness ['rɔːnis], s. **1.** Crudité f (des fruits, etc.). **2.** Inexpérience f. **3.** Écorchure f. **4.** Froid m humide; âpreté f (du temps).

ray¹ [rei], s. **1.** Ph: Rayon m. Death r., rayon de la mort. R. **of light**, rayon lumineux. Rad.-A: Soft rays, rayons mous. A r. **of hope**, une lueur d'espoir. S.a. X-RAY¹. **2.** Rayon (d'un animal ou d'une plante en étoile).

ray², s. Ich: Raie f. Electric r., torpille f.

rayon ['reiən], s. Tex: Rayonne f.

raze [reiz], v.tr. Raser (des fortifications). To r. **a building to the ground**, raser un édifice.

razor ['reizər], s. Rasoir m. Safety r., rasoir de sûreté. Electric r., rasoir électrique. R. **blade**, lame f de rasoir. **'razor-backed**, a. (Cheval) à dos tranchant; (colline f) en dos d'âne. **'razor-edge**, s. **1.** Fil m, tranchant m, de rasoir. **2.** Arête f (de montagne) en lame de couteau. **'razor-fish**, **'razor-shell**, s. Moll: (Manche de) couteau m.

razorbill ['reizəbil], s. Orn: Petit pingouin.

razz¹ [ræz], v.tr. F: U.S: Se moquer de (qn); narguer (qn).

razz², s. U.S: Son moqueur.

razzle(-dazzle) ['ræzl(dæzl)], s. P: O: To go on the r. (-d.), faire la noce, faire la nouba.

re¹ [rei], s. Mus: Ré m.

re² [riː]. Lt. s. as prep. phr. **1.** Jur: (In) re Smith v Jones, (en l')affaire Smith contre Jones. **2.** Com: Re your letter of June 10th, relativement à, au sujet de, votre lettre du 10 juin.

reabsorb ['riːəb'sɔːb], v.tr. Réabsorber.

reabsorption ['riːəb'sɔːpʃ(ə)n], s. Réabsorption f.

reaccustom ['riːə'kʌstəm], v.tr. Réhabituer, réaccoutumer (to, à).

reach¹ [riːtʃ], s. **1.** Extension f (de la main). Box: Allonge f. To have the longer r., être avantagé en allonge. Fenc: To have a long r., avoir beaucoup d'étendue. **2.** (a) Portée f, atteinte f. Within s.o.'s r., à la portée de qn. Within r. of the hand, à portée de la main; F: sous la main. Out of r., hors de portée. Beyond the r. of all suspicion, à l'abri de tout soupçon. Cars within the r. of small incomes, voitures accessibles aux petites bourses. Posts within the r. of all emplois accessibles à tous. The goal is within our r. nous touchons au but. (b) Hotel within easy r. of the station, hôtel à proximité de la gare. (c) Étendue (de l'esprit). **3.** R. of meadow, étendue de prairies **4.** Partie droite (d'un fleuve) entre deux coudes; bief m (d'un canal).

reach². **I.** v.tr. **1.** To r. out, étendre; tendre, avancer (la main). **2.** Atteindre. The law does not r. these cases, la loi ne s'étend pas jusqu'à ces cas. **3.** (a) Arriver à, parvenir à. We shall r. Paris in the evening nous arriverons à Paris dans la soirée. To r. the summit of the mountain, parvenir en haut de la montagne. To r. the age of sixty, atteindre l'âge de soixante ans. To r. perfection, atteindre, toucher, à la perfection. To r. a high price, atteindre un haut prix; se vendre cher. **The disease had reached the town,** la maladie avait gagné la ville. **Your letter reached me today,** votre lettre m'est parvenue aujourd'hui. **These rumours reached him,** ces bruits vinrent jusqu'à lui. (b) Arriver à (une conclusion). **To r. an agreement,** aboutir à un accord. 4. (a) R. me my gloves, passez-moi mes gants. (b) R. me (down) that plate, descendez-moi cette assiette. II. **reach,** v.tr. & i. Arriver, s'élever, monter, descendre, jusqu'à. To r. (down) to the bottom, atteindre le fond; descendre jusqu'au fond. She scarcely reaches up to your shoulder, c'est à peine si elle vous vient à l'épaule. III. **reach,** v.i. 1. S'étendre. As far as the eye could r., à perte de vue. 2. To r. out (with one's hand) for sth., tendre, avancer, la main pour prendre qch. He reached over to the table, il étendit la main vers la table. **'reach-me-down,** s. F: Costume m de confection; F: un décrochez-moi-ça.

reachable ['riːtʃəbl], a. Que l'on peut atteindre; accessible; à portée. Not r., inaccessible, hors de portée.

react [riˈækt], v.i. Réagir (upon, sur; against, contre).

reactance [riˈæktəns], s. El: Réactance f.

reaction [riˈækʃ(ə)n], s. Réaction f. 1. (a) The reactions of a policy, les contre-coups m d'une politique. (b) Physiol: Cutaneous r., réaction cutanée. (c) Ph: R. wheel, tourniquet m hydraulique. Atom. Ph: Nuclear r., réaction nucléaire. 2. Pol: The forces of r., le parti réactionnaire.

reactionary [riˈækʃən(ə)ri], a. & s. Pol: Réactionnaire (mf).

reactive [riˈæktiv], a. Réactif, -ive.

reactor [riˈæktər], s. El.E: Bobine f de réactance; tamponneur m; réacteur m. Atom. Ph: Atomic r., réacteur atomique. Breeder r., pile couveuse.

read¹ [riːd], s. Action f de lire. He was having a quiet r., il lisait tranquillement.

read² [riːd], v.tr. (p.t. & p.p. read [red]) 1. (a) Lire. To teach s.o. to r., enseigner la lecture à qn. To r. to oneself, lire tout bas; lire des yeux. Adm: Read [red] and approved, lu et approuvé. (b) Typ: To r. proofs, corriger des épreuves. (c) To r. up a subject, étudier un sujet. He is reading for his examination, il prépare son examen. (At university) To r. French, étudier le français. To r. law, faire son droit. Abs. To r. for the bar, faire ses études d'avocat. 2. To r. sth. aloud, lire qch. à haute voix, tout haut. To r. a report (to the meeting), donner lecture d'un rapport (à l'assemblée). To take the minutes as read [red], approuver le procès-verbal sans lecture. To r. to s.o., faire la lecture à qn. S.a. LESSON 1, RIOT¹ 1. 3. To r. s.o. to sleep, endormir qn en lui faisant la lecture. 4. (a) Lire (la musique). (b) To r. the future, lire dans l'avenir. To r. s.o.'s hand, lire dans la main de qn. To r. s.o.'s thoughts, lire dans la pensée de qn. I can r. him like a book, je le connais comme le fond de ma poche. To r. into a sentence what is not there, mettre dans une phrase ce qui n'y est pas. To r. between the lines, lire entre les lignes; F: aider à la lettre. S.a. RUN² I. 1. 5. Lire (l'horloge, le thermomètre); relever (un compteur à gaz). 6. (a) The book reads like a translation, le livre fait l'effet d'une traduction. (b) The clause reads both ways, l'article peut s'interpréter dans les deux sens. **read out,** v.tr. Lire (qch.) à haute voix. To r. out the agenda, donner lecture de l'ordre du jour. **read over,** v.tr. Relire (qch.). **read through,** v.tr. 1. Parcourir (qch.). 2. Lire (qch.) en entier. **read³** [red], a. 1. (Discours) lu. 2. (Of pers.) Well-r., instruit, savant; qui a beaucoup lu; très cultivé. F: Well-r. chap, type calé. **reading¹,** a. The r. public, le public qui lit. A r. man, un (grand) liseur. **reading²,** s. 1. (a) Lecture(s) f(pl). To be fond of r., aimer la lecture. (b) Lecture à haute voix. R. of a will, lecture, ouverture f, d'un testament. Parl: Second r., prise f en considération d'un projet de loi. (c) Explication f, interprétation f (d'une énigme). 2. (a) Lecture (d'un instrument de précision). (b) Relevé m (d'un

compteur à gaz); observation (faite avec un instrument de précision); cote (donnée par l'instrument). Barometer r., hauteur f barométrique. W.Tel: Dial readings, réglages m (du poste). Tg: Sound r., lecture au son. 3. (a) Façon f de lire. (b) Interprétation (d'un rôle). (c) Leçon f, variante f d'un texte). **'reading-book,** s. Livre m de lecture. **'reading-desk,** s. Pupitre m. Ecc: Lutrin m. **'reading-glass,** s. Loupe f. **'reading-lamp,** s. Lampe f de travail, de table, de bureau. Bedside r.-l., lampe de chevet. **'reading-room,** s. Salle f de lecture (d'une bibliothèque).

readable ['riːdəbl], a. Lisible. 1. This book is barely r., ce livre est à peine lisible. Is it r.? peut-on le lire? est-ce intéressant? 2. His handwriting is very r., son écriture est très lisible.

readdress ['riːə'dres], v.tr. Changer l'adresse (d'une lettre); faire suivre (une lettre).

reader ['riːdər], s. 1. (a) Liseur, -euse; lecteur, -trice. He is not much of a r., il n'aime guère la lecture. (b) Publisher's r., lecteur, -trice, de manuscrits. (c) Proof r., correcteur, -trice, d'épreuves. 2. (a) Lecteur, -trice (à haute voix). (b) Ecc: Lecteur m. (c) Sch: = Professeur m de faculté. 3. Sch: Livre m de lecture.

readership ['riːdəʃip], s. 1. Sch: = Professorat m de faculté. 2. A r. of two millions, deux millions de lecteurs. An educated r., un public cultivé.

readiness ['redinis], s. 1. (a) Empressement m, alacrité f (à faire qch.). (b) Bonne volonté. 2. Facilité f, vivacité f (d'esprit). R. of speech, facilité de parole. 3. To be in r., être prêt.

readjust ['riːə'dʒʌst], v.tr. Rajuster; remettre (un instrument) au point; réadapter (ses mœurs, ses habitudes).

readjustment ['riːə'dʒʌstmənt], s. Rajustement m, rectification f (d'un instrument); réadaptation f (de mœurs, du train de vie). Nau: Régulation f (des compas).

readmission ['riːəd'miʃ(ə)n] **readmittance** ['riːəd'mitəns], s. Réadmission f.

readmit ['riːəd'mit], v.tr. Réadmettre.

ready ['redi]. I. a. 1. (a) Prêt. Are you r.? êtes-vous prêt? y êtes-vous? (To racers) R.! go! préparez-vous! partez! To make r., get r., se préparer, s'apprêter, se disposer (to, à). R. for the fray, prêt au combat. (Of book) Now r., sur le point de paraître. To be r. to face s.o., attendre qn de pied ferme. Nau: All r.! (on est) paré! Typ: To make r., mettre en train. Tg: R. signal, invitation f à transmettre. (b) R. to hand, sous la main. R. money, argent comptant. 2. (a) Prêt, disposé (à faire qch.). He is a r. believer in miracles, il croit volontiers aux miracles. (b) R. to die with hunger, sur le point de mourir de faim. 3. Prompt, facile. (a) To have a r. wit, avoir l'esprit prompt. To have a r. tongue, avoir la langue agile, bien pendue. To have a r. pen, avoir la plume facile. To be r. with an answer, avoir la réplique prompte. (b) Goods that meet with a r. sale, marchandises de vente courante. -ily, adv. 1. (Faire qch.) volontiers, avec empressement. 2. (Imaginer qch.) aisément, facilement. II. ready, adv. R. dressed, tout habillé. III. ready, s. 1. Mil: To come to the r., apprêter l'arme. Artil: Guns at the r., pièces parées à faire feu. 2. P: Argent comptant. **'ready-'cooked,** a. (a) (Aliment) tout cuit. (b) Mets à emporter. **'ready-'made,** a. (Article) tout fait. R.-m. clothes, le prêt-à-porter, confection f. **'ready 'reckoner,** s. Com: Barème m (de calculs tout faits). **'ready-to-wear,** attrib. a. Prêt-à-porter. **'ready-'witted,** a. A l'esprit prompt, vif.

reaffirm ['riːə'fəːm], v.tr. Réaffirmer (qch.).

reafforestation [riːəfɔresteiʃ(ə)n], s. Reboisement m.

reagent [riˈeidʒənt], s. Ch: Réactif m.

real [riəl], a. 1. (a) Vrai. R. silk, soie naturelle. R. old nobility, noblesse de bon aloi. (b) Véritable, réel, -elle. The r. world, le monde réel. The r. value of things, le véritable prix des choses. A r. friend, un vrai ami, un véritable ami. It is the r. thing, F: it's the r. McCoy, (i) c'est authentique; (ii) F: c'est ce qu'il nous faut; (iii) F: c'est au poil. s. The r. and the ideal, le réel et l'idéal. Fin: R. value, valeur effective.

2. *Jur*; **R. estate, r. property,** propriété immobilière; biens-fonds *mpl. U.S*: **R. estate register,** cadastre *m.* 3. *adv. U.S: F:* **That's r. kind of you,** c'est très aimable de votre part. **-ly,** *adv.* Vraiment; réellement; en effet. **It was r. my fault,** c'était vraiment, franchement, de ma faute. **You r. must go there,** il faut absolument que vous y alliez. **Has he r. gone?** est-il parti pour de vrai? **Is it r. true?** est-ce bien vrai? **R.?** vraiment? *F:* sans blague? **Not r.!** pas possible!

realism ['riəlizm], *s.* Réalisme *m.*

realist ['riəlist], *a. & s.* Réaliste (*mf*).

realistic [,riə'listik], *a.* Réaliste. **-ally,** *adv.* Avec réalisme.

reality [ri'æliti], *s.* 1. La réalité; le réel. **In r.,** en réalité. 2. **We must stick to realities,** il faut s'en tenir aux réalités.

realizable ['riə'laizəbl], *a.* 1. Réalisable. (*a*) Qui peut se faire. (*b*) **Assets that are hardly r.,** biens *mpl* difficiles à réaliser. 2. Imaginable; dont on peut se rendre compte.

realization [,riəlai'zeiʃ(ə)n], *s.* 1. (*a*) Réalisation *f* (d'un projet). (*b*) *Com:* Conversion *f* en espèces. 2. Conception nette (d'un fait). **To come to the r. that . . .,** se rendre compte de ce que. . . .

realize ['riəlaiz], *v.tr.* 1. (*a*) Réaliser (un projet). (*b*) *Com:* Convertir (des biens) en espèces, réaliser (des biens). (*c*) **To r. a high price,** atteindre un prix élevé. 2. Concevoir nettement, bien comprendre (qch.); se rendre compte de (qch.); prendre conscience *f* de (qch.). **I realized it at the first glance,** je m'en suis rendu compte au premier coup d'œil.

really, *adv.* See REAL.

realm [relm], *s.* Royaume *m.* **The realms of fancy,** le domaine de l'imagination.

realtor [ri'æltər], *s. U.S:* Agent immobilier.

realty ['riəlti], *s. Jur:* Biens immobiliers; immeubles *mpl.*

ream[1] [ri:m], *s. Paperm:* Rame *f. F:* **He writes reams,** il écrit des pages et des pages.

ream[2], *v.tr.* 1. **To r. (out),** aléser (un trou). 2. Fraiser, chanfreiner (un trou). 3. Sertir (une cartouche). **reaming,** *s.* 1. Alésage *m.* 2. Fraisage *m.*

reamer(-bit) ['ri:mər(bit)], *s. Tls:* 1. Alésoir *m,* aléseuse *f.* 2. **Countersinking r.,** fraise *f.*

reanimate ['ri:'ænimeit], *v.tr.* Ranimer, réanimer.

reap [ri:p], *v.tr.* (*a*) Moissonner (le blé, un champ). *Abs.* Moissonner. *Prov:* **We r. as we sow,** on recueille ce qu'on a semé. (*b*) Recueillir (le fruit de ses travaux). **To r. laurels,** cueillir des lauriers. **To r. profit from sth.,** tirer profit de qch. **reaping,** *s.* Moisson *f;* fauchage *m;* fauchaison *f.*

reaper ['ri:pər], *s.* 1. (*Pers.*) Moissonneur, -euse. *Lit:* **The R.,** la Mort. 2. (*Machine*) Moissonneuse *f.* **R.-binder,** moissonneuse-lieuse *f, pl.* moissonneuses-lieuses.

reappear ['ri:ə'piər], *v.i.* Reparaître, réapparaître.

reappearance ['ri:ə'piərəns], *s.* (*a*) Réapparition *f.* (*b*) *Th:* Rentrée *f* (d'un acteur). (*c*) *Geol:* Résurgence *f* (d'un cours d'eau souterrain).

reapply ['ri:ə'plai]. 1. *v.tr.* Réappliquer (une couche de peinture) (**upon,** sur). 2. *v.i.* S'adresser de nouveau (**to,** à).

reappoint ['ri:ə'pɔint], *v.tr.* Réintégrer (qn) dans ses fonctions.

rear[1] ['riər]. I. *s.* 1. *Mil:* (*a*) Arrière-garde *f,* derrières *mpl* (d'une armée). **To remove a casualty to the r.,** transporter un blessé à l'arrière. (*b*) *P:* **The rear(s),** les latrines *f,* les cabinets *m,* les water. 2. (*a*) Arrière *m,* derrière *m* (d'une maison). (*b*) Dernier rang, queue *f* (d'un cortège). (*c*) *P:* **A kick in the r.,** un coup de pied au derrière. II. **rear,** *a.* D'arrière, de queue; postérieur. **R. wheel,** roue (d')arrière. *Mil:* **R. rank,** dernier rang; derrière-rang *m.* **R.-rank man,** serre-file *m.* **'rear-'admiral,** *s.* Contre-amiral *m.* **'rear-'drive,** **'rear-'engined,** *a. Aut: etc:* Propulsion *f* par les roues arrières. **'rear-'engined,** *a. Aut:* Avec moteur *m* à l'arrière; tout-à-l'arrière. **'rear(-)guard,** *s. Mil:* Arrière-garde *f.* **R.-g. action,** combat *m* d'arrière-garde; action retardatrice. **'rear-gunner,** *s. Av:* Mitrailleur *m* de queue. **'rear-light,** *s. Aut:* Feu *m* arrière. **'rear-'window,** *s. Aut:* Lunette *f* arrière.

rear[2]. 1. *v.tr.* (*a*) *O:* Élever (une cathédrale); ériger (une statue). (*b*) Dresser (un mât). 2. *v.tr.* Élever (une famille, des animaux); cultiver (des plantes). 3. *v.i.* (*Of cliff, etc.*) Se dresser (**above,** au-dessus de). 4. *v.i.* (*Of horse*) Se cabrer. **rearing,** *s.* 1. Élevage *m* (des animaux). 2. Cabrement *m* (d'un cheval).

rearm ['ri:'ɑ:m], *v.tr.* Réarmer.

rearmament ['ri:(:)'ɑ:məmənt], *s.* Réarmement *m.*

rearmost ['riəmoust], *a.* Dernier, -ière; de queue.

rearrange ['ri:ə'reindʒ], *v.tr.* (*a*) Arranger de nouveau. (*b*) Remettre en ordre.

rearrangement ['ri:ə'reindʒmənt], *s.* (*a*) Nouvel arrangement. (*b*) Remise *f* en ordre.

rearview ['riəvju:], *attrib.a. Aut:* **R. mirror,** rétroviseur *m.*

rearward ['ri:əwəd]. 1. *s.* Arrière-garde *f* (d'une armée). **In the r.,** à l'arrière. 2. *a.* (*a*) Situé à l'arrière. (*b*) (Mouvement, etc.) en arrière.

rearwards ['ri:əwədz], *adv.* 1. A l'arrière. 2. Vers l'arrière.

reason[1] ['ri:z(ə)n], *s.* 1. Raison *f,* cause *f,* motif *m.* **The r. for my absence,** la raison de mon absence. **To state one's reasons for a decision,** motiver une décision. *Jur:* **Reasons adduced,** les attendus *m* (d'un jugement). **For reasons best known to myself,** pour des raisons de moi seul connues. **He will not come, and for a very good r.,** il ne viendra pas et pour cause. **For the same r. . . .,** au même titre. . . . **For no r. at all,** sans motif, sans cause. **For the very r. that . . .,** précisément parce que. . . . **The r. why,** le pourquoi. **What's the r. for it?** à quoi cela tient-il? **You have r. to be glad,** vous avez sujet de vous réjouir. **I have r. to believe that . . .,** j'ai lieu de croire que. . . . **He complains with (good) r.,** il se plaint à bon droit. **All the more r. for going,** raison de plus pour y aller. **By r. of . . .,** à cause de. . . . 2. Raison; faculté *f* de raisonner. **He lost his r.,** il a perdu la raison. 3. Raison; bon sens. **To hear, listen to, r.,** entendre raison. **It stands to r.,** c'est évident; cela va sans dire. **Everything in r.,** il y a mesure à tout.

reason[2]. 1. *v.i.* **To r. from premises,** déduire des conclusions des prémisses. **To r. on, about, a subject,** raisonner sur un sujet. **To r. with s.o.,** raisonner qn, avec qn. 2. *v.tr.* (*a*) **To r. that . . .,** arguer que. . . . (*b*) **To r. s.o. out of doing sth.,** faire entendre raison à qn. **reasoned,** *a.* 1. Raisonné; (refus) motivé. 2. Raisonnable. **reasoning**[1], *a.* Doué de raison. **reasoning**[2], *s.* Raisonnement *m;* dialectique *f.* **There is no r. with him,** il n'y a pas moyen de lui faire entendre raison.

reasonable ['ri:z(ə)nəbl], *a.* 1. (*a*) Raisonnable; équitable. **You must try to be r.,** il faut vous raisonner. **R. offer,** offre acceptable, raisonnable. (*b*) **R. suspicions,** soupçons bien fondés. 2. **R. prices,** prix modérés, raisonnables, abordables. **-ably,** *adv.* Raisonnablement.

reasonableness ['ri:z(ə)nəblnis], *s.* 1. Caractère *m* raisonnable; raison *f.* 2. Modération *f* (des prix).

reasoner ['ri:z(ə)nər], *s.* Raisonneur, -euse. **He is a bad r.,** il raisonne mal.

reassemble ['ri:ə'sembl]. 1. *v.tr.* (*a*) Rassembler; assembler de nouveau. **School reassembles tomorrow,** c'est demain la rentrée (des classes). (*b*) Remonter, remettre en état (une machine); remboîter (un meuble). 2. *v.i.* Se rassembler. **reassembly,** *s.* Remontage *m* (d'une machine, etc.); remboîtement *m* (d'un meuble).

reassert ['ri:ə'sə:t], *v.tr.* Réaffirmer (une conviction).

reassume ['ri:ə'sju:m], *v.tr.* Reprendre (un emploi, etc.); réassumer (une responsabilité).

reassurance ['ri:ə'ʃuərəns], *s.* 1. Action *f* de rassurer (qn). 2. *Ins:* Réassurance *f.*

reassure [ri:(:)ə'ʃuər], *v.tr.* 1. Rassurer, tranquilliser (qn) (**on, about,** sur). **To feel reassured,** se rassurer. 2. *Ins:* Réassurer. **reassuring,** *a.* (*Of news*) Rassurant.

reawaken ['ri:ə'weikən]. 1. *v.tr.* Réveiller (qn) de nouveau. **To r. s.o.'s love,** ranimer l'amour de qn. 2. *v.i.* Se réveiller de nouveau, encore; se ranimer.

rebarbative [ri'bɑ:bətiv], *a.* Rébarbatif, -ive, sinistre; rebutant; menaçant.

rebate ['ri:beit], s. Com: 1. Rabais m, escompte m. 2. Ristourne f; remboursement m; (on tax) décharge f.

rebel¹ ['reb(ə)l]. 1. a. Insurgé. 2. s. Rebelle mf; révolté, -ée; insurgé, -ée. To be a confirmed r., faire toujours la mauvaise tête.

rebel² [ri'bel], v.i. (rebelled) Se rebeller, se soulever (against, contre).

rebellion [ri'beljən], s. Rébellion f, révolte f (against, contre); soulèvement m.

rebellious [ri'beljəs], a. Rebelle. R. act, acte de rébellion. -ly, adv. En rebelle; d'un ton de défi.

rebelliousness [ri'beljəsnis], s. Esprit m de rébellion; insubordination f.

rebind ['ri:'baind], v.tr. (p.t. & p.p. rebound ['ri:'baund]) Relier (un livre) de nouveau, à neuf.

rebirth ['ri:'bə:θ], s. Renaissance f; retour m à la vie.

rebore¹ ['ri:'bɔ:r], s. F: Mec.E: Réalésage m.

rebore² [ri:'bɔ:r], v.tr. Mec.E: Réaléser; reforer.

reborn ['ri:'bɔ:n], a. Réincarné; né de nouveau. A r. hope, un espoir renaissant.

rebound¹ ['ri:baund], s. Rebondissement m, retour m brusque; ricochet m (d'une balle). F: To take s.o. on the r., profiter du moment de détente de qn (après une émotion).

rebound² [ri'baund], v.i. Rebondir.

rebound³. See REBIND.

rebroadcast¹ ['ri:'brɔ:dkɑ:st], s. W.Tel: Rediffusion f.

rebroadcast², v.tr. W.Tel: Rediffuser.

rebuff¹ [ri'bʌf], s. Rebuffade f; échec m. To meet with a r., essuyer un refus.

rebuff², v.tr. Repousser, rebuter.

rebuild ['ri:'bild], v.tr. (p.t. & p.p. rebuilt ['ri:'bilt]) Rebâtir, reconstruire. rebuilding, s. Reconstruction f; réfection f (d'un pont).

rebuke¹ [ri'bju:k], s. Réprimande f, blâme m.

rebuke², v.tr. Réprimander, blâmer (qn).

rebus ['ri:bəs], s. Rébus m,

rebut [ri'bʌt], v.tr. (rebutted) 1. Réfuter (une accusation, une théorie). 2. Rebuter, repousser (qn).

rebuttal [ri'bʌtl], s. Réfutation f.

recalcitrance [ri'kælsitrəns], s. Récalcitrance f; esprit m réfractaire.

recalcitrant [ri'kælsitrənt], a. & s. Récalcitrant, réfractaire; regimbeur, -euse.

recall¹ [ri'kɔ:l], s. 1. Rappel m (de qn). Dipl: Letters of r., lettres de rappel. 2. Rétractation f, révocation f. Decision past r., décision irrévocable. Lost beyond r., perdu irrévocablement.

recall², v.tr. 1. Rappeler (un ambassadeur). To r. s.o. to his duty, rappeler qn au devoir. 2. (a) Rappeler (qch. à qn). Legends that r. the past, légendes évocatrices du passé. (b) I don't r. his name, je ne me souviens pas de son nom. How vividly I r. the scene! avec quelle netteté je revois ce spectacle! 3. Annuler (un jugement). recalling, s. 1. Rappel m. 2. Révocation f.

recant [ri'kænt], v.tr. 1. v.tr. Rétracter, revenir sur (une opinion); abjurer (une erreur de doctrine). 2. v.i. Se rétracter.

recantation [,ri:kæn'teiʃ(ə)n], s. Rétractation f, abjuration f (of, de).

recap¹ ['ri:kæp], s. F: Récapitulation f. Let's do a r., faisons le point.

recap² ['ri:kæp], v.i. F: Récapituler; faire le point.

recapitulate ['ri:kə'pitjuleit], v.tr. Récapituler; reprendre les faits; faire le point.

recapitulation ['ri:kə,pitju'leiʃ(ə)n], s. Récapitulation f.

recapture¹ ['ri:'kæptʃər], s. Reprise f.

recapture², v.tr. Reprendre, recapturer.

recast¹ ['ri:'kɑ:st], s. 1. Refonte f. 2. Th: Nouvelle distribution des rôles.

recast², v.tr. (recast; recast) 1. Metall: Refondre (une cloche, etc.); 2. Th: Faire une nouvelle distribution des rôles de (la pièce).

recce ['reki], Mil: P: 1. s. Reconnaissance f. 2. v.i. Faire une reconnaissance.

recede [ri'si:d], v.i. 1. (a) S'éloigner, reculer. The coast recedes (from the ship), la côte s'éloigne. (b) (Of forehead) Fuir. 2. Art: (Of background) Se renfoncer. receding, a. (a) Qui s'éloigne, qui recule. R. tide, marée descendante. (b) R. forehead, front fuyant.

receipt¹ [ri'si:t], s. 1. Cu: A: & U.S: Recette f. 2. (a) Com: Recette. Receipts and expenses, recettes et dépenses. (b) Perception f (des impôts). (c) Réception f. On r. of this letter, au reçu de cette lettre. To pay on r., payer à la réception. To acknowledge r. of a letter, accuser réception d'une lettre. 3. (i) Reçu m, quittance f; (ii) récépissé m, accusé m de réception. R. for loan, reconnaissance f de dette. R. in full (discharge), quittance pour solde. To give a r. for sth., donner acquit de qch. re'ceipt-book, s. Carnet m de quittances. re'ceipt-stamp, s. Timbre-quittance m.

receipt², v.tr. Com: Acquitter, quittancer, décharger (une facture).

receivable [ri'si:vəbl], a. 1. Recevable. 2. Com: Bills r., effets m à recevoir.

receive [ri'si:v], v.tr. 1. (a) Recevoir. On receiving your letter, au reçu de votre lettre. To r. money, recevoir, toucher, de l'argent. Received with thanks, pour acquit. (b) Jur: To r. stolen goods, recéler (des objets volés). 2. (a) Recevoir (des invités). To r. s.o. with open arms, accueillir qn à bras ouverts. The proposal was well received, la proposition reçut un accueil favorable. (b) To r. s.o. into the Church, admettre qn dans l'Église. 3. (a) To r. sympathy, recevoir des marques de sympathie. (b) To r. a refusal, essuyer un refus. receiving¹, s. Récepteur, -trice. receiving², s. Réception f; recel m (d'objets volés). P: To be on the r. end, prendre qch.; en prendre pour son grade. re'ceiving-order, s. Jur: (In bankruptcy) Ordonnance f de mise sous séquestre. re'ceiving-station, s. W.Tel: Poste récepteur.

receiver [ri'si:vər], s. 1. (a) Personne f qui reçoit (qch.); destinataire mf (d'une lettre). (b) Adm: Receveur m (des deniers publics). (c) R. in bankruptcy, (in Eng.) administrateur m judiciaire (en matière de faillite); (in Fr.) syndic m de faillite. (d) Receleur m (d'objets volés). 2. (a) Récepteur m (de téléphone). To lift the r., décrocher (le récepteur). (b) Ch: Ind: Récipient m.

recent ['ri:s(ə)nt], a. Récent. Event of r. date, événement de fraîche date. -ly, adv. Récemment; tout dernièrement. As r. as yesterday, pas plus tard qu'hier. Until quite r., jusque dans ces derniers temps. They are r. married, ils sont mariés depuis peu.

receptacle [ri'septəkl], s. 1. Bot: Réceptacle m. 2. Récipient m.

reception [ri'sepʃ(ə)n], s. 1. (a) Réception f (d'un candidat à une académie). (b) R. office, r. desk (of hotel, etc.), la réception. R. clerk = RECEPTIONIST. Adm: R. order, permis m d'internement. (c) R. centre (for refugees, etc.), centre m d'accueil. 2. Accueil m. To give s.o. an unfriendly r., faire mauvais accueil à qn. 3. Réception (officielle). We are going to a r., nous allons en soirée. R. room, (i) salle f de réception; salon m; (ii) pièce f (par opposition à chambre à coucher). 4. W.Tel: Réception.

receptionist [ri'sepʃənist], s. Préposé(e) à la réception (d'un hôtel); réceptionniste f (dans un salon de beauté, etc.).

receptive [ri'septiv], a. Réceptif, -ive.

receptivity [,ri:sep'tiviti], s. Réceptivité f.

recess¹ [ri'ses], s. 1. (a) Vacances fpl (des tribunaux); intersession f (parlementaire). (b) Sch: Esp. U.S: (L'heure f de) la récréation. 2. (a) Recoin m. (b) Enfoncement m; rentrant m (de muraille); embrasure f (de fenêtre); niche f. R. under a staircase, soupente f d'escalier.

recess². 1. v.tr. Évider; chambrer; pratiquer un enfoncement, une alcôve, dans (une muraille); encastrer (la tête d'une vis, etc.). 2. v.i. U.S: (Of assembly) Suspendre la séance, les séances. recessed, a. Enfoncé; en retrait. R. arch, arc renforcé. R. head, tête encastrée (d'un boulon, etc.). recessing, s. Techn: Chambrage m; évidement m; encastrement m.

recession [ri'seʃ(ə)n], s. Recul m, retraite f, régression f. Pol. Ec: Récession f.

recessional [ri'seʃ(ə)n(ə)l], a. & s. Ecc: R. (hymn), hymne m de sortie du clergé.

recessive [ri'sesiv], a. 1. Rétrograde. 2. Biol: R. characteristic, caractère récessif, dominé.

rechristen ['ri:'kris(ə)n], v.tr. Rebaptiser.

recidivism [ri'sidivizm], s. Récidivité f.
recidivist [ri'sidivist], s. Récidiviste mf.
recipe ['resipi], s. 1. Cu: Recette f. Pharm: Formule f. Med: Ordonnance f. 2. Recette; moyen m (de faire qch.).
recipient [ri'sipiənt]. 1. a. Réceptif, -ive. 2. s. Personne f qui reçoit (un don); destinataire mf (d'une lettre); bénéficiaire mf (d'un chèque); donataire mf.
reciprocal [ri'siprɔk(ə)l]. 1. a. (a) Réciproque, mutuel, -elle. (b) Gram: (Verbe) réciproque. 2. s. Log: Réciproque f, inverse f. 3. a. & s. Mth: Geom: (Fonction f) inverse; (figure f) réciproque. R. ratio, raison f inverse. -ally, adv. 1. Réciproquement, mutuellement. 2. Mth: Inversement.
reciprocate [ri'siprəkeit]. 1. v.tr. (a) Se rendre mutuellement (des services). (b) Payer de retour (un sentiment). To r. s.o.'s good wishes, souhaiter la pareille à qn. 2. v.i. (a) Retourner le compliment. (b) Mec.E: (Of piston) Avoir un mouvement alternatif, un mouvement de va-et-vient. **reciprocating**, a. Mec.E: (Mouvement) alternatif; (machine) à mouvement alternatif.
reciprocation [ri,siprə'keiʃ(ə)n], s. 1. Action f de payer de retour (un sentiment); retour m (d'un compliment); 2. Mec.E: Alternation f (de mouvement); va-et-vient m inv.
reciprocity [,resi'prɔsiti], s. Réciprocité f.
recital [ri'sait(ə)l], s. 1. Récit m, narration f (d'un incident); énumération f (des détails). 2. Récitation f (d'une poésie). 3. Jur: Exposé m (des faits). 4. Mus: Audition f; récital m, -als.
recitation [,resi'teiʃ(ə)n], s. Récitation f.
recitative [,resitə'ti:v], s. Mus: Récitatif m.
recite [ri'sait], v.tr. 1. (a) Réciter, déclamer (un poème). (b) Abs. Réciter une pièce. 2. Jur: Exposer (les faits). 3. Énumérer (des détails).
reciter [ri'saitər], s. Diseur, -euse; récituer, -euse; déclamateur m. She's a good r., elle est bonne diseuse.
reckless ['reklis], a. Insouciant (of, de); téméraire. R. gambler, homme aventureux au jeu. Aut: R. driving, conduite imprudente, téméraire. R. driver, conducteur imprudent, F: chauffard m. -ly, adv. Témérairement; avec insouciance. He spends r., il dépense sans compter.
recklessness ['reklisnis], s. Insouciance f (of, de); imprudence f, témérité f.
reckon ['rek(ə)n]. 1. v.tr. (a) Compter, calculer. Abs. Reckoning from today, à compter d'aujourd'hui. To r. sth. among, with . . ., compter, ranger, qch. parmi. . . . (b) Estimer, juger. I r. he is forty, je lui donne quarante ans. (c) To r. s.o. as . . ., regarder qn comme. . . . 2. v.i. (a) Compter, calculer. (b) To r. (up)on sth., compter sur qch. reckon up, v.tr. Compter, calculer, supputer. To r. up one's losses, dresser le bilan de ses pertes. **reckon with**, v.i. 1. To r. with s.o., demander des comptes à qn. 2. To have to r. with s.o., avoir à compter avec qn. **reckoning**, s. (a) Compte m, calcul m. To be out in one's r., s'être trompé dans son calcul. Day of r., (i) jour de règlement; (ii) Lit: jour d'expiation. (b) Estimation f. To the best of my r., autant que j'en puis juger. (c) Nau: (Dead) r., estime f (du point). By dead r., à l'estime.
reclaim¹ [ri'kleim], s. Used in the phr. Past r., beyond r., perdu à tout jamais; qui ne se corrigera jamais.
reclaim², v.tr. (a) Réformer, corriger (qn). To r. s.o. from vice, tirer qn du vice. To r. young delinquents, redresser l'enfance coupable. (b) Défricher, assécher (du terrain); mettre (un marais) en valeur. Reclaimed land, terrain amendé. (c) Récupérer (un sous-produit). **reclaiming**, s. = RECLAMATION.
reclamation [,reklə'meiʃ(ə)n], s. 1. Réforme f (de qn). 2. Défrichement m (d'un terrain); assèchement m, mise f en valeur (des marais); récupération f (de sous-produits). 3. Réclamation f.
recline [ri'klain]. 1. v.tr. Reposer, appuyer, coucher (sa tête sur qch.). 2. v.i. Être couché, se reposer (on, sur); (of head) reposer, être appuyé (on, sur). Reclining on a couch, étendu, à demi couché, sur un canapé.
reclothe ['ri:'klouð], v.tr. 1. Rhabiller (qn). 2. Fournir de nouveaux vêtements à (qn).

recluse [ri'klu:s]. 1. a. Retiré du monde; reclus. 2. s. Reclus, -use; solitaire mf; anachorète m. To live the life of a r., vivre en anachorète, en ermite.
reclusion [ri'klu:ʒ(ə)n], s. Réclusion f.
recognition [,rekəg'niʃ(ə)n], s. Reconnaissance f. 1. (a) Fact which has obtained general r., fait qui a été reconnu de tous. (b) In r. of . . ., en reconnaissance de. . . . This artist won r., cet artiste s'imposa (à l'estime publique). 2. To alter sth. beyond, past, r., changer qch. au point de le rendre méconnaissable. Smile of r., sourire de reconnaissance. Av: R. light, feu m d'identification.
recognizable [,rekəg'naizəbl], a. Reconnaissable. Not r., méconnaissable.
recognizance [ri'kɔ(g)niz(ə)ns], s. Jur: 1. Caution personnelle; engagement m (par-devant le tribunal). To enter into recognizances, donner caution. 2. Somme fournie à titre de cautionnement.
recognize ['rekəgnaiz], v.tr. 1. To r. a government, reconnaître un gouvernement. To r. s.o. as king, reconnaître qn pour roi. 2. He knows he is wrong but won't r. it, il sait qu'il a tort mais ne veut pas l'admettre, le reconnaître, l'avouer. 3. To r. s.o. by his walk, reconnaître qn à sa démarche. I do not r. you, je ne vous remets pas. **recognized**, a. Reconnu, admis, reçu; (of manner, style, etc.) classique. The r. term, le terme consacré. Com: R. agent, agent accrédité, attitré.
recoil¹ [ri'kɔil], s. 1. (a) Rebondissement m, détente f (d'un ressort). (b) Recul m (d'une arme à feu); contre-coup m (d'une explosion). 2. Mouvement m de recul, de dégoût.
recoil², v.i. 1. (a) (Of spring) Se détendre. (b) (Of firearm) Reculer, repousser. 2. (Of pers.) Reculer (from, devant); se révolter (from, contre). To r. from doing sth., reculer devant l'idée de faire qch. 3. (Of evil) Retomber, rejaillir (on, sur).
recollect¹ [rekə'lekt], v.tr. Se rappeler (qch.); se souvenir de (qch.). I don't r. you, je ne vous remets pas. As far as I r., autant qu'il m'en souvienne.
recollect² ['ri:kə'lekt], v.tr. Assembler, réunir, collectionner (des personnes, des choses) de nouveau.
recollection [,rekə'lekʃ(ə)n], s. Souvenir m, mémoire f. I have a dim r. of it, j'en ai gardé un souvenir confus. To the best of my r., autant que je m'en souviens, que je m'en souvienne. It has never occurred within my r., cela n'est jamais arrivé de mon temps.
recommence [rekə'mens, 'ri:kə'mens], v.tr. & i. Recommencer.
recommend [,rekə'mend], v.tr. 1. To r. s.o. to do sth., recommander, conseiller, à qn de faire qch. I have been recommended (to come) to you, on m'a adressé à vous. 2. To r. a candidate for a post, recommander un candidat pour un emploi. She has little to r. her, elle n'a pas grand-chose pour elle. The hotel is to be recommended for its cooking, l'hôtel se recommande par sa cuisine. Not to be recommended, à déconseiller.
recommendable [,rekə'mendəbl], a. Recommandable; (chose) à conseiller.
recommendation [,rekəmen'deiʃ(ə)n], s. Recommandation f. 1. Letter of r., (lettre f de) recommandation. 2. The recommendations of the commission, les avis rendus par la commission.
recommission ['ri:kə'miʃ(ə)n], v.tr. (a) Réarmer (un navire). (b) Réintégrer (un officier) dans les cadres.
recompense¹ ['rekəmpens], s. 1. Récompense f (for, de). 2. Dédommagement m (for, de). As a r. for his trouble, pour prix de sa peine.
recompense², v.tr. 1. Récompenser (s.o. for sth., qn de qch.). 2. Dédommager (s.o. for sth., qn de qch.). 3. Compenser, réparer (un mal). 4. Payer de retour (un service).
reconcilable [rekən'sailəbl], a. Conciliable, accordable (with, avec).
reconcile ['rekənsail], v.tr. 1. Réconcilier, raccommoder, remettre bien ensemble (deux personnes). To become reconciled, se réconcilier. To r. s.o. to sth., faire accepter qch. à qn. To r. oneself to sth., se résigner à qch. 2. Concilier, faire accorder (des faits); mettre d'accord (deux points de vue).
reconciliation [,rekənsili'eiʃ(ə)n], s. 1. Réconciliation f, rapprochement m. 2. Conciliation f (d'opinions contraires).

recondite [ri'kɔndait, 'rekəndait], a. (Of knowledge) Abstrus, profond; (of style) obscur.

recondition ['ri:kən'diʃ(ə)n], v.tr. Rénover; remettre à neuf, en état; Com: reconditionner. **Reconditioned engine**, moteur révisé, reconditionné.

reconnaissance [ri'kɔnis(ə)ns], s. Mil: etc: Reconnaissance f. **R. aircraft**, avion m, de reconnaissance. **R. party**, détachement m en reconnaissance, d'exploration. To make a r., explorer le terrain.

reconnect ['ri:kə'nekt], v.tr. El.E: etc: Rebrancher (un câble, etc.).

reconnoitre [,rekə'nɔitər], v.tr. Mil: etc: Reconnaître (le terrain). Abs. Faire une reconnaissance; éclairer le terrain. **Reconnoitring party**, détachement m en reconnaissance. **reconnoitring**, s. Reconnaissance f.

reconquer ['ri:'kɔŋkər], v.tr. Reconquérir.

reconsider ['ri:kən'sidər], v.tr. 1. Considérer de nouveau, examiner à nouveau, reconsidérer, repenser (une question); reviser, revoir (un jugement). 2. Revenir sur (une décision).

reconsideration ['ri:kən,sidə'reiʃ(ə)n], s. Examen m à nouveau; reconsidération f (d'une question); revision f (d'un jugement).

reconsolidate ['ri:kən'sɔlideit], v.tr. Reconsolider.

reconstitute ['ri:'kɔnstitju:t], v.tr. Reconstituer.

reconstitution ['ri:kɔnsti'tju:[(ə)n], s. Reconstitution f.

reconstruct ['ri:kən'strʌkt], v.tr. 1. Reconstruire, rebâtir (un édifice). 2. To r. a crime, reconstituer un crime.

reconstruction ['ri:kən'strʌkʃ(ə)n], s. 1. Reconstruction f, réfection f; refonte f. **Educational r.**, refonte de l'organisation de l'enseignement. **Financial r.**, restauration financière. 2. Reconstitution f (d'un crime).

reconversion ['ri:kən'və:ʃ(ə)n], s. Pol.Ec: Reconversion f.

reconveyance ['ri:kən'veiəns], s. Jur: Rétrocession f.

recopy ['ri:'kɔpi], v.tr. Recopier.

record¹ ['rekɔ:d], s. 1. Jur: (a) Enregistrement m (d'un fait). (Of judgment, fact) To be on r., être enregistré, être authentique. It is on r. that . . ., il est rapporté dans l'histoire que. . . . F: Off the r., en secret, entre nous. (b) R. of a court, feuille f d'audience. (c) R. of evidence, procès-verbal m de témoignage. (d) Minute f (d'un acte). 2. (a) Note f, mention f. To make, keep, a r. of an observation, faire une note d'une observation; noter une observation. (b) Registre m. R. of attendances, registre de présence. 3. pl. Archives f, annales f. Com: Archives. **The Public Records**, les Archives nationales. **Official record(s) of a society**, bulletin officiel d'une société. **The R. office**, les Archives. 4. Monument m, document m, souvenir m (de qch.). 5. Carrière f, dossier m (de qn). **Service r.**, état m de services. His past r., sa conduite passée. **Police r.**, casier m judiciaire. To have a clean r., avoir un casier judiciaire intact, vierge. 6. Sp: etc: Record m. To break, beat, the r., battre le record. To hold a r., détenir un record. **World r.**, record mondial, du monde. Ind: R. output, production constituant un record. R. figure, chiffre m record. At r. speed, à une vitesse record. 7. (Of phonograph). To listen to records by . . ., écouter des enregistrements par. . . . **Long-playing r.**, (disque) microsillon m. 'record-breaking, a. Qui bat tous les records. 'record(-)changer, s. Changeur m de disques. 'record-cutter, s. Aiguille f à graver; style m (d'enregistrement phonographique). 'record-holder, s. Sp: Recordman m, recordwoman f, pl. recordmen, recordwomen. 'record-library, s. Discothèque m; phonothèque m. 'record-player, s. Électrophone m, tourne-disques m inv.

record² [ri'kɔ:d], v.tr. 1. (a) Enregistrer (un fait); consigner (qch.) par écrit; prendre acte de (qch.); minuter (un jugement, etc.). To r. one's vote, voter. (b) Relater, narrer, rapporter (qch.). (c) (Of instrument) Enregistrer, marquer. 2. Gramophones: Enregistrer, graver (une chanson, etc.). To r. on tape, enregistrer sur bande. **recording¹**, a. 1. The r. angel, l'ange qui tient le registre des actes de chacun. 2. (Instrument) enregistreur. **recording²**, s. 1. (a) Enregistrement m; consignation f par écrit. (b) Narration f, relation f. 2. Gramophones: Enregistrement. **Recording head**, tête enregistreuse. Cin: Enregistrement, prise f de son.

recorder [ri'kɔ:dər], s. 1. Jur: Avocat nommé par la Couronne pour remplir certaines fonctions de juge. 2. (a) He was a faithful r. of what he saw, il transcrivait fidèlement ce qu'il voyait. (b) Archiviste m. 3. Appareil enregistreur. **Tape r.**, Magnétophone m (R.t.m.). Aut: Trip r., enregistreur de distance. Cin: Sound r., appareil d'enregistrement du son. 4. Mus: Flûte f à bec.

recork ['ri:'kɔ:k], v.tr. Reboucher (une bouteille).

recount¹ [ri'kaunt], v.tr. Raconter.

recount² ['ri:,kaunt], s. Nouveau dépouillement du scrutin.

recount³ ['ri:'kaunt], v.tr. Recompter.

recoup [ri'ku:p], v.tr. 1. Dédommager (qn). To r. one's losses, abs. to r., se dédommager, se rattraper, de ses pertes. 2. Jur: Défalquer.

recourse [ri'kɔ:s], s. 1. Recours m. To have r. to sth., avoir recours à qch.; recourir à qch. 2. Expédient m.

recover¹ [ri'kʌvər], v.tr. 1. Recouvrer, retrouver (un objet perdu); retrouver (son appétit). Ind: To r. by-products from coal, récupérer des sous-produits de la houille. To r. one's breath, reprendre haleine. To r. consciousness, reprendre ses sens; revenir à soi. 2. Regagner (de l'argent perdu); rentrer en possession de (ses biens); rentrer dans (ses droits, ses débours); recouvrer, récupérer (une créance). To r. one's fortunes, se refaire une situation. To r. lost time, rattraper le temps perdu. To r. lost ground, reprendre du terrain perdu; se rattraper. To r. sth. from s.o., reprendre qch. à qn. Jur: To r. damages, abs. to r., from s.o., obtenir des dommages-intérêts de qn. 3. To r. one's health, v.i. to r., guérir; recouvrer la santé; se rétablir. To r. from an illness, se remettre, guérir, d'une maladie. To be quite recovered, être tout à fait remis, rétabli. To r. from one's astonishment, revenir, se remettre, de son étonnement. Prices have recovered, les cours se sont relevés. 4. To r. oneself, abs. to r., se remettre, se ressaisir. To r. one's balance, se ressaisir; reprendre, retrouver, son équilibre.

recover², re-cover ['ri:'kʌvər], v.tr. Recouvrir; regarnir (des meubles).

recoverable [ri'kʌvərəbl], a. Recouvrable, récupérable.

recovery [ri'kʌvəri], s. 1. Recouvrement m (d'un objet perdu). Ind: Récupération f (de sous-produits). 2. Jur: Action for r. of property, (action en) revendication f. 3. (a) Rétablissement m, guérison f (de qn). The patient is making a good r., le malade est en bonne voie de guérison. To be past r., être dans un état désespéré. (b) Redressement m (économique); relèvement m, reprise f (des affaires). Sp: To make a brilliant r., se ressaisir, se raccrocher. 4. Fenc: Remise f en garde.

re-create ['ri:kri'eit], v.tr. Recréer.

recreation [,rekri'eiʃ(ə)n], s. Récréation f, divertissement m, délassement m. A few moments of r., quelques moments de détente f. **recre'ation-ground**, s. 1. Sch: Cour f de récréation. 2. Terrain m de jeux, de sports.

re-creation ['ri:kri'eiʃ(ə)n], s. Nouvelle création.

recreative ['rekrieitiv], a. Récréatif, divertissant.

recriminate [ri'krimineit], v.i. Récriminer.

recrimination [ri'krimi'neiʃ(ə)n], s. Récrimination f.

recriminatory [ri'kriminətri], recriminatory [ri'kriminətri], a. Récriminatoire; récriminateur, -trice.

recross ['ri:'krɔs], v.tr. Retraverser; repasser (une rivière).

recrudescence ['ri:kru:'des(ə)ns], s. Recrudescence f. R. of activity, regain m d'activité.

recrudescent ['ri:kru:'des(ə)nt], a. Recrudescent.

recruit¹ [ri'kru:t], s. Recrue f. A raw r., F: un bleu. R. drill, école f du soldat.

recruit², v.tr. 1. (a) Recruter (une armée, des partisans); racoler (des hommes pour l'armée). **The new party was largely recruited from the middle classes**, le nouveau parti faisait de nombreuses recrues dans la bourgeoisie. (b) To r. supplies, se réapprovisionner. 2. O: To r. one's health, abs. to r., se restaurer, se remettre, se retremper. **recruiting**, s. Mil: Recrutement m. R. officer, officier recruteur. R. board, conseil m de révision. R. station, bureau m de recrutement.

recruitment [ri'kru:tmənt], s. Recrutement m (de troupes, etc.).

rectal ['rekt(ə)l], a. Anat: Rectal, -aux. R. **injection**, lavement m.

rectangle ['rektæŋgl], s. Rectangle m.

rectangular [rek'tæŋgjulər], a. Rectangulaire.

rectifiable [ˌrekti'faiəbl], a. Rectifiable.

rectification [ˌrektifi'keiʃ(ə)n], s. 1. Rectification f, (i) d'une erreur; (ii) Dist: de l'alcool, etc. 2. El.E: Redressement m (du courant alternatif).

rectifier ['rektifaiər], s. 1. Dist: Rectificateur m. 2. El: Redresseur m, rectificateur (de courant). R. **station**, poste m de redressement.

rectify ['rektifai], v.tr. 1. (a) Rectifier, corriger (une erreur); réparer (un oubli). (b) Dist: Rectifier (l'alcool). 2. El.E: Redresser (le courant). **rectifying**, a. Rectificatif, -ive. W.Tel: R. **device**, système redresseur.

rectilineal [ˌrekti'liniəl], **rectilinear** [ˌrekti'liniər], a. Rectiligne. Phot: **Rapid r. lens**, objectif rectilinéaire.

rectitude ['rektitjuːd], s. Rectitude f (de conduite); droiture f (de caractère).

recto ['rektou], s. Typ: Recto m (de la page).

rector ['rektər], s.m. 1. (a) Ch. of Eng: = Curé. (b) R.C. Ch: Supérieur (d'un séminaire, etc.). 2. (a) Recteur (d'une université). (b) Scot: Directeur (d'une école secondaire).

rectorial [rek'tɔːriəl], a. Sch: Rectoral, -aux.

rectory ['rektəri], s. Ecc: = Presbytère m, cure f.

rectum ['rektəm], s. Anat: Rectum m.

recultivate ['riː'kʌltiveit], v.tr. Remettre en valeur, en culture (des terres).

recumbency [ri'kʌmbənsi], s. Position couchée.

recumbent [ri'kʌmbənt], a. Couché, étendu. R. **figure (on tomb)**, gisant m. Geol: R. **fold**, pli couché.

recuperate [ri'kjuːpəreit]. 1. v.tr. (a) Remettre, rétablir (qn). (b) Ind: To r. **waste heat**, récupérer la chaleur perdue. 2. v.i. Se remettre, se rétablir; reprendre des forces.

recuperation [riˌkjuːpə'reiʃ(ə)n], s. 1. Rétablissement m, guérison f. 2. Ind: Récupération f.

recuperative [ri'kjuːpəreitiv], a. 1. (Pouvoir) de rétablissement. 2. (Remède) restauratif, réparateur, régénérateur.

recuperator [ri'kjuːpəreitər], s. Ind: Artil: Récupérateur m.

recur [ri'kəːr], v.i. (**recurred**) 1. Revenir (**to a subject**, sur un sujet). 2. (a) To r. **to the memory**, revenir, se retracer, à la mémoire. (b) (Of event, etc.) Se reproduire, se renouveler; (of occasion) se représenter. **recurring**, a. Périodique. **Ever-r.**, qui revient sans cesse. Mth: R. **decimal**, fraction décimale périodique.

recurrence [ri'kʌrəns], s. Réapparition f, renouvellement m, retour m. Med: Récidive f (d'une maladie). To be of frequent r., revenir fréquemment.

recurrent [ri'kʌrənt], a. 1. Anat: Bot: Récurrent. 2. Périodique; qui revient souvent. Mth: R. **series**, série récurrente.

recusant ['rekjuz(ə)nt]. 1. s. Eng. Ecc. Hist: Récusant m. 2. a. & s. Réfractaire (mf) (**against**, à).

recut ['riː'kʌt], v.tr. Recouper; retailler (une lime).

red [red]. I. 1. a. (**redder**) (a) Rouge; (deep) pourpre. R. **lips**, lèvres vermeilles. R. (-**rimmed**) **eyes**, yeux rouges. **To turn, go, r.**, rougir; (of sky, etc.) rougeoyer. **It's like a r. rag to a bull**, c'est comme le rouge pour les taureaux. F: **It makes him see r.**, il voit rouge quand il entend (dire) cela. **To see r.**, se fâcher tout rouge. Cu: R. **meat**, (i) viande saignante; (ii) (viande de) bœuf (m). R. **granite**, granit rose. **The R. Sea**, la Mer Rouge. Art: R. **chalk**, sanguine f. Ent: R. **Admiral**, vulcain m. S.a. CENT 1, ENSIGN 1, HERRING, INDIAN 2, LIGHT[1] 2. (b) (Of hair) Roux f. rousse. (c) Pol: Rouge; de l'extrême gauche. **The r. flag**, le drapeau rouge. 2. a. & s. (In Fr. a.inv.) **Cherry r.**, rouge cerise. **Fiery r.**, rouge feu. II. s. (a) Rouge m. **Dressed in r.**, habillé de, en rouge. (b) Pol: Rouge mf. (c) Bill: **The r.**, la bille rouge. (d) F: **To be in the r.**, avoir une balance déficitaire. **'red-'blooded**, a. (Of pers.) Vigoureux, robuste. **'red-cap**, s. 1. Mil: F: Soldat m de la police militaire. 2. U.S: Rail: Porteur m. **'red-'eyed**, a. 1. Aux yeux rouges. 2. Aux yeux éraillés. **'red-'faced**, a. Rougeaud, sanguin. **'red-'haired**, a. Roux, f. rousse. **red-'handed**, a. **To be caught r.-h.**, être pris sur le fait, en flagrant délit, F: la main dans le sac.

'red-head, s. F: Rouquin, -ine. **She's a lovely r.-h.**, c'est une belle rouquine. **'red-'hot**, a. 1. (Chauffé au) rouge. **To make sth. r.-h.**, porter qch. au rouge. 2. F: R.-h. **Communist**, communiste ardent; communiste à tous crins. **'red 'lead** [led], s. Minium m. **'red-'letter**, attrib.a. F: R.-l. **day**, (i) jour de fête; (ii) jour mémorable; jour pour lequel on fait une croix à la cheminée. **'red-'nosed**, a. Au nez rouge. **'red-'roofed**, a. (Maison, etc.) à toit rouge. **'red 'tape**, s. 1. Bolduc m (rouge) (des documents officiels). 2. F: Chinoiseries administratives; bureaucratie f, paperasserie f. **Today, r. t. reigns supreme**, aujourd'hui tout est bureaucratisé.

redbreast ['redbrest], s. See ROBIN 2.

redbrick ['redbrik], attrib.a. Sch: Journ: F: R. **universities**, centres universitaires provinciaux (de conception moderne, à contraster avec Oxford et Cambridge).

redcoat ['redkout], s. Hist: Soldat anglais.

redden ['red(ə)n]. 1. v.tr. Rougir (qch.). 2. v.i. Devenir rouge; rougir; (of sky) rougeoyer; (of leaves) roussir.

reddish ['rediʃ], a. (a) Rougeâtre. (b) Roussâtre.

reddle ['redl], s. Ocre f rouge.

redecorate ['riː'dekəreit], v.tr. Peindre, tapisser (un appartement) à nouveau.

redeem [ri'diːm], v.tr. 1. Racheter, rembourser (une obligation); dégager (un nantissement); amortir (une dette); purger (une hypothèque). **To r. one's watch (from pawn)**, retirer, dégager, sa montre. 2. Tenir, accomplir (sa promesse). 3. (a) Libérer, racheter (un esclave). (b) **His good points r. his faults**, ses qualités rachètent, compensent, ses défauts. **redeeming**, a. 1. Rédempteur, -trice. 2. Qui fait compensation. R. **feature**, qualité f qui rachète les défauts.

redeemable [ri'diːməbl], a. Fin: (Of stock) Rachetable, remboursable, amortissable.

redeemer [ri'diːmər], s. Theol: **The R.**, le Rédempteur.

redemption [ri'dempʃ(ə)n], s. 1. (a) Remboursement m, amortissement m (d'une obligation); rachat m (d'un emprunt); dégagement m (d'un nantissement); purge f (d'une hypothèque). R. **fund**, caisse f d'amortissement. (b) **Sale with power of r.**, vente avec faculté de rachat. 2. Rachat (d'un esclave). Theol: Rédemption f (du genre humain). 3. Rachat (d'un crime, etc.). **Crime past r.**, crime irréparable. **Spoilt beyond (all hope of) r.**, abîmé irrémédiablement.

redemptive [ri'demptiv], a. Rédempteur, -trice.

redirect ['riːdai'rekt, -di-], v.tr. Faire suivre (une lettre).

rediscover ['riːdis'kʌvər], v.tr. Redécouvrir; retrouver.

redistribute ['riːdis'tribju(ː)t], v.tr. (a) Redistribuer. (b) Répartir à nouveau.

redistribution ['riːˌdistri'bjuːʃ(ə)n], s. (a) Redistribution f. (b) Nouvelle répartition.

redness ['rednis], s. 1. Rougeur f. 2. Rousseur f (des cheveux).

redolence ['redələns], s. 1. Odeur f suave; parfum m. 2. Odeur forte (**of**, de).

redolent ['redələnt], a. 1. Odorant, parfumé. R. **of spring**, qui exhale une odeur de printemps, qui respire le printemps. 2. Qui a une forte odeur (**of**, de). **Sauce r. of garlic**, sauce qui fleure l'ail.

redouble[1] ['riː'dʌbl], s. Cards: Surcontre m.

redouble[2] ['riː'dʌbl], v.tr. 1. Replier (un tissu, etc.); plier en quatre. 2. Cards: **To r. spades**, surcontrer pique.

redouble[3] [ri'dʌbl]. 1. v.tr. Redoubler (ses cris, ses instances, etc.). 2. v.i. Redoubler. **redoubling**, s. Redoublement m (de joie, de zèle).

redoubt [ri'daut], s. Fort: Redoute f, réduit m.

redoubtable [ri'dautəbl], a. Redoutable, formidable.

redound [ri'daund], v.i. 1. Contribuer (**to**, à). **This will r. to your credit**, votre réputation y gagnera. 2. Résulter; rejaillir (**to**, sur). **The advantages that r. to us**, les avantages qui en résultent pour nous.

redpoll ['redpoul], s. 1. Orn: Linotte f; sizerin m. 2. Husb: **Redpolls**, célèbre race de bovins roux sans cornes.

redraft ['riː'drɑːft], v.tr. Rédiger de nouveau.

re-draw ['riː'drɔː], v.tr. (-**drew** [druː]; -**drawn**) 1. Com: Faire retraite (**on s.o.**, sur qn). 2. Redessiner.

redress¹ [ri'dres], s. Redressement m, réparation f (d'un tort); réforme f (d'un abus). *Jur:* Legal r., réparation légale. **Injury beyond r., past r.,** tort irréparable.

redress² [ri'dres], v.tr. 1. Rétablir (l'équilibre). 2. Redresser, réparer (un tort); corriger, réformer (un abus).

redress³ ['ri:'dres], v.tr. *Th:* To r. a play, costumer une pièce à nouveau.

redshank ['redʃæŋk], s. *Orn:* Chevalier m gambette.

redskin ['redskin], s. *Ethn:* Peau-Rouge m.

redstart ['redstɑ:t], s. *Orn:* Rouge-queue m.

reduce [ri'dju:s], v.tr. 1. (a) Réduire, rapetisser (un dessin); amincir, amenuiser (une planche); (in length) raccourcir. v.i. Do you want to r.? voulez-vous maigrir? *Cu:* To r. a sauce, faire réduire une sauce. (b) Réduire, abaisser (la température); (ra)baisser, diminuer (le prix, etc.). **Reduced from 5 shillings,** réduction sur l'ancien prix de cinq shillings. To r. expenses, diminuer la dépense; faire des économies. To r. speed, diminuer de vitesse; ralentir la marche. *Ind:* To r. the output, ralentir la production. *El:* To r. the voltage, abaisser la tension. (c) Atténuer (un contraste). *Phot:* Affaiblir, baisser (un cliché dur). (d) (Of illness) Affaiblir (qn); amaigrir (qn). 2. (a) To r. sth. to ashes, to dust, réduire qch. en cendres, en poussière. **Clothes reduced to rags,** vêtements à l'état de guenilles. (b) To r. a fraction to its lowest terms, ramener une fraction à sa plus simple expression. To r. everything to a single principle, tout ramener à un seul principe. (c) To r. bribery to a system, ériger la corruption en système. 3. (a) To r. s.o. to silence, faire taire qn. (b) *Mil:* Réduire (une ville révoltée). 4. He was reduced to begging, il en était réduit à mendier son pain. 5. (a) To r. s.o. to the level of beasts, ravaler qn au niveau des bêtes. (b) *Mil:* Réduire (un homme) à un grade inférieur; rétrograder, casser (un sous-officier). 6. *Ch:* Réduire (un oxyde). 7. *Med:* Réduire (une fracture); remettre (une épaule démise). **reduced,** a. 1. Réduit. At (greatly) r. prices, au (grand) rabais; en solde. 2. In r. circumstances, dans l'indigence, dans la gêne.

reducer [ri'dju:sər], s. *Ch: etc:* Réducteur m.

reducible [ri'dju:sibl], a. Réductible (to, à).

reduction [ri'dʌkʃ(ə)n], s. 1. Rapetissement m (d'un dessin, etc.); amincissement m (d'une planche, etc.). R. compasses, compas m de réduction. *Automation:* Data r., traduction f des informations. 2. (a) Réduction f, diminution f (des prix); baisse f (de température). *Jur:* Relaxation f (d'une peine). *Ind:* R. of staff, compression f du personnel. *Phot:* Affaiblissement m (d'un cliché). *Mec.E:* R. of gear ratio, démultiplication f. (b) *Com:* Rabais m. To make a r. on an article, faire une remise sur un article. 3. *Mil:* Réduction (d'une ville). 4. *Mil:* Rétrogradation f (d'un sous-officier). 5. *Ch:* Réduction (d'un oxyde). 6. *Med:* Réduction (d'une fracture). Open r., réduction sanglante.

redundance [ri'dʌndəns], **redundancy** [ri'dʌndənsi], s. 1. *Lit:* Redondance f, tautologie f, pléonasme m. 2. Surabondance f. 3. Surplus m, excédent m; (of workers) surnombre m. **Redundancy payment,** compensation pour perte d'emploi faite aux ouvriers en surnombre.

redundant [ri'dʌndənt], a. 1. *Lit:* (Mot) redondant, pléonastique, tautologique, qui fait double emploi. 2. Surabondant; (ouvrier(s)) en surnombre.

reduplicate [ri'dju:plikeit], v.tr. Redoubler, répéter.

reduplication [ri,dju:pli'keiʃ(ə)n], s. Redoublement m.

redwood ['redwud], s. *Bot:* 1. Séquoia m, Wellingtonia m. 2. *Dy: etc:* (Bois m de) brésil, brésillet m.

re-echo [ri(:)'ekou]. 1. v.tr. Répéter, renvoyer (un son). 2. v.i. Retentir, résonner.

reed [ri:d], s. 1. *Bot:* Roseau m; jonc m à balais. To lean on a broken r., s'appuyer sur un roseau. 2. *Poet:* Chalumeau m, pipeau m. 3. *Mus:* (a) Anche f (de hautbois, etc.). (b) (In orchestra) The reeds, les instruments m à anche. 4. Peigne m (de métier à tisser). **'reed-bed,** s. Roselière f. **'reed-mace,** s. *Bot:* Massette f; quenouille f. **'reed-pipe,** s. *Mus:* Tuyau m à anche. **'reed-stop,** s. *Organ:* Jeu m d'anches. **'reed-warbler,** s. *Orn:* (Rousserolle f) effarvate f.

re-edit ['ri:'edit], v.tr. Rééditer (d'anciens ouvrages); donner une nouvelle édition critique (d'un texte).

re-educate ['ri:'edjukeit], v.tr. *Med:* Rééduquer (les muscles, les centres nerveux d'un paralysé, etc.).

re-education ['ri,edju'keiʃ(ə)n], s. *Med:* Rééducation f (physique) (d'un accidenté, d'un paralytique).

reedy ['ri:di], a. 1. Abondant en roseaux; couvert de roseaux. 2. R. voice, voix flûtée; voix ténue. The r. oboe, le hautbois nasillard.

reef¹ [ri:f], s. *Nau:* Ris m. To take in a r., (i) prendre un ris; (ii) agir avec circonspection. To shake out a r., larguer un ris. **'reef-knot,** s. Nœud plat, nœud droit. **'reef-point,** s. Garcette f de ris.

reef², v.tr. 1. To r. a sail, prendre un ris dans une voile. 2. Rentrer (le beaupré, etc.).

reef³, s. 1. Récif m, banc m de rochers (à fleur d'eau). Coral r., récif de corail. Submerged r., récif sous-marin; écueil m, brisant m. 2. *Gold-min:* Filon m de quartz aurifère; reef m.

reefer ['ri:fər], s. 1. *Nau:* (Pers.) Cargueur m. 2. *Cost:* Veste f quartier-maître. 3. *P: Esp. U.S:* Cigarette dopée au hachisch.

reek¹ [ri:k], s. 1. *Lit. & Scot:* (a) Fumée f. (b) Vapeur f, exhalaison f. 2. (a) Odeur forte, âcre. R. of tobacco, relent m de tabac. (b) Atmosphère f fétide.

reek², v.i. 1. *Scot:* (Of chimney) Fumer. 2. *Lit:* Exhaler des vapeurs; fumer. (Of street, etc.) To r. with crime, suer le crime. 3. Exhaler une mauvaise odeur. To r. of garlic, empester, puer, l'ail. This room is reeking of tobacco, ça empoisonne le tabac ici. **reeking,** a. 1. Fumant. 2. Empestant, puant.

Reekie ['ri:ki], s. *Scot:* Auld R., la vieille Enfumée, *i.e.* Édimbourg.

reel¹ [ri:l], s. 1. *Tex: etc:* Dévidoir m, bobine f; touret m (pour câbles). 2. Moulinet m (de canne à pêche). *F:* (Straight) off the r., d'arrache-pied; (tout) d'une traite; d'affilée. 3. Bobine (de coton). R. of paper, bobine de papier. **Paper in reels,** papier continu. *Cin:* Film r., (i) bobine; (ii) bande f, rouleau m, de film.

reel², v.tr. (a) *Tex: etc:* Dévider, bobiner (le fil, etc.). To r. off verses, réciter d'un trait, *F:* dégoiser, des vers. (b) *Nau:* To r. in, up, the log-line, remonter la ligne de loch. **reeling,** s. *Tex: etc:* Dévidage m, bobinage m.

reel³, v.i. 1. Tournoyer. My head reels, la tête me tourne. 2. Chanceler; (of drunken man) tituber. He reeled out, back, il sortit, il recula, en chancelant. The ship reeled under the force of the wave, le navire s'abattit sous le coup de la vague.

reel⁴, s. Danse écossaise (d'un mouvement très vif); branle écossais.

re-elect ['ri:i'lekt], v.tr. Réélire.

re-election ['ri:i'lekʃ(ə)n], s. Réélection f.

re-eligible ['ri:'elidʒibl], a. Rééligible.

re-embark ['ri:im'bɑ:k], v.tr. & i. Rembarquer.

re-embarkation ['ri:,emba:'keiʃ(ə)n], s. Rembarquement m.

re-employ ['ri:im'plɔi], v.tr. Remployer, réemployer (qn).

re-employment ['ri:im'plɔimənt], s. *Pol. Ec: etc:* Remploi m, réemploi m.

re-enact ['ri:i'nækt], v.tr. 1. Remettre en vigueur (une loi). 2. Reconstituer, reproduire (une scène).

re-engage ['ri:in'geidʒ], v.tr. (a) Rengager (des troupes); réintégrer (des employés). (b) *Mec.E:* Rengrener (une roue dentée). *Aut:* To re-e. the clutch, rembrayer.

re-enlist ['ri:in'list], v.i. Se rengager.

re-enlistment ['ri:in'listmənt], s. *Mil:* Rengagement m. That man is a re-e., cet homme est un rengagé.

re-enter ['ri:'entər]. 1. v.i. (a) Rentrer. (b) To re-e. for an examination, se présenter de nouveau à un examen. 2. v.tr. (a) Rentrer dans (un endroit). (b) Inscrire de nouveau (un article sur un compte).

re-entry ['ri:'entri], s. Rentrée f.

re-equip ['ri:i'kwip], v.tr. Rééquiper.

re-equipment ['ri:i'kwipmənt], s. Rééquipement m.

re-erect ['ri:i'rekt], v.tr. 1. Reconstruire; remonter (une machine). 2. Dresser (qch.) de nouveau.

re-erection ['ri:i'rekʃ(ə)n], s. 1. Reconstruction f; réédification f; remontage m (d'un appareil). 2. Remise f en place (de qch.).

re-establish ['riːisˈtæbliʃ], v.tr. **1.** Rétablir. To re-e. s.o. in public esteem, réhabiliter qn dans l'opinion. To re-e. s.o. in his possessions, réintégrer qn dans ses biens. **2.** To re-e. one's health, se rétablir.

re-establishment ['riːisˈtæbliʃmənt], s. Rétablissement m; réintégration f (in, dans).

reeve¹ [riːv], s. **1.** Hist: Premier magistrat; bailli m. **2.** (In Canada) Président m (du conseil municipal).

reeve², v.tr. (rove [rouv]; reeved, rove) Nau: To r. a rope, passer un cordage (through a block, dans une poulie). To r. a tackle, passer les garants d'un palan. To r. a rope to a yard, capeler un cordage sur une vergue.

re-examination ['riːigˌzæmiˈneiʃ(ə)n], s. **1.** Nouvel examen. **2.** Jur: Nouvel interrogatoire.

re-examine ['riːigˈzæmin], v.tr. **1.** Examiner de nouveau. **2.** Jur: Interroger de nouveau (un témoin).

re-export¹ ['riːˈekspoːt], **re-exportation** ['riːˌekspɔːˈteiʃ(ə)n], s. Réexportation f.

re-export² ['riːeksˈpoːt], v.tr. Réexporter.

ref [ref], s. F: Sp: Arbitre m.

refashion ['riːˈfæʃ(ə)n], v.tr. Refaçonner.

refasten ['riːˈfɑːsn], v.tr. Rattacher; ragrafer.

refection [riˈfek(ʃ)(ə)n], s. **1.** Réfection f (des forces, de l'esprit). **2.** A: Repas léger; collation f.

refectory [riˈfektəri], s. Réfectoire m.

refer [riˈfəːr], v. (referred) **1.** v.tr. (a) Rapporter, rattacher (un fait à une cause). (b) To r. a matter to s.o., s'en référer à qn d'une question. To r. a question to s.o.'s decision, s'en rapporter, s'en remettre, à la décision de qn. To r. a matter to a tribunal, soumettre une affaire à un tribunal. (c) To r. s.o. to s.o., renvoyer, adresser, qn à qn. 'The reader is referred to . . .,' "se reporter à. . ." (Of bank) To r. a cheque to drawer, refuser d'honorer un chèque. (d) Sch: Ajourner (un candidat). **2.** v.i. (a) Se référer (à une autorité); se reporter (à un document). Referring to your letter . . ., comme suite à votre lettre. . . . (b) (Of statement) To r. to sth., se rapporter, avoir rapport, avoir trait, à qch. (c) (Of pers.) Faire allusion (à qn). I am not referring to you, je ne parle pas de vous; ce n'est pas à vous que j'en ai. To r. to a fact, faire mention d'un fait; signaler un fait. We will not r. to it again, n'en reparlons plus.

referee¹ [refəˈriː], s. (a) Sp: Jur: Arbitre m. Board of referees, commission arbitrale. (b) Répondant m, recommandataire m.

referee², v.i. & tr. (refereed) Sp: To r. a match, arbitrer un match.

reference ['refr(ə)ns], s. **1.** (a) Renvoi m, référence f (d'une question à une autorité). (b) Compétence f, pouvoirs mpl (d'un tribunal). Terms of r. of a commission, mandat m, attributions fpl, d'une commission. Outside the r. of the commission, hors de la compétence de la commission. **2.** (a) With r. to my letter of the 20 inst. . . ., me référant à, comme suite à, ma lettre du 20 ct. . . . Surv: etc: R. mark, repère m. (b) Work of r., ouvrage à consulter, ouvrage de référence. **3.** Rapport m. To have r. to sth., avoir rapport, avoir trait, se rapporter, à qch. In r., with r., to your letter . . ., en ce qui concerne votre lettre. . . . Without r. to . . ., sans tenir compte de. . . . **4.** To make r. to a fact, faire mention d'un fait, signaler un fait. (A) r. was made to this conversation, on a fait allusion à, on a parlé de, cette conversation. **5.** Renvoi (dans un livre). (On map) R. point, point coté. Com.Corr: R. AB, référence, à rappeler (dans la réponse), AB. Typ: R. mark, renvoi. Footnote r., appel m de note. S.a. CROSS-REFERENCE. **6.** (a) To give a r. concerning s.o., fournir des renseignements sur qn. To take up s.o.'s references, prendre des renseignements sur qn. To have good references, avoir de bonnes références, de bonnes recommandations. (b) (Pers.) Référence; Jur: répondant m. To give s.o. as a r., se recommander de qn.

referendum [refəˈrendəm], s. Referendum m.

refill¹ ['riːfil], s. Objet m de remplacement, de rechange; recharge f, cartouche f (d'encre, etc.); pile f de rechange (pour lampe électrique); mine f de rechange (pour porte-mine); feuilles fpl de rechange (pour carnet à feuilles mobiles).

refill² ['riːfil], v.tr. Remplir (qch.) (à nouveau). To r. the tanks with water, regarnir les réservoirs d'eau.

refine [riˈfain]. **1.** v.tr. (a) Raffiner, affiner (les métaux); purger (l'or); raffiner (le sucre, le pétrole). (b) Raffiner (les goûts); épurer, purifier (les mœurs). **2.** v.i. Se raffiner. **refined**, a. **1.** (Or) fin, affiné (sucre) raffiné. **2.** (Goût) raffiné, délicat; (homme) distingué, cultivé. **refining**, s. Metall: Affinage m, raffinage m, affinement m; épuration f. Ind: R. furnace, four m d'affinage, à affiner.

refinement [riˈfainmənt], s. **1.** Affinage m (des métaux); raffinage m (du sucre, du pétrole). **2.** Raffinement m (du goût, de qn). O: A person of r., un(e) raffiné(e); un(e) délicat(e). **3.** Raffinement, subtilité f (de la pensée). R. of cruelty, raffinement de cruauté.

refiner [riˈfainər], s. Raffineur m (de sucre); affineur m (de métaux).

refinery [riˈfainəri], s. Raffinerie f.

refit [riːˈfit], v.tr. (refitted) **1.** Nau: (i) Radouber (un navire). Abs. (Of ship) (i) Entrer en radoub; (ii) réarmer. **2.** Rajuster (une machine, etc.). **3.** Regarnir, remonter, réaménager (une usine, etc.). **refitting**, s. Nau: (a) Radoub m. (b) Réarmement m.

reflect [riˈflekt]. **1.** v.tr. (a) (Of surface) Réfléchir, refléter (la lumière, une image); renvoyer (la chaleur, la lumière). Trees reflected in the water, arbres qui se reflètent dans l'eau. (b) Action that reflects credit on s.o., action qui fait honneur à qn. Your fame will be reflected upon your children, votre renom rejaillira sur vos enfants. **2.** v.i. (a) Méditer (on, upon, sur); réfléchir (à, sur). To r. that . . ., penser, se dire, que. . . . To r. (on) how . . ., se demander comment. . . . (b) To r. on s.o., adresser une critique, un reproche, à qn. To r. on s.o.'s honour, porter atteinte à l'honneur de qn. (c) (Of action) Faire du tort (on s.o., à qn); nuire à la réputation de (qn).

reflection [riˈflek(ʃ)(ə)n], s. **1.** Réfléchissement m, réflexion f (de la lumière, d'une image). Opt: Angle of r., angle de réflexion. **2.** Réflexion, reflet m, image f. To see one's r. in a mirror, voir son image dans un miroir. **3.** To cast reflections on s.o., censurer, critiquer, qn. This is a r. on your honour, c'est une atteinte à votre honneur. **4.** On r., (toute) réflexion faite. To do sth. without due r., faire qch. sans avoir suffisamment réfléchi. **5.** pl. **Reflections**, considérations f, pensées f.

reflective [riˈflektiv], a. **1.** (Of surface) Qui réfléchit; réfléchissant. **2.** (Homme, esprit) réfléchi; réflectif, -ive. -ly, adv. D'un air réfléchi.

reflectiveness [riˈflektivnis], s. Caractère réfléchi.

reflector [riˈflektər], s. Réflecteur m. Aut: Cy: Catadioptre m; cataphote m (R.t.m.).

reflex¹ ['riːfleks], s. **1.** Reflet m. **2.** Physiol: Réflexe m. Med: Knee r., réflexe rotulien.

reflex², a. **1.** Physiol: (Of movement) Réflexe. **2.** (Of influence) Indirect. **3.** (Of thoughts, etc.) Introspectif, -ive. **4.** Phot: R. camera, (appareil m) reflex m. **5.** Mth: R. angle, angle rentrant.

reflexion [riˈflek(ʃ)(ə)n], s. = REFLECTION.

reflexive [riˈfleksiv], a. & s. Gram: (Verbe, pronom) réfléchi. -ly, adv. Au sens réfléchi.

refloat ['riːˈflout], v.tr. Renflouer, (re)mettre à flot (un navire échoué).

reflux ['riːflʌks], s. **1.** Reflux m; refluement m. **2.** (Tide) Jusant m.

reforge ['riːˈfɔːdʒ], v.tr. Reforger.

reform¹ ['riːˈfɔːm], s. Réforme f.

reform². **1.** v.tr. (a) Réformer (un abus); apporter des réformes à (une administration). (b) Réformer, corriger (qn). **2.** v.i. Se réformer, se corriger. **reformed**, a. **1.** (Église) réformée. **2.** He's a r. character, le diable s'est fait ermite. **reforming**, a. Réformateur, -trice.

re(-)form ['riːˈfɔːm]. **1.** v.tr. Reformer (un bataillon, etc.). **2.** v.i. (Of troops) Se reformer.

reformation [refəˈmeiʃ(ə)n], s. Réformation f, réforme f. Rel.H: The R., la Réforme.

reformatory [riˈfɔːmətri], s. Maison f de correction.

reformer [riˈfɔːmər], s. Réformateur, -trice.

reformist [riˈfɔːmist], a. & s. Pol: Rel.H: Réformiste (m).

refract [ri'frækt], *v.tr. Ph:* Réfracter, briser (un rayon de lumière). **To be refracted,** se réfracter. **refracting,** *a. Ph:* Réfringent. **Double-r.,** biréfringent. *S.a.* TELESCOPE[1].

refraction [ri'frækʃ(ə)n], *s. Ph:* Réfraction *f. Opt:* **Double r.,** biréfringence *f.*

refractive [ri'fræktiv], *a.* Réfractif, -ive, réfringent. **R. index,** indice *m* de réfraction. **Doubly r.,** biréfringent.

refractoriness [ri'fræktrinis], *s.* **1.** Indocilité *f*, insoumission *f*, mutinerie *f.* **2.** (*a*) *Ch: Min: etc:* Nature *f* réfractaire. (*b*) *Med:* Opiniâtreté *f* (d'une toux, etc.).

refractory [ri'frækt(ə)ri], *a.* **1.** (*Of pers.*) Réfractaire, indocile, mutin, insoumis. **2.** *Ch:* Réfractaire; à l'épreuve du feu. **3.** (Toux, etc.) opiniâtre.

refrain[1] [ri'frein], *s. Pros: Mus:* Refrain *m* .

refrain[2], *v.i.* Se retenir, s'abstenir (**from,** de). **He could not r. from smiling,** il ne put s'empêcher, se défendre, de sourire. **It is impossible to r. from admiring this work,** on ne peut laisser d'admirer ce travail.

refrangible [ri'frændʒibl], *a. Ph:* Réfrangible.

refresh [ri'freʃ]. **1.** *v.tr.* (*a*) Rafraîchir; (*of rest*) délasser, récréer (qn). **To r. the eye,** reposer l'œil. **To awake refreshed,** s'éveiller bien reposé. (*b*) Rafraîchir (la mémoire). (*c*) (*Of rain, etc.*) Rafraîchir (l'air). **2.** *v.i.* (*a*) Se rafraîchir, se reposer. (*b*) Se restaurer. **refreshing,** *a.* Rafraîchissant. **R. sleep,** sommeil reposant, réparateur. **It was quite r. to hear him,** cela faisait du bien de l'entendre.

refresher [ri'freʃər], *s.* **1.** Chose *f* qui rafraîchit. *F:* **Let's have a r.,** on va boire quelque chose, allons boire un pot. **2.** *Sch:* **R. course,** cours *m* de perfectionnement.

refreshment [ri'freʃmənt], *s.* **1.** (*a*) Rafraîchissement *m*, délassement *m.* (*b*) **To take some r.,** manger ou boire quelque chose; se rafraîchir. *Rail:* **R. room,** buffet *m.* **2.** *pl.* **Refreshments,** rafraîchissements (servis au buffet, etc.).

refrigerant [ri'fridʒərənt], *a. & s. Med: Ind:* Réfrigérant (*m*).

refrigerate [ri'fridʒəreit], *v.tr. Ind:* Réfrigérer, frigorifier. **refrigerating**[1], *a.* Réfrigérant, frigorifique. **refrigerating**[2], *s.* Réfrigération *f*, frigorification *f.* **R. plant,** installation *f* frigorifique.

refrigeration [ri,fridʒə'reiʃ(ə)n], *s.* Réfrigération *f*; frigorification *f*; l'industrie *f* du froid.

refrigerator [ri'fridʒəreitər], *s.* (*a*) Réfrigérateur *m*; Frigidaire *m* (*R.t.m.*); *F:* frigo *m.* (*b*) Chambre *f* frigorifique. **R. car, van,** wagon *m* frigorifique.

refringent [ri'frindʒənt], *a. Ph:* Réfringent.

refuel ['ri:'fjuəl], *v.i.* (**refuelled**) *Nau: Aut: Av:* Se réapprovisionner, se ravitailler, en combustible; faire le plein d'essence, de fuel, etc. **refuelling,** *s.* Ravitaillement en combustible. *Av:* **R. point,** soute *f* à essence, à carburants, à combustibles.

refuge ['refju:dʒ], *s.* **1.** (*a*) Refuge *m*, abri *m* (**from,** contre). **Place of r.,** lieu *m* de refuge, d'asile. **Haven of r.,** port de salut. **To seek r.,** chercher refuge. **To take r.,** se réfugier (**in,** dans). **To take r. behind a pretext,** se retrancher derrière un prétexte. (*b*) **God is my r.,** Dieu est mon recours, mon refuge. **2.** Lieu de refuge, d'asile. *Mount:* Refuge. **Street r.,** refuge.

refugee [,refju(:)'dʒi:], *s.* Réfugié. ée.

refulgence [ri'fʌldʒəns], *s.* Splendeur *f*, éclat *m.*

refulgent [ri'fʌldʒənt], *a.* Resplendissant, éclatant.

refund[1] ['ri:fʌnd], *s.* (*a*) Remboursement *m.* (*b*) Ristourne *f.*

refund[2] [ri:'fʌnd], *v.tr.* **1.** (*a*) Rembourser (de l'argent) (**to s.o.,** à qn). **To have money refunded,** rencaisser de l'argent. (*b*) Ristourner (un paiement en trop); restituer (de l'argent). **2.** (*a*) **To r. s.o.,** rembourser qn. **refunding,** *s.* Remboursement *m.*

refurbish ['ri:'fə:biʃ], *v.tr.* Remettre à neuf.

refurnish ['ri:'fə:niʃ], *v.tr.* Meubler de neuf, remeubler (un appartement); remonter (sa maison).

refusal [ri'fju:z(ə)l], *s.* **1.** Refus *m.* **To give a flat r.,** refuser (tout) net. **I will take no r.,** je n'admets pas de refus. *Jur:* **R. of justice,** déni *m* de justice. **2.** Droit *m* de refuser. **To have the r. of sth.,** avoir le droit d'accepter ou de refuser qch. **To have the first r. of sth.,** avoir la première offre de qch.

refuse[1] ['refju:s]. **1.** *s.* Rebut *m* (de boucherie); déchets *mpl*; ordures *fpl* (de marché). **Household r.,** ordures ménagères. **Town r.,** résidus urbains; ordures; gadoues *fpl.* **Garden r.,** balayures *fpl*, détritus *m*, de jardin. **R. bin,** boîte *f* aux ordures; poubelle *f.* **R. dump,** voirie *f*; terrain *m* de décharge publique, la décharge (publique). **R. collection, service** *m* du nettoiement, de la voirie. **2.** *a.* De rebut. *Ind:* **R. water,** eaux-vannes *fpl.*

refuse[2] [ri'fju:z], *v.tr.* **1.** Refuser (une offre, un don). **That is not to be refused,** cela n'est pas de refus. **2.** (*a*) Rejeter, repousser (une requête). **To r. s.o. sth.,** refuser qch. à qn. **He was refused a hearing,** on refusa de l'entendre. **I have never been refused,** on ne m'a jamais rien refusé. (*b*) **To r. to do sth.,** refuser de faire qch.; se refuser à faire qch. **3.** **Horse that refuses (the fences),** cheval qui refuse, qui se dérobe (devant les obstacles).

refutable [rə'fjutəbl], *a.* Réfutable.

refutation [,refju(:)'teiʃ(ə)n], *s.* Réfutation *f.*

refute [ri'fju:t], *v.tr.* Réfuter (une opinion, qn). **To r. a statement,** démontrer la fausseté d'une dire.

refuter [ri'fju:tər], *s.* Réfutateur, -trice.

regain [ri'gein], *v.tr.* Regagner; reconquérir (une province); recouvrer (la liberté). **To r. possession of sth.,** rentrer en possession de qch. **To r. consciousness,** reprendre connaissance, revenir à soi. **To r. one's footing,** reprendre pied. **To r. strength,** reprendre des forces.

regal ['ri:g(ə)l], *a.* Royal, -aux. **-ally,** *adv.* Royalement; en roi.

regale [ri'geil], *v.tr.* Régaler. **To r. s.o. with a good meal, with a story,** regaler qn d'un bon repas, d'une anecdote.

regalia [ri'geiliə], *s.pl.* (*a*) Insignes *m* de la royauté; joyaux *m* de la Couronne. (*b*) Insignes (de franc-maçon, etc.).

regard[1] [ri'ga:d], *s.* **1. In this r.,** à cet égard, à ce point de vue. **With r. to . . .,** quant à . . .; pour ce qui concerne . . .; en ce qui se rattache à . . . **Dispute with r. to a sale,** dispute à l'occasion d'une vente. **In r. to, of . . .,** en ce qui concerne . . . . **2.** Égard *m* (**to, for,** à, pour); attention *f* (**to, for,** à). **To pay no r. to . . .,** ne faire aucune attention à. . . . **To have no r. for human life,** faire peu de cas de la vie humaine. **R. must be had, paid, to . . .,** on doit avoir égard à, faire attention à. . . . **Having r. to . . .,** si l'on tient compte de . . .; eu égard à. . . . **3.** (*a*) Égard, respect *m*, estime *f.* **To have (a) great r. for s.o., to hold s.o. in high r.,** tenir qn en haute estime. **To show r. for s.o.,** témoigner de l'estime, des égards, pour qn. **Out of r. for s.o.,** par égard pour qn. (*b*) *pl.* **To send s.o. one's kind regards,** envoyer le bonjour à qn. **Give my kind regards to your brother,** faites mes amitiés à votre frère. **With kind regards from . . .,** avec les sincères amitiés de. . . .

regard[2], *v.tr.* **1.** *A. & Lit:* Regarder (fixedly, fixement). **2.** Faire attention, prendre garde, à (qn, qch.). **To r. s.o.'s advice,** tenir compte des conseils de qn. **3.** (*a*) **To r. sth. as a crime,** regarder, considérer, qch. comme un crime. (*b*) **To r. sth. with horror,** regarder qch. avec horreur. **To r. sth. with suspicion,** avoir des soupçons au sujet de qch. **4.** Concerner. **That does not r. me,** cela ne me regarde pas. **As regards . . .,** pour ce qui regarde . . .; en ce qui concerne. . . . **As far as it regards you,** en ce qui vous touche. **regarding,** *prep.* A l'égard de; concernant; quant à. **R. your enquiry,** en ce qui concerne votre demande. **To entertain suspicions r. s.o.,** avoir des soupçons à l'endroit de qn.

regardless [ri'ga:dlis], *a.* Peu soigneux, -euse (**of,** de); inattentif, -ive (**of,** à). **R. of the consequences,** sans se soucier des conséquences. **R. of expense,** sans regarder à la dépense. *P:* **She was got up r.,** elle s'était mise sur son trente et un. **-ly,** *adv.* Avec insouciance, avec indifférence.

regardlessness, *s.* Insouciance *f*, indifférence *f* (**of,** pour).

regatta [ri'gætə], *s.* Régate(s) *f(pl).*

regency ['ri:dʒənsi], *s.* Régence *f.*

regenerate [ri'dʒenəreit]. **1.** *v.tr.* Régénérer. **2.** *v.i.* Se régénérer. **regenerating,** *a.* **1.** Régénérateur, -trice. **2.** *Tchn:* **R. furnace,** (four *m*) régénérateur *m.* **R. plant,** régénérateur.

regeneration [ri,dʒenə'reiʃ(ə)n], s. Régénération f.
regenerative [ri'dʒenərətiv], a. = REGENERATING.
regenerator [ri'dʒenəreitər], s. 1. (Pers.) Régénérateur, -trice. 2. Ind: Régénérateur m, récupérateur m.
regent ['ri:dʒənt], a. & s. Régent, -ente. **Prince r.,** prince régent.
regicidal [redʒi'saidl], a. Régicide.
regicide[1] ['redʒisaid], s. Régicide mf.
regicide[2], s. (Crime m de) régicide m.
regild ['ri:'gild], v.tr. Redorer.
regime [rei'ʒi:m], s. Régime m. **The new industrial r.,** le nouveau régime industriel.
regimen ['redʒimen], s. O: Med: etc: Régime m.
regiment[1] ['redʒ(i)mənt], s. Régiment m.
regiment[2] [redʒi'ment], v.tr. 1. Enrégimenter (des volontaires, des ouvriers). 2. Organiser, administrer (les industries, les ressources d'un pays).
regimental [,redʒi'mentl]. 1. a. Du régiment, de régiment; régimentaire. 2. s.pl. Regimentals, uniforme m. **In full regimentals,** en grand uniforme, en grande tenue.
Regina [ri'dʒainə]. Pr.n.f. Jur: **R. v. Smith,** la Reine en cause avec Smith.
regimentation [,redʒimen'teiʃ(ə)n], s. 1. Enrégimentation f. 2. Adm: Ind: Réglementation f (de l'industrie), planning (industriel).
region ['ri:dʒ(ə)n], s. Région f. **The arctic regions,** les régions, les terres f, arctiques. **The nether regions,** les enfers m. F: **This costs in the r. of £500,** cela coûte dans les, quelque chose comme, £500.
regional ['ri:dʒənl], a. Régional, -aux.
regionalism ['ri:dʒənəlizm], s. Régionalisme m.
register[1] ['redʒistər], s. 1. (a) Registre m; matricule f. Nau: **Ship's r.,** livre m de bord. **There are ten million (annuitants, etc.) on the registers,** il y a dix millions d'immatriculés. **The registers of births, marriages, and deaths,** les registres de l'état civil. **R. of voters,** liste électorale. **Trade R.,** registre du Commerce. (b) Nau: Adm: Acte m de nationalité. 2. Mus: Registre (d'un instrument, de la voix); étendue f (de la voix). 3. Registre (d'un fourneau); rideau m, trappe f (d'une cheminée). 4. Compteur m (kilométrique, etc.). S.a. CASH-REGISTER. 5. Typ: **In r.,** en registre. **Out of r.,** mal en registre.
register[2]. 1. v.tr. (a) Enregistrer; inscrire (un nom); immatriculer (une auto). (Abs.) Mil: Recenser. **To r. a birth,** déclarer une naissance. **To r. a trade-mark,** déposer une marque de fabrique. **To r. with the police,** se faire inscrire à la police (pour permis de séjour, etc.). (b) **To r. luggage,** enregistrer des bagages. **To r. a letter,** recommander une lettre. (c) (Of thermometer) Marquer (tant de degrés). (d) Typ: Engr: Repérer (les impressions). (e) Cin: Enregistrer (une émotion). **His face registered disappointment,** son visage a marqué de la déception. F: **It didn't r. (with her),** elle n'a rien pigé. 2. v.i. (a) (Of holes and pins, etc.) Coïncider exactement. Typ: Être en registre. (b) S'inscrire sur le registre (d'un hôtel, etc.). **registered,** a. (a) Enregistré, inscrit, immatriculé. Com: **R. pattern,** modèle déposé. (b) Post: **R. parcel,** paquet recommandé. **R. letter,** lettre recommandée. (c) State **r. nurse,** infirmière diplômée d'État. **registering,** a. Tchn: Enregistreur, -euse. S.a. SELF-REGISTERING.
registrar ['redʒistrɑ:r, redʒis'trɑ:r], s. 1. Jur: Greffier m. 2. Officier m de l'état civil. **The registrar's office,** le bureau de l'état civil. **The R. General,** le Conservateur des actes de l'état civil. **To get married before the r.** = se marier civilement. 3. Secrétaire m et archiviste m (d'une université).
registration [,redʒis'treiʃ(ə)n], s. 1. Enregistrement m, inscription f; immatriculation f (de matériel roulant, etc.). **R. of mortgages,** inscription hypothécaire. **R. of a letter, a parcel,** recommandation f d'une lettre, d'un colis. Mil: Recensement m. **R. of a trade-mark,** dépôt m d'une marque de fabrique. **R. of luggage,** enregistrement des bagages. (Hotel) **r. form,** fiche policière. **R. number,** numéro m matricule. Aut: **R. plate,** plaque f minéralogique, d'immatriculation. Adm: **R. number (of car),** numéro minéralogique. **A car with the r. number SPF 342,** une voiture immatriculée SPF 342. 2. Engr: Typ: Repérage m.

registry ['redʒistri], s. 1. Enregistrement m. Nau: **Certificate of r.,** certificat m d'inscription; acte m de nationalité. **Port of r.,** port d'armement; port d'attache. 2. **R.** (office). (a) Bureau m d'enregistrement; greffe m. (b) Bureau de l'état civil. **To be married at a r.** (office) = se marier civilement. (c) Bureau, agence f, de placement (de domestiques).
regrade [,ri:'greid], v.tr. Reclasser. **regrading,** s. Reclassement m (de fonctionnaires, etc.).
regress[1] ['ri:gres], s. (a) Retour m en arrière; rétrogression f. (b) Astr: Rétrogradation f.
regress[2] [ri'gres], v.i. Régresser. Astr: Rétrograder.
regression [ri'greʃ(ə)n], s. 1. = REGRESS[1]. 2. Biol: Régression f. 3. Mth: Rebroussement m (d'une courbe).
regressive [ri'gresiv], a. Régressif, -ive.
regret[1] [ri'gret], s. Regret m. **To have no regrets,** n'avoir aucun regret. **I state the fact with r.,** je le dis à regret. **Much to my r.,** I find myself constrained to . . ., à mon grand regret, je me vois forcé de. . . .
regret[2], v.tr. (regretted) Regretter. **I r. having deceived him,** j'ai regret de l'avoir trompé. **I r. to have to leave you,** je regrette d'avoir à vous quitter. **I r. to have to inform you that . . .,** j'ai le regret de vous annoncer que. . . . **We very much r. to hear . . .,** nous sommes désolés d'apprendre. . . . **It is to be regretted that . . .,** il est à regretter, il est regrettable, que + sub.
regretful [ri'gretful], a. (Of pers.) Plein de regrets. **-fully,** adv. Avec regret, à regret.
regrettable [ri'gretəbl], a. Regrettable; à regretter. **-ably,** adv. Regrettablement. **There was a r. small attendance,** il est à regretter que l'assistance ait été si peu nombreuse.
regrind ['ri:'graind], v.tr. (reground ['ri:'graund]) 1. Rebroyer, remoudre (du blé, du café). 2. (a) Remoudre, réaffuter (un outil). (b) Roder à nouveau (une soupape). **regrinding,** s. 1. Rebroyage m, remoulage m. 2. (a) Réaffutage m. (b) Rodage m à nouveau.
regroup ['ri:'gru:p], v.tr. Reclasser; regrouper. Rural Ec: Remembrer. **regrouping,** s. (a) Rural Ec: **R. of land,** remembrement m des terres. (b) Fin: **R. of shares,** regroupement m d'actions.
regrowth ['ri:'grouθ], s. Croissance nouvelle; régénération f. For: Repeuplement m.
regular ['regjulər]. I. a. Régulier, -ière. 1. **R. footsteps,** pas réguliers, mesurés. **As r. as clockwork,** exact comme une horloge; réglé comme du papier à musique. **My r. time for going to bed,** l'heure habituelle à laquelle je me couche. **To do sth. as a r. thing,** faire qch. régulièrement. Rail: **The r. travellers,** les abonnés m. **R. reader,** lecteur, -trice, fidèle. (At restaurant) **Our r. waiter,** notre garçon habituel. **R. staff,** employés permanents. 2. Réglé, rangé. **Man of r. habits,** homme rangé dans ses habitudes. 3. (a) Dans les règles; réglementaire. **The r. expression,** l'expression consacrée. (b) Ordinaire; normal, -aux. Ind: **R. model,** modèle courant; type courant. (c) Gram: (Verbe) régulier. (d) Mil: **R. troops,** troupes régulières. **R. officer,** officier de carrière. 4. F: (Intensive) Vrai, véritable. **R. rascal,** vrai coquin. **R. set-to,** bataille f en règle. **-ly,** adv. 1. Régulièrement. 2. F: Véritablement, franchement. II. regular, s. 1. Ecc: Régulier m; religieux m. 2. Mil: Soldat m de l'armée permanente. **Regulars,** troupes régulières. 3. Habitué, -ée; bon client; F: (at public house) pilier m de café.
regularity [,regju'læriti], s. Régularité f. **R. of attendance,** assiduité f.
regularization [,regjulərai'zeiʃ(ə)n], s. Régularisation f.
regularize ['regjuləraiz], v.tr. Régulariser.
regulate ['regjuleit], v.tr. 1. Régler, ajuster (une machine, etc.). 2. Régler, diriger (les affaires); réglementer (les affaires); fixer les règles pour (une procédure, etc.). **To r. one's life by s.o.,** se régler sur qn.
regulation [,regju'leiʃ(ə)n], s. 1. (a) Réglage m (d'un chronomètre, etc.); Nau: régulation f (des compas). (b) Règlement m, réglementation f (des affaires, etc.). **To bring under r.,** réglementer. 2. (a) Règlement arrêté m, ordonnance f. **Hospital regulations,** régime m des hôpitaux. (b) attrib. Réglementaire. Mil: **R. revolver,** revolver d'ordonnance. S.a. TRAFFIC[1] 2.

'egulator ['regjuleitər], s. 1. (Pers.) Régulateur, -trice, régleur, -euse. 2. (Device) Régulateur m; modérateur m (de moteur). Mch: R. lever, registre m (de prise de vapeur). S.a. DRAUGHT-REGULATOR.

'egurgitate [ri:'gə:dʒiteit]. 1. v.tr. Régurgiter, regorger. 2. v.i. (Of liquid, etc.) Refluer, regorger.

'egurgitation [ri:,gə:dʒi'teiʃ(ə)n], s. Régurgitation f.

'ehabilitate [,ri:(h)ə'biliteit], v.tr. Réhabiliter; réadapter (des réfugiés); reclasser (des ouvriers); réintégrer (des démobilisés). rehabilitating, a. (Of order, etc.) Réhabilitant, réhabilitoire.

'ehabilitation ['ri:(h)ə,bili'teiʃ(ə)n], s. 1. Réhabilitation f. 2. Assainissement m (des finances). 3. R. of disabled men, rééducation f des mutilés. R. centre, centre m de rééducation professionnelle. R. of occupied territories, reconstruction f des pays occupés. R. (of refugees), réadaptation f (de réfugiés). R. of ex-servicemen, réintégration f des démobilisés dans la vie civile.

'ehandle ['ri:'hændl], v.tr. 1. Traiter à nouveau (un sujet). 2. Remanier (un ouvrage).

'eharden ['ri:'hɑ:dn], v.tr. Metall: Retremper (le métal). rehardening, s. Retrempe f.

'ehash¹ ['ri:hæʃ], s. Réchauffé m; F: nouvelle mouture (d'un livre, etc.).

'ehash² [ri:'hæʃ], v.tr. Réchauffer (un vieux conte, etc.).

'ehear [ri:'hiər], v.tr. (reheard ['ri:'hə:d]) Entendre (une cause, etc.) de nouveau. rehearing, s. Nouvelle audition.

'ehearsal [ri'hə:s(ə)l], s. Th: Répétition f. The dress r., la (répétition) générale; l'avant-première f.

'ehearse [ri'hə:s], v.tr. Th: Répéter (une pièce).

'eheat ['ri:'hi:t], v.tr. (a) Réchauffer. (b) Metall: Recuire, récrouir.

'ehouse ['ri:'hauz], v.tr. Reloger, (se) recaser. rehousing, s. Relogement m, recasement m.

'eign¹ [rein], s. Règne m. In the r. of . . ., sous le règne de. . . .

'eign², v.i. Régner (over, sur).

'eimbursable [,ri:im'bə:səbl], a. Remboursable.

'eimburse [,ri:im'bə:s], v.tr. 1. Rembourser (une somme). 2. To r. s.o. (for) his expenses, rembourser qn de ses frais.

'eimbursement [,ri:im'bə:smənt], s. Remboursement m.

'eimport¹ [ri:'impɔ:t], s. Réimportation f.

'eimport² ['ri:im'pɔ:t], v.tr. Réimporter.

'eimportation ['ri:,impɔ:'teiʃ(ə)n], s. Réimportation f.

'eimpose ['ri:im'pouz], v.tr. Typ: Réimposer (une feuille); remanier (les pages).

'eimposition ['ri:,impə'ziʃ(ə)n], s. Réimposition f.

'eimpression ['ri:im'preʃən], s. Typ: Publ: Réimpression f.

'ein¹ [rein], s. Rêne f (de cheval monté); guide f (de cheval de voiture). To hold the reins, tenir les rênes; tenir la bride; tenir les guides. With a loose r., with a slack r., (i) (chevaucher) à bout de rênes; (ii) (mener ses gens) mollement. To give a horse the reins, lâcher la bride à un cheval. To give r. to one's anger, lâcher la bride à sa colère. To draw r., serrer la bride; s'arrêter. To keep a tight r. on, over, s.o., tenir la bride serrée, tenir la bride haute, à qn. To drop the reins, lâcher, abandonner les rênes; abandonner.

'ein², v.tr. To r. in a horse, serrer la bride à un cheval. Abs. To r. in, ramener son cheval au pas. To r. s.o. in, retenir qn; ramener qn sous la discipline. To r. up a horse, arrêter un cheval. To r. back a horse, (faire) reculer un cheval.

'eincarnate [ri:in'kɑ:neit]. 1. v.tr. Réincarner. 2. v.i. Se réincarner.

'eincarnation ['ri:inkɑ:'neiʃ(ə)n], s. Réincarnation f.

'eincorporate ['ri:in'kɔ:pəreit], v.tr. Réincorporer.

'eindeer ['reindiər], s. Z: Renne m. A herd of reindeer, un troupeau de rennes.

'einflate ['ri:in'fleit], v.tr. Regonfler (un ballon).

'einforce [,ri:in'fɔ:s], v.tr. 1. Renforcer (une armée, un son); appuyer (une demande). 2. Renforcer (un mur, etc.); consolider (des fondations); entretoiser (un bâtiment); nervurer (une tôle, etc.). Reinforced concrete, béton armé.

reinforcement [,ri:in'fɔ:smənt], s. 1. (a) Mil: Renforcement m (d'une garnison). (b) Const: etc: Renforcement, renforçage m; armature f (du béton). 2. Mil: (Usu. pl.) To await reinforcements, attendre un renfort, des renforts.

reingratiate ['ri:in'greiʃieit], v.tr. Faire rentrer en grâce (qn) (with, auprès de).

reinsert ['ri:in'sə:t], v.tr. 1. Réinsérer. 2. Remettre (une pièce) en place.

reinstall ['ri:in'stɔ:l], v.tr. Réinstaller.

reinstate ['ri:in'steit], v.tr. 1. Réintégrer (qn) (dans ses fonctions); rétablir (un fonctionnaire). 2. Remettre, rétablir (qch.).

reinstatement ['ri:in'steitmənt], s. 1. Réintégration f (de qn dans ses fonctions). 2. Rétablissement m (de qch.).

reinsurance ['ri:in'ʃuər(ə)ns], s. Ins: Réassurance f; contre-assurance f, pl. contre-assurances.

reinsure ['ri:in'ʃuər], v.tr. Ins: Réassurer.

reintegrate [,ri:'intigreit], v.tr. (a) Rétablir (qch.) dans son intégrité. (b) To r. s.o. in his possessions, réintégrer qn dans ses possessions.

reintegration ['ri:,inti'greiʃ(ə)n], s. (a) Rétablissement intégral. (b) Réintégration f (de qn dans son domaine, etc.).

reinter ['ri:in'tə:r], v.tr. (reinterred) Enterrer de nouveau, renterrer.

reinterrogate ['ri:in'terəgeit], v.tr. Réinterroger (un témoin, etc.).

reintroduce ['ri:,intrə'dju:s], v.tr. Réintroduire.

reinvent ['ri:in'vent], v.tr. Réinventer.

reinvest ['ri:in'vest], v.tr. Trouver un nouveau placement pour (des fonds).

reinvestment ['ri:in'vestmənt], s. Fin: Nouveau placement.

reinvigorate ['ri:in'vigəreit], v.tr. Revigorer, redonner de la vigueur à (qn).

reinvite ['ri:in'vait], v.tr. Réinviter.

reissue¹ ['ri:'isju:], s. 1. Nouvelle émission (de billets de banque, etc.). 2. Publ: Nouvelle édition; nouveau tirage.

reissue², v.tr. 1. Fin: Émettre de nouveau (des actions, etc.). 2. Donner une nouvelle édition, un nouveau tirage (d'un livre).

reiterate [ri:'itəreit], v.tr. Réitérer, répéter.

reiteration [ri:,itə'reiʃ(ə)n], s. Réitération f, répétition f.

reiterative [ri:'itərətiv], a. Réitératif, -ive.

reject¹ ['ri:dʒekt], s. Pièce f de rebut. Export r., article (de rebut) impropre, non destiné, à l'exportation.

reject² [ri'dʒekt], v.tr. (a) Rejeter; repousser (une offre); rejeter (un projet de loi); réprouver (une doctrine). (b) Refuser (des marchandises, un candidat). Ind: To r. a casting, mettre une pièce au rebut.

rejection [ri'dʒekʃ(ə)n], s. 1. Rejet m (d'un projet de loi, etc.); repoussement m (d'une mesure); refus m (d'une offre). 2. pl. Ind: Rejections, pièces f de rebut; rebuts m.

rejoice [ri'dʒɔis]. 1. v.tr. Réjouir (qn). I am rejoiced to hear it, je me réjouis, je suis heureux, de l'entendre. 2. v.i. (a) Se réjouir (at, over, de). (b) To r. in sth., jouir de qch.; posséder qch. Iron: He rejoiced in the name of Bloggs, il s'honorait du nom de Bloggs.

rejoicing¹, a. 1. (Of news, etc.) Réjouissant. 2. Joyeux, -euse, jubilant; plein de joie. rejoicing², s. Réjouissance f, allégresse f; la fête.

rejoin¹ [ri'dʒɔin], v.i. Répliquer, répondre.

rejoin² ['ri:'dʒɔin]. 1. v.tr. (a) Rejoindre, réunir (to, with, à). (b) Rejoindre (qn, son régiment). Mil: The scouts rejoined their unit, les éclaireurs rallièrent leur unité. To r. one's ship, rallier le bord. 2. v.i. (Of lines, etc.) Se réunir, se rejoindre.

rejoinder [ri'dʒɔindər], s. Réplique f, repartie f. Sharp r., réponse verte.

rejuvenate [ri'dʒu:vineit], v.tr. & i. Rajeunir.

rejuvenation [ri,dʒu:vi'neiʃ(ə)n], s. 1. (a) Rajeunissement m. (b) Med: Régénérescence f. 2. Cure f de rajeunissement.

rekindle ['ri:'kindl]. 1. v.tr. Rallumer (le feu); ranimer (l'espoir). 2. v.i. Se rallumer.

relapse[1] [ri'læps], s. **1. R. into sin**, rechute *f* dans le péché. **R. into crime**, récidive *f*. **2.** *Med:* Rechute. **To have a r.**, faire une rechute; rechuter.

relapse[2], *v.i.* **1. To r. into vice**, retomber dans le vice. **To r. into crime**, récidiver. *Theol:* **Relapsed heretic**, relaps, *f.* relapse. **2.** *Med:* Rechuter; faire une rechute.

relate [ri'leit]. **1.** *v.tr.* Raconter, conter (une histoire); rapporter, *Jur:* relater (les faits). **To r. one's adventures**, faire le récit de ses aventures. **Strange to r.!** chose étonnante à dire! **2.** (*a*) *v.tr. Nat.Hist: etc:* Rapporter, rattacher (une espèce à une famille); établir un rapport entre (deux faits). (*b*) *v.i.* Se rapporter, avoir rapport (to, à). **Agreement relating to . . .**, convention ayant trait à. . . . **related**, *a.* **1.** (*a*) Ayant rapport (to, à). (*b*) **R. ideas**, idées connexes. *Ch:* **R. elements**, éléments apparentés. *Mus:* **R. keys**, tons relatifs. **2.** (*Of pers.*) Apparenté (to, à); parent (to, de); (*by marriage*) allié (to, à). **He is r. to us**, il est notre parent. **They are nearly, closely, r.**, ils sont proches parents. **They are very distantly r.**, ils sont parents à un degré très éloigné. **relating**, *a.* **R. to . . .**, relatif à . . .; qui se rapporte à. . . . **Information r. to a matter**, renseignements afférents à une affaire.

relator [ri'leitər], s. Conteur, -euse; narrateur, -trice.

relation [ri'leiʃ(ə)n], s. **1.** Relation *f*, récit *m* (d'événements). **2.** (*a*) Relation, rapport *m*. **In r. to . . .**, relativement à . . .; par rapport à. . . . **To bear a r. to . . .**, avoir rapport à. . . . **That has no r. to the present situation**, cela n'a rien à faire, rien à voir, avec la situation actuelle. (*b*) *pl.* **To have (business) relations with s.o.**, être en relations (d'affaires) avec qn. **To enter into relations with s.o.**, entrer en rapport, en relations. avec qn; entamer des relations avec qn. **To break off all relations with s.o.**, rompre toutes relations, cesser tout rapport, avec qn. *Adm: Com: etc:* **Public relations**, service *m* des relations publiques, avec le public. **Public relations officer**, chef du service des relations publiques, avec le public. **3.** Parent, -ente. **Near r.** proche parent. **R. by marriage**, allié, -ée. **Distant r.**, parent éloigné. **Parents and relations**, ascendants directs et collatéraux. **What r. is he to you?** quelle est sa parenté avec vous? **Is he any r. to you?** est-il de vos parents?

relationship [ri'leiʃ(ə)nʃip], s. **1.** (*a*) Rapport *m* (entre deux choses). (*b*) (*Of pers.*) **To be in r. with s.o.**, avoir des relations avec qn; être en rapport avec qn. **2.** Parenté *f*; lien *m* de parenté. **Blood r.**, proximité *f* de sang.

relative ['relətiv]. **1.** *a.* (*a*) Relatif, qui se rapporte (to, à). (*b*) (*Of terms, etc.*) Relatif. **R. positions of two parts**, positions relatives de deux organes. **They live in r. luxury**, par rapport aux autres ils vivent dans le luxe. (*c*) *Gram:* **R. pronoun**, pronom relatif. **2.** *s.* = RELATION 3. **-ly**, *adv.* (*a*) Relativement (to, à); par rapport (à). (*b*) **She is r. happy**, somme toute elle est assez heureuse.

relativity [ˌrelə'tiviti], s. Relativité *f*. *Ph:* **Theory of r.**, théorie *f* de la relativité.

relax [ri'læks]. **1.** *v.tr.* (*a*) Relâcher (les muscles, la discipline); détendre, délasser (l'esprit); détendre, débander (un arc). **The serpent relaxed its hold**, le serpent desserra son étreinte. (*b*) **To r. the bowels**, relâcher le ventre. (*c*) Mitiger (une loi, une peine). **2.** *v.i.* (*a*) (*Of muscles, etc.*) Se relâcher, se détendre. **His face relaxed into a smile**, son visage se détendit dans un sourire. (*b*) (*Of pers.*) Se détendre, se décontracter, se relaxer. **To r. for an hour**, prendre une heure de délassement. *F:* faire une heure de relaxe. **relaxed**, *a.* (*a*) Relâché; (muscle) relaxé. *Med:* **R. throat**, pharyngite subaiguë. (*b*) Relaxé, décontracté. **relaxing**, *a.* (Climat,) énervant, débilitant, mou; (médicament) relâchant, laxatif; (séjour) décontractant, relaxant.

relaxation [ˌriːlæk'seiʃ(ə)n], s. **1.** (*a*) Relâchement *m* (des muscles, de la discipline). (*b*) Mitigation *f*, adoucissement *m* (d'une loi). **2.** Délassement *m*, repos *m*, détente *f*, relaxation *f*, décontraction *f*. **To take some r.**, se donner un peu de relâche; se délasser. **These little jobs come as a r.**, ces petits travaux me distraient. **To seek r. in books**, se délasser dans les livres.

relay[1] ['riːlei], s. **1.** Relais *m* (d'hommes, de chevaux); relève *f* (d'ouvriers). **To work in relays**, se relayer. **R. horse**, (i) cheval de relais; (ii) cheval de renfort. *Sp:* **R. race**, course de, à, relais. **2.** (*a*) *El.E:* Relais contacteur *m*. *Tg:* Répétiteur *m*. (*b*) Servo-moteur *m*. **3.** *W.Tel:* Radio-diffusion relayée. **'relay station**, *s.* Relais hertzien; poste amplificateur.

relay[2], *v.tr.* (relayed ['riːleid]) *Tg: W.Tel:* Relayer (un message, un programme); transmettre (un message par relais.

re-lay ['riː'lei], *v.tr.* (re-laid [-'leid]) **1.** Poser (un tapis, etc.) de nouveau; remettre (la nappe). **2.** Reposer (une voie ferrée); remanier (une canalisation).

relearn ['riː'lə:n], *v.tr.* Rapprendre.

release[1] [ri'liːs], s. **1.** (*a*) (*Of pers.*) Délivrance *f* (from de); décharge *f*, libération *f* (from an obligation, d'une obligation). *Mil:* Mise *f* en disponibilité. *Adm:* Démobilisation *f*. (*b*) Élargissement *m*, mise *f* en liberté, *Jur:* relaxation *f*, relaxe *f* (d'un prisonnier). **Order of r.**, (ordre de) levée *f* d'écrou. (*c*) Mise *f* en vente (d'une nouvelle auto, etc.). *Cin:* Mise en circulation (d'un film). **General r.**, passage *m* à la région. *Journ:* **Press r.**, communiqué *m* de presse. **2.** (*a*) *Ch:* Dégagement *m* (d'un gaz); *Mch:* Échappement *m* (de la vapeur). (*b*) *Av:* Lâchage *m* (d'une bombe); lancement *m* (d'une bombe). (*c*) *Mec.E. etc:* Mise en marche (d'un appareil); déclenchement *m* (d'un ressort); dégagement *m*, desserrage *m* (d'un frein). **R. gear**, déclencheur *m*, déclic *m*. *Phot:* **Shutter-r.**, déclencheur. **Trigger r.**, déclenchement au doigt. **3.** *El.E:* Disjoncteur *m*, interrupteur *m*. **4.** *Com:* Acquit *m*, quittance *f*. **5.** *Jur:* Cession *f* (de terres). **re'lease-valve**, *s.* Soupape *f* de sûreté.

release[2], *v.tr.* **1.** (*a*) Décharger, acquitter, libérer (qn d'une obligation). **To r. s.o. from his promise**, délier qn de sa promesse; rendre sa parole à qn. *Mil:* Mettre en disponibilité; démobiliser. (*b*) Libérer, élargir, relâcher (un prisonnier). **Released on bail**, remis en liberté sous caution. (*c*) Lâcher (des pigeons voyageurs). (*d*) Mettre en vente (une nouvelle auto, etc.). *Cin:* Mettre (un film) en circulation. **2.** (*a*) *Ch:* Dégager (un gaz); émettre (de la fumée). (*b*) *Av:* Lâcher (une bombe); lancer (un parachute). (*c*) Faire jouer (un ressort); décliquer (un doigt d'encliquetage); déclencher, décoller, débloquer (un organe). **To r. one's hold**, lâcher prise. **To r. the brake**, dégager, desserrer, le frein. **To r. the trigger (of a gun)**, faire jouer la gâchette. *Phot:* **To r. the shutter**, déclencher l'obturateur. **3.** *Jur:* (*a*) **To r. a debt**, faire (à qn) la remise d'une dette. (*b*) Renoncer à (un droit). (*c*) Céder (une terre).

releaser [ri'liːsər], s. **1.** (*Device*) Déclencheur *m*, démarreur *m*. **2.** *Cin:* (*Pers.*) Distributeur *m* (de films).

relegate ['religeit], *v.tr.* **1.** Reléguer (un tableau au grenier, etc.). **To r. one's wife to the position of a servant**, ravaler sa femme au rôle de servante. **2.** **To r. a matter to s.o.**, (i) remettre une question à la décision de qn; (ii) confier une affaire à qn.

relegation [reli'geiʃ(ə)n], s. **1.** (*a*) *Jur:* Relégation *f*, bannissement *m*. (*b*) Mise *f* à l'écart, *F:* mise au rancart (d'un objet inutile, etc.). **2.** Renvoi *m* (d'une affaire à qn).

relent [ri'lent], *v.i.* Se laisser attendrir; revenir sur une décision (sévère). **He would not r. (towards me)**, il me tenait rigueur.

relentless [ri'lentlis], *a.* (*a*) Implacable, impitoyable. (*b*) **R. persecution**, persécution sans rémission. **To be r. in doing sth.**, mettre de l'acharnement à faire qch. **-ly**, *adv.* (*a*) Implacablement, impitoyablement. (*b*) Sans rémission.

relentlessness [ri'lentlisnis], s. Inflexibilité *f*, implacabilité *f*; acharnement *m*.

relevance ['relivəns], **relevancy** ['relivənsi], s. Pertinence *f*, à-propos *m*; rapport *m* (to, avec).

relevant ['relivənt], *a.* Qui a rapport (to, à); pertinent (to, à); à propos (to, de). **The r. documents**, les documents qui se rapportent à l'affaire. **All r. information**, tous renseignements utiles. **-ly**, *adv.* Pertinemment.

reliability [ri‚laiə'biliti], *s.* Sûreté *f*; honnêteté *f*, véracité *f* (de qn); sécurité *f* du fonctionnement, régularité *f* de marche, fiabilité *f* (d'une machine). *Aut:* **R. trial,** épreuve *f* de régularité, d'endurance.

reliable [ri'laiəbl], *a.* Sûr; (homme) sérieux, digne de confiance; (ami) solide; (renseignement) sûr, digne de foi; (machine) d'un fonctionnement sûr. **R. firm,** maison de confiance. **R. guarantee,** garantie solide. **To have sth. from a r. source,** tenir qch. de bonne source. *F:* **R. tip,** tuyau sûr. *Jur:* **R. witness,** témoin sans reproche. **-ably,** *adv.* Sûrement; d'une manière digne de confiance.

reliance [ri'laiəns], *s.* Confiance *f.* **To place r. in,** (up)on s.o., avoir confiance en qn; se fier à qn; compter sur qn. **I put little r. in him,** je n'ai pas grande confiance en lui.

reliant [ri'laiənt], *a.* (*a*) Confiant. (*b*) Qui dépend (**on** s.o. for sth.,** de qn pour qch.). *S.a.* SELF-RELIANT.

relic ['relik], *s.* **1.** *Ecc:* Relique *f.* **2.** *pl.* **Relics, restes** *m.* (*a*) Dépouille mortelle. (*b*) **Relics of the past,** vestiges *m* du passé; survivance *f* des temps passés.

relict ['relikt], *s. Jur:* Veuve *f* (of, de).

relief¹ [ri'li:f], *s.* **1.** (*a*) Soulagement *m* (d'une douleur); allégement *m* (d'une détresse). **To heave a sigh of r.,** pousser un soupir de soulagement. **It was a r. to me when . . . ,** je fus soulagé quand. . . . (*b*) **Black costume without r.,** toilette noire sans agrément. **A comic scene follows by way of r.,** une scène comique suit pour détendre les esprits. (*c*) Décharge *f. Mch:* **R. cock,** décompresseur *m.* **2. To go to s.o.'s r.,** aller, se porter, au secours de qn, à l'aide de qn. **R. fund,** caisse *f* de secours (en cas de sinistre). **Refugee r.** (**work**), œuvre *f* de secours aux réfugiés. **R. engine,** locomotive remorqueuse. **R. train,** train *m* supplémentaire. **3.** *Mil:* (*a*) Dégagement *m* (d'une place forte). **R. troops,** troupes de secours. (*b*) Relève *f* (d'une garde, etc.). **R. party,** draft of reliefs, détachement *m* de relève; une relève. **4.** *Jur:* Réparation *f* (d'un grief); redressement *m* (d'un tort). **5.** *Mec.E:* Dégagement *m*, dépouille *f* (d'un foret, etc.). **re'lief-valve,** *s. Mch:* Soupape *f* de sûreté, de décompression; clapet *m* de décharge.

relief², *s.* **1.** *Art:* Relief *m*; modelé *m.* **High r., low r.,** haut-relief, bas-relief. **In r.,** en relief. **To stand out in r.,** ressortir, se détacher (**against,** sur). **To bring, throw, sth. into r.,** faire ressortir qch.; mettre qch. en relief. **R. map,** carte en relief. **2.** *Geog:* Relief (terrestre).

relieve [ri'li:v], *v.tr.* **1.** (*a*) Soulager, alléger (les souffrances). **To r. s.o.'s mind,** tranquilliser l'esprit de qn. **To r. one's feelings,** se décharger le cœur. **To r. oneself,** faire ses besoins; se soulager. (*b*) **Black blouse relieved with white lace,** corsage noir agrémenté de dentelle blanche. **To r. the tedium of the journey,** tromper, dissiper, l'ennui du voyage. (*c*) Soulager, décharger (une soupape, etc.). **To r. congestion,** (i) faciliter la circulation (aux heures d'affluence); (ii) *Med:* décongestionner (les poumons). **2.** Secourir, aider, assister (qn); venir en aide à (qn). **3. To r. s.o. of sth.,** soulager, délester, qn (d'un fardeau); débarrasser qn (de son manteau); dégager qn (d'une obligation); relever qn (de ses fonctions). **Relieved of anxiety,** hors d'inquiétude; allégé de souci. **To r. s.o. of his purse,** soulager qn de son porte-monnaie. **4.** (*a*) *Mil:* Dégager, débloquer (une ville). (*b*) Relever (des troupes, une sentinelle); relayer (qn). *Nau:* **To r. the watch,** faire la relève. **5.** *Mec.E:* Dépouiller, dégager (un foret, etc.). **6.** *Art:* Relever, mettre en relief, donner du relief à (un motif); faire ressortir (une couleur). **Relieved against a dark background,** qui se découpe, qui se détache, qui tranche, sur un fond noir. **relieving,** *a.* **1.** *Mil:* (Armée) de secours; **R. party,** etc.) de relève. **2.** *Arch:* **R. arch,** voûte *f* de décharge; *Civ.E:* arche *f* de soutènement.

relievo [ri'li:vou], *s. Art:* Relief *m.* **Alto r.,** haut-relief *m.* **Basso r.,** bas-relief *m.*

relight ['ri:'lait]. **1.** *v.tr.* Rallumer. **2.** *v.i.* Se rallumer.

religion [ri'lidʒən], *s.* Religion *f*; culte *m. Adm: Mil:* Confession *f.* **Established r.,** religion d'État. **To enter r.,** entrer en religion. *F:* **To get r.,** (i) se convertir; (ii) devenir bigot. **To make a r. of doing sth.,** se faire une religion de faire qch.

religiosity [ri‚lidʒi'ositi], *s.* Religiosité *f*.

religious [ri'lidʒəs]. **1.** *a.* (*a*) Religieux, -euse, pieux, -euse, dévot. (*b*) (Ordre) religieux. **R. book,** livre de piété, de dévotion. **R. minorities,** minorités de religion. (*c*) (Soin) religieux, scrupuleux. **2.** *s.* (*inv. in pl.*) *Ecc:* Religieux, -euse. **-ly,** *adv.* Religieusement. (*a*) Pieusement. (*b*) Scrupuleusement.

religiousness [ri'lidʒəsnis], *s.* (*a*) Piété *f*, dévotion *f*; caractère religieux, pieux. (*b*) Attention scrupuleuse (**in attending to sth.,** apportée à faire qch.).

re-line ['ri:'lain], *v.tr.* **1.** Remettre une doublure à (un manteau); rentoiler (un tableau, etc.). **2.** Regarnir (un frein, etc.).

relinquish [ri'liŋkwiʃ], *v.tr.* **1.** Abandonner (une habitude, tout espoir); renoncer à (un projet, un droit); se dessaisir de (ses biens). *Jur:* Délaisser (un droit, une succession). **2.** Lâcher (qch.).

relinquishment [ri'liŋkwiʃmənt], *s.* Abandon *m* (de ses biens); renonciation *f* (of a right, à un droit).

reliquary ['relikwəri], *s.* Reliquaire *m.*

relish¹ ['reliʃ], *s.* **1.** (*a*) Goût *m*, saveur *f* (d'un mets); attrait *m* (d'une idée, etc.). **His food has no more r. for him,** il ne trouve plus de goût à sa nourriture. (*b*) Assaisonnement *m.* (*c*) *Cu:* Soupçon *m*, pointe *f* (de piment, etc.). **2. To eat sth. with r.,** manger qch. de bon appétit. **He used to tell the story with great r.,** il se délectait à raconter cette histoire.

relish², *v.tr.* (*a*) Relever le goût de (qch.). (*b*) (*Of pers.*) Goûter, savourer (un mets). **To r. doing sth.,** trouver du plaisir à faire qch. **We did not r. the idea,** l'idée ne nous souriait pas.

relive ['ri:'liv], *v.tr.* Revivre (sa vie, le passé).

reload ['ri:'loud], *v.tr.* Recharger.

reluctance [ri'lʌktəns], *s.* **1.** Répugnance (**to do sth.,** à faire qch.). **To do sth. with r.,** faire qch. à regret, à contre-cœur. **To affect r.,** faire des manières. **2.** *El:* Réluctance *f.*

reluctant [ri'lʌktənt], *a.* **1.** Qui agit à contre-cœur. **To be r. to do sth.,** être peu disposé, hésiter, à faire qch. **I feel r. to . . . ,** il me répugne de. . . . **2.** (Consentement) accordé à contre-cœur. **-ly,** *adv.* Avec répugnance; à contre-cœur. **I say it r.,** il m'en coûte de le dire. **He paid up very r.,** *F:* il s'est fait tirer l'oreille pour payer.

rely [ri'lai], *v.i.* **To r.** (**up**)**on s.o.,** compter sur qn; se fier à qn. **To r. on s.o.'s evidence,** se baser sur le témoignage de qn. **I want a man I can r. on,** il me faut un homme de confiance. **We cannot r. on the weather,** le temps n'est pas sûr.

remain¹ [ri'mein], *s. Usu. pl.* Restes *m* (d'un repas, d'un édifice); vestiges *m* (d'une ancienne voie, d'un château); œuvres *f* posthumes (d'un auteur). **Mortal remains,** restes mortels; dépouille mortelle. **To discover human remains,** découvrir des ossements *m.*

remain², *v.i.* **1.** Rester. **This objection remains,** cette objection subsiste. **The fact remains that . . . ,** il n'en est pas moins vrai que. . . . **Much yet remains to be done,** il reste encore beaucoup à faire. **It remains to be seen whether . . . ,** reste à savoir si. . . . **2.** Demeurer, rester. (*a*) **To r. at home,** rester à la maison. **To r. sitting,** demeurer assis. **To r. behind,** rester; ne pas partir. (*b*) **Let it r. as it is,** laissez-le comme cela. **3.** (*a*) **The weather remains fine,** le temps se maintient au beau. (*b*) *Corr:* **I r., Sir, yours truly, agreez, Monsieur, mes salutations distinguées. **remaining,** *a.* **I have four r.,** j'en ai quatre de reste. **The r. travellers,** le reste des voyageurs.

remainder¹ [ri'meindər], *s.* **1.** (*a*) Reste *m*, restant *m* (de fortune). **The r. of his life,** le reste de sa vie. (*b*) *Ar:* Division with no r.,** division sans reste. **2.** (*a*) *Coll.* **The r.,** les autres *mf.* (*b*) *Com:* Invendus soldés. **To sell off the remainders,** liquider les invendus. *Publ:* **Remainders, r. line,** fin *f* de série; solde *m* d'édition. **3. The estate is left to A with r. to B,** la succession passe à A avec réversion sur B.

remainder², *v.tr.* Solder (une édition).

remake¹ ['ri:'meik], *s. Cin: Gramophones:* Remake *m.*

remake² ['ri:'meik], *v.tr.* (Conj. like MAKE) Refaire. **remaking,** *s.* Réfection *f*; refaçon *f.*

remand¹ [ri'mɑ:nd], *s. Jur:* Renvoi *m* (d'un prévenu) à une autre audience. **Detention under r.,** détention préventive. **R. home,** maison *f* de détention.

remand², v.tr. Jur: Renvoyer (un prévenu) à une autre audience. He was remanded for a week, son cas a été remis à huitaine. Person remanded in custody = préventionnaire mf.

remanence ['remənəns], s. Magn: Rémanence f.

remanent ['remənənt], a. (Magnétisme) rémanent, résiduel.

remark¹ [ri'mɑ:k], s. 1. Remarque f, attention f. Things worthy of r., choses dignes d'attention. 2. Remarque, observation f, commentaire m. To make a r., (i) faire une observation; (ii) F: faire une réflexion. To venture a r., se permettre un mot. After some preliminary remarks, après quelques avant-propos m. F: To pass remarks upon s.o., faire des observations sur qn.

remark². 1. v.tr. (a) Remarquer, observer. It may be remarked that . . ., constatons que. . . . (b) Faire la remarque (que . . .); faire observer (à qn que . . .). 2. v.i. Faire une remarque, faire des remarques (on, sur). I remarked upon it to my neighbour, j'en fis l'observation à mon voisin.

remarkable [ri'mɑ:kəbl], a. Remarquable; frappant. Our family has never been r., notre famille n'a jamais marqué. -ably, adv. Remarquablement.

remarry ['ri:'mæri], v.i. Se remarier; (of widow) convoler en deuxièmes noces.

remediable [ri'mi:diəbl], a. Remédiable.

remedial [ri'mi:diəl], a. Réparateur, -trice; (traitement, etc.) curatif.

remedy¹ ['remidi], s. 1. Remède m. R. for an ailment, remède pour, contre, une maladie. Old wives' r., remède de bonne femme. The evil is past r., le mal est sans remède. 2. To have no r. at law, n'avoir aucun recours contre qn.

remedy², v.tr. Remédier à (qch.). That cannot be remedied, on ne saurait y remédier.

remelt ['ri:'melt], v.tr. Refondre. remelting, s. Refonte f.

remember [ri'membər], v.tr. 1. (a) Se souvenir de (qch.); se rappeler (qch.). I r. seeing it, je me souviens, il me souvient, de l'avoir vu. I r. his going, je me rappelle son départ. If I r. rightly, si j'ai bonne mémoire. As far as I r., autant qu'il m'en souvient, qu'il m'en souvienne. I can't r. his name for the moment, son nom m'échappe pour l'instant. Don't you r. me? est-ce que vous ne me remettez pas? It will be something to r. you by, ce sera un souvenir de vous. (b) One cannot r. everything, on ne peut pas songer à tout. That is worth remembering, cela est à noter. Let it be remembered (that), n'oublions pas (que), ne l'oublions pas. (c) He remembered me in his will, il ne m'a pas oublié dans son testament. (d) To r. oneself, se ressaisir. 2. R. me (kindly) to them, rappelez-moi à leur bon souvenir.

remembrance [ri'membrəns], s. 1. Souvenir m, mémoire f. To have sth. in r., avoir qch. à la mémoire. To the best of my r., autant qu'il m'en souvienne. In r. of s.o., en souvenir, en mémoire, de qn. 2. pl. Give my kind remembrances to him, rappelez-moi à son bon souvenir.

remilitarize ['ri:'militəraiz], v.tr. Remilitariser.

remind [ri'maind], v.tr. To r. s.o. of sth., rappeler, remémorer, qch. à qn; faire souvenir qn de qch. She has reminded me that we are going there tonight, elle me rappelle que nous y allons ce soir. That reminds me of . . ., cela me rappelle. . . . That reminds me! à propos! R. me to write to him, faites-moi penser à lui écrire.

reminder [ri'maindər], s. (a) Mémento m. As a r. that . . ., pour rappeler que. . . . (b) Com: (Letter of) r., lettre de rappel. I'll send him a r., je vais lui rafraîchir la mémoire. (c) Com: Rappel m de compte; rappel d'échéance.

reminisce [remi'nis], v.i. F: Raconter ses souvenirs; échanger des souvenirs (with s.o., avec qn).

reminiscence [,remi'nis(ə)ns], s. 1. Réminiscence f, souvenir m. 2. To write one's reminiscences, écrire ses souvenirs.

reminiscent [,remi'nis(ə)nt], a. 1. Qui se souvient. 2. R. of sth., qui rappelle qch.; qui fait penser à qch. -ly, adv. De l'air de qn qui se souvient. He smiled r., il sourit à ce souvenir.

remiss [ri'mis], a. Négligent, insouciant; inexact à remplir ses devoirs.

remission [ri'miʃ(ə)n], s. 1. R. of sins, pardon m rémission f, des péchés. To grant s.o. r. of his sins, absoudre qn de ses péchés. 2. Remise f (d'une peine, d'une dette). Jur: With r. of sentence, avec sursis m. 3. (a) Relâchement m (du froid). (b) Med: Rémission (d'une fièvre).

remissness [ri'misnis], s. Négligence f.

remit [ri'mit], v.tr. (remitted) 1. (a) Remettre, pardonner (les péchés). (b) Remettre (une dette, une peine). 2. Relâcher (son zèle). 3. Renvoyer un procès à un autre tribunal. 4. Com: To r. a sum to s.o., remettre, envoyer, une somme à qn. Abs. Kindly r., prière de nous couvrir. 5. v.i. Diminuer d'intensité; (of pain, storm, etc.) se calmer, s'apaiser.

remittal [ri'mitl], s. 1. Remise f (of a debt, d'une dette). 2. Jur: Renvoi m (d'un procès à un autre tribunal).

remittance [ri'mitəns], s. Com: Remise f (d'argent); envoi m de fonds. A: R.-man, brebis galeuse, subventionnée par sa famille pour rester outre-mer.

remitter [ri'mitər], s. Com: Remetteur m, remettant m.

remnant ['remnənt], s. 1. Reste m, restant m. I found a few remnants of food, je trouvai quelques restes, quelques bribes de nourriture. 2. Vestige m (d'un usage). 3. Coupon m (d'étoffe). Remnants, soldes m. R. sale, solde de coupons.

remodel ['ri:'modl], v.tr. (remodelled) Remodeler (une statue); remanier (un ouvrage); transformer (une machine).

remonstrance [ri'monstrəns], s. Remontrance f.

remonstrate ['remənstreit]. 1. v.i. To r. with s.o., faire des remontrances à qn. To r. against sth., protester contre qch. 2. v.tr. To r. that . . ., protester que. . . .

remonstrative [ri'monstrətiv], a. (Ton, lettre) de remontrance, de protestation.

remorse [ri'mo:s], s. 1. Remords m. A feeling of r., un remords. 2. Without r., sans aucune componction; sans pitié.

remorseful [ri'mo:sf(u)l], a. Plein de remords; repentant. -fully, adv. Avec remords.

remorseless [ri'mo:slis], a. 1. Sans remords. 2. Sans pitié; impitoyable. -ly, adv. 1. Sans remords. 2 Sans pitié.

remote [ri'mout], a. 1. Éloigné, écarté. Sciences r. from each other, sciences qui n'ont rien en commun. 2. Lointain; éloigné, écarté. The house lies r. from the road, la maison est située loin de la route. In the remotest part of Asia, au fond de l'Asie. In a r. future, dans un avenir lointain, reculé. R. ancestors, lointains ancêtres. R. causes, causes lointaines. R. control, télécommande f. To operate by r. control, télécommander. 3. A r. resemblance, une vague ressemblance. I haven't the remotest idea, je n'ai pas la moindre idée. Without the remotest chance of succeeding, sans la moindre chance de réussir. R. prospect, éventualité f peu probable. -ly, adv. 1. Loin; au loin; dans le lointain. 2. We are r. related, nous sommes parents de loin. 3. Vaguement.

remoteness [ri'moutnis], s. 1. Éloignement m (d'un village). 2. (a) Degré éloigné (de parenté). (b) Faible degré (de ressemblance).

remoulding ['ri:'moulding], s. Remoulage m.

remount¹ ['ri:maunt], s. Mil: 1. Remonte f. 2. Cheval m de remonte. Army remounts, chevaux de troupe.

remount² [ri:'maunt], v.tr. Remonter; enfourcher de nouveau (son vélo). To r. one's horse, abs. to remount, remonter à cheval; se remettre en selle.

removability [ri'mu:və'biliti], s. Amovibilité f.

removable [ri'mu:vəbl], a. 1. Détachable; amovible. 2. Transportable. 3. (Fonctionnaire) amovible, révocable.

removal [ri'mu:v(ə)l], s. 1. (a) Enlèvement m (d'une tache); suppression f (d'un abus). (b) Révocation f (d'un fonctionnaire); destitution f (d'un officier). (c) F: Assassinat m (de qn). 2. Déplacement m (d'une épave); transport m (d'un colis); dépose f (de dalles, etc.). 3. Démontage m (d'un pneu); levée f (de scellés). 4. Déménagement m. Adm: R. expenses, frais de déplacement.

remove¹ [ri'mu:v], s. 1. Cu: Relevé m. 2. Sch: (a) Passage m à une classe supérieure. Not to get one's r., redoubler une classe. (b) Classe f intermédiaire. 3. It is but one r. from . . ., cela est tout près de. . . .

remove², v.tr. 1. (a) Enlever, effacer, ôter (une tache); écarter (un obstacle); résoudre (une objection); chasser (une appréhension); supprimer (un abus). To r. s.o.'s name from a list, rayer qn d'une liste. Toil: To r. make-up, démaquiller. (b) Révoquer (un fonctionnaire); destituer (un officier). (c) F: Assassiner, supprimer (qn). 2. (a) Déplacer (une machine); transporter (des colis); déménager (sa bibliothèque). To r. oneself and all one's belongings, F: faire place nette. Abs. To r., déménager. (b) Éloigner (qch., qn). (c) Enlever, retirer (son chapeau); enlever (les assiettes, etc.). Med: To r. a bandage, enlever un pansement. (d) Déplacer (un fonctionnaire). removed, a. 1. First cousin once r., cousin(e) issu(e) de germain. 2. Éloigné. Far r. from . . ., bien loin de. . . .

remover [ri'muːvər], s. 1. (Pers.) = FURNITURE-REMOVER. 2. Varnish, paint r., décapant m pour vernis, pour peinture. Superfluous hair r., pâte f épilatoire. (Nail-varnish) r., dissolvant m (pour ongles). Make-up r., démaquillant m.

remunerate [ri'mjuːnəreit], v.tr. Rémunérer.

remuneration [ri,mjuːnə'reiʃ(ə)n], s. Rémunération f (for, de).

remunerative [ri'mjuːnərətiv], a. (Travail, prix, etc.) rémunérateur, -trice.

renaissance [rə'neis(ə)ns], s. Art: Lit: Renaissance f. R. style, style (de la) Renaissance.

renal ['riːn(ə)l], a. Anat: Rénal, -aux; des reins.

rename ['riː'neim], v.tr. Rebaptiser; débaptiser (une rue, etc.).

renascence [ri'neis(ə)ns, -'næs-], s. Retour m à la vie; renouveau m.

renascent [ri'neisnt, -'næ-], a. Renaissant.

rend [rend], v.tr. (rent; rent) Lit: Déchirer. To r. sth. asunder, in two, in twain, déchirer qch. en deux. To r. one's garments, déchirer ses vêtements. A cry rent the air, un cri fendit l'air. To r. s.o.'s heart, fendre, déchirer, le cœur à qn.

render ['rendər], v.tr. Rendre. 1. (a) To r. good for evil, rendre le bien pour le mal. (b) To r. thanks to s.o., remercier qn. To r. thanks to God, rendre grâce à Dieu. 2. Lit: Rendre (une forteresse). 3. To r. a service to s.o., rendre un service à qn. To r. oneself liable to (judicial) proceedings, s'exposer à des poursuites (judiciaires). 4. (a) To r. an account of sth., rendre compte de qch. (b) Com: To r. an account to s.o., remettre un compte à qn. 'As per account rendered,' 'to account rendered,' "suivant notre compte"; "suivant compte remis." 5. Interpréter (un morceau de musique); rendre, traduire (une phrase). 6. Rendre; faire devenir. His action renders it probable that . . ., son action fait pressentir que. . . . 7. Cu: Fondre (la graisse); clarifier. rendered, a. Cu: R. fat, graisse fondue. rendering, s. 1. (a) R. of thanks, of help, remerciements mpl, assistance f. (b) Reddition f (d'un compte, d'une forteresse). 2. Rendu m (des traits de qn); interprétation f (d'un morceau de musique); traduction f (d'une phrase). 3. Fonte f, extraction f (de la graisse); clarification f.

rendezvous¹ ['rɔndivuː], s. Rendez-vous m.

rendezvous², v.i. (rendezvoused [-vuːd]; rendez-vousing [-vuːiŋ]) Se rencontrer.

rendition [ren'diʃ(ə)n], s. 1. Hist: Reddition f (d'une forteresse). 2. Esp: U.S: (a) Traduction f. (b) Th: etc: Interprétation f (d'un rôle, d'un morceau de musique etc.).

renegade ['renigeid], s. Renégat m.

renew [ri'njuː]. 1. v.tr. (a) Renouveler. To r. one's youth, rajeunir. To r. a lease, renouveler un bail. To r. one's subscription, se réabonner (to, à). Com: To r. a bill, prolonger une lettre de change. (Of bill) Unless renewed, à moins de renouvellement. Jur: To r. a title, rénover un titre. (b) To r. one's acquaintance with s.o., renouer connaissance avec qn. To r. the combat, rengager le combat. To r. a promise, renouveler une promesse. (c) Remplacer (un organe de machine); renouveler (ses vêtements). 2. v.i. Se renouveler.

renewable [ri'njuːəbl], a. Renouvelable.

renewal [ri'njuːəl], s. 1. (a) Renouvellement m. R. of subscription, réabonnement m (to, à). Com: R. of a

bill, atermoiement m, prolongation f, d'une lettre de change. Jur: Reconduction f (d'un bail). (b) R. of acquaintance, renouement m des relations. R. of negotiations, reprise f de négociations. 2. Remplacement m (d'un pneu).

rennet¹ ['renit], s. Présure f; caillette f. Vet: Anat: R. stomach, caillette f.

rennet², s. Hort: (Pomme f de) rainette f.

renounce¹ [ri'nauns], s. Cards: Renonce f.

renounce², v.tr. 1. Renoncer à, abandonner (un droit, un projet). 2. Renier (son fils); dénoncer (un traité); abjurer (sa religion). 3. Abs. Cards: Renoncer.

renouncement [ri'naunsmənt], s. Renoncement m (of, à). Jur: R. of a succession, répudiation f d'une succession.

renovate ['renoveit], v.tr. 1. Renouveler (l'air). 2. Remettre à neuf (un vêtement); rénover (des pneus). renovating, a. Rénovateur, -trice.

renovation [,reno'veiʃ(ə)n], s. Rénovation f, renouvellement m; remise f à neuf.

renovator ['renoveitər], s. Rénovateur, -trice.

renown [ri'naun], s. Renommée f, renom m, célébrité f. To win r., se faire un grand nom.

renowned [ri'naund], a. Renommé (for, pour); célèbre (for, par); illustre.

rent¹. See REND.

rent², s. 1. Déchirure f, accroc m (à un vêtement); déchirure (dans les nuages). 2. Fissure f (de terrain). 3. Rupture f, schisme m (dans une société).

rent³, s. Loyer m; (prix m de) location f (d'une maison); fermage m (d'une ferme). Quarter's r., terme m. 'rent-collector, s. Receveur m de loyers. 'rent-day, s. Jour m du terme. 'rent-free, a. To live r.-f. in a house, habiter une maison sans payer de loyer. 'rent-roll, s. (a) Montant m des loyers. (b) Hist: État m des fermages (d'une propriété).

rent⁴, v.tr. (a) (Let) Louer (une maison); affermer (une terre). (b) (Hire) Louer, prendre en location (une maison); affermer (une terre).

rental ['rentl], s. 1. (a) Loyer m; valeur locative; montant m du loyer. Yearly r., redevance annuelle. (b) Revenu m provenant des loyers. 2. Tp: Fixed r., redevances d'abonnement.

renunciation [ri,nʌnsi'eiʃ(ə)n], s. 1. Renoncement m, renonciation f (of rights, aux droits). Jur: R. of a succession, répudiation f d'une succession. Letter of r., lettre de renonciation. 2. Reniement m (of, de). R. on oath, abjuration f (of, de).

reoccupation ['riː,ɔkju'peiʃ(ə)n], s. Réoccupation f (d'un territoire, etc.).

reoccupy ['riː'ɔkjupai], v.tr. Réoccuper. reoccupying, s. Réoccupation f.

reopen ['riː'oup(ə)n]. 1. v.tr. (a) Rouvrir (un livre). To r. an old sore, raviver une plaie. (b) Reprendre (les hostilités). (c) The question cannot be reopened, il n'y a pas à y revenir. 2. v.i. (a) (Of wound) Se rouvrir. (b) (Of theatre) Rouvrir; (of school) rentrer. reopening, s. 1. Réouverture f (d'un théâtre). 2. Rentrée f (des classes, des tribunaux).

reorganization ['riː,ɔːgənai'zeiʃ(ə)n], s. Réorganisation f.

reorganize ['riː'ɔːgənaiz]. 1. v.tr. Réorganiser. 2. v.i. Se réorganiser. reorganizing, a. Réorganisateur, -trice.

reorganizer ['riː'ɔːgənaizər], s. Réorganisateur, -trice.

rep¹ [rep], s. Tex: Reps m.

rep², s. Th: (Abbr. for REPERTORY). Le théâtre m de province. To be, act, in r., faire partie d'une troupe de province.

repaid [ri'peid]. See REPAY.

repaint [riː'peint], v.tr. Repeindre.

repair¹ [ri'pɛər], v.i. O: To r. to a place, aller, se rendre, à un endroit; gagner un endroit.

repair², s. 1. Réparation f (d'une machine); rétablissement m (d'un bâtiment); Nau: radoub m (d'une coque). Road repairs, réfection f des routes. Emergency, makeshift, r., réparation d'urgence, de fortune; dépannage m. To be under r., subir des réparations. Ship under r., navire en radoub. Ruined beyond r., ruiné irréparablement. 2. To be in (good) r., être en bon état. In bad r., mal entretenu. Ind: R. shop, atelier m de réparations. re'pair outfit, s. Nécessaire m, trousse f, de réparation.

repair³, *v.tr.* **1.** Réparer, réfectionner, remettre en état (une machine); raccommoder (un vêtement); radouber (un filet, *Nau:* une coque). **2.** Réparer (un tort). **repairing,** *s.* Réparation *f*, raccommodage *m*, remise *f* en état.

repairer [ri'pɛərər], *s.* Réparateur, -trice. **Clock r.,** horologer rhabilleur. **Shoe r.,** cordonnier, -ière.

repaper ['ri:'peipər], *v.tr.* Retapisser (une pièce).

reparable ['rəpərəbl], *a.* (Machine *f*, faute *f*, tort *m*) réparable.

reparation [repə'reiʃ(ə)n], *s.* Réparation *f*.

repartee ['repɑ:'ti:], *s.* Repartie *f*. **To be quick at r.,** avoir la repartie prompte; avoir l'esprit de repartie.

repartition [repɑ'tiʃ(ə)n, -ri:pɑ:-], *s.* **1.** Répartition *f*. **2.** [ri:-] Nouveau partage.

repast [ri'pɑːst], *s. Lit:* Repas *m*.

repatriate [ri:'pætrieit], *v.tr.* Rapatrier. **repatriated,** *a.* Rapatrié. **To r.,** the r., les rapatriés *m*.

repatriation [ri:'pætri'eiʃ(ə)n], *s.* Rapatriement *m*.

repay [ri:'pei], *v.tr.* (**repaid** [ri:'peid]; **repaid**) **1.** Rendre (de l'argent). **To r. an obligation,** s'acquitter d'une obligation. **To r. an injury,** se venger d'un tort. **To r. s.o.'s kindness,** payer de retour la bonté de qn. **I owe you more than I can r.,** *F:* je vous dois une fière chandelle. **2.** (i) Rembourser (qn); (ii) récompenser (qn) (**for, de**). **To r. s.o. in full,** s'acquitter avec, envers, qn. **To r. s.o. with ingratitude,** payer qn d'ingratitude. **How can I r. you?** comment pourrai-je m'acquitter envers vous? **3.** **Book that repays reading,** livre qui vaut la peine d'être lu.

repayable [ri:'peiəbl], *a.* Remboursable.

repayment [ri:'peimənt], *s.* **1.** Remboursement *m*. **2.** Récompense *f* (d'un service).

repeal¹ [ri'pi:l], *s.* Abrogation *f* (d'une loi); révocation *f* (d'un décret).

repeal², *v.tr.* Rapporter, abroger, annuler (une loi); révoquer (un décret).

repeat¹ [ri'pi:t], *s.* **1.** *Mus:* **R.(-mark),** (barre *f* de) reprise *f*; renvoi *m*. **2.** *Tg:* **R. signal,** invitation *f* à répéter. **3.** *Com:* **R. (order),** commande renouvelée; "à nouveau" *m inv.*

repeat². **1.** *v.tr.* (*a*) Répéter; réitérer (un ordre). (*After a line of a song*) 'R.,' "bis." **To have a telegram repeated,** faire collationner un télégramme. (*b*) *Pej:* Rapporter (un méfait). *Sch:* **He repeats everything to the master,** c'est un rapporteur. (*c*) Renouveler (ses efforts). *Com:* Renouveler (une commande). *Sch:* Doubler (une classe). **2.** *v.i.* (*a*) (*Of rifle*) Être à répétition. (*b*) *Ar:* (*Of figures*) Se répéter. (*c*) (*Of food*) Revenir; donner des renvois. **repeated,** *a.* Répété, réitéré, redoublé. **R. requests,** demandes réitérées. **-ly,** *adv.* A plusieurs reprises. **repeating,** *a.* (Fusil) à répétition; (montre) à sonnerie. *Clockm:* **R. spring,** tout-ou-rien *m inv.*

repeater [ri'pi:tər], *s.* **1.** (*a*) Montre *f* à répétition, à sonnerie. (*b*) Fusil *m* à répétition. **2.** *El: Tg:* Translateur *m*. **Impulse r.,** translateur d'impulsions.

repel [ri'pel], *v.tr.* (**repelled**) **1.** Repousser (une attaque). **2.** Repousser (qn); répugner à (qn). **To be repelled by s.o.,** éprouver de la répulsion pour qn. **repelling**¹, *a.* Répulsif, -ive. **repelling**², *s.* Repoussage *m*.

repellent [ri'pelənt], *a.* **1.** Répulsif, -ive. *Ph:* **R. force,** force répulsive. **2.** Repoussant, répulsif, répugnant. **He has a r. manner,** il a l'abord antipathique. **4.** *s.* **Water r.,** (tissu *m*, surface *f*) imperméable. **Insect r.,** insectifuge *m*.

repent [ri'pent]. **1.** *v.i.* Se repentir (**of, de**). **2.** *v.tr.* **To r. having done sth.,** se repentir d'avoir fait qch. **He has bitterly repented it,** il s'en est repenti amèrement.

repentance [ri'pentəns], *s.* Repentir *m*. **Stool of r.,** sellette *f*.

repentant [ri'pentənt], *a.* **1.** Repentant, repenti. **2.** (Soupir) de repentir.

repeople ['ri:'pi:pl], *v.tr.* Repeupler. **repeopling,** *s.* Repeuplement *m*.

repercussion [,ri:pə'kʌʃ(ə)n], *s.* (*a*) Répercussion *f*; contre-coup *m* (d'une explosion). (*b*) Résonance *f*.

repercussive [,ri:pə'kʌsiv], *a.* Répercussif, -ive; répercutant.

repertoire ['repətwɑːr], *s. Th: Mus:* Répertoire *m*.

repertory ['repət(ə)ri], *s.* **1.** Répertoire *m* (de renseignements). **2.** *Th:* Répertoire. **R. theatre,** théâtre *m* de province. **R. company,** troupe *f* à demeure (dans une ville), troupe de province.

repetition [repi'tiʃ(ə)n], *s.* **1.** Répétition *f* (d'un mot). *Mus:* (*In playing*) Reprise *f*. *Tg:* Collationnement *m*. **2.** Répétition, réitération *f* (d'une action); renouvellement *m* (d'un effort).

repetitive [ri'petitiv], *a.* (Livre *m*) plein de répétitions (personne *f*) qui se répète.

repine [ri'pain], *v.i.* Être mécontent, se chagriner (**at against, de**); exhaler des plaintes. **repining**¹, *a.* **1.** Disposé à se plaindre; mécontent. **2.** (Ton) dolent (humeur) chagrine. **repining**², *s.* Mécontentement *m*, plaintes *fpl.*

replace [ri'pleis], *v.tr.* **1.** Replacer (qch.); remettre (qch.) en place. *Tp:* **To r. the receiver,** raccrocher (le récepteur). **2.** Remplacer. **I shall ask to be replaced,** je demanderai à me faire remplacer.

replaceable [ri:'pleisəbl], *a.* Remplaçable.

replacement [ri:'pleismənt], *s.* **1.** Remise *f* en place; remontage *m* (d'un pneu). **2.** (*a*) Remplacement *m*, substitution *f*. (*b*) (*Pers.*) Remplaçant *m*. (*c*) *pl. Ind:* **Replacements,** pièces *f* de rechange.

replant ['ri:'plɑ:nt], *v.tr.* Replanter.

replaster ['ri:'plɑ:stər], *v.tr.* Replâtrer; recrépir (un mur).

replate ['ri:'pleit], *v.tr.* **1.** Replaquer. **2.** **To r. with gold, silver, tin, etc.,** redorer, réargenter, rétamer (qch.).

replay¹ ['ri:plei], *s. Games: Sp:* Second match, match rejoué (après match nul).

replay² [ri:'plei], *v.tr.* Rejouer (un match).

repleat ['ri:'pli:t], *v.tr.* Replisser. **To have a skirt repleated,** faire replisser une jupe.

replenish [ri'pleniʃ], *v.tr.* Remplir (de nouveau) (**with, de**). **To r. one's wardrobe,** remonter sa garde-robe. **To r. one's supplies,** se réapprovisionner (**with, de**).

replenishment [ri'pleniʃmənt], *s.* Remplissage *m*. **R. of supplies,** réapprovisionnement *m*, ravitaillement *m*.

replete [ri'pli:t], *a.* Rempli, plein (**with, de**).

repletion [ri'pli:ʃ(ə)n], *s.* Réplétion *f*. **To eat to r.,** manger jusqu'à satiété.

replica ['replikə], *s.* (*a*) Reproduction *f*, copie *f* (d'un document). (*b*) *Art:* Réplique *f*, double *m* (d'une œuvre d'art).

reply¹ [ri'plai], *s.* **1.** Réponse *f*. **What have you to say in r.?** qu'avez-vous à répondre? *Tg:* **R. paid,** réponse payée. *Post:* **International r. coupon,** coupon-réponse international. **2.** *Jur:* Réplique *f*.

reply², *v.i. & tr.* (**replied**) Répondre, répliquer (**to, à**).

repoint ['ri:'point], *v.tr. Const:* Rejointoyer (un mur).

repolish ['ri:'poliʃ], *v.tr.* Repolir.

report¹ [ri'po:t], *s.* **1.** (*a*) Rapport *m* (on, sur); compte rendu; exposé *m* (d'une affaire). *Com: Ind:* **Annual (company's) r.,** rapport de gestion. **Progress r.,** état *m* périodique. **Stock-market r.,** bulletin *m* des cours de la Bourse. **Policeman's r.,** procès-verbal. *Sch:* **Terminal r.,** bulletin trimestriel. **Examiner's r.,** rapport des examinateurs. *Mil:* **Sick r.,** rôle *m* des malades. **Law reports,** recueil *m* de jurisprudence. *S.a.* EXPERT². (*b*) **Weather r.,** bulletin *m* météorologique. **2.** (i) Bruit *m* qui court; rumeur *f*; (ii) nouvelle *f*. **There was a r. that . . .,** le bruit courait que. . . . **To know of sth. by r.,** savoir qch. par ouï-dire. **3.** *O:* Réputation *f*, renommée *f*. **Man of good r.,** homme de bonne réputation, bien famé. **4.** Détonation *f* (d'une arme à feu); coup *m* de fusil, de canon.

report². **I.** *v.tr.* **1.** (*a*) Rapporter (un fait); rendre compte de (qch.). **To r. a speech, a meeting,** faire le compte rendu d'un discours, d'une séance. **To r. progress,** exposer l'état de l'affaire. *Parl:* **To move to r. progress,** demander la clôture des débats. **To r. to a superior,** rendre compte à un supérieur. *Parl:* **To r. a bill (to the House),** rapporter un projet de loi. *S.a.* SPEECH 5. (*b*) *Journ:* Faire le reportage de (qch.) (*for broadcast, etc.*) faire un reportage (**on, sur**). (*c*) Rapporter, dire (qch.). **It is reported that . . .,** bruit court, on dit, que. . . . *Journ:* **It is reported from Paris that . . .,** on mande de Paris que. . . **2.** (*a*) **To r. an accident to the police,** signaler un accident à la police. **To r. s.o. to the police,** dénoncer qn à la police. *Adm: Mil:* **To r. s.o. sick,** porter qn malade. **'Nothing to r.'** "rien à signaler." **Reported missing,** porté manquant. *Cust:* **To r. a vessel,** déclarer un navire; faire la déclaration d'entrée. (*b*) **To r. oneself to (s.o.),** se présenter à, devant (un supérieur). II. **report,** *v.ind.tr.* **To r. on sth.,** faire un rapport sur qch.; rendre compte de qch. **report-ing,** *s.* Reportage *m*; comptes rendus. *Journ:* **R. staff,** service *m* des informations.

reportage [ripɔː'tɑːʒ], *s. Journ:* (*a*) Reportage *m.* (*b*) Article *m* de journal.

reportedly [ri'pɔːtidli], *adv. Journ:* **The President has r. said that . . .,** le président aurait dit que. . . .

reporter [ri'pɔːtər], *s.* (*a*) Journaliste *mf*, reporter *m.* **Our r. in Brussels,** notre correspondant, notre envoyé spécial, à Bruxelles. (*b*) Sténographe *mf* (parlementaire). **The Reporters' Gallery,** la tribune de la presse.

repose¹ [ri'pouz], *v.tr.* **To r. one's trust in s.o.,** mettre sa confiance en qn.

repose², *s.* **1.** Repos *m.* (*a*) **To seek r.,** chercher du repos. (*b*) Sommeil *m.* (*c*) Calme *m*, tranquillité *f* (d'esprit). **Features in r.,** traits au repos. **2.** *Civ.E:* **Angle of r.,** angle d'éboulement (d'un talus).

repose³, *v.i.* (*a*) Se reposer; (i) se délasser; (ii) dormir. (*b*) Reposer (on, upon, sur). **The foundations r. upon rock,** les fondations reposent sur la roche.

reposeful [ri'pouzful], *a.* Reposé, reposant; calme.

repository [ri'pɔzitəri], *s.* **1.** Dépôt *m*, entrepôt *m*, magasin *m* (de marchandises). **Furniture r.,** garde-meuble *m.* **2.** Répertoire *m* (de renseignements). **He is a r. of curious information,** c'est une mine de renseignements curieux. **3.** (*Pers.*) Dépositaire *mf* (d'un secret).

repossess ['riːpə'zes], *v.tr.* Reposséder; reprendre possession (of, de).

repoussé [rə'puːsei], *a. & s.* Repoussé (*m*). **R. work,** travail *m* de repoussé, repoussage *m.*

reprehend [,repri'hend], *v.tr.* **1.** Reprendre, blâmer, réprimander (qn). **2. To r. s.o.'s conduct,** trouver répréhensible la conduite de qn.

reprehensible [,repri'hensəbl], *a.* Répréhensible, blâmable, condamnable. **-ibly,** *adv.* De façon répréhensible.

reprehension [,repri'henʃ(ə)n], *s.* Réprimande *f.*

reprehensive [,repri'hensiv], *a.* Réprehensif, -ive.

represent [,repri'zent], *v.tr.* **1.** (*a*) Représenter (qch. à l'esprit). (*b*) *Th:* Représenter (une pièce); jouer (un personnage). (*c*) **The flag represents the nation,** le drapeau symbolise la nation. **This angel represents peace,** cet ange figure la paix. **2.** Faire remarquer, signaler (**sth. to s.o., qch. à qn**). **May I r. that . . .?** puis-je vous faire observer que . . . ? **3. He represents himself as a model of virtue,** il se donne pour un modèle de vertu. **Exactly as represented,** exactement conforme à la description. **4.** Représenter (une maison de commerce, une circonscription électorale, etc.).

representation [,reprizen'teiʃ(ə)n], *s.* **1.** (*a*) Représentation *f* (de qch. à l'esprit). (*b*) *Th:* Représentation (d'une pièce); interprétation *f* (d'un rôle). **2.** (*a*) *Pol:* **Proportional r.,** représentation proportionnelle. (*b*) *Coll.* Les représentants *m.* **3. To make false representations to s.o.,** déguiser la vérité à qn. **4.** (i) Représentation; remontrance courtoise; (ii) exposé *m* des faits; (iii) *Dipl:* démarche *f.* **Joint representations,** démarche collective. **To make representations,** faire une démarche.

representative [,repri'zentətiv]. **1.** *a.* (*a*) **R. government,** gouvernement représentatif. (*b*) *Com:* **R. sample,** échantillon *m* type. (*c*) **Meeting of men r. of all classes,** réunion d'hommes représentant toutes les classes. **2.** *s.* (*a*) Représentant, -ante; délégué, -ée. (*b*) **Last r. of an illustrious race,** dernier rejeton d'une race illustre. (*c*) *Com:* Représentant (d'une maison de commerce). **District r.,** représentant régional. (*d*) *Pol:* Député *m.* *U.S:* **House of Representatives =** Assemblée Nationale.

repress [ri'pres], *v.tr.* **1.** Réprimer (une sédition). **2.** Réprimer, retenir (ses désirs). *Psy:* Refouler (ses sentiments). **To r. a sneeze,** étouffer un éternuement.

repressed, *a.* Réprimé, contenu. **A r. young man,** un jeune homme renfermé.

repression [ri'preʃ(ə)n], *s.* **1.** Répression *f.* **2.** *Psy:* **Unconscious r.,** refoulement *m.* **Conscious r.,** répression.

repressive [ri'presiv], *a.* Répressif, -ive, réprimant.

reprieve¹ [ri'priːv], *s.* **1.** (*a*) Commutation *f* de la peine capitale. (*b*) Lettre(s) *f(pl)* de grâce. **2.** Répit *m*, délai *m.*

reprieve², *v.tr.* **1.** *Jur:* Accorder à (un condamné) une commutation de la peine capitale. **2.** Donner du répit à (un débiteur); accorder un délai (à qn).

reprimand¹ ['reprimɑːnd], *s.* (*a*) Réprimande *f.* (*b*) *Adm. & Jur:* Blâme *m.*

reprimand², *v.tr* (*a*) Réprimander (qn). (*b*) *Adm. & Jur:* Blâmer publiquement (qn).

reprint¹ ['riːprint], *s.* Réimpression *f*; nouveau tirage. **Cheap r. of a book,** édition *f* populaire d'un ouvrage.

reprint² ['riː'print], *v.tr.* Réimprimer.

reprisal [ri'praiz(ə)l], *s. Usu.pl.* Représaille *f.* **To make reprisal(s),** user de représailles.

reproach¹ [ri'proutʃ], *s.* **1.** (*a*) Motif *m* de honte. **To be a r. to . . .,** être la honte, l'opprobre m, de. . . . (*b*) Honte, opprobre. **2.** Reproche *m*, blâme *m.* **Beyond r.,** irréprochable. **Term of r.,** terme injurieux.

reproach², *v.tr.* **1.** Faire, adresser, des reproches à (qn) (**about,** au sujet de). **To r. s.o. with sth.,** reprocher qch. à qn. **2.** Blâmer (l'ignorance de qn).

reproachful [ri'proutʃful], *a.* Réprobateur, -trice; plein de reproche(s). **-fully,** *adv.* D'un air, d'un ton, de reproche.

reprobate¹ ['reprobeit], *s. F:* Chenapan *m*, vaurien *m.* **Old r.,** vieux marcheur. *Ecc:* Réprouvé(e).

reprobate² ['reprobeit], *v.tr.* Réprouver (qn, un crime).

reprobation [,repro'beiʃ(ə)n], *s.* Réprobation *f.*

reproduce ['riːprə'djuːs]. **1.** *v.tr.* Reproduire. (*a*) Copier. **The features are well reproduced,** les traits sont bien rendus. (*b*) Multiplier (par génération). **2.** *v.i.* Se reproduire, se multiplier. **Print that will r. well,** estampe *f* qui se prête à la reproduction.

reproduction [,riːprə'dʌkʃ(ə)n], *s.* **1.** Reproduction *f* (d'un tableau, du genre humain). **R. rate,** taux de natalité *f.* *Cin:* **Sound r.,** reproduction sonore. *Art: Typ: etc:* **Correct r. of colour,** rendu exact des couleurs. **2.** Copie *f*, imitation *f.*

reproductive ['riːprə'dʌktiv], *a.* Reproductif, -ive; reproducteur, -trice. **The r. organs,** les organes de la reproduction.

reproof¹ [ri'pruːf], *s.* Reproche *m*, blâme *m.* **Deserving of r.,** réprimandable. **Term of r.,** Réprimande *f.*

reproof² ['riː'pruːf], *v.tr.* Réimperméabiliser.

reprove [ri'pruːv], *v.tr.* (*a*) Reprendre, réprimander (qn). (*b*) Condamner, réprouver (une action).

reproving, *a.* Réprobateur, -trice; (ton) plein de blâme. **-ly,** *adv.* D'un ton de reproche.

reprovision ['riːprə'viʒ(ə)n], *v.tr.* Rapprovisionner (une maison, une ville, de vivres, etc.).

reptile ['reptail]. **1.** *s.* Reptile *m.* **2.** *a.* (*a*) Reptile, rampant. (*b*) *F:* (Caractère) rampant.

reptilian [rep'tiliən]. **1.** *a.* Reptilien. **2.** *s.* Reptile *m.*

republic [ri'pʌblik], *s.* République *f.*

republican [ri'pʌblikən], *a. & s.* Républicain, -aine.

republicanism [ri'pʌblikənizm], *s.* Républicanisme *m.*

republicanize [ri'pʌblikənaiz], *v.tr.* Républicaniser.

republication ['riː,pʌbli'keiʃ(ə)n], *s.* **1.** Nouvelle édition, réédition *f* (d'un livre). **2.** Nouvelle publication (d'une loi, d'un décret).

republish ['riː'pʌbliʃ], *v.tr.* Rééditer (un livre).

repudiate [ri'pjuːdieit], *v.tr.* **1.** Répudier (une épouse). **2.** Répudier, désavouer (une opinion). (*Of government*) **To r. its debts,** répudier ses engagements. *Com: Jur:* **To r. (a contract),** refuser d'honorer (un contrat).

repudiation [ri,pjuːdi'eiʃ(ə)n], *s.* **1.** Répudiation *f* (d'une épouse). **2.** Répudiation, désaveu *m* (d'une opinion); reniement *m* (d'une dette).

repugnance [ri'pʌgnəns], *s.* Répugnance *f*, antipathie *f* (**to, against,** pour). **To feel r. to doing sth.,** répugner à faire qch.

repugnant [ri'pʌgnənt], *a.* **1.** Incompatible (**to, with,** avec); contraire (**to, with,** à). **2.** Répugnant (**to,** à). **To be r. to s.o.,** répugner à qn.

repulse¹ [ri'pʌls], *s.* **1.** Échec *m*; défaite *f* (de l'ennemi). **2.** Rebuffade *f*, refus *m.*

repulse², *v.tr.* **1.** Repousser, refouler (un assaut, un ennemi). **2.** Repousser (les avances de qn, une demande); refuser, renvoyer (qn).

repulsion [ri'pʌlʃ(ə)n], *s.* **1.** *Ph:* Répulsion *f.* **2.** Répulsion, aversion *f*, répugnance *f.*

repulsive [ri'pʌlsiv], *a.* **1.** *Ph:* Répulsif, -ive. **2.** Répulsif, repoussant. **To be r.-looking**, avoir l'air repoussant, répugnant. *F:* **R. job, person**, travail, type, écœurant. **-ly**, *adv.* **R. ugly**, d'une laideur repoussante.

repulsiveness [ri'pʌlsivnis], *s.* **1.** *Ph:* Force répulsive. **2.** Caractère repoussant; aspect répugnant.

repurchase¹ ['riː'pəːtʃes], *s.* Rachat *m.* *Jur:* Réméré *m.*

repurchase², *v.tr.* Racheter.

reputable ['repjutəbl], *a.* **1.** (*Of pers.*) Honorable, estimé, estimable. **2.** (Emploi) honorable. **-ably**, *adv.* Honorablement.

reputation [ˌrepju(ː)'teiʃ(ə)n], *s.* Réputation *f*, renom *m.* **To have a r. for courage**, avoir une réputation de courage. **Of bad r.**, de mauvaise réputation; *Adm:* mal noté. **Of good r.**, de bon renom. **To ruin s.o.'s r.**, perdre qn de réputation.

repute¹ [ri'pjuːt], *s.* Réputation *f*, renom *m*, renommée *f.* **To know s.o. by r.**, connaître qn de réputation. **To be held in high r.**, (i) avoir une haute réputation; (ii) *Adm:* être bien noté. **Doctor of r.**, médecin réputé. **The family is of good r.**, la famille est honorablement connue. **Place of ill r.**, endroit mal famé. **Of no r.**, sans réputation.

repute², *v.tr.* **To be reputed wealthy**, avoir la réputation d'être riche, passer pour riche. **reputed**, *a.* Réputé, censé, supposé. **A r. Hogarth**, un tableau attribué à Hogarth. *Jur:* **R. father**, père putatif. *S.a.* PINT. **-ly**, *adv.* Suivant l'opinion commune. **He is r. the best heart specialist**, il passe pour le meilleur cardiologue.

request¹ ['ri'kwest], *s.* **1.** Demande *f*, requête *f.* **Earnest r.**, sollicitation *f.* **R. for money**, demande d'argent. **At the r. of s.o.**, à la demande, sur la demande, de qn. **At the urgent r. of . . .**, sur les instances pressantes de.... **Samples sent on r.**, échantillons sur demande. **To make a r.**, faire une demande. **To grant a r.**, accéder à un désir. **To sing sth. by r.**, chanter qch. à la demande générale. *P.N:* 'R. stop,' "arrêt facultatif." *W.Tel:* **R. programme**, programme *m* des auditeurs. **2.** Recherche *f*, demande. **To be in r.**, être recherché. *Com:* **Article in great r.**, article très demandé. **He is very much in r.**, on se le dispute.

request², *v.tr.* **1.** **To r. sth. of s.o.**, demander qch. à qn; solliciter qch. de qn. *S.a.* PLEASURE 1. **2.** **To r. s.o. to do sth.**, demander à qn de faire qch.; prier qn de faire qch. **The public is requested to keep off the grass**, prière au public de ne pas marcher sur le gazon. *Com:* **As requested**, conformément à vos instructions. **3.** **To r. permission to do sth.**, demander à faire qch.

requiem ['rekwiem], *s.* **1.** **R.** (**mass**), requiem *m*; messe *f* des morts. **2.** Chant *m* funèbre.

require [ri'kwaiər], *v.tr.* **1.** **To r. sth. of s.o.**, demander, réclamer, qch. à qn; exiger qch. de qn. **What do you r. of me?** que voulez-vous de moi? **To r. s.o. to do sth.**, exiger de qn qu'il fasse qch. **I r. you to obey me**, je veux que vous m'obéissiez. **The court requires you to attend**, la cour requiert que vous comparaissiez. **2.** Exiger, réclamer. **Work that requires great precision**, travail qui nécessite une grande précision. **Ore that requires special treatment**, minerai qui comporte des traitements particuliers. **The vine requires a stony soil**, la vigne veut un terrain pierreux. **Have you all you r.?** avez-vous tout ce qu'il vous faut? **You will not r. a coat**, vous n'aurez pas besoin d'un manteau. **I shall do whatever is required**, je ferai tout ce qu'il faudra. **If required**, s'il le faut; si besoin est; au besoin. **required**, *a.* Exigé, demandé, voulu. **To cut sth. to the r. length**, couper qch. à la longueur voulue. **In the r. time**, dans le délai prescrit. **To have the money r.**, avoir l'argent nécessaire. **The qualities r. for this post**, les qualités requises pour ce poste.

requirement [ri'kwaiəmənt], *s.* **1.** Demande *f*, réclamation *f.* **2.** Exigence *f*, besoin *m.* **To meet s.o.'s requirements**, satisfaire les exigences de qn. **To make one's requirements known**, faire connaître ses besoins. **3.** Condition requise; nécessité *f.*

requisite ['rekwizit]. **1.** *a.* Requis (**to, pour**); nécessaire (**to, à**); indispensable (**to, pour**); voulu. **2.** *s.* (*a*) Condition requise (**for, pour**). (*b*) Chose *f* nécessaire. **Toilet requisites**, accessoires *m* de toilette.

requisition¹ [ˌrekwi'ziʃ(ə)n], *s.* **1.** Demande *f.* **Upon a r. by ten members**, sur la demande de dix membres. *Com:* **R. for materials, for supplies**, demande de matériaux; commande *f* pour fournitures. **R. number**, numéro de référence. **2.** *Mil:* Réquisition *f.* **His services were in constant r.**, on avait constamment recours à ses services.

requisition², *v.tr.* **1.** Réquisitionner (des vivres); mettre (des chevaux) en réquisition. **To r. s.o.'s services**, avoir recours aux services de qn. **2.** Faire des réquisitions dans (une ville).

requital [ri'kwaitl], *s.* **1.** Récompense *f*, retour *m.* **In r. for**, en récompense, en retour, de. **2.** Revanche *f*, représailles *fpl.*

requite [ri'kwait], *v.tr.* **1.** Récompenser, payer de retour (un service). **To r. s.o.'s love**, répondre à l'amour de qn. **2.** **To r. s.o. for a service**, récompenser qn d'un service. **He requites me with ingratitude**, il me paie d'ingratitude.

reredos ['riːrədɔs], *s.* *Ecc:* Retable *m.*

re-registration ['riːredʒis'treiʃ(ə)n], *s.* Réinscription *f.*

res [riːz], *s.* *Jur:* Chose *f.* **R. judicata**, chose jugée.

resaddle ['riː'sædl], *v.tr.* Resseller (un cheval).

resale ['riː'seil], *s.* Revente *f.*

rescind [ri'sind], *v.tr.* Rescinder (un acte); annuler (un vote); abroger (une loi). **rescinding**, *a.* (Clause) abrogatoire.

rescission [ri'siʒ(ə)n], *s.* Rescision *f*, abrogation *f* (d'un acte); annulation *f* (d'un contrat).

rescript ['riːskript], *s.* Rescrit *m.*

rescue¹ ['reskjuː], *s.* Délivrance *f*; (*from shipwreck, fire*) sauvetage *m.* **To the r.!** au secours! **R. party**, équipe *f* de sauvetage. **R. squad**, équipe *f* de secours. **Air Sea R.**, sauvetage aérien en mer.

rescue², *v.tr.* **1.** Sauver, délivrer, secourir. **To r. s.o. from death**, sauver qn de la mort. **To r. s.o. from drowning**, sauver qn qui se noie. **The rescued men**, *s.* **the rescued**, les rescapés *m.* **To r. s.o. from a scrape**, tirer qn d'un mauvais pas. **2.** *Jur:* Arracher (un prisonnier) aux mains de la justice.

rescuer ['reskjuər], *s.* **1.** Secoureur, -euse; libérateur, -trice. **2.** (*From shipwreck*) Sauveteur *m.*

research [ri'səːtʃ], *s.* Recherche *f* (**after, for**, de). **Scientific r.**, recherche scientifique. **R. work**, recherches, investigations; travaux *mpl* de recherche. **R. worker**, chercheur, -euse. *Ind:* **R. department**, service *m* de recherches.

reseat ['riː'siːt], *v.tr.* **1.** Rasseoir (qn); faire rasseoir (qn). **2.** Remettre un fond à (une chaise). **3.** **To r. a valve**, roder le siège d'une soupape.

resect [ri'sekt], *v.tr.* *Surg:* Réséquer (un os).

resection [ri'sekʃ(ə)n], *s.* *Surg:* Résection *f.*

reseda [ri'siːdə]. **1.** *s.* *Bot:* Réséda *m.* **2.** ['rezedə] *a. & s.* (Vert) réséda *inv.*

resell ['riː'sel], *v.tr.* (**resold** ['riː'sould]; **resold**) Revendre.

resemblance [ri'zembləns], *s.* Ressemblance *f* (**to, à**, **with**; **between, entre**). **A strong r.**, une grande ressemblance. **To bear a r. to sth.**, avoir de la ressemblance avec qch.

resemble [ri'zembl], *v.tr.* Ressembler à (qn, qch.). **To r. one another**, se ressembler.

resent [ri'zent], *v.tr.* **1.** Être offensé, froissé, de (qch.); être irrité de (qch.). **You r. my being here**, ma présence vous déplaît. **2.** S'offenser de (qch.); ressentir (une critique). **To r. a bit of fun**, se fâcher d'une badinerie. **I should r. a refusal**, un refus me blesserait.

resentful [ri'zentful], *a.* **1.** Plein de ressentiment; rancunier. **2.** Froissé, irrité (**of**, de). **-fully**, *adv.* Avec ressentiment; d'un ton, d'un air, rancunier.

resentment [ri'zentmənt], *s.* Ressentiment *m*, rancœur *f.* **To cherish a secret r. against s.o.**, ressentir un dépit secret contre qn.

reservation [ˌrezə'veiʃ(ə)n], *s.* **1.** (*a*) Réserve *f* (des places). *Rail:* **Seat reservation**(**s**), location *f* des places. (*b*) Place retenue. **2.** Réserve, restriction *f.* **To accept sth. without r.**, accepter qch. (i) sans réserve; (ii) sans arrière-pensée. **With reservations**, avec certaines réserves; *Jur:* sous bénéfice

d'inventaire. **With this r.,** à cette restriction près. *S.a.*
MENTAL. **3.** *Jur:* Réservation *f* (d'un droit). **4.** *U.S:*
Terrain réservé; parc national; réserve zoologique.
Indian r., réserve indienne.

reserve[1] [ri'zə:v], *s.* **1.** (*a*) Réserve *f* (d'argent, d'énergie).
Cash reserves, réserve de caisse. **R. fund,** fonds de
réserve, de prévision. *S.a.* GOLD. (*b*) **To have sth. in
r.,** tenir qch. en réserve. **2.** (*a*) *Mil:* **The reserves,** les
réserves. (*b*) *Mil:* **The r.,** la réserve (de l'armée
active). **R. list,** cadre *m* de réserve. (*c*) *Sp:* (Joueur
m de) réserve. **3.** Terrain réservé. *For:* Réserve.
Nature r., réserve naturelle. **4.** (*a*) Réserve, restriction
f. **Without r.,** sans réserve. (*b*) (*At sale*) **R. price,**
prix *m* minimum; mise *f* à prix. **To be sold without
r.,** à vendre sans réserve. **5.** Réserve, discrétion *f*.
When he breaks through his r. . . ., quand il sort de
sa réserve. . . .

reserve[2], *v.tr.* Réserver (sth. for s.o., qch. pour qn);
mettre (qch.) en réserve. **To r. a seat for s.o.,** retenir
une place pour qn. **To r. the right to do sth.,** se
réserver de faire qch. **I consent, reserving the right to
. . .,** je consens sauf à. . . . **reserved,** *a.* **1.** (Compartiment) réservé. **R. seats,** places réservées, louées.
Publ: **All rights r.,** tous droits (de reproduction)
réservés. **2.** *Navy: etc:* **R. list,** cadre *m* de réserve.
3. Réservé; renfermé; peu communicatif.

reservedly [ri'zə:vidli], *adv.* Avec réserve.

reservist [ri'zə:vist], *s. Mil:* Réserviste *m*.

reservoir ['rezəvwɑ:r], *s.* Réservoir *m*.

reset ['ri:'set], *v.tr.* (*p.t.* reset; *p.p.* reset; *pr.p.* resetting) **1.** Remettre en place; replacer; remonter
(des pierres précieuses); replanter (des rosiers). **2.**
Surg: **To r. a limb,** remettre un membre. **3.** Raffûter
(un outil). **4.** *Typ:* Recomposer (un livre). **resetting,**
s. **1.** (*a*) Remontage *m*. (*b*) Remise *f* en place. **2.**
Raffûtage *m*. **3.** *Typ:* Recomposition *f*.

resettle ['ri:'setl]. **I.** *v.tr.* Réinstaller. **To r. oneself,** se
rasseoir; se réinstaller. **2.** *v.i.* (*a*) Se remettre (**to an
occupation,** à une occupation); se réinstaller. (*b*) (*Of
wine after transport*) Se reposer.

resettlement ['ri:'setlmənt], *s.* (*a*) Nouvelle colonisation (d'un pays). (*b*) Recasement *m* (de la population);
transfert *m* (de population).

resharpen ['ri:'ʃɑ:p(ə)n], *v.tr.* Réaffûter, raffûter (un
outil); retailler (un crayon).

reship ['ri:'ʃip], *v.tr.* **1.** Rembarquer, réexpédier (des
marchandises). **2.** Remonter (le gouvernail, l'hélice).

reshipment ['ri:'ʃipmənt], *s.* Réembarquement *m*,
réexpédition *f*.

reshoe ['ri:'ʃu:], *v.tr.* Referrer (un cheval).

reshuffle[1] ['ri:'ʃʌfl], *s.* (*a*) Nouveau battement (des
cartes). (*b*) *F:* Cabinet r., remaniement ministériel.

reshuffle[2] ['ri:'ʃʌfl], *v.tr.* (*a*) Rebattre, remêler (les
cartes). (*b*) *F:* Remanier (un personnel).

reside [ri'zaid], *v.i.* **1.** Résider (**in a place,** dans un
endroit). **2.** (*Of quality*) Résider (**in sth.,** dans qch.).

residence ['rezidəns], *s.* **1.** Résidence *f*, demeure *f*,
séjour *m*. **To have one's r. at . . .,** résider à. . . .
During my r. abroad, pendant mon séjour à l'étranger.
To take up one's r. somewhere, fixer sa résidence,
établir sa demeure, quelque part. *Ecc:* **Canon in r.,**
chanoine en résidence. *Sch:* (Student's) **hall of r. =**
cité *f* universitaire. *S.a.* BOARD[1] **2.** Demeure,
maison *f*, habitation *f*. **Desirable r. for sale,** belle
propriété à vendre. **Gentleman's r.,** maison *f* de
maître. **Grace and favour r.,** résidence concédée à
titre gracieux, par faveur spéciale, par le souverain.

residency ['rezidənsi], *s. Adm:* Résidence officielle
(d'un haut fonctionnaire); la Résidence.

resident ['rezidənt]. **1.** *a.* (*a*) Résidant; qui réside. **To
be r. in a place,** résider dans un endroit. **The r.
population,** la population fixe. (*b*) (*In hospital*) **R.
physician,** interne *m*. *Sch:* **R. master = maître** *m*
d'internat (qui est aussi professeur). **2.** *s.* (*a*)
Habitant, -ante; pensionnaire *mf*. (*b*) *Adm:* (Ministre) résident *m* (p.ex. dans un pays sous protectorat).
(*c*) *Adm:* (*Person living in a foreign country*) Résident
-ente.

residential [,rezi'denʃ(ə)l], *a.* Résidentiel, -elle. **R.
district,** quartier résidentiel.

residual [ri'zidjuəl]. **1.** *a. Ph: etc:* Résiduel, -elle,
résiduaire. **R. magnetism,** magnétisme rémanent.
2. *s.* (*a*) *Ch:* Résidu *m*. (*b*) *Ar:* Reste *m*.

residuary [ri'zidjuəri], *a.* **1.** *Ch:* Résiduaire, résiduel.
2. Qui reste; restant. **3.** *Jur:* **R. legatee,** légataire (à
titre) universel.

residue ['rezidju:], *s.* **1.** *Ch:* Résidu *m*. **2.** Reste(s)
m(pl) (d'une armée). **3.** *Jur:* Reliquat *m* (d'une
succession). **4.** *Mth:* Résidu (d'une fonction).

residuum, *pl.* -a [ri'zidjuəm, -ə], *s. Ch: etc:* Résidu
m; reste *m*.

resign [ri'zain], *v.tr.* **1.** (*a*) Résigner (une fonction);
se démettre de, donner sa démission de (son emploi);
abs. démissionner. *Parl:* **R.! r.!** démission! démission! (*b*) Abandonner (tout espoir); renoncer à
(une tâche). *c.*) **To r. sth. to s.o.,** abandonner, céder,
qch. à qn. **2.** (*a*) **To r. oneself to sleep,** s'abandonner
au sommeil. **To r. oneself to s.o.'s guidance,** se laisser
guider par qn. (*b*) **To r. oneself to doing sth.,** se
résigner à faire qch.; en prendre son parti. **resigned,** *a.* Résigné (to, à). **To become r. to sth.,**
prendre son parti de qch.; se résigner à qch.

resignation [,rezig'neiʃ(ə)n], *s.* **1.** (*a*) Démission *f*. **To
tender one's r.,** donner sa démission. (*b*) Abandon *m*
(d'un droit, etc.). **2.** Résignation *f* (to, à); soumission *f*.

resignedly [ri'zainidli], *adv.* Avec résignation; d'un
air, d'un ton résigné.

resilience [ri'ziliəns], **resiliency** [ri'ziliənsi], *s.* **1.** (*a*)
Mec: Élasticité *f*. **Spring resilience,** bande *f* d'un
ressort. (*b*) Élasticité (de tempérament). **2.** Rebondissement *m*.

resilient [ri'ziliənt], *a.* Rebondissant, élastique. (*Of
pers.*) **To be r.,** avoir du ressort.

re-silver ['ri:'silvər], *v.tr.* Rétamer (un miroir).

resin[1] ['rezin], *s.* **1.** Résine *f*. **White r.,** galipot *m*. **2.**
Colophane *f*; poix sèche. **'resin-tapper,** *s. For:*
(*Pers.*) Résinier *m*; gemmeur *m*. **'resin-tapping,** *s.
For:* Résinage *m*, gemmage *m*.

resin[2], *v.tr.* Résiner.

resinous ['rezinəs], *a.* Résineux, -euse.

resist[1] [ri'zist], *s. Engr: Dy:* Réserve *f*.

resist[2], *v.tr.* **1.** (*a*) Résister à (une attaque). **A temptation too strong to be resisted,** une tentation irrésistible.
(*b*) **I couldn't r. telling him what I thought of him,** je
n'ai pas pu m'empêcher de lui dire son fait. **I can't
r. chocolates,** je ne peux pas résister aux chocolats.
2. (*a*) Résister à, s'opposer à (un projet). **It's best not
to r.,** mieux vaut ne pas offrir de résistance. (*b*)
Repousser (une suggestion). **To r. the evidence,** se
refuser à l'évidence. **3.** (*Of girder*) Résister à (une
pression).

resistance [ri'zistəns], *s.* Résistance *f*. **1. To offer r.,**
résister (à la police, etc.) **She made no r.,** elle s'est
laissé faire. **Passive r.,** résistance passive. *Lit:*
Weary of r., de guerre lasse. *Pol:* (*1939-45 war*) **The
R. (movement),** la Résistance. **R. fighter,** résistant,
-ante. **2.** (*a*) *Mec: Ph:* **Line of least r.,** ligne de
moindre résistance. (*Whence*) **To take the line of
least r.,** aller au plus facile, prendre la solution
paresseuse. *Mec:* **Impact r.,** résistance au choc.
High-r. steel, acier à haute résistance. (*b*) *El: Magn:*
R. coil, bobine de résistance. (*c*) *El:* **Variable r.,**
résistance variable; rhéostat *m*.

resistant, resistent [ri'zistənt], *a.* Résistant.

resistivity [,rizis'tiviti], *s. El:* Résistivité *f*.

resistless [ri'zistlis], *a.* **1.** Irrésistible. **2.** Qui se laisse
faire. **-ly,** *adv.* Irrésistiblement.

resistor [ri'zistər], *s. El:* Resistor *m*.

resnatron ['reznətrən], *s. Electronics:* Resnatron *m*.

reso-jet ['rezoudʒet], *s.* Pulsoréacteur *m*.

re-sole ['ri:'soul], *v.tr.* Ressemeler (des souliers). **re-
soling,** *s.* Ressemelage *m*.

resolute ['rezəlu:t], *a.* Résolu, déterminé. **R. tone,** ton
résolu; ton ferme. **-ly,** *adv.* Résolument; avec
détermination; avec décision, décidément.

resoluteness ['rezəlu:tnis], *s.* Résolution *f*.

resolution [,rezə'lu:ʃ(ə)n], *s.* **1.** *Ch: Mth: Mus: etc:*
Résolution *f*. **R. of water into steam,** résolution de
l'eau en vapeur. *Mec:* **R. of forces,** décomposition *f*
des forces. *T.V:* **Picture r.,** définition *f* d'une image.
2. Résolution, délibération *f* (d'une assemblée);
ordre *m* du jour. **To put a r. to the meeting,** mettre
une résolution aux voix. **3.** Résolution, détermination
f. **Good resolutions,** bonnes résolutions. **4.** Résolution, fermeté *f*, décision *f*. **Lack of r.,** manque *m* de
caractère.

resolvability [ri͵zɔlvə'biliti], s. Résolubilité f.
resolvable [ri'zɔlvəbl], a. Résoluble, réductible.
resolve[1] [ri'zɔlv], s. Résolution f; détermination f.
resolve[2]. I. v.tr. 1. (a) Résoudre (qch. en ses éléments). The water resolves itself into vapour, l'eau se résout en vapeur. Steam resolved into water, vapeur résoute en eau. Mec: To r. a velocity into its components, décomposer une vitesse en ses composantes. Mus: To r. a discord, résoudre une dissonance. (b) The House resolved itself into a committee, la Chambre se constitua en commission. 2. Résoudre (un problème); dissiper (un doute). 3. (a) (Of committee) Résoudre, décider (de faire qch.). (b) (Of individual) To r. to do sth., prendre la résolution de faire qch. II. resolve, v.i. 1. Se résoudre (en ses éléments). 2. (Of pers.) Se résoudre (upon sth., à qch.); résoudre (upon sth., de faire qch.). resolved, a. Résolu, décidé (to do sth., à faire qch.).
resolvedly [ri'zɔlvidli], adv. Résolument.
resonance ['rezənəns], s. Résonance f. Mus: Vibration f (de la voix).
resonant ['rezənənt], a. (Of sound) Résonnant. R. voice, voix sonore.
resonator ['rezəneitər], s. Ph: El: Résonateur m.
resorption [ri'sɔːpʃ(ə)n], s. Résorption f.
resort[1] [ri'zɔːt], s. 1. (a) Ressource f. To be the only r., être la seule ressource. (b) Recours m. Without r. to compulsion, sans avoir recours à la force. Last r., dernier ressort. 2. (a) Lieu de séjour, de rendez-vous. (b) Health r., station climatique, thermale. Seaside r., station balnéaire; plage f. Holiday r., (centre m de) villégiature f.
resort[2], v.i. 1. Avoir recours, recourir (to, à); user (to, de). To r. to force, faire emploi de la force. To r. to violence, recourir à la violence. To r. to blows, en venir aux coups. 2. O: To r. to a place, (i) (in numbers) se rendre, affluer, dans un endroit; (ii) fréquenter un lieu.
resound [ri'zaund], v.i. (a) Résonner; retentir (with cries, de cris). (b) (Of event) Avoir du retentissement. **resounding**, a. Résonnant, retentissant; (rire) sonore. (Of voice) Tonitruant. R. success, succès bruyant. -ly, adv. D'une manière retentissante; bruyamment; avec fracas.
resource [ɪi'sɔːs], s. 1. Ressource f. Man of r., homme de ressource. Man of no r., homme sans moyens, incapable de se débrouiller. S.a. LAST[2] 1. 2. pl. To be at the end of one's resources, être au bout de ses ressources. 3. Récréation f, distraction f.
resourceful [ri'sɔːsf(u)l], a. Fertile en ressources; F: débrouillard.
resourcefulness [ri'sɔːsf(u)lnis], s. Ressource f.
respect[1] [ris'pekt], s. 1. Rapport m, égard m. With r. to . . ., en ce qui concerne . . .; quant à. . . . In many respects, à bien des égards. In some respects, sous quelques rapports; par certains côtés. In this r., à cet égard. 2. (Heed) Égard. To have r. to sth., tenir compte de qch. Without r. of persons, sans acception de personnes. 3. (a) Respect m (for the truth, pour la vérité); considération f (for s.o., pour, envers, qn). To have r. for s.o., avoir du respect pour qn. He can command r., il sait se faire respecter. Worthy of r., respectable; digne d'estime. Out of r. for . . ., par respect, par égard, pour. . . . With (all) due r. (to you), sans vouloir vous contredire. (b) R. for the law, respect de la loi. 4. pl. Respects, respects, hommages m. To pay one's respects to s.o., présenter ses respects à qn.
respect[2], v.tr. Respecter. 1. Honorer (qn); porter respect à (qn). Respected by all, respecté de tous. 2. Avoir égard à (qch.). (a) To r. s.o.'s opinion, respecter l'opinion de qn. (b) To r. persons, faire acception de personnes. (c) To r. the law, avoir le respect des lois, obéir à la loi. (d) He was able to make himself respected, il a su se faire respecter. 3. Avoir rapport, avoir trait, à (qch.); concerner (qch.). **respecting**, prep. Relativement à; quant à; à l'égard de. Questions r. a matter, questions relatives à un sujet.
respectability [ris͵pektə'biliti], s. Respectabilité f, honorabilité f; décence f.
respectable [ris'pektəbl], a. Respectable. 1. Digne de respect. 2. (a) Honorable, convenable; de bonnes

mœurs. R. family, famille honnête. R. couple wanted, on demande un ménage recommandable. (b) Convenable, comme il faut. I'm going to put on some r. clothes, je vais mettre des vêtements convenables, comme il faut. You don't look r., vous n'avez pas l'air convenable. (c) She is of a r. age, elle est d'âge canonique; elle n'est plus jeune. 3. Passable. A r. sum (of money), une somme rondelette. -ably, adv. 1. R. dressed, convenablement vêtu. 2. Pas mal, passablement. He plays quite r., il joue passablement.
respecter [ris'pektər], s. Death is no r. of persons, la mort n'épargne personne.
respectful [ris'pektf(u)l], a. Respectueux, -euse (to, envers, pour). To keep s.o. at a r. distance, tenir qn en respect. -fully, adv. Respectueusement; avec respect. Corr: I remain yours r., je vous prie d'agréer mes salutations très respectueuses.
respectfulness [ris'pektf(u)lnis], s. Caractère respectueux; respect m.
respective [ris'pektiv], a. Respectif, -ive. -ly, adv. Respectivement.
respiration [͵respə'reiʃ(ə)n], s. Physiol: Bot: Respiration f. Artificial r., respiration artificielle.
respirator ['respəreitər], s. Respirateur m; masque m respiratoire; Mil: masque à gaz.
respiratory [ris'pirət(ə)ri, 'respireitəri], a. Respiratoire; (m only) respirateur.
respire [ris'paiər], v.tr. & i. Physiol: Bot: Respirer.
respite[1] ['respait], s. 1. Jur: Sursis m, délai m. To get a r., obtenir un délai. 2. Répit m, relâche m. To work without r., travailler sans relâche.
respite[2], v.tr. 1. (a) Accorder un sursis à (un prévenu). (b) Remettre, différer (un jugement). 2. Apporter du soulagement à (qn).
resplendence [ris'plendəns], **resplendency** [ris'plendənsi], s. Splendeur f, resplendissement m, éclat m (d'une cérémonie).
resplendent [ris'plendənt], a. Resplendissant, éblouissant. -ly, adv. Avec splendeur.
respond [ris'pɔnd], v.i. 1. (a) Répondre; faire une réponse. To r. to a toast, répondre à un toast. (b) Ecc: Réciter les répons. 2. Répondre, être sensible (à l'affection); se prêter (à une proposition). To r. to music, apprécier la musique. (Of machine) To r. to the controls, obéir aux commandes.
respondent [ris'pɔndənt]. 1. a. Répondant; qui répond. 2. s. Jur: (i) (Esp. in divorce case) Défendeur, -eresse. (ii) (Before Court of Appeal) Intimé m.
response [ris'pɔns], s. 1. (a) Réponse f, réplique f. (b) Ecc: Répons m. To make the responses at mass, répondre la messe. 2. (a) Réponse (à un appel). This appeal met with a generous r., il fut répondu largement à cet appel. The Anglo-French treaty met with a warm r., on a fait un accueil chaleureux au traité franco-anglais. To act in r. to the call of duty, répondre à l'appel du devoir. (b) Réaction f, réponse.
responsibility [ris͵pɔnsə'biliti], s. Responsabilité f. To assume a r., accepter une responsabilité. To accept r. for sth., prendre la responsabilité de qch. To do sth. on one's own r., faire qch. de son chef, sous sa propre responsabilité.
responsible [ris'pɔnsəbl], a. 1. (a) Chargé (d'un devoir). Person r. for doing sth., personne à qui il incombe de faire qch. R. to s.o., responsable devant qn. Commission r. to a government, commission relevant d'un gouvernement. To be r. to s.o. for sth., avoir à rendre compte à qn de qch. He is not r. for his actions, il n'est pas maître de ses actes. (b) Responsable (d'un accident). To hold s.o. r. (for sth.), tenir qn responsable (de qch.). Jur: To be r. for s.o.'s actions, être solidaire des actes de qn. 2. Capable, compétent. In r. quarters, dans les milieux autorisés. Situation for a r. man, situation pour homme sérieux. 3. (Poste) plein de responsabilités.
responsive [ris'pɔnsiv], a. (a) Impressionnable; sensible (to, à). They are r. to affection, ils répondent à l'affection. (b) Mec.E: Aut: (Moteur) nerveux, souple. W.Tel: (Détecteur) sensible. -ly, adv. Avec sympathie.
responsiveness [ris'pɔnsivnis], s. 1. Émotion f sympathique; sensibilité f. 2. Flexibilité f, nervosité f, souplesse f (d'un moteur). 3. Mus: Résonance f.

rest[1] [rest], s. 1. (a) Repos m. To go, retire, to r., aller se reposer. To have a good night's r., passer une bonne nuit. At r., en, au, repos. To set a question at r., régler, vider, une question. To set s.o.'s mind at r., calmer l'esprit de qn; dissiper les inquiétudes de qn. S.a. LAY[4] 3. (b) To take a r., se donner du repos; se reposer; Mil: faire la pause. The day of r., le repos dominical. (c) To come to r., s'arrêter, s'immobiliser. 2. Mus: Pause f, silence m. Semi-breve r., pause. Crotchet r., soupir m. Quaver r., demi-soupir m. 3. Abri m (pour chauffeurs de taxis); foyer m (pour matelots). R. centre, centre m d'accueil. R. home, maison f de repos. 4. Support m. Arm-r. (of chair), accoudoir m. Telescope r., affût m, support m, de télescope. Tp: Receiver-r., fourche interruptrice (du récepteur). 'rest-camp, s. Mil: Cantonnement m de repos. 'rest-cure, s. Cure f de repos. 'rest house, s. (In the East) Bungalow m à la disposition des fonctionnaires en tournée, etc. 'rest-room, s. (In shops, etc.) Toilette f.

rest[2]. I. v.i. 1. (a) Avoir du repos, de la tranquillité. He will not r. till he has succeeded, il n'aura (pas) de cesse qu'il n'ait réussi. To r. in the Lord, s'en remettre à Dieu. May he r. in peace, qu'il repose en paix. The waves never r., les vagues ne sont jamais tranquilles. (b) Se reposer. Let us r. here a little while, reposons-nous ici quelques instants. Th: F: To be resting, se trouver sans engagement. S.a. OAR[1]. (c) So the matter rests, l'affaire en reste là. And there the matter rests, les choses en sont là. I shall not let it r. at that, cela ne se passera pas ainsi. 2. (a) Se poser, s'appuyer. His hand resting on the table, sa main posée, appuyée, sur la table. To let one's glance r. on sth., reposer ses regards sur qch. A heavy responsibility rests upon them, une lourde responsabilité pèse sur eux. (b) Trade rests upon credit, le commerce repose sur le crédit. II. rest, v.tr. (a) Reposer, faire reposer (qn). To r. one's men, faire reposer ses hommes. God r. his soul! Dieu donne le repos à son âme! (b) Appuyer (ses coudes sur la table); déposer (un fardeau par terre). To r. sth. against sth., appuyer qch. contre qch. resting, a. (Homme, machine) au repos. 'resting-place, s. (Lieu m de) repos m; gîte m, abri m. Last r.-p., dernière demeure.

rest[3], s. 1. Reste m, restant m. To do the r., faire le reste. For the r., quant au reste; d'ailleurs. And all the r. of it, et tout ce qui s'ensuit, F: et patati et patata. 2. The r., les autres mf. The r. of us, nous autres; les autres d'entre nous.

rest[4], v.i. 1. Rester, demeurer. R. assured that . . ., soyez assuré que. . . . 2. It rests with you (to do sth.), il dépend de vous, il ne tient qu'à vous (de faire qch.). It does not r. with me to . . ., il est en dehors de mes pouvoirs de. . . . It rests with France to decide, il appartient à la France de décider.

restart ['ri:'stɑːt]. 1. v.tr. (a) Recommencer, reprendre (un travail). (b) (Re)mettre (une machine) en marche; relancer (un moteur). 2. v.i. (a) (Of work) Recommencer, reprendre. (b) (Of machine) Se remettre en marche.

restate ['ri:'steit], v.tr. Exposer de nouveau (une théorie); énoncer de nouveau (un problème); spécifier de nouveau (des conditions). The question needs to be restated, la question a besoin d'être mise au point.

restaurant ['rest(ə)rɔ̃], s. Restaurant m. Rail: R. car, wagon-restaurant m. Civic, municipal, r. = restaurant social, communautaire.

restaurateur [restɔːrɔ'tɜːr], s. Restaurateur, -trice.

restful ['restful], a. Qui repose; paisible, tranquille. R. spot, endroit reposant. Colour r. to the eyes, couleur reposante pour la vue. -fully, adv. Paisiblement, tranquillement.

restfulness ['restfulnis], s. Tranquillité f.

restitch ['ri:'stitʃ], v.tr. Repiquer (à l'aiguille).

restitution [ˌresti'tjuːʃ(ə)n], s. Restitution f. To make r. of sth., restituer qch. Jur: R. of conjugal rights, réintégration f du domicile conjugal.

restive ['restiv], a. 1. (Cheval) rétif, quinteux; (personne) rétive, indocile. 2. Inquiet, -ète; nerveux, -euse -ly, adv. (Of horse) D'une manière rétive; (Of pers.) indocilement; nerveusement.

restiveness ['restivnis], s. 1. Humeur rétive. 2. Humeur inquiète; nervosité f, énervement m.

restless ['restlis], a. 1. Sans repos. To have a r. night, passer une nuit blanche. 2. (a) Agité. To be r. in one's sleep, avoir le sommeil agité, troublé. (b) (Enfant) remuant. 3. Inquiet, agité. R. brain, cerveau en effervescence. He's a r. soul, c'est un agité. R. eye, regard inquiet. The audience was getting r., l'auditoire s'impatientait, s'énervait. -ly, adv. 1. Avec agitation. 2. Nerveusement, fiévreusement.

restlessness ['restlisnis], s. 1. (a) Inquiétude f, agitation f; fièvre f. (b) Turbulence f; mouvement incessant (de la mer). 2. Nervosité f; effervescence f (du peuple).

restock ['ri:'stɔk], v.tr. 1. Repeupler, rempoissonner, (un étang). 2. Com: Remonter, regarnir (un magasin). 3. Rapprovisionner, réapprovisionner (une maison, etc., de vivres).

restoration [ˌrestɔ'reiʃ(ə)n], s. 1. Restitution f (de biens); remise f (d'objets trouvés). 2. Restauration f (d'un monument); restitution (d'un texte). 3. (a) Réintégration f (d'un fonctionnaire). (b) Rétablissement m de la santé. (c) Relèvement m (d'une fortune). 4. Rétablissement sur le trône; restauration.

restorative [ris'tɔːrətiv], a. & s. Med: 1. Fortifiant (m); reconstituant (m), restoratif, -ive. 2. Cordial (m), -aux.

restore [ris'tɔːr], v.tr. 1. Restituer, rendre (qch.). To r. sth. to s.o., rendre qch. à qn. 2. (a) Restaurer (un monument); réparer (un tableau); rénover (un meuble). (b) Reconstituer, restituer (un texte). 3. (a) To r. sth. to its place, to its former condition, remettre qch. en place, en état. (b) Rétablir, réintégrer (qn dans ses fonctions). To r. the king (to the throne), rétablir le roi sur le trône. (c) To r. s.o. to health, rétablir la santé de qn. To r. s.o. to life, ramener qn à la vie. 4. (a) Rétablir (la liberté, la discipline); ramener (la confiance); faire renaître (le calme). Public order is being restored, l'ordre se rétablit. To see calm restored, voir renaître le calme. (b) To r. s.o.'s strength, redonner des forces à qn. To r. the circulation, réactiver la circulation.

restorer [ris'tɔːrər], s. 1. Restaurateur, -trice (d'un tableau); rénovateur m (de meubles); rétablisseur m (d'un texte). 2. Health r., fortifiant m.

restow ['ri:'stou], v.tr. Réarrimer (la cargaison d'un navire, d'un avion, d'un véhicule).

restrain [ris'trein], v.tr. 1. Retenir, empêcher (qn) (from, de). 2. Jur: Détenir (qn). 3. Contenir, refréner (ses passions); retenir (sa curiosité). To r. oneself, se contraindre. To r. one's mirth, se retenir de rire. To r. production, freiner la production. To r. s.o.'s activities, entraver les, mettre un frein aux, activités de qn. restrained, a. (Of anger) Contenu. In r. terms, en termes mesurés. (Of style) Tempéré. R. drawing, dessin très sobre. restraining, a. Qui retient; restrictif, -ive.

restrainedly [ris'treinidli], adv. Avec retenue. To speak r., parler avec contrainte.

restraint [ris'treint], s. 1. (a) Contrainte f, entrave f, frein m. To put a r. on s.o., tenir qn en contrainte. To fret, chafe, under r., (i) ronger son frein; (ii) ne pouvoir souffrir aucune contrainte. To break through every r., se donner libre cours. (b) Contrainte, réserve f. To put a r. upon oneself, se contenir, se contraindre. Lack of r., abandon m; manque m de réserve. To speak without r., parler en toute liberté. To fling aside all r., ne garder aucune mesure. (c) Sobriété f (de style); mesure f. 2. Contrainte par corps; interdiction f (d'un aliéné). To keep s.o. under r., tenir qn emprisonné. To put a lunatic under r., interner un aliéné.

restrict [ris'trikt], v.tr. Restreindre; réduire (les libertés publiques). I am restricted to advising, il ne m'est permis que de donner des conseils. To r. s.o.'s power, limiter le pouvoir de qn. To r. the consumption of alcohol, restreindre la consommation de l'alcool. restricted, a. Restreint, limité. R. horizon, horizon borné. R. diet, régime sévère. Adm: Aut: R. area, zone f de vitesse limitée, à limitation f de vitesse.

restriction [ris'trikʃ(ə)n], s. Restriction f. (a) R. of expenditure, réduction f des dépenses. (b) To place restrictions on the sale of . . ., apporter des restrictions à la vente de. . . . (c) Aut: R. of speed, Restriction, limitation f, de vitesse.

restrictive [ris'triktiv], *a.* Restrictif, -ive. **-ly,** *adv.* D'une façon restrictive.

restring ['ri:'striŋ], *v.tr.* 1. Enfiler de nouveau (des perles). 2. Remonter (un violon); recorder (une raquette.)

result¹ [ri'zʌlt], *s.* 1. Résultat *m* (of, de); aboutissement *m* (des efforts de qn). His infirmity is the r. of an accident, son infirmité est due à un accident. The r. is that . . ., il en résulte que. . . . What will be the r. of it all? que sortira-t-il de tout cela? As a r. of . . ., par suite de. . . . Without r., sans résultat. To give out the results (of a competition), donner le classement. 2. *Ar:* Résultat.

result², *v.i.* 1. Résulter, provenir (from, de). It results from this that . . ., il s'ensuit que. . . . Little will r. from all this, il ne sortira pas grand-chose de tout cela. Damage resulting from an accident, dommage consécutif à un accident. 2. Aboutir (in a discovery, à, dans, une découverte). It resulted in nothing, il n'en est rien résulté; cela n'a mené à rien. It resulted in a large profit, cela a donné de gros bénéfices.

resultant [ri'zʌltənt], *a.* Résultant. *Mec:* R. force, *s.* resultant, force résultante; résultante *f.* To find the r. of three forces, composer trois forces.

resume [ri'zju:m], *v.tr.* 1. Reprendre, regagner (sa vigueur). To r. one's seat, se rasseoir. 2. To r. (posession of) a territory, reprendre possession d'un territoire. 3. (*a*) Reprendre (une conversation); renouer (des relations). To r. work, se remettre au travail. If hostilities should be resumed, si les hostilités repreneaient. (*b*) "This was a great mistake," he resumed, "c'était une grosse erreur," reprit-il. 4. Reprendre, récapituler (les faits).

résumé [re'zju(:)mei], *s.* Résumé *m.*

resumption [ri'zʌm(p)ʃ(ə)n], *s.* Reprise *f* (de négociations, des travaux). *Jur:* R. of residence, réintégration *f* de domicile.

resurface ['ri:'sə:fis]. 1. *v.tr.* To r. a road, refaire le revêtement d'une route; remettre une route en état. 2. *v.i.* (*Of submarine, etc.*) Faire surface.

resurge [ri'sə:dʒ], *v.i.* Resurgir; ressusciter.

resurgence [ri'sə:dʒəns], *s.* Résurrection *f* (de l'art, d'un peuple).

resurgent [ri'sə:dʒənt], *a.* Qui resurgit; qui ressuscite.

resurrect ['rezə'rekt], *v.tr.* Ressusciter, faire revivre (qn, une mode, etc.).

resurrection ['rezə'rekʃ(ə)n], *s.* 1. Résurrection *f* (des morts). 2. *Eng.Hist:* R. man, déterreur *m* de cadavres. 3. Résurrection (d'une coutume); réchauffement *m* (d'un plat). *Cu: F:* R. pie, hachis *m* de viande aux pommes de terre.

resurrectionist [,rezə'rekʃənist], *s. Eng.Hist:* Déterreur *m* de cadavres (aux fins de dissection).

resuscitate [ri'sʌsiteit], *v.tr. & i.* Ressusciter.

resuscitation [ri'sʌsi'teiʃ(ə)n], *s.* Ressuscitation *f.*

ret [ret], *v.tr.* (retted) Rouir (le lin). **retting,** *s.* Rouissage *m* (du lin).

retable [ri'teibl, 'ri:teibl], *s. Ecc:* Retable *m.*

retail¹ ['ri:teil], *s. Com:* Détail *m*; vente *f* au détail. To sell goods r., vendre des marchandises au détail. Wholesale and r., en gros et au détail. R. dealer, détaillant *m.* R. price, prix de détail.

retail² [ri:'teil], *v.tr.* 1. Détailler, vendre au détail (des marchandises). Goods that r. at . . ., marchandises qui se vendent au détail à . . ., qui se détaillent à. . . . 2. Répéter, colporter (des commérages).

retailer ['ri:'teilər, 'ri:'teilər], *s.* 1. Détaillant *m*; marchand *m* au détail. 2. R. of news, colporteur *m* de nouvelles.

retain [ri'tein], *v.tr.* 1. Retenir, maintenir (qch. dans une position). 2. Engager, retenir (un domestique). To r. s.o.'s services, retenir, arrêter, les services de qn. 3. Conserver, garder (un bien). To r. all one's faculties, conserver toutes ses facultés. To r. hold of sth., ne pas lâcher (prise de) qch. To r. control of one's car, demeurer maître de sa voiture. 4. Garder (qch.) en mémoire; retenir (qch.) dans son souvenir. **retaining,** *a.* Rétenteur, -trice. 1. R. wall, mur de soutènement. R. dam, barrage *m* de retenue. *Surg:* R. bandage, bandage contentif. 2. R. fee = RETAINER 3.

retainer [ri'teinər], *s.* 1. (*a*) Dispositif *m* de retenue. (*b*) A brick is a r. of heat, une brique conserve la chaleur. 2. *Hist:* Serviteur *m*, suivant *m.* A lord's

retainers, la suite, les gens *m*, d'un noble. 3. (*a*) Arrhes *fpl.* (*b*) *Jur:* Honoraires versés à un avocat pour s'assurer son concours éventuel; avance *f.*

retake¹ ['ri:'teik], *s. Cin:* Réplique *f* (d'une prise de vues).

retake² ['ri:'teik], *v.tr.* (retook ['ri:'tuk]; retaken) 1. Reprendre (une place forte); rattraper (un prisonnier qui s'est sauvé). 2. *Cin:* Tourner à nouveau (une scène). **retaking,** *s.* Reprise *f* (d'une position).

retaliate [ri'tælieit], *v.i.* To r. on s.o., rendre la pareille (à qn); user de représailles (envers qn).

retaliation [ri,tæli'eiʃ(ə)n], *s.* Revanche *f*, représailles *fpl.* In r., en revanche. The law of r., la loi du talion.

retaliatory [ri'tæli'eitəri], *a.* De représailles. R. measures, représailles *f*; *Internat. Jur:* mesures *f* de rétorsion.

retard [ri'tɑ:d], *v.tr.* Retarder. *I.C.E:* To r. the spark, retarder l'allumage. *Mec:* Retarded acceleration, accélération négative. *Med:* Mentally retarded child, enfant attardé, arriéré.

retardation [,ri:tɑ:'deiʃ(ə)n], *s.* 1. (*a*) Retardement *m*; retard *m.* (*b*) *Mus:* Ralentissement *m* (de la mesure). 2. *Mec: Ph:* (*a*) Retardation *f*; accélération négative. (*b*) Freinage *m.* 3. *Nau:* Retard (des marées).

retardment [ri'tɑ:dmənt], *s.* Retardement *m*, retard *m.* Mental r., arriération mentale.

retch [retʃ, ri:tʃ], *v.i.* Faire des efforts pour vomir; avoir des haut-le-cœur. **retching,** *s.* Efforts *mpl* pour vomir; des haut-le-cœur *m.*

retell [ri:'tel], *v.tr.* (retold [ri:'tould]; retold) Raconter de nouveau.

retemper [ri:'tempər], *v.tr.* 1. *Metalw:* Retremper. 2. Regâcher, redélayer (le béton, etc.). **retempering,** *s.* 1. *Metalw:* Retrempe *f.* 2. Regâchage *m*, redélayage *m* (du béton, etc.).

retention [ri'ten(ʃ)(ə)n], *s.* 1. *Med:* Rétention *f* (d'urine, etc.). 2. Fixation *f.* *Surg:* R. of a fracture in position, contention *f* d'une luxation. 3. Conservation *f* (d'un usage); maintien *m* (d'une autorité). 4. *Psy:* (Faculté *f* de) rétention; mémoire *f.*

retentive [ri'tentiv], *a.* 1. (*a*) (Mémoire) tenace, fidèle, sûre. (*b*) To be r. of sth., retenir, garder, qch. R. soil, sol qui retient l'eau. 2. *Surg:* (Bandage) contentif.

retentiveness [ri'tentivnis], *s.* Pouvoir *m*, faculté *f*, de retenir. R. of memory, fidélité *f*, ténacité *f*, de mémoire.

reticence ['retis(ə)ns], *s.* 1. Réticence *f.* To tell a story without any r., raconter les choses sans rien cacher, voiler, sans aucune réserve. 2. Caractère peu communicatif.

reticent ['retis(ə)nt], *a.* Peu communicatif, -ive, réticent; taciturne. To be very r. about an event, faire grand mystère d'un événement. **-ly,** *adv.* Avec réticence; avec réserve.

reticle ['retikl], *s. Opt:* Réticule *m* (de télescope).

reticular [ri'tikjulər], *a.* Réticulaire; en réseau.

reticulate¹ [ri'tikjuleit], *a.* Réticulé, rétiforme.

reticulate² [ri'tikjuleit]. 1. *v.tr.* Couvrir (une surface) d'un réseau; diviser (une surface) en réseau. 2. *v.i.* Former un réseau. **reticulated,** *a.* Réticulé; rétiforme.

reticulation [ri,tikjʊ'leiʃ(ə)n], *s.* Réticulation *f*; structure maillée.

reticule ['retikju:l], *s.* 1. *A:* Réticule *m*; sac *m* à main. 2. = RETICLE.

retighten ['ri:'taitn], *v.tr.* Resserrer (une vis, etc.).

re-tile ['ri:'tail], *v.tr.* Recarreler (un mur, un plancher, etc.).

retina ['retinə], *s. Anat:* Rétine *f* (de l'œil).

retinue ['retinju:], *s.* Suite *f* (d'un prince).

retire [ri'taiər]. I. *v.i.* 1. (*a*) Se retirer (to a place, dans un endroit). To r. into oneself, se replier sur soi-même; se concentrer (en soi-même); se recueillir. (*b*) To r. from the room, quitter la salle. To r. for the night, aller se coucher. 2. Se démettre (de ses fonctions). To r. from business, se retirer des affaires. To r. (on a pension), prendre sa retraite. *Abs.* He has retired, c'est un retraité, il est en retraite. 3. (*a*) *Mil:* Reculer; se replier. (*b*) *Sp:* To r. from the race, se retirer de la partie; abandonner. (*c*) *Fenc:* Rompre. 4. *Art:* (*Of background*) S'éloigner, fuir. II. **retire,** *v.tr.* 1. *Adm:* Mettre (un fonctionnaire) à la retraite. 2. *Com:* Retirer, rembourser (un effet). **retired,** *a.*

1. (a) (Of life) Retiré. (b) (Endroit) retiré, peu fréquenté. **In a r. spot**, à l'écart. **2.** (a) En retraite, retraité, retiré (des affaires). **R. schoolmaster**, professeur m en retraite. (b) Mil: **R. pay**, (pension f de) retraite (f). **R. list**, cadre m de retraite. **On the r. list**, en retraite; retraité. **retiring**[1], a. **1.** (Of pers.) Réservé; farouche. **He is of a r. disposition**, il aime à s'effacer. **2.** (Président) sortant. **-ly**, adv. Modestement; en s'effaçant. **retiring**[2], s. **R. room**, cabinet particulier, vestiaire m (d'un magistrat).

retirement [ri'taiəmənt], s. **1.** (a) La retraite. **R. pension**, (pension f de) retraite. Adm: Mil: **Optional r.**, retraite sur demande. **Compulsory r.**, retraite d'office. **R. on** (account of) **age**, retraite par limite d'âge. (b) **To live in r.**, vivre retiré du monde. **2.** (a) Retraite, repliement m (des troupes). (b) Sp: Abandon m de la partie; abs. abandon. **3.** Com: Retrait m, remboursement m (d'un effet).

retold ['ri:'tould]. See RETELL.

retort[1] [ri'tɔ:t], s. Réplique f (to, à); riposte f. **To make an insolent r.**, répliquer par une insolence.

retort[2], v.tr. Répliquer, riposter, repartir. **'That's your business,' he retorted**, "ça c'est votre affaire," riposta-t-il.

retort[3], s. Ch: Ind: Cornue f.

retorted [ri'tɔ:tid], a. Nat.Hist: etc: **1.** Recourbé, tordu. **2.** Retourné.

retortion [ri'tɔ:ʃ(ə)n], s. **1.** Renversement m, reploiement m. **2.** Internat. Jur: Rétorsion f, représailles fpl.

retouch[1] ['ri:'tʌtʃ], s. Retouche f (à un tableau).

retouch[2], v.tr. Retoucher (un travail).

retrace [ri'treis], v.tr. **1.** Remonter à l'origine de (qch.). **2.** Reconstituer (le passé). **3.** **To r. one's steps**, revenir sur ses pas.

retract [ri'trækt], v.tr. **1.** (a) Rétracter; tirer (qch.) en arrière. Av: **To r. the under-carriage**, escamoter, rentrer, le train d'atterrissage. (b) Rétracter (ce qu'on a dit). **To r. one's confession**, revenir sur ses aveux. Abs. **To r.**, se rétracter; se dédire. Chess: **To r. a move**, déjouer. **2.** v.i. Se rétracter; se contracter; (of cat's claws, etc.) rentrer.

retractable [ri'træktəbl], a. **1.** (a) Nat.Hist: = RETRACTILE. (b) Av: **R. under-carriage**, train d'atterrissage rentrant, escamotable. **2.** (Remarque, opinion) rétractable, désavouable.

retractation ['ri:træk'teiʃ(ə)n], s. Rétractation f (de sa parole); désaveu m (d'une opinion).

retractile [ri'træktail], a. Nat.Hist: (Organe, etc.) rétractile.

retraction [ri'trækʃ(ə)n], s. **1.** Retrait m, rétraction f (des griffes). **2.** = RETRACTATION.

retranslate ['ri:træns'leit, -trɑ:ns-], v.tr. Retraduire.

retranslation ['ri:træns'leiʃ(ə)n, -trɑ:ns-], s. Nouvelle traduction. Sch: R. exercise, thème m d'imitation.

retransmission ['ri:træns'miʃ(ə)n], s. **1.** Réexpédition f, translation f (d'un télégramme). **2.** W.Tel: T.V: Retransmission f.

retransmit ['ri:træns'mit], v.tr. (retransmitted) Réexpédier (un télégramme). W.Tel: T.V: Retransmettre, rediffuser.

retread[1] ['ri:'tred], v.tr. (p.t. retrod ['ri:'trɔd]; p.p. retrodden ['ri:'trɔdn]) Repasser (dans un lieu).

retread[2], v.tr. (p.t. & p.p. retreaded) Aut: Rechaper (un pneu). **retread**, s. F: Pneu rechapé. **retreading**, s. Rechapage m.

retreat[1] [ri'tri:t], s. **1.** Mil: (a) Retraite f. **To be in r.**, battre en retraite. (b) (Evening call) La retraite. **2.** Retraite, recul m (d'un glacier, etc.). **3.** (a) Abri, asile m; retraite. Ecc: **House of r.**, maison f de retraite. (b) Repaire m (de brigands).

retreat[2]. **1.** v.i. (a) Se retirer, s'éloigner (**to a place**, vers un endroit). Box: Fenc: Rompre. (b) Mil: Battre en retraite. (c) (Of glacier) Reculer. **2.** v.tr. Chess: Ramener (une pièce en danger). **retreating**, a. (a) (Mer, etc.) qui se retire. (b) (Ennemi) en retraite.

retrench [ri'tren(t)ʃ], v.tr. Restreindre (ses dépenses). Abs. **To r.**, restreindre sa dépense; faire des économies.

retrenchment [ri'tren(t)ʃmənt], s. **1.** (a) Réduction f (des dépenses). (b) **Policy of r.**, politique f d'économies. **2.** Suppression f, retranchement m (d'un passage littéraire, etc.). **3.** Mil: Retranchement.

retrial [ri:'trai(ə)l], s. Jur: Nouveau procès.

retribution [,retri'bju:ʃ(ə)n], s. Châtiment m; jugement m. **Just r. of, for, a crime**, juste récompense f d'un crime.

retributive [ri'tribjutiv], **retributory** [ri'tribjut(ə)ri], a. Vengeur, f. vengeresse. **R. punishment**, punition justicière.

retrievable [ri'tri:vəbl], a. **1.** (Somme) recouvrable. **2.** (Perte, erreur) réparable.

retrieval [ri'tri:v(ə)l], s. **1.** Recouvrement m (de biens). **2.** Rétablissement m, relèvement m (de sa fortune). **3.** Réparation f (d'une perte, d'une erreur). **Beyond r., past r.**, irréparable. **Lost beyond r.**, perdu irréparablement.

retrieve [ri'tri:v], v.tr. **1.** (a) (Of dog) Rapporter (le gibier). (b) Recouvrer (des biens); retrouver (un objet perdu). **2.** (a) Relever, rétablir (la fortune de qn). **To r. one's honour, to r. oneself**, racheter son honneur; rétablir sa réputation. (b) **To r. s.o. from ruin**, arracher qn à la ruine. **3.** Réparer (une perte, une erreur).

retriever [ri'tri:vər], s. (Dog) Retriever m. **Golden r.**, retriever golden, doré. **A good r.**, un chien qui rapporte bien.

retrim ['ri:'trim], v.tr. (retrimmed) Regarnir; F: retaper (un chapeau, etc.).

retroact ['retrou'ækt], v.i. **1.** Réagir (**against**, contre). **2.** (Of legislation) Rétroagir.

retroaction [,retrou'ækʃ(ə)n], s. **1.** Réaction f; contrecoup m. **2.** Rétroaction f (d'une loi).

retroactive [,retrou'æktiv], a. Rétroactif, -ive.

retrocede[1] [,retrou'si:d], v.i. Rétrograder, reculer.

retrocede[2], v.tr. Rétrocéder (un territoire, etc.).

retrocession[1] [,retrou'seʃ(ə)n], s. Recul m; mouvement m rétrograde.

retrocession[2], s. Rétrocession f (d'un droit).

retrocessive [,retrou'sesiv], a. Rétrocessif, -ive.

retro(-)choir ['retrou'kwaiər], s. Ecc.Arch: Arrièrechœur m.

retrogradation [,retrougrə'deiʃ(ə)n], s. **1.** Astr: Rétrogradation f; mouvement m rétrograde. **2.** Dégénérescence f; Biol: régression f.

retrograde[1] ['retrougreid], a. (a) Rétrograde. (b) **In r. order**, en ordre inverse.

retrograde[2], v.i. Rétrograder.

retrogress [,retrou'gres], v.i. **1.** Rétrograder. **2.** Mth: (Of curve) Rebrousser.

retrogression [,retrou'greʃ(ə)n], s. **1.** = RETROGRADATION. **2.** Mth: Rebroussement m (d'une courbe).

retrogressive [,retrou'gresiv], a. **1.** Rétrogressif, -ive, rétrograde. **2.** Biol: Régressif, -ive; dégénérescent.

retro-rocket [,retrou'rɔkit], s. Rétrofusée f.

retrospect ['retrouspekt], s. Coup d'œil rétrospectif; examen rétrospectif.

retrospection [,retrou'spekʃ(ə)n], s. Examen rétrospectif (des événements, etc.), rétrospection f.

retrospective [,retrou'spektiv], a. **1.** (Examen) rétrospectif. **2.** (Loi) avec effet rétroactif. **3.** (Vue) vers l'arrière. **-ly**, adv. **1.** Rétrospectivement. **2.** Rétroactivement.

retry [ri'trai], v.tr. Jur: Juger à nouveau.

returf ['ri:'tə:f], v.tr. Regazonner.

return[1] [ri'tə:n], s. **1.** (a) Retour m. (Immediately) **on my r.**, dès mon retour, à mon retour. **On my r. home, I found . . .**, de retour à la maison j'ai trouvé. . . . **By r. of post, of mail**, par retour du courrier. **Many happy returns** (of the day), mes meilleurs vœux d'anniversaire! **R. journey**, voyage de retour. Rail: **R. ticket**, F: **r.**, (billet m d') aller et retour. (b) **R. stroke** (of piston), course de retour. **R. flue**, tube de retour de fumée, de flamme. **R. angle**, retour d'angle. El.E: **R. current**, contre-courant m. (c) Arch: Retour (d'un mur). **2.** Com: (a) pl. **Returns**, recettes f. **Quick returns**, un prompt débit. (b) Revenu m, profit m; rendement m. **To bring** (in) **a fair r.**, rapporter un bénéfice raisonnable. **3.** (a) Renvoi m, retour (de marchandises avariées, etc.). **On sale or r.**, (marchandises) vendues avec faculté de retour; en dépôt avec reprise des invendus. Post: **R. address**, adresse de l'expéditeur. (b) Restitution f (d'un objet volé, etc.); ristourne f (d'une somme payée en trop); remise f (d'un objet à sa place). (c) **Pen given in r. for a pencil**, plume donnée en échange d'un crayon. **In r. for which . . .,** moyennant quoi. . . . **If you will do sth. in r.,** si vous voulez bien faire qch. en retour. (d) pl. Com: **Returns,** rendus m, F: retours; (of books, newspapers) invendus m, F: bouillons m. **4.** (a) Renvoi, répercussion f (d'un son). **R. of a control lever,** rappel m d'un levier. **R. spring,** ressort de rappel. Typewr: **Carriage r.,** retour, rappel, de chariot. (b) Ten: etc: Renvoi (de la balle); riposte f. **5.** (a) Récompense f. **In r. for this service . . .,** en récompense, en retour, de ce service. . . . (b) Sp: **R. match,** match retour. **6.** (a) État m, exposé m; compte rendu; relevé m, relèvement m; statistique f. **Bank r.,** situation f de la banque. **Quarterly r.,** rapport trimestriel. (b) **R. of income, income tax r.,** déclaration f de revenu. Pol.Ec: **Law of diminishing returns,** loi du rendement non-proportionnel. **7.** Pol: Élection f (d'un député). **To announce the election returns,** publier les résultats m du scrutin.

return². I. v.i. **1.** (Come back) Revenir; (go back) retourner. **To r. from a journey,** rentrer de voyage. **To r.** (to one's) **home,** (i) rentrer (chez soi); (ii) regagner sa patrie. They have returned, ils sont de retour. **Her colour returned,** les couleurs lui revinrent. Nau: **To r. to port,** rentrer au port. **2. To r. to a task,** reprendre une tâche. **Let us r. to the subject,** revenons à nos moutons. **3.** Retourner, revenir (à un état antérieur). II. **return,** v.tr. **1.** (a) Rendre (un livre emprunté); restituer (un objet volé); renvoyer (un cadeau); rembourser (un emprunt). (b) **To r. a book to its place,** remettre un livre à sa place. **2.** Renvoyer (la lumière, une balle). **Spring to r. the valve to its seat,** ressort pour ramener, rappeler, la soupape sur son siège. **3.** (a) Rendre (une visite, un compliment, un coup); renvoyer (une accusation). **To r. like for like,** rendre la pareille. **To r. s.o.'s love,** répondre à l'amour de qn; aimer qn en retour. Cards: **To r. clubs,** rejouer du trèfle (après son partenaire). (b) Répondre, répliquer. **To r. a denial,** opposer une dénégation. (c) **To r. thanks to s.o.,** adresser des remerciements à qn. **4.** Rapporter, donner (un bénéfice). **5.** (a) Déclarer, rapporter; rendre compte de (qch.). (b) Jur: **Prisoner was returned guilty,** l'accusé fut déclaré coupable. **6.** Pol: Élire (un député). **returned,** a. **1.** (Of pers.) De retour. **2. R. letter,** lettre renvoyée à l'expéditeur. Com: **R. article,** (i) rendu m; (ii) laissé-pour-compte m. **3.** Sp: **R. time,** temps contrôlé, temps officiel.

returnable [ri'tə:nəbl], a. Restituable. Com: **R. goods,** marchandises de retour; marchandises en commission. **Non-r. packing,** emballage perdu, non consigné.

reunion¹ ['ri:'ju:njən], s. Réunion f, assemblée f.

Reunion² [ˌri:'ju:njən]. Pr.n. Geog: Réunion f.

reunite ['ri:ju:'nait]. **1.** v.tr. (a) Unir de nouveau; réunir. (b) Réunir, rassembler (ses partisans); réconcilier (une famille). **2.** v.i. Se réunir. (a) Se réconcilier. (b) (Of edges of wound) Se ressouder.

rev¹ [rev], s. Aut: F: (Abbr. of revolution) **Two thousand revs a minute,** deux mille tours m à la minute.

rev², v.tr. (revved) Aut: F: **1.** v.tr. **To r. up the engine,** faire emballer le moteur. **2.** v.i. **The engine began to r. up,** le moteur s'emballa.

revaccinate ['ri:'væksineit], v.tr. Revacciner.

revaccination ['ri:'væksi'neiʃ(ə)n], s. Revaccination f.

revalorize ['ri:'væləraiz], v.tr. Fin: Revaloriser.

revalue ['ri:'vælju:], v.tr. Réévaluer.

revaluation ['ri:'vælju'eiʃ(ə)n], s. Réévaluation f, ré-estimation f.

revarnish ['ri:'vɑ:niʃ], v.tr. Revernir.

reveal [ri'vi:l], v.tr. (a) Révéler, découvrir (son jeu); faire connaître (un fait). **To r. one's identity,** se faire connaître. (b) Laisser voir. (c) Révéler, découvrir, déceler (un objet caché); dévoiler (un mystère); faire voir, mettre à jour (qch.). **revealing,** a. Révélateur, -trice.

revealer [ri'vi:lər], s. Révélateur, -trice (d'un complot, etc.).

reveille [ri'væli], s. Mil: Le réveil; la diane.

revel¹ ['revl], s. Often pl. (a) Divertissement(s) m(pl); réjouissances fpl; ébats mpl. (b) Bacchanale f, orgie f. **Midnight revels,** orgies nocturnes.

revel², v. (revelled) **1.** v.i. (a) Se réjouir, se divertir. (b) F: Faire bombance, faire ripaille. (c) **To r. in sth., in doing sth.,** se délecter à qch., à faire qch.; faire ses délices de qch. **To r. in words,** se griser de mots. **2.** v.tr. **To r. away the time,** passer le temps en orgies.

revelation [ˌrevi'leiʃ(ə)n], s. **1.** Révélation f. **2.** B: **The R.,** (the Book of) **Revelations,** l'Apocalypse f.

reveller ['rev(ə)lər], s. (a) Joyeux convive. (b) Noceur, -euse, cascadeur, -euse, bambocheur, -euse.

revelry ['revlri], s. (a) Divertissements mpl, ébats mpl. (b) Bacchanale f, orgie f, bombance f.

revenge¹ [ri'vendʒ], s. **1.** Vengeance f. **To take r. for sth. on s.o.,** se venger de qch. sur qn. **To have one's r.,** se venger. **In r.,** pour se venger (for, de). **Out of r.,** par vengeance. **2.** (Esp. in games) Revanche f; contre-partie f.

revenge², v.tr. **1. To r. oneself, to be revenged,** se venger (on s.o.), tirer, prendre, vengeance (de qn). **To r. oneself for sth.,** se venger de qch. **2.** Venger (une injure). **3.** Venger (qn).

revengeful [ri'vendʒful], a. **1.** Vindicatif, -ive. **2.** Vengeur, -eresse. **-fully,** adv. Par vengeance.

revengefulness [ri'vendʒfulnis], s. Caractère vindicatif; esprit m de vengeance.

revenger [ri'vendʒər], s. Vengeur, -eresse (of, de).

revenue ['revinju:], s. **1.** Revenu m, rentes fpl; rapport m (from an estate, d'une terre). **2. The Public R.,** (i) le revenu de l'État; le Trésor public; (ii) Adm: le fisc. **(Inland) R. office,** (bureau m de) perception f. **R. stamp,** timbre fiscal. **Excise r.,** contributions indirectes. **R. officer,** employé m de la douane.

reverberate [ri'və:b(ə)reit]. **1.** v.tr. (a) Renvoyer, répercuter (le son). (b) Réverbérer, réfléchir (la lumière, la chaleur). **To be reverberated,** réverbérer. **2.** v.i. (a) (Of sound) Retentir, résonner. (b) (Of light, heat) Réverbérer.

reverberation [riˌvə:bə'reiʃ(ə)n], s. (a) Renvoi m, répercussion f (d'un son). (b) Réverbération f (de la lumière, de la chaleur).

reverberator [ri'və:bəreitər], s. Réflecteur m.

reverberatory [ri'və:bəreitəri], a. & s. Metall: **R. (furnace),** four m à réverbère.

revere [ri'viər], v.tr. Révérer, vénérer.

reverence¹ ['rev(ə)r(ə)ns], s. **1.** Respect religieux; révérence f, vénération. f. **To hold s.o. in r.,** révérer qn; éprouver de la vénération pour qn. **To pay r. to s.o.,** rendre hommage à qn. **2.** (Esp. in Ireland) **Your R.,** monsieur l'abbé.

reverence², v.tr. Révérer.

reverend ['rev(ə)r(ə)nd], a. **1.** Vénérable. **2.** Ecc: (a) **The r. gentleman,** le révérend abbé, père, pasteur. (b) (As title) **The Rev. Ch. Black,** le révérend Ch. Black. **The Rev. Father O'Malley,** le révérend père O'Malley. **The R. Mother Superior,** la révérende mère supérieure. (Of dean) **Very R.,** très révérend. (Of bishop) **Right R.,** très révérend. (Of archbishop) **Most R.,** révérendissime.

reverent ['rev(ə)r(ə)nt], a. Respectueux, -euse; plein de vénération. **-ly,** adv. Avec respect.

reverential [ˌrevə'renʃ(ə)l], a. (Respect) révérenciel. **-ally,** adv. Avec respect; avec une crainte révérencielle.

reverie ['revəri], .s. Rêverie f; songerie f.

revers [ri'viəz], s.pl. Cost: Revers mpl.

reversal [ri'və:s(ə)l], s. **1.** Jur: Réforme f, annulation f (d'un jugement). **2.** (a) Renversement m (Opt: d'une image, Log: d'une proposition); inversion f. **R. of opinion,** revirement m d'opinion. Ph: **R. of polarity,** renversement de polarité. Mec.E: **R. of motion,** renversement de marche. (b) Phot: Inversion (de l'image). **R. finder,** viseur redresseur.

reverse¹ [ri'və:s], a. Inverse, contraire, opposé (to, à). **In the r. order,** en ordre inverse. **The r. side of a medal,** le revers, l'envers m, d'une médaille. **The r. side of a picture,** le dos d'un tableau. **R. slope of a hill,** contre-pente f. **R. stroke,** contre-course f (du piston). Mec: Cin: **R. motion, action,** marche f arrière. Tp: **R. charge call,** communication f payable à l'arrivée, avec P.C.V.

reverse², s. **1.** (a) Inverse m, contraire m, opposé m. **To be quite the r. of s.o.,** être tout le contraire de qn. (b) Mil: **To take a position in r.,** prendre une position à revers. (c) Aut: **To go, get, into r.,** mettre en marche arrière. (*d*) *Typewr:* **Automatic ribbon r.,** retour automatique du ruban. **2.** (*a*) Revers *m* (d'une médaille). (*b*) Verso *m* (d'un feuillet). **3. R. of fortune,** revers de fortune. **To suffer a r.,** essuyer un revers, une défaite.

reverse³, *v.tr.* **1.** Renverser. *Mil:* **To r. arms,** renverser l'arme. **2.** (*a*) Retourner (un habit). (*b*) Renverser (un mouvement); invertir (l'ordre). **To r. a process,** avoir recours à une méthode inverse. *Tp:* **To r. the charge,** demander une communication avec P.C.V. *Phot:* **To r. a negative,** invertir un cliché (de négatif en positif). (*c*) *Aut:* **To r. one's car,** *abs.* **to r.,** faire marche arrière. **3.** *Jur:* Révoquer (une sentence). **To r. one's own judg(e)ment,** se déjuger. **4.** *v.i. Danc:* Valser de gauche à droite. **reversed,** *a.* **1.** Renversé. *Mil:* **With r. arms,** les armes renversées. **2.** Inverse, contraire, opposé. *El:* **R. current,** renverse *f* de courant. **reversing¹,** *a.* Réversible. **reversing²,** *s.* **1.** Renversement *m.* **2.** Inversion *f. Mch:* Inversion de marche. *Aut:* Marche *f* arrière. **R. light,** phare *m* de recul. *Mec.E:* **R. lever,** (levier *m* de) renvoi *m. El:* **R. switch,** inverseur *m* du courant.

reversible [ri'vɔ:səbl], *a.* **1.** (Flacon) renversable. **2.** (Drap) à deux endroits; (vêtement) à double face. **3.** (Procédé) réversible. **R. motion,** mouvement réciproque.

reversion [ri'vɔ:ʃ(ə)n], *s.* **1.** *Jur:* (*a*) Retour *m* (d'un bien); réversion *f.* (*b*) Substitution *f.* **Estate in r.,** bien grevé de droit de retour. **2.** Survivance *f* (d'un bénéfice). **3.** Retour (à un état antérieur). *Biol:* **R. to type,** réversion (au type primitif). **4.** *Phot:* Inversion *f.*

reversionary [ri'vɔ:ʃnəri], *a.* **1.** (Droit) de réversion. **R. annuity,** (i) annuité *f* réversible; (ii) rente *f* à paiement différé. **2.** *Biol:* Atavique.

revert [ri'vɔ:t], *v.i.* (*a*) (*Of property*) Revenir, retourner (**to,** à). (*Of estate*) **To r. to an ascendant,** faire retour à un ascendant. (*b*) *Biol:* **To r. to type,** revenir au type primitif. (*c*) **To r. to our subject,** pour en revenir à notre sujet.

revertible [ri'vɔ:tibl], *a. Jur:* Réversible.

revetment [ri'vetmənt], *s. Const:* Revêtement *m. Civ.E: Fort:* Fascine r., fascinage *m.*

revictual ['ri:'vitl], *v.* (**revictualled**) **1.** *v.tr.* Ravitailler, réapprovisionner. **2.** *v.i.* Se ravitailler. **revictualling,** *s.* Ravitaillement *m,* réapprovisionnement *m.*

review¹ [ri'vju:], *s.* **1.** *Jur:* Révision *f* (d'un procès). **To keep a question under r.,** suivre une question de très près. **2.** *Mil:* Revue *f.* **To hold a r.,** passer une revue. *S.a.* ORDER¹ 3. **3.** Examen *m,* revue (du passé). **4.** Critique *f* (d'un livre). **R. copy,** exemplaire fourni au critique; exemplaire de service de presse. **5.** *Publ:* Revue (périodique).

review², *v.tr.* **1.** Réviser (un procès). **2.** Passer (des faits) en revue. **3. To r. the troops,** passer les troupes en revue. **4. To r. a book,** faire la critique d'un livre.

reviewer [ri'vju:ər], *s.* Critique *m* (littéraire).

revile [ri'vail], *v.tr.* Injurier; insulter (qn). **reviling¹,** *a.* Injurieux, -euse. **reviling²,** *s.* Injures *fpl.*

reviler [ri'vailər], *s.* Insulteur *m.*

revise¹ [ri'vaiz], *s. Typ:* Épreuve *f* de révision; seconde *f.*

revise², *v.tr.* **1.** Revoir, relire (un travail); corriger, réviser (des épreuves). *Sch:* Repasser, revoir (une leçon). **2.** (*a*) Réviser (les lois). (*b*) **To r. a decision,** revenir sur une décision.

reviser [ri'vaizər], *s.* **1.** Réviseur *m;* correcteur *m* (d'épreuves d'imprimerie). **2.** Révisionniste *m* (de la constitution).

revision [ri'viʒ(ə)n], *s.* Révision *f.* **'For r.,'** "à revoir."

revisit ['ri:'vizit], *v.tr.* Visiter de nouveau; revisiter; revenir voir (sa maison natale).

revisor [ri'vaizər], *s.* = REVISER.

revisory [ri'vaizəri], *a.* Révisionniste.

revitalize ['ri:'vaitəlaiz], *v.tr.* Revivifier.

revival [ri'vaiv(ə)l], *s.* **1.** Renaissance *f* (des arts); reprise *f* (d'une pièce de théâtre); remise *f* en vigueur (d'une loi). **The r. of trade,** la reprise des affaires. *Hist:* **The r. of learning,** la renaissance des lettres; la Renaissance. **2.** (*a*) Retour *m* à la vie; retour des forces. (*b*) Reprise des sens. **3.** *Rel:* Réveil *m.* **Religious r.,** renouveau religieux.

revivalist [ri'vaiv(ə)list], *s.* Revivaliste *mf.*

revive [ri'vaiv]. **1.** *v.i.* (*a*) (*Of pers.*) Ressusciter; reprendre connaissance; reprendre ses sens. (*b*) (*Of feelings*) Se ranimer; renaître. **His spirits revived,** son courage se ranima. (*c*) (*Of custom*) Reprendre; (*of arts*) renaître. **Industry is reviving,** l'industrie reprend. **Credit is reviving,** le crédit se rétablit. **2.** *v.tr.* (*a*) Faire revivre (qn); rappeler (qn) à la vie; ressusciter (qn). **That will r. you,** voilà qui vous remontera. (*b*) Ranimer (les espérances); réveiller (un désir); rappeler (un souvenir); renouveler (un usage); ressusciter (un parti politique). **To r. an old charge,** reproduire une accusation. **To r. s.o.'s courage,** remonter le courage de qn. (*c*) Remettre (une pièce) au théâtre; ressusciter (un périodique); rénover (un genre littéraire). (*d*) **To r. leather,** redonner de la souplesse au cuir.

reviver [ri'vaivər], *s. F:* Petit verre qui ravigote, coup *m* de cognac, de whisky.

revivify [ri'vivifai], *v.tr.* Revivifier.

revocability [,revəkə'biliti], *s.* Révocabilité *f.*

revocable ['revəkəbl], *a.* Révocable. **R. post,** emploi amovible.

revocation [,revə'keiʃ(ə)n], *s.* Révocation *f;* abrogation *f* (d'un décret).

revocatory [ri'vəkətri], *a.* Révocatoire.

revoke¹ [ri'vouk], *s. Cards:* Fausse renonce.

revoke². **1.** *v.tr.* (*a*) Révoquer (un ordre); rapporter (un décret); retirer (son consentement); rétracter (une promesse). (*b*) **To r. a driving licence,** retirer un permis de conduire. **2.** *v.i. Cards:* Faire une fausse renonce.

revolt¹ [ri'voult], *s.* Révolte *f.* **To rise in r.,** se soulever, se révolter (**against,** contre).

revolt². **1.** *v.i.* Se révolter, s'insurger, se soulever, se rebeller (**from, against,** contre). **2.** *v.tr.* (*Of action*) Révolter, indigner (qn). **revolting,** *a. F:* Révoltant, dégoûtant, écœurant. **-ly,** *adv.* D'une façon révoltante.

revolution ['revə'lu:ʃ(ə)n], *s.* **1.** *Astr:* Révolution *f* (d'une planète). **2.** (*a*) Rotation *f* (autour d'un axe). (*b*) Tour *m,* révolution (d'une roue). **Maximum revolutions,** régime *m* maximum. **R. counter,** compte-tours *m inv.* **3.** *Pol: etc:* Révolution.

revolutionary [,revə'lu:ʃnəri], *a. & s.* Révolutionnaire (*mf*).

revolutionist [,revə'lu:ʃnist], *s.* Partisan *m* de la révolution; révolutionnaire *mf.*

revolutionize [,revə'lu:ʃnaiz], *v.tr.* Révolutionner.

revolve [ri'vɔlv]. **1.** *v.tr.* (*a*) Retourner, ruminer (une pensée). (*b*) Faire tourner (les roues). **2.** *v.i.* (*a*) Tourner. **To r. on a spindle,** pivoter, tourner, sur un axe. **The earth revolves round the sun,** la terre tourne autour du soleil. (*b*) **The seasons r.,** les saisons font leur révolution, reviennent. **revolving,** *a.* **1.** En rotation. **2. R. chair,** fauteuil pivotant, tournant. **R. light,** feu à éclats (d'un phare). **R. crane,** grue à pivot. *Th:* **R. stage,** scène tournante.

revolver [ri'vɔlvər], *s.* Revolver *m.*

revue [ri'vju:], *s. Th:* Revue *f.* **R. writer,** revuiste *mf.*

revulsion [ri'vʌlʃ(ə)n], *s.* **1.** Revirement *m* (de sentiments). **R. from s.o.,** réaction *f* contre qn. **2.** *Med:* Révulsion *f.* **3.** *F:* Écœurement *m.*

revulsive [ri'vʌlsiv], *a. & s. Med:* Révulsif (*m*).

reward¹ [ri'wɔ:d], *s.* Récompense *f.* **A hundred pounds r.,** cent livres de récompense. **As a r. for . . .,** en récompense de . . ., pour prix de. . . .

reward², *v.tr.* Récompenser, rémunérer (s.o. for sth., qn de qch.). **That's how he rewards me for my trouble,** voilà comment il me paie mon zèle. **rewarding,** *a.* (*a*) Rémunérateur, -trice. (*b*) Qui en vaut la peine. **A r. book,** un livre qui vaut la peine d'être lu.

re-weigh ['ri:'wei], *v.tr.* Repeser.

re-wind ['ri:'waind], *v.tr.* (**re-wound** ['ri:'waund]) (*a*) Rebobiner (la soie). (*b*) *Typewr: etc:* Rembobiner (le ruban). *Cin:* Réembobiner (le film). (*c*) Remonter (une horloge). **re-winding,** *s.* (*a*) Rebobinage *m.* (*b*) *Typewr:* Rembobinage *m. Cin:* Réembobinage *m.* (*c*) Remontage *m* (d'une horloge).

rewire ['ri:'waiər], *v.tr.* Remettre à neuf la canalisation électrique (d'une maison).

reword ['ri:'wɔ:d], *v.tr.* Recomposer, rédiger à nouveau.

rewrite¹ ['ri:'rait], *s. F:* Remaniement *m* (d'un article, etc.). *U.S:* **R. man,** remanieur *m.*

rewrite² ['riː'rait], *v.tr.* (rewrote ['riː'rout]; **rewritten** ['riː'rit(ə)n]) Récrire, remanier (un article, etc.).

Rex [reks]. *Pr.n.m. Jur:* R. v. Smith, le Roi en cause avec Smith.

Rhaetian ['riː'ʃiən], *a. Geog:* The R. Alps, les Alpes rhétiques.

rhapsodize ['ræpsədaiz], *v.i. F:* To r. over sth., s'extasier sur qch.

rhapsody ['ræpsədi], *s.* 1. Rhapsodie *f.* 2. *F:* Transports *mpl*, dithyrambe *m.*

rhea ['riə], *s. Orn:* Nandou *m.*

Rheims [riːmz]. *Pr.n. Geog:* Reims *m.*

Rhenish ['riːniʃ], *a.* Rhénan. R. wine, vin du Rhin.

rhenium ['riːniəm], *s. Ch:* Rhénium *m.*

rheostat ['riːostæt], *s. El.E:* Rhéostat *m;* résistance *f* à curseur.

rhesus ['riːsəs]. 1. *s. Z:* Rhésus *m.* 2. *attrib. Med:* R. factor, facteur *m* rhésus (du sang).

rhetoric ['retərik], *s.* 1. Rhétorique *f,* éloquence *f.* 2. *Pej:* Rhétorique; discours creux.

rhetorical [ri'torik(ə)l], *a.* (*a*) (Terme) de rhétorique. R. question, question *f* pour la forme. (*b*) *Pej:* (Style) ampoulé.

rhetorician [‚retə'riʃ(ə)n], *s.* (*a*) Rhétoricien *m.* (*b*) *Pej:* Rhéteur *m.*

rheumatic [ruː'mætik], *a.* (*Of pain*) Rhumatismal, -aux. R. person, *s.* rheumatic, rhumatisant, -ante. R. fever, rhumatisme articulaire aigu.

rheumaticky [ruː'mætiki], *a. F:* Rhumatisant.

rheumatics [ruː'mætiks], *s.pl. F:* Rhumatisme *m.*

rheumatism ['ruːmətizm], *s.* Rhumatisme *m.*

rheumatoid ['ruːmətɔid], *a.* Rhumatoïde. *S.a.* ARTHRITIS.

rheumy ['ruːmi], *a.* R. eyes, yeux chassieux.

Rhine (the) [ðə'rain]. *Pr.n.* Le Rhin.

Rhineland (the) [ðə'rainlænd]. *Pr.n.* Les pays rhénans; la Rhénanie.

rhinestone ['rainstoun], *s.* 1. Caillou *m* du Rhin (en cristal de roche). 2. Faux diamant.

rhinitis [rai'naitis], *s. Med:* Rhinite *f.*

rhino¹ ['rainou], *s. A: F:* Argent *m; F:* galette *f.*

rhino², *s. F:* Rhinocéros *m.*

rhinoceros [rai'nɔsərəs], *s.* Rhinocéros *m.*

rhinology [rai'nɔlədʒi], *s. Med:* Rhinologie *f.*

rhinoplasty ['rainouplæsti], *s. Surg:* Rhinoplastie *f.*

rhizome ['raizoum], *s. Bot:* Rhizome *m.*

Rhodesia [rou'diːziə]. *Pr.n. Geog:* Rhodésie *f.*

Rhodesian [rou'diːziən], *a. & s.* Rhodésien, -ienne.

rhodium ['roudiəm], *s. Ch:* Rhodium *m.*

rhododendron, *pl.* -ons, -a [‚roudə'dendr(ə)n, -ənz, -ə], *s. Bot:* Rhododendron *m.*

rhomb [rɔm], *s.* 1. *Geom:* Losange *m;* rhombe *m.* 2. *Cryst:* Rhomboèdre *m.*

rhombic ['rɔmbik], *a. Geom:* Rhombique.

rhombohedron, *pl.* -a [‚rɔmbou'hiːdr(ə)n, -ə], *s. Cryst:* Rhomboèdre *m.*

rhomboid ['rɔmbɔid], *a. & s. Geom:* Rhomboïde (*m*).

rhomboidal [rɔm'bɔidl], *a. Geom:* Rhomboïdal, -aux.

rhombus ['rɔmbəs], *pl.* -uses, -i ['rɔmbəs, -əsiz, -ai], *s. Geom:* Losange *m;* rhombe *m.*

Rhone (the) [ðə'roun]. *Pr.n. Geog:* Le Rhône.

rhubarb ['ruːbɑːb], *s. Bot:* Rhubarbe *f.*

rhumb [rʌm], *s. Nau:* R(h)umb *m* (de 11° 15'). 'rhumb-line, *s.* Ligne *f* de rumb; (*on chart*) loxodromie *f.*

rhyme¹ [raim], *s. Pros:* Rime *f.* Rhymes in couplets, rimes plates, suivies. Alternate rhymes, rimes croisées, alternées. Without r. or reason, sans rime ni raison. There's neither r. nor reason about it, cela ne rime à rien. *Usu. pl.* Vers (rimés); poésie *f.* In r., en vers.

rhyme². 1. *v.i.* (*a*) Rimer; faire des vers. (*b*) (*Of words*) Rimer (with, avec). 2. *v.tr.* Faire rimer (des mots). **rhyming**, *s.* 1. Recherche *f* de la rime. R. dictionary, dictionnaire de rimes. 2. Versification *f.*

rhymester ['raimstər], *s. Pej:* Rimailleur *m.*

rhythm ['rið(ə)m], *s.* Rythme *m,* cadence *f.*

rhythmic(al) ['riðmik(əl)], *a.* Rythmique, cadencé.

ria [riə], *s. Ph.Geog:* Ria *f.* R. coast, côte à rias.

rib¹ [rib], *s.* 1. *Anat:* Côte *f.* True ribs, vraies côtes. Floating ribs, fausses côtes. *Cu:* R. of beef, côte de bœuf. 2. (*a*) Nervure *f* (d'une feuille); strie *f* (d'une coquille). (*b*) *Arch:* Nervure (d'une voûte). (**Dia-**

gonal) r. (*under a groin*), ogive *f.* Transverse r., doubleau *m.* 3. (*a*) Support *m,* étançon *m* (d'un échafaudage); baleine *f* (de parapluie); brin *m* (d'éventail). *Av:* Travée *f* (d'une aile). (*b*) *N.Arch:* Membre *m,* membrure *f.*

rib², *v.tr.* (**ribbed**) 1. Garnir (qch.) de côtes, de nervures. 2. *F: U.S:* Taquiner, agacer (qn). **ribbed**, *a.* 1. (Coquillage) strié; (plafond) à nervures. *Arch:* Ribbed vault, voûte *f* d'ogives. 2. (Bas, velours) à côtes, côtelé. R. stitch, point à côtes. 3. *Bot:* (*Of leaf*) A nervures, nervuré. **ribbing**, *s.* 1. Côtes *fpl.* 2. *F: U.S:* To give s.o. a r., taquiner qn.

ribald ['ribəld], *a.* Licencieux, -euse, impudique. R. song, chanson paillarde, grivoise. R. joke, paillardise *f.*

ribaldry ['ribəldri], *s.* Paillardises *fpl,* grivoiseries *fpl.*

riband ['ribənd], *s. A:* = RIBBON.

ribband ['ribənd], *s.* 1. *Av: N.Arch:* Lisse *f.* 2.=RIBBON.

ribbon ['ribən], *s.* 1. Ruban *m.* R. trade, rubanerie *f.* Bunch of r., chou *m. Typewr:* (Inking) r., ruban (encreur). 2. (*a*) Ruban (d'une décoration); cordon *m* (d'un ordre). Blue r., ruban bleu. (*b*) *Navy:* Cap r., ruban légendé (du béret). 3. *pl. F:* Ribbons, guides *f.* 4. (*a*) Ruban (de magnésium). (*b*) Steel r., ruban d'acier; feuillard *m.* 5. Bande *f,* ruban (de route). R. development, extension urbaine en bordure de route. 6. *pl.* To tear sth. to ribbons, mettre qch. en lambeaux; déchiqueter qch. 'ribbon-saw, *s.* Scie *f* à ruban, à lame sans fin.

rice [rais], *s.* Riz *m.* Husked r., riz décortiqué. Ground r., farine *f* de riz. 'rice-grower, *s.* Riziculteur *m.* 'rice-growing, *s.* Riziculture *f.* 'rice-mill, *s.* Rizerie *f.* 'rice-paper, *s.* Papier *m* de riz. 'rice-plantation, *s.* Rizière *f.* 'rice 'pudding, *s. Cu:* Riz *m* au lait. 'rice 'shape, *s. Cu:* Gâteau *m* de riz. 'rice-straw, *s.* Paille *f* de riz. 'rice-water, *s.* Eau *f* de riz.

rich [ritʃ], *a.* 1. Riche. R. people, *s.* the r., les riches *m. F:* Disgustingly r., richissime. The newly r., les nouveaux riches. To grow r., s'enrichir. 2. (*Of soil*) Riche, fertile. R. pastures, gras pâturages. Museum r. in paintings, musée riche en tableaux. R. in hope, riche d'espérances. *S.a.* STRIKE² I. 7. 3. (*a*) R. food, (i) nourriture grasse, difficile à digérer; (ii) aliments de choix. (*b*) *I.C.E:* R. mixture, mélange riche. 4. R. colour, couleur chaude, riche. 5. *F:* (*Of incident*) Très divertissant; impayable, épatant. -ly, *adv.* 1. Richement; avec opulence. 2. (*a*) Richement, abondamment. (*b*) *F:* He r. deserves it, il l'a joliment bien mérité.

riches ['ritʃiz], *s.pl.* Richesse(s) *f(pl).* He had great r., il était très riche.

richness ['ritʃnis], *s.* 1. Richesse *f,* abondance *f.* 2. Richesse (du sol); fertilité *f.* 3. Somptuosité *f,* luxe *m.* 4. (*a*) The r. of the cooking upsets me, je ne digère pas cette cuisine grasse. (*b*) *I.C.E:* R. of the mixture, richesse du mélange. 5. Éclat *m* (d'une couleur); ampleur *f* (de la voix); richesse (du style).

rick¹ [rik], *s.* Meule *f* (de foin).

rick²,³, *s. & v.tr.* = WRICK¹,².

rickets ['rikits], *s.pl.* Rachitisme *m,* nouure *f.* To have r., être rachitique.

rickety ['rikiti], *a.* 1. *Med:* Rachitique, *F:* noué. 2. *F:* R. legs, jambes chancelantes. 3. *F:* (Escalier) branlant, délabré; (fauteuil) bancal. R. table, table boiteuse.

rickshaw ['rikʃɔː], *s.* Pousse-pousse *m inv.* Bicycle r., vélo-pousse *m.*

ricochet¹ ['rikəʃei, 'rikəʃei, 'rikəʃet], *s.* Ricochet *m.*

ricochet², *v.i.* (ricochetted ['rikəʃeid, rikə'ʃetid]) (*Of projectile*) Ricocher.

rictus ['riktəs], *s.* Rictus *m.*

rid [rid], *v.tr.* (*p.t.* ridded, rid; *p.p.* rid) Débarrasser, délivrer (s.o. of sth., qn de qch.); débarrasser (a place of sth., un endroit de qch.). To r. one's estate of debt, purger ses terres de dettes. To get r. of sth., to r. oneself of sth., se débarrasser, se défaire, de qch. *Com: F:* Article hard to get r. of, article d'écoulement difficile. *Mth:* To get r. of x, y, éliminer x, y. *F:* To get r. of s.o., (i) se débarrasser de qn; (*politely*) éconduire qn; renvoyer (un domestique); (ii) faire disparaître qn; se défaire (d'un ennemi).

riddance ['rid(ə)ns], *s.* (*a*) Débarras *m.* A good r.! bon débarras! (*b*) Délivrance *f* (from, de).

ridden. See RIDE².

riddle¹ ['ridl], s. Énigme f, devinette f. To ask s.o. a r., poser une énigme à qn. To speak in riddles, parler par énigmes.

riddle², s. Crible m, claie f.

riddle³, v.tr. 1. Cribler (le grain); passer (qch.) au crible. 2. To r. s.o. with bullets, cribler qn de balles. **riddling,** s. 1. Criblage m. 2. pl.Riddlings, criblures fpl.

ride¹ [raid], s. 1. (a) Course f, promenade f, trajet m (à cheval, à bicyclette). (b) Promenade, voyage m (en auto). To go for a r. in the car, aller se promener, faire un tour, en voiture. R. on a roundabout, tour m de chevaux de bois. It's a short r. on the bus, c'est un court trajet en autobus. F: To take s.o. for a r., (i) enlever qn (pour l'assassiner); (ii) faire marcher, duper, qn. 2. (In forest) Allée cavalière; piste; allée f.

ride², v. (rode [roud]; ridden ['rid(ə)n]) I. v.i. 1. (a) Chevaucher; se promener, monter, à cheval. abs. Can you r.? montez-vous à cheval? To r. astride, monter à califourchon. To r. side-saddle, monter en amazone. He rides well, il monte bien (à cheval); il est bon cavalier. He's riding for a fall, il court à un échec. (b) To r. on an elephant, voyager à dos d'éléphant. To r. on a bicycle, aller, se promener, monter, à bicyclette. (Of child) To r. on s.o.'s knee, être à califourchon, à cheval, sur le genou de qn. (c) Did he walk or r.? est-il venu à pied ou à cheval? He rode straight at us, il lança son cheval contre nous. To r. like mad, chevaucher à une allure folle. S.a. FALL¹ 1, HOUND¹, ROUGHSHOD. 2. He rides twelve stone, il pèse 76 kilos en selle. 3. Aller, se promener, en voiture; aller, venir, être, en autobus, etc. (With passive force) The car rides smoothly, la voiture est bien suspendue. 4. (a) The moon was riding high in the heavens, la lune voguait haut dans le ciel. (b) (Of ship) To r. at anchor, être mouillé. We were riding by the starboard anchor, nous étions sur l'ancre de tribord. To r. head to the land, être évité le cap sur la terre. II. ride, v.tr. 1. To r. a race, courir (une course). 2. (a) To r. a horse, monter un cheval. Turf: Comet ridden by Jones, Comet monté par Jones. To r. an elephant, être monté à dos d'éléphant. To r. a bicycle, aller à bicyclette. For sale: bicycle, never (been) ridden, à vendre: vélo, jamais roulé. (b) To r. one's horse at a fence, diriger son cheval sur une barrière. To r. a horse to death, crever, éreinter, un cheval. To r. an idea to death, être féru d'une idée. (c) Opprimer; (of nightmare) oppresser (qn). Ridden by fear, hanté par la peur. 3. The ship rides the waves, le navire vogue sur les flots. **ride away,** v.i. Partir, s'éloigner (à cheval, etc.). **ride back,** v.i. (S'en) retourner, s'en revenir (à cheval, etc.). **ride behind,** v.i. 1. Monter en croupe. (in car, etc.) prendre le siège arrière. 2. Suivre à cheval. **ride by,** v.i. Passer (à cheval, etc.). **ride down,** v.tr. Écraser, piétiner. The squadron rode them down, l'escadron leur passa sur le corps. **ride off,** 1. v.i. Partir, s'éloigner (à cheval, etc.). 2. v.tr. (a) (Polo) Bousculer (son adversaire. (b) Donner le change (à qn). **ride out.** 1. v.i. Sortir (à cheval, etc.). 2. v.tr. To r. out the storm, (i) Nau: étaler la tempête; (ii) surmonter la crise. **ride up,** v.i. 1. Arriver (à cheval, etc.). 2. (Of garment) Remonter. **ridden,** a. (With noun prefixed) Tyrannisé par; infesté de. Priest-ridden, sous l'empire des prêtres; infesté par les prêtres. **riding¹,** s. 1. Équitation f; exercice m à cheval. Clever r. (of jockey), monte adroite. S.a. TRICK¹ 3. R. costume, habit m de cavalier. Nau: Mouillage m. S.a. LIGHT¹ 2. 'riding-boots, s.pl. Bottes f (à l'écuyère). 'riding-breeches, s.pl. Culotte f de cheval. 'riding-coat, s. Habit m de cheval. 'riding-habit, s. Cost: Amazone f. 'riding-hood, s. A: Capuchon m. Little Red R.-H., le petit Chaperon rouge. 'riding-master, s.m. Maître, moniteur, d'équitation. 2. Mil: Écuyer instructeur. 'riding-school, s. École f d'équitation; manège m. 'riding-whip, s. Cravache f.

rider ['raidər], s. 1. Cavalier m, -ière; (in circus) écuyer, -ère. Turf: Jockey m. He is a good r., il monte bien à cheval. 2. pl. N.Arch: Riders, porques f. 3. (a) Ajouté m, annexe f (d'un document); avenant m (d'un verdict); clause additionnelle (d'un projet de loi). (b) Mth: Exercice m d'application (d'un théorème). 4. Cavalier (d'une balance).

riderless ['raidəlis], a. (Cheval) sans cavalier; (motocyclette) sans conducteur.

ridge¹ [ridʒ], s. 1. (a) Arête f, crête f (d'une chaîne de montagnes). Wind-cut r., arête vive. (b) Faîte m, faîtage m, crête (d'un comble). (c) Nau: Banc m (de rochers). 2. Chaîne f, rangée f (de coteaux); seuil m (à travers une vallée). 3. Agr: Billon m, butte f. 4. Arête, strie f (sur une surface); ride f (sur le sable). 'ridge-bar, -board, s. Const: Longeron m, longrine f, de faîtage. 'ridge-pole, s. Poutre f de faîte. 'ridge-roof, s. Comble m à deux pentes. 'ridge-tile, s. (Tuile) faîtière f, enfaîteau m.

ridge². 1. v.tr. (a) Const: To r. a roof, enfaîter un toit. (b) Agr: Disposer le terrain en sillons. (c) Sillonner, strier (une surface); rider (le sable). 2. v.i. Se sillonner, se strier; se rider.

ridicule¹ ['ridikju:l], s. Moquerie f, raillerie f, risée f, dérision f. To hold s.o. up to r., se moquer de qn; tourner qn en ridicule. To cover s.o. with r., couvrir qn de ridicule. To lay oneself open to r., s'exposer au ridicule. To invite r., prêter à rire.

ridicule², v.tr. Se moquer de, ridiculiser (qn, qch.).

ridiculous [ri'dikjuləs], a. Ridicule. It is perfectly r., c'est d'un ridicule achevé. To make oneself r., se rendre ridicule. The r. side of the situation, le ridicule de la situation. -ly, adv. Ridiculement; (se conduire) d'une façon ridicule.

ridiculousness [ri'dikjuləsnis], s. Ridicule m.

riding² ['raidiŋ], s. Adm: 1. Division administrative du comté de York. 2. (In Canada) Circonscription électorale.

rife [raif], pred.a. To be r., (of disease) régner, sévir; (of rumour) courir les rues. Distress is r., la misère sevit partout.

riff-raff ['rifræf], s. Coll. Canaille f, racaille f, gueusaille f. All the r.-r., tout le bas peuple.

rifle¹ ['raifl], v.tr. Piller (un endroit); (fouiller et) vider (les poches de qn). To r. a tomb, violer, spolier, un tombeau.

rifle², s. 1. Rayure f (d'un fusil). 2. Fusil (rayé); carabine (de chasse). Gallery r., carabine f de salon. Magazine r., fusil à répétition. R. shooting, tir m au fusil. 3. pl. Rifles, (régiment m de) fusiliers m. R. = Chasseurs à pied. 'rifle-club, s. Société f de tir. 'rifle-pit, s. Trou m de tirailleur(s); tranchée-abri f. 'rifle-range, s. 1. = RIFLE-SHOT 1. 2. (a) Champ m de tir. (b) Stand m (de tir). 'rifle-shot, s. 1. Within r.-shot, à portée de fusil. 2. Coup m de fusil.

rifle³, v.tr. Rayer (une arme à feu). **rifled,** a. Rayé. R. bore, âme rayée. **rifling,** s. 1. Rayage m (d'un fusil). 2. Coll: Rayure(s) f.

rifleman, pl. -men ['raiflmən], s.m. Mil: Fusilier m; A: = chasseur à pied.

rift [rift], s. (a) Fente f; fissure f (dans une roche); crevasse f. R. in the clouds, éclaircie f. (b) Lit: A r. in the lute, une fêlure dans le cristal de leur amitié. 'rift-valley, s. Geol: Fossé m (d'effondrement); rift m.

rig¹ [rig], s. 1. Gréement m (d'un navire). 2. F: Toilette f, tenue f. S.a. RIG-OUT. 3. Mec.E: Ind: etc: (a) Équipement m, installation f; tour f de forage, derrick m. (b) Mécanisme m de manœuvre.

rig², v.tr. (rigged). 1. Gréer, équiper (un navire). Monter, mâter (un mât de charge). **rig out,** v.tr. Équiper (qn, qch.); F: attifer, accoutrer (qn). 'rig-out, s. 1. F: Toilette f, tenue f. Evening r.-o., tenue de soirée. 2. (a) Trousseau m, équipement m. (b) Jeu complet (d'instruments). **rig up,** v.tr. Monter, installer (un appareil); mâter (un mât de charge). **rigging,¹** s. 1. (a) Gréage m (d'un navire). (b) Mec.E: Équipage m ou montage m (d'une machine). 2. Gréement m, agrès mpl (d'un navire); capelage m (d'un mât). Main r., haubans mpl de grand mât. Standing r., manœuvres dormantes.

rig³, s. 1. Mauvais tour. 2. (a) Coup monté; tripotage m. (b) St.Exch: Coup de bourse.

rig⁴, v.tr. 1. To r. the market, provoquer une hausse ou une baisse factice. 2. Cards: Apprêter, truquer (les cartes). **rigging²,** s. Agiotage m; tripotage m (de bourse).

rigger¹ ['rigər], s. Nau: 1. Gréeur m, mâteur m; (on board) gabier m. 2. Square r., navire gréé en carré.

rigger², s. St.Exch: Agioteur m, trafiqueur m, tripoteur m.

right[1] [rait]. I. *a.* **1.** *Geom:* R. **angle,** angle droit. **To meet at right angles,** se croiser à angle droit. **2.** **Bon, honnête, droit. More than is r.,** p!us que de raison. **It is only r. to tell you . . .,** il n'est que justice de vous dire. . . . **Would it be r. for me to . . .?** ferais-je bien de . . .? **I thought it r. to . . .,** j'ai cru devoir . . . . **To take a r. view of things,** voir juste. **To do the r. thing,** (i) se conduire honnêtement; (ii) faire ce qu'il fallait faire. **To do the r. thing by s.o.,** traiter qn honorablement. **3.** (*a*) **Correct, juste, exact. The r. use of words,** l'emploi correct des mots. **To give the r. answer,** répondre juste. **The sum is r.,** l'addition est exacte. **To put an account r.,** ajuster un compte. **To put an error r.,** redresser, corriger, réparer, rectifier, une erreur. **Mistake that can be put r.,** erreur réparable. **The r. time,** l'heure exacte, l'heure juste. **My watch is r.,** ma montre est à l'heure. (*b*) **To be r.,** avoir raison. **He was r. in his opinion,** il ne s'était pas trompé dans son opinion. **Are you r. in refusing?** êtes-vous fondé à refuser? (*c*) **The r. word,** le mot juste. **The r. side of a material,** l'endroit *m* d'un tissu. **R. side up,** à l'endroit. **The plank is not the r. width,** la planche n'est pas de la largeur voulue. **Have you the r. amount?** avez-vous votre compte? **Is that the r. house?** est-ce bien la maison? **The r. train,** le bon train, le train qu'il faut. **Am I r. for Paris?** suis-je bien sur la route pour, dans le train de, Paris? **To put s.o. r.,** (i) mettre qn sur la voie; (ii) détromper, désabuser, qn; (iii) rectifier les dires de qn. **To know the r. people,** (i) avoir des relations, (ii) avoir d'utiles relations. (*d*) **In the r. place,** (i) bien placé; (ii) à sa place. **The r. man in the right place,** l'homme de la situation. **You came at the r. moment,** vous êtes venu au bon moment. **To do sth. in the r. way,** s'y bien prendre pour faire qch. **The r. thing to do,** ce qu'il y a de mieux à faire. **The knack of saying the r. thing,** le don de l'à-propos. *F:* **He's one of the r. sort,** c'est un brave homme. *P:* **She sticks out in all the r. places,** elle est bien carrossée. **That's r.!** c'est bien cela! à la bonne heure! **Quite r.!** parfaitement! *F:* **R.! r. you are!** all r.! bon! entendu! d'accord! (*e*) **He is on the r. side of forty,** il n'a pas encore quarante ans. **To get on the r. side of s.o.,** s'insinuer dans les bonnes grâces de qn. **4.** (*a*) **As r. as rain,** en parfait état. **To be in one's r. mind,** être en possession de toutes ses facultés; avoir toute sa raison. **He is not r. in his head,** il est un peu détraqué. **That'll set you r.,** voilà qui vous remontera. **To set things r.,** rétablir les choses. **Things will come r.,** les affaires s'arrangeront. (*b*) **All r. Everything is all r.,** tout est très bien. **It's all r.,** c'est parfait; tout va bien. **All r.!** c'est bon! ça y est! **I'm all r. again now,** je suis tout à fait remis maintenant. **I have made it all r. for my family,** j'ai pris des arrangements en faveur de ma famille. *F:* **It's all r. for you to laugh!** permis à vous de rire! **He's all r.!** c'est un bon type! *P:* **A bit of all r.,** (i) quelque chose d'épatant; (ii) une chic fille. **5.** (Côté, etc.) droit. **On the r. side,** à droite, sur la droite. **On one's r. hand,** à sa droite. **-ly,** *adv.* **1. To act r.,** bien agir; agir sagement. **2.** (Expliquer) correctement. **To see r.,** voir juste. **R. speaking,** à bien prendre les choses. **I cannot r. say,** je ne saurais dire au juste. **R. or wrongly, I think he is guilty,** à tort ou à raison je le juge coupable. II. **right,** *s.* **1.** Le droit; la justice; le bien. **Might and r.,** la force et le droit. **R. and wrong,** le bien et le mal. *S.a.* WRONG[1] II. **To be in the r.,** avoir raison; être dans son droit. **2.** (*a*) Droit, titre *m.* **To have a r. to sth.,** avoir droit à qch. **R. of way,** (i) *Jur:* servitude *f* de passage; jouissance *f* de passage; (ii) *Aut:* priorité *f* de passage. **He has no r. to complain,** il est mal venu à se plaindre. **With r. of transfer,** avec faculté de transfert. **By what . . .?** de quel droit . . .? à quel titre . . .? **To possess sth. in one's own r.,** posséder qch. de son chef; avoir qch. en propre. (*b*) *pl.* **Rights,** droits; droit. **By rights,** en toute justice. **To be within one's rights,** être dans son droit. *Jur:* **Rights granted by contract,** droits contractuels. **3.** (*a*) **To set things to rights,** rétablir les choses; réparer le désordre. (*b*) **Not to know the rights of the case,** ne pas savoir qui a tort et qui a raison. **I want to know the rights of it,** je voudrais en avoir le cœur net. **4.** (*a*) Droite *f*; côté droit. **On the**

r., à droite. **To keep to the r.,** tenir la droite. *Mth: etc:* **From r. to left,** sinistrorsum. *Mil:* **By the r.!** guide à droite! (*b*) *Pol:* **The R.,** la Droite. (*c*) *Box:* Coup *m* du droit. III. **right,** *adv.* **1.** (*a*) Droit. **To go r. on,** continuer tout droit. (*b*) **To do sth. r. away,** faire qch. sur-le-champ. **I am going there r. away,** j'y vais de ce pas. **R. away!** *Rail:* en route! **R. away!** enlevez (les cales)! *F:* **It's r. here!** ah, c'est ici! ah, le voilà! *F:* **I'll do it r. now,** je le fais tout de suite. **2.** (*a*) **To sink r. to the bottom,** couler droit au fond. **There was a wall r. round the house,** il y avait un mur tout autour de la maison. (*b*) **R. at the top,** tout en haut. **R. in the middle,** au beau milieu. **He threw it r. in my face,** il me le jeta en pleine figure. **The wind was r. behind us,** nous avions le vent juste dans le dos. **3. To know r. well that . . . ,** savoir fort bien que. . . **R. reverend,** très révérend. **4.** (*a*) **To do r.,** bien faire; bien agir. *S.a.* SERVE I. 7. (*b*) (Répondre) correctement; (deviner) juste. **If I remember r.,** si je me souviens bien. **Nothing goes r. with me,** rien ne me réussit. **I got your letter all r.,** j'ai bien reçu votre lettre. *F:* **He is coming r. enough,** il va venir sans aucun doute. **5.** A droite. **He looks neither r. nor left,** il ne regarde ni à droite ni à gauche. **He owes money r. and left,** il doit de l'argent de tous les côtés. *Mil:* **Eyes r.!** tête à droite! **R. turn!** à droite! par le flanc droit! **R. dress!** à droite, alignement! **'right-'about.** **1.** *s.* *Mil:* Demi-tour *m* à droite. *F: A:* **To send s.o. to the r.-a.,** envoyer promener qn. **2.** *adv.* *Mil:* **R.-a. turn!** demi-tour à droite! *Nau:* **To go r.-a.,** virer court. **'right-angled,** *a.* A angle droit. **R.-a. triangle,** triangle rectangle. **'right-hand,** *attrib.a.* (*a*) (Pouce, gant) de la main droite. **R.-h. drawer,** le tiroir de droite. **On the r.-h. side,** à droite. **R.-h. man,** *F:* bras droit (de qn). **'right-'handed,** *a.* **1.** (*Of pers.*) Droitier. **2.** *Box:* **R.-h. blow, punch,** coup du droit. **3.** *adv.* **To play tennis r.-h.,** jouer au tennis de la main droite. **'right-'hander,** *s.* *Box:* Coup *m* du droit. **'right-'minded,** *a.* Bien pensant. **'right-'thinking,** *a.* Bien pensant. **'right-'wing,** *a.* *Pol:* De droite, conservateur, -trice. **'right-'winger,** *s.* *Fb:* Ailier droit.

right[2], *v.tr.* **1.** Redresser (un canot); remettre (une auto) d'aplomb. (*Of boat*) **To r. itself,** *v.i.* to r., se redresser, se relever. **2.** (*a*) Redresser, réparer (un tort). (*b*) Rendre justice à (qn). (*c*) **To r. oneself in the eyes of s.o.,** se justifier aux yeux de qn. **3.** Corriger, rectifier (une erreur).

righteous ['raitʃəs], *a.* **1.** Droit, juste; vertueux, -euse. **2.** Juste, justifié. **R. anger,** juste colère. **-ly,** *adv.* Avec droiture; vertueusement.

righteousness ['raitʃəsnis], *s.* Droiture *f*, vertu *f*.

rightful ['raitful], *a.* **1.** **R. heir,** héritier légitime. **2.** (*a*) (*Of claim*) Légitime, juste. (*b*) (*Of conduct*) Équitable. **-fully,** *adv.* Légitimement; à juste titre.

rightist ['raitist], *a.* *Pol:* De droite.

rightness ['raitnis], *s.* **1.** Rectitude *f*, droiture *f*. **2.** Justesse *f* (d'une décision).

rigid ['ridʒid], *a.* **1.** Rigide, raide. **R. member,** organe fixe (d'une machine). **2.** (*Of conduct*) Sévère, strict. **R. parsimony,** âpre parcimonie. **R. obligation,** obligation stricte. **-ly,** *adv.* **1.** Rigidement. **2.** Sévèrement.

rigidity [ri'dʒiditi], *s.* **1.** Rigidité *f*, raideur *f*. **2.** Sévérité *f*; intransigeance *f*.

rigmarole ['rigm(ə)roul], *s.* Discours sans suite, incohérent; galimatias *m*.

rigor ['rigɔːr], *s.* *Med:* **1.** Frissons *mpl.* **2.** **R. mortis,** rigidité *f* cadavérique.

rigorous ['rigərəs], *a.* Rigoureux, -euse. **-ly,** *adv.* Rigoureusement; avec rigueur.

rigour ['rigər], *s.* **1.** Rigueur *f*, sévérité *f*. **The r. of the law,** la rigueur de la loi. **2.** Rigueur, âpreté *f* (du temps). **3.** Exactitude *f* (d'une preuve). **4.** Raideur *f*, austérité *f* (d'une doctrine).

rile [rail], *v.tr.* *F:* Agacer, exaspérer (qn).

rill [ril], *s.* *Lit:* Ruisselet *m*; petit ruisseau.

rim [rim], *s.* **1.** (*a*) Jante *f* (de roue). *Aut:* **Well-base r.,** jante à base creuse. **Beaded r.,** jante à rebord. (*b*) Cercle *m* (d'un tamis). **2.** Bord *m* (d'un vase); cordon *m*, listeau *m* (d'une pièce de monnaie); rebord *m* (d'une cartouche). **Spectacle rims,** monture *f* de lunettes. *Astr:* **R. of the sun,** limbe *m* du soleil.

rime¹ [raim], s. Givre m; gelée blanche.

rime²,³, s. & v. = RHYME¹,².

rimless ['rimlis], a. (Lunettes) sans monture; (récipient) sans bordure (dépassante).

rimmed [rimd], a. A bord; bordé.

rind [raind], s. 1. Écorce f (mince), peau f (d'arbre). 2. Peau, pelure f (de fruit); pelure, croûte f (de fromage); couenne f (de lard).

rinderpest ['rindəpest], s. Peste bovine.

ring¹ [riŋ], s. 1. (Finger-)r., (symbolical of rite, office) anneau m; (for adornment) bague f. Bishop's r., anneau pastoral. Wedding r., anneau nuptial; alliance f; Fr.C: jonc m. 2. (a) Rond m, anneau (de métal, etc.); maille f (d'une cotte de mailles); (of ski-stick) rondelle f. Napkin r., rond de serviette. Umbrella r., rondelle de parapluie. Split r. (for keys), anneau brisé. R. and staple, anneau à happe. (b) (Binding-)r., frette f; (of ferrule type) virole f. (c) Mch: I.C.E: Segment m. Split r., segment fendu. 3. (a) Anneau (d'une planète); cerne m (autour des yeux); aréole f (autour de la lune); rond (de fumée). He has rings round his eyes, il a les yeux cernés. F: To make rings round s.o., courir deux fois aussi vite que qn; battre qn à plate couture. (b) Annual r. (of tree), couche annuelle, cercle annuel. (c) Orn: Collier m (d'un pigeon). 4. Cercle m (de personnes). Sitting in a r., assis en rond. 5. (a) Groupe m, petite coterie (de personnes). Com: (i) Syndicat m, cartel m. (ii) Pej: Bande noire, gang m. (c) St. Exch: The R., le Parquet; le marché officiel. 6. Arène f, piste f (de cirque). 7. Box: Wr: (a) Cercle formé par les spectateurs. F: To keep, hold, the r., laisser le champ libre aux adversaires. (b) Enceinte f ring m (d'un match de boxe). (c) F: The r., le pugilisme. 8. Turf: The R., (i) l'enceinte (du pesage); (ii) les bookmakers m. 'ring-bolt, s. (a) Anneau m à fiche. (b) Boucle f, bague f, d'amarrage. 'ring-box, -case, s. Baguier m. 'ring-dove, s. (Pigeon) ramier m; palombe f. 'ring(-)master, s.m. Maître de manège, chef m de piste (d'un cirque). 'ring-ouzel, s. Orn: Merle m à collier. 'ring-road, s. Route f de ceinture (autour d'une ville).

ring², v.tr. 1. (a) Baguer (un pigeon) (b) Boucler, anneler (un taureau). 2. To r. round, encercler; entourer.

ring³, s. 1. Son (clair); sonnerie f (de cloches); tintement m (de cloches, de pièces de monnaie); timbre m, intonation f (de la voix). The r. of truth, l'accent m de (la) vérité. 2. (a) Coup m de sonnette, de timbre. There is a r. at the door, on sonne (à la porte). (b) R. on the telephone, appel m téléphonique. I'll give you a r., je vous téléphonerai, je vous appellerai, F: je vous passerai un coup de fil.

ring⁴, v. (rang [raŋ], occ. rung [rʌŋ]; rung) 1. v.i. (a) (Of bell) Sonner, tinter. To set the bells ringing, mettre les cloches en branle. The electric bell rang, le timbre électrique résonna. (b) (Of coin) To r. true, sonner clair. His answer did not r. true, sa réponse a sonné faux. (c) Résonner, retentir (with, de). The air rang with their cries, l'air résonnait de leurs cris. (d) Words ringing with emotion, paroles vibrantes d'émotion. My ears are ringing, les oreilles me tintent. 2. v.tr. (a) Sonner, faire sonner (une cloche). R. the bell! sonnez! Abs. To r. at the door, sonner à la porte. To r. for the lift, appeler l'ascenseur. To r. for the maid, sonner la bonne. Did you r., madam? madame a sonné? To r. for (church) service, sonner l'office. To r. the alarm, sonner le tocsin. F: Does that r. a bell? est-ce que ça vous rappelle quelque chose? S.a. CHANGE¹ 5. (b) Faire sonner (une pièce de monnaie). (c) To r. the bell, (i) (at fair) faire sonner la sonnette de tête de Turc; (ii) P: réussir le coup. ring again, v.i. 1. Sonner de nouveau. 2. Résonner, retentir. To make the mountains r. again, réveiller tous les échos de la montagne. 3. Tp: Rappeler. ring back, v.i. Tp: = RING AGAIN 3. ring down, v.tr. Th: To r. down the curtain, sonner pour la chute du rideau. ring in, v.tr. To r. in the New Year, sonner le carillon pour annoncer le nouvel an. ring off, v.tr. 1. Tp: Abs. To r. off, raccrocher (l'appareil); couper la communication. 2. Nau: 'R. off the engines,' "terminé pour la machine." ring out, v.i. Sonner; retentir. A shot rang out, un coup de fusil retentit. ring up, v.tr. 1. Th: To r. up the curtain, sonner pour le lever du rideau; (in Fr.) frapper les trois coups. 2. To r. s.o. up (on the telephone), donner un coup de téléphone à qn. ringing¹, a. 1. (Of bell) Qui tinte, qui résonne. 2. Sonore, retentissant. In r. tones, d'une voix vibrante. ringing², s. 1. Son m, tintement m (de cloches). 2. (a) Tintement (dans les oreilles). (b) Retentissement m.

ringer ['riŋər], s. 1. Sonneur m; carillonneur m. 2. U.S: F: To be a dead r. for s.o., être le portrait tout craché de qn.

ringleader ['riŋli:dər], s. Chef m (d'attroupement); meneur m (de révolte); chef d'émeute.

ringlet ['riŋlit], s. 1. Petit anneau. 2. Boucle f (de cheveux); frisette f.

ringside ['riŋsaid], s. To have a r. seat, (i) (at circus, boxing match) avoir une place au premier rang; (ii) être bien placé pour tout observer, tout suivre.

ringworm ['riŋwə:m], s. Med: Teigne tonsurante, tondante.

rink [riŋk], s. Skating r., patinoire f. Roller-skating r., salle f de patinage à roulettes.

rinse¹ [rins], s. 1. Rinçage m. To give a bottle a r., rincer une bouteille. 2. Haird: Rinçage (de couleur).

rinse², v.tr. Rincer (une bouteille, le linge). rinsing, s. Rinçage m.

riot¹ ['raiət], s. 1. Émeute f; rassemblement tumultueux, bagarre f. The R. Act, la loi contre les attroupements. To read the R. Act, (i) faire les trois sommations légales; (ii) F: semoncer (qn) d'importance. 2. Orgie f (de couleurs, etc.). 3. (a) To run r., se déchaîner, ne plus connaître de frein; (of plants) pulluler. (b) F: It's, he's, a r., c'est rigolo; c'est un rigolo. The play was a r., la pièce a fait fureur.

riot², v.i. (rioted) (a) Provoquer une émeute; s'ameuter; bagarrer. (b) Faire du vacarme. rioting, s. Émeutes fpl; troubles mpl.

rioter ['raiətər], s. 1. Émeutier m, séditieux, -euse. 2. Noceur m.

riotous ['raiətəs], a. 1. Séditieux, -euse; tumultueux, -euse, turbulent. 2. (a) (Of pers.) Tapageur, -euse, bruyant. A few r. students, quelques étudiants en rupture de ban. (b) A: R. living, vie dissipée. -ly, adv. 1. Séditieusement; tumultueusement. 2. D'une manière désordonnée.

riotousness ['raiətəsnis], s. 1. Turbulence f (de la foule). 2. Désordre m.

rip¹ [rip], s. Déchirure f; fente f. 'rip-cord, s. Cordelette f de déclenchement (de parachute). 'rip-saw, s. Tls: Scie f à refendre.

rip², v. (ripped) 1. v.tr. Fendre (en long); déchirer. To r. (sth.) open, ouvrir un paquet en le déchirant; (of wild boar) découdre (un chien). 2. v.i. (a) Se déchirer, se fendre. (b) F: O: To r. (along), aller à toute vitesse. F: Aut: Let her r.! laissez-la filer! F: To let r., laisser déchaîner sa colère, etc. rip off, v.tr. Arracher, déchirer (ce qui recouvre qch.). rip out, v.tr. To r. out the lining of a coat, arracher la doublure d'un habit. rip up, v.tr. Éventrer (qn); découdre (un vêtement, le ventre). ripping, a. 1. Qui déchire, qui fend. 2. F: Épatant, fameux.

rip³, s. F: (a) Mauvais garnement. An old r., un vieux marcheur. (b) He's a bit of a r., c'est un gaillard.

rip⁴, s. Clapotis m (du courant). R. tide, courant m de retour.

riparian [rai'pɛəriən], a. & s. Riverain (m).

ripe [raip], a. 1. (a) Mûr. R. cheese, fromage (bien) fait. To grow r., mûrir. (b) A r. old age, un bel âge. 2. Plan r. for execution, projet prêt à être exécuté; projet mûr. He is r. for mischief, il est prêt à faire le mal.

ripen ['raip(ə)n]. 1. v.tr. Mûrir; faire mûrir. 2. v.i. Mûrir; venir à maturité. This cheese will r., ce fromage se fera. ripening, s. Maturation f; jaunissement m (du blé); affinage m (du fromage).

ripeness ['raipnis], s. Maturité f; état mûr

riposte¹ [ri'poust], s. Riposte f.

riposte², v.i. Riposter.

ripper ['ripər], s. 1. Hist: Jack the R., Jack l'Éventreur. 2. P: A: Type épatant; chose épatante, sensationnelle.

ripple¹ ['ripl], *s.* **1.** (*a*) Ride *f* (sur l'eau); ondulation *f.* (*b*) Gazouillement *m* (d'un ruisseau). **2.** (*In hair*) Ondulation. **3.** Murmure(s) *m(pl)* (de conversation). **4.** *Tex:* Égrugeoir *m.* **'ripple-mark,** *s.* Ride laissée sur le sable (par la marée).

ripple². 1. *v.i.* (*a*) (*Of water*) Se rider. (*b*) (*Of corn*) Onduler; (*of hair*) former des ondulations. (*c*) (*Of brook*) Murmurer; (*of the tide*) clapoter; (*of laughter*) perler. **2.** *v.tr.* (*Of wind*) Rider (le sable). **3.** *v.tr. Tex:* Égruger (le lin).

riprap¹ ['ripræp], *s. Civ.E: Hyd.E:* Enrochement *m.*

riprap², *v.tr. Civ.E: Hyd.E:* Enrocher.

rip-roaring ['ripro:riŋ], *a. F:* Débordant de gaieté tapageuse.

rise¹ [raiz], *s,* **1.** (*a*) Ascension. *f. Th:* R. of the curtain, lever *m* du rideau. (*b*) To shoot a bird on the r., tirer, un oiseau au cul levé. (*Of fish*) To be on the r., monter à la mouche. *F:* To get a r. out of s.o., mystifier qn; se payer la tête de qn. **2.** (*a*) Montée *f*, côte *f* (sur une route); rampe *f*. R. in the ground, exhaussement *m* du terrain; (*sharp*) ressaut *m* de terrain. (*b*) Éminence *f*, élévation *f*. **3.** *Arch: Civ.E:* Flèche *f*, hauteur *f* sous clef (d'un arc). **4.** (*a*) Crue *f* (des eaux); flot *m*, flux *m* (de la marée); hausse *f* (du baromètre); élévation (de température); augmentation *f* (de pression). The r. of the tide, la montée de l'eau. (*b*) Augmentation, hausse (de prix). R. in value of a possession, appréciation *f* d'un bien. To ask (one's employer) for a r., demander une augmentation. (*c*) *Mus:* R. of half a tone, hausse d'un demiton. **5.** Avancement *m*; élévation (en rang). The r. of Napoleon, l'essor *m* de Napoléon. **6.** To give r. to sth., faire naître, engendrer, occasionner, qch. To give r. to dissatisfaction, provoquer le mécontentement.

rise², *v.i.* (rose [rouz]; risen ['riz(ə)n]) **1.** (*a*) To r. (to one's feet), se lever; se mettre debout; (*after kneeling*) se relever. To r. from table, se lever de table. The horse rose on its hind legs, le cheval se dressa, se cabra. (*b*) Parliament will r. next week, le Parlement doit s'ajourner la semaine prochaine. (*c*) To r. early, se lever tôt. (*d*) To r. (again) from the dead, ressusciter d'entre les morts. **2.** To r. (in revolt), se soulever, se révolter (against, contre). To r. (up) in arms, prendre les armes. **3.** (*a*) (*Of sun, star*) Se lever; (*of smoke*) monter, s'élever. (*b*) To r. off the ground, quitter le sol. To r. to the surface, monter à la surface. (*c*) (*Of fish*) To r. to the bait, monter à la mouche; mordre. *F:* (*Of pers.*) To r. to it, se laisser provoquer. He didn't r. (to it), il n'a pas tiqué, il laissa passer l'occasion. (*d*) *Ven:* (*Of game*) To r., se lever, s'envoler. **4.** (*a*) (*Of ground*) Monter, s'élever; (*of dough*) lever; (*of sea*) (i) monter, (ii) devenir gros. The barometer is rising, le baromètre remonte, est à la hausse. (*b*) A castle rises in the distance, au loin s'élève, se dresse, un château. (*c*) A picture rises in my mind, une image se présente à mon esprit. (*d*) The wind is rising, le vent se lève. Her colour rose, ses joues s'empourpraient. (*e*) Prices are rising, les prix sont à la hausse. Everything has risen in price, tout a augmenté de prix. **5.** (*a*) To r. above vanity, être au-dessus de la vanité. (*b*) The horse rose at the fence, le cheval s'enleva pour franchir l'obstacle. To r. to the occasion, se montrer à la hauteur de la situation. **6.** To r. in the world, faire son chemin. To r. in s.o.'s esteem, monter dans l'estime de qn. He rose from nothing, il est parti de rien. *S.a.* RANK¹ 1. **7.** (*Of river*) Prendre sa source (at, à; in, dans). **rising**¹, *a.* **1.** (Soleil) levant. **2.** (*a*) (Route) qui monte; (baromètre) en hausse. R. ground, élévation *f* de terrain. R. tide, marée montante. (*b*) *Phot:* R. front, objectif à décentrement en hauteur. **3.** (*a*) (Vent) qui se lève; (colère) croissante. (*b*) R. prices, prix *m (pl)* en hausse. R. market, marché orienté à la hausse. *St. Exch:* To speculate on a r. market, jouer à la hausse. **4.** R. man, homme d'avenir. **5.** The r. generation, la nouvelle génération. **6.** *F:* To be r. five, (*of horse, of child*) aller sur (ses) cinq ans. **rising²,** *s.* **1.** (*a*) Lever *m* (du rideau). (*b*) Upon the r. of the House, quand la Chambre s'ajourna. (*c*) Not to like early r., ne pas aimer à se lever tôt. (*d*) R. from the dead, résurrection *f.* **2.** Ameutement *m*, soulèvement *m.* **3.** (*a*) Lever (d'un astre). (*b*) *Ven:*

Envol *m* (de gibier). **4.** Hausse *f* (du baromètre); crue *f* (des eaux); poussée *f* (de la sève). R. and falling, mouvement de hausse et de baisse.

riser ['raizər], *s.* **1.** To be an early r., être matinal. To be a late r., faire la grasse matinée, se lever tard tous les jours. **2.** *Const:* Contremarche *f* (d'un escaler). **3.** *Ind:* Canalisation ascendante; tuyau *m* de montée. *Petroleum Ind: etc:* Colonne montante.

risk¹ [risk], *s.* (*a*) Risque *m*, péril *m.* The risks of an undertaking, les aléas *m* d'une entreprise. To take, run, incur, a r., courir un risque. It isn't worth the r., *F:* ça ne vaut pas le coup. At one's own r., à ses risques et périls. (*b*) *Ins:* Fire r., risque d'incendie.

risk², *v.tr.* Risquer. (*a*) Aventurer, hasarder (qch.) To r. one's own skin, risquer sa peau; payer de sa personne. (*b*) I'll r. it, je vais risquer, tenter, le coup. (*c*) To r. defeat, courir les chances d'une défaite.

riskiness ['riskinis], *s.* Risques *mpl* et périls *mpl*; aléas *mpl* (d'une entreprise).

risky ['riski], *a.* **1.** Hasardeux, -euse, chanceux, -euse, aléatoire. **2.** (*Of story*) Risqué.

risotto [ri'zɔtou], *s. Cu:* Risotto *m.*

risqué ['ri:skei] *a.* Risqué, scabreux, -euse, osé.

rissole ['risoul], *s. Cu:* Croquette *f.*

rite [rait], *s.* Rite *m.* Funeral, burial rites, les rites funèbres. The last rites, les derniers sacrements. Fortified with the rites of the Church, muni des sacrements de l'Église.

ritual ['ritjuəl]. **1.** *a.* Rituel, -elle; selon le rite. **2.** *s.* (*a*) Rites *mpl.* (*b*) (*Book*) Rituel *m.* **-ally,** *adv.* Selon les rites.

ritualism ['ritjuəlizm], *s. Ecc:* Ritualisme *m.*

ritualist ['ritjuəlist], *s.* Ritualiste *mf.*

ritualistic ['ritjuə'listik], *a.* Ritualiste.

rival¹ ['raiv(ə)l]. **1.** *a.* Concurrentiel, -elle. **2.** (*a*) *a. & s.* Rival, -ale, *pl.* -aux, -ales; concurrent, -ente. (*b*) *s.* Émule *mf.*

rival², *v.tr.* (**rivalled**) (*a*) Rivaliser avec (qn). (*b*) Être l'émule de (qn).

rivalize ['raivəlaiz], *v.i.* Rivaliser (with, avec).

rivalry ['raivəlri], *s.* (*a*) Rivalité *f.* To enter into r. with s.o., entrer en rivalité avec qn; aller sur les brisées de qn. (*b*) Émulation *f.*

river ['rivər], *s.* **1.** Cours *m* d'eau; (*main r.*) fleuve *m*; (*tributary, smaller r.*) rivière *f*; (*small r. flowing into sea*) fleuve côtier. Down (the) r., en aval. Up (the) r., en amont. *F:* To sell s.o. down the r., vendre, trahir, qn. R. port, port fluvial. *S.a.* POLICE¹. **2.** Flot *m* (de sang). **'river 'bank,** *s.* Bord *m* de la rivière, du fleuve; rive *f.* **'river-'basin,** *s.* Bassin fluvial. **'river-'bed,** *s.* Lit *m* de rivière.

riverine ['rivərain], *a.* **1.** Riverain. **2.** De la rivière; fluvial, -aux.

riverside ['rivəsaid], *s.* **1.** Bord *m* de l'eau; rive *f.* **2.** *Attrib.* R. inn, auberge située au bord de la rivière.

rivet¹ ['rivit], *s.* **1.** (i) Rivet *m*; (ii) clou *m* à river. To drive a r., placer un rivet. **2.** (*For china*) Attache *f.* **'rivet-joint,** *s. Metalw:* Assemblage à rivets. **'rivet-punch, -set, -snap,** *s.* Chasse-rivet(s) *m inv;* bouterolle *f.*

rivet², *v.tr.* (**rivet(t)ed**) (*a*) River, riveter. (*b*) To r. the attention, fixer, capter, l'attention. **rivet(t)ing,** *s.* **1.** Rivetage *m.* **2.** Rivure *f.* **'riveting-hammer,** *s. Tls:* (Marteau *m*) rivoir *m.* **'riveting-machine,** *s.* Machine *f* à river, riveteuse *f*, riveuse *f.*

riveter ['rivitər], *s.* Riveteur *m*, riveur *m.*

Riviera (the) [ðə,rivi'eərə]. *Pr.n.* The French R., la Côte d'Azur. The Italian R., la Riviera.

rivulet ['rivjulit], *s.* Ruisseau *m.*

roach [rout∫], *s. Ich:* Gardon *m.*

road [roud], *s.* **1.** Route *f*, chemin *m*, voie *f*; (*in towns often = street*) rue *f.* (*a*) Across the r., de l'autre côté de la route, de la rue. High r., main r., grand chemin, grande route. Local r., chemin vicinal. Accommodation r., chemin de terre. Farmservice r., chemin; *Fr.C:* rang *m.* "A" road = route nationale. "B" road = route départementale. R. transport, transports routiers. 'It's your r.', "à vous la priorité." (*b*) To take, *F:* hit, the r., se mettre en route; partir. To be on the r., (i) être en route; (ii) *Com: F:* être représentant (d'une maison de commerce); (iii) *Com:* (*of traveller*) être en tournée. *F:* The garage man got us on the r. again quickly, le garagiste nous a vite dépannés. R. sense, sens pratique des dangers de la route. He is on the right r., il est dans la bonne voie. The r. to success, la voie du succès. (c) Voie, chemin. Rail: To whistle for the r., demander la voie. 2. Chaussée f. Car that holds the r. well, voiture qui tient bien la route. 3. Nau: Roads, rade f. 'road-bed, s. Civ.E: (a) Assiette f, encaissement m (de la route). (b) Rail: Superstructure f (de la voie). 'road-block, s. Barrage m. 'road-hog, s. F: Écraseur m, chauffard m. 'road-house, s. Auberge f, hôtel m; esp. hôtellerie f en bord de route avec piscine, dancing, etc. 'road-map, s. Carte routière. 'road-mender, s. Cantonnier m. 'road-metal, s. Matériaux mpl d'empierrement pour routes. 'road-race, s. Sp: Course f (i) cycliste, (ii) automobile, sur route. 'road-racer, s. Cy: Vélo m de course (sur route). 'road-roller, s. Civ.E: Rouleau compresseur. 'road test, s. Essai m (de voiture) sur route. 'road-trials, s.pl. Cy: Aut: Compétitions routières. 'road-user, s. Usager m de la route.

roadman, pl. -men ['roudmən], s.m. Travailleur de la voirie; cantonnier.

roadrailer ['roud,reilər], s. Rail: Wagon m rail-route.

roadside ['roudsaid], s. 1. Bord m, côté m, de la route, de la chaussée. 2. attrib. R. inn, auberge située au bord de la route. Aut: R. repairs, réparations f de fortune; dépannage m.

roadstead ['roudsted], s. Nau: Rade f. Open r., rade ouverte, foraine.

roadster ['roudstər], s. (a) Vélo m de tourisme. (b) Voiture f décapotable (à deux places).

roadway ['roudwei], s. 1. Chaussée f. 2. Voie f, tablier m (de pont).

roadworthiness ['roudwə:ðinis], s. Aut: etc: (Of vehicle) Aptitude f à rouler.

roadworthy ['roudwə:ði], a. Aut: En état de marche.

roam [roum]. 1. v.i. Errer, rôder. To r. about the world, rouler (de) par le monde; rouler sa bosse. 2. v.tr. Errer par, parcourir (les rues). roaming¹, a. Errant, vagabond. roaming², s. Course errante.

roan [roun]. 1. a. Rouan. 2. s. (Cheval) rouan m. Red r. (cheval) aubère m.

roar¹ ['rɔ:r], s. 1. (a) (Of pers.) Hurlement m; rugissement m. Roars of laughter, grands éclats de rire. (b) Rugissement (du lion); mugissement m (du taureau). 2. Grondement m (de canon); mugissement (de la mer); ronflement m (d'un fourneau).

roar². 1. v.i. (a) (Of pers.) Hurler, rugir. To r. with pain, hurler de douleur. S.a. LAUGHTER. (b) (Of lion) Rugir. (Of bull) mugir; (of camel) blatérer. (c) (Of thunder) Gronder; (of sea) mugir. (d) (Of stove) Brondir, ronfler. 2. v.tr. To r. (out) an order, vociférer un ordre. roaring¹, a. 1. (a) (Lion) rugissant. (b)(Tonnerre) grondant; (vent) mugissant. We were sitting in front of a r. fire, nous étions assis devant une belle flambée. Nau: The r. forties, zone située entre les 40e et 50e degrés de latitude sud (où soufflent les grands vents d'ouest). 2. To do a r. trade, faire un gros commerce; faire des affaires superbes. roaring², s. 1.=ROAR¹. 2. Vet: Cornage m.

roast¹ [roust], s. Cu: Rôti m. A r. of beef, un rosbif. A r. of veal, un rôti de veau.

roast², v. (p.p. in compound tenses roasted, as attrib. a. roast) 1. v.tr. (a) Rôtir, faire rôtir (la viande); rôtir (des marrons). Fire fit to r. an ox, feu à rôtir un bœuf. (b) Ind: Griller (le minerai). (c) Griller, torréfier (le café). 2. v.i. (a) (Of meat, etc.) Rôtir. (b) I was roasting in the sun, je grillais sous le soleil. roast³, a. R. meat, viande rôtie. R. beef, rôti m de bœuf; rosbif m. roasting¹, a. (Feu m, etc.) brûlant. roasting², s. 1. Rôtissage m, cuisson f (de la viande). R. chicken, poulet à rôtir. 2. Grillage m, calcination f (du minerai). 3. Torréfaction f (du café). 'roasting-jack, s. Tourne-broche m.

roaster ['roustər], s. 1. (a) Cu: Rôtissoire f. (b) Metall: Four m à griller. (c) Brûloir m, torréfacteur m (à café). 2. Volaille f (etc.) à rôtir. 3. F: Journée f torride.

rob [rɔb], v.tr. (robbed) Voler, dévaliser, détrousser (qn); piller (un verger). To r. s.o. of sth., (i) voler qch. à qn; (ii) escroquer qch. à qn. To r. the till, voler la caisse.

robber ['rɔbər], s. Voleur, -euse.

robbery ['rɔbəri], s. Vol qualifié. A: Highway r., vol de grand chemin; brigandage m. F: It's sheer highway r., c'est de l'escroquerie.

robe¹ [roub], s. 1. Robe f (d'office, de cérémonie). Magistrates in their robes, magistrats en robe. The Coronation robes, les robes et insignes du sacre (du souverain). 2. Vêtement m. Bath r., peignoir m de bain. 3. U.S: Couverture f, couvre-pied(s) m en fourrure.

robe². 1. v.tr. Revêtir (qn d'une robe d'office). 2. v.i. Revêtir sa robe.

Robin ['rɔbin]. 1. Pr.n.m. Lit: R. Goodfellow, lutin m domestique. R. Hood, Robin des bois. 2. s. (a) Orn: R. (redbreast), rouge-gorge m. (b) Bot: Ragged r., lychnide f des prés. (c) See ROUND ROBIN.

robot ['roubɔt], s. Robot m.

robust [ro'bʌst], a. (Of pers.) Robuste, vigoureux, -euse, solide. R. appetite, appétit robuste.

robustness [ro'bʌstnis], s. Nature f robuste, robustesse f, vigueur f.

rocambole ['rɔkəmboul], s. Bot: Rocambole f; échalote d'Espagne.

roche moutonnée ['rɔ:ʃmu:'tɔnei], s. Geog: Roche moutonnée.

rochet ['rɔtʃit], s. Ecc.Cost: Rochet m; surplis m (à manches étroites).

rock¹ [rɔk], s. 1. (a) Rocher m, roc m. R.-face (to be climbed), varappe f. (b) Geol: Roche f. Volcanic r., roche volcanique. 2. A r., un rocher, une roche. F: The R., le rocher de Gibraltar. Nau: To run upon the rocks, donner sur les écueils. To see rocks ahead, voir des obstacles devant soi. F: To be on the rocks, être à la côte; être dans la débine, dans la dèche. Comest: (Brighton, etc.) r., bâton m de sucrerie. Whisky on the rocks, whisky avec cubes de glace, avec glaçons. S.a. FIRM² 1. 3. (Used adjectively) (a) Rupestre. Art: R. drawings, dessins rupestres. (b) R. plant, plante f des rochers; plante alpine. 'rock-bottom, s. (a) Fond rocheux. (b) F: Le fin fond. R.-b. price, prix le plus bas. 'rock-bound, a. Entouré de rochers. R.-b. coast, côte hérissée de rochers. 'rock-cake, s. Cu: Petit gâteau pour le thé aux raisins secs. 'rock-climber, s. Varappeur m. 'rock-climbing, s. Varappe f. Rock-climbing, expedition, varappée f. ,rock-'crystal, s. Miner: Cristal m de roche. 'rock-garden, s. Jardin m de rocaille; jardin alpin. 'rock-oil, s. Miner: Huile f de roche; naphte minéral. 'rock-pigeon, s. Orn: Pigeon m biset. 'rock salt, s. Sel m gemme.

rock². 1. v.tr. (a) Bercer, balancer; basculer (un levier). To r. a child, bercer un enfant. To r. a cradle, balancer faire aller, un berceau. Ship rocked by the waves, navire ballotté, balancé, par les flots. Lever rocked by a cam, levier basculé par une came. Gold-Min: To r. the ore, travailler le minerai au berceau. (b) The earthquake rocks the house, le tremblement de terre secoue, ébranle, la maison. 2. v.i. (a) The cradle rocks, le berceau balance. (b) The house was rocking with the shock, la maison oscillait sous le choc. To r. with laughter, se tordre de rire, se désopiler. rocking¹, a. 1. Oscillant; à bascule. 2. Branlant. 'rock-and-roll, F: rock'n'roll, s. Danc: F: Rock'n'-roll m, F: rock m. 'rocking-chair, s. Fauteuil m à bascule. 'rocking-horse, s. Cheval m à bascule. 'rocking-lever, s. = ROCKER-ARM. 'rocking-stone, s. Geol: Rocher branlant. rocking², s. 1. Balancement m, bercement m; oscillation f. Mec.E: Basculage m. Rail: Mouvement m de lacet. 2. Tremblement m, branlement m.

rocker ['rɔkər], s. 1. Bascule f (de berceau). F: To be off one's r., avoir l'esprit dérangé; être un peu toqué. 2. Gold-Min: etc: Berceau m. 3. I.C.E: Culbuteur m. Aut: Valve-r. shaft, rampe f des culbuteurs. 'rocker-arm, s. (a) Mec.E: Basculeur m. I.C.E: Culbuteur m. (b) Mch: Balancier m de renvoi. 'rocker-shaft, s. Mch: Arbre m de renversement de marche.

rockery ['rɔkəri], s. Hort: Rochers artificiels; jardin m de rocaille.

rocket¹ ['rɔkit], s. Bot: Roquette f.

rocket², s. **1.** Pyr: Fusée f. **R. signal, signal r.,** signal m à fusée; fusée de signaux. **2.** Mil: Roquette f. Av: **R.(-propelled) fighter,** chasseur-fusée m, pl. chasseurs-fusées. **R. base,** base f de lancement (de fusées). **First-stage r.,** fusée mère. **3.** F: Savon m **He's just had a r. from the old man,** son père vient de lui passer un savon. **'rocket-apparatus,** s. (Fusée f) porte-amarre m inv. **'rocket-gun,** s. Lance-fusée m. **'rocket-launcher,** s. (a) Lance-fusée m, pl. lance-fusées, lance-roquette m, pl. lance-roquettes. (b) Rampe f de lancement de fusées. **'rocket-stick,** s. Baguette f de direction (d'une fusée).

rocket³, v.i. (a) (Of horse) Se lancer comme un éclair. (Of rider, etc.) **To r. into s.o.,** caramboler contre qn. (b) (Of partridge, aircraft) Monter en chandelle. (c) Pol.Ec: **Prices are rocketing,** les prix montent en flèche.

Rockies ['rɔkiz]. Pr.n.pl. Geog: See ROCKY¹ 2.

rockiness ['rɔkinis], s. Nature rocheuse, rocailleuse (of, de).

rocky¹ ['rɔki], a. **1.** Rocailleux, -euse; rocheux, -euse. **2.** De roche; rocheux. **The R. Mountains,** s. **the Rockies,** les (montagnes) Rocheuses.

rocky², a. F: Chancelant, instable.

rococo [ro'koukou], a. & s. (Style) rococo (m inv).

rod [rɔd], s. **1.** Baguette f. **2.** Verge f. **To make a r. for one's own back,** se préparer des ennuis. **To have a r. in pickle for s.o.,** garder à qn un chien œ sa chienne. Prov: **Spare the r. and spoil the child,** qui aime bien châtie bien. **3.** Verge (d'huissier). **To rule s.o. with a r. of iron,** mener qn à la baguette. **4.** (Fishing-)r., canne f à pêche. **R. and line,** ligne f de pêche. **5.** Meas: = PERCH¹ 2. **6.** (a) Tringle f. **Curtain r.,** tringle de rideau. **Stair r.,** tringle d'escalier. (b) **Copper r.,** barre f de cuivre. El: **Carbon r., zinc ɪ.,** crayon m de charbon, de zinc (de pile). (c) **Pump r.,** tige f de pompe. Aut: **Brake r.,** tige de frein; tirant m de frein. Ph: **R. of a pendulum,** verge d'un pendule. **7.** Surv: Mire f. **'rod-bac'terium,** pl. -ia, s. Biol: etc: Bâtonnet m.

rode. See RIDE².

rodent ['roud(ə)nt]. **1.** a. Rongeur, -euse. **2.** s. Z: Rongeur m.

rodeo [rou'deiou], s. U.S: Rodéo m.

Roderick ['rɔd(ə)rik]. Pr.n.m. Rodrigue.

roe¹ [rou], s. Z: **R.(-deer),** chevreuil m.

roe², s. (a) (Hard) r., œufs mpl (de poisson). (b) Soft r., laite f, laitance f.

roebuck ['roubʌk], s. Chevreuil m (mâle).

roentgen ['rʌntgən], s. Ph: Rœntgen m.

rogation [ro'geiʃ(ə)n], s. Ecc: Usu. pl. Rogations fpl. **R. days,** Rogations.

rogatory ['rɔgətəri], a. Rogatoire.

Roger ['rɔdʒər]. **1.** Pr.n.m. Roger. A: **The Jolly R.,** le pavillon noir (des pirates). **2.** W.Tel: Av: etc: (Code word) = R(eçu et compris).

rogue [roug], s. **1.** Coquin, -ine; fripon, -onne; chenapan m. F: **They formed a real rogues' gallery,** ils avaient tous une mine patibulaire. **2.** Malin, -igne; espiègle mf. **She's a little r.,** c'est une petite coquine, une petite friponne. **3.** Jur: A: Vagabond m. **4.** (Éléphant ou buffle) solitaire m.

roguery ['rougəri], s. **1.** Coquinerie f, friponnerie f, fourberie f. **2.** Malice f, espièglerie f (d'un enfant).

roguish ['rougiʃ], a. **1.** (Air) coquin, fripon, polisson; (ruses) de coquin, de fripon. **2.** (Air) malin, espiègle. **-ly,** adv. **1.** En fripon, en fourbe, en coquin. **2.** Avec espièglerie; malicieusement.

roguishness ['rougiʃnis], s. = ROGUERY 2.

roisterer ['rɔistərər], s. Tapageur, -euse; fêtard, -arde.

roistering¹ ['rɔistəriŋ], a. ᵀapageur, -euse; bruyant.

roistering², s. Tapage m; chahut m; la noce, la fête.

rôle [roul], s. Th: etc: Rôle m.

roll¹ [roul], s. **1.** (a) Rouleau m (de papier, etc.); pièce f (d'étoffe). (b) Arch: Volute f (de chapiteau ionique). (c) Cu: **Boiled jam r.,** pudding bouilli farci de confiture (en forme de bûche). **Swiss r.,** bûche f. Bak: **R. (of bread),** petit pain. **Bridge r.,** petit pain mollet. (d) Coquille f (de beurre). (e) U.S: Liasse f (de billets de banque). **2.** Adm: etc: Rôle m, contrôle m, liste f. Mil: Nau: **To put, enter, a man on the rolls,** porter un homme sur les contrôles. **To

call the r., faire l'appel. **The r. of honour,** (i) la liste de ceux qui sont morts pour la patrie; (ii) Sch: etc: le tableau d'honneur. **To strike s.o. off the rolls,** Jur: rayer qn du tableau, du barreau; Mil: etc: rayer qn des états. **3.** Canon m, bâton m (de soufre); carotte f, boudin m (de tabac). **4.** Tail: Rabat m (de col d'habit). **5.** (Roller) (a) Rouleau, cylindre m (de laminoir, etc.). (b) pl. **Rolls,** train m (de laminoir). **'roll-call,** s. Mil: Sch: Appel (nominal). **'roll-collar, -neck,** s. Cost: (Of sweater, etc.) Col roulé. **'roll-top,** attrib. a. **R.-t. desk,** pupitre m à cylindre; bureau américain.

roll², s. **1.** (a) Nau: Coup m de roulis. **To walk with a r.,** se dandiner en marchant. (b) **The r. of the sea,** la houle. **2.** (a) Roulement m (d'une balle, etc.). (b) **To have a r. on the grass,** se rouler par terre. (c) Av: Vol m en tonneau. **Flick r.,** tonneau déclenché. **Aileron r.,** tonneau lent. **3.** Roulement (de tambour, de tonnerre).

roll³. I. v.tr. **1.** Rouler (un tonneau, une bille). **To r. one's eyes,** rouler les yeux. **2.** To r. one's r's, rouler les r; grasseyer. **3.** (a) Rouler, passer au rouleau (le gazon); cylindrer (une route). (b) Laminer (les métaux); travailler (les métaux) au laminoir. (c) Cu: **To r. (out) paste,** étendre la pâte au rouleau. **4.** To r. (up) paper, (en)rouler du papier. **To r. cigarettes,** rouler des cigarettes. **II. roll,** v.i. Rouler. **1.** (a) **The ball rolls under the table,** la balle roule sous la table. **Some heads will r. in the Government,** quelques ministres vont être limogés. S.a. BALL¹ 1. (Of pers.) **To r. downhill,** faire une roulade. **To r. downstairs,** débouler l'escalier. **The tears rolled down his cheeks,** les larmes coulaient sur ses joues. (b) **His eyes were rolling,** les yeux lui roulaient dans la tête. **2.** v.i. & pr. **To r. (oneself) from side to side,** se retourner et se rouler, de côté et d'autre. F: **To be rolling in wealth,** rouler sur l'or. **3.** (Of thunder) Gronder, rouler. **To hear the drums rolling,** entendre le roulement des tambours. **4.** (Of ship, aircraft) Rouler; avoir du roulis. **To r. gunwhale under,** rouler bord sur bord; engager. **roll about. 1.** v.tr. Rouler (qch.) çà et là. **2.** v.i. Rouler çà et là. **roll back. 1.** v.tr. (a) Rouler (qch.) en arrière. (b) F: (Of government) Baisser (les prix). **2.** v.i. (a) Rouler en arrière; reculer (en roulant). (b) (Of the eyes) Chavirer. **roll by,** v.i. Passer (en roulant); (of time) s'écouler. **roll in. 1.** v.tr. Hockey: **To r. in the ball,** remettre la balle en jeu. **2.** v.i. Entrer en roulant. **To watch the waves r. in,** regarder les vagues déferler sur le rivage. **'roll-in,** s. Hockey: Touche f. **roll off. 1.** v.tr. Publ: **To r.o. 20,000 copies,** imprimer 20,000 exemplaires. **2.** v.i. Tomber (en roulant). **roll on,** v.i. Continuer de rouler; (of time) s'écouler. F: **R. o. Christmas!** vite Noel! **'roll-on,** attrib.a. **R.-on corset, belt,** s. F: **roll-on,** gaine f (élastique extensible). **roll over. 1.** v.tr. Retourner (qch₁.); culbuter (qn). **2.** v.i. Se retourner (en roulant). **To r. over and over,** rouler sur soi-même (plusieurs fois). **roll up. 1.** v.tr. (a) Rouler, enrouler (une carte); relever, retrousser (ses manches). (b) Envelopper (qch.). **To r. oneself up in a blanket,** s'enrouler dans une couverture. **2.** v.i. (a) (Of blind, etc.) S'enrouler. (Of kitten) **To r. up into a ball,** se mettre en boule. (b) F: (Of guests, etc.) Arriver, s'amener. **rolled,** a. **1.** (Papier) en rouleau. **R. (up) leaf,** feuille enroulée. **2. R. iron,** fer laminé, cylindré. **R. gold,** doublé m. **R.-gold watch,** montre en plaqué or, en doublé. **rolling¹,** a. **1.** Roulant. Prov: **A r. stone gathers no moss,** pierre qui roule n'amasse pas mousse. **He's a r. stone,** il ne s'applique à rien; il roule sa bosse. **2. To have a r. gait,** se balancer, se dandiner, en marchant. **3.** (a) **R. sea,** mer grosse, houleuse. (b) **R. country,** région ondulée, accidentée. **'rolling-stock,** s. Rail: Matériel roulant. **rolling²,** s. **1.** Roulement m. **2.** Metalw: Laminage m, cylindrage m; travail m au laminoir. **3.** Roulis (d'un navire). **4.** Roulement (du tambour, du tonnerre). **'rolling-mill,** s. Metalw: **1.** Usine f de laminage. **2.** Laminoir m. **'rolling-pin,** s. Cu: Rouleau m (pour pâtisserie).

rollback ['roulbæk], s. U.S: **1.** Baisse f de prix (par action gouvernementale). **2. The r. of the enemy forces,** le repoussement, la retraite, des armées ennemies.

roller ['roulər], s. **1.** (a) Rouleau m (de pâtissier, etc.); enrouleur m (de store). Typ: **Inking r.,** rouleau encreur. (b) (For roads) (Rouleau) compresseur; cylindre compresseur. **Garden r.,** rouleau de jardin. (c) Metalw: Cylindre (lamineur); laminoir m. Tex: Paperm: Calandre f. (d) Mec.E: Galet m, rouleau. **R. ring,** couronne f de galets. (e) Tourniquet m, tambour m (de cabestan). **2. R.-bandage,** bande roulée. **3.** Nau: Lame f de houle. **4.** Orn: (a) Pigeon culbutant. (b) Rollier m; geai bleu. **roller-'bearing,** s. Mec.E: Coussinet m, palier m, roulement m, à rouleaux. **'roller-blind,** s. Store roulant. **'roller-chain,** s. Chaîne f à galets. **'roller-'coaster,** s. esp: U.S: Montagnes f russes. **'roller-map,** s. Carte f sur rouleau. **'roller-skate,** v.i. Patiner sur roulettes. **'roller-'skating,** s. Patinage m à roulettes. **'roller-skates,** s.pl. Patins m à roulettes. **'roller-towel,** s. Essuie-main(s) m à rouleau; serviette f sans fin.

rollick ['rɔlik], v.i. Faire la fête, la noce, la bombe; rigoler. **rollicking,** a. D'une gaieté exubérante; rigoleur, -euse. **To lead a r. life,** mener une vie de patachon, de bâton de chaise.

roly-poly ['rouli'pouli], s. **1.** Cu: Pudding bouilli farci de confiture (en forme de bûche). **2.** F: **R.-p. (child, puppy,** etc.) boulot, -otte, grassouillet, -ette.

Romaic [ro'meiik], a. & s. Ling: etc: Romaïque.

Roman ['roumən], a. & s. Romain, -aine. (a) **R. numerals,** chiffres romains. **R. nose,** nez busqué, aquilin. Pyr: **R. candle,** chandelle romaine. (b) **The Holy R. Empire,** le Saint Empire (romain). (c) Typ: **R. type,** (caractère) romain. **'Roman 'Catholic,** a. & s. Catholique (mf).

romance[1] [ro'mæns], s. **1. The R. languages,** les langues romanes, néo-latines. **2.** (a) Mediev.Lit: Roman m de chevalerie, d'aventures, etc. **The age of r.,** les temps chevaleresques. (b) Histoire f romanesque; conte bleu. **Historical r.,** roman m de cape et d'épée. **It's quite a r.,** c'est tout un roman. **R. between two young people,** idylle f entre deux jeunes gens. (c) **Love of r.,** amour du romanesque. (d) **The r. of the sea,** la poésie de la mer. **3.** Mus: Romance f.

romance[2], v.i. Exagérer; lâcher la bride à son imagination; inventer à plaisir.

romancer [ro'mænsər], s. **1.** Lit: Romancier, -ière (de l'ancien temps). Pej: (i) Brodeur, -euse; (ii) menteur, -euse.

Romanesque [‚roumən'esk], a. & s. Arch: Roman m.

Romania [rou'meiniə], s. **Romanian** [rou'meiniən], a. = ROUMANIA, ROUMANIAN.

Romanic [ro'mænik]. **1.** a. & s. Ling: (Le) roman. **2.** a. Romain; qui dérive des Romains.

romanize ['roumənaiz]. **1.** v.tr. (a) Hist: Romaniser (un peuple vaincu). (b) Convertir (un pays) au catholicisme. **2.** v.i. Ecc: Romaniser.

Romans(c)h [ro'mænʃ], s. Ling: Le romanche.

romantic [ro'mæntik]. **1.** a. (a) (Histoire, etc.) romanesque; qui tient du roman. **R. young woman,** jeune fille romanesque, exaltée. (b) **R. landscape,** paysage romantique. (c) Art: Lit: Romantique. **2.** s. = ROMANTICIST. **-ally,** adv. **1.** Romanesquement; pittoresquement. **2.** En romantique.

romanticism [ro'mæntisizm], s. **1.** Idées f romanesques. **2.** Art: Lit: Romantisme m.

romanticist [ro'mæntisist], s. Romantique mf.

romanticize [ro'mæntisaiz]. **1.** v.tr. Romancer (une idée, un incident); faire tout un roman (d'un incident). **2.** v.i. Donner dans le romantique.

Romany ['rɔməni], s. **1.** Romanichel, -elle; bohémien, -ienne. **2.** Ling: Le romanichel.

Rome [roum]. Pr.n. Rome f. Prov: **When at R. (you must)** do as the Romans do, à Rome il faut vivre comme à Rome. **All roads leads to R.,** tout chemin mène à Rome. Ecc: **The Church of R.,** l'Église romaine; le catholicisme.

Romish ['roumiʃ], a. Pej: Catholique.

romp[1] [rɔmp], s. Gambades fpl; jeu turbulent.

romp[2], v.i. **1.** S'ébattre (bruyamment). **2.** Rac: F: **To r. in, home,** gagner haut la main; arriver dans un fauteuil. **To r. through an exam,** passer un examen haut la main.

romper(s) ['rɔmpər(z)], s.(pl.) Barboteuse f (pour enfants).

rondeau ['rɔndou], s. Lit: Rondeau m.

rondel ['rɔnd(ə)l], s. Lit: Rondel m, rondeau m.

rondo ['rɔndou], s. Mus: Rondeau m.

Roneo[1] ['rouniou], s. R.t.m. Appareil m à polycopier "Ronéo."

roneo[2], v.tr. Polycopier.

röntgen. See ROENTGEN.

rood [ru:d], s. **1.** (a) A: **The (Holy) R.,** la Sainte Croix. (b) Ecc: Crucifix m (au centre du jubé). **2.** Meas: Quart m d'arpent. **'rood-loft,** s. (Galerie f du) jubé. **'rood-screen.** s. Jubé m.

roof[1] [ru:f], s. **1.** Toit m, toiture f, comble m. **Tiled r.,** toit en tuiles. **Flat r.,** toit en terrasse. **Pent r.,** lean-to r., comble en appentis. F: **To lift the r.,** applaudir à tout casser. **2.** Voûte f (de tunnel, de caverne). **R. of the mouth,** dôme m du palais; le palais. **3.** Aut: Toit, capotage m. **Sunshine r.,** toit ouvrant. **R. rack,** galerie f. **4.** Min: Ciel m, plafond m, toit (d'une mine). **5.** Mch: Ciel (du foyer). **6.** Av: = CEILING **2. 'roof-garden,** s. Jardin m sur un toit en terrasse. **'roof-light,** s. Aut: Plafonnier m. **'roof-tree,** s. Charpente f de toiture; faîtage m.

roof[2], v.tr. **1.** Const: Couvrir (une maison, etc.). **Red-roofed,** à toit rouge; à toiture rouge. **2. To r. sth. (in, over),** recouvrir qch. d'un toit. **roofing,** s. Toiture f, couverture f; garniture f de comble. **Glass r.,** vitrerie f de toits. **Corrugated r.,** toiture en tôle, aluminium, polyester, ondulé; couverture en plaques ondulées. S.a. FELT[1] 2.

roofer ['ru:fər], s. Const: (Ouvrier m) couvreur m.

roofless ['ru:flis], a. **1.** Sans toit, sans toiture; à ciel ouvert. **2.** (Of pers.) (i) Sans abri, sans asile. (ii) s. Les sans-abri m inv.

rook[1] [ruk], s. Orn: Corbeau freux.

rook[2], v.tr. F: Refaire, rouler (qn). **To r. s.o. of his money,** filouter son argent à qn.

rook[3], s. Chess: Tour f.

rookery ['rukəri], s. **1.** Colonie f de freux. **2. Seal r.,** colonie de phoques. **Penguin r.,** rookerie f, F: pingouinière f.

rookie ['ruki], s. Mil: P: O: Recrue f.

room[1] [ru:m, rum], s. **1.** (a) Place f, espace m. **To take up a great deal of r.,** être très encombrant. **There is plenty of r.,** ce n'est pas la place qui manque. **You have plenty of r. here,** vous êtes au large ici. **There is still r.,** il y a encore de la place. **To be cramped for r.,** être à l'étroit. **R. taken up by a machine,** encombrement m d'une machine. **To make r. for s.o.,** faire place à qn. (b) F: **I'd rather have his r. than his company,** je me consolerais facilement de son absence. **2. There is r. for uneasiness at . . . ,** il y a lieu d'être inquiet de. . . . **No r. for dispute,** aucun sujet de désaccord. **That leaves no r. for doubt,** le doute n'est plus permis. **There is (much) r. for improvement,** cela laisse (beaucoup) à désirer. **3.** (a) (In house) Pièce f; (public room) salle f. **(Bed)r.,** chambre f (à coucher). **Double r.,** chambre à deux personnes, chambre à grand lit. **Single r.,** chambre à une personne. **Double-bedded r.,** r. with twin beds, chambre à deux lits. **R. (to r.) telephone,** téléphone intérieur, d'appartement. **(Reception) r.,** salon m; salle de séjour. **Private r.,** (in restaurant) cabinet particulier; (in hotel) salon réservé. attrib. **R. temperature,** température normale d'intérieur. (Of wine) **To be served at r. temperature,** servir bien chambré. (b) pl. (Set of) rooms, appartement m. **To live in rooms,** vivre en garni. **Bachelor's rooms,** garçonnière f. **'Furnished rooms to let,'** "chambres garnies à louer." **4.** (a) Ind: Salle, hall m. S.a. BOILER-ROOM, ENGINE-ROOM. (b) Nau: **Store-r.,** soute f. **Torpedo-r.,** magasin m des torpilles. **'room-clerk,** s. U.S: (In hotel) Employé(e) à la réception. **'room-mate,** s. Compagnon, f. compagne, de chambre.

room[2], v.i. U.S: (a) Vivre en garni. (b) Partager un logement (with s.o., avec qn). **To r. together,** partager un logement. **'rooming-house,** s. U.S: Maison f de rapport; maison, immeuble m, dont les pièces sont louées en garni; immeuble à studios.

-roomed [ru:md], a. **Four-r. flat,** appartement m de quatre pièces.

roomer ['ru:mər], s. U.S: Locataire mf (d'une pièce garnie).

roomette [ˌruːmˈet], *s. U.S: Rail:* Compartiment (privé) de wagon-lit.

roomful [ˈruːmful], *s.* Salle pleine, pleine salle (of, de).

roominess [ˈruːminis], *s.* Ample espace *m*, dimensions spacieuses (d'une maison, etc.).

roomy [ˈruːmi], *a.* Spacieux, -euse; (vêtement) ample, d'amples proportions. **This makes the cabin more r.**, cela donne plus de place dans la cabine.

roost¹ [ruːst], *s.* Juchoir *m*, perchoir *m*. **To go to r.**, (i) (*of hens*) se jucher; (ii) *F:* (*of pers.*) aller se coucher. (*Of crime, etc.*) **To come home to r.**, retourner sur son auteur. **To rule the r.**, être le maître; faire la loi chez soi.

roost², *v.i.* (*of hens*) Se percher (pour la nuit); se jucher.

rooster [ˈruːstər], *s. esp. U.S:* Coq *m*.

root¹ [ruːt], *s.* **1.** (*a*) Racine *f.* **To take r., strike r.**, pousser des racines; prendre racine; raciner. **To pull a plant up by the roots**, déraciner, arracher, une plante. **To strike at the r. of an evil**, couper un mal dans sa racine. (*b*) Racine (d'une dent). **2.** Source *f*, fondement *m.* **To lie at the r. of . . .**, être la cause première de. . . . **Money is the r. of all evil**, l'argent est la source de tous les maux. **R. ideas**, idées fondamentales. **R. cause**, cause première. **3.** *Mth:* Square r., cube r., racine carrée, cubique. **4.** *Ling:* Racine (d'un mot). **5.** *Mus:* Base *f*, son fondamental (d'un accord). ˈroot-ˈcleaner, *s. Agr:* Décrotteur *m.* ˈroot-crop, *s. Agr:* Racines alimentaires. ˈroot ˈcutter, *s. Agr:* Coupe-racines *m inv.* ˈroot-hair, *s. Bot:* Poil *m* radiculaire. ˈroot-sign, *s. Mth:* Signe radical. ˈroot-stock, *s.* (*a*) *Bot:* Rhizome *m.* (*b*) Souche *f*, origine *f.* ˈroot-word, *s. Ling:* Mot *m* racine, mot souche.

root². **1.** *v.tr.* Enraciner. **To remain rooted to the spot**, rester cloué, figé, sur place. **Principles rooted in the public mind**, principes enracinés dans l'opinion publique. **2.** *v.i.* S'enraciner, prendre racine. **root out, up**, *v.tr.* Déraciner, arracher (une plante); extirper (un abus). **rooted**, *a.* **1. Shallow-r. tree**, arbre à enracinement superficiel. *S.a.* DEEP-ROOTED. **2.** (Préjugé) enraciné, invétéré.

root³. **1.** *v.i.* (*a*) (*Of swine*) Fouiller avec le groin; fouger. (*b*) *F:* (*Of pers.*) **To r. among, in, papers**, fouiller dans des paperasses. (*c*) *U.S: F:* **To r. for one's team**, encourager, applaudir, son équipe. **To r. for a candidate**, appuyer un candidat (aux élections). **2.** *v.tr.* (*Of swine*) Fouiller (la terre). *F:* **To r. sth out, up**, dénicher qch.

rooter [ˈruːtər], *s. U.S: F:* Partisan *m*, fanatique *mf* (d'une équipe, d'un candidat).

rootle [ˈruːtl], *v.i. & v.tr. F:* Fouiller.

rootlet [ˈruːtlit], *s. Bot:* Radicelle *f*; radicule *f.*

rope¹ [roup], *s.* **1.** (*a*) Corde *f*, cordage *m. Nau:* Filin *m.* Hempen r., cordage en chanvre. **Three-, four-stranded r.**, filin en trois, en quatre. **Wire r.**, câble *m* métallique. *Nau:* **Running ropes**, manœuvres courantes. *F:* **To know the ropes**, connaître son affaire; *F:* être à la coule. **To show s.o. the ropes**, mettre qn au courant. **To give s.o. (plenty) of r.**, lâcher la bride à qn. *Mount:* Cordée *f.* **To come down on a doubled r.**, faire une descente en rappel *m.* **To put on the r.**, s'encorder. **First on the r.**, premier de cordée. (*b*) *Box: Rac:* **The ropes**, les cordes. **2.** Glane *f*, chapelet *m* (d'oignons); grand collier (de perles). **3.** *Brew:* Graisse *f* (dans la bière). ˈrope-dancer, *s.* Danseur de corde; funambule *mf*; équilibriste *mf.* ˈrope-ladder, *s.* Échelle *f* de corde. ˈrope-maker, *s.* Cordier *m.* ˈrope's-ˈend, *s.* Bout *m* de corde; *Nau:* (i) bout de manœuvre; (ii) garcette *f.* ˈrope-ˈsoled, *a.* (Espadrilles *f* etc.) à semelles de corde. ˈrope-walk, *s.* Corderie *f.* ˈrope-walker, *s.* = ROPE-DANCER. ˈrope-yard, *s.* Corderie *f.*

rope². **I.** *v.tr.* **1.** Corder (un paquet). **2.** (*a*) **To r. s.o. to a tree**, lier qn à un arbre. (*b*) *Mount:* Abs. S'encorder. **Climbers roped together**, alpinistes en cordée. **To rope down**, faire une descente en rappel, rappeler. **3.** *Nau:* Ralinguer (une voile). **4.** *U.S: F:* Prendre (un cheval) au lasso. **II. rope**, *v.i.* (*Of beer, etc.*) Devenir graisseux; (*when poured*) filer. **rope in, round**, *v.tr.* **1.** Entourer (un terrain) de cordes. **2.** *F:* **To r. s.o. in**, (i) s'assurer le concours de qn; (ii)

prendre (un filou) dans une rafle. **rope off**, *v.tr.* Réserver (une partie de la salle) au moyen d'une corde tendue.

ropeway [ˈroupwei], *s.* Câble aérien; transporteur *m* par câbles; téléphérique *m.*

ropey [ˈroupi], *a. P:* Pas fameux, camelote.

ropiness [ˈroupinis], *s.* Viscosité *f*; (*in beer*) graisse *f.*

ropy [ˈroupi], *a.* (*Of liquid*) Visqueux; (*of beer*) gras, *f.* grasse, graisseux, -euse; (*when poured*) filant, qui file. (*Of wine*) **To become r.**, tourner à la graisse.

rorqual [ˈrɔːkwəl], *s. Z:* Rorqual, -als *m.*

Rosaceae [rouˈzeisiiː], *s.pl. Bot:* Rosacées *f.*

rosarium [rouˈzɑːriəm], *s. Hort:* Roseraie *f.*

rosarian [rouˈzɛəriən], *s.* Rosiériste *f.*

rosary [ˈrouzəri], *s.* **1.** Rosaire *m.* **Lesser r.** (*of 55 beads*), chapelet *m.* **2.** *Hort:* Roseraie *f.*

rose¹ [rouz], *s.* **1.** Rose *f.* **Briar-r., wild r.**, églantine *f.* **Life is not a bed of roses**, tout n'est pas rose(s) dans ce monde. *Prov:* **No r. without a thorn**, pas de rose sans épines. *Hist:* **The Wars of the Roses**, les guerres des Deux-Roses. **Under the r.**, en cachette; en confidence; sous le manteau. **2.** (*On hat, shoe*) Rosette *f.* **3.** (*On stag's horn*) Fraise *f.* **4.** Pomme *f* (d'arrosoir); crépine *f* (de pompe). *Mch:* Reniflard *m.* **5.** *El:* Ceiling r., rosace *f* de plafond. **6.** *Tls:* R. (countersink) bit, fraise champignon. **7.** (*Colour*) Rose *m.* **Dark r. materials**, tissus (d'un) rose foncé. ˈrose-bay, *s. Bot:* **1.** Laurier-rose *m.* **2.** Rhododendron *m.* ˈrose-bed, *s.* Massif *m*, corbeille *f*, de rosiers. ˈrose-bowl, *s.* Coupe *f* à fleurs. ˈrose-bush, *s.* Rosier *m.* ˈrose-ˈcampion, *s. Bot:* Coquelourde *f.* ˈrose-coloured, *a.* Rose, rosé; couleur de rose *inv.* **To see things through r.-c. spectacles**, voir tout en rose. ˈrose-ˈdiamond, *s. Lap:* (Diamant taillé en) rose *f.* ˈrose-gall, *s. Hort:* Bédégar *m*, éponge *f.* ˈrose-garden, *s.* Roseraie *f.* ˈrose-grower, *s.* Rosiériste *m.* ˈrose-mallow, *s. Bot:* Rose trémière; passe-rose *f.* ˈrose-ˈnoble, *s. Num: A:* Noble *m* à la rose. ˈrose-pink. (*a*) *s.* Rose *m.* (*b*) *a.* (Couleur de) rose; rosé; incarnat. ˈrose-red, **1.** *a.* Vermeil. **2.** *s.* Vermillon *m.* ˈrose-tree, *s.* Rosier *m.* ˈrose-water, *s.* Eau *f* de rose. ˈrose-window, *s. Arch:* Rosace *f*, rose *f.*

rose². *See* RISE².

roseate [ˈrouziit], *a. Lit:* Couleur de rose *inv*; rose, rosé.

rosebud [ˈrouzbʌd], *s.* Bouton *m* de rose.

rosemary [ˈrouzməri], *s. Bot:* Romarin *m.*

roseola [rouˈzioulə, rouziˈoulə], *s. Med:* Roséole *f.*

rosery [ˈrouzəri], *s.* Roseraie *f.*

rosette [roˈzet], *s.* **1.** Chou *m*, -oux (de ruban); cocarde *f*; rosette *f* (de la Légion d'honneur). **2.** *Arch: Sculp:* Rosette *f.*

rosewood [ˈrouzwud], *s.* Palissandre *m*; bois *m* de rose.

rosin [ˈrɔzin], *s.* Colophane *f.*

roster [ˈrɔstər, ˈroustər], *s. Mil: etc:* (*a*) (**Duty**) r., tableau *m* de service. **By r.**, à tour de rôle. (*b*) Liste *f. Adm:* Promotion r., tableau d'avancement.

rostrum, *pl.* **-a, -ums** [ˈrɔstrəm, -ə, -əmz], *s.* (*a*) *Rom. Ant:* **The Rostra**, les rostres *m.* (*b*) Tribune *f.* (*At auction sale*) **To take the r.**, monter sur l'estrade, prendre le marteau (du commissaire-priseur).

rosy [ˈrouzi], *a.* De rose; rose, rosé. **R. cheeks**, joues vermeilles. **To paint everything in r. colours**, peindre tout en beau, en rose. **A r. prospect**, une perspective souriante, attrayante. ˈrosy-ˈfingered, *a. Lit:* (L'Aurore) aux doigts de rose.

rot¹ [rɔt], *s.* **1.** Pourriture *f*, carie *f. Vit:* Brown r., mildiou *m.* Dry-r., carie sèche. Wet-r., carie humide. **2.** *Vet:* Cachexie *f* (des moutons). *S.a.* FOOT-ROT. **3.** *F:* Blague *f*, bêtises *fpl.* **That's all r.!** tout ça c'est de la blague, des sottises! **To talk (utter) r.**, dire des imbécillités. **(What) r.!** quelle blague! allons donc! **4.** Démoralisation *f.* **A r. set in**, le moral (des joueurs, des combattants) a flanché. **To stop the r.**, parer à la démoralisation; enrayer la crise. ˈrot-proof, *a.* Imputrescible.

rot², *v.* (rotted) **1.** *v.i.* (Se) pourrir; se décomposer, se putréfier, se carier. **To r. off, away**, tomber en pourriture. **2.** *v.tr.* (*a*) Pourrir, faire pourrir; décomposer, putréfier, carier. (*b*) *Abs. F: O:* **He's only rotting**, c'est de la blague! **rotting**, *a.* En pourriture. ˈrot-gut, *s. P:* (*Spirits*) Tord-boyaux *m.*

rota ['routə], s. Liste f de roulement; tableau m de service.

rotarian [ro'tɛəriən], s. Rotarien m.

rotary ['routəri]. 1. a. Rotatif, -ive, rotatoire. (a) R. motion, mouvement de rotation. (b) R. crane, grue pivotante. R. dryer, essoreuse centrifuge. (Pers.) R. printer, rotativiste m. R. printing-press, rotative f. R. Club, Rotary (Club) m. 2. s. U.S: Rond-point m.

rotate [ro'teit]. 1. v.i. Tourner; (on pivot) basculer, pivoter. 2. v.tr. (a) Faire tourner; faire basculer. (b) Remplir (des fonctions) à tour de rôle. (c) Agr: Alterner, varier (les cultures). **rotating**, a. Tournant, rotatif, -ive, à rotation. R. body, corps en rotation.

rotation [ro'teiʃ(ə)n], s. 1. (a) (Mouvement m de) rotation f. (b) Basculage m. 2. (a) Succession f tour à tour. R. roll, (tableau m de) roulement m. By r., in r., par roulement; à tour de rôle. (b) Agr: R. of crops, assolement m. 3. Rotation, tour m. **Rotations per minute**, tours-minute mpl.

rotational [ro'teiʃən(ə)l], **rotative** ['routətiv], a. Rotatif, -ive; de rotation; (of force, etc.) rotateur, -trice.

rotatory [ro'teitəri], a. Rotatoire; de rotation, rotateur, -trice.

rote [rout], s. Routine f. To say, learn, sth. by r., dire, apprendre, qch. mécaniquement, par cœur. To do sth. by r., faire qch. par routine.

rotor ['routər], s. Mec.E: Rotor m. El.E: Rotor, induit m. Aut: Balai rotatif (du distributeur). Av: Helicoper r., rotor.

rotten ['rɔtn], a. 1. Pourri, carié. R. egg, œuf pourri, gâté. He is r. to the core, il est pourri de vices. Pol. Hist: R. borough, bourg pourri. 2. F: De mauvaise qualité; F: lamentable; F: moche. R. weather, temps de chien. R. job, sale besogne. I am feeling r., je me sens patraque. R. luck! quelle guigne! pas de veine! -ly, adv. F: D'une façon pitoyable; abominablement. **'rotten(-)stone**, s. Tripoli anglais; terre pourrie.

rottenness ['rɔtnnis], s. 1. État m de pourriture, de décomposition. 2. F: Caractère m lamentable (de qn, qch.).

rotter ['rɔtər], s. F: 1. Raté m; propre m à rien. 2. Sale type m; P: vilain coco.

rotund [ro'tʌnd], a. 1. Rond, arrondi. 2. (Discours) emphatique; (style) ampoulé.

rotunda [ro'tʌndə], s. Arch: Rotonde f.

rotundity [ro'tʌnditi], s. 1. Rondeur f, rotondité f. Hum: Embonpoint m. 2. Grandiloquence f (de style).

rouble ['ru:bl], s. Num: Rouble m.

roué ['ru:ei], s. Débauché m; F: vieux marcheur.

rouge[1] [ru:ʒ], s. 1. (a) Toil: Rouge m, fard m, carmin m. (b) Jewellers' r., rouge à polir. 2. Cards: R. et noir ['ru:ʒei'nwɑːr], trente et quarante m.

rouge[2], v.tr. To r. one's cheeks, se farder les joues. Abs. Mettre du rouge.

rough[1] [rʌf]. I. a. 1. (a) (Of surface, skin) Rêche, rugueux, -euse, rude; (of cloth) gros, grossier. R. to the touch, rude, âpre, au toucher. R. edges, tranches non ébarbées, non rognées (d'un livre). R. glass, verre dépoli. R. side of a skin, côté chair. (b) (Of road) Raboteux, -euse, rude; (of ground) inégal, accidenté. R. hair, cheveux ébouriffés. (c) In the r. state, à l'état brut. R. casting, pièce brute de fonderie. 2. Grossier, brutal, -aux; (of wind) violent. R. sea, mer agitée, mauvaise, houleuse. Nau: R. weather, gros temps. To have a r. crossing, passage, faire une mauvaise traversée. F: He's had a r. passage, P: il en a bavé. R. play, jeu brutal. F: R. music, tintamarre m, charivari m. To give s.o. a r. handling, malmener, houspiller, qn. To be r. with s.o., brutaliser, rudoyer, qn. S.a. TIME[1] 8. 3. (Of manners) Grossier, -ière, fruste; (of speech) bourru, rude; (of style) fruste. F: R. customer, sale type m, mauvais coucheur. F: To give s.o. a r. time, traiter qn avec sévérité, P: être vache avec qn. R. nursing, soins rudes, sommaires. Dom.Ec: R. work, le gros ouvrage, F: le plus gros. S.a. DIAMOND 1. 4. Approximatif. R. sketch, (i) ébauche f, esquisse f; (ii) plan m en croquis; premier jet; aperçu m. R. translation, traduction à peu près. Sch: R. work, brouillon m. R. draft, brouillon. R. calculation, calcul approximatif. At a r. guess, par aperçu; approximativement. R. estimate, évaluation en gros. 5. (a) (Of voice) Rude, rêche, rauque. (b)

Gram: R. breathing, esprit m rude. (c) (Of wine) Rude, âpre, rêche. -ly, adv. 1. Rudement, brutalement, brusquement. To treat s.o. r., malmener, rudoyer, qn. 2. R. painted, peint grossièrement. R. made, F: fait à coups de serpe. To sketch sth. r., faire un croquis sommaire de qch. 3. Approximativement; à peu près; en gros. R. speaking, en général; généralement parlant; grosso-modo. II. **rough**, adv. Rudement, grossièrement. To play r., jouer brutalement. F: To cut up r., se fâcher, se mettre en colère. III. **rough**, s. 1. Terrain accidenté. Golf: To be in the r., être dans l'herbe longue. 2. Crampon m (d'un fer à cheval). 3. One must take the r. with the smooth, il faut prendre le bénéfice avec les charges; à la guerre comme à la guerre. 4. (Pers.) Voyou m, bandit m. 5. (a) Wood in the r., bois (à l'état) brut; bois en grume. (b) Statue in the r., statue brute; ébauche f d'une statue. **'rough-and-'ready**, a. 1. Exécuté grossièrement; fait à la hâte. Done in a r.-and-r. fashion, taillé à coups de hache. R.-and-r. installation, installation de fortune. 2. (Of pers.) Cavalier, -ière; sans façon. **'rough-and-'tumble**. 1. a. (a) (Combat, jeu) où l'on n'observe pas de règles. (b) R.-and-t. life, vie mouvementée. 2. s. Mêlée f, bousculade f; corps-à-corps jovial. **'rough-cast**[1], s. 1. Const: Crépi m, gobetis m. 2. Ébauche f (d'un plan). **'rough-cast**[2], v.tr. (rough-cast) 1. Const: Crépir, hourder, gobeter (un mur); ravaler (une façade). 2. Ébaucher (un plan). **'rough-cast**[3], a. 1. Const: Crépi, hourdé. 2. Metall: Brut de fonte. 3. (Plan) à l'état d'ébauche. **'rough-coated**, a. (Cheval) hérissé, à long poil; (chien) à poil dur. **'rough-dry**, v.tr. Faire sécher (le linge) sans le repasser. **rough-'forged**, a. Brut de forge. **'rough-grained**, a. A grain grossier, à gros grain. **'rough-'handle**, v.tr. Malmener qn. **'rough-'hew**, v.tr. (rough-hewed) **rough-hewn**) Ébaucher, dégrossir (une statue, etc.). **'rough-house**, s. F: Chahut m, bousculade f. **'rough-rider**, s. Dresseur m de chevaux. **'rough-spoken**, a. 1. Bourru. 2. Au langage grossier. **'rough stuff**, s. F: 1. Bousculade f, chahut m. 2. Brutalité f; P: voyouterie f.

rough[2], v.tr. 1. To r. (up) the hair, ébouriffer (les cheveux); faire hérisser (le poil). 2. (a) Ferrer (un cheval) à glace. (b) Dépolir (le verre). (c) Const: Piquer (un mur). 3. F: To r. it, (i) vivre à la dure; en voir de dures; (ii) se passer des raffinements auxquels l'on est habitué. 4. Dégrossir (une lentille, etc.) **rough down**, v.tr. Dégrossir (une pièce de forge). **rough out**, v.tr. Ébaucher (un plan); dégrossir (une pièce, une statue). **rough up**, v.tr. esp. U.S: F: Malmener (qn). **'rough-up**, s. F: esp. U.S: Rixe f.

roughage ['rʌfidʒ], s. (a) Fourrages grossiers. (b) Matières inassimilables (excitatrices de l'intestin).

roughish ['rʌfiʃ], a. 1. Un peu rude, rugueux, -euse. 2. (Mer) assez houleuse. 3. (Individu m) un peu fruste, mal dégrossi.

roughneck ['rʌfnek], s. U.S: F: 1. Individu grossier, rustaud. 2. Voyou m, canaille f, P: fripouille f.

roughness ['rʌfnis], s. 1. (a) Rudesse f, aspérité f, rugosité f. (b) Rugosité, inégalité f (du sol). 2. (a) Grossièreté f, brusquerie f; manières bourrues. (b) Agitation f (de la mer); rudesse (du temps). 3. Rudesse (de la voix); âpreté f (de goût); qualité f fruste (du vin).

roughshod ['rʌfʃɔd], a. (a) (Cheval) ferré à glace. (b) To ride r. over s.o., fouler qn aux pieds; traiter qn sans ménagement.

roulade [ru:'lɑːd], s. 1. Mus: Roulade f. 2. U.S: Cu: Paupiette f.

roulette [ru:'let], s. 1. (Gaming) Roulette f. 2. Mth: (Courbe) cycloïde f. 3. Tls: Roulette (de graveur, etc.); molette f (à perforer).

Roumania [ru:(')meinjə]. Pr.n. Geog: La Roumanie.

Roumanian [ru:(')meinjən], a. & s. Roumain, -aine.

round[1] [raund]. I. a. 1. Rond, circulaire. The R. Table, la Table ronde. Pol: Ind: etc: R.-table conference, table ronde, réunion f paritaire. To make r., arrondir. R. shoulders, épaules voûtées. R. hand, (écriture) ronde; grosse f. Com: R. bars, fer rond; rondins. R. timber, bois rond. Tls: R. file, lime ronde. R. nut, écrou cylindrique. S.a. ARCH[1] 1. 2. R. dance, danse en rond; ronde *f. U.S:* **R. trip,** l'aller et le retour. **3.** (*a*) **R. dozen,** bonne douzaine. **In r. figures,** en chiffres ronds. **R. sum,** compte rond. (*b*) **Good r. sum,** somme rondelette. **To go at a good r. pace,** aller bon train. (*c*) **R. style,** style rond, coulant. **R. voice,** voix pleine, sonore. **R. oath,** gros juron. **-ly,** *adv.* **1.** Rondement, vivement. **To go r. to work,** mener rondement les choses; s'y mettre avec entrain. **2.** *O:* (Parler) rondement, carrément. **II. round,** *s.* **1.** (*a*) Cercle *m,* rond *m.* **Cylinder out of r.,** cylindre ovalisé. (*b*) *Art:* **Statue in the r.,** statue en bosse. **To draw from the r.,** dessiner d'après la bosse. **2.** (*a*) Barreau *m,* échelon *m* (d'échelle). (*b*) *Arch:* Rond (de moulure). (*c*) *Cu:* **R. of beef,** gîte *m.* **R. of veal,** rouelle *f* de veau. **R. of toast,** rôtie *f.* **3. The daily r.,** le train ordinaire des jours; le train-train quotidien. **One continual r. of pleasure,** une succession perpétuelle de plaisirs. **4.** (*a*) Tour *m. Sp:* Circuit *m.* **To have a r. of golf,** faire une tournée de golf. **The story went the r.,** l'histoire a passé de bouche en bouche. (*b*) Tournée *f.* **The postman's r.,** la tournée du facteur. (*Of doctor*) **To make his rounds, to go (on) his rounds,** faire sa tournée. (*c*) *Mil:* Ronde *f* (d'inspection). (*Of officer*) **To go the rounds,** faire sa ronde. **5.** (*a*) *Box:* Round *m,* reprise *f.* (*b*) *Ten:* Tour, série *f* (d'un tournoi). (*c*) *Sp:* Manche *f.* **6.** (*a*) **To stand a r. of drinks,** payer une tournée (générale). (*b*) *Cards:* Tour; levée *f.* (*c*) *Mil:* **A r. of ten shots,** une salve de dix coups. **R. of applause,** salve d'applaudissements. (*d*) *Mil:* **R. of ammunition,** cartouche *f.* (*Of company*) **To fire a r.,** tirer un coup (chacun). **7.** *Mus:* Canon *m.* **'round-'eyed.** *a.* **To stare r.-e.,** ouvrir de grands yeux étonnés. **To listen in r.-e. wonder,** écouter les yeux ouverts tout ronds. **'round(-)house,** *s.* **1.** *Nau:* Rouf *m;* dunette *f.* **2.** *Hist:* Corps *m* de garde. **3.** *Rail: U.S:* Rotonde *f.* **'round 'robin,** *s.* Pétition revêtue de signatures en rond (pour ne pas révéler le chef de bande). **'round-'shouldered,** *a.* Au dos voûté, bombé. **To be r.-s.,** avoir les dos rond. **To get r.-s.,** se voûter.

round². I. *adv.* **1.** (*a*) **To go r.,** tourner; décrire un cercle. **To turn r. and r.,** tournoyer. **To turn r.** (**about**), se retourner. (*b*) **All the year r.,** (pendant) toute l'année. **Winter came r.,** l'hiver revint, arriva. *S.a.* BRING ROUND, COME ROUND, *etc.* **2.** (*a*) **Garden with a wall right r.,** all r., jardin avec un mur tout autour. **To be six feet r.,** avoir six pieds de tour. **To show s.o. r.,** faire faire à qn le tour de sa propriété, etc. **Taken all r.,** dans l'ensemble; en général. *S.a.* ALL-ROUND. (*b*) **All the country r.** (**about**), tout le pays à l'entour. **For a mile r.,** à un mille à la ronde. **3.** **To hand r. the cakes,** faire passer, faire circuler, les gâteaux. **There is not enough to go r.,** il n'y en a pas pour tout le monde. **4.** (*a*) **It's a long way r.,** cela fait un grand détour. **To take the longest way r.,** prendre par le plus long. (*b*) **To ask s.o. r. for the evening,** inviter qn à venir passer la soirée. **If you are r. this way,** si vous passez par ici. *S.a.* GET ROUND, GO ROUND, *etc.* **II. round,** *prep.* **1.** (*a*) Autour de. **Seated r. the table,** assis autour de la table. **There was a crowd r. the church,** il y avait foule aux abords de l'église. **He is 36 inches r. the chest,** il a un tour de poitrine de 36 pouces. **It will be somewhere r. a hundred pounds,** cela fera dans les cent livres. **R.** (**about**) **midday,** sur les midi, vers midi. (*b*) (*Motion*) **To row, swim, r. the island,** faire le tour de l'île à la rame, à la nage. **To go r. the museums,** visiter les musées. **To go r.** (**and r.**) **sth.,** tourner autour de qch. **To write a book r. an incident,** écrire un livre à propos d'un incident. **2.** **To go r. an obstacle,** contourner un obstacle. *F:* **To go r. the bend,** devenir fou, louftingue. **You will find the grocer r. the corner,** vous trouverez l'épicerie en tournant le coin. *S.a.* GET ROUND 1 (*c*).

round³. 1. *v.tr.* (*a*) Arrondir; abattre (un angle). *Bookb:* Endosser (un livre). (*b*) Contourner (un obstacle). *Nau:* Doubler, franchir (un cap). **2.** *v.i.* (*a*) S'arrondir. (*b*) **To r. on one's heels,** faire demi-tour. *F:* **To r. on s.o.,** (i) dénoncer qn; (ii) s'en prendre inopinément à qn. **round off,** *v.tr.* Arrondir; adoucir (une arête). **To r. off one's sentences,** arrondir, perler, ses phrases. **To r. off the negotiations,** achever les négociations. **round up,** *v.tr.* Rassembler

(du bétail); cerner, rabattre, rafler (des filous). **'round(-)up,** *s.* (*a*) Rassemblement *m* (du bétail); grande battue (à cheval). (*b*) Rafle *f* (de filous). **rounded,** *a.* Arrondi. **R. cheeks,** joues rebondies. **R. bank,** talus curviligne, bombé.

roundabout ['raundəbaut]. **I.** *s.* **1.** (Manège *m* de) chevaux *mpl* de bois; carrousel *m.* **2.** *Aut:* Rond-point *m, pl.* ronds-points; *Adm:* carrefour *m* à giration, à sens *m* giratoire. **II. roundabout,** *a.* (Chemin) détourné, indirect. **To take a r. way,** faire un détour. *F:* prendre le chemin des écoliers. **To lead up to a question in a r. way,** aborder de biais une question. **R. phrase,** circonlocution *f.*

roundel ['raund(ə)l], *s.* **1.** *Her:* Tourteau *m. Av:* Cocarde *f.* **2.** *A: Mus: Danc:* Ronde *f.*

roundelay ['raundilei], *s. A:* (*a*) Chanson *f* à refrain; rondeau *m.* (*b*) Chant *m* d'oiseau.

rounders ['raundəz], *s.pl. Games:* Balle *f* au camp.

Roundhead ['raundhed], *s. Eng. Hist:* Tête ronde (adhérent de Cromwell).

roundish ['raundiʃ], *a.* Rondelet, -ette.

roundness ['raundnis], *s.* Rondeur *f.*

roundsman, *pl.* -men ['raundzmən], *s.m.* Homme de tournée; livreur. **Milk r.,** laitier livreur.

roup [ru:p], *s.* Diphtérie *f* des poules; angine croupeuse.

rouse [rauz]. **I.** *v.tr.* **1.** (*a*) *Ven:* Faire lever (le gibier). (*b*) **To r. s.o.** (**from sleep**), réveiller qn. **To r. the camp,** donner l'alerte au camp. **To r. s.o. from indolence, to r. s.o. up,** secouer l'indifférence, l'énergie, de qn; *F:* secouer qn. **I tried to r. him,** je voulus le faire sortir de sa torpeur. **To r. oneself,** se secouer; sortir de son apathie. **To r. s.o. to action,** inciter qn à agir. **To r. the masses,** remuer, activer, les masses. (*c*) Mettre (qn) en colère. **He is terrible when roused,** il est terrible quand il est monté. **2.** Soulever (l'indignation); susciter (l'admiration, l'opposition). *Nau:* **To r. in the cable,** haler la chaîne. **II. rouse,** *v.i.* **To r.** (**up**), se réveiller; (ii) se secouer; sortir de sa torpeur. **rousing,** *a.* **1. R. cheers,** applaudissements chaleureux. **R. speech,** discours enlevant, vibrant. **R. chorus,** refrain entraînant. **2.** (*a*) *F:* **R. lie,** gros mensonge. (*b*) **R. fire,** belle flambée.

rout¹ [raut], *s.* **1.** Bande *f* (de fêtards). **2.** *A:* Raout *m;* réception (mondaine).

rout², *s. Mil:* Déroute *f;* débandade *f.* **To put troops to r.,** mettre des troupes en déroute. **To break into a r.,** se débander.

rout³, *v.tr. Mil:* Mettre (une armée) en déroute; disperser, défaire, enfoncer (une armée). **routed,** *a.* En déroute.

rout⁴, *v.tr. & i.* = ROOT³. **rout out,** *v.tr.* **1.** Dénicher (qn, qch.); tirer (qn) de son lit, etc.; faire déguerpir (un renard). **2.** (*a*) *Carp:* Évider (une rainure). (*b*) *Engr: Typ:* Échopper. **'routing-plane,** *s. Tls:* Guimbarde *f.*

route [ru:t], *s.* (*a*) Itinéraire *m;* route *f,* voie *f,* chemin *m. Mount:* **To find the r.,** faire la trace. **Sea r.,** route maritime. **Trade routes,** routes commerciales. **Shipping routes,** routes de navigation. **Bus r.,** (i) ligne *f* d'autobus; (ii) itinéraire, parcours *m,* d'un autobus. *Nau:* **To alter one's r.,** changer de direction. (*b*) *Mil:* [raut] **Column of r.,** colonne de route. **route-map** ['ru:tmap], *s.* Carte routière. **route-march** ['rautmɑ:tʃ], *s. Mil:* Marche *f* d'entraînement.

routine [ru:'ti:n], *s.* **1.** Routine *f.* **Daily r.,** le train-train journalier. **Office r.,** travail courant du bureau. **To do sth. as a matter of r.,** faire qch. d'office. **R. work,** affaires courantes; *Adm:* service de détail. **R. enquiries,** constatations *f* d'usage. **2.** *Mil: Navy:* Emploi *m* du temps. **R. board,** tableau *m* de service. **R. patrol,** ronde *f.* **'routine-'minded,** *a.* (*Pers.*) Routinier, -ière. **He's very r.-m.,** *F:* c'est un encroûté.

roux [ru:], *s. Cu:* Roux *m.*

rove [rouv], **1.** *v.i.* Rôder, vagabonder, errer. **To r. in every land,** rouler dans tous les pays; rouler sa bosse. **His eyes roved over the pictures,** son regard parcourait les tableaux. **2.** *v.tr.* Parcourir (la campagne). (*Of pirate, etc.*) **To r. the seas,** écumer les mers. **roving¹,** *a.* Vagabond, nomade. **To have a r. commission,** avoir liberté de manœuvre. *F:* **To have a r. eye,** avoir l'œil gaillard. **roving²,** *s.* Vagabondage *m.* **R. instincts,** instincts nomades.

rove². *See* REEVE².
rover¹ ['rouvər], *s.* (*a*) Coureur *m*; vagabond *m.* (*b*)
   Scouting: Routier *m.*
rover², *s. Nau:* Écumeur *m* de mer.
row¹ [rou], *s.* 1. (*a*) Rang *m*, rangée *f*; ligne *f*; file *f*
   (de voitures). R. of pearls, rang de perles. R. of
   bricks, assise *f* de briques. R. of knitting, rang, tour
   m, de tricot. In a r., en rang, en ligne. In rows, par
   rangs. In two rows, sur deux rangs. (*b*) *Hort:* R. of
   onions, of lettuces, rang, rayon *m*, d'oignons, de
   laitues. 2. (*a*) Rang (de chaises, etc.). In the front
   r., au premier rang. (*b*) Row of houses, ligne, rangée,
   de maisons. 3. *Typewr:* Rang.
row² [rou], *s.* 1. Promenade *f* en canot; partie *f* de
   canotage. To go for a r., faire une promenade en
   canot. 2. It was a long r., il a fallu ramer longtemps.
row³ [rou]. 1. *v.i.* (*a*) Ramer. *Nau:* Nager. To r.
   hard, faire force de rames. To r. round the island, faire
   le tour de l'île en canot, à la rame. To r. a fast stroke,
   ramer vite. To r. a race, faire une course d'aviron.
   (*b*) Canoter; faire du canotage. 2. *v.tr.* (*a*) Conduire
   (un bateau) à l'aviron. (*b*) To r. s.o. over the river,
   transporter qn (en canot) sur l'autre rive. rowing, *s.*
   Conduite *f* (d'un bateau) à l'aviron. *Nau:* Nage *f.*
   Sp: Canotage *m.* To go in for r., faire du canotage,
   de l'aviron. He's a r. man, c'est un amateur de
   canotage, un canotier. 'row(ing)-boat, *s.* Bateau
   m à rames; canot *m* à l'aviron. 'rowing-club, *s.*
   Cercle *m*, club *m*, d'aviron.
row⁴ [rau], *s.* 1. Chahut *m*, tapage *m*, vacarme *m.*
   F: To make, kick up, a r., faire du chahut; chahuter;
   faire du tapage, *P:* du boucan, du chambard. *F:*
   To kick up the devil of a r., faire un bacchanal, un
   charivari, de tous les diables. *P:* Hold your r.!
   taisez-vous! *P:* la ferme! 2. Rixe *f*, dispute *f*;
   scène *f.* To be always ready for a r., *F:* ne demander
   que plaies et bosses. 3. Réprimande *f*; *F:* savon *m.*
   To get into a r., se faire attraper; se faire laver la
   tête.
row⁵ [rau]. 1. *v.tr. F:* Attraper, semoncer (qn). 2. *v.i.*
   Se quereller (with s.o., avec qn).
rowan ['rouən, 'rauən], *s. Bot:* 1. R.(-tree), sorbier *m*
   des oiseaux. 2. R.(-berry), sorbe *f.*
rowdiness ['raudinis], *s.* Turbulence *f*; tapage *m.*
rowdy ['raudi]. 1. *a.* Tapageur. 2. *s.* (*a*) Chahuteur
   m. (*b*) Voyou *m.*
rowdyism ['raudiizm], *s.* Chahutage *m*; désordre
   m.
rowel ['rauəl], *s.* Molette *f* (d'éperon).
rower ['rouər], *s.* Rameur, -euse; canotier *m. Nau:*
   Nageur *m.*
rowlocks ['rɔləks], *s.pl.* Dames *f* de nage; tolets *m.*
   Swivel r., tolets à fourche; systèmes (articulés).
royal ['rɔiəl], *a.* (*a*) Royal, -aux. His, Her, Royal
   Highness, son Altesse royale. The R. household, la
   maison du roi, de la reine. With r. consent, avec le
   consentement du roi, de la reine. R. blue, bleu *inv* de
   roi. (*b*) Royal, princier; magnifique. A r. munificence,
   munificence princière. A r. feast, un festin de roi.
   To have a (right) r. time, s'amuser follement. (*c*) *Nau:*
   R. (sail), cacatois *m.* -ally, *adv.* Royalement; en roi.
royalism ['rɔiəlizm], *s.* Royalisme *m.*
royalist ['rɔiəlist], *a. & s.* Royaliste (*mf*).
royalty ['rɔiəlti], *s.* 1. Royauté *f.* 2. (*a*) *pl.* Royalties,
   membres *m* de la famille royale. (*b*) *Coll.* Hotel
   patronized by r., hôtel fréquenté par les personnages
   royaux. 3. *pl.* Royalties, (i) redevance (due à un
   inventeur, etc.); (ii) *Publ:* droits *m* d'auteur. (iii)
   Ind: *Oil: etc:* (On patent, or for use of pipe-line)
   royalties *fpl.* Mining royalties, redevance tré-
   foncière.
rub¹ [rʌb], *s.* 1. Frottement *m*; friction *f.* To give sth.
   a r. (up), donner un coup de torchon à qch.; frotter,
   astiquer (des cuivres). 2. *Bowls:* Inégalité *f* (du
   terrain). There's the r.! c'est là la difficulté! c'est
   là le hic!
rub², *v.* (rubbed) 1. *v.tr.* (*a*) Frotter. To r. one's leg
   with oil, se frictionner la jambe avec de l'huile. To
   r. one's hands (together), se frotter les mains. To r.
   shoulders with other people, se frotter au monde;
   s'associer avec, frayer avec, d'autres gens. To r. s.o.
   up the wrong way, prendre qn à rebrousse-poil;
   contrarier, énerver, qn; échauffer la bile de qn. (*b*) To

r. sth dry, sécher qch. en le frottant. To r. a surface bare,
dénuder une surface par le frottement. (*c*) To r. sth.
through a sieve, passer qch. dans un tamis. To r. sth.
over a surface, enduire une surface de qch. To r. oil
into s.o., faire une friction d'huile à qn; frictionner
qn à l'huile. (*d*) To r. an inscription, prendre un frottis
d'une inscription. To r. a drawing, poncer un dessin.
2. *v.i.* (*a*) Frotter (against, contre); (of pers.)
se frotter (contre). (*b*) (Of clothes, etc.). S'user.
Nau: (Of hawser, etc.) Riper, raguer. rub along, *v.i.*
F: Aller son petit bonhomme de chemin; se
débrouiller. We manage to r.a., on v:t tant bien que
mal. rub away, *v.tr.* 1. User (qch.) par le frottement.
2. Faire disparaître (une douleur) par des frictions.
'rubbing a'way, *s.* Usure *f.* rub down, *v.tr.* 1. (*a*)
Panser, épousseter, (with wisp) bouchonner (un
cheval). (*b*) Frictionner (qn) (après le bain). 2.
Adoucir (une surface); regratter (un mur); poncer
(la peinture). rub-'down, *s.* Friction *f.* To give s.o.
a r.-d., faire une friction à qn; frictionner qn. To
give a horse a r.-d., bouchonner un cheval. 'rubbing-
'down, *s.* 1. Bouchonnage *m* (d'un cheval). 2.
Adoucissage *m*, usure *f* (d'une surface); ponçage *m*
(de la peinture). rub in, *v.tr.* Faire pénétrer (un
liniment, etc.) par des frictions. *F:* Don't r. it in!
n'insistez pas davantage (sur ma gaffe, etc.). rub
off, *v.tr.* Enlever (qch.) par le frottement. To r. one's
skin off, s'écorcher légèrement; s'érafler la peau.
rub out, *v.tr.* Effacer. *U.S: P:* Liquider, descendre
(qn). He was rubbed out by the gangsters, les gangsters l'ont descendu. rub up. 1. *v.tr.* Astiquer,
frotter, fourbir. *F:* To r. up one's memory, rafraîchir
sa mémoire. To r. up one's Greek, dérouiller son
grec. To r. up one's knowledge of a subject, se
remettre au courant d'un sujet. 2. *v.i.* To r. up
against other people, se frotter au monde. 'rubbing-
up, *s.* Astiquage *m.* rubbed, *a.* (Of cloth) Râpé;
qui montre la corde. R. furniture, meubles dévernis.
rubbing, *s.* 1. (*a*) Frottage *m. Med:* Frictions *fpl.*
R. compound, pâte *f* à polir. (*b*) Frottement *m* (d'un
organe de machine, etc.). 2. Calque *m* par frottement;
frottis *m.* 'rubbing-strake, *s. N.Arch:* Bourrelet *m*
de défense; liston *m.*
rub-a-dub ['rʌbə'dʌb], *s.* Rataplan *m* (d'un tambour).
rubber¹ ['rʌbər], *s.* 1. Frottoir *m.* Kitchen r., torchon
m. Blackboard r., effaceur *m.* 2. (*Pers:*) (*a*) Frotteur,
-euse. (*b*) Masseur, -euse (de hammam). 3. (*a*)
(India-)r. (eraser), gomme *f* (à effacer). (*b*) (India-)r.,
caoutchouc *m.* Crepe r., crêpe *m* de latex. Hard r.,
caoutchouc durci. Synthetic r., caoutchouc synthétique. Foam r., caoutchouc mousse. R. dinghy,
canot *m* pneumatique. (India-)r. band, (i) élastique *m*,
F: bracelet *m*; (ii) courroie *f* en caoutchouc. R.
fabric, tissu caoutchouté. *El.E:* R. cable, câble sous
caoutchouc. R. gloves, gants en caoutchouc. (*c*) *pl.*
(Overshoes) Caoutchoucs. 'rubber-covered, *a.*
(Câble) à revêtement en caoutchouc, sous (gaine de)
caoutchouc. 'rubber 'stamp, *s.* 1. Tampon *m.* 2.
U.S: F: Béni-oui-oui *m.* 'rubber-stamp, *v.i. U.S:*
F: Se conduire en béni-oui-oui; approuver à tort et
à travers. rubber-tree, *s. Bot:* Arbre *m* à gomme.
rubber², *s. Cards:* Robre *m*, rob *m.* To play a r., faire
un robre. The r. game, la belle.
rubberize ['rʌbəraiz], *v.tr.* Caoutchouter; imprégner,
enduire, (un tissu) de caoutchouc.
rubberneck¹ ['rʌbənek], *s. U.S: P:* Badaud, -aude;
touriste *mf.*
rubberneck², *v.i. U.S: P:* Badauder.
rubbery ['rʌbəri], *a.* (*a*) Caoutchouteux, -euse,
gommeux, -euse. (*b*) Coriace.
rubbish ['rʌbiʃ], *s.* 1. (*a*) Immondices *fpl*, détritus
mpl; (of buildings) décombres *mpl. Ind:* Rebuts
mpl; déchets *mpl.* Household r., ordures ménagères.
P.N: 'Shoot no r.', "défense de déposer des
ordures." (*b*) Fatras *m*; choses *fpl* sans valeur. (*c*)
Camelote *f.* 2. To talk r., débiter des absurdités;
dire des bêtises, des niaiseries. (What) r.! quelle
blague! 'rubbish-bin, *s.* Boîte *f* aux ordures;
poubelle *f.* 'rubbish-cart, *s.* Tombereau *m.*
'rubbish-dump, *s.* Décharge publique. 'rubbish-
heap, *s.* (In garden) Monceau *m* de détritus. 'rubbish-
shoot, *s.* (*a*) = RUBBISH-DUMP. 'rubbish-shoot, *s.* (*a*) = RUBBISH-
DUMP. (*b*) Vide-ordures *m inv.* (dans un immeuble).

rubbishy ['rʌbiʃi], *a.* Sans valeur; (marchandises) de camelote.

rubble ['rʌbl], *s. Const:* **1. R.(-stone)**, moellons (bruts); libages *mpl*; blocaille *f*; *Civ.E:* (*for roads*) brocaille *f.* **2. R.(-work)**, moellonage *m*, blocage *m*; maçonnerie brute, en blocaille; *Arch:* rocaille *f.* **3.** (*Result of demolition, etc.*) Décombres *mpl.*

rube [ru:b], *s. F: U.S:* Rustre *m.* **R. town**, patelin *m*, bled *m.*

rubella [ru:'belə], *s. Med:* Rubéole *f.*

rubeola [ru:bi:'oulə], *s. Med:* Rougeole *f.*

Rubicon ['ru:bikən]. *Pr.n. Geog:* Le Rubicon. **To cross the R.**, franchir le Rubicon; sauter le pas.

rubicund ['ru:bikənd], *a.* Rubicond; rougeaud.

rubric ['ru:brik], *s. Typ: Ecc:* Rubrique *f.*

ruby ['ru:bi]. **1.** *s. Miner: Lap:* (*a*) Rubis *m.* **Balas r.**, rubis balais. **Bohemian r.**, rubis de Bohême. (*b*) *Miner:* **R. silver**, argent rouge. **2.** *a. & s.* Couleur de rubis; rouge (*m*). **R. lips**, lèvres vermeilles. *F:* **R. nose**, nez vineux. *S.a.* WEDDING.

ruche¹ [ru:ʃ], *s. Dressm:* Ruche *f.*

ruche², *v.tr. Dressm:* Rucher. **ruched**, *a.* A ruches; garni de ruches. **ruching**, *s.* Ruché *m.*

ruck¹ [rʌk], *s.* **1.** *Rac:* Peloton *m* (des coureurs). **2. The (common) r.**, le commun (du peuple). **To get out of the r.**, sortir du rang, de l'ornière.

ruck²,³, *s. & v.* = RUCKLE¹,².

ruckle¹ ['rʌkl], *s.* (*In cloth*) Faux pli; godet *m*; froissure *f.*

ruckle², *v.* **To r. (up). 1.** *v.tr.* Froisser, chiffonner, friper (ses habits). **2.** *v.i.* (*Of garment*) (*a*) Se froisser. (*b*) Goder.

rucksack ['rʌksæk], *s.* Sac *m* à dos.

ruckus ['rʌkəs], *s. F: U.S:* Chahut *m*, vacarme *m.*

ruction ['rʌkʃ(ə)n], *s. F: Usu.pl.* Désordre *m*, scène *f.* **There will be ructions**, il va y avoir du grabuge. **If you come home late, there'll be ructions**, si tu rentres tard, tu te feras attraper, *P:* tu te feras engueuler.

rudd [rʌd], *s. Ich:* Gardon *m* rouge.

rudder ['rʌdər], *s.* **1.** *Nau:* Gouvernail *m.* **2.** *Av:* **Vertical r.**, gouvernail de direction. **Horizontal r.**, gouvernail de profondeur. **3.** Queue *f* (d'orientation) (de moulin à vent). **'rudder-bands, -braces**, *s.pl.* Pentures *f* du gouvernail. **'rudder-bar**, *s.* **1.** Barre *f* du gouvernail. **2.** *Av:* Palonnier *m.* **'rudder-post**, *s.* **1.** *N.Arch:* Étambot *m* arrière. **2.** *Av:* Axe *m* du gouvernail.

rudderless ['rʌdəlis], *a.* (Vaisseau) sans gouvernail, à la dérive.

ruddiness ['rʌdinis], *s.* Coloration *f* du teint.

ruddle ['rʌdl], *s.* = REDDLE.

ruddy¹ ['rʌdi], *a.* **1.** (Teint) coloré, haut en couleur, rouge de santé. **Large r. man**, gros rougeaud. (*b*) Rougeâtre. **R. glow** (*of fire*), lueur rouge, rougeoyante. **2.** *P:* (*Attenuated form of* BLOODY 2.) **He's a r. nuisance**, il est bigrement enquiquinant. **A r. liar**, un sacré menteur. **All this r. work**, tout ce sacré travail.

ruddy², *v.tr.* Rendre rouge.

rude [ru:d], *a.* **1.** (*a*) Primitif, -ive, rude; non civilisé. **R. style**, style fruste. **R. voice**, voix sans raffinement. (*b*) (Outil, etc.) grossier; rudimentaire. **R. beginnings**, commencements informes. **R. verses**, (i) vers faits sans art; (ii) vers scabreux. **R. drawing**, (i) dessin primitif, sans art; (ii) dessin obscène. **2.** Violent, brusque. **R. shock**, choc violent; rude secousse. *S.a.* AWAKENING². **3. R. health**, santé robuste. **4.** (*Of pers.*) Impoli, malhonnête; mal élevé. **To be r. to s.o.**, répondre grossièrement; dire des grossièretés à qn. **He was most r.**, il a été on ne peut plus grossier. **Would it be r. to inquire . . .**, peut-on demander sans indiscrétion. . . **-ly**, *adv.* **1.** Primitivement; grossièrement. **R. fashioned**, fabriqué sans art. **2.** Violemment; brusquement. **3.** (Parler, etc.) impoliment, malhonnêtement, grossièrement.

rudeness ['ru:dnis], *s.* **1.** Manque *m* de civilisation (d'un peuple); manque d'art; rudesse *f* (des mœurs). **2.** (*Of pers.*) Impolitesse *f*, malhonnêteté *f*, grossièreté *f.*

rudiment ['ru:dimənt], *s.* **1.** *Biol:* Rudiment *m.* **R. of a thumb**, rudiment de pouce. **2.** *pl.* Rudiments, éléments *m*, premières notions (de grammaire, etc.).

rudimentary [ˌru:di'ment(ə)ri], *a.* Rudimentaire.

rue¹ [ru:], *v.tr.* Regretter amèrement (une action); se repentir de (qch.). **You shall r. it**, vous vous en repentirez.

rue², *s. Bot:* Rue *f.* **Common r.**, rue odorante.

rueful ['ru:ful], *a.* Triste, lugubre. **-fully**, *adv.* Tristement, lugubrement.

ruefulness ['ru:fulnis], *s.* Tristesse *f*; air *m* triste, lugubre; ton *m* triste.

ruff¹ [rʌf], *s.* **1.** *A.Cost:* Fraise *f*, collerette *f.* **2.** *Z: Orn:* Collier *m*, cravate *f.*

ruff², *s. Orn:* Chevalier combattant.

ruff³, *v.tr. Whist: etc:* Couper (avec un atout).

ruffian ['rʌfjən], *s.* (*a*) Bandit *m*, brute *f.* *A:* **Hired r.**, spadassin *m* à gages. (*b*) *F:* **Little ruffians**, petits polissons.

ruffianly ['rʌfjənli], *a.* (Homme) brutal; (conduite) de brute. **R. appearance**, allure *f* de brigand, d'apache.

ruffle¹ ['rʌfl], *s.* **1.** (*a*) *A:* Trouble *m*, agitation *f.* **Life without r.**, vie que rien n'est venu agiter. (*b*) **R. on the surface of the water**, rides *fpl* sur l'eau. **2.** (*a*) *Cost:* (*At wrist*) Manchette *f* en dentelle; (*at breast*) jabot plissé; (*at neck*) fraise *f.* (*b*) *Nat.Hist:* Collier *m*; cravate *f.*

ruffle², *v.tr.* **1.** Ébouriffer (les cheveux); troubler, rider (la surface des eaux). **The bird ruffles (up) its feathers**, l'oiseau hérisse ses plumes. **To r. s.o.'s feelings**, froisser qn. **To r. s.o.'s temper**, contrarier qn. **Nothing ever ruffles him**, rien ne le trouble jamais. **2.** Rucher (des manchettes); plisser (un jabot).

rug [rʌg], *s.* **1.** Couverture *f.* **Travelling r., car r.**, couverture de voyage; plaid *m.* **2.** (**Floor**) **r.**, carpette *f.* **Bedside r.**, descente *f* de lit.

Rugby ['rʌgbi]. *Pr.n.* **1.** (Le collège de) Rugby. **2.** (*a*) **R.** (**football**), le rugby. **League R.**, rugby à treize. (*b*) **R. player**, rugbyman *m*, *pl.* rugbymen.

rugged ['rʌgid], *a.* **1.** (*Of ground*) Raboteux, -euse, accidenté, inégal; (*of rock*) anfractueux, -euse; (*of bark*) rugueux. **2. R. features**, traits rudes, irréguliers. **3.** (*Of character*) Bourru, rude; (*of style*) raboteux, fruste. **R. independence**, indépendance farouche. **R. kindness**, tendresse bourrue. **4.** *U.S:* Vigoureux, -euse, robuste.

ruggedness ['rʌgidnis], *s.* **1.** Nature raboteuse, aspérité *f*, rugosité *f* (d'une surface); anfractuosités *fpl* (d'un rocher). **2.** Rudesse *f* (de caractère).

rugger ['rʌgər], *s. Fb: F:* Le rugby.

rugosity [ru'gɔsiti], *s.* Rugosité *f.*

Ruhr (the) [ðə'ruər]. *Pr.n. Geog:* La Ruhr.

ruin¹ ['ruin], *s.* **1.** Ruine *f*; renversement *m* (d'un État). **To go to r.**, se délabrer; tomber en ruine. *S.a.* RACK². **The r. of my hopes**, la ruine, l'effondrement *m*, de mes espoirs. **R. was staring him in the face**, la ruine se dressait devant lui. **To bring s.o. to r.**, ruiner, perdre, qn. **2.** (*Often pl.*) Ruine(s); décombres *mpl.* **Ramparts fallen in ruins**, remparts dégradés. **The building is a r.**, l'édifice est en ruines. **To lay a town in ruins**, détruire une ville de fond en comble. **3. To be, prove, the r. of s.o.**, ruiner, perdre, qn. *P:* **Mother's r.** = pousse-au-crime *m inv.*

ruin², *v.tr.* Ruiner. **1.** (*a*) Abîmer (son chapeau, etc.). (*b*) **To r. one's prospects**, gâcher son avenir. **To r. one's health**, démolir sa santé. **To r. s.o.'s reputation**, perdre qn de réputation; démolir la réputation (de qn). **2.** (*a*) **Her extravagance ruined him**, ses folles dépenses l'ont ruiné. **He is utterly ruined**, *F:* il est coulé. (*b*) Séduire, tromper (une jeune fille). **ruined**, *a.* **1.** En ruines. **2.** Ruiné.

ruination [rui'neiʃ(ə)n], *s.* Ruine *f*, perte *f.* **It will be the r. of him**, ce sera sa ruine.

ruinous ['ruinəs], *a.* **1.** (Tombé) en ruines; délabré; ruineux, -euse. **2.** Ruineux. **R. expense**, dépenses ruineuses. (*Of undertaking*) **To prove r. to s.o.**, être la ruine de qn. **-ly**, *adv.* **R. expensive**, ruineux.

rule¹ [ru:l], *s.* **1.** Règle *f.* (*a*) **To set sth. down as a r.**, établir qch. en règle générale. **As a (general) r.**, en règle générale; en thèse générale; en principe. **It is the r. to . . .**, il est de règle de. . . **To do everything by r.**, tout faire suivant les règles. **R. of thumb**, méthode *f* empirique; procédé *m* mécanique. *Mth:* **R. of three**, règle de trois. (*b*) **To make it a r. to . . .**, se faire une règle de. . . **Rules of conduct**, directives *f*; normes *f* de conduite. (*c*) **Rules and regulations**, statuts *m* et règlements *m.* *Ind:* **Working**

to r., grève *f* de zèle. **The rules of the game,** les règles, les lois, du jeu. **That is against the rules,** c'est contre les règles; ce n'est pas réglementaire. **The r. of the road,** (i) *Aut:* le code de la route; (ii) *Nau:* les règles de route. 2. Empire *m*, autorité *f*. **Under the r. of a tyrant,** sous l'empire d'un tyran. **Under British r.,** sous l'autorité britannique. 3. *Jur:* Décision *f*, ordonnance *f*. **R. of court,** décision du tribunal. 4. (*a*) *Carp: etc:* Règle graduée; mètre *m*. **Folding r.,** mètre pliant. (*b*) *Surv:* **Sighting r.,** alidade *f*. 5. *Typ:* (*a*) (Brass) **r.,** filet *m*. (*b*) (Em) **r.,** tiret *m*. (En) **r.,** trait *m* d'union.

rule². I. *v.tr.* 1. Gouverner, régir (un État). **To r.** (over) **a nation,** régner sur une nation. **To r. one's passions,** contenir, commander à, ses passions. **To be ruled by s.o.,** subir la loi de qn; *F:* être sous la coupe de qn. *Jur: etc:* Décider. **To r. sth. out of order,** déclarer que qch. n'est pas en règle. 3. Régler, rayer (du papier). **To r. a line,** tracer une ligne à la règle. II. **rule,** *v.i.* **The prices ruling in Manchester,** les prix qui se pratiquent à Manchester. **rule off,** *v.tr.* 1. Tirer une ligne au-dessous (d'un paragraphe, d'un compte, etc.). 2. *Com:* Clore, régler (un compte, une affaire). **rule out,** *v.tr.* 1. Écarter, éliminer (qch.). **Possibility that cannot be ruled out,** possibilité que l'on ne saurait écarter. 2. Biffer, rayer (un mot). **ruling¹,** *a.* 1. Souverain, dominant. **The r. classes,** les classes dirigeantes. **R. passion,** passion dominante. 2. **R. price,** cours pratiqué; prix *m* du jour. **ruling²,** *s.* 1. Ordonnance *f*, décision *f*, (d'un juge, etc.) sur un point de droit. **To give a r. in favour of s.o.,** décider en faveur de qn. 2. Réglage *m*, réglure *f* (d'une feuille de papier).

ruler ['ru:lər], *s.* 1. Souverain, -aine (of, over, de). **The rulers,** les dirigeants *m*. 2. Règle *f*, mètre *m*.

rum¹ [rʌm], *s. Dist:* Rhum *m*. **R. distillery,** rhumerie *f*.

rum², *a.* (**rummer**) *F: O:* Drôle, bizarre. **That's rum!** ça c'est pas ordinaire!

Rumania [ru(:)'meiniə]. *Pr.n. Geog:* La Roumanie.

Rumanian [ru:'meiniən], *a. & s.* Roumain, -aine.

rumba ['rʌmbə], *s. Danc:* Rumba *f*.

rumble¹ ['rʌmbl], *s.* 1. Grondement *m* (du tonnerre); roulement *m* (d'une charrette); gargouillement *m*, grouillement *m* (des entrailles). 2. *Veh: A:* Siège *m* de derrière (pour domestique); *Aut:* spider *m*. 3. *U.S: P:* Rixe *f*, bagarre *f* (entre bandes de jeunes voyous).

rumble², *v.i.* (*Of thunder, etc.*) Gronder (sourdement); rouler, bruire; (*of bowels*) grouiller, gargouiller. **The cart rumbled off,** la charrette s'ébranla lourdement. **rumbling,** *s.* = RUMBLE¹ 1. *Med:* **Rumblings in the bowels,** *F:* tummy-rumblings, borborygmes *mpl*.

rumble³, *v.tr. P:* Flairer, se douter de, qch.; subodorer qch.; voir venir qn, qch.

rumen ['ru:men], *s. Z:* Rumen *m*, panse *f* (d'un ruminant).

ruminant ['ru:minənt], *a. & s. Z:* Ruminant (*m*).

ruminate ['ru:mineit]. 1. *v.i.* (*Of cow*) Ruminer. 2. *v.i. & tr.* Ruminer, méditer.

rumination [ˌru:mi'nei∫(ə)n], *s.* 1. *Physiol:* Rumination *f*. 2. Rumination, méditation *f*.

ruminative ['ru:minətiv], *a.* Méditatif, -ive.

rummage¹ ['rʌmidʒ], *s.* 1. Recherches *fpl*, fouille *f* (dans de vieux documents, etc.). 2. Vieilleries *fpl* de rebut (mises en vente). **R. sale,** vente *f* d'objets usagés (pour une œuvre charitable).

rummage². 1. *v.tr.* Fouiller, farfouiller (une armoire, dans une armoire). 2. *v.i.* **To r. in one's pockets,** fouiller dans ses poches. **To r. for sth.,** fouiller pour trouver qch. **To r. about among old papers,** fouiller, fourrager, dans de vieux documents.

rummy¹ ['rʌmi], *a. F: O:* = RUM².

rummy², *s.* Jeu *m* de cartes (pour un nombre indéterminé de joueurs).

rumour¹ ['ru:mər], *s.* Rumeur *f*, bruit *m* (qui court); on-dit *m inv*. **R. has it that . . .,** le bruit court que . . .; on dit que. . . . **Disquieting rumours are afloat,** il court des bruits peu rassurants. 'rumour(-)monger, *s.* Colporteur -euse, de fausses nouvelles. 'rumour(-)mongering, *s.* Colportage *m* de fausses nouvelles.

rumour², *v.tr.* (*Esp. in the passive*) **It is rumoured that . . .,** le bruit, la rumeur, court que. . . .

rump [rʌmp], *s.* 1. Croupe *f* (d'un quadrupède); croupion *m* (de volaille); *F:* postérieur *m*, derrière *m* (d'une personne). *Cu:* Culotte *f* (de bœuf). 2. *F: Usu. Pej:* Restes *mpl*, restant *m* (d'un parti politique, etc.). 'rump-steak, *s. Cu:* Rum(p)-steak *m*, romsteck *m*.

rumple ['rʌmpl], *v.tr.* Chiffonner, friper, froisser (une robe, etc.); ébouriffer (les cheveux).

rumpus ['rʌmpəs], *s. F:* Chahut *m*, vacarme *m*. **To kick up, make, a r.,** (i) faire un chahut à tout casser; (ii) faire du fracas, faire une scène. **To have a r. with s.o.,** avoir une prise de bec avec qn. *U.S:* **R. room,** salle *f* de jeux.

run¹ [rʌn], *s.* 1. (*a*) Action *f* de courir. **At a r.,** au pas de course. **To break into a r.,** se mettre à courir. **Prices have come down with a r.,** les prix ont dégringolé. **She is always on the r.,** elle est tout le temps à courir. *Mil:* **To keep the enemy on the r.,** ne laisser aucun répit aux fuyards. *Nau:* **To lower the yards by the r.,** amener les vergues en pagaïe. (*b*) *Course f.* **The horse had had a long r.,** le cheval avait fourni une longue course. **Criminal on the r.,** malfaiteur recherché par la police. **To have a r. for one's money,** en avoir pour son argent. (*c*) Élan *m*. **To make a r. at s.o.,** s'élancer sur qn. (*d*) *Cr:* **To make ten runs,** faire dix courses; marquer dix points. *Baseball:* **Home r.,** coup *m* de circuit. (*e*) *Fish:* Remonte *f*, montaison *f* (du saumon, etc.). 2. (*a*) Course, promenade *f*, tour *m*. *Aut: etc:* **To go for a r.,** faire une promenade. **Trial r.,** (i) course d'essai (d'un navire, d'une locomotive); (ii) *Aut:* course d'essai (que l'on fait faire à un client). (*b*) *Rail:* Trajet *m*. (*c*) *Nau:* Traversée *f*, parcours *m*. **Day's r.,** course; distance parcourue. **Full-power r.,** essai *m* à pleine puissance. *Av:* Take-off r., parcours au décollage. **Landing r.,** parcours à l'atterrissage. (*d*) Marche *f* (d'une machine). *Typ:* **R. of three thousand (copies),** tirage *m* à trois mille. 3. (*a*) *N.Arch:* Formes *fpl* arrière (d'un navire); coulée *f* arrière; façons *fpl* de l'arrière. **Ship with a clean r.,** navire à l'arrière évidé. (*b*) **R. of sea, of tide,** courant *m* de marée. (*c*) Cours *m*, marche, suite *f* (des événements); rythme *m*, cadence *f* (des vers). 4. **To have a r. of luck,** être en veine. **A r. of misfortune,** une suite de malheurs; *F:* la série noire. *Cards:* **R. of three,** séquence *f* de trois. **To have a long r.,** (*of fashion*) avoir une longue vogue, rester longtemps en vogue; *Th:* tenir longtemps l'affiche. **In the long r.,** à la longue; en fin de compte. **It will pay in the long r.,** cela rapportera avec le temps. 5. *Gaming:* **R. on the red,** série *f* à la rouge. 6. Descente *f* (sur une banque); **There was a r. on the bank,** les guichets ont été assiégés. **There is a great r. on that novel,** on demande beaucoup ce roman. 7. **The common r. of men,** le commun des hommes. 8. Libre accès *m*. **To allow s.o. the r. of one's library,** mettre sa bibliothèque à la disposition de qn. **To have the (free) r. of the house,** avoir libre accès, pouvoir aller partout, dans la maison. **We have the free r. of his house,** sa maison est nôtre. 9. (*a*) Galerie *f* (d'une taupe). **Sheep r.,** pâturage *m* de moutons; bergerie *f*. **Pigeon r.,** volière *f*. **Chicken r.,** parcours (d'un poulailler). (*b*) **Toboggan r.,** piste *f* de toboggan. **Ski r.,** descente *f* à ski. 10. *Mus:* Roulade *f*, tirade *f*, trait *m*. 11. *U.S:* LADDER 3.

run², *v.* (*p.t.* **ran** [ræn]; *p.p.* **run**; *pr.p.* **running**) I. *v.i.* 1. Courir. **To r. like a hare, like the devil,** courir comme un lièvre, comme un dératé. **To r. to meet s.o.,** courir au-devant de qn. **To r. upstairs,** monter l'escalier en toute hâte, quatre à quatre. **To r. down the street,** descendre la rue en courant. **To r. a race,** courir, disputer, une course. **To r. a mile,** courir, faire, un mille. **To r. about the streets, to r. about the fields,** courir les rues, les champs. **To r. an errand, a message,** faire une course. **To r. the blockade,** forcer le blocus. 2. Fuir, s'enfuir, se sauver. **Now we must r. for it!** maintenant sauvons-nous! 3. **To r. in a race,** courir, disputer, une épreuve, une course. **To r. for office,** se porter candidat (à une place). 4. (*Of salmon, etc.*) Remonter les rivières; faire la montaison. 5. *Nau:* Courir, filer, faire route. **To r. before the wind,** courir vent arrière; fuir devant le vent. **To r. free,** courir largue. **To r. before the sea,** fuir devant la lame. **To r. on the rocks,** donner sur les rochers. *S.a.* AGROUND. **6.** (*a*) Aller, marcher, **Vehicle that runs easily,** voiture qui roule bien, qui rend bien. **Train running at fifty miles an hour,** train qui marche à cinquante milles à l'heure, qui fait cinquante milles à l'heure. **Trains running to Paris,** trains à destination de Paris. (*b*) Circuler. **Trains running between London and the coast,** trains qui font le service entre Londres et la côte. **This train is not running to-day,** ce train est supprimé aujourd'hui. **Boats that r. daily,** bateaux qui font la traversée tous les jours. **7.** (*a*) **A whisper ran through the crowd,** un murmure courut dans la foule. **This error runs through all his work,** cette erreur se retrouve dans toute son œuvre. **The thought keeps running through my head,** cette idée me revient continuellement à l'esprit, me trotte dans la cervelle. **It runs in the family, in the blood,** cela tient de famille, cela est dans le sang. (*b*) **The talk ran on this subject,** la conversation a roulé sur ce sujet. **His life runs smoothly,** ses jours s'écoulent paisiblement. **Things must r. their course,** il faut que les choses suivent leur cours. **The lease has only a year to r.,** le bail n'a plus qu'un an à courir. **The play has been running for a year,** la pièce tient l'affiche depuis un an. (*c*) (*Of amount*) **To r. to . . .,** se monter, s'élever, à . . . **The interval sometimes runs to as much as half an hour,** l'entracte va parfois jusqu'à la demi-heure. **The manuscript ran to a great length,** le manuscrit était très long. (*d*) **The money won't r. to a car,** c'est une somme insuffisante pour acheter une auto. *F:* **I can't r. to that,** c'est au-dessus de mes moyens. **8.** (*Of engine*) Fonctionner, marcher; (*of wheel, etc.*) tourner. **The engine is running,** le moteur est en marche. **Apparatus that runs off the mains,** appareil qui se branche sur le secteur. **The drawer does not r. easily,** le tiroir ne joue pas bien. **9.** (*Of colour in fabric*) Déteindre; (*of ink on paper*) s'étendre; (*of dye*) couler (au lavage). **10.** (*a*) (*Of liquid, etc.*) Couler. **River that runs for 200 miles,** rivière qui a 200 milles de cours. **River running into the sea,** rivière qui coule, se jette, dans la mer. **The tide runs strong,** le courant de marée est fort. **A heavy sea was running,** la mer était grosse. **The wine ran over the table,** le vin se répandit sur la table. **The rivers ran blood,** les rivières coulaient rouge, étaient teintes de sang. **Our stores are running low,** nos provisions s'épuisent, tirent à leur fin. *S.a.* BLOOD[1] 1, DRY[1] 1, HIGH II. 3, SHORT[1] I. 3. (*b*) **The floor was running with water,** le parquet ruisselait. **He was running with sweat,** il était en nage. **His nose was running,** le nez lui coulait. **Her eyes were running,** ses yeux pleuraient. **Ulcer that runs,** ulcère qui suppure. **Pen that runs,** stylo qui bave, qui coule. **Casting that has r.,** pièce qui a coulé. (*c*) **Vase that runs,** vase qui coule, qui fuit. **Money runs through his fingers,** l'argent lui fond entre les mains. **11.** (*a*) **A gallery runs round the room,** il y a une galerie tout autour de la salle. **To r. north and south,** être orienté du nord au sud. **The road runs quite close to the village,** la route passe tout près du village. (*b*) **So the story runs,** c'est ainsi que l'histoire est racontée. **He runs to sentimentality,** il tombe dans la sentimentalité. **To r. to seed,** (*of plant*) monter en graine. (*Of pers.*) **To r. to fat,** prendre de la graisse. **II. run,** *v.tr.* **1.** (*a*) Chasser (le renard, etc.) *S.a.* EARTH[1] 4. (*b*) **To r. s.o. hard, close,** serrer qn de près. **You'll r. me off my legs,** à ce train-là vous me romprez les jambes. **To r. oneself out of breath,** s'essouffler (à force de courir). *S.a.* FINE[3] 6. **2.** (*a*) Pousser (un cheval) au galop. (*b*) Mettre (du bétail) au vert. **3.** (*a*) **To r. the car into the garage,** rentrer la voiture dans le garage. **To r. s.o. into town,** conduire qn en ville (en voiture). **To r. a boat ashore,** atterrir une embarcation. **To r. one's head against the door,** donner de la tête contre la porte. (*b*) **They are running an extra train today,** il y aura aujourd'hui un train supplémentaire. (*c*) Introduire (de l'alcool) en contrebande. **4.** (*a*) **I can't afford to r. a car,** je n'ai pas les moyens d'entretenir une auto. **My car is cheap to r.,** ma voiture est économique. *Av:* **To r. the engines for checking,** faire le point fixe. (*b*) *Com:* **We are running a cheap line,** nous avons en magasin, nous vendons, un article à bon marché. **5.** (*a*) Tenir (un magasin, un hôtel); exploiter (une usine); diriger

(un théâtre, une ferme); éditer, gérer (un journal). **To r. the business,** faire marcher la maison. **To r. s.o.'s house,** tenir le ménage de qn. (*b*) **To r. a (high) temperature,** faire de la température. (*c*) *Turf:* **To r. a horse,** faire courir un cheval. *F:* **To r. a candidate,** (i) mettre en avant, (ii) appuyer, un candidat. **7.** Passer; faire passer. **To r. a sword through s.o.,** **to r. s.o. through with a sword,** passer à qn une épée à travers le corps. **To r. pipes through a wall,** faire passer des tuyaux à travers un mur. **To r. a thorn into one's finger,** s'enfoncer une épine dans le doigt. **To r. one's fingers over a surface,** promener, faire glisser, ses doigts sur une surface. **To r. one's eye over sth.,** jeter un coup d'œil sur qch.; parcourir qch. des yeux. **To r. one's pen through a word,** rayer, biffer, un mot. **8. To r. lead into a joint,** couler du plomb dans un joint. **9.** Tracer (une ligne) (**round,** autour de). **run about,** *v.i.* Courir de côté et d'autre. **To let the dogs r. a.,** laisser courir les chiens. **run across,** *v.i.* **1.** Traverser (la rue) en courant. **2.** Rencontrer (qn) par hasard; tomber sur (qn) inopinément. **run after,** *v.i.* Courir après (qn). **She is much r. a. in society,** elle est très recherchée dans le monde. **run against,** (*a*) Se heurter contre (qch.). (*b*) **This runs against my interests,** cela va à l'encontre de mes intérêts. **run along,** *v.i.* **1. Road that runs along the river,** chemin qui longe la rivière. **A ditch runs along the garden,** un fossé borde le jardin. **2. R. a.!** allez-vous-en! filez! **run at,** *v.i.* Courir sur, se jeter sur (qn). **run away,** *v.i.* (*a*) (*Of pers.*) S'enfuir, se sauver; s'échapper. **To r. a. from the facts,** se refuser à l'évidence des faits. (*b*) (*Of horse*) S'emballer, s'emporter; prendre le mors aux dents. (*c*) **To r. a. with s.o.,** enlever qn. **To r. a. with sth.,** emporter, enlever, qch. **Don't r. a. with the idea that . . .,** n'allez pas vous imaginer, n'allez pas croire, que . . . **That runs away with a lot of money,** cela mange beaucoup d'argent. **run down.** I. *v.i.* **1.** (*a*) Descendre en courant. (*b*) **The rain ran down the windscreen,** la pluie ruisselait le long du pare-brise. **The sweat ran down his forehead,** la sueur lui coulait sur le front. **2.** (*Of spring*) Se détendre; (*of clock*) s'arrêter (faute d'être remonté); (*of accumulator*) se décharger à plat; (*of dynamo*) se désamorcer. II. **run down,** *v.tr.* **1. To r. d. a ship,** (i) couler (à fond) un navire, (ii) laisser porter sur un navire. **To r. s.o. down,** heurter, renverser, qn; (*of motorist*) écraser qn. **2.** (*a*) *Ven:* Mettre aux abois (un cerf). (*b*) **The police ran him down,** la police l'a dépisté. **3.** *F:* Dénigrer, déprécier, décrier, éreinter (qn); déblatérer contre (qn); éreinter (une pièce de théâtre). **'run 'down,** *a.* **1.** (Accumulateur) à plat, déchargé. **2.** *F:* (*Of pers.*) **To get r. d.,** s'anémier; se débiliter. **'running 'down,** *s.* **1.** Descente *f*; ruissellement *m* (de l'eau). **2.** *F:* Dépréciation *f*, ravalement *m*, éreintement *m*, débinage *m* (de qn). **3.** Désamorçage *m* (d'une dynamo). **run in,** *v.tr.* **1.** *F:* Conduire (qn) au poste (de police); fourrer (qn) au bloc. **To be, get, r. in,** se faire coffrer; se faire ramasser. **2.** *I.C.E:* Roder (un moteur). *Aut:* **'Running in',** "en rodage." **To r. in the gears,** permettre aux engrenages de se faire. **run into, 1.** *v.i.* (*a*) **To r. i. debt,** faire des dettes; s'endetter. **To r. i. absurdity,** tomber dans l'absurdité. (*b*) (*Of colours*) **To r. i. one another,** se fondre l'une dans l'autre. (*c*) **To r. i. sth.,** entrer en collision avec qch.; (*of vehicle*) heurter, accrocher (un autre); (*of train*) tamponner (un autre); (*of ship*) aborder (un autre). (*Of pers.*) **To r. i. s.o.,** se trouver nez à nez avec qn. (*d*) **His income runs into thousands,** son revenu s'élève à des milliers de livres. **Book that has r. i. five editions,** livre dont on a publié cinq éditions. **2.** *v.tr.* (*a*) **To r. one's car into a wall,** aller s'emboutir contre un mur. (*b*) **To r. s.o. into debt,** faire faire des dettes à qn. **run off. 1.** *v.i.* Fuir, s'enfuir, se sauver. **To r. o. with the cash,** filer avec l'argent. **2.** *v.tr.* (*a*) Réciter (qch.) tout d'une haleine; rédiger (un article) au courant de la plume. **To r. o. a letter on the typewriter,** taper une lettre en moins de rien. (*b*) Faire écouler (un liquide). **To r. o. the water from a boiler,** vider l'eau d'une chaudière. (*c*) *Sp:* **To r. o. a heat,** courir une finale éliminatoire. **'run-off,** *s.* **1.** *Hyd.E:* Écoulement *m*; *Geog:* ruissellement *m*. **2.** *Sp:* (Course) finale *f*.

run on. 1. *v.i.* (*a*) Continuer sa course. (*b*) (*Of time*) S'écouler; (*of contract, disease, etc.*) suivre son cours. (*c*) (*Of verse*) Enjamber. (*d*) *Typ:* (*Of words*) Se rejoindre; être liés; (*of text*) suivre sans alinéa. **'Run on.'** "alinéa à supprimer." (*e*) Continuer à parler; *F:* en dégoiser. 2. *v.tr. Typ:* **To r. on the matter**, faire suivre sans alinéa. **run out.** 1. *v.i.* (*a*) Sortir en courant. (*b*) **The tide is running out**, la mer se retire. (*c*) (*Of liquid*) Couler, fuir; se répandre (sur la table). (*d*) (*Of period of time*) Se terminer, expirer. **Our lease has r. o.**, notre bail est expiré. (*e*) *Cards:* (*Of player*) Gagner la partie. (*f*) (*Of supplies*) Venir à manquer; faire défaut. **Our stores are running out**, nos provisions s'épuisent, tirent à leur fin. *Lit:* **His sands are running out**, il tire à sa fin. **The sands are running out**, la dernière heure approche. (*Of pers.*) **To have r. o. of provisions**, avoir épuisé ses provisions; être à court, à bout, de provisions. (*g*) (*Of rope*) Filer, se dérouler. (*h*) **A strip of land runs out to sea**, une langue de terre s'avance dans la mer. 2. *v.tr.* (*a*) **To r. oneself out**, s'épuiser à force de courir. (*b*) (Laisser) filer (une corde). (*c*) *Nau:* Pousser dehors (une passerelle). (*d*) *Typ:* **To r. o. a line** (into the margin), sortir une ligne. **run over**, *v.i.* 1. (*a*) Parcourir (un document) du regard; passer en revue (les événements). (*b*) **To r. o. the seams of a boat**, vérifier les coutures d'une embarcation. **To r. o. s.o.'s pockets**, fouiller qn. (*c*) (*Of vehicle*) Passer sur le corps de (qn). **He has been r. o.**, il a été écrasé. 2. (*Of vessel or contents*) Déborder. **run through.** 1. *v.i.* (*a*) Traverser (la salle) en courant. (*b*) Parcourir (un document) du regard; feuilleter (un livre). **He ran through his pockets but couldn't find it**, il fouilla dans ses poches mais ne réussit pas à le trouver. (*c*) **To r. t. a fortune**, dissiper, dévorer, une fortune. 2. *v.tr.* *See* RUN² II. 7. **To r. s.o. t.** (and through), percer qn de part en part; transpercer, enfiler, qn. **run up.** 1. *v.i.* (*a*) Monter en courant. (*b*) Accourir. **To come running up**, arriver en courant. **To r. up against s.o.**, (i) rencontrer qn par hasard; (ii) *F:* être, entrer, en conflit avec qn. (*c*) (*Of amount, price*) Monter, s'élever. 2. *v.tr.* (*a*) Laisser grossir (un compte); faire monter (le prix de qch.); laisser accumuler (des dettes). (*b*) **To r. up a flag**, hisser un pavillon. (*c*) Bâtir (une maison) à la va-vite; confectionner (une robe) à la hâte; faire un point à (une déchirure). **'run-up**, *s.* 1. (*a*) *Golf:* Coup roulé d'approche. (*b*) *Fb:* Percée *f.* 2. *Fish:* Montaison *f* (du saumon). 3. *Av:* **The pilot made his r.-up to the target**, le pilote fonça sur l'objectif. **run**, *a. Tchn:* **Price per foot r.**, prix par pied courant. 2. (*Of dutiable goods*) Passé en contrebande. 3. **R. butter**, beurre fondu pour conserve. **R. honey**, miel extrait de rayons. **running¹**, *a.* 1. *Fb:* **R. kick**, coup de pied donné en courant. *Sp:* **R. jump**, saut avec élan. **To keep up a r. fight**, (i) se battre en retraite; (ii) *Navy:* soutenir, appuyer, la chasse. 2. **R. water**, eau courante, eau vive. (*In hotel*) **Bedroom with r. water**, chambre avec eau courante. **R. sore**, plaie qui suppure. **R. cold**, rhume *m* de cerveau. 3. (*a*) (Style) coulant. (*b*) **R. hand**, écriture cursive; écriture coulée. 4. (*a*) Continu. **R. accompaniment**, accompagnement soutenu. *Mil:* **R. fire**, feu roulant. *Typ:* **R. title**, titre courant. (*b*) *Meas:* **R. foot**, pied courant. (*c*) **R. expenses**, dépenses courantes. (*d*) (*Following the noun*) Consécutif; de suite. **Three days r.**, trois jours de suite. 5. (*a*) **R. block**, poulie mobile. (*b*) *Nau:* **R. rigging**, manœuvres courantes. 6. *Needlew:* **R. stitch**, point devant, point droit. 7. *W.Tel:* *T.V. etc:* **R. commentary**, reportage *m* en direct. **running²**, *s.* 1. Course(s) *f(pl).* *F:* **To make, take up, the r.**, mener la course. **To be in the r.**, avoir des chances d'arriver, de réussir. **To be out of the r.**, ne plus avoir aucune chance. 2. (*a*) Marche *f*, fonctionnement *m* (d'une machine); roulement *m* (d'une voiture). **Smooth r.**, allure régulière. **In r. order**, prêt au service. (*b*) **To alter the r. of the trains**, modifier la marche des trains. (*c*) Direction *f* (d'un hôtel, etc.); exploitation *f* (des chemins de fer). (*d*) Introduction *f* (de l'alcool) en contrebande. *S.a.* GUN-RUNNING. 3. Écoulement *m*, ruissellement *m* (de l'eau, etc.). *Med:* Suppuration *f.* **'running board**, *s.* 1. *Aut:* O: Marchepied *m.* 2. *Rail:* Tablier *m.* **'running track**, *s. Sp:* Piste *f.*

runabout ['rʌnəbaut], *s.* 1. Vagabond, -onde. 2. (*a*) *Nau:* Runabout *m.* (*b*) *Aut:* Voiturette *f.*
runagate ['rʌnəgeit], *s. A:* 1. Vagabond, -onde. 2. Fugitif, -ive.
runaway ['rʌnəwei], *attrib. a. & s.* 1. (*a*) Fuyard (*m*), fugitif (*m*). **R. slave**, esclave fugitif. (*b*) **R. horse**, cheval emballé. (*c*) *Rail:* **R. truck, wagon** (parti) à la dérive. 2. (*a*) **To make a r. match with s.o.**, enlever une jeune fille pour l'épouser; (*of girl*) se laisser enlever pour être épousée. (*b*) **R. victory**, victoire remportée haut la main.
rune [ru:n], *s. Pal:* Rune *f.*
rung¹ [rʌŋ]. *See* RING⁴.
rung², *s.* Échelon *m*, barreau *m*, (barre *f* de) traverse *f* (d'une échelle); bâton *m* (d'une chaise).
runic ['ru:nik], *a.* Runique.
runnel ['rʌn(ə)l], *s.* Ruisseau *m*; rigole *f.*
runner ['rʌnər], *s.* 1. (*a*) Coureur, -euse. *Rac:* **Five runners**, cinq partants *m.* (*b*) Messager *m*, courrier *m.* (*c*) *Hist:* (Bow-street) **r.**, sergent *m* (de police). (*d*) **Blockade-r.**, forceur *m* de blocus. (*e*) *Mil:* Agent *m* de liaison. 2. *Orn:* Râle *m* d'eau. 3. *Hort:* (*a*) Coulant *m*, stolon *m*; traînée *f* (de fraisier). (*b*) **Scarlet r., r. bean**, haricot *m* d'Espagne. 4. (Meule) courante *f* (de moulin). 5. Patin *m* (de traîneau). 6. (*a*) *Nau:* Chaîne *f* de charge. (*b*) Anneau *m* mobile. 7. Curseur *m.* *El:* **R. resistance**, résistance à curseur. 8. (*a*) Chariot *m* de roulement; trolley *m.* (*b*) Galet *m* (de roulement). (*c*) Roue *f* parasite, intermédiaire. (*d*) Roue mobile, couronne *f* mobile (d'une turbine). 9. *Mec.E:* Poulie *f* fixe. 10. *Metall:* (*a*) Trou *m*, jet *m*, de coulée. (*b*) Jet, masselotte *f.* 11. (Carpet-)r., chemin (d'escalier, de couloir). (Table-)r., chemin *m* de table. 12. **R.-up.** (i) *Sp: etc:* Second, -onde. (ii) *Sch: etc:* **The runners-up**, les premiers parmi les ajournés, les refusés.
runny ['rʌni], *a.* (*a*) (Trop) liquide. (*b*) **R. nose**, nez qui coule.
runt [rʌnt], *s.* 1. Bœuf *m* ou vache *f* de race petite. 2. (Cheval) ragot *m.* 3. Pigeon romain. 4. *F:* Nain *m*, nabot *m.* 5. Trognon *m* (de chou).
runty ['rʌnti], *a. F:* Rabougri, *F:* riquiqui.
runway ['rʌnwei], *s.* 1. *Mec.E:* Chemin *m* de roulement. **Crane r.**, pont roulant. **Overhead r.**, transporteur aérien. 2. *Av:* Piste *f* d'envol.
rupee [ru:'pi:], *s. Num:* Roupie *f.*
rupture¹ ['rʌptʃər], *s.* 1. (*a*) Rupture *f* (de négociations, etc.); brouille *f* (entre amis). (*b*) *El:* **R. of the arc**, rupture de l'arc. 2. *Med:* (*a*) Rupture (d'une veine). (*b*) Hernie *f.*
rupture². 1. *v.tr.* (*a*) Rompre (des relations). (*b*) **To r. a ligament**, se rompre un tendon; claquer un tendon. 2. *v.i.* Se rompre, **ruptured**, *a.* 1. Rompu. 2. (Intestin) hernié. (*Of pers.*) **To be r.**, avoir une hernie.
rural ['ruərəl], *a.* Rural, -aux; champêtre; de (la) campagne. **R. site**, site agreste. **R. occupation**, travaux des champs. **R. postman**, facteur rural. **-ally**, *adv.* **R. situated**, situé à la campagne.
ruse [ru:z], *s.* Ruse *f*, stratagème *m*, piège *m.*
rush¹ [rʌʃ], *s.* 1. Jonc *m.* **Plantation of rushes**, jonchaie *f.* **Sweet r.**, jonc odorant; lis *m* des marais. 2. Jonc, paille *f* (pour fonds de chaises). **'rush-bed**, *s.* Jonchaie *f.* **'rush-bottomed**, *a.* (Chaise) à fond de paille. **'rush-'candle**, **-'dip**, *s. A:* = RUSHLIGHT. **'rush-'mat**, *s.* Natte *f* de jonc; paillasson *m.*
rush², *s.* 1. (*a*) Course précipitée. **To make a r. at s.o.**, se précipiter sur qn. *Mil:* **To attack by rushes**, attaquer par bonds. (*b*) **General r.**, ruée générale; bousculade *f*, rush *m.* **There was a r. for shelter**, ce fut une ruée pour se mettre à l'abri. **There was a r. to the doors**, on se précipita vers les portes. **The r. hours**, (i) les heures d'affluence, les heures de pointe; (ii) (*in business*) le coup de feu. 2. Hâte *f.* **We had a r. to get the job done**, il a fallu nous hâter pour achever le travail. **The r. of modern life**, la vie fiévreuse d'aujourd'hui. **R. order**, commande urgente. **R.-work**, travail de première urgence. 3. **A r. of air**, un coup d'air, une chasse d'air. **R. of blood to the head**, (i) coup de sang; (ii) accès *m* de rage. *El.E:* **R. of current**, à-coup *m* de courant. 4. *Cin:* *pl.* **Rushes**, premières épreuves (d'un film); projection *f* d'essai (d'un film avant montage).

rush³. I. v.i. **1.** (a) Se précipiter; s'élancer. **To r.** about, courir çà et là. **The river rushes along,** la rivière précipite ses eaux. **To r. into the room,** faire irruption dans la salle. **To r. to the window,** se ruer à la fenêtre. **To r. in where angels fear to tread,** y aller avec audace sans avoir peur de gaffer. **To r. into an affair,** se jeter étourdiment dans une affaire. **To r. to conclusions,** conclure trop hâtivement. (b) **To r. out,** s'élancer dehors. **To r. down,** descendre impétueusement. **To r. up,** (i) monter à la hâte; (ii) accourir. **To r. upstairs,** monter l'escalier quatre à quatre. **To r. through France,** traverser la France à la galopade. **To r. through one's prayers,** expédier ses prières. (c) **To r. at, on, s.o.,** se ruer, se jeter, sur qn; fondre sur qn. **2. The wind rushes up the chimney,** le vent s'engouffre dans la cheminée. **The blood rushed to his face,** le rouge lui monta au visage. II. **rush,** v.tr. **1.** (a) Pousser, entraîner, violemment. **To r. s.o. out of the room,** chasser qn brusquement de la chambre. **They were rushed to hospital,** on les transporta d'urgence à l'hôpital. **To r. s.o. into an undertaking,** entraîner qn dans une entreprise sans lui donner le temps de réfléchir. **He rushed me through luncheon,** il me fit déjeuner au galop. **I don't want to r. you,** je ne voudrais pas vous bousculer. **Don't r. me,** laissez-moi le temps de souffler. **To r. a bill through (the House),** faire passer un projet de loi à la hâte. Th: **To r. the ending,** brusquer le dénouement. (b) F: **To r. s.o. for sth.,** faire payer à qn un prix exorbitant pour qch. **2.** Dépêcher (un travail); exécuter (une commande) d'urgence. **3. The audience rushed the platform,** le public envahit l'estrade. Mil: **To r. a position,** prendre d'assaut une position. **rush up,** v.tr. **1.** Bâtir (une maison) à la hâte. **2. To r. up the prices,** se hâter de majorer les prix. **3. To r. up reinforcements,** faire venir du renfort en toute hâte. **rushed,** a. **1.** (Pers.) Débordé de travail. **To be greatly r.,** avoir fort à faire; être débordé; en avoir par-dessus la tête. **2.** (Travail) fait à la va-vite, bâclé. **rushing¹,** a. (Vent, torrent) impétueux. **rushing²,** s. Course précipitée; ruée f, bousculade f. **All this pointless r. about,** toute cette bousculade insensée.

rushlight ['rʌʃlait], s. Chandelle f à mèche de jonc.

rusk [rʌsk], s. Cu: Biscotte f.

russet ['rʌsit]. **1.** s. (a) A: Drap m de bure de couleur brunâtre. (b) Hort: Reinette grise. **R. (pear),** rousselet m. **2.** a. & s. (Couleur f) roussâtre; feuille-morte (m) inv.

Russia ['rʌʃə]. Pr.n. La Russie. **White R.,** la Russie blanche, la Biélorussie. **R. leather,** cuir m de Russie.

Russian ['rʌʃən]. **1.** s. (a) Russe mf. (b) Ling: Le russe. **2.** a. De Russie; russe.

Russianize ['rʌʃənaiz], v.tr. Russifier.

Russophil(e) ['rʌsoufail], a. & s. Russophile (mf).

Russophobe ['rʌsoufoub], a. & s. Russophobe (mf).

russula ['rʌsjulə], s. Fung: Russule f.

rust¹ [rʌst], s. **1.** Rouille f. **To rub the r. off,** (i) enlever la rouille; (ii) F: se remettre au courant (d'une science, etc.); se dérouiller. **2.** Agr: Rouille. **Black r.,** charbon m des céréales; nielle f. **'rust-cement,** s. Mastic m de fonte. **'rust-coloured,** a. Roux, rousse. **'rust-preventer, -preventive,** s. Antirouille m inv. **'rust-proof,** a. Inoxydable.

rust². **1.** v.i. Se rouiller. **To allow one's knowledge t[o] r.,** laisser rouiller ses connaissances. **2.** v.tr. Rouille[r]. **Idleness rusts the mind,** l'oisiveté rouille l'espri[t]. **rust in,** v.i. (Of screw) Se rouiller dans son trou (of pers.) s'incruster.

rustic ['rʌstik]. **1.** a. Rustique; agreste; paysar[d]. **R. seat,** banc rustique. **2.** s. (a) Paysan, -anne[;] campagnard, -arde. (b) Rustaud, -aude; rust[aud] m.

rusticate ['rʌstikeit]. **1.** v.i. Habiter la campagne[,] être en villégiature. **2.** v.tr. Sch: Renvoyer tem[-]porairement (un étudiant).

rustication [,rʌsti'keiʃ(ə)n], s. **1.** Vie f à la campagne[.] **2.** Sch: Renvoi m temporaire (d'un étudiant).

rusticity [rʌs'tisiti], s. Rusticité f.

rustiness ['rʌstinis], s. Rouillure f; rouille f.

rustle¹ ['rʌsl], s. **1.** Bruissement m; frou-frou m (de l[a] soie); froissement m (de papiers); friselis m[,] susurrement m (de feuilles). **2.** U.S: = HUSTLE¹ 2.

rustle². **1.** v.i. (a) (Of leaves, paper) Produire u[n] bruissement; (of leaves, wind) bruire; (of garment[s]) faire frou-frou. **I heard a deer r. through the bracke[n,]** j'entendis un cerf froisser les fougères. (b) U.S: [=] HUSTLE² 2. **2.** v.tr. Faire bruire (les feuilles, de[s] papiers); faire froufrouter (la soie); froisser (l[e] papier). **3.** v.tr. U.S: Voler (du bétail, des chevaux)[.] **rustle up,** v.tr. esp: U.S: F: **She can always r. u[p] a meal,** elle sait toujours se débrouiller pour avoir d[e] quoi manger. **rustling¹,** a. Bruissant; (jupon[)] froufroutant. **rustling²,** s. **1.** = RUSTLE¹. **2.** U.S[:] Vol m de bétail.

rustler ['rʌslər], s. U.S: **1.** Voleur m de bétail. **2.** [=] HUSTLER 2.

rustless ['rʌstlis], a. **1.** Sans rouille. **2.** Inoxydable.

rusty¹ ['rʌsti], a. **1.** (a) Rouillé. **To get r.,** se rouiller[.] **My French is r.,** mon français se rouille, est rouillé[.] (b) (Of voice) Enroué, rauque, éraillé. **2.** Couleur d[e] rouille; rouilleux, -euse. **A r. black coat,** un habi[t] d'un noir rouilleux. **3.** Agr: (Blé) rouillé. **-ily,** adv[.] **The door moved r. on its hinges,** la porte grinça su[r] ses gonds rouillés.

rusty², a. (Cheval) rétif, quinteux. F: O: (Of pers[.]) **To turn r.,** to cut up r., se rebiffer; regimber.

rut¹ [rʌt], s. Ornière f. **To settle, sink, into a r.,** (o[f] pers.), s'encroûter; (of the mind) devenir routinier[.] **To move in a r.,** être routinier. **To get out of the r.[,]** sortir de l'ornière; se désencroûter.

rut², v.tr. (rutted) Sillonner (un chemin) d'ornières.

rut³, s. (Of stags, etc.) Rut m.

rut⁴, v.i. (rutted) Être en rut. **Rutting season,** saison [f] du rut.

rutabaga [rutə'bɑːgə], s. Esp. U.S: Agr: Rutabag[a] m, chou-navet m, pl. choux-navets.

ruth [ruːθ], s. A: Pitié f; compassion f.

ruthless ['ruːθlis], a. Impitoyable; sans pitié, san[s] merci; (of truth, act) brutal, -aux. **-ly,** adv. San[s] pitié, sans merci.

ruthlessness ['ruːθlisnis], s. Nature f impitoyable.

rutty ['rʌti], a. (Chemin) coupé d'ornières.

rye [rai], s. Seigle m. U.S: F: **Mine's a r.!** je prendra[i] un whisky. **'rye-bread,** s. Pain m de seigle.

rye-grass ['raigrɑːs], s. Ivraie f vivace; ray-grass m.

S, s [es], s. **1.** (La lettre) S, s m or f. Tp: S for Sammie, S comme Suzanne. Typ: Long s., s allongée. **2.** (Courbe f en) S. S-hook, esse f. S curve, courbure double. S-shaped wall-anchor, fer en S.

's¹. Signe du possessif singulier, pl. s'. The boy's father, le père du garçon. The boys' father, le père des garçons.

's². **1.** abbr. of **is.** See BE. **2.** abbr. of **has.** See HAVE. **3.** abbr. of **us.** See WE.

Sabbatarian [ˌsæbəˈtɛəriən], s. Observateur, -trice, du dimanche, Jew: du sabbat.

Sabbath [ˈsæbəθ], s. **1.** (a) Jew: B.Hist: Sabbat m. (b) Ecc: Dimanche m. To keep, break, the S., observer, violer, le sabbat, le dimanche. **2.** A: Witches' s., sabbat. 'Sabbath 'day, s. = SABBATH 1. S. day's journey, chemin m du sabbat; voyage très court. F: It's a S. day's journey from here to the station, il y a un bon bout de chemin (à pied) d'ici à la gare.

sabbatic(al) [səˈbætik(ə)l], a. Jew.Rel: Sabbatique. S. year, (i) Jew.Rel: année sabbatique; (ii) année de congé (accordée à un professeur pour voyager).

sable¹ [ˈseibl], s. **1.** Z: (Martre f) zibeline f. **2.** S. (fur), zibeline. **3.** Art: S. (brush), pinceau m en poil de martre.

sable². **1.** Her: (a) a. Sable m. (b) a. (Écusson, etc.) de sable. **2.** Poet: a. Noir; (vêtement) de deuil.

sabot [ˈsæbou], s. **1.** Cost: Sabot m. **2.** Sabot (de pieu). Artil: Sabot (de projectile).

sabotage¹ [ˈsæbɑtɑːʒ], s. Sabotage m.

sabotage², v.tr. Saboter (l'outillage, un projet).

saboteur [ˌsæbəˈtəːr], s. Saboteur, -euse.

sabre [ˈseibər], s. Mil: Sabre m. S. cut, (i) coup m de sabre; (ii) (scar) balafre f. 'sabre-rattler, s. O: Traîneur m de sabre. 'sabre-rattling, s. O: Rodomontades fpl; menaces fpl de guerre.

sac [sæk], s. Nat.Hist: Sac m, poche f.

saccharin(e) [ˈsækərin, -riːn], s. Saccharine f.

sacerdotal [ˌsæsəˈdout(ə)l], a. Sacerdotal, -aux.

sachet [ˈsæʃei], s. Toil: Sachet m. Scent s., sachet à parfums.

sack¹ [sæk], s. **1.** (Grand) sac. S. of coal, sac de charbon. To put (sth.) into sacks, ensacher (qch.). **2.** F: To give s.o. the s., congédier (un employé, etc.); F: donner son paquet à qn; débarquer, balancer, saquer, qn; mettre qn à pied. To get the s., recevoir son congé; F: se faire saquer. 'sack-race, s. Sp: Course f en sac.

sack², v.tr. **1.** Ensacher, mettre en sac (du charbon, etc.). **2.** F: To s. s.o., congédier qn. **sacking¹**, s. **1.** Mise f en sac; ensachage m (de blé, etc.). **2.** F: Congédiement m. **3.** = SACKCLOTH 1.

sack³, s. Sac m, pillage m (d'une ville, etc.).

sack⁴, v.tr. Saccager, mettre à sac, mettre au pillage. **sacking²**, s. Sac m (d'une ville, etc.).

sack⁵, s. A: (Canary) s., vin m des Canaries. Sherry s., vin de Xérès.

sackcloth [ˈsækklɔθ], s. **1.** Tex: Toile f à sacs; grosse toile; toile d'emballage. **2.** B: etc: Sac m; bure f (au sens figuré). S. and ashes, le sac et la cendre.

sackful [ˈsækful], s. Sachée f, plein sac.

sacral [ˈseikrəl], a. Anat: Sacré; du sacrum.

sacrament [ˈsækrəmənt], s. Ecc: Sacrement m. The Holy S., the Blessed S., le saint Sacrement (de l'autel); le Très Saint Sacrement. To receive, partake of, the s., s'approcher des sacrements; communier. S. of baptism, of marriage, le sacrement du baptême, du mariage.

sacramental [ˌsækrəˈmentl], a. (a) Sacramentel, -elle. (b) S. obligation, obligation sous serment; vœu m.

sacrarium, pl. -ia [səˈkrɛəriəm, -iə], s. **1.** Rom. Ant: Sacrarium m. **2.** Ecc: (a) Sanctuaire m (d'une église). (b) R.C.Ch: Piscine f.

sacred [ˈseikrid], a. **1.** (a) Sacré. (b) S. to the memory of . . ., consacré à la mémoire de. . . . (c) S. cow, (i) vache sacrée (des Hindous); (ii) F: chose sacro-sainte. **2.** (a) Ecc: Sacré, saint. S. history, l'Histoire sainte. S. books, (i) livres d'Église; (ii) livres saints. Convent of the S. Heart, couvent du Sacré-Cœur. The s. orders, les ordres majeurs. (b) S. music, musique religieuse. **3.** (Of promise, etc.) Sacré, inviolable. S. duty, devoir sacré. His S. Majesty, la personne sacrée du Souverain. Nothing was s. to him, il ne respectait rien.

sacredness [ˈseikridnis], s. **1.** Caractère sacré (d'un lieu). **2.** Inviolabilité f (d'un serment).

sacrifice¹ [ˈsækrifais], s. **1.** (a) Sacrifice m, immolation f (d'une victime). To offer (up) sth. as a s., offrir qch. en sacrifice (to, à). To win a battle at a great s. of life, remporter la victoire au prix de grands sacrifices. (b) Victime f; offrande f. **2.** Theol: Sacrifice (du Christ). The S. of the Mass, le saint sacrifice, le sacrifice de la messe. **3.** (a) Sacrifice, abnégation f (de qch.); renoncement m (à qch.). To make sacrifices to attain one's end, faire de grands sacrifices pour arriver à ses fins. He succeeded at the s. of his health, il a réussi en sacrifiant sa santé. S.a. SELF-SACRIFICE. (b) Com: Mévente f; vente f à perte. To sell sth. at a s., vendre qch. à perte.

sacrifice², v.tr. **1.** Sacrifier, immoler, offrir en sacrifice (une victime). Abs. To s. to idols, offrir des sacrifices aux idoles. **2.** (a) Sacrifier, renoncer à (qch.); faire abnégation de (ses intérêts, etc.). To s. oneself, se sacrifier (for, pour). (b) Com: Sacrifier, vendre à perte (des marchandises).

sacrificial [sækriˈfiʃ(ə)l], a. **1.** Sacrificatoire. **2.** Com: (Vente f) à perte; (prix m) au-dessous du prix coûtant.

sacrilege [ˈsækrilidʒ], s. Sacrilège m.

sacrilegious [ˌsækriˈlidʒəs], a. Sacrilège. S. person, sacrilège mf. **-ly,** adv. D'une manière sacrilège.

sacristan [ˈsækristən], s. Ecc: Sacristain m.

sacristy [ˈsækristi], s. Ecc: Sacristie f.

sacrosanct [ˈsækrosæŋkt], a. Sacro-saint.

sacrum [ˈseikrəm], s. Anat: Sacrum m.

sad [sæd], a. (sadder) **1.** (a) Triste. To become s., s'attrister. To look s., avoir l'air triste, malheureux, affligé, mélancolique. To make s.o. s., attrister, contrister, qn. To be s. at heart, avoir le cœur gros. Lit: In s. earnest, bien sérieusement. A sadder and a wiser man, (i) un homme instruit par le malheur; (ii) un homme désillusionné. (b) (Of news, etc.) Affligeant; (of loss, etc.) cruel; (of place, etc.) morne, lugubre. He came to a s. end, il a fait une triste fin. **2.** A s. mistake, une erreur déplorable. Lit: To make s. work of . . ., s'acquitter peu brillamment de. . . . **-ly,** adv. **1.** Tristement, avec tristesse. **2.** Lit: Déplorablement. I was s. puzzled, j'étais cruellement embarrassé. **3.** O: Très; beaucoup. I need it s., j'en ai bien besoin, grand besoin. You are s. mistaken, vous vous trompez fort.

sadden [ˈsæd(ə)n], (a) v.tr. Attrister, affliger. (b) v.i. S'attrister.

saddle¹ [ˈsædl], s. **1.** (a) (i) Selle f (de cheval); (ii) sellette f (de cheval de trait). Hunting s., selle anglaise. To rise in the s., faire du trot enlevé. To vault into the s., sauter en selle. To be thrown out of the s., vider les arçons. You are putting the s. on the wrong horse, votre accusation porte à faux. (b) Selle (de bicyclette). **2.** Col m (de montagne). **3.** Cu: Selle (de mouton); râble m (de lièvre). **4.** Tchn: Reposoir m (d'un cric, etc.); chevalet m (de chaudière). **5.** Nau: Croissant m, collier m (de gui, de vergue). 'saddle-backed, a. (Toit, etc.) ensellé. 'saddle-bag, s. **1.** Cy: etc: Sacoche f (de selle). **2.** Furn: Moquette f (d'ameublement). 'saddle-bow, s. Harn: Pommeau m, arçon m (de devant). 'saddle-cloth, s. Housse f de cheval; couverture f, tapis m, de selle. 'saddle-horse, s. Cheval m de selle; monture f. 'saddle-room, s. Sellerie f.

saddle², *v.tr.* (*a*) Seller (un cheval); embâter (une bête de somme). (*b*) *F:* To s. s.o. with sth., to s. sth. on s.o., charger, encombrer, qn de qch.; mettre qch. sur le dos de qn. **She is saddled with five children,** elle a cinq enfants sur le dos, sur les bras. **Saddled with a tax,** grevé d'un impôt.

saddleback ['sædlbæk]. **1.** *s.* (*a*) Toit *m* ensellé. (*b*) (*Of hill*) Ensellement *m*. (*c*) *Geol:* Pli anticlinal. **2.** *a.* = SADDLE-BACKED.

saddler ['sædlər], *s.* Sellier *m*; bourrelier *m*; harnacheur *m*.

saddlery ['sædləri], *s.* **1.** (*Trade*) Sellerie *f*, bourrellerie *f*. **2.** = SADDLE-ROOM. **3.** *Coll.* Harnachement *m* (de selle); sellerie.

Sadducee ['sædjusi:], *s.* Saducéen, -enne.

sadism ['seidizm], *s.* Sadisme *m*.

sadist ['seidist], *s.* Sadique *mf*.

sadistic [sə'distik], *a.* Sadique.

sadness ['sædnis], *s.* Tristesse *f*, mélancolie *f*.

safari [sə'fɑːri], *s.* (*In Africa*) Safari *m*, expédition *f* de chasse. **On s.,** en safari.

safe¹ [seif], *s.* **1.** Coffre-fort *m*, *pl.* coffres-forts. **S. deposit,** dépôt *m* en coffre-fort. **S. Deposit Company,** service *m* de coffres-forts. **2. Meat-s.,** garde-manger *m inv.* **3. Rifle (set) at s.,** carabine au cran de sûreté. **'safe-breaker,** *s.* Perceur *m* de coffres-forts.

safe², *a.* **1.** (*a*) En sûreté; à l'abri. **S. from sth.,** à l'abri de, en sûreté contre, qch. **To be s. from recognition,** ne pas risquer d'être reconnu. **S. (and sound),** (sain et) sauf. (*b*) **We got s. into port,** nous sommes arrivés à bon port. **To come s. home again,** rentrer sans accident. **With a s. conscience,** en toute sûreté de conscience. **His honour is s.,** son honneur est à couvert, est sauf. **2.** (*a*) Sans danger; sûr. **S. retreat,** asile assuré, sûr. **To put s.o., sth., in a s. place,** mettre qn, qch., en lieu sûr. **S. beach, s. bathing,** plage sûre. *Nau:* **S. anchorage,** bon mouillage; mouillage sain. *S.a.* CUSTODY 1. (*b*) (*Of bridge, etc.*) Solide. **Is it s. to leave him alone?** est-ce qu'il n'y a pas de danger à le laisser seul? *Tchn:* **S. load,** charge admissible; charge de sécurité. (*c*) **To be on the s. side,** être du bon côté. **In order to be on the s. side,** pour plus de sûreté. **The safest course would be to . . .,** le plus sûr serait de. . . . **To play a s. game,** avoir un jeu sûr, serré, jouer serré. **It is s. to say that . . .,** on peut dire à coup sûr que. . . . **3.** (*Of critic, politician*) Prudent, circonspect. **-ly,** *adv.* **1.** Sans accident, sans dommage. **To arrive s.,** arriver sain et sauf, sans accident; (*of ship, etc.*) arriver à bon port. **To put sth. s. away,** mettre qch. en lieu sûr. **2.** Sûrement, sans danger, sans risque. **I can s. say that . . .,** je puis dire à coup sûr que. . . . **safe(-)conduct,** *s.* Sauf-conduit *m, pl.* sauf-conduits. **safe(-)keeping,** *s.* Bonne garde. **To be in s.-k.,** être sous bonne garde, en sûreté.

safeguard¹ ['seifgɑːd], *s.* **1.** *A:* Sauvegarde *f*, sauf-conduit *m*. **2.** Sauvegarde, garantie *f* (**against,** contre).

safeguard², *v.tr.* Sauvegarder, protéger; mettre (ses intérêts) à couvert. *Pol.Ec:* **To s. an industry,** protéger une industrie.

safeness ['seifnis], *s.* **1. A feeling of s.,** un sentiment de sécurité *f*, de sûreté *f*. **2.** Solidité *f* (d'un pont). **3.** Sûreté (d'un placement, etc.).

safety ['seifti], *s.* Sûreté *f*, sécurité *f*; salut *m*. **To seek s. in flight,** chercher son salut dans la fuite. **For safety's sake,** pour plus de sûreté. **In a place of s.,** en lieu sûr. **Road s.,** sécurité de la route. **S. first!** soyez prudents! la sécurité d'abord! **S. measures,** mesures de sécurité. **To play for s.,** jouer au plus sûr. *Med:* **S. test,** essai d'innocuité. *Sm.a:* **To put one's rifle at s.,** mettre son fusil au cran de sûreté. *Ind:* **S. factor,** coefficient *m* de sécurité. **S. device,** dispositif de sécurité. *S.a.* MATCH³ 1, RAZOR. **'safety-belt,** *s.* (*a*) *Av:* Ceinture *f* de fixation. (*b*) *Aut:* Ceinture de sécurité. **'safety-catch,** *s.* **1.** Cran *m* d'arrêt. *Aut:* **Handle with a s.-c.,** poignée à condamnation. **2.** *Sm.a:* Cran de sûreté. **'safety-fuse,** *s.* *Mil: Min: etc:* Mèche lente, cordeau *m* Bickford. **'safety-glass,** *s. Aut: etc:* Verre *m* de sécurité. **'safety-net,** *s.* Filet *m.* **'safety-pin,** *s.* Épingle anglaise; épingle de nourrice, de sûreté. **'safety-valve,** *s. Mch:* Soupape *f* de sûreté.

saffron ['sæfrən], *s. Cu: Pharm:* **1.** Safran *m.* **2.** *a. & s.* (Jaune) safran *inv.*

sag¹ [sæg], *s.* **1.** (*a*) Affaissement *m*, fléchissement *m* (d'un toit). (*b*) *Com:* Baisse *f* (des valeurs, etc.). **2.** Flèche *f*, ventre *m* (d'un cordage).

sag², *v.i.* (**sagged**) **1.** (*a*) (*Of roof, etc.*) S'affaisser, fléchir, arquer (sous un poids, etc.). (*b*) (*Of gate, etc.*) Pencher d'un côté; s'incliner; gauchir. (*c*) (*Of cheeks, breasts, etc.*) Pendre. (*d*) (*Of cable*) Se relâcher, se détendre; (*of rope, beam, etc.*) fléchir au milieu; faire ventre; faire guirlande; faire flèche. **2. Prices are sagging,** les prix fléchissent. **sagging,** *a.* **1.** (*a*) (*Of roof, etc.*) Affaissé, fléchi. (*b*) (*Of gate, etc.*) Incliné; penché d'un côté; déjeté. (*c*) (*Of cheek, breast, hem of garment*) Flasque, tombant, pendant. (*d*) (*Of line*) Courbe. **2.** *Fin:* Creux, *m* creux. **S. market,** marché creux, en baisse.

saga ['sɑːgə], *s. Lit:* Saga *f.* **S. novel,** roman cycle, roman fleuve.

sagacious [sə'geiʃəs], *a.* Sagace, avisé; perspicace; entendu; (*of dog*) intelligent; (*of action*) plein de sagesse. **-ly,** *adv.* Avec sagacité.

sagaciousness [sə'geiʃəsnis], **sagacity** [sə'gæsiti], *s.* Sagacité *f*; intelligence *f* (d'un animal); sagesse *f* (d'une remarque).

sage¹ [seidʒ]. **1.** *a. Lit:* Sage, prudent. **2.** *s.* Philosophe *m*, sage *m.* **The Seven Sages,** les sept Sages. **-ly,** *adv.* (*a*) *Lit:* Sagement, prudemment. (*b*) D'un ton doctoral.

sage², *s. Bot: Cu:* Sauge *f. a. & s.* **S. green,** vert cendré *inv.*

sago ['seigou], *s. Cu:* Sagou *m.* **'sago-palm,** *s.* Sagoutier *m.*

Sahara (the) [ðəsə'hɑːrə]. *Pr.n.* Le Sahara.

Saharan [sə'hɑːrən], *a. Geog:* Saharien, -enne.

said. *See* SAY².

sail¹ [seil], *s.* **1.** *Nau:* (*a*) Voile *f.* **To hoist, lower, a s.,** hisser, amener, une voile. **To take in a s.,** carguer une voile. **To carry all sails, to have all sails set,** porter tout dessus. *S.a.* WIND¹ 1. (*b*) *Coll.* Voile(s), voilure *f*, toile *f.* **To make more s.,** augmenter de toile. **Ship under full s.,** navire toutes voiles dehors. **Vessel under s.,** navire marchant à la voile. **To get under s.,** appareiller (à la voile). **To set s.,** mettre à la voile; prendre la mer; appareiller. **To strike s.,** amener (les voiles). (*c*) (*Ship*) **S. ho!** navire en vue! *Coll. Hist:* **A fleet of twenty s.,** une flotte de vingt voiles. **2.** Aile *f*, volant *m* (de moulin). **'sail-arm,** *s.* Châssis *m* de l'aile (d'un moulin à vent). **'sail-loft,** *s.* Voilerie *f.* **'sail-maker,** *s.* Voilier *m.* **sail(-)plane,** *s. Av:* Planeur *m.*

sail², *s.* **1.** Excursion *f* en bateau à voiles; sortie *f* à la voile. **To go for a s.,** faire une promenade à la voile, en bateau. **2.** Voyage *m* sur mer. **It is a week's s. from Hull,** c'est à huit jours de traversée de Hull.

sail³. **1.** *v.i.* (*a*) (i) (*Of sailing-ship*) Aller à la voile; faire de la voile; (ii) (*of sailing-ship or steamer*) naviguer, faire route. **To s. up the coast,** remonter la côte. **To s. round a cape,** contourner un promontoire. **To s. into harbour,** entrer dans le port. **To s. to, for, America,** faire route sur l'Amérique. **To s. (at) ten knots,** filer dix nœuds. *S.a.* WIND¹ 1. (*b*) Partir, appareiller; prendre la mer. **To be about to s.,** être en partance. **The boat sails at 10 o'clock,** le bateau part à 10 heures. **2.** *v.tr. & ind.tr.* **To s. (on, over) the seas,** parcourir les mers; naviguer les mers. **3.** *v.i.* Planer (dans l'air, etc.). **The clouds sailing by,** les nuages voguant dans le ciel. **She sailed into the room,** elle fit une entrée pleine de dignité. **4.** *v.tr.* Manœuvrer (un voilier); conduire (un navire). **sailing¹**, *a.* **1.** Fleet s., flotte en mer. **2. S. ship,** (navire) voilier *m*; bâtiment *m* à voiles. **S. boat,** canot *m* à voiles. **3. Fast s. ship,** navire de bonne marche. **'sailing-barge,** *s.* Chaland *m* à voiles; gabare *f.* **'sailing-craft,** *s.* **1.** Petit bateau à voiles. **2.** *Coll.* Petits bateaux à voiles. **sailing²,** *s.* **1.** (*a*) Navigation *f.* **Plane s.,** navigation plane, loxodromique. **It's (all) plain s.,** cela va tout seul. (*b*) Marche *f*, allure *f* (d'un navire). **Fast s.,** bonne marche. *Navy:* **Order of s.,** ordre de marche. **2.** Départ *m*, appareillage *m.* **Port of s.,** port de départ.

sailcloth ['seilklɔθ], *s.* Toile *f* (à voile(s)); canevas *m.*

sailer ['seilər], s. Nau: 1. (Of sailing-ship) Voilier m. Good s., bad s., bâtiment bon, mauvais, voilier. 2. (Of any ship) Fast s., slow s., (navire) bon, mauvais, marcheur.

sailor ['seilər], s. (a) Marin m (officier ou matelot). Sailors' home, maison f, foyer m, du marin. (b) To be a bad s., être sujet au mal de mer. To be a good s., avoir le pied marin. **'sailor 'hat**, s. Cost: 1. Canotier m (pour femmes). 2. A: Jean-Bart m en paille (de petit garçon). **'sailor-'suit**, s. Costume marin (d'enfant).

sainfoin ['seinfoin], s. Sainfoin m.

saint [seint]. 1. (a) s. Saint, -e. **Saint's day**, fête f de saint. **All Saints' (Day)**, la Toussaint. **To try the patience of a s.**, lasser la patience d'un saint. (b) [s(ə)nt] Attrib.a. (abbr. St or S.) **S. Chrysostom**, saint Chrysostome. **St Peter's**, (l'église f) Saint-Pierre. 2. s. **The Communion of Saints**, la Communion des Saints. **Saint 'Bernard**, s. (Chien m) saint-bernard inv. **Saint He'lena** [he'li:nə]. Pr.n. Geog: Sainte-Hélène f. **Saint 'Lawrence**. Pr.n. Geog: Le (fleuve) Saint-Laurent. **The St L. Seaway**, La voie maritime du Saint-Laurent.

saintliness ['seintlinis], s. Sainteté f.

saintly ['seintli], a. (De) saint.

saith. See SAY².

sake¹ [seik], s. Used only in the phr. **For the s. of s.o., of sth. To do sth. for the s. of s.o., for s.o.'s s.**, faire qch. dans l'intérêt de qn, par égard pour qn, en considération de qn, à cause de qn. **I forgive you for her s.**, je vous pardonne à cause d'elle. **Do it for the s. of your family**, faites-le pour (l'amour de) votre famille. **Do it for my s.**, faites-le pour moi, pour me faire plaisir. **For God's s., for goodness(') s.**, pour l'amour de Dieu. **For the s. of example**, pour l'exemple. **For old times' s.**, en souvenir du passé. **For old acquaintance s.**, en souvenir de notre vieille amitié. **For conscience s.**, par acquit de conscience. **To talk for talking's s.**, parler pour le plaisir de parler. **Art for art's s.**, l'art pour l'art.

sake² ['sɑ:ki], s. Saké m, saki m.

sal [sæl], s. A.Ch: Sel m. **sal-am'moniac**, s. Sel ammoniac. **sal volatile** [sælvə'lætili], s. Sels volatils anglais; F: sels (à respirer).

salaam¹ [sə'lɑ:m], s. Salamalec m; grand salut.

salaam², v.tr. & i. Faire des salamalecs, un grand salut (à qn).

salacious [sə'leiʃəs], a. Lubrique, ordurier, -ière.

salaciousness [sə'leiʃəsnis], **salacity** [sə'læsiti], s. Salacité f, lubricité f.

salad ['sæləd], s. Salade f. **Mixed s.**, salade panachée. **Fruit s.**, macédoine f de fruits. **'salad-bowl**, s. Saladier m. **'salad 'cream**, s. Com: Sauce f genre mayonnaise. **'salad days**, s.pl. Années f de jeunesse, d'inexpérience. **'salad-'dressing**, s. (i) Vinaigrette f; (ii) Com: sauce f genre mayonnaise. **'salad-'oil**, s. Huile f comestible, de table. **'salad-shaker**, s. Panier m à salade.

Salamanca [ˌsæləˈmæŋkə]. Pr.n. Geog: Salamanque.

salamander ['sæləmændər], s. 1. Rept: Salamandre f. 2. Cu: Couvercle m à braiser; four m de campagne. 3. Tisonnier ardent; allumoir m.

salami [sə'lɑ:mi], s. Cu: Salami m.

salaried ['sælərid], a. 1. (Personnel) aux appointements. **High-s. officials**, fonctionnaires à forts appointements. 2. (Of post) Rétribué.

salary¹ ['sæləri], s. Traitement m, appointements mpl. **S. of a member of Parliament**, indemnité f parlementaire. **To receive a s.**, être aux appointements.

sale [seil], s. 1. Vente f. (a) Débit m, mise f en vente (de marchandises). **Cash s.**, vente au comptant. **Credit s., hire-purchase s.**, vente à crédit. **S. value**, valeur marchande. **Goods that command a sure s.**, marchandises de placement sûr. **House for s.**, maison à vendre. **To exhibit sth. for s.**, mettre qch. en vente. **On s.**, en vente. **There's a great deal of sales resistance**, la clientèle boude. Ind: **The sales department**, le service commercial, le service ventes. **Sales-book**, livre de(s) vente(s); facturier m. **Sales promotion**, campagne f de vente. (b) **S. by auction**, vente à l'enchère, aux enchères; vente à la criée. Jur: **Compulsory s.**, adjudication forcée. (c) **S. of work**, vente de charité. 2. Com: **The sales are on**,

c'est le moment des soldes m. **White s.**, exposition f de blanc. **S. goods**, soldes. **S. price**, (i) prix de vente, (ii) prix de solde. **'sale-goer**, s. 1. Habitué, -ée, amateur m, de soldes. 2. **He's a keen s.-g.**, il fréquente les salles de vente; il est grand amateur des ventes aux enchères. **'sale-room**, s. Salle f de(s) vente(s). **'sales-talk**, s. Boniment m.

saleable ['seiləbl], a. (Of goods, etc.) Vendable; de vente facile, courante.

salesclerk ['seilzklɔ:k], s. U.S: Vendeur, -euse.

salesgirl ['seilzgə:l], s.f. Vendeuse.

salesman, pl. **-men** ['seilzmən], s.m. 1. Vendeur; employé à la vente. 2. Représentant m de commerce. **Travelling s.**, voyageur de commerce; commis voyageur. **Door-to-door s.**, placier m.

salesmanship ['seilzmənʃip], s. L'art m de vendre.

saleswoman, pl. **-women** ['seilzwumən, -wimin], s.f. Vendeuse.

Salic ['seilik, sæ-], a. Hist: **The S. law**, la loi salique.

salicin ['sælisin], s. Ch: Salicine f.

salicylate [sæ'lisileit], s. Ch: Salicylate m.

salicylic [ˌsæli'silik], a. Ch: (Acide) salicylique.

salient ['seiliənt], a. 1. (a) (Of angle, etc.) Saillant; en saillie. (b) s. Mil: Saillant m. 2. (Trait) saillant, frappant.

saliferous [sə'lifərəs], a. Salifère, salicole.

saline ['seilain, sə'lain]. 1. a. (a) Salin, salé. (b) (Of medicine, etc.) Salin. **Normal s. solution**, solution f physiologique. 2. s. Purgatif salin; sel purgatif. 3. s. Marais salant; salin m; saline f.

salinity [sə'liniti], s. Salinité f.

saliva [sə'laivə], s. Salive f.

salivary [sə'laivəri, 'sæliv(ə)ri], a. Salivaire.

salivate ['sæliveit], v.i. Saliver.

sallow¹ ['sælou], s. Bot: Saule m.

sallow², a. (Teint) jaune, jaunâtre, olivâtre; occ. (teint) plombé, brouillé.

sallowness ['sælounis], s. Ton m jaunâtre (du teint).

sally¹ ['sæli], s. 1. Mil: Sortie f (des assiégés). 2. O: Excursion f, sortie. 3. (a) Saillie f, élan m (d'activité, etc.). (b) **S.** (of wit), saillie (d'esprit); boutade f; trait m d'esprit.

sally², v.i. 1. Mil: **To s. (out)**, faire une sortie. 2. O: **To s. forth**, se mettre en route; partir en promenade.

Sally³. Pr.n.f. (Dim. of Sarah) Sarah. S.a. AUNT 2. **Sally Lunn**, s. Cu: Petit pain au lait (qui se mange en rôtie beurrée).

salmi ['sælmi], s. Cu: Salmis m.

salmon ['sæmən]. 1. s. Ich: (Usu. inv.) Saumon m. **Young s.**, saumoneau m. Fish: **S. ladder, s. leap**, échelle f à saumon(s). 2. a. & s. (Colour) Saumon inv. **'salmon-'trout**, s. Ich: Truite saumonée.

salon ['sælɔ̃], s. 1. (a) Salon m. (b) Réception f (de notabilités). 2. (a) Salon d'exposition (d'une modiste, etc.). **Beauty s.**, institut m de beauté. (b) Art: **The S.**, le Salon.

saloon [sə'lu:n], s. 1. (a) Salle f, salon m. **Billiard s.**, salle de billard. **Hairdressing s.**, salon de coiffure. (b) U.S: Bar m, café m, débit m de boisson. **S. keeper**, débitant m de boissons. 2. Nau: Salon (de paquebot); cabine f. **S. passenger**, voyageur de première (classe). **S. deck**, pont des premières. 3. (a) Rail: **S. (-coach, -carriage)**, voiture-salon f, pl. voitures-salons, wagon-salon m, pl. wagons-salons. (b) Aut: **S. (car)**, conduite intérieure, berline f. **Two-door s.**, coach m. **sa'loon-bar**, s. = Bar m.

salsify ['sælsifi], s. Bot: Cu: Salsifis m.

salt¹ [sɔ:lt]. I. s. 1. (a) Cu: Sel (commun); Ch: chlorure m de sodium. **Rock s.**, sel gemme. **Kitchen s.**, sel de cuisine; sel gris; gros sel. **Table s.**, sel de table; sel blanc. **To eat s.o.'s s.**, (i) recevoir l'hospitalité de qn; (ii) être à la charge de qn. **To take a story with a grain, a pinch, of s.**, croire à une histoire avec quelques réserves; prendre l'histoire avec un grain de sel. **He is not worth his s.**, il ne vaut pas le pain qu'il mange. (b) A: = SALT-CELLAR. **To sit (at table) above, below, the s.**, être assis au haut bout, au bas bout, de la table. (c) F: **Old s.**, loup m de mer; vieux matelot; F: vieux bourlingueur. 2. (a) Ch: Sel. **Metal(lic) s.**, sel métallique. Com: **Spirit(s) of salts**, esprit m de sel; acide m chlorhydrique. (b) **Salt(s) of lemon**, sel d'oseille. S.a. EPSOM. II. **salt**, a. Salé. 1. (a) **S. water**, eau salée; eau de mer. **S. lake**, lac salé. **S. provisions**, vivres salés. *Lit:* **To weep s. tears**, pleurer à chaudes larmes. (b) (*Of food*) **Too s.**, trop salé. **2. S. plant**, plante marine, salicole. **3.** (*Of rocks, ground*) Salifère. **'salt-cellar**, s. **1.** Salière f (de table). **2.** *F:* **S.-cellars**, salières (derrière les clavicules). **'salt-free**, a. *Med:* **S.-f. diet**, régime déchloruré, sans sel. **'salt-lick**, s. *Husb:* Pain salé; salègre m. **'salt-marsh**, s. Marais salant. **'salt meadow**, s. Pré salé. **'salt-mine**, s. Mine f de sel. **'salt-pan**, s. Vase m de saunage. **'salt-pit**, s. Saline f; mine f de sel. **'salt-shaker**, s. Salière f, saupoudroir m. **'salt-spoon**, s. Cuiller f à sel; pelle f à sel. **'salt-tax**, s. *Hist:* La gabelle. **'salt-water**, attrib.a. **S.-w. fish**, poisson de mer. **'salt-works**, s. (a) Saunerie f. (b) Raffinerie f de sel.

salt², v.tr. **1.** (a) **To s. (down) meat, butter**, saler la viande, le beurre. (b) Saupoudrer (qch.) de sel. (c) Saler (un mets). **2.** *Vet:* Immuniser (un cheval). **3.** (a) *Com:* *F:* Cuisiner, truquer (les livres de comptes). (b) *F:* **To s. the bill**, saler l'addition. (c) *Min:* **To s. a mine**, saler une mine (d'or, etc.); tapisser le front d'une mine. **salting**, s. **1.** Salaison f. **2.** *Vet:* Immunisation f. **3.** pl. **Saltings**, prés salés. **'salting-tub**, s. Saloir m.

salter ['sɔːltər], s. **1.** Fabricant m de sel; ouvrier m de saunerie; saunier m. **2.** = DRYSALTER. **3.** Saleur m (de poissons, etc.).

saltire ['sɔːltaiər], s. *Her:* Sautoir m; croix f de Saint-André. **In s.**, en sautoir.

saltish ['sɔːltiʃ], a. Légèrement salé; saumâtre.

saltless ['sɔːltlis], a. Sans sel; fade, insipide.

saltness ['sɔːltnis], s. Salure f, salinité f.

saltpetre ['sɔːltpiːtər], s. Salpêtre m.

salty ['sɔːlti], a. **1. S. deposit**, grumeaux mpl de sel. **2.** Salé, saumâtre.

salubrious [sə'luːbriəs], a. Salubre, sain.

salubrity [sə'luːbriti], s. Salubrité f.

saluki [sə'luːki], s. *Z:* Sloughi m; lévrier m arabe.

salutary ['sæljut(ə)ri], a. Salutaire (**to**, à).

salutation [ˌsælju'teiʃ(ə)n], s. Salutation f.

salute¹ [sə'luːt], s. (a) Salut m, salutation f. *Fenc:* **S. with foils**, salut des armes. (b) *Mil:* *Navy:* Salut. **To give a s.**, faire, exécuter, un salut. **To return, acknowledge, a s.**, rendre un salut. **To stand at (the) s.**, garder l'attitude du salut. **To beat a s.**, battre aux champs. **To take the s. (at a march past)**, passer les troupes en revue. (c) *Mil:* *Navy:* **To fire a s.**, tirer une salve. **To fire a s. of ten guns**, saluer de dix coups.

salute², v.tr. Saluer (qn). **1.** (a) **To s. s.o. emperor**, saluer qn empereur. (b) **To s. s.o. with a smile, a kiss**, accueillir, saluer, qn par un sourire, un baiser. **2. To s. (s.o.) with the hand, with the sword**, saluer (qn) de la main, de l'épée. *Abs.* *Mil:* **To s.**, faire le salut militaire. **To s. with twenty guns**, saluer de vingt coups.

salvable ['sælvəbl], a. *Ins:* Qui peut être sauvé; susceptible de sauvetage.

salvage¹ ['sælvidʒ], s. **1.** Indemnité f, droit m, prime f, de sauvetage. **2.** Sauvetage m (d'un navire, etc.); assistance f maritime. **S. company**, société f de sauvetage (de marchandises). *Nau:* **S. plant**, appareils mpl de renflouage. **S. vessel**, navire m de relevage. **3.** Objets sauvés (d'un naufrage, d'un incendie). **4.** Récupération f (de matières pour l'industrie). **'salvage-tug**, s. Remorqueur m de sauvetage.

salvage², v.tr. (a) *Nau:* *etc:* Sauver, relever (un navire); effectuer le sauvetage (des marchandises); sauver (des objets dans un incendie). (b) Récupérer (une voiture, etc.). **Salvaged material**, matériel sauvé, récupéré.

salvation [sæl'veiʃ(ə)n], s. Salut m. **To work out one's own s.**, travailler à son (propre) salut; faire son salut. **To find s.**, faire son salut. **To seek s. in sth.**, chercher son salut dans qch. *S.a.* ARMY 1.

salvationist [sæl'veiʃ(ə)nist], s. Salutiste mf.

salve¹ [sælv], s. *Pharm:* Onguent m, baume m, pommade f.

salve², v.tr. Adoucir, apaiser, calmer (les sentiments). **To do sth. to s. one's conscience**, faire qch. par acquit de conscience.

salve³ [sælv], v.tr. = SALVAGE².

salve⁴ ['sælvei], s. *Ecc:* Salvé m.

salver ['sælvər], s. Plateau m (d'argent, etc.).

salvia [salvjа], s. *Hort:* Sauge f.

salvo¹, pl. -oes ['sælvou, -ouz], s. (a) *Com:* *Jur:* Réserve f. (b) Restriction mentale; échappatoire f.

salvo², s. Salve f. **To fire a s.**, lancer, tirer, une salve. **S. of applause**, salve d'applaudissements.

salvor ['sælvər], s. (*In salvage operations*) Sauveteur m.

Sam [sæm]. *Pr.n.m.* Samuel. *F:* **Uncle S.**, l'oncle Sam; les États-Unis. *F:* *A:* **Upon my S.**, parole d'honneur. **Sam Browne**, s. *Mil:* **S. B. (belt)**, ceinturon m et baudrier m (d'officier).

Samaria [sə'mεəriə]. *Pr.n.* La Samarie. *B:* **The woman of S.**, la Samaritaine.

Samaritan [sə'mærit(ə)n], a. & s. Samaritain, -aine. *B:* **The good S.**, le bon Samaritain.

samba ['sæmbə], s. *Danc:* Samba f.

same [seim]. **1.** a. & pron. (Le, la) même, (les) mêmes. **To repeat the s. words twice**, répéter deux fois les mêmes mots. **At the s. time that this was happening**, au moment même où cela se passait. **He is (of) the s. age as myself**, il est du même âge que moi. **They are sold the s. day they come in**, ils sont vendus le jour même de leur arrivée. **All actuated by the s. impulse**, tous poussés par un même élan. **In the s. way**, de même. **(A) Happy New Year (to you)!—The s. to you!** je vous souhaite une bonne année!—A vous de même, à vous pareillement. **I got up and I did the s.**, il se leva et j'en fis autant, et je fis de même. (*Emphatic*) **The very s. thing, one and the s. thing**, une seule et même chose; tout à fait la même chose. **At the s. time**, (i) en même temps; (ii) à la fois. **It is the s. (thing) everywhere**, il en est de même partout. **It all amounts, comes, to the s. thing**, tout cela revient au même. **It's all the s.**, **it's just the s.**, c'est tout un; *F:* c'est tout comme. **It is all the s. to me**, ça m'est égal. **If it is all the s. to you**, si cela ne vous fait rien; si ça vous est égal. **It is the s. with me**, il en va de même pour moi. **You still look the s.**, vous n'avez pas changé. **It is much the s.**, c'est à peu près la même chose. **He is much about the s.**, il va à peu près de même. *F:* **(The) s. here!** et moi aussi! et moi de même! **2.** adv. **To think, feel, act, the s.**, penser, sentir, agir, de même. **All the s.**, malgré tout; quand même; tout de même. **All the s. it has cost us dear**, n'empêche que cela nous a coûté cher. **I feel anxious all the s.**, cela ne laisse pas (que) de m'inquiéter. **When I am away things go on just the s.**, quand je suis absent tout marche comme d'habitude.

sameness ['seimnis], s. **1.** (a) Identité f (**with**, avec). (b) Ressemblance f (**with**, à). **2.** Monotonie f, uniformité f (d'un paysage, etc.).

samovar ['sæmovɑːr], s. Samovar m.

Samoyed [sæ'mɔied]. **1.** a. & s. Samoyède (mf). **2.** s. Chien m samoyède.

sampan ['sæmpæn], s. *Nau:* Sampan m.

samphire ['sæmfaiər], s. *Bot:* **1.** C(h)ristemarine f. **2.** Salicorne f.

sample¹ ['sɑːmpl], s. Échantillon m; prise f, prélèvement m (de gaz, de minerai, de sang, etc.). **True, fair, s.**, échantillon représentatif. **S. survey**, enquête f par sondage. **S. card**, carte f d'échantillons. **Up to s.**, pareil, conforme, à l'échantillon. **To be up to s.**, répondre à l'échantillon. **To send sth. as a s.**, envoyer qch. à titre d'échantillon. **To buy sth. from s.**, acheter qch. d'après l'échantillon. **To give a s. of one's knowledge**, donner un exemple de son érudition.

sample², v.tr. **1.** (a) *Com:* Prendre des échantillons de, échantillonner (une étoffe, etc.); déguster (un vin). (b) Goûter (un mets); essayer (un nouveau restaurant). **2.** Donner un échantillon de (qch.). **sampling**, s. Prise f d'échantillons; échantillonnage m; action f de goûter (un mets).

sampler ['sɑːmplər], s. Modèle m de broderie.

samurai ['sæmurai], s.inv. *Japanese Hist:* Samouraï m.

sanatorium, pl. **-ia, -iums** [ˌsænə'tɔːriəm, -iə, iəmz], s. **1.** Sanatorium m, *F:* sana m. **Open-air s.**, aérium m. **2.** *Sch:* Infirmerie f.

sanctification [ˌsæŋ(k)tifi'keiʃ(ə)n], s. Sanctification f.

sanctify ['sæŋ(k)tifai], *v.tr.* Sanctifier; consacrer. **Custom sanctified by time,** coutume consacrée par le temps. **sanctified,** *a.* (*Of pers.*) Sanctifié, saint; (*of thg*) consacré.

sanctimonious [,sæŋ(k)ti'mounjəs], *a.* Papelard, cagot, béat; *F:* bondieusard. **His s. air,** son air confit (en dévotion). **-ly,** *adv.* D'une manière béate; d'un air de petit saint.

sanctimoniousness [,sæŋ(k)ti'mounjəsnis], *s.* Papelardise *f*, cagoterie *f*, *F:* bondieuserie *f*.

sanction[1] ['sæŋ(k)ʃ(ə)n], *s.* **1.** *Jur:* Vindicatory s., punitive s., sanction pénale. *Pol:* To impose sanctions on a country, prendre des sanctions contre un pays. **2.** Sanction *f*, consentement *m*, approbation *f*. **With the s. of...,** avec le consentement de... **S. of custom,** sanction de l'usage. **3.** *Hist:* Ordonnance *f*, décret *m*. **The Pragmatic S.,** la pragmatique sanction.

sanction[2], *v.tr.* Sanctionner. **1.** *Jur:* Attacher des sanctions (pénales) à (une loi, etc.). **2.** (*a*) *Jur:* Ratifier (une loi, etc.). (*b*) Approuver, autoriser (qch.). **Sanctioned by usage,** consacré par l'usage.

sanctity ['sæŋ(k)titi], *s.* **1.** Sainteté *f*. *S.a.* ODOUR 2. **2.** Caractère sacré (d'un terrain, d'un serment); inviolabilité *f* (de la vie privée).

sanctuary ['sæŋ(k)tjuəri], *s.* **1.** (*a*) Sanctuaire *m*, temple *m*. (*b*) (*Sacrarium*) Sanctuaire; saint *m* des saints. **2.** *Ecc. Jur:* Asile (sacré); refuge *m*. **Rights of s.,** droits *m* d'asile; immunité *f*. **To take s.,** chercher asile. **3.** Refuge (de bêtes sauvages, d'oiseaux). **Wild life s.,** réserve *f* zoologique.

sanctum ['sæŋktəm], *s.* **1.** Sanctuaire *m*, sacrarium *m*. **2.** Sanctuaire; cabinet privé.

sand[1] [sænd], *s.* **1.** (*a*) Sable *m*. **Scouring s., welding s., fine s.,** sablon *m*. **To scour with s.,** sablonner. **Choked up with s.,** ensablé. **To build on s.,** bâtir sur le sable. *U.S: F:* **Man with plenty of s.,** homme qui a du cran. (*b*) *sg. or pl.* Banc *m* de sable. (*c*) *Usu. pl.* Grain(s) *m(pl)* de sable. **As numerous as the sand(s) on the sea-shore,** aussi nombreux que les grains de sable de la mer. **2.** *pl.* **Sands,** plage *f*, grève *f*. *S.a.* QUICKSAND. **'sand-bar,** *s.* Somme (à l'embouchure d'un fleuve). **'sand-blast,** *s. Glassm: Metalw: etc:* Jet *m* de sable. **S.-b. (machine),** sableuse *f*. **'sand-box,** *s. Metall:* Caisse *f* à sable. *Golf:* Boîte *f* à sable. **'sand-casting,** *s. Metall:* Coulée *f* en sable. **'sand-dune,** *s.* Dune *f*. **'sand-eel,** *s. Ich:* Équille *f*, lançon *m*. **'sand-fly,** *s. Ent:* Simulie *f*; *F:* moustique *m*. **'sand-glass,** *s.* Sablier *m*. **'sand-hill,** *s.* Dune *f*. **'sand-martin,** *s.* Hirondelle *f* de rivage. **'sand-pit,** *s.* Sablière *f*, sablonnière *f*. **'sand-soap,** *s.* Savon minéral. **'sand-spout,** *s.* Trombe *f* de sable.

sand[2], *v.tr.* **1.** Sabler (une allée). **To s. the floor,** répandre du sable sur le plancher. **2.** (*a*) (*Of alluvium*) **To s. (up),** ensabler (l'embouchure d'un fleuve). (*b*) *v.i.* **To s. up,** s'ensabler. **3.** Sablonner; sabler; nettoyer avec du sable.

sandal ['sænd(ə)l], *s.* Sandale *f*. **Rope-soled sandals,** espadrilles *f*.

sandal(wood) ['sænd(ə)l(wud)], *s.* (Bois *m* de) santal *m*.

sandbag[1] ['sæn(d)bæg], *s.* **1.** *Fort:* Sac *m* à terre. **2.** Sac de lest. **3.** *F:* Assommoir *m*; boudin *m*.

sandbag[2], *v.tr.* **1.** Protéger (un bâtiment, etc.) avec des sacs de terre, de sable. **2.** *F:* Assommer (qn) (d'un coup de boudin sur la nuque).

sandbank ['sæn(d)bæŋk], *s.* Banc *m* de sable; (*in river*) allaise *f*, *Fr.C:* batture *f*.

sandboy ['sæn(d)bɔi], *s.m. Used in phr.* **As happy as a s.,** gai comme un pinson, heureux comme un poisson dans l'eau.

sandcastle ['sændkɑːsl], *s.* Château en sable.

sander ['sændər], *s. Mch:* Sableuse *f*; ponceuse *f*.

sandman ['sæn(d)mən], *s.* (*To children*) **The s. is coming,** le marchand de sable passe.

sandpaper[1] ['sæn(d)peipər], *s.* Papier *m* de verre, papier-émeri *m*.

sandpaper[2], *v.tr.* Frotter (qch.) au papier de verre; poncer, doucir (une surface).

sandpiper ['sæn(d)paipər], *s. Orn:* Bécasseau *m*, chevalier *m*.

sandshoe ['sæn(d)ʃu], *s.* (*a*) Sandale *f* en caoutchouc (pour la plage). (*b*) Espadrille *f*.

sandstone ['sæn(d)stoun], *s. Geol:* Grès *m*. **Red s.,** grès rouge. **Bunter S., New Red S.,** grès bigarré. **S. quarry,** grésière *f*. **S. wheel,** meule *f* en grès.

sandstorm ['sæn(d)stɔːm], *s.* Simoun *m*; tempête *f* de sable.

sandwich[1] ['sænwidʒ], *s.* Sandwich *m*. **Ham sandwiches,** sandwichs au jambon. **'sandwich-board,** *s.* Panneau *m* publicitaire (porté par un homme-sandwich). **'sandwich(-)counter,** *s.* Buffet *m*. **'sandwich(-)loaf,** *s.* = Pain *m* de mie. **'sandwich-man,** *pl.* **-men,** *s.m.* Homme-sandwich, *pl.* hommes-sandwichs.

sandwich[2], *v.tr.* Serrer, intercaler (between, entre).

sandy ['sændi], *a.* **1.** Sableux, -euse, sablonneux, -euse; (*of path*) sablé. **S. stretches of coast,** longues grèves de sable. **2.** (*Of hair*) Roux pâle *inv*; blond roux *inv*.

sane [sein], *a.* Sain d'esprit; sensé; (*of views, speech*) raisonnable, sensé. **To be s.,** avoir toute sa raison. **-ly,** *adv.* Raisonnablement.

sanforize ['sænfəraiz], *v.tr. Tex: R. t. m.* Rendre (un tissu) irrétrécissable; procéder à l'opération de Sanforisage (*R. t. m.*). **sanforizing,** *s.* Sanforisage *m* (*R. t. m.*).

sang. *See* SING.

sanguinary ['sæŋgwinəri], *a.* **1.** (*a*) (*Of battle*) Sanguinaire, sanglant. (*b*) (*Of law*) Barbare. (*c*) Altéré de sang. **2.** *P:* (*Euphemism for* BLOODY 2.) Sacré.

sanguine ['sæŋgwin]. **1.** *a.* (*a*) (*Of complexion*) D'un rouge sanguin; rubicond. (*b*) (*Of temperament*) Sanguin. (*c*) Confiant, optimiste, plein d'espérance. **To be of a s. disposition,** être porté à l'optimisme. **To be, feel, s. about the future,** avoir confiance en l'avenir. **2.** *s. Art:* Sanguine *f* (crayon ou dessin). **-ly,** *adv.* Avec espoir, avec optimisme.

sanguineness ['sæŋgwinnis], *s.* Confiance *f*, espoir *m*, optimisme *m*.

Sanhedrin ['sæn'hidrin, sænidrin], *s. Jew.Ant:* Sanhédrin *m*.

sanitarium [sæni'tɛəriəm], *s U.S:* Sanatorium *m*.

sanitary ['sænit(ə)ri], *a.* Hygiénique, sanitaire. **Insufficient s. arrangements,** manque *m* d'hygiène. **S. engineering,** (i) technique *f* sanitaire; (ii) constructions *fpl* et matériel sanitaires. *S.a.* TOWEL 2.

sanitation [sæni'teiʃ(ə)n], *s.* **1.** Hygiène *f*; salubrité publique; système *m* sanitaire. **To improve the s. of a town,** assainir une ville. **2.** Aménagements *m* sanitaires.

sanity ['sæniti], *s.* Santé *f* d'esprit; jugement sain; bon sens; rectitude *f* (du jugement).

sank. *See* SINK[2].

San Marino [sænmə'riːnou], *Pr.n. Geog:* (La république de) Saint-Marin.

sanserif [sæn'serif], *s. Typ:* Caractères *mpl* sans empattements.

Sanskrit ['sænskrit], *a. & s. Ling:* (Le) sanscrit.

Santa Claus ['sæntə'klɔːz]. *Pr.n.m.* Le Père Noël.

sap[1] [sæp], *s. Bot:* Sève *f*. **'sap-wood,** *s.* Aubier *m*. *Carp:* Aubour *m*.

sap[2], *s. Mil:* Sape *f*. **To drive a s.,** exécuter une sape.

sap[3], *v.* (**sapped**) **1.** *v.tr. & i. Mil:* Saper; approcher (d'un endroit) à la sape. **To s. forward,** pousser des approches. **2.** *v.tr.* Saper, miner (les fondements d'une doctrine, etc.). **Fever has sapped his strength,** la fièvre l'a miné.

sap[4], **saphead** ['sæphed], *s. F:* Niais, -aise, idiot, -ote, nigaud, -aude.

sapless ['sæplis], *a.* Sans sève; desséché; (*of pers.*) sans vigueur.

sapling ['sæpliŋ], *s.* **1.** Jeune arbre *m*; plant *m*, baliveau *m*. *For: S.* wood, gaulis *m*. **2.** (*a*) Jeune homme *m*; adolescent *m*. (*b*) Jeune lévrier *m*.

saponaceous [sæpə'neiʃəs], *a.* Saponacé, savonneux, -euse.

saponification [səpɔnifi'keiʃ(ə)n], *s. Ind: Ch:* Saponification *f*.

saponify [sə'pɔnifai]. **1.** *v.tr. Ind:* Saponifier (la graisse, etc.). **2.** *v.i.* Se saponifier.

sapper ['sæpər], *s. Mil:* Sapeur *m*. **Engineer s.,** sapeur du génie. *F:* **The Sappers,** le génie.

sapphic ['sæfik]. *Pros:* **1.** *a.* (Strophe) saphique. **2.** *s.pl.* **Sapphics,** vers *m* saphiques.

sapphire ['sæfaiər], *s. Miner:* Saphir *m*. **S. ring,** bague de saphirs. *Gramophones:* Saphir.

sappiness ['sæpinis], *s.* **1.** Abondance *f* de sève; teneur *f* en sève (du bois). **2.** *F:* Niaiserie *f*; inexpérience *f*.

sappy ['sæpi], *a.* **1.** (*a*) Plein de sève. (*b*) (*Of timber*) Vert. **2.** *F:* Niaud; sans expérience.

saraband ['særəbænd], *s. Danc:* Sarabande *f*.

Saracen ['særəs(ə)n], *a. & s. Hist:* Sarrasin (*m*).

saratoga [,særə'tougə], *s. A:* S. (**trunk**), malle bombée.

sarcasm ['sɑːkæzm], *s.* **1.** Ironie *f*; esprit *m* sarcastique. **2.** (**Piece of**) s., sarcasme *m*.

sarcastic [sɑː'kæstik], *a.* Sarcastique; mordant. S. **remark**, sarcasme *m*. **-ally**, *adv.* D'une manière sarcastique; ironiquement.

sarcology [sɑː'kɔlədʒi], *s. Anat:* Sarcologie *f*.

sarcoma [sɑː'koumə], *s. Med:* Sarcome *m*.

sarcophagus, *pl.* **-phagi** [sɑː'kɔfəgəs, -fəgai, -fədʒai], *s.* Sarcophage *m*.

sard [sɑːd], *s. Miner:* Sardoine *f*.

sardine [sɑː'diːn], *s. Ich:* Sardine *f*. **Tinned, canned, sardines**, sardines (conservées) à l'huile. **Packed like sardines**, serrés comme des harengs.

Sardinia [sɑː'diniə]. *Pr.n.* La Sardaigne.

Sardinian [sɑː'diniən], *a. & s.* Sarde (*mf*).

sardonic [sɑː'dɔnik], *a.* (Expression, rire) sardonique. **-ally**, *adv.* Sardoniquement.

sardonyx ['sɑːdəniks], *s.* Agate *f* onyx; sardoine *f*.

sargasso [sɑː'gæsou], *s. Algae:* Sargasse *f*. **The S. Sea**, la mer des Sargasses.

sari ['sɑːri], *s. Cost:* Sari (indien).

Sark [sɑːk]. *Pr.n. Geog:* Sercq *m*.

sarky ['sɑːki], *a. P:* Sarcastique, mordant.

sarmentose [sɑː'mentous], **sarmentous** [sɑː'mentəs], *a. Bot:* Sarmenteux, -euse.

sarong [sə'rɔŋ], *s.* Sarong *m*, jupe *f* (des indigènes de la Malaisie).

sarsaparilla [,sɑːsəpə'rilə], *s.* Salsepareille *f*.

sarsen ['sɑːs(ə)n], *s.* **1.** Monolithe *m* tumulaire (des plaines du Wiltshire). **2.** *Geol:* S. **stone**, grès mamelonné.

sartorial [sɑː'tɔːriəl], *a.* De tailleur. S. **art**, l'art *m* du tailleur.

Sarum ['sɛərəm]. *Pr.n. Ecc:* (Évêché *m* de) Salisbury.

sash¹ [sæʃ], *s. Cost:* (a) *Mil:* Écharpe *f*, ceinture *f* (de tissu). (b) Large ceinture à nœud bouffant (d'enfant).

sash², *s. Const:* Châssis *m* mobile, cadre *m* (d'une fenêtre à guillotine). **'sash-cord**, *s.* Corde *f*, cordon *m* (d'une fenêtre à guillotine). **'sash frame**, *s.* (Châssis) dormant *m* (d'une fenêtre à guillotine). **sash-'window**, *s.* Fenêtre *f* à guillotine.

sassafras ['sæsəfræs], *s. Bot:* Sassafras *m*.

Sassenach ['sæsənæx], *a. & s. Scot: Irish: Usu. Pej:* Anglais, -aise.

sat. *See* SIT.

Satan ['seit(ə)n]. *Pr.n.m.* Satan.

satanic [sə'tænik], *a.* Satanique, diabolique. **-ally**, *adv.* Sataniquement, diaboliquement.

satchel ['sætʃ(ə)l], *s.* Sacoche *f. Sch:* Cartable *m*, carton *m* (d'écolier). *Cy:* **Saddle s.**, sacoche de selle.

sate [seit], *v.tr.* **1.** Assouvir (sa faim, ses passions); rassasier, satisfaire (qn, la faim). **2.** = SATIATE. **sated**, *a.* **1.** Rassasié (with, de). **2. To become s.**, se blaser (with, de).

sateen [sə'tiːn], *s. Tex:* Satinette *f*.

satellite ['sætəlait], *s. Astr: Ph: Pol: etc:* Satellite *m*. **Artificial s.**, satellite artificiel, spoutnik *m. Pol:* S. **state**, état *m*, pays *m*, satellite. *Town P:* S. **town**, agglomération *f* satellite.

satiate ['seifieit], *v.tr.* Rassasier (qn) (jusqu'au dégoût) (with, de); blaser (with, de). **satiated**, *a.* Gorgé, rassasié.

satiation [seifi'eif(ə)n], *s.* **1.** Rassasiement *m*. **2.** Satiété *f*.

satiety [sə'taiəti], *s.* Satiété *f*.

satin¹ ['sætin], *s.* **1.** *Tex:* Satin *m*. **2.** S. **finish**, apprêt satiné (du papier, etc.). S. **paper**, papier satiné. **'satin-flower**, *s. Bot:* Lunaire *f*; monnaie *f* du pape. **'satin-stitch**, *s. Needlew:* Plumetis *m*. **'satin-wood**, *s. Com:* (Bois) satiné de l'Inde.

satin², *v.tr.* Satiner (le papier, etc.).

satinette [,sæti'net], *s.* (a) (*Silk*) Satinade *f*. (b) (*Cotton*) Satinette *f*.

satiny ['sætini], *a.* Satiné.

satire ['sætaiər], *s.* **1.** *Lit:* Satire *f* (**on, upon,** contre). **2.** Satire, sarcasme *m*.

satiric(al) [sə'tirik(əl)], *a.* **1.** Satirique. **2.** (**satirical**) Sarcastique, ironique. **-ally**, *adv.* Satiriquement d'un ton moqueur.

satirist ['sætirist], *s.* **1.** (Auteur) satirique *m*. **2** Esprit mordant, malicieux.

satirize ['sætiraiz], *v.tr.* Satiriser.

satisfaction [,sætis'fækʃ(ə)n], *s.* **1.** (a) Acquittement *m*, paiement *m*, liquidation *f* (d'une dette); désintéressement *m* (d'un créancier); exécution (d'une promesse). (b) S. **for an offence**, réparation *f* expiation *f*, d'une offense. **To demand s. for an insult**, demander raison d'un affront. **To give s.o. s.** (by a duel), faire réparation à qn (par les armes). (c) Assouvissement *m* (de la faim, d'une passion). **2.** Satisfaction *f*, contentement *m* (at, with, de). **To give s.o. s.**, donner du contentement à qn; satisfaire, contenter, qn. **To express s. at a result**, se féliciter d'un résultat; exprimer sa satisfaction. **I note with s. that . . .**, je suis heureux de noter que. . . . **The work will be done to your s.**, le travail sera fait de manière à vous satisfaire. **3. That is a great s.**, c'est un grand motif de contentement.

satisfactoriness [,sætis'fækt(ə)rinis], *s.* Caractère satisfaisant (d'un travail, etc.).

satisfactory [,sætis'fækt(ə)ri], *a.* Satisfaisant. S. **pupil**, élève qui donne satisfaction. **To bring negotiations to a s. conclusion**, mener à bien des négociations. **To give a s. account of one's movements**, justifier ses mouvements. **-ily**, *adv.* De façon satisfaisante.

satisfy ['sætisfai], *v.tr.* **1.** (a) S'acquitter (d'une dette, d'une obligation); exécuter (une promesse); faire droit à (une réclamation); remplir (une condition); désintéresser (ses créanciers). (b) Satisfaire (qn); faire réparation à, satisfaire à (l'honneur). **To s. one's conscience**, par acquit de conscience. **2.** (a) Satisfaire, contenter (qn); donner sujet de satisfaction à (qn). *Sch:* **To s. the examiners**, être reçu (à un examen). (b) Satisfaire, assouvir, donner satisfaction à (un désir, un appétit). **To s. all requirements**, suffire à tous les besoins. *Abs.* **Food that satisfies**, nourriture rassasiante. **3.** Convaincre, satisfaire (qn); éclaircir (un doute, etc.). **To s. s.o. of a fact**, convaincre qn d'un fait. **I have satisfied myself that . . .**, je me suis assuré que. . . . **satisfied**, *a.* **1. To be s. with sth.**, (i) être content, satisfait, de qch.; se louer de qch.; (ii) se contenter de qch. **To rest s. with an explanation**, se contenter d'une explication; se tenir pour satisfait. *Cards:* **I am s.**, je m'y tiens. **2.** Convaincu. **satisfying**, *a.* **1.** Satisfaisant; qui contente; (*of food*) nourrissant. **2.** (Argument, etc.) convaincant. **-ly**, *adv.* De façon satisfaisante.

satrap ['sætræp], *s. Hist:* Satrape *m*.

saturate¹ ['sætjureit], *v.tr.* **1.** Saturer, tremper, imbiber (with, de). **To become saturated with . . .**, s'imprégner de. . . . **2.** *Ch: Ph:* Saturer (une solution). **saturated**, *a.* **1.** (*Terrain, etc.*) trempé. (*Of solution, etc.*) Saturé; (*of vapour*) saturant. **3.** (*Of colour*) Riche; intense.

saturate² ['sætjurit], *a. Ch: Ph: etc:* Saturé.

saturation [,sætju'reiʃ(ə)n], *s.* **1.** Imprégnation *f*. **2.** *Ch: Ph:* Saturation *f*. **To dissolve a salt to s.**, dissoudre un sel jusqu'à saturation, jusqu'à refus. *El:* S. **voltage**, tension *f* de saturation. *Com:* **The market has reached s. (point)**, le marche est saturé.

Saturday ['sætədi], *s.* Samedi *m*. (*For phrases see* FRIDAY.)

Saturn ['sætə:n]. *Pr.n. Astr: Myth:* Saturne *m*.

Saturnalia [,sætə'neiliə], *s.pl.* Saturnales *f*.

saturnine ['sætənain], *a.* Taciturne, sombre. **To be of a s. disposition**, avoir du sombre dans l'âme.

satyr ['sætər], *s. Myth:* Satyre *m*.

satyric [sə'tirik], *a. Gr.Lit:* Satyrique. S. **drama**, drame satyrique.

sauce¹ [sɔːs], *s.* **1.** (a) Sauce *f*. **Tomato s.**, sauce tomate. **Caper s.**, sauce aux câpres. (b) Assaisonnement *m*; condiment *m*. **To add a s. to sth.**, relever le goût de qch. *Prov:* **What is s. for the goose is s. for the gander**, ce qui est bon pour l'un l'est aussi pour l'autre. *S.a.* APPLE-SAUCE, BREAD-SAUCE,

HUNGER¹, MINT-SAUCE. 2. *P:* (i) Impertinence *f*, insolence *f*; (ii) culot *m*, toupet *m*. None of your s.! pas d'impertinences! What s.! quel toupet! 'sauce-boat, *s.* Saucière *f*. 'sauce-cook, *s. Cu:* (*Pers.*) Saucier *m*.

sauce², *v.tr. P:* Dire des impertinences à (qn); manquer de respect à (qn).

saucepan ['sɔːspən], *s.* Casserole *f*. Double s., bain-marie *m*, *pl*. bains-marie. 'saucepan-cleaner, -scourer, *s.* Lavette *f* (métallique); tampon *m* à récurer.

saucer ['sɔːsər], *s.* (*a*) Soucoupe *f. F: Av:* Flying s., soucoupe volante. (*b*) *Art:* Godet *m* à couleur. 'saucer-eyed, *a.* Aux yeux en soucoupe, en boules de loto.

saucerful ['sɔːsəful], *s.* Pleine soucoupe (of, de).

sauciness ['sɔːsinis], *s. F:* Impertinence *f*; toupet *m*.

saucy ['sɔːsi], *a.* (*a*) Impertinent, effronté. (*b*) Fripon, gamin. S. smile, sourire aguichant. (*c*) S. little hat, petit chapeau coquet, chic. -ily, *adv.* (*a*) D'un ton effronté. (*b*) D'un air gamin. (*c*) (Chapeau porté) coquettement, avec chic.

Saudi Arabia [ˌsaudiəˈreibiə]. *Pr.n. Geog:* L'Arabie Séoudite.

sauerkraut ['sauəkraut], *s. Cu:* Choucroute *f*.

Saul [sɔːl]. *Pr.n.m. B.Hist:* Saül.

sauna ['saunə], *s.* Sauna *m*.

saunter¹ ['sɔːntər], *s.* Promenade faite à loisir; flânerie *f*.

saunter², *v.i.* To s. (along), flâner; se balader; déambuler. To s. up to the hotel, arriver à petits pas devant l'hôtel. To s. across the road, traverser la rue sans se presser. To s. back home, s'en revenir tout doucement chez soi.

saurian ['sɔːriən], *a. & s. Rept:* Saurien (*m*).

sausage ['sɔsidʒ], *s.* 1. *Cu:* (*a*) (*Fresh, eaten hot*) Saucisse *f. Chipolata* s., chipolata *f. P:* Not a s., nib de nib. (*b*) (*Preserved, hard, dry*) Saucisson *m*. (*c*) *F:* S. dog, teckel *m*, *F:* chien à roulettes. 2. (*a*) *Min: etc:* Boudin *m* (d'explosif). (*b*) *Mil: F:* S. (balloon), ballon *m* (i) d'observation; (ii) de protection antiaérienne; *F:* saucisse. 'sausage-meat, *s.* Chair *f* à saucisse. 'sausage-'roll, *s. Cu:* = Friand *m*.

sauté¹ ['soutei], *a. & s. Cu:* Sauté (*m*).

sauté², *v.tr. Cu:* Sauter, faire sauter (des pommes de terre).

savage¹ ['sævidʒ]. 1. *a.* (*a*) Sauvage, barbare; non civilisé. (*b*) (Animal, coup) féroce; (coup) brutal, -aux; (visage) farouche. (*c*) *F:* (*Of pers.*) Furieux, -euse; en rage. To grow s., se fâcher (tout rouge). To make a s. attack on s.o., s'attaquer férocement à qn. 2. *s.* Sauvage *mf*. -ly, *adv.* Sauvagement, férocement; furieusement.

savage², *v.tr.* (*Of animals*) Attaquer, mordre (qn, les autres bêtes).

savageness ['sævidʒnis], savagery ['sævidʒri], *s.* 1. Sauvagerie *f*, barbarie *f* (d'une race, etc.). 2. Férocité *f*; brutalité *f* (d'un coup).

savanna(h) [sə'vænə], *s.* Savane *f*.

savant ['sævənt], *s.* Savant, -e.

save¹ [seiv], *s. Fb:* Arrêt *m* (du ballon). To effect a s., parer à l'attaque.

save², *v.tr.* 1. (*a*) Sauver. To s. s.o.'s life, sauver la vie à qn. He has saved several lives at sea, il a fait plusieurs sauvetages en mer. He was saved from the wreck, il a réchappé au naufrage. To s. s.o. from death, arracher qn à la mort. To s. s.o. from s.o.'s anger, préserver qn de la colère de qn. To s. s.o. from falling, empêcher qn de tomber. *Fb:* To s. the goal, arrêter le ballon. (*b*) To s. one's soul, sauver son âme. (*c*) Sauver, protéger, sauvegarder (son honneur, etc.). To s. the situation, se montrer à la hauteur de l'occasion. To s. appearances, sauver, sauvegarder les apparences. (God) s. me from my friends! Dieu me protège contre mes amis! God s. the King! Dieu sauve le Roi! S. us! Dieu nous garde!! *S.a.* BACON, FACE¹ 2. 2. (*a*) Mettre (qch.) de côté. S. a dance for me, réservez-moi une danse. (*b*) Économiser, épargner, mettre de côté (de l'argent). I have money saved, j'ai de l'argent de côté. To s. little by little, économiser sou par sou. To s. on sth., économiser sur qch. *Abs.* To s. (up), économiser pour l'avenir; thésauriser. To s.

up for one's old age, faire des économies pour ses vieux jours. (*c*) *Ind:* Recueillir, capter (les sous-produits, etc.). 3. Ménager (ses vêtements, etc.); éviter (une dépense, de la peine). To s. time, gagner, économiser, du temps. In this way you s. twenty per cent, vous faites ainsi une économie de vingt pour cent. I am saving my strength, je me ménage. To s. oneself for sth., se réserver pour qch. *S.a.* STITCH¹ 1. 4. To s. s.o. sth., éviter, épargner, qch. à qn. This has saved him much expense, cela lui a évité beaucoup de dépense. They would be saved all this labour, cela leur épargnerait tout ce travail. To s. s.o. the trouble of doing sth., épargner à qn la peine de faire qch. saving¹. I. *a.* 1. (*a*) Qui sauve; qui protège. (*b*) (Qualité) qui rachète des défauts. *S.a.* GRACE¹ 2. 2. (*a*) (*Of pers.*) Économe, ménager, -ère (of, de). (*b*) (*Of system, etc.*) Économique. 3. S. clause, clause de sauvegarde; clause restrictive; réservation *f*. II. saving. 1. *prep. & conj.* = SAVE³. 2. *prep.* Sauf; sans porter atteinte à. *A:* S. your presence, sauf votre respect. saving², *s.* 1. (*a*) Délivrance *f*, salut *m* (de qn, des âmes). This was the s. of him, cela a été son salut. (*b*) Sauvetage *m*. (*c*) Protection *f*. 2. (*a*) Économie *f*, épargne *f*. (*b*) *pl.* Savings, économies. To live on one's savings, vivre de ses épargnes. (National) savings certificate = bon *m* d'épargne. 'savings bank, *s.* Caisse *f* d'épargne. Post office s. b., = caisse (nationale) d'épargne (postale).

save³, *prep. A. & Lit:* Sauf, excepté, hormis. All is lost s. honour, *A:* tout est perdu fors l'honneur.

saveloy ['sævəloi], *s. Cu:* Cervelas *m*.

saver ['seivər], *s.* 1. (*a*) Sauveur *m*, libérateur, -trice (de sa patrie, etc.). (*b*) Sauveteur *m* (de vie, de biens). 2. Appareil économiseur. 3. Personne *f* économe.

saviour ['seivjər], *s.* Sauveur *m. Theol:* Our S., Notre Sauveur.

savoir-faire ['sævwɑːˈfeər], *s.* Adresse *f*; savoir-faire *m*.

savoir-vivre ['sævwɑːˈviːvrə], *s.* Savoir-vivre *m*.

savory ['seivəri], *s. Bot: Cu:* Sarriette *f*.

savour¹ ['seivər], *s.* 1. Saveur *f*, goût *m*, arome *m*. The s. of his humour, son humour savoureux. 2. Trace *f*, soupçon *m*, pointe *f* (d'ail, d'hérésie).

savour². 1. *v.tr.* Savourer (un mets). 2. *v.i.* (*Of thg*) To s. of sth., sentir qch.; tenir de qch. Doctrine that savours of heresy, doctrine qui sent le fagot.

savouriness ['seivərinis], *s.* Saveur *f*, succulence *f* (d'un mets, etc.).

savourless ['seivəlis], *a.* Fade; sans saveur.

savoury ['seivəri]. 1. *a.* (*a*) Savoureux, appétissant; succulent. To make a dish s., relever un plat. (*b*) (Mets) piquant ou salé. S. herbs, plantes aromatiques. S. omelette, omelette aux fines herbes. 2. *s.* Entremets non sucré (en fin de repas).

Savoy [sə'vɔi]. 1. *Pr.n. Geog:* La Savoie. 2. *s.* (*a*) Chou frisé de Milan. (*b*) Biscuit *m* à la cuillère.

savvy¹ ['sævi], *s. F:* Jugeotte *f*.

savvy², *v.tr. P:* Savoir; comprendre, *P:* piger. S.? compris?

saw¹ [sɔː], *s. Tls:* Scie *f*. Hand-s., scie à main; (small) égoïne *f*, égohine *f*. Keyhole s., pad s., compass s., scie passe-partout, à guichet, à chantourner. Cross-cut s., two-handled s., (scie) passe-partout *m inv*. Power s., scie mécanique; tronçonneuse *f*. Circular s., *U.S:* buzz s., scie circulaire. Bookbinder's s., grecque *f*. 'saw-bench, *s.* Scie *f* circulaire à table. 'saw-cut, *s.* Trait *m* de scie. 'saw-frame, *s.* Châssis *m*, monture *f*, de scie. 'saw-horse, -jack, *s.* Chevalet *m* de sciage, de scieur. 'saw-pit, *s.* Fosse *f* de scieur de long. 'saw-tooth, *s.* Dent *f* de scie. S.-t. roof, toit en dents de scie; (toit en) shed *m*. 'saw-toothed, *a.* En dents de scie; (toit) en shed.

saw², *v.tr.* (*p.t.* sawed; *p.p.* sawn, sawed) 1. Scier. To s. up wood, débiter du bois. Sawn timber, bois de sciage. To s. off a piece of wood, scier (et détacher) un morceau de bois. Sawed-off shot-gun, fusil *m* à canon tronçonné. To s. out a piece, découper un morceau à la scie; chantourner un morceau. To s. the air, battre l'air (avec les bras). To s. on the fiddle, racler du violon. *Equit:* To s. a horse's mouth, gourmander la bouche d'un cheval; scier du bridon. 2. *Bookb:* Grecquer (les feuilles).

saw³, *s.* Adage *m*, proverbe *m*, maxime *f*; dicton *m*. Wise s., aphorisme *m*.

saw⁴. *See* SEE¹.

sawbones ['sɔːbounz], *s. P:* (*Surgeon*) Charcutier *m*; carabin *m*.

sawdust ['sɔːdʌst], *s.* Sciure *f* (de bois); bran *m* de scie.

sawfish ['sɔːfiʃ], *s. Ich:* Scie *f* (de mer).

sawmill ['sɔːmil], *s.* Scierie *f*.

sawn. *See* SAW².

sawyer ['sɔːjər], *s.* Scieur *m*; *esp.* scieur de long.

sax¹ [sæks], *s. Tls:* Hache *f* d'ouvrage (de couvreur); asseau *m*, assette *f*.

sax², *s. Mus: F:* Saxo *m*.

saxatile ['sæksətail], *a. Nat.Hist:* Saxatile.

saxhorn ['sækshɔːn], *s. Mus:* Saxhorn *m*.

saxifrage ['sæksifridʒ], *s. Bot:* Saxifrage *f*.

Saxon ['sæks(ə)n], *a. & s.* Saxon, -onne.

Saxony ['sæksəni]. *Pr.n. Geog:* La Saxe.

saxophone ['sæksəfoun], *s.* Saxophone *m*.

saxophonist [sæk'səfənist], *s.* (Joueur *m* de) saxophone *m*.

say¹ [sei], *s.* Dire *m*, parole *f*, mot *m*. **To have one's s.,** dire ce qu'on a à dire; dire son mot. **To have one's s. out,** dire ce que l'on a sur le cœur. **Let me have my s.,** laissez-moi parler. **I have no s. in the matter,** je n'ai pas voix au chapitre.

say², *v.tr.* (said [sed]; said; *3rd sg. pr. ind.* says [sez], *A:* sayeth ['seiəθ], saith [seθ]) Dire. **1.** (*a*) To s. a word, dire un mot. To ask s.o. to s. a few words, prier qn de prendre la parole. To s. good morning to s.o., dire bonjour à qn. *F:* Who shall I s.? qui dois-je annoncer? To s. again, répéter, redire. It isn't said, cela ne se dit pas. What do you s.? que dites-vous? qu'est-ce que vous dites? What did you s.? (i) qu'avez-vous dit? (ii) plaît-il? To s. yes, no, dire (que) oui, (que) non. To s. yes to an invitation, accepter une invitation. What do you s. to a drink? si on buvait un verre? What do you s. to a game of bridge? si on faisait un bridge? He goes to the club.—So he says! il va au cercle.—À l'en croire! *B:* Thus saith the Lord, ainsi dit l'Éternel; ainsi parle le Seigneur. "I accept," said he, he said, "j'accepte," fit-il, dit-il. (*b*) (*Express orally or otherwise*) All of that can be said in a couple of words, tout ça tient en deux mots. As I said in my letter, comme je vous l'ai dit dans ma lettre. The Bible says..., it says in the Bible..., il est dit dans la Bible.... The text of the treaty says..., le texte du traité porte ces mots.... The church clock says ten, le cadran de l'église marque dix heures. Though I s. it who should not, *F: Hum:* though I says [sez] it as shouldn't, bien que ce ne soit pas à moi de le dire. As people say, as they say, comme on dit. So to s., pour ainsi dire. As one might s...., comme qui dirait.... One might as well s...., autant dire.... I must s...., j'avoue...; franchement.... This news surprises me, I 'must s., cette nouvelle me surprend, je l'avoue. That is to s...., c'est-à-dire... à savoir.... Have you said anything about it to him? lui en avez-vous parlé? I remember something was said about it, je me souviens qu'il en a été parlé. The less said the better, moins nous parlerons, mieux cela vaudra. S. no more! n'en dites pas davantage! To s. nothing of..., sans parler de... He has plenty to s. for himself, (i) il n'a pas sa langue dans sa poche; (ii) il sait se faire valoir, se mettre en avant. At first they would have nothing to s. to him, d'abord on refusa de le reconnaître. There is something to be said on both sides, il y a du pour et du contre. This much can be said at present, that..., on peut affirmer dès maintenant que.... There is much to be said for beginning now, il y a de bonnes raisons pour s'y mettre dès maintenant. That doesn't s. much for his intelligence, cela ne dénote pas beaucoup d'intelligence. *P:* You've said it! vous l'avez dit! You don't s. so! allons donc! pas possible! *P:* You don't s.! c'est-il possible! ça alors! S. it with flowers! dites-le avec des fleurs! (*c*) (*Report*) They s. that..., it is said that..., on dit que.... That is what people are saying, voilà ce qu'on raconte. He is said to have a large fortune, on lui attribue une grande fortune. He is said to be rich, on le dit riche. (*d*) (*Opine*) Anyone would s. that he was asleep, on dirait qu'il dort. I should s. she has intelligence, autant que j'en puis juger elle est intelligente. I

should s. not, je ne crois pas; je crois que non. What s. you? what would, do, you s.? et vous, qu'en dites-vous? Didn't I s. so! quand je vous le disais! (*e*) It was you who said I was to, c'est vous qui m'avez dit de le faire. (*f*) Come and have lunch one of these days, s. Sunday, venez déjeuner un de ces jours, disons dimanche. If I had an income of s. a thousand a year, si j'avais des rentes, mettons mille livres par an. Three times round the track, s. two miles, trois tours de piste, soit deux milles. Well, s. it were true, what then? eh bien, mettons que ce soit vrai, alors quoi? (*g*) (*Exclamatory*) I s.! dites donc! (*expressing surprise*) pas possible! fichtre! *U.S:* S. mister, can you tell me..., pardon, monsieur, pouvez-vous me dire... 2. Dire, réciter (une leçon, une prière, etc.); faire (ses prières). To s. mass, dire la messe. **saying,** *s.* 1. (*a*) Énonciation *f* (d'un fait, etc.). It goes without s. that..., il va de soi, cela va sans dire, que... That goes without s., cela va sans dire. (*b*) There is no s. ..., (il est) impossible de dire (quand..., etc.). 2. (*a*) Dit *m*. Historical s., mot *m* historique. (*b*) (*Popular*) s., adage *m*, proverbe *m*, dicton *m*, aphorisme *m*. As the s. goes, comme dit le proverbe.

scab¹ [skæb], *s.* 1. (*a*) *Vet:* Gale *f*, bouquet *m*. (*b*) (*Of plants*) Gale. 2. (*a*) (*On wound*) Croûte *f*, escarre *f*. (*b*) *Metall:* Dartre *f*. 3. *P:* (*Pers.*) (*a*) *Ind: Esp. U.S:* Renard *m*, jaune *m*. (*b*) Canaille *f*; *P:* sale type *m*; salaud *m*.

scab², *v.i.* (**scabbed**) 1. (*Of wound*) To s. (over), former une croûte; se cicatriser. 2. *Metall:* Dartrer. 3. *P: U.S:* Supplanter les grévistes; trahir ses camarades.

scabbard ['skæbəd], *s.* Fourreau *m* (d'une épée); gaine *f* (d'un poignard, etc.). To throw away the s., jurer la guerre à outrance; s'en remettre au sort des armes.

scabbiness ['skæbinis], *s.* 1. État galeux. 2. État croûteux (d'une blessure). 3. *P:* Mesquinerie *f*; pingrerie *f*.

scabby ['skæbi], *a.* 1. *Vet:* Galeux, -euse. 2. (*a*) (*Of sore*) Croûteux, -euse, scabieux, -euse. (*b*) (*Of metal casting*) Dartreux, -euse. 3. *P:* (*a*) Mesquin, sordide, méprisable. (*b*) (*Of pers.*) Ladre, pingre.

scabies ['skeibiːz], *s. Med:* Gale *f*.

scabious ['skeibiəs]. 1. *a.* = SCABBY 1, 2. 2. *s. Bot:* Scabieuse *f*.

scabrous ['skeibrəs], *a.* 1. Rugueux, -euse, raboteux, -euse. 2. (*Of topic, etc.*) Scabreux, risqué.

scads [skædz], *s. pl. U.S: P:* Grande quantité de (qch.) There's s. of it, il y en a des tas.

scaffold¹ ['skæf(ə)ld], *s.* 1. *A:* (*a*) Échafaud *m*, estrade *f* (pour représentations). (*b*) Tribunes *fpl* (pour spectateurs). 2. Échafaud (pour exécutions). To go to, to mount, the s., monter à, sur, l'échafaud. 3. *Const.* = SCAFFOLDING.

scaffold², *v.tr. Const:* Dresser un échafaudage autour de, contre (une maison). **scaffolding,** *s.* Échafaudage *m*. '**scaffolding-pole,** *s. Const:* Écoperche *f*; perche *f* d'échafaudage.

scalable¹ ['skeiləbl], *a.* (*Of cliff, wall, etc.*) Dont l'escalade est possible.

scalable², *a.* (Chaudière, etc.) que l'on peut désincruster, détartrer.

scald¹ [skɔːld], *s.* Échaudure *f*.

scald², *v.tr.* 1. Échauder, ébouillanter. To s. one's foot, s'échauder le pied. 2. Faire chauffer (le lait) juste au-dessous du point d'ébullition. Scalded cream, crème échaudée. **scalding¹,** *a.* S. (hot), tout bouillant. S. tears, larmes brûlantes. **scalding²,** *s.* Échaudage *m*, ébouillantage *m*. S. room (*of slaughter house*), échaudoir *m*.

scale¹ [skeil], *s.* 1. (*On fish, bud, etc.*) Écaille *f*. *Med:* (*On skin*) Écaille, squame *f*. *Lit:* The scales fell from his eyes, les écailles lui tombèrent des yeux. 2. *Malw:* (*a*) Barbure *f* (de pièce coulée); dartre *f*. (*b*) Écailles de fer; battitures *fpl*, pailles *fpl*. Mill s., roll s., scories *fpl* de laminoir. 3. Incrustation *f*, dépôt *m*; tartre *m* (des dents). *Mec.E: Aut: Metall:* Calamine *f*. *Mch:* Boiler s., tartre, incrustation; dépôt calcaire. S. preventer, remover, désincrustant *m*, détartrant *m*.

scale², I. *v.tr.* **1.** (*a*) Écailler (un poisson, etc.). (*b*) Détartrer, nettoyer (les dents); piquer, décrasser, détartrer, désencroûter, désincruster (une chaudière). **2.** Entartrer, incruster (une chaudière). II. **scale,** *v.i.* **1. To s.** (off), s'écailler; *Med:* (*of skin*) se desquamer; (*of bone, etc.*) s'exfolier. **2.** (*Of boiler*) S'entartrer, s'incruster. **scaling¹,** *s.* **1.** (*a*) Écaillage *m* (d'un poisson). (*b*) Détartrage *m* (des dents, d'une chaudière); désincrustation *f* (d'une chaudière). **2.** Formation *f* du tartre; incrustation *f* (d'une chaudière).

scale³, *s.* **1.** Plateau *m*, plat *m* (de balance). **To throw sth. into the s.,** jeter qch. dans la balance; mettre qch. en balance. **To turn the s.,** emporter, faire pencher, la balance. **To turn the scale(s) at …,** peser plus de.... **2.** *pl.* (Pair of) scales, balance. **Platform scales,** bascule *f*; (*with steelyard*) balance romaine. **Bathroom scales,** pèse-personne *m*. **Letter scales,** pèse-lettres *m inv.* **To hold the scales even,** tenir la balance égale. **3.** *pl.* *Astr:* **The Scales,** la Balance. '**scale-maker,** *s.* *Ind:* Balancier *m*; fabricant *m* de balances.

scale⁴, *v.i.* **To s. six pounds,** peser six livres. **scale in,** *v.i.* *Turf:* Passer au pesage.

scale⁵, *s.* **1.** Échelle *f.* (*a*) Graduation *f*, graduations (d'un thermomètre, etc.); série *f*, suite *f* (de nombres, etc.). **Fahrenheit s.,** échelle de Fahrenheit. **Standard s.** (*of machine-part sizes, etc.*), échelle des calibres. **S.** (*of salaries,* échelle, barème *m*, des traitements. *Com:* **S. of prices,** échelle, gamme *f*, des prix. **The social s.,** l'échelle sociale. *S.a.* SLIDING¹. (*b*) Cadran gradué. *W.Tel:* **Wave-length s.,** cadran des longueurs d'onde. (*c*) Règle (divisée). **Diagonal s.,** échelle de proportion. (*d*) Échelle (d'une carte, d'un plan, etc.). **To draw sth. to s.,** dessiner qch. à l'échelle. **Map on the s. of …,** carte (rapportée) à l'échelle de.... **On a large s.,** en grand. *S.a.* LARGE I. **1. Reproduction on a small s.,** reproduction en petit. (*e*) Envergure *f* (d'une entreprise, etc.); étendue *f* (d'une calamité). **To keep house on a small s.,** avoir un train de maison très simple. **2.** (*a*) *Mus:* Gamme *f.* **To sing up the s.,** monter la gamme. **To practise scales,** faire des gammes. (*b*) **S. of colours, of tones,** gamme de couleurs, de nuances. '**scale drawing,** *s.* Dessin *m* à l'échelle. '**scale 'model,** *s.* Maquette *f*, modèle réduit.

scale⁶, *v.tr.* **1.** Escalader. **To s. a mountain,** faire l'ascension d'une montagne. **2. To s. a map,** tracer une carte à l'échelle. **To s. a building,** établir le dessin d'un bâtiment à l'échelle. **3. To s. wages up, down,** augmenter, réduire, les salaires à l'échelle. **scaling²,** *s.* **1.** Escalade *f.* **2.** (*a*) Graduation *f* (des prix, des salaires, etc.). (*b*) Dessin *m* à l'échelle.

scaled [skeild], *a.* Écailleux, -euse, squameux, -euse.

scalene ['skeili:n], *a.* (Triangle) scalène.

scaler ['skeilər], *s.* **1.** (*Pers.*) (*a*) Écailleur, -euse (de poissons). (*b*) *Mch:* Nettoyeur *m* (de chaudières). **2.** *Tls:* (*a*) Écailleur *m* (de poissons). (*b*) **Boiler s.,** outil détartreur. (*c*) *Dent:* Détartreur *m.*

scaliness ['skeilinis], *s.* Squamosité *f.*

scallawag ['skæləwæg], *s.* = SCALLYWAG.

scallion ['skæljən], *s.* *Bot:* (*a*) Ciboule *f.* (*b*) Échalote *f.*

scallop¹ ['skɔləp], *s.* **1.** (*a*) *Moll:* Pétoncle *m* or *f*, peigne *m*; coquille *f* Saint-Jacques. (*b*) *Cu:* Coquille (de poisson au gratin, etc.). **2.** *Needlew:* Feston *m*, dentelure *f.*

scallop², *v.tr.* **1.** *Cu:* Faire cuire (du poisson, etc.) en coquille(s). **2.** *Needlew:* Festonner; découper, échancrer. **Scalloped handkerchief, design,** mouchoir échancré, dessin dentelé. *Arch:* **Scalloped moulding,** moulure *f* en écailles.

scallywag ['skæliwæg], *s.* *F:* **1.** Propre-à-rien *m inv*; bon-à-rien *m inv*; mauvais garnement *m.* **2.** *U.S:* Bête mal venue, rabougrie.

scalp¹ [skælp], *s.* **1.** (*a*) *Anat:* Épicrâne *m.* (*b*) *Anat:* Cuir chevelu *m.* **2.** (*In Amer. Indian warfare*) Scalp(e) *m.* **To be out for scalps,** être parti en campagne; chercher qui éreinter. '**scalp-hunter,** *s.* Chasseur *m* de têtes.

scalp², *v.tr.* **1.** (*a*) (*Of Amer. Indians*) Scalper (un ennemi). (*b*) (*Of critic*) Éreinter (un auteur). (*c*) Humilier (qn). **2.** *U.S:* (*a*) Faire le trafic (de billets de théâtre, etc.). (*b*) *St. Exch:* Boursicoter.

scalpel ['skælp(ə)l], *s.* *Surg:* Scalpel *m.*

scaly ['skeili], *a.* Écailleux, -euse, squameux, -euse; (*of metal*) paillé, lamelleux, -euse; (*of boiler*) tartreux, -euse.

scamp¹ [skæmp], *s.* *F:* Vaurien *m*; mauvais sujet; garnement *m.* **My s. of a nephew,** mon garnement de neveu. (*Of child*) **Young s.,** petit galopin, petit polisson.

scamp², *v.tr.* *F:* Bâcler, saboter (un travail); faire (un travail) au galop.

scamper¹ ['skæmpər], *s.* (*a*) Course *f* folâtre, allègre. (*b*) Course rapide.

scamper², *v.i.* (*a*) Courir allégrement, d'une manière folâtre. (*b*) **To s. away, off,** détaler; se sauver à toutes jambes; *F:* prendre ses jambes à son cou.

scamper³, *s.* *F:* Bâcleur, -euse (de travail).

scampi ['skæmpi], *s. pl.* *Cu:* Langoustines *fpl.*

scan¹ [skæn], *s.* **1.** Regard scrutateur. **2.** *Radar:* *T.V:* etc. **S. axis,** axe *m* radioélectrique. **S. frequency,** fréquence *f* de balayage.

scan², *v.tr.* (**scanned**) **1.** (*a*) Scander, mesurer (des vers). (*b*) (*Of verse*) Se scander (facilement, mal, etc.). **This line won't s.,** le vers est faux. **2.** (*a*) Examiner, scruter; sonder du regard. **To s. the horizon,** scruter l'horizon. **To s. the crowd,** promener ses regards sur la foule. (*b*) **To s. the newspaper,** parcourir rapidement le journal. (*c*) *T.V:* Balayer, explorer (l'image à transmettre). **scanning¹,** *a.* Scrutateur, -trice. **scanning²,** *s.* **1.** Scansion *f* de vers. **2.** (*a*) Examen minutieux. (*b*) *Cin:* *T.V:* etc: Balayage *m* (de l'image à transmettre, de la piste sonore). **S. apparatus,** appareil explorateur. **S. cell,** cellule exploratrice.

scandal ['skænd(ə)l], *s.* **1.** Scandale *m*; honte *f*; affaire scabreuse. **To create a s.,** faire un scandale; faire de l'éclat. **Without any s.,** sans éclat. **2.** Médisance *f*; cancans *mpl.* **To talk s.,** *F:* cancaner. **3.** *Jur:* (*a*) Allégations *f* diffamatoires. (*b*) Atteinte *f* à la dignité du tribunal. '**scandal-monger,** *s.* Cancanier, -ière; médisant, -ante; mauvaise langue.

scandalize ['skændəlaiz]. **1.** *v.tr.* Scandaliser, offusquer (qn). **To be scandalized,** se scandaliser. **2.** *v.i.* Médire, *F:* cancaner, potiner.

scandalous ['skændələs], *a.* **1.** Scandaleux, -euse, infâme, honteux, -euse. **2.** *Jur:* (*Of statement*) Diffamatoire, calomnieux, -euse. **-ly,** *adv.* Scandaleusement.

Scandinavia [ˌskændi'neivjə]. *Pr.n.* La Scandinavie.

Scandinavian [ˌskændi'neivjən], *a. & s.* Scandinave (*mf*).

scanner ['skænər], *s.* **1.** Scrutateur, -trice; sondeur, -euse (de la pensée de qn, etc.). **2. Radar s.,** déchiffreur *m* de radar.

scansion ['skænʃ(ə)n], *s.* *Pros:* Scansion *f.*

scant [skænt], *a.* (*In certain phrases*) Insuffisant, peu abondant, limité. **S. weight,** poids bien juste. **In s. attire,** en tenue plutôt sommaire. **To be s. of speech,** être peu communicatif; être avare de paroles. **With s. courtesy,** peu poliment. **S. of breath,** (i) hors d'haleine; (ii) poussif, -ive.

scantiness ['skæntinis], *s.* Insuffisance *f*, rareté *f* (de provisions, etc.); pauvreté *f* (de la végétation); étroitesse *f* (d'un vêtement). **The s. of my resources,** l'exiguïté *f* de mes ressources.

scantling ['skæntliŋ], *s.* **1.** (*a*) Menu bois de sciage; volige *f.* (*b*) Bois d'équarrissage; madrier *m.* *N. Arch:* **Ship heavy of s.,** navire fort en bois. **2.** Échantillon *m*, équarrissage *m.* **To have a s. of two by four inches,** avoir un équarrissage de deux pouces sur quatre. **3.** Chantier *m* (pour fûts).

scanty ['skænti], *a.* Insuffisant, à peine suffisant; peu abondant; (*of garment*) étroit, étriqué. **S. hair,** cheveux rares. **A s. income,** un mince revenu; un revenu bien juste. **S. meal,** maigre repas *m*; repas sommaire. **In s. attire,** en tenue (plutôt) sommaire. **-ily,** *adv.* Insuffisamment; peu abondamment. **S. clad,** à peine vêtu.

scape [skeip], *s.* **1.** *Arch:* Fût *m* (d'une colonne). **2.** (*a*) *Bot:* Hampe *f.* (*b*) *Orn:* Tuyau *m* (de plume).

scapegoat ['skeipgout], *s.* (*a*) *B:* Bouc *m* émissaire. (*b*) Bouc émissaire; souffre-douleur *m inv.*

scapegrace ['skeipgreis], *s.* **1.** Polisson *m*; mauvais sujet. **2.** Petit écervelé; enfant incorrigible.

scaphoid ['skæfɔid], *a. & s. Anat:* Scaphoïde (*m*).

scapula, *pl.* -ae ['skæpjulə, -i:], *s.* Omoplate *f.*

scapular ['skæpjulər]. **1.** *a.* Scapulaire. *Anat:* **S. arch,** ceinture *f* scapulaire. *Orn:* **S. feathers,** rémiges *f* scapulaires. *Surg:* **S. bandage,** scapulaire *m.* **2.** *s. Ecc:* Scapulaire *m.*

scapulary ['skæpjuləri], *s. Ecc:* Scapulaire *m.*

scar[1] [skɑ:r], *s.* **1.** Cicatrice *f.* **2.** *Bot:* Cicatrice, hile *m.* 'scar-face, *s.* Balafré *m.* 'scar-tissue, *s.* Tissu cicatriciel.

scar[2], *v.* (**scarred**) **1.** *v.tr.* Laisser une cicatrice sur (la peau); marquer d'une cicatrice; balafrer. **2.** *v.i. (Of wound)* To s. (over), se cicatriser. **scarred,** *a. (Of face, etc.)* Couturé (de cicatrices); portant des cicatrices; balafré. **Face scarred by smallpox,** figure grêlée (par la petite vérole).

scar[3], *s. (In mountain range)* Rocher escarpé; muraille *f.*

scarab ['skærəb], *s.* **1.** *Ent:* Scarabée sacré (de l'Égypte). **2.** *Lap:* Scarabée.

scarce [skɛəs]. **1.** *a.* Rare; peu abondant. **Good engravers are growing s.,** les bons graveurs se font rares. *F:* **To make oneself s.,** s'esquiver, décamper, filer; se défiler. **2.** *adv.* = SCARCELY. **-ly,** *adv.* **1. A peine;** presque pas. **I have s. any left,** il ne m'en reste presque plus. **She could s. speak,** c'est à peine si elle pouvait parler. **He s. thinks of anything else,** il ne pense guère à autre chose. **You'll s. believe it,** vous aurez de la peine à le croire. **I s. know what to say,** je ne sais trop que dire. **S. ever,** presque jamais. **2.** *(Expressing incredulity)* Sûrement pas. **S.!** j'en doute!

scarceness ['skɛəsnis], **scarcity** ['skɛəsiti], *s.* Rareté *f*; manque *m*, pénurie *f.* **S. of rain,** rareté des pluies. **S. of labour,** manque de main-d'œuvre.

scare[1] [skɛər], *s.* Panique *f*, alarme *f.* **War s.,** psychose *f* de guerre. **To create a s.,** semer l'alarme. **To raise a s.,** porter l'alarme dans le camp. **You did give me a s.,** vous m'avez fait rudement peur. *Journ:* **S. headline,** manchette sensationnelle.

scare[2], *v.tr.* Effrayer, effarer, alarmer; faire peur à (qn). **To s. away,** effaroucher (le gibier, etc.). **2.** *v.i.* S'effrayer, s'alarmer. **I don't s. easily,** je ne m'effraie pas facilement. **scared,** *a.* **S. look,** regard effaré; air épouvanté. **To be s. to death,** avoir une peur bleue. **They were s. out of their wits,** ils étaient affolés.

scarecrow ['skɛəkrou], *s.* **1.** Épouvantail *m.* **2.** *(Of pers.)* (i) Épouvantail; (ii) *F:* grand escogriffe. *F:* **To be dressed like a s.,** être mis à faire peur.

scaremonger ['skɛəmʌŋgər], *s.* Alarmiste *mf.*

scaremongering ['skɛəmʌŋgriŋ], *s.* Colportage *m* de nouvelles alarmistes. **She loves s.,** elle adore semer la panique.

scarf[1], *pl.* **scarfs, scarves** [skɑ:f(s), skɑ:vz], *s.* **1.** *(Woman's)* Écharpe *f*, fichu *m*; *(man's)* cache-nez, *m inv.*; *(in silk)* foulard *m.* **2.** Écharpe (d'officier, de dignitaire).

scarf[2], *s. (Also* **s.-joint**) **1.** Assemblage *m* à mi-bois, à entaille; joint *m* en sifflet; enture *f.* **2.** *Metalw:* Chanfrein *m* de soudure. 'scarf-weld(ing), *s.* Soudure *f* à chanfrein.

scarf[3], *v.tr.* **1.** *Carp: N.Arch:* Enter; assembler à mi-bois. **2.** Amorcer (deux bouts à souder).

scarify ['skɛərifai], *v.tr.* **1.** Scarifier (la peau, le sol); écroûter, ameublir (le sol). **2.** Éreinter (un auteur, etc.). **scarifying**[1] *a.* (Reproche etc.) qui touche au vif, sanglant. **scarifying**[2] *s.* **1.** *Agr:* Scarifiage *m* (du sol). **2.** Éreintement *m* (d'un auteur, d'un ouvrage).

scarlatina [skɑ:lə'ti:nə], *s.* (Fièvre) scarlatine *f.*

scarlet ['skɑ:lit], *a. & s.* Écarlate (*f*). *F:* **To go s.,** devenir cramoisi, rouge comme une pivoine. *R.C.Ch:* **S. hat,** chapeau de cardinal. *A:* **To wear the King's s.,** porter l'uniforme. *A:* **S. woman,** prostituée *f. Pej:* **The S. Woman,** l'Église catholique. *S.a.* PIMPERNEL, RUNNER 3. 'scarlet 'fever, *s. Med:* (Fièvre) scarlatine *f.*

scarp [skɑ:p], *s.* **1.** *Fort:* Escarpe *f.* **2.** Escarpement *m* (d'une colline).

scary ['skɛəri], *a. U.S: F:* **1.** Épouvantable. **2.** Timide, peureux, -euse.

---

scat [skæt], *int.* Filez! fichez le camp! allez ouste!

scatheless ['skeiðlis], *a.* Sans dommage, sans blessure; sain et sauf; indemne.

scathing ['skeiðiŋ], *a.* Acerbe, mordant, cinglant, caustique. **S. retort,** réplique cinglante. **S. irony,** ironie âpre. **To write a s. criticism of a play,** soumettre une pièce à une critique sanglante. **-ly,** *adv.* D'une manière acerbe; d'un ton cinglant.

scatological [skætə'lɔdʒik(ə)l], *a.* Scatologique.

scatology [skæ'tɔlədʒi], *s.* Scatologie *f.*

scatter[1] ['skætər], *s. (Of shot)* Éparpillement *m*; dispersion *f.*

scatter[2]. **1.** *v.tr.* (*a*) Disperser, mettre en fuite. (*b*) Éparpiller; semer (des graines) à la volée; disséminer (des nouvelles); *(of surface)* diffuser (la lumière). **To s. the floor with paper,** joncher le plancher de morceaux de papier. **Path scattered with roses,** chemin jonché de roses. *(Of gun)* **To s. the shot,** *abs.* **to s.,** éparpiller, écarter, le plomb. **2.** *v.i. (Of crowd)* Se disperser; *(of party)* se débander; *(of clouds)* se dissiper; *(of shot)* s'éparpiller, s'écarter. **scattered,** *a.* Dispersé, éparpillé; épars. **Thinly s. population,** population clairsemée. *Ph:* **S. light,** lumière diffuse. **scattering,** *s.* **1.** Dispersion *f*; éparpillement *m*; diffusion *f* (de la lumière). **2.** Petit nombre; petite quantité. **He has a mere s. of followers,** ses adhérents sont peu nombreux et sans cohésion. 'scatter-brain, *s. F:* Étourdi, -ie; écervelé, -ée. **What a s.-b.!** Quelle tête d'oiseau! 'scatter-brained, *a. F:* Étourdi, écervelé, évaporé. **To be scatter-brained,** avoir la tête légère, *F:* avoir une tête de linotte.

scattiness ['skætinis], *s. F:* Étourderie insouciante; inconséquence *f.*

scatty ['skæti], *a. F:* D'une étourderie insouciante. **-ily,** *adv.* D'une manière inconséquente.

scavenge ['skævindʒ], *v.tr.* **1.** (*a*) Ébouer, balayer (les rues). (*b*) *Abs.* Fouiller dans les ordures. **2.** *Artil:* Écouvillonner (une pièce). **3.** *I.C.E:* **To s. the burnt gases,** balayer, refouler, les gaz brûlés. **scavenging,** *s.* **1.** (*a*) Ébouage *m*, balayage *m* (des rues); enlèvement *m* des ordures. (*b*) Action *f* de fouiller dans les ordures. **2.** *Artil:* Écouvillonnage *m* à l'air. **3.** Évacuation *f*, balayage (des gaz brûlés, de la vapeur).

scavenger ['skævindʒər], *s.* **1.** Boueur *m*; balayeur *m* des rues. **2.** Insecte, animal, nécrophage, coprophage. 'scavenger-beetle, *s. Ent:* Nécrophore *m.*

scenario [si'nɑ:riou], *s.* Scénario *m*; canevas *m* (d'une pièce). (Film) *s.* writer, scénariste *m.*

scene [si:n], *s.* **1.** *Th: A:* = STAGE[1] 2. **To appear on the s.,** entrer en scène. **2.** (*a*) *Th:* *(Place of action)* Scène *f.* **The s. is laid in London,** l'action se passe à Londres. (*b*) Théâtre *m*, lieu *m* (d'un événement). **The s. of operations,** le théâtre des opérations. **The s. changes,** l'action change de lieu. **A change of s. would do him good,** un changement d'air lui ferait du bien. **The scenes of his early exploits,** les lieux de ses premiers exploits. **On the s. of the disaster,** sur le(s) lieu(x) du sinistre. **3.** (*a*) *(Sub-division of a play)* Scène. **Second s. of Act III,** deuxième scène du troisième acte. (*b*) Scène, incident *m*, spectacle *m.* **Distressing scenes,** des scènes affligeantes. **That brings the s. before you,** cela fait image. **4.** (*a*) *Th:* (Set) *s.,* décor *m.* **Behind the scenes,** derrière la toile; dans la coulisse. **To know what is going on behind the scenes,** savoir ce qui se passe dans la coulisse; voir le dessous des cartes. (*b*) **A rural s.,** un paysage champêtre. **The s. from the window,** la vue de la fenêtre. **5.** *F:* **To make a s.,** faire une scène; faire de l'esclandre. 'scene-painter, *s.* Peintre *m* de, en, décors. 'scene-shifter, *s. Th:* Machiniste *m.*

scenery ['si:nəri], *s.* **1.** (*a*) *Th:* Décors *mpl*; la mise en scène. (*b*) **You want a change of s.,** il vous faut du changement. **2.** Paysage *m*; vue *f.* **A passion for s.,** la passion des beaux paysages.

scenic ['si:nik], *a.* (*a*) Scénique; théâtral, -aux. *U.S:* **S. road,** route *f* touristique. (*b*) *(Of emotion, effect)* Théâtral; exagéré. **2.** **S. railway,** montagnes russes.

scent¹ [sent], s. 1. (a) Parfum m, senteur f; odeur ɟ agréable. (b) Bottle of s., flacon m de parfum. To use scent, se parfumer. 2. Ven: (a) Fumet m, vent m (de la bête). (b) Piste f, voie f, trace f. (Of hounds) To get on the s., to pick up the s., empaumer la voie. The hounds are on the s., les chiens ont rencontré. To be on the right s., être sur la piste. To throw the hounds off the s., dépister les chiens; mettre les chiens en défaut. To put s.o. on a false s., aiguiller qn sur une fausse piste. 3. Odorat m, flair m (d'un chien). Dog that has no s., chien qui n'a pas de nez. 'scent-bottle, s. Flacon m de parfum. 'scent-spray, s. Vaporisateur m.

scent², v.tr. 1. (Of hounds, etc.) To s. (out) game, flairer, éventer, le gibier. To s. trouble, flairer des désagréments, des ennuis. 2. (a) (Of flower, etc.) Parfumer, embaumer (l'air). (b) To s. one's handkerchief, parfumer son mouchoir. scented, a. 1. Parfumé (with, de); (of air) embaumé (with, de). 2. Odorant. 3. Keen-s. dog, chien au nez fin.

scentless ['sentlis], a. Inodore; sans odeur.

sceptic ['skeptik], s. Sceptique mf.

sceptical ['skeptik(ə)l], a. Sceptique. -ally, adv. Sceptiquement; avec scepticisme.

scepticism ['skeptisizm], s. Scepticisme m.

sceptre ['septər], s. Sceptre m.

schedule¹ ['fedju:l], s. 1. (a) Annexe f (à une loi). (b) Bordereau m; note explicative. 2. (a) Inventaire m (des machines, etc.); barème m (des prix). S. of charges, liste officielle des taux; tarif m. (b) Adm: Cédule f (d'impôts). 3. Plan m (d'exécution d'un travail, etc.). Testing s., tableau m d'épreuve. Everything went off according to s., tout a marché selon les prévisions. Up to s., (train) à l'heure. To be behind s., être en retard sur les prévisions. To be ahead of s., être en avance sur l'horaire prévu, sur les délais prévus.

schedule², v.tr. 1. (a) Ajouter (un article) comme annexe (à une loi, etc.). (b) Ajouter (une note) en bordereau. 2. Inscrire (un article) sur une liste, sur l'inventaire. To s. as a place of historic interest, classer (comme) monument m historique. 3. Dresser le programme de (qch.). The mayor is scheduled to make a speech, le maire doit prononcer un discours. The train is scheduled to arrive at noon, selon l'indicateur le train arrive à midi. scheduled, a. (a) S. prices, prix m selon le tarif. (b) S. taxes, impôts m cédulaires. (c) Rail: etc: S. services, services réguliers.

Scheldt (the), [ðə'skelt, 'felt]. Pr.n. Geog: L'Escaut m.

schema, pl. -as, -ata ['ski:mə, -əs, ski:'mɑtə], s. Schéma m, diagramme m.

schematic [ski:'mætik], a. Schématique.

schematize ['ski:mətaiz], v.tr. Schématiser; représenter (qch.) par un diagramme.

scheme¹ [ski:m], s. 1. (a) Arrangement m, combinaison f. The s. of things, l'ordre de la nature. Colour s., schéma m, combinaison, de(s) couleurs; coloris m. The colour s. is good, les couleurs sont bien agencées. Rhyme s., agencement m, disposition f, des rimes. (b) Jur: S. of composition (between debtor and creditors), concordat préventif (à la faillite). 2. Résumé m, exposé m (d'un sujet d'étude); plan m (d'un ouvrage littéraire). 3. (a) Plan, projet m. S. for a canal, étude f d'un canal. Mil: etc: Tactical s., thème m tactique. (b) Pej: Machination f, intrigue f, complot m, cabale f. Shady s., combinaison louche, F: combine f. To lay a s., ourdir, tramer, une machination.

scheme². 1. v.i. Intriguer, ruser, comploter. To s. in order to do sth., combiner de faire qch.; intriguer pour faire qch. 2. v.tr. (a) Machiner, combiner (une conspiration, etc.). (b) Projeter (de faire qch.). scheming¹, a. Intrigant, tripoteur, -euse. scheming², s. 1. Plans mpl, projets mpl. 2. Machinations fpl, intrigues fpl, combinaisons fpl; F: combines fpl.

schemer ['ski:mər], s. 1. Faiseur de projets; homme à projets. 2. Pej: Intrigant, -ante; comploteur m. He's a clever s., F: il sait nager.

schism ['sizm], s. Schisme m.

schismatic [siz'mætik], a. & s. Schismatique (mf).

schist [ʃist], s. Miner: Schiste m.

schizogenesis [,skitso'dʒenəsis], s. Biol: Ph: etc: Fissiparité f, scissiparité f.

schizoid ['skitsɔid], a. & s. Psy: etc: Schizoïde (m).

schizophrenia ['skitso'fri:niə], s. Psy: Schizophrénie f.

schizophrenic [skitso'frenik], a. Psy: Schizophrène.

schmal(t)z [ʃmɑ:lts], s. U.S: 1. F: Mus: Th: etc: (Musique f etc.) d'un sentimentalisme extrême. 2. P: Cu: Com: Graisse f de volaille fondue.

schnap(p)s [ʃnæps], s. Schnaps m.

schnorkel ['ʃnɔ:kl], s. Schnorkel m.

scholar ['skɔlər], s. 1. (a) Élève mf, écolier, -ière. (b) Personne qui apprend. At eighty he was still a s., à quatre-vingts ans il apprenait encore. 2. Savant, lettré; homme d'étude; érudit; esp. humaniste m. A fine s., un fin lettré. A s. and a gentleman, un homme cultivé et raffiné. Latin s., latiniste mf. He is no s., son éducation laisse à désirer. 3. Sch: Boursier, -ière.

scholarly ['skɔləli], a. Savant, érudit. A very s. man, un homme d'un grand savoir, un érudit.

scholarship ['skɔləʃip], s. 1. Savoir m, science f; érudition f. 2. Sch: Bourse f (d'études).

scholastic [skɔ'læstik]. 1. a. (a) (Philosophie) scolastique. (b) (Année) scolaire. The s. profession (la carrière de) l'enseignement. S. agency, bureau m de placement pour professeurs. (c) (Of manner, etc.) Pédant. 2. s. Mediev: Phil: Scolastique m.

scholasticism [skə'læstisism], s. Mediev: Phil: La scolastique; le scolasticisme.

school¹ [sku:l], s. 1. (a) École f. Nursery s., école maternelle. Infant s., école pour enfants de 5 à 7 ans. Primary, A: elementary, s., école primaire. Secondary s., établissement m d'enseignement secondaire. Secondary modern s. = collège m d'enseignement général. Grammar, high, s. = lycée m. Comprehensive s. = centre m d'études secondaires. Technical s. = collège (d'enseignement) technique. Independent, private, s., école libre. Public s., (i) Collège privé (avec internat); (ii) U.S. = state school. State s., école d'État, établissement national. Denominational s., école confessionnelle. Preparatory s., institution f pour élèves de 8 à 13 ans. Approved s., maison f (d'éducation) surveillée. Sunday s., école du dimanche. What s. were you at? Où avez-vous fait vos études? S. equipment, matériel m scolaire. S.a. BOARDING-SCHOOL, FINISHING-SCHOOL. (b) (Les élèves d'une) école. The s. was assembled, on avait réuni tous les élèves. The whole s. knew it, tous les élèves le savaient; toute l'école le savait. The upper s., les grandes classes. The lower s., les petites classes. 2. (Schooling) To go to s., aller en classe. S. begins at nine, les classes commencent à neuf heures. S. attendance, scolarisation f. Compulsory s. attendance, scolarité f obligatoire. S. leavers, jeunes gens qui ont terminé leurs études secondaires. S. year, année f scolaire. S. report, bulletin trimestriel. S. fees, frais m scolaires, scolarités f pl. U.S: To teach s., être dans l'enseignement. 3. École, académie f, institut m. S. of art, école des beaux-arts. S. of dancing, académie de danse; cours m de danse. S. of music, académie de musique, conservatoire m. Fencing s., académie d'escrime; salle f d'escrime. S. of motoring, auto-école f. Evening s., cours m pl du soir. Summer s., cours de vacances. 4. pl. Hist of Phil: The Schools, l'École; la philosophie scolastique (du moyen âge). 5. (In universities) Faculté f. 6. (a) Art: etc: The Flemish, Italian s., l'école flamande, italienne. Phil: The Platonic s., l'école de Platon. (b) S. of thought, école (de pensée). He founded no s., il n'a pas laissé de disciples; il n'a pas fait école. One of the old s., un homme de la vieille école, de la vieille roche. 'school 'bus, s. Autobus m faisant le service des écoles. S. b. service, service de ramassage m des écoliers. 'school 'hall, s. Salle f de réunion, des fêtes. 'school-'leaving, attrib. a. S.-l. age, âge m de fin de scolarité.

school², v.tr. 1. Instruire (qn); faire l'éducation de (qn). 2. Former (un enfant, l'esprit de qn); discipliner (sa voix, son geste); dresser (un cheval). To s. oneself to patience, apprendre à patienter. Schooled in adversity, formé à l'école du malheur.

schooling, s. Instruction f, éducation f. He paid for his nephew's s., il a subvenu aux frais d'études de son neveu.

school³, *s.* Bande *f* (de marsouins, etc.).
schoolbook ['sku:lbuk], *s.* Livre *m* scolaire, livre de classe.
schoolboy ['sku:lbɔi], *s.m.* Écolier, élève. **S. slang,** argot *m* scolaire.
schoolchild, *pl.* **-children** ['sku:ltʃaild, -tʃildrən], *s.* Écolier, -ière, élève *mf.*
schoolday ['sku:ldei], *s.* 1. Jour *m* de classe. 2. *pl.* **In my schooldays,** au temps où j'allais en classe.
schoolfellow ['sku:lfelou], *s.* Camarade *mf* de classe.
schoolgirl ['sku:lgə:l], *s.f.* Écolière, élève. **S. complexion,** teint *m* de jeune fille.
schoolhouse ['sku:lhaus], *s.* (a) Maison *f*, bâtiment *m*, d'école; école *f.* (b) Maison de l'instituteur, de l'institutrice (faisant corps avec l'école).
schoolma'am, schoolmarm ['sku:lmɑ:m], *s.f.* (a) *U.S:* Institutrice. (b) *F:* **She's a real s.,** (i) c'est une pédante; (ii) c'est une vraie prude.
schoolmaster ['sku:lmɑ:stər], *s.m.* Professeur; instituteur.
schoolmastering ['sku:lmɑ:striŋ], *s.* L'enseignement *m.*
schoolmistress ['sku:lmistris], *s.f.* Professeur *m*; institutrice.
schoolroom ['sku:lru:m], *s.* (Salle *f* de) classe *f.*
schoolteacher ['sku:lti:tʃər], *s.* Instituteur, institutrice.
schooner¹ ['sku:nər], *s.* *Nau:* Schooner *m*; goélette *f.*
schooner², *s.* 1. *U.S:* Grande flûte (pour bière). 2. (a) (*In Engl. approx.*) Demi-litre *m*, chope *f* (de bière). (b) Grand verre (de porto, de vin de Xérès).
schreinering ['ʃrainəriŋ], *s.* *Tex:* Similisage *m* (de cotonnades).
sciatic [sai'ætik], *a. & s.* **The s. nerve, the s.,** le nerf sciatique.
sciatica [sai'ætikə], *s.* *Med:* Sciatique *f.*
science ['saiəns], *s.* Science *f.* **Physical s.,** les sciences physiques. **Natural s.,** sciences naturelles. **To study s.,** étudier les sciences. **Social s.,** économie sociale. **To reduce betting to a s.,** ériger le pari en étude **Christian S.,** Science chrétienne. **To reduce betting to a s.,** ériger le pari en étude scientifique. 'science-'fiction, *s.* science-fiction *f.* science-master,
scienter [sai'entər], *adv.* *Jur:* A bon escient.
scientific [ˌsaiən'tifik], *a.* Scientifique. **S. instruments,** instruments de précision. **S. men,** hommes de science. **-ally,** *adv.* Scientifiquement.
scientist ['saiəntist], *s.* Savant, -ante, scientifique *mf*, homme de science. **Forensic s.,** expert *m* légiste.
scilicet ['sailiset], *adv.* A savoir; c'est-à-dire.
scilla ['silə], *s.* *Bot:* Scille *f.*
Scilly ['sili], *Pr.n. Geog:* **The S. Isles,** les Sorlingues *f.*
scimitar ['simitər], *s.* Cimeterre *m.*
scintilla [sin'tilə], *s.* Soupçon *m*, parcelle *f*; étincelle *f.*
scintillate ['sintileit], *v.i.* Scintiller, étinceler. **scintillating,** *a.* Scintillant, étincelant. **S. wit,** esprit scintillant, pétillant.
scintillation [ˌsinti'leiʃ(ə)n], *s.* Scintillation *f*, scintillement *m.*
scion ['saiən], *s.* 1. *Hort:* Scion *m*, ente *f*, greffon *m.* 2. *Descendant m.* **S. of a noble house,** rejeton *m* d'une famille noble.
scirrhus ['sirəs], *s.* *Med:* Squirr(h)e *m.*
scissile ['sisail], *a.* *Miner: etc:* Scissile, fissile.
scission ['siʃ(ə)n], *s.* 1. Coupage *m* avec un instrument tranchant; cisaillement *m.* 2. Scission *f*, division *f* (dans un parti).
scissiparous [si'sipərəs], *a.* *Biol:* Scissipare.
scissor¹ ['sizər], *s.* (a) (Pair of) **scissors,** ciseaux *mpl.* **Cutting-out scissors,** ciseaux de couturière. *Journ: etc:* **To work with scissors and paste,** travailler à coups de ciseaux. *Sp:* **S. jump,** saut en hauteur avec élan. *Skiing:* **Scissors stop,** arrêt en ciseaux. *Rail:* **scissors crossing,** traversée bretelle. (b) *Swim:* **The scissors,** le coup de ciseaux. 'scissor-bill, *s.* *Orn: F:* Bec-en-ciseaux *m.*
scissor², *v.tr.* Couper, découper, (qch.) avec des ciseaux; cisailler (qch.).
sclera ['skliərə], *s.* *Anat:* Sclérotique *f*; cornée *f* opaque; *F:* blanc *m* de l'œil.
scleritis [sklia'raitis], *s.* *Med:* Sclérite *f.*
sclerosis, *pl.* **-oses** [sklia'rousis, -'rousi:z], *s.* *Med:* Sclérose *f.*
sclerotic [sklia'rɔtik]. *Anat:* 1. *a.* Sclérotique. 2. *s.* = SCLERA.

sclerotitis [skliəro'taitis], *s.* *Med:* Sclérotite *f.*
sclerous ['skliərəs], *a.* (Tissu) scléreux.
scobs [skɔbz], *s.pl.* *Ind:* 1. Sciure *f*; copeaux *mpl*; limaille *f.* 2. Scorie *f.*
scoff¹ [skɔf], *s.* Sarcasme *m*, brocard *m*, raillerie *f.*
scoff², *v.i.* Se moquer. **To s. at s.o.,** se moquer, se gausser, de qn. **To s. at dangers,** mépriser les dangers. **To be scoffed at,** recueillir des railleries. **scoffing¹,** *a.* Moqueur, -euse; railleur, -euse. **-ly,** *adv.* En raillant; par moquerie. **scoffing²,** *s.* Moquerie *f*, raillerie *f.*
scoff³, *s.* *P:* Mangeaille *f*; *P:* boustifaille *f.*
scoff⁴, *v.tr.* *P:* Manger, avaler, *P:* bouffer (de la nourriture).
scoffer ['skɔfər], *s.* Moqueur, -euse; railleur, -euse.
scold¹ [skould], *s.f.* (Femme) criarde; mégère; *F:* bougonne, rabroueuse.
scold². 1. *v.i.* Gronder, criailler, ronchonner (**at** s.o., contre qn). 2. *v.tr.* Gronder, réprimander, *F:* tancer (qn). **scolding¹,** *a.* Grondeur, -euse. **scolding²,** *s.* 1. Gronderie *f*, réprimande *f*, semonce *f.* **To give s.o. a good s.,** tancer qn; *F:* laver la tête à qn. 2. **Constant s.,** des criailleries *f* sans fin.
scoliosis [skɔli'ousis], *s.* *Med:* Scoliose *f.*
scollop¹,² ['skɔləp], *s. & v.* = SCALLOP¹,².
Scolopendra [ˌskɔlo'pendrə], *s.* *Myr:* Scolopendre *f.*
scolopendrium [ˌskɔlo'pendriəm], *s.* *Bot:* Scolopendre *f*, langue-de-cerf *f.*
Scombridae ['skɔmbridi:], *s.pl.* *Ich:* Scombridés *mpl.*
sconce¹ [skɔns], *s.* 1. Bougeoir *m.* 2. Applique *f*; candélabre fixé au mur. 3. Bobèche *f* (d'un bougeoir).
sconce², *s.* 1. Fort détaché; blockhaus *m*, fortin *m.* 2. Coin *m* du feu (d'une grande cheminée).
scone [skɔn, skoun], *s.* Pain *m* au lait (souvent cuit en galette sur une plaque de fer).
scoop¹ [sku:p], *s.* 1. (a) *Nau:* Épuisette *f*, écope *f.* sasse *f.* (b) Pelle *f* à main. (c) *Surg:* Curette *f.* (d) **Aural s.,** cure-oreilles *m inv.* 2. (a) *Civ.E:* Cuiller *f*, godet *m* (de drague). (b) *I.C.E:* Cuiller de graissage (de tête de bielle). *Rail:* Cuiller (de locomotive pour ramasser l'eau). 3. (**Coal**) **s.,** seau *m* à charbon (coupé en biseau). 'scoop-net, *s.* *Fish:* Drague *f.*
scoop², *s.* 1. Creux *m*, excavation *f.* 2. (a) Coup *m* de pelle. **At one s.,** d'un seul coup. **A fine s.!** une belle rafle! une joli coup de filet! (b) *Journ: F:* Scoop *m*, reportage sensationnel que l'on est le premier à publier. **To make a s.,** réussir un coup.
scoop³, *v.tr.* 1. **To s.** (out), écoper (l'eau); excaver (la terre); évider (un navet, etc.); gouger (le bois). **To s. up,** (i) ramasser (du charbon, etc.) avec la pelle; (ii) épuiser, écoper (l'eau). 2. *F: Journ:* Faire un scoop. **To s. a large profit,** faire une belle rafle.
scooper ['sku:pər], *s.* 1. Celui qui puise, qui évide, qui ramasse (à la pelle). 2. Outil *m* à évider; gouge *f.* 3. *Orn:* Avocette *f.*
scoot [sku:t], *v.i.* *F:* **To s. (off, away),** détaler; filer.
scooter ['sku:tər], *s.* (a) (*Child's toy*), Trottinette *f*, patinette *f.* (b) *Aut:* Scooter *m.*
scooterist ['skutərist], *s.* Scootériste *mf.*
scope [skoup], *s.* (a) Portée *f*, étendue *f* (d'une action, du savoir de qn); rayon *m* (d'une action). **That is beyond, outside, my s.,** cela n'est pas de, ne rentre pas dans, ma compétence, n'est pas dans mes moyens. **Undertaking of wide s.,** entreprise de grande envergure. **To extend the s. of one's activities,** élargir le champ de son activité. **To fall within the s. of a work,** rentrer dans le plan d'un ouvrage. **S. of gunfire,** champ *m* d'action de l'artillerie. (b) Espace *m*, place *f* (pour les mouvements de qn, etc.). **To give s.o. s. for his abilities,** donner à qn une liberté d'action en rapport avec ses capacités. **Subject that gives s. for eloquence,** sujet qui donne carrière à l'éloquence. **To give full, free, s. to (s.o., one's imagination, etc.),** donner (libre) carrière à (qn, son imagination, etc.). **To have free, full, s. to act,** avoir toute latitude pour agir; avoir ses coudées franches.
scorbutic [skɔ:'bju:tik], *a. & s.* Scorbutique (*mf*).
scorch¹ [skɔ:tʃ], *s.* Roussissement *m*, brûlure superficielle.

scorch². **1.** *v.tr.* Roussir, brûler légèrement (le linge, etc.); (*of sun*) rôtir, flétrir, dessécher (l'herbe, etc.); (*of frost*) griller (les bourgeons). **2.** *v.i.* Roussir; brûler légèrement. **3.** *v.i.* F: **To s.** (along), brûler le pavé; conduire, pédaler, comme un fou; aller un train d'enfer. **scorched**, *a.* Roussi, légèrement brûlé; (*of grass etc.*) desséché; (visage) brûlé, hâlé. **S. earth policy** tactique *f*, politique *f*, de la terre brûlée. **scorching¹**. **1.** *a.* Brûlant, ardent. **S. heat**, chaleur torride. **S. criticism**, critique caustique. **2.** *adv.* **S. hot**, tout brûlant. F: **It's s. here**, on rôtit ici. **scorching²**, *s.* Roussissement *m*; dessèchement *m*.

scorcher ['skɔːtʃər], *s.* F: (a) Journée *f* torride. (b) Discours écrasant; riposte cinglante.

score¹ ['skɔːr], *s.* **1.** (*On skin*) Éraflure *f*, entaille *f*; (*on rock*) strie *f*; (*on cylinder*) rayure *f*. **The scores in a bearing**, les grippures *f* d'un palier. **2.** (a) Trait *m* de repère. (b) Gorge *f*, engoujure *f* (de poulie). **3.** (a) Encoche *f*, coche *f*. (b) O: **To run a s. at a public house**, F: avoir une ardoise au bistrot, au cabaret. O: **To pay one's s.**, régler son compte. **To pay off old scores**, régler de vieux comptes; vider d'anciens griefs. **4.** (a) (Nombre *m* de) points *m* (dans une partie, un match). *Golf:* Compte *m* des points. *Fb:* Marque *f*, score *m*. *Fb:* **What's the s.?** où en est le jeu? **There was no s.**, aucun but n'a été enregistré. (b) F: O: (i) Réponse bien envoyée; (ii) coup *m* de fortune; aubaine *f*. **5.** *Mus:* Partition *f*. **Full s.**, partition d'orchestre. **6.** (a) *Inv. in pl.* Vingt, vingtaine *f*. **A s. of people**, une vingtaine de gens. A: **Four s. years and ten**, quatre-vingt-dix ans. (b) *pl.* F: **Scores**, un grand nombre. **Scores of people**, une masse de gens. **7.** **Point** *m*, question *f*, sujet *m*. **Have no fear on that s.**, n'ayez aucune crainte à cet égard, sur ce chapitre. **On more scores than one**, à plus d'un titre. **On the s. of ill-health**, pour cause, pour raison, de santé. **8.**J*U.S:* F: **To know the s.**, comprendre, connaître à fond (un sujet); s'y connaître. '**score-board**, *s. Sp:* Tableau *m*. '**score-card**, *s.* **1.** (*At shooting-range*) Carton *m*. **2.** *Golf: etc:* Carte *f* du parcours. '**score-game**, *s. Golf:* Match *m* par coups. '**score-play**, *s. Golf:* Jeu *m* par coups.

score², *v.tr.* **1.** (a) Érafler; inciser (le cuir); strier; rayer. **Face scored with scars, with lines**, visage couturé de cicatrices, haché de rides. (b) Faire un trait de plume au-dessous de (qch.); souligner (un passage). **2.** (a) Entailler, (en)cocher. A: **To s. a tally**, faire des coches à une taille. (b) F: O: **To s. up the drinks**, inscrire les consommations à l'ardoise. **3.** *Games:* (a) Compter, marquer (les points). (b) Gagner (une partie); faire, marquer (trente points). **To fail to s.**, ne marquer aucun point. *Cr:* **To s. a century**, faire une centaine. *Fb:* **To s. a goal**, marquer un but. *Cards:* **To s. no tricks**, être capot. **To s. (a success)**, remporter un succès. **That's where he scores**, c'est par là qu'il l'emporte; voilà où il est avantagé. **4.** *Mus:* (a) Noter (un air). (b) Orchestrer (une composition). **score off**, *v.tr.* **To s. off s.o.**, (i) *Games:* marquer un point aux dépens de qn; (ii) F: river son clou à qn. **score out**, *v.tr.* Rayer, biffer (un mot). **scoring**, *s.* **1.** Éraflement *m*; striation *f*; grippage *m* (d'un cylindre, etc.). **2.** *Games:* Marque *f* (des points). *Bill:* **S. board**, tableau *m*, boulier *m*. *Cards:* **S.-block**, carnet-bloc *m*, *pl.* carnets-blocs. *Artil:* **S.-book**, carnet *m* de tir. **3.** *Mus:* (a) Notation *f* (d'un air). (b) Orchestration *f*. (c) *Cin:* Sonorisation *f*.

scorer ['skɔːrər], *s. Games:* Marqueur *m*.

scoria, *pl.* **-iae, -ias**, ['skɔːriə, -iːɪ, -iəz], *s. Metall: etc:* Scorie *f*, mâchefer *m*, crasse *f*.

scorn¹ [skɔːn], *s.* Dédain *m*, mépris *m*.

scorn², *v.tr.* **1.** Dédaigner, mépriser. **To s. a piece of advice**, faire fi d'un conseil. **2.** **To s. to do sth.**, trouver indigne de soi de faire qch. **scorning**, *s.* Dédain *m* (pour qn, qch.).

scorner ['skɔːnər], *s.* Contempteur, -trice (of, de); railleur, -euse.

scornful ['skɔːnf(u)l], *a.* Dédaigneux, -euse, méprisant. **To be s. of sth.**, dédaigner, mépriser, qch. **-fully**, *adv.* Dédaigneusement; avec mépris.

scornfulness ['skɔːnfulnis], *s.* Dédain *m*, mépris *m*; caractère dédaigneux (d'une réponse, etc.).

scorpion ['skɔːpjən], *s.* Scorpion *m*. '**scorpion-fish**, *s.* Rascasse *f*. '**scorpion-'spider**, *s. Arach:* Pédipalpe *m*.

scorzonera [‚skɔːzo'nɛərə], *s. Bot: Cu:* Scorsonère *f*; salsifis noir.

Scot¹ [skɔt], *s.* **1.** Écossais, -aise. **2.** *pl. Hist:* (**The Picts and**) **Scots**, (les Pictes et) les Scots.

scot², *s.* **1.** A: Écot *m*. **To pay one's s.**, payer son écot. **2.** *Hist:* **S. and lot**, taxes communales. '**scot-'free**, *a.* **1.** **To get off s.-free**, s'en tirer indemne, sain et sauf. **2.** Sans frais.

scotch¹ [skɔtʃ], *s.* Cale *f*; sabot *m* d'arrêt (placé sous une roue).

scotch², *v.tr.* Caler (une roue).

scotch³, *s. O:* Entaille *f*; trait *m* (au couteau, etc.).

scotch⁴, *v.tr.* **1.** Mettre (qn, une bête) hors de combat. **2.** Mettre à néant, faire avorter (un projet).

Scotch⁵. **1.** *a.* (*Not used of persons in Scotland*) Écossais, -aise, d'Écosse. **S. terrier**, scotch-terrier *m*. **S. broth**, soupe *f* comprenant du mouton, des légumes et de l'orge. **S. mist**, bruine *f*. **S. woodcock**, œufs aux anchois sur canapé. **S. egg**, œuf dur cuit dans une boulette de viande. (b) *s.pl.* F: **The S.**, les Écossais. **2.** *s.* (a) *Ling:* Dialecte écossais (de l'anglais). (b) Whisky écossais. **A glass of s.**, un whisky, un scotch. *See* Scots.

Scotchman, *pl.* **-men** ['skɔtʃmən], *s.m.* F: (*Not used in Scotland*) Écossais.

Scotchwoman, *pl.* **-women** ['skɔtʃwumən, -wimin], *s.f.* (*Not used in Scotland*) Écossaise.

scoter ['skoutər], *s. Orn:* Macreuse *f*.

scotia ['skouʃə], *s. Arch:* Scotie *f*, nacelle *f*.

Scotland ['skɔtlənd]. *Pr.n.* **1.** L'Écosse *f*. **2.** **S. Yard =** La Sûreté.

Scots [skɔts], *a. & s.* Écossais, -aise. **To talk S.**, parler en dialecte écossais. **To write in S.**, écrire en écossais. **S. law**, droit écossais. **The S. Guards**, la Garde écossaise.

Scotsman, *pl.* **-men** ['skɔtsmən], *s.m.* Écossais. *Rail:* **The Flying S.**, le rapide de Londres à Édimbourg.

Scotswoman, *pl.* **-women** ['skɔtswumən, -wimin], *s.f.* Écossaise.

Scotticism ['skɔtisizm], *s.* Mot écossais; idiotisme écossais.

Scottie ['skɔti], *s.* F: (i) Écossais *m*. (ii) Scotch-terrier *m*.

Scottish ['skɔtiʃ], *a. & s.* Écossais, -aise. **The S. Border**, les marches *f* d'Écosse.

scoundrel ['skaundrəl], *s.* Chenapan *m*, coquin *m* scélérat *m*, gredin *m*. **Regular s.**, franche canaille.

scoundrelly ['skaundrəli], *a.* Scélérat, vil, canaille. **A s. money-lender**, une canaille d'usurier.

scour¹ ['skauər], *s.* **1.** (a) Nettoyage *m*, récurage *m*. **To give a saucepan a good s.**, récurer à fond une casserole. (b) *Hyd.E:* (i) Chasse *f* (d'un réservoir, etc.); (ii) force érosive, force d'affouillement (d'un cours d'eau). **2.** *Tex:* Dégraissant *m*. **3.** *Vet:* Diarrhée *f*.

scour², *v.tr.* **1.** (a) Nettoyer, lessiver, frotter (le plancher, etc.). **To s. out a saucepan**, récurer une casserole. (b) *Tex:* Dessuinter, dégraisser (la laine). (c) Décaper, dérocher (une surface métallique). **2.** (a) Donner une chasse d'eau à (un égout, etc.). (b) (*Of river*) Affouiller, dégrader (les rives). (c) *Purger.* **scouring**, *s.* **1.** (a) Nettoyage *m*, récurage *m*, frottage *m*. (b) *Tex:* Dessuintage *m*, dégraissage *m*. (c) *Metalw:* Décapage *m*, dérochage *m*. **2.** (a) Nettoyage *m* à grande eau (d'un fossé). (b) Affouillement *m*, dégradation *f* (des rives d'un fleuve par les eaux). (c) Purgation *f* (des intestins).

scour³. **1.** *v.i. O:* **To s. about**, battre la campagne. **To s. after s.o.**, courir à la poursuite de qn. **To s. off**, détaler, filer. **2.** *v.tr.* Parcourir, battre (la campagne); (*of pirates*) balayer, écumer (la mer). **To s. a wood**, fouiller un bois.

scourer ['skauərər], *s.* **1.** *Pers:* (a) Nettoyeur, -euse, récureur, -euse. (b) Dégraisseur, -euse (de laine, etc.). (c) Décapeur *m* (de métal). (d) Cureur *m* (de fossés, de puits etc.). **2.** (*Device*) Pot s., éponge métallique, en nylon, etc. **3.** *Agr:* Épointeuse *f*.

scourge[1] [skə:dʒ], s. **1.** A: Fouet m; Ecc: (for self-flagellation) discipline f. **2.** Fléau m. **War is the greatest s.,** la guerre est le pire des fléaux.

scourge[2], v.tr. **1.** A: Fouetter, flageller. Ecc: **To s. oneself,** se donner la discipline. **2.** Châtier (un peuple); être un fléau pour (la population).

scout[1] [skaut], s. **1.** (a) Mil: Éclaireur m. (b) (Boy) **s.,** (Catholic) scout m; (non-Catholic) éclaireur m. U.S: **Girl s.,** guide f; éclaireuse f. (c) Dépanneur m employé par une association automobile. **2.** Navy: **S. (ship),** vedette f; (croiseur-)éclaireur m. **Submarine s.,** patrouilleur m contre sous-marins. Mil: **S. car,** véhicule m de reconnaissance. Av: **S. plane,** avion m de reconnaissance. **3.** Mil: **To be, go, on the s.,** être, aller, en reconnaissance.

scout[2], v.i. Mil: etc: (a) Aller en reconnaissance. (b) **To s. about, round, for sth.,** chercher qch. un peu partout. **scouting,** s. Mil: etc: Reconnaissance f. **S. party,** reconnaissance f. Navy: **S. vessel,** éclaireur m. **S.** (for boys), scoutisme m.

scout[3], v.tr. Repousser (une proposition, etc.) avec mépris, avec dédain.

scouter ['skautər], s.m. Scouting: (a) Chef de troupe. (b) U.S: Routier.

scoutmaster ['skautmɑːstər], s.m. Chef de troupe.

scow [skau], s. Nau: (a) Chaland m. (b) (Ferry) **s.,** toue f.

scowl[1] [skaul], s. Air menaçant, renfrogné; froncement m de(s) sourcils. **To look at s.o. with a s.,** regarder qn de travers.

scowl[2], v.i. Se renfrogner; froncer les sourcils. **To s. at, on, s.o.,** regarder qn de travers, d'un air menaçant. **scowling,** a. Renfrogné, menaçant.

scrabble ['skræbl], v.i. (a) **To s. about,** gratter (çà et là); jouer des pieds et des mains. (b) Chercher à quatre pattes (pour retrouver qch.).

scrag[1] [skræg], s. **1.** (a) Personne décharnée, maigre; bête efflanquée. (b) F: **The s. of the neck,** la nuque. **2.** Cu: **S.-(end) of mutton,** bout saigneux; collet m de mouton.

scrag[2], v.tr. (scragged) F: **1.** Tordre le cou à (qn). **2.** Fb: Saisir (un adversaire) autour du cou.

scragginess ['skræginis], s. Décharnement m, maigreur f.

scraggy ['skrægi], a. Décharné, maigre; qui n'a que la peau et les os.

scram [skræm], v.i. P: Démarrer, se carapater, ficher le camp, filer, décamper, se débiner. **S.!** Fiche-moi le camp!

scramble[1] ['skræmbl], s. **1.** Marche f, ascension f difficile, à quatre pattes; escalade f à quatre pattes. **2.** Mêlée f, lutte f, bousculade f. **The s. for a living,** la lutte pour l'existence. **The s. for office,** la curée des places.

scramble[2]. **1.** v.i. (a) **To s. up, down, in, out,** monter, descendre, entrer, sortir, à quatre pattes; jouer des pieds et des mains. **To s. up a hill,** grimper une colline à quatre pattes. **To s. through sth.,** jouer des pieds et des mains pour traverser qch. (b) **To s. for sth.,** se battre, se bousculer, pour avoir qch.; se battre à qui aura qch. **2.** v.tr. (a) Brouiller (qch). **Scrambled eggs,** œufs brouillés. (b) W.Tg: Tp: etc: Brouiller (un message). **scrambling**[1], a. **To do sth. in a s. fashion,** faire qch. sans ordre, sans méthode, F: à la gribouillette. **scrambling**[2], s. **1.** = SCRAMBLE[1] 1. **2.** Mêlée f, lutte f (for sth., pour avoir qch.). **3.** W.Tg: Tp: etc: Brouillage m (d'une télécommunication).

scrambler ['skræmblər], s. W.Tel: Tp: etc: Brouilleur m.

scrap[1] [skræp], s. **1.** (a) Petit morceau; bout m, chiffon m (de papier); fragment m (de porcelaine, etc.); parcelle f (de terrain, etc.); brin m (d'étoffe). **Not a s. of evidence,** pas une parcelle de preuve. **A little s. of a man,** un bout d'homme. **To catch scraps of conversation,** saisir des bribes de conversation. **S. of comfort,** fiche f, brin, de consolation. F: **That won't be a s. of help to you,** vous n'en tirerez pas le moindre avantage. (b) Découpure f (pour album); coupure f (de journal). **2.** pl. **Scraps** (left over), restes m, reliefs m (d'un repas); déchets m (de papeterie, d'usine, etc.). **To dine off scraps,** dîner des restes de la veille. Com: **Scraps of fur,** retailles fpl. Coll. **Mill s.,** déchets de fabrication.

'scrap-book, s. Album m (de découpures, etc.).

'scrap-heap, s. Tas m de ferraille. **To throw sth. on the s.-h.,** mettre qch. au rebut. **'scrap-merchant,** s. Ferrailleur, -euse, marchand de ferraille. **'scrap-iron, -metal, -steel,** s. Ferraille f.

scrap[2], v.tr. (scrapped) **1.** Mettre (qch.) au rebut; envoyer (un navire, etc.) à la ferraille; Ind: réformer (le matériel). **Scrapped material,** matériel hors de service. **2.** F: Mettre au rancart (une théorie, un projet).

scrap[3], s. (a) F: Querelle f, rixe f; bagarre f. (b) Box: Match m. **To have a s.,** (i) se battre; (ii) se quereller.

scrap[4], v.i. (scrapped) F: Se battre; se prendre aux cheveux; se colleter.

scrape[1] [skreip], s. **1.** (a) Coup m de grattoir, de racloir. **A s. of the pen,** (i) un trait de plume; (ii) quelques mots griffonnés; (iii) une signature, un parafe. **To give a carrot a s.,** gratter, racler, une carotte. **To give one's hand a s.,** s'érafler la main. (b) F: Mince couche f (de beurre, de confitures). (c) Coup d'archet raclé (sur le violon). (d) Grincement m (d'un violon). **2.** F: Mauvaise affaire, mauvais pas. **To get into a s.,** se mettre dans un mauvais pas, dans le pétrin, dans l'embarras; s'attirer des ennuis, une affaire. **To get out of a s.,** se tirer d'affaire; se dépêtrer. **We are in a nice s.!** nous voilà propres! nous voilà bien! nous sommes dans de beaux draps!

scrape[2]. **I.** v.tr. **1.** Érafler, écorcher. **To s. one's shins,** s'érafler les tibias. (Of ship) **To s. the bottom,** sillonner le fond; talonner. **Wine that scrapes the throat,** vin qui racle le gosier. **2.** (a) Racler, gratter (qch.); Cu: gratter (des carottes, des salsifis); Surg: ruginer (un os). **To s. one's boots,** s'essuyer les pieds. **To s. one's plate,** gratter le fond de son assiette; nettoyer son assiette. F: **To s. the barrel,** racler les fonds de tiroir. (b) (Smooth) Riper (une sculpture); racler, raturer (le parchemin). **To s. the bow across the fiddle,** faire grincer l'archet sur le violon. **To s. the fiddle,** v.i. to s. on the fiddle, racler, gratter, du violon. **To s. one's feet along the floor,** frotter, traîner, les pieds sur le plancher. S.a. BOW[1] 1. (a) **To s. acquaintance with s.o.,** trouver moyen de lier connaissance avec qn. (b) **To s. (together, up) a sum of money,** amasser petit à petit, sou par sou, une somme d'argent. **II.** v.i. **1.** (a) Gratter. **Branches that s. against the shutters,** branches qui frottent les volets. (b) Grincer. **2.** (a) **To s. against, along, the wall,** raser le mur; passer tout près du mur. (b) F: **To s. clear of prison,** échapper tout juste à la prison; friser la prison. **scrape along,** v.i. F: Vivoter péniblement; joindre péniblement les deux bouts. **scrape away,** v.tr. Enlever (qch.) en frottant, en raclant. **To s. away the dirt from sth.,** décrotter qch. **scrape off,** v.tr. Enlever (qch.) au racloir. **scrape through,** v.i. Passer tout juste par (une ouverture). **To s. through an examination,** réussir de justesse (à un examen). **scraping**[1], a. **1.** (a) Qui gratte. **A s. sound,** un bruit grinçant, un grincement. (b) **S. bow,** salut obséquieux. **2.** Avare, ladre. **scraping**[2] s. **1.** Éraflement m. **2.** (a) Raclage m, grattage m (de qch.). **S. tool,** racloir m. (b) Ripage m; raturage m. **3.** Grincement m. **4.** (Bowing and) **s.,** salamalecs mpl; courbettes fpl. **5.** pl. **Scrapings.** (a) Raclures f; grattures f. (b) Sous amassés un à un; petites économies, économies de bout de chandelle.

scraper ['skreipər], s. **1.** (Pers.) Gratteur m, racleur m. **2.** Tls: (a) Racloir m, grattoir m, racle f, raclette f. Sculp: Ripe f. Surg: Bone-s., rugine f. (c) Pipe(-bowl) s., nettoie-pipes m inv. Mch: Tube-s., nettoie-tubes m inv. **Door-, shoe-s.,** décrottoir m; gratte-pieds m inv. **'scraper-ring,** s. I.C.E: (Segment) racleur m d'huile.

scrapper ['skræpər], s. F: (i) Pugiliste m. (ii) Bagarreur m.

scrappiness ['skræpinis], s. Caractère décousu (d'un discours).

scrappy ['skræpi], a. **1.** Hétérogène, hétéroclite; (of speech, style) décousu. **S. education,** éducation hétéroclite. **S. knowledge,** bribes fpl de connaissances. **3.** **S. dinner,** dîner composé de rogatons, de restes; maigre repas.

scrapy ['skreipi], a. (Of violin, etc.) Discordant, rauque.

scratch[1] [skrætʃ], s. **1.** (a) Coup m d'ongle, de griffe; griffade f. (b) Égratignure f, éraflure f; griffure f (faite par un chat, etc.). **To go through the war without a s.**, sortir de la guerre indemne, sans une égratignure. (c) Rayure f; striation f. **2.** (a) Grattement m (de la peau). **To give one's head a s.**, se gratter la tête. (b) Grincement m (d'une plume, d'un phonographe); frottement m (d'une allumette). **3.** Sp: (a) Scratch m, ligne f de départ (d'une course). **To start (at) s.**, partir scratch. **To start from s.**, partir de zéro. **To start from s. again, again from s.**, repartir à zéro. **To come up to s.**, (i) se mettre en ligne; (ii) se montrer à la hauteur (de l'occasion); s'exécuter. F: **To bring s.o. up to s.**, (i) amener qn à se décider, à s'exécuter; (ii) chauffer un candidat (pour un examen). **When it comes to the s.**, quand on en vient au fait. (b) Sp: **S. (player)**, scratch m; champion, -ionne. **'scratch-brush**, s. Tls: Gratte-bo(e)sse f. **'scratch-pad**, s. U.S: Bloc-notes m, pl. blocs-notes. **'scratch race**, s. Sp: (Course f) scratch m. **'scratch-test**, s. Med: Test m d'allergie.

scratch[2]. I. v.tr. **1.** (a) Égratigner, griffer; donner un coup de griffe à (qn). **Cat that scratches**, chat qui griffe. (b) Écorcher, érafler, érailler (la peau). **To s. one's hands**, s'égratigner les mains. (c) Rayer (le verre, un diamant, etc.); strier (la roche). **To s. a figure on ivory**, graver (au trait) une figure sur l'ivoire. **2.** (a) Gratter; frotter (une allumette). **To s. one's head**, se gratter la tête. (b) **To s. the surface**, (i) gratter la surface; (ii) F: ne pas aller au fond (de la question, etc.). **3.** (Of animal) Gratter (le sol). **To s. a hole**, creuser un trou avec les griffes. **To s. up a bone**, déterrer un os. v.i. **To scratch at the door**, gratter à la porte. **4. To s. s.o. off a list**, rayer, biffer, qn d'une liste. Turf: Sp: (Of entrant) **To s. the race**, abs. **to s.**, déclarer forfait. Turf: Sp: Scratcher. Sp: (Of organizers) **To s. a match**, décommander un match. **To s. an engagement**, contremander un rendez-vous. **5.** Griffonner (quelques mots, sa signature). II. **scratch**, v.i. (Of pen, etc.) Grincer, gratter. **scratch along**, v.i. F: Se débrouiller; se tirer d'affaire tant bien que mal. **scratch out**, v.tr. **1.** Rayer, biffer, raturer (un mot); (with penknife) gratter, effacer. **2. To s. s.o.'s eyes out**, arracher les yeux à qn. **'scratching out**, s. Raturage m, rayage m, biffage m; grattage m (d'un mot, etc.). **scratching**, s. **1.** (a) Coups mpl d'ongle, de griffe. (b) Écorchement m, éraflement m (de la peau). (c) Rayage m, striation f. **2.** Grattement m (de la tête). **3.** Rayage m, radiation f (d'un nom sur une liste). **4.** Grincement m, grattement m (d'une plume); frottement m (d'une allumette); bruit m de surface (d'un disque de phonographe).

scratch[3], a. (Repas, etc.) improvisé, sommaire. **A s. collection**, une collection hétérogène; un ramas (de bibelots). Parl: **S. vote, s. division**, vote par surprise. Sp: **S. team**, équipe improvisée.

scratchy ['skrætʃi], a. **1.** (a) (Of drawing) Au trait maigre, peu assuré. (b) **S. writing**, pattes f d'araignée; pattes de mouche. (c) Mus: etc: **S. performance**, exécution qui manque d'ensemble. **2.** (a) (Of pen, etc.) (i) Qui gratte; (ii) qui grince (sur le papier). (b) (Tissu) rugueux. **3. To be in a s. mood**, être de mauvaise humeur.

scrawl[1] [skrɔ:l], s. Griffonnage m, gribouillage m; pattes fpl de mouche. **His writing is a s.**, il écrit comme un chat.

scrawl[2], v.tr. Griffonner, gribouiller (une lettre).

scrawler ['skrɔ:lər], s. Griffonneur, -euse; gribouilleur, -euse; barbouilleur, -euse (de papier).

scrawny ['skrɔ:ni], a. Décharné, maigre.

scream[1] [skri:m], s. **1.** (a) Cri perçant. **S. of anguish**, cri d'angoisse. **To give a s.**, pousser un cri aigu, un cri de terreur. (b) **Screams of laughter**, de grands éclats de rire. **2.** F: Chose amusante, grotesque. **It was a perfect s.**, c'était F: tordant, désopilant, P: marrant. **In that part he is a (perfect, regular) s.**, dans ce rôle il est tordant, impayable.

scream[2]. **1.** v.i. (a) Pousser un cri perçant; pousser des cris; crier. **To s. (out) with pain, for help**, hurler

de douleur; crier au secours. **Give it me or I'll s.**, F: je veux ça ou je pleure. (b) F: **To s. with laughter**, rire aux éclats. **He made us s.**, il nous a fait tordre. **2.** v.tr. **To s. oneself hoarse**, s'enrouer à (force de) crier. **screaming**, a. **1.** Criard; (of sound) perçant. **2.** F: (Of farce, etc.) Tordant. **-ly**, adv. F: **S. funny**, tordant, crevant.

scree [skri:], s. Éboulis m (sur une pente de montagne).

screech[1] [skri:tʃ], s. Cri perçant; cri rauque.

screech[2], v.i. Pousser des cris perçants, des cris rauques; (of singer) chanter d'une voix aiguë. **'screech-owl**, s. Orn: Effraie f; chouette f des clochers.

screed [skri:d], s. (a) Harangue f; F: longue tartine. (b) Longue liste (de réclamations, etc.). (c) Longue missive.

screen[1] [skri:n], s. **1.** (a) Furn: Écran m. **Draught s.**, folding s., paravent m. (b) Nau: **Canvas s.**, cloison f en toile; toile f abri. (c) **S. of trees**, rideau d'arbres. (d) **Wrought-iron s.**, grille f. Ecc.Arch: **Choir-s.**, jubé m. (e) Mec.E: **Safety s.**, écran de sécurité. Mil: Navy: **To form a s.**, former un écran (against, contre). Av: **Blast s.**, déflecteur m de souffle. S.a. SMOKE-SCREEN, WINDSCREEN. **2.** Cin: (a) Écran (de projection). **Panoramic s.**, écran panoramique. **Large s.**, écran géant. Television s., F: petit écran. (b) **The s.** (considered as profession), le cinéma. **3.** (a) W.Tel: **Anode s.**, écran de plaque. **S.-grid**, grille-écran f; grille blindée. (b) Phot: **Colour s.**, écran coloré; écran de sélection. Phot. Engr: **Ruled s.**, half-tone s., trame f, réseau m. **4.** Crible m; sas m. Gravel s., crible à gravier. **Revolving s.**, trommel m.

screen[2], v.tr. **1.** (a) Munir (qch.) d'un écran. **To s. off a corner of the room**, cacher un coin de la pièce au moyen de paravents. (b) **To s. sth. from view**, cacher, masquer, dérober, qch. aux regards. **To s. oneself behind sth.**, se cacher derrière qch. (c) Abriter, protéger; mettre à couvert, à l'abri; blinder (une machine) (against, contre); couvrir (qn) de sa protection. **To s. sth. from the wind**, garantir qch. du vent. Mil: **To s. a battery from fire**, dérober une batterie. W.Tel: **To s. a valve**, blinder une lampe. (d) **To s.** (s.o.), examiner et interroger (qn) (généralement une personne suspecte); filtrer, passer au crible. **2.** Tamiser, filtrer, cribler (le gravier, etc.); passer (du sable) au tamis, au crible; sasser (le grain). **3.** (a) Cin: Mettre (un roman, etc.) à l'écran. (b) (Of pers.) **To s. well**, être photogénique. (c) Cin: Projeter. T.V: **This programme is to be screened tomorrow**, cette émission passera sur l'écran demain. **screened**, a. **1.** (a) W.Tel: **S. valve**, lampe blindée. **S.-grid valve**, valve à grille blindée. (b) Caché, dérobé, dissimulé; voilé. (c) A l'abri (from, de). (d) (Of pers.) Examiné, interrogé. **2.** (Charbon) criblé; (sable) passé à la claie. **screening**, s. **1.** (a) Mise f (de qch.) à l'abri, derrière un écran. W.Tel: (i) Blindage m (d'une lampe, etc.); (ii) compensation f de l'antenne. (b) Dissimulation f (d'un défaut). (c) Protection f (from, contre). (d) Examen m et interrogatoire m (de personnes suspectes). **2.** (a) Criblage m; filtrage m; passage m (de qch.) à la claie.

screenplay ['skri:n,plei], s. Cin: Scénario m.

screenwriter ['skri:n,raiter], s. Dialoguiste mf.

screw[1] [skru:], s. **1.** Vis f. (a) **Right-handed s.**, left-handed s., vis à droite, à gauche. **Endless s., worm s.**, vis sans fin. **Thumb s., wing s.**, vis à ailettes; papillon m. **Capstan s.**, vis à tête percée. **Bench s.**, étau m d'établi. **S. joint**, joint vissé, joint à vis. **S. thread**, filet m de vis; pas m de vis. **S. machine**, machine f à fileter. (b) **Set s.**, vis d'arrêt; vis de réglage, de rappel. F: **To have a s. loose**, avoir le timbre fêlé; être timbré, toqué. (c) A: **The screws**, les poucettes f. F: **To put the screws on s.o., to tighten the s.**, serrer les pouces, la vis, à qn; mettre les poucettes à qn; forcer la main à qn. **2.** (a) Nau: **S.(-propeller)**, hélice f. (b) Av: **Air-s.**, hélice (propulsive). **Helicopter s.**, hélice horizontale, sustentatrice; rotor m. **3.** (a) Coup m de tournevis; tour m de vis. **Give it another s.**, serrez-le encore un peu. (b) Bill: Ten: Effet m. **To put (a) s. on the ball**, (i) Bill: faire de l'effet (de côté); (ii) Ten: couper la balle. **4.** O: Cornet m, papillote f (de bonbons, de tabac, etc.). **5.** P: Avare mf; F: grigou m; pingre mf. **An old s.**, un vieux ladre. 6. F: Mauvais cheval; F: rosse f, carcan m. 7. F: (a) Gages mpl; paye f, salaire m. (b) Appointements mpl (minimes). 8. P: The screws, rhumatisme m. 'screw-auger, s. Tls: Tarière rubanée; tarière à vis. 'screw-bolt, s. Boulon m à vis, à écrou. 'screw-'cap, s. Couvercle m à vis (d'une bouteille). 'screw-coupling, s. Mec.E: Manchon m à vis. 'screw-cutter, s. 1. (Pers.) Fileteur m; tourneur m de vis. 2. Tour m à fileter; taraudeuse f. 'screw-cutting, s. Filetage m, taraudage m, décolletage m. S.-c. machine, machine à fileter, à décolleter. 'screw-eye, s. Piton m. 'screw-jack, s. Vérin m à vis. 'screw-plug, s. Tampon m à vis; bouchon fileté. 'screw-top(ped), a. S.-t. jar, bocal à couvercle m à vis. 'screw-wheel, s. Mec.E: Roue f à dents hélicoïdales (engrenant avec une vis sans fin).

screw². I. v.tr. 1. Visser. To s. sth. (on) to sth., visser qch. à, sur, qch. Screwed together, assemblé(s) à vis. 2. (a) To s. (up), visser; (res)serrer (un tourniquet, les chevilles d'un violon). To s. up a nut, serrer un écrou. To s. sth. tight, visser qch. à bloc. (b) To s. s.o.'s neck, tordre le cou à qn. To s. one's face into a smile, grimacer un sourire. (c) Bill: Donner de l'effet à (la bille). Ten: Couper (la balle). 3. Fileter (une vis, un boulon); tarauder. II. screw, v.i. 1. (Of tap, etc.) Tourner (à droite, à gauche, etc.). The knobs s. into the drawer, les boutons se vissent sur le tiroir. 2. F: A: Faire des économies; liarder. screw back, v.i. Bill: 1. Faire de l'effet rétrograde; F: faire un rétro. 2. (Of ball) Revenir en arrière. screw down, v.tr. Visser (un couvercle, un cercueil); fermer (une boîte) à vis. screw off, v.tr. (a) Dévisser (un écrou). (b) The end screws off for cleaning, le bout se dévisse pour le nettoyage. screw on, v.tr. (a) Visser, fixer. F: His head is screwed on the right way, il a de la tête, du bon sens; c'est un homme de tête. (b) The nozzle screws on to the head of the hose, la lance se visse au bout du tuyau. screw out, v.tr. F: To s. the truth out of s.o., tirer la vérité de qn. To s. money out of s.o., arracher, extorquer, de l'argent à qn. It is hard to s. money out of him, il est dur à la détente. screw up, v.tr. 1. Visser (une boîte, etc.); condamner (une porte). 2. Entortiller, tortiller (qch.); tire-bouchonner (son mouchoir). To s. sth. up in a piece of paper, entortiller qch. dans un morceau de papier. To s. up one's eyes, plisser les yeux. To s. up one's lips, pincer les lèvres. He screwed up his face, il fit la grimace. 3. F: To s. up one's courage, prendre son courage à deux mains. To s. oneself up to do sth., se forcer à faire qch. 4. U.S: F: Bousiller, gâcher, savater, torchonner (qch., un travail). screwed, a. 1. Fileté, taraudé. 2. Pred. F: Ivre; F: gris, éméché; P: paf. 3. U.S: P: Fichu.
screwball ['skru:bɔ:l], a. & s. U.S: F: Cinglé, loufoque, marteau (m), timbré; P: dingo, dingue.
screwdriver ['skru:draivər], s. Tournevis m.
screwy ['skru:i], a. F: Cinglé, louftingue.
scribble¹ ['skribl], s. 1. Griffonnage m. 2. Écriture f illisible.
scribble², v.tr. Griffonner (quelques mots à qn). Abs. To s., (i) barbouiller du papier; (ii) faire du journalisme; écrivailler. scribbling, s. Griffonnage m. S. paper, papier à brouillon. S. block, bloc-notes m.
scribbler ['skriblər], s. 1. Griffonneur, -euse. 2. F: Écrivailleur, -euse; gratte-papier m inv.
scribe¹ [skraib], s. Scribe m.
scribe², s. Tls: S.(-awl), pointe f à tracer; tire-ligne m, pl. tire-lignes.
scribe³, v.tr. 1. Carp: Tracer, trusquiner (une ligne). 2. Mec.E: etc: Repérer, pointer (le centre). 'scribing-block, s. Trusquin m à équerre.
scriber ['skraibər], s. = SCRIBE².
scrim [skrim], s. Tex: Furn: Canevas léger.
scrimmage ['skrimidʒ], s. Mêlée f; bagarre f, bousculade f.
scrip¹ [skrip], s. A: Besace f.
scrip², s. (No pl.) Fin: 1. S. (certificate), certificat m (d'actions); actions f provisoires. 2. Coll. F: Valeurs fpl, titres mpl, actions.
scripholder ['skrip,houldər], s. Fin: Détenteur, -trice, de titres.

script [skript], s. 1. (a) Manuscrit m. (b) Sch: Copie f (d'examen). (c) Jur: (Document) original m, -aux. (d) Cin: Scénario m. 2. (a) (As opposed to print) Écriture f. (b) Typ: Cursive f. 'script-girl, s. Cin: etc: Script-girl, f, pl. script-girls. 'script(-)writer, s. Scénariste mf.
scriptural ['skriptʃ(ə)r(ə)l], a. Scriptural, -aux; biblique; des saintes Écritures.
scripture ['skriptʃər], s. Holy S., the Scriptures, l'Écriture sainte, les saintes Écritures. Sch: S. (lesson), (leçon d') histoire sainte.
scrivener ['skrivnər], s. A: (a) Scribe m, copiste m; écrivain public. (b) Notaire m. (c) Changeur m, prêteur m (d'argent).
scrofula ['skrɔfjulə], s. Med: Scrofule f; écrouelles fpl.
scrofulous ['skrɔfjuləs], a. Scrofuleux, -euse.
scroll [skroul], s. 1. Rouleau m (de parchemin, de papier). 2. (a) Art: Banderole f à inscription. (b) Her: Listel m. 3. (a) Arch: etc: Spirale f; volute f (de chapiteau ionique). (b) (In writing) Enjolivement m, arabesque f. (c) Crosse f, volute (de violon). 'scroll-saw, s. Tls: Scie f à chantourner. 'scroll-work, s. Arch: Ornementation f en volute.
scrotum, pl. -ta ['skroutəm, -tə], s. Anat: Scrotum m.
scrounge [skraundʒ]. F: 1. v.tr. (a) (Steal) Chiper, chaparder, rabioter, rabiauter (qch.). (b) (Sponge) Écornifler (un dîner, du tabac). (c) F: They were scrounging fuel in the ruins, ils récupéraient du combustible dans les ruines. 2. v.i. (a) To s. around for sth., aller à la recherche de qch. (b) To s. on s.o., vivre aux crochets de qn. scrounging, s. (a) Chipage m, chapardage m. (b) Écorniflage m. (c) F: Récupération f.
scrounger ['skraundʒər], s. F: (a) Chipeur, -euse, chapardeur, -euse; rabioteur, -euse, rabiauteur, -euse. (b) Écornifleur, -euse.
scrub¹ [skrʌb], s. 1. (a) Arbuste rabougri. (b) Broussailles fpl; brousse f. 2. Barbe f de trois jours.
scrub², s. Friction f (à la brosse); nettoyage m. To give the table a good s., bien laver la table avec une brosse dure. The saucepan wants a s., la casserole a besoin d'être récurée. 'scrub-broom, s. Nau: Goret m. 'scrub-'team, s. U.S: Sp: Équipe f de deuxième ordre.
scrub³, v.tr. (scrubbed) 1. (a) Récurer (une casserole); laver, frotter, (le plancher) avec une brosse dure. (b) Nau: (i) Goreter, (ii) briquer (le pont). 2. Ch: Laver, épurer (un gaz). 3. F: Annuler (qch.). scrubbing, s. 1. (a) Récurage m; nettoyage m, lavage m avec une brosse dure. (b) Nau: (i) Goretage m; (ii) briquetage m. 2. Ch: Lavage m, épuration m (d'un gaz). 'scrubbing-brush, s. Brosse dure.
scrubber ['skrʌbər], s. 1. (Pers.) Laveur, -euse (à la brosse dure). 2. (a) Paint s., brosse f à peinture. (b) Ch: Épurateur m; flacon laveur. Gasm: Épurateur, scrubber m. Air s., épurateur d'air.
scrubby¹ ['skrʌbi], a. 1. Rabougri. 2. (Of land) Couvert de broussailles. 3. F: (Of pers.) Insignifiant; chétif, -ive, piètre (de sa personne).
scrubby², a. F: (Of chin) Mal rasé; (of moustache) hérissé. S. beard, barbe de trois jours.
scrubwoman, pl. -women ['skrʌbwumən, -wimin], s.f. U.S: Femme de ménage.
scruff [skrʌf], s. Nuque f; peau f de la nuque. Used in To seize an animal by the s. of the neck, saisir un animal par la peau du cou.
scruffy ['skrʌfi], a. F: Mal soigné; P: mal fichu.
scrum(mage) ['skrʌm(idʒ)], s. Rugby Fb: Mêlée f. F: Bousculade f. 'scrum-cap, s. Rugby Fb: Protège-oreilles m inv. 'scrum-half, s. Demi m de mêlée.
scrumptious ['skrʌm(p)ʃəs], a. F: O: Excellent, délicieux, épatant.
scrunch¹ [skrʌn(t)ʃ], s. 1. Coup m de dents. 2. Bruit m de broiement; craquement m, grincement m.
scrunch², v.tr. 1. Croquer (avec les dents). 2. Écraser (la neige durcie).
scruple¹ ['skru:pl], s. Meas: Scrupule m (de 20 grains).
scruple², s. Scrupule m (de conscience). To have scruples about sth., about doing sth., éprouver des scrupules au sujet de qch.; se faire (un) scrupule de faire qch. To have no scruples, to make no s., about doing sth., n'avoir aucun scrupule à faire qch.; ne pas hésiter à faire qch.

scruple³, *v.i.* To s. to do sth., avoir des scrupules à faire qch. He does not s. to . . ., il n'hésite pas à. . . .

scrupulous ['skru:pjuləs], *a.* 1. Scrupuleux, -euse (about, over, as to, sur). To be s. in doing sth., faire qch. scrupuleusement. Not over-s. in one's dealings, peu délicat en affaires. 2. (Of care, work) Scrupuleux, exact, méticuleux, -euse, minutieux, -euse. -ly, *adv.* 1. Scrupuleusement. 2. Méticuleusement, minutieusement. S. exact, exact jusqu'au scrupule.

scrupulousness ['skru:pjuləsnis], *s.* 1. Scrupulosité *f.* 2. Esprit scrupuleux.

scrutineer [skru:ti'niər], *s. Adm:* Scrutateur *m* (des votes, du scrutin).

scrutinize ['skru:tinaiz], *v.tr.* (a) Scruter; examiner (qch.) minutieusement. (b) To s. votes, vérifier, pointer, des suffrages. **scrutinizing¹**, *a.* Scrutateur, -trice; investigateur, -trice; inquisiteur. **scrutinizing²**, *s.* (a) Examen minutieux (de qch.). (b) *Pol: Adm:* Vérification *f*, pointage *m* (des suffrages).

scrutiny ['skru:tini], *s.* (a) Examen minutieux. His record does not bear s., son passé ne supporte pas un examen rigoureux. (b) *Pol:* Vérification *f* (des bulletins de vote). To demand a s., contester la validité d'une élection.

scud¹ [skʌd], *s.* 1. Course précipitée; fuite *f.* 2. (a) (Of clouds) Diablotins *mpl.* (b) Rafale *f.* (c) Embrun *m.*

scud², *v.i.* (scudded) 1. Courir droit et vite; filer comme le vent. To s. away, off, s'enfuir, détaler. 2. *Nau:* To s. before the wind, fuir vent arrière; avoir (le) vent sous vergue; cingler.

scuff [skʌf]. 1. *v.tr.* (a) Frotter, racler, user (avec les pieds). (b) To s. away the tread of the tyre, user la bande de roulement. 2. *v.i.* Traîner les pieds.

scuffle¹ ['skʌfl], *s.* Mêlée *f*, échauffourée *f*, bousculade *f*; (between crowd and police) bagarre *f.*

scuffle², *v.i.* 1. Se battre, se bousculer. To s. with s.o., se colleter avec qn. 2. To s. through a job, accomplir une tâche tant bien que mal, à la hâte. 3. Traîner les pieds.

scull¹ [skʌl], *s.* 1. *Row:* (a) Aviron *m* de couple, scull *m.* (b) Aviron, rame *f.* 2. Godille *f.*

scull². 1. *v.i.* (a) Ramer, nager, en couple. (b) Godiller. (c) *F:* Ramer. 2. *v.tr.* To s. a boat, faire avancer un bateau (i) à couple, (ii) à la godille, (iii) *F:* à la rame.

sculler ['skʌlər], *s.* 1. (a) Rameur *m* de couple. (b) Godilleur *m.* 2. (Boat) Double-s., outrigger *m* à deux rameurs de couple.

scullery ['skʌləri], *s.* Arrière-cuisine *f*; souillarde *f.* 'scullery maid, *s.f.* Laveuse de vaisselle.

scullion ['skʌljən], *s. A:* Marmiton *m.*

sculpt [skʌlpt], *v.tr. & i.* Sculpter.

sculptor ['skʌlptər], *s.* Sculpteur *m.*

sculptress ['skʌlptris], *s.f.* Femme sculpteur.

sculptural ['skʌlptjur(ə)l], *a.* Sculptural, -aux. S. beauty, beauté sculpturale, plastique.

sculpture¹ ['skʌlptʃər], *s.* Sculpture *f* (l'art ou l'œuvre).

sculpture², *v.tr.* 1. Sculpter. *Abs.* Faire de la sculpture. To s. a statue out of stone, sculpter une statue dans la pierre. 2. Orner de sculptures, de bas-reliefs. **sculpturing**, *s.* Sculpture *f.*

scum¹ [skʌm], *s.* 1. (a) Écume *f*, mousse *f.* To take the s. off the pot, écumer le pot. (b) *Metall:* Scories *fpl*, crasse(s) *f(pl).* 2. The s. of society, le rebut de la société. S. of the earth, excrément *m* de la terre.

scum², *v.* (scummed) 1. *v.tr.* Écumer (le bouillon, etc.). 2. *v.i.* Écumer; se couvrir d'écume.

scummy ['skʌmi], *a.* 1. Écumeux, -euse; couvert d'écume. 2. Qui ressemble à de l'écume.

scupper¹ ['skʌpər], *s. Nau:* Dalot *m* (de pont).

scupper², *v.tr.* (a) *Mil: Nau: P: O:* Surprendre et massacrer (des troupes, l'équipage). (b) *F:* Couler à fond (un navire); saborder (un navire, un projet). To s. oneself, se saborder, se ruiner (volontairement).

scurf [skə:f], *s.* Pellicules *fpl* (du cuir chevelu); farine *f* (d'une dartre); (in boiler) tartre *m.*

scurfy ['skə:fi], *a.* (a) (Of head, etc.) Pelliculeux, -euse. (b) S. affection of the skin, dartre *f.*

scurrility [skʌ'riliti], *s.* 1. Grossièreté *f*, obscénité *f* (de langage); bassesse *f* (d'une personne, d'une action). 2. To indulge in scurrilities, prononcer, publier, des grossièretés sur le compte de qn.

scurrilous ['skʌriləs], *a.* (Of language, etc.) Grossier, -ière, injurieux, -euse, ordurier, -ière; (of pers.) ignoble, vil. To make a s. attack on s.o., se répandre en injures contre qn. S. little rag, petite feuille de chou ordurière. -ly, *adv.* Grossièrement.

scurry¹ ['skʌri], *s.* 1. Galopade *f*; débandade *f.* A regular s., un sauve-qui-peut général. A general s. towards the door, une bousculade vers la porte. 2. Tourbillon *m* (de neige, etc.).

scurry², *v.i.* Courir à pas précipités; se hâter. To s. off, away, détaler, décamper. To s. through one's work, expédier son travail.

scurvy¹ ['skə:vi], *s. Med:* Scorbut *m.*

scurvy², *a.* Bas, vil, vilain, indigne. S. trick, rosserie *f*, vilain tour, goujaterie *f.* To play s.o. a s. trick, faire une crasse à qn.

scut [skʌt], *s.* Couette *f* (de lièvre, de lapin).

scutch [skʌtʃ], *v.tr. Tex:* Écanguer, teiller (le chanvre, le lin).

scutcheon ['skʌtʃ(ə)n], *s.* Écusson *m.*

scuttle¹ ['skʌtl], *s.* Seau *m* à charbon.

scuttle², *s.* 1. *Nau:* (a) Écoutillon *m*; descente *f.* (b) Hublot *m*; lentille *f* (de cabine). 2. *U.S:* Trappe *f* (de toit).

scuttle³, *v.tr. Nau:* Saborder (un navire). To s. one's ship, s'envoyer par le fond. **scuttling**, *s.* Sabordage *m.*

scuttle⁴, *s.* Fuite *f*; course précipitée; débandade *f. Pol: F:* Policy of s., (politique *f* de) lâchage (*m*).

scuttle⁵, *v.i.* (a) Courir d'une façon affairée. To s. off, away, déguerpir, filer, détaler. (b) *Pol: F:* Renoncer à un mandat; se retirer; *F:* lâcher.

scutum, *pl.* -a ['skju:təm, -ə], *s.* 1. *Rom.Ant: Z:* Scutum *m*, bouclier *m.* 2. *Ent:* Écusson *m.* 3. *Anat:* Rotule *f.*

scythe¹ [saið], *s. Tls:* Faux *f.* 'scythe-stone, *s.* Pierre *f* à faux.

scythe², *v.tr.* Faucher (le blé, etc.).

'sdeath [zdeθ], *int. A:* (Euphemism for God's death!) Mordieu! morbleu!

sea [si:], *s.* 1. Mer *f.* (a) An arm of the s., un bras de mer. On land and s., by land and s., sur terre et sur mer. By the s., au bord de la mer. S., par (voie de) mer. Beyond, over, the sea(s), outre-mer. From beyond the s., d'outre-mer. The s. air, l'air de la mer, l'air marin. To smell of the s., sentir la mer, la marine. S. bathing, bains *mpl* de mer. (Of pers.) To put to s., s'embarquer. To go to s., to take to the s., to follow the sea., se faire marin. To serve at s., servir sur mer. S. trip, excursion *f* en mer. A long s. journey, une longue traversée. S. battle, bataille navale. (b) The open s., the high seas, le large, la haute mer. On the high seas, out at s., en pleine mer. Towards the open s., in the open s., au grand large. (Of ship) To put (out) to s., prendre la mer, le large. To remain at s., to keep the s. (in heavy weather), tenir la mer. To stand out to s., gagner le large, prendre le large. Head on to s., le cap au large. Ship at s., navire en mer. *F:* To be all at s., être tout désorienté; n'y être pas du tout; ne savoir sur quel pied danser; patauger. I am quite at s., je ne m'y reconnais plus. (c) Inland s., mer intérieure, mer fermée. The seven seas, toutes les mers du monde. 2. (a) (State of the sea) Heavy s., strong s., grosse mer; mer houleuse. There is a (heavy) s., il y a de la mer. In anything of a s . . . ., pour peu qu'il y ait de la mer. . . . (b) Lame *f*, houle *f.* To run before the s., gouverner l'arrière à la lame; fuir devant la lame. Head s., mer debout. Beam s., mer de travers. (c) Coup *m* de mer; paquet *m* de mer; (grosse) vague. To ship a (green) s., embarquer une lame, un coup de mer, un paquet de mer. To be struck by a (heavy) s., essuyer un coup de mer. To ship heavy seas, embarquer d'énormes paquets de mer. 3. Océan *m*, infinité *f*, multitude *f.* A s. of faces, of corn, un océan de visages, de blés. *Lit:* A s. of cares, une infinité, une multitude, de soucis. 'sea-anchor, *s. Nau:* Ancre flottante; ancre de cape. 'sea-a'nemone, *s. Coel:* Actinie *f*; *F:*

anémone *f* de mer. '**sea-boots**, *s.pl.* Bottes *f* de marin, de mer. '**sea-born**, *a. Myth:* Né de la mer. '**sea-borne**, *a. (Of trade)* Maritime; *(of goods)* transporté par mer. '**sea-bound**, *a. (Of land)* Borné par la mer. '**sea-breeze**, *s.* Brise *f* du large. '**sea-calf**, *s. Z:* Phoque commun; veau marin. '**sea-captain**, *s.m.* Capitaine de la marine marchande; capitaine au long cours. '**sea-chart**, *s. Nau:* Carte marine. '**sea-chest**, *s.* Coffre *m* (de marin). '**sea-cow**, *s. Z:* 1. Dugong *m, F:* vache marine. 2. Lamantin *m*, manate *m, F:* bœuf marin. 3. Morse *m.* 4.*F:* Hippopotame. '**sea-'crayfish**, *s.* Langouste *f.* '**sea-dog**, *s.* An old s.-d., un vieux marin; un vieux loup de mer. '**sea-eagle**, *s. Orn:* Pygargue *m*, orfraie *f; F:* grand aigle des mers. '**sea-elephant**, *s.* Éléphant *m* marin; phoque *m* à trompe. '**sea-fennel**, *s. Bot:* = SAMPHIRE 1. '**sea fight**, *s.* Combat naval. '**sea fish**, *s.* Poisson *m* de mer. '**sea-floor**, *s.* Fond sous-marin. '**sea-girt**, *a. Lit:* Entouré, ceint, par la mer. '**sea-god**, *s.m.* Dieu marin; triton. '**sea-going**, *a.* 1. De haute mer; affecté à la navigation maritime. S.-g. ship, navire de long cours, long-courrier *m, pl.* long-courriers; navire *m*, bâtiment *m*, de mer. 2. *(Of pers.)* = SEAFARING¹. '**sea-green**, *s. & a.* Vert *(m)* de mer *inv;* vert d'eau *inv;* glauque. '**sea-horse**, *s.* 1. *Z:* Morse *m.* 2. *Myth: Z:* Hippocampe *m; F:* cheval marin. '**sea-lawyer**, *s. F:* 1. Requin *m* (féroce). 2. Rouspéteur *m*, chicaneur *m.* '**sea legs**, *s.pl. F:* Pied marin. '**sea-level**, *s.* Niveau (moyen) de la mer. Pressure corrected to s.-l., pression (barométrique) ramenée au niveau de la mer. '**sea lion**, *s. Z:* Otarie *f.* '**sea(-)lord**, *s.* Lord *m* de l'Amirauté. First S.-L. = Ministre de la Marine. '**sea-mark**, *s. Nau:* (*a*) Amer *m.* (*b*) Balise *f.* '**sea mile**, *s.* Mille marin. '**sea-otter**, *s. Z:* Loutre *f* de mer. '**sea-pass**, *s. (For neutral ships in time of war)* Permis *m* de navigation; laissez-passer *m inv.* '**sea-power**, *s.* Puissance *f* maritime. '**sea-risk**, *s. M.Ins:* Risque *m* de mer; fortune *f* de mer. '**sea-room**, *s. Nau:* (*a*) Évitage *m;* évitée *f.* (*b*) Eau *f* à courir. To have plenty of s.-r., (i) avoir de l'évitée; (ii) avoir une belle dérive. '**sea-'rover**, *s.* Corsaire *m*, pirate *m*, flibustier *m.* '**sea-salt**, *s.* Sel marin. '**sea scout**, *s.m.* Scout marin. '**sea-serpent**, *s.* (*a*) Serpent *m* de mer. (*b*) Monstre *m* maritime. '**sea-shell**, *s.* Coquille *f* de mer; coquillage *m.* '**sea-'shore**, *s.* (*a*) Rivage *m;* bord *m* de la mer. (*b*) Plage *f.* '**sea-sick**, *a.* Qui a le mal de mer. To be s.-s., avoir le mal de mer. '**sea-sickness**, *s.* Mal *m* de mer. '**sea-trip**, *s.* (*a*) Promenade *f* en mer. (*b*) Croisière *f* d'agrément. '**sea-trout**, *s. Ich:* Truite *f* de mer. '**sea-urchin**, *s. Echin:* Oursin *m.* '**sea voyage**, *s.* Voyage *m* par mer; traversée *f.* '**sea-'wall**, *s.* Digue *f.* '**sea-water**, *s.* Eau *f* de mer. '**sea-wind**, *s.* Vent *m* de mer, du large. '**sea-wolf**, *s.* 1. *Ich:* Bar(s) *m;* loup *m.* 2. Viking *m.*

seabird ['si:bə:d], *s.* Oiseau *m* de mer.
seaboard ['si:bɔ:d], *s.* Littoral *m;* rivage *m* (de la mer). S. town, ville maritime.
seacoast ['si:'koust], *s.* Littoral *m*, -aux; côte *f* (de la mer).
seacraft ['si:krɑft], *s.* 1. Art *m* du navigateur. 2. *Coll. pl.* Petits bâtiments de mer.
seafarer ['si:ˌfɛərər], *s.* (*a*) Homme *m* de mer; marin *m.* (*b*) She had been a great s., elle avait fait de nombreux voyages sur mer.
seafaring¹ ['si:ˌfɛəriŋ], *a.* (Gens, etc.) de mer, qui naviguent. S. man, marin *m.*
seafaring², *s.* Voyages *mpl* par mer.
seafood ['si:fu:d], *s.* = Fruits *mpl* de mer.
seafowl ['si:faul], *s. inv.* Oiseau *m* de mer.
seafront ['si:frʌnt], *s.* 1. Partie *f* d'une ville qui fait face à la mer. House on the s., maison qui donne sur la mer. 2. Digue *f*, esplanade *f.*
seagull ['si:gʌl], *s.* Mouette *f;* goéland *m.*
seakale ['si:keil], *s. Bot:* Crambe *m*, crambé *m*, chou marin.
seal¹ [si:l], *s.* 1. *Z:* Phoque *m.* S. oil, huile *f* de phoque. S. fishery, (i) pêche *f* des phoques; (ii) pêcherie *f* de phoques. 2. *Com:* Con(e)y s., fourrure *f* genre loutre. 3. *Leath:* Phoque (pour gainerie).

sealing¹ ['si:liŋ], *s.* Chasse *f* au phoque; pêche *f* des phoques.
seal², *s.* 1. (*a*) Sceau *m;* *(on letter)* cachet *m. Jur:* Given under my hand and s., signé et scellé par moi. Under the s. of secrecy, sous le sceau du secret. To put one's s. to a document, marquer un document de son sceau. To set one's s. to sth., autoriser qch.; donner son approbation à qch. Book that bears the s. of genius, livre qui porte le sceau, le cachet, du génie. (*b*) Cachet (de bouteille de vin, etc.). *Ind:* S. of approval, label *m. Jur:* Official s. (affixed to property, etc.), scellé *m.* To affix, remove, the seals, apposer, lever, les scellés. *Com:* Leaden s., plomb *m* (pour sceller une caisse). Custom-house s., plomb de la douane. 2. *(Instrument)* Sceau, cachet. The Great S., le grand sceau (employé pour les actes publics). 3. *Tchn:* (*a*) Dispositif *m* d'étanchéité; joint *m* étanche; tampon *m.* (*b*) (Liquide) obturateur *m* (d'un siphon).
seal³, *v.tr.* 1. (*a*) Sceller (un acte); cacheter (une lettre). To s. a bargain, confirmer, régler une affaire, un marché. His fate is sealed, son sort est réglé; c'en est fait de lui. (*b*) Cacheter (une bouteille de porto, etc.); plomber (un colis). *Jur:* Apposer les scellés sur (une porte, un meuble). 2. (*a*) To s. (up) a letter, fermer une lettre. (*b*) To s. up the windows, fermer hermétiquement les fenêtres. (*c*) My lips are sealed, il m'est défendu de parler. (*d*) Assurer l'étanchéité (d'un joint, etc.). To s. a puncture, réparer un pneu crevé. (*e*) *(Of police)* To s. off a district, mettre un cordon autour d'un quartier. sealing², *s.* 1. (*a*) Scellage *m* (d'un acte); cachetage *m* (d'une lettre). (*b*) Plombage *m* (d'un colis). 2. S. (up), fermeture *f;* obturation *f.* '**sealing-wax**, *s.* Cire *f* à cacheter.
sealer ['si:lər], *s.* 1. Navire armé pour la chasse des phoques. 2. Chasseur *m*, pêcheur *m*, de phoques.
sealskin ['si:lskin], *s.* 1. Peau *f* de phoque. 2. *Com:* (Fourrure *f* en) loutre *f.*
seam¹ [si:m], *s.* 1. (*a*) Couture *f.* Flat s., couture rabattue. Overcast s., surjet *m.* French s., couture double. Outside-stitched s., couture piquée. Welted s., couture en baguette. (*b*) *(In metal pipe, etc.)* Couture, joint *m.* Brazed s., brasure *f.* Welded s., soldered s., joint soudé; soudure *f.* S. welding, soudage *m* à molettes. (*c*) Ship's seams, coutures d'un navire. Lapped s., couture à clin. 2. (*a*) *(On face, etc.)* Ride *f.* (*b*) *(In wood, rock)* Fissure *f*, gerçure *f.* 3. *Min:* Couche *f*, gisement *m*, gîte *m*, veine *f.*
seam², *v.tr.* 1. Faire une couture. To s. up a garment, assembler un vêtement. 2. Souder (un joint, etc.). 3. Seamed and lined face, visage ridé. Face seamed with scars, visage couturé de cicatrices.
seaman, *pl.* -men ['si:mən], *s.m.* 1. Marin, matelot. *Navy:* Matelot de la marine nationale. Ordinary s., matelot de troisième classe, de pont. Able(-bodied) s., matelot de deuxième classe. Leading s., matelot (breveté) de première classe; quartier-maître. 2. (*a*) Manœuvrier. (*b*) Navigateur. A good s., un bon manœuvrier; un bon navigateur.
seamanlike ['si:mənlaik]. 1. *a.* De marin, d'un bon marin. 2. *adv.* En bon marin.
seamanship ['si:mənʃip], *s.* Manœuvre *f* et matelotage *m;* la manœuvre.
seamew ['si:mju:], *s. Orn:* Mouette *f*, goéland *m.*
seamless ['si:mlis], *a.* 1. Sans couture. 2. Sans soudure.
seamstress ['semstris], *s.f.* Ouvrière couturière.
seamy ['si:mi], *a.* Qui montre les coutures. The s. side of life, l'envers *m*, les dessous *m*, de la vie.
séance ['seiɑ:ns], *s.* Séance *f* de spiritisme.
seaplane ['si:plein], *s. Av:* Hydravion *m.* S. base, station hydroaérienne, hydrobase *f.*
seaport ['si:pɔ:t], *s.* Port *m* de mer.
sear¹ [siər], *s. Sm.a:* Gâchette *f* (de fusil).
sear², *v.tr.* 1. *(Of heat, frost)* Flétrir, dessécher (les feuilles, le grain); faner (les feuilles). 2. (*a*) Cautériser (une blessure). Endurcir (la conscience); dessécher (le cœur). (*b*) Marquer au fer rouge. '**searing-iron**, *s.* Fer *m* à cautériser; cautère *m.*
sear³, *a.* = SERE.

search[1] [səːtʃ], *s.* **1.** Recherche(s) *f(pl)*. **To make a s.**, faire des recherches. **To make a s. for** s.o., (re)chercher qn. **In s. of . . .**, à la recherche de. . . . **2.** (*a*) *Cust:* Visite *f.* **Right of s.**, droit de visite; (*at sea*) droit de recherche. (*b*) *Jur:* Perquisition *f.* **House-s.**, visite domiciliaire; perquisition à domicile. **S. warrant**, mandat *m* de perquisition. (*c*) Fouille *f* (dans un tiroir). **'search-party**, *s.* Expédition *f* de secours.

search[2]. **1.** *v.tr.* Inspecter (un endroit); chercher dans (un endroit, une boîte); fouiller dans (un tiroir); fouiller (un suspect, les poches de qn). *Cust:* **To s. a ship**, s.o.'s trunks, visiter un navire, les malles de qn. *Jur:* **To s. a house**, faire une visite domiciliaire; perquisitionner dans une maison. **To s. men's hearts**, scruter, sonder, les cœurs. *P:* **S. me!** je n'ai pas la moindre idée! **2.** *v.i.* **To s. into the cause of sth.**, rechercher la cause de qch. **To s. after the truth**, rechercher la vérité. **To s. for sth.**, (re)chercher qch. **searching**, *a.* (Examen) minutieux, attentif; (regard) pénétrant, scrutateur; (vent) pénétrant. **To give s.o. a s. look**, scruter qn du regard. **S. questions**, questions qui vont au fond des choses. **-ly**, *adv.* (Examiner, etc.) minutieusement; (regarder, qn, etc.) d'un œil scrutateur, pénétrant. **searching**[2], *s.* = SEARCH[1].

searcher ['səːtʃər], *s.* **1.** (*a*) Chercheur, -euse, rechercheur, -euse (after, de). (*b*) *Cust:* Douanier *m.* (*c*) *Jur:* Perquisiteur *m*, perquisitionneur *m.* **2.** *Surg:* Sonde *f.*

searchlight ['səːtʃlait], *s.* (*a*) Projecteur *m.* (*b*) (*Beam*) Projection *f* électrique. **To flash a s. on sth.**, donner un coup de projecteur sur qch.

seascape ['siːskeip], *s. Art:* Marine *f.*

seaside ['siːsaid, 'siːsaid], *s.* **1.** Bord *m* de la mer. **2.** *attrib.* ['siːsaid] **S. resort**, station *f* balnéaire; plage *f.*

season[1] ['siːzn], *s.* **1.** Saison *f.* (*a*) **The rainy s.**, la saison des pluies. **Late s.**, arrière-saison *f.* **Holiday s.**, **hunting s.**, saison des vacances, de la chasse. *Ven:* **Close s.**, **open s.**, chasse, pêche, fermée, ouverte. **The dull s.**, **the dead s.**, **the off s.**, la morte-saison. **The busy s.**, le fort de la saison. **Between-s.**, demisaison *f.* (*Of oysters, etc.*) **To be in s.**, être de saison. *Husb:* **Mare in s.**, jument *f* en chaleur. (*Fruit, etc.*) **Out of s.**, hors de saison. (*b*) **The (London) s.**, la saison (mondaine de Londres). **The s. is at its height**, la saison bat son plein. **Very early in the s.**, très tôt en saison. **2.** Période *f*, temps *m. Cin:* **This film will be shown for a short s.**, ce film sera projeté pendant une courte période. **To last for a s.**, durer pendant quelque temps. **It shall be done in due s.**, cela se fera en temps voulu. **Word in s.**, mot dit à propos. **Remark out of s.**, remarque déplacée. **In and out of s.**, à tout propos et hors de propos; à tout bout de champ. **3.** *F:* = SEASONTICKET. **'(Show) all seasons, please!'** "les abonnements, s'il vous plaît!" **'season-'ticket**, *s.* Carte *f* d'abonnement. **S.-t. holder**, abonné, -ée.

season[2]. **1.** *v.tr.* (*a*) Assaisonner, relever (un mets) **Speech seasoned with irony**, discours assaisonné d'ironie. (*b*) Dessécher, étuver, conditionner (le bois); mûrir, laisser se faire (le vin); aviner (un fût). (*c*) Acclimater, endurcir (qn); aguerrir (un soldat); amariner (un matelot). (*d*) Tempérer, modérer. **Justice seasoned with goodwill**, justice tempérée de bienveillance. **2.** *v.i.* (*Of wood, etc.*) Sécher; (*of wine, etc.*) mûrir, se faire. **seasoned**, *a.* **1.** Assaisonné. **Highly s. dish**, plat relevé. **Highly s. anecdote**, anecdote relevée, épicée. **2.** (*a*) (*Of wood, cigar*) Sec, *f.* sèche; (*of wine*) mûr, fait. (*b*) **To grow, become, s.**, (*of soldier*) s'aguerrir, (*of sailor*) s'amariner. **seasoning**, *s.* **1.** (*a*) *Cu:* Assaisonnement *m.* (*b*) Séchage *m*; maturation *f.* (*c*) Acclimatement *m*; aguerrissement *m.* **2.** *Cu:* Assaisonnement, condiment *m.*

seasonable ['siːznəbl], *a.* **1.** De (la) saison. **S. weather**, temps de saison. **2.** (*Of aid, advice*) Opportun, à propos. **-ably**, *adv.* Opportunément, à propos.

seasonableness ['siːznəblnis], *s.* (*Of remark, etc.*) Opportunité *f.*

seasonal ['siːznl], *a.* (Changements, etc.) des saisons; (commerce) saisonnier. **S. worker**, saisonnier, -ière. *Med:* **S. disease**, maladie saisonnière.

seat[1] [siːt], *s.* **1.** (*a*) Siège *m*; banquette *f* (d'autobus, etc.); gradin *m* (d'amphithéâtre); selle *f* (de bicyclette); lunette *f* (de w.-c.). **Driver's s.**, siège du conducteur. **Folding s.**, pliant *m.* **Flap-s.**, **bracket-s.**, siège escamotable, strapontin *m.* (*b*) **To take a s.**, s'asseoir. **To keep one's s.**, rester assis; rester à sa place. (*c*) Place *f.* **Car with four seats**, voiture à quatre places. *Th:* **S. in the stalls**, fauteuil *m* d'orchestre. **I want two seats**, il me faut deux places. *Rail:* 'Take your seats!' "en voiture!" (*d*) **He has a s. in the House**, il siège au Parlement. **To vacate one's s.**, se démettre. **2.** (*a*) Siège, fond *m* (d'une chaise). **Rush s.**, siège en paille. (*b*) *F:* Postérieur *m*, derrière *m.* **He came down on his s.**, il s'est assis par terre. (*c*) Fond (de culotte). **3.** (*a*) Théâtre *m* (de la guerre); siège, centre *m* (du gouvernement, etc.); foyer *m* (d'une maladie, etc.). (*b*) **Country s.**, château *m*; manoir *m.* **4.** *Equit:* Assiette *f*, assise *f.* **To keep one's s.**, conserver l'assiette. **To lose one's s.**, être désarçonné. (*Of rider*) **To have a good s.**, bien se tenir en selle; avoir de l'assiette. **5.** *Tchn:* Siège (d'une soupape); chaise *f* (d'un coussinet); embase *f*, assiette, surface *f* d'appui (d'une machine). **'seat-holder**, *s. Th: etc:* Personne qui a retenu une place.

seat[2], *v.tr.* **1.** (Faire) asseoir (un enfant, etc.). **To s. oneself**, s'asseoir. **To ask s.o. to be seated**, faire asseoir qn. *O:* **Please be seated**, donnez-vous la peine de vous asseoir, veuillez vous asseoir, asseyez-vous, s'il vous plaît. **To remain seated**, rester assis. *S.a.* DEEP-SEATED. **2.** (*a*) Placer (qn); trouver place pour (qn). (*Of car, etc.*) **To s. six**, à six places (assises). **This table seats twelve**, on tient douze à cette table. **3.** (Re)mettre le siège à (une chaise). **4.** (*a*) Asseoir, poser (une machine, etc.). *Mec.E:* Faire porter, caler, (une pièce) sur son siège. *I.C.E:* **To s. a valve**, ajuster l'assise d'une soupape. (*b*) (*Of part*) **To s. on . . .**, porter, reposer, sur. . . . **seating**, *s.* **1.** (*a*) Allocation *f* des places. **The s. of the guests**, la disposition des invités. (*b*) Places assises; bancs *mpl* et sièges *mpl.* **S. capacity**, nombre *m* de places (assises). **2.** Matériaux *mpl* pour sièges de chaises. **3.** *Tchn:* Portage *m*; ber *m*, berceau *m* (de chaudière); siège *m* (de soupape); embase *f*, lit *m* de pose (d'une machine); assiette *f.* logement *m.* **4.** Montage *m*, ajustage *m* (d'une pièce).

-seater ['siːtər], *s. Aut:* **Two-s.**, voiture *f* à deux places. *Av:* **Single-s.**, **two-s.**, appareil *m* monoplace, biplace.

seaward ['siːwəd]. **1.** *adv.* = SEAWARDS. **2.** *a.* (*a*) (*Of tide*) Qui porte au large. (*b*) **S. breeze**, brise du large. **3.** *s.* **To s.**, vers le large.

seawards ['siːwədz], *adv.* Vers la mer; vers le large.

seaway ['siːwei], *s.* **1.** Route *f*, sillage *m* (d'un navire). **2.** Mer dure. **3.** (*a*) Voie *f* maritime. (*b*) **The St. Lawrence S.**, la voie maritime du Saint-Laurent.

seaweed ['siːwiːd], *s.* Algue *f*; goémon *m*; varech *m.*

seaworthiness ['siːwəːðinis], *s.* Bon état de navigabilité *f* (d'un navire).

seaworthy ['siːwəːði], *a.* (*Of ship*) En (bon) état de navigabilité; capable de tenir la mer. **2.** Balayures *fpl*

seawrack ['siːræk], *s.* **1.** Varech *m.* **2.** Balayures *fpl* de la mer.

sebaceous [si'beiʃəs], *a.* (*Of gland*) Sébacé.

seborrhea [sebə'riːə], *s. Med:* Séborrhée *f.*

sec[1] [sek], *s. F:* (= SECOND[1]) **Half a s.!** attendez un instant!

sec[2], *s. Mth:* = SECANT 2.

secant ['siːkənt, 'sek-]. *Mth:* **1.** *a.* Sécant: **2.** *s.* Sécante *f.*

secateurs ['sekətəːz], *s.pl. Hort: Tls:* Sécateur *m.*

secede [si'siːd], *v.i.* Faire scission, faire sécession (from, de); se séparer (d'un parti). **seceding**, *a.* Sécessionniste, scissionnaire.

seceder [si'siːdər], *s. Pol: etc:* Sécessionniste *mf*; scissionnaire *m. Rel:* Dissident, -e.

secession [si'seʃ(ə)n], *s.* Sécession *f*; scission *f. Rel:* Dissidence *f. U.S: Hist:* **The War of S.**, la Guerre de Sécession.

secessionist [si'seʃ(ə)nist], **1.** *a. & s.* Scissionniste (*mf*). **2.** *U.S: Hist:* Sécessionniste *mf.*

seclude [si'kluːd], *v.tr.* Tenir (qn, qch.) retiré, éloigné, écarté (from, de). **secluded**, *a.* (Endroit) écarté, retiré. **S. life**, vie retirée, cloîtrée.

seclusion [si'klu:ʒ(ə)n], s. Solitude f, retraite f. **In s.**, retiré du monde. **To live in s.**, vivre retiré; vivre dans la retraite.

second[1] ['sekənd], s. **1.** Seconde f (de temps). **I'll be back in a s.**, je reviens dans un instant. **Timed to a split s.**, chronométré à une fraction de seconde près. **In a split s.**, en un rien de temps. **2.** Seconde (de degré). 'second-hand, s. Aiguille f des secondes; trotteuse f.

second[2]. **I.** a. **1.** Second, deuxième. (a) **Twenty-s.**, vingt-deuxième. **The s. of January**, le deux janvier. **To live on the s. floor**, habiter au deuxième (étage); U.S: habiter au premier. **Charles the S.**, Charles Deux. **Every s. day**, tous les deux jours. **S. marriage**, secondes noces. Aut: **S. gear**, s. F: **second**, deuxième vitesse. Sch: **S. form** = classe de cinquième. S.a. COUSIN. (b) **The s. largest city in the world**, la plus grande ville du monde sauf une. **To travel s. class**, voyager en deuxième classe, en seconde. **In intelligence he is s. to none**, pour l'intelligence il ne le cède à personne. **To take s. place**, passer second. **To be s. in command**, commander en second. S.a. FIDDLE[1] 1, LIEUTENANT. **2.** Second; autre; nouveau. **S. nature**, seconde nature. S.a. CHILDHOOD, THOUGHT **3.** **-ly**, adv. Deuxièmement; en second lieu. **II. second**, s. **1.** (Le) second, (la) seconde; (le, la) deuxième. **To come in a good s. (to so-and-so)**, arriver bon second (derrière un tel). **2.** Mus: **Major s.**, seconde majeure. **3.** pl. Com: **Seconds**, articles m de deuxième qualité; Mill: griot m. **4.** (a) (In duel) Témoin m. (b) Box: Second m; soigneur m. 'second-best. **1.** a. **My s.-b. suit**, mon complet numéro deux. **My s.-b. umbrella**, mon parapluie de tous les jours. s. **It's a s.-b.**, c'est un pis-aller. **2.** adv. **To come off 's.-'b.**, être battu; F: écoper. 'second-class, a. (Voyageur, wagon) de seconde classe, de seconde; (marchandises) de deuxième qualité; (hôtel) de second ordre. **S.-c. mail** = tarif commercial. 'second-'rate, a. Médiocre, inférieur; de qualité inférieure. **A s.-r. artist**, un artiste de second ordre. 'second 'sight, s. Psychics: Seconde vue; voyance f.

second[3], v.tr. **1.** (a) Seconder (qn); appuyer, soutenir (des troupes, etc.). (b) (In debate) **To s. a motion**, appuyer une proposition. **2.** Mil: etc: [sə'kɔnd] Mettre (un officier) en disponibilité, hors cadre. **To be seconded for service with . . .**, être détaché auprès de. . . .

secondary ['sek(ə)nd(ə)ri], a. **1.** Secondaire. **S. meaning of a word**, sens dérivé d'un mot. Sch: **S. education**, enseignement m du second degré. S.a. SCHOOL[1] 1. El: **S. current**, courant induit, secondaire. **S. winding**, (enroulement) secondaire m. Phil: **S. causes**, causes secondes. **2.** (Rôle, etc.) peu important, de peu d'importance. **S. road** = route départementale. **-arily**, adv. Secondairement; en second.

seconder ['sekəndər], s. (a) **To be the s. of a proposal**, appuyer une proposition. (b) **Proposer and s.** (of a candidate), parrain m et deuxième parrain.

secondhand ['sekənd'hænd]. **1.** Adv. **To buy sth. s.**, acheter qch. d'occasion. **2.** a. (Nouvelles) de seconde main; (marchandises) d'occasion. **S. car**, voiture d'occasion. **S. dealer**, brocanteur, -euse. **S. bookseller**, bouquiniste mf.

secrecy ['si:krəsi], s. **1.** Discrétion f. **To rely on s.o.'s s.**, compter sur la discrétion de qn. **To tell s.o. sth. under pledge of s.**, dire qch. à qn sous le secret. **2.** **In s.**, en secret. **There is no s. about it**, on n'en fait pas mystère.

secret ['si:krit]. **1.** a. (a) Secret, -ète; caché. **To keep sth. s.**, tenir qch. secret; garder le secret au sujet de qch. F: **The S. Service** = le Deuxième Bureau. Adm: **Top s.**, très secret, ultra-secret. **S. door**, porte dérobée. **The s. places of the heart**, les replis m du cœur. (b) (Of pers.) Discret, -ète; peu communicatif, -ive. (c) (Of place) Secret, caché, retiré. **2.** s. (a) Secret m. **He can't keep a s.**, il ne peut pas garder le secret. **To tell each other secrets**, se faire des confidences f. **I make no s. of it**, je n'en fais pas mystère. Com: **Trade s.**, secret de fabrique. **To let s.o. into the s.**, mettre qn dans le secret. **Open s.**, secret de Polichinelle. **To tell sth. as a s.**, dire qch. en confidence. **As a great s.**, en

grand secret. (b) = SECRECY 2. **In s.**, en secret. (c) Ecc: Secrète (prononcée tout bas avant la Préface). **-ly**, adv. Secrètement; en secret, en cachette.

secretaire [,sekrə'tɛər], s. Furn: Secrétaire m.

secretarial [,sekrə'tɛəriəl], a. (Travail, etc.) de secrétaire.

secretariat [,sekrə'tɛəriət], s. Secrétariat m.

secretary ['sekrətri], s. Secrétaire mf. (a) **Honorary s.**, secrétaire honoraire. **Private s.**, secrétaire particulier, -ière. Pol: **(Minister's) principal private s.** = chef m de cabinet. (b) Pol: **S. of State**, (i) ministre m (à portefeuille); ministre d'État; (ii) U.S: = Ministre des Affaires étrangères. (Parliamentary) **Under S. of State**, sous-secrétaire d'Etat. Adm: **Permanent under-s.**, directeur général (d'un ministère). (c) Dipl: Secrétaire d'ambassade. S.a. FOREIGN 2, HOME III. 2. 'secretary-bird, s. Secrétaire m; serpentaire m.

secretaryship ['sekrətriʃip], s. Secrétariat m; fonction f de secrétaire.

secrete[1] [si'kri:t], v.tr. (Of gland) Sécréter.

secrete[2], v.tr. Soustraire (qch.) à la vue; cacher. Jur: Recéler (des objets volés).

secretion [si'kri:ʃ(ə)n], s. Physiol: Sécrétion f.

secretive [si'kri:tiv, 'si:krətiv], a. (Of pers.) Réservé, dissimulé; F: cachottier, -ière.

secretiveness [si'kri:tivnis], s. Dissimulation f; caractère cachottier.

secretory [si'kri:təri], **1.** a. (Of duct, etc.) Sécréteur, -trice. **2.** s. Organe sécréteur.

sect [sekt], s. Secte f.

sectarian [sek'tɛəriən], a. & s. Sectaire (m).

sectarianism [sek'tɛəriənizm], s. Esprit m sectaire; sectarisme m.

section[1] ['sekʃ(ə)n], s. **1.** Sectionnement m, section f. **2.** (a) Tranche f. **Microscopic s.**, lame f mince; lamelle f. (b) Geom: **Conic sections**, sections coniques. (c) Coupe f, profil m. **Longitudinal s.**, profil en long. **Vertical s.**, coupe verticale. **Machine shown in s.**, machine figurée en coupe. S.a. CROSS-SECTION. (d) Civ.E: etc: Profilé m (en métal). **Iron s.**, fer profilé; profilé en fer. **3.** (a) Section; partie f, division f (d'une structure); tronçon m (de tube, etc.); compartiment m (d'un tiroir). **Made in sections**, démontable. **All sections of the population**, toutes les sections de la population. (b) Typ: Section; paragraphe m, alinéa m. **S. mark (§)**, paragraphe. (c) Mil: Groupe m de combat; section f.

section[2], v.tr. Diviser (qch.) en sections; diviser (une région) par sections; sectionner.

sectional ['sekʃənl], a. **1.** (Dessin, etc.) en coupe, en profil. Ind: **S. iron**, fers profilés; profilés mpl en fer. **2.** En sections. **S. bookcase**, bibliothèque démontable, par éléments. **-ally**, adv. Par sections.

sectionalism ['sekʃənəlizm], s. U.S: Régionalisme m.

sector ['sektər], s. **1.** (a) Geom: Astr: Secteur m. (b) Mil: Secteur. Adm: **Postal s.**, secteur postal. Pol. Ec: **Private s.**, secteur privé. **2.** Mec.E: Secteur, couronne f. **S. and gate**, secteur à grille. **3.** Mth: (a) Secteur circulaire. (b) Compas m de proportion.

secular ['sekjulər], a. **1.** Séculier, -ière; (enseignement) laïque. **S. music**, musique profane. Ecc: **S. (priest)**, (prêtre) séculier m. **The s. arm**, le bras séculier; la justice temporelle. **2.** Séculaire. (a) Qui a lieu tous les siècles. (b) Très ancien.

secularity [,sekju'læriti], s. **1.** (a) Sécularité f (du clergé); laïcité f (de l'enseignement). (b) Mondanité f (des mœurs). **2.** Astr: Caractère séculaire (d'une variation, etc.).

secularization ['sekjulərai'zeiʃ(ə)n], s. Sécularisation f; désaffectation f (d'une église); laïcisation f (d'une école).

secularize ['sekjuləraiz], v.tr. Séculariser; laïciser (une école).

secularizm ['sekjulərizm], s. Laïcité f, laïcisme m.

secure[1] [si'kjuər], a. **1.** Sûr; (avenir) assuré. **S. investments**, placements sûrs, de tout repos. **To feel s. of victory**, être assuré, certain, de la victoire. **2.** En sûreté; sauf. **Now we can feel s.**, nous voilà à l'abri, hors de danger. **S. from, against, attack**, à l'abri de toute attaque. **3.** (Of plank, etc.) Fixé, assujetti. (of foundations) solide; (of foothold) ferme, sûr. **To make a plank s.**, assujettir une planche. **-ly**, adv. **1.** (a) Sûrement; avec sécurité. (b) Avec confiance. **2.** Fermement, solidement.

secure², *v.tr.* **1.** (*a*) Mettre en sûreté, à l'abri. **To s. s.o. from sth.**, garantir qn de qch. **To s. a pass**, garder un défilé. (*b*) Mettre (un prisonnier) en lieu sûr. **2.** Immobiliser; assujettir (qch. qui a du jeu); fixer, retenir (qch. à sa place). **To s. the door**, verrouiller la porte. *Nau:* **To s. the boats**, saisir les canots. **3.** *Jur:* Nantir (un prêteur). **Secured by pledges**, nanti de gages. **To s. a debt by mortgage**, garantir une créance par une hypothèque; hypothéquer une créance. **4.** Obtenir, acquérir; se procurer (qch.). **He has secured a good seat**, il s'est assuré une bonne place. **To s. acceptance of sth.**, faire accepter qch. **To s. s.o.'s services**, s'assurer de l'aide de qn.

security [si'kjuəriti], *s.* **1** (*a*) Sécurité *f*, sûreté *f*. *Pol:* **S. Council (of U.N.O.)**, Conseil *m* de sécurité (de l'O.N.U.). *Adm:* **Social s.**, sécurité sociale. **In s.**, en (toute) sécurité. **S. device**, dispositif de sûreté. (*b*) Solidité *f* (d'une fermeture, etc.). **2.** (Moyen *m* de) sécurité; sauvegarde *f*. **3.** *Com: Jur:* (*a*) Caution *f*, cautionnement *m*; (*collateral*) nantissement *m*. **S. for a debt**, garantie *f* d'une créance. **To give sth. as** (a) **s.**, donner qch. en gage. **To pay in a sum as a s.**, verser une provision; verser une somme par provision. **To lodge stock as additional s.**, déposer des titres en nantissement. **To lend money on s.**, prêter de l'argent sur nantissement, sur gage. **Without s.**, à découvert; sans couverture, sans garantie. (*b*) (*Pers.*) (Donneur *m* de) caution; garant *m*. *Jur:* Répondant *m*. **To stand s. for s.o.**, se porter caution, se porter garant, pour qn. (*c*) *pl.* **Securities**, titres *m*, valeurs *f*. **Government securities**, fonds d'État; fonds publics. **Registered securities**, titres nominatifs. **Transferable securities**, valeurs mobilières. **Securities department**, service *m* des titres (d'une banque).

sedan [si'dæn], *s.* **1.** = SEDAN-CHAIR. **2.** *Aut: U.S:* Voiture *f* à conduite intérieure. se'dan-'chair, *s. A:* Chaise *f* à porteurs.

sedate [si'deit], *a.* (*Of pers.*) Posé, reposé; (maintien) composé; (esprit) rassis. -**ly**, *adv.* Posément. **To step s. forward**, s'avancer à pas posés.

sedateness [si'deitnis], *s.* Maintien calme, posé.

sedation [si'deiʃən], *s. Med:* Sédation *f*.

sedative ['sedətiv], *a.&s. Med:* Sédatif(*m*); calmant(*m*).

sedentary ['sedəntri]. **1.** *a.* (*Of statue, posture*) Assis. (*b*) (Emploi, etc.) sédentaire. **2.** *s.* Sédentaire *mf*.

sedge [sedʒ], *s. Bot:* (*a*) Laîche *f*. **Sweet s.**, souchet odorant. (*b*) *F:* Joncs *mpl*, roseaux *mpl*. 'sedge-warbler, *s. Orn:* Phragmite *m* des joncs, *F:* fauvette *f* des roseaux, rousserolle *f* (des phragmites).

sediment ['sedimənt], *s.* Sédiment *m*, dépôt *m*; boue *f* (d'un accu, d'un encrier); lie *f* (du vin). **S. in a boiler**, vidange(s) *f(pl)* d'une chaudière. *Med:* **Urinary s.**, boue urinaire.

sedimentary [ˌsedi'mentə)ri], *a. Geol:* Sédimentaire.

sedimentation [ˌsedimen'teiʃ(ə)n], *s.* Sédimentation *f*.

sedition [si'diʃ(ə)n], *s.* Sédition *f*.

seditious [si'diʃəs], *a.* Séditieux, -euse. -**ly**, *adv.* Séditieusement.

seduce [si'djuːs], *v.tr.* **1.** Séduire, corrompre (qn). **To s. s.o. from his duty**, détourner qn de son devoir. **2.** Séduire, abuser (d'une femme).

seducer [si'djuːsər], *s.* Séducteur *m*.

seduction [si'dʌkʃ(ə)n], *s.* **1.** (*a*) Séduction *f*, corruption *f* (de qn). (*b*) Séduction (d'une femme). **2.** Attrait *m*, charme *m*, séduction (de qch.).

seductive [si'dʌktiv], *a.* Séduisant, attrayant. -**ly**, *adv.* D'une manière séduisante.

seductiveness [si'dʌktivnis], *s.* Caractère séduisant (d'une offre); charmes *mpl* (d'une femme); séduction *f* (du style, etc.).

sedulous ['sedjuləs], *a.* (Travailleur) assidu, appliqué; (soin) assidu. **To be s. in doing sth.**, s'empresser à faire qch. -**ly**, *adv.* Assidûment; avec empressement.

sedulousness ['sedjuləsnis], *s.* Assiduité *f*, application *f*; diligence *f*, empressement *m* (**in doing sth.**, à faire qch.).

see¹ [siː], *v.tr.* (saw [sɔː]; seen [siːn]) **1.** Voir. (*a*) **I saw it with my own eyes**, je l'ai vu de meṣ (propres) yeux. **To s. the sights of the town**, visiter les monuments de la ville. **There was not a house to be seen**,

il n'y avait pas une maison de visible. **Nothing could be seen of him**, il restait invisible. **To s. s.o. in the distance**, apercevoir qn dans le lointain. **'S. page 8,' "voir page 8"**; **"se reporter à la page 8."** **He is not fit to be seen**, il n'est pas présentable. *F:* **To s. things**, avoir des hallucinations. *S.a.* DAYLIGHT 2, LAST II 2, LIGHT¹ 1, RED 1, STAR¹ 1. (*b*) *Abs.* **As far as the eye can s.**, aussi loin qu'on peut voir; à perte de vue. **It was too dark to s. clearly**, il faisait trop noir pour bien distinguer. **We can't s. to read**, on n'y voit pas assez clair pour lire. (*c*) **To s. s.o. do sth.**, voir faire qch. à qn; voir qn faire qch. **I saw him fall**, je l'ai vu tomber. **He was seen to fall**, on le vit tomber. **To s. s.o. coming**, voir venir qn. **I saw him taking the apples**, je l'ai vu qui prenait les pommes. **I saw it done**, je l'ai vu faire. *F:* **I'll s. him damned first!** qu'il aille au diable! (*d*) **To s. s.o. home**, reconduire qn jusque chez lui. **I'll s. you to the door**, je vais vous accompagner jusqu'à la porte. (*e*) **He has seen a good deal of the world**, il connaît bien la vie. *F:* **He will never s. forty again**, il a quarante ans sonnés. **2.** (*a*) Comprendre, saisir (une pensée); reconnaître (ses erreurs). **I don't s. the point**, je ne saisis pas la nuance. **He cannot s. a joke**, il n'entend pas la plaisanterie. **As far as I can s. . . .**, à ce que je vois . . .; autant que j'en puis juger. . . . **I can't s. my way clear to do that**, je ne vois pas comment m'y prendre pour faire cela. **I s. what you are driving at**, je vois où vous voulez en venir. **I s.!** je comprends! **You s. . . .**, vous comprenez . . .; voyez-vous. . . . (*b*) Observer, remarquer (qch.); s'apercevoir de (qch.). **I s. that it is time to go**, je m'aperçois qu'il est temps de partir. **S. for yourself**, voyez par vous-même. **I can s. no fault in him**, je ne lui connais pas de défaut. **I don't know what you can s. in her**, je ne sais pas ce que vous pouvez trouver en elle. *S.a.* REMAIN² 1. (*c*) Voir, juger, apprécier (qch. d'une manière quelconque). **This is how I s. it**, voici comment j'envisage la chose. **To s. things wrong**, juger de travers. **If you s. fit to . . .**, si vous jugez convenable, si vous trouvez bon, de. . . . **3.** Examiner (qch.); regarder (qch.) avec attention. **Let me s. that letter again**, repassez-moi cette lettre (que je la relise). **S. if this hat suits you**, voyez si ce chapeau vous va. *Abs.* **I'll go and s.**, je vais y aller voir. **Let me s.**, (i) attendez un peu; (ii) faites voir! **4. To s.** (**to it**) **that everything is in order**, s'assurer que tout est en ordre. **S. that he has all he needs**, ayez soin qu'il ait tout ce qu'il lui faut; voyez à ce qu'il ne manque de rien. **S. that he comes in time**, faites en sorte qu'il arrive à temps. **I shall s. to it that he comes**, je me charge de le faire venir. *A:* **I will s. you righted**, je veillerai à ce qu'on vous fasse justice. **5.** (*a*) Fréquenter, avoir des rapports avec (qn). **He sees a great deal of the Smiths**, il fréquente beaucoup les Smith. **We s. less of him in winter**, nous le voyons moins l'hiver. **S. you again soon**, à bientôt. *F:* **S. you on Thursday!** à jeudi! (*b*) **To go and s. s.o.**, aller trouver qn. **To call to s. s.o.**, faire une visite à qn; passer chez qn. **I wanted to s. you on business**, je voulais vous parler d'affaires. **To s. the doctor**, consulter le médecin. (*c*) Recevoir (un visiteur). **see about**, *v.ind.tr.* S'occuper de (qch.); se charger de (qch.). **I'll s. about it**, (i) je m'en occuperai; (ii) j'y réfléchirai. **see after**, *v.ind.tr. F:* = SEE TO. **see in**, *v.tr.* Voir arriver (une nouvelle époque, etc.). *S.a.* NEW YEAR. **see into**, *v.ind.tr.* **1.** Voir dans (l'avenir); pénétrer (les motifs de qn). **2. We must s. into this**, il faudra examiner cette affaire à fond. **see off**, *v.tr.* **1.** **To s. s.o. off** (at the station), accompagner qn jusqu'à la gare (pour lui dire au revoir). **2. To s. s.o. off the premises**, (i) reconduire, éconduire, expulser qn; (ii) s'assurer du départ de qn. **see out**, *v.tr.* **1.** Accompagner (qn) jusqu'à la porte; reconduire (qn). **2.** Assister à (un opéra, etc.) jusqu'au bout; voir la fin de (qch.). *S.a.* YEAR. **see over**, *v.ind.tr.* Visiter, voir (une maison, etc.). **see through**. **1.** *v.i.* (*a*) Voir à travers (qch.). (*b*) *F:* Pénétrer les intentions de (qn); voir clair dans l'esprit de (qn); pénétrer (un mystère). **Tricks easily seen through**, finesses cousues de fil blanc. **2.** *v.tr.* **To s. s.o. safely through**, soutenir qn jusqu'au bout. **He saw the operation through without wincing**, il assista à l'opération sans broncher. **To s. a business through**, mener une affaire à bonne fin. *F:* **To s. it through**, tenir jusqu'au bout. **see to**, *v.ind.tr.* S'occuper de (qn, qch.); veiller à (qch.). **To s. to the house**, vaquer aux soins du ménage. **To s. to everything**, avoir l'œil à tout. **It must be seen to**, il faut y aviser. **seeing**[1]. 1. *a.* Voyant; qui voit. 2. *Conj.phr.* **S. (that)** . . ., puisque . . ., attendu que . . ., vu que. . . . **seeing**[2], *s.* Vue *f;* vision *f.* **S. is believing**, voir c'est croire. **It is worth s.**, cela vaut la peine d'être vu.

see[2], *s. Ecc:* Siège épiscopal; (*of bishop*) évêché *m;* (*of archbishop*) archevêché *m.* **The Holy S.**, le Saint-Siège.

seed[1] [si:d], *s.* 1. (*a*) Graine *f.* **Tomato seeds**, graines de tomates. **Seeds of an apple, of a grape**, pépins *m* d'une pomme, d'un grain de raisin. **The seeds of discord**, les germes *m* de discorde. (*b*) *Coll.* Semence *f;* graine(s). **Lawn s.**, graine pour gazon. **To go, run, to s.**, monter en graine; (*of land*) s'affricher. *F:* **He's going to s.**, il se ramollit. (*c*) Frai *m* (d'huître). 2. *B. & Lit:* Descendance *f*, lignée *f.* **'seed-bed**, *s.* Couche *f* de semis; germoir *m. For:* Semis *m*, pépinière *f.* **'seed-cake**, *s. Cu:* Gâteau au carvi, à l'anis. **'seed-corn**, *s. Agr:* Grain *m* de semence. **'seed-drill**, *s. Agr:* Plantoir *m.* **'seed-hole**, *s.* Poquet *m.* **'seed-lobe**, *s. Bot:* Cotylédon *m;* feuille germinale. **'seed-oysters**, *s.pl.* Naissain *m.* **'seed-pearls**, *s.pl.* Semence *f* de perles. **'seed-po'tatoes**, *s.pl.* Pommes *f* de terre à semence. **'seed-shop, -trade**, *s.* Graineterie *f.* **'seed-time**, *s.* (Époque *f* des) semailles *f;* la semaison.

seed[2]. 1. *v.i.* (*Of plant*) (*a*) Monter en graine; porter semence. (*b*) (*Of cereals*) Grener; venir à graine. (*c*) S'égrener. 2. *v.tr.* (*a*) Ensemencer, semer (un champ). (*b*) Enlever la graine (d'un fruit); épépiner (un concombre, etc.). (*c*) *Ten:* **To s. the players**, trier les joueurs (avant le tirage au sort). **Seeded players**, têtes *f* de série. **'seeding machine**, *s. Agr:* Semoir *m* mécanique.

seeder ['si:dər], *s.* (*a*) *Agr:* Semoir *m.* (*b*) *Ind: Com:* (*Pers.*) Épépineur, -euse; (*machine*) épépineuse *f.*

seediness ['si:dinis], *s. F:* 1. Apparence *f*, tenue *j* minable, *F:* miteuse. 2. État *m* de malaise; manque *m* d'énergie.

seedless ['si:dlis], *a.* 1. *Bot:* Asperme. 2. (Fruit, etc.) (i) sans pépins, (ii) épépiné.

seedling ['si:dliŋ], *s. Hort:* Jeune plant *m;* élève *m. Arb:* Sauvageon *m.*

seedsman, *pl.* **-men** ['si:dzmən], *s.m.* Grainetier.

seedy ['si:di], *a.* 1. Monté en graine. 2. *F:* (Vêtement) râpé, usé, *F:* miteux. **S.-looking individuals**, individus d'aspect minable. 3. *F:* (*Of pers.*) Mal en train; *F:* patraque.

seek [si:k], *v.tr.* (**sought** [sɔ:t]; **sought**) 1. Chercher (un objet perdu); rechercher, quêter (de l'avancement, etc.). **To s. employment**, être en quête d'un emploi. **To s. shelter**, se réfugier (sous un arbre, etc.). **The reason is not far to s.**, la raison est assez claire. 2. (*a*) **To s. sth. from, of, s.o.**, demander qch. à qn. **To s. advice**, demander conseil. (*b*) **To s. to do sth.**, essayer de, chercher à, faire qch. **seek after**, *v.ind.tr.* (Re)chercher, poursuivre (la gloire, etc.). **Much sought after**, très recherché, très couru. **seek for**, *v.ind.tr.* (Re)chercher (qch.). **seek out**, *v.tr.* Chercher et trouver (qn); dénicher (qn).

seeker ['si:kər], *s.* Chercheur, -euse. **Pleasure-seekers**, gens en quête de plaisir(s).

seem [si:m], *v.i.* Sembler, paraître. 1. (*a*) **To s. tired**, paraître fatigué; avoir l'air fatigué. **How does it s. to you?** que vous en semble? **It seems like a dream**, on dirait un rêve; on croirait rêver. **There seems to be some difficulty**, il semble (i) qu'il y a, (ii) qu'il y ait, quelque difficulté. (*b*) **I s. to have heard his name**, il me semble avoir entendu son nom. *F:* **I don't s. to fancy it**, je ne sais pas pourquoi, mais ça ne me dit rien. 2. *Impers.* **It seems (that)** . . ., it **would s. that** . . ., il paraît, il semble, que. . . . **It seems to me that you are right**, il me semble que vous avez raison; à mon avis vous avez raison. **It seemed as though, as if** . . ., il semblait que + *sub.*;

on aurait dit que + *ind.* **So it seems**, à ce qu'il paraît. **It seems not**, il paraît que non. **seeming**, *a.* Apparent; soi-disant. **With s. kindness**, avec une apparence de bonté. **A s. friend**, un soi-disant ami. -**ly**, *adv.* Apparemment; en apparence.

seemliness ['si:mlinis], *s. O:* 1. Décorum *m;* bienséance *f*, convenance(s) *f(pl)*. 2. Aspect *m* agréable.

seemly ['si:mli], *a.* 1. *O:* Convenable, bienséant. **It is not s. for me to go alone**, il n'est pas convenable que j'aille toute seule. 2. *A:* Agréable à voir.

seen. *See* SEE[1].

seep [si:p], *v.i.* Suinter; s'infiltrer; filtrer. **Information was seeping out**, les renseignements filtraient.

seepage ['si:pidʒ], *s.* 1. Suintement *m;* infiltration *f.* 2. Fuite *f*, déperdition *f* (par infiltration).

seer [si(:)ər], *s. O:* Prophète *m.*

seersucker ['siəsʌkər], *s. Tex:* Crépon *m* de coton.

see-saw[1] ['si:sɔ:]. 1. *s.* Bascule *f*, balançoire *f*, branloire *f;* tape-cul *m.* 2. *a.* **S.-s. motion**, (i) mouvement de bascule; (ii) va-et-vient *m.*

see-saw[2], *v.i.* 1. Jouer à la bascule. 2. (*Of machine-part, etc.*) Basculer; osciller; faire la bascule. (*Of pers.*) **To s.-s. between two opinions**, balancer entre deux opinions.

seethe [si:ð], *v.i.* (*a*) Bouillonner. (*b*) (*Of crowd, etc.*) S'agiter, grouiller. **The street is seething with people**, la foule grouille dans la rue. **Country seething with discontent**, pays en effervescence. **To be seething with anger**, bouillir, bouillonner, de colère. **The seething waters**, les eaux tourmentées.

segment[1] ['segmənt], *s.* (*a*) Segment *m.* **S. of an orange**, quartier *m*, tranche *f*, d'orange. (*b*) *Ann:* Segment, anneau *m* (d'un ver). (*c*) *El:* **Commutator s.**, segment, lame *f*, touche *f*, du commutateur.

segment[2]. 1. *v.tr.* Couper, partager, en segments; segmenter. 2. *v.i. Biol:* Se segmenter. **segmented**, *a.* Segmentaire; formé de segments; (miroir) à facettes.

segmental [seg'mentl], *a.* Segmentaire. *Arch:* **S. arch**, arc surbaissé.

segmentation [,segmən'teiʃ(ə)n], *s.* Segmentation *f.*

segregate ['segrigeit]. 1. *v.tr.* Isoler, mettre à part (qch.). **To s. the sexes**, séparer les deux sexes. 2. *v.i.* (*a*) Se désunir (**from**, de). (*b*) Se grouper à part (**from**, de).

segregation [,segri'geiʃ(ə)n], *s.* Ségrégation *f;* séparation *f*, isolement *m. Pol:* Ségrégation raciale.

segregationist [segri'geiʃ(ə)nist], *s. Pol:* Partisan *m* de la ségrégation raciale.

seigniorial [sei'njɔ:riəl], *a.* Seigneurial, -aux.

seigniory ['seinjəri], *s. Hist:* Seigneurie *f.*

seine [sein], *s. Fish:* Seine *f*, senne *f.*

seise [si:z], *v.tr. Jur:* **To s. s.o. of, with, an estate** mettre qn en possession d'un bien. **To be, stand, seised of a property**, posséder une propriété de droit.

seismic ['saizmik], *a.* Séismique, sismique.

seismograph ['saizmogræf, -gra:f], *s.* Sismographe *m.*

seismology [saiz'mɔlədʒi], *s.* Sismologie *f.*

seizable ['si:zəbl], *a.* (*of goods etc.*) Saisissable.

seize [si:z]. I. *v.tr.* 1. *Jur:* = SEISE. 2. (*a*) *Jur:* Confisquer, saisir (qch.); opérer la saisie de (qch.). **To s. goods (in transit)**, faire arrêt sur des marchandises. **Three nationalist papers were seized**, on a saisi trois journaux nationalistes. (*b*) **To s. s.o.**, appréhender qn (au corps). 3. (*a*) Se saisir, s'emparer de (qn, qch.). **To s. an enemy ship**, capturer un navire ennemi. (*b*) **To s. (hold of) s.o., sth.**, saisir, empoigner, s'emparer de, qn, qch. **To s. s.o. by the throat**, prendre qn à la gorge. (*c*) **To be seized with fear**, être saisi, frappé, d'effroi. **He was seized with a fit of rage**, il fut pris d'un accès de colère. **To be seized with a desire to do sth.**, être pris du désir de faire qch. **To s. the opportunity**, saisir l'occasion. (*d*) *v.ind.tr.* **They seized upon the newcomer**, ils ont happé, accaparé, le nouvel arrivant. **To s. (up)on a pretext**, saisir un prétexte, se saisir d'un prétexte. 4. *Nau:* Amarrer, faire un amarrage à, aiguilleter (deux cordages). II. **seize**, *v.i. Mec.E: etc:* (*Of part*) Gripper, coincer. **To s. up**, (se) caler. **seizing**, *s.* 1. (*a*) Saisie *f;* prise *f* (d'une forteresse); capture *f* (d'un vaisseau ennemi). (*b*) Empoignement *m.* 2. *Nau:* Amarrage *m.* 3. Grippage *m*, coincement *m*, calage *m* (d'un piston, etc.); blocage *m.*

seizure ['si:ʒər], *s.* **1.** *Jur:* (*a*) Appréhension *f* au corps; mainmise *f* (of s.o., sur qn). (*b*) Saisie *f* (de marchandises). **2.** *Med:* (**Apoplectic**) s., attaque *f* (d'apoplexie). **To have a s.,** tomber en apoplexie, *F:* avoir une attaque.

seldom ['seldəm], *adv.* Rarement; peu souvent. **I s.** see him now, je ne le vois plus guère. **He s. if ever goes out,** il sort rarement, pour ne pas dire jamais.

select¹ [si'lekt], *a.* **1.** Choisi. (*a*) **S. passages from . . .,** morceaux choisis de. . . . (*b*) *Parl:* **S. committee,** commission d'enquête. **2.** De (premier) choix; d'élite. **S. club,** club très fermé. **S. audience,** public choisi.

select², *v.tr.* Choisir (**from,** parmi); sélectionner; trier (des minerais, etc.). **To s. a specimen at random,** prélever un spécimen au hasard.

selection [si'lek∫(ə)n], *s.* **1.** Choix *m*, sélection *f.* *Biol:* Natural s., sélection naturelle. *Sp:* **S. match,** match *m* de sélection. **2. A good s. of wines,** un bon choix de vins fins. **To make a s.,** faire un choix. **Selections from Byron,** morceaux choisis de Byron. *Mus:* **S. from 'Faust,'** fantaisie *f* sur "Faust." *Turf:* **Selections for the Derby,** pronostics *m* pour le Derby.

selective [si'lektiv], *a.* Sélectif, -ive, sélecteur, -trice. *W.Tel:* Sélectif. **My radio is not s. enough,** mon poste n'est pas assez sélectif. *Phot:* **S. filters,** écrans sélecteurs. *Biol: Husb: etc:* **S. breeding,** élevage *m* à base de sélection; *Nat. Hist:* sélection naturelle.

selectivity [,selek'tiviti], *s.* *W.Tel: El.E: Biol: etc:* Sélectivité *f.*

selector [si'lektər], *s.* **1. One of the selectors of the team,** un des sélectionneurs de l'équipe. **2.** (*a*) *Mec.E: Aut: etc:* Sélecteur *m*; dispositif *m* de sélection. **S.-rod,** baladeur *m.* (*b*) *W.Tel: Tp:* Sélecteur *m.* *El.E:* **S. switch,** combinateur *m.*

selenite ['selinait], *s.* *Miner:* Sélénite *f.*

selenium [si'li:niəm], *s.* *Ch:* Sélénium *m.* **S. cell,** cellule au sélénium; cellule photo-résistante.

selenography [,seli'nɔgrəfi], *s.* Sélénographie *f.*

self, *pl.* **selves** [self, selvz]. **1.** *s.* Le moi. **S. is his god,** il se fait un dieu de lui-même. **One's better s.,** notre meilleur côté. **He's my second s.,** c'est un autre moi-même, c'est mon alter ego. **He is quite his old s. again,** il est complètement rétabli. **All by one's very s.,** absolument tout seul. *Com:* **Your good selves,** vous-mêmes; vous. **2.** *pron. Bank:* **Pay s., selves . . . ,** payez à moi-même, à nous-mêmes. . . . *P:* **I require accommodation for wife and s.,** il me faut une chambre pour ma femme et pour moi-même. **3.** *a.* **Wooden tool with s. handle,** outil en bois avec manche de même. **S. carnation,** œillet de couleur uniforme. **4.** (*In compound pronouns*) (*a*) (*Emphatic*) **Myself,** moi(-même); *A: Ecc:* **thyself,** toi(-même); **himself, herself, itself, oneself,** lui(-même), elle(-même), soi(-même); **yourself,** vous(-même); **ourselves,** nous(-mêmes); **yourselves,** vous(-mêmes); **themselves,** eux(-mêmes) *m*, elles(-mêmes) *f.* **I drive the car myself,** je tiens le volant moi-même. **I, myself, do not believe it,** (quant à) moi, pour ma part, je ne le crois pas. **They themselves continued to enjoy independence,** eux-mêmes continuèrent à jouir de l'indépendance. **Myself and my two brothers,** mes deux frères et moi. **We saw John himself,** nous avons vu Jean en personne, lui-même. **I am not (quite) myself to-day,** je ne suis pas dans mon assiette aujourd'hui. **I am quite myself again,** je suis tout à fait rétabli. **She is kindness itself,** elle est la bonté même. *F:* **He's a 'do it yourself' enthusiast,** c'est un bricoleur passionné. **A 'do it yourself' kit,** panoplie de construction (d'une table, d'un canot, etc.). (*b*) (*Reflexive*) **Myself,** me; *A:* **thyself,** te; **himself, herself, itself, oneself,** se; **ourselves,** nous; **yourself, -selves,** vous; **themselves,** se. **I have hurt myself,** je me suis fait mal. **Are you enjoying yourself?** vous amusez-vous? (*Emphatic*) **Door that shuts itself,** porte qui se ferme d'elle-même. (*c*) (*After prep.*) **To say sth. to oneself,** (se) dire qch. à part soi. **To speak of oneself,** parler de soi. **He has to look after himself,** il est obligé de faire le ménage lui-même. **To keep oneself to oneself,** se tenir sur son quant-à-soi. **I am keeping it for myself,** je le garde pour moi(-même). **I am not speaking for myself,** je ne parle pas en mon propre nom. **He thinks for himself,** il pense de son chef. **See for yourselves,** voyez vous-mêmes. **Everyone for himself,** chacun pour soi. **To come to oneself,** revenir à soi. **The thing in itself,** la chose en elle-même. **She lived by herself,** elle vivait seule. **To do sth. (all) by oneself,** faire qch. tout seul. (*d*) (*Reciprocal*) **They whispered among themselves,** ils chuchotaient entre eux. **'self-a'basement,** *s.* Humiliation *f* de soi-même. **'self-ab'sorbed,** *a.* Égoïste. **'self-a'buse,** *s.* Onanisme *m.* **'self-accu'sation,** *s.* Auto-accusation *f.* **'self-'acting,** *a.* (Appareil) automatique. *Rail:* **S.-a. points,** aiguille *f* à contrepoids. **'self-a'djusting,** *a. Techn:* A autoréglage. **'self-ad'vertisement,** *s.* Mise en avant de sa personne; *F:* battage. **'self-a'pparent,** *a.* Évident; de toute évidence. **'self-a'pproval,** *s.* Suffisance *f.* **'self-a'ssertion,** *s.* Caractère impérieux; affirmation *f* de sa volonté; outrecuidance *f.* **'self-a'ssertive,** *a.* Autoritaire; impérieux, -euse; outrecuidant. **'self-a'ssurance,** *s.* Confiance *f* en soi; assurance *f*; aplomb *m.* **'self-a'ssured,** *a.* = SELF-CONFIDENT. **'self-'binder,** *s. Ag:* Moissonneuse-lieuse *f,* *pl.* moissonneuses-lieuses. **'self-'centred,** *a.* Égocentrique. **'self-'centring,** *a. Mec.E:* (Mandrin *m*, etc.) à centrage automatique; autocentreur, -euse. **'self-'closing,** *a.* A fermeture *f* automatique. **S.-c. door,** porte battante. **'self-'colour,** *s.* **1.** Couleur uniforme. *Tex:* **S.-c. material,** tissu uni. **2.** Couleur naturelle. **'self-'coloured,** *a.* (Tissu) uni. **'self-co'mmand,** *s.* Maîtrise *f* de soi; empire *m* sur soi-même. **self-com'placency,** *s.* Satisfaction *f* de soi-même; (*of a man*) fatuité *f.* **'self-com'placent,** *a.* Satisfait, content, de soi. **'self-con'ceit,** *s.* Suffisance *f,* vanité *f*; infatuation *f* (de soi). **He is eaten up with s.-c.,** il est pourri d'orgueil. **'self-'confidence,** *s.* Confiance *f* en soi; assurance *f.* **He is full of s.-c.,** il ne doute de rien. **'self-'confident,** *a.* Sûr de soi; plein d'assurance. **'self-'conscious,** *a.* **1.** *Phil:* Conscient. **2.** Embarrassé, gêné; (*of manner*) emprunté, contraint; (*of pers.*) intimidé. **To make s.o. s.-c.,** intimider qn. **self-'consciousness,** *s.* **1.** *Phil:* Conscience *f.* **2.** Contrainte *f*, embarras *m*, gêne *f*; timidité *f.* **'self-con'tained,** *a.* **1.** (*Of pers.*) Peu communicatif, -ive. **2.** (Appareil) indépendant, complet par lui-même. *Ind:* (Industrie) autonome. **S.-c. flat,** appartement *m* avec entrée particulière. **'self-con'trol,** *s.* Sang-froid *m*; empire *m* sur soi-même; maîtrise *f* de soi; possession *f* de soi-même. **To exercise s.-c.,** faire un effort sur soi-même. **To lose one's s.-c.,** ne plus se maîtriser. **'self-'criticism,** *s.* Autocritique *f.* **'self-de'ception,** *s.* Illusion *f*; déception *f* de soi-même. **'self-de'fence,** *s.* Défense personnelle. *Jur:* Légitime défense. **'self-de'nial,** *s.* (*a*) Abnégation *f* de soi; renoncement(s) *m(pl).* (*b*) Frugalité *f.* **'self-de'nying,** *a.* (*a*) Qui fait abnégation de soi. (*b*) Frugal, -aux. **'self-depreci'ation,** *s.* Modestie exagérée. **'self-determi'nation,** *s.* Auto-détermination *f.* **Right of peoples to s.-d.,** droit des peuples de disposer d'eux-mêmes. **'self-di'rectional,** *a.* Auto-guidé. **'self-'discipline,** *s.* Discipline personnelle. **'self-'drive,** *a.* **S.-d. cars for hire,** location *f* de voitures sans chauffeur. **'self-'educated,** *a.* Auto-didacte. **'self-e'ffacing,** *a.* Modeste. **'self-em'ployed,** *a.* **S.-e. worker,** travailleur indépendant. **'self-es'teem,** *s.* Respect *m* de soi; amour-propre *m.* **'self-'evident,** *a.* Évident en soi; qui saute aux yeux. **It is s.-e.,** cela va, parle, de soi; cela parle tout seul. **'self-exami'nation,** *s.* Examen *m* de conscience. **'self-ex'planatory,** *a.* Qui s'explique de soi-même. **'self-'feeding,** *a. Mec.E:* A alimentation automatique, continue. **'self-fertili'zation,** *s. Biol:* Autofécondation *f. Bot:* Pollinisation directe. **'self-'filling,** *a.* A remplissage automatique. **'self-'governing,** *a.* (Territoire) autonome. **'self-'government,** *s.* Autonomie *f.* **'self-'heal,** *s. Bot:* Brunelle *f.* **'self-'help,** *s.* Efforts personnels. **'self-ig'nition,** *s. I.C.E:* Allumage spontané; auto-allumage *m.* **'self-im'portance,** *s.* Suffisance *f*, présomption *f.* **'self-im'portant,** *a.* Suffisant,

présomptueux, -euse, important. **self-im'posed,**
a. (Tâche) dont on a pris de soi-même la responsabilité. **'self-in'duction,** *s. El:* Self-induction *f*;
auto-induction *f*. **'self-in'dulgence,** *s.* Sybaritisme
m; satisfaction *f* égoïste de ses appétits. **'self-
in'dulgent,** *a.* Sybarite; qui se dorlote; qui ne se
refuse rien. **'self-in'flicted,** *a.* (Punition *f*, blessure
f) volontaire. **'self-'interest,** *s.* Intérêt (personnel);
égoïsme *m*. **'self-'knowledge,** *s.* Connaissance *f*
de soi. **'self-'locking,** *a.* 1. *Mec.E:* A blocage
automatique. S.-l. nut, écrou indesserrable. 2. A
verrouillage automatique. **'self-'love,** *s.* Égoïsme
m; amour *m* de soi. **'self-'lubricating,** *a. Mch:*
Autolubrifiant; (palier, etc.) autograisseur. **'self-
'made,** *a.* (Homme) qui est (le) fils de ses œuvres,
l'artisan de sa fortune, qui est arrivé par lui-même.
'self-o'pinionated, *a.* Opiniâtre, entêté. **'self-
'portrait,** *s.* Portrait *m* de l'artiste par lui-même.
'self-po'ssessed, *a.* Maître de soi; qui a de l'aplomb,
du sang-froid. **'self-po'ssession,** *s.* Aplomb *m*,
sang-froid *m*, flegme *m*. To lose one's s.-p., perdre
son aplomb. To regain one's s.-p., se ressaisir.
'self-preser'vation, *s.* Conservation *f* de soi-même.
'self-pro'pelled, *a.* Autopropulsé. **'self-pro-
'pelling,** *a. Veh:* Automoteur, -trice; autopro-
pulseur, -euse. **'self-pro'pulsion,** *s.* Autopropul-
sion *f*. **'self-'raising,** *a. Cu:* S.-r. flour, farine
préparée à la levure chimique. **'self-'recording,**
-'registering, *a.* (Appareil) enregistreur. **'self-
'regulating,** *a.* Autorégulateur, -trice. **'self-
re'liance,** *s.* Indépendance *f*. **'self-re'liant,** *a.*
Indépendant. **'self-re'spect,** *s.* Respect *m* de soi;
amour-propre *m*. **'self-re'specting,** *a.* Qui se
respecte, qui a de l'amour-propre. **'self-re'straint,**
s. Retenue *f*; modération *f*. To exercise s.-r.,
se contenir. **'self-'righteous,** *a.* Pharisaïque.
'self-'righting, *a.* (Of lifeboat, etc.) A redressement
automatique; inchavirable. **'self-'sacrifice,** *s.*
Abnégation *f* (de soi). **'self-same,** *attrib. a.*
Identique; absolument le même. **'self-satis'faction,** *s.* Contentement *m* de soi; fatuité *f*, suffisance
f. **'self-'satisfied,** *a.* Content de soi; suffisant.
S.-s. air, air avantageux. **'self-'sealing,** *a.* (Dispositif *m*) à obturation automatique. **'self-'seeking¹,**
a. Égoïste, intéressé. **'self-'seeking²,** *s.* Égoïsme
m. **'self-'service,** *s. Com:* Libre-service *m*.
S.-s. store, magasin libre-service. **'self-'starter,**
s. Aut: Démarreur *m*. **'self-su'fficient,** *a.* (Of
thg.) Indépendant; (of pers.) suffisant. Country
s.-s. in wheat, pays qui subvient à ses propres besoins
en blé. **'self-su'fficiency,** *s.* Indépendance *f*.
National s.-s., autarcie *f*. **'self-su'pporting,** *a.*
Indépendant. (Of pers.) Qui vit de son travail;
(of business) qui couvre ses frais. **'self-'taught,** *a.*
Autodidacte. **'self-'timing,** *a.* (a) S.-t. apparatus,
oven, etc., appareil *m*, four *m*, etc., avec minuterie *f*.
(b) Phot: (Appareil) à cellule photo-électrique
incorporée. **'self-'willed,** *a.* Opiniâtre, volontaire,
obstiné. **'self-'winding,** *a.* (Montre *f*, etc.) à
remontage automatique.
selfish ['selfiʃ], *a.* Égoïste, intéressé. To act from
a s. motive, agir dans un but intéressé. -ly, *adv.*
Égoïstement; en égoïste.
selfishness ['selfiʃnis], *s.* Égoïsme *m*.
selfless ['selflis], *a.* Désintéressé.
selflessness ['selflisnis], *s.* Désintéressement *m*;
altruisme *m*.
sell¹ [sel], *s. F:* Déception *f*; *F:* attrape *f*; *F:*
carotte *f*. What a s.! quelle sale blague!
sell², *v.tr.* (sold [sould]; sold) 1. (a) Vendre (to, à).
To s. back, again, revendre. Difficult to s., de vente
difficile; d'écoulement difficile. What are you
selling plums at today? combien faites-vous les
prunes aujourd'hui? He sold it me for ten shillings,
il me l'a vendu dix shillings. To s. s.o. an idea,
faire accepter une idée à qn. St. Exch. To s. short,
vendre à découvert. (b) (With passive force) Goods
that s. easily, marchandises qui se placent facilement,
d'écoulement facile. This book sells well, ce livre
est de bonne vente. What are plums selling at?
combien valent les prunes? à combien se vendent
les prunes? Land to s., to be sold, terrain à vendre.
2. (a) Vendre, trahir (un secret, etc.); trafiquer de

(sa conscience). (b) F: Duper, tromper (qn). You
have been sold, on vous a refait. Sold again! attrapé!
(c) F: He is completely sold on the idea, il est entiché
de l'idée. sell off, *v.tr.* Solder, écouler à bas prix
(des marchandises); liquider (son écurie, etc.);
F: bazarder (ses effets). selling off, *s.* Liquidation
f. sell out, *v.tr.* (a) Fin: Réaliser (tout un portefeuille d'actions). (b) Com: Vendre tout son stock
de (qch.). The edition is sold out, l'édition est épuisée.
We are sold out of this article, nous sommes démunis
de cet article. sell up, *v.tr.* Vendre, faire saisir
(un failli). selling, *s.* Vente *f*; écoulement *m*,
placement *m* (de marchandises). Publ: Instalment s.,
vente par fascicules. S. price, prix *m* de vente.
Turf: S. race, plate, course *f*, prix, à réclamer.
seller ['selər], *s.* 1. (a) Vendeur, -euse. St. Exch:
Réalisateur *m* (de titres). (b) Marchand, -ande;
débitant, -ante (of, de). 2. (Of book, etc:) Good s.,
livre (etc.) de bonne vente. Quick sellers, articles
m, livres, d'écoulement facile. S.a. BEST-SELLER.
seltzer ['seltsər], *s. O:* S.(-water), eau *f* de seltz.
selvage, selvedge ['selvidʒ], *s. Tex:* Lisière *f*; cordeau
m (de lainages épais).
selves. See SELF.
semantic [se'mæntik], *a. Ling:* Sémantique.
semantics [se'mæntiks], *s.pl.* Sémantique *f*.
semaphore¹ ['seməfɔ:r], *s.* Sémaphore *m*.
semaphore², *v.tr.* Transmettre par sémaphore.
semblance ['sembləns], *s.* Apparence *f*, semblant *m*,
simulacre *m*. To bear the s. of sth., ressembler à
qch. To put on a s. of gaiety, faire semblant d'être
gai.
semen ['si:men], *s. Physiol:* Sperme *m*, semence *f*.
semester [sə'mestər], *s. U.S:* Semestre *m* (scolaire).
semi- ['semi], *pref.* 1. Semi-. S.-historic, semi-
historique. 2. Demi-. Semicircle, demi-cercle.
S.-opaque, demi-opaque. 3. S.-civilized, à moitié
civilisé. S.-barbarous, à demi barbare. S.-portable,
mi-fixe. **'semi-'conscious,** *a.* A demi conscient.
'semi-de'tached, *a.* S.-d. houses, maisons jumelles,
villas jumelles, maisons doubles, maisons jumelées.
'semi-'final, *s. Sp:* Demi-finale *f*. **'semi-'finalist,**
s. Sp: Joueur, -euse, équipe *f*, de demi-finale.
'semi-'invalid, *s.* Demi-valétudinaire *mf*. **'semi-
'literate,** *a.* Semi-illettré. **'semi-ob'scurity,** *s.*
Pénombre *f*. **'semi-o'fficial,** *a.* Semi-officiel,
-elle; officieux, -euse. **'semi-'precious,** *a. Lap:*
Fin. **'semi-'profile,** *attrib.a.* (Portrait) de trois
quarts. **'semi-'tran'sparent,** *a.* Semi-transparent,
à demi transparent. **'semi-'tropical,** *a.* Subtropical,
-aux.
semibreve ['semibri:v], *s. Mus:* Ronde *f. S.a.* REST¹ 2.
semicircle ['semi,sə:kl], *s.* Demi-cercle *m*.
semicircular ['semi'sə:kjulər], *a.* Demi-circulaire,
semi-circulaire; en demi-cercle. S.a. ARCH¹ 1.
semicolon ['semi'koulən], *s.* Point-virgule *m*.
seminar ['semina:r], *s. Sch:* Cycle *m* d'études;
séminaire *m* (d'études).
seminarist ['seminərist], *s. R.C.Ch:* Séminariste *m*.
seminary ['seminəri], *s.* 1. R.C.Ch: Séminaire *m*.
2. A: Young ladies' s., pensionnat *m* de jeunes filles.
semiquaver ['semi,kweivər], *s. Mus:* Double croche *f*.
Semite ['si:mait], *a. & s. Ethn:* Sémite (*mf*).
Semitic [se'mitik], *a.* Sémitique.
semitone ['semitoun], *s. Mus:* Demi-ton *m*.
semivowel ['semi'vaul], *s. Ling:* Semi-voyelle *f*.
semolina [semə'li:nə], *s. Cu:* Semoule *f*.
sempiternal [,sempi'tə:nl], *a.* Sempiternel, -elle.
sempstress ['sem(p)stris], *s.f.* = SEAMSTRESS.
senate ['senit], *s.* Sénat *m*. (At university) Conseil
m de l'université. **'senate-house,** *s.* Sénat *m*.
senator ['senətər], *s.* Sénateur *m*.
senatorial [senə'tɔ:riəl], *a.* Sénatorial, -aux.
send [send], *v.tr.* (sent [sent]; sent) 1. (a) Envoyer
(qn). To s. a child to school, envoyer, mettre, un
enfant à l'école. To s. for sth., envoyer qn
chercher qch.; envoyer qn à la recherche de qch.
(b) Envoyer, faire parvenir (qch.); expédier (un
colis, etc.). I am sending you by post the sum of ten
pounds, je vous fais tenir par la poste la somme de
dix livres. To s. word to s.o., faire savoir qch. à
qn. To s. clothes to the wash, donner du linge à
blanchir. 2. It sent a shiver down my spine, cela m'a

fait passer un frisson dans le dos. **The blow sent him sprawling,** le coup l'envoya rouler. *F:* **To s. s.o. packing,** envoyer promener qn; flanquer qn à la porte. **3.** *A:* **God s. that I may arrive in time,** Dieu veuille que j'arrive à temps. (God) s. him **victorious,** que Dieu lui accorde la victoire. **4.** *Abs.* Envoyer un message, un messager. **To s. for s.o.,** sth., envoyer chercher qn, qch. **I shall s. for it,** je vais l'envoyer prendre. **The doctor was sent for,** on fit venir le médecin. **To s. for de Gaulle,** faire appel à de Gaulle. **send along,** *v.tr.* **S. him a.!** dites-lui de venir me trouver! **send away,** *v.tr.* (a) Renvoyer, congédier (qn). (b) Expédier (qch.). **send back,** *v.tr.* Renvoyer. **send down,** *v.tr.* **1.** Envoyer en bas; faire descendre (qn). (c) *Sch:* (i) Expulser (un étudiant de l'université); (ii) renvoyer temporairement (un étudiant). **2.** *Nau:* Dégréer (une vergue). **send forth,** *v.tr.* *O:* (a) Répandre, exhaler (une odeur); lancer, jeter (des étincelles); émettre (des rayons). (b) (*Of plant*) Pousser (des feuilles). **send in,** *v.tr.* **1.** (a) Faire (r)entrer (qn). (b) **To s. in one's card,** faire passer sa carte. **To s. in one's name,** se faire annoncer. **2.** (a) Livrer, rendre (un compte); remettre (une demande). (b) **To s. in one's resignation,** donner sa démission. **send off,** *v.tr.* (a) Renvoyer (qn) (en mission, etc.). (b) Expédier (une lettre, etc.). **'send-off,** *s.* Démonstration *f* d'amitié (au départ de qn). **To give s.o. a good s.-o.,** assister en nombre au départ de qn (pour lui souhaiter bon voyage). **The press has given the play a good s.-o.,** la presse a été unanime à saluer de ses éloges la nouvelle pièce. **send on,** *v.tr.* (a) Faire suivre (une lettre). (b) Transmettre (un ordre). **send out,** *v.tr.* (a) Envoyer (qn) dehors; faire sortir (qn). (b) Lancer (des circulaires). (c) Jeter, vomir (des nuages de fumée, etc.). (d) Émettre (des signaux, de la chaleur). **send round,** *v.tr.* **1.** Faire circuler, faire passer (la bouteille, etc.). **2.** Envoyer (qn). **I'll s. r. tomorrow,** j'enverrai quelqu'un demain (pour reprendre qch., pour prendre des ordres, etc.). **send up,** *v.tr.* **1.** Faire monter. **To s. up a balloon,** mettre un ballon en ascension. **2.** *Nau:* Passer, guinder (un mât). **3.** Faire hausser (les prix, etc.). **4.** *F:* Mettre (qn) en prison, *P:* en taule. **5.** *F:* Se moquer de, parodier (qn, qch.).

sender ['sendər], *s.* **1.** Envoyeur, -euse; expéditeur, -trice (d'une lettre). **2.** *Tg:* *Tp:* (*Device*) Manipulateur *m*, transmetteur *m*.

Seneca ['senikə]. *Pr.n.m. Lt.Lit:* Sénèque.

Senegal [ˌseni'gɔ:l]. *Pr.n. Geog:* Le Sénégal.

Senegalese ['senigə'li:z], *a. & s.* Sénégalais, -aise.

senescence [se'nesns], *s.* Sénescence *f*.

seneschal ['seniʃ(ə)l], *s. Hist:* Sénéchal *m*, -aux.

senile ['si:nail], *a.* Sénile. **S. decay,** sénilité *f*.

senility [sə'niliti], *s.* Sénilité *f*.

senior ['si:njər]. **1.** *a.* (a) **Jones s.,** Jones aîné. **William Jones s.,** William Jones père. **He is two years s. to me,** il est mon aîné de deux ans. (b) **S. in rank,** de grade supérieur. **To be s. to s.o.,** être l'ancien, le doyen, de qn. **The S. Service,** la marine. *Sch:* **The s. boys,** les grands (élèves). **S. clerk,** premier commis, commis principal. **The s. officer,** le doyen des officiers. **My s. officer,** mon officier supérieur. *Sch:* **S. master** = professeur principal. *U.S:* **S. year,** dernière année d'études. **2.** *s.* (a) Aîné, -ée; doyen, -enne (d'âge). (b) (Le plus) ancien, (la plus) ancienne. **To be s.o.'s s.,** être l'ancien, le doyen, de qn. *Sch:* **The seniors,** les grands. (c) *Sch:* *U.S:* Étudiant(e) en dernière année.

seniority [ˌsi:ni'ɔriti], *s.* **1.** Priorité *f* d'âge; supériorité *f* d'âge. **2.** Ancienneté *f* (de grade), doyenneté *f*. **To be promoted by s.,** avancer à l'ancienneté.

senna ['senə], *s.* Séné *m.* **S. pods,** follicules *m* de séné.

sensation [sen'seiʃ(ə)n], *s.* **1.** Sensation *f*; sentiment *m* (de malaise, etc.). **I had a s. of falling,** j'avais l'impression que je tombais. **2.** Sensation; effet sensationnel. **To create, make, a s.,** faire sensation. **Book that made a s.,** livre qui a fait du fracas, du bruit.

sensational [sen'seiʃ(ə)nl], *a.* Sensationnel, -elle; (roman) à sensation. **S. happening,** événement qui a fait sensation. **S. writer,** auteur à gros effets, à effets corsés.

sensationalism [sen'seiʃ(ə)nəlizm], *s.* **1.** Recherche *f* du sensationnel, *P:* de l'épate. **2.** *Phil:* Sensualisme *m*.

sense[1] [sens], *s.* **1.** (a) Sens *m.* **The five senses,** les cinq sens. **To have a keen s. of smell, of hearing,** avoir l'odorat fin, l'ouïe fine. (b) Les sens. **Errors of s.,** erreurs des sens. **S. organs,** organes des sens. **2.** *pl.* (a) **To be in one's senses,** être sain d'esprit. **Are you in your right senses?** avez-vous votre raison? **Any man in his senses,** tout homme jouissant de son bon sens. **Have you taken leave of your senses?** est-ce que vous perdez la tête? vous perdez la raison? **To bring s.o. to his senses,** ramener qn à la raison. **To frighten s.o. out of his senses,** effrayer qn jusqu'à lui faire perdre la raison. **To come to one's senses,** revenir à la raison. (b) **To lose one's senses,** perdre connaissance. **To come to one's senses,** revenir à soi; reprendre ses sens. **3.** (a) Sensation *f*, sens. **A s. of pleasure,** une sensation de plaisir. **To labour under a s. of injustice,** nourrir un sentiment d'injustice. (b) Sentiment, conscience *f*. **S. of colour,** sentiment des couleurs. **To have a s. of time,** avoir le sentiment de l'heure. **Keen s. of humour,** sentiment très vif de l'humour. **4.** Bon sens, intelligence *f*, jugement *m*. **Common s., good s.,** sens commun; bon sens. **To show good s.,** faire preuve de jugement. **To talk s.,** parler raison. **There is no s. in that,** tout cela n'a pas le sens commun; cela ne rime à rien. **To have the (good) s. to** + *inf.,* avoir l'intelligence de + *inf.* **5.** Sens, signification *f* (d'un mot). **I can't make s. of this passage,** je n'arrive pas à comprendre ce passage. **In the literal s.,** au sens propre. **In the full s. of the word,** dans toute la force, l'acception, du terme. **To take a word in the wrong s.,** prendre un mot à contre-sens. **In a s.,** dans un (certain) sens; d'un certain point de vue.

sense[2], *v.tr.* **1.** Sentir (qch.) intuitivement; pressentir (qch.). **2. I had sensed as much,** c'est bien ce que j'avais compris.

senseless ['senslis], *a.* **1.** (*Of pers.*) Sans connaissance; inanimé. **To fall s.,** tomber sans connaissance. **To knock s.o. s.,** assommer qn. **2.** Qui n'a pas le sens commun; insensé, stupide, déraisonnable. **A s. remark,** une bêtise. **3.** Dépourvu de ses facultés, de sens; insensible. **-ly,** *adv.* Insensément, déraisonnablement, stupidement.

senselessness ['senslisnis], *s.* **1.** Manque *m* de bon sens; stupidité *f*. **2.** Insensibilité *f*.

sensibility [ˌsensi'biliti], *s.* **1.** Sensibilité *f* (d'un organe, etc.). **2.** (*Emotional*) Sensibilité, émotivité *f*. **Mawkish s.,** sensiblerie *f*.

sensible ['sensəbl], *a.* **1.** Sensible, perceptible. **S. heat,** chaleur sensible. **2.** (*Of difference, etc.*) Sensible, appréciable. **3.** Conscient (of, de). **To be s. of one's danger,** se rendre compte du danger. **To be s. of a fact,** apprécier un fait. **S. of an honour,** sensible à un honneur. **4.** Sensé, raisonnable; (choix) judicieux. **S. people,** les esprits sages. **Be s.,** soyez raisonnable. **S. clothing,** vêtements pratiques. **-ibly,** *adv.* **1.** Sensiblement, perceptiblement. **2.** Sensément, raisonnablement, judicieusement. **To be s. dressed,** porter des vêtements pratiques.

sensibleness ['sensiblnis], *s.* Bon sens; jugement (sain); raison *f*.

sensitive ['sensitiv], *a.* **1.** *Bot:* **S. plant,** sensitive *f*. **2.** (a) (*Of skin, tooth*) Sensible, sensitif, -ive. **S. to sth.,** sensible à qch. (*Of pers.*) **To be s. to cold,** être frileux. (b) (*Of pers.*) Susceptible; impressionnable. **S. on questions of honour,** chatouilleux sur l'honneur. (c) *Ph:* **S. scales,** balance sensible. *Com: Fin:* **S. market,** marché instable, prompt à réagir. *Phot:* **S. plate,** plaque impressionnable. **S. paper,** papier sensible, sensibilisé. **-ly,** *adv.* Sensiblement; d'une manière sensible.

sensitiveness ['sens(i)tivnis], **sensitivity** [ˌsensi'tiviti], *s.* **1.** Sensibilité *f*; faculté *f* de sentir; promptitude *f* à réagir. **2.** (a) Sensibilité (de caractère); susceptibilité *f*. (b) Sensibilité (d'une machine, etc.) (to, à, pour). **3.** *Ch: Phot:* Impressionnabilité *f*.

sensitize ['sensitaiz], *v.tr. Phot: Med: Biol:* etc. Sensibiliser. **sensitized,** *a.* (Papier) sensible, impressionnable. **sensitizing,** *a.* Sensibilisateur, -trice.

sensitizer ['sensitaizər], *s. Phot: etc:* (Agent) sensibilisateur *m.*

sensorial [sen'sɔ:riəl], *a. Physiol:* Sensoriel, -elle.
S. power, énergie vitale.

sensory ['sensəri], *a. Physiol:* (*a*) Sensoriel, -elle.
S. organs, organes *m* des sens. (*b*) Sensorial, -aux.

sensual ['sensjuəl], *a.* **1.** Sensuel, -elle; (instinct)
animal. **2.** Sensuel; voluptueux, -euse. **S. enjoyment,**
jouissances des sens; volupté *f.* **-ally,** *adv.* Avec
sensualité; sensuellement.

sensualist ['sensjuəlist], *s.* Sensualiste *mf*; jouisseur,
-euse, voluptueux, -euse.

sensuality [sensju'æliti], *s.* Sensualité *f.*

sensuous ['sensjuəs], *a.* (*Of pleasure*) Sybaritique,
voluptueux, -euse; (*of charm*) capiteux, -euse.
-ly, *adv.* Avec volupté.

sensuousness ['sensjuəsnis], *s.* Sybaritisme *m*; volupté *f.*

sent. *See* SEND[1].

sentence[1] ['sentəns], *s.* **1.** *Jur:* (*a*) Jugement *m*;
sentence *f*, condamnation *f.* **Life s.,** condamnation à
vie. **S. of death,** arrêt *m*, sentence, de mort. **Under
s. of death,** condamné à mort. **To pass (a) s.,** prononcer une sentence. (*b*) Peine *f.* **While he was undergoing
his s.,** pendant la durée de sa peine. **To serve one's s.,**
purger sa peine. **2.** *Gram:* Phrase *f.*

sentence[2], *v.tr. Jur:* Condamner (qn). **To s. s.o. to a
month's imprisonment, to death,** condamner qn à
un mois de prison, à mort.

sententious [sen'tenʃəs], *a.* Sentencieux, -euse. **-ly,**
adv. Sentencieusement.

sententiousness [sen'tenʃəsnis], *s.* Caractère, ton,
sentencieux; prudhommerie *f.*

sentient ['senʃiənt], *a.* Sensible.

sentiment ['sentimənt], *s.* **1.** Sentiment *m.* (*a*) Mouvement *m* de l'âme. **Noble sentiments,** sentiments
nobles. (*b*) Opinion *f*, avis *m.* **Those are my sentiments,** voilà mon sentiment; voilà comme je pense.
2. Sentimentalité *f*; (*mawkish*) sensiblerie *f.*

sentimental [senti'mentl], *a.* (*a*) Sentimental, -aux.
(*b*) D'une sensiblerie romanesque. **-ally,** *adv.*
Sentimentalement.

sentimentalism [senti'mentəlizm], *s.* Sentimentalisme
m, sensiblerie *f.*

sentimentalist [senti'mentəlist], *s.* Personne sentimentale. **He's, she's, a s.,** c'est un(e) sentimental(e).

sentimentality [sentimen'tæliti], *s.* Sentimentalité *f*,
sensiblerie *f.*

sentimentalize [senti'mentəlaiz]. **1.** *v.i.* Faire du
sentiment. **2.** *v.tr.* Apporter du sentiment, de la
sensiblerie dans (une œuvre, etc.).

sentinel ['sentinl], *s. O:* (i) (*Guard*) Factionnaire *m*;
(ii) (*outpost*) sentinelle *f.* **To stand s.,** monter la
garde; être posté en sentinelle. *Lit:* **The mountain
stands s. over the lake,** le pic monte la garde, veille,
sur le lac.

sentry ['sentri], *s.* **1.** (*a*) (*Guard*) Factionnaire *m.*
To relieve a s., relever qn de faction. (*b*) (*Outpost*)
Sentinelle *f.* **2.** Faction *f.* **To stand s.; to be on
s.(-go),** faire sa faction; être en, de, faction; monter
la garde. **To do s.-go before s.o.'s door,** faire les
cent pas devant la porte de qn. **To force a s.,** forcer la
consigne. **'sentry-box,** *s. Mil:* Guérite *f.*

sepal ['sepəl], *s. Bot:* Sépale *m.*

separability [sepə'rə'biliti], *s.* Séparabilité *f.*

separable ['sep(ə)rəbl], *a.* Séparable (**from,** de).

separate[1] ['sep(ə)rət], *a.* (*a*) (*Of parts*) Séparé, détaché
(**from,** de). (*b*) (*Of existence, etc.*) Distinct, indépendant; (*of room, etc.*) particulier, -ière; individuel,
-elle. **Entered in a s. column,** inscrit dans une colonne
à part. (*c*) *s. Com: Cost:* **Separates,** (rayon des)
dépareillés. **-ly,** *adv.* Séparément; à part.

separate[2] ['sepəreit]. **1.** *v.tr.* Séparer. (*a*) Désunir,
détacher, décoller (**from,** de). **To s. truth from error,**
dégager la vérité de l'erreur. *Husb:* **To s. the milk,**
écrémer le lait. (*b*) Désunir (une famille, etc.).
He is separated from his wife, il est séparé de sa femme.
(*c*) **This river separates the two countries,** ce fleuve
sépare les deux pays. **2.** *v.i.* (*a*) (*Of thg*) Se séparer,
se détacher, se désunir (**from,** de). (*b*) (*Of pers.*)
When we separated for the night, quand nous nous
sommes quittés pour la nuit. **To s. from s.o.,** se
séparer de, rompre avec, qn. (*c*) (*Of man and wife*)
Se séparer de corps et de biens.

separation [sepə'reiʃ(ə)n], *s.* **1.** Séparation *f. Min:*
Classement *m* (du minerai). **S. from s.o.,** séparation
d'avec qn. *Mil:* **S. allowances,** allocations faites
aux femmes (des soldats). *Judicial:* **S.,** séparation de
corps (et de biens); séparation judiciaire. **S. order,**
jugement *m* de séparation. **2.** Écart *m*, distance *f.*

separator ['sepəreitər], *s.* (*Device*) Séparateur *m.*
Cream-s., écrémeuse *f.*

sepia ['si:pjə], *s. Moll:* Sépia *f*, seiche *f. Art:* Sépia.
Phot: **S. paper,** papier bistre.

sepoy ['si:pɔi], *s. Mil.Hist:* Cipaye *m.*

sepsis ['sepsis], *s. Med:* (*a*) Putréfaction *f.* (*b*)
Septicémie *f*; infection *f* putride.

September [sep'tembər], *s.* Septembre *m.* **In S.,** en,
au mois de, septembre. (**On) the fifth of S.,** le cinq
septembre.

septennial [sep'tenjəl], *a.* Septennal, -aux.

septet(te) [sep'tet], *s. Mus:* Septuor *m.*

septic ['septik], *a.* (*a*) *Med:* Septique. **S. poisoning,**
septicémie *f. F:* **To become, go, s.,** s'infecter. (*b*)
Hyg: **S. tank,** fosse *f* septique. (*c*) *P:* Moche,
infecte.

septicaemia [septi'si:miə], *s.* Septicémie *f*; infection
f putride.

septuagenarian ['septjuədʒi'nɛəriən], *s. & a.* Septuagénaire (*mf*).

Septuagesima [septjuə'dʒesimə], *s. Ecc:* (Dimanche
de) la Septuagésime.

septuagint ['septjuədʒint], *s.* Version *f* (de la Bible)
des Septante.

septum, *pl.* **-a** ['septəm, -ə], (*a*) *Anat:* Septum *m.*
(*b*) *Bot:* Cloison *f.*

sepulchral [si'pʌlkr(ə)l], *a.* Sépulcral, -aux. **S. vault,**
caveau *m.* **S. stone,** pierre *f* tumulaire. **S. voice,**
voix caverneuse.

sepulchre ['sep(ə)lkər], *s.* Sépulcre *m*, tombeau *m.*

sepulture ['sep(ə)ltʃər], *s.* Sépulture *f.* **1.** Mise *f* au
tombeau. **2.** *A:* Tombeau *m.*

sequel ['si:kw(ə)l], *s.* Suite *f* (d'un roman, etc.).
Action that had an unfortunate s., acte qui entraîna
des suites malheureuses.

sequence ['si:kwəns], *s.* **1.** (*a*) Succession *f*; ordre
naturel. **In s.,** en série; en succession. *Cin:* Séquence
f (de liaison). *T.V:* **S. of interlace,** séquence d'entrelacement. (*b*) Suite *f*, série *f*, chaîne *f* (d'événements,
etc.). (*c*) *Gram:* **S. of tenses,** concordance *f* des
temps. **2.** *Cards:* Séquence *f.* **3.** *Cin: F:* Scène *f*
(de film).

sequester [sə'kwestər]. **1.** *v.pr. Lit:* **To s. oneself
(from the world, etc.),** se retirer (du monde, etc.).
2. *v.tr. Jur:* Séquestrer; mettre (un bien) sous
séquestre. **sequestered,** *a.* **1.** *Lit:* (*Of life, etc.*)
Retiré, isolé; (*of spot, etc.*) retiré, perdu. **2.** *Jur:*
(*Of property*) Sous séquestre.

sequestrate [sə'kwestreit], *v.tr. Jur:* Séquestrer,
confisquer. **Three nationalist papers were seques-
trated,** on a saisi trois journaux nationalistes.

sequestration [sekwes'treiʃ(ə)n, -se-], *s.* **1.** *Lit:*
Retraite *f*; éloignement *m* du monde. **2.** *Jur:*
Séquestration *f*; mise *f* sous séquestre.

sequin ['si:kwin], *s.* Sequin *m.*

sequoia [se:'kwɔiə], *s. Bot:* Sequoia *m.*

sérac ['seræk], *s. Geog:* Sérac *m.*

seraglio [se'rɑ:liou], *s. Mil:* Sérail *m*, -ails.

seraph, *pl.* **seraphs, seraphim** ['serəf(s), 'serəfim], *s.*
Séraphin *m.*

seraphic [se'ræfik], *a.* Séraphique.

Serbo-Croat ['sə:bou'krouæt], **1.** *a. & s. Geog:
Ethn:* Serbo-croate (*mf*). **2.** *s. Ling:* Le serbo-
croate.

sere ['siər], *a. Poet:* Flétri, desséché, fané.

serenade[1] [serə'neid], *s.* Sérénade *f.*

serenade[2], *v.tr.* Donner une sérénade à (qn).

serenader [serə'neidər], *s.* Donneur *m*, joueur *m*,
de sérénades.

serene [sə'ri:n], *a.* **1.** Serein, calme, tranquille; (ciel)
clair. **2.** **His S. Highness,** son Altesse sérénissime.
-ly, *adv.* Tranquillement; avec sérénité.

serenity [sə'reniti], *s.* Sérénité *f*, calme *m*, tranquillité
f.

serf [sə:f], *s.* Serf, *f.* serve.

serfdom ['sə:fdəm], *s.* Servage *m.*

serge [sə:dʒ], *s. Tex:* Serge *f.* **Cotton s.,** sergé *m.*

sergeant ['sɑ:dʒənt], s. (a) Mil:Av: Sergent m; (cavalry, artillery) = maréchal m des logis; (women's services, W.R.A.C., W.R.A.F.) cinquième catégorie ʳ. Av: Flight s., sergent-chef m, pl. sergents-chefs; (W.R.A.F.) quatrième catégorie. (b) Police s., brigadier m. S.a. COLOUR-SERGEANT, QUARTER-MASTER 2. 'sergeant-'major, s. Mil: (Company) s.-m. = sergent major, adjudant m; (W.R.A.C.) deuxième catégorie. Regimental s.-m. = adjudant chef; (W.R.A.C.) première catégorie.

serial ['siəriəl], a. 1. S. number, numéro de série; numéro matricule (d'un moteur, etc.). 2. S. story, s. serial, (roman-)feuilleton m. S. writer, feuille-toniste m. S. rights, droit de reproduction en feuille-ton. -ally, adv. 1. En, par, série. 2. Journ: T.V: etc: En feuilleton.

serialize ['siəriəlaiz], v.tr. Journ: T.V: etc: Publier (un roman), présenter (un film), en feuilleton.

seriatim [siəri'eitim], adv. Successivement; au fur et à mesure.

seri(ci)culture ['seri(si)kʌltʃər], s. Séri(ci)culture f.

series ['siəri:z], s.inv. 1. Série f, suite f; échelle f, gamme f (de couleurs, etc.). Ch: S. of reactions, réactions f caténaires, réactions en chaîne. Mth: S. of numbers, of terms, suite, série, de nombres, de termes. Infinite s., série infinie. 2. Adv.phr. In s., en série, en succession. Reservoirs arranged in s., réservoirs en chapelet. El: To connect cells in s., grouper des éléments en série, en tension.

serif ['serif], s. Typ: Empattement m.

seringa [sə'riŋgə], s. Bot: Seringa m.

serious ['siəriəs], a. Sérieux, -euse. 1. S. wound, blessure grave, grave blessure. S. mistake, grosse faute. 2. (a) S. promise, promesse sérieuse, sincère. (b) Réfléchi. I am s., je ne plaisante pas. -ly, adv. Sérieusement. 1. S. ill, gravement malade. S. wounded, griève-ment blessé. 2. To take sth. (too) s., prendre qch. (trop) au sérieux. 'serious-'minded, a. Réfléchi, sérieux, -euse.

seriousness ['siəriəsnis], s. 1. Gravité f (d'une maladie, etc.). 2. Sérieux m (de maintien, etc.). 3. In all s., sérieusement.

serjeant ['sɑ:dʒənt], s. m. 1. Mil: A: = SERGEANT. S. of the watch, sergent de nuit. 2. (a) A: S. at law, avocat (d'un ordre supérieur du barreau). (b) Common S. (at law), magistrat de la corporation de Londres. (c) S. at Arms (also Sergeant at Arms) = huissier (au Parlement, etc.).

sermon ['sə:mən], s. 1. Ecc: Sermon m; homilie f; B: The S. on the Mount, le Sermon sur la montagne. 2. F: Sermon, semonce f.

sermonize ['sə:mənaiz], 1. v.i. Pej: Sermonner, prêcher. 2. v.tr. F: Sermonner, chapitrer (qn); faire la morale à (qn).

serosity [siə'rositi], s. Sérosité f.

serous ['siərəs], a. Séreux, -euse.

serpent ['sə:p(ə)nt], s. (a) Serpent m. (b) Pyr: Serpen-teau m.

serpentine ['sə:p(ə)ntain], 1. a. Serpentin; sinueux, -euse, tortueux, -euse. 2. s. Min: Serpentine f.

serrate ['sereit], **serrated** [se'reitid], a. Denté en scie; dentelé. Knife with a serrated edge, couteau-scie m.

serration [se'reiʃ(ə)n], s. Dentelure f.

serried ['serid], a. Lit: Serré. In s. ranks, en rangs serrés, pressés.

serum ['siərəm], s. Physiol: Sérum m. Med: Truth s., sérum de vérité. Med: Vet: Protective s., immunisant m.

serval ['sə:vəl], s. Z: Serval m, pl. servals.

servant ['sə:v(ə)nt], s. 1. (a) (Domestic) s., domestique mf; servante f, bonne f. General s., bonne à tout faire. To keep a s., avoir une domestique. Mil: Officer's s., ordonnance f. (b) Serviteur m, servante (de Dieu, etc.). (c) Corr: (Formal) Your (most) obedient s., (usual equivalent) je vous prie d'agréer mes salutations empressées. A: Your humble s., votre (très) humble serviteur. 2. Employé, -ée (du chemin de fer, etc.). Civil s., fonctionnaire m (de l'État). Jur: Servants and agents, préposés.

serve [sə:v]. I. v.tr. 1. (a) (Of pers.) Servir (un maître, une cause, etc.). Abs. To s. (at table), servir (à table). To s. in the army, servir dans l'armée; être au service militaire. To have served ten years, avoir dix ans de service. Jur: To s. on the jury, être du jury. (b) To s. one's apprenticeship, faire son apprentissage. To have served one's time, (i) avoir fait son temps de service; (ii) sortir d'apprentissage. To s. one's sentence, subir, purger, sa peine. 2. (a) (Of thg) Être utile à (qn); suffire à (qn). It will s. the purpose, abs. it will s., cela fera l'affaire. If my memory serves me right, si j'ai bonne mémoire. 3. Desservir. Localities served by a railway line, localités desservies par un chemin de fer. 4. (a) To s. s.o. with a pound of butter, servir une livre de beurre à qn. Are you being served? est-ce qu'on vous sert? (b) Tradesman who has served us for ten years, marchand qui nous sert, qui fournit chez nous, depuis dix ans. (c) (At table) To s. s.o. with soup, servir du potage à qn. 5. (a) To s. a dish, (i) servir un mets; (ii) servir (aux convives) d'un mets. "Dinner, lunch, is served," "Monsieur, Madame, est servi(e)." (b) Ten: To s. the ball, abs. to s., servir (la balle). 6. Jur: To s. a writ on s.o., to s. s.o. with a writ, délivrer, signifier, notifier, une assignation à qn. 7. Traiter (qn) (bien, mal). He served me very badly, il a très mal agi envers moi. It serves you right! c'est bien fait! vous ne l'avez pas volé! It serves him right for being . . ., ça lui apprendra à être . . . 8. Breed: (Of stallion, bull) Saillir, couvrir (une jument, une vache). II. serve, v.i. To s. for sth., servir à qch. To s. as sth., servir de qch.; faire fonction de qch. To s. as a pretext, as an example, servir de prétexte, d'exemple. **serve out**, v.tr. 1. Distribuer (des pro-visions, etc.); servir (la soupe, etc.) à la ronde. 2. F: To s. s.o. out for sth., revaloir qch. à qn; se venger. **serve up**, v.tr Servir, mettre sur la table (un plat). F: To s. up an old tale, resservir une vieille rengaine. **serving**[1], a. Servant; (soldat) au service. 'serving-man, s.m. A: Domestique. 'serving-woman, s.f. A: Domestique. **serving**[2], s. 1. Service m (d'un maître). 2. Service (du dîner, etc.). 3. Nau: Fourrage m garniture f (d'un cordage).

server ['sə:vər], s. 1. (a) Serveur, -euse. (b) Ecc: (At mass) Acolyte m, répondant m; servant m. 2. pl. Salad-servers, fish-servers, service m à salade, à poisson.

service[1] ['sə:vis], s. 1. Service m. Length of s., ancienneté f. To do one's military s., faire son service militaire. To be on active s., être en activité (de service). Killed on active s., tué en service com-mandé. To have seen long s., avoir vieilli dans le service. 2. (a) Public services, services publics. The Public S., l'Administration f. Postal s., tele-graph s., administration (publique) des postes, des télégraphes. Mil.Hist: Royal Army S. Corps = service de l'Intendance. (b) Distribution f, installation f (de gaz, d'électricité, d'eau). El.E: S. tension, tension de distribution. (c) Entretien m et dépannage m (d'automobiles, etc.). 3. (a) Emploi m (d'un fonctionnaire, etc.). The military and civil services, les administrations militaires et civiles de l'État. To be in the civil s., être fonctionnaire (de l'État). The Foreign S., la diplomatie, le service diplomatique. (b) The three services, l'armée f, la marine et l'armée de l'air. The armed services, les forces armées. S. families, les familles de militaires. To use s. labour, avoir recours à la main-d'œuvre militaire. A: Av: S. pilot, pilote militaire. The Senior S., la marine. 4. (a) (Domestic) s., service (domestique). O: To be in s., être en service, F: en condition. (b) S. flat, appartement avec service. (In restaurant, etc.) S. charge, service. 5. (a) To render, do, s.o. a s., rendre (un) service à qn. His services to education, les services qu'il a rendus à l'enseignement. (b) I am at your s., je suis à votre disposition. Always at your s., toujours, à votre disposition, à votre service. (Motto) 'S.,' 'servir!' Social services, institutions sociales. (c) Utilité f. To be of some s., être de quelque utilité. To be of s. to s.o., être utile à qn. (Of thg) To do s., servir. To do good s., faire un bon usage; faire de l'usage. 6. Ecc: Office m; (in Protestant churches) service, culte m. Open-air s., Mil: drum-head s., office divin en plein air. 7. Ten: Service. 8. Jur: Délivrance f, signification f (d'un acte, d'une assignation). 9. Tea s., service à thé. 'service-lift, s. Monte-plats m inv. 'service-line, *s. Ten:* Ligne *f* de service, de fond. **'service-pipe,** *s.* Branchement *m* (pour le gaz, etc.). **'service-rifle,** *s. Mil:* Fusil *m* d'ordonnance. **'service-station,** *s. Aut:* Station-service *f*, *pl.* stations-service. **'service-'uniform,** *s. Mil: etc:* Uniforme *m* réglementaire.

service², *v.tr.* Entretenir et réparer (les automobiles, etc.). **servicing,** *s.* Entretien *m* (d'une auto, etc.).

serviceable ['sə:visəbl], *a.* 1. (*Of pers.*) Serviable. 2. (*Of thg*) (*a*) En état de fonctionner; utilisable. (*b*) Utile; de bon usage; avantageux. (*c*) Pratique, commode.

serviceableness ['sə:visəblnis], *s.* 1. Utilité *f*, commodité *f* (d'un outil, etc.). 2. Solidité *f*, utilité *f* (d'un vêtement).

serviceman, -men [sə:vismən], *s.m.* Soldat *m*, mobilisé *m.* **National s.,** soldat (qui fait son service militaire), appelé *m*, militaire *m* du contingent. **Disabled ex-s.,** mutilé *m* de guerre.

servicewoman, -women ['sə:viswumən, -wimin], *s.f.* Femme-soldat.

serviette [,sə:vi'et], *s.* = NAPKIN 1.

servile ['sə:vail], *a.* 1. Servile; d'esclave. **S. imitation,** imitation servile. 2. (*Of pers.*) Servile; bas *f*. basse. **-ly,** *adv.* 1. Servilement; avec servilité; bassement. 2. (Traduire) servilement, trop exactement.

servility [sə:'viliti], *s.* 1. Servilité *f*, exactitude trop étroite (d'une copie, etc.). 2. (*Of pers.*) Servilité; bassesse *f.*

servitude ['sə:vitju:d], *s.* 1. Servitude *f*, esclavage *m.* 2. *Jur:* **Penal s.,** travaux forcés; prison *f* cellulaire.

servo-brake ['sə:vou'breik], *s. Aut:* Servofrein *m.*

servo-mechanism ['sə:vou'mekənizm], *s. Mec.E:* Servomécanisme *m.*

servo-motor ['sə:vou'moutər], *s. Mec.E:* Servo-moteur *m.*

sesame ['sesəmi], *s.* 1. *Bot:* Sésame *m.* 2. **Open S.!** Sésame, ouvre-toi! **A good open s.,** un bon passe-partout.

sessile ['sesail], *a.* (*Of leaf, etc.*) Sessile.

session ['se∫(ə)n], *s.* 1. *A:* Tenue *f* (d'une assemblée, des assises, etc.). 2. Session *f*; séance *f.* **To have a long s.,** faire une longue séance. *F:* **To have a s. on sth.,** discuter le coup. *Parl:* **The House is now in s.,** la Chambre siège actuellement. **To go into secret s.,** se former en comité secret. **During this (legislative) s.,** pendant cette législature. 3. (*a*) *Sch: U.S:* Trimestre *m* scolaire, universitaire. (*b*) *U.S. & Scot:* Année *f* universitaire. 4. *Jur:* *pl.* **Petty sessions,** session du tribunal (d'instance).

sestet [ses'tet], *s.* 1. *Pros:* Les deux tercets (d'un sonnet). 2. *Mus:* = SEXTET(TE).

set¹ [set], *s.* 1. Ensemble *m.* (*a*) Jeu *m* (d'outils, de dominos); série *f* (de casseroles); batterie *f* (d'ustensiles de cuisine); collection complète (des œuvres de qn); service *m* (de porcelaine). **Construction s.,** jeu de construction. **S. of golf-clubs,** jeu de crosses. **S. of tyres,** train *m* de pneus. **S. of furniture,** ameublement *m.* **S. of fire-irons,** garniture *f* de foyer. **Toilet s.,** garniture de toilette. *El:E:* **Generating s.,** groupe *m* électrogène. *Com:* **Bill drawn in a s. of three,** lettre de change tirée à trois exemplaires. *S.a.* TOOTH¹ 1. (*b*) **Wireless, radio, s.,** poste *m* de radio, de T.S.F. **Receiving-s.,** poste récepteur. **Television s.,** poste de télévision. (*c*) *Ten:* **Manche** *f*, **set** *m.* (*d*) Groupe *m* (de personnes). **S. of thieves,** bande *f* de voleurs. **Literary s.,** coterie *f* littéraire. **The smart s.,** le monde élégant. **We don't move in the same s.,** nous ne fréquentons pas les mêmes milieux. 2. (*a*) *Poet:* **At s. of sun,** au coucher du soleil. (*b*) *Ven:* (*Of dog*) Arrêt *m.* **To make a dead s.,** tomber en arrêt. *F:* **To make a (dead) s. at s.o.,** (i) attaquer furieusement qn (à la tribune); (ii) (*of woman*) se jeter à la tête d'un homme. (*c*) *Hairdr:* Mise *f* en plis. 3. (*a*) Assiette *f* (d'une poutre); attitude *f*, posture *f* (de corps); port *m* (de tête); tournure *f* (d'un vêtement); disposition *f* des plis (d'une draperie). **S. of a saw,** voie *f*, chasse *f*, d'une scie. *Nau:* **S. of the sails,** (i) orientation *f* des voiles; (ii) façon *f* dont les voiles sont établies. (*b*) **Direction** *f* (du courant); *Nau:* lit *m* (du vent). 4. (*a*) *Hort:* **Plant** *m* à repiquer. (*b*) **(Paving-)s.,** pavé *m* d'échantillon. (*c*) *Nat.Hist:* **Badger's s.,**

terrier m de blaireau. (*d*) *Th: Cin: etc:* Décor *m*; mise *f* en scène. **Rehearsal on the s.,** répétition *f* sur le plateau. 5. *Tls:* (*a*) Saw-s., tourne-à-gauche *m inv.* (*b*) **Cold s.,** tranche *f* à froid.

set², *v.* (**set; set; setting**) I. *v.tr.* 1. (*a*) Asseoir, placer (qn sur le trône). **To s. sth. above rubies,** priser qch. plus que des rubis. (*b*) **To s. a hen,** mettre une poule à couver. 2. (*a*) Mettre, poser (qch. sur qch., devant qn). **To s. one's glass on the table,** poser son verre sur la table. **To s. a dish on the table,** servir un plat. **To s. one's seal to a document,** apposer son sceau à un acte. (*Usu. in neg.*) **I haven't s. eyes on him for a long time,** il y a long-temps que je ne l'ai vu. *S.a.* FIRE¹ 1, HAND¹ 1, (*b*) **To s. one's affections on s.o.,** fixer ses affections sur qn. *S.a.* HEART¹ 2 (*c*). 3. (*a*) **To s. chairs (for the company),** placer, avancer, des chaises. (*b*) **To s. the table,** mettre le couvert, la table. **To s. (the table) for two,** mettre deux couverts. 4. (*a*) **To s. a piano too high,** accorder un piano trop haut. (*b*) **To s. words to music,** mettre des paroles en musique. **To s. 'Othello' to music,** écrire une partition sur *Othello.* 5. (*a*) **To s. a stake in the ground,** enfoncer, planter, un pieu dans la terre. (*b*) **To s. seeds,** planter des graines. 6. (*a*) **To s. the clock,** régler la pendule. **To s. the alarm for five o'clock,** mettre le réveille-matin sur cinq heures. *Aut:* **To s. the speedometer to zero,** ramener le compteur à zéro. *Navy:* **To s. a torpedo,** régler une torpille. *Av:* **To s. the controls,** régler, repérer, les commandes. (*b*) *El.E:* **To s. the brushes,** ajuster, caler, les balais. (*c*) **To s. the iron of a plane,** régler, ajuster, le fer d'un rabot. **To s. (the teeth of) a saw,** donner de la voie à une scie. (*d*) **To have one's hair s.,** se faire faire une mise en plis. 7. (*a*) **To s. a butterfly,** monter un papillon. (*b*) *Th:* **To s. a scene,** monter un décor. (*c*) **To s. a gem,** sertir, enchatonner, enchâsser, une pierre. **Ring s. with rubies,** bague ornée de rubis. **Panes s. in lead,** vitres serties de plomb. *Mec.E:* **To s. the shaft in its bearings,** loger l'arbre dans les paliers. (*d*) *Nau:* **To s. a sail,** déployer, établir, une voile. **(With) all sails s.,** toutes voiles dehors. 8. **To s. a snare,** dresser, tendre, un piège. 9. (*a*) **To s. a razor,** affiler un rasoir. **To s. a chisel,** affûter un ciseau. 10. *Typ:* **To s. type,** composer. 11. **To s. a date, a day,** fixer une date. **To s. limits to sth.,** assigner des limites à qch. *S.a.* WATCH¹ 4. 12. **To s. the fashion,** fixer, mener, la mode; donner le ton. *Row:* **To s. the stroke,** régler l'allure. *Nau:* **To s. the course (on the chart),** tracer la route. 13. **To s. a bone,** remettre un os. **To s. one's teeth,** serrer les dents. 14. **To s. one's teeth,** serrer les dents. 15. **Cold sets jellies,** le froid fait prendre les gelées. 16. **To s. s.o. on his way,** mettre qn dans le bon chemin. 17. (*a*) **To s. s.o. doing sth.,** mettre qn à faire qch. **To s. the dog barking,** faire aboyer le chien. **This incident s. everybody's tongue wagging,** cet incident a mis toutes les langues en branle. (*b*) **To s. sth. going,** mettre qch. en train. 18. **To s. a man to work,** mettre un homme au travail. *S.a.* THIEF 1. 19. **To s. a good example,** donner un bon exemple. **To s. a problem,** donner un problème à résoudre. *Sch:* **To s. a book,** mettre un livre au programme (d'études). **To s. a paper,** établir les questions d'une composition. II. **set,** *v.i.* 1. (*a*) (*Of sun*) Se coucher. (*b*) (*Of fame*) S'éteindre. 2. (*Of dress*) **To s. well, badly,** bien, mal, tomber. 3. (*Of broken bone*) Se ressouder; *F:* se recoller. 4. (*a*) (*Of white of egg*) Se coaguler; (*of blood*) se figer; (*of milk*) se cailler; (*of jelly*) prendre. (*b*) (*Of cement*) Prendre, durcir. 5. *Ven:* (*Of dog*) Tomber en arrêt. 6. *Danc: A:* **To s. (to partners),** balancer; faire chassé-croisé. 7. (*Of current*) **To s. southwards,** porter au sud. **The tide has s. in his favour,** ses actions remontent. 8. **To s. to work,** se mettre au travail, à l'œuvre. **set about.** 1. *v.i.* (*a*) **To s. about doing sth.,** se mettre à faire qch. **I don't know how to s. about it,** je ne sais pas comment m'y prendre. (*b*) *F:* **To s. about s.o.,** attaquer qn. 2. *v.tr.* **To s. a rumour about,** donner cours à un bruit. **set against,** *v.tr.* (*a*) **To s. s.o. against s.o.,** prévenir qn contre qn. (*b*) **To s. one's face against sth.,** s'opposer résolument à qch. **set apart,** *v.tr.* 1. **To s. the women a.,** isoler les femmes. 2. Mettre (qch.) à part. **set aside,**

v.tr. 1. = SET APART 2. 2. (*a*) Rejeter; mettre (qch.) au rebut. (*b*) Écarter (une proposition). **Setting aside my expenses . . .,** sans compter :nes frais. . . . (*c*) **To s. a will a.,** annuler un testament. **set back,** *v.tr.* 1. (*a*) Renfoncer (une façade). **House s. b. (from the alignment),** maison en retrait. (*b*) (*Of horse*) **To s. b. its ears,** coucher les oreilles. 2. (*a*) **To s. b. the trip-recorder to 0,** remettre le compteur de trajet à 0. (*b*) Retarder (la pendule, le travail, le progrès). *F:* **This car s. me b. a packet,** cette voiture m'a coûté les yeux de la tête. **'set-back,** *s.* (*pl.* **set-backs).** (*a*) Recul *m* (dans les affaires). (*b*) Déconvenue *f*; revers *m* de fortune. **set before,** *v.tr.* (*a*) **To s. a dish b. s.o.,** servir un plat à qn. (*b*) **To s. a plan b. s.o.,** exposer un projet à qn. **set down,** *v.tr.* 1. Poser, déposer. **I shall s. you down at your door,** je vous déposerai à votre porte. (*Of train*) **To s. d. passengers at . . .,** débarquer, déposer, des voyageurs à. . . . 2. **To s. sth. d. (in writing),** consigner, coucher, qch. par écrit. **set forth.** 1. *v.tr.* Énoncer; exposer; faire valoir (ses raisons); avancer (une théorie). 2. *v.i. O:* Se mettre en route, en voyage; partir (for, pour). **set in,** 1. *v.i.* Commencer. **Before winter sets in,** avant le début de l'hiver. **It's setting in for rain,** le temps se met à la pluie. **A reaction is setting in,** une réaction se dessine. **If no complications s. in,** s'il ne survient pas de complications. 2. *v.tr.* (*a*) Encastrer (une pierre); emboîter (une mortaise); poser (une vitre). (*b*) *Dressm: Tail:* Monter (les manches). **Set-in sleeve,** manche rapportée. **set off.** I. *v.tr.* 1. (*a*) **To s. o. a debt,** compenser une dette. (*b*) Faire ressortir, faire valoir (une couleur). **Her dress sets off her figure,** sa robe fait valoir sa taille. 2. *Surv:* Rapporter (un angle). 3. Faire partir (une fusée). **This answer s. them off laughing,** cette réponse a déclenché les rires. II. *v.i.* 1. Partir; se mettre en route; se mettre en voyage. 2. *Typ:* (*Of wet ink*) Maculer. **'set-off,** *s.* 1. Contraste *m.* **S.-o. to beauty,** (i) ornement *m* de la beauté; (ii) repoussoir *m* à la beauté. **As a s.-o. to . . .,** comme contraste à. . . . 2. (*a*) Compensation *f* (d'une dette). *Book-k:* Écriture *f* inverse. (*b*) *Jur:* (*Counter-claim*) Reconvention *f.* 3. *Typ:* Maculage *m.* **set on,** *v.tr.* **To s. a dog on s.o.,** lancer un chien contre qn. **I was s. on by a dog,** j'ai été attaqué par un chien. **set out.** I. *v.tr.* 1. (*a*) Mettre (qch.) dehors, déposer (qch.) à la porte. (*b*) Mettre en terre (des plants). 2. Arranger, disposer. **To s. o. one's ideas clearly,** ordonner clairement ses idées. **His work is well s. o.,** son travail est bien présenté. **To s. goods out on the counter,** disposer, étaler, des marchandises sur le comptoir. 3. *Mth: Surv: etc:* **To s. o. a curve,** faire le tracé d'une courbe. 4. *Typ:* Espacer (les mots). II. *v.i.* (i) Se mettre en route, en chemin; (ii) s'embarquer; faire voile. **To s. o. for France,** partir pour la France. **To s. o. in pursuit of s.o.,** se mettre à la poursuite de qn. **set to,** *v.i.* 1. Se mettre (résolument) au travail. **We must s. to!** allons-y! *F:* (*Of two pers.*) En venir aux coups. **'set-to,** *s.* 1. Assaut *m* (de boxe). 2. *F:* Lutte *f*, combat *m*, empoignade *f.* **To have a s.-to,** en venir aux mains. **set up.** I. *v.tr.* 1. (*a*) Placer, fixer (un objet). (*b*) Élever, ériger (une statue); planter (un drapeau); monter (une machine); armer (un appareil). (*c*) *Typ:* **To s. up a MS.,** composer un MS. 2. Exalter, élever (qn). 3. (*a*) Instaurer (un culte). (*b*) Établir (une agence, une école, un record); fonder (une maison de commerce); monter (un magasin). **To s. up house somewhere,** établir son domicile quelque part. (*c*) **Food that sets up irritation,** aliment qui occasionne de l'irritation. (*d*) **To s. up a king,** instaurer une monarchie. (*e*) **To s. s.o. up in business,** établir qn dans un commerce. (*f*) **To s. s.o. up as a model,** proposer qn comme modèle. **To s. up ridiculous pretentions,** afficher des prétentions ridicules. 4. **To s. up a shout,** pousser une clameur. 5. Donner, rendre, de la vigueur à (qn). **This medicine will s. you up,** ce remède va vous remettre d'aplomb. II. *v.i.* 1. **To s. up in business,** s'établir dans le commerce. 2. *v.i. & pr.* **To s. (oneself) up as a critic,** se poser en critique. **'set-up,** *s. F:* Organisation *f.* **setting up,** *s.* 1. (*a*) Montage *m*, installation *f.*

(*b*) *Typ:* Composition *f.* 2. **S. up of a new order,** établissement *m*, instauration *f*, d'un nouveau régime. **S. up housekeeping,** entrée *f* en ménage. **set upon,** *v.i.* **To s. u. the enemy,** attaquer l'ennemi. **setting¹,** *a.* (Astre) baissant, couchant; (gloire) sur son déclin. **setting²,** *s.* 1. (*a*) Mise *f*, pose *f* (de qch.). (*b*) Disposition *f*, arrangement *m.* **S. to music,** mise en musique. (*c*) Plantation *f* (de graines). (*d*) Réglage *m*; mise à l'heure (d'une horloge); ajustage *m.* (*e*) Montage *m* (d'un spécimen); armement *m* (d'un piège); mise en plis (des cheveux). (*f*) Aiguisage *m*, affûtage *m* (d'un outil). (*g*) *Typ:* Composition *f.* **Page-s.,** mise en pages. (*h*) Fixation *f* (d'une date). (*i*) Réduction *f* (d'une fracture). (*j*) Imposition *f* (d'une tâche). 2. (*a*) Coucher *m* (du soleil). (*b*) Recollement *m* (d'un os brisé). (*c*) Nouure *f* (du fruit). (*d*) Prise *f* (du ciment); coagulation *f* (de l'albumine). 3. (*a*) Cadre *m* (d'un récit). *Th:* Mise en scène. (*b*) Monture *f* (d'un diamant). (*c*) *Mus:* (i) Ton *m* (d'un morceau). (ii) **S. for piano,** arrangement pour piano. **set³,** *a.* 1. (*a*) **S. face,** visage immobile, aux traits rigides. **S. smile,** sourire figé. *S.a.* FAIR² I. 6. (*b*) (Ressort) bandé, tendu. *Sp:* (*To runners*) **(Get) s.!** en position! *F:* **To be all s.,** être prêt à commencer. (*c*) **Hard s.,** ferme, figé. (*d*) **The fruit is s.,** le fruit est formé, noué. 2. (*a*) **S. price,** prix fixe. **S. time,** heure fixée. **At s. hours,** à des heures réglées. **S. purpose,** ferme intention. (*b*) **S. phrase,** cliché *m*; expression consacrée. **S. phrases,** expressions toutes faites. **S. speech,** discours composé à l'avance, discours en forme. (*c*) *Cu: Pyr:* **S. piece,** pièce montée. *Th:* **S. scene,** décor (monté). (*d*) **S. task,** tâche assignée. *Sch:* **S. subject,** sujet imposé aux candidats. **The s. books,** les auteurs *m* du programme. 3. **To be s. on sth.,** être résolu, déterminé, à qch. **Since you are s. upon it . . .,** puisque vous y tenez. . . . **His mind is s.,** son parti est pris. **To be dead s. against s.o.,** s'acharner contre qn. **'set square,** *s.* Équerre *f* (à dessin).

setaceous [si(:)'teiʃəs], *a. Nat.Hist:* Sétacé.
setness ['setnis], *s.* 1. Rigidité *f* (des traits). **S. of purpose,** détermination *f.* 2. Opiniâtreté *f.*
settee [se'ti:], *s. Furn:* Canapé *m*; causeuse *f.* **set'tee-bed,** *s.* Canapé-lit *m, pl.* canapés-lits.
setter ['setər], *s.* 1. (*Pers.*) (*a*) Monteur *m*, sertisseur *m* (de diamants). (*b*) Affûteur *m* (de scies). 2. Chien *m* d'arrêt; setter *m.*
settle¹ ['setl], *s. Furn:* Banc *m* à dossier.
settle². I. *v.tr.* 1. (*a*) Établir, installer (qn) (dans un pays). (*b*) Coloniser (un pays). (*c*) Rendre stable. (*d*) Mettre bien en place. 2. (*a*) **To s. an invalid for the night,** arranger un malade pour la nuit. (*b*) **To s. one's children,** établir ses enfants. (*c*) **To s. one's affairs,** mettre ordre à ses affaires. 3. (*a*) Clarifier, laisser rasseoir (un liquide). (*b*) **To s. s.o.'s doubts,** dissiper les doutes de qn. 4. Concerter, préparer (son attitude); calmer (les nerfs). **Give me something to s. my stomach,** donnez-moi quelque chose pour me remettre l'estomac. 5. Fixer, déterminer (un jour, un endroit). **The terms were settled, on** convint des conditions. **It's as good as settled,** *F:* l'affaire est dans le sac. **It's all settled,** c'est une affaire faite. **That's settled then,** alors c'est dit. 6. (*a*) Résoudre, décider (une question); trancher, aplanir (un différend); vider (une querelle); arranger, liquider (une affaire). **Questions not yet settled,** questions en suspens. **That settles it!** (i) voilà qui tranche la question! (ii) cela me décide! **S. it among yourselves,** arrangez cela entre vous. *Jur:* **To s. an affair out of court,** transiger avant jugement. **Settled between the parties,** arrangé à l'amiable. (*b*) Conclure, terminer (une affaire); régler, solder (un compte); payer (une dette). *Abs.* **To s. (up) with s.o.,** régler son compte avec qn. **Shall I s. for everyone?** voulez-vous que je règle toute l'addition? (*c*) *F:* **To s. s.o.,** régler son compte à qn. *S.a.* HASH¹ 2. 7. **To s. an annuity on s.o.,** constituer une annuité à qn. II. *v.i.* 1. *v.i. & pr.* (*a*) **To s. (down) in a locality,** s'établir dans un lieu. (*b*) **To s. (oneself) in an armchair,** s'installer commodément dans un fauteuil. (*c*) (*Of bird*) Se percher, se poser (sur un arbre). (*d*) **The snow is settling,** la

neige prend, ne fond pas. (*e*) **The wind is settling in the north**, le vent s'établit au nord. (*f*) **To s. (down) to work**, se mettre sérieusement au travail. **2.** (*Of liquid*) Se clarifier, déposer; (*of sediment*) se précipiter. **To let (sth.) s.**, laisser déposer (un précipité); laisser rasseoir (le vin). **3.** (i) (*Of ground, pillar*) Prendre son assiette; se tasser; (ii) (*of foundation*) s'affaisser. **Things are settling into shape**, (i) les choses commencent à prendre tournure; (ii) l'ordre se rétablit. **4.** (*Of passion*) S'apaiser, se calmer. **The weather is settling**, le temps se calme. **settle down**, *v.i.* **1.** *See* SETTLE² II. 1 (*a*), (*f*). **2.** (*a*) (*Of pers.*) Se ranger; devenir sérieux. **To s. down for life**, se marier; se caser. **Marriage has made him s. down**, le mariage l'a rangé. (*b*) **Since the war things have settled down**, depuis la guerre tout s'est tassé. **3.** **He is beginning to s. down at school**, il commence à s'habituer à l'école. **settle upon**, *v.i.* **1. To s. upon sth.**, choisir qch.; se décider pour qch. **2.** (*Of affections*) Se poser sur (qn). **settled**, *a.* **1.** (*a*) Invariable, sûr; (*of idea*) fixe, enraciné. **S. intention**, intention bien arrêtée. **S. policy**, politique continue. **S. weather**, temps fait, fixe. (*b*) (*Of pers.*) Rassis, réfléchi. (*c*) (*Of pers.*) Rangé; *esp.* marié. **2.** (*a*) (*Of question*) Arrangé, décidé. (*b*) (*On bill*) **'S.,'** "pour acquit." **3.** (*Of pers.*) Domicilié, établi; (*of thg*) bien assis. **4.** (*Of country*) Colonisé. **settling**, *s.* **1.** = SETTLE-MENT 1. **2.** (*a*) Apaisement *m* (d'une agitation). (*b*) Clarification *f* (d'un liquide). (*c*) Précipitation *f* (du sédiment). (*d*) Tassement *m*; affaissement *m* (du terrain). **3.** = SETTLEMENT 2 (*a*). **4.** Conclusion *f*, terminaison *f* (d'une affaire). **S. (up)**, règlement *m* (d'un compte).

settlement ['setlmənt], *s.* **1.** (*a*) Établissement *m*; installation *f*. (*b*) Colonisation *f*, peuplement *m* (d'un pays). **2.** (*a*) Règlement *m* (d'une affaire); résolution *f* (d'une question). (*b*) *Com:* Règlement, paiement *m* (d'un compte). **In (full) s.**, pour solde de tout compte. *St.Exch:* **S. day**, jour *m* du règlement. (*c*) **They have reached a s.**, ils sont arrivés à un accord amical. (*d*) **(Deed of) s.**, acte *m* de disposition; contrat *m* de constitution. **Family s.**, pacte *m* de famille. **Marriage s.**, contrat de mariage. **3.** (*a*) Colonie *f* (de peuplement). (*b*) Œuvre sociale (dans les quartiers pauvres d'une grande ville).

settler ['setlər], *s.* Colon *m*, immigrant *m*, défricheur, -euse (dans un pays nouvellement découvert).

settlor ['setlər], *s. Jur:* Disposant *m*, constituteur, -trice (d'une annuité, etc.).

seven ['sevn], *num. a. & s.* Sept (*m*). **Fourteen is s. times as much as two**, quatorze est le septuple de deux. *S.a.* SIX. (*For other phrases see* EIGHT.) **'seven-league(-)**, *attrib.a.* **S.-l. boots**, bottes de sept lieues.

sevenfold ['sevnfould]. **1.** *a.* Septuple. **2.** *adv.* Sept fois autant. **To increase s.**, septupler.

seventeen ['sevn'ti:n], *num. a. & s.* Dix-sept (*m*). (*For other phrases see* EIGHT).

seventeenth ['sevn'ti:nθ]. **1.** *num. a. & s.* Dix-septième. **Louis the S.**, Louis Dix-sept. **2.** *s.* (*Fractional*) Dix-septième *m*.

seventh ['sevnθ]. **1.** *num. a. & s.* Septième. **To be in the s. heaven (of delight)**, être au septième ciel; être aux anges. (*For other phrases see* EIGHTH.) **2.** *s.* (*Fractional*) Septième *m*. (*b*) *Mus:* Septième *f*. **-ly**, *adv.* Septièmement; en septième lieu.

seventieth ['sevntiiθ], *num. a. & s.* Soixante-dixième.

seventy ['sevnti], *num. a. & s.* Soixante-dix (*m*); (*Belgium, Switzerland*) septante (*m*). **S.-one, -nine**, soixante et onze, soixante-dix-neuf. **To be in the seventies**, être septuagénaire.

sever ['sevər], *v.tr.* Désunir, disjoindre (les parties d'un tout); rompre (une amitié, une liaison). **To s. one's connections with s.o.**, se désassocier d'avec qn. **To s. a beam**, sectionner une poutre.

several ['sevrəl], *a.* **1.** (*a*) Séparé; différent. **The s. members of the committee**, les divers membres du comité. (*b*) *Jur:* (Bien) individuel. **Joint and s. bond**, obligation *f* solidaire. *S.a.* LIABILITY 1. (*c*) **Our s. rights**, nos droits respectifs. **They went their s. ways**, ils s'en allèrent, chacun de son côté. **2.** (*a*) Plusieurs, divers; quelques. **He and s. others**, lui et quelques autres. (*b*) **I have s.**, j'en ai plusieurs. **S. of them**, plusieurs d'entre eux. **-ally**, *adv.*

Séparément, individuellement. **Jointly and s.**, conjointement et solidairement.

severance ['sev(ə)rəns], *s.* Séparation *f* (**from**, de); rupture *f* (des relations). **S. of communications**, interruption complète des communications.

severe [si'viər], *a.* **1.** (*a*) Sévère, strict, rigoureux, -euse (**with**, envers). **S. sentence**, sentence rigoureuse. **Unduly s. regulations**, règlements draconiens. A **s. reprimand**, une verte réprimande. (*b*) **To be s. on s.o.'s failings**, être sévère pour les défauts de qn. **2.** (*a*) (Temps) rigoureux, dur. **The cold was s.**, le froid sévissait. (*b*) **S. blow**, coup rude. **S. pain**, vive douleur. *Med:* **S. cold**, gros rhume. **3.** (Style, etc.) sévère, austère. **-ly**, *adv.* **1.** Sévèrement; avec sévérité. **I was left s. alone**, personne ne m'a accordé la moindre attention. **2.** Grièvement, gravement (blessé). **3.** **S. plain**, d'une simplicité sévère.

severity [si'veriti], *s.* **1.** Sévérité *f*, rigueur *f*. **To use s.**, sévir. **2.** (*a*) Rigueur, inclémence *f* (du temps). (*b*) Gravité *f* (d'une maladie); violence *f* (d'une douleur). (*c*) Rigueur (d'un examen). **3.** Sévérité, austérité *f* (de style).

sew [sou], *v.tr.* (**sewed** [soud]; **sewn** [soun]) Coudre. *Bookb:* Brocher, coudre (les feuilles d'un livre). **sew on**, *v.tr.* Coudre, attacher (un bouton). **sew up**, *v.tr.* Coudre (un ourlet); faire (une couture). *Surg:* Coudre, suturer (les lèvres d'une plaie). **sewn**, *a.* Cousu. **Hand-s.**, cousu (à la) main. **Machine-s.**, cousu piqué, à la machine. **sewing**, *s.* **1.** Couture *f*. *Bookb:* Brochage *m*. **Plain s.**, couture simple. **S. needle**, aiguille *f* à coudre. **S. cotton**, fil *m* à coudre. **S. silk**, fil soie. **2.** Ouvrage *m* (à l'aiguille). **'sewing-bee**, *s.* Réunion *f* de couture (pour œuvre sociale). **'sewing-machine**, *s.* Machine *f* à coudre. **'sewing-press**, *s. Bookb:* Cousoir *m*.

sewage ['sju(:)idʒ], *s.* Eau(x) *f(pl)* d'égout. **S. system**, système du tout-à-l'égout. **S. farm**, champs *mpl* d'épandage.

sewer¹ ['souər], *s. Bookb:* Brocheur, -euse.

sewer² ['sjuər], *s. Civ.E:* Égout *m*. **Main s.**, égout collecteur. **S. gases**, miasme égoutier.

sewerage ['sjuəridʒ], *s.* **1.** Système *m* d'égouts. **2.** = SEWAGE.

sewerman, *pl.* **-men** ['sjuəmən], *s.m.* Égoutier.

sex¹ [seks], *s.* (*a*) Sexe *m*. A: **The fair s.**, le beau sexe. **The sterner s.**, le sexe fort. (*b*) *F:* Le désir sexuel; rapports sexuels. **'sex(-)appeal**, *s.* Charme sensuel, *F:* sex-appeal *m*. **'sex(-)kitten**, *s.f. U.S: F:* Pin-up particulièrement aguichante.

sex², *v.tr.* Déterminer le sexe (d'un animal). **sexed**, *a.* (*a*) Sexué. (*b*) **To be highly s.**, avoir du tempérament, *F:* du chien. **Under-s.**, froid, frigide.

sexagenarian [,seksədʒe'nɛəriən], *a. & s.* Sexagénaire (*mf*).

Sexagesima [seksə'dʒesimə], *s. Ecc:* **S. (Sunday)**, (le dimanche de) la Sexagésime.

sexennial [seks'enjəl], *a.* Sexennal, -aux.

sexiness ['seksinis], *s.* Tendances sexuelles prononcées.

sexless ['sekslis], *a.* (*a*) Asexué. (*b*) *F:* Froid, frigide.

sextant ['sekstənt], *s.* Sextant *m*.

sextet(te) [seks'tet], *s. Mus:* Sextuor *m*.

sexton ['sekst(ə)n], *s. Ecc:* (*a*) Sacristain *m*. (*b*) Sonneur *m* (de cloches). (*c*) Fossoyeur *m*. **'sexton-beetle**, *s. Ent:* Nécrophore *m*; enfouisseur *m*.

sextuple¹ ['sekstjupl], *a. & s.* Sextuple (*m*).

sextuple², *v.tr.* Sextupler.

sexual ['seksjuəl], *a.* Sexuel, -elle. **S. characteristics**, caractères sexués. **S. intercourse**, rapports sexuels. **S. reproduction**, reproduction sexuée. **S. perversion**, inversion sexuelle. **-ally**, *adv.* **1.** D'une manière sexuelle. **2.** Quant au sexe.

sexuality [,seksju'æliti], *s.* **1.** Sexualité *f*. **2.** Tendances sexuelles prononcées.

sexy ['seksi], *a. F:* Excitant, capiteux, -euse, affriolant, aguichant. A **s. little piece**, une petite femme croustillante. **To be s.**, avoir du chien, du tempérament.

sez you [sez'ju:], *int. P:* (= *says you*) Tu parles!

sgraffito, *pl.* **-ti** [sgræ'fi:tou, -ti:], *s. Art:* Sgraffite *m*.

sh [ʃ], *int.* Chut!

shabbiness ['ʃæbinis], *s.* **1.** État râpé, usé (d'un habit, etc.); état défraîchi (d'un meuble); apparence pauvre, miteuse (de qn). **2.** (*a*) Mesquinerie *f* (de conduite). (*b*) Parcimonie *f*.

shabby ['ʃæbi], *a.* **1.** (Habit) râpé, usé; (mobilier, etc.) pauvre, minable. **S. room,** pièce tristement meublée. (*Of pers.*) **To look s.,** avoir l'air râpé. **2.** (*a*) Mesquin; peu honorable. **To do s.o. a s. turn,** faire une mesquinerie à qn. (*b*) Chiche; parcimonieux, -euse. **-ily,** *adv.* **1.** Pauvrement. S. dressed, miteux, -euse, râpé. **2.** (*a*) (Se conduire) mesquinement. (*b*) Chichement. **'shabby-gen'teel,** *a.* A s.-g. **appearance,** dignité miséreuse. **S.-g. aristocracy,** aristocratie dédorée, miteuse. **'shabby-looking,** *a.* De pauvre apparence; minable.

shack [ʃæk], *s.* Cabane *f*, hutte *f*.

shackle¹ ['ʃækl], *s.* **1.** *pl.* **Shackles,** fers *m* (d'un prisonnier). **The shackles of convention,** les entraves *f* des conventions sociales. **2.** Maillon *m* de liaison (d'une chaîne); anse *f* (d'un cadenas); cigale *f* (d'une ancre).

shackle², *v.tr.* **1.** Mettre les fers à, entraver (un prisonnier). **2.** Maniller, mailler (une chaîne); étalinguer (une ancre).

shad [ʃæd], *s. Ich:* Alose *f*.

shade¹ [ʃeid], *s.* **1.** (*a*) Ombre *f*. **Temperature in the s.,** température à l'ombre. **To put s.o. in(to) the shade,** éclipser qn; faire ombre à qn. **A s. of annoyance on his face,** une ombre de contrariété sur son visage. **The shades of night,** les ombres de la nuit; les ténèbres *f*. **The Shades,** les enfers *m*. (*b*) *Art:* Ombre (dans un tableau). **2.** (*a*) Nuance *f* (de couleur, d'opinion); teinte *f*. (*b*) Nuance; petit peu. **He is a s. better,** il va un tout petit peu mieux. **3.** (*a*) Pâle reflet *m*, ombre (de qch.). (*b*) Ombre, fantôme *m* (d'un mort). **4.** (*a*) (**Lamp-**)s., abat-jour *m inv. Opt: Phot:* Lens s., sky s., parasoleil *m*. *Opt:* Eye-glass s. (of telescope), bonnette *f*. (*b*) *U.S:* Store *m* (de fenêtre). **'shade-card,** *s. Com:* Carte *f* de coloris.

shade². I. *v.tr.* **1.** (*a*) Ombrager; couvrir (qch.) d'ombre. **To s. sth. from the sun,** abriter qch. du soleil. **To s. one's eyes with one's hand,** mettre la main en abat-jour. **To s. a light,** (i) voiler une lumière; (ii) masquer une lumière. (*b*) Obscurcir, assombrir (le visage). **2.** (*a*) *Art:* Ombrer (un dessin). (*b*) *Mapm:* Hachurer. **3.** Nuancer (un tissu). **To s. away, s. off, colours,** dégrader des couleurs. II. **shade,** *v.i.* Blue that shades (off) into green, bleu qui se fond en vert. **shaded,** *a.* **1.** (*a*) *Art:* (Dessin) ombré. (*b*) *Mapm:* Hachuré. **2.** (*Of embroidery, etc.*) Nuancé. **shading,** *s.* **1.** Projection *f* d'une ombre (sur qch.); protection *f* (de qch.) contre la lumière. *Hort:* S. mat, paillasson *m* à ombrer. **2.** (*a*) *Art:* Dessin *m* des ombres. *Mapm:* Hachuré *m*, modelé *m*. (*b*) Ombres (d'un dessin). **3.** Nuancement *m* (de couleurs). **S. off,** dégradation *f* (d'une couleur); estompage *m*; dégradé *m*. **4.** *T.V:* Tache *f*.

shadiness ['ʃeidinis], *s.* **1.** Ombre *f*, ombrage *m* (d'un sentier). **2.** *F:* Aspect *m* louche (d'une affaire).

shadow¹ ['ʃædou], *s.* Ombre *f*. **1.** (*a*) Obscurité *f*. **The s. of death,** l'ombre de la mort. **Under the s. of a terrible accusation,** sous le coup d'une accusation terrible. (*b*) Noir *m* (d'un tableau). **To have shadows under one's eyes,** avoir les yeux cernés. **2.** **To cast a s.,** projeter une ombre; faire ombre. **Coming events cast their shadows before,** les événements à venir se font pressentir. **In the s. of . . .,** à l'ombre de. . . . **May your s. never grow less!** tous mes vœux pour votre prospérité! **Not the s. of a doubt,** pas l'ombre d'un doute. **3.** (*a*) Compagnon inséparable (de qn). (*b*) **To wear oneself to a s.,** (i) se manger les sangs; (ii) s'épuiser (de travail). **He's a mere s. of his former self,** il n'est plus que l'ombre de lui-même. **4.** *Pol:* **S. government,** gouvernement *m* fantôme. **S. cabinet,** conseil *m* des ministres fantôme. **'shadow-boxing,** *s. Box:* Assaut *m* d'entraînement contre un adversaire fictif.

shadow², *v.tr.* **1.** (*a*) *Poet:* Ombrager (qch.); couvrir (qch.) de son ombre. (*b*) *Tex:* Chiner (un tissu). **2.** Filer (qn). **shadowing,** *s.* Filature *f* d'une personne suspecte.

shadowy ['ʃædoui], *a.* (Songe) chimérique; (projet) indécis, vague. **The s. form seen by X,** l'ombre aperçue par X.

shady ['ʃeidi], *a.* **1.** (*a*) Qui donne de l'ombre; ombreux, -euse. (*b*) Ombragé; couvert d'ombre. **S. walk,** allée couverte. **2.** (*Of transaction*) Louche. **S. public house,** cabaret borgne. **S.-looking customer,** individu *m* aux allures louches. **The s. side of politics,** les dessous *m* de la politique.

shaft¹ [ʃɑːft], *s.* **1.** (*a*) Hampe *f*, bois *m* (d'une lance). (*b*) Manche *m* (de crosse de golf). **2.** (*a*) Flèche *f*, trait *m*. (*b*) *A:* Javelot *m*. **The shafts of Cupid, of satire,** les traits de l'Amour, de la satire. **3.** Rayon *m* (de lumière). **4.** (*a*) Tige *f* (de plume d'oiseau). *Anat:* Corps *m* (du tibia). (*b*) *Arch:* Tige, fût *m* (d'une colonne). *Const: Ind:* Souche *f* (de cheminée d'usine). **5.** *Mec.E:* Arbre *m*. **Driving s.,** arbre de transmission. **Driven s.,** arbre commandé. **Coupling s.,** arbre d'accouplement. **6.** *Veh:* Brancard *m*, limon *m*. **'shaft-case, -casing,** *s. Aut: etc:* Carter *m* d'arbre. **'shaft-horse,** *s.* Cheval *m* de brancard; limonier *m*.

shaft², *s.* **1.** *Min:* Puits *m*. **Ventilating s., air s.,** puits d'aérage; cheminée *f* d'appel. **Hoisting s.,** puits d'extraction. **2.** Cage *f* (d'un ascenseur). **'shaft-sinker,** *s. Min:* Puisatier *m*.

shag¹ [ʃæg], *s.* Tabac fort (coupé fin).

shag², *s. Orn:* Cormoran huppé.

shagged ['ʃægd], *a. F:* Fourbu, exténué; *F:* éreinté; claqué, crevé.

shagginess ['ʃæginis], *s.* Rudesse *f*, longueur *f* de poil (d'un animal); état mal peigné, ébouriffé (des cheveux).

shaggy ['ʃægi], *a.* Poilu; (poney) à longs poils, à poils rudes; (barbe) hirsute, touffue; (sourcils) en broussailles. **S. dog story** = histoire *f* de fous.

shagreen¹ [ʃæ'griːn], *s. Leath:* (*a*) (Peau *f* de) chagrin *m*. (*b*) Galuchat *m*.

shagreen², *v.tr.* Chagriner (le cuir).

shah [ʃɑː], *s.* Chah *m* (de Perse).

shake¹ [ʃeik], *s.* **1.** (*a*) Secousse *f*. **To give sth. a good s.,** bien secouer, bien agiter, qch. **A s. of the head,** un hochement de tête. **To answer with a s. of the head,** répondre d'un mouvement de tête. *F:* **In a s., in a brace of shakes,** in two shakes of a lamb's tail, en un rien de temps. (*b*) Tremblement *m*. **To be all of a s.,** trembler de tous ses membres. *pl. F:* **The shakes,** tremblement *m* alcoolique. (*c*) *Mus:* Trille *m*. (*d*) **With a s. in his voice,** d'une voix mal assurée. **2.** **Egg s.,** lait *m* de poule. **3.** (*In wood*) Gerçure *f*. **4.** *F:* **To be no great shakes,** n'être pas grand-chose; ne pas valoir grand-chose.

shake², *v.* (**shook** [ʃuk]; **shaken** [ʃeikn]) I. *v.tr.* **1.** Secouer; agiter (un liquide, etc.). **'S. the bottle,' "agiter le flacon."** **To s. one's head,** (i) secouer, hocher, la tête; (ii) (*in dissent*) faire non de la tête. **To s. one's fist at s.o.,** menacer qn du poing. **To s. s.o. by the hand,** to shake hands with s.o., serrer la main à qn; donner une poignée de main à qn. **They shook hands on it,** ils ont topé. **To s. oneself free (from sth.),** se dégager (de qch.) d'une secousse. **2.** Ébranler. **Threats cannot s. my purpose,** les menaces ne sauraient m'ébranler. **It has shaken his health,** sa santé a reçu une secousse. **To feel shaken after a fall,** se ressentir d'une chute. **Voice shaking with emotion,** voix émue. II. *v.i.* **1.** Trembler; (*of building*) chanceler, branler; (*of voice*) trembloter, chevroter. **His hand was shaking,** la main lui tremblait. *S.a.* LAUGHTER. **To s. all over,** trembler de tout son corps. **To s. in one's shoes,** trembler dans sa peau. **2.** *Nau:* (*Of sail*) Ralinguer. **To keep the sails shaking,** tenir les voiles en ralingue. **shake down. 1.** *v.tr.* Secouer, faire tomber (des fruits). **2.** *v.i.* (*a*) S'installer. (*b*) Se tasser. **The team is shaking down,** l'équipe se forme. **3.** *U.S: P:* Faire chanter (qn); extorquer de l'argent (à qn). **'shake-down,** *s.* **1.** *F:* Lit improvisé. **2.** *U.S: P:* Chantage *m*; extorsion *f*. **shake off, v.tr. 1.** **To s. off the dust from one's feet,** secouer la poussière de ses pieds. **To s. off the yoke,** secouer le joug; s'affranchir du joug. **To s. off a cold,** venir à bout d'un rhume. **2.** Se débarrasser, se défaire, de (qn). **I can't s. him off,** il ne me lâche pas d'un cran. **shake out, v.tr. 1.** (*a*) Secouer; faire sortir (la poussière). (*b*) Vider (un sac) en le secouant. **2.**

Nau: To s. out a reef, larguer un ris. **shake up,**
v.tr. 1. Secouer, brasser (un oreiller). 2.(*a*) Agiter
(le contenu d'une bouteille). (*b*) *F:* Éveiller, secouer,
stimuler (qn). ′**shake-up,** *s.* 1. *esp. U.S: F:*
Mélange *f* d'alcools, de vin, avec du whisky. 2. A big
s.-up, grand remaniement du personnel (administratif, etc.). **shaking**[1], *a.* Tremblant, branlant. **S.
voice,** voix tremblotante, chevrotante. **shaking**[2], *s.*
(*a*) Secouement *m.* To give sth. a good s., bien
secouer (un tapis, etc.). (*b*) Ébranlement *m* (d'une
maison); tremblement *m* (du sol); tremblotement
m (de la voix).
shaker [′ʃeikər], *s.* 1. *Rel.H:* Trembleur *m,* shaker *m.*
2. (*a*) (Appareil *m*) secoueur. **Salad s.,** panier *m* à
salade. (*b*) **Cocktail s.,** shaker *m.*
Shakespearian [ʃeiks′piəriən], *a.* Shakespearien,
-ienne; de Shakespeare.
shakiness [′ʃeikinis], *s.* Manque *m* de stabilité;
tremblement *m* (de la main); chevrotement *m* (de
la voix).
shako [′ʃækou], *s. Mil.Cost:* Shako *m.*
shaky [′ʃeiki], *a.* (Bâtiment) peu solide; (santé)
faible, chancelante. **S. hand,** main tremblante.
S. writing, écriture tremblée. **S. voice,** voix mal
assurée. **To be s. on one's legs,** avoir les jambes
qui flageolent. **I feel s. today,** je ne suis pas d'aplomb
aujourd'hui, je suis tout patraque aujourd'hui.
His English is s., il est faible en anglais. **-ily,** *adv.*
Peu solidement; faiblement; (marcher) à pas
chancelants; (écrire) d'une main tremblante.
shale [ʃeil], *s.* Schiste (argileux); argile schisteuse.
Oil s., schiste bitumineux. ′**shale-oil,** *s.* Huile *f*
de schiste.
shall [ʃæl, ʃ(ə)l], *modal aux. v.* (*pr.* **shall, shalt** [ʃælt],
shall; *p.t. & condit.* **should** [ʃud], **shouldst** [ʃudst].
No other parts. '**Shall not**' *is often contracted into*
shan't [ʃɑ:nt]) I. 1. *Denotes duty or a command.*
(*a*) (*In general precepts*) **Ships s. carry three lights,**
les navires sont tenus de porter trois feux. **Everybody
should go to the poll,** tout le monde devrait aller aux
urnes, voter. **All is as it should be,** tout est très bien.
Which is as it should be, ce qui n'est que justice.
(*b*) **He s. do it if I order it,** il devra le faire si je l'ordonne. **He s. not die!** il ne faut pas qu'il meure!
He s. not do it, je défends qu'il le fasse. **You ′shall
do it!** vous le ferez, je le veux! (*c*) **You should do it
at once,** vous devriez le faire tout de suite. **It was an
accident that should have been foreseen,** c'était un
accident à prévoir. **You should have seen him!** il
fallait le voir! **This inquiry should be taken up
again,** c'est une question à reprendre. (*d*) **He should
have arrived by this time,** il devrait être arrivé à
l'heure qu'il est. **That should suit you!** voilà qui
fera sans doute votre affaire! **I should think so!**
je crois bien! 2. **S. I open the window?** voulez-
vous que j'ouvre la fenêtre? **I'll call the children,
s. I?** je vais appeler les enfants, hein? **Let us go in,
s. we?** rentrons, voulez-vous? 3.(*a*) (*Exclamative and
rhetorical questions*) **Why should you suspect me?**
pourquoi me soupçonner (, moi)? **Whom should I
meet but Jones!** voilà que je rencontre Jones!
Who s. describe their surprise? comment décrire leur
surprise? (*b*) **He ordered that they should be released,**
il ordonna qu'on les relâchât. (*c*) (*In conditional
clauses*) **If he should come (you will) let me know,**
si par hasard il vient faites-le-moi savoir. **Should I be
free I s. come,** si je suis libre je viendrai. **Should the
occasion arise, should it so happen,** le cas échéant.
In case he should not be there . . ., au cas où il
n'y soit pas . . .; dans le cas où il n'y serait pas. . . .
II. **shall** *used as an auxiliary verb forming the
future tenses.* 1. (*Assurance, promise, threat*) **You
shan't have any!** tu n'en auras pas! **You s. pay for
this!** vous me le payerez! 2. (*Simple futurity*) (*a*)
(*Used in the 1st pers. For the 2nd and 3rd pers. see*
WILL[2].) **Tomorrow I s. go and he will arrive,** demain,
moi je partirai et lui arrivera. **We s. hope to see you
again,** nous espérons avoir l'occasion de vous
revoir. **Will you be there?—I s.,** y serez-vous?—
Oui (, j'y serai). **No, I s. not; no, I shan't,** non
(, je n'y serai pas). **He had promised that I should be
there,** il avait promis que je serais là. **I s. explain
the situation to you and you will listen,** je vais vous

expliquer la situation et vous allez m'écouter. (*b*)
(*In interrogation*) **S. you come tomorrow?** vous
viendrez demain? (*Cp.* **Will you come tomorrow?**
voulez-vous venir demain?) 3. **If he comes I s. speak
to him,** s'il vient je lui parlerai. **We should come
if we were invited,** nous viendrions si on nous invitait.
I shouldn't do it if I were you, à votre place je n'en
ferais rien. 4.(*In softened affirmation*) **I should like a
drink,** je prendrais bien quelque chose. **I shouldn't
be surprised (if . . .),** cela ne me surprendrait pas
(que . . .).
shallot [ʃə′lɔt], *s. Hort:* Échalote *f.*
shallow [′ʃælou]. 1. *a.* (*a*) (*Of water*) Peu profond,
bas de fond; (*of dish*) plat. *Nau:* **S. water,** hauts-
fonds *m.pl.* **S. draft,** faible tirant *m* (d'un navire). (*b*)
(*Of mind, pers.*) Superficiel, -elle, frivole. **S. intellect,**
esprit superficiel. **S. steps, stairs,** marches peu
hautes. 2. *s.* (*In sea, river*) (*often in pl.*) Bas-fond *m,*
haut-fond *m.*
shallowness [′ʃælounis], *s.* (*a*) (Le) peu de profondeur
(de l'eau, etc.). (*b*) Caractère superficiel; manque
m de fond (de qn, de l'esprit).
sham[1] [ʃæm]. I. *a.* (*Of illness*) Simulé, feint; (*of
jewel*) faux, *f.* fausse, postiche, *F:* en toc. **S. title,** titre
d'emprunt. **A s. colonel,** un faux colonel. **S. fight,**
combat d'exercice; simulacre *m* de combat. II.
sham, *s.* 1. Feinte *f,* trompe-l'œil *m inv, F:* chiqué
m. **That's all s.,** *F:* tout ça c'est de la frime. **His
love was a mere s.,** son amour était une imposture.
He is all s., tout en lui est artificiel. 2. (*Of pers.*)
He's a s., c'est un imposteur.
sham[2], *v.tr.* (**shammed**) Feindre, simuler. **To s. sickness,** feindre une maladie. **To s. modesty,** faire le, la,
modeste, *P:* faire des chichis. **To s. sleep,** faire
semblant de dormir. *Abs.* **He is only shamming,**
tout ça c'est de la frime. *Pred.* **He shammed dead,** il
fit le mort.
shamble[1] [′ʃæmbl], *s.* Démarche traînante.
shamble[2], *v.i.* **To s. (along),** aller à pas traînants;
s'avancer en traînant le pas.
shambles [′ʃæmblz], *s.pl.* (*With sg. const.*) (*a*) Abattoir
m. (*b*) Scène *f* de carnage, de boucherie. (*c*) *F:*
Désordre *m,* gâchis *m.* **What a s.!** Quelle pagaille!
shame[1] [ʃeim], *s.* (*a*) Honte *f.* **To put s.o. to s.,** (i)
confondre qn; (ii) faire honte à qn. **S. on you!**
honte à vous! **All the more s. to you!** c'est d'autant
plus honteux à vous! **For s.!** fi! quelle honte!
To blush for s., (i) rougir de honte; (ii) rougir
pudiquement. **Without s.,** éhonté. **To be lost to all
(sense of) s.,** avoir perdu toute honte, toute pudeur.
(*b*) **It was a s. of you to . . .,** c'était honteux de votre
part de. . . . **It is a s. to laugh at him,** ce n'est pas
bien de se moquer de lui. **It's a (great) s.!** c'est
honteux! **It's a sin and a s.!** c'est une indignité!
What a s.! quel dommage!
shame[2], *v.tr.* Faire honte à, humilier (qn); couvrir
(qn) de honte. **To be shamed into doing sth.,** faire
qch. par amour-propre.
shamefaced [′ʃeimfeist], *a.* 1. (A l'air) honteux;
embarrassé, penaud. 2. Timide, pudique.
shamefacedly [′ʃeimfeistli, ʃeim′feisidli], *adv.* 1.
D'une manière embarrassée; honteusement; d'un air
penaud. 2. Timidement, pudiquement, modestement.
shamefacedness [′ʃeimfeistnis, ʃeim′feisidnis], *s.* 1.
Fausse honte; mauvaise honte; embarras *m.* 2.
Timidité *f* pudique; modestie *f.*
shameful [′ʃeimf(u)l], *a.* Honteux, -euse, scandaleux,
-euse, indigne. **-fully,** *adv.* Honteusement, scandaleusement.
shamefulness [′ʃeimf(u)lnis], *s.* Honte *f,* infamie *f.*
shameless [′ʃeimlis], *a.* 1. (*Of pers., conduct*) Éhonté,
effronté, cynique. 2. (*Of action*) Honteux, -euse,
scandaleux, -euse. **-ly,** *adv.* Immodestement,
effrontément. **To lie s.,** mentir impudemment.
shamelessness [′ʃeimlisnis], *s.* 1. Immodestie *f,*
impudeur *f.* 2. Effronterie *f,* impudence *f.*
shammy(-leather) [′ʃæmi(′leðər)], *s.* = CHAMOIS-
LEATHER.
shampoo[1] [ʃæm′pu:], *s.* Shampooing *m.* **Dry s.,**
friction *f.* **To buy a s.,** acheter un shampooing.
shampoo[2], *v.tr.* **To s. one's hair,** se laver la tête.
To s. s.o., faire un shampooing à qn. *Dom.Ec:* **To s.
a carpet,** nettoyer un tapis avec un savon spécial.

shamrock ['ʃæmrɔk], s. Trèfle m d'Irlande.
shandy(gaff) ['ʃændi(gæf)], s. Bière panachée, F: panaché m.
Shanghai¹ [ʃæŋ'hai], Pr.n. Geog: Changhai.
shanghai², v.tr. (a)Nau: F: To s. a man, enivrer, droguer, un homme pour l'embarquer contre sa volonté. (b) I was shanghaied into doing it, on m'a forcé à le faire.
shank [ʃæŋk], s. 1. (a) Le devant de la jambe. pl. F: Shanks, jambes f, P: quilles f. F: To go, come, on shanks's pony, mare, prendre le train onze. (b) (i) Tibia m; (ii) Farr: canon m (du membre antérieur). (c) Cu: Manche m (de gigot de mouton); jarret m (de bœuf). 2. (a) Branche f, bras m (de ciseaux). (b) Tige f (de clef, etc.); fût m (d'une colonne); hampe f (d'hameçon); Typ: corps m, tige (de lettre); Anchor s., verge f (d'ancre). (c) Queue f (d'un bouton). 'shank-bone, s. Tibia m.
shan't. See SHALL.
Shantung [ʃæn'tʌŋ], 1. Pr.n. Geog: Chantoung. 2. s. Tex: Chantoung m.
shanty¹ ['ʃænti], s. Hutte f, cabane f, baraque f. 'shanty-town, s. Bidonville m.
shanty², s. Sea s., chanson f de bord.
shape¹ [ʃeip], s. 1. (a) Forme f, configuration f (de la terre, etc.); façon f, coupe f (d'un habit, etc.). Trees of all shapes, des arbres de toutes les formes. My hat was knocked out of s., mon chapeau a été déformé. To get out of s., to lose s., se déformer; (of boots, etc.) s'avachir. Journ: etc: To put an article into s., mettre un article au point. F: To be in good, bad, shape, être en bonne, mauvaise, forme. To keep in s., garder sa forme. S.a. LICK² 1. (b) Taille f, tournure f. (c) Forme indistincte; apparition f. 2. To take s., prendre forme. Our plans are taking s., nos projets se dessinent. 3. No communication in any s. or form, aucune communication de n'importe quelle sorte. 4. (a) (i) Dom.Ec: (For jellies, etc.) Moule m. (ii) Cu: Rice s., gâteau m de riz. (b) (i) Forme (pour chapeau); (ii) carcasse f (de chapeau). (c) Phot: Cutting s., calibre m à découper.
shape², v. 1. v.tr. (a) Façonner, modeler (de l'argile); tailler (un bloc de pierre); Cer: Contourner (un vase). To s. the clay into an urn, donner à l'argile la forme d'une urne. To s. a coat to the figure, ajuster un habit à la taille. To s. one's life, régler sa vie. (b) Former, inventer (un plan). (c) To s. one's course, diriger ses pas, se diriger (towards, vers); Nau: faire route (for, sur). To s. the course of public opinion, imprimer une direction à l'opinion. 2. v.i. Se développer. To s. well, promettre. The affair is shaping well, l'affaire prend bonne tournure. He is shaping well at Latin, il mord au latin. The crops are shaping well, la récolte s'annonce bien. shape up, v.i. To s. up to s.o., avancer sur qn en posture de combat. shaped, a. 1. Façonné, taillé. 2. Well-s., ill-s., bien, mal, formé. Heart-s., wedge-s., en forme de cœur, de coin. shaping, s. 1. Façonnement m, façonnage m (d'un bloc de pierre); contournement m (d'un vase). 2. Formation f, conception f (d'un projet); mise f au point.
shapeless ['ʃeiplis], a. Informe; difforme. S. legs, jambes toutes d'une venue.
shapelessness ['ʃeiplisnis], s. Manque m de forme; manque de galbe.
shapeliness ['ʃeiplinis], s. Beauté f de forme; galbe m.
shapely ['ʃeipli], a. Bien fait, bien tourné.
shard [ʃɑːd], s. Tesson m (de poterie). To break into shards, se briser (en fragments).
share¹ [ʃɛər], s. Soc m (de charrue).
share², s. 1. (a) Part f, portion f. In equal shares, par portions égales. The lion's s., la part du lion. S. in profits, participation f aux bénéfices; tantième m (des bénéfices). To go shares, partager (with, avec). To go half-shares with s.o., mettre qn de part à demi. S. and s. alike, en partageant également. (b) (Fair) s., portion juste; lot m. To come in for one's full s. of sth., avoir sa bonne part de qch. To each one his due s., à chacun ce qui lui revient. To Contribution f, écot m. To pay one's s., payer sa (quote-)part, son écot. To take a s. in the conversation, contribuer (sa part) à la conversation. To bear one's s. of the

burden, prendre sa part du fardeau. He doesn't do his s., il n'y met pas du sien. To have a s. in an undertaking, avoir un intérêt dans une entreprise. 3. Com: (In a company) Action f, titre m. Ordinary s., action ordinaire. Qualification s., action statutaire. Founder's s., part de fondateur. To hold shares, posséder, détenir, des actions. 'share-certificate, s. Fin: Titre m d'action(s). 'share-list, s. Cours m de la Bourse. 'share-pusher, s. Courtier marron. 'share-warrant, s. Titre m au porteur.
share³. 1. v.tr. Partager. (a) Donner une partie de (ce que l'on a). To s. sth. with s.o., partager qch. avec qn. (b) Avoir part à (qch.). To s. s.o.'s opinion, partager l'avis de qn. To s. and s. alike, partager entre tous également. 2. v.tr. & ind.tr. To s. (in) sth., prendre part à, participer à, qch. To s. (in) s.o.'s grief, partager la douleur de qn. share out, v.tr. Partager, répartir (le butin). 'share-out, s. Partage m, distribution f, répartition f (du travail, des bénéfices, du butin). sharing, s. 1. Partage m. 2. Participation f. 'share-cropper, s. Agr: Métayer, -ère. 'share-cropping, s. Agr: Métayage m.
shareholder ['ʃɛə,houldər], s. Actionnaire mf.
shareholding ['ʃɛə,houldiŋ], s. 1. Actionnariat m. 2. Possession f d'actions, de titres.
sharer ['ʃɛərər], s. Partageant, -ante; participant, -ante.
shark¹ [ʃɑːk], s. 1. Ich: Requin m. Basking s., pèlerin m. 2. Escroc m; requin; (esp. of lawyer) brigandeau m; affairiste m. Financial sharks, les aigrefins m de la finance. 'shark-skin, s. Peau f de requin; galuchat m.
shark², v.tr. & i. Escroquer, exploiter, dépouiller, P: carotter (qn). sharking, s. Escroquerie f; P: carottage m.
sharp¹ [ʃɑːp]. I. a. 1. (a) Tranchant, aiguisé, affilé; (of point) aigu, pointu. S. edge of a sword, tranchant m d'un sabre. (b) (Of features) Anguleux, tiré; (of angle) saillant, aigu; (of curve) prononcé. S. edge, vive arête. S. turn, tournant brusque. (c) (Of outline, Phot: of image) Net, f. nette. (d) S. contrast, contraste marqué. 2. (a) (Of pers.) Fin, éveillé, (of sense of hearing) fin, subtil; (of sight) perçant; (of glance) pénétrant. A s. child, un enfant vif, futé. He is as s. as a needle, il est malin comme un singe. S.a. LOOK-OUT 1. (b) (Of pers., etc.) Rusé, malin; peu scrupuleux, -euse. S. practice(s), procédés peu honnêtes. To be too s. for s.o., être trop malin pour qn. 3. (a) (Combat) vif, acharné. (b) (Orage) violent. S. shower, forte averse. (c) (Hiver) rigoureux; (vent) vif, perçant; (froid) vif, pénétrant. S. pain, vive douleur. (d) Rapide; (trot) vif. That was s. work! ça n'a pas pris longtemps! (e) S. rebuke, verte réprimande. S. tongue, langue acérée. In a s. tone, d'un ton acerbe, cassant. 4. (Of sauce) Piquant; (of apple) aigre, acide; (of wine) vert. S. to (Of sound) Pénétrant, aigu. A s. whistle, un coup de sifflet perçant. (b) Mus: (Fa, etc.) dièse. (c) Ling: S. consonant, consonne forte. 6. U.S: F: Chic. A s. suit, un costume chic, dernier cri. -ly, adv. 1. S. divided into two classes, partagé nettement en deux classes. 2. The road dips s., la route plonge brusquement. 3. (a) (Marcher) vivement; (geler) fort. (b) He looked s. at her, il dirigea sur elle un regard pénétrant. (c) (Réprimander) sévèrement. To speak s. to s.o., rudoyer qn. To answer s., répondre avec brusquerie. 4. (Sonner) sec. II. sharp, s. 1. Mus: Dièse m. 2. U.S: F: = SHARPER. III. sharp, adv. 1. S.-cut outline, profil nettement découpé. S.-pointed pencils, des crayons taillés fin. 2. (a) (S'arrêter) brusquement, court. (b) (Tourner) brusquement. Turn s. right, prenez à droite à angle droit. 3. Ponctuellement, exactement. At four o'clock s., à quatre heures sonnantes, précises, tapantes; F: à quatre heures pile. 4. F: Look s.! faites vite! Now then, look s. about it! allons, et plus vite que ça! Grouille-toi! 'sharp-'edged, a. Tranchant, affilé. 'sharp-'eyed, a. Aux yeux perçants, à la vue perçante. 'sharp-'faced, a. Au visage en lame de couteau. 'sharp-'featured, a. 1. Aux traits tirés, amaigris. 2. = SHARP-FACED. 'sharp-looking, a. 1. (Of pers.) Éveillé, vif, intelligent. 2. U.S: F: Chic. A s.-l. outfit, une toilette dernière mode, un complet de coupe impeccable.

'sharp-'set, *a.* 1. To be s.-s., avoir l'estomac creux. 2. (*Of tool*) Bien aiguisé; affilé. 'sharp-'sighted, *a.* 1. A la vue perçante. 2. Perspicace. 'sharp-'tongued, *a.* Qui a la langue acérée. 'sharp-'toothed, *a.* Aux dents aiguës. 'sharp-'witted, *a.* Intelligent, éveillé, dégourdi.

sharp², *v.tr.* (*a*) *F:* Duper (qn). (*b*) *Abs.* Tricher (au jeu). sharpen ['ʃɑːp(ə)n]. I. *v.tr.* 1. (*a*) Affiler, affûter, aiguiser. Knife that wants sharpening, couteau qui a perdu son fil. (*b*) Tailler en pointe, aiguiser (un bâton). To s. a pencil, tailler un crayon. *S.a.* CLAW¹ 1. 2. *F:* To s. (the wits of) s.o., dégourdir qn. The wine had sharpened his wits, le vin lui avait éveillé l'esprit. 3. Aviver, aggraver (la douleur); aviver, exciter (un désir). To s. one's voice, prendre un ton plus cassant. 4. Relever (une sauce) (au vinaigre). 5. *Mus:* Diéser (une note). II. sharpen, *v.i.* 1. (*Of faculties, etc.*) S'aiguiser. 2. (*Of the voice*) Devenir plus acerbe, plus âpre. 3. (*Of sound*) Devenir plus perçant, plus aigu.

sharpener ['ʃɑːpnər], *s.* Dispositif *m* d'affûtage; aiguisoir *m.* *S.a.* PENCIL-SHARPENER.
sharper ['ʃɑːpər], *s.* *F:* 1. Aigrefin *m;* chevalier *m* d'industrie. 2. (*At cards*) Tricheur *m.*
sharpness ['ʃɑːpnis], *s.* 1. (*a*) Acuité *f,* finesse *f* (du tranchant d'un couteau); acuité (d'une pointe). (*b*) *Nau:* Finesse (des formes d'un navire). (*c*) *Aut:* S. of the turn, raccourci *m* du virage. (*d*) Netteté *f* (des contours). (*e*) Caractère marqué (d'un contraste). 2. (*a*) S. of sight, acuité de la vue. (*b*) Intelligence *f* (d'un enfant). 3. (*a*) Acuité (de la douleur). (*b*) There is a s. in the air, il y a une fraîcheur dans l'air; il fait frisquet. (*c*) Sévérité *f,* acerbité *f* (du ton). 4. (Goût) piquant *m* (d'une sauce); acidité *f,* aigreur *f* (d'une pomme). 5. Acuité (d'un son).
sharpshooter ['ʃɑːpˌʃuːtər], *s.* *Mil:* Tirailleur *m;* tireur *m* d'élite.
shatter ['ʃætər]. 1. *v.tr.* (*a*) Fracasser; briser en éclats. The glass was shattered, le verre a volé en éclats. (*b*) Briser (des espérances). (*c*) Détraquer (les nerfs). 2. *v.i.* Se briser (en éclats); se fracasser.
shattering, *a.* 1. (Coup) écrasant. 2. *Exp:* S. charge, charge brisante.
shave¹ [ʃeiv], *s.* 1. To have a s., (i) se faire raser; (ii) se raser. Hair-cut or s., sir? les cheveux ou la barbe? 2. Coup effleurant, à fleur de peau. *F:* To have a close, narrow, s., l'échapper belle. It was a narrow shave! *P:* il était moins cinq!
shave², *v.tr.* (*p.p. in comp. tenses* shaved; *as adj.* shaven ['ʃeiv(ə)n]) 1. (*a*) Raser; faire la barbe à (qn). (*b*) To s. (oneself), se raser, se faire la barbe. 2. Planer (le bois). 3. Friser, raser, effleurer (qch.). shaven, *a.* (*Of monk*) Tonsuré; (*of head, chin*) rasé. shaving, *s.* 1. (*a*) Action *f* de raser ou de se raser. (*b*) Planage *m* (du bois). 2. Copeau *m,* planure *f* (de bois, de métal); rognure *f* (de métal). *pl.* Shavings, copeaux, raboture(s) *f.* 'shaving-brush, *s.* Blaireau *m.* 'shaving-cream, *s.* Crème *f* à raser. 'shaving-glass, *s.* Miroir *m* à barbe. 'shaving-soap, -stick, *s.* Savon *m* à barbe; bâton *m* de savon pour la barbe.
shaveling ['ʃeivliŋ], *s.* *A: Pej:* Tonsuré *m.*
shaven. *See* SHAVE².
shaver ['ʃeivər], *s.* 1. (*a*) Raseur *m,* barbier *m.* (*b*) Electric s., rasoir *m* électrique. 2. *F: O:* Young s., gosse *m,* gamin *m,* *P:* moutard *m.*
shavetail ['ʃeivteil], *s.* *U.S: P:* Sous-lieutenant *m,* *pl.* sous-lieutenants.
shawl [ʃɔːl], *s.* Châle *m.*
she [ʃi, ʃiː], *pers. pron. nom. f.* 1. (*Unstressed*) Elle. (*a*) (*Of pers.*) What is s. doing? que fait-elle? Here s. comes, la voici qui vient. (*b*) *F:* (i) (*Of female animals, motor cars, etc.*) Elle. (ii) (*Of ships*) Il. S. sails tomorrow, il appareille demain. 2. (*Stressed*) (*a*) Elle. S. and I, elle et moi. It is s., c'est elle. (*Emphatic*) 'S. knows nothing about it, elle n'en sait rien, elle. (*b*) (*Antecedent to a rel. pron.*) (i) Celle. S. that, s. who, believes, celle qui croit. (ii) It is s. who did it, c'est elle qui l'a fait. 3. (*As substantive*) *F:* Femelle, femme. S.-ass, ânesse *f.* S.-bear, ours *m* femelle; ourse *f.* S.-cat, chatte *f.* S.-devil, diablesse *f.* S.-monkey, guenon *f.*

sheaf, *pl.* -ves [ʃiːf, -vz], *s.* 1. Gerbe *f* (de blé, de fleurs). Loose s. (of corn), javelle *f.* 2. Liasse *f* (de papiers).
shear¹ [ʃiər], *s.* *Usu.pl.* 1. (Pair of) shears, cisaille(s) *f(pl);* (grands) ciseaux. Garden shears, cisailles à haie. 2. *Mec.E:* Shears, s.-legs, bigue *f;* chèvre *f* à haubans. 'shear-hulk, *s.* *Nau:* Ponton-mâture *m;* mâture flottante.
shear², *s.* 1. Tonte *f* (de laine). 2. (*a*) Cisaillement *m* (de métaux, etc.). Wind s., cisaillement du vent. (*b*) *Mec:* (Effort *m* de) cisaillement *m.*
shear³, *v.tr.* (*p.t.* sheared; *p.p.* shorn [ʃɔːn], sheared) 1. (*a*) To s. (off), couper (une branche). To s. through sth., trancher qch. (*b*) *Metalw:* Cisailler (une tôle). 2. Tondre (un mouton). To be shorn of sth., être dépouillé, privé, de qch. 3. *Mec:* Cisailler; faire subir un effort de cisaillement à (une poutre). shorn, *a.* 1. *A:* (*Of monk*) Tonsuré. 2. (Mouton) tondu. S. of all his belongings, dépouillé de tout ce qu'il possédait. shearing, *s.* 1. (*a*) Taille *f* (d'une haie); cisaillement *m* (d'une tôle); tonte *f,* tondaison *f* (des moutons). (*b*) *Mec:* S. stress, (effort *m* de) cisaillement. 2. *pl.* Shearings, tontes (de laine).
shearer ['ʃiərər], *s.* Tondeur *m* (de moutons).
shearling ['ʃiəliŋ], *s.* *Husb:* Mouton *m* d'un an.
shearwater ['ʃiəwɔːtər], *s.* *Orn:* Puffin *m.*
sheath [ʃiːθ], *s.* (*pl.* [ʃiːðz] *or* [ʃiːθs]) (*a*) Manchon protecteur; fourreau *m* (d'épée); étui *m* (de ciseaux); gaine *f* (de couteau). (*b*) *Anat:* Enveloppe *f* (d'un organe). (*c*) *Biol:* Enveloppement *m* (d'une graine, etc.) (*d*) *Cost:* (Robe *f*) fourreau. 'sheath-knife, *s.* Couteau *m* à gaine.
sheathe [ʃiːð], *v.tr.* 1. (Re)mettre au fourreau, rengainer (une épée). 2. (*a*) Revêtir, recouvrir, doubler (un navire) (with, de, en). (*b*) *El.E:* Armer (un câble). sheathing, *s.* 1. (*a*) Mise *f* au fourreau. (*b*) Armement *m* (d'un câble). 2. (*a*) Revêtement *m* (de, en, métal). *N.Arch:* Doublage *m.* S. felt, ploc *m.* (*b*) *Mec.E: etc:* Enveloppe *f;* chemise *f* (d'un cylindre). (*c*) Armure *f* (d'un câble).
sheave [ʃiːv], *s.* Réa *m,* rouet *m* (de poulie).
sheaves. *See* SHEAF.
Sheba ['ʃiːbə], *Pr.n.* *A.Geog:* Saba.
she'd = *she had, she would.*
shed¹ [ʃed], *s.* (*a*) Hangar *m.* Lean-to s., appentis *m.* Building s., atelier *m* de construction. *Rail:* Engine s., remise *f* de locomotives; garage *m,* dépôt *m,* des machines.
shed², *v.tr.* (*p.t. & p.p.* shed; *pr.p.* shedding) 1. (*a*) Perdre (ses dents, ses feuilles); (*of animal*) jeter (sa peau). *S.a.* HORN 1. (*b*) *F:* Se défaire de (qn); semer (un importun). (*c*) To s. one's clothes, se dévêtir, se dépouiller de ses vêtements. (*d*) *El:* To s. the load, délester. 2. Répandre, verser (des larmes, le sang). The lamp s. a soft light, la lampe versait une douce lumière. To s. light on a matter, éclairer une affaire. shedding, *s.* 1. Perte *f,* chute *f* (des feuilles, des dents). (*Of animals*) S. of skin, mue *f.* 2. Effusion *f* (de sang, etc.).
sheen [ʃiːn], *s.* Luisant *m,* lustre *m* (de la soie); chatoiement *m* (d'une étoffe). To take the s. off sth., délustrer qch.
sheeny ['ʃiːni], *s.* *P: Pej:* Youpin, -ine.
sheep [ʃiːp], *s. inv.* 1. Mouton *m.* Black s., brebis noire. The black s. (of the family), la brebis galeuse. To feel like a lost s., se sentir dépaysé. They follow one another like s., ce sont les moutons de Panurge. *S.a.* EYE¹ 1. 2. *Bookb:* = SHEEPSKIN 2. 'sheep-dip, *s.* Bain *m* parasiticide (pour moutons). 'sheep-farmer, *s.* Éleveur *m* de moutons. 'sheep-farming, *s.* Élevage *m* de moutons. 'sheep-pox, *s. Vet:* Clavelée *f* (des moutons). 'sheep-run, -walk, *s.* Pâturage *m* (pour moutons). 'sheep-shearing, *s.* Tonte *f,* tondaison *f.*
sheepdog ['ʃiːpdɔg], *s.* Chien *m* de berger.
sheepfold ['ʃiːpfould], *s.* 1. Parc *m* à moutons; bercail *m.*
sheepish ['ʃiːpiʃ], *a.* 1. Penaud; interdit. To look s., rester penaud. 2. Timide; gauche. -ly, *adv.* 1. D'un air penaud. 2. D'un air timide.
sheepishness ['ʃiːpiʃnis], *s.* 1. Timidité *f;* fausse honte. 2. Air penaud.
sheepshank ['ʃiːpʃæŋk], *s.* (Nœud *m* en) jambe *f* de chien.

sheepskin ['ʃiːpskin], s. 1. Peau f de mouton. 2. *Bookb:* Basane f. 3. Parchemin m.

sheer[1] [ʃiər], s. *Nau:* Embardée f.

sheer[2], v.i. *Nau:* Embarder. **sheer off,** v.i. 1. *Nau:* Larguer les amarres. 2. *F:* S'écarter; prendre le large.

sheer[3], s. *N.Arch:* Tonture f (du pont). **'sheer-rail,** s. Liston m, listeau m, listel m.

sheer[4]. 1. a. (a) Pur, véritable, franc, f. franche. It's s. robbery, c'est un véritable vol. A s. impossibility, une impossibilité absolue. A s. waste of time, une pure perte de temps. (b) Perpendiculaire; (rocher) à pic. S. coast, côte accore. (c) *Tex:* Léger, -ère, fin; transparent, diaphane. 2. adv. (a) Tout à fait; complètement. (b) Hill that descends s. to the town, colline qui descend abruptement à la ville.

sheer-hulk ['ʃiəhʌlk], s. = SHEAR-HULK.

sheer-legs ['ʃiəlegz], s.pl. = SHEAR[1] 2.

sheet[1] [ʃiːt], s. 1. Drap m (de lit). **Waterproof s.,** drap d'hôpital. *S.a.* WHITE[1] I. 2. 2. (a) Feuille f, feuillet m (de papier). **Loose s.,** feuille volante. *Publ:* Books in sheets, livres en feuilles. *Com:* **Order s.,** bulletin m de commande. (b) *F:* Journal m, -aux; feuille. 3. Feuille (de verre, de plomb, etc.); tôle f. 4. (a) Nappe f (d'eau); couche f (de neige). (b) Lame d'eau (embarquée à bord). **'sheet-copper,** s. Cuivre m en feuilles, en lames. **'sheet-glass,** s. Verre m à vitres. **'sheet-iron,** s. (Fer m en) tôle f. **'sheet-lead** [led], s. Plomb laminé; plomb en feuilles. **'sheet-lightning,** s. Éclairs mpl diffus; éclairs en nappe(s). **'sheet-mill,** s. *Ind:* Metalw. Laminoir m à tôles. **'sheet-steel,** s. *Metalw:* Tôle f d'acier.

sheet[2], v.tr. 1. Couvrir, garnir, (qch.) d'un drap, d'une bâche. Ensevelir (un mort). 2. River sheeted with ice, rivière couverte de glace. **sheeting,** s. 1. Toile f pour draps. **Waterproof s.,** drap m d'hôpital. 2. *Coll:* Tôlerie f, tôles fpl.

sheet[3], s. *Nau:* Écoute f. **S. bend,** nœud m d'écoute. *F:* **To be three sheets in the wind,** avoir un peu de vent dans les voiles, avoir beaucoup bu. 2. **Stern-sheets,** arrière m, chambre f (d'un canot).

sheet-anchor ['ʃiːtæŋkər], s. *Nau:* Ancre f de veille. It is our s.-a., c'est notre ancre de salut.

sheik(h) [ʃeik, ʃiːk], s.m. Cheik.

shekel ['ʃek(ə)l], s. 1. *A. Jew. Meas. & Num:* Sicle m. 2. pl. *F:* Shekels, argent m; *P:* galette f, pognon m.

sheldrake ['ʃeldreik], f. **sheld-duck** ['ʃeldʌk], s. *Orn:* Tadorne m de Belon.

shelf[1], pl. **shelves** [ʃelf, ʃelvz], s. 1. Tablette f (de rayonnage); planche f (d'armoire); rayon m (de bibliothèque). **S. space,** rayonnage m. **Set of shelves,** étagère f. *F:* **To be on the s.,** être au rancart. She is on the s., elle a coiffé sainte Catherine. 2. (a) Rebord m, corniche f (d'un rocher). *Mount:* Replat m. (b) *Continental* s., plateau m, banc, continental. (c) Haut-fond m, bas-fond m; banc m de sable. **'shelf-rail,** s. Galerie f.

shell[1] [ʃel], s. 1. (a) Coquille f (de mollusque); carapace f (de tortue); écaille f (d'huitre). (Empty) shells, coquillages m. **To come out of one's s.,** sortir de sa chrysalide, de sa coquille. **To retire into one's s.,** rentrer dans sa coquille. (b) Coquille (d'œuf, de noix); coque f (d'œuf plein); gousse f, cosse f (de pois, etc.). *Ent:* Enveloppe f (de nymphe). (c) Forme f vide; simple apparence f. 2. (a) *Mch:* Paroi f, coque (de chaudière). (b) Enveloppe extérieure. *Metall:* Manteau m (de moule). 3. (a) Carcasse f, coque (de navire); carcasse f, cage f (d'un édifice). (b) *Row:* Canot m de course. 4. *Artil:* Obus m. **Live s.,** obus de combat. **High-explosive s.,** obus brisant. **To clear (ground) of shells,** désobuser. **Shell clearance,** désobusage m. 5. *O: Sch:* Classe f intermédiaire. **'shell-back,** s. *Nau: P:* Vieux loup de mer. **'shell-fire,** s. Tir m à obus. **To be under s.-f.,** subir un bombardement. **'shell-hole,** s. Trou m d'obus; cratère m; entonnoir m. **'shell-proof,** a. Blindé. **'shell-shock,** s. *Med:* Psychose f traumatique; syndrome commotionnel.

shell[2], v.tr. 1. Écaler (des noix); écosser (des pois). **To s. green walnuts,** cerner des noix. 2. *Mil:* Bombarder. **shell out,** v.tr. *F:* **To s. out one's money,** abs. **to s. out,** payer la note; débourser; *P:* casquer, abouler. **shelled,** a. 1. (*Of creatures*) A coquille; testacé. 2. (*Of nuts*) Écalé; (*of peas*) écossé. **shelling,** s. 1. Égrenage m (de pois); décorticage m (d'amandes). 2. *Mil:* Bombardement m.

shellfish [ʃelfiʃ], s. 1. Testacé m (moule, etc.); *F:* coquillage m. (b) Crustacé m (homard, etc.). 2. *Coll.* Mollusques m et crustacés; fruits m de mer.

she'll = she will.

shellac[1] ['ʃelæk], s. Gomme-laque f; shellac m.

shellac[2], v.tr. (**shellacked**) 1. Gommelaquer. 2. *U.S: P:* Rouer (qn de coups), rosser, *P:* tabasser (qn). **shellacking,** s. 1. Traitement m (de qch.) à la gomme-laque. 2. *U.S: P:* Rossée f, raclée f.

shelter[1] ['ʃeltər], s. 1. Lieu m de refuge; abri m; asile m. *Prehist:* Rock s., abri sous roche. 2. **Under s.,** à l'abri, à couvert. **To take s.,** s'abriter, se mettre à l'abri (under, sous; from, de, contre). **'shelterdeck,** s. *Nau:* Pont-abri m; pont-promenade abrité. **'shelter-tent,** s. *Mil:* Tente-abri f, pl. tentes-abris.

shelter[2]. 1. v.tr. (a) Abriter. (b) Donner asile à, recueillir (un malheureux). **To s. s.o. from blame,** tenir qn à l'abri de la censure. 2. v.i. & pr. S'abriter, se mettre à l'abri (from, contre). **To s. from the rain,** se mettre à couvert (de la pluie). **sheltered,** a. Abrité (against, from, contre). **sheltering,** a. Protecteur, -trice.

shelve[1] [ʃelv], v.tr. 1. Munir, garnir, (une bibliothèque) de rayons. 2. Mettre (des livres) sur les rayons. 3. Ajourner, enterrer (une question); mettre (qn) au rancart; remiser (qn); mettre (qch.) sur une voie de garage. **My request has been shelved,** ma demande est restée dans les cartons. **shelving**[1], s. 1. Enterrement m, ajournement m (d'une question); mise f au rancart (de qn). 2. (Ensemble m de) rayons mpl; rayonnage m. **Adjustable s.,** rayons mobiles.

shelve[2], v.i. Aller en pente. **The shore shelves down to the sea,** le rivage s'incline vers la mer. **shelving**[2], a. En pente; incliné.

shelves. See SHELF[1].

shepherd[1] ['ʃepəd], s.m. (a) Berger, pâtre. **S. boy,** petit pâtre. (b) *B:* **The Good S.,** le bon Pasteur. *S.a.* PIE[2]. **shepherd's 'check, 'plaid,** s. *Tex:* Tissu m (de laine) en damier. **shepherd's 'purse,** s. *Bot: F:* Bourse-à-pasteur f.

shepherd[2], v.tr. 1. Garder, soigner (les moutons). 2. **To s. school children through the town,** piloter des écoliers à travers la ville.

shepherdess ['ʃepədis], s.f. Bergère.

sherardizing ['ʃerədaiziŋ], s. *Ind:* Galvanisation f au gris de zinc; shérardisation f.

sherbet ['ʃəːbət], s. Sorbet m.

shereef, sherif [ʃe'riːf], s. Chérif m (titre arabe).

sheriff ['ʃerif], s.m. 1. *Eng.Adm:* Shériff (d'un comté). *S.a.* OFFICER[1] 1. 2. (*Scot.*) *Jur:* Premier président (d'un comté). 3. *U.S:* Chef de la police (d'un comté). **sheriff 'substitute,** s.m. (*Scot.*) *Jur:* = Juge de grande instance.

sherry ['ʃeri], s. Vin m de Xérès; xérès m. **'sherryglass,** s. Verre m à madère.

she's = she is, she has.

Shetland ['ʃetlənd]. 1. *Pr.n.* **The S. Islands,** les îles Shetland. **'Shetland 'pony,** s. Poney shetlandais.

Shetlander ['ʃetləndər], s. *Geog:* Shetlandais, -aise.

shew[1], [2] [ʃou], s. & v. = SHOW[1].

shewbread ['ʃoubred], s. *Jew.Rel:* Pain m de proposition.

shibboleth ['ʃibəleθ], s. (a) *B.Hist:* S(c)hibboleth m. (b) Mot m d'ordre (d'un parti). **Outworn shibboleths,** doctrines désuètes.

shield[1] [ʃiːld], s. 1. (a) Bouclier m. *A.Arms:* **Body-s.,** pavois m. (b) *Her:* Écusson m. 2. *Tchn:* Tôle protectrice. **Sun-s.,** pare-soleil m inv. *Artil:* Bouclier (d'une pièce d'artillerie). 3. (a) *Z:* Carapace f. *Ent:* Écu m, écusson. (b) *Hort:* Écusson (de greffe). **'shield-bearer,** s. *Hist:* Écuyer m. **'shield-bud, s.** *Hort:* Écusson m. **'shield-budding,** s. *Hort:* Écussonnage m; greffe f en écusson. **'shield-shaped,** a. Scutiforme.

shield², *v.tr.* **1.** Protéger **(from, against, contre)**; couvrir (qn) de sa protection. **2.** (*a*) To s. one's eyes, se protéger les yeux. (*b*) *El.E: Ind: etc:* Blinder (un transformateur, etc.). **shielding,** *s.* Protection *f* **(against, from,** contre).

shieling ['ʃiːliŋ], *s. Scot:* **1.** Pâturage *m.* **2.** Abri *m* (pour moutons, chasseurs).

shier ['ʃaiər], **shiest** ['ʃaiist]. *See* SHY³.

shift¹ [ʃift], *s.* **1.** (*a*) Changement *m* de position; renverse *f* (de la marée). **To make a s.,** changer de place. **S. of the wind,** saute *f* du vent. *Nau:* **S. of cargo,** désarrimage *m. Ling:* **Consonant s.,** mutation *f* consonantique. (*b*) *Mus:* (*In violinplaying*) Démanchement *m.* **2.** *Ind:* (*a*) Équipe *f,* poste *m* (d'ouvriers). **To work in shifts,** se relayer; travailler par équipes. **S. work,** travail par équipes. (*b*) Journée *f* de travail; **shift** *m.* **They work an eight-hour s.,** ils se relaient toutes les huit heures. **3.** (*a*) *A:* Chemise *f.* (*b*) *Cost:* S. (**dress**), (robe *f*) fourreau *m.* **4.** (*a*) Expédient *m.* **To be at one's last s.,** être aux abois, à sa dernière ressource. **To make s. to do sth.,** trouver moyen de faire qch. **To make s. with sth.,** s'arranger, s'accommoder, de qch. **I can make s. without it,** je peux m'en passer. (*b*) **Nothing but shifts and excuses,** rien que des échappatoires et des excuses. **'shift-key,** *s. Typewr:* Touche *f* majuscules. **'shift-lock,** *s. Typewr:* Touche *f* fixe-majuscules.

shift². **I.** *v.tr.* (*a*) Changer (qch.) de place; déplacer. **To s. the furniture,** remuer, déplacer, les meubles. **To s. the responsibility of sth. upon s.o.,** rejeter la responsabilité de qch. sur qn. (*b*) Changer. *Th:* **To s. the scenery,** changer le décor. **To s. one's quarters,** changer de résidence. *Rail:* **To s. all the trains by one hour (forward, back),** décaler tous les trains d'une heure. *S.a.* GROUND² 5. (*c*) *Nau:* **To s. a sail,** changer une voile. (*d*) *Aut: esp.U.S:* **To s. gears,** passer les vitesses. (*e*) *Abs.* (*In violin playing*) Démancher. **II. shift,** *v.i.* **1.** (*a*) Changer de place; se déplacer. *Nau:* (*Of cargo*) Se désarrimer. (*b*) Changer. **The scene shifts,** la scène change. **The wind has shifted,** le vent a tourné, sauté. **2.** *F:* **To s. for oneself,** se débrouiller. **He can s. for himself,** il est débrouillard. **shift about,** *v.tr. & i.* Changer continuellement de place. **shift round,** *v.i.* Changer de place. (*Of wind*) Virer. **shifting,** *a.* **1.** Qui se déplace. **S. sand,** sables mouvants. **2.**(*Of scene*)Changeant; (*of wind*) inégal,-aux.

shiftiness ['ʃiftinis], *s.* Sournoiserie *f*; astuce *f*; manque *m* de franchise.

shiftless ['ʃiftlis], *a.* **1.** Paresseux, -euse; sans énergie. **2.** Peu débrouillard; qui manque d'initiative; (action *f*) inefficace. **-ly,** *adv.* D'une manière inefficace, futile.

shiftlessness ['ʃiftlisnis], *s.* **1.** Paresse *f*; manque *m* d'énergie. **2.** Manque de ressource, d'initiative; inefficacité *f.*

shiftwork ['ʃiftwəːk], *s. Ind:* Travail *m* par équipes.

shifty ['ʃifti], *a.* Roublard, retors; (regard) chafouin, sournois. **S. eyes,** yeux fuyants. *S.a.* CUSTOMER 2.

shillelagh [ʃi'leilə], *s.* Gourdin irlandais.

shilling ['ʃiliŋ], *s. Num:* Shilling *m.* **To cut s.o. off with a s.,** déshériter qn. *A:* **To take the King's s.,** s'engager.

shilly-shally¹ ['ʃiliʃæli], *s.* Barguignage *m,* vacillation *f.* **No more s.-s.!** plus d'hésitations!

shilly-shally², *v.i.* Barguigner, lanterner, vaciller. **'shilly-'shallying,** *v. =* SHILLY-SHALLY¹.

shimmer¹ ['ʃimər], *s.* Lueur *f*; chatoiement *m.* **The s. of the moon on the lake,** les reflets *m* de la lune sur le lac.

shimmer², *v.i.* Miroiter, luire, chatoyer.

shimmy ['ʃimi], *s.* **1.** *Danc: A:* Shimmy *m.* **2.** *Aut:* Shimmy.

shin¹ [ʃin], *s.* (*a*) *Anat:* (i) Le devant du tibia, de la jambe; (ii) canon *m* (du cheval). *S.a.* BARK². (*b*) *Cu:* Jarret *m* (de bœuf). **'shin-bone,** *s. Anat:* Tibia *m.* **'shin-guard, -pad,** *s. Fb:* Jambière *f.*

shin², *v.i.* (**shinned**) *F:* **To s. up a tree,** grimper à un arbre (à la force des bras et des jambes). **To s. down,** dégringoler.

shindig ['ʃindig], *s. U.S: F:* **1.** Fête (publique ou privée); sauterie *f.* **2.** = SHINDY 1.

shindy ['ʃindi], *s.* **1.** *F:* Tapage *m,* chahut *m,* boucan *m.* **To kick up a s.,** chahuter; faire du chahut, du tapage. **2.** *U.S: F:* = SHINDIG 1.

shine¹ [ʃain], *s.* **1.** Éclat *m,* lumière *f.* **Rain or s.,** par tous les temps. **2.** (*On boots*) Brillant *m;* (*on material*) luisant *m.* **To give a s. to the brass-work,** faire reluire les cuivres. **To take the s. off sth.,** défraîchir, délustrer, qch. *P:* **To take the s. out of s.o.,** éclipser, surpasser, qn. **3.** *U.S: P:* **To take a s. to s.o.,** s'enticher, se toquer, de qn.

shine², *v.i.* (**shone** [ʃɔn]; **shone**) **1.** Briller; reluire. **The moon is shining,** il fait clair de lune. **The sun is shining,** il fait du soleil. **Joy shines in his face,** la joie rayonne sur son visage. **His face shone with happiness,** sa figure rayonnait de bonheur. **He does not s. in conversation,** il ne brille pas dans la conversation. **2.** **To s. on sth.,** éclairer, illuminer, qch. **3.** *v.tr.* (**shined**; **shined**) Polir, cirer (les chaussures etc.) **To s. (sth.) up,** relustrer (qch.). **shining,** *a.* Brillant, (re)luisant. **S. example,** exemple brillant, insigne (**of,** de). *S.a.* IMPROVE 1.

shingle¹ ['ʃiŋgl], *s.* **1.** *Const:* Bardeau *m.* **2.** *U.S:* Petite enseigne (de magasin, de bureau). **3.** *Hairdr: A:* Coupe *f* à la garçonne.

shingle², *v.tr.* **1.** *Const:* Couvrir (un toit) de bardeaux. **2.** *A:* **To s. s.o.'s hair,** couper les cheveux de qn coiffer qn, à la garçonne.

shingle³, *s.* Galets *mpl;* (gros) cailloux *mpl.* **S. beach,** plage *f* de galets.

shingle⁴, *v.tr. Metall:* Cingler (le fer); faire ressuer (la loupe).

shingles ['ʃiŋglz], *s.pl. Med:* Zona *m.*

shingly ['ʃiŋgli], *a.* Couvert de galets; caillouteux, -euse. **S. beach,** plage *f* de galets.

shiny ['ʃaini], *a.* (*a*) Brillant, luisant. (*b*) **Clothes made s. by long wear,** vêtements lustrés par l'usage.

ship¹ [ʃip], *s.* (*Usu. referred to as* **she, her**) Navire (marchand); bâtiment *m;* bateau *m. Navy:* **Capital s.,** grosse unité, capital ship. **His, Her Majesty's ships,** les vaisseaux de la marine royale. **Merchant s.,** navire de commerce, navire marchand. **Ore s.,** minéralier *m.* **Sailing s.,** bâtiment à voiles. *A:* **Convict s.,** bagne flottant. *S.a.* HOSPITAL 1., LINE¹ 4, PARENT SHIP, SISTER 3, TAR¹ 1, TRAINING-SHIP, TROOP-SHIP, WARSHIP, WEATHER¹ 2. **The ship's company,** l'équipage *m.* **On board s.,** à bord. **To take s.,** (s')embarquer. **When my s. comes home,** dès que j'aurai fait fortune. *Lit:* **The S. of State,** le char de l'État. **The s. of the desert,** le chameau. *S.a.* BOOK¹ 2, PAPER¹ 3, REGISTER¹ 1. **'ship-breaker,** *s.* Démolisseur *m* de navires. **'ship-broker,** *s.* Courtier *m* maritime. **'ship-canal,** *s.* Canal *m* maritime, *pl.* canaux maritimes. **'ship('s) chandler,** *s.* Fournisseur *m,* approvisionneur *m,* de navires. **'ship(-)owner,** *s.* Armateur *m.* **ship's 'carpenter,** *s.* Charpentier *m* du bord. **'ship-worm,** *s. Moll:* Taret *m.*

ship², *v.* (**shipped**) **I.** *v.tr.* **1.** Embarquer (une cargaison, etc.). **2.** *Com:* (i) Mettre (des marchandises) à bord. (ii) Envoyer, expédier (des marchandises). **3. To s. a sea,** embarquer une lame; *abs.* embarquer. **4.** *Nau:* (*a*) Monter, mettre en place (l'hélice, etc.). (*b*) **To s. oars,** (i) armer les avirons; (ii) rentrer les avirons. **II. ship,** *v.i.* (*a*) (*Of passenger*) S'embarquer. (*b*) (*Of sailor*) **To s. on (board) a vessel,** embarquer sur un bateau, *F:* mettre son sac à bord d'un bateau. **shipping,** *s.* **1.** (*a*) Embarquement *m.* **S. charges,** frais *m* de mise à bord. **S. -bill,** connaissement *m.* *Com:* Expédition *f,* envoi *m* (de marchandises). (*c*) Montage *m,* mise *f* en place (de l'hélice, etc.). **2.** *Coll.* Navires *mpl,* vaisseaux *mpl* (d'un pays, d'un port). **Idle s.,** tonnage désarmé. **3. Dangerous for, to, s.,** dangereux pour la navigation. **S. routes,** routes de navigation. **S. company,** compagnie *f* de navigation. *S.a.* LINE¹ 5. **4.** Marine marchande. **S. intelligence, s. news,** nouvelles *f* maritimes. **S. articles,** contrat *m,* conditions *fpl.* d'engagement (de l'équipage). **'shipping-'agency,** *s.* Agence *f* maritime. **'shipping-agent,** *s.* Agent *m* maritime; (*for goods*) expéditeur *m.* **'shipping-clerk,** *s.* Expéditionnaire *m.* **'shipping-office,** *s.* **1.** (*For sailors*) L'Inscription *f* maritime. **2.** Bureau *m* de réception des marchandises. **3.** Agence *f* maritime.

-ship, *s.suff.* **1.** État ou qualité. **Authorship,** qualité d'auteur. **Ownership,** propriété. **2.** (*a*) Emploi ou dignité; ou période d'exercice de l'emploi. **Professorship,** professorat. (*b*) **His Lordship,** Sa Seigneurie.

shipboard ['ʃipbɔːd], *s.* Bord *m* (de navire). **On s.,** à bord.

shipbuilder ['ʃip,bildər], *s.* Constructeur *m* de navires.

shipbuilding ['ʃip,bildiŋ], *s.* Architecture navale; construction navale.

shipload ['ʃiploud], *s.* Chargement *m*; cargaison *f*; fret *m*.

shipmaster ['ʃip,mɑːstər], *s.* **1.** Capitaine marchand. **2.** Patron *m*.

shipmate ['ʃipmeit], *s.* Compagnon *m*, camarade *m*, de bord.

shipment ['ʃipmənt], *s.* **1.** (*a*) Embarquement *m*; mise *f* à bord. (*b*) Expédition *f* (de marchandises); envoi *m* par mer. **2.** (*Goods shipped*) Chargement *m*.

shipper ['ʃipər], *Com:* **1.** Chargeur *m*, expéditeur *m.* **2.** Affréteur *m.*

shipshape ['ʃipʃeip], *Nau:* **1.** *a.* Bien tenu; en bon ordre; fin prêt. **All's s.,** tout est à sa place. **2.** *adv.* En marin; comme il faut.

shipway ['ʃipwei], *s.* **1.** = SLIPWAY 2. **2.** = SHIP-CANAL.

shipwreck¹ ['ʃiprek], *s.* Naufrage *m.* (*Of ship*) **To suffer s.,** faire naufrage. **The s. of one's hopes,** le naufrage, la ruine, de ses espérances.

shipwreck², *v.tr.* Faire naufrager (un navire); faire échouer (une entreprise). **To be ship-wrecked,** faire naufrage. **shipwrecked,** *a.* Naufragé.

shipwright ['ʃiprait], *s.* Charpentier *m* de navires.

shipyard ['ʃipjɑːd], *s. N.Arch:* Chantier *m*, atelier *m*, de constructions navales; chantier naval.

shire ['ʃaiər; *termination* ʃ(i)ər], *s.* Comté *m.* **Ayrshire** ['ɛəʃ(i)ər], le comté d'Ayr. **The shires,** les comtés centraux (de l'Angleterre). **'shire horse,** *s.* Cheval (anglais) de gros trait; trait anglais Shire.

shirk [ʃəːk], *v.tr.* Manquer à, se dérober à (une obligation); esquiver (un devoir). *Mil: F:* Carotter (le service). *Sch: F:* Sécher (l'école). *Abs.* Négliger son devoir. **He is shirking,** *F:* il se défile.

shirker ['ʃəːkər], *s. F:* Carotteur, -euse; *Mil:* (i) tireur *m* au flanc; (ii) embusqué *m.* **To be no s.,** être franc du collier.

shirr [ʃəːr], *v.tr. Dressm:* Bouillonner (une jupe, des manches). **shirred,** *a.* **1.** *Tex:* etc: (Ruban, etc.) caoutchouté. **2.** *Dressm:* Bouillonné. **3.** *Cu:* **S. egg,** œuf poché à la crème. **shirring,** *s. Dressm:* Bouillonné *m.*

shirt [ʃəːt], *s.* Chemise *f* (d'homme); chemisier *m* (de femme). **Dress s., starched, stiff, s.,** *F:* **boiled s.,** chemise empesée, de soirée. **To put on a clean s.,** changer de chemise. **To be in one's s.-tails,** *F:* être en bannière. *F:* **Keep your s. on!** ne vous emballez pas! ne vous fâchez pas! *Turf:* **To put one's s. on a horse,** parier tout ce qu'on possède sur un cheval. *Arm:* **S. of mail,** chemise de mailles. **'shirt-'button,** *s.* Bouton *m* de chemise. **'shirt-'collar,** *s.* Col *m* de chemise. **'shirt-'front,** *s.* Plastron *m.* **'shirt-maker,** *s.* Chemisier, -ière. **'shirt-'sleeve,** *s.* Manche *f* de chemise. **To be in one's shirt-sleeves,** être en bras de chemise. **'shirt-'waist,** *s.* Chemisier *m.* **'shirt-'waister,** *s.* Robe *f* (de forme) chemisier.

shirting ['ʃəːtiŋ], *s.* Toile *f* pour chemises; shirting *m.*

shirty ['ʃəːti], *a. P: O:* Irritable; *P:* en rogne. **To get s.,** se fâcher.

shit¹ [ʃit], *s. V:* **1.** Merde *f.* **The s.-house,** *V:* les chiottes *fpl.* **2.** (*Pers:*) Salaud *m*, merdeux *m.*

shit², *v.i. V:* Chier.

shiver¹ ['ʃivər], *s.* Éclat *m*, fragment *m.* **To break into shivers,** se briser; voler en éclats.

shiver². **1.** *v.tr.* Fracasser; briser (qch.) en éclats. **2.** *v.i.* Se fracasser; voler en éclats.

shiver³, *s.* Frisson *m.* **It sent cold shivers down my back,** cela m'a donné froid dans le dos. *F:* **To have the shivers,** avoir la tremblote, le frisson.

shiver⁴. **1.** *v.i.* **To s.** (**with cold**), frissonner, grelotter, trembler (de froid). **To have a shivering fit,** être pris de frissons. **2.** *Nau:* (*a*) *v.i.* (*Of sail*) Ralinguer. (*b*) *v.tr.* Faire ralinguer (les voiles).

shivery ['ʃiv(ə)ri], *a.* **To feel s.,** (i) grelotter de froid; (ii) se sentir fiévreux.

shoal¹ [ʃoul]. **1.** *a.* **S. water,** eau peu profonde. *Nau:* **To be in s. water,** raguer le fond. **2.** *s.* Haut-fond *m.*

shoal², *v.i.* **The water shoals,** le fond diminue.

shoal³, *s.* Banc voyageur (de poissons); grande quantité, tas *m* (de lettres, etc.).

shoal⁴, *v.i.* (*Of fish*) Se réunir en bancs; voyager par bancs.

shock¹ [ʃɔk], *s. Agr:* Moyette *f*, meulette *f.*

shock², *s.* **S. of hair,** tignasse *f*; toison *f.* **'shock-headed,** *a.* A la tête ébouriffée.

shock³, *s.* **1.** (*a*) Choc *m*, heurt *m*; secousse *f*; à-coup *m.* (*b*) *Geol:* Séisme *m.* **Distant s.,** téléséisme *m.* **2.** (*a*) Coup *m*, atteinte *f.* **It gave me a dreadful s.,** cela m'a porté un coup terrible. **The s. killed him,** il mourut de saisissement. (*b*) *Med:* Choc; traumatisme *m*, commotion *f.* **Electric s. treatment,** traitement *m* par électrochocs. (*c*) *El:* **Electric s.,** secousse électrique. **'shock-absorber,** *s.* *Aut: Av:* etc: Amortisseur *m.* **'shock-proof,** *a.* **1.** Antichoc *inv.* **2.** (Homme *m*) inébranlable. **'shock-'tactics,** *s.pl. Mil:* Tactique *f* de choc. **'shock-'therapy,** *s. Med:* Thérapeutique *f* du choc. **'shock troops,** *s.pl. Mil:* Troupes *f* d'assaut, de choc.

shock⁴, *v.tr.* **1.** (*a*) Choquer, scandaliser (qn). **Easily shocked,** pudibond. (*b*) Bouleverser (qn). **I was shocked to hear that . . .,** j'ai été atterré, choqué, d'apprendre que. . . . (*c*) **To s. the ear,** blesser l'oreille. **2.** (*a*) Donner une secousse électrique à (qn). (*b*) *Med: Surg:* **To be shocked,** être commotionné. **shocking,** *a.* **1.** (*Of spectacle*) (i) Choquant; (ii) révoltant, affreux, -euse. **S. news,** nouvelle atterrante. **How s.!** quelle horreur! **2.** (*Of weather*) Abominable, exécrable. **-ly,** *adv.* **1.** Abominablement, affreusement. **2. S. dear,** terriblement cher.

shocker ['ʃɔkər], *s. F:* **1.** Chose affreuse. **Her hat was a s.,** elle était coiffée d'un chapeau affreux. **That woman is a s.!** quelle catastrophe que cette femme! quelle femme! (i) affreuse, (ii) impossible. **2.** *Publ: O:* Roman *m* à gros effets, à sensations. **3.** *O:* Surprise *f* pénible; rude coup *m.*

shod. *See* SHOE².

shoddiness ['ʃɔdinis], *s.* Mauvaise qualité.

shoddy¹ ['ʃɔdi], *s. Tex:* Drap *m* de laine d'effilochage.

shoddy², *a.* **1.** (*Of cloth*) D'effilochage. **2.** (Marchandises) de pacotille, de camelote.

shoe¹ [ʃuː], *s.* **1.** Soulier *m*, chaussure *f.* **Court shoes,** escarpins *m.* **Strap shoes,** souliers à barrette. **Wooden shoes,** sabots *m.* **Plain front s.,** chaussure sans bout rapporté. **Lace-up s.,** richelieu *m.* **Gym s.,** chaussure de gymnastique. **I buy my shoes at Smith's,** je me chausse chez Smith. **To put on one's shoes,** se chausser. **To take off one's shoes,** se déchausser. **To step into s.o.'s shoes,** prendre la place de qn. **I should not like to be in his shoes,** je ne voudrais pas être à sa place. **To be waiting for dead men's shoes,** attendre la mort de qn (pour le remplacer). **That's another pair of shoes,** ça c'est une autre paire de manches. *S.a.* SHAKE² II. 1. **2.** Fer *m* (de cheval). **To cast a s.,** perdre un fer, se déferrer. **My horse has a s. loose,** mon cheval a un fer qui lâche. **3.** *Tchn:* Sabot *m* (d'un pieu, etc.); patin *m* (de traîneau). **'shoe-brush,** *s.* Brosse *f* à souliers. **'shoe-buckle,** *s.* Boucle *f* de soulier. **'shoe-cream,** *s.* Crème *f* à chaussures. **'shoe-horn,** *s.* Chausse-pied *m.* **'shoe-lace,** *s.* Lacet *m.* **'shoe-leather,** *s.* Cuir *m* pour chaussures. **You might as well save your s.-l.,** autant vous épargner le trajet. **'shoe-polish,** *s.* Cirage *m.* **'shoe-shop,** *s.* Magasin *m* de chaussures. **'shoe-strap,** *s.* Barrette *f* de soulier. **'shoe-tree,** *s.* Forme *f.* tendeur *m*, embauchoir *m* (pour chaussures).

shoe², *v.tr.* (**shod** [ʃɔd]; shod; *pr.p.* shoeing) **1.** Chausser. **To be well shod,** être bien chaussé. **2.** Ferrer; mettre un fer à (un cheval). **3.** Garnir d'une ferrure, d'un sabot; armer (un pieu).

shoeblack ['ʃuːblæk], *s.* Décrotteur *m*, cireur *m* (de chaussures).

shoemaker ['ʃuːmeikər], *s.* **1.** Cordonnier *m*; bottier *m.* **2.** Fabricant *m* de chaussures. *S.a.* LAST¹.

shoemaking ['ʃuːmeikiŋ], *s.* **1.** Cordonnerie *f.* **2.** Fabrication *f* de chaussures.

shoestring [ˈʃuːstriŋ], s. **1.** = SHOE-LACE. **2.** F: **On a s.**, à peu de frais. **To set up in business on a s.**, s'établir avec de minces capitaux.

shone. See SHINE².

shoo¹ [ʃuː], int. (a) (To chickens) Ch-ch! (b) (To children) Allez! filez!

shoo², v.tr. **To s. (away, off,) the chickens**, chasser les poules.

shook. See SHAKE².

shoot¹ [ʃuːt], s. **1.** Bot: Pousse f (d'une plante); rejeton m. Vit: Sarment m. **2.** (In river) Rapide m. **3.** (a) Ind: Couloir m; glissière f; (for water, coal, etc.) goulotte f. Min: Ore-s., cheminée f à minerai. Ind: **Coal-s.**, manche f à charbon; trémie f de chargement. (b) Dépôt m (d'immondices). **4.** (a) Partie f de chasse. (b) Concours m de tir. **5.** Chasse gardée. **To rent a s.**, louer une chasse. **6.** F: **The whole s.**, tout le bataclan, le tremblement.

shoot², v. (shot [ʃɔt]; shot) I. v.i. **1.** Se précipiter; se lancer; s'élancer; (of star) filer. **The dog shot past us**, le chien passa près de nous comme un éclair. **To s. ahead**, aller rapidement en avant. **To s. ahead of s.o.**, devancer qn rapidement. **2.** (Of pain) Lanciner, élancer. **My corns are shooting**, mes cors m'élancent. **3.** (Of tree, bud) Pousser, bourgeonner; (of plant) germer. II. **shoot**, v.tr. **1.** Franchir (un rapide); passer rapidement sous (un pont). Aut: **To s. the (traffic) lights**, brûler le feu rouge. **2.** (a) Précipiter, lancer (qch.); pousser vivement (un verrou). (b) Verser, décharger (des décombres). **To s. coal into the cellar**, déverser du charbon dans la cave. P: **To s. the cat**, vomir, dégobiller, jeter son lest. F: **To s. a line**, (i) exagérer son importance; (ii) baratiner; (iii) P: monter un bobard. (c) Fish: Jeter (un filet). **3.** Darder, faire jaillir (des rayons). **4.** (a) Décocher (une flèche); lancer, tirer (une balle). **To s. a glance at s.o.**, lancer, décocher, un regard à qn. S.a. BOLT¹ 1. (b) Décharger (un fusil). Abs. **Don't s.!** ne tirez pas! **To s. straight**, bien viser. **To s. wide of the mark**, (i) mal viser; (ii) être loin de la vérité. **To s. at s.o.**, tirer, faire feu, sur qn. S.a. SUN¹. **To s. s.o. with a revolver**, atteindre qn d'un coup de revolver. (d) Tuer (qn) d'un coup de fusil; fusiller (un espion). **To s. s.o. through the head**, tuer qn d'une balle à la tête. Mil: **To s. a deserter**, passer un déserteur par les armes. (e) Chasser (le gibier). **To s. a partridge**, abattre une perdrix. Abs. **To s. over an estate**, chasser dans un domaine. **5.** Phot: Prendre un instantané de (qn). Cin: **To s. a film**, tourner un film. Esp. U.S: P: **S.! Allez-y! commencez! 6.** Fb: **To s. the ball**, abs. **to s.**, shooter. **To s. a goal**, marquer un but. **shoot away**, v.tr. **1. He had an arm shot away**, il eut un bras emporté. **2. To s. away all one's ammunition**, épuiser ses munitions. **shoot down**, v.tr. Abattre, descendre (le gibier, un avion). **shoot off. 1.** v.i. Partir comme un trait. **2.** v.tr. **He had a foot shot off**, il eut un pied emporté par un obus. **3.** v.tr. P: **To s. one's mouth off**, (i) bavarder (indiscrètement), caqueter, jacasser; (ii) gueuler. **shoot out. 1.** v.i. Sortir comme un trait. **The sun shot out**, le soleil s'est montré tout à coup. **The flames were shooting out of the window**, les flammes jaillissaient de la fenêtre. **2.** v.tr. (a) Lancer (des étincelles). **The snake shoots out its tongue**, le serpent darde sa langue. (b) (Of tree) Pousser (des branches). **shoot up. 1.** v.i. (a) (Of flame) Jaillir. (Of aircraft) **To s. up like a rocket**, monter en chandelle. (b) (Of prices) Augmenter rapidement. (c) (Of plant) Pousser. **To s. up into a young man**, devenir jeune homme. **2.** v.tr. (a) Mil.Av: Mitrailler, arroser (un aérodrome, etc.). (b) F: Révolvériser (qn).

shot¹, a. **1.** (Poisson) qui a déposé ses œufs. **To fall like a s. rabbit**, tomber raide. **3.** (a) Tex: Chatoyant. **S. silk**, taffetas changeant; soie gorge-de-pigeon, chatoyée. T.V: **Shot-silk effect**, moirure f. (b) Beard s. with grey, barbe parsemée de gris.

shooting¹, a. **1.** Qui s'élance; jaillissant. **S. star**, étoile filante. **S. pains**, douleurs lancinantes. **2.** F: **S. war**, guerre chaude. **shooting²**, s. **1.** (a) Élancement m (d'une blessure, etc.). (b) Bourgeonnement m. **2.** Franchissement m (d'un rapide).

3. Déchargement m (de décombres). Fish: Jet m (d'un filet). **4.** (a) Décochement m (d'une flèche); action f de tirer (un coup de revolver). S. affray, bagarre f avec coups de feu. (b) Tir m (au pistolet). Fusillade f (d'un espion, etc.). **Rabbit s.**, chasse f aux lapins. **Pigeon s.**, tir aux pigeons. **To go s.**, aller à la chasse. **The s. season has begun**, la chasse est ouverte. **5.** Cin: **S. of a film**, tournage m, prise f de vues. **'shooting-box**, s. Pavillon m de chasse. **'shooting-brake**, s. Aut: Break m (de chasse), canadienne f. **'shooting-gallery**, s. Tir m; stand m. **'shooting-party**, s. Partie f de chasse. **'shooting-range**, s. (a) Champ m de tir; F: tir m. (b) Polygone m d'artillerie. **'shooting-script**, s. Cin: T.V: Découpage m. **'shooting-stick**, s. Canne-siège f.

shooter [ˈʃuːtər], s. **1.** (a) Tireur, -euse. (b) Fb: etc: Marqueur m de but. **2.** U.S: Arme f à feu; esp. revolver m.

shop¹ [ʃɔp], s. **1.** Magasin m; (small) boutique f; (for wine, tobacco) débit m. Com: Maison f. **The Pen S.**, la Maison du Porte-plume. **Grocer's s.**, épicerie f, (magasin d')alimentation f. **Baker's s.**, boulangerie f. **Mobile, travelling s.**, camionnette-boutique f, pl. camionnettes-boutiques. **To keep a s.**, tenir (un) magasin, un commerce. **To go round the shops**, courir les magasins. **You have come to the wrong s.**, vous vous adressez mal; vous tombez mal. F: **Everything was all over the s.**, tout était en confusion. **2.** Ind: Atelier m. **Pattern s.**, atelier de modelage. **Closed s.**, atelier fermé aux (ouvriers) non-syndiqués. **Open s.**, atelier ouvert aux non-syndiqués. S.a. STEWARD 4. **3.** F: (a) Bureau m, maison f, où l'on travaille; F: boîte f. (b) **To talk s.**, parler métier. **'shop-assistant**, s. Employé, -ée, de magasin; vendeur, -euse. **'shop-fitter**, s. Agenceur m, installateur m, de magasins. **'shop-foreman**, s. Ind: Chef m d'atelier. **'shop-front**, s. Devanture f de magasin. **'shop-girl**, s.f. Vendeuse. **'shop-lifter**, s. Voleur, -euse, à l'étalage. **'shop-lifting**, s. Vol m à l'étalage. **'shop-soiled**, a. (Article) défraîchi. **'shop(-)walker**, s. **1.** Chef m de rayon. **2.** Inspecteur, -trice (du magasin). **'shop-window**, s. Vitrine f; devanture f (de magasin); étalage m. **The goods displayed in the s.-w.**, la montre.

shop², v. (shopped) **1.** v.i. Faire des achats, des emplettes. **2.** v.tr. P: Coffrer (qn). **shopping**, s. Achats mpl, emplettes fpl. **To go s.**, faire ses emplettes; faire ses courses; Fr.C: magasiner, faire du magasinage. **I have some s. to do**, j'ai des courses à faire. **To go window-s.**, faire du lèche-vitrines m. **S. centre**, quartier commerçant, centre commercial. **S. bag**, sac à provisions.

shopkeeper [ˈʃɔpkiːpər], s. Commerçant, -ante; boutiquier, -ière.

shopkeeping [ˈʃɔpkiːpiŋ], s. Le commerce.

shopman, pl. **-men** [ˈʃɔpmən], s.m. Vendeur.

shopper [ˈʃɔpər], s. Acheteur, -euse.

shore¹ [ʃɔːr], s. (a) Rivage m, littoral m; bord m (de la mer, d'un lac). (b) Nau: **The s.**, la terre. **On s.**, à terre. **Off s.**, au large. **In s.**, près de la côte. (Of ship) **To keep close to the s.**, côtoyer. Nau: **S. clothes**, frusques f d'escale. (c) pl. Poet: **Distant shores**, de lointains rivages. **To return to one's native shores**, rentrer dans son pays natal. **'shore-boat**, s. Nau: Bateau m de passage. **'shore-dinner**, s. U.S: **To eat a s. d.**, manger un repas composé de fruits de mer; se régaler de fruits de mer.

shore², s. Const: etc: Étai m, étançon m; contreboutant m. Nau: Béquille f, épontille f.

shore³, v.tr. **To shore (up)**, étayer, étançonner; contrebouter, arc-bouter (un mur). Nau: Épontiller, accorer (un navire).

shorn. See SHEAR³.

short¹ [ʃɔːt]. I. a. **1.** Court. **To go by the shortest road**, prendre par le plus court. **A s. way off**, à peu de distance. **S. steps**, petits pas. **A s. man**, un homme de petite taille. **To be s. in the arm**, avoir les bras courts. **Your coat is s. in the arms**, votre habit est trop court des manches. S.a. CUT¹ 9, HEAD¹ 1, SIGHT¹ 1. **2.** Court, bref, f. brève. (a) De peu de durée. **Days are getting shorter**, les jours raccourcissent.

For a **s. time**, pour peu de temps. **In a s. time**, sous peu; bientôt. **A s. time ago**, il y a peu de temps. **A s. sleep**, un petit somme. *Ling:* **S. vowel**, voyelle brève. *Com:* **S. bills**, traites à courte échéance. **Deposit at s. notice**, dépôt à court terme. **To make s. work of it**, ne pas y aller par quatre chemins; mener rondement les choses. **To make s. work of sth.**, expédier qch. (b) **S. story**, nouvelle *f*, conte *m*. **S. story writer**, auteur *m* de contes, de nouvelles. **Harrap's Shorter French and English Dictionary**, édition abrégée du Dictionnaire Harrap français-anglais. **S. list**, liste choisie (d'aspirants à un poste). **In s. . . .**, bref . . ., en un mot . . ., en somme. . . . **He is called Bob for s.**, on l'appelle Bob pour abréger. *F:* **A s. (one)**, un petit verre. *S.a.* SHRIFT. (c) (Pouls) rapide. (d) (Style) concis, serré. (e) (*Of reply*) Brusque; sec, *f.* sèche. **To be s. with s.o.**, être sec, cassant, avec qn. **S. temper**, caractère brusque, vif. 3. (*Of weight*) Insuffisant. **To give s. weight**, ne pas donner le poids. **It is two francs s.**, il s'en faut de deux francs. **I am twenty francs s.**, il me manque vingt francs. *Ind:* **To be on s. time**, être en chômage partiel. *S.a.* COMMONS 2. **Little, not far, s. of it**, peu s'en faut. **It is little s. of folly**, cela confine à la folie. **Nothing s. of violence would compel him**, la violence seule le contraindrait. (b) **To be s. of sth.**, être à court de qch. **S. of petrol**, à bout d'essence. **To be s. of hands**, manquer de main-d'œuvre. *Cards:* **To be s. of spades**, avoir une renonce à pique. **To go s. of sth.**, se priver de qch. **We ran s. of butter**, le beurre vint à manquer. 4. *Cu:* **S. pastry**, pâte brisée. **-ly**, *adv.* 1. (Raconter qch.) brièvement, en peu de mots. 2. (Répondre) brusquement, sèchement. 3. Bientôt, prochainement; sous peu. **S. after(wards)**, peu (de temps) après; bientôt après. II. **short**, *s.* 1. (a) **The long and the s.** *See* LONG[1] II. 1. (b) *pl.* **Shorts**, culotte *f* de sport, short *m*. 2. (a) *Pros:* (Syllabe) brève *f*. (b) *Ling:* Voyelle brève. (c) *Artil:* Coup court. 3. *El.* = SHORT-CIRCUIT[1]. 4. *Cin:* Court métrage *m*. III. **short**, *adv.* 1. **To stop s.**, s'arrêter pile. **To cut s.o. s.**, couper la parole à qn. 2. **To fall s. of the mark**, ne pas atteindre le but. **To fall, come, s. of sth.**, être, rester, au-dessous de qch. **It falls far s. of it**, il s'en faut de beaucoup. **S. of burning it . . .**, à moins de le brûler. . . . **To stop s. of crime**, s'arrêter au seuil du crime. **short-'circuit[1]**, *s.* *El:* Court-circuit *m.* **short-'circuit[2]**. 1. *v.tr.* (a) *El:* Court-circuiter. **To s.-c. a resistance**, mettre une résistance hors circuit. (b) *F:* Court-circuiter (qn, un service). 2. *v.i.* *El.E:* (*Of current*) Se mettre en court-circuit. **'short-date[1]**, *a.* *Fin:* (Billet) à courte échéance; (papier) court. **short-'handed**, *a.* A court de main-d'œuvre, de personnel. **short-'headed**, *a.* *Anthr:* Brachycéphale. **'short-'lived**, *a.* (*of pers.*) Qui meurt jeune; (*of joy*) éphémère, de courte durée. **'short-'range**, *attrib.a.* (Tir) à courte portée. **short-'sighted**, *a.* 1. Myope; à la vue basse. **I am getting s.-s.**, ma vue baisse. 2. Imprévoyant. **short-'sightedness**, *s.* 1. Myopie *f.* 2. Imprévoyance *f.* **'short-'tempered**, *a.* Vif, *f.* vive; d'un caractère emporté. **'short-term**, *attrib.a.* *Fin:* (Placement, etc.) à court terme. **short-'winded**, *a.* Poussif, -ive; à l'haleine courte. **short[2]**, *v.tr. & i.* *El.E:* = SHORT-CIRCUIT[2]. **shortage** ['ʃɔːtidʒ], *s.* 1. (a) Insuffisance *f*, manque *m* (de poids). **S. of staff**, pénurie *f* de personnel. (b) *pl.* *Com:* Manquants *m*. 2. Crise *f*, disette *f*. **Food s.**, disette. **The paper s.**, la crise du papier. **shortbread** ['ʃɔːtbred], *s.* *Cu:* = Sablé *m*. **shortcoming** ['ʃɔːtkʌmiŋ], *s.* *usu.pl.* **Shortcomings**, défauts *m*, imperfections *f*. **shorten** ['ʃɔːt(ə)n]. 1. *v.tr.* (a) Raccourcir, rapetisser; abréger (un texte, une tâche, *Pros:* une syllabe). *Mil:* **To s. step**, raccourcir le pas. (b) *Nau:* **To s. sail**, diminuer de voile. (c) *Cu:* **Baby not yet shortened**, bébé encore en robes (longues). 2. *v.i.* (*Of days*) Raccourcir, décroître. 3. *Cu:* **To s. pastry**, travailler une pâte (avec du beurre, etc.). **shortening**, *s.* 1. Raccourcissement *m*; décroissance *f* (des jours). 2. *Cu:* Matière grasse, employée pour travailler une pâte.

shorthand ['ʃɔːthænd], *s.* Sténographie *f*, *F:* sténo *f.* **S. writing**, écriture *f* sténographique. **To take a speech down in s.**, sténographier un discours. (*Pers.*) **S. typist**, sténodactylographe *mf*; *F:* sténo(dactylo) *mf*. **shorthorn** ['ʃɔːthɔːn], *s.* *Breed:* (a) Race bovine Shorthorn. (b) Bovin *m* (de race) Shorthorn. **shortness** ['ʃɔːtnis], *s.* 1. (a) Peu *m* de longueur. (b) Brièveté *f*, courte durée (de la vie). **S. of memory**, manque *m* de mémoire. *Pros:* **S. of a vowel**, brièvité *f* d'une voyelle. (c) Brusquerie *f* (d'humeur). 2. Manque, insuffisance *f* (de vivres). **shot[1]**. *See* SHOOT[2]. **shot[2]** [ʃɔt], *s.* 1. *Artil:* (a) Boulet *m.* (b) *Sp:* Poids *m.* *S.a.* PUT[2] I. 6. (c) *Coll.* Projectiles *mpl.* 2. *Sm.a:* (a) A: Balle *f.* *S.a.* POWDER[1]. (b) *Ven:* Plomb *m.* **Small s.**, menu plomb. **Bird s., dust s.**, cendrée *f.* 3. (a) Coup *m* de feu. **Pistol s.**, coup de pistolet. **Without firing a s.**, sans brûler une cartouche. **To take a (flying) s. at a bird**, tirer un oiseau (au vol). **To be off like a shot**, partir comme un trait. **He accepted like a s.**, il accepta avec empressement. (b) (*Pers.*) Tireur, -euse. **He's a good s.**, il est bon chasseur. *S.a.* DEAD I. 5. 4. Coup. (a) *F:* **I'll have a s. (at it)**, je vais essayer; je vais tenter le coup. **To make a s. at an answer**, répondre au petit bonheur. *F:* **To make a long s.**, prendre un (gros) risque. (b) *Fb:* **S. (at the goal)**, shot *m.* *Ten: etc:* **Drop s.**, amortie *f.* *Cin:* **Prise *f* de vue. Dolly s., follow s.**, travelling *m* en poursuite. (d) *F:* **Piqûre *f.* S. in the arm**, (i) piqûre au bras; (ii) *F:* stimulant *m*, coup de fouet. 5. *Min:* **To fire a s.**, tirer un coup de mine. 6. *F:* **Big s.**, gros bonnet, grosse légume. **'shot-gun**, *s.* Fusil *m* de chasse. *F:* **S.-g. wedding**, mariage forcé. **'shot-proof**, *a.* A l'épreuve des balles. **shott** [ʃɔt], *s.* *Geog:* Chott *m.* **should**. *See* SHALL. **shoulder[1]** ['ʃouldər], *s.* 1. (a) Épaule *f.* **Round shoulders**, dos rond, voûté. **Breadth of shoulders**, carrure *f.* *F:* **He's got broad shoulders**, il a bon dos. **Slung across the s.**, en bandoulière. **To bring the gun to the s.**, épauler le fusil. **To hit out straight from the s.**, frapper directement, en plein. **To square one's shoulders**, raidir sa volonté. **I let him have it straight from the s.**, je ne le lui ai pas envoyé dire. **To stand head and shoulders above the rest**, dépasser les autres de la tête. **To stand s. to s.**, se soutenir les uns les autres. **To put one's s. to the wheel**, (i) pousser à la roue; (ii) se mettre à l'œuvre. *S.a.* COLD[1], HEAD[1] 2, RUB[2] 1. (b) *Cu:* Épaule (de mouton). *Nau:* **S. of mutton sail**, (voile *f* à) houari *m.* (c) Épaulement (de colline); contrefort *m* (de montagne); ressaut *m* (de terrain); bas-côté *m* (d'une route). 2. Embase *f* (de boulon, etc.); talon *m* (de lame d'épée); ressaut *m* (d'un projectile). **'shoulder-bag**, *s.* Sac *m* en bandoulière. **'shoulder-belt**, *s.* Baudrier *m.* **'shoulder-blade**, *s.* (i) Omoplate *f*; (ii) paleron *m* (de cheval, etc.). **'shoulder-joint**, *s.* *Anat:* Articulation *f* de l'épaule. **'shoulder-knot**, *s.* Nœud *m* d'épaule; aiguillette *f.* **'shoulder-strap**, *s.* 1. (a) Bretelle *f*; bandoulière *f.* **Shoulder-straps** (*of rucksack*), brassière *f.* (b) (*On women's underclothing*), Bretelle. 2. *Mil:* Patte d'épaule. **shoulder[2]**, *v.tr.* 1. Pousser avec l'épaule. **To s. one's way through the crowd**, se frayer un chemin à travers la foule. **To s. s.o. out of the way**, écarter qn d'un coup d'épaule. 2. Charger qch. sur l'épaule. **To s. one's gun**, mettre son fusil sur l'épaule. **To s. the responsibility**, endosser la responsabilité. 3. *Mil:* **S. arms!** portez armes! **shout[1]** [ʃaut], *s.* (a) Cri *m* (de joie, etc.). **Shouts of laughter**, éclats *m* de rire. (b) Clameur *f.* **Shouts of applause**, acclamations *f.* **shout[2]**. 1. *v.i.* Crier; pousser des cris. *v.pr.* **To s. oneself hoarse**, s'enrouer à force de crier. 2. *v.tr.* Crier (qch.); vociférer (des injures). **shout down**, *v.tr.* Huer (un orateur). **shout out**. 1. *v.i.* Crier, s'écrier. 2. *v.tr.* Crier (un nom). **shouting**, *s.* Cris *mpl*; acclamations *fpl.* **shove[1]** [ʃʌv], *s.* *F:* Coup *m* (d'épaule); poussée *f.* **To give s.o. a s. off**, aider qn au départ, au démarrage.

shove[2], *v.tr. F:* Pousser. **To s. (one's way) through the crowd,** se frayer un chemin à travers la foule. **To s. sth. into a drawer,** fourrer qch. dans un tiroir. **shove aside,** *v.tr. F:* Écarter d'une poussée; pousser (qch.) de côté. **shove away,** *v.tr. F:* 1. Repousser (qn, qch.). 2. *Abs.* Continuer à pousser. **S. a.!** poussez donc! allez-y! **shove back,** *v.tr. F:* Repousser, faire reculer. **shove forward.** *F:* 1. *v.tr.* Pousser en avant. 2. *v.i.* (a) Se frayer un chemin. (b) Se pousser; faire son chemin. **shove off,** *v.tr. Nau:* Pousser (une embarcation) au large. *Abs.* **S. off!** (i) laissez aller! poussez! (ii) *P:* fiche-moi le camp! *P:* **I'm shoving off home,** je file, je m'en vais chez moi. **shove out,** *v.tr. F:* Pousser dehors. **To s. out one's hand,** étendre le bras. **shoving,** *s. F:* Poussée *f.* **'shove-ha'penny,** *s.* = Jeu *m* de galets.

shovel[1] ['ʃʌv(ə)l], *s.* Pelle *f.* **Fire-s.,** pelle à feu. **'shovel 'hat,** *s. A:* Chapeau *m* ecclésiastique.

shovel[2], *v.tr.* (shovelled) Pell(et)er (le charbon, etc.); prendre, jeter (le charbon, etc.) à la pelle. **shovel away,** *v.tr.* Enlever (qch.) à la pelle. **shovel up,** *v.tr.* Ramasser, entasser (qch.) à la pelle. *P:* **To s. up one's food,** bâfrer sa mangeaille. **shovelling,** *s.* Ramassage *m* à la pelle.

shovelboard ['ʃʌvlbɔːd], *s.* = Jeu *m* de galets.

shovelful ['ʃʌv(ə)lful], *s.* Pellée *f,* pelletée *f.*

shoveller ['ʃʌv(ə)lər], *s.* 1. Pelleteur *m.* 2. *Orn:* S. (duck), (canard *m*) souchet *m.*

show[1] [ʃou], *s.* 1. Mise *f* en vue; étalage *m* (de qch.). **S. of hands,** vote *m* à main(s) levée(s). **The s. pupil of the class,** l'élève *mf* vedette. *Com:* **On s. on our premises,** exposé dans nos magasins. *Mus:* **S. piece,** morceau de facture. *Organ:* **The s. pipes,** montre *f* d'orgue. **S. house,** **s. flat,** maison *f,* appartement *m,* témoin. 2. (a) Exposition *f* (de marchandises); exhibition *f* (d'animaux sauvages), comice *m* (agricole). **S. breeder,** **s. breeding,** éleveur *m,* élevage *m,* de bêtes à concours. **Motor s.,** salon *m* de l'automobile. **Fashion s.,** présentation *f* de collections. (b) **Film s.,** séance *f* de cinéma; spectacle *m.* **Wild-beast s.,** ménagerie *f.* **To make a s. of oneself,** se donner en spectacle. **To go to a s.,** aller au spectacle. *S.a.* DUMB. (c) Étalage *m. F:* **Good s.!** Très bien! Compliments! Bravo! **Our furniture makes a poor s.,** notre mobilier fait triste figure. (d) **To give s.o. a (fair) s.,** laisser franc jeu à qn. 3. (a) (i) Apparence *f;* (ii) semblant *m.* **With some s. of reason,** avec quelque apparence de raison. **S. of resistance,** simulacre *m* de résistance. **To make a great s. of friendship,** faire de grandes démonstrations d'amitié. (b) Parade *f,* ostentation *f,* affichage *m.* **To be fond of s.,** aimer l'éclat, la parade. **To make a s. of learning,** faire parade d'érudition. **To do sth. for show,** faire qch. pour la galerie. **4.** *F:* Affaire *f.* **To run the s.,** diriger l'affaire. *S.a.* GIVE AWAY 3. **'show-bill,** *s.* Affiche *f* (de spectacle). **'show-boat,** *s. U.S: A:* Bateau-théâtre *m* (sur le Mississipi). **'show business,** *s.* **To be in (the) s. b.,** appartenir au monde des spectacles. **'show-card,** *s. Com:* 1. Pancarte *f.* 2. Étiquette *f* (de vitrine). 3. Carte *f* d'échantillons. **'show-case,** *s. Com:* Montre *f,* vitrine *f.* **'show-girl,** *s.f.* Girl. **'show-ground,** *s.* (a) Champ *m* de foire. (b) Terrain *m* de concours hippique. **'show-place,** *s.* Endroit *m,* monument *m,* d'intérêt touristique. **'show-ring,** *s.* Arène *f* (i) d'exposition; (ii) de vente; (iii) de concours hippique, etc.

show[2], *v.* (p.t. showed [ʃoud]; p.p. showed, shown [ʃoun]) I. *v.tr.* 1. Montrer. (a) Faire voir, exhiber (qch.). **To s. s.o. sth.,** montrer, faire voir, qch. à qn. *Com:* **What can I s. you, madam?** madame désire? **Picture shown at the Academy,** tableau exposé au Salon de Londres. **To s. a picture on the screen,** projeter une image (sur l'écran). **We're going to s. some films this evening,** on va passer des films ce soir. **To s. one's passport,** montrer, présenter, son passeport. **To s. one's cards, one's hand,** (i) jouer cartes sur table; (ii) découvrir ses batteries. *Nau:* **To s. a light,** porter un feu. **To have sth. to s. for one's money,** en avoir pour son argent. **He won't s. his face here again,** il ne se montrera plus ici. **To s. oneself,** se montrer; (*at a reception*) faire acte de

présence. (*Of thg*) **To s. itself,** devenir visible; se révéler. *S.a.* HEEL[1] 1. (b) Représenter, figurer (qch.). **Machine shown in section,** machine figurée en coupe. (c) Indiquer. **As shown in the illustration,** comme l'indique l'illustration. (*Of watch*) **To s. the time,** indiquer, marquer, l'heure. **The indicator shows a speed of . . .,** l'indicateur accuse une vitesse de. . . . **To s. a profit,** faire ressortir un bénéfice. 2. (a) **To s. s.o. the way,** indiquer, tracer, le chemin à qn. *S.a.* DOOR 1. (b) **To s. s.o. to his room,** conduire qn à sa chambre. **Let me s. you round,** laissez-moi vous piloter. **To s. s.o. round the house, etc.,** faire visiter la maison, etc. à qn. **To s. s.o. to his seat,** placer qn. **To s. s.o. into a room,** faire entrer qn dans une pièce. 3. (a) **To s. intelligence,** faire preuve d'intelligence. **To s. an interest in s.o.,** témoigner de l'intérêt à qn. **His face showed his delight,** son visage annonçait sa joie. **Selection that shows s.o.'s tastes,** choix qui déclare, qui accuse, les goûts de qn. **He shows his age,** il fait (bien) son âge. **To s. one's true character,** se démasquer. *Abs.* **Time will s.,** qui vivra verra. *S.a.* FIGHT[1] 2, HOSPITALITY. (b) Révéler, montrer. **Garment that shows the figure,** vêtement qui dessine la taille. (c) **To s. s.o. to be a rogue,** prouver la coquinerie de qn. *Abs. P:* **I'll s. you!** je vous apprendrai! **To s. cause, reason,** exposer ses raisons. II. **show,** *v.i.* Se montrer. (ap)paraître; se laisser voir. **The buds are beginning to s.,** les bourgeons commencent à se montrer, à paraître. **Your slip's showing,** votre jupon dépasse. **To s. to advantage,** faire bonne figure. *F:* **To s. willing,** faire preuve de bonne volonté. **'show-down,** *s.* 1. *Cards:* Étalement *m* de son jeu (sur la table). 2. *F:* Déballage *m.* **A forces B to a s.-d.,** A force B à montrer ses cartes. **To call for a s.-d.,** sommer qn de mettre cartes sur table. **If it comes to a s.-d.,** s'il faut en venir au fait. **show in,** *v.tr.* S. **him, them,** in, faites entrer. **show off.** 1. *v.tr.* (a) Faire valoir, mettre en valeur (qch.). (b) Faire parade, étalage, de (qch.). 2. *v.i.* Parader, poser; se pavaner. **To s. off before s.o.,** chercher à épater qn. **'show-off,** *s. F:* Poseur, -euse; *P:* m'as-tu-vu *m inv.* **show out,** *v.tr.* Reconduire (qn); escorter (qn) jusqu'à la porte. **show through,** *v.i.* Transparaître. **show up.** I. *v.tr.* 1. *Sch:* Donner (sa copie). 2. Démasquer (un imposteur); dévoiler (une imposture); révéler (un défaut). II. *v.i.* 1. Se détacher, ressortir (sur un fond). 2. *F:* Se présenter; faire acte de présence. **showing,** *s.* Exposition *f,* mise *f* en vue (de qch.). *Cin:* **First s.,** en première vision. **On your own s.,** à ce que vous dites vous-même.

shower[1] ['ʃauər], *s.* 1. (a) Averse *f.* **Heavy s.,** ondée *f.* **Sudden s.,** averse; (*with hail or snow*) giboulée *f.* (b) **Shower of stones,** volée *f* de pierres. **S. of sparks,** gerbe *f* d'étincelles. (c) *Toil:* Douche *f.* 2. *U.S:* **Pluie** *f* de cadeaux (de noce, etc.) **S. (party),** réception où chacun apporte un cadeau. **'shower-bath,** *s.* Bain-douche *m,* pl. bains-douches.

shower[2]. 1. *v.tr.* (a) Verser; faire pleuvoir (de l'eau). (b) **To s. blows,** frapper dru (on s.o., sur qn). **To s. invitations on s.o.,** accabler qn d'invitations. 2. *v.i.* (*of rain*) Tomber par ondées.

showery ['ʃauəri], *a.* (Temps) de giboulées, à ondées; (temps) pluvieux.

showiness ['ʃouinis], *s.* Prétention *f,* clinquant *m,* faste *m;* luxe criard; ostentation *f.*

showman, *pl.* **-men** ['ʃoumən], *s.m.* (a) Directeur (d'un spectacle de la foire); forain. **He's a great s.,** c'est un as pour la mise en scène. (b) Montreur de curiosités (à la foire).

showmanship ['ʃoumənʃip], *s.* Art *m* de la mise en scène.

showpiece ['ʃoupiːs], *s.* Article *m* d'exposition, de vitrine; objet *m,* monument *m,* etc. de grand intérêt.

showroom ['ʃourum], *s.* Salle *f,* salon *m,* magasin *m,* d'exposition (d'une maison de commerce); salle de démonstration (d'automobiles).

showy ['ʃoui], *a.* (*Of appearance*) Prétentieux, -euse, voyant. **S. hat,** chapeau à effet; chapeau criard. **He does s. work,** *F:* il fait du tape-à-l'œil. **-ily,** *adv.* (Habillé) d'une façon prétentieuse; avec ostentation; (meublé) avec un luxe criard.

shrank. *See* SHRINK.

shrapnel ['ʃræpn(ə)l], s. 1. Shrapnel m; obus m à balles. 2. F: Éclats mpl d'obus.

shred¹ [ʃred], s. Brin m; lambeau m, fragment m (d'étoffe). **To tear sth. (in)to shreds,** déchiqueter qch.; mettre qch. en lambeaux. **Her dress was all in shreds,** sa robe était tout en lambeaux. **There isn't a s. of evidence,** il n'y a pas la moindre preuve.

shred², v.tr. (shredded) Couper (qch.) par languettes; déchirer (qch.) en lambeaux; effilocher; déchiqueter.

shrew¹ (-mouse, pl. -mice) ['ʃru:(maus, -mais)], s. Z: Musaraigne f.

shrew², s.f. Femme criarde, acariâtre; mégère.

shrewd [ʃru:d], a. 1. Sagace, perspicace; qui a du flair. **S. business man,** homme d'affaires très entendu. **S. reasoning,** raisonnement judicieux. 2. (a) A: (Of cold) Sévère, âpre. (b) S. blow, coup bien placé. 3. (Intensive) **I have a s. idea that . . .,** je suis porté à croire que. . . . **To make a s. guess . . .,** avoir de fortes raisons pour deviner. . . . **-ly,** adv. Sagacement; avec finesse; avec perspicacité.

shrewdness ['ʃru:dnis], s. Sagacité f; perspicacité f; finesse f.

shrewish ['ʃru(:)iʃ], a. (Femme) acariâtre, criarde. **-ly,** adv. D'une façon acariâtre, querelleuse; en mégère.

shrewishness ['ʃru(:)iʃnis], s. Humeur acariâtre.

shriek¹ [ʃri:k], s. 1. Cri déchirant; cri perçant. **S. of anguish,** cri d'angoisse. **Shrieks of laughter,** grands éclats de rire. **The s. of a locomotive,** le cri strident d'une locomotive. **To give a s.,** pousser un cri. 2. F: Point m d'exclamation.

shriek². 1. v.i. Pousser des cris aigus; (of locomotive) siffler, déchirer l'air. **To s. with laughter,** rire aux éclats; s'esclaffer (de rire). 2. v.tr. **To s. out a warning,** avertir qn d'un cri. **shrieking,** s. Cris stridents.

shrift [ʃrift], s. A: Ccnfession f et absolution f. (b) **To give s.o. short s.,** expédier vite son homme.

shrike [ʃraik], s. Orn: Pie-grièche f.

shrill¹ [ʃril], a. (Of voice) A note aiguë; aigu, strident. **In a s. voice,** d'une voix perçante. **S. whistle,** coup de sifflet strident. **-lly** ['ʃrilli], adv. D'un ton aigu, criard.

shrill², v.i. Lit: Pousser un son aigu. **A whistle shrilled,** un coup de sifflet déchira l'air.

shrillness ['ʃrilnis], s. Stridence f.

shrimp¹ [ʃrimp], s. Crevette (grise). F: **S. (of a man),** petit bout d'homme; gringalet m.

shrimp², v.i. Pêcher la crevette. **shrimping,** s. Pêche f à la crevette.

shrimper ['ʃrimpər], s. Pêcheur, -euse, de crevettes.

shrine [ʃrain], s. 1. Châsse f, reliquaire m. 2. Tombeau m de saint, de sainte. 3. Chapelle f, autel m, consacré(e) à un saint.

shrink [ʃriŋk], v. (shrank [ʃræŋk]; shrunk [ʃrʌŋk]; as adj. shrunken ['ʃrʌŋk(ə)n]) 1. v.i. (a) Se contracter; (se) rétrécir; se rétracter. **His gums are shrinking,** ses dents se déchaussent. **To s. in the wash,** (se) rétrécir au lavage. **He is beginning to s. (with age),** il commence à se tasser. (b) Faire un mouvement de recul; se dérober. **To s. away,** s'éloigner timidement. **To s. (back) from (sth.),** reculer devant (un danger). **To s. from doing sth.,** répugner à faire qch. **His mind shrank from painful memories,** son esprit se dérobait aux souvenirs pénibles. (c) **To s. into oneself,** rentrer dans sa coquille. 2. v.tr. Rétrécir, faire rétrécir (un tissu). **shrinking**¹, a. 1. Qui se contracte. **S. capital,** capital qui diminue. 2. Timide, craintif, -ive. **-ly,** adv. Timidement. **shrinking**², s. 1. = SHRINKAGE. 2. **S. (away, back) from sth.,** reculement m devant qch. **shrunk(en),** a. Contracté; ratatiné. **S. with age,** tassé par l'âge. Anthr: **Shrunken heads,** têtes réduites.

shrinkage ['ʃriŋkidʒ], s. Contraction f (du métal); rétrécissement m (d'une étoffe).

shrive [ʃraiv], v.tr. (shrove [ʃrouv]; shriven ['ʃriv(ə)n]) A: Confesser, absoudre (un pénitent).

shrivel ['ʃriv(ə)l], v. (shrivelled) 1. v.tr. **To s. (up),** rider, ratatiner (la peau); (of sun) brûler, hâler (les plantes). 2. v.i. **To s. (up),** se rider, se ratatiner.

shroud¹ [ʃraud], s. 1. Linceul m, suaire m. **In a s. of mystery,** enveloppé de mystère. 2. Mec.E: Bouclier m, blindage m.

shroud², s. Nau: Civ.E: Hauban m.

shroud³, v.tr. 1. (a) Ensevelir; envelopper (un cadavre) d'un linceul. (b) Envelopper, voiler (qch.). 2. W.Tel: Blinder (un transformateur). **shrouded,** a. 1. (a) Enveloppé d'un suaire. (b) Enveloppé, voilé (in, de). **S. in mist,** enveloppé de brume. **S. in gloom,** enténébré; (of pers.) endeuillé, plongé dans la tristesse. 2. W.Tel: (Transformateur) blindé.

shrove [ʃrouv]. 1. See SHRIVE. 2. **S. Tuesday,** (le) mardi gras.

Shrovetide ['ʃrouvtaid], s. Ecc: Les jours gras.

shrub¹ [ʃrʌb], s. Arbrisseau m, arbuste m.

shrub², s. Grog m à l'orange, au citron.

shrubbery ['ʃrʌbəri], s. Bosquet m; plantation f d'arbustes, massif m d'arbustes.

shrubby ['ʃrʌbi], a. 1. Qui ressemble à un arbuste. **S. tree,** arbrisseau m. 2. Couvert d'arbustes.

shrug¹ [ʃrʌg], s. Haussement m d'épaules. **S. of resignation,** geste m de résignation.

shrug², v.tr. (shrugged) **To s. (one's shoulders),** hausser les épaules.

shrunk, shrunken. See SHRINK.

shuck¹ [ʃʌk], U.S: 1. Cosse f, gousse f (de pois, etc.); écale f (de noix); bogue f (de châtaigne); spathe f (de maïs). 2. int. **Shucks!** allons donc! chansons!

shuck², v.tr. U.S: Écosser (des pois); écaler (des noix); éplucher (le maïs).

shudder¹ ['ʃʌdər], s. Frisson m (d'horreur); frémissement m. **A s. passed over him,** il fut pris d'un frisson.

shudder², v.i. **To s. with horror,** frissonner d'horreur; frémir d'horreur.

shuffle¹ ['ʃʌfl], s. 1. (a) Mouvement traînant des pieds; marche traînante. (b) Danc: Frottement m de pieds. 2. Battement m, mélange m (des cartes). 3. (a) Tergiversation f, barguignage m. (b) Faux-fuyant m.

shuffle². 1. v.tr. & i. **To s. (one's feet),** traîner les pieds. 2. v.tr. (a) (Entre)mêler (des papiers). (b) **To s. the dominoes,** brasser les dominos. (c) Battre, mêler (les cartes). 3. v.i. Équivoquer, tergiverser, se dérober, barguigner. **shuffle off.** 1. v.tr. (a) Se débarrasser de (la responsabilité, etc.). (b) Ôter (ses vêtements) à la hâte, n'importe comment. 2. v.i. S'en aller en traînant le pas. **shuffling**¹, a. 1. (Of gait) Traînant. 2. (Of pers.) Tergiversateur, -trice; (of conduct) équivoque, évasif, -ive. **shuffling**², s. = SHUFFLE¹.

shuffle-board ['ʃʌflbɔːd], s. = SHOVEL-BOARD.

shuffler ['ʃʌflər], s. Tergiversateur, -trice.

shun¹ [ʃʌn], v.tr. (shunned) Fuir, éviter (qn, qch.). **To s. everybody,** s'éloigner de tout le monde.

'shun² [ʃ(ʌ)n], int. Mil: F: (= attention!) Garde à vous!

shunt¹ [ʃʌnt], s. 1. Rail: Garage m, manœuvre f (d'un train). 2. El: Shunt m, dérivation f. **To put in s.,** mettre en dérivation; shunter. **'shunt circuit,** s. El: Circuit dérivé. **'shunt line,** s. Rail: Voie f de garage. **shunt-wound,** ['ʃʌntwaund], a. El.E: Excité en dérivation, en shunt.

shunt² v.tr. 1. Rail: Garer, manœuvrer (un train). **'S. with care,'** "défense de tamponner." 2. El: Shunter, dériver (un circuit); monter (un condensateur) en dérivation. **shunting,** s. 1. Rail: Garage m, manœuvre f; aiguillage m. **S. operations,** manœuvres de triage m. **S. yard,** chantier m, gare f, de manœuvre et de triage. 2. El: Dérivation f, shuntage m.

shush [ʃʌʃ], 1. v.tr. F: Faire taire (un enfant, etc.). 2. Int: [ʃ] Chut!

shut [ʃʌt], v. (p.t. shut; p.p. shut; pr.p. shutting) 1. v.tr. (a) Fermer (une porte, une boîte). **To s. the door against s.o.,** refuser de recevoir qn. **To find the door s.,** trouver porte close; trouver visage de bois. S.a. EYE¹ 1. **To s. one's mouth,** (i) fermer la bouche; (ii) se taire. **To keep one's mouth shut (tight),** F: avoir la bouche cousue. P: **S. your trap!** ferme ton bec! la ferme! (b) **To s. one's finger, one's dress, in the door,** se pincer le doigt, laisser prendre sa robe, dans la porte. 2. v.i. (Of door) (Se) fermer. **The door won't s.,** la porte ne ferme pas. **shut down.** 1. v.tr. (a) Rabattre (un couvercle). (b) Ind: Fermer (une usine). 2. v.i. Tchn: Couper (la vapeur). 2. v.i. (Of lid) Se rabattre. **shut in,** v.tr. (a) Enfermer. (b) (Of hills) Entourer, encercler (un endroit). **shut off,** v.tr. 1. Couper, interrompre (la vapeur); fermer (l'eau). Aut: **To s. off the engine,** couper le moteur.

2. Séparer, isoler (**from**, de). **shut out**, *v.tr.* (*a*) Exclure (qn, l'air). The trees s. out the view, les arbres bouchent la vue. (*b*) **To s. s.o. out (of doors)**, fermer la porte à qn. **S. the dog out!** *F:* mets le chien dehors! **shut up. 1.** *v.tr.* (*a*) Enfermer. **To s. oneself up**, se renfermer; se reclure. (*b*) **To s. s.o. up (in prison)**, emprisonner qn. (*c*) Fermer (une maison). **To s. up shop**, fermer boutique. *F:* **We'll have to s. up shop for a bit**, il va falloir suspendre nos activités pendant quelque temps. (*d*) *P:* Réduire (qn) au silence; clouer le bec à (qn). **2.** *v.i.* *P:* Se taire; ne plus dire mot. **S. up!** ta ferme! ta gueule! **shutting**, *s.* Fermeture *f.* **'shut-eye**, *s.* *P:* Somme *m;* *P:* roupillon *m.*

shutter ['ʃʌtər], *s.* **1.** Volet *m.* **Outside s.**, contrevent *m.* **Venetian shutters**, persiennes *f.* **Folding shutters**, volets brisés. **To take down the shutters**, enlever les volets (d'un magasin). **To put up the shutters (of a shop)**, mettre les volets. **2.** *Phot:* Obturateur *m.* **Diaphragm s.**, obturateur au diaphragme. **Focal-plane s.**, obturateur focal. **'shutter-release**, *s.* *Phot:* Déclencheur *m* d'obturateur.

shuttering ['ʃʌt(ə)riŋ], *s.* *Const:* Coffrage *m* (pour le béton armé).

shuttle¹ ['ʃʌtl], *s.* **1.** Navette *f.* **2.** *Mec.E:* **S. movement**, mouvement alternatif. **Line over which a s. service is run**, ligne de chemin de fer exploitée en navette. **'shuttle-winder**, *s.* Dévidoir *m* (de machine à coudre).

shuttle², *v.tr.* & *i.* Faire la navette; aller et venir. **shuttling**, *s.* Va-et-vient *m*, navette *f.*

shuttlecock ['ʃʌtlkɔk], *s.* *Games:* Volant *m.*

shy¹ [ʃai], *s.* Écart *m*, faux bond (d'un cheval).

shy², *v.i.* (**shied**; **shying**) (*Of horse*) Faire un écart; broncher. **To s. at sth.**, prendre ombrage de qch. **shying**, *s.* Écart *m*, bronchement *m.* **Horse given to s.**, cheval ombrageux.

shy³, *a.* (**shyer**, **shyest**; *occ.* **shier**, **shiest**) Sauvage, farouche, timide; (*of horse*) ombrageux. **To make s.o. s.**, intimider qn. **She's not at all s.**, *F:* elle n'a pas froid aux yeux. **To fight s. of sth.**, se défier, se méfier, de qch. **To fight s. of a job**, éviter une besogne. **Don't pretend to be s.**, ne faites pas le, la, timide. **The fish are s.**, les poissons ne mordent pas. *S.a.* BITE² 1, WORK-SHY. **-ly**, *adv.* Timidement.

shy⁴, *s.* *F:* **1.** Jet *m*, lancement *m* (d'une pierre). (*At fairs*) **Three shies a shilling**, trois coups *m* pour un shilling. **2.** *O:* Essai *m*, tentative *f* (pour atteindre qch.).

shy⁵, *v.* (**shied**; **shying**) *F:* **1.** *v.i.* Lancer une pierre, une balle, etc. (**at**, à). **2.** *v.tr.* **To s. a stone at s.o.**, lancer une pierre à qn.

shyness ['ʃainis], *s.* Timidité *f*, réserve *f*; sauvagerie *f.*

shyster ['ʃaistər], *s.* *U.S:* *P:* Homme d'affaires, etc., véreux.

Siamese [,saiə'mi:z], *a.* & *s.* Siamois, -oise. **S. twins**, frères siamois, sœurs siamoises. **S. cat**, (chat) siamois.

Siberia [sai'biəriə]. *Pr.n.* La Sibérie.

Siberian [sai'biəriən], *a.* & *s.* Sibérien, -ienne.

sibilant ['sibilənt]. **1.** *a.* Sifflant. **2.** *s.* *Ling:* (Lettre) sifflante *f.*

sibyl ['sibil], *s.* Sibylle *f.*

sibylline ['sibilain], *a.* Sibyllin.

sic [sik], *Lt. adv.* Sic, ainsi.

siccative ['sikətiv], *a.* & *s.* Siccatif (*m*).

Sicilian [si'siljən], *a.* & *s.* Sicilien, -ienne.

Sicily ['sisili]. *Pr.n.* La Sicile.

sick¹ [sik], *a.* **1.** Malade. *s.pl.* **The s.**, les malades. *Mil:* **To report s.**, se faire porter malade. **2. To be s.**, vomir, rendre. **To feel s.**, avoir mal au cœur. **A s. feeling**, un malaise. **3. To be s. at heart**, être abattu. **He did look s.!** il en faisait une tête! *F:* **To be s. of sth.**, être las, dégoûté, de qch. *F:* **It makes me s.**, cela me donne la nausée. *F:* **I'm s. of it**, j'en ai assez, j'en ai plein le dos. *F:* **I'm s. and tired of telling you**, je me tue à vous le dire. **'sick-'bay**, *s.* *Navy:* Infirmerie *f*; poste *m* des malades. **S.-b. attendant**, infirmier *m.* **'sick-'bed**, *s.* Lit *m* de malade; lit de douleur. **'sick-'headache**, *s.* Migraine *f.* **'sick-'leave**, *s.* Congé *m* de maladie; de réforme. **'sick-list**, *s.* *Mil:* Rôle *m* des malades; état *m* des malades. **To be on the s.-l.**, être malade. **'sick-room**, *s.* Chambre *f* de malade.

sick², *v.tr.* *F:* **To s. sth. up**, vomir qch.

sicken ['sik(ə)n]. **1.** *v.i.* (*a*) Tomber malade (**of**, **with**, de). **To be sickening for an illness**, couver une maladie. (*b*) **To s. of sth.**, se lasser de qch. **2.** *v.tr.* (*a*) Rendre malade; donner mal au cœur à (qn). *F:* **His business methods s. me**, ses procédés me soulèvent le cœur. (*b*) **To s. s.o. of sth.**, dégoûter qn de qch. **sickening**, *a.* Écœurant, navrant. **S. fear**, crainte qui serre le cœur. **-ly**, *adv.* De façon à vous soulever le cœur, à vous écœurer.

sickener ['siknər], *s.* *F:* **1.** Déception *f*; aventure écœurante. **2.** Spectacle écœurant.

sickle ['sikl], *s.* *Agr:* Faucille *f.* **'sickle-feather**, *s.* Faucille *f* (de la queue du coq).

sickliness ['siklinis], *s.* **1.** État maladif. **2.** Pâleur *f* (du teint). **3.** Fadeur *f* (d'un goût); sentimentalité outrée (d'un roman).

sickly ['sikli], *a.* **1.** (*a*) Maladif, -ive, souffreteux, -euse, égrotant. (*b*) (*Of light*) Faible, pâle. **A s. white**, un blanc terreux. (*c*) **S. smile**, sourire pâle. **2.** (*Of climate*) Malsain, insalubre. **3.** (*Of taste*) Fade. **S.-sweet**, douceâtre.

sickness ['siknis], *s.* **1.** Maladie *f.* **Bed of s.**, lit de malade, de misère. **Is there any s. on board?** avez-vous des malades à bord? **2.** Mal *m*, maladie. **Mountain s.**, mal des montagnes. **Air s.**, mal de l'air, de l'avion. **Car s.**, mal de voiture. **3.** Mal de cœur; nausées *fpl.*

side¹ [said], *s.* Côté *m.* **1.** (*a*) Flanc *m.* (*Of animal*) **To lash its sides**, se battre les flancs. **By the s. of s.o.**, à côté de qn. **S. by s. (with s.o.)**, côte à côte (avec qn). *F:* **To split one's sides (with laughter)**, se tenir les côtes de rire. (*b*) **S. of bacon**, flèche *f* de lard. **2.** Côté (d'un triangle); flanc *m*, versant *m* (d'une montagne); paroi *f* (d'un fossé, d'un vase). **S. of a ship**, bord *m*, flanc. **3.** (*Surface*) (*a*) **The right s.**, wrong s. (of sth.), le bon, mauvais, côté (de qch.); l'endroit *m*, l'envers *m* (d'une étoffe). (*Of garment*) **Right s. out**, à l'endroit. **Wrong s. out**, à l'envers. *Bookb:* **Cloth sides of a book**, plats *m* toile d'un livre. *Gramophones:* Face *f* (d'un disque). *S.a.* BREAD. (*b*) **The bright s. of things**, le bon côté des choses. **The other s. of the picture**, le revers de la médaille. **To get on the soft s. of s.o.**, prendre qn par son endroit faible. **To get on the wrong s. of s.o.**, prendre qn à rebrousse-poil. **To hear both sides (of a question)**, entendre le pour et le contre. **To take sides**, sortir de la neutralité. **The weather's on the cool s.**, il fait plutôt froid. *S.a.* SEAMY. **4.** (*a*) **On this s.**, de ce côté-ci. **On the left-hand s.**, à (main) gauche. **On both sides**, des deux côtés, de part et d'autre. **On all sides**, de tous côtés. **To be on the right s. of forty**, avoir moins de quarante ans. **To move to one s.**, se ranger. **To put sth. on one s.**, mettre qch. à l'écart. (*b*) *F:* **To put on s.**, se donner des airs; poser; *P:* faire sa poire. **He puts on s.**, il est poseur. *F:* **To make sth. on the s.**, faire de la gratte. **5.** (*a*) Parti *m.* **He is on our s.**, il est de notre parti. **To change sides**, changer de camp. **You have the law on your s.**, vous avez la loi pour vous. **Mistakes made on both sides**, erreurs commises de part et d'autre. **Time is on our s.**, le temps travaille pour nous. (*b*) Section *f*, division *f.* (*c*) *Games:* Camp *m*, équipe *f.* **To pick sides**, tirer les camps. *Rugby Fb:* **No s.**, fin *f* de partie. (*d*) **Well connected on his mother's s.**, avoir de la bonne parenté par sa mère, du côté maternel. **6.** *attrib.* Latéral, de côté. **S. entrance**, entrée de côté. **S. door**, porte latérale. **To enter a profession through the s. door**, entrer dans une profession par la petite porte. *Ecc.Arch:* **S. aisle**, nef latérale; bas-côté *m.* **S. altar**, autel latéral. **S. street**, rue latérale, transversale. **S. road**, chemin latéral. **S. issue**, question d'intérêt secondaire. *Med:* **S. effect**, résultat secondaire. **'side-drum**, *s.* Tambour *m*, caisse *f.* **'side-face**, *s.* Profil *m.* **2.** *adv.* Taken s.-f., photographié de profil. **'side-glance**, *s.* Regard *m* de côté; coup *m* d'œil oblique. **'side-saddle**, *s.* Selle *f* de dame. **To ride s.-s.**, monter en amazone. **'side-show**, *s.* **1.** Spectacle, jeu, forain. **2.** *F:* Affaire *f* d'importance secondaire. **'side-splitting**, *a.* *F:* Désopilant, tordant; *P:* marrant. **'side-step. 1.** *v.i.* Faire un pas de côté

Box. esquiver. **2.** *v.tr.* Éviter (une question). **'side-table,** *s.* Petite table, desserte *f.* **'side-track,** *v.tr.* **1.** *Rail:* Garer (un train). **2.** Détourner l'attention (de qn). **'side-view,** *s.* Vue *f* de profil, de côté. **'side-whiskers,** *s.pl.* Favoris *m.*

side², *v.i.* To s. with s.o., se ranger du côté de qn.

sideboard ['saidbɔ:d], *s. Furn:* Buffet *m;* desserte *f.*

sideburns ['saidbə:nz], *s.pl. U.S: F:* Favoris *m.*

sidecar ['saidkɑ:r], *s. Aut:* Sidecar *m.*

-sided ['saidid], *a.* Five-s., à cinq faces, à cinq pans.

sidekick ['saidkik], *s. U.S: F:* Associé *m;* sous-fifre *m.*

sidelight ['saidlait], *s.* **1.** *Phot: etc:* Lumière *f* oblique. To throw a s. on a subject, donner un aperçu indirect sur un sujet. **2.** *Aut: Nau:* Feu *m* de position.

sideline ['saidlain], *s.* (a) Occupation *f* secondaire; violon d'Ingres. (b) *Com:* Article *m* à côté. (c) *Sp:* Ligne *f* de touche.

sidelong ['saidlɔŋ]. **1.** *adv.* (Se mouvoir) obliquement, de côté. **2.** *a.* (Regard) oblique, en coulisse.

sidereal [sai'diəriəl], *a.* Sidéral, -aux. **S.** time, heure *f* astronomique.

sidesman, *pl.* -men ['saidzmən], *s.m. Ecc:* = Marguillier adjoint.

sidewalk ['saidwɔ:k], *s. U.S:* Trottoir *m.*

sideways ['saidweiz]. **1.** *adv.* De côté; latéralement. To jump s., faire un saut de côté. To walk s., marcher en crabe. **To stand s.,** s'effacer. **2.** *a.* Latéral, -aux; de côté.

siding ['saidiŋ], *s. Rail:* (a) Voie *f* de garage, de service. (b) Embranchement *m,* voie privée. **Goods s.,** voie de chargement.

sidle ['saidl], *v.i.* **To s. along,** s'avancer de côté, de guingois. **To s. up to s.o.,** se couler auprès de qn.

siege [si:dʒ], *s. Mil:* Siège *m.* **To lay s. to a town,** assiéger une ville. **'siege-ar'tillery,** *s. Mil.Hist:* Artillerie *f* de siège.

Siena [si'enə]. *Pr.n. Geog:* Sienne *f.*

sienna [si'enə], *s.* Terre *f* de Sienne. **Raw, burnt, s.,** terre de Sienne naturelle, brûlée.

sierra [si'erə], *s.* Sierra *f.*

siesta [si'estə], *s.* Sieste *f,* méridienne *f.*

sieve¹ [siv], *s.* Crible *m;* tamis *m. Ind:* Sas *m,* crible. *S.a.* MEMORY 1. **2.** Personne qui ne sait pas garder le secret.

sieve², *v.tr.* = SIFT 1 (a).

sift [sift]. **1.** *v.tr.* (a) Passer (qch.) au tamis, au crible; tamiser; vanner (le blé); sasser (la farine). (b) Examiner minutieusement. **To s. a matter to the bottom,** éplucher une affaire. **To s. (out) the true from the false,** dégager le vrai du faux. **2.** *v.i.* (Of dust) Filtrer (through, à travers). **sifting,** *s.* **1.** (a) Tamisage *m,* criblage *m.* (b) Examen minutieux (des preuves). **2.** *pl.* **Siftings,** criblure(s) *f(pl).*

sifter ['siftər], *s.* **1.** (*Pers.*) Tamiseur *m,* cribleur *m; Ind:* sasseur *m.* **2.** (a) Tamis *m,* crible *m.* (b) Appareil *m* à cribler; cribleuse *f. Mill:* Sasseur *m.* **3.** Saupoudroir *m* (à sucre).

sigh¹ [sai], *s.* Soupir *m.* **To breathe a s.,** laisser échapper un soupir. **To heave a s.,** pousser un soupir.

sigh², *v.i.* (a) Soupirer; pousser un soupir. (b) **To s. for, after, sth.,** soupirer pour, après, qch. **sighing,** *s.* Soupirs *mpl.*

sight¹ [sait], *s.* **1.** (*Faculty of vision*) Vue *f.* (a) To have long s., avoir la vue longue. **Short s.,** myopie *f.* To lose one's s., perdre la vue; devenir aveugle. (b) To catch s. of s.o., apercevoir qn. **To lose s. of s.o.,** perdre qn de vue. *Nau:* To lose s. of land, perdre terre. **To lose s. of the fact that . . .,** perdre de vue que. . . . *F:* I can't bear the s. of him, je ne peux pas le sentir. **At s.,** à vue. **To translate at s.,** traduire à livre ouvert. *Mus:* **To play at s.,** jouer à vue. **To shoot s.o. at s.,** faire feu sur qn à première vue. *Com:* Bill payable at s., effet payable à vue. **At first s.,** à première vue; au premier abord. **Love at first s.,** coup *m* de foudre. **To know s.o. by s.,** connaître qn de vue. **2.** To come into s., (ap)paraître. **To come in s. of . . .,** arriver en vue de. . . . **To be within s.,** être à portée de la vue; être en vue. **Land in s.!** terre! **My goal is in s.,** j'approche de mon but. **Keep him in s.,** ne le perdez pas de vue. **Out**

of s., caché aux regards. He didn't let her out of his s., il ne la perdait pas de vue. *Prov:* Out of s., out of mind, loin des yeux, loin du cœur. **3.** *Surv:* Coup *m* de lunette. *Artil: Sm.a:* Visée *f. Nau:* To take a s. at the sun, observer le soleil. **4.** (a) Appareil *m* de visée; œilleton *m* (de viseur). (b) *Sm.a: Artil:* (Back-)s., hausse *f.* (Fore-)s., (i) *Sm.a:* guidon *m;* (bouton *m* de) mire *f;* (ii) *Artil:* fronteau *m* de mire. **With open sights,** à bout portant. **5.** (a) Spectacle *m.* **Sad s.,** spectacle navrant. It is a s. well worth seeing, cela vaut la peine d'être vu. It was a s. for sore eyes, c'était réjouissant à voir. (b) *F:* His face was a s., si vous aviez vu son visage! **What a s. you are!** comme vous voilà fait! (c) Chose digne d'être vue. **The sights,** les monuments *m,* les curiosités *f* (de la ville). **6.** *F:* A s. of . . ., énormément de. . . . He's a s. too clever for you, il est de beaucoup trop fort pour vous. **'sight-reading,** *s.* Déchiffrement *m* (de la musique); lecture *f* à vue. **'sight-testing,** *s.* Examen *m* de la vue.

sight², *v.tr.* **1.** Apercevoir, aviser (qn, qch.). *Nau:* To s. land, reconnaître la terre; relever la terre. **2.** Viser, observer (un astre). **3.** Pointer (un fusil). **sighting,** *s.* **1.** Vue *f.* **2.** Visée *f,* pointage *m.* **S. slit,** voyant *m* (d'un instrument scientifique). *Mil: etc:* **S.-shot,** coup *m* (préliminaire) de réglage, de visée.

sighted ['saitid], *a.* Qui voit. **The s.,** les voyants. **Weak-s.,** à la vue faible.

sightless ['saitlis], *a.* Aveugle; privé de la vue. **S. eyes,** yeux éteints.

sightlessness ['saitlisnis], *s.* Cécité *f.*

sightly ['saitli], *a.* Agréable à voir; avenant, séduisant.

sightseeing ['saitsi:iŋ], *s.* **To go s.,** visiter les monuments, les curiosités (d'une ville, etc.).

sightseer ['saitsi:ər], *s.* Touriste *mf;* excursionniste *mf.*

siglum, *pl.* **sigla** ['sigləm, 'siglə], *s. Pal:* Sigle *m.*

sign¹ [sain], *s.* **1.** Signe *m.* (a) To make a s. to s.o., faire (un) signe à qn. **To make an affirmative s.,** faire signe que oui. (b) **S. of recognition,** signe de reconnaissance. **2.** (a) Indice *m,* indication *f.* **Sure s.,** indice certain. **S. of rain,** signe de pluie. **S. of the times,** marque *f,* signe, des temps. **There is no s. of his coming,** rien n'annonce sa venue. (b) Trace *f.* **No s. of . . .,** nulle, aucune, trace de. . . . **To show no s. of life,** ne donner aucun signe de vie. **There was no s. of him,** il restait invisible. **3.** (a) Enseigne *f* (d'auberge). (b) (Shop-)s., enseigne. **Neon s.,** réclame *f* au néon. (c) *Aut: etc:* Panneau indicateur. **International road signs,** signalisation routière internationale. (d) *W.Tel: etc:* Studio warning s., indicateur *m* d'occupation. (e) **S. of the Zodiac,** signe du zodiaque. **4.** (*Written sign*) *Mth: Mus: etc:* Symbole *m.* **Positive s.,** signe positif. **5.** **S. of the cross,** signe de la croix. **sign-'manual,** *s.* Seing *m,* signature *f, esp.* la signature du souverain. **'sign-painter,** *s.* Peintre *m* d'enseignes. **'sign-writer,** *s.* Peintre *m* en lettres; peintre d'enseignes.

sign², *v.tr.* (a) Signer; marquer d'un signe. **To s. oneself,** se signer. (b) Signer (son nom); souscrire (une lettre de change). (*Countersign*) **S. please!** visa, s'il vous plaît! *S.a.* PLEDGE¹ 3. **sign away,** *v.tr.* Céder par écrit (une propriété). **sign off,** *v.i.* **1.** (*Of workmen*) Pointer au départ. **2.** *W.Tel:* Terminer l'émission. **sign on. 1.** *v.tr.* Embaucher (un ouvrier); engager (un matelot). **2.** *v.i.* (a) (*Of workmen*) S'embaucher; (*of seamen*) s'engager. (b) Pointer à l'arrivée. **sign up,** *v.i.* S'inscrire (à un cours, etc.). **signing,** *s.* Signature *f* (d'un document); souscription *f* (d'un acte).

signal¹ ['signəl], *s.* **1.** (*Sign*) Signal, -aux *m.* **To give the s. (for departure),** donner le signal (du départ). *W.Tel:* **Station s.,** indicatif *m* du poste (émetteur). *S.a.* CONTROL¹ 1, READY I. 1. **2.** (*Apparatus*) (a) (Visual) s., signal optique; voyant *m.* **Semaphore s.,** signal à bras. **S. bell,** avertisseur *m.* (b) *Rail:* **Home s.,** signal d'arrivée. (c) *Aut:* **Traffic signals,** feux *mpl* de circulation. **3.** *Navy:* **S. officer,** officier de transmissions. **Yeoman of the signals,** maître-timonier *m. Mil: F: pl.* **Signals,** les transmissions *fpl.* **'signal-book,** *s. Nau:* Code *m* de signaux. **'signal-box,** *s. Rail:* Cabine *f* à signaux; poste *m* d'aiguillage. **'signal-flag,** *s. Navy:* Pavillon *m* pour signaux. **'signal-lamp,** *s.* **1.** Lampe *f* de

signal. **2.** *Ind:* Lampe indicatrice, lampe témoin.
'**signal-light,** *s.* *Nau: etc:* Fanal *m*, -aux.
Signal-lights, feux *m* de route. '**signal-rocket,** *s.*
Fusée *f* de signalisation. '**signal-station,** *s. Nau:*
(*On board*) Poste *m* de timonerie; (*on land*) sémaphore *m.*
signal², *v.* (**signalled**) **1.** *v.i.* Donner un signal (to, à);
signaler. *Aut:* To s. before stopping, avertir avant
de stopper. **2.** *v.tr.* (*a*) Signaler (un train). (*b*)
Aut: To s. a turn, signaler un changement de
direction. (*c*) To s. to s.o. to stop, faire signe
à qn de s'arrêter. (*d*) *Rail:* **Track signalled for two-
way working,** voie banalisée. **signalling,** *s.* Signalisation *f*; transmission *f* de signaux. *Nau:* Timonerie
f. S.-flag, fanion-signal *m.*
signal³, *a.* (Service) signalé, insigne; (succès) éclatant.
-ally, *adv.* Remarquablement.
signalize ['signəlaiz], *v.tr.* Signaler, marquer (une
victoire).
signaller ['signələr], *s.* Signaleur *m.*
signalman, *pl.* -men ['signəlmən], *s.m.* **1.** *Rail:*
Aiguilleur *m.* **2.** *Navy:* Timonier.
signatory ['signət(ə)ri], *a. & s.* Signataire (*mf*).
signature ['signətər], *s.* **1.** Signature *f*; *Adm:* visa
m. Stamped s., griffe *f.* **2.** *Typ:* (*a*) Signature *f*
(d'un cahier). (*b*) **We are sending you the first four
signatures,** nous vous envoyons les quatre premiers
cahiers. **3.** *Mus:* Key-s., armature *f*, armure *f* (de
la clef). '**signature tune,** *s. W.Tel:* Indicatif musical.
signboard ['sainbɔːd], *s.* Enseigne *f* (d'auberge, etc.).
signet ['signit], *s.* **1.** Sceau *m*, cachet *m.* **2.** *Scot:*
Writer to the s. = avoué *m.* '**signet-ring,** *s.* (Bague
f) chevalière *f.*
significance [sig'nifikəns], *s.* **1.** Signification *f.* Look
of deep s., regard très significatif. **2.** Importance *f*,
conséquence *f.*
significant [sig'nifikənt], *a.* **1.** (Mot) significatif.
2. *Ar:* S. figure, chiffre significatif. **3.** (Événement)
important, de grande portée. -ly, *adv.* (Regarder)
d'une manière significative.
signification [signifi'keiʃ(ə)n], *s.* Signification *f*,
sens *m* (d'un mot, d'une phrase, etc.).
signify ['signifai]. **1.** *v.tr.* Signifier. (*a*) Être (le)
signe de (qch.). (*b*) Vouloir dire. **What does this
word s.?** que signifie ce mot? (*c*) Déclarer, faire
connaître (ses intentions). **2.** *v.i.* Importer. **It
doesn't s.,** cela n'importe guère.
signpost¹ ['sainpoust], *s.* Poteau indicateur.
signpost², *v.tr.* *F:* Signaliser (une route). **Road
inadequately signposted,** route dont la·signalisation
est défectueuse.
silage ['sailidʒ], *s.* *Husb:* Fourrage ensilé.
silence¹ ['sailəns], *s.* **1.** Silence *m.* (*a*) Dead s., silence
absolu. **A breathless s.,** un ·silence ému, anxieux.
Calls for s., des chut réitérés. **S.!** silence! du silence!
(*notice in reading-room*) silence *f* de parler. **S. gives
consent,** qui ne dit mot consent. (*b*) To pass over
sth. in s., passer qch. sous silence. (*c*) **The s. of the
night,** le silence de la nuit.
silence², *v.tr.* (*a*) Réduire (qn) au silence; faire taire
(un adversaire); étouffer (les plaintes). To s.
criticism, fermer la bouche à la critique. (*b*) Amortir,
étouffer (un bruit). *I.C.E:* To s. the exhaust,
assourdir l'échappement.
silencer ['sailənsər], *s.* Amortisseur *m* de son. *I.C.E:*
Silencieux *m*; pot *m* d'échappement.
silene [sai'liːni], *s.* *Bot:* Silène *m.*
silent ['sailənt], *a.* **1.** Silencieux, -euse. (*a*) To keep
s., (i) observer le silence; (ii) garder le silence,
se taire (**about,** sur). To become s., se taire. S. as
the tomb, muet comme la tombe. *U.S: Com:*
S. partner, (associé) commanditaire. (*b*) A s. man, un
homme silencieux, taciturne. **2.** (*a*) Silencieux,
insonore. S. running of the engine, allure silencieuse
du moteur. (*b*) *Ling:* S. letter, lettre muette. -ly,
adv. Silencieusement; en silence.
Silesia [sai'liːziə], *Pr.n. Geog:* La Silésie.
Silesian [sai'liːziən], *a. & s.* Silésien, -ienne.
silex ['saileks], *s.* *Miner:* Silex *m.*
silhouette¹ [silu(ː)'et], *s.* Silhouette *f.*
silhouette², *v.tr.* Silhouetter.
silica ['silikə], *s.* *Ch:* Silice *f.*
silicate ['silikit], *s.* *Ch:* Silicate *m.*

siliceous [si'liʃəs], *a. Ch:* Siliceux, -euse.
silicic [si'lisik], *a. Ch:* (Acide) silicique.
silicon ['silikən], *s. Ch:* Silicium *m.*
silicone ['silikoun], *s. Ch:* Silicone *f.*
silicosis [,sili'kousis], *s. Med:* Silicose *f*, chalicose
f.
silk [silk], *s.* **1.** Soie *f.* (*a*) Raw s., soie grège. **Thrown
s.,** soie moulinée; organsin *m.* **Sewing s.,** soie à
coudre. **S. stockings,** bas de soie. **The s. trade,** la
soierie. (*b*) *Tex:* Oiled s., taffetas *m* imperméable.
Artificial s., soie artificielle. **S. fabrics, silks,** soierie.
S.a. PURSE¹ 1, SOFT I. 1. **2.** *Jur:* To take s., être
nommé conseiller du roi, de la reine. '**silk-'finish,**
v.tr. Tex: Similiser. **S.-finished cotton,** *F:* simili *m.*
'**silk-moth,** *s. Ent:* Bombyx *m* du ver à soie.
silken ['silk(ə)n], *a. Lit:* **1.** Soyeux, -euse. S. tresses,
boucles de soie. **2.** (*Of voice*) Doucereux, -euse.
silkiness ['silkinis], *s.* **1.** Nature soyeuse (d'un tissu).
2. Moelleux *m* (de la voix).
silkworm ['silkwəːm], *s.* Ver *m* à soie. S. breeder,
sériciculteur *m*; magnanier, -ière.
silky ['silki], *a.* (*a*) Soyeux, -euse. (*b*) S. voice, voix
moelleuse. (*c*) *Pej:* Doucereux, -euse.
sill [sil], *s.* **1.** *Const:* Seuil *m* (de porte). **2.** (Window-)
s., tablette *f*, appui *m*, de fenêtre. **3.** *Min:* Sole *f*,
semelle *f* (d'une galerie). **4.** (*a*) *Geol:* Filon-couche
m. (*b*) *Oc:* Seuil.
silliness ['silinis], *s.* Sottise *f*, niaiserie *f.*
silly ['sili], *a.* **1.** Sot, *f.* sotte; niais. **S. answer,**
réponse *f* stupide, ridicule. **You s. boy!** petit nigaud!
s. You little s.! petite niaise! **S. ass!** imbécile!
gros bêta! To do sth. s., faire une bêtise. **2.** To
knock s.o. s., étourdir, assommer, qn.
silo¹ ['sailou], *s.* **1.** *Agr:* Silo *m.* **2.** *Ball:* **Launching
s.,** puits *m* de lancement.
silo², *v.tr. Agr:* Ensiler (du fourrage).
silt¹ [silt], *s.* Dépôt (vaseux); vase *f.* *Geol:* Limon *m.*
silt², *v.* To s. (up). **1.** *v.tr.* Envaser, ensabler (un port).
2. *v.i.* (*Of harbour*) S'envaser, s'ensabler. **silting
(up),** *s.* Envasement *m.*
Silurian [sai'ljuəriən], *a. Geol:* Silurien, -enne.
silver¹ ['silvər], *s.* **1.** Argent *m.* **2.** *attrib.* (*a*) D'argent,
en argent. **S. inkstand,** encrier en argent. **S. spoon,**
cuiller d'argent. **He was born with a s. spoon in his
mouth,** il est né coiffé. (*b*) *Cin: A:* S. screen,
écran argenté. *S.a.* CLOUD¹ 1. **3.** Argent monnayé.
S. coin, pièce *f* d'argent. **4.** *Coll.* Argenterie *f*;
vaisselle *f* d'argent. '**silver-'foil,** *s.* Feuille *f*
d'argent. '**silver 'fox,** *s. Z:* Renard argenté.
'**silver-gilt. 1.** *s.* Vermeil *m.* **2.** *a.* En vermeil.
'**silver-'headed,** *a.* **1.** *Lit:* Aux cheveux argentés.
2. (Canne) à pomme d'argent. '**silver-mounted,** *a.*
Monté en argent. '**silver 'paper,** *s.* Feuille *f*
d'étain; papier *m* d'étain. *F:* papier argent.
silver-'plate, *v.tr.* Argenter. **silver-'plated,** *a.*
Argenté. **S.-p. wares,** doublé *m* d'argent. '**silver-
plating,** *s.* Argenture *f*, argentage *m.* '**silver-
'tongued,** *a. Lit:* Éloquent; à la langue dorée.
'**silver-work,** *s.* Orfèvrerie *f.*
silver², *v.tr.* (*a*) Argenter. (*b*) Étamer (un miroir).
silvering, *s.* **1.** (*a*) Argentage *m.* (*b*) Étamage *m* (de
miroirs). **2.** (*a*) Argenture *f.* (*b*) Tain *m* (de miroir).
silverside ['silvəsaid], ,*s. Cu:* Gîte *m* à la noix.
silversmith ['silvəsmiθ], *s.* Orfèvre *m.*
silverware ['silvəweər], *s.* Argenterie *f* (de table).
silvery ['silvəri], *a.* (*a*) (Nuage) argenté; (écailles)
d'argent. (*b*) (Rire) argentin.
simian ['simiən], *a. & s.* Simien (*m*).
similar ['similər], *a.* (*a*) Semblable, pareil (to, à).
Geom: S. triangles, triangles semblables. (*b*) *Mth:*
S. products, produits similaires. -ly, *adv.* Pareillement, semblablement.
similarity [,simi'læriti], *s.* Ressemblance *f*, simi-
larité *f.* *Geom:* Similitude *f* (de triangles).
simile ['simili], *s. Rh:* Comparaison *f*, image *f.*
similitude [si'militjuːd], *s.* Similitude *f.*
simmer ['simər]. **1.** *v.i.* (*a*) (*Of liquid*) Frémir; (*of food
in pot*) mijoter, cuire à petit feu. To let the soup s.,
mitonner la soupe. (*b*) (*Of revolt, etc.*) Fermenter.
(*Of pers.*) To s. down, s'apaiser peu à peu. **2.** *v.tr.*
(Faire) mijoter (un ragoût). **simmering,** *s.* **1.**
Frémissement *m* (d'un liquide); cuisson à petit
feu. **2.** Ferment *m* (de révolte).

simnel cake ['simn(ə)lkeik], *s.* Gâteau *m* de Pâques.
Simon ['saimən]. *Pr.n.m.* Simon. *F:* **Simple S.,** niais *m. Esp. U.S:* The (real) S.(-)Pure, la véritable personne; l'objet *m* authentique.
simoniac [sai'mouniæk], **simoniacal** [ˌsaimə'naiək(ə)l], *a. Ecc:* Simoniaque.
simony ['saiməni,], *s. Ecc:* Simonie *f.*
simoon [si'mu:n], *s. Meteor:* Simoun *m.*
simper¹ ['simpər], *s.* Sourire affecté, minaudier.
simper², *v.i.* Minauder, mignarder. **simpering¹**, *a.* Minaudier, -ière. **simpering²**, *s.* Minauderie(s) *f(pl)*; grimaces *fpl.*
simple ['simpl]. **1.** *a.* (*a*) (*Of pers.*) Simple, naturel (de caractère); sans affectation. S. folk, les humbles, les petits. A s. soul, une bonne âme. (*b*) *Pej:* Naïf, *f.* naïve; crédule, niais. What a s. soul he is! ce qu'il est candide, naïf. *S.a.* SIMON. (*c*) S. problem, problème simple, peu difficile. As s. as ABC, as shelling peas, simple comme bonjour. (*d*) *Com:* S. interest, intérêts simples. *Gram:* S. sentence, proposition indépendante. (*e*) *Jur:* S. contract, convention verbale, tacite. (*f*) *F:* It's s. robbery, c'est du vol pur et simple. **2.** *s. Med: Bot: A:* **Simples,** simples *m*, herbes médicinales. **-ply,** *adv.* **1.** (Parler) simplement. **2.** (*a*) Absolument. You look s. lovely! vous êtes absolument parfaite! You s. must, il le faut absolument. *F:* The weather's s. ghastly! il fait un temps de chien. (*b*) Uniquement; tout simplement. He did it s. to test you, il l'a fait uniquement pour vous éprouver. I s. observed that . . ., je me suis borné à faire remarquer que. . . . **'simple-'hearted,** *a.* Simple, ingénu. **'simple-'minded,** *a.* Simple d'esprit; naïf, *f.* naïve. **'simple-'mindedness,** *s.* Simplicité *f* d'esprit; naïveté *f*; candeur *f.*
simpleness ['simplnis], *s.* = SIMPLICITY.
simpleton ['simpltən], *s.* Nigaud, -aude; niais, -aise; *F:* bêta, -asse.
simplicity [sim'plisiti], *s.* **1.** (*a*) Candeur *f*, simplicité *f* (d'un enfant). (*b*) Bêtise *f*, niaiserie *f.* **2.** (*a*) Simplicité (d'un problème). It is s. itself, c'est simple comme bonjour. (*b*) Absence *f* de recherche; simplicité (dans la mise).
simplification [ˌsimplifi'keiʃ(ə)n], *s.* Simplification *f.*
simplify ['simplifai], *v.tr.* Simplifier. To become simplified, se simplifier.
simply ['simpli], *adv. See* SIMPLE.
simulacrum, *pl.* **-a** [ˌsimju'leikrəm, -ə], *s.* Simulacre *m*, semblant *m.*
simulate ['simjuleit], *v.tr.* Simuler, feindre (une maladie); affecter (de l'enthousiasme).
simulation [ˌsimju'leiʃ(ə)n], *s.* Simulation *f*, feinte *f.*
simulator ['simjuleitər], *s.* **1.** Simulateur, -trice. **2.** *Av:* Simulateur (de vol).
simultaneity [ˌsimʌltən'i:iti], **simultaneousness** [ˌsimʌl-'teiniesnis], *s.* Simultanéité *f.*
simultaneous [ˌsim(ə)l'teiniəs], *a.* (*a*) Simultané. (*b*) S. with . . ., qui a lieu en même temps que. . . . **-ly,** *adv.* (*a*) Simultanément. (*b*) En même temps (with, que).
sin¹ [sin], *s.* (*a*) Péché *m.* **Original s.,** péché originel. The forgiveness of sins, le pardon des offenses *f.* To fall into s., tomber dans le péché. To live in s., *F:* vivre dans le collage. For my sins, I was appointed to . . ., pour mes péchés je fus nommé à. . . . As ugly as s., laid comme un singe. *F: O:* Like s., furieusement, violemment. (*b*) Offense (contre les convenances, le goût).
sin², *v.i.* (sinned) (*a*) Pécher. (*b*) To s. against propriety, manquer aux convenances. **sinning,** *s.* Le péché.
since [sins]. **1.** *adv.* Depuis. (*a*) Ever s., depuis (lors). (*b*) (*Ago*) Many years s., il y a bien des années. Long s., (i) depuis longtemps; (ii) il y a longtemps. How long is it s.? il y a combien de cela? **2.** *prep.* Depuis. He has been there since five o'clock, il est là depuis cinq heures. *F:* Since when do children answer their mothers back like that? Depuis quand répond-on comme ça à sa mère? S. that time, s. then, depuis lors. **3.** *conj.* (*a*) Depuis que; que. S. I have been here, depuis que je suis ici. It is just a week s. he came, il y a juste huit jours qu'il est arrivé. (*b*) Puisque. S. he is not of age, puisqu'il est mineur.

sincere [sin'siər], *a.* (*a*) Sincère; franc, -che. (*b*) (Sentiment) sincère. **-ly,** *adv.* Sincèrement. Yours s., cordialement à vous.
sincerity [sin'seriti], *s.* Sincérité *f*; bonne foi. In all s., de la meilleure foi du monde. Speaking in all s., en toute sincérité.
sine [sain], *s. Mth:* Sinus *m* (d'un angle). S. wave, onde sinusoïdale.
sinecure ['sainikjuər], *s.* Sinécure *f*; prébende *f.*
sinecurist ['sainikjuərist], *s.* Sinécuriste *mf.*
sinew ['sinju:], *s.* **1.** (*a*) Tendon *m.* (*b*) A man of s., un homme musclé; un homme fort. **2.** *pl.* Sinews, nerf *m*, force *f.* The sinews of war, le nerf de la guerre.
sinewy ['sinju(:)i], *a.* **1.** (*Of meat*) Tendineux, -euse. **2.** (Bras) musclé, nerveux.
sinful ['sinful], *a.* S. person, pécheur, *f.* pécheresse. S. pleasure, plaisir coupable. S. world, monde de pécheurs. S. waste, gaspillage scandaleux. **-fully,** *adv.* D'une façon coupable.
sinfulness ['sinfulnis], *s.* **1.** Caractère criminel (d'un acte); culpabilité *f.* **2.** Le péché.
sing [sin], *v.* (sang [san]; sung [sʌn]) **1.** *v.tr.* Chanter. *F:* To sing small, (i) déchanter; (ii) filer doux. To s. s.o. to sleep, endormir qn en chantant. **2.** *v.i.* (*a*) (*Of the wind, etc.*) Siffler; (*of the ears*) tinter, bourdonner. The kettle sings, la bouilloire chante. (*b*) *U.S: P:* Informer contre (qn); *P:* moucharder. **sing out. 1.** *v.tr. Nau: etc:* Crier (le fond, etc.). **2.** *F:* S.o. if you need me, appelez si vous avez besoin de moi. **singing¹,** *a.* (Oiseau) chanteur; qui chante. **'singing-buoy,** *s. Nau:* Bouée *f* sonore, à sifflet. **singing²,** *s.* **1.** Chant *m.* S. lesson, leçon de chant. *S.a.* COMMUNITY 3. **2.** Sifflement *m* (du vent, etc.). S. in the ears, bourdonnement *m*, tintement *m*, d'oreilles.
Singapore [ˌsingə'pɔːr]. *Pr.n.* Singapour.
singe¹ [sindʒ], *s.* **1.** Légère brûlure. **2.** *Hairdr:* Brûlage *m* (de la pointe des cheveux).
singe², *v.tr.* **1.** Brûler (qch.) légèrement; roussir (du linge, etc.). To s. one's wings, se brûler à la chandelle. **2.** Passer (qch.) à la flamme; flamber (une volaille). *Hairdr:* Brûler (la pointe des cheveux).
singer ['sinər], *s.* **1.** Chanteur; *f.* chanteuse, (*operatic etc.*) cantatrice. *Ecc:* Chantre *m.*
Singhalese [ˌsingə'li:z], *a. & s.* = SINHALESE.
single¹ ['singl], *s. Ten: Golf:* Partie *f* simple; simple *m. Ten:* Men's singles, simple messieurs.
single², *a.* **1.** (*a*) Seul, unique. Not a s. one, pas un seul; pas un. I haven't seen a s. soul, je n'ai pas vu âme qui vive. He hasn't a s. penny, il n'a pas le premier sou. *Fin:* S. premium, prime unique. (*b*) Individuel, -elle, particulier, -ière. Every s. day, tous les jours que Dieu fait. **2.** (*a*) S. bed, lit à une place, pour une personne. S. bedroom, chambre à un lit. In s. rank, sur un rang. (*b*) (*Of pers.*) Célibataire; non marié(e). To lead a s. life, vivre dans le célibat. **3.** Sincère, honnête, simple. **-gly,** *adv.* **1.** Séparément; un à un. **2.** Seul; sans aide. **'single-'barrelled,** *a.* (Fusil) à un canon, à un coup. **'single-'breasted,** *a. Cost:* (Veston) droit. **'single-cylinder,** *attrib.a.* Monocylindrique. **single-'handed,** *a.* **1.** (Arme, instrument) qui se manie d'une main. **2.** (Accomplir une tâche) seul, sans aide, tout seul. **single-'hearted,** *a.* (*Of pers.*) Sincère, honnête, droit; loyal, -aux. **single-'heartedness,** *s.* Sincérité *f*; loyauté *f.* **single-'minded,** *a.* **1.** = SINGLE-HEARTED. **2.** Qui ne vise qu'un but. **single-'mindedness,** *s.* **1.** = SINGLE-HEARTEDNESS. **2.** Unité *f* d'intention. **'single-phase,** *attrib.a. El.E:* Monophasé. **'single-'track,** *attrib.a. Rail:* (Ligne) à voie unique. To have a s.-t. mind, être incapable d'envisager deux idées à la fois.
single³, *v.tr.* To s. out s.o., sth., (i) choisir qn, qch., (ii) remarquer, distinguer, qn, qch. (for, pour; as, comme).
singleness ['singlnis], *s.* **1.** Sincérité *f*, droiture *f.* **2.** Unicité *f.* With s. of purpose, avec un seul but en vue. **3.** Célibat *m.*
singlestick ['singlstik], *s. Sp:* Canne *f.*
singlet ['singlit], *s.* **1.** Gilet *m* de corps. **2.** *Sp:* Maillot fin.

singleton ['siŋglt(ə)n], s. Cards: Singleton m.
singsong ['siŋsɔŋ]. 1. a. S. voice, voix f monotone. 2. s. (a) Chant m monotone; psalmodie f. (b) F: Concert improvisé (entre amis).
singular ['siŋgjulər], a. 1. Gram: Singulier. s. In the s., au singulier. 2. (a) Rare, remarquable, surprenant. (b) Singulier, bizarre. -ly, adv. Singulièrement. (a) Remarquablement. (b) Bizarrement.
singularity [,siŋgju'læriti], s. Singularité f. 1. Particularité f. 2. Bizarrerie f.
singularize ['siŋgjuləraiz], v.tr. Singulariser.
Sinhalese [,sin(h)ə'liːz], a. & s. inv. Cingalais, -aise.
sinister ['sinistər], a. 1. Sinistre. With a s. purpose, dans un mauvais dessein. A man of s. appearance, un homme de mauvaise mine. 2. Her: Sénestre.
sink¹ [siŋk], s. 1. (a) Évier m (de cuisine). S. trap, siphon m d'évier. S. basket, (passoire f de) coin m d'évier. To pour (sth.) down the s., jeter (qch.) à l'égout. (b) S. of iniquity, cloaque m, bourbier m, sentine f, de tous les vices. 2. = SINK-HOLE 2. 3. Th: Trappe f (de plateau). 'sink-hole, s. 1. Souillard m (de dallage, etc.); puisard m. 2. Geol: Aven m.
sink², v. (sank [sæŋk]; sunk [sʌŋk], A: & a. sunken ['sʌŋkən]) I. v.i. 1. Tomber au fond (des eaux); aller au fond; (of ship) couler au fond; couler bas; sombrer. (Of ship) To s. by the bow, couler de l'avant. He was left to s. or swim, il fut abandonné à la grâce de Dieu. Here goes! s. or swim! allons-y! advienne que pourra! 2. To s. into sth. (a) S'enfoncer, pénétrer (dans la boue, etc.). The dye must be allowed to s. in, il faut donner à la teinture le temps de pénétrer. (Of words) To s. into the memory, se graver dans la mémoire. His words begin to s. in, ses paroles commencent à faire impression. (b) Tomber (dans le vice, dans l'oubli). To s. deep(er) into crime, s'enfoncer dans le crime. To s. into insignificance, devenir insignifiant. (c) To s. into oneself, rentrer en soi-même; se recueillir. 3. (Subside) (a) To s. (down), s'affaisser; (of building) se tasser. (b) (Of pers) s'enfoncer, se renfoncer. To s. (down) into a chair, se laisser tomber, s'affaler, dans un fauteuil. To s. on one's knees, (se laisser) tomber à genoux. His legs sank under him, ses jambes se plièrent sous lui. His heart sank, son cœur se serra; le cœur lui manqua. His spirits sank, son courage s'abattit. 4. Descendre; aller en descendant; s'abaisser. To s. out of sight, disparaître. The sun is sinking, le soleil baisse. 5. Baisser (en valeur); diminuer; s'affaiblir, décliner. The patient is sinking, le malade baisse. He has sunk in my estimation, il a baissé, diminué, dans mon estime. II. sink, v.tr. 1. (a) Couler, faire sombrer (un navire); envoyer (un navire) au fond. (b) Mouiller (une mine). 2. Baisser (la voix); enfoncer (un pieu, etc.). 3. (a) Creuser, foncer (un puits). To s. a bore-hole, opérer un sondage. (b) Engr: To s. a die, graver un coin en creux. 4. Supprimer (une objection, etc.). They sank their differences, ils ont fait table rase de leurs différends. 5. Fin: Éteindre, amortir (une dette). 6. (a) To s. money in an annuity, placer de l'argent en viager. (b) To s. money in an unfortunate undertaking, enterrer, engloutir, de l'argent dans une entreprise malheureuse. **sinking¹**, a. (Navire) qui coule; (navire) en perdition. With s. heart, avec un serrement de cœur. **sinking²**, s. 1. (a) Enfoncement m (des pieds dans la boue, etc.); enlisement m (de qn dans une fondrière); engloutissement m (d'un navire). (b) The s. of a ship (in war), le torpillage d'un navire. 2. Affaissement m, abaissement m (du sol, etc.); oppression f (du cœur). F: That s. feeling, ce sentiment de défaillance. 3. Affaiblissement m, déclin m (des forces, etc.); abaissement m (de la voix, etc.). 4. Creusage m, foncement m (d'un puits). 5. (a) Amortissement m, extinction f (d'une dette). (b) Placement m (d'une somme) à fonds perdu. 'sinking-fund, s. Caisse f d'amortissement.
sinker ['siŋkər], s. 1. Well-s., shaft-s., fonceur m de puits; puisatier m. 2. (a) Navy: Crapaud m d'amarrage (d'une mine). (b) Plomb m (d'une ligne de pêche). (c) U.S: F: (i) Mauvaise pièce (de monnaie). (ii) Gâteau lourd; beignet soufflé.

sinless ['sinlis], a. Sans péché; innocent.
sinlessness ['sinlisnis], s. Innocence f, pureté f.
sinner ['sinər], s. (a) Pécheur, f. pécheresse. (b) F: Mauvais sujet.
sinuosity [,sinju'ɔsiti], s. Sinuosité f; lacet m (de la route).
sinuous ['sinjuəs], a. 1. Sinueux, -euse. 2. (Of pers.) Souple, agile.
sinus ['sainəs], s. Anat: Sinus m, antre m. Med: Fistule f. S. tract, trajet fistuleux.
sinusitis [,sainə'saitis], s. Med: Sinusite f.
sinusoid ['sainəsɔid], s. Mth: Sinusoïde f.
sip¹ [sip], s. Petit coup; petite gorgée; F: goutte f.
sip², v.tr. (sipped) Boire à petits coups, à petites gorgées. To s. one's coffee, siroter, déguster, savourer, humer, son café.
siphon¹ ['saif(ə)n], s. Siphon m. (a) S. barometer, baromètre à siphon. (b) Siphon à eau de seltz, à soda.
siphon², v.tr. Siphonner (un liquide).
sir¹ [səːr, sər], s. 1. (a) Monsieur m. Yes, s., (i) oui, monsieur; (ii) Mil: (to superior officer) oui, mon capitaine; oui, mon colonel, etc.; (iii) Navy: oui, commandant; oui, amiral. Dinner is served, s., monsieur est servi. (b) Corr: S., (my) dear S., Monsieur. 2. Sir (titre d'un baronet et d'un knight); ne s'emploie jamais sans le prénom.
sir², v.tr. F: Appeler qn Monsieur. Don't s. me, ne m'appelez pas Monsieur. He was sirring me all the time, il m'appelait Monsieur gros comme le bras.
sire¹ [saiər], s. 1. (a) A. & Poet: Père m, aïeul m. (b) Breed: Père m (en parlant des quadrupèdes); esp. étalon m. 2. (In addressing sovereigns) Sire m.
sire², v.tr. Breed: Engendrer (un poulain, etc.).
siren ['saiərən], s. 1. (a) Myth: Sirène f. (b) F: O: Femme fatale; tentatrice f; sirène. 2. Ind: Nau: etc: Sirène (de navire, d'usine, d'alarme).
sirloin ['səːlɔin], s. Cu: Aloyau m (de bœuf); faux-filet m.
sirocco [si'rɔkou], s. Meteor: Sirocco m.
sisal ['sais(ə)l], s. Bot: Agave f d'Amérique; sisal m.
sissy ['sisi], s. F: Pej: 1. (a) Homme, garçon, efféminé. (b) Enfant, etc., peureux; poule mouillée.
sister ['sistər], s.f. 1. Sœur f. 2. (a) Ecc: Religieuse; sœur. S. Ursula, la sœur Ursule. (b) (In hospital) (Ward-)s., surveillante; infirmière-major. 3. attrib. S. nations, nations sœurs. S. ships, navires-jumeaux m. 'sister-in-law, s.f. Belle-sœur, pl. belles-sœurs.
sisterhood ['sistəhud], s. Communauté religieuse.
sisterly ['sistəli], a. De sœur.
Sistine ['sistain, -tiːn], a. The S. chapel, la chapelle Sixtine.
sit [sit], v. (p.t. sat [sæt]; p.p. sat; pr.p. sitting) I. v.i. 1. (a) (Of pers.) S'asseoir; être assis, rester assis; se tenir (dans une pièce, etc.). She is a s.-by-the-fire, elle ne quitte pas le coin du feu; elle est casanière. To s. still, rester sans bouger; rester tranquille. P: He does nothing but s. on his behind, F: il ne bouge pas d'une semelle! To s. with s.o., tenir compagnie à qn. To s. at home, se tenir chez soi. To s. at table, être à table. To s. over one's work, rester attablé à son travail. To s. over a pipe, rester (assis) à savourer une pipe. To s. over a book, s'absorber dans la lecture d'un livre. F: To s. tight, ne pas bouger de sa place; ne pas se laisser ébranler; ne pas céder. F: To s. on s.o., rabrouer qn; rabaisser le caquet à qn. S.a. EXAMINATION 2. (b) To s. for one's portrait, poser pour son portrait. To s. for an artist, poser chez un artiste. (c) To s. on the committee, on the jury, être du comité, du jury. To s. in Parliament, siéger au parlement. 2. (Of assemblies) Siéger; être en séance. A committee is sitting on the question, une commission discute la question. Jur: (Of judge) To s. on a case, juger une affaire. F: To s. on a project, laisser dormir un projet. 3. (a) (Of bird) (Se) percher; être perché, posé. (b) (Of hen) To s. (on eggs), couver (des œufs). (c) To find a hare sitting, trouver un lièvre au gîte. To shoot a pheasant sitting, tirer un faisan à terre, un faisan posé. 4. O: How sits the wind? d'où vient le vent? This food sits heavy on the stomach, cette nourriture pèse sur l'estomac. His responsibilities s. heavy upon him, ses responsabilités lui sont à charge. (b) (Of garments) Tomber (bien, mal);

(bien ou mal) aller. II. **sit**, *v.tr.* **1. To s. a horse well, badly,** se tenir bien, mal, à cheval; avoir une bonne, mauvaise, assiette. **2. To s. a child on the table,** asseoir un enfant sur la table. **To s. (oneself) down,** s'asseoir. **sit back,** *v.i.* **To s. b. in one's chair,** se renverser dans sa chaise, son fauteuil; *F:* se relaxer. **sit down,** *v.i.* S'asseoir; prendre un siège. **Please s. d.,** asseyez-vous; veuillez vous asseoir. **To s. d. to table,** s'attabler; se mettre à table. **To s. d. under an insult,** empocher, avaler, une insulte. *F:* **To s. d. hard on a plan,** s'opposer résolument à un projet. **'sit-down,** *attrib.a.* **S.-d. strike,** grève *f* sur le tas. **sit out,** *v.tr.* **1.** Ne pas prendre part à (un jeu etc.). **To s. o. a dance (with s.o.),** faire la causette (avec son cavalier) pendant que les autres dansent. **2.** (*a*) **To s. a lecture o.,** rester (patiemment) jusqu'à la fin d'une conférence. (*b*) **To s. s.o. out,** rester jusqu'après le départ de qn. **sit up,** *v.i.* **1.** (*a*) Se tenir droit; se redresser (sur sa chaise). *F:* **To make s.o. s. up,** étonner qn. (*b*) **To s. up (in bed),** se mettre, se lever, sur son séant. **He is beginning to s. up and take notice,** il est en train de se remettre. **2. To s. up late,** veiller tard; se coucher tard. **To s. up for s.o.,** (rester levé à) attendre qn. **To s. up with a sick person,** veiller un malade. **3. To s. up to the table,** approcher sa chaise de la table. **sitting¹,** *a.* **1.** Assis. *F:* **To be s. pretty,** avoir une bonne place, *F:* tenir le filon. **2.** (*Of tribunal, etc.*) En séance; siégeant. **3.** (*a*) (*Gibier*) posé, au repos. (*b*) **S. hen,** poule en train de couver. **sitting²,** *s.* **1.** (*a*) Posture assise. **S. and standing room,** places assises et places debout. (*b*) **To paint a portrait in three sittings,** faire un portrait en trois séances *f.* **2.** (*a*) **To serve 500 people at one s.,** servir 500 personnes à la fois. **To write two chapters at one s.,** écrire deux chapitres d'un seul jet, d'arrache-pied. (*b*) Séance, réunion *f* (d'une commission, etc.); tenue *f* (d'une assemblée). **S. of a court,** audience *f.* **3.** *Husb:* (*a*) (*Of hen*) Couvaison *f*, incubation *f.* (*b*) Couvée *f* (d'œufs). **'sitting room,** *s.* **1.** Salle *f* de séjour, living-room *m*, *pl.* living-rooms, *F:* living *m.* **2.** (*Space*) Place *f* pour s'asseoir; (*in bus, etc.*) places assises. **site** [sait], *s.* **1.** Emplacement *m* (d'un édifice, d'une ville); assiette *f* (d'un camp). **Caravan, camp(ing), s.,** camping *m.* *Archeol:* **Prehistoric s.,** gisement *m* préhistorique. **2.** Chantier *m.* **Building s.,** (i) terrain *m* à bâtir; (ii) chantier de construction. **sitter** ['sitər], *s.* **1.** (*a*) Personne assise. (*b*) **Baby s., s. in,** garde-bébé *mf*, *pl.* gardes-bébés. **2.** *Art:* (*a*) Modèle *mf.* (*b*) Client, -ente. **3.** (*a*) (*Poule*) couveuse *f.* (*b*) **To fire at a s.,** tirer sur le gibier posé. **situate** ['sitjueit], *v.tr.* Situer (une maison, etc.). **situated,** *a.* **1. Pleasantly s. house,** maison bien située. **2.** (*Of pers.*) **This is how I am s.,** voici la situation dans laquelle je me trouve. **Awkwardly s.,** dans une position embarrassante. **situation** [ˌsitjuˈeiʃ(ə)n], *s.* **1.** Situation *f*, emplacement *m* (d'un édifice). **2.** Situation (politique, financière). **3.** Emploi *m*, (*of servant*) place *f.* **To get a s.,** obtenir un emploi. **To be out of a s.,** être sans place; se trouver sans emploi. **Situations vacant,** offres *fpl* d'emplois. **six** [siks], *num.* *a.* & *s.* Six (*m*). **I have s.,** j'en ai six. **Two and s.,** deux shillings et six pence. **Coach and s.,** carrosse à six chevaux. (*At dominoes*) **The double s.,** le double six. **It is s. of one and half a dozen of the other,** c'est bonnet blanc et blanc bonnet; *P:* c'est kif-kif. **Everything is at sixes and sevens,** tout est désorganisé, en désordre; tout est sens dessus dessous, *F:* en pagaille. (*For other phrases see* EIGHT.) **'six-'eight,** *s.* *Mus:* (Mesure *f* à) six-huit *m.* **'six-foot,** *attrib.a.* *Rail:* **The s.-f. way,** l'entre-voie *f.* **six-'footer,** *s.* *F:* Homme (haut) de six pieds. **'six-'shooter,** *s.* Revolver *m*, pistolet *m* à six coups. **sixfold** ['siksfould]. **1.** *a.* Sextuple. **2.** *adv.* Six fois autant; au sextuple. **sixpence** ['sikspəns], *s.* **1.** Six pence. **2.** Pièce *f* de six pence. **sixpenny** ['sikspəni], *attrib.a.* (Journal, etc.) qui coûte, qui vaut, six pence; à, de, six pence. **S. piece, bit,** pièce *f* de six pence. **sixpennyworth** [siksˈpeniwəːθ], *s.* **To buy s. of chocolate,** acheter pour six pence de chocolat.

sixteen ['siksˈtiːn], *num.* *a.* & *s.* Seize (*m*). **She is s.,** elle a seize ans. (*For other phrases see* EIGHT.) **sixteenth** ['siksˈtiːnθ], *num.* *a.* & *s.* Seizième (*mf*). **Louis the S.,** Louis Seize. **(On) the s. (of August),** le seize (août). **sixth** [siksθ]. **1.** *num.* *a.* & *s.* Sixième (*mf*). *Sch:* **The s.** (form), *approx.* = la classe de première. **2.** *s.* (*a*) (*Fractional*) Sixième *m.* (*b*) *Mus:* Sixte (majeure, mineure). **-ly,** *adv.* Sixièmement, en sixième lieu. **sixtieth** ['sikstiiθ], *num.* *a.* & *s.* Soixantième (*mf*). **sixty** ['siksti], *num.* *a.* & *s.* Soixante (*m*). **S.-one,** soixante et un. **He is in the sixties,** il a passé la soixantaine. **In the sixties (of our century),** pendant les années soixante (de notre siècle). **sizable** ['saizəbl], *a.* = SIZEABLE. **size¹** [saiz], *s.* **1.** (*a*) Grandeur *f*, dimension *f*, grosseur *f*, volume *m.* **All of a s.,** tous de la même grosseur; tous de même taille. **Drawn full s., life s.,** dessiné à grandeur naturelle. *F:* *O:* **That's about the s. of it,** c'est à peu près cela. (*b*) *Ind:* **To cut a piece to s.,** tailler une pièce à la dimension, à la cote. **2.** (*a*) (*Of pers., horse, etc.*) Taille *f.* (*b*) *Com:* Numéro *m* (d'un article); taille (de vêtements); encolure *f* (de chemises); pointure *f* (de chaussures, de gants). **Small s.,** petit modèle. **What s. do you take?** (*in dresses, etc.*) quelle est votre taille? (*in shoes*) quelle pointure chaussez-vous? (*in hats*) du combien coiffez-vous? (*c*) Format *m* (d'un livre, etc.). (*d*) Calibre *m* (d'un fusil); grosseur (du plomb de chasse). **size²,** *v.tr.* **1.** Classer (des objets) par grosseur, par dimension. **2.** *Ind:* (*a*) Calibrer. (*b*) Mettre (une pièce) à la cote, à dimension. **size up,** *v.tr.* Jauger; prendre les dimensions de (qch.). **To s. s.o. up,** classer, juger, qn. **I have sized him up,** j'ai pris sa mesure. **sized,** *a.* **Fair-s.,** assez grand. **Large-s.,** de grande taille; de grandes dimensions. **size³,** *s.* *Tchn:* Apprêt *m.* (*a*) Colle *f.* **Animal s.,** colle animale. (*b*) *Tex:* Empois *m.* **size⁴,** *v.tr.* Apprêter, coller, encoller (le papier, etc.). **sizeable** ['saizəbl], *a.* D'une belle taille; assez grand. **sizzle¹** ['sizl], *s.* Grésillement *m.* **sizzle²,** *v.i.* Grésiller. (*of gas*) chuinter. **Sizzling hot,** tout chaud. **skate¹** [skeit], *s.* *Ich:* Raie *f.* **skate²,** *s.* Patin *m.* *S.a.* ROLLER-SKATES. **skate³,** *v.i.* Patiner. **To s. over sth.,** effleurer un sujet. **To s. round sth.,** tourner autour du pot. **To s. on thin ice,** toucher à un sujet délicat; manier habilement une situation délicate. **skating,** *s.* Patinage *m.* **'skating-rink,** *s.* (*a*) Patinoire *f.* (*b*) Skating *m*; piste *f*, salle *f*, de patinage. **skater** ['skeitər], *s.* Patineur, -euse. **skedaddle¹** [skiˈdædl], *s.* *F:* *O:* (i) Fuite précipitée; (ii) débandade *f.* **skedaddle²,** *v.i.* *F:* *O:* (*a*) Se sauver à toutes jambes; déguerpir. (*b*) S'enfuir à la débandade. **skein** [skein], *s.* (*a*) Écheveau *m* (de fil de soie, de laine). (*b*) **Tangled s.,** confusion *f*, *F:* (em)brouillamini *m.* (*c*) Vol *m* (d'oies sauvages). **skeletal** ['skelit(ə)l], *a.* Squelettique. **skeleton** ['skelit(ə)n], *s.* **1.** Squelette *m*, ossature *f.* **The s. in the cupboard,** le secret honteux de la famille. **The s. at the feast,** le rabat-joie. **2.** (*a*) Charpente *f*, carcasse *f*, ossature *f* (d'un navire, etc.). **S. key,** crochet *m* (de serrurier); fausse clef; *F:* rossignol *m.* (*b*) Monture *f*, carcasse (d'un parapluie). (*c*) Canevas *m*, esquisse *f* (d'un roman, etc.). (*d*) **S. map,** carte muette. (*d*) **S. staff,** personnel réduit. **A s. staff of three is always on duty,** la permanence comprend trois employés. **S. army,** armée-cadre *f.* **skep** [skep], *s.* **1.** Panier *m*; harasse *f.* **2.** *Ap:* Ruche *f* en paille. **sketch¹** [sketʃ], *s.* **1.** (*a*) Croquis *m*, esquisse *f.* (**Rough) s.,** griffonnement *m*, griffonnage *m.* **Free-hand s.,** dessin *m* à main levée. (*b*) *Mil:* Levé *m* topographique. (*c*) *Ind:* **Dimensioned s.,** croquis coté. **2.** (*a*) **S. of procedure to be adopted,** exposé *m* de la procédure à adopter. (*b*) *Th:* Saynète *f.* **'sketchbook,** *s.* Cahier *m*, album *m*, de croquis. **'sketchmap,** *s.* Carte-croquis *f*, *pl.* cartes croquis; plan *m* sommaire d'un terrain; *F:* topo *m.*

sketch², *v.tr.* Esquisser, dessiner à grands traits, croquer (un paysage, etc.); faire le croquis de (qch.). **sketch in**, *v.tr.* Dessiner sommairement (les détails, etc.). **sketching**, *s.* Prise *f* de croquis; dessin *m* à main levée.

sketcher ['sketʃər], *s.* Artiste *m* (peintre), aquarelliste *mf*, amateur.

sketchiness ['sketʃinis], *s.* Manque *m* de précision, de perfection.

sketchy ['sketʃi], *a.* F: (Ouvrage) qui manque de précision, de perfection. S. knowledge, connaissances superficielles. -ily, *adv.* D'une manière imprécise, incomplète, vague.

skew¹ [skju:], *s.* Biais *m*, obliquité *f* (d'un pont, d'une arche). On the s., en biais; obliquement.

skew². 1. *a.* Arch: Mec: etc: (Pont, mur) biais; (section) oblique. 2. *adv.* (also F: **skew-'whiff**) En biais; de travers. **'skew-eyed**, *a.* F: Aux yeux louches.

skew³. 1. *v.i.* Biaiser, obliquer. 2. *v.tr.* Couper en sifflet.

skewbald ['skju:bɔ:ld], *a.* (Cheval) blanc et roux.

skewer¹ ['skju(:)ər], *s.* 1. Cu: Brochette *f*, hâtelet *m*. 2. F: Baïonnette *f*, épée *f*.

skewer², *v.tr.* Brocheter (une volaille); embrocher (un gigot).

ski¹ [ski:], *s.* Ski *m*. S.-runner, skieur, -euse. S. tip, spatule *f*. **'ski-binding**, *s.* Fixation *f*. **'ski-jump**, *s.* 1. (Action) Saut *m* à, en, ski(s). 2. Skiing: (Obstacle) Civ.E: (Overflow device) Saut de ski. **'ski-lift**, *s.* Sp: (Re)monte-pente *m inv*, téléski *m*.

ski², *v.i.* (ski'd; ski'd; *pr.p.* ski-ing, skiing) Faire du ski; skier. **ski-ing, skiing**, *s.* Le ski.

skid¹ [skid], *s.* Aut: etc: Dérapage *m*.

skid², *v.i.* (skidded) (a) Aut: etc: Déraper, glisser. (b) Av: Glisser sur l'aile. **skidding**, *s.* Dérapage *m*. **'skid-pan**, *s.* Aut: Piste savonnée.

skier ['ski:ər], *s.* Skieur, -euse.

skiff [skif], *s.* 1. Nau: (a) Esquif *m*, yole *f*. (b) Youyou *m*. 2. Row: Skiff *m*.

skilful ['skilful], *a.* Adroit, habile. -fully, *adv.* Habilement, adroitement.

skilfulness ['skilfulnis], *s.* Habileté *f*, adresse *f*.

skill [skil], *s.* Habileté *f*, adresse *f*, dextérité *f*. Technical s., compétence *f* (technique). S. in doing sth., talent *m* pour faire qch. Want, lack, of s., maladresse *f*.

skilled [skild], *a.* Habile. S. labour, main-d'œuvre spécialisée, professionnelle. To be s. in an art, in business, être fort en, versé dans, un art; se connaître en affaires.

skillet ['skilit], *s.* Cu: 1. Poêlon *m* à trois pieds. 2. U.S: Poêle *f*.

skilly ['skili], *s.* Cu: = Lavasse *f*.

skim¹ [skim], *s.* (a) Vol plané (d'un oiseau, d'un avion). (b) To take, have, a s. through a book, parcourir rapidement un livre. **'skim-milk**, *s.* Lait écrémé.

skim², *v.tr. & i.* (skimmed) 1. Écumer (le bouillon); écrémer (le lait, etc.); dégraisser (la soupe). To s. the cream off sth., prendre la meilleure partie de qch. 2. Effleurer, raser (une surface). To s. along, passer légèrement; glisser. To s. (over, through) a novel, parcourir rapidement, feuilleter, un roman.

skimmer ['skimər], *s.* 1. (For soup) Écumoire *f*; (for milk) écrémoir(e) *m(f)*, écrémeuse *f*.

skimp [skimp], *v.tr.* 1. (a) To s. s.o. for food, mesurer la nourriture à qn; compter les morceaux à qn. (b) To s. the food, lésiner sur la nourriture. To s. the material in making a dress, être parcimonieux, -euse de tissu. Skimped coat, habit étriqué. 2. F: To s. one's work, saboter, bâcler, son ouvrage.

skimpiness ['skimpinis], *s.* Insuffisance *f*, manque *m*. S. of a skirt, aspect étriqué d'une jupe.

skimpy ['skimpi], *a.* S. skirt, jupe étriquée, (bien) juste. S. meal, maigre repas. -ily, *adv.* Insuffisamment, parcimonieusement (meublé, etc.).

skin¹ [skin], *s.* 1. Peau *f*. (i) Outer s., épiderme *m*. (ii) True s., derme *m*. To have a thin s., être susceptible. To have a thick s., avoir la peau dure. (Of snake, etc.) To cast, throw, its s., faire peau neuve. Next (to) one's s., à même, sur, la peau. To strip to the s., F: se mettre à poil. He is nothing but s. and bone, il n'a que la peau et les os. To come out of it with a whole s., s'en tirer sain et sauf, indemne. By the s. of one's teeth, de justesse. To save one's (own) s., sauver sa peau, se tirer d'affaire, échapper au désastre. F: To get under s.o.'s s., donner sur les nerfs à qn; échauffer les oreilles à qn. P: I've got her under my s., je l'ai dans la peau. 2. (a) Dépouille *f*, peau (d'un animal). Fur skins, pelleterie *f*. Raw skins, peaux vertes. (b) (For wine, etc.) Outre *f*. (c) Feuille *f* (de parchemin). 3. (a) Bot: Tunique *f* (d'une graine); pellicule *f* (d'un grain de café). (b) Peau (de fruit, de saucisson). Cu: Potatoes boiled in their skins, pommes de terre en robe de chambre. 4. Nau: Bordé extérieur (d'un canot). Av: Revêtement *m* (du fuselage). 5. (a) Crème *f*, peau (sur le lait, etc.). (b) Metall: Croûte *f* (de la fonte). **'skin-'deep**, *a.* (Of wound, emotions) A fleur de peau; superficiel. **'skin-'dip**, *s.* U.S: Bain *m* de minuit. **'skin-disease**, *s.* Maladie de (la) peau. **'skin-diver**, *s.* Plongeur, -euse autonome. **'skin-diving**, *s.* Plongée *f* autonome. **'skin-dresser**, *s.* Peaussier *m*, pelletier *m*. **'skin-game**, *s.* F: Escroquerie *f*; exploitation *f* malhonnête. **'skin-grafting**, *s.* Med: Greffe cutanée. **'skin-test**, *s.* Med: Cuti-réaction *f*. **'skin-tight**, *a.* (Vêtement) collant.

skin², *v.tr.* (skinned) 1. (a) Écorcher, dépouiller, (un lapin, etc.). F: To s. s.o., dépouiller, écorcher, plumer, qn (au jeu). To s. a flint, tondre un œuf. (b) Peler, éplucher (un fruit, etc.). 2. (a) N.Arch: To s. a ship, revêtir un navire. (b) Nau: To s. up a sail, faire la chemise d'une voile. 3. *v.i.* Med: (Of wound) Se cicatriser. **skinned**, *a.* Dark-s., à peau brune; qui a la peau brune. Clean-s., qui a la peau saine. S.a. EYE¹ 1. **skinning**, *s.* 1. (a) Écorchement *m* (d'un lapin). (b) Épluchage *m* (d'un fruit). 2. Med: S. over, cicatrisation *f* (d'une blessure). 3. Desquamation *f*.

skinflint ['skinflint], *s.* Avare *mf*; rapiat *m*.

skinful ['skinful], *s.* 1. (Pleine) outre (de vin, etc.). 2. P: He's got a good s., il a son plein (de boisson), il a pris la, une, cuite.

skinniness ['skininis], *s.* F: Maigreur *f*, décharnement *m*.

skinny ['skini], *a.* 1. F: Décharné; maigre; (of child) maigrichon, -onne; maigriot, -ote. 2. Membraneux, -euse. 3. Avare, ladre.

skip¹ [skip], *s.* (Petit) saut; gambade *f*.

skip², *v.* (skipped [skipt]) 1. *v.i.* (a) Sauter, sautiller, gambader. To s. for joy, sauter de joie. (b) Sauter à la corde. (c) To s. from one subject to another, bondir d'un sujet à un autre; papillonner, voleter, de sujet en sujet. To s. a few items, F: en passer. (d) F: To s. (off), filer; décamper. 2. *v.tr. & i.* To s. (over) a passage in a book, sauter, passer, un passage d'un livre. Sch: To s. a form, sauter une classe. P: S. it! ça suffit! **skipping**, *s.* 1. Gambades *fpl*, sauts *mpl*. 2. Saut à la corde. 3. Omission *f* (de qch.). Typew: Sautage *m* (d'un espace). **'skipping-rope**, *s.* Corde *f* à sauter.

skipper¹ ['skipər], *s.* Sauteur, -euse.

skipper², *s.* 1. Nau: Patron *m* (de bateau). 2. Sp: F: Chef *m* d'équipe.

skirl [skə:l], *s.* Scot: Son aigu (de la cornemuse). To set up a s., se mettre à jouer de la cornemuse.

skirmish¹ ['skə:miʃ], *s.* Mil: Escarmouche *f*, échauffourée *f*.

skirmish², *v.i.* (a) Escarmoucher. (b) Combattre en tirailleurs; tirailler (with, contre).

skirmisher ['skə:miʃər], *s.* Mil: Tirailleur *m*.

skirt¹ [skə:t], *s.* 1. Cost: (a) Jupe *f* (de femme). Divided s., jupe-culotte *f*. To be always hanging on to s.o.'s skirts, être toujours pendu aux basques de qn. (b) Pans *mpl*, basque *f* (de pardessus, etc.). (c) P: (i) Femme *f*; (ii) poule *f*. 2. *pl.* O: Skirts, bord *m* (d'un village, etc.); lisière *f*, bordure *f* (d'un bois). **'skirt-hanger**, *s.* Porte-jupe *m inv*.

skirt², *v.tr. & i.* Contourner (un village, une colline); (of pers.) longer, serrer (le mur, etc.). The path skirts (along, round) the wood, le sentier côtoie, contourne, le bois. **skirting**, *s.* (a) Bord *m*, bordure *f*. (b) Const: S. (-board), plinthe *f*.

skit [skit], *s. Lit: Th:* Pièce *f* satirique; charge *f*; satire *f* (**on**, de).

skittish ['skitiʃ], *a.* **1.** (*a*) (Cheval) ombrageux, peureux. (*b*) (Femme) capricieuse. **2.** (Femme) évaporée, folâtre, coquette. **-ly**, *adv.* D'un air, d'un ton espiègle; en faisant la coquette.

skittishness ['skitiʃnis], *s.* **1.** Inégalité *f* d'humeur (d'un cheval, d'une femme). **2.** Pétulance *f*, légèreté *f*.

skittle ['skitl], *s.* **1.** Quille *f*. **2.** *pl.* (**Game of**) **skittles**, jeu *m* de quilles. **S.-alley**, quillier *m*, (terrain *m* de) jeu de quilles.

skive [skaiv], *v.tr.* Doler, drayer (les peaux); fendre (le caoutchouc) en feuilles minces.

skiver ['skaivər], *s.* **1.** *Tls:* Doloir *m.* **2.** *Bookb:* Parchemin *m* mince; mouton scié.

skivvy ['skivi], *s.f. F: now usu. Hum: Pej:* Boniche; petite bonne à tout faire.

skua ['skju(:)ə], *s. Orn:* Stercoraire *m*; mouette pillarde.

skulk [skʌlk], *v.i.* **1.** Se cacher; se tenir caché. **2.** Rôder furtivement. **3.** *F:* Se défiler; fainéanter; se dérober (au devoir). *Mil:* Tirer au flanc.

skulker ['skʌlkər], *s.* Fainéant *m. Mil:* Tireur *m* au flanc; embusqué *m.*

skull [skʌl], *s.* Crâne *m.* **S. and cross-bones**, tête *f* de mort et tibias (du pavillon des pirates). **'skull-cap**, *s.* Calotte *f* (de prêtre, etc.).

skunk [skʌŋk], *s.* **1.** *Z:* Mouffette *f*. **2.** (*Fur*) Skunks *m*, sconse *m.* **3.** *F:* (*Pers.*) Mufle *m*, rosse *f*.

sky[1] [skai], *s.* **1.** Ciel *m, pl.* cieux, ciels. **Under the open s.**, au grand air; (dormir) à la belle étoile. **To laud, praise, s.o. to the skies**, élever, porter, qn aux nues. *Art:* **Turner's skies**, les ciels de Turner. *Th:* **S. pieces**, frises *f*. *S.a.* SHADE[1] 4. **2.** Ciel, *pl.* ciels; climat *m.* **'sky blue, 1.** *s.* Bleu *m* céleste; bleu ciel. **2.** *a.* Azuré. **S.-b.** dresses, robes *f* bleu ciel. **'sky-'high**, *adv.* (Faire sauter qn, qch.) jusqu'aux cieux, aux nues. **'sky 'pilot**, *s. F:* Prêtre *m*, pasteur *m. Nau:* Aumônier *m.*

sky[2], *v.tr.* (**skied**; **skying**) (*a*) *Cr: Ten: etc:* Lancer (la balle) en chandelle. (*b*) *Art: F:* Jucher (un tableau); exposer (un tableau) au plafond.

Skye [skai]. *Pr.n.Geog:* (L'île *f* de) Skye. **S. terrier**, skye-terrier *m.*

skylark[1] ['skailɑ:k], *s. Orn:* Alouette *f* (des champs).

skylark[2], *v.i. F:* Rigoler; faire des farces. **sky-larking**, *s. F:* Rigolade *f.*

skylight ['skailait], *s.* Châssis vitré; lucarne *f*; (*hinged*) abattant *m*; châssis à tabatière; (*in cellar*) soupirail, **-aux** *m.*

skyline ['skailain], *s.* (Ligne *f* d') horizon *m.*

skyman, *pl.* **-men** ['skaimən], *s. F:* Parachutiste *m.*

sky(-)rocket[1] ['skairɔkit], *s. Pyr:* Fusée volante.

skyrocket[2], *v.i. F:* (*Of prices, etc.*) Monter en flèche.

skyscraper ['skaiskreipər], *s.* Gratte-ciel *m inv.*

skyward(s) ['skaiwədz], *adv.* Vers le ciel.

skyway ['skaiwei], *s.* **1.** Route aérienne. **The sky ways of the world**, les voies aériennes mondiales. **2.** *U.S: Aut:* Route surélevée.

slab [slæb], *s.* **1.** (*a*) Plaque *f*, tranche *f* (de marbre); dalle *f* (de pierre). *Metall:* Brame *f*, lopin *m* (de fer). (*b*) **S. of gingerbread**, pavé *m* de pain d'épice. **S. of cake**, grosse tranche de gâteau. **S. of chocolate**, tablette *f* de chocolat. **2.** *Typ:* Marbre *m* (pour broyer les couleurs).

slack[1] [slæk], *s.* (i) Menus *mpl* (de houille); charbonnaille *f*; (ii) poussier *m.*

slack[2], *s.* **1.** (*a*) Mou *m*, ballant *m*, étale *m* (d'un câble). **To take up the s. in a cable**, mettre un câble au raide. (*b*) *Mec.E:* Jeu *m.* **To take up the s.**, rattraper le jeu. **2.** *pl.* **Slacks**, pantalon *m.*

slack[3], *a.* **1.** (*a*) (Cordage) mou, lâche, flasque; mal tendu; (pneu) dégonflé, détendu; (écrou) desserré. (*Of rope*) **To hang s.**, avoir du mou. (*b*) (Main, prise) faible, sans force. **2.** (*Of pers.*) Négligent; mou, *f.* molle; *P:* flemmard. **To be s. in, about, doing sth.**, être lent, paresseux, à faire qch. **She has got very slack**, elle s'est avachie. **3.** Peu vif; faible. **S. oven**, four modéré. **S. business**, affaires languissantes. **S. time**, accalmie *f.* **The s. season**, la morte-saison. *Nau:* **S. water**, mer étale; étale *m* de la marée. *Ind: etc:* **S. hours**, heures creuses. **-ly**, *adv.* **1.** (Agir) négligemment, nonchalamment;

sans énergie. **2.** (Lier qch.) mollement, lâchement. **'slack-rope**, *s.* Corde *f* lâche; voltige *f.*

slack[4]. **1.** *v.tr.* (*a*) Détendre, relâcher (un cordage); desserrer (un écrou). (*b*) **To s. lime**, éteindre, amortir, la chaux. **2.** *v.i.* (*a*) (*Of cable, sail*) Prendre du lâche, du mou. (*b*) (*Of lime*) S'éteindre, s'amortir. (*c*) *F:* (*Of pers.*) Se relâcher. **To s.** (**about**), fainéanter. **slack off. 1.** *v.tr.* Relâcher (la pression, etc.). **2.** *v.i.* Se relâcher; diminuer d'efforts; mollir. **slacking**, *s.* **1.** Relâchement *m.* **2.** Extinction *f* (de la chaux). **3.** *F:* Manque *m* d'application au travail; paresse *f.*

slacken ['slæk(ə)n]. **1.** *v.tr.* (*a*) Ralentir (le pas, son ardeur). **To s. speed**, diminuer de vitesse; ralentir. *Nau:* **To s. a ship's way**, casser l'erre d'un navire. (*b*) Détendre, relâcher (un cordage); détendre (les muscles); desserrer (un écrou). **To s. the reins**, lâcher la bride, les rênes. **2.** *v.i.* (*a*) (*Of pers.*) **To s.** (**off, up**), se relâcher; devenir négligent. (*b*) (*Of rope*) Prendre du mou. (*c*) (*Of speed*) Ralentir; (*of energy, etc.*) diminuer. (*d*) (*Of the tide*) Mollir. **slackening**, *s.* Ralentissement *m*; diminution *f* (de zèle); relâchement *m* (d'un cordage); desserrage *m* (d'un écrou); détente *f* (des muscles, etc.).

slacker ['slækər], *s. F:* Paresseux, **-euse**; *F:* flemmard, **-arde.**

slackness ['slæknis], *s.* **1.** (*a*) Manque *m* d'énergie; négligence *f*, mollesse *f*; inexactitude *f* (à remplir ses devoirs); fainéantise *f.* (*b*) Désœuvrement *m.* (*c*) Relâchement *m* (de la discipline). **2.** Détente *f* (des muscles, etc.); mou *m* (d'un cordage). **3.** *Com:* Stagnation *f*, marasme *m* (des affaires); manque d'affaires.

slag [slæg] *s.* **1.** *Metall:* Scorie(s) *f(pl)*, crasse(s) *f (pl)*, laitier *m*, mâchefer *m* (de haut fourneau). **S.-heap**, crassier *m.* **S. wool**, coton minéral, ouate minérale. **2.** Volcanic s., scories volcaniques.

slain. See SLAY.

slake [sleik]. **1.** *v.tr.* (*a*) **To s. one's thirst**, étancher sa soif; se désaltérer. (*b*) Éteindre, amortir (la chaux). **2.** *v.i.* (*of lime*) S'éteindre, s'amortir. **slaking**, *s.* **1.** Étanchement *m*, assouvissement *m* (de la soif). **2.** = SLACKING 2.

slalom ['slɑləm], *s. Skiing:* Slalom *m.*

slam[1] [slæm], *s.* Claquement *m* (d'une porte, etc.).

slam[2], *v.* (**slammed**) **1.** *v.tr.* **To s. a door** (**to**), claquer, faire claquer, une porte. **2.** *v.i.* Se fermer avec bruit; claquer.

slam[3], *s. Cards:* (*At bridge*) Chelem *m.* **To make a s.**, faire (le) chelem.

slander[1] ['slɑ:ndər], *s.* Calomnie *f.* **S. and libel**, diffamation *f.*

slander[2], *v.tr.* Calomnier. *Jur:* Diffamer. **slandering**, *a.* **She has a s. tongue**, c'est une mauvaise langue, une langue de vipère.

slanderer ['slɑ:ndərər], *s.* Calomniateur, **-trice.** *Jur:* Diffamateur, **-trice.**

slanderous ['slɑ:nd(ə)rəs], *a.* (Propos) calomnieux. *Jur:* Diffamatoire. **-ly**, *adv.* Calomnieusement.

slang[1] [slæŋ], *s.* Argot *m.*

slang[2], *v.tr. F:* (*a*) Injurier (qn); *F:* enguirlander (qn). (*b*) Réprimander vivement (qn); *P:* engueuler (qn). **slanging**, *s. F:* (*a*) Pluie *f* d'injures. (*b*) Verte réprimande; *P:* engueulade *f.*

slangy ['slæŋi], *a.* **1.** (*Of pers.*) Qui aime à s'exprimer en argot. **2.** (Style, langage) argotique; (terme) d'argot. **-ily**, *adv.* (S'exprimer, etc.) en termes d'argot.

slant[1] [slɑ:nt], *s.* **1.** Pente *f*, inclinaison *f.* **2.** Biais *m*, biseau *m.* **On the s.**, en écharpe. **3.** Point *m* de vue. **He has an interesting s. on the question**, il envisage la question d'une manière intéressante.

slant[2], *a.* Oblique; d'écharpe; en écharpe. **'slant-eyed**, *a.* Aux yeux bridés.

slant[3]. **1.** *v.i.* (*a*) Être en pente; (s')incliner. (*b*) Être oblique. **2.** *v.tr.* Incliner (qch.); mettre (qch.) en pente; déverser (un mur). **slanting**, *a.* (*a*) (Toit) en pente, incliné. (*b*) (Direction) oblique. **S. rain**, pluie qui tombe en oblique. **S. hand(writing)**, écriture couchée, inclinée. **-ly**, *adv.* Obliquement, en biais.

slantways ['slɑ:ntweiz], **slantwise** ['slɑ:ntwaiz], *adv.* Obliquement; de biais; en écharpe.

slap[1] [slæp]. I. *s.* **1.** Claque *f*, tape *f*, *F:* calotte *f*. **S. in the face,** (i) soufflet *m*, gifle *f*; (ii) *F:* affront *m*. **2.** *I.C.E:* Piston s., claquement *m* du piston. II. **slap,** *adv.* **To run s. into s.o., sth.,** se heurter en plein contre qn, qch. **'slap-bang,** *adv.* Brusquement; de but en blanc. **'slap-'happy,** *a. F:* (*a*) *Box:* Sonné. (*b*) *F:* (i) Exalté, transporté; (ii) toqué, fêlé. **'slap-up,** *a. F:* Fameux, -euse, soigné, chic, de premier ordre.

slap[2], *v.* (slapped [slæpt]) **1.** *v.tr.* Frapper (qn) avec la main (ouverte); donner une fessée à (un enfant, etc.). **To s. s.o.'s face,** gifler, souffleter, *F:* calotter, qn. **To s. s.o. on the back,** donner à qn une tape sur l'épaule. **2.** *v.i. I.C.E:* (*Of piston*) Claquer. **slap down,** *v.tr. F:* **To s. s.o. down,** (re)mettre qn à sa place, rembarrer, rebuffer qn; rabattre le caquet de qn. **slapping,** *s.* **1.** (*a*) Claques *fpl*; jeu *m* de mains. (*b*) Fouettée *f*, fessée *f*. **2.** *I.C.E:* Claquement *m* (du piston).

slapdash ['slæpdæʃ], *a. & adv.* Sans soin. **S. work,** travail bâclé. **To do sth. in a s. fashion,** faire qch. au petit bonheur.

slapjack ['slæpdʒæk], *s. Cu: U.S:* Crêpe *f*.

slapstick ['slæpstik], *s.* **1.** Batte *f* (d'Arlequin). **2.** **S. (comedy),** farce bouffonne.

slash[1] [slæʃ], *s.* **1.** Estafilade *f*, entaille *f*; (*on the face*) balafre *f*. **2.** *Cost: A:* Crevé *m*, taillade *f*.

slash[2], *v.tr.* **1.** (*a*) Taillader (la chair); balafrer, écharper (le visage). (*b*) Cingler (un cheval, etc. d'un coup de fouet); fouailler (un cheval). (*c*) *Abs.* Frapper à droite et à gauche; ferrailler, sabrer. **To cut and s.,** frapper d'estoc et de taille. (*d*) *F:* (*Criticize*) Éreinter, esquinter (un ouvrage littéraire). (*e*) **To s. a speech,** faire des amputations dans un discours. *Com: F:* **Articles sold at slash(ed) prices,** articles sacrifiés. **2.** *A: Cost:* Faire des crevés, des taillades, dans (un vêtement). **3.** Faire claquer (un fouet). **slashed,** *a.* (*Visage*) balafré. **2.** *A: Cost:* (Pourpoint) à crevés, à taillades. **slashing**[1], *a.* (*a*) (*Of criticism, etc.*) Mordant, cinglant. (*b*) **S. rain,** pluie cinglante. **slashing**[2], *s.* **1.** Taillades *fpl*; coups *mpl* de sabre, de fouet. **2.** *A: Cost:* Crevé *m*. **3.** Critique incisive, cinglante.

slat [slæt], *s.* Lame *f*, lamelle *f* (de jalousie, etc.); traverse *f* (de lit).

slate[1] [sleit], *s.* **1.** (*a*) *Geol:* Ardoise *f*; schiste ardoisier. (*b*) *Const:* (Feuille *f* d') ardoise. **S. industry,** ardoiserie *f*. *F:* **To have a s. loose,** être un peu toqué; avoir la tête fêlée. **2.** Ardoise (pour écrire). **To wipe, clean, the s.,** passer l'éponge sur le passé. **To start with a clean s.,** commencer une nouvelle vie. **3.** *U.S: Pol:* Liste *f* provisoire de candidats. **'slate-blue,** *a.* Bleu ardoise *inv.* **'slate-coloured,** **-grey,** *a.* Ardoisé; (gris) ardoise *inv.* **'slate-pencil,** *s.* Crayon *m* d'ardoise. **'slate-quarry,** *s.* Ardoisière *f*.

slate[2], *v.tr.* **1.** Ardoiser (un toit). **Slated roof,** toit en ardoise. **2.** *U.S: Pol:* Inscrire (un candidat) sur la liste; adopter un candidat.

slate[3], *v.tr. F:* **1.** Tancer, réprimander vertement (qn); laver la tête à (qn). **2.** Critiquer (qn); éreinter (un livre). *F:* **To s. a play,** déshabiller une pièce. **slating,** *s. F:* **1.** Verte réprimande; *F:* savon *m*. **2.** Dure critique; éreintement *m*.

slater ['sleitər], *s.* **1.** (*Pers.*) Couvreur *m* (en ardoises). **2.** *Crust:* Cloporte *m*.

slattern ['slætə:n], *s.f.* Femme mal soignée; traîne-savates *inv*; souillon *m* or *f*.

slatternly ['slætənli], *a.* (*Of woman*) Mal soignée, mal peignée; qui manque d'ordre.

slaty ['sleiti], *a.* **1.** *Geol:* Ardoiseux, -euse, schisteux, -euse. **2.** (*Of colour*) Ardoisé.

slaughter[1] ['slɔːtər], *s.* **1.** (*a*) Abattage *m* (de bêtes de boucherie). (*b*) Abattis *m* (de gibier). **2.** Tuerie *f*, carnage *m*, massacre *m*. **'slaughter-house,** *s.* Abattoir *m*.

slaughter[2], *v.tr.* **1.** Abattre (des bêtes de boucherie). **2.** Tuer, massacrer (des gens). **slaughtering,** *s.* **1.** Abattage *m*. **2.** Tuerie *f*, massacre *m*.

slaughterer ['slɔːtərər], *s.* **1.** Tueur *m*, massacreur *m*, égorgeur *m*. **2.** = SLAUGHTERMAN.

slaughterman, *pl.* **-men** ['slɔːtəmən], *s.m.* Tueur *m* (aux abattoirs).

Slav [slɑːv], *a. & s. Ethn:* Slave (*mf*).

slave[1] [sleiv], *s.* Esclave *mf*. **To be the s. of, a s. to, a passion,** être l'esclave d'une passion. **To be a s. to duty,** ne connaître que son devoir. **'slave-dealer,** *s.* Marchand *m* d'esclaves. **'slave-driver,** *s. F:* (i) Maître, maîtresse, qui traite durement ses domestiques; (ii) patron, patronne, sans merci. **'slave-trade, -traffic,** *s.* Traite *f* des noirs, des nègres. **White s.-t.,** traite des blanches; proxénétisme *m*. **'slave-trader,** *s.* = SLAVE-DEALER.

slave[2], *v.i.* Travailler comme un nègre; peiner, bûcher. **To s. away at (sth.),** s'échiner, s'éreinter, à (un travail).

slaver[1] ['slævər], *s.* **1.** Bave *f*, salive *f*. **2.** Flatterie grossière; flagornerie *f*.

slaver[2], *v.i.* Baver (over, sur). **slavering,** *a.* Baveur.

slaver[3] ['sleivər], *s.* **1.** *Nau: Hist:* (Bâtiment) négrier *m*. **2.** = SLAVE-DEALER. **White s.,** proxénète *mf*.

slaverer ['slævərər], *s.* **1.** Baveur, -euse. **2.** Flagorneur, -euse.

slavery ['sleivəri], *s.* **1.** Esclavage *m*. **To reduce a nation to s.,** asservir une nation. **2.** Asservissement *m* (à une passion, une habitude). **3.** Travail tuant.

slavey ['sleivi], *s. F: O:* Boniche *f*; petite bonne à tout faire.

slavish ['sleiviʃ], *a.* (Soumission) d'esclave; (imitation) servile. **-ly,** *adv.* (Obéir) en esclave; (imiter) servilement.

slavishness ['sleiviʃnis], *s.* Servilité *f*.

Slavonian [slə'vounjən]. **1.** *a. & s.* Slavon, -onne. **2.** *s. Ling:* Le slavon.

Slavonic [slə'vɔnik], *a. & s. Ling:* Slave (*m*).

slaw [slɔː], *s. U.S:* (Cole) s., salade *f* de chou cru.

slay [slei], *v.tr.* (slew [sluː]; slain [slein]) *Lit:* Tuer; mettre à mort. **slaying,** *s.* Tuerie *f*; massacre *m*.

slayer ['sleiər], *s.* Tueur *m*; meurtrier *m* (of, de).

sleazy ['sliːzi], *a. Pej:* **1.** *Tex:* Léger, sans consistance; *F:* de camelote, de pacotille. **2.** *F:* Sordide, répugnant; mal soigné.

sled[1,2] [sled], *s. & v:* = SLEDGE[1,2].

sledge[1] [sledʒ], *s.* Traîneau *m*; (*dans les Alpes*) ramasse *f*.

sledge[2]. **1.** *v.i.* Aller en traîneau. **2.** *v.tr.* Transporter (qch.) en traîneau.

sledge(-hammer) ['sledʒ(hæmər)], *s.* Marteau *m* de forgeron; marteau à deux mains; marteau à frapper devant. **S.-h. argument,** argument coup de massue.

sleek[1] [sliːk], *a.* **1.** Lisse; luisant (de santé). **S. hair,** cheveux lisses. **2.** (*Of manner*) Mielleux, -euse; onctueux, -euse.

sleek[2], *v.tr.* Lisser (les cheveux); polir (qch.).

sleekness ['sliːknis], *s.* **1.** Luisant *m* (d'une peau, etc.). **2.** Onctuosité *f* (de ton).

sleep[1] [sliːp], *s.* **1.** Sommeil *m*. **Short s.,** somme *m*. **Sound s.,** sommeil profond. **Winter s.,** sommeil hibernal (de certains animaux). **To go, drop off, to s.,** s'endormir, s'assoupir. **He has gone to s.,** il dort. **To send s.o. to s.,** endormir, assoupir, qn. **To put a child to s.,** endormir un enfant. **To put an animal to s.** (= *kill*), endormir, piquer, un animal. **To put s.o.'s suspicions to s.,** endormir les soupçons de qn. **I lose s. over it,** j'en perds le sommeil. **To come out of one's s.,** s'éveiller. **To rouse s.o. from his s.,** réveiller qn. **To have a good s.,** faire un bon somme. **I didn't have a wink of s. all night,** je n'ai pas fermé l'œil de (toute) la nuit; j'ai passé une nuit blanche. **To walk in one's s.,** être noctambule, somnambule. **2.** **My foot has gone to s.,** j'ai le pied engourdi; j'ai des fourmis dans le pied. **'sleep-walker,** *s.* Somnambule *mf*; noctambule *mf*. **'sleep-walking,** *s.* Somnambulisme *m*; noctambulisme *m*.

sleep[2], *v.i. & tr.* (slept [slept]; slept) **1.** Dormir. (*a*) **To s. like a log,** dormir à poings fermés; dormir comme un sabot. **To s. soundly,** dormir profondément; (*without fear*) dormir sur les deux oreilles. **To s. lightly,** avoir le sommeil léger. **I have not slept a wink all night,** je n'ai pas fermé l'œil de (toute) la nuit. **To s. on a question; to s. on it,** prendre conseil de son oreiller. (*b*) **To s. the sleep of the just,** dormir du sommeil du juste. **2.** Coucher. **To s. at an hotel,** coucher à un hôtel. **To s. away from home,** découcher. **3.** **To s. in the churchyard,**

with one's fathers, reposer dans le cimetière. **sleep away,** *v.tr.* Passer (le temps) à dormir. **sleep in,** *v.i.* (*a*) Être logé dans la maison. (*b*) Faire la grasse matinée. **sleep off,** *v.tr.* Faire passer (une migraine, etc.) en dormant. **To s. off the effects of wine,** cuver son vin. **sleep out,** *v.i.* 1. Découcher. 2. (*Of servant*) Ne pas coucher à la maison. **sleeping**[1], *a.* 1. Dormant, endormi. *Prov:* **Let s. dogs lie,** ne réveillez pas le chat qui dort. 2. (*Of limb*) Engourdi. 3. *Com:* **S. partner,** (associé *m*) commanditaire *m*; bailleur *m* de fonds. **sleeping**[2], *s.* Sommeil *m*. **S. accommodation,** logement *m*. **'sleeping-bag,** *s.* Sac *m* de couchage. **'sleeping-car,** *s.* *Rail:* Wagon-lit *m*, *pl.* wagons-lits; voiture-lit *f*, *pl.* voitures-lits. **'sleeping draught, pills,** *s.* Potion assoupissante; soporifique *m*; narcotique *m*, somnifère *m*. **'sleeping-quarters,** *s.pl.* Dortoir *m*. **'sleeping 'sickness,** *s.* *Med:* Trypanosomiase *f*; *F:* maladie *f* du sommeil. **'sleeping-suit,** *s.* Pyjama *m*.

sleeper ['sli:pər], *s.* 1. Dormeur, -euse. **To be a light, a heavy, s.,** avoir le sommeil léger, profond. 2. (*a*) Poutre horizontale; sole *f*; lambourde *f* (de parquet, etc.). (*b*) *Rail:* (Cross-)s., traverse *f*. Longitudinal s., longrine *f*. 3. *Rail: F:* = SLEEPING-CAR.

sleepiness ['sli:pinis], *s.* 1. Somnolence *f*. 2. Indolence *f*, léthargie *f*.

sleepless ['sli:plis], *a.* 1. Sans sommeil. **S. night,** nuit blanche. 2. (*Of mind*) Sans cesse en éveil.

sleeplessness ['sli:plisnis], *s.* Insomnie *f*.

sleepy ['sli:pi], *a.* 1. (*a*) Somnolent. **To be, feel, s.,** avoir envie de dormir; avoir sommeil. (*b*) **S. look,** air endormi. **S. little town,** petite ville endormie. 2. (*a*) Apathique, engourdi. (*b*) *Med:* **S. sickness,** (i) encéphalite *f* léthargique; (ii) *F:* trypanosomiase *f*. 3. (*Of fruit*) Blet, -ette, cotonneux, -euse. **-ily,** *adv.* (Répondre, etc.) d'un air endormi, somnolent. **'sleepy-head,** *s.* *F:* Endormi, -ie.

sleet[1] [sli:t], *s.* Grésil *m*.

sleet[2], *v.impers.* Grésiller. **It's sleeting,** il grésille.

sleeve [sli:v], *s.* 1. Manche *f*. *Dressm:* **Short s.,** manche courte, mancheron *m*. **Set-in s.,** manche rapportée. *S.a.* SHIRT-SLEEVE. **To put sth. up one's s.,** mettre qch. dans sa manche. **To have a plan up one's s.,** avoir un expédient en réserve. **To have more than one trick up one's s.,** avoir plus d'un tour dans son (bis)sac. 2. (*a*) *Mec.E:* Manchon *m*, douille *f*; bague *f* d'assemblage; virole *f*. (*b*) (*Of gramophone record*) Pochette *f*. **'sleeve-board,** *s.* 1. *Laund:* Pied *m* à manche, à repasser; *F:* jeannette *f*. 2. *Tail:* Passe-carreau *m*; cifran *m*. **'sleeve-nut,** *s.* Manchon taraudé. **'sleeve-valve,** *s.* *I.C.E:* Soupape *f* à fourreau; fourreau *m* de distribution.

sleeved [sli:vd], *a.* (Vêtement) à manches. **Long-s. dress,** robe *f* à manches longues.

sleeveless ['sli:vlis], *a.* (Robe *f*, etc.) sans manches.

sleigh[1] [slei], *s.* Traîneau *m*. *S.a.* BOB-SLEIGH. **'sleigh-bell,** *s.* Grelot *m*; clochette *f*. **'sleigh-ride,** *s.* Promenade *f* en traîneau.

sleigh[2]. 1. *v.i.* Aller en traîneau. 2. *v.tr.* Transporter en traîneau.

sleight [slait], *s.* **S. of hand,** prestidigitation *f*; tours *mpl* de passe-passe.

slender ['slendər], *a.* 1. Mince, ténu; (*of figure*) svelte, élancé; (*of finger*) fuselé. **To grow, become, more s.,** s'amincir. 2. (*Of intelligence, etc.*) Maigre; (*of hope, etc.*) faible; (*of income, etc.*) exigu, mince. **S. voice,** filet *m* de voix. **Our s. means,** nos ressources exiguës. **-ly,** *adv.* 1. **S. made, s. built, person,** personne fluette. 2. Maigrement, faiblement.

slenderize ['slendəraiz], *v.tr.* *U.S:* Amincir.

slenderness ['slendənis], *s.* 1. Minceur *f*, ténuité *f*; sveltesse *f*. 2. Exiguïté *f* (d'une fortune, etc.); faiblesse *f* (des ressources).

slept. *See* SLEEP[2].

sleuth ['slu:θ], *v.i.* *F:* Faire le détective.

sleuth(-hound) ['slu:θ(haund)], *s.* 1. Limier *m*. 2. *F:* **The sleuths,** la police de sûreté; les limiers de la police.

slew[1] [slu:]. 1. *v.tr.* **To s. (over) a mast,** dévirer, trévirer, un mât. 2. *v.i.* Pivoter, virer. **slew round.** 1. *v.tr.* Faire pivoter (qch.). 2. *v.i.* (*a*) (*Of crane, etc.*) Pivoter, tourner. (*b*) *Aut:* Faire (un) tête-à-queue.

slew[2]. *See* SLAY.

slice[1] [slais], *s.* 1. Tranche *f*; darne *f* (de gros poisson). (Round) s. (*of sausage, etc.*) rond *m*, rondelle *f*. **S. of bread and butter,** tartine *f* de beurre. **S. of (good) luck,** coup *m* de veine. 2. *Cu:* Fish-s., truelle *f* (à poisson). 3. Coup *m* en biseau ou en sifflet. *Golf:* Coup qui fait dévier la balle à droite.

slice[2], *v.tr.* 1. Découper (qch.) en tranches. **To s. thinly,** émincer (la viande, etc.). 2. (*a*) *Ten:* Couper (la balle). (*b*) *Abs.* (i) *Golf:* Faire dévier la balle à droite. (ii) *Row:* Attaquer en sifflet. **slice off,** *v.tr.* Trancher, couper, détacher (un morceau).

slicer ['slaisər], *s.* Machine *f* à trancher le pain, etc. *S.a.* VEGETABLE.

slick [slik]. *F:* 1. *a.* (*a*) Habile, adroit. (*b*) Bien rangé; en bon ordre; lisse; luisant. (*c*) **You'd better look s. about it,** vous ferez bien de vous dépêcher. (*d*) **A s. customer,** une fine mouche, un fin matois. 2. *adv.* (*a*) Habilement, adroitement. (*b*) **To cut s. through sth.,** couper qch. net. **S. in the middle,** en plein milieu. (*c*) Prestement; vite.

slick[2], *v.tr.* *U.S:* Lisser (ses cheveux); mettre (une chambre) en ordre. **To s. oneself up,** faire un bout de toilette, se pomponner.

slicker ['slikər], *s.* *U.S:* 1. Imperméable *m*, *F:* imper *m* (en toile huilée). 2. *P:* Escroc adroit.

slickness ['sliknis], *s.* *F:* Habileté *f*, dextérité *f*, adresse *f*.

slid. *See* SLIDE[2].

slide[1] [slaid], *s.* 1. (*a*) Glissade *f*, glissement *m*. (*b*) *Mus:* Coulé *m*. 2. (*Slipway, runner*) Glissière *f*, coulisse *f*. 3. (*a*) (*On snow or ice*) Glissoire *f*, glissade. (*b*) Plan *m* de glissement; piste *f* en pente. 4. (*a*) Glissoire; coulant *m* (d'une bourse, etc.); curseur *m* (d'un compas, etc.). *Row:* Glissière. **S. fastener,** fermeture *f* à glissière. **S. of a slide-rule,** réglette *f*, tiroir *m*, d'une règle à calcul. *Opt:* **Focusing s., draw-s.,** tube *m* à tirage. (*b*) *Mus:* Coulisse (de trombone, etc.). 5. (*a*) *Microscopy:* **Object-s.,** (plaque *f*, lame *f*) porte-objet *m inv*; lamelle *f*. (*b*) *Phot:* Diapositive *f*. *O:* **Lantern-s.,** diapositive *f* de projection; vue *f* (de projection). **Lecture illustrated with slides,** conférence avec projections. **Stereo s.,** plaque *f* stéréoscopique. 6. *Phot:* **Dark s.,** châssis *m* porte-plaques. 7. *Toil:* (Hair-)s., barrette *f*. **'slide-rule,** *s.* Règle *f* à calcul (logarithmique).

slide[2], *v.* (slid [slid]; slid) 1. *v.i.* (*a*) Glisser, coulisser. (*b*) (*Of pers.*) **To s. (on ice),** faire des glissades. (*c*) **He slid on the floor and fell,** il glissa sur le parquet et tomba. (*d*) **To s. into sin,** glisser dans le péché. (*e*) *F:* **To let a thing s.,** se désintéresser de qch. **To let things s.,** laisser tout aller à vau-l'eau. 2. *v.tr.* (Faire) glisser. **To s. sth. into s.o.'s hand,** glisser qch. dans la main à, de, qn. **slide down,** *v.i.* 1. Descendre en glissant. 2. **To s. down the banisters,** glisser le long de la rampe. **To s. down the wall,** se laisser couler en bas du mur. **slide off,** *v.i.* *F:* Décamper; filer (sans bruit). **sliding**[1], *a.* Glissant; coulissant. **S. door,** porte coulissante, roulante, à glissières. **S. panel,** panneau mobile. **S. sash,** châssis à coulisse. **S. seat,** (i) *Row:* banc à glissières, à coulisses; (ii) *Aut:* Siège *m* amovible. *Opt:* **S. tube,** tube à tirage. *El:* **S. contact,** curseur *m*, frotteur *m*. *Pol.Ec: Mth:* **S. scale,** échelle *f* mobile. **sliding**[2], *s.* Coulissement *m*, glissement *m*.

slider ['slaidər], *s.* 1. (*Pers.*) Glisseur, -euse. 2. Curseur *m* (d'une bobine électrique, etc.).

slight[1] [slait], *a.* 1. Mince, ténu; (*of figure*) frêle; menu, svelte. 2. (*Of pain, etc.*) Léger, -ère, petit; (*of intelligence, etc.*) maigre, faible; (*of occasion, etc.*) de peu d'importance. **To make a s. gesture,** faire un léger geste; esquisser un geste. **There is a s. improvement,** il y a un léger mieux. **To some s. extent,** quelque peu. **Not the slightest danger,** pas le moindre danger. **To take offence at the slightest thing,** se piquer d'un rien. **Not in the slightest (degree),** pas le moins du monde. **-ly,** *adv.* 1. **S. built,** (i) au corps frêle; (ii) à la taille mince, svelte. 2. Légèrement, faiblement. **S. better,** un petit peu mieux. **I know him s.,** je le connais un peu.

slight[2], *s.* Manque *m* de considération, d'égards; affront *m*. **To put, pass, a s. on s.o.,** infliger un affront à qn; manquer d'égards envers qn.

slight³, *v.tr.* Traiter (qn) sans considération; manquer d'égards envers (qn); négliger (qn). **slighting,** *a.* (Air) de mépris. **-ly,** *adv.* Avec peu d'égards; dédaigneusement.

slightness ['slaitnis], *s.* **1.** Minceur *f*, ténuité *f*; sveltesse *f* (de la taille). **2.** Légèreté *f*, petitesse *f* (d'une faute, etc.); peu *m* d'importance, insignifiance *f* (des dégâts, etc.).

slim¹ [slim], *a.* (slimmer) **1.** (*a*) Svelte, élancé, délié, mince. **S.-waisted,** à la taille svelte. (*b*) (*Of chance, hope, etc.*) Mince, léger, -ère. **The slimmest of evidence,** les preuves les moins concluantes. **2.** *F: O:* Rusé; malin, -igne; astucieux, -euse.

slim², *v.* (slimmed) **1.** *v.tr.* Amincir. **Slimming remedy, diet,** médicament, régime, amaigrissant. **2.** *v.i.* Suivre un régime amincissant.

slime [slaim], *s.* **1.** Limon *m*, vase *f*. **2.** Humeur visqueuse (qui couvre les poissons, etc.); bave *f* (de limace, etc.). **3.** Bitume *m* (liquide).

sliminess ['slaiminis], *s.* **1.** (*a*) État vaseux. (*b*) Viscosité *f*. **2.** Servilité *f*.

slimness ['slimnis], *s.* **1.** Taille *f* mince; sveltesse *f*, gracilité *f*. **2.** *F: O:* Astuce *f*.

slimy ['slaimi], *a.* **1.** (*a*) Limoneux, -euse, vaseux, -euse. (*b*) Visqueux, -euse, gluant. **2.** Couvert de vase, de limon. **3.** Servile, obséquieux, -euse. **S.-tongued,** doucereux, -euse.

sling¹ [sliŋ], *s.* **1.** Fronde *f*. **2.** (*a*) *Med:* Écharpe *f*. **To carry one's arm in a s.,** porter le bras en écharpe. (*b*) Bandoulière *f* (de harpe); courroie *f* (de bidon). (*c*) (*For hoisting*) Élingue *f* (pour barriques); cravate *f* (pour mât). *Nau:* **Boat slings,** pattes *f* d'embarcation; saisines *f*. **Yard s.,** suspente *f* de vergue.

sling², *v.tr.* (slung [slʌŋ]; slung) **1.** Lancer, jeter ((i) avec une fronde, (ii) avec la main). **2.** Suspendre. **To s. a hammock,** suspendre, gréer, un hamac. **To s.** (sth.) **over one's shoulder,** jeter (son pardessus) sur l'épaule; passer la bandoulière (d'une harpe, etc.) sur son épaule; mettre (une harpe, etc.) en bandoulière. **3.** Élinguer, brayer (un fardeau).

sling³, *s.* Grog *m*.

slinger ['sliŋər], *s.* **1.** Frondeur *m*. **2.** Lanceur *m* (d'une pierre, etc.).

slingshot ['sliŋʃɔt], *s.* *U.S:* Fronde *f*.

slink [sliŋk], *v.i.* (slunk [slʌŋk]; slunk) **To s. off, away,** partir furtivement, *F:* en catimini. **To s. in,** entrer furtivement. **slinking,** *a.* Furtif, -ive.

slinky ['sliŋki], *a.* *F:* (Forme) svelte; (allure) séduisante; (vêtement) collant.

slip¹ [slip], *s.* **1.** (*a*) Glissade *f*, glissement *m*, faux pas. (*b*) **To give s.o. the s.,** se dérober à qn; faire faux bond à qn. (*c*) Faute *f*, erreur *f* d'inattention; inadvertance *f*. **S. of the tongue, of the pen,** lapsus *m*; mot *m* de travers. **It was a s. of the tongue,** la langue lui a fourché. (*d*) Écart *m* (de conduite); peccadille *f*. (*e*) Glissement, patinage *m*. *Aut:* **Clutch s.,** patinage de l'embrayage. **Propeller s.,** (i) *N.Arch: Av:* recul *m* de l'hélice; (ii) *Av:* vent *m* de l'hélice. **2.** Laisse *f* (de chien de chasse). **3.** *Rail:* **S.(-portion),** rame *f* remorque. **4. Pillow s.,** taie *f* d'oreiller. **5.** *Cost:* (*a*) Combinaison *f* (de femme). (*b*) Slip *m* (d'homme). (*c*) *O:* **Gym s.,** tunique *f* (d'écolière). **6.** (*a*) Cale *f* de chargement (pour bacs, etc.). (*b*) *N.Arch:* **Building s.,** cale, chantier *m* (de construction). **Ship on the slips,** navire sur cale(s), en chantier. (*c*) **Launching slip(s)** = SLIPWAY 2. **7.** *pl. Th:* **The slips,** les coulisses *f*. **'slip-carriage, -coach,** *s. Rail:* Voiture *f* remorque; wagon détaché. **'slip-knot,** *s.* Nœud coulant. **'slip-noose,** *s.* Nœud coulant. **'slip-ring,** *s. El.E:* Bague collectrice (de dynamo, etc.); collecteur *m*. **'slip-stitch,** *s. Knitting:* Maille glissée. (*b*) *Needlew:* Point perdu. **'slip-stream,** *s. Aut: Av:* Sillage *m*, remous *m* (d'air).

slip², *v.* (slipped [slipt]) **I.** *v.i.* **1.** (*a*) Glisser; (*of knot*) couler; *Nau:* (*of rope*) choquer; (*of earth, etc.*) s'ébouler. *Mec.E:* (*Of belt, etc.*) Patiner, glisser. **His foot slipped,** son pied glissa. **To s. from s.o.'s hands, through s.o.'s fingers,** échapper des mains de qn; glisser entre les doigts de qn. (*b*) Se glisser, se couler. **To s. into the room,** se glisser dans la salle; entrer furtivement dans la salle. **To s. into bed,** se couler, se glisser, entre les draps, dans son lit. (*c*) *F:* **Just s. round to the post,**

faites un saut jusqu'au bureau de poste. (*d*) (*Of bolt*) **To s. home,** fermer à fond. **2.** (*a*) Faire une faute d'étourderie, une bévue. (*b*) Faire un écart de conduite. **3. To let s.,** lâcher (un lévrier); laisser échapper (une belle occasion, un secret). **II. slip,** *v.tr.* **1.** (*a*) Se dégager de (qch.). (*Of animal*) **To s. its chain,** se détacher. (*b*) **Your name has slipped my memory,** votre nom m'échappe. **To s. s.o.'s notice,** échapper à l'attention de qn. **2.** (*a*) *Ven:* Lâcher, découpler (les chiens). **To s. the hounds,** laisser courre. (*b*) *Nau:* **To s. a cable,** larguer, filer, une amarre par le bout. **To s. one's moorings,** filer le corps mort. (*c*) *Rail:* Décrocher (un wagon en marche). (*d*) *Husb:* (*Of animal*) **To s. its young,** mettre bas avant terme. **3.** Pousser (un verrou); couler, glisser (qch. dans la main de qn). **To s. the bolt home,** pousser le verrou à fond. **4.** *Aut:* **To s. the clutch,** laisser patiner l'embrayage. **slip away,** *v.i.* **1.** (*Of pers.*) Filer à l'anglaise; s'esquiver. **2.** (*Of time*) S'écouler, (se) passer, fuir. **slip by,** *v.i.* = SLIP AWAY 2. **slip down,** *v.i.* **1.** (*Of pers.*) Tomber (du fait d'avoir glissé). **2.** Descendre en glissant; se couler en bas (de l'arbre, etc.). **'slip-in,** *attrib.a.* (Album, etc.) passe-partout *inv.* **slip off,** *v.tr.* Enlever, ôter (un vêtement). **slip on,** *v.tr.* Enfiler, passer, mettre (une chemise, etc.). **'slip-on,** *a. & s. F:* (*a*) (Vêtement *m*) à enfiler. (*b*) *s.* Gaine *f* (élastique). (*c*) *s.* Pull-over *m*. **slip out,** *v.i.* (*a*) S'échapper. **The secret slipped out,** le secret se fit jour. (*b*) Sortir (à la dérobée). **slip over,** *v.tr.* **To s. a dress over one's head,** enfiler une robe par-dessus la tête. **'slip-over,** *s. F:* Pull-over *m* (sans manches). **slip up,** *v.i.* **1.** Se tromper; faire une bourde. **2.** (*Of plan*) Échouer; ne pas aboutir. **'slip-up,** *s. F:* Erreur *f*, bévue *f*. **That's a bad s.-up!** en voilà (i) une gaffe! (ii) un contretemps! (iii) un désastre!

slip³, *s.* **1.** (*a*) *Hort:* Bouture *f*, plançon *m*, plant *m*; (*for grafting*) scion *m*. (*b*) **S. of a girl,** jeune fille fluette. **Tall s. of a woman,** jeune femme élancée. **Fine s. of a girl,** beau brin de fille. (*c*) *Ich: Com:* Petite sole. **2.** (*a*) Bande étroite (de toile, de terre). **S. of paper,** bande, fiche *f*, de papier; bout *m* de papier. **Detachable s.,** volant *m* (d'un carnet, etc.). (*b*) Billet *m*, bordereau *m*. (*c*) *Typ:* **S.(proof),** placard *m*. **To pull matter in slips,** placarder des épreuves. **3.** *pl. Th:* **Slips,** couloir *m* du balcon.

slip⁴, *v.tr.* (slipped) Bouturer (une plante).

slip⁵, *s. Cer:* Barbotine *f*, engobe *m*. **To coat with s.,** engober.

slippage ['slipidʒ], *s. Mec.E: etc:* Glissement *m*, patinage *m*; décalage *m*. *El.E:* **Frequency s.,** décalage de fréquence.

slipper ['slipər], *s.* **1.** Pantoufle *f*; *Fr.C:* chaussette *f*. **Turkish slippers,** babouches *f*. *P:* (*To child*) **I'll take the s. to you!** je vais te donner une fessée! **2.** (*a*) *Mec.E:* Patin *m*, savate *f* (de frein). (*b*) **Piston rod s.,** glissière *f* de bielle. **3.** *Med:* Bassin *m* lit. **'slipper-bath,** *s.* Baignoire *f* (en) sabot.

slippered ['slipəd], *a.* En pantoufles.

slipperiness ['slipərinis], *s.* **1.** Nature glissante (du sol, etc.). **2.** Caractère rusé.

slipperwort ['slipəwəːt], *s. Bot:* Calcéolaire *f*.

slippery ['slipəri], *a.* **1.** Glissant. **It is s. walking,** on glisse en marchant. **The roads are s.** (**with frost**), il y a, il fait, du verglas. **2.** (*a*) Instable, incertain; sur lequel on ne peut compter. **To be on s. ground,** être sur un terrain glissant. (*b*) (Sujet) délicat, scabreux. **3.** Fin, rusé, matois. **He's as s. as an eel,** il est souple comme une anguille; il vous coule entre les doigts. **He's a s. customer,** on ne sait par où le prendre.

slippy ['slipi], *a. P:* **To be, look, s.,** se dépêcher. **Look s.!** grouille-toi!

slipshod ['slipʃɔd], *a.* **1.** *A:* En savates. **2. S. person,** personne (i) mal soignée, (ii) négligente. **She looks s.,** elle a l'air débraillé. **S. work,** travail négligé, bâclé. **S. English,** anglais peu correct. **I don't like s. definitions,** je n'aime pas les à peu près.

slipslop ['slipslɔp], *s. F:* **1.** (*a*) Aliments *m* liquides. (*b*) Lavasse *f*. **2.** Conversation *f*, écriture *f*, d'une sentimentalité fade; sensiblerie *f*.

slipway ['slipwei], *s.* **1.** Cale *f* (d'un bac). **2.** *N.Arch:* Cale (de lancement); slipway *m*, slip *m*; chantier *m* de construction.

slit¹ [slit], s. Fente f; fissure f, rainure f; (between curtains) entrebâillement m; Surg: incision f. The s. of the letter-box, le guichet de la boîte aux lettres. S.-eyed, (i) aux yeux bridés; (ii) aux yeux en amande.

slit², v. (slit; slit; slitting) 1. v.tr. (a) Fendre. To s. s.o.'s throat, couper la gorge à qn; égorger qn. To s. open a sack, éventrer un sac. (b) Surg: Faire une incision dans (les chairs, etc.). The blow s. his cheek, le coup lui a déchiré la joue. (c) Refendre (le cuir, le bois). 2. v.i. Se fendre, se déchirer (en long). slitting, s. Fendage m.

slither¹ ['sliðər], s. Glissement m, glissade f; dégringolade f.

slither². 1. v.i. (a) Glisser; manquer de tomber. To s. into the room, glisser en entrant dans la pièce. (b) (Of snake, worm) Ramper. 2. v.tr. Traîner (les pieds).

slitter ['slitər], s. Ind: 1. (Pers.) Fendeur m. 2. Tls: Fendoir m.

sliver¹ ['slivər, 'slaivər], s. 1. (a) Tranche f. Fish: Tranche de poisson montée en appât. (b) Éclat m (de bois). 2. Tex: Ruban m (de lin cardé); mèche f.

sliver². 1. v.tr. (a) Couper (qch.) en tranches. (b) Tex: Établir les rubans (de lin cardé). 2. v.i. (Of wood) Éclater.

slob [slɔb], s. 1. (a) Vase f, limon m. (b) Plage f de boue (dans un estuaire). 2. U.S: F: Rustaud m, goujat m, manant m.

slobber¹ ['slɔbər], s. (a) Bave f. (b) Sentimentalité larmoyante.

slobber², v.i. (a) Baver. (b) Larmoyer. To s. over s.o., témoigner une tendresse exagérée envers qn; s'attendrir sur qn.

slobbery ['slɔbəri], a. Baveux, -euse.

sloe [slou], s. Bot: 1. Prunelle f. S. gin, (liqueur f de) prunelle. 2. Prunellier m; épine noire.

slog¹ [slɔg], s. F: 1. Coup violent. 2. Corvée f; P: turbin m, boulot m.

slog², v. (slogged) F: 1. v.tr. Cogner violemment; rouer (qn) de coups. Abs. Box: Cogner dur (mais sans science). 2. v.i. (a) Cr: To s. at the ball, donner de grands coups de batte. (b) P: Turbiner. To s. away at sth., travailler avec acharnement à qch. (c) To s. along, marcher d'un pas lourd.

slogan ['slougən], s. 1. Hist: Cri m de guerre (de clan écossais). 2. (a) Cri de guerre, mot m d'ordre, slogan m (d'un parti politique). (b) Com: Devise f; slogan.

slogger ['slɔgər], s. F: 1. Box: Cr: Cogneur m (qui frappe au hasard). 2. Travailleur, -euse, acharné(e); abatteur, -euse, de besogne; bûcheur, -euse.

sloop [slu:p], s. Nau: Navy: Sloop m.

slop¹ [slɔp], s. 1. Boue f, bourbe f. 2. pl. Slops, (a) Boissons renversées (sur la table, etc.). (b) (Tasteless drink) Lavasse f, P: bibine f. (c) Aliments m liquides. (Of invalid) To be on slops, être réduit au bouillon. (d) Eaux ménagères; eaux sales. 3. F: Sensiblerie f. 4. Cer: = SLIP⁵. 'slop-basin, s. Vide-tasses m inv. 'slop-pail, s. (a) Seau m de ménage. (b) Seau de toilette; seau hygiénique.

slop², v. (slopped) 1. v.tr. To s. beer over the table, répandre de la bière sur la table. 2. v.i. (a) To s. (over), (i) (of liquids) déborder; (ii) F: se répandre en effusions de tendresse; faire de la sensiblerie. (b) To s. about in the mud, patauger dans la boue.

slop³, s. 1. A: Blouse f; sarrau m. 2. pl. Slops. (a) A: Pantalon m de marin. (b) Effets m (d'habillement), frusques f (d'un matelot). (c) Pej: Vêtements m de confection. 'slop-room, s. Nau: Magasin d'habillement.

slope¹ [sloup], s. 1. (a) Pente f, inclinaison f. Steep s., pente rapide. S. down, descente f; déclivité f. S. up, montée f. Angle of s., angle de déclivité. S. of a wall, dévers m d'un mur. Street on the s., rue en pente. Mil: Rifle at the s., l'arme sur l'épaule. Civ.E: Natural s., pente naturelle de talus. (b) Dégagement m (d'un outil). (c) Cut on the s., coupé en biais. 2. Pente; talus m; (in railway) rampe f; (in road) côte f. Half-way down, up, the s., à mi-pente. Mountain slope, versant m de montagne.

slope². 1. v.i. (a) Être en pente; incliner, pencher. To s. down, descendre. To s. up, monter. (Of writing) To s. forward, backward, pencher à droite, à gauche. (b) Aller en pente. The garden slopes down to the river, le jardin dévale vers le fleuve. 2. v.tr. (a) Couper (qch.) en pente. (b) Mil: To s. arms, mettre l'arme sur l'épaule. sloping, a. (a) En pente; incliné; (jardin) en talus. S. shoulders, épaules tombantes. Typ: S. letters, lettres couchées. (b) En biais. -ly, adv. (a) En pente. (b) De biais, en biais.

slope³, v.i. F: 1. O: To s. about, flâner. 2. To s. (off), filer, se défiler.

sloppiness ['slɔpinis], s. 1. État détrempé. 2. (a) (Of pers.) Mollesse f; avachissement m. S. of mind, manque m de netteté dans les idées. (b) Manque de soin; négligence f (de style). (c) Sentimentalité larmoyante.

sloppy ['slɔpi], a. 1. (a) (Chemin) détrempé, bourbeux, plein de flaques. (b) (Plancher) encore mouillé; (table) qui n'a pas été essuyée. 2. (a) (Of pers.) Mou, f. molle; flasque. (b) (Travail) fait sans soin; (style) négligé. (c) (Vêtement) mal ajusté. F: S. joe, pullover m de très amples proportions. (d) (Roman) larmoyant. S. sentimentality, sensiblerie f.

slosh [slɔʃ], v.tr. P: 1. Flanquer un coup à (qn). 2. Flanquer une (bonne) pile à (qn). sloshed, a. P: Ivre, gris, pompette.

slot¹ [slɔt], s. 1. Entaille f, encoche f, rainure f, mortaise f; cannelure f; fente f (de la tête d'une vis). Cotter s., logement m de clavette. To cut slots, mortaiser des rainures. S.-drilling machine, fraiseuse f à rainer. To put a penny in the s., introduire un penny dans la fente (d'un distributeur). 2. Th: Trappillon m (dans le plateau). 'slot-machine, s. (a) Distributeur m automatique. (b) Appareil m à jetons (pour jeux, etc.). 'slot-meter, s. Compteur m à paiement préalable. 'slot-winding, s. El.E: Enroulement m (d'induit) à rainures.

slot², v.tr. (slotted) Tailler une fente, une rainure, dans (qch.); entailler, encocher, mortaiser. Slotted screw, vis à filets interrompus. Av: Slotted wing, aile à fente. 'slotting-machine, s. Mortaiseuse f.

slot³, s. Ven: Foulées fpl, voies fpl (d'une bête).

sloth [slouθ], s. 1. Paresse f, fainéantise f, indolence f. To become sunk in s., s'avachir, s'aveulir. 2. Z: (a) Paresseux m. (b) S.(-bear), ours jongleur.

slothful ['slouθful], a. Paresseux, -euse, fainéant; indolent. -fully, adv. Paresseusement; avec indolence.

slouch¹ [slautʃ], s. 1. (a) Lourdaud m. (b) Fainéant m. U.S: F: He's no s., il n'est pas empoté. 2. Démarche f mollasse; lourdeur f d'allure. To walk with a s., traîner le pas. S. of the shoulders, épaules arrondies. 'slouch-'hat, s. Grand chapeau mou; sombrero m.

slouch². 1. v.i. Se laisser aller en marchant; manquer de tenue; avoir une allure lourde. Don't s.! tenez-vous droit! To s. away, s'en aller d'un pas traînant, le dos courbé. 2. v.tr. Rabattre le bord de (son chapeau). slouching, a. (a) (Of pers.) (i) Qui traîne le pas; (ii) aux épaules arrondies. (b) (Allure) mollasse.

slough¹ [slau], s. (a) Bourbier m, fondrière f. The sloughs of vice, le bourbier du vice. S.a. DESPOND¹. (b) Terrain marécageux.

slough² [slʌf], s. 1. (Of reptile, insect) Dépouille f, mue f. (Of serpent) To cast its s., quitter sa peau; jeter sa dépouille. 2. Med: Escarre f, croûte f (sur une plaie).

slough³ [slʌf]. 1. v.i. (a) (Of reptile, etc.) Se dépouiller; muer. (b) (Of scab) To s. off, away, tomber; se détacher. (c) (Of wound) Se couvrir d'une escarre. 2. v.tr. (Of reptile) To s. its skin, jeter sa dépouille.

Slovak ['slouvæk], a. & s. Slovaque (mf).

sloven ['slʌv(ə)n], s. 1. Mal peigné, -ée; mal soigné, -ée; maritorne f; souillon m or f. 2. Gâcheur de besogne.

Slovene ['slouvi:n], a. & s. Slovène (mf).

slovenliness ['slʌv(ə)nlinis], s. 1. Négligence f (de mise); manque m de tenue; laisser-aller m inv. 2. Manque de soin.

slovenly ['slʌv(ə)nli], *a.* **1.** (*Of pers.*) Mal peigné, mal soigné. **S. gait,** allure déhanchée; (*of soldier*) allure peu martiale. **S. voice,** voix débraillée. **2.** (*a*) Négligent; sans soin. (*b*) (Travail) négligé, *F:* bousillé.

slow¹ [slou]. **I.** *a.* **1.** (*a*) Lent. **At a s. trot,** au trot ralenti. **S. speed,** petite vitesse; ralenti *m. Cin: etc:* **S. motion,** ralenti. *Mch: Mec.E:* **S. running,** ralenti. **Trees of s. growth,** arbres longs à pousser. **He was a s. speaker,** il avait la parole lente. **It is s. work,** ça ne va pas vite. **S. and sure!** hâtez-vous lentement! *Cu:* **Cook in a s. oven,** faites cuire à feu doux. *Med:* **S. digestion,** digestion paresseuse. **S. pulse,** pouls lent. *Rail:* **S. train,** train omnibus. (*b*) **To be s. to start sth., in starting sth.,** être lent, être peu empressé, à commencer qch. **To be s. to act,** être lent à agir. **He was not s. to . . .,** il ne tarda pas à (agir, répondre, etc.). (*c*) **S. (of intellect),** à l'esprit lourd. **He's frightfully s.,** il a l'intelligence très lourde. **S. child,** enfant tardif, arriéré. (*d*) (Spectacle) ennuyeux, qui manque d'entrain. **Business is s.,** les affaires traînent. **2.** (*Of clock*) **En retard. Your watch is five minutes s.,** votre montre retarde de cinq minutes. **-ly,** *adv.* Lentement; (écrire) à main posée. **Engine running s.,** moteur au ralenti. **Drive s.!** ralentir! **II. slow,** *adv.* (*In certain set phrases*) Lentement. *P.N:* **S.!** Ralentir! **To go slower,** ralentir sa marche. **To go s.,** (i) aller lentement; (ii) ne pas agir à la hâte; (iii) *Ind:* faire la grève perlée. **To go s. with one's provisions,** ménager ses vivres. *Nau:* **S. ahead!** en avant doucement! **'slow-'acting,** *a.* A action lente. **'slow-burning,** *a.* **1.** A combustion lente. **2.** Peu combustible. **'slow-'motion,** *attrib.a. Cin:* **S.-m. film,** film tourné au ralenti. **S.-m. projection,** ralentissement *m* de la projection. **'slow-'witted,** *a.* A l'esprit lent, lourd.

slow². 1. *v.i.* (*a*) **To s. down, to s. up,** ralentir (son allure); diminuer de vitesse. **I have slowed down somewhat,** j'ai un peu ralenti de mes efforts. (*b*) **To s. down (to a stop),** s'arrêter. **2.** *v.tr.* **To s. down, up,** ralentir qch.

slowcoach ['sloukoutʃ], *s. F:* Lambin, -ine.

slowness ['slounis], *s.* **1.** (*a*) Lenteur *f.* **S. to answer,** lenteur à répondre. (*b*) Lourdeur *f,* lenteur (d'esprit). **2.** Retard *m* (d'une pendule).

slowpoke ['sloupouk], *s. U.S: F:* Lambin, -ine.

slow-worm ['slouwə:m], *s.* Orvet *m; F:* serpent *m* de verre.

sludge [slʌdʒ], *s.* Vase *f,* fange *f;* neige à demi fondue. *Ind:* Boue *f* d'émoulage; tartres boueux. (Sewage) **s.,** vidanges *fpl.*

sludgy ['slʌdʒi], *a.* Vaseux, -euse, fangeux, -euse. *Ind:* Boueux, -euse.

slug¹ [slʌg], *s.* Limace *f.*

slug², *s.* **1.** *Sm.a:* Lingot *m.* **2.** *Typ:* (*a*) Lingot. (*b*) Ligne-bloc *f* (de linotype). (*c*) *U.S:* Jeton *m* (pour distributeur automatique). **3.** *U.S: F:* Goutte *f, F:* coup *m* (d'eau-de-vie, etc.).

slug³, *v.tr. P:* (*a*) Amocher (qn). (*b*) Assommer (qn) raide.

sluggard ['slʌgəd], *s.* Paresseux, -euse, fainéant *m.*

sluggish ['slʌgiʃ], *a.* **1.** Paresseux, -euse, léthargique; (esprit) lourd, inerte. **2. S. river,** rivière lente, paresseuse. **S. liver,** foie paresseux, engorgé. **S. digestion,** digestion laborieuse. *Aut:* **S. engine,** moteur mou, peu nerveux. **-ly,** *adv.* **1.** Paresseusement. **2.** (*Of river*) **To flow s.,** couler lentement.

sluggishness ['slʌgiʃnis], *s.* **1.** (*a*) Paresse *f.* (*b*) Lourdeur *f,* pesanteur *f* (de l'esprit). **2.** Lenteur *f* (d'une rivière); paresse (du foie, de l'intestin).

sluice¹ [slu:s], *s.* **1.** *Hyd.E:* (*a*) Écluse *f;* bonde *f* (d'étang). **To open the sluices,** lâcher les écluses. (*b*) Canal *m,* -aux, de décharge. **2.** = SLUICE-VALVE. **3. To give (sth.) a s. down,** laver (le plancher, etc.) à grande eau. **'sluice-gate,** *s.* Porte *f* d'écluse; vanne *f.* **'sluice-valve,** *s.* Vanne *f* (de communication). **'sluice-way,** *s.* Canal *m,* -aux, à vannes.

sluice², *v.tr.* (*a*) *Hyd.E:* Vanner (un cours d'eau). (*b*) **To s. out the water in a reservoir,** laisser échapper l'eau d'un réservoir (par les vannes). (*c*) Laver à grande eau; débourber (un égout).

slum¹ [slʌm], *s.* (*a*) Bas quartier. (*b*) Rue *f,* impasse *f,* sordide. (*c*) Taudis *m.* **S. clearance,** suppression *f* des taudis, lutte *f* contre les taudis; curetage *m.*

slum², *v.i.* (slummed) (*a*) **A: To go slumming,** faire des visites (i) de charité, (ii) de curiosité, dans les quartiers pauvres. (*b*) *F:* **To go slumming with s.o.,** s'abaisser à faire qch. en compagnie de qn. **slumming,** *s. F:* **Intellectual s.,** abaissement intellectuel.

slumber¹ ['slʌmbər], *s.* (*a*) Sommeil *m* (paisible); assoupissement *m;* somme *m.* (*b*) *Com:* **S. wear,** vêtements *mpl* de nuit.

slumber², *v.i.* Sommeiller; être assoupi; dormir (paisiblement).

slummy ['slʌmi], *a.* (Quartier) de taudis. **S. street,** rue *f* sordide.

slump¹ [slʌmp], *s. Com:* Baisse soudaine, effondrement *m* (des cours); crise *f.* **The s. in the book trade,** la crise du livre. **S. in the franc,** dégringolade *f* du franc. **The s.,** la crise, la dépression. économique.

slump², *v.i.* **1.** Tomber lourdement, comme une masse. **2.** *Com: Ind: etc:* (*Of prices, etc.*) Baisser tout à coup; s'effondrer, dégringoler.

slung. *See* SLING².

slunk. *See* SLINK.

slur¹ [slə:r], *s.* **1.** (*a*) Affront *m.* **To put, cast, a s. on s.o.,** infliger un affront à qn. (*b*) Tache *f,* flétrissure *f.* **To cast a s. on s.o.'s reputation,** entamer, porter atteinte à, la réputation de qn. **2.** *Typ:* Frison *m,* macule *f.* **3.** *Mus:* (*a*) (*Sign*) Liaison *f.* (*b*) (*Slurred passage*) Coulé *m.* **4.** (*In speech*) Mauvaise articulation.

slur², *v.* (slurred) **1.** *v.tr.* (*a*) **To s. one's words** (in speaking), mal articuler ses mots; bredouiller. **To s. a word,** *v.i.* **to s. over a word,** bredouiller un mot; escamoter un mot. **To s. (over) a fact,** passer légèrement sur un fait; glisser sur un fait. (*b*) *Mus:* Lier (deux notes); couler (un passage). (*c*) *Typ:* Maculer, friser (une page). **2.** *v.i.* (*Of outline, etc.*) Se brouiller; s'estomper. **slurred,** *a.* (*a*) Brouillé, indistinct. (*b*) *Mus:* (Passage) coulé.

slush [slʌʃ], *s.* **1.** (*a*) Neige à demi fondue. **To tramp through the s.,** patauger dans la neige. (*b*) Fange *f,* bourbe *f.* **2.** *F:* Sensiblerie *f.*

slushy ['slʌʃi], *a.* (*a*) (i) Détrempé par la neige; (ii) boueux, -euse, bourbeux, -euse, fangeux, -euse. (*b*) **S. sentimentality,** sentimentalité fadasse.

slut [slʌt], *s.f.* **1.** Souillon *m* or *f; F:* salope. **2.** Coureuse; *F:* catin.

sluttish ['slʌtiʃ], *a.* (*Of woman*) Malpropre, sale; mauvaise ménagère. **-ly,** *adv.* Malproprement, en salope.

sly [slai], *a.* (slyer, slyest) **1.** (*a*) Matois, rusé, madré. (*b*) Cauteleux, -euse, sournois; en dessous. *F:* **S. dog,** (i) fin matois; (ii) retors *m.* (*c*) *a.* **To do sth. on the s.,** faire qch. furtivement, à la dérobée. **2.** Malin, -igne, malicieux, -euse, espiègle, futé. **-ly,** *adv.* **1.** (*a*) Avec finesse; adroitement. (*b*) Sournoisement, cauteleusement. **2.** D'une manière espiègle.

slyness ['slainis], *s.* **1.** (*a*) Finesse *f.* (*b*) Sournoiserie *f.* **2.** Malice *f,* espièglerie *f.*

smack¹ [smæk], *s.* Léger goût, saveur *f,* soupçon *m* (d'ail, etc.).

smack², *v.i.* **To s. of sth.,** avoir un léger goût de qch. **Opinions that s. of heresy,** opinions qui sentent l'hérésie, le fagot, le brûlé.

smack³. I. *s.* **1.** Claquement *m,* clic-clac *m* (d'un fouet). **2.** Claque *f.* **S. in the face,** (i) gifle *f;* (ii) affront *m.* **He gave the ball a hard s.,** il frappa vigoureusement la balle. **3.** *P:* Gros baiser retentissant. **II. smack,** *adv.* **1. S. went the whip,** le fouet claqua. **2. He fell s. on the floor,** il est tombé paf! **To bump s. into a tree,** donner en plein contre un arbre. **S. in the middle,** en plein milieu, vlan!

smack⁴. 1. *v.tr.* (*a*) Faire claquer (un fouet). **To s. one's lips,** *F:* se lécher les babines. (*b*) Frapper, taper (avec le plat de la main). **To s. s.o.'s face,** donner une gifle à qn. **2.** *v.i.* (*Of whip*) Claquer. **Smacking kiss,** baiser retentissant.

smack⁵, *s.* (Fishing-)s., bateau pêcheur.

smacker ['smækər], *s.* **1.** *P:* Gifle retentissante. (*b*) Gros baiser. **2.** *P:* (*a*) Livre *f* sterling. (*b*) *U.S:* Dollar *m.*

small [smɔːl]. I. *a.* Petit. **1.** (*a*) Menu. **S. stature,** petite taille. **Dress that makes one look s.,** robe qui vous amincit. **To make oneself s.,** se faire tout petit, rentrer le cou dans, entre, les épaules. **S. shot,** menu plomb. **A s. coffee,** une petite tasse de café. **He is a s. eater,** il n'est pas gros mangeur. *Ven:* **S. game,** menu gibier. *Typ:* **S. letters, minuscules** *f.* *Journ:* **S. ads.,** petites annonces. *S.a.* ARM¹ 1, END¹ 1, HOUR 2. (*b*) **In s. numbers,** en petit nombre. **S. party,** réunion peu nombreuse. **S. committee,** comité restreint. **2.** (*a*) **S. beer,** petite bière. **He thinks no s. beer of himself,** il se croit sorti de la cuisse de Jupiter. (*b*) **S. voice,** voix fluette. **3.** **S. resources,** faibles ressources. **S. income,** mince revenu. **S. harvest,** maigre récolte. **Not the smallest difference,** pas la moindre différence. **He failed, and s. blame to him,** il échoua, et ce n'était nullement sa faute. **It is s. wonder that . . .,** ce n'est guère étonnant que + *sub.* **4.** Peu important; peu considérable. **S. matter,** bagatelle *f.* **S. hotel,** hôtel *m* modeste. **S. change,** menue monnaie. **The smaller industries,** la petite industrie. **S. shopkeeper,** petit commerçant. **S. landowner,** petit propriétaire. **The smallest possible number of people,** le moins de gens possible. **In a s. way,** en petit; modestement. **Great and s.,** les grands et les petits. *S.a.* FRY¹ 1, 2, TALK¹ 1. **5.** Mesquin, chétif, -ive. **S. mind,** petit esprit. **To look s.,** avoir l'air penaud. **To feel rather s.,** ne pas être fier. **To make s.o. look s.,** humilier qn. II. **small,** *s.* **1.** **S. of the back,** creux *m,* chute *f,* des reins. *Sm.a:* **S. of the butt,** poignée *f* de la crosse. **2.** *pl.* **Smalls,** sous-vêtements *mpl.* III. **small,** *adv.* **1.** (Hacher) menu, en petits morceaux. **2.** *See* SING 1. **small-'minded,** *a.* A l'esprit mesquin; qui manque de largeur d'esprit. **'small-scale,** *a.* **1.** **S.-s. model,** modèle réduit. **2.** **S.-s. operations, business,** affaire(s) peu importante(s), de peu d'étendue. **'small-'time,** *a.* *Esp. U.S:* F: De troisième ordre. **S.-t. crook,** petit escroc. **'small-'timer,** *s.* *U.S:* F: Personnage insignifiant. **'small-'town,** *a.* *U.S:* F: Provincial, -aux, de province.

smallholder ['smɔːlhouldər], *s.* Paysan *m,* petit fermier.

smallholding ['smɔːlhouldiŋ], *s.* Petite ferme.

smallish ['smɔːliʃ], *a.* Assez petit; plutôt petit.

smallness ['smɔːlnis], *s.* **1.** Petitesse *f;* exiguïté *f;* faiblesse *f* (d'une somme). **2.** **The s. of his mind,** sa petitesse d'esprit.

smallpox ['smɔːlpɔks], *s.* Petite vérole; variole *f.*

smarm [smɑːm], *v.* F: **1.** *v.tr.* **To s. one's hair down,** s'aplatir les cheveux à la pommade. **2.** *v.i.* **To s. over s.o., up to s.o.,** flagorner qn.

smarmy ['smɑːmi], *a.* F: Doucereux, -euse, flagorneur, -euse.

smart¹ [smɑːt], *s.* Douleur cuisante; cuisson *f* (d'une blessure); cinglure *f* (d'une lanière).

smart², *v.i.* (*a*) (Of wound, etc.) Cuire, brûler. **My eyes are smarting,** les yeux me picotent. (*b*) **To s. under an injustice,** souffrir sous le coup d'une injustice. **He will make you s. for it,** il vous le fera payer cher. **You shall s. for this,** il vous en cuira. **smarting,** *s.* Douleur cuisante.

smart³, *a.* **1.** (Coup de fouet) cinglant; (coup de marteau) sec. **S. box on the ear,** bonne gifle. **2.** Vif, *f.* vive, prompt; alerte. **S. attack,** vive attaque. **S. pace,** vive allure. **That's s. work!** vous allez vite en besogne! **Look s.** (about it)! dépêchez-vous! **3.** (*a*) Habile; à l'esprit éveillé; débrouillard, dégourdi. *P:* **He's a s. one,** c'est une fine mouche. **S. answer,** réponse adroite. (*b*) *Pej:* Malin, madré. **To try to be s.,** faire le malin. **S. practice,** escroquerie *f.* *S.a.* ALEC(K). **4.** Élégant, distingué, chic. **S. dress,** (i) robe habillée; (ii) robe du dernier chic. **To make oneself s.,** se faire beau. **He thinks it smart to . . .,** il croit chic de . . . . **-ly,** *adv.* **1.** Promptement, vivement. **2.** Habilement, adroitement. **3.** (S'habiller) élégamment.

smarten ['smɑːt(ə)n]. **1.** *v.tr.* (*a*) **To s.** (up), accélérer (la production); animer (le dialogue). **To s. s.o. up,** dégourdir qn. (*b*) **To s. oneself up,** se faire beau. **2.** *v.i.* **To s. up.** (*a*) S'animer. (*b*) Se dégourdir; prendre du chic.

smartness ['smɑːtnis], *s.* **1.** (*a*) Vivacité *f* (d'esprit); débrouillardise *f.* (*b*) A-propos *m* (d'une réponse). **2.** Habileté peu scrupuleuse; finesse *f.* **3.** Élégance *f,* coquetterie *f* (de toilette); chic *m.*

smash¹ [smæʃ]. I. *s.* **1.** (*a*) F: Coup écrasant. **He fell with an awful s.,** il est tombé comme une masse. (*b*) *Ten:* Coup écrasé; smash *m.* (*c*) *attrib.* *Th: etc:* **S. hit,** succès fou. **The film was a s. hit,** le film a fait fureur. **2.** (*a*) Mise *f* en morceaux, en miettes; fracassement *m.* (*b*) Désastre *m,* sinistre *m* (de chemin de fer). **Car s.,** accident *m;* collision *f,* tamponnement *m* (de voitures). **3.** Débâcle *f;* faillite (commerciale); krach *m* (d'une banque). II. **smash,** *adv.* **1.** **To go s.,** (i) (of firm) faire faillite, tomber en faillite; (of bank) sauter. **2.** **To run s. into sth.,** se heurter de front contre qch.

smash². I. *v.tr.* **1.** (*a*) **To s. sth. against sth.,** heurter qch. contre qch. avec violence. (*b*) *Ten:* Écraser, massacrer, smasher (la balle). **2.** (*a*) **To s. sth. to pieces,** briser qch. en morceaux. **To s. the door open,** enfoncer la porte. **S.-and-grab raid,** rafle *f* (de bijoux) après bris de devanture. (*b*) Détruire; écraser (une armée). (*c*) Ruiner (qn); faire échouer (un projet). II. **smash,** *v.i.* **1.** Se heurter violemment (contre qch.). **2.** Éclater en morceaux; se briser. **3.** Faire faillite; (of bank) sauter. **smash in,** *v.tr.* Enfoncer, défoncer (une boîte); enfoncer (une porte). *F:* **To s. s.o.'s face in,** casser la figure à qn. **smash up,** *v.tr.* Briser en morceaux; fracasser. **'smash-up,** *s.* **1.** Destruction complète. *Aut: Rail:* Collision *f.* **2.** Débâcle *f;* faillite *f.* **smashing,** *a.* **1.** (Coup) écrasant, assommant. **2.** *F:* **That's s.!** ça, c'est formidable! c'est sensas!

smasher ['smæʃər], *s.* (*a*) Coup écrasant. (*b*) *F:* **To come a s.,** faire une violente culbute. (*c*) *F:* **She's a s.!** c'est une jolie pépée!

smattering ['smætəriŋ], *s.* Légère connaissance (d'une langue, etc.). **To have a s. of chemistry,** avoir des notions de chimie.

smear¹ [smiər], *s.* **1.** Tache *f,* souillure *f.* *attrib.* **S. campaign,** campagne *f* de diffamation. **2.** (For microscopic slide) Frottis *m* (de sang, etc.).

smear², *v.tr.* **1.** (*a*) Barbouiller, salir (with, de). (*b*) Enduire (with, de). **2.** Maculer, barbouiller (une page écrite). (Of outline) **To get smeared,** s'estomper. **3.** *Esp. U.S:* **To s.s.o., s.o.'s reputation,** diffamer, calomnier qn.

smeary [smiəri], *a.* **1.** Taché, barbouillé; aux contours brouillés. **2.** Graisseux, -euse.

smell¹ [smel], *s.* **1.** (Sense of) s., odorat *m;* flair *m* (d'un chien). **To have a keen sense of s.,** avoir l'odorat fin. **2.** (*a*) Odeur *f;* parfum *m.* **Unpleasant s.,** relent *m.* (Good) **s. of cooking,** fumet *m* de cuisine. (*b*) Mauvaise odeur.

smell², *v.* (*p.t. & p.p.* smelt, *occ.* smelled) **1.** *v.tr. & ind.tr.* (*a*) Flairer (qch.); sentir (une fleur). **To s. a bottle of salts,** respirer un flacon de sels. **The dog smelt at my shoes,** le chien flaira mes souliers. (*b*) *Abs.* Avoir de l'odorat. (*c*) Sentir l'odeur de (qch.); sentir (une odeur). (*d*) Sentir, flairer, pressentir (le danger). **2.** *v.i.* (*a*) (Of flower, etc.) Sentir. **To s. nice,** sentir bon. **Room that smells damp,** pièce qui sent l'humidité. (*b*) Sentir (mauvais); avoir une forte odeur. **smell out,** *v.tr.* (*a*) (Of dog) Flairer, dépister (le gibier). (*b*) Découvrir (un secret). **'smelling-bottle,** *s.* *O:* Flacon *m* de sels. **'smelling-salts,** *s.pl.* *O:* Sels (volatils) anglais; *F:* sels.

smelliness ['smelinis], *s.* Mauvaise odeur; puanteur *f,* fétidité *f* (d'un taudis, etc.).

smelly ['smeli], *a.* *F:* Malodorant.

smelt¹ [smelt], *v.tr.* *Metall:* **1.** Fondre (le minerai). **2.** Extraire (le métal) par fusion. **smelting,** *s.* (*a*) Fonte *f,* fonderie *f,* fusion *f.* (*b*) Extraction *f* (du métal). **S. works,** fonderie *f.*

smelt², *s.* *Ich:* (*a*) Éperlan *m.* (*b*) *pl.* Smelts, *Fr.C:* poissons des chenaux.

smelt³. *See* SMELL².

smilax ['smailæks], *s.* *Bot:* Smilax *m.*

smile¹ [smail], *s.* Sourire *m.* **Scornful s.,** sourire de mépris. **With a s. on his lips,** le sourire aux lèvres. **To give a faint s.,** sourire du bout des lèvres; esquisser un sourire. **Fixed s.,** sourire stéréotypé. **To be all smiles,** être tout souriant. **Face wreathed in smiles,** visage rayonnant.

smile². **1.** *v.i.* Sourire. **He smiled disdainfully,** il eut un sourire dédaigneux. **To s. (up)on, at, s.o.,** sourire à qn. (*Of child*) **To s. in his sleep,** rire aux anges. **To keep smiling,** garder le sourire. **2.** *v.tr.* (*a*) **To s. a bitter smile,** sourire amèrement. (*b*) **To s. a welcome to s.o.,** accueillir qn avec, par, un sourire. **smiling,** *a.* Souriant. **He always comes up s.,** il garde toujours le sourire. **-ly,** *adv.* En souriant.

smirch¹ [sməːtʃ], *s.* Tache *f*; salissure *f*, souillure *f*.

smirch², *v.tr.* Tacher; salir, souiller.

smirk¹ [sməːk], *s.* Sourire affecté, minaudier.

smirk², *v.i.* Sourire d'un air affecté; minauder. **smirking,** *a.* Affecté; minaudier, -ière.

smite [smait], *v.tr.* (smote [smout]; smitten [smitn]) Frapper. **1.** *Lit:* **To s. one's thigh,** se taper la cuisse avec la main. *S.a.* HIP¹ 1. **My conscience smote me,** je fus frappé de remords. **2.** (*a*) *A:* **To be smitten with blindness,** être frappé de cécité. (*b*) **To be smitten with a desire to do sth.,** être pris du désir de faire qch. *F:* **He's quite smitten with her,** il est épris d'elle. **3.** *v.i. Lit:* **A sound smote upon his ear,** un son lui frappa l'oreille.

smith [smiθ], *s.* Forgeron *m.* **Shoeing s.,** maréchal ferrant.

smithereens ['smiðə'riːnz], *s.pl. F:* Morceaux *m*; miettes *f.* **To smash, knock, sth. (in)to s.,** briser, réduire, qch. en éclats, en mille morceaux, atomiser qch.

smithy ['smiði], *s.* Forge *f.*

smitten. *See* SMITE.

smock¹ [smɔk], *s. Cost:* Blouse *f*, sarrau *m.*

smock², *v.tr. Needlew:* Orner, broder (un vêtement) de smocks. **smocking,** *s. Needlew:* Smocks *mpl.*

smog [smɔg], *s. F:* Brouillard enfumé.

smoke¹ [smouk], *s.* **1.** Fumée *f.* (*Of project*) **To end in s.,** s'en aller en fumée; n'aboutir à rien. **There's no s. without fire,** il n'y a pas de fumée sans feu. **2.** (*a*) Action de fumer (du tabac). **Will you have a s.?** voulez-vous fumer? (*b*) Quelque chose à fumer; pipe *f*, cigare *m*, cigarette *f.* **'smoke-bomb,** *s.* Bombe *f* fumigène. **'smoke-blackened,** *a.* Noirci de fumée. **'smoke-cured, -dried,** *a.* (Jambon, etc.) fumé. **'smoke-free,** *a.* (Air *m*) pur, sans fumée. **'smoke-grey,** *a.* Gris fumé *inv.* **'smoke-screen,** *s. Mil: etc:* Rideau *m* de fumée; nuage artificiel. **'smoke-stack,** *s.* Cheminée *f* (de locomotive, d'usine, de bateau à vapeur).

smoke². **1.** *v.i.* Fumer. **2.** *v.tr.* (*a*) Fumer (le jambon). (*b*) Noircir de fumée, enfumer (le plafond). (*c*) Fumer (du tabac, une cigarette). **To s. too much,** abuser du tabac. *Abs.* **Do you s.?** êtes-vous fumeur? **Do you mind if I s.?** la fumée vous gêne-t-elle? *S.a.* PIPE¹ 4. **smoke out,** *v.tr.* Enfumer (un guêpier). **smoked,** *a.* **1.** (*a*) (Jambon etc.) fumé; *Fr.C:* (viande) boucanée. (*b*) (Plafond) enfumé. (*c*) .S. **glass,** verre *m* à teinte fumée. **2.** *Ch:* Qui a un goût de fumée. **smoking,** *s.* **1.** Émission *f* de fumée. **2.** Fumage *m* (du jambon); *Fr.C:* boucanage *m* (de la viande). **3.** Action *f*, habitude *f* de fumer (le tabac). **No s. (allowed),** défense *f* de fumer. **'smoking-compartment,** *s. Rail:* Compartiment *m* pour fumeurs. **'smoking-jacket,** *s. A. Cost:* Veston *m* d'intérieur. **'smoking-mixture,** *s.* Mélange *m* de tabacs pour la pipe. **'smoking-room,** *s.* Fumoir *m.* **S.-r. stories,** histoires égrillardes.

smokeless ['smouklis], *a.* (Combustible) sans fumée.

smoker ['smoukər], *s.* **1.** Fumeur *m* (de tabac). **Heavy s.,** grand fumeur. **2.** *F:* = SMOKING-COMPARTMENT.

smokiness ['smoukinis], *s.* Condition fumeuse (de l'atmosphère).

smoky ['smouki], *a.* **1.** (*Of atmosphere*) Fumeux, -euse; fuligineux, -euse; (*of room*) plein de fumée. **2.** (Plafond) noirci par la fumée. **3.** S. **lamp,** lampe qui fume.

smooth¹ [smuːð], *a.* **1.** (*a*) (Surface) lisse; (chemin) uni, égal. **S. as glass,** poli, uni, comme la glace. **S. forehead,** front sans rides. **S. skin,** peau douce, satinée. **Sea as s. as a mill-pond,** mer calme comme un lac; mer d'huile. (*b*) (Menton) glabre. **2.** (*a*) Doux, *f.* douce; sans heurts. **S. running,** marche douce (d'une machine); roulement silencieux (d'une voiture). (*b*) **S. voice,** voix moelleuse. (*c*) Doucereux, -euse, mielleux, -euse. **He has a s.**

tongue, c'est un beau parleur. (*d*) *Pej:* **S. young man,** beau parleur; jeune homme à l'air doucereux. **-ly,** *adv.* **1.** Uniment; sans inégalités; sans secousses. **2.** (Marcher, travailler) doucement. **Everything is going on s.,** tout va comme sur des roulettes. **Things aren't going s.,** il y a du tirage. **3.** (Parler) doucereusement. **'smooth-bore,** *a. & s.* (Canon *m*) à âme lisse. **S.-b. gun,** fusil *m* à canon lisse. **'smooth-'chinned,** *a.* **1.** Au menton rasé de près. **2.** Imberbe. **'smooth-faced,** *a.* A l'air doucereux. **'smooth-'running,** *a.* (*Of machine, etc.*) A marche douce, régulière. **'smooth-'shaven,** *a.* Rasé de près. **'smooth-'spoken, -'tongued,** *a.* Aux paroles doucereuses.

smooth², *s.* **1. To give one's hair a s.,** lisser ses cheveux. **2.** Partie lisse (de qch.); terrain uni. *See* ROUGH¹ III. 3.

smooth³, *v.tr.* **1.** Lisser (ses plumes, ses cheveux); aplanir (une planche); égaliser (le terrain). **To s. one's brow,** se dérider. **To s. s.o.'s ruffled spirits,** apaiser l'irritation de qn. **To s. the way for s.o.,** aplanir la voie pour qn. **2.** Adoucir (un angle). **smooth away,** *v.tr.* Aplanir (un obstacle). **smooth down, 1.** *v.tr.* (*a*) Lisser (ses plumes, etc.). (*b*) Enlever (une rugosité, etc.). **To s. things down for s.o.,** aplanir les difficultés pour qn. (*c*) Calmer, radoucir (qn). **2.** *v.i.* (*Of sea, anger*) Se calmer, s'apaiser. **smooth out,** *v.tr.* Faire disparaître (un faux pli); défriper, défroisser (un vêtement). **smooth over,** *v.tr.* **1.** Aplanir (une difficulté). **2.** (*a*) Pallier (une faute). (*b*) **To s. things over,** arranger les choses.

smoothie ['smuːði], *s. U.S: F: Pej:* **1.** Personne trop polie. **2.** Individu doucereux, mielleux.

smoothness ['smuːðnis], *s.* **1.** (*a*) Égalité *f* (d'une surface); satiné *m* (de la peau). (*b*) Calme *m* (de la mer). **2.** Douceur *f* (de la marche d'une machine). **3.** (*Of pers.*) Douceur feinte; air doucereux.

smote. *See* SMITE.

smother ['smʌðər]. **1.** *v.tr.* (*a*) Étouffer (qn, le feu); suffoquer (qn). **To s. a curse,** étouffer un juron. (*b*) Recouvrir. **Strawberries smothered with cream,** fraises enrobées de crème. **Pedestrian smothered in dust,** piéton enfariné de poussière. **2.** *v.i.* Suffoquer. **smothered,** *a.* (Cri) sourd. **smothering¹,** *a.* (*Of atmosphere, etc.*) Étouffant, suffocant. **smothering²,** *s.* Étouffement *m*, suffocation *f.*

smoulder ['smouldər], *v.i.* (*a*) Brûler lentement, sans flamme. (*b*) (*Of fire, rebellion*) Couver (sous la cendre). **smouldering¹,** *a.* (*a*) Qui brûle sans fumée. (*b*) Qui couve (sous la cendre). **smouldering²,** *s.* Combustion lente.

smudge¹ [smʌdʒ], *s.* Tache *f* (de suie, etc.); noircissure *f*; bavure *f* de plume.

smudge², *v.tr.* Salir, souiller; barbouiller, maculer (son écriture).

smudgy ['smʌdʒi], *a.* **1.** Taché, souillé; (*of writing*) barbouillé, maculé. **2.** (Contour) estompé.

smug [smʌg], *a.* (Ton, air) suffisant; satisfait de soi-même. **S. optimism,** optimisme béat. **-ly,** *adv.* D'un air suffisant. **'smug-faced, -looking,** *a.* A l'air suffisant.

smuggle ['smʌgl], *v.tr.* (Faire) passer (des marchandises) en contrebande, en fraude. *Abs.* Faire la contrebande. **To s. sth. into the room,** apporter qch. dans la salle furtivement. **To s. sth. away,** escamoter (une lettre, etc.). **smuggling,** *s.* Contrebande *f*; fraude *f* (aux droits de douane).

smuggler ['smʌglər], *s.* Contrebandier *m*; fraudeur *m* (à la douane).

smugness ['smʌgnis], *s.* Suffisance *f*; fatuité *f.*

smut [smʌt], *s.* **1.** Tache *f* de suie; flocon *m* de suie. **2.** *Coll:* Grivoiseries *fpl*, indécences *fpl*, ordures *fpl.* **To talk s.,** dire des saloperies, des cochonneries. **3.** *Agr:* Charbon *m*, nielle *f* (des céréales).

smuttiness ['smʌtinis], *s.* **1.** Noirceur *f*, saleté *f.* **2.** Obscénité *f*, grivoiserie *f.* **3.** *Agr:* État niellé, charbonné (du blé).

smutty ['smʌti], *a.* **1.** (*a*) Noirci; sali (de suie). (*b*) (*Of conversation*) Malpropre, ordurier, grivois. **A s. story,** une histoire cochonne. **2.** *Agr:* Niellé.

snack [snæk], *s.* Léger repas; casse-croûte *m inv*; (*for emergencies*) en-cas *m inv.* **To have a s.,** casser la croûte; manger sur le pouce. **'snack-bar,** *s.* Snack-bar *m.*

snaffle[1] [snæfl], s. *Harn:* Filet *m*; mors *m* de bridon. **'snaffle-'bridle**, s. Filet *m*, bridon *m*.

snaffle[2], v.tr. *P:* S'emparer de (qch.); chiper (qch.).

snafu [snɑːˈfuː], a. *U.S:* *P:* (Situation, etc.) extrêmement confuse, chaotique; *P:* bousillé, amoché.

snag[1] [snæg], s. (a) Chicot *m* (d'arbre); souche *f* au ras d'eau; entrave *f* à la navigation fluviale. (b) Écueil *m*; obstacle caché. **That's the s.**, voilà le hic. **To strike, to come on, a s.**, se heurter à un obstacle, avoir un pépin. **There's a s.**, il y a un cheveu. (c) (i) Accroc *m* (dans un vêtement); (ii) maille partie (dans un bas).

snag[2], v.tr. (**snagged**; **snagging**) (a) (*Of boat*) Se heurter contre un chicot; toucher un écueil. (b) Accrocher, faire un accroc à sa robe, son bas.

snail [sneil], s. Limaçon *m*, escargot *m*, colimaçon *m*. **Edible s.**, escargot comestible. **To go at a s.'s pace**, aller à pas de tortue.

snake[1] [sneik], s. Serpent *m*. **Common s.**, couleuvre *f* à collier; serpent d'eau. **A s. in the grass**, (i) une anguille sous roche; (ii) *F:* individu *m* louche, équivoque; séducteur *m*, tombeur *m* de femmes. *Games:* **Snakes and ladders** = le jeu de l'oie. **'snake-bite**, s. Morsure *f* de serpent. **'snake-charmer**, s. Charmeur, -euse, de serpents. **'snake-fence**, s. *U.S:* Clôture *f* en zig-zag. **'snake-root**, s. *Bot: Pharm:* Serpentaire *f*.

snake[2], v.i. Serpenter.

snaky ['sneiki], a. **1.** (a) De serpent. (b) (Langue) perfide, de vipère. **2.** (*Of road*) Serpentant.

snap[1] [snæp], s. **1.** s. (a) Coup *m* de dents. (*Of dog*) **To make a s. at s.o.**, essayer de mordre qn. (b) Coup sec, claquement *m* (des dents, des doigts, d'un fouet). **The box shut with a s.**, la boîte se ferma avec un bruit sec. **2.** Cassure *f*; rupture soudaine. **3. Cold s.**, courte période de temps froid; coup *m* de froid. **4.** *F:* Énergie *f*, vivacité *f*. *O:* **Put some s. into it!** un peu d'énergie! **5.** *Cu:* **Ginger s.**, biscuit croquant au gingembre. **6. S.(-fastener)**, fermoir *m* (de valise); agrafe *f*, fermoir *m* (de collier, de bracelet); bouton *m* à pression. *El:* **S. contact**, contact à languette. **7.** *Phot:* = SNAPSHOT[1]. **8.** Jeu de cartes enfantin. **9.** *U.S:* *F:* **Soft s.**, chose *f*, emploi *m*, facile. **II. snap**, *attrib.a.* Instantané, imprévu. *Parl:* **S. division**, vote *m* de surprise. **To make a s. decision**, se décider sur le coup. **III. snap**, *adv.* Crac. **To go s.**, se casser net. **'snap-lock**, s. Serrure *f* à ressort.

snap[2], v. (**snapped** [snæpt]) **I.** v.i. **1. To s. at s.o.**, (i) (*of dog*) chercher à mordre qn; (ii) (*of pers.*) rembarrer qn. **2.** (*Of whip*) Claquer; faire un bruit sec; (*of fastener*) se fermer avec un bruit sec; (*of pistol*) partir. **3. To s. (asunder)**, se casser net. **II. snap**, v.tr. **1.** (*Of dog*) Happer (qch.). **2.** (a) Faire claquer (un fouet). **To s. one's fingers**, faire claquer ses doigts. **To s. one's fingers at s.o.**, narguer qn. (b) *Phot:* *F:* **To s. s.o.**, prendre un instantané de qn. **3.** Casser, rompre (une canne). **Snapped tendon**, tendon claqué. **4. To s. out an order**, donner un ordre d'un ton sec. **5.** v.tr. & i. *F:* **To s. out of it** se secouer. **snap off. 1.** v.tr. (a) Enlever (qch.) d'un coup de dents. *F:* **Don't s. my head off!** ne m'avalez pas! (b) Casser (le bout d'une canne). **2.** v.i. Se détacher brusquement. **snap up**, v.tr. Saisir, happer (qch.). **To s. up a bargain**, saisir une occasion.

snapdragon ['snæpdrægən], s. *Bot:* Muflier *m*, gueule-de-loup *f*, pl. gueules-de-loup.

snappish ['snæpiʃ], a. Irritable; hargneux, -euse. **-ly**, adv. D'un ton hargneux; avec mauvaise humeur.

snappishness ['snæpiʃnis], s. Humeur hargneuse; irritabilité *f*.

snappy ['snæpi], a. **1.** = SNAPPISH. **2.** (Style) vif, plein d'allant. **S. phrase**, locution pleine de sel. **3.** *F:* **Make it s.!** look s.!** dépêchez-vous! *F:* grouille-toi! **4.** *F:* (Voiture *f*, toilette *f*) chic, dernier cri.

snapshot ['snæpʃɔt], s. *Phot:* *F:* Instantané *m*.

snare[1] [snɛər], s. **1.** (a) *Ven:* Lacet *m*, collet *m*; lacs *m*, filet *m*. (*Of rabbit*) **To be caught in a s.**, être pris au lacet. (b) Piège *m*. (*Of pers.*) **To be caught in the s.**, être pris au piège. **A s. and a delusion**, qch. de trompeur, de décevant. **2.** pl. **Snares of a drum**, timbre *m* d'un tambour. **'snare-drum**, s. Tambour *m* à timbre; caisse claire.

snare[2], v.tr. Prendre (un lapin) au collet, au lacet; attraper (qn).

snarky ['snɑːki], a. *F:* Désagréable, maussade, hargneux, -euse.

snarl[1] [snɑːl], s. Grondement *m*, grognement *m*, (*of tiger*) feulement *m*.

snarl[2], v.i. Grogner, gronder; (*of tiger*) feuler. **snarling**[1], a. Grondant, grognant; (*of pers., dog*) hargneux. **snarling**[2], s. Grondement *m*, grognement *m*.

snarl[3], s. **1.** Enchevêtrement *m*. **2.** *U.S:* *Aut:* Embouteillage *m*.

snarl[4], v.tr. **1.** Enchevêtrer. **2.** *U.S:* *F:* (*Of traffic*) **Snarled up**, pris dans un embouteillage.

snatch[1] [snætʃ], s. **1.** (a) Mouvement vif pour saisir qch. **To make a s. at sth.**, chercher à saisir qch. (b) *U.S:* *P:* Kidnapping *m*. **2.** (a) Courte période. **S. of sleep**, petit somme. **To work by snatches**, travailler à bâtons rompus. (b) **Snatches of song**, fragments *m* de chanson. **'snatch-block**, s. Poulie coupée; galoche *f*. **'snatch-crop**, s. *Agr:* Récolte dérobée.

snatch[2], v.tr. & i. **1.** Saisir, empoigner (qch.). **He snatched (up) his revolver off the table**, il saisit son revolver sur la table. **To s. (at) an opportunity**, saisir une occasion. **To s. a meal**, manger un morceau sur le pouce. **2.** (a) **To s. sth. out of s.o.'s hands**, arracher qch. des mains de qn. **She had her handbag snatched**, on lui a volé son sac à main. (b) *U.S:* *P:* Kidnapper (qn).

sneak[1] [sniːk], s. **1.** Pleutre *m*; pied plat; capon, -onne. **2.** *Sch:* *F:* Cafard, mouchard *m*; rapporteur, -euse. **'sneak-thief**, s. Chapardeur, -euse; chipeur, -euse.

sneak[2], v.i. (a) **To s. off, away**, partir furtivement; s'éclipser. **To s. in, out**, se faufiler dans un endroit, hors d'un endroit; entrer, sortir, à pas de loup. (b) *Sch:* *F:* Moucharder, cafarder. **2.** v.tr. *P:* Chiper, chaparder. **sneaking**, a. **1.** (a) Furtif. **To have a s. liking for sth.**, avoir un penchant inavoué pour qch. (b) Sournois, dissimulé. **2.** Rampant, servile.

sneakers ['sniːkəz], s. pl. = Espadrilles *fpl*.

sneer[1] [sniər], s. **1.** Sourire *m* de mépris; ricanement *m*. **2.** Sarcasme *m*.

sneer[2], v.i. Sourire, rire, d'un air moqueur; ricaner. **To s. at s.o.**, parler de qn d'un ton méprisant. **To s. at riches**, dénigrer les richesses. **sneering**[1], a. Ricaneur, -euse; moqueur, -euse; sarcastique. **-ly**, adv. D'un air méprisant; en ricanant. **sneering**[2], s. **1.** Ricanerie *f*. **2.** Sarcasme *m*.

sneeze[1] [sniːz], s. Éternuement *m*. **To stifle a s.**, réprimer une envie d'éternuer.

sneeze[2], v.i. Éternuer. *F:* **That's not to be sneezed at**, cela n'est pas à dédaigner, *F:* ce n'est pas à cracher dessus.

snick[1] [snik], s. **1.** Entaille *f*, encoche *f*. **2.** Coup *m* de ciseaux; entaille (dans un tissu).

snick[2], v.tr. **1.** Faire une entaille dans (le drap). **2.** *Cr:* **To s. the ball**, couper légèrement la balle.

snicker[1] ['snikər], s. (*Of horse*) (Petit) hennissement (amical).

snicker[2], v.i. **1.** = SNIGGER[2]. **2.** (*Of horse*) Hennir.

snide [snaid], a. *F:* **1. S. remark**, remarque offensante. **2.** Faux, *f.* fausse, factice.

sniff[1] [snif], s. Reniflement *m*. **To get a s. of fresh air**, prendre une bouffée d'air frais.

sniff[2], v.i. & tr. **1.** (a) Renifler. (b) *F:* **To s. at a dish**, renifler sur un plat. **The offer is not to be sniffed at**, l'offre n'est pas à dédaigner. **2.** Flairer (un danger). **3.** Humer, renifler (une prise de tabac). *Med:* 'To be sniffed up the nostrils,' "aspirer par les narines."

sniffle[1] ['snifl], s. *F:* Petit rhume (de cerveau).

sniffle[2], *F:* v.i. **1.** Être enchifrené; renifler. **2.** Larmoyer, pleurnicher.

sniffy ['snifi], a. *F:* **1.** (a) Dédaigneux, -euse. (b) De mauvaise humeur. **2.** D'odeur suspecte.

snifter ['sniftər], s. *P:* Petit verre. **To have a s.**, prendre une goutte.

snigger[1] ['snigər], s. (a) Rire intérieur, en dessous; léger ricanement. (b) Petit rire grivois.

snigger[2], v.i. Rire sous cape; ricaner tout bas. **sniggering**, s. Rires *mpl* en dessous; petits rires.

snip¹ [snip], *s.* **1.** Morceau coupé; petit morceau (de papier, de toile). **2.** (*a*) Petite entaille. (*b*) Coup *m* de ciseaux. **3.** P: (*a*) Certitude *f.* Turf: Gagnant sûr. (*b*) Affaire avantageuse.

snip², *v.tr.* (snipped [snipt]) Couper avec des ciseaux.

snipe¹ [snaip], *s.* Bécassine *f.* **The moor was full of snipe,** la lande abondait en bécassines.

snipe², *v.i. & tr.* **To s. (at) the enemy,** canarder l'ennemi. **To be sniped at,** essuyer les coups de feu de tireurs isolés. **sniping,** *s.* Tir *m* à tuer.

sniper ['snaipər], *s. Mil:* Tireur d'élite embusqué, canardeur *m.*

snippet ['snipit], *s.* **1.** Bout *m,* morceau (coupé). **2.** Court extrait (de journal).

snitch¹ [snitʃ], *s. P:* Nez *m,* P: pif *m.*

snitch², *v.i. P:* **1.** Vendre la mèche; P: moucharder. **2.** Chaparder.

snivel¹ ['sniv(ə)l], *s.* (*a*) Reniflement larmoyant. (*b*) Pleurnicherie *f.*

snivel², *v.i.* (snivelled) Pleurnicher, larmoyer. **snivelling¹,** *a.* Pleurnicheur, -euse; larmoyant. **snivelling²,** *s.* **1.** Reniflement *m.* **2.** Pleurnicherie *f.*

sniveller ['snivlər], *s.* Pleurnicheur, -euse.

snob [snɔb], *s.* (*a*) Prétentieux, -euse. (*b*) Snob *m.* (*c*) (Intellectual) *s.,* poseur, -euse.

snobbery ['snɔbəri], *s.* (*a*) Morgue *f.* (*b*) Pose *f.* (*c*) Snobisme *m.*

snobbish ['snɔbiʃ], *a.* (*a*) Poseur, -euse. (*b*) Snob.

snobbishness ['snɔbiʃnis], *s.* = SNOBBERY.

snood [snu:d], *s. Cost:* Résille *f.*

snook [snu:k], *s. P:* Pied *m* de nez. **To cock a s. at s.o.,** faire un pied de nez à qn.

snooker ['snu:kər], *s.* (Sorte de) jeu *m* de billard.

snoop [snu:p], *v.i.* Fureter, fouiner.

snooper ['snu:pər], *s. F:* Inquisiteur *m;* F: fouineur, -euse, fureteur, -euse.

snootiness ['snu:tinis], *s. P:* Morgue *f.*

snooty ['snu:ti], *a. P:* Prétentieux, -euse, suffisant.

snooze¹ [snu:z], *s. F:* Petit somme, P: roupillon *m.*

snooze², *v.i. F:* Sommeiller; faire un petit somme, P: piquer un roupillon. **snoozing,** *a.* Endormi, assoupi.

snore¹ ['snɔ:r], *s.* Ronflement *m.*

snore², *v.i.* Ronfler. **snoring,** *s.* Ronflement *m.*

snorer ['snɔ:rər], *s.* Ronfleur, -euse.

snorkel ['snɔ:kl], *s.* (i) Schnorchel *m,* schnorkel *m;* (ii) masque sous-marin.

snort¹ [snɔ:t], *s.* **1.** Reniflement *m;* ébrouement *m* (d'un cheval). **2.** P: = SNIFTER.

snort². **1.** *v.i.* Renifler fortement; (*of horse*) s'ébrouer. **2.** *v.tr.* **To s. defiance at s.o.,** lancer un défi à qn avec un reniflement de mépris. **snorting,** *s.* Reniflement *m;* ébrouement *m.*

snorter ['snɔ:tər], *s. P:* (*a*) Chose épatante. (*b*) **Problem that is a regular s.,** problème qui va nous donner du fil à retordre. (*c*) Nau: Vent carabiné. (*d*) = SNIFTER.

snot [snɔt], *s. P:* Morve *f.*

snotty ['snɔti]. P: **1.** *a.* (*a*) Morveux, -euse, roupieux, -euse. (*b*) Sale, dégoûtant. **2.** *s. Navy:* = MIDSHIPMAN.

snout [snaut], *s.* **1.** (*a*) Museau *m;* mufle *m* (de taureau); groin *m* (de porc). (*b*) P: Nez *m,* P: pif *m.* **2.** Ind: Tech: Bec *m,* buse *f,* ajutage *m* (de tuyère, etc.); tuyère *f* (de haut fourneau).

snow¹ [snou], *s.* **1.** Neige *f.* **There has been a fall of s.,** il est tombé de la neige. **Driven s.,** neige vierge. **S. shower,** chute *f* de neige. **Flurry of s.,** rafale *f* de neige. **S. report,** (bulletin d')enneigement *m.* **S. surveying,** relevé *m* d'enneigement, sondage *m* nivométrique. **S. gauge,** nivomètre *m.* Mount: Skiing: **Crusted s.,** (neige) tôlée (*f*). **2.** Cu: **Apple s.,** pommes meringuées. **3.** P: (Drug) Cocaïne *f,* P: coco *f.* '**snow-blind,** *a.* Atteint de la cécité des neiges. '**snow-blindness,** *s.* Cécité *f* des neiges. '**snow-blink,** *s.* Reflet *m,* clarté *f,* des glaces (à l'horizon). '**snow-boots,** *s.pl.* Snow-boots *m;* après-ski *m inv.* '**snow-capped, -clad, -covered,** *a.* Couronné, encapuchonné de neige. '**snow-field,** *s.* Champ *m* de neige. '**snow-leopard,** *s. Z:* Léopard *m* des neiges; once *f.* '**snow-plough,** *s.* Chasse-neige *m inv.* '**snow-white,** *a.* D'un blanc de neige.

snow². **1.** *v. impers.* Neiger. **It is snowing,** il neige; il tombe de la neige. **2. To be snowed in, up,** être retenu, bloqué, pris, par la neige. F: **Snowed under with work,** submergé de besogne.

snowball¹ ['snoubɔ:l], *s.* **1.** Boule *f,* pelote *f,* de neige. **2.** Bot: S.(-tree), boule-de-neige *f;* rose *f* de Gueldre.

snowball², **1.** *v.tr.* **To s. s.o.,** lancer des boules de neige à qn. **2.** *v.i.* (Of crowd, debts, etc.) Faire boule de neige.

snowbound ['snoubaund], *a.* (Of pers.) Retenu par la neige; (of road) bloqué par la neige.

snowdrift ['snoudrift], *s.* Amoncellement *m* de neige, congère *f.*

snowdrop ['snoudrɔp], *s. Bot:* Perce-neige *f inv.*

snowfall ['snoufɔ:l], *s.* (*a*) Chute *f* de neige. (*b*) (Profondeur d') enneigement *m.*

snowflake ['snoufleik], *s.* Flocon *m* de neige.

snowline ['snoulain], *s.* Limite *f* des neiges perpétuelles.

snowman ['snoumæn], *s.* (*a*) Bonhomme *m* de neige. (*b*) **The Abominable S.,** l'abominable homme des neiges.

snowmobile ['snoumo'bi:l], *s.* Tracteur *m* automobile pour expéditions polaires.

snowshoes ['snouʃu:z], *s.pl.* Raquettes *fpl.*

snowstorm ['snoustɔ:m], *s.* Tempête *f* de neige.

snowy ['snoui], *a.* Neigeux, -euse; de neige. **S. hair,** cheveux de neige.

snub¹ [snʌb], *s.* Mortification *f,* avanie *f,* rebuffade *f.* **He got a good s.,** F: il a été mouché de belle façon.

snub², *v.tr.* (snubbed) (*a*) Faire sentir à (qn) qu'il a pris une liberté; remettre (qn) à sa place. (*b*) Infliger un affront à (qn).

snub³, *a.* (Nez) camus, retroussé. '**snub-nosed,** *a.* (Au nez) retroussé.

snuff¹ [snʌf], *s.* Tabac *m* à priser. **To take s.,** priser. **A pinch of s.,** une prise. '**snuff-box,** *s.* Tabatière *f.* '**snuff-coloured,** *a.* (Couleur) tabac *inv.*

snuff², *v.i.* Priser.

snuff³, *v.tr.* A: Moucher (une chandelle). **snuff out.** **1.** *v.tr.* Éteindre (une chandelle) avec des mouchettes. **2.** *v.i. P:* Mourir.

snuffer ['snʌfər], *s.* **1.** A: Moucheur (de chandelles). **2.** *pl.* (Pair of) snuffers, mouchettes *f.*

snuffle¹ ['snʌfl], *s.* **1.** (*a*) Reniflement *m.* (*b*) *pl.* F: **To have the snuffles,** être enchifrené, légèrement enrhumé. **2.** Ton nasillard.

snuffle², *v.i.* **1.** (*a*) Renifler. (*b*) Être enchifrené; avoir le nez bouché. **2.** Nasiller. **snuffling,** *a.* **1.** Qui renifle; enchifrené. **2.** Nasillard.

snuffy ['snʌfi], *a. F:* (Of pers.) Au nez, au linge, barbouillé de tabac. **A s. old man,** un petit vieux malpropre.

snug [snʌg], *a.* **1.** Nau: (Navire) paré (à tout événement). **2.** (Of house) Confortable; (of pers.) bien abrité; bien au chaud. **It is very s. in here,** on est bien ici. F: **S. little job,** emploi *m* pépère. F: **S. little fortune,** fortune rondelette. **To lie s. in bed,** être bien au chaud dans son lit. F: **As s. as a bug in a rug,** tranquille comme Baptiste. **3. To lie s.,** rester coi. **-ly,** *adv.* Confortablement, douillettement.

snuggery ['snʌgəri], *s. F:* (i) Pièce confortable, douillette. (ii) Petit fumoir (du maître de maison); (iii) Rendez-vous *m* des intimes (derrière le bar du bistrot).

snuggle ['snʌgl]. **1.** *v.i.* **To s. up to s.o.,** se pelotonner contre qn. **To s. down in bed,** se blottir dans son lit. **2.** *v.tr.* **To s. a child close to one,** serrer un enfant dans ses bras.

snugness ['snʌgnis], *s.* Confortable *m;* ambiance *f* de bien-être.

so [sou]. **I.** *adv.* **1.** (*a*) Si, tellement. **He is so (very) kind,** il est si aimable. **She isn't so very old,** elle n'est pas tellement vieille. **I am not so sure of that,** je n'en suis pas bien sûr. **He is not so feeble as he appears,** il n'est pas aussi faible qu'il en a l'air. **Would you be so kind as to . . .?** voudriez-vous avoir la bonté de . . .? **What man would be so mean as not to admire him?** quel est l'homme assez mesquin pour ne pas l'admirer? **So greatly, so much,** tellement, tant. **I loved him so (much),** je l'aimais tant. **We enjoyed ourselves so much,** on

s'est joliment bien amuses. **Loving her so, he could
not blame her,** l'aimant à ce point, il ne puovait la
blamer. **The young and the not so young,** les jeunes
et les moins jeunes. *S.a.* EVER 3, FAR[1] 1, LONG[1] III. 1.
(*b*) **If it takes so many men so long to do so much
work** . . ., s'il faut à tant d'hommes tant de temps
pour faire tant de travail. . . . **2.** (*a*) Ainsi; de
cette façon; de cette manière. **Stand so,** tenez-
vous comme ça. **Why do you cry so?** pourquoi
pleurez-vous ainsi? **As X is to Y, so is Y to Z,**
comme X est à Y, Y est à Z. **As the father is so is the
son,** tel père, tel fils. **So many men so many minds,**
autant de têtes autant d'avis. **They are so many
rogues,** ce sont autant de filous. **She so arranged
things that** . . ., elle fit en sorte que + *ind. or sub.*
It so happened that I was there, le hasard a voulu
que je fusse là. **And so forth, and so on,** et ainsi du
reste; et ainsi de suite. **So to say, so to speak,**
pour ainsi dire. **So saying he departed,** ce disant il
partit. (*b*) **I think so,** je le crois. **I suppose so, I
expect so,** je le suppose; sans doute. **I hope so,** je
l'espère bien. **I fear so,** j'en ai bien peur. *S.a.*
SAY[2] 1 (*d*). **So it seems,** à ce qu'il paraît. **I told you so!**
je vous l'avais bien dit! **So much so that** . . ., à
tel point que . . .; tellement que. . . . **Much more
so,** bien plus encore. **It is so; so it is; that's so,**
il en est ainsi; parfaitement; effectivement. **Is that
so?** vraiment? **It's not so,** il n'en est rien. **So be it!**
qu'il en soit ainsi! soit! (*c*) **How so?** comment cela?
Why so? pourquoi cela? **If so,** s'il en est ainsi.
Perhaps so, cela se peut. **Not so,** pas du tout. **Quite
so! just so!** très juste! parfaitement! **A shilling or
so,** un shilling ou à peu près. **A hundred pounds
or so,** une centaine de livres. **In a month or so,**
dans un mois ou deux. (*d*) **He's right and so are you,**
il a raison et vous aussi. **He quickened his pace
and so did I,** il hâta le pas et j'en fis autant. **I thought
you were French.—So I am,** je pensais que vous
étiez Français.—(Je le suis) en effet; mais parfaitement! (*e*) **You're late.—So I am!** vous êtes en
retard.—C'est vrai! (*f*) **A little girl 'so high,** une
petite gamine pas plus haute que ça. **3.** *Conj.phr.*
So that. (*a*) **He stepped aside so that I could come in,**
il s'effaça pour que je puisse entrer. **Speak so that you
are understood,** parlez de (telle) sorte qu'on vous
comprenne. (*b*) **He tied me up so that I could not
move,** il m'a ligoté de (telle) sorte que je ne pouvais
pas bouger. **4.** *Conj.phr.* **So as to.** (*a*) Afin de.
We hurried so as not to be late, nous nous sommes
dépêchés pour ne pas être en retard. (*b*) **Speak so
as to be understood,** parlez de (telle) sorte qu'on vous
comprenne. **To behave so as to annoy one's neighbours,** se conduire de façon à incommoder ses voisins.
II. **so,** *conj.* **1.** Donc; c'est pourquoi. **He did not
reappear so he was thought dead,** il ne reparut
plus, si bien qu'on le crut mort. **2. So there you are!**
vous voilà donc! **So you are not coming?** ainsi
vous ne venez pas? **So, my dear, I am reduced
to** . . ., enfin, mon petit, me voilà réduit à. . . .
So(,) that's what it is?(!) ah! c'est comme ça?(!)
P: **S. what?** (i) et puis quoi? (ii) ça te regarde, toi?
qu'est-ce que ça te fait? 'so-and-so, *s.* F: (*a*) **Mr
So-and-so, Mrs So-and-so,** Monsieur un tel, Madame
une telle; Monsieur, Madame, Chose, Machin. F:
Pej: **The so-and-so played me a shabby trick,** ce sale
type m'a joué un vilain tour. (*b*) **I was asked to do
so-and-so,** on me priait de faire ceci et cela. 'so-
called, *a.* **1.** Ainsi nommé. **The so-c. temperate zone**
la zone dite tempérée. **2. A so-c. doctor,** un soi-disant
docteur. **So-c. improvements,** prétendus progrès.
'so so, 'so-so, *a. & adv.* Médiocre(ment), comme ci
comme ça; F: couci-couça. **I'm only so so,** ça ne va
qu'à moitié. **Business is so so,** les affaires vont
doucement. **It's so-so,** c'est entre les deux.
soak[1] [souk], *s.* **1.** Trempe *f.* **To put (sth.) in s.,** (i)
(faire) tremper (le linge sale); (ii) faire macérer (des
cornichons, etc.); dessaler (le poisson etc.). **2.** *P:*
Ribote *f*, cuite *f.* **3.** *P:* Ivrogne *m*, soûlard *m*,
soûlaud *m.*
soak[2]. **1.** *v.tr.* (*a*) Tremper, détremper. **The rain
soaked me to the skin,** la pluie m'a trempé jusqu'aux
os. (*b*) **To s. sth. in sth.,** tremper qch. dans qch.
To s. a sponge, imbiber une éponge. (*c*) F: Écorcher

(un client). **To s. the rich,** faire payer les riches. **2.**
v.i. (*a*) (*Of thg. in soak*) Baigner, tremper (**in sth.,**
dans qch.). (*b*) S'infiltrer, s'imbiber (**into,** dans).
(*c*) *P:* Boire comme une éponge; s'ivrogner.
soak through, *v.i.* S'infiltrer à travers (qch.).
soak up, *v.tr.* Absorber, boire, imbiber. **soaked,** *a.*
Trempé. **S. to the skin,** trempé jusqu'aux os. **S.
ground,** sol détrempé. **Oil-s. rag,** linge imbibé
d'huile. **soaking[1],** *a.* **1.** Trempé. **2. S. downpour,**
pluie battante. **soaking[2],** *s.* (*a*) Trempage *m*,
trempe *f.* (*b*) Trempée *f.* **To get a s.,** se faire tremper.
F: **A good s.,** un bon arrosage.
soakage ['soukidʒ], *s.* Eau *f* d'infiltration.
soakaway ['soukə'wei], *s.* *Civ.E:* Puisard *m.*
soaker ['soukər], *s.* F: **1.** Biberon, -onne; ivrogne
m, *f;* soiffard *m.* **2.** Déluge *m* de pluie. **Yesterday
was a (regular) s.,** hier il a plu du matin au soir.
soap[1] [soup], *s.* Savon *m.* **Cake of s.,** (pain *m* de)
savon; savonnette *f.* **Household s.** = savon de
Marseille. **S. manufacturer,** fabricant *m* de savon.
S. factory, savonnerie *f.* **The s. industry,** l'industrie
savonnière. *F: U.S:* **S. opera,** feuilleton mélodramatique, sentimental, de radio, de télévision
(diffusé aux frais d'une maison commerciale). *S.a.*
SHAVING-SOAP, SOFT-SOAP[1]. 'soap-box, *s.* Caisse *f* à
savon. F: **S.-b. orator,** orateur de carrefour.
'soap-bubble, *s.* Bulle *f* de savon. 'soap-dish, *s.*
Porte-savon *m inv.* 'soap-powder, *s.* *Dom. Ec:*
Savon *m* en poudre.
soap[2], *v.tr.* **1.** Savonner. **2.** *P:* Flagorner (qn).
soapflakes ['soupfleiks], *s.pl.* Savon *m* en paillettes.
soapiness ['soupinis], *s.* **1.** Caractère savonneux,
nature savonneuse, de qch.; goût *m*, odeur *f*, de
savon. **2.** *Pej:* (*Of pers.*) Onction *f.*
soapstone ['soupstoun], *s.* *Miner:* Stéatite *f;* talc *m.*
soapsuds ['soupsʌdz], *spl.* Eau *f* de savon.
soapwort ['soupwəːt], *s.* *Bot:* Saponaire *f.*
soapy ['soupi], *a.* **1.** (*a*) Savonneux, -euse; couvert,
imprégné de savon. (*b*) **S. taste,** goût de savon.
(*c*) **S. potatoes,** pommes de terre cireuses. **2.** (*Of
pers.*) Doucereux, -euse, onctueux, -euse.
soar ['sɔːr], *v.i.* (*a*) Prendre son essor; monter,
s'élever (dans les airs). **Prices soared,** les prix ont
subi une hausse vertigineuse, ont monté en flèche.
Rents have soared, les loyers ont fait un bond. (*b*)
To s. above the common herd, planer sur la foule.
soaring[1], *a.* **1.** (*a*) Qui monte dans les airs. **S.
steeple,** clocher élancé. (*b*) **S. flight,** vol plané
(d'un oiseau). **2.** (*Ambition*) sans bornes. **soaring[2],**
s. **1.** (*a*) Essor *m.* (*b*) Hausse *f* (des prix). **2.** Plane-
ment *m* (d'un oiseau).
sob[1] [sɔb], *s.* Sanglot *m.* F: **S.-stuff,** littérature
(d'une sentimentalité) larmoyante. 'sob(-)sister,
s.f. F: *U.S: Journ:* Journaliste spécialisé(e) en
reportages d'histoires larmoyantes. 'sob-story, *s.*
F: (*a*) Histoire *f* qui tire les larmes. (*b*) Histoire,
généralement fausse, racontée pour susciter la pitié.
To tell a s.s., raconter ses malheurs pour inspirer
la pitié.
sob[2], *v.* (**sobbed**) **1.** *v.i.* Sangloter; pousser des sanglots.
2. *v.tr.* (*a*) **To s. (out) sth.,** dire qch. en sanglotant.
(*b*) **She was sobbing her heart out,** elle pleurait à
chaudes larmes. **sobbing,** *a.* **In a s. voice,** d'une
voix sanglotante.
sober[1] ['soubər], *a.* **1.** (*a*) Sobre, modéré, tempéré.
(*b*) Calme, posé. **As s. as a judge,** sérieux comme un
juge. **In s. earnest,** bien sérieusement. (*c*) **In his s.
senses,** jouissant de son bon sens. (*d*) **S. fact,** fait
réel. **In s. fact,** en réalité. (*e*) **S. colours,** couleurs
sobres, peu voyantes. **2.** (*a*) Qui n'est pas ivre. **He
is never s.,** il est toujours ivre. **To sleep oneself s.,** cuver
sa boisson, son vin. (*b*) Qui ne s'enivre jamais;
tempérant. **-ly,** *adv.* (*a*) Sobrement, modérément.
(*b*) Avec calme; tranquillement. 'sober-'minded,
a. Sérieux, -euse; pondéré.
sober[2]. **1.** *v.tr.* Dégriser, dessoûler. **This news
sobered him,** cette nouvelle l'a dégrisé. **2.** *v.i.* **To s.
down.** (*a*) S'assagir. (*b*) Se dégriser; se dessoûler.
soberness ['soubənis], *s.* **1.** (*a*) Sobriété *f*, modération
f, tempérance *f.* (*b*) Calme *m*, tranquillité *f.* **2.
To return to a state of s.,** se dessoûler.
sobersides ['soubəsaidz], *s.* Personne grave, pondérée.
sobriety [sou'braiəti], *s.* = SOBERNESS.

soccer ['sɔkər], s. F: Football m.
sociability [,souʃə'biliti], s. Sociabilité f.
sociable ['souʃəbl], a. (a) Sociable. To become more s., s'apprivoiser. (b) Z: S. animals, (animaux) sociétaires (mpl). -ably, adv. Sociablement, amicalement.
sociableness ['souʃəblnis], s. Sociabilité f.
social ['souʃ(ə)l], a. 1. Social, -aux. (a) S. problems, problèmes sociaux. S. sciences, sciences humaines. S. security, sécurité sociale. S. worker, assistante sociale. S. reformer, réformateur, -trice, de la société. S. service, œuvres fpl d'amélioration sociale. S. system, société f. S. insurance, assurances sociales. A S. History of England, Histoire f de la société en Angleterre. (b) S. events, mondanités f. S. gathering, (i) soirée f; (ii) réception f. The top of the s. ladder, le sommet de l'échelle sociale. S. climber, parvenu m. S.a. ENGAGEMENT 1. (c) S. evening, petite soirée intime; réunion f. 2. Man is an essentially s. animal, l'homme est essentiellement sociable. -ally, adv. Socialement.
socialism ['souʃəlizm], s. Socialisme m. State s., étatisme m.
socialist ['souʃəlist], a. & s. Socialiste (mf).
socialistic [souʃə'listik], a. Socialiste.
socialite ['souʃəlait], s. F: Membre m de la haute société; mondain m.
socialize ['souʃəlaiz], 1. v.tr. Socialiser (la propriété, etc.) 2. v.i. U.S: (a) Frayer (with s.o., avec qn). (b) Prendre part aux activités d'une société, d'un club.
society [sə'saiəti], s. 1. Société f. (a) Compagnie f (de qn). He is fond of s., il aime la compagnie. (b) Duties towards s., devoirs envers la société. (c) (High) s., la haute société. Fashionable s., le beau monde. To go into, move in, s., aller dans le monde. S. woman, mondaine f. Journ: S. news, mondanités f. 2. Société (de la Croix rouge, etc.); association f. Charitable s., œuvre f de bienfaisance.
sociological [,souʃiə'lɔdʒik(ə)l], a. Sociologique.
sociologist [,souʃi'ɔlədʒist], s. Sociologue mf.
sociology [,souʃi'ɔlədʒi], s. Sociologie f.
sock¹ [sɔk], s. 1. Chaussette f. (Girls') ankle socks, socquettes f. S.a. PULL UP 1. 2. Semelle intérieure (en liège, etc.). 3. A.Th: S. and buskin, le socque et le cothurne.
sock², s. P: Coup m, gnon m; (in the eye) pochon m. To give s.o. socks, flanquer à qn une bonne raclée.
sock³, v.tr. & i. P: 1. To s. a brick at s.o., lancer un briqueton à qn. 2. To s. (into) s.o., flanquer une beigne à qn.
socket ['sɔkit], s. 1. (a) Emboîture f, douille f; godet m (de pied de machine). El: Lamp s., douille de lampe. (b) Crapaudine f (de gouvernail). (c) Bobèche f (de chandelle). (d) Emplanture f (d'aile d'avion). (e) Cuissard m (de jambe artificielle). 2. Anat: (a) Alvéole m (de dent). (b) Eye-s., orbite f de l'œil; (of horse) salière f. (c) Cavité f articulaire, glène f (d'un os). S.a. BALL¹ 1. 'socket-joint, s. Joint m à rotule.
socle ['sɔkl], s. Arch: Socle m.
Socrates ['sɔkrəti:z]. Pr.n.m. Socrate.
Socratic [sə'krætik], a. Socratique.
sod¹ [sɔd], s. 1. Gazon m. Under the s., enterré. 2. Motte f de gazon. To cut the first s., donner le premier coup de bêche.
sod², v.tr. (sodded) To s. over, up, gazonner (un terrain).
sod³, s. V: Bougre m.
soda ['soudə], s. 1. (a) Ch: Soude f. Caustic s., soude caustique. (b) Com: Washing s., common s., soude du commerce; carbonate m de soude; F: cristaux mpl (de soude). (c) Cu: Cooking s., baking s., bicarbonate m de soude. S.-bread, -cake, pain m, gâteau m, au bicarbonate de soude. U.S: S. biscuit, cracker, biscuit dur. 2. = SODA-WATER. Ice-cream s., limonade f, etc. contenant une glace. 'soda-fountain, s. U.S: Bar m pour glaces et rafraîchissements. 'soda-jerk(er), s. U.S: F: Serveur m dans un soda-fountain. 'soda-water, s. Eau f de seltz; soda m.
sodality [sou'dæliti], s. Ecc: Confrérie f.
sodden ['sɔdn], a. 1. (a) (Of field) (Dé)trempé. (b) (Of bread) Mal cuit; pâteux. 2. S. with drink, abruti par l'alcool.

sodium ['soudiəm], s. Ch: Sodium m. S. nitrate, nitrate m de soude. S. chloride, chlorure m de sodium.
sodomite ['sɔdəmait], s. Sodomite m; pédéraste m.
sodomy ['sɔdəmi], s. Sodomie f; pédérastie f.
soever [sou'evər], adv. Lit: In any way s., n'importe comment. How great s. it may be, quelque grand que ce soit.
sofa ['soufə], s. Furn: Canapé m.
soffit ['sɔfit], s. Arch: Soffite m, intrados m.
soft [sɔft]. I. a. 1. Mou, f. molle. (a) As s. as butter mou comme le beurre. S. iron, fer doux. S. coal houille grasse. S. pencil, crayon tendre. Com: S. fruit, fruits rouges. S.a. CORN² 1, FOOD 1, PALATE ROE². (b) S. to the touch, mou, doux, au toucher moelleux. S. hair, cheveux flous. As s. as silk, doux comme du satin. Pol.Ec: Fin: S. currency, devises faibles. Com: S. goods, matières f textiles; tissus m. S.a. HAT. (c) S. muscles, muscles mous, flasques 2. Doux, f. douce. (a) S. rain, pluie douce. S. water, eau qui n'est pas dure. S. outline, contour mou, flou. S. voice, voix douce. S.a. PEDAL¹ 2. S. step, pas feutré, ouaté. Ling: S. consonant consonne douce. F: S. job, emploi facile et agréable. F: emploi m pépère. F: To have a s. time of it, se la couler douce. S. drinks, boissons non alcooliques. (b) S. words, mots doux, tendres. S. heart, cœur tendre. To have a s. place in one's heart for s.o., avoir un faible pour qn. P: To be s. on s.o., être épris de qn. S.a. SIDE¹ 3. 3. a. & s. F: S. (person), niais, -aise. He's s.! il a perdu la boule! Don't be s. ne fais pas l'imbécile! -ly, adv. 1. (a) Doucement. To tread s., marcher sans bruit. (b) Tendrement. 2. Mollement. II. soft, adv. Doucement. 'soft-'boiled, a. (Œuf) mollet, à la coque. 'soft-'headed, a. F: Faible de cerveau, d'esprit. He's getting s.-h., il se ramollit. 'soft-'hearted, a. Au cœur tendre; compatissant. 'soft-'pedal, v.tr. 1. Mus: Se servir de la pédale douce (d'un piano). 2. F: (a) To s.-p. an incident, etc., atténuer, amoindrir, un incident; obscurcir une histoire. (b) Ralentir (son progrès); marcher doucement (dans une affaire). (c) Abs. You'd better s.-p., tu ferais bien d'y aller doucement, de te méfier. 'soft-'sawder, s. F: O: Flatterie f, patelinage m. 'soft-'skinned, a. A peau tendre. Mil: S.-s. vehicles, véhicules non blindés. 'soft-'soap¹, s. 1. Savon vert, noir. 2. F: Flatterie f, flagornerie f. soft-soap², v.tr. F: Flatter (qn), faire du plat à (qn). 'soft-'spoken, a. Mielleux, -euse, doucereux, -euse. 'soft-'witted, a. = SOFT-HEADED.
soften ['sɔfn]. 1. v.tr. (a) Amollir, ramollir, mollifier. (b) Assouplir (le cuir). (c) Affaiblir, énerver. Softened by idleness, (r)amolli par l'oisiveté. (d) Adoucir (sa voix). Curtains that s. the light, rideaux qui tamisent la lumière. (e) Attendrir, émouvoir (qn). (f) Soulager (la douleur). 2. v.i. (a) S'amollir, se ramollir. (b) S'attendrir. softening, s. (a) Amollissement m. S. of the brain, ramollissement m du cerveau. (b) Assouplissement m (du cuir). (c) Adoucissement m du caractère. (d) Attendrissement m.
softener ['sɔfnər], s. Substance amollissante; ramollissant m. S.a. WATER-SOFTENER.
softness ['sɔftnis], s. 1. Douceur f (de la peau, du climat); tiédeur f (de l'air). 2. (a) Mollesse f (de caractère); manque m d'énergie. (b) Flou m (des contours). 3. Niaiserie f, simplicité f.
softwood ['sɔftwud], s. 1. Carp: Bois m tendre. 2. For: Essences mpl conifères.
softy ['sɔfti], s. F: Niais, -aise.
soggy ['sɔgi], a. 1. Détrempé; saturé (d'eau). 2. (Of bread, etc.) Pâteux, -euse; lourd.
soil¹ [sɔil], s. (a) Sol m, terrain m, terre f. Rich s., terre grasse. Light s., loose s., terre meuble. (b) One's native s., le sol, le pays, natal. Lit: Son of the s., fils de la terre.
soil², v.tr. (a) Souiller, salir. (b) Material that soils easily, tissu qui se salit facilement. soiled, a. Souillé, sali, défraîchi. S. linen, linge sale.
sojourn¹ ['sɔdʒə(:)n, 'sʌdʒə(:)n], s. A. & Lit: 1. Séjour m. 2. Lieu m de séjour.
sojourn², v.i. Lit: Séjourner. sojourning, s. Séjour m.

sol [sɔl], s. Mus: Sol m. 'sol-'fa¹, s. Mus: Solfège m. 'sol-'fa², v.tr. Mus: Solfier.

solace¹ ['sɔləs], s. Lit: Consolation f, soulagement m. solace², v.tr. Lit: Consoler (qn); soulager, adoucir (la douleur de qn).

solan(-goose) ['sɔulən('gu:s)], s. Orn: Fou m.

Solanaceae [sɔlə'neisii:], s.pl. Bot: Solan(ac)ées f.

solar ['soulər], a. (Système) solaire. Anat: S. plexus, plexus m solaire.

solarium [sɔ'lɛəriəm], s. Med: Solarium m.

sold. See SELL².

solder¹ ['sɔldər], s. Soudure f. Soft s., soudure tendre. Hard s., soudure forte; brasure f.

solder², v.tr. Souder; ressouder. 'soldering-bit, s. Tls: Fer m à souder; soudoir m. 'soldering-lamp, s. Lampe f à souder, à braser.

soldier¹ ['sɔuldʒər], s. 1. (a) Soldat m. Three soldiers and two civilians, trois militaires m et deux civils. Private s., simple soldat. Old s., ancien soldat; vétéran m. Tin, toy, s., soldat de plomb. S. of fortune, soldat, officier m, de fortune. (b) Tacticien m, stratégiste m. (c) Nau: F: (i) Faınéan⁺ m; (ii) marin m d'eau douce. 2. (a) Ent: S. (-ant), so'dat (de termites). (b) Crust: S. (-crab), bernard-l'ermite m.

soldier², v.i. Faire le métier de soldat. soldiering, s. Le métier de soldat, des armes.

soldierly ['sɔuldʒəli], a. De soldat. S. bearing, allure martiale, militaire.

soldiery ['sɔuldʒəri], s. Coll. Soldats mpl, militaires mpl.

sole¹ [soul], s. 1. Plante f (du pied). 2. Semelle f (de chaussure). 3. Semelle (de rabot, de crosse de golf, etc.).

sole², v.tr. (a) Mettre une semelle à (un soulier). (b) Ressemeler. soling, s. (a) Pose f d'une semelle. (b) Ressemelage m.

sole³, s. Ich: Sole f.

sole⁴, a. Seul, unique. The s. management, l'entière direction. S. right, droit exclusif. S. agent, agent exclusif. S. legatee, légataire universel. -ly, adv. Uniquement. S. responsible, seul responsable.

solecism ['sɔlisizm], s. 1. Gram: Solécisme m; faute f de grammaire. 2. S. (in conduct), solécisme (de conduite); impair m.

solemn ['sɔləm], a. 1. Solennel, -elle. S. fact, réalité sérieuse. S. duty, devoir sacré. S. ceremony, solennité f. It is the s. truth, je vous jure que c'est vrai. 2. (Of pers.) Grave, sérieux, -euse. To keep a s. face, composer son visage. -ly, adv. 1. Solennellement. 2. Gravement, sérieusement.

solemness ['sɔlemnis], s. = SOLEMNITY 1.

solemnity [sɔ'lemniti], s. 1. (a) Solennité f. (b) Gravité f (de maintien). 2. Fête solennelle.

solemnization [,sɔləmnai'zeif(ə)n], s. Sclennisation f; célébration f (d'un mariage).

solemnize ['sɔləmnaiz], v.tr. 1. Solenniser (une fête); célébrer (un mariage). 2. Prêter de la solennité à (une occasion).

solenoid ['sɔlinɔid], s. El: Solénoïde m.

solfatara [,sɔlfə'ta:rə], s. Geol: Solfatare f, soufrière f.

solfeggio [sɔl'fedʒiou], s. Mus: Solfège m.

solicit [sɔ'lisit], v.tr. Solliciter (une faveur). To s. s.o. for sth., solliciter qch. de qn. To s. votes, solliciter, briguer, des voix. 2. (Of prostitute) Raccrocher. Jur: To s. in a public place, racoler sur la voie publique. soliciting, s. (Of prostitute) Jur: Raccrochage m, racolage m.

solicitation [sɔ,lisi'teif(ə)n], s. 1. Sollicitation f. 2. (Of prostitute) Raccrochage m; racolage m.

solicitor [sɔ'lisitər], s. Jur: = Avoué m. The S. General, le conseiller juridique de la Couronne.

solicitous [sɔ'lisitəs], a. Soucieux, -euse, désireux, -euse (of, de). S. about sth., préoccupé de qch. To be s. for s.o.'s comfort, avoir à cœur le confort de qn. To be s. of sth., désirer qch. -ly, adv. Avec sollicitude; soucieusement.

solicitousness [sɔ'lisitəsnis], solicitude [sɔ'lisitju:d], s. Sollicitude f, souci m, préoccupation f.

solid ['sɔlid], 1. a. Solide. (a) S. food, aliment solide. To become s., se solidifier. (b) To build on s. foundations, bâtir sur le solide. Steps cut in the s. rock, escalier taillé dans la pierre vive. (c) S. common

sense, solide bɔn sens. (d) Plein, massif, -ive. S. contents, volume plein. S. mahogany table, table en acajou massif. Pond frozen s., étang gelé jusqu'au fond. Typ: Matter set s., texte non interligné. S. measures, mesures de volume. S.a. GEOMETRY. To sleep for nine s. hours, dormir neuf heures d'affilée. S. vote, vote unanime. (e) En une seule pièce. Parts cast s., parties (coulées) monobloc. 2. s. Solide m. -ly, adv. 1. Solidement. 2. To vote s. for sth., voter qch. à l'unanimité.

solidarity [,sɔli'dæriti], s. Solidarité f.

solidification [sə,lidifi'keif(ə)n], s. (i) Solidification f; (ii) congélation f (de l'huile).

solidify [sə'lidifai]. 1. v.tr. Solidifier; concréter (l'huile). 2. v.i. (i) Se solidifier; (ii) se figer; se congeler.

solidity [sə'liditi], s. Solidité f.

solidness ['sɔlidnis], s. 1. Solidité f. 2. Unanimité f (d'un vote).

solidungular [,sɔlid'ʌŋgjulər], solidungulate [,sɔlid-'ʌŋgjuleit], a. Z: Solipède.

soliloquist [sə'liləkwist], s. Monologueur m.

soliloquize [sə'liləkwaiz], v.i. Monologuer; se parler à soi-même.

soliloquy [sə'liləkwi], s. Soliloque m; monologue (intérieur).

soliped ['sɔliped], s. Z: Solipède m.

solitaire [,sɔli'tɛər], s. 1. Solitaire m (diamant de bague). 2. Games: Solitaire.

solitary ['sɔlit(ə)ri], a. (a) Solitaire; qui est ou qui se sent seul. Not a s. one, pas un seul. S.a. CONFINEMENT 1. (b) (Lieu) solitaire, retiré. -ily, adv. Solitairement.

solitude ['sɔlitju:d], s. 1. Solitude f, isolement m. 2. (a) Lieu m solitaire. (b) Lieu inhabité.

solo, pl. -os, ['soulou, -ouz], s. 1. Mus: Solo m. To play s., jouer en solo. Violin s., solo de violon. S. violin, violon solo. 2. Cards: S. whist, whist m de Gand. To go s., jouer solo. 3. Av: To make a s. flight, voler seul.

soloist ['soulɔist], s. Mus: Soliste mf.

Solomon ['sɔləmən]. Pr.n.m. Salomon. Geog: The S. Islands, les îles Salomon. 'Solomon's 'seal, s. Bot: Sceau m de Salomon.

solstice ['sɔlstis], s. Astr: Solstice m.

solubility [,sɔlju'biliti], s. 1. Solubilité f (d'un sel). 2. To question the s. of a problem, mettre en doute la résolution d'un problème.

soluble ['sɔljubl], a. 1. Soluble. 2. (Problème) soluble, résoluble.

solution [sə'lu:ʃ(ə)n], s. Solution f. 1. (a) Dissolution f. (b) Ch: Standard s., liqueur titrée; solution normale. (Rubber) s., (dis)solution (de caoutchouc). 2. (a) (Ré)solution f (d'une équation). (b) (Answer) Solution. 3. S. of continuity, solution de continuité.

solvability [,sɔlvə'biliti], s. 1. Solvabilité f (d'un commerçant). 2. Résolubilité f (d'un problème).

solvable ['sɔlvəbl], a. (Problème) résoluble.

solve [sɔlv], v.tr. Résoudre (un problème). To s. a riddle, trouver le mot d'une énigme. Problem not yet solved, problème encore en suspens. Mth: To s. an equation, résoudre une équation.

solvency ['sɔlvənsi], s. Solvabilité f.

solvent ['sɔlvənt]. 1. a. Com: Solvable. 2. a. & s. Dissoluant (m). Ch: Solvant m.

Somali, pl. -alis, -ali [sə'mɑ:li, -ɑ:li:z, -ɑ:li], a. & s. Ethn: Somali (m).

Somalia [sə'mɑ:liə]. Pr.n. Geog: La République démocratique de Somalie.

Somaliland [sə'mɑ:lilænd]. Pr.n. (a) French S., la Côte française des Somalis. (b) Hist: La Somalie. British S., Italian S., la Somalie britannique, italienne.

sombre ['sɔmbər], a. Sombre, morne. -ly, adv. Sombrement.

some [sʌm]. I. a. 1. Quelque, quelconque. (a) S. other solution will have to be found, il faudra trouver quelque autre solution. In s. form or (an)other, sous une forme ou sous une autre. He will arrive s. day, il arrivera un de ces jours. I shall see you s. day this week, je vous verrai dans le courant de la semaine. S. way or another, d'une manière ou d'une autre. To make s. sort of reply, répondre d'une façon quelconque. (b) Give it to s. lawyer or

other, remettez-le aux mains de n'importe quel notaire. **To ask s. experienced person,** se rapporter à l'avis de quelqu'un qui a, qui ait, de l'expérience. **2.** (*Partitive*) De. **To drink s. water,** boire de l'eau. **To eat s. fruit,** manger des fruits. **Can you give me s. lunch?** pouvez-vous me donner à déjeuner? **3.** (*a*) Quelque. **S. distance away,** à quelque distance de là. **After s. time,** après un certain temps. **It takes s. time,** cela prend pas mal de temps. **At s. length,** assez longuement. (*b*) (*In the pl.*) **There are s. others,** il y en a d'autres. **S. days ago,** il y a quelques jours. **S. days he is better,** certains jours il va mieux. **4.** *F:* (*Intensive*) **He's s. doctor,** (i) c'est un médecin à la hauteur; (ii) *Iron:* comme médecin il est plutôt quelconque. **It was s. dinner,** c'était un chic dîner. **II.** some, *pron.* **1.** *Pers.* Certains. **S. agree with us, and s. disagree,** les uns sont de notre avis, d'autres ne le sont pas. **We scattered, s. one way, s. another,** on se dispersa, qui d'un côté, qui de l'autre. **2. I have s.,** j'en ai. **Take s.!** prenez-en! **Give me s. of that wine,** donnez-moi de ce vin. **S. of them,** quelques-uns d'entre eux. **I agree with s. of what you say,** je suis d'accord avec une partie de ce que vous dites. *F:* **He's up to all the tricks and then s.,** il les sait toutes et une par-dessus. **III.** some, *adv.* **1.** (*a*) Environ, quelque *inv.* **S. twenty pounds,** une vingtaine de livres. **S. five hundred people,** environ cinq cents personnes; quelque cinq cents personnes. (*b*) **I waited s. few minutes,** j'ai attendu quelques minutes. **2.** *U.S: F:* **It amused me s.,** ça m'a pas mal amusé.
somebody ['sʌmbədi], *s. or pron.* Quelqu'un. **1.** *pron.* **S. told me so,** quelqu'un, on, me l'a dit. **S. is knocking,** on frappe. **S. passing at the time,** un passant. **I was speaking to s. I know,** je parlais à une personne que je connais, avec une connaissance, avec une personne de ma connaissance. **S. or other has told him . . .,** je ne sais qui lui a dit. . . . **Mr S. or other,** Monsieur Chose. **2.** *s. or pron. F:* (*pl.* somebodies ['sʌmbədiz]) **He's** (*a*) **s.,** c'est un personnage. **He thinks he's s.,** il se croit quelqu'un.
somehow ['sʌmhau], *adv.* **1.** De façon ou d'autre, d'une manière ou d'une autre. **We'll manage s.,** on se débrouillera. **2. I never liked him s.,** je ne sais pourquoi mais il ne m'a jamais été sympathique.
someone ['sʌmwʌn], *pron.* = SOMEBODY 1.
someplace ['sʌmpleis], *adv. U.S:* = SOMEWHERE 1.
somersault ['sʌməsɔːlt], *s.* (*a*) (*Accidental*) **To turn a s.,** (*of pers.*) faire la culbute; *Aut: Av:* capoter, faire panache. (*b*) *Gym:* Saut périlleux. (*c*) Cabriole *f.* **To turn somersaults,** faire des cabrioles.
something ['sʌmθiŋ]. **I.** *s. or pron.* Quelque chose *m.* **1.** (*a*) **Say s.,** dites quelque chose. **S. or other,** une chose ou une autre. **S. or other went wrong,** je ne sais quoi a cloché. **There's s. the matter with him,** il a quelque chose. **S. to drink,** de quoi boire, quelque chose à boire. **To ask for s. to drink,** demander à boire. *F:* **Will you take s.?** voulez-vous boire, manger, quelque chose? **To give s.o. s. to live for,** donner à qn une raison de vivre. **I have s. else to do,** j'ai autre chose à faire. **The four s. train,** le train de quatre heures et quelque chose. (*b*) **An indefinable s.,** un je ne sais quoi d'indéfinissable. **2.** (*a*) **To speak with s. of a foreign accent,** parler avec un accent plus ou moins étranger. **He's s. of a miser,** il est un peu, tant soit peu, avare. **Perhaps we shall see s. of you now,** peut-être que maintenant on vous verra un peu. (*b*) **There's s. in what you say;** there's s. in that, il y a un fond de vérité dans ce que vous dites. **There's s. in him,** il a du fond. **Well, that's s.!** c'est toujours quelque chose! **II.** something. *adv.* (*a*) Quelque peu, tant soit peu. **S. after the French style,** un peu dans le style français. *F:* **That's s. 'like a cigar!** voilà un vrai cigare! *S.a.* LIKE[1] I. 2. (*b*) *P:* **He treated me s. shocking,** il m'a traité d'une façon abominable.
sometime ['sʌmtaim], *adv.* **1.** (*a*) *O:* Autrefois, jadis. **S. priest of this parish,** autrefois, ci-devant, prêtre de cette paroisse. (*b*) *adj.* **Mr X, my s. tutor,** M. X, autrefois mon précepteur. **2. S.** (or other), tôt ou tard. **S. before dawn,** avant l'aube. **S. last year,** au cours de l'année dernière. **S. soon,** bientôt; un de ces quatre matins; un de ces jours.

sometimes ['sʌmtaimz], *adv.* Quelquefois, parfois. **S. the one, s. the other,** tantôt l'un, tantôt l'autre.
someway(s) ['sʌmwei(z)], *adv. U.S: F:* De façon ou d'autre.
somewhat ['sʌmwɔt]. **1.** *adv.* Quelque peu; un peu tant soit peu. **It is s. difficult,** c'est assez difficile. **To be s. surprised,** être passablement étonné. **We treat him s. as he treated us,** nous le traitons à peu près de la même façon qu'il nous a traités. **2.** *s.* **He was s. of a coward,** il était quelque peu poltron.
somewhere ['sʌmwɛər], *adv.* **1.** Quelque part. **S. near us,** pas bien loin de chez nous. **S. in the world,** de par le monde. **S. else,** ailleurs; autre part. **S. or other,** je ne sais où. *P:* **I'll see him s. first!** qu'il aille au diable! **2. He is s. about fifty,** il a environ cinquante ans.
somnambulism [sɔm'næmbjulizm], *s.* Somnambulisme *m*, noctambulisme *m.*
somnambulist [sɔm'næmbjulist], *s.* Somnambule *mf*; noctambule *mf.*
somnambulistic [sɔm,næmbju'listik], *a.* Somnambule.
somnolence ['sɔmnələns], *s.* Somnolence *f.*
somnolent ['sɔmnələnt], *a.* Somnolent.
son [sʌn], *s.m.* Fils. **How is your son?** comment va votre fils? *S.a.* MOTHER[1] 1. **'son-in-law,** *s.m.* Gendre, beau-fils.
sonant ['sounənt]. *Ling:* **1.** *a.* Sonore. **2.** *s.* Consonne *f* sonore.
sonar ['sounɑːr], *s. U.S: Nau:* Sonar *m.*
sonata [sə'nɑːtə], *s. Mus:* Sonate *f.*
sonatina [,sɔnə'tiːnə], *s. Mus:* Sonatine *f.*
sonde [sɔnd], *s. Meteor: etc:* Sonde *f.*
song [sɔŋ], *s.* **1.** Chant *m.* **To burst into s.,** se mettre tout à coup à chanter. **2.** (*a*) Chanson *f.* **Give us a s.,** chantez-nous quelque chose. *Mus:* **S. without words,** romance *f* sans paroles. *Mil:* **Marching s.,** chanson de route. *Nau:* **Capstan s.,** chanson à virer. **Hauling s.,** chanson à hisser. *F:* **To buy sth. for a s.,** acheter qch. à vil prix. **To make a s. about sth.,** faire des embarras, des histoires, à propos de qch. **He made a great s. and dance about it,** il en faisait un foin de tous les diables. (*b*) *Lit:* **S. of victory,** chant de victoire. **The S. of Roland,** la Chanson de Roland. *Gr.Ant:* **S. of triumph,** péan *m.* (*c*) *B:* **The S. of Songs,** le Cantique des Cantiques. **'song-bird,** *s.* Oiseau chanteur. **'song-book,** *s.* Recueil *m* de chansons; chansonnier *m.* **'song-thrush,** *s.* Grive musicienne. **'song-writer,** *s.* Chansonnier, -ière.
songster ['sɔŋstər], *s.m.* **1.** Chanteur. **2.** Oiseau chanteur.
songstress ['sɔŋstris], *s.f.* Chanteuse; cantatrice.
sonic ['sɔnik], *a.* Sonique. *Oc: Nau:* **S. depth-finder,** sondeur *m* à écho. *Av: etc:* **S. barrier, s. wall,** mur sonique, du son.
sonnet ['sɔnit], *s. Pros:* Sonnet *m.* **S. writer,** sonnettiste *mf.*
sonny ['sʌni], *s.m. F: O:* Mon petit, (mon) fiston.
sonority [sə'nɔriti], *s.* Sonorité *f.*
sonorous ['sɔnərəs, sə'nɔːrəs], *a.* Sonore. **-ly,** *adv.* D'un ton sonore.
sonorousness ['sɔnərəsnis, sə'nɔːrəsnis], *s.* Sonorité *f.*
soon [suːn], *adv.* **1.** (*a*) Bientôt, tôt. **S. after,** bientôt après; peu après. **See you again s.!** à bientôt! **It will s. be three years since . . .,** voici bientôt trois ans que. . . . **How s. may I expect you?** quand devrai-je vous attendre? **How s. can you be ready?** en combien de temps serez-vous prêt? **Too s.,** trop tôt; avant le temps. **I got out of the house none too s.,** je m'échappai de la maison juste à temps. *S.a.* MEND[2] I. 3. (*b*) **As s. as, so s. as,** aussitôt que, dès que. **As s. as possible,** le plus tôt possible; aussitôt que possible. (*c*) **I would as s. stay,** j'aime autant rester. **2.** (*a*) **The sooner the better,** le plus tôt sera le mieux. **Sooner or later,** tôt ou tard. **No sooner said than done,** aussitôt dit, aussitôt fait. **No sooner had he finished than he was seized,** à peine eut-il fini qu'il fut arrêté. (*b*) **Death sooner than slavery,** plutôt la mort que l'esclavage. **I would sooner die,** j'aimerais mieux mourir; plutôt mourir!
soot[1] [sut], *s.* Suie *f.*

soot², *v.tr. I.C.E:* **To s. up the plugs**, encrasser les bougies. (*Of plugs*) **To s. up**, s'encrasser. . . .

sooth [su:θ], *s. A:* Vérité *f.* **S. to say . . .**, à vrai dire. . . .

soothe [su:ð], *v.tr.* Calmer, apaiser (la douleur); tranquilliser (l'esprit). **soothing**, *a.* Calmant, apaisant. *Med:* Lénitif, -ive. **-ly**, *adv.* Avec douceur.

soothsayer ['su:θˌseiər], *s. Lit:* Devin *m, f.* devineresse.

soothsaying ['su:θˌseiiŋ], *s. Lit:* Divination *f.*

sooty ['suti], *a.* **1.** Couvert de suie; noir de suie. **2.** Qui contient de la suie; fuligineux, -euse. **S. deposit**, dépôt *m* de suie.

sop¹ [sɔp], *s.* **1.** Morceau de pain trempé. **2.** (*a*) Pot-de-vin *m, pl.* pots-de-vin. (*b*) **S. (to Cerberus)**, don *m* propitiatoire.

sop², *v.tr.* (sopped [sɔpt]). **1.** Tremper (le pain). **2. To s. up a liquid**, éponger un liquide. **sopping**, *a.* **S. wet**, tout trempé.

sophism ['sɔfizm], *s.* Sophisme *m.*

sophist ['sɔfist], *s.* Sophiste *m.*

sophistical [sə'fistikl], *a.* Sophistique; (argument) captieux.

sophisticated [sə'fistikeitid], *a.* **1.** Aux goûts compliqués; blasé. **2. She is more s. now,** (i) elle a plus de savoir-vivre à présent; (ii) elle est devenue mondaine, blasée.

sophistication [səˌfisti'keiʃ(ə)n], *s.* **1.** Sophistication *f.* **2.** Raisonnements sophistiques, captieux. **3.** Savoir-vivre *m inv*; usage *m* du monde. **S. of manners**, urbanité *f.*

sophistry ['sɔfistri], *s.* **1.** Sophistique *f.* **To indulge in s.**, sophistiquer. **2.** Sophisme *m.*

sophomore ['sɔfəmɔ:r], *s. U.S: Sch:* Étudiant, -ante de seconde année.

soporific [ˌsɔpə'rifik], *a. & s.* Somnifère (*m*), soporifique (*m*).

soppy ['sɔpi], *a.* **1.** (Terrain) détrempé. **2.** *F:* (*a*) (*Of pers.*) Mou, *f.* molle; flasque. (*b*) (*Of sentiment*) Fadasse; larmoyant.

soprano, *pl.* -os, -i [sə'prɑ:nou, -ouz, -i:], *s. Mus:* Soprano *m.* **S. voice**, voix de soprano.

sorbet ['sɔ:bet], *s.* Sorbet *m.*

sorcerer ['sɔ:s(ə)rər], *s.m.* Sorcier; magicien.

sorceress ['sɔ:s(ə)ris], *s.f.* Sorcière; magicienne.

sorcery ['sɔ:s(ə)ri], *s.* Sorcellerie *f.*

sordid ['sɔ:did], *a.* Sordide. (*a*) Sale, crasseux, -euse. (*b*) Bas, *f.* basse, vil. **-ly**, *adv.* Sordidement.

sordidness ['sɔ:didnis], *s.* Sordidité *f.* (*a*) Saleté *f.* (*b*) Bassesse *f.* (*c*) Avarice *f* sordide.

sore¹ [sɔ:r]. **I.** *a.* **1.** (*a*) Douloureux, -euse, endolori. **To be s. all over**, avoir mal partout. **He's like a bear with a s. head**, il est d'une humeur massacrante. (*b*) Enflammé, irrité. **S. eyes**, yeux malades. *S.a.* SIGHT¹ 5. **S. throat**, mal *m* de gorge. (*c*) Ulcéré. **To have a s. finger**, avoir un ulcère, *F:* un bobo, au doigt. **To put one's finger on the s. place**, mettre le doigt sur la plaie. (*d*) **That's his s. spot**, c'est son endroit sensible. **2.** Chagriné. **To be s. at heart**, être désolé. **To be s. about sth.**, être chagriné, *F:* fâché, au sujet de qch. **3. To be in s. need of sth.**, avoir grandement besoin de qch. **S. trial**, cruelle épreuve. **S. temptation**, tentation difficile à vaincre. **-ly**, *adv.* **S. wounded**, gravement, grièvement, blessé. **S. tried**, fort éprouvé; cruellement éprouvé. **II.** **sore**, *adv.* *A: & Lit:* **S. distressed**, dans une grande détresse.

sore², *s.* (*a*) Plaie *f*; (*chafe*) blessure *f*, écorchure *f.* **To (re)open an old s.**, évoquer un souvenir pénible; raviver une ancienne plaie. (*b*) Ulcère *m.*

sorehead ['sɔ:hed], *a. & s. F:* Frustré (*m*); grincheux (*m*), rouspéteur (*m*).

soreness ['sɔ:nis], *s.* **1.** Endolorissement *m.* **2.** (*a*) Chagrin *m*, peine *f.* (*b*) Sentiment *m* de rancune.

sorority [sə'rɔriti], *s. U.S:* Cercle féminin.

sorghum ['sɔ:gəm], *s. Bot:* Sorg(h)o *m.*

sorrel¹ ['sɔrəl], *s. Bot:* Oseille *f.* **Salts of s.**, sel *m* d'oseille.

sorrel², *a. & s.* (Cheval) rouan roux (*m*), aubère (*m*).

sorrow¹ ['sɔrou], *s.* Peine *f*, chagrin *m*, tristesse *f.* **To be s.-stricken**, être accablé de douleur. **To my s.**, à mon regret.

sorrow², *v.i.* S'affliger, être affligé (over, at, about, sth., de qch.). **To s. after s.o.**, pleurer qn. **sorrowing**, *a.* Affligé.

sorrowful ['sɔrəf(u)l], *a.* Affligé, chagriné; triste; (*of news, etc.*) attristant, pénible. **S. look**, regard attristé, mélancolique, désolé. **-fully**, *adv.* Tristement; avec chagrin.

sorry ['sɔri], *a.* **1.** (*a*) Fâché, chagriné, désolé, peiné. **He is s. (that) he did it**, il se repent de l'avoir fait. **You will be s. for it**, il vous en cuira. **I am extremely s.**, je regrette infiniment. **I'm s. for that**, j'en suis bien fâché. **S. to have kept you**, pardon de vous avoir retenu. **S.!** pardon! je regrette! (*b*) **I am s. for him**, je le plains. **To look s. for oneself**, faire piteuse mine. **2.** *O:* Mauvais; misérable. **S. steed**, méchant cheval. **S. jest**, mauvaise plaisanterie. **S. excuse**, piètre excuse. **To cut a s. figure**, faire piteuse figure. **-ily**, *adv.* Misérablement, pauvrement, piteusement, tristement.

sort¹ [sɔ:t], *s.* **1.** (*a*) Sorte *f*, genre *m*, espèce *f.* **What s. of tree is it?** quelle sorte d'arbre est-ce? **What s. of car have you (got)?** quelle marque de voiture avez-vous? **Wines of different sorts**, vins *m* de différents crus. **Of all sorts**, de toutes sortes. **All sorts of men**, des hommes de toutes sortes. **This s. of people**, les gens de cette espèce. **A strange s. of fellow**, un type bizarre. **That's the s. of man he is**, il est comme ça. *F:* **She's a (real) good s.**, c'est une brave fille. **He looks a good s.**, il a l'air bon garçon. **That's the sort of thing I mean**, c'est à peu près ce que je veux dire. **I can't stand that s. of thing**, je ne peux pas souffrir tout ça. **Something of that s.**, quelque chose dans ce genre-là. **Nothing of the s.**, (i) rien de semblable; (ii) pas du tout! **I shall do nothing of the s.**, je n'en ferai rien. **A writer of some s.**, quelque vague écrivain. **What s. of day is it?** quel temps fait-il? **To make some s. of excuse**, faire des excuses quelconques. **There is no s. of reason for this**, il n'y a aucune raison pour cela. **I have a s. of idea that . . .**, j'ai comme une idée, j'ai une sorte d'idée, que . . . **A s. of sour taste**, un goût plutôt aigre. *F:* **I s. of feel that . . .**, j'ai comme une impression que. . . . (*b*) *Pej:* **We had coffee of sorts, of a s.**, on nous a donné du soi-disant café. **A translation of a s.**, ce qui peut passer pour une traduction. (*c*) *Typ:* Sorte. **Missing s., short s.**, sorte manquante. (*d*) **To be out of sorts**, (i) être indisposé; ne pas être dans son assiette; *F:* être patraque; (ii) être de mauvaise humeur. **2. In some s.**, à un certain degré; jusqu'à un certain point.

sort², *v.tr.* (*a*) Trier, assortir; débrouiller (des papiers, etc.). **To s. rags**, séparer des chiffons; faire le tri des chiffons. *Post:* **To s. the letters**, trier, router, les lettres. (*b*) **To s. out sth. from sth.**, faire le départ entre qch. et qch. **To s. out the bad ones**, trier les mauvais; faire le tri des mauvais. **sorting**, *s.* Triage *m*, tri *m*; classement *m.* *Hort:* **S. board (for seeds, etc.)**, volet *m.* *Post:* Routage *m* (de lettres). **S.-office**, bureau *m* de tri.

sorter ['sɔ:tər], *s.* (*a*) (*Pers.*) Trieur, -euse; classeur, -euse. *Post:* **Letter s.**, trieur de lettres. (*b*) (*Device*) Trieur (de minerai). *Automation:* Trieuse *f.*

sortie ['sɔ:ti(:)], *s. Mil:* Sortie *f.* *Av:* Vol *m.*

sot [sɔt], *s.* Alcoolique *mf*; ivrogne *m, f.* ivrognesse; *P:* soûlard, -arde.

sottish ['sɔtiʃ], *a.* Abruti par l'alcool; (air) d'ivrogne.

sottishness ['sɔtiʃnis], *s.* Abrutissement *m* (causé par l'alcoolisme).

sotto voce ['sɔtou'voutʃi], *adv.* (*a*) (Causer) tout bas, à demi-voix. (*b*) *Mus:* Sotto-voce; (chanter) à demi-voix; (jouer) à demi-jeu.

soubrette [su:'bret], *s.f. Th:* Soubrette.

Soudan (the) [ðəsu:(:)'dɑ:n]. *Pr.n. Geog:* = SUDAN.

Soudanese [ˌsu:də'ni:z], *a. & s. Geog: Ethn:* = SUDANESE.

soufflé ['su:flei], *s. Cu:* Soufflé *m.* **Cheese s., chocolate s.**, soufflé au fromage, au chocolat.

sough¹ [sau, sʌf], *s. Lit:* Murmure *m*, susurration *f*, frémissement *m* (du vent, etc.).

sough², *v.i. Lit:* (*Of wind, etc.*) Murmurer, susurrer.

sought. *See* SEEK.

soul [soul], s. Âme f. **1.** (a) With all my s., de tout mon cœur; de toute mon âme. O: Upon my s.! sur mon âme! He has a s. above money, il est au-dessus des préoccupations d'argent. S.a. BODY 1, HEART¹ 2 (d), LIFE 1. (b) He is the s. of the enterprise, c'est lui qui mène, fait marcher, l'affaire. S.a. HONOUR¹ 3. **2.** Departed souls, les âmes des trépassés. God rest his s.! que Dieu ait son âme! All Souls' Day, la fête des Morts. **3.** (a) Population of a thousand souls, population de mille âmes. Ship lost with all souls, navire perdu corps et biens. Without meeting a living s., sans rencontrer âme qui vive. (b) He's a good s., c'est une bonne âme; F: c'est une bonne pâte (d'homme). Poor s.! pauvre créature f! 'soul-destroying, -killing, a. (Emploi) abrutissant.

soulful ['soulful], a. (a) Plein d'âme. S. eyes, yeux expressifs. S. music, musique qui émeut l'âme. (b) Sentimental, -aux. -fully, adv. (a) (Chanter) avec âme, avec expression. (b) Sentimentalement.

soulless ['soullis], a. **1.** Sans âme; terre à terre. **2.** (Emploi) abrutissant.

sound¹ [saund], s. (a) Son m, bruit m. Not a s. was heard, on n'entendait pas le moindre bruit, le moindre son. S. barrier, mur m du son, mur sonique. S. engineer, ingénieur m du son. (b) Within (the) s. of . . ., à portée du son de. . . . To catch the s. of sth., entendre qch. à demi. I don't like the s. of it, cela ne me dit rien qui vaille. (c) (The science of) s., l'acoustique f. 'sound-board, s. (a) Table f d'harmonie (de piano). (b) Tamis m (d'orgue). 'sound-box, s. **1.** Mus: Caisse f de résonance (d'un instrument à cordes). 2. O: Diaphragme m (de phonographe). 'sound-dampening, -deadening. **1.** a. (Of material) Insonore. **2.** s. Cin: W.Tel: etc: Insonorisation f. 'sound-de'tector, s. Géophone m. 'sound-effects, s.pl. Bruitage m. 'sound-hole, s. Mus: Ouïe f (de violon, de guitare). 'sound-locator, s. Mil: Appareil m de repérage par le son. 'sound-post, s. L'âme f (d'un violon). 'sound-proof¹, a. Impénétrable au son; isolant; (of film studio) insonore. 'sound-proof², v.tr. Insonoriser. 'sound-proofed, a. Insonorisé. 'sound-proofing, s. Insonorisation f; isolation f phonique. 'sound-track, s. Cin: Bande f sonore. 'sound-wave, s. Onde f sonore.

sound². **I.** v.i. **1.** Sonner, résonner; retentir. **2.** (a) To s. like a drum, avoir le son du tambour. To s. hollow, sonner creux; rendre un son creux. (b) Paraître, sembler. Name that sounds French, nom qui a une apparence française. It sounded a long way off, on aurait dit que cela venait de loin. That sounds well in a speech, cela fait bon effet dans un discours. That sounds like heresy, cela a l'air d'une hérésie. He doesn't s. like a man to . . ., d'après ce que vous dites, il ne serait pas homme à . . . It sounds like Mozart, on dirait du Mozart. **II.** sound, v.tr. **1.** (a) Sonner (la cloche, le tocsin). To s. the trumpet, sonner de la trompette. Aut: To s. the horn, klaxonner. (b) Proclamer (une vérité, etc.). S.a. PRAISE¹. **2.** Prononcer (une lettre). To sound one's r's, faire sonner les r. **3.** (a) Med: Ausculter; (by percussion) percuter. (b) Rail: Vérifier (une roue) au marteau. **sounding¹,** a. **1.** (Of style, etc.) Sonore, pompeux, -euse; ronflant. **2.** Sharp-s., au son aigu. S.a. HIGH-SOUNDING. **sounding²,** s. **1.** Résonnement m; retentissement m (du tambour, etc.). **2.** The s. of the retreat, le signal de la retraite. **3.** Med: Auscultation f; percussion f. 'sounding-board, s. **1.** Abat-voix m inv. **2.** = SOUND-BOARD.

sound³, s. Surg: Sonde f.

sound⁴. **1.** v.tr. (a) Nau: Sonder. Abs. Prendre le fond. (b) Surg: Sonder (une plaie). (c) To s. s.o. (about sth.), sonder qn (relativement à qch.); tâter le pouls à qn. To s. one's conscience, interroger sa conscience. **2.** v.i. (Of whale) Faire la sonde, foncer. **sounding³,** s. Nau: **1.** Sondage m, brassiage m. **2.** pl. (a) To be in soundings, être sur les sondes. To be out of soundings, être hors des sondes. (b) To take soundings, sonder; prendre le fond. What are the soundings? quel est le fond? 'sounding-balloon, s. Meteor: Ballon m de sondage, ballon-sonde m. 'sounding-lead [led], s. Nau: (Plomb m de) sonde f. 'sounding-machine, s. Nau: Sondeur m.

sound⁵, s. (i) Détroit m; goulet m; (ii) bras m de mer. Geog: The S., le Sund.

sound⁶. **I.** a. **1.** (a) Sain. S. constitution, santé f solide, robuste. S. in body and mind, sain de corps et d'esprit. Of s. mind, sain d'esprit. Vet: S. horse, cheval sans tare. (Of pers.) To be s. in wind and limb, avoir bon pied bon œil; F: avoir le coffre solide. I'm as s. as a bell, je suis en parfaite santé. S.a. SAFE² 1. (b) En bon état; non endommagé. S. timber, bois sans tare. S. fruit, fruits sains. **2.** (a) S. financial position, situation financière solide. To be a s. man, avoir du crédit sur la place; être solide. S. statesman, homme d'état au jugement sain. (b) (Argument) valide, irréfutable; (raisonnement) juste. It is a s. rule to . . ., la bonne règle est de. . . . It isn't s. finance, ce n'est pas de la finance sérieuse. S.a. JUDG(E)MENT 3. **3.** S. sleep, sommeil profond. To give s.o. a s. thrashing, rosser qn d'importance. -ly, adv. **1.** Sainement; judicieusement. To argue s., raisonner avec justesse. **2.** To sleep s., dormir profondément, à poings fermés, sur les deux oreilles. To thrash s.o., rosser qn d'importance, de la belle manière. **II.** sound, adv. To sleep s., dormir à poings fermés. S.a. ASLEEP 1.

sounder¹ ['saundər], s. Nau: (Man or apparatus) Sondeur m.

sounder², s. (Of wild boar) Harde f, bande f, troupe f, de sangliers.

soundless¹ ['saundlis], a. Muet, f. muette; silencieux, -euse. -ly, adv. Sans bruit.

soundless², a. (Mer, etc.) insondable; sans fond.

soundness ['saundnis], s. **1.** État sain (de l'esprit); bon état (des poumons, des marchandises). **2.** Solidité f (d'une maison de commerce). **3.** Solidité (d'un argument); sûreté f, justesse f (d'un jugement).

soup [su:p], s. **1.** Soupe f, potage m. Thick s., crème f. Clear s., consommé m. Vegetable s., potage m de légumes. Onion s., soupe à l'oignon. F: To be in the soup, être dans le pétrin, dans la purée, dans la sauce. **2.** F: (a) U.S: Nitroglycérine f. (b) Brouillard m. 'soup-kitchen, s. Soupe f populaire. 'soup-ladle, s. Louche f. 'soup-plate, s. Assiette creuse. 'soup-tureen, s. Soupière f.

soup up ['su:p'ʌp], v.tr. P: **1.** Gonfler, agrandir (la puissance de qch.). Aut: Souped up engine, moteur gonflé. **2.** Exagérer, rendre plus intéressant (une publicité, etc.).

soupy ['su:pi], a. (a) Qui ressemble à de la soupe. (b) U.S: Très brumeux, -euse. (c) F: Sentimental, -aux.

sour¹ ['sauər], a. **1.** (a) (Fruit) aigre, acide. S.a. GRAPE. (b) (Lait, pain) aigre, suri; (vin) suret, verjuté. To turn s., tourner à l'aigre; surir. To turn sth. s., (faire) aigrir qch. To smell s., sentir l'aigre. (c) Agr: (Sol) trop humide. **2.** (Of pers.) Revêche; aigre. F: She's a s.-face, c'est une chipie. -ly, adv. (Répondre) avec aigreur, d'un ton revêche. 'sour-faced, a. Au visage morose. 'sour(-)puss, s. F: Rabat-joie m inv, trouble-fête mf inv; grincheux, -euse.

sour². **1.** v.i. (a) Surir; (s')aigrir. (b) Her temper has soured, son caractère a aigri. **2.** v.tr. Aigrir (le lait, le caractère).

source [sɔːs], s. Source f (d'un fleuve, de malheurs, etc.). To trace a tradition back to its s., remonter aux sources, à l'origine, d'une tradition. S. of infection, foyer m d'infection. I know it from a good s., je le sais de bonne source, de bonne part.

sourish ['sauəriʃ], a. Aigrelet, suret.

sourness ['sauənis], s. **1.** Aigreur f, acidité f (d'un fruit). **2.** Aigreur (de qn); humeur f revêche.

souse¹ [saus], s. **1.** Cu: Marinade f. **2.** To get a s., recevoir une saucée; être trempé jusqu'aux os. **3.** P: (a) Soûlerie f. (b) Ivrogne m.

souse². **1.** v.tr. (a) Cu: Faire mariner (le poisson, etc.). (b) Plonger, immerger (in, dans). (c) Tremper, noyer (with water, d'eau). (d) To s. water over sth., répandre de l'eau sur qch. **2.** v.i. Mariner. **soused,** a. **1.** Cu: Mariné. **2.** P: To be s., avoir une cuite.

south¹ [sauθ]. **1.** s. Sud m, midi m. On the s., to the s. (of), au sud (de); du côté du sud. To live in the s. of England, demeurer dans le sud de l'Angleterre.

The S. of France, le Midi (de la France). 2. *adv.*
(*a*) Au sud. To travel s., voyager vers le sud. (*b*)
To go s., aller dans le sud, dans le midi. 3. *a.* Sud
inv; (vent) du sud; (pays) du sud, méridional,
-aux; (mur) qui fait face au sud, exposé au midi.
South 'Africa. *Pr.n.* *Geog:* (The Republic of)
S.A., la République d'Afrique du sud, la République
sud-africaine. *Hist:* The Union of S.A., l'Union
sud-africaine. **South-'African,** *a.* & *s.* Sud-
africain, -aine. **'south(-)bound,** *a.* (Train, autobus,
car, etc.) en direction sud. **south-'east.** 1. *s.*
Sud-est *m.* 2. *adv.* Vers le sud-est. 3. *a.* Du sud-est.
south-'easter, *s.* Vent du sud-est. **south-'easterly,**
a. Du sud-est. **south-'eastern,** *a.* Du sud-est.
south-'eastward. 1. *s.* Sud-est *m.* 2. *a.* Au, du,
sud-est. 3. *adv.* = SOUTH-EASTWARDS. **south-'eastwards,** *adv.* Vers le sud-est. **'South 'Sea (the).**
Pr.n. *Geog:* Le Pacifique sud. **The S. S. Islands,** les
îles *f* du Pacifique; l'Océanie *f.* **south-'west,** *Nau:*
sou''west. 1. *s.* Sud-ouest *m.* 2. *adv.* Vers le sud-
ouest. 3. *a.* Du sud-ouest. *Geog:* S.-W. Africa, le
Sud-Ouest africain. **south-'wester,** *Nau:* sou'
'wester, *s.* 1. Vent *m* du sud-ouest; le suroît. 2.
Chapeau *m* imperméable; suroît *m.* **south-
'westerly,** *Nau:* sou''westerly, *a.* Du sud-ouest.
south-'western, *a.* Du sud-ouest. **south-'westward.**
1. *s.* Sud-ouest *m.* 2. *a.* Du, au, sud-ouest. 3.
adv. = SOUTH-WESTWARDS. **south-'westwards,** *adv.*
Vers le sud-ouest.

south², *v.i.* 1. (*Of star*) Passer le méridien. 2. (*Of ship*)
Faire route au sud. **southing,** *s.* 1. *Astr:* Passage
m au méridien. 2. *Nau:* Chemin *m* sud.

southdown ['sauθdaun], *s.* *Husb:* Race *f* de moutons
southdown.

southerly ['sʌðəli], *a.* 1. (*a*) (i) (Vent) du sud, qui
vient du sud; (ii) (courant) qui se dirige vers le
sud. (*b*) S. aspect, exposition au midi. *Nau:* To
steer a s. course, faire route au sud; mettre le cap
au sud. 2. *adv.* (*a*) Vers le sud. (*b*) The wind blows
s., le vent souffle du sud.

southern ['sʌðən], *a.* (Du) sud; du midi; méridional,
-aux. The s. counties, les comtés du sud. S. lights,
aurore australe. *Astr:* The S. Cross, la Croix du
Sud.

southerner ['sʌðənər], *s.* 1. Habitant, -ante, du sud;
(*in Fr.*) méridional, -e. 2. *U.S:* *Hist:* Sudiste *mf.*

southernmost ['sʌðənmoust], *a.* (Point etc.) le plus au
sud.

southron ['sʌðrən], *a.* & *s.* *Scot:* *Pej:* Anglais, -aise.

southward ['sauθwəd]. 1. *s.* To the s., vers le sud.
2. *a.* Au, du, sud; du côté du sud.

southwards ['sauθwədz], *adv.* Vers le sud.

souvenir ['su:v(ə)niər, su:və'niər], *s.* Souvenir *m.*

sovereign ['sɔvrin]. 1. *a.* Souverain; suprême. S.
rights, droits de souveraineté. The s. good, le
souverain bien. S. remedy, remède souverain,
infaillible. 2. *s.* (*a*) Souverain, -aine. (*b*) *Num:*
A: Souverain *m* (pièce d'or de la valeur de 20
shillings).

sovereignty ['sɔvrənti], *s.* Souveraineté *f.*

Soviet ['souviet], *s.* Soviet *m.* S. Union, Union soviétique. **The Union of S. Socialist Republics,** l'Union
des Républiques socialistes soviétiques.

sovietize ['souvietaiz], *v.tr.* Soviétiser (un pays).

sow¹ [sou], *v.tr.* (sowed [soud]; sowed, sown [soun])
Semer (des graines, un champ). To s. land with
wheat, ensemencer une terre en blé. *Abs.* To s.
broadcast, semer à la volée, à tout vent. To s. discord,
semer, répandre, la discorde. The seeds of revolution
were being sown, la révolution se préparait. *S.a.*
OAT, REAP. **sowing,** *s.* Semailles *fpl,* semis *m.*
'sowing-machine, *s.* Semoir *m.* **'sowing-season,** *s.*
La semaison; le temps des semailles.

sow² [sau], *s.* 1. (*a*) Truie *f.* (*b*) *Ven:* Laie *f* (sanglier
femelle). 2. *Metall:* (*a*) Gueuse *f.* (*b*) S.(-channel),
mère-gueuse *f.*

sower ['souər], *s.* Semeur, -euse.

sow-thistle ['sau,θisl], *s.* *Bot:* Laiteron *m.*

soy [sɔi], *s.* 1. *Cu:* Sauce piquante (de soya). 2.
= SOYA-BEAN.

soya-bean ['sɔiə,bi:n], *s.* *Bot:* Soya *m,* soja *m;* pois
chinois.

sozzled ['sɔzld], *a.* *F:* Ivre, parti.

spa [spɑː], *s.* 1. Source minérale. 2. Ville *f* d'eau;
station thermale.

space¹ [speis], *s.* 1. Espace *m,* intervalle *m* (de temps).
For a s., pendant quelque temps. 2. (*a*) L'espace.
Staring into s., le regard perdu dans le vide. *attrib.*
Spatial, -iaux. S. race, course interplanétaire. (*b*)
In a confined s., dans un espace restreint. To take
up a lot of s., occuper beaucoup de place; être
encombrant. To leave s. for . . ., laisser de la place
à. . . . (*c*) Étendue *f;* surface *f.* The aerodrome
occupies a large s., l'aérodrome occupe un vaste
terrain. To clear a s. in the middle of the room,
débarrasser le milieu de la pièce. 3. (*a*) Espace libre;
espacement *m,* intervalle. S. between two things,
écartement *m* de deux choses; (*between windows*)
entre-deux *m inv;* (*between lines of writing, etc.*)
entre-ligne *m,* interligne *m.* Blank s., blanc *m.*
To write one's name in the s. indicated, écrire son
nom dans la case indiquée. (*b*) *Typ:* Espace *f,*
(en métal); blanc *m.* Thick s., espace forte. *S.a.*
LINE-SPACE. **'space-bar,** *s.* *Typewr:* Barre *f*
d'espacement. **'space-fiction,** *s.* Romans *mpl* de
l'espace. **'space-flight,** *s.* Voyage interstellaire,
interplanétaire, spatial. **'space-lines,** *s.pl.* *Typ:*
Interlignes *m.* **'space-platform,** *s.* = SPACE-STATION.
'space-port, *s.* Base *f* de lancement de fusées
spatiales, d'astronefs. **'space-rocket,** *s.* Fusée *f*
interplanétaire. **'space-saving,** *a.* Compact. **'space
station,** *s.* Station spatiale. **'space-suit,** *s.* Scaphandre
m d'astronaute; vêtement *m* anti-g. **'space-time,** *s.*
Espace-temps *m.* S.-t. co-ordinates, coordonnées
espace-temps. **'space-travel,** *s.* Astronautique *f.*
'space-traveller, *s.* Astronaute *m.* **'space-writer,**
s. Journaliste payé(e) à la ligne.

space², *v.tr.* (*a*) To s. (out), espacer; disposer (des
objets) de distance en distance; échelonner (des
troupes, des paiements). *Typ:* To s. (out) the lines,
espacer les lignes. To s. out the matter, blanchir la
composition. (*b*) To s. off, (sub)diviser (une ligne);
répartir (des trous). **spaced,** *a.* 1. Écarté; espacé.
2. *Typ:* Close-s., aux espaces fines. **spacing,** *s.*
(*a*) Espacement *m,* écartement *m;* échelonnement *m*
(des troupes, des paiements). *Typ:* Espacement.
Typewr: In single, double, s., à interligne simple,
double. (*b*) Pas *m;* répartition *f* (de rivets, etc.).

spacecraft ['speiskrɑːft], *s.inv.* Astronef *m,* navire
spatial.

spaceless ['speislis], *a.* Sans bornes, illimité.

spaceman, *pl.* -men ['speismæn], *s.* (*a*) Habitant *m* de
l'espace. (*b*) Cosmonaute *m.*

spacer ['speisər], *s.* 1. *Typ:* Espace *f.* 2. *Typewr:*
Barre *f* d'espacement. *S.a.* LINE-SPACER. 3. *Mec.E:*
Pièce *f* d'épaisseur; entretoise *f.*

spaceship ['speisʃip], *s.* Astronef *m,* navire spatial.

spacious ['speiʃəs], *a.* (*a*) Spacieux, -euse, vaste.
(*b*) Ample (vêtement).

spaciousness ['speiʃəsnis], *s.* (*a*) Vaste étendue *f.*
(*b*) Proportions *f* spacieuses (d'un appartement, etc.).

spade¹ [speid], *s.* 1. *Tls:* Bêche *f;* (*child's*) pelle *f.*
To call a s. a s., appeler les choses par leur nom. 2.
Artil: Trail *s.,* bêche de crosse. **'spade-work,**
s. 1. Travaux *mpl* à la bêche; le gros travail. 2.
Travaux préliminaires, déblaiement *m* de terrain (en
vue d'une enquête, etc.).

spade², *v.tr.* Bêcher (la terre, etc.).

spade³, *s.* *Cards:* Pique *m.* Ace of spades, as de
pique. To play a s., to play spades, jouer pique.

spadeful ['speidful], *s.* Pleine bêche; pelletée *f.*

spaghetti [spə'geti], *s.* *Cu:* Spaghetti *mpl.*

spahi ['spɑːhiː], *s.* *Mil:* Spahi *m.*

Spain [spein], *Pr.n.* L'Espagne *f.*

spake. See SPEAK.

spallation [spə'leiʃ(ə)n], *s.* *Atom.Ph:* Spallation *f.*

span¹ [spæn], *s.* 1. (*a*) (i) Empan *m* (de la main);
(ii) *Meas:* neuf *inches* (229 mm.). (*b*) Wing-s.
(*of bird, aircraft*), envergure *f.* 2. (*a*) Portée *f*
(entre deux appuis); ouverture *f,* largeur *f* (d'une
arche); écartement *m* (de deux piliers). Sixty
foot s., soixante pieds de portée. (*b*) Travée *f* (d'un
pont, d'un comble). 3. (*a*) Petite étendue (de terre).
(*b*) Court espace de temps. Our mortal s., notre
séjour *m* terrestre. **'span-roof,** *s.* *Const:* Comble
m à deux versants, à double pente.

span², *v.tr.* (spanned) 1. Mesurer à l'empan. 2. (*Of bridge, etc.*) Franchir, enjamber (une rivière, etc.). His life spans nearly the whole century, sa vie embrasse presque tout le siècle.

span³, *s.* (*a*) *U.S:* Paire *f*, couple *m* (de chevaux, de bœufs). (*b*) (*S. Africa*), Attelage *m* (de bœufs).

span⁴. *See* SPIN².

spandrel ['spændr(ə)l], *s. Arch:* Écoinçon *m.*

spangle¹ ['spæŋgl], *s. Tex:* Paillette *f*; (*large*) paillon *m.* Gold spangles, paillettes d'or.

spangle², *v.tr.* Pailleter (with, de). Spangled with silver, lamé d'argent.

spangly ['spæŋgli], *a.* (*a*) Pailleté; (robe, etc.) parsemée de paillettes. (*b*) Étincelant.

Spaniard ['spæniəd], *s.* Espagnol, -ole.

spaniel ['spæniəl], *s.* Épagneul *m.*

Spanish ['spæniʃ]. 1. *a.* Espagnol. S. onion, oignon d'Espagne. *Hist:* The S. Main, (i) la Terre-ferme; (ii) la mer des Antilles. 2. *s. Ling:* L'espagnol *m.* **Spanish-A′merican,** *a.* Hispano-américain, ibéro-américain.

spank¹ [spæŋk], *s.* Claque *f* (sur le derrière).

spank², *v.tr.* Fesser (un enfant); administrer une fessée, une fouettée, à (un enfant). **spanking¹,** *s.* Fessée *f.*

spank³, *v.i. O:* To s. along, aller bon train; filer à bonne allure. **spanking²,** *a.* 1. *A:* F: De premier ordre; *P:* chic, épatant. 2. To go at a s. pace, filer raide; brûler le terrain.

spanker ['spæŋkər], *s.* 1. *Nau:* Brigantine *f.* 2. *A: F:* (*a*) Cheval *m* qui va bon train. (*b*) Chose épatante.

spanner ['spænər], *s.* 1. Clef *f* (à écrous). Bolt-s., serre-écrou *m inv.* Screw, adjustable, s., clef anglaise; clef à molette. F: To throw a s. in the works, mettre des bâtons dans les roues. 2. *Civ.E:* Entretoise *f.*

spar¹ [spɑːr], *s.* 1. *Nau:* (*a*) Espar *m*; bout *m* de mât. (*b*) *pl.* The spars, la mâture. 2. *Av:* Wing s., poutrelle *f*; bras *m* d'aile. ′spar-deck, *s. Nau:* Spardeck *m.*

spar², *s. Miner:* Spath *m.* Diamond s., spath adamantin.

spar³, *s.* 1. *A:* Combat *m* de coqs. 2. (*a*) Assaut de boxe amical. (*b*) Assaut de paroles; *F:* prise *f* de bec.

spar⁴, *v.i.* (sparred) 1. (*Of cocks*) Se battre. 2. (*Of pers.*) To s. with s.o., (i) faire un assaut de boxe amical avec qn; (ii) s'escrimer contre qn. To s. up to s.o., se mettre en posture de combat. Sparring match, (i) assaut de boxe amical, de démonstration; (ii) *F:* prise *f* de bec. Sparring partner, partenaire *m* (d'un boxeur).

spare¹ ['spɛər], *a.* 1. (*a*) S. diet, régime frugal. (*b*) (*Of pers.*) Sec, *f.* sèche; maigre, fluet. 2. S. time, (i) temps disponible; (ii) moments perdus; loisir(s) *m(pl).* S.-time activities, les loisirs *mpl.* In my s. time, à mes heures perdues. S. capital, fonds disponibles. S. bedroom, chambre d'ami. A yard of s. rope, trois pieds de corde de reste, en surplus. 3. S. parts, *s.* spares, pièces *f* de rechange, de réserve, pièces détachées; rechanges *m.* S. machine, machine de remplacement. *Aut:* S. wheel, roue de secours. S. tyre, (i) *Aut:* pneu *m* de rechange; (ii) *F:* bourrelet *m* de graisse. *Nau:* S. bunker, soute de réserve. -ly, *adv.* 1. (*a*) (Manger) frugalement. (*b*) (*Of pers.*) S. built, sec, *f.* sèche; mince. 2. = SPARSELY.

spare², *v.tr.* 1. Épargner, ménager. To s. no expense, ne pas regarder à la dépense. To s. no pains, ne pas ménager, ne pas marchander, sa peine. He will s. no pains to do it, rien ne lui coûtera pour le faire. 2. (*a*) Se passer de (qch.). Can you s. it? pouvez-vous vous en passer? je ne vous prive pas? We can s. him, nous pouvons nous passer de lui, nous n'avons pas besoin de lui. To have nothing to s., n'avoir que le strict nécessaire. Three yards to s., neuf pieds de trop, de reste. To have enough and to s. of sth., avoir plus qu'il n'en faut de qch. He has money and to s., il a de l'argent de reste. (*b*) I cannot s. the time, le temps me fait défaut. To have no time to s., (i) ne pas avoir de temps de libre; (ii) n'avoir que juste le temps (pour attraper le train, etc.). (To catch a train) with five minutes to s., (prendre un train) avec cinq minutes de bon. I have a minute to s., je peux disposer d'un instant. (*c*) To s. s.o. sth., donner, céder, qch. à qn. Can you s. me a few moments? voulez-vous m'accorder quelques minutes?

Can you s. me a hundred francs? pouvez-vous me prêter cent francs? 3. (*a*) Faire grâce à (qn). To s. s.o.'s life, épargner la vie de qn. If he is spared a few weeks longer, s'il lui est donné de vivre encore quelques semaines. Death spares no one, la mort ne pardonne à personne. The fire spared nothing, le feu ne respecta rien. He spares nobody, il ne fait de quartier à personne. To s. s.o.'s feelings, ménager qn. (*b*) Ménager (qn, son cheval). (*c*) To s. s.o. the trouble of doing sth., épargner, éviter, à qn la peine de faire qch. **sparing,** *a.* 1. Ménager, -ère; économe. To be s. with the butter, épargner, ménager, le beurre. He is s. of praise, il est chiche, avare, de louanges. S. of words, sobre de paroles. 2. S. use of sth., emploi modéré, restreint, de qch. -ly, *adv.* Frugalement; (manger) sobrement. To use sth. s., ménager qch.

spare-rib ['spɛərib], *s. Cu:* Côte découverte de porc.

spark¹ [spɑːk], *s.* (*a*) Étincelle *f*; (*of fire*) flammèche *f.* A s. of wit, un trait d'esprit. He hasn't a s. of generosity in him, il n'a pas pour deux sous de générosité. (*b*) *El:* Étincelle. S. resistance, résistance de la distance explosive. S. discharge, étincelle disruptive. *I.C.E:* S. ignition, allumage par étincelle. To advance the s., mettre de l'avance à l'allumage. ′spark-arrester, *s. El.E:* Déchargeur *m*; parafoudre *m.* ′spark-gap, *s. El:* 1. Distance explosive. 2. Pont *m* d'éclatement. ′spark plug, *s. I.C.E: U.S:* = SPARKING-PLUG.

spark², *v.i.* (*a*) Émettre des étincelles; (*of dynamo, etc.*) cracher. (*b*) (*Of current*) To s. across the terminals, jaillir entre les bornes. **sparking,** *s. El:* 1. Émission *f* d'étincelles; (*accidental*) jaillissement *m* d'étincelles; crachement *m.* 2. Allumage *m* par étincelle électrique. **spark off,** *v.tr.* Mettre le feu aux poudres. ′sparking-distance, *s.* Distance explosive. ′sparking-plug, *s. I.C.E:* Bougie *f* (d'allumage).

spark³, *s. O:* 1. Élégant *m*; *A:* petit-maître *m.* 2. Gay s., gaillard *m*; gai luron.

sparkle¹ ['spɑːkl], *s.* 1. Brève lueur. 2. Étincellement *m*; éclat *m*, pétillement *m* (des yeux); feux *mpl* (d'un diamant). 3. Vivacité *f* d'esprit.

sparkle², *v.i.* 1. (*a*) Étinceler, scintiller; (*of jewel*) chatoyer, miroiter. Book sparkling with wit, livre qui pétille d'esprit. (*b*) (*Of wine*) Pétiller, mousser. 2. (*Of fire*) Émettre des étincelles; pétiller. **sparkling¹,** *a.* (*a*) Étincelant, brillant. S. wit, vivacité *f* d'esprit. S. conversation, conversation pétillante d'esprit. (*b*) (Vin) mousseux; (limonade) gazeuse. Semi-s. wine, vin pétillant. **sparkling²,** *s.* 1. Étincellement *m*; scintillement *m*, scintillation *f.* 2. Pétillement *m.*

sparklet ['spɑːklit], *s.* 1. Petite étincelle. 2. *R.t.m:* Sparklet *m* (pour siphon à soda).

sparling ['spɑːliŋ], *s. Ich:* Éperlan *m.*

sparrow ['spærou], *s.* 1. Moineau *m*, passereau *m.* 2. Hedge s., fauvette *f* des haies. ′sparrow-hawk, *s. Orn:* Épervier *m.*

sparse [spɑːs], *a.* Clairsemé, épars, éparpillé. S. hair, cheveux rares, clairsemés. -ly, *adv.* Peu abondamment. S. populated, qui a une population clairsemée. S. covered with trees, aux arbres clairsemés.

sparseness ['spɑːsnis], *s.* Absence relative. S. of vegetation, végétation clairsemée.

Sparta ['spɑːtə]. *Pr.n. A.Geog:* Sparte *f.*

Spartan ['spɑːt(ə)n], *a. & s.* Spartiate (*mf*). To live a s. life, vivre en spartiate.

spasm ['spæz(ə)m], *s.* 1. *Med:* Spasme *m.* 2. Accès *m* (de toux, de jalousie). In a s. of temper, dans un mouvement de colère. To work in spasms, travailler par à-coups.

spasmodic [spæz'mɔdik], *a.* 1. (*a*) *Med:* Spasmodique. (*b*) (Saut) involontaire, convulsif. 2. Qui se produit par saccades; fait par à-coups. -ally, *adv.* (Travailler, etc.) par à-coups.

spastic ['spæstik]. *Med:* 1. *a.* (Paralysie) spasmodique. 2. *s.* Personne atteinte de paralysie spasmodique.

spat¹ [spæt], *s.* Frai *m*, naissain *m* (d'huîtres, de moules).

spat², *v.i.* (spatted) (*Of oysters*) Frayer.

spat³, *s. Cost:* Demi-guêtre *f*; guêtre *f* de ville.

spat⁴. See SPIT⁴.
spat⁵, s. U.S: 1. Prise f de bec. 2. Bruit sec, claquement m (d'une balle, etc.).
spate [speit], s. Crue f. River in s., rivière en crue. To have a s. of work, être débordé de travail.
spathe [speið], s. Bot: Spathe f.
spatial ['speiʃ(ə)l], a. Spatial, -aux; dans l'espace; concernant l'espace.
spatter¹ ['spætər], s. Éclaboussure f. Ind: Projection f (de soudure).
spatter². 1. v.tr. To s. s.o. with mud, éclabousser qn de boue. 2. v.i. (Of liquid) Jaillir, gicler.
spatula ['spætjulə], s. Spatule f.
spatulate ['spætjuleit], a. Nat.Hist: Spatulé. S. fingers, doigts en spatule.
spavin ['spævin], s. Vet: Éparvin m.
spawn¹ [spɔːn], s. 1. Frai m; œufs mpl (de poisson, etc.). 2. F: Progéniture f; rejeton m. 3. Mushroom s., blanc m de champignon.
spawn², v.i. (a) (Of fish, etc.) Frayer. (b) Se multiplier. (c) To s. from sth., naître de qch. **spawning,** s. Le frai. **'spawning-ground,** s. Frayère f. **'spawning-season,** s. Époque f du frai; fraie f, fraieson f.
spay [spei], v.tr. Vet: Châtrer (une bête femelle).
speak [spiːk], v. (spoke [spouk], A: spake [speik]; spoken) I. v.i. 1. (a) Parler. Without speaking, sans parler; sans rien dire. (b) To s. to s.o., parler à qn; adresser la parole à qn; s'adresser à qn. I will s. to him about it, je lui en toucherai un mot. To s. rudely to s.o., tenir un langage grossier à qn. I know him to s. to, (i) je le connais assez bien pour lui parler; (ii) nous nous disons bonjour. Speaking for myself . . ., pour ma part . . .; quant à moi. . . . F: S. for yourself, parle pour toi. Roughly speaking, approximativement. So to s., pour ainsi dire. Tp: Who's speaking? Qui est à l'appareil? c'est de la part de qui? 'Mr. Smith?' 'Yes, speaking,' "M. Smith? Lui-même." (c) The facts s. for themselves, ces faits se passent de commentaire. (d) (Of gun, organ) Parler. Suddenly the guns spoke, tout à coup le canon se fit entendre. 2. Faire un discours; prendre la parole. Mr X rose to s., M. X a demandé la parole. II. speak, v.tr. 1. (a) Dire (un mot, ses pensées). To s. the truth, dire la vérité. Not to s. a word, ne pas dire, ne pas prononcer, un mot. (b) To s. one's mind, dire sa façon de penser; avoir son franc parler. 2. Indiquer, accuser (qch.). 3. Parler (une langue). Do you s. French? parlez-vous français? 'English spoken,' "on parle anglais." 4. Nau: Héler, arraisonner (un navire). **speak for,** v.i. 1. (a) To s. for s.o., parler, plaider, pour qn. (b) That speaks well for your courage, cela en dit long sur votre courage; cela fait honneur à votre courage. 2. O: That is already spoken for, cela est déjà réservé, retenu. **speak of,** v.i. 1. Parler de (qch.). Speaking of . . ., à propos de. . . . There's nothing to s. of, ce n'est rien; cela ne vaut pas la peine d'en parler. She has no voice to s. of, elle n'a pour ainsi dire pas de voix. To s. well, highly, of s.o., sth., dire du bien de qn; parler en termes très flatteurs de qn; vanter qch. 2. Être significatif de (qch.). His pinched features spoke of privation, ses traits hâves trahissaient les privations. **speak out,** v.i. (a) Parler à haute voix. (b) Parler franchement, sans détours; trancher le mot. **speak up,** v.i. 1. Parler plus fort, plus haut. 2. To s. up for s.o., parler en faveur de qn. **spoken,** a. 1. The s. word, la parole. S. language, langue parlée. To be loud-s. man, un homme à la parole courtoise. To be loud-s., avoir le verbe haut. S.a. PLAIN-SPOKEN. **speaking¹,** a. 1. Expressif, -ive, éloquent. A s. likeness, un portrait parlant, vivant. 2. Evil-s., médisant. English-s. (races), (races) de langue anglaise; anglophone. French-speaking, francophone. **speaking²,** s. 1. Parler m, discours m, parole f. Plain s., franchise f, franc-parler m. To be on s. terms, se connaître assez pour se parler. We are no longer on s. terms, nous sommes brouillés. S.a. DISTANCE 1. 2. Public s., l'éloquence f; l'art m oratoire. **'speaking-trumpet,** s. Porte-voix m inv. **'speaking-tube,** s. Tuyau m acoustique. Nau: etc: Porte-voix m inv (communiquant avec la chambre des machines). **'speakeasy,** s. U.S: P: Débit, bar, clandestin.

speaker ['spiːkər], s. 1. Parleur, -euse; (in dialogue) interlocuteur, -trice. The last s., celui qui a parlé le dernier. Plain s., qn qui appelle les choses par leur nom; paysan m du Danube. 2. (In public) Orateur m. To be a fluent s., avoir la parole facile. 3. Parl: The S. = le Président (des Communes). 4. W.Tel: S. (unit), haut-parleur m.
spear¹ [spiər], s. 1. (a) Lance f. (b) (For throwing) Javelot m, javeline f. 2. Fish: Foëne f, trident m. (Underwater) s. fishing, pêche, chasse, (sous-marine) au harpon. **'spear-shaped,** a. Lancéolé. **'spearthrust,** s. Coup m de lance.
spear², v.tr. (a) (Trans)percer d'un coup de lance. (b) Prendre (un poisson) à la foëne.
spearhead ['spiəhed], s. 1. Fer m, pointe f, de lance. 2. Mil: Pointe. To launch a s. against . . ., pousser une pointe sur. . . .
spearmint ['spiəmint], s. Bot: Menthe verte.
spearwort ['spiəwɔːt], s. Bot: Renoncule f langue; douve f.
spec [spek], s. F: = SPECULATION 2.
special ['speʃ(ə)l]. 1. a. (a) Spécial, -aux; particulier, -ière. S. feature, particularité f. Journ: S. correspondent, envoyé spécial. To make a s. study of sth., se spécialiser en qch. S. tool, outil façonné exprès. Com: S. price, prix de faveur, F: prix d'ami. Post: U.S: 'By s. delivery,' "par exprès." S. (marriage) licence = dispense f de publication du mariage par le Procureur de la République. S.a. CONSTABLE 2. (b) (Especial) To take s. care over sth., apporter des soins particuliers à qch. S. friend, ami intime. A s. case, un cas d'espèce. I have nothing s. to tell you, je n'ai rien de particulier à vous dire. (c) Com: (Article) hors série. 2. s. (a) Train spécial. (b) Édition spéciale (d'un journal). (c) F: = special constable. **-ally,** adv. Spécialement, particulièrement; surtout. I went there s. to see them, j'y ai été dans le seul but de les voir.
specialist ['speʃəlist], s. Spécialiste mf. To become a s. (in sth.), se spécialiser (en, dans, qch.). Med: Heart s., cardiologue m.
speciality [ˌspeʃi'æliti], s. 1. Spécialité f. To make a s. of sth., se faire une spécialité de qch. That's my s., ça c'est mon fort. 2. Qualité particulière; particularité f. 3. Jur: = SPECIALTY 1.
specialization [ˌspeʃəlai'zeiʃ(ə)n], s. Spécialisation f.
specialize ['speʃəlaiz]. 1. v.tr. (a) Particulariser, spécialiser. (b) Désigner à un but spécial. Hospital with specialized wards, hôpital aux salles spécialisées. 2. v.i. Se spécialiser (in, dans). To s. in a subject, faire sa spécialité d'un sujet.
specialty ['speʃəlti], s. 1. Jur: Contrat formel sous seing privé. 2. = SPECIALITY 1.
specie ['spiːʃiː], s. (No pl.) Espèces monnayées; numéraire m. To pay in s., payer en espèces.
species ['spiːʃiːz], s. inv. 1. Nat.Hist: Espèce f. Closely related s., espèces voisines. 2. Espèce, sorte f, genre m. 3. R.C.Ch: Les saintes espèces.
specific [spi'sifik]. 1. a. (a) Spécifique. Ph: S. gravity, poids m spécifique. Jur: In each s. case, dans chaque cas d'espèce. (b) (Of statement) Précis; (of order) explicite. S. aim, but déterminé. 2. s. Med: Spécifique m (for, contre). **-ally,** adv. 1. Spécifiquement. 2. Précisément.
specification [ˌspes(i)fi'keiʃ(ə)n], s. 1. Spécification f (des détails, etc.). 2. Devis descriptif. **Specifications of a patent,** mémoire descriptif d'une invention; description f de brevet. **Specifications of a car,** caractéristiques f d'une voiture. **Specifications of a contract,** stipulations f d'un contrat.
specify ['spesifai], v.tr. Spécifier, déterminer; préciser (des conditions). Specified load, charge prévue, prescrite. Unless otherwise specified, sauf indication contraire.
specimen ['spesimin], s. (a) Spécimen m. The finest specimens in his collection, les plus belles pièces de sa collection. (b) Exemple m, échantillon m. S. page, page spécimen; page type. S. copy (of book), livre à l'examen. Med: To take a s. of s.o.'s blood, prélever une goutte de sang à qn. Med: F: A s., un échantillon d'urine. (c) F: (Of pers.) Queer s., drôle m de type.

specious ['spi:ʃəs], *a.* (*Of appearance*) Spécieux, -euse, trompeur, -euse; (*of argument*) captieux, -euse, spécieux.

speciousness ['spi:ʃəsnis], *s.* Spéciosité *f*; apparence trompeuse.

speck [spek], *s.* **1.** Petite tache; point *m*, goutte *f* (de couleur); moucheture *f*, tacheture *f*. **2.** (*a*) Grain *m*, atome *m* (de poussière). **S. on the horizon,** point noir à l'horizon. (*b*) **Not a s. of generosity,** pas un brin de générosité. **3.** Défaut *m*; tavelure *f* (sur un fruit).

specked [spekt], *a.* Tacheté, moucheté; (fruit) tavelé.

speckle ['spekl], *s.* Petite tache; point *m* (de couleur); moucheture *f*, tacheture *f*.

speckled ['spekld], *a.* Tacheté, moucheté, tiqueté, truité; (*of plumage*) grivelé. **S. with white,** tacheté de blanc.

specs [speks], *s.pl.* *F:* Lunettes *fpl.*

spectacle ['spektəkl], *s.* **1.** Spectacle *m.* **To make a s. of oneself,** se donner en spectacle. **2.** *pl.* **Spectacles,** lunettes *f.* **S. frame,** monture *f* (de lunettes). **3.** *Cin:* Superproduction *f.* **'spectacle-case,** *s.* Étui *m* à lunettes. **'spectacle-maker,** *s.* Lunet(t)ier *m.*

spectacled ['spektəkld], *a.* Qui porte des lunettes; à lunettes.

spectacular [spek'tækjulər], *a.* Spectaculaire. **S. play,** pièce à grand spectacle. **S. effect,** effet impressionnant.

spectator [spek'teitər], *s.* Spectateur, -trice; assistant, -ante. **The spectators,** l'assistance *f.*

spectral ['spektrəl], *a.* (*a*) Spectral, -aux. *Opt:* **The s. colours,** les couleurs du spectre. (*b*) Spectral; fantomatique.

spectre ['spektər], *s.* Spectre *m*, fantôme *m*, apparition *f.*

spectrometer [spek'trɔmitər], *s.* *Opt:* Spectromètre *m.*

spectroscope ['spektrəskoup], *s.* *Opt:* Spectroscope *m.*

spectroscopic [spektrə'skɔpik], *s.* Spectroscopique.

spectroscopy [spek'trɔskəpi], *s.* Spectroscopie *f.*

spectrum, *pl.* **-tra** ['spektrəm, -trə], *s.* *Ph:* Spectre *m.* **Solar s.,** spectre solaire. **The colours of the s.,** les couleurs du spectre. **'spectrum a'nalysis,** *s.* *Ch:* Analyse spectrale.

specular ['spekjulər], *a.* (Minéral) spéculaire.

speculate ['spekjuleit], *v.i.* **1.** **To s. (up)on, about, sth.,** (i) spéculer, méditer, sur qch.; (ii) faire des conjectures sur qch. **2.** *Fin:* Spéculer (in, sur). **To s. on the Stock Exchange,** jouer à la Bourse. **To s. in mining securities,** jouer sur les mines. **speculating,** *s.* Spéculation *f.*

speculation [spekju'leiʃ(ə)n], *s.* **1.** (*a*) Spéculation *f*, méditation *f* (on, sur). (*b*) Conjecture *f.* **To be the subject of much s.,** donner lieu à bien des conjectures. **2.** (*a*) *Fin:* Spéculation. **To buy sth. on s.,** (i) acheter qch. à titre de spéculation; (ii) acheter qch. à tout hasard. (*b*) Entreprise spéculative. *St.Exch:* Coup *m* de bourse. **Good s.,** bonne affaire.

speculative ['spekjulətiv], *a.* **1.** (*a*) Spéculatif, -ive, contemplatif, -ive. (*b*) Conjectural, -aux. **This is a s. assumption,** c'est une pure hypothèse. **2.** *Fin:* Spéculatif; fait par spéculation. **-ly,** *adv.* **1.** D'un air méditatif. **2.** Par spéculation.

speculator ['spekjuleitər], *s.* Spéculateur, -trice. *St.Exch:* Joueur *m* à la Bourse; agioteur *m.* **Small s.,** boursicoteur, -euse.

speculum *pl.* **-a, -ums** ['spekjuləm, -ə, -əmz], *s.* **1.** *Surg:* Spéculum *m.* **2.** Miroir *m* (d'un télescope, etc.). **3.** *Orn:* Miroir.

sped. See SPEED².

speech [spi:tʃ], *s.* **1.** (*a*) (**Faculty of) s.,** la parole. **To lose the power of s.,** perdre la parole. (*b*) **To be slow of s.,** parler lentement; avoir l'articulation lente; avoir un débit très lent. **Abruptness of s.,** brusquerie de langage. *S.a.* IMPEDIMENT 1. (*c*) **Figure of s.,** figure *f* de rhétorique. *Gram:* **Parts of s.,** parties *f* du discours. **2.** Paroles, propos *mpl.* **Fair speeches,** belles paroles. **3.** Langue *f* (d'un peuple); parler *m* (d'une région, d'une classe sociale). **4.** Discours *m*, harangue *f*; (*to subordinates*) allocution *f.* **To make, deliver, a s.,** faire, prononcer, un discours. **After-dinner s.,** discours d'après-dîner. *S.a.* MAIDEN. **5.** *Gram:* **Direct s.,** discours direct. **Indirect, reported s.,** discours oblique, indirect. **'speech-day,** *s.* *Sch:* Distribution *f* des prix.

speechifier ['spi:tʃifaiər], *s.* *Pej:* Discoureur, -euse; phraseur, -euse.

speechify ['spi:tʃifai], *v.i.* *Pej:* Discourir, pérorer; *F:* laïusser. **speechifying,** *s.* *Pej:* Beaux discours.

speechless ['spi:tʃlis], *a.* **1.** Incapable de parler. **2.** Interdit, interloqué. **S. with surprise,** muet de surprise. **Emotion left him s.,** l'émotion lui coupa la parole. **-ly,** *adv.* Sans dire un mot; d'un air interdit.

speechlessness ['spi:tʃlisnis], *s.* **1.** Mutisme *m.* **Emotion reduced him to s.,** l'émotion lui coupa la parole. **2.** Aphonie *f.*

speed¹ [spi:d], *s.* **1.** (*a*) Vitesse *f*; marche *f* (rapide); rapidité *f*, célérité *f.* **At full s., at top s.,** à toute vitesse; (*of car*) à toute vitesse, à toute allure, à fond de train; (*of runner*) à toutes jambes; (*of horseman*) à bride abattue, ventre à terre. *Nau:* **Full s. ahead!** en avant (à) toute (vitesse)! **Maximum s.,** vitesse limite; pleine allure; *Aut:* (vitesse) plafond (*m*). *Av:* **Ground s.,** vitesse vraie. **Air s.,** vitesse propre. **To pick up s.,** prendre de la vitesse. *Aut: F:* **S.-hog,** chauffard *m.* (*b*) *Mec.E:* **Normal running s.,** vitesse de régime. **To attain s.,** atteindre sa vitesse de régime. **Keep to this s.,** gardez ce régime. (*c*) *Phot:* Rapidité *f* (d'une émulsion, d'un objectif). **2.** *A: & Lit:* **To wish s.o. good s.,** souhaiter bonne chance à qn. **'speed(-)cop,** *s.* *Aut: F:* Motard *m.* **'speed-indicator,** *s.* *Aut: etc:* Indicateur *m* de vitesse. *Av:* Badin *m.* **'speed-limit,** *s.* Vitesse *f* maxima. **'speed-trial,** *s.* Essai *m* de vitesse.

speed², *v.* (**sped** [sped]; **sped**) **1.** *v.i.* Se hâter, se presser; aller vite. **He sped down the street,** il descendit vite la rue. **To s. off,** partir à toute vitesse. **2.** *v.tr.* *A: & Lit:* (*a*) **To s. the parting guest,** (i) souhaiter bon voyage à l'hôte qui part; (ii) l'encourager à partir plus vite. (*b*) **God s. you!** que Dieu vous fasse prospérer!

speed³, *v.* (**speeded**) **1.** *v.tr.* (*a*) **To s. an engine,** régler la vitesse d'une machine. (*b*) **To s. (up) the work,** activer, accélérer, les travaux. **2.** *v.i.* *Aut: etc:* **To s. along,** faire de la vitesse, foncer. **speeding,** *s.* **1.** *Aut:* Excès *m* de vitesse. **2.** **S. (up),** accélération *f* (d'un travail, d'un service).

speedboat ['spi:dbout], *s.* Canot-automobile *m*; (*with outboard motor*) hors-bord *m inv:* (*cabin-cruiser type*) cabin-cruiser *m.*

speeder ['spi:dər], *s.* **1.** *Techn:* (*Device*) Contrôleur *m* de vitesse. **2.** *Aut: F:* (*Pers.*) Chauffard *m.*

speediness ['spi:dinis], *s.* Rapidité *f*, célérité *f.*

speedometer [spi'dɔmitər], *s.* **1.** *Aut: etc:* Indicateur *m* de vitesse; compteur *m.* **2.** *Mec.E:* Tachymètre *m.*

speedway ['spi:dwei], *s.* *Aut:* **1.** *U.S:* Autoroute *f.* **2.** Piste *f* (d'autodrome).

speedwell ['spi:dwel], *s.* *Bot:* Véronique *f.*

speedy ['spi:di], *a.* Rapide, prompt. **S. revenge,** prompte vengeance. **-ily,** *adv.* Vite; promptement; en toute hâte.

spel(a)eological [spi:liə'lɔdʒikl], *a.* Spéléologique.

spel(a)eologist [spi:li'ɔlədʒist], *s.* Spéléologue *mf.*

spel(a)eology [spi:li'ɔlədʒi], *s.* Spéléologie *f.*

spell¹ [spel], *s.* **1.** Incantation *f*; formule *f* magique. **2.** Charme *m*, maléfice *m.* **To cast a s. over s.o., to lay s.o. under a s.,** jeter un sort sur qn; ensorceler, envoûter, qn. **Under a s.,** sous un charme; ensorcelé.

spell², *v.tr.* (**spelt** *or* **spelled**) **1.** Épeler; (*in writing*) orthographier (un mot). **He can't s.,** il ne sait pas l'orthographe. **To s. badly,** faire des fautes d'orthographe. **To s. out sth.,** déchiffrer, lire, qch. péniblement. **Spelt in full,** écrit en toutes lettres. **How is it spelt?** comment cela s'écrit-il? **2. What do these letters s.?** quel mot forment ces lettres? **3.** Signifier. **That would s. disaster!** ce serait le désastre! **spelling,** *s.* Épellation *f*; (*in writing*) orthographe *f.* **Reformed s.,** néographie *f.* **'spelling-bee,** *s.* Concours (oral) d'orthographe. **'spelling-book,** *s.* Syllabaire *m*, alphabet *m.*

spell³, *s.* **1.** Tour *m* (de travail, etc.). **To do a s. of duty,** faire un tour de service. **To take spells at the pumps,** se relayer aux pompes. **Three hours at a s.,** trois heures de suite, d'arrache-pied. **2.** (Courte) période. **To rest for a (short) s.,** se reposer pendant quelque temps. **A long s. of cold weather,** une longue période de froid. **During the cold s.,** pendant le coup de froid. **A new s. of cold,** une reprise du froid.

spell⁴, *v.tr. U.S:* Relayer, relever (qn) (dans son travail).

spellbinder ['spelbaindər], *s. F:* Orateur entraînant; chanteur, -euse, qui séduit les auditeurs.

spellbound ['spelbaund], *a.* Retenu par un charme; magnétisé; figé sur place.

speller ['spelər], *s.* To be a good, a bad, s., savoir, ne pas savoir, l'orthographe.

spelter ['speltər], *s. Com:* Zinc *m.*

spencer ['spensər], *s. Cost:* Tricot *m.*

spend [spend], *v.tr.* (spent [spent]; spen.) **1.** Dépenser (de l'argent). To s. money on s.o., faire des dépenses pour qn. I am always spending, j'ai toujours l'argent à la main. Without spending a penny, sans bourse délier, sans rien débourser. *F:* To s. a penny, aller faire une petite commission, aller faire pipi. **2.** To s. care, time, on sth., consacrer, employer, du soin, du temps, à qch. **3.** Passer, employer (son temps). To s. Sunday in the country, passer le dimanche à la campagne. **4.** To s. oneself in a vain endeavour, s'épuiser dans un vain effort. The bullet had spent its force, la balle avait perdu (de) sa force. **spent**, *a.* **1.** *Lit:* The day was far s., c'était tard dans la journée. **2.** (*a*) *O:* Épuisé (de fatigue). The horses are s., les chevaux n'en peuvent plus. (*b*) The storm is s., l'orage est calmé. S. bullet, balle morte. S. cartridge, cartouche vide, brûlée. *I.C.E:* S. oil, huile décomposée. **spending**, *s.* Dépense *f. Pol.Ec:* S. power, pouvoir d'achat.

spendthrift ['spend θrift], *s.* Dépensier, -ière; dilapidateur, -trice; dissipateur, -trice; gaspilleur, -euse; *F:* panier percé. *attrib.* S. habits, habitudes dépensières.

spent. See SPEND.

sperm¹ [spə:m], *s. Physiol:* Sperme *m.*

sperm², *s.* S.(-whale), cachalot *m.* 'sperm oil, *s.* Huile *f* de baleine; huile de spermaceti.

spermaceti [spə:mə'seti], *s.* Spermaceti *m*; blanc *m* de baleine.

spermatozoon, *pl.* -zoa ['spə:mətə'zouən, -zouə], *s. Biol/Physiol: etc:* Spermatozoïde *m.*

spew [spju:]. **1.** *v.tr. & i.* Vomir. *A: & Lit:* To s. out, forth, rejeter (avec dégoût).

sphagnum ['sfægnəm], *s. Bot:* Sphaigne *f.*

sphenoid ['sfi:nɔid], *a. & s. Anat:* Sphénoïde (*m*).

sphenoidal [sfi'nɔidl], *a. Anat:* Sphénoïdal, -aux.

sphere [sfiər], *s.* **1.** Sphère *f. S.a.* MUSIC. **2.** (*a*) Milieu *m*, sphère. To be out of one's s., être hors de sa sphère; se sentir dépaysé. In the mental s., dans le domaine de l'esprit. (*b*) To extend one's s. of activity, étendre sa sphère d'activité, le champ de son activité. Limited s., cadre restreint. That does not come within my s., cela ne rentre pas dans ma compétence; cela n'est pas de mon domaine, de mon ressort. S. of influence, sphère, zone *f*, d'influence. In the political s., sur le plan politique.

spherical ['sferik(ə)l], *a.* Sphérique. *Mec.E:* S. joint, joint à rotule.

spheroid ['sfiərɔid], *s.* Sphéroïde *m.*

spherometer [sfiə'rɔmitər], *s.* Sphéromètre *m.*

sphincter ['sfiŋ(k)tər], *s. Anat:* Sphincter *m.*

sphinx [sfiŋks], *s. Myth: Ent:* Sphinx *m.* 'sphinx-like, *a.* (Sourire, etc.) de sphinx.

sphygmograph ['sfigmɔgræf, -ɑ:f], *s. Med:* Sphygmographe *m.*

sphygmomanometer [ˌsfigmɔmə'nɔmitər], *s. Med:* Tensiomètre.

spica ['spaikə], *s.* **1.** *Bot:* Épi *m.* **2.** *Surg:* S. bandage, spica *m*, épi.

spicate ['spaikeit], *a. Bot:* Épié; en épi, à épi.

spice¹ [spais], *s.* (*Coll. sg. preferred to pl.*) **1.** Épice *f*, aromate *m.* Mixed spice(s), épices mélangées. **2.** (*a*) *A:* Teinte *f* (de fourberie); nuance *f* (d'hypocrisie); soupçon *m* (de jalousie). (*b*) To give s. to a story, pimenter un récit. The s. of adventure, le piment de l'aventure.

spice², *v.tr.* **1.** Épicer (un mets). **2.** Épicer, pimenter (un récit, etc.).

spiciness ['spaisinis], *s.* **1.** Goût épicé. **2.** Piquant *m*, sel *m* (d'un récit).

spick and span ['spikən'spæn], *adj.phr.* Reluisant de propreté; propre comme un sou neuf; (*of pers.*) tiré à quatre épingles.

spicy ['spaisi], *a.* **1.** Épicé; (goût) relevé. **2.** Aromatique, parfumé. **3.** (*Of story, etc.*) (i) Piquant, croustillant; (ii) salé, épicé, poivré. S. expressions, termes pimentés, égrillards. **-ily**, *adv.* D'une manière piquante; avec du piquant; lestement.

spider ['spaidər], *s.* **1.** Araignée *f.* Spider's web, toile *f* d'araignée. **2.** *U.S:* (i) Trépied *m*; (ii) poêle *f* à frire. 'spider-crab, *s.* Araignée *f* de mer. 'spider monkey, *s. Z:* Atèle *m*, singe-araignée *m.*

spidery ['spaidəri], *a.* **1.** Qui ressemble à une araignée. S. handwriting, pattes *fpl* d'araignée. **2.** (Grenier) infesté d'araignées.

spiel¹ [spi:l], *s. F:* Boniment *m*, *P:* baratin *m.*

spiel², *v. F:* (*a*) *v.i.* Discourir, pérorer, *F:* en dégoiser. (*b*) *v.tr.* To s. off a whole list of names, débiter, *F:* dégoiser, toute une liste de noms.

spieler ['spi:lər], *s.* **1.** Beau parleur, bonimenteur *m*, *P:* baratineur *m.* **2.** (*a*) Tricheur *m*, fileur *m* de cartes. (*b*) Chevalier *m* d'industrie, escroc *m.*

spiffing ['spifiŋ], *a. F: O:* Épatant.

spifflicate ['spiflikeit], *v.tr. F: O:* Écraser, démolir (un adversaire).

spigot¹ ['spigət], *s.* **1.** Fausset *m*, broche *f*, cannelle *f* (de tonneau). **2.** (*a*) Clef *f*, carotte *f* (de robinet). (*b*) *U.S:* Robinet *m.* **3.** Pipe s., bout *m* mâle (d'un tuyau). 'spigot-joint, *s.* Assemblage *m* à emboîtement.

spigot², *v.i.* S'encastrer (into, dans).

spike¹ [spaik], *s.* **1.** Pointe *f* (de fer); piquant *m* (de fil barbelé); (*on railing*) lance *f.* **2.** (*a*) S.(-nail), clou *m* à large tête; broche *f.* (*b*) Rail: etc: Crampon *m* (d'attache). Screw s., tire-fond *m inv.* **3.** *Bot:* (*a*) Épi *m*; hampe (florale). (*b*) S.(-lavender), lavande commune; spic *m.* S. oil, essence *f* de spic. **4.** *Ven:* S.(-horn), dague *f* (de cerf de deux ans).

spike². **1.** *v.tr.* (*a*) Clouer, cheviller. (*b*) Armer (qch.) de pointes. (*c*) *Artil: A:* Enclouer (un canon). *F:* I spiked his guns for him, je lui ai damé le pion. (*d*) *U.S:* To s. a drink, corser (une bière, etc.) d'alcool. **2.** *v.i.* (*Of plants*) Former des épis. **spiked**, *a.* Garni de pointes; barbelé. S. shoes, chaussures à pointes.

spikenard ['spaiknɑ:d], *s.* Nard (indien).

spiky ['spaiki], *a.* A pointe(s) aiguë(s).

spile¹ [spail], *s.* **1.** Cheville *f*, fausset *m*, broche *f* (d'un tonneau). **2.** Pilot *m*, pieu *m.*

spile², *v.tr.* Piloter (les fondements d'un édifice).

spill¹ [spil], *s.* To have a s., culbuter; (*in car*) faire panache; (*from bicycle, horse*) *F:* ramasser une pelle, une bûche.

spill², *v.* (spilt [spilt] *or* spilled) I. *v.tr.* **1.** Répandre, renverser; verser (du sang). Much ink has been spilt about this question, on a fait couler beaucoup d'encre autour de cette question. **2.** Désarçonner (un cavalier); verser (les occupants d'une voiture). **3.** *F:* To s. the beans, (i) mettre les pieds dans le plat; (ii) gaffer; (iii) vendre la mèche. II. *v.i.* (*Of liquid*) Se répandre; s'épancher, s'écouler.

spill³, *s.* Allume-feu *m inv* en papier roulé, en bois.

spillikin ['spilikin], *s.* Jonchet *m.* To play (at) spillikins, jouer aux jonchets.

spillway ['spilwei], *s. Hyd.E:* Évacuateur *m* de crues; déversoir *m.*

spin¹ [spin], *s.* **1.** (*a*) Tournoiement *m*; (mouvement *m* de) rotation *f* (d'une balle). *Games:* To put s. on the ball, donner de l'effet à la balle. (*b*) *Av:* (Tail) s., vrille *f.* Steep s., vrille serrée. Flat s., (i) *Av:* tonneau *m*; (ii) *F:* panique *f.* To get into a s., descendre en vrille. *F:* To get into a flat s., ne pas savoir où donner de la tête. **2.** *O:* To go for a s., aller faire une promenade (en auto, etc.); faire une randonnée.

spin², *v.* (*p.t.* span [spæn], spun [spʌn]; *p.p.* spun; *pr.p.* spinning) **1.** *v.tr.* (*a*) Filer (la laine, etc.). *S.a.* YARN¹ 2. (*b*) To s. a top, faire aller une toupie. *Fb: etc:* To s. the coin, tirer au sort. To s. s.o. round, faire tourner, faire tournoyer, qn. (*c*) *Fish:* Pêcher à la cuiller. (*d*) *Metalw:* Emboutir, repousser, au tour. **2.** *v.i.* (*a*) (*Of top, etc.*) Tourner; (*of aircraft*) descendre en vrille; (*of compass*) s'affoler. To s. round and round, tournoyer; toupiller. My head is spinning, la tête me tourne. (*Of pers.*) To s. round, (i) pivoter, virevolter; (ii) se retourner vivement. Blow that sent him spinning, coup qui l'a

envoyé rouler. (b) (*Of wheel*) Patiner (sur place).
spin out, *v.tr.* Délayer (un discours); faire traîner
(une affaire) en longueur. **To make one's money
s. out**, ménager son argent. **spun**, *a.* (a) *Tex:*
Câblé. (b) *Metalw:* (Cuivre) repoussé. *S.a.* GLASS
1. **spinning**[1], *a.* Tournoyant. *Fb:* S. ball, ballon
tourbillonnant. **spinning**[2], *s.* 1. (a) Filage *m*
(au rouet). (b) *Ind:* Filature *f.* 2. Tournoiement *m*;
(mouvement *m* de) rotation *f*; affolement *m* (de
l'aiguille magnétique). *Av:* Vrille *f.* S. top, toupie
f. 3. Pêche *f* à la cuiller. **'spinning-frame**, *s.*
'spinning-mill, *s.* Filature *f.*
'spinning-wheel, *s.* Rouet *m.* **'spin 'drier**, *s.*
Dom.Ec: Essoreuse *f.*
spinach ['spinidʒ], *s. Bot:* Épinard *m; Cu:* épinards
mpl. **'spinach-beet**, *s. Bot: Cu:* Blète *f*, blette *f*,
bette *f* à couper.
spinal ['spain(ə)l], *a.* Spinal, -aux. S. column, colonne
vertébrale. S. complaint, maladie *f* de la moelle
épinière. S. curvature, déviation *f* de la colonne
vertébrale. *S.a.* CORD[1].
spindle ['spindl], *s.* 1. *Tex:* Fuseau *m.* 2. *Mec.E:
etc:* Mandrin *m*; axe *m* (de pompe); arbre *m*,
broche *f* (de tour, etc.). Valve s., tige *f* de soupape.
Nau: S. of the capstan, mèche *f* du cabestan. *Veh:*
Axle s., fusée *f* d'essieu. **'spindle-berry**, *s. Bot:*
Baie *f* du fusain. **'spindle(-)shanks**, *s.pl.* F: 1.
Jambes *f* de fuseau; mollets *m* de coq. 2. (With
sg. const.) Type grand et maigre. **'spindle-shaped**, *a.*
Fusiforme, fuselé. **'spindle-tree**, *s. Arb:* Fusain *m.*
spindrift ['spindrift], *s.* Embrun courant; poussière *f*
d'eau; poudrin *m.*
spine [spain], *s.* 1. *Nat.Hist:* Épine *f*; piquant *m*
(de hérisson). 2. *Anat:* Épine dorsale; colonne
vertébrale. 3. *Bookb:* Dos *m* (d'un livre).
spinel ['spin(ə)l], *s. Miner:* Spinelle *m.*
spineless ['spainlis], *a.* F: (*Of pers.*) Mou, *f.* molle;
qui manque de caractère.
spinelessness ['spainlisnis], *s.* F: Mollesse *f*; manque
m de caractère.
spinet [spi'net], *s. Mus:* Épinette *f.*
spinnaker ['spinəkər], *s. Nau:* Spinnaker *m. S.a.*
BOOM[1] 2.
spinner ['spinər], *s.* 1. Araignée fileuse. 2. (a) *Tex:*
Fileur, -euse. Master s., filateur *m.* (b) S. of yarns,
of theories, débiteur, -euse, conteur, -euse, d'histoires;
faiseur, -euse, de systèmes. 3. Machine *f* à filer;
métier *m* à filer. 4. = SPINNERET.
spinneret ['spinəret], *s.* Filière *f* (de ver à soie, etc.).
spinney ['spini], *s.* Petit bois; bosquet *m*; breuil *m.*
spinster ['spinstər], *s.f.* (a) Fille non mariée; *Adm:*
célibataire *f.* (b) Vieille fille.
spinsterhood ['spinstəhud], *s.* 1. État *m* de fille;
célibat *m.* 2. *Coll:* Les vieilles filles.
spinule ['spinju:l], *s.. Nat.Hist:* Spinule *f.*
spiny ['spaini], *a.* Épineux, -euse; couvert d'épines,
de piquants. *S.a.* LOBSTER.
spiracle ['spaiərəkl], *s.* (a) Évent *m* (d'un cétacé).
(b) *Ent:* Stigmate *m.*
spiraea [spai'ria], *s. Bot:* Spirée *f.*
spiral[1] ['spaiər(ə)l]. 1. *s.* (a) Spirale *f*, hélice *f.* **In a
s.**, en spirale. (b) Spire *f*; tour *m* (de spirale).
(c) *Av:* Montée *f* ou descente *f* en spirale. Vicious
s., cycle infernal. (d) *Pol.Ec:* Wage-price s., montée
en flèche des prix et des salaires. 2. *a.* Spiral, -aux;
hélicoïdal, -aux; en spirale; vrillé; (ressort) en
boudin; (mouvement) spiroïdal, -aux. S. gear,
engrenage hélicoïdal. *Surg:* S. bandage, bandage
rampant. *S.a.* CONVEYOR, STAIRCASE. **-ally**, *adv.*
En spirale, en hélice.
spiral[2], *v.i.* (**spiralled**) Former une spirale; tourner
en spirale; monter en spirale; (*of smoke*) tire-
bouchonner. *Av:* To s. up, vriller.
spirant ['spaiər(ə)nt], *s. Ling:* Spirante *f.*
spire[1] ['spaiər], *s.* Aiguille *f*, flèche *f* (d'église).
spire[2], *s.* Spire *f*, tour *m* (d'une hélice, etc.).
spirit[1] ['spirit], *s.* 1. Esprit *m*, âme *f. B: Lit:* **He was
vexed in his s.**, il avait l'esprit tourmenté. **Peace to
his s.**, la paix soit de son âme. 2. (a) **The Holy S.**,
le Saint-Esprit. **Evil s.**, esprit malin, mauvais génie.
S.a. MOVE[2] I. 3. (b) **To raise a s.**, évoquer un esprit.
To believe in spirits, croire aux esprits, aux revenants.
3. (*Pers.*) The leading s., (i) l'âme, le chef (d'une

entreprise); (ii) le meneur (d'une révolte). 4
Esprit, disposition *f.* **The s. of the age**, l'esprit d
siècle. **Party s.**, esprit de parti. *S.a.* PUBLIC 1. T
follow out the s. of s.o.'s instructions, se conforme
à l'intention des ordres de qn. **To take sth. in :
wrong s.**, prendre qch. en mauvaise part, de travers
In a s. of mischief, par espièglerie. **To enter into the s
of sth.**, entrer de bon cœur dans (la partie). F
That's the s.!, à la bonne heure! 5. (a) Caractère *m*
cœur *m*, courage *m; F:* cran *m.* **Man of s.**, homm
de caractère. **To show s.**, montrer du caractère
du courage. (b) Ardeur *f*, entrain *m*, fougue *f*
He went on playing with s., il continua de joue
avec entrain, avec brio. (c) **He is full of spirits**, i
est très remuant, très diable. **To be in good spirits**
être gai, dispos; être de bonne humeur. **To be i:
high spirits**, être en train, en verve; être d'un
gaieté folle. **To be in low spirits**, être abattu, accablé
se sentir tout triste. **To keep up one's spirits**, n
pas perdre courage; ne pas se laisser abattre. T
recover one's spirits, reprendre courage; se remonter
Their spirits rose, ils reprenaient courage, leu
moral se relevait. 6. *Usu. pl.* (a) Spiritueux *mpl*
liqueurs spiritueuses, alcooliques; alcool *m.* (b.
Surgical s. = alcool *m* à 90°. **'spirit-lamp**, *s*
Lampe *f*, réchaud *m*, à alcool. **'spirit-level**, *s*
Niveau *m* à bulle d'air, à alcool. **'spirit-rapping**, *s*
Communication *f* avec des esprits frappeurs. **'spirit-
stove**, *s.* Réchaud *m* à alcool.
spirit[2], *v.tr.* (**spirited**) To s. s.o. away, faire disparaîtr
qn comme par enchantement. **To s. sth. away**, F.
subtiliser, escamoter, qch.
spirited ['spiritid], *a.* 1. (High-)s., (*of pers.*) vif, *f*
vive, animé; plein de verve, d'ardeur; (*of horse*
fougueux, -euse, ardent, vif. 2. (*Of style*) Chaleureux
-euse, entraînant, plein de verve. **To give a s. per
formance**, jouer avec verve. **-ly**, *adv.* Ardemment
avec verve, avec entrain.
spiritedness ['spiritidnis], *s.* Ardeur *f*, entrain *m*
verve *f*; fougue *f*, ardeur (d'un cheval).
spiritless ['spiritlis], *a.* 1. Sans vie; terne; qu
manque d'entrain. 2. Sans courage, sans caractère
lâche. 3. Abattu, déprimé. 4. Sans force, san:
vigueur; mou, *f.* molle. **-ly**, *adv.* Sans vigueur;
sans entrain; mollement.
spiritlessness ['spiritlisnis], *s.* Manque *m* de courage
de verve, d'entrain; léthargie *f.*
spiritual ['spiritjuəl]. 1. *a.* (a) Spirituel, -elle; de
l'esprit. S. court, tribunal ecclésiastique. (b) S.
features, traits purs, raffinés. (c) Spirituel, immatériel.
2. *s.* Negro spiritual, negro spiritual *m, pl.* negro
spirituals.
spiritualism ['spiritjuəlizm], *s.* 1. *Psychics:* Spiritisme
m. 2. *Phil:* Spiritualisme *m.*
spiritualist ['spiritjuəlist], *s. & a.* 1. *Psychics:* Spirite
(*mf*). 2. *Phil:* Spiritualiste (*mf*).
spirituality [spiritju'æliti], *s.* 1. Spiritualité *f* (de
l'âme). 2. *pl.* Spiritualities, biens *m* et bénéfices *m*
ecclésiastiques.
spirituous ['spiritjuəs], *a.* Spiritueux, -euse, alcoolique.
spirochaete ['spaiərəki:t], *s. Bac:* Spirochète *m.*
spirometer [spai(ə)'rɔmitər], *s.* Spiromètre *m.*
spirt[1,2] [spə:t], *s. & v.* = SPURT[1,2].
spit[1] [spit], *s.* 1. *Cu:* Broche *f.* Electric s., rôtissoire *f.*
2. *Ph.Geog:* Flèche *f.*
spit[2], *v.tr.* (**spitted**) (a) Embrocher, brocheter, mettre à
la broche (un rôti). (b) Embrocher (qn).
spit[3], *s.* 1. (a) Crachat *m*, salive *f. F:* He's the dead
s. of his father, c'est son père tout craché. *F:* S.
and polish, fourbissage *m*; astiquage *m.* (b) Crachement *m.* 2. Crachin *m* (de pluie).
spit[4], *v.* (**spat** [spæt]; **spat**; **spitting**) 1. *v.i.* Cracher.
I.C.E: (*Of engine*) To s. back, avoir des retours de
flamme (au carburateur). **It is spitting (with rain)**,
il crachine; il tombe quelques gouttes. 2. *v.tr.*
Cracher (du sang). **To s. sth. out**, cracher qch. *F:*
S. it out! dis-le! **spitting**, *s.* (a) Crachement *m*
(i) Expectoration *f. P.N:* No s., défense de cracher.
(ii) S. of blood, crachement de sang. (b) *I.C.E:*
S. back, retour *m* de flamme au carburateur.
spit[5], *s.* Profondeur *f* de fer de bêche. **To dig two-
spit(s) deep**, labourer la terre à deux fers de bêche.

spite¹ [spait], *s.* **1.** (*a*) Rancune *f.* (*b*) Malveillance *f.* (*c*) Pique *f*, dépit *m.* **From s., out of spite,** (i) par rancune; (ii) par dépit; (iii) par malveillance, par méchanceté. **To have a s. against s.o.,** en vouloir à qn; garder rancune à qn. **2.** *Prep.phr.* **In s. of . . .,** en dépit de . . .; malgré. . . .

spite², *v.tr.* Vexer, contrarier (qn).

spiteful ['spaitful], *a.* Rancunier, -ière, vindicatif, -ive, méchant, malveillant. **S. tongue,** langue venimeuse. **-fully,** *adv.* **1.** Par dépit; par rancune; par méchanceté. **2.** Méchamment.

spitefulness ['spaitfulnis], *s.* Méchanceté *f*; rancœur *f*; malveillance *f.*

spitfire ['spit'faiər], *s.* F: Rageur, -euse.

spittle ['spitl], *s.* Salive *f*, crachat *m*; bave *f* (du crapaud).

spittoon [spi'tu:n], *s.* Crachoir *m.*

spiv [spiv], *s.* F: (*a*) Profiteur *m*, trafiquant *m* du marché noir, chevalier *m* d'industrie. (*b*) Parasite *m.*

splash¹ [splæʃ], *s.* **1.** Éclaboussement *m*; clapotis *m* (des vagues). **To fall into the water with a s.,** tomber dans l'eau en faisant flac. F: **To make a splash,** (i) faire sensation; (ii) jeter l'argent par les fenêtres. *Journ:* **S. headline,** grosse manchette. **2.** (*a*) Éclaboussure *f* (de boue, etc.). (*b*) Tache *f* (de couleur, de lumière). (*c*) Flaque *f* (d'eau). **3.** F: **Whisky and s.,** whisky-soda *m.* **Just a s., please,** très peu (d'eau, etc.), s'il vous plaît.

splash². **1.** *v.tr.* (*a*) Éclabousser (**with,** de). (*b*) **To s. water about,** faire rejaillir l'eau. F: **To s. one's money about,** prodiguer son argent, jeter son argent par les fenêtres. *Journ:* **To s. a piece of news,** mettre une nouvelle en (grosse) manchette. **2.** *v.i.* (*a*) (*Of liquid*) Rejaillir en éclaboussures; (*of waves*) clapoter; (*of tap*) cracher. **To s. up,** gicler. (*b*) Barboter; patauger. **To s. into the water,** entrer dans l'eau en faisant rejaillir des éclaboussures. **To s. about in the water,** s'agiter dans l'eau. **'splash-down,** *s.* Amerrissage *m* (d'un engin spatial).

splatter ['splætər], *s. & v.* = SPATTER¹,².

splay¹ [splei], *s.* **1.** (*a*) *Arch:* Embrasure *f.* (*b*) (*Bevelled edge*) Chanfrein *m*; coupe *f* oblique. **2.** (*Of bowl, etc.*) Évasement *m*, évasure *f.*

splay². **1.** *v.tr.* (*a*) **To s. the sides of a window,** ébraser une fenêtre. **To s. out an embrasure,** épanouir une embrasure. (*b*) *Carp:* Couper en biseau, en sifflet; chanfreiner. (*c*) *Vet:* **To s. a horse's shoulder,** épauler un cheval; démettre l'épaule d'un cheval. **2.** *v.i.* **To s. out,** s'évaser. **splayed,** *a.* **1.** (*Of opening*) Ébrasé; évasé. **S. wheel,** roue désaxée. **2.** *Carp:* En sifflet.

splay³, *a.* **Bricks cut s.,** briques biaises. **'splay-footed,** *a.* Aux pieds plats tournés en dehors; (cheval) panard.

spleen [spli:n], *s.* **1.** *Anat:* Rate *f.* **2.** O: (*a*) Spleen *m*; humeur noire. **In a fit of s.,** dans un moment d'humeur noire. (*b*) Mauvaise humeur. **To vent one's s. (up)on s.o.,** décharger sa bile sur qn.

splendid ['splendid], *a.* Splendide; superbe; magnifique. **A s. friend,** un excellent ami, F: un ami épatant. **She's simply s.!** elle est vraiment merveilleuse! **That's s.!** à la bonne heure! **-ly,** *adv.* Splendidement; magnifiquement. **I am getting on s.,** ça marche comme sur des roulettes.

splendiferous [splen'difərəs], *a.* F: O: Magnifique, F: mirobolant.

splendour ['splendər], *s.* Splendeur *f*; magnificence *f*, éclat *m.*

splenic ['splenik], *a.* *Anat:* Splénique.

splice¹ [splais], *s.* **1.** (*In rope*) Épissure *f*; (*in wire cable*) ligature *f*; joint épissé. **2.** (*a*) *Carp:* Enture *f.* (*b*) *Cin:* Collure *f*, point *m* de collage (d'un film). (*c*) Soudure *f* (d'un pneu).

splice², *v.tr.* **1.** Épisser (un cordage, un câble). *S.a.* MAIN-BRACE. **2.** *Carp:* Enter. *Tex:* **Nylon spliced,** renforcé nylon. **3.** *Cin:* Réparer (un film cassé). **4.** F: **To get spliced,** se marier.

spline¹ [splain], *s. Mec.E:* **1.** (*a*) Languette *f*; clavette *f* linguiforme. (*b*) Saillie *f* (d'un arbre); ergot *m.* **2.** Cannelure *f*, rainure *f.* **Two-s. hole,** trou à deux rainures.

spline², *v.tr. Mec.E:* **1.** Claveter. **2.** Canneler, rainurer.

splint¹ [splint], *s.* **1.** *Surg:* Éclisse *f*, attelle *f*; (*cradle-shaped*) gouttière *f.* **To put a limb in splints,** éclisser un membre. **2.** *Vet:* Suros *m.* **'splint-bone,** *s.* Os métacarpien (du cheval).

splint², *v.tr. Surg:* Éclisser (un membre fracturé). **splinting,** *s. Med:* Éclissage *m*, clissage *m.*

splinter¹ ['splintər], *s.* **1.** Éclat *m* (de bois, d'obus); picot *m* (de bois). **S. lodged under the skin,** écharde *f.* **2.** *Surg:* Esquille *f* (d'os). **3.** **S. group,** groupe *m* fractionnaire (d'un parti politique). **'splinter-deck,** *s. N.Arch:* Pont *m* pare-éclats. **'splinter-proof,** *a.* **1.** A l'épreuve des éclats (d'obus). **2.** **S. glass,** verre *m* de sécurité; verre durci, incassable.

splinter². **1.** *v.tr.* (*a*) Briser en éclats; faire voler en éclats. (*b*) Éclater (un mât, etc.). **2.** *v.i.* (*a*) Voler en éclats. (*b*) Éclater. **splintered,** *a.* (Bois) en éclats; (os) en esquilles, esquilleux.

split¹ [split], *s.* **1.** Fente *f*; fissure *f*; crevasse *f* (dans une roche); déchirure *f*; gerçure *f* (de la peau). **2.** Division *f*, séparation *f*; rupture *f*, scission *f* (dans un parti politique, etc.). **3.** F: Quart *m* de bouteille; demi-bouteille *f.* **4.** *Cu:* Devonshire s., brioche fourrée à la crème. **5.** *pl.* **To do the splits,** faire le grand écart.

split², *v.* (**split**; **split**; **splitting**) **1.** *v.tr.* (*a*) Fendre; refendre (l'ardoise); cliver (la roche). *Leath:* **To s. a hide,** dédoubler une peau. *Ph:* **To s. the atom,** désintégrer, désagréger, diviser, l'atome. *S.a.* HAIR 1, SIDE¹ 1. (*b*) Déchirer (sa jupe, etc.). (*c*) Diviser; partager. (*d*) *Pol:* **To s. a party (on a question),** diviser un parti (sur une question); provoquer une rupture dans le parti. *Pol:* **To s. one's vote,** panacher un bulletin de vote. *Fin:* **To s. shares,** fractionner, scinder, des actions. (*e*) *Gram:* **To s. an infinitive,** intercaler un adverbe entre *to* et le verbe. *S.a.* DIFFERENCE 2. **2.** *v.i.* (*a*) Se fendre, se crevasser; (*of rock*) se cliver; (*of paint, skin*) se gercer. **The ship s. in two,** le navire s'est cassé en deux. **To s. open,** se fendre largement. (*b*) (*Of cloth*) Se déchirer. (*c*) F: **My head is splitting,** j'ai un mal de tête fou. (*d*) F: **To s. on s.o.,** dénoncer qn; vendre (un complice); F: cafarder. **split up.** **1.** *v.tr.* Fractionner; décomposer (une fraction). **2.** *v.i.* Se fractionner. **The party split up into three groups,** le parti se divisa en trois groupes. **split³,** *a.* **1.** Fendu. **S. peas,** pois cassés. **In a s. second,** en un rien de temps. *S.a.* RING¹ 2, SECOND¹ 1. **2.** *Psy:* **S. personality,** dédoublement *m* de la personnalité. **S. mind,** esprit dédoublé, schizophrène. **splitting,** *s.* **1.** Fendage *m*, éclatement *m*; refente *f* (des ardoises); délitement *m* (de la pierre). **2.** (*a*) *Pol:* Panachage *m* (d'un bulletin de vote). (*b*) *Ph:* **The s. of the atom,** fission *f* de l'atome.

splotch¹ [splotʃ], *s.* F: Tache *f* (de couleur, etc.).

splotch², *v.tr.* Barbouiller (**with,** de); tacher.

splotchy ['splotʃi], *a.* Barbouillé; taché.

splurge¹ [splə:dʒ], *s.* F: Esbroufe *f*; F: épate *f*; démonstration bruyante.

splurge², *v.i.* F: Faire des dépenses extravagantes; faire de l'esbroufe, de l'épate.

splutter¹ ['splʌtər], *s.* **1.** Bredouillement *m.* **2.** Crachement *m* (d'une plume); bafouillage *m* (d'un moteur).

splutter². **1.** *v.tr.* **To s. (out) a threat,** bredouiller une menace. **2.** *v.i.* (*a*) Lancer de la salive (en parlant); *P:* envoyer des postillons, postillonner. **Pen that splutters,** plume qui crache. (*b*) Bredouiller, bafouiller. (*c*) *I.C.E:* (*Of engine*) Bafouiller.

spoil¹ [spoil], *s.* **1.** (*Usu. pl.*) Dépouilles *fpl*; butin *m.* **To claim one's share of the spoils,** demander sa part du gâteau. *Min: etc:* Déblai(s) *m* (*pl*).

spoil², *v.* (*p.t. & p.p.* **spoiled** or (*except in sense* 2) **spoilt**) **1.** *v.tr.* (*a*) Gâter, endommager, abîmer (qch.); avarier (des marchandises). **To get spoiled,** spoilt, s'abîmer. **To s. a piece of work,** gâcher un travail. **To s. a lock,** fausser une serrure. **To s. the beauty of sth.,** déparer qch.; détruire la beauté de qch. F: **It spoils her,** ça lui fait tort. **To s. a sauce,** rater une sauce. **The news spoilt his appetite,** la nouvelle lui a coupé l'appétit. (*b*) Gâter (un enfant). **2.** *v.tr.* A. & *Lit:* (*a*) Dépouiller, spolier (s.o. of sth., qn de qch.). (*b*) Piller, saccager (une ville). **3.** *v.i.* (*Of fruit, etc.*) Se gâter, s'abîmer;

s'avarier, s'altérer. *F:* **To be spoiling for a fight,** brûler du désir de se battre. **spoilt,** *a.* **1.** (*a*) Gâté, gâché, abîmé, manqué. **S. voting paper,** bulletin nul. (*b*) Avarié, gâté, corrompu. **S. goods,** marchandises détériorées. **2. S. child,** enfant gâté. **'spoil-sport,** *s. F:* Trouble-fête *m inv,* rabat-joie *mf inv,* gâte-tout *m inv.*

spoilage ['spɔilidʒ], *s. Ind:* Déchets *mpl.*

spoke[1] [spouk], *s.* **1.** (*a*) Rayon *m,* rai(s) *m* (de roue). (*b*) *Nau:* Poignée *f,* manette *f* (de roue de gouvernail). **2.** (*a*) Échelon *m* (d'échelle). (*b*) Bâton *m* (à enrayer). **To put a spoke in s.o.'s wheel,** mettre des bâtons dans les roues à qn.

spoke[2], *v.tr.* Enrayer (une roue).

spoke[3], **spoken.** See SPEAK.

spokeshave ['spoukʃeiv], *s. Tls:* Vastringue *f,* racloire *f.*

spokesman, *pl.* -**men** ['spouksmən], *s.* Porte-parole *m inv.* **To act as s. for one's fellow-citizens,** prendre la parole pour ses concitoyens.

spoliation [,spouli'eiʃ(ə)n], *s.* **1.** (*a*) Spoliation *f,* dépouillement *m.* (*b*) Pillage *m.* **2.** *Jur:* Destruction *f,* altération *f* (de documents probants).

spondaic [spɔn'deiik], *a. Pros:* Spondaïque.

spondee ['spɔndi:], *s. Pros:* Spondée *m.*

spondulix [spɔn'dju:liks], *s. U.S: P:* Argent *m,* pognon *m.*

sponge[1] [spʌn(d)ʒ], *s.* **1.** (*a*) Éponge *f.* **To throw up the s.,** (i) *Box:* jeter l'éponge; abandonner; (ii) s'avouer vaincu; quitter la partie. (*b*) *Artil: A:* Écouvillon *m.* **2.** (*a*) *Cu:* Pâte molle. (*b*) *Metall:* Éponge métallique. **3.** = SPONGER 2. **4.** Ivrogne *m.* **'sponge-bag,** *s.* Sac *m* à éponge. **'sponge-cake,** *s. Cu:* **1.** Gâteau *m* de Savoie; gâteau mousseline. **2.** = Madeleine *f.* **'sponge-cloth,** *s. Tex:* Tissu-éponge *m.* **'sponge-'finger,** *s.* = Biscuit *m* à la cuiller. **'sponge-'fisher,** *s.* Pêcheur *m* d'éponges. **'sponge-holder,** *s.* Porte-éponge(s) *m inv.*

sponge[2], *s.* Coup *m* d'éponge. **To give sth. a s.,** passer l'éponge sur qch.

sponge[3]. **1.** *v.tr.* (*a*) Éponger (qch.); nettoyer (qch.) avec une éponge. (*b*) *Med:* Lotionner (une plaie). (*c*) *F:* Écornifler (un dîner, etc.). **2.** *v.i.* (*a*) Pêcher les éponges. (*b*) *F:* Écornifler; *F:* écumer les marmites. **To s. on s.o.,** vivre aux crochets de qn. **To s. on s.o. for drinks,** se faire payer des tournées par qn. **sponge down,** *v.tr.* Passer l'éponge sur le corps de (qn); éponger (un cheval). **sponge off,** *v.tr.* **1.** Effacer (une tache) à l'éponge. **2.** *Artil: A:* Écouvillonner (une pièce) à l'eau. **sponging**[1], *a. F:* (*Of pers.*) Parasite, écornifleur. **sponging**[2], *s.* **1.** (*a*) Nettoyage *m* à l'éponge. (*b*) *Med:* Lotionnement *m.* **2.** *F:* Écorniflage *m.*

sponger ['spʌn(d)ʒər], *s.* **1.** Pêcheur *m* d'éponges. **2.** *F:* Parasite *m;* écornifleur, -euse; pique-assiette *m inv;* pieuvre *f.*

sponginess ['spʌn(d)ʒinis], *s.* Spongiosité *f.*

spongy ['spʌn(d)ʒi], *a.* Spongieux, -euse.

sponsion ['spɔnʃ(ə)n], *s. Jur:* Garantie (personnelle) (**on behalf of,** en faveur d'un État, etc.).

sponsor[1] ['spɔnsər], *s.* **1.** Garant *m,* caution *f,* répondant *m* (**for s.o.,** de qn). **2.** (*a*) (*At baptism*) Parrain *m,* marraine *f.* **To stand s. to a child,** tenir un enfant sur les fonts (baptismaux). (*b*) (*Introducing new member to club, etc.*) Parrain.

sponsor[2], *v.tr.* Être le garant de, répondre pour (qn); parrainer (qn). *W.Tel: T.V: etc:* Offrir un programme; subventionner des programmes (de ses fonds personnels).

sponsorship ['spɔnsəʃip], *s.* Parrainage *m.*

spontaneity [,spɔntə'ni:iti], *s.* Spontanéité *f.*

spontaneous [spɔn'teinjəs], *a.* Spontané; (i) (mouvement) automatique; (ii) (acte) volontaire. **-ly,** *adv.* Spontanément; (i) automatiquement; (ii) de son propre mouvement.

spontaneousness [spɔn'teinjəsnis], *s.* Spontanéité *f.*

spoof[1] [spu:f], *s. F:* Attrape *f;* mystification *f;* blague *f.*

spoof[2], *v.tr. F:* Mystifier, duper (qn). **You've been spoofed,** on vous a eu.

spook [spu:k], *s. F:* Spectre *m,* revenant *m,* apparition *f.*

spooky ['spu:ki], *a. F:* (Histoire *f,* etc.) de revenants, de spectres; (maison) hantée.

spool[1] [spu:l], *s.* **1.** *Tex:* Bobine *f,* can(n)ette *f.* **S. of a sewing-machine,** can(n)ette. *U.S:* **S. of thread,** bobine de coton (à coudre). **2.** *Fish:* Tambour *m* (de moulinet). **3.** *Phot:* Bobine (de film). *Typewr:* **Ribbon spools,** bobines du ruban.

spool[2], *v.tr.* Bobiner; dévider, envider (du fil, etc.).

spoon[1] [spu:n], *s.* **1.** Cuiller *f,* cuillère *f.* **Dessert s., soup s.,** cuillère à dessert, à soupe. **Wooden s.,** cuillère *f* en bois, mouvette *f, Fr.C:* micoine *f.* **2.** *Metall: etc:* **Assay s.,** éprouvette *f.* **'spoon-bit,** *s. Tls:* Mèche *f* à cuiller. **'spoon-feed,** *v.tr.* Nourrir (un enfant) à la cuiller. *F:* **To s.-feed a pupil,** mâcher les morceaux à un élève. **Spoon-fed industries,** industries subventionnées. **'spoon-net,** *s. Fish:* Épuisette *f.*

spoon[2]. **1.** *v.tr.* (*a*) **To s. (up) one's soup,** manger sa soupe (avec la cuiller). **To s. off the cream,** enlever la crème (avec la cuiller). (*b*) *Cr: Golf:* Prendre (la balle) en cuiller. **2.** *v.i. P:* (*Of couple*) Se faire des mamours.

spoonbill ['spu:nbil], *s. Orn:* Spatule *f.* **S. duck,** souchet *m.*

spoonerism ['spu:nərizm], *s. F:* Contre-petterie *f,* contre(-)pèterie *f.*

spoonful ['spu:nful], *s.* Cuillerée *f.* **Two dessert-spoonfuls,** deux cuillerées à dessert.

spoor[1] [spuər], *s. Ven:* Foulées *fpl,* erre *f* (d'un cerf, etc.).

spoor[2], *v.tr. Ven:* Suivre (un animal) à la piste.

sporadic [spə'rædik], *a.* **1.** Sporadique. **2.** Isolé; rare. **-ally,** *adv.* **1.** Sporadiquement. **2.** Dans des cas isolés; par-ci par-là.

sporangium, *pl.* -**ia** [spo'rændʒiəm, -iə], *s. Bot:* Sporange *m.*

spore ['spo:r], *s.* Spore *f.* **'spore-case,** *s. Bot:* Sporange *m.*

sporran ['spɔrən], *s. Scot:* Bourse en peau brute (portée par les Écossais sur le devant du kilt); sporran *m.*

sport[1] [spɔ:t], *s.* **1.** (*a*) Jeu *m,* divertissement *m.* **In s., pour rire;** par plaisanterie; en badinant. **To make s. of . . .,** se moquer de . . ., se jouer de . . . (*b*) **To have good s.,** (*hunting*) faire bonne chasse; (*fishing*) faire bonne pêche. **2.** Sport *m.* **School sports,** fête sportive. **To go in for sports,** s'adonner aux sports. *Aut:* **Sports model,** modèle *m* grand sport. *Journ:* **Sports edition,** édition sportive. **3. To be the s. of fortune,** être le jouet de la fortune. **4.** *Biol:* Variété anormale. **5.** *F:* **He's a (good) s.,** (i) c'est un beau joueur; (ii) c'est un chic type. **Be a s.!** sois chic! **'sports car,** *s. Aut:* Voiture *f* grand sport. **'sports coat,** *s.* Veston sport. **'sports day,** *s. Sch:* Fête sportive. **'sports e'quipment,** *s. Com:* Accessoires *mpl,* fournitures *fpl,* articles *mpl,* de sport. **'sports ground,** *s.* Terrain de jeux; stade *m.* **'sports jacket,** *s.* Veston sport. **'sports requisites,** *spl. Com:* = SPORTS EQUIPMENT.

sport[2]. **1.** *v.i.* (*a*) Jouer; se divertir. (*b*) *Biol:* Produire une variété anormale. **2.** *v.tr. F:* Arborer (sa cravate rouge, etc.); exhiber (un manteau de fourrure). *S.a.* OAK. **sporting,** *a.* **1.** Amateur de la chasse ou de la pêche. **2.** De sport; sportif. **S. man,** amateur *m,* fervent *m,* de sport. **In a s. spirit,** sportivement. **S. behaviour,** conduite digne d'un sportsman. **You have a s. chance,** ça vaut la peine d'essayer le coup. **I'll make you a s. offer,** je vais vous faire une offre à laquelle vous ne perdrez rien.

sportive ['spɔ:tiv], *a.* Badin; folâtre. **-ly,** *adv.* En badinant; en plaisantant.

sportiveness ['spɔ:tivnis], *s.* Folâtrerie *f,* folichonnerie *f.*

sportsman, *pl.* -**men** ['spɔ:tsmən], *s.m.* **1.** Chasseur *m;* pêcheur. **2.** Amateur de sport, sportsman, *pl.* sportsmen. **3. He's a real s.,** il est animé de l'esprit sportif; c'est un beau joueur.

sportsmanlike ['spɔ:tsmənlaik], *a.* (Conduite) digne d'un sportsman.

sportsmanship ['spɔ:tsmənʃip], *s.* **1.** Habileté *f,* qualités *fpl,* de sportsman; pratique *f* des sports. **2.** Conduite *f* digne d'un sportsman; sportivité *f,* esprit sportif.

sportswear [ˈspɔːtswɛər], s. Com: Vêtements mpl sport.

sportswoman, pl. **-women** [ˈspɔːtswumən, -wimin], s.f. 1. Femme amateur de la chasse, etc. 2. Femme sportive, amateur de sport.

sporty [ˈspɔːti], a. 1. F: (a) Sportif, -ive. (b) (Femme) qui se vante de son allure sportive. (c) O: It's awfully s. of you to . . ., c'est très chic de votre part de . . . 2. F: (a) O: The s. set, les viveurs. (b) (Veston, etc.) de couleurs criantes, voyantes. 3. (Of dog) A s. little fellow, un petit chien courageux, résolu.

sporule [ˈspɔrjuːl], s. Sporule f.

spot[1] [spɔt], s. 1. (a) Endroit m, lieu m. I was standing on the very s., je me trouvais sur les lieux mêmes. The manager should always be on the s., le gérant doit toujours être là. Rely on the man on the s., faites confiance à la personne qui est sur place. To have a soft s. for s.o., avoir un faible pour qn. To hit the high spots, faire la noce. F: To be in a (tight) s., (i) être dans le pétrin; (ii) avoir des ennuis pécuniaires. (b) F: To be on the s., (i) être ìrès éveillé; (ii) être dans une situation dangereuse. P: To put s.o. on the s., (i) assassiner qn; (ii) mettre qn dans une situation difficile, embarrassante. (c) Adv.phr. On the s., sur-le-champ; immédiatement. To be killed on the s., être tué net, raide; F: y rester. To fall dead on the s., tomber raide mort. (d) Com: S. cash, argent comptant. (e) To put one's finger on a weak s., mettre le doigt sur un point faible. To touch the s., aller jusqu'à la racine du mal. 2. (a) Tache f, macule f. F: There are spots on the sun, il y a du vilain dans l'air. Th: Cin: F: Hot s., tache f de lumière. (b) (On face) Bouton m. 3. (a) Pois m (de couleur). Blue tie with red spots, cravate bleue à pois rouges. A panther's spots, la tacheture, la moucheture, d'une panthère. F: To knock spots off s.o., battre qn à plate(s) couture(s). (b) The blind s., (i) Anat: la papille optique; (ii) Aut: angle m aveugle. F: That's your blind s., c'est là où vous refusez de voir clair. (c) Bill: (i) Mouche f (sur la bille ou la table). (ii) Bille marquée d'une mouche. Radar: Scanning s., spot explorateur. 4. (a) Goutte f (de pluie). (b) F: Just a s. of whisky, deux doigts de whisky. What about a s. of lunch? si nous allions déjeuner ? A s. of trouble, un petit ennui; une anicroche. ˈspot-ˈcheck[1], s. Contrôle-surprise m. ˈspot-ˈcheck[2], v.tr. Contrôler, vérifier (qch.) à intervalles irréguliers. ˈspot height, s. Surv: Point coté. ˈspot ˈnews, s. Journ: Dernière heure. ˈspot-on. F: 1. a. Exact, approprié, au point. 2. adv. Au poil. ˈspot remover, s. Com: Détachant m. ˈspot-welder, s. 1. (Pers.) Soudeur m par points. 2. Machine f à souder par points. ˈspot-welding, s. Soudure f par points.

spot[2], v.tr. (spotted) 1. (a) Tacher, souiller (qch.). (b) Tacheter, moucheter (qch.). v.impers. It's spotting with rain, il commence à pleuvoir. 2. F: (a) Repérer; apercevoir (qn, qch.). He spotted me from his box, il m'a repéré de sa loge. (b) Reconnaître. Turf: To s. the winner, prédire le gagnant. **spotted**, a. 1. (a) Tacheté, moucheté. (b) Tex: A pois. 2. F: O: S. fever, méningite cérébro-spinale. 3. F: S. dog, (i) chien m de Dalmatie; (ii) pudding m aux raisins de Corinthe. **spotting**, s. 1. Taches fpl; tachetures fpl. 2. (a) Repérage m. (b) (i) Artil: Aircraft s., réglage m (de tir) par avions. (ii) Av: Mil: Observation f (de défense contre avions).

spotless [ˈspɔtlis], a. Sans tache; immaculé; pur. S. snow, neige vierge. **-ly**, adv. S. clean, d'une propreté irréprochable.

spotlessness [ˈspɔtlisnis], s. Propreté f; netteté f; pureté f.

spotlight[1] [ˈspɔtlait], s. Th: Cin: etc: (a) Feu m de projecteur. (b) Projecteur m. F: To put the s. on sth., mettre qch. en vedette.

spotlight[2], v.tr. Th: etc: Diriger les projecteurs sur (une vedette). F: Mettre qch. en vedette.

spotter [ˈspɔtər], s. 1. Av: Avion m de réglage de tir. 2. Av: Mil: Observateur m (de défense contre avions). F: Train s., car s., enfant mf qui regarde passer les trains, les voitures (pour repérer les différents modèles).

spotty [ˈspɔti], a. Moucheté, tacheté; (visage) couvert de boutons.

spouse [spauz], s. Lit: Époux, f. épouse. Jur: Conjoint, -ointe.

spout[1] [spaut], s. 1. (a) Rair -water s., (i) tuyau m de décharge; (ii) gargouille f, goulotte f (de gouttière). P: Down the s., perdu. (b) Bec m (de théière); jet m, dégorgeoir m (de pompe). 2. P: To put one's watch up the s., mettre sa montre au clou. 3. Meteor: Trombe f. ˈspout-hole, s. Z: Évent m (de baleine).

spout[2]. 1. v.i. (a) (Of liquid) Jaillir, rejaillir. (b) (Of whale) Souffler. 2. v.tr. (a) Faire jaillir, lancer (de l'eau). (b) F: Dégoiser (des discours). Abs. To s., parler à jet continu. **spouting**, s. 1. Jaillissement m. 2. F: Déclamation f.

spouter [ˈspautər], s. F: Déclamateur m, péroreur m.

sprain[1] [sprein], s. Entorse f, foulure f.

sprain[2], v.tr. To s. one's wrist, se fouler le poignet. To s. one's ankle, se donner une entorse.

sprang. See SPRING[2].

sprat [spræt], s. 1. Ich: Sprat m, harenguet m. 2. F: Gringalet m.

sprawl [sprɔːl], v.i. (a) S'étendre, s'étaler. (b) To go sprawling, s'étaler par terre; P: ramasser une pelle. To send s.o. sprawling, envoyer rouler, P: bouler, qn par terre. **sprawling**, a. 1. (a) Vautré. (b) Étendu les quatre fers en l'air. 2. S. hand-writing, grosse écriture informe; gribouillage m.

spray[1] [sprei], s. Brin m, ramille f. S. of flowers, rameau fleuri. S. of diamonds, aigrette f de diamants.

spray[2], s. 1. Poudroiement m d'écume; embrun m. 2. (a) Poussière f d'eau. (b) Jet pulvérisé (de parfum). 3. (a) Liquide m pour vaporisation. (b) Coup m de vaporisateur; jet (de parfum). (c) Gicleur m; vaporisateur m. ˈspray-gun, s. Paint: Hort: etc: Pulvérisateur m, pistolet m (à peinture, aux insecticides, etc.). ˈspray-painting, s. Peinture f au pistolet.

spray[3], v.tr. 1. Pulvériser, vaporiser, atomiser (un liquide). 2. Asperger, arroser. Hort: To s. a tree, passer un arbre au vaporisateur. **spraying**, s. 1. Pulvérisation f, vaporisation f (d'un liquide); Hort: seringage m. S. machine, pulvérisateur m, vaporisateur m. Metal s., métallisation f par projection. 2. Arrosage m.

sprayer [ˈspreiər], s. (a) Hort: Vaporisateur m (d'insecticide); pulvérisateur m, atomiseur m. (b) S. (for fuel oil), brûleur m (de mazout). (c) Foam s., extincteur m à mousse.

spread[1] [spred], s. 1. (a) Étendue f (de pays, etc.). (b) (Of bird's wings, of aircraft) Envergure f. F: To develop a middle-age s., prendre de l'embonpoint avec l'âge. 2. (a) Diffusion f (de l'éducation, d'une maladie); propagation f (d'une doctrine); expansion f (des idées). (b) Ball: Dispersion f (du tir). 3. F: Régal m, festin m. Cold s., repas froid. 4. Journ: Double-page s., annonce f sur deux pages. 5. Fromage m, pâté m, à tartiner.

spread[2], v. (spread; spread) I. v.tr. 1. Étendre. To s. a net, tendre un filet. To s. the sails, déployer les voiles. To s. out goods for sale, étaler des marchandises. To s. oneself on a subject, s'étendre sur un sujet. 2. (a) Répandre (du sable, des nouvelles, la terreur). S. it abroad! qu'on se le dise! (b) Instalments s. over several months, versements échelonnés sur plusieurs mois. 3. To s. butter on a slice of bread, tartiner une tranche de pain. 4. To s. a surface with sth., couvrir une surface de qch. II. spread, v.i. 1. S'étendre, s'étaler. The plain spreads out a mile wide, la plaine s'étend sur un mille. 2. (Of news) Se disséminer; se répandre; (of disease) se propager, gagner. The swelling has s. to the throat, l'enflure f a gagné la gorge. The fire is spreading, le feu gagne. His fame had s., sa renommée s'était répandue. 3. (Of small shot) S'écarter, se disperser. **spread-'eagle**[1], s. Her: Aigle éployée.

spread-'eagle[2], v.tr. Étaler (qch.). Bathers lying spread-eagled on the sand, baigneurs vautrés sur la plage. **spreading**, s. 1. (a) Déploiement m, développement m. (b) Colportage m (d'une nouvelle); propagation f (d'une maladie); diffusion f (de l'éducation). 2. (a) Extension f (d'une industrie). (b) Dispersion f.

spreader ['spredər], s. 1. (a) Étendeur, -euse, étaleur, -euse. (b) Propagateur, -trice (d'une idée); colporteur, -euse, semeur, -euse (d'une nouvelle). 2. Arrosoir m (d'une machine à arroser); diffuseur m (d'une lance d'arrosage). Agr: Épandeur m.

spree [spri:], s. F: Partie f de plaisir; bombe f. To go on the s., faire la fête, la bombe; Nau: tirer une bordée. To go on a shopping, spending, s., faire des achats extravagants.

sprig [sprig], s. 1. (a) Brin m, brindille f; petite branche. (b) Needlew: Ramage m. 2. F: Usu. Pej: Rejeton m (d'une race illustre).

sprightliness ['spraitlinis], s. Vivacité f, enjouement m, sémillance f.

sprightly ['spraitli], a. Éveillé, enjoué, sémillant.

spring¹ [spriŋ], s. 1. (a) Source f (d'eau). Hot s., source d'eau chaude. Thermal spring(s), source thermale; thermes mpl; station thermale. (b) Source, origine f. (c) Arch: Naissance f (de voûte); apophyge f (de colonne). 2. Printemps m. In (the) s., au printemps. S. is in the air, on respire le printemps dans l'air. S. flowers, fleurs printanières. F: To have a s. fever, Fr.C: avoir la fièvre du printemps. Cu: S. chicken, poussin m. F: She's no s. chicken, elle n'est plus jeune. S.a. ONION. 3. Saut m, bond m. To make a s., prendre son élan; faire un bond. 4. Élasticité f. 5. (a) Ressort m. Spiral s., ressort en boudin. Cin: S.-drive camera, appareil avec moteur à ressort. The springs of human action, les mobiles m qui font agir les hommes. S.a. BINDING² 2. (b) pl. Springs, suspension f (d'une auto, etc.). Cart without springs, charrette non suspendue. 'spring-balance, s. Peson m (à ressort). spring-'clean, v.tr. Nettoyer à fond (au printemps). spring-'cleaning, s. Grand nettoyage (fait au printemps); Fr.C: le grand ménage. 'spring-gun, s. Piège m à fusil. spring-'head, s. Source f. spring-'mattress, s. Matelas m à ressorts. spring-tide, s. 1. Lit: ['spriŋtaid] = SPRINGTIME. 2. ['spriŋ'taid] Grande marée; marée de syzygie; vive-eau f. 'spring water, s. Eau f de source.

spring², v. (sprang [spræŋ]; sprung [sprʌŋ]) I. v.i. 1. (a) Bondir, sauter. To s. to one's feet, se dresser vivement sur ses pieds. To s. over a ditch, sauter un fossé. To s. out of bed, sauter du lit. To s. to s.o.'s help, se précipiter au secours de qn. To s. at s.o., s'élancer sur qn. F: Where did you s. from? d'où sortez-vous? (b) O: If you could s. to a thousand pounds, si vous pouviez aller jusqu'à mille livres. (c) The lid sprang open, le couvercle se releva instantanément. 2. (a) (Of water) Jaillir, sourdre. (b) The blood sprang to her cheeks, une rougeur subite lui monta aux joues. Hope springs eternal, l'espérance reste toujours vivace. To s. into existence, naître; (ap)paraître (soudainement). (c) (Of plant) Pousser. 3. (Of mast) Craquer. II. spring, v.tr. 1. (a) Fendre (une raquette); faire craquer (un aviron). (b) To s. a leak, (i) Nau: (of ship) (se) faire une voie d'eau; (ii) U.S: P: uriner. 2. (a) Faire jouer (un piège); faire sauter (une mine). (b) F: To s. a surprise on s.o., prendre qn à l'improviste. To s. a question on s.o., poser à qn une question inattendue. 3. Suspendre (une voiture). 4. U.S: P: Lâcher, relâcher, faire (re)lâcher un prisonnier. spring aside, v.i. Faire un bond de côté. spring back, v.i. 1. Faire un bond en arrière. 2. Faire ressort. The branch sprang back, la branche se redressa. spring up, v.i. 1. (a) Sauter en l'air. (b) Se lever précipitamment. 2. (a) (Of plant) Pousser. (b) A breeze sprang up, une brise se leva. An intimacy sprang up between them, l'intimité s'établit entre eux. sprung, a. 1. Aut: S. weight, poids suspendu. 2. Nau: S. mast, mât craqué. springing, s. 1. Bonds mpl, sauts mpl. 2. (a) Jaillissement m (d'une source). (b) Germination f (de plantes). 3. Craquement m (d'un mât). 4. Aut: Suspension f (d'une voiture). 5. Arch: Retombée f (d'un arc).

springboard ['spriŋbɔ:d], s. Gym: Tremplin m.

springbok ['spriŋbɔk], s. Z: Springbok m.

springe [sprin(d)ʒ], s. 1. (For birds) Lacet m, lacs m. 2. (For rabbits) Collet m.

springer ['spriŋər], s. 1. Sauteur, -euse. 2. Z: (a) (Épagneul m) springer m. (b) Springbok m. 3. Arch: Coussinet m (d'une arcade); claveau m de naissance (de voûte).

springless ['spriŋlis], a. 1. Sans ressort(s). S. gait, démarche lourde. 2. Sans printemps. 3. Sans sources; sans eau; aride.

springiness ['spriŋinis], s. Élasticité f.

springlike ['spriŋlaik], a. Printanier, -ière.

springtime ['spriŋtaim], s. Printemps m.

springy ['spriŋi], a. 1. Élastique; qui fait ressort; flexible. S. carpet, tapis moelleux. 2. Alerte; dansant. S. step, pas alerte.

sprinkle¹ ['spriŋkl], s. 1. A s. of rain, quelques gouttes f de pluie. 2. A s. of salt, quelques grains m de sel; une pincée de sel.

sprinkle², v.tr. (a) Répandre, jeter (de l'eau, du sel). (b) Asperger, arroser, (with water, d'eau); saupoudrer (with salt, de sel). To s. the floor with sand, répandre du sable sur le plancher. Lawn sprinkled with dew, gazon parsemé de gouttes de rosée. (c) Bookb: Jasper (les tranches). sprinkling, s. 1. Aspersion f, arrosage m; saupoudrage m. 2. (a) S. of gravel, légère couche de gravier. (b) A s. of knowledge, quelques connaissances f. 3. Bookb: Jaspure f. 'sprinkling-can, s. U.S: Arrosoir m. 'sprinkling-cart, s. U.S: Voiture f d'arrosage; arroseuse f (de rues).

sprinkler ['spriŋklər], s. 1. Arroseuse f à jet tournant, arroseur m automatique rotatif, tourniquet m. 2. Ecc: Goupillon m, aspersoir m, aspergès m. 3. Saupoudroir m.

sprint¹ [sprint], s. Pointe f de vitesse, sprint m.

sprint², v.i. Faire une course de vitesse, sprinter. sprinting, s. Course f de vitesse, sprint m.

sprinter ['sprintər], s. Coureur, -euse, de vitesse; sprinter m.

sprit [sprit], s. Nau: Livarde f, baleston m.

sprite [sprait], s. Lutin m; esprit follet; farfadet m.

spritsail ['spritseil, 'spritsl], s. Nau: Voile f à livarde.

sprocket ['sprɔkit], s. 1. Dent f (de pignon). 2. S.(wheel), pignon m de chaîne; barbotin m. S. chain, chaîne f à barbotin.

sprout¹ [spraut], s. Bot: 1. (a) Jet m, rejeton m, pousse f. (b) Germe m, bourgeon m. 2. (Brussels) sprouts, choux m de Bruxelles.

sprout². 1. v.i. (a) (Of plant) Pousser, pointer. (b) (Of branch) Bourgeonner. (c) (Of seed) Germer. 2. v.tr. (Of animal) To s. horns, pousser des cornes. sprouting, s. Germination f, pointement m, bourgeonnement m.

spruce¹ [spru:s], a. Pimpant; soigné; tiré à quatre épingles.

spruce², v.tr. To s. oneself up, se faire beau, belle; se pomponner. All spruced up, sur son trente et un.

spruce³, s. Bot: S.(fir), sapin m, épinette f. White s., sapinette f. Norway s., épicéa m.

spruceness ['spru:snis], s. Mise pimpante.

sprung. See SPRING².

spry [sprai], a. (spryer, spryest) Vif, f. vive, actif, -ive; plein d'allant; plein d'entrain.

spud¹ [spʌd], s. 1. Petite bêche; sarcloir m; béquillon m; arrache-racine(s) m inv. 2. F: Pomme f de terre.

spud², v.tr. (spudded) Agr: Béquiller, sarcler (un terrain).

spume [spju:m], s. Lit: Écume f (de la mer).

spumy ['spju:mi], a. Lit: Écumeux, -euse, spumeux, -euse.

spun. See SPIN².

spunk [spʌnk], s. 1. Amadou m. 2. F: Courage m, cran m.

spunky ['spʌŋki], a. F: Qui a du cran.

spur¹ [spə:r], s. 1. Éperon m. To win one's spurs, faire ses preuves. Geog: The s. of Italy, l'éperon de la botte. 2. Coup m d'éperon; stimulant m. The s. of necessity, l'aiguillon m de la nécessité. To do sth. on the s. of the moment, faire qch. sous l'impulsion du moment, à l'impromptu. 3. (a) Ergot m (de coq). (b) Éperon d'ergot (d'un coq de combat). 4. (a) Éperon, contrefort m (d'une chaîne de montagnes). (b) Embranchement m (de chemin de fer). 5. N.Arch: Arc-boutant m de soutien. 6. Fort: Éperon m.

spur², *v.tr.* (spurred) 1. Éperonner (un cheval); donner de l'éperon à (un cheval). *Abs.* To s. on, piquer des deux. 2. To s. s.o. on, aiguillonner, stimuler, qn. Spurred on by desire, fouetté par le désir. 3. Éperonner (un coq de combat).

spurge [spɔːdʒ], *s. Bot:* Euphorbe *f.* **'spurge-flax,** *s. Bot:* Sainbois *m,* garou *m.* **'spurge-laurel,** *s. Bot:* Daphné *m,* lauréole *f.*

spurious ['spjuəriəs], *a.* 1. Faux, *f.* fausse; contrefait, falsifié. S. coin, pièce de monnaie fausse. 2. (*Of writings*) Apocryphe. **-ly,** *adv.* Faussement; par contrefaçon.

spuriousness ['spjuəriəsnis], *s.* 1. Fausseté *f;* nature falsifiée (of, de). 2. Caractère *m* apocryphe (d'un texte).

spurn [spɔːn], *v.tr.* 1. Repousser, écarter, (qch.) du pied. 2. Rejeter (une offre) avec mépris; traiter (qn) avec mépris.

spurr(e)y ['spʌri], *s. Bot:* Spergule *f.*

spurt¹ [spɔːt], *s.* 1. Jaillissement *m;* rejaillissement *m;* jet *m.* S. of petrol, giclée d'essence. 2. (*a*) Effort soudain; coup *m* de collier. (*b*) *Sp:* Démarrage *m.* Row: Enlevage *m.* To put on a s., démarrer. Final s., pointe finale.

spurt², 1. *v.i.* To s. up, jaillir. To s. out, saillir, gicler. To s. back, rejaillir. 2. *v.tr.* To s. (out) a liquid, faire jaillir, faire gicler, un liquide. Pen that spurts, plume qui crache. 3. *v.i. Sp:* Démarrer; faire un effort de vitesse, un sprint.

sputnik ['sputnik], *s. Astr: Ph:* Spoutnik *m,* satellite artificiel.

sputter ['spʌtər]. 1. *v.tr.* Débiter (qch.) en bredouillant. 2. *v.i. (a)* Lancer des postillons en parlant, postillonner; bredouiller. (*b*) (*Of pen*) Cracher. (*c*) (*Of candle flame*) Grésiller, crépiter. **sputtering,** *s.* 1. Bredouillement *m.* 2. Crachement *m* (d'une plume). 3. Crépitement *m.*

sputum, *pl.* -a ['spjuːtəm, -ə], *s. Med:* Crachat *m;* expectorations *fpl.*

spy¹, *pl.* **spies** [spai, -aiz], *s.* Espion, -onne; *F: Pej:* mouchard *m.*

spy², (**spied** *or* **spying**) 1. *v.tr. (a) A:* Apercevoir, remarquer. (*b*) To s. out the ground, explorer le terrain. 2. *v.i.* Espionner. To s. on s.o., espionner qn. **spying,** *s.* Espionnage *m.* **'spy-glass,** *s.* Lunette *f* d'approche; longue-vue *f.* **'spy-hole,** *s.* (*a*) Trou *m* (dans un rideau). (*b*) Judas *m* (de porte). (*c*) Regard *m* (de machine).

squab [skwɔb], *s.* 1. Pigeonneau *m* (sans plumes). S. pie, pâté *m* en croûte contenant (i) du pigeon; (ii) du mouton, des pommes et des oignons. 2. *Aut:* Coussin *m* (de siège). 3. Ottomane *f.*

squabble¹ ['skwɔbl], *s.* Querelle *f,* chamaillerie *f;* prise *f* de bec.

squabble². 1. *v.i.* Se chamailler, se quereller. 2. *v.tr. Typ:* Faire chevaucher (les caractères). **squabbling,** *s.* Chamaillerie *f;* querelles *fpl.*

squabbler ['skwɔblər], *s.* Chamailleur, -euse; querelleur, -euse.

squad [skwɔd], *s.* 1. *Mil: etc:* Escouade *f.* Defaulters' s., peloton *m* de punition; *F:* la pelote. Firing s., peloton d'exécution. 2. (*a*) Brigade *f* (de cheminots). (*b*) The Flying S. (of Scotland Yard), la brigade mobile (de la police). (*c*) Rescue s., équipe *m* de secours.

squadron ['skwɔdrən], *s.* 1. (*a*) *Mil:* Escadron *m.* (*b*) *Mil.Av:* Escadron *m,* groupe *m.* S. leader, commandant *m* de groupe. 2. *Navy:* Escadre *f.* Flying s., escadre volante.

squalid ['skwɔlid], *a.* Sale; misérable. S. dwellings, demeures sordides.

squalidity [skwɔ'iditi], **squalidness** ['skwɔlidnis], *s.* = SQUALOR.

squall¹ [skwɔːl], *s.* Cri *m* (rauque).

squall², *v.i.* Crier, brailler, piailler. **squalling,** *a.* Criard, braillard.

squall³, *s. Nau:* Grain *m;* coup *m* de vent; bourrasque *f;* rafale *f.* Light s., risée *f.* Look out for squalls! (i) veille au grain! (ii) *F:* il va y avoir du grabuge.

squally ['skwɔːli], *a.* (Temps) à grains, à rafales.

squalor ['skwɔlər], *s.* Saleté *f;* misère *f;* aspect *m* sordide. Born in s., né dans la crasse. To die in s., mourir sur le fumier.

squama, *pl.* -ae ['skweimə, -iː], *s.* 1. *Z:* Squame *f.* 2. *Bot:* Pellicule *f.* 3. *Med:* Squame.

squamose ['skweimous], **squamous** ['skweiməs], *a.* Squameux, -euse.

squander ['skwɔndər], *v.tr.* Gaspiller, prodiguer (l'argent); dissiper, dilapider (sa fortune). **squandering,** *s.* Gaspillage *m.*

squanderer ['skwɔndərər], *s.* Gaspilleur, -euse; dilapidateur, -trice; prodigue *mf.*

square¹ [skweər]. I. *s.* 1. Carré *m. Mil.Hist:* To form into a s., former le carré. *Mil:* Terrain *m* de manœuvre. To be on the s., être passé en revue. *F:* S. bashing = l'exercice. 2. (*a*) Carreau *m* (de figure quadrillée); case *f* (d'échiquier). To divide a map into squares, quadriller une carte. (*b*) Silk s., foulard *m,* carré *m.* 3. (*Of town*) Place *f;* (*with garden*) square *m.* 4. Équerre *f.* Set s., équerre à dessin. T s., tee-s., équerre en T. *Surv:* Optical s., équerre d'arpenteur. To cut sth. on the s., couper qch. à angles droits. Out of s., hors d'équerre. *F:* To act on the s., agir carrément, honnêtement. 5. *Mth:* Carré (d'une expression). II. **square,** *a.* 1. Carré. (*a*) S. table, table carrée. S. game, partie à quatre. S. measure, mesure de surface. *S.a.* PEG¹ 1. (*b*) S. shoulders, épaules carrées. S. chin, menton carré. S. toe, carre *f* (de chaussure). *Cost:* S. neck, décolleté (en) carré. 2. *Mth:* S. root, racine carrée. 3. To get things s., mettre tout en ordre. *S.a.* MEAL² 1. S. dealings, procédés honnêtes. He always gives you a s. deal, il est toujours loyal en affaires. To be s. with s.o., être quitte envers qn. *Golf:* To be all s., être à égalité. 4. *a. & s. F:* Vieux jeu *inv;* (personne) empesé(e). **-ly,** *adv.* 1. Carrément. 2. Loyalement, honnêtement. III. **square,** *adv.* 1. A angles droits (to, with, avec). Set s. upon its base, d'aplomb sur sa base. 2. Fair and s., loyalement, carrément. **'square-'built,** *a.* 1. Bâti en carré. 2. (*Of pers.*) Trapu. **'square-'toed,** *a.* 1. (Souliers) à bouts carrés. 2. *U.S: F:* Conservateur, -trice (de la vieille roche).

square². I. *v.tr.* 1. (*a*) Carrer, équarrir (la pierre, le bois). (*b*) *Nau:* To s. the yards, brasser carré. (*c*) To s. one's shoulders, (i) effacer les épaules; (ii) raidir sa volonté. 2. (*a*) How do you s. it with your conscience? comment arrangez-vous cela avec votre conscience? (*b*) Balancer, régler (un compte). To s. matters, arranger les choses. (*c*) *F:* Graisser la patte à (qn); acheter, suborner (qn). 3. *Mth:* Élever (une expression) au carré; carrer (un nombre). 4. Quadriller (une carte). II. **square,** *v.i.* 1. His practice does not s. with his principles, ses actions ne s'accordent pas, ne cadrent pas, avec ses principes. 2. *Golf:* To s. with one's opponent, égaliser la marque. **square up.** 1. *v.tr. (a)* Affranchir d'équerre (le bout d'une planche). (*b*) *Abs.* To s. up with s.o., régler ses comptes avec qn. 2. *v.i.* To s. up to s.o., s'avancer vers qn en posture de combat. **squared,** *a.* 1. (Bois, etc.) équarri. S. stone, pierre carrée. 2. *Mth:* (Élevé) au carré. 3. (Papier) quadrillé. **squaring,** *s.* 1. Équarrissage *m,* dressage *m* (d'un bloc de pierre, etc.). 2. Quadrillage *m* (d'une carte, etc.).

squareness ['skweənis], *s.* 1. Forme carrée. 2. Honnêteté *f,* loyauté *f* (dans les affaires).

squash¹ [skwɔʃ], *s.* 1. Écrasement *m,* aplatissement *m.* 2. Cohue *f,* presse *f.* 3. Pulpe *f.* Lemon, orange, s., citronnade *f,* orangeade *f.* 4. *Sp:* Squash *m.* **'squash-court,** *s. Sp:* Terrain *m* de squash. **'squash-rackets,** *s.* = SQUASH 4.

squash². 1. *v.tr. (a)* Écraser, aplatir (un fruit). (*b*) Aplatir, écraser (qn). (*c*) *F:* Remettre (qn) à sa place; *F:* s'asseoir sur (qn). 2. *v.i. (a) (Of fruit)* S'écraser. (*b*) Se serrer, se presser.

squash³, *s. Hort: (a)* Gourde *f.* (*b*) *Esp. U.S:* Courge *f;* courgette *f.*

squashy ['skwɔʃi], *a.* Mou (et humide); détrempé.

squat¹ [skwɔt], *v.i.* (squatted) 1. (*a*) To s. (down), s'accroupir. (*b*) *Ven: (Of game)* Se tapir. 2. To s. on a piece of land, s'approprier un terrain. **squatting,** *a.* 1. Accroupi. 2. Qui occupe un terrain comme squatter.

squat², *a.* (*Of pers.*) Ramassé, trapu.
squatter ['skwɔtər], *s.* Squatter *m.*
squaw [skwɔː], *s.f.* Femme peau-rouge.
squawk¹ [skwɔːk], *s.* Cri *m* rauque; couac *m.*
squawk², *v.i.* 1. Pousser des cris rauques; faire des couacs. 2. *U.S: P:* (*a*) Rouspéter. (*b*) Avouer, confesser (à la police).
squeak¹ [skwiːk], *s.* Petit cri aigu; couic *m* (de souris); crissement *m*, grincement *m* (de choses mal huilées). *F:* To have a narrow s., l'échapper belle.
squeak², *v.i.* (*a*) Pousser des cris aigus; (*of mouse*) faire couic; (*of shoes*) crier. Pen that squeaks, plume qui grince sur le papier. (*b*) *P:* Moucharder.
squeaking, *s.* Couics *mpl*; grincements *mpl.*
squeaker ['skwiːkər], *s.* (*a*) Celui qui pousse des petits cris. (*b*) *P:* Mouchard *m.*
squeaky ['skwiːki], *a.* Criard, qui crie; qui grince; qui fait couic. S. voice, voix aiguë.
squeal¹ [skwiːl], *s.* (*a*) Cri aigu; cri perçant. (*b*) Grincement *m.*
squeal², *v.i.* (*a*) Pousser des cris aigus. (*b*) *F:* Protester; pousser les hauts cris. (*c*) *P:* Trahir ses complices. To s. on s.o., dénoncer qn. (*d*) Grincer.
squealing¹, *a.* Criard. **squealing²**, *s.* Cris aigus; hauts cris.
squealer ['skwiːlər], *s.* 1. Criard, -arde. 2. *P:* Dénonciateur, -trice, *F:* cafard *m*, mouchard *m.*
squeamish ['skwiːmiʃ], *a.* 1. Sujet aux nausées. To feel s., avoir mal au cœur. 2. (*a*) Difficile, délicat, dégoûté. (*b*) Scrupuleux à l'excès. (*c*) Pudique à l'excès. Don't be so s.! ne faites pas tant de façons!
squeamishness ['skwiːmiʃnis], *s.* 1. Disposition *f* aux nausées. 2. Délicatesse exagérée.
squeegee ['skwiːˈdʒiː], *s.* 1. Balai *m* en caoutchouc; racloir *m. Nau:* Râteau de pont.
squeeze¹ [skwiːz], *s.* 1. (*a*) Compression *f.* (*b*) Étreinte *f.* To give s.o. a s., serrer qn dans ses bras. 2. Presse *f*, cohue *f.* It was a tight s., on tenait tout juste. 3. Empreinte *f* au carton mouillé (d'une médaille, etc.). 4. *F:* credit s., restriction *f*, resserrement *m*, du crédit.
squeeze², *v.tr.* 1. Presser (une éponge, un citron). To s. s.o.'s hand, serrer la main à qn. To s. one's finger, se pincer le doigt (dans la porte). He was squeezed to death in the crowd, il fut étouffé dans la foule. 2. To s. sth. into a box, faire entrer qch. de force dans une boîte. To s. the juice out of a lemon, exprimer le jus d'un citron. To s. (oneself) through a hole in the fence, se faufiler par un trou dans la clôture. To s. up, se serrer, se tasser. 3. (*a*) Exercer une pression sur (qn); *F:* serrer les pouces à (qn). (*b*) To s. money out of s.o., extorquer de l'argent à qn. **squeezing**, *s.* 1. (*a*) Compression *f.* (*b*) Étreinte *f.* 2. Expression *f* (du jus d'un citron). 3. Extorsion *f*, exaction *f.*
squeezer ['skwiːzər], *s.* Machine *f* à compression; presse *f. S.a.* LEMON-SQUEEZER.
squelch¹ [skwel(t)ʃ], *s.* 1. Giclement *m* (de boue); gargouillement *m*, gargouillis *m* (de souliers détrempés, etc.). 2. Lourde chute (sur qch. de mou).
squelch². 1. *v.tr.* (*a*) Écraser (qch.) (en le faisant gicler). (*b*) *F:* Aplatir (qn); réprimer (une rébellion). 2. *v.i.* The water squelched in his shoes, l'eau gargouillait dans ses chaussures. To s. through the mud, patauger dans la boue.
squib [skwib], *s.* 1. *Pyr:* Pétard *m*, serpenteau *m. F:* Damp s., affaire ratée. 2. *Min:* Charge explosive, cartouche *f* de mine. *Expl:* Amorce *f* électro-pyrotechnique. 3. Satire *f*, brocard *m.*
squid [skwid], *s. Moll:* Calmar *m*, encornet *m.*
squiffy ['skwifi], *a. F:* Gris, ivre, éméché, pompette.
squiggle ['skwigl], *s.* (*a*) Fioriture *f*, enjolivure *f*; (*after signature*) parafe *m.* (*b*) Écriture *f* illisible.
squint¹ [skwint], *s.* 1. Strabisme *m*, louchement *m.* He has a slight s., il louche légèrement. 2. Coup d'œil furtif. 3. *F:* Regard *m*; coup d'œil. Let's have a s. at it! faites voir! 4. *Ecc.Arch:* Guichet (de lépreux, etc.).
squint², *v.i.* 1. Loucher. 2. To s. at sth., regarder qch. de côté, furtivement. **squinting¹**, *a.* Strabique, louche. **squinting²**, *s.* Strabisme *m*; louchement *m*, loucherie *f.*
squint³, *a.* S. eyes, yeux louches. 'squint-eyed, *a.* Au regard louche; strabique.

squinter ['skwintər], *s.* Loucheur, -euse. *Med:* Strabique *mf.*
squire¹ ['skwaiər], *s.* 1. *Hist:* Écuyer (attaché à un chevalier). 2. O: (*a*) Propriétaire terrien. (*b*) The s., le châtelain (de l'endroit).
squire², *v.tr.* Servir de cavalier à (une dame).
squirearchy ['skwaiərɑːki], *s. Hist: Coll:* Les (gros) propriétaires terriens.
squireen [ˌskwaiəˈriːn], *s.* (*Esp. in Ireland*) Hobereau *m.*
squirm [skwəːm], *v.i.* (*a*) (*Of worm*) Se tordre, se tortiller. (*b*) Ne savoir comment se tenir; être au supplice. To make s.o. s., mettre qn au supplice.
squirrel ['skwir(ə)l], *s.* 1. Écureuil *m. Siberian s.*, petit-gris *m.* 2. S. (fur), *Com:* petit-gris; *Her:* vair *m.*
squirt¹ [skwəːt], *s.* 1. Seringue *f.* 2. Jet *m*, giclée *f* (de liquide). 3. *F:* (*a*) Little s., riquiqui *m*, gringalet *m.* (*b*) Jeune insolent *m.*
squirt². 1. *v.tr.* Faire jaillir, lancer en jet (un liquide). To s. in oil, injecter de l'huile. 2. *v.i.* (*Of liquid*) Jaillir, gicler.
squishy ['skwiʃi], *a. F:* Détrempé; pulpeux, -euse; mou, *f* molle. S. ground, terrain détrempé.
squit [skwit], *s. P:* Little s. (of a man), avorton *m.*
stab¹ [stæb], *s.* 1. Coup *m* de poignard, de couteau. S. in the back, (i) coup porté dans le dos; (ii) attaque déloyale, coup de Jarnac. S. of pain, élancement *m.* 2. *Golf:* S. shot, coup sec. 3. *F:* To have a s. at sth., essayer le coup.
stab², *v.* (stabbed) 1. *v.tr.* (*a*) Poignarder; donner un coup de couteau à (qn). To s. s.o. in the back, (i) poignarder qn dans le dos; (ii) calomnier qn. (*b*) *Bookb:* Piquer (un cahier). Stabbed pamphlet, piqûre *f.* 2. *v.i.* To s. at s.o., porter un coup de couteau, de poignard, à qn. **stabbing**, *a.* Qui perce, qui frappe. S. pain, douleur lancinante.
stability [stəˈbiliti], *s.* Stabilité *f*, solidité *f* (d'une construction). Man of no s., homme de peu de fermeté; homme inconstant.
stabilization [ˌsteibilaiˈzeiʃ(ə)n], *s.* 1. Stabilisation *f* (d'un avion, etc.). 2. *Fin:* Stabilisation, valorisation *f* (des cours, etc.).
stabilize ['steibilaiz], *v.tr.* Stabiliser. *Com:* To s. prices, revaloriser les prix. **stabilizing**, *a.* Stabilisateur, -trice. *Fin:* S. factors of the market, éléments pondérateurs du marché. S. policy, politique *f* de stabilité.
stabilizer ['steibilaizər], *s. Av: Nau: etc:* Stabilisateur *m*, équilibreur *m.*
stable¹ ['steibl], *s.* 1. (*For horses*) Écurie *f.* 2. (*a*) Chevaux *mpl* d'une certaine écurie. *S.a.* RACING. (*b*) *Sp: Aut: etc:* Écurie. 'stable-boy, *s.* Valet, garçon, d'écurie, palefrenier *m*; *Rac:* lad *m.* 'stable companion, *s.* 1. Cheval *m* de la même écurie. 2. *F:* Membre *m* de la même entreprise. 'stable-keeper, *s.* Loueur *m* de chevaux. 'stable-litter, *s. Husb:* (*a*) Clean s.-l., paille *f*, litière *f.* (*b*) Old s.-l., (i) paillé *m*, (ii) fumier *m* d'écurie.
stable², *v.tr.* Loger (un cheval). We can s. three horses, nous avons de la place pour trois chevaux. **stabling**, *s.* 1. Logement *m*, installation *f* (de chevaux). 2. *Coll.* Écuries *fpl.*
stable³, *a.* 1. Stable; solide, fixe. To become s., se stabiliser. 2. (*Of pers.*) Constant, ferme. **-bly**, *adv.* D'une manière stable.
stableman, *pl.* -men ['steiblmən], *s.m.* Palefrenier.
staccato [stəˈkɑːtou], *a., adv. & s.* (*a*) *Mus:* Staccato (*m*). S. note, note piquée, détachée. (*b*) S. style, style haché. In a s. voice, d'une voix saccadée.
stachys ['stækis], *s. Bot:* Épiaire *m.*
stack¹ [stæk], *s.* 1. (*a*) Meule *f* (de foin); (*of corn*) gerbier *m.* (*b*) Pile *f*, tas *m* (de bois). *F:* I've stacks of work, j'ai de quoi faire, j'ai du pain sur la planche. 2. (*a*) Souche *f* (de cheminée). (*b*) Cheminée *f* (d'une locomotive, etc.). (*c*) *U.S:* Étagère *f*, bibliothèque *f.*
stack², *v.tr.* 1. Mettre (le foin) en meule. Stacking machine, gerbeuse *f.* 2. To s. (up), empiler, entasser. The villages are stacked with food, les villages regorgent de denrées alimentaires. 3. To s. the cards, tricher au jeu.
stadium, *pl.* -ia ['steidiəm, -iə], *s.* Stade *m.*

staff[1] [stɑːf], s. **1.** (a) Bâton m. **Pilgrim's s.**, bourdon m de pèlerin. **Bread is the s. of life**, le pain est le soutien de la vie. (b) Hampe f (de bannière). Nau: Mât m (de pavillon). (c) Surv: Jalon m, mire f. **2.** (a) Mil: Navy: État-major m. **S. College =** École supérieure de Guerre. (b) Personnel m. **The domestic s.**, les domestiques m. **Teaching s.**, personnel enseignant. Journ: **Editorial s.**, la rédaction. **3.** Mus: (pl. **staves** [steivz]) Portée f. **S. notation**, notation figurée sur la portée. **'staff officer**, s. Officier m d'état-major.

staff[2], v.tr. Pourvoir (un bureau) de personnel. **To be over-staffed**, avoir un personnel trop nombreux. **To be under-staffed**, manquer de personnel.

staffwork ['stɑːfwəːk], s. Travail m d'organisation.

stag[1] [stæg], s. **1.** Cerf m. **2.** St.Exch: F: **A s.**, un loup. **'stag-beetle**, s. Ent: Lucane m, cerf-volant m. **'stag-hunt(ing)**, s. Chasse f (au cerf). **'stag-party**, s. F: Réunion f entre hommes.

stag[2], v.tr. St.Exch: Spéculer sur (des valeurs).

stage[1] [steidʒ], s. **1.** (a) Estrade f, échafaud m, échafaudage m. **Hanging s.**, échafaud volant. Nau: **Floating s.**, plate-forme flottante. S.a. LANDING-STAGE. (b) Platine f (d'un microscope). Ph: etc: Étage m (d'une fusée à exploration spatiale). **2.** (a) Th: Scène f; F: les planches f. **S. play** (as opposed to film), pièce f de théâtre. **Front of the s.**, avant-scène f. **To come on the s.**, entrer en scène. **To go on the s.**, se faire acteur, actrice. **To put a play on the s.**, monter une pièce. **To write for the s.**, écrire pour le théâtre. **S. lights, herses** f. **S. directions**, indications scéniques. S.a. HOLD[2] I. 3. (b) Champ m d'action. **3.** Phase f, période f, stade m. **The stages of an evolution**, les étapes f, les stades, d'une évolution. **At this s. an interruption occurred**, à ce point une interruption se produisit. **To rise by successive stages**, monter par échelons. **At what s. of his development . . .** à quel moment de son développement. . . . **4.** (a) Étape f. **To travel by easy stages**, voyager à petites étapes. (b) A: Relais m. (c) **Fare s.**, section f (de l'itinéraire d'un autobus). **'stage-box**, s. Th: Loge f d'avant-scène. **stage-'carpenter**, s. Th: Machiniste m. **'stage-coach**, s. A: Diligence f. **'stage-'door**, s. Th: Entrée f des artistes. **'stage-effect**, s. Th: Effet m scénique. **'stage-fright**, s. Th: Trac m. **'stage-hand**, s. Th: Machiniste m. **'stage-'manager**, s. Th: Régisseur m. **'stage-name**, s. Th: Nom m de théâtre. **'stage-'property**, s. Th: Accessoire m de théâtre. **'stage-rights**, s.pl. Droits m de production (d'une pièce). **'stage-struck**, a. Entiché, enamouré, du théâtre. **'stage-'whisper**, s. Th: Aparté m. **In a s.-w.**, en aparté.

stage[2], v.tr. (a) Monter (une pièce); mettre (un roman) à la scène. (b) Organiser (une démonstration); monter (un coup). **staging**, s. **1.** Mise f à la scène (d'une pièce, d'un roman). **2.** (a) Échafaud m, échafaudage m. (b) Nau: Appontement m (d'un quai).

stagecraft ['steidʒkrɑːft], s. Th: Technique f de la scène.

stager ['steidʒər], s. F: **Old s.**, vieux routier.

stagger[1] ['stægər], s. **1.** (a) Titubation f. (b) Allure chancelante. **2.** pl. Vet: Vertigo m.

stagger[2]. **I.** v.i. Chanceler, tituber. **To s. along**, avancer en chancelant; (when drunk) faire des zigzags. **To s. to one's feet**, se (re)lever en chancelant. **II.** v.tr. **1.** (a) Faire chanceler (qn). (b) Confondre, consterner (qn); frapper (qn) de stupeur. **To be staggered**, être saisi d'étonnement). **2.** (a) Av: Décaler (les ailes). (b) Mec.E: Disposer (des rivets) en chicane. (c) El: Échelonner (les balais). (d) Étaler, échelonner (les vacances). **staggered**, a. Décalé; (of rivets) en chicane. **S. holidays**, congés échelonnés. **staggering**[1], a. **1.** (Pas) chancelant, titubant. **2.** (a) **S. blow**, coup d'assommoir. (b) (Of news) Renversant, atterrant. **staggering**[2], s. **1.** Titubation f. **2.** (a) Décalage m. (b) Disposition f en quinconce. (c) Échelonnement m. (d) Échelonnage m, échelonnement m, étalement m (des vacances).

staghound ['stæghaund], s. Lévrier m d'Écosse.

stagnancy ['stægnənsi], s. Stagnation f.

stagnant ['stægnənt], a. Stagnant; (of trade) en stagnation.

stagnate ['stægneit, stæg'neit], v.i. (Of water, trade) Être, devenir, stagnant; (of water) croupir.

stagnation [stæg'neiʃ(ə)n], s. Stagnation f.

stagy ['steidʒi], a. Théâtral, -aux; histrionique. (a) De cabotin. (b) Peu sincère.

staid [steid], a. Posé, sérieux, -euse, sage. **-ly**, adv. Posément, sérieusement, sagement.

staidness ['steidnis], s. Caractère posé, sérieux, sage; air posé.

stain[1] [stein], s. **1.** (a) Tache f, souillure f. (b) **He came out of the business without a s. on his character**, il est sorti de l'affaire sans atteinte à sa réputation. **To cast a s. on s.o.'s honour**, ternir l'honneur de qn. **2.** Couleur f, colorant m. **Wood-s.**, couleur pour bois. **S. remover**, détacheur m, détachant m.

stain[2], v.tr. **1.** (a) Tacher; souiller (with, de). **Hands stained with blood**, mains souillées de sang. **Cloth that stains easily**, tissu m qui se tache facilement. (b) Tacher, ternir (la réputation de qn). **2.** Teindre, teinter (le bois); peindre (le verre). **Stained floor**, parquet teinté. S.a. GLASS 1.

stainless ['steinlis], a. **1.** Sans tache; immaculé, pur. **2.** **S. steel**, acier m inoxydable.

stair ['stɛər], s. **1.** Marche f, degré m (d'un escalier). **2.** (Usu. pl.) Escalier. **Spiral stairs**, escalier tournant, en vis. **To meet s.o. on the stairs**, rencontrer qn dans l'escalier. **'stair-carpet**, s. Tapis m d'escalier. **'stair-rod**, s. Tringle f d'escalier.

staircase ['stɛəkeis], **stairway** ['stɛəwei], s. Escalier m. **External s., turret s.**, escalier extérieur. **Winding, spiral, corkscrew, s.**, escalier tournant; escalier en vis, en (co)limaçon.

stairwell ['stɛəwel], s. Cage f d'escalier.

stake[1] [steik], s. **1.** (a) Pieu m, poteau m; (rod) jalon m, fiche f. Hort: Tuteur m; échalas m (de vigne). (b) Surv: Jalon, piquet m. F: U.S: **To (pull) up stakes**, déménager, quitter le pays, partir (avec toutes ses possessions). **2.** (Poteau du) bûcher. **To be burnt at the s.**, mourir sur le bûcher. **3.** (a) Gaming: Mise f, enjeu m. **To lay the stakes**, faire le jeu. **Put down your stakes!** faites vos jeux! **To hold the stakes**, tenir les enjeux. **The interests at s.**, les intérêts en jeu. **To have a s. in sth.**, avoir des intérêts dans une affaire. S.a. HIGH I. 2 (d). (b) pl. Turf: **Stakes**, prix m. **Maiden Stakes**, prix de l'avenir. **'stake money**, s. Mise f, enjeu m.

stake[2], v.tr. **1.** **To s. (off, out)**, (i) jalonner (une concession); enclore (une concession) de pieux; (ii) Surv: jalonner (une ligne). **2.** Ramer (des haricots); tuteurer (des tomates, etc.). **3.** (Of horse) **To be staked on a jump**, s'éventrer sur une haie. **4.** Mettre (une somme) en jeu; jouer (une somme). **To s. twenty francs**, miser vingt francs. **To s. one's all**, jouer son va-tout; y aller de son reste. **I'd s. my life on it**, j'y mettrais ma tête à couper. **5.** U.S: **To s. s.o.**, fournir (qn) d'argent; fournir aux besoins de qn. **staking**, s. **1.** S. (out), jalonnement m, bornage m, piquetage m (d'une concession, etc.). **2.** Échalassage m (d'une vigne); tuteurage m (des plants de tomate). **3.** Mise f (en jeu d'une somme).

stakeholder ['steik,houldər], s. Celui qui tient les enjeux.

stakhanovism [stæk'hɑːnovizm], s. Stakhanovisme m.

stakhanovite [stæk'hɑːnovait,-it], s. Stakhanoviste m.f.

stalactite ['stæləktait], s. Stalactite f.

stalagmite ['stæləgmait], s. Stalagmite f.

stale[1] ['steil], a. **1.** (a) (Pain) rassis. **To get s.**, rassir. (b) (Œuf) qui n'est pas frais. (c) (Air) vicié, croupi. **S. smell**, odeur de renfermé; remugle m. **2.** (a) Vieux, f. vieille; passé. **S. goods**, articles défraîchis. **S. joke**, vieille plaisanterie; plaisanterie rebattue. **S. news**, nouvelle déjà connue. (b) **S. cheque**, chèque prescrit. **3.** Fatigué, éreinté. **I'm s.**, je n'ai plus d'enthousiasme; rien ne va plus. F: **It's gone s. on me**, ça ne me plaît plus; je n'arrive plus à m'y mettre. (Of athlete) **To go s.**, se surentraîner, se surmener.

stale[2]. **1.** v.tr. Rendre (qch.) banal. **2.** v.i. (a) (Of beer) S'éventer. (b) (Of news, etc.) Perdre son intérêt. Lit: **Pleasure that never stales**, plaisir toujours nouveau.

stale[3], v.i. (Of cattle, horses) Uriner.

stalemate[1] ['steilmeit], s (a) Chess: Pat m. (b) Impasse f.

stalemate², *v.tr.* Faire pat (son adversaire).

staleness ['steilnis], *s.* **1.** (*a*) État rassis (du pain). (*b*) Évent *m* (de la bière). (*c*) Odeur *f* de renfermé. **2.** Manque *m* de fraîcheur (d'une nouvelle); banalité *f* (d'une plaisanterie).

stalinism ['stɑːlinizm], *s.* Stalinisme *m.*

stalinist ['stɑːlinist], *a. & s.* Stalinien, -ienne.

stalk¹ [stɔːk], *s.* **1.** Démarche fière. **2.** *Ven:* Chasse *f* à l'approche.

stalk², **1.** *v.i.* To s. (along), (i) marcher d'un pas majestueux; (ii) marcher à grands pas. **2.** *v.tr.* (*a*) Traquer (la bête) à l'approche. *Abs.* Chasser à l'approche. (*b*) To s. s.o., filer qn. **stalking,** *s.* *Ven:* = STALK¹ 2. *S.a.* DEER-STALKING. 'stalking-horse, *s.* **1.** *Ven:* Cheval *m* d'abri. **2.** Prétexte *m,* masque *m.*

stalk³, *s.* **1.** Tige *f* (de plante); queue *f* (de fruit); trognon *m* (de chou). **2.** Pied *m* (de verre à vin).

stalker ['stɔːkər], *s.* *Ven:* Chasseur *m* à l'approche.

stall¹ [stɔːl], *s.* **1.** (*a*) Stalle *f* (d'écurie); case *f* (d'étable). Garage s., box *m.* (*b*) Étable *f.* **2.** Étalage *m* (en plein vent); échoppe *f*; (*at exhibitions*) stand *m.* Market stalls, boutiques *f* en plein vent. Newspaper s., kiosque *m.* To have a s. (*at a bazaar*), tenir un stand. *S.a.* BOOKSTALL, COFFEE-STALL. **3.** (*a*) *Ecc:* Stalle. (*b*) *Th:* (Orchestra) stalls, fauteuils *m* d'orchestre. Seat in the stalls, fauteuil. **'stall-fed,** *a.* Engraissé à l'étable. **'stall-holder,** *s.* **1.** Marchand, -ande, aux halles; étalagiste *mf.* **2.** (*At charity bazaar*) Vendeuse *f.*

stall², **I.** *v.tr.* **1.** Établer (des bestiaux); mettre (des chevaux) à l'écurie. **2.** (*a*) *Aut: etc:* Caler, bloquer (le moteur). (*b*) *Av:* Mettre (l'appareil) en perte de vitesse. **II.** stall *v.i.* **1.** S'embourber; s'enfoncer dans la boue. **2.** (*a*) *Aut:* (*Of engine*) (Se) caler, se bloquer. (*b*) *Av:* Se mettre en perte de vitesse. (*of plane*) s'engager. **3.** To s. (for time), chercher à gagner du temps. **stalling,** *s.* **1.** Stabulation *f* (des bêtes). **2.** (*a*) Calage *m,* blocage *m,* arrêt *m* (du moteur). (*b*) *Av:* Perte *f* de vitesse. S. point, vitesse *f* minimum de sustentation.

stallion ['stæljən], *s.* Étalon *m*; cheval entier.

stalwart ['stɔːlwət], *a.* **1.** Robuste, vigoureux, -euse, *F:* costaud. **2.** Vaillant, résolu. **3.** *s.* The stalwarts of the market = les forts *m* des Halles. One of the old stalwarts, un vieux de la vieille.

stamen ['steimen], *s.* *Bot:* Étamine *f.*

stamina ['stæminə], *s.* Vigueur *f*, résistance *f.* Man of great s., homme qui a du fond.

staminate ['stæminit], *a.* *Bot:* Staminé *a.*

stammer¹ ['stæmər], *s.* (*a*) Bégaiement *m.* (*b*) Balbutiement *m.*

stammer², **1.** *v.i.* (*a*) Bégayer. (*b*) Balbutier. **2.** *v.tr.* To s. (out) sth., bégayer, balbutier, qch. **stammering¹,** *a.* (Personne) bègue. **-ly,** *adv.* En bégayant. **stammering²,** *s.* = STAMMER¹.

stammerer ['stæmərər], *s.* Bègue *mf*; balbutieur, -euse.

stamp¹ [stæmp], *s.* **1.** Battement *m* de pied (d'impatience); trépignement *m.* With a s. (of the foot), en frappant du pied. **2.** (*a*) Timbre *m*, empreinte *f.* Signature s., griffe *f.* Date-s., timbre à date. Self-inking s., timbre à encrage automatique. Rubber s., tampon *m.* (*b*) Découpoir *m* (à emporte-pièce). (*c*) Étampe *f*, poinçon *m.* (*d*) *Minting:* Coin *m.* **3.** (*a*) Timbre; marque (apposée). Official s., estampille officielle. (*b*) To bear the s. of genius, porter l'empreinte, le cachet, du génie. Men of his s., les hommes de sa trempe, de sa sorte, *Pej:* de son acabit. **4.** Revenue s., timbre du fisc. Adhesive s., timbre mobile. Embossed s., timbre à empreinte; timbre fixe. Postage s., timbre(-poste) *m.* Postage-due s., timbre-taxe *m,* *pl.* timbres-taxe. Used s., timbre oblitéré. National Insurance s. = cotisation *f* de la sécurité sociale. Savings-Bank s., timbre-épargne *m.* *Com:* Trading s., timbre-prime *m.* **5.** *Metalw:* Étampeuse *f.* **6.** *Min:* Bocard *m* (pour écraser les minerais); pilon *m*; broyeuse *f.* **'stamp-album,** *s.* Album *m* de timbres. **'stamp-collector,** *s.* Collectionneur *m* de timbres-poste; philatéliste *mf.* **'stamp-dealer,** *s.* Marchand *m* de timbres-poste pour philatélistes. **'stamp-duty,** *s.* Droit *m* de timbre. **'stamp-machine,** *s.* Distributeur *m* automatique de timbres-poste. **'stamp office,** *s.* = Bureau *m* de l'Enregistrement.

stamp², *v.tr.* **1.** (*a*) To s. one's foot, frapper du pied. To s. one's feet, (i) trépigner; (ii) (*for warmth*) battre la semelle. (*b*) *Abs.* To s. (about), piétiner. To s. on sth., fouler qch. aux pieds. **2.** Frapper, imprimer, une marque sur (qch.); frapper, estamper (la monnaie, une médaille, le cuir); contrôler, poinçonner (l'or, l'argent). **3.** Timbrer (un document); viser (un passeport); timbrer, affranchir (une lettre); estampiller (un document). The letter is insufficiently stamped, l'affranchissement est insuffisant. **4.** *Min:* Broyer, bocarder (le minerai). **5.** *Metalw:* Étamper, matricer (des objets en métal). **6.** His manners s. him a gentleman, ses manières indiquent un homme comme il faut. **7.** To s. sth. on the mind, imprimer, empreindre, qch. sur l'esprit. **stamp out,** *v.tr.* **1.** *Metalw:* Découper (qch.) à la presse. **2.** To s. out the fire, piétiner sur le feu pour l'éteindre. To s. out an epidemic, étouffer, juguler, une épidémie. **stamped,** *a.* **1.** (*a*) Broyé, concassé. (*b*) S. earth, terre battue. **2.** S. paper, papier timbré. S.-addressed envelope, enveloppe timbrée. *S.a.* SIGNATURE 1. **3.** (Acier) estampé, embouti; (cuir) gaufré. **stamping,** *s.* **1.** Piétinement *m.* **2.** (*a*) Timbrage *m* (de documents); estampillage *m.* (*b*) *Metalw:* Estampage *m,* matriçage *m.* (*c*) *Min:* Bocardage *m,* broiement *m* (du minerai). **3.** *Metalw:* Pièce estampée, emboutie. **'stamping-ground,** *s.* *F:* Terrain *m* d'élection, lieu favori. This is our favourite s.-g., nous aimons beaucoup venir ici. **'stamping-mill,** *s.* *Min:* Moulin *m* à bocards; bocard *m.* **'stamping-press,** *s.* Estampeuse *f,* emboutisseuse *f.*

stampede¹ [stæm'piːd], *s.* **1.** (*a*) Fuite précipitée; panique *f.* (*b*) Débandade *f* (de troupes). **2.** Ruée *f.* There was a s. for the door, on se précipita vers la porte.

stampede², **1.** *v.i.* (*a*) Fuir en désordre, à la débandade. (*b*) Se ruer, se précipiter (for, towards, vers, sur). **2.** *v.tr.* Jeter la panique parmi (des bêtes).

stamper ['stæmpər], *s.* **1.** (*Pers.*) Timbreur *m.* **2.** (*Machine*) Estampeuse *f.*

stance [stæns], *s.* *Sp:* Position *f* des pieds; posture *f.* To take up one's s., se mettre en posture (pour jouer).

stanch [stɑːn(t)ʃ, stɔːn(t)ʃ], *v.tr.* **1.** Étancher (le sang). **2.** Étancher le sang (d'une blessure).

stanchion ['stɑːnʃ(ə)n], *s.* **1.** Étançon *m*, étai *m*, béquille *f.* **2.** *Nau:* Épontille *f* (de cale).

stand¹ [stænd], *s.* **1.** (*a*) Manière *f* de se tenir (debout). To take a firm s., (i) se camper solidement sur ses jambes; (ii) se montrer résolu. (*b*) Arrêt *m,* halte *f.* To be brought to a s., être forcé de s'arrêter. (*c*) *Th:* One-night s., représentation *f* unique. **2.** Résistance *f.* To make a s. against s.o., résister à qn. **3.** Situation *f*, position *f.* (*a*) To take one's s. near the door, se placer près de la porte. (*b*) To take one's s. on a principle, se fonder sur un principe. **4.** Station *f,* stationnement *m* (de voitures). **5.** Support *m*, pied *m* (de lampe); affût *m* (de télescope); dessous *m* (de carafe); (*for vase, etc.*) présentoir *m.* Milliner's s., champignon *m.* *Motor-Cy:* Back-wheel s., béquille *f.* **6.** Étalage *m*, étal *m* (en plein air); (*at exhibition*) stand *m.* **7.** (*a*) *Sp:* Tribune *f*; stand. (*b*) Estrade *f.* **8.** *U.S: Jur:* = Barre *f* des témoins. **'stand-pipe,** *s.* Tuyau montant; colonne *f* d'alimentation (d'eau, d'essence).

stand², *v.* (stood [stud]; stood) **I.** *v.i.* **1.** (*a*) Être debout; se tenir debout; rester debout. I could hardly s., je pouvais à peine me tenir. To s. on one's own feet, ne dépendre que de soi, voler de ses propres ailes. I didn't leave him a leg to s. on, j'ai détruit ses arguments de fond en comble. *For:* To leave a tree standing, réserver un arbre. *S.a.* EASE¹ 1, HAIR 1, SENTRY 2. (*b*) To s. six feet high, avoir six pieds de haut. (*c*) Se lever. **2.** (*a*) Se trouver; être. The chapel stands on a hill, la chapelle se dresse sur une hauteur. The village stands against the hill, le village s'adosse à la colline. The tears stood in his eyes, il avait les larmes aux yeux. To let sth. s. in the sun, laisser qch. exposé au soleil. To buy the house as it stands, acheter la maison telle quelle. Nothing stands between you and success, rien ne s'oppose à votre succès. (*b*) A man stood in the doorway, un homme se tenait à la porte. To s. talking, rester à causer. He left her standing in the middle of the room, il la laissa plantée au milieu de la salle. 3. *A:* S'arrêter; faire halte. S.! halte! halte-là! **S. and deliver!** la bourse ou la vie! 4. Rester, durer. **To s. fast,** tenir (pied); tenir bon. **I shall s. or fall by the issue,** je suis prêt à engager ma fortune sur le résultat. 5. **The contract stands,** le contrat tient. **The objection stands,** cette objection subsiste. *S.a.* REASON[1] 3. 6. (*a*) **To s. convicted of . . .,** être déclaré coupable de. . . . *S.a.* CONVICT[2]. **To s. in need of . . .,** avoir besoin de. . . . **You s. in danger of getting killed,** vous vous exposez à vous faire tuer. *S.a.* CORRECT[1] 3. **To s. to lose nothing,** n'avoir rien à perdre. (*b*) **To s. as security for a debt,** assurer une créance. **To s. as candidate,** se porter candidat. (*c*) **He stands first on the list,** il vient en tête de (la) liste. **The thermometer stood at 30°,** le thermomètre marquait 30°. (*d*) **The house does not s. in his name,** la maison n'est pas portée à son nom. (*e*) **The amount standing to your credit,** votre solde créditeur. **How do we s.?** où en sont nos comptes? **The matter stands thus,** voici, voilà, où en est l'affaire. **As matters s., as it stands,** au point où en sont les choses. **I don't know where I s.,** j'ignore quelle est ma position. **To s. well with s.o.,** être estimé de qn. *S.a.* CEREMONY. 7. **I'll s. by the window,** je me mettrai à la fenêtre. *Nau:* **To s. to the south,** avoir, mettre, le cap au sud. *S.a.* CLEAR[1] II. 8. **To allow a liquid to s.,** laisser reposer un liquide. **To let the tea s.,** laisser infuser le thé. **Taxis may s. here,** les taxis peuvent stationner ici. II. *v.tr.* 1. Mettre, poser. **To s. sth. against the wall,** dresser qch. contre le mur. 2. **To s. one's ground,** tenir bon, ferme. 3. Supporter, subir. **To s. the cold,** supporter le froid. **To s. a shock,** soutenir un choc. (*Of car*) **To s. rough handling,** résister à des manipulations brutales. **We had to s. the loss,** la perte a porté sur nous. **Utensils that will s. the fire,** ustensiles qui vont au feu. *F:* **I can't s. him at any price,** je ne peux pas le sentir. **I can't s. it any longer,** je n'y tiens plus; j'en ai assez. 4. *F:* Payer, offrir. **To s.o. a drink,** payer à boire à qn. **I am standing this one,** c'est ma tournée. **stand about,** *v.i.* (*Of one pers.*) Rester debout; (*of several pers.*) (i) se trouver là; (ii) rester à regarder, flâner par là. **stand aside,** *v.i.* 1. (*a*) Se tenir à l'écart. (*b*) S'écarter, se ranger. (*c*) **To s. aside in favour of s.o.,** se désister en faveur de qn. **stand back,** *v.i.* (i) Se tenir en arrière; (ii) reculer. **House standing back from the road,** maison en retrait (de la route). **stand by,** *v.i.* 1. (*a*) Se tenir prêt. *Mil:* **The troops are standing by,** les troupes sont consignées. (*b*) *Nau:* Se tenir paré; veiller. **S. by below!** paré à manœuvrer! (*c*) Se tenir là (sans intervenir). 2. (*a*) Se tenir près de, à côté de (qn). (*b*) Soutenir, défendre (qn). (*c*) Rester fidèle à (sa promesse). **I s. by what I said,** j'en tiens, j'en suis, pour ce que j'ai dit. (*d*) *Nau:* **S. by the anchors!** paré à mouiller! **'stand-by,** *s.* 1. (*Pers.*) Appui *m,* soutien *m.* 2. Ressource *f.* **S.-by engine,** locomotive de réserve. **To have a small sum as a s.-by,** avoir une petite somme d'argent comme en-cas. **stand down,** *v.i.* 1. (*Of witness*) Quitter la barre. 2. Retirer sa candidature (in favour of, en faveur de). **stand for,** *v.ind.tr.* 1. Défendre, soutenir (une cause). 2. Tenir lieu de (qch.). 3. Signifier, vouloir dire (qch.). **To s. for nothing,** ne compter pour rien. **stand in,** *v.i.* 1. **To s. in with others,** s'associer à d'autres (pour une cotisation). 2. *Nau:* **To s. in to land,** rallier la terre. 3. **To s. in for s.o.,** remplacer qn (au travail dans une équipe). *Th: etc:* Doubler (qn). **'stand-in,** *s.* Remplaçant *m* (temporaire). *Th: etc:* Doublure *f.* **stand off,** 1. *v.i.* (*a*) Se tenir éloigné, à l'écart. (*b*) S'éloigner. *Nau:* Courir au large. **To s. off and on,** (i) courir des bordées près de terre; louvoyer; (ii) *F:* louvoyer. 2. *v.tr.* (*Of employer*) Mettre à pied (des employés). **stand out,** *v.i.* 1. Résister (against, à); tenir bon (against, contre). 2. **To s. out for sth.,** s'obstiner à demander qch. 3. Faire saillie. **To s. out in relief,** ressortir. **To s. out against sth.,** se détacher sur qch. **Mountains that s. out on the horizon,** montagnes qui se dessinent à l'horizon. **The qualities that s. out in his work,** les qualités marquantes de son œuvre. **His character**

makes him s. out from the crowd, sa personnalité le détache de la foule. 4. *Nau:* **To s. out to sea,** gagner le large. **stand over,** *v.i.* 1. Rester en suspens. **To let a question s. over,** remettre une question à plus tard. **To let an account s. over,** laisser traîner un compte. 2. **If I don't s. over him he does nothing,** si je ne suis pas toujours sur son dos il ne fait rien. **stand to,** *v.i.* (*a*) *Nau:* **To s. to the south,** avoir le cap au sud. (*b*) *Mil:* **To s. to one's arms,** se tenir sous les armes. *Abs.* **To s. to,** être en état d'alerte. (*c*) **To s. to one's promise,** ne pas renier sa promesse. *S.a.* MIL: etc: Alerte *f.* **stand up,** *v.i.* 1. (*a*) Se lever; se mettre debout. (*b*) Se dresser, se tenir droit. 2. (*a*) **To s. up against . . .,** résister à . . .; tenir tête à. . . . (*b*) **To s. up for s.o.,** défendre qn; prendre fait et cause pour qn. (*c*) **To s. up to s.o.,** affronter bravement qn; tenir pied à qn. **To s. up to one's work,** être courageux au travail. *P:* **To s. s.o. up,** (i) planter là qn; (ii) plaquer (un amoureux). **'stand-up,** *attrib.a.* 1. *Cost:* S.-up collar, col droit, montant. 2. **S.-up buffet,** buffet-bar *m;* comptoir *m.* 3. **S.-up fight,** combat en règle. **standing[1],** *a.* 1. (*a*) (Qui se tient) debout. *Rac: F:* **To leave a competitor s.,** brûler un concurrent. **To be left s.,** être laissé sur place. *S.a.* START[1] 2. (*b*) **S. crops,** récoltes sur pied. 2. (*a*) **S. water,** eau stagnante, dormante. (*b*) *Typ:* **S. type,** conservation *f.* 3. (*a*) *Mil:* **S. camp,** camp permanent. (*b*) *Tchn:* **S. block,** poulie *f* fixe. 4. *adv.phr. Nau:* **To be brought up all s.,** rester en panne. 5. (*a*) *Com:* **S. expenses,** frais généraux. **S. rule,** règle fixe. **S. joke,** plaisanterie courante, traditionnelle. **'standing 'stone,** *s. Prehist:* Menhir *m.* **standing[2],** *s.* 1. Fait de se tenir debout; station *f* debout. *Aut: U.S:* **No s.,** stationnement interdit. 2. Durée *f.* **Friend of long s.,** ami de longue main, de longue date. **Officer of six months' s.,** officier qui a six mois de service. 3. Rang *m,* position *f;* standing *m.* **Social s.,** position sociale. **Man of high s.,** homme haut placé. **Man of good s.,** homme estimé. **Man of no s.,** homme sans consistance. **It would mean a loss of s.,** ce serait déchoir. **S. of a firm,** importance *f* d'une maison. **Firm of recognized s.,** maison d'une honorabilité reconnue. **'standing room,** *s.* (*In bus, etc.*) Place(s) *f(pl)* debout. **There wasn't even any s. r.,** il n'y avait pas où mettre le pied.

standard ['stændəd], *s.* 1. Bannière *f. Mil:* Étendard *m. Nau:* Pavillon *m.* 2. Étalon *m* (de poids). **The metre is the s. of length,** le mètre est l'unité de longueur. *Fin:* **The gold s.,** l'étalon (d')or. 3. Modèle *m,* type *m.* **S. of living,** niveau *m* de vie. **Judged by that s. . . .,** à cette mesure. . . . 4. (*a*) Degré *m* (d'excellence); qualité *f.* **The s. of wages,** le taux des salaires. **To aim at a high s.,** viser à un haut degré d'excellence. *Com:* **Up to s.,** conforme à l'échantillon. *Sch:* **Your papers are up to s.,** vos compositions sont à la hauteur. (*b*) **S. (of purity) of gold,** titre *m* de l'or. 5. *A:* (*In primary schools*) Classe *f.* 6. (*a*) Support *m* (d'un instrument scientifique); montant *m* (d'une machine). (*b*) Pylône *m* d'éclairage. *S.a.* LAMP 2. 7. *Hort:* **S. (tree),** arbre *m* de plein vent. 8. *attrib.* Standard. **S. measure,** mesure-étalon *f.* **S. metre,** étalon *m* du mètre. **S. gold,** or au titre. *Rail:* **S. gauge,** voie normale. **Of s. size,** de taille courante. *Ind:* **Of s. dimensions,** de dimensions normales. **Car of s. model,** voiture de série. **The s. authors,** les auteurs classiques. **A S. French Dictionary,** un dictionnaire général de la langue française. **S. English,** l'anglais des gens cultivés. **One of his s. jokes,** une de ses plaisanteries classiques, traditionnelles. **'standard-bearer,** *s. Mil. Hist:* Porte-étendard *m inv,* porte-drapeau *m inv.*

standardization [ˌstændədaiˈzeiʃ(ə)n], *s.* Étalonnage *m,* étalonnement *m* (des poids); unification *f* (des méthodes d'essai). *Ind:* Standardisation *f* (d'une machine). *Ch:* Titrage *m.*

standardize ['stændədaiz], *v.tr.* Étalonner, unifier (des méthodes d'essai). *Ind:* Standardiser (des voitures). *Ch:* Titrer (une solution).

standee ['stændi:], *s. U.S: F:* Voyageur *m* debout.

stand-offish [stændˈɔfiʃ], *a. F:* (*Of pers.*) Peu accessible, distant, réservé.

stand-offishness [ˌstænd'ɔfiʃnis], s. F: Raideur f, réserve f, morgue f.

standpoint ['stændpɔint], s. Point m de vue.

standstill ['stændstil], s. Arrêt m, immobilisation f. **To come to a s.**, s'arrêter, s'immobiliser; (of car) rester en panne. **To bring a train to a s.**, arrêter un train. **Trade is at a s.**, le commerce ne va plus. **Many factories are at a s.**, beaucoup d'usines chôment.

stank. See STINK².

stanza, pl. **-as** ['stænzə, -əz], s. Stance f, strophe f.

staphylococcus, pl. **-cocci** [ˌstæfilə'kɔkəs, kɔkai], s. Bac: Staphylocoque m.

staple¹ ['steipl], s. 1. Crampon m (à deux pointes). Wire s., (i) (clou) cavalier m en fil de fer, clou à deux pointes; (ii) Bookb: etc: broche f (en fil métallique), agrafe f. 2. (Bolt-)s., gâche f, gâchette f; auberon m d'une serrure de malle). 'staple-press, s. Bookb: Brocheuse f.

staple², v.tr. 1. Const: etc: Agrafer, cramponner (qch). 2. Bookb: Brocher. **stapling**, s. Agrafage m; fixage m à l'aide de crampons. Bookb: Brochage m.

staple³, s. (a) Produit principal (d'un pays). Attrib. **S. commodities**, (i) denrées principales; (ii) produits m de première nécessité. **S. diet**, nourriture f de base. **S. industry**, industrie principale. (b) Matière première, matière brute.

staple⁴, s. Tex: Brin m, fibre f (de laine); soie f (de coton). **Long-s. cotton**, coton longue soie. S.a. FIBRE 2.

stapler ['steiplər], s. Tls: Agrafeuse f.

star¹ [stɑːr], s. 1. (a) Étoile f; astre m. **Shooting s.**, étoile filante. **The pole s.**, l'étoile polaire. **To be born under a lucky s.**, naître sous une bonne étoile. **I thank my (lucky) stars that . . .**, je bénis mon étoile de ce que + ind. **To see stars**, voir trente-six chandelles. F: **There's a s. in the east**, votre braguette est déboutonnée. (b) Bot: **S. of Bethlehem**, ornithogale · m (à ombelle); F: belle f d'onze heures. 2. (a) **S. of an order**, plaque f d'un ordre; décoration f. (b) Mil: Étoile (servant à indiquer les grades). 3. (a) **The stars and stripes** (of the U.S.A.), la bannière étoilée. (b) (On horse's forehead) Étoile. (c) (Star-shaped crack) Étoile, étoilement m. (d) Typ: F: Astérisque m. **Four s. hotel**, hôtel m de grand luxe, palace m. 4. Cin: Th: (Pers.) Étoile, vedette f, star f. **S. part**, rôle de vedette. **S. turn**, (i) numéro m de vedette; (ii) F: clou m (d'une fête, etc.). s. Pol.Hist: **S. of David**, Yellow S., l'Étoile de David, l'étoile jaune. 'Star-chamber (the), s. Hist: La Chambre étoilée. 'star-gaze, v.i. F: 1. Faire de l'astronomie. 2. Bayer aux corneilles; rêvasser. 'star-gazing, s. Rêvasserie(s) f(pl). 'star-gazer, s. (a) F: Pej: Astronome m; astrologue m. (b) Rêvasseur, -euse. 'star-spangled, a. (Par)semé d'étoiles. **The s.-s. banner**, la bannière étoilée (des États-Unis).

star², v. (starred) 1. v.tr. (a) Étoiler; (par)semer d'étoiles. (b) Étoiler, fêler (une glace). 2. v.i. (a) (Of glass) Se fêler, s'étoiler. (b) Th: Cin: Être en vedette; tenir le premier rôle; avoir un rôle d'étoile, de star. **starred**, a. (a) Étoilé; parsemé d'étoiles. (b) F: Marqué d'un astérisque.

starboard¹ ['stɑːbəd], s. Nau: Tribord m. **On the s. side**, to s., à tribord. **S. tack**, tribord amures. **On the s. bow**, par tribord devant. **Hard a-s.!** à droite toute!

starboard². Nau: 1. v.tr. **To s. the helm**, mettre la barre à tribord. 2. v.i. (Of ship) Venir sur tribord.

starch¹ [stɑːtʃ], s. 1. (a) Amidon m. **Potato s.**, fécule f de pommes de terre. (b) S.(-paste), colle f d'amidon. 2. F: O: (a) Manières empesées, guindées; raideur f. (b) **To take the s. out of s.o.**, démonter qn. 'starch-reduced, a. Débarrassé de matières féculentes.

starch², v.tr. Empeser, amidonner. **starched**, a. 1. Empesé. S.a. SHIRT. 2. F: O: (Of pers.) Empesé; guindé; raide.

starchiness ['stɑːtʃinis], s. Manières guindées; raideur f.

starchy ['stɑːtʃi], a. 1. Ch: Amylacé; féculent. **S. foods**, féculents mpl. 2. = ˈSTARCHED.

stardom ['stɑːdəm], s. Cin: etc: **To rise to s.**, devenir une vedette.

stare¹ [stɛər], s. Regard fixe; regard appuyé. **Glassy s.**, regard terne, vitreux. **Set s.**, regard fixe. **Stony s.**, regard dur. **Vacant s.**, regard vague; regard ahuri. **To give s.o. a s.**, dévisager qn. **With a s. of astonishment**, les yeux écarquillés; les yeux ébahis. **With a s. of horror**, les yeux grands ouverts d'horreur.

stare². 1. v.i. (a) Regarder fixement. **To s. into the distance**, regarder au loin. **To s. in s.o.'s face**, dévisager qn. (b) Écarquiller les yeux; ouvrir de grands yeux. 2. v.ind.tr. **To s. at s.o.**, (i) regarder qn fixement; fixer ses yeux sur qn; fixer qn; (ii) regarder qn effrontément; dévisager qn; (iii) regarder qn d'un air hébété. 3. v.tr. **To s. s.o. in the face**, dévisager qn. **Ruin stares him in the face**, sa ruine est imminente. F: **It's staring you in the face**, ça vous saute aux yeux. **To s. s.o. out (of countenance)**, faire baisser les yeux à qn; faire perdre contenance à qn. **staring**, a. 1. **S. eyes**, (i) yeux fixes; (ii) yeux grands ouverts; yeux effarés; regard ébahi. 2. **Stark s. mad**, complètement fou.

starfish ['stɑːfiʃ], s. Echin: Astérie f; étoile f de mer.

stark [stɑːk]. 1. a. Lit: (a) Raide, rigide. **He lay in death**, il gisait dans la rigidité de la mort. (b) Poet: Fort, vigoureux. (c) Poet: Résolu, inflexible. (d) **S. nonsense**, pure bêtise. **The s. desolation of the whole region**, la désolation absolue de toute cette région. 2. adv. **S. naked**, tout nu; nu comme un ver, comme la main.

starless ['stɑːlis], a. Sans étoiles.

starlet ['stɑːlit], s. Cin: etc: Starlette f.

starlight ['stɑːlait], s. 1. Lumière f des étoiles; lumière stellaire. **In the s.**, by s., à la lueur, à la clarté, des étoiles. 2. attrib. **A s. night**, une nuit étoilée.

starling ['stɑːliŋ], s. Orn: Étourneau m; sansonnet m.

starlit ['stɑːlit], a. **S. night**, nuit étoilée.

starry ['stɑːri], a. (Ciel) étoilé, (par)semé d'étoiles. 'starry-'eyed, a. (a) Idéaliste. (b) (Esprit m) romanesque. **She's a bit s.-e.**, elle n'a pas beaucoup de sens pratique.

start¹ [stɑːt], s. 1. (a) Tressaillement m, sursaut m, soubresaut m. **To wake with a s.**, se réveiller en sursaut. **He gave a s.**, il tressaillit, sursauta. **To give a s. of joy**, tressaillir de joie. **To give s.o. a s.**, faire tressaillir qn. (b) Saut m; mouvement m brusque. S.a. FIT² 2. (a) Commencement m, début m. **To make an early s.**, commencer de bonne heure. **You will work here for a start**, vous travaillerez ici pour débuter. **For a s.**, his data are wrong, d'abord, pour commencer, ses données sont fausses. **At the s.**, au début. **At the very s.**, de prime abord. **From s. to finish**, du commencement à la fin. **To give s.o. a s.**, lancer qn (dans les affaires, etc.). **To give an artist, a play, a good s.**, lancer un artiste, une pièce. **To make a good s.**, bien commencer. **To make a fresh s. (in life)**, recommencer (sa vie); repartir sur nouveaux frais. (b) Départ m. Av: **Envol m. To make an early s.**, partir de bonne heure. Rac: **Flying s.**, départ lancé. **Standing s.**, départ arrêté. **False s.**, faux départ. (c) Sp: **To give s.o. a s.**, donner un peu d'avance à qn. **To get the s. of s.o.**, prendre les devants; devancer qn.

start². I. v.i. 1. (a) Tressaillir, tressauter, sursauter; avoir un haut-le-corps; (of horse, etc.) soubresauter. **The report made him s.**, la détonation le fit (sur)sauter. **He started with surprise**, il eut un mouvement de surprise. **To s. out of one's sleep**, se réveiller en sursaut. (b) **To s. aside**, se jeter de côté; s'écarter brusquement; (of horse) faire un écart. **To s. back**, se jeter en arrière. **To s. to one's feet**, se lever tout à coup. **To s. from one's chair**, se lever vivement de sa chaise. **Tears started from his eyes**, les larmes jaillirent de ses yeux. **His eyes were starting out of his head**, les yeux lui sortaient de la tête. 2. (Of rivets) Se détacher; sauter. Nau: (Of ship's seams) Se délier, s'ouvrir. 3. (a) Commencer; débuter. **To s. with soup**, commencer par un potage. **The play starts (off) with a prologue**, la pièce débute par un prologue. **To s. at the beginning**, commencer par le commencement. S.a. END¹ 1. **To s. afresh**, recommencer. **To s. in life**, débuter dans la vie. **To s. in business**, se mettre, se lancer, dans les affaires. **There were only six members to s. with**, il n'y avait que six membres au début. **To s. with we must . . .,** en premier lieu il va falloir. . . . **To s. by doing sth.,** commencer par faire qch. **Starting Monday . . .,** à partir de lundi. (*b*) **To s.** (away, off, out, on one's way), partir; se mettre en route. **We s. to-morrow,** nous partons demain. **He started back the next day,** il reprit le chemin de la maison le lendemain. **He started out to write a novel,** il se mit en devoir d'écrire un roman. *Rac:* **Only six horses started,** six chevaux seulement sont partis. (*c*) **To s.** (off), (*of car*) démarrer; (*of train*) s'ébranler. (*d*) **To s.** (up), (*of engine*) se mettre en marche; (*of injector, dynamo*) s'amorcer. **The engine won't s.,** le moteur refuse de partir. II. *v.tr.* **1.** Commencer (un travail); entamer (une conversation). **To s. a fresh loaf,** entamer un nouveau pain. **To s. negotiations,** entamer, engager, des négociations. **To s. life afresh,** recommencer sa vie. *Fb: etc:* **To s. an attack,** amorcer une attaque. **To s. doing sth.,** commencer à, de, faire qch.; se mettre à faire qch. **To s. crying again,** se remettre à pleurer. **It's just started raining,** voilà qu'il commence à pleuvoir. **2.** (*a*) **To s.** (off) **a horse at a gallop,** faire partir un cheval au galop. (*b*) *Rac:* Donner le signal du départ à (des coureurs). (*c*) *Ven:* Lancer (un cerf, un sanglier); lever, faire partir (une perdrix, etc.). **3.** (*a*) Lancer, donner le branle à (une entreprise); fonder (un commerce); fonder, lancer (un journal); ouvrir (une école); mettre en train (une affaire). (*b*) **To s. a fire,** provoquer un incendie. **4.** (*a*) Mettre en marche, faire marcher (une horloge). (*b*) **To s.** (up) **a machine,** mettre une machine en marche, en train. *Av:* **S. up!** mettez en route! **5.** **To s. s.o. on a career,** lancer qn dans une carrière. **Once you s. him talking . . .,** quand on le met à causer. . . . **6.** Disjoindre (des tôles); faire craquer (les coutures d'un vêtement). **start up,** *v.i.* **1.** (*Of pers.*) Se lever brusquement; se lever en sursaut. **2.** Pousser rapidement. **Mushroom towns starting up everywhere,** partout des villes qui surgissent du jour au lendemain. (*c*) Se produire; naître. **starting,** *s.* **1.** Tressaillement *m*; sursaut *m*, soubresaut *m*. **2.** (*a*) Commencement *m*, début *m*. (*b*) Départ *m*. **3.** (*a*) Mise *f* en train (d'une entreprise, etc.). (*b*) **S.** (up), mise en mouvement, mise en marche, lancement *m* (d'une machine); amorçage *m* (d'une dynamo). 'starting-block,' *s. Sp: F:* Starting-block *m*. 'starting-engine,' *s.* Moteur *m* de lancement. 'starting-gate,' *s. Rac:* Barrière *f*, starting-gate *m*. 'starting-gear,' *s.* Appareil *m* de démarrage; mise *f* en train. 'starting-handle,' *s.* Manivelle *f* (de mise en marche). 'starting-lever,' *s.* Levier *m* de mise en marche. 'starting-line,' *s. Sp:* Ligne *f* de départ. 'starting-place, -point,' *s.* Point *m* de départ. *Rail: etc:* Tête *f* de ligne. 'starting-post,' *s. Sp:* Poteau *m* de départ; barrière *f*. 'starting-pistol,' *s. Sp:* Pistolet *m* de starter. 'starting-price,' *s.* **1.** *Com:* Prix initial. **2.** *Rac:* Dernière cote avant le départ.

starter ['stɑːtər], *s.* **1.** (*a*) **You are an early s.,** vous partez de bonne heure. (*b*) *Sp:* Partant *m.* **2.** (*a*) *Rac:* Starter *m* (qui donne le signal du départ). (*b*) Auteur *m* (d'un projet, etc.); lanceur, -euse (d'une affaire, etc.). **3.** (*Device*) *Aut: El.E:* Appareil *m* de mise en marche; démarreur *m.* **S.**-button, bouton *m* du démarreur. *Aut:* Self-s., démarreur.

startle ['stɑːtl], *v.tr.* Effrayer, alarmer (qn); faire tressaillir, faire sursauter (qn). **To s. s.o. out of his sleep,** éveiller qn en sursaut. **startling,** *a.* Effrayant, saisissant; foudroyant. **S. events,** événements sensationnels. **S. get-up,** toilette ébouriffante. **S. resemblance,** ressemblance saisissante.

starvation [stɑːˈveiʃ(ə)n], *s.* Privation *f*, manque *m* de nourriture. *Med:* Inanition *f.* **To die of s.,** mourir de faim, d'inanition. **S. wages,** salaire de famine; salaire de meurt-de-faim. *S.a.* DIET[1] 2.

starve [stɑːv]. **1.** *v.i.* (*a*) **To s. to death,** mourir de faim. (*b*) Manquer de nourriture; endurer la faim. **I'm starving,** je meurs de faim. (*c*) *A: & Dial:* **To be starving with cold,** être tout transi (de froid); être gelé. (*d*) *O: Dial:* (*Of tree, plant*) Dépérir; s'étioler. **2.** *v.tr.* (*a*) Faire mourir (qn) de faim. **To s. out a town,** prendre, réduire, une ville par la

famine. **Trade would have been starved out of existence,** le commerce serait mort d'inanition. (*b*) Priver (qn) de nourriture. **To s. a fever,** traiter une fièvre par la diète. **starved,** *a.* (*a*) Affamé. **S. looking,** à l'aspect famélique. (*b*) **S. of affection,** privé d'affection. **starving,** *a.* Mourant de faim; famélique.

starveling ['stɑːvliŋ], *s.* Famélique *mf*; meurt-de-faim *m inv.*

stash [stæʃ], *v.tr. F:* Cacher (un trésor, etc.); mettre (son argent) en sécurité, à l'abri. **Stashed away for future use,** bien caché pour l'avenir.

state[1] [steit], *s.* **1.** (*a*) État *m*, condition *f*; situation *f.* **In a good s.,** en bon état; en bonne condition. *F:* **Here's a nice, a pretty, s. of things,** nous voilà bien! c'est du joli, du propre! *F:* **What a s. you are in!** dans quel état vous êtes! *F:* **To get into a terrible s.,** (i) se mettre dans tous ses états; (ii) se trouver dans un état lamentable. (*b*) **Body in a s. of rest,** corps à l'état de repos; corps au repos. **S. of health,** état de santé. **People in a savage s.,** peuple à l'état sauvage. **The married s.,** le mariage. **The single s.,** le célibat. **S. of mind,** disposition *f* d'esprit. **2.** (*a*) Rang *m*, dignité *f.* **In a style befitting his s.,** sur un pied digne de son rang. (*b*) Pompe *f*, parade *f*, apparat *m.* **To keep great s.,** to live in s., mener grand train. **To travel in s.,** voyager en grand apparat, en grand équipage. **To dine in s.,** dîner en grand gala. (*Of body*) **To lie in s.,** être exposé (sur un lit de parade). **Lying in s.,** exposition *f* (d'un corps). *F:* **To sit in s. in one's carriage,** car, se pavaner, se prélasser, dans sa voiture. **He was in his robes of s.,** il était en costume d'apparat. **Bed of s.,** lit de parade. (*c*) **S. carriage, s. coach,** voiture d'apparat; voiture de gala. **S. reception of a prince,** réception solennelle d'un prince. **S. ball,** grand bal officiel; grand bal de cour. **S. apartments,** salons d'apparat. **3.** (*a*) = ESTATE 3. *Fr.Hist:* **The States General,** les États généraux. (*b*) (*Channel Is.*) **The States,** l'assemblée législative. **4.** (*a*) **The S.,** l'État. **Church and S.,** l'Église et l'État. **Secretary of S.,** (i) secrétaire d'État; (ii) *U.S:* = Ministre *m* des Affaires étrangères. *U.S:* **S. Department,** Ministère *m* des Affaires étrangères. **Affairs of S.,** affaires d'État. **S. trial,** procès politique. **S. forest,** forêt domaniale; forêt de l'État. **To establish s. control,** étatiser. **Establishment of s. control,** étatisation *f. S.a.* WELFARE. (*b*) État, nation *f.* **Every s. was represented,** tous les états étaient représentés. **The United States (of America),** les États-Unis (d'Amérique). **S. aided,** *a.* Subventionné par l'État. 'state-controlled,' *a.* Étatisé. 'state-'managed,' *a.* (Théâtre, etc.) en régie. 'state-room,' *s.* **1.** Chambre *f* d'apparat; salle *f* de réception (d'un palais). **2.** *Nau: O:* Cabine *f* (de luxe). *U.S: Rail:* (Compartiment *m* de) wagon-lit *m.*

state[2], *v.tr.* **1.** (*a*) Énoncer, déclarer, affirmer, faire connaître (qch.). **To s. sth. definitely,** spécifier qch. **This condition was expressly stated,** cette condition était énoncée expressément. **Please s. below . . .,** veuillez noter en bas. . . . **As stated above,** (i) ainsi qu'il est dit plus haut; (ii) (*on official form*) voir déclaration *f* ci-dessus. **It should also be stated that . . .,** nous devons ajouter que. . . . **I have stated my opinion,** j'ai donné mon opinion. **He states positively that he heard it,** il affirme l'avoir entendu. **It is stated that he has been found . . .,** on affirme l'avoir trouvé. . . . **I have seen it stated that . . .,** j'ai lu quelque part que. . . . (*b*) Exposer (une réclamation). *Jur:* **To s. the case,** faire l'exposé des faits. **To s. a case,** soumettre les faits au tribunal. (*c*) *Mth:* Poser, énoncer (un problème). **2.** Régler, arrêter, fixer (une heure, une date). **stated,** *a.* **At s. intervals,** à des époques fixées; à intervalles réglés. **On s. days,** à jours fixes.

statecraft ['steitkrɑːft], *s.* Habileté *f* politique; diplomatie *f.*

stateless ['steitlis], *a. Adm:* **S. person,** apatride *mf.*

statelessness ['steitlisnis], *s.* Apatridie *f*, heimatlosat *m.*

stateliness ['steitlinis], *s.* Majesté *f*; aspect imposant; dignité *f.*

stately ['steitli], *a.* **1.** Majestueux, -euse; imposant. **2.** Plein de dignité; noble, élevé.

statement ['steitmənt], s. **1.** (a) Exposition f, exposé m, énoncé m (des faits); rapport m, compte rendu, relation f. **Official s.** (to the press), communiqué m. **Certified s.,** constatation f. **To make, publish, a s.,** émettre une déclaration. **Full s. of the position,** exposé complet de la situation. **According to his own s.,** suivant sa propre déclaration. **To make a signed s.,** U.S: **to make a s. over one's signature,** faire une déclaration. Jur: **The statements made by the witnesses,** les dépositions f des témoins. **Written s. of a case,** instruction écrite; mémoire m. (b) Affirmation f. **To contradict a s.,** nier une affirmation. **2.** Com: **S. of account,** état m de compte; relevé m de compte. **S. of affairs** (in bankruptcy), bilan m de liquidation.

statesman, pl. **-men** ['steitsmən], s.m. Homme d'État. Pol: F: **The Elder Statesmen,** les vétérans m (de la politique).

statesmanlike ['steitsmənlaik], a. D'homme d'État. **He acted in a s. manner,** il se conduisit en homme d'État.

statesmanship ['steitsmənʃip], s. Science f du gouvernement.

static ['stætik], a. Statique. **S. electricity,** électricité f statique.

statice ['stætis(i)], s. Bot: Statice m.

statics ['stætiks], s.pl. **1.** Mth: Ph: etc: La statique. **2.** W.Tel: Perturbations f atmosphériques; parasites mpl.

station[1] ['steiʃ(ə)n], s. **1.** (a) Position f, place f, poste m. **To take up a s.,** (i) prendre une place; se placer; (ii) se rendre à un poste. Navy: **Action stations,** postes de combat. (Of ship) **To be in s., out of s.,** être, ne pas être, à son poste. (b) Station f, poste. **Naval s.,** station navale; port m de guerre. **Ship on s.,** navire en station. Av: R.A.F. s., base aérienne. **Military s.,** poste militaire. **The battalion is about to change s.,** le bataillon va changer de garnison. **Broadcasting s.,** poste émetteur, de radio-diffusion. (c) (In Austr.) (Sheep-)s., élevage m (de moutons). (d) **Lifeboat s.,** station de sauvetage. **Frontier s.,** poste de frontière. El.E: **Transformer s.,** transformateur m, poste abaisseur de tension. Hyd.E: **Pumping s.,** centrale f de pompage. Aut: **Service s.,** station-service f, pl. stations-service. S.a. POLICE[1]. **2.** Position, condition f; rang m. **S. in life,** situation sociale. **3.** (a) Rail: **Gare** f. **Passenger s.,** gare de voyageurs. **Goods s.,** gare de marchandises. **Euston S.,** la gare de Euston. **S. hotel,** hôtel de la gare. **S. bus,** l'autobus qui va à la gare. (b) **Coach, bus, s.,** gare routière. **4.** Ecc: **The Stations of the Cross,** le chemin de (la) Croix. 'station-signal, s. W.Tel: etc: Indicatif m du poste. 'station-wagon, s. Aut: Familiale f, break m.

station[2], v.tr. (a) Placer, mettre (qn dans un endroit). (b) **To s. troops,** poster des troupes. Mil: Navy: **To s. the officers and men,** désigner leurs postes aux officiers et aux hommes. (c) **To be stationed at . . .,** (i) Mil: être en garnison à . . . (ii) Navy: être en station à . . . .

stationary ['steiʃənəri], a. **1.** Stationnaire; immobile. **S. car,** voiture en stationnement. **2.** (a) **S. engine,** machine fixe. (b) **S. troops,** troupes sédentaires.

stationer ['steiʃənər], s. Papetier m. **Stationer's shop,** papeterie f. **Stationers' Hall,** Hôtel de la Corporation des libraires, relieurs, et papetiers (à Londres). **Entered at Stationers' Hall,** (livre) déposé.

stationery ['steiʃənəri], s. Papeterie f. **Office s.,** school s., fournitures fpl de bureau, d'école.

stationmaster ['steiʃ(ə)nmɑːstər], s. Chef m de gare.

statism ['steitizm], s. Pol: Étatisme m.

statistical [stə'tistik(ə)l], a. Statistique. **S. tables,** statistiques f pl.

statistician [,stætis'tiʃ(ə)n], s. Statisticien, -ienne.

statistics [stə'tistiks], s.pl. La statistique. **Compiled from s.,** établi d'après des statistiques. **Vital s.,** (i) Pol.Ec: statistiques démographiques; (ii) F: (woman's measurements) mensurations fpl.

stator ['steitər], s. Stator m (d'une turbine, d'un moteur électrique).

statuary ['stætjuəri]. **1.** a. Statuaire. **2.** s. (Pers.) Statuaire mf. **3.** s. (a) La statuaire; l'art m statuaire. (b) Coll. Statues fpl.

statue ['stætjuː], s. Statue f.

statuesque [,stætju'esk], a. Sculptural, -aux; plastique.

statuette [,stætju'et], s. Statuette f.

stature ['stætjər, -ʃər], s. Stature f; taille f. **To be short of s.,** avoir la taille courte.

status ['steitəs], s. (a) Statut légal (de qn). **Personal s.,** statut personnel. (b) Adm: **Civil s.,** état civil. (c) **Condition** f, **position** f, rang m. **Social s.,** rang social. **S. symbol,** marque f de standing. **Without any official s.,** sans titre officiel.

status quo ['steitəs'kwou], s. Statu quo m inv.

statute ['stætjuːt], s. **1.** Acte m du Parlement; loi f, ordonnance f. **The S. of Limitations,** la loi de prescription. **To bar a debt by the S. of Limitations,** prescrire une dette. **2.** pl. Statuts m, règlements m (d'une société, d'une compagnie). **3.** Internat. Jur: **Personal s.,** statut personnel. 'statute-book, s. Code m (des lois). 'statute law, s. Droit écrit; jurisprudence f.

statutory ['stætjut(ə)ri], a. **1.** Établi, imposé, par la loi; réglementaire; (of offence) prévu par la loi. **S. holiday,** fête légale. **S. declaration,** (i) attestation f (tenant lieu de serment); (ii) acte m de notoriété. **2.** Statutaire; conforme aux statuts.

staunch[1] [stɔːn(t)ʃ], a. **1.** (Of pers.) Sûr, dévoué; ferme. **S. friend,** ami à toute épreuve; ami solide. **S. courage,** courage inébranlable. **2.** (Of ship) Étanche. -ly, adv. Avec fermeté; avec résolution; avec dévouement.

staunch[2], v.tr. = STANCH.

staunchness ['stɔːn(t)ʃnis], s. **1.** Fermeté f; dévouement m. **2.** Étanchéité f.

stave[1] [steiv], s. **1.** (a) Coop: **Barrel staves,** douves f pour tonneaux. (b) Bâton m. **2.** Pros: **Stance** f, strophe f (d'un poème). **3.** Mus: (a) Portée f. (b) (Barre f de) mesure f.

stave[2], v.tr. (p.t. **staved**; p.p. **staved,** Nau: **stove** [stouv]) **1.** Coop: Assembler les douves (d'un tonneau). **2.** = STAVE IN. **stave in,** v.tr. Défoncer, enfoncer (une barrique, un bateau). **stave off,** v.tr. Détourner, écarter (un ennui, etc.); prévenir (un danger); conjurer (un désastre). **To s. off hunger,** tromper la faim.

stay[1] [stei], s. **1.** Séjour m; visite f (chez un ami). **Fortnight's s.,** séjour de quinze jours. **2.** (a) Lit: Retard m; entrave f. (b) Jur: **S. of proceedings,** suspension f d'instance. **S. of execution,** sursis m; ordonnance f de surseoir (à un jugement).

stay[2]. **I.** v.i. **1.** A: (a) S'arrêter. (b) (In imp.) **S.!** attendez! **2.** (a) Rester; demeurer sur les lieux. **S. here till I return,** restez ici jusqu'à ce que je revienne. **S. there!** tenez-vous là! F: **To s. put,** rester sur place. **To s. at home,** se tenir chez soi; rester à la maison. **To s. in bed,** rester au lit; garder le lit. **To s. to dinner, for dinner,** rester à dîner. **To make s.o. s. to lunch,** retenir qn à déjeuner. **He has come to s.,** il est venu (i) passer quelques jours, (ii) habiter, chez nous. **Book that has come to s.,** livre m qui restera. (b) Séjourner, demeurer quelque temps (dans un endroit). **To s. at an hotel,** (i) descendre à un hôtel; (ii) s'installer à un hôtel. **3.** Rac: **He was not able to s.,** il n'a pas pu soutenir l'allure. **He can s. three miles,** il peut fournir une course de trois milles. **II.** v.tr. **1.** O: Arrêter (le progrès de qn); enrayer (une épidémie). **To s. s.o.'s hand,** retenir le bras de qn. **To s. one's hand,** se retenir. **2.** Jur: etc: Remettre, ajourner (une décision); surseoir à (un jugement). **stay away,** v.i. Ne pas venir; s'absenter. **stay down,** v.i. Sch: Redoubler. **stay in,** v.i. (a) Ne pas sortir; rester à la maison; garder le logis. (b) Sch: Être en retenue. (c) **S.-in strike,** grève f sur le tas. **stay on,** v.i. Rester encore quelque temps, rester. **stay out,** v.i. Rester dehors; ne pas rentrer. **To s. out all night,** découcher; ne pas rentrer. **stay up,** v.i. Ne pas se coucher; veiller. **To s. up late,** veiller tard. **staying**[1], s. **1.** Séjour m. **2.** **S. power,** résistance f; endurance f. (Of horse) **To have good s. power,** avoir du fond. **3.** (a) O: Arrêt m (du progrès de qch.); enrayage m, enraiement m (d'une épidémie, etc.). (b) Jur: etc: Remise f, ajournement m. 'stay-at-home, a. & s. Casanier, -ière.

stay³, *s.* **1.** (*a*) Support *m*, soutien *m*. *O:* The s. of his old age, le soutien de sa vieillesse. (*b*) *Const: Mec.E:* Support, appui *m*, étai *m*, étançon *m*; jambe *f* de force; arc-boutant *m*; accore *m* (de navire en construction). **2.** (*Brace, tie*) Tirant *m* (de chaudière); entretoise *f.* **3.** *pl. Cost: A:* Stays, corset *m*.

stay⁴, *v.tr.* **1.** Étayer, étançonner, arc-bouter (un mur, une maison); accorer (un navire). **2.** Entretoiser; ancrer (une cheminée). **staying**², *s.* **1.** Étayage *m*. **2.** Entretoisement *m*.

stay⁵, *s.* **1.** Hauban *m*. **2.** (*Of ship*) To be in stays, to hang in stays, être pris vent devant. To be slack in stays, être lent à virer (de bord). To go about in stays, virer vent devant. **'stay-rope**, *s.* Hauban *m*.

stay⁶, *v.tr.* Hauban(n)er (un mât, un poteau). **2.** *Nau:* (*a*) *v.tr.* Faire virer de bord (un navire) vent devant. (*b*) *v.i.* Virer de bord vent devant.

stayer ['steiər], *s. Sp:* (*a*) Coureur *m* de fond; stayer *m*. (*b*) Cheval *m* qui a du fond. (*c*) *F:* He's a terrible s., il ne sait pas partir.

staysail ['steisl], *s. Nau:* Voile *f* d'étai.

stead [sted], *s.* **1.** To stand s.o. in good s., être fort utile à qn; être d'un grand secours à qn. **2.** In s.o.'s s., à la place de qn. To act in s.o.'s s., remplacer qn.

steadfast ['stedfəst], *a.* Ferme; inébranlable. S. in danger, ferme en face du danger. S. in love, in adversity, constant en amour, dans l'adversité. **-ly**, *adv.* Fermement; avec constance.

steadfastness ['stedfəstnis], *s.* Fermeté *f* (d'esprit); constance *f.* S. of purpose, ténacité *f* de caractère.

steadiness ['stedinis], *s.* **1.** Fermeté *f.* S. of hand, sûreté *f* de main. **2.** Assiduité *f*, persévérance *f*, application *f.* S. of gaze, fermeté du regard. **3.** Stabilité *f.* S. of prices, tenue *f* des prix. **4.** (*Of pers.*) Conduite rangée; sagesse *f.*

steady¹ ['stedi]. **1.** *a.* (*a*) Ferme, solide; fixe, rigide. To make a table s., caler une table. To keep s., ne pas bouger; rester en place. To have a s. hand, avoir la main sûre. With a s. hand, step, d'une main assurée; d'un pas assuré. *Equit:* To have a s. seat, avoir une bonne assiette. *Mil:* S. fire, feu nourri. Ship s. in a sea, navire qui tient bien la mer. (*b*) Continu, soutenu; persistant; régulier, -ière. To play a s. game, avoir un jeu régulier. S. progress, progrès ininterrompus, soutenus. S. pace, allure réglée. S. trot, trot soutenu. S. pulse, pouls égal. S. weather, temps établi. S. downpour, pluie persistante. S. barometer, baromètre stationnaire. *Com:* S. demand for . . ., demande suivie pour. . . . (*c*) S. worker, travailleur assidu, régulier. (*d*) (*Of pers.*) Rangé, posé; sérieux, -euse, sage. **2.** *adv. & int.* (*a*) S.! (i) ne bougez pas! (ii) *Mil:* fixe! S. (on)! (i) doucement! du calme! (ii) attention (de ne pas tomber)! (*b*) *Nau:* Steady! comme ça! **3.** *s.* (*a*) Support *m* (pour la main, etc.). (*b*) Lunette *f* (d'un tour). **-ily**, *adv.* **1.** Fermement. To walk s., marcher d'un pas ferme. **2.** (*a*) Régulièrement; sans arrêt. His health grows s. worse, sa santé va (en) empirant. (*b*) Uniment; sans à-coups. **3.** Assidûment. To work s. at sth., travailler assidûment, d'arrache-pied, à qch. **4.** (Se conduire) d'une manière rangée, posée; avec sagesse. **'steady-'going**, *a.* (*Of pers.*) (i) Rangé, sage, sérieux; (ii) pondéré; méthodique.

steady² **1.** *v.tr.* (*a*) Raffermir, affermir. To s. a table-leg, caler le pied d'une table. To s. one's hand, assurer sa main. To s. oneself against sth., s'étayer contre qch. To s. the nerves, raffermir les nerfs. (*b*) Assagir (un jeune homme). **2.** *v.i.* Se raffermir; reprendre son aplomb. **steady down. 1.** *v.tr.* Assagir (qn). **2.** *v.i.* The market has steadied down, le marché a repris son aplomb. Young man who has steadied down, jeune homme qui s'est rangé.

steak [steik], *s. Cu:* (*a*) Tranche *f* (de viande, de poisson); darne *f* (de saumon). (*b*) Bifteck *m*; (*cut from the ribs*) entrecôte *f.* Fillet s., tournedos *m*. Thin grilled s., entrecôte *f* minute.

steal [sti:l], *v.* (*stole* [stoul]; *stolen* ['stoul(ə)n]) **1.** *v.tr.* (*a*) Voler, dérober, soustraire (sth. from s.o., qch. à qn). To s. money from the till, voler de l'argent dans la caisse. (*b*) To s. s.o.'s heart, séduire le cœur de qn. To s. a few hours from one's work, dérober quelques heures à son travail. (*c*) To s. a glance at s.o., jeter furtivement un regard à qn; regarder qn à la dérobée, d'un œil furtif. (*d*) To s. a march on the enemy, on s.o., gagner une marche sur l'ennemi; devancer qn; circonvenir qn. **2.** *v.i.* To s. away, down, in, out, s'en aller, descendre, entrer, sortir, à la dérobée, furtivement. He stole away, il s'esquiva. He stole into the room, il se faufila, se glissa, dans la pièce. To s. along, marcher à pas de loup. A smile stole across her lips, elle eut un sourire furtif. **stealing**, *s.* Vol *m*.

stealer ['sti:lər], *s.* Voleur, -euse (of, de). Sheep-s., voleur de moutons.

stealth [stelθ], *s.* (*Only in the phr.*) By s., à la dérobée; furtivement.

stealthiness ['stelθinis], *s.* Caractère furtif (d'une action).

stealthy ['stelθi], *a.* Furtif, -ive. S. glance, regard dérobé. **-ily**, *adv.* A la dérobée; furtivement; *F:* à la sauvette. To creep in s., entrer à pas de loup.

steam¹ [sti:m], *s.* (*a*) Vapeur *f* (d'eau); buée *f.* Room full of s., salle remplie de buée. (*b*) *Ph: Mch:* Wet s., vapeur mouillée. Dry s., vapeur sèche. Heated by s., chauffé à la vapeur. To work by s., fonctionner à la vapeur. To get up s., to raise s., mettre (la chaudière) sous pression. To keep up s., rester sous pression. To let off, blow off, s., (i) lâcher la vapeur; (ii) *F:* dépenser son superflu d'énergie; (iii) *F:* épancher sa bile. Engine under s., machine sous pression. To put on full s., mettre à toute vitesse. To make all s., pousser les feux. At full s., à toute vapeur. *Nau:* Full s. ahead! en avant à toute vapeur! en avant toute! (*Of damaged ship*) To proceed under its own s., marcher par ses seuls moyens. **'steam-'boiler**, *s.* Chaudière *f* (à vapeur); générateur *m*. **'steam-cock**, *s.* Prise *f* de vapeur. **'steam-'crane**, *s.* Grue *f* à vapeur. **'steam-driven**, *a.* Actionné par la vapeur; à vapeur. **'steam-engine**, *s.* **1.** Machine *f* à vapeur. **2.** *F:* Locomotive *f.* **'steam-gauge**, *s.* Manomètre *m* de pression. **'steam-'hammer**, *s.* Marteau-pilon *m* à vapeur. **'steam-heating**, *s.* Chauffage *m* à la vapeur. **'steam-'jacket**, *s. Mch:* Chemise *f* de vapeur. **'steam-'pressure**, *s.* Tension *f* de vapeur. **'steam(-)'radio**, *s. F:* (*As opposed to television*) Radio *f.* **'steam-'roller**, *s.* (*a*) *Civ.E:* Cylindre *m* compresseur à vapeur; rouleau *m* compresseur. (*b*) Force *f* irrésistible. **'steam-'shovel**, *s. O:* Pelle *f* à vapeur; excavateur *m*.

steam² **1.** *v.tr.* (*a*) *Cu:* Cuire (des légumes) à la vapeur, à l'étuvée. (*b*) Passer (qch) à la vapeur. *Tex:* Délustrer (le drap). To s. open an envelope, décacheter une lettre à la vapeur. **2.** *v.i.* (*a*) Jeter, exhaler, de la vapeur; fumer. The soup steams on the table, la soupe fume sur la table. Horses steaming with sweat, chevaux fumants (de sueur). (*b*) Marcher (à la vapeur). To s. ahead, (i) avancer (à la vapeur); (ii) faire des progrès rapides. The train steamed away, steamed off, le train partit. The ship steamed out of port, le navire sortit du port. To s. at ten knots, filer dix nœuds. **steam up**, *v.i.* (*a*) Mettre la vapeur. (*b*) (*Of window, etc.*) S'embuer. **steaming** *a.* Fumant. Steaming hot, tout chaud.

steamboat ['sti:mbout], *s.* Bateau *m*, navire *m*, à vapeur; vapeur *m*; steamboat *m*.

steamer ['sti:mər], *s.* **1.** = STEAMSHIP. **2.** *Cu:* Marmite *f* à vapeur.

steamship ['sti:mʃip], *s.* Navire *m* à vapeur; vapeur *m*; paquebot *m*.

steamy ['sti:mi], *a.* Plein de vapeur, de buée; (*of atmosphere*) humide.

stearate ['stiəreit], *s. Ch:* Stéarate *m*.

stearic [sti'ærik, 'stiərik], *a. Ch:* Stéarique.

stearin(e) ['stiərin], *s. Ch:* Stéarine *f.* S. candle, bougie *f* stéarique.

steatite ['stiətait], *s. Miner:* Stéatite *f.*

steatosis [stiə'tousis], *s. Med:* Stéatose *f.*

steed [sti:d], *s. Lit:* Coursier *m*.

steel¹ [sti:l], *s.* **1.** *Metall:* Acier *m*. *Metalw:* The iron and s. industry, l'industrie *f* sidérurgique. Heat-resisting s., acier indétrempable. Rolled s., acier laminé. Bar s., acier en barres. Cold-drawn s., acier

étiré à froid. Tungsten s., acier au tungstène. **Spring s.,** acier à, de, ressort. **S. edge** (*of a tool*), acérure *f*. *Electro-Ch:* **S. bath,** bain d'aciérage. *Dom.Ec:* **S. wool,** laine *f* d'acier. **Grip of s.,** poigne d'acier. **Heart of s.,** cœur *m* de fer. *S.a.* STAINLESS 2. **2.** *Lit:* Fer *m*, épée *f*; lame *f*. **To fight with cold s.,** se battre à l'arme blanche. **3.** (*a*) (*For sharpening knives*) Fusil *m*; affiloir *m*. (*b*) A: (*For striking light*) Briquet *m*. **4.** Busc *m* (de corset). **'steel-clad,** *a.* Couvert, revêtu, d'acier; (*of ancient knight*) bardé de fer. **'steel-en'graving,** *s.* **1.** Gravure *f* sur acier. **2.** Estampe *f* sur acier. **steel-'plate,** *s.* **1.** Tôle *f* d'acier. **2.** *Engr:* Planche *f* d'acier. **steel-'plated,** *a.* Cuirassé.
steel², *v.tr.* **1.** (*a*) Aciérer, acérer, armer (un outil). (*b*) *Electro-Ch:* To s.(-face) a copper plate, aciérer une plaque de cuivre. (*c*) *Metall:* Aciérer (le fer). **3. To s. oneself, to s. one's heart, to do sth.,** (i) s'endurcir à faire qch.; (ii) s'armer de courage pour faire qch. **To s. oneself against sth.,** se raidir, se cuirasser, contre qch. *Lit:* **Selfishness had steeled his heart,** l'égoïsme lui avait endurci le cœur. **steeling,** *s. Metall:* Aciérage *m*.
steeliness ['sti:linis], *s.* Dureté *f*; inflexibilité *f* (de caractère, etc).
steelwork ['sti:lwə:k], *s.* **1.** (*a*) Constructional s., profilés *mpl* pour constructions. (*b*) *Aut: etc:* Tôleries *fpl.* **2.** *pl.* **Steelworks,** aciérie *f*.
steely ['sti:li], *a.* **1.** D'acier; (fer) aciéreux, aciéré. **2.** D'acier; dur, inflexible. **To flash a s. glance at s.o.,** lancer un regard dur à qn.
steelyard ['sti:lja:d, 'stiljəd], *s.* (Balance) romaine *f*; peson *m* à contrepoids.
steenbok ['sti:nbɔk], *s. Z:* Steinbock *m*.
steep¹ [sti:p]. **1.** (*a*) Escarpé; à pic; raide. **S. gradient,** forte pente; pente raide, rapide. **The slopes grow steeper,** les pentes s'escarpent. **S. path,** chemin ardu. **S. climb,** rude montée; montée raide. *Nau:* **S. shore,** côte accore. *Av:* **S. start,** départ en chandelle. **Too s. a dive,** descente trop piquée. (*b*) *F:* **That's a bit s.!** c'est un peu fort! c'est un peu raide! **S. price,** prix exorbitant; prix salé. **2.** *s.* Pente *f* rapide; escarpement *m*; à-pic *m*. **-ly,** *adv.* En pente rapide; à pic.
steep², *s. Ind:* **1.** = STEEPING. **To put sth. in s.,** mettre qch. à tremper. **2.** Bain *m* (de macération).
steep³. 1. *v.tr.* (*a*) Baigner, tremper; mettre (qch.) à tremper, à macérer; mouiller (le linge); infuser (des herbes) à froid. **To s. flax,** rouir le lin. (*b*) Saturer, imbiber (**sth. in sth.,** qch. de qch.). **Steeped in the classics,** nourri des (auteurs) classiques. **To s. oneself in the atmosphere of the Middle Ages,** se tremper, se plonger, dans l'atmosphère du moyen âge. **Steeped in ignorance, in prejudice,** croupi dans l'ignorance; imbibé de préjugés. **2.** *v.i.* (*Of soiled linen, etc.*) Tremper; (*of flax*) rouir; (*of herbs*) infuser (à froid). **steeping,** *s. Ind: etc:* Trempage *m*, macération *f*, trempée *f*; mouillage *m* (du linge); rouissage *m* (du chanvre); infusion *f* à froid.
steepen ['sti:p(ə)n]. **1.** *v.i.* (*a*) (*Of road, etc.*) S'escarper; devenir plus raide. (*b*) (*Of prices*) Augmenter. **2.** *v.tr.* *F:* Augmenter, hausser (un prix, un impôt).
steeple ['sti:pl], *s.* (*a*) Clocher *m*. (*b*) Flèche *f* (de clocher).
steeplechase ['sti:pltʃeis], *s. Rac:* Steeple-chase *m*, *F:* steeple *m*.
steeplechaser ['sti:pltʃeisər], *s. Rac:* **1.** Cheval *m* de steeple(-chase), steeple-chaser *m*. **2.** Jockey *m* de steeple *m*.
steepled ['sti:pld], *a.* (*Of church*) A clocher; surmonté d'un clocher.
steeplejack ['sti:pldʒæk], *s.* Réparateur *m* de clochers, de cheminées d'usines.
steepness ['sti:pnis], *s.* Raideur *f*, rapidité *f*, escarpement *m* (d'une pente). *Mth:* **S. of a curve,** degré *m* d'inclinaison d'une courbe.
steer¹ ['stiər], *v.tr.* Gouverner (un navire); conduire, diriger, mener (un bateau, une auto); barrer (un yacht). *Abs.* **To s.,** gouverner; tenir la barre, le gouvernail; *Row:* barrer. **To s. by the wind,** gouverner d'après le vent. **To s. the course,** faire route; gouverner en route. **To s. north,** faire route au nord. **To s. (one's course) for . . .,** faire route,

mettre le cap, sur. . . . **To s. clear of sth.,** éviter, s'écarter de, qch. (*With passive force*) **Ship that steers well, badly,** navire qui gouverne bien, mal. **The ship refused to s.,** le navire ne gouvernait plus. **steering,** *s.* **1.** (*a*) Direction *f*, conduite *f* (d'un bateau, d'une auto). *Aut:* **Ease of s.,** facilité *f* de braquage. *Pol: etc:* **S. committee,** comité *m* d'organisation (d'une association, etc.). (*b*) = STEERING-GEAR. **2.** *Nau:* Manœuvre *f* de la barre. (*Of ship*) **To have lost s. control,** n'être plus maître de sa manœuvre. **'steering-column,** *s. Aut:* Colonne *f* de direction. **'steering-gear,** *s.* Appareil *m* à gouverner. *Aut:* (i) *Coll:* Ensemble *m* des organes de direction; (ii) boîte *f* de direction. *Av:* Direction *f*. *Nau:* Servomoteur *m* de gouvernail. **'steering-wheel,** *s.* **1.** (*a*) *Nau:* Roue *f* de gouvernail. (*b*) *Aut:* Volant *m*. **2.** *Cy:* Roue directrice.
steer², *s.* **1.** Jeune bœuf *m*; bouvillon *m*. **2.** *U.S:* Bœuf; taureau *m*.
steerage ['stiəridʒ], *s. Nau: A:* Emménagements *mpl* pour passagers de dernière classe, pour émigrants; entrepont *m*. **To travel s.,** faire la traversée en dernière classe. **'steerage-way,** *s.* Erre *f* pour gouverner. (*Of ship*) **To have good s.-w.,** sentir la barre.
steersman, *pl.* **-men** ['stiəzmən], *s.m. Nau:* Homme de barre; timonier.
stein [stain], *s. U.S:* Chope *f*.
steinbok ['stainbɔk], *s.* = STEENBOK.
stele, *pl.* **-ae** ['sti:li, -i:], *s.* Stèle *f*.
stellar ['stelər], *a.* Stellaire.
stellate ['steleit], **stellated** [ste'leitid], *a. Nat. Hist:* Étoilé; en étoile; radié.
stem¹ [stem], *s.* **1.** (*a*) *Bot:* Tige *f* (de plante, de fleur); queue *f* (de fruit, de feuille); pétiole *m*, hampe *f* (de fleur); tronc *m*, souche *f* (d'arbre); stipe *m* (de palmier). **Underground s.,** rhizome *m*. (*b*) Régime *m* (de bananes). (*c*) Dague *f* (de cerf de deux ans). (*a*) *Pied m*, patte *f* (de verre à boire); tige, queue (de soupape); tige (de vis); broche *f* (de serrure); tuyau *m* (de pipe de fumeur); arbre *m* (de grue). (*b*) *Mus:* Queue (d'une note). **3.** (*a*) Souche (de famille). (*b*) *Ling:* Thème *m*, radical *m* (d'un mot). **4.** *N.Arch:* Étrave *f*, avant *m*; *A. & Lit:* proue *f*. **Cutwater s.,** étrave à guibre. **From s. to stern,** de l'avant à l'arrière. **5.** *Skiing:* Chasse-neige *m inv*; stembogen *m*. **'stem-turn,** *s. Skiing:* Virage *m* en chasse-neige; stembogen *m*.
stem² (**stemmed**) **1.** *v.tr.* Égrapper (des raisins); écôter (des feuilles de tabac). **2.** *v.i.* **To s. from,** être issu de; être le résultat de.
stem³, *v.tr.* **1.** Contenir, arrêter, endiguer (un cours d'eau); enrayer (une épidémie). **To s. the course of events,** endiguer la marche des événements. **2.** Aller contre, lutter contre (la marée); refouler, remonter (le courant); (*of ship*) étaler (le courant); refouler, résister à (une attaque). **To s. the tide of popular indignation,** endiguer le flot de l'indignation publique.
stemmed [stemd], *a.* **1.** (Fleur, etc.) à tige, à queue; (verre) à pied, à patte. **2.** *Bot:* **Long-s.,** longicaule. **Thick-s.,** crassicaule.
stembogen ['stemboug(ə)n], *s. Skiing:* Stembogen *m*.
stemless ['stemlis], *a. Bot:* Sans tige; acaule.
stench [sten(t)ʃ], *s.* Odeur infecte; puanteur *f*.
stencil¹ ['stensl], *s.* **1.** (*a*) Patron (ajouré); poncif *m*; pochoir *m*. **S.-plate,** pochoir. (*b*) Cipher-s., grille *f*. **2.** Peinture *f*, décoration *f*, au poncif, au pochoir. **3.** *Typewr: etc:* Stencil *m*. **'stencil-brush,** *s.* Pinceau *m*, brosse *f*, à poncer. **'stencil-paper,** *s.* Papier *m* stencil.
stencil², *v.tr.* (**stencilled**) (*a*) Peindre, marquer, imprimer, (qch.) au patron ou au pochoir; passer (un dessin) au pochoir. *Ind:* Marquer (une caisse, un ballot). (*b*) Polycopier (une circulaire); tirer (une circulaire) au stencil.
sten-gun ['stengʌn], *s. Mil: etc:* = Fusil-mitrailleur *m*, *pl.* fusils-mitrailleurs.
stenographer [ste'nɔgrəfər], *s.* Sténographe *mf*, *F:* sténo *mf*.
stenography [ste'nɔgrəfi], *s.* Sténographie *f*.
stenotype¹ ['stenotaip], *s.* Sténotype *m*.
stenotype², *v.tr.* Sténotyper.
stenotypist ['steno'taipist], *s.* Sténotypiste *mf*.

stenotypy ['steno'taipi], s. Sténotypie f.

Stentor ['stentɔːr]. 1. Pr.n.m. Stentor. 2. s. (a) Prot: Stentor m. (b) Z: S. (monkey), stentor.

stentorian [sten'tɔːriən], a. (Voix) de Stentor.

step[1] [step], s. 1. Pas m. To take a s., faire un pas. To take a s. back, forward, faire un pas en arrière, en avant. To turn, bend, one's steps towards . . ., se diriger vers . . .; diriger ses pas vers. . . . S. by s., pas à pas; petit à petit. To fall back s. by s., reculer pied à pied. To retrace one's steps, revenir sur ses pas. Within a s. of the house, à deux pas de la maison. It is a good s., c'est un bon bout de chemin; il y a une bonne trotte. That is a great s. forward, c'est déjà un grand pas de fait. To tread in the steps of s.o., marcher sur les traces de qn. 2. (a) Pas, cadence f. Mil: Mus: Quick s., pas redoublé; pas accéléré. To keep s., to be in s., marcher au pas; être au pas. To fall into s., se mettre au pas. To break s., rompre le pas. (b) El.E: Alternators in s., alternateurs accrochés, en phase. (c) Waltz s., pas de valse. 3. Démarche f. Untimely s., démarche inopportune. To take a rash s., commettre une imprudence. If you take such a s. . . ., si vous agissez de la sorte. . . . To take the necessary steps, all useful steps, faire les démarches nécessaires; prendre toutes les dispositions utiles. To take steps to do sth., aviser, se préparer, à faire qch. A s. in the right direction, un pas dans la bonne voie. The first s. will be to . . ., la première chose à faire, ce sera de. . . . His first steps in this career, ses débuts m dans cette carrière. 4. (a) Marche f, degré m, pas (d'un escalier); échelon m, barreau m (d'une échelle); marchepied m (d'un véhicule). Cellar steps, descente f. Top s. (of a stair), palière f. The steps of the altar, le marchepied de l'autel. The steps of the throne, les marches du trône. Flight of steps, (i) escalier; (ii) perron m. (b) Gradin m, étage m (de cône-poulie). 5. (Pair, set, of) steps, escabeau m; échelle f double. Folding steps, escabeau pliant. Av: Steps, passerelle f. 6. (a) Cran m. Steps of a key, dents f d'une clef. (b) Redan m (d'hydroglisseur). 'step-dance, s. Danse f de caractère. 'step-ladder, s. Escabeau m; échelle f double.

step[2], v. (stepped [stept]) I. v.i. Faire un pas, des pas; marcher pas à pas; marcher, aller. S. this way, venez par ici. II. step, v.tr. 1. (a) To s. (off, out) a distance, mesurer une distance au pas. (b) To s. a minuet, danser un menuet. 2. Disposer en échelons; échelonner. 3. Nau: Mettre (un mât) dans son emplanture. step across, v.i. Traverser (la rue, etc.). step aside, v.i. 1. S'écarter, se ranger. 2. Se détourner de son chemin. step back, v.i. Faire un pas en arrière; reculer. step down. 1. v.i. Descendre. 2. v.tr. (a) El.E: To s. down the current, the voltage, réduire la tension; dévolter le courant. (b) Mec.E: To s. down the gear, démultiplier la transmission. step forward, v.i. S'avancer; faire un pas en avant. step in, v.i. 1. Entrer; (into car, etc.) monter (en voiture). 2. F: Intervenir; s'interposer. 'step-'in, s. Vêtement m facile à mettre. step off, v.i. (a) To s. off with the left foot, partir du pied gauche. (b) Descendre (de voiture, d'autobus, etc.). step on, v.i. 1. Mettre le pied sur, marcher sur (qch.). Someone stepped on my foot, on m'a marché sur le pied. F: Aut: To s. on the gas, to s. on it, écraser le champignon; mettre tous les gaz. To s. on the brakes, donner un coup de frein. 2. Nau: To s. on board, monter à bord. step out, v.i. 1. Sortir; descendre (de voiture). As we stepped out into the sunshine . . ., tandis que nous débouchions au soleil. . . . 2. (a) Allonger le pas. (b) Marcher avec entrain. step over, v.i. 1. Franchir; enjamber (un obstacle). 2. To s. o. to s.o.'s house, faire un saut jusque chez qn (qui habite en face). step up. 1. v.i. (a) Monter. (b) S'approcher (to, de). 2. v.tr. El.E: To s. up the current, survolter le courant; augmenter la tension. S.-up transformer, survolteur m. stepped, a. A gradins, en gradins, à étages; échelonné, en échelons. S. gear(ing), engrenage en échelon. 'stepping-stone, s. 1. Marchepied m. To take a job as a s.-s. (to a better position), prendre un poste comme tremplin. 2. pl. S.-stones, pierres de gué.

stepbrother ['step'brʌðər], s.m. Frère consanguin, frère utérin; demi-frère.

stepchild, pl. -children ['steptʃaild, -'tʃildr(ə)n], s. Enfant mf d'un autre lit.

stepdaughter ['step'dɔːtər], s.f. Belle-fille (née d'un lit antérieur), pl. belles-filles.

stepfather ['step'fɑːðər], s.m. Beau-père (second mari de la mère), pl. beaux-pères.

Stephen ['stiːvn]. Pr.n.m. Étienne.

stepmother ['step'mʌðər], s.f. Belle-mère (seconde femme du père), pl. belles-mères.

steppe [step], s. Ph.Geog: Steppe f.

stepsister ['step'sistər], s.f. Sœur consanguine, sœur utérine; demi-sœur.

stepson ['stepsʌn], s.m. Beau-fils (né d'un lit antérieur), pl. beaux-fils.

stereo ['steriou], s. & a. F: 1. = STEREOTYPE[1] 1. 2. = STEREOSCOPE, STEREOSCOPIC. 3. = STEREO-PHONY, STEREOPHONIC.

NOTE. For words beginning stereo- an alternative pronunciation [stiər-] is also acceptable.

stereochemistry ['steriou'kemistri], s. Stéréochimie f.

stereographic [steriə'græfik], a. Stéréographique.

stereography [steri'ogrəfi], s. Stéréographie f.

stereometry [steri'omitri], s. Stéréométrie f.

stereophonic [sterio'fonik], a. Stéréophonique.

stereophony [steri'ofoni], s. Stéréophonie f.

stereophotography ['sterioufə'togrəfi], s. Stéréophoto-graphie f.

stereoscope ['steriəskoup], s. Opt: Stéréoscope m.

stereoscopic ['steriə'skopik], a. Stéréoscopique. S. camera, appareil m stéréoscopique. S. television, télévision f en relief. -ally, adv. Stéréoscopiquement.

stereotomy ['steri'otəmi], s. Geom: Stéréotomie f.

stereotype[1] ['sterioutaip]. Typ: 1. s. Cliché m. 2. a. Stéréotypé, cliché. S. printing, stéréotypie f.

stereotype[2], v.tr. Typ: Stéréotyper, clicher. stereo-typed, a. Typ: Stéréotypé. F: S. phrase, cliché m.

stereotypy ['steriətaipi], s. Stéréotypie f.

sterile ['sterail], a. 1. Stérile; (d'un animal) bréhaigne. 2. Bac: Stérile, aseptique.

sterility [ste'riliti], s. Stérilité f.

sterilization [sterilai'zeiʃ(ə)n], s. Stérilisation f. S. of milk, stérilisation f du lait.

sterilize ['sterilaiz], v.tr. Stériliser. Sterilized milk, lait stérilisé. Sterilized gauze, gaze stérilisée.

sterilizer ['sterilaizər], s. Stérilisateur m; autoclave m.

sterling ['stəːliŋ], a. 1. (Monnaie, or) de bon aloi, d'aloi. 2. Pound s., livre f sterling. Fin: S. area, zone f sterling. 3. De bon aloi, vrai, véritable, solide. S. qualities, qualités solides.

stern[1] [stəːn], a. Sévère, rigide, dur. S. countenance, visage austère. -ly, adv. Sévèrement; durement.

stern[2], s. 1. Nau: (a) Arrière m; poupe f. (Of ship) To sink s. foremost, couler par l'arrière. To go out s. first, appareiller en culant. To anchor by the s., mouiller en croupière. To be (down) by the s., être enfoncé par l'arrière. S. ladder, échelle de poupe. (b) Arrière-bec m (d'un ponton). (c) F: Postérieur m, derrière m. (b) Ven: Queue f (d'un chien courant). 'stern-chase, s. Navy: Chasse f dans les eaux du navire chassé. 'stern-chaser, s. Navy: Canon m, pièce f, de retraite. 'stern-fast, s. Nau: Amarre f (de l')arrière; croupière f. 'stern-light, s. Nau: Feu m d'arrière; feu de poupe. 'stern-oar, s. Nau: Aviron m de queue; godille f. 'stern-post, s. Nau: Étambot m. 'stern-sheet(s), s. Nau: Arrière m, chambre f (d'une embarcation). 'stern-way, s. Nau: Marche f arrière; aculée f. To gather s.-w., culer; aller de l'arrière.

sternmost ['stəːnmoust], a. Le plus à l'arrière ((i) à bord, (ii) de l'escadre).

sternness ['stəːnnis], s. Sévérité f; austérité f; dureté f.

sternum ['stəːnəm], s. Anat: Sternum m.

sternutation [stəːnju'teiʃ(ə)n], s. Sternutation f, éternuement m.

stertorous ['stəːtərəs], a. Med: Stertoreux, -euse, ronflant.

stet[1] [stet], Lt.imp. Typ: Bon; à maintenir.

stet[2], v.tr. (stetted) Typ: Maintenir (un mot sur l'épreuve, sur le MS.).

stethoscope ['steθəskoup], *s. Med:* Stéthoscope *m.*

stetson ['stetsn], *s.* Chapeau à larges bords (pour hommes).

stevedore ['stiːvdɔːr], *s. Nau:* 1. (*Labourer*) Arrimeur *m*; déchargeur *m.* 2. Entrepreneur *m* d'arrimage; entrepreneur de chargement et de déchargement.

stew[1] [stjuː], *s.* 1. *A:* (*a*) Maison *f* de bains. (*b*) *pl.* Lieu *m* de débauche. 2. (*a*) *Cu:* Ragoût *m*; civet *m* (de chevreuil, etc.); *Mil: P:* ratatouille *f*, rata *m.* Mutton s., ragoût de mouton; navarin *m.* Irish s., ragoût de mouton à l'irlandaise. (*b*) *F:* To be in a s., être sur des charbons ardents; être dans tous ses états. (*c*) *F:* What a s.! quelle chaleur ici! quelle étuve!

stew[2]. 1. *v.tr. Cu:* Faire cuire (la viande) en ragoût, à la casserole. To s. some mutton, faire un ragoût de mouton. To s. a rabbit, fricasser un lapin. To s. fruit, faire cuire des fruits en compote. 2. *v.i.* (*a*) *Cu:* Cuire à la casserole; mijoter. *F:* To let s.o. s. in his own juice, laisser qn mijoter (dans son jus). (*b*) *F:* Étouffer; manquer d'air. stewed, *a.* (*a*) S. mutton, ragoût *m* de mouton. S. beef, bœuf (à la) mode; bœuf en daube. S. fruit, compote *f* de fruits; fruits en compote. S. prunes, pruneaux au jus. S. apples, marmelade *f* de pommes. (*b*) S. tea, thé trop infusé.

stew[3], *s.* 1. Vivier *m.* 2. Huîtrière *f*; parc *m* à huîtres.

steward ['stjuəd], *s.* 1. Économe *m*, régisseur *m*, intendant *m* (d'une propriété). 2. (*a*) Maître *m* d'hôtel (d'une maison, d'un cercle). (*b*) *Nau:* Commis *m* aux vivres. Steward's room, cambuse *f.* (*c*) *Nau:* Garçon *m* (de cabine); *Nau: Av:* steward *m.* Chief s., maître d'hôtel. 3. Commissaire *m* (d'une réunion sportive, d'un bal). 4. *Ind:* Shop s., délégué *m* d'atelier, d'usine, du personnel; délégué syndical.

stewardess ['stjuədis], *s.f. Nau:* Femme de chambre.

stewardship ['stjuədʃip], *s.* Économat *m*, intendance *f*; charge *f* de régisseur. To give an account of one's s., rendre compte de sa gestion.

stewpan ['stjuːpæn], stewpot ['stjuːpɔt], *s.* Braisière *f*; daubière *f*; cocotte *f*, faitout *m*; *esp.U.S:* (grande) casserole *f.*

stick[1] [stik], *s.* 1. (*a*) Bâton *m.* To get the s., recevoir des coups de bâton. The big s., le recours à la force; la politique de la force. *S.a.* CLEAVE[1] 1. *Hort:* Pea sticks, rames *f.* Hop sticks, vine sticks, échalas *m.* (*b*) Walking s., canne *f.* Loaded stick, canne plombée. (*c*) Manche *m* (à balai); canne, manche (de parapluie); baguette *f* (de fusée volante). S. of a violin bow, baguette d'archet. *Av:* Direction s., manche à balai. S. full back, manche au ventre. To ease the s., rendre la main. To ease the s. back, tirer sur le manche. (*d*) *Sp:* Crosse *f* (de hockey). (*At hockey*) To give sticks, couper; donner des crosses. (*e*) Morceau *m* de bois. To gather sticks, ramasser du bois sec, du petit bois. Cherry s., bâtonnet *m* (pour cerise de cocktail). *S.a.* ORANGE-STICK. *F:* Not a s. was saved, on n'a pas sauvé une allumette. Without a s. of furniture, sans un meuble. *f*) *Typ:* (Setting-)s., composteur *m.* 2. *F:* (*Of pers.*) (*a*) Queer s., drôle de type, drôle d'oiseau. Old s., vieille perruque. (*b*) Personne *f* sans entrain, sans talent; acteur *m* au jeu raide; *P:* godiche *mf.* 3. Bâton (de sucre d'orge, de cire à cacheter, etc.); doigt *m* (de chocolat); *El:* baguette *f* (de charbon). *Cu:* Bread s., gressin *m.* S. sulphur, soufre en canons. *S.a.* LIPSTICK, SHAVING-STICK. 4. S. of celery, branche *f* de céleri. S. of rhubarb, tige *f* de rhubarbe. 5. *Av: Mil:* A s. of bombs, un chapelet de bombes. 'stick-insect, *s. Ent:* Phasme *m.*

stick[2], *v.* (stuck [stʌk]; stuck) I. *v.tr.* 1. (*a*) Piquer, enfoncer (into, dans). To s. a dagger into s.o., percer qn d'un poignard. To s. a stake in the ground, ficher un pieu en terre. To s. a pin through sth., passer une épingle à travers qch. (*b*) To s. s.o. with a bayonet, enfoncer une baïonnette dans le corps de qn. To s. a pig, (*of butcher*) égorger, saigner, un porc. To s. s.o. with a bayonet, (*of butcher*) saigner un porc. (*c*) Planter, fixer (sth. on a spike, qch. sur une pointe). 2. *F:* (= *put, place*) To s. a rose in one's buttonhole, mettre une rose à sa boutonnière. To s. one's hat on one's head, planter son chapeau sur sa tête. To s. a candle in a bottle, ficher une bougie dans une bouteille. S. it in your pocket,

fourrez-le dans votre poche. S. in a few commas, insérez quelques virgules. 3. Coller. To s. photographs in an album, fixer, coller, des photographies dans un album. Trunk stuck all over with labels, malle bardée d'étiquettes. To s. a postage stamp (on a letter), timbrer (une lettre). *S.a.* BILL[4] 3. 4 *F:* Supporter, endurer, souffrir (qn, qch.). To s. it, tenir le coup; tenir. I can't s., je ne peux pas le sentir. 5. *Hort:* Ramer (des pois, etc.). II. *v.i.* 1. Se piquer, s'enfoncer, se ficher, se planter. The arrows s. in the target, les flèches se piquent dans la cible. 2. (*a*) (Se) coller, s'attacher, tenir, adhérer (to, à); happer (aux lèvres, à la langue). The envelope will not s., l'enveloppe ne veut pas (se) coller. The vegetables have stuck to the pan, les légumes ont attaché. The name stuck to him, ce nom lui (en) est resté. It sticks like pitch, cela colle comme poix. To s. by, to, a friend, s'attacher à un ami; ne pas abandonner un ami. He has stuck to me, il m'est resté fidèle. To s. together, faire preuve de solidarité. To s. like a limpet, like a leech, like glue, like a burr (to s.o.), se cramponner à qn); *F:* cramponner (qn). To s. to one's post, rester à son poste. S. to it! persévérez! ne lâchez pas! *F:* To s. to one's guns, to one's opinions, ne pas en démordre. To s. to (the) facts, s'en tenir aux faits. To s. to it, il ne veut pas en démordre. *S.a.* LAST[1]. (*b*) *F:* To s. to sth., garder qch. pour soi. S. to what you've got! ne lâchez pas ce que vous avez! (*c*) *F:* Rester. Here I am and here I s., j'y suis, j'y reste. He sticks to his room, il ne sort pas de sa chambre. 3. (*a*) To s., to be stuck, to become stuck, être pris, engagé; (*in mud, etc.*) s'embourber, être embourbé, s'enliser. To get stuck in a bog, s'embourber dans un marécage. (*Of boat*) To s. fast, s'enliser. To s., to be stuck (in a speech), *F:* rester en carafe, en panne. (*b*) (*To be caught, jammed*) Être pris, être engagé, rester pris, s'empêtrer; (*of machine parts*) (se) coincer, gommer; *Aut:* (*of valve, etc.*) rester collé. It sticks in my throat, je ne peux pas avaler ça. The lift has stuck, l'ascenseur est en panne. *Aut:* The switch was stuck, le contact était collé. stick around, *v.i. F:* Attendre. He always sticks a., ce qu'il est collant. S. a.! I'll be back in 10 minutes, bouge pas! je reviens dans dix minutes. To s. a. the house all day, traîner dans la maison toute la journée. stick at, *v.i.* 1. To s. at a difficulty, s'arrêter devant, achopper contre, une difficulté. To s. at doing sth., se faire scrupule de faire qch. To s. at nothing, ne reculer devant rien. 2. To s. at a job for six hours, travailler à qch. pendant six heures d'arrache-pied. stick down, *v.tr.* 1. *F:* (*a*) S. it down anywhere, mettez-le, collez-le, n'importe où. To s. sth. down in a note-book, inscrire qch. sur un carnet. 2. To s. down an envelope, fermer, coller, une enveloppe. stick on. 1. *v.tr.* (*a*) Coller, fixer (un timbre, etc.). (*b*) *F:* To s. it on, (i) surfaire, saler, l'addition, la note; (ii) *O:* se donner de grands airs; faire l'important. 2. *v.i.* Rester collé; adhérer; s'agripper. 'stick-on, *attrib.a.* S.-on label, étiquette adhésive. stick out. 1. *v.tr.* (*a*) Faire dépasser (qch.); sortir (qch.). To s. out one's tongue, tirer la langue. To s. o. one's chest, bomber la poitrine. *F:* To s. o. one's neck, prendre des risques. I've stuck my neck out, je l'ai cherché, je me suis avancé. (*b*) *F:* To s. it out, tenir jusqu'au bout. 2. *v.i.* (*a*) Faire saillie; ressortir. To s. out beyond sth., dépasser qch. (*b*) *F:* To s. out for sth., s'obstiner à demander qch. stick up. 1. *v.tr.* (*a*) *F:* Dresser (une cible, etc.). *P:* S. 'em up! haut les mains! (*b*) To s. up a bill, a notice, afficher un avis. 2. *v.i.* (*a*) Se dresser; se tenir debout. His hair sticks straight up, il a les cheveux en brosse. The end keeps sticking up, le bout persiste à se relever. (*b*) *F:* To s. up for s.o., prendre la défense de qn. sticking, *s.* 1. Adhésion *f* (to, à); collage *m*, collement *m* (de deux choses). 2. Arrêt *m*, coincement *m. Mch:* Blocage *m. I.C.E:* Gommage *m* (du piston); grippage *m* (du moteur). 'sticking-plaster, *s. Pharm:* Taffetas gommé, sparadrap *m.* 'stick-in-the-mud, *s. F:* An old s.-in-the-m., un vieux routinier. 'stick-jaw, *s. P:* Bonbons collants; caramels *mpl.*

sticker ['stikər], s. **1.** Tueur m (de porcs). **2.** (a) Couteau m de boucher. (b) Couteau de chasse. **3.** Colleur, -euse (d'affiches). S.a. BILL-STICKER. **4.** F: (a) Rude travailleur. (b) Cr: Batteur prudent. **5.** P: (Of pers.) Crampon m. **6.** Sch: F: Colle f. **7.** Étiquette gommée.

stickiness ['stikinis], s. Viscosité f; nature gluante (d'un produit); adhésivité f.

stickleback ['stiklbæk], s. Ich: Épinoche f.

stickler ['stiklər], s. Rigoriste mf (for sth., à l'égard de qch.). To be a s. for etiquette, être à cheval sur l'étiquette. S. over trifles, tatillon, -onne.

stickpin ['stikpin], s. U.S: Épingle f de cravate.

sticky ['stiki], a. **1.** Collant, gluant, visqueux, -euse, adhésif, -ive. To make one's hands s., s'engluer les mains. Cr: S. wicket, terrain m (de guichet) qui ne rend pas. F: To be on a s. wicket, être dans une situation difficile. **2.** F: (a) Peu accommodant; difficile, désagréable. (b) I had a s. ten minutes, j'ai passé un mauvais quart d'heure. He will come to a s. end, il finira mal.

stiff [stif]. I. a. **1.** (a) Raide, rigide, dur, inflexible. S. shirt-front, plastron empesé. S. brush, brosse dure, rude. (b) S. joint, articulation ankylosée. (Of joint) To grow s., s'ankyloser. To be quite s., (i) (with sitting still) être engourdi; (ii) (after exercise) être tout courbaturé. F: (Of pers.) S. as a poker, raide, droit, comme un piquet. The body was already s., le cadavre était déjà raide. (c) (Of pers.) Raide, contraint, guindé, compassé. S. bow, salut contraint, froid. S. style, style guindé, empesé. (d) (Of pers.) Inflexible, obstiné. To offer a s. resistance, résister opiniâtrement. **2.** (a) (Of door-handle, etc.) Qui fonctionne mal. The handle is s., le bouton est dur. (b) (Of paste, batter) Ferme; (of lubricant) consistant; (of soil) tenace. (c) Nau: S. wind, forte brise. **3.** (a) S. climb, montée rude, pénible, raide. S. examination, examen difficile. S. piece of work, besogne ardue. The book is very s. reading, ce livre est dur à lire. (b) F: S. price, prix salé. (c) A s. whisky, un whisky bien tassé. **-ly,** adv. **1.** Raidement; avec raideur. **2.** D'un air guindé. **3.** (Résister) obstinément II. **stiff,** s. P: **1.** Cadavre m; mac(c)habée m. **2.** Big s., gros bêta. **'stiff-necked,** a. Obstiné, entêté, intraitable.

stiffen ['stifn]. I. v.tr. **1.** (a) Raidir, renforcer (une poutre, etc.); donner plus de rigidité à (qch.). Aut: To s. the springs, durcir la suspension. (b) Age has stiffened his joints, l'âge lui a raidi les membres. (c) Raidir, rendre obstiné (qn). (d) Mil: To s. a battalion, renforcer un bataillon (avec des éléments aguerris). **2.** (a) Donner de la consistance à (une pâte). (b) To s. a drink, corser une boisson. **3.** Rendre (un examen) plus difficile, plus dur. II. v.i. **1.** (a) (Se) raidir; devenir raide. The body had stiffened, le cadavre était déjà raide. (b) (Of pers.) Se raidir; se guinder. **2.** (a) (Of paste, etc.) Prendre de la consistance. (b) Nau: (Of wind) Fraîchir. **3.** (Of examination) Devenir plus difficile. **stiffening,** s. **1.** Raidissement m, consolidation f (de qch.). Aut: etc: S. of the springs, durcissement m de la suspension. Tex: S. of fabrics, apprêt m des étoffes. Mec.E: etc: S. piece, plate, plaque f, tôle f, de renfort. **2.** (a) Empois m; Tex: cati m. Bootm: Contrefort m. (b) Carp: Étrésillons mpl, entretoises fpl.

stiffener ['stifnər], s. **1.** (Pierre f de) renfort m; entretoise f. **2.** F: Verre m d'alcool, etc. Have a s.? Tu prendras un petit verre?

stiffish ['stifiʃ], a. F: **1.** Assez, plutôt, raide. **2.** S. exam paper, composition f assez difficile.

stiffness ['stifnis], s. **1.** (a) Raideur f, rigidité f. (b) S. of manner, raideur, contrainte f; air guindé. (c) Obstination f, opiniâtreté f. **2.** Fermeté f, consistance f (d'une pâte); ténacité f (du sol). **3.** (a) Raideur (d'une pente). (b) Difficulté f (d'un examen).

stifle¹ ['staifl]. **1.** v.tr. (a) Étouffer, suffoquer. To be stifled by the smoke, être asphyxié par la fumée. To s. a revolt at birth, étouffer une révolte dans son germe. (b) Étouffer (un son, les cris de qn). To s. a scandal, étouffer un scandale. (c) Réprimer (une émotion, un éternuement). To s. one's laughter, pouffer dans son mouchoir. To s. one's grief, faire

taire sa douleur. **2.** v.i. Suffoquer, étouffer. **stifling,** a. Étouffant, suffocant. It is s. here! on étouffe ici!

stifle², s. **1.** Z: S.(-joint), grasset m. **2.** Vet: Affection f du grasset.

stigma, pl. **-as, -ata** ['stigmə, -əz, -ətə], s. **1.** (pl. stigmas) (a) A: Flétrissure f (au fer rouge). (b) Stigmate m, tache f; flétrissure (morale). **2.** (pl. stigmata) (a) Nat.Hist: Stigmate (d'un insecte, etc.). (b) Med: Stigmate (de l'hystérie). (c) pl. Stigmates (d'un saint). **3.** Bot: (pl. stigmas) Stigmate (du pistil).

stigmatic [stig'mætik]. **1.** a. Opt: (Objectif) stigmatique. **2.** s. Rel.H: Stigmatisé, -ée.

stigmatize ['stigmətaiz], v.tr. **1.** Marquer de stigmates. **2.** Stigmatiser, flétrir (qn).

stile¹ [stail], s. Échalier m. S.a. DOG¹ 1.

stile², s. Montant m (de porte, etc.).

stiletto, pl. **-os, -oes** [sti'letou, -ouz], s. **1.** (Dagger) Stylet m. **2.** Needlew: Poinçon m. S.a. HEEL¹ 1.

still¹ [stil]. **1.** a. Tranquille. S. Immobile. To keep s., ne pas bouger; se tenir tranquille. To stand s., (i) ne pas bouger; (ii) s'arrêter. There is no standing s., qui n'avance pas recule. His heart stood s., son cœur cessa de battre. (b) Silencieux, -euse. Lit: In the s. watches of the night, pendant les veilles silencieuses de la nuit. S. water, eau tranquille. S.a. DEEP II. 1. B: The s. small voice, la voix de la conscience. (c) S. wines, vins non mousseux. S. champagne, champagne non champagnisé. (d) Art: S. life, nature morte. **2.** s. (a) In the s. of the night, dans le calme de la nuit. (b) Cin: etc: Photographie f publicitaire (tirée d'un film, d'une pièce). **'still(-)birth,** s. Mise f au monde d'un enfant mort-né. Rate of s.(-)births, mortinatalité f. **'still-born,** a. Mort-né, pl. mort-nés.

still². 1. v.tr. Tranquilliser, calmer, apaiser. Lit: To s. s.o.'s fears, calmer les craintes de qn. **2.** v.i. Lit: Se calmer.

still³. 1. adv. (a) Encore. He is s. here, il est toujours ici. I s. have five francs, il me reste cinq francs. In spite of his faults, I love him s., malgré ses fautes je l'aime toujours. (b) S. more, s. less, encore plus, encore moins. **2.** conj. Cependant, pourtant, encore, toutefois, malgré cela. S. the fact remains that . . ., toujours est-il que. . . .

still⁴, s. Alambic m, cornue f. Tar s., cornue à goudron. Oil s., purificateur m d'huile. **'still-room,** s. **1.** A: Laboratoire m de distillerie. **2.** Office f.

stillness ['stilnis], s. Tranquillité f, calme m, repos m, silence m.

stilt [stilt], s. **1.** Échasse f. To be on stilts, (i) être monté sur des échasses; (ii) F: être guindé, ampoulé. **2.** Civ.E: Pilotis m, pieu m. **3.** Manche m, mancheron m (de charrue). **4.** The s. birds, les échassiers m.

stilted ['stiltid], a. **1.** Arch: (Arc) surhaussé, surélevé. **2.** (Of style, etc.) Guindé, tendu.

stiltedness ['stiltidnis], s. Manière guindée; air, ton, guindé, emphatique, ampoulé.

stimulant ['stimjulənt]. **1.** a. & s. Med: Stimulant (m); remontant (m). **2.** s. Surexcitant m.

stimulate ['stimjuleit], v.tr. (a) Stimuler; aiguillonner, activer, exciter (to, à); aiguiser (l'esprit, l'appétit). To s. s.o. to do sth., encourager qn à faire qch. To s. production, encourager, activer, la production. (b) Med: Stimuler (le foie, etc.). **stimulating,** a. **1.** Stimulant, encourageant; (désir) aiguillonnant; (musique) entraînante; (livre) qui donne à penser. **2.** Med: etc: (Régime) stimulant, excitant, remontant.

stimulation ['stimju'leiʃ(ə)n], s. Stimulation f.

stimulative ['stimjulətiv], a. Stimulateur, -trice.

stimulus, pl. **-i** ['stimjuləs, -ai], s. **1.** (a) Stimulant m; aiguillon m. To give a s. to trade, donner de l'impulsion f au commerce. To give a s. to the circulation, donner un coup de fouet à la circulation. (b) Physiol: Stimulus m; incitation motrice. **2.** Bot: Stimule m.

stimy ['staimi], s. & v.tr. = STYMIE¹,².

sting¹ [stiŋ], s. **1.** (a) Dard m, aiguillon m (d'abeille). (b) Dard; poil piquant (d'ortie); poil urticant. (c) Crochet venimeux (d'un serpent). **2.** (a) Piqûre f (de guêpe, etc.). (b) Pointe f (d'une épigramme). The s. of remorse, l'aiguillon du remords. (c) Douleur cuisante (d'une blessure); cinglure f (d'une lanière). (d) Vigueur f, mordant m (d'une attaque). 'sting-bull, s. Ich: Vive commune. 'sting-fish, s. Ich: Petite vive. 'sting-ray, s. Ich: Pastenague f.

sting², v. (stung [stʌŋ]; stung) 1. v.tr. (a) (Of bees, nettles) Piquer. His conscience stings him, sa conscience le tourmente. That reply stung him (to the quick), cette réponse l'a piqué (au vif). Smoke that stings the eyes, fumée qui picote les yeux. (b) P: To s. s.o. for sth., faire payer qch. à qn (à) un prix exorbitant. To be stung, attraper, essuyer, le coup de fusil. 2. v.i. (Of parts of the body) Cuire; sentir des élancements. My eyes were stinging, les yeux me cuisaient. stinging, a. Piquant, cuisant, mordant. S. plant, plante piquante, urticante. S.a. NETTLE¹. S. blow, coup cinglant, coup raide.

stinger ['stiŋər], s. F: O: Coup m raide, qui cingle.

stinginess [stin(d)ʒinis], s. Mesquinerie f, ladrerie f; pingrerie f.

stingy ['stin(d)ʒi], a. Mesquin, chiche, ladre, regardant. S. fellow, pingre m. **-ily,** adv. Chichement, mesquinement.

stink¹ [stiŋk], s. 1. (a) Puanteur f; odeur f fétide; mauvaise odeur. (b) P: To raise a s., faire de l'esclandre; rouspéter. 2. pl. Sch: F: O: Stinks, la chimie. 'stink-bomb, s. P: Boule puante.

stink², v. (p.t. stank [staŋk], stunk [stʌŋk]; p.p. stunk) 1. v.i. Puer; sentir mauvais; F: empester. To s. of garlic, puer l'ail. P: He (positively) stinks! c'est un type infect! 2. v.tr. To s. s.o. out, chasser qn par la mauvaise odeur. To s. out a fox, enfumer un renard. stinking, a. Puant, nauséabond, empesté, infect. P: What a s. fellow! Quel type infect!

stinkbug ['stiŋkbʌg], s. Ent: U.S: Punaise f des bois.

stinker ['stiŋkər], s. P: 1. (a) Individu m méprisable, sale type m. (b) Individu qui pue. 2. (a) To write s.o. a s., écrire, (i) une verte réprimande, (ii) une lettre carabinée, à qn. (b) The algebra paper was a s., on a eu une sale composition d'algèbre.

stint¹ [stint], s. 1. Restriction f. Without s., sans restriction; sans limite; à discrétion. To spend money without s., dépenser sans compter. 2. Besogne assignée. To do one's daily s., accomplir sa tâche quotidienne.

stint², v.tr. 1. Réduire (qn) à la portion congrue. To s. oneself, se refuser le nécessaire. To s. oneself for one's children, se priver pour ses enfants. To s. s.o. of sth., priver qn de qch.; refuser qch. à qn. 2. Réduire (la nourriture); être chiche de (qch.); lésiner sur (qch.). To give without stinting, donner sans compter.

stipend ['staipend], s. Traitement m, appointements mpl (d'un ecclésiastique, d'un magistrat).

stipendiary [stai'pendjəri], a. Qui reçoit des appointements fixes. Esp. S. magistrate, s. stipendiary, juge m d'un tribunal d'instance (à Londres et dans les grandes villes).

stipple¹ ['stipl], s. Art: Pointillé m; Engr: grenure f.

stipple², v.tr. (a) Figurer (un dessin) en pointillé. (b) Engr: Graver au pointillé; grener (une planche).

stipulate ['stipjuleit]. 1. v.i. To s. for sth., stipuler, énoncer expressément (une condition obligatoire). To s. for a reward of a hundred pounds, stipuler une récompense de cent livres. 2. v.tr. To s. (in writing) that . . ., stipuler (par écrit) que. . . . **stipulated,** a. Stipulé, convenu. The s. quality, la qualité prescrite.

stipulation [ˌstipjuˈleiʃ(ə)n], s. Jur: Stipulation f (d'une condition). On the s. that . . ., à condition que. . . .

stipule ['stipju:l], s. Bot: Stipule f.

stir¹ [stə:r], s. 1. Remuement m. To give one's coffee, the fire, a s., remuer son café; tisonner le feu. 2. Mouvement m. S. of warm wind, souffle m d'air chaud. 3. (a) Remue-ménage m inv. (b) Agitation f, émoi m. To make a s., faire du bruit, de l'éclat; faire événement; faire sensation. To make (very) little s., avoir peu de retentissement.

stir², v. (stirred) 1. v.tr. (a) Remuer, mouvoir. (Usu. neg.) Not a breath stirs the leaves, pas un souffle ne remue, ne fait trembler, les feuilles. He could not s. a foot, (i) il était incapable de faire un pas; (ii) on ne lui laissait aucune liberté. I will not s. a foot, je ne

bougerai pas d'ici. (b) Activer, tisonner, fourgonner (le feu); agiter (un mélange); Cu: tourner, touiller (une crème). To s. one's tea, remuer son thé. To s. heaven and earth, remuer ciel et terre. (c) Émouvoir, troubler (qn). To s. s.o. to pity, émouvoir la compassion de qn. 2. v.i. Bouger, remuer; se mettre en mouvement. (Usu. neg.) To sit without stirring, rester assis sans bouger. Don't s. from here, ne bougez pas d'ici. He did not s. out of the house, il n'est pas sorti de la maison. There is not a breath of air stirring, on ne sent pas un souffle d'air. stir up, v.tr. 1. Remuer, agiter, touiller (un liquide); ranimer, activer (le feu). 2. Fomenter (les dissensions); ameuter (le peuple); exciter, éveiller (la curiosité, l'attention); susciter (l'admiration). To s. up hatred, attiser les haines. To s. s.o. up to mutiny, pousser qn à la sédition. He wants stirring up, il a besoin d'être secoué. stirring, a. 1. Actif, -ive, remuant. To lead a s. life, mener une vie très active. S. times, époque mouvementée. 2. Émouvant, empoignant. S. speech, discours vibrant, entraînant.

stir³, s. P: Prison f, P: taule f, tôle f.

stirrer ['stə:rər], s. 1. (Pers.) S.(-up), incitateur, -trice; instigateur, -trice (of, de). S.-up of strife, fomentateur, -trice, de dissensions. 2. (Device) Agitateur m. Cu: Mouvette f, spatule f. 3. (Pers.) A: To be an early s., être matinal.

stirrup ['stirəp], s. 1. Étrier m. To put one's feet in the stirrups, chausser les étriers. To lose one's stirrups, perdre ses étriers. 2. Nau: Étrier (de marchepied de vergue). 3. Tire-pied m (de cordonnier). 4. Surg: Étrier (de la table d'opération). 5. (a) Const: Étrier (de fixation); armature f en étrier. (b) (Of rowlock) Lyre f. (c) (Of leaf-spring) Bride f de ressort. 'stirrup-bone, s. Anat: Étrier m (de l'oreille). 'stirrup-cup, s. Coup m de l'étrier. 'stirrup-leather, s. Étrivière f. 'stirrup-pump, s. Pompe à main portative.

stitch¹ [stitʃ], s. 1. (a) Needlew: Point m. Darning s., point de reprise. Running s., point glissé, point coulé. Knot s., point noué. Machine s., piqûre f à la machine. To put a few stitches in a garment, faire un point à un vêtement. Prov: A s. in time saves nine, un point à temps en épargne cent. Nau: With every s. of canvas set, couvert de toile; toutes voiles dehors. He has not a dry s. on him, il est complètement trempé. (b) (In knitting, crochet) Maille f. To drop a s., sauter, laisser échapper, une maille. 2. Surg: (Point de) suture f. To put stitches in a wound, suturer, faire une suture à, une plaie. 2. Med: S. (in the side), point de côté.

stitch², v.tr. 1. (a) Coudre (un vêtement, etc.). (b) To s. leather, piquer le cuir. 2. Surg: Suturer (une plaie). 3. Bookb: Brocher (un livre). stitch down, v.tr. Needlew: Rabattre (une couture). stitch on, v.tr. Coudre (qch.) sur qch.; appliquer (une poche, etc.); coudre (qch.) en place. stitch up, v.tr. 1. Recoudre (une déchirure, etc.); faire un point à (qch.). 2. Surg: Suturer (une plaie). stitched, a. 1. Piqué. 2. Bookb: Broché. stitching, s. 1. (a) Needlew: Couture f. Leath: Piqûre f. (b) Surg: Suture f. (c) Bookb: Brochage m, brochure f. 2. Points mpl, piqûres.

stitchwort ['stitʃwə:t], s. Bot: Stellaire f.

stiver ['staivər], s. F: O: Sou m. He hasn't a s., il n'a pas le sou; P: il n'a pas un radis.

stoat [stout], s. Z: Hermine f d'été.

stock¹ [stɔk], s. 1. (a) Bot: Tronc m (d'arbre). (b) Souche f (d'arbre); bloc m; billot m (d'enclume). Lit: Stocks and stones, objets inanimés; personnes stupides. S.a. LAUGHING-STOCK. (c) Hort: Sujet m. ente f; porte-greffe m inv. (d) Race f, famille f, lignée f. True to s., fortement racé. 2. (a) Fût m, bois m, monture f (de fusil); manche m (de fouet). Anchor s., jas m d'ancre. (b) Bit-s., vilebrequin m. Die-s., tourne-à-gauche m inv; filière f (à coussinets). 3. pl. Stocks, pilori m, tabouret m (en place publique). 4. pl. N.Arch: Stocks, chantier m; cale f de construction. Ship on the stocks, navire en construction, sur cales. To have a piece of work on the stocks, avoir un ouvrage en chantier. 5. (a) Provision f, approvisionnement m. S. of wood, provision de bois. S. of plays, répertoire m. To lay in a s. of . . ., faire (une) provision de . . .; s'approvisionner de. . . . To lay in a good s. of linen, se monter en linge. (b) *Com:* Marchandises *fpl*; stock *m*. Old s., dead s., fonds *mpl* de boutique; vieux rossignols. Surplus s., soldes *mpl*. S. in hand, s.-in-trade, marchandises en magasin; stock. To buy the whole s. of a business, acheter un fonds en bloc. In s., en magasin, en stock, en dépôt. (*Of goods*) To be out of s., manquer en magasin. To take s., faire, dresser, l'inventaire. To take s. of s.o., scruter, toiser, qn. To take s. (of a situation), faire le point. (c) (*At cards, dominoes*) Talon *m*. (d) *Husb:* Grazing s., bétail *m*; bestiaux *mpl*; cheptel *m*. Fat s., bétail de boucherie. *Breed:* S. mare, jument de haras. (e) *Ind:* Dotation *f*. *Rail:* Locomotive s., effectif *m* en locomotives. 6. *Cu:* Bouillon *m*. 7. *Fin:* Fonds *mpl*, valeurs *fpl*, actions *fpl*. Government s., fonds d'État; fonds publics; rentes *fpl* (sur l'État). Bank s., valeurs de banque. Fully paid s., titres libérés. Stocks and shares, valeurs mobilières; valeurs de bourse. To take up s., lever des actions. His s. is going up, going down, ses actions montent, baissent. *U.S:* To take no s. in s.o., faire peu de cas de qn. 8. *Bot:* Matthiole *f*; giroflée *f* des jardins. Virginia s., julienne *f* de Mahon. 9. *Cost:* (a) *A:* Cravate *f* ample. (b) *Mil:* *A:* Col droit (d'uniforme). (c) Col-cravate *m* (d'équitation). (d) Plastron *m* en soie noire (des ecclésiastiques). 10. *attrib.* (a) *Com:* S. size, taille courante. S. car, (i) voiture de série; (ii) stock-car, *pl.* stock-cars. S.(-)car racing, course *f* à obstacles pour stock-cars. (b) *Th:* S. play, pièce du répertoire. S. argument, argument habituel, bien connu. S. phrase, phrase toute faite; cliché *m*. 'stock-account, *s. Book-k:* Compte *m* de capital. 'stock-book, *s.* 1. Livre *m* de magasin; magasinier *m*. 2. *Husb:* Livre *m* généalogique des races chevalines, ovines, etc.; herd-book *m* (des bovins). stock-breeder, *s.* Éleveur *m*. 'stock-breeding, *s.* Élevage *m*. 'stock-dove, *s. Orn:* Petit ramier; pigeon colombin *m*. 'stock exchange, *s.* Bourse *f* (des valeurs). The S. E., la Bourse (de Londres). 'stock-farm, *s.* Élevage *m* (de bestiaux). 'stock-in-'trade, *s.* 1. See STOCK¹ 5 (b). 2. (a) Outils essentiels (d'un artisan). (b) Fonds *m*, répertoire *m* (de phrases à effet, etc.). 'stock-keeper, *s.* Magasinier *m*. 'stock-list, *s.* 1. *Com:* Inventaire *m*. 2. *St.Exch:* Bulletin *m* de la cote. 'stock-market, *s.* 1. Marché *m* des valeurs; marché financier. 2. Marché aux bestiaux. 'stock-raiser, *s.* Éleveur *m*. 'stock-raising, *s.* Élevage *m*. 'stock-room, *s. Ind:* Magasin *m*. 'stock-rider, *s.* (*In Austr.*) Cowboy *m*. 'stock solution, *s. Ch: Phot:* Solution concentrée (et de bonne garde). 'stock-'still, *a.* To stand s.-s., rester complètement immobile, sans bouger; demeurer immobile. 'stock-whip, *s.* (*In Austr.*) Fouet *m* de bouvier (à manche court).

stock², *v.tr.* 1. (a) Monter (un fusil). (b) *Nau:* Enjaler (une ancre). 2. Monter (une ferme) en bétail; approvisionner (une maison) (with, de); empoissonner (un étang); peupler (une forêt). Shop well stocked with . . ., magasin bien monté en . . .; bien approvisionné de, en. . . ., *F:* bien achalandé en. . . . Memory stocked with facts, mémoire meublée de faits. 3. Tenir, garder (des marchandises) en magasin, en dépôt; stocker (des marchandises).

stockade¹ [stɔ'keid], *s.* 1. Palissade *f*, palanque *f*. 2. Estacade *f*.

stockade², *v.tr.* 1. Palissader, palanquer. 2. Garnir (une berge) d'une estacade.

stockbroker ['stɔk,broukər], *s. Fin:* Agent *m* de change. Outside s., coulissier *m*.

stocker ['stɔkər], *s.* Stockiste *m* (de pièces détachées d'automobiles, etc.).

stockfish ['stɔkfiʃ], *s.* Morue séchée; merluche *f*.

stockholder ['stɔk,houldər], *s.* Actionnaire *mf*; porteur *m*, détenteur *m*, de titres.

stockinet(te) [,stɔki'net], *s.* Tissu *m* à mailles, tissu en jersey de coton (pour sous-vêtements, bandages, etc.).

stocking ['stɔkiŋ], *s.* 1. *Cost:* Bas *m*. Open-work stockings, bas à jour(s). Ribbed stockings, bas à côtes. Fully-fashioned s., bas diminué. *Surg:*

Elastic stockings, bas pour varices. *S.a.* BLUE-STOCKING. 2. White s. (of a horse), balzane *f*. Horse with white stockings, cheval balzan. 'stocking-frame, -loom, *s.* Métier *m* à bas. 'stocking-stitch, *s. Knitting:* Point *m* (de) jersey.

stockinged ['stɔkiŋd], *a.* In one's s. feet, sans chaussures.

stockist ['stɔkist], *s. Com:* Stockiste *m*.

stockman, *pl.* -men ['stɔkmən], *s.m.* (*In Austr.*) Gardeur de bestiaux; bouvier.

stockpile¹ ['stɔkpail], *s.* Stocks *m* de réserve.

stockpile². 1. *v.i.* Stocker, constituer des stocks de réserve. 2. *v.tr.* Stocker. stockpiling, *s.* Stockage *m*, constitution *f* de réserves.

stockpot ['stɔkpɔt], *s. Dom.Ec: Cu:* Pot *m* à bouillon; pot-au-feu *m inv.*

stocktaking ['stɔk,teikiŋ], *s. Com: Ind:* Inventaire *m*.

stocky ['stɔki], *a.* Trapu; ragot, -ote; (*of horse*) goussaut, ragot.

stockyard ['stɔkjɑːd], *s.* 1. Parc *m* à bestiaux. 2. Parc à matériau.

stodge¹ [stɔdʒ], *s. F:* (a) Aliment bourrant, *esp.* pudding *m*. (b) Littérature *f* indigeste.

stodge², *v.i. & pr. F:* Se bourrer, s'empiffrer de nourriture; bâfrer.

stodgy ['stɔdʒi], *a.* (Repas) lourd; (aliment) qui bourre; (livre) indigeste; *F:* (personne) lourde, rasoir.

stoep [stuːp], *s.* (*In S. Africa*) Véranda *f.*

stoic ['stouik], *a. & s.* Stoïcien, -ienne; stoïque *mf.*

stoical ['stouik(ə)l], *a.* Stoïque. -ally, *adv.* Stoïquement.

stoicism ['stouisizm], *s.* Stoïcisme *m.*

stoke [stouk], *v.tr.* 1. Charger (un foyer); chauffer (un four); entretenir, alimenter, le feu (d'un four); chauffer le foyer (d'une machine à vapeur). 2. *Abs.* To s. (up). (a) Pousser les feux. (b) *F:* Manger, bouffer, bâfrer. 'stoke-hole, *s.* 1. (a) Ouverture *f* de foyer; *Ind:* tisard *m*. (b) *Nau:* Enfer *m* (devant le tisard). 2. = STOKEHOLD.

stokehold ['stoukhould], *s. Nau:* Chaufferie *f*; chambre *f* de chauffe.

stoker ['stoukər], *s. Nau: Rail:* 1. (*Pers.*) Chauffeur *m*. Head s., chef *m* de chauffe. 2. Mechanical s., chauffeur automatique; grille *f* mécanique.

stole¹ [stoul], *s.* 1. *Rom.Ant:* Stole *f*. 2. *Ecc:* Étole *f*. 3. *Cost:* Écharpe *f*, étole (de fourrure, etc.).

stole², *s.* = STOLON.

stole³. See STEAL.

stolen. See STEAL.

stolid ['stɔlid], *a.* Lourd, lent, flegmatique, impassible. -ly, *adv.* Avec flegme.

stolidity [stɔ'liditi], **stolidness** ['stɔlidnis], *s.* Flegme *m.*

stolon ['stoulən], *s. Biol:* Stolon *m*; *Bot:* coulant *m* (de fraisier).

stoma, *pl.* **stomata** ['stoumə, 'stoumətə], *s. Bot:* Stomate *m.*

stomach¹ ['stʌmək], *s.* 1. Estomac *m*. Pain in the s., mal *m* d'estomac. *Pharm:* To be taken on an empty s., prendre à jeun. On a full s., aussitôt après un repas; au moment de la digestion. To turn s.o.'s s., soulever le cœur à qn; écœurer qn. It makes my s. rise, cela me donne des nausées. 2. *F:* (Euphémisme pour désigner le) ventre. To crawl on one's s., ramper à plat ventre. 3. (a) Envie *f*, goût *m* (for, de); inclination *f* (for, pour); cœur *m*, courage *m* (pour faire qch.). He had no s. for a fight, il n'avait aucune envie de se battre. (b) *A:* To be of a proud, of a high, s., être plein de morgue. 'stomach-ache, *s.* (a) Douleurs *fpl* d'estomac. (b) *F:* Mal *m* de ventre. To have a s.-a., avoir mal au ventre; avoir la colique. 'stomach-cough, *s.* Toux *f* gastrique. 'stomach-pump, *s. Med:* Pompe stomacale. 'stomach-tube, *s. Med:* Sonde œsophagienne.

stomach², *v.tr. F:* Endurer, supporter, tolérer (qch.); *F:* digérer (une insulte, etc.). He won't s. that affront, il n'avalera pas, ne digérera pas, cet affront. I can't s. it any longer, j'en ai plein le dos.

-stomached ['stʌməkt], *a.* Weak-s., fragile de l'estomac.

stomacher ['stʌmətʃər], *s. A.Cost:* (Pièce *f* d')estomac (*m*) (d'un costume de femme).

stomachful ['stʌməkf(u)l], *s.* Plein estomac (de nourriture, etc.). *F:* I've had a s., j'en ai soupé.

stomatitis [ˌstəumə'taitis], s. Med: Stomatite f. Angular s., perlèche f, pourlèche f.

stomatology [ˌstəumə'tɔlədʒi], s. Stomatologie f.

stone¹ [stoun], s. 1. Pierre f. (a) Meteoric s., aérolithe m. To leave no s. unturned (to . . .), ne rien négliger (pour . . .); mettre tout en œuvre, remuer ciel et terre, faire l'impossible (pour . . .). To throw, cast, stones at s.o., (i) lancer des pierres à qn; (ii) F: jeter des pierres dans le jardin de qn. To throw stones at a dog, lapider un chien. To clear of stones, épierrer. (b) Const: etc: Moellon m; pierre de taille. Not to leave a s. standing, ne pas laisser pierre sur pierre. (c) Typ: (Imposing-)s., marbre m. (d) Meule f (à repasser, de moulin). Honing s., oil-s., pierre à huile. 2. Precious stones, pierres précieuses; pierreries f. 3. (Material) Pierre (à bâtir, etc.). Broken s., pierraille f, cailloutis m. 4. Med: Calcul m, pierre (de la vessie, du rein). 5. Noyau m (de fruit). 6. inv. Meas: Stone m (= 6 kg, 348). He weighs 12 s., il pèse 76 kilos. 7. attrib. S. jug, pot m, cruche f, de grès. 'Stone Age, s. Prehist: Âge m de pierre. Old S. A., âge de la pierre taillée. New S. A., âge de la pierre polie. 'stone-axe, s. Const: Marteau m à dresser. 'stone-'blind, a. Complètement aveugle. 'stone-breaker, s. 1. (Pers.) Casseur m de pierres. 2. (Machine) Concasseur m. 'stone-'cold, a. Froid comme (le) marbre. The tea is s.-c., le thé est complètement froid. F: I've got him s.-c.! je le tiens (à ma merci)! 'stone-coloured, a. (De) couleur pierre inv. 'stone-crusher, s. Civ.E: Concasseur m. 'stone(-)curlew, s. Orn: Grand pluvier; courlis m de terre. 'stone-cutter, s. Tailleur m, équarrisseur m, de pierres. 'stone-'dead, a. Raide mort. 'stone-'deaf, a. Complètement sourd; F: sourd comme un pot. 'stone-dresser, s. Dresseur m de pierres. 'stone falcon, s. Orn: Émerillon m. 'stone-fruit, s. Fruit m à noyau. 'stone-plover, s. Orn: = STONE CURLEW. 'stone-quarry, s. Carrière f (de pierre). 'stone's throw, s. Jet m de pierre. Within a s.'s t., à quelques pas, à deux pas.

stone², v.tr. 1. Lapider; assaillir (qn) à coups de pierres. To s. s.o. to death, lapider qn. 2. To s. fruit, enlever les noyaux des fruits; énoyauter, dénoyauter, épépiner, les fruits. 3. Revêtir de pierres (un édifice); paver de pierres (une allée). 4. Empierrer, caillouter (une route).

stonechat ['stountʃat], s. Orn: 1. Traquet m; tarier m saxicole. 2. F: = WHEATEAR.

stonecrop ['stounkrɔp], s. Bot: Orpin m.

stonemason ['stounmeis(ə)n], s. Maçon m.

stonewall ['stoun'wɔːl], v.i. 1. (a) Cr: Jouer un jeu prudent pour tenir jusqu'à la fin. (b) Fenc: Parer au mur. 2. Parl: etc: F: Faire de l'obstruction.

stonewaller ['stoun'wɔːlər], s. 1. Cr: Joueur prudent, qui ne risque rien. 2. Parl: F: Obstructionniste mf.

stoneware ['stounwɛər], s. Grès m (cérame); poterie f de grès.

stonework ['stounwəːk], s. 1. (a) Maçonnage m; maçonnerie f. (b) Ouvrage m en pierre. 2. Typ: Correction f sur le marbre.

stoniness ['stouninis], s. 1. Nature pierreuse (du sol). 2. Dureté f (de cœur).

stony ['stouni], a. 1. Pierreux, -euse; couvert, rempli, de pierres; rocailleux, -euse; pétré. 2. Dur comme la pierre. 3. S. heart, cœur de roche, de marbre. S. look, regard glacial. S. politeness, politesse glacée. 4. F: = STONY-BROKE. -ily, adv. (Regarder) d'un air glacial. 'stony-'broke, a. P: Dans la dèche; décavé; à sec. I'm s.-b., je n'ai pas le sou. 'stony-'hearted, a. (Of pers.) Au cœur de roche, de marbre; dur, insensible.

stood. See STAND².

stooge¹ [stuːdʒ], s. F: (a) Th: Faire-valoir m inv. (b) Souffre-douleur mf inv. (c) Subalterne m, nègre m. (d) Espion, -ionne; P: (of police) casserole f.

stooge², v.i. F: 1. (a) Th: Servir de faire-valoir (à un acteur). (b) To s. (for s.o.), faire le nègre. 2. To s. around, faire un tour, flâner. Av: To s. about, attendre pour atterrir; patrouiller sans s'en faire. Av: To s. around (a target), rôder autour (d'un objectif). F: To s. around (the office), bricoler (au bureau).

stook [stuːk], s. Agr: Tas m de gerbes; meulette f, moyette f.

stool [stuːl], s. 1. (a) Tabouret m. Folding s., pliant m. Piano s., music s., tabouret de piano. S. of repentance, sellette f. To fall between two stools, demeurer entre deux selles (le cul à terre). (b) (Three-legged) Escabeau m. 2. (a) A: Garde-robe f. Night-s., close s., chaise percée. To go to s., aller à la selle. (b) pl. Med: Stools, selles. 3. (a) For: etc: Souche f (d'un arbre abattu). (b) Hort: Pied m mère; plante f mère. 4. = STOOL PIGEON. 'stool pigeon, s. 1. Ven: Pigeon appelant; chanterelle f. 2. F: (a) Mouchard m. (b) Compère m (d'un escroc).

stoop¹ [stuːp], s. Inclination f en avant (du corps); attitude voûtée. To walk with a s., marcher le dos voûté; marcher penché.

stoop². 1. v.i. (a) Se pencher, se baisser. He had to s. to go through the door, il lui fallait se baisser pour passer par la porte. (b) S'abaisser, s'avilir, descendre (to do sth., à, jusqu'à, faire qch.). He stooped to a lie, il s'abaissa jusqu'au mensonge. I refuse to s. to such a thing, je ne veux pas déroger jusqu'à faire une chose pareille. (c) Avoir le dos rond; être voûté. 2. v.tr. Pencher, incliner, courber (la tête); courber, arrondir (le dos). stooping, a. Penché, courbé; voûté.

stoop³, s. U.S: Canada: (a) Terrasse surélevée (devant une maison). (b) Véranda f.

stop¹ [stɔp], s. 1. (a) Arrêt m, interruption f. To put a s. to sth., arrêter, faire cesser, qch.; mettre fin à qch. It ought to be put a s. to, il faudrait y mettre fin. (b) Arrêt, halte f, pause f. Short s., moment m d'arrêt. Ten minutes' s., dix minutes d'arrêt. To come to a s., s'arrêter; faire halte; (of car) stopper. Traffic s., arrêt de circulation. To bring sth. to a s., arrêter qch. S.a. DEAD 5. (c) Bus s., arrêt m d'autobus. Regular s., arrêt fixe. Request s., arrêt facultatif. (d) Av: (On long-distance flight) Escale f. 2. Signe m de ponctuation; point m. Full s., point (final). To put in the stops, mettre les points et les virgules. 3. Mus: (a) Jeu m, registre m (d'orgue). To pull out a stop, tirer un registre. F: To pull out all the stops, y aller à plein, donner son maximum. (b) Trou m (de flûte, etc.). (c) Clé f (de clarinette, etc.). (d) Touche f, touchette f (de la guitare). (e) Barré m (sur la guitare, le violon). 4. Dispositif m de blocage; arrêt, taquet m, butée f, toc m; heurtoir m (d'une porte, etc.); arrêtoir m (de vis, de boulon); (on moving part of machine) mentonnet m. Carp: Bench s., crochet m, griffe f, d'établi. Typewr: Margin(al) s., margeur m (réglable). 5. (a) Cards: Carte f d'arrêt. (b) Box: Coup bloqué. 6. Opt: Phot: Diaphragme m (de l'objectif). 7. Ling: Plosive f; explosive f. 'stop-gear, s. Appareil m d'arrêt. 'stop-hit, s. Fenc: Coup m d'arrêt. 'stop-light, s. Aut: The s.-l., le (feu) stop, le (feu) rouge; le signal d'arrêt. 'stop-press, attrib. Journ: S.-p. news, (informations de) dernière heure. 'stop-screw, s. Vis-butoir f; vis f de butée. 'stop-signal, s. Rail: Signal m d'arrêt. 'stop-watch, s. Compte-secondes m inv; chronomètre m.

stop², v. (stopped [stɔpt]) I. v.tr. 1. Boucher, aveugler (une voie d'eau); plomber, obturer (une dent). To s. (up), boucher, fermer (un trou); obstruer, obturer (un tuyau). (Of pipe) To get stopped (up), se boucher, s'obstruer. To s. one's ears, se boucher les oreilles. To s. one's ears against entreaties, rester sourd aux requêtes. To s. a gap, (i) boucher un trou; (ii) combler une lacune. To s. the way, fermer, barrer, le passage. 2. (a) Arrêter (un cheval, une balle, etc.). To s. s.o. short, arrêter qn (tout) court. S. thief! au voleur! To s. the traffic, interrompre la circulation. To s. s.o.'s breath, couper la respiration à qn. To s. a blow, parer un coup; Box: bloquer. Fb: To s. the ball, bloquer. To s. the light, intercepter la lumière. (b) To s. s.o.'s doing sth., to s. s.o from doing sth., empêcher qn de faire qch. To s. sth. being done, empêcher que qch. (ne) se fasse. There is no one to s. him, il n'y a personne pour l'en empêcher. Com: To s. (payment of) a cheque, bloquer, stopper, un chèque; frapper un chèque d'opposition. (c) Arrêter (une pendule); arrêter, stopper (une machine). (d) Mettre fin à (qch.).

enrayer (un abus). **It ought to be stopped,** il faudrait y mettre fin. 3. (*a*) Cesser (ses efforts, ses visites). *Com:* **To s. payment,** cesser ses paiements. **To s. doing sth.,** s'arrêter de faire qch. **To s. playing,** cesser de jouer. **She never stops talking,** elle n'arrête jamais de parler. **S. that noise!** assez de bruit! **S. it!** assez! finissez! (*b*) *Impers:* **It has stopped raining,** il a cessé de pleuvoir; la pluie a cessé. 4. **To s. s.o.'s supply of electricity,** couper l'électricité à qn. **To s. s.o.'s wages,** retenir le salaire de qn. **To s. s.o.'s allowance,** couper les vivres à qn. *Mil:* **All leave is stopped,** toutes les permissions sont suspendues. 5. *Mus:* **To s. (down) a string,** presser une corde. 6. *Nau:* Genoper (un amarrage). II. **stop,** *v.i.* 1. (*a*) S'arrêter. *Nau:* (*Of ship*) Stopper. (*Of pers.*) **To s. short, dead,** s'arrêter (tout) court; s'arrêter net; *F:* s'arrêter pile. (*Of car*) **To s. at the kerb,** s'arrêter, stopper, le long du trottoir. **'Buses s. by request,'** "arrêt facultatif." **'All buses s. here,'** "arrêt fixe, obligatoire." *Rail:* **How long do we s. at Aix?** combien d'arrêt à Aix? **To pass a station without stopping,** brûler une gare. *Nau:* **To s. at a port,** faire escale à un port. (*b*) Cesser (de parler, de fonctionner, etc.). **My watch has stopped,** ma montre (s')est arrêtée. **To work fifteen hours without stopping,** travailler pendant quinze heures d'arrache-pied. **To s. short in one's speech,** rester court dans son discours. **Once on this subject he never stops,** une fois sur ce sujet il ne tarit pas. **He did not s. at that,** il ne s'en tint pas là. **To s. for s.o.,** (rester à) attendre qn. **S. a moment,** arrêtez un instant. **S. there!** (i) restez-en là! (ii) demeurez là! restez là! **The matter will not s. there,** l'affaire n'en demeurera pas là. **The rain has stopped,** la pluie a cessé. **All their knowledge stops there,** toute leur science se borne à cela. **He'll s. at nothing,** rien, aucune considération, ne l'arrêtera. 2. *F:* = STAY² I. 2. **stop away,** *v.i.* 1. Ne pas venir; ne pas y aller. 2. S'absenter. **stop by,** *v.i. F:* Entrer en passant; passer chez qn. **stop off,** *v.i. F: esp. U.S:* **To s. o. in London,** s'arrêter, faire étape, à Londres. **stop-off.** *F: U.S:* 1. *a.* **A good s.-o. place for travellers,** une bonne étape. 2. *s.* Arrêt *m.* **stopping,** *s.* 1. (*a*) Arrêt *m.* **S. device,** dispositif d'arrêt (de mouvement). (*b*) Suspension *f*; cessation *f.* (*c*) S. of a cheque, arrêt de paiement d'un chèque. (*d*) S. (up), obturation *f. Dent:* Plombage *m*, obturation, d'une dent. (*e*) *Gram:* Ponctuation *f.* 2. (*a*) Bouchon *m*, tampon *m.* (*b*) *Dent:* Plombage *m*, mastic *m.* **'stopping-place,** *s.* (Point m d')arrêt *m*; halte *f. Av:* Escale *f.*

stopcock ['stɔpkɔk], *s.* Robinet *m* d'arrêt, de fermeture.

stope¹ [stoup], *s. Min:* 1. Gradin *m.* 2. Chantier *m* en gradins.

stope², *v.tr. Min:* 1. Exploiter (une mine) en gradins. 2. Abattre (le minerai).

stopgap ['stɔpgæp], *s.* Bouche-trou *m.* **It will serve as a s.,** cela servira à boucher un trou.

stopover ['stɔp'ouvər], *s. F: U.S:* = STOP-OFF 2.

stoppage ['stɔpidʒ], *s.* 1. Arrêt *m*; mise *f* au repos; suspension *f* (du travail, etc.). **S. of the traffic,** suspension de la circulation. **S. of payments,** suspension de paiements. **S. of pay,** retenue *f* sur les appointements; *Mil:* suppression *f* de solde. *Mil:* **S. of leave,** consigne *f*; suppression des permissions. 2. Obstruction *f*, engorgement *m. Med:* **Intestinal s.,** occlusion intestinale. 3. Arrêt, pause *f*, halte *f*; interruption *f* (du travail).

stopper¹ ['stɔpər], *s.* 1. (*a*) Bouchon *m* (en verre). **Screw s.,** fermeture *f* à vis. (*b*) Obturateur *m*; pointeau *m* d'arrêt (de citerne). 2. (*a*) *Mec.E:* Taquet *m* (d'arrêt de mouvement). *F:* **To put a s. on s.o.'s activities,** enrayer les activités de qn. (*b*) *Nau:* Bosse *f.* **Cat-head s.,** bosse de bout.

stopper², *v.tr.* 1. Boucher (un flacon). 2. *Nau:* Bosser.

storage ['stɔːridʒ], *s.* 1. Accumulation *f* (*of power, energy*); emmagasinage *m*, emmagasinement *m*, entreposage *m.* **To take goods out of s.,** sortir des marchandises. **S. tank,** réservoir d'emmagasinage. *Hyd.E:* **S. basin,** réservoir de barrage. *S.a.* BATTERY 3, COLD¹ 1. 2. Caves *fpl*, greniers *mpl*; entrepôts *mpl*, magasins *mpl* (d'une maison de

commerce); espace *m* disponible. *Furn:* **S. unit,** meuble *m* de rangement. 3. Frais *mpl* d'entrepôt. **'storage bin,** *s.* Coffre *m*, récipient *m.* **'storage cell,** *s. El:* Élément *m* d'accumulateur.

storax ['stɔːræks], *s. Bot:* Styrax *m.*

store¹ [stɔːr], *s.* 1. (*a*) Provision *f*, approvisionnement *m.* (*b*) Abondance *f. Ind:* **S. of energy,** énergie disponible. **To lay in a s. of sth.,** faire une provision de qch.; s'approvisionner de qch. **To lay in stores,** s'approvisionner. **To hold, keep, sth. in s.,** tenir, garder, qch. en réserve. **What the future holds in s. for us,** ce que l'avenir nous réserve. **I have a surprise in s. for him,** je lui ménage une surprise. **That is a treat in s.,** c'est un plaisir à venir. **To set great s. by sth.,** faire grand cas de qch.; attacher beaucoup de prix à qch. **To set little s. by sth.,** faire peu de cas de qch. 2. *pl.* (*a*) Stores, provisions, approvisionnements, vivres *m.* (*b*) **Marine stores,** (i) approvisionnements, matériel, de navires; (ii) maison *f* d'approvisionnements de navires. **Marine-s. dealer,** approvisionneur, -euse. 3. (*a*) Entrepôt *m*, magasin *m*; réserve *f*; (*for furniture*) garde-meuble *m. Mil: Navy:* Magasin *m*; (*for whole district*) manutention *f.* (*b*) Magasin. **The village s.,** l'alimentation *f*, l'épicerie *f*, du village. (*c*) (*Department*) s., grand magasin. **'store-room,** *s.* (*a*) (*In private house*) Office *f*, dépense *f. Ind:* Halle *f* de dépôt. (*c*) *Nau:* (i) Soute *f* aux vivres; soute à provisions; (ii) cambuse *f.*

store², *v.tr.* 1. Pourvoir, munir, approvisionner (**with,** de). **To have a well-stored mind,** avoir la tête bien meublée. 2. **To s. sth. (up),** amasser, accumuler, qch. **To s. up electricity, heat,** emmagasiner l'électricité, la chaleur. 3. (*a*) Emmagasiner, mettre en dépôt (des meubles); mettre en grange (le foin, le blé). (*b*) Prendre en dépôt. **Stored furniture,** mobilier au garde-meuble.

storehouse ['stɔːhaus], *s.* Magasin *m*, entrepôt *m. Mil:* Manutention *f.* **He is a s. of information,** c'est une mine de renseignements.

storekeeper ['stɔːkiːpər], *s.* 1. (*a*) Garde-magasin *m*, *pl.* gardes-magasin; magasinier *m.* (*b*) (*In hospital, convent, etc.*) Dépensier, -ière. *Nau:* Cambusier *m.* 2. *U.S:* Boutiquier, -ière.

storey ['stɔːri], *s.* Étage *m* (d'une maison). **To add a s. to a house,** exhausser une maison d'un étage. **On the third s.,** *U.S:* **on the fourth s.,** au troisième (étage). *F:* **To be weak in the upper s.,** avoir une araignée dans le plafond.

storeyed ['stɔːrid], *a.* A étage(s). **Two-s. house,** maison à un étage; *U.S:* maison à deux étages.

storied¹ ['stɔːrid], *a.* 1. *Arch:* **S. window,** vitrail historié. 2. *Lit:* Célébré dans l'histoire, dans la légende.

storied², *a.* = STOREYED.

stork [stɔːk], *s. Orn:* Cigogne *f. O: F:* **A visit from the s.,** l'arrivée *f* d'un bébé.

storm¹ [stɔːm], *s.* 1. Orage *m. Meteor:* Tempête *f*, dépression *f.* **Rain s.,** tempête de pluie; *Nau:* fort grain de pluie. **Magnetic s.,** orage magnétique. **A s. in a tea-cup,** une tempête dans un verre d'eau. **Political s.,** tourmente *f* politique. **To stir up a s.,** soulever une tempête. 2. Pluie *f* (de projectiles); bordée *f* (de sifflets). **S. of abuse, of applause,** tempête d'injures, d'applaudissements. **To bring a s. about one's ears,** s'attirer une véritable tempête d'ennuis, d'indignation; soulever un tollé général. 3. **To take a stronghold by s.,** emporter, prendre d'assaut, une place forte. **To take the audience by s.,** emporter l'auditoire. **'storm-area,** *s.* Étendue *f* d'une dépression. **'storm-beaten,** *a.* Battu par les tempêtes. **'storm-bell,** *s.* Tocsin *m.* **'storm-belt,** *s.* Zone *f* des tempêtes. **'storm-bird,** *s.* Oiseau *m*, pétrel *m*, des tempêtes. **'storm-bound,** *a.* Retenu par la tempête; en relâche forcée. **'storm centre,** *s.* (*a*) *Meteor:* Centre *m* de dépression. (*b*) Foyer *m* d'agitation. **'storm-cloud,** *s.* (*a*) Nuée *f* (d'orage). (*b*) Nuage *m* à l'horizon; nuage menaçant. **'storm-cone,** *s. Nau:* Cône *m* de tempête. **'storm-jib,** *s. Nau:* Tourmentin *m.* **'storm-lantern,** *s.* Lampe-tempête *f*, *pl.* lampes-tempête. **'storm-proof,** *a.* 1. A l'épreuve de la tempête. 2. Inexpugnable. **'storm-tossed,** *a.* Ballotté par la tempête. **'storm-troops,** *s.pl.* Troupes *f* d'assaut.

storm². 1. *v.i.* (a) (*Of wind, rain*) Se déchaîner; faire rage. (b) (*Of pers.*) Tempêter, pester. 2. *v.tr.* (i) Livrer l'assaut à (une place forte); (ii) prendre d'assaut, emporter d'assaut (une place forte). **storming,** *s.* 1. Violence *f*, emportements *mpl*. 2. *Mil:* (i) Assaut *m*; (ii) prise *f* d'assaut. **'storming party,** *s. Mil:* Troupes *fpl* d'assaut.

storminess ['stɔːminis], *s.* Caractère orageux (du temps, d'une réunion).

stormy ['stɔːmi], *a.* (Vent) tempétueux; (temps, ciel) orageux, d'orage. **S. sea,** mer démontée. **S. discussion,** discussion orageuse. **S. meeting,** réunion houleuse.

story¹ ['stɔːri], *s.* 1. Histoire *f*, récit *m*, conte *m*. **Idle s.,** conte en l'air. **Tall s.,** galéjade *f*. **To tell a s.,** raconter, conter, une histoire. **To tell tall stories,** galéjer. **According to his own s.,** à croire ce qu'il raconte; d'après lui. **There is a s. that . . .,** on raconte que. . . . **That's quite another s.,** ça c'est une autre paire de manches. **It's the (same) old s.,** c'est toujours la même rengaine, la même chanson. **It's a long s.,** c'est toute une histoire. **The best of the s. is that . . .,** le plus beau de l'histoire, c'est que. . . . **These bruises tell their own s.,** ces meurtrissures en disent long. **Have you read the s. of his life?** avez-vous lu l'histoire de sa vie? 2. *Lit:* **Short s.,** nouvelle *f*; conte. 3. Intrigue *f* (d'un roman, d'une pièce de théâtre). 4. *O: F:* Conte; mensonge *m*, menterie *f*. **To tell stories,** dire des mensonges; raconter des blagues *f*. 5. *A:* L'histoire; la légende. **Famous in s.,** célèbre dans l'histoire, dans la fable. **'story-book,** *s.* Livre *m* de contes; livre d'histoires. **'story-teller,** *s.* 1. Conteur, -euse. 2. *O: F:* Menteur, -euse. **'story-telling,** *s.* 1. L'art *m* de conter. 2. *O: F:* Mensonges *mpl*.

story², *s.* = STOREY.

stoup [stuːp], *s.* 1. *A:* Cruche *f*. 2. *Ecc:* Bénitier *m*.

stout¹ [staut], *a.* 1. (i) Fort, vigoureux, -euse, *F:* costaud; (ii) brave, vaillant; (iii) ferme, résolu. **S. fellow,** (i) homme vaillant; (ii) gaillard *m* solide. **To put up a s. resistance,** se défendre vaillamment. **S. heart,** cœur vaillant. 2. (*Of thg*) Fort, solide; (*of cloth, etc.*) renforcé, résistant. *Bootm:* **S. sole,** semelle forte. 3. Gros *f*, grosse; corpulent. **To grow s.,** devenir adipeux, -euse; engraisser; prendre de l'embonpoint. **-ly,** *adv.* 1. Fortement, vigoureusement, vaillamment. **To deny sth. s.,** nier qch. (fort et) ferme. **He s. maintained that . . .,** il affirmait énergiquement que. . . . 2. **S. built,** solidement bâti. **'stout-'hearted,** *a.* Intrépide, vaillant. **'stout-'heartedness,** *s.* Intrépidité *f*, courage *m*.

stout², *s.* Stout *m*; bière brune forte.

stoutish ['stautiʃ], *a.* 1. Assez corpulent; replet, -ète. 2. Assez solide.

stoutness ['stautnis], *s.* Embonpoint *m*, corpulence *f*.

stove [stouv], *s.* 1. (a) Poêle *m*, fourneau *m*. **Slow-combustion s.,** poêle à feu continu, calorifère *m*. *Dom.Ec:* Oil s., poêle à mazout. (b) Fourneau de cuisine; cuisinière *f*. *S.a.* GAS-STOVE. 2. *Ch: Ind:* Étuve *f*, four *m*. **'stove-pipe,** *s.* 1. Tuyau *m* de poêle. 2. *O: F:* Chapeau haut de forme; *F:* huit-reflets *m inv*.

stove². See STAVE².

stow [stou], *v.tr.* 1. **To s. (away),** mettre en place, ranger, serrer (des objets). *P:* **S. it!** ferme ça! la barbe! 2. *Nau:* Arrimer (des marchandises, le charbon). **To s. the cargo,** faire l'arrimage. **To s. the anchor, the boats,** mettre l'ancre à poste; saisir les canots.

stowage ['stouidʒ], *s. Nau:* (a) Arrimage *m*. (b) Capacité *f* utilisable pour marchandises; espace *f* utile. (c) Frais *mpl* d'arrimage.

stowaway¹ ['stouəwei], *s. Nau:* Voyageur *m* de fond de cale; passager clandestin.

stowaway², *v.i.* **To s. on board a ship,** s'embarquer clandestinement à bord d'un navire.

stower ['stouər], *s. Nau:* Arrimeur *m*.

strabismus [strə'bizməs], *s.* Strabisme *m*.

straddle¹ ['strædl], *s.* 1. (a) Écartement *m* des jambes. (b) Position *f* à califourchon. 2. *Artil:* Encadrement *m* (du but).

straddle². 1. *v.i.* Se tenir (debout) les jambes écartées. 2. *v.tr.* (a) Enfourcher (un cheval); se mettre à califourchon sur (une chaise); chevaucher (un mur). *Mil:* **To s. a river,** être à cheval sur un fleuve. (b) *Artil:* **To s. a target,** encadrer un objectif. (c) **To s. (out) one's legs,** écarter les jambes.

strafe [strɑːf], *v.tr. F:* 1. *Mil:* (i) Mitrailler, (ii) bombarder, *P:* marmiter (l'ennemi). 2. *F:* Rosser (qn); donner une bonne correction (à qn). **strafing,** *s.* 1. *Mil:* Bombardement *m*, *P:* marmitage *m*. 2. *F:* Verte semonce, bonne correction.

straggle ['strægl], *v.i.* 1. **To s. (along),** marcher sans ordre, à la débandade. 2. **Houses that s. round the lake,** maisons qui s'éparpillent autour du lac. **The guests s. off,** les invités s'en vont par petits groupes. **straggling,** *a.* 1. Disséminé. **S. village,** village aux maisons éparses. **S. hairs,** cheveux épars. 2. **S. plants,** plantes qui traînent.

straggler ['stræglər], *s.* Celui qui reste en arrière. *Mil:* Traînard *m*.

straight [streit]. I. *a.* 1. (a) Droit, rectiligne. **S. as a ram-rod,** droit comme un i. **S. line,** ligne droite; droite *f*. **S. up and down,** tout d'une venue. **S. hair,** cheveux (i) plats, (ii) raides. *Carp:* **S. joint,** assemblage à plat. *Geom:* **S. angle,** angle plat. (b) (Mouvement) en ligne droite. 2. Juste, honnête; loyal, -aux. **Man who does a s. deal,** homme sérieux et rond en affaires; homme loyal en affaires. **S. answer,** réponse franche, sans équivoque. **To be s. with s.o.,** agir loyalement avec qn. **To play a s. game,** jouer bon jeu bon argent. 3. Net, *f.* nette; tout simple. *Pol:* **S. fight,** campagne électorale à deux candidats. *Th:* **S. play,** pièce de théâtre proprement dite. **S. part,** rôle *m* sans complications. **S. drink,** verre *m* (de vin, d'alcool) pur, sans eau. **S. whisky,** whisky sec. 4. (a) Droit; d'aplomb. **To put sth. s.,** redresser, ajuster, qch. **Your tie isn't s.,** votre cravate est de travers. (b) En ordre. **To put the room s.,** remettre de l'ordre dans la chambre. **To put things s.,** arranger les choses; débrouiller l'affaire. **The accounts are s.,** les comptes sont en ordre. *S.a.* FACE¹ II. **straight,** *s.* 1. (a) **To be out of the s.,** n'être pas d'aplomb; être de travers. **To cut material on the s.,** couper un tissu de droit fil. (b) *F:* **To act on the s.,** agir loyalement. 2. (a) *Rac:* **The s.,** les dernières centaines de mètres (avant le poteau d'arrivée), le finish. (b) *Rail:* Alignement droit. III. **straight,** *adv.* 1. Droit. **To shoot s.,** tirer juste. **To go s.,** (i) aller droit; (ii) vivre honnêtement. **Keep s. on,** continuez tout droit. **The bullet went s. through his leg,** la balle lui a traversé la jambe de part en part. **To read a book s. through,** lire un livre d'un bout à l'autre. 2. Directement. **I shall come s. back,** je ne ferai qu'aller et (re)venir. **To go s. to the point,** aller droit au fait. **To drink s. from the bottle,** boire à même la bouteille. **To walk s. in,** entrer sans frapper. **S. away,** immédiatement, aussitôt; tout de suite; (deviner) du premier coup. **S. off,** sur-le-champ; tout de suite; d'emblée. *F:* **It's s. from the horse's mouth,** j'ai ça de source sûre; c'est un tuyau increvable. 3. **To go s. across the road,** traverser la rue tout droit. **S. above sth.,** juste au-dessus de qch. **To look s.o. s. in the face,** regarder qn bien en face. **I tell you s.,** je vous le dis tout net. **S. out,** franchement; sans détours, sans ambages; (parler) carrément, franchement, sans détours. **'straight-'edge,** *s.* Règle *f* (à araser); limande *f*.

straighten ['streit(ə)n]. 1. *v.tr.* (a) Rendre (qch.) droit; (re)dresser (qch.). **To s. (out) an iron bar,** défausser, dégauchir, une barre de fer. (b) **To s. (up),** ranger; mettre en ordre. **To s. one's tie,** arranger sa cravate. **To s. (out) one's affairs,** mettre ses affaires en ordre. 2. *v.i.* Se redresser; devenir droit. (*Of pers.*) **To s. up,** se redresser. **I expect things will s. out,** *F:* je pense que ça s'arrangera.

straightforward [streit'fɔːwəd], *a.* Loyal, -aux; franc, *f.* franche. **To give a s. answer,** répondre sans détours. **-ly,** *adv.* (i) avec droiture, loyalement; (parler) carrément, franchement, sans détours.

straightforwardness [streit'fɔːwədnis], *s.* Droiture *f*, honnêteté *f*, franchise *f*.

straightness ['streitnis], *s.* 1. Rectitude *f* (d'une ligne). 2. Droiture *f*, rectitude (de conduite).

straightway ['streitwei], *adv. Lit:* Immédiatement, tout de suite, aussitôt.

strain¹ [strein], s. **1.** Rapport m de la déformation, allongement m unitaire; tension f, surtension f. The s. on the rope, la tension de la corde. To take the s. off a beam, soulager une poutre. *Mec.E:* Breaking s., effort m de rupture. Bending s., effort à la flexion. To impose a s. on (a machine), fatiguer (une machine). Parts under s., pièces de contrainte. It would be too great a s. on my purse, ce serait trop demander à ma bourse. The s. of a long match, l'effort soutenu d'un match prolongé. The s. of modern life, la tension de la vie moderne. Mental s., surmenage intellectuel. To write without s., écrire sans effort. **2.** (a) *Med:* Entorse f, foulure f. S. in the back, tour m de reins. (b) *Mec.E:* Rapport de la déformation f (d'une pièce). **3.** pl. *Poet:* Accents mpl. Sweet strains, doux accords. **4.** Ton m, sens m (d'un discours, etc.). He said much more in the same s., il s'est étendu longuement dans ce sens.

strain². I. v.tr. **1.** Tendre, surtendre (un câble). To s. one's ears, tendre l'oreille. To s. one's eyes, se fatiguer, s'abîmer, les yeux (doing sth., à faire qch.). To s. the law, faire violence à la loi. To s. s.o.'s friendship, exiger trop de l'amitié de qn. To s. a point, faire une exception; faire violence à ses principes. *S.a.* NERVE¹ **3. 2.** (a) To s. one's back, se donner un tour de reins. To s. one's heart, one's shoulder, se forcer le cœur; se fouler l'épaule. (b) Forcer (un mât, une poutre). *Mec.E:* Déformer (une pièce). (c) To s. oneself, se surmener, F: s'éreinter (doing sth., à faire qch.). **3.** *Lit:* To s. s.o. to one's bosom, serrer qn sur son cœur. **4.** (a) Filtrer, passer, couler (un liquide) (à travers un linge, etc.); passer au tamis; tamiser. (b) To s. sth. out (of a liquid), enlever qch. d'un liquide (en se servant d'une passoire). To s. the vegetables, faire égoutter les légumes. II. v.i. **1.** Faire un (grand) effort. To s. at a rope, tirer sur une corde. To s. after sth., faire tous ses efforts pour atteindre qch. **2.** (Of beam, etc.) Fatiguer, travailler. (Of ship) To s. in a seaway, fatiguer, bourlinguer, par une mer dure. **3.** (Of machine part) Se déformer; gauchir; se fausser. **strained,** a. **1.** (a) S. relations, rapports tendus. (b) S. ankle, cheville foulée. S. heart, cœur claqué, fatigué. **2.** S. laugh, rire forcé, contraint. **3.** Filtré, tamisé.

strain³, s. **1.** Qualité héritée, inhérente; tendance (morale). A s. of weakness, un héritage, un fond, de faiblesse. **2.** Race f, lignée f. *Biol:* (Of virus) Souche f. He _as a s. of Irish blood, il y a en lui une trace de sang irlandais.

strainer ['streinər], s. **1.** (a) Filtre m; tamis m. *Cu:* Passoire f. Conical s., chinois m. *Ind:* Épurateur m. Soup s., passe-bouillon m inv. (b) Crépine f (d'une pompe). *Mch:* Reniflard m. (Over drain-pipe) Pommelle f. **2.** Tendeur m, tenseur m, raidisseur m.

strait [streit]. **1.** a. (a) A: Étroit. B: The s. gate, la porte étroite. (b) S. jacket, s. waistcoat, camisole f de force. **2.** s. (a) Détroit m. The Straits of Dover, le Pas de Calais. (b) *Anat:* Straits of the pelvis, détroits du bassin. (c) To be in (great, dire) straits, être dans l'embarras, dans la (plus grande) gêne; être aux abois. 'strait-'laced, a. Prude; collet monté inv.

straitened ['streitnd], a. To be in s. circumstances, être dans la gêne, dans le besoin, dans l'embarras.

strake [streik], s. Virure f de bateau. Binding s. (of deck), virure d'hiloires.

stramonium [strə'mouniəm], s. **1.** *Bot:* Stramoine f. **2.** *Pharm:* Stramonine f.

strand¹ [strænd], s. Rive f, grève f.

strand². **1.** v.tr. Échouer (un navire); jeter (un navire) à la côte. **2.** v.i. (Of ship) Échouer. **stranded¹,** a. **1.** (Of ship) Échoué. **2.** To leave s.o. s., laisser qn en plan; laisser qn le bec dans l'eau. To be s., être en panne.

strand³. **1.** (a) Brin m, toron m (de cordage); cordon m (d'aussière); brin (de fil à coudre). (b) Brin, corde f. Four-s. pulley-block, palan à quatre brins. **2.** Fil m (de perles); tresse f (de cheveux).

stranded² ['strændid], a. A torons à brins. Three-s. rope, filin commis en trois; corde à trois torons.

strange [strein(d)ʒ], a. **1.** (a) A: In a s. land, dans un pays étranger. (b) This writing is to me, je ne connais pas cette écriture. S. faces, visages nouveaux,

inconnus. **2.** Singulier, -ière, bizarre, étrange. S. beasts, bêtes curieuses. S. to say . . ., chose étrange (à dire). . . . It is s. that he has not arrived yet, il est singulier, étonnant, qu'il ne soit pas encore arrivé. **3.** I am s. to the work, je suis nouveau dans le métier. To feel s., se sentir dépaysé. -ly, adv. Étrangement, singulièrement.

strangeness ['strein(d)ʒnis], s. **1.** Étrangeté f, singularité f. **2.** The s. of the work, la nouveauté du travail.

stranger ['strein(d)ʒər], s. **1.** (a) Étranger, -ère; inconnu, -ue. I am a s. here, je ne suis pas d'ici. He is a complete s. to me, il m'est tout à fait étranger, inconnu. You are quite a s.! on ne vous voit plus! vous vous faites rare! quel revenant vous faites! He is a s. to fear, il ne connaît pas la peur. (In House of Commons) I spy strangers, je demande le huis clos. Strangers' gallery, tribune réservée au public. *U.S: F:* Say, s.! pardon, monsieur! (b) *Jur:* Tiers m (qui n'est pas partie à un fait). **2.** (In a cup of tea) Chinois m.

strangle ['stræŋgl], v.tr. Étrangler; serrer le cou à (qn). To s. a sneeze, réprimer un éternuement. To s. evil at its birth, étouffer le mal au berceau. Strangled voice, voix étranglée. **strangling,** s. Étranglement m; *Jur:* strangulation f.

stranglehold ['stræŋglhould], s. To have a s. on s.o., tenir qn à la gorge. The s. of restrictions, l'étau m des restrictions.

strangles ['stræŋglz], s.pl. *Vet:* Gourme f.

strangulate ['stræŋgjuleit], v.tr. *Med:* Étrangler (l'intestin). Strangulated hernia, hernie étranglée.

strangulation [ˌstræŋgju'leiʃ(ə)n], s. Strangulation f. *Med:* Étranglement m (herniaire). Economic s., asphyxie f économique.

strap¹ [stræp], s. **1.** (a) Courroie f. Watch s., bracelet m pour montre. Harn: Stirrup-s., étrivière f. (b) *F:* To give a child the s., corriger un enfant avec une courroie. **2.** (a) Bande f, sangle f (de cuir, de toile). (b) Cost: Bande, patte f (de tissu). Bootm: Barrette f (de soulier). Cost: Trouser s., sous-pied m. **3.** (a) Lien m, attache f, armature f, plate-bande f (en métal); (for pipe) collier m. (b) *Mch:* Chape f, bride f (de bielle); bague f (d'excentrique). *Mec.E:* Ruban m, bande (de frein). 'strap-hang, v.i. *F:* Voyager debout (en se tenant à la courroie). 'strap hinge, s. Penture f.

strap², v.tr. (strapped [stræpt]) **1.** To s. sth. (up), attacher, lier, qch. avec une courroie; cercler (une caisse); sangler (un paquet). **2.** *F:* Administrer une correction à (un enfant) avec le bout d'une courroie. **3.** *Med:* Mettre des bandelettes, de l'emplâtre adhésif, à (une blessure). **strapping¹,** a. *F:* S. fellow, grand gaillard; gaillard solide; jeune homme bien découplé. Tall s. girl, beau brin de fille. **strapping²,** s. **1.** *F:* Correction (administrée avec une courroie). **2.** (a) Courroies fpl, liens mpl, armatures fpl. (b) *Med:* Emplâtre adhésif. (c) *Dressm:* Bandes fpl.

straphanger ['stræphæŋər], s. *F:* Voyageur m debout (dans le métro).

strapper ['stræpər], s. **1.** *F:* Grand gaillard. **2.** Groom m, panseur m (de chevaux).

strata. See STRATUM.

stratagem ['strætədʒem], s. Ruse f (de guerre); stratagème m.

strategic(al) [strə'tiːdʒik(əl)], a. Stratégique. -ally, adv. Stratégiquement.

strategist ['strætədʒist], s. Stratégiste m.

strategy ['strætədʒi], s. Stratégie f.

stratification [ˌstrætifi'keiʃ(ə)n], s. Stratification f.

stratify ['strætifai], v.tr. Stratifier.

strato-cirrus ['straːtou'sirəs], s. *Meteor:* Cirro-stratus m.

stratocruiser ['strætoukruːzər], stratoliner ['strætolainər], s. Avion m (de ligne) stratosphérique.

strato-cumulus ['straːtou'kjuːmjuləs], s. *Meteor:* Cumulo-stratus m.

stratosphere ['strætosfiər], s. Stratosphère f.

stratum, pl. -a ['straːtəm, 'streitəm, -ə], s. (a) *Geol:* Couche f. (b) Social strata, étages m de la société; couches sociales. (c) *Hyd.E:* Foundation s., sol m de fondation.

stratus ['straːtəs, streitəs], s. *Meteor:* Stratus m.

straw[1] [strɔː], s. 1. Paille f. **Loose s.**, paille de litière. **Man of s.**, homme de paille; prête-nom m. **S. roof**, toiture en paille. **S. case (for bottle)**, paillon m. 2. Paille; chalumeau m. **To drink lemonade through a s.**, boire de la limonade avec une paille. **It is not worth a s.**, cela ne vaut pas un fétu. **To cling to a s.**, se raccrocher à un brin d'herbe. **S. in the wind**, indication f de l'opinion publique. F: **It's the last s.!** c'est le comble! il ne manquait plus que cela! c'est la dernière goutte qui fait déborder le vase. 'straw-board, s. Carton m paille. 'straw-bottomed, a. A fond de paille; (chaise) de paille. 'straw-coloured, a. (Jaune) paille inv; paillé. 'straw-cutter, s. Hache-paille m inv. 'straw 'hat, s. Chapeau m de paille; canotier m. 'straw 'mat, s. Paillasson m. 'straw 'mattress, s. Paillasse f. 'straw 'vote, s. Pol: U.S: Sondage m de l'opinion publique. 'straw-yard, s. Pailler m.

straw[2], v.tr. (a) Enchausser (des légumes, etc.). (b) Couvrir (la cour, etc.) de paille. (c) Pailler, rempailler (une chaise).

strawberry ['strɔːb(ə)ri], s. (i) Fraise f; (ii) (plant) fraisier m. **Wild s.**, (petite) fraise des bois. **S. jam**, confiture de fraises. **S. ice**, glace à la fraise. 'strawberry mark, s. Fraise f (sur la peau); tache f de vin (congénitale). 'strawberry-tree, s. Arbousier commun.

stray[1] [strei]. I. s. 1. (a) Animal égaré; bête perdue. (b) **Waifs and strays**, enfants abandonnés. 2. El: (a) Dispersion f. (b) pl. W.Tel: Bruissements m parasites; (bruits m de) friture f. II. stray, a. 1. (Of animal) Égaré, errant. 2. **S. bullets**, balles perdues, égarées. **S. thoughts**, pensées détachées. **A few s. houses**, quelques maisons isolées, éparses.

stray[2], v.i. (a) S'égarer, errer; (of sheep) s'écarter du troupeau. **To s. from the right path**, s'écarter du bon chemin; se dévoyer. **To let one's thoughts s.**, laisser vaguer ses pensées. (b) El: (Of current) Se disperser.

streak[1] [striːk], s. 1. Raie f, rayure f, bande f, strie f; sillon m (de feu); trait m, filet m (de lumière); coulée f (de soleil); traînée f (de vapeur). **The first s. of dawn**, la première lueur du jour. **Like a s. of lightning**, comme un éclair. 2. **There is in him a s. of Irish blood**, il y a en lui une trace de sang irlandais. F: **There was a yellow s. in him**, il y avait de la lâcheté dans sa nature. **A s. of irony**, une pointe, un filet d'ironie.

streak[2]. 1. v.tr. Rayer, strier, zébrer. **Sky streaked with shooting stars**, ciel sillonné d'étoiles filantes. **Panes streaked with water**, vitres hachurées d'eau. 2. v.i. F: Passer comme un éclair. **He streaked off**, il se sauva à toutes jambes. **streaked**, a. Rayé, strié, bariolé, panaché; lardé. **streaking**, s. Raies fpl., rayures fpl., bandes fpl., stries fpl; T.V: traînage m.

streaky ['striːki], a. 1. En raies, en bandes. 2. Rayé, strié, zébré; vergeté. Tex: Vergé. Geol: Rubané. 3. (Of bacon) Entrelardé.

stream[1] [striːm], s. 1. (a) Cours m d'eau; fleuve m, rivière f. (b) Ruisseau m. (c) Flot m (d'eau); ruissellement m. **In a thin s.**, en mince filet. 2. Coulée f (de lave); flot(s), jet m (de lumière, de sang). **S. of abuse**, torrent m d'injures. **People entered in streams**, les gens entraient à flots. **S. of cars**, défilé ininterrompu de voitures. **In one continuous s.**, à jet continu. 3. Courant m. **With the s.**, dans le sens du courant; au fil de l'eau. **To go with the s.**, suivre le mouvement. **Against the s.**, à contre-courant.

stream[2]. 1. v.i. (a) (Of liquid) Couler (à flots); ruisseler. **The fugitives were streaming over the meadows**, les fuyards traversaient les prés à flot continu. (b) (Of hair, banner) Flotter (au vent). 2. v.tr. (a) Verser à flots, laisser couler (un liquide). (b) Nau: Mouiller (une bouée). S.a. LOG[1] 2. **stream forth**, v.i. Jaillir. **stream in**, v.i. (Of sunlight) Pénétrer à flots; (of crowd) entrer à flots. **stream out**, v.i. Sortir à flots. **streaming**, a. Ruisselant. **Face s. with tears**, visage baigné de larmes. **To be s. with perspiration**, être en nage.

streamline[1] ['striːmlain], s. 1. Courant naturel (d'un fluide). 2. Aut: Av: Ligne fuyante, fuselée.

streamline[2], v.tr. (a) Caréner (une auto), (b) Moder niser, rationaliser (des méthodes, etc.). **We hav streamlined our catalogue**, nous avons rénové allégé, refondu, notre catalogue. 'streamlined, a Caréné, fuselé, profilé; aux formes élancées aérodynamique. Pol.Ec: **S. economy**, économi réduite à l'essentiel. **streamlining**, s. (a) Aut Av: etc: Carénage m, profilage m. (b) Modernisa tion f (des méthodes, etc.).

streamer ['striːmər], s. Banderole f. Nau: Flamm f. **(Paper) streamers**, serpentins m.

street [striːt], s. (a) Rue f. **The main streets, le grandes artères. To turn s.o. into the streets**, mettr qn sur le pavé. **To walk the streets**, courir les rues bâttre le pavé; (of prostitute) faire la retape, le trottoir. **The man in the s.**, l'homme moyen; l grand public. F: **Not to be in the same s. with s.o.** n'être pas de taille avec qn. **He's streets above you** il vous dépasse du tout au tout. **He's streets ahea of them**, il les a devancés de beaucoup. F: **That' right up my s.**, c'est dans ma ligne, c'est mo rayon. **That's not up his s. at all**, cela est tout à fa hors de sa compétence. **S. level**, rez-de-chaussé m inv. **S. accidents**, accidents de la circulation. **S. cries**, cris des marchands ambulants. **S. musician** musicien de carrefour. (b) (Opposed to footway) L chaussée. 'street-'arab, s. O: Gamin m des rues 'street-'door, s. Porte f sur la rue; porte d'entrée 'street-'guide, s. Indicateur m des rues. 'street 'lamp, s. Réverbère m. street-'lighting, s. Éclairag m des rues. 'street-sweeper, s. 1. (Pers.) Balayeur m des rues. 2. (Machine) Balayeuse f (de rues). 'street walker, s.f. Raccrocheuse f, racoleuse f.

streetcar ['striːtkɑːr], s. U.S: Tramway m.

strength [streŋθ], s. 1. (a) Force(s) f(pl). **S. of body** force corporelle. **S. of a current**, force d'un courant El: intensité f d'un courant. Art: **S. of a colour** intensité d'une couleur. **Alcoholic s.**, teneur f e alcool. Ch: **S. of a solution**, titre m d'une solution **S. of mind**, fermeté f d'esprit. **S. of will**, résolutio f. **By sheer s.**, de vive force. **To recover, regai s.**, reprendre des forces; se retremper; se remonter **On the s. of . . .**, sur la foi de . . ., se fiant à . . (b) Solidité f; rigidité f, résistance f (d'une poutre etc.); robustesse f (d'un meuble). Mec: **Breakin s.**, ultimate s., résistance à la rupture; résistanc limite. 2. **To be present in great s.**, être présents e grand nombre. 3. Mil: Effectif(s) m(pl) (d'u régiment). **Fighting s.**, effectif mobilisable. **To brin a battalion up to s.**, compléter un bataillon. **Squadro at full s.**, escadron au grand complet. **Under s. incomplet, -ète; à effectif insuffisant. To be taker on the s.**, être porté sur les contrôles. **Not on th s.**, hors cadre. **To strike s.o. off the s.**, rayer qn de cadres.

strengthen ['streŋθ(ə)n], v.tr. Consolider, assure (un mur); renforcer (une poutre); remonter, fortifie (qn, le corps); (r)affermir (l'autorité de qn). **To s. solution**, augmenter la concentration d'une solution **strengthening**[1], a. Fortifiant; (of drink, etc.) remontant. **strengthening**[2], s. Renforcement m renforçage m; consolidation f; armement m (d'un poutre, etc.).

strenuous ['strenjuəs], a. 1. (Of pers.) Actif, -iv agissant, énergique. 2. (Travail) acharné, ardu (effort) tendu. **S. profession**, métier dur, pénible **S. life**, vie toute d'effort. **To offer s. opposition** faire une opposition vigoureuse (to, à). **-ly**, adv Vigoureusement; avec acharnement; énergiquement

strenuousness ['strenjuəsnis], s. Ardeur f, vigueur f acharnement m.

streptococcal [ˌstreptoˈkɔk(ə)l], a. Med: Streptococ cique.

streptococcus, pl. -i [ˌstreptoˈkɔkəs, -ai], s. Med Streptocoque m.

streptomycin [ˌstreptoˈmaisin], s. Med: Streptomy cine f.

stress[1] [stres], s. 1. Force f, contrainte f. **S. of weather** gros temps. **Under s. of poverty**, poussé par la misèr 2. (a) Mec: Effort (subi); tension f, travail m **S. diagram**, épure f des contraintes. **Bending s.** contrainte de flexion. **Yield s.**, limite f élastiqu résistance élastique. (Of beam) **To be in s.**, travaille

(b) Period of storm and s., période de trouble et d'agitation. 3. (a) Insistance f. To lay s. on a fact, insister sur un fait; faire ressortir un fait. To lay s. on a word, on a syllable, peser sur un mot; appuyer sur une syllabe. (b) Ling: S.(-accent), accent m (d'intensité); accent tonique. 4. Med: Stress m. 'stress-mark, s. Ling: Accent écrit.

stress², v.tr. 1. Mec: Charger, faire travailler (une poutre, etc.). 2. Appuyer, insister, sur (qch.); faire ressortir (un fait); souligner, peser sur (un mot); accentuer (une syllabe). Mus: To s. the melody, faire sentir la mélodie; faire ressortir le chant.

stretch¹ [stretʃ], s. 1. (a) Allongement m, extension f. S. of the arm, extension du bras. Rac: At full s., à [toute allure; ventre à terre. (b) Allongement, élargissement m par traction; tension f, étirage m. By a s. of the imagination, par un effort d'imagination. (c) Étendue f, portée f (du bras, etc.). S. of wing, envergure f. (d) Élasticité f. attrib. S. nylons, bas extensibles. 2. (a) Étendue (de pays, d'eau). Level s. (of road), palier m. Rac: The (home-)s., la ligne droite, le finish. (b) For a long s. of time, longtemps. At a s., (tout) d'un trait, (tout) d'une traite. He has been working for hours at a s., voilà des heures qu'il travaille d'arrache-pied, d'affilée. F: He is doing a s., il tire, fait, de la prison, P: il fait de la taule.

stretch². 1. v.tr. (a) Tendre (de l'élastique); tendre, tirer, bander (un câble, un ressort); élargir (des souliers); détirer (le linge). (b) To s. (oneself), s'étirer. To s. one's legs, se dégourdir, se dérouiller, les jambes. Stretched on the ground, étendu de tout son long par terre. (c) Forcer (le sens d'un mot, etc.). To s. a privilege, abuser d'un privilège. To s. veracity too far, (outre)passer les bornes de la vérité. To stretch a point, faire une concession. 2. v.i. (a) S'élargir; s'allonger; (of elastic) s'étendre; (of gloves) s'élargir. Material that stretches, tissu m qui prête. (b) S'étendre. The valley stretches southward, la vallée s'étend, se déroule, vers le sud. stretch out. 1. v.tr. (a) Allonger (le bras). To s. s.o. out (on the ground), (i) étendre qn par terre tout de son long; (ii) assommer qn raide. (b) Tendre, avancer (la main). Abs: To s. out to reach sth., tendre la main pour atteindre qch. 2. v.i. (Of column on the march, etc.) S'étirer.

stretchable ['stretʃəbl], a. (Bas, etc.) extensible.

stretcher ['stretʃər], s. 1. (a) Tendeur m; tenseur m (de hauban). Trouser-s., extenseur m. S.a. GLOVE-STRETCHER. (b) Art: Canvas-s., châssis m (de toile). 2. (a) Bois m d'écartement (de hamac); traverse f (de tente); arc-boutant m (d'un parapluie). (b) Barreau m, bâton m (de chaise). 3. Brancard m, civière f. To carry (s.o.) on a s., brancarder (qn). 4. Row: Marchepied m, barre f des pieds, traversin m. 5. (In masonry) Carreau m; panneresse f. S.-bond, appareil m en panneresses. 'stretcher-bearer, s. Brancardier m, ambulancier m. 'stretcher-party, s. Détachement m de brancardiers.

stretchy ['stretʃi], a. Élastique, qui donne, qui prête.

strew [stru:], v.tr. (p.p. strewed [stru:d] or strewn [stru:n]) 1. To s. sand over the floor, jeter, répandre, du sable sur le plancher. Fragments strewn about the pavement, débris qui jonchent le pavé. 2. To s. the floor with flowers, joncher, parsemer, le plancher de fleurs. The ground was strewn with rushes, une jonchée de roseaux recouvrait le sol.

strewth [stru:θ], int. P: Ça alors! mince (alors)!

stria, pl. -ae ['straiə, -i:], s. Strie f, striure f.

striated [strai'eitid], a. Strié.

stricken. See STRIKE².

strickle ['strikl], s. 1. Meas: Racloire f. 2. Metall: Trousse f, gabarit m, râble. 3. Husb: Pierre f à (aiguiser les) faux.

strict [strikt], a. 1. Exact; strict. (a) Précis. In the strictest sense of the word, au sens précis, dans le sens le plus étroit, du mot. (b) Rigoureux, -euse. S. neutrality, neutralité rigoureuse. In strictest confidence, à titre tout à fait confidentiel. 2. S. orders, ordres formels. S. discipline, discipline sévère. S. etiquette, étiquette rigide. Jur: S. time-limit, délai péremptoire. 3. (Of pers.) Sévère. To be s. with s.o., être sévère avec, envers, pour, qn; traiter qn avec beaucoup de rigueur. -ly, adv. 1.

Exactement, rigoureusement. S. speaking, à proprement parler. 2. Étroitement; strictement. Smoking (is) s. prohibited, défense formelle, défense expresse, de fumer. It is s. forbidden, c'est absolument défendu. 3. Sévèrement; (élevé) avec rigueur.

strictness ['striktnis], s. 1. Exactitude rigoureuse, précision f (d'une traduction). 2. Rigueur f (des règles); sévérité f (de la discipline).

stricture ['striktʃər], s. 1. Med: Rétrécissement m; étranglement m (de l'intestin). 2. To pass strictures (up)on sth., exercer sa critique sur qch.; trouver à redire à qch.

stride¹ [straid], s. (Grand) pas m; enjambée f. To make great strides, faire de grands progrès. To take sth. in one's s., faire qch. sans le moindre effort. To get into one's s., prendre son allure normale; attraper la cadence (d'un travail).

stride², v. (strode [stroud]; stridden [strid(ə)n]) 1. v.i. (a) To s. along, avancer à grands pas, à grandes enjambées. To s. away, s'éloigner à grands pas. To s. up and down the room, arpenter la salle. Science is striding ahead, la science avance à pas de géant. (b) To s. over sth., enjamber qch. 2. v.tr. (a) A: Arpenter (les rues). (b) Lit: Enjamber (un fossé).

stridency ['straidnsi], s. Stridence f.

strident ['straid(ə)nt], a. Strident.

stridulant ['stridjulənt], a. Ent: Stridulant.

stridulate ['stridjuleit], v.i. (Of insect) Striduler.

stridulation [,stridju'leiʃ(ə)n], s. Stridulation f.

strife [straif], s. Lutte f. To be at s., être en conflit, en lutte (with, avec). To cease from s., mettre bas les armes. Domestic s., querelles fpl de ménage.

strike¹ [straik], s. 1. (a) Coup (frappé). (b) Mil: Av: Raid m, intervention aérienne. Air s., opération f de soutien aérien. S. aircraft, avion m d'assaut. 2. Ind: Grève f. To go, to come out, on s., se mettre en grève. To call a s., ordonner une grève. To be on s., faire grève, être en grève. Staggered s., grève tournante. Unofficial s., grève désapprouvée par les autorités syndicales. Sympathy s., grève de solidarité. Token s., grève d'avertissement, symbolique. Lightning s., grève surprise. Sit-down s., grève sur le tas. Go-slow s., grève perlée. Wildcat s., grève sauvage. 3. Min: Rencontre f (de minerai, de pétrole). F: Lucky s., coup de veine. 4. Geol: Direction f (d'un filon). 'strike-breaker, s. Ind: Renard m, jaune m. 'strike-pay, s. Allocation f de grève.

strike², v. (struck [strʌk]; struck, A: stricken [strik(ə)n]) I. v.tr. & ind.tr. 1. (a) Frapper. Jur: Porter la main sur (qn). To s. at s.o., porter un coup à qn. S.a. BLOW⁶ 1. (Of ship) To be struck by a heavy sea, essuyer un coup de mer. Abs. To s. home, frapper juste, F: dans le mille. To s. one's fist on the table, frapper du poing sur la table. Nau: To s. the hour, piquer l'heure. Prov: S. while the iron is hot, il faut battre le fer quand il est chaud. (b) Frapper (une monnaie, une médaille). (c) Frapper (les touches du piano); toucher de la harpe). To s. a chord, plaquer un accord. (d) To s. a bargain, faire, conclure, un marché. 2. (a) To s. sparks from a flint, faire jaillir des étincelles d'un silex. To s. a match, a light, frotter une allumette. (b) El: To s. the arc, amorcer l'arc (entre les charbons). 3. (a) To s. a knife into s.o.'s heart, enfoncer un couteau dans le cœur de qn. Abs. (Of serpent) To s., foncer. To s. terror into s.o., frapper qn de terreur. The plant strikes root, abs. strikes, la plante prend racine; la plante prend. (b) Fish: Ferrer, piquer (le poisson). 4. To s. s.o. with wonder, frapper qn d'étonnement. Struck with terror, saisi d'effroi. S.a. DUMB 1, LIGHTNING. 5. Percer; pénétrer. The rays s. through the mist, les rayons percent le brouillard. 6. (a) To s. (against) sth., heurter, donner, buter, contre qch. His head struck the pavement, sa tête a porté sur le trottoir. (Of ship) To s. (the) bottom, abs. to s., toucher (le fond); talonner. To s. a mine, heurter une mine. The ship strikes (on) the rocks, le navire donne, touche, sur les écueils. A sound struck my ear, un bruit me frappa l'oreille. The thought strikes me that . . ., l'idée me vient que. . . . (b) How did she s. you? quelle impression vous a-t-elle faite? He strikes me as (being) sincere, il me paraît sincère. That is how it struck me, voilà l'effet que

cela m'a fait. **It strikes me that . . .,** il me semble, il me paraît, que. . . . (c) Faire impression à (qn); impressionner (qn); frapper (l'œil, l'imagination). **What struck me was . . .,** ce qui m'a frappé, c'est. . . . F: **To get struck on s.o.,** s'enticher de qn. 7. Tomber sur, découvrir (une piste, etc.). **To s. oil,** (i) rencontrer, toucher, le pétrole; (ii) F: faire une bonne affaire; trouver le filon. **I struck upon an idea,** j'ai eu une idée. 8. (a) Nau: Amener (une voile); abaisser (un mât). **To s. one's flag, one's colours,** amener, baisser, son pavillon. (b) **To s. tents,** abattre, plier, détendre, les tentes. **To s. camp,** lever le camp. (c) Const: **To s. the centre of an arch,** décintrer une voûte. 9. Abs. Ind: Se mettre en grève. 10. **To s. an attitude,** prendre une attitude dramatique; poser. 11. (a) Tirer (une ligne); décrire (un cercle). (b) **To s. an average,** établir, prendre, une moyenne. S.a. BALANCE[1] 3. II. v.i. 1. (Of clock) Sonner. **The clock struck six,** six heures sonnèrent. **It has just struck ten,** dix heures viennent de sonner. **His hour has struck,** son heure a sonné. 2. **To s. across country,** prendre à travers champs. **To s. into the jungle,** s'enfoncer, pénétrer, dans la jungle. **The road strikes off to the right,** la route tourne à droite. **strike down,** v.tr. Abattre, renverser (d'un coup de poing, etc.). **He was struck down by apoplexy,** l'apoplexie l'a foudroyé. **Stricken down by disease,** terrassé par la maladie. **strike in.** 1. v.tr. Enfoncer (un clou). 2. v.i. (Of pers.) S'interposer (dans une querelle). **She struck in with the remark that . . .,** elle est intervenue pour faire observer que. . . . **strike off,** v.tr. 1. Trancher, abattre (la tête de qn). 2. **To s. a name off a list,** rayer, radier, un nom d'une liste. S.a. ROLL[1] 2. 3. Typ: Tirer (tant d'exemplaires). **strike out.** 1. v.tr. (a) Rayer, radier, biffer, barrer (un mot); retrancher (un passage). (b) Faire jaillir (des étincelles). (c) Tracer, ouvrir (une route). 2. v.i. (a) **To s. out at s.o.,** allonger un coup à qn. (b) **I struck out for the shore,** je me mis à nager dans la direction du rivage. (c) F: **To s. out for oneself,** voler de ses propres ailes. **strike up,** v.tr. 1. Entonner (une chanson); commencer de jouer (un morceau). Abs. **On his arrival the band struck up,** à son arrivée la fanfare attaqua un morceau. 2. **To s. up an acquaintance, a friendship, with s.o.,** lier connaissance avec qn; se lier d'amitié avec qn. **stricken,** a. Lit: 1. Ven: (Daim) blessé. 2. **S. with grief,** accablé de douleur; en proie à la douleur. **S. with fever,** atteint d'une fièvre. 3. A: **S. in years,** avancé en âge; écrasé sous le poids des ans. 4. A: **S. field,** champ m de carnage. 5. **S. measure,** mesure rase. **striking**[1], s. 1. (a) Mil: **S. power,** puissance f de frappe. **S. force,** force f de frappe. (b) **S. clock,** pendule à sonnerie; horloge sonnante. 2. (Spectacle) remarquable, frappant, saisissant; (trait) saillant. -ly, adv. **S. beautiful,** d'une beauté frappante. **striking**[2], s. 1. (a) Frappement m; coups mpl. **Within s. distance,** à portée; à (la) portée de la main. Row: **Rate of s.,** cadence f de nage. (b) Frappe f (de la monnaie). (c) El: Amorçage m (de l'arc). 2. Sonnerie f (d'une horloge). **S. mechanism,** sonnerie. **'striking-distance,** s. Portée f.
strikebound ['straikbaund], a. Paralysé par la grève.
striker ['straikər], s. 1. Frappeur, -euse. 2. Ten: Relanceur, -euse. 2. Ind: Gréviste mf. 3. (Device) (Of clock) Marteau m; (of firearm) percuteur m.
strikingness ['straikiŋnis], s. Caractère frappant, saisissant (d'un spectacle, etc.).
string[1] [striŋ], s. 1. (i) Ficelle f; (ii) corde f, cordon m. **A ball of s.,** une pelote de ficelle. F: **To have s.o. on a s.,** (i) tenir qn en lisière; (ii) se payer la tête de qn; faire marcher qn. **To pull the strings,** tirer les fils, les ficelles. 2. (a) **String** (in beans), fils mpl (des haricots). (b) Anat: Filet m, frein m (de la langue). S.a. APRON-STRINGS, HEART-STRINGS, PURSE-STRINGS. 3. (a) Mus: Corde. **Catgut s.,** corde à boyau. (Of violin) **First s.,** E s., le mi; la chanterelle. (In orchestra) **The strings,** les instruments m à cordes. (b) Corde (d'un arc, etc.). **Strings of a tennis-racket,** cordes, cordage m, d'une raquette. S.a. BOW[1] 4. 4. **S. of beads,** (i) collier m; (ii) Ecc: chapelet m. **S. of onions,** chapelet d'oignons. **S. of medals,** brochette f de décorations. **S. of vehicles,** file f de véhicules.

S. of barges, train m de bateaux. **A long s. of tourists,** une longue procession de touristes. **'string 'bag,** s. Filet m à provisions. **'string-bean,** s. U.S: (a) Haricot vert; mange-tout m inv. (b) F: (Of pers.) Une asperge (montée). **string-'orchestra,** s. Mus: Orchestre m à cordes. **string-piece,** s. Const: etc: Longeron m, longrine f.
string[2], v.tr. (strung [strʌŋ]; strung) 1. (a) Mettre une ficelle, une corde, à (qch.); ficeler (un paquet). (b) Garnir (qch.) de cordes; corder (une raquette); monter (un violon). 2. Bander (un arc). **Highly strung,** nerveux, -euse, impressionnable. 3. Enfiler (des perles). **To s. sentences together,** enfiler des phrases. 4. Cu: Effiler (les haricots). 5. Esp. U.S: F: (i) **To s. s.o. along,** faire marcher qn; (ii) v.i. **To s. along with s.o.,** suivre qn, être copain avec qn. **string up,** v.tr. 1. Pendre (qn) haut et court. **String him up!** à la lanterne! 2. F: **To s. oneself up to do sth.,** tendre toute sa volonté pour faire qch. **stringed,** a. Mus: (Instrument) à cordes.
stringency ['strin(d)ʒənsi], s. Rigueur f, sévérité f (des règles, etc.).
stringent ['strin(d)ʒənt], a. 1. (Règlement) rigoureux, strict. 2. Fin: (Argent) serré; (marché) tendu.
stringer ['striŋər], s. 1. (Pers.) Monteur m de cordes (d'un piano). 2. (a) Const: Tirant m, entrait m (d'une ferme de comble). (b) Longeron m, longrine f; sommier m (d'un pont).
stringiness ['striŋinis], s. 1. Caractère fibreux, filandreux (de la viande, etc.). 2. Caractère visqueux (d'un liquide).
stringy ['striŋi], a. 1. Fibreux, -euse, filandreux, -euse. **S. meat,** viande tendineuse, filandreuse. 2. (Liquide) visqueux, qui file.
strip[1] [strip], s. Bande f (d'étoffe, de papier). **Narrow s.,** bandelette f. **Metal s.,** ruban m métallique. **S. of land,** bande, langue f, de terre. Hort: **S. of onions,** planche f d'oignons. Journ: **S. cartoon, comic s.,** bande illustrée, comics mpl. **S. lighting,** éclairage fluorescent, par fluorescence. Av: **Ground s.-signal,** panneau m. Mil: **Loading s.** (of machine-gun), bande-chargeur f. P: **To tear s.o. off a s.,** laver la tête à qn, donner un savon à qn. **'strip-iron,** s. (Fer) feuillard m; fer en barres.
strip[2], v. (stripped [stript]) I. v.tr. 1. Mettre (qn) tout nu; dépouiller (qn) de ses vêtements. **Stripped to the waist,** nu jusqu'à la ceinture; le torse nu. 2. (a) **To s. s.o. of sth.,** dépouiller qn de qch. **To s. an apple tree,** défruiter un pommier. **Trees stripped of their leaves, of their bark,** arbres dépouillés de leurs feuilles, dénudés de leur écorce. **To s. s.o. of his money,** dévaliser qn. (b) Dégarnir (un lit, une maison); défaire (un lit); démeubler (une maison). El.E: Dépouiller (un câble). Aut: **Stripped chassis,** châssis nu. **To s. a wall,** arracher le papier d'un mur. **Stripped tobacco-leaf,** tabac écôté. Tex: **To s. flax,** teiller le lin. Mec.E: **To s. a nut,** arracher le filet d'un écrou. Metall: **To s. a casting,** démouler une pièce coulée. **To s. sth. off, from, sth.,** ôter, enlever, qch. de qch. II. v.i. 1. (Of pers.) Se dépouiller de ses vêtements; dépouiller ses vêtements; se dévêtir. **To s. to the skin,** F: se mettre à poil. 2. (Of bark, etc.) **To s. (off),** s'enlever, se détacher. **strip down,** v.tr. Démonter (un moteur). **'strip(-)tease,** s. (Mus. Hall.) Acte m de déshabillage m; striptease m. **S.(-)t. artiste,** strippeuse f, stripteaseuse f.
stripe[1] [straip], s. (a) Raie f, barre f (d'un tissu); raie, rayure f, zébrure f (sur le pelage). **Black with a red s.,** noir rayé de rouge. **Table linen with coloured stripes,** linge m de table à liteaux. (b) Bande f (de pantalon). (c) Mil: etc: **Sergeant's stripes,** galons m de sergent. **Long-service s.,** chevron m. **To lose one's stripes,** être dégradé.
stripe[2], v.tr. Rayer, barrer. **striped,** a. (a) (Chaussettes, etc.) à raies; à barres; (pantalon) rayé; (pelage) rayé, tigré. Nat.Hist: Zébré, rubané. (b) Anat: (Muscle) strié.
stripling ['striplin], s. Tout jeune homme; adolescent m.
strive [straiv], v.i. (strove [strouv]; striven [strivn]) 1. **To s. to do sth.,** tâcher, s'efforcer, de faire qch. **To s. for sth.,** essayer d'obtenir qch. **What are you striving after?** à quoi tendent vos efforts? **To s. after effect,** rechercher l'effet. 2. **To s. with, against, s.o.,** lutter, se débattre, contre qn.

strode. *See* STRIDE[2].

stroke[1] [strouk], *s.* Coup *m.* **1. To receive twenty strokes,** recevoir vingt coups (de férule, etc.). **To fell a tree at a s.,** abattre un arbre d'un seul coup. **Finishing s.,** coup de grâce. **2.** (*a*) Coup (d'aile, d'aviron). *Bill: etc:* **Whose s. is it?** à qui de jouer? *Row:* **To lengthen the s.,** allonger la nage. **'Keep s.!' "**nagez ensemble!" (*b*) *Swim:* Brassée *f.* **The swimming strokes,** les nages *f.* **Stroke's length,** nagée *f.* *S.a.* BACK-STROKE 3, BREAST-STROKE, OVERARM. (*c*) *Mec.E:* Mouvement *m,* course *f* (du piston). *I.C.E:* **Two-s. engine,** moteur à deux temps. (*d*) *F:* **He hasn't done a s. of work,** il n'a rien fait de ses dix doigts. (*e*) **S. of (good) luck,** coup de chance. **S. of genius,** trait *m* de génie. **A good s. of business,** une bonne affaire. **3.** Coup (d'horloge, etc.). **On the s. of nine,** sur le coup de neuf heures; à neuf heures sonnant(es). **To arrive on the s. (of time),** arriver à l'heure juste. **4. S. of apoplexy,** attaque *f* d'apoplexie; coup de sang; congestion cérébrale. *F:* **To have a s.,** avoir une attaque. **5.** Coup de crayon, de pinceau; trait de plume. *Typ:* **Thin s.,** délié *m* (d'une lettre). **Thick s.,** plein *m.* **With a s. of the pen,** d'un trait de plume. **6.** *Row:* (*a*) (*Pers.*) Chef *m* de nage. (*b*) **To row s.,** donner la nage. **'stroke-play,** *s. Golf:* Concours *m* par coups.

stroke[2], *v.tr. Row:* **To s. a boat,** être chef de nage d'un canot; donner la nage.

stroke[3], *s.* Caresse *f* de la main.

stroke[4], *v.tr.* Passer la main sur, caresser de la main. **To s. the cat the wrong way,** caresser le chat à contre-poil, à rebrousse-poil. *F:* **To s. s.o. the wrong way,** prendre qn à contre-poil, à rebrousse-poil. **To s. s.o. down,** (i) apaiser la colère de qn; (ii) câliner, cajoler, qn.

stroll[1] [stroul], *s.* Petit tour; bout *m* de promenade; *F:* balade *f.* **To take, go for, a s.,** (aller) faire un tour.

stroll[2], *v.i.* Errer à l'aventure; flâner; déambuler; *F:* se balader. **strolling,** *a.* Vagabond, errant. **S. player,** comédien ambulant; acteur forain.

stroller ['stroulər], *s.* **1.** Flâneur, -euse; promeneur, -euse. **2.** *U.S:* Voiture *f* d'enfant, poussette *f.*

strong [strɔŋ], *a.* (**stronger** ['strɔŋgər]) Fort. **1.** (*a*) Solide. **S. cloth,** drap fort, solide, résistant, qui a du corps. **S. conviction,** ferme conviction. *Com:* **S. market,** marché ferme. **S. character,** caractère fort, ferme. (*b*) **S. constitution,** tempérament robuste. **S. nerves,** nerfs bien équilibrés. **He is not very s.,** il est peu robuste. **2.** (*a*) **S. fellow,** solide gaillard. **S. horse,** cheval vigoureux. **S. voice,** voix forte, puissante. **To be s. in the arm,** avoir le bras fort. **The s. arm of the law,** l'autorité publique. **S. measures,** mesures énergiques. **He is s. enough to overthrow you,** il est de force, de taille, à vous renverser. **S. in Greek,** fort en grec. **Politeness is not his s. point,** la politesse n'est pas son fort. **S. in numbers,** en grand nombre. *Cards:* **S. suit,** couleur longue. **S. partisan,** partisan ardent. **He is s. against . . .,** il s'oppose énergiquement à. . . . **Company two hundred s.,** compagnie forte de deux cents hommes. **S. evidence,** preuves convaincantes. **S. argument,** argument puissant. **S. reason,** forte raison. **S. features,** traits accusés. **S. spring,** ressort puissant. **S. wind,** grand vent. *El:* **S. current,** courant intense. *Mus:* **S. beat,** temps fort. *S.a.* LANGUAGE 2. (*b*) **S. drink,** boissons fortes. **S. solution,** solution concentrée. **S. light,** vive lumière. (*c*) **S. cheese,** fromage qui pique. **S. butter,** beurre rance. (*Of food*) **To have a s. smell,** sentir fort. **3.** *Gram:* (Verbe, etc.) fort. **4.** *adv. F:* **It's still going s.,** ça marche toujours à merveille. **Going s.?** ça marche? **-ly,** *adv.* Fortement. **1.** Solidement, fermement. **2.** Vigoureusement, énergiquement. **S. worded letter,** lettre en termes énergiques. **S. marked,** accentué, prononcé. **I don't feel s. about it,** je n'y attache pas une grande importance. **'strong-arm[1],** *s. F: U.S:* Homme fort, *F:* fortiche *m;* brute *f, F:* battant *m.* **'strong-arm[2],** *v.tr. F: U.S:* Attaquer (qn); *P:* tabasser (qn). **strong-'armed,** *a.* Aux bras forts. **'strong-box,** *s.* Coffre-fort *m.* **strong-'minded,** *a.* A l'esprit solide, résolu, décidé. **S.-m. person,** forte tête. **strong-'mindedness,** *s.* Force *f* de caractère. **'strong(-)room,** *s.* Cave *f* des coffres-forts. *Nau:* Soute *f* aux valeurs.

stronghold ['strɔŋhould], *s.* Forteresse *f;* place forte. **S. of free trade,** citadelle *f* du libre-échange.

strongish ['strɔŋiʃ], *a.* Assez fort.

strontia ['strɔnʃə], *s. Ch:* Strontiane *f.*

strontium ['strɔnʃəm], *s. Ch:* Strontium *m.*

strop[1] [strɔp], *s.* **1.** (Razor-)s., cuir *m,* affiloir *m* (à rasoir). **2.** *Nau:* Estrope *f* (de poulie).

strop[2], *v.tr.* (**stropped** [strɔpt]) Affiler, repasser sur le cuir (un rasoir).

strophanthin [strɔ'fænθin], *s. Pharm:* Strophantine *f.*

strophe ['stroufi], *s. Gr.Lit:* Strophe *f.*

strove. *See* STRIVE.

struck. *See* STRIKE[2].

structural ['strʌktʃərəl], *a.* **1.** De construction. **S. iron,** steel, fer, acier, de construction; charpentes *f* métalliques. **S. engineer,** ingénieur-constructeur *m.* **2.** Structural, -aux.

structure ['strʌktʃər], *s.* **1.** Structure *f;* facture *f* (d'un drame). **2.** (*a*) Édifice *m,* structure, bâtiment *m.* (*b*) *Civ.E:* Ouvrage *m* d'art; travail, -aux *m* d'art. **The social s.,** l'édifice social.

structureless ['strʌktʃəlis], *a. Biol: etc:* Amorphe.

struggle[1] ['strʌgl], *s.* Lutte *f.* **1. Desperate s.,** lutte désespérée; combat acharné. **He gave in without a s.,** il n'a fait aucune résistance. **In the death s.,** à l'agonie; dans les affres *f* de la mort. **2.** *Biol:* **The s. for life,** la lutte pour l'existence; la concurrence vitale.

struggle[2], *v.i.* Lutter (**with, against,** avec, contre); se débattre, se démener. **To be struggling with adversity,** être aux prises avec l'adversité. **To s. hard to succeed,** faire tous ses efforts, faire des pieds et des mains, pour réussir. **They s. for the prize,** ils se disputent le prix. **He struggled to his feet,** il réussit à se relever. **We struggled through,** nous avons surmonté tous les obstacles. **struggle in, out,** *v.i.* Se frayer un passage (à grand-peine). **struggle up,** *v.i.* **1.** (*Adv. use*) Se hisser avec peine jusqu'au sommet (de qch.). **2.** (*Prep. use*) Gravir, escalader, péniblement (une côte, un rocher). **struggling,** *a.* (Artiste) qui vit péniblement, qui cherche à percer.

struggler ['strʌglər], *s.* Lutteur *m.*

strum [strʌm], *v.tr.* (**strummed**) **To s.,** *v.i.* **to s. on, the piano, the guitar,** taper sur le piano; s'escrimer, *F:* jouailler, sur le piano; gratter de la guitare. *Abs.* **To s.,** pianoter. **To s. a tune,** tapoter un air (au piano).

strumpet ['strʌmpit], *s.f. O:* Catin.

strung. *See* STRING[2].

strut[1] [strʌt], *s.* Démarche orgueilleuse, affectée; pas mesuré.

strut[2], *v.i.* (**strutted**) **To s. (about),** se pavaner, se rengorger. **To s. along,** se carrer en marchant. **To s. in, out,** entrer, sortir, d'un air important.

strut[3], *s.* Entretoise *f,* étrésillon *m;* montant *m,* cale *f,* support *m,* étai *m,* traverse *f;* (*spur*) arc-boutant *m,* jambe *f* de force; (*of roof-truss*) contre-fiche *f.*

strut[4], *v.tr.* (**strutted**) *Const: etc:* Entretoiser, étrésillonner; étayer (une tranchée).

struth [struːθ], *int. P:* Ça alors! mince (alors)!

strychnine ['strikniːn], *s.* Strychnine *f.*

stub[1] [stʌb], *s.* **1.** Souche *f* (d'arbre); chicot *m* (d'arbre, de dent); bout *m* (de crayon, de cigare); tronçon *m* (de mât); *P:* mégot *m* (de cigare, de cigarette). *Mec.E:* **S. teeth,** denture tronquée. **2.** *Tchn:* Mentonnet *m* (de serrure). **3.** Souche, talon *m* (de chèque).

stub[2], *v.tr.* (**stubbed**) **1. To s. (up)** roots, extirper des racines. **To s. (out) a field,** essoucher un champ. **2. To s. one's toe against sth.,** se cogner le pied, heurter du pied, contre qch. **3. To s. out a cigarette,** éteindre une cigarette (en l'écrasant le bout).

stubble ['stʌbl], *s.* **1.** Chaume *m;* éteule *f.* **2.** Barbe de trois jours. **'stubble-field,** *s.* Chaume *m.*

stubbly ['stʌbli], *a.* **1.** (Champ) couvert de chaume. **2. S. beard,** (i) barbe de trois jours; (ii) barbe courte et raide.

stubborn ['stʌbən], *a.* **1.** Obstiné, opiniâtre, entêté, têtu; (volonté) tenace; (cheval) rétif. **As s. as a mule,** têtu comme un mulet, comme une mule. **2. S. ore,** minerai réfractaire. **S. fever,** fièvre rebelle. **S. soil,** terre ingrate. **-ly,** *adv.* Obstinément, opiniâtrement.

stubbornness ['stʌbənnis], s. Entêtement m, obstination f, opiniâtreté f; ténacité f (de volonté).

stubby ['stʌbi], a. **1.** (*Of plant, etc.*) Tronqué; (*of pers.*) trapu. **2.** (Terrain) couvert de chicots.

stucco[1] ['stʌkou], s. *Const:* Stuc m. **'stucco-work**, s. Stucage m.

stucco[2], v.tr. (stuccoed) Stuquer; enduire de stuc, de stucage.

stuck [stʌk], a. (a) S. pig, porc égorgé. *F:* **To look like a s. pig**, avoir l'air d'un hibou empaillé. √(b) *F:* Immobilisé; en panne. **'stuck-'up**, a. Prétentieux, -euse, guindé.

stud[1] [stʌd], s. **1.** (a) Clou m à grosse tête, clou doré (pour ornement). (b) Clou (de passage clouté). **2.** Collar s., bouton m de col. Shirt s., bouton de plastron (de chemise). **S.-hole**, boutonnière f. *S.a.* PRESS-STUD. **3.** *Tchn:* (a) Goujon m, tourillon m. Spring s., verrou m à ressort. Locking s., ergot m d'arrêt. (b) *El:* Plot m (de contact); goutte-de-suif f. **4.** *Const:* Poteau m, montant m (de cloison). **'stud-bolt**, s. Goujon m; (goujon) prisonnier m.

stud[2], v.tr. (studded) **1.** Garnir de clous; clouter. **2.** *Const:* Établir la charpente (d'une cloison). **studded**, a. **1.** Garni de clous; clouté. **2.** Parsemé (with, de). Sky s. with stars, ciel piqué d'étoiles. **S. with jewels**, constellé de pierreries. **Style s. with metaphors**, style émaillé de métaphores.

stud[3], s. **1.** Écurie f (de chasse, etc.). **2.** Breeding s., haras m. **'stud-book**, s. Livre m généalogique, registre m (des chevaux, etc.); stud-book m. **'stud-farm**, s. Haras m. **'stud-horse**, s.m. Étalon. **'stud-mare**, s. f (Jument) poulinière.

student ['stju:d(ə)nt], s. **1.** Étudiant, -ante. **Medical s.**, étudiant en médecine. *attrib.* **S. organization**, organisation étudiante, estudiantine. **2.** He is a great s., il est très studieux; il étudie beaucoup.

studentship ['stju:dəntʃip], s. Bourse f d'études.

studio ['stju:diou], s. *Art:* Atelier m. *Cin:* Studio m. *W.Tel: T.V:* Broadcasting s., studio d'émission. **Photographer's s.**, salon m, atelier, de pose.

studious ['stju:diəs], a. **1.** (*Of pers.*) Studieux, -euse, appliqué; adonné à l'étude. **2.** *O:* **S. to do sth.**, attentif à, empressé à, faire qch. **With s. politeness**, avec une politesse étudiée. **-ly**, adv. **1.** Studieusement. **2.** Avec empressement. **He s. avoided me**, il s'étudiait à m'éviter.

studiousness ['stju:diəsnis], s. **1.** Caractère m de celui qui est studieux; attachement m à l'étude. **2.** *O:* Empressement m (in doing sth., à faire qch.).

study[1] ['stʌdi], s. **1.** *A:* Soin(s) m(pl), attention f. **2.** Brown s., rêverie f. **To be (lost) in a brown s.**, être plongé, absorbé, dans ses réflexions, dans de vagues rêveries. **3.** Étude f. **The s. of mathematics**, l'étude des mathématiques. **To make a s. of sth.**, étudier qch. **To finish one's studies**, achever ses études. **His face was a s.**, il fallait voir son visage! **4.** *Art: Mus:* Étude. **5.** (a) Cabinet m de travail. (b) *Sch:* Salle f d'étude. **'study-'bedroom**, s. *Sch:* Chambre f d'étudiant(e).

study[2], v.tr. (studied) **1.** Étudier; observer (les astres); faire des études de (philologie). **He had studied under Professor X**, il avait suivi les cours du professeur X. **To s. for an examination**, préparer un examen. **To s. hard**, travailler ferme. **2.** S'occuper de, se préoccuper de (qn, qch.). **To s. economy**, viser à l'économie. **3.** S'étudier, s'appliquer, chercher (to do sth., à faire qch.). **studied**, a. Étudié, recherché; prémédité, calculé. **S. carelessness**, négligence voulue.

stuff[1] [stʌf], s. **1.** (a) Matière f, substance f, étoffe f. *Carp:* Thick s., planches fpl de doublage. **He is of the s. that heroes are made of**, il est du bois, de la pâte, dont on fait les héros. **You will see what s. I am made of**, vous verrez de quel bois je me chauffe. **There is good s. in him**, il a de l'étoffe. *F:* **He writes nasty s.**, il écrit des saletés fpl. *F:* **Rough s.**, (i) jeu brutal; (ii) *Sp:* cyclo-cross m. *F:* **He knows his s.**, il s'y connaît. *F:* **That's the s.!** c'est du bon! **That's the s. to give him!** c'est comme ça qu'il faut le traiter. *F:* **Come on, do your s.!** allons! montre-nous ce que tu sais faire! *S.a.* HOT 1. (b) *F:* Fatras m. **Silly s.**, sottises fpl, balivernes fpl. **S. and nonsense!** quelle bêtise! allons donc! **2.** *Tex:* Étoffe f, tissu m (de

laine). *Jur: A:* **A s. gownsman**, un avocat en second (qui ne porte pas de soie).

stuff[2], v.tr. **1.** (a) Bourrer (with, de); rembourrer (un meuble). **To s. a child with cakes**, bourrer, gaver, un enfant de gâteaux. *F:* **To s. (oneself)**, se bourrer; bâfrer. (b) *Cu:* Farcir (une volaille). (c) *F: O:* **To s. s.o. for an exam**, chauffer qn en vue d'un examen. (d) Empailler (un animal). **2.** *F:* **To s. s.o. (up)**, bourrer le crâne à qn; faire marcher qn. **3.** **To s. up a hole**, boucher un trou. **My nose is stuffed up**, je suis enchifrené. **4.** **To s. sth. into sth.**, fourrer qch. dans qch. **stuffed**, a. Rembourré; empaillé; *Cu:* farci. *F:* **He's a s. shirt**, c'est un individu (i) suffisant, prétentieux; (ii) collet monté, vieux jeu. **stuffing**, s. **1.** (a) Bourrage m, rembourrage m. (b) Empaillage m. **2.** (a) Bourre f. *Mch:* Garniture f, étoupe f. *F:* **To knock the s. out of s.o.**, flanquer une tripotée à qn. **To take the s. out of s.o.**, dégonfler qn. (b) *Cu:* Farce f. **'stuffing-box**, s. *Mch:* Boîte f à étoupe; presse-étoupe m inv.

stuffiness ['stʌfinis], s. **1.** Manque m d'air; odeur f de renfermé. **2.** Préjugés vieillots. **3.** *Med:* Enchifrènement m.

stuffy ['stʌfi], a. **1.** Mal ventilé; mal aéré. **Room that smells s.**, pièce qui sent le renfermé. **2.** (*Pers.*) *F:* (a) Collet monté inv; aux préjugés vieillots. **Don't be s.!** il n'y a pas de quoi te scandaliser! (b) Lourd, rasoir; ennuyeux, -euse.

stultify ['stʌltifai], v.tr. **1.** Enlever toute valeur à (un argument); infirmer (un décret); rendre inutile (une mesure). **2.** Rendre ridicule (qn); faire ressortir l'absurdité (d'une action). *Jur:* **To s. oneself**, se démentir.

stumble[1] ['stʌmbl], s. Trébuchement m: faux pas; bronchement m (d'un cheval).

stumble[2], v.i. **1.** Trébucher; faire un faux pas; (*of horse*) broncher. **To s. along**, avancer en trébuchant. **To s. over sth.**, buter contre qch. **That is where all have stumbled**, voilà où tous ont achoppé. **2.** **To s. in one's speech**, hésiter en parlant. **To s. through one's lesson**, ânonner sa leçon. **3.** **To s. across, upon, s.o., sth.**, rencontrer qn, qch., par hasard; tomber sur qn, qch. **stumbling**[1], a. Qui trébuche; (*of horse*) qui bronche; (*of speech*) hésitant. **-ly**, adv. **1.** D'un pas mal assuré. **2.** En hésitant. **stumbling**[2], s. **1.** Trébuchement m, faux pas m; bronchement m. **2.** Hésitation f; ânonnement m. **'stumbling-block**, s. Pierre f d'achoppement.

stumer ['stju:mər], s. *F:* **1.** (a) Chèque m sans provision. (b) Faux billet de banque. **2.** Chose qui ne vaut rien.

stump[1] [stʌmp], s. **1.** Tronçon m, souche f (d'arbre); chicot m (de dent); moignon m (de bras, de jambe); bout m (de cigare, de crayon); mégot m (de cigare, cigarette); tronçon (de queue, de mât); trognon m (de chou). **2.** pl. *F:* Jambes, *P:* guiboles f. **You must stir your stumps**, il faut vous remuer. **3.** *F:* **S. orator**, orateur de carrefour; harangueur m. **4.** *Cr:* Piquet m (du guichet). **To draw stumps**, cesser la partie. **5.** *Draw:* Estompe f.

stump[2]. **1.** v.i. **To s. along**, clopiner. **To s. in, out**, entrer, sortir, clopin-clopant. **2.** v.tr. (a) *F:* Coller (un candidat); réduire (qn) à quia. **To s. s.o. on a subject**, faire sécher qn sur un sujet. **This stumped me**, sur le coup je n'ai su que répondre. (b) *Cr:* Mettre hors jeu (un batteur qui est sorti de son camp). (c) *Draw:* Estomper (un dessin). **stump up**, v.i. *F:* Payer, casquer, s'exécuter.

stumper ['stʌmpər], s. *F:* Question embarrassante; *F:* colle f.

stumpy ['stʌmpi], a. (*Of pers.*) Trapu, ragot, ramassé. **S. umbrella**, tom-pouce m.

stun [stʌn], v.tr. (stunned) **1.** Étourdir, assommer. **2.** Renverser, abasourdir. **The news stunned us**, ce fut un coup de massue. **stunning**, a. **1.** (a) (Coup) étourdissant, d'assommoir. (b) (Malheur) accablant. **2.** *F: O:* Renversant; épatant, formidable, sensationnel, -elle, du tonnerre.

stung. See STING[2].

stunk. See STINK[2].

stunner ['stʌnər], s. *F: O:* **1.** Type épatant, formidable, sensationnel, du tonnerre. **She's a s.**, elle est épatante. **2.** Chose épatante.

stunt¹ [stʌnt], *v.tr.* Arrêter (qn, qch.) dans sa croissance; rabougrir. **stunted**, *a.* (Arbre) rabougri, chétif; (esprit) noué. **To become s.**, (se) rabougrir.

stunt², *s.* F: 1. Coup *m*, affaire *f* de publicité. 2. Tour *m* de force. *Av:* **S. flying**, vol de virtuosité. **To perform stunts**, faire des acrobaties (en vol). '**stunt man**, *s.m. Cin: etc: F:* Acrobate *f* (-doublure).

stunt³, *v.i. Av:* Faire des acrobaties (en vol).

stuntedness ['stʌntidnis], *s.* État rabougri.

stupefaction [ˌstjuːpiˈfækʃ(ə)n], *s.* Stupéfaction *f*; stupeur *f*, ahurissement *m*.

stupefier ['stjuːpifaiər], *s. Med:* Stupéfiant *m*.

stupefy ['stjuːpifai], *v.tr.* 1. (*a*) *Med:* Stupéfier, engourdir. (*b*) Hébéter, abrutir. **Stupefied with grief**, hébété par la douleur. 2. Abasourdir, stupéfier. **I am absolutely stupefied (by what has happened)**, je n'en reviens pas; les bras m'en tombent.

stupendous [stjuːˈpendəs], *a.* Prodigieux, -euse; F: formidable. **-ly**, *adv.* Prodigieusement.

stupid ['stjuːpid], *a.* Stupide; sot, *f.* sotte; F: bête. **My pupils are very s.**, mes élèves ont la tête dure, F: j'ai une classe de crétins. **Don't be s.!** ne faites pas la bête! **How s. of me!** que je suis bête! **To drink oneself s.**, s'hébéter, s'abrutir, à force de boire. **-ly**, *adv.* Stupidement, sottement; F: bêtement.

stupidity [stjuːˈpiditi], *s.* Stupidité *f.* (*a*) Lourdeur *f* d'esprit; béotisme *m.* (*b*) Sottise *f*, niaiserie *f*, bêtise *f*; butorderie *f*.

stupor ['stjuːpər], *s.* Stupeur *f.*

sturdiness ['stəːdinis], *s.* 1. Vigueur *f*, robustesse *f*. 2. Résolution *f*, fermeté *f*.

sturdy ['stəːdi], *a.* (*a*) Vigoureux, -euse, robuste. (*b*) (*Of opposition, etc.*) Hardi, résolu, ferme. **-ily**, *adv.* 1. Fortement; avec robustesse. 2. Hardiment, vigoureusement.

sturgeon ['stəːdʒ(ə)n], *s. Ich:* Esturgeon *m.*

stutter¹ ['stʌtər], *s.* Bégaiement *m.*

stutter², *v.i. & tr.* Bégayer, bredouiller. **stuttering¹**, *a.* Bègue. **-ly**, *adv.* En bégayant. **stuttering²**, *s.* Bégaiement *m.*

stutterer ['stʌtərər], *s.* Bègue *mf.*

sty¹, *pl.* **sties** [stai, staiz], *s.* (*a*) Étable *f* (à porcs); porcherie *f.* (*b*) Taudis *m.*

sty², **stye** [stai], *s. Med:* Orgelet *m*, F: compère-loriot *m*, *pl.* compères-loriots.

Stygian [ˈstidʒiən], *a.* Stygien, -ienne. **S. gloom**, (i) nuit noire, (ii) humeur noire, comme le Styx.

style¹ [stail], *s.* 1. (*a*) *Ant:* Style *m* (pour écrire). (*b*) *Engr:* Style, burin *m.* (*c*) *Surg:* Stylet *m* (à bout olivaire). (*d*) (*Of sundial*) Style, gnomon *m.* (*e*) *Bot:* Style. 2. (*a*) Style, manière *f*, façon *f.* **S. of living**, manière de vivre; train *m* de maison. **To live in (grand, great) s.**, mener grand train. **They drove up in s.**, ils ont fait leur entrée en grand équipage. **In good s.**, dans le bon genre; de bon goût, de bon ton. **To win in fine s.**, gagner haut la main. F: **That's the s.!** bravo! à la bonne heure! **Furniture in the Empire s.**, meubles style Empire. **In the s. of the last century**, dans le goût du siècle dernier. (*b*) Style, genre; type *m*, modèle *m.* **Made in three styles**, fabriqué en trois genres, sur trois modèles. **Something in that s.**, quelque chose de ce genre; quelque chose dans ce goût-là. (*c*) **In the latest s.**, à la dernière mode; F: dernier cri. 3. Style; manière d'écrire. **Written in a humorous s.**, écrit sur un ton de plaisanterie. **Writer who lacks s.**, écrivain qui n'a pas de style. 4. Ton *m*, chic *m*, cachet *m.* **She has s.**, elle a de l'allure, du chic, du genre. **There is no s. about her**, elle manque de chic. 5. Titre *m*, nom *m*; *Com:* raison sociale; firme *f.* 6. *Hist:* **March 14th, old s., new s.**, le 14 mars, vieux style, nouveau style.

style², *v.tr.* 1. Dénommer; appeler. **To s. oneself Doctor**, se donner le titre de docteur; se faire appeler docteur. 2. *Com:* Créer.

stylish ['stailiʃ], *a.* Élégant, chic; coquet, -ette; (chapeau) habillé, qui a du chic. **-ly**, *adv.* Élégamment; avec chic.

stylishness ['stailiʃnis], *s.* Élégance *f*, chic *m.*

stylist ['stailist], *s. Lit:* Styliste *mf.*

stylistic [staiˈlistik], *a.* Du style.

stylistics [staiˈlistiks], *s.pl.*, Stylistique *f.*

stylization [ˌstailaiˈzeiʃ(ə)n], *s.* Stylisation *f.*

stylize ['stailaiz], *v.tr. Art:* Styliser.

stylobate ['stailəbeit], *s. Arch:* Stylobate *m*; soubassement *m* (de colonnade).

stylus ['stailəs], *s.* Style *m.*

stymie¹ ['staimi], *s. Golf:* Trou barré.

stymie², *v.tr. Golf:* Barrer le trou (à son adversaire). F: **I'm completely stymied**, je suis dans une impasse.

styptic ['stiptik], *a. & s. Med:* Styptique (*m*).

suasion ['sweiʒ(ə)n], *s. O:* Persuasion *f.*

suave [swɑːv, sweiv], *a.* 1. Suave; doux, *f.* douce. 2. (*a*) (Accueil) affable. (*b*) *Pej:* **S. manners**, manières doucereuses. **-ly**, *adv.* 1. Suavement. 2. (*a*) Avec affabilité. (*b*) *Pej:* Doucereusement.

suavity ['swɑːviti, 'swæv-], *s.* (*a*) Affabilité *f.* (*b*) *Pej:* Politesse mielleuse.

sub¹ [sʌb], *s. F:* (*Abbreviation for:*) 1. SUBSCRIPTION. 2. SUB-EDITOR. 3. SUBALTERN 2. 4. SUBMARINE 2.

sub², *v. F:* (*Abbreviation for:*) 1. SUB-EDIT. 2. SUB-STITUTE² 2. **To s. for s.o.**, remplacer qn.

subacetate [sʌbˈæsiteit], *s. Ch:* Sous-acétate *m.*

subacid [sʌbˈæsid], *a.* 1. Aigrelet, -ette. 2. (Ton) aigre-doux.

subacute [ˈsʌbəˈkjuːt], *a. Med:* Subaigu, -uë.

sub-agency [sʌbˈeidʒ(ə)nsi], *s.* Sous-agence *f.*

sub-agent [sʌbˈeidʒ(ə)nt], *s.* Sous-agent *m.*

subalpine [sʌbˈælpain], *a.* Subalpin.

subaltern ['sʌblt(ə)n], 1. *a.* Subalterne, subordonné. 2. *s. Mil:* Lieutenant *m*; sous-lieutenant *m.*

subarctic [sʌbˈɑːktik], *a.* Presque arctique.

subatomic [ˈsʌbəˈtɒmik], *a.* Subatomique.

subchloride [sʌbˈklɔːraid], *s. Ch:* Sous-chlorure *m.*

subclass ['sʌbklɑːs], *s. Nat.Hist:* Sous-classe *f.*

sub-commission [ˈsʌbkəˈmiʃ(ə)n], *s.* Sous-commission *f.*

subcommittee ['sʌbkəˌmiti], *s.* Sous-comité *m*; sous-commission *f.*

subconscious ['sʌbˈkɒnʃəs], *a. Psy:* Subconscient. **The s. self**, *s.* **the subconscious**, l'inconscient *m.* **-ly**, *adv.* Inconsciemment.

subconsciousness ['sʌbˈkɒnʃəsnis], *s. Psy:* Subconscience *f.*

subcontinent ['sʌbˈkɒntinənt], *s.* **The Indian s.**, la péninsule indienne. **The s. of Greenland**, l'île de Groenland, le Groenland.

subcontract¹ ['sʌbˈkɒntrækt], *s.* Sous-traité *m.*

subcontract² [ˈsʌbkənˈtrækt], *v.tr.* Sous-traiter (une affaire).

subcontractor ['sʌbkənˈtræktər], *s.* Sous-entrepreneur *m*, sous-traitant *m.*

subculture¹ ['sʌbˈkʌltʃər], *s. Bac:* Repiquage *m.*

subculture², *v.tr. Bac:* Repiquer.

subcutaneous [ˌsʌbkjuːˈteiniəs], *a.* Sous-cutané.

subdeacon [sʌbˈdiːk(ə)n], *s. Ecc:* Sous-diacre *m.*

subdivide ['sʌbdiˈvaid]. 1. *v.tr.* Subdiviser. 2. *v.i.* Se subdiviser.

subdivision ['sʌbdiˌviʒ(ə)n], *s.* Subdivision *f*; sous-division *f.*

subdominant ['sʌbˈdɒminənt], *s. Mus:* Sous-dominante *f.*

subdue [səbˈdjuː], *v.tr.* 1. Subjuguer, soumettre, assujettir (une tribu); maîtriser (un incendie); dompter (ses passions); 2. Adoucir (la lumière, la voix); assourdir (une couleur); amortir, atténuer (la lumière, la douleur). **subdued**, *a.* 1. (Peuple) vaincu, subjugué. 2. (*Of pers.*) Déprimé. 3. **S. light**, demi-jour *m*; lumière tamisée, atténuée. **S. conversation**, conversation à voix basse. **In a s. voice**, à voix basse; à mi-voix.

sub-edit ['sʌbˈedit], *v.tr. Journ:* Corriger, mettre au point (un article).

sub-editor ['sʌbˈeditər], *s. Journ:* Secrétaire *m* de la rédaction.

subfusc ['sʌbˈfʌsk], *a.* (*a*) Sombre. *s.* **In s.**, habillé de couleurs sombres. (*b*) F: (*Of pers.*) Insignifiant, terne.

subgenus, *pl.* **-genera** ['sʌbˈdʒiːnəs, -ˈdʒenərə], *s. Nat.Hist:* Sous-genre *m.*

subgrade ['sʌbgreid], *s. Civ.E:* Hérisson *m* (d'une route).

subheading ['sʌbˈhediŋ], *s.* Sous-titre *m.*

subhuman ['sʌbˈhjuːmən], *a.* 1. Pas tout à fait humain. F: **He's positively s.**, il est bête comme ses pieds. 2. Presque humain.

subjacent ['sʌb'dʒeis(ə)nt], *a.* Sous-jacent, subjacent.

subject¹ ['sʌbdʒikt], *s.* 1. Sujet, -ette (d'un souverain). British s., sujet britannique. 2. *Gram:* Sujet (du verbe). 3. (*a*) Sujet (de conversation, etc.); objet *m* (de méditation). S. picture, tableau de genre. Let us return to our s., revenons au sujet, à notre texte, à nos moutons. On the s. of . . ., au sujet de. . . . To change the s., parler d'autre chose; changer de sujet. (*b*) *Sch:* What subjects do you teach? quelles matières enseignez-vous? 4. To be a s. of experiment, servir de sujet d'expérience. Good hypnotic s., sujet facile à hypnotiser. 'subject-matter, *s.* contenu *m* (d'un livre); contenu *m* (d'une lettre); objet *m* (d'un contrat réel).

subject², *a.* 1. (Pays) assujetti, soumis (to, à); sous la dépendance (to, de). S. to the laws of nature, soumis aux lois de la nature. S. to military law, justiciable des tribunaux militaires. 2. (*a*) Sujet, exposé (à des accès de fièvre, etc.). He is s. to extraordinary whims, il lui prend des lubies impossibles. (*b*) Prices s. to 5 % discount, prix qui comportent 5 % d'escompte. S. to stamp duty, passible du droit de timbre. The plan is s. to modifications, ce projet pourra subir des modifications. 3. (*Conditional*) S. to ratification, sous réserve de ratification. S. to alteration, sauf nouvel avis; sauf correction.

subject³ [səb'dʒekt], *v.tr.* 1. Assujettir, subjuguer (un peuple). 2. To s. s.o. to an operation, soumettre qn à une opération. To s. s.o., sth., to an examination, faire subir un examen à qn; soumettre qch. à un examen. To s. s.o. to criticism, critiquer qn. To be subjected to much criticism, être en butte à de nombreuses critiques.

subjection [səb'dʒekʃ(ə)n], *s.* Sujétion *f*, soumission *f*, assujettissement *m* (to, à). To hold s.o. in s., tenir qn sous sa dépendance. To be in s. to s.o., être soumis à qn. To bring into s., soumettre, assujettir.

subjective [sʌb'dʒektiv], *a.* 1. *Phil:* Subjectif, -ive. 2. *Gram:* The s. case, le cas sujet; le nominatif. -ly, *adv.* Subjectivement.

subjoin ['sʌb'dʒɔin], *v.tr.* Ajouter, adjoindre (une liste, etc.). The subjoined details, les détails ci-joints.

sub judice ['sʌb'dʒuː'disi]. *Lt.phr. Jur:* The case is s. j., l'affaire n'est pas encore jugée, est encore devant les tribunaux.

subjugate ['sʌbdʒugeit], *v.tr.* Subjuguer, soumettre, assujettir (un peuple); dompter (un animal, ses passions).

subjugation [,sʌbdʒu'geiʃ(ə)n], *s.* Subjugation *f*, assujettissement *m*.

subjunctive [səb'dʒʌŋ(k)tiv], *a. & s. Gram:* Subjonctif (*m*). In the s. (mood), au subjonctif.

sublease¹ ['sʌb'liːs], *s.* Sous-bail *m*, sous-location *f*.

sublease² *v.tr.* Sous-louer (un appartement); sous-affermer (une terre).

sublessee ['sʌble'siː], *s.* Sous-locataire *mf*.

sublessor ['sʌble'sɔːr], *s.* Sous-bailleur, -bailleresse.

sublet¹ ['sʌblet], *s. F:* Sous-bail *m*, sous-location *f*.

sublet² ['sʌb'let], *v.tr.* (-let; -letting) Sous-louer (un appartement); sous-affermer (une terre).

sub-librarian ['sʌblai'breəriən], *s.* Sous-bibliothécaire *mf*.

sub-lieutenant ['sʌblef'tenənt], *s. Navy:* Enseigne *m* (de vaisseau).

sublimate¹ ['sʌblimit], *s. Ch:* Sublimé *m.* Corrosive s., sublimé corrosif.

sublimate² ['sʌblimeit], *v.tr.* 1. Sublimer (le soufre). 2. Raffiner, idéaliser (un sentiment).

sublimation [,sʌbli'meiʃ(ə)n], *s.* Sublimation *f*.

sublime [sə'blaim]. 1. *a.* (*a*) Sublime. (*b*) S. indifference, suprême indifférence. S. impudence, impudence sans pareille. 2. *s.* The s., le sublime. -ly, *adv.* 1. Sublimement. 2. To be s. unconscious of . . ., être dans une ignorance absolue de. . . .

subliminal [sʌb'liminl], *a. Psy:* Subliminal, -aux. *Com:* S. advertising, publicité insidieuse.

sublimity [sə'blimiti], *s.* Sublimité *f*.

sub-machine-gun ['sʌbmə'ʃiːngʌn], *s.* Mitraillette *f*.

sub-manager ['sʌb'mænidʒər], *s.* Sous-directeur *m*, sous-gérant *m*.

sub-manageress ['sʌb,mænidʒə'res], *s.f.* Sous-directrice, sous-gérante.

submarine ['sʌbməriːn]. 1. *a.* Sous-marin. 2. *s.* (Navire) sous-marin *m. S.a.* PEN¹.

submerge [sʌb'məːdʒ]. 1. *v.tr.* (*a*) Submerger, immerger. (*b*) Inonder, noyer (un champ). 2. *v.i.* (*Of submarine*) Plonger; effectuer sa plongée.

submerged, *a.* 1. (*a*) Submergé. *I.C.E:* The jet is s., le gicleur est noyé. S. vessel, navire englouti par les flots. (*b*) S. submarine, sous-marin en plongée. S. speed, vitesse en plongée. (*c*) S. reef, écueil sous-marin. 2. *a. & s.* The s. (tenth), les nécessiteux *m*; les économiquement faibles.

submergence [sʌb'məːdʒ(ə)ns], *s.* Submersion *f*; plongée *f* (d'un sous-marin).

submersible [sʌb'məːsəbl], *a. & s.* Submersible (*m*); sous-marin (*m*).

submersion [sʌb'məːʃ(ə)n], *s.* Submersion *f*; plongée *f*.

submission [səb'miʃ(ə)n], *s.* 1. (*a*) Soumission *f* (à une autorité); résignation *f* (à une défaite). To starve s.o. into s., réduire qn par la famine. (*b*) Docilité *f*; humilité *f*. 2. Soumission (d'une question à un arbitre). 3. *Jur:* Plaidoirie *f*. In my s., selon ma thèse.

submissive [səb'misiv], *a.* Soumis, humble, résigné. -ly, *adv.* D'un ton soumis; avec docilité.

submissiveness [səb'misivnis], *s.* Soumission *f*, docilité *f*. In all s., très humblement.

submit [səb'mit], *v.* (submitted) 1. *v.i. & pr.* Se soumettre (to, à); se plier (à une nécessité); s'astreindre (à la discipline); se résigner (à un malheur). 2. *v.tr.* (*a*) Soumettre. To s. sth. to s.o.'s inspection, soumettre, présenter, qch. à l'inspection de qn. To s. proofs of identity, présenter des pièces d'identité. To s. a question to a court, saisir un tribunal d'une question. (*b*) To s. that . . ., représenter, alléguer, que . . .; poser en thèse que . . .

submultiple ['sʌb'mʌltipl], *a. & s. Mth:* Sous-multiple (*m*) (of, de).

subnormal ['sʌb'nɔːm(ə)l], 1. *a.* (Température, etc.) au-dessous de la normale. 2. *s. Geom:* Sous-normale *f*, sous-perpendiculaire *f* (d'une courbe).

sub-office ['sʌb,ɔfis], *s. Com:* Succursale *f*; filiale *f*; bureau *m* auxiliaire.

suborder ['sʌb,ɔːdər], *s. Nat.Hist:* Sous-ordre *m*.

subordinate¹ [sə'bɔːdinit]. 1. *a.* (*a*) (Rang, etc.) inférieur, subalterne; (rôle) secondaire, accessoire. (*b*) Subordonné (to, à). *Gram:* S. clause, proposition subordonnée. 2. *s.* Subordonné, -ée. -ly, *adv.* D'une façon secondaire; en sous-ordre.

subordinate² [sə'bɔːdineit], *v.tr.* Subordonner (to, à).

subordination [sə,bɔːdi'neiʃ(ə)n], *s.* 1. Subordination *f* (to, à). 2. Soumission *f* (to, à).

suborn [sə'bɔːn], *v.tr. Jur:* Suborner, corrompre, séduire (un témoin). **suborning**, *s.* = SUBORNATION.

subornation [,sʌbɔː'neiʃ(ə)n], *s.* Subornation *f*, corruption *f*, séduction *f* (de témoins).

suborner [sə'bɔːnər], *s.* Suborneur, -euse.

subpoena¹ [səb'piːnə], *s. Jur:* Citation *f*, assignation *f* (de témoins) (sous peine d'amende).

subpoena², *v.tr.* (subpoenaed) To s. s.o. to appear, citer, assigner, qn à comparaître (sous peine d'amende). To s. a witness, signifier une assignation à un témoin.

subpolar ['sʌb'poulər], *a.* Subpolaire.

subrent ['sʌb'rent], *v.tr.* Sous-louer; prendre (un appartement) en sous-location.

subrogate ['sʌbrogeit], *v.tr. Jur:* Subroger.

subrogation [,sʌbro'geiʃ(ə)n], *s. Jur:* Subrogation *f* (d'un créancier); substitution *f* (de créancier).

sub rosa ['sʌb'rousə], *Lt. adv. phr.* Secrètement, confidentiellement; sub rosa.

subscribe [səb'skraib], *v.tr.* 1. (*a*) Souscrire (son nom). To s. one's name to a document, apposer sa signature à un document. (*b*) *Abs.* To s. to an opinion, souscrire à une opinion. 2. (*a*) To s. ten pounds, souscrire pour (la somme de) dix livres. To s. to a charity, verser sa cotisation à une œuvre de charité. *Fin:* To s. shares, souscrire des actions. To s. to a loan, souscrire à un emprunt. Subscribed capital, capital souscrit. (*b*) To s. to a newspaper, (i) s'abonner, prendre un abonnement, à un journal; (ii) être abonné à un journal. (*c*) *Publ:* To s. a book, (i) (*of publisher*) offrir un livre en souscription; (ii) (*of bookseller*) acheter un livre en souscription.

subscriber [səbˈskraibər], *s.* **1.** Signataire *mf*, souscripteur *m* (d'un document). **The s.,** (i) le soussigné; (ii) le contractant. **2. S. to a charity, for shares,** cotisant, -ante, souscripteur, à une œuvre de charité, souscripteur à des actions. **3.** Abonné, -ée (à un journal, au téléphone).

subscription [səbˈskrip∫(ə)n], *s.* **1.** (*a*) Souscription *f* (de son nom); signature *f*. (*b*) Adhésion *f* (**to,** à); approbation *f* (**to, de**). **2. To pay a s.,** verser une cotisation. **To get up a s.,** se cotiser. *Fin:* **S. to a loan,** souscription à un emprunt. **S. list,** liste des souscripteurs. **S. dance,** bal par souscription. **3.** Abonnement *m* (à un journal, etc.). **To take out a s. to a paper,** s'abonner à un journal. **S. to a club,** cotisation (annuelle) à un cercle. **To withdraw one's s.,** se désabonner.

subsequence [ˈsʌbsikwəns], *s.* **1.** Postériorité *f.* **2.** Événement subséquent; conséquence *f.*

subsequent [ˈsʌbsikwənt], *a.* (Chapitre, etc.) subséquent, qui suit. **At a s. meeting,** dans une séance ultérieure. **S. to . . .,** postérieur, consécutif, à . . . **-ly,** *adv.* Plus tard; dans la suite; postérieurement (to, à).

subservience [səbˈsəːviəns], *s.* **1.** Utilité *f* (**to,** à). **2.** Soumission *f*, servilité *f.* **S. to fashion,** asservissement *m* à la mode.

subservient [səbˈsəːviənt], *a.* **1.** Utile, qui aide (**to,** à). **To make sth. s. to sth.,** faire servir qch. à qch. **2.** Subordonné (**to,** à). **3.** Obséquieux, -euse, servile.

subside [səbˈsaid], *v.i.* **1.** (*a*) (*Of sediment*) Tomber au fond; se précipiter. (*b*) (*Of liquid*) Déposer. **2.** (*Of ground, building*) S'affaisser, se tasser, s'enfoncer. **To s. into an armchair,** s'affaler, s'effondrer, dans un fauteuil. **3.** (*Of water, etc.*) Baisser. **The flood is subsiding,** la crue diminue. **4.** (*a*) (*Of storm, anger, fever, etc.*) S'apaiser, se calmer, tomber. (*b*) (*Of pers.*) Se taire.

subsidence [ˈsʌbsid(ə)ns], *s.* **1.** (*a*) Affaissement *m*; dénivellation *f*, dénivellement *m*; effondrement *m*; tassement *m* (des fondations). (*b*) Décrue *f*, baisse *f* (d'une rivière). (*c*) Apaisement *m* (d'une fièvre, d'une colère). **2.** *Geol:* Effondrement.

subsidiary [səbˈsidjəri], *a.* Subsidiaire, auxiliaire. *Book-k:* **S. account,** sous-compte *m. Fin:* **S. company,** *s.* **subsidiary,** filiale *f.* **-ily,** *adv.* Subsidiairement; en second lieu.

subsidize [ˈsʌbsidaiz], *v.tr.* Subventionner; primer (une industrie). **To be subsidized by the State,** recevoir une subvention de l'État.

subsidy [ˈsʌbsidi], *s.* Subvention *f; Ind:* prime *f.*

subsist [səbˈsist], *v.i.* Subsister. (*a*) Continuer d'être. **Custom that still subsists,** coutume qui existe encore, qui persiste. (*b*) S'entretenir, vivre (**on, de**). **To s. on vegetables,** se nourrir de légumes.

subsistence [səbˈsist(ə)ns], *s.* **1.** Existence *f.* **2. Means of s.,** moyens de subsistance *f.* **A bare s. wage,** un salaire à peine suffisant pour vivre.

subsoil [ˈsʌbsɔil], *s. Geol: Agr:* Sous-sol *m.* **To sell soil and s.,** vendre le fonds et le tréfonds. **S. plough,** fouilleuse *f.*

subsonic [ˈsʌbˈsɔnik], *a. Aer:* Subsonique.

subspecies [ˈsʌbˈspiːʃiːz], *s. Nat.Hist:* Sous-espèce *f.*

substance [ˈsʌbst(ə)ns], *s.* **1.** *Phil: Ch:* Substance *f*, matière *f.* **2.** Substance, fond *m*, essentiel *m* (d'un article, d'un argument). **3.** Solidité *f.* **Book of s.,** livre solide. **Argument of little s.,** argument qui n'a rien de solide. **4.** Avoir *m*, bien *m*, fortune *f.* **Man of s.,** homme à de quoi, qui a du bien; *F:* homme cossu, aisé.

substandard [ˈsʌbˈstændəd], *a.* Inférieur au niveau acceptable, au niveau normal, à la norme. *Com: Ind:* **S. goods,** marchandises inférieures.

substantial [səbˈstæn∫(ə)l], *a.* **1.** Substantiel, -elle, réel, *f.* réelle. **2.** Important. **S. reasons,** raisons sérieuses. **S. proof,** preuve concluante. **A s. difference,** une différence appréciable, sensible. **3.** (*a*) **S. food,** nourriture substantielle. **S. meal,** repas copieux, solide. (*b*) Solide; (drap) résistant. **S. furniture,** ameublement solide et riche. **Man of s. build,** homme bien taillé. **4.** (Bourgeois) cossu, aisé; (maison de commerce) bien assise. **-ally,** *adv.* Substantiellement. **1.** Réellement; en substance. **2.** Solidement. **3.** Fortement. **This contributed s. to our success,** cela a contribué pour une grande part à notre succès.

substantiality [səbˌstænʃiˈæliti], *s.* **1.** Solidité *f*, caractère *m* solide (d'une construction, etc.). **2.** Réalité *f.* **3.** *Jur:* Bien-fondé *m* (d'une accusation etc.).

substantiate [səbˈstænʃieit], *v.tr.* Établir, justifier (une affirmation). **To s. a claim,** établir le bien-fondé d'une réclamation.

substantiation [səbˌstænʃiˈeiʃ(ə)n], *s.* Justification *f* (d'une affirmation); énumération *f* des faits à l'appui (d'une accusation).

substantive [ˈsʌbst(ə)ntiv]. **1.** *a.* (*a*) *Gram:* Substantif, -ive. (*b*) Réel, *f.* réelle, indépendant. *Jur:* **S. law,** droit positif. **2.** *s. Gram:* Substantif *m*, nom *m.* **-ly,** *adv.* Substantivement.

sub-station [ˈsʌbˌsteiʃ(ə)n], *s.* Sous-station *f; El.E:* sous-centrale *f.*

substitute[1] [ˈsʌbstitjuːt], *s.* **1.** (*Pers.*) (*a*) Suppléant, -ante; intérimaire *mf*; remplaçant(e). **To find a s.,** se faire suppléer. (*b*) Mandataire *mf*; représentant(e). **2.** (*a*) (*Of food-stuffs, etc.*) Succédané *m* (**for, de**). **Coffee s.,** café ersatz. (*b*) **Beware of substitutes,** se méfier des contrefaçons *f.*

substitute[2]. **1.** *v.tr.* Substituer. **To s. margarine for butter,** substituer la margarine au beurre; remplacer le beurre par la margarine. **2.** *v.i.* **To s. for s.o.,** remplacer, suppléer, qn.

substitution [ˌsʌbstiˈtjuːʃ(ə)n], *s.* Substitution *f*, remplacement *m.*

substratum, *pl.* **-a, -ums** [ˈsʌbˈstreitəm, -ə, -əmz, -ˈstrɑː-], *s.* Couche inférieure; sous-couche *f. Agr:* Sous-sol *m.* **A s. of truth,** un fond de vérité.

substructure [ˈsʌbˌstrʌktiər], *s. Const:* Substruction *f*, fondement *m* (d'un édifice). *Civ.E:* Infrastructure *f.* **The social s.,** les bases *f* de la société.

subtangent [ˈsʌbˈtæn(d)ʒ(ə)nt], *s. Geom:* Sous-tangente *f.*

subtenancy [ˈsʌbˈtenənsi], *s.* Sous-location *f.*

subtenant [ˈsʌbˈtenənt], *s.* Sous-locataire *mf.*

subtend [səbˈtend], *v.tr. Geom:* Sous-tendre (un arc).

subterfuge [ˈsʌbtəfjuːdʒ], *s.* Subterfuge *m*; faux-fuyant *m.* **To resort to s.,** user de subterfuge.

subterranean [ˌsʌbtəˈreiniən], *a.* Souterrain.

subtilization [ˌsʌbtilaiˈzeiʃ(ə)n], *s.* Tendance *f* à subtiliser; raffinement *m*, ergotage *m.*

subtilize [ˈsʌbtilaiz]. **1.** *v.tr.* Subtiliser; raffiner (son style); *Pej:* alambiquer (sa pensée). **2.** *v.i.* Subtiliser, raffiner; discuter sur des vétilles.

subtitle[1] [ˈsʌbˌtaitl], *s.* Sous-titre *m.*

subtitle[2], *v.tr. Cin:* Sous-titrer. **subtitling,** *s.* Sous-titrage *m.*

subtle [ˈsʌtl], *a.* Subtil. **1.** (*a*) (Parfum) délicat. (*b*) (Charme) qui échappe à l'analyse. **S. distinction,** distinction subtile. **2.** (Esprit) fin, raffiné; (dispositif) ingénieux. **S. irony,** fine ironie. (*b*) Rusé, astucieux, -euse. **-tly,** *adv.* Subtilement; avec finesse.

subtlety [ˈsʌtlti], *s.* **1.** Subtilité *f.* (*a*) Raffinement *m*, finesse *f.* (*b*) Distinction subtile. **2.** Ruse *f*, astuce *f.*

subtonic [ˈsʌbˈtɔnik], *s. Mus:* (Note *f*) sensible *f.*

subtract [səbˈtrækt], *v.tr. Mth:* Soustraire; retrancher (**from, de**).

subtraction [səbˈtrækʃ(ə)n], *s. Mth:* Soustraction *f.*

subtropical [ˈsʌbˈtrɔpik(ə)l], *a.* Subtropical, -aux.

suburb [ˈsʌbəːb], *s.* Banlieue *f.* **In the suburbs,** dans la banlieue. **Garden s.,** cité-jardin *f.*

suburban [səˈbəːb(ə)n], *a.* (*a*) Suburbain; (maison, pavillon, train) de banlieue. (*b*) *Pej:* (*Of pers.*) A l'esprit étroit.

suburbanite [səˈbəːbənait], *s. F: Often Pej:* Banlieusard, -arde.

suburbia [səˈbəːbiə], *s.* (*a*) La banlieue. (*b*) La manière de pensée qui caractérise un banlieusard.

subversion [sʌbˈvəːʃ(ə)n], *s. Pol: etc:* Subversion *f*; renversement *m* (d'un système).

subversive [sʌbˈvəːsiv], *a.* Subversif, -ive.

subvert [sʌbˈvəːt], *v.tr.* Renverser, subvertir.

subway [ˈsʌbwei], *s.* (*a*) Passage, couloir souterrain. (*b*) *El.E:* **Cable s.,** tunnel *m* de câbles. (*c*) *U.S:* Métro *m.*

succeed [səkˈsiːd], *v.tr. & i.* **1.** (*a*) Succéder (à qn, à qch.). **To s. to the throne,** succéder à la couronne. **To s. to an estate,** hériter d'une propriété. **To s. a minister,** prendre la succession d'un ministre. **George**

III **was succeeded by George IV,** George III eut pour successeur George IV. (b) **Day succeeds day,** les jours se suivent. **Winter is succeeded by spring,** le printemps suit l'hiver. 2. *v.i.* Réussir; atteindre son but; venir à bien. **How to s.,** le moyen de parvenir. **To s. in doing sth.,** réussir, parvenir, arriver, à faire qch.; venir à bout de faire qch. **succeeding,** *a.* 1. Suivant, subséquent. 2. A venir; futur. 3. Successif.

success [sək'ses], *s.* 1. A: Succès *m*, issue *f* (d'une affaire). 2. (a) Succès, réussite *f*; issue heureuse. **To meet with s.,** avoir, obtenir, remporter, du succès; réussir. **Man who has achieved s.,** homme qui a réussi. **Without s.,** sans succès; sans y parvenir. (b) (Of venture) **To be, turn out, a s.,** réussir; (of play) avoir du succès. **The evening was a great s.,** la soirée a été très réussie. **He was a s. as Hamlet,** il était excellent dans le rôle de Hamlet. **To make a s. of sth.,** réussir qch.

successful [sək'sesf(u)l], *a.* (Projet) couronné de succès; (résultat) heureux; (portrait) réussi. **S. play,** pièce qui a du succès. **To be entirely s.,** remporter un succès complet. **To be s. in doing sth.,** réussir à faire qch. **He is s. in everything,** tout lui réussit. **S. candidates,** (i) candidats élus; (ii) *Sch:* candidats reçus. **-fully,** *adv.* Avec succès.

succession [sək'se∫(ə)n], *s.* Succession *f.* 1. (a) Suite *f.* **In s.,** successivement; à la file. **For two years in s.,** pendant deux années successives, consécutives. **In rapid s.,** coup sur coup. (b) Série *f*, suite (de victoires, etc.). **After a s. of losses,** après des pertes successives. 2. (a) Succession (à la couronne, etc.). **In s. to s.o.,** en remplacement de qn. (b) *Jur:* **Title by s.,** titre par droit de succession. **S. duties,** droits de succession, de mutation. **To tie up a s.,** rendre un legs inaliénable. (c) Héritage *m.* (d) Lignée *f*; descendance *f*, descendants *mpl.*

successive [sək'sesiv], *a.* Successif, -ive, consécutif, -ive. **-ly,** *adv.* Successivement; (i) à mesure; (ii) tour à tour.

successor [sək'sesər], *s.* Successeur *m* (to, of, de). **To appoint a s. to s.o.,** remplacer qn.

succinct [sək'siŋ(k)t], *a.* Succinct, concis. **-ly,** *adv.* Succinctement; en peu de mots.

succinctness [sək'siŋktnis], *s.* Concision *f*; brièveté *f.*

succour[1] ['sʌkər], *s. Lit:* Secours *m*; aide *f.*

succour[2], *v.tr. Lit:* Secourir, soulager (les malheureux); venir en aide à, venir à l'aide de (qn).

succulence ['sʌkjuləns], *s.* Succulence *f.*

succulent ['sʌkjulənt], *a.* (a) Succulent. (b) *Bot:* **S. leaf,** feuille charnue. (c) *s. Bot:* Plante grasse.

succumb [sə'kʌm], *v.i.* Succomber; céder. **To s. to temptation,** succomber à la tentation. **To s. to force,** succomber sous le nombre. **To s. to one's injuries,** succomber à, mourir de, ses blessures.

such [sʌt∫]. I. *a.* Tel *f.* telle, pareil, -eille, semblable. 1. (a) **Poets s. as Keats, s. poets as Keats,** des poètes tels que Keats. **S. men as he and I,** des gens comme lui et moi. **S. food is very unwholesome,** les aliments de cette nature sont très malsains. **S. a man,** un tel homme. **S. things,** de telles choses. **In s. cases,** en pareils cas. **Did you ever see s. a thing!** a-t-on jamais vu chose pareille! **How can you tell s. lies?** comment pouvez-vous mentir de la sorte? **All s. errors are to be avoided,** toutes les erreurs de ce genre sont à éviter. **Some s. plan,** un projet de ce genre. **No s. body exists,** il n'existe aucun corps de cette nature. **There are no s. things as fairies,** les fées n'existent pas. **I said no s. thing,** je n'ai rien dit de semblable, de la sorte. **No s. thing!** il n'en est rien! pas du tout! *S.a.* ANOTHER 2. (b) **S. is not my intention,** ce n'est pas là mon intention. **S. is not the case,** il n'en est pas ainsi. **S. were his words,** tel furent ses paroles. **S. is the world!** ainsi va le monde! 2. **In s. (and s.) a place,** en tel endroit. **We are told that on s. a date he lived in s. and s. a street,** on nous dit qu'à une certaine date il demeurait dans telle et telle rue. **S. a one,** un tel, une telle. 3. **In s. a way that . . .,** de telle sorte que . . .; de manière, de façon, que . . . **His pain was s. that . . .,** telle était sa douleur que . . . **S. is his strength,** tant il est fort. **To take s. steps as shall be considered necessary,** prendre telles mesures qui paraîtront nécessaires. **Until s. time as . . .,** jusqu'à ce que . . .

4. (*Intensive*) **S. large houses,** de si grandes maisons. **I had never heard s. good music,** je n'avais jamais entendu d'aussi bonne musique. **S. a clever man,** un homme si habile. **S. courage,** un tel courage tant de courage. **S. an industrious person as yourself,** une personne aussi travailleuse que vous. **I had s. a fright!** j'ai eu une de ces peurs! **You do use s. expressions!** vous avez de ces expressions! II. **such,** *pron.* 1. **Down with traitors and all s.,** à bas les traîtres et tous ceux qui leur ressemblent. 2. **Let (all) s. as are of my opinion raise their hands,** que (tous) ceux qui sont de mon opinion lèvent la main. **I will send you s. as I have,** je vous en ai je vous les enverrai. 3. **History as s. is too often neglected,** l'histoire en tant que telle est trop souvent négligée.

suchlike ['sʌt∫laik]. 1. *a. F:* Semblable, pareil; de ce genre. 2. *pron. Usu. pl.* **Beggars, tramps. and s.,** mendiants, clochards et autres gens de la sorte, de cette espèce.

suck[1] [sʌk], *s.* 1. (a) Action *f* de sucer. **To have, take, a s. at a sweet,** sucer, suçoter, un bonbon. (b) *Hyd.E:* Succion *f*, aspiration *f* (d'une pompe). 2. **To give a child a s.,** donner à téter, la tétée, à un enfant.

suck[2]. 1. *v.tr.* (a) Sucer (le lait, etc.). (*Of horse*) **To s. wind,** avaler de l'air. (b) Sucer, suçoter (des bonbons); mordiller (le coin de son mouchoir); sucer, tirer sur (sa pipe). **To s. one's fingers,** se sucer les doigts. **To s. a raw egg,** gober un œuf. *F:* **To s. s.o.'s brains,** exploiter les connaissances, l'intelligence, de qn. **To s. s.o. dry,** sucer qn jusqu'à la moelle, jusqu'au dernier sou. 2. *v.i.* (a) (*Of pers.*) **To s. at sth.,** sucer, suçoter (un bonbon); sucer, tirer sur (une pipe). (b) (*Of pump*) Super. **suck down,** *v.tr.* Engloutir; entraîner au fond. **suck in,** *v.tr.* 1. (a) Sucer, absorber; aspirer. (b) Engloutir (dans un tourbillon). (c) Faire rentrer (ses joues). 2. *P:* Duper, rouler, refaire (qn). **You were quite sucked in,** on vous a complètement refait. **suck up.** 1. *v.tr.* Sucer, aspirer, pomper (un liquide, de l'air); (*of sponge*) absorber, boire (l'eau). 2. *v.i. P:* **To s. up to s.o.,** faire de la lèche à qn; lécher les bottes à qn. **sucking**[1], *a.* (*Animal*) qui tette. **S. calf,** veau de lait. **S. child,** enfant à la mamelle. *A:* **S. poet,** poète en herbe. **'sucking-fish,** *s.* Rémora *m.* **'sucking-pig,** *s.* Cochon *m* de lait. **sucking**[2], *s.* Succion *f*; aspiration *f. Nat.Hist:* **S. disk,** ventouse *f.*

sucker[1] ['sʌkər], *s.* 1. Suceur, -euse. 2. *F:* (a) Écornifleur, -euse. (b) Blanc-bec *m*; gogo *m*, poire *f.* 3. (a) *Nat.Hist:* Suçoir *m*; ventouse *f* (de sangsue). (b) Piston *m* (de pompe aspirante). 4. *Hort:* Rejeton *m*; drageon *m*, accru *m*, surgeon *m* (d'arbre); stolon *m* (de fraisier). **Stem s.,** bouture *f.*

sucker[2], *v. Hort:* 1. *v.tr.* Enlever les drageons (d'un arbre). 2. *v.i.* (*Of plant*) Rejetonner; (*of tree*) pousser des drageons.

suckle ['sʌkl], *v.tr.* Allaiter (un enfant, un veau); donner le sein, donner à téter, à (un enfant).

suckling[1] ['sʌkliŋ], *s.* Allaitement *m.* **S. pig,** cochon *m* de lait.

suckling[2], *s.* (a) Nourrisson *m*; enfant à la mamelle. (b) Jeune animal *m* qui tette encore.

suction ['sʌk∫(ə)n], *s.* 1. Succion *f*; aspiration *f* (de l'eau); appel *m* (d'air). **To adhere by s.,** faire ventouse. **S.-grip ash-tray,** cendrier à ventouse. **S. apparatus,** appareil aspirateur. **S. pump,** pompe aspirante. **'suction-dredger,** *s.* Drague suceuse, aspirante. **'suction-fan,** *s.* Ventilateur aspirant; aspirateur *m.* **'suction-shaft,** *s. Min:* Puits *m* d'appel d'air. **'suction-valve,** *s.* Clapet *m* d'aspiration.

suctorial [sʌk'tɔːriəl], *a. Nat.Hist:* Suceur, -euse. **S organ,** suçoir *m.*

Sudan [suː'dɑːn, -'dæn]. *Pr.n. Geog:* Le Soudan. *Hist:* **Anglo-Egyptian S.,** Soudan anglo-égyptien.

Sudanese [ˌsuːdəˈniːz], *a. & s. Geog: Ethn: Ling:* Soudanais, -aise.

sudden ['sʌdn], *a.* (a) Soudain, subit. **S. shower,** averse soudaine. (b) (Mouvement) brusque. **S. turning,** tournant brusque. *Adv.phr.* **All of a s.,** soudain, subitement; tout à coup. **-ly,** *adv.* Soudain, soudainement; subitement; tout à coup. **The door s. opened,** la porte s'ouvrit brusquement.

suddenness ['sʌdnnis], s. (a) Soudaineté f. **With startling s.**, en coup de théâtre. (b) Brusquerie f (d'un départ).

sudoriferous [ˌsjuːdəˈrifərəs], a. Sudoripare.

sudorific [ˌsjuːdəˈrifik], a. & s. Sudorifique (m).

suds [sʌdz], s.pl. (Soap-)s., eau f de savon; mousse f (de savon).

sue [sjuː]. 1. v.tr. (a) **To s. s.o. at law**, intenter un procès à qn; poursuivre qn en justice. **To s. s.o. for damages**, poursuivre qn en dommages-intérêts. (b) **To s. for a writ**, obtenir une ordonnance de la cour. **To s. out a pardon for s.o.**, obtenir la grâce de qn (à la suite d'une requête). 2. v.i. **To s. for peace**, demander la paix. O: **To s. (to s.o.) for sth.**, solliciter qch. (de qn). **He sued for her hand**, il demanda sa main.

suède [sweid]. s. (a) (For shoes) Daim m. (b) (For gloves, etc.) Peau f de suède; suède m.

suet ['sjuː)it], s. Cu: Graisse f de rognon; gras m de rognon. F: **S. face**, visage terreux.

Suez ['suː(ː)iz]. Pr.n. Suez. **The S. Canal**, le canal de Suez.

suffer ['sʌfər]. I. v.tr. 1. Éprouver, souffrir (une perte); subir (une peine, etc.). **To s. defeat**, essuyer, subir, une défaite. **To s. death**, subir la peine de mort. 2. O: Permettre, supporter, tolérer. **He will s. no retort**, il ne souffre, ne supporte, aucune réplique. F: **He does not s. fools gladly**, il ne supporte pas les imbéciles. II. v.i. 1. Souffrir. **To s. from rheumatism**, souffrir de rhumatismes; être affligé de rhumatismes. **To s. for one's misdeeds**, supporter la conséquence de ses méfaits. **You will s. for it**, il vous en cuira. 2. **To s. from neglect**, souffrir d'un manque de soins. **Country suffering from labour troubles**, pays en proie à l'agitation ouvrière. 3. Subir une perte, un dommage. **The battalion suffered severely**, le bataillon a essuyé de fortes pertes. **The vines have suffered from the frost**, les vignes ont souffert de la gelée. **suffering¹**, a. Souffrant; qui souffre. **suffering²**, s. (a) Souffrance f. (b) pl. **Sufferings**, souffrances; douleurs f.

sufferance ['sʌfərəns], s. Tolérance f, souffrance f (of, de); permission f (tacite). Esp. **On s.**, par tolérance.

sufferer ['sʌfərər], s. (From a calamity) Victime f; (from an accident) accidenté m; (from an illness) malade mf. **Fellow-s.**, compagnon m d'infortune.

suffice [sə'fais]. 1. v.i. Suffire. **That will s. for me**, cela me suffira. **S. it to say that . . .**, qu'il (nous) suffise de dire que . . .; F: suffit que . . . 2. v.tr. Suffire à (qn). **One meal a day suffices him**, il lui suffit d'un repas par jour.

sufficiency [sə'fiʃ(ə)nsi], s. (a) Suffisance f. **A s. of provisions**, une quantité suffisante de vivres. (b) Fortune suffisante. **To have a s.**, jouir de l'aisance; être dans l'aisance.

sufficient [sə'fiʃ(ə)nt], a. Assez; suffisant. **This is s. to feed them**, cela suffit pour les nourrir. **A hundred francs will be s.**, j'aurai assez de cent francs. **One lamp is s.**, il suffit d'une lampe. Prov: **S. unto the day is the evil thereof**, à chaque jour suffit sa peine. -ly, adv. Suffisamment; assez.

suffix ['sʌfiks], s. Gram: Suffixe m.

suffocate ['sʌfəkeit]. 1. v.tr. Étouffer, suffoquer, asphyxier. **In a suffocated voice**, d'une voix étranglée. 2. v.i. Étouffer, suffoquer. **suffocating**, a. Suffocant, étouffant, asphyxiant. **It is s. in this room**, on étouffe dans cette pièce.

suffocation [ˌsʌfə'keiʃ(ə)n], s. Suffocation f; étouffement m, asphyxie f.

suffragan ['sʌfrəgən], a. & s. Ecc: (Évêque) suffragant (m).

suffrage ['sʌfridʒ], s. Suffrage m. (a) Vote m, voix f. (b) Droit m de vote. **Universal s.**, suffrage universel.

suffragette [ˌsʌfrə'dʒet], s.f. Pol.Hist: Suffragette; militante.

suffragist ['sʌfrədʒist], s. Pol.Hist: Partisan m du droit de vote des femmes.

suffuse [sə'fjuːz], v.tr. (Of light, colour, tears) Se répandre sur (qch.). **A blush suffused her cheeks**, une rougeur se répandit sur ses joues. **Eyes suffused with tears**, yeux baignés de larmes. **Suffused with light**, inondé de lumière.

sugar¹ ['ʃugər], s. 1. Sucre m. **S. industry**, l'industrie sucrière. **Granulated s.**, sucre cristallisé. **Lump s.**, sucre en morceaux. **Castor s.**, sucre en poudre; sucre semoule. **Icing s.**, sucre à glacer. **Brown s.**, **moist s.**, cassonade f. Cu: **Burnt s.**, caramel m. **Help yourself to s.**, F: sucrez-vous. 2. (a) A.Ch: **S. of lead**, acétate m de plomb. (b) **S. of milk**, sucre de lait; lactose f. 3. U.S: P: Argent m, P: pognon m. 4. Esp. U.S: F: Belle fille; petite amie. **'sugar-almond**, s. Dragée f. **'sugar-basin, -bowl**, s. Sucrier m. **'sugar-beet**, s. Betterave f à sucre. **'sugar-'candy**, s. Sucre candi. **'sugar-cane**, s. Canne f à sucre. **'sugar-'coated**, a. Dragéifié. **S.-c. pill**, dragée f. **S.-c. tablet**, comprimé dragéifié, dragée. **'sugar-daddy**, s.m. P: Vieux protecteur; papa-gâteau. **She's got a s.-d.**, elle s'est trouvé un vieux. **'sugar-dredger**, s. = SUGAR-SIFTER. **'sugar-loaf**, s. Pain m de sucre. **S.-l. mountain**, montagne f en pain de sucre. **'sugar-maple**, s. Bot: Érable m à sucre. **'sugar-mill**, s. 1. Moulin à broyer la canne à sucre. 2. Ind: = SUGAR-REFINERY. **'sugar-pea**, s. Hort: Mange-tout m inv. **'sugar-plantation**, s. Plantation f de cannes à sucre. **'sugar-plum**, s. A: Bonbon m. **'sugar-refiner**, s. Raffineur m (de sucre). **'sugar-refinery**, s. Raffinerie f (de sucre). **'sugar-refining**, s. Raffinage m (du sucre). **'sugar-sifter**, s. Saupoudroir m. **'sugar-tongs**, s.pl. Pince f à sucre.

sugar², v.tr. Sucrer; saupoudrer (un gâteau) de sucre; lisser (des amandes). **To s. the pill**, dorer la pilule.

sugariness ['ʃugərinis], s. (a) Goût sucré. (b) Douceur mielleuse (d'un discours, etc.).

sugary ['ʃugəri], a. 1. (a) Sucré; (gâteau) saupoudré de sucre. (b) Trop sucré. 2. (Sourire) mielleux, sucré; (ton) doucereux. **S. eloquence**, éloquence mielliflue.

suggest [sə'dʒest], v.tr. 1. Suggérer, proposer (qch. à qn). **A solution suggested itself to me**, une solution me vint à l'esprit, se présenta à mon esprit. 2. Inspirer, faire naître (une idée). **Prudence suggests a retreat**, la prudence conseille la retraite. 3. Insinuer. **Do you s. that I am lying?** est-ce que vous insinuez que je mens? Jur: **I s. that . . .**, n'est-il pas vrai que . . .? 4. Évoquer. **His nose and ears s. a rabbit**, son nez et ses oreilles donnent, évoquent, l'idée d'un lapin.

suggestibility [sə,dʒesti'biliti], s. Psy: etc: Suggestibilité f.

suggestible [sə'dʒestəbl], a. 1. (Projet, etc.) que l'on peut suggérer. 2. Psy: etc: (Sujet) influençable par la suggestion; (sujet) suggestible.

suggestion [sə'dʒestʃən], s. 1. Suggestion f. **To make, offer, a s.**, faire une suggestion, une proposition. **Suggestions for improvement**, suggestions en vue d'une amélioration. Jur: **My s. is that . . .**, n'est-il pas vrai que . . .? 2. **It conveys the s. that . . .**, cela donne l'idée que. . . . **To speak with just a s. of a foreign accent**, parler avec une pointe d'accent étranger. **S. of regret**, nuance f de regret. 3. **Hypnotic s.**, suggestion hypnotique. S.a. AUTO-SUGGESTION.

suggestive [sə'dʒestiv], a. (a) Suggestif, -ive; évocateur, -trice. **S. of sth.**, qui évoque qch. (b) Qui frise l'obscénité. -ly, adv. De façon suggestive.

suicidal [ˌsuː(ː)i'said(ə)l], a. **S. tendencies**, tendances au suicide. **It would be s. to do so**, ce serait un véritable suicide, ce serait courir à la ruine, que d'agir de la sorte.

suicide¹ ['suː(ː)isaid], s. (Pers.) Suicidé, -ée.

suicide², s. (Crime m du) suicide. **To commit s.**, se suicider; (of murderer) se faire justice. **To attempt s.**, attenter à ses jours. **Attempted s.**, tentative f de suicide.

suit¹ [suːt], s. 1. Jur: **S. at law**, procès (civil); poursuites f pl (en justice). **To bring a s. against s.o.**, intenter un procès à qn. **To be a party to a s.**, être en cause. 2. O: Prière f, demande f, requête f. **At the s. of s.o.**, à la requête de qn. 3. O: Recherche f, demande, en mariage. 4. Cost: (a) S. of clothes, costume m, complet m (pour homme). **Lounge s.**, complet veston. S.a. ARMOUR¹ 1. (b) Ensemble m (pour femme); tailleur m. C: A: **Sailor-s.**, costume marin (pour enfant). 5. Nau: **S. of sails**, jeu m de voiles; voilure f. 6. Cards: Couleur f. **To lead from one's long s.**, attaquer dans sa longue. **Politeness is**

not his long suit, la politesse n'est pas son fort. To follow s., (i) Cards: donner de la couleur; (ii) en faire autant, faire de même.

suit², v.tr. **1.** Accommoder, adapter, approprier (to, à). To be suited to, for, sth., être adapté, apte, à qch.; être fait pour qch. Th: He is not suited to these parts, ces rôles ne lui conviennent pas. They are suited to each other, ils sont faits l'un pour l'autre. S.a. ACTION 1. **2.** Convenir à, aller à, accommoder (qn). That suits me best, c'est ce qui m'arrange le mieux. I am not easily suited, je suis difficile à satisfaire. That just suits me, ça me va à merveille; c'est juste mon affaire. I shall do it when it suits me, je le ferai quand cela me conviendra. S. yourself, arrangez cela à votre gré; faites comme vous voudrez. This climate does not s. me, ce climat ne me va pas, ne me vaut rien. This hat suits you, ce chapeau vous va, vous coiffe bien. **suiting,** s. **1.** Adaptation f, appropriation f (de qch. à qch.). 2. pl. Com: Gentlemen's suitings, tissus m pour complets.

suitability [ˌsuːtəˈbiliti], s. Convenance f; à-propos m (d'une remarque); accord m (de caractères). S. of a candidate to, for, a post, aptitude f d'un candidat à un poste.

suitable [ˈsuːtəbl], a. **1.** Convenable, qui convient; (exemple) approprié. S. marriage, union bien assortie. We have found nothing s., nous n'avons rien trouvé qui nous convienne. The most s. date, la date qui conviendrait le mieux. It seemed more s. to laugh, il semblait plus à propos de rire. **2.** S. to, for, sth., bon à qch.; propre, approprié, adapté, à qch. S. to the occasion, qui convient à la circonstance. **-ably,** adv. Convenablement; (répondre) à propos; (agir) comme il convient. S. matched, bien assortis.

suitableness [ˈsuːtəblnis], s. = SUITABILITY.

suitcase [ˈsuːtkeis], s. Mallette f, valise f.

suite [swiːt], s. **1.** Suite f, cortège m (d'un prince). **2.** (a) S. of rooms, appartement m; pièces fpl en enfilade. (b) S. of furniture, ameublement m; mobilier m, ensemble m. Dining-room s., salle f à manger. Bathroom s., salle de bain(s). Hyg: Low-down, low-level, s., W.C. à aspiration, à action syphonique. **3.** Orchestral s., suite d'orchestre.

suitor [ˈsuːtər], s. **1.** Jur: Plaideur, -euse. **2.** Prétendant m, soupirant m.

sulk¹ [sʌlk], s. Usu. pl. To have (a fit of) the sulks, bouder; faire la mine.

sulk², v.i. Bouder; faire la mine; être maussade.

sulkiness [ˈsʌlkinis], s. Bouderie f, maussaderie f.

sulky¹ [ˈsʌlki], a. Boudeur, maussade. To be s., bouder. To look s., faire la mine. To be s. with s.o., bouder (contre) qn. **-ily,** adv. En boudant; d'un air bouder, maussade.

sulky², s. Veh: Sulky m.

sullage [ˈsʌlidʒ], s. **1.** Eaux fpl d'égout; eaux usées. **2.** Metall: Scories fpl, crasses fpl.

sullen [ˈsʌlən], a. (Of pers.) Maussade, renfrogné, morose; (of thg) sombre, morne. S. silence, silence obstiné. **-ly,** adv. D'un air maussade, renfrogné; (obéir) de mauvaise grâce.

sullenness [ˈsʌlənnis], s. (a) Maussaderie f; air renfrogné. (b) Obstination f à ne pas parler.

sully [ˈsʌli], v.tr. Souiller, salir, ternir; flétrir, tacher (la réputation de qn).

sulpha [ˈsʌlfə], a. Ch: The s. series, la série des sulfamides. S. drug, sulfamide m.

sulphate¹ [ˈsʌlfeit], s. **1.** Ch: Sulfate m. Iron s., sulfate ferreux, de fer; vitriol vert. Copper s., sulfate de cuivre. **2.** Com: Sulfate de soude.

sulphate² [ˈsʌlfeit]. **1.** v.tr. Ch: Ind: Sulfater. **2.** v.i. El: (Of battery) Se sulfater. Sulphated accumulator, accu encrassé de sulfate. **sulphating,** s. **1.** Ch: Ind: Sulfatage m. **2.** El: Sulfatation f (des plaques d'accumulateur).

sulphide [ˈsʌlfaid], s. Ch: Sulfure m. Hydrogen s., hydrogène sulfuré; acide m sulfhydrique.

sulphite [ˈsʌlfait], s. Ch: Sulfite m. Sodium s., sulfite de soude.

sulphonamide [sʌlˈfɒnəmaid], s. Ch: Sulfamide m.

sulphur¹ [ˈsʌlfər], s. Soufre m. Roll s., stick s., soufre en canon(s), en bâtons. Plastic s., soufre mou. Flowers of s., fleur(s) f de soufre. S. dioxide, anhydrique sulfureux. **ˈsulphur mine,** s. Soufrière f.

sulphur², v.tr. Soufrer. **sulphuring,** s. Soufrage m.

sulphurate [ˈsʌlfjureit], v.tr. Sulfurer (un métal); soufrer (la laine).

sulphuration [sʌlfjuˈreiʃ(ə)n], s. (a) Sulfurage m (des vignes). (b) Soufrage m.

sulphurator [ˈsʌlfjureitər], s. Hort: Soufreuse f.

sulphureous [sʌlˈfjuəriəs], a. (a) Sulfureux, -euse. (b) Couleur de soufre inv; soufré. (c) Bleuâtre (comme le soufre qui brûle).

sulphuretted [ˈsʌlfəretid], a. Ch: Sulfuré. S. hydrogen, hydrogène sulphuré; acide m sulfhydrique.

sulphuric [sʌlˈfjuərik], a. Ch: Sulfurique.

sulphurous [ˈsʌlfərəs], a. Ch: (Acide, etc.) sulfureux.

sultan [ˈsʌltən], s. **1.** Sultan m. **2.** Bot: Sweet s., ambrette f.

sultana [sʌlˈtɑːnə], s. **1.** Sultane f. **2.** Raisin sec de Smyrne.

sultanate [ˈsʌltəneit], s. Sultanat m.

sultriness [ˈsʌltrinis], s. Chaleur étouffante; lourdeur f (de l'atmosphère).

sultry [ˈsʌltri], a. (Of heat, etc.) Étouffant, suffocant. It is s., il fait très lourd. S. voice, voix chaude.

sum¹ [sʌm], s. **1.** (a) Somme f, total m; montant m. To find the s. of the terms of a series, sommer les termes d'une série. (b) The s. and substance of the matter, le fond, l'essence f, de l'affaire. (c) S. of money, somme d'argent. **2.** Problème m, exercice m (d'arithmétique). To do a s. in one's head, faire un calcul de tête. To do sums, faire du calcul, des problèmes. **ˈsum ˈtotal,** s. Somme totale, globale.

sum², v.tr. (summed) (a) Additionner. (b) Mth: To s. a series, sommer une série. **sum up,** v.tr. (a) Résumer, faire un résumé de (qch.), récapituler. To s. up the matter, abs. to s. up, en résumé. (b) Jur: (Of judge) To s. up (the case), résumer les débats. (c) To s. up the situation at a glance, se rendre compte de la situation d'un coup d'œil. To s. s.o. up, juger, classer, qn. **summing up,** s. (a) Jur: Résumé m des débats (par le juge). (b) Évaluation f (de la situation, etc.).

sumac(h) [ˈsjuːmæk, ˈʃuːmæk], s. Bot: Sumac m. Venetian s., (sumac) fustet m.

summarize [ˈsʌməraiz], v.tr. Résumer sommairement (un ouvrage). **summarized,** a. (Of report, etc.) Compendieux, -euse; en résumé.

summary [ˈsʌməri]. **1.** a. Sommaire. S. account, (i) récit sommaire, succinct; (ii) récit récapitulatif. Jur: S. proceedings, affaire f sommaire. **2.** s. Sommaire m, résumé m (d'un livre); récapitulation f, relevé m (d'opérations commerciales, etc.). Mil: Jur: To take a s. of evidence, prendre des informations. **-ily,** adv. Sommairement.

summer¹ [ˈsʌmər], s. Été m. In s., en été. A s.('s) day, un jour d'été. St. Martin's s., Indian s., l'été de la Saint-Martin. S. time, l'heure f d'été. S. clothes, habits d'été. S. residence, résidence estivale; résidence d'été. S. visitor, estivant, -ante. The s. holidays, les grandes vacances. **ˈsummer-house,** s. Pavillon m, kiosque m. **ˈsummer-time,** s. L'été m.

summer², v.i. (a) Passer l'été, estiver (au bord de la mer, etc.). (b) (Of cattle) Estiver.

summer³, s. Const: S.(-beam, -tree), poutre f de plancher.

summit [ˈsʌmit], s. Sommet m, cime f, faîte m (d'une montagne); point m de partage (d'un canal). The s. of greatness, le faîte, le comble, des grandeurs. Pol: S. meeting, conférence f au sommet.

summon [ˈsʌmən], v.tr. **1.** (a) Appeler, faire venir (un domestique); mander (un ministre); convoquer (une assemblée). To be summoned to the peerage, être appelé à la pairie. (b) Jur: Sommer (qn) de comparaître. To s. a defendant, a witness, to attend, citer, assigner, un défendeur, un témoin. To s. s.o. for debt, assigner qn en paiement d'une dette. **2.** Sommer, requérir. To s. a town to surrender, sommer une place de se rendre. **3.** To s. up one's courage, faire appel à, s'armer de, tout son courage.

summons¹, pl. -ses [ˈsʌmənz, -ziz], s. **1.** Appel (fait d'autorité); convocation urgente. **2.** Jur: Citation f (à comparaître); assignation f; mandat m de comparution; sommation f (de comparaître); procès-verbal m, pl. procès-verbaux. To serve a s. on s.o., signifier une citation, une assignation, à qn. To take out a s. against s.o., faire assigner qn. 3. *Mil:* S. to surrender, sommation.

summons², *v.tr. Jur:* Citer (qn) à comparaître; assigner (qn); appeler (qn) en justice.

sump [sʌmp], s. 1. Puisard *m*; dépotoir *m*. 2. *Mec.E: Aut:* Fond *m* de carter (formant réservoir d'huile); cuvette *f* d'égouttage. Dry sump, carter sec. To drain the s. (and change the oil), faire la vidange.

sumpter ['sʌmptər], s. *A:* Bête *f* de somme, de charge; sommier *m*. S. mule, mulet *m* de somme, de charge.

sumptuary ['sʌmptjuəri], a. *(Of law)* Somptuaire.

sumptuous ['sʌmptjuəs], a. Somptueux, -euse, fastueux, -euse. -ly, adv. Somptueusement.

sumptuousness ['sʌmptjuəsnis], s. Somptuosité *f*, faste *m*; richesse *f* (du mobilier).

sun¹ [sʌn], s. (a) Soleil *m*. The s. is shining, il fait (du) soleil. *Nau:* To take, shoot, the s., observer le soleil; faire le point. With the s., against the s., de gauche à droite, de droite à gauche. (b) To have one's place in the sun, avoir sa place au soleil. Full in the s., au grand soleil. To take the s., s'insoler; prendre le soleil. *F:* To get a touch of the s., prendre un coup de soleil. **'sun-baked**, a. Brûlé par le soleil; cuit au soleil. **'sun-blind**, s. Store *m*. **'sundeck**, s. *Nau:* Pont-promenade supérieur; sundeck *m*. **'sun-dog**, s. Parhélie *m*; faux soleil. **'sun-dress**, s. Robe *f* de plage. **'sun-dried**, a. (a) Séché au soleil. (b) (Fruit) confit au soleil. **'sun-glasses**, s.pl. Lunettes fumées, verres fumés, lunettes solaires, de soleil. **'sun-hat**, s. Chapeau *m* à larges bords. **'sun-helmet**, s. Casque colonial. **'sun(-)lamp**, s. 1. *Cin:* Sunlight *m*. 2. *Med:* S.(-)l. treatment, traitement *m* par rayons ultraviolets. **'sun lounge**, *U.S:* **'sun parlor, porch,** s. Solarium *m* (de maison particulière). **'sun-ray**, *attrib. a. Med:* S.-r. treatment, héliothérapie *f*. **'sun-spot**, s. *Astr:* Tache *f* solaire. **'sun-tan**, s. Hâle *m*. **'sun-tanned**, a. Hâlé, basané. **'sun-trap**, s. *F:* Endroit très ensoleillé. **'sun-up**, s. *U.S:* Lever *m* du soleil. **'sun-visor**, s. *Aut:* Pare-soleil *m.inv.* **'sun-worship**, s. Culte *m* du soleil. **'sun-worshipper**, s. Adorateur, -trice, du soleil.

sun², v.tr. (sunned) Exposer au soleil; insoler. To s. oneself, prendre le soleil; se chauffer au soleil; *F:* faire le lézard; lézarder.

sunbath ['sʌnbɑ:θ], s. Bain *m* de soleil.

sunbathe ['sʌnbeið], v.i. Prendre des bains de soleil; s'insoler. **sunbathing**, s. Bains *mpl* de soleil; insolation *f*.

sunbather ['sʌnbeiðər], s. Personne *f* qui prend des bains de soleil.

sunbeam ['sʌnbi:m], s. Rayon *m* de soleil.

sunburn ['sʌnbə:n], s. 1. Hâle *m*. 2. *Med:* Coup *m* de soleil.

sunburned, -burnt ['sʌnbə:nd, -bə:nt], a. Brûlé par le soleil, hâlé, basané. To get s., se hâler, se basaner.

sunburst ['sʌnbə:st], s. (a) Échappée *f* de soleil. (b) Bijou *m* (en forme de) soleil.

sundae ['sʌndei], s. Glace *f* aux fruits.

Sunday ['sʌndi], s. Dimanche *m*. S. calm, le repos dominical. S. paper, journal du dimanche. As long as a month of Sundays, long comme un jour sans pain. In one's S. clothes, in one's S. best, dans ses habits du dimanche; endimanché. *(For other phrases see* FRIDAY*.)*

sunder ['sʌndər], v.tr. (a) Séparer, disjoindre (from, de). (b) Couper, fendre (qch.) en deux.

sundew ['sʌndju:], s. *Bot:* Drosère *f*, drosera *m*, rossolis *m*.

sundial ['sʌndail], s. Cadran *m* solaire.

sundown ['sʌndaun], s. = SUNSET.

sundowner ['sʌndaunər], s. 1. *Austr:* Clochard *m* (qui règle sa journée pour arriver à une habitation au soleil couchant). 2. *F:* Consommation prise au coucher du soleil.

sundry ['sʌndri]. 1. a. Divers. S. expenses, frais divers. On s. occasions, à différentes occasions. 2. s. (a) All and s., tous sans exception; le monde et son père. He told all and s. about it, il le racontait à tout venant. (b) pl. Sundries, (i) articles divers; (ii) frais divers; faux frais.

sunfish ['sʌnfiʃ], s. Poisson-lune *m*; môle *f*.

sunflower ['sʌnflauər], s. *Bot:* Hélianthe annuel; tournesol *m*, soleil *m*; girasol *m*.

sung. *See* SING.

sunk [sʌŋk], a. (a) (Navire) sombré, coulé. S. in thought, plongé dans ses pensées. (b) *F:* Perdu, ruiné. *S.a.* SINK².

sunken ['sʌŋk(ə)n], a. (a) (Rocher) noyé, submergé. S. wreck, épave sous-marine. (b) Affaissé, enfoncé. S. cheeks, joues creuses. (c) S. road, chemin creux. S. garden, jardin *m* en contrebas. *S.a.* SINK².

sunless ['sʌnlis], a. Sans soleil.

sunlight ['sʌnlait], s. Lumière *f* du soleil. In the s., au (grand) soleil. *Med:* S. treatment, héliothérapie *f*; traitement *m* solaire.

sunlit ['sʌnlit], a. Éclairé par le soleil; ensoleillé.

sunniness ['sʌninis], s. 1. Situation ensoleillée (d'un endroit, etc.). 2. Gaieté *f* (de caractère); naturel heureux; rayonnement *m* (du visage).

sunny ['sʌni], a. 1. (Journée) de soleil; (endroit) ensoleillé; (côté) exposé au soleil. It is s., il fait (du) soleil. The s. side of the picture, le bon côté de l'affaire. 2. (Visage) radieux, rayonnant; (caractère) heureux.

sunproof ['sʌnpru:f], a. (Tissu) inaltérable au soleil.

sunrise ['sʌnraiz], s. Lever *m* du soleil. At s., au soleil levant; au lever du soleil.

sunset ['sʌnset], s. Coucher *m* du soleil. At s., au soleil couchant; au coucher du soleil. The s. of life, le déclin de la vie.

sunshade ['sʌnʃeid], s. Ombrelle *f*; *(for table, etc.)* parasol *m*.

sunshine ['sʌnʃain], s. 1. (Clarté *f*, lumière *f*, du) soleil. In the s., au soleil. In (the) bright s., au grand soleil; en plein soleil. 2. Bonheur *m*, gaieté *f*, rayonnement *m* (du visage, de la vie). 3. *Aut:* S. roof, toit ouvrant.

sunshiny ['sʌnʃaini], a. *F:* = SUNNY.

sunstroke ['sʌnstrouk], s. *Med:* Insolation *f*; coup *m* de soleil. To get (a touch of) s., attraper un coup de soleil.

sunsuit ['sʌnsu:t], s. Costume *m* bain de soleil.

sup¹ [sʌp], s. *Esp. Scot:* Petite gorgée. To take a sup of soup, prendre une goutte de bouillon. *S.a.* BITE¹ 3.

sup², v. (supped [sʌpt]) 1. v.tr. *Esp. Scot:* Prendre à petites gorgées. 2. v.i. Souper (off, on, de).

super ['su:pər], s. *F:* 1. = SUPERNUMERARY 2. 2. = SUPERINTENDENT. 3. a.Superbe, sensationnel, -elle.

superable ['su:pərəbl], a. Surmontable.

superabound [su:pərə'baund], v.i. Surabonder (in, with, de, en); foisonner (de).

superabundance [su:pərə'bʌndəns], s. Surabondance *f*, foisonnement *m*, pléthore *f* (of, de).

superabundant [su:pərə'bʌndənt], a. Surabondant, pléthorique. -ly, adv. Surabondamment.

superannuate [su:pər'ænjueit]. 1. v.tr. (a) Mettre (qn) à la retraite; retraiter (qn). (b) *F:* Mettre au rancart (une vieille auto). 2. v.i. *Jur: (Of power of attorney, etc.)* Périmer. **superannuated**, a. 1. Suranné; démodé. 2. En retraite; retraité.

superannuation ['su:pər,ænju'eiʃ(ə)n], s. Retraite *f* par limite d'âge. S. fund, caisse *f* des retraites. S. contribution, retenue *f* pour la retraite.

superb [su'pə:b], a. Superbe, magnifique; *F:* sensationnel, -elle. -ly, adv. Superbement, magnifiquement.

supercargo ['su:pə,kɑ:gou], s. *Nau:* Subrécargue *m*.

supercharged ['su:pə'tʃɑ:dʒd], a. *I.C.E:* (Moteur) suralimenté, surcomprimé, à compresseur.

supercharger ['su:pə'tʃɑ:dʒər], s. *I.C.E:* Compresseur *m*; surcompresseur *m*.

supercharging ['su:pə'tʃɑ:dʒiŋ], s. *I.C.E:* Suralimentation *f*, surcompression *f*.

superciliary [su:pə'siliəri], a. *Anat:* Sourcilier. The s. arches, les arcades sourcilières.

supercilious [su:pə'siliəs], a. Sourcilleux, -euse, hautain; (air) pincé, dédaigneux. -ly, adv. Avec une nuance de dédain.

superciliousness [su:pə'siliəsnis], s. Hauteur *f*; air dédaigneux.

superduper ['su:pə'du:pər], a. *U.S: P:* Sensas, formidable.

supererogation ['su:pər,ero'geiʃ(ə)n], s. Surérogation *f*; superfétation *f*.

supererogatory ['su:pərε'rɔgt(ə)ri], a. Surérogatoire.

superficial [ˌsuːpəˈfiʃ(ə)l], *a.* Superficiel, -elle. **1.** S. measurement, mesure *f* de superficie. S. foot, pied carré. **2.** To have a s. knowledge of sth., avoir des connaissances superficielles de qch. **His knowledge is entirely s.,** son savoir est tout en surface, tout en superficie. **She has a s. mind,** elle manque de profondeur. **-ally,** *adv.* Superficiellement.

superfine [ˈsuːpəfain], *a.* **1.** Superfin; *Com:* surfin. **2.** S. distinctions, distinctions raffinées.

superfluity [ˈsuːpəˈfluiti], *s.* **1.** Superfluité *f.* S. of good things, embarras *m* de richesses. **2.** To have a s. of labour, avoir un excédent de main-d'œuvre. To give of one's s., donner de son superflu.

superfluous [suˈ(ː)pəˈfluəs], *a.* Superflu; superfétatoire. **-ly,** *adv.* D'une manière superflue; inutilement.

superheat [ˈsuːpəˈhiːt], *v.tr. Mch:* Surchauffer (la vapeur).

superheater [ˈsuːpəˈhiːtər], *s. Mch:* Surchauffeur *m* (de vapeur).

superhet(erodyne) [ˈsuːpəˈhet(ərədain)], *s. W.Tel:* Superhétérodyne *m*; *F:* super *m*.

superhighway [ˈsuːpəˌhaiwei], *s. U.S:* Autoroute *f.*

superhuman [ˈsuːpəˈhjuːmən], *a.* Surhumain.

superimpose [ˌsjuːpərimˈpouz], *v.tr.* Superposer, surimposer. *Cin: etc:* Surimprimer.

superimposition [ˌsuːpərimpəˈziʃ(ə)n], *s.* Superposition *f* (de couleurs, etc.); surimpression *f.*

superintend [ˈsuːpərinˈtend], *v.tr.* Diriger, surveiller. To s. an election, présider au scrutin.

superintendence [ˌsuːpərinˈtendəns], *s.* Direction *f,* surveillance *f,* contrôle *m*; conduite *f* (des travaux).

superintendent [ˌsuːpərinˈtendənt], *s.* **1.** Directeur, -trice; surveillant, -ante; chef *m* (des travaux). **2.** Police s. = commissaire *m* de police. **Railway s.,** commissaire *m* des chemins de fer. **3.** *Hist:* Surintendant *m.*

superior [suˈpiəriər]. **1.** *a.* (*a*) Supérieur, -eure. To be s. in numbers to the enemy, être supérieur en nombre à l'ennemi; avoir la supériorité du nombre sur l'ennemi. **My gardener is a s. sort of man,** mon jardinier est d'une classe supérieure. Thanks to your s. wealth, grâce à la supériorité de vos richesses. **To be s. to flattery,** être au-dessus de la flatterie. (*b*) (*Of pers.*) Sourcilleux, -euse, superbe. With a s. smile, avec un sourire suffisant, condescendant. (*c*) *Typ:* S. letter, lettre supérieure; lettrine *f.* S. figure, appel *m* de note. **2.** *s.* (*a*) Supérieur, -eure. He is your s., il est votre supérieur. (*b*) *Ecc:* The Father S., le père supérieur. *S.a.* MOTHER[1] 3. **-ly,** *adv.* **1.** *Bot: etc:* S. placed, placé plus haut. **2.** D'une manière supérieure. **S. armed,** mieux armé. **3.** D'un air suffisant; avec un air de supériorité.

superiority [suːˌpiəriˈɔriti], *s.* Supériorité *f. Mil: etc:* S. in men and materials, supériorité en hommes et en matériel.

superlative [suːˈpəːlətiv]. **1.** *a.* Suprême; d'une excellence suprême. **2.** *a. & s. Gram:* Superlatif (*m*). **In the s.,** au superlatif. **-ly,** *adv. F:* Au suprême degré. **S. ugly,** d'une laideur sans pareille.

superman, *pl.* **-men** [ˈsuːpəmæn, -men], *s.m.* Surhomme.

supermarket [ˈsuːpəˌmɑːkit], *s. Com:* Supermarché *m*, libre-service *m.*

supernational [ˈsuːpəˈnæʃ(ə)nəl], *a.* Supranational.

supernatural [ˌsuːpəˈnætʃ(ə)rəl], *a.* Surnaturel. *s.* The s., le surnaturel.

supernormal [ˈsuːpəˈnɔːm(ə)l], *a.* Au-dessus de la normale.

supernumerary [ˌsuːpəˈnjuːmərəri]. **1.** *a.* Surnuméraire; en surnombre. S. officer, officier à la suite. **2.** *s.* (*a*) Surnuméraire *m.* (*b*) *Th:* Figurant, -ante.

superpanchromatic [ˈsuːpəˌpænkroˈmætik], *a. Phot:* Superpanchromatique *m.*

superphosphate [ˈsuːpəˈfɔsfeit], *s. Ch: Agr:* Superphosphate *m.*

superpose [ˌsuːpəˈpouz], *v.tr.* Superposer (upon, on, à); étager (des planchettes).

superposition [ˈsuːpəpəˈziʃ(ə)n], *s.* Superposition *f.*

supersaturate [ˈsuːpəˈsætʃəreit], *v.tr.* Sursaturer.

supersaturation [ˈsuːpəˌsætʃəˈreiʃ(ə)n], *s.* Sursaturation *f.*

superscribe [ˌsuːpəˈskraib], *v.tr.* **1.** Marquer d'une inscription, d'une suscription. **2.** Écrire son nom en tête (d'un document).

superscription [ˌsuːpəˈskripʃ(ə)n], *s.* Inscription *f;* (*on coin*) légende *f;* (*on letter*) adresse *f,* suscription *f;* (*on document*) en-tête *m.*

supersede [ˌsuːpəˈsiːd], *v.tr.* (*a*) Remplacer. **This catalogue supersedes previous issues,** ce catalogue annule les précédents. **To s. an official,** relever un employé de ses fonctions. **Method now superseded,** méthode périmée. (*b*) Prendre la place de (qn); supplanter (qn).

supersensitive [ˈsuːpəˈsensitiv], *a.* Hypersensible.

supersensitiveness [ˈsuːpəˈsensitivnis], *s.* Hypersensibilité *f.*

supersonic [ˌsuːpəˈsɔnik], *a.* **1.** *Ph:* Ultra-sonore. **2.** Supersonique. **S. boom, bang,** double bang *m.* **S. bomber,** bombardier *m* supersonique.

superstition [ˌsuːpəˈstiʃ(ə)n], *s.* Superstition *f.*

superstitious [ˌsuːpəˈstiʃəs], *a.* Superstiteux, -euse. **-ly,** *adv.* Superstitieusement.

superstratum, *pl.* **-a** [ˈsuːpəˈstreitəm, -ə, -ˈstrɑː-], *s. Geol:* Couche supérieure.

superstructure [ˈsuːpəˈstrʌktʃər], *s.* Superstructure *f;* tablier *m* (d'un pont).

supertax [ˈsuːpətæks], *s. Adm:* Impôt *m* supplémentaire sur le revenu; surtaxe *f.*

supertonic [ˈsuːpəˈtɔnik], *s. Mus:* Sus-tonique *f.*

supervene [ˌsuːpəˈviːn], *v.i.* Survenir. **Tetanus supervened on the wound,** le tétanos se déclara à la suite de la blessure.

supervise [ˈsuːpəvaiz], *v.tr.* **1.** Avoir l'œil sur, surveiller (une entreprise). **2.** Diriger, conduire (une entreprise).

supervision [ˌsuːpəˈviʒ(ə)n], *s.* **1.** Surveillance *f.* **Under police s.,** sous la surveillance de la police. **To keep s.o. under strict s.,** exercer une surveillance sévère sur la conduite de qn. **2.** Direction *f* (d'une entreprise).

supervisor [ˈsuːpəvaizər], *s.* Surveillant, -ante; directeur, -trice. **To act as s.,** exercer la surveillance.

supinator [ˈsuːpineitər], *a. & s. Anat:* (Muscle *m*) supinateur (*m*).

supine[1] [ˈsuːpain], *a.* **1.** (*Of pers*) Couché, étendu, sur le dos. *Med:* En supination. **2.** Mou, *f.* molle; indolent, inerte. **-ly,** *adv.* **1.** (Couché) sur le dos. **2.** Avec indolence; mollement; nonchalamment.

supine[2], *s. Lt.Gram:* Supin *m.* **In the s.,** au supin.

supineness [ˈsuːpainnis], *s.* Mollesse *f,* indolence *f,* inertie *f.*

supper [ˈsʌpər], *s.* Souper *m.* **To have s.,** souper. **The Last S.,** la (Sainte) Cène. *Ecc:* **The Lord's S.,** la communion, l'eucharistie *f.* **'supper-time,** *s.* Heure *f* du souper.

supperless [ˈsʌpəlis], *a.* **To go to bed s.,** se coucher sans souper.

supplant [səˈplɑːnt], *v.tr.* Supplanter; prendre la place de (qn); évincer (qn).

supplanter [səˈplɑːntər], *s.* Supplanteur *m.*

supple[1] [ˈsʌpl], *a.* Souple. **1.** Liant, pliable, flexible; (cordage) maniable. **S. figure,** taille souple, déliée, libre. **To become s.,** s'assouplir. **2.** Complaisant. **-ply,** *adv.* Souplement; avec souplesse.

supple[2], *v.tr.* Assouplir (un membre, l'esprit, le cuir); dresser (un cheval).

supplement[1] [ˈsʌplimənt], *s.* Supplément *m*; appendice *m* (d'un livre). *Geom:* Supplément (d'un angle). *Journ:* **Literary s.,** supplément littéraire.

supplement[2] [ˈsʌpliˈment], *v.tr.* Ajouter à (un livre, etc.). **To s. one's income by journalism,** augmenter ses revenus en faisant du journalisme.

supplementary [ˌsʌpliˈment(ə)ri], *a.* Supplémentaire (to, de); additionnel (to, à). **S. income,** revenus *mpl* annexes. *Geom:* **S. angle,** angle supplémentaire.

suppleness [ˈsʌplnis], *s.* **1.** Souplesse *f,* flexibilité *f.* **2.** Complaisance *f.*

suppliant [ˈsʌpliənt]. **1.** *a.* Suppliant; de supplication. **2.** *s.* Suppliant, -ante.

supplicant [ˈsʌplikənt], *s.* Suppliant, -ante.

supplicate [ˈsʌplikeit]. **1.** *v.i.* Supplier. **2.** *v.tr.* **To s. s.o. to do sth.,** supplier qn de faire qch. **To s. protection,** solliciter humblement la protection de qn.

supplicating, *a.* Suppliant. **-ly,** *adv.* D'un air, d'un ton, suppliant.

supplication [sʌpli'keiʃ(ə)n], s. **1.** Supplication f. **2.** Supplique f.

supplier [sə'plaiər], s. Fournisseur, -euse; pourvoyeur, -euse (of, de); approvisionneur, -euse (of, en, de).

supply¹ [sə'plai], s. **1.** (a) Approvisionnement m, fourniture f. Mil: etc: **S. column**, convoi de ravitaillement. Navy: **S. ship**, (transport) ravitailleur m. Electric **s. service**, alimentation f électrique. **S. pressure**, tension f de distribution. (b) Parl: **Bill of S.**, projet m de crédit supplémentaire. **To vote supplies**, voter des crédits m. (c) Occupation f (d'une place) par intérim; suppléance f. **2.** (a) Provision f. **To take in, lay in, a s. of sth.**, se faire une provision, s'approvisionner, de qch. **To get (in) a fresh s. of sth.**, se remonter en qch. Pol.Ec: **S. and demand**, l'offre f et la demande. Com: **Goods in short s.**, marchandises en manque. (b) pl. **Supplies.** (i) Fournitures f (de photographie, etc.). (ii) Approvisionnements; réserves fpl; stocks mpl. **Food supplies**, vivres m. **To obtain, get, one's supplies from X**, s'approvisionner chez X; se fournir chez X. **To cut off, stop, the enemy's supplies**, couper les vivres à l'ennemi. (c) Suppléant, -ante; intérim m. **To arrange for a s.**, se faire suppléer. **S. teacher**, remplaçant, -ante (d'un professeur). su′pply-circuit, s. El.E: **The local s.-c.**, le secteur. su′pply-main, -pipe, s. Hyd.E: Canalisation f; tuyau m d'alimentation.

supply², v.tr. (supplied) **1.** (a) **To s. s.o. with sth.**, fournir, pourvoir, munir, approvisionner, qn de qch. **To s. s.o. with food**, alimenter qn. **To s. a town (with provisions)**, approvisionner, ravitailler, une ville. Com: **Families supplied daily**, livraisons f à domicile tous les jours. **To s. a machine** (with fuel, etc.), alimenter une machine. (b) **To s. sth.**, fournir, apporter, qch.; amener (l'eau, le gaz, etc.). **2.** (a) Réparer (une omission); combler (un déficit); répondre à (un besoin). **To s. s.o.'s needs**, fournir, pourvoir, subvenir, aux besoins de qn. (b) abs. **To s. for s.o.**, remplacer, suppléer, qn; assurer l'intérim.

supply³ ['sʌpli], adv. See SUPPLE¹.

support¹ [sə'pɔːt], s. **1.** (a) Appui m, soutien m. **Moral s.**, appui moral. **To give s. to the proposal**, venir à l'appui de, appuyer, la proposition. **To get, obtain, no s.**, ne trouver aucun appui. **Documents in s. of an allegation**, pièces à l'appui d'une allégation. **Troops in s.**, troupes de soutien. **A collection in s. of Foreign Missions**, une quête à l'intention (de l'œuvre) des Missions à l'étranger. (b) Soutènement m (d'une voûte, etc.). (c) **To be without means of s.**, être sans ressources. Jur: **To be without visible means of s.**, être sans moyens d'existence connus. **2.** (a) **The sole s. of his old age**, son seul soutien dans sa vieillesse. (b) Appui, support m, soutien (d'une voûte, etc.); pied m (de sustentation); console f, soupente f (de treuil); assiette f (de pied de colonne, etc.); potence f. Mec.E: Mch: Chaise f. Hort: Tuteur m.

support², v.tr. **1.** (a) Supporter, soutenir, appuyer, maintenir (une voûte, etc.). Hort: Tuteurer (un arbuste). (b) Mec.E: Supporter, résister à (un effort, une charge). **2.** Appuyer (qn); soutenir, corroborer (une théorie); patronner (un, un bal de charité); faire une donation à (une œuvre de charité, etc.). **Proofs that s. a case**, preuves à l'appui d'une cause. Parl: etc: **To s. the motion**, soutenir la motion. **He supported my statement**, il est venu à l'appui de mon dire. **To be supported by s.o.** (in a proposal), être secondé par qn. **3.** Entretenir (la vie, la combustion, etc.). **To s. a family**, faire vivre, faire subsister, une famille. **To s. oneself**, se suffire (à soi-même); gagner sa vie. **4.** Supporter, tolérer (une injure, etc.). supporting, a. (Mur) d'appui, de soutènement. Th: **The s. cast**, la troupe qui seconde les premiers rôles.

supportable [sə'pɔːtəbl], a. **1.** Supportable, tolérable. **2.** (Of theory, etc.) Soutenable.

supporter [sə'pɔːtər], s. **1.** (Device) Soutien m, support m. **2.** (Pers.) Défenseur m, tenant m (d'une opinion); adhérent m (d'une cause); partisan m (d'un homme politique); supporter m (d'une équipe sportive, d'un gouvernement). **3.** Her: Support (de l'écu).

suppose [sə'pouz], v.tr. Supposer. (a) **Let us s. the two things equal**, supposons les deux choses égales. **S. ABC an equilateral triangle**, soit ABC un triangle équilatéral. **S. you are right, supposing (that) you are right**, supposons, supposé, que vous ayez raison; en supposant, à supposer, que vous ayez raison. **Supposing he came back**, si par supposition il revenait. **S. we change the subject**, si nous changions de sujet. (b) **That supposes the perfectibility of man**, cela (pré)suppose la perfectibilité humaine. (c) S'imaginer; croire, penser. **You will do it, I s.**, je suppose que vous le ferez. **I don't s. he will do it**, je ne suppose pas, il est peu probable, qu'il le fasse. **Will you go?**—**I s. so**, irez-vous?—Probablement; sans doute. **I declined, as you may s.**, vous pensez bien que j'ai refusé. **I don't s. I have ridden in a bus for two years**, autant que je sache, voilà deux ans que je n'ai pris l'autobus. **He is supposed to be wealthy**, on le suppose riche; il est censé être riche. **I am not supposed to know**, je suis censé ne pas le savoir. supposed, a. Supposé, prétendu; soi-disant. **The s. culprit**, le présumé coupable.

supposedly [sə'pouzidli], adv. Censément; soi-disant.

supposition [sʌpə'ziʃ(ə)n], s. Supposition f, hypothèse f. **Why should I make such a s.?** pourquoi irais-je supposer cela?

suppositional [sʌpə'ziʃənl], a. Supposé; imaginaire.

supposititious [səpɔzi'tiʃəs], a. Faux, f. fausse. Jur: (Enfant) supposé, substitué; (testament) supposé.

suppository [sə'pɔzitəri], s. Pharm: Suppositoire m.

suppress [sə'pres], v.tr. **1.** (a) Réprimer (une révolte). (b) Supprimer (un journal); interdire (une publication); faire disparaître (un abus). **2.** Étouffer (un bâillement, un scandale); réprimer, refouler (ses sentiments); faire taire (un interrupteur). **To s. one's feelings**, se contenir. **3.** Cacher, dissimuler (qch.); ne pas révéler (un fait); taire (un nom). Jur: Supprimer (un fait). **4.** T.V: etc: Antiparasiter. suppressed, a. **S. anger**, colère réprimée, rentrée, refoulée. **S. excitement**, agitation contenue. **In a s. voice**, en baissant la voix.

suppressible [sə'presibl], a. **1.** Supprimable. **2.** Réprimable. **3.** Que l'on peut passer sous silence.

suppression [sə'preʃ(ə)n], s. **1.** Répression f (d'une émeute, d'un abus); suppression f (d'un livre). T.V: etc: Antiparasitage m. **2.** Étouffement m (d'un scandale); refoulement m (des émotions). **3.** Dissimulation f (de la vérité).

suppressor [sə'presər], s. **1.** (a) Étouffeur m (d'une émeute, etc.). (b) Dissimulateur m (d'un fait). **2.** W.Tel: **S. grid**, grille f de freinage. T.V: etc: Antiparasite m; appareil m, dispositif m, antiparasite.

suppurate ['sʌpjureit], v.i. Suppurer.

suppuration [sʌpju'reiʃ(ə)n], s. Suppuration f.

supranational ['suːprə'næʃənl], a. Supranational, -aux.

supremacy [su(ː)'preməsi], s. Suprématie f (over, sur).

supreme [su(ː)'priːm], a. Suprême. **The S. Being**, l'Être suprême, Dieu. **To make the s. sacrifice**, mourir (pour qn, pour son pays). **To reign s.**, régner en maître, en souverain absolu. Jur: **S. court**, cour souveraine. Pol: **The S. Soviet**, le Soviet suprême. **S. happiness**, bonheur suprême. **To hold s.o. in s. contempt**, avoir un souverain mépris pour qn. -ly, adv. Suprêmement; au suprême degré.

sura(h) ['sjuərə], s. Surate f (du Coran).

surah, s. Tex: Surah m.

surcharge¹ ['sɜːtʃɑːdʒ], s. **1.** (Overload) Surcharge f; charge excessive. **2.** Droit m supplémentaire, surtaxe f. **3.** Surcharge (sur un timbre-poste).

surcharge², v.tr. **1.** (Overload) Surcharger (with, de). **2.** (Sur)taxer (une lettre, etc.). **3.** Post: Surcharger (un timbre-poste).

surd [sɜːd], s. (a) Mth: Quantité f incommensurable; racine irrationnelle. (b) Ling: Consonne sourde.

sure ['ʃuər]. **1.** a. Sûr, certain. (a) **To be s. of sth.**, être sûr, certain, de qch. **I am s. of it**, j'en suis convaincu; j'en ai la certitude. **I am not so s. of that**, je n'en suis pas bien sûr. **To be s. of oneself**, être sûr de soi(-même). **I'm s. I don't know**, ma foi, je ne sais pas. **To make s. of a fact**, s'assurer d'un fait. **To make s. of a seat**, s'assurer une place. **To make s.o. s. of sth.**, assurer qch. à qn. (b) Infaillible;

(jugement, tireur) sûr; (asile) assuré; (remède) sûr, infaillible. (c) Indubitable; (succès) sûr, assuré. *F:* S. thing, chose certaine; *Rac:* certitude *f.* *U.S: P:* S. thing! bien sûr! I do not know for s., je n'en suis pas bien sûr. To-morrow for s., demain sans faute. (d) It is s. to be fine, il fera sûrement beau. He is s. to come, il viendra à coup sûr; il viendra sûrement. Be s. to come early, ne manquez pas d'arriver de bonne heure. Be s. not to lose it, prenez garde de le perdre. (Yes,) to be s.! certainement! bien sûr! It's John, to be s.! tiens, c'est Jean! *O:* Well, to be s.! tiens, tiens! par exemple! 2. *adv.* (a) *U.S:* Vraiment; certainement. It s. was a cold night, il faisait vraiment froid cette nuit-là. (b) As s. as death, as fate ; *F:* as s. as eggs is eggs, aussi sûr que deux et deux font quatre. S. enough, he was there, il était bien là; c'était bien lui. He will come s. enough, il viendra à coup sûr. S. enough! c'est (bien) vrai! bien sûr! assurément! *Esp. U.S:* S.! mais oui! bien sûr! -ly, *adv.* 1. Sûrement. To work slowly but s., travailler lentement mais sûrement. 2. (a) *Lit:* Assurément. (b) S. you don't believe that! vous ne croyez pas cela, voyons! I know something about it s.! j'en sais quelque chose peut-être! 3. Will you help me? — S.! voulez-vous m'aider ? — Assurément! 'sure-'fire, *a. F:* Infaillible, certain. 'sure-'footed, *a.* Au pied sûr. sure-'sighted, *a.* A l'œil juste.
sureness ['ʃuənis], *s.* 1. Sûreté *f* (de main, de pied). 2. Certitude *f.*
surety ['ʃuəti], *s.* 1. *A:* Sûreté *f,* certitude *f.* 2. (a) *A:* Garantie *f,* cautionnement *m.* (b) (*Pers.*) Caution *f;* garant, -ante; *Com:* donneur *m* d'aval. To stand, go, s. for s.o., se rendre caution, se porter garant pour qn. 'surety-bond, *s.* Cautionnement *m.*
surf[1] [sə:f], *s.* Barre *f* (de plage); ressac *m;* déferlement *m,* brisants *mpl* sur la plage. 'surf(-)board, *s. Sp:* (a) Aquaplane *m.* (b) Planche *f* de surfing. 'surf(-)boat, *s.* Surf-boat *m;* pirogue *f* de barre. 'surf-rider, *s. Sp:* Aquaplaniste *mf.* 'surf-riding, *s.* (a) Sport *m* de l'aquaplane. (b) Surf *m,* surfing *m.*
surf[2], *v.i.* (a) Se baigner dans le ressac. (b) Faire du surfing.
surface[1] ['sə:fis], *s.* 1. (a) Surface *f.* (*Of submarine*) To proceed on the s., marcher en surface. To break s., revenir en surface. *Post:* To send a letter by s. mail, envoyer une lettre par voie *f* de terre, de mer. *Min:* Work at the s., travail au jour. *Mec.E:* Bearing s., working s., surface d'appui; portée *f.* (b) Extérieur *m,* dehors *m.* On the s. everything was well, tout allait bien en apparence. His faults are all on the s., never goes below the s., il s'arrête à la surface des choses. 2. (a) *Geom:* S. of revolution, surface de révolution. (b) Aire *f,* étendue *f,* superficie *f.* 'surface-coated, *a. Paperm:* (Papier) couché. 'surface-drain, *s.* Tranchée *f* à ciel ouvert. 'surface-plate, *s. Mec.E:* Marbre *m* à dresser; plaque *f* de dressage. 'surface-tension, *s. Ph:* Tension superficielle, de surface.
surface[2], *v.tr.* 1. Apprêter, polir, la surface de (qch.). *Paperm:* Calandrer, glacer (le papier). 2. *Civ.E:* Revêtir (une route, etc.) (with, de). 3. *v.i. Navy:* (*Of submarine*) Faire surface, revenir en surface. -surfaced, *a.* Mat(t)-s., à surface mate. Smooth-s., à surface lisse. surfacing, *s.* 1. (a) Apprêtage *m* polissage *m* (de la surface de qch.); surfaçage *m.* *Paperm:* Calandrage *m,* glaçage *m.* (b) *Carp:* Dégauchissage *m* (d'une planche). 2. *Civ.E:* Revêtement *m* (d'une route).
surfaceman, *pl.* **-men** ['sə:fismən], *s.m.* 1. *Min:* Ouvrier du jour. 2. *Rail:* Cheminot.
surfeit[1] ['sə:fit], *s.* 1. Surabondance *f.* 2. (a) Réplétion *f;* satiété *f.* To have a s. of oysters, être rassasié d'huîtres. To have a s. of advice, être comblé, accablé, de conseils. (b) Dégoût *m;* nausée *f.*
surfeit[2]. 1. *v.i.* Se gorger, se repaître. 2. *v.tr.* Gorger, rassasier (s.o. with good cheer, qn de bonne chère); blaser (qn). To s. oneself with sth., se gorger de qch. jusqu'à la nausée.
surfing ['sə:fiŋ], *s. Sp:* Surf *m,* surfing *m.*
surfy ['sə:fi], *a.* (Plage *f*) à brisants, à ressac; (brisants) écumants, écumeux.

surge[1] [sə:dʒ], *s.* 1. (a) *Nau:* Levée *f* de la lame; houle *f.* A s. of anger, une vague de colère. (b) *El.E:* S. of current, vague, à-coup *m,* de courant; onde *f* de surtension. *El/Rail:* S. absorber, para-surtension *m.* (c) *Hyd.E:* S. tank, shaft, cheminée *f* d'équilibre (d'un barrage). 2. *Nau:* Saut *m* (d'un cordage); choc *m,* coup *m* de fouet (au cabestan).
surge[2], *v.i.* 1. (*Of sea*) Être houleux; (*of waters*) se soulever. The crowd surged along the street, la foule se répandit en flots dans la rue. The crowd surged back, la foule reflua. The blood surged to her cheeks, le sang lui reflua au visage. 2. *El.E:* The current surges, il y a des surtensions de courant. *I.C.E:* The engine surges, le moteur pompe, galope. 3. (*Of wheel*) Glisser. *Nau:* (*Of cable*) Choquer brusquement. **surging,** *a.* S. sea, mer houleuse; forte mer. A s. mass of people, un flot (pressé) d'êtres humains.
surgeon ['sə:dʒən], *s.* (a) Chirurgien, -ienne. Plastic s., chirurgien plastique, esthétique. Orthopaedic s., chirurgien orthopédiste. (b) *Mil: etc:* Médecin *m.* *S.a.* DENTAL, HOUSE-SURGEON, VETERINARY.
surgery ['sə:dʒəri], *s.* 1. Chirurgie *f.* 2. Cabinet *m* de consultation (chez un médecin); dispensaire *m* (d'un hôpital). S. hours, heures de consultation.
surgical ['sə:dʒik(ə)l], *a.* Chirurgical, -aux. S. instruments, instruments de chirurgie. S. appliances, (i) appareils chirurgicaux; (ii) appareils orthopédiques.
surliness ['sə:linis], *s.* Air bourru; maussaderie *f.*
surly ['sə:li], *a.* (a) Bourru. (b) Hargneux, -euse, maussade. S. disposition, humeur rébarbative.
surmise[1] ['sə:maiz], *s.* Conjecture *f,* supposition *f.*
surmise[2] [sə:'maiz], *v.tr.* Conjecturer, deviner; soupçonner. I surmised as much, je m'en doutais bien.
surmount [sə:'maunt], *v.tr.* 1. Surmonter. Column surmounted by a cross, colonne surmontée d'une croix. 2. Surmonter (un obstacle); triompher (d'une difficulté).
surmullet [sə:'mʌlit], *s. Ich:* Surmulet *m.*
surname[1] ['sə:neim], *s.* Nom *m* de famille. Christian names and s., nom et prénoms *m.*
surname[2], *v.tr.* 1. He is surnamed Smith, il se nomme Smith, son nom de famille est Smith. 2. *A:* William surnamed Longsword, Guillaume surnommé Longue-Épée.
surpass [sə:'pɑːs], *v.tr.* 1. Surpasser. You have surpassed yourself, vous vous êtes surpassé. 2. The result surpassed my hopes, le résultat a excédé mes espérances, a dépassé mon attente. surpassing, *a.* Sans pareil. Of s. beauty, d'une beauté incomparable. -ly, *adv.* Extrêmement, excessivement. He was s. ugly, il était d'une laideur sans égale.
surplice ['sə:plis], *s. Ecc.Cost:* Surplis *m.*
surpliced ['sə:plist], *a.* En surplis.
surplus ['sə:pləs], *s.* 1. Surplus *m,* excédent *m. Fin:* Boni *m.* To have a s. of sth., avoir qch. en excès; avoir (des livres) en surnombre. 2. *attrib.* S. population, surplus, excédent, de la population. *Com:* Sale of s. stock, vente de soldes *m,* de surplus.
surprise[1] [sə'praiz], *s.* Surprise *f.* 1. To take s.o. by s., prendre qn à l'improviste, au dépourvu. *Mil:* S. attack, attaque brusquée; coup *m* de main. S. visit, visite à l'improviste. 2. To give s.o. a s., faire une surprise à qn. It was a great s. to me, j'en ai été grandement surpris. 3. Étonnement *m.* To my great s., much to my s., à ma grande surprise. I paused in s., je m'arrêtai surpris.
surprise[2], *v.tr.* Surprendre. 1. Prendre (une place) par surprise, par coup de main. To s. s.o. in the act, prendre qn sur le fait, en flagrant délit. 2. Étonner. To be surprised at sth., être surpris de qch. I am surprised to see you, je m'étonne de vous voir. I should not be surprised if . . ., cela ne me surprendrait pas si. . . . I am surprised at you! vous m'étonnez! surprising, *a.* Surprenant, étonnant. It is s. that you (should) know it, il est surprenant que vous le sachiez. -ly, *adv.* Étonnamment. I found him looking s. young, j'ai été surpris de lui trouver l'air si jeune.
surprisedly [sə'praizidli], *adv.* D'un air de surprise; avec surprise.
surrealism [sə'riəlizm], *s.* Surréalisme *m.*
surrealist [sə'riəlist], *a. & s.* Surréaliste.
surrealistic [sə,riə'listik], *a.* Surréaliste.

surrender[1] [sə'rendər], *s.* **1.** (*a*) Reddition *f* (d'une forteresse). (*b*) No s.! on ne se rend pas! (*c*) *Jur:* S. of a defendant to his bail, décharge *f* de ses cautions par un accusé. **2.** Abandon *m*, abandonnement *m*, cession *f* (de biens); remise *f* (des armes à feu, etc.). To make a s. of principle(s), transiger avec ses principes. **3.** *Ins:* Rachat *m* (d'une police).

surrender[2]. **1.** *v.tr.* (*a*) Rendre, livrer (une forteresse, etc.). (*b*) *Jur: etc:* Abandonner, céder (un droit, ses biens, etc.). To s. one's office, démissionner. To s. all hope of sth., abandonner, renoncer à, tout espoir de qch. (*c*) *Ins:* Racheter (une police). **2.** *v.pr. & i.* To s. (oneself), se rendre; *Mil:* faire (sa) soumission; rendre les armes. To s. (oneself) to justice, se livrer à la justice.

surreptitious [ˌsʌrəp'tiʃəs], *a.* Subreptice, clandestin. **-ly,** *adv.* Subrepticement, clandestinement, furtivement.

surround[1] [sə'raund], *s.* Encadrement *m*, bordure *f.*

surround[2], *v.tr.* Entourer. (*a*) To s. a town with walls, entourer, ceinturer, ceindre, une ville de murs. Surrounded by, with, dangers, entouré, environné, de dangers. (*b*) *Mil:* Entourer, cerner (l'ennemi, etc.); investir (une ville, etc.). **surrounding,** *a.* Entourant, environnant. The s. countryside, le pays d'alentour. **surroundings,** *s.pl.* **1.** Entourage *m*, milieu *m*, ambiance *f.* **2.** Environs *mpl*, alentours *mpl* (d'une ville, etc.).

surtax[1] ['sɔːtæks], *s.* Surtaxe *f*; *Adm:* surtaxe progressive sur le revenu.

surtax[2], *v.tr.* Surtaxer.

surveillance [sə(ː)'veiləns], *s.* *Adm:* Surveillance *f*, contrôle *m.*

survey[1] ['sɔːvei], *s.* **1.** (*a*) Aperçu *m*; vue générale, exposé *m* sommaire (d'un sujet). (*b*) Examen attentif; étude *f* (de la situation); enquête *f.* To take, make, a s. of sth., (i) jeter un coup d'œil sur qch.; (ii) se rendre compte de (la situation actuelle, etc.). To make a sample s., faire une enquête par sondage. Political s., tour *m* d'horizon politique. (*c*) Inventaire *m* (de monuments historiques, etc.). **2.** *Surv:* (*a*) Levé *m* des plans; relevé *m.* (*b*) Plan *m*, levé (du terrain). Trigonometrical s., levé trigonométrique. Aerial s., levé aérophotogrammétrique. To make, effect, a s., lever un plan. S. vessel, navire *m* hydrographe. **3.** Inspection *f*, visite *f*; expertise *f.*

survey[2] [sə(ː)'vei], *v.tr.* **1.** (*a*) Regarder, contempler, promener ses regards sur (le paysage, etc.). (*b*) Mettre (une question) à l'étude; passer (la situation) en revue. **2.** *Surv:* Relever, faire le (re)levé de, lever le(s) plan(s) de (la ville, etc.); cadastrer (une commune); arpenter (un champ). To s. a railway, faire les études d'une ligne de chemin de fer. *Nau:* To s. a coast, faire l'hydrographie d'une côte. *Civ.E:* To s. for quantities, métrer, toiser. **3.** Inspecter; visiter; faire l'expertise de l'état (d'un navire). **surveying,** *s.* **1.** *Surv:* Levé *m* de plans. (**Land-)s.,** arpentage *m*, géodésie *f*; topographie *f.* **Naval s.,** hydrographie *f.* **2.** Inspection *f*, visite *f*; expertise *f.*

surveyor [sə'veiər], *s.* **1.** (**Land-)s.,** géomètre expert; arpenteur *m* (géomètre). **Naval s.,** (ingénieur) hydrographe *m.* **Highways s.,** agent *m* voyer. *Arch:* (Architecte) expert *m.* **2.** *Adm:* (*a*) Surveillant *m*, inspecteur *m.* S. of taxes, contrôleur, inspecteur, des contributions directes. (*b*) **Ship s.,** visiteur *m*, inspecteur, de navires; expert *m.*

survival [sə'vaiv(ə)l], *s.* (*a*) Survivance *f.* S. of the fittest, survivance des mieux adaptés, du plus apte. (*b*) *Jur: Ins:* Survie *f.*

survive [sə'vaiv]. **1.** *v.i.* (*a*) Survivre; (*of custom*) subsister; passer à la postérité. (*b*) *Jur:* (*Of estate*) To s. to X, passer aux mains de X (qui est le survivant). **2.** *v.tr.* (*a*) Survivre à (qn). (*b*) To s. an injury, survivre à une blessure. To s. a disease, a shipwreck, réchapper d'une maladie, d'un naufrage.

survivor [sə'vaivər], *s.* Survivant, -ante. The survivors of the disaster, les rescapé(e)s.

survivorship [sə'vaivəʃip], *s.* *Jur:* Survie *f.*

Susan ['suːz(ə)n]. *Pr.n.f.* Suzanne. *U.S: Furn:* (**Lazy) S.,** (i) plateau tournant, (ii) table (desserte) roulante.

susceptibility [səˌsepti'biliti], *s.* **1.** Susceptibilité *f.* (*a*) *El:* (**Magnetic) s.,** susceptibilité (magnétique). (*b*) **S. to a disease,** prédisposition *f* à une maladie. **S. to impressions,** suggestibilité *f.* **2.** Sensibilité *f*, susceptibilité. These people have their susceptibilities, ces gens-là ont leurs délicatesses *f.* To avoid wounding any susceptibilities, éviter tout froissement.

susceptible [sə'septibl], *a.* **1.** Susceptible. (*a*) S. of proof, susceptible d'être prouvé. (*b*) S. to a disease, prédisposé à une maladie. **2.** (*a*) Sensible, impressionnable. To be s., avoir la fibre sensible. S. to good influences, ouvert, sensible, accessible, aux bonnes influences. (*b*) Qui se froisse facilement; susceptible.

suspect[1] ['sʌspekt], *a. & s.* Suspect, -e. To hold s.o. s., tenir qn pour suspect.

suspect[2] [sə'spekt], *v.tr.* **1.** To s. s.o. of a crime, soupçonner qn d'un crime. To be suspected, être suspect. To be suspected by s.o. of sth., être suspect à qn de qch. I s. him of drinking, je le soupçonne d'être ivrogne. **2.** Soupçonner, s'imaginer (qch.). To suspect sth., subodorer qch. I s. that he is, I s. him to be, the perpetrator of the joke, j'ai idée que c'est lui l'auteur de cette farce. I suspected as much, je m'en doutais; j'en avais le soupçon. To s. danger, flairer le danger. He suspects nothing, il ne se doute de rien. I s. he is inclined to be selfish, je lui soupçonne un peu d'égoïsme. **suspected,** *a.* A s. person, un suspect, une suspecte.

suspend [sə'spend], *v.tr.* Suspendre. **1.** Pendre (un trophée, etc.). **2.** Suspendre (son jugement, les paiements, le travail). *Jur:* To s. judgment, surseoir au jugement. **3.** Suspendre (un fonctionnaire); mettre à pied. *Parl:* Exclure temporairement (un député). *Aut:* To s. a driving licence, suspendre un permis de conduire. **suspended,** *a.* Suspendu. **1.** S. particles, particules en suspension. **2.** (*a*) (*Of traffic*) Interrompu. *Jur:* (*Of proceedings*) En suspens. S. animation, arrêt momentané des fonctions vitales; syncope *f.* (*b*) *Mus:* S. cadence, cadence suspendue.

suspender [səs'pendər], *s.* (*a*) Suspensoir *m.* (*b*) (**Stocking) suspenders,** jarretelles *f.* **Sock suspenders,** fixe-chaussettes *m. S.a.* BELT[1] 1. (*c*) *U.S:* Suspenders, bretelles *f.*

suspense [sə'spens], *s.* (*a*) Suspens *m.* After a long period of s., après une longue incertitude. To keep, hold, s.o. in s., tenir qn en suspens. (*b*) *F:* Suspense *m.* **S.-film, -novel,** film *m*, roman *m*, à suspense. (*c*) *Bookk:* S. item, suspens *m.*

suspension [sə'spenʃ(ə)n], *s.* **1.** (*a*) *Mec.E: etc:* Suspension *f.* S. bridge, pont suspendu. S. cable, câble porteur. (*b*) *Ch:* In s., en suspension. **2.** (*a*) Suspension (de la circulation, etc.). To the s. of all other business, toute affaire cessante. (*b*) *Gram:* Points of s., points de suspension. **3.** Suspension (d'un fonctionnaire, etc.); mise *f* en non-activité (d'un officier); *F:* mise à pied. *Parl:* Exclusion *f* temporaire (d'un député). **S. of a driving licence,** retrait *m* temporaire d'un permis de conduire.

suspensory [sə'spensəri], *a.* (*a*) *Anat:* (*Of ligament, etc.*) Suspenseur (*m.*) (*b*) S. bandage, suspensoir *m.*

suspicion[1] [sə'spiʃ(ə)n], *s.* **1.** Soupçon *m.* *Jur:* Suspicion *f.* Not the shadow, not the ghost, of a s., pas l'ombre *f* d'un soupçon. With s., avec défiance. My s. is that . . ., je soupçonne que . . ., j'ai dans l'idée que. . . . To have suspicions about s.o., avoir des doutes sur qn; soupçonner qn. To hold s.o. in s., tenir qn pour suspect. To cast s. on s.o.'s good faith, suspecter la loyauté de qn. To lay oneself open to s., s'exposer aux soupçons. To arouse s., éveiller, faire naître, les soupçons. To arouse, awaken, s.o.'s suspicions, éveiller la défiance de qn; donner l'éveil à qn. Above s., au-dessus de tout soupçon. Evidence not beyond s., témoignages sujets à caution. To be right in one's suspicions, soupçonner juste. *Jur:* To arrest, detain, s.o. on s., arrêter, détenir, qn préventivement. **2.** I had my suspicions about it, je m'en doutais. **3.** Très petite quantité, soupçon (of, de).

suspicion[2], *v.tr.* *U.S: F:* Soupçonner (that . . ., que + *ind.*).

suspicious [sə'spiʃəs], *a.* 1. Soupçonnable, suspect; (*of conduct, etc.*) louche, équivoque. To look s., avoir l'air louche, suspect. 2. Méfiant, soupçonneux, -euse. To be, feel, s. about s.o., of s.o., avoir des soupçons à l'endroit de qn, à l'égard de qn. -**ly**, *adv.* 1. D'une manière suspecte, équivoque, louche. It looks to me s. like measles, ça m'a tout l'air d'être la rougeole. 2. D'un air méfiant; soupçonneusement.

suspiciousness [sə'spiʃəsnis], *s.* 1. Caractère suspect, louche, équivoque (of, de). 2. Caractère soupçonneux; méfiance *f.*

sustain [sə'stein], *v.tr.* Soutenir, supporter. 1. (*a*) Enough to s. life, de quoi entretenir la vie; de quoi vivre. To s. the body, soutenir, sustenter, le corps. Evidence to s. an assertion, témoignages pour soutenir une affirmation. *Th: O:* To s. a part, soutenir, tenir, remplir, un rôle. *Mus:* To s. a note, soutenir, prolonger, une note. (*b*) *Jur:* (*Of court*) To s. an objection, admettre une réclamation. 2. (*a*) *Mil:* To s. an attack, soutenir une attaque. (*b*) To s. a loss, éprouver, essuyer, souffrir, subir, une perte. To s. an injury, recevoir une blessure; être blessé. **sustained**, *a.* (*Of effort, attention, etc.*) Soutenu. S. applause, applaudissements prolongés, nourris. *Ph:* S. oscillations, oscillations entretenues. **sustaining**, *a.* Soutenant. 1. S. food, nourriture fortifiante. 2. *Mec:* S. force, force portante. *Arch: Constr:* S. wall, mur m de soutènement.

sustainable [sə'steinəbl], *a.* Soutenable.

sustenance ['sʌstinəns], *s.* (*a*) Sustentation *f.* Means of s., moyens de subsistance; moyens de vivre. (*b*) Aliments *mpl*, nourriture *f.*

suture ['suːtjər, 'suːtʃər], *s. Anat: Bot: Surg:* Suture *f.*

suzerain, *f.* -**aine** ['suːzərein], *s.* Suzerain, -aine.

suzerainty ['suːzəreinti], *s.* Suzeraineté *f.*

svelte [svelt], *a.* Svelte.

swab[1] [swɔb], *s.* 1. (*a*) Torchon *m*; toile *f* à laver, serpillière *f*, wassingue *f*. (*b*) *Artil:* Écouvillon *m*. (*c*) *Nau:* Fauber(t) *m*. (*d*) *Surg:* S. of cotton wool, tampon *m* d'ouate. *Med:* To take a s. (of s.o.'s throat), faire un prélèvement dans la gorge de qn. 2. *P:* Lourdaud *m*, andouille *f*; propre m à rien.

swab[2], *v.tr.* (**swabbed**) 1. Nettoyer, essuyer (avec un torchon, etc.). *Nau:* Fauberter, essarder (le pont). 2. *Artil:* To s. (out), écouvillonner (une pièce). 3. To s. (down), laver à grande eau. 4. To s. up, éponger (une flaque, etc.).

swaddle ['swɔdl], *v.tr.* Emmailloter (with, de). '**swaddling-clothes**, *s.pl.* Maillot m, langes m.

swag [swæg], *s.* 1. *A:* Balancement *m*, ballottement *m*. 2. *Furn: Arch:* Bouillon *m*, guirlande *f*. 3. *P:* (*a*) Rafle *f*, butin *m* (d'un cambrioleur). (*b*) (*In Austr.*) Baluchon *m*, paquet *m* (de clochard).

swage[1] [sweidʒ], *s. Tls:* Étampe *f*, emboutissoir *m*. Bottom s., sous-chasse *f*, contre-étampe *f*.

swage[2], *v.tr.* Étamper, emboutir.

swagger[1] ['swægər], *a. F:* Élégant; ultra-chic.

swagger[2], *s.* 1. (*a*) Air important. To walk with a s., marcher avec un air avantageux; faire la roue. (*b*) Air cavalier, désinvolte. 2. Rodomontades *fpl*; crâneries *fpl*. '**swagger-cane**, -**stick**, *s. Mil:* Jonc *m*, stick *m* (d'officier). '**swagger-coat**, *s. Cost: O:* Manteau *m* raglan trois-quarts (de femme).

swagger[3], *v.i.* (*a*) Crâner; se pavaner; plastronner; poser (insolemment). (*b*) Fanfaronner; faire de l'esbroufe. (*c*) To s. in, out, entrer, sortir, d'un air important. To s. along, se carrer en marchant. **swaggering**, *a.* (Air, etc.) important, crâneur, glorieux, conquérant.

swaggerer ['swægərər], *s.* Crâneur, -euse.

swain [swein], *s.m. A. & Poet:* Jeune berger; amoureux (de pastorale); soupirant.

swallow[1] ['swɔlou], *s.* 1. Gosier *m*, gorge *f*. 2. Gorgée *f* (d'eau, etc.). To drink sth. at one s., boire qch. d'un seul coup. '**swallow-hole**, *s. Geol:* Aven *m*, gouffre *m*.

swallow[2], *v.tr.* 1. To s. sth. (down), (i) avaler, ingurgiter, qch.; (ii) gober (une huître). To s. the bait, (i) (*of fish*) avaler l'appât; (ii) (*of pers.*) se laisser prendre à l'appât. To s. sth. hook, line and sinker, avaler la pilule. To s. one's tears, dévorer ses larmes. To s. one's pride, mettre son orgueil dans sa poche. To s. a story, gober, avaler, une histoire. To s. an affront,

avaler, boire, un affront. To s. one's words, se rétracter. 2. *Abs.* Avaler sa salive (pour faire passer une émotion). **swallow up**, *v.tr.* (i) Dévorer, avaler (qch.); (ii) (*of the sea, etc.*) engloutir, engouffrer (qch.).

swallow[3], *s.* Hirondelle *f.* Common, house, s., hirondelle de cheminée. *Prov:* One s. does not make a summer, une hirondelle ne fait pas le printemps. '**swallow dive**, *s. Swim:* Saut *m* de l'ange. '**swallow-tail**, *s.* 1. Queue fourchue; queue d'hirondelle. 2. *Ent:* S.-t. (butterfly), machaon *m.* '**swallow-tailed**, *a.* A queue fourchue.

swam. See SWIM[2].

swamp[1] [swɔmp], *s.* Marais *m*, marécage *m*, bas-fond *m.* '**swamp-fever**, *s. Med: A:* = MALARIA.

swamp[2], *v.tr.* 1. Inonder, submerger (un pré); inonder (une pièce, la cave). 2. (*a*) Remplir d'eau (une embarcation). (*b*) To be swamped with work, être débordé de travail.

swampy ['swɔmpi], *a.* Marécageux, -euse.

swan [swɔn], *s.* Cygne *m. Swim: U.S:* S. dive, saut *m* de l'ange. '**swan-neck**, *s. Mec.E:* Cou *m*, col *m*, de cygne. '**swan-necked**, *a.* 1. Au cou de cygne. 2. *Tls: etc:* En col de cygne. '**swan-song**, *s.* Chant *m* du cygne. It was his s.-s., ce fut pour lui le chant du cygne. '**swan-upping**, *s.* Recensement annuel des cygnes (de la Tamise).

swank[1] [swæŋk], *s. F:* 1. Prétention *f*, gloriole *f*, épate *f.* 2. = SWANKER.

swank[2], *v.i. F:* Se donner des airs; crâner; faire de l'épate; faire le fier.

swanker ['swæŋkər], *s. F:* Épateur, -euse; poseur, -euse; crâneur, -euse.

swanky ['swæŋki], *a. F:* Prétentieux, -euse, poseur, -euse, *F:* snob. That's very s., ça fait très snob.

swannery ['swɔnəri], *s.* Centre *m* d'élevage de cygnes.

swansdown ['swɔnzdaun], *s.* 1. Duvet *m* de cygne. 2. *Tex:* Molleton *m.*

swanskin ['swɔnskin], *s.* 1. Peau *f* de cygne. 2. *Tex: U.S:* Molleton *m*; flanelle *f* de laine.

swap[1] [swɔp], *s. F:* (*a*) Troc *m*, échange *m.* (*b*) *pl.* (*In stamp-collecting, etc.*) Swaps, doubles *m.*

swap[2], *v.tr.* (**swapped** [swɔpt]) *F:* To s. sth. for sth., échanger, troquer, qch. contre, pour, qch. To s. places with s.o., changer de place avec qn. **swapping**, *s.* Échange *m*, troc *m.*

sward [swɔːd], *s. Lit:* (Tapis *m* de) gazon *m*; pelouse *f.*

sware. See SWEAR[2].

swarm[1] [swɔːm], *s.* Essaim *m*, jetée *f*, jeton *m* (d'abeilles). A s. of locusts, un vol de sauterelles. (*Of bees*) To send out a s., jeter un essaim. *F:* S. of children, essaim, troupe *f*, *f*; ribambelle *f*, d'enfants.

swarm[2], *v.i.* 1. (*a*) (*Of bees*) Essaimer; faire l'essaim. (*b*) (*Of pers.*) Accourir en foule, se presser (autour de, dans, qch.). (*c*) *F:* Pulluler, grouiller. 2. To s. with . . ., fourmiller, grouiller, de. . . . The streets are swarming with people, les rues grouillent, regorgent, de monde.

swarm[3], *v.tr. & i.* To s. (up) a tree, monter, grimper, à un arbre.

swarthiness ['swɔːðinis], *s.* Teint basané, bistré.

swarthy ['swɔːði], *a.* (Teint) basané, bistré, boucané.

swash [swɔʃ], 1. *s.* Clapotage *m*, clapotement *m*, clapotis *m* (des vagues). 2. *adv.* To fall s., faire flac en tombant (dans l'eau).

swashbuckler ['swɔʃbʌklər], *s.* Rodomont *m*, brétailleur *m*, matamore *m.*

swashbuckling[1] ['swɔʃbʌkliŋ], *a.* Brétailleur, bretteur, fanfaron.

swashbuckling[2], *s.* Rodomontades *fpl*; fanfaronnades *fpl.*

swastika ['swɔstikə], *s.* Svastika *m*; croix gammée.

swat [swɔt], *v.tr. F:* Frapper (qn, qch.). S. that fly! écrasez donc cette mouche!

swath [swɔːθ], *s. Husb:* Andain *m.*

swathe[1] [sweið], *v.tr.* Emmailloter; envelopper (in, de). **swathing**, *s.* 1. Emmaillotement *m*, enveloppement *m.* 2. *pl.* Swathings, bandages *m*; bandelettes *f* (de momie). '**swathing-bands**, *s.pl. A:* Langes *mpl*, maillot *m.*

swathe[2], *s.* = SWATH.

swatter ['swɔtər], *s.* (Fly-)s., (balai *m*) tue-mouches *m inv*, tapette *f* (à mouches).

sway[1] [swei], s. **1.** Balancement m, oscillation f; mouvement m de va-et-vient. Aut: Roulis m (de la voiture). **2.** Empire m, domination f. **Under his s.,** sous son empire; sous son influence. **To bring a people under one's s.,** réduire un peuple sous sa puissance.

sway[2]. **1.** v.i. (a) Se balancer; osciller; ballotter; (of drunkard) vaciller. (Of trees) **To s. in the wind,** se balancer au vent. (b) Rester indécis; balancer. (c) (Of balance, etc.) Pencher; incliner. **2.** v.tr. (a) Faire osciller; balancer, agiter (les arbres, etc.). (b) Porter, tenir (le sceptre). (c) Gouverner, diriger, influencer. (d) **To s. s.o. from his course,** détourner qn de ses projets. (e) Nau: **To s. up,** hisser, guinder (un mât de hune, etc.). **swaying,** a. Oscillant. S. **gait,** dandinement m. S. **crowd,** foule ondoyante.

swear[1] [swɛər], s. F: Jurons mpl. **To indulge in, to have, a good s.,** lâcher une bordée de jurons. **'swear-word,** s. F: Gros mot; juron m.

swear[2], v. (p.t. swore [swɔːr], A: sware [swɛər]; p.p. sworn [swɔːn]) **1.** v.tr. (a) Jurer. **To s. sth. on the Bible,** jurer qch. sur la Bible. **To s. to do sth.,** jurer de faire qch. **We could have sworn we heard cries,** on aurait juré entendre des cris. (b) **To s. (in) a witness,** faire prêter serment, déférer le serment, à un témoin. (Of juryman) **To be sworn (in),** prêter serment. **To s. s.o. to secrecy,** faire jurer le secret à qn. (c) Déclarer (qch.) sous la foi du serment. **2.** v.i. Jurer; proférer un juron. **To s. like a trooper,** jurer comme un charretier. **It's enough to make a saint s.,** il y a de quoi faire jurer un saint. **swear at,** v.ind.tr. Maudire, injurier (qn). **swear by,** v.i. **To s. by one's honour,** jurer sur l'honneur. **2.** Préconiser, vanter. **swear off,** v.i. Jurer de renoncer à (l'alcool, etc.). **swear to,** v.ind.tr. Attester, certifier, (qch.) sous serment. **I s. to it,** j'en mettrais ma main au feu. **I would s. to it,** j'en jurerais. **sworn,** a. **1.** S. **official,** fonctionnaire assermenté. **S. enemies,** ennemis jurés, acharnés. **2.** S. **statement,** déclaration sous serment. **swearing,** s. **1.** (a) Attestation f sous serment. (b) Prestation f de serment. **2.** S. **(in) of the jury,** assermentation f du jury. **3.** Jurons mpl; gros mots.

swearer ['swɛərər], s. **1.** Celui qui prête serment; jureur m. **2.** Homme mal embouché; jureur.

sweat[1] [swet], s. **1.** Sueur f, transpiration f. **To be in a cold s.,** (i) souffrir d'une sueur froide; (ii) F: s'inquiéter, avoir le trac. **By the s. of one's brow,** à la sueur de son front. **To be in a s.,** (i) être trempé de sueur; suer à grosses gouttes; (ii) être tout en émoi. **2.** **To give a horse a s.,** donner une suée à un cheval. **3.** F: Corvée f; suée f. **It's an awful s.,** c'est un drôle de travail, c'est un fichu travail. **4.** Mil: P: **An old s.,** un vieux troupier. **'sweat-band,** s. Cuir intérieur (d'un chapeau). **'sweat-duct,** s. Anat: Conduit m sudorifère. **'sweat-gland,** s. Anat: Glande f sudoripare. **'sweat-shirt,** s. Cost: Blouson m de sport, d'entraînement.

sweat[2]. **I.** v.i. **1.** (a) Suer, transpirer; F: être en nage. **To s. profusely,** suer à grosses gouttes. (b) (Of worker) Peiner; P: turbiner. **2.** (Of walls) Suer, suinter. **II.** sweat, v.tr. **1.** (a) Suer (du sang). (b) Faire suer (qn). Med: Faire transpirer (qn). (c) Exploiter (la main-d'œuvre). **2.** (a) Metall: Suer, faire ressuer (le minerai). (b) Metalw: **To s. (in, on),** souder (qch.) à l'étain, à la soudure tendre; ressuer (une jointure). **sweat out. 1.** v.tr. (a) **To s.o. the moisture from a wall,** faire exsuder l'humidité d'un mur. (b) Guérir (un rhume) par des sudorifiques. **2.** v.i. (Of moisture) Exsuder. **sweated,** a. (Travail) mal rétribué. **sweating**[1], a. En sueur; suant; (mur) suintant. **sweating**[2], s. **1.** (a) Transpiration f; Med: sudation f. (b) Suintement m (d'un mur). **2.** (a) Med: Suée f. (b) Exploitation f (de la main-d'œuvre).

sweater ['swetər], s. **1.** Cost: Chandail m; tricot m, sweater m. **U.S:** P: S. **girl,** jeune femme bien moulée.

sweatiness ['swetinis], s. Moiteur f (du corps); humidité (d'un vêtement) due à la transpiration.

sweaty ['sweti], a. Couvert de sueur, en sueur. S. **hands,** mains moites.

Swede [swiːd], s. **1.** (Pers.) Suédois, -oise. **2.** Agr: Rutabaga m; navet m de Suède.

Sweden ['swiːd(ə)n]. Pr.n. La Suède.

Swedish ['swiːdiʃ]. **1.** a. Suédois. **2.** s. Ling: Le suédois.

sweep[1] [swiːp], s. **1.** (a) Coup m de balai, de faux. **At one s.,** d'un seul coup. (b) Mil: Av: etc: Balayage m. F: **To make a clean s. of sth.,** faire table rase de qch. **To make a clean s. of one's staff,** balayer tout son personnel. Gaming: **To make a clean s.,** rafler le tout. **2.** Mouvement m circulaire (du bras, du regard). **With a wide s. of the arm,** d'un geste large. **Within the s. of the net,** dans le cercle du filet. **3.** Course f rapide (d'un fleuve). **4.** (a) Courbe f; boucle f (d'une rivière); Arch: courbure f (d'un arc); façons fpl (d'un navire); flèche f (des ailes d'un avion). **To make a (wide) s.,** décrire une (grande) courbe; prendre un virage large. (b) **Fine s. of grass,** belle étendue de gazon. (c) Artil: T.V: Balayage. (d) Envergure f. **5.** (i) Aviron m (de galère); (ii) aviron de queue (d'une embarcation). **6.** Nau: Câble balayeur; drague f (pour mines). **7.** (Chimney-)s., ramoneur m. **8.** F: Sweepstake m. S. **ticket,** billet m de sweepstake. **'sweep-net,** s. Fish: Seine f.

sweep[2], v. (swept [swept]; swept) **I.** v.tr. **1.** (a) Balayer (une chambre); ramoner (une cheminée). **A storm swept the town,** un orage balaya la ville. **The deck was swept by a sea,** une grosse vague balaya le pont. **To s. the horizon with a telescope,** parcourir l'horizon avec une lunette. **To s. the seas of one's enemies,** purger la mer de ses ennemis. F: **To s. the board,** tout rafler; faire table rase; remporter un succès complet. S.a. BROOM 2. (b) Draguer (un chenal). Abs. **To s. for mines,** draguer des mines. **2.** (a) Balayer (la poussière). (b) Emporter, entraîner. **A wave swept him overboard,** une lame le jeta à la mer. **To be swept off one's feet by the tide,** être entraîné par la marée; perdre pied. **3.** **To s. one's hand over sth.,** passer la main sur qch. **II.** sweep, v.i. **1.** **The plain sweeps (away) towards the north,** la plaine s'étend vers le nord. **2.** **To s. (along),** avancer d'un mouvement rapide et uni. **She swept into the room,** elle entra dans la salle d'un air majestueux. (Of car) **To s. round the corner,** tourner le coin de la rue en faisant un large virage. **The road sweeps round the lake,** la route décrit une courbe autour du lac. **sweep along,** v.tr. (Of current) Entraîner, emporter (qch.). **sweep aside,** v.tr. Écarter (les rideaux, etc.) d'un geste large. **sweep away,** v.tr. Balayer (la neige); supprimer, détruire (un abus). **Bridge swept away by the torrent,** pont emporté, balayé, par le torrent. **sweep by,** v.i. Passer (i) rapidement, (ii) majestueusement. **sweep down. 1.** v.tr. **The current sweeps the logs down with it,** le courant entraîne, charrie, le bois. **2.** v.i. (a) **The enemy swept down upon us,** l'ennemi s'abattit sur nous. (b) **Hills sweeping down to the sea,** collines qui dévalent vers la mer. **sweep in,** v.i. (a) **The wind sweeps in,** le vent s'engouffre par la porte. (b) **She swept in,** elle entra d'un air majestueux. **sweep off,** v.tr. Enlever, emporter, avec violence. **sweep on,** v.i. Continuer d'avancer (irrésistiblement). **sweep out,** v.tr. Balayer (une chambre). **sweep past,** v.i. = SWEEP BY. **sweep round,** v.i. Nau: Virer. **sweep up. 1.** v.tr. (a) Balayer, ramasser (la poussière). (b) Rassembler (la poussière) en tas. **2.** v.i. **The avenue sweeps up to the front door,** l'allée décrit une courbe jusqu'au perron. **sweeping**[1], a. **1.** (Of stream) Rapide, impétueux. **2.** (a) S. **gesture,** geste large. S. **curtsy,** révérence profonde. (b) S. **flight,** vol plané (des grands oiseaux). (c) Art: **The s. lines of the drapery,** les lignes dégagées des draperies. **3.** S. **statement,** déclaration par trop générale. S. **reform,** réforme complète. S. **changes,** changement de fond en comble. **-ly,** adv. **1.** Rapidement. **2.** Sans distinction; d'une façon générale. **sweeping**[2], s. **1.** Balayage m; ramonage m (d'une cheminée). **2.** pl. Sweepings, balayures f, ordures f.

sweeper ['swiːpər], s. **1.** (Pers.) Balayeur, -euse. **2.** (Machine) Balayeuse f (mécanique). **Rotary street-s.,** balayeuse f mécanique. **S. and sprinkler,** balayeuse-arroseuse f.

sweepstake ['swiːpsteik], s. Turf: Sweepstake m.

sweet [swiːt]. I. *a.* Doux, *f.* douce. **1.** Sucré. **As s. as honey,** doux comme le miel. **S. stuff,** bonbons, *mpl.* friandises *fpl.* **My tea is too s.,** mon thé est trop sucré. **To have a s. tooth,** aimer les douceurs. **S. morsel,** morceau succulent. *S.a.* CHESTNUT 1, POTATO 2. **2. S. violet,** violette odorante. **To smell s.,** sentir bon, *(of flower)* embaumer. **It doesn't smell exactly s.,** ça ne sent pas la rose. *S.a.* BRIAR, PEA 2. **3.** *(Of food)* Frais, *f.* fraîche. **S. breath,** haleine saine, fraîche. **4.** *(Son)* doux, mélodieux. **5.** *(a)* **S. temper,** caractère doux, aimable. **Revenge is s.,** la vengeance est douce. *(b)* Charmant; gentil, -ille. **She's a s. person,** c'est une personne charmante, exquise. **What a s. kitten!** quel petit chat adorable! **That's very s. of you!** c'est bien gentil à vous! **To say s. nothings to s.o.,** dire des gentillesses, des douceurs, à qn. *(c)* **To keep s.o. s.,** cultiver la bienveillance de qn. **6.** *F:* **To be s. on s.o.,** être amoureux de qn, avoir un béguin pour qn. **-ly,** *adv.* **1.** *(a)* Doucement; avec douceur. *(b)* *(Chanter)* mélodieusement. **2.** Agréablement, gentiment. *S.a.* PRETTY 1. **3.** *(Of machine)* **To run s.,** fonctionner sans à-coups; avoir une allure douce. II. **sweet,** *s.* *(a)* Bonbon *m.* **Sweets,** sucreries *f,* confiseries *f.* *(b)* *(At dinner)* Entremets sucré. **'sweet(-)corn,** *s.* *Cu:* Maïs doux, vert. **'sweet-'scented,** *a.* Qui sent bon, qui embaume; au parfum délicieux. **'sweet-shop,** *s.* Confiserie *f.* **'sweet-'smelling,** *a.* = SWEET-SCENTED. **'sweet-talk¹,** *s.* *U.S:* Flatterie *f,* flagornerie *f.* **'sweet-'talk²,** *v.tr.* *U.S:* Flatter, flagorner (qn). **'sweet-'tempered,** *a.* Au caractère doux. **'sweet-'toothed,** *a.* Qui aime les douceurs, le sucre. **sweet-'william,** *s.* *Bot:* Œillet *m* de poète.

sweetbread ['swiːtbred], *s.* *Cu:* Ris *m* de veau, d'agneau.

sweeten ['swiːt(ə)n]. **1.** *v.tr.* *(a)* Sucrer (un plat). *(b)* Purifier (l'air, l'eau). *(c)* Adoucir (la vie). *(d)* *F:* Graisser la patte (à qn). **2.** *v.i.* S'adoucir. **sweetening,** *s.* **1.** Adoucissement *m;* sucrage *m.* **2.** Substance *f* pour sucrer.

sweetener ['swiːtnər], *s.* **1.** Édulcorant *m.* **2. Friendship is the s. of life,** c'est l'amitié qui rend la vie douce. **3.** *F:* **I had to give him a s.,** j'ai dû lui graisser la patte.

sweetheart ['swiːthɑːt], *s.* **1.** Amoureux, -euse. **(My) s.!** mon amour! **2.** Fiancé, -ée.

sweetie ['swiːti], *s.* *F:* **1.** Bonbon *m.* **2.** = SWEET-HEART. **'sweetie-pie,** *s.* *F:* Chéri(e), chouchou, -oute.

sweetish ['swiːtiʃ], *a.* Douceâtre.

sweetmeat ['swiːtmiːt], *s.* *A:* Bonbon *m.* **Sweetmeats,** sucreries *f.* **S. box,** bonbonnière *f.*

sweetness ['swiːtnis], *s.* **1.** Douceur *f.* **2.** Gentillesse *f,* charme *m.*

swell¹ [swel]. I. *s.* **1.** *(a)* Bosse *f;* renflement *m.* *(b)* **S. of ground,** éminence *f,* ondulation *f.* *(c)* *Mus:* Crescendo *m* et diminuendo. *Lit:* **The majestic s. of the organ,** les accents majestueux du grand orgue. **2.** *Nau:* Houle *f;* levée *f* (de la lame). **There is a heavy s.,** il y a une forte houle. **3.** *Mus:* Soufflet *m* (d'un orgue). *S.a.* PEDAL¹ 2. **4.** *(a)* *F:* *O:* Élégant *m;* *F:* faraud *m.* *(b)* *P:* Gros personnage. **The swells,** les gens chics; la (haute) gomme; le gratin. II. **swell,** *a.* *F:* *(a)* Chic, élégant. *(b)* De premier ordre. *(c)* *Esp.* *U.S:* *P:* (i) Épatant; (ii) chic; rupin. **'swell-box,** *s.* *(Of organ)* Caisse *f* d'expression; le récit. **'swell-manual,** *s.* *(Of organ)* Clavier expressif.

swell², *v.* (*p.t.* swelled [sweld]; *p.p.* swollen ['swoul(ə)n], *occ.* swelled) **1.** *v.tr.* *(a)* (R)enfler, gonfler. **Eyes swollen with tears,** yeux gonflés de larmes. **To s. the crowd,** augmenter la foule. *(b)* *Mus:* Enfler (une note). **2.** *v.i.* *(a)* **To s. (up),** (s')enfler, se gonfler; *Med:* se tuméfier; *(of lime)* foisonner; *(of debt)* augmenter, grossir. **The murmur swells into a roar,** le murmure s'enfle jusqu'à devenir un rugissement. **To s. with importance, to s. like a turkey-cock,** enfler, gonfler le jabot. *(b)* *(Of sea)* Se soulever; houler. **Hate swelled up within him,** la haine montait en lui. *(c)* To s. out, être bombé; bomber. **swollen,** *a.* Enflé, gonflé. **1.** *(a)* **The river is s.,** la rivière est en crue. *(b)* **To have a s. face,** (i) avoir le visage bouffi; (ii) avoir une fluxion à la joue. *S.a.* GLAND¹ **2.** *F:* **To suffer from a s. head, a swelled head,**

être pénétré de sa propre importance; *F:* s'en croire, se croire. **'swollen-'headed,** *a.* *F:* Vaniteux, -euse, suffisant. **swelling¹,** *a.* *(Of sails)* Enflé, gonflé. *Med:* Tumescent. **S. with importance,** gonflé d'importance. **swelling²,** *s.* **1.** *(a)* Enflement *m,* gonflement *m;* crue *f* (d'un fleuve). *(b)* Renflement *m* (d'une colonne). *(c)* *Aut:* *Cy:* Hernie *f* (du bandage). **2.** *Med:* Tuméfaction *f;* boursouflement *m* (du visage). **3.** Bosse *f,* enflure *f* (au front); tumescence *f,* tumeur *f;* fluxion *f* (à la joue). **To have a s. on the neck,** avoir une grosseur au cou.

swellhead ['swelhed], *s.* *U.S:* *F:* Vaniteux, -euse, prétentieux, -euse.

swelter¹ ['sweltər], *s.* Chaleur lourde et humide. **To be in a s.,** étouffer de chaleur; être en nage.

swelter², *v.i.* *(a)* Étouffer de chaleur. *(b)* Être en nage. **sweltering,** *a.* **1.** En nage. **2. S. heat,** chaleur étouffante, accablante.

swept. *See* SWEEP².

swerve¹ [swəːv], *s.* Écart *m,* déviation *f.* *Fb:* Crochet *m.* *Aut:* Embardée *f.*

swerve², *v.i.* Faire un écart, un crochet; *(of horse)* se dérober; *(of car)* faire une embardée; *(of footballer)* crocheter.

swift [swift]. I. *a.* *(a)* Rapide. **As s. as thought,** rapide comme la pensée. *(b)* Prompt. **S. of wit,** vif d'esprit; à la repartie prompte. **S. to action,** prompt à agir. **-ly,** *adv.* Vite, rapidement. **To fly s. away,** s'envoler à tire-d'aile. II. **swift,** *adv.* Vite, rapidement. III. **swift,** *s.* *Orn:* (Black) s., martinet (noir). **Alpine s.,** martinet alpin. **'swift-flowing,** *a.* *(Rivière)* au cours rapide. **'swift-footed,** *a.* Au pied léger.

swiftness ['swiftnis], *s.* **1.** Rapidité *f,* vitesse *f.* **2.** Promptitude *f.*

swig¹ [swig], *s.* *P:* Grand trait, lampée *f* (de bière). **To take a s. at the bottle,** boire à même la bouteille.

swig², *v.tr.* *P:* Boire (un verre) à grands traits, à grands coups. *Abs.* Lamper. **To s. off a glass,** siffler un verre.

swill¹ [swil], *s.* **1.** Lavage *m* à grande eau. **To give a pail a s. out,** rincer un seau. **2.** *(a)* Pâtée *f* pour les porcs; eaux grasses. *(b)* *P:* Mauvaise boisson; rinçure *f.*

swill², *v.tr.* **1.** Laver (le plancher) à grande eau. **To s. out a basin,** rincer une cuvette. **2.** *P:* *(a)* Boire avidement (qch.). *(b)* *Abs.* Riboter.

swim¹ [swim], *s.* **1.** Action *f* de nager. **To have a s.,** faire un peu de nage, nager un peu. **The s. across the river,** la traversée du fleuve à la nage. **2.** *F:* **To be in the s.,** être dans le mouvement, dans le train. **'swim-suit,** *s.* Costume de bain(s) (pour dame).

swim², *v.* (swam [swæm]; swum [swʌm]; *pr.p.* swimming) I. *v.i.* **1.** *(a)* Nager. **To s. like a fish,** nager comme un poisson. **To start to s.,** se mettre à nager. **To s. for one's life, to s. for it,** se sauver à la nage. **To s. under water,** nager sous l'eau. **To s. like a brick,** nager comme une clef. **To s. across a river,** traverser une rivière à la nage. **To s. with the tide,** (i) nager dans le sens du courant; (ii) aller dans le sens de la foule. *S.a.* SINK² I. 1. *(b)* **To s. a stroke,** faire une brasse. *F:* **He can't s. a stroke,** il nage comme un chien de plomb. *(c)* **Meat swimming in gravy,** viande noyée dans la sauce. *(d)* Surnager, flotter. **2. Eyes swimming with tears,** yeux inondés de larmes. **3.** *(a)* **My head is swimming,** la tête me tourne. **Everything swam before my eyes,** tout semblait tourner autour de moi. II. *v.tr.* **1.** Traverser, passer, (une rivière) à la nage. **2.** Faire nager (un cheval). **swimming¹,** *a.* **1.** (Animal) nageant, qui nage. **2. S. eyes,** yeux noyés de larmes. **3. S. head,** tête qui tourne. **-ly,** *adv.* *F:* Comme sur des roulettes; à merveille. **swimming²,** *s.* Nage *f,* natation *f.* **'swimming-bath,** *s.* Piscine *f.* **'swimming-bell,** *s.* *Coel:* Ombrelle *f.* **'swimming-pool,** *s.* Piscine *f* (en plein air).

swimmer ['swimər], *s.* Nageur, -euse.

swindle¹ ['swindl], *s.* **1.** Escroquerie *f,* filouterie *f.* **2.** Duperie *f.* **3.** Déception *f.*

swindle², *v.tr.* Escroquer, filouter (qn); *F:* rouler (qn). **To s. s.o. out of sth.,** escroquer qch. à qn.

swindler ['swindlər], *s.* Filou *m,* escroc *m.*

swine [swain], *s.inv.* **1.** Cochon *m*, porc *m*; pourceau *m*. **2.** *P:* Dirty s.! sale cochon! He's a s., c'est un salaud. '**swine-fever**, *s. Vet:* Peste porcine. '**swine(-)herd**, *s.m. A: & Lit:* Porcher; gardeur de cochons.

swing¹ [swiŋ], *s.* **1.** *(a)* Balancement *m*. **To give a hammock a s.**, faire aller un hamac. *(b)* Tour *m*. *Aut: Mec.E:* **To give the starting-handle a s.**, donner un tour à la manivelle. *(c)* Coup balancé. *Box:* Swing *m*. *(d) Golf:* **Upward s., downward s.**, ballant ascendant, descendant. *(e) Mus:* Swing *m*. **2.** *(a)* Oscillation *f* (d'un pendule). *Pol:* **The s. of the pendulum**, le flux et le reflux des partis. **To be in full s.**, *(of fête)* battre son plein; *(of factory)* être en plein travail. **Sudden s. of public opinion**, revirement inattendu de l'opinion publique. **S.-to of the door**, rabattement *m* de la porte. *(b)* **To give a child a s.**, pousser un enfant sur l'escarpolette; balancer un enfant. **3.** *(a)* Amplitude *f* (d'une oscillation). *(b) Nau:* Évitage *m* (d'un navire à l'ancre). **4. To walk with a s.**, marcher d'un pas rythmé. **Song that goes with a s.**, chanson très rythmée; chanson entraînante. *F:* **Everything went with a s.**, tout a très bien marché. **When you have got into the s. of things**, quand vous serez au courant. **5.** Escarpolette *f*, balançoire *f*. '**swing-boat**, *s. (At fairs)* (Bateau *m*) balançoire (*f*). '**swing-bridge**, *s.* Pont tournant, pivotant. '**swing-door**, *s.* Porte battante; porte va-et-vient. '**swing-gate**, *s.* **1.** Barrière battante, tournante. **2.** Counterpoise s.-g., tape-cul *m*. '**swing-round**, *s. Aut: etc:* Tête-à-queue *m*. '**swing shift**, *s. U.S: Ind:* Équipe *f* de relève mi-jour, mi-nuit (dans une usine travaillant jour et nuit). **swing-wing**, *a. Av:* à ailes variables.

swing², *v.* (swung [swʌŋ]; swung) I. *v.i.* **1.** *(a)* **To s. to and fro**, se balancer; *(of bell)* branler; *(of pendulum)* osciller. **To set the bells swinging**, mettre les cloches en branle. **Door that swings to and fro in the wind**, porte qui ballotte au vent. *F:* **To s. for a crime**, être pendu pour un crime. *(b)* Tourner, pivoter (sur un axe); basculer. **The door swung on its hinges**, la porte tourna sur ses gonds. *(Of door)* **To s. open**, s'ouvrir. **To s. to**, se refermer. *(c) (Of ship)* **To s. (at anchor)**, éviter (sur l'ancre). *(d) Games:* Se balancer. **2.** Faire un mouvement de conversion; changer de direction. *(a)* **To s. round**, faire volte-face. **The car swung right round**, la voiture a fait un tête-à-queue. *(b) Mil:* **The whole line swung to the left**, toute la ligne fit une conversion vers la gauche. *(Of fleet)* **To s. to starboard**, faire un crochet sur la droite. **3.** **To s. along**, marcher d'un pas rythmé. II. *v.tr.* **1.** *(a)* (Faire) balancer (qch.); faire osciller (un pendule). **To s. one's arms**, balancer les bras (en marchant). **To s. the hips** (*in walking*), se dandiner. *S.a.* CAT 1, LEAD¹ 3. *(b) P:* **To s. it on s.o.**, duper, essayer de duper qn; tirer une carotte à qn. **2.** *(a) Nau:* Boat swung out, embarcation parée au dehors. *(b)* **To s. a car round**, faire faire un brusque virage à une auto. *(c) Fai.:*e tourner. *Av:* **To s. the propeller**, mettre en marche à l'hélice. **3.** **To s. a hammock**, pendre, (ac)crocher, un hamac. **4.** *v.pr. & i.* **To s.** (oneself) **into the saddle**, monter vivement à cheval, en selle. **swing back**, *v.i.* **1.** Basculer; se rabattre. **2.** *(Of pendulum)* Revenir. **Public opinion swung back**, il y eut un revirement d'opinion. '**swing-back**, *s.* Retour *m* en arrière; revirement *m* (d'opinion). **swinging¹**, *a.* **1.** Balançant, oscillant; (bras) ballants. **2.** *(a)* **S. stride**, allure rythmée, cadencée. **-ly**, *adv.* Avec rythme; d'un pas cadencé; avec entrain. **swinging²**, *s.* **1.** *(a)* Balancement *m*, oscillation *f*. *(b)* Mouvement *m* de bascule, de rotation. *(c) Nau:* Évitage *m*. *(d)* **S. round**, tête-à-queue *m inv.* **2.** *Av:* Mise *f* en marche (de l'hélice).

swinish ['swainiʃ], *a.* De cochon, de pourceau; sale. **-ly**, *adv.* Salement; comme un pourceau. **To eat s.**, manger comme un pourceau; manger en goinfre.

swinishness ['swainiʃnis], *s.* **1.** Saleté *f*, grossièreté *f*. **2.** Goinfrerie *f*.

swipe¹ [swaip], *s.* **1.** *Cr: Golf:* Coup *m* à toute volée. **2.** *F:* Taloche *f*.

swipe², *v.tr. & ind.tr.* **1.** *Cr: etc:* **To s.** (at) **the ball**, frapper la balle à toute volée. **2.** *F:* Donner une taloche à (qn). **3.** *P:* Chiper, chaparder (qch. à qn).

swipes [swaips], *s.pl. F:* Petite bière.

swirl¹ [swəːl], *s.* Remous *m* (de l'eau). **A s. of dust**, un tourbillon de poussière.

swirl², *v.i.* Tournoyer, tourbillonner. *(Of dust)* **To s. up**, monter en tourbillons.

swish¹ [swiʃ], *s.* **1.** Bruissement *m* (de l'eau); froufrou *m* (d'une robe); sifflement *m* (d'un fouet); crissement *m* (d'une faux). **2.** Coup *m* de fouet.

swish². **1.** *v.i. (Of water)* Bruire; susurrer. *(Of wheels)* **To s. through the mud**, faire gicler la boue. **2.** *v.tr.* *(a)* Fouetter. *(b)* Faire siffler (sa canne). *(c) (Of animal)* **To s. its tail**, battre l'air de sa queue. **swishing**, *s. Sch: F:* **To get a s.**, recevoir une bonne correction.

Swiss [swis]. **1.** *a.* Suisse; helvétique. **The S. Government**, le gouvernement helvétique. **2.** *s.* Suisse, -esse. **The S.**, les Suisses.

switch¹ [switʃ], *s.* **1.** *(a)* Badine *f*; houssine *f* (pour battre les meubles). **Riding s.**, cravache *f*, stick *m*. *(b)* Coup *m* de baguette. **2.** *(a) Rail:* Aiguille *f*; changement *m* de voie. *Cards:* Changement *m* de couleur (dans les annonces). *(b) El.E:* Interrupteur *m*; commutateur *m*. **Isolating s.**, sectionneur *m*. **Tumbler s.**, interrupteur à culbuteur. **Two-way s.**, commutateur à deux départs; interrupteur d'escalier. *Aut:* **The starting s.**, le contact. **3.** *Toil:* Tresse *f* de cheveux postiches. '**switch-bar**, *s. Rail:* Tringle *f* de manœuvre. '**switch-plate**, *s. Rail:* Plaque *f* de manœuvre. '**switch-rail**, *s. Rail:* Rail *m* mobile.

switch², *v.tr.* **1.** *(a)* Donner un coup de badine à (qn); houssiner (des meubles). *(b) (Of animal)* **To s. its tail**, battre l'air de sa queue. **2.** **To s. a train on to a branch line**, aiguiller, dériver, un train sur un embranchement. **switch off**, *v.tr.* *(a) El:* Interrompre, couper (le courant); *abs.* ouvrir le circuit. **To s. off the light**, couper la lumière. *I.C.E:* **To s. off the ignition, the engine**, couper l'allumage. **To s. off the radio, the television**, *abs.* **to s. off**, fermer le poste. *(b) Tp:* Couper la communication. **switch on**, *v.tr.* **To s. on the current**, *abs.* **to s. on**, donner du courant. **To s. on the light**, allumer (l'électricité). **To s. on the radio, the television**, ouvrir le poste. *Aut:* **To s. on the ignition**, mettre le contact. **switch over**, *v.tr. El:* Commuter (le courant). *Abs. W.Tel:* **To s. over (to another station)**, changer de réglage. *F: Mil: etc:* **To s. over to the offensive**, passer à l'offensive. *Ind:* **To s. over production**, changer la production.

switchback ['switʃbæk], *s.* Montagnes *f* russes. **S. road**, route qui monte et descend.

switchboard ['switʃbɔːd], *s.* *(a) El.E:* Tableau *m* de distribution. *(b) Tp:* Office s., standard *m*. **S. operator**, standardiste *mf*.

switchman, *pl.* -men ['switʃmən], *s.m. Rail: U.S:* Aiguilleur.

Swithin ['swiðin]. *Pr.n.m.* St S.'s day, (15th July) = la Saint-Médard (le huit juin).

Switzerland ['switsələnd]. *Pr.n.* La Suisse. **French-, German-, Italian-speaking S.**, la Suisse romande, allemande, italienne.

swivel¹ ['swiv(ə)l], *s.* *(a)* Émerillon *m*; maillon tournant. *(b)* Pivot *m*; tourillon *m*. **Ball s.**, pivot à rotule. **S. block**, poulie *f* à émerillon. *S.a.* ROWLOCKS. '**swivel-eyed**, *a. F:* Louche, bigle. '**swivel-gun**, *s.* Canon *m* à pivot. '**swivel-seat**, *s.* Siège tournant.

swivel², *v.i.* (swivelled) Pivoter, tourner.

swizz(le) ['swiz(l)], *s. Sch: O: F:* *(a)* Déception *f*. *(b)* Duperie *f*.

swizzle ['swizl], *s. Esp.U.S: F:* (Sorte de) cocktail. '**swizzle-stick**, *s. F:* Fouet à champagne.

swollen. See SWELL².

swoon¹ [swuːn], *s. O:* Évanouissement *m*, défaillance *f*. *Med:* Syncope *f*. **To go off in a s.**, s'évanouir; tomber évanoui.

swoon², *v.i. O:* S'évanouir, défaillir; se trouver mal. *Med:* Avoir une syncope. **swooning**, *a. O:* *(a)* Défaillant. *(b)* Évanoui.

swoop¹ [swuːp], *s.* Descente *f* (d'un faucon sur sa proie); attaque *f* en piqué (d'un avion) (upon, sur); attaque brusquée. *F:* **At one (fell) s.**, d'un seul coup (fatal).

swoop², *v.i.* **To s. down upon sth.**, s'abattre, foncer, sur qch.

swop[1,2] ['swɔp], s. & v.tr. = SWAP[1,2].

sword [sɔːd], s. (a) Épée f. **To wear a s.**, porter l'épée. **To draw one's s.**, tirer son épée; dégainer. **To draw the s.**, commencer les hostilités. **To cross swords with s.o.**, (i) croiser le fer avec qn; (ii) mesurer ses forces avec qn. (b) Sabre m. **With drawn s.**, sabre au clair. '**sword-arm**, s. Le bras droit. '**sword-bearer**, s. Officier municipal qui porte le glaive. '**sword-belt**, s. Ceinturon m. '**sword-cut**, s. Coup m de sabre; (on face) balafre f. '**sword-dance**, s. Danse f du sabre. '**sword-play**, s. 1. Maniement m de l'épée; escrime f. 2. (Verbal) s.-p., joute f oratoire. '**sword-stick**, s. Canne f à épée. '**sword-thrust**, s. Coup m de pointe; coup d'épée.

swordfish ['sɔːdfiʃ], s. Ich: Espadon m.

swordsman, pl. **-men** ['sɔːdzmən], s.m. Escrimeur m. **Fine s.**, fine lame.

swordsmanship ['sɔːdzmənʃip], s. Habileté f au maniement de l'épée; escrime f.

swore, sworn. See SWEAR[2].

swot[1] [swɔt], s. Sch: F: 1. (a) Travail m intense. (b) Corvée f. 2. (Pers.) Bûcheur, -euse; potasseur m.

swot[2], v.tr. & i. (swotted) Sch: F: Bûcher, piocher. **To s. for an exam**, potasser un examen. **To s. up one's maths**, potasser ses maths.

swum. See SWIM[2].

swung. See SWING[2].

sybarite ['sibərait], a. & s. Sybarite (mf).

sybaritic [,sibə'ritik], a. Sybarite.

sycamore ['sikəmɔːr], s. (Érable m) sycomore (m); faux platane.

sycophancy ['sikəfənsi], s. Flagornerie f.

sycophant ['sikəfənt], s. 1. Gr.Ant: Sycophante m. 2. Flagorneur, -euse.

syllabic [si'læbik], a. Syllabique.

syllable ['siləbl], s. Syllabe f.

syllabus, pl. **-uses, -i** ['siləbəs, -əsiz, -ai], s. Programme m, sommaire m (d'un cours).

syllogism ['silədʒizm], s. Syllogisme m.

sylph [silf], s. 1. Sylphe m, sylphide f. 2. (Applied to woman) Sylphide f. '**sylph-like**, a. (Taille, etc.) de sylphide.

sylvan ['silvən], a. Lit: Sylvestre.

symbiosis [,simbi'ousis], s. Biol: Symbiose f.

symbol ['simb(ə)l], s. 1. Symbole m, emblème m. 2. Ch: Mth: Symbole.

symbolic(al) [sim'bɔlik(əl)], a. Symbolique. **-ally**, adv. Symboliquement.

symbolism ['simbəlizm], s. Symbolisme m.

symbolist ['simbəlist], s. Symboliste mf.

symbolization [,simbəlai'zeiʃ(ə)n], s. Symbolisation f.

symbolize ['simbəlaiz], v.tr. Symboliser.

symmetrical [si'metrik(ə)l], a. Symétrique. **-ally**, adv. Symétriquement.

symmetry ['simitri], s. Symétrie f.

sympathetic [,simpə'θetik], a. 1. (a) (Of pain, nerve) Sympathique. **The s. nerve**, le grand sympathique. (b) S. ink, encre sympathique. 2. (a) Compatissant. **S. glance**, regard compatissant. **He's always very s.**, il est toujours prêt à vous écouter. (b) S. audience, auditoire bien disposé. **S. words**, paroles de condoléance. (c) Dicté par la solidarité. **S. strike**, grève f de solidarité. **-ally**, adv. D'une manière compatissante.

sympathize ['simpəθaiz], v.i. 1. **To s. with s.o.** (in his sorrow), avoir de la compassion pour qn. **The Smiths called to s.**, les Smith sont venus exprimer leurs condoléances. 2. **To s. with s.o.'s point of view**, comprendre le point de vue de qn (sans l'approuver). **sympathizing**, a. Compatissant.

sympathizer ['simpəθaizər], s. 1. **To be a s. in s.o.'s grief**, compatir au chagrin de qn. 2. Partisan, -ane (with a cause, d'une cause); sympathisant, -e.

sympathy ['simpəθi], s. 1. Compassion f. **Accept my deep s.**, agréez mes condoléances. 2. (a) Sympathie f, solidarité f (for s.o., à l'égard de qn). **Popular sympathies are on his side**, il a l'opinion pour lui. **I know you are in s. with them**, je sais que vous êtes de leur côté. **To strike in s.**, se mettre en grève par solidarité. (b) Prices went up in s., les prix sont montés par contre-coup. Ph: **String that vibrates in s.**, corde qui vibre par résonance.

symphonic [sim'fɔnik], a. Symphonique.

symphony ['simfəni], s. Symphonie f. **S. concert**, concert m symphonique.

symposium, pl. **-ia** [sim'pouziəm, -iə], s. 1. Gr.Ant: Banquet m. 2. (a) Discussion f (académique); colloque m. (b) Recueil m d'articles.

symptom ['simptəm], s. Symptome m; indice m. **To show symptoms of . . .**, présenter des indices de. . . .

symptomatic [,simptə'mætik], a. Symptomatique.

synagogue ['sinəgɔg], s. Synagogue f.

syncroflash ['siŋkro'flæʃ], a. Phot: **S. (device)**, dispositif syncroflash.

synchromesh ['siŋkromeʃ], s. Aut: (Boîte f de vitesses) synchromesh (m).

synchronism ['siŋkrənizm], s. Synchronisme m. **In s.**, en synchronisme; El.E: en phase. T.V: **Irregular s.**, drapeau m.

synchronization [,siŋkrənai'zeiʃ(ə)n], s. Synchronisation f. El.E: Accrochage m. Cin: T.V: etc: **S. of sound and image**, synchronisation du son et de l'image.

synchronize ['siŋkrənaiz], 1. v.tr. (a) Synchroniser (deux mouvements, deux horloges); El.E: coupler en phase; accrocher (un alternateur). (b) Établir le synchronisme de (différents événements). 2. v.i. (a) (Of events) Arriver, avoir lieu, simultanément. (b) El.E: **When the generators s.**, lorsque les générateurs sont en phase.

synchronizer ['siŋkrənaizər], s. Synchroniseur m; dispositif m, mécanisme m, de synchronisation.

synchrotron ['siŋkrotrən], s. Atom.Ph: Synchrotron m.

synclinal [siŋ'klain(ə)l], a. Geol: Synclinal, -aux.

syncopate ['siŋkəpeit], v.tr. Gram: Mus: Syncoper.

syncopation [,siŋkə'peiʃ(ə)n], s. Mus: Syncope f.

syncope ['siŋkəpi], s. Med: Syncope f.

syndic ['sindik], s. Syndic m.

syndical ['sindik(ə)l], a. Syndical, -aux.

syndicalism ['sindikəliz(ə)m], s. Syndicalisme m.

syndicalist ['sindikəlist], s. Syndicaliste (mf).

syndicate[1] ['sindikit], s. 1. Com: Syndicat m. 2. Conseil m de syndics.

syndicate[2] ['sindikeit], v.tr. (a) Syndiquer (des ouvriers, une industrie). (b) Publier (un article) simultanément dans plusieurs journaux.

syndrome ['sindroum, 'sindrəmi], s. Med: Syndrome m.

synergy ['sinədʒi], s. Synergie f.

synod ['sinəd], s. Ecc: Synode m, concile m.

synonym ['sinənim], s. Synonyme m.

synonymous [si'nɔniməs], a. Synonyme (with, de).

synonymy [si'nɔnimi], s. Synonymie f.

synopsis, pl. **-opses** [si'nɔpsis, -ɔpsiːz], s. Résumé m, sommaire m; tableau m synoptique. **S. of chemistry**, mémento m de chimie.

synoptic(al) [si'nɔptik(əl)], a. Synoptique. **The Synoptic Gospels**, les Évangiles m synoptiques.

synovia [si'nouviə, sai-], s. Anat: Synovie f.

synovial [si'nouviəl, sai-], a. Synovial, -aux.

synovitis [si'nou'vaitis, sai-], s. Med: Synovite f.

syntactic(al) [sin'tæktik(əl)], a. Syntactique, syntaxique.

syntax ['sintæks], s. Syntaxe f.

synthesis, pl. **-es** ['sinθesis, -iːz], s. Synthèse f.

synthesize ['sinθisaiz], v.tr. Synthétiser.

synthetic(al) [sin'θetik(əl)], 1. a. Synthétique. **Synthetic rubber**, caoutchouc artificiel, synthétique. 2. s. Usu. pl. **Synthetics**, (i) (tissus, etc.), synthétiques m; (ii) la matière plastique, F: les plastiques m. **-ally**, adv. Synthétiquement.

synthetize ['sinθətaiz], v.tr. = SYNTHESIZE.

syntonic [sin'tɔnik], a. W.Tel: Syntonique.

syntonism ['sintənizm], s. W.Tel: Syntonie f.

syntonization [,sintənaiz'eiʃ(ə)n], s. W.Tel: Syntonisation f.

syntonize ['sintənaiz], v.tr. W.Tel: Syntoniser, accorder.

syntony ['sintəni], s. Syntonie f, accord m.

syphilis ['sifilis], s. Med: Syphilis f.

syphilitic [,sifi'litik], a. Syphilitique.

Syria ['siriə]. Pr.n. La Syrie.

Syriac ['siriæk], s. Ling: Le syriaque.

Syrian ['siriən], a. & s. Syrien, -ienne.

syringa [si'riŋgə], s. Bot: Seringa m.

syringe[1] [si'rindʒ], s. Seringue f.

syringe², *v.tr.* Seringuer (des fleurs, etc.). **To s. (out) the ears**, laver les oreilles avec une seringue. **syringing**, *s. Hort:* Seringage *m.*
syrup [ˈsirəp], *s.* **1.** Sirop *m.* **2. Golden s.**, mélasse raffinée; sirop de sucre.
syrupy [ˈsirəpi], *a.* Sirupeux, -euse.
system [ˈsistəm], *s.* **1.** (*a*) Système *m.* **The feudal s.**, le régime féodal. **To establish sth. on a s.**, établir qch. d'après un système. *Astr:* **The solar s.**, le système solaire. *Anat:* **The digestive s.**, l'appareil digestif. **The s.**, l'organisme *m.* (*b*) Réseau ferré (de chemin de fer); réseau télégraphique. **River s., road s.**, réseau fluvial, routier. **2.** Méthode *f* (de travail). **To lack s.**, manquer de méthode, d'organisation.
systematic [ˌsistəˈmætik], *a.* (*a*) Systématique, méthodique. **He is s.**, il a de l'ordre, de la méthode. (*b*) **S. opposition**, opposition systématique. **-ally,** *adv.* Systématiquement. **She does her work s.**, elle travaille avec méthode.
systematization [ˌsistimətaiˈzeiʃ(ə)n], *s.* Systématisation *f*; action *f* de systématiser.
systematize [ˈsistəmətaiz], *v.tr.* Réduire en système; systématiser.
systole [ˈsistəli], *s. Physiol:* Systole *f.*
systolic [sisˈtɔlik], *a.* Systolique.
syzygy [ˈsizidʒi], *s. Astr:* Syzygie *f.*

T,t [tiː], *s.* **1.** (La lettre) T, t *m.* **To cross one's t's,** (i) barrer ses t; (ii) mettre les points sur les i. *Tp:* **T for Tommy,** T comme Thérèse. *Adv.phr.* **To a T,** exactement; à la perfection. **That suits me to a T,** cela me va à merveille. **2.** (*a*) *Mec.E:* **Union T, union tee,** raccord *m* en T. (*b*) En (forme de) **T. T section,** T iron, fer *m* à, en, T. **T-shaped,** en T, en potence. **3.** *Cost:* **T. shirt,** tee-shirt *m*, T-shirt *m*. *S.a.* SQUARE[1] I. 4.

ta [taː], *int.* (*Nursery speech*) Merci.

tab [tæb], *s.* **1.** (*a*) Patte *f* (de vêtement). (*b*) Écusson *m*, insigne *m* (d'officier d'état-major). (*c*) Shoe-lace t., ferret *m* de cordon de soulier. (*d*) (*For hanging up coat*) Attache *f.* (*e*) Onglet *m* (de dictionnaire, de fichier). **2.** Étiquette *f* (pour bagages). *F:* **To keep tabs on s.o., sth.,** tenir qn, qch., à l'œil.

tabard ['tæbəd], *s.* Tabar(d) *m* (de héraut).

tabby ['tæbi], *s.* **1. T. cat,** (i) chat tigré, moucheté; (ii) *O:* F: chatte *f.* **2.** F: Vieille fille cancanière; vieille chipie.

tabernacle ['tæbənækl], *s.* Tabernacle *m.*

tabes ['teibiːz], *s. Med:* Tabès *m.*

table¹ ['teibl], *s.* Table *f.* **1.** (*a*) Occasional t., petite table; guéridon *m.* **Nest of tables,** table gigogne. **Card-t., gaming t.,** table de jeu. **Picnic t.,** table pliante, de camping. *Parl:* **To lay a measure on the t.,** déposer un projet de loi sur le bureau. (*b*) **To lay the t.,** mettre la table; dresser le couvert. **T. laid for twelve,** table de douze couverts. **To clear the t.,** desservir. **To sit down to t.,** se mettre à table. *Sch:* **High t.** (*at a university*) = table d'honneur. **T. wine,** vin de table. *Ecc:* **The Lord's T.,** the Communion T., la Sainte Table. *S.a.* CLOTH 2. (*c*) *Geog:* **T. Mountain,** Montagne *f* de la Table. **2.** *pl. A:* **Tables,** trictrac *m. F:* **To turn the tables on s.o.,** renverser les rôles; retourner la situation. **3.** *Tchn:* Table *f*, plateau *m* (de machine-outil); entablement *m* (de laminoir). **4.** (*a*) Table (d'un diamant). (*b*) Tablier (de pont à bascule). **5.** Plaque *f*, tablette *f* (de marbre). *B:* **The Tables of the Law,** les Tables de la loi. **6.** (*List*) Table, tableau *m.* **Multiplication t.,** table de multiplication. *Ch:* **T. of chemical equivalents,** abaque *m* des équivalents chimiques. *Nau:* **Tide t.,** annuaire *m* des marées. 'table(-)centre, *s.* Jeté *m* de table. 'table-cover, *s.* Tapis *m* de table. 'table diamond, *s.* Diamant (taillé) en table. 'table-flap, *s.* Abattant *m* de table. 'table-fork, *s.* Fourchette *f.* 'table(-)land, *s. Ph.Geog:* Plateau *m.* 'table-leaf, *s.* **1.** = TABLE-FLAP. **2.** Rallonge *f* (de table). 'table-linen, *s.* Linge *m* de table. 'table-mat, *s.* Dessous *m* de plat, d'assiette. 'table-rapping, *s. Psychics:* Tables parlantes. 'table-talk, *s.* Propos *mpl* de table. 'table-tennis, *s.* Tennis *m* de table; ping-pong *m.* 'table-top, *s.* Dessus *m* de table. 'table-turning, *s. Psychics:* Tables tournantes.

table², *v.tr.* **1.** *Parl:* **To t. a bill,** (i) saisir la Chambre d'un projet de loi; (ii) *U.S:* ajourner (indéfiniment) un projet de loi. **2.** *Carp:* Emboîter. **3.** *Nau:* Doubler les bords (d'une voile).

tablecloth ['teiblklɔθ], *s.* Nappe *f.*

table d'hôte ['taːblə'dout], *s.* Table *f* d'hôte; repas *m* à prix fixe.

tablespoon ['teiblspuːn], *s.* Cuiller *f* à servir, à ragoût.

tablespoonful ['teiblspuːnful], *s.* Cuillerée *f* à bouche.

tablet ['tæblit], *s.* **1.** Plaque commémorative. **Votive t.,** ex-voto *m inv.* **2.** (*a*) *Pharm: etc:* Comprimé *m.* (*b*) **T. of soap,** savonnette *f.* **3.** *U.S:* Bloc-correspondance *m.*

tabloid ['tæbloid], *s. Pharm: R.t.m:* (*applied to drugs, made by Burroughs, Wellcome & Co.*) Comprimé *m.*

taboo¹ [tə'buː]. **1.** *s.* Tabou *m*, -ous. **2.** *Pred. a.* Interdit, proscrit (comme étant tabou). **It's t.,** c'est une chose qui ne se fait pas.

taboo², *v.tr.* **1.** *Anthr:* Tabouer; déclarer tabou. **2.** *F:* Proscrire, interdire (qch.).

tabor ['teibər], *s.A:* Tambourin *m*; tambour *m* de basque.

tabular ['tæbjulər], *a.* Tabulaire.

tabulate ['tæbjuleit], *v.tr.* Disposer (des chiffres) en forme de table(s); classifier (des résultats); cataloguer.

tabulator ['tæbjuleitər], *s.* Tabulateur *m.*

tachometer [tæ'kɔmitər], *s. Mec.E:* Tachymètre *m*, compte-tours *m.* **Recording t.,** tachygraphe *m.*

tachymeter [tæ'kimətər], *s. Surv:* Tachéomètre *m.*

tacit ['tæsit], *a.* (Consentement) tacite, implicite. **-ly** *adv.* Tacitement.

taciturn ['tæsitəːn], *a.* Taciturne.

taciturnity [ˌtæsi'təːniti], *s.* Taciturnité *f.*

Tacitus ['tæsitəs]. *Pr.n.m.* Tacite.

tack¹ [tæk], *s.* **1.** Petit clou; broquette *f*; semence *f* (de tapissier). *F:* **To get down to brass tacks,** en venir au fait. **2.** *Needlew:* Point de bâti. **3.** *Nau:* (*a*) (*Clewline*) Amure *f.* **Tacks and sheets of a sail,** les lofs *m.* (*b*) **To make a t.,** tirer un bord, une bordée. *F:* **To be on the right t.,** être sur la bonne voie.

tack², **1.** *v.tr.* (*a*) **To t. sth. (down),** clouer qch. avec des semences. *F:* **To t. sth. (on) to sth.,** attacher qch. à qch. (*b*) *Needlew:* Faufiler, bâtir. **2.** *v.i. Nau:* **To t. (about),** (i) virer (de bord); (ii) tirer des bordées; louvoyer. **tacking,** *s.* **1.** (*a*) Clouage *m.* (*b*) *Needlew:* Bâtissage *m*; faufilure *f.* **To take out the t.,** défaufiler. **2.** *Nau:* Virement *m* de bord.

tack³, *s. O:* Nourriture *f*, aliment *m.* **Hard-t.,** biscuit *m* de mer.

tackle¹ ['tækl], *s.* **1.** Attirail *m*, appareil *m*, engins *mpl.* **Fishing t.,** (i) attirail, engins de pêche; (ii) *Com:* articles *mpl* de pêche. **2.** Appareil de levage. **Rope t.,** agrès *mpl*, apparaux *mpl. Nau:* Pulley t., les palans *m.* **Boat tackles,** garants *m* de canot. **3.** Action *f* de saisir (qn). *Fb:* Placage *m.* 'tackle-block, *s.* Moufle *f.* 'tackle-fall, *s.* Garant *m.*

tackle², *v.tr.* (*a*) Empoigner; saisir (qn) à bras-le-corps; s'attaquer à (une question); aborder (un problème). (*b*) *Rugby Fb:* Plaquer (un adversaire).

tacky ['tæki], *a.* Collant; (vernis) presque sec.

tact [tækt], *s.* Tact *m*, savoir-faire *m*; doigté *m.*

tactful ['tæktf(u)l], *a.* (Homme) de tact; délicat. **To be t.,** avoir du tact. **-fully,** *adv.* Avec tact. **To deal t. with s.o.,** ménager qn.

tactical ['tæktik(ə)l], *a.* **1.** Tactique. **2.** (*Of pers.*) Adroit.

tactician [tæk'tiʃ(ə)n], *s.* Tacticien *m*; manœuvrier *m.*

tactics ['tæktiks], *s.pl.* Tactique *f.*

tactile ['tæktail], *a.* Tactile, tangible.

tactless ['tæktlis], *a.* (*a*) Dépourvu de tact; maladroit. (*b*) **T. question,** question indiscrète. **-ly,** *adv.* Sans tact.

tactlessness ['tæktlisnis], *s.* Manque *m* de tact; maladresse *f.*

tadpole ['tædpoul], *s. Amph:* Têtard *m.*

tael [teil], *s. Num:* Tael *m.*

taenia, *pl.* **-iae** ['tiːniə, -iː], *s. Med:* Ténia *m*; ver *m* solitaire.

taenifuge ['tiːnifjuːdʒ], *s. Med:* (Médicament) ténifuge.

taffeta ['tæfitə], *s.* Taffetas *m.*

taffrail ['tæfreil], *s. N.Arch:* (Lisse *f* de) couronnement *m* (de la poupe).

taffy ['tæfi], *s. U.S:* **1.** (Pâte *f* à) berlingot(s). **2. T. coloured,** marron.

tag¹ [tæg], *s.* **1.** (*a*) Morceau *m* (d'étoffe) qui pend. (*b*) Attache *f*; tirant *m* (de botte). (*c*) Ferret *m* (de lacet). (*d*) Étiquette *f.* **2.** (*a*) Citation banale; cliché *m.* **One of his favourite tags,** une de ses expressions favorites. (*b*) Refrain *m.* **3.** (Jeu *m* du) chat *m.* 'tag day, *s. U.S:* = FLAG DAY.

tag², *v.tr.* (**tagged**) **1. To t. a shoe-lace,** ferrer un lacet. **2. To t. sth. on to sth.,** attacher, ajouter, qch. à qch. **3. To t. along behind s.o.,** traîner derrière qn.

Tagus (the) [ðə'teigəs]. *Pr.n. Geog:* Le Tage.

Tahiti [taˈ(h)iːti, taiˈ(h)iːti]. *Pr.n. Geog:* Tahiti *m.*

tail¹ [teil], *s.* **1.** (*a*) Queue *f* (d'animal); (*Of peacock*) **To spread its t.,** faire la roue. **With his t. between his legs,** (i) (*of dog*) la queue entre les jambes; (ii) *F:*

(*of pers.*) l'oreille basse. *F:* **To keep one's t. up,** ne pas se laisser abattre. **To turn t.,** s'enfuir; tourner les talons. (*b*) Queue (de note musicale); empennage *m,* queue (d'avion). **T. of a shirt,** pan *m* de chemise. *pl.* Tails of a coat, coat-tails, basques *f,* pans, d'un habit. **To wear tails,** porter l'habit. *S.a* SPIN¹ 1. (*c*) Arrière *m* (d'une charrette). **There was another car close on my t.,** il y avait une autre voiture qui me suivait de près. **T. of a procession,** queue d'un défilé. (*d*) *F:* **The t. of the class,** la queue de la classe. 2. (*Of coin*) Pile *f,* revers *m. S.a.* HEAD¹ 8. **'tail-board,** *s. Veh:* Layon *m.* **'tail-'coat,** *s. Cost:* Habit *m, F:* queue-de-pie *f.* **'tail-end,** *s.* Bout *m;* queue *f* (d'un défilé); fin *f* (d'un orage, etc.). *Turf:* **To come in at the t.-e.,** arriver en queue, *F:* dans les choux. **'tail-lamp, -light,** *s. Rail: etc:* Feu *m* (d')arrière; lanterne *f* arrière. **'tail-piece,** *s.* 1. Queue *f.* 2. Cordier *m* (de violon). 3. *Typ:* Cul-de-lampe *m.* **'tail-plane,** *s. Av:* Plan stabilisateur. **'tail-shaft,** *s. N.Arch:* Extrémité *f* de l'arbre. **'tail-skid,** *s. Av:* Béquille *f.* **'tail-stock,** *s.* Poupée *f* mobile (de tour).

tail², 1. *v.tr.* **To t. sth. on to sth.,** attacher qch. derrière qch. 2. *v.tr.* Enlever les queues (des groseilles, etc.). 3. *v.i. & tr. F:* **To t. (after) s.o.,** (i) suivre qn de près; (ii) suivre qn à la queue leu leu. **tail off,** *v.i.* (*Of voice*) S'éteindre. **tailed,** *a.* A queue.

tail³, *s. Jur:* **Heir, estate, in t.,** héritier par substitution; bien substitué.

tailor¹ ['teilər], *s.* Tailleur *m* (d'habits). **T.-made costume,** (costume *m*) tailleur.

tailor², *v.tr.* Faire, façonner (un complet). **Well-tailored overcoat,** pardessus de façon soignée. **tailoring,** *s.* 1. Métier *m* de tailleur. 2. Ouvrage *m* de tailleur.

taint¹ [teint], *s.* 1. (*a*) Corruption *f,* infection *f.* (*b*) **The t. of sin,** la tache, la souillure, du péché. 2. Tare *f* héréditaire (d'insanité). 3. Trace *f* (d'infection).

taint², *v.tr.* 1. Infecter, vicier (l'air); gâter, corrompre (la nourriture). 2. (*With passive force*) Se corrompre; se gâter. **tainted,** *a.* Infecté, corrompu. **T. meat,** viande gâtée. **T. heredity,** hérédité chargée. **To be t. with insanity,** avoir une tare d'insanité. *Jur:* **T. with fraud,** entaché de dol.

take [teik], *v.* (took [tuk]; taken ['teik(ə)n]) Prendre. **I.** *v.tr.* 1. (*a*) **To t. sth. on one's back,** prendre, charger, qch. sur son dos. (*b*) **To t. sth. from s.o.,** enlever, prendre, qch. à qn. **Someone has taken my umbrella,** on m'a pris mon parapluie. **To t. sth. from the table,** prendre qch. sur la table. **To t. a saucepan off the stove,** retirer une casserole du feu. **To t. the lid off sth.,** enlever, ôter, le couvercle de qch. **T. your hands out of your pockets,** ôtez, sortez, les mains de vos poches. (*c*) **To t. hold of s.o.,** saisir, empoigner, qn. **He took her in his arms,** il la prit dans ses bras. **She took my arm,** elle me prit le bras. **To t. one's courage in both hands,** prendre son courage à deux mains. **To t. an opportunity,** saisir une occasion. *S.a.* CHANCE¹ 2, WHEEL¹ 1. (*d*) Prendre (une ville). **To t. s.o. prisoner,** faire qn prisonnier. **To be taken ill,** tomber malade. **He was very much taken with the idea,** l'idée lui souriait beaucoup. **I was not taken with him,** il ne m'a pas été sympathique; il ne m'a pas fait bonne impression. *S.a.* ABACK. (*e*) **To t. a passage from a book,** emprunter un passage à un livre. **To t. an idea from an author,** puiser une idée chez un auteur. 2. (*a*) Louer, prendre (une maison). (*b*) **To t. tickets,** prendre des billets. (*Of seat, table*) **'Taken,'** "occupé." **To t. a paper,** s'abonner à un journal. **To t. paying guests,** recevoir, prendre, des pensionnaires. **To t. pupils,** donner des leçons particulières. *S.a.* WIFE 1. (*c*) Prendre (le train). **To t. a seat,** prendre un siège; s'asseoir. **T. your seats!** prenez vos places! *Rail:* en voiture! (*d*) **T. the turning on the left,** prenez à gauche. **To t. the wrong road,** se tromper de chemin. *Sp:* **To t. an obstacle,** franchir, sauter, un obstacle. (*e*) **To t. legal advice** = consulter un avocat. (*f*) **To t. holy orders,** recevoir les ordres. *S.a.* COURSE¹ 1, 3, FIELD¹ 1. 3. (*a*) Gagner, remporter (le prix). *Cards:* **To t. a trick,** faire une levée. (*b*) **To t. one's degree,** recevoir ses diplômes. **To t. an examination,** se présenter à un examen. (*c*) *Com:* **To t. so much a week,** se faire tant

par semaine. 4. Prendre (de la nourriture). **To t. a meal,** faire un repas. **I cannot t. whisky,** je ne supporte pas le whisky. **'Not to be taken internally,'** "médicament pour usage externe." *P:* **I'm not taking any (of that)!** je ne marche pas! 5. (*a*) **To t. a walk,** faire une promenade. **To t. a bath,** prendre un bain. *S.a.* STEP¹ 3. **Mr X is taking the sixth form,** M. X prend la classe de première. **To t. a print from a negative,** tirer une épreuve d'un cliché. *Surv:* **To t. an angle,** observer un angle. **To t. breath,** reprendre haleine. **To t. effect,** produire son effet. *S.a.* OATH 1, PLACE¹ 2, PLUNGE¹, POSSESSION 1, STAND¹ 1, 3, STOCK¹ 5. (*b*) **To t. a photograph,** faire une photo. **To have one's photograph taken,** se faire photographier. (*c*) **To t. sth. apart, to pieces,** démonter qch. 6. (*a*) Prendre, recevoir. *Ten:* **To t. the service,** recevoir le service. **T. that (and that)!** attrape ça (et ça)! **To t. no denial,** ne pas accepter de refus. **What will you t. for it?** combien en voulez-vous? **To t. a bet,** tenir un pari. **To t. all responsibility,** assumer toute la responsabilité. **Taking one thing with another,** l'un dans l'autre. **Taking all in all,** à tout prendre. **We must t. things as we find them,** il faut prendre les choses comme elles sont. **T. it from me!** croyez-m'en! **I wonder how he will t. it,** *F:* je me demande quelle tête il fera. *S.a.* GIVE¹ I. 1, HINT¹ 1, LAMB¹. (*b*) **Bus that takes twenty passengers,** autobus qui tient vingt voyageurs. (*Of crane*) **To t. heavy loads,** supporter de fortes charges. *Mec:* **To t. a stress,** résister à une tension. 7. (*a*) Prendre, attraper (une maladie, un rhume). (*b*) **To t. a dislike to s.o.,** prendre qn en grippe. *S.a.* EXCEPTION 2. 8. (*a*) **We t. the will for the deed,** l'intention est réputée pour le fait. **How old do you t. him to be?** quel âge lui donnez-vous? **I t. it that . . .,** je suppose que. . . . (*b*) **I took you for an Englishman,** je vous croyais anglais. *F:* **What do you t. me for?** pour qui me prenez-vous? 9. (*Require*) (*a*) **That will t. some explaining,** voilà qui va demander des explications. **The work took some doing,** le travail a été difficile, dur. **The journey takes five days,** le voyage prend, demande, cinq jours. **It won't t. long,** ce sera tôt fait. **It took four men to hold him,** il a fallu le tenir à quatre. **It takes a clever man to do that,** bien habile qui peut le faire. (*b*) *Gram:* **Verb that takes a preposition,** verbe qui veut la préposition. (*c*) **I t. sixes (in gloves, etc.),** j'ai six de pointure. 10. (*a*) **To t. s.o. somewhere,** mener, conduire, qn dans un endroit. **To take s.o. abroad,** emmener qn à l'étranger. **To t. s.o. over a house,** faire visiter une maison à qn. **To t. s.o. out of his way,** écarter qn de sa route. *F:* **What (ever) took him there?** qu'allait-il faire dans cette galère? (*b*) **To t. sth. to s.o.,** porter qch. à qn. **To t. s.o. to the hospital,** transporter qn à l'hôpital. **II. take,** *v.i.* (*a*) Avoir du succès; réussir; prendre. (*b*) *Med:* **The vaccine has not taken,** le vaccin n'a pas pris. **take after,** *v.i.* Tenir de (qn). **His daughter does not t. after him,** sa fille n'a rien de lui. **take away,** *v.tr.* 1. Enlever, emporter (qch.); emmener (qn). (*Of book in library*) **'Not to be taken away,'** "exclu du prêt." 2. (*a*) **To t. away a knife from a child,** ôter un couteau à un enfant. (*b*) *Mth:* Soustraire. **To t. a child away from school,** retirer un enfant du collège. **take back,** *v.tr.* 1. (*a*) Reconduire (qn). (*b*) **To t. a book back to s.o.,** reporter un livre à qn. 2. (*a*) Reprendre (un employé). (*b*) **I t. back what I said,** je retire ce que j'ai dit. **I t. it all back,** mettons que je n'aie rien dit. **take down,** *v.tr.* 1. (*a*) **To t. down a picture,** descendre, décrocher, un tableau. (*b*) **To t. down a machine,** démonter une machine. **To t. down a wall,** abattre, démolir, un mur. (*c*) *F:* **To t. s.o. down (a peg or two),** remettre qn à sa place. 2. **To t. down a few notes,** prendre quelques notes. **To t. down in shorthand,** sténographier. **'take-down,** *s. F:* Mortification *f,* humiliation *f.* **take in,** *v.tr.* 1. (*a*) **To t. in s.o.'s card,** faire passer la carte de qn. (*b*) **To t. in the harvest,** rentrer la moisson. *Nau:* **To t. in (a supply of) water,** faire de l'eau. (*Of boat*) **To t. in water,** faire eau; prendre l'eau. (*c*) **To t. in an orphan,** recueillir un orphelin. **To t. in lodgers,** prendre des locataires. **To t. in washing,** faire des lessives. **To t. in the washing,** rentrer le linge. (*e*) *Sch:* **To t. in the marks,** relever les notes. 2. (*a*) **To t. in a dress at the waist,** reprendre une robe à la taille.

(b) **To t. in sail**, diminuer de voile(s). **3.** Comprendre, inclure. **The empire took in all these countries**, l'empire englobait tous ces pays. **4.** (a) Comprendre, se rendre compte de (qch.). **To t. in the situation**, se rendre compte de la situation; juger la situation. **To t. in everything at a glance**, tout embrasser d'un coup d'œil. (b) *F:* (*Believe*) **He takes it all in**, il prend tout ça pour argent comptant. (c) *F:* (*Cheat*) Mettre (qn) dedans; *F:* rouler (qn). **To be taken in**, se laisser attraper. **He is easily taken in**, il est très jobard. **To be taken in by appearances**, se laisser tromper aux apparences. 'take-in, *s.* Duperie *f*; attrape *f*. take into, *v.tr.* **1. To t. s.o. into one's confidence**, mettre qn dans sa confidence. **2. To t. it into one's head to do sth.**, se mettre dans la tête de faire qch. take off. 1. *v.tr.* **1. To t. s.o.'s attention off sth.**, distraire l'attention de qn. **To t. one's eye off sth.**, quitter qch. des yeux. *S.a.* CHILL[1] 2. **2.** (a) Enlever, ôter. *Aut:* Déjanter (le pneu). **To t. off one's clothes**, quitter ses vêtements; se déshabiller. *S.a.* HAT. *Tp:* **To t. off the receiver**, décrocher le récepteur. (b) Emmener (qn). **He was taken off to gaol**, il fut emmené en prison. *F:* **To t. oneself off**, s'en aller, s'éloigner, *F:* filer. (c) **To t. so much off (the price of sth.)**, rabattre tant (sur le prix de qch.). (d) **To t. off a train**, supprimer un train. (e) *F:* Imiter, singer (qn). II. take off, *v.i.* Prendre son élan, s'élancer (*from*, de). *Av:* Décoller, s'envoler. 'take-off, *s.* (a) Élan *m*. (b) *Av:* Décollage *m*. (c) *F:* Caricature *f*, charge *f*. take on. 1. *v.tr.* (a) Se charger de, entreprendre (un travail). (b) Accepter le défi de (qn). **I'll t. you on at billiards!** je vais vous faire une partie de billard! **To t. on a bet**, accepter un pari. (c) Engager, embaucher (un ouvrier). (d) Prendre, revêtir (une qualité). (e) (*Of train*) **To t. on passengers**, prendre des voyageurs. (f) Mener (qn) plus loin, au delà de sa destination. **2.** *v.i.* (a) *P:* **Don't t. on so!** ne vous désolez pas comme ça! (b) *F:* Devenir populaire; réussir. **This fashion has taken on**, cette mode a pris. take out, *v.tr.* **1.** (a) **To t. out one's pipe**, sortir sa pipe. **To t. out a tooth**, arracher une dent. **To t. out a stain**, enlever une tache. (b) *F:* **I'll t. it out of him**, je me vengerai. **Don't t. it out on me**, ne vous en prenez pas à moi. **The heat takes it out of me**, la chaleur m'épuise. **2.** Faire sortir (qn). **He is going to t. me out to dinner**, il va m'emmener dîner. **He's always taking girls out**, il est toujours à sortir avec des jeunes filles. **3.** Prendre, obtenir (un brevet). **To t. out an insurance policy**, contracter une assurance. *S.a.* SUMMONS[1] 2. take over, *v.tr.* **1. To t. over a business**, prendre la suite des affaires. **To rent a flat and t. over the furniture**, louer un appartement avec une reprise de meubles. **To t. over the liabilities**, prendre les dettes à sa charge. *Abs.* **To t. over from s.o.**, remplacer qn (dans ses fonctions); relever qn. **2.** (a) Transporter (qn, qch.). (b) Passer (qn) (dans un bateau). (c) *W.Tel:* Mettre en communication. **We t. you over to Rome**, nous vous mettons en communication avec Rome. 'take-over, *s.* Reprise *f* (d'une maison de commerce, etc.); prise de possession (du pouvoir). **T.-o. bid**, offre *m* de rachat. take round, *v.tr.* **To t. round the plate**, faire la quête. **To t. s.o. round the town**, faire faire le tour de la ville à qn. take to, *v.i.* **1. To t. to flight**, prendre la fuite. **To t. to the woods**, se réfugier dans les bois. *S.a.* BED[1] 1, HEEL[1] 1. **To t. to drink**, se mettre à boire. **3.** (a) **To t. to s.o.**, se prendre de sympathie pour qn; prendre qn en amitié. (b) **To t. to a game**, prendre goût à un jeu. **I don't t. to the idea**, cette idée ne me dit rien. **I shall never t. to it**, je ne m'y ferai jamais. take up. I. *v.tr.* **1.** (a) Relever, ramasser (qch.). (b) **To t. up a carpet**, enlever un tapis. **To t. up a street**, dépaver une rue. *S.a.* ARM[2] 1. (c) *Rail:* **To stop to t. up passengers**, s'arrêter pour prendre des voyageurs. (d) *Dressm:* **To t. up a sleeve**, (i) raccourcir une manche; (ii) (*at the shoulder*) remonter une manche. (e) *Mec.E:* **To t. up the wear**, compenser l'usure. **2.** (a) Absorber (de l'eau). (b) *Aut:* **To t. up the bumps**, absorber les chocs. **3.** (a) *Com:* **To t. up a bill**, honorer un effet. *St.Exch:* **To t. up an option**, lever une prime. **To t. up shares**, souscrire à des actions. (b) **To t. up a challenge**, relever un défi. (c) **To t. up an idea**,

adopter une idée. **4.** (a) **To t. up a question**, prendre une question en main. *S.a.* REFERENCE 6. (b) Embrasser, (une carrière); s'adonner à (une occupation); épouser (une querelle). **To t. up new studies**, aborder de nouvelles études. **To t. up one's duties again**, reprendre ses fonctions. (c) Prendre (qn) sous sa protection. **5.** Arrêter (qn). **He was taken up by the police**, il a été arrêté. **6. To t. s.o. up sharply**, reprendre qn vertement. **To t. s.o. up short**, couper la parole à qn. **7. To t. s.o. up wrongly**, mal comprendre les paroles de qn. **8.** Occuper. (a) **To t. up too much room**, occuper trop de place. (b) **To t. up all s.o.'s attention**, absorber l'attention de qn. **It takes up all my evenings**, cela remplit toutes mes soirées. (c) **He is entirely taken up with his business**, il est tout à son commerce, il ne songe qu'à son commerce. *F:* **He is quite taken up with her**, il ne pense plus qu'à elle. II. take up, *v.i.* **To t. up with s.o.**, (i) se lier d'amitié avec qn; (ii) se mettre à fréquenter (des vauriens); (iii) *F:* se mettre (en ménage) avec qn, *P:* se coller avec qn. take upon, *v.tr.* **To t. it upon oneself to do sth.**, prendre sur soi de faire qch. **He takes a good deal upon himself**, il se permet bien des choses. taking, *a.* (Style) attrayant; (visage) séduisant. **T. manners**, manières engageantes. takings, *s.pl. Com: etc:* Recette *f*, produit *m*.

taker ['teikər], *s.* (a) Preneur, -euse (d'un bail, etc.). (b) *St.Exch:* **T. of an option**, optant *m*. **T. of a bill**, preneur d'une lettre de change. (c) **T. of a bet**, tenant *m* d'un pari. *Turf:* **The takers of odds**, les preneurs.

talc [tælk], *s.* **1.** Talc *m*. **2.** *Com:* Mica *m*.

talcum ['tælkəm], *s. Toil:* **T. powder**, (poudre *f* de) talc *m*.

tale [teil], *s.* **1.** Conte *m*. (a) Récit *m*, histoire *f*. **Old wives' tales**, contes de bonne femme. **His drawn face told the t. of his sufferings**, ses traits tirés en disaient long sur ses souffrances. **I've heard that t. before**, je connais des paroles sur cet air-là. (b) *Lit:* Nouvelle *f*, conte. **2.** *Pej:* (a) Racontar *m*. **I've heard a fine t. about you**, j'en ai appris de belles sur votre compte. (b) Rapport *m*, *F:* cafardage *m*. **To tell tales (out of school)**, rapporter; *F:* cafarder. *S.a.* DEAD I. 1. **3.** *A:* Nombre *m*; quantité *f*; compte *m*.

talebearer ['teilbɛərər], *s.* Rapporteur, -euse; *F:* cafard, -arde.

talent ['tælənt], *s.* **1.** *A:* **Gold t., silver t.**, talent *m* d'or, d'argent. **2.** (a) Talent; capacité (naturelle); aptitude *f*. **To have a t. for doing the right thing**, avoir le don d'agir à propos. (b) **Man of t.**, homme de talent. **3.** *Coll:* Gens *mpl* de talent. **Exhibition of local t.**, exposition des œuvres d'artistes régionaux. **T. scout**, dénicheur *m* de vedettes.

talented ['tæləntid], *a.* Doué.

talion ['tæliən], *s.* **The law of t.**, la loi du talion.

talisman ['tælizmən], *s.* Talisman *m*.

talk[1] [tɔ:k], *s.* **1.** (a) Paroles *fpl.* **He is all t.**, ce n'est qu'un bavard. (b) Bruit *m*, dires *mpl*, racontages *mpl*. **There is some t. of his returning**, il est question qu'il revienne. **It's all t.**, ce ne sont que des on-dit. (c) Propos *mpl*; bavardage *m*. **Idle t.**, paroles en l'air. **Small t.**, menus propos. **To indulge in small t.**, parler de la pluie et du beau temps. **To have plenty of small t.**, ne pas manquer de sujets de conversation. **Double t.**, propos *mpl* nègre-blanc. **2.** (a) Entretien *m*; causerie *f*. **To have a t. with s.o.**, causer, s'entretenir, avec qn. (b) Causerie. **3. It is the t. of the town**, on ne parle, il n'est bruit, que de cela. **She's the t. of the town**, elle défraie la chronique. *S.a.* COMMON[1] 1.

talk[2]. I. *v.i.* **1.** (a) Parler. **To learn to t.**, apprendre à parler. (b) Parler, discourir. **It was only for the sake of talking**, c'était histoire de parler. **To t. in riddles**, parler par énigmes. **To t. big**, se vanter. *F:* **To t. through one's hat**, débiter des sottises. **It's easy to t.!** cela vous plaît à dire! *F:* **Now you're talking!** voilà qui s'appelle parler! **I am not talking of you**, il ne s'agit pas de vous. **Talking of that . . .**, à propos de cela. . . . **He knows what he is talking about**, il parle en connaissance de cause; il sait ce qu'il dit. *F:* **T. about luck!** tu parles d'une chance! (c) **To t. of doing sth.**, parler de faire qch. **2.** (a) **To t. to, with, s.o.**, causer, s'entretenir, avec qn. **To t. freely to s.o.**, s'ouvrir à qn. **To t. to oneself**, se parler à soi-même.

F: parler tout seul. *F:* Who do you think you are talking to! à qui croyez-vous donc parler? (*b*) To t. (severely) to s.o., faire des remontrances à qn; réprimander qn. I'll t. to him! je vais lui dire son fait! 3. (*a*) Jaser, bavarder. (*b*) To get oneself talked about, faire parler de soi. The whole town was talking about it, toute la ville en jasait. II. talk, *v.tr.* 1. (*a*) To t. French, parler français. (*b*) To t. politics, parler politique. To t. (common) sense, parler raison. *S.a.* RUBBISH 2, SCANDAL 2. 2. (*a*) To t. oneself hoarse, s'enrouer à force de parler. I've talked myself blue in the face telling you! je m'époumone à vous le dire! (*b*) To t. s.o. into doing sth., amener qn à faire qch. *S.a.* HEAD¹ 1. talk at, *v.i.* To t. at s.o., faire des allusions voilées à qn (qui se trouve présent). talk away, 1. *v.tr.* Passer (le temps) à causer. 2. *v.i.* Parler sans arrêt. talk down. 1. *v.i. Pej:* To t. down to one's audience, se mettre à la portée de son auditoire. 2. *v.tr.* Réduire (qn) au silence (en parlant plus haut et plus longtemps que lui). 3. *v.tr. Av:* To t. down (an aircraft), donner des instructions d'atterrissage. talk on, *v.i.* Continuer à parler. talk over, *v.tr.* 1. Discuter, débattre (une question). 2. = TALK ROUND 1. talk round. 1. *v.tr.* Enjôler (qn); amener (qn) à changer d'avis. I talked them round at last, j'ai fini par les persuader. 2. *v.i.* To t. round a question, tourner autour du pot. talking¹, *a.* Parlant. *Cin:* T. film, film parlant. talking², *s.* 1. Discours *mpl*, propos *mpl*. 2. (*a*) Conversation *f*. (*b*) Bavardage *m*. To do all the t., faire tous les frais de la conversation. No t. please! pas de bavardage! 3. To give s.o. a good t.-to, semoncer qn.

talkative ['tɔ:kətiv], *a.* Causeur, -euse; bavard, loquace.

talkativeness ['tɔ:kətivnis], *s.* Loquacité *f*.

talker ['tɔ:kər], *s.* 1. Causeur, -euse; parleur, -euse. 2. To be a great t., être bavard; *F:* avoir la langue bien pendue; avoir du bagou(t).

talkie ['tɔ:ki], *s. Cin: F: O:* Film parlant.

tall¹ [tɔ:l], *a.* 1. (*Of pers.*) (*a*) Grand; de haute taille. (*b*) How t. are you? combien mesurez-vous? She is taller than I, elle est plus grande que moi. He was taller by a head than I, il me dépassait de la tête. She is growing t., elle se fait grande. 2. (*Of thg*) Haut, élevé. How t. is that mast? quelle hauteur a ce mât? 3. *F:* (Histoire) incroyable, invraisemblable. That's a t. story, celle-là est raide. *S.a.* ORDER¹ 10.

tallboy ['tɔ:lbɔi], *s. Furn:* Grande commode à deux corps superposés.

tallness ['tɔ:lnis], *s.* (*a*) (*Of pers.*) Grande taille. (*b*) Hauteur *f* (d'un édifice).

tallow ['tælou], *s.* Suif *m*. *S.a.* CANDLE 1. 'tallowchandler, *s.* Fabricant *m* ou marchand *m* de chandelles.

tally¹ ['tæli], *s.* 1. *A:* Taille *f* (de boulanger, etc.). 2. Pointage *m*. To keep t. of goods, pointer des marchandises (sur une liste). 3. Étiquette *f* (pour plantes, etc.). 'tally-clerk, *s.* Pointeur *m*. 'tally-sheet, *s.* Feuille *f* de pointage; bordereau *m*. 'tally-stick, *s.* = TALLY¹ 1.

tally², *v.tr.* 1. Pointer, contrôler (des marchandises). 2. *v.i.* Correspondre (with, à); s'accorder (with, avec). These accounts do not t., (i) ces comptes ne s'accordent pas; (ii) ces comptes-rendus ne s'accordent pas.

tally-ho ['tæli'hou], *int. & s.* Taïaut (*m*).

Talmud (the) [ðə'tælmud]. *Pr.n. Jew.Rel:* Le Talmud.

Talmudic(al) [tæl'mudik(əl)], *a.* Talmudique.

Talmudist ['tælmudist], *s.* Talmudiste *m*.

talon ['tælən], *s.* 1. Serre *f* (d'oiseau de proie); griffe *f* (de lion). 2. *Arch:* Talon *m*, doucine *f*. 3. (*a*) Talon (d'une feuille de coupons); talon de souche. (*b*) (*At cards*) Talon.

tamarind ['tæmərind], *s. Bot:* 1. Fruit *m* du tamarinier. 2. Tamarinier *m*.

tamarisk ['tæmərisk], *s. Bot:* Tamaris *m*.

tambour ['tæmbuər], *s.* 1. *Mus:* Grosse caisse. 2. *Needlew:* Métier *m*, tambour *m*, à broder. 3. Tambour (de vestibule). 'tambour-lace, *s.* Dentelle *f* sur tulle.

tambourine ['tæmbə'ri:n], *s. Mus:* Tambour *m* de basque.

tame¹ [teim], *a.* 1. (Animal) apprivoisé, domestiqué. 2. (*a*) (*Of pers.*) Soumis, docile. (*b*) (Style) monotone, terne.

tame², *v.tr.* (*a*) Apprivoiser. (*b*) Domestiquer (une bête). (*c*) Mater (qn, une passion); dompter (un lion). taming, *s.* 1. (*a*) Apprivoisement *m*. (*b*) Domestication *f*. 2. Domptage *m*.

tameness ['teimnis], *s.* 1. (*a*) Nature douce (d'un animal). (*b*) Caractère soumis, docilité *f* (de qn). 2. Monotonie *f*, fadeur *f* (du style, etc.); insipidité *f*, banalité *f* (d'un conte).

tamer ['teimər], *s.* Apprivoiseur, -euse; dompteur, -euse (d'animaux sauvages).

Tamil ['tæmil], *s. Ling: Ethn:* Tamil *m*, tamoul *m*.

tammy ['tæmi], *s. F:* = TAM O'SHANTER.

tam o'shanter [tæmo'ʃæntər], *s. Scot:* Béret écossais.

tamp [tæmp], *v.tr.* 1. *Civ.E:* Damer, pilonner, tasser (la terre, etc.). 2. Bourrer (un fourneau de mine).

tamper ['tæmpər], *v.i.* (*a*) To t. with sth., toucher à (un mécanisme); altérer (un document); falsifier (un registre); fausser, brouiller (une serrure). To t. with the cash, tripoter dans la caisse. (*b*) To t. with a witness, suborner un témoin.

tampon ['tæmpən], *s. Surg:* Tampon *m* (d'ouate).

tan¹ [tæn]. 1. *s.* (*a*) Tan *m*. Spent t., tannée *f*. (*b*) Couleur *f* du tan; (i) tanné *m*; (ii) hâle *m* (du teint). To lose one's t., *F:* débronzer. 2. *a.* Tanné; tan *inv.* T. leather shoes, souliers jaunes. Black and t. dog, chien noir et feu *inv.* 'tan(-)bark, *s.* Écorce *f* à tan. 'tan(-)yard, *s.* Tannerie *f*.

tan², *v.* (tanned) 1. *v.tr.* (*a*) Tanner (les peaux). *F:* To t. s.o., s.o.'s hide, tanner le cuir à qn; étriller qn. (*b*) (*Of sun*) Hâler, bronzer (la peau). 2. *v.i.* (*Of complexion*) Se hâler, se basaner. tanning, *s.* 1. Tannage *m*. 2. *F:* Tannée *f*, raclée *f*.

tandem ['tændəm]. 1. *s. Veh: Cy:* Tandem *m*. 2. *adv.* To drive t., conduire en flèche, en tandem.

tang¹ [tæŋ], *s.* 1. Soie *f* (d'un couteau, d'une épée, d'une lime). 2. Goût vif; saveur *f*. T. of the soil, native t., goût *m* de terroir. The t. of the morning air, le piquant de l'air matinal. The t. of the sea, la senteur de l'air marin.

tang², *s.* Son aigu, tintement *m* (d'une cloche).

tang³. 1. *v.tr.* Faire retentir, faire résonner (une cloche, etc.). 2. *v.i.* (*Of bell*) Rendre un son aigu; retentir.

tangency ['tæn(d)ʒ(ə)nsi], *s.* Tangence *f*.

tangent ['tæn(d)ʒ(ə)nt]. 1. *a.* (Plan) tangent, tangentiel (to, à). T. screw, vis tangentielle; vis sans fin. 2. *s.* Tangente *f*. To fly off at a t., prendre la tangente.

tangential [tæn'dʒenʃ(ə)l], *a. Geom:* Tangentiel, -elle, tangent (to, à).

tangerine [,tæn(d)ʒə'ri:n], *s.* Mandarine *f*.

tangibility [,tæn(d)ʒi'biliti], *s.* Tangibilité *f*.

tangible ['tæn(d)ʒəbl], *a.* 1. Tangible. T. assets, valeurs matérielles. 2. Réel. T. difference, différence sensible.

Tangier(s) [tæn'dʒiər, -iəz]. *Pr.n.* Tanger *m*.

tangle¹ ['tæŋgl], *s. Algae:* Laminaire *f*; baudrier *m* de Neptune.

tangle², *s.* Embrouillement *m*; emmêlement *m* (de cheveux); fouillis *m* (de broussailles). The string is all in a t., la ficelle est tout embrouillée. *F:* To be in a t., ne plus savoir où on en est. To get into a t., (i) s'embrouiller; (ii) se mettre dans le pétrin. It's a hopeless t., *F:* c'est le pot au noir.

tangle³. 1. *v.tr.* To t. (up) sth., embrouiller, (em)mêler (des fils); embrouiller (une affaire). To get tangled (up), (*of thgs*) s'emmêler; (*of thgs, pers.*) s'embrouiller, *F:* (*of pers.*) se mettre dans le pétrin. Tangled web, trame compliquée. 2. *v.i.* S'embrouiller, s'emmêler.

tanglefoot ['tæŋglfut], *s. U.S: F:* Whisky *m* (de mauvaise qualité); *P:* casse-pattes *m*.

tango¹ ['tæŋgou], *s. Danc:* Tango *m*.

tango², *v.i.* Danser le tango.

tank¹ [tæŋk], *s.* 1. (*a*) Réservoir *m*. Water t., réservoir à eau; citerne *f*; *Rail:* château *m* d'eau; (on locomotive) caisse *f* à eau. *Hyg:* Septic t., fosse *f* septique. *I.C.E:* Petrol t., réservoir à essence. (*Of submarine*) To blow the tank, chasser aux ballasts.

(b) **Air t.**, caisson m à air. *Phot:* **Washing t.**, cuve f à lavage. *Cin: etc:* **Cooling t.**, cuvette f de refroidissement. 2. (a) *Mil:* Char m de combat; **tank** m. (b) *Rail:* **T. car, t. wagon**, wagon-citerne m. (c) *Aut: U.S:* **T. truck**, camion-citerne m. **'tank-engine**, s. *Rail:* Locomotive f tender; machine f tender. **'tank-trans'porter**, s. *Mil:* Porte-chars m.

tank², v.i. *Aut: etc:* **To t. up**, faire le plein.

tankard ['tæŋkəd], s. Pot m, chope f, en étain.

tanker ['tæŋkər], s. Bateau-citerne m, pl. bateaux-citernes; pétrolier m; butanier m. *Veh:* Camion-citerne m.

tannate ['tænit], s. *Ch:* Tannate m.

tanner¹ ['tænər], s. Tanneur m.

tanner², s. *P:* (Pièce f de) six pence.

tannery ['tænəri], s. Tannerie f.

tannic ['tænik], a. *Ch:* Tannique.

tannin ['tænin], s. Tan(n)in m.

tansy ['tænzi], s. *Bot:* Tanaisie f.

tantalize ['tæntəlaiz], v.tr. Infliger le supplice de Tantale à (qn); taquiner (qn); mettre (qn) au supplice. **tantalizing**, a. Tentant (sourire) provocant. **-ly**, adv. (a) Cruellement. (b) D'un air provocant.

tantalum ['tæntələm], s. *Ch:* Tantale m.

Tantalus ['tæntələs]. 1. *Pr.n.m.* Tantale. 2. s. Cave à liqueurs.

tantamount ['tæntəmaunt], a. Équivalent (to, à). **To be t. to sth.**, équivaloir à qch.

tantrum ['tæntrəm], s. Accès m de mauvaise humeur, de colère. **To get into a t.**, se mettre en colère; sortir de ses gonds.

Tanzania [tæn'zeiniə]. *Pr.n. Geog:* La Tanzanie.

Taoism ['tɑːouizm], s. *Rel.Hist:* Taoïsme m.

Taoist ['tɑːouist], a. & s. *Rel.Hist:* Taoïste mf.

tap¹ [tæp], s. 1. (a) Fausset m (de fût). (b) Robinet m; (of cask) cannelle f. **To turn on, turn off, the t.**, ouvrir, fermer le robinet. (c) **On t.**, (i) (of cask) en perce, en vidange; (ii) (of liquor) au tonneau. **To be on t.**, être toujours disponible. 2. *F: O:* Boisson f, esp. bière f. 3. = TAP-ROOM. 4. *El:* Dérivation f (d'une canalisation); prise f intermédiaire (d'une bobine). 5. *Tls:* (Screw-)t., taraud m. 6. *Metall:* Coulée f (de métal fondu). **'tap-hole**, s. *Metall:* Trou m de coulée. **'tap-nozzle**, s. Brise-jet m inv. **'tap-room**, s. Bar m. **'tap-root**, s. *Bot:* Racine pivotante; pivot m. **'tap-water**, s. Eau f du robinet; eau de la ville.

tap², v.tr. **(tapped)** 1. (a) Percer, mettre en perce (un fût). (b) **To t. a tree (for resin)**, inciser, gemmer, un arbre. *Metall:* **To t. the furnace**, percer le haut fourneau. *Surg:* **To t. a lung**, ponctionner, faire une ponction à, un poumon. **To t. (capital, talent, etc.)**, faire appel à, drainer. (c) **To t. wine**, tirer du vin. (d) **To t. a stream**, faire une prise à un cours d'eau. **To t. a main**, brancher une conduite (de gaz, d'eau). **To t. a telegraph wire**, faire une prise sur un fil télégraphique; capter un message. **To t. the phone**, écouter, passer à la table d'écoute. 2. Tarauder, fileter. **tapping**, s. (a) Mise f en perce, perçage m (d'un tonneau); incision f, gemmage m (d'un arbre). *Surg:* Ponction f. (b) Tirage m (du vin). *El:* Dérivation f (d'une canalisation). 3. Taraudage m.

tap³, s. Tape f; petit coup. **There was a t. at the door**, on frappa doucement à la porte. **'tap dancing**, s. (Danse f à) claquettes (fpl.).

tap⁴, v. **(tapped)** 1. v.tr. Frapper légèrement; taper, tapoter. 2. v.ind.tr. **To t. at, on, the door**, frapper doucement à la porte. **To t. off a message**, envoyer un message en Morse. **To t. out a pin**, chasser une goupille. **To t. out one's pipe on one's heel**, débourrer sa pipe sur son talon.

tape¹ [teip], s. 1. (a) Ruban m; ganse f; (for parcels) bolduc m. **Paper t.**, bande f de papier; esp. bande de papier gommé. **Self-adhesive (cellulose) t.**, ruban adhésif, Scotch (R.t.m). *El:* **Insulating t.**, chatterton m. *F:* **Red t.**, fonctionnarisme m. (b) *Sp:* Bande d'arrivée, fil m (de laine). (c) *Turf:* **The tapes** (at the starting-post), les rubans. 2. **Steel t.**, ruban d'acier. **Surveyor's t.**, roulette f d'arpenteur. 3. *Tg:* Bande ruban, du récepteur. **Recording t.**, ruban magnétique. **'tape-machine**, s. Téléimprimeur m. **'tape(-) measure**, s. (a) Mètre m (à ruban). (b) Centimètre

m (de couturière). **'tape-re'corder**, s. Magnétophone m (R.t.m.). **'tape recording**, s. Enregistrement m sur bande magnétique.

tape², v.tr. 1. *Dressm:* Garnir d'une ganse; border (un vêtement). *El:* Guiper (un conducteur). 2. *Bookb:* Coudre sur ruban (les cahiers d'un livre). 3. Mesurer (un terrain) au cordeau. *F:* (Of pers.) **I've got him taped**, j'ai pris sa mesure. **I've got it all taped**, j'ai la situation bien en main. 4. Enregistrer sur bande.

taper¹ ['teipər], s. Bougie filée. *Ecc:* Cierge m.

taper², s. *Mec.E:* Conicité f.

taper³. 1. v.tr. Effiler; tailler en cône. *Mec.E:* Ajuster en cône, côner (une fusée, etc.). 2. v.i. **To t. (off, away)**, s'effiler; aller en diminuant. **tapered**, a. *Mec.E: etc:* (Calibre, taraud) conique, diminué; effilé, en forme de fuseau. **tapering**, a. En pointe; (doigt) effilé, fuselé. *Arch:* **T. column**, colonne diminuée.

tapestry ['tæpistri], s. Tapisserie f. **To hang a wall with t.**, tendre un mur avec des tapisseries. **'tapestry-carpet**, s. Tapis bouclé. **'tapestry-work**, s. Tapisserie f.

tapeworm ['teipwəːm], s. Ténia m; ver m solitaire.

tapioca [ˌtæpi'oukə], s. Tapioca m.

tapir ['teipər], s. *Z:* Tapir m.

tappet ['tæpit], s. *Mch:* Came f (de distribution); taquet m, heurtoir m, mentonnet m. *I.C.E:* Poussoir m (de tige de culbuteur, de soupape). **'tappet-rod**, s. Tige-poussoir f.

tapster ['tæpstər], s. *A:* 1. Garçon m de cabaret. 2. Cabaretier m.

tar¹ [tɑːr], s. 1. (a) Goudron m. (b) *A:* Bitume m, brai m. **To spoil the ship for a ha'p'worth of t.**, faire des économies de bouts de chandelle. *S.a.* COAL-TAR. 2. *Nau: F:* (Jack) t., loup m de mer; mathurin m. **'tar-brush**, s. Brosse f à goudronner; *Nau:* guipon m. *Pej:* To have a touch of the t.-b., avoir un peu de sang nègre. **'tar-sprayer**, s. (Pers.) Goudronneur m. **'tar-spraying**, s. Goudronnage m. **T.-s. machine**, goudronneuse f.

tar², v.tr. **(tarred)** Goudronner (une route, un cordage); bitumer (du carton); *Nau:* brayer (un bateau). *F:* **They are all tarred with the same brush**, ils sont à mettre dans le même panier. **Tarred felt**, feutre bitumé. **tarring**, s. Goudronnage m, bitumage m.

tarantella [tærən'telə], s. *Danc:* Tarentelle f.

Taranto [tə'ræntou]. *Pr.n. Geog:* Tarente f.

tarantula [tə'ræntjulə], s. *Arach:* Tarentule f.

tarboosh [tɑː'buːʃ], s. Tarbouch(e) m.

Tardigrada [tɑː'digrədə], s.pl. *Arach:* Tardigrades mpl.

tardiness ['tɑːdinis], s. 1. Lenteur f, nonchalance f (in doing sth., à faire qch.). 2. (a) Tardiveté f (d'un fruit, etc.). (b) *U.S:* Manque m de ponctualité.

tardy ['tɑːdi], a. 1. Lent, nonchalant, paresseux, -euse. 2. (a) Tardif, -ive. (b) *U.S:* (Belated) En retard.

tare¹ ['teər], s. *Bot:* 1. Vesce f. 2. *B:* Ivraie f.

tare², s. (a) *Com:* Tare f; poids m à vide. **To allow for t.**, faire la tare. (b) Poids net (des voitures automobiles).

target ['tɑːgit], s. 1. *A.Arms:* Targe f. 2. (a) Cible f; but m, objectif m. **Disappearing t., vanishing t.**, cible, but, à éclipse. (b) To be the t. for popular ridicule, être en butte aux risées. 3. *X-rays:* Anticathode f. 4. *U.S: Rail:* = SIGNAL¹. 5. *Cu:* Épaulée f (d'agneau, de mouton).

tariff ['tærif], s. 1. Tarif m. **T. walls**, barrières douanières. **T. reform**, réforme f des tarifs douaniers. 2. Tableau m, liste f, des prix.

tarlatan ['tɑːlətən], s. *Tex:* Tarlatane f.

tarmac ['tɑːmæk], s. 1. *Civ.E:* Goudron m, bitume m. 2. *Av:* (a) Aire f de stationnement. (b) Aire d'embarquement. (c) Piste f d'envol.

tarn [tɑːn], s. Petit lac (de montagne).

tarnish¹ ['tɑːniʃ], s. Ternissure f.

tarnish². 1. v.tr. Ternir (un métal, la réputation de qn). 2. v.i. (Of metal, etc.) Se ternir; (of picture-frame) se dédorer.

tarpaulin [tɑː'pɔːlin], s. (a) *Nau:* Toile goudronnée. (b) Bâche f; *Nau:* prélart m; banne f.

tarpon ['tɑːpɔn, -pən], s. *Ich:* Tarpon m.

tarragon ['tærəgən], s. Estragon m.

tarry ['tɑːri], a. 1. Goudronneux, bitumineux. 2. Couvert, souillé, de goudron.

tarry² ['tæri], *v.i. Lit:* **1.** Rester, demeurer (dans un endroit). **2.** Tarder, s'attarder.

tarsus, *pl.* -i ['tɑ:səs, -ai], *s. Anat:* Tarse *m*.

tart¹ [tɑ:t], *s.* **1.** *Cu:* (a) (*Open*) Tarte *f*. **Small jam t.,** tartelette *f* aux confitures. (b) (*Covered*) Tourte *f*. **2.** *P:* Fille *f*, cocotte *f*, grue *f*, poule *f*. '**tart-dish,** -**plate,** *s.* Tourtière *f*.

tart², *v.i. F:* To t. sth. up, attifer qch. To t. oneself up, s'attifer.

tart³, *a.* (a) Acerbe, aigrelet; (*of wine*) vert, piquant. (b) (*Of answer*) Acerbe; acrimonieux, -euse.

tartan¹ ['tɑ:t(ə)n], *s. Tex: Cost:* Tartan *m*.

tartan², *s. Nau:* Tartane *f*.

tartar¹ ['tɑ:tər], *s. Ch: Dent:* Tartre *m*.

Tartar². **1.** *a. & s. Ethn:* Tatar, -e; Tartare. **2.** *s. F:* Homme *m* intraitable; (*of woman*) mégère *f*.

tartaric [tɑ:'tærik], *a. Ch:* Tartrique.

Tartary ['tɑ:təri]. *Pr.n. A.Geog:* La Tartarie.

tartlet ['tɑ:tlit], *s. Cu:* Tartelette *f*.

tartness ['tɑ:tnis], *s.* Acerbité *f*; verdeur *f* (d'un vin); acidité *f*, aigreur *f*, causticité *f* (du ton).

tartrate ['tɑ:treit], *s. Ch:* Tartrate *m*.

task [tɑ:sk], *s.* **1.** Tâche *f*. (a) *Sch:* **Holiday t.,** devoir *m* de vacances. (b) Travail, -aux *m*, ouvrage *m*, besogne *f*. **2. To take s.o. to t. for sth.,** prendre qn à partie, réprimander qn, pour avoir fait qch. **3.** *Mil:* T. force, corps *m* expéditionnaire, force *f* tactique. **taskmaster** [tɑ:skmɑ:stər], *s.m.* Chef de corvée; surveillant. **Hard t.,** véritable tyran.

Tasmania [tæz'meiniə]. *Pr.n. Geog:* La Tasmanie.

Tasmanian [tæz'meiniən], *a. & s.* Tasmanien, -ienne.

tassel ['tæs(ə)l], *s.* **1.** *Cost: Furn: etc:* Gland *m*, pompon *m*, houppe *f* (de rideau, etc.). **2.** *Bookb:* Signet *m*. **3.** *Bot:* Aigrette *f*.

tasselled ['tæsld], *a.* A glands; à houppes.

Tasso ['tæsou]. *Pr.n.m. Lit.Hist:* Le Tasse.

taste¹ [teist], *s.* **1.** (a) (Sense of) t., goût *m*. T. bud, papille gustative. (b) Saveur *f*, goût. It has a burnt t., cela sent le brûlé. This drink has no t., cette boisson n'a pas de goût, est insipide. (c) A t. of sth., un petit peu (de fromage, etc.); une petite gorgée (de vin, etc.). (d) He gave us a t. of his bad temper, il nous a donné un échantillon de son mauvais caractère. *F:* You'll get a t. of it one of these days, vous en tâterez un de ces jours. **2.** Goût, penchant (particulier), prédilection *f* (for, pour). To have a t. for sth., avoir du goût pour qch.; avoir le goût de (la musique, etc.). To have. no t. for . . ., n'avoir pas de goût pour . . .; *F:* être fermé à (la musique, etc.). To acquire, develop, a t. for sth., prendre goût à qch. To find sth. to one's t., trouver qch. à son goût. To add sugar to t., ajouter du sucre selon son goût, à volonté. Tastes differ; everyone to his t., chacun (à) son goût. **3.** (a) To have t., avoir du goût. People of t., les gens de goût. (b) Furnished in perfect t., meublé avec un goût parfait. It is (in) bad t. to . . ., il est de mauvais goût de. . . .

taste². I. *v.tr.* **1.** Percevoir la saveur de (qch.); sentir (qch.). I can't t. any garlic in the salad, je ne sens pas (de goût) d'ail dans la salade. **2.** (a) (*Of cook*) Goûter (un mets). (b) Déguster (des vins, etc.); sonder (un fromage). **3.** (a) Goûter de, à (qch.); manger un petit morceau (d'un mets); tâter de (qch.); boire une petite gorgée (d'un liquide). He had not tasted food for three days, il ne s'était rien mis sous la dent depuis trois jours. (b) To t. happiness, ill fortune, connaître, goûter, le bonheur, la malchance. To t. power, goûter, tâter, du pouvoir. II. taste, *v.i.* To t. of sth., avoir un goût de qch. To t. like honey, avoir un goût qui rappelle le miel. To t. of honey, avoir un goût de miel.

tasteful ['teistf(u)l], *a.* De bon goût; (vêtement) élégant. **-fully,** *adv.* (Habillé, etc.) avec goût.

tasteless ['teistlis], *a.* **1.** Sans saveur; fade, insipide. **2.** (Ameublement) qui manque de goût, de mauvais goût.

tastelessness ['teistlisnis], *s.* (a) Insipidité *f*, fadeur *f*, manque *m* de goût (d'un mets, etc.) (b) Manque *m* de goût.

taster ['teistər], *s.* **1.** Dégustateur, -trice (de vins, de thés, etc.). **2.** Wine-t., tâte-vin *m inv*. Cheese-t., sonde *f* à fromage.

tastiness ['teistinis], *s.* Saveur *f*, goût *m* agréable (d'un mets).

tasty ['teisti], *a.* **1.** *O:* (Mets) savoureux; (morceau) succulent, *P:* (mets) relevé. **2.** *P:* Chic, élégant.

tat [tæt], *v.tr. & i.* (tatted) *Needlew:* Faire de la frivolité. **Tatted insertion,** entre-deux en frivolité. **tatting,** *s.* Frivolité *f*.

ta-ta ['tæ'tɑ:], *int. Nursery & P:* Au revoir!

tatter ['tætər], *s.* Lambeau *m.* Garment in tatters, vêtement en lambeaux, en loques.

tatterdemalion [,tætədi'meiljən], *s.* Loqueteux, -euse; déguenillé, -ée; va-nu-pieds *mf inv*.

tattered ['tætəd], *a.* (Vêtement) dépenaillé, en loques; (homme) déguenillé, loqueteux.

tattle¹ ['tætl], *s.* **1.** Bavardage *m,* commérage *m.* **2.** Cancans *mpl*; commérages.

tattle², *v.i.* **1.** Bavarder; jaser; commérer. **2.** Cancaner; faire des cancans.

tattler ['tætlər], *s.* **1.** Bavard, -arde; babillard, -arde. **2.** Cancanier, -ière.

tattoo¹ [tə'tu:], *s. Mil:* **1.** Retraite *f* (du soir). To beat, sound, the t., battre, sonner, la retraite. T. roll-call, appel *m* du soir. To beat a t. (on the table, etc.), tambouriner, pianoter (sur la table, etc.). **2.** (a) Torchlight t., retraite aux flambeaux. (b) Carrousel *m*, revue *f*, militaire.

tattoo², *s.* Tatouage *m*.

tattoo³, *v.tr.* Tatouer (le corps). **tattooing,** *s.* Tatouage *m*.

tatty ['tæti], *a. F:* Défraîchi.

taught. *See* TEACH.

taunt¹ [tɔ:nt], *s.* Reproche méprisant; injure *f* (en paroles); sarcasme *m*, brocard *m*.

taunt², *v.tr.* (a) Accabler (qn) de sarcasmes; se gausser de (qn). (b) To t. s.o. with sth., reprocher qch. à qn (avec mépris). **taunting,** *a.* (Ton, air) de sarcasme.

taut [tɔ:t], *a. Nau: etc:* (a) (Cordage) tendu, raide, raidi. To haul a rope t., raidir, embraquer, un cordage. T. situation, situation tendue. (b) T. and trim, (navire) paré, en bon état.

tauten ['tɔ:t(ə)n], *v.tr.* Raidir, embraquer (un câble); étarquer (une voile).

tautness ['tɔ:tnis], *s.* Raideur *f* (d'un câble).

tautology [tɔ:'tɔlədʒi], *s.* Tautologie *f*.

tavern ['tæv(ə)n], *s. A:* Taverne *f*, cabaret *m*.

taw¹ [tɔ:], *s. Games:* Grosse bille (de verre); calot *m*.

taw², *v.tr.* Mégir, mégisser (les peaux), passer (les peaux) en mégie. **tawing,** *s.* Mégisserie *f*.

tawdriness ['tɔ:drinis], *s.* Clinquant *m*; faux brillant.

tawdry ['tɔ:dri], *a.* D'un mauvais goût criard. T. jewellery, clinquant *m*, toc *m*.

tawer ['tɔ:ər], *s.* Mégissier *m*.

tawery ['tɔ:əri], *s.* (Établissement *m* de) mégisserie *f*.

tawny ['tɔ:ni], *a.* (i) *A:* Tanné, basané; (ii) fauve; tirant sur le roux. **Old t. port,** porto qui a jauni dans le fût. **T. owl,** (i) *Orn:* chouette *f* hulotte, hulotte *f* chat-huant; (ii) *Scouting:* assistante *f* (des Jeannettes).

tax¹ [tæks], *s.* **1.** (a) Impôt *m*, contribution *f*, taxe *f*. Direct taxes, assessed taxes, contributions directes; impôts. Indirect taxes, contributions indirectes. Land t., impôt foncier. Emergency t., impôt extraordinaire. Purchase tax = taxe à la production. Value added t., taxe à la valeur ajoutée. To lay, levy, a t. on sth., mettre un impôt sur qch.; frapper qch. d'un impôt; imposer qch. To collect a t., percevoir un impôt. To reduce the t. on sth., dégrever partiellement (un produit, etc.). Free of t., t. free, exempt d'impôts. (b) *Hist:* Taille *f*. **2.** Charge *f*; fardeau (imposé à qn). To be a t. on s.o., être une charge pour qn; être à charge à qn. '**tax-collector,** *s.* Percepteur *m* (des contributions directes); receveur *m* (des contributions indirectes). '**tax-evasion,** *s.* Fraude fiscale. '**tax-payer,** *s.* Contribuable *mf*.

tax², *v.tr.* **1.** (a) Taxer (les objets de luxe, etc.); frapper (qch.) d'un impôt; mettre un impôt sur (qch.). (b) Imposer (qch.). (c) Mettre à l'épreuve (l'adresse, la patience, de qn). **2.** *Jur:* Taxer (les dépens d'un procès). **Taxed bill of costs,** mémoire taxé (par le juge). **Taxing-master,** (juge) taxateur *m*. **3.** To t. s.o. with doing sth., accuser qn d'avoir fait qch. To t. s.o. with ingratitude, taxer qn d'ingratitude.

taxable ['tæksəbl], *a.* **1.** Imposable. To make sth. t., imposer qch. **2.** *Jur:* Costs t. to s.o., frais à la charge de qn.

taxation [tæk'seiʃ(ə)n], s. **1.** (a) Imposition f (de la propriété, etc.). **The t. authorities,** le fisc. (b) Charges fiscales; prélèvement fiscal. (c) Revenu réalisé par les impôts; les impôts m. **2.** Jur: **T. of costs,** taxation f, taxe f, des frais.

taxi[1] ['tæksi], s. Taxi m. **'taxi-driver,** s. Conducteur m, chauffeur m, de taxi. **'taxi-girl,** s. Entraîneuse f. **'taxi-rank,** U.S: **'taxi-stand,** s. Station f de taxis.

taxi[2], v.i. (**taxied**; **taxying**) (Of aircraft) Rouler au sol.

taxidermist ['tæksi,də:mist], s. Empailleur m, naturaliste m, taxidermiste m.

taxidermy ['tæksi,də:mi], s. Taxidermie f, naturalisation f d'animaux.

taximeter ['tæksimi:tər], s. Taximètre m.

taxiplane ['tæksiplein], s. Avion-taxi m.

tea [ti:], s. Thé m. (a) **To drink t.,** boire, prendre, du thé. **China t.,** thé de Chine. **Indian t.,** thé de Ceylan. **Weak t., strong t.,** thé léger, fort. (b) (i) (In Austr.) Dîner m. (ii) (**Afternoon**) **t.,** thé; goûter m. **High t.,** repas du soir (arrosé de thé). **2.** Tisane f, infusion f. **'tea-bag,** s. Sachet m de thé. **'tea-basket,** s. Mallette f de pique-nique. **'tea-break,** s. = Pause-café f. **'tea-caddy,** s. Boîte f à thé. **'tea-cake,** s. Brioche plate (se mange grillée et beurrée). **'tea-chest,** s. Caisse f à thé. **'tea-cloth,** s. **1.** Nappe f à thé; napperon m. **2.** Torchon m; essuie-verres m. **'tea-cosy,** s. Couvre-théière m. **'tea-garden,** s. **1.** Établissement m où l'on sert le thé en plein air. **2.** Plantation f de thé. **'tea-infuser,** s. Boule f à thé. **'tea-merchant,** s. Négociant m en thés. **'tea-party,** s. Thé m. **To give a t.-p.,** donner un thé. **'tea-plant,** s. Arbre m à thé. **'tea-planter,** s. Planteur m de thé. **'tea-room,** s. Salon m de thé. **'tea-rose,** s. Hort: Rose f thé, pl. roses thé. **'tea-service, -set,** s. Service m à thé. **'tea-shop,** s. Pâtisserie f (où l'on sert le thé); salon m de thé. **'tea-strainer,** s. Passe-thé m inv. **'tea-table,** s. Table f à thé. **'tea-things,** s.pl. F: Service m à thé. **'tea-towel,** s. Torchon m; essuie-verres m. **'tea-trolley,** s. Table roulante. **'tea-urn,** s. = Samovar m. **'tea-wagon,** s. Table roulante.

teach [ti:tʃ], v.tr. (**taught** [tɔ:t]; **taught**) Enseigner, instruire (qn); enseigner (qch.). **To t. s.o. sth.,** enseigner, apprendre, qch. à qn. **He is being taught all sorts of things,** on lui apprend toutes sortes de choses. **He teaches French,** il enseigne, il professe, le français. U.S: **To t. school,** être dans l'enseignement. **He teaches,** il est dans l'enseignement. **The teaching staff,** les professeurs (d'un lycée); les instituteurs (d'une école primaire). **The teaching profession,** (i) le corps enseignant; (ii) l'enseignement m. **To t. s.o. (how) to do sth.,** apprendre à qn à faire qch. **To t. oneself sth.,** apprendre qch. tout seul. S.a. SELF-TAUGHT. **I had been taught never to tell a lie,** on m'avait appris à ne jamais mentir. F: **To t. s.o. a lesson,** donner à qn une leçon (qu'il n'oubliera pas de si tôt). **That will t. him!** ça lui apprendra! **To t. s.o. a thing or two,** dégourdir qn. F: **I'll t. you to speak to me like that!** je vous apprendrai à me parler de la sorte! **teaching,** s. **1.** Enseignement m, instruction f. **To go in for t.,** entrer dans l'enseignement. **2.** Doctrine f.

teachable ['ti:tʃəbl], a. **1.** Qui apprend facilement; docile. **2.** (Sujet) enseignable.

teacher ['ti:tʃər], s. (i) Instituteur, -trice; maître, f. maîtresse (d'école); (ii) maître (au sens large). **He's a good t.,** c'est un bon professeur. **Student t.,** étudiant(e) qui fait un stage comme instituteur (-trice) ou comme professeur. **The t. and his disciples,** le maître et ses disciples.

teacup ['ti:kʌp], s. Tasse f à thé.

teacupful ['ti:kʌpful], s. Pleine tasse à thé (of, de).

teak [ti:k], s. Teck m.

teal [ti:l], s.inv. Orn: Sarcelle f. **The moorland is full of t.,** la lande abonde en sarcelles.

team[1] [ti:m], s. **1.** (Inv. after numeral) Attelage m (de chevaux, de bœufs). **2.** Équipe f (de joueurs, d'ouvriers); camp m (de joueurs). **Football t.,** équipe de football. **Home t.,** équipe qui reçoit. **T. games,** jeux d'équipe. **The t. spirit,** l'esprit d'équipe. **'team-work,** s. Travail m en équipe; collaboration f. Sp: Jeu m d'ensemble.

team[2]. **1.** v.tr. Atteler (des chevaux, des bœufs). **2.** v.i. **To t. up with s.o.,** se joindre à qn, faire équipe avec qn (pour un travail).

teamster ['ti:mstər], s. U.S: Camionneur m.

teapot ['ti:pɔt], s. Théière f.

tear[1] [tiər], s. Larme f. **To shed tears,** verser des larmes. **To shed a perfunctory t.,** y aller de sa larme. **To burst into tears,** fondre en larmes. **To move s.o. to tears,** attendrir qn (jusqu'aux larmes). **To be easily moved to tears,** avoir la larme facile. **She was in tears,** elle était (tout) en larmes. **To laugh till the tears come,** rire (jusqu')aux larmes. **'tear-drop,** s. Larme f. **'tear-duct,** s. Conduit lacrymal. **'tear-gas,** s. Gaz m lacrymogène. **'tear-stained,** a. (Visage) portant des traces de larmes, barbouillé de larmes.

tear[2] [tɛər], s. **1.** Déchirement m (d'une étoffe). **2.** Déchirure f, accroc m (dans un vêtement). **T.-proof,** indéchirable. **3.** A: F: (a) **To go full t.,** aller à toute vitesse, à fond de train. (b) Rage f, agitation f.

tear[3] [tɛər], v. (tore [tɔ:r]; torn [tɔ:n]) **1.** v.tr. (a) Déchirer. **To t. sth. open,** ouvrir qch. en le déchirant éventrer (un paquet). S.a. PIECE[1]. **To t. a hole in sth.,** faire un trou, faire un accroc, à (un vêtement) **Material that tears easily,** tissu qui se déchire facilement. Paperm: **To t. rags,** effilocher les chiffons **To t. a muscle,** claquer un muscle. **Country torn by civil war,** pays déchiré par la guerre civile. **Torn between two emotions,** tiraillé entre deux émotions. (b) **Arracher (from, à** qn, de qch.). **To t. (out) one's hair,** s'arracher les cheveux. **To t. each other's hair,** se prendre aux cheveux, F: se crêper le chignon **2.** v.i. (a) **To t. at sth.,** déchirer ou arracher qch. avec des doigts impatients; tirer de toutes ses forces sur qch. (b) F: **To t. along,** aller à fond de train, (of horse) ventre à terre; brûler le pavé. **He was tearing along (the road),** il dévorait la route. **tear away,** Arracher. **I could not t. myself away from this scene,** je ne pouvais pas m'arracher de, à, cette scène. **He could not t. himself away,** il ne pouvait se décider à partir. **tear down,** v.tr. Arracher (une affiche, etc.). **tear off,** v.tr. Arracher. **A shell tore off his arm,** un obus lui emporta le bras. S.a. CALENDAR 1. **tear out,** v.tr. Arracher. **To t. s.o.'s eyes out,** arracher les yeux à qn. **tear up,** v.tr. **1.** Déchirer; mettre en pièces. **2.** **To t. up a tree by the roots,** déraciner un arbre. **To t. up the road,** défoncer la route. **tearing**[1], a. **1.** Déchirant; (vent) à écorner les bœufs. F: **T. rage,** colère bleue. **2.** F: **To be in a t. hurry,** être terriblement pressé. **tearing**[2], s. **1.** Déchirement m. **2.** **T. away, off, out,** arrachement m. Mec: **T. stress,** travail m à l'arrachement.

tearful ['tiəf(u)l], a. Éploré; tout en pleurs; Pej: larmoyant. **In a t. voice,** (i) avec des larmes dans la voix; (ii) Pej: en pleurnichant. **-fully,** adv. En pleurant; les larmes aux yeux.

tease[1] [ti:z], s. **1.** Taquin, -ine. **He's a t.,** il est taquin. **2.** O: Taquinerie f.

tease[2], v.tr. **1.** (a) **To t. (out),** effiler, effilocher (un tissu); démêler (la laine). (b) = TEASEL[2]. (c) Carder (la laine). **2.** Taquiner, tourmenter, faire enrager (qn); faire des taquineries à (qn). **3.** **To t. the salad,** F: fatiguer, touiller, la salade. **teasing**[1], a. Taquin. **teasing**[2], s. **1.** (a) **T. (out),** effilage m, effilochage m; démêlage m (de la laine). (b) Cardage m. **2.** Taquinerie f.

teasel[1] ['ti:zl], s. **1.** Bot: Cardère f. S.a. FULLER[1]. **2.** Tex: Carde f.

teasel[2], v.tr. (**teaseled**) Tex: Lainer, gratter (le drap). **teaseling,** s. Grattage m, lainage m.

teaser ['ti:zər], s. **1.** = TEASE[1] 1. **2.** F: Problème m difficile; question embarrassante; colle f.

teaspoon ['ti:spu:n], s. Cuiller f à thé, à café.

teaspoonful ['ti:spu:n,ful], s. Cuiller(ée) f à café.

teat [ti:t], s. **1.** (a) Mamelon m; bout m de sein; tétin m (de femme); tette f, trayon m (de vache). (b) Tétine f (de biberon). **2.** Tchn: Téton m.

teazle[1],[2] ['ti:zl], s. & v.tr. = TEASEL[1],[2].

tec [tek], s. P: = DETECTIVE 2.

technical ['teknik(ə)l], a. **1.** Technique. **T. difficulty,** difficulté d'ordre technique. **T. terms,** termes techniques; termes de métier. Jur: **Judgment quashed on a t. point,** arrêt cassé pour vice de forme, de procédure. **2.** Jur: **T. offence,** quasi-délit m. **-ally,** adv. Techniquement.

technicality [ˌtekni'kæliti], s. Détail m technique; considération f d'ordre technique; technicité f.

technician [tek'niʃ(ə)n], s. Technicien m.

Technicolor ['teknikʌlər], s. Cin: R.t.m: Technicolor m.

technics ['tekniks], s.pl. Technologie f.

technique [tek'niːk], s. Technique f.

technocracy [tek'nɔkrəsi], s. Pol.Éc: Technocratie f.

technocrat ['teknokræt], s. Technocrate mf.

technological [ˌteknə'lɔdʒik(ə)l], a. Technologique.

technologist [tek'nɔlədʒist], s. Technologue m.

technology [tek'nɔlədʒi], s. Technologie f.

tectrices [tek'traisiːz], s.pl. Orn: (Plumes) tectrices f.

ed [ted], v.tr. (tedded) Faner, sauter (le foin).

edder ['tedər], s. 1. Faneur, -euse. 2. (Machine) Faneuse f.

Teddy ['tedi]. Pr.n.m. (Dim.) = Édouard, Edmond, Théodore. **T. bear**, ours m en peluche, F: nounours m. **'teddy-boy**, s. F: Blouson noir.

tedious ['tiːdiəs], a. (Travail) fatigant, pénible; (discours) ennuyeux, fastidieux. **T. tale**, histoire à dormir debout.

tediousness ['tiːdiəsnis], **tedium** ['tiːdiəm], s. Ennui m; manque m d'intérêt (d'un travail).

tee¹ [tiː], s. Golf: (a) Dé m (de sable); tee m. (b) = TEEING-GROUND.

tee², v.tr. Golf: Surélever (la balle). Abs. **To t. up**, placer la balle sur le dé. **To t. off**, jouer sa balle (du tertre de départ). **'teeing-ground**, s. (Tertre m de) départ m.

teem [tiːm], v.i. Abonder (**with**, en); foisonner, regorger, fourmiller (**with**, de). **Streets that t. with people**, rues qui regorgent, qui grouillent, de monde. **His brain is teeming with new ideas**, son cerveau est fertile en idées neuves. **teeming**, a. **T. crowd**, foule grouillante. **T. rain**, pluie torrentielle.

teenage ['tiːneidʒ], a. Adolescent; de l'adolescence.

teenager ['tiːneidʒər], s. Adolescent, -e.

teens [tiːnz], s.pl. F: L'âge m entre treize et vingt ans. **To be in one's t.**, être adolescent(e). **To be out of one's t.**, avoir plus de vingt ans.

teeny(-weeny) ['tiːni('wiːni)], a. F: Minuscule; tout petit.

teeter¹ ['tiːtər], s. U.S: = SEE-SAW.

teeter², v.i. Se balancer; chanceler.

teeth [tiːθ]. See TOOTH¹.

teethe [tiːð], v.i. (Only in pr.p. and progressive tenses) Faire ses (premières) dents. **teething**, s. Dentition f. attrib. **T. troubles**, difficultés initiales.

teetotal [tiː'toutl], a. Antialcoolique; qui ne boit que de l'eau.

teetotalism [tiː'toutəlizm], s. Abstention f des liqueurs alcooliques; antialcoolisme m.

teetotaller [tiː'toutlər], s. Abstinent, -ente; buveur, -euse, d'eau.

teetotum [tːː'toutəm], s. Toton m.

tegument ['tegjumənt], s. Tégument m.

telecast¹ ['telikɑːst], s. F: Émission f de télévision.

telecast², v.tr. Téléviser.

telecine [ˌteli'siːni], s. Télécinéma m.

telecommunications ['telikəˌmjuːni'keiʃ(ə)nz], s.pl. Post: Télécommunications f.pl. **T. specialist**, télémécanicien m.

telecontrol [ˌtelikən'troul], s. Télécommande f, commande f à distance.

teledynamics ['telidai'næmiks], s. El.E: Télédynamie f.

teleferic [ˌteli'ferik], s. Téléphérique.

telegram ['teligræm], s. Télégramme m; dépêche f. **Wireless t.**, radio t., radiotélégramme m.

telegraph¹ ['teligrɑːf], s. 1. Télégraphe m. **Recording t.**, télégraphe enregistreur. **T. office**, bureau télégraphique. **2. Nau: (Ship's) t.**, transmetteur m d'ordres. **Engine-(room) t.**, chadburn m. **3. Sp: T. (board)**, tableau m d'affichage (des résultats). **'telegraph boy, messenger**, s.m. Facteur télégraphiste; petit télégraphiste. **'telegraph operator**, s. Télégraphiste mf. **'telegraph-pole**, s. Poteau m télégraphique.

telegraph². 1. v.i. Télégraphier; envoyer un télégramme, une dépêche. 2. v.tr. Télégraphier (une nouvelle, etc.).

telegraphic [ˌteli'græfik], a. Télégraphique.

telegraphist [ti'legrəfist], s. Télégraphiste mf

telegraphy [ti'legrəfi], s. Télégraphie f. **Wireless t.**, télégraphie sans fil, abbr. T.S.F.

telekinesis ['teliki'niːsis], s. Psychics: Télékinésie f.

telelens ['telilenz], s. Phot: Téléobjectif m.

telemark ['telimɑːk], s. Skiing: Télémark m.

telemechanics ['telimi'kæniks], s.pl. Télémécanique f.

telemeter [ti'lemitər], s. Télémètre m.

teleological [ˌteliə'lɔdʒik(ə)l], a. Téléologique.

teleology [ˌteli'ɔlədʒi], s. Téléologie f.

telepathic [ˌteli'pæθik], a. Télépathique.

telepathy [ti'lepəθi], s. Télépathie f.

telephone¹ ['telifoun], s. Téléphone m. **Automatic t.**, (téléphone) automatique m. **House t.**, téléphone intérieur. **Desk t.**, poste m mobile. **Are you on the t.?** avez-vous le téléphone? **You are wanted on the t.**, on vous demande au téléphone. **Order by t.**, commande f téléphonique. **T. number**, numéro m de téléphone; numéro d'appel. S.a. CALL¹ 2, EXCHANGE¹ 3. **'telephone-booth, -box**, s. Cabine f téléphonique. **'telephone operator**, s. Téléphoniste mf; standardiste mf.

telephone². 1. v.i. Téléphoner (**to**, à). 2. v.tr. (a) Téléphoner (un message). (b) Téléphoner à (qn).

telephonic [ˌteli'fɔnik], a. Téléphonique.

telephonist [ti'lefənist], s. Téléphoniste mf; standardiste mf.

telephony [ti'lefəni], s. Téléphonie f. **Wireless t.**, téléphonie sans fil.

telephoto [teli'foutou], a. **T. lens**, téléobjectif m.

telephotograph [teli'foutəgrɑːf], s. Bélinogramme m.

telephotography ['telifə'tɔgrəfi], s. Téléphotographie f; photographie f au téléobjectif.

teleprinter ['teli'printər], s. Tg: (Appareil) télétype m, téléimprimeur m, téléscripteur m.

teleprinting ['teli'printiŋ], s. Télétypie f.

telerecording [teliri'kɔːdiŋ], s. Émission de télévision enregistrée.

telescope¹ ['teliskoup], s. (a) **Refracting t.**, lunette f (d'approche); longue-vue f; Astr: réfracteur m. (b) **Reflecting t.**, lunette astronomique, télescope m.

telescope². 1. v.tr. Télescoper (un train, etc.). 2. v.i. (a) (Of trains, etc.) (Se) télescoper. (b) **Parts made to t.**, pièces qui s'emboîtent.

telescopic [ˌtelis'kɔpik], a. 1. Télescopique. Phot: **T. lens**, téléobjectif m. **2. T. leg (of tripod)**, branche coulissante, à coulisse.

televiewer ['teli,vjuər], s. Téléspectateur, -trice.

televise ['telivaiz], v.tr. Téléviser.

television ['teli'viʒ(ə)n], s. Télévision f. **T. set**, poste m de télévision, téléviseur m, F: télévision f. **T. screen**, écran m de télévision, le petit écran. **On t.**, à la télévision.

telewriter ['teli'raitər], s. Tg: Télautographe m.

tell [tel], v. (told [tould]; told) I. v.tr. 1. (a) Dire (une nouvelle, etc.). S.a. LIE¹, TRUTH 1. (b) **To t. s.o. sth.**, dire, apprendre, qch. à qn; faire savoir qch. à qn. **I cannot t. you how pleased I am**, je ne saurais vous dire combien je suis content. **I have been told that . . ., on m'a dit que. . . . I t. you no!** je vous dis que non! **Don't let me have to t. you that again**, tenez-vous cela pour dit. **I told you so!** je vous l'avais bien dit! **quand je vous le disais!** F: **You're telling me!** (i) allons donc! (ii) à qui le dites-vous? F: **tu parles!** I'll t. you what! écoute(z)! (c) Raconter, conter (une histoire). **I will t. you what happened**, je vais vous raconter ce qui est arrivé. **He told his adventures**, il nous a fait le récit de ses aventures. F: **T. me another!** à d'autres! **More than words can t.**, plus qu'on ne saurait dire. (d) Annoncer, proclamer (un fait); révéler (un secret). **The sign-post tells the way to . . .**, le poteau indique le chemin pour aller à. . . . (Of clock) **To t. the time**, marquer l'heure. S.a. FORTUNE 1. 2. (a) **To t. s.o. about s.o., sth.**, parler de qn, de qch., à qn. (b) (Emphatic) **It is not so easy, let me t. you**, ce n'est pas si facile, je vous assure. **He will be furious, I (can) t. you!** il va être furieux, je vous en réponds! 3. **To t. s.o. to do sth.**, ordonner, dire, à qn de faire qch. **Do as you are told**, faites comme on vous l'ordonne, comme on vous dit. **I told him not to**, je le lui ai défendu. 4. (a) Discerner, distinguer, reconnaître. **To t. right from wrong**, discerner le bien du mal. **You can't t. her from her sister**, elle ressemble à sa sœur à s'y tromper. **One can t. him by his voice**, on le reconnaît à sa voix. **One can t. she is intelligent,** on sent qu'elle est intelligente. (b) Savoir. **How can I t. that he will do it?** quelle certitude ai-je qu'il le fera? **Who can t.?** qui sait? **You never can t.,** il ne faut (jamais) jurer de rien; on ne sait jamais. **I cannot t.,** je n'en sais rien. **5.** Abs. (a) To t. of sth., annoncer, révéler, qch. **The lines on his face told of suffering,** son visage sillonné de rides révélait, disait, ses souffrances. (b) P: **I'll t. Mum of, on, you!** je m'en vais le dire à maman! **6. To t.** (over), compter (un troupeau, etc.); compter, énumérer (les voix). **All told,** tout compris; somme toute. **There were twenty people all told,** il y avait en tout vingt personnes. S.a. BEAD¹ 1. **II. tell,** v.i. (a) Produire son effet; porter. **Blood will t.,** bon sang ne saurait mentir. **Words that t.,** mots à l'emporte-pièce. **Every shot tells,** chaque coup porte. **These drugs t. upon one in time,** l'effet de ces drogues se fait sentir à la longue. (b) **This tells in his favour,** cela milite en sa faveur. **Everything told against him,** tout témoignait contre lui. **tell off,** v.tr. **1.** Désigner, affecter (qn pour une corvée). **To t. off one's men,** désigner leurs postes à ses hommes. **2.** F: Rembarrer, moucher (qn); dire son fait à (qn). **'telling-off,** s. F: Engueulade f. **telling¹,** a. Fort, efficace; qui fait de l'effet. **T. blow,** coup qui porte; coup bien asséné. **T. style,** style énergique. **With t. effect,** avec un effet marqué. **telling²,** s. **1.** Récit m; narration f (d'une histoire). **2.** Divulgation f (d'un secret). **3. There's no t.,** on ne sait pas; qui sait? **4. T.** (over), dénombrement m; énumération f (des votes). **'tell(-)tale,** s. **1.** (a) Rapporteur, -euse; Sch: F: cafard, -arde. (b) T.-t. **signs,** signes révélateurs. **2.** Mec.E: etc: Aiguille indicatrice; indicateur m. Aut: **Petrol-tank t.-t.,** indicateur m, jauge f, d'essence. El.E: Ind: **T.-t. (lamp),** lampe témoin, F: loupiote f. **3.** Nau: (a) Axiomètre m (du gouvernail). (b) Compas renversé.

teller ['telər], s. **1.** (Ra)conteur, - euse; narrateur, -trice. **2.** (a) Caissier m, payeur m (de banque). (b) Parl: Scrutateur m; recenseur m.

telluric [te'ljuərik], a. Tellurique.

telluride ['teljuraid], s. Ch: Tellurure f.

tellurium [te'ljuəriəm], s. Ch: Tellure m.

telly (the) [ðə'teli], s. T.V: P: La télé.

telpher ['telfər], a. Ind: **T. (rail)way,** s. **telpher,** (ligne) téléphérique m.

telpherage ['telfəridʒ], s. Téléphérage m.

temerity [ti'meriti], s. Témérité f.

temper¹ ['tempər], s. **1.** Metall: Coefficient m de dureté (de l'acier); trempe f. **To draw, let down, the t.** (of a tool), recuire après trempe. (Of steel) **To lose its t.,** se détremper. **2.** (Of pers.) Sang-froid m. **To keep one's t.,** rester calme; garder, conserver, son sang-froid. **To lose one's t.,** perdre son sang-froid; s'emporter, se fâcher. **To be out of t.,** être de mauvaise humeur. **To try s.o.'s t.,** énerver qn. **3.** Humeur f. (a) Caractère m, tempérament m. **Even t.,** caractère égal, calme. **To have a good t.,** avoir bon caractère. **To have a bad t.,** avoir le caractère mal fait. (b) **In a vile t.,** d'une humeur massacrante. **To be in a good, a bad, t.,** être de bonne, de mauvaise, humeur. (c) Mauvaise humeur. **Outburst of t.,** mouvement m d'humeur. **To be in a t.,** être en colère. **To get s.o.'s t. up,** mettre qn en colère; fâcher qn.

temper², v.tr. **1.** (a) Gâcher, délayer (le mortier, etc.); broyer (les couleurs). (b) Metall: (i) Tremper; donner la trempe à (l'acier). (ii) Recuire, adoucir (un métal). **2.** Tempérer; modérer (son ardeur, une passion). **tempered,** a. **1.** (Acier) trempé, recuit. **2.** Mus: **Equally t. scale,** gamme tempérée. **3.** Mild-t.,** d'un caractère doux. S.a. BAD-TEMPERED, etc.

tempera ['tempərə], s. Art: Détrempe f.

temperament ['temp(ə)rəmənt], s. **1.** (Of pers.) Tempérament m, humeur f, complexion f. **2.** Mus: Tempérament. **Equal t., even t.,** tempérament égal.

temperamental [,temp(ə)rə'mentl], a. (a) Capricieux, -euse, fantasque. (b) Qui s'emballe ou se déprime facilement.

temperance ['temp(ə)r(ə)ns], s. Tempérance f. **1.** Modération f, retenue f. **2.** (a) Sobriété f (à table). (b) Abstention f des boissons alcooliques. **T. society,** ligue f antialcoolique.

temperate ['temp(ə)rit], a. **1.** (a) (Of pers.) Tempérant, sobre. **T. habits,** habitudes de sobriété. (b) (Of language) Modéré, mesuré. **2.** (Of climate) Tempéré. **-ly,** adv. Sobrement; avec modération.

temperateness ['temp(ə)ritnis], s. **1.** Modération f, retenue f; sobriété f. **2.** Douceur f (du climat).

temperature ['temprit∫ər], s. Température f. Med: **To have a high t.,** F: to have, to run, a t., avoir de la température, de la fièvre. **T. chart,** feuille f de température.

tempest ['tempist], s. Tempête f, tourmente f.

tempestuous [tem'pestjuəs], a. **1.** Tempétueux, -euse; de tempête. **2.** (Of meeting) Orageux, -euse.

Templar ['templər], s. Hist: (Knight) T., Templier m; chevalier m du Temple.

template ['templit], s. = TEMPLET.

temple¹ ['templ], s. Temple m.

temple², s. Anat: Tempe f.

templet ['templit], s. **1.** Gabarit m, calibre m, patron m, jauge f. **2.** Const: Sablière f.

tempo, pl. **-i** ['tempou, -iː], s. (a) Mus: Tempo m. (b) Rythme m. **Breakdowns which upset the t. of production,** pannes qui interrompent le rythme de la production.

temporal¹ ['temp(ə)r(ə)l], a. Anat: (Os, etc.) temporal, -aux.

temporal², a. Temporel. Ecc: **T. power,** pouvoir temporel. **T. affairs,** les affaires séculières.

temporary ['temp(ə)rəri], a. (a) Temporaire, provisoire. **T. officer,** fonctionnaire m à titre temporaire; intérimaire. **T. appointment,** emploi amovible. **T. apparatus, installation,** installation de fortune. **T. measures,** mesures f transitoires. **T. post,** situation f intérimaire, par intérim. (b) Momentané. **The improvement is only t.,** l'amélioration n'est que passagère. **-ily,** adv. (a) Temporairement, provisoirement. (b) Momentanément; pour le moment.

temporization [,tempərai'zei∫(ə)n], s. **1.** Temporisation f. **2.** Transaction f; compromis m.

temporize ['tempəraiz], v.i. **1.** Temporiser; chercher à gagner du temps. **2.** Transiger provisoirement (with, avec).

temporizer ['tempəraizər], s. Temporisateur m.

tempt [tem(p)t], v.tr. Tenter. **1. To t. s.o. to do sth.,** induire qn à faire qch.; tenter qn pour lui faire faire qch. **To allow oneself to be tempted,** se laisser tenter; céder à la tentation. **I was greatly tempted,** l'occasion était bien tentante. **I am strongly tempted to accept,** j'ai bien envie d'accepter. **2.** (a) A: Mettre (qn) à l'épreuve. B: **God did t. Abraham,** Dieu tenta Abraham. (b) **To t. providence,** tenter la providence. **tempting,** a. Tentant, alléchant; (of offer) séduisant, attrayant; (of dish) appétissant.

temptation [tem(p)'tei∫(ə)n], s. Tentation f. **To throw t. in s.o.'s way,** exposer qn à la tentation. **To yield to t.,** succomber à la tentation; se laisser tenter.

tempter ['tem(p)tər], s. Tentateur m; séducteur m.

temptress ['tem(p)tris], s.f. Tentatrice.

ten [ten], num. a & s. Dix (m). **About t. years ago,** il y a une dizaine d'années. **To count in tens,** compter par dizaines. F: **T. to one he'll find it out,** je vous parie qu'il le découvrira. (For other phrases see EIGHT.)

tenable ['tenəbl], a. (Position) tenable; (théorie) soutenable.

tenacious [ti'nei∫əs], a. Tenace. **To be t.,** tenir à son opinion. **-ly,** adv. Obstinément; avec ténacité.

tenacity [ti'næsiti], s. Ténacité f.

tenancy ['tenənsi], s. **1.** Location f. **Expiration of t.,** expiration de bail. **2. During my t.,** pendant que j'étais locataire.

tenant ['tenənt], s. Locataire mf. **Sub.-t.,** sous-locataire mf. **T.'s repairs,** réparations locatives. **tenant-'farmer,** s. Tenancier m; cultivateur m à bail.

tenantry ['tenəntri], s. Coll. O: Les fermiers m et tenanciers (d'un domaine).

tench [ten(t)∫], s. Ich: Tanche f.

tend¹ [tend], v.tr. Soigner (un malade); panser (un blessé); surveiller (des enfants, une machine); garder (les moutons); entretenir (un jardin).

tend², v.i. **1.** (a) (Of course, etc.) Tendre, se diriger (towards, vers). **The road tends downwards,** la route va en descendant. **Doctrine that tends towards**

socialism, doctrine qui penche vers le, qui tend au, socialisme. **Blue tending to green,** bleu tirant sur le vert. (*b*) **Examples that t. to undermine morality,** exemples qui tendent à ébranler les mœurs. **To t. to the success of an enterprise,** contribuer au succès d'une entreprise. 2. **To t. to do sth.,** être sujet à faire qch. **Woollens that t. to shrink,** lainages qui ont tendance à rétrécir.

tendency ['tendənsi], *s.* Tendance *f*, inclination *f*, disposition *f* (**to,** à). **T. to drink,** penchant *m* à la boisson. **There is a t. for the weak vowels to disappear,** les voyelles faibles tendent à disparaitre. **Rheumatic t.,** diathèse rhumatismale. *Com:* **Strong upward t.,** forte poussée vers la hausse.

tendential [ten'denʃ(ə)l], **tendentious** [ten'denʃəs], *a.* Tendanciel, -elle, tendancieux, -euse.

tender¹ ['tendər], *s.* 1. *Esp. U.S:* Garde *m*, gardien *m* (d'un pont à bascule, etc.). **Bar t.,** garçon *m* de comptoir, barman *m.* 2. (*a*) *Nau:* Bateau *m* annexe, ravitailleur *m.* (*b*) *Rail:* Tender *m.*

tender², *a.* 1. Tendre; peu résistant. **T. meat,** viande tendre. 2. Tendre, sensible. **T. to the touch,** sensible, douloureux, au toucher. **Horse with a t. mouth,** cheval qui a la bouche sensible, délicate. **T. heart,** cœur tendre, sensible. 3. (*a*) (*Of plant, etc.*) Délicat, fragile. (*b*) Jeune, tendre. **Child of t. years,** enfant en bas âge. 4. (*Of pers.*) Tendre, affectueux. **T. parents,** parents aimants, indulgents. **To have a t. recollection of s.o.,** conserver un souvenir ému de qn. 5. Soigneux, soucieux, jaloux (**of,** de). **-ly,** *adv.* 1. (Toucher qch.) doucement. 2. Tendrement; avec tendresse. **'tender(-)'hearted,** *a.* Compatissant; au cœur tendre, sensible. **'tender(-)'heartedness,** *s.* Sensibilité *f.*

tender³, *s.* 1. *Com:* Soumission *f,* offre *f.* **To invite tenders for a piece of work,** mettre un travail en adjudication. **To make, put in, send in, a t. for sth.,** faire une soumission pour qch.; soumissionner un travail. **By t.,** par voie d'adjudication. 2. **Legal t.,** cours légal; monnaie *f* libératoire. (*Of money*) **To be legal t.,** avoir cours; avoir force libératoire.

tender⁴. 1. *v.tr.* Offrir (ses services, une somme, etc.). **To t. one's resignation,** offrir de démissionner. 2. *v.i. Com:* **To t. for sth.,** soumissionner (pour) qch.; faire une soumission pour qch.

tenderer ['tendərər], *s.* 1. Offreur *m* (**of,** de). 2. *Ind: etc:* Soumissionnaire *m.* **Successful t.,** adjudicataire *m.*

tenderfoot ['tendəfut], *s. U.S:* (*a*) Nouveau venu; novice *m.* (*b*) *Scouting:* Novice.

tenderloin ['tendələin], *s. Cu:* Filet *m* de bœuf, de porc. **Double t.,** châteaubriand *m.*

tenderness ['tendənis], *s.* 1. Sensibilité *f* (de la peau, etc.). 2. Délicatesse *f,* fragilité *f* (d'une plante, etc.). 3. Tendresse *f* (des sentiments); affection *f* (**for,** pour). 4. Tendreté *f* (des aliments).

tendon ['tendən], *s. Anat:* Tendon *m.*

tendril ['tendril], *s. Bot:* Vrille *f;* crampon *m.*

Tenebrae ['tenibrei], *s.pl. Ecc:* Ténèbres *fpl.*

tenement ['tenimənt], *s.* 1. *Jur:* Fonds *mpl* (de terre). 2. (*a*) *Pej:* Appartement *m* dans une maison de rapport. (*b*) *Scot:* Maison de rapport. **'tenement house,** *s. Pej:* Maison *f* de rapport; logements ouvriers.

tenet ['ti:net, 'te-], *s.* (*a*) Doctrine *f,* dogme *m;* principe *m.* (*b*) Opinion *f.*

tenfold ['tenfould]. 1. *a.* Décuple. 2. *adv.* Dix fois autant; au décuple. **To increase t.,** décupler.

tennis ['tenis], *s.* 1. (**Lawn-)tennis,** (lawn-)tennis *m.* **Table t.,** ping-pong *m inv* (*R.t.m*). 2. (Jeu *m* de) paume *f.* **'tennis-ball,** *s.* Balle *f* de tennis. **'tennis-court,** *s.* 1. (*a*) Court *m* (de tennis). (*b*) (Terrain *m* de) tennis *m.* 2. (i) Salle *f,* (ii) terrain *m,* de) jeu *m* de paume. **'tennis-racket,** *s.* Raquette *f* de tennis.

tenon¹ ['tenən], *s. Carp:* Tenon *m.*

tenon², *v.tr. Carp: etc:* Tenonner; assembler à tenon (des pièces de bois). **To t. and mortise,** assembler à tenon et mortaise.

tenor ['tenər], *s.* 1. (*a*) *Jur:* Copie *f* conforme. (*b*) Teneur *f* (d'un acte); contenu *m,* sens général (d'une lettre). (*c*) Cours *m,* marche *f* (des affaires, de la vie). 2. *Mus:* (*a*) Ténor *m.* **T. voice,** voix de ténor. **T. clef,** clé d'ut quatrième ligne. (*b*) **T. (bell),** bourdon *m* (d'une sonnerie).

tenpin ['tenpin], *s. esp. U.S:* **Tenpins,** jeu *m* de quilles. **T. bowling alley,** bowling *m.*

tense¹ [tens], *s. Gram:* Temps *m.* **In the future t.,** au (temps) futur.

tense², *a.* 1. Tendu, rigide, raide. 2. (*Of nerves, relations, etc.*) Tendu. **T. moment,** moment angoissant. **T. silence,** silence impressionnant. **T. voice,** voix étranglée (par l'émotion).

tenseness ['tensnis], *s.* 1. Rigidité *f;* (état *m* de) tension *f* (des muscles). 2. Tension (de relations, etc.).

tensile ['tensail, -sil], *a.* 1. Extensible, élastique; (*of metal*) ductile. 2. *Mec:* **T. stress, load,** effort *m* de traction. **T. stretch,** allongement *m* (à l'essai). **High-t. steel,** acier de, à, haute tension.

tension ['tenʃ(ə)n], *s.* 1. (*a*) Tension *f,* raideur *f,* rigidité *f* (d'une corde, des muscles, etc.). (*b*) Tension, état tendu (des nerfs, etc.). (*c*) Tension, pression *f* (d'un gaz). (*d*) *El:* Tension, voltage *m.* **High-, low-t. circuit,** circuit de haute, basse, tension. 2. *Mec.E:* Traction *f.* **To be in t., under stress of t.,** travailler à la traction. 3. (*Device*) Tendeur *m* (d'une machine à coudre). **'tension-pulley, -roller,** *s. Mec.E: etc:* Galet tendeur, de tension.

tent¹ [tent], *s.* Tente *f.* **To pitch (the) tents,** dresser les tentes. **'tent-peg,** *s.* Piquet *m* de tente.

tent², *s. Surg:* Mèche *f,* tampon *m.*

tentacle ['tentəkl], *s. Nat.Hist:* (*a*) Tentacule *m.* (*b*) Cirre *m.*

tentative ['tentətiv]. 1. *a.* Expérimental, -aux; d'essai. **T. offer,** ouverture *f.* 2. *s.* Tentative *f,* essai *m.* **-ly,** *adv.* A titre d'essai; avec une certaine hésitation.

tenter¹ ['tentər], *s. Tex:* Élargisseur *m.* **'tenter-hook,** *s. Tex:* (Clou *m* à) crochet *m.* **To be on tenter-hooks,** être au supplice, sur des charbons ardents. **To keep s.o. on tenter-hooks,** faire languir qn.

tenter², *s. Ind:* Soigneur *m* (de machines); machiniste *m.*

tenth [tenθ]. 1. *num. a. & s.* Dixième. 2. *s.* (*Fractional*) Dixième *m.* **-ly,** *adv.* Dixièmement; en dixième lieu; décimo.

tenuity [te'nju:iti], **tenuousness** ['tenjuəsnis], *s.* 1. Ténuité *f,* finesse *f* (d'un fil). 2. Ténuité (d'un liquide); raréfaction *f* (de l'air, d'un gaz).

tenuous ['tenjuəs], *a.* 1. Ténu; délié; mince. 2. (*a*) (Gaz) raréfié. (*b*) Subtile.

tenure ['tenjər], *s.* 1. *Hist: & Jur:* Tenure (féodale). 2. *Jur:* (Période *f* de) jouissance *f,* (période d')occupation *f.* **Stability of t.,** (i) bail assuré; (ii) stabilité *f* d'un emploi. **During his t. of office,** (i) sous son ministère; (ii) lorsqu'il était en fonctions.

tepid ['tepid], *a.* Tiède. **-ly,** *adv.* Tièdement; sans ardeur.

teratological [,terətə'lɔdʒik(ə)l], *a.* Tératologique.

teratology [,terə'tɔlədʒi], *s.* Tératologie *f.*

tercel ['tə:s(ə)l], **tercelet** ['tə:s(ə)lit], *s. Orn:* Tiercelet *m;* faucon *m* mâle.

tercentenary [,tə:sen'ti:nəri], *a. & s.* Tricentenaire (*m*).

tercet ['tə:sit], *s.* 1. *Pros:* Tercet *m.* 2. *Mus:* Triolet *m.*

teredo [ti'ri:dou], *s. Moll:* Taret (naval); perce-bois *m inv.*

tergiversation [,tə:dʒivə'seiʃ(ə)n], *s.* Tergiversation *f.*

term¹ [tə:m], *s.* 1. (*a*) Terme *m,* borne *f,* fin *f,* limite *f.* **To set, put, a t. to sth.,** fixer une limite à qch.; assigner une fin, un terme, à qch. (*b*) *Com:* (Terme d') échéance *f* (d'une lettre de change). 2. (*a*) Terme, période *f,* durée *f.* **Banishment for a t. of years,** bannissement à temps. **During his t. of office,** lorsqu'il était, tout le temps qu'il a été, en fonctions. **To owe a t.'s rent,** devoir trois mois de loyer; devoir un terme. **Long-t., short-t., transaction,** opération à long, à court, terme. *Sch:* Trimestre *m.* **To keep one's terms,** (i) (*in universities*) *approx.* = prendre ses inscriptions; (ii) (*of law students*) remplir les obligations matérielles et pécuniaires incombant à un étudiant. (*c*) *Jur:* Session *f.* 3. *pl.* **Terms.** (*a*) Conditions *f;* clauses *f,* termes, teneur *f* d'un contrat). *Fin:* **Terms and conditions of an issue,** modalités *f* d'une émission. **On these terms I accept,** à ces conditions j'accepte. **I'll take it on your terms,** je le prends à vos conditions. **Make, name, your own terms,** faites vos conditions vous-même. **By the terms**

of article **49** ..., aux termes de l'article 49.... **To dictate, fix, terms,** imposer des conditions. **To come to terms, make terms,** en venir à un accommodement; venir à composition. *S.a.* REFERENCE 1. (*b*) **Terms of payment,** conditions de paiement. **Inclusive terms,** tout compris. **To buy sth. on easy terms,** acheter qch. avec facilités de paiement. **Not on any terms,** à aucun prix. **4.** *pl.* Relations *f*, termes, rapports *m*. **To be, live, on friendly, on good, terms with s.o.,** vivre en bonne intelligence, en bons termes, avec qn. **To be on bad terms with s.o.,** être mal avec qn. **To be on the best of terms with s.o.,** être au mieux, dans les meilleurs termes, avec qn. **5.** (*a*) **Terme** (d'une équation, d'un syllogisme). **To express one quantity in terms of another,** exprimer une quantité en fonction d'une autre. (*b*) **Terms of a problem,** énoncé *m* d'un problème. **6.** (*a*) Terme, mot *m*, expression *f*, appellation *f*. **Legal terms,** termes de droit, de pratique. (*b*) *pl.* Langage *m*, termes. **How dare you speak to me in such terms?** c'est à moi que vous osez tenir un pareil langage? '**term-time,** *s.* *Sch:* Période *f* des cours, trimestre *m*.

term², *v.tr.* Appeler, désigner, nommer.

termagant ['tə:məgənt], *s.f.* Mégère, virago.

terminable ['tə:minəbl], *a.* Terminable; (*of contract*) résiliable.

terminal ['tə:min(ə)l]. **I.** *a.* **1.** Qui borne, qui termine (une région, etc.). *Mil:* **T. leave,** permission *f*, congé *m*, libérable. **2.** (*a*) *Nat.Hist:* Terminal, -aux; distal, -aux. (*b*) *Geol:* **T. moraine,** moraine frontale. (*c*) *s. Rail:* (Gare) terminus, tête de ligne. *Aer:* Aérogare *f*. (*d*) *El:* **Tg:** (Isolateur, poteau) d'arrêt. (*e*) (*Of letter, etc.*) Final, -als; dernier, -ière. (*f*) *W.Tel:* **T. amplifier,** ampli terminal, de sortie. **3.** Trimestriel, -elle. **II. terminal,** *s. El:* Borne *f* (de prise de courant). (**Cable**) **t.,** cosse *f*.

terminate ['tə:mineit]. **I.** *v.tr.* Terminer. **1.** (*Of boundary*) Délimiter (une région). **2.** (*a*) Résoudre, résilier (un contrat, etc.); mettre fin à (un engagement). (*b*) Être à la fin de (qch.). **II. terminate,** *v.i.* **1.** (*Of word, etc.*) Se terminer, finir (**in, en,** par). **2.** Aboutir (**in, at, à**).

termination [tə:mi'neiʃ(ə)n], *s.* **1.** Terminaison *f*, fin *f* (d'un procès, etc.); cessation *f* (de relations). **2.** *Gram:* Terminaison, désinence *f*.

terminological [tə:minə'lɔdʒik(ə)l], *a.* Terminologique. **T. inexactitude,** inexactitude de termes.

terminology [tə:mi'nɔlədʒi], *s.* Terminologie *f*.

terminus ['tə:minəs], *s.* **1.** (Gare *f*) terminus *m*; (gare) tête *f* de ligne. **2.** *Sculp:* Terme *m*; dieu *m* Terme.

termitary ['tə:mitəri], *s. Ent:* Termitière *f*.

termite ['tə:mait], *s. Ent:* Termite *m*; fourmi blanche.

tern [tə:n], *s. Orn:* Sterne *m*; hirondelle *f* de mer.

ternary ['tə:nəri], *a. Mth: etc:* Ternaire.

terrace¹ ['terəs], *s.* **1.** *Const:* Terrasse *f*; terre-plein *m*, *pl.* terre-pleins. **2.** Rangée de maisons de style uniforme.

terrace², *v.tr.* Disposer (un jardin, etc.) en terrasse(s). **terraced,** *a.* (Jardin) suspendu, étagé, en terrasse.

terra-cotta ['terə'kɔtə], *s.* Terre cuite.

terra firma ['terə'fə:mə], *s.* Terre *f* ferme.

terrain [tə'rein], *s.* Terrain *m*.

terramycin [terə'maisin], *s. Med: Pharm:* Terramycine *f*.

terrapin ['terəpin], *s.* Tortue *f* diamant, terrapin *m*.

terrestrial [ti'restriəl], *a.* Terrestre.

terrible ['teribl], *a.* Terrible, affreux, -euse, épouvantable; atroce. *F:* **He's a t. talker,** c'est un terrible bavard. *F:* **T. prices,** prix *m* formidables. **-bly,** *adv.* (*a*) Terriblement, affreusement, atrocement. (*b*) *F:* **T. dangerous,** terriblement dangereux. **T. rich,** diablement riche.

terrier ['teriər], *s.* (Chien *m*) terrier *m*. **Bull-t.,** bull-terrier *m*.

terrific [tə'rifik], *a.* **1.** Terrifiant, épouvantable. **2.** *F:* Terrible; énorme; formidable. **T. pace,** allure vertigineuse. **-ally,** *adv.* **1.** D'une manière terrifiante. **2.** *F:* Terriblement.

terrify ['terifai], *v.tr.* Terrifier, effrayer, épouvanter. **To t. s.o. into doing sth.,** faire faire qch. à qn sous le coup de la peur. **To t. s.o. out of his wits,** rendre qn fou de terreur. **terrifying,** *a.* Terrifiant, épouvantable.

terrine [te'ri:n], *s.* Terrine *f*.

territorial [teri'tɔ:riəl]. **1.** *a.* (*a*) Territorial, -aux. (*b*) Terrien, foncier. **2.** *s. Mil:* Territorial *m*.

territoriality ['teri'tɔri'æliti], *s.* Territorialité *f*.

territory ['terit(ə)ri], *s.* **1.** Territoire *m*. **2.** *Austr:* **The Northern T.,** le Territoire du Nord. **3.** **Commercial traveller's t.,** région assignée à un représentant (de commerce).

terror ['terər], *s.* **1.** Terreur *f*, effroi *m*, épouvante *f*. **To be in t.,** être dans la terreur. **To be in t. of one's life,** craindre pour sa vie. **To go in t. of s.o.,** avoir une peur bleue de qn. *F:* **To have a holy t. of sth.,** craindre qch. comme le feu. *Fr.Hist:* **The (Reign of) T.,** la Terreur. **2.** (*a*) **He was the t. of the countryside,** c'était la terreur du pays. (*b*) *F:* **He's a little t., a holy t.,** c'est un enfant terrible. **He was a t. for always being late,** il était d'une inexactitude désespérante. '**terror-stricken, -struck,** *a.* Saisi de terreur; épouvanté.

terrorism ['terərizm], *s.* Terrorisme *m*.

terrorist ['terərist], *a. & s.* Terroriste (*m*).

terrorize ['terəraiz], *v.tr.* Terroriser.

terry ['teri], *a. Tex:* (Velours, etc.) bouclé, épinglé, frisé. **T. towelling,** tissu *m* éponge.

terse [tə:s], *a.* (*a*) (*Of style, language*) Concis, net; élégant et précis. (*b*) Brusque. **-ly,** *adv.* Avec concision.

terseness ['tə:snis], *s.* (*a*) Concision *f*; netteté *f* (de style). (*b*) Brusquerie *f* (d'une réponse).

tertiary ['tə:ʃiəri], *a.* Tertiaire.

terylene ['terili:n], *s. R.t.m:* Térylène *m*.

tessellated ['tesileitid], *a.* (Pavage) en mosaïque; disposé en damier.

tessellation [tesi'leiʃ(ə)n], *s.* Arrangement *m* en damier; mosaïque *f*.

test¹ [test], *s.* **1.** (*a*) Épreuve *f*. **To put s.o. to the t., through a t.,** mettre qn à l'épreuve, à l'essai. **To pass, stand, the t.,** soutenir, supporter, l'épreuve; subir victorieusement l'épreuve. (*b*) *Ind: Ch:* Essai *m*, épreuve; réaction *f*. **Boiler t.,** épreuve des chaudières. **Endurance t.,** épreuve d'endurance. **Control t., check t.,** essai contradictoire; contre-épreuve *f*. **The acid t.,** l'épreuve à la pierre de touche; l'épreuve concluante. **Blood t.,** analyse *f* du sang. *Aut:* **T. run,** course d'essai. **T. engine, t. car,** moteur, voiture, d'étude. (*c*) *Ch:* Réactif *m* (of, for, de). **2.** (*a*) Examen *m* (d'un malade, etc.). **Eye t.,** examen des yeux. *Mil: etc:* **To fail to pass the eye t.,** être refusé, réformé, pour la vue. *Aut:* **Driving t.,** examen pour permis de conduire. (*b*) *Sch:* Composition *f*. **Oral t.,** épreuve orale. (*c*) *Psy: Ind:* Test *m*. **Intelligence t.,** test mental. *Ch:* Têt *m*, test (de coupellation); coupelle *f*. '**test-bar,** *s. Mec.E: Metall:* Barreau *m* d'essai; éprouvette *f*. '**test-bench,** *s.* Banc *m* d'essai; banc d'épreuve. '**test case,** *s. Jur:* Précédent *m*. '**test-match,** *s. Cr:* Rencontre internationale, grand match (entre l'Angleterre et l'Australie, etc.). '**test-paper,** *s.* **1.** *Ch:* Papier réactif. **2.** *Sch:* Composition *f*. '**test-piece,** *s. Mus:* Morceau imposé (dans un concours de fanfares, d'orphéons). *Metall:* Éprouvette *f*. '**test-pilot,** *s.* Pilote *m* d'essais. '**test-strip,** *s. Cin:* Bout *m* d'essai. '**test-tube,** *s. Ch:* Éprouvette *f*, tube *m* à essais. *F:* **T.-t. baby,** bébé éprouvette *m*.

test², *v.tr.* **1.** (*a*) Éprouver; tester; mettre (qn, qch.) à l'épreuve, à l'essai. (*b*) Essayer (un ciment, une machine); contrôler, vérifier (des poids et mesures); examiner (la vue de qn, etc.); expérimenter (un procédé); analyser (l'eau, etc.). **To t. a boiler,** éprouver une chaudière. **2.** (*a*) Coupeller (l'or). (*b*) *Ch:* Déterminer la nature (d'un corps) au moyen d'un réactif. **To t. with litmus paper,** faire la réaction au papier de tournesol.

test³, *s. Nat.Hist:* Test *m* (d'un oursin, d'une graine); carapace *f* (du tatou).

testacean [tes'teiʃən], *s. Z:* Testacé *m*.

testaceous [tes'teiʃəs], *a. Z:* Testacé.

testament ['testəmənt], *s.* **1.** Testament *m*; dernières volontés *f.* **2.** *B:* **The Old, the New, T.,** l'Ancien, le Nouveau, Testament.

testamentary [testə'ment(ə)ri], *a.* Testamentaire.

testate ['testit], *a. & s.* (Personne) qui est morte en laissant un testament valable.

testator [tes'teitər], *s.m.* Testateur.

testatrix [tes'teitriks], *s.f.* Testatrice.

tester[1] ['testər], *s. A.Furn:* Baldaquin *m*, ciel *m* (de lit). **'tester-bed**, *s.* Lit *m* à baldaquin.

tester[2], *s.* 1. *Ind:* (*Pers.*) Essayeur, -euse; contrôleur, -euse. 2. Appareil de contrôle, à essais. **Battery t.**, vérificateur *m* d'accus.

testicle ['testikl], *s.* Testicule *m.*

testify ['testifai]. 1. *v.tr.* Témoigner (son regret, sa foi). 2. *Jur:* (*a*) *v.tr.* Déclarer, affirmer (qch.) (sous serment). *Abs.* **To t. in s.o.'s favour**, rendre témoignage en faveur de qn. **To t. against s.o.**, déposer contre qn. (*b*) *v.ind.tr.* **To t. to a fact**, attester un fait; se porter garant d'un fait; témoigner d'un fait.

testimonial [‚testi'mouniəl], *s.* 1. Certificat (délivré par une maison, un chef); (lettre de) recommandation *f*; attestation *f.* **To show one's testimonials**, exhiber ses certificats. 2. Témoignage *m* d'estime; cadeau (offert à qn par cotisation).

testimony ['testiməni], *s.* Témoignage *m* (des sens); *Jur:* attestation *f*; déposition *f* (d'un témoin). **To bear t. to sth.**, rendre témoignage de qch. **In t. whereof . . .**, en foi de quoi. . . . *Jur:* **To produce t. of, to, a statement**, apporter des preuves testimoniales à l'appui d'une affirmation.

testiness ['testinis], *s.* (*a*) Irritabilité *f*, irascibilité *f.* (*b*) Susceptibilité *f.*

testudo [tes'tju:dou], *s.* 1. Tortue *f.* 2. *Rom.Ant:* (*a*) Tortue (de siège). (*b*) Tortue (de boucliers).

testy ['testi], *a.* (*a*) Irritable, irascible; peu endurant. (*b*) Susceptible. **-ily**, *adv.* D'un air irrité; avec humeur.

tetanus ['tetənəs], *s. Med:* Tétanos *m.*

tête-à-tête ['teita:'teit]. 1. *adv.* Tête-à-tête. 2. *s.* (*pl.* **tête-à-têtes**) Tête-à-tête *m inv.* **T.-a-t. dinner**, dîner en tête-à-tête.

tether[1] ['teðər], *s.* Longe *f*, attache *f* (d'un cheval, etc.). **To be at the end of one's t.**, (i) être à bout de forces; n'en plus pouvoir; (ii) être à bout de ressources; *F:* être au bout de son rouleau.

tether[2], *v.tr.* Attacher, mettre à l'attache (un cheval, etc.).

tetrachord ['tetrəkɔ:d], *s. Mus:* Tétracorde *m.*

tetraethyl ['tetrə'eθil], *a. Ch:* Tétraéthyle.

tetragon ['tetrəgən], *s.* Tétragone *m*, quadrilatère *m.*

tetragonal [te'trægən(ə)l], *a.* Tétragone, quadrilatère. *Cryst:* Quadratique.

tetrahedral ['tetrə'hi:dr(ə)l], *a. Geom:* Tétraédrique.

tetrahedron ['tetrə'hi:dr(ə)n], *s.* Tétraèdre *m.*

tetralogy [te'trælədʒi], *s. Gr.Th:* Tétralogie *f.*

tetrameter [te'træmitər], *s.* Tétramètre *m.*

tetrarch ['tetra:k], *s.* Tétrarque *m.*

tetrarchy ['tetra:ki], *s.* Tétrarchie *f.*

tetrasyllabic ['tetrəsi'læbik], *a. Gram:* Tétrasyllabe, tétrasyllabique.

tetravalent [tetrə'veilənt], *a. Ch:* Tétravalent.

tetrode ['tetroud], *s.* Lampe *f* à quatre électrodes; tétrode *f.*

Teuton ['tju:tən], *s.* Teuton, -onne.

Teutonic [tju:'tɔnik], *a.* Teuton, teutonique.

Texan ['teksən], *a. & s. Geog:* Texan, -ane.

text [tekst], *s.* 1. Texte *m* (d'un manuscrit, d'un auteur). 2. (*Scripture*) t., citation tirée de l'Écriture sainte. **To stick to one's t.**, ne pas s'écarter de la question; s'en tenir au sujet. **'text-book**, *s. Sch:* Manuel *m.* **A t.-b. on, of, algebra**, une algèbre.

textile ['tekstail]. 1. *a.* Textile. 2. *s.* (*a*) Tissu *m*, étoffe *f.* **The t. industry**, l'industrie textile. (*b*) Matière *f* textile; textile *m.*

textual ['tekstjuəl], *a.* (*a*) Textuel, -elle. (*b*) **T. error**, erreur de texte.

texture ['tekstʃər], *s.* Texture *f* (d'un tissu); texture, grain *m* (de la peau, du bois).

Thai [tai], *a.* Thaï. *s. Ling:* Le thaï.

Thailand ['tailænd]. *Pr.n. Geog:* La Thaïlande.

thalidomide [θə'lidəmaid], *s. Med:* Thalidomide *f. Journ:* **T. baby**, bébé malformé (à cause de l'emploi de la thalidomide chez la mère).

thallium ['θæliəm], *s. Ch:* Thallium *m.*

thallus ['θæləs], *s. Bot:* Thalle *m.*

Thames (the) [ðə'temz]. *Pr.n.* La Tamise. *F:* **He will never set the T. on fire**, il n'a pas inventé la poudre.

than [ðæn, ðən], *conj.* (*a*) (*In comparison of inequality*) Que; (*with numbers*) de. **I have more, less, t. you**, j'en ai plus, moins, que vous. **More t. twenty**, plus de vingt. **More t. once**, plus d'une fois. **You had better speak to him t. write**, vous feriez mieux de lui parler que de lui écrire. **She would do anything rather t. let him suffer**, elle ferait n'importe quoi plutôt que de le laisser souffrir. **No sooner had we entered t. the music began**, nous étions à peine entrés que la musique commença. (*b*) **Any person other t. himself**, tout autre que lui.

thane [θein], *s. Eng. Hist:* = Baron *m.*

thank[1] [θæŋk], *s.* Thanks, remerciement(s) *m.* **Give him my best thanks**, remerciez le bien de ma part. *F:* **Thanks!** je vous remercie; merci. **Many thanks!** merci bien! **To give thanks to s.o. for sth.**, rendre grâces à qn de qch. **To pass a vote of thanks to s.o.**, voter des remerciements à qn. **Thanks be to God!** rendons grâces, grâce, à Dieu! **Thanks to . . .**, grâce à. . . . *F:* **That's all the thanks I get!** voilà comme on me remercie! **'thank-offering**, *s. B:* Sacrifice *m* d'actions de grâces.

thank[2], *v.tr.* 1. (*a*) Remercier (qn); dire merci à (qn); rendre grâce(s) à (Dieu). **To t. s.o. for sth.**, remercier qn de qch. **To t. s.o. effusively**, se confondre en remerciements. **T. God!** t. **heaven!** t. **goodness!** Dieu merci! grâce au ciel! *S.a.* STAR[1] 1. (*b*) **T. you**, je vous remercie; merci. **Will you have some tea?—No, t. you**, prenez-vous du thé?—Merci! 2. **I will t. you to close the door**, je vous demanderai de vouloir bien fermer la porte. **I'll t. you to mind your own business!** occupez-vous donc de ce qui vous regarde! 3. **To have s.o. to t. for sth.**, devoir qch. à qn. *F:* **You have only yourself to t. for it**, c'est à vous seul qu'il faut vous en prendre.

thankful ['θæŋkf(u)l], *a.* Reconnaissant. **Let us be t. that our lives have been spared**, félicitons-nous de ce que nous avons la vie sauve. **-fully**, *adv.* Avec reconnaissance.

thankfulness ['θæŋkf(u)lnis], *s.* Reconnaissance *f*, gratitude *f.*

thankless ['θæŋklis], *a.* Ingrat. **A t. task**, une tâche ingrate, une vraie corvée.

thanklessness ['θæŋklisnis], *s.* 1. Ingratitude *f.* 2. Caractère ingrat, peu profitable (d'une tâche).

thanksgiving ['θæŋks'giviŋ], *s.* Action *f* de grâce(s). **T. Day**, fête célébrée (i) *U.S:* le 4e jeudi de novembre; (ii) (*in Canada*) le 2e lundi d'octobre, *Fr.C:* le jour de l'action de grâces.

that[1] [ðæt]. I. *Dem. pron., pl.* those [ðouz]. 1. Cela, *F:* ça; ce. (*a*) **Give me t.**, donnez-moi cela. **What is t.?** qu'est-ce (que c'est) que cela, que ça? **Who is t.?** qui est-ce là? **That's Mr. Smith**, c'est M. Smith. **Are those your children?** sont-ce là vos enfants? **T. is my opinion**, voilà mon avis. **After t.**, après cela. **With t.**, **she took out her handkerchief**, là-dessus elle a sorti son mouchoir. **What do you mean by t.?** qu'entendez-vous par-là? **They all think t.**, c'est ce qu'ils pensent tous. **Have things come to t.?** les choses en sont-elles arrivées là? *S.a.* ALL I. 1, FOR[1] I. 9. **T. is . . .**, c'est-à-dire. . . . (*b*) (*Stressed*) **And so 't. is settled**, alors quant à cela, c'est décidé. **He is only a fiddler, and a poor one at t.**, ce n'est qu'un violoneux, et encore assez piètre. *F:* **Will you help me?—T. I will!** voulez-vous m'aider?—Volontiers! **That's right!** that's it! c'est cela! **That's all**, voilà tout. **That's curious!** voilà qui est curieux! **That's it!** et voilà! **And t. was t.**, plus rien à dire. 2. (*Opposed to* '*this*', '*these*') Celui-là, *f.* celle-là; *pl.* ceux-là, *f.* celles-là. **This is new and t. is old**, celui-ci est neuf et celui-là est vieux. *S.a.* THIS I. 2. 3. Celui, *f.* celle; *pl.* ceux, *f.* celles. **All those t. I saw**, tous ceux que j'ai vus. **Those of whom I speak**, ceux dont je parle. **There are those who think t. . . .**, certains pensent que. . . . II. **that**, *dem.a., pl.* those. (*a*) Ce, (*before vowel or h 'mute'*) cet; *f.* cette; *pl.* ces; (*for emphasis and in opposition to* '*this*', '*these*') ce . . . -là. **T. book, those books**, ce livre(-là), ces livres(-là). **T. one**, celui-là, celle-là. **Everybody is agreed on t. point**, tout le monde est d'accord là-dessus. **I only saw him t. once**, je ne l'ai vu que cette fois-là. *S.a.* THIS II. (*b*) (*Followed by* '*of mine*', '*of his*', *etc.*) *F:* **Well, how's t. leg of yours?** eh bien, et cette jambe? (*c*) Those people who take an interest in these things, les gens, ceux, qui s'intéressent à ces choses-là. I am not one of those people who . . ., je ne suis pas de ceux qui. . . . III. that, *dem.adv. F:* 'T. high, aussi haut que ça. *S.a.* MUCH 3. He was 't. tall, il était tellement grand. . . .

that² [ðæt], *rel. pron. sg. & pl.* **1.** (*For subject*) Qui; (*for object*) que. The house t. stands at the corner, la maison qui se trouve au coin. The letter t. I sent you, la lettre que je vous ai envoyée. *F:* Idiot t. I am! idiot que je suis! **2.** (*Governed by prep.*) Lequel, *f.* laquelle; *pl.* lesquels, *f.* lesquelles. The envelope t. I put it in, l'enveloppe dans laquelle je l'ai mis. The man t. we are speaking of, about, l'homme dont nous parlons. No one has come t. I know of, personne n'est venu que je sache. **3.** Où; que. The night t. we went to the theatre, le soir où nous sommes allés au théâtre. During the years t. he had languished in prison, pendant les années qu'il avait langui en prison.

that³ [ðæt, ðət], *conj.* **1.** (*Introducing subordinate clause*) Que. (*a*) It was for this t. they fought, c'est pour cela qu'on s'est battu. Never a year goes by t. he does not write to us, il ne se passe jamais une année qu'il ne nous écrive. Not that, *see* NOT 4. But that, *see* BUT 1. (*b*) I hope t. you will have good luck, j'espère que vous aurez de la chance. (*c*) (Afin) que, pour que, + *sub.* Come nearer (so) t. I may see you, approchez, que je vous voie. I am telling you, (so) t. you may know, je vous préviens pour que vous soyez au courant. **2.** (*a*) T. he should behave like this! dire qu'il se conduit comme cela! (*b*) Oh t. it were possible! oh, si c'était possible!

thatch¹ [θætʃ], *s.* Chaume *m* (de toiture). *F:* He's lost his t., il n'a plus de cresson sur la fontaine, le caillou.

thatch², *v.tr.* Couvrir (un toit) de, en, chaume. thatched, *a.* (Toit) de chaume. T. cottage, chaumière *f.*

thatcher ['θætʃər], *s.* Couvreur *m* en chaume.

thaumaturgy [ˌθɔːməˈtɜːdʒi], *s.* Thaumaturgie *f.*

thaw¹ [θɔː], *s.* Dégel *m*; fonte *f* des neiges. Silver t., verglas *m*. The t. is setting in, le temps est au dégel, il se met à dégeler.

thaw². **1.** *v.tr.* Dégeler; décongeler (la viande frigorifiée). **2.** *v.i.* (*a*) (*Of snow*) Fondre; (*of frozen meat*) se décongeler. (*b*) *Impers.* It is thawing, il dégèle. (*c*) *F:* (*Of pers.*) Se réchauffer. (*d*) *F:* (*Of pers.*) S'humaniser. thawing, *s.* **1.** Dégèlement *m* (des conduites d'eau); décongélation *f* (de la viande). **2.** Dégel *m*; fonte *f* (des neiges).

the¹ [ðə; *before vowel* ði], *def. art.* **1.** Le, *f.* la; (*before vowel or h 'mute'*) l'; *pl.* les. (*a*) (*Particularizing*) The father and (the) mother, le père et la mère. On the other side, de l'autre côté. The Alps, les Alpes. I spoke to the postman, j'ai parlé au facteur. Give it to the maid, donnez-le à la bonne. He has gone to the fields, il est allé aux champs. The roof of the house, le toit de la maison. The arrival of the guests, l'arrivée des invités. The Smiths, les Smith. Edward the Seventh, Édouard Sept. *P:* The wife, ma femme, *P:* la bourgeoise. Well, how's the throat? eh bien, et cette gorge? (*b*) He is not the person to do that, ce n'est pas une personne à faire cela. The impudence of it! quelle audace! He hasn't the patience to wait, il n'a pas la patience d'attendre. (*c*) The beautiful, le beau. Translated from the Russian, traduit du russe. *Coll.* The poor, les pauvres. (*d*) *F:*| He's got the toothache, the measles, il a mal aux dents; il a la rougeole. (*e*) (*Generalizing*) The dog is our best friend, le chien est notre meilleur ami. (*f*) (*Distributive*) To be employed by the day, travailler à la journée. Twenty-five miles to the gallon, = 11 litres aux 100 kilomètres. **2.** (*Demonstrative in French*) Ce, cet, *f.* cette, *pl.* ces. I was absent at the time, j'étais absent à cette époque, à ce moment-là. I shall see him during the summer, je le verrai cet été. (*In café, etc.*) And what will the ladies take? et ces dames, que prendront-elles? **3.** (*Stressed*) [ðiː] Her father is Professor X, 'the Professor X, son père est le professeur X, le grand, le célèbre, professeur X. He is 'the surgeon here, c'est lui le grand chirurgien ici. Smith's is 'the shop for furniture, la maison Smith est la meilleure pour les meubles.

the², *adv.* (*Preceding an adj. or adv. in the comparative degree*) (*a*) It will be all the easier for you as you are young, cela vous sera d'autant plus facile que vous êtes jeune. (*b*) The sharper the point the better the needle, les aiguilles sont d'autant meilleures que leur pointe est plus fine. The sooner the better, le plus tôt sera le mieux. The less said about it the better, moins on en parlera mieux cela vaudra. *S.a.* MORE 4, WORSE 1.

thé-dansant [tei'dã(n)sã(n)], *s.* Thé dansant *m.*

theatre ['θiətər], *s.* **1.** (*a*) Théâtre *m*; salle *f* de spectacle. Open-air t., théâtre de verdure. (*b*) News t., ciné-actualités *m.* (*c*) The t., l'art *m* dramatique; le théâtre. **2.** (*a*) (*In universities*) Amphithéâtre *m.* (*b*) = OPERATING-THEATRE. **3.** The t. of war, le théâtre de la guerre. 'theatre-goer, *s.* Amateur *m* du théâtre.

theatrical [θi'ætrik(ə)l], *a.* **1.** Théâtral, -aux. T. performance, représentation théâtrale. T. company, troupe *f* d'acteurs. **2.** (*Of attitude*) Théâtral, histrionique. -ally, *adv.* **1.** Théâtralement (parlant). **2.** De façon théâtrale.

theatricals [θi'ætrik(ə)lz], *s.pl.* Amateur t., spectacle *m* d'amateurs. Private t., comédie *f* de salon.

thee [ðiː], *pers. pron., objective case. A: Ecc: Poet:* **1.** Te; (*before a vowel sound*) t'. We beseech t., nous te supplions. **2.** (*Stressed*) Toi. T. and me, toi et moi.

theft [θeft], *s.* (*a*) Vol *m.* (*b*) *Jur:* Aggravated t., vol qualifié. Petty t., larcin *m.* 'theft-proof, *a.* Muni d'un dispositif antivol.

their [ðeər], *poss.a.* **1.** (*a*) Leur, *pl.* leurs. T. father and mother, leur père et leur mère, leurs père et mère. (*b*) T. Majesties, leurs Majestés. **2.** *F:* Nobody in t. senses . . ., personne jouissant de son bon sens.

theirs [ðeəz], *poss.pron.* Le leur, la leur, les leurs. This house is t., cette maison est la leur, est à eux, à elles, leur appartient. He is a friend of t., c'est un de leurs amis.

them [ðem], *pers. pron., pl., objective case.* **1.** (*a*) (*Direct*) Les *mf*; (*indirect*) leur *mf*. I like them, je les aime. I shall tell t. so, je le leur dirai. Call t., appelez-les. Speak to t., parlez-leur. *F:* When anyone comes she says to t . . ., quand quelqu'un vient elle lui dit. . . . (*b*) (*Refl.*) They took the keys away with t., ils ont emporté les clefs avec eux. **2.** (*Stressed*) Eux, *f.* elles. It's t.! c'est eux, elles! I don't like 'them, je ne les aime pas, eux. *F:* Them's my sentiments, voilà ce que je pense, moi. *P:* T. there sheep, ces moutons-là. **3.** Many of t., nombre d'entre eux. Both of t. saw me, ils m'ont vu tous (les) deux. Give me half of t., donnez-m'en la moitié. Every one of t. was killed, ils furent tous tués. Neither of t., ni l'un ni l'autre. None of t., aucun d'eux. Lay the tables and put some flowers on t., préparez les tables et mettez-y des fleurs.

theme [θiːm], *s.* **1.** Sujet *m*, thème *m* (d'un discours). **2.** *Mus:* Thème, motif *m.* 'theme-song, *s.* Chanson leitmotiv.

themselves [ðəm'selvz], *pers.pron. See* SELF 4.

then [ðen], I. *adv.* **1.** Alors; en ce temps-là. The t. existing system, le système qui existait à cette époque. T. and there, séance tenante. *S.a.* NOW I. 1. **2.** Puis, ensuite, alors. They travelled in France and t. in Spain, ils voyagèrent en France et ensuite en Espagne. What t.? et puis? et (puis) après? **3.** D'ailleurs; aussi (bien); et puis. I haven't the time, and t. it isn't my business, je n'ai pas le temps, d'ailleurs, aussi bien, ce n'est pas mon affaire. II. **then**, *conj.* En ce cas, donc, alors. Go, t., soit, allez. But t . . ., mais c'est que. . . . You knew all the time t.? vous le saviez donc d'avance? *S.a.* NOW I. 2. III. **then**, *quasi-s.* Ce temps-là; cette époque-là. Before t., avant cela. By t. they had gone, ils étaient déjà partis. Till t., (i) jusqu'alors; (ii) jusque-là. (*Ever*) since t., dès lors; depuis ce temps-là. Between now and t., d'ici là. ''then'-clause, *s. Gram: F:* Apodose *f.*

thence [ðens], *adv. A. & Lit:* **1.** De là. **2.** Pour cette raison; par conséquent.

thenceforth ['ðens'fɔːθ], **thenceforward** ['ðens'fɔːwəd], *adv. A. & Lit:* Dès lors; désormais.

theocracy [θi'ɔkrəsi], *s.* Théocratie *f.*

theocratic [ˌθi(ː)o'krætik], *a.* Théocratique.

theodolite [θiˈɔdəlait], s. Surv: Théodolite m.
theologian [ˌθi(ː)əˈloudʒiən], s. Théologien m.
theological [ˌθi(ː)əˈlɔdʒik(ə)l], a. Théologique.
theology [θiˈɔlədʒi], s. Théologie f.
theorem [ˈθiərəm], s. Théorème m.
theoretic(al) [θiəˈretik(əl)], a. Théorique. -ally, adv. Théoriquement.
theoretician [ˌθiəreˈtiʃ(ə)n], s., **theorist** [ˈθiːərist], s. Théoricien, -ienne.
theorize [ˈθiəraiz], v.tr. & i. Faire de la théorie, se lancer dans des théories.
theorizer [ˈθiəraizər], s. Théoricien, -ienne.
theory [ˈθiəri], s. Théorie f. In t., en théorie. Plan which is all right in t., projet qui est beau sur le papier.
theosophical [ˌθiəˈsɔfik(ə)l], a. Théosophique.
theosophist [θiˈɔsəfist], s. Théosophe mf.
theosophy [θiˈɔsəfi], s. Théosophie f.
therapeutic(al) [ˌθerəˈpjuːtik(əl)], a. Med: Thérapeutique.
therapeutics [θerəˈpjuːtiks], s.pl. La thérapeutique.
therapeutist [θerəˈpjuːtist], s. Med: Thérapeutiste m, thérapeute m.
therapist [ˈθerəpist], s. Occupational t., spécialiste mf de thérapie rééducative.
therapy [ˈθerəpi], s. Med: Thérapie f. Occupational t., thérapie rééducative. Speech t., traitement m par un phoniatre.
there [ðɛər]. I. adv. 1. (a) Là, y. Put it t., mettez-le là. He is still t., il y est toujours. We are t., nous voilà arrivés. F: To be all t., être avisé, dégourdi. He's all t., c'est un homme capable; c'est un malin. He is not all t., il n'a pas toute sa tête. S.a. HERE 6, THEN I. 1. (b) I am going t., j'y vais. A hundred miles t. and back, cent milles aller et retour. S.a. GET II. 2. (c) F: (Emphatic) -là. That man t. always comes, cet homme-là vient toujours. Hurry up t.! dépêchez-vous là-bas! (d) (Calling attention to s.o., sth.) T. is, are . . ., voilà. . . . There's the bell ringing, voilà la cloche qui sonne. T. they are! les voilà! T. she comes, la voilà qui vient. There's a good boy! tu seras bien gentil! and t. you are! Et ça y est! 2. (Unstressed) (a) T. is, are . . ., il est, il y a. . . . T. was once a king . . ., il était, il y avait, une fois un roi. . . . T. was singing and dancing, on a chanté et dansé. T. is a page missing, il manque une page. (b) T. comes a time when . . ., il arrive un moment où. . . . 3. (Stressed) Quant à cela; en cela. T. you are mistaken, quant à cela vous vous trompez. There's the difficulty, c'est là qu'est la difficulté. F: T. you have me! ça, ça me dépasse. II. there, int. (Stressed) Voilà! T. now! (i) voilà! (ii) allons bon! T., I told you so! Là! je vous l'avais bien dit! T., take this book, tenez! prenez ce livre. T.! t.! don't worry! là là, ne vous inquiétez pas! But t., what is the good of talking! mais à quoi bon en parler! I shall do as I like, so t.! Je ferai comme il me plaira, voilà! III. there, quasi-s. He left t. last night, il est parti (de là) hier soir. In t., là-dedans; là.
thereabouts [ˈðɛərəbauts], adv. 1. Près de là; dans le voisinage. Somewhere t., quelque part par là. 2. A peu près; environ. It is four o'clock or t., il est à peu près quatre heures.
thereafter [ðɛərˈɑːftər], adv. A. & Lit: Après (cela); par la suite.
thereat [ðɛərˈæt], adv. A. & Lit: Là-dessus; à ce sujet.
thereby [ˈðɛəˈbai], adv. Par ce moyen; de ce fait; de cette façon.
therefore [ˈðɛəfɔːr], adv. Donc; par conséquent. I should be glad, t., if you would . . ., par conséquent, je vous serais reconnaissant de vouloir bien. . . .
therefrom [ðɛəˈfrɔm], adv. A. & Lit: Jur: De là.
therein [ðɛərˈin], adv. A. & Lit: Jur: 1. En cela; à cet égard. T. you are mistaken, en cela vous faites erreur. 2. (Là-)dedans.
thereof [ðɛərˈov], adv. A. & Lit: Jur: De cela; en. Jur: In lieu t., au lieu de cela.
thereon [ðɛərˈon], adv. A. & Lit: Jur: (Là-)dessus.
thereto [ðɛəˈtuː], adv. A. & Lit: Jur: He put his signature t., il y apposa sa signature.
thereupon [ðɛərəˈpon], adv. 1. Sur ce. 2. Lit: There is much to be said t., il y aurait beaucoup à dire là-dessus, à ce sujet.

therewith [ðɛəˈwið, ˈwiθ], adv. A. & Lit: Jur: 1. Avec cela. 2. = THEREUPON 1. 3. En outre.
therm [θəːm], s. (a) A: (= British thermal unit, B.T.U.) = 252 petites calories. (b) (In gas industry) = 100 000 B.T.U.
thermal [ˈθəːm(ə)l], a. 1. Thermal, -aux. T. baths, thermes m. 2. Ph: Thermal, thermique. T. efficiency, rendement m thermique.
thermic [ˈθəːmik], a. Ph: = THERMAL 2.
thermionic [ˌθəːmiˈɔnik], a. W.Tel: T. tube, lampe f thermoïonique.
thermistor [ˈθəːmistəːr], s. Thermistance f.
thermite [ˈθəːmait], s. Metall: Thermite f.
thermochemical [ˈθəːmouˈkemik(ə)l], a. Thermo-chimique.
thermochemistry [ˈθəːmouˈkemistri], s. Thermo-chimie f.
thermo-couple [ˈθəːmouˈkʌpl], s. Couple m thermo-électrique; thermocouple m.
thermodynamics [ˈθəːmoudaiˈnæmiks], s.pl. Thermo-dynamique f.
thermo-electric [ˈθəːmouiˈlektrik], a. Thermo-électrique.
thermo-electricity [ˈθəːmouˌelikˈtrisiti], s. Thermo-électricité f.
thermo-electronic [ˈθəːmouˌelekˈtrɔnik], a. Ph: Thermo-électronique.
thermogene [ˈθəːmodʒiːn], s. R.t.m. Ouate f thermo-gène.
thermograph [ˈθəːməgræf, -grɑːf], s. Ph: Thermo-graphe m.
thermometer [θəˈmɔmitər], s. Thermomètre m. Maximum and minimum t., thermomètre à maxima et minima. Meteor: Wet-bulb t., thermomètre mouillé. Alcohol t., thermomètre à alcool. The t. stood at 100° (Fahrenheit), le thermomètre indiquait 38° (centigrades).
thermometric [θəːmoˈmetrik], a. Thermométrique.
thermo-motion [ˈθəːmouˈmouʃ(ə)n], s. Thermopro-pulsion f.
thermo-motive [ˈθəːmouˈmoutiv], a. Thermopropulsé.
thermonuclear [ˈθəːmouˈnjuːkliər], a. Atom Ph: Ther-monucléaire.
thermopile [ˈθəːmopail], s. Pile f thermo-électrique; thermopile f.
Thermos [ˈθəːmos], s. R.t.m: "T." vacuum flask, F: T., bouteille Thermos.
thermoscope [ˈθəːməskoup], s. Ph: Thermoscope m.
thermostat [ˈθəːməstæt], s. Thermostat m.
thesaurus [θiˈsɔːrəs], s. Thesaurus m; trésor m (de la langue grecque, etc.).
these [ðiːz]. See THIS.
thesis, pl. **theses** [ˈθiːsis, ˈθiːsiːz], s. Thèse f. Sch: To defend a t., soutenir une thèse.
thews [θjuːz], s.pl. Muscles m; F: nerfs m.
they [ðei]. 1. Pers. pron. nom. pl. (a) Ils, f. elles. T. are dancing, ils, elles, dansent. Here t. come, les voici (qui viennent). T. are rich people, ce sont des gens riches. (b) (Stressed) Eux f. elles. T. alone, eux seuls. It is t., ce sont eux. If I were t., (si j'étais) à leur place. They know nothing about it, quant à eux, ils n'en savent rien. (c) T. who believe, ceux, celles, qui croient. 2. (a) Indef. pron. On. T. say that . . ., on dit que. . . . (b) F: Nobody ever admits t. are to blame, on ne veut jamais reconnaître ses torts.
they'd [ðeid] = they had, they would.
they'll [ðeil] = they will.
they're [ðeiər] = they are.
they've [ðeiv] = they have.
thick [θik]. I. a. 1. Épais, f. épaisse, (of book, thread) gros, f. grosse. Wall that is two feet t., mur qui a deux pieds d'épaisseur. F: To have a t. skin, être peu sensible, peu susceptible. Typ: etc: T. stroke, plein m. S.a. SPACE¹ 3. 2. (Of forest, etc.) Épais, serré, touffu dru. T. beard, barbe fournie. 3. (a) (Of liquid) Épais, consistant; (of wine) trouble; (of mist) dense, épais; (of weather) couvert, bouché; (of darkness) profond. T. mud, boue grasse. Cu: T. sauce, sauce courte. T. soup, potage m) crème (f). (b) (Of voice) Pâteux, -euse; embarrassé. To have a t. head, (i) avoir la tête lourde; (ii) (from drinking) P: avoir mal aux cheveux; (iii) F: être obtus. (c)

F: (*Of pers.*) Obtus. **4.** *F:* **To be very t. with s.o.,** être très lié, être à tu et à toi, avec qn. **They're as t. as thieves,** ils s'accordent comme larrons en foire, *F:* ils sont amis comme cochons. **5.** *F:* **That's a bit t.!** ça c'est raide! ça c'est un peu fort! **-ly,** *adv.* **1.** En couche épaisse. **2. Snow fell t.,** la neige tombait dru. **3.** (Parler) d'une voix empâtée. **II. thick,** *s.* **1.** (*a*) (La) partie charnue, le gras (de la jambe, etc.). (*b*) **In the t. of the fight,** au (plus) fort de la mêlée. **2. To stick to s.o. through t. and thin,** rester fidèle à qn à travers toutes les épreuves. **III. thick,** *adv.* **1.** En couche épaisse. **Don't spread the butter too t.,** ne mettez pas trop de beurre sur les tartines. **To cut the bread t.,** couper le pain en tranches épaisses. *S.a.* LAY ON 2. **2. His blows fell t. and fast,** il frappait à coups redoublés; les coups pleuvaient dru. **'thick-'headed,** *a. F:* Bête, stupide; à l'esprit obtus. **'thick-'lipped,** *a.* Lippu; à grosses lèvres. **'thick-'set,** *a.* **1.** (*Of hedge*) Épais, *f,* épaisse; dru. **2.** (*Of pers.*) (Short and) t.-s., trapu. **'thick-'skinned,** *a.* **1.** A la peau épaisse; *Z:* pachyderme. **2.** *F:* (*Of pers.*) Qui n'a pas l'épiderme sensible; peu susceptible.

thicken ['θik(ə)n]. **1.** *v.tr.* Épaissir; lier (une sauce). **2.** *v.i.* (*a*) (S')épaissir. (*b*) (*Of sauce*) Se lier. **The crowd thickens,** la foule augmente. (*c*) (*Of plot*) Se compliquer, se corser.

thicket ['θikit], *s.* Hallier *m,* fourré *m.*

thickness ['θiknis], *s.* **1.** (*a*) Épaisseur *f* (d'un mur); grosseur *f* (des lèvres). (*b*) Épaisseur (d'une forêt); abondance *f* (de la chevelure). (*c*) Consistance *f* (d'un liquide); épaisseur (du brouillard). (*d*) Empâtement *m* (de la voix); grasseyement *m.* **2.** Couche *f,* épaisseur (de papier).

thief, *pl.* **thieves** [θiːf, θiːvz], *s.* **1.** Voleur, -euse. **Thieves** (*as a class*), *F:* la pègre. **Stop t.!** au voleur! *Prov:* **Set a t. to catch a t.,** à voleur, voleur et demi. **There's honour among thieves,** les loups ne se mangent pas entre eux. *S.a.* KITCHEN 1, THICK I. 4. **2.** *F:* (*In candle*) Champignon *m,* larron *m.*

thieve [θiːv], *v.tr.* Voler (qch.). *Abs.* Être voleur; voler. **thieving¹,** *a.* Voleur, -euse. **thieving²,** *s.* Vol *m,* volerie *f.* Petty t., larcin(s) *m(pl.).*

thievish ['θiːviʃ], *a.* Voleur, -euse. **-ly,** *adv.* En voleur. **thievishness** ['θiːviʃnis], *s.* Penchant *m* au vol.

thigh [θai], *s.* Cuisse *f. S.a.* HIP¹ 1. **'thigh-bone,** *s.* Fémur *m.* **'thigh-boots,** *s.pl.* Bottes cuissardes, bottes d'égoutier.

thill [θil], *s. Veh:* Limon *m.*

thimble ['θimbl], *s.* **1.** Dé *m* (à coudre). **2.** *Mch:* Bague *f;* virole *f.* **3.** *Nau:* Cosse *f* (de câble).

thimbleful ['θimblful], *s. F:* Doigt *m* (de cognac, etc.).

thimblerigger ['θimblrigər], *s.* **1.** Escamoteur *m.* **2.** *F:* Escroc *m.*

thimblerigging ['θimblrigiŋ], *s. F:* Escroquerie *f.*

thin¹ [θin], *a.* (**thinner**) **1.** (*a*) Peu épais; (*of paper*) mince; (*of thread*) ténu; (*of stuff*) léger. **To cut the bread thin,** couper le pain en tranches minces. *Typ:* **T. stroke,** délié *m. Phot:* **T. negative,** cliché faible. (*b*) (*Of pers.*) Maigre, mince. **To grow thinner,** maigrir; s'amaigrir. **As t. as a lath,** maigre comme un clou. *S.a.* ICE¹ 1. **2.** (*Of hair, population*) Clairsemé, rare. *Th: etc:* **There was a t. house,** le théâtre était presque vide. **3.** (*a*) (*Of liquid*) Fluide, clair; (*of blood*) appauvri. (*b*) **T. voice,** voix fluette, grêle. **4.** *F:* (*a*) Peu convaincant. **T. excuse,** pauvre excuse. **That's a bit t.!** c'est peu convaincant! (*b*) **To have a t. time of it,** passer un temps peu agréable. **5.** *s. See* THICK II. 2. **-ly,** *adv.* **1.** A peine. **T. clad,** vêtu insuffisamment. **T. veiled allusion,** allusion à peine voilée. **2.** D'une manière éparse. **To sow t.,** semer clair. **Country t. populated,** pays peu peuplé. **'thin-'lipped,** *a.* Aux lèvres minces. **'thin-'skinned,** *a.* **1.** A la peau mince. **2.** A l'épiderme sensible; susceptible; qui se froisse facilement.

thin², *v.* (**thinned**) **1.** *v.tr.* (*a*) Amincir. **To t. (down) a board,** amincir, alléger, une planche. (*b*) **To t. (down) the paint,** a sauce, délayer la peinture; allonger une sauce. (*c*) Éclaircir (les arbres). **To t. (out) seedlings,** éclaircir les jeunes plants. **2.** *v.i.* (*a*) Maigrir. (*b*) S'amincir, s'amaigrir. (*c*) (*Of crowd*) S'éclaircir. **thinning,** *s.* **1.** **T. (down),** amincissement *m,* amaigrissement *m.* **2.** **T. (out),** éclaircissage *m* (de jeunes plants). *For:* **Thinnings,** bois *m* de déchet.

thine [ðain]. **A.** *& Poet:* **1.** *Poss.pron.* (*a*) Le tien, la tienne, les tiens, les tiennes. (*b*) (*Thy kindred*) For **thee and t.,** pour toi et les tiens. (*c*) (*Thy property*) **What is mine is t.,** ce qui est à moi est à toi. **2.** *Poss.a.* **When I look into t. eyes,** quand je regarde dans tes yeux.

thing [θiŋ], *s.* **1.** Chose *f.* (*a*) Objet *m,* article *m.* **Things to be washed,** du linge à faire laver. **To go the way of all things,** aller où va toute chose; mourir. (*b*) **What's that t.?** qu'est-ce que c'est que ce machin-là? (*c*) *Usu. pl.* **Tea things,** service *m* à thé. **To clear away the things,** desservir. **To wash up the tea things, the dinner things,** faire la vaisselle. (*d*) *pl.* Vêtements *m,* effets *m.* **To take off one's things,** (i) se déshabiller; (ii) (= *outdoor things*) enlever son manteau, etc. (*e*) *pl.* Affaires *f,* effets. **To pack up one's things,** faire ses malles. **To put one's things away,** ranger ses affaires. **2.** Être *m,* créature *f.* **Poor little things!** pauvres petits! *F:* **He's a nice old t.,** c'est un bon vieil homme bien sympathique. *A O:* **I say, old t.!** dis donc mon vieux, ma vieille! **3.** (*a*) **You take the t. too seriously,** vous prenez la chose trop au sérieux. **To expect great things of the new treatment,** attendre grand bien du nouveau traitement. **To be all things to all men,** être tout à tous. **She was wearing nylon stockings, a silk dress, and of all things a top hat!** elle portait des bas de nylon, une robe de soie et, tenez-vous bien, un chapeau haut de forme! **Of all things to do!** comme si vous ne pouviez pas faire autre chose! **To talk of one t. and another,** parler de choses et d'autres. **That's the very t.,** c'est juste ce qu'il faut. **That's the t. for me,** voilà mon affaire. **The t. is to find a substitute,** le difficile c'est de trouver un remplaçant. **The play's the t.,** la pièce c'est ce qui compte. **The t. is this,** voici ce dont il s'agit. **That's quite another t.,** c'est tout autre chose, *F:* ça, c'est une autre paire de manches. **It's just one of those things,** ce sont de ces choses qui arrivent! **Neither one t. nor another,** ni l'un ni l'autre; mi-figue, mi-raisin. **What with one t. and another . . .,** tant et si bien que . . ., *F:* entre une chose et l'autre. . . . **For one t. it's too good to be true,** en premier lieu c'est trop beau pour être vrai. **For another t. I know it's false,** d'autre part je sais que c'est faux. **It's one t. to talk, another to write,** autre chose est de parler, autre chose d'écrire. **He makes a good t. out of it,** *F:* ça lui rapporte pas mal. **It would be a good t. to make sure of it,** il serait bon, intéressant, de s'en assurer. *S.a.* GOOD I 1. **I don't know a t. about algebra,** je n'entends rien à l'algèbre. *F:* **To know a t. or two,** être malin; *F:* être à la coule. *F:* **To put s.o. up to a t. or two,** mettre qn sur la voie d'une affaire, etc. **To put s.o. wise to a t. or two,** mettre qn au courant des choses. *F:* **I could tell you a t. or two,** je pourrais vous en conter. *S.a.* FIRST I. 1, LAST² I. 1, RIGHT¹ I. 2. (*b*) *pl.* **Things are going badly,** les affaires vont mal. **As things are,** dans l'état actuel des choses. **Since that is how things are . . .,** puisqu'il en est ainsi. . . . *F:* **How's things?** comment ça va? **4. The latest t. in ties,** cravate(s) dernier cri. **5.** *F:* **It's not the t.,** cela ne se fait pas. **It's quite the t.,** c'est tout à fait correct; c'est la mode. **He is not feeling quite the t. this morning,** il ne se sent pas dans son assiette ce matin.

thingamy(bob) ['θiŋəmi(bɔb)], **thingumbob** ['θiŋəm-bɔb], **thingummy** ['θiŋəmi], *s. F:* Chose *m,* machin *m.*

think¹ [θiŋk], *s.* **To have a quiet t.,** réfléchir. *F:* **You've another t. coming!** tu peux toujours courir!

think², *v.* (**thought**) [θɔːt]; **thought** I. *v.tr. & i.* **1.** Penser, réfléchir. **He thinks for himself,** il pense par lui-même. **To t. hard,** réfléchir profondément. **I can't t. why,** je me demande pourquoi. **He does not say much, but he thinks a lot,** il ne dit pas grand-chose mais il n'en pense pas moins. **I know what you are thinking,** je connais vos pensées. **To act without thinking,** agir sans réflexion. **T. before you speak,** pesez vos paroles. **Give me time to t. (and remember)** laissez-moi réfléchir. **His name was—let me t.—there, I've forgotten!** il s'appelait—voyons—allons, bon! j'ai oublié! **To t. again,** se raviser. *F:* **T. again!** réfléchissez! *S.a.* TWICE. **2.** Songer, s'imaginer. **I can't t. what you mean,** je n'arrive pas à voir ce que vous voulez dire. **One would have thought that . . .,** c'était à croire que. . . . **Anyone would t. that he was asleep,** on dirait qu'il dort. **Who'd have thought it!** qui l'aurait dit? **Only t.!** songez donc! **To t. that he is only twenty!** et dire qu'il n'a que vingt ans! 3. (a) **I have been thinking that . . .,** l'idée m'est venue que. . . . **Thinking to . . .,** dans l'intention de. . . ., avec l'idée de. . . . **I t. I'll go too,** ma foi! j'y vais aussi. (b) **Did you t. to bring any money?** avez-vous pensé à apporter de l'argent? 4. (a) **Then you t. that . . .,** il vous semble donc que. . . . **It is better, don't you t., to get it over?** il vaut mieux, n'est-ce pas, en finir? **What do you t. I ought to do?** que pensez-vous que je doive faire? **I thought all was over,** je me disais que tout était fini. **He thinks he may do anything,** il se croit tout permis. **I t. she is pretty,** je la trouve jolie. **Everyone thought he was mad,** on le jugeait fou. **I t. he is looking off colour,** je lui trouve mauvaise mine. **I t. so,** je pense que oui; c'est ce qui me semble. **I should hardly t. so,** c'est peu probable. **I should (just) t. so!** je crois bien! P: **I don't t.!** jamais de la vie! (b) Pred. Juger, trouver, penser. **I think her pretty,** je la trouve jolie. **I hardly t. it likely that . . .,** il n'est guère probable que + sub. **You thought her a fool,** vous l'avez prise pour une sotte. **They were thought to be rich,** ils passaient pour (être) riches. S.a. BEST[1] 2. 5. **I little thought to see him again,** je ne m'attendais guère à le revoir. **I thought as much, I thought so,** je m'y attendais; je m'en doutais (bien). II. **think of, about,** v.ind.tr. 1. Penser à (qn, qch.); songer à (qch.). **We are thinking of you,** nous pensons à vous. **One can't t. of everything,** on ne s'avise jamais de tout; on ne saurait penser à tout. **I have so much to t. about, of,** j'ai tant de choses auxquelles il me faut songer. **I can't t. of the right word,** le mot propre m'échappe. **The best thing I can t. of,** ce que je vois de mieux. **When you come to t. of it,** à la réflexion. **That is worth thinking about,** cela mérite réflexion. **What 'am I thinking about?** où ai-je la tête? 2. S'imaginer, se figurer, songer. **T. of me having to beg!** (i) dire que je suis obligé de mendier! (ii) me voyez-vous réduit à mendier! F: **T. of that!** ça, c'est pas banal! 3. Considérer. **To t. of s.o.'s feelings,** avoir égard aux sentiments de qn. **To t. of the expense,** regarder à la dépense. 4. **To t. of, about, doing sth.,** méditer, projeter, de faire qch.; penser à faire qch. **I couldn't t. of it!** il n'y a pas à y songer! 5. (a) v.tr. Penser (qch.) de (qch., qn). **What do you t. of it, about it?** qu'en pensez-vous? **To t. a great deal of oneself,** avoir une haute idée de sa personne. **To t. too much of sth.,** attacher trop d'importance à qch. **I told him what I thought of him,** je lui ai dit son fait. **To t. well of s.o.,** estimer qn. **To t. ill of s.o.,** tenir qn en médiocre estime. **He is thought well of,** il est bien vu. S.a. BETTER[1] 3, MUCH 3 (c). **think out,** v.tr. 1. Imaginer, méditer (qch.). **To t. out a plan,** élaborer un plan. **Carefully thought-out answer,** réponse bien pesée. **That wants thinking out,** cela demande mûre réflexion. 2. **He thinks things out for himself,** il juge des choses par lui-même. **think over,** v.tr. Réfléchir sur, aviser à (une question). **T. it over,** réfléchissez-y bien. **This wants thinking over,** cela mérite réflexion. **thinking**[1], a. Pensant; qui pense. **thinking**[2], s. Pensée(s) f(pl), réflexion(s) f(pl). F: **To put on one's t. cap,** méditer une question. **To my t.,** à mon avis. **That is my way of t.,** voilà ma façon de penser.

thinkable ['θiŋkəbl], a. Concevable, imaginable. **Is it t. that . . .?** est-il admissible que+ sub.

thinker ['θiŋkər], s. Penseur, -euse.

thinness ['θinnis], s. 1. (a) Peu m d'épaisseur; minceur f; légèreté f (d'un voile). (b) Maigreur f. 2. Rareté f (des cheveux). 3. Fluidité f (d'un liquide); manque m de corps (d'un vin). 4. F: Faiblesse f (d'une excuse).

thinnish ['θiniʃ], a. F: 1. (a) Plutôt mince. (b) Assez maigre, F: maigrichon, -onne. 2. (Cheveux) assez rares. 3. (Voix) fluette.

third [θəːd]. 1. num.a. Troisième. **T. person,** (i) Jur: tierce personne, tiers m; (ii) Gram: troisième personne. **Edward the T.,** Édouard Trois. (On) **the t. of March,** le trois mars. Rail: **To travel t.,** voyager en troisième (classe). S.a. DEGREE 2. 2. s. (a) Mus:

Tierce f. (b) Aut: F: Troisième vitesse f. 3. s. (Fractional) Tiers m. -ly, adv. Troisièmement; en troisième lieu; tertio. **'third-'class,** a. (a) (Wagon) de troisième (classe). (b) De qualité inférieure; (hôtel) d'ordre inférieur. **'third-'hand,** adv.phr. **T.-h. information,** renseignements de troisième main. **'third-'rate,** a. De troisième qualité; très inférieur.

thirst[1] [θəːst], s. Soif f. **Great t.,** altération f. S.a. QUENCH 3. **The t. for knowledge,** la soif de savoir.

thirst[2], v.i. A: Avoir soif; être altéré. Lit: **To t. after sth.,** avoir soif de qch. **To t. for blood,** être altéré de sang. **thirsting,** a. Altéré, assoiffé (for, de).

thirsty ['θəːsti], a. 1. Altéré. **To be t.,** avoir soif. **To make s.o. t.,** donner soif à qn; altérer qn. F: **So much talking is t. work,** de tant parler, cela donne soif. **T. for blood, for riches,** assoiffé, avide, de sang, de richesses. 2. (Of earth) Desséché; sec, f. sèche. -ily, adv. Avidement.

thirteen ['θəː'tiːn], num. a. & s. Treize (m).

thirteenth ['θəː'tiːnθ]. 1. num. a. & s. Treizième. (On) **the t. of May,** le treize mai. 2. s. (Fractional) Treizième m.

thirtieth ['θəːtiiθ], num. a. & s. Trentième (m). (On) **the t. of June,** le trente juin.

thirty ['θəːti], num. a. & s. Trente (m). **T.-one,** trente et un. **T.-first,** trente et unième. **The t.-first of March,** le trente et un mars. **T.-two,** trente-deux. **About t. people,** une trentaine de personnes. **She is in the thirties,** elle a passé la trentaine. **The thirties (1930-39),** les années trente.

this [ðis]. I. Dem.pron., pl. **these** [ðiːz]. 1. Ceci; ce. **T. I knew,** ceci, je le savais. **Who is t.?** quelle est cette personne? **You will be sorry for t.,** vous le regretterez. **After t.,** après cela, ensuite, désormais. **It ought to have been done before t.,** cela devrait être déjà fait. **T. is a free country,** nous sommes dans un pays où l'on est libre. **T. is curious,** voilà qui est curieux. **T. is Mr Smith,** je vous présente M. Smith. **T. is where he lives,** c'est ici qu'il habite. **It was like t.,** voici comment les choses se sont passées. **The thing is t.,** voici ce dont il s'agit. **In t. their first campaign,** dans cette campagne, qui était leur première. 2. (Opposed to 'that') **Will you have t. or that?** voulez-vous ceci ou cela? **To put t. and that together,** rapprocher les faits. **Speaking of t. and that,** parlant de choses et d'autres. 3. Celui-ci, f. celle-ci, pl. ceux-ci, f. celles-ci. **I prefer these to those,** je préfère ceux-ci à ceux-là. II. **this,** dem.a., pl. **these.** (a) Ce, (before vowel or h 'mute') cet, f. cette, pl. ces; (for emphasis) ce (etc.) . . . -ci. **T. book,** these books, ce livre(-ci), ces livres(-ci). **In these days,** de nos jours. **T. day last year,** l'an dernier à pareil jour. **To run t. way and that,** courir de-ci, de-là. **There's a nip in the air these mornings,** le matin, en cette saison, l'air est piquant. S.a. ONE III. (b) **I've been watching you these ten minutes,** voilà dix minutes que je vous observe. III. **this,** dem.adv. **T. high,** aussi haut que ceci, que ça. **T. far,** jusqu'ici. S.a. MUCH 3.

thistle ['θisl], s. Bot: Chardon m. **Scotch t.,** acanthe f sauvage.

thistledown ['θisldaun], s. Duvet m de chardon.

thither ['ðiðər]. A. & Lit: 1. adv. (Expressing motion) Là; y. **To run hither and t.,** courir çà et là. 2. a. Plus lointain. **On the t. side of the mountains,** de l'autre côté des montagnes.

tho' [ðou], adv. & conj. = THOUGH.

thole(-pin) ['θoul(pin)], s. Nau: (a) Tolet m. (b) pl. = ROWLOCKS.

thong [θoŋ], s. Lanière f de cuir.

thoracic [θoːˈræsik], a. Thoracique.

thorax ['θoːræks], s. Anat: Ent: Thorax m.

thorite ['θoːrait], s. Miner: Thorite f.

thorium ['θoːriəm], s. Ch: Thorium m.

thorn [θoːn], s. (a) Épine f. F: **To be on thorns,** être sur des épines, être au supplice. **To be on a bed of thorns,** être dans une situation épineuse. **A t. in the flesh,** une épine au pied. (b) Arbrisseau épineux; épine. S.a. BLACKTHORN, HAWTHORN. **'thorn-apple,** s. Pomme épineuse; stramoine f. **'thorn-bush,** s. Buisson m d'épines. **'thorn-hedge,** s. Haie f d'épines; esp. haie d'aubépine.

thornback ['θoːnbæk], s. Ich: Raie bouclée.

thorny ['θoːni], a. Épineux, -euse.

thorough ['θʌrə], a. (a) (Of search) Minutieux, -euse; (of knowledge) profond; (of work) consciencieux, -euse. T. enquiry, enquête approfondie. To give a room a t. cleaning, nettoyer une chambre à fond. (b) A t. Frenchman, un vrai Français. A t. republican, un républicain convaincu. A t. scoundrel, un coquin achevé. -ly, adv. (Épuiser) tout à fait; (comprendre) parfaitement; (renouveler) complètement; (nettoyer) à fond. To know sth. t., savoir qch. sur le bout du doigt.

thoroughbred ['θʌrəbred]. 1. a. (Cheval) pur sang inv; (chien) de (pure) race. 2. s. (a) Cheval pur sang. (b) Animal de race. (Of pers.) She is a real t., elle est très racée.

thoroughfare ['θʌrəfɛər], s. Voie f de communication. Public t., voie publique. One of the main thoroughfares of the town, une des principales artères de la ville. Busy t., rue très passante. P.N: No t., passage interdit; rue barrée.

thoroughgoing ['θʌrəgouiŋ], a. 1. (Of rascal) Accompli, fieffé; (of socialist, etc.) enragé, à tous crins. 2. (Travailleur, etc.) consciencieux.

thoroughness ['θʌrənis], s. Caractère approfondi (des recherches); perfection f (du travail).

those [ðouz]. See THAT[1] I., II.

thou [ðau], pers. pron. A: Poet: Ecc: (a) Tu. T. seest, tu vois. (b) (Stressed) Toi. T. and I, toi et moi.

though [ðou]. I. conj. 1. Quoique, bien que, encore que, + sub. T. he is poor he is generous, quoiqu'il soit pauvre, quoique pauvre, il est généreux. I am sorry for him, t. he is nothing to me, je le plains, encore qu'il ne me soit rien. T. I am a father . . ., tout père que je suis. . . . T. small he is none the less brave, pour être petit il n'en est pas moins brave. 2. (With sub.) (a) Strange t. it may appear . . ., si étrange que cela paraisse. . . . I will do it (even) t. it cost me my fortune, je le ferai quand (bien même) cela me coûterait toute ma fortune. Even t. I could . . ., alors même que je le pourrais. . . . Lit: Vice is infamous t. it be in a prince, le vice est infâme fût-ce chez un prince. (b) Lit: What t. the way be long! qu'importe que le chemin soit long! 3. As t., comme si. It looks as t. he had gone, il semble qu'il soit parti. As t. nothing had happened . . ., comme si de rien n'était. . . . II. though, adv. (a) Cependant, pourtant. (b) (Exclamatory) Did he t.! vraiment! il a dit, fait, cela?

thought[1] [θɔːt], s. (La) pensée. 1. T. is free, la pensée est libre. Capable of t., capable de penser. 2. (a) Idée f. Happy t., heureuse idée. (b) Gloomy thoughts, pensées sombres. A penny for your thoughts, à quoi pensez-vous? To read s.o.'s thoughts, lire dans la pensée de qn. (c) The mere t. of it, rien que d'y penser. I did not give it another t., je n'y ai pas repensé. (d) pl. Esprit m, pensée. To collect one's thoughts, rassembler ses idées, ses esprits. Her thoughts were elsewhere, son esprit était ailleurs. 3. (a) Réflexion f, considération f. Want of t., irréflexion f. After much t., après mûre réflexion. He has no t. for his mother, il n'a pas de considération pour sa mère. On second thoughts, (toute) réflexion faite. Lit: To take no t. for the morrow, ne pas songer au lendemain. (b) Pensées, rêverie f, méditation f. Lost, deep in t., perdu dans ses pensées, plongé dans ses méditations. 4. (a) Intention f, dessein m. To have thoughts of doing sth., avoir la pensée de faire qch.; songer à faire qch. I had no t. of offending you, je n'avais pas l'intention de vous offenser. His one t. is to get money, il ne pense qu'à l'argent. With the t. of . . ., dans le dessein de. . . . (b) (Usu. neg.) I had no t. of meeting you here, je ne m'attendais pas à vous rencontrer ici. 5. Adv.phr. F: A t., un tout petit peu, un tantinet. The ribbon is a t. too blue, le ruban est d'un rien trop bleu. 'thought-reader, s. Liseur, -euse, de pensées. 'thought-reading, s. Lecture f de la pensée; télépathie f. 'thought-transference, s. Télépathie f.

thought[2], v. See THINK[2].

thoughtful ['θɔːtf(u)l], a. 1. (a) Pensif, -ive, méditatif, -ive; rêveur, -euse. (b) Réfléchi, prudent. 2. Prévenant (of, pour). To be t. of others, être plein d'égards pour les autres. He was t. enough to notify me, il a eu la prévenance de m'avertir. 3. (Of book) Profond. -fully, adv. 1. Pensivement. 2. D'une manière réfléchie. 3. Avec prévenance.

thoughtfulness ['θɔːtf(u)lnis], s. 1. Méditation recueillement m. 2. Réflexion f, prudence f. Prévenance f, égards mpl (of, pour, envers).

thoughtless ['θɔːtlis], a. 1. Irréfléchi, mal avisé étourdi. T. action, étourderie f. 2. T. of others, pe soucieux des autres. -ly, adv. Étourdiment; (agir à la légère.

thoughtlessness ['θɔːtlisnis], s. 1. Irréflexion f étourderie f. 2. Manque m d'égards (of, pour envers).

thousand ['θauz(ə)nd], num. a. & s. Mille (m) inv; s millier m. A t. men, mille hommes. Com: A t needles, un mille d'aiguilles. About a t. men, u millier d'hommes; quelque mille hommes. F: paid five t. for it, je l'ai payé cinq mille (livres). Th year 4000 B.C., l'an quatre mille avant J.-C. Jur The year one thousand nine hundred and thirty, l'a mil neuf cent trente. A t. years, un millénaire Thousands of people, des milliers de gens. Thousand upon thousands, des milliers. He is one in a t., c'es un homme entre mille. A t. apologies! (je vou demande) mille fois pardon! mille pardons! No, no a t. times no! non, non, et cent fois non!

thousandfold ['θauzənd,fould]. 1. a. Multiplié pa mille. 2. adv. Mille fois autant.

thousandth ['θauz(ə)n(t)θ], num. a. & s. Millième.

thraldom ['θrɔːldəm], s. Lit: Esclavage m, servitude f

thrall [θrɔːl], s. Lit: 1. Esclave m, serf m (of, to, de) 2. = THRALDOM.

thrash [θræʃ], v.tr. 1. (a) Battre (qn); F: rosser étriller (qn). (b) Battre (un adversaire) à plate coutures. 2. (a) Husb: = THRESH. (b) Swim: To t the water, battre l'eau (avec les jambes). 3. Abs. (a Nau: To t. to windward, marcher vent debout. (b Mec.E: Vibrer. thrash out, v.tr. Débattre, creuse (une question); démêler (la vérité). thrashing, s. 1 (a) Rossée f, correction f. To give s.o. a t., administre une raclée à qn. (b) F: Sp: Défaite f. 2. (a) Husb: = THRESHING. (b) Battement m (de la pluie). (c) Mec.E Vibration (d'un vilebrequin) due à la torsion.

thread[1] [θred], s. 1. Filament m, fil m (de soie). T hang by a t., ne tenir qu'à un fil. 2. (a) Needlew: Fi (de coton); esp. fil de lin. Sewing t., fil à coudre Gold t., fil d'or. (b) Tex: Fil (de trame ou de chaîne) The t. of life, la trame de la vie. To lose the t. of one' discourse, perdre le fil de son discours. (c) (Length of) t., brin m, bout m (de coton, etc.). 3. Tchn: File m, filetage m, pas m (de vis). Worn t., filetage usé mangé. 'thread-cutter, s. Metalw: Tour m à fileter; taraudeuse f. 'thread-like, a. Filiforme.

thread[2], v.tr. 1. Enfiler (une aiguille, des perles) passer, enfiler (un élastique). 2. To t. one's way through the crowd, se faufiler à travers la foule. 3 Fileter (une vis); tarauder (un tuyau).

threadbare ['θredbɛər], a. (a) (Of clothes) Râpé élimé; qui montre la corde. (b) (Of argument) Usé (jusqu'à la corde).

threadworm ['θredwəːm], s. 1. Ann: Nématode m. 2 Med: Ascaride m, trichine f.

threat [θret], s. Menace f. (a) To utter a t., proférer une menace. To be under the t. of expulsion, être sous le coup d'un arrêté d'expulsion. (b) There is a t. of rain, la pluie menace.

threaten ['θretn], v.tr. 1. Menacer. Jur: Intimider. To t. s.o. with sth., menacer qn de qch. He threatened him with dismissal, il menaça de le renvoyer. To t. to do sth., menacer de faire qch. 2. The sky threatens rain, le ciel annonce la pluie. Abs. A storm is threatening, la tempête, l'orage, menace. threatening, a. (Ton) menaçant. T. letter, lettre de menaces; Jur: lettre comminatoire. The weather looks t., le temps menace. To put a t. tone into one's voice, faire la grosse voix. -ly, adv. D'un air menaçant.

three [θriː], num. a. & s. Trois (m). Number t., le numéro trois. Pol: The Big T., Les Trois (Grands). To enter t. by t., entrer par trois. S.a. R. (For other phrases, see EIGHT.) 'three-act, attrib.a. Th. (Pièce) en trois actes. 'three-colour(ed), a. Phot: Trichrome. 'three-'cornered, a. Triangulaire; (of hat) tricorne. Pol: T.-c. fight, élection f triangulaire. S.a. FILE[1] 1. 'three-di'mensional, a. Tridimensionnel, -elle, à trois dimensions. 'three-'decker,

Nau: A: Trois-ponts *m.* 'three-element, 'three-e'lectrode, *attrib.a. W.Tel:* (Lampe) triode. 'three-'engined, *a. Av:* (Avion) trimoteur. 'three-'four, *a. Mus:* T.-f. time, trois-quatre *m.* three-halfpence [θriː'heipəns], *s.* Un penny et demi. 'three-'handed, *a. Cards:* T.-h. game, partie à trois. 'three-'legged, *a.* (Tabouret, etc.) à trois pieds. 'three-'masted, *a. Nau:* (Vaisseau) à trois mâts. 'three-'master, *s. Nau:* Trois-mâts *m.* 'three-'party, *a.* Tripartite. T.-p. government, coalition, tripartisme *m.* 'three-phase, *attrib.a. El.E:* Triphasé. 'three-piece, *attrib.a.* En trois pièces. (Lady's) t.-p. suit, trois-pièces *m.* 'three-ply, *attrib.a.* 1. T.-ply wood, contre-plaqué *m* à trois épaisseurs. 2. (*Of wool*) A trois fils, à trois brins. three-'quarter, *attrib.a.* (Portrait) de trois quarts. T.-q. fiddle, trois-quarts *m. Fb:* T.-q. back, *s.* three-quarter, trois-quarts. (Ladies') t.-q. length coat, trois-quarts *m.* 'three-speed, *attrib.a.* A trois vitesses. 'three-way, *attrib.a.* (Soupape, robinet) à trois voies. *El:* (Commutateur) triple. 'three-'wheeled, *a.* A trois roues. 'three-'wheeler, *s. Aut:* (Petite) voiture à trois roues.

threefold ['θriːfould]. 1. *a.* Triple. 2. *adv.* Trois fois autant. **To increase t.**, tripler.

threepence ['θrep(ə)ns, 'θri-, 'θrʌ-], *s.* (La somme de) trois pence *m.*

threepenny ['θrep(ə)ni, 'θri-, 'θrʌ-], *attrib.a.* (Article) coûtant trois pence. **T. bit**, pièce *f* de trois pence.

threescore ['θriːskɔːr], *a. Lit:* Soixante.

threesome ['θriːsəm], *s. Golf:* Partie *f* à trois.

thresh [θreʃ], *v.tr.* 1. Battre (le blé). 2. (*Of ship's screw*) To t. the water, battre l'eau. **threshing**, *s.* Battage *m* (des blés). 'threshing-floor, *s.* Aire *f.* 'threshing-machine, *s.* Batteuse *f.*

thresher ['θreʃər], *s.* 1. *Husb:* (a) Batteur *m* en grange. (b) (*Machine*) Batteuse *f.* 2. *Ich:* Renard marin.

threshold ['θreʃ(h)ould], *s.* 1. Seuil *m*, pas *m* (d'une porte). To cross the t., franchir le seuil. 2. *Psy: Physiol:* Seuil (de la perception, de l'excitation, etc.).

threw. See THROW².

thrice [θrais], *adv. Lit:* 1. Trois fois. **T. as great**, trois fois plus grand. 2. **T.-told tale**, histoire rebattue.

thrift [θrift], *s.* 1. Économie *f*, épargne *f.* 2. *Bot:* Statice *m.* Sea-t., gazon *m* d'Olympe.

thriftiness ['θriftinis], *s.* Économie *f.*

thriftless ['θriftlis], *a.* 1. Dépensier, -ière, prodigue. 2. Sans soin; imprévoyant.

thriftlessness ['θriftlisnis], *s.* 1. Prodigalité *f.* 2. Manque *m* de soin; imprévoyance *f.*

thrifty ['θrifti], *a.* Économe, ménager, -ère. *U.S:* (*Of plant*) Vigoureux, -euse; de belle venue; (*of pers.*) prospère. **-ily**, *adv.* Avec économie. To live t., vivre frugalement.

thrill¹ [θril], *s.* (a) Frisson *m*, tressaillement *m.* (b) (Vive) émotion. It gave me quite a t., ça m'a fait quelque chose.

thrill². 1. *v.tr.* (a) Faire frissonner, faire frémir (qn). To be thrilled with joy, tressaillir de joie. (b) Émouvoir, empoigner (qn); *F:* électriser (son auditoire). To be thrilled at the sight of sth., ressentir une vive émotion à la vue de qch. 2. *v.i.* Tressaillir, frissonner, frémir. **thrilling**, *a.* (Spectacle) empoignant, émouvant; (roman) sensationnel. *Rac:* T. finish, arrivée palpitante.

thriller ['θrilər], *s.* (a) Roman *m*, film *m*, pièce *f*, à sensation. (b) *Occ:* Roman policier.

thrive [θraiv], *v.i.* (*p.t.* throve [θrouv], thrived; *p.p.* thriven ['θrivn], thrived) (a) (*Of child, plant*) Se (bien) développer; (*of plant*) réussir, bien venir; (*of business*) bien marcher. **Children who t. on milk**, enfants à qui le lait profite bien. **Plant that thrives in all soils**, plante qui s'accommode de tous les sols. He thrives on it, il s'en trouve bien. (b) (*Of pers.*) Prospérer. To t. on other people's misfortunes, s'engraisser des misères d'autrui. **thriving**, *a.* Vigoureux, -euse; (*of pers., business*) prospère, florissant.

throat [θrout], *s.* 1. (a) *Anat:* Gorge *f.* To grip s.o. by the t., empoigner qn à la gorge. To cut s.o.'s t., couper la gorge à qn; égorger qn. *F:* He is cutting

his own t., il travaille à sa propre ruine. (b) Gorge, gosier *m.* To have a fish-bone in one's t., avoir une arête dans le gosier. I have a sore t., j'ai mal à la gorge. To clear one's t., s'éclaircir le gosier, la voix; tousser un coup. *F:* He's always ramming it down my t., il m'en rabat toujours les oreilles. *S.a.* JUMP² I. 1, STICK² II. 3. 2. *Nau:* Mâchoire *f* (de corne, de gui). 3. Gueulard *m* (de haut fourneau). 'throat spray, *s.* Vaporisateur *m* (pour la gorge).

throatiness ['θroutinis], *s.* Qualité gutturale (de la voix).

throaty ['θrouti], *a.* (*Of voice*) D'arrière-gorge; guttural, -aux.

throb¹ [θrɔb], *s.* Pulsation *f*, battement *m* (du cœur); vrombissement *m* (d'une machine).

throb², *v.i.* (throbbed) (a) (*Of heart*) Battre fort; palpiter; (*of engine, etc.*) vrombir. His heart throbbed with joy, son cœur tressaillit de joie. (b) My finger is throbbing, le doigt me lancine, j'ai des élancements dans le doigt. **throbbing**, *s.* (a) Battement *m*, pulsation *f*, palpitation *f* (du cœur); vrombissement *m* (d'une machine). (b) Lancination *f*, élancement *m* (d'un panaris).

throes [θrouz], *s.pl.* Douleurs *fpl*, angoisse *f*, agonie *f.* The t. of death, les affres *f* de la mort; l'agonie. England was in the t. of a general election, l'Angleterre était au beau milieu des élections.

thrombosis [θrɔm'bousis], *s. Med:* Thrombose *f.* Coronary t., infarctus *m* du myocarde.

thrombus ['θrɔmbəs], *s. Med:* Thrombus *m*; caillot sanguin.

throne [θroun], *s.* Trône (royal ou épiscopal). To come to the t.; to mount the t., venir au trône; monter sur le trône.

throng¹ [θrɔŋ], *s.* (a) Foule *f*, affluence *f.* (b) Cohue *f.*

throng². 1. *v.i.* S'assembler en foule; affluer (à, dans, un endroit). To t. round s.o., se presser autour de qn. 2. *v.tr.* Encombrer (les rues). **thronged**, *a.* (*Of street, etc.*) Plein de gens; (*of hall*) comble, bondé. Everywhere was t., la foule se pressait partout. **thronging**, *a.* (*Of crowd*) Serré, compact.

throstle ['θrɔsl], *s.* 1. Grive musicienne. 2. *Tex:* Métier continu.

throttle¹ ['θrɔtl], *s.* 1. *F:* Gosier *m.* 2. *Mch: I.C.E:* Papillon *m.* To open out the t., mettre les gaz. 'throttle-chamber, *s. I.C.E:* Boisseau *m.* 'throttle-lever, *s. I.C.E:* Manette *f* des gaz.

throttle², *v.tr.* 1. Étrangler; serrer (qn) à la gorge. 2. *Mch: I.C.E:* Étrangler (la vapeur, le moteur). *Abs.* To t. down, mettre le moteur au ralenti; fermer le(s) gaz. **throttling**, *s.* Étranglement *m.*

through [θruː]. I. *prep.* 1. (a) A travers; par. T. a hedge, au travers d'une haie. A narrow path leads t. the forest, un chemin étroit traverse la forêt. To look t. the window, regarder par la fenêtre. To look t. a telescope, regarder dans un télescope. *F:* To go t. s.o.'s pockets, fouiller qn. *F:* He's been t. it, il en a vu de dures. To speak t. one's nose, parler du nez. *F:* He is t. his examination, il a été reçu à son examen. I am half t. this book, j'ai lu la moitié de ce livre. I have got t. this book, j'ai fini ce livre. *S.a.* PUT² I. 5. (b) Pendant, durant. All t. his life, sa vie durant. To sleep the night t., faire la nuit tout d'un somme. To sleep t. a thunderstorm, ne pas se réveiller pendant toute la durée d'un orage. 2. T. s.o., par qn; par l'entremise de qn. To send sth. t. the post, envoyer qch. par la poste. (c) *U.S:* Monday t. Friday, de lundi à vendredi; du lundi au vendredi. 3. (a) En conséquence de, à cause de (qch.). T. ignorance, par ignorance. Absent t. illness, absent par suite, pour cause, de maladie. To act t. fear, agir sous le coup de la peur. (b) Par l'action de (qn, qch.). It all happened t. him, il est cause de tout. II. through, *adv.* 1. (a) A travers. The water poured t., l'eau coulait à travers. To let s.o. t., laisser passer qn. (b) T. (and t.), de bout en bout; de part en part. To run s.o. t. (with one's sword), transpercer qn. *S.a.* WET¹ 1. (c) D'un bout à l'autre; jusqu'au bout. To see sth. t., mener qch. à bonne fin. The lesson is half t., la leçon est à moitié finie. *U.S: Tp:* Are you t.? terminé? I am t. with you, j'en ai fini avec vous. *S.a.* SEE THROUGH 2. 2. (a) The train runs t. to Paris, le train va directement à Paris. (b) *Tp:* To get t. to s.o., obtenir la communication avec qn. I can't get t. to him, je ne peux pas l'avoir. I'm putting you t. to the secretary, je vous passe le secrétaire. You are t., vous avez la communication. III. **through**, *attrib.a. Rail:* T. **carriage for** . . ., voiture directe pour. . . . T. **coach**, wagon *m* de groupage. T. **traffic**, transit *m. U.S:* T. **street**, rue à circulation prioritaire. **'through-stone**, s. *Const:* Parpaing *m.*

throughout [θru'aut]. 1. *prep.* (a) T. **the country**, d'un bout à l'autre du pays, dans tout le pays. T. **France**, partout en France. (b) T. **the year**, pendant toute l'année. 2. *adv.* (a) **House with central heating t.**, maison avec chauffage central dans toutes les pièces. **Leather-lined t.**, doublé entièrement en peau. (b) Tout le temps.

throughway ['θru:wei], s. *U.S:* Autoroute *f.*

throve. *See* THRIVE.

throw¹ [θrou], s. 1. (a) Jet *m*, lancement *m*, lancer *m* (de qch.). T. **of dice**, coup *m* de dés. (b) **Long t.**, jet d'une longue portée. *S.a.* STONE'S THROW. (c) *Wr:* Mise *f* à terre (de l'adversaire). 2. *Geol:* Rejet *m* (dans une stratification). 3. *Mec.E:* T. **of the piston**, course *f*, du piston.

throw², *v.r.* (threw [θru:]; thrown [θroun]) 1. (a) Jeter, lancer (une balle). *Abs.* **He can t. a hundred yards**, il est capable de lancer à cent mètres. **To t. s.o. a kiss**, envoyer un baiser à qn. **To t. a glance at s.o.**, jeter un coup d'œil à, sur, qn. **To t. oneself backwards**, se rejeter en arrière. **To t. temptation in s.o.'s way**, exposer qn à la tentation. **To t. the blame on s.o.**, rejeter la faute sur qn. *S.a.* MONEY 1, MUD, WATER¹ 1. (b) **To t. a sheet over sth.**, couvrir qch. d'un drap. **To t. oneself into the fray**, s'élancer à l'assaut. **To t. oneself on s.o.'s generosity**, s'en remettre à la générosité de qn. **To be thrown upon one's own resources**, n'avoir plus à compter que sur soi-même. **To t. two rooms into one**, de deux pièces n'en faire qu'une. **To t. open the door**, ouvrir la porte toute grande. *S.a.* GEAR¹ 3, WORK¹ 4. 2. (a) Projeter (des éclaboussures). (b) **To t. a picture on the screen**, projeter une image sur l'écran. **To t. light on the matter**, jeter de la lumière sur une question. 3. *F:* **To t. a fit**, tomber en convulsions; piquer une attaque de nerfs. *F:* **To t. a party**, inviter des amis à une réunion. 4. (a) *Wr:* **To t. an opponent**, terrasser un adversaire. (b) (*Of horse*) **To t. its rider**, démonter son cavalier. (*Of rider*) **To be thrown**, être désarçonné. 5. *Cer:* Tourner (un pot). **throw about**, *v.tr.* 1. Jeter (des objets) çà et là; éparpiller. **To t. one's money about**, gaspiller son argent. 2. (a) **To t. one's arms about**, faire de grands gestes. **To t. oneself about**, se démener. (b) **To be thrown about**, être ballotté, cahoté. **throw aside**, *v.tr.* Jeter (qch.) de côté. **throw away**, *v.tr.* 1. Jeter (son cigare); rejeter (qch.); mettre (qch.) au rebut. 2. Donner (qch.) inutilement; gaspiller. **To t. away a chance**, laisser passer une occasion. **To t. away one's life**, se sacrifier inutilement. (*Of girl*) **To t. herself away**, se marier avec un homme indigne d'elle. **throw back**, 1. *v.tr.* (a) Rejeter (un poisson dans l'eau); renvoyer (une balle); réverbérer (la lumière). (b) **To t. back one's shoulders**, effacer les épaules. (c) Retarder (un travail). (d) **To be thrown back upon s.o.**, être forcé de se rabattre sur qn. 2. *v.i.* (*Of breed*) Retourner à un type antérieur. **'throw-back**, s. 1. Recul *m* (dans le progrès); échec *m.* 2. *Biol:* Retour *m* atavique, régression *f.* **throw down**, *v.tr.* (a) Jeter (qch.) de haut en bas. (b) Jeter (qch.) à terre; abattre (ses cartes). (c) **To t. down one's arms**, (i) abandonner ses armes; (ii) se rendre. *Ind:* **To t. down one's tools**, se mettre en grève. **throw in**, *v.tr.* 1. Jeter (qch.) dedans. 2. (a) Ajouter (qch.); donner (qch.) par-dessus le marché. (b) Placer (un mot). **To t. in one's lot with s.o.**, partager le sort de qn. 4. (a) **To t. in one's hand, one's cards**, abandonner la partie. (b) *Fb:* **To t. in**, remettre en touche. **'throw-in**, s. *Fb:* Remise *f* en jeu, en touche. **throw off**, *v.tr.* 1. (a) Jeter, rendre (de la vapeur). (b) Enlever, quitter (ses vêtements); se débarrasser de (qn, qch.); abandonner (un déguisement); lever (le masque). **To t. off a bad habit**, se défaire d'une mauvaise habitude. *S.a.* YOKE¹ 1. 2. (a) **To t. a train off the rails**, faire dérailler un train. (b) **To t. the dogs off the scent**,

dépister les chiens. *S.a.* GUARD¹ 1. **throw out**, *v.tr.* 1. Jeter (qch.) dehors; expulser (qn). 2. Répandre, émettre (de la chaleur). 3. (a) Rejeter (un projet de loi). *Cards:* Se défausser (d'une carte), écarter (une carte). (b) *Aut:* **To t. out the clutch**, débrayer. 4. (a) **To t. out one's chest**, bomber la poitrine. (b) *Mil:* T. **t. out skirmishers**, envoyer des tirailleurs en avant. 5. Lancer, laisser entendre (des insinuations). **'throw-outs**, *s.pl. Com:* Rebuts *m.* **throw over**, *v.tr.* 1. Abandonner (ses confédérés). 2. *Mec.E:* Renverser (un levier). *S.a.* POINT II. 4. **throw together**, *v.tr.* 1. Assembler (qch.) à la hâte. 2. **Chance had thrown us together**, le hasard nous avait réunis. **throw up**, *v.tr.* 1. Jeter (qch.) en l'air. *S.a.* SPONGE¹ 1. 2. (a) Vomir, rejeter, rendre. **Volcano that throws up lava**, volcan qui vomit de la lave. (b) *Abs. P:* (*Of pers*) Vomir, rejeter. 3. Lever haut, mettre haut (les mains). 4. Construire à la hâte (une maison). 5. Renoncer à, abandonner. **To feel like throwing everything up**, avoir envie de tout plaquer. **To t. up one's job**, se démettre de son poste.

throwaway ['θrouǝwei]. 1. *a. Th: etc:* (*Phrase*) énoncée avec une indifférence calculée. 2. *s. F U.S:* Prospectus *m.*

thrower ['θrouǝr], s. Lanceur, -euse. **Discus t.**, discobole *m.*

thru [θru:], *U.S: F:* = THROUGH.

thrum¹ [θrʌm], s. *Tex:* (*Usu. pl.*) Penne(s) *f(pl)*, bouts laissés à la fin de la pièce.

thrum², *v.tr. & i.* = STRUM.

thrush¹ [θrʌʃ], s. *Orn:* Grive *f.*

thrush², s. 1. *Med:* Muguet *m.* 2. *Vet:* Échauffement *m* de la fourchette (du cheval).

thrust¹ [θrʌst], s. 1. (a) Poussée *f.* (b) Coup *m* de pointe. *Fenc:* Coup d'estoc. **T. and parry**, la botte et la parade. **A shrewd t.**, un trait, une critique, une frappe juste. 2. (a) *Arch: Mec:* Poussée, butée *f.* (b) *Geol:* Chevauchement *m* (des plissements). **'thrust-block**, s. Palier *m* de butée.

thrust², *v.* (thrust; thrust) 1. *v.tr.* (a) Pousser (avec force). **To t. one's hands into one's pockets**, fourrer les mains dans ses poches. **To t. a dagger into s.o.'s back**, enfoncer un poignard dans le dos de qn. (b) **To t. oneself upon s.o.**, s'imposer à qn, chez qn. (c) **To t. (one's way) through the crowd**, se frayer un chemin à travers la foule. **To t. past s.o.**, écarter qn pour passer. 2. *v.i.* **To t. at s.o.**, porter un coup de pointe à qn; *Fenc:* porter, pousser, une botte à qn. **To t. in tierce**, tirer en tierce. **thrust aside, away**, *v.tr.* Repousser, écarter (qn, qch.). **thrust back**, *v.tr.* Repousser violemment (la porte). **thrust forward**, *v.tr.* 1. Pousser (qn, qch.) en avant; avancer (la main). 2. **To t. oneself forward**, (i) se mettre en avant; (ii) s'ingérer dans une affaire.

thruster ['θrʌstǝr], s. (a) Chasseur *m* à courre qui pousse de l'avant. (b) *F:* Arriviste *mf.*

thud¹ [θʌd], s. Bruit sourd; son mat; floc *m.*

thud², *v.i.* (thudded) Tomber avec un bruit sourd; émettre un bruit mat.

thug [θʌg], s. 1. *Hist:* Thug *m*, étrangleur *m.* 2. *F:* Apache *m*, assassin *m*, bandit *m.*

thumb¹ [θʌm], s. 1. Pouce *m.* **To hold sth. between finger and t.**, tenir qch. entre le pouce et l'index. *F:* **His fingers are all thumbs**, il est maladroit de ses mains. **To be under s.o.'s t.**, être sous la domination, sous la coupe, de qn. **To twiddle one's thumbs**, se tourner les pouces. *F:* **Thumbs up!** (i) chic alors! (ii) on les eus! *S.a.* RULE¹ 1. **'thumb-index**, s. 1. Bound with t.-i., relié avec encoches. 2. Répertoire *m* à onglets. **'thumb-nail**, s. Ongle *m* du pouce. T.-n. sketch, croquis *m* minuscule, hâtif. **'thumb-piece**, s. Poucier *m*, poussoir *m* (d'un loquet). **'thumb-print**, s. Marque *f* de pouce. **'thumb-screw**, s. 1. Vis *f* à ailettes; papillon *m.* 2. *Hist:* Poucettes *fpl* (de torture). **'thumb-stall**, s. Poucier *m* (de cordonnier); *Med:* Doigtier *m* pour pouce.

thumb², *v.tr.* 1. Manier (qch.) maladroitement. 2. **Well-thumbed book**, livre fatigué; livre souvent feuilleté. 3. *F:* **To t. a lift**, faire de l'auto-stop.

thumbtack ['θʌmtæk], s. *U.S:* Punaise *f* (pour planche à dessin).

thump¹ [θʌmp], s. 1. Coup sourd; cognement *m* (d'un mécanisme). 2. Coup de poing; bourrade *f.*

thump², *v.tr. & i.* Bourrer (qn) de coups. **To t. (on) the table,** frapper du poing sur la table. **To t. out a tune,** taper un air (au piano). **My heart was thumping,** mon cœur battait fort. **thumping,** *a.* *F: O:* Énorme. **This is a t. lie,** le mensonage est de taille.

thunder¹ ['θʌndər], *s.* 1. (*a*) Tonnerre *m.* **Peal of t.,** coup *m* de tonnerre. **There is t. in the air,** (i) le temps est à l'orage; (ii) l'atmosphère (d'une réunion) est orageuse. (*b*) **T. of applause,** tonnerre d'applaudissements. 2. (*a*) La foudre. (*b*) **To steal s.o.'s t.,** couper l'herbe sous le pied à qn, *F:* couper ses effets à qn. *S.a.* BLACK¹ I. 1. **'thunder-clap,** *s.* Coup *m* de tonnerre. **'thunder-cloud,** *s.* Nuage orageux. **'thunder-storm,** *s.* Orage *m.*

thunder², *v.i. & tr.* 1. Tonner. **It is thundering,** il tonne. **The artillery is thundering past us,** l'artillerie passe devant nous avec un bruit de tonnerre. **The sea thunders under our windows,** la mer gronde sous nos fenêtres. 2. (*Of pers.*) Tonitruer. **To t. (out) threats,** fulminer des menaces. **To t. out an order,** donner un ordre d'une voix tonnante. **thundering¹,** *a.* 1. Tonnant; fulminant. 2. *F:* **To be in a t. rage,** être dans une rage à tout casser. *F: O:* **What a t. nuisance!** ce que c'est embêtant! *adv. F: O:* **A t. great fish,** un poisson formidable. **thundering²,** *s.* 1. Tonnerre *m.* 2. Bruit retentissant.

thunderbolt ['θʌndəboult], *s.* 1. (Coup *m* de) foudre *f. S.a.* JOVE. 2. Nouvelle foudroyante. 3. *A:* Météorite *m.*

thunderous ['θʌnd(ə)rəs], *a.* 1. Orageux, -euse. 2. (*Of voice*) Tonnant; (*of applause*) à tout rompre.

thunderstruck ['θʌndəstrʌk], *a.* Confondu, abasourdi, sidéré. **To be t.,** tomber des nues; être atterré.

thundery ['θʌndəri], *a.* Orageux, -euse.

thurible ['θjuəribl], *s. Ecc:* Encensoir *m.*

thurifer ['θjuərifər], *s. Ecc:* Thuriféraire *m.*

Thursday ['θə:zdi], *s.* Jeudi *m.* **Maundy T.,** le jeudi saint. (*For other phrases see* FRIDAY.)

thus [ðʌs], *adv.* 1. Ainsi; de cette façon. **If you do it t.,** si vous le faites comme ceci, comme cela. 2. Ainsi, donc. **T., when he arrived . . .,** donc, lorsqu'il arriva. . . . 3. **T. far,** jusqu'ici; jusque-là. **Having gone t. far,** arrivé là.

thuya ['θju:jə], *s. Bot:* Thuya *m.*

thwack¹,² [θwæk], *s. & v.tr.* = WHACK¹,².

thwart¹ [θwɔ:t], *s.* Banc *m* de nage (d'une embarcation).

thwart², *v.tr.* Contrecarrer (qn); déjouer les menées de (qn). **To t. s.o.'s plans,** se mettre en travers des projets de qn. **To be thwarted,** essuyer un échec.

thy [ðai], *poss.a.* (**thine** *before a vowel sound*) *A: Ecc: Lit:* Ton, *f.* ta, *pl.* tes. **T. service,** ton service. **T. glory,** ta gloire. **T. friendship,** ton amitié *f.* **Thine own son,** ton propre fils.

thyme [taim], *s. Bot:* Thym *m.* **Wild t.,** serpolet *m.*

thymol ['θaiməl], *s. Pharm:* Thymol *m.*

thymus ['θaiməs], *s.* **T. (gland),** thymus *m.*

thyratron ['θaiərətron], *s. El:* Thyratron *m.*

thyroid ['θaiərɔid], *a. Anat:* (Glande *f,* cartilage *m*) thyroïde.

thyroidal [θai'rɔid(ə)l], *a. Med:* Thyroïdien, -ienne.

thyroidism ['θaiərɔidizm], *s. Med:* Thyroïdisme *m.*

thyself [ðai'self], *pron. See* SELF 4.

tiara [ti'ɑ:rə], *s.* Tiare *f.*

Tiber (the) [ðə'taibər], *Pr.n. Geog:* Le Tibre.

Tiberius [tai'biəriəs], *Pr.n.m. Hist:* Tibère.

Tibet [ti'bet], *Pr.n. Geog:* Le Tibet.

Tibetan [ti'bet(ə)n], *a. & s.* Tibétain, -aine.

tibia, *pl.* -ae ['tibii:, -i:], *s.* Tibia *m.*

tic [tik], *s. Med:* 1. Tic *m.* 2. Tic douloureux.

tick¹ [tik], *s.* 1. (*a*) Tic-tac *m. F:* **On the t.,** à l'heure tapante. **On the t. of seven,** à sept heures tapant. (*b*) *F:* Moment *m,* instant *m.* **Half a t.!** un instant! **He'll do it in two ticks,** il fera ça en moins de rien. 2. Marque *f,* pointage *m,* trait *m.* **To put a t. against a name,** pointer, cocher, un nom. **'tick-'tack, 'tick-'tock,** *s.* Tic-tac *m.*

tick², *v.i.* (*Of clock*) Faire tic-tac, tictaquer. *F:* **I'd like to know what makes him t.,** je voudrais bien savoir ce qui le pousse. 2. *v.tr.* = TICK OFF 1. **tick off,** *v.tr.* 1. Pointer (une liste). **To t. off a name,** cocher un nom. 2. *F:* Rembarrer (qn). **tick out,** *v.tr.* (*Of telegraph*) Enregistrer (un message). **tick**

over, *v.i. I.C.E:* (*Of engine*) Tourner au (grand) ralenti. **The business is just ticking over,** l'affaire marche tout doucement. **ticking¹,** *s.* Tic-tac *m.*

tick³, *s.* 1. *Arach:* Tique *f* (du bétail). 2. *Ent:* Hippobosque *m,* mouche *f* araignée. 3. *P:* **A nasty little t.,** un petit salaud.

tick⁴, *s. F:* Crédit *m.* **To buy sth. on t.,** acheter qch. à crédit.

tick⁵, *s.* 1. Enveloppe *f,* toile *f* (à matelas). 2. = TICKING².

ticker ['tikər], *s.* 1. (*a*) *F:* Montre *f; P:* tocante *f.* (*b*) *F:* Le cœur. 2. Téléimprimeur *m.* **'ticker-tape,** *s. Tg:* Bande *f* (de téléimprimeur).

ticket¹ ['tikit], *s.* 1. Billet *m* (de chemin de fer); ticket *m* (d'autobus). **Complimentary t.,** billet de faveur. **Cloak-room t.,** numéro *m* de vestiaire. *Rail:* **Single t.,** aller *m.* **Return t.** (billet d')aller et retour. **Left-luggage t., cloak-room t.,** bulletin *m* de consigne. **Platform t.,** billet de quai; laissez-passer *m inv.* **Reader's t.,** carte *f* de lecteur. *Adm:* Papillon *m.* **To fix a t.** (*on a windscreen for a fine*), coller un papillon (sur le pare-brise pour une contravention). **To get a t.,** attraper une contravention. 2. *Com:* (Price-)t., étiquette *f;* fiche *f.* 3. *Pol: U.S: F:* (*a*) Liste électorale. **To vote a straight t.,** voter pour la liste entière. **To vote a split t.,** faire du panachage. **The democratic t.,** le programme du parti démocrate. 4. (*a*) *Mil: Nau:* **To get one's t.,** être libéré. (*b*) *Nau: F:* **To get one's (master's) t.,** passer capitaine. *Av:* **To get one's (pilot's) t.,** obtenir son brevet de pilote. (*c*) *See* LEAVE¹ 2. 5. *P:* **That's the t.!** voilà qui fera l'affaire! à la bonne heure! *F:* Ça colle! **'ticket-collector,** *s. Rail:* Contrôleur *m* (de billets). **'ticket-holder,** *s.* Voyageur, spectateur, muni d'un billet. **Season-ticket-holder,** abonné(e). **'ticket-inspector,** *s.* Contrôleur *m* (d'autobus). **ticket-office,** *s. U.S:* = BOOKING-OFFICE. **'ticket-punch,** *s. Rail:* Poinçon *m* de contrôleur.

ticket², *v.tr.* (ticketed) Étiqueter, marquer (des marchandises).

ticking² ['tikiŋ], *s.* Toile *f,* coutil *m,* à matelas.

tickle¹ ['tikl], *s.* Chatouillement *m.*

tickle². 1. *v.tr.* (*a*) Chatouiller. (*Of food*) **To t. the palate,** chatouiller le palais. **To t. s.o.'s fancy,** amuser qn. (*b*) *F:* Amuser. **To be tickled to death at sth.,** se tordre de rire à l'idée de qch. (*c*) *Aut:* **To t. the carburettor,** amorcer, *F:* titiller, le carburateur. (*d*) Pêcher (la truite) à la main. 2. *v.i.* **My hand tickles,** la main me démange. **tickle up,** *v.tr. F:* Exciter, stimuler. **tickling¹,** *a.* Qui chatouille. **T. cough,** toux d'irritation. **tickling²,** *s.* 1. Chatouillement *m.* 2. *Fish:* Pêche *f* à la main.

tickler ['tiklər], *s.* 1. *I.C.E:* Poussoir *m* (du carburateur). 2. (*a*) Question embarrassante. (*b*) Sujet délicat. 3. *F:* **Memory t.,** pense-bête *m, pl.* pense-bêtes.

ticklish ['tikliʃ], *a.* 1. Chatouilleux, -euse. **To be t.,** craindre les chatouilles. 2. (*a*) (*Of pers.*) Susceptible. (*b*) (*Of task*) Délicat; (*of undertaking*) scabreux, -euse. **A t. subject,** un sujet brûlant.

ticklishness ['tikliʃnis], *s.* 1. Sensibilité *f* au chatouillement. 2. (*a*) Susceptibilité *f.* (*b*) Délicatesse *f* (d'une tâche).

tidal ['taid(ə)l], *a.* 1. Qui relève de la marée. **T. wave,** (i) raz *m* de marée; vague *f* de fond; (*in estuary*) mascaret *m;* (ii) vague d'enthousiasme, d'indignation). 2. (*Of river, harbour*) A marée. **T. basin,** bassin à flot. **T. power station,** usine *f* marémotrice.

tiddler ['tidlər], *s.* **T.** = STICKLEBACK.

tiddly ['tidli], *a. F:* Ivre, *F:* pompette.

tiddlywinks ['tidliwiŋks], *s.* Jeu *m* de la puce.

tide¹ [taid], *s.* 1. *A:* Temps *m,* époque *f,* saison *f. S.a.* EASTERTIDE. 2. Marée *f.* **Flood t.,** marée montante; *Nau:* (marée de) flot *m.* **High t.,** marée haute; haute marée. **Low t.,** marée basse. **Spring t.,** maline *f,* grande marée. **Neap t.,** marée de morte-eau. **Against the t.,** à contre-marée. **To go with the t.,** suivre le courant. **To go against the t.,** prendre le contre-sens de la marée. **The t. of battle turned,** le sort de la bataille tourna. **'tide-gate,** *s.* Porte *f* à flot; écluse *f* (de bassin). **'tide-gauge,** *s.* Échelle *f* de marée. **'tide-mark,** *s.* (*a*) Ligne *f* de marée haute. (*b*) Laisse *f* de marée. (*c*) *F:* Ligne de crasse (sur la peau, la baignoire). **'tide-race,** *s.* Raz *m* de marée. **'tide-rip,** *s.* 1. Revolin *m* de lame; clapotis *m* de marée. 2. Raz *m* de marée.

tide², *v.i. Nau:* To t. (it) into port, out of port, entrer au port avec le flot, sortir du port avec le jusant. **tide over**, *v.tr.* Venir à bout (d'une difficulté). This sum will t. us over, cette somme nous permettra de tenir le coup, *F:* va nous dépanner.
tideless ['taidlis], *a.* Sans marée.
tideway ['taidwei], *s.* Lit *m* de la marée.
tidiness ['taidinis], *s.* Bon ordre; (*of dress*) bonne tenue.
tidings ['taidiŋz], *s.pl. O:* Nouvelle(s) *f(pl)*.
tidy¹ ['taidi], *a.* 1. (*a*) (*Of room, etc.*) Bien rangé, en bon ordre; (*of dress*) bien tenu. Make yourself t., faites-vous propre. (*b*) (*Of pers.*) Ordonné; qui a de l'ordre. 2. *F:* Assez bon; passable. At a t. pace, à un bon petit train. A t. fortune, une jolie fortune. A t. sum, une somme rondelette. -ily, *adv.* Proprement; avec ordre. T. dressed, mis avec soin.
tidy², *s.* Vide-poche(s) *m inv.* Sink t., coin *m* d'évier.
tidy³, *v.tr.* Ranger; mettre de l'ordre dans. To t. one's hair, s'arranger les cheveux. To t. oneself (up), faire un brin de toilette. To t. away the books, ranger les livres. T. up the room a bit, mettez un peu d'ordre dans la pièce. *Abs.* To t. up, tout remettre en place.
tie¹ [tai], *s.* 1. (*a*) Lien *m*; attache *f*. Ties of friendship, liens d'amitié. (*b*) Assujettissement *m*. Her children are a t. on her, ses enfants sont pour elle une entrave continuelle. 2. (*a*) Lien (de corde, etc.). (*b*) *Nau:* Itague *f*. (*c*) Lacet *m*, cordon *m* (de soulier). (*d*) (Neck-)t., nœud *m*, cravate *f*. (*On invitation*) Black t. = Smoking. 3. *Const: etc:* Chaîne *f*, ancre *f*, moise *f*, entretoise *f*; tirant *m*. *U.S: Rail:* Traverse *f*. 4. *Mus:* Liaison *f*. 5. (*a*) *Sp:* Match *m* nul. T. award, prix ex æquo. (*b*) Match de championnat. *S.a.* CUP-TIE. (*c*) The election has ended in a t., les candidats sont à égalité de voix. 'tie-beam, *s. Const:* Entrait (de toit). 'tie-clip, *s.* Pince *f* à cravate. 'tie-pin, *s.* Épingle *f* de cravate. 'tie-rod, *s.* Tirant *m*; barre *f* d'accouplement.
tie², *v.* (tied ; tying) I. *v.tr.* 1. (*a*) Attacher; lier (qn à un poteau). To t. s.o.'s hands, enlever à qn toute liberté d'action, lier les mains à qn. To be tied (and bound), (i) être ligoté; (ii) avoir les mains liées. To be tied to one's bed, être cloué au lit (par la maladie). To be tied to one's work, être toujours à l'attache, *F:* être rivé à la chaîne. (*b*) Lier, nouer (un lacet, etc.); faire (un nœud, sa cravate). To t. an artery, ligaturer une artère. 2. Renforcer (une chaudière, etc.) avec des tirants; entretoiser. 3. *Mus:* Lier (deux notes). II. tie, *v.i. Sp: etc:* Être, arriver, à égalité (with, avec). *Sch: etc:* To t. for first place, être premier ex æquo (with, avec). tie down, *v.tr.* 1. Immobiliser (qn) en l'attachant contre terre, sur son lit; assujettir (qch.). 2. Tied down to one's duties, assujetti à ses fonctions. To t. s.o. down to a task, asservir, astreindre, qn à une tâche. tie in, *v.tr.* Attacher avec une ficelle. T.-on label, étiquette *f* à œillet(s). tie up, *v.tr.* 1. Attacher, ficeler (un paquet); bander, panser (un bras blessé). 2. Attacher (un animal); ligoter (qn). 3. Rendre (un legs) inaliénable; immobiliser (des capitaux). 4. (*a*) *F:* To get tied up, (i) s'empêtrer, s'embrouiller; (ii) se marier, *F:* se mettre la corde au cou. *F:* At the moment I'm tied up, pour l'instant je suis (très) occupé; je ne suis pas disponible. (*b*) *U.S:* The traffic was tied up, il y avait un embouteillage. 5. *v.i.* S'associer à (une maison de commerce). They are tied up with the firm of X., ils ont des accords avec la maison X. That ties up with what I've just said, ça se rapporte à ce que je viens de dire. 6. *v.i. Nau:* Amarrer. 'tie-up, *s.* 1. *U.S: Nau:* Amarrage *m*. 2. *U.S:* Embouteillage *m* (de la circulation); arrêt *m* (du travail). 3. *F:* Association *f*; rapport *m*; lien *m*. 'tying-up, *s.* 1. Ficelage *m* (d'un paquet). 2. Immobilisation *f* (des capitaux). tied, *a.* 1. To keep s.o. close t., ne laisser aucune liberté à qn. 2. T. (public-)house, débit de boissons qui est astreint à ne vendre que les produits d'une certaine brasserie. 2. *Mus:* T. notes, notes liées.
tier [tiər], *s.* Rangée *f* (de sièges, etc.); étage *m*. Tiers of an amphitheatre, gradins *m* d'un amphithéâtre. In tiers, en amphithéâtre. To arrange in tiers, disposer par étages; étager. To rise in tiers, s'étager.
tierce [tiəs], *s.* 1. *Ecc:* Tierce *f*. 2. *Cards: Fenc:* Tierce.
tiered ['tiəd], *a.* A gradins, à étages. Three-t. cake, pièce montée à trois étages.

tiff [tif], *s.* Petite querelle; fâcherie *f*. They have had a t., ils se sont chamaillés.
tig¹ [tig], *s.* (Jeu *m* du) chat *m*.
tig², *v.tr.* (tigged) Toucher (qn) (au jeu du chat).
tiger ['taigər], *s.* Tigre *m*. 'tiger-cat, *s.* Chat-tigre *m*; serval, -als *m*; ocelot *m*. 'tiger-lily, *s.* Lis tigré. 'tiger-moth, *s. Ent:* Arctie *f*.
tigerish ['taigəriʃ], *a.* 1. De tigre. 2. Cruel, -elle, sanguinaire, féroce.
tight [tait], I. *a.* 1. Imperméable (à l'eau, etc.); à l'épreuve (du gaz, etc.); (*of ship, container*) étanche; (*of joint*) hermétique. *S.a.* AIR-TIGHT, WATERTIGHT. 2. (*a*) (*Of cord, etc.*) Raide, tendu. To draw a cord t., serrer un cordon. *F:* To keep a t. hand, a t. hold, over s.o., tenir qn serré; brider qn. (*b*) (*Of clothes*) (Skin-)t., collant. (Too) t., étriqué; trop juste. My shoes are too t., mes souliers me gênent. *F:* To be in a t. corner, être en mauvaise passe; n'en pas mener large. *S.a.* FIT². (*c*) (*Of mortise, etc.*) Bien ajusté; (*of knot, screw*) serré. The nut is t., l'écrou est serré à bloc, à refus. 3. (*Of money*) Resserré, rare. 4. *F:* To be t., être ivre, gris, soûl. To get t., prendre une cuite. -ly, *adv.* 1. Eyes t. shut, yeux bien fermés. 2. (*a*) (Tendre, etc.) fortement. (*b*) Étroitement. To hold sth. t., tenir qch. serré; serrer qch. dans ses mains, dans ses bras. To fit t., être bien ajusté. II. tight, *adv.* 1. Hermétiquement. Shut t., t. shut, (porte) hermétiquement close; (yeux) bien fermés. 2. (*a*) Fortement, fermement. To hold sth. t., tenir qch. serré; serrer qch. dans ses bras. To screw a nut up t., serrer un écrou à bloc, à refus. *S.a.* HOLD² II. 1, SIT I. 1. (*b*) Étroitement. To fit t., être bien ajusté. 'tight-'fisted, *a. F:* Serré; ladre; dur à la détente. To be t.-f., être très près de ses sous. 'tight-fitting, *a.* 1. (Vêtement) collant. 2. (*Of joint, etc.*) Bien ajusté. 'tight-'laced, *a. O:* 1. Serré dans son corset. 2. *F:* Prude. 'tight rope, *s.* Corde tendue; corde raide. T.-r. walker, danseur de corde; funambule *mf*.
tighten ['tait(ə)n]. 1. *v.tr.* (*a*) Serrer, resserrer (une vis, un nœud); retendre (une courroie, un ressort); raidir (un cordage). *Aut:* To t. (up) the steering, rattraper le jeu de la direction. *F:* To t. one's belt, se serrer le ventre, la ceinture. (*b*) To t. (up) a blockade, restrictions, renforcer un blocus, des restrictions. 2. *v.i.* (*a*) Se (res)serrer. (*b*) (*Of cable, etc.*) Se tendre; raidir.
tightness ['taitnis], *s.* 1. Étanchéité *f* (d'un vaisseau); imperméabilité *f*. 2. (*a*) Tension *f*, raideur *f* (d'un cordage). (*b*) *Med:* To feel a t. across the chest, avoir la poitrine oppressée. (*c*) Étroitesse *f* (d'un lien, d'un vêtement). 3. *Fin:* Resserrement *m*, rareté *f* (de l'argent).
tights [taits], *s.pl.* Collant *m*.
tigress ['taigris], *s.f.* Tigresse.
Tigris (the) [ðə'taigris]. *Pr.n. Geog:* Le Tigre.
tike [taik], *s.* = TYKE.
tilde ['tild(ə)], *s. Typ: etc:* Tilde *m*.
tile¹ [tail], *s.* 1. Tuile *f* (de toiture). Crest t., tuile faîtière. *F:* He spends his nights on the tiles, il traîne dehors toute la nuit. *F:* To have a t. loose, être toqué, timbré. 2. *P:* Chapeau *m*; *esp.* chapeau haut de forme; *P:* galurin *m*. 3. Carreau *m*. Paving t., carreau (de carrelage).
tile², *v.tr.* 1. Couvrir (un comble) de tuiles, en tuiles. 2. Carreler (un plancher, etc.). tiled, *a.* 1. (Toit) de, en, tuiles. 2. (Pavage) carrelé, en carreaux; (paroi) à carreaux vernissés. tiling, *s.* 1. (*a*) Pose *f* des tuiles. (*b*) Carrelage *m*. 2. Coll. (*a*) Couverture *f* en tuiles. (*b*) Carreaux *mpl*, carrelage.
tiler ['tailər], *s.* Couvreur *m* (en tuiles).
till¹ [til], *v.tr.* Labourer, cultiver. tilling, *s.* Labourage *m*, culture *f*.
till², *s. Com:* Tiroir-caisse *m*. *F:* To be caught with one's hand in the t., être pris en flagrant délit, la main dans le sac.
till³. 1. *prep.* (*a*) Jusqu'à. T. now, t. then, jusqu'ici, jusque-là. From morning t. night, du matin au soir. (*b*) Not t., pas avant. He will not come t. after dinner, il ne viendra qu'après le dîner. He did not begin t. 1880, ce ne fut qu'en 1880 qu'il commença. 2. *conj.* (*a*) Jusqu'à ce que + *sub.* T. the doors are shut, jusqu'à ce que les portes soient fermées. To laugh t.

one cries, rire aux larmes. (b) Not t., pas avant que +sub. He will not come t. you invite him, t. he is invited, il ne viendra pas avant que vous (ne) l'invitiez, avant d'être invité.

tillage ['tilidʒ], s. (a) Labour m, labourage m, culture f. (b) Terre en labour, terre cultivée.

tiller[1] ['tilər], s. Nau: Barre franche (de direction). To put the t. hard over, donner un brusque coup de barre. **'tiller-rope,** s. Drosse f (du gouvernail).

tiller[2], s. Laboureur m, cultivateur m.

tilt[1] [tilt], s. 1. Inclinaison f, pente f; dévers m. To be on the t., être penché, incliné. To give a cask a t., incliner un tonneau. 2. (a) A: Joute f, tournoi m. (b) A: Coup m de lance. F: To have a t. at s.o., jouter avec qn (dans un débat). (c) (At) full t., à fond de train. To run full t. into sth., se jeter tête baissée, à corps perdu, contre qch. To ride (at) full t., aller à franc étrier, à bride abattue. **'tilt-hammer,** s. Metall: Martinet m; marteau m à bascule. **'tilt-yard,** s. A: Lice f; champ clos.

tilt[2]. I. v.i. 1. To t. (up), s'incliner; pencher. To t. backwards, incliner vers l'arrière. To t. over, (i) se pencher, s'incliner; (ii) se renverser. (Of bench) To t. up, basculer. 2. A: (a) Jouter (avec qn). (b) To t. at s.o., (i) courir sur qn la lance en arrêt; (ii) attaquer qn; critiquer qn. II. tilt, v.tr. Pencher, incliner. To t. one's chair back, se balancer, se renverser, sur sa chaise. To t. over a table, renverser une table. **tilting**[1], a. (i) Incliné; (ii) basculant; (iii) (mouvement) de bascule. **tilting**[2], s. 1. Inclinaison f, pente f. 2. A: Joute f. T. at the ring, jeu m de bagues.

tilt[3], s. Veh: Bâche f, banne f. Nau: Tendelet m.

tilt[4], v.tr. Couvrir d'une bâche; bâcher (une charrette); couvrir (une embarcation) d'un tendelet.

tilth [tilθ], s. 1. Labour m, culture f. 2. Couche f arable.

Tim [tim]. Pr.n.m. F: (a) (abbr. for TIMOTHY) Timothée. (b) Tp: L'horloge parlante.

timber[1] ['timbər], s. 1. (a) Bois m d'œuvre. Building t., bois de construction, de charpente. T. merchant, marchand m de bois. (b) Standing t., bois sur pied; arbres mpl de haute futaie. 2. (a) (Piece of) t., poutre f, madrier m. (b) N.Arch: Couple m, membre m, allonge f. (c) A: Shiver my timbers! mille tonnerres! **'timber-hitch,** s. Nœud m de bois, d'anguille. **'timber-work,** s. 1. Construction f en bois. 2. Charpente f. **'timber-yard,** s. Chantier m (de bois de charpente).

timber[2], v.tr. Boiser, blinder, cuveler (un puits de mine, etc.). **timbered,** a. (a) (Maison, etc.) en bois. (b) (Of land) Boisé. **timbering,** s. 1. Boisage m. 2. (i) Blindage m (d'un puits de mine); (ii) armature f (de bois).

timbre [tɛ̃mbr, timbə], s. Timbre m (de la voix, etc.).

Timbuctoo, Timbuktu [,timbʌk'tu:]. Pr.n. Tombouctou.

time[1] [taim], s. 1. Temps m. Work of t., ouvrage de longue haleine. (Father) T., le Temps. T. will show, qui vivra verra. In (the course) of t., in process of t., as t. goes on, avec le temps; à la longue. It was a race against t., il importait d'agir vite. 2. In a short t., en peu de temps; sous peu. In three weeks' t., dans trois semaines. To do sth. in no t., faire qch. en un rien de temps, en moins de rien. Within the required t., dans les délais voulus. To take a long t. over sth., mettre un temps interminable à faire qch. For a long t. to come, d'ici (à) longtemps. We haven't seen him for a long t., voilà longtemps que nous ne l'avons vu. For some t. (past), depuis quelque temps. For some t. (to come), pendant quelque temps. A short t. after, peu (de temps) après. After a short t., au bout d'un moment; un moment après; peu après. After a long t., longtemps après. All the t., (i) pendant tout ce temps; (ii) continuellement. Sp: Official t., temps chronométré. 3. (a) My t. is my own, je suis libre de mon temps. To have t. on one's hands, avoir du temps de reste. To have no t. to do sth., ne pas avoir le temps de faire qch. F: I've no t. for him, il m'embête; ce n'est pas un type intéressant. F: You have heaps of t., vous avez tout le temps voulu. To lose t., perdre du temps. To make up for lost t., rattraper le temps perdu. To lose no t. in doing sth., s'empresser de faire qch.; faire qch. sans perdre de temps. To gain t., gagner du temps. Sp: etc: To play for t., chercher à gagner du temps. It takes t.,

cela prend du temps. To take one's t. over sth., mettre le temps à faire qch. Take your t., prenez votre temps. F: It will take you all your t. to . . ., vous aurez fort à faire pour. . . . T.'s up! l'heure a sonné! c'est l'heure! Box: T.! allez! (In public house) T., gentlemen, please! on ferme! (b) P: To do t., faire de la prison. To serve one's t. (of apprenticeship), faire son apprentissage. F: She is near her t., elle est près d'accoucher. The house will last our t., la maison durera autant que nous. 4. Usu. pl. Époque f. (a) A sign of the times, un signe des temps. In times past, in olden times, autrefois, (au temps) jadis. The good old times, le bon vieux temps. Those were happy times, c'était le bon temps. In time(s) to come, à l'avenir; dans l'avenir. In my t. it was different, de mon temps c'était différent. In our t., de nos jours. The times we live in, notre époque. (b) To be behind the times, ne plus être de son siècle; être arriéré, attardé. To move with the times, to be abreast of the times, marcher avec son temps. As times go, par le temps qui court. 5. Moment m. (a) At the t. of delivery, au moment de la livraison. I was absent at the t., j'étais absent alors, à ce moment. At that t., en ce temps-là. At the present t., à l'heure qu'il est; actuellement. At a given t., à un moment donné. At the t. fixed, à l'heure dite. At one t. . . ., at another t. . . ., tantôt . . . tantôt. . . . At any other t., en d'autres temps. At one t., it used not to be so, autrefois, dans le temps, il n'en était pas ainsi. At one t. priest of this parish, ancien prêtre de cette paroisse. Lit: T. was when . . ., il fut un temps où. . . . At no t., jamais; à aucun moment. At times, parfois. At various times, à diverses reprises. At all times, (i) en tout temps; (ii) à n'importe quel moment. Between times, entre temps. (At) any t. (you like), n'importe quand. He may turn up at any t., il peut arriver d'un moment à l'autre. If at any t. . . ., si jamais. Some t. or other, un jour ou l'autre. This t. next year, l'an prochain à pareille époque. By the t. (that) I got there . . ., (i) lorsque je suis arrivé . . .; (ii) lorsque je serais arrivé. . . . From t. to t., de temps en temps. From that t., dès lors; depuis lors. To do sth. when the t. comes, faire qch. en son temps, en temps utile. Now is the t. to . . ., voilà le moment de. . . . To choose one's t., choisir son heure. This is no t. for trifling, ce n'est pas le moment de badiner. (b) In due t. and place, en temps et lieu. You will hear from me in good t., je vous écrirai le moment venu. In his own good t., à son heure. 6. Heure f. (a) Greenwich mean t., l'heure de Greenwich. Standard t., l'heure légale. Summer t., l'heure d'été, Fr.C: l'heure avancée. (b) What is the t.? quelle heure est-il? What t. do you make it? quelle heure avez-vous? To look at the t., regarder (à) sa montre. Watch that keeps (good) t., montre qui est exacte, qui est bien réglée. He turns up at any t., il n'a pas d'heure. F: To pass the t. of day with s.o., échanger quelques mots avec qn. At this t. of day, à cette heure du jour. (c) Dinner-t., l'heure du dîner. To be before (one's) t., être en avance. To be behind (one's) t., être en retard. To arrive on t., arriver à l'heure. To arrive in t. for dinner, arriver à temps pour dîner. I was just in t. to see it, je suis arrivé juste à temps pour le voir. It was only just in t., il n'était que temps. To start in good t., (i) s'y prendre bien à temps; (ii) se mettre en route de bonne heure. F: And about t. too! c'est pas trop tôt! (d) T. of the year, époque de l'année; saison f. At my t. of life, F: of day, à mon âge. Sowing t., la saison, le temps, des semailles. In the day-t., de jour. At night-t., de nuit. (e) To die before one's t., mourir avant l'âge. 7. Ind: To be paid by t., être payé à l'heure. To put t. in, faire des heures. 8. To have a good t., s'amuser; F: se la couler douce. We had a good t., on s'est bien amusé. To have a bad t., a rough t., (of it), (i) souffrir; en voir de dures; manger de la vache enragée; (ii) passer un mauvais quart d'heure. 9. Fois f. Five times, cinq fois. Next t., la prochaine fois. At other times, d'autres fois. The first t. I saw him, la première fois que je l'ai vu. To do sth. several times over, faire qch. à plusieurs reprises, plusieurs fois. T. and t. again, t. after t., à maintes reprises; maintes et maintes fois. To do two things at a t., faire deux choses à la fois. **To run upstairs four at a t.,** monter l'escalier quatre à quatre. **For weeks at a t.,** des semaines durant. **Three times running,** trois fois de suite, à trois reprises. **Four times two is eight,** quatre fois deux font huit. **Three times as big as . . .,** trois fois plus grand que. . . . **10.** *adv.phr.* **At the same t.** (a) En même temps. **You cannot be in two places at the same t.,** on ne peut pas être au four et au moulin. (b) **At the same t. you must not forget . . .,** d'autre part il ne faut pas oublier. . . . **11.** (a) *Mus:* Durée *f* (d'une note). (b) *Mus:* Mesure *f.* **Common t.,** (i) (*also* **quadruple t.**) mesure à quatre temps; (ii) (*also* **duple t.**) mesure à deux temps. **To beat t.,** battre la mesure. (c) **In strict t.,** en mesure. **To keep t.,** jouer, danser, en mesure. **To get out of t.,** perdre la mesure. *I.C.E:* **The ignition is out of t.,** l'allumage est déréglé, décalé. (d) *Mus:* **To quicken the t.,** presser le mouvement. *Gym:* **To march in quick t.,** marcher au pas accéléré. **'time-belt,** *s.* (Standard) t.-b., fuseau *m* horaire. **'time-bomb,** *s.* Bombe *f* à retardement. **'time-clause,** *s. Gram:* Proposition temporelle. **'time-expired,** *a.* (Soldat) libérable. **'time-exposure,** *s. Phot:* Pose *f.* **'time-fuse,** *s.* Fusée fusante. **'time-honoured,** *a.* Consacré (par l'usage). **'time-lag,** *s. El.E:* Retard *m.* **'time-limit,** *s.* **1.** Limite de temps (imposée à un orateur, etc.). **2.** Délai *m* (de payement, etc.). **'time-server,** *s.* Complaisant *m* (envers le pouvoir, etc.); opportuniste *m.* **'time-serving,** *s.* Basse complaisance (envers le pouvoir); opportunisme *m.* **'time-sheet,** *s. Ind:* Feuille *f* de présence. **'time-signal,** *s. W.Tel:* etc: Signal *m* horaire, *pl.* signaux horaires. **'time-switch,** *s.* Minuterie *f* (d'escalier, etc.). **'time-work,** *s.* Travail *m* à l'heure. **'time-worker,** *s.* Ouvrier, -ère, qui travaille à l'heure. **'time-worn,** *a.* **1.** Usé par le temps. **2.** Séculaire, vénérable.

time², *v.tr.* **1.** (a) Fixer l'heure de (qch.). (b) **To t. a blow,** choisir le moment de porter un coup; mesurer un coup. **Well-timed remark,** observation opportune, à propos. **Well-timed stroke,** coup bien calculé, bien jugé. (c) Régler (une horloge). (d) *I.C.E:* Régler, ajuster (l'allumage, etc.); caler (la magnéto). (e) *Row:* **To t. the stroke,** régler la nage. **2.** Calculer la durée de (qch.). **3.** *Sp:* etc: Chronométrer (qn, une course). **To t. how long it takes s.o. to do sth.,** mesurer le temps que qn met à faire qch. **timing,** *s.* **1.** (a) *I.C.E:* Réglage *m* (de l'allumage). *Mch:* Calage *m* (d'une soupape). (b) *I.C.E:* Distribution *f.* **T. gear,** (engrenage(s) *m(pl)* de) distribution. **2.** *Phot:* Calcul *m* (du temps de pose). **3.** *Sp:* Chronométrage *m.* **4. Error of t.,** mauvais calcul; erreur *f* de jugement.

timekeeper ['taimkiːpər], *s.* **1.** *Sp:* etc: Chronométreur *m.* **2. Good t.,** (i) montre *f* qui est toujours à l'heure; (ii) personne *f* qui est toujours à l'heure.
timeless ['taimlis], *a.* Éternel, -elle; sans fin.
timeliness ['taimlinis], *s.* Opportunité *f*; à-propos *m* (d'une intervention, etc.).
timely ['taimli], *a.* Opportun, à propos.
timepiece ['taimpiːs], *s.* Pendule *f*; montre *f.*
timesaver ['taimseivər], *s.* Appareil *m*, méthode *f*, qui économise le temps.
timesaving ['taimseiviŋ], *a.* Qui économise le temps.
timetable ['taimteibl], *s.* **1.** Horaire *m*; indicateur *m* (des chemins de fer). **2.** *Sch:* Emploi *m* du temps.
timid ['timid], *a.* Timide, timoré, peureux, -euse. **-ly,** *adv.* Timidement.
timidity [ti'miditi], *s.* Timidité *f.*
timorous ['timərəs], *a.* Timoré, peureux, -euse, craintif, -ive. **-ly,** *adv.* Peureusement, craintivement.
timpani ['timpəni(ː)], *s.pl. Mus:* Timbales *f.*
timpanist ['timpənist], *s.* Timbalier *m.*
tin¹ [tin], *s.* **1.** Étain *m. Fin:* **T. shares,** valeurs *f* stannifères. **2.** (a) = TINPLATE¹. **T. hat,** casque *m* (de tranchée). *F:* **That puts the t. hat, lid, on it,** ça c'est le comble. **T. whistle,** flageolet *m.* (b) Boîte *f* (en fer-blanc). **Petrol-t.,** bidon *m* à essence. **Cake-t.,** moule *m* à gâteaux. **Baking t.,** plat *m* à rôtir. **T. loaf,** pain moulé. **3.** *P: O:* (Money) Galette *f*, pognon *m*, fric *m.* **'tin-bearing,** *a.* Stannifère. **'tin-opener,** *s.* Ouvre-boîte(s) *m inv.* **'Tin Pan 'Alley.** *Pr.n. F:* (a) Quartier des éditeurs de musique populaire. (b) Les compositeurs de musique populaire.

tin², *v.tr.* (tinned) **1.** Étamer. **2.** Mettre (des sardines, etc.) en boîtes (de fer-blanc). **tinned,** *a.* **1.** Étamé. **2.** Conservé (en boîtes métalliques). **T. foods,** conserves *f* alimentaires (en boîte). *P:* **T. music,** musique enregistrée.
tinctorial [tiŋk'tɔːriəl], *a.* Tinctorial, -aux.
tincture¹ ['tiŋ(k)tʃər], *s.* **1.** *Pharm:* Teinture *f* (d'iode, etc.). **2.** Teinte *f*, nuance *f.* **3.** *Her:* Émail *m*, -aux.
tincture², *v.tr.* Teindre, teinter.
tinder ['tindər], *s.* Mèche *f* de briquet. **German t.,** amadou *m.* **'tinder-box,** *s.* Briquet *m* (à silex).
tine [tain], *s.* **1.** Dent *f*, fourchon *m* (de fourche). **2.** Andouiller *m* (de bois de cerf).
tinfoil ['tinfɔil], *s.* **1.** Feuille *f* d'étain. **2.** Papier *m* (d')étain, *F:* papier d'argent.
ting¹ [tiŋ], *s.* Tintement *m* (d'une cloche).
ting², *v.i.* Tinter.
ting-a-ling ['tiŋəliŋ], *s.* Drelin drelin *m.*
tinge¹ [tin(d)ʒ], *s.* Teinte *f*, nuance *f.*
tinge², *v.tr.* Teinter, nuancer. **Words tinged with malice,** paroles teintées de malice.
tingle¹ ['tiŋgl], *s.* **1. T. in the ears,** tintement *m* d'oreilles. **2.** Picotement *m*, fourmillement *m* (de la peau).
tingle², *v.i.* **1.** (Of ears) Tinter. **2.** Picoter. **To t. with impatience,** vibrer d'impatience. **Her cheeks tingled,** les joues lui picotaient, lui cuisaient. **My legs are tingling,** j'ai des fourmis dans les jambes. **My fingers are tingling to box his ears,** la main me démange de lui flanquer une gifle. **tingling,** *s.* = TINGLE¹.
tinker¹ ['tiŋkər], *s.* (a) Chaudronnier ambulant; rétameur *m.* (b) *Scot:* = GIPSY. (c) *F:* Bousilleur *m*, savetier *m*; gâcheur *m* (d'ouvrage).
tinker². **1.** *v.tr.* **To tinker (sth.) up,** retaper, rafistoler (une machine, etc.); replâtrer (un contrat, etc.). **To t. up a car,** rafistoler une voiture. **2.** *v.i.* Bricoler. **tinkering,** *s.* **1.** (Petite) chaudronnerie; rétamage *m.* **2.** (a) Petites besognes d'entretien, de réparation. (b) Rafistolage *m.*
tinkle¹ ['tiŋkl], *s.* Tintin *m*, tintement *m*, drelin *m.* *F: Tp:* **To give s.o. a tinkle,** donner un coup de fil à qn.
tinkle². **1.** *v.i.* Tinter; *Lit:* tintinnabuler. **2.** *v.tr.* Faire tinter (une sonnette). **tinkling,** *s.* = TINKLE¹.
tinner ['tinər], *s.* Étameur *m.*
tinniness ['tininis], *s.* Timbre grêle, métallique, fêlé (d'un piano, etc.).
tinny ['tini], *a.* **1.** (Of earth, etc.) Stannifère. **2.** (Goût) d'étain. **3. To sound t.,** sonner grêle; rendre un son fêlé. **4.** *F:* (Of car, etc.) **It's a very t. job,** ce n'est qu'un tas de ferraille.
tinplate¹ ['tinpleit], *s.* Fer-blanc *m*; ferblanterie *f.*
tinplate², *v.tr. Metalw:* Étamer (le fer).
tinpot ['tinpɔt], *attrib.a. F:* Mesquin, misérable, méprisable, inférieur.
tinsel¹ ['tins(ə)l], *s.* **1.** (a) *Dressm:* Lamé *m*, paillettes *fpl.* (b) Clinquant *m.* (c) Faux éclat, clinquant (du style). **2.** *attrib.* Faux, *f.* fausse; de clinquant.
tinsel², *v.tr.* (tinselled) Garnir (une robe) de lamé, de paillettes. **Tinselled finery,** oripeaux *mpl.*
tinsmith ['tinsmiθ], *s.* Ferblantier *m.*
tint¹ [tint], *s.* **1.** Teinte *f*, nuance *f.* **To paint t. upon t.,** peindre ton sur ton. *S.a.* FLESH-TINTS, HALF-TINT. **2.** (In line engraving) Grisé *m.* **'tint-drawing,** *s.* **1.** Camaïeu *m.* **2.** (Épure *f* au) lavis.
tint², *v.tr.* **1.** Teinter, colorer. **2.** *Engr:* Ombrer; hachurer.
tintack ['tintæk], *s.* Broquette *f*; clou *m* de tapisserie.
tinware ['tinwɛər], *s.* Articles *mpl* en fer-blanc; ferblanterie *f.*
tiny ['taini], *a.* Minuscule. **A t. bit,** un tout petit morceau.
tip¹ [tip], *s.* **1.** Bout *m*, extrémité *f*, pointe *f*; dard *m* (de flamme). **On the tips of the toes,** sur la pointe des pieds. **Artist to the finger-tips,** artiste jusqu'au bout des ongles. **To have sth. on the t. of one's tongue,** avoir qch. sur le bout de la langue. *El:* **Platinum t.,** grain *m* de platine. *Cu:* **Asparagus tips,** pointes d'asperges. **2.** (a) Bout ferré, embout *m* (d'une canne, etc.). *Bootm:* bout (de fer, de caoutchouc). (b) *Bill:* Procédé *m* (de la queue). **'tip-tilted,** *a.* À bout relevé; (nez) retroussé.

tip², *v.tr.* (tipped [tipt]) Mettre un bout à (un soulier); mettre un embout à (une canne, etc.). **tipped**, *a.* Gold-t., silver-t., à bout doré, d'argent.

tip³, *s.* 1. Pente *f*, inclinaison *f*. 2. Coup léger; tape *f*. 3. (*a*) Pourboire *m*, gratification *f*. **The t.** is included, le service est compris. (*b*) *F:* Don *m* d'argent de poche (à un neveu, etc.). 4. *Turf: etc:* Tuyau *m*. If you take my t. . . . , si vous m'en croyez. . . . 5. *Civ.E: etc:* (*a*) Chantier *m* de versage. **Rubbish t.**, dépotoir *m*. (*b*) Tas *m*, monceau *m* (de déblais, etc.). **'tip-cart,** *s.* Tombereau *m* (à bascule). **'tip-cat,** *s.* *Games:* Bâtonnet *m*. **'tip-lorry,** *s.* Camion *m* à benne basculante.

tip⁴, *v.* (tipped [tipt]) I. *v.tr.* 1. (*a*) To t. (over), renverser (qch.); chavirer, verser (un canot, etc.). (*b*) To t. (up), soulever (un strapontin); faire basculer (une charrette). (*c*) To t. (out), déverser, décharger. To t. **one's passengers into the ditch**, verser, renverser, ses voyageurs dans le fossé. (*d*) Faire pencher, faire incliner. To t. **the scale(s) at a hundred pounds**, peser tout juste cent livres. 2. (*a*) Toucher légèrement, effleurer (qch. du pied). **T.-and-run raid**, raid de surprise avec fuite précipitée. (*b*) *P:* Donner, passer, lancer (qch. à qn). (*c*) Donner un pourboire, une gratification, à (qn). 3. *Turf: etc:* Tuyauter (qn). II. **tip**, *v.i.* (*a*) To t. (over), se renverser, basculer; (*of boat, etc.*) chavirer, verser. (*b*) To t. (up), (*of plank, etc.*) se soulever, basculer. **'tip-up,** *attrib.a.* (Charrette, cuvette, etc.) à bascule, à renversement. **T.-up seat**, strapontin *m*. **tipping¹**, *a.* Basculant, culbutant, à bascule. **tipping²**, *s.* 1. (*a*) Inclinaison *f*. (*b*) **T.** (over), renversement *m*; chavirement *m* (d'un canot). (*c*) Basculage *m*; versage *m*. *P.N:* Tipping **(of rubbish) prohibited**, décharge interdite. 2. (Système *m* des) pourboires *m*; distribution *f* de pourboires. 3. *Turf:* Tuyautage *m*.

tippet ['tipit], *s. Cost:* 1. Collet *m* de fourrure. 2. *Ecc:* Étole *f*.

tipple¹ ['tipl], *s.* Boisson *f* (alcoolique).

tipple², *v.i.* Se livrer à la boisson; picoler, pinter. **tippling**, *s.* Ivrognerie *f*.

tippler ['tiplər], *s.* Ivrogne *m*; *F:* poivrot *m*.

tipsiness ['tipsinis], *s.* Ivresse *f*.

tipstaff ['tipsta:f], *s. Jur:* Huissier *m*.

tipster ['tipstər], *s. Turf: etc:* Donneur *m* de tuyaux.

tipsy ['tipsi], *a.* 1. Gris, éméché, *F:* pompette. To get t., se griser. 2. (Rire, etc.) d'ivrogne. **-ily,** *adv.* D'une voix, avec une démarche, qui accuse l'ivresse. **'tipsy-cake,** *s. Cu:* = Diplomate *m*.

tiptoe¹ ['tiptou], *s. & adv.* (On) t., sur la pointe des pieds. To be on **tiptoes of expectation**, être dans l'angoisse de l'attente; attendre fiévreusement.

tiptoe², *v.i.* Marcher sur la pointe des pieds. To t. in, out, entrer, sortir, sur la pointe des pieds.

tiptop ['tiptɔp], *a. F:* De premier ordre; excellent, extra.

tirade [tai'reid], *s.* Tirade *f*. **T.** of invective, bordée *f* d'injures. **A violent t. against s.o.**, une diatribe contre qn.

tire¹ ['taiər]. 1. *v.tr.* (*a*) Fatiguer, lasser. (*b*) To t. s.o. out, (i) épuiser, rompre, qn de fatigue; (ii) excéder qn. 2. *v.i.* Se fatiguer, se lasser. To t. of sth., se lasser, se fatiguer, de qch. **tired**, *a.* Fatigué. (*a*) Las, *f* lasse. **T.** out, t. to death, rompu de fatigue; exténué, éreinté, fourbu. (*b*) (*Sleepy*) To be t., être fatigué, avoir sommeil. *F:* You make me t., tu m'ennuies; tu m'embêtes. (*c*) To be t. of sth., être las de qch. To get, grow, t. of doing sth., se lasser de faire qch. *F:* I'm t. of you, tu me fais suer. **tiring**, *a.* 1. Lassant, fatigant. 2. Ennuyeux, -euse.

tire², *s. A:* (*a*) Atours *mpl*. (*b*) Coiffure *f*. **'tire-woman**, *pl.* -women, *s.f. A:* Demoiselle, dame, d'atour.

tire³, *v.tr. A:* Parer. **'tiring-room**, *s. A:* Chambre *f* d'atours.

tire⁴, *s. U.S:* = TYRE.

tiredness ['taiədnis], *s.* Lassitude *f*, fatigue *f*.

tireless ['taiəlis], *a.* Inlassable, infatigable. **-ly,** *adv.* Infatigablement, inlassablement.

tiresome ['taiəsəm], *a.* 1. Fatigant, lassant; (discours) fastidieux, ennuyeux. 2. Exaspérant; (*of child*) fatigant, assommant. How t.! que c'est assommant!

tiro, *pl.* -o(e)s ['taiərou, -ouz], *s.* Novice *mf*; néophyte *m*.

'tis [tiz] = **it is.**

tissue ['tisju:], *s.* 1. (*a*) Tissu *m* (de coton, etc.); étoffe *f*. (*b*) Face t., serviette *m* à démaquiller. *Com:* **Toilet t.**, (i) papier *m* hygiénique; (ii) serviette à démaquiller. (*c*) T. of lies, tissu de mensonges. 2. *Biol:* Tissu (musculaire, etc.). **'tissue-paper**, *s.* (*a*) Papier *m* de soie. (*b*) Papier pelure.

tit¹ [tit], *s. Orn:* (= TITMOUSE, *q.v.*) Mésange *f*.

tit², *s. In the phr.* T. for tat, un prêté pour un rendu; à bon chat bon rat. To give s.o. t. for tat, rendre à qn la pareille; riposter du tac au tac.

tit³, *s. V:* Mamelle *f*.

Titan ['tait(ə)n], *s. Myth:* Titan *m*. *Const:* **T.** crane, (grue *f*) titan (*m*).

titanic [tai'tænik], *a.* Titanique, titanesque.

titanium [tai'teiniəm], *s. Ch:* Titane *m*.

titbit ['titbit], *s.* Morceau friand; friandise *f*.

titfer ['titfər], *s. P:* Chapeau *m*.

tithe¹ [taið], *s.* 1. Dîme *f*. 2. Dixième *m*.

tithe², *v.tr.* 1. Payer la dîme de (ses récoltes). 2. Soumettre (un champ, qn) à la dîme. **tithing**, *s.* (*a*) Paiement *m* de la dîme. (*b*) Prélèvement *m* de la dîme; levée *f* de la dîme. **'tithe-barn**, *s.* Grange *f* de la dîme.

Titian ['tiʃiən]. *Pr.n.m.* Le Titien.

titillate ['titileit], *v.tr.* (*a*) Titiller, chatouiller. (*b*) Chatouiller (le palais); émoustiller (les sens).

titillation [ˌtiti'leiʃ(ə)n], *s.* Titillation *f*, chatouillement *m*.

titivate ['titiveit]. 1. *v.tr.* Faire (qn) beau; pomponner (qn). 2. *v.i. & pr.* Se faire beau; faire un brin de toilette; se bichonner.

titlark ['titlɑ:k], *s. Orn:* Pipit *m*. **Meadow t.**, farlouse *f*.

title¹ ['taitl], *s.* 1. (*a*) Titre *m*. To have a t., avoir un titre, une qualification. To deprive s.o. of his t., déqualifier qn. (*b*) Titre de noblesse. 2. Titre (d'un livre); intitulé *m* (d'un journal, d'un acte). *Typ:* **Bastard t.**, faux titre. *S.a.* HALF-TITLE. (*c*) *Cin:* **Credit titles**, générique *m*. 3. (*a*) Titre, droit *m*. **T.** to property, droit de propriété. **Clear t.**, titre incontestable. To have a t. to sth., avoir droit, avoir des titres, à qch. **Titles to fame**, titres de gloire. (*b*) = TITLE-DEED. 4. Titre (de l'or). **'title-deed**, *s. Jur:* Titre (constitutif) de propriété. **'title-page**, *s. Typ:* Page *f* de titre; titre *m*. **'title-part, -rôle**, *s. Th:* Rôle *m* qui donne le titre à la pièce.

title², *v.tr.* Intituler (un livre, etc.). **titled**, *a.* Titré. I noticed several t. people, j'ai remarqué (dans l'assistance) plusieurs personnes titrées.

titmouse, *pl.* -mice ['titmaus, -mais], *s. Orn:* Mésange *f*. **Great t.**, (mésange) charbonnière *f*. **Coal t.**, (mésange) petite charbonnière; mésange noire. **Crested t.**, mésange huppée.

titrate ['taitreit], *v.tr.* Titrer, doser (une solution).

titter¹ ['titər], *s.* 1. Rire étouffé. 2. Petit rire bête, nerveux.

titter², *v.i.* 1. Avoir un petit rire étouffé. 2. Rire nerveusement, bêtement. **tittering**, *s.* Petits rires.

tittle ['titl], *s.* 1. *A:* Point *m*. 2. La moindre partie. Not one t., pas un iota. To a t., exactement; trait pour trait.

tittle-tattle¹ ['titlˌtætl], *s.* Potins *mpl*, cancans *mpl*, racontars *mpl*, commérages *mpl*. The t.-t. of the day, la chronique scandaleuse du jour.

tittle-tattle², *v.i.* Potiner, cancaner.

tittup ['titəp], *v.i.* (*Of horse*) Aller au petit galop; fringuer.

titty ['titi], *s. V:* = TIT³.

titubation [ˌtitju'beiʃ(ə)n], *s. Med:* Titubation *f*.

titular ['titjulər], *a.* (*a*) (Évêque, etc.) titulaire, in partibus. (*b*) (*Of function, etc.*) Nominal, -aux. (*c*) **T.** possessions, terres attachées à un titre.

tizzy ['tizi], *s. F:* Affolement *m*.

tmesis ['tmi:sis], *s. Gram:* Tmèse *f*.

to [tu:]. I. *prep.* A, à. 1. (*a*) They go to church, ils vont à l'église. What school do you go to? à quelle école allez-vous? He went to France, to Japan, to the United States, il est allé en France, au Japon, aux États-Unis. She returned home to her family, elle est rentrée auprès de sa famille. I am going to the grocer's, je vais chez l'épicier. From town to town, from flower to flower, de ville en ville, de fleur en fleur.

Air-lines to and from the Continent, lignes aériennes à destination ou en provenance du Continent. (b) The road to London, la route de Londres. The road to ruin, le chemin de la ruine. The shortest way to the station, le plus court (chemin) pour aller à la gare. It is twenty miles to London, il y a vingt milles d'ici Londres. To horse! à cheval! 2. (a) Vers, à. To the east, vers l'est. (At marine station) 'To the boat,' "vers le bateau." 'To the trains,' "Accès aux quais." 'To the station,' "Direction de la gare." To the right, à droite. (b) Feet to the fire, les pieds au feu. 3. Elbow to elbow, coude à coude. To fight man to man, se battre homme à homme. To clasp s.o. to one's heart, serrer qn sur son cœur. 4. (Of time) (a) From morning to night, du matin au soir. From day to day, de jour en jour. (b) Ten minutes to six, six heures moins dix. 5. (a) Wet to the skin, trempé jusqu'aux os. Shaken to the foundations, ébranlé jusque dans les fondements. To see s.o. to the end of the street, accompagner qn jusqu'au bout de la rue. To this day, jusqu'à ce jour. To count up to ten, compter jusqu'à dix. Killed to a man, tués jusqu'au dernier. (b) To a high degree, à un haut degré. Generous to a fault, généreux à l'excès. Accurate to a millimetre, exact à un millimètre près. A year to the day, un an jour pour jour. 6. (a) To this end, à cet effet, dans ce but. To come to s.o.'s aid, venir à l'aide de qn. To sentence s.o. to death, condamner qn à mort. (b) To my despair, à mon grand désespoir. To the general surprise, à la surprise de tous. 7. (a) En. To run to seed, monter en graine. To go to ruin, tomber en ruine. To put to flight, mettre en fuite. (b) To take s.o. to wife, prendre qn pour femme. 8. To sing sth. to the tune of . . ., chanter qch. sur l'air de. . . . 9. Charles brother to John, Charles frère de Jean. Heir to s.o., to an estate, héritier de qn, d'une propriété. Ambassador to the King of Sweden, ambassadeur auprès du roi de Suède. Secretary to the manager, secrétaire du directeur. 10. (a) (Effecting a comparison) Superior to, supérieur à. That's nothing to what I have seen, cela n'est rien auprès de, à côté de, ce que j'ai vu. (b) Three is to six as six is to twelve, trois est à six ce que six est à douze. Six votes to four, six voix contre quatre. Three goals to nil, trois buts à zéro. To bet ten to one, parier dix contre un. It's ten to one that . . ., Il y a dix à parier contre un que. . . . One house to the square mile, une maison par mille carré. One glass of wine to a pint of soup, un verre de vin par, pour un, demi-litre de bouillon. Thirteen to the dozen, treize à la douzaine. 11. To all appearances, selon toute apparence. To write to s.o.'s dictation, écrire sous la dictée de qn. To the best of my remembrance, autant qu'il m'en souvienne. 12. To build an altar to s.o., ériger un autel à qn. To drink to s.o., boire à la santé de qn. 13. (a) (Concerning) What did he say to my suggestion? qu'est-ce qu'il a dit de ma proposition? That's all there is to it, c'est tout ce qu'il y a à dire. There's nothing to it, ça ne vaut pas la peine; cela ne rapporte rien. (b) (On bill) To repairing boiler . . ., réparations à la chaudière. . . . To taking out jets . . ., pour avoir démonté les gicleurs. . . . 14. (Used to form the dative) (a) To give sth. to s.o., donner qch. à qn. The man I gave it to, l'homme à qui je l'ai donné. What is that to you? qu'est-ce que cela vous fait? What is life to me? que m'importe la vie? To keep sth. to oneself, garder qch. pour soi. I said to myself . . ., je me suis dit (en moi-même). . . . (b) Envers, pour. Favourable to s.o., favorable à qn. Good to all, bon pour tous, envers tous. Kind to me, aimable à mon égard; aimable pour, envers, moi. (c) Known to the ancients, connu des anciens. Those who are born to a fortune, ceux qui naissent héritiers d'une fortune. II. to. With the infinitive. 1. (a) (Purpose, result) Pour. He came to help me, il est venu (pour) m'aider. We must eat (in order) to live, il faut manger pour vivre. So to speak, pour ainsi dire. I have not done anything to rouse his anger, je n'ai rien fait pour provoquer sa colère. (b) Happy to do it, heureux de le faire. Ready to listen, prêt à écouter. Old enough to go to school, assez âgé pour aller à l'école. You are foolish to believe that, vous êtes bien sot de croire cela. What a queer chap to be a mayor! quel drôle d'homme pour

un maire! Good to eat, bon à manger. Too hot to drink, trop chaud pour qu'on puisse le boire. (c) (i) To look at her one would never imagine that . . ., à la voir on ne s'imaginerait pas que. . . . (ii) (Expressing subsequent fact) He woke to find the lamp still burning, en s'éveillant il trouva la lampe encore allumée. These times are gone never to return, ces temps sont passés et ne reviendront plus. 2. (a) (Infin. with adjectival function) To have a letter to write, avoir une lettre à écrire. To have much to do, avoir beaucoup à faire. Nothing to speak of, rien qui vaille la peine qu'on en parle. There is no one to see us, il n'y a personne qui puisse nous voir. He is not a man to forget his friends, il n'est pas homme à oublier ses amis. He is not a man to be trusted, ce n'est pas un homme à qui on puisse se fier. The first to complain, le premier à se plaindre. The third to arrive, le troisième à venir. House to be sold, maison à vendre. The English Plato is still to be, un Platon anglais est encore à naître. (b) Tendency to do sth., tendance à faire qch. Desire to do sth., désir de faire qch. This is the time to do it, c'est le moment de le faire. 3. (Infin. used as noun) To be or not to be . . ., être ou ne pas être. . . . To lie is shameful, it is shameful to lie, il est honteux de mentir. 4. (Infin. = finite clause) I wish him to do it, je veux qu'il le fasse. You would like it to be true, vous voudriez bien que cela soit vrai. 5. (Expressing futurity, obligation) (In headline) A hundred employees to go, cent employés vont recevoir leur congé. 6. (With ellipsis of verb) I did not want to look, I 'had to, je ne voulais pas regarder mais il le fallut bien, mais je ne pus m'en défendre. Take it; it would be absurd 'not to, prenez-le; ce serait absurde de ne pas le faire, de manquer l'occasion. You ought to, vous le devriez. I want to, je voudrais bien. III. to, adv. (Stressed) 1. Ship moored head to (= to the wind), navire amarré vent debout. To put the horses to (= to the carriage), atteler les chevaux. To come to (= to one's senses), reprendre connaissance. 2. To and fro. To go to and fro, aller et venir. Two journeys to and fro, deux voyages d'aller et retour. Mec.E: To-and-fro movement, mouvement m de va-et-vient. to-'do, s. F: Remue-ménage m. To make a to-do, faire des histoires, des chichis. What a to-do! quelle affaire!

toad [toud], s. 1. (a) Crapaud m. Lit: To treat s.o. like a t. under the harrow, fouler qn aux pieds. (b) P: Type répugnant; sale type. 2. Cu: T. in the hole, morceau de viande ou saucisses qu'on fait cuire au four dans de la pâte à crêpes. 'toad spit, s. Bot: Crachat m de coucou.

toadflax ['toudflæks], s. Bot: Linaire f.

toadstone ['toudstoun], s. Crapaudine f.

toadstool ['toudstu:l], s. Champignon, esp. champignon vénéneux.

toady[1] ['toudi], s. Flagorneur, -euse; lèche-bottes m.

toady[2], v.tr. & i. (toadied) To t. (to) s.o., lécher les bottes à qn; flagorner qn.

toadyism ['toudiizm], s. Flagornerie f.

toast[1] [toust], s. 1. Pain grillé, toast m. Piece, round, of t., rôtie f. Anchovies on t., anchois sur canapé. P: To have s.o. on t., avoir qn à sa merci; tenir qn. 2. (a) (i) Personne à qui on porte un toast; esp. (ii) Hist: beauté f à la mode. (b) Toast m. To give, propose, a t., porter un toast; boire à la santé de qn. 'toast-list, s. Liste f des toasts (à un banquet). 'toast-master, s. Annonceur m des toasts. 'toast-rack, s. Porte-rôties m inv., porte-toasts m inv.

toast[2]. 1. v.tr. (a) Rôtir, griller (du pain). F: To t. one's feet (before the fire), se chauffer les pieds. (b) To t. s.o., porter un toast à (la santé de) qn; boire à la santé de qn. 2. v.i. Rôtir, griller. 'toasting-fork, s. Fourchette f à rôties.

toaster ['toustər], s. Grille-pain m inv.

tobacco, pl. -os [tə'bækou, -ouz], s. Tabac m (à fumer). Cut t., tabac haché. to'bacco-heart, s. Maladie de cœur due à l'abus du tabac. to'bacco-jar, s. Pot m à tabac. to'bacco-pouch, s. Blague f à tabac.

tobacconist [tə'bækənist], s. Marchand m de tabac, buraliste m f. Tobacconist's (shop), débit m de tabac.

toboggan[1] [tə'bɔg(ə)n], s. Toboggan m; luge f. to'boggan-run, -shoot, s. Piste f de toboggan.

toboggan², v.i. Faire du toboggan.
tobogganer [tə'bɔgənər], s. Tobogganniste mf; lugeur, -euse.
Toby ['toubi]. **1.** Pr.n.m. Tobie. **2.** T. jug, pot m à bière (en forme de gros bonhomme à tricorne). **3.** s. Chien (vivant) du guignol anglais.
toccata [tɔ'kɑːtə], s. Mus: Toccata f.
tocsin ['tɔksin], s. Tocsin m.
today [tə'dei], adv. & s. Aujourd'hui (m). T. week, d'aujourd'hui en huit. Today's paper, le journal d'aujourd'hui, du jour. He is here t. and gone tomorrow, il est comme l'oiseau sur la branche.
toddle¹ ['tɔdl], s. **1.** Allure chancelante (d'un enfant). **2.** F: Petite promenade.
toddle², v.i. **1.** Marcher à petits pas chancelants. **2.** Marcher à petits pas; trottiner. To t. in, out, entrer, sortir, à petits pas. To t. off, F: se trotter. F: I must be toddling, il faut que je me trotte, que je file.
toddler ['tɔdlər], s. Enfant qui commence à marcher. The toddlers, les tout petits.
toddy ['tɔdi], s. **1.** Toddy m, vin m de palmier. **2.** Grog chaud.
toe¹ [tou], s. **1.** Orteil m; doigt m de pied. Great t., big t., gros orteil. Little t., petit orteil. To come down on (the points of) one's toes, retomber sur la pointe des pieds. To stand on the tips of one's toes, se dresser sur la pointe des pieds. To dance on one's toes, faire des pointes. To be on one's toes, être alerte. To tread on s.o.'s toes, (i) marcher sur les pieds de qn; (ii) F: offenser, froisser qn. P: To turn up one's toes, mourir, F: casser sa pipe. **2.** (a) Bout m, pointe f (de soulier, chaussette, etc.). (b) Farr: Pince f (de sabot ou de fer à cheval). (c) Golf: Pointe (de la crosse). **3.** (a) Mch: Touche f (de distribution Corliss). (b) Ergot (actionné par une came). **4.** Éperon m, saillie f (d'un arc-boutant). **'toe-cap**, s. Bootm: Bout rapporté; bout de pied (d'un soulier de football). **'toe-clip**, s. Cy: Cale-pied m, pl. cale-pieds.
toe², v.tr. To t. a sock, (i) tricoter, (ii) refaire, la pointe d'une chaussette. To t. a shoe, mettre ou remettre un bout à un soulier. **2.** To t. the line, the mark, (i) s'aligner; (ii) F: s'aligner avec son parti; se conformer au mot d'ordre. **3.** (a) Fb: Botter (le ballon) avec la pointe du pied. (b) F: Enlever le ballon à (qn); botter (qn). **5.** Golf: Frapper (la balle) avec la pointe de la crosse. **toed**, a. **1.** Two-t., three-t., à deux, trois, orteils. **2.** (Soulier) à bout rapporté.
toehold ['touhould], s. F: Mount: etc: Prise f précaire.
toenail ['touneil], s. Ongle m du pied.
toff [tɔf], s. P: Dandy m, aristo m. The toffs, les gens huppés, le gratin.
toffee ['tɔfi], s. Caramel m au beurre. Almond t., walnut t., caramel aux amandes, aux noix.
tog [tɔg], v.tr. & i. (togged) F: O: Attifer, fringuer. To t. (oneself) up, out, se faire beau; se mettre sur son trente-et-un.
toga ['tougə], s. Rom.Ant: Toge f.
together [tə'geðər], adv. Ensemble. (a) To go t., belong t., aller ensemble. We stand or fall t., nous sommes tous solidaires. (Of ships) To sail t., naviguer de conserve. T. with, avec; en même temps que.... (b) To gather t., (i) réunir, rassembler; (ii) se réunir, se rassembler. To strike two things t., frapper deux choses l'une contre l'autre. To bring t., rassembler, réunir. (c) To act t., agir de concert. All t., tout le monde ensemble; tous à la fois; tous en chœur. (d) For months t., pendant des mois entiers. For hours t., des heures durant.
toggle ['tɔgl], s. **1.** Nau: Cabillot m (d'amarrage). **2.** (a) Barrette f (de chaîne de montre). (b) Brake t., clef f de frein. (c) Halter-rope t., billot m de longe de licou. **'toggle-joint**, s. Mec.E: Genouillère f. **'toggle-lever**, s. Levier articulé; I.C.E: levier-bascule m (du carburateur). **'toggle-pin**, s. = TOGGLE 1.
Togo ['tougou]. Pr.n. Geog: (The Republic of) T., (la République du) Togo.
togs [tɔgz], s.pl. F: O: Nippes f, frusques f. Nau: Harbour t., long t., frusques d'escale.
toil¹ [tɔil], s. Travail dur, pénible; labeur m, peine f. **'toil-worn**, a. Usé par le travail.

toil², v.i. Travailler, peiner; se donner du mal. To t. and moil, peiner; travailler dur. To t. up a hill, gravir péniblement une colline.
toiler ['tɔilər], s. Travailleur, -euse.
toilet ['tɔilit], s. **1.** (= Washing, make-up) Toilette f. **2.** (In hotels, etc.) Les toilettes, les cabinets m. **'toilet-case**, s. Nécessaire m de toilette; trousse f de voyage. **'toilet-paper**, s. Papier m hygiénique. **'toilet-roll**, s. Rouleau m de papier hygiénique. **T.-r. fitting**, porte-papier m inv hygiénique. **'toilet-soap**, s. Savon m de toilette. **'toilet-table**, s. Coiffeuse f.
toils [tɔilz], s.pl. Ven: Filet m, lacs m. To be taken, get caught, in the t., se laisser prendre au filet; se laisser prendre au piège. Caught in his own t., pris à son propre piège.
toilsome ['tɔilsəm], a. Lit: Pénible, fatigant.
token ['touk(ə)n], s. **1.** Signe m, marque f, témoignage m (d'amitié, de respect, etc.). In t. of ..., as a t. of ..., en signe de ..., en témoignage de ..., comme marque de.... It gives t. of intelligence, cela annonce, indique, de l'intelligence. By the same t...., de plus.... T. payment, paiement symbolique. T. strike, grève d'avertissement. **2.** (a) Love t., gage m d'amour. (b) Jeton m (pour cabine téléphonique, etc.). (c) Book t., bon pour l'achat d'un livre. Flower t., chèque-fleurs m, pl. chèques-fleurs. **'token-money**, s. Monnaie f fiduciaire.
told. See TELL.
Toledo [tɔ'leidou]. Pr.n. Tolède.
tolerable ['tɔl(ə)rəbl], a. (a) Tolérable, supportable. (b) Passable; assez bon, F: potable. They enjoy a t. amount of freedom, ils jouissent d'une assez grande liberté. **-ably**, adv. **1.** Tolérablement. **2.** Passablement. It is t. certain that..., il est à peu près certain que....
tolerance ['tɔlər(ə)ns], s. **1.** Med: Tolérance f (d'un médicament); accoutumance (à un médicament). **2.** Tolérance (religieuse, etc.). To show great t., faire preuve de beaucoup de tolérance, d'une grande indulgence. **3.** Mec.E: T. of two thousandths, tolérance de deux millièmes (de pouce).
tolerant ['tɔlər(ə)nt], a. Tolérant (of, à l'égard de). **-ly**, adv. Avec tolérance.
tolerate ['tɔləreit], v.tr. Tolérer, supporter (la douleur, la contradiction). I can't t. him, je ne puis pas le souffrir.
toleration [,tɔlə'reiʃ(ə)n], s. Tolérance f (en matière de religion).
toll¹ [toul], s. **1.** (a) Droit m de passage; péage m. To pay t., payer un droit de passage. To pay the t., acquitter le péage. (b) Droit de place (au marché). **2.** Rent takes heavy t. of one's income, le loyer mange une grande partie de nos revenus. The t. of the roads, les accidents m, les hécatombes f, de la route. **'toll-bar**, s. Barrière f (de péage). **'toll-bridge**, s. Pont m à péage. **'toll call**, s. A: Tp: Communication interurbaine (entre villes peu éloignées). **'toll-collector**, s. Péager. -ère. **'toll-gate**, s. = TOLL-BAR. **'toll-house**, s. Bureau m de péage; péage m. **'toll-keeper**, s. Péager, -ère. **'toll road**, s. (Auto)-route f à péage.
toll², s. Tintement m, son m (de cloche).
toll³. 1. v.tr. Tinter, sonner (une cloche). Abs. To t. for the dead, sonner pour les morts. To t. s.o.'s death, sonner le glas (pour la mort de qn). **2.** v.i. (Of bell) (a) Tinter, sonner. (b) Sonner le glas. **tolling**, s. (a) Tintement m (de cloche). (b) Glas m.
Tom [tɔm]. **1.** Pr.n.m. (Dim. of Thomas) Thomas. F: Any T., Dick, or Harry, n'importe qui; le premier venu. **2.** T. cat, F: a tom, matou m. **'Tom 'Thumb.** Pr.n.m. Le petit Poucet; Tom Pouce. **'tom-tit**, s. Orn: Mésange bleue.
tomahawk¹ ['tɔməhɔːk], s. Hache f de guerre (des Peaux-Rouges); tomahawk m.
tomahawk², v.tr. Frapper (qn) avec un tomahawk; assommer (qn).
tomato, pl. -oes [tə'mɑːtou, -ouz], s. Tomate f. T. sauce, sauce f tomate.
tomb [tuːm], s. Tombe f; (with monument) tombeau m.
tombola ['tɔmbələ], s. Tombola f.

tomboy ['tɔmbɔi], s. Fillette f d'allures garçonnières. She's a regular t., c'est un garçon manqué.

tombstone ['tuːmstoun], s. Pierre tombale.

tome [toum], s. Tome m; gros volume.

tomfool ['tɔm'fuːl]. F: 1. s. Nigaud m, serin m. 2. attrib.a. Stupide, idiot. T. scheme, projet insensé.

tomfoolery [tɔm'fuːləri], s. F: Bêtise(s) f(pl); niaiserie(s) f(pl).

Tommy ['tɔmi]. 1. Pr.n.m. (Dim. of Thomas) Thomas. 2. Pr.n. F: O: T. Atkins, sobriquet du soldat anglais. s. A t., pl. tommies, un simple soldat, F: un troufion. **'tommy-gun,** s. Mitraillette f. **'tommy-'rot,** s. F: Bêtises fpl, inepties fpl.

tomorrow [tə'mɔrou], adv. & s. Demain (m). T. morning, demain matin. T. week, de demain en huit. The day after t., après-demain.

tomtom ['tɔmtɔm], s. Tam-tam m.

ton [tʌn], s. Meas: 1. Tonne f. Long t., gross t. (of 2240 lb.), tonne forte. Short t., net t. (of 2000 lb.), tonne courte. Metric t. (of 1000 kg. or 2204·6 lb.), tonne métrique. F: There's tons of it, il y en a des tas. F: Tons of money, un argent fou. 2. Nau: (a) Tonneau m (de jauge); tonne (de 100 pieds cubes). Per net register t., par tonne de jauge nette. (b) Measurement t., measured t., tonne d'arrimage, d'encombrement (de 40 pieds cubes). 3. P. To do the t., faire cent milles à l'heure (en moto).

tonal ['toun(ə)l], a. Ac: Mus: Tonal, -aux.

tonality [to'næliti], s. Tonalité f.

tone¹ [toun], s. 1. Son m, accent m; timbre m (de la voix, d'une cloche). T. quality, qualité f de la note (d'un instrument). Tp: Ringing t., signal m d'appel. 2. (a) Ton m, voix f. In an impatient t., d'un ton d'impatience. To alter one's t., changer de ton, de note. (b) To give a serious t. to a discussion, donner un ton sérieux à une discussion. Fin: The prevailing t., la tendance générale. The t. of the market, la tenue, l'allure f, du marché. (c) Med: Tonicité f (des muscles). Want of t., atonie f. (Of pers.) To lose t., faiblir; s'avachir. To recover t., se retremper. 3. Mus: Ac: Ton. Whole t., ton entier. 4. Ton, nuance f (d'une couleur). Warm tones, tons chauds. S.a. HALF-TONE. 5. Ling: Ton; accent m tonique. **'tone-arm,** s. Bras m acoustique (d'un phonographe). **'tone-'deafness,** s. Surdité musicale. **'tonepoem,** s. Mus: Poème m symphonique.

tone². 1. v.tr. (a) Régler la tonalité (d'un instrument). (b) Modifier la tonalité (d'un tableau). (c) Phot: Virer (une épreuve). (d) Tonifier (la peau, etc.). 2. v.i. To t. (in) with sth., s'harmoniser avec qch. **tone down.** 1. v.tr. Adoucir, atténuer (une expression, un contraste, une couleur); Art: estomper. 2. v.i. (Of pers.) Se radoucir; le prendre sur un ton plus doux. **tone up.** 1. v.tr. Tonifier (le système nerveux); retremper, F: remonter (qn). 2. v.i. Se tonifier. **'toning-up,** s. Tonification f. **toned,** a. Low-t., high-t., à ton bas, élevé. Low-t. conversation, conversation à voix basse. Full-t. voice, voix grave. **toning,** s. Phot: Virage m.

toneless ['tounlis], a. 1. (Couleur) sans éclat. 2. (Personne) veule; (voix) blanche, atone.

tonga¹ ['tɔŋgə], s. Voiture légère à deux roues (en usage aux Indes).

Tonga². Pr.n. The T. Islands, l'archipel m de Tonga; les îles f des Amis.

tongs [tɔŋz], s.pl. 1. (Fire-)t., pincettes f. 2. Ind: Pince(s) f, tenailles fpl.

tongue¹ [tʌŋ], s. 1. Langue f. (a) To put out one's t., montrer, tirer, la langue (at s.o., à qn). (b) To have a ready, a glib, t., avoir la langue bien pendue. To keep a watch on one's t., surveiller sa langue. To hold one's t., tenir sa langue. To find one's t. again, retrouver la parole. To keep a civil t. in one's head, rester courtois. To compliment s.o. with one's t. in one's cheek, faire des compliments ironiques à qn. He always has his t. in his cheek, il ne fait que blaguer. (Of hounds) To give t., donner de la voix. 2. Langue, idiome m (d'un peuple). The German t., la langue allemande. The gift of tongues, le don des langues. 3. Langue f (de terre, de feu); patte f, languette f (de soulier); battant m (de cloche); ardillon m (de boucle); soie f (de couteau, de lime); flèche f (de chariot). Mus: Languette, anche f (de hautbois). Carp: Languette.

S.a. GROOVE¹. **'tongue-depressor,** s. Surg: Abaisse-langue m. **'tongue-rail,** s. Rail: Aiguille f. **'tongue-tied,** a. Qui a la langue liée. 1. Muet, -ette (d'étonnement, etc.); interdit. 2. Tenu au silence. **'tongue-twister,** s. Mot m ou phrase f difficile à prononcer, phrase à décrocher la mâchoire.

tongue², v.tr. (a) Carp: Langueter (le bord d'une planche). S.a. GROOVE². (b) Mus: To t. a passage (on the flute, etc.), détacher les notes d'un passage. **tongued,** a. A langue, à languette.

tonic ['tɔnik]. 1. a. (a) Med: Tonique, remontant, réconfortant. (b) Gram: (Accent) tonique. (c) Med: T. spasm, convulsion f tonique. 2. s. (a) Med: Tonique m, reconstituant m, fortifiant m. (Of news, etc.) To act as a t. on s.o., réconforter qn; remonter qn. (b) Mus: Tonique f.

tonicity [to'nisiti], s. Tonicité f.

tonight [tə'nait], adv. & s. Cette nuit; ce soir.

tonka ['tɔŋkə], s. T. (bean), tonka f.

Tonkin ['tɔŋ'kin], **Tongking** ['tɔŋ'kiŋ]. Pr.n. Le Tonkin.

Tonkin(g)ese [tɔŋki'niːz], a. & s. Geog: Tonkinois, -oise.

tonnage ['tʌnidʒ], s. 1. Nau: Tonnage m, jauge f. Register(ed) t., tonnage officiel. Gross t., tonnage brut. 2. Tonnage (d'un port, d'un pays).

tonsil ['tɔnsl], s. Amygdale f. Med: Enlarged tonsils, hypertrophie f des amygdales.

tonsillectomy [tɔnsi'lektəmi], s. Surg: Amygdalectomie f.

tonsillitis [tɔnsi'laitis], s. Med: Angine f (tonsillaire); amygdalite f.

tonsorial [tɔn'sɔːriəl], a. F: Hum: De barbier. T. artist, artiste capillaire.

tonsure¹ ['tɔnʃər], s. Tonsure f.

tonsure², v.tr. Tonsurer.

tontine [tɔn'tiːn], s. Ins: Tontine f.

tonus ['tounəs], s. Med: 1. Tonicité f, tonus m. 2. Contraction f tonique.

Tony ['touni]. Pr.n.m. (Dim. of Antony) Antoine.

too [tuː], adv. 1. Trop, par trop. T. difficult a job, travail (par) trop difficile. T. much money, trop d'argent. To work t. much, too little, travailler trop, trop peu. Ten shillings t. much, dix shillings de trop. The task is t. much for me, la tâche est au-dessus de mes forces. He was t. much, F: one t. many, for me, il était trop fort pour moi. F: To have had one t. many, être gris, pompette. The hole was t. narrow for a rat to come in by, le trou était trop étroit pour laisser passer un rat. I know him all t. well, je ne le connais que trop. 2. (Also) Aussi; également. I t. want some, il m'en faut également; moi aussi il m'en faut. 3. (Moreover) D'ailleurs; de plus; en outre. The prisoner, t., inspired little sympathy, le prisonnier, d'ailleurs, inspirait peu de sympathie.

took. See TAKE.

tool¹ [tuːl], s. 1. Outil m; instrument m, ustensile m. Garden tools, gardening tools, outils, matériel m, de jardinage. A bad workman always finds fault with his tools, à méchant ouvrier point de bon outil. 2. F: Instrument, créature f. To make a t. of s.o., se servir de qn (dans un but intéressé). He was a mere t. in their hands, il était devenu leur créature. 3. V: Membre viril. **'tool-bag,** s. Sac m à outils; (of car, etc) sacoche f. **'tool-basket,** s. Cabas m. **'toolbox, -chest,** s. Coffre m à outils. **'tool-holder,** s. Porte-outil(s) m inv. **'tool-outfit,** s. Outillage m. **'tool-rest,** s. Support m d'outil; porte-outil(s) m inv (de tour).

tool², v.tr. 1. (a) Bookb: Ciseler, dorer (une tranche, une reliure). (b) Stonew: Bretteler (une pierre). (c) Usiner, travailler (une pièce venue de fonte). 2. U.S: Équiper (une usine). **tooling,** s. 1. (a) Ciselage m. (b) Usinage m. 2. Bookb: Ciselure f, dorure f (du dos ou des plats). Blind t., dorure à froid. Gold t., dorure à chaud. 3. Outillage m.

toot¹ [tuːt], s. 1. Son m, appel m (de clairon, etc.). 2. Nau: Coup m de sirène. Aut: Coup de klaxon.

toot². 1. v.tr. F: To t. a horn, a trumpet, sonner du cor, de la trompette. Aut: To t. the horn, corner; klaxonner. 2. v.i. (Of pers.) Sonner du cor. Aut: Corner, klaxonner; avertir. To t. on the trumpet, sonner de la trompette.

tooth[1], *pl.* **teeth** [tu:θ, ti:θ], *s.* **1.** Dent *f.* **Second teeth,** dentition définitive. **Front teeth,** dents de devant. **A fine set of teeth,** une belle denture. **False t.,** fausse dent. **(Set of) false teeth,** dentier *m,* F: râtelier *m.* To cut one's teeth, faire, percer, ses dents. To have a t. out, se faire arracher une dent. To knock a t. out of s.o.'s mouth, faire sauter une dent à qn; édenter qn. F: To cast, throw, sth. in s.o.'s teeth, jeter qch. à la figure de qn, reprocher qch. à qn. In the teeth of all opposition, en dépit de toute opposition. To show one's teeth, montrer les dents. Armed to the teeth, armé jusqu'aux dents. To fight t. and nail, se battre avec acharnement. He went at it t. and nail, il y allait de toutes ses forces. Sth. to get one's teeth into, qch. de substantiel. To set one's teeth, serrer les dents. To mutter sth. between one's teeth, grommeler qch. entre ses dents. To be long in the t., n'être plus jeune; P: avoir de la bouteille. To have a sweet t., aimer les sucreries. T. powder, poudre *f* dentifrice. **2.** Dent (de scie, de peigne, de fourche); dent, alluchon *m* (de roue d'engrenage). The teeth of a wheel, la denture. To break the teeth of a comb, édenter un peigne. **3.** *Const.* = TOOTHING-STONE. **4.** Grain *m* (du papier).

tooth[2]. **1.** *v.tr.* (*a*) Denter, créneler. (*b*) Bretteler (une pierre). **2.** *v.i.* (*Of cog-wheels*) S'engrener. **toothed,** *a.* **1.** T. wheel, roue dentée; roue d'engrenage. T. plate (*of safety razor, etc.*), peigne *m.* **2.** *Bot:* Dentelé. **3.** White-t., aux dents blanches. **toothing,** *s.* (*a*) Dents *fpl* (d'une roue); crénelage *m.* (*b*) *Const:* Arrachement *m.* (*c*) *Stonew:* Bretture *f.* **'toothing-stone,** *s. Const:* Pierre *f* d'attente; harpe *f.*

toothache ['tu:θeik], *s.* Mal *m* de dents. To have t., avoir mal aux dents.

toothbrush ['tu:θbrʌʃ], *s.* Brosse *f* à dents. T. moustache, moustache taillée en brosse. T. holder, porte-brosses (à dents) *m inv.*

toothless ['tu:θlis], *a.* Sans dents; édenté.

toothpaste ['tu:θpeist], *a.* Pâte *f* dentifrice.

toothpick ['tu:θpik], *s.* Cure-dents *m inv.*

toothsome ['tu:θsəm], *a.* Savoureux; agréable au goût. T. morsel, morceau friand, fin morceau.

tootle[1] ['tu:tl], *v.i.* F: Corner, klaxonner, doucement (et de façon continue). To t. on the flute, flûter; seriner un air de flûte.

top[1] [tɔp]. **I.** *s.* **1.** Haut *m,* sommet *m,* cime *f,* faîte *m* (d'une montagne, d'un arbre); haut (de la tête). At the t. of the tree, (i) en haut de l'arbre; (ii) au premier rang de sa profession. From t. to bottom, de haut en bas; de fond en comble. From t. to toe, de la tête aux pieds; de pied en cap. To put the best apples on t., mettre les plus belles pommes sur le dessus (du panier). To come out on t., avoir le dessus. One thing happens on t. of another, the other, les événements se précipitent. To go to bed on t. of one's supper, se coucher sitôt dîné. On t. of it all he wanted . . ., pour comble il a voulu. . . . **2.** Surface *f* (de l'eau, de la terre); dessus *m* (d'une table, etc.); impériale (d'un autobus). Oil always comes to the t., l'huile surnage toujours. **3.** Dessus (d'un soulier); revers *m* (d'un bas, etc.); scion *m* (d'une canne à pêche); capote *f* (d'une voiture). *Aut:* Hard t., berline *f.* F: To blow one's t., s'emporter, F: sortir de ses gonds. **4.** Tête *f* (de page, etc.). *Bookb:* Gilt t., tête dorée. **5.** Haut bout (de la table). The t. of the street, le haut de la rue. *Sch:* To be at the t. of the form, être à la tête de la classe. **6.** To shout at the t. of one's voice, crier à tue-tête. I was feeling on t. of my form, je me sentais tout à fait en train, en pleine forme. *Aut:* To climb a hill in t., prendre une montée en prise (directe). *Nau:* The t. of the flood, of the tide, le haut de l'eau; l'étale *m* du flot. **7.** *Bot:* Flowering t., sommité fleurie. Turnip tops, carrot tops, fanes *f* de navets, de carottes. **8.** *Nau:* Hune *f.* Main t., grand-hune *f.* Fore t., hune de misaine. *Navy:* Director t., hune de télépointage. (*In circus*) Big t., chapiteau *m.* **II.** *a, attrib.a.* **1.** Supérieur; du dessus, du haut, d'en haut. The t. floor, storey, le dernier étage, l'étage du haut. F: To be weak in the t. storey, être faible d'esprit, timbré. T. stair, dernière marche (en montant). *Mus:* The t. notes, les notes hautes. *Aut:* T. gear, prise directe. *Adm:* T. secret, très secret, ultra-secret. *Cu:* T. ribs

(of beef), plat *m* de côtes; plates côtes. *S.a.* HAT. **2.** Premier, -ière; principal, -aux. T. people, personnalités *fpl,* gens éminents. F: T. brass, (i) *Mil:* les officiers supérieurs, les huiles; (ii) les gros bonnets, les grosses légumes. *Sch:* The t. boy, le premier de la classe. **'top-'boots,** *s.pl.* Bottes *f* à revers. **'top coat,** *s.* **1.** Pardessus *m.* **2.** Couche *f* de finition (de peinture). **'top 'dog,** *s.* F: Vainqueur *m.* To be t. d., avoir le dessus. **top-'dressing,** *s. Agr:* Fumure *f* en surface. **'top-'hamper,** *s.* Superstructure *f* (d'un pont, etc.). *Nau:* Fardage *m.* **'top-'heavy,** *a.* Trop lourd du haut; peu stable. (*Of ship*) Trop chargé dans les hauts. **'top-'notch,** *attrib.a.* F: De premier ordre. The t.-n. people of Paris, le gratin de la société parisienne. **'top-'notcher,** *s.* F: Crème *f.* He's a t.-n., c'est la crème, un as.

top[2], *v.tr.* (**topped** [tɔpt]) **1.** Écimer, étêter (un arbre). To t. and tail gooseberries, éplucher des groseilles à maquereau. **2.** (*a*) Surmonter, couronner, coiffer (with, de). A statue tops the column, une statue surmonte la colonne. (*b*) He topped off his dinner with a cup of coffee, il a couronné son dîner d'une tasse de café. And to t. it all . . ., et pour comble . . .; et brochant sur le tout. . . . **3.** Dépasser, surpasser. To t. sth. in height, dépasser qch. en hauteur. The takings have topped a thousand pounds, les recettes dépassent mille livres. To t. s.o. by a head, dépasser qn de la tête. **4.** To t. a hill, atteindre le sommet d'une colline. The squadron topped the ridge, l'escadron franchit l'arête. **5.** To t. a list, a class, être à la tête d'une liste, de la classe. **6.** *Golf:* Calotter, topper (la balle). **top up,** *v.tr.* Remplir (complètement). *Aut:* To t. up (*battery, oil, etc.*), faire l'appoint. T. her up, faites le plein. (*When serving drinks*) Let me t. it up! encore un peu? **-topped,** *a.* Cloud-t. peaks, sommets couronnés de nuages. Ivory-t. walking stick, canne à pomme d'ivoire. **topping,** *a.* F: *O:* Excellent, chic. A t. idea, une riche idée.

top[3], *s.* (**Spinning, peg**) t., toupie *f.* **To spin a t.,** faire aller une toupie.

topaz ['toupæz], *s.* Topaze *f.* Pink t., topaze brûlée.

tope [toup], *v.i.* F: Boire, pinter.

topee ['toupi(:)], *s.* Casque colonial.

toper ['toupər], *s.* F: Ivrogne *m,* buveur *m,* soiffard *m.*

topgallant [tɔp'gælənt, tə'gælənt], *a. & s. Nau:* (Voile *f,* mât *m*) de perroquet.

tophole ['tɔphoul], *a.* F: *O:* Épatant, chic.

topi ['toupi(:)], *s.* Casque colonial.

topiary ['toupjəri], *a. & s. Hort:* T.(work), taille ornementale des arbres.

topic ['tɔpik], *s.* Matière *f* (d'un écrit, d'une discussion); sujet *m,* thème *m* (de conversation). Topics of the day, questions *f* d'actualité.

topical ['tɔpik(ə)l], *a.* **1.** Qui se rapporte au lieu; topique; local, -aux. **2.** T. allusion, allusion aux événements du jour. T. song, chanson d'actualités.

topicality [,tɔpi'kæliti], *s.* Actualité *f.*

topknot ['tɔpnɔt], *s.* **1.** *A.Cost:* Fontange *f.* **2.** (*a*) Aigrette *f* (d'un oiseau). (*b*) Chignon (porté sur le front) topknot.

topmast ['tɔpma:st], *s.* Mât *m* de hune; mât de flèche.

topmost ['tɔpmoust], *a.* Le plus haut; le plus élevé. Having reached the t. height . . ., arrivé au faîte. . . .

topographer [tə'pɔgrəfər], *s.* Topographe *m.*

topography [tə'pɔgrəfi], *s.* Topographie *f.*

topper ['tɔpər], *s.* F: **1.** *O:* Type épatant, chose épatante, formidable. **2.** Chapeau haut de forme.

topple ['tɔpl]. **1.** *v.i.* (*a*) To t. (down, over), tomber, s'écrouler, culbuter. To bring the Government toppling down, faire tomber le gouvernement. (*b*) Chanceler, vaciller, branler. **2.** *v.tr.* To t. sth. down, over, faire tomber qch.; jeter qch. à bas.

tops [tɔps], *a.* F: *esp. U.S:* To be t., être la crème de la crème, le dessus du panier.

topsail ['tɔpsl], *s. Nau:* Hunier *m;* (*of cutter*) flèche *f.* Main t., grand hunier.

topside ['tɔp'said], *s. Cu:* Tende *f* de tranche (de bœuf).

topsides ['tɔpsaidz], *s.pl. Nau:* Hauts *m,* œuvres mortes, accastillage *m* (d'un navire).

topsy-turvy ['tɔpsi'tɜ:vi], *adv. & adj.* Sens dessus dessous. **To turn sth. t.-t.,** mettre qch. sens dessus dessous; renverser qch. **To turn everything t.-t.,** tout bouleverser. *F:* tout chambouler. **Everything is t.-t.,** tout est en désarroi, en l'air.

toque [touk], *s. Cost:* Toque *f*,

tor [tɔ:r], *s.* Pic rocheux, éminence *f* conique (dans le sud-ouest de l'Angleterre).

torch [tɔ:tʃ], *s.* 1. Torche *f*, flambeau *m. Lit:* **To hand on the t.,** transmettre le flambeau (à la génération suivante). 2. (Electric) t., lampe *f* électrique, de poche; torche électrique. '**torch-bearer,** *s.* Porte-flambeau *m inv.* '**torch-light,** *s.* Lueur *f* de(s) flambeaux. **T.-l. procession, tattoo,** retraite *f* aux flambeaux; défilé *m* aux flambeaux.

tore. *See* TEAR².

toreador ['tɔriədɔ:r], *s.* Toréador *m.*

torment¹ ['tɔ:ment], *s.* Tourment *m*, torture *f*, supplice *m.* **He suffered torments,** il souffrait le martyre. **To be in t.,** être au supplice. *F:* **That child is a positive t.,** cet enfant est assommant.

torment² [tɔ:'ment], *v.tr.* Tourmenter, torturer (qn). **To be tormented by hunger,** éprouver les tourments de la faim. **Tormented with remorse,** tourmenté par les remords; en proie aux remords. **Tormented with suspense,** angoissé par l'attente.

tormentil ['tɔ:məntil], *s. Bot:* Tormentille *f.*

tormentor [tɔ:'mentər], *s.* (*a*) *Hist:* Tourmenteur *m*, bourreau *m.* (*b*) **The dog and its tormentors,** le chien et les gamins qui étaient après.

torn. *See* TEAR².

tornado, *pl.* -oes [tɔ:'neidou, -ouz], *s.* Tornade *f*, ouragan *m*, cyclone *m.* **Political t.,** ouragan politique.

torpedo¹, *pl.* -oes [tɔ:'pi:dou, -ouz], *s.* 1. *Ich:* Torpille *f.* 2. *Navy: Mil.Av:* Torpille *f.* **To make a t. attack,** attaquer à la torpille. **T. officer,** officier torpilleur. *Navy:* **T. boom,** hampe *f* porte-torpille. **T. tube,** (tube *m*) lance-torpille (*m*). **Motor t. boat,** vedette *f* lance-torpilles. *Av:* **Aerial t.,** torpille aérienne. **T. bomber, carrier, plane,** avion torpilleur.

torpedo², *v.tr.* Torpiller.

torpid ['tɔ:pid], *a.* (*a*) Engourdi, inerte, torpide. (*b*) Endormi, nonchalant; léthargique. **T. liver,** foie paresseux.

torpidity [tɔ:'piditi], **torpidness** ['tɔ:pidnis], *s.* Engourdissement *m*, inertie *f*, torpeur *f*; léthargie *f*, lenteur *f.*

torpor ['tɔ:pər], *s.* Torpeur *f.* **To arouse oneself from one's t.,** sortir de sa torpeur.

torque¹ [tɔ:k], *s. Archeol:* Torque *f* (des Gaulois).

torque², *s. Mec:* Couple *m* de torsion; couple moteur. **Starting t.,** couple de démarrage. *El:* **Armature t.,** couple d'induit.

torrefaction [,tɔri'fækʃ(ə)n], *s.* Torréfaction *f.*

torrefy ['tɔrifai], *v.tr.* Torréfier.

torrent ['tɔrənt], *s.* Torrent *m.* **Mountain t.,** torrent de montagne. (*Of rain*) **To fall in torrents,** tomber à torrents, à verse. **T. of abuse,** torrent d'injures.

torrential [tɔ'renʃ(ə)l], *a.* Torrentiel, -elle; torrentueux, -euse.

torrid ['tɔrid], *a.* Torride.

torridity [tɔ'riditi], *s.* Chaleur *f*, caractère *m* torride (of, de).

torsion ['tɔ:ʃ(ə)n], *s.* Torsion *f. Mec: Aut:* **T. bar,** barre *f* de torsion. **T. balance,** balance *f* de torsion.

torsional ['tɔ:ʃənl], *a. Mec:* De torsion. **T. stress, strain,** effort *m* de torsion.

torso, *pl.* -os ['tɔ:sou, -ouz], *s.* Torse *m.*

tort [tɔ:t], *s. Jur:* Acte *m* dommageable; dommage *m*; préjudice *m.*

torticollis [,tɔ:ti'kɔlis], *s. Med:* Torticolis *m.*

tortoise ['tɔ:təs], *s.* 1. *Z:* Tortue *f.* 2. *Rom.Ant:* Tortue (de boucliers).

tortoiseshell ['tɔ:təʃel], *s.* Écaille *f* de tortue. **Imitation t.,** simili-écaille. **T. (-rimmed) spectacles,** lunettes en écaille. **T. cat,** chat écaille de tortue. **T. butterfly,** (vanesse *f*) tortue.

Tortuga [tɔ:'tu:gə]. *Pr.n.* (L'île *f* de) la Tortue.

tortuosity [,tɔ:tju'ɔsiti], *s.* Tortuosité *f.*

tortuous ['tɔ:tjuəs], *a.* Tortueux, -euse. **T. descent,** descente sinueuse. **T. style,** style contourné. **T. mind,** esprit tortu.

torture¹ ['tɔ:tʃər], *s.* 1. *Hist:* Torture *f*, question *f.* **To put s.o. to the t.,** mettre qn à la torture; appliquer la question à qn. 2. Torture, tourment *m*, supplice *m.* **Gout is a real t.,** la goutte est un supplice.

torture², *v.tr.* (*a*) *Hist:* Appliquer la question à (qn); mettre (qn) à la question. (*b*) Torturer (qn); mettre (qn) à la torture, au supplice. **Tortured by remorse,** tenaillé par le remords. **torturing,** *a.* Tourmenteur, -euse.

torturer ['tɔ:tʃərər], *s.* 1. *Hist:* Bourreau *m.* 2. Harceleur, -euse.

Tory ['tɔ:ri], *a. & s. Pol:* Tory (*m*).

Toryism ['tɔ:riizm], *s. Pol:* Torysme *m.*

tosh [tɔʃ], *s. F:* Bêtises *fpl*, blague(s) *f(pl)*.

toss¹ [tɔs], *s.* 1. Action *f* de jeter (qch.) en l'air. (*a*) Lancement *m*, jet *m* (d'une balle, etc.). (*b*) Coup *m* de pile ou face. *Sp:* Tirage *m* au sort. **To win the t.,** gagner à pile ou face; *Sp:* gagner le toss. 2. **T. of the head,** mouvement de tête impatient, dédaigneux. 3. Chute *f* de cheval. **To take a t.,** faire une chute de cheval; vider les arçons.

toss², *v.* (tossed) [tɔst]) 1. *v.tr.* (*a*) Lancer, jeter, (une balle, etc.) en l'air; (*of bull*) lancer (qn) en l'air; (*of horse*) démonter (un cavalier). **To t. a pancake,** (faire) sauter, retourner, une crêpe. **To t. sth. to s.o.,** jeter qch. à qn. **To t. s.o. in a blanket,** berner qn; *F:* passer qn à la couverture. *Nau:* **To t. (the) oars,** mâter les avirons. (*b*) **To t. (up) a coin,** jouer à pile ou face. *Abs.* To t. for sth., jouer qch. à pile ou face. **To t. for sides,** choisir les camps (à pile ou face). (*c*) **To t. one's head,** relever la tête d'un air dédaigneux, méprisant. (*Of horse*) **To t. its head,** hocher de la tête; encenser. (*d*) Agiter, secouer, ballotter. **Tossed on the waves,** ballotté par les flots. 2. *v.i.* (*a*) **To t. (about) in bed,** se tourner et se retourner dans son lit. **To t. in one's sleep,** s'agiter dans son sommeil. (*b*) **To t. on the waves,** être ballotté par les flots. (*Of ship*) **To pitch and t.,** tanguer. (*c*) (*Of the waves*) S'agiter. **toss aside, away,** *v.tr.* Jeter (qch.) de côté. **toss off,** *v.tr.* Avaler d'un trait, lamper (un verre de vin); expédier (une tâche); écrire (un article) au pied levé. **toss-'up,** *s.* 1. (*Of coin*) Coup *m* de pile ou face. 2. Affaire *f* à issue douteuse. **It is a t.-up,** les chances sont égales. **tossing,** *s.* 1. Lancement *m* en l'air. 2. Agitation *f*, ballottement *m.* **We had a t. in the Channel,** nous avons été secoués dans la Manche.

tot¹ [tɔt], *s.* 1. Tout(e) petit(e) enfant. **Tiny t.,** bambin, -ine, petit marmot. 2. *F:* Goutte *f*, petit verre (de whisky, etc.).

tot², *v.* (totted) 1. *v.tr.* **To t. up a column of figures,** additionner une colonne de chiffres. **To t. up expenses,** faire le compte des dépenses. 2. *v.i.* (*Of expenses, etc.*) **To t. up,** s'élever, se monter (to, à).

total¹ ['toutl]. 1. *a.* Total, -aux; complet, -ète; global, -aux. (*a*) **T. amount,** somme totale, globale. **T. tonnage,** tonnage global (d'un port, etc.). (*b*) **The t. loss of his fortune,** la perte totale de sa fortune. **They were in t. ignorance of it,** ils l'ignoraient complètement. **T. failure,** échec complet. *Astr:* **T. eclipse,** éclipse totale. 2. *s.* Total *m*; montant *m*; tout *m.* **Grand t.,** total global. **-ally,** *adv.* Totalement, entièrement, complètement.

total², *v.tr. & i.* (totalled) 1. Totaliser, additionner (les dépenses). 2. **To t. up to . . .,** to t. . . ., s'élever à, se monter à (une somme, un nombre).

totalitarian [,toutæli'tɛəriən], *a.* Totalitaire.

totalitarianism [,toutæli'tɛəriənizm], *s.* Totalitarisme *m.*

totality [tou'tæliti], *s.* Totalité *f.*

totalization [,toutəlai'zeiʃ(ə)n], *s.* Totalisation *f.*

totalizator ['toutəlaizeitər], *s. Turf:* Totaliseur *m*, totalisateur *m* (des paris).

totalize ['toutəlaiz], *v.tr.* Totaliser, additionner.

tote¹ [tout], *s. F:* = TOTALIZATOR.

tote², *v.tr. U.S:* Transporter (des marchandises, etc.); porter (qch.).

totem ['toutəm], *s.* Totem *m.* **T. pole,** poteau qui porte une représentation du totem.

t'other, tother ['tʌðər], *a. & pron. F:* = the other.

totter¹ ['tɔtər], *s.* Chancellement *m.*

totter², *v.i.* **1.** (*Of pers.*) (*a*) Chanceler. To t. to one's feet, se relever en chancelant. To t. in, out, entrer, sortir, d'un pas mal assuré, d'un pas chancelant. (*b*) Tituber (sous le coup de l'ivresse). **2.** (*Of building, etc.*) Menacer ruine; chanceler, branler. **tottering**, *a.* Chancelant; (*of drunken pers.*) titubant. T. steps, pas mal assurés. T. empire, empire qui menace ruine, qui croule.

tottery ['tɔtəri], *a.* Chancelant.

toucan ['tu:kæn], *s. Orn:* Toucan *m.*

touch¹ [tʌtʃ], *s.* **1.** (*a*) Attouchement *m.* To give s.o. a t., toucher qn. I felt a t. on my arm, je sentis qu'on me touchait le bras. (*b*) *Mil:* T. of elbows, le coude à coude. **2.** (Le sens du) toucher; tact. To know sth. by the t., reconnaître qch. au toucher. **3.** (*Feel*) The cold t. of marble, le contact froid du marbre. **4.** (*a*) Léger coup. To give one's horse a t. of the spurs, toucher son cheval de l'éperon. (*b*) Touche *f* (de pinceau); coup *m* (de crayon). To add a few touches to a picture, faire quelques retouches *f* à un tableau. To give the finishing touch(es), the final t. to sth., mettre la dernière main à qch. **5.** (*a*) Sculptor with a bold t., sculpteur au ciseau hardi. Delicate t. (with the brush), coup de pinceau délicat. To write with a light t., avoir la plume légère, le style léger. (*b*) *Mus:* Toucher *m. Typewr:* Frappe *f.* **6.** (*a*) T. of salt, of garlic, pointe *f* de sel, d'ail. T. of satire, pointe de satire. T. of rouge, soupçon *m* de rouge. The first touches of autumn, les premières atteintes de l'automne. There was a t. of bitterness in his reply, il répondit avec une nuance d'amertume. T. of nature, trait naturel. (*b*) T. of fever, of flu, of gout, soupçon, brin, de fièvre; un peu de grippe; légère attaque de goutte. **7.** Contact *m.* To be in t. with s.o., être en contact avec qn; être en rapport avec qn. To get in(to) t. with s.o., joindre, contacter, qn; prendre contact avec qn. To get in t. with the police, se mettre en communication avec la police. To put s.o. in t. with s.o., mettre qn en relations avec qn. To lose t. with s.o., perdre qn de vue; perdre contact avec qn. The personal t., les rapports personnels (avec les clients, etc.). **8.** *Fb:* Touche. Kick into t., envoi *m* en touche. **9.** *F:* It was a near t., cela n'a tenu qu'à un fil. 'touch-in-'goal, *s. Rugby Fb:* Touche *f* de but. 'touch-line, *s. Fb:* Ligne *f* de touche. 'touch-type, *v.i.* Taper à la machine au toucher. 'touch-typist, *s.* Dactylo *mf* qui tape au toucher; dactylo accompli(e).

touch². I. *v.tr.* **1.** (*a*) Toucher. To t. sth. with one's finger, toucher qch. du doigt. To t. s.o. on the shoulder, toucher l'épaule à qn. To t. one's hat, porter, mettre, la main à son chapeau. *F:* T. wood! touche du bois! Don't t. those eggs, ne touchez pas à ces œufs. To t. land, atterrir, aborder. *S.a.* BARGE-POLE, BOTTOM¹ 1, GROUND² 1. (*b*) His garden touches mine, son jardin touche au mien. (*c*) Effleurer (les cordes de la harpe). To t. a spring, faire jouer un ressort. (*d*) *v.ind.tr.* To t. on a subject, toucher, effleurer, un sujet. (*e*) Toucher, atteindre, The law can't t. him, la loi ne peut rien contre lui. No one can t. him in comedy, personne ne l'approche dans la comédie. (*f*) I never t. wine, jamais je ne bois de vin. **2.** (*a*) Produire de l'effet sur (qch.). The file will not t. it, la lime ne mord pas dessus. *S.a.* RAW II. (*b*) I couldn't t. the history paper, je n'ai pas pu répondre à la moindre question en histoire. **3.** Toucher, émouvoir (qn). To be touched by s.o.'s kindness, être touché de la bonté de qn. **4.** The question touches you nearly, la question vous touche de près. **5.** Flowers touched by the frost, fleurs atteintes, touchées, par la gelée. *F:* To t. s.o. for a fiver, taper qn de cinq livres. II. **touch**, *v.i.* **1.** (*Of persons, thgs*) Se toucher. (*a*) Être en contact. (*b*) Venir en contact. **2.** *Nau:* To t. at a port, faire escale à un port. **touch down**, *v.i. Av:* Atterrir; faire escale. *Rugby Fb:* Toucher dans les buts. 'touch-down, *s.* Touché *m.* **touch off**, *v.tr.* Faire jouer, faire exploser (une mine). **touch up**, *v.tr.* Faire des retouches à (un tableau); badigeonner (un vieux meuble); (*of paintwork*) faire des raccords (en peinture). 'touching-'up, *s. Art:* Repeint *m.* **touched**, *a. F:* Toqué, timbré. He's slightly t., il a un grain (de folie). **touching**. **1.** *a.* Touchant, émouvant, attendrissant.

2. *prep.* Touchant, concernant. -ly, *adv.* D'une manière touchante. 'touch and 'go, *s.* It was t. and go whether we should catch the train, nous courions grand risque de manquer le train. That was t. and go! *F:* il était moins cinq!

touchiness ['tʌtʃinis], *s.* Susceptibilité *f*, irascibilité *f.*

touchstone ['tʌtʃstoun], *s.* Pierre *f* de touche.

touchwood ['tʌtʃwud], *s.* Amadou *m.*

touchy ['tʌtʃi], *a.* Susceptible, ombrageux, -euse. To be t., se piquer, se froisser, facilement. He is very t. on that point, il n'entend pas raillerie là-dessus. To be t. on a point of honour, être chatouilleux sur le point d'honneur.

tough [tʌf], *a.* **1.** Dur, résistant. T. meat, viande coriace. **2.** (*Of pers.*) Fort, solide. To become t. (through training), s'endurcir. **3.** (*Of pers.*) Raide, inflexible. *F:* He's a t. customer! il est peu commode! **4.** *F:* (*a*) (*Of task*) Rude, difficile. (*b*) That's t.! c'est dur pour vous! **5.** *s. F:* Voyou *m*, bandit *m*; *F:* un dur. -ly, *adv.* **1.** Avec ténacité. **2.** Vigoureusement. **3.** Avec opiniâtreté.

toughen ['tʌfn], **1.** *v.tr.* (*a*) Durcir (qn). (*b*) Endurcir (qn). **2.** *v.i.* (*a*) Durcir. (*b*) (*Of pers.*) S'endurcir.

toughish ['tʌfiʃ], *a.* **1.** Plutôt dur; (*of meat*) peu tendre. **2.** (Travail) assez dur, peu facile.

toughness ['tʌfnis], *s.* **1.** Dureté *f*; résistance *f*; (*of meat*) coriacité *f.* **2.** (*a*) Force *f*, solidité *f.* (*b*) Résistance *f* à la fatigue. **3.** Caractère *m* peu commode (de qn). **4.** Difficulté *f* (d'un travail).

tour¹ [tuər], *s.* **1.** Tour *m*; voyage *m* circulaire. Conducted tours, voyages organisés. Walking t., excursion à pied. Motor t., randonnée (en auto, en car). **2.** T. of inspection, tournée *f* de visite. *Th:* To take a company on t., emmener une troupe en tournée.

tour², *v.tr. & i.* To t. a country, faire le tour d'un pays; voyager dans un pays. *Th:* To t. the provinces, faire une tournée en province. *Th:* Touring company, troupe *f* en tournée.

tourist ['tuərist], *s.* Touriste *mf.* T. agency, bureau *m* de tourisme. T. centre, centre *m*, ville *f*, de tourisme. The t. trade, le tourisme. T. class, classe touriste. T. information, renseignements *m* touristiques.

touristic [tuə'ristik], *a.* Touristique.

tourmalin(e) ['tuəməlin, -i:n], *s.* Tourmaline *f.*

tournament ['tuənəmənt], *s.* **1.** *Hist:* (*a*) Tournoi *m.* (*b*) Carrousel *m.* **2.** Tennis t., tournoi de tennis. Chess t., concours *m* d'échecs. Bridge t., tournoi de bridge.

tournedos ['tuənədou], *s. Cu:* T. (steak), tournedos *m.*

tourniquet ['tuənikei], *s. Surg:* Tourniquet *m*, garrot *m.*

tousle ['tauzl], *v.tr.* **1.** Houspiller, tirailler (qn). **2.** Ébouriffer (les cheveux).

tout¹ [taut], *s.* **1.** Racoleur *m*; bonisseur *m*; démarcheur *m*; (*for hotels*) rabatteur *m*, pisteur *m.* **2.** *Turf:* Espion *m.*

tout², *v.i.* **1.** *Turf:* Espionner dans les écuries. **2.** To t. for customers, courir après la clientèle; racoler des clients.

tow¹ [tou], *s.* **1.** (Câble *m* de) remorque *f.* **2.** To take a boat in t., prendre un bateau à la remorque. To be taken in t., se mettre à la remorque. **3.** (*a*) (*Vessel towed*) Remorque. (*b*) A t. of barges, une rame de péniches. 'tow-boat, *s.* Remorqueur *m*; toueur *m.* 'tow-line, -rope, *s.* Remorque *f*; corde *f* de halage. 'tow-path, *s.* Chemin *m* de halage.

tow², *v.tr.* Remorquer (un navire, une auto); touer (un chaland); (*from tow-path*) haler (un chaland). **towing**, *s.* Remorque *f*, remorquage *m*; touage *m*; (*from tow-path*) halage *m.*

tow³, *s.* Étoupe (blanche), filasse *f.* 'tow-'headed, *a. F:* Aux cheveux blond filasse.

towage ['touidʒ], *s.* **1.** Remorquage *m*; touage *m*; halage *m.* **2.** (Frais *mpl* de) remorquage.

toward. **1.** ['touəd] *A: a.* (*Pred.*) Proche; tout près. **2.** [tə'wɔ:d] *prep.Lit:* = TOWARDS.

towards [tə'wɔ:dz], *prep.* **1.** (*Of place*) Vers; du côté de. **2.** Envers, pour, à l'égard de (qn). His feelings t. me, ses sentiments envers, pour, moi. **3.** Pour. To save t. the children's education, économiser pour l'éducation des enfants. **4.** (*Of time*) Vers, sur. T noon, vers midi. T. the end of his life . . ., sur la fin de sa vie. . . .

towel¹ ['tauəl], s. **1.** Serviette f (de toilette); essuie-main(s) m inv. **Turkish t.**, **rough t.**, serviette éponge. **Roller t.**, serviette sans fin. **2. Sanitary t.**, serviette hygiénique. **'towel-horse,** s. Chevalet m. **'towel-rail,** s. Porte-serviettes m inv.

towel², v.tr. (towelled) Essuyer, frotter, avec une serviette. **towelling,** s. **1.** Friction f avec une serviette. **2.** Toile f pour serviettes; tissu-éponge m.

tower¹ ['tauər], s. **1.** (a) Tour f. (b) **Church t.**, clocher m. **Observation t.**, belvédère m. **Water t.**, château m d'eau. (c) **He is a t. of strength,** c'est un puissant appui. **2.** Civ.E: Pylône m (de réseau électrique, etc.). **T.-crane,** grue sur pylône. **3.** Av: **Control t.**, tour de contrôle. **4.** Nau: Conning t., kiosque m (de sous-marin).

tower², v.i. **1.** Dominer. **He towered above the others,** il dominait les autres par la taille. **2.** (a) Monter très haut (en l'air). (b) (Of bird) Planer. **towering,** a. **1.** (a) Très haut. **At a t. height,** une très grande hauteur. (b) **T. ambition,** ambition sans bornes. (b) F: **In a t. passion, rage,** au paroxysme de la colère.

tower³ ['tauər], s. Haleur, -euse (de péniches, etc.).

towered ['tauəd], a. **1.** Surmonté d'une tour, flanqué de tours. **2. High-t.,** aux tours élevées.

town [taun]. **1.** Ville f. **County t.** = chef-lieu m (de département). **Country t.** = bourg m; bourgade m. F: **One-horse t.,** patelin m, bled m. **2.** (a) **He works in T.,** il travaille à Londres. **A man about t.,** un mondain. (b) **To go into t.,** aller, se rendre, à la ville. **She's in t. shopping this morning,** elle fait ses courses en ville ce matin. (c) F: **They really went to t.,** (i) ils se sont drôlement bien amusés; (ii) ils ont dépensé à pleines mains. Sch: **T. and gown,** les habitants de la ville et les étudiants. **3.** Attrib. De la ville, urbain, municipal, -aux. **T. life,** vie urbaine. **'town 'clerk,** s. = Chef m du secrétariat de l'hôtel de ville. **'town-council,** s. Conseil municipal. **'town-'councillor,** s. Conseiller municipal. **town-'hall,** s. Hôtel m de ville; mairie f. **'town-'planner,** s. (Architecte m) urbaniste (m). **'town-'planning,** s. Urbanisme n ; aménagement m des villes; urbanification f.

townsfolk ['taunzfouk], s.pl. Habitants m de la ville; citadins m.

township ['taunʃip], s. Commune f. Geog: **The Eastern Townships,** Fr.C: les cantons de l'Est.

townsman, pl. **-men** ['taunzmən], s.m. Habitant de la ville; citadin. **Fellow t.,** concitoyen m.

townspeople ['taunzpi:pl], s.pl. **1.** Habitants m de la ville; citadins m. **2.** Concitoyens m.

townswoman, pl. **-women** ['taunswumən, -wimin], s.f. **1.** Habitante de la ville; citadine. **2.** Concitoyenne.

toxaemia [tɔk'si:miə], s. Med: Toxémie f.

toxic ['tɔksik], a. & s. Med: Toxique (m); intoxicant (m).

toxicological [ˌtɔksikə'lɔdʒik(ə)l], a. Toxicologique.

toxicologist [ˌtɔksi'kɔlədʒist], s. Toxicologue m.

toxicology [ˌtɔksi'kɔlədʒi], s. Toxicologie f.

toxin ['tɔksin], s. Toxine f.

toy¹ [tɔi], s. **1.** Jouet m; F: joujou m, -oux. **2.** attrib. (a) **T. trumpet,** trompette d'enfant. **T. theatre,** théâtre de marionnettes. (b) Tout petit. **T. dog,** bichon m, chien de salon. (c) **A t. army,** une armée pour rire.

toy², v.i. **1.** **To t. with sth.,** s'amuser, jouer, avec qch. **To t. with one's food,** manger du bout des dents, chipoter. **To t. with an idea,** caresser une idée. **To t. with the idea of work,** avoir des velléités de travail. **2. To t. with s.o.,** badiner avec qn.

toyshop ['tɔiʃɔp], s. Magasin m de jouets.

trace¹ [treis], s. **1.** (Usu. pl.) Trace(s) f(pl) (de qn, d'un animal); empreinte f (d'un animal). **2.** Trace, vestige m. **To find a t. of s.o.,** retrouver trace de qn. **There is no t. of it,** il n'en reste pas trace. Biol: **T. element,** oligo-élément m, pl. oligo-éléments.

trace³, v.tr. **1.** Tracer (un plan). **To t. out a scheme,** esquisser un projet. **2.** (a) **To t. (out) a plan,** faire le tracé d'un plan. (b) Calquer (un dessin). **3. To t. an animal,** suivre une piste d'une bête. **He has been traced to Paris,** on a suivi sa piste jusqu'à Paris. **To t. lost goods,** recouvrer des objets perdus. **4. I cannot t. any reference to the event,** je ne trouve trace d'aucune mention du fait. **5.** Suivre (un chemin). **trace back,** v.tr. **To t. sth. back to its source,** remonter jusqu'à l'origine de qch. **To t. one's family back to the Conqueror,** faire remonter sa famille à Guillaume le Conquérant. **tracing,** s. **1.** (a) Tracé m. (b) Calquage m. **2.** Dessin calqué; calque m. **'tracing-cloth, -paper,** s. Toile f, papier m, à calquer. **'tracing-wheel,** s. Dressm: Roulette f (à piquer).

trace³, s. Harn: Trait m. **In the traces,** attelé. F: (Of pers.) **To kick over the traces,** (i) s'insurger; F: ruer dans les brancards; (ii) s'émanciper.

tracer ['treisər], s. **1.** Rad A: Traceur m. **2.** Mil: **T. shell,** traçant m. **T. bullet,** traçante f.

tracery ['treisəri], s. **1.** Arch: Remplage m (d'une rosace); découpures fpl. **2.** Réseau, nervures fpl (d'une feuille).

trachea, pl. **-eae** [trə'ki(:)ə, -i:i:], s. (a) Anat: Trachée-artère f; F: trachée f. (b) Trachée (d'insecte).

tracheitis [ˌtræki'aitis], s. Med: Trachéite f.

tracheotomy [ˌtræki'ɔtəmi], s. Surg: Trachéotomie f.

trachoma [trə'koumə], s. Med: Trachome m.

track¹ [træk], s. **1.** (a) Voie f, foulées fpl, trace(s) f(pl), piste f (d'une bête). (b) Trace(s), piste (de qn); sillage m (d'un navire). **To follow in s.o.'s t.,** suivre la voie tracée par qn. **To be on s.o.'s t.,** être sur la trace de qn. **To keep t. of s.o.,** ne pas perdre qn de vue. **To throw s.o. off the t.,** dépister qn. **To cover up one's tracks (from the police),** dépister la police. F: **To make tracks,** filer, s'éclipser. **To make tracks for . . .,** se diriger vers . . . **2.** (a) **Mule t.,** piste muletière. **Sheep t.,** sentier battu par les moutons. **Cart t.,** chemin m de terre. S.a. BEATEN 1. (b) Mec.E: Chemin m, piste (de glissement). **3.** Route ɪ, chemin. **To put s.o. on the right t.,** mettre qn sur la voie. **To be on the wrong t.,** faire fausse route. **4.** Rac: Piste. **Motor-racing t.,** autodrome m. (On road) **Cycle t.,** piste cyclable. **5.** Rail: Voie (ferrée). **Single t.,** voie unique. F: **A one t. mind,** un esprit obsédé par une seule idée. **The train left the t.,** le train a déraillé. **6.** Chenille f (de tracteur). **'track-racing,** s. Courses fpl sur piste. **'track-suit,** s. Sp: Survêtement m.

track², v.tr. Suivre (une bête) à la piste; traquer (un malfaiteur). **To t. down,** dépister (le gibier, un malfaiteur). **tracking-down,** s. Dépistage m.

tracker ['trækər], s. Traqueur m (de gibier).

trackless ['træklis], a. Sans chemins. **T. forest,** forêt vierge.

tract¹ [trækt], s. **1.** Étendue f (de pays); nappe f (d'eau); région (montagneuse). **2.** Anat: Respiratory t., appareil m respiratoire. **Digestive t.,** les voies digestives.

tract², s. Petit traité; brochure f; esp. petite brochure de piété; tract m.

tractability [ˌtræktə'biliti], **tractableness** ['træktəblnis], s. Humeur f traitable; docilité f.

tractable ['træktəbl], a. **1.** (Of pers.) Docile; traitable. **2.** (Of material) Facile à ouvrer; ouvrable.

traction ['træk(ʃə)n], s. Traction f, tirage m. **Motor t.,** traction automobile. **T. wheels,** roues motrices (d'une locomotive). **'traction-engine,** s. Machine routière; tracteur m.

tractive ['træktiv], a. Tractif, -ive; (force) de traction.

tractor ['træktər], s. **1.** Tracteur m. S.a. PLOUGH¹ 1. Mil: **T. drawn artillery,** artillerie tractée. **2.** Av: **T. propeller,** hélice tractive.

trad [træd], a. F: = TRADITIONAL.

trade¹ [treid], s. **1.** État m, emploi m; métier manuel; commerce m. **To carry on a t.,** exercer un métier, un commerce. **Everyone to his t.,** chacun son métier. S.a. JACK¹ II. 1. **2.** Commerce, négoce m, affaires fpl. **T. in cotton,** commerce du coton. **Foreign t.,** commerce étranger, extérieur. Nau: **Coasting t.,** cabotage m. **To be in t.,** être dans le commerce. **It's good for t.,** cela fait marcher le commerce. S.a. FREE TRADE, ROARING¹ 2. **3.** Corps m de métier. **To be in the t.,** être du métier. **4.** pl. **Trades** = TRADE-WINDS. **5.** attrib. **T. card,** carte d'affaires. **T. catalogue,** tarif-album m, pl. tarifs-albums. **T. disputes,** conflits m du travail. **T. name,** appellation f. **T. price,** prix marchand. **T. secret,** secret m de fabrique. Pol.Ec: **T. cycle,** cycle m économique. **'trade-mark,** s. Marque f de fabrique. **Registered t.-m.,** marque déposée. **trade-'union,** s. Syndicat (ouvrier). **trade-'unionism,** s. Syndicalisme (ouvrier). **trade-'unionist,** s. Syndiqué, -ée; syndicaliste mf. **'trade-wind,** s. Vent alizé; alizé m.

trade². **1.** *v.i.* (*a*) Faire le commerce, le négoce (**in, de**); trafiquer (**in, en**). (*b*) To t. on s.o.'s **ignorance**, exploiter l'ignorance de qn. **2.** *v.tr.* (*a*) Faire trafic de (son honneur). (*b*) To t. sth. for sth., troquer qch. contre qch. **trade in**, *v.tr.* To t. **in a used car**, donner sa vieille auto en reprise. **'trade in**, *s.* F: Reprise *f*. **'trading-'in**, *s.* Vente *f* de qch. en reprise. **trading**, *s.* Commerce *m*, négoce *m*. **T. stamp**, timbre-prime *m*, *pl.* timbres-prime(s). **T. vessel**, navire marchand. *Fin:* **T. capital**, capital de roulement. *Book-k:* This month's t., l'exercice *m* du mois.
trader ['treidər], *s.* **1.** Négociant, -ante; commerçant, -ante; marchand, -ande. **2.** Navire marchand.
tradesfolk ['treidzfouk], *s.pl.* O: Commerçants *m*.
tradesman, *pl.* -men ['treidzmən], *s.m.* **1.** Marchand, fournisseur. **Tradesmen's entrance**, entrée des fournisseurs. **2.** *Scot: U.S:* Artisan *m*. *Mil:* Spécialiste *m*.
tradition [trə'dif(ə)n], *s.* Tradition *f*.
traditional [trə'difənl], *a.* Traditionnel, -elle. **-ally**, *adv.* Traditionnellement.
traduce [trə'dju:s], *v.tr.* Calomnier, diffamer.
traducer [trə'dju:sər], *s.* Calomniateur, -trice.
traffic¹ ['træfik], *s.* **1.** Trafic *m*, négoce *m*, commerce *m* (**in, de**). *Pej:* T. in arms, trafic d'armes. **Ocean t.**, navigation *f* au long cours. **2.** Mouvement *m*, circulation *f*. **Road t.**, circulation routière. **Road carrying heavy t.**, route à circulation intense. **T. congestion**, embouteillage *m* (de la circulation). *Aut:* **T. indicator**, indicateur *m* de direction. **T. island**, refuge *m*. **T. accident**, accident de la circulation. **'Beware of t.!'** "attention aux voitures!" **T. regulations**, règlements sur la circulation. **Road fit for t.**, route viable. **3.** Rail t., trafic ferroviaire. *S.a.* POLICEMAN, THROUGH III. **'traffic-jam**, *s.* Encombrement *m* (de circulation), embouteillage *m*. **'traffic-lights**, *s.pl.* Feux *mpl* de circulation. **'traffic-manager**, *s.* *Rail:* Chef *m* de mouvement. **'traffic-signals**, *s.pl.* Feux *mpl* de circulation.
traffic², *v.* (**trafficked** ['træfikt]) **1.** *v.i.* Trafiquer (**in, en**); faire le commerce (**in, de**). **2.** *v tr.* *Usu. Pej:* Trafiquer de (qch.).
trafficator ['træfikeitər], *s.* *Aut:* Indicateur *m*, flèche *f*, de direction.
trafficker ['træfikər], *s.* *Pej:* Trafiquant *m* (**in, de, en**).
tragedian [trə'dʒi:diən], *s.* **1.** Auteur *m* tragique. **2.** *Th:* Tragédien, -ienne.
tragedienne [trə,dʒi:di'en], *s.f.* *Th:* Tragédienne.
tragedy ['trædʒidi], *s.* (*a*) Tragédie *f*. (*b*) The final t. of his death, le drame final de sa mort.
tragic(al) ['trædʒik(əl)], *a.* Tragique. **-ally**, *adv.* Tragiquement. To take things t., prendre les choses au tragique.
tragi-comedy ['trædʒi'kɔmidi], *s.* Tragi-comédie *f*.
trail¹ [treil], *s.* **1.** (*a*) Traînée *f* (de fumée). **T. of fire** (of rocket), sillon *m* de feu. **T. of a meteor**, queue *f* d'un météore. (*b*) *Av: Ball:* Traînée (de la bombe). (*c*) *Artil:* Flèche *f*, crosse *f* (d'affût). **2.** (*a*) Piste *f*, trace *f*, voie *f* (d'une bête). To pick up the t., retrouver la piste. **False t.**, fausse piste. (*b*) Sentier (battu); piste (dans une forêt). **'trail-bridge**, *s.* (Bac *m* à) traille *f*. **'trail-net**, *s.* *Fish:* Chalut *m*. **'trail-rope**, *s.* **1.** *Artil:* Prolonge *f*. **2.** *Aer:* Guide-rope *m*.
trail². **I.** *v.tr.* **1.** (*a*) To t. sth. (**along**), traîner qch. après soi. F: To t. one's coat, chercher noise à tout le monde; traîner son sabre. (*b*) *Mil:* To t. arms, porter l'arme avec le canon parallèle au sol. **2.** Traquer (une bête). **II.** **trail**, *v.i.* **1.** (*a*) Traîner. (*b*) **With a boat trailing behind**, avec un bateau à la traîne. **2.** (*Of pers.*) To t. along, se traîner. **Her voice trailed off in the distance**, sa voix se perdit dans le lointain. **3.** (*Of plant*) Grimper; ramper. **trailing**, *a.* **1.** (*Of plant*) Grimpant; rampant. **2.** *Rail:* T. wheel, roue porteuse arrière (de locomotive). *Av:* T. edge, bord de fuite.
trailer ['treilər], *s.* **1.** (*Pers.*) Traqueur *m*. **2.** Plante grimpante. **3.** *Veh:* Remorque *f*; *U.S:* roulotte *f* (de camping). **4.** *Cin:* Film *m* annonce.
train¹ [trein], *s.* **1.** Traîne *f*, queue *f* (d'une robe). **2.** (*a*) Suite *f*, équipage *m* (d'un prince). **To be in s.o.'s t.**, être à la suite de qn. (*b*) War brings famine in its t., la guerre amène la disette (à sa suite). **3.** (*a*) Train, convoi *m* (de wagons); **succession** *f*, **série** *f* (d'événe-

ments). **T. of thought**, enchaînement *m* d'idées. (*b*) *Min:* To fire a t., allumer une traînée de poudre. **4.** *Tchn:* Système *m* d'engrenages; rouage(s) *m(pl)* (d'une montre). **Wheel t.**, train de roues. **5.** *Rail:* (*a*) Train. **Slow t.**, train omnibus. **Fast, express t.**, train express, train rapide. **Relief t.**, train supplémentaire. **Breakdown t.**, train de secours. **Main-line t.**, train de grande ligne. **Winter sports, ski, t.**, train de neige. **To go by t.**, aller par le train. **To get into the t.**, monter en wagon. **We had dinner on the t.**, nous avons dîné dans le train. **The t. is in**, le train est en gare, à quai. *S.a.* GOOD II 2. (*b*) Rame *f* (du Métro). **'train-bearer**, *s.* (*Pers.*) Porte-queue *m inv.* **'train-ferry**, *s.* Ferry-(boat) *m*.
train². **I.** *v.tr.* **1.** (*a*) Former, instruire (qn); dresser (un animal); exercer (l'oreille). To t. a child, élever un enfant. **Engineers who have been trained at . . .**, les ingénieurs sortis de. . . . To t. a youth for the navy, préparer un jeune homme pour la marine. To t. s.o. to business, rompre qn aux affaires. (*b*) *Sp:* Entraîner (un coureur). *Box:* He is being trained by so-and-so, c'est le poulain d'un tel. (*c*) *Hort:* Diriger, conduire (une plante); palisser (un arbre fruitier). **2.** Pointer (un canon), braquer (une lunette) (**on, sur**). *Navy:* Orienter (un canon). **II.** **train**, *v.i.* (*a*) S'exercer. *Mil:* Faire l'exercice. (*b*) *Sp:* S'entraîner. (*Of athlete*) To t. down, réduire son poids. **trained**, *a.* **1.** (*a*) (Soldat) instruit; (chien) dressé; (domestique) stylé; (œil) exercé. **Well-t. child**, enfant bien élevé. **T. nurse**, infirmière diplômée. (*b*) *Sp:* Entraîné. **2.** (Rosier) palissé, mis en espalier. **training**, *s.* **1.** (*a*) Éducation *f*, instruction *f*. Character t., formation *f* du caractère. **Physical t.**, éducation physique. To have had a business t., être formé aux affaires. (*b*) *Military t.*, instruction *f* militaire. To keep troops in t., tenir des troupes en haleine. *Navy:* **T. squadron**, escadre d'instruction. (*c*) *Sp:* Entraînement *m* (d'un boxeur, etc.). **To go into t.**, s'entraîner. **To be out of t.**, ne plus être en forme. (*d*) Dressage (d'un animal). **2.** *Hort:* Palissage *m*. **3.** *Artil:* Pointage *m* en direction. **'training-college**, *s.* *Sch: A:* École normale. **'training-ship, -vessel**, *s.* Navire *m* école; vaisseau-école *m*.
trainee [trei'ni:], *s.* *Sch:* Élève *mf*; stagiaire *mf*.
trainer ['treinər], *s.* **1.** Dresseur *m* (d'animaux). **2.** *Sp:* Entraîneur *m*.
train-oil ['treinɔil], *s.* Huile *f* de baleine; thran *m*.
traipse ['treips], *v.i.* Traîner çà et là; se balader.
trait [trei], *s.* Trait *m* (de caractère).
traitor ['treitər], *s.* Traître *m*. **To turn t.**, passer à l'ennemi; se vendre.
traitorous ['treitərəs], *a.* Traître, *f.* traîtresse; perfide. **-ly**, *adv.* En traître; traîtreusement.
traitress ['treitris], *s. f.* Traîtresse.
trajectory [trə'dʒektəri], *s.* Trajectoire *f*.
tram [træm], *s.* **1.** Tramway *m*. **T. driver**, conducteur *m* de tramway; wattman *m*. **T. conductor**, receveur *m*. **2.** *Min:* Benne *f*, berline *f*.
tramcar ['træmkɑ:r], *s.* (Voiture *f* de) tramway *m*.
tramline ['træmlain], *s.* **1.** *Usu.pl.* Tramlines, les rails du tramway. **2.** *Ten:* The tramlines, le couloir.
trammel¹ ['træm(ə)l], *s.* **1.** *Fish:* T.(-net), tramail *m*, -ails. **2.** *pl.* Contrainte *f*, entraves *fpl*.
trammel², *v.tr.* (**trammelled**) Entraver.
tramp¹ [træmp], *s.* **1.** Bruit *m* de pas marqués. **I heard the (heavy) t. of the guard**, j'entendis le pas lourd de la garde. **2.** (*a*) Marche *f*; promenade *f* à pied. (*b*) To be on the t., *P:* être sur le trimard. **3.** (*Pers.*) (*a*) Chemineau *m*, vagabond *m*; clochard *m*; *P:* trimardeur *m*. (*b*) *U.S:* *P:* Prostituée *f*. **4.** *Nau:* (Ocean) t., t. steamer, navire *m*, cargo *m*, sans ligne régulière; tramp *m*.
tramp², *v.i.* **1.** Marcher à pas marqués; marcher lourdement. **2.** = TRAMPLE 1. **3.** (*a*) Marcher; voyager à pied. *v.tr.* To t. the country, parcourir le pays à pied. (*b*) Vagabonder, *P:* trimarder. *v.tr.* To t. the streets, battre le pavé.
trample ['træmpl]. **1.** *v.i.* To t. on sth., s.o., piétiner, écraser, qch., qn. To t. on s.o.'s feelings, fouler aux pieds les susceptibilités de qn. **2.** *v.tr.* To t. sth. under foot, fouler qch. aux pieds. To t. down the grass, fouler, piétiner, l'herbe. **trampling**, *s.* Piétinement *m*; bruit *m* de pas.

tramway ['træmwei], s. Voie f de tramway.
trance [trɑːns], s. (a) Med: (i) Extase f; (ii) catalepsie f. To fall into a t., tomber en extase; F: piquer une crise d'hystérie. (b) (Hypnotic) t., transe f, hypnose f.
tranquil ['træŋkwil], a. Tranquille (et serein); calme, paisible. -illy, adv. Tranquillement, paisiblement; avec sérénité.
tranquillity [træŋ'kwiliti], s. Tranquillité f, calme m, sérénité f.
tranquillize ['træŋkwilaiz], v.tr. Tranquilliser, calmer, apaiser.
tranquillizer ['træŋkwilaizər], s. Med: Tranquillisant m, calmant m.

NOTE. For the words beginning trans- [træns], an alternative pronunciation [trɑːns] is usually acceptable.

transact ['træn'zækt], v.tr. To t. business with s.o., faire des affaires avec qn; traiter une affaire, une opération, avec qn.
transaction [træn'zækʃ(ə)n], s. 1. Conduite f (d'une affaire). The t. of business, le commerce, les affaires f. 2. Opération (commerciale). Cash t., opération au comptant. 3. pl. Transactions, (i) transactions f, (ii) procès-verbaux m des séances (d'une société savante).
transalpine ['trænz'ælpain], a. Transalpin.
trans-American ['trænzə'merikən], a. Transaméricain.
transatlantic ['trænzət'læntik], a. Transatlantique.
transceiver [træn'siːvər], s. Émetteur-récepteur m.
transcend [træn'send], v.tr. 1. Dépasser les bornes de (la raison); aller au delà de (ce que l'on peut concevoir), transcender. 2. Surpasser (qn).
transcendence [træn'sendəns], transcendency [træn'sendənsi], s. Transcendance f.
transcendent [træn'sendənt], a. Transcendant.
transcendental [ˌtrænsen'dentl], a. 1. Phil: Transcendantal, -aux. 2. Mth: (Of quantity) Transcendant.
transcontinental ['trænz,kɔ̃nti'nentl], a. Transcontinental, -aux.
transcribe [træns'kraib], v.tr. Transcrire.
transcriber [træns'kraibər], s. Transcripteur m.
transcript ['trænskript], s. Transcription f, copie f.
transcription [træns'kripʃ(ə)n], s. Transcription f.
transept ['trænsept], s. Ecc.Arch: Transept m. Arm of the t., croisillon m.
transfer¹ ['trænsfə(ː)r], s. 1. (a) Translation f, transport, renvoi m (de qch. à un autre endroit); déplacement m (d'un fonctionnaire). Fb: T. fee, somme payée pour le transfert d'un joueur. (b) Jur: Transfert m (d'un droit); mutation f (de biens). T. of power, passation f des pouvoirs. St.Exch: T. of shares, transfert, assignation f, d'actions. (c) Book-k: Transport (d'une somme). Bank: T. of funds, virement m de fonds. 2. Jur: (Deed of) t., acte m de cession. 3. (a) Lith: Report m. (b) Needlew: Décalque m. (c) T.(-picture), décalcomanie f. 'transfer-paper, s. 1. Papier m à décalquer f. Lith: Phot: Papier à report.
transfer² [træns'fəːr], v.tr. (transferred) 1. Transférer. (a) To t. a civil servant, déplacer un fonctionnaire. To t. a soldier, muter un soldat. (b) Jur: Transmettre, céder (une propriété). (c) Book-k: Contre-passer (une écriture). Bank: Virer (une somme). 2. (a) Lith: Phot: Reporter. (b) Needlew: etc: Calquer.
transferability [trænsˌfəːrə'biliti], s. Transmissibilité f.
transferable [træns'fəːrəbl], a. Transmissible. Jur: (Droit) cessible. Fin: T. securities, valeurs mobilières. 'Not t,' (on railway ticket, etc.) strictement personnel.
transferee [ˌtrænsfə(ː)'riː], s. Jur: Cessionnaire mf.
transference ['trænsf(ə)r(ə)ns], s. Transfert m.
transferor [ˌtræns'fə(ː)rər], s. Cédant, -ante.
transfiguration [ˌtrænsfigju(ə)'reiʃ(ə)n], s. Transfiguration f.
transfigure [træns'figər], v.tr. Transfigurer.
transfix [træns'fiks], v.tr. 1. Transpercer. 2. He stood transfixed (with fear), il resta cloué au sol (par la peur).
transform [træns'fɔːm], v.tr. 1. Transformer; métamorphoser. 2. (a) Ch: etc: Convertir (into, en). To t. heat into energy, convertir la chaleur en énergie. (b) El.E: Transformer (le courant). transforming, s. Transformation f. conversion f (into, en).

transformable [træns'fɔːməbl], a. 1. Transformable. 2. Convertissable (into, en).
transformation [ˌtrænsfə'meiʃ(ə)n], s. 1. (a) Transformation f; métamorphose f. Th: T. scene, (i) changement à vue; (ii) apothéose f (d'une féerie). (b) T. of heat into energy, conversion f de la chaleur en énergie. 2. Haird: O: Faux toupet; transformation.
transformer [træns'fɔːmər], s. El.E: Transformateur m (de tension). T. station, poste m de transformateurs.
transfuse [træns'fjuːz], v.tr. (a) Transfuser (du sang). (b) Faire une transfusion à (un malade).
transfuser [træns'fjuːzər], s. Med: Transfuseur m (de sang).
transfusion [træns'fjuːʒ(ə)n], s. Blood t., transfusion f de sang.
transgress [træns'gres], v.tr. Transgresser, enfreindre (la loi). Abs. Pécher. To t. a rule, violer une règle.
transgression [træns'greʃ(ə)n], s. (a) Transgression f, violation f (d'une loi); infraction f (of the law, à la loi). (b) Péché m, faute f.
transgressor [træns'gresər], s. Transgresseur m; pécheur, f. pécheresse.
tranship [træn'ʃip]. 1. v.tr. Transborder (des voyageurs). 2. v.i. (Of passenger) Changer de bateau.
transhipment [træn'ʃipmənt], s. Transbordement m.
transhumance [træns'hjuːməns], s. Husb: Transhumance f.
transient ['trænziənt], a. (a) Transitoire; (bonheur) passager, éphémère. U.S: T. guest, s. transient, hôte m, client, -ente, de passage. (b) (Espoir) momentané. (c) Mus: T. note, note de passage. -ly, adv. Transitoirement, passagèrement; en passant.
transistor [træn'zistər], s. El: Transistor m. W.Tel: F: T. (set), transistor m.
transit ['trænsit], s. 1. Passage m (à travers un pays). 2. Transport m (de marchandises). Damage in t., avarie(s) f(pl) en cours de route. Loss in t., freinte f de route. 3. Cust: Transit m. 4. Astr: Passage (i) d'une planète sur le disque du soleil, (ii) d'un astre au méridien).
transition [træn'siʒ(ə)n], s. 1. Transition f; passage m (du jour à la nuit). T. period, période de transition. 2. Mus: Modulation f.
transitive ['trænsitiv], a. Gram: (Verbe) transitif. -ly, adv. Transitivement.
transitory ['trænsit(ə)ri], a. Transitoire; (bonheur) fugitif.
translatable [træns'leitəbl], a. Traduisible.
translate [træns'leit], v.tr. 1. Traduire. Book translated from (the) German, livre traduit de l'allemand. 2. (a) Transférer (un évêque) (to, à). (b) Enoch was translated (to heaven), Énoch fut enlevé au ciel.
translation [træns'leiʃ(ə)n], s. 1. (a) Traduction f. (b) Traduction; ouvrage traduit. Sch: Version (latine, etc.). 2. (a) Translation f (d'un évêque). (b) Mec: Movement of t., mouvement de translation. (c) B: Enlèvement m au ciel.
translator [træns'leitər], s. 1. Traducteur m. 2. El: Tg: Translateur m.
transliterate [træns'litəreit], v.tr. Transcrire (en caractères différents).
transliteration [trænslitə'reiʃ(ə)n], s. Translit(t)ération f.
translucence [trænz'luːsns], s. Translucidité f.
translucent [trænz'luːsnt], a. Translucide.
transmigrate [ˌtrænzmai'greit], v.i. Transmigrer.
transmigration [ˌtrænzmai'greiʃ(ə)n], s. 1. Transmigration f (d'un peuple, etc.). 2. T. of souls, métempsycose f.
transmissibility [trænzˌmisə'biliti], s. Transmissibilité f.
transmissible [trænz'misəbl], a. Transmissible.
transmission [trænz'miʃ(ə)n], s. 1. Transmission f (d'un ordre). Ph: Transmission (de la chaleur, etc.). El.E: T. of power, transport m de force. 2. Mec.E: (Système m d'arbres de) transmission.
transmit [trænz'mit], v.tr. (transmitted) Transmettre (un ordre, etc.). Ph: Transmettre (la lumière, etc.). El.E: Transporter (la force). transmitting, a. (a) Transmetteur. (b) W.Tel: T. station, poste émetteur.
transmitter [trænz'mitər], s. (a) T. of motive power, communicateur m de mouvement. (b) Tg: Transmetteur m. (c) W.Tel: (Poste) émetteur m. (d) Microphone m (d'un téléphone).

transmogrification [ˌtrænzmɔgrifiˈkeiʃ(ə)n], *s. F:* Métamorphose *f.*

transmogrify [trænzˈmɔgrifai], *v.tr. F:* Transformer, métamorphoser.

transmutation [ˌtrænzmjuˈteiʃ(ə)n], *s.* Transmutation *f.*

transmute [trænzˈmju:t], *v.tr.* (*a*) Transformer (into, en). (*b*) Transmuer (un métal).

transoceanic [ˌtrænzouʃiˈænik], *a.* Transocéanique.

transom ['trænsəm], *s.* **1.** *Const:* (*a*) Traverse *f*, linteau *m* (de fenêtre, de porte). (*b*) Meneau horizontal (de croisée). **2.** *N.Arch:* (Barre *f* d')arcasse *f.* **3.** = TRANSOM-WINDOW. **'transom-window**, *s.* **1.** Fenêtre *f* à meneau horizontal. **2.** *U.S:* Vasistas *m*, imposte *f* (de porte).

transparency [trænsˈpɛər(ə)nsi, -ˈpær-], *s.* **1.** (*a*) Transparence *f* (du verre). (*b*) Limpidité *f* (de l'eau). **2.** (*a*) (*Picture*) Transparent *m.* (*b*) *Phot:* Diapositive *f* (de projection).

transparent [trænsˈpɛər(ə)nt, -ˈpær-], *a.* **1.** Transparent; (eau) limpide. **T. window-panes**, vitres claires. **2.** Évident, clair. **T. deception**, tromperie cousue de fil blanc. **-ly**, *adv.* D'une manière transparente; clairement.

transpierce [trænsˈpiəs], *v.tr.* Transpercer.

transpiration [ˌtrænspiˈreiʃ(ə)n], *s.* Transpiration *f.*

transpire [trænˈspaiər]. **1.** *v.tr.* (*Of plants, etc.*) Exsuder (un fluide); exhaler (une odeur). **2.** *v.i.* (*a*) Transpirer. (*b*) (*Of news*) Transpirer, s'ébruiter. (*c*) **His account of what transpired**, sa version de ce qui s'était passé.

transplant [trænsˈplɑ:nt]. **1.** *v.tr.* (*a*) Transplanter, repiquer (des plants). (*b*) Transplanter (une population). (*c*) *Surg:* Greffer (du tissu). **2.** *s.* Greffe *f* (du cœur).

transplantation [ˌtrænsplənˈteiʃ(ə)n], *s.* Transplantation *f.*

transport¹ ['trænspɔ:t]. **1.** Transport *m* (de marchandises). **T. worker**, employé *m* des entreprises de transport. **T. agent**, transitaire *m.* **T. cafe**, restaurant *m*, casse-croûte *f*, des routiers. *Com:* **Door to door t.**, le porte à porte *m.* **2.** *Nau:* **Transport-(ship)**, (bâtiment *m* de) transport. *Av:* **T. plane**, (avion *m* de) transport; avion-cargo *m.* **3.** Transport (de joie, de colère); élancement *m* (de l'esprit).

transport² [trænsˈpɔ:t], *v.tr.* **1.** Transporter. **2. To be transported with joy**, être transporté de joie; être ravi.

transportation [ˌtrænspɔ:ˈteiʃ(ə)n], *s.* (*a*) *Jur: A:* Déportation *f*; (*for life*) relégation *f.* **Convict sentenced to t.**, relégué *m.* (*b*) *U.S:* Transport *m*, transportation *f.*

transporter [trænsˈpɔ:tər], *s.* Transporteur *m.* **T.-bridge**, (pont) transbordeur *m.* *Mil:* **Tank t.**, portechars *m inv.*

transposable [trænsˈpouzəbl], *a.* Transposable.

transpose [trænsˈpouz], *v.tr.* Transposer. **transposing¹**, *a. Mus:* Transpositeur. **transposing²**, *s. Mus:* Transposition *f.*

transposition [ˌtrænspəˈziʃ(ə)n], *s.* Transposition *f.*

trans-Siberian ['træn(z)saiˈbiəriən], *a.* Transsibérien, -ienne. **The T.-S. Railway**, le transsibérien.

trans-sonic [træns'sɔnik], *a. Av:* Transsonique.

transubstantiate [ˌtrænsəbˈstænʃieit], *v.tr. Ecc:* Transsubstantier.

transubstantiation ['trænsəbˌstænʃiˈeiʃ(ə)n], *s. Theol:* Transsubstantiation *f.*

transude [trænˈsju:d], *v.tr. & i.* Transsuder.

transversal [trænzˈvə:s(ə)l], *a.* Transversal, -aux.

transverse [trænzˈvə:s], *a.* Transversal, -aux; en travers. **T. muscle**, *s.* **transverse**, (muscle) transverse *m.* **-ly**, *adv.* Transversalement.

trap¹ [træp], *s.* **1.** (*a*) Piège *m*; (*for big game*) trappe *f*; (*for wolves*) chausse-trape *f*; (*for small game*) traquenard *m*; (*for hares, etc.*) panneau *m.* **To set a t.**, dresser, tendre, un piège. **To catch an animal in a t.**, prendre une bête au piège. (*b*) Piège, ruse *f.* **Police t.**, (i) souricière *f*; (ii) *Aut:* zone *f* de contrôle de vitesse. **To be caught in the t.**, se laisser prendre au piège, donner dans le panneau. **2.** (*a*) = TRAP-DOOR. (*b*) *Th:* Trappe. (*c*) *P:* Bouche *f*, *P:* gueule *f.* **3.** Boîte *f* de lancement (pour pigeons vivants). **4.** *Tchn:* (*a*) Collecteur *m* (d'huile). *Mch:* **Steam-t.**, purgeur *m* de vapeur. (*b*) (Air-, gas-)t., siphon *m*, coupe-air *m inv*, garde *f* d'eau (d'un égout, etc.). **5.** *Veh:* Charrette anglaise; cabriolet *m.* **'trap-'door**, *s.* **1.** Trappe *f.* **T.-d. spider**, mygale *f.* **2.** *Min:* Porte *f* d'aérage. **'trap-shooting**, *s. Sp:* Tir *m* aux pigeons (artificiels), ball-trap *m.* **'trap-valve**, *s.* Soupape *f* à clapet.

trap², *v.tr.* (trapped) **1.** (*a*) Prendre (une bête) au piège, piéger. **Trapped by the flames**, cerné par les flammes. (*b*) Tendre des pièges dans un bois. (*c*) *Abs.* Trapper. *Fb:* Bloquer (le ballon) avec la plante du pied. **3.** *Tchn:* To t. a drain, disposer un siphon dans une conduite d'eaux ménagères. **trapped**, *a.* Pris dans un piège; pris au piège.

trap³, *s. Geol:* Trapp *m.*

trapeze [trəˈpi:z], *s.* Trapèze *m.* **Flying t.**, trapèze volant. **T. artist**, trapéziste *mf.*

trapezium [trəˈpi:zjəm], *s. Geom:* Trapèze *m.*

trapezoid ['træpizɔid], *s. Geom:* Trapézoïde *m.*

trapezoidal [ˌtræpiˈzɔidl], *a.* Trapézoïdal, -aux.

trapper ['træpər], *s. Ven:* Trappeur *m.*

trappings ['træpiŋz], *s.pl.* **1.** Harnachement *m*, caparaçon *m.* **2.** Atours *mpl*; apparat *m.*

trappist ['træpist], *s. Ecc:* Trappiste *m.* *attrib.* **T. monastery**, trappe *f.*

trappistine ['træpistin], *s.f. Ecc:* Trappistine.

traps [træps], *s.pl. F:* Effets (personnels). **To pack up one's t.**, faire ses paquets, plier bagage.

trapse [treips], *v.i.* Traîner çà et là; se balader.

trash [træʃ], *s.* (*a*) Chose(s) *f(pl)* sans valeur; camelote *f.* (*b*) Littérature *f* de camelote. (*c*) *U.S:* Détritus *mpl*, immondices *fpl.* (*d*) To talk t., dire des sottises. (*e*) *U.S:* White t., les pauvres *m* de race blanche.

trashy ['træʃi], *a.* (Marchandises) sans valeur; (littérature) de camelote.

trauma ['trɔ:mə], *s. Med:* Traumatisme *m.*

traumatic [trɔ:ˈmætik], *a. Med:* (Fièvre, choc) traumatique.

traumatology [ˌtrɔ:məˈtɔlədʒi], *s. Med:* Traumatologie *f.*

travail ['træveil], *s.* **1.** *A:* Dur travail. **2.** *A. & Lit:* Douleurs *fpl* de l'enfantement. **Woman in travail**, femme en travail.

travel¹ ['trævl], *s.* (*a*) Voyages *mpl.* **To be fond of t.**, aimer à voyager. **T. agency**, bureau *m* de tourisme, agence *f* de voyages. (*b*) *pl.* **Is he still on his travels?** est-il toujours en voyage? **'travel-warrant**, *s. Mil: etc:* Feuille *f* de route.

travel², *v.i.* (travelled) **1.** (*a*) Voyager; faire des voyages. **He is travelling**, il est en voyage. **To t. round the world**, faire le tour du monde. **To t. over a country**, parcourir un pays. **To t. a long way**, faire un long trajet. (*b*) Aller, marcher; (*of news*) circuler. **Light travels faster than sound**, la lumière va, se propage, plus vite que le son. **Train travelling at sixty miles an hour**, train qui marche à, *F:* fait du, soixante milles à l'heure. *Aut:* **We travelled two hundred miles in one day**, nous avons fait une étape de deux cents milles. **2.** Être voyageur de commerce. **To t. in lace**, être représentant en dentelles. **3.** *Mec.E:* (*Of part*) Se mouvoir, se déplacer. **travelled**, *a.* (*Of pers.*) (Much-, well-)t., qui a (beaucoup) voyagé. **travelling¹**, *a.* **1.** *Rail:* **T.** post-office, bureau ambulant. **2. T. crane**, grue *f* mobile. *Ind:* **T. apron**, tablier *m* mobile. **travelling²**, *s.* Voyages *mpl.* **T. bag**, sac de voyage. **T. expenses**, frais de voyage, de route, de déplacement. *S.a.* RUG 1.

traveller ['trævlər], *s.* **1.** Voyageur, -euse. **Fellow-t.**, compagnon de voyage, de route; *Pol:* communisant, -ante. **Traveller's cheque**, chèque de voyage. **2.** (**Commercial**) **t.**, voyageur de commerce; représentant *m.* **T. in lace**, représentant en dentelles. **'Our t. is out'**, "notre voyageur est en tournée." **3.** Curseur *m* (de règle à calcul). **'traveller's 'joy**, *s. Bot:* Clématite *f* des haies.

travelogue ['trævəlɔg], *s.* Documentaire *m* de voyage.

traverse¹ ['trævəs], *s.* **1.** (*a*) *Mount:* Vire *f*; traversée *f.* (*b*) Translation latérale (d'un chariot de tour, etc.). (*c*) *Artil:* Pointage *m* en direction. **2.** *Geom:* (Ligne) transversale *f.* **3.** *Mec.E:* Traverse, entretoise *f* (de châssis). **4.** (*a*) *Fort:* Traverse *f.* (*b*) *Mil:* Pareéclats *m inv.* (de tranchée).

traverse² [trəˈvə:s], *v.tr.* **1.** (*a*) Traverser, passer à travers (une région); passer (la mer). (*b*) *Abs. Mount:* Prendre une vire. **2.** *Artil:* Braquer pointer en direction (un canon).

travesty¹ ['trævisti], s. Parodie f; travestissement m.
travesty², v.tr. Parodier, travestir.
trawl¹ [trɔːl], s. 1. Fish: T.(-net), chalut m, traille f; filet m à la trôle. 2. (For mines) Câble balayeur.
trawl². 1. v.i. Fish: Pêcher au chalut; chaluter. 2. v.tr. Traîner (un chalut). **trawling**, s. Pêche f au chalut.
trawler ['trɔːlər], s. Chalutier m,
tray [trei], s. 1. (a) Plateau m; Fr.C: cabaret m. (b) Châssis m (d'une malle, etc.); tablette f mobile (d'un classeur). (c) Boîte f, corbeille f, à correspondance. 2. Phot: Developing t., cuvette f de développement. S.a. ASH-TRAY. 'tray(-)cloth, s. Dessus m, napperon m, de plateau.
treacherous ['tretʃərəs], a. (Homme) traître; infidèle; (action) perfide. -ly, adv. (Agir) en traître, perfidement.
treachery ['tretʃəri], s. Trahison, f perfidie f. An act of t., une perfidie.
treacle ['triːkl], s. Mélasse f.
tread¹ [tred], s. 1. (a) Pas m. To walk with measured t., marcher à pas comptés. (b) Bruit m de pas. 2. (a) T. of a stair, giron m d'une marche d'escalier. (b) Semelle f (d'un soulier). (c) Échelon m (d'échelle). (d) Aut: Bande f de roulement, chape f (d'un pneu). Non-skid t., roulement antidérapant. 3. Cy: Distance f entre pédales. 4. Veh: Largeur f de voie; voie f.
tread², v. (trod [trɔd]; trodden [trɔdn]) 1. v.i. Marcher; poser les pieds. To t. softly, marcher doucement, à pas feutrés. To t. on sth., marcher sur qch.; mettre le pied sur qch. S.a. CORN² 1, DELICATE 2, FOOTSTEP 2 RUSH² I. 1. 2. v.tr. (a) Well-trodden path, chemin battu. To t. sth. under foot, écraser qch. du pied; fouler qch. aux pieds. (b) To t. (out) grapes, fouler la vendange. Swim: To t. water, nager debout. (c) Orn: Côcher, couvrir (la poule). **tread down**, v.tr. Écraser du pied, fouler aux pieds; opprimer (le peuple). **treading**, s. (a) Piétinement m. (b) Foulage m (des raisins). (c) T. water, nage f debout.
treadle ['tredl], s. Pédale f (de tour, etc.).
treadmill ['tredmil], s. (a) A: (In prisons) Écureuil m; treadmill m. (b) Besogne ingrate quotidienne; le collier de misère.
treason ['triːzn], s. Jur: Trahison f. To talk t., tenir des propos séditieux. High t., haute trahison; lèse-majesté f.
treasonable ['triːznəbl], a. 1. De trahison. 2. Traître, perfide. -ably, adv. Traîtreusement.
treasure¹ ['treʒər], s. Trésor m. To hoard t., thésauriser. Art treasures, richesses f artistiques. 'treasure-house, s. Trésor m. 'treasure hunt, s. Chasse f au(x) trésor(s). 'treasure-trove, s. Jur: Trésor (découvert par hasard).
treasure², v.tr. 1. Priser, tenir beaucoup à (qch.). 2. To t. sth., garder qch. soigneusement.
treasurer ['treʒ(ə)rər], s. Trésorier, -ière; économe m, intendant m (d'un collège).
treasury ['treʒ(ə)ri], s. 1. Trésor (public); trésorerie f. Adm: The T., = Ministère m des Finances. First Lord of the T. = Président m du Conseil (des ministres). S.a. BENCH 1. 2. Lit: T. of verse, anthologie f poétique. 'treasury-bill, s. Bon m du Trésor.
treat¹ [triːt], s. 1. (a) Régal m, -als; festin m; fête f. (b) P: I'll stand t. all round, je paie une tournée générale. 2. Plaisir m. It is quite a t. to me to listen to him, cela m'est un vrai régal de l'écouter. To give oneself a t., faire un petit extra. A t. in store, un plaisir à venir. 3. Adv.phr. P: A (fair) t., parfaitement; vachement bien.
treat². I. v.i. 1. To t. with s.o., traiter, négocier, avec qn. To t. for peace, traiter la paix. 2. To t. of a subject, traiter d'un sujet. II. treat, v.tr. 1. Traiter. To t. s.o. well, se conduire bien avec qn; bien agir avec qn. Is that how you t. him? est-ce ainsi que vous en agissez avec lui? To t. sth. as a joke, considérer qch. comme une plaisanterie. 2. Régaler (qn); payer à boire (à qn). To t. oneself to an ice, s'offrir, se payer, une glace. 3. (a) Med: Traiter (un malade). He was treated in hospital, il a reçu des soins à l'hôpital. To t. s.o. for rheumatism, soigner qn pour le rhumatisme. (b) Ch: To t. a metal with an acid, traiter un métal par un acide. 4. Traiter (un thème).
treatise ['triːtiz], s. Traité m (on, de).

treatment ['triːtmənt], s. 1. (a) Traitement m (de qn). His t. of his friends, sa manière d'agir envers ses amis. Special t. (of prisoners), régime spécial. (b) Traitement (d'un sujet). 2. Traitement médical. Fresh air t., cure f d'air. To take a course of ten treatments, subir un traitement de dix séances.
treaty ['triːti], s. 1. Traité m (de paix); convention f. T. obligations, obligations conventionnelles. Hist: T. port, port ouvert (au commerce étranger). (b) Accord m, contrat m. To sell sth. by private t., vendre qch. à l'amiable. (b) To be in t. with s.o. for . . ., être en pourparlers avec qn pour. . . .
treble¹ ['trebl]. I. a. 1. Triple. 2. Mus: T. voice, (voix f de) soprano m. T. clef, clef f de sol. II. treble, adv. Trois fois autant. He earns t. my salary, il gagne trois fois plus que moi. III. treble, s. 1. Triple m. 2. Mus: (a) To sing the t., chanter le dessus. (b) (Pers., voice) Soprano m.
treble². 1. v.tr. Tripler. 2. v.i. (Se) tripler.
trebly ['trebli], adv. Triplement; trois fois autant.
tree [triː], s. 1. Arbre m. Apple t., pommier m. Rose t., rosier m. To climb a t., grimper sur, monter à, un arbre. To be at the top of the t., être au haut de l'échelle. To get to the top of the t., arriver. F: To be up a t., être dans le pétrin. S.a. BARK¹ 1. The t. of life, l'arbre de vie. 2. Family t., arbre généalogique. 3. (a) A: Gallows t., gibet m, potence f. (b) B: La Croix (du Christ). 4. (a) Const: Poutre f. Min: Étai m, butte f. (b) (Shoe) t., tendeur m (pour chaussures). 'tree-calf, s. Bookb: Veau raciné. 'tree-fern, s. Fougère arborescente. 'tree-frog, s. Amph: Rainette f.
treeless ['triːlis], a. Dépourvu d'arbres; sans arbres.
treetop ['triːtɔp], s. Cime f (d'un arbre). Av: To fly at t. height, voler en rase-mottes.
trefoil ['triːfoil,'tre-], s. 1. Bot: Trèfle m. Bird's-foot t., lotier m. Marsh t., trèfle d'eau. 2. Arch: Trèfle.
trek¹ [trek], s. 1. (In S. Africa) (a) Voyage m en chariot; étape f d'un voyage. (b) Migration f. 2. Voyage long et difficile (surtout à pied). Day's t., étape f. It's quite a t., c'est bien loin.
trek², v.i. 1. (In S. Africa) Voyager en chariot. 2. Faire un voyage long et difficile (surtout à pied).
trellis¹ ['trelis], s. Treillis m, treillage m. 'trellis-work, s. Treillis m, treillage m.
trellis², v.tr. Treillisser, treillager.
tremble¹ ['trembl], s. Frisson m; (in voice) tremblotement m. F: To be all of a t., être tout tremblant, F: avoir la tremblote.
tremble², v.i. 1. Trembler, vibrer. 2. Trembler, frissonner. To t. before s.o., trembler devant qn. **trembling¹**, a. Tremblant, tremblotant. **trembling²**, s. Tremblement m; tremblotement m. In fear and t., tout tremblant.
trembler ['tremblər], s. 1. Trembleur, -euse. 2. El.E: Trembleur m.
tremendous [tri'mendəs], a. 1. Terrible, épouvantable. 2. Immense, énorme. There was a t. crowd, il y avait un monde fou. T. success, succès formidable. T. blow, coup d'assommoir. -ly, adv. 1. Terriblement. 2. F: Énormément; démesurément.
tremolo ['treməlou], s. Mus: Trémolo m. T. stop (of organ), trémolo m. T. notes, notes tremblées.
tremor ['tremər], s. 1. Tremblement m, frémissement m. 2. Trépidation f (des vitres). Meteor: Earth f., secousse f sismique.
tremulous ['tremjuləs], a. Tremblotant, frémissant. T. smile, sourire timide, craintif. T. voice, voix chevrotante. -ly, adv. En tremblant; timidement, craintivement.
trench¹ [tren(t)ʃ], s. 1. (a) Agr: Tranchée f, fossé m; saignée f. (b) El.E: Covered-in t. (for wiring), canalisation f. 2. Mil: Tranchée. 'trench-coat, s. Mil: Manteau m imperméable; trench-coat m. 'trench-fever, s. Med: Fièvre f des tranchées, typhus récurrent. 'trench-mortar, s. Mortier m de tranchée.
trench². 1. v.tr. (a) Creuser un fossé, une tranchée, dans (le sol). Abs. To t., creuser des fossés. (b) Hort: Planter (le céleri) dans une rigole. 2. v.i. To t. (up)on s.o.'s property, s.o.'s rights, empiéter sur la propriété, sur les droits, de qn. **trenching**, s. Fossoyage m.

trenchant ['tren(t)ʃənt], a. 1. Poet: (Of sword) Tranchant, coupant. 2. (a) (Ton) tranchant, incisif. (b) (Réponse) mordante, caustique. -ly, adv. D'une manière tranchante.

trencher ['tren(t)ʃər], s. Dom.Ec: A: Tranchoir m, tailloir m.

trencherman, pl. -men ['tren(t)ʃəmən], s. (Good) t., (gros) mangeur.

trend[1] [trend], s. Direction f; tendance f (de l'opinion publique). The t. of my thoughts, le cours de mes pensées.

trend[2], v.i. Se diriger, tendre (to, towards, vers).

trepan[1] [tri'pæn], s. Surg: Min: Trépan m.

trepan[2], v.tr. (trepanned) Trépaner. **trepanning**, s. Trépanation f.

trepang [tri'pæŋ], s. Echin: Tripang m, trépang m; F: bêche-de-mer f.

trephine [tri'fi:n], s. Surg: Tréphine f.

trepidation [,trepi'deiʃ(ə)n], s. Trépidation f.

trespass[1] ['trespəs], s. 1. (a) Infraction f à la loi; délit m. (b) Theol: Offense f, péché m. 2. Jur: Violation f des droits de qn; trouble m de jouissance.

trespass[2], v.i. 1. A. & Lit: Pécher (against, contre). To t. against the law, enfreindre la loi. 2. (a) To t. (up)on s.o.'s rights, violer les droits de qn. (b) To t. on s.o.'s property, abs. to t., s'introduire sans autorisation sur la propriété de qn. To t. on s.o.'s preserves, empiéter sur le domaine de qn, F: marcher sur les plates-bandes de qn. (c) To t. on s.o.'s kindness, abuser de la bonté de qn.

trespasser ['trespəsər], s. 1. Theol: Pécheur m. 2. Auteur m d'une violation de propriété (foncière); intrus m. 'Trespassers will be prosecuted,' "défense d'entrer sous peine d'amende."

tress [tres], s. (a) Tresse f, boucle f (de cheveux). (b) Lit: pl. Tresses, chevelure f (d'une femme).

trestle ['tresl], s. Tréteau m, chevalet m. 'trestle-bed, s. Lit m de sangle. 'trestle-bridge, s. Pont m sur chevalets. 'trestle-table, s. Table f à tréteaux.

trews [tru:z], s.pl. Pantalon m en tartan (de certains régiments écossais).

trey [trei], s. Cards: Dice: (Le) trois.

triad ['traiæd], s. Triade f. Ch: Élément trivalent. Mus: Accord parfait.

trial ['traiəl], s. 1. Jur: (a) Jugement m (d'un litige, d'un accusé). To bring s.o. to t., faire passer qn en jugement. They were sent for t., ils furent renvoyés en jugement. T. by jury, jugement par jury. S.a. COMMIT 2. (b) Procès m. Famous trials, causes f célèbres. (c) Hist: T. by combat, combat m judiciaire. T. by combat, combat m judiciaire. 2. Essai m. (a) Épreuve f. Lit: To make t. of s.o.'s courage, mettre à l'épreuve le courage de qn. Sp: T. game, match m de sélection. (b) To give sth. a t., faire l'essai de qch. On t., à l'essai. Mth: To proceed by t. and error, procéder par tâtonnements. Com: T. order, commande d'essai. Book-k: T. balance, balance de vérification. Aut: Com: T. run, course d'essai. Av: T. flight, vol d'essai. Nau: etc: Speed t., essai de vitesse. Artil: Gun trials, expériences f de tir. (c) Sheep-dog trials, concours m de chiens de berger. 3. Épreuve douloureuse. He has met with sad trials, il a été cruellement éprouvé. That child is a great t. to his parents, cet enfant fait le martyre de ses parents.

triangle ['traiæŋgl], s. 1. Triangle m. The eternal t., le ménage à trois. 2. Mus: Triangle.

triangular [trai'æŋgjulər], a. Triangulaire; en triangle. Nau: T. flag, triangle f.

triangulate [trai'æŋgjuleit], v.tr. Surv: Trianguler.

triangulation [traiæŋgju'leiʃ(ə)n], s. Surv: Triangulation f.

trias ['traiæs], s. Geol: Trias m.

triassic [trai'æsik], a. & s. Geol: Triasique (m).

triatomic [,traiə'tɔmik], a. Ch: Triatomique.

tribal ['traib(ə)l], a. 1. (Of race) Qui vit en tribus. 2. Tribal, -aux; de tribu.

tribasic [trai'beisik], a. Ch: Tribasique.

tribe [traib], s. 1. Tribu f. F: Father with a whole t. of children, père avec toute une smala d'enfants. 2. Nat.Hist: Tribu, espèce f.

tribesman, pl. -men ['traibzmən], s.m. Membre de la tribu.

tribrach ['traibræk], s. Pros: Tribraque m.

tribulation [,tribju'leiʃ(ə)n], s. Tribulation f, affliction f; épreuves fpl.

tribunal [tri'bju:nl, trai-], s. Tribunal m, -aux. 1. Siège m du juge. 2. Cour f de justice; la cour.

tribune[1] ['tribju:n], s. Rom.Hist., etc: Tribun m.

tribune[2], s. Tribune f (d'orateur).

tributary ['tribjut(ə)ri]. 1. a. Tributaire. 2. s. Tributaire m. (b) Affluent m (d'un fleuve).

tribute ['tribju:t], s. 1. Tribut m. To pay t., payer tribut (to, à). 2. Tribut, hommage m. To pay a last t. of respect to s.o., rendre à qn les derniers devoirs. Journ: Floral tributes, (i) bouquets m de fleurs (offerts à une actrice, etc.); (ii) gerbes f et couronnes f (à un enterrement).

tricar ['traika:r], s. Veh: Tri-car m; (commercial) triporteur m.

trice[1] [trais], s. Only in the phr. In a t., en un clin d'œil, en moins de rien.

trice[2], v.tr. Nau: To t. (up) a sail, hisser, remonter, une voile.

tricephalous [trai'sefələs], a. Tricéphale.

triceps ['traiseps], s. Anat: Triceps m.

trichina, pl. -ae [tri'kainə, -i:], s. Med: Trichine f.

trichord ['traikɔ:d], s. Mus: Tricorde m.

trichology [tri'kɔlədʒi], s. Trichologie f.

trichromatic [,traikro'mætik], a. Phot: etc: (Procédé) trichrome.

trick[1] [trik], s. 1. (a) Tour m, ruse f; supercherie f. To play a t. on s.o., jouer un tour à qn. To obtain sth. by a t., obtenir qch. par ruse. Tricks and jokes, farces et attrapes. (b) Truc m. Tricks of writing, artifices m de style. The tricks of the trade, les trucs, les recettes f, les astuces f, du métier. He knows a t. or two, he's up to every t., il est roublard. I know a t. worth two of that, je connais un truc encore meilleur que celui-là. To know the t. of it, avoir le truc, le chic. That'll do the t., ça fera l'affaire. F: To play a t. on s.o., faire une farce à qn. You have been up to your old tricks, vous avez encore fait des vôtres. 3. Tour d'adresse. Card t., tour de cartes. F: The whole bag of tricks, toute la boutique; tout le bataclan. F: To do the t., réussir le coup. T. riding, voltige f. S.a. FLYING[2] 1, PARLOUR. 4. Manie f, habitude f. He has a t. of (doing sth.), il a la manie de (faire qch.). 5. Cards: Levée f. The odd t., le trick; la levée supplémentaire. To take a t., faire une levée. 6. Nau: T. at the wheel, tour de barre.

trick[2], v.tr. 1. Attraper, duper (qn). Fb: Mystifier (un adversaire). I've been tricked, on m'a refait. To t. s.o. out of sth., escroquer qch. à qn. 2. O: To t. s.o. out, parer qn (with, in, de).

trickery ['trikəri], s. 1. Fourberie f, tricherie f. Piece of t., fraude f, supercherie f.

trickiness ['trikinis], s. 1. Fourberie f. 2. F: Complication f, délicatesse f. (d'un mécanisme).

trickle[1] ['trikl], s. Filet m (d'eau). 'trickle charger, s. El.E: Chargeur m (d'accu) à régime lent.

trickle[2]. 1. v.i. (a) Couler (goutte à goutte). Waters that t. from the rock, eaux qui suintent de la roche. Tears trickled down her cheeks, les larmes coulaient le long de ses joues. To t. in, s'infiltrer. (b) The ball just trickled into the hole, la balle roula tout doucement dans le trou. 2. v.tr. Laisser dégoutter (un liquide); laisser tomber (un liquide) goutte à goutte. **trickling**, s. Dégouttement m; écoulement m goutte à goutte.

trickster ['trikstər], s. Fourbe m, escroc m. F: carotteur, -euse.

tricky ['triki], a. 1. Rusé, astucieux, -euse, fin. 2. F: (Mécanisme) d'un maniement délicat; compliqué; (situation) délicate.

tricolo(u)r ['trikələr]. 1. a. Tricolore. 2. s. The T., le drapeau tricolore (français), les trois couleurs.

tricycle ['traisikl], s. Tricycle m.

tricyclist ['traisiklist], s. Tricycliste mf.

tridactyl(ous) [trai'dæktil(əs)], a. Z: Tridactyle.

trident ['traid(ə)nt], s. Trident m (de Neptune).

tried. See TRY[2].

triennial [trai'enjəl], a. 1. Trisannuel. 2. T. plants, s. triennials, plantes trisannuelles.

trier ['traiər], s. 1. F: He's a t., il fait toujours de son mieux. 2. Tail: T.-on, essayeur, -euse.

trifle¹ ['traifl], s. 1. (a) Bagatelle f, vétille f. **The merest t. puts him out**, il se fâche pour un rien. **Ten pounds, a mere t.!** dix livres, une misère! **To stick at trifles**, s'arrêter à des vétilles. **It's no t.**, ce n'est pas une petite affaire. (b) **He gave the beggar a t.**, il donna quelques sous au mendiant. (c) *Adv.phr:* **A t.**, un tout petit peu. **A t. too narrow**, un soupçon trop étroit. 2. *Cu:* = Diplomate m.
trifle². 1. v.i. (a) Jouer, badiner (with, avec). **To t. with s.o.**, se jouer de qn. **To t. with one's health**, jouer avec sa santé. (b) **To t. with sth.**, manier nonchalamment (sa canne). **To t. with one's food**, manger du bout des dents. (c) Vétiller; s'occuper à des riens. 2. v.tr. **To t. one's time away**, gâcher son temps.
trifling¹, a. 1. (*Of pers.*) Futile, léger, -ère. 2. (*Of thg*) Insignifiant; peu important. **T. incidents**, menus incidents. **Of t. value**, d'une valeur minime.
trifling², s. 1. Légèreté f d'esprit; manque m de sérieux; badinage m. 2. Futilités fpl.
trifler ['traiflər], s. Personne f frivole; baguenaudier m.
triforium, pl. -ia [trai'fɔːriəm, -iə], s. *Arch:* Triforium m.
trig¹ [trig], s. 1. Cale f (pour empêcher une roue, un tonneau, de rouler). 2. Sabot m d'enrayage.
trig², v.tr. (**trigged**) 1. Caler (une roue, un tonneau). 2. Enrayer (une roue).
trig³, s. *Mth: F:* Trigonométrie f, *F:* trigo f.
trigger ['trigər], s. (a) Poussoir m à ressort. **T. action**, déclenchement m. (b) *Sm.a:* Détente f; *F:* gâchette f. **'trigger-finger**, s. Index m (de la main droite). **'trigger-guard**, s. *Sm.a:* Pontet m; sous-garde f. **'trigger-happy**, a. *F:* **To be t.-h.**, avoir la gâchette facile.
trigger², v.tr. Déclencher. **trigger off**, v.tr. Déclencher.
trigonometric(al) [,trigənə'metrik(əl)], a. Trigonométrique. **-ally**, adv. Trigonométriquement.
trigonometry [,trigə'nɔmitri], s. Trigonométrie f. **Plane t.**, trigonométrie rectiligne.
trigynous ['tridʒinəs], a. *Bot:* Trigyne.
trihedral [trai'hiːdrəl, -'hedrəl], a. & s. (Angle) trièdre; trièdre m.
trilateral [trai'læt(ə)rəl], a. Trilatéral, -aux.
trilby ['trilbi], s. *Cost:* Chapeau mou.
trilinear [trai'liniər], a. *Geom:* Trilinéaire.
trilingual [trai'liŋgw(ə)l], a. Trilingue.
trill¹ [tril], s. 1. *Mus:* (a) Trille m. (b) Cadence perlée. 2. Chant perlé (des oiseaux). 3. *Ling:* Consonne roulée.
trill². 1. v.i. (a) *Mus:* Faire des trilles. (b) (*Of bird*) Perler son chant. 2. v.tr. (a) *Mus:* Triller (une note). (b) *Ling:* Rouler (les r).
trillion ['triljən], s. Trillion m.
trilobate [trai'loubeit], a. *Bot: etc:* Trilobé.
trilogy ['trilədʒi], s. Trilogie f.
trim¹ [trim], s. 1. Bon ordre. (a) **Everything was in perfect t.**, tout était en parfait état. **Ship in fighting t.**, navire paré pour le combat. (b) **To be in good t.**, être gaillard; (*of boxer*) être en forme. 2. *Nau:* Assiette f, arrimage m (d'un navire). *Av:* Équilibrage m. 3. *Hairdr:* Coupe f.
trim², a. Soigné; en bon état; tiré à quatre épingles. **A t. figure**, une tournure élégante. **-ly**, adv. En bon ordre; proprement.
trim³, v.tr. (**trimmed**) 1. (a) Arranger; mettre en ordre. (b) Tailler (une haie); émonder (un arbre); dégrossir (le bois); rafraîchir (la barbe). *Phot:* Calibrer (une épreuve). **To t. one's nails**, se faire les ongles. **To t. a lamp**, émécher une lampe. *Bookb:* **To t. (down) the edges of a book**, rogner les tranches d'un livre. *Cu:* **To t. meat**, parer la viande. 2. *Dressm: etc:* Orner, parer (with, de). **Underclothes trimmed with lace**, linge de corps garni de dentelles. 3. *Nau:* (a) Équilibrer (un navire). **Trimmed by the head**, chargé sur le nez. **To t. the cargo**, arrimer le chargement. (b) Orienter (les voiles). **trim up**, v.tr. 1. Garnir à neuf (un chapeau). **To t. oneself up**, faire un brin de toilette. 2. *Carp:* Dresser (une poutre). **trimming**, s. 1. (a) Arrangement m, mise f en état (de qch.). (b) Taille f (des haies). *Phot:* Calibrage m (des épreuves). *Bookb:* **T. (down) of the edges**, ébarbage m des tranches. (a) Garnissage m (de chapeaux). (b) Garniture f, ornement m (de vêtements, de chapeaux). **Bead t.**, motif perlé. **Lace t.**,

garniture de dentelles. 3. (a) *Nau:* Arrimage m. (b) *Av:* **T. tab**, flettner m, compensateur m. 4. pl. **Trimmings.** (a) Rognures fpl (de papier); parure f (de viande). (b) Passementerie f (pour vêtements); fournitures fpl (pour chapeaux). *Cu: F:* Accompagnements mpl, garniture (d'un gigot, etc.).
trimeter ['trimitər], a. & s. *Pros:* Trimètre (m).
trimmer ['trimər], s. 1. (a) *Ind:* Appareilleur m. (b) Garnisseur, -euse (de chapeaux). (c) *Nau:* Arrimeur m. **Coal-t.**, soutier m. (d) *Av:* Compensateur m. (e) *Pol: F:* Opportuniste m. 2. (a) Machine f à trancher. *Bookb:* Massicot m. (b) *Const:* Chevêtre m.
trimness ['trimnis], s. Air soigné, air bien tenu (de qn); élégance f (de mise). **The t. of her figure**, sa jolie tournure.
tringle ['triŋgl], s. *Arch: Furn:* Tringle f.
Trinidad ['trinidæd]. *Pr.n.* (Ile de) la Trinité.
trinitrotoluene ['trainaitrou'tɔljuːin], s. *Exp:* Trinitrotoluène m.
Trinity ['triniti], s. 1. (a) *Theol:* **The (blessed) T.**, la (sainte) Trinité. **T. Sunday**, (fête f de) la Trinité. (b) Groupe m de trois (personnes). 2. *Nau:* **T. House**, corporation chargée de l'entretien des phares, du balisage et du pilotage.
trinket ['triŋkit], s. (a) Petit objet de parure; breloque f. (b) Bibelot m.
trinomial [trai'noumiəl], a. & s. *Mth:* Trinôme (m).
trio, pl. -os ['triːou(z)], s. Trio m.
triode ['traioud], s. *El:* Lampe f à trois électrodes.
triolet ['traiolit], s. *Pros:* Triolet m.
trip¹ [trip], s. 1. Excursion f; voyage m d'agrément. **To go for a short sea t.**, faire une sortie en mer. **Cheap t.**, excursion à prix réduit. *Aut:* **T. recorder** (*of speedometer*), (totalisateur) journalier m. *Nau:* **Maiden t.**, première sortie (d'un navire). **Round t.**, croisière f. 2. (a) Faux pas; trébuchement m. (b) Faute f; faux pas. (c) Croc-en-jambe m, croche-pied m, pl. croche-pieds. *Box:* Enlaçage m de jambe. **trip-gear**, s. *Mec.E:* Déclic m; modificateur instantané. **'trip-hammer**, s. Marteau m à bascule. **'trip-wire**, s. *Mil:* Fil tendu (en guise de traquenard ou d'avertisseur).
trip², v. (**tripped** [tript]) 1. v.i. (a) **To t. (along)**, aller d'un pas léger. (b) Trébucher; faire un faux pas. (c) Se tromper; commettre une faute. *F:* **To catch s.o. tripping**, prendre qn en défaut. (d) (*Of anchor*) Déraper. 2. v.tr. (a) **To trip s.o. (up)**, (i) donner un croc-en-jambe à qn; (*of obstacle*) faire trébucher qn; (ii) prendre qn en défaut. (b) *Nau:* **To t. the anchor**, déraper l'ancre.
tripe [traip], s. (a) *Cu:* Tripe(s) f(pl); gras-double m. (b) *F:* Fatras m, bêtises fpl. **To publish t.**, publier des ouvrages sans valeur, de la littérature de camelote. **This is t.**, c'est un navet. **'tripe-dealer, -seller**, s. Tripier, -ière.
triphase ['traifeiz], a. *El:* (Courant) triphasé.
triplane ['traiplein], a. & s. *Av:* Triplan (m).
triple¹ ['tripl], a. Triple. *Mus:* **T. time**, mesure ternaire, à trois temps. *Hist:* **The T. Alliance**, la Triplice; la triple Alliance. **T.-expansion engine**, machine à triple expansion. **T. screw steamer**, vapeur à trois hélices. **-ply**, adv. Triplement.
triple². 1. v.tr. Tripler. 2. v.i. (Se) tripler.
triplet ['triplit], s. 1. Trio m; réunion f de trois personnes, de trois choses. *Esp:* (a) *Mus:* Triolet m. (b) *Pros:* Tercet m. (c) *Opt:* **T. lens**, triplet m. 2. pl. **Triplets**, triplés mpl. **Birth of triplets**, accouchement m trigémellaire.
triplex ['tripleks], a. (Planche) en trois épaisseurs; (machine) à trois cylindres. **T.(glass)**, (verre) triplex (*R.t.m.*).
triplicate¹ ['triplikit]. 1. a. Triplé; triple. 2. s. Triple m; triplicata m. **Agreement in t.**, traité en triple exemplaire, en triple expédition.
triplicate² ['triplikeit], v.tr. 1. Tripler. 2. Rédiger (un document) en triple expédition.
tripod ['traipɔd], s. Trépied m; pied m (à trois branches). **T. stand**, pied à trois branches; support m à trois pieds. *Nau:* **T. mast**, (mât m) tripode m.
Tripoli ['tripɔli]. *Pr.n.* (a) Tripoli m. (b) La Tripolitaine.
tripos ['traipɔs], s. *Sch:* = (Examen de) licence ès lettres, ès sciences, etc. (à Cambridge).

tripper ['tripər], *s.* Excursionniste *mf.*

tripperish ['tripəriʃ], **trippery** ['tripəri], *a. F:* Envahi de touristes.

triptych ['triptik], *s. Art:* Triptyque *m.*

triptyque ['triptik], *s. Aut:* Triptyque *m* (pour passage en douane).

trireme ['trairi:m], *s. Gr.Ant:* Trirème *f.*

trisect [trai'sekt], *v.tr. Geom: etc:* Triséquer. **trisecting**, *a.* Trisecteur, -trice.

trisection [trai'sekʃ(ə)n], *s.* Trisection *f.*

trisyllabic['traisi'læbik], *a.* Tris(s)yllabique, tris(s)yllabe.

trisyllable ['trai'siləbl], *s.* Tris(s)yllabe *m.*

trite [trait], *a.* Banal, -als. **T. subject,** sujet usé, rebattu. **-ly,** *adv.* Banalement.

triteness ['traitnis], *s.* Banalité *f.*

triton ['traitən], *s. Myth:* Triton *m.*

triturate ['tritjureit], *v.tr.* Triturer. **'triturating-machine,** *s. Ind:* Triturateur *m.*

trituration [tritju'reiʃ(ə)n], *s.* Trituration *f.*

triumph[1] ['traiəmf], *s.* **1.** *Rom.Ant:* Triomphe *m.* **2.** *(a)* Triomphe, succès *m.* **To achieve great triumphs,** remporter de grands succès. *(b)* Air *m* de triomphe; jubilation *f.*

triumph[2], *v.i.* **1.** *Rom.Ant:* Triompher. **2.** Triompher; remporter un succès éclatant. **To t. over one's enemies,** triompher de ses ennemis; l'emporter sur ses ennemis.

triumphal [trai'ʌmf(ə)l], *a.* Triomphal, -aux; de triomphe. **T. arch,** arc *m* de triomphe.

triumphant [trai'ʌmfənt], *a.* Triomphant. **The Church T.,** l'Église triomphante. **-ly,** *adv.* Triomphalement; d'un air, d'un ton, de triomphe.

triumvir, *pl.* **-virs, -viri** [trai'ʌmvə(:)r, -və(:)z, -viri:] *s. Rom.Hist:* Triumvir *m.*

triumvirate ['trai'ʌmvirit], *s.* Triumvirat *m.*

triune ['traiju:n], *a.* D'une unité triple; trois en un. *Esp.* **T. godhead,** divinité *f* une en trois personnes.

trivalence [trai'veiləns], *s. Ch:* Trivalence *f.*

trivalent [trai'veilənt], *a. Ch:* Trivalent.

trivet ['trivit], *s.* Trépied *m,* chevrette *f* (pour bouilloire etc.).

trivia ['triviə], *s.pl.* Des vétilles *f,* des riens *m.*

trivial ['triviəl], *a.* **1.** *(a)* Insignifiant; sans importance. *(b)* *(Of pers.)* Superficiel, léger, futile. **2.** Banal, -als. **The t. round,** le train-train de tous les jours.

triviality [ˌtrivi'æliti], *s.* *(a)* Insignifiance *f* (d'une perte, d'une offense, etc.). *(b)* Banalité *f* (d'une observation, etc.). *(c)* Bagatelle *f;* pl des riens.

tri-weekly ['trai'wi:kli]. **1.** *(a) a.* De toutes les trois semaines. *(b) adv.* Toutes les trois semaines. **2.** *(a) a.* Trihebdomadaire. *(b) adv.* Trois fois par semaine.

troat[1] [trout], *s. Ven:* Bramement *m* (du cerf).

troat[2], *v.i. Ven: (Of stag)* Bramer.

trocar ['troukər], *s. Surg:* Trocart *m.*

trochaic [tro'keiik], *a. & s. Pros:* Trochaïque (*m*).

trochee ['trouki:], *s. Pros:* Trochée *f.*

trochlea, *pl.* **-eae** ['troklia, -ii:], *s. Anat:* Trochlée *f.*

trochoid ['troukoid]. **1.** *a. (a) Anat:* (Articulation) trochoïde. *(b) Geom:* Cycloïdal, -aux. **2.** *s. Geom:* (i) *A:* Cycloïde *f,* roulette *f.* (ii) Courbe cycloïdale.

trod [trod], **trodden** ['trodn]. *See* TREAD[2].

troglodyte ['trogloдait], *s.* Troglodyte *m.*

Trojan ['troudʒən], *a. & s.* Troyen, -enne; de Troie. **The T. War,** la guerre de Troie. **To work like a T.,** travailler comme un nègre.

troll[1] [troul], *s.* **1.** Chanson *f* à reprises; canon *m.* **2.** *Fish:* *(a)* Cuiller *f.* *(b)* Moulinet *m* (de canne à pêche).

troll[2]. **1.** *v.tr. (a) A:* Chanter (un air) en canon. *(b)* Chantonner (un air); *abs.* chantonner. **2.** *v.i. Fish:* To t. for pike, pêcher le brochet à la cuiller. **trolling,** *s. Fish:* Pêche *f* à la cuiller.

troll[3], *s. Norse Myth:* Troll *m.*

trolley ['troli], *s.* **1.** *(a) Veh: (Four-wheeled)* Fardier *m,* chariot *m; (two-wheeled)* diable *m.* **Porter's luggage t.,** chariot à bagages. *(b) Dinner t.,* table desserte, table roulante. **2.** *Ind:* Overhead t., chariot (de pont roulant, etc.); transporteur aérien à câbles. **3.** *(a)* Moufle *f* (de transport sur câble aérien). *(b) El.E:* Trolley *m* (d'un tramway). *U.S:* t. (car), tramway. **'trolley-bus,** *s.* Trolleybus *m.*

trollop ['troləp], *s.f. O:* Souillon *f.*

trolly ['troli], *s.* = TROLLEY.

trombidium [trɔm'bidiəm], *s. Ent:* Trombidion *m.*

trombone [trɔm'boun], *s.* Trombone *m.* **Valve t.,** trombone à pistons.

troop[1] [tru:p], *s.* **1.** Troupe *f,* bande *f* (de personnes). **In troops,** par bandes. **2.** *Mil: (a)* pl. **Troops,** troupes. **To raise troops,** lever des soldats. *S.a.* STORM-TROOPS. *(b)* Escadron *m* (de cavalerie). **To get one's t.,** passer capitaine. **3.** *Scouting:* Troupe. **'troop-ship,** *s.* Transport *m* (de troupes). **'troop-train,** *s.* Train *m* militaire.

troop[2]. **1.** *v.i. (a)* To t. together, s'attrouper, s'assembler. *(b)* To t. in, out, off, entrer, sortir, partir, en troupe, en bande. **2.** *v.tr. Mil:* To t. the colour(s), faire la parade du drapeau; présenter le drapeau. **trooping,** *s.* **1.** T. (together), attroupement *m,* assemblement *m;* rassemblement *m* (de troupes). **2.** *Mil:* **T. the colour(s),** présentation *f* du drapeau; salut *m* au drapeau.

trooper ['tru:pər], *s.* **1.** *Mil: (a)* Cavalier *m;* soldat *m* de cavalerie. *S.a.* SWEAR[2] 2. *(b)* Cheval *m* de cavalerie. **2.** *U.S: Austr:* Membre *m* de la police montée.

trope [troup], *s. Rh:* Trope *m.*

trophy ['troufi], *s.* *(a)* Trophée *m.* *(b)* Panoplie *f.*

tropic ['tropik]. **1.** *s. (a) Astr: Geog:* Tropique *m.* *(b)* **The tropics,** les tropiques; les pays chauds. **In the tropics,** sous les tropiques. **2.** *a.* Tropical, -aux.

tropical ['tropik(ə)l], *a.* **1.** *Astr:* (Année) tropique. **2.** (Climat) tropical, -aux; des tropiques.

troposphere ['troposfi:ər], *s. Meteor:* Troposphère *f.*

trot[1] [trot], *s.* Trot *m.* **Gentle t.,** petit trot. **Full t.,** grand trot. **Close t.,** trot assis. **To go at a t.,** aller au trot. **At a slow t., at an easy t.,** au petit trot. **To break into a t.,** se mettre au trot. **F:** To keep s.o. on the t., faire trotter qn. *S.a.* JOG-TROT.

trot[2], *v.* (trotted) **1.** *v.i. (a) (Of horse)* Trotter; aller au trot. **To t. away, off,** partir au trot. **To t. five miles,** faire cinq milles au trot. **To t. short,** trottiner. *(b)* *(Of pers.)* Trotter; *(of child, etc.)* trottiner; *(of athlete)* courir au pas gymnastique. **2.** *v.tr. (a)* Faire trotter (un cheval). *(b) F: O:* To t. s.o. round, balader qn; faire voir la ville à qn; servir de guide à qn. **trot out.** **1.** *v.i.* Allonger le pas; aller au grand trot. **2.** *v.tr. (a)* To t. out a horse, faire trotter un cheval (devant un client). *(b) F:* To t. out one's knowledge, exhiber, faire étalage de, ses connaissances. **'trotting race,** *s.* Course *f* au trot; course attelée.

troth [trouθ], *s. A. & Lit:* **1.** Foi *f.* **By my t.!** sur ma foi! *S.a.* PLIGHT[2]. **2.** In t., en vérité.

Trotskyist ['trotskiist], *s. Pol.Hist:* Trotskiste *mf.*

trotter ['trotər], *s.* **1.** *(a) (Horse)* Trotteur *m.* *(b) See* GLOBE-TROTTER. **2.** pl. *(a) Cu:* Sheep's trotters, pigs' trotters, pieds *m* de mouton, de cochon; pieds panés. *(b) Hum:* Les pieds.

trouble[1] ['trʌbl], *s.* **1.** Peine *f,* chagrin *m;* affliction *f,* malheur *m.* **To be in t.,** être dans la peine; avoir du chagrin. *(Cp. 2 (b).)* **They are in great t.,** ils sont tout désemparés. **His troubles are over,** il est au bout de ses peines. **2.** Ennui *m,* difficulté *f.* *(a)* **Money troubles,** soucis *m* d'argent. **Family troubles,** ennuis de famille. **The t. is that . . . ,** l'ennui, la difficulté, c'est que. . . . **You will have t. with him,** il vous donnera du fil à retordre. **The child must be a great t. to you,** cet enfant doit vous donner bien du tracas. *Prov:* **Troubles never come singly,** un malheur ne vient jamais seul. *(b)* To get into t., s'attirer une mauvaise affaire, des désagréments, des ennuis. **To get into t. with the police,** avoir affaire à, des démêlés avec, la police. **To get s.o. into t., to make t. for s.o.,** créer, susciter, des ennuis à qn. *P:* To get a girl into t., rendre une fille enceinte. **To get s.o. out of t.,** tirer qn d'affaire. **To be in t.,** avoir des ennuis (avec la police, etc.). **He's asking for t.,** il fait tout ce qu'il faut pour s'attirer une affaire; il se prépare des ennuis. *(c)* To make t., semer la discorde, la mésentente. **If you do not consent he will make t.,** si vous ne consentez pas il va se montrer désagréable. **There is going to be t.,** il y aura du vilain, du grabuge. **3.** Dérangement *m,* peine. **To take the t. to do sth.; to go to the t. of doing sth.,** prendre, se donner, la peine de faire qch. **It is not worth the t.,** ce n'est pas la peine; cela n'en vaut pas la peine. **To give s.o. t.,** déranger qn. **I am putting you to a lot of t.,** je vous donne beaucoup d'embarras. **To give oneself a lot of t., to go to a lot of t., to take a great deal of t.,** se donner beaucoup de mal, beaucoup de peine, F: se mettre en frais, en quatre. **To spare no t. in order to . . .,** ne pas ménager sa peine pour. . . . **He thinks nothing too much t.,** rien ne lui coûte. **To have a certain amount of t. in doing sth.,** avoir quelque peine à faire qch. **It is no t. to make,** cela ne donne aucun mal; cela se fait tout seul. **It is no t.,** cela ne me dérange pas; ce n'est rien! **It won't be much t. to copy it again,** il n'en coûtera guère de le recopier. **To have (had) all one's t. for nothing, for one's pains,** en être pour sa peine. 4. (a) Med: Dérangement, trouble m, troubles. **He's having t. with his eyesight,** il a des troubles de vision. **Eye t.,** affection f de l'œil. **Digestive troubles,** embarras digestifs. **To have heart t.,** souffrir du cœur, être cardiaque. **What's the t.?** qu'est-ce qui ne va pas? où avez-vous mal? (b) Aut: etc: **Engine t.,** panne f du moteur. (c) Ind: **Labour troubles,** conflits sociaux, conflits entre ouvriers et patrons.

trouble². 1. v.tr. (a) Affliger, tourmenter, chagriner (qn); inquiéter, préoccuper (qn). **To be troubled about s.o.,** se tourmenter au sujet de qn. **He has been much troubled about his son,** son fils lui a causé bien du tourment. **That does not t. him much,** ça lui donne fort peu de soucis; cela ne le préoccupe guère. (b) (Of disease, ailment) Affliger, faire souffrir (qn). (c) Déranger, incommoder, gêner, ennuyer, embarrasser (qn); donner de la peine à (qn). **I am so sorry to t. you,** toutes mes excuses pour la peine que je vous donne. **I shall not t. you with the details,** je vous fais grâce de tous les détails. **May I t. you to shut the door?** cela vous dérangerait-il de fermer la porte? Vous seriez bien aimable de fermer la porte. **May I t. you for the mustard?** voudriez-vous, s'il vous plaît, me passer la moutarde? puis-je vous demander la moutarde? **To t. oneself about sth.,** se mettre en peine de qch. **To t. oneself to do sth.,** se donner la peine de faire qch. 2. v.i. (a) S'inquiéter, F: se tracasser (about, au sujet de, à propos de). **Don't t. about it,** ne vous inquiétez pas de cela; que cela ne vous inquiète pas. (b) Se déranger; se mettre en peine. **Don't t. to write,** ne vous donnez pas la peine d'écrire. **troubled,** a. 1. (Of liquid) Trouble. **To fish in t. waters,** pêcher en eau trouble. S.a. OIL¹ 1. 2. (a) Inquiet, -ète; agité. (b) T. **period (of history),** époque de troubles.

troublemaker ['trʌblmeikər], s. Fomentateur, -trice, de troubles; factieux m; F: troublion m.

troubleshooter ['trʌblʃuːtər], s. 1. Mec.E: Dépanneur m. 2. Ind: Conciliateur m.

troublesome ['trʌblsəm], a 1. Ennuyeux, -euse, gênant, incommode, embarrassant. **T. child,** enfant fatigant, énervant. **T. rival,** rival gênant. **T. asthma,** asthme pénible. **How t.!** quel ennui! 2. (Tâche) difficile, pénible.

troublous ['trʌbləs], a. A: Troublé, agité. **T. times,** époque f de troubles.

trough [trɔf], s. 1. Auge f; (small) auget m, augette f. Husb: **Drinking t.,** abreuvoir m. **Feeding t.,** auge, mangeoire f. Ph: **Mercury t.,** cuvette f, cuve f, à mercure. **Accumulator t.,** bac m d'accumulateur. S.a. HORSE-TROUGH, KNEADING-TROUGH. 2. Caniveau m (en bois, etc.); chéneau m. 3. Geol: Fond m de bateau. 4. **T. of the wave,** creux m de la lame. Ph: **T. of a wave,** point bas, creux, d'une onde. 5. (Of low pressure, of depression) Dépression f, zone f dépressionnaire. **'trough-battery,** s. El: Pile f à auge.

trounce [trauns], v.tr. 1. (a) Rosser, étriller (qn); rouer (qn) de coups. (b) Games: Écraser (ses adversaires); battre (ses adversaires) à plates coutures. 2. Réprimander, semoncer. **trouncing,** s. Raclée f; étrillage m. **To give s.o. a t.,** (i) administrer une raclée à qn; étriller qn; (ii) battre (un adversaire) à plates coutures.

troupe [truːp], s. Troupe f (de comédiens, etc.).

trouser ['trauzər], s. **(Pair of) trousers,** pantalon m. **Turn-up trousers,** pantalon à revers. **Skiing trousers,** fuseaux mpl. F: **She wears the trousers,** c'est elle qui porte la culotte. **'trouser-clip,** s. Pince f à pantalon (pour cycliste, etc.). **'trouser-press,** s. Presse f pour pantalons; presse-pantalon m.

trousseau ['truːsou], s. Trousseau m.

trout [traut], s. inv. (a) Ich: Truite f. **River full of trout,** rivière pleine de truites. **T. stream,** ruisseau à truites. S.a. SALMON-TROUT, SEA-TROUT. (b) P: **An old t.,** une vieille rombière. **'trout-coloured,** a. (Cheval) truité. **'trout-fly,** s. Fish: Mouche f pour la pêche à la truite.

trow [trou], v.tr. A: Croire, penser.

trowel ['trau(ə)l], s. 1. Truelle f. S.a. LAY ON 2. 2. Hort: Déplantoir m.

trowelful ['trau(ə)lful], s. Clapée f (de mortier); truellée f.

troy¹ [trɔi], s. T. **(weight),** poids m troy (pour la pesée de l'or et de l'argent). S.a. OUNCE¹ 1.

Troy². Pr.n. A.Geog: Troie f.

truant ['truːənt], a. & s. Élève absent de l'école sans permission. **To play t.,** faire l'école buissonnière.

truce [truːs], s. Trêve f. Hist: **The T. of God,** la trêve de Dieu. S.a. FLAG⁴ 1. **'truce-bearer,** s. Mil: Parlementaire m. **'truce-breaker,** s. Violateur m de la trêve.

truck¹ [trʌk], s. 1. Troc m, échange m. 2. Hist: **T. Act,** loi f interdisant le paiement des ouvriers en nature. 3. **I have no t. with him,** (i) je n'ai pas affaire à lui; (ii) je n'ai rien à faire avec lui. 4. (a) Articles divers. (b) Camelote f. 5. U.S: Produits maraîchers. **'truck farmer,** s. U.S: Maraîcher m. **'truck farming,** s. U.S: Culture maraîchère.

truck². 1. v.i. (a) Troquer, faire un échange (with s.o., avec qn). (b) Trafiquer (in sth., en qch.). 2. v.tr. (a) Troquer, échanger (sth. for sth., qch. contre qch.) (b) Troquer, échanger (des marchandises).

truck³, s. 1. (a) (Four-wheeled) Fardier m, camion m, chariot m. (b) Min: Benne f. (c) (Porter's) luggage t., (four-wheeled) chariot à bagages; (two-wheeled) diable m. (d) Aut: U.S: Camion. **Delivery t.,** light t., camionnette f. **Tow t.,** dépanneuse f. 2. Rail: Wagon à marchandises ouvert. **'truck driver,** s. U.S: Camionneur m.

truckful ['trʌkful], s. Plein wagon, plein camion (of, de).

trucking ['trʌkiŋ], s. U.S: Camionnage m.

truckle ['trʌkl], v.i. **To t. to s.o.,** ramper, s'abaisser, devant qn; faire des platitudes à qn.

truckle-bed ['trʌkl'bed], s. O: Lit bas à roulettes.

truckler ['trʌklər], s. Flagorneur m; plat valet.

truculence ['trʌkjuləns], **truculency** ['trʌkjulənsi], s. Férocité f; truculence f.

truculent ['trʌkjulənt], a. Féroce; brutal, -aux; truculent. **-ly,** adv. Férocement; avec truculence.

trudge¹ [trʌdʒ], s. Marche f pénible.

trudge², v.i. Marcher lourdement, péniblement.

trudgen ['trʌdʒən], s. Swim: T. **(stroke),** trudgeon m.

true¹ [truː]. I. a. 1. Vrai; exact. **If it be t. that . . .,** s'il est vrai que + sub.; si tant est que + sub. **So t. is it that . . .,** tant il est vrai que + ind. **T.! c'est** (bien) vrai! c'est juste! **To come t.,** se réaliser; se vérifier. **The same holds t. in respect of . . .,** il en est de même pour. . . . S.a. BILL⁴ 6, LIFE 1. 2. Véritable; vrai, réel, authentique. **To form a t. estimate of the situation,** se faire une idée juste de la situation. Nau: **T. longitude,** longitude vraie. 3. Mec.E: etc: Juste, droit; rectifié, ajusté. **To make a piece t.,** ajuster une pièce. **The (billiard) table is not t.,** le billard n'est pas d'aplomb. 4. (a) Fidèle, loyal, -aux (to, à). (b) **T. repentance,** repentir sincère. (c) A: (Of pers.) Honnête. 5. (Of voice, instrument) Juste. 6. Biol: **T. to type,** conforme au type ancestral. II. **true,** adv. 1. Vraiment; F: vrai. 2. (a) **To sing t.,** chanter juste. **To aim t.,** viser juste. **The wheel is not running t.,** la roue ne tourne pas rond, est désaxée. (b) **To breed t.,** se reproduire suivant un type invariable. III. **true,** s. Adj. phr. & adv. phr. **Out of t.,** (i) (of vertical post, etc.) hors d'aplomb; (ii) (of horizontal member, etc.) dénivelé; (iii) (of metal plate) gauchi, gondolé; (of wheel) voilé; (of axle) faussé, dévoyé; (of timber) déjeté, dévié; (iv) (of cylinder, etc.) ovalisé; (of wheel) décentré, excentré. **To run out of t.,** être décentré; tourner à faux. **A t.-b. Englishman,** un vrai Anglais d'Angleterre. **'true-hearted,** a. (a) Au cœur fidèle; loyal, -aux. (b) Sincère, honnête.

true², *v.tr.* To t. (up), ajuster (les pièces d'une machine); défausser, dégauchir (un essieu, etc.); rectifier, (re)dresser (une surface); dégauchir (une planche, etc.); mettre (bien) d'équerre (le bord d'une planche).

truffle ['trʌfl], *s.* Truffe *f.* **'truffle-dog, -hound,** *s.* Chien truffier.

truffled ['trʌfld], *a. Cu:* Truffé; aux truffes.

trug [trʌg], *s. Hort:* Corbeille *f* en bois éclaté.

truism ['truːizm], *s.* Truisme *m,* axiome *m;* vérité *f* de La Palisse.

truly ['truːli], *adv.* **1.** *(a)* Vraiment, véritablement. I am t. grateful, je vous suis sincèrement reconnaissant. *(b) Corr:* (I am) yours (very) t., je vous prie de croire à mes sentiments distingués; veuillez agréer mes salutations distinguées. *F:* No one knows it better than yours t., personne ne le sait mieux que votre serviteur. **2.** En vérité. T., I should be puzzled to say . . ., en vérité, ma foi, je serais embarrassé de dire. . . . *F:* Really t.? Vrai de vrai? **3.** (Servir qn, etc.) fidèlement, loyalement. **4.** Avec vérité; justement.

trump¹ [trʌmp], *s. A. & Lit:* Trompette *f.* The last t., the t. of doom, la trompette du jugement dernier.

trump², *s.* **1.** *Cards:* Atout *m.* To play trumps, jouer atout. To call no trumps, annoncer, demander, sans-atout. *F:* He always turns up trumps, (i) il a toujours la chance; (ii) il est toujours là pour donner un coup de main. To play one's t. card, jouer son atout. **2.** *F:* (a) Bon type; brave garçon, brave fille. (b) Chic type.

trump³, *v.tr.* **1.** *Cards:* Couper (une carte). *Abs.* To t., jouer atout. **2.** To t. up an excuse, inventer une excuse. To t. up a charge against s.o., forger une accusation contre qn.

trumpery ['trʌmpəri]. **1.** *s.* (a) Friperie *f,* camelote *f.* (b) Bêtises *fpl,* fadaises *fpl.* **2.** *a* (a) (Marchandises) sans valeur, de camelote, de pacotille. (b) (Argument, etc.) mesquin, spécieux.

trumpet¹ ['trʌmpit], *s.* **1.** Trompette *f.* Valve t., trompette d'harmonie. Flourish of trumpets, fanfare *f* de trompettes. To publish sth. with a flourish of trumpets, publier qch. à cor et à cri. **2.** *(Pers:)* Trompette *f.* **3.** *(Ear-)*t., cornet *m* acoustique. *S.a.* SPEAKING-TRUMPET. **'trumpet-call,** *s.* Coup *m* de trompette; sonnerie *f* de trompette. **'trumpet-'major,** *s. Mil:* Trompette-major *m.* **'trumpet-player,** *s. Mus:* Trompettiste *m.* **'trumpet-shell,** *s. Moll:* Triton *m;* buccin *m.*

trumpet², *v.* (trumpeted) **1.** *v.i.* (a) Sonner de la trompette. (b) *(Of elephant)* Barrir. **2.** *v.tr.* Publier (qch.) à son de trompe. To t. forth, abroad, s.o.'s great deeds, proclamer les hauts faits de qn. **trumpeting,** *s.* **1.** Sonnerie *f* de trompette. **2.** *(Of elephant)* Barrit *m,* barrissement *m.*

trumpeter ['trʌmpitər], *s.* (a) *Mil:* Trompette *m* (b) *(Member of the orchestra)* Trompettiste *m.*

truncate [trʌŋ'keit], *v.tr.* Tronquer (un arbre, etc.). **truncated,** *a.* Tronqué. *Geom:* T. cone, tronc *m* de cône; cône tronqué.

truncheon ['trʌn(t)ʃ(ə)n], *s.* Bâton *m* (d'agent de police). Rubber t., matraque *f* en caoutchouc.

trundle¹ ['trʌndl], *s.* **1.** Roulette *f* (de meuble). **2.** *Mec.E:* Lanterne *f.* T.(-wheel), (roue *f* à) lanterne *f.* (b) *(Stave)* Fuseau *m,* alluchon *m* (de lanterne).

trundle², *v.tr.* (a) Faire rouler, faire courir (un cerceau, etc.). (b) Pousser (une brouette).

trunk [trʌŋk], *s.* **1.** *(a)* Tronc *m* (d'arbre). (b) Tronc (du corps). (c) *Rail:* Artère principale (d'un réseau). *Tp:* T. connections, relations interurbaines. (d) *Arch:* Fût *m* (d'une colonne). **2.** Malle *f,* coffre *m.* Wardrobe t., malle-armoire *f.* To pack one's t., faire sa malle. *S.a.* CABIN-TRUNK. **3.** Trompe *f* (d'éléphant). **4.** *pl.* Trunks, (i) *Cost:* Caleçon court; slip *m;* (ii) *Tp: F:* inter *m.* **'trunk-call,** *s. Tp:* Appel interurbain. **'trunk-hose,** *s. A.Cost:* Haut-de-chausse(s) *m.* **'trunk-line,** *s. Rail:* Grande ligne. *Tp:* Ligne interurbaine. **'trunk-maker,** *s.* Malletier *m.* **'trunk-road,** *s.* Grande route, route nationale.

truss¹ [trʌs], *s.* **1.** Botte *f* (de foin). **2.** *(a) Const:* (i) Armature *f* (de poutre, etc.); (ii) ferme *f* (de comble, de pont). (b) *Arch:* Console *f,* encorbellement *m.* **3.** *Nau:* Drosse *f* (de vergue). **4.** *Med:* Bandage *m* herniaire. **'truss-bridge,** *s.* Pont *m* métallique à poutres en treillis. **'truss-girder,** *s.* Poutre armée.

truss², *v.tr.* **1.** Botteler (le foin); mettre (le foin) en bottes. **2.** *Const:* Armer, renforcer (une poutre). Trussed roof, comble *m* sur fermes. **3.** *Cu:* Trousser, brider (une volaille); *F:* ligoter (qn).

trust¹ [trʌst], *s.* **1.** Confiance *f* (in, en). To put one's t. in s.o., avoir confiance en qn; mettre sa confiance en qn. To take sth. on t., (i) accepter qch. de confiance; (ii) ajouter foi à qch. sans examen. **2.** Espérance *f,* espoir *m.* **3.** *Com:* To supply goods on t., fournir des marchandises à crédit. **4.** (a) Responsabilité *f,* charge *f.* Position of t., poste de confiance. (b) Garde *f;* dépôt *m.* To commit sth. to the t. of s.o., confier qch. à qn, aux soins de qn, à la garde de qn. *S.a.* BREACH¹ 1. **5.** *Jur:* Fidéicommis *m,* fiducie *f.* To hold sth. in t., tenir qch. par fidéicommis. **6.** *Ind:* Trust *m,* syndicat *m,* cartel *m.*

trust². **1.** *v.tr.* Se fier à (qn, qch.); mettre sa confiance en (qn). He is not to be trusted, on ne peut pas se fier à lui. If we may t. his account, s'il faut en croire son compte-rendu. I can scarcely t. my own eyes, my own ears, c'est à n'en pas croire mes yeux, mes oreilles. To t. s.o. with sth., confier qch. à qn. To t. s.o. to do sth., se fier à qn pour que qch. se fasse. T. him! laissez-le faire! I could not t. myself to speak, j'étais trop ému pour me risquer à rien dire. *F:* She won't t. him out of her sight, elle ne le perd jamais de vue. (b) To t. sth. to, with, s.o., confier qch. à qn, aux soins de qn. (c) *Com: F:* Faire crédit à (un client). (d) Espérer (que + ind.); exprimer le vœu (que + sub.). *Com: Corr:* I t. to hear from you soon, j'espère avoir de vos nouvelles sous peu. **2.** *v.i.* (a) Se confier (in, en); se fier (in, à); mettre sa confiance (in, en). (b) Mettre ses espérances, son espoir (to sth., en qch.). To t. to chance, to luck, s'en remettre au hasard. **trusted,** *a.* (Serviteur, etc.) de confiance. **trusting,** *a.* Plein de confiance.

trustee [trʌs'tiː], *s.* **1.** *Jur:* (a) *(Of estate)* Fidéicommissaire *m;* curateur, -trice. The Public T., le curateur de l'État aux successions. (b) Dépositaire *m,* consignataire *m.* (c) *(With powers of attorney)* Mandataire *mf.* T. (in bankruptcy), syndic *m* (de faillite). In the hands of trustees, en régie. **2.** Administrateur *m,* curateur (d'un musée, etc.). Board of trustees, conseil *m* d'administration.

trusteeship [trʌs'tiːʃip], *s.* **1.** Fidéicommis *m.* **2.** Administration *f,* curatelle *f.* *Pol:* Tutelle *f.*

trustful ['trʌstf(u)l], *a.* Plein de confiance; confiant. **-fully,** *adv.* Avec confiance.

trustiness ['trʌstinis], *s.* Fidélité *f,* loyauté *f.*

trustworthiness ['trʌst,wəːðinis], *s.* **1.** *(Of pers.)* Loyauté *f,* fidélité *f.* **2.** Crédibilité *f,* exactitude *f* (d'un témoignage, etc.).

trustworthy ['trʌst,wəːði], *a.* **1.** *(Of pers.)* (Digne) de confiance, digne de foi; honnête, fidèle. T. witness, témoin irrécusable. **2.** (Renseignement, etc.) digne de foi, exact.

trusty ['trʌsti], *a.* **1.** *Lit:* Sûr, fidèle; loyal, -aux. **2.** *s.* Forçat bien noté (à qui sont accordés certains privilèges).

truth [truːθ], *s.* (a) Vérité *f.* The t. (of the matter) is, to tell the t., I forgot it, pour dire la vérité, à dire vrai, je l'ai oublié. There is some t. in what you say, il y a du vrai dans ce que vous dites. T. will out, tôt ou tard la vérité se découvre, se fait jour. *Jur:* The t., the whole t., and nothing but the t., la vérité, rien que la vérité, toute la vérité. (b) Vérité; chose vraie. To tell s.o. some home truths, dire ses quatre vérités à qn; dire son fait à qn.

truthful ['truːθf(u)l], *a.* **1.** *(Of pers.)* Véridique. **2.** (Témoignage, etc.) vrai; (portrait, etc.) fidèle. **-fully,** *adv.* **1.** Véridiquement; sans mentir. **2.** Fidèlement.

truthfulness ['truːθf(u)lnis], *s.* **1.** *(Of pers.)* Véracité *f,* véridicité *f.* **2.** Véracité (d'une assertion, etc.); fidélité *f* (d'un portrait, etc.).

try¹ [trai], *s.* **1.** Essai *m,* tentative *f.* To have a t. at (doing) sth., s'essayer à qch.; essayer de faire qch. Let's have a t.! essayons toujours! At the first t., du premier coup. **2.** *Rugby Fb:* Essai. To score a t., marquer un essai. To convert a t., transformer un essai.

try², v. (tried [traid]) I. v.tr. **1.** (a) Éprouver (qn); mettre (qn, qch.) à l'épreuve. To be tried and found wanting, ne pas supporter l'épreuve. (b) Éprouver; affliger. A people sorely tried, une nation durement éprouvée. (c) To t. one's eyes by reading too much, se fatiguer les yeux à trop lire. **2.** Essayer, expérimenter (qch.); faire l'essai de (qch.). To t. a dish, goûter un mets. To t. (out) a medicine on an animal, faire l'essai d'un médicament sur une bête. **3.** Vérifier (un mécanisme); ajuster (des poids); essayer (un cordage, une voiture). **4.** Jur: Juger (une cause, un accusé). To be tried for theft, passer en correctionnelle pour vol; être jugé pour vol. **5.** Essayer, tenter. T. your hand at it, essayez par vous-même. To t. one's strength against s.o., se mesurer avec qn. T. and see how far you can throw the ball, essayez (pour) voir à quelle distance vous pouvez lancer la balle. **6.** To t. to do sth., F: to t. and do sth., tâcher, essayer, de faire qch. She tried to smile, elle essaya, s'efforça, de sourire. He tried his best, his hardest, to save them, il a fait tout son possible pour les sauver. To t. again, tenter un nouvel effort; essayer de nouveau. F: You had better not t.! ne vous en avisez pas! II. try, v.i. To t. for sth., tâcher d'obtenir qch. try on, v.tr. **1.** Essayer (un vêtement). **2.** F: To t. it on with s.o., chercher à mettre qn dedans; bluffer. 'try-on, s. F: **1.** Tentative f de déception; bluff m. **2.** Ballon m d'essai. try out, v.tr. (a) Essayer à fond (une machine, etc.); soumettre (qn, une invention) à une épreuve prolongée. (b) Ind: Épurer, affiner (un métal). 'try-out, s. Essai m à fond (d'une machine, etc.). try over, v.tr. Essayer (un morceau de musique, etc.). **tried,** a. Éprouvé. Well-t. remedy, remède éprouvé. **trying¹,** a. **1.** Difficile, rude, dur. A t. position, une position pénible. **2.** Vexant; contrariant. He is very t., il est insupportable. **3.** T. light, lumière fatigante (pour la vue). **trying²,** s. **1.** Essai m, épreuve f. **2.** Jur: Jugement m (d'une cause).

trysail ['traiseil, traisl], s. Nau: Voile f goélette, (voile de) senau m. Main t., grande voile goélette.

tryst [trist], s. Lit: Rendez-vous m.

trysting-place ['tristiŋpleis], s. Lit: (Lieu m de) rendezvous m.

tsar [zɑ:r], s.m. Tsar.

tsarevitch ['zɑːrəvitʃ], s.m. Tsarévitch.

tsarina [zɑː'riːnə], s.f. Tsarine.

tsarism ['zɑːrizm], s. Tsarisme m.

tsarist ['zɑːrist], a. & s. Tsariste (mf).

tsetse ['tsetsi], s. Ent: T.(-fly), (mouche f) tsé-tsé f.

tub¹ [tʌb], s. **1.** (a) Baquet m, bac m. Nau: Baille f. (b) (Wash-)t., baquet, cuvier m (à lessive). **2.** (Bath-)t., tub m. **3.** Min: (a) Benne f. (b) Berline f, wagonnet m. **4.** (a) Nau: F: Old t. (of a boat), vieux rafiau, rafiot. (b) Row: Canot m d'entraînement. 'tub-seat, s. Aut: etc: Baquet m. 'tub-thumper, s. F: Orateur m de carrefour.

tub², v. (tubbed) **1.** v.tr. (a) Encaisser (une plante). (b) Donner un tub à (qn). **2.** v.i. Prendre un tub.

tuba ['tjuːbə], s. Mus: (a) (Organ) Trompette f. (b) Contrebasse f à vent; bombardon m, tuba m.

tubby ['tʌbi], a. F: (Of pers.) Boulot; gros et rond; pansu. A t. little man, un petit pot à tabac.

tube¹ [tjuːb], s. **1.** (a) Tube m, tuyau m. W.Tel: Lead-in t., pipe f d'entrée (de l'antenne). (b) Tube (de pâte dentrifrice, etc.). (c) W.Tel: Rad.-A: Lampe f, tube. Cathode-ray t., oscillographe m cathodique. (d) Aut: Cy: Inner t., chambre f à air (de pneu). (e) Surg: Drain m (de plaie profonde). Med: T.-fed, nourri à la sonde. **2.** Anat: Tube; canal, -aux m; conduit m. P: Hum: It's my tubes [mi'tjubz], c'est mes bronches. **3.** F: = Le Métro. We came by t. = nous avons pris le Métro. 'tube-station, s. = Station f du Métro.

tube², v.tr. Civ.E: Tuber, garnir de tubes (un sondage). Surg: Tuber (le larynx); drainer (une plaie profonde). **tubing,** s. **1.** Tubage m. **2.** (a) Coll. Tuyautage m, tuyauterie f, tubes mpl. (b) Tube m, tuyau m. Rubber t., tuyau en caoutchouc.

tubeless ['tjuːblis], a. Aut: T. tyre, pneu m sans chambre, f: tubeless m.

tuber ['tjuːbər], s. **1.** Bot: (a) (i) Racine tubéreuse; (ii) tubercule m. (b) Tubéracée f, truffe f. **2.** (a) Anat: Tubérosité f. (b) Med: Tubercule.

tubercle ['tjuːbəːkl], s. Tubercule m.

tubercular [tju(:)'bəːkjulər], a. Bot: Tuberculeux, -euse.

tuberculin [tju(:)'bəːkjulin], s. Med: Tuberculine f. T. tested milk, lait garanti exempt de tuberculose, = lait cru certifié.

tuberculinize [tju:'bəːkjulinaiz], v.tr. Vet: Tuberculiner.

tuberculosis [tju(:)bəːkju'lousis], s. Med: Tuberculose f. T. test, tuberculination f.

tuberculous [tju(:)'bəːkjuləs], a. Tuberculeux, -euse.

tuberosity [,tjuːbə'rositi], s. Tubérosité f.

tuberous ['tjuːbərəs], a. Bot: Tubéreux, -euse.

tubular ['tjuːbjulər], a. (a) Tubulaire. Mus: T. bells, carillon m (d'orchestre). (b) Mch: (Chaudière) tubulaire, à tubes. (c) T. breathing, souffle m tubaire.

tuck¹ [tʌk], s. **1.** Dressm: (Petit) pli; rempli m, plissé m; (to shorten a garment) troussis m. To make, take up, a t. in a garment, faire un rempli à, remplier, un vêtement; (to shorten) faire un troussis à un vêtement. **2.** Sch: F: Gâteaux mpl, friandises fpl; mangeaille f. T. box, boîte à provisions. 'tuck-shop, s. Sch: F: Boutique f du marchand de gâteaux, de bonbons.

tuck², v.tr. **1.** Dressm: (a) Faire des plis à, remplier (un vêtement); plisser, froncer (l'étoffe). (b) Raccourcir (un vêtement). **2.** Replier, rentrer, serrer, mettre; F: fourrer. To t. a rug round s.o., envelopper qn d'une couverture. To t. a table-napkin under one's chin, rentrer un coin de sa serviette sous son menton. To t. sth. (away) in a drawer, serrer qch. dans un tiroir. Village tucked away at the far end of the valley, village caché au fond de la vallée. **tuck in. 1.** v.tr. (a) Serrer, rentrer; replier (le bord d'un vêtement, etc.). To t. in a flap (in folding document, etc.) rentrer un quartier. To t. in the bed-clothes, border le lit. (b) To t. s.o. in, border qn (dans son lit). **2.** v.i. F: Manger à belles dents; s'en mettre jusque-là. Tuck in! allez-y! 'tuck-'in, s. F: Bombance f ripaille f. To have a good t.-in, s'en mettre jusqu'au menton. **tuck into,** v.i. F: To t. into a good, square meal, attaquer un repas copieux. **tuck up,** v.tr. (a) Relever, retrousser (sa jupe). To t. up one's dress (at the waist), se trousser. (b) Border (qn) (dans son lit).

tucker ['tʌkər], s. **1.** A.Cost: Fichu m, guimpe f, chemisette f. **2.** Austr: F: Mangeaille f.

Tuesday ['tjuːzdi], s. Mardi m. (For phrases cf. FRIDAY.) S.a. SHROVE 2.

tufa ['tjuːfə], s. Geol: (a) Tuf m calcaire. (b) = TUFF.

tuff [tʌf], s. Geol: Tuf m volcanique.

tuffet ['tʌfit], s. **1.** Pouf m. **2.** A: = TUFT 1 (a).

tuft¹ [tʌft], s. **1.** (a) Touffe f (d'herbe). (b) Touffe (de plumes); houppe f (de soie); mèche f, flocon m (de laine); huppe f, aigrette f (d'un oiseau). **2.** (a) Barbiche f. (b) Toupet m (de cheveux). **3.** (a) Gland m, houppe (d'un bonnet); pompon m. (b) A: Étudiant m noble (qui portait un gland en or à sa toque).

tuft², v.tr. (a) Houpper (la laine); piquer, capitonner (un matelas). (b) Garnir (qch.) de touffes. **tufted,** a. **1.** (a) Garni de houppes, de glands. (b) En touffe, en houppe. **2.** Orn: Muni d'une aigrette; huppé.

tug¹ [tʌg], s. **1.** (a) Traction (subite); saccade f. To give a good t., tirer fort; (of horse, etc.) donner un bon coup de collier. T. of war, (i) Sp: lutte f de traction (à la corde); (ii) lutte acharnée et prolongée. (b) To feel a t. at one's heartstrings, avoir un serrement de cœur. **2.** (a) (Bateau) remorqueur m. (b) Av: Avion remorqueur. **3.** Harn: (a) Trait m (d'attelage). (b) Porte-brancard m. 'tug-boat, s. (Bateau) remorqueur m.

tug², v. (tugged [tʌgd]) **1.** v.tr. & i. Tirer avec effort. To t. sth. along, traîner qch. To t. at sth., tirer sur qch. To t. at the oars, tirer sur les rames; souquer (ferme). To t. s.o. this way and that, tirailler qn de côté et d'autre. **2.** v.tr. Nau: Remorquer (un bateau).

tuition [tju(:)'iʃ(ə)n], s. Instruction f, enseignement m. Private t., leçons particulières. Postal t., enseignement par correspondance.

tulip ['tjuːlip], s. Tulipe f. 'tulip-tree, s. Bot: Tulipier m.

tulle [tju:l], s. *Tex:* Tulle m.

tumble¹ ['tʌmbl], s. 1. Culbute f, chute f, dégringolade f. 2. *Gym:* Culbute (d'acrobate). 3. Désordre m; masse confuse.

tumble². 1. v.i. (a) To t. (down, over), tomber (par terre); dégringoler; faire la culbute. **Building that is tumbling down,** édifice qui s'écroule, qui tombe en ruine. **Her hair came tumbling down,** ses cheveux se déroulèrent. (b) To t. (about), s'agiter. **To toss and t. in bed,** s'agiter dans son lit. (c) Se jeter (précipitamment) (into, dans). To t. into bed, se jeter dans son lit; se mettre au lit. **To t. into one's clothes,** enfiler ses vêtements à la hâte. To t. out, tomber (de la voiture, par la fenêtre, etc.). *F:* To t. on sth., trouver qch. par hasard. (d) (Of acrobat, pigeon) Faire des culbutes. (e) *F:* To t. to an idea, comprendre, saisir, une idée. 2. v.tr. (a) To t. sth. down, over, culbuter, jeter à bas, renverser, qch. (b) Bouleverser, déranger; mettre en désordre. **'tumble-down,** attrib.a. *F:* Croulant, délabré. **Old t.-d. house,** maison qui tombe en ruine.

tumbler ['tʌmblər], s. 1. *A:* Jongleur m, acrobate mf. 2. *Orn:* T. pigeon (pigeon) culbutant (m). 3. Verre m (à boire) sans pied; gobelet m. 4. (Device) (a) *El.E:* Culbuteur m (d'interrupteur, etc.). (b) Gorge f (mobile), arrêt m (de serrure). **T. lock,** serrure à gorge(s).

tumbrel ['tʌmbrəl], **tumbril** ['tʌmbril], s. Tombereau m.

tumefaction [ˌtju:mi'fækʃ(ə)n], s. Tuméfaction f.

tumefy ['tju:mifai]. 1. v.tr. Tuméfier. 2. v.i. Se tuméfier.

tumescence [tju:'mesns], s. *Med:* Tumescence f.

tumescent [tju:'mesnt], a. *Med:* Tumescent.

tumid ['tju:mid], a. 1. *Med:* Enflé, gonflé. 2. (Style) ampoulé.

tummy ['tʌmi], s. *F:* (a) Estomac m, ventre m. **T. ache,** mal m au ventre. (b) Bedaine f.

tumour ['tju:mər], s. Tumeur f.

tumult ['tju:mʌlt], s. 1. Tumulte m; fracas m. 2. Tumulte, agitation f, trouble m, émoi m (des passions).

tumultuous [tju:(:)'mʌltjuəs], a. Tumultueux, -euse.

tumulus, pl. **-i** ['tju:mjuləs, -ai], s. Tumulus m.

tun [tʌn], s. 1. Tonneau m, fût m, foudre m. 2. *Brew:* Cuve f (de fermentation).

tuna ['tu:nə], s. *Ich:* T.(fish), thon m.

tundra ['tʌndrə], s. *Ph.Geog:* Toundra f.

tune¹ [tju:n], s. 1. Air m (de musique). *F:* **Give us a t.!** faites-nous un peu de musique! *S.a.* PIPER. **To change one's t.,** changer de ton, de langage. *F:* **To be fined to the t. of fifty pounds,** être mis à l'amende pour la somme pas mal salée de cinquante livres. 2. (a) Accord m. **The piano is in t.,** le piano est d'accord. **The piano is out of t.,** le piano est désaccordé. **To get out of t.,** se désaccorder; perdre l'accord. (Of singer) **To be out of t.,** détonner. **To sing in t.,** out of t., chanter juste, faux. (b) **Engine in perfect t.,** moteur au point. 3. (a) Accord, harmonie f. **To be in t. with one's surroundings,** être en bon accord avec son milieu. (b) *W.Tel:* **To be in t.,** être en résonance. **To get into t.,** accrocher la longueur d'onde.

tune², v.tr. 1. Accorder, mettre d'accord (un instrument). 2. *El.E:* *W.Tel:* **To t. one circuit to another,** accorder, syntoniser, un circuit sur un autre. *W.Tel:* **To t. in (to) a station,** accrocher, capter, un poste. *Abs:* **To t. in,** syntoniser le poste; accorder le récepteur. **To t. out a station,** éliminer un poste émetteur. 3. *I.C.E: Mch: etc:* **To t. (up),** caler, régler, (re)mettre au point (un moteur). **tune up,** v.i. 1. (Of orchestra) S'accorder. 2. Se mettre à chanter. **tuning,** s. 1. *Mus:* Accordage m, accord m (d'un piano, etc.). 2. *I.C.E: Mch:* T. (up), calage m, réglage m; (re)mise f au point. 3. *W.Tel:* T. (in), accordage, réglage, syntonisation f. **'tuning condenser,** s. *W.Tel:* Condensateur m d'accord, de syntonisation. **'tuning-fork,** s. *Mus:* Diapason m. **'tuning-hammer,** s. *Mus:* Accordoir m; clef f d'accordage, d'accordeur. **'tuning-slide,** s. *Mus:* Pompe f d'accord (d'un instrument à vent).

tuneful ['tju:nf(u)l], a. Mélodieux, harmonieux. **-fully,** adv. Mélodieusement, harmonieusement.

tuneless ['tju:nlis], a. Discordant, inharmonieux, -euse; inharmonique.

tuner ['tju:nər], s. Accordeur m (de pianos, etc.).

tungsten ['tʌŋstən], s. *Ch:* Tungstène m. **T. steel,** acier m au tungstène.

tunic ['tju:nik], s. 1. *Cost:* Tunique f. 2. *Nat. Hist:* Tunique, enveloppe f (d'un organe).

Tunis ['tju:nis]. *Pr.n.* Tunis.

Tunisia [tju:'niziə]. *Pr.n. Geog:* La Tunisie.

Tunisian [tju:'niziən], a. Tunisien, -ienne.

tunnel¹ ['tʌnl], s. Tunnel m; passage souterrain. *Rail:* Tunnel. *Min:* Galerie f (d'accès) à flanc de coteau. **To drive a t. through . . .,** percer un tunnel à travers, sous. . . . *Mec:* **Wind t.,** tunnel aérodynamique; soufflerie f.

tunnel², v.tr. & i. (tunnelled ['tʌnld]) **To t. a hill; to t. through, into, a hill,** percer un tunnel, à travers, dans, sous, une colline. **tunnelling,** s. Percement m d'un tunnel, de tunnels.

tunny(-fish) ['tʌni(fiʃ)], s. *Ich:* Thon m. **Tunny boat,** thonier m.

tup [tʌp], s. *Husb:* Bélier m.

tuppence ['tʌp(ə)ns], s. *F:* = TWOPENCE.

tuppenny ['tʌp(ə)ni], a. *F:* = TWOPENNY.

turban ['tə:bən], s. *Cost:* Turban m. **'turban-shell,** s. *Conch:* Turbo m.

turbid ['tə:bid], a. 1. (Liquide) trouble, bourbeux. 2. (Esprit) brouillon.

turbidity [tə:'biditi], **turbidness** ['tə:bidnis], s. Turbidité f.

turbinate ['tə:binit], a. *Nat.Hist:* Turbiné.

turbine ['tə:bain], s. (a) Turbine f. **Steam t.,** turbine à vapeur. (b) Turbine à vapeur; turbomoteur m.

turbo-blower ['tə:bou'blouər], s. *Ind:* Turbosoufflante f.

turbo-compressor ['tə:boukəm'presər], s. *Mec.E: Av:* Turbocompresseur m.

turbo-dynamo ['tə:bou'dainəmou], s. *El.E:* Turbodynamo f.

turbo-jet ['tə:bou'dʒet], s. *Av:* Turboréacteur m.

turbo-motor ['tə:bou'moutər], s. *Mch:* Turbomoteur m.

turbo-prop ['tə:bou'prɔp], a. **T.-p. aircraft,** avion à turbopropulseur m.

turbo-propeller ['tə:boupro'pelər], s. *Av:* Turbopropulseur m.

turbo-pump ['tə:bou'pʌmp], s. *Mch:* Turbopompe f.

turbo-supercharger ['tə:bousupə'tʃɑ:dʒər], s. Turbocompresseur m.

turbot ['tə:bət], s. *Ich:* Turbot m. **'turbot-kettle,** s. *Cu:* Turbotière f.

turbotrain ['tə:bou'trein], s. Turbotrain m.

turbulence ['tə:bjuləns], s. 1. (a) Turbulence f, trouble m tumulte m. (b) Indiscipline f. 2. *I.C.E:* (High) t. **combustion chamber,** chambre de combustion à (haute) turbulence.

turbulent ['tə:bjulənt], a. 1. (a) Turbulent, tumultueux, -euse. (b) Insubordonné. 2. *I.C.E:* T. **cylinder-head,** culasse f à turbulence.

Turcoman, pl. **-mans** ['tə:kəmæn, -mænz], s. 1. *Ethn:* Turcoman m. 2. *Ling:* Le turcoman.

tureen [tə'ri:n], s. Soupière f.

turf¹, pl. **turves, turfs** [tə:f, tə:vz, tə:fs], s. 1. (a) Gazon m. (b) Motte f de gazon. 2. (a) (In Ireland) Tourbe f. **T. moor,** marais tourbeux, tourbière f. (b) A t. of peat, une motte de tourbe. 3. *Rac:* The t., le turf; le monde des courses. **T. accountant,** bookmaker m. **'turf-cutter,** s. *Tls:* 1. Tranche-gazon m inv. 2. Louchet m (pour couper les mottes de tourbe).

turf², v.tr. 1. Gazonner (un terrain). 2. *F:* **To t. s.o out,** flanquer qn dehors.

turgescence [tə:'dʒesns], s. 1. Turgescence f. 2. Emphase f.

turgid ['tə:dʒid], a. 1. Turgide, enflé, gonflé. 2. (Style) boursouflé, ampoulé.

turgidity [tə:'dʒiditi], s. 1. Enflure f. 2. Emphase f (de style).

Turk [tə:k], s. (a) Turc, f. Turque. (b) **Turk's head** (long broom), tête-de-loup f. *Nau:* Turk's head knot, nœud m de bonnet turc.

Turkey¹ ['tə:ki]. *Pr.n.* La Turquie. **T. carpet,** tapis m d'Orient, de Smyrne. **T. red,** rouge m d'Adrinople.

turkey², s. 1. Dindon m. Hen t., dinde f. **Young t.,** dindonneau m. 2. *Cu:* Dinde, dindonneau. **'turkey-cock,** s.m. Dindon. **Red as a t.-c.,** rouge comme une pivoine, une tomate.

Turkish ['tə:kiʃ]. 1. *a.* Turc, *f.* turque; de Turquie. **T. bath,** bain turc. **T. cigarettes,** cigarettes d'Orient. **T. delight,** rahat loukoum *m.* **T. towel,** serviette *f* éponge. 2. *s. Ling:* Le turc.

turmeric ['tə:mərik], *s.* Curcuma *m*; safran *m* des Indes.

turmoil ['tə:mɔil], *s.* (*a*) Trouble *m*, tumulte *m*, agitation *f.* (*b*) Remous *m* (des eaux); tourbillon *m*.

turn[1] [tə:n], *s.* 1. Tour *m*, révolution *f* (d'une roue). **Meat done to a t.,** viande cuite à point. 2. (*a*) Changement *m* de direction. *Nau:* Giration *f. Aut:* Virage *m.* **To take a short t.,** virer court. **To make, take, a t. to the right,** tourner à droite. **T. of the wind,** saute *f* de vent. **At every t.,** à tout bout de champ. *Av:* **Aileron t.,** tonneau *m* en descendant. (*b*) Tournure *f* (des affaires). **The matter was taking a tragic t.,** l'affaire tournait au tragique. **Things are taking a t. for the better,** les affaires prennent meilleure tournure. **The weather is taking a t. for the worse,** le temps se gâte. (*c*) **T. of the tide,** renversement *m*, changement *m*, de (la) marée. **The tide is on the t.,** la mer est en étale, la marée change. **The milk is on the t.,** le lait est en train de tourner. **T. of the scale,** trait *m* de balance. **At the t. of the year,** (i) à la fin de l'année; (ii) au commencement de l'année. (*d*) *F:* **The sight gave me quite a t.,** ce spectacle m'a donné un (vrai) coup, *F:* ça m'a fait un effet de voir ça. (*e*) *F:* **She had one of her turns yesterday,** elle a eu une de ses crises, une de ses attaques, hier. **You gave me such a t.!** vous m'avez fait une belle peur! 3. **To take a t. in the garden,** faire un tour dans le, de, jardin. 4. (*a*) **Tour** (de rôle). **It is your t.,** c'est votre tour. **It is your t. (to play),** c'est à vous de jouer. **It will be my t. some day,** (i) mon tour viendra un de ces jours; (ii) je prendrai ma revanche un jour. **In t., by turns,** tour à tour; à tour de rôle. **To play out of one's t.,** jouer avant son tour. **T. and t. about,** chacun son tour. **To take turns in, at, doing sth.,** faire qch. à tour de rôle. **To take it in turns to steer,** se relayer à la barre. **To take one's t.** (*at work, etc.*), prendre son tour. (*b*) **Music-hall t.,** numéro *m* de music-hall. *Th:* **Short t.,** flash *m.* 5. (*a*) (Bon ou mauvais) procédé. **To do s.o. a (good) t.,** rendre un service, rendre service, à qn. **To do s.o. a bad t.,** jouer un mauvais tour à qn; desservir qn. **One good t. deserves another,** à charge de revanche; un service en vaut un autre. **T. for t.,** échange de bons procédés. (*b*) Intention *f*, but *m.* **It will serve my t.,** cela fera mon affaire pour le moment. 6. (*a*) Disposition *f* d'esprit. **His t. of mind,** son tour d'esprit. (*b*) Forme *f.* **T. of phrase,** tournure *f* de phrase. (*c*) **Car with a good t. of speed,** auto rapide, qui roule bien. 7. (*a*) Tournant *m*, coude *m* (d'un chemin, etc.). **Sudden t., sharp t.,** crochet *m*, virage *m* brusque. **The path is full of twists and turns,** le sentier fait beaucoup de tours et de détours. (*b*) **Tour** (d'une corde); tour, spire *f* (d'une spirale). *Nau:* **A round t. and two half-hitches,** un tour mort et deux demi-clefs. 8. *Mus:* Gruppetto *m*, *pl.* gruppetti. 9. *Typ:* Caractère retourné; blocage *m*.

turn[2]. I. *v.tr.* 1. Tourner, faire tourner (une roue). **To t. the key in the lock,** donner un tour de clef à la porte. **To t. the knife in the wound,** retourner le fer dans la plaie. (*Passive force*) **The tap won't t.,** le robinet ne marche pas. 2. **To t. (over) a page,** tourner une page. **Newly turned soil,** terre fraîchement retournée. **To t. a garment inside out,** retourner un vêtement. **To t. the hay,** retourner le foin. *F:* **Without turning a hair,** sans sourciller, sans broncher. 3. **He turned his steps homewards,** il dirigea ses pas vers la maison. **He never turned a beggar from the door,** jamais il ne renvoyait un mendiant. **To t. a blow,** faire dévier un coup; détourner un coup. **To t. the conversation,** détourner la conversation. 4. Tourner, retourner (la tête); diriger (les yeux) (**towards,** vers). **To t. a telescope on a star,** braquer une lunette sur une étoile. 5. **To t. the laughter against s.o.,** retourner les rires contre qn. **To t. everyone against one,** se mettre tout le monde à dos. 6. (*a*) **To t. the corner,** tourner le coin. (*b*) **He is, has, turned forty,** il a passé la quarantaine. **It is turned seven (o'clock),** il est sept heures passées. 7. (*a*) Changer, convertir, transformer (**into,** en). **His love**

was turned to hate, son amour a tourné en haine. **The drawing-room was turned into a study,** le salon fut transformé, converti, en bureau. (*b*) Faire devenir; rendre. **The storm has turned the milk (sour),** l'orage a fait tourner le lait. **Autumn turns the leaves (yellow),** l'automne fait jaunir les feuilles. (*c*) **Success has turned his head,** le succès lui a tourné la tête. 8. Tourner, façonner au tour (un pied de table, etc.). **Well-turned sentence,** phrase bien tournée. II. **turn,** *v.i.* 1. Tourner. (*a*) **The wheel turns,** la roue tourne. **The door turns on its hinges,** la porte tourne, pivote, sur ses gonds. (*b*) **Everything turns on your answer,** tout dépend de votre réponse. **The conversation turned on a variety of subjects,** la conversation a roulé sur une variété de sujets. 2. (*a*) **To toss and t. in bed,** se tourner et se retourner dans son lit. (*b*) **To t. upside down,** (i) (*of boat*) chavirer; (ii) (*of vehicle*) capoter, se retourner. 3. Se tourner, se retourner. **To t. short,** se retourner brusquement. *Mil:* **Right t.! left t.!** à droite, marche! à gauche, marche! 4. (*a*) Tourner, se diriger. **He turned to the left,** il tourna, il prit, à gauche. **I turned down Regent Street,** j'ai pris (par) Regent Street. *Nau:* **To t. to the east,** venir cap à l'est. **To t. sixteen points, to turn a half-circle,** virer de bord cap pour cap; venir de seize quarts. **The wind is turning,** le vent change. (*b*) Se diriger (vers qch.); s'adresser (à qn). **My thoughts often t. to this subject,** mes réflexions se portent souvent sur ce sujet. **To t. to a document,** se reporter à un document. **I don't know which way, where, to t.,** je ne sais de quel côté (me) tourner; je ne sais (plus) où donner de la tête, sur quel pied danser. **To t. to s.o.,** recourir à qn, à l'aide de qn; avoir recours à qn. 5. (*a*) **The tide is turning,** la marée change. **His luck has turned,** sa chance a tourné. (*b*) **To t. against s.o.,** se retourner contre qn. 6. (*a*) Se changer, se convertir, se transformer (**into,** en). **It is turning to rain,** le temps se met à la pluie. **Everything he touches turns to gold,** tout ce qu'il touche se change en or. **The caterpillar turns into a butterfly,** la chenille se transforme en papillon. (*b*) **To t. acid,** tourner au vinaigre. **The milk has turned (sour),** le lait a tourné. **The leaves are beginning to t.,** les feuilles commencent à tourner, à jaunir. **To t. all the colours of the rainbow,** passer par toutes les couleurs de l'arc-en-ciel. (*c*) **To t. socialist,** devenir socialiste; embrasser le socialisme. **To t. informer,** *F:* moucharder. **turn about.** 1. *v.i.* (*a*) Se tourner, se retourner. (*b*) Se tourner d'un côté et de l'autre; s'agiter. 2. *v.tr.* Tourner (qch.) dans l'autre sens; faire faire demi-tour à (un cheval, etc.). **turn aside.** 1. *v.tr.* Détourner, écarter (qch., qn). 2. *v.i.* Se détourner, s'écarter. **turn away.** 1. *v.tr.* (*a*) Détourner (les yeux, la colère). (*b*) Renvoyer, congédier (qn). 2. *v.i.* Se détourner. **turn back.** 1. *v.tr.* (*a*) Faire revenir, faire retourner (qn) sur ses pas. (*b*) Relever, retrousser (ses manches); rabattre (le col de son pardessus, etc.). (*c*) *Nau:* Dévirer (le treuil, etc.). 2. *v.i.* S'en retourner; retourner sur ses pas; rebrousser chemin; (*of horseman*) tourner bride. **turn down,** *v.tr.* 1. (*a*) Rabattre. **To t. down the bed (clothes),** faire la couverture; ouvrir le lit. (*b*) Faire un pli, une corne, à (une page). 2. Retourner (une carte) (face à la table). 3. Baisser (le gaz). 4. **To t. down a candidate, a claim,** refuser un candidat; écarter une réclamation. **To t. down an offer,** repousser une offre. 'turn-down, *attrib.a.* **T.-down collar,** col rabattu. **turn in.** 1. *v.tr.* (*a*) Rentrer (les bouts de qch.); replier (le bord d'un vêtement, etc.). (*b*) **To t. one's toes in,** tourner les pieds en dedans. (*c*) **To t. in one's equipment on leaving the army,** rendre son équipement en quittant l'armée. 2. *v.i.* (*a*) **His toes t. in,** il a les pieds tournés en dedans. (*b*) *F:* **To t. in,** (aller) se coucher. **turn off.** I. *v.tr.* 1. Fermer, couper (l'eau, le gaz); éteindre (le gaz); fermer (un robinet). 2. Renvoyer, congédier (un employé). II. **turn off,** *v.i.* 1. Changer de route; tourner (à droite, à gauche). 2. **The car turned off the main road,** l'auto quitta la grande route. **Chancery Lane turns off High Holborn,** Chancery Lane fait le coin avec High Holborn. **turn on.** 1. *v.tr.* Donner (la vapeur); ouvrir, faire couler (l'eau); allumer (l'électricité); allumer, ouvrir (le gaz). **Shall I t. on the light?**

voulez-vous que j'allume? **2.** *v.i.* (*Prep. use*) **To t. on s.o.,** attaquer qn, s'en prendre à qn. **turn out.** I. *v.tr.* **1.** (*a*) **To t. s.o. out** (**of doors**), mettre qn dehors, à la porte. **T. him out!** A la porte! **To t. out a tenant,** déloger, évincer, un locataire. **To t. out the government,** renverser le gouvernement. (*b*) Mettre (le bétail) au vert. *S.a.* GRASS¹ 2. (*c*) *Nau:* Réveiller (les hommes). *Mil:* Alerter (les troupes). **To t. out the guard,** faire sortir la garde. **T. out the guard!** A la garde! (*d*) *Cu:* Démouler (une crème, etc.). **2.** Vider (un tiroir, ses poches); retourner (ses poches); nettoyer, faire, (une chambre) à fond. **3.** Produire, fabriquer (des marchandises). **Turned out to order,** confectionné sur demande. **4.** (*Of pers.*) **Well turned out,** élégant; soigné dans sa mise. **5.** Couper, éteindre (le gaz, etc.). **6. To t. out one's toes,** tourner les pieds en dehors. II. **turn out,** *v.i.* **1.** (*a*) Sortir; paraître en public. **Guard t. out!** aux armes! (*b*) (*Of workmen*) **To t. out** (**on strike**), se mettre en grève. (*c*) *F:* Sortir du lit; se lever. **2. His toes t. out,** il a les pieds tournés en dehors. **3.** (*a*) **Things have turned out well,** les choses ont bien tourné. **It will t. out all right,** cela s'arrangera. **I don't know how it will t. out,** je ne sais pas comment cela finira. **As it turned out . . .,** comme il arriva . . .; en l'occurrence. . . . **His son turned out badly,** son fils a mal tourné. **The weather has turned out fine,** le temps s'est mis au beau. (*b*) **The dog turned out to be mine,** il se trouva que le chien m'appartenait. **It turns out that . . .,** il apparaît, il se trouve, que. . . . **'turn-out,** *s.* **1.** Concours *m*, assemblée *f* (de gens). **There was a great t.-o. at his funeral,** il y avait foule à son enterrement. **2.** (*a*) Tenue *f*, uniforme *m* (d'un régiment, etc.). (*b*) Attelage *m*, équipage *m*. **3.** Rendement *m*; production *f*. **turn over. 1.** *v.tr.* (*a*) Retourner (qch.); tourner (une page). **To t. over the pages, the leaves, of a book,** feuilleter un livre. *S.a.* LEAF¹ 2. *Agr:* **To t. over the soil,** retourner le sol. **To t. an idea over in one's mind,** ruminer une idée. (*b*) **He turns over £500 a week,** son chiffre d'affaires est de 500 livres par semaine. (*c*) **To t. sth. over to s.o.,** transférer, référer, remettre, qch. à qn. **2.** *v.i.* Se tourner, se retourner; (*of vehicle*) verser, capoter; (*of aircraft*) capoter. **To t. right over,** faire panache. **'turn-over,** *s.* **1.** (*a*) Renversement *m*, culbute *f.* (*b*) *Parl: etc:* **T.-o. of four votes,** déplacement *m* de quatre voix. **2.** *Com:* (*a*) Chiffre *m* d'affaires. (*b*) **Rapid t.-o. of goods,** écoulement *m* rapide de marchandises. **3.** *Cu:* **Apple t.-o.,** chausson *m* aux pommes. **turn round. 1.** *v.tr.* Retourner. **2.** *v.i.* (*a*) Tourner; (*of crane, etc.*) virer, pivoter. **To t. round and round,** tourner, tournoyer; (*on one's toes*) pirouetter. (*b*) Se retourner; faire volte-face; (*in one's opinions, etc.*) tourner casaque. (*c*) (*Of ship in port*) Se retourner (pour repartir). (*d*) *F:* **To t. round on s.o.,** se retourner contre qn; s'en prendre à qn. **turn-round,** *s. Com:* Rotation *f* (de navires, de camions). **turn to,** *v.i. F:* Se mettre au travail; s'y mettre. **turn up.** I. *v.tr.* **1.** (*a*) Relever (le col de son pardessus); retrousser (ses manches). **Turned-up nose,** nez retroussé. *F:* **To t. up one's nose at sth.,** renifler sur qch.; faire le dégoûté. (*b*) Retourner (le sol). **The gardener turned up some human bones,** le jardinier a déterré des ossements humains. (*c*) Trouver, se reporter à (une citation). **To t. up a word in the dictionary,** consulter le dictionnaire. (*d*) *P:* Écœurer, faire vomir (qn). **2.** Remonter (une lampe). II. **turn up,** *v.i.* **1.** Se relever, se retrousser, se replier; se rebrousser. **2.** (*a*) **The ten of diamonds turned up,** le dix de carreau est sorti. (*b*) Arriver, se présenter (inopinément); faire son apparition. **To t. up at s.o.'s house,** arriver (à l'improviste) chez qn. **If any patients t. up,** s'il se présente des malades. **He will t. up one of these days,** il reparaîtra un de ces jours. **Something is sure to t. up,** il se présentera sûrement une occasion. **Till something better turns up,** en attendant mieux. **'turn-up,** *s.* (*a*) Revers *m* (d'un pantalon, etc.). (*b*) (*At cards*) Retourne *f.* **turned,** *a.* **1.** (**Lathe-, machine-**) **t.,** façonné au tour; fait au tour; tourné. **2.** Retourné. **turning**¹, *a.* Tournant; qui tourne, giratoire, rotatif, -ive. **turning²,** *s.* **1.** (*a*) Mouvement *m* giratoire; rotation *f*, giration *f.* (*b*) Virage *m* (d'une auto, etc.); changement *m* de

direction. (*c*) Retournage *m* (d'un vêtement, de la terre). (*d*) **T. of the tide,** renversement *m* de la marée. (*e*) Changement, conversion *f* (**into,** en). **2.** Travail *m* au tour; tournage *m.* **3.** Tournant *m* (d'une route); coude *m. Aut:* Virage. **Take the t. on the left,** prenez à gauche. **Take the first t. to the right,** prenez la première (route, rue) à droite. **4.** *pl.* Tournures *f*; copeaux *m* de tour. **5.** *Dressm:* *pl.* Rentrés *m,* remplis *m.* **'turning-lathe,** *s.* = LATHE. **'turning-point,** *s.* Point décisif; moment *m* critique. **The turning-points of history,** les tournants *m* de l'histoire.

turncoat ['tə:nkout], *s.* Renégat *m,* apostat *m.* **Don't be a t.,** n'allez pas tourner casaque.

turncock ['tə:nkɔk], *s.* (*a*) *Adm:* Fontainier *m*; l'employé *m* de la compagnie des eaux. (*b*) Clef *f* (pour ouvrir, fermer, l'eau).

turner ['tə:nər], *s. Ind:* Tourneur *m.*

turnery ['tə:nəri], *s.* **1.** (*a*) Tournage *m*; travail *m* au tour). (*b*) Articles façonnés au tour. **2.** Atelier *m* de tourneur; tournerie *f.*

turnip ['tə:nip], *s.* Navet *m.* **'turnip-cutter,** *s. Agr:* Coupe-racines. **'turnip-tops,** *s.pl.* Fanes *f* de navets.

turnkey ['tə:nki:], *s.* Guichetier *m* (d'une prison); porte-clefs *m.*

turnpike ['tə:npaik], *s.* **1.** *Hist:* Barrière *f* de péage. **2.** *Hist:* Route *f* à barrière, à péage. **3.** *U.S:* Autoroute *f* à péage.

turnsole ['tə:nsoul], *s. Bot:* Tournesol *m.*

turnspit ['tə:nspit], *s. A:* Tournebroche *m.*

turnstile ['tə:nstail], *s.* Tourniquet(-compteur) *m* (pour entrées).

turntable ['tə:nteibl], *s.* **1.** *Rail:* Plaque tournante. **2.** *Gramophones:* Plateau *m* tourne-disques.

turpentine ['tə:p(ə)ntain], *s.* Térébenthine *f.* **Oil of t.,** essence *f* de térébenthine. **'turpentine tree,** *s.* Térébinthe *m.*

turpitude ['tə:pitju:d], *s.* Turpitude *f.*

turps [tə:ps], *s. Com: F:* (Essence *f* de) térébenthine.

turquoise ['tə:kwɑ:z, -kwɔiz], *s.* **1.** Turquoise *f.* **2.** *a. & s.* **T.(-blue),** turquoise (*m*) *inv.*

turret ['tarit], *s.* **1.** *Arch:* Tourelle *f.* **2.** *Mil: Navy:* (Gun-)t., tourelle. **Twin t.-guns,** pièces couplées en tourelles. **3.** *Mec.E:* Tourelle; (porte-outil(s)) revolver *m.* **turret-ship,** *s.* Cuirassé *m* à tourelles.

turtle ['tə:tl], *s.* Tortue *f* de mer. *U.S:* **Land t.,** tortue. **T. soup,** consommé *m* à la tortue. *S.a.* MOCK TURTLE. **To turn t.,** (i) (*of boat*) chavirer; capoter; (ii) (*of car, etc.*) capoter; faire panache. *Nau:* **T.-back** (**deck**), pont *m* en carapace de tortue.

turtle-dove ['tə:tldʌv], *s. Orn:* Tourterelle *f.*

Tuscan ['tʌskən], *a. & s.* Toscan, -ane.

Tuscany ['tʌskəni]. *Pr.n.* La Toscane.

tush [tʌʃ], *int. A:* Bah! chansons!

tusk [tʌsk], *s.* **1.** Défense *f* (d'éléphant, etc.); croc *m* (de loup, etc.). **2.** *Carp:* Renfort *m* (de tenon).

tusker ['tʌskər], *s.* Éléphant *m* ou sanglier *m* adulte, qui a ses défenses.

tussle¹ ['tʌsl], *s.* Lutte *f*, bagarre *f*, mêlée *f*, corps-à-corps *m.* **To have a t.,** en venir aux mains (avec qn); (*of women*) se prendre aux cheveux, *F:* se crêper le chignon.

tussle², *v.i.* **To t. with s.o.,** lutter avec qn; s'escrimer contre qn, *F:* se bagarrer avec qn.

tussock ['tʌsɔk], *s.* Touffe *f* d'herbe.

tussore (**silk**) ['tʌsɔ:r, 'tʌsɔ:silk], *s. Tex:* Tussor(e) *m.*

tut [tʌt], *int.* (*a*) Quelle bêtise! allons donc! **T., t.!** ta, ta, ta! (*b*) (*of impatience*) Zut!

tutelage ['tju:tilidʒ], *s.* Tutelle *f.*

tutelar ['tju:tilər], **tutelary** ['tju:tiləri], *a.* Tutélaire.

tutor¹ ['tju:tər], *s.* **1.** *Sch:* Directeur *m* des études d'un groupe d'étudiants. **2. Private t.,** précepteur *m.* **Army t.,** préparateur *m* aux écoles militaires. **3.** Méthode *f* (de piano, etc.).

tutor², *v.tr.* Instruire (qn). **To t. a boy in Latin,** donner à un élève des leçons particulières de latin. *A:* **To t. oneself to endure poverty,** s'entraîner à supporter la pauvreté.

tutorial [tju:(')tɔ:riəl]. **1.** *a.* (Cours) d'instruction. **2.** *s. Sch:* Cours individuel fait par le directeur d'études. *s.pl. Sch: Med: etc:* **Tutorials,** travaux pratiques.

tutorship ['tju:təʃip], *s.* Préceptorat *m.*

tutu [tutu], *s. Ballet: Cost:* Tutu *m.*

tu-whit, tu-whoo [tu'wittu'wuː]. 1. *int.* Hou hou! 2. *s.* Ululement *m* (du hibou).

tuxedo [tʌk'siːdou], *s. Cost: U.S:* Smoking *m.*

twaddle¹ ['twɔdl], *s.* Fadaises *fpl*; futilités *fpl.* To talk t., débiter des balivernes; parler pour ne rien dire.

twaddle², *v.i.* Dire, conter, des sottises, des balivernes, des fadaises; radoter.

twain [twein], *a. & s. Poet:* Deux. In t., en deux.

twang¹ [twæŋ], *s.* 1. Bruit sec (de la corde d'un arc); son vibrant (d'une harpe). 2. Nasal t., ton nasillard. To speak with a t., parler du nez; nasiller.

twang.² 1. *v.tr.* Faire frémir, faire résonner (les cordes d'une harpe). To t. a guitar, *v.i.* to t. on a guitar, pincer, *F:* gratter, de la guitare. 2. *v.i. (Of string)* Vibrer, résonner, frémir. *(b) (Of pers.)* Nasiller.

'twas [twɔz] = it was.

tweak [twiːk], *v.tr.* Pincer; serrer entre les doigts (en tordant). To t. a boy's ears, tirer les oreilles à un gamin.

twee [twiː], *a. F: Pej:* Gentillet, -ette (de goût douteux).

tweed [twiːd], *s.* 1. *Tex:* Tweed *m*; cheviot(t)e écossaise. 2. *pl.* Tweeds, complet *m*, costume *m*, de cheviot(t)e.

'tween [twiːn], *adv. & prep. A. & Poet:* = BETWEEN. **'tween-decks.** *Nau:* 1. *s.* Le faux-pont; l'entrepont *m.* 2. *adv.* Dans l'entrepont.

tweet¹ [twiːt], *s.* Pépiement *m*, gazouillement *m.*

tweet², *v.i. (Of bird)* Pépier; gazouiller.

tweezers ['twiːzəz], *s.pl.* Petite pince; brucelles *fpl*; pince à épiler; pince de philateliste.

twelfth [twelfθ]. 1. *num. a. & s.* Douzième. The T., le douze août (ouverture de la chasse au grouse). **Louis the T.,** Louis Douze. **T. Night,** le jour des Rois. **T. Night cake,** gâteau *m* des Rois. 2. *s. (Fractional)* Douzième *m.*

twelve [twelv], *num. a. & s.* Douze (*m*). T. o'clock, (i) midi *m*; *Adm: Rail:* douze heures; (ii) minuit *m. Rail:* zéro heure. Half past t., midi, minuit, et demi. **About t. handkerchiefs,** une douzaine de mouchoirs. *B.Hist:* The T., les Douze (apôtres *m*). *(For other phrases see* EIGHT.)

twelvemo ['twelvmou], *a. & s. Typ:* In-douze (*m*) *inv.*

twelvemonth ['twelvmʌnθ], *s. O:* Année *f.* This day t., (i) d'aujourd'hui en un an; (ii) il y un an aujourd'hui.

twelve-tone ['twelvtoun], *a. Mus:* Dodécaphoniste, dodécaphonique. **T.-t. system,** dodécaphonisme *m.*

twentieth ['twentiiθ], *num. a. & s.* Vingtième (*m*).

twenty ['twenti], *num. a. & s.* Vingt (*m*). T.-one, vingt et un. T.-two, vingt-deux. T.-first, vingt et unième. The t.-first of May, le vingt et un mai. **About t. people,** une vingtaine de gens. **The twenties (1920-29),** les années vingt. *(For other phrases see* EIGHT.)

twentyfold ['twentifould]. 1. *a.* Vingtuple. 2. *adv.* Vingt fois autant. To increase t., vingtupler.

twentyfourmo ['twenti'fɔːmou], *a. & s. Typ:* In-vingt-quatre (*m*) *inv.*

twerp [twɔːp], *s. P:* Nouille *f*, pauvre type *m.*

twice [twais], *adv.* Deux fois. T. as big as . . ., deux fois grand comme. . . . I am t. your age, j'ai deux fois votre âge; j'ai le double de votre âge. T. as slow, deux fois plus lent. T. over, à deux reprises. To think t. before doing sth., y regarder à deux fois avant de faire qch. That made him think t., cela lui a donné à réfléchir. He did not have to be asked t., il ne se fit pas prier; il ne se fit pas tirer l'oreille.

twiddle ['twidl], *v.tr. & i.* Tourner (ses pouces); tortiller (sa moustache).

twig¹ [twig], *s.* 1. Brindille *f* (de branche); ramille *f.* 2. **(Dowser's hazel)** t., baguette *f* de sourcier.

twig², *v.tr.* (twigged) *P:* Comprendre, saisir; *P:* piger. Now I t. it! j'y suis maintenant!

twilight ['twailait], *s.* 1. Crépuscule *m*, demi-jour *m.* In the (evening) t., au crépuscule; entre chien et loup; à la brune. 2. *attrib.* Crépusculaire.

twilit ['twailit], *a.* Crépusculaire; éclairé par le crépuscule.

twill [twil], *s. Tex:* Twill *m.* T. (weave), croisé *m*, sergé *m.*

'twill [twil] = it will.

twin¹ [twin], *a. & i.* 1. Jumeau, -elle. T.(-)brother (-)sister, frère jumeau, sœur jumelle. Siamese twins frères siamois, sœurs siamoises. *Astr:* The Twins les Gémeaux *m.* 2. *a. (a)* T. beds, lits jumeaux. T. tyres, pneus jumelés. *El:* T. wire, fil torsadé. *(b) Bot:* Géminé. 3. T. (crystal), macle *f.* **twin-cylinder,** *s. Aut:* Moteur *m* à deux cylindres. **'twin-engine,** *attrib.a. Av:* T.-e. machine, (appareil) bimoteur (*m*). **'twin-'jet,** *a.* T.-j. plane, biréacteur *m.* **'twin-screw,** *attrib.a.* T.-s. steamer, vapeur à hélices jumelles, à deux hélices.

twin², *v.tr.* Jumeler. **twinning,** *s.* Jumelage *m* (de villes).

twine¹ [twain], *s.* 1. Ficelle *f.* 2. Twines of a snake, replis *m* d'un serpent.

twine². 1. *v.tr.* Tordre, tortiller (des fils); entrelacer. To t. sth. round sth., (en)rouler qch. autour de qch.; entourer qch. de qch. 2. *v.i. (a)* Se tordre, se tortiller. To t. round sth., s'enrouler, s'enlacer, autour de qch. *(b) (Of road)* Serpenter. **twining,** *a. (a) Bot:* Volubile. *(b)* (Sentier) sinueux.

twinge¹ [twin(d)ʒ], *s. (a)* Élancement *m* (de douleur); légère atteinte (de goutte, etc.). *(b)* T. of conscience, remords *m.*

twinge², *v.i. (a)* Élancer. His finger twinges, le doigt lui élance. *(b)* His conscience twinges, sa conscience le tourmente. **twinging,** *a. (Of pain)* Lancinant, cuisant.

twinkle¹ ['twiŋkl], *s.* 1. Scintillement *m*, clignotement *m* (des étoiles). 2. Pétillement *m* (du regard). A mischievous t. in the eye, un éclair, une lueur, de malice dans les yeux.

twinkle², *v.i. (a) (Of light)* Scintiller, papilloter, clignoter. 2. His eyes twinkled (with mischief), ses yeux pétillaient (de malice). **Twinkling eyes,** yeux pétillants d'esprit, de malice. **twinkling,** *s.* = TWINKLE¹ 1. In a t., in the t. of an eye, en un clin d'œil, en un tour de main.

twirl¹ ['twɔːl], *s.* 1. *(a)* Tournoiement *m*; *(of dancer)* pirouette *f. Fenc:* Moulinet *m.* 2. Volute *f* (de fumée, etc.). *Conch:* Spire *f. (In writing)* Enjolivure *f* en spirale; fioriture *f.*

twirl². 1. *v.tr. (a)* Faire tournoyer; faire des moulinets avec (une canne, etc.). *(b)* Tortiller, friser (sa moustache). To t. one's thumbs, se tourner les pouces. 2. *v.i.* Toupiller, tournoyer; *(of dancer)* pirouetter.

twist¹ [twist], *s.* 1. *(a)* Fil *m* retors; cordon *m*; cordonnet *m. (b)* T. of hair, torsade *f* de cheveux. T. of paper, tortillon *m*; cornet *m* de papier; papillote *f. (c)* T.(-tobacco), tabac (mis) en corde. T. of tobacco, rouleau *m*, boudin *m*, de tabac. 2. *(a)* (Effort *m* de) torsion *f.* To give sth. a t., exercer une torsion sur qch. To give one's ankle a t., se fouler la cheville; se donner une entorse. *(b)* Tors *m*, torsion (des brins d'un cordage). *Sm.a:* Pas *m* (des rayures). *(c)* Effet (donné à une balle). With a t. of the wrist, avec un tour de poignet. 3. *(a)* Spire *f.* T. of rope round a post, tour *m* de corde autour d'un poteau. The twists of a serpent, les replis *m* d'un serpent. *(b)* The road takes a t., la route fait un coude. Twists and turns, tours et détours. 4. *(a)* Dévers *m*, gauchissement *m* (d'une pièce de bois); gondolage *m* (d'une tôle). *(b)* Perversion *f* (du sens d'un texte). *(c)* (i) Prédisposition *f* (à qch). Criminal t., prédisposition au crime. (ii) Mental t., perversion, déformation *f*, d'esprit. His queer t. of mind, sa singulière tournure d'esprit. 5. *F: O:* To have a t., avoir l'estomac creux; *F:* avoir la fringale. 6. *Danc:* Twist *m.* **'twist-bit,** *s. Tls:* Mèche hélicoïdale.

twist². 1. *v.tr. (a)* Tordre, tortiller. *Tex:* Retordre (le fil). **To t. together,** torsader, cabler (des fils). **To t. (up) one's handkerchief,** tire-bouchonner son mouchoir. **To t. flowers into a garland,** tresser des fleurs en guirlande. **To t. sth. round sth.,** rouler, entortiller qch. autour de qch. *F:* She can t. him round her little finger, elle lui fait faire ses quatre volontés; elle le mène par le bout du nez. *(b)* Se tordre (le bras, etc.). To t. one's ankle, se donner une entorse; se fouler la cheville. To t. s.o.'s arm, tordre le bras à qn. Face twisted by pain, visage tordu par la douleur. *(c)* Dénaturer, altérer, fausser (le sens d'un texte). To t. the truth, donner une entorse à la vérité. (*d*) Donner de l'effet à (une balle). **2.** *v.i.* (*a*) (*Of worm, etc.*) Se tordre; se tortiller. (*b*) Se mettre en spirale; (*of smoke*) former des volutes; (*of tendril, rope*) vriller. (*c*) (*Of road*) Tourner; faire des détours, des lacets. To t. and turn, serpenter; décrire de nombreuses boucles. **twisted,** *a.* Tordu, tors; *Tex:* (fil) retors. **T. hair,** cheveux en torsade. *El.E:* **T. joint,** joint par torsade. **twisting,** *a.* (Sentier) tortueux, en lacet.

twister ['twistər], *s.* **1.** Tordeur, -euse (de chanvre, etc.). **2.** *P:* Faux bonhomme. He's a t., il est ficelle. **3.** *F:* Question déconcertante. That's a t. for you! voilà qui vous donnera du fil à retordre.

twit¹ [twit], *v.tr.* (**twitted**) **1.** Taquiner (qn); railler (qn) d'une manière sarcastique. **2.** To t. s.o. with sth., reprocher qch. à qn; railler qn de qch.

twit², *s. P:* Salopard *m.*

twitch¹ [twitʃ], *s.* **1.** Saccade *f*; petit coup sec. **2.** Élancement *m* (de douleur). **T. of conscience,** remords *m.* **3.** (*a*) Crispation nerveuse (des mains); mouvement convulsif. (*b*) Facial t., tic (convulsif). **4.** *Vet:* Serre-nez *m inv,* tord-nez *m inv.*

twitch², **1.** *v.tr.* (*a*) Tirer vivement; donner une saccade à (qch.). (*b*) Contracter (ses traits); crisper (les mains). He twitches his leg, il a un mouvement nerveux de la jambe. Horse that twitches its ears, cheval qui dresse les oreilles. **2.** *v.i.* (*a*) (*Of face*) Se contracter nerveusement; (*of hands*) se crisper nerveusement (*b*) His face twitches, il a un tic. That made him t., ça l'a fait tiquer.

twitch³, *s. Bot:* Chiendent officinal.

twitter¹ ['twitər], *s.* **1.** Gazouillement *m,* gazouillis *m.* **2.** *F:* To be all of a t., être tout en émoi.

twitter², *v.i.* Gazouiller. **twittering,** *s.* Gazouillement *m.*

'twixt [twikst], *prep. A: = BETWIXT 1.*

two [tuː], *num. a. & s.* Deux (*m*). The t. of us, you, them; us t., you t., nous deux, vous deux. *Gym:* One t.! une deux! To break sth. in t., casser qch. en deux. To walk in twos, t. by t., t. and t., t. abreast, marcher deux à deux, (deux) par deux. To put t. and t. together, tirer ses conclusions (après avoir rapproché les faits). *Mus:* **T. four time,** deux-temps *m.* To have t. of everything, avoir tout en double. *S.a.* GAME¹ 1, MIND¹ 2. (*For other phrases see* EIGHT.) **two-bladed,** *a. Av:* Bipale. **'two-edged,** *a.* (Épée, *F:* argument) à deux tranchants, à double tranchant. **'two-faced,** *a. = DOUBLE-FACED.* **'two-footed,** *a.* Bipède. **'two-'handed,** *a.* **1.** (Épée) à deux mains. **2.** *Z: etc:* Bimane. **3.** *Cards:* (Jeu) qui se joue à deux. **'two-'legged,** *a.* Bipède. **'two-phase,** *attrib.a. El.E:* (Courant) biphasé, diphasé. **'two-'piece,** *attrib.a.* En deux pièces. (Lady's) t.-p. (costume), deux-pièces *m.* **'two-ply,** *attrib.a.* **1.** (Cordage) à deux brins. **2.** T.-p. wood, contre-plaqué *m* à deux épaisseurs. **'two-pole,** *attrib.a. El:* Bipolaire. **'two-'seater,** *s.* Avion *m,* voiture *f,* à deux places; *F:* un biplace. **'two-step,** *s. Danc:* Pas *m* de deux. **'two-stroke,** *attrib.a. I.C.E:* (Moteur) (à) deux-temps. *Aut: F:* T.-stroke mixture, deux-temps *m.* **'two-time,** *v.tr. Esp. U.S:* Duper, tromper. **'two-'timer,** *s. Esp. U.S:* (Associé, etc.) malhonnête, trompeur. **'two-way,** *attrib.a.* (*a*) (Robinet) à deux voies. (*b*) T.-w. street, rue à deux sens. *S.a.* SWITCH¹ **2.** **'two-'yearly,** *a.* Biennal, -aux.

twofold ['tuːfould]. **1.** *a.* Double; (cordage) à deux brins. **2.** *adv.* Doublement. **Kindnesses returned t.,** bontés rendues au double.

twopence ['tʌpəns], *s.* Deux pence *m.* It isn't worth t., ça ne vaut pas deux sous, pas chipette.

twopenny ['tʌp(ə)ni], *a.* A, de, deux pence. **'two-penny-'halfpenny,** *attrib.a.* (*a*) A t.-h. stamp, un timbre de deux pence et demi. (*b*) *F:* Insignifiant; sans importance; de quatre sous.

tycoon [tai'kuːn], *s. Com: Ind:* Magnat *m,* grand manitou.

tying. *See* TIE².

tyke [taik], *s. P:* **1.** Vilain chien; sale cabot *m.* **2.** Rustre *m.* **3.** (Yorkshire) t., homme *m* du Yorkshire.

tympan ['timpən], *s. Typ: Arch:* Tympan *m.*

tympanic [tim'pænik], *a. Anat:* **T. membrane,** membrane *f* tympanique; membrane du tympan (de l'oreille).

tympanist ['timpənist], *s. Mus:* Timbalier *m.*

tympanitis [timpə'naitis], *s. Med:* **1.** Tympanisme *m,* tympanite *f*; gonflement *m* de l'abdomen. **2.** Tympanite; otite moyenne.

tympanum, *pl.* **-a** ['timpənəm, -ə], *s. Anat: Arch: Mus:* Tympan *m.*

type¹ [taip], *s.* **1.** Type *m.* **People of this t.,** les individus de ce genre. **2.** *Typ:* (*a*) Caractère *m,* type. (*b*) *Coll.* Caractères. **Printed, displayed, in bold t.,** en vedette. **To set t.,** composer. *S.a.* STANDING¹ **2.** **'type area,** *s. Typ:* Justification *f.* **'type-caster, -founder,** *s.* Fondeur *m* de caractères (d'imprimerie); fondeur typographe. **'type-metal,** *s.* Alliage *m* pour caractères d'imprimerie. **'type-setter,** *s. Typ:* Compositeur *m.* **'type-setting,** *s. Typ:* Composition *f.*

type², *v.tr.* Taper à la machine; dactylographier. **typing¹,** *s.* Dactylographie *f,* F: dactylo *f.*

typescript ['taipskript], *s.* Manuscrit dactylographié.

typewrite ['taiprait], *v.tr.* (*p.p.* typewritten ['taipritn] *no p.t.*) = TYPE². **Typewritten document,** document dactylographié, tapé à la machine. **typewriting,** *s.* Dactylographie *f.*

typewriter ['taipraitər], *s.* Machine *f* à écrire.

typhoid ['taifoid], *a. Med:* Typhoïde. **T. fever,** *s.* t., (fièvre *f*) typhoïde (*f*).

typhoon [tai'fuːn], *s. Meteor:* Typhon *m.*

typhus ['taifəs], *s. Med:* Typhus *m.* **Scrub t.,** fièvre fluviale du Japon, typhus rural.

typical ['tipik(ə)l], *a.* Typique. **The t. Frenchman,** le Français typique. **That is t. of him,** c'est bien de lui. **That is t. of France,** c'est un trait caractéristique de la France. **-ally,** *adv.* D'une manière typique, typiquement.

typify ['tipifai], *v.tr.* **1.** Représenter (qch.); symboliser (qch.). **2.** Être caractéristique de (sa classe); être le type de (l'officier, etc.).

typing² ['taipiŋ], *s.* Identification *f,* détermination *f* des types (de bactéries ou de virus). **Blood t.,** détermination du groupe sanguin.

typist ['taipist], *s.* Dactylographe *mf,* F: dactylo *mf.* **Typist's error,** erreur de frappe. *S.a.* SHORTHAND.

typographer [tai'pɔgrəfər], *s.* Typographe *m. F:* typo.

typographic(al) [taipo'græfik(əl), ti-], *a.* Typographique.

typography [tai'pɔgrəfi], *s.* Typographie *f.*

tyrannical [ti'rænik(ə)l, tai-], *a.* Tyrannique. **-ally,** *adv.* Tyranniquement; en tyran.

tyrannize ['tirənaiz], *v.i.* Faire le tyran. **To tyrannize over s.o.,** tyranniser qn.

tyrannous ['tirənəs], *a.* Tyrannique.

tyranny ['tirəni], *s.* Tyrannie *f.*

tyrant ['taiər(ə)nt], *s.* Tyran *m.* **Petty t.,** tyranneau *m.*

tyre ['taiər], *s.* (*a*) Bandage *m,* cercle *m* (de roue). *Rail:* Flanged t., bandage à boudin. (*b*) *Aut: Cy:* (Pneumatic) t., pneu *m.* **Balloon t.,** pneu ballon, pneu confort. **Non-skid t.,** (pneu) antidérapant *m.* **Radial-ply t.,** pneumatique *m* à carcasse radiale. *S.a.* PRESSURE **1.** **'tyre-cement,** *s. Aut: Cy:* Dissolution *f.* **'tyre-cover,** *s.* Enveloppe *f* (pour pneu). **'tyre-gauge,** *s.* Manomètre *m* (pour pneus). **'tyre-inflator, -pump,** *s.* Gonfleur *m,* pompe *f* (pour pneus). **'tyre-lever,** *s.* Démonte-pneus *m inv.*

tyro ['taiərou], *s.* Novice *mf*; néophyte *m.*

Tyrolean [tiro'liːən], *a.* Tyrolien, -ienne.

Tyrolese [ˌtiro'liːz], *s.* Tyrolien, -ienne.

tzigane [tsi'gɑːn], *a. & s.* Tzigane (*mf*).

U, u [ju:], *s.* (La lettre) U, u *m.* U and non-U, ce qui est bien, chic, comme il faut, et ce qui ne l'est pas. *Tp:* U for uncle, U comme Ursule. U-bolt, boulon *m* en U. *Aut:* U-turn, demi-tour *m, pl.* demi-tours. *P.N:* No U-turns, demi-tour interdit. 'U-boat, *F:* Sous-marin allemand.

ubiquitous [ju:'bikwitəs], *a.* Qui se trouve partout; que l'on rencontre partout. I am not u., je n'ai pas le don d'ubiquité.

ubiquity [ju:'bikwiti], *s.* Ubiquité *f.*

udder ['ʌdər], *s.* Mamelle *f*, pis *m* (de vache).

ugh [ʌx, uh], *int.* 1. Pouah! 2. U., it's cold! brrr, il fait froid!

ugliness ['ʌglinis], *s.* Laideur *f.*

ugly ['ʌgli], *a.* Laid; disgracieux, -euse. To grow u., enlaidir. U. piece of furniture, vilain meuble. *F:* U. customer, vilain type. *P:* To cut up u., se fâcher. **ugly fish**, *s. Ich: Fr.C:* Maskinonge *m.*

uhlan ['u:lɑ:n], *s.* Uhlan *m.*

ukase [ju:'keiz], *s. Mil:* Ukase *m*, oukase *m.*

ukulele [,ju:kə'leili], *s. Mus:* Ukulélé *m.*

ulcer ['ʌlsər], *s.* Ulcère *m.*

ulcerate ['ʌlsəreit]. 1. *v.tr.* Ulcérer. 2. *v.i.* S'ulcérer. **ulcerated**, *a.* Ulcéré, ulcéreux, -euse.

ulceration [ʌlsə'reiʃ(ə)n], *s.* Ulcération *f.*

ulcerous ['ʌlsərəs], *a.* Ulcéreux, -euse.

ulex ['ju:leks], *s. Bot:* Ulex *m; F:* ajonc *m.*

ullage ['ʌlidʒ], *s. Winem: Dist:* (Dry) u., vidange *f*, coulage *m; Cust:* manquant *m.* **Filling up of the u.**, ouillage *m.*

ulna ['ʌlnə], *s. Anat:* Cubitus *m.*

ulnar ['ʌlnər], *a. Anat:* Ulnaire; cubital, -aux.

ult. [ʌlt], *adv. Com:* = ULTIMO.

ulterior [ʌl'tiəriər], *a.* 1. Ultérieur, -eure. 2. U. motive, motif secret, caché. Without u. motive, sans arrière-pensée. -ly, *adv.* Ultérieurement; plus tard.

ultimate ['ʌltimit], *a.* (*a*) Final, -als. U. purpose, but final. U. decision, décision définitive. (*b*) *Mth:* U. ratio, extrême raison *f.* (*c*) U. truth, vérité fondamentale. (*d*) (*Of syllable, etc.*) Ultime, dernier. -ly, *adv.* A la fin; en fin de compte.

ultimatum, *pl.* **-tums, -ta** [,ʌlti'meitəm, -təmz, -tə], *s.* Ultimatum *m.*

ultimo ['ʌltimou], *adv. Com:* Du mois dernier.

ultra ['ʌltrə]. 1. *a.* Extrême. *Ph:* Ultra-short waves, Ondes ultra-courtes. 2. *s: Pol:* Ultra *m.* U. conservatism, immobilisme *m.*

ultra-fashionable ['ʌltrə'fæʃənəbl], *a.* Tout dernier cri, ultra-chic.

ultramarine ['ʌltrəmə'ri:n]. 1. *a.* (Pays, etc.) d'outre-mer. 2. *a. & s.* (Bleu *m* d')outremer *m inv.*

ultramicroscope ['ʌltrə'maikrəskoup], *s.* Ultramicroscope *m.*

ultramontane ['ʌltrə'məntein], *a. & s. Theol: Pol:* Ultramontain, -aine.

ultra-rich ['ʌltrə'ritʃ], *a.* Richissime.

ultrasonic ['ʌltrə'sɔnik], *a.* Ultrasonique; ultra-sonore.

ultra-violet ['ʌltrə'vaiəlit], *a. Opt:* Ultra-violet, -ette.

ultra vires ['ʌltrə'vaiəritz]. *Lt.adj. & adv.phr.* Au-delà des pouvoirs. Action u. v., excès *m* de pouvoir.

ululate ['ju:ljuleit], *v.i.* (*Of owl*) Ululer, huer; (*of jackal*) hurler.

ululation [,ju:lju'leiʃ(ə)n], *s.* Ululation *f*, ululement *m* (du hibou); hurlement *m* (du chacal).

Ulysses ['ju(:)lisi:z, ju'lisi:z]. *Pr.n.m.* Ulysse.

umbel ['ʌmb(ə)l, -bel], *s. Bot:* Ombelle *f.*

umbellate ['ʌmbeleit], *a.* (Fleur) ombellée, en ombelle.

umbellifer [ʌm'belifər], *s. Bot:* Ombellifère *f.*

umbelliferous [,ʌmbe'lifərəs], *a. Bot:* Ombellifère.

umber¹ ['ʌmbər], *s. Ich:* Ombre *m.*

umber², *s. Paint:* (Terre *f* d')ombre (*f*).

umbilical [ʌm'bilik(ə)l], *a. Anat:* Ombilical, -aux.

umbra, *pl.* **-ae** ['ʌmbrə, -i:], *s. Astr:* (*a*) Cône *m* d'ombre (dans une éclipse). (*b*) Obscurité centrale (d'une tache solaire).

umbra² ['ʌmbrə], **umbrine** ['ʌmbri:n], *s. Ich:* Ombrine *f.*

umbrage ['ʌmbridʒ], *s.* Ombrage *m*, ressentiment *m.* He took no u. at their friendship, il ne s'offensait pas de leur amitié.

umbrella [ʌm'brelə], *s.* (*a*) Parapluie *m.* Stumpy u., tom-pouce *m.* Beach u., parasol *m.* (*b*) Parasol *m* (de chef de tribu nègre). (*c*) *Av:* Aerial u., (ombrelle *f* de) protection aérienne. um'brella-frame, *s.* Monture *f*, carcasse *f*, de parapluie. um'brella-stand, *s.* Porte-parapluies *m inv.* um'brella-stick, *s.* Manche *f*, canne *f*, de parapluie. um'brella-tree, *s. Bot:* Magnolier *m* (en) parasol.

Umbria ['ʌmbriə]. *Pr.n. Geog:* L'Ombrie *f.*

umlaut ['umlaut], *s. Ling:* Umlaut *m*; métaphonie *f.*

umph [mh], *int.* Hum! hmm!

umpire¹ ['ʌmpaiər], *s.* Arbitre *m*, juge *m.*

umpire², *v.tr.* Arbitrer (un différend, *Sp:* un match). **umpiring**, *s.* Arbitrage *m.*

umpteen ['ʌmp'ti:n], *a. & s. F:* Je ne sais combien. To have u. reasons for doing sth., avoir trente-six raisons de faire qch.

'un [ən], *pron. P:* (= one) A little 'un, un petiot.

unabashed ['ʌnə'bæʃt], *a.* 1. Sans perdre contenance. U., he replied . . ., il répondit sans aucune confusion. . . . 2. Aucunement ébranlé.

unabated ['ʌnə'beitid], *a.* Non diminué. With u. speed, toujours avec la même vitesse.

unabating ['ʌnə'beitiŋ], *a.* Persistant, soutenu.

unable [ʌn'eibl], *a.* Incapable. U. to do sth., impuissant à faire qch.; hors d'état de faire qch. We are u. to help you, nous ne pouvons pas vous aider. U. to attend, empêché.

unabridged ['ʌnə'bridʒd], *a.* Non abrégé. U. edition, édition intégrale.

unaccented ['ʌnək'sentid], *a.* Sans accent; (*of syllable*) non accentué; atone.

unacceptable ['ʌnək'septəbl], *a.* Inacceptable; (théorie) irrecevable. A glass of beer wouldn't be u., un verre de bière ne serait pas de refus.

unaccommodating ['ʌnə'kɔmədeitiŋ], *a.* Peu accommodant; désobligeant.

unaccompanied ['ʌnə'kʌmp(ə)nid], *a.* 1. Non accompagné, seul; sans escorte. 2. *Mus:* Sans accompagnement.

unaccomplished ['ʌnə'kɔmpliʃt, -'kʌm-], *a.* (*a*) (Projet) inaccompli, non réalisé. (*b*) (Travail, etc.) inachevé.

unaccountable ['ʌnə'kauntəbl], *a.* (*a*) (Phénomène) inexplicable. It is u., explique cela qui pourra. (*b*) (Conduite) bizarre. -ably, *adv.* Inexplicablement, sans qu'on sache pourquoi.

unaccounted ['ʌnə'kauntid], *a.* U. for. 1. (Phénomène) inexpliqué. 2. Five of the passengers are still u. for, on reste sans nouvelles de cinq voyageurs.

unaccredited ['ʌnə'kreditid], *a.* (Agent) non accrédité, sans pouvoirs.

unaccustomed ['ʌnə'kʌstəmd], *a.* 1. (Événement) inaccoutumé. 2. (*Of pers.*) U. to sth., peu habitué à qch.

unacknowledged ['ʌnək'nɔlidʒd], *a.* 1. (*a*) (Enfant) non reconnu. (*b*) (Péché) non avoué. 2. (Lettre) demeurée sans réponse.

unacquainted ['ʌnə'kweintid], *a.* 1. To be u. with s.o., ne pas connaître qn. 2. To be u. with sth., ignorer (un fait, etc.).

unadaptable ['ʌnə'dæptəbl], *a.* (*Of pers.*) Inadaptable.

unadapted ['ʌnə'dæptid], *a.* Inadapté (to sth., à qch.).

unaddressed ['ʌnə'drest], *a.* (Colis) sans adresse, qui ne porte pas d'adresse.

unadorned ['ʌnə'dɔ:nd], *a.* Sans ornement; naturel. Beauty u., la beauté sans parure, sans fard. U. truth, la pure vérité, la vérité toute nue.

unadulterated ['ʌnə'dʌltəreitid], *a.* Pur; sans mélange; non frelaté.

unadvisable ['ʌnəd'vaizəbl], *a.* (*a*) (*Of action*) Peu sage; imprudent. (*b*) Alcohol is u. for people suffering from heart complaints, l'alcool est à déconseiller aux cardiaques.

unadvisedly ['ʌnəd'vaizidli], *adv.* Imprudemment; sans réflexion.

unaesthetic ['ʌnis'θetik], *a.* Inesthétique.

unaffected ['ʌnə'fektid], *a.* 1. Sans affectation. (*a*) Véritable, sincère. (*b*) (*Of pers.*) Sans pose. U. style, style sans recherche. 2. U. by air, inaltérable à l'air. Metal u. by acids, métal inattaquable par les acides. Organism u. by poison, organisme réfractaire au poison. -ly, *adv.* Sans affectation. (*a*) Sincèrement. (*b*) Simplement.

unaffectedness [,ʌnə'fektidnis], *s.* Absence *f* de toute affectation, simplicité *f*, naturel *m*.

unaffiliated ['ʌnə'filieitid], *a.* Non affilié (to, à).

unaided ['ʌn'eidid], *a.* Sans aide. He did it u., il l'a fait tout seul. To see sth. with the u. eye, voir qch. à l'œil nu.

unallayed ['ʌnə'leid], *a.* Lit: (*Of grief*) Inapaisé; sans soulagement.

unallotted ['ʌnə'lɔtid], *a.* 1. (Temps) disponible. 2. U. shares, actions non réparties.

unalloyed ['ʌnə'lɔid], *a.* (Métal) pur, sans alliage. U. happiness, bonheur parfait, sans nuages.

unalterable [ʌn'ɔ:lt(ə)rəbl], *a.* Immuable, invariable. -ably, *adv.* Immuablement, invariablement.

unaltered ['ʌn'ɔ:ltəd], *a.* Toujours le même; inchangé; sans changement; tel quel.

unambiguous ['ʌnæm'bigjuəs], *a.* Non équivoque. U. terms, termes précis, clairs.

unambitious ['ʌnæm'biʃəs], *a.* 1. Sans ambition. 2. (Projet) sans prétention.

unamenable ['ʌnə'mi:nəbl], *a.* Réfractaire, rebelle. U. to reason, qui ne veut pas entendre raison.

unamended ['ʌnə'mendid], *a.* Sans modification; tel quel.

un-American ['ʌnə'merikn], *a.* Contraire à l'esprit américain.

unanimity [,ju:nə'nimiti], *s.* Unanimité *f*. With u., d'un commun accord.

unanimous [ju(:)'nænimos], *a.* Unanime. -ly, *adv.* A l'unanimité; unanimement.

unannounced ['ʌnə'naunst], *a.* He marched in u., il entra sans se faire annoncer.

unanswerable [ʌn'ɑ:ns(ə)rəbl], *a.* Qui n'admet pas de réponse; (argument) sans réplique.

unanswered ['ʌn'ɑ:nsəd], *a.* 1. Sans réponse. 2. Irréfuté. 3. Inexaucé.

unanticipated ['ʌnæn'tisipeitid], *a.* Imprévu.

unappeasable ['ʌnə'pi:zəbl], *a.* (Faim) inapaisable; (appétit) insatiable; (haine) implacable.

unappeased ['ʌnə'pi:zd], *a.* Inapaisé; (*of passion*) inassouvi.

unappetizing ['ʌn'æpitaiziŋ], *a.* Peu appétissant.

unappreciated ['ʌnə'pri:ʃieitid], *a.* Inapprécié; peu estimé. U. poet, poète méconnu.

unappreciative ['ʌnə'pri:ʃiətiv], *a.* (Public) insensible; (compte rendu) peu favorable.

unapproachable ['ʌnə'prout∫əbl], *a.* 1. Inaccessible; (côte) inabordable; (*of pers.*) inabordable, distant. 2. Incomparable; sans pareil.

unappropriated ['ʌnə'prouprieitid], *a.* 1. (Argent) inutilisé, disponible. U. funds, fonds sans application déterminée. 2. (Siège) libre.

unarmed ['ʌn'ɑ:md], *a.* (*a*) Sans armes. (*b*) *Nat.Hist:* Inerme.

unascertainable ['ʌnæsə'teinəbl], *a.* Non vérifiable; indéterminable.

unascertained ['ʌnæsə'teind], *a.* Non vérifié. U. facts, faits non établis.

unashamed ['ʌnə'ʃeimd], *a.* Sans honte, éhonté; sans pudeur; cynique.

unasked ['ʌn'ɑ:skt], *a.* To do sth. u., faire qch. spontanément, sans y être invité.

unassailable ['ʌnə'seiləbl], *a.* (Droit) inattaquable; (conclusion) indiscutable.

unassertive ['ʌnə'sə:tiv], *a.* Modeste, timide.

unassimilated ['ʌnə'simileitid], *a.* (Aliment) inassimilé.

unassisted ['ʌnə'sistid], *a.* = UNAIDED.

unassuaged ['ʌnə'sweidʒd], *a.* (Souffrance) que rien ne vient calmer; (appétit) inassouvi.

unassuming ['ʌnə'sju:miŋ], *a.* Sans prétention(s); simple, modeste.

unattached ['ʌnə'tætʃt], *a.* 1. Qui n'est pas attaché (to, à); indépendant (to, de). 2. (Officier) en disponibilité. (*Of bachelor*) To be u., être garçon seul.

unattainable ['ʌnə'teinəbl], *a.* Inaccessible (by, à); hors de la portée (by, de); impossible.

unattended ['ʌnə'tendid], *a.* (*a*) Seul; sans escorte. (*b*) Sport not u. by danger, sport non dépourvu de danger. (*c*) U. to, négligé, sans soins.

unattractive ['ʌnə'træktiv], *a.* Peu attrayant; (personne) peu sympathique.

unauthorized [ʌn'ɔ:θəraizd], *a.* (*a*) Non autorisé; sans autorisation; (commerce) illicite. (*b*) (Fonctionnaire) sans mandat.

unavailable ['ʌnə'veiləbl], *a.* 1. Non disponible. 2. Qu'on ne peut se procurer; (article) épuisé.

unavailing ['ʌnə'veiliŋ], *a.* Inutile; (*of tears*) vain; (*of efforts*) infructueux. -ly, *adv.* En vain.

unavoidable ['ʌnə'vɔidəbl], *a.* (*a*) Inévitable. (*b*) (Événement) qu'on ne peut prévenir. -ably, *adv.* 1. Inévitablement. 2. U. absent, absent pour raison majeure, empêché.

unavowed ['ʌnə'vaud], *a.* Inavoué.

unaware [ʌnə'wεər], *a.* Ignorant, pas au courant (of sth., de qch.). To be u. of sth., ignorer qch. I am not u. that . . ., je ne suis pas sans savoir que + *ind.*

unawares ['ʌnə'wεəz], *adv.* 1. Inconsciemment; par inadvertance. 2. To take s.o. u., prendre qn au dépourvu.

unbaked ['ʌn'beikt], *a.* (*Of brick*) Cru.

unbalance ['ʌn'bæləns], *v.tr.* Déranger, déséquilibrer (l'esprit de qn).

unbalanced ['ʌn'bælənst], *a.* 1. (*a*) *Ph:* En équilibre instable. (*b*) (Esprit) déséquilibré, désaxé. 2. U. forces, forces non équilibrées.

unballasting ['ʌn'bæləstiŋ], *s. Nau:* Délestage *m*.

unbearable [ʌn'bεərəbl], *a.* Insupportable, intolérable. U. agony, douleur atroce. *F:* He made himself u., il s'est rendu odieux. -ably, *adv.* Insupportablement.

unbeatable ['ʌn'bi:təbl], *a.* Imbattable.

unbeaten ['ʌn'bi:tn], *a.* 1. Non battu. U. path, sentier non battu, non frayé. 2. U. champion, champion qui n'a pas encore été battu.

unbecoming ['ʌnbi'kʌmiŋ], *a.* 1. Peu convenable; déplacé. U. of s.o., déplacé chez qn. 2. (*Of garment*) Peu seyant. -ly, *adv.* D'une manière peu séante.

unbeknown ['ʌnbi'noun]. 1. *a.* Inconnu (to, de). 2. *adv.* To do sth. u. to anyone, faire qch. à l'insu de tous.

unbelief ['ʌnbi'li:f], *s.* Incrédulité *f*; mécréance *f*; incroyance *f*.

unbelievable ['ʌnbi'li:vəbl], *a.* Incroyable.

unbeliever ['ʌnbi'li:vər], *s.* Incrédule *mf*; incroyant, -ante; mécréant, -ante.

unbelieving ['ʌnbi'li:viŋ], *a.* Incrédule; incroyant.

unbend ['ʌn'bend], *v.* (unbent ['ʌn'bent]; unbent) I. *v.tr.* 1. Détendre, débander (un arc); détendre (son esprit). 2. Rendre (qch.) droit; redresser. 3. *Nau:* Défrapper, larguer (un câble). II. unbend, *v.i.* S'abandonner un petit peu; se détendre. He never unbends, son caractère ne se déraidit jamais. **unbending**, *a.* Inflexible, ferme, raide; intransigeant.

unbias(s)ed ['ʌn'baiəst], *a.* Impartial, -aux; sans parti pris; sans prévention; objectif, -ive.

unbidden ['ʌn'bid(ə)n], *a.* O: 1. Non invité; (hôte) intrus. 2. Spontané.

unbind ['ʌn'baind], *v.tr.* (unbound ['ʌn'baund]; unbound) Délier; débander (une plaie).

unbleached ['ʌn'bli:t∫t], *a. Tex:* Écru.

unblemished ['ʌn'blemi∫t], *a.* Sans défaut; immaculé. U. career, carrière sans tache.

unblock ['ʌn'blɔk], *v.tr.* 1. (*a*) Dégager, désencombrer. (*b*) *Cards:* To u. a suit, affranchir une couleur. 2. Décaler (une roue).

unblushing ['ʌn'blʌ∫iŋ], *a.* Sans vergogne; éhonté. -ly, *adv.* (*a*) Sans rougir. (*b*) Sans vergogne; (mentir) impudemment, cyniquement.

unbolt ['ʌn'boult], *v.tr.* 1. Déverrouiller (la porte). 2. Déboulonner.

unborn ['ʌn'bɔ:n], *a.* Qui n'est pas encore né. Generations yet u., générations à venir; générations futures.

unbosom [ʌn'buzəm], *v.tr.* Découvrir, révéler (ses sentiments). To u. oneself to s.o., ouvrir son cœur à qn, se confier à qn.

unbound ['ʌn'baund]. I. *See* UNBIND. II. unbound, *a.* 1. Délié. To come u., se délier. 2. (*Of book*) Non relié; broché.

unbounded [ʌn'baundid], a. Sans bornes; illimité; (*of conceit*) démesuré.

unbreakable [ʌn'breikəbl], a. Incassable.

unbreathable ['ʌn'bri:ðəbl], a. Irrespirable.

unbribable ['ʌn'braibəbl], a. Incorruptible.

unbridled ['ʌn'braidld], a. (*Of passion*) Débridé, effréné; sans retenue.

unbroken ['ʌn'brouk(ə)n], a. 1. (*a*) Non brisé, non cassé. (*b*) Intact. U. spirit, courage inentamé. (*Cp.* 2 (*b*).) (*c*) (*Of rule*) Toujours observé. Sp: Record still u., record qui n'a pas été battu. (*d*) (*Of silence*) Ininterrompu, continu. U. sheet of ice, nappe de glace continue. 2. (*a*) (Cheval) non rompu, non dressé. (*b*) U. spirit, esprit insoumis, indompté. (*Cp.* 1 (*b*).) 3. *Agr:* U. ground, terre vierge.

unbuckle ['ʌn'bʌkl], v.tr. Déboucler.

unburden [ʌn'bə:d(ə)n], v.tr. 1. (*a*) Alléger (qn) d'un fardeau. (*b*) To u. the mind, soulager, alléger, l'esprit. To u. oneself, s'épancher. To u. oneself of a secret, se soulager du poids d'un secret. 2. To u. one's sorrows to s.o., raconter ses peines à qn.

unburied ['ʌn'berid], a. 1. Déterré. 2. Sans sépulture; non enseveli.

unbusinesslike ['ʌn'biznislaik], a. 1. Peu commerçant. 2. U. proceeding, procédé irrégulier. To conduct one's affairs in an u. way, manquer de méthode.

unbutton ['ʌn'bʌtn], v.tr. Déboutonner. (*Of pers.*) All unbuttoned, tout débraillé.

uncalled ['ʌn'kɔ:ld], a. 1. *Fin:* U. capital, capitaux non appelés. 2. U. for, (*of remark*) déplacé; (*of rebuke*) immérité, injustifié. U. for insult, insulte gratuite.

uncanny [ʌn'kæni], a. D'une étrangeté inquiétante; mystérieux, -euse. U. noise, bruit inquiétant. U. light, lueur sinistre. -ily, adv. D'une manière étrange.

uncared-for ['ʌn'kɛədfɔ:r], a. Peu soigné. U.-f. child, enfant délaissé. To leave a garden u.-f., laisser un jardin à l'abandon.

unceasing [ʌn'si:siŋ], a. (*a*) Incessant, continu. (*b*) (Travail) assidu; (effort) soutenu. -ly, adv. Sans cesse, sans arrêt.

uncensored ['ʌn'sensəd], a. 1. (Article) qui n'a pas été soumis à la censure. 2. (Passage) non expurgé (par la censure).

unceremonious ['ʌnseri'mouniəs], a. (*Of pers.*) Sans façon, sans gêne. -ly, adv. 1. Sans cérémonie. 2. Sans façons; brusquement.

uncertain [ʌn'sə:t(ə)n], a. Incertain. 1. (*a*) (*Of time, amount*) Indéterminé. (*b*) (Résultat) douteux. (*c*) U. outline, contour mal défini. 2. (*a*) U. steps, pas mal assurés. U. temper, humeur inégale. U. health, santé vacillante. (*b*) His memory is u., sa mémoire vacille. To be u. of, as regards, the future, être incertain de l'avenir. To be u. whether . . ., ne pas savoir au juste si. . . . -ly, adv. D'une façon incertaine.

uncertainty [ʌn'sə:t(ə)nti], s. 1. Incertitude f. To remove any u., pour dissiper toute équivoque. . . . 2. To prefer a certainty to an u., préférer le certain à l'incertain.

uncertificated ['ʌnsə:'tifikeitid], a. Sans diplôme, non diplômé.

unchain ['ʌn'tʃein], v.tr. Déchaîner; délivrer (un prisonnier). *Lit:* To u. one's passions, donner libre cours à ses passions.

unchallenged ['ʌn'tʃælin(d)ʒd], a. 1. (*a*) Que personne ne vient contredire. To continue u., continuer sans être contredit. (*b*) (Droit) incontesté. To let (sth.) go, pass, u., ne pas relever (une affirmation). 2. *Mil:* To let s.o. pass u., laisser passer qn sans interpellation.

unchangeable [ʌn'tʃein(d)ʒəbl], a. Immuable, inchangeable.

unchanged ['ʌn'tʃein(d)ʒd], a. Inchangé; toujours le même.

unchanging [ʌn'tʃein(d)ʒiŋ], a. Invariable, immuable.

uncharitable [ʌn'tʃæritəbl], a. Peu charitable.

uncharted ['ʌn'tʃɑ:tid], a. 1. (*Of island*) Non porté sur la carte. 2. (*Of sea*) Inexploré.

unchecked ['ʌn'tʃekt], a. 1. Auquel rien n'a été opposé; sans frein. U. advance, avance qui ne rencontre pas d'obstacles. U. anger, colère non contenue. 2. (*Of account*) Non pointé, non vérifié.

unchivalrous ['ʌn'ʃiv(ə)lrəs], a. Peu chevaleresque; peu courtois, peu loyal.

unchristened ['ʌn'kris(ə)nd], a. 1. Non baptisé. 2. Sans nom.

unchristian ['ʌn'kristjən], a. 1. Infidèle, païen, -enne. 2. Peu chrétien. 3. *F:* At this u. hour, à cette heure indue.

uncial ['ʌnsiəl], a. (*Of letter*) Oncial, -aux. s. Lettre onciale.

uncircumcised ['ʌn'sə:kəmsaizd], a. Incirconcis.

uncivil ['ʌn'sivil], a. Discourtois, impoli. -illy, adv. Impoliment.

uncivilized ['ʌn'sivilaizd], a. Incivilisé, barbare.

unclaimed ['ʌn'kleimd], a. Non réclamé. U. right, droit non revendiqué. *Post:* U. letter, lettre au rebut.

unclasp ['ʌn'klɑ:sp], v.tr. (*a*) Dégrafer, défaire (un bracelet). (*b*) Desserrer (le poing).

unclassified ['ʌn'klæsifaid], a. Non classé.

uncle ['ʌŋkl], s. 1. Oncle m. Yes, u.! oui, mon oncle! To talk to s.o. like a Dutch u., faire la morale à qn. 2. *P:* My watch is at my uncle's, ma montre est chez ma tante, au clou.

unclean ['ʌn'kli:n], a. 1. Impur, immonde. 2. Malpropre, sale.

uncleared ['ʌn'kliəd], a. 1. U. ground, terrain indéfriché. 2. (*a*) (*Of debt*) Non acquitté, en souffrance. (*b*) (Chèque) non compensé.

unclench ['ʌn'klen(t)ʃ], v.tr. Desserrer (le poing, les dents).

uncloak ['ʌn'klouk], v.tr. (*a*) Dépouiller (qn) de son manteau. (*b*) Découvrir (des projets); démasquer, dévoiler (une imposture).

unclothe ['ʌn'klouð], v.tr. Déshabiller, dévêtir (qn); mettre (qn) à nu. unclothed, a. 1. Déshabillé. 2. Nu; sans vêtements.

unclouded ['ʌn'klaudid], a. (*Of sky*) Sans nuage, serein; (*of vision*) clair; (*of liquid*) limpide.

uncoil ['ʌn'kɔil]. 1. v.tr. Dérouler. *Nau:* Délover. 2. v.i. (*Of snake*) Se dérouler.

uncoloured ['ʌn'kʌləd], a. (*a*) Non coloré. U. account of sth., rapport fidèle de qch. (*b*) Incolore.

uncombed ['ʌn'koumd], a. (*Of hair*) Non peigné, mal peigné, ébouriffé; (*of wool*) non peigné.

uncomely ['ʌn'kʌmli], a. Peu gracieux, -euse; disgracieux, -euse; laid.

uncomfortable [ʌn'kʌmf(ə)təbl], a. 1. Inconfortable, peu confortable; incommode, incommodant. This is a very u. bed, on est très mal dans ce lit. 2. (*a*) Désagréable. To make things u. for s.o., créer des ennuis à qn; faire des histoires à qn. It makes things u., c'est très gênant. (*b*) (*Of news*) Inquiétant. 3. To feel u., être mal à l'aise. To be, feel, u. about sth., être inquiet au sujet de qch. -ably, adv. 1. Peu confortablement; incommodément. 2. Désagréablement. The enemy was u. near, la proximité de l'ennemi était inquiétante.

uncommitted [ʌnkə'mitid], a. (*a*) Non engagé, libre, indépendant. (*b*) *Pol:* Neutraliste.

uncommon [ʌn'kɔmən]. 1. a. Peu commun. (*a*) U. word, mot rare, peu usité. (*b*) Peu ordinaire; singulier, -ière. 2. adv. *P:* = UNCOMMONLY 2. -ly, adv. 1. Not u., assez souvent. 2. Singulièrement. U. good, excellent.

uncommunicative ['ʌnkə'mju:nikətiv], a. Peu communicatif, -ive; renfermé, taciturne.

uncompanionable ['ʌnkəm'pænjənəbl], a. Peu sociable.

uncomplaining ['ʌnkəm'pleiniŋ], a. Qui ne se plaint pas; patient, résigné. -ly, adv. Sans se plaindre.

uncomplimentary ['ʌn,kɔmpli'ment(ə)ri], a. Peu flatteur, -euse.

uncompromising [ʌn'kɔmprəmaiziŋ], a. Intransigeant; intraitable. U. sincerity, sincérité absolue.

unconcealed ['ʌnkən'si:ld], a. Qui n'est pas caché; fait à découvert. U. opinions, opinions avouées.

unconcern ['ʌnkən'sə:n], s. Insouciance f; indifférence f.

unconcerned ['ʌnkən'sə:nd], a. 1. (*a*) Insouciant, indifférent. U. air, air dégagé. U., he went on speaking, sans se troubler, il continua de parler. (*b*) Sans inquiétude. 2. Neutre, impartial, -aux.

unconcernedly ['ʌnkən'sə:nidli], adv. D'un air indifférent, dégagé; avec insouciance.

unconciliatory [ˈʌnkənˈsiliət(ə)ri], a. Peu conciliant; intraitable.

unconditional [ˈʌnkənˈdiʃən(ə)l], a. Inconditionnel; absolu. U. refusal, refus m catégorique. -ally, adv. To accept u., accepter sans réserve. To surrender u., se rendre sans conditions.

unconditioned [ˈʌnkənˈdiʃ(ə)nd], a. Inconditionné.

unconfirmed [ˈʌnkənˈfɔːmd], a. Non confirmé. 1. (Of news) Qui n'est pas confirmé; sujet à caution. 2. Ecc: Qui n'a pas reçu le sacrement de la confirmation.

uncongenial [ˈʌnkənˈdʒiːniəl], a. 1. (Of pers.) Peu sympathique. 2. (a) (Climat) peu favorable (to, à). (b) U. job, travail ingrat.

unconnected [ˈʌnkəˈnektid], a. (a) Sans rapport, sans lien. The two events are totally u., les deux événements n'ont aucun rapport entre eux. (b) (Style) décousu, sans suite.

unconquerable [ʌnˈkɔŋk(ə)rəbl], a. Invincible; (curiosité, etc.) irrésistible; (difficulté) insurmontable; (défaut) incorrigible.

unconscionable [ʌnˈkɔnʃənəbl], a. 1. A: Sans conscience. 2. To take an u. time doing sth., mettre un temps inconcevable à faire qch.

unconscious [ʌnˈkɔnʃəs], a. 1. Inconscient. To be u. of sth., (i) ne pas avoir conscience de qch.; (ii) ignorer qch. He remained blissfully u. of it all, F: il n'y a vu que du bleu. 2. Sans connaissance; évanoui, inanimé. To become u., perdre connaissance. 3. s. Psy: The u., l'inconscient m. -ly, adv. Inconsciemment.

unconsciousness [ʌnˈkɔnʃəsnis], s. 1. Inconscience f, (of, de). 2. Évanouissement m, état m d'inconscience.

unconsidered [ˈʌnkənˈsidəd], a. 1. (Of remark) Inconsidéré, irréfléchi. 2. (Petit objet) auquel on n'attache aucune valeur.

unconsoled [ˈʌnkənˈsould], a. Inconsolé.

unconstitutional [ˈʌnˌkɔnstiˈtjuːʃən(ə)l], a. Anticonstitutionnel, -elle.

unconstrained [ˈʌnkənˈstreind], a. Non contraint; libre; (acte) spontané. U. manner, allure aisée, désinvolte.

unconstrainedly [ˈʌnkənˈstreinidli], adv. Sans contrainte, sans aucune gêne; librement.

unconsummated [ˈʌnˈkɔnsəmeitid], a. (Mariage) inconsommé.

uncontaminated [ˈʌnkənˈtæmineitid], a. Incontaminé; non corrompu.

uncontested [ˈʌnkənˈtestid], a. (Droit) incontesté. Jur: U. owner, possesseur m pacifique. Pol: U. seat, siège (à la Chambre) qui n'est pas disputé.

uncontradicted [ˈʌnˌkɔntrəˈdiktid], a. Non contredit.

uncontrollable [ˈʌnkənˈtrouləbl], a. 1. (Pouvoir) absolu. 2. (Enfant) ingouvernable; (désir) irrésistible. U. laughter, fou rire. Fits of u. temper, emportements m. -ably, adv. Irrésistiblement.

uncontrolled [ˈʌnkənˈtrould], a. 1. Indépendant; irresponsable. 2. U. liberty, liberté absolue. U. passions, passions effrénées.

unconventional [ˈʌnkənˈvenʃən(ə)l], a. Non-conformiste; original, -aux. U. life, vie f de bohème, vie irrégulière. -ally, adv. A l'encontre des conventions.

unconventionality [ˈʌnkənˌvenʃəˈnæliti], s. Indépendance f à l'égard des conventions sociales, artistiques, etc.; originalité f; liberté f d'allures.

unconversant [ˈʌnkənˈvəːs(ə)nt], a. U. with sth., peu versé dans (une science, etc.); peu familier avec (un sujet).

unconvinced [ˈʌnkənˈvinst], a. Sceptique (of, à l'égard de).

unconvincing [ˈʌnkənˈvinsiŋ], a. (Récit) peu probant, peu convaincant; (excuse) peu vraisemblable.

uncooked [ˈʌnˈkukt], a. (Aliment) non cuit, inapprêté, cru.

uncooperative [ˈʌnkouˈɔp(ə)rətiv], a. Peu coopératif, -ive.

uncoordinated [ˈʌnkouˈɔːdineitid], a. Non coordonné; (récit) décousu.

uncork [ˈʌnˈkɔːk], v.tr. Déboucher (une bouteille). uncorking, s. Débouchage m.

uncorrected [ˈʌnkəˈrektid], a. 1. (Of proof) Non corrigé. 2. (Of error) Non rectifié. Ph: Result u. for temperature and pressure, résultat brut.

uncouple [ʌnˈkʌpl], v.tr. 1. Découpler (les chiens). 2. Débrayer (une machine); désaccoupler (des piles). Rail: Dételer, découpler (des wagons).

uncouth [ʌnˈkuːθ], a. 1. Grossier, rude. 2. Malappris, gauche. An u. (and shy) girl, une sauvageonne. -ly, adv. 1. Grossièrement. 2. (Se conduire) gauchement.

uncouthness [ʌnˈkuːθnis], s. 1. Rudesse f (de mœurs). 2. Gaucherie f, lourdeur f.

uncover [ʌnˈkʌvər], v.tr. (a) Découvrir (son visage); mettre à découvert. (b) Chess: To u. a piece, dégarnir une pièce. uncovered, a. 1. Mis à découvert; découvert. 2. Com: (Achat) à découvert. U. balance, découvert m.

uncreasable [ʌnˈkriːsəbl], a. Infroissable.

uncritical [ʌnˈkritik(ə)l], a. Dépourvu de sens critique; sans discernement. U. audience, auditoire peu exigeant.

uncrossed [ˈʌnˈkrɔst], a. 1. U. cheque, chèque non barré. 2. Que personne n'a franchi.

uncrowned [ˈʌnˈkraund], a. 1. Découronné. 2. Non couronné.

uncrushable [ʌnˈkrʌʃəbl], a. Tex: etc: Infroissable.

unction [ˈʌŋkʃ(ə)n], s. (a) Onction f. Ecc: To administer extreme u. (to s.o.), donner l'extrême-onction (à qn), extrémiser (qn). (b) To speak with u., parler avec onction. (c) To relate a scandal with u., raconter un scandale en se délectant.

unctuous [ˈʌŋktjuəs], a. 1. Onctueux, -euse, graisseux, -euse. 2. (a) (Prédicateur) onctueux. (b) Pej: Mielleux, -euse. -ly, adv. Onctueusement.

unctuousness [ˈʌŋktjuəsnis], s. Onctuosité f.

uncultivated [ʌnˈkʌltiveitid], a. (Terrain) inculte; (personne) sans culture.

uncultured [ˈʌnˈkʌltʃəd], a. (Esprit) incultivé, inculte; (personne) sans culture.

uncurbed [ˈʌnˈkəːbd], a. (a) Libre; (autorité) sans restriction. (b) (Of passion) Débridé; sans frein.

uncurl [ˈʌnˈkəːl], v.i. F: (D'un chat, etc.) Se dépelotonner.

uncut [ˈʌnˈkʌt], a. 1. U. crops, récoltes sur pied. 2. (Of hedge) Non taillé. U. diamond, diamant brut. U. book, (i) livre non coupé; (ii) Bookb: livre non rogné.

undamaged [ˈʌnˈdæmidʒd], a. Non endommagé; indemne. U. reputation, réputation intacte.

undamped [ˈʌnˈdæmpt], a. 1. Ph: Non amorti. W.Tel: U. waves, ondes entretenues. 2. (Courage) persistant, soutenu.

undated [ˈʌnˈdeitid], a. Non daté; sans date.

undaunted [ʌnˈdɔːntid], a. (a) Intrépide. (b) Aucunement intimidé. -ly, adv. Intrépidement.

undecaying [ˈʌndiˈkeiiŋ], a. Impérissable.

undeceive [ˈʌndiˈsiːv], v.tr. Désabuser (of, de); détromper (qn), dessiller les yeux (à qn). To u. oneself, se désabuser. undeceived, a. 1. Désabusé; détrompé. 2. Aucunement trompé (by, par).

undecided [ˈʌndiˈsaidid], a. Indécis. (a) (Of colour) Mal défini. (b) (Of pers.) Irrésolu, hésitant.

undecipherable [ˈʌndiˈsaif(ə)rəbl], a. Indéchiffrable.

undeciphered [ˈʌndiˈsaifəd], a. Indéchiffré.

undefeated [ˈʌndiˈfiːtid], a. Invaincu.

undefended [ˈʌndiˈfendid], a. 1. Sans défense. 2. Jur: U. suit, cause où le défendeur s'abstient de plaider.

undefiled [ˈʌndiˈfaild], a. Pur; sans souillure.

undefinable [ˈʌndiˈfainəbl], a. Indéfinissable, indéterminable.

undefined [ˈʌndiˈfaind], a. 1. Non défini. 2. Indéterminé; vague.

undelivered [ˈʌndiˈlivəd], a. Non délivré. U. letter, lettre au rebut. If u. please return to sender, en cas de non-délivrance prière de retourner à l'expéditeur.

undemonstrative [ˈʌndiˈmɔnstrətiv], a. Peu expansif, -ive, peu démonstratif, -ive; réservé.

undeniable [ˈʌndiˈnaiəbl], a. Indéniable, incontestable. -ably, adv. Incontestablement; indiscutablement.

undenominational [ˈʌndiˌnɔmiˈneiʃən(ə)l], a. Non confessionnel; (école) laïque.

undenominationalism [ˈʌndiˌnɔmiˈneiʃənəlizm], s. Laïcité f (des écoles, etc.).

under ['ʌndər]. I. *prep.* 1. Sous; au-dessous de. (*a*) U. water, sous l'eau. *S.a.* SWIM² I.1. Put it u. that, mettez-le là-dessous. Here is a table, get u. it, voici une table, mettez-vous dessous. The village lies u. the mountain, le village est situé au pied de la montagne. *S.a.* FOOT¹ 1 (*c*), NOSE¹ I.1. (*b*) To speak u. one's breath, parler à demi-voix. He is u. thirty, il a moins de trente ans. The u.-thirties, les moins de trente ans. 2. (*a*) U. lock and key, sous clef. Visible u. the microscope, visible au microscope. To be u. sentence of death, être condamné à mort. U. these circumstances, dans ces conditions. U. the terms of the treaty, aux termes du traité. U. his father's will, d'après le testament de son père. Look u. the word 'fire', cherchez au mot 'fire'. To be classified u. . . ., être classé parmi. . . . To be u. the necessity of . . ., être dans la nécessité de. . . . *S.a.* FIRE¹ 4, OBLIGATION, SAIL¹ 1 (*b*), SPELL¹ 2, WAY¹ 1. (*b*) To be u. s.o., être sous le commandement de qn. U. government control, assujetti au contrôle de l'État. *F:* To be u. the doctor, être entre les mains du médecin. (*c*) To be u. a violent emotion, être en proie à une violente émotion., 3. (*a*) U. repair, en (voie de) réparation. Patients u. treatment, malades en traitement. (*b*) *Agr:* Field u. corn, champ mis en blé. II. under, *adv.* 1. (Au-)dessous. As u., comme ci-dessous. *S.a.* DOWN³ I.2. 2. To keep s.o. u., tenir qn dans la soumission. *S.a.* KEEP UNDER. 3. (*In compounds*) Trop peu; insuffisamment. To underpay, mal rétribuer. III. under, *attrib. a. & comb.fm.* 1. De dessous; inférieur. Under-strata, couches inférieures. Underlip, lèvre inférieure. 2. Subalterne. Under-gardener, aide-jardinier *m.* 3. Insuffisant. Under-dose, dose *f* trop faible. 'under-de'veloped, *a.* 1. *Phot:* (Cliché) insuffisamment développé. 2. (Enfant) retardé. 3. (Pays) sous-développé, économiquement arriéré. 'under-em'ployment, *s.* Sous-emploi *m.* 'under-ex'posure, *s. Phot:* Sousexposition *f;* manque *m* de pose. 'under-garment, *s.* Sous-vêtement *m.* 'under-keeper, *s.* Garde-chasse *m* auxiliaire, *pl.* gardes-chasse(s). 'under-'nourished, *a.* Insuffisamment nourri; sous-alimenté. 'under-pants, *s.* Caleçon *m,* slip *m.* 'under-'ripe, *a.* Pas assez mûr. 'under-'secretary, *s.* Sous-secrétaire *mf.* Permanent u.-s., directeur général (d'un Ministère). 'under-'sized, *a.* D'une taille au-dessous de la moyenne. 'under-skirt, *s.* Jupon *m;* sous-jupe *f.* 'under-'staffed, *a.* The office is u.-s., le bureau manque de personnel. 'under-sub'scribed, *a. Fin:* (Emprunt) non couvert.

underbid ['ʌndə'bid], *v.tr.* (underbid; underbid(den)) 1. *Com:* Demander moins cher que (qn). 2. *Cards:* To u. one's hand, demander au-dessous de son jeu.

underbred ['ʌndə'bred], *a.* Mal appris; mal élevé.

underbrush ['ʌndəbrʌʃ], *s.* = UNDERGROWTH..

undercall ['ʌndə'kɔ:l], *v.tr. Cards:* = UNDERBID 2.

undercarriage ['ʌndəkæridʒ], *s.* 1. *Av:* (Retractable) u., train *m* d'atterrissage (escamotable). 2. *Aut:* Dessous *m* (de la voiture).

undercharge ['ʌndə'tʃɑːdʒ], *v.tr.* Ne pas faire payer assez à (qn).

underclothes ['ʌndəklouðz], *s.pl.*, **underclothing** ['ʌndəklouðiŋ], *s.* Vêtements *mpl* de dessous; linge *m* de corps; (*for women*) lingerie *f.* Set of u., parure *f.*

undercoat ['ʌndəkout], *s.* 1. Sous-poil *m* (d'un chien, etc.). 2. *Paint:* Couche *f* de fond.

undercurrent ['ʌndəkʌrənt], *s.* 1. Courant *m* de fond; (*in sea*) courant sous-marin. 2. U. of discontent, courant profond de mécontentement.

undercut¹ ['ʌndəkʌt], *s.* 1. *Cu:* Filet *m* (de bœuf). 2. *Box:* Coup *m* de bas en haut; undercut *m.*

undercut² ['ʌndə'kʌt], *v.tr.* (undercut; undercut; undercutting) 1. *Sculp:* Fouiller (une sculpture); creuser. 2. *Golf:* Couper (la balle). 3. (*a*) Faire des soumissions plus avantageuses que (qn). (*b*) Vendre moins cher que (qn).

underdog ['ʌndədɔg], *s.* To feel for the u., se pencher sur les souffrances du peuple. To plead for the u., plaider la cause des opprimés.

underdone ['ʌndə'dʌn], *a.* 1. Pas assez cuit. 2. Pas trop cuit; (bœuf) saignant.

underestimate¹ ['ʌndər'estimeit], *v.tr.* (*a*) Sous-estimer. *Artil:* To u. the range, apprécier court. (*b*) To u. the importance of . . ., faire trop peu de cas de . . .

underestimate², *s.* Sous-évaluation *f.*

underfeed ['ʌndə'fi:d], *v.tr.* (*p.t. & p.p.* underfed [-fed]) Nourrir insuffisamment, sous-alimenter; mal nourrir. **underfed**, *a.* Mal nourri; sous-alimenté. **underfeeding**, *s.* Sous-alimentation *f.*

underfelt ['ʌndəfelt], *s. Furn:* Assise *f* de feutre (pour tapis).

underfoot ['ʌndə'fut], *adv. See* FOOT¹ 1 (*c*).

undergo ['ʌndə'gou], *v.tr.* (underwent [-went]; undergone [-gɔn]) 1. (*a*) Passer par, subir (un changement). Undergoing repairs, en réparation. (*b*) Subir (une épreuve). To u. an operation, se soumettre à une intervention chirurgicale; *F:* être opéré. 2. Supporter (des souffrances); essuyer, éprouver (une perte).

undergraduate ['ʌndə'grædjuit], *s.* Étudiant, -ante (qui n'a pas encore ses diplômes).

underground ['ʌndə'graund]. 1. *adv.* (*a*) Sous terre. To work u., travailler sous (la) terre. To rise from u., surgir de dessous terre. (*b*) Secrètement; sous main. (*c*) *F:* To go u., prendre le maquis. 2. *a.* ['ʌndəgraund] (*a*) Qui est sous le sol; souterrain. U. dwelling, habitation sous terre. U. passage, passage souterrain. U. gallery, souterrain *m.* U. worker, *Min:* ouvrier du fond. (*b*) Clandestin. U. forces, armée clandestine. 3. *s.* The U. = le Métro.

undergrown ['ʌndəgroun], *a.* (*Of child*) Mal venu; chétif, -ive, rabougri.

undergrowth ['ʌndəgrouθ], *s. For:* Broussailles *fpl;* sous-bois *m.*

underhand ['ʌndə'hænd]. 1. *adv.* (*a*) *Ten:* (Servir) par en dessous. (*b*) (Agir) sous main, sournoisement. 2. *a.* ['ʌndəhand] (*a*) *Ten: etc:* U. service, service par en dessous. (*b*) Secret, -ète; (*of pers.*) sournois. U. dealings, menées clandestines. U. trick, sournoiserie *f.*

underhung ['ʌndə'hʌŋ], *a.* U. jaw, menton *m* prognathe; *F:* mention en galoche.

underlay ['ʌndəlei], *s.* 1. *Typ:* Hausse *f.* 2. *Furn:* Assise *f* de feutre (pour tapis).

underlie ['ʌndə'lai], *v.tr.* (underlay [-lei]; underlain [-lein]; underlying) 1. Être sous (qch.); être au-dessous de (qch.). 2. Être à la base de (qch.). **underlying**, *a.* 1. Au-dessous; (*of rock*) sous-jacent. 2. (Principe) fondamental, -aux. U. causes of an event, raisons profondes d'un événement.

underline ['ʌndə'lain], *v.tr.* Souligner.

underlinen ['ʌndə,linin], *s. A:* Linge *m* de corps, de dessous.

underling ['ʌndəliŋ], *s. Usu. Pej:* Subalterne *m;* subordonné, -ée, sous-ordre *m; F:* sous-fifre *m.*

undermanned ['ʌndə'mænd], *a.* A court de personnel. *Nau:* A court d'équipage.

undermentioned ['ʌndə'menʃ(ə)nd], *a.* Mentionné ci-dessous; sous-mentionné.

undermine ['ʌndə'main], *v.tr.* Miner, saper (une muraille); (*of river*) affouiller (les berges). To u. one's health, s'abîmer lentement la santé. **undermining**, *s.* Affouillement *m.*

undermost ['ʌndəmoust], *a.* Le plus bas, *f.* la plus basse; inférieur.

underneath ['ʌndə'ni:θ]. 1. *prep.* Au-dessous de; sous. From u. sth., de dessous qch. 2. *adv.* Au-dessous; dessous; par-dessous. 3. *a.* De dessous; inférieur.

undernourished ['ʌndə'nʌriʃt], *a. & s.* Sous-alimenté.

underpaid ['ʌndə'peid], *a.* Mal rétribué.

underpass ['ʌndəpɑːs], *s. Civ.E:* Passage inférieur.

underpin ['ʌndə'pin], *v.tr.* (underpinned) 1. Étayer; étançonner (un mur). 2. Reprendre en sous-œuvre (des fondations); rechausser. **underpinning**, *s.* 1. (*a*) Étayage *m,* étançonnement *m.* (*b*) Reprise *f* en sous-œuvre. 2. (*a*) Étais *mpl.* (*b*) Maçonnerie *f* en sous-œuvre.

underprivileged [ʌndə'privəlidʒd], *a.* Déshérité, défavorisé. *s.* The u., les économiquement faibles.

underproduction ['ʌndəprə'dʌkʃ(ə)n], *s.* Sous-production *f.*

underrate ['ʌndə'reit], *v.tr.* Mésestimer, sous-estimer (l'importance de qch.).

undersell ['ʌndə'sel], *v.tr.* (*p.t. & p.p.* undersold [-sould]) Vendre à meilleur marché, moins cher, que (qn).

undershirt ['ʌndəʃəːt], s. *U.S:* Gilet m de corps, *Fr.C:* camisole f.

undershoot[1] ['ʌndəˌʃuːt], s. *Av:* Présentation trop courte.

undershoot[2] ['ʌndəˌʃuːt], v.tr. *Av:* To u. (the runway), se présenter trop court (sur la piste).

undershot ['ʌndəʃət], a. *Hyd.E:* U. wheel, roue en dessous, à aubes. 2. = UNDERHUNG.

undersigned ['ʌndəˈsaind], a. & s. Soussigné, -ée. I, the u. . . ., je, soussigné. (. . .)

underslung ['ʌndəˈslʌŋ], a. (Ressort) sous l'essieu, surbaissé. U. car, voiture à châssis surbaissé.

undersold ['ʌndəˈsould]. *See* UNDERSELL.

understand ['ʌndəˈstænd], v.tr. (p.t. & p.p. understood [-stud]) 1. Comprendre. (a) I don't u. French, je ne comprends pas le français. To u. one's business, bien connaître son affaire. To u. business, s'entendre aux affaires. To u. horses, se, s'y, connaître en chevaux. Nobody has ever understood me, je suis un(e) incompris(e). To u. driving a car, s'entendre à conduire une auto. To u. sth., se rendre compte de qch. *Abs.* Now I u.! je comprends, j'y suis, maintenant! I am at a loss to u. it, je n'y comprends rien. I can't u. why . . ., je ne m'explique pas pourquoi. . . . That's easily understood, cela se comprend facilement. (b) To give s.o. to u. sth., donner à entendre qch. à qn. Am I to u. that . . .? ai-je bien compris que . . .? I. u. that he will consent, je crois savoir qu'il consentira. Now u. me, I am determined to . . ., sachez-le bien, je suis résolu à . . . 2. *Gram:* Sous-entendre (un mot). 3. v.i. To u. about sth., savoir ce qu'il faut faire à propos de qch. **understood**, a. 1. Compris. 2. Convenu. That is understood, cela va sans dire. 3. *Gram:* Sous-entendu. **understanding**[1], s. 1. Entendement m, appréhension f, compréhension f. To have reached the age of u., être arrivé à l'âge de discernement m. A person of good u., quelqu'un d'intelligent. It's beyond u., c'est à n'y rien comprendre. 2. (a) Accord m, entente f. Friendly u., entente cordiale. (b) Arrangement m. To have an u. with s.o., avoir un arrangement, être d'intelligence, avec qn. To come to an u. with s.o., s'accorder, s'entendre, avec qn. (c) On the u. that . . ., à condition que . . .; étant bien entendu que. . . **understanding**[2], a. An u. father, un père qui comprend, compréhensif.

understandable ['ʌndəˈstændəbl], a. Compréhensible. That is u., cela se comprend.

understate ['ʌndəˈsteit], v.tr. Minimiser (les faits).

understatement ['ʌndəˈsteitmənt], s. 1. Amoindrissement m, atténuation f (des faits). 2. Affirmation f qui reste au-dessous de la vérité, de la réalité.

understudy[1] ['ʌndəˌstʌdi], s. *Th:* Doublure f.

understudy[2], v.tr. Doubler (qn).

undertake [ˌʌndəˈteik], v.tr. (undertook [-tuk]; undertaken [-teik(ə)n]) 1. Entreprendre (un voyage). 2. (a) Se charger de, assumer (une tâche). (b) To u. to do sth., se charger de faire qch.; se faire fort de faire qch. **undertaking**, s. 1. (a) Entreprise f (de qch.). (b) Métier m d'entrepreneur de pompes funèbres. 2. Entreprise (commerciale). It is quite an u., c'est toute une affaire. 3. Engagement m, promesse f.

undertaker ['ʌndəˌteikər], s. Entrepreneur m de pompes funèbres.

undertone ['ʌndətoun], s. To speak in an u., parler bas; parler à demi-voix. An u. of discontent, un courant sourd de mécontentement.

undertook. *See* UNDERTAKE.

undertow ['ʌndətou], s. 1. Contre-marée f; courant m de fond. 2. Ressac m.

undervalue [ˌʌndəˈvæljuː], v.tr. 1. Sous-estimer, sous-évaluer. 2. Mésestimer, faire trop peu de cas de (qn).

underwater ['ʌndəˈwɔːtər], attrib. a. Sous-marin. U. fishing, pêche sous-marine.

underwear ['ʌndəwɛər], s. = UNDERCLOTHES.

underwent. *See* UNDERGO.

underwood ['ʌndəwud], s. Sous-bois m, broussailles fpl, taillis m.

underworld ['ʌndəwəːld], s. 1. (Les) enfers m. 2. (Les) bas-fonds de la société; *F:* le Milieu.

underwrite ['ʌndərait], v.tr. (underwrote [-rout]; underwritten [-ˌritn]) (a) *Fin:* Garantir, souscrire (une émission). (b) *Ins:* To u. a risk, souscrire un risque. **underwriting**, s. 1. *Fin:* Garantie f d'émission; souscription éventuelle à forfait. 2. (a) Souscription f (d'une police d'assurance). (b) Assurance f maritime.

underwriter ['ʌndəˌraitər], s. 1. *Fin:* Membre m d'un syndicat de garantie. The underwriters, le syndicat de garantie. 2. *Ins:* Assureur m; esp. assureur maritime.

undescribable ['ʌndisˈkraibəbl], a. Indescriptible.

undeserved ['ʌndiˈzəːvd], a. Immérité.

undeservedly ['ʌndiˈzəːvidli], adv. A tort; injustement.

undeserving ['ʌndiˈzəːviŋ], a. (a) Peu méritant; sans mérite. (b) U. of attention, indigne d'attention. U. case, cas peu intéressant.

undesigned ['ʌndiˈzaind], a. (Of action) Involontaire, non prémédité; (of result) imprévu.

undesirable ['ʌndiˈzaiərəbl], a. & s. Indésirable (mf), peu désirable; inopportun. U. alien, étranger indésirable.

undetected ['ʌndiˈtektid], a. 1. Qui a échappé à l'attention. (Of mistake) To pass u., passer inaperçu. 2. (Malfaiteur) insoupçonné.

undetermined ['ʌndiˈtəːmind], a. 1. (Of quantity) Indéterminé, incertain. 2. (Of question) Indécis. 3. (Of pers.) Irrésolu, indécis.

undeterred ['ʌndiˈtəːd], a. Non découragé, aucunement ébranlé (by, par).

undeveloped ['ʌndiˈveləpt], a. Non développé. U. land, terrains inexploités. Industry still u., industrie encore dans son enfance.

undeviating [ʌnˈdiːvieitiŋ], a. 1. (Cours, chemin) droit, direct. 2. Constant; (honnêteté) rigide.

undid. *See* UNDO.

undies ['ʌndiz], s.pl. *F:* Lingerie f, dessous mpl (de femme).

undigested ['ʌndiˈdʒestid], a. (Mets, ouvrage) mal digéré. U. knowledge, connaissances confuses, mal assimilées.

undignified [ʌnˈdignifaid], a. (a) Peu digne. (b) To be u., manquer de dignité, de tenue.

undiluted ['ʌndaiˈljuːtid], a. Non dilué; non étendu (d'eau); (vin) pur; (acide) concentré. To talk u. nonsense, divaguer.

undine ['ʌndiːn], s.f. *Myth:* Ondine.

undiplomatic ['ʌnˌdiplə'mætik], a. Peu diplomatique; peu politique, peu adroit.

undiscernible ['ʌndiˈsəːnəbl], a. Indiscernable.

undiscerning ['ʌndiˈsəːniŋ], a. (Esprit) sans discernement, peu pénétrant.

undischarged ['ʌndisˈtʃɑːdʒd], a. 1. *Jur:* U. bankrupt, failli non réhabilité. 2. U. debt, dette non acquittée. 3. (Devoir) inaccompli.

undisciplined [ʌnˈdisiplind], a. Indiscipliné.

undiscountable ['ʌndisˈkauntəbl], a. *Fin:* Inescomptable.

undiscovered [ˌʌndisˈkʌvəd, 'ʌn-], a. Non découvert; caché. Land at that time u., terre inconnue à cette époque.

undiscriminating ['ʌndisˈkrimineitiŋ], a. (Of pers.) Sans discernement; (of taste) peu averti. U. praise, éloges prodigués sans discernement.

undiscussed ['ʌndisˈkʌst], a. Indiscuté.

undisguised ['ʌndisˈgaizd], a. (Of voice) Non déguisé; (of feelings) non dissimulé. To show u. satisfaction, témoigner franchement sa satisfaction.

undismayed ['ʌndisˈmeid], a. Sans peur, sans terreur; aucunement ébranlé; *Lit:* impavide.

undisputed ['ʌndisˈpjuːtid], a. Incontesté, indisputé, incontroversé.

undistinguishable ['ʌndisˈtiŋgwiʃəbl], a. 1. Indiscernable (from, de). 2. Imperceptible; indistinct.

undistinguished ['ʌndisˈtiŋgwiʃt], a. Médiocre, banal, -als. An u. performance, une représentation tout à fait quelconque.

undisturbed ['ʌndisˈtəːbd], a. 1. (Of pers.) Tranquille; (of sleep, etc.) paisible. 2. (Of peace) Que rien ne vient troubler; (of the ground) qui n'a pas été remué. We found everything u., rien n'avait été dérangé.

undivided ['ʌndiˈvaidid], a. 1. Indivisé; entier. 2. Non partagé. Give me your u. attention, donnez-moi toute votre attention. 3. U. opinion, opinion unanime.

undo ['ʌn'duː], *v.tr.* (undid [-'did]; undone [-'dʌn]) 1. Détruire (une œuvre). To u. the mischief, réparer le mal. What is done cannot be undone, ce qui est fait est fait. 2. Défaire, dénouer (un nœud, ses cheveux). To u. one's dress, dégrafer, défaire, sa robe. 3. *O:* Perdre, ruiner (qn). undoing, *s.* 1. Action *f* de défaire. 2. Ruine *f*, perte *f*.

undone ['ʌn'dʌn]. I. *See* UNDO. II. undone, *a.* 1. (*a*) Défait. To come u., (*of button*) se défaire. My shoe has come u., le lacet de mon soulier est défait. (*b*) *O:* Ruiné; perdu. 2. Inaccompli; non accompli. To leave some work u., laisser du travail inachevé. To leave nothing u. which might help, ne rien négliger qui puisse être utile.

undoubted [ʌn'dautid], *a.* (Fait) indubitable, incontestable. -ly, *adv.* Indubitablement, assurément. U. he is wrong, sans aucun doute il a tort.

undreamt ['ʌn'dremt], *a.* U. of, (i) dont on ne s'aviserait jamais; insoupçonné; (ii) qui passe l'imagination.

undress[1] ['ʌn'dres], *s.* 1. *O:* (*For women*) Déshabillé *m*, négligé *m*. 2. *Mil: Navy:* U. (uniform), petite tenue.

undress[2] [ʌn'dres], *v.* (undressed ['ʌn'drest]) 1. *v.i & pr.* Se déshabiller, se dévêtir. 2. *v.tr.* Déshabiller, dévêtir.

undressed [ʌn'drest], *a.* 1. (*a*) Déshabillé, dévêtu. (*b*) En déshabillé; en négligé. 2. ['ʌn'drest] (*a*) Non préparé; brut. U. leather, cuir inapprêté. (*b*) *Agr:* (Terre) qui n'a reçu aucune façon. (*c*) U. wound, blessure non pansée.

undrinkable ['ʌn'driŋkəbl], *a.* Imbuvable, non potable.

undue ['ʌn'djuː], *a.* (*a*) U. influence, influence *f* illégitime; intimidation *f*; (*upon testator*) manœuvres *f* captatoires. (*b*) (*Of haste*) Exagéré, indu. U. optimism, optimisme excessif, peu justifié.

undulate ['ʌndjuleit]. 1. *v.tr.* Onduler. 2. *v.i.* Onduler, ondoyer. undulating, *a.* Onduleux, -euse; (*blé*) ondoyant. U. country, pays ondulé, vallonné.

undulation [ʌndju'leiʃ(ə)n], *s.* Ondulation *f*; accident *m* de terrain.

undulatory [ʌndju'leitəri], *a.* 1. Ondulatoire. 2. Ondulé, onduleux, -euse.

unduly [ʌn'djuːli], *adv.* 1. (*a*) (Réclamer) indûment. (*b*) Sans raison. 2. A l'excès, outre mesure. U. high price, prix exagéré.

undutiful ['ʌn'djuːtif(u)l], *a.* Qui ne remplit pas ses devoirs (filiaux, conjugaux).

undying [ʌn'daiiŋ], *a.* Immortel, -elle, impérissable.

unearned ['ʌn'əːnd], *a.* 1. (*Of reward*) Immérité. 2. Non gagné par le travail. U. income, rente(s) *f(pl.)*.

unearth ['ʌn'əːθ], *v.tr.* (*a*) Déterrer, exhumer. (*b*) To u. an old manuscript, déterrer, dénicher, un vieux manuscrit.

unearthly [ʌn'əːθli], *a.* (*a*) Qui n'est pas de ce monde; surnaturel. (*b*) U. pallor, pâleur mortelle. U. light, lueur sinistre, blafarde. (*c*) *F:* At an u. hour, à une heure indue. U. din, vacarme de tous les diables.

uneasiness [ʌn'iːzinis], *s.* 1. Gêne *f*, malaise *m*. 2. Inquiétude *f*.

uneasy [ʌn'iːzi], *a.* (*a*) Mal à l'aise; gêné. U. feeling, sentiment de malaise. (*b*) Inquiet, -ète; anxieux. To be u. in one's mind about . . ., avoir l'esprit inquiet au sujet de. . . . To pass an u. night, passer une nuit tourmentée. U. sleep, sommeil agité. (*c*) (*Of situation*) Incommode, gênant. -ily, *adv.* (*a*) D'un air gêné. (*b*) Avec inquiétude.

uneatable ['ʌn'iːtəbl], *a.* Immangeable.

uneconomic ['ʌniːkə'nɔmik], *a.* 1. Non économique. 2. (Travail, loyer) peu rémunérateur, non rentable.

uneconomical ['ʌniːkə'nɔmikl], *a.* (*a*) (*Pers.*) Peu économe, peu ménager. (*b*) (*Method, etc.*) Peu économique.

uneducated ['ʌn'edjukeitid], *a.* 1. (*Of pers.*) Sans instruction; ignorant. 2. (*Of pronunciation*) Vulgaire.

unemotional ['ʌni'mouʃən(ə)l], *a.* Peu émotif, -ive; peu impressionnable. -ally, *adv.* Avec impassibilité.

unemployable ['ʌnim'plɔiəbl], *a.* Inemployable.

unemployed ['ʌnim'plɔid], *a.* 1. (*Of pers.*) (*a*) Désœuvré. (*b*) *Ind:* Sans travail; sans emploi. The u., les chômeurs *m*, les sans-travail *m*. 2. (*Of capital*) Inemployé.

unemployment ['ʌnim'plɔimənt], *s. Ind:* Chômage *m* (involontaire); manque *m* de travail. U. fund, caisse *f* contre le chômage. U. benefit, allocation *f* de chômage.

unencumbered ['ʌnin'kʌmbəd], *a.* 1. Non encombré (by, with, de). 2. Non embarrassé (by, with, par). U. estate, propriété franche d'hypothèques.

unended ['ʌn'endid], *a.* Inachevé.

unending [ʌn'endiŋ], *a.* 1. Interminable. U. complaints, plaintes sans fin, sempiternelles. 2. Éternel, -elle.

unendurable ['ʌnin'djuərəbl], *a.* Insupportable, intolérable.

un-English ['ʌn'iŋgliʃ], *a.* Peu anglais; contraire à l'esprit anglais.

unenlightened [ʌnin'laitənd], *a.* Ignorant.

unenterprising ['ʌn'entəpraiziŋ], *a.* Peu entreprenant; (*homme*) mou.

unenviable [ʌn'enviəbl], *a.* Peu enviable.

unequal [ʌn'iːkwəl], *a.* 1. (*a*) Inégal, -aux. (*b*) To be u. to the task, ne pas être à la hauteur de sa tâche. To be u. to doing sth., ne pas être de force à faire qch. 2. Inégal, irrégulier, -ière. -ally, *adv.* Inégalement.

unequalled [ʌn'iːkwəld], *a.* Inégalé; sans égal, -aux.

unequivocal [ʌni'kwivək(ə)l], *a.* (*Of language*) Clair, net, *f.* nette; sans équivoque. -ally, *adv.* Sans équivoque.

unerring [ʌn'əːriŋ], *a.* (Jugement) infaillible, sûr. To fire with u. aim, ne jamais manquer le but. -ly, *adv.* Infailliblement, sûrement.

Unesco [juː'neskou]. *Pr.n.* Unesco *f*.

unessential [ʌni'senʃ(ə)l], *a.* Non essentiel; peu important. *s.* The unessential(s), l'accessoire *m*.

unethical [ʌn'eθikl], *a.* Qui manque de probité.

uneven [ʌn'iːv(ə)n], *a.* 1. Inégal, -aux. (*a*) Rugueux, -euse; (chemin) raboteux. (*b*) (Terrain) accidenté; (contour) anfractueux. (*c*) Irrégulier. U. temper, humeur inégale. 2. (Nombre) impair. -ly, *adv.* 1. Inégalement. 2. Irrégulièrement.

unevenness [ʌn'iːv(ə)nnis], *s.* Inégalité *f*. (*a*) Caractère raboteux (d'une route). (*b*) Irrégularité *f* (du pouls).

uneventful ['ʌni'ventf(u)l], *a.* Sans incidents. U. life, vie calme, unie, peu mouvementée.

unexampled ['ʌnig'zɑːmpld], *a.* Sans exemple, sans égal, sans pareil; unique.

unexcelled ['ʌnik'seld] *a.* Qui n'a jamais été surpassé.

unexceptionable ['ʌnik'sepʃ(ə)nəbl], *a.* Irréprochable; (conduite) inattaquable; (témoignage) irrécusable. U. person, personne tout à fait bien.

unexcitable ['ʌnik'saitəbl], *a. Physiol: etc:* Inexcitable; (*of pers*). peu émotionnable.

unexciting ['ʌnik'saitiŋ], *a.* Insipide; peu passionnant. U. life, vie monotone.

unexpected ['ʌnik'spektid], *a.* (Visiteur) inattendu; (résultat) imprévu; (secours, etc.) imprévu. U. meeting, rencontre inopinée. *s.* The u., l'imprévu *m*. -ly, *adv.* De manière inattendue; inopinément.

unexpired ['ʌnik'spaiəd], *a.* (Bail) non expiré; (passeport, billet) non périmé, encore valable.

unexplained ['ʌniks'pleind], *a.* Inexpliqué; (mystère) inéclairci.

unexploded ['ʌniks'ploudid], *a.* (Obus) non éclaté.

unexplored ['ʌniks'plɔːd], *a.* (Pays) inexploré, encore inconnu.

unexposed ['ʌniks'pouzd], *a.* 1. *Phot:* (Film) vierge. 2. U. crime, crime caché.

unexpurgated ['ʌn'ekspəːgeitid], *a.* (Livre) non expurgé. U. edition, édition intégrale.

unfailing ['ʌn'feiliŋ], *a.* 1. Qui ne se dément pas; (moyen) infaillible, sûr. U. good humour, bonne humeur inaltérable. 2. (Source) intarissable, inépuisable (of, de). -ly, *adv.* 1. Infailliblement. 2. Intarissablement.

unfair ['ʌn'fɛər], *a.* 1. (*Of pers.*) Injuste; peu équitable. To be u. (to s.o.), défavoriser (qn). It's u.! ce n'est pas juste! 2. (*a*) Inéquitable. U. price, prix déraisonnable. (*b*) U. play, jeu déloyal. -ly, *adv.* 1. Injustement; inéquitablement. 2. To act u., commettre une déloyauté.

unfairness ['ʌn'fɛənis], *s.* 1. Injustice *f*; partialité *f*. 2. Déloyauté *f*; mauvaise foi.

unfaithful [ʌn'feiθful], *a.* Infidèle. (*a*) Déloyal, -aux (to, envers). To be u. to one's wife, tromper sa femme. (*b*) (Compte rendu) inexact.

unfaithfulness [ʌn'feiθfulnis], *s.* Infidélité *f.* 1. Déloyauté *f* (to, envers). 2. Inexactitude *f.*

unfaltering ['ʌn'fɔ:ltəriŋ], *a.* U. voice, voix ferme, résolue. U. steps, pas assurés.

unfamiliar ['ʌnfə'miljər], *a.* 1. Peu familier, -ière. U. face, visage étranger, inconnu. 2. (*Of pers.*) To be u. with sth., être peu familier avec qch. To be u. with the customs, ne pas être au courant des usages.

unfamiliarity ['ʌnfə,mili'æriti], *s.* 1. Nouveauté (d'un lieu). 2. Ignorance *f* (with, de).

unfashionable ['ʌn'fæʃ(ə)nəbl], *a.* (Vêtement) démodé, qui n'est pas de mode.

unfasten ['ʌn'fɑ:sn], *v.tr.* 1. To u. sth. from sth., détacher qch. de qch. 2. Défaire (un vêtement); ouvrir, déverrouiller (la porte).

unfathomable [ʌn'fæðəməbl], *a.* (Abîme) insondable; (mystère) impénétrable.

unfathomed ['ʌn'fæðəmd], *a.* Insondé. U. depths, profondeurs inexplorées.

unfavourable [ʌn'feiv(ə)rəbl], *a.* Défavorable, peu favorable; (vent) impropice; (*of terms*) désavantageux (to, à). U. criticism, critique *f* adverse.

unfeeling [ʌn'fi:liŋ], *a.* Insensible, impitoyable. U. heart, cœur sec, indifférent. **-ly,** *adv.* Sans pitié; froidement.

unfeigned ['ʌn'feind], *a.* Sincère; non simulé.

unfeignedly [ʌn'feinidli], *adv.* Sincèrement; vraiment.

unfermentable ['ʌnfə'mentəbl], *a.* Infermentescible.

unfermented ['ʌnfə'mentid], *a.* Non fermenté.

unfettered ['ʌn'fetəd], *a.* Libre de tous liens; (cheval) sans entraves.

unfilial ['ʌn'filjəl], *a.* Indigne d'un fils, d'une fille.

unfinished ['ʌn'finiʃt], *a.* 1. Inachevé; (ouvrage) imparfait. 2. (*a*) *Ind:* Brut; non façonné. (*b*) Qui manque de fini.

unfit ['ʌn'fit], *a.* 1. (*a*) Impropre, peu propre (for, à). U. for human consumption, impropre à la consommation. Story u. for publication, histoire qu'on ne peut décemment publier. Road u. for motor traffic, chemin impraticable aux automobiles. (*b*) U. for military service, inapte au service (militaire). U. to rule, indigne de régner. 2. (*a*) To be u., être en mauvaise santé. (*b*) Faible de constitution. *Mil:* To be discharged as u., être réformé.

unfitness ['ʌn'fitnis], *s.* 1. Manque *m* d'à-propos (d'une observation). U. for sth., inaptitude *f* à qch. 3. Mauvaise santé.

unfitted ['ʌn'fitid], *a.* 1. Impropre (for sth., to do sth., à qch., à faire qch.); inapte (à faire qch.). 2. Non équipé (with, de).

unfitting ['ʌn'fitiŋ], *a.* Peu convenable; peu séant; mal à propos; déplacé.

unfix ['ʌn'fiks], *v.tr.* Détacher, défaire. *Mil:* To u. bayonets, remettre la baïonnette.

unflagging [ʌn'flægiŋ], *a.* (Courage, vigueur) inlassable, infatigable; (intérêt) soutenu.

unflattering ['ʌn'flætəriŋ], *a.* Peu flatteur, -euse.

unfledged ['ʌn'fledʒd], *a.* 1. (Oiseau) sans plumes. 2. Sans expérience de la vie; jeune.

unflinching [ʌn'flin(t)ʃiŋ], *a.* 1. Qui ne recule pas; qui ne bronche pas. 2. Stoïque; impassible. **-ly,** *adv.* 1. Sans reculer; sans broncher. 2. Stoïquement.

unfold¹ [ʌn'fould]. 1. *v.tr.* (*a*) Déplier (un journal). (*b*) Dérouler, déployer. (*c*) Exposer (une doctrine, un projet). 2. *v.i. & pr.* Se déployer, se dérouler. The landscape unfolds before us, le paysage se déroule devant nous.

unfold², *v.tr.* Déparquer (des moutons).

unforbearing ['ʌnfɔ:'bɛəriŋ], *a.* Peu endurant; impatient, intolérant; sans indulgence.

unforced ['ʌn'fɔ:st], *a.* Naturel, -elle, spontané. U. laugh, rire franc.

unfordable ['ʌn'fɔ:dəbl], *a.* Impassable à gué.

unforeseeable ['ʌnfɔ:'si:əbl], *a.* Imprévisible.

unforeseen ['ʌnfɔ:'si:n], *a.* Imprévu, inattendu; inopiné. U. circumstances, force majeure.

unforgettable ['ʌnfə'getəbl], *a.* Inoubliable.

unforgivable ['ʌnfə'givəbl], *a.* Impardonnable.

unforgiving ['ʌnfə'giviŋ], *a.* Implacable, rancunier,-ière.

unforgotten ['ʌnfə'gɔtn], *a.* Inoublié.

unformulated ['ʌn'fɔ:mjuleitid], *a.* Informulé.

unfortified ['ʌn'fɔ:tifaid], *a.* Sans fortifications. U. town, ville ouverte.

unfortunate [ʌn'fɔ:tʃ(ə)nit]. 1. *a.* (*a*) Malheureux, -euse infortuné. To be u., avoir de la malchance. (*b*) (Événement) malencontreux; (erreur) regrettable. It is u. that . . ., il est fâcheux, malheureux, que + *sub.* How u.! quel malheur! quel dommage! 2. *s.* Malheureux, -euse. **-ly,** *adv.* Malheureusement; par malheur.

unfounded ['ʌn'faundid], *a.* (Accusation) sans fondement, sans base. U. rumour, bruit dénué de fondement. U. supposition, supposition gratuite.

unfreeze ['ʌn'fri:z], *v.tr.* Dégeler. *Fin:* Débloquer.

unfrequented ['ʌnfri'kwentid], *a.* Peu fréquenté. U. spot, endroit écarté, solitaire.

unfriendliness ['ʌn'frendlinis], *s.* Inimitié *f* (towards, pour); hostilité *f* (towards, contre).

unfriendly ['ʌn'frendli], *a.* Peu amical, -aux. U. action, acte hostile. To be u. towards s.o., être mal disposé pour, envers, qn.

unfrock ['ʌn'frɔk], *v.tr.* Défroquer (un prêtre).

unfruitful ['ʌn'fru:tf(u)l], *a.* 1. Stérile, infécond. 2. U. labour, travail improductif.

unfulfilled ['ʌnful'fild], *a.* (*a*) U. prophecy, prophétie irréalisée. (*b*) (Désir) non satisfait, inassouvi, inexaucé. (*c*) U. promise, promesse non tenue.

unfurl ['ʌn'fɔ:l], *v.tr.* *Nau:* Déferler (une · voile); déployer (un drapeau).

unfurnished ['ʌn'fɔ:niʃt], *a.* 1. Non fourni, dépourvu (with, de). 2. (Appartement) non meublé.

ungainly [ʌn'geinli], *a.* Gauche, lourd; dégingandé.

ungallant [ʌn'gælənt, 'ʌngə'lænt], *a.* Peu galant; indigne d'un galant homme.

ungenerous ['ʌn'dʒen(ə)rəs], *a.* Peu généreux, -euse.

ungentlemanly ['ʌn'dʒentlmənli], *a.* Pas comme il faut; (homme) mal élevé. U. conduct, conduite indélicate. It is u. to . . ., il n'est pas poli de. . . .

ungetattable ['ʌnget'ætəbl], *a.* *F:* Inaccessible.

unglazed ['ʌn'gleizd], *a.* 1. (*Of window*) Non vitré; sans vitres. 2. (*a*) (Fil, papier) non glacé, non lustré. *Phot:* U. paper, papier mat. (*b*) *Cer:* Non verni. U. china, biscuit *m.*

ungodliness [ʌn'gɔdlinis], *s.* Impiété *f.*

ungodly [ʌn'gɔdli], *a.* 1. Impie. *F:* They were making an u. row, ils faisaient un bruit de tous les diables.

ungovernable [ʌn'gʌv(ə)nəbl], *a.* 1. Ingouvernable. 2. (Désir) irrésistible. U. passion, passion effrénée, déréglée.

ungraceful ['ʌn'greisf(u)l], *a.* Disgracieux, -euse; gauche. **-fully,** *adv.* Sans grâce; gauchement.

ungracious [ʌn'greiʃəs], *a.* Malgracieux, -euse; peu aimable. It would be u. to refuse, il serait de mauvaise grâce de refuser. **-ly,** *adv.* De mauvaise grâce.

ungraciousness ['ʌn'greiʃəsnis], *s.* Mauvaise grâce; manque *m* d'amabilité.

ungrammatical ['ʌngrə'mætik(ə)l], *a.* Peu grammatical, -aux; incorrect. **-ally,** *adv.* Incorrectement.

ungrateful [ʌn'greitf(u)l], *a.* Ingrat. (*a*) Peu reconnaissant. (*b*) U. soil, sol ingrat. **-fully,** *adv.* Avec ingratitude.

ungratefulness ['ʌn'greitf(u)lnis], *s.* Ingratitude *f.*

ungratified ['ʌn'grætifaid], *a.* (Désir) inassouvi, non satisfait; (vœu) inexaucé.

ungrounded ['ʌn'graundid], *a.* = UNFOUNDED.

ungrudging ['ʌn'grʌdʒiŋ], *a.* 1. Donné de bon cœur. To give s.o. u. praise, ne pas ménager ses louanges à qn. 2. Libéral, -aux; généreux, -euse. **-ly,** *adv.* De bonne grâce; libéralement.

unguarded ['ʌn'gɑ:did], *a.* 1. (*a*) Non gardé; (ville) sans défense. (*b*) *Cards:* (Roi) sec, non gardé. 2. (*Of pers.*) Qui n'est pas sur ses gardes; (*of speech*) inconsidéré. In an u. moment, dans un moment d'inattention. **-ly,** *adv.* Inconsidérément.

unguent ['ʌngwənt], *s.* Onguent *m.*

ungulate ['ʌngjuleit], *a. & s.* *Z:* Ongulé (*m*). *s.pl.* The Ungulata, les ongulés.

unhallowed [ʌn'hæloud], *a.* 1. Non béni, profane. 2· (*Of joy, etc.*) Impie.

unhampered ['ʌn'hæmpəd], *a.* Libre (de ses mouvements). U. by rules, sans être gêné, qui n'est pas gêné, par des règles.

unhand [ʌn'hænd], *v.tr.* *A. & Lit:* Lâcher.

unhandy ['ʌn'hændi], *a.* 1. (*Of pers.*) Maladroit, gauche. 2. (Outil) peu maniable, malcommode.

unhanged ['ʌn'hæŋd], *a.* Non pendu. **One of the greatest rogues u.,** un vrai gibier de potence.

unhappiness [ʌn'hæpinis], *s.* 1. Chagrin *m*; infélicité *f*; soucis *mpl.* 2. Inopportunité *f* (d'une expression).

unhappy [ʌn'hæpi], *a.* 1. Malheureux, -euse, triste; infortuné. **To make s.o. u.,** causer du chagrin à qn. **To be u. about leaving s.o.,** avoir du chagrin de, à, quitter qn. 2. Mal inspiré; peu heureux, -euse. **-ily,** *adv.* (*a*) Malheureusement; par malchance. (*b*) Tristement. **To live u. together,** faire mauvais ménage.

unharmed [ʌn'hɑ:md], *a.* Sain et sauf; indemne.

unharness [ʌn'hɑ:nis], *v.tr.* (*a*) Déharnacher (un cheval). (*b*) Dételer (un cheval).

unhealthiness [ʌn'helθinis], *s.* 1. Insalubrité *f* (du climat). 2. (*a*) Mauvaise santé; état maladif. (*b*) **U. of mind,** esprit malsain; morbidité *f* d'esprit.

unhealthy [ʌn'helθi], *a.* 1. Malsain, insalubre. 2. (*a*) (*Of pers.*) Maladif, -ive. **U. complexion,** visage terreux. (*b*) **U. influence,** influence malsaine. **U. curiosity,** curiosité morbide.

unheard [ʌn'hə:d], *a.* 1. **To condemn s.o. u.,** condamner qn sans l'entendre. 2. **U. of,** (i) inouï; (ii) (auteur) inconnu, ignoré.

unheeded [ʌn'hi:did], *a.* (*Of warning*) Négligé, dédaigné. **To pass u.,** passer inaperçu.

unheeding [ʌn'hi:diŋ], *a.* 1. Insouciant, distrait. 2. Inattentif, -ive (of, à); insouciant (of, de).

unhelped [ʌn'helpt], *a.* Sans aide, sans secours. **To do sth. u.,** faire qch. tout seul.

unhelpful [ʌn'helpf(ə)l], *a.* (Critique, etc.) peu utile; (conseil) vain; (personne) peu secourable. **Don't be so u.!** tâche donc un peu de nous aider!

unhesitating [ʌn'heziteitiŋ], *a.* Qui n'hésite pas; ferme, résolu. **U. reply,** réponse faite sans hésitation; réponse prompte, du tac au tac. **-ly,** *adv.* Sans hésiter.

unhindered [ʌn'hindəd], *a.* Sans encombre, sans obstacle, sans empêchement; librement.

unhinge [ʌn'hindʒ], *v.tr.* 1. Enlever (une porte) de ses gonds. 2. Ébranler, détraquer (l'esprit). **His mind is unhinged,** il a le cerveau détraqué.

unholy [ʌn'houli], *a.* 1. Profane. **U. desires,** convoitises *f.* 2. *F:* **U. muddle,** désordre invraisemblable, affreux.

unhonoured [ʌn'ɔnəd], *a.* Sans être honoré; qui n'est pas honoré; dédaigné.

unhook [ʌn'huk], *v.tr.* (*a*) Décrocher. (*b*) Dégrafer (un vêtement).

unhoped [ʌn'houpt], *a.* **U. for,** inespéré.

unhorse [ʌn'hɔ:s], *v.tr.* Désarçonner, démonter (un cavalier). **To be unhorsed,** vider les arçons, les étriers.

unhurt [ʌn'hə:t], *a.* 1. (*Of pers.*) Sans mal; indemne. **To escape u.,** s'en tirer sans aucun mal; s'en tirer sain et sauf. 2. (*Of thg*) Intact.

Uniat(e) ['ju:nieit], *s. & a. Ecc:* Uniate (*m*).

unicellular ['ju:ni'seljulər], *a.* Unicellulaire.

unicorn ['ju:nikɔ:n], *s.* (*a*) *Myth:* Licorne *f.* (*b*) *Z:* Sea-u., licorne de mer.

unidentified [ʌnai'dentifaid], *a.* Non identifié.

unidirectional ['ju:nidai'rekʃən(ə)l, -di-], *a. El:* (Courant) continu, redressé

unification [ju:nifi'keiʃ(ə)n], *s.* Unification *f.*

uniform ['ju:nifɔ:m]. 1. *a.* Uniforme. **U. temperature,** température constante. **U. velocity,** vitesse uniforme. 2. *s.* (*a*) Uniforme *m.* **Field-service u.,** tenue *f* de campagne. **Full-dress u.,** tenue *f* numéro un. **In u.,** en uniforme. **In full(-dress) u.,** en grande tenue. (*b*) Costume *m* (d'infirmière, etc.). **-ly,** *adv.* Uniformément.

uniformity [ju:ni'fɔ:miti], *s.* 1. Uniformité *f*, unité *f* (de style). (*b*) Régularité *f* (de fonctionnement).

unify ['ju:nifai], *v.tr.* Unifier.

unilateral ['ju:ni'læt(ə)rəl], *a.* Unilatéral, -aux.

unimaginable [ʌni'mædʒinəbl], *a.* Inimaginable.

unimaginative [ʌni'mædʒinətiv], *a.* Dénué d'imagination; peu imaginatif, -ive.

unimpaired [ʌnim'pɛəd], *a.* Non affaibli; inaltéré. **U. health,** santé non altérée; santé intacte. **U. strength,** forces non diminuées. **With faculties u.,** en possession de toutes ses facultés.

unimpassioned [ʌnim'pæʃ(ə)nd], *a.* Sans passion; tranquille. **U. speech,** discours mesuré.

unimpeachable [ʌnim'pi:tʃəbl], *a.* (*a*) Incontestable. **I have it from an u. source,** je le tiens de source sûre. (*b*) (Témoignage) inattaquable, irrécusable.

unimpeded [ʌnim'pi:did], *a.* Libre; aucunement entravé; sans empêchement.

unimportant [ʌnim'pɔ:t(ə)nt], *a.* Sans importance; peu important. **It is quite u.,** cela ne tire pas à conséquence.

unimpressed [ʌnim'prest], *a.* **I was u. by his speech,** son discours m'a laissé froid.

unimpressive [ʌnim'presiv], *a.* Peu émouvant; (discours) terne.

uninformed [ʌnin'fɔ:md], *a.* 1. **To be u. on a subject,** ne pas connaître un sujet. 2. (Homme) ignorant; (esprit) inculte.

uninhabitable [ʌnin'hæbitəbl], *a.* Inhabitable.

uninhabited [ʌnin'hæbitid], *a.* Inhabité, désert.

uninitiated [ʌni'niʃieitid], *a.* Non initié (in, dans). *s.* **The u.,** les profanes *m.*

uninjured [ʌn'indʒəd], *a.* 1. (*Of pers.*) Sain et sauf; sans mal; indemne. 2. (*Of thg*) Intact; sans dommage.

uninspired [ʌnin'spaiəd], *a.* Sans inspiration; (style) banal, qui rampe.

uninsured [ʌnin'ʃuəd], *a.* Non assuré (**against,** contre).

unintelligent [ʌnin'telidʒənt], *a.* Inintelligent; à l'esprit borné.

unintelligible [ʌnin'telidʒəbl], *a.* Inintelligible. **-ibly,** *adv.* D'une manière peu intelligible.

unintelligibility ['ʌnin,telidʒə'biliti], *s.* Inintelligibilité *f.*

unintentional ['ʌnin'tenʃən(ə)l], *a.* Involontaire; fait sans intention. **-ally,** *adv.* Involontairement; sans le vouloir; intentionnellement.

uninterested ['ʌn'intristid], *a.* Non intéressé; indifférent.

uninteresting ['ʌn'intristiŋ], *a.* Peu intéressant; sans intérêt; inintéressant.

uninterrupted ['ʌnintə'rʌptid], *a.* 1. Ininterrompu. 2. Continu. **U. correspondence,** correspondance suivie. **-ly,** *adv.* Sans interruption.

uninvited ['ʌnin'vaitid], *a.* Sans être invité. **U. guest,** hôte inattendu; *F:* resquilleur, -euse.

uninviting ['ʌnin'vaitiŋ], *a.* (*Of appearance*) Peu attrayant; peu engageant; (*of food*) peu appétissant.

union ['ju:njən], *s.* 1. Union *f.* (*a*) (*Marriage*) Well-assorted u., union bien assortie. (*b*) Concorde *f*, harmonie *f.* 2. (*a*) **The (American) U.,** les États-Unis. **Customs u.,** union douanière. (*b*) = TRADE-UNION. **U. regulations,** règles syndicales. **Non u. men,** ouvriers non syndiqués. (*c*) *Adm: A:* **U. workhouse,** *F:* **U.,** asile *m* des pauvres. 3. (*a*) Soudure *f* (des os); raccordement *m* (de fils). (*b*) *Mec.E: etc:* **U.(-joint),** raccord *m* "Union." **'Union 'Jack,** *s.* Le pavillon britannique.

unionist ['ju:njənist], *s.* 1. *Pol:* Unioniste *mf.* 2. *Ind:* = TRADE-UNIONIST.

uniparous [ju:'nipərəs], *a. Biol:* Unipare.

unipolar ['ju:ni'poulər], *a. El:* Unipolaire; (lampe) à plot central.

unique [ju:'ni:k], *a.* Unique.

unisexed ['ju:ni'sekst], **unisexual** ['ju:ni'seksjuəl], *a. Biol:* Unisexué, unisexuel, -elle.

unison ['ju:niz(ə)n, -s(ə)n], *s.* 1. *Ph: Mus:* Unisson *m.* **In u.,** à l'unisson (**with,** de). 2. **To act in u. with s.o.,** agir de concert avec qn.

unissued [ʌn'isju:d], *a. Fin:* **U. shares,** actions non encore émises; actions à la souche.

unit ['ju:nit], *s.* 1. Unité *f.* *Com:* **U. price,** prix unitaire. *Fin:* **U. trust,** société *f* de gestion de portefeuille. 2. (*a*) Unité (de longueur, etc.). **Standard u.,** module *m.* (*b*) *Mil:* Self-contained u., unité organique. (*c*) *Mec.E:* Élément *m*, bloc *m.* **Motor u.,** bloc moteur. **U. furniture,** mobilier *m* par éléments. **Kitchen u.,** bloc cuisine. *Cin:* **Sound u.,** bloc sonore. (*d*) *Rail:* **Electric multiple u.,** électrotrain *m.*

Unitarian [ju:ni'tɛəriən], *a. & s. Rel.H:* Unita(i)rien.

unite [ju:'nait]. 1. *v.tr.* (*a*) Unir (une chose à une autre). *Surg:* **To u. a wound,** suturer une blessure. (*b*) Mettre (les gens) d'accord; unifier (un parti). 2. *v.i.* (*a*) S'unir; se joindre (**with,** à). (*b*) (*Of companies*) S'amalgamer; (*of states*) se confédérer. *Ch:* (*Of atoms*) S'unir, se combiner.

To u. in doing sth., se mettre d'accord pour faire qch.
Pol: To u. against a party, faire bloc contre un parti.
united, *a.* Uni, réuni. U. efforts, efforts conjugués.
To present a u. front, faire front unique. U. we stand,
divided we fall, l'union fait la force. The U. Kingdom,
le Royaume-Uni. The U. States (of America), les
États-Unis (d'Amérique).

unity ['juːniti], *s.* Unité *f.* 1. *Mth:* To reduce a coefficient to u., réduire un coefficient à l'unité. 2.
Concorde *f*, accord *m.* 3. *Lit:* The dramatic unities,
les unités dramatiques. U. of place, unité de lieu.

univalent ['juːniˈveilənt], *a.* *Ch:* Univalent, monovalent.

universal [ˌjuːniˈvɔːs(ə)l]. 1. *a.* Universel. He is a
u. favourite, tout le monde l'aime. *S.a.* JOINT[1] 1. 2.
s. Log: Proposition universelle. -ally, *adv.* Universellement.

universe ['juːnivəːs], *s.* Univers *m.* The wonders of the
u., les merveilles de la création.

university [ˌjuːniˈvəːs(i)ti], *s.* Université *f.* To have
had a u. education, avoir fait des études supérieures.
U. professor, professeur de faculté. U. town, ville
universitaire.

unjust ['ʌnˈdʒʌst], *a.* Injuste (to, envers, avec, pour).
My suspicions were u., mes soupçons étaient mal
fondés. -ly, *adv.* Injustement.

unjustifiable [ʌnˈdʒʌstifaiəbl], *a.* Injustifiable, inexcusable.

unjustified [ʌnˈdʒʌstifaid], *a.* Non justifié; (of verdict)
non motivé.

unkempt ['ʌnˈkem(p)t], *a.* 1. (Of hair) Mal peigné;
(of appearance) dépeigné, hirsute. 2. (Of garden, etc.)
Peu soigné; mal tenu.

unkind ['ʌnˈkaind], *a.* (i) Dur; cruel; (ii) peu aimable.
U. fate, sort cruel. That's very u. of him, c'est peu
aimable de sa part. Her aunt is u. to her, sa tante la
traite mal. He was u. enough to . . ., il a eu la
méchanceté de. . . . -ly[1], *adv.* (i) Méchamment,
durement; (ii) sans bienveillance. Don't take it u.
if . . ., ne le prenez pas en mauvaise part si. . . .

unkindly[2] [ʌnˈkaindli], *a.* 1. Peu aimable, peu bienveillant. 2. (Temps) peu favorable; (climat) rude.

unkindness [ʌnˈkain(d)nis], *s.* Méchanceté *f*; rudesse
f (du climat). 2. Manque *m* de bienveillance.

unknot ['ʌnˈnɔt], *v.tr.* (unknotted) Dénouer.

unknowable ['ʌnˈnouəbl], *a.* Inconnaissable.

unknowing ['ʌnˈnouiŋ], *a.* Ignorant (of, de). -ly, *adv.*
Inconsciemment; sans le savoir.

unknown ['ʌnˈnoun]. 1. *a.* (a) Inconnu (to, à, de);
ignoré (to, de). U. writer, écrivain obscur. *adv.* He
did it u. to me, il l'a fait à mon insu. (b) *Mth:* U.
quantity, inconnue *f.* 2. *s.* (a) (Pers.) Inconnu, -ue.
(b) *Mth:* Inconnue *f.* (c) The u., l'inconnu.

unlace ['ʌnˈleis], *v.tr.* Délacer, défaire (ses souliers,
etc.).

unladen ['ʌnˈleidn], *a.* *Nau:* A vide.

unladylike ['ʌnˈleidilaik], *a.* Indigne d'une femme bien
élevée; peu distingué.

unlaid ['ʌnˈleid], *a.* U. ghost, esprit non exorcisé.
Carpets still u., tapis pas encore posés.

unlatch ['ʌnˈlætʃ], *v.tr.* Ouvrir (le loquet).

unlawful [ʌnˈlɔːful], *a.* (a) Illégal, -aux. *S.a.* ASSEMBLY
1. (b) (Moyen) illicite. -fully, *adv.* (a) Illégalement.
(b) Illicitement.

unlearned ['ʌnˈləːnid], *a.* 1. Ignorant; illettré. 2.
[ʌnˈləːnd] *a.* Peu versé (in, dans). (b) To leave a
lesson u., ne pas apprendre une leçon.

unleash ['ʌnˈliːʃ], *v.tr.* Lâcher, découpler (des chiens).

unleavened ['ʌnˈlev(ə)nd], *a.* (Pain) sans levain, azyme.
Jew.Rel: The feast of u. bread, la fête des azymes.

unless [ʌnˈles], *conj.* A moins que + *sub.* U. it be
you . . ., à moins que ce ne soit vous. . . . You will
be late u. you start at once, vous arriverez trop tard
à moins de partir immédiatement. U. I am mistaken . . ., si je ne me trompe (pas). . . . U. I hear
to the contrary, à moins d'avis contraire.

unlettered [ʌnˈletəd], *a.* Peu lettré; illettré.

unlicensed [ʌnˈlaisənst], *a.* (a) Non autorisé; illicite.
(b) Sans patente. U. broker, courtier marron. U.
hotel, hôtel *m* où la vente des boissons alcooliques
n'est pas autorisée.

unlike ['ʌnˈlaik], *a.* Différent, dissemblable. (a) *Mth:*
U. quantities, quantités dissemblables. (b) U. sth.,

différent de qch. Portrait quite u. the sitter, portrait
peu ressemblant. Not u. s.o., assez ressemblant à qn.
He, u. his father . . ., lui, à la différence de son
père. . . . (c) That was very u. him! je ne le reconnais
pas là!

unlik(e)able [ʌnˈlaikəbl], *a.* Peu sympathique.

unlikelihood [ʌnˈlaiklihud], unlikeliness [ʌnˈlaiklinis]
s. Invraisemblance *f*, improbabilité *f.*

unlikely [ʌnˈlaikli], *a.* 1. (a) Invraisemblable; peu
probable. Most u., très peu probable. It is not at all
u. that . . ., il se pourrait bien que + *sub.* (b) He is
u. to come, il est peu probable qu'il vienne. 2. The
most u. man to do such a thing, l'homme le moins fait
pour agir de la sorte.

unlimited [ʌnˈlimitid], *a.* Illimité; sans bornes.

unload [ʌnˈloud], *v.tr.* 1. (a) Décharger (un bateau,
des marchandises). *Mil. Av:* Lâcher (des bombes).
Abs. Décharger (un camion, un bateau). (b) *St.
Exch:* To u. stock on the market, se décharger d'un
paquet d'actions. 2. Enlever la charge; décharger
(un fusil). unloading, *s.* Déchargement *m.*

unloaded [ʌnˈloudid], *a.* 1. (a) Déchargé. (b) (Fusil)
désarmé. 2. (a) Non chargé. (b) (Fusil) sans charge.

unlock [ʌnˈlɔk], *v.tr.* 1. Ouvrir (la porte); faire jouer
la serrure de (la porte). 2. (a) Débloquer (une roue).
Typ: Desserrer (la forme). (b) *Aut:* To u. the steering-gear, déverrouiller la direction.

unlocked [ʌnˈlɔkt], *a.* Qui n'est pas fermé à clef.

unlooked [ʌnˈlukt], *a.* U. for, (événement) inattendu,
imprévu.

unloose [ʌnˈluːs], unloosen [ʌnˈluːsn], *v.tr.* 1. To
unloose(n) one's hold, lâcher prise. To unloose(n) one's
tongue, délier sa langue. 2. Délier, dénouer (ses
souliers).

unlovable ['ʌnˈlʌvəbl], *a.* Peu aimable; peu sympathique.

unlovely ['ʌnˈlʌvli], *a.* Sans charme, disgracieux, -euse.

unlucky [ʌnˈlʌki], *a.* 1. (a) Malheureux, -euse, infortuné. To be u., ne pas avoir de chance; jouer de
malheur. (b) (Of thg) Malheureux, malencontreux,
-euse. U. day, jour néfaste. How u. that he came!
quelle malchance qu'il soit venu! 2. U. star, étoile
maléfique. It is u., cela porte malheur. U. omen,
mauvais augure. -ily, *adv.* Malheureusement.

unmaidenly [ʌnˈmeidnli], *a.* *O:* Qui ne sied pas à
une jeune fille; immodeste.

unman [ʌnˈmæn], *v.tr.* (unmanned) (a) Amollir (une
nation). (b) Attendrir (qn). (c) Abattre, décourager
(qn).

unmanageable [ʌnˈmænidʒəbl], *a.* 1. Intraitable; (of
child) intenable; (of ship) difficile à manœuvrer. 2.
Difficile à manier.

unmanly [ʌnˈmænli], *a.* Indigne d'un homme; peu
viril.

unmannerliness [ʌnˈmænəlinis], *s.* Mauvaises manières,
impolitesse *f*, grossièreté *f.*

unmannerly [ʌnˈmænəli], *a.* Qui a de mauvaises
manières; malappris; grossier, -ière.

unmarketable ['ʌnˈmɑːkitəbl], *a.* Invendable; d'un
placement difficile.

unmarriageable ['ʌnˈmæridʒəbl], *a.* (Fille) que l'on
n'arrive pas à marier.

unmarried ['ʌnˈmærid], *a.* Célibataire; non marié.
U. state, célibat *m.* U. mother, fille-mère *f.*

unmask [ʌnˈmɑːsk]. 1. *v.tr.* (a) Démasquer. (b) To
u. a conspiracy, dévoiler un complot. 2. *v.i.* Se
démasquer.

unmatched ['ʌnˈmætʃt], *a.* 1. Sans égal, *pl.* sans égaux;
incomparable. 2. Désassorti, dépareillé.

unmeaning [ʌnˈmiːniŋ], *a.* Qui ne signifie rien; vide
de sens.

unmeant [ʌnˈment], *a.* (Of insult) Involontaire; fait
sans intention.

unmeasured [ʌnˈmeʒəd], *a.* 1. (a) Non mesuré. (b)
Infini, immense. 2. (Langage) qui manque de
retenue.

unmentionable [ʌnˈmenʃnəbl], *a.* (Mot) qu'on n'ose
pas prononcer; (chose) dont il ne faut pas parler.

unmerciful [ʌnˈməːsif(u)l], *a.* Impitoyable; sans pitié.
-fully, *adv.* Impitoyablement.

unmerited [ʌnˈmeritid], *a.* Immérité.

unmethodical ['ʌnmiˈθɔdik(ə)l], *a.* 1. Peu méthodique;
(travail) décousu. 2. (Of pers.) Brouillon, -onne.

unmindful [ʌn'maindf(u)l], a. U. of one's duty, oublieux de son devoir. U. of one's own interests, sans penser à ses propres intérêts.

unmistakable ['ʌnmis'teikəbl], a. (a) Qui ne prête à aucune erreur; clair; évident. (b) Facilement reconnaissable. -ably, adv. Nettement, évidemment; à ne pas s'y méprendre.

unmitigated [ʌn'mitigeitid], a. 1. (Mal) non mitigé 2. Dans toute la force du terme. F: U. ass, âne bâté, parfait imbécile. U. lie, pur mensonge.

unmixed ['ʌn'mikst], a. Sans mélange; pur. It is not an u. blessing, cela ne va pas sans quelques inconvénients.

unmolested ['ʌnmo'lestid], a. Sans être inquiété; (voyager) sans obstacle.

unmoor ['ʌn'muər], v.tr. Nau: Démarrer, désamarrer (un navire). unmooring, s. Démarrage m, désamarrage m.

unmounted ['ʌn'mauntid], a. Non monté. 1. (a) (Of gem) Non serti. (b) (Of photograph) Non collé. 2. (Soldat) à pied.

unmoved ['ʌn'mu:vd], a. Impassible. U. by sth., aucunement ému, touché, de, par, qch. He remained u. by all entreaties, il resta insensible à toutes les prières.

unmusical [ʌn'mju:zik(ə)l], a. 1. Peu mélodieux, -euse. 2. (a) (Of ear) Peu musicien, -enne. (b) Qui n'aime pas la musique.

unnamable ['ʌn'neiməbl], a. Innommable.

unnamed ['ʌn'neimd], a. 1. Au nom inconnu; anonyme. 2. Innom(m)é; sans nom.

unnatural [ʌn'nætʃr(ə)l], a. Non naturel. (a) Anormal, -aux. (b) Contre nature; monstrueux, -euse. U. father, père dénaturé. (c) U. laugh, rire forcé.

unnaturalized ['ʌn'nætʃrəlaizd], a. (Of alien) Non naturalisé.

unnavigable ['ʌn'nævigəbl], a. Innavigable.

unnecessary [ʌn'nesis(ə)ri], a. Peu nécessaire; inutile, superflu. (It is) u. to say that . . ., inutile de dire que. . . . -ily, adv. 1. Sans nécessité; inutilement. 2. Plus que de raison.

unneeded ['ʌn'ni:did], a. Inutile; dont on n'a pas besoin.

unneighbourly ['ʌn'neibəli], a. Peu obligeant; (conduite) de mauvais voisin. To behave in an u. manner, se conduire en mauvais voisin.

unnerve ['ʌn'nə:v], v.tr. Faire perdre son courage, son sang-froid, à (qn); effrayer (qn). Entirely unnerved, tout à fait démonté.

unnoticed ['ʌn'noutist], a. 1. Inaperçu, inobservé. To pass u., passer inaperçu. 2. To let an interruption pass u., ne pas relever une interruption. To leave a fact u., passer un fait sous silence.

unnumbered ['ʌn'nʌmbəd], a. 1. (a) Qui n'est pas compté. (b) Sans nombre; innombrable. 2. Non numéroté.

unobjectionable [ʌnəb'dʒekʃnəbl], a. (Personne) à qui on ne peut rien reprocher; (chose) à laquelle on ne peut trouver à redire.

unobservant [ʌnəb'zə:v(ə)nt], **unobserving** [ʌnəb'zə:viŋ], a. Peu observateur, -trice.

unobserved ['ʌnəb'zə:vd, ʌn-], a. Inobservé, inaperçu. To go out u., sortir sans être vu.

unobstructed ['ʌnəb'strʌktid], a. 1. Non-obstrué; (of street) non encombré; (of view) libre. 2. Sans rencontrer d'obstacles.

unobtainable ['ʌnəb'teinəbl], a. Impossible à obtenir, à se procurer.

unobtrusive ['ʌnəb'tru:siv], a. Discret, -ète; (rôle) effacé, modeste. -ly, adv. Discrètement.

unoccupied ['ʌn'ɔkjupaid], a. Inoccupé. 1. Sans occupation. 2. Inhabité. 3. (Of seat) Libre, disponible.

unoffending ['ʌnə'fendiŋ], a. Innocent.

unofficial ['ʌnə'fiʃ(ə)l], a. Non officiel; (i) (renseignement) officieux; (ii) (nouvelle) non confirmée. -ally, adv. A titre officieux.

unopened ['ʌn'oup(ə)nd], a. Qui n'a pas été ouvert; (of letter) non décacheté.

unopposed ['ʌnə'pouzd], a. Sans opposition.

unorthodox ['ʌn'ɔ:θədɔks], a. Peu orthodoxe.

unostentatious ['ʌn,ɔsten'teiʃəs], a. 1. (Of pers.) Peu fastueux, -euse; simple. 2. Fait sans ostentation. -ly, adv. Sans ostentation, sans faste.

unpack ['ʌn'pæk], v.tr. 1. Déballer, dépaqueter (des objets). 2. Défaire (une malle). Abs. Défaire sa malle, sa valise. unpacking, s. Déballage m, dépaquetage m.

unpaid ['ʌn'peid], a. Non payé. 1. Qui ne reçoit pas de salaire; (of post) non rétribué. U. secretary, secrétaire sans traitement. U. services, services à titre gracieux, bénévoles. 2. (Of bill) Impayé; (of debt) non acquitté.

unpalatable [ʌn'pælətəbl], a. (a) D'un goût désagréable. (b) (Of truth) Désagréable.

unparalleled [ʌn'pærəleld], a. Incomparable; sans pareil, sans égal; (of action) sans précédent.

unpardonable [ʌn'pɑ:dnəbl], a. Impardonnable; irrémissible.

unparliamentary ['ʌnpɑ:lə'ment(ə)ri], a. (Langage) (i) peu parlementaire; (ii) F: grossier, injurieux.

unpatriotic ['ʌn,pætri'ɔtik], a. (Of pers.) Peu patriote; (of action) peu patriotique; anti-patriotique. To be u., être mauvais patriote.

unpen ['ʌn'pen], v.tr. Déparquer (le bétail).

unperceivable ['ʌnpə'si:vəbl], a. Imperceptible.

unperceived ['ʌnpə'si:vd], a. Inaperçu.

unperforated ['ʌn'pə:fəreitid], a. Non perforé.

unperturbed ['ʌnpə(:)'tə:bd], a. 1. Impassible. 2. U. by this event, peu ému de cet événement.

unpick ['ʌn'pik], v.tr. Défaire (une couture, etc.).

unpickable ['ʌn'pikəbl], a. (a) (Couture) qu'on peut défaire. (b) (Serrure) incrochetable.

unpitying [ʌn'pitiiŋ], a. Impitoyable.

unplaced ['ʌn'pleist], a. 1. (Cheval) non placé; (candidat) non classé. 2. (Of pers.) Sans poste; sans place.

unpleasant [ʌn'plez(ə)nt], a. Désagréable, déplaisant; fâcheux, -euse. -ly, adv. Désagréablement; déplaisamment.

unpleasantness [ʌn'plez(ə)ntnis], s. 1. Caractère m désagréable (de qch.). 2. Désagrément m, ennui m. There has been some u., F: il y a eu de la brouille, du grabuge.

unpleasing ['ʌn'pli:ziŋ], a. Peu agréable; qui manque de grâce.

unplumbed ['ʌn'plʌmd], a. Lit: U. depths, profondeurs insondées.

unpoetic(al) ['ʌnpou'etik(əl)], a. Peu poétique.

unpolished ['ʌn'pɔliʃt], a. 1. Non poli; mat; (of stone) brut. 2. Rude, grossier. U. style, style fruste.

unpolluted ['ʌnpə'lu:tid], a. Non pollué; pur; (atmosphère) vierge de fumée.

unpopular ['ʌn'pɔpjulər], a. Impopulaire. To make oneself u. with everybody, se faire mal voir de tout le monde.

unpopularity ['ʌn,pɔpju'læriti], s. Impopularité f.

unpopulated ['ʌn'pɔpjuleitid], a. Non peuplé; sans population.

unpractical ['ʌn'præktik(ə)l], a. 1. (Of pers.) Peu pratique. 2. (Projet) impraticable.

unpractised ['ʌn'præktist], a. Inexercé, inexpert (in, à, dans); inexpérimenté (in, dans).

unprecedented ['ʌn'presidentid], a. (i) Sans précédent; (ii) sans exemple; inouï; inédit.

unprejudiced [ʌn'predʒudist], a. Sans préjugés, sans préventions; impartial, -aux; désintéressé.

unpremeditated ['ʌnpri'mediteitid], a. (Départ) inopiné. Jur: (Délit) non prémédité.

unprepared ['ʌnpri'pɛəd], a. 1. (Of food) Inapprêté. U. speech, discours improvisé. Sch: U. translation, traduction à livre ouvert. 2. To catch s.o. u., prendre qn au dépourvu. 3. Sans préparatifs. To go u. into an undertaking, se lancer sans préparation dans une affaire, F: s'embarquer sans biscuit.

unprepossessing ['ʌn,pri:pə'zesiŋ], a. (Of pers.) Peu engageant. A man of u. appearance, un homme de méchante mine.

unpresuming ['ʌnpri'zju:miŋ], a. Modeste; sans présomption.

unpretentious ['ʌnpri'tenʃəs], a. Sans prétentions; modeste. -ly, adv. Modestement.

unprincipled [ʌn'prinsipld], a. (Of pers.) Sans principes; sans scrupule.

unprintable ['ʌn'printəbl], a. Que l'on rougirait d'imprimer.

unprocurable ['ʌnprə'kjuərəbl], a. Impossible à obtenir; que l'on ne peut se procurer; introuvable.

unproductive ['ʌnprə'dʌktiv], a. Improductif, -ive; (travail) stérile; (capital) qui dort.

unprofessional ['ʌnprə'feʃnl], a. (a) U. conduct, manquement m aux devoirs de la profession. (b) For an architect he's very u., comme, en tant qu'architecte, il est plutôt amateur. -ally, adv. (a) Contrairement aux usages du métier. (b) En amateur, d'une façon gauche.

unprofitable [ʌn'prɔfitəbl], a. Peu lucratif; sans profit; peu rentable; (travail) inutile. -ably, adv. Sans profit; inutilement.

unpromising ['ʌn'prɔmisiŋ], a. Peu prometteur, -euse. (Of weather) To look u., s'annoncer mal.

unprompted ['ʌn'prɔm(p)tid], a. (Of answer) Spontané. To do sth. u., faire qch. spontanément, sans y être incité.

unpronounceable ['ʌnprə'naunsəbl], a. Imprononçable.

unpropitious ['ʌnprə'piʃəs], a. Impropice, défavorable, peu favorable (to, à).

unprotected ['ʌnprə'tektid], a. 1. Inabrité; sans protection, sans défense. 2. Ind: (Of moving part, etc.) Exposé; nu; sans carter; sans garde-fou.

unproved ['ʌn'pru:vd], **unproven** ['ʌn'pru:v(ə)n], a. 1. (Of accusation) Improuvé; non prouvé. 2. (Of fidelity) Inéprouvé.

unprovided ['ʌnprə'vaidid], a. U. with sth., dépourvu, dénué, de qch. To be left u. for, être laissé sans ressources.

unprovoked ['ʌnprə'voukt], a. Non provoqué; fait sans provocation. U. abuse, insultes gratuites. S.a. ASSAULT[1] 2.

unpublished ['ʌn'pʌbliʃt], a. 1. Inédit; non publié. 2. The u. facts, les faits qui n'ont pas été livrés au public.

unpunctual ['ʌn'pʌŋ(k)tju(ə)l], a. (a) Inexact; peu ponctuel. (b) En retard; pas à l'heure.

unpunctuality ['ʌn,pʌŋ(k)tju'æliti], s. Inexactitude f; manque m de ponctualité.

unpunished ['ʌn'pʌniʃt], a. Impuni. To go u., (i) (of pers.) échapper au châtiment; (ii) (of crime) rester impuni.

unqualified [ʌn'kwɔlifaid], a. 1. (a) Incompétent. Jur: U. to vote, inhabile à voter. (b) Sans diplômes. 2. U. statement, déclaration générale. U. praise, éloges sans réserve.

unquenchable [ʌn'kwen(t)ʃəbl], a. (Feu, soif) inextinguible; (cupidité) inassouvissable.

unquenched [ʌn'kwen(t)ʃt], a. (Feu) non éteint; (désir, etc.) inassouvi. U. thirst, soif non étanchée.

unquestionable [ʌn'kwestʃənəbl], a. Indiscutable, indubitable. U. fact, fait hors de doute. -ably, adv. Indubitablement, incontestablement, sans aucun doute.

unquestioned [ʌn'kwestʃ(ə)nd], a. 1. (Droit) indisputé, incontesté. 2. To let a statement pass u., laisser passer une affirmation sans la relever. To let s.o. in u., laisser entrer qn sans interpellation, sans le questionner.

unquestioning [ʌn'kwestʃəniŋ], a. (Obéissance) aveugle; inconditionnel, -elle; sans hésitation ni murmure. -ly, adv. Aveuglément; sans question.

unquiet ['ʌn'kwaiət], a. Inquiet, -ète; agité.

unquote [ʌn'kwout], v.i. Fermer les guillemets. Quote . . . u., début m de citation . . . fin f de citation. **unquoted**, a. 1. Non cité. 2. St.Exch: U. securities, valeurs non cotées.

unratified ['ʌn'rætifaid], a. (Traité, etc.) sans ratification; qui n'a jamais été ratifié.

unrationed ['ʌn'ræʃ(ə)nd], a. War Adm: En vente libre.

unravel [ʌn'ræv(ə)l], v. (unravelled) 1. v.tr. (a) Effiler, effilocher (un tissu). (b) Débrouiller démêler (des fils). 2. v.i. (a) (Of cloth) S'effiler. (b) Of tangle) Se débrouiller, se démêler. **unravelling**, s. (1. Effilage m, effilochement m (d'un tissu). 2. Débrouillement m, démêlement m; éclaircissement m (d'un mystère).

unread ['ʌn'red], a. 1. Non lu. To leave sth. u., ne pas lire qch. 2. (Of pers.) Sans instruction; illettré.

unreadable ['ʌn'ri:dəbl], a. Illisible.

unreal ['ʌn'riəl], a. Irréel, -elle; sans réalité.

unreality ['ʌnri'æliti], s. Irréalité f.

unrealized ['ʌn'riəlaizd], a. Irréalisé.

unreasonable [ʌn'ri:znəbl], a. Déraisonnable. 1. Don't be u., soyez raisonnable. 2. (a) U. demands, demandes exorbitantes. (b) At this u. hour, à cette heure indue. -ably, adv. Déraisonnablement; d'une manière peu raisonnable.

unreasoning [ʌn'ri:zniŋ], a. Qui ne raisonne pas. U. hatred, haine irraisonnée.

unreceipted ['ʌnri'si:tid], a. Non acquitté.

unrecognizable ['ʌn'rekəgnaizəbl], a. Méconnaissable.

unrecognized ['ʌn'rekəgnaizd], a. 1. (Of genius) Méconnu. 2. (Of ruler) Non reconnu (by, par).

unrecorded ['ʌnri'kɔ:did], a. Non enregistré; dont on ne trouve aucune mention.

unredeemed ['ʌnri'di:md], a. 1. (Péché) non racheté. Town of u. ugliness, ville uniformément laide. 2. (a) U. promise, promesse non remplie. (b) (From pawn) Non dégagé. (c) Fin: (Emprunt) non amorti.

unrefined ['ʌnri'faind], a. 1. Brut; (sucre) non raffiné. 2. (Homme) peu raffiné, grossier.

unreformable ['ʌnri'fɔ:məbl], a. Irréformable; incorrigible.

unreformed ['ʌnri'fɔ:md], a. Non réformé; qui ne s'est pas corrigé. U. characters, les incorrigibles m.

unrefreshed ['ʌnri'freʃt], a. 1. Non rafraîchi. 2. To wake u., se réveiller encore fatigué.

unregenerate ['ʌnri'dʒenərit], a. (Of pers.) Non régénéré; inconverti.

unregistered ['ʌn'redʒistəd], a. Non enregistré, non inscrit. U. birth, naissance non déclarée. Post: Non recommandé.

unregretted ['ʌnri'gretid], a. To die u., mourir sans laisser de regrets.

unrehearsed ['ʌnri'hə:st], a. (Discours, etc.) impromptu. U. play, pièce jouée sans répétitions préalables. U. effect, effet non préparé.

unrelated ['ʌnri'leitid], a. (a) (Of phenomena) Sans rapport (one to another, l'un avec l'autre). (b) (Of pers.) They are entirely u., il n'y a aucun lien de parenté entre eux.

unrelaxing ['ʌnri'læksiŋ], a. (Assiduité) sans relâche; (effort) assidu, soutenu.

unrelenting ['ʌnri'lentiŋ], a. (a) (Of pers.) Implacable, impitoyable (towards, à, pour, à l'égard de). (b) (Of persecution) Acharné.

unreliability ['ʌnrilaiə'biliti], s. 1. Inexactitude f (des résultats d'une expérience, etc.). 2. Instabilité f (de qn).

unreliable ['ʌnri'laiəbl], a. (Homme) sur lequel on ne peut pas compter; (renseignement) sujet à caution; (machine) d'un fonctionnement incertain. U. map, carte peu fidèle.

unrelieved ['ʌnri'li:vd], a. 1. (a) (Of pers.) Laissé sans secours. (b) (Of pain) Non soulagé. (c) U. boredom, ennui mortel. 2. (Of landscape) Qui manque de relief; monotone.

unremembered ['ʌnri'membəd], a. Oublié; Lit: immémoré.

unremitting ['ʌnri'mitiŋ], a. 1. Ininterrompu; sans intermission. U. efforts, efforts soutenus. 2. He was u. in his attentions, son assiduité ne s'est pas démentie un instant. -ly, adv. Sans cesse, sans relâche.

unremunerative ['ʌnri'mju:nərətiv], a. Peu rémunérateur, -trice; peu lucratif, -ive.

unrepentant ['ʌnri'pentənt], **unrepenting** ['ʌnri'pentiŋ], a. Impénitent. To die u., mourir dans le péché.

unrepresentative ['ʌnrepri'zentətiv], a. Peu typique. U. legislature, législature f qui représente mal le peuple. U. sample, échantillon mal choisi, mauvais échantillon.

unrequited ['ʌnri'kwaitid], a. 1. (Of service) Non récompensé. 2. U. love, amour non partagé.

unreserved ['ʌnri'zə:vd], a. 1. Sans réserve. (a) Franc, f. franche; expansif, -ive. (b) (Of approval) Complet, -ète; entier, -ière. 2. U. seats, places non réservées. -edly ['ʌnri'zə:vidli], adv. Sans réserve. (a) Franchement; à cœur ouvert. (b) Entièrement; sans restriction.

unresisting ['ʌnri'zistiŋ], a. Qui ne résiste pas; soumis, docile.

unresponsive ['ʌnris'pɔnsiv], a. (a) Difficile à émouvoir; froid. (b) *I.C.E:* U. **engine**, moteur peu sensible, mou, plat.

unrest ['ʌn'rest], s. 1. Inquiétude *f.* 2. **Social u.**, le malaise social. **Labour, industrial, u.**, agitation ouvrière.

unrestrained ['ʌnris'treind], a. Non restreint; libre; immodéré.

unrestrainedly ['ʌnris'treinidli], adv. Librement; sans contrainte.

unrestricted ['ʌnris'triktid, ʌn-], a. Sans restriction; (pouvoir) absolu. U. **prospect**, vue dégagée. U. **road**, voie publique sans restriction de vitesse.

unretentive ['ʌnri'tentiv], a. U. **memory**, mémoire courte, peu fidèle.

unrevenged ['ʌnri'ven(d)ʒd], a. Invengé. 1. Sans être vengé. 2. Sans s'être vengé.

unrewarded ['ʌnri'wɔ:did], a. Sans récompense.

unrighteous [ʌn'raitʃəs], a. 1. Impie. 2. Inique, injuste. **-ly**, adv. Iniquement, injustement.

unrighteousness [ʌn'raitʃəsnis], s. Iniquité *f*, injustice *f.*

unripe ['ʌn'raip], a. (Of fruit) Vert; qui n'est pas mûr; (of corn) en herbe.

unrivalled [ʌn'raiv(ə)ld], a. Sans rival; sans pareil; incomparable. **Our goods are u.**, nos articles sont hors ligne, sans concurrence.

unroadworthy [ʌn'roudwə:ði], a. (Of vehicle) Inapte à rouler.

unroll ['ʌn'roul]. 1. *v.tr.* Dérouler. 2. *v.i. & pr.* Se dérouler.

unromantic ['ʌnro'mæntik], a. Peu romanesque; terre à terre *inv.*

unruffled ['ʌn'rʌfld], a. 1. (Of temper) Calme, serein, placide. **An u. composure**, un calme imperturbable. 2. (Of sea) Calme, uni.

unruly [ʌn'ru:li], a. (Of child) Indiscipliné, insoumis, mutin; (of horse) fougueux; (of tongue, passions) déréglé.

unsaddle ['ʌn'sædl], *v.tr.* 1. Desseller (un cheval). 2. (Of horse) Désarçonner (le cavalier).

unsafe ['ʌn'seif], a. 1. (Of action) Dangereux, -euse; (of ice) peu sûr; (of undertaking) hasardeux, -euse; (of business) véreux, -euse. *Nau:* U. **anchorage**, mauvais mouillage. 2. Exposé au danger.

unsaid ['ʌn'sed]. 1. *See* UNSAY. 2. a. **To leave sth. u.**, passer qch. sous silence.

unsalaried ['ʌn'sælərid], a. 1. (Fonctionnaire) sans traitement. 2. (Emploi) non rétribué.

unsaleable ['ʌn'seiləbl], a. (Of goods) Invendable.

unsanitary ['ʌn'sænit(ə)ri], a. Peu hygiénique; insalubre.

unsated ['ʌn'seitid], **unsatiated** ['ʌn'seiʃieitid], a. Inassouvi; non rassasié.

unsatisfactory ['ʌn,sætis'fækt(ə)ri], a. Peu satisfaisant; qui laisse à désirer; (of explanation) peu convaincant. **-ily**, adv. D'une manière peu satisfaisante.

unsatisfied ['ʌn'sætisfaid], a. 1. Mécontent, peu satisfait (**with**, de). 2. Inconvaincu. 3. (Of appetite) Inassouvi.

unsatisfying ['ʌn'sætisfaiiŋ], a. 1. Peu satisfaisant; peu convaincant. 2. (Of meal) Peu rassasiant.

unsavoury ['ʌn'seiv(ə)ri], a. 1. (a) (Goût) désagréable; (plat) d'un goût désagréable. (b) U. **smell**, mauvaise odeur. 2. (Scandale) répugnant. U. **business**, vilaine affaire. U. **reputation**, réputation *f* équivoque.

unsay ['ʌn'sei], *v.tr.* (**unsaid** [-'sed]; **unsaid**) Se dédire de, rétracter (ses paroles).

unscathed [ʌn'skeiðd], a. Sans dommage, sain et sauf.

unscholarly [ʌn'skɔləli], a. 1. Indigne d'un savant. 2. Peu savant; illettré.

unscientific ['ʌn,saiən'tifik], a. (a) Non scientifique. (b) Peu scientifique.

unscratched ['ʌn'skrætʃt], a. Sans égratignure.

unscreened ['ʌn'skri:nd], a. 1. (a) (Of place) Exposé. (b) Sans écran. *El:* (Condensateur) non blindé. 2. (Of coal) Non criblé. 3. Non examiné (par les services de contre-espionnage).

unscrew ['ʌn'skru:], *v.tr.* Dévisser.

unscrupulous [ʌn'skru:pjuləs], a. Indélicat; sans scrupules. **Man of u. ambition**, arriviste *m.* **-ly**, adv. Peu scrupuleusement; sans scrupule.

unseasonable [ʌn'si:z(ə)nəbl], a. 1. (Of fruit, etc.) Hors de saison. U. **weather**, temps qui n'est pas de saison. 2. (Of action) Inopportun; intempestif; déplacé. **-ably**, adv. 1. Hors de saison. **It is u. warm**, il fait chaud pour la saison. 2. Mal à propos.

unseasoned ['ʌn'si:znd], a. 1. (Of food) Non assaisonné. 2. (a) U. **timber**, bois vert. (b) Inacclimaté; (of troops) inaguerri.

unseat ['ʌn'si:t], *v.tr.* 1. Désarçonner (un cavalier). 2. Invalider (un membre élu); *Parl:* faire perdre son siège à (un député).

unseaworthy ['ʌn'si:,wə:ði], a. (Navire) hors d'état de prendre la mer; incapable de tenir la mer.

unsecured ['ʌnsi'kjuəd], a. 1. Mal assujetti; non assujetti. 2. (Of loan) Non garanti; à découvert.

unseeing ['ʌn'si:iŋ], a. Qui ne voit pas; aveugle. **To look at sth. with u. eyes**, regarder qch. sans (le) voir.

unseemliness [ʌn'si:mlinis], s. Inconvenance *f*, incongruité *f* (d'une remarque).

unseemly [ʌn'si:mli], a. (Of behaviour) Inconvenant; peu convenable.

unseen ['ʌn'si:n], a. (a) Inaperçu, invisible. (b) *Sch:* U. **translation**, s. u., version *f.*

unselfconscious ['ʌnself'kɔnʃəs], a. Naturel, -elle, sans contrainte.

unselfish ['ʌn'selfiʃ], a. (Of pers.) Généreux, -euse; sans égoïsme. U. **motive**, motif désintéressé. **-ly**, adv. Généreusement.

unselfishness ['ʌn'selfiʃnis], s. Générosité *f*; désintéressement *m.*

unserviceable ['ʌn'sə:visəbl], a. (a) (Cadeau) inutilisable. (b) (Vêtement) de mauvais service, peu pratique. (c) Hors d'état de servir.

unset ['ʌn'set], a. 1. (Of diamond) Non serti; hors d'œuvre. 2. **Cement still u.**, ciment qui n'a pas encore pris.

unsettle ['ʌn'setl], *v.tr.* Ébranler (les convictions); troubler le repos de (qn). **unsettling**, a. (Of news) Troublant.

unsettled ['ʌn'setld], a. 1. (Pays, gouvernement) troublé; (temps) variable; (esprit) (i) inquiet, (ii) dérangé, détraqué. **The u. state of the weather**, l'incertitude *f* du temps. 2. (Of pers.) Sans domicile fixe. 3. (Esprit) indécis. 4. (a) (Of question) Indécis, en suspens. (b) (Of bill) Impayé, non réglé. 5. (Pays) sans habitants.

unshackle ['ʌn'ʃækl], *v.tr.* 1. Désentraver (un cheval, etc.); ôter les fers à (un prisonnier). 2. Démaniller (une chaîne); détalinguer (une ancre).

unshackled ['ʌn'ʃækld], a. Libre; sans entraves.

unshakeable ['ʌn'ʃeikəbl], a. Inébranlable; (amitié) à toute épreuve.

unshaken ['ʌn'ʃeik(ə)n], a. Inébranlé, ferme; (of faith) inentamé; (of perseverance) constant. (Of troops) **To remain u.**, tenir bon.

unshapely ['ʌn'ʃeipli], a. 1. Mal fait; difforme, disgracieux, -euse. 2. Informe.

unshaven ['ʌn'ʃeivn], a. Non rasé.

unsheathe ['ʌn'ʃi:ð], *v.tr.* Dégainer.

unsheltered ['ʌn'ʃeltəd], a. Sans abri, non abrité (**from**, contre); exposé (**from the wind**, au vent).

unship ['ʌn'ʃip], *v.tr.* (**unshipped** [-'ʃipt]) *Nau:* Décharger (les marchandises). 2. (a) Enlever (un mât); démonter (le gouvernail, etc.). (b) U. **oars!** rentrez!

unshod ['ʌn'ʃɔd], a. 1. (Of pers.) Déchaussé. (Of horse) Déferré. 2. (a) (Of pers.) Nu-pieds *inv.* (b) (Of horse) Sans fers.

unshrinkable ['ʌn'ʃriŋkəbl], a. (Of cloth) Irrétrécissable.

unshrinking [ʌn'ʃriŋkiŋ], a. 1. Hardi; qui ne bronche pas. **-ly**, adv. Hardiment; sans broncher.

unshriven ['ʌn'ʃrivn], a. **To die u.**, mourir sans confession; mourir sans absolution.

unsightly [ʌn'saitli], a. Peu agréable à la vue; laid, vilain.

unsigned ['ʌn'saind], a. Non signé; sans signature.

unsinkable ['ʌn'siŋkəbl], a. (Of boat) Insubmersible.

unskilful ['ʌn'skilf(u)l], a. Malhabile, inhabile (**in, at, à**).

unskilled ['ʌn'skild], a. (Of pers.) Inexpérimenté (**in, à**); inexpert (**in,** dans, en). *Ind:* U. **workman**, manœuvre *m.* U. **labour**, main-d'œuvre non spécialisée.

unslaked ['ʌn'sleikt], a. 1. U. **lime**, chaux vive, non éteinte. 2. (Of thirst) Non étanché.

unsleeping [ʌn'sli:piŋ], a. Lit: Toujours en éveil; vigilant.

unsling ['ʌn'sliŋ], v.tr. (p.t. & p.p. **unslung** [-'slʌŋ]) Nau: 1. Décrocher (un hamac). 2. Enlever les élingues (d'un ballot).

unsmirched ['ʌn'smə:tʃt], a. (Of reputation) Sans tache, sans souillure.

unsociable [ʌn'souʃəbl], a. Insociable; sauvage, farouche.

unsoiled ['ʌn'sɔild], a. Propre; sans tache. Com: A l'état (de) neuf.

unsold ['ʌn'sould], a. Invendu. Journ: U. **copies**, invendus m, bouillon m.

unsoldierly ['ʌn'sould ʒəli], a. Peu martial, -aux; peu militaire.

unsolicited ['ʌnsə'lisitid], a. Non sollicité; (of action) volontaire, spontané. To do sth. u., faire qch. spontanément.

unsolved ['ʌn'sɔlvd], a. (Problème) non résolu; (mystère) impénétré.

unsophisticated ['ʌnsə'fistikeitid], a. 1. Non frelaté, naturel, -elle. 2. (Of pers.) Ingénu, naïf, -ïve, simple, candide.

unsound ['ʌn'saund], a. 1. (a) (Of pers.) Malsain, maladif, -ive. Of u. **mind**, non sain d'esprit; qui a le cerveau dérangé. Vet: U. **horse**, cheval taré. (b) Gâté; en mauvais état. 2. (a) (Of ice) Peu solide; (of position) mal affermi; (of business) périclitant. (b) U. **opinions**, opinions perverties. Theory that is fundamentally u., théorie qui pèche par la base. Ins: U. **life**, mauvais sujet d'assurance. -ly, adv. Défectueusement; (raisonner) à faux.

unsoundness ['ʌn'saun(d)nis], s. 1. (a) U. **of mind**, faiblesse f d'esprit. (b) Mauvais état (du bois, des fruits). 2. (a) Manque m de solidité (d'un bâtiment). (b) Fausseté f (d'une doctrine).

unsparing [ʌn'spɛəriŋ], a. 1. Prodigue (of, de). U. **in one's efforts**, infatigable. To be u. of one's strength, ne pas ménager ses forces. 2. U. **of others**, impitoyable, sans pitié, pour les autres. -ly, adv. 1. Avec prodigalité; généreusement. To use sth. u., ne pas ménager, user largement de, qch. 2. Impitoyablement.

unspeakable [ʌn'spi:kəbl], a. 1. (Douleur) inexprimable. U. **confusion**, désordre sans nom. 2. F: Détestable, inqualifiable. It is u.! ça n'a pas de nom! -ably, adv. Ineffablement, indiciblement.

unspecified ['ʌn'spesifaid], a. Non spécifié.

unspoiled, unspoilt ['ʌn'spɔilt], a. (a) (Of child) Non gâté; bien élevé. (b) Inaltéré. U. **countryside**, campagne non encore profanée.

unspoken ['ʌn'spouk(ə)n], a. Non prononcé; sous-entendu; (accord) tacite.

unsportsmanlike ['ʌn'spɔ:tsmənlaik], a. Indigne d'un sportsman; antisportif, -ive; peu loyal, -aux.

unstable ['ʌn'steibl], a. 1. Instable; (of position) peu sûr. Mec: U. **equilibrium**, équilibre instable. 2. (Of pers.) Peu consistant; (of character) changeant, inconstant; (of mind) déséquilibré.

unstained ['ʌn'steind], a. 1. Propre; sans tache. 2. Non teint, non mis en couleur. 3. (Of reputation) Sans tache.

unstamped ['ʌn'stæm(p)t], a. (a) (Of letter) Sans timbre; non affranchi. (b) (Of document) Non estampillé.

unsteadiness ['ʌn'stedinis], s. 1. Instabilité f; manque m d'aplomb (d'une table); manque de sûreté (de la main). 2. (a) Irrésolution f, indécision f. (b) Manque de conduite. 3. Irrégularité f, variabilité f (du vent, des prix).

unsteady ['ʌn'stedi], a. 1. (Of table) Peu stable, peu solide; (of footsteps) chancelant; (of voice) mal assuré. To be u. on one's legs, vaciller; tituber. 2. (a) (Of purpose) Vacillant, irrésolu. (b) (Of pers.) Dissipé; déréglé. 3. Irrégulier, -ière; (of barometer) variable. -ily, adv. 1. (Marcher) d'un pas chancelant. 2. D'une façon irrégulière, inégale.

unstick ['ʌn'stik], v.tr. (p.t. & p.p. **unstuck** [-'stʌk]) Décoller (qch.). To come **unstuck**, (i) se décoller; (ii) F: (of plan) s'effondrer.

unstinted [ʌn'stintid], a. (a) (Of supplies) Abondant; à discrétion. (b) To give s.o. u. **praise**, ne pas ménager ses louanges à qn.

unstitch [ʌn'stitʃ], v.tr. Dépiquer, découdre (un vêtement); débrocher (un livre). To come **unstitched**, se découdre.

unstop ['ʌn'stɔp], v.tr. (**unstopped** [-'stɔpt]) Déboucher, dégorger (un tuyau).

unstopped ['ʌn'stɔpt], a. 1. (a) Débouché, dégorgé. (b) (Of tooth) To come u., se déplomber. 2. (Tuyau) non bouché; ouvert.

unstressed ['ʌn'strest], a. (Of syllable) Sans accent; inaccentué; atone.

unstring ['ʌn'striŋ], v.tr. (p.t. & p.p. **unstrung** [-'strʌŋ]) 1. (a) Enlever les ficelles de (qch.). (b) Débander (un arc). 2. Défiler, désenfiler (des perles).

unstudied ['ʌn'stʌdid], a. 1. U. **in . . .**, ignorant de. . . . 2. (Style) inapprêté, sans apprêt; (langage) naturel.

unsubdued ['ʌnsəb'dju:d], a. Non subjugué, inassujetti; (of horse, passion) non maîtrisé; indompté.

unsubmissive ['ʌnsəb'misiv], a. Insoumis, rebelle.

unsubsidized ['ʌn'sʌbsidaizd], a. Non subventionné; sans subvention, sans prime.

unsubstantial [ʌnsəb'stæn ʃ(ə)l], a. Insubstantiel, -elle; immatériel, -elle.

unsubstantiated ['ʌnsəb'stænʃieitid], a. (Of accusation) Non prouvé; (of rumour) sans confirmation.

unsuccessful ['ʌnsək'sesf(u)l], a. 1. Non réussi; infructueux, -euse. U. **attempt**, tentative sans succès; F: coup manqué, raté. The negotiations were u., les pourparlers n'ont pas abouti. 2. (Of pers.) Qui n'a pas réussi; qui a échoué; (of candidate) refusé, (at election) non élu, malheureux. To be u., échouer; ne pas réussir. -fully, adv. Sans succès; vainement.

unsuitability ['ʌns(j)u:tə'biliti], s. 1. Inaptitude f (de qn) (to, for, à); incapacité f. 2. Disconvenance f (du climat, etc.); inopportunité f (d'une observation); impropriété f (d'un terme); caractère mal assorti (d'un mariage).

unsuitable ['ʌn's(j)u:təbl], a. 1. (Of pers.) Peu fait (to, for, pour); inapte (à). 2. (Of thg) Impropre, mal adapté (à); (of remark) déplacé; inopportun; (of marriage) mal assorti. U. to the occasion, qui ne convient pas à la circonstance. -ably, adv. D'une manière qui ne convient pas. U. **matched**, mal assorti(s).

unsuited ['ʌn's(j)u:tid], a. U. to, for, sth., (of pers.) peu fait pour qch.; inapte à qch.; (of thg) impropre, mal adapté, mal approprié, à qch.

unsullied ['ʌn'sʌlid], a. Sans souillure; sans tache; immaculé.

unsupported ['ʌnsə'pɔ:tid], a. 1. (a) (Of statement) Non confirmé, sans preuves. (b) (Of pers.) Non appuyé, non soutenu; (agir) seul, sans encouragement. 2. Civ.E: etc: Sans support, sans appui; non étayé.

unsure [ʌn'ʃuə:r], a. Peu sûr, incertain (about, de). I'm u. whether . . ., je ne sais trop si. . . . To be u. of oneself, se défier de soi-même, manquer de confiance en soi-même.

unsurpassed ['ʌnsə(:)'pɑ:st], a. Qui n'a jamais été surpassé; sans égal, -aux; sans pareil, -eille.

unsuspected ['ʌnsəs'pektid], a. Insoupçonné (by, de); (i) non suspect; (ii) dont on ne soupçonnait pas l'existence.

unsuspecting ['ʌnsəs'pektiŋ], a. 1. Qui ne se doute de rien; sans soupçons; sans défiance. 2. Naturally u., peu soupçonneux, -euse. -ly, adv. Sans rien soupçonner; sans défiance.

unsuspicious ['ʌnsəs'piʃəs], a. 1. = UNSUSPECTING. 2. To be u. of sth., ne pas douter de qch.

unsweetened ['ʌn'swi:tnd], a. Non sucré.

unswerving [ʌn'swə:viŋ], a. 1. Constant, ferme. 2. U. **flight**, vol rectiligne, qui ne s'écarte pas de la ligne droite. To pursue an u. **course**, ne pas s'écarter de son chemin, du but. -ly, adv. Sans s'écarter du but.

unsymmetrical ['ʌnsi'metrik(ə)l], a. Asymétrique.

unsympathetic ['ʌn,simpə'θetik], a. Peu compatissant; froid; indifférent. -ally, adv. Sans compassion; froidement.

unsystematic [ˈʌnˌsistiˈmætik], a. Non systématique; sans méthode. **-ally**, adv. Sans méthode; au petit bonheur.

untainted [ˈʌnˈteintid], a. Non gâté; non corrompu; (of food) frais, f. fraîche.

untalented [ˈʌnˈtælǝntid], a. Sans talents.

untam(e)able [ˈʌnˈteiməbl], a. Inapprivoisable; indomptable.

untamed [ˈʌnˈteimd], a. Inapprivoisé, sauvage; indompté.

untapped [ˈʌnˈtæpt], a. (Of barrel) Non mis en perce; encore plein. U. resources, ressources inutilisées, inexploitées.

untarnishable [ˈʌnˈtɑːniʃǝbl], a. Internissable.

untarnished [ˈʌnˈtɑːniʃt], a. 1. Non terni. 2. (Réputation) sans tache, sans souillure.

untaught [ˈʌnˈtɔːt], a. (a) (Of pers.) Sans instruction; illettré, ignorant. (b) (Of skill) Naturel, -elle.

unteachable [ˈʌnˈtiːtʃǝbl], a. (Of pers.) Incapable d'apprendre; à qui l'on ne peut rien apprendre.

untenable [ˈʌnˈtenǝbl], a. 1. (Of position) Intenable. 2. (Of theory) Insoutenable.

untenanted [ˈʌnˈtenǝntid], a. Sans locataire(s); vide; inoccupé; inhabité.

untested [ˈʌnˈtestid], a. Pas encore essayé, inéprouvé; qui n'a pas encore été mis à l'épreuve.

untether [ˈʌnˈteðǝr], v.tr. Détacher (un cheval).

unthinkable [ʌnˈθiŋkǝbl], a. Inimaginable; impensable. It is u. that he should be acquitted, il est inconcevable qu'il soit acquitté.

unthinking [ˈʌnˈθiŋkiŋ], a. Irréfléchi, étourdi. In an u. moment, dans un moment d'inadvertance, par étourderie. **-ly**, adv. Sans (y) penser; étourdiment; (prendre un engagement) à la légère.

unthought [ˈʌnˈθɔːt], a. U. of, imprévu, inattendu.

unthread [ˈʌnˈθred], v.tr. Désenfiler (une aiguille, des perles).

untidiness [ˈʌnˈtaidinis], s. Désordre m; manque m d'ordre, de soin.

untidy [ʌnˈtaidi], a. (a) (Of room) En désordre; mal tenu; (of hair) ébouriffé, mal peigné. U. dress, tenue négligée, débraillée. (b) (Of pers.) Désordonné. **-ily**, adv. Sans ordre, sans soin.

untie [ˈʌnˈtai], v.tr. (untied; untying) Dénouer (sa ceinture); défaire, délier (un nœud, un paquet); détacher (un chien); déficeler (un paquet). To come untied, se défaire, se délier.

until [ǝnˈtil]. 1. prep. (a) Jusqu'à. U. evening, jusqu'au soir. (b) Not u., pas avant. He won't come u. after dinner, il ne viendra qu'après le dîner. 2. conj. (a) Jusqu'à ce que + sub. I'll wait u. he comes, j'attendrai jusqu'à ce qu'il vienne. (b) Not u., pas avant que + sub. He won't come u. you invite him, il ne viendra pas avant que vous (ne) l'invitiez, avant d'être invité.

untilled [ˈʌnˈtild], a. (Of land) 1. Inculte. 2. Non labouré; en friche.

untimely¹ [ʌnˈtaimli], a. 1. (a) Prématuré. To come to an u. end, mourir avant l'âge. (b) (Of fruit) Précoce. 2. (Of rain, etc.) Hors de saison. 3. (Of action) Inopportun, intempestif, -ive. 4. At an u. hour, à une heure indue.

untimely², adv. 1. Prématurément; avant l'heure. 2. Inopportunément; mal à propos.

untiring [ʌnˈtaiǝriŋ], a. Inlassable, infatigable; (travail) assidu. **-ly**, adv. Inlassablement, infatigablement.

unto [ˈʌntu(ː)], prep. A. & B.Lit: (= 'to' in certain uses) 1. U. us a child is born, un enfant nous est né. To be like u. sth., ressembler à qch. And I say u. you . . ., et je vous dis. . . . Let us u. our ships, allons à nos vaisseaux. 2. Vers. To turn u. s.o., se tourner vers qn. To come nigh u. sth., s'approcher de qch. 3. Jusqu'à. U. this day, jusqu'à ce jour même.

untold [ˈʌnˈtould], a. 1. (Richesse, etc.) immense, énorme, incalculable. It is worth u. gold, cela vaut une somme fabuleuse. U. losses, pertes incalculables. U. suffering, souffrances inouïes. 2. (Of tale, etc.) Non raconté; passé sous silence.

untouchable [ʌnˈtʌtʃǝbl]. (a) a. Intouchable. (b) s. (In India) The untouchables, les intouchables.

untouched [ˈʌnˈtʌtʃt], a. 1. (a) Non touché. (Of food) U. by hand, non manié. (b) He had left the food u., il n'avait pas touché à la nourriture. 2. (a) To leave sth. u., laisser qch. intact. (b) (Of pers.) Sain et sauf. 3. (Of subject) U. (upon), non mentionné; non discuté. 4. (Of pers.) Non ému; indifférent; insensible (by, à).

untoward [ˈʌntǝwɔːd, ʌnˈtouǝd], a. 1. O: (Of pers.) Indocile; rétif, -ive; (of thg) incommode; difficile (à façonner). 2. (Événement) fâcheux, malencontreux. I hope nothing u. has happened, il n'est pas arrivé un malheur, j'espère. 3. (Of season) Impropice. 4. (Of behaviour) Malséant.

untraceable [ˈʌnˈtreisǝbl], a. Introuvable.

untrained [ˈʌnˈtreind], a. Inexpert, inexercé, inexpérimenté; (animal domestique) non dressé, non formé.

untrammelled [ˈʌnˈtræm(ǝ)ld], a. Sans entraves, sans contrainte; non empêtré (by, de); libre (by, de).

untransferable [ˈʌntrɑːnsˈfǝːrǝbl, -træns-], a. Intransférable. Jur: (Droit, propriété) incessible, inaliénable. (On tickets) Strictement personnel.

untranslatable [ˈʌntrɑːnsˈleitǝbl, -træns-], a. Intraduisible.

untravelled [ˈʌnˈtræv(ǝ)ld], a. 1. (Of pers.) Qui n'a jamais voyagé. 2. (Pays) inexploré, peu connu.

untried [ˈʌnˈtraid], a. 1. Non essayé. We left no remedy u., il n'y a pas de remède qu'on n'ait essayé. 2. Qui n'a pas été mis à l'épreuve. U. troops, troupes qui n'ont pas encore vu le feu.

untrodden [ˈʌnˈtrɔdn], a. (Chemin) non frayé; (région) inexplorée. U. forest, forêt vierge. U. paths, des sentiers nouveaux. U. snow, neige immaculée, vierge.

untroubled [ˈʌnˈtrʌbld], a. Calme, tranquille, paisible; (of water) limpide.

untrue [ˈʌnˈtruː], a. 1. (Of statement, etc.) Faux, f. fausse; mensonger, -ère; erroné. 2. Tchn: Inexact, faux; qui n'est pas juste. 3. (Of pers.) Infidèle, déloyal, -aux (to, à). 4. adv. Mec.E: Shaft that runs u., arbre m qui tourne à faux.

untrustworthiness [ˈʌnˈtrʌst,wǝːðinis], s. 1. (Of pers.) Manque m de probité. 2. Caractère douteux (d'un renseignement).

untrustworthy [ˈʌnˈtrʌst,wǝːði], a. 1. (Of pers.) Indigne de confiance; (témoin) récusable. U. memory, mémoire infidèle, peu sûre. 2. (Renseignement) douteux, peu sûr, sujet à caution.

untruth [ˈʌnˈtruːθ], s. Mensonge m; contre-vérité f. To tell an u., dire, faire, un mensonge.

untruthful [ˈʌnˈtruːθf(u)l], a. 1. (Of pers.) Menteur, -euse. 2. (Of news, etc.) Mensonger, -ère; faux, f. fausse. **-fully**, adv. Menteusement, mensongèrement.

untruthfulness [ˈʌnˈtruːθf(u)lnis], s. 1. (Of pers.) Caractère menteur. 2. Fausseté f, caractère mensonger (d'une histoire).

untuck [ˈʌnˈtʌk], v.tr. Déborder (un lit). F: He untucked his legs (from under him), il se déplia les jambes.

untuned [ˈʌnˈtjuːnd], a. 1. Mus: Non accordé; désaccordé; discordant. 2. (Of pers.) Peu disposé (to, à).

untuneful [ˈʌnˈtjuːnf(u)l], a. Peu harmonieux, -euse.

unturned [ˈʌnˈtǝːnd], a. Non (re)tourné. S.a. STONE¹.

untutored [ˈʌnˈtjuːtǝd], a. 1. (a) Sans instruction; illettré, ignorant; (esprit, goût) non formé. (b) To be u. in the art of . . ., ignorer l'art de. . . . 2. (Talent) naturel.

untwist [ˈʌnˈtwist]. 1. v.tr. Détordre (un cordage); détortiller. To come untwisted, se détordre; se détortiller. 2. v.i. Se détordre; se détortiller.

unusable [ˈʌnˈjuːzǝbl], a. Inutilisable.

unused, a. 1. [ˈʌnˈjuːzd], (a) Inutilisé; non employé; (mot) inusité. U. building, bâtiment inhabité, vide, (of public building) désaffecté. (b) Qui n'a pas encore servi; neuf, f. neuve, à l'état de neuf. 2. [ˈʌnˈjuːst] (Of pers.) Peu habitué (to, à). To get u. to sth., se déshabituer, perdre l'habitude, de qch.

unusual [ʌnˈjuːʒju(ǝ)l], a. (a) Peu commun; exceptionnel, -elle, insolite; qui sort de l'ordinaire; inhabituel, -elle. It is u., (i) cela se fait peu; ce n'est pas l'usage; (ii) cela se voit rarement. Nothing u., rien d'anormal. (b) (Mot) peu usité. **-ally**, adv. U. tall, d'une taille exceptionnelle. He was u. attentive, il s'est montré plus attentif que d'habitude.

unusualness [ʌn'juːʒ‌ju(ə)lnis], s. Nature exceptionnelle, extraordinaire, insolite (of, de); rareté f.

unutilized ['ʌn'juːtilaizd], a. Inutilisé.

unutterable [ʌn'ʌt(ə)rəbl], a. Inexprimable, indicible. **F: U. fool**, parfait imbécile. **-ably,** adv. Indiciblement; ineffablement.

unvalued ['ʌn'væljuːd], a. 1. Peu estimé. 2. Non évalué.

unvanquished ['ʌn'væŋkwiʃt], a. Invaincu.

unvaried [ʌn'vɛərid], a. Uniforme, constant; (nourriture) sans variété, qui manque de variété; monotone.

unvarnished ['ʌn'vɑːniʃt], a. Non verni; (of pottery) non vernissé. **Plain u. wood,** bois cru. 2. [ʌn'vɑːniʃt] (Of statement) Simple. **To tell a plain u. tale,** raconter les choses sans fard.

unvarying [ʌn'vɛəriiŋ], a. Invariable; uniforme, constant; monotone.

unveil [ʌn'veil], v.tr. Dévoiler. **To u. a statue,** inaugurer une statue. **unveiling,** s. Inauguration f (d'une statue).

unverifiable ['ʌnveri'faiəbl], a. Invérifiable.

unverified ['ʌn'verifaid], a. Invérifié.

unversed ['ʌn'vəːst], a. Peu versé (in, dans); ignorant (de).

unvoiced ['ʌn'vɔist], a. 1. Non exprimé. 2. Ling: (Of vowel, consonant) Sourd, soufflé, dévoisé.

unwanted ['ʌn'wɔntid], a. 1. Non désiré, non voulu. 2. Superflu.

unwariness [ʌn'wɛərinis], s. Imprudence f, imprévoyance f; manque m de précaution.

unwarrantable [ʌn'wɔrəntəbl], a. (Action) injustifiable, inexcusable; (assertion) insoutenable.

unwarranted a. 1. ['ʌn'wɔrəntid] Sans garantie. 2. [ʌn'wɔrəntid] Injustifié; peu justifié. **U. insult,** injure gratuite. **U. remark,** observation déplacée. **I should be u. in supposing that . . .,** je n'ai aucune raison de supposer que. . . .

unwary ['ʌn'wɛəri], a. Imprudent, imprévoyant. **-ily,** adv. Imprudemment; sans précaution.

unwashed ['ʌn'wɔʃt], a. Non lavé; malpropre, sale. s. **P: The Great U.,** les prolétaires m; les pouilleux m.

unwavering [ʌn'weivəriŋ], a. Constant, ferme, résolu. **U. fortitude,** fermeté qui ne se dément jamais. **U. policy,** politique ferme et suivie.

unwearied [ʌn'wiərid], a. (a) Non fatigué. (b) Infatigable.

unwearying [ʌn'wiəriiŋ], a. Inlassable, infatigable.

unweathered ['ʌn'weðəd], a. (Of stone, etc.) Inaltéré (par les intempéries).

unwelcome [ʌn'welkəm], a. (a) (Visiteur) mal venu, importun. **A not u. visit,** une visite opportune. (b) **U. news,** nouvelle fâcheuse, désagréable. **A not u. addition to our stores,** un surcroît de provisions très utile.

unwell ['ʌn'wel], a. Indisposé; souffrant.

unwholesome ['ʌn'houlsəm], a. (a) (Aliment) malsain; (climat) insalubre; (air) vicié. (b) **U. doctrines,** doctrines malsaines, pernicieuses.

unwieldiness [ʌn'wiːldinis], s. Lourdeur f; pesanteur f; difficulté f de maniement (d'un colis, etc.).

unwieldy [ʌn'wiːldi], a. 1. (Of pers.) Lourd, gauche; à la démarche lourde. 2. (Outil, colis) peu portatif; peu maniable; difficile à porter ou à manier.

unwilling ['ʌn'wiliŋ], a. 1. Peu serviable; de mauvaise volonté. 2. **To be u. to do sth.,** être peu disposé à faire qch. **U. acquiescence,** assentiment donné à contre-cœur. **I was u. for my wife to accept the invitation,** je ne voulais pas que ma femme accepte l'invitation. **-ly,** adv. A contre-cœur; de mauvaise grâce; à regret.

unwillingness ['ʌn'wiliŋnis], s. 1. Mauvaise volonté; mauvaise grâce. 2. Répugnance f (à faire qch.).

unwind ['ʌn'waind], v.tr. (unwound ['ʌn'waund]). Dérouler; dépelotonner. Tex: Dévider (un cocon). El: Débobiner (une bobine). **To come unwound,** se dérouler.

unwise ['ʌn'waiz], a. Imprudent; peu prudent, peu sage; malavisé. **-ly,** adv. Imprudemment.

unwitting [ʌn'witiŋ], a. 1. Inconscient (of, de). 2. (Of action) Non intentionnel, -elle; accidentel, -elle. **-ly,** adv. Sans le savoir; sans le vouloir; inconsciemment.

unwonted [ʌn'wountid], a. Inaccoutumé, inhabituel, -elle; (événement) peu commun, insolite.

unworkable ['ʌn'wəːkəbl], a. 1. (a) (Projet) inexécutable, impraticable. (b) Difficile à mener. 2. (a) Min: (Gisement) inexploitable. (b) **U. material,** matière rebelle.

unworked ['ʌn'wəːkt], a. 1. (Métal, etc.) non ouvré, non travaillé. 2. Min: (Gisement) inexploité.

unworldly ['ʌn'wəːldli], a. 1. (a) Peu mondain; détaché de ce monde. (b) Simple, candide. 2. Céleste; (beauté) qui n'est pas de ce monde.

unworthiness [ʌn'wəːðinis], s. Démérite m, indignité f.

unworthy [ʌn'wəːði], a. Indigne. 1. **U. of sth., to do sth.,** indigne de qch., de faire qch. **U. of notice,** qui ne mérite pas qu'on y fasse attention. 2. (Conduite) méprisable. 3. (Travail) peu méritoire.

unwounded ['ʌn'wuːndid], a. Non blessé; sans blessure; indemne; sain et sauf. **There were only ten u. men left,** il ne restait que dix hommes valides.

unwrap ['ʌn'ræp], v.tr. (unwrapped) Défaire, désenvelopper (un paquet); enlever l'enveloppe de (qch.).

unwrinkled [ʌn'riŋkld], a. Sans rides; lisse.

unwritten ['ʌn'ritn], a. Non écrit; (of tradition) oral, -aux. **The u. law,** (i) le droit coutumier; esp. (ii) le droit de tuer pour venger son honneur ou celui d'une femme.

unyielding [ʌn'jiːldiŋ], a. Qui ne cède pas; raide, ferme; (of pers.) inébranlable, opiniâtre; inflexible. **U. grip,** prise indesserrable.

unyoke ['ʌn'jouk], v.tr. Dételer, découpler (des bœufs).

up¹ [ʌp]. I. adv. 1. (a) En montant; vers le haut. **To go up,** monter. **Up went his stick,** il leva son bâton. **My room is three flights up,** ma chambre est au troisième (palier). **To throw sth. up (in the air),** jeter qch. en l'air. **All the way up,** jusqu'au haut (de la colline, etc.); jusqu'en haut (de l'escalier). **Half-way up,** jusqu'à mi-hauteur. S.a. HAND¹ 1. (b) **To walk up and down,** se promener de long en large. **To go up north,** aller dans le nord. **To go up to town,** aller à la capitale, à Londres. **To go up to the university,** aller à l'université. **To go up for an examination,** se présenter à un examen. (c) Nau: **Hard up with the helm!** la barre au vent toute! (d) **From five pounds up,** à partir de cinq livres. **From my youth up,** dès ma jeunesse. 2. (a) Haut; en haut. **What are you doing up there?** que faites-vous là-haut? **Up above,** en haut. **Up above sth.,** au-dessus de qch. **The moon is up,** la lune est levée. **Bill: Game of a hundred up,** partie en cent. **The blinds are up,** on a relevé les stores. **The shops had their shutters up,** les magasins avaient leurs volets mis. **The new building is up,** le nouveau bâtiment est fini. Turf: **Comet with Jones up,** Comet monté par Jones. **The tide is up,** la marée est haute. **Road up,** route en réfection, en réparation, travaux. (b) En dessus. **Face up,** face en dessus. (On packing-case) **This side up,** haut; dessus. (c) **Up in London,** à Londres. **Up in Yorkshire,** au nord, dans le Yorkshire. **Relations up from the country,** parents de province en visite à la ville. 3. (a) **To go up in price,** subir une hausse de prix. **Bread is up again,** le pain a encore augmenté. **The thermometer has gone up,** le thermomètre a monté. **Things are looking up,** les affaires f sont à la hausse. **To be one game up,** être en avance d'une partie. Fb: **To be one goal up,** mener par un but. (b) **To screw up,** visser, serrer (un tourniquet, etc.). Mch: **Steam is up,** nous sommes sous pression. **His blood was up,** il était monté; le sang lui bouillait. (c) **To be well up in a subject,** connaître un sujet à fond; être versé dans une matière. **To be well up in geography,** être fort, F: calé, en géographie. (d) (Intensive) **To praise s.o. up,** vanter, prôner, qn. **To speak up,** parler plus fort, plus haut. **Sing up!** plus fort! 4. **Put it up beside, close up to,** the other one, mettez-le tout près de l'autre. **To follow s.o. up,** suivre qn de près. **To be up with sth.,** être au niveau de qch. **He came up with me,** il me rejoignit. 5. (a) Debout, levé. **To get up,** (from bed) se lever; (from seat) se lever, se mettre debout. **To be up and about,** être sur pied. **Let us be up and doing,** mettons-nous à la besogne. **Hold yourself up!** tenez-vous droit! **Up, guards!** debout, les gardes! (b) **At midnight I was still up,** à minuit je n'étais pas encore couché. **To be up all night,** ne pas se coucher de la nuit. **To stay, wait, up,** veiller. **I was up late last night,** je me suis couché tard hier soir. **I was up late this morning,** je me suis levé tard ce matin. (c) **You are up against a strong man,** vous avez affaire à forte partie. **To be up against diffi- culties,** se heurter à, être aux prises avec, des diffi- cultés. F: **To be up against it,** avoir la déveine, la guigne. 6. (a) **To stir up sediment,** remuer, agiter, un dépôt. **To be up in arms,** se révolter, s'insurger. (b) F: **What's up?** que se passe-t-il? qu'y a-t-il? de quoi retourne-t-il? **There is something up,** il y a quelque chose. **What's up with you?** qu'est-ce qui vous prend? 7. **Time is up,** il est l'heure (de finir, de fermer); c'est l'heure. **His time is up,** il a fini son temps (de service militaire, etc.). **His leave is up,** sa permission est expirée. F: **The game is up, it's all up,** tout est perdu. F: **It's all up with him,** son affaire est faite; P: il est fichu, flambé. F: **I thought it was all up with me,** j'ai cru que ma dernière heure était venue. 8. **Up to.** (a) **They advanced up to the walls of the city,** ils s'avancèrent jusque devant les murs de la ville. **To come, go, up to s.o.,** s'approcher de, s'avancer vers qn. **I'm up to you,** je vous ai rattrapé. **What page are you up to?** où en êtes vous (du livre que vous lisez)? **To be covered with mud up to the ears,** être crotté jusqu'aux oreilles. *S.a.* EAR[1] 1, NECK 1. (b) **Up to now, up to here,** jusqu'ici. **Up to this day,** jusqu'à ce jour. **Up to £500,** jusqu'à concurrence de 500 livres. **To live up to one's income,** dépenser tout son revenu. (c) **To be up to sth.,** être capable de qch. F: **She is up to anything,** elle n'a pas froid aux yeux. **To be up to a job,** être à la hauteur d'une tâche. **I don't feel up to it,** je ne m'en sens pas le courage, la force. **To be up to s.o.'s tricks,** être de force à lutter avec qn. (d) *Sch:* **He's up to Mr. Martin for Latin,** il est dans la classe de latin de M. Martin. (e) F: **What are you up to?** qu'est-ce que vous faites? qu'est-ce que vous fabriquez? qu'est-ce que vous mijotez? **He is up to something,** il a quelque chose en tête. (f) F: **It is up to him to . . .,** c'est à lui de . . .; c'est affaire à lui de. . . . **It's up to you to accept,** il ne tient qu'à vous d'accepter. II. **up,** *prep.* 1. **To go up the stairs, a hill,** monter l'escalier, une côte. **The cat is up the tree,** le chat est en haut de l'arbre. 2. (a) **Up the river,** en remontant le fleuve; en amont. **Further up the street,** plus loin dans la rue. **To walk up and down the platform,** faire les cent pas sur le quai; arpenter le quai. (b) **Up the yard,** au fond de, dans, la cour. *S.a.* COUNTRY 1. III. **up,** *attrib.a.* **Up motion,** mouvement de montée. *Rail:* **Up line,** voie descen- dante, paire; la voie en direction de Londres. **Up train,** train descendant, de retour. IV. **up,** *s.* **Ups and downs,** ondulations f (du terrain). F: **The ups and downs of life,** les vicissitudes f, les péripéties f, les hauts et les bas, de la vie. **A life of ups and downs,** une vie cahotée, mouvementée. **'up-and-'coming,** *a.* (Jeune homme) d'avenir. **'up-and-'down,** *attrib.a.* **Up-and-down motion,** (i) mouvement de haut en bas et de bas en haut; (ii) jeu vertical (d'une pièce). **'up-and-'up,** *s.* F: **To be on the up-and-up,** (i) être en bonne voie, prospérer; (ii) être honnête. **'up-'end,** *v.tr.* Dresser (qch.) debout; mettre (un tonneau) à cul. **'up-grade.** 1. *s.* Pente ascendante; rampe f, montée f (d'une route). F: **To be on the up-g.,** (i) (of prices) monter; tendre à la hausse; (ii) (of business) reprendre, se relever. 2. *attrib.a.* (Traction, etc.) en rampe. **'up-'river.** 1. *Attrib.a.* D'amont. 2. *adv.* En amont. **'up-'stream,** 1. *adv.* (a) En amont. (b) En remontant le courant; à contre-fil de l'eau. 2. *attrib.a.* (a) (Bief, etc.) d'amont. (b) (Vent) d'aval. **'up-stroke,** *s.* 1. (In writing) Délié m. 2. (Of violin bow) Poussé m. 3. *Mch:* Course ascendante, levée f (du piston). **'up- to-'date,** *attrib.a.* 1. (Of pers.) Moderne; de son temps; F: à la page. 2. Au goût du jour; moderne. **Up-to-d. hat,** chapeau dernier cri, à la mode. **More up-to-d. model,** modèle plus récent. *S.a.* DATE[2].

up[2], *v.* (upped) *v.tr.* **To up the swans,** recenser les cygnes. **upping,** *s.* **Swan u.,** recensement m des cygnes.

upas ['juːpəs], *s. Bot:* Upas m.

upbeat ['ʌpbiːt], *s. Mus:* Levé m; temps m faible.

upbraid [ʌp'breid], *v.tr.* Réprimander (qn), faire des reproches à (qn). **To u. s.o. with, for, sth.,** reprocher vertement qch. à qn.

upbringing ['ʌp,briŋiŋ], *s.* Éducation f. **What sort of (an) u. has he had?** comment a-t-il été élevé?

upgrade ['ʌp'greid], *v.tr.* Placer à un niveau supérieur.

upheaval [ʌp'hiːv(ə)l], *s.* 1. *Geol:* (a) Soulèvement m. (b) Commotion f, bouleversement m. 2. Boulverse- ment, agitation f. **Political u.,** convulsion f politique.

uphill. 1. *a.* ['ʌp'hil] (a) (Of road, etc.) Montant; en rampe. (b) (Of task) Ardu, rude. 2. *adv.* [ʌp'hil] **To go u.,** monter; aller en montant. *S.a.* HILL 1.

uphold [ʌp'hould], *v.tr.* (**upheld** [-'held]; **upheld**) Supporter, soutenir, maintenir. **To u. the law,** faire observer la loi. **To u. s.o. (in an action),** prêter son appui à qn. **To u. a decision,** confirmer une décision.

upholder [ʌp'houldər], *s.* Partisan m (d'un usage, etc.); défenseur m (d'une opinion).

upholster [ʌp'houlstər], *v.tr.* (i) Capitonner, garnir, rembourrer; (ii) tapisser, couvrir (un canapé, etc.) (**with, in,** de). F: (Of pers.) **Well upholstered,** rondelet, -ette.

upholsterer [ʌp'houlstərər], *s.* Tapissier m (en ameublement).

upholstery [ʌp'houlstri], *s.* 1. Capitonnage m, rem- bourrage m (d'un fauteuil, etc.). 2. (i) Tapisserie f d'ameublement; (ii) garniture f d'intérieur (d'une voiture). **Leather u.,** garniture en cuir. 3. Métier m de tapissier; tapisserie.

upkeep ['ʌpkiːp], *s.* (Frais mpl d')entretien m.

upland ['ʌplənd]. 1. *s.* *Usu. pl.* Région montagneuse. **The uplands,** les hautes terres. 2. *attrib.a.* (Village, etc.) des montagnes.

uplift[1] ['ʌplift], *s.* 1. (a) Élévation f (du terrain). *Geol:* Soulèvement m. *Civ.E:* (Dams) Sous-pression f, *pl.* sous-pressions. (b) a. **U. brassière,** soutien-gorge m au maintien parfait, pigeonnant. 2. **Moral u.,** élévation morale.

uplift[2] [ʌp'lift], *v.tr.* 1. Soulever, élever (qch.); hausser (les sourcils). 2. Élever (l'âme, la voix).

upon [ə'pɔn], *prep.* = ON I.

upper ['ʌpər]. I. *a.* 1. (a) Supérieur, -eure; (plus) haut, (plus) élevé; de dessus; d'au-dessus. **The u. jaw,** la mâchoire supérieure. **U. part of sth.,** dessus m de qch. **The u. storey,** l'étage supérieur. F: **To be weak in the u. storey,** avoir le timbre fêlé. *S.a.* DECK[1] 1, LIP 1. (b) **U. end of a hall,** fond m d'une salle. **U. waters of a river,** amont m d'une rivière. **The u. Rhine,** le haut Rhin. **U. Egypt,** la Haute- Égypte. 2. Supérieur (en rang, etc.). **U. end of the table,** haut bout de la table. *Parl:* **The U. House,** la Chambre Haute. **The u. classes,** la haute société; P: la haute. **To get, gain, have, the u. hand,** prendre, avoir, le dessus; prédominer, prévaloir; F: tenir la corde. **To allow s.o. to get the u. hand,** se laisser tyranniser, mener, par qn. **To get the u. hand of s.o.,** avoir raison de qn. *Sch:* **The u. forms,** les grandes classes. II. **uppers,** *s.pl.* *Bootm:* (a) Empeignes f. (b) Tiges f (de bottes). F: **To be (down) on one's u.,** être dans la débine, dans la dèche.

uppermost ['ʌpəmoust]. 1. *a.* (a) Le plus haut, le plus élevé. (b) De la plus grande importance; premier, -ière. **To be u.,** prédominer; tenir le premier rang; avoir l'avantage. 2. *adv.* (a) (Le plus) en dessus. **Face u.,** face en dessus. (b) **His friend's fate was u. in his thoughts,** ce qui le préoccupait le plus, c'était le sort de son ami.

uppish ['ʌpiʃ], *a.* F: Présomptueux, -euse, arrogant, rogue; suffisant. **Don't be so u.!** ne le prenez pas de si haut!

uppishness ['ʌpiʃnis], *s.* F: Présomption f, arrogance f; suffisance f; grands airs.

upright ['ʌprait]. I. *a.* 1. Vertical, -aux; perpendicu- laire; droit. **U. joint,** joint montant. **To set sth. u.,** mettre qch. debout, d'aplomb. **'To be kept u.,''** "tenir debout." 2. (Of conduct) Droit, intègre, honnête, probe. II. **upright,** *s.* 1. **Out of u.,** hors d'aplomb. 2. *Const:* Montant m; pied-droit m, *pl.* pieds-droits; jambage m. *Fb: etc:* **The up- rights,** les montants de but.

uprightness ['ʌpraitnis], *s.* Droiture f, intégrité f, rectitude f, honnêteté f.

uprising ['ʌp'raiziŋ], s. 1. A: Lever m (de qn). 2. Soulèvement m (du peuple); insurrection f.

uproar ['ʌprɔ:r], s. Vacarme m, tapage m, grand bruit; F: chahut m. The town is in an u., la ville est en effervescence.

uproarious [ʌp'rɔ:riəs], a. Tumultueux, -euse, tapageur, -euse. To burst into u. laughter, partir d'un grand éclat de rire. -ly, adv. Tumultueusement. S.a. LAUGH² 1.

uproot [ʌp'ru:t], v.tr. Déraciner, extirper, arracher (une plante, un mal). To u. s.o. from his home, arracher qn de son foyer.

upset¹ ['ʌpset], s. 1. Renversement m (d'une voiture); chavirement m (d'un bateau). 2. (a) Désorganisation f, bouleversement m, désordre m; remue-ménage m inv. (b) Anicroche f, ennui m. (c) Bouleversement (d'esprit). She has had a dreadful u., elle vient d'avoir un coup terrible. (d) Dérangement m (de corps).

upset² [ʌp'set], v. (upset; upset; upsetting) 1. v.tr. (a) Renverser (un vase, etc.); (faire) verser (une voiture); (faire) chavirer (un bateau); culbuter (qn). (b) Désorganiser, bouleverser, déranger (les plans de qn); tromper (les calculs de qn). (c) Troubler, bouleverser, démonter (qn); mettre (qn) en émoi, impressionner (qn); F: tournebouler (qn). He is easily u., il s'émeut d'un rien. Don't u. yourself, ne vous laissez pas émouvoir; F: ne vous frappez pas. (d) Indisposer (qn); dérégler, déranger (l'estomac); troubler (la digestion). Beer upsets me, la bière me rend malade, ne me vaut rien. 2. v.i. (Of cup, etc.) Se renverser; (of carriage) verser; (of boat) chavirer.

upset³, a. 1. (a) Bouleversé, ému. Don't be so u., ne vous désolez pas comme cela. To get u., se laisser démonter, se frapper. He looked very much u., il avait l'air tout bouleversé, F: tout chaviré. (b) My digestion is u., j'ai l'estomac dérangé. 2. (At auction) U. ['ʌpset] price, mise f à prix; prix de départ; prix demandé.

upshot ['ʌpʃɔt], s. Résultat m, issue f, dénouement m (d'une affaire, etc.). What will be the u. of it? à quoi cela aboutira-t-il, mènera-t-il?

upside down ['ʌpsaid'daun]. 1. adv.phr. (a) Sens dessus dessous; la tête en bas. He was holding the barometer u. d., il tenait le baromètre renversé, à l'envers. (b) F: En désordre; bouleversé. To turn everything u. down, tout bouleverser; tout mettre sens dessus dessous. 2. a. Renversé. U.-d. ideas, idées biscornues, paradoxales.

upstairs ['ʌp'stɛəz]. 1. adv. En haut (de l'escalier). To go u., monter (l'escalier); aller en haut. To call s.o. u., faire monter qn. 2. a. (Of room, etc.) D'en haut; situé à l'étage supérieur.

upstanding [ʌp'stændiŋ], a. 1. Debout inv. A fine u. fellow, un gaillard bien campé. 2. (Of pers.) Honnête, probe, sincère.

upstart ['ʌpstɑ:t], s. Nouveau riche; parvenu, -ue.

upsurge ['ʌpsə:dʒ], s. Poussée f.

uptake ['ʌpteik], s. 1. F: To be slow in the u., avoir la compréhension lente. He is quick in the u., il a l'esprit vif, éveillé. 2. U. pipe, tuyau ascendant, montant. Min: U. (shaft), puits m de retour d'air.

upthrow ['ʌpθrou], s. Geol: Rejet m en haut.

upthrust ['ʌpθrʌst], s. Geol: Soulèvement m.

upturned ['ʌptə:nd, ʌp'tə:nd], a. (Bord) relevé; (nez) retroussé; (yeux) tournés vers le ciel. I looked into the child's u. face, je regardai le visage que l'enfant levait vers moi.

upward ['ʌpwəd]. 1. a. U. movement, mouvement ascensionnel, ascendant. U. gradient, rampe f, montée f. Prices show an u. tendency, les prix sont à la hausse. 2. adv. = UPWARDS. Faces turned u., visages levés vers le ciel.

upwards ['ʌpwədz], adv. 1. De bas en haut; vers le haut; en montant. The road runs u., la route va en montant. 2. En dessus. To lay sth. face u. on the table, mettre qch. à l'endroit sur la table. To look u., regarder en haut, en l'air. 3. Au-dessus. £100 and u., cent livres et au-dessus, et au-delà. U. of fifty pupils, plus de cinquante élèves. From ten years of age u., à partir de dix ans.

uraemia [ju(ə)'ri:miə], s. Med: Urémie f.

Ural ['juərəl]. Pr.n. The U. (river), l'Oural m. The U. mountains, les monts Oural.

uranium [ju(ə)'reiniəm], s. Ch: Uranium m. U. oxide, urane m. U. bearing, uranifère.

urban ['ə:bən], a. Urbain.

urbane [ə:'bein], a. Courtois, poli, civil. -ly, adv. Courtoisement; avec urbanité.

urbanity [ə:'bæniti], s. Urbanité f; courtoisie f.

urbanization [ˌə:bənai'zeif(ə)n], s. Urbanisation f.

urchin ['ə:tʃin], s. 1. F: (a) Galopin, gamin; petit polisson. (b) Gosse mf; marmot m; P: moutard m. 2. = SEA-URCHIN.

Urdu [ə:'du:], s. Ling: L'ourdou m.

urea [ju'riə], s. Ch: Urée f.

ureter [ju(ə)'ri:tər], s. Anat: Uretère m.

urethra [ju(ə)'ri:θrə], s. Anat: Urètre m.

urge¹ [ə:dʒ], s. Incitation f, impulsion f; poussée f. To feel an u. to do sth., se sentir poussé à faire qch. U. to write, démangeaison f d'écrire.

urge², v.tr. 1. (a) To u. s.o. (on), encourager, exhorter, exciter, qn. To u. a horse forward, on, pousser, enlever, talonner, un cheval. To u. s.o. to do sth., pousser, exhorter, qn à faire qch.; prier instamment qn de faire qch. (b) Hâter, pousser; activer (le feu). To u. on, forward, a piece of work, hâter, activer, un travail. 2. Mettre en avant, alléguer, objecter (une raison); faire valoir (une excuse); insister sur (un point). 3. Conseiller fortement, recommander (une démarche). To u. that sth. should be done, insister pour que qch. se fasse.

urgency ['ə:dʒ(ə)nsi], s. 1. Urgence f; extrémité f (d'un besoin). 2. Besoin pressant; nécessité urgente.

urgent ['ə:dʒ(ə)nt], a. Urgent, pressant. U. need, besoin pressant. The matter is u., l'affaire presse. It is most u. that the doctor should come, il y a grande urgence à ce que le docteur vienne. U. entreaty, prière instante. -ly, adv. Avec instance; avec insistance. A doctor is u. required, on demande instamment un médecin.

uric ['juərik], a. (Acide, etc.) urique.

urinal ['juərin(ə)l], s. 1. Med: (Bed) u., urinal m, -aux. 2. Urinoir m. Street u., vespasienne f, F: pissotière f.

urinate ['juərineit], v.i. Uriner.

urine ['juərin], s. Urine f.

urn [ə:n], s. 1. Urne f. 2. (Tea-)urn, fontaine f (à thé); samovar m.

urologist [juə'rɔlədʒist], s. Urologiste mf, urologue mf.

Ursa ['ə:sə]. Pr.n. Astr: U. major, le grand chariot, la grande ourse. U. minor, le petit chariot, la petite ourse.

Ursuline ['ə:sjulin], a. & s.f. Ecc: Ursuline f.

Urticaceae [ˌə:ti'keisii], s.pl. Bot: Urticacées f.

urticaria [ˌə:ti'kɛəriə], s. Med: Urticaire f.

urus ['juərəs], s. Z: Urus m, aurochs m.

us [əs], pers.pron., objective case. 1. [əs] (a) Nous. He sees us, il nous voit. Give us some, donnez-nous-en. There are three of us, nous sommes trois. (b) We will take the boxes with us, nous prendrons les boîtes avec nous. 2. (Stressed) [ʌs] Nous. Between you and us, entre vous et nous. You cannot deceive us engineers, on ne peut pas nous tromper, nous autres ingénieurs. 3. (Stressed: as a nominative) F: He would not believe that it was us, il ne voulait pas croire que c'était nous. 4. (With sg. meaning, = me) (a) (Of majesty) Nous. Cf. WE 2. (b) F: Let us, let's, have a look, laissez-moi regarder.

usable ['ju:zəbl], a. Utilisable.

usage ['ju:zidʒ], s. 1. (Usu. pej.) Traitement m. Book damaged by rough u., livre qui a été maltraité. His u. of me, sa manière d'agir envers moi. 2. (a) Usage m, coutume f; pratique consacrée. (b) Jur: Droit m de passage. 3. Emploi m, usage (d'un mot, etc.).

usance ['ju:z(ə)ns], s. Com: Usance f.

use¹ [ju:s], s. 1. (a) Emploi m, usage m. A new u. for radio, une nouvelle utilisation de la radio. I'll find a u. for it, j'en trouverai l'emploi. To make u. of sth., se servir de qch.; faire usage de qch.; tirer parti de qch. To make good, bad, u. of sth.; to put sth. to good u., to (a) bad u., faire bon usage, mauvais usage, de qch. Article of everyday u., article d'usage courant. Word in everyday u., mot très usité. Not in u., (i) pas en service; (ii) disponible. Machine that has been in u. for ten years, machine qui sert depuis dix ans. **Out of u.**, hors de service; hors d'usage; (mot) désuet, tombé en désuétude. **Fit for u.**, en état de servir. **Ready for u.**, prêt à servir. **For the u. of schools**, à l'usage des écoles. **'Directions for u.'**, "mode *m* d'emploi". **For u. in case of fire**, à employer en cas d'incendie. (b) **To improve with u.**, s'améliorer à l'usage. **2.** Jouissance *f*, usage. (a) **To have the full u. of one's faculties**, jouir de toutes ses facultés. **He has lost the u. of his left leg**, il est impotent de la jambe gauche. (b) **To have the u. of the bathroom**, avoir le droit de faire usage de la salle de bains. **I should like to have the u. of it**, je voudrais pouvoir en disposer. (c) *Jur*: **Full right of u. of sth.**, plein usufruit de qch.; pleine jouissance de qch. **3.** Utilité *f*. **To be of u.** (for sth.), être utile (à qch.). **Can I be of any u.** (to you)? puis-je vous être utile à quelque chose? **It is of no u.**, cela ne sert à rien. **That will be of little u.**, of great u., cela ne servira pas à grand-chose; cela sera d'une grande utilité. **For all the u. it is to me**, pour ce que j'en fais. *F*: **He's no u.**, c'est une non-valeur; il est incapable. **To have no u. for sth.**, n'avoir que faire, ne savoir que faire, de qch. **To have no further u. for sth.**, n'avoir plus besoin de qch. *F*: **I've no u. for him**, je ne peux pas le voir. **It is no u. discussing the question**, rien ne sert de, inutile de, discuter la question. **It is no u. his writing to me**, il est inutile qu'il m'écrive. **What's the u. of, in, making plans?** à quoi sert de faire des projets? à quoi bon faire des projets? **4.** Usage, coutume *f*, habitude *f*.

use² [juːz], v.tr. **1.** (a) Employer, se servir de (qch.); emprunter (une route). **Are you using this knife?** vous servez-vous de ce couteau? (Of thg) **To be used for sth.**, servir à qch.; être employé à qch. **I used the money to rebuild my house**, j'ai utilisé l'argent à rebâtir ma maison. **Word no longer used**, mot désuet. **The root is used as food**, on emploie la racine comme aliment. **I u. that as a hammer**, cela me sert de marteau. **You may u. my name** (as a reference), vous pouvez vous réclamer de moi. (b) **To u. force**, employer la force. **To u. discretion**, agir avec discrétion. **To u. every means**, mettre en œuvre tous les moyens. **To u. one's influence**, user de son influence. **2. To u. s.o. well, ill**, en user bien, mal, avec qn; bien, mal, agir envers qn. **To u. s.o. roughly**, maltraiter, rudoyer, qn. **3. To u. sth.** (up). (a) **User, épuiser, qch. To u. up all one's provisions**, consommer toutes ses provisions. **It is all used up**, il n'en reste plus. (b) **To u. up the scraps**, tirer parti des restes. (c) **To u. up one's horse**, surmener, épuiser, son cheval. **4.** (As aux., only in p.t.; often *translated by imperfect*.) **As children we used** [juːst] **to play together**, quand nous étions petits nous jouions ensemble. **I used to do it**, j'avais l'habitude, j'avais coutume, de le faire. **Things aren't what they used to be**, ce n'est plus comme autrefois. **You don't practise as much as you used to**, vous ne vous exercez pas autant que vous en aviez l'habitude. **She used not to like tobacco**, autrefois elle n'aimait pas le tabac. **used**, a. **1.** [juːzd] Usagé; (timbre-poste) oblitéré. **U. cars**, voitures d'occasion. **Hardly u.**, à l'état de neuf. **2. U. up** ['juːzd'ʌp], (of supplies) fini, épuisé. **3.** [juːst] **To be u. to sth., to doing sth.**, être habitué, accoutumé, à qch., à faire qch. **I am not u. to it**, je n'en ai pas l'habitude. **To get u. to sth.**, s'habituer, s'accoutumer à qch. **You will get u. to it in time**, vous vous y ferez à la longue.

useful ['juːsf(u)l], a. **1.** Utile; (vêtement, etc.) pratique. **This book was very u. to me**, ce livre m'a été d'une grande utilité, m'a rendu grand service. **To make oneself u.**, se rendre utile. **2.** (a) *P*: **He's pretty u. with his fists**, il sait se servir de ses poings. (b) **He made a u. goalkeeper**, il s'est très bien acquitté comme gardien de but. **-fully**, adv. Utilement.

usefulness ['juːsf(u)lnis], s. Utilité *f*. **Institution that has outlived its u.**, institution *f* qui a perdu sa raison d'être.

useless ['juːslis], a. Inutile; bon à rien; (effort) vain. **To be u.**, ne servir à rien. **U. regrets**, regrets superflus. **U. remedy**, remède inefficace. **-ly**, adv. Inutilement; en vain, en pure perte.

uselessness ['juːslisnis], s. Inutilité *f*.

user¹ ['juːzər], s. **1.** Usager, -ère (d'une bicyclette, etc.). **2.** *Jur*: Usufruitier *m*.

user², s. *Jur*: Droit *m* d'usage continu. **Full right of u. of sth.**, plein usufruit de qch.

Ushant [ʌʃ(ə)nt]. Pr.n. Geog: Ouessant.

usher¹ ['ʌʃər], s. **1.** (a) (Gentleman) u., huissier *m*; introducteur *m* (à une réception). *Jur*: Court u., huissier audiencier. (b) Theatre u., ouvreuse *f*. (c) (At wedding) **The ushers**, les garçons d'honneur. **2.** Sch: A: Surveillant *m* d'études; F: pion *m*.

usher², v.tr. **To u. s.o. in, into, a drawing-room**, introduire qn, faire entrer qn, dans un salon. **To u. in a new epoch**, inaugurer une époque. **To u. s.o. out**, reconduire qn (jusqu'à la porte).

usherette [ʌʃəˈret], s.f. Cin: Ouvreuse.

usual ['juːʒu(ə)l], a. Usuel, -elle, habituel, -elle, ordinaire. **At the u. hour**, à l'heure accoutumée. **The u. terms**, les conditions d'usage. **It is u. to pay in advance**, il est d'usage de payer d'avance. **It is the u. practice**, c'est la pratique courante. **Earlier than u.**, plus tôt que de coutume, que d'habitude, que d'ordinaire. **As u.**, comme à l'ordinaire, comme d'ordinaire, comme d'habitude; comme d'usage. *P.N*: **Business as u.**, les affaires continuent, la vente continue (à l'intérieur). *s. F*: (In bar, etc.) **Are you having your u.?** est-ce que vous prenez (votre demi) comme d'habitude? **-ally**, adv. Ordinairement, habituellement; d'ordinaire, d'habitude; à l'ordinaire. **He was more than u. polite**, il s'est montré encore plus poli que d'habitude.

usufruct ['juːzjufrʌkt], s. *Jur*: Usufruit *m* (of, de).

usufructuary [juːzjuˈfrʌktjəri], a. & s. *Jur*: Usufruitier, -ière.

usurer ['juːʒ(ə)rər], s. Usurier, -ière.

usurious [juːˈzjuəriəs], a. **1.** (Intérêt) usuraire. **2.** (Banquier, etc.) usurier.

usurp [juːˈzəːp]. **1.** v.tr. Usurper (from, sur); voler (un titre) (from, à). **2.** v.i. **To u. (up)on s.o.'s rights**, empiéter, usurper, sur les droits de qn. **usurping**, a. Usurpateur, -trice.

usurpation [juːzəːˈpeiʃ(ə)n], s. Usurpation *f*.

usurper [juːˈzəːpər], s. Usurpateur, -trice.

usury ['juːʒuri], s. Usure *f*. **To practise u.**, pratiquer l'usure. **To repay a service with u.**, rendre un bienfait avec usure.

utensil [juˈ(ː)tensl], s. (a) Ustensile *m*. **Household utensils**, ustensiles de ménage. **Set of kitchen utensils**, batterie *f* de cuisine. (b) Outil *m*, instrument *m*.

uterus, pl. -ri ['juːtərəs, -riː], s. Anat: Utérus *m*, matrice *f*.

utilitarian [juːtiliˈtɛəriən], a. Utilitaire.

utilitarianism [juːtiliˈtɛəriənizm], s. Utilitarisme *m*.

utility [juˈtiliti], s. **1.** (a) Utilité *f*. **To be of great u.**, être d'une grande utilité. Adm: Com: **U. goods**, articles *m* d'utilité sociale. **U. car**, voiture *f* à carrosserie canadienne. (b) **Public utility** U.S: utility, service public, service de ville. **2.** Th: **To be a u.** (man), jouer les utilités.

utilizable ['juːtilaizəbl], a. Utilisable.

utilization [juːtilaiˈzeiʃ(ə)n], s. Utilisation *f*; mise *f* en valeur; exploitation *f* (d'une invention).

utilize ['juːtilaiz], v.tr. Utiliser, se servir de (qch.); tirer parti de, tirer profit de, mettre en valeur (qch.).

utmost ['ʌtmoust]. **1.** a. Extrême; dernier, -ière. **The u. ends of the earth**, les (derniers) confins, les extrémités *f*, de la terre. **To make the u. efforts to . . .**, faire tout son possible pour. . . . **It is of the u. importance that . . .**, il est de toute importance, de la dernière importance, que + *sub*. **With the u. ease**, avec la plus grande facilité. **2.** s. Dernière limite; dernier degré. **To the u.**, le plus possible; au suprême degré. **I shall assist you to the u. of my ability**, je vous aiderai dans toute la mesure de mes moyens. **Fifty at the u.**, cinquante au plus, tout au plus. **To do one's u. to . . .**, faire tout son possible, faire l'impossible, pour. . . .

Utopia [juːˈtoupiə]. **1.** Pr.n. L'Utopie *f*. **2.** s. **To create utopias**, créer des utopies.

Utopian [juːˈtoupiən]. **1.** a. Utopique. **2.** s. Utopiste *mf*.

utricularia [jutrikjuˈlɛəriə], s. Bot: Utriculaire *f*.

utter¹ [ˈʌtər], a. Complet, -ète; absolu. **He is an u. stranger to me,** il m'est complètement étranger. **U. fool,** sot achevé; maître sot; parfait imbécile. **U. want of breeding,** manque complet de savoir-vivre. **-ly,** adv. Complètement, absolument, tout à fait.

utter², v.tr. **1.** (a) Pousser, faire entendre (un cri, etc.); prononcer, proférer (un mot); lancer (un juron). **Not to u. a word,** ne pas souffler mot, ne pas desserrer les dents. (b) Dire; exprimer (ses sentiments); débiter (des mensonges). **2.** Émettre, mettre en circulation (de la fausse monnaie).

utterance [ˈʌt(ə)r(ə)ns], s. Expression f (des sentiments, etc.); émission f (d'un son). **To give u. to one's feelings,** exprimer ses sentiments. **2.** Articulation f, prononciation f. **To have a clear u.,** avoir la parole nette. **3.** pl. **Utterances,** propos m, paroles f (de qn).

uttermost [ˈʌtəmoust], a. & s. = UTMOST.

uvula [ˈjuːvjulə], s. Uvule f; luette f.

uvular [ˈjuːvjulər], a. Uvulaire. Ling: **U. r,** r vélaire.

uxorious [ʌkˈsɔːriəs], a. (Mari) (i) très attaché à sa femme, (ii) dominé par sa femme.

V, v [viː], s. (La lettre) V, v m. Tp: V for Victor, V comme Victor. **V-shaped,** en (forme de) V. I.C.E: **V-type engine,** moteur (à cylindres) en V. Mec.E: **V gear,** engrenage à chevrons. Dressm: **V neck,** décolleté en pointe.

vac [væk], s. Sch: F: Vacances fpl. **The long v.,** les grandes vacances.

vacancy ['veikənsi], s. **1.** Vide m, vacuité f. **To stare into v.,** regarder dans le vide, dans le vague. **2.** Nullité f d'esprit; absence f d'idées. **3.** Vacance f; poste vacant. (Boarding-house) **No vacancies!** Complet!

vacant ['veikənt], a. **1.** Vacant, vide, libre. **V. space, place vide. V. room,** chambre libre, inoccupée. S.a. POSSESSION 1, SITUATION 3. **2.** (Esprit) inoccupé; (regard) distrait, vague, sans expression. **V. expression,** air hébété. **-ly,** adv. D'un air distrait, le regard perdu.

vacate [və'keit], v.tr. (a) Quitter (un emploi). **To v. office,** se démettre; donner sa démission. (b) Quitter, laisser libre (un siège); évacuer (un appartement); (at hotel) quitter (une chambre). Jur: **To v. the premises,** vider les lieux. **vacating,** s. (a) **V. of office,** démission f. (b) Évacuation f (d'une maison).

vacation[1] [və'keiʃ(ə)n], s. **1.** Vacances fpl. Jur: Vacations fpl. **The long v.,** (at university) les grandes vacances; Jur: les vacances judiciaires. **2.** = VACATING.

vacation[2], v.i. U.S: Prendre des vacances.

vaccinate ['væksineit], v.tr. Vacciner (esp. contre la variole).

vaccination [ˌvæksi'neiʃ(ə)n], s. Vaccination f (esp. contre la variole).

vaccinator ['væksineitər], s. Vaccinateur m.

vaccine ['væksiːn], s. Vaccin m. **V. point,** plume f pour vaccination.

vacillate ['væsileit], v.i. Vaciller; hésiter (entre deux opinions). **vacillating,** a. Vacillant, irrésolu.

vacillation [ˌvæsi'leiʃ(ə)n], s. Vacillation f, hésitation f.

vacuity [və'kju(ː)iti], s. **1.** Vacuité f, vide m (de l'espace, de la pensée). **2.** Espace m vide; vide.

vacuole ['vækjouəl], s. Biol: Vacuole f.

vacuous ['vækjuəs], a. Vide de pensée, d'expression. **V. remark,** observation dénuée de bon sens. **V. laugh,** rire niais, bête. **V. look,** air hébété.

vacuousness ['vækjuəsnis], s. Vacuité f, vide m (de la pensée).

vacuum, pl. **-ua, -uums** ['vækjuəm, -juə, -juəmz], s. Ph: Vide m. **Very high v.,** vide très poussé. **To create a v.,** faire le vide. Aut: **V.(-feed) tank,** réservoir à élévateur. **'vacuum-brake,** s. Frein m à vide. **'vacuum-clean,** v.tr. Dépoussiérer; passer à l'aspirateur. **'vacuum-cleaning,** s. Nettoyage m par le vide; dépoussiérage m par aspirateur. **'vacuum-cleaner,** s. Aspirateur m (de poussière); dépoussiéreur m. **'vacuum-fan,** s. Ventilateur négatif; ventilateur aspirant. **'vacuum-flask,** s. Bouteille isolante; bouteille Thermos (R.t.m.). **'vacuum-lamp,** s. El: Lampe f à vide. **'vacuum-packed,** a. Emballé sous vide. **'vacuum-pump,** s. Pompe f à vide.

vagabond ['vægəbənd]. **1.** a. Vagabond, errant. **2.** s. (a) Vagabond, -onde; chemineau m. (b) F: Vaurien m.

vagabondage ['vægəbəndidʒ], s. Vagabondage m.

vagary ['veigəri], s. Caprice m, fantaisie f, lubie f. **The vagaries of fashion,** les caprices de la mode.

vagina [və'dʒainə], s. Vagin m.

vagrancy ['veigrənsi], s. (a) Jur: Vagabondage m; mendicité f. (b) Vie f errante.

vagrant ['veigrənt]. **1.** a. Vagabond, errant. **2.** s. (a) Jur: Vagabond, -onde. (b) Homme sans aveu; mendiant, -ante; chemineau m.

vague [veig], a. Vague; imprécis; (of outline) indécis, estompé, flou. **I haven't the vaguest idea,** je n'en ai pas la moindre idée. **-ly,** adv. Vaguement.

vagueness ['veignis], s. Vague m, imprécision f.

vain [vein], a. Vain. **1.** (Of hope, etc.) Mensonger, creux. **V. promises,** vaines promesses. **2.** Inutile, infructueux. **V. efforts,** efforts vains, futiles, stériles. **It is v. (for you) to try, you will never succeed,** vous aurez beau essayer, vous n'y arriverez jamais. **3.** Vaniteux, glorieux. **She was v. of her beauty,** elle était fière de sa beauté. **4. In v.,** en vain. (a) Vainement. **We protested in v., it was in v. that we protested,** nous avons eu beau protester, l'arbre a été abattu. **To labour in v.,** travailler inutilement; perdre sa peine. (b) **To take God's name in v.,** prendre le nom de Dieu en vain; blasphémer le nom de Dieu. **-ly,** adv. **1.** Vainement, en vain, inutilement. **2.** Vaniteusement; avec vanité.

vainglorious [vein'glɔːriəs], a. Lit: Vaniteux, glorieux, orgueilleux. **-ly,** adv. Vaniteusement.

vainglory [vein'glɔːri], s. Vaine gloire; gloriole f.

vainness ['veinnis], s. Vanité f.

vair ['veər], s. Her: Vair m.

valance ['væləns], s. Furn: Frange f de lit; tour m de lit; lambrequin m (d'un ciel de lit, d'une fenêtre).

vale [veil], s. Poet: Vallon m; val m, pl. vals, occ. vaux. **This v. of tears,** cette vallée de larmes, de misère.

valediction [ˌvæli'dikʃ(ə)n], s. Adieu(x) m(pl).

valedictory [ˌvæli'diktəri]. a. (Allocution, dîner) d'adieu.

valence[1] ['veiləns], s. = VALENCY.

valence[2] ['væləns], s. = VALANCE.

valency ['veilənsi], s. Ch: Valence f; atomicité f.

Valentine ['væləntain]. **1.** Pr.n. **Saint V.'s day,** la Saint-Valentin (le 14 février). **2.** s. Carte envoyée le jour de la Saint-Valentin.

valerian [və'liəriən], s. Bot: Valériane f.

valet[1] ['vælei, 'vælit], s. Valet m de chambre.

valet[2] ['vælei], v.tr. (valeted ['vælitid]). **1.** Servir (qn) comme valet de chambre. **2.** Remettre en état (un vêtement d'homme).

valetudinarian ['væliˌtjuːdi'nɛəriən], a. & s. Valétudinaire (mf).

valiant ['væljənt], a. Vaillant, valeureux, brave. **-ly,** adv. Vaillamment.

valid ['vælid], a. (Contrat, etc.) valide, valable; (passeport) régulier; (argument) solide. **Ticket v. for three months,** billet valable, bon pour, trois mois. **No longer v.,** périmé.

validate ['vælideit], v.tr. Valider; rendre valable.

validity [və'liditi], s. Validité f (d'un contrat, d'un passeport, etc.). **V. of an argument,** justesse f, force f, d'un argument.

valise [və'liːs, -iːz], s. **1.** U.S: Sac m de voyage; mallette f. **2.** Mil: Sac de voyage (d'officier).

Valkyrie ['vælkiəri], s.f. Walkyrie, Valkyrie.

valley ['væli], s. **1.** Vallée f; (small) vallon m. **U-, V-shaped v.,** vallée (à profil) en u, v. **The Rhone V.,** la vallée du Rhône. **2.** Const: Noue f, cornière f (de toit). **V. tile,** tuile cornière.

valorization [ˌvælərai'zeiʃ(ə)n], s. Fin: Com: Valorisation f.

valorous ['vælərəs], a. Lit: Valeureux, -euse, vaillant.

valour ['vælər], s. Lit: Valeur f, vaillance f.

valuable ['væljuəbl]. **1.** a. (a) Précieux, -euse; de valeur, de prix. Jur: **For a v. consideration,** à titre onéreux. (b) Évaluable. **2.** s.pl. **Valuables,** objets m de valeur, de prix.

valuation [ˌvælju'eiʃ(ə)n], s. **1.** (a) Évaluation f, estimation f. Jur: Expertise f. **At a v.,** à dire d'expert. **To make a v. of the goods,** faire l'expertise des marchandises. (b) Inventaire m. **2.** Valeur estimée. (a) **To set too high a v. on goods,** surestimer des marchandises. (b) **To take s.o. at his own v.,** estimer, coter, qn selon l'opinion qu'il a de lui-même.

value[1] ['vælju:], s. Valeur f. **1. To be of v.,** avoir de la valeur. **To be of little v.,** valoir peu de chose. **Of no v.,** sans valeur. **He doesn't seem to know the v. of time,** il semble ignorer le prix du temps. **To set a low v. on sth** attacher peu de prix à qch. **To set a high

v. on sth., faire grand cas de qch., attacher un grand prix à qch. *Ins:* Aliment *m*; risque *m*; intérêt *m*. *Com:* **Market v.**, valeur marchande. **Increase in v.**, plus-value *f*. **Decrease in v.**, moins-value *f*. **To fall in v.**, se dévaloriser. **2. To pay s.o. the v. of the lost umbrella**, rembourser à qn le prix du parapluie perdu. *Com:* **For v. received**, valeur reçue. **To get good v. for one's money**, *F:* en avoir pour son argent. **This article is very good v.**, cet article est très avantageux. **value**[2], *v.tr.* **1.** *Com:* **To v. goods**, évaluer, estimer, priser, des marchandises. **2.** Estimer, faire grand cas de (qn, qch.). **To v. one's life**, tenir à la vie. **He doesn't v. his skin**, il fait bon marché de sa peau. **3.** *v.i. Com:* **To v. upon s.o.**, disposer, faire traite, sur qn. **valued**, *a.* Estimé, précieux.

valueless ['væljulis], *a.* Sans valeur.

valuer ['væljuər], *s.* Estimateur *m*, commissaire-priseur *m*, expert *m*.

valve [vælv], *s.* **1.** Soupape *f.* (*a*) **Ball-v.**, clapet *m* sphérique. **Needle-v.**, soupape à pointeau. **Clack-v., flap-v.**, soupape à clapet, à charnière. *S.a.* AIR-VALVE, CHECK-VALVE, SAFETY-VALVE, etc. (*b*) *I.C.E:* **Exhaust, outlet, v.**, soupape d'échappement. **Inlet v.**, soupape d'admission. **Mushroom v., poppet v.**, soupape en champignon; soupape circulaire; clapet. (*c*) **Stop-v.**, obturateur *m*. **Butterfly v.**, (soupape à) papillon *m*; volet *m* (de carburateur). (*d*) *Mch:* **Slide-v.**, tiroir *m*. (*e*) *Aut: Cy:* **Valve** *f* (de pneu). **2. Valvule** *f* (du cœur, etc.). **3.** (*a*) *El:* **Rectifying v.**, soupape électrique; valve redresseuse (de courant). (*b*) *W.Tel: etc:* **Lampe** *f* radio-électrique; lampe valve; tube *m*. **Five-electrode v.**, pentode *f*. **4.** *Bot: Moll:* **Valve. 5.** *Hyd.E:* **(Gate,-sluice-)v.**, vanne (de communication). '**valve-box, -case, -chest**, *s.* **1.** *Hyd.E:* Boîte *f* à clapet. **2.** *Mch:* (*Of slide-valve*) Boîte à vapeur; boîte de distribution (de vapeur). '**valve-cap**, *s.* Capuchon *m*, chapeau *m* (d'une valve de pneu). '**valve-gear**, *s.* **1.** *Mch:* (Steam) v.-gear, mécanisme *m* de distribution (de la vapeur). **2.** *I.C.E:* (Organes *mpl* de) distribution *f*. '**valve-holder**, *s. W.Tel:* Douille *f*, support *m*, de lampe. '**valve-rocker**, *s. I.C.E:* Culbuteur *m*.

valvular ['vælvjulər], *a.* Valvulaire.

valvule ['vælvju:l], *s.* Valvule *f*.

vamoose [və'mu:s], *v.i. P:* Décamper; filer.

vamp[1] [væmp], *s.* **1.** *Bootm:* Empeigne *f*, claque *f*. **2.** *Mus: F:* Accompagnement tapoté, improvisé.

vamp[2], *v.tr.* **1.** *Bootm:* Remonter (un soulier). **2.** *Mus: F:* Tapoter au piano (un accompagnement ad hoc).

vamp[3], *s.f. F: O:* (*Abbrev. of* vampire) (*a*) Aventurière; femme fatale. (*b*) Flirteuse, allumeuse, vamp.

vamp[4], *v.tr. F: O:* (*Of woman*) Ensorceler, envoûter (un homme). (*b*) *Abs.* Flirter.

vampire ['væmpaiər], *s.* **1.** (*a*) *Myth:* Vampire *m*; strige *f*. (*b*) *F:* Vampire; extorqueur, -euse. **2.** *Z:* **V.(-bat)**, vampire.

van[1] [væn], *s.* (*a*) Avant-garde *f*. (*b*) Front *m* (de bataille). **To be in the v. of progress**, être un pionnier du progrès.

van[2], *s. Veh:* **1.** (*a*) Fourgon *m*. **Furniture v., removal v.**, voiture *f*, fourgon, de déménagement. **Bullion v.**, fourgon bancaire. **Delivery v.**, camion *m* de livraison; (*light*) camionnette *f*. (*b*) **Gipsy v.**, roulotte *f*. **2.** (*a*) *Cin:* **Recording v.**, camion d'enregistrement. (*b*) *W.Tel:* **Outside broadcasting v.**, car *m* de radio-reportage. (*c*) **Police loud-speaker v.**, camionnette de police. **3.** *Rail:* Wagon *m*, fourgon *m*. **Luggage v.**, fourgon à bagages. **Guard's v.**, fourgon du chef de train, de queue. '**van-man**, *pl.* -**men**, *s.m.* Livreur.

van[3], *s. Ten: F:* **V. in, out** = advantage **in, out**, *q.v. under* ADVANTAGE[1] **1.**

vanadium [və'neidiəm], *s. Ch:* Vanadium *m*.

vandal ['vænd(ə)l], *s.* Vandale *m*.

vandalism ['vændəlizm], *s.* Vandalisme *m*. **Piece of v.**, acte *m* de vandalisme.

vane [vein], *s.* **1.** (*a*) **(Wind-, weather-)v.**, girouette *f*. (*b*) Moulinet *m* (d'un anémomètre, etc.); turbine *f* (d'un compteur à eau). **2.** Bras *m* (de moulin à vent); aube *f*, ailette *f* (de turbine); ailette, pale *f* (de venti-lateur). **3.** *Surv:* **(Sight-)v.**, pinnule *f* (d'une alidade); viseur *m* (de compas). **Slide v.**, voyant *m* (d'une mire de nivellement). **4.** *W.Tel:* Lamette *f* (de condensateur variable).

vanguard ['vænga:d], *s. Mil:* Tête *f* d'avant-garde. **To be in the v. of a movement**, être un des pionniers d'un mouvement.

vanilla [və'nilə], *s.* Vanille *f*. **V. ice**, glace à la vanille.

vanish ['vænif], *v.i.* Disparaître; (*of visions, suspicions, etc.*) se dissiper, s'évanouir. *Mth:* (i) Tendre vers zéro; (ii) s'évanouir. **At the moment of danger he vanished**, au moment du danger il s'est éclipsé. **To v. into thin air**, se volatiliser. **vanishing**, *s.* Disparition *f*. **Profits have dwindled to v. point**, les bénéfices se sont réduits à néant. *Art:* **V. line**, ligne d'horizon; ligne de fuite. *Toil:* **V. cream**, crème *f* de jour.

vanity ['væniti], *s.* **1.** Vanité *f*, vide *m* (des grandeurs humaines, etc.); futilité *f* (d'une tentative). **All is v.**, tout est vanité. **2.** Vanité; orgueil *m*. **To do sth. out of v.**, faire qch. par vanité.

vanquish ['væŋkwif], *v.tr.* Vaincre.

vanquisher ['væŋkwiʃər], *s. Lit:* Vainqueur *m*.

vantage ['va:ntidʒ], *s.* **1.** **(Coign, point, of) v.**, position avantageuse; avantage *m* du terrain. **2.** *Ten:* = VAN[3].

vapid ['væpid], *a.* Plat, insipide; (*of conversation, etc.*) fade.

vapidity [və'piditi], **vapidness** ['væpidnis], *s.* Fadeur *f*, insipidité *f*.

vaporization [,veipərai'zeiʃ(ə)n], *s.* **1.** Vaporisation *f*. **2.** Pulvérisation *f* (d'un liquide).

vaporize ['veipəraiz]. **1.** *v.tr.* (*a*) Vaporiser, gazéifier. (*b*) Pulvériser (un liquide); vaporiser. *I.C.E:* Carburer (le combustible). **2.** *v.i.* Se vaporiser, se gazéifier.

vaporizer ['veipəraizər], *s.* (*Device*) Vaporis(at)eur *m*; pulvérisateur *m*; atomiseur *m*.

vaporous ['veipərəs], *a.* Vaporeux.

vapour ['veipər], *s.* **1.** Vapeur *f*; buée *f* (sur les vitres). **2.** *pl. Med: A:* Vapeurs. '**vapour-bath**, *s.* **1.** Bain *m* de vapeur. **2.** Étuve *f* humide (de hammam).

variability [,veəriə'biliti], *s.* Variabilité *f* (du temps, etc.). *Biol:* Inconstance *f* (de type).

variable ['veəriəbl]. **1.** *a.* (*a*) Variable; changeant, inconstant. *Mth:* **V. quantity**, quantité variable. (*b*) *Mec.E:* Réglable. **2.** *s. Mth:* Variable *f*.

variance ['veəriəns], *s.* **1.** Désaccord *m*; discorde *f*. **To be at v. with s.o.**, être en désaccord avec qn; être brouillé avec qn. **To set two people at v.**, mettre la discorde entre deux personnes. **Theory at v. with the facts**, théorie incompatible, en désaccord, en contradiction, avec les faits. **2.** (*a*) Variation *f* (de température, de volume, etc.). (*b*) *Ch:* Variance *f*.

variant ['veəriənt]. **1.** *a.* (*a*) *Lit:* **V. reading**, variante *f*. (*b*) *Biol:* Qui s'écarte du type, aberrant. **2.** *s.* Variante *f*.

variation [,veəri'eiʃ(ə)n], *s.* **1.** Variation *f*, changement *m. El:* **Current v.**, variation de courant. *Magn:* **Magnetic v.**, déclinaison magnétique (locale). **2.** Différence *f*; écart *m*. **3.** *Mus:* **Theme with varia-tions**, thème varié; thème avec variations.

varicose ['værikous], *a. Med:* **1.** Variqueux, -euse. **V. vein**, varice *f*. **2.** **V. stocking**, bas *m* à varices.

varied ['veərid], *a.* See VARY.

variegate ['veərigeit], *v.tr.* **1.** Varier, diversifier (les couleurs). **2.** Bigarrer, barioler; diaprer. **varie-gated**, *a.* **1.** Varié; divers. **2.** Bigarré, bariolé; diapré, versicolore. *Nat.Hist:* Panaché.

variegation [,veəri'geiʃ(ə)n], *s.* Diversité *f* de couleurs; bigarrure *f*, bariolage *m. Bot:* Panachure *f*, diaprure *f*.

variety [və'raiəti], *s.* **1.** (*a*) Variété *f*, diversité *f*. **To lend v. to the menu**, donner de la variété au menu. (*b*) **A v. of patterns**, un assortiment d'échantillons. **For a v. of reasons**, pour toutes sortes de raisons. **2.** (*a*) *Nat.Hist:* Variété (de fleur, etc.). (*b*) *Th:* **V. entertainment, varieties**, attractions *f.* **V. turns, numéros** *m* de music-hall. **V. theatre**, théâtre de variétés, music-hall *m*.

variometer [,veəri'ɔmitər], *s. Av: El:* Variomètre *m*.

various ['veəriəs], *a.* **1.** Varié, divers. **Of v. kinds**, de diverses sortes. **To talk about v. things**, parler de chose(s) et d'autre(s). **2.** (*a*) Différent, dissemblable; divers. *Lit:* **V. reading**, variante *f*. (*b*) Plusieurs; plus d'un. **For v. reasons**, pour plusieurs raisons. **At v. times**, à différentes reprises. **-ly**, *adv.* Diverse-ment; de diverses manières.

varlet ['vɑːlit], *s.m.* **1.** *Hist:* Varlet, page. **2.** *A:* Coquin; vaurien.

varmint ['vɑːmint], *s. P:* **1.** (a) Vermine *f.* (b) *Ven:* Renard *m.* **2. Young v.,** petit polisson, petite peste.

varnish[1] ['vɑːniʃ], *s.* **1.** Vernis *m.* **Spirit v.,** vernis à l'alcool. *Toil:* Nail v., vernis à ongles. **2.** (Enduit *m* de) vernis; vernissure *f.* **'varnish-remover,** *s.* (a) *Ind:* Décapant *m* pour vernis. (b) *Toil:* Dissolvant *m.*

varnish[2], *v.tr.* **1.** Vernir; vernisser (la poterie). **2.** *F:* **To v. (over),** farder (les faits); glisser sur (les défauts de qn). **varnishing,** *s.* Vernissage *m.* **'varnishing-day,** *s.* Vernissage *m* (au Salon de peinture).

varsity ['vɑːs(:)ti], *s. O: F: =* UNIVERSITY.

vary ['vɛəri]. **1.** *v.tr.* Varier, diversifier; faire varier. **To v. one's methods,** varier de méthode. **2.** *v.i.* (a) Varier, changer; être variable. (b) **To v. from . . .,** dévier, s'écarter, de . . .; différer de. . . . (c) Différer (d'avis). **As to the date, authors v.,** quant à la date, les auteurs ne sont pas d'accord. **varied,** *a.* Varié; divers. **varying,** *a.* Variable, changeant; varié, divers.

vascular ['væskjulər], *a.* Vasculaire.

vasculum, *pl.* **-a** ['væskjuləm, -ə], *s.* **1.** *Bot:* Ascidie *f.* **2.** Boîte *f* en fer blanc (de botaniste).

vase [vɑːz], *s.* Vase *m.* **Flower v.,** vase à fleurs.

Vaseline ['væsəliːn], *s. R.t.m.* Vaseline. *f.* **To smear, coat, sth. with v.,** enduire qch. de vaseline; vaseliner qch.

vaso-motor ['veizou'moutər], *a. & s. Anat:* Vaso-moteur (*m*).

vassal ['væs(ə)l], *a. & s.* Vassal (*m*), -aux; feudataire (*m*) (**to, de**).

vassalage ['væsəlidʒ], *s.* (a) Vassalité *f,* vasselage *m.* (b) Sujétion *f.*

vast [vɑːst], *a.* Vaste, immense. **To spend a v. amount of money,** dépenser énormément d'argent. **-ly,** *adv.* Vastement; immensément.

vastness ['vɑːstnis], *s.* Vastitude *f,* immensité *f;* amplitude *f.*

vat[1] [væt], *s.* Cuve *f;* (*small*) cuveau *m;* bac *m;* bain *m.* *Leath:* Tan v., fosse *f* de tannage.

vat[2], *v.tr.* Mettre en cuve; encuver.

vatful ['vætful], *s.* Cuvée *f.*

Vatican ['vætikən]. *Pr.n.* **The V.,** le Vatican. **V. Council,** Concile *m* du Vatican.

vaudeville ['voudəvil], *s. Th:* **1.** Vaudeville *m.* **2.** Spectacle *m* de music-hall.

vault[1] [vɔːlt, vɔlt], *s.* **1.** (a) Voûte *f.* **Barrel v.,** voûte en berceau, en plein cintre. **Groined vault,** voûte d'arêtes. **Ribbed v.,** voûte d'ogives. *Lit:* **The v. of heaven,** le dôme des cieux; la voûte céleste. (b) *Const:* Chapelle *f* (de four de boulangerie); voûte (d'un fourneau). **2.** (a) Souterrain *m.* (*Of bank, etc.*) **Safety v.,** chambre forte. (b) **Wine-v.,** cave *f,* cellier *m.* (c) (Sepulchral) v., caveau *m.* **Family v.,** caveau de famille.

vault[2], *v.tr.* **To v. (over) a cellar,** voûter une cave. **vaulted,** *a.* Voûté, voussé; en voûte. **vaulting**[1], *s.* **1.** Construction *f* de voûtes. **2.** *Coll:* Voûte(s) *f(pl).* **Fan v.,** voûtes en éventail.

vault[3], *s. Gym: etc:* Saut *m* (de barrière, etc.); saut au cheval de bois.

vault[4]. **1.** *v.i.* (a) **To v. over a gate,** sauter une barrière, franchir une barrière d'un saut (en s'aidant des mains). **To v. over a stream,** sauter un ruisseau à la perche. (b) **To v. into the saddle,** sauter en selle. **2.** *v.tr.* Sauter (une barrière, etc.). **vaulting**[2], *a. Lit:* **Vaulting ambition,** ambition qui vise trop haut. **vaulting**[3], *s. Gym:* Exercice *m* du saut; voltige *f* (sur le cheval de bois). *S.a.* HORSE 3.

vaunt[1] [vɔːnt], *s. Lit:* Vanterie *f;* fanfaronnade *f.*

vaunt[2], *v.tr. Lit:* (a) Vanter (qch.). (b) Se vanter de (qch.); se faire gloire de (qch.). **vaunting**[1], *s.* Vantard. **vaunting**[2], *s.* Vanterie *f;* jactance *f.*

veal [viːl], *s. Cu:* Veau *m.* *S.a.* LEG[1] 2.

vector[1] ['vektər], *s.* **1.** *Mth:* Vecteur *m.* **Radius v.,** rayon vecteur. **2.** *Med:* Porteur, -euse (d'une maladie).

vector[2], *v.tr. Av:* Diriger (un avion) par radio.

vectorial [vek'tɔːriəl], *a. Mth:* Vectoriel, -elle.

veer[1] [viər], *s.* **1.** Changement *m* de direction, saute *f* (de vent). **2.** (*Of ship*) Virage *m* vent arrière. **3.** Revirement *m* (d'opinion).

veer[2]. **1.** *v.i.* (a) (*Of wind*) Tourner, sauter. **To v. aft, abaft,** adonner. **To v. ahead,** venir debout. **To v. forward,** refuser. (b) (*Of ship*) Virer (vent arrière); changer de bord. (c) (*Of pers.*) **To v. round,** changer d'opinion, *F:* donner un coup de barre. **2.** *v.tr.* (Faire) virer (un navire) vent arrière. **veering,** *s.* *Nau:* Tacking and v., virement *m* de bord.

veer[3], *v.tr. Nau:* **To v. out the cable,** filer du câble.

vegetable ['vedʒitəbl]. **1.** *a.* Végétal, -aux. **V. life,** vie végétale. *F:* **V. existence,** (i) (*of invalid, etc.*) existence végétative; (ii) vie monotone. **2.** *s.* (a) *Bot:* Végétal *m,* -aux. (b) Légume *m.* **Early vegetables,** primeurs *f.* **Green vegetables,** légumes verts. **Dried vegetables,** légumes secs. **V. garden,** (jardin) potager *m.* **V. slicer,** coupe-légumes *m inv.* **'vegetable-dish,** *s.* Légumier *m.*

vegetal ['vedʒit(ə)l], *a. & s. Bot:* Végétal (*m*), -aux.

vegetarian [vedʒi'tɛəriən], *a. & s.* Végétarien, -ienne.

vegetarianism [vedʒi'tɛəriənizm], *s.* Végétarisme *m.*

vegetate ['vedʒiteit], *v.i.* Végéter. **To v. in an office,** moisir, végéter, dans un bureau.

vegetation [vedʒi'teiʃ(ə)n], *s.* Végétation *f.*

vegetative ['vedʒiteitiv], *a.* Végétatif, -ive.

vehemence ['viːəmǝns], *s.* Véhémence *f;* impétuosité *f.*

vehement ['viːəmǝnt], *a.* Véhément; (vent) impétueux; passionné. **-ly,** *adv.* Véhémentement; impétueusement; passionnément.

vehicle ['viːikl], *s.* **1.** Véhicule *m,* voiture *f.* *Aut:* **Commercial v.,** véhicule utilitaire. *Mil:* Engin *m.* **2. Air is the v. of sound,** l'air est le véhicule du son. **The newspaper as a v. for advertising,** le journal comme moyen de réclame. *Med:* **V. of disease,** agent vecteur. **3.** *Pharm:* Excipient *m.*

vehicular [vi'hikjulər], *a.* **V. traffic,** circulation *f* des voitures.

veil[1] [veil], *s.* **1.** (a) Voile *m* (de religieuse, etc.). **Bridal v.,** voile de mariée. *Ecc:* **To take the v.,** prendre le voile. (b) Hat-v., eye v., voilette *f.* **2.** *A:* Voile, rideau *m.* *Lit:* **Beyond the v.,** au delà de la tombe. **3. To draw, throw, a v. over sth.,** jeter un voile sur qch. **4.** *Phot:* Léger voile.

veil[2], *v.tr.* **1.** Voiler. **2.** Voiler, cacher, dissimuler (ses sentiments). **veiled,** *a.* **1.** Voilé; couvert d'un voile. **2.** Voilé, caché, dissimulé. **Hardly v. hostility,** hostilité à peine déguisée. **In thinly v. terms,** en termes peu voilés. **veiling,** *s. Coll:* Voile(s) *m(pl).* *S.a.* NUN'S VEILING.

vein[1] [vein], *s.* **1.** *Anat:* Veine *f.* **2.** Nervure *f* (de feuille). **3.** *Geol: Min:* Veine, filon *m.* **4.** (*In wood, marble*) Veine. **5.** Veine, disposition *f,* humeur *f.* **In humororous v.,** en veine de plaisanterie. **The poetic v.,** la veine poétique.

vein[2], *v.tr.* Veiner, marbrer (une porte).

veined [veind], *a.* **1.** Veiné; à veines. **2.** *Bot: Ent:* Nervuré.

velar ['viːlər], *a. & s. Ling:* Vélaire (*f*).

veld(t) [velt], *s.* (*In S. Afr.*) Veld(t) *m.*

velleity [vi'liːiti], *s.* Velléité *f.*

vellum ['veləm], *s.* Vélin *m.* **Rough v.,** parchemin *m* en cosse. **'vellum paper,** *s.* Papier *m* vélin.

velocipede [vi'lɔsipiːd], *s. A:* Vélocipède *m.*

velocity [vi'lɔsiti], *s.* Vitesse *f.* *Mec:* **Accelerated v.,** vitesse accélérée.

velour(s) [və'luər], *s. Com:* **1.** *Tex:* Velouté *m;* velours *m* de laine. **2. V. hat,** chapeau (en feutre) taupé.

velum ['viːləm], *s. Anat:* Voile *m* du palais.

velvet ['velvit], *s.* **1.** *Tex:* Velours *m.* **Plain v.,** velours plain, uni. **Uncut v., terry v.,** velours bouclé, frisé, épinglé. **Ribbed v., corduroy v.,** velours à côtes. **The v. glove,** le gant de velours. *F:* **To be on v.,** jouer sur le velours. *F:* **Black v.,** mélange de champagne et de stout. **2.** *Nat.Hist:* Velouté *m.* **2.** *Attrib.* **V. coat,** habit de velours. **With v. tread,** à pas feutrés.

velveteen [velvi'tiːn], *s.* **1.** *Tex:* Velours *m* de coton; velours de chasse; velvantine *f.* **Ribbed v., corduroy v.,** velours (de coton) côtelé, à côtes. **2.** *pl. O:* **Velveteens,** pantalon *m* en velours de chasse.

velvety ['velviti], *a.* Velouté, velouteux, -euse. **V. wine,** vin velouté, vin moelleux.

venal ['viːnl], a. Vénal, -aux; mercenaire. **-ally**, adv. Vénalement.

venality [viːˈnæliti], s. Vénalité f.

vend [vend], v.tr. (a) Jur: Vendre. (b) Faire le commerce de (choses de peu de valeur); vendre (des journaux). **Vending machine**, distributeur m automatique.

vendetta [venˈdetə], s. Vendetta f.

vendor ['vendɔːr, -ər], s. Vendeur, -euse. Fin: **V.'s shares**, actions d'apport, de fondation.

veneer¹ [vəˈniər], s. **1.** (a) Placage m, revêtement m (de bois mince). (b) Bois m de placage. **2.** Masque m; apparence extérieure; vernis m (de connaissances). **A mere v. of politeness**, une politesse toute en surface.

veneer², v.tr. Plaquer (le bois).

venerability [ˌven(ə)rəˈbiliti], s. Vénérabilité f.

venerable ['ven(ə)rəbl], a. Vénérable.

venerate ['venəreit], v.tr. Vénérer.

veneration [ˌvenəˈreiʃ(ə)n], s. Vénération f (**for**, pour). **To hold s.o. in v.**, avoir de la vénération pour qn.

venereal [viˈniəriəl], a. Vénérien, -ienne.

venery ['venəri], s. A: Vénerie f; la chasse.

Venetian [viˈniːʃən], a. & s. Geog: Vénitien, -ienne. Needlew: **V. lace**, point m de Venise. S.a. BLIND³ 1, SHUTTER 1.

Venezuela [ˌveneˈzweilə]. Pr.n. Geog: Le Vénézuela.

Venezuelan [ˌveneˈzweilən], a. & s. Vénézuélien, -ienne.

vengeance ['ven(d)ʒ(ə)ns], s. Vengeance f. **To take v. on s.o.**, se venger sur qn; se venger de qn. **Crime that cries for v.**, crime qui crie vengeance. F: **With a v.**, furieusement; à outrance; pour de bon. **It is raining with a v.**, voilà qui s'appelle pleuvoir. **He's a gambler with a v.**, c'est un joueur s'il en fut jamais.

vengeful ['ven(d)ʒf(u)l], a. Vindicatif, -ive.

venial ['viːniəl], a. (Péché) véniel. (Of fault) Léger, -ère, pardonnable, véniel, -ielle.

veniality [ˌviːniˈæliti], s. Caractère léger, véniel (d'une faute).

Venice ['venis]. Pr.n. Venise f.

venison ['venizn], s. Venaison f. **Haunch of v.**, quartier m de chevreuil.

vennel ['ven(ə)l], s. Scot: Ruelle f, venelle f.

venom ['venəm], s. (a) Venin m. (b) **Tongue full of v.**, mauvaise langue; langue de vipère.

venomous ['venəməs], a. **1.** Venimeux; (of plant) vénéneux. **2. V. tongue**, langue de vipère. **-ly**, adv. D'une manière venimeuse; méchamment.

venomousness ['venəməsnis], s. **1.** Nature venimeuse (d'un animal); nature vénéneuse (d'une plante). **2.** Méchanceté f (de langue).

venous ['viːnəs], a. Veineux, -euse.

vent¹ [vent], s. **1.** (a) Trou m, orifice m, lumière f, passage m (pour laisser entrer ou échapper l'air); évent m. (b) Lumière (d'une arme à feu). (c) **Vents of a flute**, trous d'une flûte. (d) Cheminée f (de volcan). **2. To give v. to one's grief, to one's anger**, donner libre cours à sa douleur, à sa colère. **To give v. to a sigh**, laisser échapper un soupir. **'vent-hole**, s. Trou m de fausset (d'un tonneau); évent m (d'un volcan).

vent², v.tr. **To v. one's anger on s.o.**, passer sa colère sur qn.

vent³, s. Cost: Fente f (derrière un pardessus).

ventilate ['ventileit], v.tr. **1.** Aérer (une chambre); ventiler (un tunnel). **Ventilating fan**, ventilateur m. **2.** F: Agiter (une question) (au grand jour).

ventilation [ˌventiˈleiʃ(ə)n], s. **1.** Aération f, aérage m, ventilation f. Ind: **V. plant**, installation f d'aérage. **2.** Mise f en discussion publique (d'une question). **venti'lation-shaft**, s. Min: Puits m d'aérage.

ventilator ['ventileitər], s. **1.** Ventilateur m; ventouse f (d'une cheminée); soupirail, -aux m (d'une cave). Nau: Manche f à air. **2.** (Over door) Vasistas m. **3.** Aut: Volet m d'aération (de capot); déflecteur m.

Ventimiglia [ˌventiˈmiːljə]. Pr.n. Geog: Vintimille.

ventricle ['ventrikl], s. Ventricule m (du cœur).

ventriloquial [ˌventriˈloukwiəl], a. Ventriloque.

ventriloquism [venˈtriləkwizm], s. Ventriloquie f.

ventriloquist [venˈtriləkwist], s. Ventriloque mf.

ventriloquy [venˈtriləkwi], s. Ventriloquie f.

venture¹ ['ventʃər], s. **1.** Entreprise risquée. **To be ready for any v.**, être prêt aux entreprises les plus hasardeuses. **2.** Com: Entreprise, spéculation f. **3. At a v.**, à l'aventure, au hasard. **To answer at a v.**, répondre au petit bonheur. **To draw a bow at a v.**, plaider le faux pour savoir le vrai.

venture². **1.** v.tr. (a) **To v. to do sth.**, oser faire qch.; se risquer à faire qch. **I will v. to affirm that . . .**, j'ose affirmer que. . . . **I v. to write to you**, je me permets de vous écrire. (b) **To v. a guess**, hasarder une conjecture. (c) Hasarder, aventurer, risquer (sa vie, son argent). **2.** v.i. (a) **To v. upon sth.**, se risquer à faire qch. **To v. on an opinion**, hasarder une opinion. (b) **To v. into an unknown country**, s'aventurer en pays inconnu. **To v. out of doors**, se risquer à sortir.

venturesome ['ventʃəsəm], a. **1.** Aventureux, osé. **2.** (Of action) Aventuré, risqué.

venturesomeness ['ventʃəsəmnis], s. Esprit aventureux.

venue ['venjuː], s. **1.** Jur: Lieu m du jugement; juridiction f. **To change the v. (of a trial)**, renvoyer l'affaire devant une autre cour. **2.** Lieu de réunion; rendez-vous m.

Venus ['viːnəs]. Pr.n.f. Vénus. **'Venus's 'fly-trap**, s. Bot: Dionée f gobe-mouches. **'Venus's 'slipper**, s. Bot: cypripède m; sabot m de Vénus.

veracious [vəˈreiʃəs], a. Véridique. **-ly**, adv. Véridiquement; avec véracité.

veraciousness [vəˈreiʃəsnis], **veracity** [vəˈræsiti], s. Véracité f.

veranda(h) [vəˈrændə], s. Véranda f.

verb [vəːb], s. Gram: Verbe m.

verbal ['vəːb(ə)l], a. **1.** (a) Verbal, -aux; oral, -aux. **V. agreement**, convention verbale. (b) **V. dispute**, dispute de mots. (c) (Of translation) Mot à mot, mot pour mot; littéral, -aux. **2.** Gram: **V. noun**, nom verbal. **-ally**, adv. **1.** Verbalement; de vive voix. **2.** Littéralement.

verbatim [vəːˈbeitim]. **1.** adv. Mot pour mot; textuellement. **2.** a. **V. report of the proceedings**, compte-rendu sténographique des débats.

verbena [və(ː)ˈbiːnə], s. Verveine f.

verbiage ['vəːbiidʒ], s. Verbiage m.

verbomania [ˌvəːbouˈmeiniə], s. Psy: Verbomanie f.

verbose [vəːˈbous], a. Verbeux, -euse; diffus, prolixe. **-ly**, adv. Avec verbosité.

verboseness [vəːˈbousnis], **verbosity** [vəːˈbositi], s. Verbosité f, prolixité f.

verb. sap. ['vəːbˈsæp]. Lt.phr. (= verbum sapienti sat est) À bon entendeur salut.

verdant ['vəːd(ə)nt], a. Lit: Vert, verdoyant.

verdict ['vəːdikt], s. **1.** Jur: (a) Verdict m; réponse f du jury. **To return a v.**, prononcer, rendre, un verdict. (b) (In coroner's court) **The jury returned a v. of suicide**, le jury a conclu au suicide. **Open v.**, jugement m qui conclut au crime sans désigner le coupable. **2.** Jugement, décision f. **To stick to one's v.**, maintenir le bien-fondé de son jugement.

verdigris ['vəːdigris], s. Vert-de-gris m. **To become coated with v.**, se vert-de-griser.

verdure ['vəːdjər], s. (a) Verdure f; (i) couleur verte; (ii) herbage m, feuillage m. (b) Lit: Verdeur f, jeunesse f, vigueur f.

verge¹ [vəːdʒ], s. **1.** (a) Bord m (d'un fleuve); accotement m (d'une route), orée f (d'une forêt). (b) Bordure f (d'une plate-bande). (c) **To be on the v. of forty**, friser la quarantaine. **He is on the v. of ruin**, il est à deux doigts de la ruine. **On the v. of war**, à la veille de la guerre. **On the v. of tears**, au bord des larmes. **2.** Ecc: Verge (portée devant l'évêque).

verge², v.i. (a) **To v. on sth.**, toucher à, être contigu à, qch. (b) **That verges on disingenuousness**, cela frise la mauvaise foi.

verger ['vəːdʒər], s. (a) Ecc: Bedeau m. (b) Huissier m à verge.

veridical [veˈridik(ə)l], a. Véridique.

verification [ˌverifiˈkeiʃ(ə)n], s. Vérification f, contrôle m.

verify ['verifai], v.tr. **1.** (Of evidence) Confirmer (un fait). **2.** Vérifier, contrôler (des renseignements, des comptes).

verily. See VERY¹ I.

verisimilitude [ˌverisiˈmilitjuːd], *s.* Vraisemblance *f.*
veritable [ˈveritəbl], *a.* Véritable. **-ably,** *adv.* Véritablement.
verity [ˈveriti], *s. Lit:* Vérité *f.* **1.** The eternal verities, les vérités éternelles. **2.** Fait réel.
verjuice [ˈvəːdʒuːs], *s. Cu:* Verjus *m.*
vermicelli [ˌvəːmiˈseli], *s.* Vermicelle *m.*
vermicular [vəːˈmikjulər], *a.* Vermiculaire, vermiforme.
vermiculation [vəːˌmikjuˈleiʃ(ə)n], *s.* Vermiculure *f.*
vermiform [ˈvəːmifɔːm], *a.* Vermiforme.
vermifuge [ˈvəːmifjuːdʒ], *a. & s.* Vermifuge (*m*).
vermilion [vəˈmiljən]. **1.** *s.* Vermillon *m,* cinabre *m.* **2.** *a.* (De) vermillon; vermeil.
vermin [ˈvəːmin], *s.* **1.** (*Body parasites, etc.; Pej: of people*). Vermine *f.* **2.** (*Weasels, etc.*) Bêtes puantes; nuisibles *mpl.*
verminous [ˈvəːminəs], *a.* Couvert de vermine; *F:* grouillant de vermine.
vermouth [ˈvəːməθ, ˈvəːmuːt], *s.* Vermout(h) *m.*
vernacular [vəˈnækjulər]. *Ling:* **1.** *a.* Vernaculaire; indigène; (idiome) national. **V. Arabic,** l'arabe vulgaire. **2.** *s.* (*a*) Langue *f* du pays; idiome national. (*b*) La langue vulgaire. (*c*) Langage *m* (d'un métier).
vernal [ˈvəːnl], *a. Lit:* Printanier, -ière; du printemps, *Astr: Bot:* Vernal, -aux.
vernier [ˈvəːniər], *s.* Vernier *m.* **V. calliper,** jauge *f* micrométrique.
veronal [ˈverənl], *s. Pharm:* Véronal *m.*
Veronica [vəˈrɔnikə], *s.* **1.** *Pr.n.f.* Véronique. **2.** *s.* (*a*) *Bot:* Véronique *f.* (*b*) *Ecc:* Véronique, suaire *m.*
versant [ˈvəːs(ə)nt], *s. Geog:* **1.** Versant *m* (d'une montagne). **2.** Pente *f* (de terrain).
verruca [veˈruːkə], *s. Med:* Verrue *f.*
versatile [ˈvəːsətail], *a.* **1.** (*a*) Aux talents variés. **He is a v. writer,** il écrit dans tous les genres. (*b*) **V. mind,** esprit souple. **2.** (*a*) Pivotant; capable de tourner. (*b*) *Nat.Hist:* Versatile.
versatility [ˌvəːsəˈtiliti], *s.* **1.** Souplesse *f,* universalité *f* (d'esprit); (faculté *f* d')adaptation *f.* **2.** *Nat.Hist:* Versatilité *f.*
verse [vəːs], *s.* **1.** Vers *m.* **2.** (*Of song*) Couplet *m;* (*of poem*) strophe *f.* **3.** *Coll.* Vers *mpl.* **Light v.,** poésie légère. **Free v.,** vers libres. **4.** *Ecc:* Verset *m* (de la Bible). *S.a.* CHAPTER 1.
versed[1] [vəːst], *a.* Versé (**in,** en, dans). **To be well v. in business matters,** être entendu aux affaires.
versed[2], *a. Mth:* Versed sine, sinus *m* verse.
versification [ˌvəːsifiˈkeiʃ(ə)n], *s.* Versification *f.*
versify [ˈvəːsifai], *v.tr. & i.* Versifier; mettre en vers.
version [ˈvəːʃ(ə)n], *s.* **1.** Version *f,* traduction *f.* **2.** Version (des faits); interprétation *f* (d'un fait). **According to his v.,** selon son dire...; d'après lui... **3.** Version (d'une voiture, etc.).
verso [ˈvəːsou], *s.* Verso *m* (d'une page); revers *m* (d'une médaille).
versus [ˈvəːsəs], *Lt.prep. Esp. Jur: Sp:* Contre. **Smith v. Robinson,** Smith contre Robinson.
vert [vəːt], *s. Her:* Sinople *m,* vert *m.*
vertebra, *pl.* **-ae** [ˈvəːtibrə, -iː], *s.* Vertèbre *f.*
vertebral [ˈvəːtibr(ə)l], *a.* Vertébral, -aux.
vertebrate [ˈvəːtibrit], *a. & s.* Vertébré (*m*). *pl.* **Vertebrates, the Vertebrata,** les vertébrés.
vertex, *pl.* **-tices** [ˈvəːteks, -tisiːz], *s.* Sommet *m* (d'un angle, d'une courbe).
vertical [ˈvəːtik(ə)l]. **1.** *a.* (*a*) Vertical, -aux. **V. elevation,** altitude *f.* **V. cliff,** falaise à pic. (*b*) Du zénith; situé au zénith. (*c*) **V. angles,** angles opposés par le sommet. **2.** *s.* Verticale *f.* **-ally,** *adv.* Verticalement; d'aplomb.
vertices [ˈvəːtisiːz], *s.pl. See* VERTEX.
vertiginous [vəːˈtidʒinəs], *a.* Vertigineux, -euse.
vertigo [ˈvəːtigou], *s. Med:* Vertige *m.*
vervain [ˈvəːvein], *s. Bot:* Verveine *f.*
verve [vəːv], *s.* Verve *f.* **To play, act, with v.,** jouer avec verve.
very[1] [ˈveri]. **I.** *a.* **1.** Vrai, véritable. **The veriest fool knows that,** le plus parfait nigaud sait cela. **2.** (*a*) Même. **He lives in this v. place,** il habite ici même. **You are the v. man I wanted to see,** vous êtes justement l'homme que je voulais voir. **We shall appoint X, he is the v. man,** nous nommerons X, il est tout indiqué. **At that v. moment,** à cet instant même.

It was a year ago to the v. day, c'était il y a un an jour pour jour. **These are his v. words,** ce sont là ses propres paroles. **That's the v. thing,** c'est juste ce qu'il faut; cela fait juste mon affaire. **That's the v. thing I was going to say,** c'est (tout) juste ce que j'allais dire. (*b*) **At the v. beginning,** tout au commencement. **He knows our v. thoughts,** il connaît jusqu'à nos pensées. **The v. children knew of it,** les enfants mêmes le savaient. (*c*) **The v. thought frightens me,** la seule pensée m'effraie. **I shudder at the v. thought of it,** je frémis rien que d'y penser. **-ily,** *adv. B:* **For v. I say unto you...,** car je vous dis en vérité.... **II. very,** *adv.* **1.** Très; fort, bien. **Very good,** (i) très bon, (ii) très bien, fort bien. **You are not very polite,** vous êtes peu poli. **Not v. well pleased,** médiocrement satisfait. **That's v. nice of you,** c'est bien gentil de votre part. **Not so v. small,** déjà pas si petit. **So v. little,** si peu. **It isn't so v. difficult,** ce n'est pas tellement difficile. **I was v. much surprised,** *F:* **v. surprised,** j'en ai été très surpris. **I feel v. much better,** je me sens beaucoup mieux. **2.** **The v. first,** le tout premier. **The v. best,** tout ce qu'il y a de meilleur, de mieux. **I did the v. best I could,** j'ai fait tout mon possible. **The v. next day,** dès le lendemain. **At the v. most,** tout au plus. **At the v. latest,** au plus tard. **The v. same,** absolument le même. **For your v. own,** pour vous seul.
Very[2]. *Pr.n. Mil:* **V. light,** fusée éclairante. **Very (-light) pistol,** pistolet *m* lance-fusée; pistolet Very.
vesical [ˈvesikl], *a. Anat: Med:* Vésical, -aux.
vesicatory [ˈvesikeitəri, veˈsikətəri], *a. & s. Med: Pharm:* Vésicatoire (*m*), vésicant (*m*).
vesicle [ˈvesikl], *s.* **1.** (*a*) *Anat: Bot:* Vésicule *f.* (*b*) *Med:* Vésicule; phlyctène *f.* **2.** *Geol:* Vacuole *f.*
vesper [ˈvespər]. **1.** *s. Poet:* Le soir. **2.** *s.pl. Ecc:* Vespers, vêpres *f.*
vessel [ˈvesl], *s.* **1.** Récipient *m.* **2.** Navire *m,* bâtiment *m.* **3.** *Anat: Bot:* Vaisseau *m.* **4.** *B.Lit:* Vaisseau, vase, instrument *m.* **Chosen v.,** vase d'élection. **Weaker v.,** le sexe faible.
vest[1] [vest], *s.* **1.** *Com: & U.S:* Gilet *m.* **2.** (*a*) (*For men*) (Under-)v., maillot *m,* tricot *m,* de corps, gilet de dessous. **Short-sleeved v.,** gilet à manches courtes. **Sleeveless v.,** gilet athlétique. *Sp:* (Running) v., maillot. (*b*) (*For women*) Chemise américaine, *Fr.C:* camisole *f.* **'vest-'pocket,** *s.* **1.** Poche *f* du gilet. **2.** *Attrib.* De petites dimensions. **V.-p. camera,** (appareil) vest-pocket (*m*).
vest[2]. **1.** *v.tr.* (*a*) **To v. s.o. with authority,** investir, revêtir, qn de l'autorité. *Jur:* **To v. s.o. with an inheritance,** saisir qn d'un héritage. (*b*) **Right vested in the Crown,** droit dévolu à la Couronne. **Authority vested in the people,** autorité exercée par le peuple. *Jur:* **Vesting order,** envoi *m* en possession. (*c*) **Vêtir,** revêtir (un dignitaire, le prêtre, etc.). **2.** *v.i.* (*Of property*) **To v. in s.o.,** échoir à qn. **vested,** *a. Jur:* **V. interests,** droits acquis.
vestal [ˈvestl], *a. & s. Rom.Ant:* **V. (virgin),** vestale *f.*
vestibule [ˈvestibjuːl], *s.* Vestibule *m,* antichambre *f.*
vestige [ˈvestidʒ], *s.* Vestige *m,* trace *f.* **Not a v. of...,** pas la moindre trace de...; pas un grain de (bon sens, etc.).
vestment [ˈvestmənt], *s.* (*a*) Vêtement *m* (de cérémonie). (*b*) *Ecc:* Vêtement sacerdotal, *esp.* chasuble *f.* *pl.* **Vestments,** vêtements sacerdotaux; ornements sacerdotaux.
vestry [ˈvestri], *s. Ecc:* **1.** Sacristie *f.* **2.** = Conseil paroissial.
Vesuvius [viˈsuːviəs, -sjuː-]. *Pr.n. Geog:* Le Vésuve.
vet[1] [vet], *s. F:* Vétérinaire *m.*
vet[2], *v.tr.* (vetted) *F:* (*a*) Examiner, traiter (une bête). **To have a horse vetted,** faire examiner un cheval par le vétérinaire. (*b*) Examiner (qn) (médicalement). (*c*) Revoir, corriger (l'œuvre littéraire de qn).
vetch [vetʃ], *s. Bot:* Vesce *f.*
vetchling [ˈvetʃliŋ], *s. Bot:* Gesse *f* des prés, des bois.
veteran [ˈvet(ə)rən]. **1.** *s.* Vétéran *m; F:* vieux *m* de la vieille. *U.S:* Ancien combattant. **2.** *a.* De(s) vétéran(s); aguerri. **A v. golfer,** un vétéran du golf. **V. car,** (vetted) voiture (1914-1930).
veterinary [ˈvetrənri], *a.* Vétérinaire. **V. surgeon,** vétérinaire *m.*

veto[1], *pl.* **-oes** ['vi:tou, -ouz], *s.* Veto *m*. **To put a v. on sth.**, mettre le veto, son veto, à qch. **To have the right of v.**, avoir le veto. **To exercise one's v.**, opposer son veto.

veto[2], *v.tr.* Mettre son veto à (qch.); interdire (qch.); s'opposer à (qch).

vex [veks], *v.tr.* **1.** Vexer, fâcher, chagriner. **2.** *Lit:* Troubler, tourmenter, agiter. **vexed**, *a.* **1.** Vexé, contrarié, chagrin. **To be v. at sth.**, être vexé, fâché de qch. **To be v. with s.o.**, être fâché contre qn. **To be v. with oneself**, s'en vouloir. **He was v. that he could not find out anything**, il se dépitait de ne rien découvrir. **2. Vexed question**, question souvent débattue, non résolue. **vexing**, *a.* Vexant, ennuyeux, -euse, contrariant.

vexation [vek'seiʃ(ə)n], *s.* **1.** Vexation *f*, tourment *m*. **V. of spirit**, tourment. **2.** (*a*) Contrariété *f*, ennui *m*. (*b*) Chagrin *m*, dépit *m*.

vexatious [vek'seiʃəs], *a.* **1.** Fâcheux, -euse, ennuyeux, -euse, contrariant. **2.** *Jur:* Vexatoire. **-ly**, *adv.* A seule fin de contrarier; de façon vexatoire.

via ['vaiə], *prep.* Via; par la voie de; par (une route).

viability [ˌvaiə'biliti], *s.* Viabilité *f*; aptitude *f* à vivre.

viable ['vaiəbl], *a.* Viable; apte à vivre.

viaduct ['vaiədʌkt], *s.* Viaduc *m*.

vial ['vaiəl], *s.* Fiole *f*. *Lit:* **To pour out the vials of one's wrath**, lâcher la bonde à sa colère.

viand ['vaiənd], *s.* *Lit:* Mets *m*. *Usu.pl.* **Viands**, aliments *m*.

viaticum [vai'ætikəm], *s.* *Ecc:* Viatique *m*.

vibrant ['vaibrənt], *a.* Vibrant.

vibrate [vai'breit]. **1.** *v.i.* (*a*) Vibrer; trépider. (*b*) *Ph:* Vibrer, osciller. **2.** *v.tr.* Faire vibrer. **vibrating**, *a.* Vibrant; (mouvement) vibratoire, oscillant. **Voice v. with emotion**, voix vibrante d'émotion.

vibration [vai'breiʃ(ə)n], *s.* **1.** Vibration *f*; oscillation *f*. **2.** *Mch:* Trépidation *f*.

vibrator [vai'breitər], *s.* *El.E:* Vibrateur *m*; trembleur *m* (de bobine); (*for massage*) vibromasseur *m*. *W.Tel:* Oscillateur *m*.

vibratory [vai'breitəri], *a.* Vibratoire.

viburnum [vai'bə:nəm], *s.* *Bot:* Viorne *f*.

vicar ['vikər], *s.* **1.** *Ch. of Eng:* = Curé *m*. **2.** *R.C.Ch:* **V. apostolic**, vicaire apostolique. **3. V. of Christ**, le Pape. **'vicar-'general**, *s.* *Ecc:* Vicaire général; grand vicaire.

vicarage ['vikəridʒ], *s.* = Presbytère *m*; cure *f*.

vicarious [vai'kɛəriəs, vi-], *a.* **1.** (*Of authority*) Délégué. **2.** (*a*) (Châtiment) souffert (i) par un autre, (ii) pour un autre. (*b*) (Méthode) de substitution. **-ly**, *adv.* **1.** Par substitution. **2.** A la place d'un autre; par procuration.

vice[1] [vais], *s.* **1.** Vice *m*. (*a*) **To live in v.**, vivre dans le vice. (*b*) **Avarice is a v.**, l'avarice est un vice. **2.** Défaut *m*. **3.** Vice (d'un cheval). **Stable v.**, tic *m*. **'vice-squad**, *s.* *Adm:* Brigade *f* des mœurs.

vice[2], *s.* *Tls:* Étau *m*. **Bench-v.**, étau d'établi.

vice[3], *s.* *F:* = VICE-CHAIRMAN, VICE-PRESIDENT.

vice[4] ['vaisi], *prep.* A la place de (qn). *Treasurer:* **Mr B, v. Mr A**, resigned, trésorier: M. B, qui succède à M. A, démissionnaire.

vice-admiral ['vais'ædm(ə)r(ə)l], *s.* Vice-amiral, -aux *m*.

vice-chairman, *pl.* **-men**, ['vais'tʃɛəmən], *s.* Vice-président *m*.

vice-chairmanship, [vais'tʃɛəmənʃip], *s.* Vice-présidence *f*.

vice-chancellor ['vais'tʃɑ:nsələr], *s.* **1.** Vice-chancelier *m*. **2.** Recteur *m* (d'une université).

vice-chancellorship ['vais'tʃɑ:nsələʃip], *s.* **1.** Fonction *f*, dignité *f*, de vice-chancelier. **2.** Rectorat *m* (d'université).

vice-consul ['vais'kɔnsəl], *s.* Vice-consul *m*.

vice-consulate ['vais'kɔnsjəlit], *s.* Vice-consulat *m*.

vice-marshal ['vais'mɑ:ʃ(ə)l], *s.* *Mil.Av:* **Air v.-m.**, général *m*, -aux, de division (aérienne).

viciennial ['vi'senjəl], *a.* Vicennal, -aux.

vice-presidency ['vais'prezidənsi], *s.* Vice-présidence *f*.

vice-president ['vais'prezidənt], *s.* Vice-président *m*.

vice-principal ['vais'prinsip(ə)l], *s.* *Sch:* Sous-directeur, -trice; sous-principal, -aux *m*; préfet *m* des études.

viceregal ['vais'ri:g(ə)l], *a.* Du vice-roi.

viceroy ['vaisrɔi], *s.m.* Vice-roi.

vice versa ['vaisi'və:sə], *Lt.adv.phr.* Vice versa; réciproquement.

Vichy ['vi:ʃi]. *Pr.n.Geog:* **1.** Vichy. **2.** *attrib.* **V. water**, eau *f* de Vichy. *Pol:* **The V. Government**, le Gouvernement de Vichy.

Vichyist ['vi:ʃi:ist], *a.* & *s.* *Pol: Pej:* Vichyste (*m*), (homme (*m*)) de Vichy.

vicinity [vi'siniti], *s.* **1.** Voisinage *m*, proximité *f* (**to**, **with**, de). **2.** Abords *mpl*, alentours *mpl* (d'un lieu). **In the v. of ...**, à proximité de ...; *Nau:* dans les parages de....

vicious ['viʃəs], *a.* **1.** Vicieux, corrompu. **V. tastes**, goûts pervers. **2.** (*Of horse*) Vicieux, rétif. **3.** (*Of language*) Vicieux, défectueux. *S.a.* CIRCLE[1] **1. 4.** (*a*) Méchant, haineux, -euse. *F:* **criticism**, critique méchante. (*b*) Rageur, -euse. **To give a v. tug at the bell**, tirer rageusement la sonnette. **-ly**, *adv.* **1.** Vicieusement. **2.** Incorrectement. **3.** Méchamment; rageusement.

viciousness ['viʃəsnis], *s.* **1.** Nature vicieuse; vice *m*. **2.** Méchanceté *f*.

vicissitude [vi'sisitju:d], *s.* Vicissitude *f*; péripétie *f*. **The vicissitudes of fortune**, les retours *m* de la fortune.

victim ['viktim], *s.* **1.** Victime (offerte en sacrifice) **2. To be the v. of s.o.**, être la victime de qn. **V. of an accident**, accidenté, -ée. **To fall a v. to s.o.'s charm**, succomber au charme de qn. **To make a v. of oneself**, se poser en victime.

victimization [ˌviktimai'zeiʃ(ə)n], *s.* **1.** Oppression *f*; sévices *mpl*; représailles *fpl*. **2. A case of v.**, une duperie.

victimize ['viktimaiz], *v.tr.* **1.** Prendre (qn) comme victime; exercer des représailles contre (les meneurs d'une grève, etc.). **2.** Tromper, escroquer (qn).

victor ['viktər], *s.* Vainqueur *m*.

Victoria [vik'tɔ:riə]. **1.** *Pr.n.f.* Victoire. **Queen V.**, la reine Victoria. **2.** *s.* (*a*) *Veh:* Victoria *f*. (*b*) **V.** (plum), (sorte de) prune *f* rouge. **Vic'toria 'Cross**, *s.* (*Abbr.* V.C. ['vi:'si:]) Croix *f* de Victoria (décernée pour un acte de bravoure insigne).

Victorian [vik'tɔ:riən], *a.* & *s.* **1.** Victorien, -ienne; du règne de la reine Victoria. **2.** *Geog:* (Natif, habitant) du Victoria (Australie).

victorious [vik'tɔ:riəs], *a.* Victorieux; vainqueur *m*. **To be v. over s.o.**, être victorieux de qn. **-ly**, *adv.* Victorieusement; en vainqueur.

victory ['vikt(ə)ri], *s.* Victoire *f*. **To gain a v.**, **the v.**, remporter la victoire (**over**, sur). *S.a.* PYRRHIC[2].

victual ['vitl], *v.* (**victualled** ['vitld]) **1.** *v.tr.* Approvisionner; ravitailler (un navire). **2.** *v.i.* Se ravitailler. **victualling**, *s.* Approvisionnement *m*, ravitaillement *m*.

victualler ['vitlər], *s.* (*a*) Pourvoyeur *m*; fournisseur *m* de vivres. (*b*) **Licensed v.**, (hôtelier) débitant *m* de boissons.

victuals ['vitlz], *s.pl.* (*a*) Vivres *m*, provisions *f*. (*b*) Victuailles *f*.

vicugna, vicuña [vi'ku:njə], *s.* Vigogne *f*.

video-tape ['vidjouteip], *s.* *T.V:* Bande *f* magnétique vidéo. **V.-t. recorder**, magnétoscope *m*.

vie [vai], *v.i.* (**vied**; **vying**) Le disputer (**with s.o.**, à qn); rivaliser (**with s.o.**, avec qn). **To vie with s.o. in politeness**, faire assaut de politesse avec qn. **They v. with one another as to who shall speak**, c'est à qui parlera.

Vietnam ['vjet'næm], *Pr.n. Geog:* Le Vietnam.

Vietnamese [ˌvjetnə'mi:z], *a.* & *s.* Vietnamien, -ienne.

view[1] [vju:], *s.* Vue *f*. **1.** Regard *m*; coup *m* d'œil. **At first v.**, à première vue. **I should like to get a nearer v. of it**, je voudrais l'examiner de plus près. **On v.**, exposé; ouvert au public. **Private v.**, entrée *f* sur invitation personnelle; avant-première *f*; vernissage *m* (d'une exposition de peinture). **2.** (*a*) **Exposed to v.**, exposé aux regards, à la vue de tous. **In view**, en vue. **At last a hotel came into v.**, enfin nous aperçûmes un hôtel. **We were in v. of land**, nous étions en vue de la terre. **Land in v.!** terre! (*b*) **Field of v.** (*of telescope*), champ *m*. **3.** (*Prospect*) (*a*) Vue, perspective *f*. **Front v. of the hotel**, l'hôtel vu de face. **You will get a better v. from here**, vous verrez mieux d'ici. **It was worth while coming up for the v.**, le panorama valait le déplacement. **Point**

of v., point m de vue. (b) Arch: Front v., élévation f du devant. (c) To keep sth. in v., ne pas perdre qch. de vue. 4. Aperçu m, exposé m. To offer a general v. of the subject, donner un aperçu général de la question. 5. Manière f de voir; opinion f. To take a right v. of things, voir juste. To hold extreme views, avoir des idées extrémistes. To have very decided views on . . ., avoir des idées arrêtées au sujet de.... What are your views on the matter? comment envisagez-vous la question? In my v., à mon avis. To share s.o.'s views, partager les sentiments de qn. 6. In v. of . . ., en considération de . . .; eu égard à.... étant donné . . . en raison de . . . In v. of these facts . . ., en présence de ces faits.... In v. of the distance . . ., vu l'éloignement.... 7. Vue, intention f. To fall in with s.o.'s views, entrer dans les vues de qn. Will this meet your views? cela vous conviendra-t-il? To have sth. in v., avoir qch. en vue; méditer (un voyage). With a special object in v., avec, dans, un but précis. With this in v., à cette fin. With a v. to . . ., en vue de . . ., dans le but de . . ., avec l'idée de . . . Whom have you in v.? à qui pensez-vous? vous avez un candidat (à proposer)? Negotiations with a v. to an alliance, négociations visant une alliance. 'view-finder, s. Phot: Viseur m. 'view-ha'lloo, s. Ven: "Vue f" (du renard) (cri ou fanfare). 'view-point, s. Point m de vue; (of beauty-spot) belvédère m.

view², v.tr. 1. Regarder (qn, qch.); examiner, inspecter (qn, qch.); visiter (une maison à louer). 2. Envisager (qch.). 3. Voir, apercevoir. Ven: To v. the fox away, voir débucher le renard. 4. v.i. T.V: Regarder.

viewer ['vju:ər], s. 1. Spectateur, -trice. T.V: Téléspectateur, -trice. 2. Cin: Phot: Visionneuse f.

vigil ['vidʒil], s. 1. Veille f. To keep v., veiller. 2. Ecc: Vigile f.

vigilance ['vidʒiləns], s. Vigilance f. U.S: V. committee, comité de surveillance des mœurs.

vigilant ['vidʒilənt], a. Vigilant, éveillé, alerte.

vigilante [vidʒi'lænti:], s. U.S: Membre m du comité de surveillance.

vignette¹ [vi'njet], s. 1. Vignette f. 2. Phot: Photo-(graphie) f en dégradé. 3. Lit: Saynète f.

vignette², v.tr. Phot: Dégrader (un portrait).

vigorous ['vig(ə)rəs], a. Vigoureux, -euse, robuste. -ly, adv. Vigoureusement. F: To go at it v., F: y aller d'attaque.

vigour ['vigər], s. 1. Vigueur f, énergie f. To die in the full v. of manhood, mourir dans la force de l'âge. 2. (a) Vigueur (de style). (b) Mus: Brio m.

Viking ['vaikiŋ], a. & s. Hist: Viking (m).

vile [vail], a. 1. Vil; sans valeur. 2. Vil; bas, infâme. The vilest of men, le dernier des hommes. 3. F: Abominable, exécrable. V. weather, un sale temps. He's in a v. temper, il est d'une humeur massacrante. -ly, adv. 1. Vilement; bassement. 2. Abominablement.

vileness ['vailnis], s. 1. Bassesse f, caractère m ignoble (de qn, d'un sentiment). 2. F: The v. of the weather, le temps abominable.

vilification [vilifi'keiʃ(ə)n], s. Dénigrement m.

vilify ['vilifai], v.tr. Vilipender, diffamer, dénigrer (qn); dire des infamies de (qn).

villa ['vilə], s. Villa f. Roman v., villa romaine.

village ['vilidʒ], s. 1. Village m; bourgade f; bourg m. Village inn, auberge de campagne. 2. U.S: Petite municipalité.

villager ['vilidʒər], s. Villageois, -oise.

villain ['vilən], s. (a) Scélérat m; bandit m, gredin m. F: You little v.! petit coquin! (b) Th: The v. (of the piece), le traître.

villainous ['vilənəs], a. 1. Vil, infâme; scélérat; de scélérat. 2. F: = VILE 3. -ly, adv. 1. D'une manière infâme; en scélérat. 2. F: D'une manière exécrable.

villainy ['viləni], s. 1. Scélératesse f, infamie f (d'une action). 2. Action scélérate; infamie.

villein ['vilin], s. Hist: Vilain m; serf m.

villosity [vi'lositi], s. Anat: Villosité f.

vim [vim], s. F: Vigueur f, énergie f.

vinculum, pl. -la ['viŋkjuləm, -lə], s. 1. Lien m. 2. Typ: (a) = BRACE¹ 6. (b) Mth: Barre tirée au-dessus d'un groupe de symboles.

vindicate ['vindikeit], v.tr. 1. Défendre, soutenir (qn, sa foi); justifier (qn, sa conduite); prouver, maintenir (son dire). To v. one's character, se justifier. 2. To v. one's rights, faire valoir son bon droit.

vindication [,vindi'keiʃ(ə)n], s. 1. Défense f, apologie f. In v. of his conduct, pour justifier sa conduite. 2. Revendication f (d'un droit).

vindicative ['vindikətiv, vin'dik-], a. Justificatif, -ive.

vindicator [,vindi'keitər], s. Défenseur m.

vindicatory [,vindi'keit(ə)ri], a. = VINDICATIVE.

vindictive [vin'diktiv], a. 1. Vindicatif; vengeur, -eresse. 2. (Of pers.) Vindicatif, rancunier. -ly, adv. Par rancune; par esprit de vengeance; avec une méchanceté rancunière.

vindictiveness [vin'diktivnis], s. Esprit m de vengeance; esprit rancunier.

vine [vain], s. 1. (Grape-)v., vigne f. Wild v., lambruche f, lambrusque f. 2. Sarment m, tige f (de houblon). 3. U.S: Plante grimpante. 'vine-arbour, s. Treille f. 'vine-branch, s. Rameau m de vigne. 'vine-dresser, s. Vigneron m. 'vine-grower, s. Viticulteur m; vigneron m. 'vine-growing¹, a. (Pays) vignoble, vinicole. 'vine-growing², s. Viticulture f. 'vine-plant, -stock, s. Cep m de vigne. 'vine-prop, s. Échalas m.

vinegar ['vinigər], s. Vinaigre m. Wine v., vinaigre de vin. Tarragon v., vinaigre à l'estragon. Mother of v., mère f de vinaigre. 'vinegar-cruet, s. Burette f à vinaigre; vinaigrier m.

vinery ['vainəri], s. Serre f à vignes, forcerie f de raisin.

vineyard ['vinjəd], s. Clos m (de vigne); vigne f, vignoble m. The best vineyards, les meilleurs crus.

vinous ['vainəs], a. 1. (a) (Goût) vineux. (b) Couleur inv de vin. 2. (a) Aviné. (b) Ivrogne.

vintage ['vintidʒ], s. 1. (a) Récolte f du raisin; vendanges fpl. (b) (Crop) Vendange. (c) Temps m de la vendange. 2. Année f (de belle récolte). Of the v. of 1964, de l'année 1964. V. year, année de bon vin; bonne année, grande année. V. wine, vin de marque; vin cacheté; grand vin. V. champagne, champagne m d'origine. V. burgundies, (i) des bourgognes d'appellation; (ii) des bourgognes de la bonne année. Guaranteed v., appellation contrôlée. 3. (a) V. car, vieille voiture d'avant 1914. (b) This is v. Shaw, c'est du Shaw et du meilleur.

vintager ['vintidʒər], s. Vendangeur, -euse.

vintner ['vintnər], s. Négociant m en vins.

viol [vaiəl], s. A.Mus: Viole f. Bass-v., basse f de viole.

viola¹ [vi'oulə], s. Mus: Alto m (à cordes). V. player, altiste mf.

viola² ['vaiələ], s. Bot: 1. Pensée f (unicolore). 2. (Genus) Viola m.

Violaceae [vaiou'læsii:], s.pl. Bot: Violacées fpl.

violate ['vaiəleit], v.tr. Violer (un serment): profaner (un sanctuaire); manquer à (une règle). To v. the law, violer, enfreindre, la loi.

violation [,vaiəleiʃ(ə)n], s. 1. Violation f (d'un serment); profanation f (d'un sanctuaire). V. of an order, infraction f à un ordre. V. of s.o.'s privacy, intrusion f auprès de, chez, qn. 2. Viol m (d'une femme).

violator ['vaiəleitər], s. 1. Violateur, -trice. V. of the law, contrevenant, -ante. 2. Violateur, F: violeur m (d'une femme).

violence ['vaiələns], s. 1. (a) Violence f, intensité f (du vent). (b) To die by v., mourir de mort violente. To do v. to one's feelings, se faire violence. 2. Jur: To resort to v., se livrer, se porter, à des voies de fait. Robbery with v., vol m à main armée.

violent ['vaiələnt], a. 1. Violent. Aut: V. braking, freinage brutal. To lay v. hands on s.o., attaquer brutalement qn. To lay v. hands on oneself, attenter à ses jours. To become v., se livrer à des actes de violence; s'emporter. 2. (a) Violent, aigu, fort. V. dislike, vive aversion. In a v. hurry, extrêmement pressé. V. cold, gros rhume, F: rhume carabiné. (b) V. colours, couleurs criardes, crues. -ly, adv. 1. Violemment; avec violence. 2. Vivement; extrêmement. To fall v. in love with s.o., tomber follement amoureux, -euse, de qn.

violet ['vaiəlit]. **1.** s. Bot: Violette f. **2.** a. & s. (Colour) Violet (m).

violin [,vaiə'lin], s. Violon m.

violinist [,vaiə'linist], s. Violoniste mf.

violoncellist [,vaiələn'tʃelist], s. Violoncelliste mf.

violoncello [,vaiələn'tʃelou], s. Violoncelle m.

viper ['vaipər], s. (a) Vipère f. **Young v.,** vipereau m. S.a. BUGLOSS 2. (b) F: (Of pers.) Vipère.

viperine ['vaipərain], a. Vipérin V. **snake,** vipérine f.

viperish ['vaipəriʃ], a. F: V. **tongue,** langue de vipère.

virago [vi'rɑ:gou, -'rei-], s.f. Mégère, virago.

virgin ['və:dʒin]. **1.** s. Vierge f. **The Blessed V.,** la Sainte Vierge. a. **The V. Birth,** la maternité divine. Biol: V. **birth,** parthénogénèse f. Ap: V. **queen,** reine non fécondée. **2.** a. (a) De vierge; virginal, -aux. (b) V. **forest,** forêt vierge.

virginal ['və:dʒinl], a. Virginal, -aux.

Virginia [və'dʒinjə]. **1.** Pr.n. Virginie. Geog: La Virginie. Bot: V. **creeper,** vigne f vierʒe. **2.** s. Tabac m de Virginie; virginie m.

virginity [və:'dʒiniti], s. Virginité f.

virile ['virail], a. Viril, mâle. A v. **old age,** une mâle vieillesse.

virilism ['virilizm], s. Path: Virilisme m.

virility [vi'riliti], s. Virilité f.

virtu [və:'tu:], s. O: Objects of v., objets m d'art.

virtual ['və:tjuəl], a. **1.** De fait; en fait. He is the v. head of the business, c'est lui le vrai chef de la maison. This was a v. admission of guilt, de fait, c'était un aveu. **2.** Tchn: Virtuel. Opt: V. **image,** image virtuelle. -ally, adv. Virtuellement; de fait; en pratique.... I am v. certain of it, j'en ai la quasi-certitude.

virtue ['və:tju:], s. **1.** Vertu f. **Woman of easy v.,** femme de petite vertu. To make a v. of necessity, faire de nécessité vertu. **2.** Qualité f; avantage m. **3.** Plants that have healing virtues, plantes qui ont des propriétés curatives. **4.** Prep.phr. By v. of, en vertu de; en raison de. By v. of one's office, de par ses fonctions.

virtuosity [,və:tju'ɔsiti], s. Virtuosité f.

virtuoso [,və:tju'ouzou], s. **1.** A: Amateur m d'art; connaisseur m. **2.** Mus: Virtuose mf.

virtuous ['və:tjuəs], a. Vertueux, -euse. -ly, adv. Vertueusement.

virulence ['viruləns], s. Virulence f.

virulent ['virulənt], a. Virulent. -ly, adv. Avec virulence.

virus ['vaiərəs], s. **1.** Med: Virus m. V. **disease,** virose f. **2.** Venin m; poison (moral).

visa¹ ['vi:zə], s. Adm: Visa m.

visa², v.tr. Adm: Viser; apposer un visa à (un passeport).

visage ['vizidʒ], s. Lit: Visage m, figure f.

vis-à-vis ['vi:za:'vi:]. **1.** s. Danc: etc: Vis-à-vis m. **2.** adv. Vis-à-vis (to, with, de).

viscera ['visərə], s.pl. Viscères m.

visceral ['visər(ə)l], a. Viscéral, -aux.

viscid ['visid], a. Visqueux.

viscidity [vi'siditi], s. Viscosité f.

viscose [vis'kous], s. Tex: Viscose f.

viscosity [vis'kɔsiti], s. Viscosité f.

viscount ['vaikaunt], s.m. Vicomte.

viscountcy ['vaikauntsi], s. Vicomté f.

viscountess ['vaikauntis], s.f. Vicomtesse.

viscounty ['vaikaunti], s. Vicomté f.

viscous ['viskəs], a. Visqueux; mucilagineux; gluant.

visé¹,² ['vi:zei], s. & v.tr. = VISA¹,².

visibility ['vizi'biliti], s. Visibilité f. Nau: Av: Good v., bonne visibilité. (In car) Good v., vue dégagée.

visible ['vizəbl], a. Visible. To become v., apparaître. V. **horizon,** horizon visuel. V. **signal,** signal optique. F: I'm not v., je ne suis pas présentable. -ibly, adv. Visiblement, manifestement; (grandir) à vue d'œil.

Visigoth ['vizigɔθ], s. Hist: Wisigoth m.

vision ['viʒ(ə)n], s. **1.** (a) Vision f, vue f. **Within the range of v.,** à portée de vue. **Beyond our v.,** au delà de notre vue. **Field of v.,** champ visuel. (b) **Man of v.,** homme d'une grande perspicacité, qui voit loin dans l'avenir. **2.** (a) Imagination f, vision. **Visions of wealth,** visions de richesses. (b) Apparition f, fantôme m. He sees visions, il a des visions.

visionary ['viʒən(ə)ri]. **1.** a. (a) (Of pers.) Visionnaire. (b) (Projet) chimérique, fantastique. (c) (Mal) imaginaire. **2.** s. Visionnaire mf: idéologue m; illuminé, -ée.

visit¹ ['vizit], s. **1.** (a) (Social) v., visite f. **Courtesy v.,** visite de politesse. To pay s.o. a v., rendre visite à qn; faire une visite à qn. F: To pay a v., aller faire pipi. To return s.o.'s v., rendre sa visite à quelqu'un. (b) **Doctor's round of visits,** tournée f de visites d'un médecin. V. **of a (commercial) traveller,** passage m d'un représentant voyageur. **2.** Visite, séjour m. To be on a v. to friends, être en visite chez des amis. **3.** Tournée f d'inspection; visite d'inspection. Jur: V. **to the scene** (of a crime), descente f sur les lieux. **Domiciliary v.,** visite domiciliaire.

visit², v.tr. **1.** (a) Rendre visite à (qn); aller voir (qn). (b) To v. the sick, visiter les malades. (c) Com: (Of traveller) Passer chez (un client). (d) Visiter, aller voir (un endroit). We visited the museums, nous avons vu les musées. **2.** (Of official) Visiter, inspecter. **3.** B: To v. the sins of the fathers upon the children, punir les enfants pour les péchés des pères; faire retomber sur les enfants les péchés des pères.

visiting¹, a. **1.** En visite. Sp: V. **team,** les visiteurs m. **2.** Sch: V. **master,** maître externe; professeur particulier. **visiting²**, s. Visites fpl. To go v., faire des visites. To be on v. terms with s.o., être en relations de visites avec qn. They are not on v. terms, ils ne se voient pas. V. **hours** (at hospital), heures de visite. 'visiting-card, s. Carte f de visite.

visitation [,vizi'teiʃ(ə)n], s. **1.** (a) Visite f (d'inspection); (of bishop) visite pastorale. (b) Tournée f (d'inspection). **2.** (a) Ecc: V. (of the Blessed Virgin Mary), la Visitation. (b) Apparition (surnaturelle). **3.** (a) A: V. **of God,** affliction f, épreuve f. (b) F: Visite fâcheuse, trop prolongée. (c) Calamité f.

visitor ['vizitər], s. (a) Visiteur, -euse. She has visitors, elle a du monde. (b) **Summer visitors, winter visitors,** (at a seaside resort) estivants m, hivernants m, (d'une station balnéaire). **Visitors' book,** livre des voyageurs (à un hôtel); registre m des visiteurs (à un musée); livre m d'or.

visor ['vaizər], s. **1.** A: Arm: Visière f (de casque). **2.** Visière (de casquette).

vista ['vistə], s. **1.** Échappée f (de vue); (in forest) percée f, éclaircie f, trouée f. **2.** A long v. of beech-trees, une longue perspective de hêtres. Arch: To open vistas, dégager les vues. To open up new vistas, ouvrir de nouvelles perspectives.

visual ['vizju(ə)l], a. **1.** Visuel, -elle; perceptible à l'œil. V. **distance,** distance de visibilité. Mil: Nau: V. **signalling,** télégraphie optique. Sch: Teaching by v. aids, enseignement m par l'image. **2.** Anat: The v. nerve, le nerf optique. -ally, adv. Visuellement.

visualize ['vizjualaiz], v.tr. **1.** Rendre (qch.) visible. **2.** Se représenter (qch.); évoquer l'image de (qch.).

vital ['vaitl], a. **1.** Vital, -aux; essentiel à la vie. V. **force,** force vitale. **2.** Essentiel; capital, -aux. **Question of v. importance,** question d'importance capitale. **3.** Mortel, fatal, -als. V. **error,** erreur fatale, irrémédiable. S.a. STATISTICS. **4.** O: s.pl. Organes vitaux. -ally, adv. D'une manière vitale.

vitality [vai'tæliti], s. **1.** Vitalité f (d'un organisme); vitalité, vigueur f (d'une race). **2.** Vie f, animation f, vigueur (de style).

vitalize ['vaitəlaiz], v.tr. Vitaliser, vivifier.

vitamin ['vitəmin], s. Bio-Ch: Vitamine f. V. **deficiency,** avitaminose f.

vitaminised ['vitəminaizd], a. Vitaminé.

vitellus, pl. -i [vi'teləs, -ai], s. Biol: Vitellus m.

vitiate ['viʃieit], v.tr. **1.** Vicier, corrompre. **2.** Jur: Vicier (un contrat). To v. a transaction, rendre une opération nulle.

vitiation ['viʃi'eiʃ(ə)n], s. Viciation f.

viticultural ['viti'kʌltʃur(ə)l], a. Viticole.

viticulture ['vitikʌltʃər], s. Viticulture f.

vitreous ['vitriəs], a. **1.** Vitreux, -euse; hyalin. **2.** Anat: V. **body,** corps vitré (de l'œil).

vitrify ['vitrifai]. **1.** v.tr. Vitrifier. **2.** v.i. Se vitrifier.

vitriol ['vitriəl], s. **1.** Vitriol m. **Blue v.,** sulfate m de cuivre. **2.** (Oil of) v., acide m sulfurique. To throw v. at s.o., vitrioler qn. V. **throwing,** vitriolage m.

vitriolic [ˌvitri'ɔlik], a. (Acid, etc.) Vitriolique. V. pen, plume trempée dans du vitriol.

vituperate [vi.tjuːpəreit, vai-], v.tr. Injurier, vilipender (qn).

vituperation [viˌtjuːpə'reiʃ(ə)n, vai-], s. Injures fpl, insultes fpl, invectives fpl.

vituperative [vi'tjuːpərətiv, vai-], a. Injurieux; mal embouché.

Vitus ['vaitəs]. Pr.n.m. St. V., Saint-Guy. Med: Saint V.'s dance, chorée f; danse f de Saint-Guy.

viva ['vaivə], s. F: = VIVA VOCE 3.

vivacious [vi'veiʃəs], a. Vif, f. vive, animé, enjoué. -ly, adv. Avec enjouement; avec verve.

vivaciousness [vi'veiʃəsnis], vivacity [vi'vasiti], s. Vivacité f; animation f; enjouement m.

viva voce ['vaivə'vousi, 'viːvə'voutʃi]. 1. adv. De vive voix; oralement. 2. a. Oral, -aux. 3. s. Sch: Examen oral; épreuves orales; l'oral m.

vivid ['vivid], a. 1. Vif, f. vive, éclatant. V. flash of lightning, éclair aveuglant. 2. V. imagination, imagination vive. V. description, description vivante. V. recollection, souvenir très net. -ly, adv. 1. Vivement; avec éclat. 2. To describe sth. v., décrire qch. d'une manière vivante.

vividness ['vividnis], s. 1. Vivacité f, éclat m (des couleurs). 2. The v. of his style, la vigueur de son style.

vivify ['vivifai], v.tr. Vivifier, animer.

Vivipara [vi'vipərə], s.pl. Z: Vivipares m.

viviparous [vi'vipərəs], a. Z: Vivipare.

vivisect [ˌvivi'sekt], v.tr. Pratiquer des vivisections sur (des animaux). Abs. Faire de la vivisection.

vivisection [ˌvivi'sekʃ(ə)n], s. Vivisection f.

vixen ['viksn], s.f. 1. Z: Renarde. 2. F: Mégère; femme acariâtre; P: teigne.

vixenish ['viksəniʃ], a. 1. (Of woman) Acariâtre, méchante. 2. (Of disposition) De mégère.

viz. [viz], adv. A savoir . . .; c'est à dire . . . ('Namely' is generally substituted when reading aloud).

Vizier [vi'ziər], s. Vizir m.

vocab [və'kæb], s. Sch: F: Vocabulaire m.

vocable ['voukəbl], s. Vocable m.

vocabulary [və'kæbjuləri], s. Vocabulaire m; lexique m. Molière's v., le lexique de Molière. Sch: Look it up in the v.! consultez le vocabulaire!

vocal ['vouk(ə)l], a. 1. (a) Vocal, -aux. Anat: V. cords, cordes vocales. (b) V. communication, communication verbale. (c) Ling: = VOICED 2. 2. (a) Doué de voix; capable de produire des sons. The most v. member of the audience, celui des membres de l'auditoire qui s'est fait le plus entendre. (b) Bruyant, sonore. -ally, adv. 1. Vocalement, oralement, verbalement. 2. Par des chants; à l'aide du chant.

vocalic [vou'kælik], a. 1. (Langue) qui a beaucoup de voyelles. 2. (Son) vocalique.

vocalist ['voukəlist], s. Chanteur, -euse, cantatrice f.

vocalization [ˌvoukəlai'zeiʃ(ə)n], s. Vocalisation f.

vocalize ['voukəlaiz]. 1. v.tr. (a) Prononcer (un mot); chanter (un air). (b) Ling: Vocaliser (une consonne). 2. v.i. Mus: Faire des vocalises.

vocation [vo'keiʃ(ə)n], s. 1. (a) Vocation f (to the ministry, sacerdotale). (b) A v. for literature, la vocation littéraire. 2. Vocation, profession f. To miss one's v., manquer sa vocation.

vocational [vo'keiʃənl], a. (Enseignement, cours) professionnel. Sch: V. adviser, orienteur, -euse. V. guidance, orientation professionnelle. V. bias, déformation professionnelle.

vocative ['vɔkətiv], a. & s. Gram: V. (case), (cas) vocatif m. In the v., au vocatif.

vociferate [vo'sifəreit], v.i. & tr. Vociférer, crier (against, contre).

vociferation [voˌsifə'reiʃ(ə)n], s. 1. Cri m, clameur f. 2. Vociférations fpl, cris, clameurs.

vociferous [vo'sifərəs], a. Vociférant, bruyant, criard, braillard. -ly, adv. En vociférant; bruyamment.

vodka ['vɔdkə], s. Vodka f.

vogue [voug], s. Vogue f, mode f. To be in v., être en vogue, à la mode; avoir de la vogue. To bring into v., mettre en vogue.

voice[1] [vɔis], s. 1. Voix f. To raise one's v., hausser la voix. To lose one's v., attraper une extinction de voix. In a gentle v., d'une voix douce. In a low v., à voix basse; à mi-voix; à demi-voix. He likes to hear his own v., il aime à s'entendre parler. S.a. RAISE 4, TOP[1] I. 6. 2. (a) Voix, suffrage m. (b) To give v. to one's indignation, exprimer son indignation. We have no v. in the matter, nous n'avons pas voix au chapitre. With one v., à l'unanimité. 3. Gram: Voix (du verbe). In the active v., à la voix active; à l'actif. 'voice-production, s. Élocution f; diction f.

voice[2], v.tr. 1. Exprimer, énoncer (une opinion). 2. Ling: Voiser (une consonne). 3. Harmoniser (un orgue, un tuyau d'orgue). voiced, a. 1. Sweet-v., low-v., à la voix douce, à la voix basse. 2. Ling: Voisé; (consonne) sonore.

voiceless ['vɔislis], a. 1. Sans voix; muet; aphone. 2. Ling: Sourd; non voisé.

voicer ['vɔisər], s. Mus: (Pers.) Harmoniste m (d'un orgue).

void [vɔid]. I. a. 1. Vide. V. space, espace vide; vide m. 2. (Of office) Vacant, inoccupé. 3. Jur: (Of deed) Nul, f. nulle. To make a clause v., annuler une clause. S.a. NULL. 4. Poet: Vain, inutile. 5. Dépourvu, dénué (of, de). Proposal v. of reason, proposition dénuée de raison. II. void, s. Vide m. To fill the v., combler le vide. F: To have an aching v., avoir l'estomac creux, dans les talons.

voile [vɔil], s. Tex: Voile m.

volatile ['vɔlətail], a. 1. Ch: Volatil, gazéifiable. 2. (a) Vif, f. vive, gai. (b) Volage, inconstant.

volatility [ˌvɔlə'tiliti], s. Ch: Volatilité f.

volatilize [və'lætilaiz]. 1. v.tr. Volatiliser. 2. v.i. Se volatiliser.

volcanic [vɔl'kænik], a. Volcanique.

volcano, pl. -oes [vɔl'keinou, -ouz], s. Volcan m. Active v., volcan en activité.

vole [voul], s. Z: (Field-)v., campagnol m (des champs). Water v., rat m d'eau.

volition [vo'liʃ(ə)n], s. Volition f, volonté f. To do sth. of one's own v., faire qch. de son propre gré.

volley[1] ['vɔli], s. 1. Volée f, salve f (d'armes à feu); grêle f (de pierres). 2. Volée, bordée f (d'injures). 3. Ten: (Balle prise de) volée.

volley[2]. 1. v.tr. (a) Mil: Tirer une volée, une salve, de (projectiles). (b) Ten: To v. the ball, abs. to volley, reprendre la balle de volée. 2. v.i. (a) (Of guns) Partir ensemble. (b) Tonner.

volley-ball ['vɔlibɔ:l], s. Sp: Volley-ball m. V.-b. player, volleyeur m, -euse.

volplane[1] ['vɔl'plein], s. Av: Vol plané.

volplane[2], v.i. Av: 1. Faire du vol plané; planer. 2. Descendre en vol plané.

volt[1] [vɔlt], s. Equit: Fenc: Volte f.

volt[2] [voult], s. El.Meas: Volt m. volt-'ampere, s. El: Voltampère m; watt m.

voltage ['voultidʒ], s. El.E: Voltage m; tension f (en volts). High v., haute tension. High v. test, essai m de claquage. V. drop, perte f de charge. V. recorder, voltmètre enregistreur.

volte [voult], s. = VOLT[1].

voltmeter ['voultˌmiːtər], s. El: Voltmètre m.

volubility [ˌvɔlju'biliti], s. Volubilité f.

voluble ['vɔljubl], a. (Of speech) Facile, aisé; (langue) déliée, bien pendue; (of pers.) volubile. To be a v. talker, parler avec volubilité. -bly, adv. Avec volubilité.

volume ['vɔljum], s. 1. Volume m, livre m; tome m. Volume one, tome premier. A large v., un gros livre. F: It speaks volumes for him, cela en dit long en sa faveur. 2. pl. Volumes of smoke, nuages m de fumée. Volumes of water, torrents m d'eau. 3. (a) Ch: Ph: Volume. Densities for equal volumes, densités à volume égal. (b) The v. of the brain, le volume du cerveau. V. of a reservoir, cubage m d'un réservoir 4. Volume (d'un son); ampleur f (de la voix). Mus: To give v. to the tone, nourrir le son.

volumetric [ˌvɔlju'metrik], a. Ch: (Analyse) volumétrique.

voluminous [və'ljuːminəs], a. 1. (Auteur) volumineux, abondant. 2. (Paquet) volumineux.

voluntary ['vɔlənt(ə)ri]. **1.** *a.* (*a*) Volontaire, spontané. **V. offer,** offre spontanée. **V. confession of guilt,** confession volontaire; aveu spontané. **V. discipline,** discipline librement consentie. (*b*) **V. organization,** organisation bénévole. (*c*) **V. army,** armée de volontaires. **2.** *s.* *Ecc.Mus:* Morceau d'orgue (joué avant, pendant, ou après l'office). **-ily,** *adv.* Volontairement, spontanément; de (son) plein gré.

volunteer¹ [ˌvɔlən'tiər], *s.* (*a*) *Mil:* Volontaire *m.* (*b*) **To call for volunteers,** demander des volontaires.

volunteer². **1.** *v.tr.* Offrir volontairement, spontanément (ses services). *Abs.* S'offrir (pour une tâche). **To v. some information,** donner spontanément des renseignements. **2.** *v.i.* *Mil:* S'engager comme volontaire.

voluptuary [və'lʌptjuəri], *s.* Voluptueux, -euse; sybarite *m;* épicurien, -ienne.

voluptuous [və'lʌptjuəs], *a.* Voluptueux, -euse. **-ly,** *adv.* Voluptueusement.

voluptuousness [və'lʌptjuəsnis], *s.* Sensualité *f.*

volute [və'lju:t], *s.* *Arch: Conch: Moll:* Volute *f.*

voluted [və'lju:tid], *a.* **1.** A volutes. **2.** Enroulé en spirale.

vomit¹ ['vɔmit], *s.* Vomissure *f;* vomissement *m.*

vomit², *v.tr. & i.* (*a*) Vomir, rendre. **He began to v.,** il fut pris de vomissements. (*b*) (*Of chimney*) **To v. smoke,** vomir de la fumée. **vomiting,** *s.* Vomissement *m.*

vomitory ['vɔmitəri]. **1.** *a. & s. Med:* Vomitif (*m*). **2.** *s. Rom.Ant:* Vomitoire *m.*

voodoo¹ ['vu:du:], *s. Anthr:* **1.** Vaudou *m.* **2.** V. (doctor, priest), vaudou, *pl.* -ous; sorcier *m* (nègre).

voodoo², *v.tr. Anthr:* Envoûter.

voracious [vɔ'reiʃəs], *a.* Vorace, dévorant. **V. appetite,** appétit de loup. **V. reader,** lecteur vorace. **-ly,** *adv.* Avec voracité; goulûment.

voraciousness [vɔ'reiʃəsnis], **voracity** [vɔ'ræsiti], *s.* Voracité *f.*

vortex, *pl.* **-ices, -exes** ['vɔ:teks, -isi:z, -eksiz], *s.* (*a*) *Ph:* Tourbillon *m.* **V. ring,** vortex *m.* (*b*) Tourbillonnement *m* (d'air); tourbillon (de fumée). (*c*) (*Whirlpool*) Tourbillon, gouffre *m.* **The v. of politics,** le tourbillon de la politique.

vortical ['vɔ:tik(ə)l], *a.* Tourbillonnaire.

votaress ['voutəris], *s.f.* Fervente (of, de); adoratrice (of, de); sectatrice (de).

votary ['voutəri], *s.* Fervent *m* (of, de); adorateur *m* (de); sectateur *m;* partisan zélé.

vote¹ [vout], *s.* **1.** *a.* Vote *m,* scrutin *m.* **Secret v.,** scrutin secret. **Popular v.,** consultation *f* populaire. **V. of an assembly,** délibération *f* d'une assemblée. **To put a question to the v.,** mettre une question aux voix. **To take the v.,** procéder au scrutin. (*b*) **(Individual) v.,** voix *f,* suffrage *m.* **To give one's v. to, for, s.o.,** donner sa voix à qn. **To have a v.,** avoir le droit de vote. **To record one's v.,** voter. **2.** Motion *f,* résolution *f.* **V. of censure,** motion de censure. **To carry a v.,** adopter une résolution. *S.a.* CONFIDENCE 1.

vote². **1.** *v.i.* Voter (**for, against,** pour, contre); *abs.* prendre part au vote. **2.** *v.tr.* (*a*) To v. a sum, voter une somme; *Parl:* voter un crédit. **To v. down a motion,** repousser une motion. (*b*) **I v. that we go,** je propose que nous y allions. **voting,** *s.* (Participation *f* au) vote; scrutin *m.* **Voting paper,** bulletin *m* de vote.

voter ['voutər], *s.* (*a*) Votant *m.* (*b*) Électeur, -trice.

votive ['voutiv], *a.* Votif, -ive. **V. offering,** offrande votive; ex-voto *m.*

vouch [vautʃ]. **1.** *v.tr.* (*a*) Affirmer, garantir (qch.). (*b*) Prouver, confirmer (une affirmation). **2.** *v.i.* **To v. for the truth of sth.,** témoigner de, répondre de, la vérité de qch. **To v. for s.o.,** répondre de qn; se porter garant de qn.

voucher ['vautʃər], *s.* (*a*) Justification produite à l'appui de dépenses; pièce justificative. *Book-k:* Pièce comptable. (*b*) *Com:* Fiche *f;* reçu *m,* bon *m.* **Cash v.,** bon de caisse. **Gift v.,** bon *m* d'achat. *Adm:* **Issue v.,** facture *f* de sortie. (*c*) *Th:* Contremarque *f.*

vouchsafe [vautʃ'seif], *v.tr. Lit:* (*a*) **To v. s.o. sth.,** accorder, octroyer, qch. à qn. (*b*) **To v. to do sth.,** daigner faire qch.

voussoir ['vu:swɑ:r], *s. Arch:* Voussoir *m,* vousseau *m,* claveau *m.*

vow¹ [vau], *s.* Vœu *m,* serment *m.* **Monastic vows,** vœux monastiques. **To take one's vows,** entrer en religion. **To be under a v. to do sth.,** avoir fait le vœu de faire qch. **To fulfil a v.,** accomplir un vœu.

vow², *v.tr.* Vouer, jurer. **To v. obedience,** jurer obéissance. **To v. vengeance against s.o.,** faire vœu de se venger de, sur, qn.

vow³, *v.tr. A:* Affirmer, déclarer (that, que).

vowel ['vauəl], *s.* Voyelle *f.* **V. sound,** son *m* vocalique.

vox humana ['vɔkshju'mɑ:nə], *s.* Voix humaine (d'un orgue).

voyage¹ ['vɔiidʒ], *s.* Voyage *m* sur mer. **On the v. out, home,** à l'aller, au retour.

voyage², *v.i.* Voyager sur mer; naviguer.

voyager ['vɔiədʒər], *s.* Voyageur, -euse, par mer; passager, -ère; navigateur *m.*

vulcanite ['vʌlkənait], *s.* Vulcanite *f,* ébonite *f.*

vulcanization [ˌvʌlkənai'zeiʃ(ə)n], *s. Ind:* Vulcanisation *f* (du caoutchouc).

vulcanize ['vʌlkənaiz]. **1.** *v.tr. Ind:* Vulcaniser (le caoutchouc). **2.** *v.i.* Se vulcaniser. **vulcanizing,** *s.* Vulcanisation *f.*

vulgar ['vʌlgər], *a.* **1.** Vulgaire, commun. **V. display of wealth,** gros luxe de mauvais goût. *A:* **The v. herd,** *s.* **the v.,** le vulgaire; le commun des hommes. **2.** (*a*) Vulgaire; communément reçu. **V. errors,** erreurs très répandues. (*b*) **The v. tongue,** la langue commune, la langue vulgaire. (*c*) *Ar:* **V. fraction,** fraction ordinaire. **-ly,** *adv.* **1.** Vulgairement, grossièrement. **2.** Vulgairement, communément.

vulgarian [vʌl'geəriən], *s.* (*a*) Personne vulgaire, commune. (*b*) Parvenu(e) mal décrassé(e).

vulgarism ['vʌlgərizm], *s.* Expression *f* vulgaire, vulgarisme *m.*

vulgarity [vʌl'gæriti], *s.* Vulgarité *f,* trivialité *f.* **To lapse into v.,** donner dans le vulgaire.

vulgarization [ˌvʌlgərai'zeiʃ(ə)n], *s.* Vulgarisation *f.*

vulgarize ['vʌlgəraiz], *v.tr.* Vulgariser.

Vulgate ['vʌlgeit], *s. B.Lit:* **The V.,** la Vulgate.

vulnerability [ˌvʌln(ə)rə'biliti], *s.* Vulnérabilité *f.*

vulnerable ['vʌln(ə)rəbl], *a.* (*a*) Vulnérable. **That is his v. spot,** c'est son point faible, son talon d'Achille. (*b*) *Cards:* (*At bridge*) Vulnérable.

vulpine ['vʌlpain], *a.* **1.** Qui a rapport au renard. **2.** Qui tient du renard; rusé, astucieux, -euse.

vulture ['vʌltʃər], *s.* Vautour *m.*

vulva ['vʌlvə], *s. Anat:* Vulve *f.*

vying ['vaiiŋ]. *See* VIE.

W, w [ˈdʌblju:], s. (La lettre) W, w m. Tp: W for William, W comme William.

wad¹ [wɔd], s. 1. (a) Tampon m, bouchon m (d'ouate, etc.). (b) Liasse f (de billets de banque). 2. Bourre f (de cartouche).

wad², v.tr. (wadded) Dressm: Ouater, capitonner (un vêtement). **wadding**, s. 1. Ouatage m, rembourrage m. 2. (a) Ouate f (pour vêtements); bourre f (pour armes à feu). (b) Tampon m d'ouate.

waddle¹ [ˈwɔdl], s. Dandinement m; démarche f de canard.

waddle², v.i. Se dandiner (comme un canard); marcher en canard.

wade [weid]. 1. v.i. Marcher dans l'eau. To w. **across a stream**, passer à gué un cours d'eau. F: To w. **through a book**, venir péniblement à bout d'un livre. To w. **in**, (i) entrer dans l'eau; (ii) F: intervenir; prendre part (à qch.). 2. v.tr. Passer à gué (un cours d'eau). **wading**, a. Orn: W. **bird** = WADER 1.

wader [ˈweidər], s. 1. Orn: Échassier m. 2. Personne f qui marche dans l'eau. 3. pl. Waders, bottes f d'égoutier, de pêcheur.

wadi [ˈwɔdi], s. Oued m.

wafer [ˈweifər], s. 1. Cu: Gaufrette f. 2. Ecc: Hostie f. Unconsecrated w., pain m à chanter. 3. (a) O: Pain à cacheter. (b) Disque m de papier rouge (collé sur un document en guise de cachet). 4. Pharm: Cachet m (de quinine, etc.).

waffle¹ [ˈwɔfl], s. Cu: Gaufre f. **ˈwaffle-iron**, s. Gaufrier m; moule m à gaufres.

waffle², s. F: Laïus m.

waffle³, v.i. F: Laïusser.

waffler [ˈwɔflər], s. F: Laïusseur m.

waft¹ [wɑ:ft], s. 1. Lit: Bouffée f, souffle m (de vent). 2. Coup m d'aile (d'un oiseau).

waft², v.tr. Lit: To w. **a sound, a scent, through the air**, porter, transporter, un son, un parfum, dans les airs. Music wafted on the breeze, musique apportée par la brise. (Of the wind) To w. **the ship along**, faire avancer le navire.

wag¹ [wæg], s. O: Farceur m, blagueur m; F: loustic m.

wag², s. Agitation f, frétillement m (de la queue); hochement m (de la tête). (Of dog) With a w. of its tail, en remuant la queue.

wag³, (wagged) 1. v.tr. (Of dog) To w. **its tail**, remuer la queue; (of bird) hocher la queue. To w. **one's tongue**, jaser; jacasser. To w. **one's finger at s.o.**, menacer qn du doigt. To w. **one's head**, hocher, branler, la tête. S.a. CHIN. 2. v.i. S'agiter, se remuer. His tongue was beginning to w., sa langue se déliait. To set (people's) tongues wagging, faire jaser.

wage¹ [weidʒ], s. Usu.pl. (a) Gages mpl (de domestique); salaire m, paie f (d'ouvrier). To receive one's day's wage(s), toucher sa journée. To earn good wages, être bien rétribué. Minimum w., (i) salaire minimum interprofessionnel garanti; (ii) minimum vital. W. freeze, blocage m des salaires. (b) Lit: Prix m, salaire. The wages of sin is death, la mort est le salaire du péché. **ˈwage-earner**, s. 1. Salarié, -ée. 2. Le soutien (de la famille). **ˈwage(s)-sheet**, s. Ind: Feuille f de paie.

wage², v.tr. To w. **war**, faire la guerre (with, on, à).

wager¹ [ˈweidʒər], s. Pari m; gageure f. To lay, make, a w., faire un pari; parier.

wager², v.tr. Parier, gager. I'll w. that..., je parie, je gage, que...

waggish [ˈwægiʃ], a. Plaisant, badin; blagueur, facétieux, -euse. W. **remarks**, facéties f.

waggle [ˈwægl], v.tr. & i. F: = WAG³.

Wagnerian [vɑːgˈniːəriən], a. & s. Wagnérien, -ienne.

wag(g)on [ˈwæg(ə)n], s. 1. Charrette f (à quatre roues); chariot m; camion m. F: To be on the (water) w., s'abstenir de boissons alcooliques. 2. Rail: Wagon découvert (à marchandises). Covered goods w., fourgon m. **ˈwag(g)on-load**, s. Charretée f, enlevée f (de foin, etc.). Rail: (Charge f de) wagon m.

wag(g)oner [ˈwægənər], s. Roulier m, voiturier m, charretier m.

wag(g)onette [wægəˈnet], s. Veh: Wagonnette f, break m.

wagtail [ˈwægteil], s. Orn: Bergeronnette f, hoche-queue m, branle-queue m.

waif [weif], s. (a) Jur: Épave f. (b) Waifs and strays, (enfants) abandonnés.

wail¹ [weil], s. (a) Cri plaintif; plainte f, gémisse-ment m. (b) Vagissement m (de nouveau-né).

wail², v.i. (a) Gémir; (of new-born child) vagir. (b) To w. **over sth.**, se lamenter sur qch. **wailing**, a. (Cri) plaintif; (of pers.) gémissant.

wain [wein], s. 1. A: Charrette f (à quatre roues). 2. Astr: Charles's W., le Grand Chariot.

wainscot¹ [ˈweinskət], s. Lambris m; boiserie f (d'une salle).

wainscot², v.tr. Lambrisser. **Wainscot(t)ed room**, pièce lambrissée.

wainscot(t)ing [ˈweinskətiŋ], s. 1. Lambrissage m. 2. = WAINSCOT¹.

waist [weist], s. 1. (a) (Of pers.) Taille f, ceinture f. Down to the w., up to the w., jusqu'à mi-corps. W. **measurement**, tour m de taille. To put one's arm round s.o.'s w., prendre qn par la taille. Wr: Grip round the w., la ceinture. (b) Étranglement m, rétrécissement m (d'un sablier, d'un violon). (c) Nau: Embelle f; passavant m. 2. Dressm: Dress with a short w., robe à taille courte. **ˈwaist-belt**, s. Mil: Ceinturon m. **ˈwaist-ˈdeep, -ˈhigh**, adv. Jusqu'à la ceinture; jusqu'à mi-corps. **ˈwaist-lock**, s. Wr: Ceinture f.

waistband [ˈweis(t)bænd], s. Ceinture f (de jupe, de pantalon).

waistcoat [ˈweis(t)kout, ˈweskət], s. 1. Gilet m. S.a. POCKET¹ 1. 2. Strait w., camisole f de force.

waisted [ˈweistid], a. Long-w., short-w., long, court, de taille.

waistline [ˈweistlain], s. Dressm: Taille f. Natural w., taille normale. To keep, watch, one's w., garder, soigner, sa ligne.

wait¹ [weit], s. 1. (a) Attente f; (of train) arrêt m. Twenty minutes' w. between the two trains, battement m de vingt minutes entre les deux trains. (b) To lie in w., se tenir en embuscade; être à l'affût. To lie in w. **for s.o.**, attendre qn au passage; tendre un guet-apens à qn. 2. pl. Waits, chanteurs m de noëls (qui vont de porte en porte).

wait². 1. v.i. (a) Attendre. W. **a moment**, F: w. **a bit**, attendez un moment. To keep s.o. waiting, faire attendre qn. He is keeping us waiting, il se fait attendre. To w. **for s.o.**, attendre qn. Not to w. for s.o., brûler la politesse à qn. We are waiting to be served, nous attendons qu'on nous serve. He did not w. to be told twice, il ne se le fit pas dire deux fois. Parcel waiting (to be called for) at the station, colis en souffrance à la gare. Com: Repairs while you w., réparations à la minute. Prov: Everything comes to him who waits, tout vient à point à qui sait attendre. To w. **and see**, voir venir, se réserver. W.-and-see policy, attentisme m. (b) To w. **at table**, servir (à table); faire le service. 2. v.tr. (a) Attendre, guetter (une occasion). (b) Don't w. **dinner for me**, ne m'attendez pas pour vous mettre à table. **wait on, upon**, v.ind.tr. (a) Servir (qn). To w. on s.o. **hand and foot**, être aux petits soins pour, avec, qn. (b) Se présenter chez (qn). (c) Lit: Être la conséquence de (qch.); suivre (qch.). **wait up**, v.i. To w. **up for s.o.**, rester levé à attendre qn. **waiting**, s. 1. Attente f. We shall lose nothing by w., nous ne perdrons rien pour attendre. W. **list**, liste f d'attente. Aut: No w., stationnement interdit. 2. Service m. Lady in w., dame d'honneur. **ˈwaiting-room**, s. Salle f d'attente.

waiter [ˈweitər], s. 1. Garçon m (de restaurant). Head w., maître m d'hôtel. W.! garçon! 2. Plateau m.

waitress [ˈweitris], s.f. Serveuse (de restaurant). W.! mademoiselle!

waive [weiv] *v.tr.* Renoncer à, abandonner (ses prétentions); déroger à (un principe); ne pas insister sur (une condition).

waiver ['weivər], *s. Jur:* W. of a right, abandon *m* d'un droit. W. of a claim, désistement *m* (de revendication).

wake[1] [weik], *s.* (*a*) *Nau:* Sillage *m*, houache *f.* To be in the w. of a ship, être dans les eaux d'un bâtiment. (*b*) To follow in s.o.'s w., marcher à la suite de, sur les traces de, qn. In the w. of the storm, à la suite de la tempête.

wake[2], *s.* 1. (*In Ireland*) Veillée *f* mortuaire. 2. (*a*) *Hist:* Fête de la dédicace (d'une église). (*b*) (*N. of Eng.*) *Usu. pl.* Congé annuel.

wake[3], *v.* (*p.t.* woke [wouk], waked [weikt]; *p.p.* woken ['wouk(ə)n]) 1. *v.i.* (*a*) Être éveillé. Waking or sleeping, that thought never left her, éveillée ou endormie, cette pensée ne la quittait jamais. (*b*) To w. (up), se réveiller. Come on, w. up! allons, réveille-vous! To w. up with a start, se réveiller en sursaut. To wake up to find oneself famous, se réveiller célèbre. He is waking up to the truth, la vérité commence à lui apparaître. 2. *v.tr.* (*a*) To w. s.o. (up), réveiller qn. *F:* He wants something to w. him up, il lui faut quelque chose qui l'émoustille. (*b*) (*In Ireland*) Veiller (un mort). **waking**[1], *a.* Éveillé. W. hours, heures de veille. *S.a.* DREAM[1]. **waking**[2], *s.* 1. Veille *f.* Between sleeping and w., entre la veille et le sommeil. 2. Réveil *m.* On w., au réveil.

wakeful ['weikf(u)l], *a.* 1. (*a*) Éveillé; peu disposé à dormir. (*b*) Sans sommeil. W. night, nuit blanche. 2. Vigilant.

wakefulness ['weikf(u)lnis], *s.* 1. (*a*) Insomnie *f.* (*b*) État *m* de veille. 2. Vigilance *f.*

waken ['weik(ə)n]. 1. *v.tr.* (*a*) Éveiller, réveiller (qn). (*b*) Éveiller, exciter (une émotion). 2. *v.i.* Se réveiller, s'éveiller. **wakening**, *s.* Réveil *m.*

waker ['weikər], *s.* To be an early w., se réveiller (habituellement) de bonne heure.

wale[1] [weil], *s.* 1. Marque *f*, trace *f* (d'un coup de fouet). 2. *Nau:* The wales, les préceintes.

wale[2], *v.tr.* Marquer (d'un coup de fouet); zébrer (de coups de fouet).

Wales [weilz]. *Pr.n.* Le pays de Galles. North W., la Galles du Nord. *S.a.* NEW SOUTH WALES. The Prince of W., le Prince de Galles.

walk[1] [wɔːk], *s.* 1. Marche *f.* It is half an hour's w. from here, c'est à une demi-heure de marche d'ici. It's only a short w. (from here), ce n'est qu'une promenade. 2. Promenade (à pied). To go for a w., aller se promener; faire un tour, une promenade. To take s.o. for a w., emmener qn en promenade. 3. (*a*) Démarche *f.* I know him by his w., je le reconnais à sa marche, à sa démarche. (*b*) (*Of horse*) To fall into a w., se mettre au pas. 4. (*a*) Allée *f* (de jardin); avenue *f*, promenade. (*b*) Trottoir *m.* (*c*) Covered w., allée couverte; promenoir *m.* 5. Walk of life, (i) position sociale; milieu *m*; (ii) métier *m*, carrière *f.*

walk[2]. I. *v.i.* 1. Marcher, cheminer. To w. on the road, cheminer sur la chaussée. To w. on to the road, s'engager sur la chaussée. To w. in one's sleep, être somnambule. To w. with s.o., accompagner qn. W. a little way with me, faites-moi un bout de conduite. 2. (*As opposed to ride, drive*) Aller à pied. To w. home, rentrer à pied. I had to w., j'ai dû faire le trajet à pied. You can w. it in ten minutes, vous en avez pour dix minutes à pied. (*b*) (*For pleasure*) Se promener (à pied). To be out walking, être en promenade. 3. (*Of horse, etc.*) Aller au pas. 4. (*Of ghost*) Revenir. II. *v.tr.* 1. To w. the streets, courir les rues; battre le pavé; (*of prostitute*) faire le trottoir. (*Of sentry*) To w. one's round, faire sa faction. To w. the boards, être sur les planches; faire du théâtre. *S.a.* PLANK[1]. 2. (*a*) Faire marcher (un stupéfié). (*b*) To w. s.o. off his legs, exténuer qn à force de le faire marcher. (*c*) To w. a horse, conduire, promener, un cheval (au pas). **walk about**, *v.i.* Se promener; circuler. **walk along**, *v.i.* 1. Marcher; s'avancer. 2. To w. along the kerb, suivre le bord du trottoir. **walk away**, *v.i.* S'en aller; partir. *Sp: F:* To w. away from a competitor, distancer facilement, *F:* semer, un concurrent. **'walk-away**, *s. F:*

Victoire *f* facile. **walk in**, *v.i.* Entrer. To ask s.o. to walk in, faire entrer qn. (*On office door*) (Please) walk in, entrez sans frapper. **walk into**, *v.i.* 1. To w. into the room, entrer dans la salle. 2. (*a*) Se heurter à (qch.); se trouver nez à nez avec (qn). (*b*) *F:* S'attaquer à (qn); faire une sortie contre (qn); *P:* enguirlander (qn). **walk off**. 1. *v.i.* S'en aller; partir. *F:* To w. o. with sth., décamper avec (un objet volé, etc.). 2. *v.tr.* (*a*) To w. s.o. off to prison, emmener qn en prison. (*b*) To w. o. one's lunch, faire une promenade de digestion. **walk on**, *v.i.* 1. Continuer sa marche. 2. *Th:* Remplir un rôle de figurant(e). **'walking-'on**, *attrib.a. Th:* W.-o. part, rôle de figurant(e). **walk out**, *v.i.* (*a*) Sortir. *F:* To w.o. on s.o., (i) abandonner qn; (ii) quitter qn en colère. (*b*) *P:* To w.o. with a young man, (i) sortir, (ii) être avec, un jeune homme. (*c*) (*Of workmen*) Se mettre en grève. **'walk-out**, *s. F:* Grève *f.* **walk over**, *v.i. Sp:* To w. o. (the course), gagner d'office (en l'absence d'autres concurrents); *F:* gagner dans un fauteuil. **'walk-over**, *s.* Victoire *f* facile; *Sp: F:* walk-over *m.* **walk round**, *v.i.* 1. Faire le tour de (qch.). 2. Faire le tour; faire un détour. **walk up**. 1. *v.i.* To w. up to s.o., s'avancer vers qn; s'approcher de qn. To w. up and down, se promener de long en large; faire ses cent pas. He walked up to the fifth floor, il est monté (à pied) jusqu'au cinquième (étage). 2. *v.tr.* To w. a horse up and down, promener un cheval. **walking**[1], *a.* (Voyageur) ambulant. *Mil: Med:* W. case, blessé qui peut marcher. **walking**[2], *s.* Marche *f*; promenades *fpl* à pied. To like w., aimer la marche. It is within w. distance, on peut aisément s'y rendre à pied. **'walking-boots, -shoes**, *s.pl.* Chaussures *f* de marche. **'walking-pace**, *s.* Allure *f* du pas. *Aut:* To drive at a w.-p., rouler au pas. **'walking-race**, *s.* Épreuve *f* de marche. **'walking-stick**, *s.* Canne *f.*

walker ['wɔːkər], *s.* 1. Marcheur, -euse; promeneur, -euse; piéton *m.* He is a fast w., il marche vite. To be a good w., être bon marcheur, avoir de bonnes jambes. I am not the w. I used to be, je n'ai plus mes jambes de quinze ans. 2. *Th:* Walker-on, figurant,-ante.

walkie-talkie ['wɔːki'tɔːki], *s. W.Tel: F:* Émetteur-récepteur *m*, *pl.* émetteurs-récepteurs, poste de radio portatif.

wall[1] [wɔːl], *s.* 1. (*a*) Mur *m.* Main walls, gros murs. Surrounding w., mur d'enceinte. Dry wall, perré *m.* Dry-stone w., mur en pierres sèches. W. to w. carpet, tapis ajusté. *El.E:* W. switchboard, tableau de distribution mural. To leave only the bare walls standing, ne laisser que les quatre murs. *F:* To come up against a blank w., se heurter à un mur. You might just as well talk to a brick w., autant vaut parler à un sourd. Walls have ears, les murs ont des oreilles. *F:* To run one's head against a (brick) w., donner de la tête contre un mur; se buter à l'impossible. *F:* He can see through a brick w., il a le nez fin. *F:* To go to the w., succomber; perdre la partie. The weakest always goes to the w., le plus faible est toujours écrasé. (*b*) Muraille *f.* W. of rocks, muraille de rochers. Within the walls (of the town), dans la ville; intra muros. Outside the walls, extra muros. The Great W. of China, la muraille de Chine. *Pol.Ec:* High tariff walls, hautes barrières douanières. 2. *Anat:* Paroi *f* (de la poitrine, d'une cellule); joue *f* (d'un pneu). **'wall-bracket**, *s.* Console murale. **'wall-clock**, *s.* Cartel *m*; pendule murale; (*round*) œil-de-bœuf *m*, *pl.* œils-de-bœuf. **'wall-drill**, *s. Tls:* Tamponnoir *m.* **'wall-'face**, *s.* 1. Surface *f* d'un mur. 2. *Min:* Paroi *f* (d'une galerie). **'wall fern**, *s.* Polypode *m* vulgaire. **'wall-map**, *s.* Carte murale. **'wall-painting**, *s.* Peinture murale. **'wall-seat**, *s.* Banquette *f.* **'wall-walk**, *s. Fort:* Chemin *m* de ronde.

wall[2], *v.tr.* 1. To w. (in), entourer de murs; murer. 2. Murailler (un talus, etc.). **wall up**, *v.tr.* To w. up the windows of a house, murer les fenêtres d'une maison. **walled**, *a.* 1. W. (in), muré; clos de murs. 2. Brick-w. house, maison en brique.

walling ['wɔːliŋ], *s.* (*a*) Muraillement *m.* (*b*) Maçonnerie *f*; murs *mpl.*.

wallaby ['wɔləbi], *s.* 1. *Z:* Wallaby *m.* 2. *F:* Australien *m.*

wallah ['wɔlə], s. O: (Anglo-Indian) Employé m, garçon m. **Punkah-w.**, tireur m de panka.

wallboard ['wɔːlbɔːd], s. Constr: Panneau m de revêtement.

wallet ['wɔlit], s. Portefeuille m.

wall-eyed ['wɔːl'aid], a. 1. (Of horse, pers.) Vairon. 2. (Of pers.) A strabisme divergent.

wallflower ['wɔːlflauər], s. 1. Bot: Giroflée f jaune, des murailles; ravenelle f. 2. F: (At a dance) To be a w., faire tapisserie.

Walloon [wɔ'luːn]. 1. a. & s. Wallon, -onne. 2. s. Ling: Le wallon.

wallop[1] ['wɔləp], s. F: 1. Gros coup; P: torgn(i)ole f. 2. **And down he went with a w.!** et patatras, le voilà par terre! 3. F: Bière brune.

wallop[2], v.tr. F: Rosser (qn); flanquer une tournée à (qn). **walloping**[1], a. P: Énorme; épatant. **walloping**[2], s. P: Volée f (de coups); rossée f, tannée f.

wallow[1] ['wɔlou], s. Trou bourbeux (où se roulent les buffles); souille f, bauge f (de sanglier).

wallow[2], v.i. (Of animals) Se vautrer; se rouler dans la boue. (Of pers.) **To w. in blood**, se plonger dans le sang. **To w. in vice**, croupir dans le vice. F: **He's wallowing in money**, il roule sur l'or, P: il est plein aux as.

wallpaper ['wɔːlpeipər], s. Papier peint.

walnut ['wɔːlnʌt], s. 1. Noix f. **Green w.**, cerneau m. 2. Bot: **W.(-tree)**, noyer m. 3. (Bois m de) noyer. **'walnut-shell**, s. Coquille f de noix. **'walnut-stain**, s. Brou m de noix.

walrus ['wɔːlrəs], s. Z: Morse m. F: **W. moustache**, moustache f à la gauloise.

Walter ['wɔːltər]. Pr.n.m. Gauthier.

waltz[1] [wɔːls], s. 1. Valse f. 2. Mus: Air m de valse.

waltz[2], v.i. Valser. **waltzing**, s. Valse f.

wan [wɔn], a. Pâlot, -otte; blême. **W. light**, lumière blafarde. **W. smile**, pâle sourire. **-ly**, adv. (Sourire) d'un air triste.

wand [wɔnd], s. 1. Baguette f (de fée). 2. (Staff of office) Bâton m (de commandement); verge f (d'huissier).

wander ['wɔndər]. 1. v.i. (a) Errer (sans but); se promener au hasard. **To w. about**, aller à l'aventure; vaguer. **To let one's thoughts w.**, laisser vaguer ses pensées. (b) **To w. (away) from the subject**, s'écarter du sujet. **My thoughts were wandering**, je n'étais pas à la conversation. **His mind wanders at times**, il a des absences. (c) (Of pers.) **To w. in one's mind**, divaguer; avoir le délire; battre la campagne. 2. v.tr. Lit: **To w. the world**, errer de par le monde. **wandering**[1], a. 1. (a) Errant, vagabond. **W. tribes**, nomades m. (b) (Esprit) distrait. 2. (a) Med: Qui a le délire. (b) (Discours) incohérent. **wandering**[2], s. 1. (a) Vagabondage m; errance f. (b) Usu. pl. Voyages mpl; pérégrinations fpl. 2. (a) Rêverie f. (b) Med: Égarement m (de l'esprit). **In his wanderings, dans ses divagations. 3. W. from the subject**, digression(s) f.

wanderer ['wɔndərər], s. Vagabond, -onde. Our w. has returned, notre voyageur nous est revenu.

wanderlust ['wɔndəlʌst], s. La passion des voyages; l'esprit d'aventure.

wane[1] [wein], s. Déclin m. **Moon on the w.**, lune à son décours. **To be on the w.**, (of moon) décroître; (of pers.) être à, sur, son déclin. **His star is on the w.**, son étoile pâlit.

wane[2], v.i. (Of the moon, of power, etc.) Décroître, décliner; (of beauty) être sur le retour; (of enthusiasm) s'attiédir. **waning**, s. Décours m (de la lune); déclin m.

wangle[1] ['wæŋgl], s. F: Moyen détourné; truc m.

wangle[2], v.tr. F: 1. Obtenir (qch.) par subterfuge; resquiller. **To w. a week's leave**, carotter huit jours de congé. 2. Cuisiner (des comptes). **wangling**, s. Fricotage m; resquille f.

wangler ['wæŋglər], s. F: Resquilleur, -euse.

wanness ['wɔnnis], s. Pâleur f.

want[1] [wɔnt], s. 1. (a) Manque m, défaut m. **W. of judgment**, défaut de jugement. **W. of imagination**, manque d'imagination. **For w. of sth.**, faute de qch.; par manque de (prévoyance, etc.). **For w. of something better**, faute de mieux. **For w. of something to do**, par désœuvrement. **To make up for the w. of sth.**,

suppléer à l'absence de qch. (b) **To be in w. of sth.**, avoir besoin de qch. **To be in w. of money**, être à court d'argent. **I am in w. of . . .**, il me manque. . . . 2. Indigence f, misère f. **To be in w.**, être dans le besoin, dans la gêne. **To be living in w.**, vivre dans la misère. 3. Besoin m. **To attend to s.o.'s wants**, pourvoir aux besoins de qn. **A long-felt w.**, une lacune à combler.

want[2]. 1. v.i. (a) Manquer (for, de); être dépourvu (de). **To w. for nothing**, ne manquer de rien. (b) **His family will see to it that he does not w.**, sa famille veillera à ce qu'il ne se trouve pas dans le besoin. 2. v.tr. (a) Manquer de, ne pas avoir (qch.). **To w. patience**, manquer de patience. Impers: **It wanted only a few days to Christmas**, c'était juste quelques jours avant Noël. (b) (Of pers.) Avoir besoin de (qch.); (of thg) exiger, réclamer (qch.). **To w. rest**, avoir besoin de repos. **That work wants a lot of patience**, ce travail exige beaucoup de patience. **Have you all you w.?** avez-vous tout ce qu'il vous faut? **You shall have as much as you w.**, vous en aurez autant que vous voudrez. **I've had all I want(ed)**, j'en ai assez. **That's the very thing I w.**, c'est juste ce qu'il me faut; c'est juste mon affaire. **To w. a job**, être en quête d'un emploi. **Wanted, a good cook**, on demande une bonne cuisinière. (c) **Your hair wants cutting**, vous avez besoin de vous faire couper les cheveux. **It wants some doing**, ce n'est pas (si) facile à faire. (d) Désirer, vouloir. **He knows what he wants**, il sait ce qu'il veut. **How much for this armchair?—I w. five pounds**, combien ce fauteuil?—J'en demande cinq livres. Iron: **You don't w. much!** tu n'es pas difficile! **You are wanted**, on vous demande. **We are not wanted here**, nous sommes de trop ici. **We don't w. you**, nous n'avons que faire de vous. **What does he w. with me?** que me veut-il? **I w. to tell you that . . .**, je voudrais vous dire que. . . . **To w. to see s.o., to speak to s.o.**, demander qn; avoir à parler à qn. **I w. him to come**, je désire qu'il vienne. **I don't w. it known**, je ne veux pas que cela se sache. **wanted**, a. 1. Désiré, voulu, demandé. 2. Recherché par la police. **wanting**, pred.a. (a) Manquant, qui manque. **To be w.**, faire défaut. **One sheet is w.**, il manque une feuille. **There is something w.**, le compte n'y est pas. (b) **W. in intelligence**, dépourvu d'intelligence. **He was tried and found w.**, il ne supporta pas l'épreuve. (c) F: Faible d'esprit. **He is slightly w.**, il lui manque un petit quelque chose.

wanton ['wɔntən]. 1. a. (a) (Of woman) Licencieuse, impudique. (b) **W. winds**, vents folâtres. (c) Gratuit; sans motif. **W. cruelty**, cruauté gratuite. **W. destruction**, destruction pour le simple plaisir de détruire. 2. s.f. Femme légère. **-ly**, adv. 1. Impudiquement. 2. De gaieté de cœur. 3. (Blesser, insulter) gratuitement.

wantonness ['wɔntənnis], s. 1. Libertinage m. 2. **To do sth. in sheer w.**, faire qch. de gaieté de cœur, par étourdie.

wapiti ['wɔpiti], s. Z: Wapiti m.

war[1] [wɔːr], s. Guerre f. **Total w.**, guerre totale. **Cold w.**, guerre froide. **Shooting w.**, guerre chaude. **W. of nerves**, guerre des nerfs. **W. of movement**, guerre de mouvement. **The w. to end all wars**, F: la der des der. **The First, Second, World W., World W. One, Two**, la première, deuxième, guerre mondiale. **The Great W.**, la Grande Guerre. F: **The phoney w.** (1939–40), la drôle de guerre. **To go to w.**, se mettre en guerre. **To make w. on s.o.**, faire la guerre à, contre, qn. **W. of the elements**, conflit m des éléments. **W. of words**, dispute f de mots. F: **You look as if you had been in the wars**, vous avez l'air de vous être battu. **On a w. footing**, sur le pied de guerre. **W. zone**, zone militaire. **W. crimes tribunal**, tribunal militaire international. S.a. ARTICLE[1] 2, MEMORIAL 2. **'war-cloud**, s. Menace f de guerre. **'war-correspondent**, s. Correspondant m de guerre. **'war-cry**, s. Cri m de guerre. **'war-dance**, s. Danse guerrière. **'war-fever**, s. Psychose f de guerre. **'war-horse**, s. 1. A: Destrier m; cheval m de bataille. 2. F: **An old w.-h.**, (i) un vieux soldat; (ii) un vétéran de la politique. **'war-loan**, s. Fin: Emprunt m de guerre. **'war-lord**, s.m. (Esp. in

China). Seigneur de la guerre. **'war-paint**, *s.* **1.** Peinture *f* de guerre (des Peaux-Rouges). **2.** *F:* Decked out in all one's w.-p., en grande toilette, en grand tralala, sur son trente et un. **'war-path**, *s.* *F:* To be on the w.-p., (i) être parti en campagne; (ii) en vouloir à tout le monde: chercher noise à tout le monde. The boss is on the w.-p., le patron est d'une humeur massacrante. **'war-time**, *s.* Temps *m* de guerre. **W.-t. regulations**, règlements du temps de guerre. **'war-weary**, *a.* Fatigué, las, de la guerre. **'war-worn**, *a.* Usé par la guerre.

war², *v.i.* (warred) To w. against s.o., mener une campagne contre qn; lutter contre qn. To w. **against abuses**, faire la guerre aux abus. **warring**, *a.* W. **nations**, nations en guerre. W. **interests**, intérêts contraires.

warble¹ ['wɔːbl], *s.* Gazouillement *m*, gazouillis *m*, ramage *m* (des oiseaux).

warble². **1.** *v.i.* (*a*) Gazouiller. (*b*) *F:* (*Of pers.*) Chanter. **2.** *v.tr.* Chanter (qch.) en gazouillant. **warbling**, *s.* = WARBLE¹.

warbler ['wɔːblər], *s.* **1.** (Oiseau) chanteur. **2.** *Orn:* Fauvette *f*; bec-fin *m*.

ward¹ [wɔːd], *s.* **1.** (*a*) *A:* Guet *m.* To keep watch and w., faire le guet; faire bonne garde. (*b*) (*Pers.*) Pupille *mf.* *Jur:* W. **in Chancery**, w. **of Court**, pupille sous tutelle judiciaire. **2.** (*a*) **Hospital w.**, salle *f* d'hôpital. **Emergency w.**, salle d'urgence. **W. maid**, fille *f* de salle. (*b*) Quartier *m* (d'une prison). **3.** Circonscription électorale. **4. Wards of a lock**, gardes *f* d'une serrure.

ward², *v.tr.* (*a*) *A. & Lit:* Garder (from, de); défendre (from, contre). (*b*) To w. **off a blow**, parer un coup. To w. **off an illness**, prévenir une maladie.

warden ['wɔːdn], *s.* **1.** (*a*) Directeur *m* (d'une institution). (*b*) *Freemasonry:* Surveillant *m.* (*c*) Gardien *m*; conservateur *m* (d'un parc national). (*d*) Gouverneur *m* (d'une ville). (*e*) *War. Adm:* Air-raid w., chef *m* d'îlot. (*f*) *Aut:* Traffic w., contractuel *m* (qui surveille le stationnement des voitures). **2.** = CHURCHWARDEN 1.

warder ['wɔːdər], *s.* Gardien *m* (de prison). **Female w.**, gardienne *f.*

wardress ['wɔːdris], *s.f.* Gardienne de prison.

wardrobe ['wɔːdroub], *s.* **1.** *Furn:* Armoire *f*, garderobe; *f* penderie *f.* **2.** (= *clothing*) Garde-robe. W. **dealer**, fripier, fripière. *Th:* W.-keeper, costumier *m.*

wardroom ['wɔːdrum], *s.* *Navy:* Carré *m* des officiers.

ware¹ [wɛər], *s.* **1.** *Coll.* (*a*) Articles fabriqués. Aluminium w., ustensiles *mpl* en aluminium. (*b*) Faïence *f.* **China w.**, porcelaine *f.* **2.** *pl.* Wares, marchandise(s)*f.*

ware², *v.tr.* *Esp. Ven:* W. wire! gare le fil de fer! W. wheat! attention au blé!

warehouse¹ ['wɛəhaus], *s.* Entrepôt *m*; magasin *m.* **Bonded w.**, entrepôt en douane. *Com:* Ex w., à prendre en entrepôt.

warehouse² [wɛəhauz], *v.tr.* Emmagasiner; mettre en magasin. **warehousing**, *s.* (*a*) (Em)magasinage *m*; mise *f* en magasin. (*b*) *Cust:* Entreposage *m* (de marchandises).

warehouseman, *pl.* -men ['wɛəhausmən], *s.m.* (*a*) Entrepositaire; magasinier. (*b*) Garde-magasin.

warfare ['wɔːfɛər], *s.* La guerre. **Trench w.**, la guerre de tranchées. **Naval w.**, guerre maritime. **Aerial w.**, guerre aérienne. **Total w.**, guerre totale. **Global w.**, guerre mondiale. **Static w.**, guerre de positions. **Class w.**, la lutte des classes.

warhead ['wɔːhed], *s.* (*a*) Cône *m* de charge (d'une torpille). (*b*) Tête *f*; ogive *f* (de fusée). **Nuclear w.**, tête nucléaire.

wariness ['wɛərinis], *s.* Circonspection *f*, prudence *f*; défiance *f.*

warlike ['wɔːlaik], *a.* (Exploit) guerrier; (air) martial; (peuple) belliqueux.

warm¹ [wɔːm], *a.* **1.** (*a*) Chaud (mais non brûlant). To be w., (i) (*of water*) être chaud; (ii) (*of pers.*) avoir chaud. I can't get w., je ne peux pas me réchauffer. (*At games*) You are getting w.! vous brûlez! To keep oneself w., se tenir au chaud, se vêtir chaudement. *Com:* 'To be kept in a w. place,' 'tenir au chaud.' *S.a.* FIRE¹ 1. (*b*) (Vêtement) chaud. *s.* *Mil:* British w., pardessus (court) d'officier. (*c*) (*Of the weather*) It is w., il fait chaud. (*d*) *Ven:*

W. **scent**, piste toute chaude. **2.** (*a*) Chaleureux, -euse; ardent. W. **thanks**, remerciements chaleureux. W. **applause**, vifs applaudissements. (*b*) W. **heart**, cœur généreux, chaud. To meet with a w. **reception**, (i) être accueilli chaleureusement; (ii) *Iron:* être accueilli par des huées. (*c*) The argument was getting w., la discussion s'animait. W. **contest**, lutte acharnée, chaude. The warmest spot (of the battle), le coin où ça chauffait le plus. It is w. work, c'est une rude besogne, *F:* To make it w. for s.o., en faire voir de dures à qn *F:* en faire baver à qn. (*d*) (*Of colour*) W. **tints**, tons chauds. **3.** *F:* A w. man, un homme riche, cossu, qui a de quoi. -ly, *adv.* **1.** (Vêtu) chaudement. **2.** (*a*) (Applaudir) chaudement. To thank s.o. w., remercier qn chaleureusement, en termes chaleureux. (*b*) (Répondre) vivement, avec chaleur. **'warm-'blooded**, *a.* *Z:* (Animal) à sang chaud. **'warm-'hearted**, *a.* Au cœur chaud, généreux.

warm², *s.* *F:* Action *f* de chauffer. Come and have a w., venez vous réchauffer.

warm³. **1.** *v.tr.* (*a*) Chauffer. To w. **oneself at the fire**, **in the sun**, se chauffer au feu, au soleil. To w. **oneself walking**, se réchauffer en marchant. (*b*) That will w. **the cockles of your heart**, voilà qui vous réchauffera. *P:* To w. **s.o.'s ears**, frotter les oreilles à qn. **2.** *v.i.* (*a*) (Se) chauffer; se réchauffer. To w. **to s.o.**, se prendre de sympathie pour qn. (*b*) S'animer. The lecturer was warming to his subject, le conférencier s'échauffait peu à peu. **warm up. 1.** *v.tr.* (*a*) Chauffer; réchauffer. The wine will w. **him up**, le vin le réchauffera. (*b*) (Faire) réchauffer (la soupe, etc.). **2.** *v.i.* (*a*) S'échauffer; s'animer. The game was warming up, la partie s'animait. (*b*) (*Of company*) Devenir plus cordial; *F:* se dégeler. **warming**, *s.* **1.** Chauffage *m.* **2.** *F:* Rossée *f*, raclée *f.* **'warm-ing-pan**, *s.* Bassinoire *f.*

warmonger ['wɔːmʌŋgər], *s.* Belliciste *m*; fauteur, -trice, de guerre.

warmongering ['wɔːmʌŋgriŋ], *s.* Propagande *f* de guerre; bellicisme *m.*

warmth [wɔːmθ], *s.* **1.** Chaleur *f.* **2.** (*a*) Ardeur *f*, zèle *m*; ferveur *f.* (*b*) Cordialité *f*, chaleur (d'un accueil). (*c*) Emportement *m*, vivacité *f.*

warn [wɔːn], *v.tr.* Avertir; prévenir. To w. **s.o. of a danger**, prémunir qn contre un danger; avertir qn d'un danger. To w. **s.o. against sth.**, mettre qn en garde contre qch. He warned her not to go, il lui conseilla fortement de ne pas y aller. You have been warned! vous voilà prévenu! I shall not w. you again, tenez-vous-le pour dit. **warn off**, *v.tr.* *Turf:* To w. **s.o. off the course**, exclure qn des champs de course. **warning¹**, *a.* (Geste) avertisseur d'avertissement. W. **lamp**, lampe *f* témoin. *Aut:* W. **sign**, (plaque *f*, écriteau *m*, d')avertissement (*m*). *Nau:* W. **shot**, coup *m* de semonce. **warning²**, *s.* Avertissement *m.* **1.** Action *f* d'avertir. (Air-raid) w., alerte *f.* **Danger w.**, signalisation *f* des dangers. W. **device**, avertisseur *m.* **2.** (*a*) Avis *m*, préavis *m.* To give w. **of danger to s.o.**, avertir qn d'un danger. Without w., sans préavis; *F:* sans crier gare. (*b*) To give s.o. **fair w.**, donner à qn un avertissement formel. (*c*) Let this be a w. to you, que cela vous serve de leçon, d'exemple. Let this be a fair w.! que ce soit bien entendu et bien compris!

warp¹ [wɔːp], *s.* **1.** *Tex:* Chaîne *f*; (*for tapestry*) lisse *f*, lice *f.* **2.** *Nau:* Amarre *f*; grelin *m*, aussière *f* de halage; touée *f.* **3.** Voilure *f*, courbure *f*, gauchissement *m* (d'une planche). **'warp-end**, *s.* *Tex:* Fil *m* de chaîne.

warp². **I.** *v.tr.* **1.** (*a*) Déjeter, (faire) voiler (le bois, une tôle). (*b*) Fausser, pervertir (l'esprit). **2.** *Av:* Gauchir (les ailes). **2.** *Tex:* Ourdir (l'étoffe). **3.** *Nau:* Haler, touer (un navire). To w. **off a ship**, déhaler un navire. **II.** **warp**, *v.i.* **1.** Se déformer; (*of timber*) se déjeter, gauchir; (*of wheel*) se voiler. The wood warps, le bois joue, travaille. **2.** *Nau:* To w. **out of port**, sortir du port à la touée; déhaler. **warped**, *a.* (*a*) (Bois) déjeté, gauchi, déversé. W. **wheel**, roue voilée. (*b*) (Esprit) perverti, faussé. W. **nature**, caractère mal fait. **warping**, *s.* **1.** (*a*) Gauchissement *m* (du bois, etc.), gondolage *m* (de la tôle); voile *m* (d'une roue). (*b*) Perversion *f* (de l'esprit). **2.** *Tex:* Ourdissage *m.* **3.** *Nau:* Touage *m.*

warrant[1] ['wɔr(ə)nt], s. 1. Garantie f. 2. Autorisation f; justification f. 3. (a) Mandat m, ordre m. W. of arrest, mandat d'arrêt, mandat d'amener. A w. is out against him, il est sous le coup d'un mandat d'amener. (b) Autorisation écrite; autorité f. S.a. ATTORNEY. (c) Certificat m. Warehouse, dock, w., certificat d'entrepôt; warrant m. To issue a warehouse w. for goods, warranter des marchandises. (d) W. for payment, ordonnance f de paiement. Mil: Adm: (Travel) w., feuille f de route. (e) Brevet m. Royal w., brevet de fournisseur du roi, de la reine. Warrant-officer, (i) Mil: = adjudant-chef; (ii) Navy: = maître principal.

warrant[2], v.tr. 1. Garantir, certifier (qch.). It won't happen again, I w. you! cela n'arrivera pas deux fois, je vous en réponds! 2. Justifier. Nothing can w. such conduct, rien ne justifie une pareille conduite. **warranted**, a. Com: Garanti. Colours w. fast, couleurs garanties bon teint.

warrantor ['wɔr(ə)ntɔːr], s. Jur: Répondant m, garant m.

warranty ['wɔr(ə)nti], s. 1. Autorisation f; justification f (for doing sth., pour faire qch.). Have you any w. for such an accusation, êtes-vous fondé à porter une telle accusation? 2. Garantie f. Jur: W. of title, attestation f du titre.

warren ['wɔrən], s. (Rabbit-)w., garenne f.

warrior ['wɔriər], s. Guerrier m, soldat m. The Unknown W., le Soldat inconnu. W. tribes, tribus guerrières.

Warsaw ['wɔːsɔː]. Pr.n. Varsovie f.

warship ['wɔːʃip], s. Navire m, bâtiment, m de guerre.

wart [wɔːt], s. Verrue f; F: poireau m. 'wart-hog, s. Z: Phacochère m.

wary ['wɛəri], a. (a) Avisé, prudent, circonspect. To keep a w. eye on s.o., surveiller qn attentivement. (b) To be w. of sth., se méfier de qch. -ily, adv. Avec circonspection; prudemment.

was. See BE.

wash[1] [wɔʃ], s. 1. (a) Lavage m, savonnage m. To give sth. a w., laver qch. (b) (Of pers.) To have a w. (and brush-up), faire un brin de toilette. (c) Lessive f, blanchissage m. To send clothes to the w., donner du linge à blanchir. F: It will all come out in the w., ça se tassera. 2. (a) Hair-w., lotion f capillaire. (b) Hort: Lessive, bouillie f (insecticide). 3. (a) Colour w. (for walls), badigeon m. (b) Couche légère (de couleur sur une surface). (c) Art: Lavis m (d'aquarelle). W.-drawing, épure f au lavis. 4. (a) The w. of the waves, le bruit des flots qui passent. (b) Nau: Sillage m, houache f, remous m (d'un navire). Av: Propeller w., souffle m de l'hélice. 'wash-basin, s. (Cuvette f de) lavabo m. 'wash-house, s. (a) Buanderie f. (b) Laverie f. 'wash-leather, s. Peau f de chamois. W.-l. gloves, gants chamois. 'wash-tint, s. Art: Lavis m. 'wash-tub, s. Cuvier m; baquet m (à lessive).

wash[2]. I. v.tr. 1. (a) Laver. To w. one's face, se débarbouiller. To w. one's hair, se laver la tête. To w. one's hands, se laver les mains. F: To w. one's hands of sth., se laver les mains de qch. (b) v.pr. & i. To w. (oneself), se laver. (c) Med: Lotionner (une plaie). 2. (a) Blanchir, lessiver, laver (le linge). (b) Material that washes well, étoffe très lavable. Material that won't w., étoffe qui ne se lave pas, qui déteint. F: That story won't w.! ça ne prend pas! 3. Ind: Débourber (le minerai); épurer (le gaz). 4. (a) To w. the walls, badigeonner les murs (with, de). (b) To w. a metal with gold, donner un métal au trempé. (c) Art: Laver (un dessin). 5. (Of river, sea) Baigner, arroser (les côtes, un pays). 6. (Of sea) To w. sth. ashore, rejeter qch. sur le rivage. Sailor washed overboard, matelot enlevé par une lame. II. wash, v.i. The waves washed over the deck, les vagues balayaient le pont. wash away, v.tr. 1. Enlever (une tache) par le lavage. 2. (a) River-bank washed away, berge affouillée, dégradée. (b) Emporter, entraîner. Washed away by the tide, emporté par la mer. wash down, v.tr. 1. Laver (les murs) à grande eau. 2. F: To w. down one's dinner with a glass of beer, faire descendre son dîner avec un verre de bière. 'wash-down, s. (a) Toilette complète. (b) Av: Aire f de lavage. wash off, v.tr. Enlever,

effacer, (qch.) par le lavage. It will w. off, cela s'en ira au lavage. wash out, v.tr. 1. (a) Enlever (une tache). Lit: To w. out an insult in blood, laver un affront dans le sang. F: We must w. out the whole business, mieux vaut passer l'éponge là-dessus. You can wash that right out, il ne faut pas compter là-dessus. (b) Laver, rincer (une bouteille). (c) Min: To w. out the gold, extraire l'or (en lavant le sable). 2. (Of stain) Partir au lavage. 'wash-out, s. F: (a) Fiasco m, four m. The business is a w.-o., l'affaire est manquée, loupée. The play was a w.-o., la pièce a fait four. (b) (Of pers.) He's a w.-o., c'est un raté. (c) Affouillement m de terrain; Rail: effondrement m de la voie (causé par l'eau). washed out, a. 1. (a) (Of colour) Délavé. (b) F: W.-o. complexion, teint de papier mâché. 2. F: (Of pers.) Flapi, vanné. To feel w. o., se sentir à plat. wash up, v.tr. (a) To w. up the dishes, abs. to w. up, laver la vaisselle; faire la vaisselle. (b) (Of sea) Rejeter (qn, qch.) sur le rivage. (c) F: To be washed up, être ruiné, fichu. 'washing-'up, s. (Lavage m de la vaisselle; (in restaurant) plonge f. W.-up machine, machine f à laver la vaisselle. W.-up bowl, bassine f à vaisselle. **washing,** s. 1. (a) Lavage m. Colour that won't stand any w., couleur qui ne se lave pas. (b) Ablutions fpl. 2. (a) Blanchissage m, lessive f (du linge). To do a little w., faire un petit savonnage. W. is included, le blanchissage est compris. (b) Linge (à blanchir ou blanchi); le blanchissage. F: To take in one another's w., se rendre mutuellement service. 3. Ind: (a) Débourbage m (du minerai), épuration f, épurage m (du gaz). (b) pl. Washings, produits m de lavage. 4. (a) Badigeonnage m. (b) Art: Lavis m (d'un dessin). 'washing-bay, s. Aut: Installation f de lavage. 'washing-bottle, s. Ch: Flacon laveur. 'washing-day, s. Jour m de lessive. 'washing-machine, s. Dom.Ec: Machine f à laver. 'washing-place, s. Laverie f.

washable ['wɔʃəbl], a. Lavable.

washboard ['wɔʃbɔːd], s. Planche f à laver.

washcloth ['wɔʃklɔθ], s. U.S: = Gant m de toilette.

washer[1] ['wɔʃər], s. 1. (Pers.) (a) Laveur, -euse. (b) W.-up, laveur, -euse, de vaisselle; (in restaurant) plongeur m. 2. (a) Laund: Machine f à laver. (b) Phot: Plate-w., print-w., cuve f de lavage. (c) Aut: Wind-screen w., lave-glace m, pl. lave-glaces.

washer[2], s. Mec.E: etc: Rondelle f. Spring w., rondelle élastique.

washerwoman, pl. -women ['wɔʃəwumən, -wimin], s.f. Blanchisseuse.

washrag ['wɔʃræg], s. U.S: = Gant m de toilette.

washroom ['wɔʃruːm], s. U.S: (a) Cabinet m de toilette. (b) Cabinets mpl.

washstand ['wɔʃstænd], s. 1. Furn: Table f de toilette. 2. U.S: Aut: WASHING-BAY.

washy ['wɔʃi], a. F: (a) Fade, insipide. This coffee's pretty w.! quelle lavasse que ce café! (b) (Of colour) Délavé.

wasp [wɔsp], s. Guêpe f. Wasps' nest, guêpier m. 'wasp-waisted, a. À taille de guêpe.

waspish ['wɔspiʃ], a. F: Irascible; irritable; méchant. W. tone, ton aigre. -ly, adv. D'un ton irrité.

waspishness ['wɔspiʃnis], s. F: Irritabilité f; méchanceté f (d'une réponse).

wast. See BE.

wastage ['weistidʒ], s. 1. (a) Déperdition f, perte f (de chaleur). (b) Gaspillage m. 2. Coll: Déchets mpl, rebuts mpl.

waste[1] [weist], a. 1. (a) W. land, w. ground, (i) terre f inculte; (ii) (in town) terrains m vagues. (Of ground) To lie w., rester en friche. (b) To lay w., dévaster, ravager (un pays). 2. (a) (Matière) de rebut. W. products of nutrition, déchets m de la nutrition. W. paper, papier de rebut; vieux papiers. W.-paper basket, corbeille f à papier(s). Typ: W. sheets, maculatures f. W. water(s), (i) Ind: eaux f résiduaires; (ii) Dom.Ec: eaux ménagères. (b) Mch: W. steam, vapeur perdue. S.a. WOOL 1.

waste[2], s. 1. Région f inculte; désert m. 2. Gaspillage m (d'argent). House where there is a lot of w., maison où on gaspille beaucoup. W. of time, perte f de temps. To run to w., (i) (of liquids) se perdre; (ii) (of garden) se couvrir d'herbes; (of land) s'affricher.

3. (a) Déchets *mpl*, rebut *m*. **Cotton w.**, déchets, bourre *f*, de coton; chiffons *mpl* de nettoyage. **Printing w.**, maculatures *fpl*. **Radioactive w.**, *mpl* radio-actifs. *Dom.Ec:* **W. disposal unit**, broyeur *m* à ordures. (b) *Hyd.E:* Trop-plein *m*. 'waste-pipe, *s. Hyd.E: etc:* Tuyau *m* d'écoulement du tropplein; (tuyau de) trop-plein. 'waste-weir, *s.* Déversoir *m*.

waste³. I. *v.tr.* 1. Consumer, user, épuiser (le corps). Patient **wasted** by disease, malade miné, amaigri, par la maladie. *A:* **Wasting disease**, maladie de langueur; consomption *f*. 2. Gaspiller; gâcher (du papier). **Nothing is wasted**, rien ne se perd. **To w. one's time**, perdre son temps. **Wasted life**, vie manquée. **All my advice was wasted** on him, tous mes conseils ne lui ont servi à rien. **To w. one's words**, prêcher dans le désert. **W. not, want not**, qui épargne gagne. II. **waste**, *v.i.* 1. Se perdre; s'user. 2. (*Of living being*) **To w. (away)**, dépérir; (*of pers.*) se miner, se décharner; maigrir. **wasted**, *a.* 1. (Pays) dévasté, ravagé. 2. (Malade) affaibli, amaigri. 3. (Argent) gaspillé. **Time w.**, temps perdu. *Tchn:* **W. energy**, dépense *f* à vide. **wasting**, *s.* 1. Gaspillage *m*, perte *f* (de ses ressources). 2. **W. (away)**, dépérissement *m*, marasme *m*; atrophie *f* (d'un membre); *Med: A:* consomption *f*.

wasteful ['weistf(u)l], *a.* Gaspilleur, -euse; prodigue. **W. expenditure**, gaspillage *m*. **W. habits**, habitudes de gaspillage. **-fully**, *adv.* Avec prodigalité; (dépenser une somme) en pure perte.

wastefulness ['weistf(u)lnis], *s.* Prodigalité *f*; (habitudes *fpl* de) gaspillage *m*.

waster ['weistər], *s.* (*Pers.*) (a) Gaspilleur, -euse. **Time w.**, (i) personne qui perd son temps; (ii) chose, travail, qui vous fait perdre votre temps. (b) = WASTREL.

wastrel ['weistrəl], *s.* Rebut *m* de la société; vaurien *m*; propre *m* à rien.

watch¹ [wɔtʃ], *s.* 1. *A:* Veille *f*. **In the watches of the night**, pendant les heures de veille. 2. Garde *f*; surveillance *f*. **To be on the w.**, (i) être en observation; se tenir aux aguets; (ii) être sur ses gardes. **To be on the w. for s.o.**, guetter qn. **To keep w.**, monter la garde. **To keep (a) good w.**, faire bonne garde. **To keep a close w. on s.o.**, surveiller qn de près. **To set a w. on s.o.**, faire surveiller qn. 3. *Hist:* **The w.**, la garde, le guet; la ronde de nuit. 4. *Nau:* (a) Quart *m*. **To set the watches**, régler les quarts. **The officer of the w.**, l'officier de quart. **To be on w.**, être de quart. **To have w. and w.**, faire le quart par bordées. *S.a.* RELIEVE 4. (b) (*Men*) Bordée *f*. **The w. on deck**, la bordée de quart. 5. Montre *f*. **It is six by my w.**, il est six heures à ma montre. 'watchband, *s.* Bracelet *m* de montre. 'watch-case, *s.* Boîtier *m* de montre. 'watch-chain, *s.* Chaîne *f* de montre. 'watch committee, *s.* Comité *m* qui veille au maintien de l'ordre public de la commune, etc. 'watch-dog, *s.* Chien *m* de garde. 'watch-fire, *s.* Feu *m* de bivouac. 'watch-glass, *s.* Verre *m* de montre. 'watch-keeper, *s. Nau:* 1. Homme *m* de quart. 2. Chef *m* de quart. 'watchnight, *s. Ecc:* Office *m* de minuit (à la veille du jour de l'an); veillée *f* du 31 décembre. 'watchpocket, *s. Cost:* Gousset *m* (de montre). 'watchtower, *s.* Tour *f* d'observation, de guet; (*in prison camp*) mirador *m*.

watch². 1. *v.i.* (a) Veiller. (b) **To w. by a sick person**, veiller un malade. **To w. over a flock**, garder un troupeau. **He needs watching**, il a besoin d'être surveillé. (c) **To w. (out)**, être aux aguets; être sur ses gardes. **W. out!** ouvrez l'œil! prenez garde! (d) **To w. for s.o.**, attendre qn; guetter qn. 2. *v.tr.* (a) Veiller (un mort); garder, veiller sur (qn, qch.). (b) Observer; regarder attentivement. **To w. s.o. narrowly**, surveiller qn de près; ne pas quitter qn des yeux. **We are being watched**, on nous observe. (c) **We shall have to w. the expenses**, il nous faudra avoir l'œil sur la dépense. **W. your step!** prenez garde de tomber! **I had to w. my step throughout the discussion**, pendant toute la discussion il m'a fallu éviter tout faux pas. (d) Regarder; voir. **I watched her working**, je la regardais travailler. **To w. a football match**, assister à un match de football. *Jur:* **To w.**

a case, veiller (en justice) aux intérêts de qn. (e) **To w. one's opportunity, one's time**, guetter l'occasion, le moment propice.

watcher ['wɔtʃər], *s.* 1. Veilleur, -euse (d'un malade). 2. **Bird w.**, observateur des mœurs des oiseaux.

watchful ['wɔtʃf(u)l], *a.* Vigilant; alerte; attentif, -ive. **To be w.**, être sur ses gardes. **To keep a w. eye on, over, s.o.**, surveiller qn de près. **-fully**, *adv.* Avec vigilance.

watchfulness ['wɔtʃf(u)lnis], *s.* Vigilance (méfiante).

watchmaker ['wɔtʃmeikər], *s.* Horloger *m*.

watchmaking ['wɔtʃmeikiŋ], *s.* Horlogerie *f*.

watchman, *pl.* -men ['wɔtʃmən], *s.m.* Gardien, garde. *Nau:* Homme *m* de garde (au mouillage). *Ind:* **Night w.**, veilleur de nuit.

watchword ['wɔtʃwəːd], *s.* Mot *m* d'ordre.

water¹ ['wɔːtər], *s.* Eau *f*. 1. (a) **Cold w.**, eau fraîche. **Fresh w.**, eau douce. **To throw cold w. on a scheme**, décourager un projet. **Drinking w.**, eau potable. **To take the horses to w.**, conduire les chevaux à l'abreuvoir. **To take in w.**, (*of locomotive, etc.*) faire de l'eau. (*Of ship*) **To make w.**, (i) faire de l'eau; (ii) (*leak*) avoir une voie d'eau, faire eau. *S.a.* HOLD² 7, HOT¹ 1. (b) (*For domestic needs*) Eaux ménagères. **To turn on the w.**, ouvrir l'eau. **To have w. laid on**, (i) faire mettre l'eau courante; (ii) avoir l'eau courante. **W. supply**, service *m* des eaux, distribution *f* d'eau (de la ville); adduction *f* d'eau. **The W. Company**, la Compagnie des eaux. (c) **To wash sth. in two or three waters**, laver qch. dans deux ou trois eaux. 2. *Usu. pl.* **Iron waters**, eaux ferrugineuses. **To take, drink, the waters**, prendre les eaux. **To take the waters at Bath**, faire la cure à Bath. 3. (a) **The waters of the Danube**, les eaux du Danube. **Pirate-infested waters**, parages infestés par les pirates. (b) **On land and w.**, sur terre et sur mer. **By w.**, par mer; par bateau; *Com:* par voie d'eau. (*Of water fowl, etc.*) **To take the w.**, se mettre à la nage. *S.a.* FISH¹ 1, TREAD² 2. (c) **To be under w.**, (*of land*) être inondé, submergé. **To swim under w.**, nager entre deux eaux. **Above w.**, à flot; surnageant. **To keep one's head above w.**, (i) se maintenir à la surface; (ii) faire face à ses engagements. (d) **High w.**, marée haute; haute mer. **High-w. mark**, = TIDE-MARK. **Low w.**, marée basse. *F:* **He is in low w.**, (i) il est dans la dèche; (ii) il est dans le marasme; il est bien bas. (e) *Nau:* **Shallow w.**, hauts fonds. **In home waters**, dans les eaux de la Métropole. (f) *Nau:* **What w. does the ship draw?** quel est le tirant d'eau du navire? **There are a hundred fathoms of w.**, il y a cent brasses de fond. 4. (a) *Med:* **W. on the brain**, hydrocéphalie *f*. **W. on the knee**, hydarthrose *f* du genou; épanchement *m* de synovie. *S.a.* BLISTER¹. (b) **To bring the w. to one's eyes**, faire venir les larmes aux yeux. (c) **It brings the w. to one's mouth**, cela fait venir l'eau à la bouche. (d) **To make, pass, w.**, uriner. 5. Transparence *f*, eau (d'un diamant). **The w. of a pearl**, l'orient *m* d'une perle. **Of the first w.**, de la plus belle eau. 'water-bag, *s.* Outre *f*, vache *f*, à eau. 'waterbailiff, *s.* Garde-pêche *m*. 'water-ballast, *s. Nau:* Lest *m* d'eau; lest liquide. **W.-b. tanks**, ballasts *m* (d'un sous-marin). 'water-bath, *s. Ch:* Bainmarie *m*. 'water-bearing, *a. Geol:* (Couche) aquifère. 'water-bed, *s. Med:* Matelas *m* d'eau. 'water-beetle, *s. Ent:* 1. Dytique *m*. 2. Gyrin *m*, tourniquet *m*. 'water-biscuit, *s.* Galette salée. 'water-borne, *a.* (*Of goods*) Transporté par voie d'eau. **W.-b. transport**, transport par eau. 'water bottle, *s.* 1. Carafe *f*. 2. Gourde *f. Mil:* Bidon *m*. 3. Hot-w. b., bouillotte *f*; boule *f*; (*of earthenware*) cruchon *m*. 'water-butt, *s.* Tonneau *m* (pour recueillir l'eau de pluie). 'water-can, *s.* Broc *m*. 'water-carrier, *s.* (a) Porteur, -euse, d'eau. (b) Canvas w.-c., vache *f* à eau. 'water-cart, *s.* Tonneau *m* d'arrosage; arroseuse *f*. 'water-cask *s. Nau:* Baril *m* de galère. 'water-closet, *s.* (*Abbr.* W.C. ['dʌblju'siː]) Cabinets *mpl*, toilettes *fpl*, *F:* les W.C., les waters *m*. 'water-cock, *s.* Robinet *m* d'arrivée d'eau. 'water-colour, *s. Art:* 1. *pl.* Water-colours, couleurs *f* pour l'aquarelle. **To paint in watercolours**, faire de l'aquarelle. 2. A w.-c., une aquarelle. 'water-colourist, *s.* Aquarelliste *mf*. 'water-cooled, *a. I.C.E:* (Moteur) à refroidissement d'eau. 'water-crane, *s. Rail:* Grue *f* d'alimentation, prise *f* d'eau. 'water-cress, *s.* Cresson *m* de fontaine. 'water-diviner, *s.* Sourcier *m,* radiesthésiste *m.* 'water-divining, *s.* Radiesthésie *f.* 'water-front, *s.* Bord *m* de l'eau, de mer; les quais *m. U.S:* On the w.-f., chez les dockers. 'water-gate, *s.* 1. Porte *f* d'écluse; vanne *f* (d'écluse). 2. Grille *f* d'accès donnant sur le fleuve. 'water-gauge, *s.* (Indicateur *m* de) niveau *m* d'eau; hydromètre *m;* (*in river*) échelle *f* d'étiage. 'water-glass, *s. Com:* Silicate *m* de potasse ou de soude; *F:* verre *m* soluble. 'water-heater, *s.* Chauffe-eau *m.inv.* 'water-hen, *s.* Poule *f* d'eau. 'water-hole, *s.* Mare *f* (dans un cours d'eau à sec). 'water-ice, *s. Cu:* Sorbet *m.* 'water-jacket, *s. I.C.E: etc:* Chemise *f* d'eau. 'water-jug, *s.* 1. Pot *m,* cruche *f,* à eau. 2. *Toil:* Broc *m.* 'water-jump, *s. Rac:* Douve *f,* brook *m.* 'water-level, *s.* (*a*) Niveau *m* d'eau. (*b*) *Geol:* Niveau piézométrique. 'water-lily, *s.* Nénuphar *m.* 'water-line, *s. Nau:* (Ligne *f* de) flottaison *f.* 'water-main, *s. Hyd.E:* Conduite principale (d'eau). 'water-mark, *s.* 1. *Nau:* Laisse *f* (de marée). 2. (*In paper*) Filigrane *m.* 'water-marked, *a.* (Papier) à filigrane. 'water-meadow, *s.* Prairie susceptible d'être inondée; noue *f.* 'water-melon, *s.* Pastèque *f.* 'water-mill, *s.* Moulin *m* à eau. 'water-nymph, *s. Myth:* Naïade *f.* 'water-ouzel, *s. Orn:* Merle *m* d'eau, cincle plongeur. 'water-pipe, *s.* Tuyau *m* d'eau, conduite *f* d'eau. 'water-polo, *s. Sp:* Water-polo *m;* polo *m* nautique. 'water-power, *s.* Force *f* hydraulique; énergie *f* hydraulique; houille blanche. 'water-rat, *s. Z:* Rat *m* d'eau; campagnol nageur. 'water-rate, *s.* Taux *m* de l'abonnement aux eaux de la ville. 'water-rights, *s.pl.* Droits *m* de captation d'eau. 'water-repellent, (*a*) *s.* Substance *f* imperméable. (*b*) *a.* Imperméable. 'water-skiing, *s.* Ski *m* nautique. 'water-softener, *s.* 1. Adoucisseur *m* d'eau. 2. *Ind:* Installation *f* d'épuration chimique de l'eau. 'water-softening, *attrib.a. Ind:* W.-s. plant, épurateur *m* d'eau. 'water-spout, *s.* 1. Tuyau *m,* descente *f* (d'eau). 2. Gouttière *f,* gargouille *f.* 3. *Meteor:* Trombe *f.* 'water-sprite, *s.* Ondin, -ine. 'water-system, *s.* Canalisation *f* d'eau. 'water-table, *s. Geol:* Nappe *f* phréatique. 'water-tower, *s. Hyd.E:* Château *m* d'eau. 'water-wheel, *s.* Roue *f* hydraulique; turbine *f* hydraulique; roue à aubes. 'water-wings, *s.pl.* Flotteur *m* de natation.

water², 1. *v.tr.* (*a*) Arroser (une plante, une région). (*b*) To w. one's wine, mouiller, couper, *F:* baptiser, son vin. *Fin:* To w. the capital, diluer le capital (d'une société). (*c*) Faire boire, abreuver (des bêtes). (*d*) *Tex:* Moirer (la soie). 2. *v.i.* (*a*) My right eye is watering, mon œil droit pleure, larmoie. *S.a.* MOUTH¹ 1. (*b*) *Nau:* (*Of ship*) Faire de l'eau; faire provision d'eau. (*c*) (*Of horses, etc.*) Être à l'abreuvoir. water down, *v.tr.* (*a*) = WATER² 1 (*b*). (*b*) To w. down an expression, a statement, atténuer une expression, une affirmation. watered, *a.* 1. Arrosé. 2. Étendu d'eau, mouillé. 3. *Tex:* W. silk, moire *f.* watering, *s.* 1. Arrosage *m.* 2. Dilution *f* (d'un breuvage). *Fin:* W. of stock, dilution de capital (social). 3. Abreuvage *m* (des bêtes). 4. *Tex:* Moirage *m.* 5. W. of the eyes, larmoiement *m.* 'watering-can, *s.* Arrosoir *m.* 'watering-cart, *s.* = WATER-CART. 'watering-place, *s.* 1. (*For cattle*) Abreuvoir *m.* 2. Station *f* balnéaire. (*a*) Ville *f* d'eau. (*b*) Bains *mpl* de mer; plage *f.*

watercourse ['wɔːtəkɔːs], *s.* 1. Cours *m* d'eau. 2. Conduit *m.*

waterfall ['wɔːtəfɔːl], *s.* Chute *f* d'eau; cascade *f.*

waterfowl ['wɔːtəfaul], *s.* (*a*) Oiseau *m* aquatique. (*b*) *Coll.* Gibier *m* d'eau; sauvagine *f.*

waterless ['wɔːtəlis], *a.* Sans eau.

waterlogged ['wɔːtəlɔgd], *a.* 1. (*a*) *Nau:* (Navire) plein d'eau, entre deux eaux. (*b*) (Bois) alourdi par absorption d'eau. 2. (Terrain) imbibé d'eau, détrempé.

Waterloo [wɔːtəˈluː]. *Pr.n.* The battle of W., la bataille de Waterloo. To meet one's W., arriver au désastre.

waterman, *pl.* -men ['wɔːtəmən], *s.m.* Batelier, marinier.

waterproof¹ ['wɔːtəpruːf]. 1. *a.* (Tissu) imperméable (à l'eau), caoutchouté. W. varnish, vernis hydrofuge. *S.a.* SHEETING 1. 2. *s. Cost:* Imperméable *m, F:* imper *m.*

waterproof², *v.tr.* Imperméabiliser; hydrofuger (un enduit); caoutchouter (un vêtement). waterproofing, *s.* Imperméabilisation *f.*

watershed ['wɔːtəʃed], *s. Ph.Geog:* Ligne *f* de partage des eaux.

waterside ['wɔːtəsaid], *s.* Bord *m* de l'eau. *U.S:* W. workers, les dockers *m.*

watertight ['wɔːtətait], *a.* (Cloison) étanche (à l'eau). (*Of vessel*) To be w., retenir l'eau. W. regulations, règlement qui a prévu tous les cas.

waterway ['wɔːtəwei], *s.* Voie *f* d'eau; voie navigable.

waterworks ['wɔːtəwəːks], *s.pl.* 1. Usine *f* de distribution d'eau. The town w., le service des eaux de la ville. 2. (*a*) *A:* Jeux *mpl* d'eaux. (*b*) *F:* To turn on the w., (i) se mettre à pleurer, *P:* à chialer; (ii) faire pipi.

watery ['wɔːtəri], *a.* 1. (*a*) Aqueux, -euse; qui contient de l'eau; noyé d'eau. W. clouds, nuages (chargés) de pluie. W. eyes, yeux larmoyants. W. potatoes, pommes de terre aqueuses. (*b*) (Temps) pluvieux. W. sun, soleil qui annonce la pluie. (*c*) *Poet:* To find a w. grave, avoir les flots pour tombeau. 2. (*a*) (*Of soup*) Peu consistant; clair; "à l'eau." (*b*) (*Of colour*) Pâle, déteint.

watt [wɔt], *s. El.Meas:* Watt *m.* 'watt-hour, *s. El.E:* Watt-heure *m.*

wattage ['wɔtidʒ], *s. El.E:* Puissance *f,* consommation *f* en watts.

wattle¹ ['wɔtl], *s.* (*a*) W.(-work), clayonnage *m.* (*b*) Claie *f.*

wattle², *v.tr.* Clayonner.

wattle³, *s.* 1. Caroncule *f* (d'un dindon); fanon *m* (d'un porc, d'un dindon); barbillon *m,* barbe *f* (d'un poisson, d'un coq). 2. *Bot: Austr:* (*a*) Acacia *m.* (*b*) Mimosa *m.*

wattmeter ['wɔtmiːtər], *s. El.E:* Wattmètre *m.*

wave¹ [weiv], *s.* 1. (*a*) Vague *f; Nau:* lame *f.* (*b*) The waves, *Lit:* les flots *m.* (*c*) W. of enthusiasm, vague d'enthousiasme. The new w., la nouvelle vague. *S.a.* BRAIN-WAVE, HEAT-WAVE. 2. *Ph:* Onde *f.* Long waves, grandes ondes. Medium waves, ondes moyennes, petites ondes. Short waves, petites ondes, ondes courtes. *Aer:* Shock w., onde de choc. 3. Ondulation *f* (des cheveux). To have a natural w. in one's hair, avoir les cheveux ondulés naturellement. 4. (*a*) Balancement *m,* ondoiement *m.* (*b*) With a w. of his hand, d'un geste, d'un signe, de la main. 'wave-detector, *s. W.Tel:* Détecteur *m* d'ondes. 'wave-length, *s. Ph:* Longueur *f* d'onde. 'wave-meter, *s.* Onde-mètre *m.*

wave². I. *v.i.* 1. S'agiter; (*of flag*) flotter (au vent); (*of wheat*) ondoyer, onduler. 2. To w. to s.o., faire signe à qn (en agitant le bras). 3. My hair waves naturally, mes cheveux ondulent naturellement. II. wave, *v.tr.* 1. Agiter (le bras, un mouchoir); brandir (un parapluie). To w. one's hand, faire signe de la main. 2. (*a*) He waved us good-bye, il nous fit un signe d'adieu. (*b*) To w. s.o. aside, écarter qn d'un geste. He waved us on, de la main il nous fit signe de continuer. To w. aside an objection, écarter une objection. 3. *Hairdr:* To have one's hair waved, se faire onduler, se faire faire une mise en plis. waved, *a.* Ondé, ondulé. waving, *s.* 1. (*a*) Agitation *f* (d'un mouchoir). W. of the hand, geste *m* de la main. (*b*) Ondoiement *m* (du blé). 2. *Hairdr:* Ondulation *f* (des cheveux). 'waving-iron, *s.* Fer *m* à friser, à onduler.

wavelet ['weivlit], *s.* Petite vague.

waver ['weivər], *v.i.* Vaciller. 1. (*Of flame*) Trembloter. 2. (*a*) Hésiter; être indécis; (*of the voice*) se troubler; (*of courage*) défaillir. (*b*) (*Of troops*) Fléchir. wavering¹, *a.* 1. (*Of flame*) Vacillant, tremblotant. 2. (*a*)· (Homme) irrésolu, hésitant; (voix) défaillante. (*b*) W. line of battle, ligne de bataille flottante. -ly, *adv.* Avec indécision; irrésolument. wavering², *s.* 1. Tremblement *m,* vacillement *m* (d'une flamme). 2. (*a*) Vacillation *f,* irrésolution *f* (de l'esprit); défaillance *f* (du courage). (*b*) Flottement *m* (d'une ligne de troupes).

waverer ['weivərər], s. Indécis, -ise; hésitant, -ante.

waviness ['weivinis], s. Caractère onduleux, ondulé (d'une surface, des cheveux).

wavy ['weivi], a. Onduleux, -euse. **W. line**, ligne tremblée. **W. hair**, chevelure ondoyante.

wax¹ [wæks], s. 1. Cire f. S.a. BEESWAX. 2. Fossil w., mineral w., cire fossile, minérale; ozokérite f. 3. Skiing: Fart m. '**wax-bill**, s. Orn: Bec-de-cire m. '**wax 'candle**, s. Bougie f de cire; (in church) cierge m. '**wax-'end**, s. Bootm: Fil poissé. '**wax-myrtle**, s. Bot: Cirier m. '**wax-paper**, s. Papier ciré. '**wax 'taper**, s. 1. Rat m de cave; (small) queue-de-rat f. 2. Ecc: Cierge m.

wax², v.tr. 1. Cirer, enduire de cire, encaustiquer (un meuble). 2. Bootm: Empoisser (le fil). 3. Skiing: Farter. **waxed**, a. 1. Ciré; enduit de cire. **W. moustache**, moustache cosmétiquée. 2. **W. thread**, fil poissé. **waxing**, s. 1. Encaustiquage m. 2. Skiing: Fartage m.

wax³, v.i. 1. (Of the moon) Croître. **To w. and wane**, croître et décroître. 2. Lit: Devenir, se faire. **He waxed indignant**, il s'indigna. **waxing**, s. Croissement m (de la lune).

wax⁴, s. F: Rage f, colère f. **To be in a w.**, être en colère. **To get into a w.**, se mettre en colère.

waxen ['wæks(ə)n], a. (a) De cire, en cire. (b) Cireux, -euse. **W. complexion**, teint m de cire.

waxwing ['wækswiŋ], s. Orn: Jaseur m.

waxwork ['wækswə:k], s. 1. Modelage m en cire. 2. (a) Figure f de cire. (b) pl. **Waxworks**, (musée m de) figures de cire.

waxy¹ ['wæksi], a. Cireux, -euse. Med: **W. (degeneration of the) liver**, amylose f du foie.

waxy², a. F: En colère; P: en rogne.

way¹ [wei], s. 1. Chemin m, route f, voie f. **The public w.**, la voie publique. **Over, across, the w.**, de l'autre côté de la route, de la rue. **The house across the w.**, la maison d'en face. Rail: **Six-foot w.**, entre-voie f. S.a. COMPANION², PERMANENT. 2. (a) **The w. to the station**, le chemin de la gare. **To show s.o. the w.**, montrer la route à qn. **To ask one's w.**, demander son chemin. **To lose one's w.**, s'égarer, se perdre. **To go the wrong w.**, se tromper de chemin; faire fausse route. **To go the shortest w.**, prendre par le plus court. **To know one's w. about (a house)**, connaître les aîtres. F: **He knows his w. about**, il sait se débrouiller. **To prepare the w.**, préparer les voies. **To start on one's w.**, se mettre en route. **On the w.**, chemin faisant; en chemin; en cours de route. **On my w. home**, en revenant chez moi; en rentrant. **To go the w. of all things**, aller où va toute chose; mourir. **To go one's w.**, passer son chemin. **To go one's own w.**, (i) faire à sa guise; (ii) faire bande à part. **To go out of one's w. to oblige s.o.**, se déranger pour être agréable à qn. **He seems to go out of his w. to look for difficulties**, il a l'air de rechercher la difficulté. **Village that is rather out of the w.**, village un peu écarté. **That talent is nothing out of the w.**, son talent n'est pas extraordinaire. (b) **W. in**, entrée f. **W. out**, sortie f. **W. through**, passage m. **W. up**, montée f. **W. down**, descente f. **To find a w. in**, trouver moyen d'entrer. **To find a w. out**, trouver une issue. (c) **To find one's w. to a place**, parvenir à un endroit. **To find one's w. into . . .**, s'introduire dans. . . . **To make one's w. towards a place**, se diriger vers un endroit. **To make one's w. through the crowd**, se frayer un chemin à travers la foule. **To make one's w. back**, retourner, revenir. **To make a w. for oneself**, se faire jour. **How to make one's w. in the world**, le moyen de parvenir. **To work one's w. up**, s'élever à force de travail. **To pay one's w.**, se suffire. **I can't see my w. to doing it now**, je ne vois pas pour le moment comment le faire. **As soon as I see my w. to something better**, dès que je trouverai mieux. S.a. CLEAR² I. 3, FEEL² 1. (d) **To stand in s.o.'s w.**, barrer le passage à qn; faire obstacle à qn. **To put difficulties in s.o.'s w.**, créer des difficultés à qn. **To get in one another's w.**, se gêner (les uns les autres). **To be in s.o.'s w.**, gêner, embarrasser, qn. F: **To put s.o. out of the w.**, se débarrasser de qn; faire disparaître qn. **To get out of the w.**, se ranger, s'effacer. **Get out of the w.!** laissez passer! rangez-vous! **To keep out of the w.**, se tenir à l'écart. **To keep out of s.o.'s w.**, se cacher de qn; éviter qn. **To make w. for s.o.**, faire place à qn. S.a. HARM¹. (e) See RIGHT¹ II. 2. 3. (Distance) **To go a little w. with s.o.**, faire un bout de chemin avec qn. **All the w.**, tout le long du chemin; jusqu'au bout. **I flew part of the w.**, j'ai fait une partie du trajet en avion. **It's a long w. from here**, c'est loin d'ici. **To have a long w. to go**, avoir beaucoup de chemin à faire. **A little, a short, w. off**, à peu de distance; pas trop loin. **He will go a long w.**, il ira loin; il fera son chemin. **His name goes a long w.**, son nom est d'un grand poids. **A little sympathy goes a long w.**, un peu de sympathie fait grand bien. **To make a penny go a long w.**, savoir ménager les sous. **By a long w.**, de beaucoup. **Not by a long w.**, pas à beaucoup près; il s'en faut de beaucoup. **You are a long w. out**, vous êtes loin de compte. 4. (a) Côté m, direction f. **Which w. is the wind blowing?** d'où vient le vent? **This w. out**, par ici la sortie. **Which w. did you come?** par où êtes-vous venu? **This w. and that**, de-ci de-là. **Not to know which w. to look**, être tout décontenancé. **To look the other w.**, détourner les yeux. **I have nothing to say one w. or the other**, je n'ai rien à dire pour ou contre. **I am going your w.**, je vais de votre côté. F: **Down our w.**, chez nous. **He lived Hampstead w.**, il habitait du côté de Hampstead. **Such people have not often come my w.**, je n'ai pas souvent eu affaire à des gens pareils. **I undertake anything that comes my w.**, j'entreprends n'importe quoi. **If the opportunity comes your w.**, si vous en trouvez l'occasion. S.a. INCLINED 2, PARTING² 1. (b) Sens m. **(In) the wrong w.**, à contre-sens. **The wrong w. up**, sens dessus dessous; à l'envers. **Right w. up**, dans le bon sens. 5. (Means) Moyen m. **To find a w.**, trouver (le) moyen (to, de). Adm: **Ways and means**, voies et moyens. Parl: **Committee of Ways and Means** = Commission f du Budget. S.a. WILL¹ 1. 6. (a) Façon f, manière f. **In this w.**, de cette façon. **In a friendly w.**, en ami; amicalement. **In the French w.**, à la française. **Speaking in a general w.**, d'une façon générale. **In no w.**, en aucune façon; nullement. **Without in any w. wishing to criticize . . .**, sans aucunement vouloir critiquer. . . . **That's the w. the money goes!** voilà comme l'argent file! **That's the w.!** à la bonne heure! **To go the right w. to work**, s'y prendre bien. **In one w. or another**, de façon ou d'autre. **There are no two ways about it**, il n'y a pas à discuter. **To go on the same old w.**, aller toujours son train. **The w. things are going**, au train dont vont les choses. **It's the w. of the world**, ainsi va le monde. **Well, it is this w.**, voici ce que c'est. **Our w. of living**, notre train m, genre m, de vie. **The American w. of life**, la vie américaine. **His w. of looking at things**, sa manière de voir. **That's his w.**, voilà comme il est. **That is always the w. with him**, il est toujours comme ça; il n'en fait jamais d'autres. **To do things in one's own w.**, faire les choses à sa guise. **He is a genius in his w.**, c'est un génie dans son genre. **I help them in my small w.**, je les aide dans la mesure de mes moyens. **To be in the w. of doing sth.**, avoir l'habitude de faire qch. **To get into the w. of doing sth.**, (i) prendre l'habitude de faire qch.; (ii) apprendre à faire qch. **You will get into the w. of it**, vous vous y ferez. (b) **Engaging ways**, petites façons engageantes; gentillesses f. **I know his little ways**, je connais ses petites manies. **He has a w. with him**, il est insinuant. **He has a w. with children**, il sait prendre les enfants. (c) **The good old ways**, les usages m du bon vieux temps. (d) **To get one's (own) w.**, arriver à ses fins. **He wants his own w.**, il veut n'en faire qu'à sa tête. **He had it all his own w.**, il n'a pas rencontré de résistance. **If I had my w.**, si ce n'était que de moi. **You can't have it both ways**, on ne peut pas être et avoir été. 7. **In many ways**, à bien des égards. **In some ways . . .**, à certains points de vue. . . . **He was a gentleman in every w.**, c'était un parfait gentleman. **She is certainly clever in a w.**, elle ne manque pas d'une certaine adresse. 8. Cours m; course f. **I met him in the ordinary w. of business**, je l'ai rencontré dans le courant, au cours, de mes affaires. **In the ordinary w.**, I am home by five o'clock, d'habitude je suis rentré à cinq heures

9. (*a*) **The flood is making w.**, l'inondation fait des progrès. (*b*) **Erre** *f* (d'un navire). **Ship under w.**, navire en marche, faisant route. **To get (a ship) under w.**, appareiller; se mettre en route. **To gather w.**, prendre de l'erre. (*In rowing*) **Give w.**, avant partout. (*Cp.* GIVE[2] I. 10.) **10.** (*a*) **To be in a good w.**, être bien en point. **Things seem in a bad w.**, les choses ont l'air d'aller mal. **He is in a bad w. of health**, sa santé est chancelante; *F:* il file un mauvais coton. **He is in a bad w. of business**, les affaires vont mal; il est dans de vilains draps. (*b*) *F:* **He is in a fine w. about it**, (i) il ne décolère pas; (ii) il a pris la chose très à cœur. (*c*) **In a fair w. to succeed**, en bonne voie pour réussir. **11. W. of business**, genre *m* d'affaires; métier *m*. **To be in a small w. of business**, avoir un petit commerce. **He lives in a small w.**, il vit petitement, modestement. **12.** (*a*) **By the w.** (i) Chemin faisant; en route. (ii) Incidemment; en passant. **All this is by the w.**, tout ceci est par parenthèse. (iii) A (ce) propos. **By the w.!** ah, j'y pense! (*b*) **By w. of.** (i) Par la voie de, par (un endroit). (ii) En guise de, à titre de. **By w. of warning**, à titre d'avertissement. (iii) **What have you got in the w. of ties?** qu'est-ce que vous avez en fait de cravates? (iv) **He's by w. of being a socialist**, il est vaguement socialiste. **13.** *pl. N.Arch:* Ways, couettes *f*. **'way-bill**, *s. Com:* Lettre *f* de voiture; feuille *f* de route; bordereau *m*. **'way-leave**, *s.* **1.** *Min: etc:* Droit *m* de passage. **2.** *Av:* Droit de survol (**over a territory**, d'un territoire).

way[2], *adv. Esp. U.S: F:* = AWAY. **It was w. back in 1890**, cela remonte à 1890.

wayfarer ['weifɛərər], *s.* Voyageur *m* (à pied); passant *m*.

waylay [wei'lei], *v.tr.* (**waylaid** [wei'leid]; **waylaid**) **1.** Attirer (qn) dans une embuscade; tendre un guet-apens à (qn). **2.** Arrêter (qn) au passage.

wayside ['weisaid], *s.* Bord *m* de la route. **To fall by the w.**, rester en chemin. **W. flowers**, fleurs qui croissent en bordure de route.

wayward ['weiwəd], *a.* (*a*) Volontaire, rebelle. (*b*) Capricieux, -euse, fantasque.

waywardness ['weiwədnis], *s.* (*a*) Entêtement *m*, obstination *f*. (*b*) Caractère *m* fantasque.

we [wi(:)], *pers. pron. nom. pl.* **1.** (*a*) Nous. **We are playing**, nous jouons. **Here we are**, nous voici. (*b*) (*Stressed*) Nous. **We are English, they are French**, nous, nous sommes anglais, eux, ils sont français. **We Englishmen**, nous autres Anglais. (*c*) On. **As we say**, comme on dit. *F:* **We are sure to catch it**, on est sûrs de se faire attraper. **2.** (*Plural of majesty*) **We are persuaded that . . .**, nous sommes persuadé que . . .

weak [wi:k], *a.* **1.** Faible; (*of health*) débile; (*of body*) infirme, chétif. **To have w. eyesight**, avoir la vue faible. **W. stomach**, estomac peu solide. **To grow w.**, s'affaiblir. **The weaker sex**, le sexe faible. **W. style**, style sans vigueur. **2.** (*a*) **W. decision**, décision qui dénote de la faiblesse. (*b*) **W. character**, caractère faible. **S.o.'s w. side**, le côté faible, le faible, de qn. **3.** (*a*) (*Of solution*) Dilué, étendu. **W. tea**, thé léger. (*b*) *I.C.E:* **W. mixture**, mélange pauvre. **4.** *Gram:* **W. conjugation**, conjugaison faible. **-ly**, *adv.* (*a*) Faiblement; sans force. (*b*) Sans résolution. **'weak-'headed**, *a.* Faible d'esprit. **'weak-'hearted**, *a.* Sans courage. **'weak-'kneed**, *a. F:* Sans caractère. **'weak-'minded**, *a.* **1.** (*a*) Faible d'esprit. (*b*) (Action) qui dénote de la faiblesse d'esprit. **2.** Qui manque de résolution. **weak-'sighted**, *a.* A la vue faible.

weaken ['wi:k(ə)n]. **1.** *v.tr.* Affaiblir; amollir (l'esprit). *I.C.E:* **To w. the mixture**, appauvrir le mélange. **2.** *v.i.* S'affaiblir, faiblir; (*of current*) fléchir. **weakening**[1], *a.* **1.** Affaiblissant; *Med:* anémiant. **2.** Faiblissant; qui faiblit. **weakening**[2], *s.* Affaiblissement *m*, amollissement *m*; fléchissement *m* (de courant). *I.C.E:* Appauvrissement *m* (du mélange).

weakling ['wi:kliŋ], *s.* (*a*) Être *m* faible, débile. (*b*) Homme faible de caractère.

weakly ['wi:kli], *a.* (Enfant) débile, faible (de santé).

weakness ['wi:knis], *s.* (*a*) Faiblesse *f*. **The w. of his argument**, le peu de solidité de son argument. *I.C.E:* **W. of the mixture**, pauvreté *f* du mélange.

(*b*) **To have a w. for sth., s.o.**, avoir un faible pour qch., qn.

weal[1] [wi:l], *s. Lit:* **W. and woe**, bonheur et malheur. **For w. or (for) woe**, quoi qu'il arrive; advienne que pourra. **The common w.**, le bien de tous.

weal[2], *s.* Marque *f*, trace *f* (d'un coup de fouet).

weald [wi:ld], *s. Geog:* Région partiellement boisée.

wealth [welθ], *s.* **1.** Richesse(s) *f(pl)*; opulence *f*. **He is rolling in w.**, il roule sur l'or. **2.** Abondance *f*, profusion *f* (de détails, etc.). **Her w. of hair**, sa chevelure abondante.

wealthy ['welθi], *a.* Riche, opulent. **W. heiress**, grosse héritière. *s.* **The w.**, les riches *m*.

wean [wi:n], *v.tr.* **1.** Sevrer (un nourrisson). **2.** **To w. s.o. from his bad habits**, faire perdre à qn ses mauvaises habitudes. **weaning**, *s.* Sevrage *m*.

weapon ['wepən], *s.* Arme *f*. **To beat s.o. with his own weapons**, battre qn avec ses propres armes.

wear[1] ['wɛər], *s.* **1.** (*a*) Usage *m*. **Dresses for evening w.**, toilettes pour le soir. **Ladies' w.**, articles *m* pour dames. (*b*) **Material that will stand hard w.**, étoffe d'un bon usage. **These shoes still have some w. in them**, ces souliers sont encore mettables. (*Of dress, etc.*) **To be the worse for w.**, être usé, défraîchi. *F:* **To feel the worse for w.**, avoir la gueule de bois. **2.** Usure *f*; fatigue *f* (d'une machine); dégradation *f* (d'une route). **W. and tear**, (i) usure; avaries *fpl*; (ii) frais *mpl* d'entretien. *Jur:* **Fair w. and tear**, usure normale.

wear[2], *v.* (**wore** ['wɔːr]; **worn** [wɔːn]) **1.** *v.tr.* Porter (un vêtement). **He was wearing a large hat**, il portait un grand chapeau. **To w. black**, porter du noir. **To have nothing fit to w.**, n'avoir rien de mettable. **What shall I w.?** qu'est-ce que je vais mettre? **A lounge suit may be worn**, le veston est, sera, de mise. **To w. one's hair long**, porter les cheveux longs. **To w. a sour look**, avoir un air revêche. **2.** *v.tr.* User. **To w. one's coat threadbare**, user son veston jusqu'à la corde. **To w. sth. into holes, to w. holes in sth.**, faire des trous à qch. (à force d'usage). **To w. oneself to death**, se tuer à force de travail. **3.** (*With passive force*) (*a*) (*Of garment*) **To w. into holes**, se trouer. (*Of stone*) **To w. smooth**, se lisser par le frottement. (*b*) **To w. well**, (i) (*of material*) faire bon usage; (ii) (*of pers.*) être bien conservé. **This friendship has worn well**, cette amitié a tenu bon. **Tyres that w. for ever**, pneus inusables. **4.** *v.i.* (*Of time*) Traîner. **The year was wearing to its close**, l'année tirait à sa fin. **wear away. 1.** *v.tr.* (*a*) User, ronger. **He is worn away to a shadow**, il n'est plus que l'ombre de lui-même. (*b*) Effacer, détruire. **2.** *v.i.* (*a*) S'user. (*b*) S'effacer. (*c*) (*Of time*) S'écouler. **wear down. 1.** *v.tr.* User. **To w. one's heels down**, éculer ses souliers. **To w. down the enemy's resistance**, user à la longue la résistance de l'ennemi. **2.** *v.i.* S'user. **wear off. 1.** *v.tr.* Faire disparaître (par l'usure). **2.** *v.i.* S'effacer, disparaître; (*of pain*) se calmer. **The novelty of the sight soon wore off**, la nouveauté de ce spectacle passa vite. **wear on**, *v.i.* (*Of time*) S'écouler (lentement). **As the evening wore on . . .**, à mesure que la soirée s'avançait. . . . **wear out. 1.** *v.tr.* (*a*) User (ses habits). **To w. oneself out**, s'user, s'épuiser. **Worn out with work**, usé par le travail. (*b*) Épuiser, lasser (la patience de qn). (*c*) **To w. out one's days in captivity**, passer le reste de ses jours dans la captivité. **2.** *v.i.* S'user. **Material that will not w. out**, étoffe inusable. **worn out**, *a.* **1.** Usé. **W. out shoes**, souliers usés, finis. **2.** (*Of pers.*) (i) Épuisé; exténué; (ii) usé (par le travail). **The horses are w. out**, les chevaux n'en peuvent plus. **3.** (*Of idea*) Rebattu. **wearing**[1], *a.* **1.** Fatigant, lassant, épuisant. **2.** Destructeur, -trice. **3. W. parts** (*of a machine*), organes sujets à l'usure. **4. Good-w. material**, étoffe de bon usage. **wearing**[2], *s.* **1.** Port *m* (de vêtements). **W. apparel**, vêtements *mpl*, habits *mpl*. **2.** Usure *f*. **W. surface**, surface d'usure.

wear[3], *v.* (**wore**; **wore**) *Nau:* **1.** *v.i.* (*Of ship*) Virer lof pour lof; virer vent arrière. **2.** *v.tr.* Virer (un navire) lof pour lof.

wearable ['wɛərəbl], *a.* (Vêtement) mettable.

wearer ['wɛərər], *s.* Personne qui porte qch. (sur elle).

weariness ['wiǝrinis], s. **1.** Lassitude f, fatigue f. **2.** Dégoût m, lassitude.

wearisome ['wiǝris(ǝ)m], a. Ennuyeux, -euse, fastidieux, -euse; F: assommant. **W. task**, tâche ingrate.

weary[1] ['wiǝri], a. **1.** Fatigué; las, f. lasse. F: A w. Willie, un fainéant, un traîne-la-patte. **2.** Las, dégoûté (of, de). **To grow w. of sth.**, se dégoûter de qch. **3.** Fatigant, obsédant. **-ily,** adv. **1.** D'un air, d'un ton las, fatigué. **2.** Avec fatigue; (cheminer) péniblement.

weary[2], v. (wearied) **1.** v.i. (a) Se lasser, se fatiguer. **To w. of s.o.**, se fatiguer de la compagnie de qn. (b) Trouver le temps long. (c) O: **To w. for sth.**, désirer ardemment qch.; languir après qch. **2.** v.tr. (a) Lasser, fatiguer. (b) **To w. s.o. with one's requests**, importuner qn de ses sollicitations. **wearied,** a. Las, f. lasse; fatigué. **wearying,** a. Ennuyeux, -euse, fastidieux, -euse, F: assommant.

weasel ['wi:z(ǝ)l], s. Z: Belette f. **'weasel-faced,** a. A la mine chafouine.

weather[1] ['weðǝr], s. **1.** Temps m (qu'il fait). **In all weathers,** par tous les temps. **It is settled w.,** le temps est au beau fixe. **In this, in such, w.,** par le temps qu'il fait. **In the hot w.,** pendant les grandes chaleurs. **It is awful w.,** il fait un temps de chien. **(Wind and) w. permitting,** si le temps le permet. **If there is a break in the w.,** s'il y a changement de temps. **What is the w. like?** quel temps fait-il? (Of ship) **To make heavy w.,** bourlinguer. **To make heavy w. of a job,** compliquer les choses. F: (Of pers.) **To be under the w.,** être indisposé, F: patraque. S.a. CLERK 3. **2.** Attrib. (a) **W. forecast,** bulletin m météorologique; prévisions fpl du temps. **W. conditions,** conditions atmosphériques. **W. ship,** navire m, frégate f, météorologique. (b) Nau: Du côté du vent. **On the w. beam,** par le travers au vent. **'weather-beaten,** a. **1.** Battu des vents; battu par la tempête. **2.** (a) (Of complexion) Bronzé, hâlé, basané. (b) (Of thg) Dégradé par le temps. **'weather-bound,** a. Retenu, arrêté, par le mauvais temps. **'weather bureau, centre,** s. Bureau m météorologique. **'weather-chart,** s. Carte f météorologique; carte du temps. **'weather-deck,** s. Nau: Partie du pont exposée aux vents et à la mer. **'weather-eye,** s. **To keep one's w.-e. open,** veiller au grain. **'weather-gauge,** s. Nau: Avantage m du vent. **'weather-glass,** s. Baromètre m (à cadran). **'weather-proof,** a. A l'épreuve du gros temps; (vêtement) imperméable; (édifice) étanche. **'weather-report,** s. Bulletin m météorologique, F: la météo. **'weather-shore,** s. Nau: Côte f du vent. **'weather-side,** s. **1.** Côté m (d'une maison) exposé au vent. **2.** Nau: Bord m du vent. **'weather-strip,** s. Bourrelet m étanche. **'weather-worn,** a. Usé, rongé, par les intempéries.

weather[2]. I. v.tr. **1.** Geol: Désagréger, altérer. Furn: Weathered oak, chêne patiné. **2.** Nau: (a) **To w. a headland,** doubler un cap (à la voile). **To w. a ship,** passer au vent d'un navire. (b) **To w. (out) a storm,** (i) survivre à une tempête; (ii) (of pers.) se tirer d'affaire. **II. weather,** v.i. **1.** (Of rock) Se désagréger, s'altérer. **2.** (Of building, bronze) Prendre de la patine. **weathering,** s. (a) Altération f, désagrégation f (des roches). **W. agents,** intempéries fpl. (b) Patine f.

weatherboard ['weðǝbɔ:d], s. (a) (For roofs) Planche f à recouvrement. (b) (For window) Jet m d'eau. (c) Row: Hiloire f.

weathercock ['weðǝkɔk], s. (a) Girouette f. (b) Personne inconstante; girouette.

weave[1] ['wi:v], s. Tex: **1.** Armure f. **2.** Tissage m.

weave[2], v. (wove [wouv]; woven ['wouv(ǝ)n]) **1.** v.tr. (a) Tex: Tisser (une étoffe). Abs. Faire le métier de tisserand. (b) **To w. a plot,** tramer un complot. (c) Tresser (une guirlande, un panier); entrelacer (des fils, des fleurs). **2.** v.i. **To w. through the traffic,** se frayer un chemin à travers les encombrements. **3.** v.i. P: **To get weaving,** s'y mettre. **Get weaving!** vas-y! **weaving,** s. **1.** Tissage m. Hand-loom w., tissage à la main. Power-loom w., tissage mécanique. **2.** Entrelacement m (de rameaux).

weaver ['wi:vǝr], s. **1.** Tisserand m. **2.** W.(-bird), tisserin m.

web [web], s. **1.** Tex: Tissu m. **W. of lies,** tissu de mensonges. **2.** Spider's w., toile f d'araignée. **3.** Nat.Hist: Palmure f, membrane f (d'un palmipède). **4.** Tchn: Joue f, flasque m; bras m (de manivelle); âme f (d'une poutre, d'un rail). **5.** Pièce f, rouleau m (d'étoffe). **'web-fingered,** a. Z: Syndactyle. **'web-footed, -toed,** a. Palmipède; aux pieds palmés.

webbed [webd], a. Palmé, membrané.

webbing ['webiŋ], s. **1.** Sangles fpl (de chaise). **2.** Toile f à sangles; ruban m à sangles.

wed [wed], v. (wedded) **1.** v.tr. (a) Épouser (qn); se marier avec (qn). (b) (Of priest) **To w. a couple,** marier un couple. (c) Unir (to, with, à). **To be wedded to an opinion,** être entiché d'une opinion. **To become wedded to an opinion,** se fixer à une opinion. **2.** v.i. Se marier. **wedded,** a. **1.** Marié. **2.** Conjugal, -aux. **wedding,** s. **1.** Noce(s) f(pl); mariage m. **Church w.,** mariage à l'église. **Silver, ruby, golden, diamond w.,** noces d'argent, de vermeil, d'or, de diamant. **2.** Attrib. Nuptial, -aux; de noce(s); de mariage. **W. breakfast,** repas m de noces. **W. cake,** gâteau m de mariage. **W. day,** jour m des noces. **W. dress,** robe f de mariée. **W. guest,** invité, -ée (à un mariage). **W. march,** marche nuptiale. **W. present,** cadeau m de mariage. **W. ring,** alliance f.

we'd = we had, we would.

wedge[1] [wedʒ], s. Coin m. **1.** (a) **Fixing w.,** coin de serrage; cale f de fixation; Mec.E: clavette f, clef f. (b) **Splitting w.,** coin à fendre. **To drive in a w.,** enfoncer un coin. **It is the thin end of the w.,** c'est un premier empiétement; c'est un pied de pris. **2.** Chose de forme triangulaire. **W. of a tennis racket,** cœur m d'une raquette. **W. of cake,** morceau m (triangulaire) de gâteau. **'wedge-shaped,** a. En (forme de) coin.

wedge[2], v.tr. **1.** Coincer, assujettir; caler (des rails); claveter (une roue sur son axe). **2. To w. (up) a piece of furniture,** caler un meuble. **To w. a door open,** maintenir une porte ouverte avec une cale. **3. To w. sth. in sth.,** enclaver, insérer, implanter, enfoncer, serrer, qch. dans qch. **Traveller wedged in between two fat women,** voyageur coincé entre deux grosses femmes.

wedged [wedʒd], a. Cunéiforme; en forme de coin.

wedlock ['wedlɔk], s. Lit. & Jur: (a) Mariage m. **Born in, out of, w.,** (enfant) légitime, illégitime. (b) La vie conjugale.

Wednesday ['wed(n)zdi], s. Mercredi m. **Ash W.,** le mercredi des Cendres. (For phrases see FRIDAY.)

wee [wi:], a. F: Petit; tout petit; minuscule. **A w. bit,** un tout petit peu.

weed[1] [wi:d], s. **1.** Bot: Mauvaise herbe; herbe folle. **2.** O: (a) **The w.,** le tabac. (b) F: Cigare m. **3.** F: Personne étique, malingre, chétive. **'weed-killer,** s. Herbicide m, désherbant m.

weed[2], v.tr. Sarcler; désherber. **weed out,** v.tr. **1.** Éclaircir (des laitues, etc.). **2.** Éliminer; extirper (des préjugés, etc.). **'weeding out,** s. **1.** Éclaircie f. **2.** Élimination f. **weeding,** s. Sarclage m; désherbage m.

weeder ['wi:dǝr], s. **1.** Sarcleur, -euse; extirpateur m. **2.** Tls: Sarcloir m.

weediness ['wi:dinis], s. F: Maigreur f; apparence f malingre.

weeds [wi:dz], s.pl. O: Vêtements m de deuil (de veuve).

weedy ['wi:di], a. **1.** Couvert de mauvaises herbes. **2.** F: (Homme) malingre, poussé en asperge.

week [wi:k], s. Semaine f. **1.** (a) **What day of the w. is it?** quel jour de la semaine sommes-nous? **Twice a w.,** deux fois par semaine. **P: To knock s.o. into the middle of next w.,** donner à qn un fameux coup. **W. in w. out,** d'un bout de la semaine à l'autre. **I haven't seen him for weeks,** je ne l'ai pas vu depuis des semaines. **F: A w. of Sundays,** une éternité. (b) **Huit jours. Once a w.,** une fois par semaine; tous les huit jours. **Every w.,** tous les huit jours. **Within the w.,** dans la huitaine. **A w. from now, this day w., today w.,** d'aujourd'hui en huit. **Tomorrow w., Tuesday w.,** de demain, de mardi, en huit. **Yesterday w.,** il y a eu hier huit jours. **In a w. or so,** dans une huitaine. **Forty hour w.,** semaine de quarante heures. **2. What I can't get done in the w. I do on Sundays,** ce que je n'arrive pas à faire en semaine je le fais le dimanche.

weekday ['wiːkdei], *s.* Jour *m* ouvrable; jour de semaine. **On weekdays,** en semaine.

weekend ['wiːk'end], *s.* Fin *f* de semaine, weekend *m*. **To have one's weekends free,** être libre le samedi et le dimanche; faire la semaine anglaise. **I stayed with them for the w.,** j'ai passé le weekend chez eux.

weekly ['wiːkli]. **1.** (*a*) (Salaire) de la semaine; (visite, paiement) hebdomadaire. (*b*) (Pensionnaire) à la semaine. **2.** *s.* Journal *m*, revue *f*, hebdomadaire. **3.** *adv.* Par semaine; tous les huit jours. **Twice w.,** deux fois par semaine.

weeny ['wiːni], *a.* *F:* Minuscule.

weep¹ [wiːp], *s.* Crise *f* de larmes. **To have a good w.,** pleurer à chaudes larmes; pleurer tout son soûl. 'weep-hole, *s.* Chantepleure *f* (dans un mur).

weep², *v.* (wept [wept]) **1.** *v.i.* (*a*) Pleurer. **To w. bitterly,** pleurer à chaudes larmes. **To w. for joy,** pleurer de joie. **That's nothing to w. over, about,** (i) il n'y a pas de quoi pleurer; (ii) *Iron:* tant mieux! **I could have wept to see them …,** j'en aurais pleuré de les voir…. (*With cogn. acc.*) **To w. tears,** répandre, verser, des larmes. (*b*) (*Of wall, etc.*) Suinter, suer; (*of tree*) pleurer; (*of sore*) couler, exsuder. *v.tr.* **To w. oneself to sleep,** s'endormir en pleurant, dans les larmes. **To w. one's heart, one's eyes, out,** pleurer à chaudes larmes, *F:* comme une madeleine. **To w. away the time,** passer son temps à pleurer. **weeping¹,** *a.* **1.** (Enfant) qui pleure. **2.** (*Of rock, etc.*) Suintant, humide. **3.** *Bot:* **W. willow,** saule pleureur. **weeping²,** *s.* **1.** Pleurs *mpl*, larmes *fpl*. **2.** Suintement *m*; exsudation *f*.

weeper ['wiːpər], *s.* Pleureur, -euse.

weepy ['wiːpi], *a.* *F:* (*a*) (Ton, air) larmoyant. (*b*) **To feel w.,** se sentir envie de pleurer.

weever ['wiːvər], *s.* *Ich:* Vive *f*.

weevil ['wiːv(i)l], *s.* *Ent:* Charançon *m*.

wee-wee ['wiːwiː], *s.* *F:* **To do w.-w.,** faire pipi.

weft [weft], *s.* *Tex:* (*a*) Trame *f*. (*b*) = WEFT-YARN. 'weft-yarn, *s.* *Tex:* Fil *m* de trame.

weigh¹ [wei], *s.* *Nau:* **To get a ship under w.,** appareiller; se mettre en route.

weigh². **1.** *v.tr.* (*a*) Peser (un paquet, etc.); faire la pesée de (qch.). **To w. sth. in one's hand,** soupeser qch. (*b*) **To w. one's words,** peser, mesurer, ses paroles. **To w. sth. (up) in one's mind,** considérer qch. **To w. (up) the consequences of sth.,** calculer les conséquences de qch. **To w. the pros and cons,** peser le pour et le contre. (*c*) *Nau:* **To w. anchor,** lever l'ancre; appareiller. **2.** *v.i.* (*a*) Peser; avoir du poids. **To w. heavy, light,** peser lourd *inv*; peser peu. (*b*) **The debt is weighing on his mind,** cette dette le tracasse. **Fate weighs heavily on us,** la fatalité s'appesantit sur nous. **To w. heavily on the finances,** obérer les finances. (*c*) **The point that weighs with me is …,** ce qui a du poids pour moi c'est…. **weigh down,** *v.tr.* **1.** Peser plus que (qch.); l'emporter en poids sur (qch.). **2.** Faire pencher (la balance). **3.** Surcharger. **Branch weighed down with fruit,** branche surchargée de fruits. **Weighed down with sorrow,** accablé de chagrin, par le chagrin. **weigh in,** *v.i.* (*a*) (*Of jockey, boxer*) Se faire peser avant la course, le match. *Turf:* **The weighing-in room,** le pesage. (*b*) **To w. in (with an argument),** intervenir avec un argument. 'weigh-in, *s.* *Turf: Box:* Pesage *m*. **weigh out,** *v.tr.* Peser (du sucre, etc.) en petites quantités. **weighing,** *s.* **1.** Pesée *f* (de denrées, etc.). *Turf:* Pesage *m*. **2.** *Nau:* Levage *m* (de l'ancre); appareillage *m*. 'weighing-enclosure, *s.* *Turf:* (Enceinte *f* du) pesage; enceinte des balances. 'weighing-machine, *s.* Appareil *m* de pesage; bascule *f*. 'weigh-beam, *s.* **1.** Fléau *m*, verge *f* (d'une balance romaine). **2.** Balance romaine. 'weighbridge, *s.* Pont-bascule *m*, bascule *f*.

weighman, *pl.* -men ['weimən], *s.m.* Peseur.

weight¹ [weit], *s.* **1.** (*a*) Poids *m*. **To sell by w.,** vendre au poids. **To give good w.,** faire bon poids. **Two pounds in w.,** d'un poids de deux livres. **It is worth its w. in gold,** cela vaut son pesant d'or. (*Of pers.*) **To lose w.,** perdre de son poids. **To gain w.,** prendre du poids. **To throw one's w. about,** faire du volume, de l'esbrouffe. **To pull one's w.,** (i) *Row:* fournir un effort en rapport avec son poids; (ii) y mettre du sien. (*b*) Poids, pesanteur *f*, lourdeur *f*. **To try, feel,** the w. of sth., soupeser qch. **Specific w.,** poids spécifique, volumique. **Atomic w.,** poids atomique. **2.** (*a*) Poids (en cuivre, etc.). **Set of weights,** série *f* de poids. **Weights and measures,** poids et mesures. (*b*) Corps lourd. **Letter-w., paper-w.,** presse-papiers *m inv*. **Weights of a clock,** poids d'une horloge. *Sp:* **Putting the w.,** lancement *m* du poids. *Gym:* **Heavy w.,** gueuse *f* d'athlétisme. *F:* **To hang a w. round one's own neck,** se mettre la corde au cou. **3.** **Charge** *f.* **To put the w. on a beam,** charger une poutre. **That's a w. off my mind,** voilà qui me soulage (l'esprit). **The w. of years,** le fardeau, le faix, le poids, des ans, des années. **He feels the w. of his responsibilities,** sa responsabilité lui pèse. **4.** Force *f* (d'un coup). **Blow with no w. behind it,** coup sans force. **5.** Importance *f.* **To give w. to an argument,** donner du poids à un argument. **His word carries w.,** sa parole a du poids, de l'autorité. **People of w.,** gens influents. **Of no w.,** (i) sans conséquence, sans importance; (ii) (*of pers.*) sans influence. 'weight-lifter, *s.* *Gym:* Haltérophile *m.* 'weight-lifting, *s.* *Gym:* (Travail *m* aux) poids et haltères, haltérophilie *f*.

weight², *v.tr.* **1.** Attacher un poids à (qch.); charger, alourdir, (qch.) d'un poids; lester, plomber (un filet, etc.); plomber (une canne). **2.** *Paperm:* Charger (le papier).

weightiness ['weitinis], *s.* **1.** Pesanteur *f*, lourdeur *f* (d'un paquet, etc.). **2.** Importance *f*, force *f* (d'une opinion).

weightlessness ['weitlisnis], *s.* Apesanteur *f*.

weighty ['weiti], *a.* **1.** Pesant, lourd. **2.** (Motif, etc.) grave, important, sérieux. **W. arguments,** arguments puissants, d'un grand poids. **-ily,** *adv.* **1.** Pesamment. **2.** (Raisonner) avec force.

weir [wiər], *s.* **1.** Barrage *m* (dans un cours d'eau). **2.** Déversoir *m* (d'un étang, etc.).

weird [wiəd], *a.* (*a*) Surnaturel, -elle; mystérieux, -euse; d'une étrangeté inquiétante. (*b*) Étrange, singulier, -ière. **-ly,** *adv.* Étrangement.

weirdie ['wiədi], *s.* *P:* Excentrique *mf*.

weirdness ['wiədnis], *s.* **1.** Étrangeté inquiétante (d'un spectacle, etc.). **2.** Caractère singulier (d'un costume, etc.).

welcome¹ ['welkəm], *a.* **1.** Bienvenu. (*a*) **To make s.o. w.,** faire bon accueil à qn. (*b*) *As int.* **W. (to you)!** soyez le bienvenu, la bienvenue! **2.** (*Of thg*) **A w. change,** un changement bienvenu. **This cheque is most w.,** ce chèque tombe à merveille. **3.** **You are w. to try,** libre à vous d'essayer. **You are w. to it,** (i) c'est à votre service, à votre disposition; (ii) *Iron:* je ne vous l'envie pas; grand bien vous fasse! *F:* **Thank you very much—You're w.,** merci bien, monsieur—Il n'y a pas de quoi.

welcome², *s.* (*a*) Bienvenue *f.* **To overstay one's w.,** lasser l'amabilité de ses hôtes, s'incruster. (*b*) Accueil *m.* **To give s.o. a hearty w.,** faire bon accueil à qn. **To meet with a cold w.,** être reçu froidement.

welcome³, *v.tr.* **1.** Souhaiter la bienvenue à (qn); faire bon accueil à (qn). **2.** Recevoir avec plaisir. **To w. a piece of news,** se réjouir d'une nouvelle.

weld¹ [weld], *s.* Soudure *f*; joint *m*, ligne *f*, de soudure.

weld². **1.** *v.tr.* (*a*) Souder (deux pièces) au blanc soudant; unir (deux pièces) à chaud. (*b*) Corroyer (l'acier). (*c*) Unir, joindre, étroitement. **2.** *v.i.* (*Of metals*) (i) Se souder; (ii) se corroyer. **welding,** *s.* Soudage *m*, soudure *f.* **(Oxy)acetylene w.,** soudure autogène. **W. heat,** (température *f* du) blanc soudant.

welder ['weldər], *s.* **1.** (*Pers.*) Soudeur *m*. **2.** Machine *f* à souder.

welfare ['welfɛər], *s.* Bien-être *m*; prospérité *f.* **Social w.,** sécurité sociale. **Child w., infant w.,** protection *f* de l'enfance. **Infant w. centre,** consultation *f* de nourrissons. **W. work,** assistance sociale. **W. worker,** assistante sociale. **W. State,** État providence.

welkin (the) [ðə'welkin], *s.* *Poet:* Le firmament; la voûte céleste. **To make the w. ring,** faire retentir l'air.

well¹ [wel], *s.* **1.** Puits *m.* **To drive, sink, a w.,** forer, creuser, un puits. **2.** (*a*) (*Shaft*) Puits, cage *f* (d'un ascenseur). (*b*) Partie encaissée, creux *m* (de qch.). *Nau:* Vivier *m* (d'un bateau de pêche). *Jur:* **The w.**

of the court, le parquet. (c) **W. of a yacht,** cockpit m d'un yacht. (d) Fond m de carter, etc. (formant réservoir d'huile). (e) Nau: Puisard m, archipompe f, sentine f (d'un navire). **'well-boring,** s. (i) Sondage m, forage m, (ii) fonçage m, de puits. **'well-deck,** s. N.Arch: Coffre m. **'well-digger,** s. Puisatier m.

well², v.i. **To w. (up, out, forth),** (of liquid) jaillir; (of spring) sourdre; (of tears) jaillir. **welling,** s. Jaillissement m.

well³. (Comp. **better,** sup. **best,** q.v.) I. adv. Bien. **1.** (a) **To work w.,** bien travailler. **This boy will do w.,** ce garçon fera son chemin, ira loin. **To do as w. as one can,** faire de son mieux. **W. done!** bravo! très bien! bien joué! F: **To do oneself w.,** bien se soigner; bien se nourrir. **You would do w. to be quiet,** vous feriez bien de vous taire. **He accepted, as w. he might,** il accepta, et rien d'étonnant. **One might as w. say that...,** autant dire que.... **You may (just) as w. stay,** (i) autant (vaut) rester; (ii) vous n'êtes pas de trop. **You could just as w. have stayed till to-morrow,** vous auriez tout aussi bien pu rester jusqu'à demain. **I can't very w. do it,** il ne m'est guère possible de le faire. **Very w.!** très bien! (c'est) entendu! (b) **To receive s.o. w.,** faire bon accueil à qn. **It speaks w. for...,** cela fait honneur à.... **To do w. by s.o.,** se montrer généreux envers qn. **She deserves w. of you,** elle mérite bien votre reconnaissance. **W. intended,** fait à bonne intention. (c) (Happily) **You are w. out of it,** soyez heureux d'en être quitte. **To come off w.,** (i) avoir de la chance; (ii) (of event) bien se passer. **2.** (Intensive) **It is w. worth trying,** cela vaut vraiment la peine d'essayer. F: ça vaut le coup. **W. after six,** six heures bien sonnées. **W. on into the small hours,** bien avant dans la nuit, (jusqu') à une heure avancée de la nuit. **W. on in the fifties,** qui a dépassé la cinquantaine, qui a cinquante ans bien sonnés. **To be w. up in a subject,** bien posséder un sujet. **W. up in history,** ferré, F: calé, en histoire. **W.-away,** (i) F: bien en train; (ii) P: ivre, pompette. **3.** (With qualifying adv.) **Pretty w. all,** presque tout. F: **It serves him jolly w. right,** c'est joliment bien fait pour lui. **4.** (a) **As w.,** aussi. **Take me as w.,** emmenez-moi aussi. **I want some as w.,** il m'en faut également. (b) **As w. as,** de même que; comme; non moins que. **By day as w. as by night,** de jour comme de nuit. **5.** (a) (To introduce a remark) **W., as I was telling you...,** donc, comme je vous disais.... **W., and what of that?** eh bien, et après? (b) (Expressing astonishment, relief, etc.) **W.!** ça alors! P: **W. I never!** pas possible! **W., it can't be helped,** ma foi! on n'y peut rien. **W., w.!** (i) que voulez-vous! (ii) vous m'en direz tant! (c) (Summarizing) **W. then, why worry about it?** eh bien, alors, pourquoi vous faire de la bile? II. **well,** pred.a. **1. To be w.,** être en bonne santé, être bien portant. **To look w.,** avoir bonne mine. **W. and strong,** robuste; F: vaillant. **Not to feel w.,** ne pas se sentir bien. **2.** (a) (Advisable) **It is w. to...,** il est opportun de.... **It would be w. to...,** il serait bon, utile, à propos, de.... **It would be just as w. if you were present,** il y aurait avantage à ce que vous soyez présent. (b) (Lucky) **It was (just as) w. that you were there,** c'est bien heureux, bien tombé, que vous vous soyez trouvé là. (c) (Satisfactory) **All's w. that end's w.,** tout est bien qui finit bien. **All's w.!** tout va bien! Nau: bon quart! (d) **That's all very w., but...,** tout cela est bel et bon, mais.... **It is all very w. for you to say that...,** libre à vous, c'est bien gentil à vous, de dire que.... **He is all very w. in his way, but...,** il n'y a rien à dire contre lui, mais.... **W. and good!** soit! bon! **That's all very w. and good, but...,** tout ça c'est très bien, F: c'est pas tout ça. mais.... III. **well,** s. **1.** pl. **The w. and the sick,** les bien portants et les malades. **2. To wish s.o. w.,** vouloir du bien à qn. **'well ad'vised,** pred.a. (a) (Of pers.) Bien avisé. (b) (Of action) Sage, prudent, judicieux, -euse. **'well-'balanced,** a. Bien équilibré; (of pers.) posé. **'well-be'haved,** a. (Enfant) sage; (chien) bien dressé. **'well-being,** s. Bien-être m. **'well 'born,** a. Bien né; de bonne famille. **'well-'bred,** a. **1.** (Of pers.) Bien élevé, bien appris. **2.**

(Of dog, etc.) De (bonne) race. **'well-con'ducted,** a. **1.** Qui se conduit bien; sage. **2.** (Commerce) bien dirigé; (expérience) bien menée. **'well di'rected,** a. (Tir, etc.) bien ajusté. **'well dis'posed,** a. **1.** Bien arrangé, bien disposé. **2.** (Of pers.) Bien disposé (**to, towards,** envers). **'well 'earned,** a. Bien mérité. **'well 'educated,** a. Instruit. **'well 'found,** a. (Of ship, etc.) Bien équipé; bien pourvu (**in,** de); bien monté (**in,** en). **'well 'founded,** a. Bien fondé; (appréhension) légitime. **'well-'grown,** a. (Enfant) bien venu. **'well in'formed,** a. (Of pers.) Bien renseigné, bien informé, instruit; (of committee) documenté. **To keep w. i.,** se tenir au courant. **To be w. i. on a subject,** connaître un sujet à fond. **In w. i. quarters,** en lieu compétent. **'well 'kept,** a. (a) (Of garden) Bien tenu. (b) (Of secret) Bien gardé. **'well-'knit,** a. Compact, solide, bien bâti. **'well 'known,** a. (Bien) connu; célèbre; réputé; renommé (**for, pour**). **As is w. k.,** comme chacun sait. **'well 'made,** a. (Article) soigné. **'well-'mannered,** a. Qui a de bonnes manières, du savoir-vivre; (enfant) bien élevé. **'well-'marked,** a. (Of change) Bien marqué; évident; accusé. **W.-m. differences,** différences tranchées. **W.-m. outlines,** contours nets. **'well-'matched,** a. (Ménage) bien assorti. **The two teams are w.-m.,** les deux équipes sont de force (égale). **'well-'meaning,** a. Bien intentionné. **'well-'meant,** a. Fait avec une bonne intention. **'well-nigh,** adv. Lit: Presque. **'well 'off,** adj. phr. **1.** (a) **To be w. o.,** être dans l'aisance, à l'aise; être riche; F: avoir de quoi. (b) Prospère. **You don't know when you are w. o.,** vous ne connaissez pas votre bonheur. **2. To be w. o. for sth.,** être bien pourvu, bien fourni, de qch. **'well-'oiled,** a. F: Pompette; rétamé. **'well-'ordered,** a. Bien ordonné; (of mind) méthodique. **'well 'read,** a. **1.** (Of pers.) cultivé; qui a de la lecture. **2.** (Volume) qui porte les traces de nombreuses lectures. **'well-'spoken,** a. (a) Qui parle bien; qui a un accent cultivé. (b) A la parole affable. **'well-'timed,** a. Bien calculé, opportun. **'well-to-'do,** a. **To be w.-to-do,** être dans l'aisance; être à son aise. **W.-to-do appearance,** air prospère, cossu. **'well-wisher,** s. Ami, -ie, partisan m (de qn, d'une cause). **'well-'worn,** a. (a) (Vêtement) fortement usagé. (b) (Argument) rebattu, usé jusqu'à la corde.

we'll = **we will, we shall.**

Wellingtons ['weliŋtənz], s.pl. Cost: (Also **Wellington boots**). Bottes f en caoutchouc.

Welsh¹ [welʃ]. **1.** a. Gallois; du pays de Galles. **2.** s. (a) pl. **The W.,** les Gallois m. (b) Ling: Le gallois.

welsh², v.i. (Of bookmaker) Décamper, filer; lever le pied.

welsher ['welʃər], s. Turf: Bookmaker marron.

Welshman, pl. **-men** ['welʃmən], s.m. Gallois.

Welshwoman, pl. **-women** ['welʃ,wumən, -,wimin], s.f. Galloise.

welt¹ [welt], s. **1.** (a) Bootm: Trépointe f (de semelle). (b) Bordure f (de gant). **2.** Marque f (d'un coup de fouet).

welt², v.tr. **1.** (a) Mettre des trépointes à (des souliers). (b) Border (un gant). **2.** F: Rosser, battre (qn). **welted,** a. (Soulier, semelle) à trépointes.

welter¹ ['weltər], s. **1.** Confusion f, désordre m. **2.** Masse confuse, fouillis m (de choses disparates); ramassis m, fatras m (d'idées).

welter², v.i. Se vautrer, se rouler (dans la boue, etc.). **To be weltering in one's blood,** baigner dans son sang.

welter³ weight ['weltəweit], s. Box: (Poids) mi-moyen.

wen [wen], s. Med: Kyste sébacé; F: loupe f.

wench¹ [wen(t)ʃ], s.f. (a) A: Jeune fille, jeune femme. **Strapping w.,** grande gaillarde. (b) A: Prostituée. (c) Hum: F: (Jeune) fille, jeunesse.

wench², v.i. F: Courir les filles, le jupon.

wend [wend], v.tr. Lit: **To w. one's way,** porter, diriger, ses pas (**to,** vers). **To w. one's way back,** s'en revenir.

went. See GO².

wept. See WEEP².

were. See BE.

we're [wiər] = **we are.**

werewolf, pl. **-wolves** ['wiəwulf, -wulvz], s. Loup-garou m, pl. loups-garous.

wert   W : 13   **what**

wert. *See* BE.

Wesleyan ['wezliən, 'wes-], *a. & s.* Wesleyen, -enne.

west [west]. **1.** *s.* (*a*) Ouest *m*, occident *m*, couchant *m*. **House facing (the) w.,** maison exposée à l'ouest. **On the w., to the west,** à l'ouest, au couchant (of, de). (*b*) *Pol:* The W., l'Occident; l'Ouest. (*c*) *U.S:* The W., les États occidentaux (des États-Unis). **The Far W.,** le Far West. **2.** *adv.* A l'ouest, à l'occident. **W. of here,** à l'ouest d'ici. **To travel w.,** voyager vers l'ouest. **To go w.,** (i) se diriger vers l'ouest; (ii) *F:* mourir; *F:* casser sa pipe. **3.** *a.* Ouest *inv;* (vent) d'ouest; (pays) de l'ouest, occidental, -aux; (mur, fenêtre) qui fait face à l'ouest. **The w. side,** le côté ouest. **'west-bound,** *a.* (*Of traffic*) Qui se dirige vers l'ouest. **'West 'End,** *s.* The W. End, le quartier chic (de Londres). **'West 'Indian,** *a.* Des Antilles; antillais. **'West 'Indies (the).** *Pr.n. Geog:* Les Antilles *f.*

wester ['westər], *v.i.* **1.** (*Of sun, moon, stars*) Passer à l'ouest. **The westering sun,** le soleil couchant. **2.** (*Of wind*) Sauter à l'ouest.

westerly ['westəli]. **1.** *a.* **W. wind,** vent d'ouest. **W. current,** courant qui se dirige vers l'ouest. **2.** *adv.* Vers l'ouest.

western ['westən]. *a.* **1.** Ouest, de l'ouest; occidental, -aux. **W. Europe,** l'Europe occidentale. **The W. Church,** l'Église d'Occident, latine. **2.** *s. F: Cin:* Western *m*.

westerner ['westənər], *s.* Occidental, -ale, -aux.

westernize ['westənaiz], *v.tr.* Occidentaliser.

Westphalia [west'feiljə]. *Pr.n. Geog:* La Westphalie.

westward ['westwəd]. **1.** *s.* Direction *f* de l'ouest. **To w.,** vers l'ouest. **2.** *a.* A l'ouest, de l'ouest.

westwards ['westwədz], *adv.* Vers l'ouest, à l'ouest.

wet¹ [wet], *a.* (**wetter**) **1.** (*a*) Mouillé, humide; imbibé d'eau. **To get w.,** se mouiller. **To get one's feet w.,** se mouiller les pieds. **To be w. through, w. to the skin, dripping w.,** être trempé (jusqu'aux os). **Wringing w., sopping w., soaking w.,** (*of clothes, etc.*) mouillé à tordre; (*of pers.*) trempé comme une soupe, jusqu'aux os. **Ink still w.,** encre encore fraîche. (*b*) **W. weather,** temps humide, pluvieux; temps de pluie. **It is going to be w.,** il va pleuvoir. **We had three w. days,** nous avons eu trois jours de pluie. **The w. season,** la saison des pluies; la saison humide. (*c*) *Ch:* **W. process,** (procédé d'analyse par) voie humide. *El:* **W. cell,** pile à élément humide. (*d*) *P:* **He's a bit w.,** c'est une nouille. **2.** *F:* (*Of country, state*) Anti-prohibitionniste. **'wet 'blanket,** *s. F:* **1.** To throw a w. b. over the meeting, jeter un froid sur l'assemblée. **2.** Rabat-joie *m inv*, trouble-fête *m inv*. **'wet nurse,** *s.* Nourrice *f*.

wet², *s.* **1.** Humidité *f*. **2.** Pluie *f*. **To go out in the w.,** sortir sous la pluie. **3.** *P:* To have a w., boire un coup; se rincer la dalle. **4.** *P:* (*Pers.*) Nouille *f*.

wet³, *v.tr.* (**wetted**) **1.** Mouiller, humecter (une éponge). **2.** *F:* To w. one's whistle, boire un coup; se rincer la dalle. **wetting,** *s.* Mouillage *m*. **To get a w.,** se faire tremper.

wether ['weðər], *s. Husb:* Bélier châtré; mouton *m*.

wetness ['wetnis], *s.* Humidité *f*.

we've = *we have.*

whack¹[(h)wæk]. **1.** *s.* (*a*) Coup (de bâton) bien appliqué. (*b*) Action de battre (qch.). *F:* To have a w. at sth., (i) tenter l'aventure; essayer de faire qch.; (ii) s'attaquer à (un pâté, etc.). (*c*) *F:* Part *f*, portion *f*; (grand) morceau. **To give s.o. a w. of cake,** donner à qn un gros morceau de gâteau. **2.** *int. F:* V'lan!

whack², *v.tr. F:* (*a*) Donner des coups à (qn, qch.); fesser (un enfant). (*b*) Battre (ses adversaires) à plates coutures. (*c*) *Nau:* To w. her up to twenty knots, pousser l'allure à vingt nœuds. **whacked,** *a. F:* Éreinté. **whacking¹,** *a. F:* Énorme; colossal, -aux. **W. lie,** mensonge de taille. **whacking²,** *s. F:* Rossée *f*, raclée *f*.

whacker ['(h)wækər], *s. P:* **1.** Quelque chose de colossal; chose énorme. **2.** Gros mensonge. What a w.! en voilà une forte!

whacko ['(h)wæk'ou], *int. P:* Magnifique! épatant!

whacky ['(h)wæki], *a. P:* Fou, *f.* folle, fêlé.

whale¹ [(h)weil], *s.* **1.** *Z:* Baleine *f*; cétacé *m.* Right w., baleine franche. **White w.,** bél(o)uga *m.* **W. calf,** baleineau *m. S.a.* KILLER 1. **2.** *F:* He's a w. at

tennis, au tennis! c'est un as. **He's a w. for work,** il abat du travail. **It's a w. of a crop,** c'est une récolte fantastique. **He has a w. of a cold,** il a un rhume carabiné. **We had a w. of a time,** on s'est drôlement bien amusés. **'whale-boat,** *s.* Baleinière *f*. **'whale-oil,** *s.* Huile *f* de baleine.

whale², *v.i.* Faire la pêche à la baleine. **whaling,** *s.* Pêche *f* à la baleine. **W. ship,** baleinier *m.* **W. industry,** industrie baleinière. **'whaling-ground,** *s.* Parages fréquentés par les baleines.

whaleback ['(h)weilbæk], *s. Nau:* W. deck, pont *m* en dos de baleine.

whalebone ['(h)weilboun], *s.* Fanon *m* de baleine; baleine *f* (d'un corset, etc.).

whaler ['(h)weilər], *s.* **1.** (*Pers.*) Baleinier *m*; pêcher *m* de baleines. **2.** (*a*) (*Ship*) Baleinier. (*b*) (*Boat*) Baleinière *f.*

wharf¹ [(h)wɔ:f], *s. Nau:* Appontement *m*, débarcadère *m*, embarcadère *m*; wharf *m*, quai *m. Com:* Ex w., à prendre sur quai. **'wharf-rat,** *s.* **1.** *Z:* Surmulot *m*, rat *m* d'égout. **2.** *P:* Rôdeur *m* (qui fréquente les quais).

wharf², *v.tr.* **1.** (*a*) Déposer (des marchandises) sur le quai. (*b*) Débarquer (les marchandises). **2.** *v.i.* (*Of ship*) Amarrer à quai.

wharfage['(h)wɔ:fidʒ], *s.* Quayage *m*; droits *mpl* de quai.

wharfinger ['(h)wɔ:fin(d)ʒər], *s.* (*a*) Propriétaire *m* d'un quai, d'un wharf. (*b*) Gardien *m* de quai.

what [(h)wɔt]. **I.** *a.* **1.** (*Relative*) (Ce, la chose) que, qui. **He took away from me w. little I had left,** il m'a pris le peu qui me restait. **He traded with w. capital he had,** il faisait le commerce avec ce qu'il possédait de capital. **2.** (*Interrogative*) Quel, *f.* quelle. **W. time is it?** quelle heure est-il? **Tell me w. time it is,** dites-moi l'heure qu'il est. **W. right has he to give orders?** de quel droit donne-t-il des ordres? **W. good is this?** à quoi cela est-il bon? **W. news?** quoi de nouveau? **W. day of the month is it?** le combien sommes-nous? **3.** (*Exclamatory*) **W. an idea!** quelle idée! **W. a fool he is!** qu'il est bête! **W. silly fools we have all been!** comme nous avons tous été bêtes! **W. a lot of people!** que de gens! **II. what,** *pron.* **1.** (*Relative,* = *that which*) Ce qui, ce que. **W. is done cannot be undone,** ce qui est fait est fait. **W. I like is music,** ce que j'aime c'est la musique. **W. is most remarkable is that . . .,** ce qu'il y a de plus remarquable c'est que. . . . **He had a key, and w. is more, he has it still,** il avait une clef, et qui plus est, il l'a encore. **This is w. it is all about,** voici ce dont il s'agit. **Come w. may,** advienne que pourra. **Say w. he will . . .,** quoi qu'il dise . . .; il a beau dire. . . . **W. with golf and w. with tennis,** I have no time to write, entre le golf et le tennis, il ne me reste pas une minute pour écrire. *P:* **To give s.o. w. for,** laver la tête à qn; flanquer une bonne raclée à qn. **2.** (*Interrogative*) (*a*) Qu'est-ce qui? qu'est-ce que? que? quoi? **W. on earth are you doing here?** qu'est-ce que vous pouvez bien faire ici? **W. is it?** (i) qu'est-ce? qu'est-ce que c'est? (ii) qu'est-ce qu'il y a? **What's that?** qu'est-ce que cela? qu'est-ce que c'est que ça? **W. is he?** qu'est-ce qu'il est? qu'est-ce qu'il fait? **What's the matter?** qu'y a-t-il? de quoi s'agit-il? **What's his name?** comment s'appelle-t-il? **W. is that to you?** qu'est-ce que cela vous fait? **What's the good, the use?** à quoi bon? **W. is to be done?** comment faire? que faire? **What's the French for dog?** comment dit-on "dog" en français? **W. do seven and eight make?** combien font sept et huit? **W. are potatoes today?** (à) combien (sont) les pommes de terre aujourd'hui? **What's the rent?** de combien est le loyer? **W. is he like?** comment est-il? **W. d'you take me for?** pour qui me prenez-vous? **What's it all about?** de quoi s'agit-il? **W. about a game of bridge?** si on faisait une partie de bridge? **W. about you?** et vous? **Well, w. about it?** (i) eh bien, quoi? et puis après? (ii) eh bien, qu'en dites-vous? **W. is that for?** à quoi sert cela? *F:* à quoi ça sert? **W. (on earth) for?** mais pourquoi donc? **And w. if she comes to hear of it?** et si elle vient à l'apprendre? **W. then?** et après? et alors? *F:* So w.? et puis après? alors? **Paper, pens, pencils and w. not,** du papier, des plumes, des crayons, et que sais-je encore? **W. (did you say)?** plaît-il? pardon? *F:* comment? **W. of that?** qu'est-ce que cela fait? (*b*) (*Indirect*) Ce qui, ce que.

Tell me w. is happening, dites-moi ce qui se passe. I don't know w. to do, je ne sais que faire. **Tell me w. you are crying for,** dites-moi pourquoi vous pleurez. **I'll tell you w. . . .,** je vais vous dire . . .; écoutez. . . . He knows w.'s w., il la connaît; il s'y connaît; c'est un malin. **3.** (*Exclamatory*) (*a*) **W. he has suffered!** ce qu'il a souffert! **W. next!** ça, par exemple! (*b*) **W.! you can't come!** comment! vous ne pouvez pas venir! *F: O:* **Nice girl, w.!** joli brin de fille, hein! '**what-d'ye-call-'em, -her, -him, -it,** *s. F:* Machin *m*; (*of pers.*) chose *mf*. **Mr. W.-d'ye-call-him,** monsieur Machin. '**what-'ho,** *int. F:* Eh bien! Eh alors!

whatever [(h)wɒt'evər], (*Cf.* '*what ever*' *under* EVER 3.) **1.** *pron.* (*a*) (*Relative*) **W. you like,** tout ce qui vous plaira; tout ce que vous voudrez; n'importe quoi. (*b*) Quoi qui, quoi que + *sub.* **W. it may be . . .,** quoi que ce soit. . . . **2.** *a.* (*a*) Quelque . . . qui, que + *sub.* **W. mistake he has made . . .,** quelque faute qu'il ait commise . . . **Every treaty of w. character . . .,** tout traité de quelque nature que ce soit. . . . (*b*) (i) Aucun. **He has no chance w.,** il n'a pas la moindre chance. **None w.,** pas un seul. **Nothing w.,** absolument rien. **He won't say anything w.,** il refuse de dire quoi que ce soit. (ii) **Has he any chance w.?** a-t-il une chance quelconque?

whatnot['(h)wɒtnɒt],*s.***1.** *Furn:* Étagère *f*. **2.** *F:*Machin *m*.

whatsoever ['(h)wɒtsou'evər], *pron.* & *a.* = WHATEVER.

wheat [(h)wiːt], *s.* Blé *m*, froment *m*. **Grain of wheat,** grain de blé. **W.-growing area,** région à blé.

wheatear ['(h)wiːtiər], *s. Orn:* Traquet motteux *m*, *F:* cul-blanc *m*.

wheaten ['(h)wiːtn], *a.* (Pain) de froment, de blé.

wheatmeal ['(h)wiːtmiːl], *s.* Grosse farine (de froment).

wheatsheaf ['(h)wiːtʃiːf], *s.* Gerbe *f* de blé.

wheedle ['(h)wiːdl], *v.tr.* Enjôler, cajoler, embobiner (qn). **To w. money out of s.o.,** soutirer de l'argent à qn. **wheedling,** *a.* (*Of manner*) Enjôleur, câlin. **W. voice,** voix pateline.

wheedler ['(h)wiːdlər], *s.* Enjôleur -euse.

wheel¹ [(h)wiːl], *s.* **1.** Roue *f.* (*a*) **To run on wheels,** (i) marcher sur (des) roues; (ii) *F:* aller comme sur des roulettes. *Aut:* **Wire w.,** roue à rayons métalliques. **Disc w.,** roue à voile plein. *Av:* **Ground wheels, landing wheels,** roues (du train d'atterrissage.) *S.a.* FLY² (*a*), SHOULDER¹. (*b*) *Mec.E:* **Fixed w.,** roue calée. **Loose w.,** roue folle, décalée. **Toothed w.,** roue dentée; roue d'engrenage. **There are wheels within wheels,** c'est une affaire compliquée, il y a toutes sortes de forces en jeu. **The wheels of government,** les rouages *m* de l'administration. *S.a.* SPROCKET 2. (*c*) *Aut:* **Steering w.,** volant *m* (de direction). *Aut:* **He was killed at the w.,** il a été tué au volant. *Nau:* **The (steering) w.,** la roue du gouvernail; la barre. **To take the w.,** *Aut:* se mettre au volant; *Nau:* prendre la barre. **The man at the w.,** (i) *Nau:* le timonier, l'homme de barre; (ii)*Aut:* l'homme au volant; (iii) *F:* l'homme à la tête des affaires. (*d*) (Grinding-)w., meule *f* (*e*) Potter's w., tour *m* de potier. (*f*) **Cutting w.,** (i) molette *f* (à couper le verre); (ii) roulette *f* (à couper la pâte). **2.** *Hist:* **To break s.o. on the w.,** rouer qn. **3.** *U.S: F:* Vélo *m f*. **4.** *Mil:* Conversion *f*. **Left w.,** conversion à gauche. '**wheel-chair,** *s.* Fauteuil roulant; voiture *f* de malade. '**wheel-disc,** *s. Aut:* Enjoliveur *m*. '**wheel-gear,** *s. Mec.E:* Transmission *f* par engrenage(s). '**wheel-house,** *s. Nau:* La timonerie. '**wheel(-)spin,** *s. Aut:* Patinage *m*. '**wheel-track,** *s.* **1.** Ornière *f.* **2.** Trace *f* de roues. '**wheel-train,** *s. Mec.E:* Train *m* de roues.

wheel². **1.** *v.tr.* (*a*) Tourner; faire pivoter. (*b*) Rouler (une brouette); pousser (une bicyclette) à la main. **2.** *v.i.* (*a*) Tourner en rond; tournoyer. (*b*) *Mil:* Faire une conversion. **Left w.!** à gauche, marche! (*c*) (*Of pers.*) **To wheel round,** faire demi-tour; se retourner (brusquement). (*d*) *Rugby Fb:* **To w. the scrum,** tourner la mêlée.

wheelbase ['(h)wiːlbeis], *s. Veh: Rail:* Empattement *m*.

wheelbarrow ['(h)wiːlbærou], *s.* Brouette *f*.

wheeled [(h)wiːld], *a.* A roues; muni de roues.

wheelwright ['(h)wiːlrait], *s.* Charron *m*.

wheeze¹[(h)wiːz],*s.***1.** Respiration asthmatique, sifflante. **2.** *P:* Truc *m*.

wheeze². **1.** *v.i.* (*a*) Respirer péniblement, en asthmatique. (*b*) (*Of horse*) Corner. **2.** *v.tr.* **To w. out sth.,** dire qch. d'une voix asthmatique. **wheezing,** *s.* (*a*) Respiration *f* asthmatique; sifflement gras (d'asthmatique). (*b*) (*Of horse*) Cornage *m*.

wheezy ['(h)wiːzi], *a.* (*a*) (*Of pers.*) Asthmatique; *F:* poussif, -ive. (*b*) (*Of horse*) Cornard.

whelk [(h)welk], *s. Moll:* Buccin *m*.

whelp¹ [(h)welp], *s.* **1.** (*a*) = PUPPY. (*b*) Petit *m* d'un fauve. **Lion's w.,** lionceau *m*. (*c*) *F:* Mauvais garnement; drôle *m*. **2.** *Nau:* Flasque *m*, taquet *m* (de cabestan).

whelp², *v.i.* & *tr.* (*Of lion, dog, etc.*) Mettre bas.

when [(h)wen]. **I.** *adv.* Quand? **W. will you go? quand** partirez-vous? **I wonder when he will go,** je me demande quand il partira. **W. is the meeting?** pour quand est la réunion? **W. ever, w. on earth, will he come?** quand donc viendra-t-il? (*When pouring drink*) **Say w.!** dites-moi quand (je devrai arrêter de verser); comme ça? **II.** **when,** *conj.* **1.** Quand, lorsque. **W. I entered the room . . .,** lorsque j'entrai dans la pièce. . . . **W. he was born, married,** lors de sa naissance, de son mariage. **W. I was young, du** temps que j'étais jeune. **W. one is young,** quand on est jeune; lorsqu'on est jeune. **We shall try again w. you are rested,** nous essaierons de nouveau quand vous serez reposé. **He will speak w. I have done,** il parlera après que j'aurai fini. **He looks in w. passing,** il nous fait une petite visite en passant. **2.** (*Relative*) (*a*) **The day w. I met you,** le jour où je vous ai rencontré. **One day w. I was on duty . . .,** un jour que j'étais de service. . . . **At the very time w. . . .,** alors même que . . .; au moment même où. . . . **Now is w. I need him most,** c'est maintenant que j'ai le plus besoin de lui. **W.** (= *and then*) **The king will arrive on the 10th, w. he will open the new building,** le roi arrivera le dix, pour l'inauguration du nouvel édifice. **III.** **when,** *s.* Tell me the w. and the how of it, dites-moi quand et comment la chose est arrivée.

whence [(h)wens], *adv. A.* & *Lit:* D'où. **Do you know (from) w. he comes?** savez-vous d'où il vient? **W. I conclude that . . .,** d'où je conclus que. . . .

whenever [(h)wen'evər], *adv.* (*a*) Toutes les fois que; chaque fois que. **I go w. I can,** j'y vais aussi souvent que (cela m'est) possible. (*b*) **You may come w. you like,** vous pouvez venir quand vous voudrez.

where [(h)weər], *adv.* **1.** (*Interrogative*) (*a*) Où? **W. am I?** où suis-je? **Tell me w. he is,** dites-moi où il est. **W. ever have you been?** où diable étiez-vous (donc)? **mais d'où venez-vous? W. did we leave off** (reading, etc.)? où en sommes-nous restés? (*b*) **W. is the way out?** par où sort-on? (*c*) **W. do you come from?** (i) d'où venez-vous? (ii) de quel pays êtes-vous? **W. are you going to?** où allez-vous? **2.** (*Relative*) (*a*) (**There) w.,** (là) où. **I shall stay w. I am,** je resterai (là) où je suis. **Go w. you like,** allez où vous voudrez. (*b*) **That is w. we've got to,** voilà où nous en sommes. **That is w. you are mistaken,** voilà où vous vous trompez. **W. you are mistaken is . . .,** ce en quoi vous vous trompez c'est. . . . (*c*) **He came to w. I was fishing,** il est venu à l'endroit où je pêchais. **I can see it from w. we stand,** je le vois d'où nous sommes. (*d*) **The house w. I was born,** la maison où, dans laquelle, je suis né. **3.** *s.* **The w. and when of his birth are unknown,** on ne sait ni le lieu ni la date de sa naissance. *S.a.* ANYWHERE, ELSEWHERE, EVERYWHERE, NOWHERE, SOMEWHERE.

whereabouts ['(h)weərəbauts]. **1.** *adv.* Où (donc)? **W. are you?** où donc êtes-vous? **2.** *s.* Lieu *m* où se trouve qn, qch. **No one knows his w.,** personne ne sait où il demeure, où il est.

whereafter [(h)weər'ɑːftər], *rel.adv. A: or formal:* Après quoi; à la suite de quoi.

whereas [(h)weər'æz], *conj.* **1.** Attendu que, vu que, puisque + *ind.*; *Jur:* considérant que + *ind.* **2.** Alors que, tandis que, au lieu que + *ind.*

whereat [(h)weər'æt], *adv. Lit:* A quoi, sur quoi, de quoi, etc. **He said something, w. everyone laughed,** il a dit quelque chose, sur quoi tout le monde a ri.

whereby [(h)weə'bai], *adv.* **1.** *A:* (*Interrogative*) Par quoi? par quel moyen? **2. Decision w. . . .,** décision par laquelle. . . .

wherefore [ʹ(h)wɛəfɔːr]. **1.** *adv. A:* (*a*) Pourquoi? pour quelle raison? **W. do you laugh?** pourquoi riez-vous? (*b*) = THEREFORE. **2.** *s.* **The whys and wherefores,** les pourquoi et les comment.

wherefrom [(h)wɛəˈfrɔm], *adv. A:* D'où.

wherein [(h)wɛərˈin], *adv. A:* **1.** En quoi? **W. have we offended you?** en quoi vous avons-nous offensé? **2.** Dans lequel; où. **The month w. the event took place,** le mois où l'événement eut lieu.

whereof [(h)wɛərˈɔv], *adv. A:* **1.** En quoi? de quoi? **W. is it made?** en quoi est-ce fait? **2.** De quoi; dont. **Metals w. jewellery is made,** métaux dont on fait les bijoux.

whereon [(h)wɛərˈɔn], *adv. A:* **1.** Sur quoi? **2.** Sur quoi, sur lequel. **That is w. we differ,** c'est sur quoi nous ne sommes pas du même avis.

wheresoever [ˌ(h)wɛəsouˈevər], *adv. Lit:* = WHEREVER.

whereupon [ˌ(h)wɛərəˈpɔn], *adv.* **1.** = WHEREON 1. **2.** (*a*) = WHEREON 2. (*b*) **W. he left us,** sur quoi il nous quitta.

wherever [(h)wɛərˈevər], *adv.* (*Cp.* 'where ever' *under* EVER 3.) **1.** Partout où...; n'importe où.... **W. I go I see...,** partout où je vais je vois.... **I will go w. you want me to,** j'irai où vous voudrez. **2. W. you are, may be, do write to me,** où que vous soyez, ne manquez pas de m'écrire. **W. they come from they have done very well,** d'où qu'ils viennent ils se sont très bien acquittés (de leur tâche, etc.).

wherewith [(h)wɛəˈwiθ], *adv. A:* **1.** Avec quoi? **2.** (*a*) Avec lequel; avec quoi; au moyen duquel. (*b*) = WHEREUPON 2 (*b*).

wherewithal [ʹ(h)wɛəwiθɔːl]. **1.** *adv. A:* = WHEREWITH. **2.** *s.* **The w.,** le nécessaire; les moyens *m.* **I hadn't the w. to pay for a dinner,** je n'avais pas de quoi me payer un dîner. **To have the time and the w.,** avoir le temps et l'argent, et les moyens.

wherry [ʹ(h)weri], *s.* **1.** Esquif *m.* **2.** Bachot *m* (de rivière).

whet[1] [(h)wet], *s. F:* (*a*) Stimulant *m*, aiguillon *m*, excitant *m.* **W. to the appetite,** stimulant de l'appétit. (*b*) Apéritif *m*, petit verre.

whet[2], *v.tr.* (**whetted**) **1.** Aiguiser, affûter, affiler, repasser (un outil). **2.** *F:* Stimuler, aiguiser, exciter, aiguillonner (l'appétit, les désirs, etc.). **To w. one's whistle,** se rincer la dalle.

whether [ʹ(h)weðə], *conj.* **1.** (*Introducing an indirect question*) Si. **I don't know w. it is true,** je ne sais pas si c'est vrai. **It depends upon w. you are in a hurry or not,** cela dépend de si vous êtes pressé ou non. **The question was w. or not to take David with him,** la question était de savoir si, oui ou non, il devait emmener David. **2. W. it rains or (w. it) blows, he always goes out,** qu'il vente ou qu'il pleuve, il sort toujours. **We shall all die, w. today or tomorrow,** nous mourrons tous, que ce soit aujourd'hui, ou demain. **W. he comes or not, or no, we shall leave,** qu'il vienne ou non, qu'il vienne ou qu'il ne vienne pas, nous allons partir. **W. or not...,** qu'il en soit ainsi ou non....

whetstone [ʹ(h)wetstoun], *s.* Pierre *f* à aiguiser.

whew [hju], *int.* **1.** (*Of fatigue, relief*) Ouf! **2.** (*Astonishment*) Fichtre!

whey [(h)wei], *s.* Petit lait. **ʹwhey-faced,** *a.* A figure de papier mâché.

which [(h)witʃ]. **I.** *a.* **1.** (*Interrogative*) Quel, *f.* quelle; *pl.* quels, *f.* quelles? **W. colour do you like best?** quelle couleur aimez-vous le mieux? **W. way do we go?** par où allons-nous? **W. way is the wind?** d'où vient le vent? **W. one?** lequel? laquelle? **W. ones?** lesquels? lesquelles? **W. one of us?** lequel d'entre nous? **2.** (*Relative*) Lequel, *f.* laquelle; *pl.* lesquels, lesquelles. **He came at noon, at w. time I am usually in the garden,** il est arrivé à midi, heure à laquelle je suis d'habitude au jardin. **Look w. way you will...,** de quelque côté que vous regardiez.... **II.** *which, pron.* **1.** (*Interrogative*) Lequel, *f*, laquelle; *pl.* lesquels, *f*, lesquelles? **W. have you chosen?** lequel avez-vous choisi? **W. of the ladies has come?** laquelle des dames est venue? **W. of you can answer?** lequel d'entre vous peut répondre? **To w. is he speaking?** auquel, duquel, parle-t-il? **Tell me w. is w.,** dites-moi comment les distinguer. **I don't mind w.,** cela m'est égal. **2.** (*Relative*) (*a*) (*Adj. clauses*) Qui; que; lequel. **The house w. is to be sold,** la maison qui est à vendre. **The books w. I possess,** les livres que je possède. **The thing w. I need,** la chose dont j'ai besoin. **B:** *Our Father, w. art in Heaven,* notre père qui es aux cieux. (*b*) (*Continuative clauses*) Ce qui, ce que. **He looked like a retired colonel, w. indeed he was,** il avait l'air d'un colonel en retraite, ce qu'il était en effet. **He went over many incidents of my youth, all of w. were true,** il a rappelé nombre d'incidents de ma jeunesse, qui étaient tous exacts. **If this happens, w. God forbid...,** si cela arrive, ce qu'à Dieu ne plaise.... **She tickles my neck, w. I hate,** elle me chatouille le cou, chose que je déteste. **3.** (*Relative pron. governed by a prep.*) (*a*) **To w., at w.,** auquel, *f.* à laquelle, *pl.* auxquels, auxquelles. **Of w., from w.,** duquel, *f.* de laquelle; *pl.* desquels, desquelles; dont. **The house of w. I speak,** la maison dont je parle. **The book on the cover of w. there is a picture,** le livre sur la couverture duquel il y a une image. **The countries to w. we are going, w. we are going to,** les pays où nous irons. **The hotels at w. we stayed,** les hôtels où nous sommes descendus. **I have nothing with w. to write,** je n'ai pas de quoi écrire. (*b*) (*Continuative clauses*) **He demands that actors should have talent, in w. he is right,** il exige que les acteurs aient du talent, (ce) en quoi il a raison. **There are no trains on Sunday, w. I hadn't thought of,** il n'y a pas de trains le dimanche, ce à quoi je n'avais pas pensé. **After w. he went out,** après quoi il est sorti.

whichever [(h)witʃˈevər], *rel. pron. & a.* **1.** (*a*) *pron.* Celui qui, celui que, n'importe lequel. **Take w. you like,** prenez celui que vous voudrez; prenez n'importe lequel. (*b*) *a.* Le...que; n'importe quel. **Take w. book you like,** prenez le livre que vous voudrez, prenez n'importe quel livre. **2.** *a.* N'importe quel; quelque...que. **W. way I turn I see nothing but sand,** de quelque côté que je me tourne, n'importe de quel côté je me tourne, je ne vois (rien) que du sable.

whiff[1] [(h)wif], *s.* **1.** (*a*) Bouffée *f* (de vent, de fumée, etc.). **There wasn't a w. of wind,** il n'y avait pas un souffle de vent. **To go out for a w. of fresh air,** sortir pour respirer un peu, pour prendre l'air. (*b*) *F:* Mauvaise odeur. **2.** Petit cigare. **3.** *Row:* Skiff *m.*

whiff[2]. **1.** *v.i.* (*a*) Souffler par bouffées. (*b*) *F:* Puer. **2.** *v.tr.* To w. smoke, émettre des bouffées de fumée.

whiffy [(h)wifi], *a. F:* Qui pue.

whig [(h)wig], *s. Hist:* Whig *m*; libéral *m*, -aux (de vieille roche).

while[1] [(h)wail], *s.* **1.** (*Espace m de*) temps *m.* **After a w.,** quelque temps après, au bout de quelque temps. **In a little w.,** sous peu; avant peu. **For a (short) w.,** pendant quelque temps. **A little w. ago,** il n'y a pas bien longtemps; il y a peu de temps. **A long w.,** longtemps. **A good w.,** pas mal de temps. **It will be a good w. before you see him again,** vous ne le reverrez pas de si tôt. **It will take me quite a w. to do,** cela me prendra pas mal de temps. **Stay a (little) w.,** restez un (petit) peu. (*b*) *Adv.phr. O:* **The w.,** en attendant; pendant ce temps. **2. To be worth (one's) w.,** valoir la peine. **I will come if it is worth (my) w.,** je viendrai si cela en vaut la peine. **I will make it worth your w.,** vous serez bien payé de votre peine. **It is perhaps worth w. pointing out that...,** il n'est peut-être pas oiseux de faire remarquer que....

while[2], *v.tr.* **To w. away,** faire passer (le temps); tuer (une heure, le temps).

while[3], *conj.* **1.** (*a*) Pendant que, tandis que. **W. he was here, w. here,** he studied a great deal, pendant qu'il était ici il a beaucoup étudié. **He died w. eating his dinner,** il est mort en dînant. **W. reading I fell asleep,** tout en lisant, je me suis endormi. **W. this was going on,** sur ces entrefaites. (*b*) (*As long as*) Tant que. **W. I live you shall lack nothing,** tant que je vivrai vous ne manquerez de rien. **2.** (*Concessive*) Quoique, bien que, tout en.... **W. I admit, w. admitting, the thing is difficult, I do not think it impossible,** quoique j'admette, tout en reconnaissant, que la chose est difficile, je ne la crois pas impossible. **3.** (*Whereas*) Tandis que. **One of the sisters was dressed in white, w. the other was all in black,** une des sœurs était en blanc tandis que l'autre était tout en noir.

whilom [ʹ(h)wailəm], *a. A:* = FORMER.

whilst [(h)wailst], *conj.* = WHILE[3].

whim [(h)wim], *s.* **1.** Caprice *m*; fantaisie *f*, lubie *f*. A mere w., une simple lubie. **Passing w.**, toquade *f*. **It is a sudden w.** of his, c'est un caprice qui lui a pris. **2.** *Veh: Austr:* Triqueballe *m*.

whimbrel [('h)wimbrəl], *s. Orn:* Petit courlis, courlieu *m*.

whimper¹ [('h)wimpər], *s.* (*a*) Pleurnicherie *f*, pleurnichement *m*. (*b*) Geignement *m*, plainte *f*.

whimper². **1.** *v.i.* (*a*) Pleurnicher, geindre. (*b*) (*Of dog*) Pousser des petits cris plaintifs. **2.** *v.tr.* Dire (qch.) en pleurnichant. **whimpering,** *s.* = WHIMPER¹.

whims(e)y [('h)wimzi], *s.* Fantaisie *f*, lubie *f*.

whimsical [('h)wimzik(ə)l], *a.* **1.** Capricieux, -euse, fantasque; lunatique. **2.** (*Of thg*) Bizarre, baroque. **-ally,** *adv.* Capricieusement, bizarrement.

whimsicality [,(h)wimzi'kæliti], *s.* **1.** Caractère *m* fantasque. **2.** Bizarrerie *f* (de caractère).

whin¹ [(h)win], *s. Bot:* Ajonc *m*.

whin², *s.* = WHINSTONE.

whinberry [('h)winbəri], *s. Bot:* Airelle *f*, myrtille *f*.

whinchat [('h)wint∫æt], *s. Orn:* Tarier *m*.

whine¹ [(h)wain], *s.* **1.** Plainte *f*; cri dolent; geignement *m*. **2.** Jérémiade *f*.

whine². **1.** *v.i.* (*Of pers.*) Se plaindre; (*of infant*) pleurnicher, piauler; (*of dog*) geindre. **2.** *v.tr.* Dire (qch.) d'un ton dolent, plaintif, pleurard. **whining¹,** *a.* (*a*) Geignant; (enfant) pleurnicheur; (ton) plaintif, pleurard; (voix) dolente. (*b*) Geignard. **whining².** *s.* (*a*) Geignement *m*; piaulement *m*. (*b*) Jérémiades *fpl*; plaintes *fpl*.

whinny¹ [('h)wini], *s.* Hennissement *m* (de cheval).

whinny², *v.i.* (*Of horse*) Hennir.

whinstone [('h)winstoun], *s. Geol:* Trapp *m*.

whip¹ [(h)wip], *s.* **1.** Fouet *m*. *S.a.* HORSEWHIP¹, RIDING-WHIP. **2.** *Parl:* (*a*) (Membre désigné par un parti comme) chef *m* de file; whip *m*. (*b*) Appel *m* aux membres d'un groupe. **Four-line w.**, appel urgent souligné quatre fois. **3.** Fouettement *m*, coup *m* de fouet (d'un câble, etc.). **4.** Aile *f*, bras *m* (de moulin à vent). **5.** *Nau:* Cartahu *m*. **6.** *Cu:* (Sorte de) mousse *f*. **'whip (-)hand,** *s.* Main *f* du fouet; main droite. **To have the w.-h.,** avoir l'avantage. **To have the w.-h. of s.o.,** avoir barre(s) sur qn. **'whip-lash,** *s.* Mèche *f* de fouet. **Tongue like a w.-l.,** langue cinglante. **'whip-stock,** *s.* Manche *m* de fouet. **'whip-top,** *s. Toys:* Sabot *m*.

whip², *v.* (whipped [wipt]) **I.** *v.tr.* **1.** (*a*) Fouetter; donner le fouet à (un enfant). **To w. a top,** fouetter, faire aller, un sabot. **The rain whipped the window-panes,** la pluie fouettait, cinglait, les vitres. (*b*) *Cu:* Battre (les œufs); fouetter, faire mousser (la crème). **Whipped cream,** crème fouettée. (*c*) *Fish:* Fouetter (un cours d'eau). **2.** (*a*) *Nau:* Surlier, garnir (un cordage). (*b*) Ligaturer (un brancard, etc.). (*c*) **To w. a seam,** surjeter une couture; faire un surjet. **3.** Mouvoir vivement (qch.). **He whipped the revolver out of his pocket,** il sortit vivement le revolver de sa poche. **4.** *Nau:* Hisser (une vergue) avec un cartahu. **II.** whip, *v.i.* **1.** Fouetter. **The rain whipped against the panes,** la pluie fouettait, cinglait, contre les vitres. **2.** (*Of pers.*) **To w. behind the door,** se jeter derrière la porte. **To w. down the stairs,** dévaler l'escalier. **To w. round the corner,** tourner vivement le coin. **3.** *Mec.E:* (*Of shaft, etc.*) Fouetter. **whip back,** *v.i.* (*of cable, etc.*) Fouetter. **whip in,** *v.tr. Ven:* Ramener, rassembler (les chiens) (avec le fouet). *Abs.* **To w. in,** être piqueur. **whip off,** *v.tr.* Enlever vivement (qch. de la table, etc.). **To w. off one's hat,** se découvrir d'un geste rapide. **whip round. 1.** *v.tr. Abs.* **To w. round for subscriptions,** faire passer à la ronde une invitation à participer à une souscription. **2.** *v.i.* (*Of pers.*) Se retourner vivement; (*of horse*) faire (un) tête-à-queue. **'whip-round,** *s.* Appel *m* en faveur d'une souscription. **whip up,** *v.tr.* **1.** Activer, stimuler (un cheval). **2.** *Parl:* Faire passer un appel urgent (aux membres d'un parti). *F:* **To w. up one's friends,** rallier ses amis. **whipping,** *s.* (*a*) Fouettage *m.* (*b*) Fouettée *f. Jur:* (Châtiment *m* du) fouet; peine *f* du fouet. **To give a child a w.,** donner le fouet à un enfant. **To get a w.,** être fouetté. **2.** (*a*) Fouettement *m* (de la pluie, etc.). (*b*) *Mec.E:* Fouettement. **'whipping-boy,** *s.* Bouc *m* émissaire. **'whip-poor-'will,** *s. Orn:* Engoulevent *m* de la Virginie, *Fr.C:* bois-pourri *m*.

whipcord [('h)wipkɔ:d], *s.* **1.** (*a*) Mèche *f* de fouet. (*b*) Corde *f* à fouet. **2.** *Tex:* Whipcord *m*.

whipper-in [('h)wipər'in], *s. Ven:* Piqueur *m*; valet *m* de chiens.

whipper-snapper [('h)wipəsnæpər], *s. F:* Freluquet *m*, paltoquet *m*; jeune fat.

whippet [('h)wipit], *s.* **1.** (*Dog*) Whippet *m*. **2.** *Mil: A:* Char *m* d'assaut de modèle léger.

whirl¹, ² [(h)wə:r], *s. & v.i.* = WHIRR¹, ².

whirl¹ [(h)wə:l], *s.* (*a*) Mouvement *m* giratoire, giration *f* (d'une roue, etc.). (*b*) Tourbillon *m*, tourbillonnement *m*, tournoiement *m*. **My head is in a w.,** la tête me tourne.

whirl². **1.** *v.i.* (*a*) **To w.(round),** tourbillonner, tournoyer; (*of dancer*) pirouetter. **My head whirls,** la tête me tourne; j'ai le vertige. (*b*) **To w. along,** rouler, filer, à toute vitesse, à toute allure. **To come whirling down,** descendre en tournoyant. **2.** *v.tr.* (*a*) Faire tournoyer, faire tourbillonner (les feuilles mortes, etc.). (*b*) **The train whirled us along,** le train nous emportait à toute vitesse.

whirligig [('h)wə:ligig], *s.* **1.** (*a*) *Toys:* Tourniquet *m*. (*b*) Manège *m* de chevaux de bois. **2.** Tournoiement *m*.

whirlpool [('h)wə:lpu:l], *s.* Tourbillon *m* (d'eau); remous *m*; gouffre *m*.

whirlwind [('h)wə:lwind], *s.* Tourbillon *m* (de vent); trombe *f*. **To come in like a w.,** entrer en trombe, en coup de vent.

whirr¹ [(h)wə:r], *s.* Bruissement *m* (d'ailes); ronflement *m*, ronronnement *m* (de machines); sifflement *m* (d'obus); vrombissement *m* (d'une hélice d'avion).

whirr², *v.i.* (*Of machinery, etc.*) Tourner à toute vitesse; ronfler, ronronner; (*of air-screw, etc.*) vrombir; (*of shell*) siffler.

whisk¹ [(h)wisk], *s.* **1.** Mouvement *m* en coup de fouet. **A w. of the tail, of a duster,** un coup de queue, de torchon. **2.** (**Dusting**) **w.,** époussette *f*. (**Furniture**) **w.,** plumeau *m*. **3.** *Dom. Ec:* Batteur *m*, fouet *m* (à œufs, etc.).

whisk². **1.** *v.i.* S'élancer. **To w. away,** filer comme un trait. **To w. past,** passer comme le vent. **2.** *v.tr.* (*a*) (*Of cow*) **To w. its tail,** agiter sa queue; se battre les flancs avec la queue. (*b*) **To w. sth. away, off,** enlever qch. d'un geste rapide; escamoter qch. **To w. away a fly,** chasser une mouche. **I was whisked up in the lift,** l'ascenseur m'emporta rapidement. (*c*) *Cu:* Battre (des œufs); fouetter (la crème).

whisker [('h)wiskər], *s. Usu. pl.* **Whiskers,** favoris *m* (d'homme); moustache(s) *f* (de chat, de souris, etc.).

whisk(e)y [('h)wiski], *s.* Whisk(e)y *m*.

whisper¹ [('h)wispər], *s.* **1.**(*a*) Chuchotement *m*. **To speak in a w., in whispers,** parler tout bas. **To say sth. in a w.,** chuchoter qch.; dire qch. tout bas. **This was said in a w.,** ceci fut dit dans un souffle. *S.a.* STAGE-WHISPER. (*b*) *Lit:* Bruissement *m* (des feuilles); murmure *m* (de l'eau). **2.** Rumeur *f*, bruit *m* (que l'on se transmet à voix basse).

whisper². **1.** *v.i.* Chuchoter; parler bas; susurrer; (*of water*) murmurer. **To whisper to s.o.,** chuchoter à l'oreille de qn; dire, souffler, qch. à l'oreille de qn. **2.** *v.tr.* (*a*) **To w. a word to s.o.,** dire, glisser, souffler, un mot à l'oreille de qn. **Whispered conversation,** conversation à voix basse. (*b*) **It is whispered that . . . ,** il court un bruit que. . . . **whispering,** *s.* **1.** (*a*) Chuchotement *m*. (*b*) *Pej:* Chuchoterie(s) *f(pl)*. **W. campaign,** campagne sournoise, de chuchoteries. **2.** Bruissement *m*; murmure *m*. **'whispering-gallery,** *s.* Galerie *f* à écho; voûte *f* acoustique.

whisperer [('h)wispərər], *s.* Chuchoteur, -euse.

whist [(h)wist], *s.* Whist *m*. **Dummy w.,** whist à trois avec un mort. **W. drive,** tournoi *m* de whist. *S.a.* SOLO 2.

whistle¹ [('h)wisl], *s.* **1.** Sifflement *m*; coup *m* de sifflet. **The blackbird's w.,** le sifflement du merle. **2.** Sifflet *m*. **'Pea' w.,** sifflet à roulette. **To blow a w.,** donner un coup de sifflet. **3.** *P:* **To wet, whet, one's w.,** s'humecter le gosier; se rincer la dalle. **'whistle stop,** *s. U.S:* (*a*) *Rail:* Halte *f* (à arrêt facultatif). *attrib.* **W.s. tour,** tournée électorale faite par train spécial. (*b*) *F:* Patelin *m*, bled *m*.

whistle². 1. *v.i.* (a) Siffler. **To w. for one's dog,** siffler son chien. *F:* **He may w. for his money,** il peut courir après son argent. *F:* **You can w. for it!** tu peux te fouiller, te brosser! **The bullet whistled past his ear,** la balle passa en sifflant près de son oreille. (b) Donner un coup de sifflet. *Rail:* **To w. for the road,** demander la voie; siffler au disque. **2.** *v.tr.* Siffler, siffloter (un air, etc.)

whistler ['(h)wislər], *s.* **1.** (a) Siffleur, -euse. (b) Cheval cornard. **2.** Oiseau siffleur. **3.** Marmotte canadienne, *Fr.C:* siffleur *m.*

whit¹ [(h)wit], *s.* Brin *m*, iota *m*, petit morceau. (*Only in a few adv. phrs.*) **He is not a w. the better for it,** il ne s'en porte aucunement mieux. **He is no w. the happier for it,** il n'en est pas plus heureux (pour ça).

Whit², *a.* **W. Sunday,** (dimanche de) la Pentecôte. **W. Monday,** le lundi de la Pentecôte.

white [(h)wait]. **I.** *a.* **1.** Blanc, *f.* blanche. **He is going w.,** il commence à blanchir. *Cu:* **W. sauce,** sauce blanche. *Com:* **W. ware,** faïence fine. *Parl:* **W. paper,** livre blanc. *Geog:* **The W. Sea,** la Mer Blanche. **2.** (a) De couleur claire. **W. bread,** pain blanc. **W. wine,** vin blanc. (b) **The w. races,** les races blanches. **A w. man,** (i) un blanc; (ii) *U.S:* un homme loyal. (c) **W. with fear,** blanc de peur. **To turn, go, w.,** pâlir, blêmir. **As w. as a ghost, as a sheet,** pâle comme la mort, blanc comme un linge. **In a w. rage,** blême de colère. **3.** (*Of reputation, etc.*) Sans tache. *S.a.* LIE¹. **II. white,** *s.* **1.** Blanc *m*; couleur blanche. **Dead w.,** blanc mat. **2.** *Com:* **Zinc w.,** blanc de zinc. **3. Dressed in w.,** habillé en blanc, de blanc. *Com:* **W. sale,** vente de blanc. *Com:* **Wash your whites with X,** lavez votre linge avec X. *Sp:* **Whites,** pantalon blanc. **4.** (*Pers.*) Blanc, *f.* blanche; homme, femme, de la race blanche. **Poor w.** (*in U.S.A., etc.*), petit blanc. **5.** (a) **W. of egg,** blanc d'œuf. (b) **W. of the eye,** blanc de l'œil; cornée *f. F:* **To turn up the whites of one's eyes,** (i) faire des yeux de carpe pâmée, *P:* de merlan frit; (ii) tourner de l'œil. **'white-'collar,** *attrib.a.* **W.-c. worker,** employé de bureau. **'white-'haired,** *a.* Aux cheveux blancs. **'white-'headed,** *a.* **1.** *Z:* À tête blanche. **2.** (*Of pers.*) (a) Aux cheveux blancs. (b) *F:* **The w.-h. boy,** l'enfant gâté, le chouchou, de la famille. **'white-heart,** *attrib.a.* See CHERRY 1. **'white 'hot,** *a. Metall:* Chauffé à blanc; porté au blanc. **'white-'lipped,** *a.* **1.** Aux lèvres pâles. **2.** Blême, livide (de peur). **'white-'livered,** *a. F:* Poltron. **To be w.-l.,** *P:* avoir les foies (blancs). **'white 'metal,** *s.* **1.** Métal blanc. **2.** Antifriction *f*, régule *m.*

white², *v.tr.* Blanchir. *Now only in* **Whited sepulchre,** sépulchre blanchi.

whitebait ['(h)waitbeit], *s.* Blanchaille *f.* **A dish of w.,** une friture.

whitebeam ['(h)waitbi:m], *s. Bot:* Alisier blanc.

whitefish ['(h)waitfiʃ], *s. Com:* Poisson blanc, *esp.* le merlan et l'aiglefin *m.*

Whitehall ['(h)waitho:l], *Pr.n.* (a) Rue *f* et quartier *m* des Ministères (à Londres). (b)*F:* L'Administration *f.*

whiten ['(h)wait(ə)n]. **1.** *v.tr.* (a) Blanchir. **To w. s.o.'s reputation,** blanchir la réputation de qn. (b) Blanchir à la chaux; badigeonner en blanc. (c) *Metalw:* Étamer (un métal). **2.** *v.i.* (a) Blanchir. (b) (*Of pers.*) Pâlir, blêmir. **whitening,** *s.* **1.** Blanchiment *m* (des textiles, du papier, d'un mur, etc.). **2.** Blanchissement *m* (des cheveux, etc.).

whiteness ['(h)waitnis], *s.* (a) Blancheur *f.* (b) Pâleur *f* (du teint, du visage, etc.).

whitethorn ['(h)waitθɔːn], *s. Bot:* Aubépine *f.*

whitethroat ['(h)waitθrout], *s. Orn:* **Common w.,** grisette *f.* **Lesser w.,** fauvette babillarde.

whitewash¹ [(h)waitwɔʃ], *s.* Blanc *m* de chaux, lait *m* de chaux; badigeon blanc. **W. brush,** badigeon *m.*

whitewash², *v.tr.* (a) Badigeonner en blanc; blanchir à la chaux, disculper (qn). (b) Blanchir, disculper (qn) (un failli). **whitewashing,** *s.* (a) Peinture *f* à la chaux; badigeonnage *m* en blanc. (b) Réhabilitation *f.*

whitewood ['(h)waitwud], *s. Com:* Bois blanc.

whither ['(h)wiðər], *adv. A: & Lit:* **1.** Où? vers quel lieu? **W. will all this lead?** où tout cela nous mènera-t-il? **2.** (Là) où. **I shall go w.** Fate leads me, j'irai là où me mènera le Destin.

whithersoever [ˌ(h)wiðəsou'evər], *adv. A: & Lit:* N'importe vers quel endroit; n'importe où; où que + *sub.*

whiting¹ ['(h)waitiŋ], *s. Com:* Blanc *m* d'Espagne, blanc de Meudon.

whiting², *s. Ich:* Merlan *m.*

whitish ['(h)waitiʃ], *a.* Blanchâtre.

whitlow ['(h)witlou], *s. Med:* Panaris *m.* **'whitlow-grass,** *s. Bot:* Drave printanière.

Whitsun(tide) ['(h)wits(ə)n(taid)], *s.* Pentecôte *f.*

whittle [(h)witl], *v.tr.* **To w. (down),** amenuiser (un bâton, etc.). **To w. down, away, s.o.'s allowance,** rogner la pension de qn.

whizz¹ [wiz]. **1.** *int.* Pan! **2.** *s. F:* Sifflement *m* (d'une balle).

whizz², *v.i.* (*Of bullet, etc.*) Siffler. **To w. past,** passer en sifflant; (*of motor cycle*) passer à toute vitesse.

who [hu:], *pron. nom.* **1.** (a) Qui? qui est-ce qui? **W. is that lady?** qui, quelle, est cette dame? *F:* **W. on earth is it?** qui cela peut-il bien être? **Ask him w. found it,** demandez-lui qui l'a trouvé. **He is there.—W.?** il est là.—Qui ça? qui donc? **Tell me who's w.,** dites-moi les noms des personnes présentes. *Publ:* **Who's W.,** annuaire *m* des notabilités. *F:* **W. does he think he is?** pour qui se prend-il? **W. are in the running?** quels sont les candidats ayant des chances? **W. of us can still remember ...?** lequel d'entre nous se rappelle encore ...? *S.a.* ELSE 2, EVER 3. (b) *F:* (*Used incorrectly for whom*). **W. do you want?** qui voulez-vous? **2.** (*Relative*) (a) Qui. **Those w. do not know their lessons ...,** ceux qui ne sauront pas leurs leçons.... **My friend w. came yesterday,** mon ami qui est venu hier. (b) (*To avoid ambiguity in the French*) Lequel. **Three witnesses were called, w. declared ...,** ont comparu trois témoins, lesquels ont déclaré.... **The father of this girl, w. is very rich,** le père de cette jeune fille, lequel est très riche. (c) **W. eats must pay,** celui qui mange doit payer. **Deny it w. may ...,** le nie qui voudra....

whoa [wou], *int.* (a) (*To horse*) Ho! (signal d'arrêt). (b) *F:* (*To pers.*) Holà! doucement! attendez!

whodunit [hu:'dʌnit], *s. F:* Roman policier.

whoever [hu(:)'evər], *pron. nom.* (*Cp. 'who ever' under* EVER 3.) **1.** Celui qui; quiconque. **W. finds it may keep it,** celui qui le trouvera, quiconque le trouvera, pourra le garder. **2.** Qui que + *sub.* **W. you are, speak!** qui que vous soyez, parlez! **W. wrote that letter is a fool,** qui que ce soit qui ait écrit cette lettre, c'est un sot. **3.** *acc.* **W. she marries will be lucky,** celui qu'elle épousera sera heureux.

whole [houl]. **I.** *a.* **1.** *A:* Sain; en bonne santé. (b) (*Of pers.*) Sain et sauf; (*of thg*) intact. **2.** (a) Intégral, -aux; entier, -ière; complet, -ète. **Ox roasted w.,** bœuf rôti entier. **He swallowed it w.,** (i) il l'a avalé sans le mâcher; (ii) *F:* il a pris ça pour de l'argent comptant. *Mth:* **W. number,** nombre entier. **W. length,** longueur totale. **W. leather binding,** reliure pleine peau. (b) **To tell the w. truth,** dire toute la vérité. **The w. world,** le monde entier. **To last a w. week,** durer toute une semaine. **The w. thing is to ...,** le tout est de.... *F:* **The w. lot of you,** vous tous. **W. families died of it,** des familles entières en sont mortes. **II. whole,** *s.* Tout *m*, totalité *f*, ensemble *m.* **The w. of the school,** l'école entière; toute l'école. **Nearly the w. of our resources,** la presque totalité de nos ressources. **The w. amounts to ...,** le total se monte à.... **As a w.,** dans son ensemble; en totalité. **Taken as a w.,** pris dans sa totalité. **On the w.,** à tout prendre; en somme; somme toute. **The work on the w. is good,** dans l'ensemble le travail est bon. **'whole-'hearted.** *See* -HEARTED. **'whole-'hoggism,** *s. F:* Jusqu'au-boutisme *m.* **'whole-'length,** *attrib. a.* (Portrait) en pied. **'whole-'time,** *attrib. a.* = FULL-TIME.

wholemeal ['houlmi:l], *a.* (Pain) complet.

wholesale ['houlseil]. **1.** *s.* (Vente *f* en) gros *m.* **W. and retail,** gros et détail. **2.** *a.* (a) **W. trade,** commerce de gros, en gros. **W. warehouse, firm,** maison *f* de gros. **W. dealer,** grossiste *m.* **W. price,** prix de, en, gros. (b) **A w. slaughter,** une tuerie en masse, un massacre. **3.** *adv.* (Vendre acheter) en gros.

wholesaler ['houlseilər], s. Grossiste m.
wholesome ['houlsəm], a. (Aliment) sain; (air, climat) salubre; (remède) salutaire.
wholesomeness ['houlsəmnis], s. Nature saine (de la nourriture, d'un jeu); salubrité f (du climat).
wholly ['houl(l)i], adv. 1. Tout à fait; complètement, entièrement. 2. Intégralement; en totalité. W. or partly, en tout ou en partie.
whom [hu:m], pron., objective case, used of pers. 1. (Interrogative) Qui? W. did you see? qui avez-vous vu? qui est-ce que vous avez vu? Of w. are you speaking? de qui parlez-vous? W. else? qui d'autre? 2. (Relative) (a) (Direct obj.) Que; lequel, f. laquelle; pl. lesquels, f. lesquelles. The man w. you saw, l'homme que vous avez vu. (b) (Indirect obj. and after prep.) Qui. The beggar to w. you gave a penny, le mendiant à qui vous avez donné deux sous. The two officers between w. she was sitting, les deux officiers entre lesquels elle était assise. The friend of w. I speak, l'ami dont je parle. These two men, both of w. were quite young, ces deux hommes, qui tous deux étaient tout jeunes. 3. Celui que; qui. W. the gods love die young, qui est aimé des dieux meurt jeune.
whomsoever ['hu:msou'evər], pron. Lit: 1. Celui (quel qu'il soit) que . . .; W. they choose will have the right to . . ., celui qu'on choisira aura le droit de . . . . 2. N'importe qui que . . .; qui que ce soit que . . . .
whoop[1] [(h)wu:p]. 1. int. Houp! 2. s. (a) Houp m. Ven: Huée f. (b) Med: Quinte f (de la coqueluche).
whoop[2], v.i. 1. Pousser des "houp". Ven: Huer. 2. Med: Faire entendre la toux convulsive de la coqueluche, le chant du coq. '**whooping-cough**, s. Med: Coqueluche f.
whoopee ['(h)wu:pi:], s. F: To make w., (i) faire la noce, la bombe; (ii) bien s'amuser.
whop [(h)wɔp], v.tr. (whopped) P: (a) Rosser, battre (qn). (b) Battre, rouler (une équipe, etc.). **whopping**. 1. a. F: W. lie, gros mensonge. 2. s. P: Rossée f, raclée f.
whopper ['(h)wɔpər], s. P: 1. Chose énorme. 2. Gros mensonge.
whore[1] [hɔ:r], s.f. Prostituée f; V: putain.
whore[2] [hɔ:r], v.i. V: Putasser; courir la gueuse. **whoring**, s. V: Putasserie f.
whorl [(h)wɔ:r], (h)wə:l], s. 1. Bot: Verticille m. 2. Tour m (d'une spirale); spire f, volute f.
whorled [(h)wɔ:ld, (h)wə:ld], a. Bot: Verticillé. Conch: Turbiné. Arch: etc: Voluté.
whortleberry ['(h)wɔ:tlbəri], s. Airelle f, myrtille f.
whose [hu:z], poss.pron. 1. De qui? (ownership) à qui? W. are these gloves? à qui sont ces gants? W. daughter are you? de qui êtes-vous la fille? W. fault is it? à qui la faute? W. book did you take? quel livre avez-vous pris? 2. (Relative) (a) Dont. The pupil w. work I showed you, l'élève dont je vous ai montré le travail. (b) (After prep.) De qui; duquel, f. de laquelle; pl. desquels, f. desquelles. The man to w. wife I gave the money, l'homme à la femme de qui, duquel, j'ai donné l'argent.
whosoever ['hu:sou'evər], pron. = WHOEVER.
why [(h)wai]. 1. adv. (a) Pourquoi? pour quelle raison? W. didn't you say so? que ne le disiez-vous? il fallait le dire! W. not? pourquoi pas? W. so? pourquoi cela? (b) That is (the reason) w. . . ., voilà pourquoi . . .; c'est ce qui fait que. . . . W. he should always be late I do not understand, qu'il soit toujours en retard, je ne me l'explique pas. 2. s. (pl. whys) Pourquoi m. S.a. WHEREFORE 2. 3. int. W., it's Jones! tiens, mais c'est Jones! W., of course! mais bien sûr! W., you are not afraid, are you? voyons, vous n'avez pas peur? W., what's the matter? mais qu'avez-vous donc?
wick [wik], s. Mèche f (d'une lampe, etc.).
wicked ['wikid], a. 1. (Of pers.) Mauvais, méchant, pervers. 2. (a) (Of temper, etc.) Méchant, dangereux, -euse; (of weather, etc.) très mauvais; affreux, -euse; (of pain) cruel. It's a w. climate, le climat est atroce. (b) Malicieux, -euse, espiègle, fripon, -onne. You w. little thing! petite friponne! -ly, adv. 1. Méchamment. 2. (a) Terriblement, affreusement. (b) Malicieusement.
wickedness ['wikidnis], s. Méchanceté f, perversité f.

wicker ['wikər]. 1. s. = WICKERWORK. 2. Attrib. D'osier, en osier. W. chairs, fauteuils en vannerie.
wickerwork ['wikəwə:k], s. (a) Vannerie f; osier tressé. (b) Fort: etc: Clayonnage m.
wicket ['wikit], s. 1. Guichet m (d'une porte, etc.). 2. (a) (In large door) Porte à piétons. (b) (Into garden, etc.) Petite porte à claire-voie; barrière f. (c) Portillon m (de passage à niveau, etc.). 3. Cr: Guichet. Wickets pitched at twelve o'clock, la partie commence à midi. '**wicket-gate**, s. = WICKET 2. '**wicket-keeper**, s. Cr: Gardien m de guichet, garde-guichet m.
wide [waid]. I. a. 1. Large. To make wider, élargir. The road is twelve feet w., la route a douze pieds de large, de largeur; la route est large de douze pieds. How w. is the room? quelle est la largeur de la pièce? 2. (Of range, etc.) Étendu, vaste, ample. The w. world, le vaste monde. There is a w. difference between . . ., il y a une grande différence entre. . . . In a wider sense, par extension. 3. (a) (Vêtement) ample, large. (b) (Opinions) larges, libérales, sans étroitesse. 4. (a) Éloigné, loin. To be w. of the mark, être loin de compte. S.a. BERTH[1] 1. (b) Cr: W. (ball), balle écartée. 5. P: Retors. -ly, adv. Largement. W. read newspaper, journal très lu, à grande circulation. To be w. read, (i) (of author) avoir un public très étendu; (ii) (of pers.) avoir de la lecture. W. known, très connu. W. held opinion, opinion largement répandue. He has travelled w., il a beaucoup voyagé. W. different versions, versions qui diffèrent du tout au tout. II. wide, adv. 1. Loin. Far and wide, see FAR[1] 1. W. apart, espacé. 2. (Ouvrir, etc.) largement. To fling the door open w., w. open, ouvrir la porte toute grande. W. open eyes, yeux grands ouverts. '**wide-awake**, a. & s. 1. Chapeau m de feutre à larges bords. 2. See AWAKE[2] 1. '**wide-'eyed**, a. Les yeux grands ouverts, en écarquillant les yeux. He looked at me in w.-e. amazement, il m'a regardé les yeux écarquillés par la stupeur. '**wide-'mouthed**, a. 1. (a) (Of pers.) A la bouche grande. (b) (Of receptacle) Évasé. 2. F: (Of pers.) Bouche béante; bouche bée. '**wide-spread**, a. 1. Étendu. 2. Répandu; universel, -elle; général, -aux. W.-s. opinion, opinion largement répandue.
widen ['waidn]. 1. v.tr. (a) Élargir; rélargir; agrandir en large; donner plus d'ampleur à (un vêtement). (b) Évaser (un trou). (c) Étendre (les limites de qch.). To w. the terms of a law, donner plus d'extension aux termes d'une loi. 2. v.i. S'élargir; s'agrandir (en large). The breach is widening, la rupture s'accentue. **widen out**, v.i. S'élargir; s'évaser; s'épanouir.
widgeon ['widʒən], s. Orn: (Canard) siffleur m.
widow ['widou], s.f. Veuve. Mrs Green, w. of (the late) A. B. Green, Mme veuve Green. S.a. GRASS WIDOW.
widowed ['widoud], a. (Homme) veuf; (femme) veuve. She was w. early, elle devint veuve de bonne heure. He lives with his w. mother, il habite avec sa mère qui est veuve.
widower ['widouər], s.m. Veuf.
widowhood ['widouhud], s. Veuvage m.
width [widθ], s. 1. Largeur f; ampleur f (d'un vêtement); grosseur f (d'un pneu). The footpath is four feet in w., le trottoir a quatre pieds de large. 2. Largeur (des vues, d'idées). 3. Tex: Lé m, largeur. Double w., grande largeur.
wield [wi:ld], v.tr. Manier (l'épée, la plume); tenir (le sceptre). To w. power, exercer le pouvoir.
wife, pl. **wives** [waif, waivz], s.f. 1. Femme, épouse. She was his second w., il l'avait épousée en secondes noces. The general's w., (Madame) la générale. The farmer's w., la fermière. F: To take a w., se marier; F: prendre femme. To take s.o. to w., prendre qn pour femme; épouser qn. P: The w., la ménagère, la bourgeoise. 2. A: Femme. The Merry Wives of Windsor, les Joyeuses Commères de Windsor. S.a. FISHWIFE, HOUSEWIFE, MIDWIFE, OLD 1.
wifely ['waifli], a. (Qualités, devoirs) d'épouse, qui conviennent à une femme mariée.
wig [wig], s. (a) Perruque f. (b) Postiche m. '**wig-block**, **-stand**, s. Tête f à perruque; champignon m. '**wig-maker**, s. Perruquier m.

wigged [wigd], *a.* (Juge, etc.) à perruque, portant (une) perruque.

wigging ['wigiŋ], *s.* F: Verte semonce; P: savon *m.* To give s.o. a good w., tancer vertement qn. To get a good w., se faire laver la tête; se faire attraper.

wiggle ['wigl], *v.i. & tr.* (*a*) (Se) tortiller, (se) remuer. F: To w. one's hips, chalouper. (*b*) F: To w. out of sth., se tirer de qch. par des moyens évasifs.

wight [wait], *s.* A: Être *m*, individu *m.*

wigwam ['wigwæm], *s.* Wigwam *m.*

wild [waild], *a.* 1. Sauvage. W. country, pays inculte, sauvage. (*Of plants*) To run w., retourner à l'état sauvage. 2. (*a*) (Vent) furieux, violent; (torrent) impétueux. It was a w. night, c'était une nuit de tempête. (*b*) (Cheval, etc.) farouche, inapprivoisé. W. beast, bête sauvage, F: W. horses wouldn't draw, drag, it out of me, rien au monde ne me le ferait dire. (*c*) (*Of pers.*) Dissipé, dissolu; (*of conduct*) déréglé. To lead a w. life, mener une vie déréglée, F: une vie de patachon, de bâton de chaise. To run w., (i) faire des farces; s'émanciper; (ii) (*of children*) courir en liberté. 3.(*a*) (*Of pers.*) Affolé. W. eyes, yeux égarés. W. with joy, fou, éperdu, de joie. To be w. to do sth., avoir une envie folle de faire qch. It makes, drives, me w., cela me fait rager. F: To be w. with s.o., être furieux contre qn. (*b*) (Idée) fantasque; (projet) insensé; (conjecture) au hasard. W. talk, propos en l'air. W. exaggeration, exagération insensée. 4. *s.pl.* Wilds, région sauvage. To go out into the wilds, pénétrer dans des régions inexplorées, dans la brousse. -**ly**, *adv.* 1. D'une manière extravagante. To talk w., dire des folies. W. inaccurate, complètement inexact. To clap w., applaudir frénétiquement. Her heart was beating w., son cœur battait à se rompre. 2. (Répondre) au hasard, au petit bonheur. '**wild-cat**, *attrib. a.* F: W.-c. scheme, projet dénué de bon sens. W.-c. finance, finance extravagante. W.-c. strike, grève non officielle. '**wild-fowl**, *s.* Coll. (*a*) Gibier *m* à plume. Gibier d'eau, sauvagine *f.* au gibier d'eau. '**wild fowler**, *s.* Chasseur *m.* au gibier d'eau.

wildebeest ['wildibi:st], *s.* Z: Gnou *m.*

wilderness ['wildənis], *s.* Désert *m*; lieu *m* sauvage; pays *m* inculte. To preach in the w., prêcher dans le désert.

wildfire ['waild,faiər], *s.* (*a*) A: Feu grégeois. (*b*) To spread like w., se répandre comme une traînée de poudre.

wilding ['waildiŋ], *s.* 1. Plante *f* sauvage; Arb: sauvageon *m.* 2. Pommier *m* sauvage.

wildness ['waildnis], *s.* 1. État *m* sauvage (d'un pays, d'un animal). 2. (*a*) Fureur *f* (du vent); déchaînement *m* (de la tempête). (*b*) Dérèglement *m* (de mœurs); égarements *mpl* (de conduite). 3. Extravagance *f* (d'idées, de paroles).

wile¹ [wail], *s.* Usu. pl. Ruses *f*, artifices *m*, finasseries *f.*

wile², *v.tr* Séduire, charmer (qn).

wilful ['wilf(u)l], *a.* 1. (*Of pers.*) Entêté, volontaire. 2. (*Of action*) Fait exprès, de propos délibéré, à dessein. Jur: W. murder, homicide volontaire, prémédité. -**fully**, *adv.* 1. Exprès, à dessein, avec intention. 2. Avec entêtement; volontairement.

wilfulness ['wilf(u)lnis], *s.* 1. Obstination *f*, entêtement *m.* 2. Préméditation *f.*

wiliness ['wailinis], *s.* Astuce *f.*

will¹ [wil], *s.* 1. (*a*) Volonté *f.* W. of iron, iron w., volonté de fer. He has a w. of his own, il est volontaire; il veut bien ce qu'il veut. Man lacking strength of w., homme qui manque de caractère. To exercise one's w., faire acte de volonté. The w. to victory, to win, la volonté de vaincre. To take the w. for the deed, accepter l'intention *f* pour le fait. Where there's a w. there's a way, vouloir c'est pouvoir; qui veut la fin veut les moyens. S.a. FREE WILL. (*b*) To work with a w., travailler de bon cœur, avec ardeur, avec courage. 2. (*a*) Décision *f*; volonté. B: Thy w. be done, que ta volonté soit faite. To work one's w. upon s.o., imposer sa volonté à qn. (*b*) Bon plaisir; gré *m.* At w., à volonté; à discrétion. To have one's w., (i) obtenir ce qu'on veut; (ii) (en) faire à sa tête, à sa guise. To do sth. of one's own free w., faire qch. de son plein gré. I did it

against my w., je l'ai fait malgré moi, à contrecœur. To act against s.o.'s w., aller à l'encontre des volontés de qn. 3. Good w., ill w., bonne, mauvaise, volonté. With the best w. in the world, avec la meilleure volonté du monde. S.a. GOODWILL, ILL-WILL. 4. Jur: Testament *m.* The last w. and testament of..., les dernières volontés de.... To make one's w., faire son testament. To mention s.o. in one's w., mettre, coucher, qn sur son testament. '**will-power**, *s.* Volonté *f.* Lack of w.-p., manque *m* de volonté; aveulissement *m.*

will², *v.tr.* (*p.t.* willed [wild]; *p.p.* willed) 1. (*a*) God has willed it so, Dieu l'a voulu ainsi. Fate willed (it) that he should die, le sort voulut qu'il mourût. Those who willed the war, ceux qui ont voulu la guerre. (*b*) To w. s.o. to do, into doing, sth., faire faire qch. à qn par un acte de volonté; (*in hypnotism*) suggestionner qn. 2. Léguer (qch.); disposer de (qch.) par testament. To w. one's property away from s.o., déshériter qn.

will³, *modal aux. v. def.* (*Used only as follows:* I w., thou wilt [wilt], he, we, etc., w.; *p.t. & condit.* would [wud], thou wouldst [wudst] *or* wouldest ['wudəst]) I. Vouloir. 1. (*a*) A: What wilt thou? que désires-tu? What would they? que désirent-ils? (*b*) Do as you w., faites comme vous voudrez, comme vous l'entendrez. What would you have me do? que voulez-vous que je fasse? I would have it understood that..., je voudrais qu'il soit bien entendu que.... Say what you w., you w. not be believed, quoi que vous disiez, vous aurez beau dire, on ne vous croira pas. Look which way you w...., de quelque côté que vous regardiez.... (*c*) (*Optative*) (I) would (that) I were a bird! je voudrais être (un) oiseau! Would to God, would to heaven, it were not true! plût à Dieu, plût au ciel, que cela ne fût pas vrai! 2. (*Consent*) The great 'I w.,' le grand oui. I w. not have it said that..., je ne veux pas qu'on dise que.... He could if he would, il le pourrait s'il le voulait. The wound would not heal, la blessure ne voulait pas se cicatriser. The engine won't start, le moteur ne veut pas démarrer. Just wait a moment, w. you? attendez un instant, voulez-vous? Would you kindly pass the mustard? voudriez-vous s'il vous plaît me passer la moutarde? He w. have none of it, (i) il n'en veut à aucun prix; (ii) il refuse d'en entendre parler. I w. not have it! je ne le veux pas! Won't you sit down? veuillez (donc) vous asseoir. 'W. you hold your tongue! voulez-vous bien vous taire! 3. (*Emphatic*) Accidents 'w. happen, on ne peut pas éviter les accidents. He 'w. have it that I was wrong, il veut absolument que je me sois trompé. He 'w. have his little joke, w. the doctor, il aime à plaisanter, le docteur. I quite forgot!—You 'would (forget)! j'ai oublié!—C'est bien de toi (d'avoir oublié)! 4. (*Habit*) This hen w. lay up to six eggs a week, cette poule pond jusqu'à six œufs par semaine. She would often return home exhausted, elle rentrait souvent très fatiguée. 5. (*Of conjecture*) This w. be your cousin? c'est là sans doute votre cousin? II. will *as an auxiliary forming the future tenses.* 1. (*Still expressing something of the speaker's will. So used in the 1st pers.*) I w. not be caught again, on ne m'y reprendra plus. 2. (*Expressing a simple future. Used in the 2nd and 3rd persons. For the 1st pers. see* SHALL.) (*a*) W. he be there?—He w., y sera-t-il?—Oui (, il y sera). No, he w. not, no, he won't, non (, il n'y sera pas). But I shall starve!—No, you won't, mais je mourrai de faim!—Pas du tout. You won't forget, w. you? vous n'oublierez pas, hein? You w. write to me, won't you? vous m'écrirez, n'est-ce pas? He told me he would be there, il m'a dit qu'il serait là. I don't think he w. come, je ne crois pas qu'il vienne. (*b*) (*Immediate future*) I shall dictate and you w. write, je vais dicter et vous allez écrire. (*c*) (*In injunctions*) You w. be here at three o'clock, soyez ici à trois heures. 3. He would come if you invited him, il viendrait si vous l'invitiez.

willing, *a.* 1. (*a*) De bonne volonté; bien disposé; serviable. A few w. men, quelques hommes de bonne volonté. W. hands, mains empressées. (*b*) Consentant. 2. Used pred. To be w. to do sth., vouloir bien faire qch. W. to oblige, prêt à rendre service;

complaisant. **I am quite w. for him to come,** je veux bien qu'il vienne. **To be able and w.,** avoir à la fois le pouvoir et la volonté. **W. or not,** bon gré mal gré. **God w.,** s'il plaît à Dieu. F: **To show w.,** faire preuve de bonne volonté. -ly, adv. 1. Spontanément; de plein gré. 2. De bon cœur; volontiers.

Will², Pr.n.m. (Dim. of William) Guillaume. 'will-o'-the-'wisp, s. Feu follet.

willed [wild], a. 1. Disposé (à faire qch.). 2. **Strong-willed,** de forte volonté; volontaire.

William ['wiljəm], Pr.n.m. Guillaume. Hist: **W. the Conqueror,** Guillaume le Conquérant.

willingness ['wiliŋnis], s. 1. Bonne volonté. **With the utmost w.,** de très bon cœur. 2. Consentement m.

willow ['wilou], s. 1. Bot: W.(-tree), saule m. **Weeping w.,** saule pleureur. **Water w.,** osier m. 2. Cr: F: **The w.,** la batte. 'willow-bed, s. Saulaie f. 'willow-pattern, s. Cer: Décoration chinoise en teinte bleue à motif de saule pleureur. 'willow-warbler, s. Orn: Pouillot m.

willowy ['wiloui], a. Souple, svelte, élancé.

willy-nilly ['wili'nili], adv. Bon gré mal gré; de gré ou de force.

wilt¹ [wilt], v.i. (a) (Of plant) Se flétrir, se faner. (b) (Of pers.) Dépérir, languir; sécher sur pied.

wilt². See WILL³.

wily ['waili], a. Rusé, astucieux, -euse; malin, -igne; F: ficelle. **He's a w. old bird,** c'est un vieux roublard.

wimple ['wimpl], s. Guimpe f (de religieuse).

win [win], v.tr. & i. (p.t. & p.p. won [wʌn]; pr.p. winning) 1. Gagner; remporter (une victoire). **To w. the prize,** remporter le prix. Rac: **To w. by a length,** gagner d'une longueur. **To w. by a short head,** coiffer d'une tête; gagner de justesse. 2. Acquérir (de la popularité); captiver (l'attention). **To w. glory,** (re)cueillir des lauriers. **To w. a reputation,** se faire une réputation. **This gallant action won him the cross,** cette action d'éclat lui a valu la croix. **To w. s.o.'s love,** se faire aimer de qn. 3. **To w. all hearts,** gagner, conquérir, se concilier, tous les cœurs. 4. **To w. one's way to . . . ,** parvenir à (un endroit). 5. Extraire (le charbon, le minerai). **win back,** v.tr. 1. Reconquérir (from, sur). 2. Regagner (son argent). **win over,** v.tr. Gagner (qn). **To w. o. the audience,** se concilier les auditeurs. **win through,** v.i. Venir à bout de (ses difficultés); parvenir à son but. **winning¹,** a. 1. **W. number,** numéro gagnant; (in lottery) numéro sortant. **W. stroke,** coup décisif. 2. Attrayant, séduisant; (sourire) engageant. **W. manners,** manières avenantes. **winning²,** s. 1. Victoire f (au jeu, etc.); acquisition f (de qch.). **The w. of the war,** le fait d'avoir gagné la guerre. 2. pl. **Winnings,** gains m (au jeu). 'winning-post, s. Turf: Sp: Poteau m d'arrivée.

wince¹ [wins], s. Crispation (nerveuse, de douleur); tressaillement m. **Without a w.,** sans sourciller.

wince², v.i. Faire une grimace de douleur; tressaillir de douleur. **Not to w.,** ne pas sourciller; ne pas broncher.

winch [win(t)ʃ], s. 1. Manivelle f. 2. Treuil m (de hissage). **Hand-w.,** treuil à bras. **Steam w.,** haleur m.

wind¹ [wind], s. 1. Vent m. (a) **The north w.,** le vent du nord; Lit: l'aquilon m, la bise. **A north-east w.,** un vent de nord-est. **High w.,** vent fort, violent. **The w. is high,** il fait grand vent. **To see which way the w. blows,** regarder de quel côté vient le vent. F: **There's something in the w.,** il y a anguille sous roche; il se manigance quelque chose. **To go like the w.,** aller comme le vent. **To sow the w. and reap the whirlwind,** semer le vent et récolter la tempête. P: **To raise the w.,** se procurer de l'argent; battre monnaie. F: **To have, get, the w. up,** avoir le trac, la frousse. P: la trouille. F: **To put the w. up s.o.,** faire une peur bleue à qn. (b) Nau: **Head w.,** vent debout. **To sail, run, before the w.,** courir vent arrière. **To sail with w. and tide,** avoir vent et marée. **In the teeth of the w.,** contre le vent. **To sail into the w.,** venir, aller, au luf. **To sail off the w.,** naviguer vent largue. **To sail on a w.,** close to the w., pincer, serrer, le vent; courir au plus près. F: **To sail close to the w.,** friser l'indécence ou la malhonnêteté. F: **To take the w. out of s.o.'s sails,** déjouer les plans

de qn; couper l'herbe sous le pied de qn. **Between w. and water,** à fleur d'eau. (c) F: Du vent. **These promises are merely w.,** ce sont des promesses en l'air. 2. Ven: **To have the w. of one's game,** avoir le vent de son gibier. F: **To get w. of sth.,** avoir vent de qch.; éventer (un secret). 3. Med: Vent(s); flatuosité f. **To break w.,** lâcher un vent. **To bring up w.,** roter. 4. Souffle m, respiration f, haleine f. **To be in good w., to have plenty of w.,** être en haleine; avoir du souffle. **To get one's second w.,** reprendre haleine. 5. Mus: **The w.,** les instruments m à vent. S.a. WOOD-WIND. 'wind-bound, a. Nau: Retenu par des vents contraires. 'wind-brace¹, s. Const: Contrevent m. 'wind-brace², v.tr. Contreventer. **wind-break,** s. Brise-vent m. 'wind(-)cheater, s. Cost: Blouson m (de golf). 'wind-chest, s. Sommier m (d'un orgue). 'wind-gauge, s. Anémomètre m. 'wind-instrument, s. Mus: Instrument m à vent. 'wind(-)jammer, s. Nau: Grand voilier. 'wind-proof, a. À l'épreuve du vent. 'wind-sail, s. Nau: Manche f à vent, à air (en toile). 'wind-sock, s. Av: Manche f à air, biroute f. 'wind-storm, s. Tempête f de vent; tourbillon m. 'wind(-)swept, a. (Endroit) balayé par le vent, venteux. 'wind-tunnel, s. Tunnel m aérodynamique; soufflerie f.

wind², v.tr. 1. [waind] (p.t. & p.p. **winded** ['waindid] or **wound** [waund]) **To w. the horn,** sonner du cor. 2. [wind] (**winded** ['windid]) (a) (Of hounds) Éventer, flairer (le gibier); avoir vent (du gibier). (b) Couper la respiration, le souffle, à (qn); essouffler (qn, un cheval). (c) Laisser souffler (un cheval). **winded** ['windid], a. 1. Hors d'haleine; essoufflé; à bout de souffle. 2. See LONG-WINDED, SHORT-WINDED.

wind³ [waind], v. (p.t. & p.p. **wound** [waund]) I. v.i. Tourner; faire des détours; (of path, river) serpenter; (of staircase) monter en colimaçon. **The plant winds round the pole,** la plante s'enroule, s'entortille, autour de la perche. **The road winds up, down, the hill,** le chemin monte, descend, en serpentant. II. v.tr. 1. Enrouler. Tex: Dévider (le fil). **To w. the wool into a ball,** enrouler la laine en pelote. **To w. cotton on a reel,** bobiner du coton. Fish: **To w. in the line,** ramener la ligne. 2. **To w. a bobbin,** enrouler le fil sur une bobine. El.E: **To w. a dynamo,** armer une dynamo. 3. **To w. the clock,** remonter l'horloge. 4. Min: Hisser, remonter (le minerai). **wind up. 1.** v.tr. (a) Enrouler (un cordage). (b) Bander (un ressort); remonter (l'horloge). F: (Of pers.) **To be all wound up,** avoir les nerfs en pelote. (c) Terminer (qch.); Com: liquider (une société); régler, clôturer (un compte). **To w. up a meeting,** clore une séance. 2. v.i. (a) F: Finir; terminer. **How does the play w. up?** comment la pièce finit-elle? (b) **The company wound up,** la société se mit en liquidation. **winding¹,** a. (Chemin) sinueux, plein de détours, qui serpente; (route) en lacet. **W. streets,** rues tortueuses. S.a. STAIRCASE. **winding²,** s. 1. Mouvement sinueux; cours sinueux; replis mpl. 2. Tex: Bobinage m. El: Enroulement m, bobinage. S.a. COIL¹. 3. Remontage m (d'une horloge); bandage m (d'un ressort). 4. (a) pl. **Windings,** sinuosités f, replis, méandres m (d'une rivière). (b) Spires fpl, enroulement (d'une bobine). **Armature w.,** enroulement d'induit. 'winding-gear, s. 1. Min: Machine f d'extraction. 2. Treuil m (d'un ascenseur). 'winding-machine, s. El.E: Tex: Bobineuse f. 'winding-plant, s. Chevalement m (de puits de mine). 'winding-shaft, s. Min: Puits m d'extraction. 'winding-sheet, s. Linceul m, suaire m.

windbag ['win(d)bæg], s. 1. Outre f (d'une cornemuse). 2. F: Orateur verbeux. **He's a w.,** il parle pour ne rien dire.

windbreaker ['windbreikər], U.S: R.t.m. Blouson m.

winder ['waindər], s. (a) Tex: Bobinoir m, dévidoir m. (b) Fish: Plioir m. (c) Remontoir m (d'une montre). (d) Aut: Lève-glace(s) m inv (de portière).

windfall ['win(d)fɔ:l], s. 1. (a) A: Bois gisant; chablis m. (b) Fruit abattu par le vent; fruit tombé. 2. Aubaine f; bonne fortune.

windhover ['wind,hɔvər, -,hʌvər], s. Orn: Crécerelle f, émouchet m.

windlass ['windləs], *s.* Treuil *m*, (*on dray, etc.*) pouliot *m*. *Nau:* Guindeau *m*.
windmill ['windmil], *s.* Moulin *m* à vent; (*for pumping*) aéromoteur *m*, éolienne *f*. To tilt at windmills, se battre contre des moulins à vent.
window ['windou], *s.* **1.** (*a*) Fenêtre *f*. To look out of the w., regarder par la fenêtre. To look in at the w., regarder à la fenêtre. Dormer w., fenêtre en mansarde. To break the windows, casser les vitres, les carreaux. *Jur:* To block up the windows, condamner les vues. *F:* You make a better door than a w., tu n'es pas transparent. *S.a.* BOW-WINDOW, FRENCH WINDOW, etc. (*b*) Stained-glass w., verrière *f*; vitrail, -aux *m* (d'église). (*c*) Guichet *m* (d'un bureau de délivrance de billets). (*d*) *Com:* Vitrine *f*, devanture *f*. To put sth. in the w., mettre qch. à l'étalage, en montre. **2.** *Rail: Veh:* Glace *f*. To lower, open, the w., baisser la glace. To raise, close, the w., remonter la glace. *Aut:* Rear w., lunette *f* arrière. Wrap-round rear w., lunette arrière panoramique. **3.** Fenêtre (d'une enveloppe). **'window-box**, *s.* Caisse *f*, bac *m*, à fleurs, jardinière *f*. **'window-display**, *s.* Étalage *m*. **'window-dresser**, *s.* Étalagiste *mf*. **'window-dressing**, *s.* **1.** Art *m* de l'étalage. **2.** *F:* That's all w.-d., tout ça, c'est du camouflage, du truquage, un trompe-l'œil; ce n'est qu'une façade. **'window-envelope**, *s.* Enveloppe *f* à fenêtre, à panneau transparent. **'window-frame**, *s.* Dormant *m*, châssis *m*, de fenêtre; chambranle *m*. **'window-glass**, *s.* Verre à vitres. **'window-ledge**, *s.* Rebord *m*, appui *m*, de fenêtre. **'window-pane**, *s.* Vitre *f*, carreau *m*. **'window-sash**, *s.* Châssis *m* (de fenêtre à guillotine). **'window-seat**, *s.* Banquette *f* (dans l'embrasure d'une fenêtre). **'window-shopping**, *s.* *F:* Lèche-vitrines *m*. To go w.-s., faire du lèche-vitrines. **'window-sill**, *s.* Appui *m*, rebord *m*, tablette *f*, de fenêtre.
windpipe ['windpaip], *s.* *Anat:* Trachée-(artère) *f*; *F:* gosier *m*.
windrow ['windrou], *s.* *Agr:* Andain *m*.
windscreen ['windskri:n], *s.* **1.** (*a*) Abri *m* contre le vent. (*b*) *Hort:* Abat-vent *m inv*, brise-vent *m inv*. **2.** *Aut:* Pare-brise *m inv*. **W. washer**, lave-glace *m*.
windshield ['windʃi:ld], *s.* *Aut: U.S:* Pare-brise *m inv*.
windward ['windwəd]. **1.** *a. & adv.* Au vent. The W. Islands, les îles *f* du Vent. **2.** *s.* Côté *m* au vent. *Nau:* To work to w., louvoyer. To fetch to w., gagner (dans) le vent, au vent. To (the) w. of . . ., au vent de. . . .
windy ['windi], *a.* **1.** Venteux, -euse. W. day, journée de grand vent. It is very w., il fait beaucoup de vent. **2.** (*Of place*) Balayé par le vent; exposé aux quatre vents. **3.** *F:* To keep on the w. side of the law, se tenir hors de l'atteinte de la loi. **4.** (*a*) *Med:* Venteux, -euse, flatueux, -euse. (*b*) *P:* To be w., avoir le trac, la frousse. **5.** *F:* (*Of speech*) Ampoulé, enflé, verbeux, -euse.
wine[1] [wain], *s.* Vin *m*. Dry w., sweet w., vin sec, doux. Dessert w., vin de liqueur. W. in the wood, vin logé. To take (a glass of) w. with s.o., trinquer avec qn. *F:* To be in w., être pris de vin. *Prov:* Good w. needs no bush, à bon vin point d'enseigne. **'wine-bibber**, *s.* *Lit:* Buveur *m*; *F:* sac *m* à vin. **'wine-bin**, *s.* Porte-bouteilles *m inv*. **'wine-butler**, *s.* Sommelier *m*. **'wine-cellar**, *s.* Cave *f* au vin. **'wine-coloured**, *a.* Couleur de vin; lie de vin *inv*; vineux, -euse. **'wine-cooler**, *s.* Seau *m* à frapper; glacière *f*. **'wine-cooper**, *s.* (i) Embouteilleur *m*, (ii) dégustateur *m*, (iii) débitant *m*, de vins. **'wine-glass**, *s.* Verre *m* à vin. **'wine-grower**, *s.* Viticulteur *m*; vigneron *m*. **'wine-growing**[1], *a.* (Région) viticole, vignoble. **'wine-growing**[2], *s.* Viticulture *f*. **'wine-list**, *s.* (*At restaurant*) Carte *f* des vins. **'wine-merchant**, *s.* Négociant *m* en vins; marchand *m* de vins (en gros). **'wine-press**, *s.* Pressoir *m*. **'wine-taster**, *s.* (*a*) (*Pers.*) Dégustateur, -trice, piqueur *m* de vins. (*b*) (*Instrument*) (i) Tasse *f* à déguster; (ii) sonde *f* à vin, tâte-vin *m inv*. **'wine-vault(s)**, *s* (*pl.*) **1.** Cave *f*, caveau *m* (à vin). **2.** Cabaret *m* (en sous-sol). **'wine-waiter**, *s.* Sommelier *m*.
wine[2], *v.tr.* To (dine and) w. s.o., fêter qn.

wing[1] [wiŋ], *s.* **1.** Aile *f*. Fear lent him wings, la peur lui donnait des ailes. To take s.o. under one's w., prendre qn sous son aile, sous sa protection. **2.** Vol *m*, essor *m*. To shoot a bird on the w., tirer un oiseau au vol, à la volée. (*Of bird*) To be on the w., voler. To take w., s'envoler; prendre son vol, son essor. **3.** (*a*) Aile (d'un bâtiment); pavillon *m* (d'un hôpital). (*b*) *Mil.Av:* Escadre (aérienne). **4.** (*a*) Aile (d'un avion, d'une auto, etc.). *Av:* The wings, la voilure. W. area, surface *f* alaire. W. load(ing), charge alaire. (*b*) Oreille *f*, ailette *f* (d'une vis à main). **5.** *Th:* The wings, les coulisses *f.pl.* In the wings, (i) dans la coulisse; (ii) à la cantonade. **6.** *Fb:* (*Pers.*) Ailier *m*. **'wing-beat**, *s.* Coup *m* d'aile. **'wing-case**, *s.* *Ent:* Élytre *m*. **'wing-'chair**, *s.* *Furn:* Fauteuil *m* à oreillettes, bergère *f* à oreilles. **'wing-commander**, *s.* *Mil.Av:* Lieutenant-colonel *m*. **'wing-float**, *s.* *Av:* Ballonnet *m* (d'hydravion). **'wing-rib**, *s.* *Cu:* Côte *f* d'aloyau. **'wing-span**, **-spread**, *s.* Envergure *f*. **'wing-tip**, *s.* *Av:* Bout *m*, extrémité *f*, de l'aile.
wing[2], *v.tr.* **1.** (*a*) Empenner (une flèche). (*b*) *Lit:* Fear winged his flight, la peur lui donnait des ailes. (*c*) (*Of bird*) *Lit:* To w. the air, its way, voler. **2.** Frapper, blesser, (un oiseau) à l'aile. I have winged him, je lui ai mis du plomb dans l'aile. **winged**, *a.* **1.** (*a*) Ailé. *Ven:* W. game, gibier à plume. *Mil:* W. bomb, bombe empennée. (*b*) White-w., aux ailes blanches. **2.** (*Of bird*) To be w., être blessé à l'aile; en avoir dans l'aile.
winger ['wiŋər], *s.* *Fb:* Ailier *m*.
wingless ['wiŋlis], *a.* Sans ailes; aptère.
wink[1] [wiŋk], *s.* Clignement *m* d'œil; clin *m* d'œil. To give the w. to s.o., *F:* to tip so. the w., faire signe de l'œil à qn. With a w., en clignant de l'œil. Without a w. of the eyelid, sans sourciller. *F:* To have forty winks, faire un petit somme; faire une courte sieste.
wink[2]. **1.** *v.i.* (*a*) Cligner les yeux. (*b*) To w. at s.o., cligner de l'œil, faire signe de l'œil, *F:* faire de l'œil, à qn. (*c*) *F:* To w. at an abuse, fermer les yeux sur un abus. (*d*) (*Of light*) Vaciller, clignoter. *Aut:* Winking indicator, clignotant *m*. **2.** *v.tr.* (*a*) To wink one's eye, cligner de l'œil. (*b*) To w. assent, signifier son assentiment par un clin d'œil. **winking**, *s.* Clignement *m* de l'œil. *F:* Like w., en un clin d'œil; en un rien de temps. Easy as w., simple comme bonjour.
winkle ['wiŋkl], *s.* *Moll:* Bigorneau *m*.
winner ['winər], *s.* (*a*) Gagnant, -ante. The w. of the race, le vainqueur de l'épreuve. Every time a w.! à tous les coups l'on gagne! (*b*) *F:* Roman *m*, pièce *f*, à grand succès.
winnow ['winou], *v.tr.* (*a*) Vanner (le grain). (*b*) Éplucher, passer au crible (des témoignages, etc.). To w. (out) the true from the false, séparer, démêler, le vrai d'avec le faux. **winnowing**, *s.* **1.** (*a*) Vannage *m*. W.-basket, van *m*. (*b*) Examen minutieux. **2.** *pl.* Winnowings, vannure *f*. **'winnowing-machine**, *s.* = WINNOWER 2.
winnower ['winouər], *s.* **1.** (*Pers.*) Vanneur, -euse. **2.** (*Machine*) Tarare *m*.
winsome ['winsəm], *a.* Captivant, séduisant.
winter[1] ['wintər], *s.* Hiver *m*. In w., en hiver. W. clothing, vêtements d'hiver. W. resort, station d'hiver. W. visitors, hivernants *m*. W. sports, sports d'hiver. *Mil:* W. quarters, quartiers d'hiver; hivernage *m*. **'winter-time**, *s.* Saison *f* d'hiver. **'winter-'weight**, *a.* (Sous-vêtements, etc.) d'hiver.
winter[2], *v.i.* Hiverner, passer l'hiver (at, à). **wintering**, *s.* Hivernage *m*.
wintergreen ['wintəgri:n], *s.* *Bot:* Gaulthérie *f* du Canada. *Pharm:* Oil of w., essence *f* de wintergreen.
wintry ['wintri], *a.* D'hiver; hivernal, -aux. W. smile, sourire glacial.
wipe[1] [waip], *s.* **1.** (*a*) Coup *m* de torchon, de mouchoir, d'éponge. To give sth. a w., essuyer qch., donner un coup de torchon, etc., à qch. (*b*) *Cin:* (Fermeture en) fondu *m*. **2.** *F:* Tape *f*, taloche *f*. **3.** *P:* Mouchoir *m*; *P:* tire-jus *m*.

wipe², v.tr. **1.** (a) Essuyer. **To w. the blackboard**, passer une éponge sur le tableau. **To w. one's face**, s'essuyer la figure. **To w. one's nose**, se moucher. **To w. one's eyes**, s'essuyer les yeux. **To w. sth. dry**, bien essuyer qch. S.a. FLOOR¹ 1. (b) El.E: **Wiping contact**, contact à frottement. **2.** Plumb: Ébarber (un joint). **3.** v.i. P: **To w. at s.o. with one's stick**, allonger un coup de canne à qn. **wipe away**, v.tr. Essuyer (ses larmes). **wipe off**, v.tr. (a) Enlever, essuyer (une éclaboussure); régler, liquider (une dette). (b) Phot: Essorer (un cliché). **wipe out**, v.tr. (a) Liquider, amortir (une dette); effacer (une injure). **He has wiped out his past**, il a liquidé, racheté, son passé. (b) F: Exterminer, anéantir (une armée, etc.). **wipe up**, v.tr. Nettoyer, enlever (une saleté, etc.). Abs. Essuyer la vaisselle.

wiper ['waipər], s. **1.** Torchon m, tampon m, éponge f. **Windscreen w.**, essuie-glace m. **2.** Mec.E: Came f, mentonnet m; levée f; alluchon m. I.C.E: **Ignition w.**, came d'allumage. **3. W. lubrication**, graissage m par frotteur. **'wiper-shaft**, s. Mec.E: Arbre m à cames.

wire¹ ['waiər], s. **1.** Fil m métallique; F: fil de fer. (a) **Copper w.**, fil de laiton. **Stranded w.**, câble m métallique. **Twin w.**, fil torsadé. **W. mattress**, sommier métallique. **W. brush**, brosse f métallique; carde f. Mil: **W. entanglement**, réseau(x) m(pl) de (fil de fer) barbelé. (b) **Cheese-w.**, fil à couper le beurre. **Telegraph wires**, fils télégraphiques. **Puppet-wires**, ficelles f de marionnettes. F: **To pull the wires**, tirer les ficelles. Aut: **W. of a tyre**, tringle f d'un pneu. S.a. LIVE¹ 2, PIANO-WIRE, etc. **2.** F: Télégramme m, dépêche f. **'wire-cutter**, s. Tls: **1.** Coupe-fil m inv. **2.** (Pair of) **w.-cutters**, pince(s) coupante(s); cisaille(s) f(pl). **'wire-draw**, v.tr. **1.** Metalw: Tréfiler; travailler (un métal) à la filière. **2.** Mch: Étrangler, laminer (la vapeur). **'wire-drawing**, s. Tréfilage m; tréfilerie f. **W.-d. mill**, tréfilerie f. **'wire 'edge**, s. Morfil m, bavure f (d'un outil). **'wire-'gauze**, s. Toile f métallique. **'wire-glass**, s. Verre armé; verre à fil de fer noyé. **'wire-haired**, a. (Chien terrier) à poil dur. **'wire-mark**, s. Paperm: Vergeure f. **'wire-'netting**, s. Treillis m métallique; treillage m en fil de fer. **'wire-puller**, s. F: Intrigant, -ante; meneur. **'wire-pulling**, s. Art m de tirer les ficelles; intrigues fpl. **'wire-strainer**, s. Tendeur m pour fil de fer; raidisseur m. **'wire-tapping**, s. Captage m de messages télégraphiques; écoute f téléphonique. **'wire-wove**, a. (Papier) vergé.

wire², v.tr. **1.** (a) Munir (qch.) d'un fil métallique. (b) Rattacher (une pièce) avec du fil de fer. (c) Monter (des fleurs) sur fil de fer. (d) Grillager (une ouverture). **2.** El.E: Faire l'installation électrique; poser l'électricité (dans une maison). **3.** F: Télégraphier. **wire in. 1.** v.tr. Grillager (un terrain). **2.** v.i. F: S'y mettre de tout son cœur. **To w. into a meal**, abs. to w. in, s'attaquer à un repas. **wire up**, v.tr. El.E: Monter, accoupler (des piles). **wired**, a. **1.** Monté sur fil de fer. **2.** (Of enclosure) Grillagé; clôturé de fils de fer. **wiring**, s. (a) Montage m sur fil de fer. (b) El.E: Pose f de fils électriques; canalisation f. (c) W.Tel: Montage (du poste).

wireless¹ ['waiəlis], a. **1.** a. Sans fil. **2.** s. Télégraphie f, téléphonie f, sans fil, F: radio f. **W. set**, s. F: **wireless**, (poste m de) T.S.F. (f), radio f. **I heard it on the w.**, je l'ai entendu à la T.S.F. S.a. TELEGRAPHY, TELEPHONY.

wireless², v.tr. Envoyer (un message) par la radio.

wirework ['waiəwə:k], s. Tréfilerie f, tréfilage m.

wireworm ['waiəwə:m], s. Ent: Larve f de taupin. F: ver m fil de fer.

wiriness ['waiərinis], s. (a) Raideur f (des cheveux). (b) Vigueur (alliée à un corps sec).

wiry ['waiəri], a. (a) (Of hair) Raide, rude. (b) (Of pers.) Sec et nerveux.

wisdom ['wizdəm], s. Sagesse f. **To have the w. of the serpent**, avoir la prudence du serpent. **W. tooth**, dent de sagesse.

wise¹ [waiz], a. **1.** Sage; prudent; sagace. **The seven w. men**, les sept sages. **The W. Men (of the East)**, les Rois Mages m. **He would be a w. man that could tell**, bien avisé qui saurait le dire. **To grow**

wise(r), (i) s'assagir; (ii) acquérir de l'expérience. S.a. SAD 1, WORD¹ 1. **2.** (a) **To look w.**, prendre un (petit) air entendu. (b) **He is none the wiser (for it)**, il n'en est pas plus avancé. **To do sth. without anyone being the wiser**, faire qch. à l'insu de tout le monde. **If you hold your tongue no one will be any the wiser**, si tu te tais, ni vu ni connu. (c) F: **To get w. to a fact**, saisir un fait. **Put me w. about it**, expliquez-moi ça; mettez-moi au courant. **-ly**, adv. Sagement, prudemment.

wise², s. Manière f, façon f; guise f. **In no w.**, en aucune manière, d'aucune façon; nullement. **In some w.**, de quelque manière. Com: F: **Fashion w.**, du point de vue de la mode.

wiseacre ['waizeikər], s. Prétendu sage; pédant m.

wisecrack ['waizkræk], s. Bon mot.

wish¹ [wiʃ], s. (a) Désir m; vœu m. **He has no wish to go**, il n'a pas envie d'y aller. **Everything succeeds according to his wishes**, tout lui réussit à souhait. **You shall have your w.**, votre désir sera exaucé. (b) Souhait m, vœu m. **To send all good wishes to s.o.**, adresser tous ses vœux de bonheur à qn. **'wish-bone**, s. Lunette f, fourchette f (d'une volaille).

wish². 1. v.ind.tr. **To w. for sth.**, désirer, souhaiter, qch. **To have everything one can w. for**, avoir tout à souhait. **What more can you w. for?** que voudriez-vous de plus? **2.** v.tr. Vouloir. (a) **I do not w. it**, je ne le veux pas; je n'y tiens pas. **To w. to do sth.**, désirer, vouloir, faire qch. (b) **I w. I were in your place**, je voudrais bien être à votre place. **I w. I had seen it!** j'aurais bien voulu voir cela! **I w. I hadn't left so early**, je regrette d'être parti si tôt. **I w. he would come!** que ne vient-il? (c) **It is to be wished that . . .**, il est à souhaiter que. . . . F: **Don't you w. you may get it!** (i) tu peux te fouiller; (ii) je vous en souhaite! F: **It's been wished on me**, c'est une chose que je n'ai pas pu refuser. (d) **He wishes me well**, il est bien disposé envers moi. **He wishes nobody ill**, il ne veut de mal à personne. **To wish s.o. good night**, souhaiter une bonne nuit à qn; dire bonsoir à qn. S.a. JOY. **wishing**, s. Désirs mpl, souhaits mpl.

wishful ['wiʃf(u)l], a. Désireux, -euse (of sth., de qch.). **That's a piece of w. thinking** = c'est prendre ses désirs pour des réalités. **-fully**, adv. Avec désir.

wishy-washy ['wiʃiwɔʃi], a. F: Fade, insipide.

wisp [wisp], s. (a) Bouchon m, poignée f (de paille). (b) Tortillon m (de paille). **W. of smoke**, traînée f de fumée. **W. of hair**, mèche folle. **Little w. of a man**, tout petit bout d'homme.

wist See WIT³.

wistaria, wisteria [wis'tiəriə], s. Bot: Glycine f.

wistful ['wistf(u)l], a. (Regard, air) plein d'un vague désir, d'un vague regret; désenchanté. **W. smile**, (i) sourire désenchanté; (ii) sourire pensif. **-fully**, adv. D'un air songeur et triste; d'un air de regret.

wit¹ [wit], s. **1.** (Often pl.) Esprit m, entendement m; intelligence f. **He has slow wits, quick wits**, il a l'esprit lent, vif. **To be out of one's wits, to have lost one's wits**, avoir perdu l'esprit, la raison. **To collect one's wits**, se ressaisir. **To sharpen s.o.'s wits**, aiguiser l'intelligence de qn; F: dessaler qn. **To have, keep, one's wits about one**, avoir, conserver, toute sa présence d'esprit. **To be at one's wit's end**, ne plus savoir de quel côté se tourner; à quel saint se vouer. **To have a battle of wits**, jouer au plus fin. **To live by one's wits**, vivre d'expédients. **To set one's wits to work to get out of a difficulty**, s'ingénier à se tirer d'affaire. **2.** (Vivacité f d')esprit. **Flash of w.**, trait m d'esprit.

wit², s. (Pers.) Bel esprit; homme m, femme f, d'esprit.

wit³, v.tr. A: (The only parts used are: pr. ind. I wot, thou wottest, he wot; p.t. wist; pr.p. witting) Savoir. Jur: **To w. . . .**, à savoir . . .; c'est-à-dire. . . . **God wot**, en vérité; Dieu sait (comme). **witting**, a. (Of insult, etc.) Fait de propos délibéré. **-ly**, adv. Sciemment; à dessein.

witch [witʃ], s.f. (a) Sorcière. (b) F: **Old w.**, vieille bonne femme (déplaisante). (c) F: Jeune charmeuse; ensorceleuse. **'witch-doctor**, s. Anthr: Sorcier guérisseur.

witching ['witʃiŋ], a. **1.** Enchanteur, -eresse; charmant, séduisant. **2.** Magique. **The w. hour**, l'heure f propice à la sorcellerie.

witchcraft ['witʃkrɑːft], s. Sorcellerie f; magie noire.
witchery ['witʃəri], s. **1.** = WITCHCRAFT. **2.** (a) Ensorcellement m, enchantement m. (b) Fascination f; charme m magique.
witch-hazel ['witʃheiz(ə)l], s. Bot: Hamamélis m.
with [wið], prep. Avec. **1.** (a) (Expressing accompaniment). To travel, work, w. s.o., voyager, travailler, avec qn. He is staying w. friends, il est chez des amis. Is there someone w. you? êtes-vous accompagné? Here I am w. nobody to speak to, je suis là sans personne à qui parler. W. the colours, sous les drapeaux. I shall be w. you in a moment, je serai à vous dans un moment. Question that is always w. us, question qui est toujours d'actualité. (b) Knife w. a silver handle, couteau à manche d'argent. Girl w. blue eyes, jeune fille aux yeux bleus. Child w. a cold, w. measles, enfant enrhumé(e), atteint(e) de rougeole. W. his hat on, le chapeau sur la tête. He came w. his overcoat on, il est venu en pardessus. Have you a pencil w. you? avez-vous un crayon sur vous? W. your intelligence, you will easily understand that . . ., intelligent comme vous l'êtes, vous comprendrez facilement que. . . . (c) W. child, enceinte. (Of animal) W. young, pleine. (d) To leave a child w. s.o., laisser un enfant à la garde de qn, aux soins de qn. This decision rests, lies, w. you, c'est à vous de décider. Ecc: He rests w. God, il repose en Dieu. (e) W. him all men are equal, tous les hommes sont égaux à ses yeux. (f) (In spite of) W. all his faults . . ., malgré tous ses défauts. . . . (g) What will happen to her, w. both her parents dead? que va-t-elle devenir maintenant que son père et sa mère sont morts (tous les deux)? **2.** (Expressing association) (a) To trade w. France, faire du commerce avec la France. To have to deal w. s.o., avoir affaire avec qn. To have nothing to do w. s.o., n'avoir rien à faire avec qn. I can do nothing w. him, je ne peux rien en faire. To be patient w. s.o., être patient avec qn. To be sincere w. oneself, être sincère envers soi-même. It is a habit w. me, c'est une habitude chez moi. To be in favour w. the queen, être en faveur auprès de la reine. The difficulty, w. poetry, is to read it well, le plus difficile, en ce qui concerne la poésie, c'est de bien la lire. (b) I sympathize w. you, je vous plains de tout cœur. I do not agree w. you, je ne suis pas de votre avis. I am w. you there! j'en conviens! F: To be w. it, être dans le vent, le mouvement, à la page. To vote w. a party, voter avec un parti. (c) W. these words he dismissed me, là-dessus, ce disant, il me congédia. (d) To wrestle w. s.o., lutter avec qn. To fight w. s.o., se battre contre qn. **3.** (Dissociation) To part w. sth., se dessaisir, se défaire, de qch. **4.** (Instrument) (a) To cut sth. w. a knife, couper qch. avec un couteau, au couteau. To walk w. (the aid of) a stick, marcher avec une canne. To fight w. swords, se battre à l'épée. To take sth. w. both hands, prendre qch. à deux mains. To look at sth. w. the naked eye, regarder qch. à l'œil nu. To strike w. all one's might, frapper de toutes ses forces. (b) To tremble w. rage, trembler de rage. To be stiff w. cold, être engourdi par le froid. To be ill w. typhoid (fever), être malade de la fièvre typhoïde. (c) To fill a vase w. water, remplir un vase d'eau. It is pouring w. rain, il pleut à verse. **5.** (Forming adv. phr.) To work w. courage, travailler avec courage. To advance w. great strides, (s')avancer à grands pas. To receive s.o. w. open arms, recevoir qn à bras ouverts. W. all due respect, sauf votre respect. W. the object of . . ., dans l'intention de. . . . I say so w. regret, je le dis à regret. W. a few exceptions, à part quelques exceptions; à peu d'exceptions près. **6.** (Elliptical) Away w. care! bannissons les soucis! Down w. the President! à bas le président!
withal [wi'ðɔːl], adv. A: Aussi, en même temps; d'ailleurs, en outre, de plus.
withdraw [wið'drɔː], v. (withdrew [-'druː]; withdrawn [-'drɔːn]) **1.** v.tr. (a) Retirer (sa main); enlever (un étai). (b) Ramener (des troupes) en arrière; faire replier (des troupes). To w. s.o. from an influence, soustraire qn à une influence. (c) To w. coins from circulation, retirer des pièces de la circulation. To w. (a sum of) money, retirer une somme d'argent (de la caisse d'épargne, etc.). (d) Retirer (une offre, une promesse); reprendre (sa parole); revenir sur

(une décision); renoncer à (une réclamation). To w. a charge, se rétracter. To w. an order, Com: annuler une commande; Adm: rapporter un décret. Jur: To w. an action, abandonner un procès; retirer sa plainte. **2.** v.i. Se retirer (from, de); s'éloigner. Mil: (Of outposts) Se replier. (Of candidate) To w. in favour of s.o., se désister en faveur de qn. To w. into oneself, into silence, se renfermer en soi-même, dans le silence.
withdrawal [wið'drɔːəl], s. **1.** (a) Retrait m (de troupes, d'une somme d'argent). W. of capital, retrait de fonds. (b) Rappel m (d'un décret); rétractation f (d'une promesse); retrait (d'une plainte). (c) Med: W. symptoms, symptômes m d'abstinence. **2.** (a) Retraite f. Mil: Repli m, repliement m, reploiement m. (des troupes). (b) W. of a candidate, désistement m d'un candidat.
withe ['wiði, wið, waið], s. Brin m d'osier; hart f.
wither ['wiðər], **1.** v.i. To w. (up, away), (of plant) se dessécher, se faner; (of flowers, beauty) passer; (of pers.) dépérir. **2.** v.tr. (a) Dessécher, flétrir, faner, faire dépérir (une plante, etc.). (b) To w.s.o. with a look, foudroyer qn du regard. Withered arm, bras atrophié.
withering[1], a. (a) Qui dessèche, qui flétrit; (vent) desséchant. (b) (Regard) foudroyant, écrasant. **-ly**, adv. D'un regard foudroyant; d'un ton de mépris.
withering[2], s. Desséchement m; flétrissement m.
withers ['wiðəz], s.pl. Garrot m (du cheval).
withershins ['wiðəʃinz], adv. Scot: A contre-sens; de droite à gauche.
withhold [wið'hould], v.tr. (withheld [-'held]; withheld) (a) Refuser (son consentement) (from s.o., à qn). (b) To w. the truth from s.o., cacher la vérité à qn. (c) To w. property, détenir des biens.
within [wi'ðin]. **1.** adv. (a) A. & Lit: A l'intérieur; dans la maison, chez soi. Ecc: Make me pure w., purifiez mon âme, mon cœur. (b) Th: A la cantonade. (c) Seen from w., vu de l'intérieur, du dedans. **2.** prep. (a) A l'intérieur de, en dedans de. W. four walls, entre quatre murs. Within the frontier, en deçà des frontières. He thought w. himself that . . ., il pensait dans son for intérieur que. . . . W. the committee, au sein de la commission. (b) To keep w. the law, rester dans les bornes de la légalité; se tenir dans les marges du code. To come w. the provisions of the law, tomber sous le coup de la loi. To keep, live, w. one's income, ne pas dépenser plus que son revenu. W. reason, dans des limites raisonnables. To be well w. the truth, être en deçà, au-dessous, de la vérité. Weight w. a pound, poids à une livre près. (c) W. sight, en vue. W. call, à (la) portée de la voix. Situated w. two miles of the town, situé à moins de deux milles de la ville. W. a radius of ten miles, dans un rayon de dix milles. W. an inch of death, à deux doigts de la mort. (d) W. an hour, dans, avant, une heure, en moins d'une heure. W. the week, avant la fin de la semaine, dans la semaine. W. a year of his death, (i) moins d'un an avant sa mort; (ii) moins d'un an après sa mort. W. the next five years, d'ici cinq ans. W. the required time, dans le délai prescrit. W. a short time, (i) à court délai; (ii) peu de temps après. They are w. a few months of the same age, ils sont du même âge à quelques mois près. Within living memory, de mémoire d'homme.
without [wi'ðaut]. **1.** adv. A. & Lit: A l'extérieur, au dehors. Seen from w., vu de l'extérieur, du dehors. **2.** prep. (a) A. & Lit: En dehors de. W. the walls, hors des murs. (b) Sans. To be w. friends, être sans amis. To be w. food, manquer de nourriture. He arrived w. money or luggage, il arriva sans argent ni bagages. Not w. difficulty, non sans difficulté. W. end, sans fin. Ecc: World w. end, pour les siècles des siècles. He passed by w. seeing me, without being seen, il passa sans me voir, sans être vu. It goes w. saying that . . ., il va sans dire que. . . . That goes w. saying, cela va sans dire. A year never passes w. his writing to us, il ne se passe jamais une année sans qu'il nous écrive. To go, do, w. sth., se passer de qch.
withstand [wið'stænd], v.tr. (withstood [-'stud]; withstood) Résister à (qn, la douleur). To w. pressure, supporter, résister à, la pression. Mil: To w. an attack, soutenir une attaque.
withy ['wiði], s. **1.** Osier m. **2.** = WITHE.

witless ['witlis], *a.* (*a*) Sans intelligence; sot, *f.* sotte. (*b*) Imbécile; faible d'esprit.

witness[1] ['witnis], *s.* 1. Témoignage *m.* **To bear w. to, of, sth.,** rendre, porter, témoignage de qch.; témoigner de qch.; attester qch. *Jur:* In w. whereof, en témoignage de quoi, en foi de quoi. **I call you to w.,** j'en appelle à votre témoignage, je vous prends à témoin. 2. (*Pers.*) (*a*) Témoin *m* (d'un incident). (*b*) **W. to a document,** témoin à un acte. (*c*) Témoin judiciaire. **W. for the defence, for the prosecution,** témoin à décharge, à charge. **To call s.o. as a w.,** citer qn comme témoin. 3. **They are not all stay-at-homes; w. the three brothers who went to America,** ils ne sont pas tous casaniers; témoin les trois frères qui sont allés en Amérique. **'witness-box,** *s. Jur:* = Barre *f* des témoins.

witness[2]. 1. *v.tr.* (*a*) Être spectateur, témoin (d'une scène); assister à (une entrevue, etc.). (*b*) Attester (un acte); certifier (une signature). 2. *v.i.* **To w. to sth.,** témoigner de qch. **To w. against s.o.,** témoigner contre qn.

-witted ['witid], *a.* **Slow-w., quick-w.,** à l'esprit lourd, vif.

witticism ['witisizm], *s.* Trait *m* d'esprit; bon mot.

wittiness ['witinis], *s.* Esprit *m*; sel *m* (d'une observation, etc.).

wittingly ['witiŋli]. *See* WIT[3].

witty ['witi], *a.* (*Of pers.*) Spirituel, -elle; (*of remark*) spirituel, piquant. **-ily,** *adv.* Spirituellement; avec esprit.

wives. *See* WIFE.

wizard ['wizəd], *s.* Sorcier *m*, magicien *m. a. F:* Épatant, excellent, chic, *P:* au poil.

wizardry ['wizədri], *s.* Sorcellerie *f*, magie *f*.

wizened ['wiz(ə)nd], *a.* Desséché, ratatiné; (*of cheeks, etc.*) parcheminé; (*of face*) vieillot.

wo [wou], *int.* (*To horse*) Ho!

woad [woud], *s.* 1. *Bot:* (**Dyer's**) **w.,** pastel *m* des teinturiers; guède *f.* 2. Guède; teinture bleue.

wobble[1] ['wobl], *s.* (*a*) Branlement *m*, oscillation *f*; tremblement *m; Rail: Av: A:* (mouvement de) lacet (*m*). *Aut:* **Front-wheel w.,** dandinement *m*, shimmy *m.* (*b*) (*Of singer*) Chevrotement *m*.

wobble[2], *v.i.* 1. (*a*) Ballotter; brimbaler; (*of pers. or car in motion*) zigzaguer, tanguer; (*of pers.*) tituber; (*of jelly, etc.*) trembler; (*of table*) branler. (*b*) (*Of voice*) Chevroter. 2. *F:* (*Of pers.*) Hésiter, vaciller. **wobbling,** *s.* = WOBBLE[1].

wobbler ['woblər], *s.* Tergiversateur, -trice; personne *f* sans opinions stables.

wobbly ['wobli], *a.* Branlant, vacillant; hors d'aplomb. **W. chair,** chaise bancale. **W. voice,** voix tremblante, chevrotante. **My legs are w.,** mes jambes flageolent, *F:* j'ai les jambes en coton.

wodge [wodʒ], *s. F:* Gros morceau.

woe [wou], *s.* Malheur *m*, chagrin *m*, peine *f.* **To tell one's tale of w.,** faire le récit de ses malheurs, de ses infortunes; conter ses doléances. *O:* **W. is me!** pauvre de moi! **'woe-begone,** *a.* (*Of looks*) Triste, désolé, abattu; (*of pers.*) à l'air désolé, abattu.

woeful ['wouful], *a. O:* 1. (*Of pers.*) Triste, affligé, malheureux, -euse. 2. (*Époque*) de malheur, de misère; (nouvelle) déplorable, attristante. **-fully,** *adv.* Tristement.

wog [wog], *s. P: Pej:* Levantin *m*; Égyptien *m*; Arabe *m, P:* bico(t) *m; P:* bougnoule *m*.

woke. *See* WAKE[3].

wold [would], *s.* Région onduleuse, vallonnée. **The Wolds,** les régions vallonnées (du comté d'York, etc.).

wolf[1], *pl.* **wolves** [wulf, wulvz], *s.* 1. Loup *m.* **She-wolf,** louve *f.* **Wolf('s) cub,** louveteau *m.* **Prairie w.,** coyote *m.* **To cry w.,** crier au loup. **To have the w. by the ears,** tenir le loup par les oreilles. **That will keep the w. from the door,** cela vous mettra à l'abri du besoin. **A w. in sheep's clothing,** un loup déguisé en brebis. 2. *F:* Tombeur *m* (de femmes). **'wolf-cub,** *s.m. Scouting:* Louveteau. **'wolf-dog, 'wolf-hound,** *s.* Chien *m* de chasse au loup; *esp.* lévrier *m* d'Irlande. **'wolf's-bane,** *s. Bot:* Aconit *m.* **wolf-whistle,** *s. F:* Sifflement admiratif (au passage d'une jolie femme).

wolf[2], *v.tr.* **To w. (down) one's food,** avaler sa nourriture à grosses bouchées, bâfrer.

wolfish ['wulfiʃ], *a.* De loup; rapace, vorace, cruel.

wolfram ['wulfrəm], *s.* (*a*) *Miner:* Wolfram *m.* (*b*) Tungstène *m*.

wolverine ['wulvəri:n], *s. Z:* Glouton *m*.

wolves. *See* WOLF[1].

woman, *pl.* **women** ['wumən, 'wimin], *s.f.* 1. Femme. **A young w.,** une jeune femme; une jeune personne. **An old w.,** une vieille femme; une vieille. *P:* **The old w.,** la bourgeoise. **There's a w. in it,** cherchez la femme. **To be always (running) after women,** courir les filles, *F:* courir la gueuse. 2. *attrib.* **W. doctor,** *pl.* **woman doctors,** *or* **women doctors,** femme médecin. **W. friend,** amie. 3. **Apple-woman, 'woman-hater,** *etc.* **W.** Misogyne *m*.

womanhood ['wumənhud], *s.* 1. État *m*, qualité *f*, de femme. **She had now grown to w.,** c'était maintenant une femme (faite). 2. *Coll.* Les femmes.

womanish ['wuməniʃ], *a.* Efféminé.

womankind ['wumənkaind], *s. Coll:* Les femmes *f*.

womanlike ['wumənlaik]. 1. *a.* De femme. 2. *adv.* En femme; comme une femme.

womanliness ['wumənlinis], *s.* (*a*) Caractère *m* de femme; caractère féminin; féminité *f.* (*b*) Charme féminin.

womanly ['wumənli], *a.* De femme, des femmes; féminin. **She is so w.,** elle est si femme.

womb [wu:m], *s. Anat:* Matrice *f.* **In the w. of the earth,** dans le sein, dans les entrailles, de la terre.

wombat ['wombæt], *s. Z:* Phascolome *m*.

women. *See* WOMAN.

womenfolk ['wiminfouk], *s.pl. F:* **My w.,** mes femmes, les femmes de ma famille.

won. *See* WIN.

wonder[1] ['wʌndər], *s.* 1. Merveille *f*, prodige *m.* **To work, do, wonders,** faire, accomplir, des merveilles, des prodiges; faire merveille. **To promise wonders,** promettre monts et merveilles. **The seven wonders of the world,** les sept merveilles du monde. **A nine-days' w.,** la merveille d'un jour. **It is a w. (that) he has not lost it,** il est étonnant, c'est miracle, qu'il ne l'ait pas perdu. **The w. is that he found it,** ce qu'il y a d'étonnant c'est qu'il l'ait retrouvé. **No w., little w., that the scheme failed,** il n'est guère étonnant que la chose n'ait pas réussi. **For a w. he was in time,** par extraordinaire, il était à l'heure. **He is ill, and no w.,** il est malade, et rien d'étonnant. 2. (*a*) Étonnement *m*, surprise *f.* (*b*) Émerveillement *m.* **To fill s.o. with w.,** émerveiller qn; étonner qn. 3. *attrib.a. F:* **W. product,** produit merveilleux *a. inv.*

wonder[2]. 1. *v.i.* S'étonner, s'émerveiller (at, de). **I don't w. at it,** cela ne m'étonne pas, ne me surprend pas. **That isn't to be wondered at,** ce n'est pas étonnant; rien d'étonnant à cela. **I shouldn't w.,** cela ne m'étonnerait pas. **That set me wondering,** cela m'a intrigué. 2. *v.tr.* (*a*) **I w. he didn't kill you,** je m'étonne qu'il ne vous ait pas tué. (*b*) Se demander. **I w. whether he will come,** je me demande s'il viendra. **I w. why!** Je voudrais bien savoir pourquoi! **I w. who invented that,** je suis curieux de savoir qui a inventé cela. *Abs.* **Their son will help them.—I w.!** leur fils leur viendra en aide.—Est-ce bien sûr? **Are you going out tonight?—Why?—I just wondered,** Sortez-vous ce soir?—Pourquoi?—Oh, pour rien! **One wonders!** sait-on jamais! **wondering,** *a.* Étonné, émerveillé. **-ly,** *adv.* D'un air étonné; avec étonnement.

wonderful ['wʌndəf(u)l], *a.* Merveilleux, -euse, prodigieux, -euse, admirable. **W. to relate . . .,** chose étonnante, chose remarquable. . . . **We had a w. time,** nous nous sommes rudement bien amusés. **It was w.!** *F:* c'était épatant! **-fully,** *adv.* Merveilleusement. **W. well,** à merveille.

wonderland ['wʌndəlænd], *s.* Pays *m* des merveilles.

wonderment ['wʌndəmənt], *s.* Étonnement *m*; ébahissement *m*.

wondrous ['wʌndrəs], *a. Lit:* Étonnant; merveilleux, -euse. **W. dexterity,** dextérité prestigieuse. **-ly,** *adv.* Merveilleusement. **W. well,** à merveille.

wonky ['wɔŋki], *a. F:* (*a*) Branlant. (*b*) Patraque.

wont[1] [wount], *pred.a. Lit:* **To be w. to do sth.,** avoir coutume, avoir l'habitude, de faire qch.

wont², s. *Lit:* Coutume f, habitude f. **Use and w.,** l'usage m; les us m et coutumes. **It is my w. to . . .,** c'est mon habitude de. . . . **Oftener than was his w.,** plus souvent que d'habitude, que de coutume.

wont³, *aux.v.* (*p.t.* wont; *p.p.* wont *or* wonted) A: **To w. to do sth.,** avoir coutume, avoir l'habitude, de faire qch. **wonted,** a. *Lit:* Habituel, -elle, accoutumé.

won't [wount]. F: = will not.

woo [wu:], *v.tr.* 1. *O:* Faire la cour à, courtiser (une femme); rechercher (une femme) en mariage. 2. *O:* Rechercher, courtiser (la fortune). 3. Solliciter (s.o. to do sth., qn de faire qch.). **wooing,** s. *O:* Cour f; recherche f en mariage.

wood [wud], s. 1. Bois m; *For:* peuplement m. **Pine w.,** bois de pins. **You can't see the w. for the trees,** les arbres empêchent de voir la forêt. **We are not yet out of the w.,** nous ne sommes pas encore tirés d'affaire. **To take to the woods,** s'enfuir, se sauver; (*of animals*) gagner le taillis. **W. anemone,** anémone f des bois. 2. (*Material*) Bois. **W. shavings,** copeaux mpl. **W. pavement,** pavé de bois. **W. ash,** cendre de bois. F: **Touch w.!** touchons du bois! F: **He's w. from the neck up,** il est bouché à l'émeri. 3. *Wine-m:* **The w.,** le tonneau, la pièce, le fût. **Wine in the w.,** vin en fût. **Beer (drawn) from the w.,** bière tirée au fût. 4. *Bowls:* Boule f. 5. = WOOD-WIND. **'wood-'block,** s. 1. *Engr:* Planche f, bois m. 2. Pavé m de bois. **'wood-carving,** s. Sculpture f sur bois. **'wood-cutter,** s. Bûcheron m. **'wood-cutting,** s. 1. Coupe f des bois. 2. Gravure f sur bois. **'wood-engraver,** s. Graveur m sur bois. **'wood-engraving,** s. (*Process or print*) Gravure f sur bois. **'wood-lark,** s. *Orn:* (Alouette f) lulu (m); alouette des bois. **'wood-louse,** pl. -lice, s. Cloporte m; F: porcelet m. **'wood-nymph,** s.f. Nymphe des bois; hamadryade; dryade. **'wood-pigeon,** s. *Orn:* (Pigeon m) ramier m; palombe f. **'wood-pile,** s. Tas m, monceau m, de bois. S.a. NIGGER. **'wood-pulp,** s. *Paperm:* Pâte f de bois. **'wood-sorrel,** s. *Bot:* (Oxalis f) petite oseille, F: pain m de coucou. **'wood-spirit,** s. Alcool m méthylique. **'wood-stack,** s. = WOOD-PILE. **'wood-wind** [-wind], s. *Mus:* Les bois m.

woodbine ['wudbain], s. *Bot:* (a) Chèvrefeuille m des bois. (b) *U.S:* Vigne f vierge.

woodchuck ['wudtʃʌk], s. Marmotte f d'Amérique.

woodcock ['wudkɔk], s. (*Usu. inv.*) Bécasse f.

woodcraft ['wudkrɑ:ft], s. Connaissance f (i) de la forêt, (ii) de la chasse à courre.

woodcraftsman, pl. -men ['wudkrɑ:ftsmən], s.m. Trappeur; veneur.

woodcut ['wudkʌt], s. Gravure f sur bois; F: bois m; estampe f.

wooded ['wudid], a. Boisé.

wooden ['wud(ə)n], a. 1. De bois, en bois. *Dom.Ec:* **W. spoon,** mouvette f; cuillère f à ragoût. **Wooden shoes,** sabots m. 2. F: (*Of movement, etc.*) Raide, gauche. (b) Sans intelligence; à l'esprit obtus. **'wooden-'headed,** a. Stupide.

woodenness ['wudnnis], a. (a) Maintien compassé; raideur f. (b) Stupidité f.

woodland ['wudlənd], s. 1. Pays boisé; bois m. 2. attrib. Des bois; sylvestre.

woodman, pl. -men ['wudmən], s.m. Bûcheron.

woodpecker ['wudpekər], s. *Orn:* Pic m. **Green w.,** pivert m.

woodruff ['wudrʌf], s. *Bot:* Aspérule odorante, F: reine f des bois.

woodshed ['wudʃed], s. Bûcher m. F: **There's something nasty in the w.,** il se passe du vilain.

woodsman, pl. -men ['wudzmən], s.m. *Esp: U.S:* Chasseur (en forêt); trappeur; homme des bois.

woodwork ['wudwɔ:k], s. 1. Travail m du bois. (a) Construction f en bois; charpenterie f. (b) Menuiserie f, ébénisterie f. 2. Bois travaillé. (a) Boiserie f, charpente f. (b) Menuiserie, ébénisterie.

woody ['wudi], a. 1. Boisé. 2. *Bot:* Ligneux, -euse.

wooer ['wu:ər], s. *O:* Amoureux m; prétendant m.

woof [wu:f], s. = WEFT 1.

wool [wul], s. 1. Laine f. (a) **Waste w.,** ploc m. *Tex:* **Dyed in the w., w. dyed,** teint en laine. F: **A dyed-in-the-wool conservative,** un conservateur intransigeant. F: **Keep your w. on!** ne te fâche pas! F: **To**

pull the w. over s.o.'s eyes, donner le change à qn. **The w. trade,** le commerce des laines. **W. mill,** fabrique f de lainages. (b) **Knitting w.,** laine à tricoter. **Crochet w.,** laine perlée. 2. (a) Pelage m (d'animal). (b) *Bot:* Laine, duvet m. (c) Cheveux crépus, laine (des nègres). 3. **Mineral w.,** laine minérale; laine de laitier. **Steel w.,** paille f de fer. S.a. COTTON¹ 1, GLASS-WOOL. **'wool-bearing,** a. Lanifère. **'wool-fat,** s. 1. Suint m. 2. *Com:* Lanoline f. **'wool-fell,** s. Peau f de mouton. **'wool-gathering,** F: (a) s. Rêvasserie f. (b) a. & v. Distrait. **Your wits have gone w.-g.,** you're w.-g., vous rêvassez; F: vous êtes dans la lune. **You've been w.-g.,** vous avez l'air de revenir de Pontoise. **'wool-grower,** s. Éleveur m de moutons (pour la laine). **wool-merchant,** s. Lainier m. **'wool-waste,** s. Bourre f de laine.

woollen ['wulən], a. De laine. **W. stockings,** bas de laine. **W. cloth,** drap m. **W. goods,** s. woollens, lainages m.

woolliness ['wulinis], s. 1. Nature laineuse (of, de). 2. F: Imprécision f (de raisonnement, etc.); manque m de netteté. **W. of outline,** flou m.

woolly ['wuli]. 1. a. (a) Laineux, -euse; de laine. F: **W. hair,** cheveux laineux, crépus. **W. clouds,** nuages ouatés. (b) (*Of fruit*) Cotonneux, -euse. F: **Wild and w.,** rude, mal léché; hirsute. (c) (*Of style*) Mou, f. molle; lâche. **W. outlines,** contours flous, gras. *W.Tel:* **W. reproduction,** reproduction peu nette. (d) F: Vaseux, -euse. **W. thoughts,** pensées vaseuses. 2. s. (Vêtement m en) tricot m. F: **Winter woollies,** sous-vêtements chauds d'hiver. F: **Put on your w.!** mets ta laine. **'woolly-'bear,** s. *Ent:* F: Hérissonne f.

woolsack ['wulsæk], s. 1. Sac m de laine. 2. *Parl:* **The Woolsack,** le siège du Lord Chancelier.

woolwork ['wulwɔ:k], s. Tapisserie f.

wop [wɔp], s. P: *Pej:* Italien m., P: macaroni m.

word¹ [wɔ:d], s. 1. Mot m. (a) Vocable m. **W. for w.,** (répéter qch.) mot pour mot; (traduire qch.) mot à mot. **In a w.,** en un mot; bref; pour tout dire. **In other words,** en d'autres termes; autrement dit. **I told him in so many words that . . ,** je lui ai dit expressément que. . . . **Bad is not the w. for it,** mauvais n'est pas assez dire. (b) **Spoken words,** paroles f. **Song without words,** romance sans paroles. **In the words of . . .,** selon (l'expression) de. . . . **To put a wish into words,** formuler un souhait. **To call upon s.o. to say a few words,** prier qn de prendre la parole. **A man of few words,** un homme qui parle peu, un homme sobre de paroles. **He never said a w.,** il n'a pas soufflé mot. **I can't get a w. out of him,** je ne peux en tirer un mot. **To put one's w. in,** intervenir; placer son mot. **Without a w.,** sans mot dire. **With these words he dismissed me,** ce disant, là-dessus, il me congédia. **You have taken the words out of my mouth,** c'est justement ce que j'allais dire. **Conduct beyond words,** conduite inqualifiable, qui n'a pas de nom. **He is too silly for words,** il est d'une bêtise indicible. **Fair words, fine words, belles paroles;** F: eau bénite (de cour). S.a. LAST² 1. 1. (c) **I want (to have) a w. with you,** j'aurais un mot à vous dire. **I'll have a w. with him about it,** je lui en toucherai deux mots. **To put in a good w. for s.o.,** dire, glisser, un mot en faveur de qn. **He never has a good w. for anyone,** il ne peut s'empêcher de dire du mal de son prochain. **A w. in season,** un conseil opportun. *Prov:* **A w. to the wise (is sufficient),** à bon entendeur salut. (d) F: **To have words with s.o.,** avoir une altercation avec qn; se disputer avec qn. **Words passed between them,** ils ont eu une dispute. **Words ran high,** la querelle s'échauffait. 2. (*Speech*) **In w. or in thought,** par la parole ou par la pensée. **By w. of mouth,** vive voix; verbalement. 3. **To send s.o. w. of sth.,** faire dire, faire savoir, qch. à s.o.; prévenir qn de qch. **W. came that . . .,** on apporta la nouvelle que. . . **To bring w. of sth. to s.o.,** venir dire qch. à qn. **To leave w. that . . ,** faire dire (à qn . . . 4. **To give s.o. one's w.,** donner sa parole à qn. **To keep one's w., to be as good as one's w.,** tenir (sa) parole. **To break one's w.,** manquer à sa parole. **I give you my w. for it,** (you may) take my w. for it, croyez-m'en; je vous en réponds. **I take your w. for it,** j'en crois votre parole; je m'en rapporte à vous.

He is a man of his w., c'est un homme de parole. To take s.o. at his w., prendre qn au mot. His w. is as good as his bond, sa parole vaut sa signature; il n'a qu'une parole. Upon my w.! ça c'est trop fort! ça c'est raide! My w.! fichtre! 5. W. of command, ordre m, commandement m. To give the w. (to do sth.), (i) donner l'ordre, (ii) donner le signal (de faire qch.). The w. has gone round, on s'est donné le mot. F: Sharp's the w.! (faites) vite! 6. Theol: (a) The W. of God, la parole de Dieu. (b) The W. was made flesh, le Verbe s'est fait chair. 'word-book, s. Vocabulaire m, lexique m. 'word-'perfect, a. Qui connaît parfaitement son rôle, sa leçon. 'word-picture, s. Description imagée. 'word-play, s. Jeu m sur les mots, jeu de mots.

word², v.tr. Formuler par écrit; énoncer (un problème); rédiger (un télégramme); libeller (un document) Thus worded, ainsi conçu. Well worded, bien exprimé. wording, s. 1. Rédaction f, libellé m (d'un document); énoncé m (d'un problème). 2. Mots mpl; langage m; termes mpl (d'un acte, etc.). Form of w. for a cheque, formule f de chèque.

wordiness ['wə:dinis], s. Verbosité f.

wordy ['wə:di], a. 1. Verbeux, -euse, prolixe, diffus; (style) délayé. 2. W. warfare, lutte f oratoire.

wore. See WEAR².

work¹ [wə:k], s. 1. Travail m. To be at w., être au travail; travailler. He was hard at w., il était en plein travail. They were hard at w. ploughing, gardening, ils étaient en plein labour, en plein jardinage. The forces at w., les forces en jeu. To set to w., se mettre au travail, à l'œuvre, à l'ouvrage. To set s.o. to w., mettre qn à l'ouvrage. To set a machine to w., mettre une machine en marche. To go the right way to w., s'y prendre bien. The w. is suspended, on a suspendu les travaux. 2. (Work to be done) (a) Travail, ouvrage m, besogne f, tâche f. I have so much w. to do, j'ai tellement (de travail) à faire. To have plenty of w. to do, avoir du pain sur la planche. A piece of w., un travail, un ouvrage, une œuvre. The brandy had done its w., l'eau-de-vie avait fait son effet. I have my w. cut out, j'ai de quoi faire. You have your w. cut out with him, il vous donnera du fil à retordre. To do s.o.'s dirty w., faire les sales besognes de qn. Day's w., (travail d'une) journée. F: It's all in a day's w., c'est l'ordinaire de mon existence. (b) It was bloody w., ç'a été une sanglante affaire. It was thirsty w., c'était un travail qui donnait soif. S.a. SHORT¹ I. 2. 3. (a) The works of God, les œuvres f de Dieu. Good works, (les) bonnes œuvres. (b) Ouvrage, œuvre. A(n) historical work, un ouvrage historique. The works of Shakespeare, les œuvres f de Shakespeare; l'œuvre m de Shakespeare. A w. of art, une œuvre d'art. (c) F: (All) the works, tout le fourbi, tout le bataclan. P: To give s.o. the works, (i) battre, tabasser qn; (ii) tuer qn; (iii) passer qn à tabac. 4. To be out of w., être sans travail, sans emploi; chômer. To throw s.o. out of w., priver qn de travail; réduire qn au chômage. 5. pl. Mil: Defensive works, ouvrages défensifs. Field works, travaux de campagne. 6. pl. Civ.E: Constructive works, ouvrages d'art. Public works, travaux publics. P.N: Road works ahead! (attention,) travaux! attention, chantier! 7. pl. Rouages mpl, mécanisme m, mouvement m (d'une horloge). 8. pl. (Often with sg. const.) Usine f, atelier m. Dye-works, teinturerie f. Steelworks, aciérie f. Works committee, comité d'entreprise. Com: pl. Ex works, pris à l'usine. 9. Chased w., ouvrage ciselé. Stucco w., ouvrage de stuc. 10. Nau: Upper works, œuvres mortes, le(s) haut(s). 'work-bag, s. Sac m à ouvrage. 'work-basket, s. Corbeille f, nécessaire m, à ouvrage. 'work-bench, s. Établi m. 'work-box, s. Boîte f à ouvrage. 'work-day, s. Jour m ouvrable. 'work-room, s. (a) Atelier m. (b) (For needlework) Ouvroir m (d'une communauté). 'work-shy, a. F: Qui boude à la besogne; P: qui a un poil (dans la main); flemmard. 'work-table, s. Table f à ouvrage, travailleuse f.

work², v. (p.t. & p.p. worked [wə:kt], A: and in a few set phrases wrought [rɔːt]) I. v.i. 1. (a) Travailler. To w. hard, travailler dur, ferme. To w. like a slave, like a horse, travailler comme un nègre; peiner comme un cheval. I am working at a shawl, je travaille à un châle. He is working on a history of the war, il travaille à une histoire de la guerre. To w. to rule, faire la grève du zèle. (b) To w. for an end, travailler pour atteindre un but. Working from the principle that . . ., partant du principe que. . . . 2. (a) (Of machine, etc.) Fonctionner, aller. System that works well, système qui fonctionne bien. The pump isn't working, la pompe ne marche pas. These tools w. by compressed air, ces outils sont actionnés par l'air comprimé. (b) Medicine that works, médicament qui produit son effet, qui agit. His scheme did not w., son plan a échoué, n'a pas réussi. F: That won't w. with me, ça ne prend pas avec moi. I'll w. it so that . . ., je m'arrangerai pour que. . . . 3. (Of yeast, etc.) Fermenter. 4. (a) His mouth was working, il se tordait la bouche; sa bouche se crispait. (b) (Of sailing ship) To w. southwards, remonter vers le sud (contre le vent). (Of angler) To w. upstream, remonter le courant. II. work, v.tr. 1. Faire travailler. He works his men too hard, il surmène ses hommes. To w. oneself to death, se tuer de travail. 2. (a) Faire fonctionner, faire marcher (une machine); faire jouer (un ressort); actionner (le frein). (Of machine) To be worked by electricity, marcher à l'électricité. (b) Diriger (un service de voitures). (c) To w. a scheme, mettre un plan à exécution. 3. (a) Faire, opérer (un miracle) (une guérison); amener (un changement). To w. mischief, semer la discorde. His keys worked a hole in his pocket, ses clefs ont fini par faire un trou dans sa poche. The destruction wrought by the fire, la dévastation causée par l'incendie. (b) To w. a sum, faire un calcul; résoudre un problème. 4. Broder (un dessin). Worked with silver, lamé d'argent. 5. (a) To w. an incident into a book, introduire un incident dans un livre. (b) To w. one's hands free, parvenir à dégager ses mains. (c) He worked his way to the front of the crowd, il se fraya un chemin jusqu'au premier rang de la foule. He was working his way through college, il travaillait pour payer ses études. 6. (a) Travailler, façonner (les bois); ouvrer (les métaux précieux). (b) To w. the iron into a horseshoe, façonner, forger, le fer en fer à cheval. (c) He worked himself into a rage, il se mit peu à peu en colère. 7. (a) Exploiter (une mine). (b) Com: Traveller working the south-eastern area, représentant voyageur, qui fait le sud-est. 8. Nau: To w. one's passage, gagner son passage en travaillant. work in. 1. v.tr. Faire entrer (qch.) peu à peu. 2. v.i. Pénétrer peu à peu. work off. 1. v.tr. Se dégager de (qch.); cuver (sa colère). To w. off one's fat, se débarrasser de sa graisse par le travail. To w. off one's bad temper on s.o., passer sa mauvaise humeur sur qn. 2. v.i. (Of nut, etc.) Se détacher. work on, v.i. 1. Continuer à travailler. 2. (a) We have no data to w. on, nous n'avons pas de données sur lesquelles nous baser. (b) To w. on s.o., agir sur qn. work out. 1. v.tr. (a) Mener à bien. To w. o. one's salvation, faire son salut. To w. o. one's time, (of apprentice) finir son temps. (b) Développer (une idée); élaborer (un projet). The plan is being worked out, le projet est à l'étude. (c) Supputer (un compte); résoudre (un problème). Nau: To w. o. one's position, calculer le point. 2. v.i. Sortir peu à peu. (b) It worked out very well for me, je m'en suis bien trouvé. How will things w. o.? à quoi tout cela aboutira-t-il? (c) How much does it w. o. at? par combien cela se chiffre-t-il? The total works out at six pounds, le total s'élève à six livres. 'work-out, s. Sp: Séance f d'entraînement. work up. 1. v.i. (a) (Of garment) Remonter. (b) What are you working up to? à quoi voulez-vous en venir? S.a. CLIMAX 2. 2. v.tr. (a) Préparer (la matière première). Phot: To w. up a negative, travailler, retoucher, un cliché. (b) Développer (une situation dramatique); élaborer (un article). Com: To w. up a connexion, se faire une clientèle. (c) Préparer (un sujet). (d) Exciter, émouvoir (qn). To be worked up, être emballé. Public opinion is very much worked up, l'opinion publique est très travaillée. working¹, a. 1. (a) Qui travaille; ouvrier. The w. classes, la classe ouvrière. W. man, ouvrier m. (b) W. party, atelier m; équipe f. 2. Qui fonctionne. (a) W. parts of a machine, parties (d'une machine) qui travaillent.

(b) Not working, hors d'action; au repos. *S.a.* SUR-FACE[1] 1. (c) W. agreement, modus vivendi *m.* W. majority, majorité suffisante. W. theory, théorie qui donne des résultats. working[2], *s.* 1. Travail *m.* W. clothes, vêtements de travail. W. day, (i) jour ouvrable; (ii) journée *f* (de travail). 2. (a) Manœuvre *f* (d'une machine). W. gear, organes *mpl* de manœuvre. (b) Mise *f* en œuvre (d'un procédé); exploitation *f* (d'une mine). W. expenses, frais d'exploitation. W. capital, fonds *m* de roulement. (c) Fonctionnement *m.* Difficult in the w., difficile dans la pratique. 3. Marche *f,* fonctionnement (d'un mécanisme). To alter the w. of the trains, modifier la marche des trains. *El.E:* W. voltage, tension *f* de régime. In w. order, en état de marche. To be in good w. order, bien fonctionner; être au point. 4. The workings of the mind, le travail, le cheminement, de l'esprit. 5. *pl. Min:* Workings, chantiers *m* d'exploitation. 'work(ing)-to-'rule, *s. Ind: etc:* Grève *f* du zèle.

workable ['wəːkəbl], *a.* 1. (Bois) ouvrable. 2. (Mine) exploitable. 3. (Projet) réalisable.

workaday ['wəːkədei], *a.* (a) De tous les jours. (b) This workaday world, ce monde prosaïque.

worker ['wəːkər], *s.* 1. (a) Travailleur, -euse. Heavy w., travailleur de force. To be a hard w., travailler dur; *F:* être un piocheur. (b) Ouvrier, -ère. The workers, les classes laborieuses. *Adm:* Workers, employés et ouvriers. *S.a.* BLACK-COATED. 2. W.-(bee), abeille ouvrière. 3. W. of miracles, faiseur *m* de miracles. 'worker-'priest, *s.* Prêtre-ouvrier *m, pl.* prêtres-ouvriers.

workhouse ['wəːkhaus], *s. A:* Asile *m* des pauvres; hospice *m.*

workman, *pl.* -men ['wəːkmən], *s.m.* Ouvrier; artisan.

workmanlike ['wəːkmənlaik], *a.* 1. Bien fait, bien travaillé. 2. To do sth. in a w. manner, faire qch. en bon ouvrier.

workmanship ['wəːkmənʃip], *s. Ind:* Exécution *f;* fini *m* de l'exécution; façon *f,* facture *f.* Sound w., construction soignée. A fine piece of w., un beau travail.

workpeople ['wəːkpiːpl], *s.pl.* Ouvriers *m;* ouvriers et ouvrières.

workshop ['wəːkʃɔp], *s.* Atelier *m.* Mobile w., camion-atelier *m, pl.* camions-ateliers.

world [wəːld], *s.* Monde *m.* 1. (a) In this w., en ce bas monde; ici-bas. The other w., the next w., the w. to come, l'autre monde. He is not long for this w., il n'en a pas pour longtemps à vivre; il ne fera pas de vieux os. To go to a better w., partir pour l'autre monde. W. without end, pour les siècles des siècles. (b) To be alone in the w., être seul au monde. Nothing in the w., rien au monde; rien du tout. What in the w. is the matter with you? mais qu'est-ce que vous avez donc? I would not do it for (all) the w., je ne le ferais pour rien au monde. He was for all the w. like . . ., il avait exactement l'air de. . . . I would give the w. to know . . ., je donnerais n'importe quoi pour savoir. . . . 2. To go round the w., faire le tour du monde. He has seen the w., il a vu du pays. *F:* To knock about the w., rouler sa bosse. Map of the w., carte générale; (*in two hemispheres*) mappemonde *f.* The Old W., the New W., l'ancien Continent, le Nouveau Continent, le Nouveau Monde. The Ancient W., l'Antiquité *f.* All the w. over, dans le monde entier. It's a small w.! que le monde est petit! W. congress, congrès mondial. W. politics, politique mondiale. W. power, puissance mondiale. W. war, guerre mondiale. 3. (*Human affairs*) It's the way of the w., ainsi va le monde. Man of the w., homme qui connaît la vie. He has gone down in the w., il a connu des jours meilleurs. To have the w. before one, avoir la vie devant soi. *Ecc:* To live apart from the w., vivre loin du siècle. *F:* It's something out of this w., c'est quelque chose d'extra-ordinaire, d'épatant. 4. (a) The theatrical w., le milieu, le monde, du théâtre. The sporting w., le monde du sport. (b) That will do you a w. of good, ça vous fera énormément de bien. To give oneself a w. of trouble, se donner un mal de chien. To think the w. of s.o., avoir une très haute opinion de qn. 'world-'famous, *a.* De renommée mondiale. 'world-weary, *a.* Fatigué du monde. 'world-'wide, *a.* Universel; répandu partout; mondial, -aux.

worldliness ['wəːldlinis], *s.* Mondanité *f.*

worldling ['wəːldliŋ], *s.* Mondain, -aine.

worldly ['wəːldli], *a.* 1. Du monde, de ce monde, d'ici-bas. All his w. goods, toute sa fortune. W. wisdom, la sagesse du monde, du siècle. W. interests, soucis matériels. 2. Mondain. 'worldly-'minded, *a.* Attaché aux choses matérielles.

worm[1] [wəːm], *s.* Ver *m.* 1. (a) (Earth)worm, ver de terre; lombric *m.* To fish with worms, pêcher au ver. *F:* The w. has turned, il en a assez de se laisser mener par le bout du nez. *F:* He's a worm, c'est un pauvre type. (b) *Ent:* (i) Larve *f;* (ii) mite *f. S.a.* BLIND-WORM, BOOK-WORM, SILKWORM, *etc.* *Med: Vet:* To have worms, avoir des vers. 2. (a) Filet *m* (de vis). (b) Vis *f* sans fin. Conveyor w., hélice transporteuse. (c) Serpentin *m* (d'alambic). 'worm-bit, *s. Tls:* Mèche *f* à vis. 'worm-cast, *s.* Déjection *f* de ver de terre. 'worm-drive, *s. Aut: etc:* Transmission *f* par vis sans fin. 'worm-eaten, *a.* Rongé des vers, piqué des vers; (*of wood*) vermoulu. 'worm-gear, *s. Mec.E:* Engrenage *m* à vis sans fin. 'worm-hole, *s.* (*In cloth, wood*) Piqûre *f,* trou *m,* de ver. 'worm-like, *a.* Vermiforme, vermiculaire. 'worm-powder, *s.* Poudre *f* vermifuge.

worm[2], *v.tr.* (a) To w. (oneself, one's way) through the undergrowth, se glisser, se faufiler, à travers les buissons. To w. oneself into s.o.'s favour, s'insinuer dans les bonnes grâces de qn. (b) To w. a secret out of s.o., tirer un secret de qn. I'll w. it out of him, je vais lui tirer les vers du nez.

wormwood ['wəːmwud], *s. Bot:* Armoise amère; absinthe *f.* Life to him was gall and w., la vie pour lui n'était qu'amertume et dégoût.

worn. *See* WEAR[2].

worry[1] ['wʌri], *s.* Ennui *m,* souci *m,* tracas *m.* Financial worries, soucis *m* d'argent. He has always been a w. to me, il a fait le tourment de ma vie. *F:* What's your w.? qu'est-ce qu'il y a qui cloche?

worry[2], *v.* (worried) 1. *v.tr.* (a) (*Of dog*) Harceler (les moutons); (prendre avec les dents et) secouer (un rat). (b) To w. out a problem, s'évertuer à résoudre un problème. (c) Tourmenter, tracasser, harceler, *P:* asticoter (qn). Baby has a cough and it rather worries me, mon bébé tousse, cela m'inquiète. To w. oneself, se tourmenter, se tracasser; se faire du mauvais sang, de la bile. He worries me to death, il est assommant. 2. *v.i.* Se tourmenter, se tracasser, s'inquiéter; se faire de la bile, du mauvais sang. Don't (you) w.! soyez tranquille! *F:* vous en faites pas! Don't w. about me, ne vous inquiétez pas de moi. We'll w. along somehow, on se débrouillera. worried, *a.* To be w., (i) être en proie à l'inquiétude; (ii) avoir du souci, des ennuis. To look w., avoir l'air soucieux, préoccupé.

worse [wəːs]. 1. *a. & s.* Pire; plus mauvais. I am a w. player than he (is), je joue plus mal que lui. In w. condition, en plus mauvais état. This is w. and w., c'est de mal en pis. To make matters w. . . ., pour comble de malheur. . . . That only made matters w., cela n'a pas arrangé les choses. It might have been w., ce n'est qu'un demi-mal. I'm none the w. for it, je ne m'en porte pas plus mal. He escaped with nothing w. than a fright, il en fut quitte pour la peur. He is in a w. way than you, il est plus malade que vous. So much the w. for him, tant pis pour lui. He escaped none the w., il s'en est tiré sans aucun mal. I think none the w. of him because he accepted, je n'ai pas moins bonne opinion de lui parce qu'il a accepté. *S.a.* DRINK[1] 3, LUCK 1, WEAR[1] 1. 2. *s.* (a) But there was w. to come, mais il y eut plus grave. I have been through w. than that, j'en ai vu bien d'autres. (b) To change for the w., s'altérer. He has taken a sudden turn for the w., son état s'est subitement aggravé. *S.a.* BETTER[1] 2. 3. *adv.* (a) Pis; plus mal. He behaves w. than ever, il se conduit plus mal que jamais. You might do w., vous pourriez faire pis. To think w. of s.o., avoir plus mauvaise opinion de qn. He is w. off than before, sa situation a empiré. (b) The noise went on w. than ever, le vacarme recommença de plus belle.

worsen ['wəːs(ə)n]. 1. *v.tr.* Empirer (un mal); aggraver. 2. *v.i.* Empirer; (*of evil*) s'aggraver.

worship[1] ['wəːʃip], s. **1.** Culte m, adoration f. W. of images, idolâtrie f. **Divine w.**, le culte divin. **Public w.**, l'exercice m du culte. **Hours of w.**, heures des offices. **Place of w.**, édifice m du culte; église f, temple m. **To be an object of w.**, être un objet d'adoration. **2.** His W. the Mayor, monsieur le maire. Yes, your W., oui, monsieur le maire, monsieur le juge.

worship[2], v.tr. **(worshipped) 1.** Rendre un culte à, adorer (un dieu). **2.** Adorer (qn); avoir un culte pour (qn). **To w. money**, faire son idole de l'argent. **He worships the ground she treads on**, il baise la trace de ses pas. **3.** *Abs.* Where does he w.? à quelle église va-t-il?

worshipful ['wəːʃipful], a. *(a)* Honorable. *(b)* (*Free-masonry*) Vénérable.

worshipper ['wəːʃipər], s. Adorateur, -trice. **The wor-shippers** (*in a church*), les fidèles m.

worst[1] [wəːst]. **1.** a. (Le) pire, (le) plus mauvais. **His w. mistake**, sa plus grave erreur. **His w. enemy**, son pire ennemi. **2.** s. **The w. of the storm is over**, le plus fort de la tempête est passé. **That's the w. of cheap shoes**, c'est l'inconvénient des souliers bon marché. **When things are at their w.**, quand les choses sont au pire. **To get the w. of it** (*in a fight*), avoir le dessous. **At the w.**, au pis aller. **If the w. comes to the w.**, en mettant les choses au pis. **The w. is soon over**, le plus mauvais moment est vite passé. **The w. has happened**, c'est la catastrophe. **Do your w.**, allez-y! **3.** adv. (Le) pis, (le) plus mal. **The w. educated**, le moins instruit. **That frightened me w. of all**, c'est cela qui m'a effrayé le plus.

worst[2] v.tr. Battre, vaincre.

worsted ['wustid], s. *(a)* Laine peignée. *(b)* Laine à tricoter, à tapisserie.

worth [wəːθ]. **1.** pred. a. Valant. *(a)* **To be w. so much**, valoir tant. **That is w. something**, cela a de la valeur. **It is not worth much**, cela ne vaut pas grand-chose, pas cher. **Whatever it may be w.**, vaille que vaille. **W. the money**, avantageux. **I'm telling you this for what it's w.**, je vous passe ce renseignement sans y attribuer grande valeur. **It would be as much as my life is w.**, ce serait risquer ma vie. *(b)* **It is not w. the trouble**, cela ne, n'en, vaut pas la peine. **Is it w. while?** is it w. it? cela (en) vaut-il la peine? **Book w. reading**, livre qui mérite d'être lu. **A thing w. having**, une chose précieuse. **It is w. thinking about**, cela mérite ré-flexion. **It's w. knowing**, c'est bon à savoir. *(c)* He is w. money, il a de l'argent. He's w. millions, il est riche à millions. **To die w. a million**, mourir en laissant un million. **That is all I am w.**, voilà tout mon avoir. F: **For all one is w.**, de toutes ses forces. **2.** s. Valeur f. **People of (sterling) w.**, personnes de valeur, de mérite. **Give me two shillings' w. of choco-late**, donnez-moi pour deux shillings de chocolat. **To want one's money's w.**, en vouloir pour son argent.

worthiness ['wəːðinis], s. Mérite m.

worthless ['wəːθlis], a. Sans valeur; mauvais. **W. fellow**, vaurien m.

worthlessness ['wəːθlisnis], s. Peu m de valeur; nature f méprisable (de qn).

worthwhile ['wəːθ'wail], a. Qui en vaut l'effort, la peine, F: le coup.

worthy ['wəːði]. **1.** a. Digne. *(a)* A w. man, un digne homme; un homme estimable. O: Our w. friend, notre brave ami. *(b)* To be w. of sth., être digne de qch. The town has no museum w. of the name, la ville n'a aucun musée digne du nom. To be w. of death, mériter la mort. It is w. of note that . . ., il est à noter que. . . . **2.** s. O: The village worthies, les notables du village. **-ily**, adv. **1.** Dignement. **2.** A juste titre.

wot, v.i. See WIT[3].

wotcher ['wɔtʃər], int. P: W., mate! comment ça gaze, mon vieux?

would. See WILL[3]. **'would-be**, a. Prétendu, soi-disant.

wound[1] [wuːnd], s. *(a)* Blessure f. Bullet w., blessure par balle. *(b)* Plaie f. The w. is festering, la plaie s'envenime.

wound[2], v.tr. Blesser; faire une blessure à (qn). Wounded in the shoulder, atteint à l'épaule. To w. s.o.'s pride, blesser qn dans son amour-propre. To w. s.o.'s feelings, froisser qn. The wounded, les blessés.

wound[3] [waund]. *See* WIND[2,3].

wove [wouv], a. W. paper, (papier) vélin m. Cream w. paper, vélin blanc.

woven ['wouv(ə)n], a. Tissé. Closely w., d'un tissu serré.

wow [wau], s. F: It's a w.! c'est épatant! c'est du tonnerre!

wrack [ræk], s. Varec(h) m.

wraith [reiθ], s. *(a)* Apparition spectrale (d'un mort). *(b)* Double spectral d'une personne (présage de sa mort).

wrangle[1] ['ræŋgl], s. Dispute f, querelle f.

wrangle[2], v.i. Se disputer, se quereller. **wrangling**, s. Disputes fpl, querelles fpl, chamailleries fpl.

wrangler ['ræŋglər], s. **1.** Querelleur, -euse. **2.** (*At Cambridge University*) Étudiant sorti dans la pre-mière classe à l'examen de mathématiques.

wrap[1] [ræp], s. *(a)* (*Usu. pl.*) Wraps, couvertures f (de voyage); châles m. *(b)* Pèlerine f; manteau m. *(c)* O: Morning w., saut-de-lit m. Evening w., manteau du soir; sortie f de bal.

wrap[2], v.tr. **(wrapped** [ræpt]) **1.** *(a)* Envelopper. To w. sth. (up) in paper, envelopper qch. dans du papier. *(b)* To w. oneself up, abs. to w. up, se couvrir (de vêtements chauds), s'emmitoufler. *(c)* To w. up one's meaning in obscure language, envelopper sa pensée de paroles obscures. **2.** To w. sth. round sth., enrouler qch. autour de qch. **3.** El.E: To w. a cable (in cotton), guiper un câble. **wrapped**, a. **1.** *(a)* W. in paper, roulé dans du papier. *(b)* (*Of pers.*) W. up, bien enveloppé; emmitouflé. *(c)* Affair w. in mystery, affaire entourée de mystère. **2.** *(a)* W. in meditation, plongé dans ses pensées; absorbé dans ses réflexions. *(b)* To be w. up in s.o., vivre entièrement pour qn. He is w. up in his work, il est entièrement absorbé par son travail. **wrapping**, s. **1.** Emballage m; mise f en paquet(s); (*of newspaper*) mise sous bande. **2.** *(a)* Enveloppe f, couverture f. *(b)* Papier m, toile f, d'emballage. *(c) pl.* Bandelettes f (de momie). **'wrapping-paper**, s. Papier m d'emballage. **'wrap-round**, a. Aut: W.-r. rear window, lunette f arrière panoramique.

wrapper ['ræpər], s. **1.** Toiled'em f ballage; feuille f de papier d'emballage. **2.** *(a)* Chemise f (d'un dossier). *(b)* Couverture f (d'un livre); couvre-livre m; liseuse f. **3.** Bande f (de journal). **4.** Tchn: Couvre-joint m; fourrure f. **5.** O: Robe f de chambre (de dame); saut-de-lit m.

wrath [rɔθ, rɔːθ], s. Lit: Colère f; courroux m.

wrathful ['rɔθful, 'rɔːθful], a. Lit: Courroucé.

wreak [riːk], v.tr. To w. one's wrath upon s.o., passer sa colère sur qn. To w. vengeance on s.o., se venger de qn.

wreath [riːθ, pl. riːðz], s. **1.** Couronne f, guirlande f (de fleurs). (Funeral) w., couronne mortuaire. **2.** Volute f, panache m (de fumée).

wreathe [riːð]. **1.** v.tr. *(a)* Enguirlander; couronner de fleurs (le front de qn). Mountain wreathed with mist, montagne couronnée de brouillard. Face wreathed in smiles, visage rayonnant. *(b)* Entrelacer, tresser (des fleurs). *(c)* To w. sth. round sth., enrouler qch. autour de qch. **2.** v.i. (*Of smoke*) Tourbillonner; s'élever en volutes.

wreck[1] [rek], s. **1.** *(a)* Jur: W. of the sea, épaves fpl de mer. *(b)* Navire naufragé; épave. Ins: Total w., navire entièrement perdu. **The building is a mere w.**, le bâtiment n'est qu'une ruine. He is a perfect w., c'est une ruine. Human w., épave humaine. **To be a nervous w.**, avoir les nerfs détraqués. **To collect the w. of one's fortune**, recueillir les débris m de sa fortune. **2.** *(a)* Naufrage m (d'un navire). To suffer w., faire naufrage. To be saved from the w., échapper au naufrage. *(b)* Attrib. U.S: Rail: W. train, convoi m de secours.

wreck[2], v.tr. *(a)* Faire faire naufrage à (un navire); causer le naufrage d'un navire). To be wrecked, faire naufrage. *(b)* Faire dérailler (un train); démolir, détruire, ruiner (un édifice). To w. one's digestion, se détraquer l'estomac. *(c)* Faire échouer, saboter (une entreprise); détruire, ruiner (les espérances de qn). **wrecked**, a. (Vaisseau) naufragé, qui a fait naufrage; (marin) naufragé. **W. life**, existence brisée. **W. health**, santé ruinée. **wrecking**, s. Destruction f (d'un navire); déraillement m (d'un train); ruine f (des espérances de qn). **W. policy**, politique de sabotage. U.S: W. crew, équipe f de secours.

wreckage ['rekidʒ], s. Épaves éparses; débris *mpl.* Piece of w., épave.

wrecker ['rekər], s. 1. Naufrageur *m*; pilleur *m* d'épaves. 2. Destructeur *m* (of, de); dérailleur *m* (de trains). 3. *Aut: U.S:* Camion *m* de dépannage; dépanneuse *f.*

wren [ren], s. *Orn:* 1. Troglodyte mignon; *F:* roitelet *m.* 2. **Golden-crested w.,** roitelet huppé. 3. *F:* Membre du *Women's Royal Naval Service.*

wrench¹ [ren(t)ʃ], s. 1. Mouvement violent de torsion. To give sth. a w., tordre qch. violemment. With a w. he pulled off the knocker, d'un effort violent il arracha le marteau. He gave his ankle a w., il s'est donné une entorse. It will be a w. to leave them, il m'en coûtera de les quitter. 2. *Tls:* Clef *f* (à écrous); tourne-à-gauche *m inv.* (Adjustable) w., clef à molette.

wrench², v.tr. 1. (a) Tordre; tourner violemment. To w. the lid open, forcer le couvercle. To w. off, out, arracher, enlever (avec un violent effort de torsion). (b) To w. sth. from s.o., arracher qch. à qn. She wrenched herself free, d'une secousse elle se dégagea. (c) To w. one's ankle, se fouler la cheville. To w. one's shoulder, se démettre l'épaule. 2. Forcer, fausser (le sens d'un passage).

wrest¹ [rest], s. *Mus:* Clef *f* d'accordeur. **'wrest-block,** s. Sommier *m* (de piano). **'wrest-pin,** s. Cheville *f* (d'accordage) (d'un piano).

wrest², v.tr. 1. Arracher (from, à). 2. Forcer, fausser, tordre (le sens d'un passage); donner une entorse à (la vérité).

wrestle¹[resl], s. Lutte *f*(corps à corps); assaut *m* de lutte.

wrestle². 1. v.i. (a) To w. with s.o., lutter avec, contre, qn. To w. for a prize, disputer un prix à la lutte. (b) To w. with sth., lutter contre (les difficultés); résister à (la tentation); être aux prises avec (l'adversité); s'attaquer à (un problème); s'escrimer à (un sujet). 2. v.tr. Lutter avec, contre (qn). To wrestle a fall with s.o., faire un assaut de lutte avec qn. **wrestling,** s. Sport *m* de la lutte; lutte (corps à corps). All-in wrestling, (combat *m* en) lutte libre; catch *m.* **Wrestling match,** assaut *m* (de lutte).

wrestler ['reslər], s. Lutteur *m.*

wretch [retʃ], s. 1. Malheureux, -euse; infortuné, -ée. Poor w., pauvre diable *m.* Miserable w., traîne-misère *m inv.* 2. (a) Scélérat, -ate. You wretch! misérable! (b) You little w.! petit fripon!

wretched ['retʃid], a. 1. (Of pers.) Misérable, malheureux, infortuné. To feel w., être mal en train; *P:* avoir le cafard. To look w., avoir l'air malheureux; faire triste mine. 2. (a) Pitoyable; tout à fait mauvais; lamentable. What w. weather! quel temps de chien! (b) W. lodgings, appartement minable. W. little shop, petite boutique de rien du tout. (c) I can't find that w. umbrella! je ne retrouve pas ce diable de parapluie! **-ly,** adv. 1. (Vivre) misérablement. 2. (S'acquitter) de façon pitoyable, lamentable. 3. To be w. poor, être dans la misère. I was w. ill between Calais and Dover, entre Calais et Douvres j'ai été malade comme un chien.

wretchedness ['retʃidnis], s. Misère *f*, malheur *m*, infortune *f.*

wrick¹ [rik], s. To give oneself a w., se donner un effort. W. in the neck, torticolis *m.*

wrick,² v.tr. To w. oneself, a muscle, se donner un effort. To w. one's ankle, se fouler la cheville; se donner, *F:* se flanquer, une entorse.

wriggle¹ ['rigl], s. 1. Tortillement *m* (du corps). 2. Détour *m*, sinuosité *f.*

wriggle². 1. v.i. (a) (Of worm) Se tortiller; (of fish) frétiller; (of pers.) se tortiller, s'agiter, se remuer. To w. through a hedge, se faufiler à travers une haie (en se tortillant). (b) To w. into s.o.'s favour, s'insinuer dans les bonnes grâces de qn. To w. out of a difficulty, se tirer, s'extraire, d'une position difficile. To try to w. out of it, chercher une échappatoire. (c) *F:* Tortiller; tergiverser. 2. v.tr. (a) To w. one's body, one's legs, remuer, tortiller, le corps; agiter les jambes; se contorsionner. (b) To w. one's way into . . ., se faufiler, s'insinuer, dans. . . . **wriggling,** s. 1. Tortillement *m.* 2. *F:* Tergiversation *f.*

wriggler ['riglər], s. 1. (a) Ver *m*, etc., qui se tortille. (b) Enfant qui ne sait pas se tenir tranquille. 2. *F:* Tergiversateur, -trice.

wring¹ [riŋ], s. 1. (Mouvement *m* de) torsion *f.* To give the clothes a w., tordre le linge. 2. He gave my hand a w., il m'étreignit la main.

wring², v.tr. (wrung [rʌŋ]; wrung) 1. Tordre. To w. (out) the linen, tordre, essorer, le linge. To w. s.o.'s hand, étreindre la main de qn. To w. one's hands in despair, se tordre les mains, les bras, de désespoir. To w. a bird's neck, tordre le cou à une volaille. It wrings my heart to . . ., cela me déchire le cœur de. . . . 2. To w. sth. out of, from, sth., s.o., exprimer, faire sortir (l'eau d'un vêtement mouillé); arracher (un secret à qn); extorquer (de l'argent à qn). 3. (a) Forcer, déformer (une plaque métallique, etc.). (b) *Lit:* Donner une entorse à (la vérité). To w. s.o.'s words into an admission of guilt, dénaturer en aveu les paroles de qn. **wringing,** a. W. wet (of clothes) mouillé à tordre; (of pers.) trempé comme une soupe; trempé jusqu'aux os.

wringer ['riŋər], s. Dom.Ec: Essoreuse *f* (à rouleaux).

wrinkle¹ ['riŋkl], s. 1. (a) (On face) Ride *f.* (b) Rugosité *f*; (on water) ondulation *f*, ride. (c) (In garment) Faux pli. Dress that fits without a w., robe qui ne fait pas un pli. 2. *F:* Renseignement *m* utile; *F:* tuyau *m.*

wrinkle². 1. v.tr. Rider, plisser. To w. one's forehead, froncer les sourcils. Her stockings were wrinkled, ses bas tire-bouchonnaient. 2. v.i. To w. (up), se rider; se plisser; faire des plis. The skin of these apples wrinkles, la peau de ces pommes se ratatine.

wrist [rist], s. 1. Poignet *m.* 2. = WRIST-PIN. **'wrist-bone,** s. *Anat:* Os *m* du carpe; le carpe. **'wrist-pin,** s. *Mch:* Tourillon *m* de crosse, axe *m* de piston. 2. Bouton *m* de manivelle, de bielle; maneton *m.* **'wrist-watch,** s. Montre-bracelet *f.*

wristband ['ris(t)bænd], s. *Cost:* Poignet *m*, manchette *f.*

wristlet ['ris(t)lit], s. (a) Bracelet *m.* W. watch, montre-bracelet *f.* (b) Woollen w., miton *m.*

writ¹ [rit], s. 1. Holy w., les saintes Écritures; l'Écriture sainte. 2. *Jur:* Acte *m* judiciaire; mandat *m*, ordonnance *f.* W. of summons, assignation *f*, citation *f.* To serve a w. on s.o., assigner qn (en justice); signifier une assignation, un exploit, à qn. A w. is out for his arrest, il est sous le coup d'un mandat d'arrêt.

writ². See WRITE.

write [rait], v.tr. (p.t. wrote [rout]; p.p. written ['rit(ə)n], A: writ) 1. (a) Écrire. That was not written by me, cela n'est pas écrit de ma main. How is it written? comment cela s'écrit-il? He writes a good hand, il a une belle écriture, une belle main. His guilt was written in his eyes, on lisait dans ses yeux qu'il était coupable. There's detective written all over him, il sent le policier à une lieue. Writ large, écrit en grosses lettres. (b) *M.Ins:* = UNDERWRITE (b). 2. Écrire (un roman, une lettre); rédiger (un article). To w. for a paper, faire du journalisme, écrire dans un journal. He writes, il fait profession d'écrire; il est écrivain. *F:* That's nothing to w. home about, ce n'est pas bien extraordinaire, bien épatant. He wrote to me yesterday, il m'a écrit hier. I have written to ask him to come, je lui ai écrit de venir. I will w. (off) for it at once, je vais le commander tout de suite. **write back,** v.tr. 1. *Abs.* Répondre (par écrit). 2. *Book-k:* Contrepasser, ristourner (un article). **write down,** v.tr. 1. Coucher, consigner, (qch.) par écrit; inscrire (son nom); marquer, noter. 2. *F:* Décrier, *F:* éreinter (qn, une pièce). 3. *Fin:* Réduire (le capital). **write in,** v.tr. Insérer (un mot). **write off,** v.tr. 1. Écrire (un article) d'un trait, au courant de la plume. 2. (a) *Fin:* To w. off capital, réduire le capital; amortir du capital. (b) *Com:* Défalquer (une mauvaise créance), passer une créance par profits et pertes. To w. so much off for wear and tear, déduire tant pour l'usure. Three machines were written off, il y a eu trois appareils de détruits. **'write-off,** s. Perte totale. The car is a w.-o., la voiture est une perte totale. **write out,** v.tr. 1. Transcrire (qch.); mettre (une copie) au net. 2. To w. sth. out in full, écrire qch. en toutes lettres. 3. (a) *Med:* Formuler, rédiger (une ordonnance). (b) Libeller, remplir (un chèque). **write up,** v.tr. 1. *Journ:* (a) Écrire, rédiger (un fait-divers). (b) Prôner, *F:* faire mousser

(qn, qch.). **2.** Mettre (son agenda) au courant, à jour. **3.** To w. sth. up, faire un papier sur qch. *Sch:* W. up your notes, recopiez vos notes. **'write-up,** *s. Journ:* Article *m.* A good w.-up, un article élogieux. **writing,** *s.* **1.** Écriture *f.* (*a*) The art of w., l'art d'écrire. At the time of w., au moment où j'écris. (*b*) His w. is bad, il a une mauvaise écriture. To answer in w., répondre par écrit. *Jur:* Evidence in w., preuve littérale. **2.** (*a*) The w. profession, le métier d'écrivain. (*b*) Ouvrage *m* littéraire. *pl.* The writings of Bossuet, les écrits *m* de Bossuet. **'writing-case,** *s.* Nécessaire *m* (contenant ce qu'il faut pour écrire). **'writing-desk,** *s.* Pupitre *m*, bureau *m*; secrétaire *m.* **'writing-pad,** *s.* **1.** Sous-main *m*, buvard *m.* **2.** Bloc correspondance *m.* **'writing-paper,** *s.* Papier *m* à lettres. **'writing-table,** *s.* Bureau *m.*
writer ['raitər], *s.* **1.** To be a good, bad, w., avoir une belle, une mauvaise, écriture. Writer's cramp, crampe *f* des écrivains. **2.** The (present) w., celui qui écrit; l'auteur *m* de cette lettre. **3.** (*a*) Auteur (d'un roman, etc.). (*b*) Écrivain *m.* Woman w., femme auteur; femme écrivain. **4.** (*a*) *Navy:* Fourrier *m.* (*b*) *Scot:* = SOLICITOR. *S.a.* SIGNET.
writhe [raið], *v.i.* (*a*) Se tordre (de douleur). (*b*) He writhed under the insult, il ressentit vivement cette injure. To make s.o. writhe, crisper les nerfs à qn. **writhing,** *s.* Contorsions *fpl.*
written ['rit(ə)n], *a.* Écrit. W. consent, consentement par écrit. W. law, loi écrite.
wrong[1] [rɔŋ]. **I.** *a.* **1.** Mauvais; mal *inv.* It is w. to steal, stealing is w., c'est mal de voler. That was very w. of you! c'était très mal de votre part! *P:* A w. 'un, un mauvais sujet; un vaurien. **2.** (*a*) Incorrect, inexact; erroné; faux, *f.* fausse. My watch is w., ma montre n'est pas à l'heure. A w. calculation, un calcul faux. W. use of a word, emploi abusif, vicieux, d'un mot. His ideas are all w., il a des idées toutes de travers. (*b*) (*Of pers.*) To be w., avoir tort; se tromper. That's just where you are w., c'est justement ce qui vous trompe. **3.** "Qu'il ne faut pas." (*a*) To be in the w. place, ne pas être à sa place. Picture in the w. light, tableau dans un faux jour. *F:* To get out of bed on the w. side, se lever du pied gauche. The w. side of a material, l'envers *m* d'un tissu. Your shirt is w. side out, votre chemise est à l'envers. To be w. side up, être sens dessus dessous. To brush a hat the w. way, brosser un chapeau à rebours, à contre-poil. To stroke the cat the w. way, caresser le chat à rebrousse-poil. *S.a.* END[1] **1.** You set about it in the w. way, vous vous y prenez mal. (*Of food*) It went down the w. way, je l'ai avalé de travers. *F:* To be on the w. side of forty, avoir (dé)passé la quarantaine. *S.a.* LAUGH[2] **1.** (*b*) I went to the w. house, je me suis trompé de maison. That is the w. book, ce n'est pas là le livre qu'il faut. To take the w. road, se tromper de chemin, faire fausse route. I was sent the w. way, on m'a mal dirigé. To be on the w. track, suivre une mauvaise piste. To do, say, the w. thing, commettre un impair. *Tp:* W. number, erreur *f* de numéro.

You have been given the w. number, on vous a mal branché. *Mus:* W. note, fausse note. *Typ:* W. fount, lettre *f* d'un autre œil. *S.a.* SHOP[1] **1.** **4.** (*Amiss*) What's w. with you? qu'avez-vous? qu'est-ce qu'il y a qui ne va pas? What's w. with that? qu'avez-vous à redire à cela? What do you find w. with this book? qu'est-ce que vous reprochez à ce livre? Something is w., il y a quelque chose qui ne va pas. There's something w. somewhere, il y a quelque chose qui cloche. I hope there is nothing w., j'espère qu'il n'est rien arrivé (de malheureux). Things are all w., tout va mal, de travers. **-ly,** *adv.* **1.** A tort, à faux. Rightly or w., à tort ou à raison. **2.** Mal. **II.** **wrong,** *s.* **1.** Mal *m.* To know right from w., distinguer le bien et le mal. Two wrongs do not make a right, deux noirs ne font pas un blanc. **2.** (*a*) Tort *m*, injustice *f.* Right and w., le juste et l'injuste. To labour under a sense of w., nourrir un sentiment d'injustice. (*b*) *Jur:* Dommage *m*, préjudice *m.* **3.** To be in the w., être dans son tort; avoir tort. To put s.o. in the w., mettre qn dans son tort. **III.** **wrong,** *adv.* Mal. **1.** (*a*) Inexactement, incorrectement. To answer w., répondre mal, de travers. (*b*) A tort; à faux. You did w., vous avez mal agi. *F:* You've got me w., vous m'avez mal compris. **2.** To go w. (*a*) (i) Faire fausse route; (ii) se tromper; (iii) *F:* mal tourner. (*b*) (*Of mechanism*) Se déranger, se détraquer; (*of business*) aller mal. Something went w. with the electric light, nous avons eu une panne d'électricité. Things are going w., les affaires se gâtent; tout est à l'envers. **'wrong-'headed,** *a.* Qui a l'esprit pervers, mal fait. **'wrong-'headedness,** *s.* Perversité *f* de jugement; mauvaise tête.
wrong[2], *v.tr.* (*a*) Faire (du) tort à (qn); faire injure à (qn); léser (qn). (*b*) Être injuste pour, envers (qn).
wrongdoer ['rɔŋduər], *s.* (*a*) Auteur *m* d'une injustice. Wrongdoers, les méchants. (*b*) Celui qui commet une infraction à la foi; délinquant(e).
wrongdoing ['rɔŋduiŋ], *s.* (*a*) Mal *m*; injustice *f.* (*b*) Infraction *f* à la loi.
wrongful ['rɔŋf(u)l], *a.* **1.** Injuste. W. dismissal, renvoi injustifié (d'un employé). **2.** *Jur:* Illégal, -aux. **-fully,** *adv.* Injustement; à tort.
wrote. *See* WRITE.
wroth [rɔθ], *pred.a. Lit:* Courroucé, en colère (at, contre). To wax w., se courroucer, se mettre en colère.
wrought [rɔːt], *a.* (*a*) Travaillé, ouvré, façonné. (*b*) (*Of metals*) Ouvré, forgé, battu. W. iron, fer forgé. **'wrought up,** *a. Lit:* Excité, agité.
wrung. *See* WRING[2].
wry [rai], *a.* Tordu; de travers. To pull a w. face, faire la grimace. He gave a w. smile, il grimaça un sourire.
wryneck ['rainek], *s. Orn:* Torcol *m.*
wych-elm ['witʃ'elm], *s. See* ELM.
Wykehamist ['wikəmist], *a. & s.* (Élève *m* ou ancien élève) du collège de Winchester.
wyvern ['waivə(ː)n], *s. Her:* Dragon *m.*

X, x [eks], *s.* **1.** (La lettre) X, x *m. F: U.S:* Billet de dix dollars. *Tp:* X for Xmas, X comme Xavier. *Mth:* **The x-axis,** l'axe *m* des abscisses. *Cin:* **X certificate,** certificat délivré par le censeur interdisant le spectacle aux moins de seize ans. **2.** (*a*) **XX,** *F: U.S:* = DOUBLE-CROSS. (*b*) **Treble X, XXX,** bière extra-forte. **3.** *Ph:* **X rays,** rayons *m* X. **Deep X-rays,** rayons X pénétrants. **X-'ray¹,** *attrib.a.* (Appareil) radiologique. **X-ray examination,** examen radiographique. **X-ray photograph,** radiogramme *m.* **X-ray treatment,** radiothérapie *f.* **X-ray diagnosis,** radiodiagnostic *m.* **X-'ray²,** *v.tr. Med:* Radiographier (qn), passer (qn) aux rayons X.

xanthin ['zanθin], *s. Ch:* Xanthine *f.*

xanthous ['zænθəs], *a. Anthr:* Jaune; mongoloïde.

xenon ['zenɔn], *s. Ch:* Xénon *m.*

xenophobe ['zenəfoub], *a. & s.* Xénophobe (*mf*).

xenophobia [ˌzenə'foubjə], *s.* Xénophobie *f.*

xeranthemum [ˌzi(:)ə'rænθiməm], *s. Bot:* Xéranthème *m.*

xerography [zer'ɔgrəfi], *s.* Xérographie *f.*

xerophyte ['zerəfait], *s. Bot:* Xérophyte *f.*

xeroderm(i)a [ˌzi(:)ərou'də:m(i)ə], *s. Med:* Xérodermie *f;* ichtyose *f.*

Xerxes ['zə:ksi:z]. *Pr.n.m. A.Hist:* Xerxès.

xi [gzai], *s. Gr.Alph:* Xi *m.*

xiphias ['zifiæs], *s. Ich:* Xiphias *m,* espadon *m.*

xiphoid ['zifɔid], *a. Anat:* Xiphoïde.

Xmas ['krisməs], *s. F:* (= *Christmas*) Noël *m.*

xylograph ['zailəgrɑ:f], *s.* Xylographie *f;* gravure sur bois; estampe *f.*

xylographer [zai'lɔgrəfər], *s.* Xylographe *m;* graveur *m* sur bois.

xylography [zai'lɔgrəfi], *s.* Xylographie *f.*

xylonite ['zailənait], *s. R.t.m:* Xylonite *f.*

xylophagous [zai'lɔfəgəs], *a. Ent:* Xylophage.

xylophone ['zailəfoun], *s. Mus:* Xylophone *m.*

xylophonist [zai'ləfənist], *s. Mus:* Joueur, -euse, de xylophone.

xyster ['zistər], *s. Surg: Dent:* Xystre *m,* rugine *f.*

Y

Y, y, *pl.* **Y's, ys** [wai, waiz], *s.* (La lettre) Y, y *m*; i grec. *Tp:* Y for yellow, Y comme Yvonne. *Mth:* The y-axis, l'axe *m* des ordonnées. *Tchn:* Y joint, raccord *m* en Y. *Hyd.E:* Y branch, culotte *f*. *El.E:* Y-connection, montage *m* en étoile. **'Y-shaped,** *a.* Fourchu; à fourche; en Y.

yacht¹ [jɔt], *s.* Yacht *m*, plaisancier *m*. Pleasure y., yacht de plaisance. **'yacht-club,** *s.* Yacht-club *m*. **yacht-race,** *s.* Course *f* de yachts.

yacht², *v.i.* Faire du yachting. **yachting,** *s.* Yachting *m*. Y. cruise, croisière *f* en yacht. Y. cap, casquette *f* de yachtman. Y. jacket, vareuse *f*.

yachtsman, *pl.* **men** ['jɔtsmən], *s.m.* Plaisancier *m*, yachtman, *pl.* yachtmen.

yachtsmanship ['jɔtsmənʃip], *s.* Qualités *fpl* du bon yachtman; habileté *f* à manier un yacht.

yaffle ['jæfl], *s.* *Orn: Dial:* Pic vert; pivert *m*.

yah [jɑː], *int.* 1. (*Disgust*) Pouah! 2. (*Derision*) Oh, là, là!

yak [jæk], *s.* Z: Ya(c)k *m*; vache *f* de Tartarie.

yam [jæm], *s.* *Bot:* Igname *f*.

yammer ['jæmə(r)], *v.i.* 1. *F:* Gémir, geindre; pousser des cris; brailler. 2. (*D'une machine*) Ronfler, bourdonner, vrombir.

yank¹ [jæŋk], *s.* *U.S:* Secousse *f*, saccade *f*.

yank², *v.tr.* *F:* Tirer (d'un coup sec). To y. the bed-clothes off s.o., découvrir qn d'une secousse. To y. out a tooth, arracher une dent d'un seul coup.

Yank³, Yankee ['jæŋki], *s.* (*In U.S.A.*) *often Pej:* Habitant des États du Nord. *F:* Américain, -aine (des États-Unis); Yankee *m*.

yankeeism ['jæŋkiizm], *s.* *F:* Mot américain; locution américaine; américanisme *m*.

yap¹ [jæp], *s.* Jappement *m*, glapissement *m* (d'un chien).

yap², *v.i.* (**yapped**) (*a*) Japper. (*b*) *F:* (*Of pers.*) Crailler; en dégoiser. **yapping** (*a*) *s.* = YAP¹. (*b*) *a.* Jappeur, -euse; glapissant.

yarborough ['jɑːb(ə)rə], *s.* *Cards:* Main *f* qui ne contient aucune carte au-dessus du neuf.

yard¹ [jɑːd], *s.* 1. *Meas:* Yard *m* (0 mètre 914). How many yards do you want? quel métrage désirez-vous? *F:* Words a y. long, mots longs d'une toise. Statistics by the y., des statistiques *f* à n'en plus finir. Face a y. long, figure longue d'une aune. 2. *Nau:* Vergue *f*. **'yard-arm,** *s.* *Nau:* Bout *m* de vergue. **'yard-measure,** *s.* Mesure *f* d'un yard. **'yard-stick,** *s.* Yard *m* (en bois, en métal). *F:* To measure others by one's own y.-s., mesurer les autres à son aune.

yard², *s.* 1. (*a*) Cour *f* (de maison); *Sch:* cour, préau *m*. Back-y., cour de derrière, arrière-cour *f*. (*b*) Scotland Y., *F:* the Y., see SCOTLAND 2. 2. (*a*) Chantier *m*. *Nau:* Repair y., chantier de radoub. Naval (dock)y., *U.S:* Navy y., arsenal *m* maritime, *pl.* arsenaux. (*b*) Dépôt *m*. Coal y., dépôt de charbon. *Rail:* Goods y., cour, dépôt, de marchandises. *S.a.* MARSHALLING 2. Contractor's, builder's y., dépôt de matériaux. **yard-bird,** *s.* *U.S:* *P:* (i) *Mil:* = bleu *m*; (ii) = CONVICT. **yard-dog,** *s.* (*a*) Chien *m* de garde. (*b*) *U.S:* *P:* Malappris *m*. **yard-master,** *s.* *Rail:* Chef *m* de dépôt.

yardage¹ [jɑːdidʒ], *s.* Métrage *m*. **yardage²,** *s.* (*a*) Parcage *m*. (*b*) Frais *mpl.* de dépôt. (*c*) *Rail:* Manœuvres *fpl*.

yard(s)man, *pl.* **-men** ['jɑːd(z)mən, -mən], *s.m.* 1. Manœuvre de chantier. 2. *Rail:* Gareur, classeur, de trains. 3. (*In stables*) Garçon d'écurie.

yarn¹ [jɑːn], *s.* 1. (*a*) *Tex:* Fil *m*; filé *m* (de coton). Woollen y., laine filée; filé de laine. (*b*) *Nau:* Spun y., bitord *m*. **yarn-dyed,** *a.* Teint avant tissage. 2. *F:* (i) Histoire *f*, conte *m*, de matelot; (ii) longue histoire. To spin a y., raconter, débiter, une histoire.

yarn², *v.i.* *F:* Débiter des histoires.

yarrow ['jærou], *s.* *Bot:* Mille-feuille *f*, achillée *f*.

yashmak ['jæʃmæk], *s.* *Cost:* Yachmak *m*.

yataghan ['jætəgən], *s.* Yatagan *m*.

yatter ['jætər], *v.i.* *F:* Bavarder.

---

yaw¹ [jɔː], *s.* (*a*) *Nau:* Embardée *f*. (*b*) *Av:* Mouvement *m* de lacet.

yaw², *v.i.* (*a*) *Nau:* Embarder; faire des embardées. (*b*) *Av:* Faire un mouvement de lacet.

yawl [jɔːl], *s.* *Nau:* 1. Yole *f* (à rames). 2. Sloop *m* à tapecul.

yawn¹ [jɔːn], *s.* Bâillement *m*. To give a y., bâiller. To stifle a y., étouffer un bâillement.

yawn². 1. *v.i.* (*a*) Bâiller (de sommeil). (*b*) Être béant. The gulf yawned at his feet, le gouffre s'ouvrait à ses pieds. 2. *v.tr.* *F:* To y. one's head off, bâiller à se décrocher la mâchoire. **yawning¹,** *a.* (*a*) Bâillant, qui bâille. (*b*) (*Gouffre*) béant, ouvert. **yawning²,** *s.* Bâillement *m*.

yawp [jɔːp], *v.i.* *U.S:* *F:* Criailler.

yaws [jɔːz], *s.pl.* *Med:* Pian *m*.

yclept [i'klept], *a.* *A:* Appelé; nommé.

ye [jiː]. 1. *pers.pron.* *A:* Vous. Where were ye? où étiez-vous? 2. *def.art.* *Pseudo A:* Ye olde shoppe, la Vieille Boutique. *S.a.* GOD 1.

yea [jei]. *B:* 1. *adv.* (*a*) Oui. (*b*) En vérité; voire. Y. though I walk through the valley of the shadow of death, même quand je marcherais dans la vallée de l'ombre de la mort. 2. *s.* Oui *m*.

year [jiər, jəːr], *s.* An *m*, année *f*. (*a*) *Usu.* An. In the y. 1850, en l'an 1850. Sentenced to ten years' imprisonment, condamné à dix ans de prison. A y. last September, il y a eu un an au mois de septembre. Last y., l'an dernier; l'année dernière. To have a thousand a y., avoir mille livres de rente. To be ten years old, avoir dix ans. To see the old y. out, réveillonner. (*b*) *Usu.* Année. Calendar y., année civile. Leap y., année bissextile. Financial y., année d'exercice; exercice (financier). School y., année scolaire. He is in my y., il est de ma promotion. To rent sth. by the y., louer qch. à l'année. From year's end to year's end, d'un bout de l'année à l'autre. Y. in (and) y. out, y. after y., une année après l'autre. Years ago, il y a bien des années. In after years, dans la suite. From his earliest years, dès son âge le plus tendre. Old for his years, plus vieux que son âge; (*enfant*) précoce. Disparity in years, différence *f* d'âge. To be getting on in years, to advance in years, prendre de l'âge. Advanced in years, âgé. (*c*) *Vit:* Millésime *m*. **'year-book,** *s.* Annuaire *m*; almanach *m*; recueil annuel (de jurisprudence).

yearling ['jiəliŋ, 'jəːliŋ], *a. & s.* (*Animal m*) d'un an. *Esp.* Y. colt, poulain *m* d'un an; yearling *m*.

yearly ['jiəli, 'jəːli]. 1. *a.* (*a*) Annuel. (*a*) Qui se fait, qui revient, chaque année. (*b*) Qui dure un an. Y. letting, location à l'année. 2. *adv.* Annuellement; (i) une fois par an; (ii) tous les ans.

yearn [jəːn], *v.i.* To y. for, after, sth., languir pour, après, qch. To y. for the sight of one's native land, brûler de revoir son pays natal. To y. to do sth., avoir bien envie de faire qch. **yearning¹,** *a.* (*Désir*) vif, ardent; (*regard*) plein d'envie. -ly, *adv.* Avec envie. **yearning²,** *s.* Désir ardent; envie *f* (for, de).

yeast [jiːst], *s.* Levure *f*.

yeasty ['jiːsti], *a.* (*Goût m*) de levure.

yell¹ [jel], *s.* Hurlement *m*; cri aigu. To give a y., pousser un cri. *Sch:* *F:* College y., cri de guerre (des étudiants).

yell². 1. *v.i.* Hurler; crier à tue-tête. To y. with laughter, rire aux éclats; s'esclaffer. 2. *v.tr.* To y. out abuse, vociférer, hurler, des injures. **yelling,** *s.* Hurlements *mpl*.

yellow¹ ['jelou]. 1. *a.* (*a*) Jaune. *F:* Y. as a guinea, jaune comme un coing. To turn, go, y., jaunir. Y. metal, cuivre *m* jaune; laiton *m*. The y. races, les races jaunes. Lemon y., jaune citron *inv.* *S.a.* LEAD¹ 1. (*b*) *F:* Poltron, lâche. *S.a.* STREAK² 2. 2. *s.* Jaune *m*. Chrome y., jaune de chrome. **'yellow-band,** *attrib.a.* *Aut:* Yellow-band area = zone à parcage interdit ou limité. **'yellow-belly,** *s.* *U.S:* *P:* Froussard *m*, trouillard *m*. **'yellow 'bunting,** *s.* = YELLOW-HAMMER. **'yellow-dog,** *s.* *U.S:* 1. Sale type *m*. 2. *Attrib. Ind:* Y.-d. contract, convention *f* qui n'est pas conforme aux règlements syndicaux. 'yellow 'fever, *s*. Fièvre *f* jaune. 'yellow-hammer, *s*. *Orn:* Bruant *m* jaune. 'yellow 'jack, *s*. 1. *Nau:* Pavillon *m* de quarantaine. 2. *F:* = YELLOW FEVER. yellow jacket, *s*. *U.S:* 1. Petite guêpe américaine. 2. *P:* Pilule *f* à base de barbital qu'emploient les toxicomanes aux États-Unis. 'yellow 'soap, *s*. *O:* Savon *m* de Marseille.

yellow², *v.tr.* & *i*. Jaunir.

yellowish ['jelouiʃ], *a*. Jaunâtre; jaunet, -ette.

yellowness ['jelounis], *s*. Ton *m* jaune, teinte *f* jaune (de qch.); teint *m* jaune (de qn).

yelp¹ [jelp], *s*. Jappement *m*, glapissement *m*.

yelp², *v.i.* Japper, glapir. **yelping** (*a*) *s*. Jappement *m*, glapissement *m*. (*b*) *a*. Jappeur, -euse, glapissant.

yen¹ [jen], *v.i.* *U.S:* *F:* = YEARN.

yen², *s*. *U.S:* *F:* = YEARNING¹.

yeoman, *pl.* -men ['joumən, -mən], *s.m.* 1. Petit propriétaire; franc-tenancier; gros fermier. *F:* To do yeoman('s) service, fournir un effort précieux. 2. Y. of the Guard, hallebardier, (i) de la garde du corps, (ii) de service à la Tour de Londres. 3. *Navy:* Gardien; magasinier. *U.S:* Sous-officier, commis, aux écritures. *S.a.* SIGNAL¹ 3.

yeomanry ['joumənri], *s*. *Coll.* (*a*) Petits propriétaires. (*b*) *Mil: A:* Corps de cavalerie composé de volontaires.

yes [jes], *adv.* (*a*) Oui; parfaitement; (*contradicting negation*) si; si fait. To answer y. or no, répondre par oui ou non. Y., certainly, mais oui. You didn't hear me?—Y., I did, vous ne m'avez pas entendu?—Si (fait). (*b*) (*Interrogatively*) Y.? (i) vraiment? (ii) et puis après? 'yes-man, *s*. *F:* Béni-oui-oui, *m inv*.

yesterday ['jestədi], *adv.* & *s*. Hier (*m*). The day before y., avant-hier (*m*). Y. week, il y a eu hier huit jours. Y. was the sixteenth, c'était hier le seize. Y. morning, hier (au) matin.

yet [jet]. I. *adv.* 1. (*a*) Encore. I can see him y., je le vois encore. (*b*) Y. more, encore plus. Y. again, encore une fois. 2. Déjà; jusqu'ici. Need you go y.? faut-il que vous partiez déjà? Not y., pas encore. It will not happen just y., nous n'en sommes pas encore là. As y. nothing has been done, jusqu'à présent, jusqu'ici, on n'a rien fait. 3. Malgré tout. He will win y., malgré tout il gagnera. I'll do it y.! j'y arriverai! II. yet, *conj.* Néanmoins, cependant; tout de même. And y. I like him, et cependant, et malgré tout, il me plaît.

yew [ju:], *s*. *Bot:* Y.(-tree), if *m*.

Yid [jid], *s*. *Pej:* Youpin, -ine.

Yiddish ['jidiʃ], *a*. & *s*. *Ling:* Judéo-allemand (*m*), yiddish (*m*).

yield¹ [ji:ld], *s*. 1. Production *f* (d'une mine); rapport *m* (d'un arbre fruitier); rendement *m*, récolte *f* (d'un champ). If there is a good y. of wheat this year, si les blés donnent cette année. The y. on these shares is large, ces actions rapportent beaucoup. Net y., revenu net. 2. Fléchissement *m*. 'yield-ca'pacity, *s*. Productivité. 'yield-point, *s*. *Mec:* Limite *f* de résistance. 'yield-stress, *s*. Résistance *f* (élastique) des matériaux.

yield². 1. *v.tr.* (*a*) Rendre, donner. (*b*) Rapporter, produire. Land that yields no return, terre qui ne rend rien. Money that yields interest, argent qui rapporte. *Abs.* Ground that yields well, terre qui donne un bon rendement. *Lit:* To y. (up) the ghost, rendre l'âme. (*c*) Céder (une forteresse, un droit). To y. ground, céder du terrain. *P.N:* 'Y. right of way' = "Priorité *f* à droite." 2. *v.i.* (*a*) Se rendre; faire sa soumission; céder (to, à). To y. to temptation, succomber à la tentation. The frost is yielding, la gelée s'adoucit. To y. to nobody in courage, ne le céder à personne en courage. (*Of ship*) To y. to the helm, obéir à la barre. (*b*) S'affaisser, fléchir, plier. The plank yielded under our weight, la planche céda sous notre poids. **yielding¹**, *a*. 1. (*Of pers.*) Facile, complaisant. In a y. moment, dans un moment de faiblesse. 2. (*a*) Mou, *f*. molle. Y. ground, sol mou, peu résistant. (*b*) Souple, élastique. **yielding²**, *s*. 1. Rendement *m*. 2. (*a*) Soumission *f*. (*b*) Reddition *f* (d'une forteresse); cession *f* (d'un droit); abandon *m* (d'un argument). 3. Affaissement *m*, fléchissement *m*.

yod [jɔd], *s*. *Ling:* Yod *m*.

yodel¹ ['joudl], *s*. *Mus:* Ioulement *m*, tyrolienne *f*.

yodel², *v.i.* (yodel(l)ed) *Mus:* Iouler, yodler; chanter à la tyrolienne.

yod(e)ler, yodeller ['joudlə(r)], *s*. Chanteur, -euse, tyrolien, -ienne.

yoga ['jougə], *s*. Yoga *m*.

yogi ['jougi], *s*. Yogi *m*.

yogurt, yoghurt, yoghourt ['jɔgə:t], *s*. Yaourt *m*, yogourt *m*.

yo-heave-ho ['jouhi:v'hou], **yoho** [jo'hou], *int.* *Nau:* O(h), hisse!

yoicks [jɔiks], *int.* *Ven:* = Taïaut!

yoke¹ [jouk], *s*. 1. Joug *m*. Y. oxen, bœufs d'attelage. Y. of oxen, couple *f*, attelage *m* (de bœufs). To throw off, cast off, the y., secouer le joug; s'affranchir du joug. 2. (*For carrying two pails*) Palanche *f*. 3. *Dressm:* Empiècement *m*. 4. (*a*) *El:* Culasse *f* (d'aimant); carcasse *f*, bâti *m* (de dynamo). (*b*) *Mch:* (*Cross-head*) Joug. 'yoke-elm, *s*. *Bot:* Charme *m*.

yoke², *v.tr.* 1. Accoupler (des bœufs); mettre (des bœufs) au joug; atteler (des bœufs) (to the plough, à la charrue). 2. Accoupler (les pièces d'un appareil). 3. Unir.

yokel ['jouk(ə)l], *s*. Rustre *m*; campagnard *m*.

yolk [jouk], *s*. Jaune *m* d'œuf. 'yolk-bag, -sac, *s*. *Biol:* Membrane vitelline.

yon [jɔn], *a*. & *adv*. A: = YONDER.

yonder ['jɔndər]. 1. *adv.* Over y., là-bas. 2. *A:* *a*. Ce . . . -là, *f*. cette . . . -là, *pl.* ces . . . -là. Y. elms, ces ormes là-bas.

yore ['jɔ:r], *s*. *A:* Of y., (d')autrefois. In days of y., au temps jadis; autrefois.

Yorkshire ['jɔ:kʃiər]. *Pr.n.* Le comté d'York. Y. pudding, pâte cuite au-dessous du rôti.

you [ju:], *pers. pron.* (i) *Voc:* (ii) *sg.* (*addressing relatives, children, etc.*) tu, te, toi. 1. (*a*) (*Nom.*) Vous; tu. Y. are very kind, vous êtes bien aimable(s); tu es bien aimable. There y. are, vous voilà, te voilà. *Tp:* Are y. there? allô! (*b*) (*As object*) Vous; te. I hope to see y. to-morrow, j'espère vous voir, te voir, demain. I will give y. some, je vous en donnerai; je t'en donnerai. (*c*) Between y. and me, (i) entre vous et moi, entre toi et moi; (ii) entre nous soit dit. Away with y.! allez-vous-en! va-t'en! 2. (*a*) Y. and I will go by train, vous et moi, nous irons par le train. It is y., c'est vous, toi. If I were y., (si j'étais) à votre place. Y. are the master, c'est vous le maître. *F:* Hi! y. there! eh! dites donc, là-bas! (*b*) (*In the imperative*) Now 'y. make a speech, à votre tour de parler. Don't y. talk so much! N'en dis pas tant, toi! (*c*) Y. lawyers, y. Englishmen, vous autres avocats, vous autres Anglais. Y. idiot (, y.)! idiot que vous êtes! imbécile, va! 3. *A:* Sit y. down, asseyez-vous. Get y. gone, allez-vous-en. 4. (Indefinite) On. Y. never can tell, on ne sait jamais. When y. ask a girl to be your wife, quand on demande à une jeune fille d'être votre femme. . . . The joy y. feel when y. meet a friend, la joie qui vous saisit quand on rencontre un ami.

you'd [ju:d] = you would, you had.

you'll [ju:l] = you will.

young [jʌŋ]. 1. *a*. (*a*) Jeune; (*of animal*) petit. Younger, plus jeune. Pliny the Younger, Pline le Jeune. Younger son, younger daughter, fils cadet, fille cadette. Youngest, le, la, plus jeune; le cadet, la cadette. When I was twenty years younger, quand j'avais vingt ans de moins. We are only y. once, jeunesse n'a qu'un temps. I am not so y. as I was, je n'ai plus mes jambes de vingt ans. Y. men, jeunes gens *m*. *S.a.* LADY 1, 4, MAN¹ 3. Y. Mr Smith, (i) M. Smith fils; (ii) le jeune M. Smith. (*b*) To grow y. again, to grow younger, rajeunir. You are looking years younger! comme vous avez rajeuni! (*c*) The night is still y., la nuit n'est que peu avancée. (*d*) *F:* Lake like a y. sea, lac grand comme une petite mer. 2. *s. pl. inv.* (*a*) Les jeunes gens; la jeunesse. The y. and the not so y., les jeunes et les moins jeunes. Books for the y., livres pour la jeunesse. (*b*) Animal and its y., animal et ses petits. (*c*) *Husb:* Sow with y., truie pleine.

youngish ['jʌŋiʃ], *a*. Assez jeune; jeunet, jeunette.

youngling ['jʌŋliŋ], *s*. *U.S:* Jeune homme *m*; jeune fille *f*; jeune femme *f*; (*animal*) petit, -ite.

youngster ['jʌŋstər], s. (a) Jeune personne f; esp. jeune homme m. (b) Petit, -ite; garçon m, fillette f, F: gosse mf.

your ['jɔːr], poss.a. 1. (i) Votre, pl. vos; (ii) sg. (when addressing relatives, children, etc.) ton, f. ta, pl. tes. Y. house, votre maison, ta maison. Y. friends, vos ami(e)s, tes ami(e)s. Is it the most recent of y. books? c'est votre livre le plus récent? Have you hurt y. hand? vous vous êtes fait mal à la main? Games: Y. turn! à vous! Y. worship, (i) monsieur le maire, (ii) occ. monsieur le juge. 2. (Indefinite. Cf. you 4.) Son, f. sa, pl. ses. You cannot alter y. nature, on ne peut pas changer son caractère. 3. (Ethic) Y. true reformer is unconscious of distinctions, le vrai réformateur ne sait pas distinguer.

you're [juər] = you are.

yours ['jɔːz], poss.pron. (i) Le vôtre; (ii) sg. (when addressing relatives, children, etc.) le tien, la tienne. (a) This is y., ceci est à vous, à toi. The idea is y., l'idée est de vous. I should like to read something of y., je voudrais bien lire quelque chose de vous. He is a friend of y., c'est un de vos amis. That pride of y., votre orgueil. S.a. FAITHFULLY 1, TRULY 1. (b) You and y., vous et les vôtres; toi et les tiens.

yourself [jɔːˈself], **yourselves** [jɔːˈselvz], pers. pron. See SELF 4.

yourt, yurt [juət], s. Iourte f, yourte f.

youth [juːθ, pl. juː̃ðz], s. 1. Jeunesse f, adolescence f, jeune âge m. From y. upwards he showed talent, dès sa jeunesse, il a fait preuve de talent. Myth: The fountain of Y., la Fontaine de Jouvence. Prov: Y. will have its way, il faut que jeunesse se passe. 2. Jeune homme, adolescent m. 3. Coll. Jeunes gens m (garçons et filles); jeunesse (du village, etc.). 'youth-'hostel, s. Auberge f de la Jeunesse. 'youth-'hosteller, s. Ajiste mf (from initials A.J.). 'youth-'hostelling, s. Ajisme m.

youthful ['juːθf(u)l], a. 1. Jeune; juvénile. To look y., avoir l'air jeune. 2. Y. indiscretions, erreurs f de jeunesse. -fully, adv. En jeune homme, en jeune fille.

youthfulness ['juːθf(u)lnis], s. Jeunesse f; juvénilité f; air m de jeunesse.

you've [juːv] = you have.

yowl[1] [jaul], s. Hurlement m (de chien); miaulement m (de chat).

yowl[2], v.i. (Of dog) Hurler; (of cat) miauler.

yttrium ['itriəm], s. Ch: Yttrium m.

yucca ['jʌkə], s. Bot: Yucca m.

Yugoslav ['juːgouˈslɑːv], a. & s. Yougoslave (mf).

Yugoslavia ['juːgouˈslɑːviə]. Pr.n. Yougoslavie f.

Yukon ['juːkɔn]. Pr.n. Geog: Le Yukon.

Yule [juːl], s. A: Noël m. 'yule-log, s. Bûche f de Noël. 'yule-tide, s. A: L'époque f de Noël; les fêtes f de Noël.

Z, z [zed, *U.S:* zi:], *s.* (La lettre) Z, z *m.* *Tp:* Z for zebra, Z comme Zoë.

zabaglione [ˌzæbæl'jouni], *s.* *Cu:* Sabayon *m.*

Zambezi (the) [ðəzæm'bi:zi]. *Pr.n.* *Geog:* Le Zambèze.

Zambia ['Zæmbiə], *pr.n.* *Geog:* La Zambie.

zambo ['zæmbou], *s.* *Ethn:* *U.S:* Métis, -isse.

zany ['zeini], *s.* 1. *A.Th:* Zan(n)i *m*, bouffon *m.* 2. *A:* Sot, *f.* sotte; niais, -aise.

Zanzibar ['zænzibɑ:(r), 'zænzi'bɑ:(r)], *Pr.n.* *Geog:* Zanzibar.

zareba, zariba [zə'ri:bə], *s.* (*In Africa*) Clôture fortifiée de ronces; camp *m* de fortune.

zeal [zi:l], *s.* Zèle *m*, ardeur *f*; empressement *m.* **To make a show of z.**, faire du zèle.

Zealand ['zi:lənd]. *Pr.n.* La Zélande.

zealot ['zelət], *s.* 1. *Hist:* Zélateur, -trice; zélote *m.* 2. Fanatique *mf*, zélateur (for, de).

zealous ['zeləs], *a.* Zélé; empressé. **Z. for sth.**, plein de zèle pour qch. **-ly**, *adv.* Avec zèle; ardemment.

zebra ['zi:brə, 'zebrə], *s.* Zèbre *m.* **Striped like a z.**, zébré. **Z.-markings**, zébrure *f.* **Z. (crossing) =** passage *m*, pour piétons.

zebu ['zi:bu:], *s.* *Z:* Zébu *m*; bœuf *m* à bosse.

zemindar ['zemindɑːr], *s.* (*India*) *Hist:* Zémindar *m*; propriétaire foncier.

zenana [ze'nɑːnə], *s.* (*India*) Zénana *m*, harem *m.* *Tex:* **Z. cloth**, zénana.

zenith ['zeniθ], *s.* *Astr:* Zénith *m.* **At the z. of his fame**, à l'apogée, au sommet, de sa gloire.

zenithal ['zeniθ(ə)l], *a.* Zénithal, -aux.

zephyr ['zefər], *s.* 1. (*Wind*) Zéphire *m*, zéphyr(e) *m.* 2. *Tex:* **Z. (wool)**, laine zéphire.

zeppelin ['zepəlin], *s.* *Aer:* *Hist:* Zeppelin *m.*

zero ['ziərou], *s.* Zéro *m.* 1. *Ph:* **Absolute z.**, zéro absolu. *Mth:* *Surv:* **Z. point**, point *m* zéro, (point) origine *f.* **Determination of the z. point**, zérotage *m.* **Z. tension**, tension nulle. **'zero hour'**, *s.* *Mil:* L'heure *f* (de l'attaque); l'heure H.

zest [zest], *s.* (*a*) Enthousiasme *m*, entrain *m.* **To fight with a z.**, combattre avec élan. **To eat with z.**, manger avec appétit. (*b*) Saveur *f*, goût *m.* **To add z. to the adventure**, donner du piquant à l'aventure.

zeta ['zi:tə], *s.* *Gr.Alph:* (D)zêta *m.*

Zeus [zju:s]. *Pr.n.m.* *Myth:* Zeus.

zigzag[1] ['zigzæg], *s.* Zigzag *m.* **In zigzags**, en zigzag. *Nau:* **To steer a z. course**, faire route en zigzag, en zigzaguant; faire des zigzags. **Z. riveting**, rivetage en quinconce *adv.* **The road runs z.**, le chemin fait des zigzags.

zigzag[2], *v.* (zigzagged) 1. *v.i.* Zigzaguer; faire des zigzags, des s. 2. *v.tr.* Disposer (des rivets) en quinconce. **zigzagging**, *s.* Zigzaguement *m*, zigzagure *f*; lacets *mpl*; tournées *fpl* et virées *fpl.*

zinc [ziŋk], *s.* Zinc *m.* 1. **To cover a roof with z.**, zinguer un toit. *S.a.* OINTMENT. 2. **Z. block**, zincogravure *f*; *F:* zinc. **zinc-bearing**, *a.* Zincifère. **zinc-'plate**, *s.* *Com:* Zinc *m* en feuilles. **zinc-'plating**, *s.* Zingage *m.* **'zinc-trade**, *s.* Zinguerie *f.* **'zinc-ware**, *s.* Zinguerie *f.* **'zinc-worker**, *s.* Zingueur *m.* **'zinc-works**, *s.* Zinguerie *f.* **'zinc-yellow**, *s.* Jaune *m*, chromate *m*, de zinc.

zincograph ['ziŋkogræf, -grɑ:f], *s.* *Phot.Engr:* Zincogravure *f*; gravure *f* sur zinc.

zincographer [ziŋ'kogrəfər], *s.* Zincographe *m*, zincograveur *m.*

zincography [ziŋ'kogrəfi], *s.* *Phot.Engr:* Zincographie *f.* **To reproduce by z.**, zincographier (un dessin).

zing [ziŋ], *s.* *U.S:* *F:* Vitalité *f.*

zinnia ['ziniə], *s.* *Bot:* Zinnia *m.*

Zion ['zaiən]. 1. *Pr.n.* Sion *m* ((i) la colline; (ii) Jérusalem). 2. *s.* Chapelle *f*, temple *m* (non-conformiste).

Zionism ['zaiənizm], *s.* *Pol:* Sionisme *m.*

Zionist ['zaiənist], *a.* & *s.* *Pol:* Sioniste (*mf*).

zip[1] [zip], *s.* 1. Sifflement *m* (d'une balle). 2. *F:* Énergie *f.* **Put a z. into it**, mettez-y du nerf. 3. **Z. fastener**, Fermeture *f* Éclair *inv.* (*R.t.m.*); fermeture à curseur; (*in Belgium*) tirette-éclair *f.*

zip[2], 1. *v.i.* (zipped) Siffler (comme une balle). (*Of car*) **To z. past**, passer comme un éclair. 2. *v.tr.* *F:* **Can you z. me up?** peux-tu fermer ma Fermeture Éclair?

zipper ['zipər], *s.* *F:* = Zip fastener.

zippy ['zipi], *a.* *F:* Plein d'énergie; plein d'entrain. **Look z.!** grouille-toi!

zircon ['zə:kən], *s.* *Miner:* Zircon *m.*

zirconium [zə:'kounjəm], *s.* *Metall:* *Ch:* Zirconium *m.*

zither ['ziθər], *s.* *Mus:* Cithare *f.*

zodiac ['zoudiæk], *s.* *Astr:* Zodiaque *m.*

zodiacal [zou'daiək(ə)l], *a.* Zodiacal, -aux.

zombi(e) ['zombi], *s.* Zombi *m.*

zonal ['zoun(ə)l], *a.* Zonal, -aux.

zone[1] [zoun], *s.* Zone *f.* 1. *A.Cost:* *Lit:* Zone; ceinture *f.* 2. *Geom:* **Spherical z.**, zone sphérique. *Geog:* **Torrid z.**, zone torride. **Frigid zones**, les zones glaciales. **The Canal Z.**, la Zone du Canal (de Panama). *Chr:* **Z. time**, l'heure *f* du fuseau. *Adm:* **Frontier z.**, zone frontière. *U.S:* **Postal delivery z.**, zone de livraison postale. *Aut:* **Pink z.** = zone bleue. **No parking z.**, zone d'interdiction de stationner. **No passing z.**, zone de dépassement interdit. *U.S:* **Slow-drive z.** (*round a town, etc.*), périmètre *m* de marche lente. *Mil:* **War z.**, **Army z.**, zone des Armées. **Danger z.**, zone dangereuse. **Neutral z.**, zone démilitarisée. **Evacuation z.**, zone de l'arrière. **Z. of fire**, zone de tir. *W.Tel:* **Skip, silent, z.**, zone de silence.

zone[2], *v.tr.* Répartir (une ville, etc.) en zones. *Com:* Distribuer (des produits) par régions. **zoning**, *s.* *Town P:* Répartition *f* en zones.

zoo [zu:], *s.* *F:* Jardin *m* zoologique; *esp.* **the Z.**, le Jardin zoologique de Londres. *F:* Zoo *m.*

zoobiology [zouəbai'olədʒi], *s.* Zoobiologie *f.*

zoochemistry [zouə'kemistri], *s.* Zoochimie *f.*

zoography [zou'ogrəfi], *s.* Zoographie *f.*

zooid ['zouid], *s.* *Z:* Zooïde *m.*

zoolite ['zouəlait], *s.* *Paleont:* Zoolit(h)e *m.*

zoological [ˌzouə'lodʒik(ə)l], *f.* ˌzuə'lodʒik(ə)l], *a.* Zoologique. **The Z. [zu-] Gardens**, = THE ZOO.

zoologist [zou'olədʒist], *s.* Zoologiste *m.*

zoology [zou'olədʒi], *s.* Zoologie *f.*

zoom[1] [zu:m], *s.* 1. Bourdonnement *m*; vrombissement *m.* 2. *Av:* Montée *f* en chandelle.

zoom[2], *v.i.* 1. Bourdonner; vrombir. 2. *Av:* Monter en chandelle; (se) cabrer. 3. *F:* **To z. up**, arriver en trombe.

zoophaga [zou'ofəgə], *s.pl.* Zoophages *m.*

zoophagous [zou'ofəgəs], *a.* Zoophage.

zoophyta [zouə'faitə], *s.pl.* *Biol:* Zoophytes *m.*

zooplankton [ˌzouə'plæŋktən], *s.* *Biol:* Zooplancton *m.*

zoot-suit ['zu:t,su:t], *s.* *Cost:* *U.S:* Costume *m* zazou. **zoot-suiter**, *s.* *P:* *U.S:* = zazou *m.*

zostera ['zostərə], *s.* *Bot:* Zostère *f.*

zouave [zwɑ:v], *s.* Zouave *m.*

zounds [zaundz], *int:* *A:* Morbleu!

Zulu ['zu:lu:], *a.* & *s.* *Ethn:* Zoulou *m*, *pl.* -ous.

Zululand ['zu:lulænd]. *Pr.n.* Le Zoulouland.

zygoma, *pl.* **-ata** [zai'goumə, -ətə], *s.* *Anat:* Zygoma *m*; os *m* malaire; os de la pommette.

zygomatic [ˌzaigo'mætik], *a.* *Anat:* Zygomatique.

zymosis [zai'mousis], *s.* Fermentation *f.*

zymotic [zai'motik], *a.* (Maladie) zymotique.

a 1. *answer.* 2. *acre.* 3. *ampere.*
A.A. 1. *Associate in Arts.* 2 *Alcoholics Anonymous.* 3. *Anti-Aircraft*=D.C.A., Défense contre avions.
AAA *American Automobile Association*=A.C.F., Automobile Club de France.
AATA (F, G, I, SP) *American Association of Teachers of Arabic (French, German, Italian, Spanish and Portuguese).*
AAU *Amateur Athletic Union.*
A.B. *Bachelor of Arts*=L. ès L.
ABA *American Bar (Booksellers, Bankers, others) Association.*
ABC *American Broadcasting Company.*
abr *abridged.*
a-c, AC *El: alternating current,* C.A., courant alternatif.
acct *account.*
ACLU *American Civil Liberties Union.*
AD *anno Domini,* apr. J.-C., après Jésus-Christ.
adj 1. *adjective.* 2. *Mil: adjutant.*
ad lib. *ad libitum, q.v.*
adm *Navy: admiral.*
ADP *automatic data processing.*
ADT *Atlantic (or Alaska) Daylight Time,* heure légale d'été (fuseau de l'Atlantique ou de Alaska).
AEA *American Economic Association.*
AEC *Atomic Energy Commission.*
AF 1. *Air Force.* 2. *Air France.*
AFL-CIO *American Federation of Labor and Congress of Industrial Organizations*=C.G.T., Confédération générale du Travail.
agt *agent.*
AHA *American Historical Association.*
AID *Agency for International Development.*
AK *Alaska.*
Ala (AL) *Alabama.*
Alta *Alberta.*
a.m. *before noon.*
A & M *Sch: agricultural and mechanical.*
A.M. 1. *Master of Arts.* 2. *amplitude modulation.*
AMA *American Medical (Management, others) Association.*
AME *African Methodist Episcopal Church.*
amp *ampere.*
AMS *American Mathematical Society.*
amt *amount.*
anon. *anonymous, q.v.*
ans *answer.*
ante *before.*
AP *Associated Press.*
APA *American Psychological (Philological, Philosophical, others) Association.*
APO *army post office.*
approx *approximately, q.v.*
Apr *April.*
APSA *American Political Science Association.*
ARC *American Red Cross.*
Ariz (AZ) *Arizona.*
Ark (AR) *Arkansas*
art *article.*
ASA *American Standards (Sociological, Statistical), Association.*
ASAP *as soon as possible.*
ASPCA *American Society for the Prevention of Cruelty to Animals* = S.P.A., Société protectrice des Animaux.
assn *association.*
assoc *associate.*
asst *assistant.*
AST *Atlantic (or Alaska) Standard Time,* heure légale de l'Atlantique (de Alaska).
ATA *American Translators Association.*
atm *Ph Meas: atmosphere,* a.t.m.
atty *attorney.*
Aug *August.*
AV 1. *audiovisual.* 2. *ad valorem.* 3. *Authorized Version.*
Av(e) *avenue.*

b 1. *born,* né(e). 2. *billion,* milliard.
B.A. 1. *Bachelor of Arts*=L. ès L. 2. *Buenos Aires.*
bal *balance.*
Bart *baronet.*

BBC *British Broadcasting Corporation.*
bbl *barrel.*
BC 1. *before Christ,* av. J.-C., avant Jésus-Christ. 2. *British Columbia.*
B.C.E. *Bachelor of Chemical or Civil Engineering.*
BDT *Bering Daylight Time,* heure légale d'été (fuseau de la mer de Béring).
bf *boldface.*
b/f *Book-k: brought forward,* report.
bhp *Aut: brake horse power.*
bk 1. *book.* 2. *bank.*
bldg *building.*
B.L.S. 1. *Bachelor of Library Science.* 2. *Bureau of Labor Statistics.*
blvd *boulevard.*
bo 1. *P: body odor.* 2. *back order.*
BOAC *British Overseas Airways Corporation.*
BRD *Federal Republic of Germany,* R.F.A., République fédérale d'Allemagne.
brig gen *Mil: brigadier general,* général de brigade.
bro(s) *brother(s).*
B.S. *Bachelor of Science*=L. ès Sc.
BST 1. *Bering Standard Time,* heure légale du fuseau de la mer de Béring. 2. *British Summer Time,* heure légale d'été en G.-B.
btu *British thermal unit.*
bu *bushel.*

c. 1. (also **ca.**) *circa.* 2. *cent, centimeter, century.* 3. *copyright.* 4. *cup.*
C 1. *Centigrade.* 2. *one hundred.*
CAB *Civil Aeronautics Board.*
Calif (CA) *California.*
Can *Canada.*
cap(s) *capital(s).*
capt *Mil: captain.*
CARE *Cooperative for American Remittances to Everywhere.*
CB *Cape Breton.*
CBC *Canadian Broadcasting Corporation.*
CBE *Commander of the Order of the British Empire.*
CBS *Columbia Broadcasting System.*
CBW *chemical and biological warfare.*
cc 1. *cubic centimeter.* 2. *copy, copies.*
CD 1. *Civil Defense*=D.P., défense passive. 2. *Congressional district.*
CDT *Central Daylight Time,* heure légale d'été (fuseau central).
CEA *Council of Economic Advisers.*
C.E. *Civil or Chemical Engineer.*
CEEB *College Entrance Examination Board.*
cent *century,* siècle.
cf. *compare,* conférez.
c/f *Book-k: carried forward,* report.
ch *chapter,* chapitre.
Chas *Charles.*
CIA *Central Intelligence Agency*=Deuxième Bureau.
cif *cost, insurance, and freight,* c.a.f., coût, assurance, fret.
C in C *Mil: commander-in-chief,* commandant en chef.
cm *centimeter.*
co 1. *Com: company-* X & Co., X et Cie. 2. *county,* comté.
CO 1. *Mil: commanding officer,* officier commandant. 2. *conscientious objector.*
c/o *care of,* a/s, aux soins de.
C.O.D. *cash (or collect) on delivery,* contre remboursement.
col 1. *Mil: colonel.* 2. *column.*
Colo (CO) *Colorado.*
comdr *Navy: commander.*
Conn (CT) *Connecticut.*
Cons *Pol: conservative,* conservateur, -trice.
CONUS *Continental United States.*
CORE *Congress of Racial Equality.*
corp *corporation.*
CP *Communist Party,* P.C., parti communiste
CPA *Certified Public Accountant.*
cpl *Mil: corporal,* caporal.
cr *Book-k:* 1. *credit.* 2. *creditor.*
CST *Central Standard Time,* heure légale du fuseau central.

ct *court.*
cu *cubic.*
CWO *Mil: chief warrant officer,* adjutant.
cwt(s) *Meas hundredweight(s), q.v.*
CZ *Canal Zone.*

d 1. *died, mort.* 2. *pence.*
DA *district attorney.*
DAB *Dictionary of American Biography.*
DAH *Dictionary of American History.*
DAR *Daughters of the American Revolution.*
db *decibel.*
DBE *Dame Commander of the Order of the British Empire.*
d-c, DC *El: direct current.*
D.C. *District of Columbia.*
d/c *Book-k: double column.*
D.D. *Doctor of Divinity.*
DDR *German Democratic Republic,* R.D.A., République démocratique allemande.
DDS *Doctor of Dental Surgery.*
DDT *dichloro-diphenyl-trichloroethane* (insecticide), D.D.T.
d/e *Book-k: double-entry.*
deb *debenture.*
Dec *December.*
Del (DE) *Delaware.*
Dem *Democrat.*
dept *department.*
diss *dissertation.*
dist *district.*
div *dividend.*
D. Lit(t) *Doctor of Literature.*
DM *Deutsche Mark.*
DNB *Dictionary of National Biography.*
do. *ditto.*
DOA *dead on arrival.*
DOD *Department of Defense.*
doz *dozen.* d.z., douzaine.
DP *displaced person,* personne déplacée.
dr 1. *debtor.* 2. *debit.*
Dr. 1. *Doctor.* 2. *drive.*
DSB *Dictionary of Scientific Biography.*
D. Sc. *Doctor of Science.*
DT's *delerium tremens.*
D.V.M. *Doctor of Veterinary Medicine.*
dwt *Meas:* 1. *pennyweight, q.v.* 2. *deadweight tons.*
dz dozen.

E *east,* est.
ea *each.*
ECSC *European Coal and Steel Community* C.E.C.A., Communauté européenne du charbon et de l'acier.
ed 1. *editor.* 2. *edition*
Ed.D. *Doctor of Education.*
EDP electronic data processing.
EDT *Eastern Daylight Time,* heure légale d'été (fuseau de l'est).
EE *electrical engineer.*
EEC *European Economic Community (Common Market),* C.E.E., Communauté économique européenne.
EFTA *European Free Trade Association.*
e.g. *exempli gratia,* p. ex., par exemple.
enc, encl *enclosure.*
ENE *east-northeast,* est-nord-est.
ens *Nav: ensign.*
e & oe *errors and omissions excepted,* e.o.o.e., s.e. ou o.
ESE *east-southeast,* est-sud-est.
esp *especially.*
ESP *extrasensory perception.*
Esq. *V.* ESQUIRE.
est *estimated.*
EST *Eastern Standard Time,* heure légale de l'est.
ETA *estimated time of arrival.*
et al. *et alii, and others.*
etc. *et cetera.*
ETD *estimated time of departure.*
ETS *Educational Testing Service.*
et seq. *et sequens, and the following,* et qui s'ensuit.
ex *example,* exemple.

ex div. *without dividend,* exD., ex-dividende.

f 1. *feminine.* 2. *and the following (page or line).* 3. *Phot: focal distance,* distance focale.
F 1. *Ph: Fahrenheit.* 2. *franc.*
FAA *Federal Aviation Agency.*
fac. *facsimile.*
FAO *Food and Agriculture Organization,* OAA, Organisation des Nations Unies pour l'alimentation et l'agriculture.
FBI *Federal Bureau of Investigation.*
FCC *Federal Communications Commission.*
FDA *Food and Drug Administration.*
FDIC *Federal Deposit Insurance Corporation.*
FDR *Pres. Franklin Delano Roosevelt.*
Feb *February.*
ff. *and following (pages or lines),* qui suivent.
FHA *Federal Housing Administration.*
FICA *Federal Insurance Contributions Act.*
fifo *first in first out.*
fig. *figure.*
fl. *flourished.*
Fla (FL) *Florida.*
fl oz *fluid ounce. V.* OUNCE¹ 2.
FM *frequency modulation.*
fn *footnote.*
f.o.b. *free on board,* f.à.b., franco à bord.
fpm *feet per minute.*
fps *feet per second.*
Fri *Friday.*
ft *foot, feet.*
FTC *Federal Trade Commission.*
fwd *forward.*
FYI *for your information.*

g 1. *gram.* 2. *gravity.*
Ga (GA) *Georgia.*
gal *gallon, q.v.*
GATT *General Agreement on Tariffs and Trade,* Accord général sur les tarifs douaniers et le commerce.
GB *Great Britain,* Grande-Bretagne.
gen *Mil: general,* général d'armée.
Geo *George.*
GHQ *Mil: general headquarters,* G.Q.C.
GI 1. *government issue.* 2. *Mil: enlisted soldier,* U.S. Army, mobilisé américain.
GMT *Greenwich mean time,* heure (du méridien) de Greenwich.
GNP *gross national product.*
GOP *Grand Old Party (Republican).*
gov *governor.*
govt *government.*
GP *Med: general practitioner.*
GPO *Government Printing Office.*
gr 1. *grain.* 2. *gross.*
GU *Guam.*

hcf *Mth: highest common factor.*
HEW *Department of Health, Education, and Welfare.*
hf 1. *half.* 2. *high frequency.*
HI *Hawaii.*
hi-fi *high fidelity.*
hon. 1. *Honorable.* 2. *honorary.*
hp *horsepower,* c.v., ch., cheval-vapeur.
HQ *Mil: headquarters* = E.M.
hr *hour.*
HR *House of Representatives.*
HRH *His (Her) Royal Highness.*
HST *Pres. Harry S. Truman.*
HUD *Department of Housing and Urban Development.*

IA *Iowa.*
ibid. *ibidem.*
IBM *International Business Machines* (Inc.).
ICBM *intercontinental ballistic missile,* fusée intercontinentale.
ICC *Interstate Commerce Commission.*
ICJ *International Court of Justice,* CIJ, Cour internationale de Justice.
id. *idem.*
ID *Idaho.*

i.e. *id est, that is,* c.-à-d., c'est-à-dire.
IHS *Jesus (from Greek* IHΣOYΣ).
Ill (IL) *Illinois.*
illus **1.** *illustration.* **2.** *illustrated.*
ILO *International Labor Organization,* O.I.T., Organisation internationale du Travail.
IMF *International Monetary Fund,* F.M.I., Fonds monétaire international.
in *inch.*
inc. *incorporated, q.v.*
incl *inclusive.*
Ind (IN) *Indiana.*
inst. *instant,* ct., cour., courant.
Inst **1.** *Institute.* **2.** *Institution.*
int *interest.*
IOU *F:* "*I owe you*".
IQ *intelligence quotient,* quotient intellectuel.
IRA *Irish Republican Army.*
IRS *Internal Revenue Service.*
ital *italic.*
IUD *intrauterine device.*
IWW *International Workers of the World.*

j *Ph Meas:* **joule.**
J/A *joint account.*
Jan *January.*
JC *Jesus Christ.*
JCS *Joint Chiefs of Staff.*
J.D. *Doctor of Law.*
JFK **1.** *Pres. John Fitzgerald Kennedy.* **2.** *John F. Kennedy International Airport, New York.*
jour *journal.*
JP *Justice of the Peace.* V. PEACE **2.**
Jr. *junior.*

k *kilo.*
K **1.** *Kelvin.* **2.** *Com (want ads): thousand.* **3.** *Mus: Köchel (listing of Mozart's works).*
Kans (KS) *Kansas.*
KC **1.** *Kansas City.* **2.** *Knights of Columbus.*
kg *kilogram.*
KKK *Ku Klux Klan.*
kl *kiloliter.*
km *kilometer.*
K.O. *knock out.*
kw *kilowatt.*
Ky (KY) *Kentucky.*

l **1.** *left,* g., gauche. **2.** *liter.* **3.** *pl* **ll** *line.*
L *pound sterling,* livre sterling.
La *Louisiana.*
LA **1.** *Los Angeles.* **2.** *Louisiana.*
LAFTA *Latin American Free Trade Association.*
lat *latitude.*
lb(s) *pound(s).*
LBJ *Pres. Lyndon Baines Johnson.*
lc *Typ: lower case,* minuscules.
lcd *Mth: lowest common denominator.*
lcm *Mth: least common multiple.*
L.H.D. *Doctor of Humane Letters.*
Lib *Pol: liberal,* libéral.
lifo *last in first out.*
Litt. D. *Doctor of Letters.*
ll *lines.*
LL.B. *Bachelor of Laws* = L. en D.
LL.D. *Doctor of Laws.*
loc. cit. *loco citato, in the passage quoted.*
log *logarithm.*
long. *longitude.*
LP *long playing (record).*
LSD **1.** *Nav: an assault landing craft.* **2.** *a hallucinogenic drug.* **3.** *pounds, shillings, and pence.*
l.s.t. *local standard time.*
lt *Mil: lieutenant.*
ltd *limited.*

m **1.** *male,* masculin. **2.** *mile.* **3.** *meter,* mètre. **4.** *million.*
M **1.** *thousand.* **2.** *Monsieur.*
M.A. **1.** *Master of Arts.* **2.** *Massachusetts.*
maj *Mil: major,* commandant.
Man *Manitoba.*
Mar *March.*

Mass *Massachusetts.*
max *maximum.*
M.B.A. *Master of Business Administration.*
MBE *Member of the Order of the British Empire.*
MC **1.** *Master of Ceremonies.* V. MASTER[1]. **1.** **2.** *Member of Congress.*
Md (MD) *Maryland.*
M.D. *Doctor of Medicine* = D.M.
mdse *merchandise.*
MDT *Mountain Daylight Time,* heure légale d'été (fuseau des Rocheuses).
Me (ME) *Maine.*
M.E. **1.** *mechanical or mining engineer.* **2.** *Master of Engineering.* **3.** *Maine.*
mfd **1.** *manufactured.* **2.** *El: microfarad.*
mfg *manufacturing.*
mfr *manufacturer.*
mg *milligram.*
mgr *manager.*
mi *mile.*
Mich (MI) *Michigan.*
min *minute,* mn.
Minn (MN) *Minnesota.*
misc *miscellaneous.*
Miss *Mississippi.*
ml *milliliter.*
MLA *Modern Language Association.*
mm *millimeter.*
Mo (MO) *Missouri.*
Mon *Monday.*
Mont (MT) *Montana.*
MP **1.** *military police.* **2.** *Member of Parliament.*
mpg *miles per gallon.*
mph *miles per hour.*
Mr. *Mister*
Mrs. *Missus.*
ms, *pl* **mss.** *manuscript,* manuscrit.
MS **1.** *Mississippi.* **2.** *pl,* **MSS,** *manuscript.* **3.** *Master of Science.*
M.S. *Master of Science.*
Msgr. *R.C. Ch: Monsignor,* Mgr., Monseigneur.
m sgt *Mil:* master sergeant.
MST *Mountain Standard Time,* heure légale des Rocheuses.

n *pl.* **nn** *note.*
N *north,* nord.
na *not available.*
NAACP *National Association for the Advancement of Colored People.*
NASA *National Aeronautics and Space Administration.*
NATO *North Atlantic Treaty Organization,* O.T.A.N., Organisation du Traité de l'Atlantique Nord.
n.b. *nota bene.*
NB *New Brunswick.*
NBC *National Broadcasting Company.*
NC *North Carolina.*
NCAA *National Collegiate Athletic Association.*
NCO *Mil: non-commissioned officer.*
n.d. *no date,* sans date.
N Dak (ND) *North Dakota.*
NE *northeast,* nord-est.
Nebr (NB) *Nebraska.*
Nev (NV) *Nevada.*
NF *new franc.*
NH *New Hampshire.*
NJ *New Jersey.*
NKVD *Russian: Soviet secret police.*
NLRB *National Labor Relations Board.*
N Mex (NM) *New Mexico.*
NNE *north-northeast,* nord-nord-est.
NNW *north-northwest,* nord-nord-ouest.
no. *number,* n°, numéro.
Nov *November.*
n.p. *no place.*
NS **1.** *Nova Scotia.* **2.** *(of dates) New Style.*
nsf *Bank: not sufficient funds,* compte insuffisamment approvisionné.
NSF *National Science Foundation.*
NW *northwest,* nord-ouest.
NWT *Northwest Territories.*

NY   *New York.*
NYC   *New York City.*

OAH   *Organization of American Historians.*
OAS   *Organization of American States.*
OB   *Med:* obstetrics.
OBE   (Officer of the) Order of the British Empire.
obs   *obsolete.*
Oct   *October.*
OED   *Oxford English Dictionary.*
OEEC   *Organization for European Economic Co-operation,* O.E.C.E.
OH   *Ohio.*
OJ   *F: orange juice.*
OJT   *on-the-job training.*
Okla (OK)   *Oklahoma.*
Ont   *Ontario.*
op.   *out of print.*
op. cit.   *work cited.*
OR   **1.** *Oregon.*   **2.** *operations research.*
Oreg   *Oregon.*
os.   *out of stock.*
OS   *(of dates) Old Style.*
oz   *ounce(s).*

p   *pl*   pp *pages.*
p.a.   *per annum.*
Pa (PA)   *Pennsylvania.*
PA   *public-address (system).*
PAA   *Pan American World Airways.*
par   *paragraph.*
pat   *patent,* breveté.
pd   *paid.*
PD   *police department.*
PDT   *Pacific Daylight Time,* heure légale d'été (fuseau du Pacifique).
PEI   *Prince Edward Island.*
PERT   *Program Evaluation Review Technique.*
pfc   *Mil:* private first class.
pfd   *Com:* preferred.
PGA   *Professional Golfers' Association.*
Ph.D.   *Doctor of Philosophy.*
PIO   *public information officer,* chef du service des relations avec le public.
pk   *peck.*
pl(s)   *plate(s),* planche(s).
Pl   *place.*
P & L   *Book-k: profit and loss,* p.p., p. et p., pertes et profits.
p.m.   *after noon.*
PM   *Prime Minister,* Premier ministre.
PO   **1.** *post office,* bureau de poste.   **2.** *Nav:* petty officer, contremaître.
POE   *port of entry.*
POW   *prisoner of war,* P.G., prisonnier de guerre.
pp   *pages.*
PQ   *Province of Quebec,* le Québec.
pr   *pair.*
PR   **1.** *Puerto Rico.*   **2.** *public relations.*
pref   *preface by.*
pres   *president.*
Prof.   *Professor.*
pro tem   *pro tempore, temporarily.*
P.S.   *postscript.*
PST   *Pacific Standard Time,* heure légale du Pacifique.
pt   **1.** *part.*   **2.** *point.*   **3.** *pint.*
PT   **1.** *Nav: motor torpedo (boat),* (vedette) lance-torpilles.   **2.** *physical training,* éducation physique.
PTA   *Parent-Teacher Association.*
pto.   *please turn over. V.* OVER II. 3 (b).
pvt   *Mil:private,* soldat de 2e classe.
PX   *Mil: post exchange.*

Q   *pl*   QQ   *query, queries.*
QED   *quod erat demonstrandum, which was to be demonstrated,* C.Q.F.D., Ce qu'il fallait démontrer.
QM   *Mil: quarter master.*
qt   *quart.*
q.t.   *P: quiet (used in "On the q.t.").*
Que   *Quebec,* Québec.
q.v.   *quod vide,* voir.

r   *right,* dr., droit.
RAF   *Brit: Royal Air Force.*
RC   **1.** *Red Cross.*   **2.** *Roman Catholic.*
RCAF   *Royal Canadian Air Force.*
RCMP   *Royal Canadian Mounted Police,* la Gendarmerie royale du Canada.
RCN   *Royal Canadian Navy.*
rd   *road.*
R & D   *research and development.*
re   *in regard to.*
REA   *Rural Electrification Administration.*
recd   *received,* pour acquit.
reg   **1.** *registered.*   **2.** *regulation.*
Rep   **1.** *Representative.*   **2.** *Republican.*
rept   *report.*
res   *resolution.*
resp   *respectively.*
retd   *returned.*
rev   *revised.*
Rev.   *Ecc: See* REVEREND 2.
RFD   *rural free delivery.*
RI   *Rhode Island.*
RIP   *requiescat in pace.*
RMN   *Pres. Richard Milhous Nixon.*
R.N.   **1.** *Registered Nurse,* infirmière diplômée.   **2.** *Brit: Royal Navy*
ROTC   *Reserve Officers Training Corps.*
rpm   *revolutions per minute,* t.p.m., tours par minute.
RR   **1.** *railroad,* ch. de f., chemin de fer.   **2.** *Right Reverend. See* REVEREND 2.
R & R   *Mil: rest and recreation.*
RSVP   Répondez, s'il vous plaît.
Rt. Hon.   *Right Honorable. V.* HONOURABLE 2.
Ry   *railway,* ch. de f., chemin de fer.

S   **1.** *south,* sud.   **2.** *Senate.*   **3.** *shillings.*
s/   *signed.*
SAE   *Society of Automotive Engineers.*
Sask   *Saskatchewan.*
Sat   *Saturday.*
sc   *scene.*
S.C.   *small caps.*
SC   *South Carolina.*
SCLC   *Southern Christian Leadership Conference.*
s.d.   *sine die,* indéfiniment.
S Dak (SD)   *South Dakota.*
SDS   *Students for a Democratic Society.*
SE   *southeast,* sud-est.
s/e   *Book-k: single-entry.*
SEATO   *Southeast Asia Treaty Organization,* O.T.A.S.E., Organisation du Traité de l'Asie du Sud-Est.
sec   **1.** *second.*   **2.** *secretary.*   **3.** *section.*
SEC   *Securities and Exchange Commission.*
Sept   *September.*
ser   *series.*
SF   **1.** *San Francisco.*   **2.** *science fiction.*
sgt   *Mil: sergeant,* sergent.
sh   *shilling.*
sic   *thus, so.*
S.J.   *Society of Jesus (Jesuits).*
SM   *Master of Science.*
SNCC   *Student Nonviolent Coordinating Committee.*
Soc   *society.*
SOP   *standard operating procedure.*
SOS   *Nau: S.O.S.,* signal de détresse.
sp. gr.   *Ph: specific gravity,* masse spécifique.
sq   *square.*
sq. ft.   *square feet.*
Sr.   *senior.*
SRO   **1.** *single room occupancy*   **2.** *standing room only.*

SS   *Nau: steamship,* s/s, vapeur.
SSE   *south-southeast,* sud-sud-est.
SSW   *south-southwest,* sud-sud-ouest.
St   **1.** *street,* r. rue.   **2.** *Saint.*
stat   **1.** *statute.*   **2.** *photostatic copy* ("Photostat", a trademark).
std   *standard.*
stet   *Lt: let it stand.*

Sun   *Sunday.*
supt   *superintendent.*
SW   *southwest,* sud-ouest.

TB   *Med: tuberculosis.*
tbsp   *tablespoon.*
tel   1. *telephone.*   2. *telegraph.*   3. *telegram.*
Tenn (TN)   *Tennessee.*
Ter   *terrace.*
Tex (TX)   *Texas.*
THI   *temperature humidity index.*
Thos   *Thomas.*
Thurs   *Thursday.*
tr   *transpose.*
trans   1. *translation, translator, translated by.*   2.
   transportation.
treas   *treasurer.*
tsp   *teaspoon.*
Tues   *Tuesday.*
TV   *television.*
TVA   *Tennessee Valley Authority.*
TWA   *Trans World Airlines.*

U   *University.*
UAR   *United Arab Republic,* R.A.U.
UCMJ   *Uniform Code of Military Justice.*
UFO   *unidentified flying object.*
uhf   *ultra high frequency,* ultra haute fréquence.
UJA   *United Jewish Appeal.*
UK   *United Kingdom,* Royaume Uni.
ult.   *ultimo, q.v.*
UN   *United Nations,* O.N.U., Organisation des
   Nations unies.
UNESCO   *United Nations Educational, Scientific and*
   Cultural Organization, Organisation des Nations
   unies pour l'Education, la Science et la Culture.
UPI   *United Press International.*
USA   *United States Army*
U.S.(A.)   *United States (of America),* E.-U., États-
   Unis.
USAF   *United States Air Force.*
USDA   *United States Department of Agriculture.*
USIA   *United States Information Agency.*
USIS   *United States Information Service.*
USMC   *United States Marine Corps.*
USN   *United States Navy.*

USS   *United States Ship.*
USSR   *Union of Soviet Socialist Republics,* U.R.S.S
UT   *Utah.*

v.   1. *vide,* voir.   2. *verse.*   3. *El: volt.*
Va   *Virginia.*
VA   1. *Veteran Administration.*   2. *Virginia.*
VD   *Venereal Disease, M.D.,* maladie vénérienne.
vhf   *very high frequency,* o.t.c., onde très courte.
VI   *Virgin Islands.*
VIP   *Very Important Person,* huile f. *To give s.o.* VIP
   treatment, recevoir qn avec la croix et la bannière.
VISTA   *Volunteers in Service to America.*
viz.   *videlicet, namely.*
vol(s)   *volume(s).*
vs.   *versus,* c., contre.
Vt (VT)   *Vermont.*

w   1. *watt.*   2. *with.*
W   *west,* ouest.
WAC   *Women's Army Corps.*
Wash (WA)   *Washington.*
WASP   *white Anglo-Saxon Protestant.*
WC   *water-closet, toilet.*
Wed   *Wednesday.*
WHO   *World Health Organization,* O.M.S., Organi-
   sation mondiale de la santé.
whsle   *wholesale.*
WI   *West Indies.*
Wm   *William.*
WNW   *west-northwest,* ouest-nord-ouest.
wpm   *words per minute.*
WSW   *west-southwest,* ouest-sud-ouest.
wt   *weight,* poids.
W Va (WV)   *West Virginia.*
Wis (Wisc., WI)   *Wisconsin.*
Wyo (WY)   *Wyoming.*

yd   *yard(s).*
YDT   *Yukon Daylight Time,* heure légale d'été
   (fuseau du Yukon).
YMC(H)A   *Young Men's Christian (Hebrew) Associ-*
   ation.
yr   *year.*
YST   *Yukon Standard Time,* heure légale du Yukon.
YWC(H)A   *Young Women's Christian (Hebrew)*
   Association.